THE WORLD ALMANAC®

AND BOOK OF FACTS

2016

WORLD ALMANAC BOOKS

THE WORLD ALMANAC®

AND BOOK OF FACTS

2016

Senior Editor: Sarah Janssen
Editor: M. L. Liu **Associate Editor:** Shmuel Ross
Index Editor: Nan Badgett
Contributors: Robert Famighetti, Marshall Gerometta, Jacqueline Laks Gorman, Richard Hantula, Michael J. Kaufman, Donhae Koo, John Mastroberardino, William A. McGeveran Jr., Janet M. Olson, John Rosenthal, Helene Salmon, Peter J. Schmidtke, George W. Smith, Edward A. Thomas, Lori P. Wiesenfeld, Dale Williams

Production: Newgen North America
Design and Production, Year in Pictures: Q2A/Bill Smith
Design, Cover: Takeshi Takahashi
Photo Research: Edward A. Thomas

For Infobase Learning:
Editorial Director: Laurie E. Likoff
Project Editor: Edward A. Thomas

Photo credits. Front cover: Lupita Nyong'o: Newscom, Abaca Press/Lionel Hahn/Sipa USA; Tom Brady: Newscom, Rich Graessle/Icon Sportswire CGV; Pluto: NASA; other photos: Shutterstock. **Back cover/tabs:** Shutterstock (unless otherwise noted); Pope Francis: AP Images, Cliff Owen; American Pharoah: Newscom: Jon Durr/Cal Sport Media; Science tab: ESA/Hubble & NASA.
Interior pages: AP Images unless otherwise noted. **Jimmy Carter Library and Museum:** Carter, 500. **City of St. Petersburg:** same-sex marriage, 455. **Federal Emergency Management Agency:** Oklahoma City bombing, 451. **Gerald R. Ford Presidential Library and Museum:** Ford, 500. **Lyndon Baines Johnson Library and Museum:** Vietnam War protesters, 447; Johnson, 499. **Library of Congress:** 436, 438, 439, 441, 442, 444, 445; 493-501 (U.S presidents, unless otherwise noted); 654, 660, 661; Harding, 814. **NASA:** Moon landing, 448; Pluto, JHUAPL/SwRI, 809; water on Mars, JPL-Caltech/Univ. of Arizona, 809. **Natl. Archives and Records Administration:** 459, 461; Grant, 496. **Newscom:** Hobbit skull, Peter Brown/KRT, 646; Lumumba, DALMAS/SIPA, 665; Saigon, Hugh Van Es/UPI Photo Service, 666; Popes, Eric Vandeville/ABACA, 673; Late Show marquee, MM/ABACAUSA.COM, 813; Royal family, EPN, 815; Cuomo, Arthur Grace/ZUMAPRESS, 816; Gifford, Terry Lilly/ZUMAPRESS, 816; Meara, Henry McGee/ZUMAPRESS, 816; O'Hara, Album, 816; Sacks, Xander Remkes/ANP, 816. **Orange County Archives:** 443. **Public domain:** 437, 440, 446; Adams, 494; Taylor, 495; McKinley, 497; 656, 657, 658, 662, 663. **Reuters:** ISIS, Stringer, 672. **Ronald Wilson Reagan Library and Museum:** Sandra Day O'Connor, 449. **Shutterstock:** Refugees, 194; 647, 648, 650, 652, 655. **U.S. Army:** Capt. Kristen Griest, Spc. Nikayla Shodeen, 815. **U.S. Coast Guard:** Hurricane Katrina, 453. **U.S. Dept. of State:** Iran negotiations, 195. **U.S. Navy:** Brian Williams, Journalist Seaman David Senn, 814. **U.S. Strategic Bombing Survey:** Hiroshima, 664. **White House:** George W. Bush, Eric Draper, 501; Obama, Pete Souza, 502. **White House Historical Society:** Madison, 493. **Wikipedia Commons:** 471.

World Almanac® Books
An imprint of Infobase Learning
132 West 31st Street
New York, NY 10001

Hardcover
ISBN-13: 978-1-60057-199-2
ISBN-10: 1-60057-199-9

International Standard Serial Number
0084-1382

Paperback
ISBN-13: 978-1-60057-201-2
ISBN-10: 1-60057-201-4

The World Almanac® and Book of Facts is distributed to the trade by Simon & Schuster, and in paperback and hardcover to schools and libraries at special discounts by Infobase Learning. For further information, contact (800) 322-8755 or visit www.Infobase.com.

You can find The World Almanac® and Book of Facts on the Internet at www.worldalmanac.com.
Email: almanac@infobaselearning.com

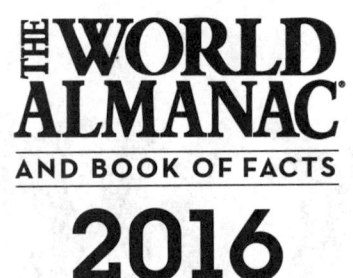

The World Almanac® and Book of Facts 2016
Book printed and bound by RR Donnelly, Kendallville, IN
Date printed: November 2015
Printed in the United States of America
RRD 10 9 8 7 6 5 4 3 2 1

CONTENTS

2015: SPECIAL FEATURES AND YEAR IN REVIEW

Top 10 News Topics 4
World at a Glance 5
Election 2016 6
Coming to America: Immigration in History and Today 8
Chronology of the Year's Events 12
Obituaries 34
State Government 37
U.S. Supreme Court Decisions 38
Notable Quotes 39
Offbeat News 40
Historical Anniversaries 41
Time Capsule 42

2015: YEAR IN PICTURES 193, 809

ECONOMY, BUSINESS, & ENERGY
- Economics 43
- Trade 73
- Transportation & Travel 79
- Agriculture 92
- Employment 101
- Energy 109

CRIME 116

MILITARY AFFAIRS 128

HEALTH & VITAL STATISTICS
- Health 141
- Vital Statistics 164

PERSONALITIES, ARTS, & MEDIA
- Noted Personalities 173
- Arts & Media 243
- Awards, Medals, & Prizes 259

SCIENCE & TECHNOLOGY
- Science 279
- Computers & Telecommunications . . . 294
- Environment 302
- Meteorology 308
- Disasters 317
- Aerospace 329
- Astronomy 337
- Calendar 354
- Weights & Measures 361

CONSUMER INFORMATION
- Postal Information 366
- Social Security & Medicare 368
- Taxes 375
- Education 380
- Directory 407

U.S. FACTS & HISTORY
- U.S. Facts 422
- Chronology of Events in U.S. History 436
- Historical Documents & Speeches . . . 458
- National Symbols 471

WORLD MAPS & FLAGS 473

U.S. GOVERNMENT
- Presidents of the U.S. 491
- Presidential Elections 505
- Obama Administration & Cabinet Departments 539
- Congress 548
- U.S. Supreme Court 559

U.S. CITIES, STATES, & POPULATION
- States & Other Areas of the U.S. 563
- 100 Most Populous U.S. Cities 594
- U.S. Population 605

WORLD HISTORY & CULTURE
- World History 646
- Historical Figures 674
- World Exploration & Geography 683
- Religion 697
- Language 708
- Buildings, Bridges, & Tunnels 716

NATIONS OF THE WORLD 730

SPORTS
- Sports Highlights, 2015 853
- Editors' Picks:
  - Memorable Super Bowls 854
- Olympic Games 855
- College Sports 877
  - College Football 877
  - College Basketball 884
  - Other College Sports 888
- Professional Sports
  - Football 890
  - Baseball 907
  - Basketball 933
  - Hockey 943
  - Soccer 948
  - Golf 952
  - Tennis 955
  - Auto Racing 959
  - Boxing 962
  - Thoroughbred Racing 966
  - Other Sports 971

GENERAL INDEX 980
- Quick Reference Index 1008

THE WORLD ALMANAC AND BOOK OF FACTS 2016

Top 10 News Topics of 2015

1. ISIS Conflict, Syrian Civil War Continue. Syria's civil war, in its fifth year, had claimed more than 320,000 lives by mid-2015, and 11-12 mil Syrians were refugees or internally displaced. Forces under Syrian Pres. Bashar al-Assad fought dozens of rebel groups, including the Sunni extremist Islamic State in Iraq and Syria (ISIS), which controlled large areas of Syria and neighboring Iraq. Airstrikes by U.S.-led coalitions against ISIS targets in Iraq and Syria entered their second year in Aug. and Sept. 2015, respectively. Russia, which backed Assad, began airstrikes Sept. 30 against anti-Assad forces.

2. Large Numbers of Migrants Seek Refuge in Europe. By late Oct., more than 700,000 refugees and other migrants—escaping war, oppression, or extreme poverty in the Middle East, Africa, and SW and S Asia—had reached Europe by sea in 2015, a dramatic increase from the estimated 216,000 who arrived in all of 2014. Syrians fleeing their country's civil war made up a majority of the 2015 total. More than 3,200 people had died at sea. Most migrants headed north—through countries including Serbia, Hungary, Croatia, Slovenia, and Austria—in order to reach Germany or other countries in N or W Europe. Large numbers from the Balkans joined the flow. Germany estimated that it had received 557,000 migrants Jan.-Aug., about 164,000 in Sept., and expected 1-1.5 mil for all of 2015. The EU adopted a plan, Sept. 22, to resettle 120,000 refugees in more than 20 EU countries despite opposition from Hungary and other Eastern European members.

3. U.S.-Led Talks Produce Iran Nuclear Agreement. After almost two years of U.S.-led negotiations, a six-nation group (the UK, France, Germany, Russia, and China, as well as the U.S.) and Iran concluded, July 14, a 15-year agreement to limit Iran's ability to produce nuclear weapons. Under the accord, Iran would reduce its capacity to develop enriched uranium and plutonium, send almost all its stockpile of enriched uranium out of the country, and allow international inspectors to verify its compliance. In return, sanctions against Iran would be lifted in stages. Critics, including members of Congress, contended the agreement did not go far enough to block Iran's nuclear program.

4. Supreme Court Upholds Same-Sex Marriage and Obamacare Subsidies. In a landmark 5-4 ruling June 26, the U.S. Supreme Court held that the Constitution guarantees same-sex couples the right to marry and that, under the 14th Amendment, states cannot prohibit same-sex marriages or refuse to recognize such marriages performed in other states. At the time of the ruling, same-sex marriage was banned in 15 states. In a June 25 decision, the Supreme Court upheld a key aspect of the Affordable Care Act—subsidies for lower-income people buying health insurance on the federal insurance marketplace. The Court held that, despite language in the statute providing for subsidies to people using exchanges "established by the State," the intent of the law was not to exclude people using the federal exchange in the 36 states that had not set up their own marketplaces.

5. Crowded Fields Seek 2016 Presidential Nominations; Ryan Replaces Boehner as House Speaker. In the run-up to the 2016 U.S. presidential election, some two dozen candidates sought the Republican or Democratic nomination. Democratic presumptive front-runner Hillary Clinton faced a stronger-than-expected challenge from Sen. Bernie Sanders (I, VT). Other declared Democratic candidates as of late Oct. included former Maryland Gov. Martin O'Malley, but Vice Pres. Joe Biden announced, Oct. 21, that he would not run. The Republican field reached a high of 17 declared candidates before former Texas Gov. Rick Perry and Wisconsin Gov. Scott Walker dropped out in Sept. Political outsiders who apparently appealed to the GOP's right wing, including businessman Donald Trump and retired surgeon Ben Carson, performed strongly in early national and state polls. Former Florida Gov. Jeb Bush placed lower in early polls than many analysts had expected. Facing opposition from the right in the Republican caucus, House Speaker John Boehner announced, Sept. 25, that he would resign his leadership post and vacate his Ohio House seat. Rep. Paul Ryan (R, WI) was elected speaker Oct. 29.

6. Mass Shootings in Charleston and Elsewhere Take Hundreds of Lives. A white gunman fatally shot a pastor and eight parishioners, all African-American, June 17 at a Charleston, SC, church. A website linked to accused shooter Dylann Roof, arrested June 18, included a racist manifesto and photo of him holding a Confederate flag. South Carolina legislation signed July 9 removed the Confederate flag from the grounds of the Capitol. The Charleston attack was one of almost 300 mass shootings in the U.S. Jan. 1-Oct. 1 according to the crowd-sourced Mass Shooting Tracker. On Oct. 1, a man identified as Christopher Harper-Mercer fatally shot nine people at Umpqua Community College in Roseburg, OR, before killing himself.

7. Deaths of African Americans Raise Questions About Police. Police shootings of unarmed African Americans or deaths in custody of African Americans raised concerns about police training, use of excessive force, and racial bias. In North Charleston, SC, Apr. 4, a black man, Walter Scott, was fatally shot as he ran away from a traffic stop; Michael Slager, the white officer who shot Scott, was charged with murder Apr. 7. Freddie Gray, an African American arrested in Baltimore, Apr. 12, suffered severe injuries while restrained in a police van; he died Apr. 19. Six police officers were indicted May 21. Near Houston, TX, African-American motorist Sandra Bland was stopped by state trooper Brian Encinia July 10 for allegedly failing to signal; the stop resulted in Bland's arrest, and she was found dead in her jail cell July 13, of an apparent suicide. A white Univ. of Cincinnati police officer, July 19, fatally shot an unarmed black man, Samuel DuBose, during a traffic stop; the officer, Ray Tensing, was indicted on murder charges July 29. Demonstrations protesting, at least in part, alleged police brutality, were held in a number of U.S. cities in 2015, some organized by the Black Lives Matter movement, founded in 2012.

8. Greece Receives New Bailout, Agrees to Further Austerity. Facing default on its debt in 2015, Greece reached agreement in Aug. with the European Central Bank and eurozone countries (known, with the Intl. Monetary Fund, as the "troika") on an 86-bil-euro bailout package, the country's third financial bailout tied to austerity measures since 2010. With Greece's economy having contracted by about 25% since 2007, Alexis Tsipras's Syriza party won Jan. 25 elections on an anti-austerity platform. As prime min., Tsipras resisted further austerity in negotiations with the troika and called a July 5 referendum in which Greek voters rejected austerity proposals. But with Greek banks forced to close (June 29-July 20) for lack of funds and the government having missed an IMF debt payment July 1, Tsipras accepted, in July-Aug. negotiations, tougher austerity measures than those previously proposed. He won reelection Sept. 20.

9. Terrorists Kill 17 in Paris, Sparking Concern About Islamist Extremist Attacks in the West. Two terrorist gunmen claiming affiliation with al-Qaeda in the Arabian Peninsula attacked, Jan. 7, the Paris office of the magazine *Charlie Hebdo*, which had published satirical cartoons showing the prophet Muhammad; 12 people were killed. In coordinated attacks, a terrorist claiming loyalty to ISIS killed a police officer Jan. 8 and four people at a kosher supermarket in Paris Jan. 9. The events increased concerns about attacks in Western nations by terrorists affiliated with or inspired by Islamist extremist groups. Western intelligence and other estimates in early 2015 indicated that perhaps 3,000-5,000 Europeans and about 150 Americans had traveled to Syria or Iraq in recent years to fight with militant groups including ISIS; some were believed to have since returned home.

10. U.S. Wins Soccer's Women's World Cup; Serena Williams and American Pharoah Among Other Stand-Outs in Sports. With a 5-2 victory in the final, July 5, over defending champion Japan, the U.S. women's soccer team won its third World Cup title. In tennis, Serena Williams completed a consecutive Grand Slam when she won the Wimbledon women's singles final July 11, after having won the 2014 U.S. Open and the 2015 Australian and French Opens. Horse racing had its first Triple Crown winner since 1978 when American Pharoah won the Belmont Stakes June 6 after having led the field in the Kentucky Derby May 2 and the Preakness May 16.

THE WORLD AT A GLANCE

Number Ones

World's most populous country . . . . China, 1.37 billion population in 2015 *(p. 731)*

World's most populous urban area. . . . . Tokyo, Japan, 38.0 million population in 2015 *(p. 730)*

World's wealthiest person. . . . . Bill Gates, U.S., $79.2 billion net worth as of Mar. 2015 *(p. 48)*

Most-visited U.S. social networking website. . . . . Facebook, 211.3 million unique visitors in June 2015 *(p. 298)*

Most-used U.S. search engine . . . . Google, 11.2 billion searches (64.0% of all searches) in June 2015 *(p. 298)*

Most-visited National Park Service site . . . . Golden Gate Natl. Recreation Area, California, 15.0 million recreation visits in 2014 *(p. 428)*

U.S. airline that carried the most passengers. . . . . American/US Airways, 145.6 million in 2014 *(p. 88)*

World's busiest airport by passenger traffic . . . . . .Hartsfield-Jackson Atlanta Intl. Airport, 96.2 million passengers in 2014 *(p. 88)*

Top U.S. state by traveler spending . . . . California, $116.0 billion in 2013 *(p. 86)*

Nation with the most paid days off of work per year. . . . . .Austria, 38 paid days off *(p. 89)*

Most popular recording artist by digital sales . . . . Rihanna, 100 million units sold as of Aug. 2015 *(p. 252)*

Most pirated movie. . . . . *Interstellar*, 35.3 million torrent downloads in Jan.-June 2015 *(p. 244)*

Surprising Facts

The number of refugees in the world has increased from 8.7 million in 2005 to 14.4 million in 2014. The number of internally displaced persons (IDPs) has increased even more steeply, from 6.6 million in 2005 to 32.3 million in 2014. *(p. 735)*

The U.S. violent crime rate dropped by more than 50% between 1991 and 2013. The murder rate in 2013 was exactly half of that in 1994. *(p. 116)*

In 1950, the U.S. produced 75.7% of the world's motor vehicles; by 2014, that number had dropped to 13.0% (up from a low of 9.5% in 2009). *(p. 79)*

Only two U.S. states (Arizona and Montana) have no laws in place that address texting while behind the wheel for at least some drivers. *(p. 83)*

Visitors to the U.S. from Mexico in 2013 spent an average of $733 per person; from Canada, $1,156; from France, $3,907; and from Brazil, $5,085. *(p. 86)*

Americans paid an average of 24.8% of their gross wage earnings in income tax and Social Security contributions in 2014; Belgians, who had some of the highest personal-income tax rates, paid 42.3%. *(p. 734)*

Among the 50 most populous nations, the U.S. has long led in spending on health expenses, at $8,845 per capita in 2012. Australia came closest to matching U.S. spending, at $6,097 per capita. *(p. 142)*

U.S. workers with professional degrees had a lower unemployment rate (1.9%) and higher median weekly earnings ($1,639) than workers with any other level of education in 2014 (including those with doctoral degrees). *(p. 106)*

21.0% of female high school students reported being bullied electronically in 2013; the rate for high school boys was 8.5%. *(p. 382)*

Milestone Birthdays, 2016

90

Jerry Lewis, Mar. 16
Hugh Hefner, Apr. 9
Harper Lee, Apr. 28
Cloris Leachman, Apr. 30
Don Rickles, May 8
Mel Brooks, June 28
Tony Bennett, Aug. 3
Chuck Berry, Oct. 18

80

Alan Alda, Jan. 28
Burt Reynolds, Feb. 11
John Madden, Apr. 10
Glen Campbell, Apr. 22
Kris Kristofferson, June 22
Robert Redford, Aug. 18
John McCain, Aug. 29
Pope Francis, Dec. 17
Mary Tyler Moore, Dec. 29

70

Diane Keaton, Jan. 5
Dolly Parton, Jan. 19
David Lynch, Jan. 20
Tim Curry, Apr. 19
Cher, May 20
Donald Trump, June 14
George W. Bush, July 6
Sylvester Stallone, July 6
Bill Clinton, Aug. 19
Tommy Lee Jones, Sept. 15
Susan Sarandon, Oct. 4
Suzanne Somers, Oct. 16
Sally Field, Nov. 6
Steven Spielberg, Dec. 18

60

Mel Gibson, Jan. 3
Nathan Lane, Feb. 3
Bryan Cranston, Mar. 7
Joe Montana, June 11
Anthony Bourdain, June 25
Tom Hanks, July 9
Martina Navratilova, Oct. 18
Carrie Fisher, Oct. 21
Steve Harvey, Nov. 23
David Sedaris, Dec. 26

50

Cindy Crawford, Feb. 20
Robin Wright, Apr. 8
Janet Jackson, May 16
Julianna Margulies, June 8
John Cusack, June 28
Mike Tyson, June 30
Halle Berry, Aug. 14
Salma Hayek, Sept. 2
Adam Sandler, Sept. 9
Troy Aikman, Nov. 21
Kiefer Sutherland, Dec. 21

40

Reese Witherspoon, Mar. 22
Keri Russell, Mar. 23
Peyton Manning, Mar. 24
David Oyelowo, Apr. 1
Tim Duncan, Apr. 25
Blake Shelton, June 18
Benedict Cumberbatch, July 19
Anna Faris, Nov. 29

30

Lady Gaga, Mar. 28
Lena Dunham, May 13
Robert Pattinson, May 13
Rafael Nadal, June 3
Ashley Olsen, June 13
Mary-Kate Olsen, June 13
Lindsay Lohan, July 2
Usain Bolt, Aug. 21
Drake, Oct. 24

ELECTION 2016

Key Election Dates, 2016

Nominating conventions	Date, location
Constitution Party	Apr. 13-16, Salt Lake City, UT
Libertarian Party	May 27-29, 2016, Orlando, FL
Republican Party	July 18-21, Cleveland, OH
Democratic Party	July 25-28, Philadelphia, PA
Green Party	Aug. 4-7, Houston, TX

Election Day
Nov. 8, 2016

Inauguration Day
Jan. 20, 2017

Primary Debate Schedules, 2015-16

Hosts, dates, and locations are subject to change. As of Oct. 31, 2015.

Republican

Host	Date, location
Fox News	Aug. 6, 2015, Cleveland, OH
CNN/Salem Radio	Sept. 16, 2015, Simi Valley, CA
CNBC	Oct. 28, 2015, Boulder, CO
Fox Business/*Wall Street Journal*	Nov. 10, 2015, Milwaukee, WI
CNN/Salem Radio	Dec. 15, 2015, Las Vegas, NV
Fox News	Jan. 2016, Des Moines, IA
ABC News	Feb. 6, 2016, New Hampshire
CBS News	Feb. 13, 2016, South Carolina
National Review	Feb. 26, 2016, Houston, TX
Fox News	Mar. 2016, TBD
CNN/Salem Radio	Mar. 10, 2016, Florida

Democratic

Host	Date, location
CNN	Oct. 13, 2015, Las Vegas, NV
CBS/KCCI/*Des Moines Register*	Nov. 14, 2015, Des Moines, IA
ABC/WMUR	Dec. 19, 2015, Manchester, NH
NBC/Congressional Black Caucus Institute	Jan. 17, 2016, Charleston, SC
Univision/*Washington Post*	Feb./Mar. 2016, Miami, FL
PBS	Feb./Mar. 2016, Wisconsin

Presidential Primaries and Caucuses, 2016

Source: Frontloading HQ, Federal Election Commission

Primaries for some state or local races may occur on other dates. Dates subject to change. As of Oct. 31, 2015.

State	Primary/caucus date
Alabama	Mar. 1
Alaska	Mar. 1 (R)/Mar. 26 (D)
Arizona	Mar. 22
Arkansas	Mar. 1
California	June 7
Colorado	Mar. 1
Connecticut	Apr. 26
Delaware	Apr. 26
Florida	Mar. 15
Georgia	Mar. 1
Hawaii	Mar. 8 (R)/Mar. 26 (D)
Idaho	Mar. 8 (R)/Mar. 22 (D)
Illinois	Mar. 15
Indiana	May 3
Iowa	Feb. 1
Kansas	Mar. 5
Kentucky	Mar. 5 (R)/May 17 (D)
Louisiana	Mar. 5
Maine	Mar. 5 (R)/Mar. 6 (D)
Maryland	Apr. 26
Massachusetts	Mar. 1
Michigan	Mar. 8
Minnesota	Mar. 1
Mississippi	Mar. 8
Missouri	Mar. 15
Montana	June 7
Nebraska	Mar. 5 (D)/May 10 (R)
Nevada	Feb. 20 (D)/Feb. 23 (R)
New Hampshire	Feb. 9
New Jersey	June 7
New Mexico	June 7
New York	Apr. 19
North Carolina	Mar. 15
North Dakota	Mar. 1 (R)/June 7 (D)
Ohio	Mar. 15
Oklahoma	Mar. 1
Oregon	Mar. 5 (R)/May 17
Pennsylvania	Apr. 26
Puerto Rico	Mar. 6 (R)/Mar. 13 (D)
Rhode Island	Apr. 26 (D)
South Carolina	Feb. 20 (R)/Feb. 27 (D)
South Dakota	June 7
Tennessee	Mar. 1
Texas	Mar. 1
Utah	Mar. 22
Vermont	Mar. 1
Virginia	Mar. 1
Washington	Feb. 20 (R)/Mar. 26 (D)
West Virginia	May 10
Wisconsin	Apr. 5
Wyoming	Mar. 1 (R)/Apr. 9 (D)
Wash., DC	Mar. 12 (R)/June 14 (D)

2016 Presidential Campaign Finances

Source: Federal Elections Commission

Financial information reported to the FEC as of Sept. 30, 2015. Super PAC financial disclosure dates vary.

	Campaign funds					
Candidate	Total contributions[1]	Contributions from individuals	Disbursements	Cash on hand	Debt	Affiliated super PAC(s) funds
Hillary Clinton (D)	$76,051,160	$75,131,206	$43,055,988	$32,995,172	$647,245	$17,109,588
Bernie Sanders (D)	41,179,952	39,671,766	14,060,230	27,119,722	0	8,795
Ben Carson (R)	31,274,992	31,247,904	20,002,458	11,272,534	25,000	3,927,445
Ted Cruz (R)	26,437,929	26,139,614	12,659,025	13,778,904	0	38,425,902
Jeb Bush (R)	24,765,380	24,244,543	14,494,251	10,271,129	404,737	103,167,846
Marco Rubio (R)	13,597,764	13,557,574	6,687,639	10,975,989	75,902	16,057,755
Rand Paul (R)	9,348,900	7,677,329	7,221,129	2,124,156	365,359	6,237,784
Carly Fiorina (R)	8,447,720	8,439,064	2,898,526	5,549,194	0	3,492,728
*Scott Walker (R)	7,356,771	7,338,291	6,371,557	985,213	161,133	20,220,077
Donald J. Trump (R)	5,735,514	3,825,880	5,440,691	254,773	1,804,747	—
Lindsey Graham (R)	4,745,811	2,967,250	3,094,501	1,651,309	0	2,897,457
John Kasich (R)	4,374,838	4,235,566	1,732,889	2,641,950	0	—
Chris Christie (R)	4,188,864	4,126,264	2,802,417	1,386,447	246,347	11,003,305
Mike Huckabee (R)	3,234,967	3,209,467	2,473,556	761,411	133,104	3,604,987
Martin O'Malley (D)	3,203,744	3,153,572	2,397,757	805,987	20,608	289,443
*Rick Perry (R)	1,266,811	1,259,770	1,564,346	44,554	0	12,815,326
Bobby Jindal (R)	1,158,092	1,148,092	897,153	260,939	0	3,685,919
Rick Santorum (R)	1,013,315	992,221	779,145	226,526	450,408	—
*Lawrence Lessig (D)	1,012,067	1,011,447	438,131	573,936	0	—
*Jim Webb (D)	696,972	691,972	380,207	316,765	0	—
George Pataki (R)	409,309	389,309	395,738	13,571	20,000	859,244

— = No disclosure available. * = Candidate had withdrawn from the race as of Nov. 2, 2015. **Note:** Campaigns with under $100,000 in total contributions not shown. Super PACs cannot coordinate with individual candidates; some candidates have publicly spoken against the super PACs established to support them. (1) Includes campaign contribution categories not shown separately here.

Looking Toward Election 2016

On Nov. 8, 2016, Americans will elect a new president, at least 34 U.S. senators, and all 435 members of the U.S. House of Representatives, along with governors in at least 12 states.

As of Oct. 2015, Republicans had 54 Senate seats—a majority, though not the 60 needed to prevent filibusters under prevailing Senate rules; Democrats held 44 seats, with 2 others held by independents who vote with the Democratic caucus. To gain a majority, Democrats would thus need just five additional seats. Of the 34 Senate seats up for election (barring additional vacancies), 24 are held by Republicans, including 5 in states that Pres. Barack Obama carried by at least 5 percentage points in 2012. In the House, Republicans held 247 seats to the Democrats' 188 in late 2015. The vast majority of districts are either strongly Democratic or strongly Republican.

The Electoral Map

Most public attention, however, has focused on the race for the White House. The winning ticket will need to accumulate a simple majority of 270 of the 538 total Electoral College votes.

The non-partisan Cook Political Report, in late 2015, rated 18 states (mostly Northeast, Middle Atlantic, or West Coast states) and the District of Columbia, with 217 electoral votes, as "blue," or in some degree likely Democratic; 24 states (mostly in the West and South), with 206 electoral votes, were rated "red," or likely Republican. The remaining nine swing states, with 115 votes, were Colorado, Florida, Iowa, Nevada, New Hampshire, Ohio, Pennsylvania, Virginia, and Wisconsin. These generalizations vary and evolve over time; a strong current can still sweep one party's ticket to victory in nearly all states. In any case, political operatives and campaigns were expected to concentrate their time, money, and ads on what they considered to be swing states, where an investment may have the best chance of making a difference.

Issues and Concerns

Through early fall 2015, with an open presidential election about a year away, Pres. Obama's approval rating, highly polarized by party, averaged around 45%—higher than Pres. George W. Bush at the same point in his two-term presidency, but well below Pres. Bill Clinton, who had ratings around 60% at that stage. Only three out of ten Americans believed the country was on the right track, according to poll aggregator Real Clear Politics. Polls put approval for Congress below 20%, whether because it could not compromise to get things done or because it failed to advance a particular agenda.

Opinion polls in 2015 generally showed that the economy was the top election issue for Americans, with no clear advantage to either party, and foreign policy seeming to take a back seat. Polling by the Pew Research Center in July did not give either party a significant edge on handling the economy, the deficit, immigration, or foreign policy. The July polling gave Democrats a strong advantage on policies related to the environment, abortion and contraception, and education. Republicans had a clear advantage on gun control and dealing with terrorism within the U.S. Polling by Pew Research typically has found that the GOP was considered more extreme in its positions, while Democrats were "more concerned with the needs of people like me."

Money

According to one estimate, the 2016 presidential campaign could cost $5 bil or more, fueled by the multiplicity of candidates and loosened spending restrictions. Unions, corporations, and so-called social welfare organizations, such as the National Rifle Association and the Sierra Club, can now contribute to candidates and run advertising targeted for or against a candidate without having to disclose donors ("dark money"), so long as they do not coordinate with candidates and their overall purpose can be interpreted as nonpolitical. Outside organizations known as super PACs can receive unlimited contributions from corporations, unions, and individuals and spend unrestricted amounts, though they cannot give directly to candidates and must by and large disclose donors. While super PACs are also barred from coordinating with candidates, nearly every 2016 presidential contender had a super PAC dedicated to his or her campaign, and most were run by a former aide or close associate of the candidate.

Getting Ready

By the time of the first Republican debate, in Aug., there were 17 GOP candidates—requiring the debate to be split into two events. In Sept., however, the GOP field began to shrink slightly as two candidates, both with experience as governors, Rick Perry (TX) and Scott Walker (WI), dropped out because of sagging poll numbers and financial support. The Democratic field was smaller, dominated by former Sec. of State Hillary Clinton and Sen. Bernie Sanders (VT). Candidates in both parties wooed potential big donors and toured early primary/caucus states like Iowa and New Hampshire. The race began to shape up, though no one could predict how it would be affected by the series of debates and primaries to come.

Establishment and Anti-Establishment

On the GOP side, former Florida Gov. Jeb Bush had strong name recognition and a super PAC heavily supported by big donors early on. However, many linked the Bush name to the Iraq War and economic failure. Jeb Bush had difficulty finding a compelling voice of his own, and many Republicans also found him insufficiently conservative—for example, he favored a path to lawful status for undocumented immigrants. Moreover some distrusted government experience and liked the idea of fresh leadership that would battle for a strong agenda. Hence the success, at least in many early polls, of candidates like real-estate billionaire Donald Trump, retired neurosurgeon Ben Carson, and former Hewlett-Packard CEO Carly Fiorina, none of whom had any experience in public office. Blasting Bush as a "low-energy" candidate, Trump claimed to be a straight talker from the outside, whose business career showed he knew how to get things done; at the same time, Trump was condemned for harsh rhetoric and allegedly superficial solutions.

Among the Republican contenders with some political experience, Sen. Ted Cruz (TX) stood out as an anti-establishment figure, ready to denounce fellow Republicans for any compromise with Democrats. Sen. Marco Rubio (FL) stressed foreign policy early on, criticizing the Obama administration as passive and ineffective; he positioned himself as the voice of a younger generation and someone who might especially appeal to fellow Hispanics. New Jersey Gov. Chris Christie pointed to the 2001 attack on the World Trade Center as an influence on his political career, while Gov. John Kasich (OH) stressed his credentials as a pro-growth budget hawk, with a nonconfrontational approach that might appeal to moderates. Sen. Rand Paul (KY) represented libertarianism and a foreign policy leaning toward nonintervention. A few GOP contenders, including former Arkansas Gov. Mike Huckabee, put particular stress on their social conservatism, appealing especially to the party's evangelical Christian wing.

Former First Lady Hillary Clinton was a polarizing figure but the clear Democratic front-runner in most 2015 polls. She had extensive ties with party insiders, and her experience as a U.S. senator (NY) and secretary of state was a plus to many Democrats, who tended to dismiss as political the controversies over the 2012 Benghazi attack and her use of a private email server. Vice Pres. Joe Biden declared in Oct. that he would not be a candidate, but she still faced opposition from many progressives in the party—angry over income inequality, distrustful of money and connections in politics, and hostile to government-as-usual. Sen. Sanders, a self-described democratic socialist, spearheaded this challenge, drawing financial support from small donors. Calling herself a "progressive who likes to get things done," Clinton came out against the Keystone XL pipeline and Trans-Pacific Partnership trade agreement, while differing with Sanders on issues such as single-payer health insurance and the U.S. role in the Middle East.

COMING TO AMERICA: IMMIGRATION IN HISTORY AND TODAY

Immigration to the U.S. has played a major role in shaping the country's history—and has often been a hot-button political issue. For the colonial era and early decades of the nation, records are incomplete, and it is difficult to know exactly how many immigrants arrived. This period includes the large-scale forced migration of African slaves—an estimated 388,000-450,000 people. Since 1820, when the U.S. government began keeping records of the number of immigrants entering the country, some 80 mil have arrived in accordance with U.S. law. Most immigrants came from Europe through the 1950s, but in recent years, larger numbers of immigrants have come to the U.S. from Latin America and Asia.

Current U.S. law requires an immigrant to obtain a visa allowing him or her to be a **lawful permanent resident (LPR)** and sets annual limits on the numbers and types of immigrants permitted to become LPRs. A person with an **LPR visa** (or **green card**) is entitled to live and work in the U.S. for an unlimited period of time and generally is eligible (after 5 years) to become a naturalized U.S. citizen.

The U.S. population also includes more than 11 mil residents who are undocumented immigrants—people who have no green cards and are not legally entitled to live in the U.S. Many entered the U.S. with a time-limited visa—allowing them to attend school, work temporarily, or visit as a tourist—and stayed in the country after their visa expired. Millions of others crossed a border, most often the southern border with Mexico, without any U.S. documents.

Waves of Immigration

Immigration to the U.S. has tended to come in waves. The mid-1800s saw the first major wave after record keeping began. Spurred by the Irish potato famine (1845-49) and continuing harsh poverty in Ireland, almost 1.7 mil people emigrated from Ireland to the U.S. in the 1840s and 1850s. Fleeing political instability, religious persecution, and economic hardship, nearly 4.5 mil Germans came to the U.S. in the latter half of the 19th century. Demand for unskilled labor in U.S. factories, farms, and mines absorbed many European immigrant workers. Others helped build the eastern section of the first U.S. transcontinental railroad (completed in 1869). The California Gold Rush (beginning in 1849) and a need for workers on the western section of the transcontinental railroad brought the first wave of immigrants to the U.S. Pacific Coast from China—about 289,000 people (mostly men) from the 1850s through the 1880s.

By the 20th century, most immigrants were coming from Southern and Eastern Europe. Largely fleeing poverty and persecution, 8.2 mil immigrants arrived in the decade from 1900 to 1909, including 2 mil from the Austro-Hungarian Empire, more than 1.9 mil from Italy, and 1.5 mil from the Russian Empire. These immigrants filled a need for factory, construction, and other labor, largely in the Northeast and Upper Midwest.

The outbreak of World War I in Europe in 1914 led to a sharp drop in immigration. After U.S. legislation, beginning in the 1920s, set immigration quotas, new lawful arrivals remained relatively low for much of the 20th century. The first decade in which the number of LPRs passed the level of 1900-09 was the 1990s (attributable in part to a 1992 increase in immigration quotas). The past quarter-century has seen more people become LPRs than any prior 25-year period in U.S. history. In relation to the total population size, however, the percentage of LPRs in each of the two most recent complete decades was lower than in any decade between 1840 and 1919.

By the late 20th century, most LPRs were non-Europeans. The top-five countries of origin for documented immigrants in the period 1990-2013 were Mexico (5 mil people); China, including Hong Kong (1.4 mil); the Philippines (1.3 mil); India (1.2 mil); and the Dominican Republic (834,000).

Analyzing recent trends in both documented and undocumented immigration, the Pew Research Center estimated that the foreign-born portion of the U.S. population in 2015 was about 14%—close to the historic high of almost 15% in the early 20th century. In part because of country-of-origin trends, Pew estimated that the non-Hispanic white portion of the U.S. population went down from 84% in 1965 to 62% in 2015. The Hispanic portion increased from 4% to 18% in that 50-year period, the Asian portion from less than 1% to 6%. (The African-American portion stayed almost constant, increasing from 11% to 12%.)

Welcome (Sort of)—Laws and Attitudes

Throughout U.S. history, immigration has largely been more readily accepted when immigrant labor was needed. And many immigrants have found that they could live more safely, practice their religion more openly, and do better for themselves and their families economically than in the countries they left behind. Tens of millions of immigrants and their descendants have assimilated into American life.

At the same time, since the first major wave of immigration in the mid-1800s, the immigrant experience has been difficult for millions of new Americans. Immigrant workers have often been exploited and have had to do the hardest work for the lowest pay. Beyond economics, immigrants in many periods of history have often faced prejudice and discrimination because they are viewed as "different" by longer-term residents. For example, in the largely Protestant America of the 1850s, anxiety about large-scale immigration of Roman Catholics from Ireland and Germany allowed the anti-immigration, anti-Catholic Know Nothing Party to flourish.

Immigrants Becoming Lawful Permanent Residents (LPRs), 1820-2013

Source: U.S. Dept. of Homeland Security

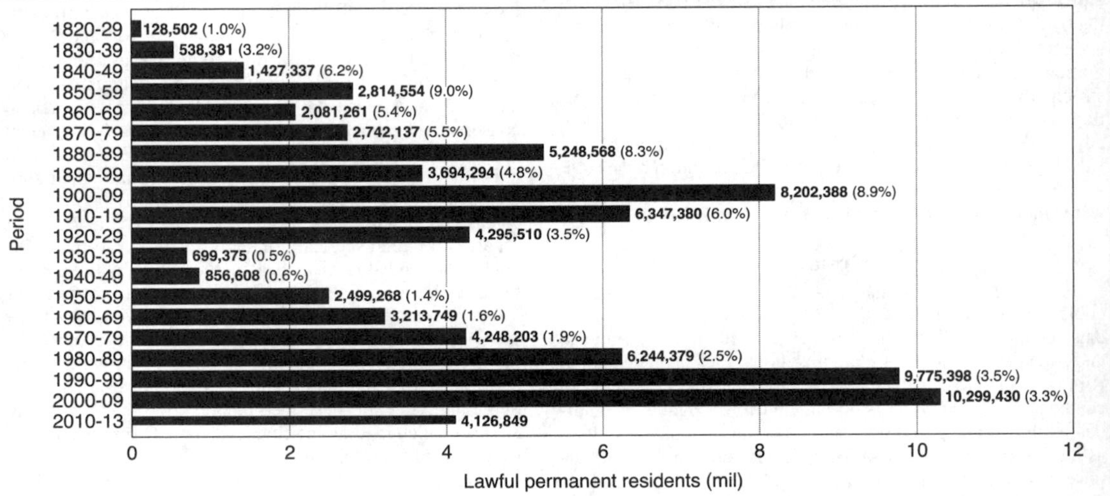

Note: All LPR data are for the fiscal years in effect at the time. Percentages are the 10-fiscal-year LPR totals as a proportion of the whole U.S. population at the next Census (for example, 1820-29 LPR total as a percentage of the 1830 national population).

Top Five Countries of Origin for LPRs in Selected Decades
Source: U.S. Dept. of Homeland Security

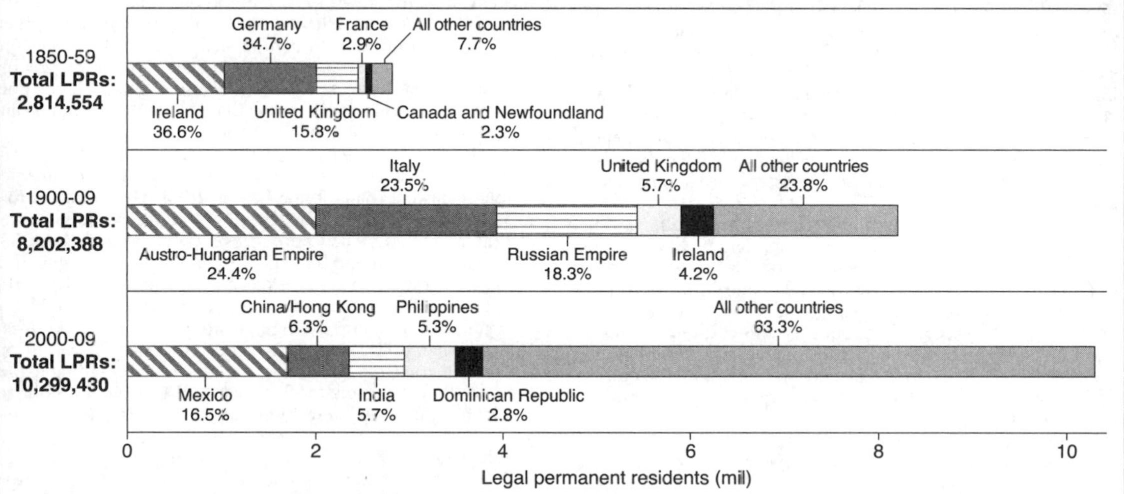

Though virtually all immigrant groups have faced challenges, they have generally been worse for non-European, nonwhite immigrants. As early as 1790, an act of Congress provided only for immigrants who were "free white persons" to become U.S. citizens. In the 19th and early 20th centuries, special efforts were made to prevent immigration from Asia. The 1882 Chinese Exclusion Act, renewed in 1892 and 1902, barred virtually all immigration from China. The 1907 Gentlemen's Agreement between the U.S. and Japan essentially blocked immigration from Japan, and the Immigration Act of 1917 established an Asiatic Barred Zone, prohibiting immigration from most of the rest of the continent. The Chinese Exclusion Act was not repealed until 1943, when China was a U.S. ally in World War II. And it was only in 1952 that legislation made people of all racial and ethnic backgrounds eligible for immigration and U.S. citizenship.

In response to the large numbers of Southern and Eastern Europeans in the immigration wave of the early 20th century, a 1921 law capped annual immigration from any country at 3% of the number of foreign-born people from that country residing in the U.S. in 1910. This law was replaced by the more restrictive Immigration Act of 1924, which lowered the annual quota to 2% and changed the reference year to 1890. Since that was before the largest immigration from Southern and Eastern Europe, the 1924 act in effect gave strong preference to immigrants from Northern Europe. An overall limit of 150,000 immigrants per year went into effect in 1927, as well as changes in the quota system that retained the Northern European preference.

Immigration limits based on national origin remained the law of the land for four decades, until the Immigration Act of 1965 dramatically changed U.S. policy. The 1965 statute set two new preferences for immigrants to be allowed permanent residency: uniting families (that is, giving priority to family members of citizens and LPRs) and admitting people with occupational or other skills needed by the U.S. The new priorities and elimination of the former quota system paved the way for much greater immigration from regions other than Europe. However, overall ceilings on annual immigration remained relatively low—less than 300,000 per year—until rising to 540,000 under 1986 legislation and to 700,000 in 1992. (Separate legislation in the second half of the 20th century permitted the entry of hundreds of thousands of Cubans and other refugees.)

The Law Today

Current U.S. immigration law is a modified version of the 1965 Immigration Act. For 2013, the official ceiling on LPR visas was 675,000, and no more than 7% of those could go to people from any single country. Because of various exceptions, the actual number of LPR visas issued was more than 315,000 higher than the ceiling, and both Mexico and China (13.6% and 7.2%, respectively) accounted for more than 7% of all visas.

LPR visas are distributed in four broad categories: family-reunification immigrants, employment-based preference immigrants, diversity immigrants, and refugees and people granted asylum (asylees). Family-reunification immigrants make up the largest group. In theory this group is limited to 480,000 people each year, but since some immediate family members (spouses and minor children of U.S. citizens and parents of adult U.S. citizens) are exempt from the numerical limit, in practice the number of family members admitted can be much higher. In 2013, some 650,000 family-reunification immigrants received LPR visas.

There is a ceiling of 140,000 LPR visas per year for employment-based preference immigrants. There are various categories (with different levels of preference and sublimits) of such immigrants. They include people of extraordinary ability in the arts, science, business, education, or sports; people with advanced professional degrees; skilled and unskilled workers in occupations where the U.S. economy faces a worker shortage; and entrepreneurs prepared to make a sizable investment in a business that will create at least 10 new jobs.

To encourage geographic distribution in the countries of origin of immigrants to the U.S., up to 55,000 LPR visas per year can be given to diversity immigrants. People from countries with low immigration to the U.S. in the previous five years, meeting certain requirements, can apply to enter an annual lottery run by the U.S. State Dept. to become eligible for an LPR visa.

The fourth major group of LPR visa recipients—refugees and asylees (generally eligible for a green card after one year of residency)—accounted for 12% of LPR visas in 2013. Refugees (outside the U.S.) and asylees (already in the U.S.) are people who have been determined to be fleeing persecution or a well-founded fear of persecution. There is no annual numerical limit in U.S. immigration law on the number of refugee/asylee LPR visas. The president sets a ceiling on the number of refugees the U.S. will admit each fiscal year. The 2015 ceiling of 70,000 was expected to increase to 85,000 in 2016 and 100,000 in 2017—in large part to allow the admission of more Syrians fleeing that country's civil war.

Once a person's LPR visa application is approved, he or she does not necessarily immediately receive a green card. Because of the overall and country ceilings on some types of LPR visas, the number of approved applicants can exceed the annual ceiling. Applicants then go on a waiting list, and in some cases, the wait can be long. For example, the average wait time for approved applicants who are siblings of U.S. citizens was more than 12 years as of late 2014; for such siblings from the Philippines, the wait time was over 23 years. Approved applicants from Mexico or the Philippines who were married sons or daughters of U.S. citizens had 20-year wait times. For employment-based immigrants, wait times are generally shorter or nonexistent, but there are exceptions. In Nov. 2014, the wait time for professional and skilled workers from India was 11 years. The long delays have prompted calls for higher immigration ceilings. Higher ceilings could bring in needed workers, reunite families more quickly, and discourage people from going outside the system. Opponents of higher ceilings have expressed concern about increased competition for jobs.

Undocumented Immigrants

Recent decades have seen millions of undocumented immigrants enter the U.S. Economists talk of "push" and "pull" factors contributing to undocumented immigration. Poverty and high unemployment in developing countries are major push factors encouraging people to leave. Pull factors include the relative strength of the U.S. economy (in most years) and the relatively high wages (even in low-wage jobs) available in the U.S. compared to many other countries. Recently, the largest numbers of undocumented immigrants have come from Mexico and Central America. Men seeking work are often the first in a family to emigrate. In many cases, family members later try to join the immigrant worker.

Some undocumented immigrants return home after a time. However, millions of undocumented immigrants have become long-term U.S. residents. According to Pew Research Center estimates, over 60% have lived in the country for 10 years or more. Under the 14th Amendment to the U.S. Constitution, children born in the U.S. are U.S. citizens (this is known as **birthright citizenship**), regardless of the citizenship or immigration status of their parents. In 2012, there were 4.5 mil U.S. citizens under age 18 living with 4 mil parents without legal permission to be in the U.S.

Undocumented immigrants are sometimes said to live in the shadows. They cannot be denied emergency medical care, and under a 1982 Supreme Court decision, undocumented children have a right to attend school. However, undocumented immigrants are not eligible for many government programs—including, for example, federal food assistance, disability payments, the Affordable Care Act (or Obamacare), and most aspects of Medicaid. In most states (38 as of July 1, 2015), undocumented immigrants cannot obtain a driver's license. They cannot legally be hired and may be paid less than minimum wage "off the books." If they are crime victims, they may refrain from calling the police for fear that their undocumented status will become known and they will face deportation. Some local governments have passed legislation or adopted policies making themselves **sanctuary cities**—in essence, government employees will not inquire about a person's immigration status when providing services and will not inform federal officials if they become aware of a person's undocumented status—but this is far from a nationwide practice.

Calls for stronger government action against undocumented immigrants have a number of motivations. Some are economic. Such immigrants are said to take work away from citizens and LPRs. They may use some government services while often not paying income taxes. (Undocumented immigrants pay sales taxes and perhaps other federal, state, and local taxes.) Undocumented immigrants are also said to have unfairly jumped the line rather than waiting to get an LPR visa. Since they do not go through the same checks as LPR applicants, it is claimed that some may be criminals or even terrorists, though hard evidence is lacking.

Congress last took substantial action to deal with undocumented immigration in the Immigration Reform and Control Act of 1986. The law allowed most undocumented immigrants who had lived in the U.S. continuously since 1982 to become legal residents; as a result of this amnesty program, 2.7 mil people obtained legal status. The law also established penalties for employers knowingly hiring undocumented workers and included steps to tighten border security.

The last two measures apparently had limited effects. The Pew Research Center has estimated that some 3.5 mil undocumented immigrants were living in the U.S. in 1990. The estimates rose to 5.7 mil in 1995, 8.6 mil in 2000, 11.1 mil in 2005, and peaked at 12.2 mil in 2007. The severe recession that began in late 2007 apparently reversed the trend. With jobs scarce, undocumented immigrants returning home exceeded new entrants. By 2012, the number of undocumented immigrants was estimated to be 11.2 mil. Of that number, slightly more than half (52%) were from Mexico, down from 59% in 1990. About 15% were from Central America, the same portion as in 1990. According to preliminary Pew estimates for 2013 and 2014, about 11.3 undocumented immigrants were living in the U.S. in each of those years.

While a slow U.S. economy provided less of a pull factor for undocumented immigrants after 2007, tougher security, especially at the U.S.-Mexico border, probably also played a role in the declining numbers. By mid-2015, about 650 miles of security fencing had been completed along the southern border. The number of U.S. Border Patrol agents almost doubled from 10,800 (9,500 of them at the southern border) in 2004 to more than 20,800 (including over 18,100 at the southern border) by 2014. The number of undocumented immigrants expelled each year (officially known as removals) by the Dept. of Homeland Security (DHS) also increased sharply for most of the early 21st century. Those removed include people apprehended both at the border and within the country. Expedited judicial proceedings and improved technology to check fingerprint records may account for the number of removals increasing from some 165,000 in 2002 (the lowest annual total since the turn of the century) to a high of more than 438,000 in 2013. Removals dipped somewhat, to just under 414,500 in 2014, as DHS emphasized the removal of criminals and recent border crossers.

Undocumented immigrants live throughout the U.S., but about 72% live in one of the 10 states with the largest undocumented populations: California (about 2,450,000 in 2012), Texas (1,650,000), Florida (925,000), New York (750,000), New Jersey (525,000), Illinois (475,000), Georgia (400,000), North Carolina (350,000), Arizona (300,000), and Virginia (275,000). The undocumented-immigrant portion of the population is highest in Nevada (7.6%), followed by California and Texas (6.3% each).

Undocumented Immigrants Living in the U.S., 1990-2012

Source: Pew Research Center

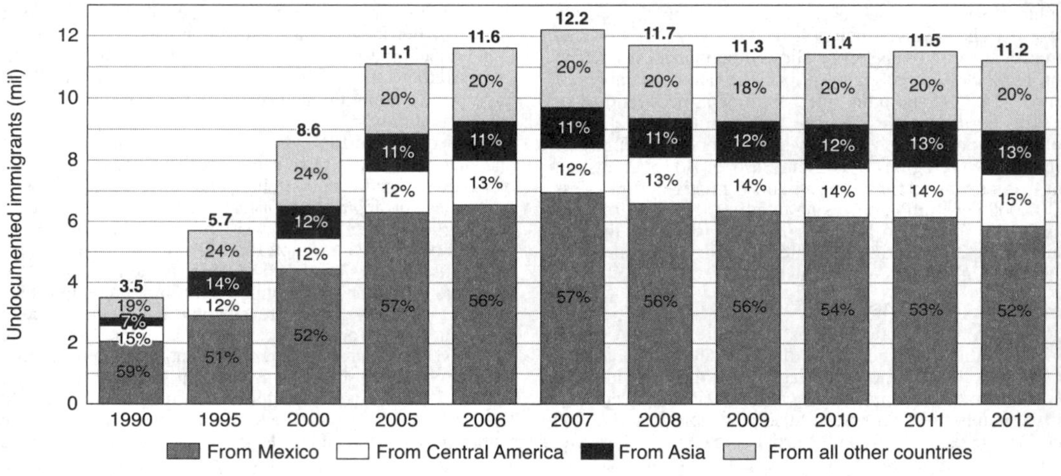

Note: Percent distribution of the estimated undocumented population is by country or region of birth.

Immigrant Removals and Returns, 1990-2014

Source: U.S. Dept. of Homeland Security

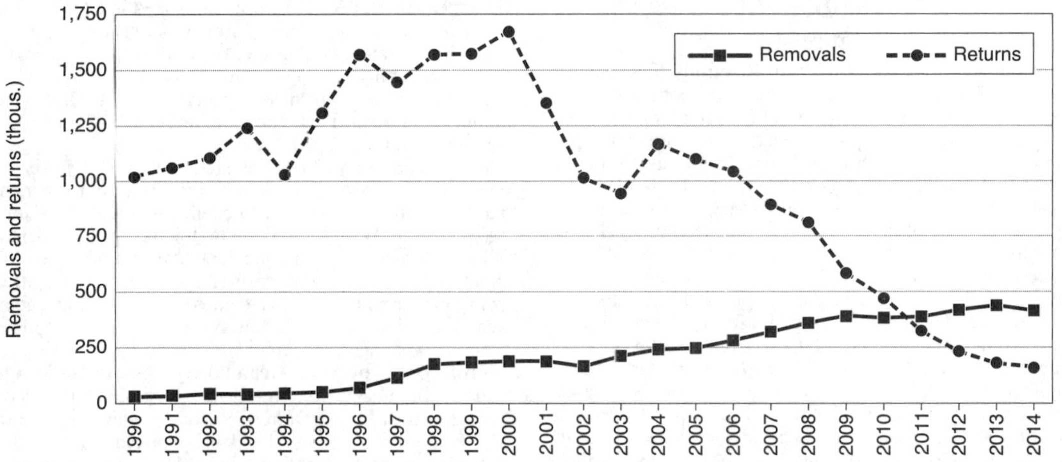

Note: Removals are inadmissible or deportable immigrants expelled from the U.S. based on an order of removal and may include some legal residents, such as those who have committed crimes, as well as undocumented immigrants. Returns are inadmissable or deportable immigrants leaving voluntarily and/or without a formal order of removal.

Some 8.1 mil undocumented immigrants were estimated to be in the workforce in 2012, making up about 5% of all U.S. workers. They accounted for more than 8% of workers in four states—Nevada (10.2%), California (9.4%), Texas (8.9%), and New Jersey (8.2%). Undocumented immigrants are disproportionately concentrated in some industries and occupations. An estimated 26% of farm workers, 14% of construction workers, and 17% of cleaning and maintenance workers are undocumented. Overall, about one-third of undocumented immigrants in the labor force are service workers.

Under federal law, employers generally are barred from hiring people they know are undocumented, must verify that prospective employees can legally work in the U.S. (new hires must provide proof of legal status and complete an I-9 form), and are subject to fines for violations. But not all employers are following the law. The federal government's E-Verify program, initiated in 1997, allows employers to electronically check I-9 form information against federal Social Security and other databases. As of July 2015, almost 603,000 employers were using E-Verify, but in 2015 the program remained voluntary for most private employers who were not government contractors.

Immigration Reform

In recent years, various plans have been introduced in Congress or implemented by executive action to deal with the country's large undocumented immigrant population or, more broadly, to revise immigration policies. One legislative initiative, first introduced in 2001, was the **DREAM Act** (Development, Relief, and Education for Alien Minors), which was intended to provide a path to legal status for undocumented immigrants who came to the U.S. as children and had lived in the country for at least five years. This group became known informally as Dreamers, and it included some people who were so young when they arrived in the U.S. that they knew no other country of residence.

With the DREAM Act unable to win congressional approval, Pres. Barack Obama implemented a variation of it by executive action in 2012. The **DACA** (Deferred Action for Childhood Arrivals) program, which went into effect June 15, 2012, affected undocumented immigrants who met the following conditions:

- came to the U.S. before their 16th birthday
- were under age 31 as of June 15, 2012
- had lived continuously in the country since June 15, 2007
- did not have a criminal record
- were in school, had a high school education, or had served in the military

People in this group could obtain a permit to work in the U.S. for renewable two-year periods and would essentially be exempt from deportation (although they would still not be legal residents, since such a status change could not be made without congressional action). By the beginning of 2015, almost 639,000 people had received DACA work permits.

A wide-ranging, bipartisan immigration reform bill passed the U.S. Senate on June 27, 2013. Among its many provisions, the measure called for an increase in the number of Border Patrol agents to more than 38,000, required completion of the planned 700 miles of border fence, and made E-Verify mandatory for private employers. The bill also spelled out a variety of category revisions, numerical-ceiling modifications, and other changes in the LPR visa program intended to give greater priority to applicants with high levels of education and occupational skills and to reduce waiting times for certain groups. In one of its most controversial sections, the bill provided for provisional legal status and a 13-year path to citizenship for most undocumented immigrants, provided they met a number of requirements and paid fines and back taxes.

After the Senate bill failed to make progress in the House of Representatives, Pres. Obama took executive actions, Nov. 20, 2014, including the following:

- Expanding the DACA program to make applicants of any age who had lived in the U.S. at least since Jan. 1, 2010, eligible for three-year renewable work permits and effective exemption from deportation
- Allowing most undocumented parents of U.S. citizens and LPRs to obtain three-year renewable work authorizations and deportation exemptions.

It was estimated that at least 4 mil undocumented immigrants could benefit from these two actions. A lawsuit initiated by the state of Texas and later joined by 25 other states challenged the president's legal authority to take the executive actions. On Feb. 16, 2015, a federal district judge blocked implementation of the new programs while the lawsuit proceeded.

What Next?

Although the original DACA remained in effect in 2015, many other potential changes in U.S. immigration policy were stalled, and whoever is elected president in 2016 would have discretion to dispose of or continue any immigration measures instituted by executive action. Regarding undocumented immigrants, 2016 presidential candidates advocated a wide range of actions, from providing a path toward citizenship to promising large-scale deportation and revoking birthright citizenship. In spite of the challenges and uncertainties of its immigration policy, the U.S. remained a destination of choice for emigrants from many other countries.

CHRONOLOGY OF EVENTS

Nov. 1, 2014, to Oct. 31, 2015

The Chronology of Events reports the top National, International, and General news stories, month by month.

November 2014

National

Republicans Dominate Midterm Elections, Take Senate Majority—Republicans gained control of both houses of Congress for the first time since 2006 in midterm elections Nov. 4. The GOP picked up nine Senate seats—including five held by incumbent Democrats in Alaska, Arkansas, Colorado, Louisiana (after a Dec. runoff), and North Carolina—to claim a 54-seat majority. Five-term Sen. Mitch McConnell (R, KY)—who received 56% of the vote and defeated Kentucky Sec. of State Alison Lundergan Grimes (D) by a 15% margin—was expected to replace Sen. Harry Reid (R, NV) as majority leader when the 114th Congress convened in Jan. 2015. Republicans also increased their control of the House by 13 seats to 247, the largest majority since the 71st Congress (1929-31).

Republican candidates won 24 of 36 gubernatorial races, including several in states that commonly support Democratic candidates like Illinois, Maryland, and Massachusetts. Florida Gov. Rick Scott (R) narrowly defeated former Gov. Charlie Crist (D) in what became this election cycle's costliest gubernatorial race, with Scott and his supporters spending around $98.1 mil. Republicans also gained 11 state legislative chambers for a total of 68 nationwide.

According to the U.S. Elections Project, run by a Univ. of Florida professor, only 35.9% of eligible voters—down from 40.9% in 2010—participated in the 2014 elections.

Unemployment Rate Falls to Six-Year Low—The Labor Dept. announced Nov. 7 that the Oct. unemployment rate had dipped to 5.8%, its lowest level since July 2008. The economy added 214,000 jobs in Oct.—the ninth consecutive month of 200,000+ job growth—and figures for the previous two months were revised slightly upwards. Despite continued job growth, private-sector nonfarm hourly wages increased by 2% over the past year, barely ahead of inflation. Major stock indexes rose for a sixth consecutive week in spite of plunging oil prices, with the Dow Jones Industrial Average finishing Nov. at 17,828.24, up 2.5% from Oct. The S&P 500 closed the month at 2,067.56, gaining 2.5% from the month before, and the Nasdaq Composite Index finished Nov. at 4,791.63, climbing 3.5%.

Home Depot, the world's largest home improvement chain, said Nov. 7 that hackers had stolen some 53 mil customer email addresses in addition to data on 56 mil debit/credit cards in a breach first disclosed by the company in Sept.

Obama Announces Executive Action on Immigration, Could Shield up to 5 Million From Deportation—Citing Congress's inability to pass comprehensive immigration reform, Pres. Barack Obama Nov. 20 announced a series of executive actions that could prevent the deportation of some 5 mil undocumented immigrants. Along with removing the upper age limit from a 2012 program delaying deportation of immigrants who had entered the U.S. illegally as children, the orders offered relief to undocumented parents of U.S. citizens and ended the Secure Communities program, which had compelled police to detain undocumented immigrants stopped for minor violations. Obama argued that deporting the more than 11 mil immigrants currently in the U.S. illegally would be "impossible and contrary to our character," but he refrained from establishing a path to citizenship. Republican congressional leadership denounced the executive actions as unconstitutional. Texas originated and filed a lawsuit Dec. 3 on behalf of 18 states to prohibit the orders from going into effect. More states joined the suit in subsequent weeks (26 as of Jan. 2015). The U.S. Senate passed a comprehensive immigration reform bill in 2013, but the legislation stalled in the House.

Defense Secretary Resigns; U.S. Troops Allegedly Exposed to Chemical Weapons in Iraq—Under White House pressure, Defense Sec. Chuck Hagel announced his resignation Nov. 24 after less than two years in the position. Following the announcement, administration officials said that the president had lost confidence in Hagel's management of U.S. military actions against ISIS rebels in Iraq and Syria. (In a memo to the White House that leaked in late Oct., Hagel had argued for a more defined strategy in dealing with Syrian Pres. Bashar al-Assad.) Hagel, a Vietnam War veteran and former Republican senator, said he would continue to serve until the Senate confirmed a replacement. Obama Dec. 5 nominated former Pentagon official Ashton Carter. (Carter was sworn in Feb. 17, 2015.)

A *NY Times* report Nov. 6 alleged that the U.S. government failed to investigate claims made by 629 military personnel that they had been exposed to chemical weapons during the 2003-11 Iraq War. According to the report, the Pentagon failed to provide adequate medical care, did not warn troops about the possibility of exposure, and forbade those affected from speaking about possible incidents involving chemical weapons. The exposé followed earlier *Times* stories on chemical weapons exposures.

Protests Erupt After Grand Jury Fails to Indict Police Officer in Ferguson Shooting—A grand jury decided Nov. 24 not to indict Darren Wilson, a white police officer who fatally shot unarmed black 18-year-old Michael Brown in Ferguson, MO. Gov. Jay Nixon (D) had declared a state of emergency in advance of the jury's decision, activating the National Guard and deploying 700 troops to Ferguson. He sent an additional 1,500 troops following the decision. Sometimes-violent protests occurred that night in Ferguson and included looting, rioting, and fires. County police made 82 arrests related to area unrest that night. Wilson resigned from the Ferguson Police Dept. Nov. 29.

After the announcement, Pres. Obama urged acceptance of the jury's decision and spoke broadly on racial issues. Demonstrations were held in numerous communities across the U.S., with some protesters occupying roadways and staging mock "die-ins"; by Nov. 27, authorities had arrested more than 300 in Los Angeles alone.

In Cleveland, a deadly shooting by police Nov. 22 of Tamir Rice—a 12-year-old black boy who had been playing in a park with a pellet gun—was already drawing protests when the police released video of the shooting Nov. 26.

International

ISIS Rebels Maintain Hold on Iraq's Anbar Province But Lose Territory in North—The Sunni extremist group known as the Islamic State of Iraq and Syria (ISIS) continued its bloody offensive against a resistant Sunni tribe in the western Iraqi province of Anbar. Mass executions in late Oct. and early Nov. ended months of resistance from Albu Nimr tribesmen, with tribal leaders reporting a death toll of more than 600. In control of roughly 80% of Anbar province by Nov. 1, ISIS had surrounded a major airbase and the strategic Haditha Dam on the Euphrates River. Militants also increased attacks on government buildings in Ramadi in an effort to take over the provincial capital, located about 70 mi from Baghdad.

U.S. officials Nov. 16 confirmed the authenticity of a video showing the ISIS beheading of U.S. aid worker Peter Kassig, the third American and fifth Westerner whose decapitation was documented in footage posted online. Although U.S.-led airstrikes failed to break ISIS's hold on Anbar, the campaign helped Kurdish forces to regain some territory in northern Iraq and to blunt an ongoing siege by militants on Kobani, a Syrian city on the border with Turkey. Iraqi officials confirmed Nov. 18 that government troops had broken ISIS's hold on the Baiji oil refinery—the nation's largest—in northern Iraq.

Pres. Obama Nov. 7 approved the sending of an additional 1,500 military personnel to Iraq, approximately doubling the number of non-combatant advisory personnel serving there. The White House also said it would ask Congress for $5.6 bil in added spending to fight ISIS, including $1.6 bil to train and supply security forces. According to the BBC World Service and King's College London, ISIS was responsible for at least 2,206 deaths in Nov. The UK-based Syrian Observatory for Human Rights reported that as of Nov. 22, U.S.-led airstrikes in Syria had killed at least 785 militants and 52 civilians since Sept.

Mexican Authorities Detain Mayor Over Mass Kidnapping—Mexican federal police arrested fugitive Iguala mayor José Luis Abarca and wife María de los Ángeles Pineda Nov. 4 for allegedly ordering the abduction of 43 college students from the Ayotzinapa Normal School in late Sept. Authorities said they believed local police and the Guerreros Unidos organized crime group, beholden to the mayor, intercepted the students in Iguala to prevent them from disrupting a speech being given by Pineda. By early Nov., officials had arrested more than 50 people—mostly local police and Guerreros Unidos members—in connection with the incident, and three cartel members confessed Nov. 7 to killing the students and burning their bodies. The disappearances sparked protests throughout Mexico—including a violent Nov. 12 demonstration at the Guerrero state congress and another in Mexico City Nov. 21 attended by tens of thousands—over alleged government complicity with drug cartels.

The search for the missing students also uncovered numerous mass grave sites and focused attention on the tens of thousands of people who had disappeared because of the drug cartels over the past decade.

Islamist Rebels Continue Terror in Nigeria—A man suspected of belonging to the Islamist insurgent group Boko Haram set off a suicide bomb at a Nigerian boarding school Nov. 10, killing nearly 50 boys. The bombing was the latest in a string of attacks on non-Islamic schools in northern Nigeria alleged to have been carried out by Boko Haram over the last three years. On Nov. 28, suspected Boko Haram suicide bombers and gunmen killed at least 120 people in Kano at a mosque where a high-ranking religious official had called for anti-militant action. Nigerian officials had claimed to have reached a cease-fire with Boko Haram Oct. 17. But in a video released Nov. 1, Boko Haram leader Abubakar Shekau denied a cease-fire and claimed that the more than 200 girls the group kidnapped from a school in Apr. 2014 had been converted to Islam and married off. According to the Council on Foreign Relations, Boko Haram-related violence had killed more than 10,000 people between Nov. 2013 and Nov. 2014.

U.S. and China Reach Historic Climate Agreement—Chinese Pres. Xi Jinping and U.S. Pres. Barack Obama, the leaders of the world's two largest carbon-emitting countries, announced Nov. 12 a landmark deal to limit their countries' carbon outputs in an effort to fight climate change. The plan called for the U.S. to reduce its emissions by 26%-28% below 2005 levels by 2025; China, which agreed to cap its carbon output for the first time, would reach peak emissions by 2030 and make renewable sources 20% of its primary energy consumption by the same year. Opponents of the deal, particularly congressional Republicans, argued the agreement threatened the economy and U.S. autonomy. Global proponents hoped it would invigorate United Nations climate change treaty talks set to take place in Paris in Dec. 2015.

Taiwan's Ruling Party Suffers Massive Defeat—Taiwanese Prime Min. Jiang Yi-huah resigned Nov. 29 after his ruling Nationalist Party (the Kuomintang, or KMT) experienced major losses in local elections, in which about 67.5% of eligible voters participated. The pro-China KMT lost its 16-year grip on the mayoral seat of the capital, Taipei, and it held onto just 6 of the 15 (out of 22) counties/municipalities under its control before the election. The Democratic Progressive Party, which advocates for Taiwan as an independent nation, won 13 counties/municipalities. Officials representing China and Taiwan met in Feb. 2014 for the first direct talks since Taiwan split from the mainland in 1949.

Egyptian Court Absolves President of Murder—A court in Egypt Nov. 29 dismissed charges against ailing 86-year-old former Pres. Hosni Mubarak over the killing of 239 protesters during the 2011 uprising against his 30-year rule. The court acquitted Mubarak's security chief and six police officials while absolving Mubarak and his two sons of corruption charges. (Mubarak was sentenced to life in prison in 2012 for conspiracy to commit murder, but the verdict was overturned in Jan. 2013 on a technicality.) Following the court's decision, about 1,000 protesters attempted to gather at Cairo's Tahrir Square, the birthplace of the revolution, but at least two were killed when police fired tear gas and bird shot. At least 846 demonstrators were killed in protests leading up to Mubarak's Feb. 2011 resignation.

Libyan Clashes Kill Hundreds in Benghazi—Edging Libya closer to civil war, about 400 people were killed in six weeks of large-scale fighting between pro-government forces and Islamist militias in Benghazi, the country's second-largest city, according to a source cited in a Nov. 29 Reuters report. After Libyan troops in mid-Oct. drove rebels out of the area near the city's airport, fighting throughout Nov. was concentrated in Benghazi's commercial port, forcing its closure. In Aug., an alliance of Islamist militia groups known as Operation Dawn or Dawn of Libya had taken control of the national capital of Tripoli where they declared their own government and forced the country's newly elected parliament into exile. Galvanized by Islamic factions losing official legislative power, the militias' actions had plunged Libya into its worst violence since the Oct. 2011 ouster and killing of Muammar al-Qaddafi. The United Nations Nov. 18 announced that the violence had displaced nearly 400,000 people since May.

General

Bayern Wins Breeders' Cup Classic—Before a crowd of 66,114 at Santa Anita Park in Arcadia, CA, Bayern took an early lead and held off 18-1 long shot Toast of New York to win the 31st Breeders' Cup Classic by a nose Nov. 1. The 1.25-mi race with a $5-mil purse featured a controversial start that saw Bayern, with 6-1 odds, slam into undefeated favorite Shared Belief, who placed fourth. It was the first victory in the Breeders' Cup Classic for both jockey Martin Garcia and trainer Bob Baffert.

One World Trade Center Opens—New York City's One World Trade Center officially welcomed its first tenants Nov. 3, 13 years after the terrorist attacks of Sept. 11, 2001, destroyed the World Trade Center's twin towers. Developed by the Port Authority of New York and New Jersey, the $3.9-bil, 1,776-ft structure is recognized as the tallest building in the Western Hemisphere.

European Spacecraft Lands on Comet—The European Space Agency (ESA) made history Nov. 12 when—more than 10 years and 4 bil miles into its mission—the unmanned *Rosetta* spacecraft released a washing machine-sized probe to perform the first-ever controlled landing on a comet. The 220-lb *Philae* lander deployed to the 2.5-mi-wide mass of ice, rock, and dust dubbed 67P/Churyumov-Gerasimenko as they traveled through space at over 40,000 mph some 317 mil mi from Earth. The ESA hoped *Philae*'s instruments would continue to collect data about the comet—a remnant from the formation of the solar system some 4.5 bil years ago—until at least Mar. 2015. Rosetta was expected to remain in the comet's orbit until the end of 2015.

Comedian Faces Multiple Rape Allegations—Grammy, Emmy, and Golden Globe Award-winning actor and comedian Bill Cosby was at the center of a string of highly publicized rape and sexual abuse allegations throughout Nov. A Nov. 13 *Washington Post* op-ed by a former aspiring actress, whose account first appeared in *People* magazine in 2006, detailed being drugged and sexually abused by Cosby in 1986. At least two dozen other women had made similar accusations public by mid-Dec. 2014. Although Cosby had settled a lawsuit on assault charges in 2006, the allegations had mostly failed to sustain national attention until Oct. 2014, when a video clip of comedian Hannibal Buress calling the 77-year-old Cosby a rapist went viral.

December 2014

National

Senate Releases Report on CIA Interrogation Tactics, Accountability—The Senate Intelligence Committee Dec. 9 released a landmark 500-page report on the detention and interrogation of terrorism suspects following the Sept. 11, 2001, attacks. The report, part of a 6,700-plus-page study that has yet to be declassified, concluded that the Central Intelligence Agency's use of enhanced interrogation techniques (EITs) in secret overseas prisons was both ineffective in uncovering unique life-saving information and "far more brutal" than the agency had acknowledged. According to the report, the result of a half-decade inquiry, at least 39 detainees endured EITs such as confinement in boxes, exposure to cold temperatures, and sleep deprivation; one detainee likely died of hypothermia. In violation of the Geneva Conventions, at least three prisoners were subjected multiple times to waterboarding, a technique that creates the sensation of drowning. (Khalid Sheikh Mohammed, the self-described architect of the Sept. 11 attacks, was waterboarded at least 183 times in a single month.) At least 26 of 119 known detainees were determined to be wrongfully held, with some imprisoned for months after the CIA made the determination.

The Senate report concluded that CIA officials had withheld and provided false information to Congress about coercive tactics and did not fully brief Pres. George W. Bush on program details until 2006, the same year he officially disclosed the program's existence to the public. The CIA said it ceased its use of EITs in 2007, and Pres. Barack Obama issued executive orders in 2009 revoking the CIA's detention authority and banning the future use of EITs. The CIA and former Vice Pres. Dick Cheney denounced the report, but its release reignited debate about U.S. policies on detention and interrogation.

Oil Prices Fall to Five-Year Low as Wall Street Ends 2014 in the Black—U.S. monthly average crude oil prices—in decline since mid-year—fell to a five-year low in Dec. of $59 per barrel of West Texas Intermediate (WTI) crude (a key U.S. benchmark), from a high of $105 per barrel in June. Other global benchmark oil prices saw similar declines in the second half of 2014, but Saudi Arabia in late Nov. pressured members of the 12-nation Organization of Petroleum Exporting Countries (OPEC) to maintain current production levels. The *Wall Street Journal* Dec. 29 reported industry analysis that predicted the loss of as many as 40,000 U.S. oil industry-support jobs in 2015 if oil prices remained around $56 per barrel or under. WTI crude closed 2014 at $53 per barrel on Dec. 31.

In spite of falling energy stocks, the Dow Jones Industrial Average was flat for the month (down 0.02%) and closed Dec. 31 at 17,823.07, up 7.5% for the calendar year, its sixth straight year of growth. The S&P 500 closed at 2,058.90, –0.4% for the month but up 11.4% for the year. The Nasdaq Composite Index closed 2014 at 4,736.05, up 13.4% over 2013 but down 1.2% for the month. The U.S. Dept. of Labor's Dec. 5 jobs report showed that the economy had added 321,000 jobs in Nov., the 10th straight month of at least 200,000 jobs gained, and the unemployment rate held steady at 5.8%. The Bureau of Economic Analysis Dec. 23 released revised figures for third quarter 2014 showing that real GDP grew by 5.0%—the highest rate since 2003—a substantial increase over its initial 3.5% estimate.

Congress Passes $1.1-Trillion Spending Bill—Pres. Obama Dec. 16 signed into law a $1.1-tril appropriations bill that funded most of the federal government through the fiscal year ending in Sept. 2015. After contentious debate in both chambers, the spending bill was approved by the House (219-206) Dec. 11 and the Senate (56-40) Dec. 13. In voting for the bill, 57 House Democrats broke ranks with Minority Leader Nancy Pelosi (D, CA), who along with a Senate faction led by Sen. Elizabeth Warren (D, MA), had objected to provisions that loosened some banking restrictions imposed by the Dodd-Frank financial reform law. The Senate vote took place during a rare Saturday session, which was forced by Senate procedures following a maneuver led by Sen. Ted Cruz (R, TX) in symbolic protest of Obama's recent executive orders on immigration. A continuing resolution passed with the omnibus spending bill funded the Dept. of Homeland Security only through Feb. 27, 2015.

Two NYPD Officers Killed Amid Anti-Police Protests—A 28-year-old black man shot and killed New York City police officers Wenjian Liu and Rafael Ramos as they sat in a patrol car in Brooklyn Dec. 20. The shooter, Ismaaiyl Brinsley, who had traveled from Baltimore, then fled to a subway station, where he fatally shot himself. He had posted on social media before the ambush that he planned to kill cops in retribution for the police killings of unarmed black men Michael Brown and Eric Garner in 2014.

The incident escalated strained tensions between police unions and New York City Mayor Bill de Blasio, who had pledged to reform the NYPD and end its controversial stop-and-frisk tactics. Many officers and police union officials physically turned their backs on the mayor in public, including at the two officers' funerals. In the two weeks after the officers' deaths, the number of arrests made and criminal summonses and parking tickets issued were down drastically over the same weeks in 2013.

Officers Liu and Ramos were killed less than three weeks after a grand jury, Dec. 3, decided not to indict a white NYPD officer for placing a chokehold on 43-year-old Garner prior to Garner's death, which a city medical examiner had ruled a homicide. (Footage of Garner telling officers he could not breathe as he was being arrested went viral online after his death in July 2014.) Protests broke out in New York City in response to the grand jury verdict; large numbers of activists blocked access to key roads and bridges. Mostly peaceful demonstrations took place in other major U.S. cities, though protests in Seattle, WA, and Berkeley, CA, turned violent, with Berkeley police using tear gas on crowds Dec. 6-7. More than 25,000 people participated in an organized New York City protest Dec. 13.

International

Pro-European Parties Increase Power in Moldova—In the midst of pro-Russian separatist strife in neighboring Ukraine, Moldova's three main Western-leaning political parties Dec. 4 agreed to form a coalition that saw them win a combined 55 of 101 seats to the pro-Russia bloc's 46 seats following Nov. 30 parliamentary elections. The pro-Russia Socialist party garnered nearly 21% of votes, the most of any single party. Just under 56% of voters participated in the election, which was widely viewed as a referendum on Moldova's moves toward economic integration with the European Union. Moldova's Central Election Commission had banned the Russia-aligned Patria (Homeland) party on Nov. 26 over illegal funds received from outside the country. The country's Russia-backed breakaway region of Trans-Dniester did not participate in the election.

Hong Kong Democracy Protests End—Police in Hong Kong, China, Dec. 15 cleared protesters from the last remaining site they had occupied, in the city's Causeway Bay district. The activists had been campaigning for the right in 2017 to publicly nominate candidates for Hong Kong chief executive. The candidates are currently chosen by a 1,200-member committee, whose members are seen as largely pro-Beijing. Discussions between student leaders and the Hong Kong government had been deadlocked since Oct. Pro-democracy demonstrators experienced a setback overnight Nov. 30 when they tried to block government offices, and police responded with pepper spray and water cannons. Armed with a court order, authorities Dec. 11 faced little opposition as they began to dismantle the movement's main encampment, located in the city's Admiralty district.

Taliban Attack Kills Scores at Pakistani School—In the deadliest Taliban attack in Pakistan to date, at least seven armed militants Dec. 16 killed around 150 people, at least 132 of whom were children, at a military-run public school in Peshawar in northwestern Pakistan. Militants attacked students and teachers with gunfire and grenades before detonating suicide vests as Pakistani army commandos attempted to retake control of the school. A Taliban official told the BBC that the group had targeted the school, where most of the students were children of military personnel, in retaliation for government actions against the Taliban and their allies in North Waziristan. In a military offensive beginning Dec. 16, Pakistan killed more than 200 suspected extremists, including the alleged planner of the attack. (U.S. drone strikes killed nine suspected militants Dec. 26 in North Waziristan.) Pakistan Prime Min. Nawaz Sharif announced Dec. 17 that a moratorium on the death penalty in terror cases would be lifted.

After More Than 50 Years, Cuba and U.S. Seek to Normalize Relations—U.S. Pres. Barack Obama and Cuban Pres. Raúl Castro Dec. 17 announced their countries would reestablish diplomatic relations for the first time since 1961, when the U.S. severed its relationship with the island nation after the 1959 communist revolution that placed Fidel Castro in power. Earlier that day, Cuba released USAID subcontractor Alan Gross, who in 2009 had been sentenced to 15 years in prison for distributing illegal telecommunications equipment. Officials also secured the release of a U.S. spy in exchange for three Cuban agents. Along with reestablishing an embassy in the Cuban capital of Havana, Obama said he would take executive actions to increase financial remittance limits, permit U.S. and Cuban financial institutions to conduct transactions, and allow travelers to use U.S. credit and debit cards in Cuba. The administration also planned to review Cuba's status as a state sponsor of terrorism.

In his announcement, Obama argued that "isolation has not worked" and urged Congress to debate lifting the U.S. trade embargo against Cuba. Many Republican lawmakers expressed disapproval, and all three U.S. senators of Cuban descent—Ted Cruz (R, TX), Marco Rubio (R, FL), and Robert Menendez (D, NJ)—sharply criticized the policy shift.

U.S. Accuses North Korea of Movie Studio Hacking—The U.S. Federal Bureau of Investigation Dec. 19 publicly blamed North Korea for a series of hacks in late Nov. that targeted Sony Pictures Entertainment. Sony Dec. 17 canceled the Christmas Day theatrical release of its comedy *The Interview*, which focused on a fictional assassination attempt on North Korean leader Kim Jong Un, after the group that claimed responsibility for the hacking threatened to attack theaters showing the film. The studio announced Dec. 23 that the film would have a limited release in theaters beginning Dec. 25 and simultaneously be made available on demand. North Korea officially disclaimed involvement in the cyberattacks even as it blamed the U.S. for causing Internet outages beginning Dec. 20 within that country.

U.S., NATO End War in Afghanistan—A U.S.-led operation and a multinational NATO alliance formally ended combat missions in Afghanistan Dec. 28 after more than 13 bloody years, during which troops toppled a Taliban regime accused of harboring terrorists. The conclusion of NATO mission Intl. Security Assistance Force (ISAF), which involved 51 nations at its height, and the U.S.-led Operation Enduring Freedom, the longest war in U.S. history, marked the turnover of security to Afghanistan's own 350,000-member force.

Even as the war formally ended, violence continued. The United Nations, in its annual report released Feb. 18, 2015, estimated that 10,548 Afghan civilians were killed or injured in 2014, a 22% increase over the year before. NATO's new non-combat mission, known as Resolute Support, began Jan. 1, 2015, and consisted of about 13,000 coalition personnel (including close to 7,000 from the U.S.), who would provide ongoing training and support for Afghan forces.

NATO's presence in the country peaked in 2011 at approximately 140,000 troops, including around 100,000 from the U.S. In total, 3,485 allied troops, including 2,215 Americans, were killed in Afghanistan since Oct. 2001, and more than 20,000 U.S. personnel were wounded. According to a Congressional Research Service report published Dec. 8, 2014, Congress has appropriated a combined $1.6 tril for U.S. military operations in Afghanistan ($686 bil), Iraq ($815 bil), and other Global War on Terror operations since the attacks of Sept. 11, 2001.

General

Deadly Stampede Kills Dozens at Shanghai New Year Celebration—A stampede Dec. 31 in Shanghai, China, killed 36 people and injured 49. Some 300,000 New Year's Eve revelers had gathered near Chen Yi Square on the Bund, a waterfront in central Shanghai, where a fireworks show had been scheduled to be held until they were canceled Dec. 30. A government inquiry blamed the stampede on local authorities for failing to anticipate the large turnout and for dramatically reducing police presence from the year before.

Scientists Uncover World's Earliest Known Engraving—According to findings reported Dec. 3 in the journal *Nature*, zigzag lines carved into the shell of a freshwater mussel dating to an estimated 430,000 to 540,000 years ago represent the oldest known abstract markings. Scientists believe the now-extinct hominid *Homo erectus* etched the pattern using a shark's tooth. The pattern on the shell, one of hundreds Dutch scientist Eugene Dubois collected in Java, Indonesia, in the 1890s, was not apparent until the shell was photographed digitally in 2007. It predates the previous earliest known engravings—in Blombos Cave, South Africa—by over 300,000 years.

L.A. Galaxy Wins MLS Championship—The L.A. Galaxy became the first team in Major League Soccer history to win five championships when they defeated the New England Revolution, 2-1 in extra time, before a sellout crowd Dec. 7 at StubHub Center in Carson, CA. A goal by the Revolution's Chris Tierney had tied the game with 11 minutes of regulation play remaining, but Galaxy forward Robbie Keane, who was named the match's MVP, kicked the winning goal from a long pass in the game's 111th minute. The match marked the third time L.A. defeated New England in an MLS Cup Final as well as the last professional game for the Galaxy's Landon Donovan, the league's all-time scoring leader.

Two Hostages Killed in Sydney Standoff—An Iranian-born, self-described Muslim cleric held 18 people at gunpoint—some for more than 16 hours—in a café in Sydney, Australia, Dec. 15-16. The gunman, Man Haron Monis, was fatally shot by police, who stormed the café after Monis executed a hostage. (Another hostage was killed by ricochet from police gunfire when they broke the siege.)

Indonesian Airliner Crashes, Killing 162—AirAsia Indonesia Flight 8501 crashed Dec. 28 into the Java Sea off Borneo, killing all 162 people aboard. Officials lost radar contact with the Airbus A320-200 a little over 40 minutes into its flight from Surabaya, Indonesia, to Singapore. Wreckage and human remains were found in the sea two days later. A week after searchers recovered the airplane's black box—a flight data recorder and cockpit voice recorder—Indonesia's transportation minister announced, Jan. 20, that the jet had performed a maneuver that would have caused it to stall.

January 2015

National

114th Congress Convenes With Republicans at Helm—With a Republican majority in both the House (246-188, 1 vacancy) and Senate (54-44, 2 independents), for the first time in eight years, the 114th Congress convened Jan. 6. The new Congress included a record number of women (104) and Hispanic legislators (38). Mitch McConnell (R, KY) was elected Senate majority leader, and Harry Reid (D, NV) was elected minority leader; each had led his party's caucus prior to the election. House Minority Leader Nancy Pelosi (D, CA) and House Speaker John Boehner (R, OH) retained their leadership roles, though 25 Republican members—most representing the Tea Party faction—did not vote for Boehner.

Former Virginia Governor Sentenced in Corruption Case—A federal district court judge sentenced former Virginia Gov. Bob McDonnell (R) to two years in federal prison Jan. 6. McDonnell had been convicted in Sept. 2014 on 11 of 13 corruption charges for trading access to his office for $165,000 in loans and luxury gifts. His wife, Maureen McDonnell—who was tried concurrently and from whom he was reportedly estranged—was sentenced Feb. 20 to one year and a day in prison for her role, which included solicitation of a Rolex watch and a shopping spree.

Honda and BP See Record Penalties; Stock Market Declines With Oil Prices; Other Economic Developments—The Natl. Highway Traffic Safety Administration Jan. 8 fined Honda $70 mil for not reporting over 1,700 death and injury claims between 2003 and 2014 and for underreporting warranty claims. A federal judge Jan. 16 reduced the maximum fine energy company BP could be liable for, from $17.6 bil to a still record $13.7 bil, because it had spilled 3.2 mil barrels of crude oil into the Gulf of Mexico, not 4.1 mil barrels, following the 2010 *Deepwater Horizon* blowout.

The Labor Dept. reported Jan. 9 that 252,000 jobs had been added to the U.S. economy in Dec. 2014, bumping that year's average monthly job growth to 246,000 compared with the 2013 monthly average of 194,000 new jobs. The monthly unemployment rate in Dec. fell to 5.6% from 5.8% in Nov.

Oil prices fell to a six-year-low $45 per barrel Jan. 13 then rebounded, ending the month at nearly $53 per barrel for global benchmark Brent crude. Oil price uncertainty was partly to blame for poor Jan. stock performances: the Dow Jones Industrial Average fell 3.7%, losing 658.12 points and closing at 17,164.95; the S&P 500 fell 3.1%, closing at 1,994.99; and the Nasdaq Composite Index dropped 2.1%, closing at 4,635.24. The Bureau of Economic Analysis Jan. 30 announced that U.S. gross domestic product grew by 2.6% in fourth quarter 2014, which fell short of predictions.

Obama Outlines Agenda in State of the Union Address—In his Jan. 20 State of the Union Address, Pres. Barack Obama credited his administration's economic policies with helping the U.S. economy improve from the 2007-09 recession and called on Congress to approve proposed measures he said would benefit the middle class. This agenda included a 10-year, $60-bil plan making two years of community college free for most students; paid sick leave for workers; enhanced childcare tax credits; and a new tax break for working couples. These new initiatives would be funded through increased taxes on inherited wealth and raising the highest capital gains tax rate.

Obama pledged to veto any legislation that sought to repeal key accomplishments from his six years in office, including health care reform, financial regulatory reform, and his executive actions on undocumented immigrants. He also sought congressional authorization of U.S.-led military campaigns in Iraq and Syria against the extremist group known as ISIS and urged lawmakers to lift the trade embargo against Cuba and approve the closing of the U.S. military prison at Guantánamo Bay.

International

Boko Haram Attacks Leave up to 2,000 Dead in Nigeria—At least 150 (and as many as 2,000, according to Amnesty Intl.) were killed in attacks Jan. 3-7 by the Islamic extremist group Boko Haram in and around the northeastern Nigerian city of Baga. The militants razed most of the city, displacing some 10,000 residents, and seized a nearby military base. Neighbors Chad and Cameroon also came under attack, and soldiers killed 143 Boko Haram fighters at a Cameroon military camp Jan. 12. According to Human Rights Watch, Boko Haram had killed some 3,750 civilians in 2014. More than 1.5 mil Nigerians had been displaced since the group launched a military campaign in 2009 to create a caliphate under Sharia.

Meeting in Addis Ababa, Ethiopia, Jan. 30-31, the African Union agreed to send 7,500 troops to fight Boko Haram.

Extremists Kill 17 in France's Deadliest Terror Attacks in 50 Years—Two gunmen, who claimed to be aligned with the Sunni extremist organization al-Qaeda in the Arabian Peninsula (AQAP), stormed the Paris offices of French magazine *Charlie Hebdo*, Jan. 7, and systematically executed its editor-in-chief and four other cartoonists in retaliation for the magazine's satirical representations of the Prophet Muhammad. Chérif and Saïd Kouachi—brothers born in France to Algerian immigrants—killed seven others, including two police officers, then fled to a printing plant about 25 mi north of Paris. Both were killed in a shootout with police Jan. 9.

During the standoff, a gunman whom authorities linked to the brothers and identified as Amedy Coulibaly entered a Jewish supermarket in Paris, killing four people and taking at least 15 hostages. Police killed Coulibaly when they raided the market. Coulibaly's partner reportedly fled to Syria before police could detain her. Authorities also attributed the fatal shooting of a police officer in Paris the previous day to Coulibaly, who had pledged loyalty to the Sunni extremist group Islamic State in Iraq and Syria (ISIS) in a video. An AQAP leader released a video Jan. 14 claiming his group had planned and funded the *Charlie Hebdo* attacks.

Some 3.7 mil people participated in Jan. 11 unity marches around France, including up to 1.6 mil in Paris. Three days later, the cover of *Charlie Hebdo* featured a caricature of a tearful Muhammad. Some 8 mil copies of the issue eventually sold compared to the magazine's typical circulation of 60,000.

French Prime Min. Manuel Valls Jan. 21 announced comprehensive new anti-terrorism measures, including proposals to fight "jihadist indoctrination." France is home to more than 4.7 mil Muslims, or 7.5% of its population.

Election Shifts Rule in Sri Lanka—Former Sri Lanka health minister Maithripala Sirisena was sworn in Jan. 9, a day after he unexpectedly defeated two-term incumbent Pres. Mahinda Rajapaksa of the United People's Freedom Alliance 51.3% to 47.6% in elections participated in by a record 81.5% of eligible voters. Sirisena pledged to root out corruption and reverse a constitutional amendment that had abolished presidential term limits and increased presidential power. Rajapaksa's increasingly authoritarian rule, his apparent support for anti-Muslim violence, and his unpopularity with Sri Lanka's Tamil minority were cited as other key factors in the election results. Though hailed in 2009 for overseeing the end of a 26-year civil war with Tamil separatists, Rajapaksa was criticized for failing to adequately address war crimes allegations.

Haitian President Rules by Decree After Parliament Is Dissolved—Pres. Michel Martelly began governing Haiti by executive order Jan. 13 after he and opposition lawmakers were unable to agree on election legislation before the expiration of most lawmakers' mandates to hold their offices. A U.S.-backed Martelly proposal, which would have allowed current lower-house members to remain in office through Apr. 24 and upper-house members through Sept. 9, was rejected in a dispute over the electoral council's makeup. Prime Min. Laurent Lamothe had vacated his office Dec. 14, 2014, amidst sometimes violent protests calling for long-overdue national and local elections and for Martelly's resignation. On Jan. 16, Martelly publicly assumed responsibility for failing to hold elections and installed former Port-au-Prince Mayor Evans Paul as prime minister. The president retained 8 members of his old cabinet and named 12 new ministers; all were sworn in Jan. 18.

Under Rebel Assault, Yemen's Government Collapses—Yemeni Pres. Abd Rabbuh Mansur Hadi, Prime Min. Khaled Bahah, and other cabinet ministers resigned Jan. 22, five days after Houthi rebels—minority Zaidi Shiites—abducted the president's chief of staff. Houthis, who protested government corruption, limited job opportunities, and high fuel prices, were in control of much of northern Yemen even before they seized the nation's capital of Sanaa in Sept. 2014. But they had weak representation in the majority-Sunni south, where Hadi's support was strongest.

A suicide bomber suspected to be aligned with the AQAP killed 49 people Dec. 31 at a celebration in the mostly Sunni southern city of Ibb, which was held by Houthi militia. Opposed to both Houthi rebels and the Hadi-led government, AQAP was suspected a week later of detonating a car bomb outside a Sanaa police academy that killed at least 40 people. AQAP had killed two hostages—including a U.S. photojournalist—Dec. 6 during a failed rescue effort by U.S. forces.

Eurozone Bond Buying Aims to Spur Growth—In an attempt to boost sluggish economies throughout the eurozone, the European Central Bank (ECB) Jan. 22 initiated a program to buy at least 1.1 tril euros ($1.3 tril) in government and private bonds through Sept. 2016. Bond purchases would be in proportion to member nations' economies, with the ECB purchasing no more than one-third of a country's bonds. Countries that had already received international bailouts would need to fulfill stricter criteria before participating. Greece, which received bailouts in 2010 and 2012, was not immediately eligible.

Saudi Arabian King Dies—King Abdullah bin Abdul Aziz al-Saud of Saudi Arabia died Jan. 23 at the age of 90, a decade after he officially took power and 20 years after he became de facto leader when his predecessor suffered a stroke. During his rule, Abdullah took steps to loosen certain restrictions on women, including establishing a coed research university and allowing women to vote in municipal elections beginning in 2015. He was criticized for suppressing public protests but lauded for all but eliminating al-Qaeda's Saudi Arabian network. Abdullah's 79-year-old half-brother, Salman, ascended a throne that faced many challenges, including falling oil prices, regional turmoil, and demands for additional reform.

Bloodshed Spurs Collapse of Ukrainian Peace Talks—Pro-Russian separatists waging a more than nine-month-old insurgency in eastern Ukraine were blamed for Jan. 24 rocket attacks on the coastal city of Mariupol that killed at least 30 people and injured at least 100. Six Ukrainian soldiers died defending the Donetsk airport, which rebels overtook Jan. 22. Earlier that week, Ukrainian troops allegedly came under fire from Russian forces in northern Luhansk, bolstering longstanding claims Russia was escalating the conflict.

The attacks followed repeated fruitless diplomatic efforts to reestablish a collapsed cease-fire. Standard & Poor's, Jan. 26, downgraded Russia's credit rating—weakened by international sanctions and falling oil prices—to junk status. Amid ongoing bloodshed, both rebels and Ukrainian officials canceled another round of peace talks scheduled for Jan. 30 in Belarus. The United Nations estimated that more than 5,000 people had been killed and over 920,000 displaced in the conflict as of Jan. 23.

Anti-Austerity Party Takes Power in Greece—Greek voters Jan. 25 rejected the ruling conservative New Democracy (ND) party in favor of far-left Syriza in national elections in which 63.7% of eligible voters participated. Syriza won 36.3% of the vote and captured 149 of 300 parliamentary seats, while ND garnered 27.8% and 76 seats. The vote was seen to reflect dissatisfaction with the stringent austerity measures imposed in 2010 as conditions of Greece's financial bailout. Syriza's Alexis Tsipras was sworn in the next day as prime minister to head an anti-austerity coalition with the center-right Independent Greeks (13 seats). Despite assertions that his government would not cooperate with international lenders, Tsipras in late Feb. agreed to enact some financial reforms mandated by eurozone officials to extend bailout aid for another four months.

General

Four Elected to Baseball Hall of Fame—The Baseball Writers' Assn. of America announced Jan. 6 that it had elected seven-time All-Star position player Craig Biggio and pitchers Randy Johnson, Pedro Martínez, and John Smoltz to the Natl. Baseball Hall of Fame. All three pitchers were chosen in their first year of eligibility; Biggio was on his third ballot. Johnson, a five-time Cy Young Award-winner, was elected with 97.3% of the vote. Eight-time All-Star Martínez received 91.1%, and Smoltz, the only pitcher in league history to surpass both 200 wins (213) and 150 saves (154), received 82.9%. Four-time Gold Glove Award-winner Biggio received 82.7% of the vote.

Buckeyes Win Inaugural College Football Playoff—The Ohio State Buckeyes claimed a fifth national championship and the first-ever title of the four-team College Football Playoff—which replaced the Bowl Championship Series in place the last 16 seasons—when the team scored a 42-20 victory over the Oregon Ducks Jan. 12 in Arlington, TX. Ohio State running back Ezekiel Elliott, the game's offensive MVP, ran for 246 yards, the most in NCAA championship history. Buckeye head coach Urban Meyer won his first national title with Ohio State; he had previously won two with Florida.

Flooding Kills Hundreds in Southern Africa—Heavy seasonal rains—falling since Dec. 2014 in Madagascar, Malawi, and Mozambique—culminated in tropical cyclone Chezda in mid-Jan., triggering floods, landslides, and building collapses that killed up to 400 people and displaced more than 300,000 by the end of the month. The government of Malawi declared more than half the country a disaster area Jan. 13.

Scientists Rank 2014 Hottest Year on Record—Independent analyses released Jan. 16 by scientists at both NASA and the Natl. Oceanic and Atmospheric Administration concluded that 2014 was Earth's warmest year since record collecting began in 1880. According to the data, the 9 of the 10 hottest years on record have occurred since 2000 (the exception being 1998). Earth's average surface temperature has increased about 1.4°F since 1880.

Papal Visit Draws Record Crowds—Wrapping up a six-day trip to Asia Jan. 18, Pope Francis celebrated an outdoor mass in the Philippines capital of Manila in front of a rain-soaked crowd estimated at 6 mil, a record for a papal gathering. The visit, which was Francis's second to the continent, also included a visit to Sri Lanka, where he visited a Buddhist temple.

Earlier in the month, the leader of the world's 1.2 bil Roman Catholics named 20 new cardinals—including the first-ever cardinals from Cabo Verde, Myanmar, and Tonga. The cardinals' formal appointment Feb. 14 marked the first time non-European members represented a majority in the Church's electoral body.

Williams, Djokovic Win Australian Open Titles—Serena Williams overcame illness Jan. 31 to win her sixth Australian Open title when she defeated Maria Sharapova of Russia (6-3, 7-6 (7-5)) in a 1 hr., 51-min. match at Rod Laver Arena in Melbourne. The following night, Serbian Novak Djokovic became the first man in the Open era to win five Australian championships, besting the UK's Andy Murray in a 3 hr., 39-min. match, 7-6 (7-5), 6-7 (4-7), 6-3, 6-0.

Eight Elected to Football Hall of Fame—A Pro Football Hall of Fame panel Jan. 31 elected six-time All-Pro linebacker Junior Seau, who committed suicide in 2012 while suffering from degenerative brain disease believed to be caused by repeated head trauma. The panel also elected receiver Tim Brown; running back Jerome Bettis; guard Will Shields, who played in 224 consecutive games over 14 years; Charles Haley, the only player to appear on five Super Bowl-winning teams; Vikings center Mick Tingelhoff; Packers general manager Ron Wolf; and NFL executive Bill Polian.

February 2015

National

Obama Proposes Budget; Miscellaneous Leadership Changes—Pres. Barack Obama Feb. 2 proposed a $4-tril federal budget for fiscal year 2016 (which begins Oct. 1, 2015) that would spend $478 bil on transportation and infrastructure over six years and continue deficit reduction, with a projected $474-bil deficit for 2016—the lowest since 2008. The budget included new outlays directed at middle- and low-income earners, including a childcare tax-credit expansion, a two-working-adult household tax break, and a program that would make two years of community college tuition-free. The proposal also included a 7% (or $74-bil) increase to spending levels set by automatic spending cuts approved in 2011. To offset increased spending, Obama's plan called for at least $1.5 tril in new taxes—most of which would come from corporations and wealthy taxpayers—over the next decade.

The Senate Feb. 12 confirmed Ashton Carter as the new secretary of defense, replacing Chuck Hagel. Obama Feb. 18 named interim Secret Service director Joseph Clancy as the agency's permanent leader. Clancy had led the agency since Oct. 2014, when director Julia Pierson resigned after a series of high-profile security lapses.

S&P, Morgan Stanley to Pay Billions in Subprime Mortgage-Related Fines; Other Economic Developments—The credit rating agency Standard & Poor's agreed Feb. 2-3 to pay $1.5 bil to settle charges that it knowingly issued inflated ratings to the subprime mortgage bonds at the center of the financial crisis that peaked in 2008. Morgan Stanley agreed Feb. 25 to pay $2.6 bil to resolve Justice Dept. claims that the investment firm misrepresented the quality of mortgage-backed securities that it sold. As of late Feb., major U.S. financial institutions had paid about $130 bil in settlements and fines connected with the mortgage crisis.

The nation's second largest health insurer, Anthem, reported Feb. 4 that some 80 mil personal records, including those of up to 18.8 mil non-customers, had been illegally accessed. While hackers were able to download names, Social Security numbers, birth dates, addresses, and income data, Anthem said it did not believe credit card or medical information had been compromised.

The Jan. jobs report, released Feb. 6 by the Labor Dept., showed that 257,000 jobs had been added to the U.S. economy during the month. The unemployment rate rose slightly to 5.7% from 5.6%. Wall Street rebounded from an anemic Jan. as Apple share prices rose, Feb. 10, to set a market capitalization record of more than $710 bil. (Apple would replace AT&T on the Dow Jones Industrial Average on Mar. 19.) The Dow Jones achieved a new closing high of 18,224.57 Feb. 25 and ended the month at 18,132.70, up 5.6% from Jan. The S&P 500 finished Feb. at 2,104.50, up 5.5% from the month before, and the Nasdaq Composite Index closed at 4,963.53, climbing 7.1%.

Judicial Injunction Blocks Actions on Immigration; DHS Shutdown Threats in Congress—A federal judge Feb. 16 temporarily blocked Pres. Obama's executive orders offering a reprieve from deportation to some 5 mil undocumented immigrants in the U.S. In halting the program, parts of which were set to go into effect two days later, U.S. District Judge Andrew Hanen ruled that a Texas-led lawsuit, which was joined by 25 other states challenging the legality of Obama's orders, had sufficient merit to proceed.

With Dept. of Homeland Security (DHS) funding set to expire Feb. 27, a partial DHS shutdown was narrowly averted when a one-week extension passed late that night. For weeks, conservative-bloc House Republicans had demanded that any DHS funding bill include amendments that would block Obama's executive orders on immigration. Such a bill had easily passed in the House in Jan., 236-191, but was obstructed in the Senate. House Speaker John Boehner (R, OH) had tried to buy more time to win over the Senate, but ultimately facilitated a vote on a bill, stripped of the amendments, to fully fund the DHS through Sept. 30. That passed Mar. 3, 257-167, with the support of just 75 Republicans.

Oregon Governor Resigns Amid Influence-Peddling Scandal—Just weeks after he was sworn into his fourth term, Oregon Gov. John Kitzhaber (D) resigned his office Feb. 18 following allegations his fiancée Cylvia Hayes had used her role as an unpaid energy policy adviser to Kitzhaber to obtain lucrative consulting work with renewable energy organizations. Oregon Sec. of State Kate Brown (D) was sworn in as governor Feb. 18; she was the country's first openly bisexual governor.

Obama Issues Rare Veto on Keystone Pipeline Bill—Using his veto power for only the third time since taking office in 2009, Pres. Obama Feb. 24 rejected a bill approving construction of the 1,179-mi Keystone XL oil pipeline that would link the Canadian province of Alberta with Midwest and Gulf Coast refineries. The administration said the president vetoed the bill because it bypassed an ongoing State Dept. review. Despite lacking the votes to overturn a veto, Republican lawmakers—who touted the pipeline's job-creating potential—had made passing Keystone a priority after convening the new Congress in Jan. The bill's opponents cited the potential for spills as well as its promotion of Alberta's highly polluting tar-sands oil. The vetoed bill had been passed by the Senate (62-36) Jan. 29 and House (270-152) Feb. 11.

Strict Net Neutrality Rules Approved—Categorizing broadband Internet as a telecommunications service, the Federal Communications Commission by a 3-2 vote Feb. 26 approved regulations requiring that wired and mobile Internet service providers (ISPs) give equal access to all legal content and applications. Supported by content providers such as Google, Netflix, and Amazon, the "net neutrality" rules were opposed by many ISPs and cable companies. While the rules barred broadband providers from creating "fast lanes" in favor of certain Internet content, they did not prevent ISPs from charging customers differing rates for corresponding speeds.

Measles Outbreak Calls Attention to Vaccination Rates—According to the Centers for Disease Control (CDC), nearly 75% of 170 measles cases reported in 2015 as of Feb. 27 were linked to a late-Dec. 2014 outbreak at Disneyland Park in Anaheim, CA. (Illinois, Nevada, and Washington also faced unrelated flare-ups, with 13 Illinois cases linked to a daycare facility.) Though the U.S. vaccination rate for MMR (measles, mumps, and rubella) was 92%, the CDC said the majority of those sickened by measles in 2015 had not been immunized. The CDC confirmed 668 measles cases in 2014, a record high since public health officials declared the highly contagious disease eliminated from the U.S. in 2000.

International

ISIS Execution Videos Draw Attacks From Jordan, Egypt; Other Developments—The Sunni extremist group known as the Islamic State of Iraq and Syria (ISIS) released a video Feb. 3 showing militants burning alive a captured Jordanian fighter pilot. Jordan, in retaliation, executed two ISIS prisoners and launched additional airstrikes against the militants in their de facto capital of Raqqa and elsewhere in Syria. ISIS Feb. 15 released footage showing the beheadings of 21 Egyptian Christians in Libya; Egypt launched airstrikes against ISIS targets in Libya the next day. Militants on Feb. 23 allegedly kidnapped more than 200 Syrian Christians. The *Washington Post* Feb. 26 identified "Jihadi John"—a masked man who killed at least six hostages in ISIS videos—as Kuwaiti-born Londoner Mohammed Emwazi.

U.S. Pres. Barack Obama Feb. 11 formally sought congressional approval for use of military force against ISIS. The U.S. had been participating in airstrikes against ISIS targets in Iraq and Syria since Aug. and Sept. 2014, respectively. ISIS continued to hold about one-third of the territory in both Iraq and Syria. According to the UN Assistance Mission for Iraq's year-end report, 2014 was Iraq's deadliest year since 2006-07, the peak years of fighting there, with at least 12,282 civilians killed.

Ukraine Peace Talks Bring Cease-Fire Deal; Putin Critic Assassinated—Russia, Ukraine, Germany, and France agreed to a new cease-fire deal Feb. 12 in Minsk, Belarus, as part of a 13-point roadmap aimed at halting months of fighting between pro-Russian separatists and Ukrainian forces in eastern Ukraine. The plan, which followed a failed Sept. 2014 truce, went into effect Feb. 15. The cease-fire reportedly took hold in parts of the region, but fierce clashes continued to rage in Debaltseve. Earlier in Feb., the U.S. reportedly engaged in talks about supplying arms to Ukrainian forces, a tactic German Chancellor Angela Merkel rejected. The UN reported that at least 5,809 people had died in the conflict as of Feb. 28.

Russian physicist and former Deputy Prime Min. Boris Nemtsov was shot and killed in Moscow Feb. 27. An outspoken critic of Russian Pres. Vladimir Putin, Nemtsov had been preparing a report on Russia's alleged military involvement in Ukraine and planning to host an opposition rally Mar. 1. Police arrested five Chechen suspects, but speculation over the assassination continued, with some Nemtsov supporters accusing the Kremlin of involvement.

Misconduct Allegations Against Argentina President Follow Prosecutor's Death—A prosecutor Feb. 13 charged Argentinean Pres. Cristina Fernández de Kirchner with trying to block an inquiry into Iran's alleged involvement in the 1994 bombing of a Buenos Aires Jewish center that killed 85 people. The formal accusation came less than a month after the case's original prosecutor, Alberto Nisman, was found shot dead. Nisman had drafted a request for Kirchner's arrest and was scheduled to appear before Argentina's congress regarding allegations that Kirchner had promised to cancel warrants against Iranian suspects. Nisman's case against the president was formally dismissed by a three-judge panel on May 12.

Yemeni President Rescinds Resignation as Rebels Reach Compromise—Kept under house arrest for a month by Shiite Houthi rebels, Yemen's ousted president Abd Rabbuh Mansur Hadi retracted his Jan. 22 resignation on Feb. 24 after escaping to the south. Houthis—who seized the Yemeni capital of Sanaa in Sept. 2014—had dissolved the nation's parliament Feb. 6 and appointed several of Hadi's former ministers to a national security committee Feb. 8. Demanding a more representative government, Houthi leaders Feb. 20 reached a UN-mediated compromise that would retain the parliament but add, as something of an upper chamber, a council comprised of Houthis and other underrepresented groups. Claiming his resignation was forced, Hadi denounced the Houthi reforms and called on government ministers to convene in Aden, the capital of formerly independent South Yemen. Citing security concerns, the U.S., UK, and France closed their embassies in Sanaa Feb. 10-13.

General

Patriots Defeat Seahawks in Super Bowl XLIX—The New England Patriots edged the Seattle Seahawks, 28-24, at Univ. of Phoenix Stadium in Glendale, AZ, Feb. 1 to win Super Bowl XLIX. The Seahawks built up a 24-14 lead by the end of the third quarter and looked likely to repeat as champions. But Patriots quarterback Tom Brady—the game's eventual MVP—led two touchdown drives and gained the lead with only 2:02 remaining. The Seahawks returned to within one yard of the end zone and attempted a slant pass that was intercepted by Patriot Malcolm Butler. Brady threw for four touchdowns and 328 yards, completing 37 of 50 passes with 2 interceptions. An average 114.4 mil viewers tuned in, making it the most watched in history; the halftime show, starring Katy Perry, also set an all-time high, with 118.5 mil viewers.

In late Jan., the NFL launched an investigation into allegations that the Patriots used underinflated footballs during the AFC championship game Jan. 18 against the Indianapolis Colts.

TransAsia Plane Crash Kills 43 in Taiwan—Taiwan's TransAsia Airways Flight 235 crashed into the Keelung River shortly after takeoff from Taipei Feb. 4, killing 43 of 58 on board. Video taken from a vehicle dashboard showed the plane dipping sharply to the left, its wing crushing a taxi. A preliminary investigation revealed one of the ATR-72's two engines had lost power, and the crew accidentally turned off the functioning engine while attempting to restart the other.

Sam Smith and Beck Big Winners at Grammy Awards—British crooner Sam Smith and multi-genre American musician Beck were the top winners at the 57th annual Grammy Awards ceremony Feb. 8 in Los Angeles, CA. Smith won record of the year and song of the year for the ballad "Stay With Me"; he also claimed awards for best new artist and best pop vocal album. Beck claimed best rock album and beat out Beyoncé and Pharrell Williams (who each won three Grammys), Smith, and Ed Sheehan for album of the year.

NBC Suspends Top News Anchor—NBC suspended *NBC Nightly News* managing editor and anchor Brian Williams for six months Feb. 10 for misrepresenting his experiences covering the Iraq War. On the Jan. 30 program, Williams said that he'd been on a helicopter in 2003 that was struck by a grenade. But according to crew members on another helicopter interviewed by *Stars and Stripes*, Williams's helicopter was never fired upon (it trailed by about an hour three others that took fire). Williams had reported the incident accurately in 2003, but misreported it multiple times on radio and TV as early as 2008.

Killing of Three Muslims Sparks Outrage—The Feb. 10 killing of three young Muslims—a newlywed man and woman and her sister—in Chapel Hill, NC, attracted national attention when relatives alleged the slayings were fueled by anti-Muslim hate. Local police said the killings appeared to have been motivated by a parking dispute. The assailant, a neighbor of the victims, had confessed and was charged with three counts of first-degree murder. The FBI Feb. 12 launched a preliminary hate crime investigation into the incident.

***Birdman* a Surprise Favorite at Oscars; "American Sniper" Killer Sentenced**—The black comedy *Birdman* received the Oscar for best picture at the 87th Academy Awards ceremony in Los Angeles, CA, Feb. 22, with the movie's Alejandro G. Iñárritu also claiming awards for best director and best original screenplay. Eddie Redmayne won best actor as ALS-afflicted physicist Stephen Hawking in *The Theory of Everything*, and veteran character actor J. K. Simmons won his first Oscar for best supporting actor as an abusive teacher in *Whiplash*. Julianne Moore received best actress as an Alzheimer's sufferer in *Still Alice*, and *Boyhood* matriarch Patricia Arquette won best supporting actress. First-time Oscar host Neil Patrick Harris received mixed reviews; the ceremony drew 36.6 mil viewers and its lowest ratings since 2009.

Despite receiving nominations for six Oscars, the war drama *American Sniper*—the top-grossing U.S. film of 2014—won just one, for best sound editing. Directed by Clint Eastwood, the film told the story of U.S. Navy SEAL Chris Kyle, who was fatally shot at a Texas gun range in early 2013 by a former Marine whom Kyle was mentoring. A jury Feb. 24 found Eddie Ray Routh guilty of the murders of Kyle and another man, and sentenced him to life in prison.

Logano Wins Daytona 500—Joey Logano won the Daytona 500 Feb. 22 in Daytona Beach, FL, holding off 2014 Sprint Cup champion Kevin Harvick on the restart of a two-lap overtime. Logano claimed victory under a caution flag following a last-lap pileup involving eight cars, including three-time Daytona winner Jeff Gordon's. Defending Daytona 500 winner Dale Earnhardt Jr. finished third, while Denny Hamlin and Jimmie Johnson placed fourth and fifth, respectively. The 43-year-old Gordon, who led for a race-high 87 laps, completed what he said was his final Daytona 500 in 33rd place.

March 2015

National

Petraeus Reaches Plea Over Classified Data Leak; CIA Announces Reorganization—Former Central Intelligence Agency Dir. David Petraeus reached a plea deal Mar. 3 with the Justice Dept. over charges that he shared highly classified information with Paula Broadwell, his biographer, with whom he had an extramarital affair while heading the agency. In pleading guilty, Petraeus admitted he disclosed security codes, war strategy, intelligence capabilities, and covert officers' identities and was sentenced in late Apr. to two years' probation and a $100,000 fine. The former four-star general and commander of U.S. forces in Iraq and Afghanistan resigned from the CIA in 2012.

CIA Dir. John Brennan Mar. 6 announced a major restructuring of the intelligence agency. Its operations and analytical teams would be combined into 10 new centers, each led by an assistant director and devoted to a particular subject or region.

Justice Dept. Releases Damning Report on Ferguson But Declines to Prosecute Officer; Other Police Shootings—The U.S. Dept. of Justice Mar. 4 released a scathing review of the Ferguson, MO, police department, which had received international attention following the Aug. 2014 fatal shooting of unarmed black 18-year-old Michael Brown by one of its officers. The review concluded officers and city officials, in particular municipal court employees, had routinely discriminated against African Americans—who made up 67% of the suburban St. Louis city's population but 93% of arrests—and engaged in ticketing practices aimed at increasing city revenue at the expense of civil rights. The report noted police frequently used unnecessary force; 88% of incidents involving force impacted black residents. The Justice Dept. mandated that Ferguson make sweeping policy changes or face a federal lawsuit. Ferguson police chief Thomas Jackson resigned Mar. 12; two Ferguson police officers were shot and seriously injured in the wake of demonstrations that greeted the announcement of his resignation. A suspect admitted to the shootings but claimed he was not aiming at the officers.

The Justice Dept. Mar. 4 declined to file federal charges against Ferguson officer Darren Wilson, reporting their forensic analysis showed Wilson did not act "unreasonably" or with the criminal intent required to prosecute and that Brown had not been running away when he was shot.

A fatal shooting by three Los Angeles police officers of an unarmed homeless black man Mar. 1 was caught on video by a bystander; police officials said the man attempted to take an officer's gun when they fell to the ground during a struggle. Later that week, a police officer in Madison, WI, shot dead an unarmed biracial teen after the young man allegedly knocked him down, setting off large-scale demonstrations.

Secret Service Agents Crash Into White House Barricade—Two senior-level Secret Service agents Mar. 4 drove a car into White House security barricades. The incident disturbed an ongoing investigation into a package left nearby by a woman claiming it was a bomb. At the behest of an agency supervisor, the agents were allowed to leave without having to undergo a sobriety test. The incident occurred two weeks after Joseph Clancy became the permanent director of the Secret Service, which was beset by security lapses in 2014, including two incidents in Sept. and Oct. in which an individual breached security and made it into the White House before being stopped.

Unemployment Rate Reaches Seven-Year Low; Mortgage-Related Lawsuits Settled; Other Economic News—The Labor Dept. reported Mar. 6 that the economy had added 295,000 jobs in Feb.; the unemployment rate fell to 5.5%, its lowest level since 2008. Shares in Kraft surged 36% Mar. 25 after Heinz announced it would acquire Kraft in a blockbuster merger that would create the world's fifth-largest food-and-beverage company; it expected to take in $28 bil in sales annually. The U.S. Bureau of Economic Analysis reported Mar. 27 that the real gross domestic product grew by an annual rate of 2.2% in fourth quarter 2014 and by 2.4% in 2014. The Dow Jones Industrial Average closed the month at 17,776.12, down 2.0% from Feb., while the S&P 500 finished Mar. at 2,067.89, a 1.7% decline from the month before. The Nasdaq Composite Index closed at 4,900.88, down 1.3%.

A New York appellate court Mar. 5 approved an $8.5-bil settlement between Bank of America and investors who had purchased $174 bil in mortgage securities issued by the former Countrywide Financial Corp., which Bank of America bought in 2008. In the largest-ever non-criminal/regulatory class-action settlement in history, American International Group won approval Mar. 20 for a $970.5-mil deal resolving shareholder claims related to high-risk subprime mortgage loans that contributed to the financial crisis that peaked in 2008.

International

Iraqi and Iranian Forces Retake Much of Tikrit From ISIS; Other Regional Developments—After about nine days of heavy fighting, a 30,000-strong force of Iraqi troops fighting alongside Shiite militias—including many Iranian groups—by Mar. 11 retook most of the strategic Iraqi city of Tikrit from the Sunni extremist group known as Islamic State of Iraq and Syria (ISIS). The offensive, the largest by Iraqi forces since ISIS seized much of northern Iraq and Syria in 2014, stalled in late Mar., at which point the central Iraqi government requested U.S. air support. U.S.-led airstrikes commenced in Tikrit Mar. 25 over the objections of Iranian and Iraqi fighters. With the city in ruins, ISIS was forced out of Tikrit Apr. 1 in a victory that was viewed as a key step towards reclaiming Iraq's second largest city of Mosul to the north.

Iraqi officials Mar. 7 said ISIS militants had bulldozed the ancient Assyrian city of Nimrud and destroyed the 2,000-year-old UNESCO-designated ruins of Hatra. ISIS was blamed for the deaths of at least 120 people in Syria on Mar. 20 alone, including 45 killed while celebrating the Kurdish new year in Hasakeh, according to the UK-based Syrian Observatory for Human Rights.

According to the UN Assistance Mission for Iraq (UNAMI) figures released Apr. 1, at least 729 Iraqi civilians (and 268 security forces and allied militias) were killed in Mar. 2015 alone.

Israeli Prime Minister Wins Fourth Term After Voicing Opposition to Iran Nuclear Deal in U.S.—Israeli Prime Min. Benjamin Netanyahu's conservative Likud party Mar. 17 achieved a strong victory in parliamentary elections in which 72.3% of eligible voters participated despite pre-election polls giving Zionist Union a slight advantage. Claiming 30 of 120 seats—12 more than it won in 2013—Likud easily bested the center-left Zionist Union's 24 seats. The day before voting, Netanyahu had said he would not support a Palestinian state—a reversal of a 2009 declaration—and claimed that foreign-funded left-wing organizations were "distorting the true will of the Israeli citizens" by busing Arab Israelis to polls. His remarks caused concern in the international community, including in the U.S., which had pursued a two-state solution for two decades. Appearing to backtrack, Netanyahu Mar. 19 declared he supported a Palestinian state under demilitarized conditions. Netanyahu May 6 scraped together a 61-seat coalition of right-leaning and religious parties, formalizing his fourth—and third consecutive—term as prime minister.

At the invitation of U.S. House Speaker John Boehner (R, OH), Netanyahu Mar. 3 had addressed a joint session of the Republican-led U.S. Congress, where he argued against a pending U.S.-negotiated agreement with Iran that would attempt to limit rather than dismantle that country's nuclear program. Netanyahu criticized the negotiations, claimed the proposed deal would not prevent Iran from acquiring nuclear weapons, and said that Iran could not be trusted. White House officials asserted Boehner violated diplomatic protocol by inviting Netanyahu without first contacting the administration; Pres. Barack Obama and Vice Pres. Biden declined to attend the address, as did 58 Democratic lawmakers. Sen. Tom Cotton (R, AR) Mar. 9 sent a letter to Iranian leaders cosigned by 46 other GOP senators warning that a nuclear deal might be reversed by the next president. The White House said the letter was an inappropriate attempt to undercut its foreign policy.

Militants Kill 22 in Tunisian Museum Attack—Three gunmen raided Tunisia's National Bardo Museum Mar. 18 in the capital of Tunis, killing 21 foreigners and 1 Tunisian police officer and injuring dozens more. Two of the assailants were killed by security forces; one escaped. Although ISIS claimed responsibility, officials speculated the militants may have acted independently. The assault raised concerns that Tunisia, which held its first democratic elections since its 1956 independence in 2014, would adopt more autocratic rule to combat terror fears.

Sunni Coalition Launches Strikes Against Yemeni Rebels—A Saudi Arabia-led alliance of 10 majority-Sunni countries began airstrikes Mar. 25 against minority Houthi rebels, who took over Sanaa, the Yemeni capital, and deposed Yemeni Pres. Abd Rabbuh Mansur Hadi in Jan. Hours after Hadi fled to Saudi Arabia, the airstrikes targeted Sanaa military bases and other Houthi positions across Yemen. The alliance cited the objective of reinstalling Hadi, but international observers cautioned that the operation could devolve into a proxy war between Saudi Arabia and Iran, which was widely believed to be supporting the Houthis. Further complicating the conflict, former Yemeni Pres. Ali Abdullah Saleh, toppled in the 2011 revolt that left then-Vice Pres. Hadi in power, aligned himself with the Houthis in an attempt to regain the presidency; he retained the loyalty of multiple Yemeni military groups.

ISIS claimed its Yemeni affiliate was responsible for Mar. 20 suicide bombings that killed at least 130 people at two Sanaa mosques affiliated with the Houthis. Leaders of the 22-nation Arab League agreed Mar. 29 to form a 40,000 member joint military force to help member nations deal with crises.

Nigerian Election Brings First Power Shift in 16 Years—Ex-military ruler Muhammadu Buhari defeated incumbent Pres. Goodluck Jonathan of the People's Democratic Party (PDP) in Nigerian presidential elections Mar. 28-29. Pledging to root out corruption, improve the country's sagging economy, and take a firmer stance against the Islamist militant group Boko Haram, Buhari, of the All Progressives Congress, won 54% of 29 mil votes cast, to the PDP's 45%. Boko Haram militants reportedly killed at least 43 people in election-related attacks Mar. 28. Both parties were accused of vote-rigging in the election, which followed a six-week postponement that some critics claimed was orchestrated in the name of security. Five suspected Boko Haram suicide bombers Mar. 7 killed 58 people in Maiduguri in northeastern Nigeria; neighboring Chad and Niger the next day launched a joint offensive against militants there.

According to an audio message claiming to be from Boko Haram leader Abubakar Shekau released Mar. 7, the Nigeria-based group was pledging allegiance to ISIS and its leader, Abu Bakr al-Baghdadi.

General

Fossil Pushes Human Origins Back 400,000 Years—The journal *Science* Mar. 4 reported the 2013 discovery of a 2.8-mil-year-old human jawbone that researchers said may serve as a plausible evolutionary link between the extinct apelike hominid *Australopithecus afarensis*, represented by the iconic 3.2-mil-year-old skeleton nicknamed Lucy, and the early human species *Homo habilis*, whose oldest remains date to about 2.35 mil years ago. Uncovered in the Afar region of Ethiopia (near where Lucy was found), the bone seemed to combine features of the genus *Homo* and more primitive attributes of *Australopithecus*, but further research was needed to determine its significance and place in the human evolutionary tree.

Oklahoma Fraternity Slurs Spark Outrage—A video recorded Mar. 7 showing members of the Univ. of Oklahoma's Sigma Alpha Epsilon fraternity singing a racist chant went viral, leading to widespread backlash and the chapter's closure. The university expelled two students who led the chant, which referenced lynching. Sigma Alpha Epsilon's national office

Mar. 27 admitted the students likely learned the chant while attending one of its conferences.

South Pacific Cyclone Cripples Vanuatu—Cyclone Pam battered the low-lying South Pacific island nation of Vanuatu—one of the world's poorest—Mar. 13, leaving around 30% of its 267,000 residents in need of emergency shelter. The category 5 storm packed wind gusts of up to 200 mph and destroyed 96% of the country's crops. Officials attributed the relatively low death toll of 11 people to a text message-based alert system, lightweight building materials, and porous construction designs.

HBO Documentary Subject Charged With Murder—Real estate heir Robert Durst, the subject of the HBO documentary series *The Jinx*, was arrested Mar. 14 for the 2000 murder of Susan Berman. Authorities alleged Durst killed Berman, a longtime friend, to prevent detectives from questioning her about the 1982 disappearance of his wife, in which he was a suspect. The 71-year-old Durst was acquitted in 2003 in the killing of a Texas neighbor, which Durst claimed was in self-defense. The series ended with an audio recording of Durst muttering to himself, "What ... did I do? Killed them all, of course," while in a bathroom still wearing a microphone.

Pilot Intentionally Crashes Germanwings Jet, Killing 150—En route from Barcelona, Spain, to Dusseldorf, Germany, Germanwings Flight 9525 crashed Mar. 24 in the French Alps, killing all 144 passengers and six crew. Cockpit recordings revealed the plane's 27-year-old copilot, Andreas Lubitz, deliberately locked the captain out of the cockpit of the Airbus A320 and initiated a controlled eight-minute fatal descent from 38,000 ft. Although Lufthansa, the parent company of Germanwings, initially declared Lubitz to have been "100 percent flightworthy," investigators found multiple doctors' notes in his apartment declaring him unfit to work.

NSA Shooting Kills One Intruder—Guards Mar. 30 fatally shot the driver of a stolen vehicle in a restricted area of the National Security Agency campus in Fort Meade, MD, less than 30 mi from Washington, DC. Security officers fired on the car when the driver failed to obey directions for leaving the campus, killing the driver and injuring the sole passenger. The car then crashed into an NSA police vehicle.

April 2015

National

California Imposes Water Restrictions—Facing a fourth consecutive year of severe drought, California Gov. Jerry Brown (D) issued the state's first-ever mandatory water restrictions Apr. 1. The executive order mandated a 25% reduction in potable urban water use across California's cities and towns—with lower targets for areas that had already cut back—and set penalties of up to $10,000 per day for local agencies that did not comply. The order followed Brown's call for voluntary 20% reductions, a goal most of the state failed to meet, when he declared a drought emergency in Jan. 2014. The restrictions notably did not target California's agriculture industry, which consumed an estimated 80% of available water resources.

Indiana, Arkansas Revise Religious Freedom Measures Amid Outcry—Indiana Gov. Mike Pence (R) signed amendments to the state's newly enacted religious freedom law Apr. 2 in the wake of boycott threats and criticism that the law would be used to deny services, jobs, and housing to lesbian, gay, bisexual, and transgender (LGBT) people. Pence denied that the Religious Freedom Restoration Act (RFRA), which he signed Mar. 26, was intended to promote discrimination, citing the federal government's 1993 religious freedom law and legislation in 19 other states. But critics contended Indiana's law went beyond other RFRAs—including the federal government's, which protects the rights of religious minorities from government intrusion—by allowing businesses to claim violations by individuals and permitting lawsuits by private parties. Under public pressure, Indiana's Republican-controlled legislature revised the law to forbid its use to deny service based on sexual orientation or gender identity.

Arkansas experienced backlash against its own RFRA, with the CEO of Arkansas-based Walmart speaking out against a bill that passed the Republican-led state legislature Mar. 31. Arkansas Gov. Asa Hutchinson (R) called on lawmakers to revise the measure before he signed it Apr. 2.

Clinton Launches Presidential Campaign Amidst Impropriety Allegations—Ending years of speculation, former first lady, U.S. senator, 2008 presidential contender, and secretary of state Hillary Clinton officially launched her campaign for the 2016 Democratic presidential nomination Apr. 12, notifying supporters via email, YouTube video, and Facebook; she filed official documents with the Federal Election Commission Apr. 13.

Ahead of the announcement, the presumed frontrunner faced scrutiny over several accusations of impropriety. The *NY Times* reported Mar. 2 that Clinton had used a private email account for correspondence during her four-year tenure as Obama's secretary of state, a practice interpreted by some as a violation of federal recordkeeping laws. After the State Dept. requested access to the emails in 2014, Clinton and staff deleted about half of the approximately 60,000 messages, deeming them private, before submitting the other half to officials. Beginning in Apr., Clinton was dogged by accusations that donors to the Clinton Foundation—a charity founded by her husband, former U.S. Pres. Bill Clinton—had received special treatment in exchange for donations while she served in the Obama administration. Clinton denied the claims of impropriety, but foundation officials admitted tax filing errors.

Blackwater Contractors Sentenced in Iraq Killings; U.S. Admits It Killed Hostages in Pakistan—A federal judge Apr. 13 sentenced one ex-guard from the security firm Blackwater (now Academi) to life in prison for firing the first shots in a mass shooting that killed 17 in Baghdad, Iraq, in 2007; three other former employees received 30-year sentences for their involvement. The men had claimed that they were fired upon while driving in a convoy, but an FBI investigation ruled that 14 of the 17 deaths were unjustified by the rules of engagement. The incident highlighted the U.S. military's dependence on private contractors and fueled anti-occupation sentiment among Iraqis.

The Obama administration Apr. 23 said that a Jan. 15 CIA drone strike in Pakistan had accidentally killed two aid workers from the U.S. and Italy who were being held hostage by al-Qaeda. Officials said the agency did not know the hostages were present when it launched the attack.

Google Faces Antitrust Challenge; Job Growth Slows; Other Developments—After a five-year investigation, the 28-nation European Union Apr. 15 charged U.S. web giant Google with manipulating search results to boost its own shopping business. The European Commission also initiated an antitrust investigation into Google, over whether smartphone makers were required to pre-install Google apps on phones that used the company's Android operating system. The U.S. had investigated similar allegations in 2012 but had not brought domestic antitrust charges after Google agreed to modify business practices in Jan. 2013.

Deutsche Bank Apr. 23 agreed to pay a record $2.5 bil to settle allegations by U.S. and UK regulators that it plotted to manipulate global interest rate benchmarks. The third-largest U.S. ice cream maker, Blue Bell Creameries, recalled its entire line of products Apr. 20 after the Food and Drug Administration reported the company's Broken Arrow, OK, facility was contaminated with listeria; officials believed three people died in the past year in connection with the outbreak.

The Labor Dept. reported Apr. 3 that 126,000 jobs had been added to the U.S. economy in Mar., less than half the monthly average of 269,000 jobs created in the preceding 12 months. The unemployment rate for Mar. remained steady at 5.5%. Wall Street revived from a weak Mar., with the Dow Jones Industrial Average finishing Apr. at 17,840.52, up 0.4% from the month before. The S&P 500—which had reached a record closing Apr. 27—ended the month at 2,085.51, a 0.9% increase from Mar., and the NASDAQ, which also achieved a closing high Apr. 24, finished Apr. at 4,941.42, up 0.8%.

Death of Black Man in Baltimore Police Custody Sparks Unrest; South Carolina Officer Charged With Murder; Other Developments—Twenty-five-year-old Freddie Gray died in Baltimore Apr. 19 from a spinal cord injury sustained

Apr. 12 while being transported in a police van. Gray's death added fuel to an ongoing protest movement against racial bias and mistreatment by police. Rioting erupted in Baltimore Apr. 27 after Gray's funeral, and Maryland Gov. Larry Hogan (R) declared a state of emergency; Mayor Stephanie Rawlings-Blake (D) ordered a citywide curfew beginning Apr. 28. Police arrested at least 486 in connection with the unrest, which injured at least 113 police officers. The U.S. Justice Dept. Apr. 21 opened a civil rights investigation into Gray's death, and a Baltimore grand jury May 21 indicted six police officers on charges ranging from assault to second-degree murder.

In North Charleston, SC, a white police officer was charged Apr. 7 with the murder of Walter Scott, a 50-year-old unarmed black man whom he shot eight times Apr. 4 after Scott ran away from him during a traffic stop. The actions of the officer, Michael Slager, were caught on video by a bystander and contradicted the official report, in which the officer claimed he had acted in self-defense. North Charleston Mayor Keith Summery ordered all city police officers to wear body cameras, and the U.S. Justice Dept. announced it would investigate the killing.

Robert Bates, a 73-year-old white reserve deputy in Tulsa, OK, was charged Apr. 13 with manslaughter for fatally shooting a prostrate, unarmed black suspect, Eric Harris. Bates claimed that he mistook his handgun for his Taser. The incident, caught on video, raised questions about the estimated 400,000 volunteer law enforcement reservists around the country, who receive less training than regular officers.

Senate Confirms New Attorney General—After months of delay, the U.S. Senate Apr. 23 confirmed Loretta Lynch as the nation's attorney general by a 56-43 vote. Lynch, the first black woman to hold the post, drew criticism from Republicans during her confirmation hearing in Jan. 2015 when she voiced support for Pres. Barack Obama's executive actions on undocumented immigrants. Lynch was sworn in Apr. 27, replacing Eric Holder Jr., who had served since 2009.

International

Iran Reaches Preliminary Nuclear Agreement With International Powers—Iran and six world powers led by the U.S. agreed Apr. 2 on the framework for a deal that would limit Iran's nuclear capacity and ability to build a nuclear weapon. Brokered largely by U.S. Sec. of State John Kerry over 18 months of talks, the framework agreed to in Lausanne, Switzerland, would cut Iran's supply of centrifuges by two-thirds and substantially reduce the amount of enriched uranium it could stockpile. Along with agreeing not to build new enrichment facilities, Iran consented to regular international inspections of its nuclear program, which it claimed was for peaceful purposes only. Israeli Prime Min. Benjamin Netanyahu and U.S. Republican congressional leadership criticized the framework, which left many issues unresolved, including the pace at which economic sanctions against Iran would be lifted. U.S. Pres. Barack Obama May 22 signed a bill granting Congress the right to review and block the deal.

Terror Attack on Kenyan Univ. Kills 148—Four gunmen stormed Garissa Univ. College Apr. 2 in northeastern Kenya, killing 148 people, mostly students, before they were killed by security forces. The attack was the deadliest terrorist incident in Kenya since al-Qaeda's 1998 U.S. embassy bombing in Nairobi. Somalia-based Islamist group al-Shabab claimed responsibility for the attack, which they claimed was in retaliation for the presence in southern Somalia of Kenyan soldiers, who had been deployed in 2011 in response to kidnappings allegedly perpetrated by the group. Al-Shabab militants were believed to have killed more than 600 people in Kenya since 2012, including 67 at the Westgate shopping mall in Nairobi in 2013.

U.S., Cuban Leaders Meet for First Time Since Cuban Revolution—U.S. Pres. Barack Obama sat down with Cuban Pres. Raúl Castro Ruz Apr. 11 in the first formal talks between leaders of the two countries in over 50 years. Occurring on the sidelines of the Summit of the Americas in Panama City, Panama, the brief meeting followed the White House's Dec. 2014 declaration that it would seek to normalize relations with the communist country. Castro called for the U.S. to lift its longstanding trade embargo against Cuba—a move that required congressional approval—and return Guantánamo Bay to Cuban control. Addressing a major obstacle towards normalization, the U.S. May 29 dropped Cuba from its list of state sponsors of terrorism.

Hundreds of Migrants Drown in Mediterranean En Route to Europe—The United Nations confirmed that at least 800 undocumented migrants drowned Apr. 19 after the boat in which they were traveling capsized about 70 mi off the Libyan coast. The incident was thought to be the deadliest yet amidst a surge of people trying to escape northern Africa by boat; it occurred five days after 400 migrants leaving Libya drowned in a separate capsizing. The drownings sparked criticism of the European Union's decision in Nov. 2014 to replace a comprehensive Italian-led water rescue operation with an EU-backed program dubbed "Triton" that emphasized border security. EU officials Apr. 20 approved a 10-point plan on migrants, including the destruction of trafficking boats and creation of an EU-wide resettlement program. EU leaders Apr. 23 pledged ships to Triton and tripled its budget.

In the first four months of 2015, nearly 1,800 migrants were known to have been killed in attempted Mediterranean crossings and some 51,000 successfully reached Europe. EU ships carried out major rescue efforts, saving some 7,000 people over three days in early May and another 4,200 during a 24-hour period ending May 30. Officials said teams were on pace to surpass 2014's count of 170,000 rescued.

The mass drownings also directed attention to Libya, where traffickers took advantage of political instability and lawlessness to establish smuggling hubs. Following the 2011 ouster and death of longtime dictator Muammar al-Qaddafi, Libya descended into civil war. Islamists took control in 2014 of the national capital of Tripoli, declaring their own government and forcing the newly elected parliament into exile, where it remained throughout 2015.

Sunni Coalition Ends, Then Resumes, Yemen Airstrikes—Reportedly facing pressure from the U.S., Saudi Arabia Apr. 21 announced it would end a nearly month-long bombing campaign against Shiite Houthi rebels who had ousted Yemeni Pres. Abd Rabbuh Mansur Hadi in Jan. The airstrikes had failed to dislodge the Houthis and forces loyal to former president Ali Abdullah Saleh killed scores of civilians. But within hours, the Saudi-led coalition of 10 Sunni nations resumed airstrikes, targeting rebels in Taiz in central Yemen and in the southern port of Aden. According to the United Nations, fighting and airstrikes in Yemen killed at least 1,244 people and displaced some 300,000 between Mar. 19 and Apr. 27.

General

Duke, UConn Win NCAA Basketball Tournaments—The Duke Univ. Blue Devils defeated the Univ. of Wisconsin Badgers, 68-63, to win both coach Mike Krzyzewski's and the school's fifth NCAA men's division I basketball championship Apr. 6 in Indianapolis, IN. The lead in the back-and-forth game changed 13 times in the first 20 min. of play, with the top-seeded teams tied 31-31 at the half. Duke shut down Wisconsin's chance at its first title since 1941. Duke guard Tyus Jones, who scored 23 points, became just the fifth freshman in history to be named the most outstanding player of the men's Final Four.

At the women's tournament final Apr. 7, the Univ. of Connecticut Huskies defeated the Notre Dame Fighting Irish for the second consecutive year, 63-53, at Amalie Arena in Tampa, FL. The title was the third in a row for the school and its 10th overall. The win also gave coach Gene Auriemma his 10th title, tying him with legendary UCLA men's coach John Wooden. UConn forward Breanna Stewart was designated most outstanding player of the Final Four a record third time, with 8 points, 15 rebounds, and 4 blocked shots.

Spieth Wins First Masters Tournament—Jordan Spieth became the second-youngest player ever to win the Masters Tournament when the 21-year-old finished four strokes ahead of veterans Phil Mickelson and Justin Rose Apr. 12 at the Augusta Natl. Golf Club in Augusta, GA. Speith tied but did not break Tiger Woods's 1997 18-under-270 scoring record.

Earthquakes Kill Over 8,500 in Nepal—A 7.8-magnitude earthquake struck Nepal shortly before noon Apr. 25, killing more than 8,000 people and displacing some 2.8 mil. Its epicenter was less than 50 mi northwest of the capital of Kathmandu at the relatively shallow depth of 9.3 mi, making it especially destructive. Rural districts Gorkha and Sindhupalchowk experienced massive housing destruction. Avalanches triggered on Mt. Everest killed at least 17. Aftershocks complicated rescue efforts already hampered by heavy rains. The government faced allegations of blocking and taxing foreign aid, and survivors Apr. 29 protested lagging emergency services outside the Nepali parliament.

Another 7.3-magnitude earthquake in Nepal May 12, centered east of Kathmandu, pushed the death toll to at least 8,669, making the combined quakes the deadliest disasters in the nation's history. According to the United Nations, up to 600,000 homes were damaged along with historic temples and UNESCO World Heritage sites.

NFL Gives up Tax-Exempt Status—The National Football League announced Apr. 28 that its central office would become a taxable corporate entity. The NFL as a whole (including its 32 teams, all of which were taxable for-profit entities) generates over $10 bil in annual revenue, though most NFL income was already taxed at the team level. Congress's Joint Committee on Taxation estimated the change in status would generate $109 mil over the next decade.

May 2015

National

Texas Police Halt Gunmen at Anti-Islam Event—A local police officer May 3 fatally shot two men who opened fire outside an event in Garland, TX, that displayed cartoon depictions of the Prophet Muhammad. Authorities identified Twitter messages between prominent jihadists and one of the shooters, who had been convicted on terrorism-related charges in 2011. But they did not definitively conclude the attack was organized by the Sunni extremist group Islamic State of Iraq and Syria (ISIS), which May 5 claimed responsibility for the attempted attack. The "Muhammad Art Exhibit and Cartoon Contest" was staged by the American Freedom Defense Initiative, an anti-Muslim group, and featured a keynote from anti-Islam Dutch politician Geert Wilders.

Amtrak Crash Kills Eight, Intensifies Train Budget Debate—An Amtrak passenger train derailed May 12 in Philadelphia, killing 8 of 243 on board and injuring more than 200 others. The locomotive and all seven passenger cars of the train, en route from Washington, DC, to New York, went off the rails traveling at 102 mph through a sharp curve with a speed limit of 50 mph. Injured in the crash, the train's engineer claimed to have no memory of the derailment. Amtrak and incident investigators said the derailment could not have occurred if positive train control, mandated by the end of 2015 for almost all U.S. railroads, had been installed to automatically slow or stop the train.

Besides drawing attention to railroad safety, the crash heightened debates in Congress over Amtrak funding, with Pres. Barack Obama and some Democratic lawmakers calling for increased financial support of the passenger rail service. The House Appropriations Committee May 13 voted 30-21 to cut 18% of Amtrak's $1.4-bil annual budget.

Boston Marathon Bomber Sentenced to Death—A federal jury May 15 sentenced Dzhokhar Tsarnaev to death for his role in the 2013 Boston Marathon bombings that killed 3 people and injured more than 260. During the sentencing phase of the trial, Tsarnaev's lawyers attempted to portray the 21-year-old Chechen immigrant as under the sway of older brother Tamerlan Tsarnaev, whom they accused of masterminding the attacks. The same jury had convicted Tsarnaev Apr. 8 on all 30 counts against him, including the killing of a campus police officer after the attack.

Air Bag Maker Issues Largest-Ever Auto Recall; Currency-Rigging Banks Fined; Other Economic News—Japanese auto parts supplier Takata Corp. May 19 increased its air-bag recall to 33.8 mil vehicles—nearly 14% of all U.S. vehicles. The faulty air bags, installed by 11 automakers, were prone to exploding and had killed 8 and injured more than 100 worldwide as of June 2015. In other regulatory action, the U.S. Justice Dept. May 20 imposed $5.8 bil in fines on six global banks for currency rigging. Barclays, Royal Bank of Scotland, Citicorp, and JPMorgan Chase pleaded guilty to rigging. Bank of America was fined but avoided a guilty plea, and UBS pleaded guilty to interest-rate manipulation.

Cable and telecommunications provider Charter Communications May 26 announced it had agreed to acquire larger rival Time Warner Cable for $55 bil in cash and stock. In another telecom merger, Verizon agreed May 12 to acquire Internet pioneer AOL Inc. Drugstore giant CVS Health agreed May 21 to acquire Omnicare, a provider of pharmacy services to long-term care facilities in a merger worth about $12.7 bil; the deal was finalized Aug. 18.

The Labor Dept. reported May 8 that the unemployment rate fell to a near seven-year-low of 5.4%, as 223,000 jobs had been added to the economy in Apr. U.S. stocks maintained steady growth, with the Dow Jones Industrial Average closing at a record high 18,312.39 May 19 and ending the month at 18,010.68, up 1.0% from Apr. The S&P 500 achieved a record closing at 2,130.82 May 21 and ended the month at 2,107.39—a 1.0% increase from Apr.—while Nasdaq finished May at 5,070.03, up 2.6% after hitting a historic high of 5,106.59 May 27.

Retired House Leader Indicted—A federal grand jury May 28 charged former U.S. House Speaker Dennis Hastert (R, IL) with trying to evade financial reporting requirements on large-sum cash withdrawals and with lying to the FBI. The indictment alleged that Hastert, the longest-serving Republican speaker of the House, had paid over $1.7 mil over four years to a man whom, the *L.A. Times* reported May 29, Hastert had allegedly sexually abused while working as a high-school wrestling coach and teacher in Yorkville, IL. (Hastert was not charged with sexual abuse.) Hastert pleaded guilty to trying to evade banking laws Oct. 28.

Presidential Candidate Fields Begin to Take Shape for 2016—Nine months ahead of the first primaries, the fields of candidates for the 2016 Republican and Democratic presidential nominations began to take shape by the end of May. The first Republicans to announce included single-term U.S. senators Ted Cruz (TX), who declared his candidacy Mar. 23; Rand Paul (KY), Apr. 7; and Marco Rubio (FL), Apr. 13. Retired neurosurgeon Ben Carson and former Hewlett-Packard CEO Carly Fiorina each announced Republican bids May 4; former Arkansas Gov. Mike Huckabee declared his candidacy a day later. Former Sen. Rick Santorum (PA) announced his campaign May 27, and former New York Gov. George Pataki—at 69, the oldest of the group—announced May 28. Prominent Republicans who declined to run included 2012 GOP nominee Mitt Romney and running mate U.S. Rep. Paul Ryan (WI), former Minnesota Gov. Tim Pawlenty, and former House Speaker Newt Gingrich.

Along with former First Lady and Sec. of State Hillary Clinton, who announced her candidacy Apr. 12, Democrats seeking nomination by the end of May were Sen. Bernie Sanders (VT), who kicked off his campaign May 26, and former Maryland Gov. Martin O'Malley, who announced May 30. Vice Pres. Joe Biden had neither declared nor declined, but Sen. Elizabeth Warren (MA) was among prominent Democrats who had declined to run.

International

Conservatives Win Surprise Majority in British Elections; New British Royal Born—Confounding poll predictions, UK Prime Min. David Cameron of the center-right Conservative Party secured a second term May 7 after Tories emerged with a slim majority of seats in the House of Commons, the lower chamber of Parliament. Cameron's Tories won 36.9% of votes and 331 of 650 seats, up 24, in an election participated in by 66% of eligible voters. The center-left Labour Party won 34.0% and 232 seats, a 26-seat decline, while centrist Liberal Democrats—Cameron's coalition partner since 2010—won just 7.9% of votes and 8 seats, down from 57. (The far-right UK Independence Party won 12.6% but only one seat.) Cameron said he would delegate more taxation and governing powers to Scotland, whose separatist Scottish National Party (SNP) won 56 of 59 of that country's seats, up from 6 seats before the election. Despite losing a 2014 independence referendum, the SNP had surged in popularity, and calls for Scottish sovereignty continued. Cameron also said he would honor his party's pledge to hold a referendum on UK secession from the European Union if he could not secure better terms within the EU.

Prince William and Catherine Middleton, Duke and Duchess of Cambridge, welcomed May 2 a second child, a girl named Charlotte Elizabeth Diana, who became fourth in line for the throne.

Ebola Epidemic Ends in Liberia—The World Health Organization (WHO), May 9, declared Liberia free of Ebola 42 days after the last lab-confirmed case was buried. The disease had killed over 4,700 people in Liberia since the Dec. 2013 start of the West African epidemic, which had claimed over 11,000 lives. Six more cases were diagnosed in Liberia in June-July, but the nation was again declared Ebola-free Sept. 3.

WHO officials May 6 reported just nine cases each over the previous week in Guinea and Sierra Leone—the lowest 2015 weekly totals thus far—but cautioned that the agency faced difficulties tracking transmissions in Guinea.

ISIS Seizes Ramadi; U.S. Raid Kills Senior ISIS Leader in Syria—ISIS May 17 seized Ramadi, capital of Iraq's Anbar province, after the last Iraqi and other pro-government forces fled. The takeover, the group's largest victory yet in 2015, came several days after militants reportedly charged the city during a sandstorm, unleashing multiple car bombings and other attacks. An Iraqi government official said militants killed or executed about 500 civilians and security personnel. The United Nations reported some 55,000 residents had left the city in the week after the takeover, largely for Baghdad, 70 mi to the east. About 114,000 others had fled in Apr.

In the first known successful ground operation by U.S. troops against ISIS in neighboring Syria, U.S. special forces May 16 reportedly killed ISIS commander Abu Sayyaf—reputed overseer of the group's black-market oil activities—during a nighttime raid. ISIS was believed to occupy over half of Syria after claiming another victory May 20, when it occupied the 2,000-year-old city Palmyra, a World Heritage Site. According to the UK-based Syrian Observatory for Human Rights, ISIS over the next week killed at least 240 people in the city, including 25 men in a public execution. Militants in June destroyed two of Palmyra's shrines.

Irish Voters Approve Same-Sex Marriage—Ireland became the first country to legalize same-sex marriage through popular referendum May 22 after over 62% of those voting chose to amend the country's constitution. Participated in by more than 60% of 3.2 mil eligible voters, the measure passed in all but one of the predominantly Roman Catholic nation's 43 electoral districts. At the time of the vote, same-sex marriage was legal in 19 other countries and 37 U.S. states.

Summit Seeks Humanitarian Solutions on Southeast Asian Refugee Crisis—In the Special Meeting on Irregular Migration in the Indian Ocean held May 29 in Bangkok, Thailand, more than 17 attending nations sought ways to facilitate the international humanitarian response to a surge in migration as the stateless Muslim minority Rohingya ethnic group fled Myanmar and Bangladesh on boats bound for Malaysia and elsewhere. Some 25,000 Rohingya and Bangladeshis had left Jan.-Mar. 2015—twice the level in the same period in 2014—many allegedly to escape religious persecution by radical Buddhists and mistreatment by the two nations' governments, which do not recognize the Rohingya as citizens. Some 6,000-8,000 migrants were stranded by mid-May in ships off the coasts of Thailand, Indonesia, and Malaysia. All three countries initially refused entry, but Indonesia and Malaysia agreed May 20 to provide temporary shelter to 7,000 migrants; Thailand maintained they would assist them at sea.

General

Mayweather Defeats Pacquiao in Welterweight Title Fight—Undefeated five-division American world champion Floyd Mayweather Jr. outscored eight-division Filipino world champion Manny Pacquiao for the World Boxing Organization's welterweight title May 2 in Las Vegas, NV. After the fight, Pacquiao's camp announced he had been denied a legal painkilling injection by fight officials despite hurting his shoulder in Apr. The bout, considered lackluster by many boxing fans, generated at least $550 mil, including more than $350 mil in payments to the fighters. The WBO stripped Mayweather of the title July 6 after he failed to pay a $200,000 sanctioning fee and to relinquish two junior middleweight titles.

American Pharoah Sweeps Kentucky Derby and Preakness Stakes—Three-year-old colt American Pharoah surged in the final stretch past Firing Line and third-place finisher Dortmund to win the 141st Kentucky Derby in 2:03.02 May 2 at Churchill Downs in Louisville, KY. Jockey Victor Espinoza claimed his third derby win in front of the record crowd of 170,513. American Pharoah stayed on course to win the Triple Crown by clinching the 140th Preakness Stakes May 16 at Pimlico Race Course in Baltimore, MD. Facing torrential rains and stiff winds, Espinoza brought the horse to an early lead, fending off a late-race surge by a trailing pack.

NFL Punishes Patriots Quarterback in "Deflategate"—National Football League officials May 11 suspended New England Patriots quarterback Tom Brady for four games after it determined he was probably aware of two team employees intentionally deflating game balls before the AFC championship game Jan. 18. The NFL also fined the Patriots $1 mil and said the 2015 Super Bowl champions would forfeit their 2016 first-round draft choice and 2017 fourth-round pick. Denying wrongdoing, Brady had declined to voluntarily turn over emails and texts, and the team refused to make one of its employees available for further interview.

Painting, Sculpture Set Auction Records—Pablo Picasso's *Women of Algiers*, part of a 15-part series created 1954-55, became the most expensive artwork sold at auction when it went for nearly $179.4 mil May 11 at Christie's in New York. Alberto Giacometti's *Pointing Man* (1947) commanded almost $141.3 mil at the same auction, setting a record for sculpture.

Biker Melee Kills Nine in Texas—Nine were killed and 18 injured May 17 during an altercation involving five biker gangs brawling outside a sports bar in Waco, TX. Riders shot at one another and fought with other weapons. Police at the scene exchanged gunfire with the gangs and arrested at least 170 participants on organized criminal activity charges.

Montoya Wins Second Indy 500—Colombian driver Juan Pablo Montoya emerged victorious at Indianapolis Motor Speedway May 24 after passing his Penske teammate Will Power on the outside with three laps remaining and holding him off by .105 sec. in the fourth-tightest Indy 500 finish ever. Montoya's first win came in 2000, with the 15 years between victories setting an Indy record. The race saw several accidents, including a chain-reaction crash with 25 laps left, but none as serious as crashes earlier in the month when three cars were separately wreckled after going airborne. Teams had agreed before the Indy 500 to reduce engine power and abandon new "aero kits" suspected in the crashes.

Oklahoma, Texas Floods Turn Deadly—Weeks of heavy precipitation preceded a slow-moving storm that dumped torrential rains across central and eastern Texas and large swaths of Oklahoma in late May, producing record floods that killed at least 31 people by the month's end. First-responders in the Houston area undertook some 530 water rescues. Also hard hit was Hays County, south of Austin, where the Blanco River crested more than 30 ft above flood stage. The same set of storms generated a tornado that killed 14 people in Ciudad Acuña, Mexico. Rain over the month—the wettest on record for Oklahoma and Texas by wide margins—eased longstanding drought in both states.

June 2015

National

NSA Bill Passes New Surveillance Policy—Pres. Barack Obama June 2 signed a bill ending the National Security Agency's bulk collection of phone data. By the end of a six-month transition period beginning with the signing, responsibility for the collected data would shift to telecom companies. The NSA must obtain a targeted warrant before accessing the data, and Internet and telecom companies were permitted to publicly report on the NSA's requests. The bill passed just after the expiration of the USA Patriot Act, the legal bulwark of the NSA's sweeping post-9/11 surveillance powers, and about two years after former NSA contractor Edward Snowden revealed information about the data collection to media. Congressional leaders were at odds on the NSA's phone data collection, with Senate Majority Leader Mitch McConnell (R, KY) opposing the new restraints and House Speaker John Boehner (R, OH) supporting them, but the bill received bipartisan support. House lawmakers passed the bill May 13, 338-88, followed by a 67-32 vote in the Senate June 2.

Job Growth Continues; Obama Wins Fast-Track Trade Authority; Other Economic News—The Labor Dept. reported June 5 that the economy had added 280,000 jobs in May. The unemployment rate rose slightly, to 5.5% from 5.4%, but the uptick reflected the addition of some 397,000 people to the workforce. Los Angeles June 13 became the largest U.S. city to enact a $15 minimum hourly wage when Mayor Eric Garcetti (D) signed a measure mandating the change over five years. Pres. Obama announced June 29 that the upper annual income limit for those eligible for mandated time-and-a-half overtime pay would increase from $23,660 to about $50,440.

The Federal Communications Commission June 17 said it would fine AT&T $100 mil for allegedly slowing data speeds for millions of smartphone consumers who had purchased "unlimited data" plans. The fine against the nation's second-largest mobile service provider would be the largest ever levied by the commission though AT&T was appealing.

The Senate June 24 voted 60-38 to approve "fast-track" trade promotion authority (TPA) that would allow Pres. Barack Obama to complete negotiations on the Trans-Pacific Partnership, a trade pact with 12 Asia-Pacific nations that together account for some 60% of global GDP. The Dow Jones Industrial Average closed the month at 17,619.51, down 2.2% from May, while the S&P 500 finished June at 2,063.11, a 2.1% decline. The Nasdaq Composite Index closed at 4,986.87, down 1.6%.

Shooting at Historic Black Church Kills Nine; Confederate Flag Removed From South Carolina Capitol—A 21-year-old white gunman fatally shot nine African Americans including South Carolina state Sen. Clementa Pinckney (D) June 17 at Emanuel African Methodist Episcopal Church, one of the nation's oldest black churches, in Charleston, SC. The three survivors—one of whom pretended to be dead and shielded her granddaughter with her body—reported that the gunman had shouted racial epithets. Police arrested the shooter, identified as Dylann Roof, the next day. The FBI revealed July 10 that a background check error on the agency's part allowed Roof to purchase a gun despite a felony indictment.

A website linked to the shooter included a racist manifesto and showed him with the Confederate flag, reviving debate over the symbol. Several major retailers, including Walmart and Amazon, announced they would discontinue sales of Confederate banner merchandise, and several Southern states, including Alabama and Virginia, removed the flag from state grounds or symbols. South Carolina Gov. Nikki Haley (R) June 22 requested its removal from a war memorial on the state's Capitol grounds. The South Carolina senate July 7 voted, 36-3, to remove the flag, and the assembly July 9 followed, 94-20. Haley signed the bill later that day.

Trump Declares Presidential Candidacy in Controversial Announcement; Other Candidacies Declared—Billionaire real estate mogul Donald Trump June 16 announced his candidacy for the 2016 Republican presidential nomination in a 45-min. speech during which he referred to undocumented Mexican immigrants as rapists and drug traffickers. NBCUniversal on June 29 announced it had severed its ties with Trump, the host of business-themed reality shows on NBC since 2004. Fellow 2016 Republican contenders, including former Florida Gov. Jeb Bush and former Texas Gov. Rick Perry, criticized Trump's remarks.

Others who announced their candidacy in June for the 2016 Republican nomination were Sen. Lindsey Graham (SC), June 1; Rick Perry, June 4; Jeb Bush, June 15; Louisiana Gov. Bobby Jindal, June 24; and New Jersey Gov. Chris Christie, June 30. Wisconsin Gov. Scott Walker and Ohio Gov. John Kasich, the sixteenth Republican candidate, declared bids July 13 and July 21, respectively. Former Rhode Island Gov. Lincoln Chafee and former Sen. Jim Webb (D, VA) declared their candidacies for the Democratic nomination June 3 and July 2, respectively.

Supreme Court Ends Term With Rulings on Same-Sex Marriage, Obamacare, Lethal Injection—The U.S. Supreme Court June 29 concluded its 2014-15 term with a 5-4 decision in *Glossip v. Gross*, ruling against plaintiffs' claims that the use of the drug midazolam in lethal injections constituted cruel and unusual punishment. Writing for the majority, Associate Justice Samuel Alito said the plaintiffs had not proven the drug carried a "substantial risk of severe pain" and failed to provide an alternative method of execution.

The Court June 25 ruled 6-3 in *King v. Burwell* that some 6.4 mil Americans could legally retain federal subsidies for health-care coverage provided for by the 2010 Affordable Care Act. Based on the law's language, plaintiffs had argued that such subsidies should be available only to those using marketplaces "established by the State," thereby excluding residents in 36 states that had not set up exchanges who used the federal exchange. Writing for the majority, Chief Justice John Roberts acknowledged the ambiguity, but argued that "Congress meant for those provisions to apply in every State as well."

In a landmark decision June 26, the Court in *Obergefell v. Hodges* ruled that states could not ban same-sex marriages and must recognize those unions. The widely watched 5-4 decision effectively invalidated bans in 15 states and made same-sex marriage a legal option in all 50 U.S. states. The majority opinion was written by Associate Justice Anthony Kennedy and cited the due process and equal protection clauses of the U.S. Constitution's 14th Amendment.

International

G7 Summit Addresses Greek Debt, Russian Aggression, Climate Change—Greece's $360-bil debt crisis was a main topic of discussion as leaders of the G7 (Canada, France, Germany, Great Britain, Italy, Japan, and the U.S.) met June 7-8 in Schloss Elmau, Germany, for their annual summit. While German Chancellor Angela Merkel voiced her desire for Greece to remain in the eurozone, she reiterated the indebted nation's need to enact further economic reforms as a condition of the European Commission releasing more bailout funds. Along with agreeing to toughen economic sanctions on Russia—suspended from the G8 in 2014—if it continued to support pro-Moscow rebels in Ukraine, the G7 called for substantial reductions of greenhouse gas emissions and a complete halt to fossil fuel use by 2100.

Turkey's Ruling Party Loses Majority, Pro-Kurdish Candidates Gain Seats—Turkey's ruling Justice and Development Party (AKP) lost its majority in the country's 550-seat parliament, winning 40.9% of the June 7 vote and 258 seats, down from 327. The surprise result was a blow to Turkish Pres. Recep Tayyip Erdogan, who had campaigned for a supermajority in order to pass legislation that would expand the president's mostly ceremonial role. The election, in which 86.6% of eligible voters participated, gave the pro-Kurdish Peoples' Democratic Party (HDP) a parliamentary voice for the first time. The HDP won 13.1% of votes and 80 seats by appealing to voters seeking to curtail the AKP, which was viewed by critics as promoting an Islamist agenda over secular democracy. The Republican People's Party (CHP) took 25% of votes and 132 seats.

Prime Min. Ahmet Davutoglu of the AKP failed to form a coalition ahead of an Aug. 24 deadline, prompting Erdogan to call repeat elections for Nov. 1.

Egypt Approves Death Sentences for Morsi, Other Islamists—An Egyptian court confirmed a death sentence June 16 against deposed Egyptian Pres. Mohammed Morsi. The decision also upheld death sentences against more than 100 other defendants, mostly Muslim Brotherhood members, many for allegedly organizing attacks on police during the country's 2011 uprising against former Pres. Hosni Mubarek. Morsi, Egypt's first democratically elected president, who was ousted by the military in 2013, also received a life sentence on espionage allegations.

ISIS Launches Assault on Kobani; Other Developments—The Sunni extremist group known as the Islamic State of Iraq and Syria (ISIS) reportedly massacred at least 146 civilians June 25-26 in the northern Syrian Kurdish city of Kobani, which Kurds had recaptured in Jan. According to the Syrian Observatory for Human Rights, as of June 8, over 230,000 people had been killed in Syria since conflict erupted more than three years earlier. By late June, fighters loyal to

ISIS had for the first time reportedly seized considerable Afghan territory from the Taliban.

Expanding the U.S.'s 3,100-troop contingent in Iraq., U.S. Pres. Barack Obama June 10 ordered up to 450 additional troops to train Sunni tribes fighting ISIS. Two weeks later, the White House said it would overhaul the U.S. government's hostage policy, stating that while officials would still make "no concessions," they would be allowed to communicate with kidnappers. The administration also said it would not prosecute families of kidnapping victims who pay ransoms. At the time of the announcement, more than 30 Americans were being held abroad, and three U.S. citizens had been beheaded by ISIS.

Same-Day Terror Attacks in Tunisia, Kuwait, France Kill Dozens—A man at a resort in Sousse, Tunisia, fatally shot 38 foreign tourists—including 30 from the UK—and injured 39 others June 26. Police killed the gunman soon after. ISIS, which had appealed to its followers to increase attacks during the Muslim holy month of Ramadan, claimed responsibility for the massacre, the deadliest in recent history in Tunisia. Officials revealed the 24-year-old shooter had trained in Libya with the two Tunisians who had attacked a Tunis museum in Mar., killing 21.

Also on June 26, a Saudi suicide bomber killed 27 people and wounded at least 227 at a Shia mosque in Kuwait City, for which ISIS claimed responsibility. On the same day, a French deliveryman, whom police had linked several years prior to radical Islamist groups, decapitated his supervisor before driving into gas canisters at a chemical facility, causing an explosion.

General

Chinese Cruise Ship Capsizes, Killing Hundreds—The cruise ship Eastern Star capsized and sank June 1 on the Yangtze River in Hubei province, China. Of 456 on board, most of whom were elderly, 442 were confirmed dead. The deadliest boating disaster in China in almost 70 years, the incident occurred in stormy weather that had unleashed a tornado. The government as of mid-June was unable to explain why the captain had maintained course despite severe weather.

FIFA President Announces Resignation Amidst Corruption Scandal—Four days after he was elected to a fifth term, embattled world soccer governing body FIFA Pres. Sepp Blatter June 2 said he would step down. The pronouncement came after the U.S. Justice Dept. May 27 charged 14 officials from FIFA and FIFA-umbrella organizations and sports marketing executives with accepting or paying more than $150 mil in bribes over the previous 24 years. Switzerland the same day launched a criminal investigation into the body's awarding of the 2018 World Cup to Russia and the 2022 Cup to Qatar.

American Pharoah Wins Triple Crown—American Pharoah became the first horse in 37 years (and 12th of all time) to claim thoroughbred racing's Triple Crown after winning the 147th Belmont Stakes on June 6 in Elmont, NY. Ridden by jockey Victor Espinoza, American Pharoah burst to the front of the eight-horse field early and led the entire 1½-mi race, finishing five-and-a-half lengths ahead of runner-up Frosted in 2:26.65. The Mexico-born Espinoza was the first Hispanic rider to clinch the Triple Crown.

Williams and Wawrinka Take French Open—Despite a lingering flu, No. 1-seed Serena Williams defeated 13-seed Lucie Safarova of the Czech Republic (6-3, 6-7 (2), 6-2) June 6 at Roland Garros to win her third French Open and 20th Grand Slam title, two titles shy of the all-time women's singles record. The next day, 8-seed Stan Wawrinka of Switzerland claimed his first French Open and second Grand Slam title when he beat No. 1-seed Serbian Novak Djokovic (4-6, 6-4, 6-3, 6-4).

Chicago Blackhawks Hoist Stanley Cup—The Chicago Blackhawks defeated the Tampa Bay Lightning in six games to win the NHL's Stanley Cup Championship June 15 at Chicago's United Center. The series included closely matched play, with the first five games decided by one goal. The win marked Chicago's third championship in six years and sixth overall. Chicago's Duncan Keith won the Conn Smythe Trophy as the playoff MVP.

The NHL June 24 announced it was formally initiating the process of expanding the league. Commissioner Gary Bettman said Las Vegas, Seattle, and Quebec City had expressed the most interest.

Golden State Warriors Win NBA Title—Oakland, CA's Golden State Warriors won Game 6, 105-97, over the Cleveland Cavaliers June 16 at Quicken Loans Arena in Cleveland, OH, to claim the NBA Finals championship. Golden State's first championship in 40 years capped the team's best regular season in franchise history. Finals MVP Andre Iguodala of the Warriors, in the starting lineup only from Game 4 on, was lauded for his defense against LeBron James, the Cavaliers' prodigal superstar, who led the Finals in scoring with 35.8 points per game.

Pope Francis Calls for Climate Change Action; Vatican Creates Abuse Tribunal—Pope Francis June 18 released a landmark encyclical urging people to fight climate change and blaming governments, special interests, and individuals alike for pursuing financial gain over the common good. Francis asserted that human activity and excessive consumerism was chiefly responsible for rising temperatures in recent decades.

The Vatican June 10 announced the formation of a tribunal to hold accountable bishops who cover up sex abuse by priests. The creation of this permanently staffed judicial section came after years of criticism that church leadership had failed to punish bishops who did not remove or report abusive priests.

Spieth Wins U.S. Open Golf Tournament—Jordan Spieth won the 115th U.S. Open golf tournament June 21 at Chambers Bay in University Place, WA. The youngest U.S. Open winner since 1923, 21-year-old Spieth emerged from a four-way tie in the final round and scored three birdies, including a 25-ft putt on the 16th to finish with a five-under-par 275, one stroke ahead of Dustin Johnson and Louis Oosthuizen.

Heat Kills Thousands in Pakistan, India—By June 27, a week-long wave of stifling heat had killed over 1,200 mostly poor and homeless people in Karachi, Pakistan. Hit with nearly 113°F temperatures during Ramadan, when many Muslims observe a daytime fast, some 65,000 heatstroke victims overwhelmed hospitals. Pre-monsoon heat in neighboring India had killed some 2,300 people May 24-30 in the world's fifth-deadliest heat wave on record. Residents in Khammam in the southern state of Telangana wilted under 118°F heat—the highest there in 67 years—and the neighboring state Andhra Pradesh, where most deaths occurred, saw its humid coastal climate push heat indexes near 140°F.

July 2015

National

Five Years After Spill, BP Pays Hefty Penalties; Other Economic News—BP agreed July 2 to pay $18.7 bil to settle federal, state, and local claims from the massive 2010 *Deepwater Horizon* blowout and oil spill, which killed 11 workers and spilled millions of gallons of oil into the Gulf of Mexico. Under the largest environmental settlement in U.S. history, BP would pay $12.6 bil for Clean Water Act penalties and natural resource damages and $4.9 bil to settle economic claims with the states of Alabama, Florida, Louisiana, Mississippi, and Texas (along with about $1 bil to 400 local entities). The fine brought BP's total pretax bill for the spill (including its cleanup costs and the company's civil/criminal penalties) to $53.8 bil.

AT&T acquired DirecTV in a $48.5-bil transaction July 24, making it the largest pay-TV provider in the U.S. The Labor Dept. July 2 reported that the U.S. economy had added 223,000 jobs in June as the unemployment rate fell to a seven-year low of 5.3%, but the work force participation rate of 62.6% was at its lowest since 1977. The Bureau of Economic Analysis's final analysis of the gross domestic product for the first quarter of 2015 showed July 30 that real GDP had increased 0.6%, compared with 2.2% growth the previous quarter.

A technical glitch July 8 forced the New York Stock Exchange to shut down for nearly four hours, interrupting the trading day. The Dow Jones Industrial Average closed the month at 17,689.86, up 0.4% from June, while the S&P 500 finished July at 2,103.84, a 2.0% gain from the month before. The Nasdaq Composite Index closed at 5,128.28, up 2.8%.

Government Database Hacks Compromise Millions of Americans' Data—Office of Personnel Management (OPM) director Katherine Archuleta July 9 announced hackers had stolen the personal information of about 22.1 mil people—

nearly 7% of the U.S. population—in two separate but related 2014 data breaches. Agency officials in early June had estimated the first discovered breach affected some 4.2 mil people. Archuleta, whose agency had been struggling to deal with the extent of the smaller breach, resigned July 10. The hacking represented the largest-ever data breach of the U.S. government. The stolen information included social security numbers and other sensitive data for 19.7 mil current, past, and prospective federal employees and contractors and 1.8 mil non-applicants (mostly spouses or cohabitants).

Black Woman's Death in Texas Jail Sparks Inquiries; Cincinnati Officer Charged in Murder of Black Motorist—State and federal officials launched investigations into the July 13 death of Sandra Bland, a 28-year-old black woman who was found dead in a jail cell in Hempstead, TX, three days after her arrest by a white officer during a traffic stop. The arresting trooper in dashcam video footage appeared to have escalated his interaction with Bland, including threatening use of his stun gun when Bland refused to exit her vehicle. Bystander video showed an officer pushing his knee into a prostrate Bland's back before she was arrested for allegedly assaulting the officer off-camera. Although Bland in a booking questionnaire admitted she had tried to take her own life in 2014, her friends and relatives disagreed with the county's finding of suicide.

A jury in late July indicted a white Univ. of Cincinnati police officer on murder charges for fatally shooting an unarmed black man following a traffic stop. The officer said he shot the motorist because he was being dragged as the man attempted to drive away, but the prosecution contended the officer's body camera footage contradicted his account.

International

Greece Moves to Renew Financial Bailout—Paving the way for its third financial bailout in five years, Greece reached a deal July 13 with international lenders that would secure about $96 bil over three years and likely allow it to remain part of the EU. The nation would face even harsher loan terms than those offered in an earlier proposal rejected by 61% of voters participating in a July 5 referendum put forward by Greek Prime Min. Alexis Tsipras. In the face of its staggering debt, Greece in 2010 and 2012 had accepted $273 bil in loans from the International Monetary Fund (IMF), European Central Bank (ECB), and the EU's European Commission that included financial austerity conditions believed by many in Greece to contribute to recession and unemployment.

Germany had held firm against further debt relief, and the parties had engaged in months-long talks. Greece became the first developed country to miss an IMF repayment when it was unable to extend the earlier bailout note beyond its July 1 deadline. The ECB had halted assistance to Greek banks leading up to the deadline, causing them to limit cash withdrawals and close to most business until July 20, when the ECB supplied emergency funding. Greek lawmakers July 16 ratified the austerity requirements by a vote of 229-64 despite opposition from Tsipras's own left-wing party. Tsipras, who had campaigned against austerity, insisted it was the best agreement he could strike that kept Greece in the EU.

Iran Reaches Historic Nuclear Agreement With World Powers—Iran and six world powers led by the U.S. formally agreed July 14 on a deal to limit Iran's nuclear capability for the next 15 years and reportedly lengthen the amount of time it would take Iran to make a nuclear weapon—its so-called breakout capacity—to about one year from current estimates of two or three months. Under the agreement, Iran would reduce its uranium stockpile by 98% and its enriched uranium centrifuge supply by over two-thirds. The agreement permitted uranium enrichment at only one facility, which would be accessible to International Atomic Energy Agency (IAEA) inspectors. The UN, U.S., and European Union would in turn drop all nuclear-related sanctions against Iran following IAEA certification of its compliance.

Approval of the deal by the Republican-dominated U.S. Congress was not assured; House Speaker John Boehner (R, OH) pledged he and his party would "do everything we can to stop it." Pres. Barack Obama said he would veto any legislation that blocked the deal.

Japanese Parliament Approves Military Expansion—The lower house of Japan's parliament easily approved bills July 16 easing post-WWII restrictions on the country's military despite public opposition. The change would extend the military's constitutional right to defend Japan to include providing aid to allies under attack. The shift had been approved earlier in the month by Prime Min. Shinzo Abe's cabinet and had the support of his Liberal Democratic Party (LDP). Boycotting lawmakers and other opponents argued that the reinterpretation violated the constitution's "peace clause" and illegally bypassed the public's right to a referendum on the issue; some 100,000 people demonstrated outside parliament in Tokyo. In an upper parliament committee meeting, Sept. 17, lawmakers on both sides swarmed the committee chair and physically scuffled over the calling of a vote on the bills. The full upper house passed the bills early Sept. 19 by a 148-90 vote.

Boko Haram Attacks Kill Scores—Suicide bombings July 16-17 in northeastern Nigeria by Islamist insurgent group Boko Haram killed more than 60 people. Twin blasts killed at least 50, many of whom were shopping for the Eid al-Fitr holiday, at a Gombe marketplace. Multiple explosions near prayer grounds in Damaturu the following day killed 13. Attacks July 5 had killed 44 civilians at a restaurant and mosque in Jos in central Nigeria, bringing that week's death toll by the group to over 200. The Sunni extremist group known as Islamic State of Iraq and Syria (ISIS), with which Boko Haram allied itself in Mar. 2015, had issued an edict to increase bloodshed during Islam's holy month of Ramadan. According to Amnesty International, some 17,000 people had been killed in northeastern Nigeria since Boko Haram began its insurgency in 2009.

U.S., Cuba Renew Long-Severed Diplomatic Ties—U.S. and Cuba reopened embassies in their respective countries July 20, formally reestablishing diplomatic relations for the first time since 1961. Sec. of State John Kerry presided Aug. 14 over a flag-raising ceremony at the U.S. embassy in Havana that was criticized by some U.S. lawmakers, including Cuban-American senators Bob Menendez (D, NJ) and Marco Rubio (R, FL), for its exclusion of anti-Castro dissidents. The actions were the latest in the process of normalization that began in Dec. 2014. Substantial hurdles to rapprochement nonetheless remained, including U.S. congressional opposition to closing the U.S. military base at Guantánamo Bay and to ending the longstanding trade embargo against the island nation.

Turkey Joins Anti-ISIS Fight; U.S. Claims Slow Progress Against ISIS—An apparent ISIS suicide bombing killed at least 32 people and injured more than 100 others July 20 in Suruç, Turkey, near the Syrian border. The first alleged attack on Turkish soil by ISIS seemed to contribute to Turkey's July 23 decisions to send ground forces into combat with militants on the Syrian border and to grant the U.S. access to Incirlik Air Base outside of Adana, Turkey, to launch strikes against ISIS in Syria and Iraq. Turkey began airstrikes against ISIS July 24, but it drew criticism for its simultaneous crackdown on Kurdish militants in Turkey and for bombing raids against Kurdish targets in Iraq. After a month-long assault assisted by U.S. airstrikes, Kurdish militia members July 27 captured the strategic northern Syrian city of Sarrin. Egypt July 2 launched airstrikes in the Sinai Peninsula against ISIS-affiliated militants who killed 17 Egyptian soldiers the day before.

U.S. Defense Sec. Ashton Carter July 7 told a Senate committee that a three-year, $500-mil program to train some 15,000 Syrian moderate opposition fighters against ISIS had achieved limited results, with just 60 recruits in training. Carter's testimony came one day after Pres. Obama stated the necessity of strong local forces in the battle against ISIS. The U.S. had trained about 10,000 Iraqi soldiers, the first 3,000 of which were deployed near Ramadi by July 23, but that program faced recruitment shortages.

Sunni Forces Recapture Major Yemeni Port; Cease-Fires Fail—Forces opposed to Yemen's minority Zaidi Shiite Houthi rebels retook the country's second largest city of Aden July 23, the insurgents' first major loss since forcing Yemeni Pres. Abd Rabbuh Mansur Hadi into exile in early 2015. The reversal came with the support of Sunni coalition airstrikes, which Saudi Arabia had initiated nearly four months earlier against the Houthis, who were believed to be backed by Iran. The United Nations reported that over 3,260 people—including more than 1,500 civilians—had been killed and nearly 1.3 mil displaced since heavy clashes between pro-Hadi forces and Houthis began in late Mar. The UN negotiated two humanitarian cease-fires, to start July 10 and July 26, but both quickly fell apart.

Taliban Leader Declared Dead—The Sunni extremist Taliban, now operating mostly in Pakistan and Afghanistan, confirmed July 30 that its founder and elusive figurehead Mullah Mohammad Omar had died; it named former Omar deputy Mullah Akhtar Mohammad Mansour as its new leader. The announcement came one day after Afghan officials said Omar had died in a Pakistan hospital in Apr. 2013, but the Taliban said he had not left Afghanistan since the Taliban was ousted from power in 2001.

General

U.S. Triumphs in Women's World Cup—The U.S. women's national soccer team won its third World Cup title July 5 in Vancouver, BC, Canada, defeating Japan 5-2. U.S. team captain Carli Lloyd scored two goals within the championship game's first five minutes and again from midfield less than 10 minutes later to achieve the first hat trick in a Women's World Cup final. Some 25.4 mil U.S. viewers tuned in to watch the final, exceeding U.S. TV viewership for any previous men's or women's soccer game.

Williams and Djokovic Take Wimbledon Championships—For the second time in her career, No. 1-ranked Serena Williams won four consecutive Grand Slam titles when she defeated No. 20-seed Garbiñe Muguruza of Spain (6-4, 6-4) at the women's final of the Wimbledon Championships in London July 11. The next day, No. 1-seed and defending champion Novak Djokovic of Serbia beat No. 2-seed Roger Federer of Switzerland (7-6 [1], 6-7 [10], 6-4, 6-3) to win the men's title.

Mexican Drug Kingpin Escapes Prison—Notorious Mexican drug kingpin Joaquín "El Chapo" Guzmán escaped from a maximum security prison in Mexico July 11, allegedly by slipping undetected into a hole underneath his video-monitored cell's shower and fleeing through a nearly mile-long tunnel. Guzmán, head of the Sinaloa cartel, one of the world's largest and most powerful drug trafficking organizations, also escaped prison in 2001 and evaded authorities until 2014.

NASA Craft First to Reach Pluto—NASA's *New Horizons* spacecraft carried out the first-ever flyby of Pluto July 14, traveling within 7,800 mi of the dwarf planet and capturing images of its surface. The mission took more than nine years to reach Pluto and covered some 3 bil miles. The approximately 8-ft-wide craft collected data revealing that Pluto—demoted officially to dwarf planet status in 2006—has an icy northern cap and a diameter of about 1,473 mi. Because of the immense distance between the spacecraft and Earth, scientists will not finish downloading all of *New Horizons*'s data until late 2016.

Shooters Kill Tennessee Military Personnel, Louisiana Moviegoers; Colorado Theater Shooter Sentenced—A 24-year-old naturalized U.S. citizen born in Kuwait opened fire July 16 on two military facilities in Chattanooga, TN, killing four Marines and a Navy petty officer before he was shot dead by police. Mohammod Youssuf Abdulazeez began his rampage at a strip mall recruiting center, where he fired 25-30 shots from his vehicle. He then drove to a U.S. Navy reserve center, where he evaded the shots of at least one service member before killing five.

That same day, a Colorado jury convicted James Holmes in the mass-shooting murder of 12 people at an Aurora, CO, movie theater in 2012. The jury in Aug. recommended life without parole; a judge sentenced Holmes to 12 life sentences for the homicides and imposed an additional 3,318 years for his other crimes, including attempted murder of 140 and wounding 70.

A 59-year-old man gunman killed two people and wounded nine others July 23 at a movie theater in Lafayette, LA. The shooter, identified later as John Russell Houser, tried to flee but fatally shot himself when the police arrive. Houser had a history of mental illness but passed a required federal background check in order to legally purchase the gun used.

Johnson, Park Win Golf British Opens—Zach Johnson emerged the victor of a three-way, four-hole playoff at the 144th British Open golf championship July 20 at the Old Course in St. Andrews, Scotland. Tied with Marc Leishman of Australia and South African Louis Oosthuizen at 15-under-273 at the end of regulation, the 39-year-old American made birdies on the first two playoff holes to finish one stroke ahead of Oosthuizen and two ahead of Leishman.

Inbee Park of South Korea shot 12-under-276 Aug. 2 to win the 40th Women's British Open at Trump Turnberry in South Ayrshire, Scotland. It was the seventh major victory for the 27-year-old Park, who became the seventh female golfer to win four different majors.

British Racer Wins Second Tour de France—Chris Froome, a 30-year-old Briton born in Kenya, won the 102nd Tour de France, his second victory in three years, in Paris July 26. Slovakia's Peter Sagan claimed the green jersey as the race's best sprinter for the fourth straight year. Froome, who crashed out in 2014, finished the 2,088-mi course in 84 hr., 46 min., 14 sec. Nairo Quintana of Colombia finished 1 min., 12 sec. behind Froome, and Spaniard Alejandro Valverde came in third, 5 min., 25 sec., out of first.

August 2015

National

U.S. Proposes Final Carbon Emissions Regulations for Power Plants; Other Environment News—Pres. Barack Obama Aug. 3 unveiled the Environmental Protection Agency's final plan for imposing the first-ever nationwide limits on carbon dioxide output from the U.S. electric power sector, which produce about one-third of the nation's carbon emissions. Seeking to curb climate change connected to atmospheric carbon emissions, the Clean Power Plan mandated states develop strategies to cut power-plant carbon emissions by 32% from 2005 levels by 2030. Coming four months ahead of international climate talks in Paris, the $8.4-bil plan was hailed by environmentalists and criticized by the energy industry. Senate Majority Leader Mitch McConnell (R, KY) urged noncompliance, and 15 states announced they would challenge the regulations in court. Later in the month, the Natl. Oceanic and Atmospheric Admin. reported that July 2015 had been the hottest month to date since global average temperature recordkeeping began 135 years ago.

EPA contractors Aug. 5 accidentally spilled some 3 mil gallons of toxic wastewater from an abandoned gold mine into the Animas River in southwestern Colorado, turning the river a deep yellow color. The U.S. and Navajo Nation EPAs predicted no serious health or environmental effects based on preliminary tests, but some local residents remained unconvinced.

Federal Court Rules on Texas Voting Law—A federal appeals court unanimously ruled Aug. 5 that Texas's voter ID law discriminated against minorities and violated the 1965 Voting Rights Act. The strict 2011 measure mandated voters show one of seven specific government-issued IDs, excluding state college IDs and some other forms of identification. While the appeals court upheld the 2014 finding of discrimination by a Texas federal court, it disagreed with the lower court's conclusion that the law was effectively a poll tax. Instead, the three-judge panel instructed the Texas court to revisit the question of whether the law had been passed with discriminatory intent.

Violence Blemishes Ferguson Protests—A St. Louis county official declared a four-day-long state of emergency Aug. 10, a day after protests marking the one-year anniversary of the fatal police shooting of unarmed black teenager Michael Brown were marred by violence and disorder. Peaceful demonstrations Aug. 9 became tense after protesters confronted police responding to a break-in at a nearby store. Later that evening, police shot and critically wounded an 18-year-old black suspect who they claimed had fired on them. Several businesses were looted that same night, but while some demonstrators reportedly threw rocks and bottles at officers, protests over the next several days were mostly peaceful. Police arrested over 100 people, including about 60 trying to shut down an interstate. St. Louis police Aug. 19 used tear gas on demonstrators protesting the fatal police shooting that same day of an 18-year-old who had allegedly pointed a gun at police.

China Economic Fears Rattle Markets; Other Business News—Shaken along with other global stock markets for a second straight week by China's apparent economic slowdown, the Dow Jones Industrial Average plunged 1,089 points within the first six minutes of trading Aug. 24. The dramatic fall was the Dow's largest-ever point loss during a trading day, and the index closed the day with a loss of 588 points, the biggest one-day decline since Aug. 2011. The Dow closed the month at 16,528.03, down 6.6% from July, while the S&P 500 finished at 1,972.18, a 6.3% loss from the month before. The Nasdaq Composite Index closed at 4,776.51, down 6.9%. Stock prices of the tech giant Google rose 6% in after-hours trading Aug. 11 after Google announced it was restructuring and creating a public company, Alphabet, Inc., to house all of its ventures.

By a 3-2 vote, the federal Securities and Exchange Commission Aug. 5 approved a rule requiring most public companies disclose their CEO's salary in relation to their employees' median salary. The Labor Dept. reported Aug. 7 that the economy had added 215,000 jobs in July and that unemployment had held steady at 5.3%.

International

China Devalues Currency Following Stock Crisis—Following a 30% drop in Chinese stocks from mid-June through early July, the People's Bank of China unexpectedly devalued China's currency Aug. 11, leading to speculation the world's second largest economy was slowing more than predictions indicated. The yuan's 1.9% drop in value against the U.S. dollar was its largest downward adjustment since 1994 and caused global stock markets to contract; over the next two days the yuan's value dropped further, for a total 4.4% decline. The move favored Chinese exports, which were down 8.3% in July from 2014, and negatively impacted U.S. companies importing to China. China's central bank asserted the devaluing reflected their decision to tie the value of the yuan to the closing price of the previous day's trading. The Chinese stock bubble, which had peaked June 12, was thought by some analysts to have been partly fueled by amateur investing, as many new investors had bought on margin. Others pointed to the market's downturn as a signal and symptom of China's overall economic slowdown. The International Monetary Fund July 9 had forecast that China's previously explosive growth would slow to 6.8% in 2015, down from 7.4% the year before.

Iraqi Lawmakers Overhaul Government—Iraq's parliament Aug. 11 unanimously approved measures to reduce corruption in the country's political system. Proposed two days earlier by Prime Min. Haider al-Abadi, the measures did away with three deputy prime minister posts and three vice presidencies, one of which was held by Abadi's rival and predecessor Nouri al-Maliki. Although Maliki, the country's preeminent Shiite cleric Grand Ayatollah Ali al-Sistani, and most of Iraqi's Sunni leadership backed the plan, many questioned how ordinary minority Sunnis would respond to measures eliminating sectarian and party quotas and abolishing several top positions held by Sunnis, who had the power to create patronage jobs for supporters. Militants from the Sunni extremist group known as Islamic State of Iraq and Syria (ISIS), which captured large swaths of the country in 2014, had appealed to Sunnis' feelings of marginalization under Maliki's rule.

ISIS claimed responsibility for an early morning bomb blast at a Baghdad market that killed 76 people Aug. 13.

Eurozone Backs Third Greek Bailout; Prime Minister Survives Snap Election—Finance ministers from the 19-member nation eurozone Aug. 14 approved a three-year, $96-bil bailout loan package for debt-burdened Greece, allowing it to remain in the currency zone and ending more than half a year of contentious negotiations between the Greek government and international creditors that demanded that Greece expand austerity measures. Greece's parliament earlier that day passed the bailout—its third in five years—by a contentious 222-64 vote that saw 31 members of its ruling Syriza party side against the loan package and 11 abstain. Attempting to strengthen his position, Prime Min. Alexis Tsipras, who was elected seven months earlier on an anti-austerity platform, resigned Aug. 20 and called for early elections. He was returned to office Sept. 20 after Syriza won an unexpected 35.5% of the vote, giving it 145 of 300 parliamentary seats.

Yemeni Forces Continue Gains Against Houthis—Forces allegiant to exiled Yemeni Pres. Abd Rabbuh Mansur Hadi expelled minority Zaidi Shiite Houthi rebels from Yemen's southern province of Shabwa Aug. 15. Supported by a coalition of Sunni nations, pro-Hadi forces had achieved multiple victories in recent weeks, including the retaking of Lahj, Dalea, and Abyan provinces. In early Aug., 1,500 troops mostly from the United Arab Emirates arrived in the liberated southern port city of Aden. Although troops loyal to Hadi had made significant gains since the Houthis, believed to be backed by Iran, seized much of Yemen in Mar., fighting continued to kill scores of people. Houthi rocket attacks reportedly killed 14 civilians in the country's third-largest city of Taiz Aug. 21, three days after Saudi-led airstrikes killed 65 noncombatants there. Coalition strikes also killed 36 factory employees in northern Yemen in late Aug. The United Nations Aug. 19 reported that the conflict had killed about 4,500 people, including nearly 400 children and 1,950 civilians, since Mar. 26, and internally displaced 1.8 mil Yemenis.

Violent Civil War Persists in Syria—In one of the bloodiest air raids of Syria's four-year-old civil war, airstrikes by government forces loyal to Syrian Pres. Bashar al-Assad killed more than 80 people at a market in the rebel-occupied Damascus suburb of Douma during rush hour Aug. 16. Opposed to both Assad and more moderate rebels, ISIS militants in early Aug. seized the strategic central Syrian transport hub of Al-Qaryatain; they were blamed by the UK-based Syrian Observatory for Human Rights (SOHR) for kidnapping at least 230 people. ISIS militants also beheaded an 81-year-old former director of antiquities of the ancient city of Palmyra, where the group had destroyed multiple shrines and temples since first occupying it in May. Syria's civil war had killed over 240,000 people and displaced more than 11 mil according to SOHR as of Aug. 5.

Terrorists Attack Bangkok Shrine—A bomb blast in central Bangkok near Erawan Shrine, a Hindu temple popular with tourists, dispersed shrapnel up to 100 meters, killing 20 people and injuring more than 120 others, Aug. 17. The next day, a similar bomb was apparently thrown into a Bangkok river, where it exploded without causing injuries. Malaysian police by Sept. 23 had arrested two suspects and eight additional people over possible connections to activities surrounding the blast; on Sept. 25, they claimed that the first suspect arrested was the principal bomber, who had been captured on surveillance video placing a backpack under a bench near the shrine. He had yet to be charged as of Oct. 5.

South Sudan Signs Peace Agreement; Fighting Resumes—Threatened with international sanctions, South Sudanese Pres. Salva Kiir and rebel fighters signed a peace agreement Aug. 26 aimed at ending 20 months of conflict that had killed more than 10,000 people and displaced some 2.2 mil. Fighting in the fledgling country, which gained independence from Sudan in 2011, broke out after Kiir accused former Vice Pres. Riek Machar of organizing a coup. The charge, which Machar denied, spurred armed conflict along ethnic lines. Forces loyal to Machar denounced the president as well as parliament's decision in Mar. 2015 to extend Kiir's rule by three years. Both sides blamed one another for the collapse of earlier cease-fires, and Kiir voiced multiple reservations with the current agreement, including his displeasure at having to turn over the office of first vice president to the rebels. The deal also required the two factions to jointly control South Sudan's oil fields and called for a transitional unity government to take office in 90 days and govern for 30 months.

General

Industrial Explosions Kill Scores in China—Two powerful explosions killed at least 170 people and injured some 800 in the port city of Tianjin, China, about 90 mi northeast of Beijing, Aug. 12. The explosions, which occurred late in the evening, destroyed an industrial warehouse operated by Rui Hai International Logistics and damaged at least 17,000 homes. Chinese officials initiated an investigation into the company's reported storage of 700 tons of toxic sodium cyanide—70 times the legal amount—just 2,000 ft from residential buildings. Two detained Rui Hai executives reportedly told Xinhua, China's state-run news agency, that they improperly obtained warehouse licenses, and China in late Aug. fired its workplace safety chief over corruption allegations.

Jason Day Takes PGA Championship—Jason Day won the 97th PGA Championship—his first victory in a major—at Whistling Straights in Kohler, WI, Aug. 16. The 27-year-old Australian made seven birdies in the final round to finish atop the leaderboard with a 20-under-268, breaking Tiger Woods's 19-under-par majors record set in 2000. Day began the final 18 holes with a two-shot lead and maintained his position throughout, finishing three strokes ahead of Jordan Spieth.

Indonesian Plane Crash Kills All On Board; Officials Identify Wing Fragment From MH370—Indonesian Trigana Air Service Flight 257 crashed Aug. 16, killing all 49 passengers and 5 crew. The twin turboprop ATR 42-300, which departed from the capital of Papua province, went down in a remote mountainous area after it lost contact with the destination airport nine minutes before it was scheduled to land. It was Indonesia's third air disaster in nine months—AirAsia Flight QZ8501 crashed into the Java Sea in Dec., killing all 162 on board, and a military transport aircraft crashed shortly after takeoff in June, killing over 140 people, including more than a dozen on the ground.

Malaysian Prime Min. Najib Razak Aug. 5 announced that part of an aircraft wing that had washed up on France's Réunion Island in the Indian Ocean near Madagascar the week before was from Malaysian Airlines Flight 370, which lost contact with air traffic controllers Mar. 8, 2014, with 239 people on board. The six-ft-long fragment was the first physical evidence from the missing Boeing 777.

Passengers Overpower Gunman on European Train—A British man and three Americans, including two off-duty military personnel, apprehended a heavily armed gunman with alleged Islamic extremist ties on a high-speed train in Belgium bound for Paris Aug. 21. A French passenger initially tried to detain the 25-year-old Moroccan national; a French-American was shot in the neck when he attempted to wrestle away his rifle. The gunman also used a box cutter to slash a British passenger as well as one of the three Americans, who together tackled him after his gun jammed. All six were awarded the Legion of Honor, France's highest civilian medal.

Wildfires Rage in Washington State—Pres. Barack Obama declared a state of emergency Aug. 21 in northeastern and central Washington in response to an array of wildfires. Wildfires in the state had charred over 900,000 acres since June—more than double last year's total in Washington—and had sometimes pitted firefighters against erratic gusty winds that grounded firefighting aircraft. Some 1,250 firefighters battled a group of five wildfires known as the Okanogan Complex, which was the largest in state history at over 400 sq mi. Three firefighters died and four others were injured Aug. 19 at another fire.

A slew of fires struck drought-stricken western U.S. states in 2015. Including Alaska, where over 5 mil acres had been scorched, more than 8.2 mil acres had burned in the U.S. as of Sept. 1, far above the past 10-year average.

Disgruntled Gunman Kills TV Journalists—A former TV reporter shot and killed a reporter and camera operator from the Roanoke, VA, CBS affiliate Aug. 26. The pair were shot during a live-TV interview with a local official; the official was also shot and injured. The gunman, identified as Vester Lee Flanagan II, posted self-shot footage of the murders to social media. He was later pronounced dead of a self-inflicted gunshot wound. Fired two years earlier from the affiliate, where he had appeared on air as Bryce Williams, the assailant had filed a racial discrimination lawsuit against the station that had been dismissed.

September 2015

National

Kentucky Clerk Refuses to Grant Same-Sex Marriages—Elected county clerk Kim Davis of Rowan County, KY, was jailed Sept. 3 for ignoring a federal judge's orders to issue marriage licenses to same-sex couples following a U.S. Supreme Court decision that legalized same-sex marriage nationwide in late June. Davis was released Sept. 8 on the condition that she not interfere with her deputy clerks, who had begun issuing licenses to same-sex couples. Citing her religious conviction, Davis altered the licenses to remove her name and mentions of Rowan County upon her return to work. Davis's jailing generated protests on both sides, with the White House stating that Davis was "subject to the rule of law" and several Republican presidential candidates, including former Arkansas Gov. Mike Huckabee and Sen. Ted Cruz (TX), publicly supporting her.

Senate Resolution Against Iran Nuclear Deal Fails—Following weeks of fierce lobbying, Senate opponents of the nuclear accord between Iran and six world powers failed Sept. 10, in a 58-42 vote, to pass a resolution blocking it. The resolution's failure effectively authorized implementation of the two-month-old accord, which would lift crippling economic sanctions in Iran in exchange for it greatly restricting uranium quantities, enrichment potential, and nuclear research for 15 years. The House the following day defeated a symbolic resolution approving the deal by a bipartisan 269-162 vote.

Volkswagen Admits Cheating U.S. Emissions Tests; Other Economic News—The EPA accused Volkswagen Sept. 18 of fitting 482,000 of its 2009-15 model-year U.S. diesel engine cars with "defeat devices" that turned on emission controls during testing only, allowing the cars at other times to emit nitrogen oxide pollutants up to 40 times over allowable limits. The German automaker faced up to $18 bil in federal penalties and admitted that about 11 mil of its cars globally, including the VW-manufactured Audi A3, had the software. VW's stock fell about 30% as of Sept. 23, and CEO Martin Winterkorn resigned.

General Motors agreed Sept. 17 to pay $900 mil to settle a Justice Dept. criminal investigation into its failure to recall an ignition switch defect that shut off cars while in use, including systems like power steering and braking, leading to at least 124 deaths.

Marking the most severe punishment for a food-safety crime, Stewart Parnell, owner of the defunct Peanut Corp. of America, was sentenced Sept. 21 to 28 years in prison for knowingly shipping salmonella-contaminated peanut products linked to more than 700 cases of salmonella that killed nine people in 2008-09.

The Labor Dept. announced Sept. 4 that 173,000 jobs had been added to the U.S. economy in Aug.—45,000 fewer than the monthly average in 2015. Unemployment fell to 5.1%—its lowest rate since 2008—from 5.3% in July. In light of cascading global stock prices in Aug., the Federal Reserve said Sept. 17 that it would maintain interest rates at the near-zero levels they have been at since late 2008. The BEA's revised estimate of the second quarter 2015 GDP showed it increased at an annual rate of 3.9%, up from 0.6% in the first quarter. The Dow Jones Industrial Average closed the month at 16,284.70, down 1.5% from Aug., while the S&P 500 finished Sept. at 1,920.03, a 2.6% loss from the month before. The Nasdaq Composite Index closed at 4,620.16, down 3.3%.

Pope Addresses Congress on Five-Day U.S. Trip—Appearing before a joint session of Congress, Roman Catholic leader Pope Francis implored U.S. lawmakers Sept. 24 to come together to break impasses on immigration reform and climate change action. He pointedly called for the abolition of the death penalty and an end to arms dealing but didn't directly reference abortion or the U.S. Supreme Court's legalization of same-sex marriage. Pres. Barack Obama Sept. 22 greeted the pontiff at Joint Base Andrews as he arrived in the U.S. for the first time and met with him at the White House the following day. Francis also visited New York City, where he addressed the UN General Assembly Sept. 25 and celebrated mass at Madison Square Garden, and Philadelphia, where he appeared at the World Meeting of Families and held an outdoor mass with a crowd estimated at hundreds of thousands.

The Vatican Sept. 1 released a letter from Francis allowing priests in the Jubilee year the discretion to forgive "contrite" women who had abortions. A week later, the pope announced changes making it easier to obtain annulments.

Boehner Resigns as House Speaker; Congress Averts Government Shutdown—Embattled House Speaker John Boehner (R, OH) Sept. 25 announced he would resign both his speakership and his congressional seat at the end of Oct. Boehner, who had served in the House since 1991 and as speaker since 2011, had faced nearly constant challenges from increasingly conservative members of his party to confront the White House and House Democrats over issues such as immigration reform, Obamacare, government spending, and abortion. Leading up to Boehner's resignation announcement, a group of House Republicans withheld votes on a critical spending bill over Planned Parenthood funding, insisting the reproductive health care provider be banned from receiving federal financing.

Narrowly avoiding another government shutdown, the House Sept. 30 voted 277-151 to pass a stopgap measure funding federal agencies and Planned Parenthood through Dec. 11. The Senate ahead of the House approved the bill 78-20, which Pres. Barack Obama signed hours before current funding expired.

International

Refugee Crisis Sparks Discord in Central Europe and Balkans—Hungary Sept. 15 closed its southern border with Serbia to thousands of refugees and migrants mostly headed for Germany and other northern and western European countries. Arguing that the migrants—many of whom were fleeing war, oppression, or poverty—should apply for asylum when reaching Greece or Serbia, Hungary Sept. 16 began criminal proceedings against detained migrants. That same day, Hungarian police drew condemnation for using batons, pepper spray, tear gas, and water cannons against crowds that broke through a border barrier. Publicly critical of Hungary's response, Croatian officials initially permitted migrants to pass through but by Sept. 17 had closed seven of the nation's eight crossings with Serbia. The border closures came less than a week after officials announced border controls in Germany, which had already taken in 450,000 refugees in 2015 and expected 1-1.5 mil total by the end of the year.

The European Union Sept. 22 approved a disputed plan to take in 120,000 refugees and relocate them throughout the bloc's 28 member nations. While the plan addressed only a fraction of the nearly half-million people who had arrived since the beginning of 2015, some nations objected to being forced to accept migrant quotas. EU leaders Sept. 24 agreed to give $1.1 bil to UN organizations aiding refugees and another $1.1 bil in aid to countries closer to Syria, like Turkey and Jordan, who were already hosting millions of refugees.

The EU actions came in the wake of multiple incidents involving migrant deaths, including one in which 71 decomposing bodies were discovered in the back of a locked truck abandoned by an Austrian highway Aug. 27. According to the International Organization for Migration, 498,931 had crossed the Mediterranean during 2015 through Sept. 25, but at least 2,873 migrants had died or gone missing attempting to reach southern Europe by sea.

Military Coup Fails in Burkina Faso—The impoverished West African nation of Burkina Faso struggled through a weeklong coup attempt that began Sept. 16 when Gen. Gilbert Diendéré led military forces loyal to former Pres. Blaise Compaoré, who had resigned in Oct. 2014 after 27 years in power, in arresting interim Pres. Michel Kafando and Prime Min. Isaac Zida. Accusing Kafando of barring Compaoré's supporters from seeking office, military spokesman Lt. Col. Mamadou Bamba the next day declared the transitional government dissolved, instituted a nationwide curfew, and closed its borders. Mediators from the Economic Community of West African States (ECOWAS) negotiated a settlement that included Kafando's reinstatement as interim president Sept. 23 and participation of Compaoré-linked candidates in Nov. 2015 elections. At least 10 people were killed and more than 100 others injured in coup-related violence.

Taliban Seizes, Loses Afghan Regional Capital—In one of its largest gains since it was ousted by a U.S.-led military campaign in 2001, the Taliban Islamic extremist movement seized the northern Afghan provincial capital of Kunduz in an early morning surprise attack Sept. 28. Hundreds of prison inmates were freed in the assault, and some 6,000 residents fled. Backed by U.S. airstrikes and advisors on the ground, Afghan security forces fought the insurgents, reportedly retaking most of Kunduz by Oct. 1. The initial loss of the country's fifth-largest city had been a significant and symbolic blow to the one-year-old government of Pres. Ashraf Ghani and raised questions about the U.S.-led coalition's decision to formally end its combat mission in Afghanistan at the end of 2014 and current U.S. troop levels. At the time of the attack, the U.S. had 9,800 troops in Afghanistan serving primarily in a training and advisory role.

Russia Enters Syrian Civil War, Backing Assad—At the request of longtime ally Syrian Pres. Bashar al-Assad, Russia Sept. 30 began airstrikes in Syria that it claimed targeted the Sunni extremist group Islamic State of Iraq and Syria (ISIS). The U.S. alleged the strikes instead appeared to target groups that included U.S.-backed moderate rebels opposing Assad, who was accused of using brutal tactics against civilians and insurgents in the bloody civil war, in which an estimated 320,000 people have died since Mar. 2011. Russian Pres. Vladimir Putin said that Russia was providing heavy weaponry and training support to the Syrian Army, but some sources reported it had also deployed combat troops. France in late Sept. carried out its first airstrikes against ISIS in Syria.

The United Nations Aug. 31 said it had used satellite images to confirm that ISIS militants had destroyed the ancient Temple of Bel in Palmyra, Syria.

Separatist Conflict Escalates in Turkey—Violence between Turkish security forces and the separatist Kurdistan Workers Party (PKK) continued throughout Sept. in the midst of an air campaign the government launched in late July against militant strongholds in southeastern Turkey and neighboring northern Iraq. After bomb attacks claimed by the PKK killed at least 30 police officers and soldiers in Turkey, Sept. 6-8, Turkey sent troops into Iraq for the first time in two years. Airstrikes Sept. 11 reportedly hit 64 PKK targets in northern Iraq, killing at least 60 militants. Two Turkey cabinet ministers affiliated with the pro-Kurdish People's Democratic Party resigned Sept. 22 over the the rising violence. According to Turkish Pres. Recep Tayyip Erdogan, the conflict had killed about 2,000 PKK militants and some 100 Turkish security forces since July, when a two-year cease-fire ended. PKK-related violence had killed some 40,000 people since 1984, when the group first launched its insurgency.

General

Brady Suspension Void as NFL Loses Deflategate Case—A federal judge Sept. 3 nullified the four-game suspension imposed on New England Patriots quarterback Tom Brady by NFL Commissioner Roger Goodell, ruling that the league did not notify Brady of potential disciplinary actions for his supposed misconduct (related to the Patriots' alleged intentional underinflation of footballs for the AFC championship game in Jan. 2015). Brady, who had led the Patriots to a fourth Super Bowl win, consistently asserted that he did not play any role in "Deflategate." Goodell in May had concluded that Brady was "generally aware" of the conspiracy and suspended him for his role and for not cooperating with the NFL's investigation.

Pennetta and Djokovic Victorious at U.S. Open—Italian tennis player Flavia Pennetta won her first major title Sept. 12, when the 26-seed handily beat unseeded fellow countrywoman Roberta Vinci (7-6 [4], 6-2) at the Billie Jean King Natl. Tennis Center at Flushing Meadows-Corona Park in New York City. In an upset the day before, Vinci defeated three-time defending champion Serena Williams in three sets, dashing her bid to become the first player to win a calendar-year Grand Slam since 1988. On Sept. 13, top-seeded Novak Djokovic of Serbia defeated (6-4, 5-7, 6-4, 6-4) No. 2 seed Roger Federer of Switzerland, winning his second U.S. Open and 10th Grand Slam crown.

***Game of Thrones*, Viola Davis Claim Emmy Firsts**—HBO's fantasy series *Game of Thrones* won the Emmy for outstanding drama series along with 11 other awards—the most for a show in a single year—at the 67th Primetime Emmy Awards Sept. 20 at Microsoft Theater in Los Angeles, CA. Among other highlights, Viola Davis became the first African American to win outstanding lead actress in a drama series for her role in ABC's *How to Get Away With Murder*. Jon Hamm, empty-handed after seven earlier nominations, was awarded best actor in a drama series for AMC's *Mad Men*. The HBO political comedy *Veep*—whose star Julia Louis-Dreyfus picked up outstanding lead actress in a comedy series for a fourth straight year—won its first Emmy for outstanding comedy series.

Wildfires Turn Deadly in Drought-Stricken California—Pres. Barack Obama declared a major disaster Sept. 22 for a blaze known as the Valley Fire that had killed at least three people and burned more than 118 sq mi in Lake, Napa, and Sonoma Counties north of San Francisco. Since breaking out Sept. 12, the fire had forced the evacuation of about 12,000 people and burned nearly 2,000 buildings. Two other northern

California fires claimed three more lives in Sept.—two people were overcome by the Butte Fire, which was largely contained and had burned some 110 sq mi since Sept. 9; a third caused the thousand-acre Tassajara Fire in Monterey County when he committed suicide.

Hundreds Die in Hajj Stampede; Crane Collapse Crushes Scores—Overcrowding at the annual five-day Islamic hajj pilgrimage in Saudi Arabia contributed to a stampede in which 2,177 worshippers were killed in Mina near the holy city of Mecca, Sept. 24. Saudi Arabia, whose official death toll was about one-third of the number compiled by the Associated Press, faced criticism over its management of the event, which went awry as two large groups of pilgrims converged at a crossroads. The incident, the deadliest at the hajj since a 1990 stampede killed 1,426, came less than two weeks after a construction crane collapsed Sept. 11 amidst strong winds and heavy rain at Mecca's Grand Mosque, killing at least 107 people.

NASA Reports Surface Water on Mars—NASA announced Sept. 28 there was evidence of the seasonal flow of liquid water on the surface of Mars in the present day. Based on images and findings from the Mars Reconnaissance Orbiter, researchers determined that seasonal streaks along Mars's slopes contain hydrated salts that demonstrate the presence of liquid water. Although researchers had long known that the planet's poles contained frozen water, liquid water occurring on the surface of the Red Planet was believed to boost the possibility of researchers finding life beyond Earth.

October 2015

National

Dell, EMC Announce Mega Merger; Other Economic Developments—Texas-based computer giant Dell Inc. agreed Oct. 12 to buy software and data storage developer EMC Corp. for $67 bil in cash and stock. If authorized by shareholders and regulators, it would be the largest-ever merger between tech companies. The proposed acquisition would position Dell as the world's largest privately-held tech firm and give it a controlling stake in the virtualization software developer VMWare Inc.

The Labor Dept. reported Oct. 2 that 142,000 jobs had been added to the U.S. economy in Sept., far less than forecast. The unemployment rate nonetheless held at 5.1% in Sept., the same as the month before. After a weak Sept., stocks saw large gains as the Dow Jones Industrial Average rose 8.5% in Oct., closing at 17,663.54, and the S&P 500 rose 8.3%, closing at 2,079.36. The Nasdaq Composite Index rose 9.4%, closing at 5,053.75.

The World Bank Oct. 4 projected the world's extreme poverty rate was set to fall to 9.6% of the world's population, or 702 mil people, in 2015; the rate had never before fallen below 10%.

Clinton Weathers Benghazi Questioning; Other 2016 Presidential Race Developments—Democratic presidential contender Hillary Clinton largely held her ground for more than eight hours of questioning Oct. 22 by a House committee investigating the 2012 attack on two U.S. facilities in Benghazi, Libya, that killed four Americans while Clinton served as secretary of state. Although seven prior congressional investigations had found no intentional fault with the administration, committee Republicans raised a newly revealed phone conversation and email in which Clinton labeled the incident a terror attack days before the administration publicly said otherwise. Clinton said she sent the emails before a terror group rescinded taking credit. Committee Democrats said the questioning was politically motivated.

Ending months of conjecture, Vice Pres. Joe Biden Oct. 21 announced he would not run for president. Former Rhode Island Gov. Lincoln Chafee and former Sen. Jim Webb (VA) dropped out of the Democratic race in Oct. The month before, Wisconsin Gov. Scott Walker and former Texas Gov. Rick Perry had withdrawn from the Republican Party's crowded presidential race.

Ryan Claims House Speaker Gavel; Congress Passes Budget Bill—U.S. Rep. Paul Ryan (R, WI), the GOP's 2012 vice presidential candidate, was elected the 54th speaker of the House of Representatives Oct. 29, replacing House speaker John Boehner (R, OH), who had announced his resignation the month before. In formal voting, Ryan won the support of 236 representatives, Rep. Daniel Webster (R, FL) received nine votes, and House Minority Leader Nancy Pelosi (D, CA) won the backing of all but three Democratic members. The 45-year-old Ryan, the youngest speaker since 1869, appealed for unity among the splintered Republican caucus as well as between Democrats and Republicans in the institution, which he called "broken." Boehner's heir-apparent, House Majority Leader Kevin McCarthy (R, CA), withdrew from consideration Oct. 8 after some conservative House members, who linked McCarthy with Boehner, opposed his candidacy. Those Republicans provided Webster with 43 votes in the party's internal nomination vote but largely cast their final votes for Ryan, who had initially refused to run.

Clearing a major obstacle for Ryan, the House Oct. 28 voted 266-167 to pass a budget bill that would increase spending by $80 bil through 2017 and raise the government's debt ceiling ahead of a Nov. 3 debt-default deadline. The bill had the support of Democrats, but less than one-third of the Republican caucus supported it. The Senate voted, on similar ideological lines, 64-35, to approve the bill Oct. 30.

International

U.S. Bombs Hospital in Afghanistan; Taliban Makes Gains—A U.S. plane conducting airstrikes against suspected Taliban militants in Kunduz in northeastern Afghanistan repeatedly bombed a hospital there Oct. 3, killing at least 30. The hospital was operated by the international nonprofit Doctors Without Borders, which Oct. 7 called for an impartial, independent investigation into the bombing by the Intl. Humanitarian Fact-Finding Commission, in addition to those being conducted by U.S., NATO, and Afghan military officials. Pres. Barack Obama formally apologized, and the Pentagon pledged payments to victims' families. Afghanistan's defense minister Oct. 19 said insurgents had been using the hospital as a safe haven, which Doctors Without Borders staff denied. U.S. officials said analysts had uncovered evidence prior to the bombings suggesting the hospital had been used by the Taliban and may have contained weaponry.

Taliban militants Oct. 14 reportedly killed 29 border officers in the southern province of Helmand near Kandahar. Threatening the province's capital of Lashkar Gah, militants were repelled by security forces in the suburbs of Babaji and Toghi and reportedly suffered 35 fatalities. Militants had killed at least 22 officers by Oct. 20, within days of occupying a primary district in the northwestern province of Faryab. In light of the escalating violence, Obama Oct. 15 said he would keep 5,500 U.S. troops in Afghanistan into 2017, down from the current level of 9,800 but dashing his pledge to bring all but 1,000 home before he left office.

Agreement Reached on Sweeping Pacific Trade Deal—Officials from the U.S., Japan, Australia, and nine other nations settled Oct. 5 on an agreement known as the Trans Pacific Partnership (TPP) that would eliminate thousands of tariffs between member countries, who accounted for about 40% of global trade. Capping five years of talks, the agreement did not include China and still required approval from several signatories' legislatures, including the U.S. Congress. Advocates claimed that TPP, a cornerstone of Obama's trade agenda, would boost U.S. access to foreign markets and result in domestic job growth, but U.S. lawmakers critical of the deal—including numerous Democrats—said it would cause businesses and jobs to move overseas. Obama in June had gained fast-track authority, which permitted him to submit the agreement to Congress for approval without amendments.

Explosions Kill Scores at Turkish Peace Rally—Two bomb blasts detonated at the start of a scheduled peace demonstration in Turkey's capital of Ankara Oct. 10, killing at least 95 people and injuring hundreds. Pro-Kurdish party demonstrators believed they were the primary targets of the violence. The rally, staged three weeks ahead of national elections, was held to protest renewed violence between the government and separatist Kurdistan Workers' (PKK) party militants. Turkish planes bombed PKK targets in southeastern Turkey and northern Iraq, reportedly killing 30-35 militants Oct. 11, one day after PKK officials declared a cease-fire. Conflict between separatists and the Turkish government had killed more than 40,000 people since 1984.

Liberals Gain Majority in Canadian Parliament—Denying a fourth term to incumbent Canadian Prime Min. Stephen Harper of the Conservative party, who had led since 2006, voters Oct. 19 elected Liberal candidates to an outright majority (184 of 338 seats) in the nation's parliament. Participated in by 68.5% of eligible voters, the election elevated Liberal party leader Justin Trudeau, the son of former Prime Min. Pierre Trudeau, to prime minister. Harper's party won 99 seats, down from 159 before the election, and the New Democratic Party won 44, down from 95. The Liberals won the largest number of seats of any party since 1984, and its 148-seat gain was the greatest single-election increase ever. Among Trudeau's campaign pledges were increasing infrastructure spending, legalizing marijuana, taking action on climate change, accepting more Syrian refugees, and withdrawing Canada from the U.S.-led air campaign against ISIS.

Violence Flares in Jerusalem, West Bank—A deadly rash of stabbing attacks by Palestinians against Israelis, primarily in Jerusalem and the West Bank, killed at least 11 Israelis and injured more than 100 in Oct. The attacks were met with violence; Israel by Oct. 29 reportedly fatally shot at least 62 Palestinians at the scene of Oct. attacks or protests, including 35 alleged to have been armed assailants. Tensions ran high over Jerusalem's Al-Aqsa mosque compound, sacred to both Muslims and Jews, starting with clashes in Sept. over the Jewish High Holy Days. Israeli Prime Min. Benjamin Netanyahu Oct. 24 announced measures to maintain the status quo barring non-Muslim prayer there. Palestinian leaders had called instead for Jordan to control access to the mosque, as it had until 2000.

Conservatives Win Big in Polish Elections—Poland's right-wing opposition Law and Justice Party (PiS) won 235 of 460 lower house parliament seats in Oct. 25 elections, marking the first time a single party won enough votes to govern alone since Poland shed communism in 1989. Beata Szydlo was slated to become prime minister after the elections, which were participated in by 50.9% of eligible voters. The centrist Civic Platform, which had led coalition governments since 2007 and sought closer links to Europe, won 138 seats, down from 197, and a new right-wing party, Kukiz'15, claimed 42 seats. The economically protectionist PiS campaigned with an anti-immigrant stance, putting it at odds with future mandatory migrant quotas aimed at addressing Europe's refugee crisis.

EU, Balkan Nations Address Migrant Crisis—Eleven European Union and Balkan leaders meeting in Brussels, Belgium, agreed Oct. 25 on a 17-point plan aimed at managing a growing flood of refugees and migrants; almost 700,000 had reached Europe since the start of 2015. The leaders pledged to provide United Nations-aided temporary shelter to 50,000 refugees at Greek reception centers and 50,000 more in northern countries, as well as increase efforts to register migrants in Greece and repatriate those not in need of international protection. Turkey had agreed Oct. 15 to enact measures to stem the tide of refugees entering Europe in exchange for talks on its joining the EU.

Reflecting the internal tensions of some countries where migrant numbers were high, Germany's southern state of Bavaria Oct. 9 threatened to sue the government if it did not limit the influx of refugees, over 225,000 of whom were estimated to have entered since Sept 1. Bavaria also announced a plan to deport asylum seekers to Austria, challenging German Chancellor Angela Merkel's refusal to put limits on arrivals. Thousands of refugees and migrants surged into Croatia Oct. 19 after it reopened its border with Serbia; Croatia had closed entry after neighboring Hungary sealed its southern border in Sept. The UN Oct. 22 accused the Czech Republic of human rights violations by holding refugees up to 90 days and strip-searching them for money to pay for detention.

U.S., Other Nations Expand Roles in Iraq and Syria—Foreign participation in Syria's four-year-old civil war intensified in Oct., with U.S. Pres. Barack Obama declaring Oct. 30 that he would for the first time deploy dozens of special operations forces to help fight ISIS. The shift followed an Oct. 9 announcement by the U.S. that it was suspending its unsuccessful $500-mil Syrian rebel training program in favor of aiding a select group of vetted leaders. An Oct. 22 joint mission by U.S. and Iraqi forces freed about 70 hostages held by ISIS in the Iraqi province of Kirkuk but left one U.S. soldier fatally wounded—the first killed in action since U.S. began anti-ISIS operations in 2014.

British Defense Sec. Michael Fallon said Oct. 2 that his agency's intelligence suggested that since Russia began conducting airstrikes Sept. 30, only 5% of Russian strikes had hit ISIS targets—Russia's stated mission—and most were instead deployed against civilians and Western-supported groups who opposed Syrian Pres. Bashar al-Assad. Russia said it had launched airstrikes against ISIS's de facto capital of Raqqa along with ISIS positions elsewhere. The U.S. and Russia reached an agreement Oct. 20 on protocols aimed at avoiding midair incidents between their forces over Syria.

Representatives of the EU, UN, and 17 countries including Iran—present at a Syria summit for the first time—met Oct. 30 in Vienna, Austria, seeking a solution to the conflict the UN said had left some 13.5 mil in need of aid and protection. Though they failed to reach consensus on Assad's future role, participants agreed on some points, inviting the UN to broker a political process that would lead to a new constitution, and agreed to hold more talks in Nov. 2015.

General

Mudslide Buries Hundreds in Guatemala—Heavy rains set off a landslide Oct. 1 that engulfed most of the southern Guatemalan village of El Cambray Dos, killing at least 280 people and covering some dwellings in about 50 ft of earth from a collapsed hillside. Some 1,800 firefighters, soldiers, and volunteers searched for victims, but about 70 people remained missing as of mid-Oct.

Oregon Gunman Kills Nine, Sparks Further Gun Control Debate—A heavily armed 26-year-old student opened fire Oct. 1 at Umpqua Community College in Roseburg, OR, killing an instructor and eight students and injuring nine others. One of the injured, Army veteran Chris Mintz, was shot five times while reportedly preventing the gunman, identified as Christopher Harper-Mercer, from reaching a second classroom. The shooter fatally shot himself after he was injured by responding police. Pres. Barack Obama continued earlier pleas for stricter gun control, which drew criticism from Republican presidential candidates; all six weapons the shooter brought to school were purchased legally. Leaders of nine national law enforcement groups Oct. 26 called for Congress to broaden background checks to cover all gun sales, including private and gun show purchases not currently covered.

Flooding in Carolinas Turns Deadly—Historically high rainfall in North and South Carolina brought flooding that killed at least 19 people by Oct. 7. Aggravated by Hurricane Joaquin in the Caribbean, the storm system Oct. 3-4 dumped up to 14 in. on the Columbia area, which had rainfall every day but one since Sept. 23. Pres. Barack Obama declared a state of emergency in South Carolina Oct. 3.

Lynx Clinch WNBA Championship—The Minnesota Lynx won Game 5, 69-52, over the Indiana Fever Oct. 14 at Target Center in Minneapolis, MN, to claim the Women's National Basketball Association Championship. It was Minnesota's third title in five years and the league's first finals to reach a deciding Game 5 since 2009. Minnesota center Sylvia Fowles was named Finals MVP, with 20 points and 11 rebounds in Game 5.

Hundreds Die in South Asia Earthquake—A magnitude-7.5 earthquake struck northeastern Afghanistan's mountainous Hindu Kush region Oct. 26, killing at least 115 in Afghanistan and 272 in neighboring Pakistan and injuring more than 2,000 others. The quake's epicenter was about 132 mi below the surface, making it less destructive than the much shallower 7.6 magnitude quake that killed more than 70,000 people in Kashmir in 2005.

Russian Airline Disaster Kills 224 in Egypt—A Russian Airbus A-321 crashed in Egypt's central Sinai region Oct. 31, killing all 217 passengers and seven crew on board. Bound for St. Petersburg, Kogalymavia Flight 9268 disappeared from radar 23 min. after taking off in clear weather from Sharm el-Sheikh, an Egyptian resort area. Although ISIS-allied militants claimed responsibility for the crash, Russia's transportation minister rejected the group's pronouncement, asserting the militants did not have the technical capability to down the jetliner.

OBITUARIES

(Nov. 1, 2014-Oct. 31, 2015)

A

Abdullah bin Abdulaziz, 90, Saudi Arabian king who sought to modernize the country; Riyadh, Saudi Arabia, Jan. 23, 2015.

Adelson, Merv, 85, TV producer and cofounder of Lorimar production company, which created *The Waltons* (1972-81) and *Dallas* (1978-91); Los Angeles, CA, Sept. 8, 2015.

Anderson, Brad, 91, cartoonist who created the comic strip *Marmaduke*; The Woodlands, TX, Aug. 30, 2015.

Anderson, Lynn, 67, Grammy Award-winning country singer best known for "(I Never Promised You a) Rose Garden" (1970); Nashville, TN, July 30, 2015.

Antonelli, Laura, 73, Italian actress and sex symbol of the 1970s known for *Till Marriage Do Us Part* (1974) and *The Innocent* (1976); Ladispoli, Italy, June 22, 2015.

Arbour, Al, 82, Hall of Fame Canadian hockey defenseman who went on to coach the NY Islanders to four Stanley Cups (1980-83); Sarasota, FL, Aug. 28, 2015.

B

Baer, Ralph, 92, German-born inventor of the first home video game system (sold as Magnavox Odyssey, 1972); Manchester, NH, Dec. 6, 2014.

Bailey, Jim, 77, female impersonator best known for performances as Judy Garland and Barbra Streisand; Los Angeles, CA, May 30, 2015.

Banks, Ernie, 83, Hall of Fame Chicago Cubs infielder (1953-71) and two-time MVP; Chicago, IL, Jan. 23, 2015.

Barry, Marion, 78, civil rights activist and Washington, DC, mayor (D, 1979-91, '95-'99); FBI surveillance showed him using crack cocaine (1990) and he was jailed for six months; Washington, DC, Nov. 23, 2014.

Bednarik, Chuck, 89, Hall of Fame linebacker for the Philadelphia Eagles (1949-62); Richland, PA, Mar. 21, 2015.

Béliveau, Jean, 83, Canadian hockey player; Longueuil, QC, Can., Dec. 2, 2014.

Berger, Sy, 91, Topps employee credited with designing the modern-day baseball card (1952); Rockville Centre, NY, Dec. 14, 2014.

Berra, Yogi, 90, Hall of Fame catcher for the NY Yankees and later Yankees and NY Mets manager; known for Yogi-isms including "It ain't over till it's over"; West Caldwell, NJ, Sept. 22, 2015.

Biden, Beau, 46, Delaware attorney general (2007-15) and son of Vice Pres. Joe Biden; Bethesda, MD, May 30, 2015.

Big Bank Hank (Henry Jackson), 58, founding member of hip-hop's Sugarhill Gang, known for "Rapper's Delight" (1979); Englewood, NJ, Nov. 11, 2014.

Bikel, Theodore, 91, Austrian-American actor and musician who played Tevye in *Fiddler on the Roof* onstage; Los Angeles, CA, July 21, 2015.

Bing, Elisabeth, 100, German-born physical therapist who cofounded Lamaze Intl. (1960); New York, NY, May 15, 2015.

Boggs, Grace Lee, 100, Chinese-American writer and human rights activist; Detroit, MI, Oct. 5, 2015.

Bond, Julian, 75, civil rights activist who served in the Georgia legislature (1967-87) and as head of the NAACP (1998-2010); Fort Walton Beach, FL, Aug. 15, 2015.

Brady, Sarah, 73, gun control advocate; wife of James Brady, the White House press secretary shot and disabled in an assassination attempt on Pres. Ronald Reagan (1981); Alexandria, VA, Apr. 3, 2015.

Bridwell, Norman, 86, author and illustrator who created Clifford the Big Red Dog in dozens of children's books; Oak Bluffs, MA, Dec. 12, 2014.

Brooke, Edward, III, 95, first African-American U.S. senator (R, MA, 1967-79) elected by popular vote; Coral Gables, FL, Jan. 3, 2015.

Brown, Bobbi Kristina, 22, media personality and daughter of singers Whitney Houston and Bobby Brown; Duluth, GA, July 26, 2015.

Bugliosi, Vincent, 80, prosecutor in Manson family murder trials (1969); *Helter Skelter* (1974) was his best-selling account of the case; Los Angeles, CA, June 6, 2015.

Burgdorfer, Willy, 89, Swiss-born entomologist who discovered the cause of Lyme disease; Hamilton, MT, Nov. 17, 2014.

Byrne, Jane, 81, first woman mayor of Chicago (D, 1979-83); known for promoting arts and tourism during a single tumultuous term; Chicago, IL, Nov. 14, 2014.

C

Carawan, Guy, 87, musician who introduced the 18th-cent. folk song "We Shall Overcome" to the civil rights movement; New Market, TN, May 2, 2015.

Carr, David, 58, *NY Times* media columnist who also chronicled his drug and alcohol addiction; New York, NY, Feb. 12, 2015.

Casper, Billy, 83, Hall of Fame golfer who won 51 PGA tournaments; Springville, UT, Feb. 7, 2015.

Charbonnier, Stéphane, 47, French editor and cartoonist at satirical magazine *Charlie Hebdo*; killed with 11 others in a terrorist attack; Paris, France, Jan. 7, 2015.

Clark, Eugenie, 92, marine biologist who studied shark behavior; Sarasota, FL, Feb. 25, 2015.

Cocker, Joe, 70, British-born Grammy Award-winning singer known for "You Are So Beautiful" (1975) and "Up Where We Belong" (1982); Crawford, CO, Dec. 22, 2014.

Coleman, Ornette, 85, jazz saxophonist and composer who innovated the controversial free jazz movement of the 1960s; New York, NY, June 11, 2015.

Collins, Jackie, 77, British-born author who wrote best-selling romance novels, with over 500 mil in print; Los Angeles, CA, Sept. 19, 2015.

Conquest, Robert, 98, British-born historian of Soviet history, best known for *The Great Terror: Stalin's Purge of the Thirties* (1968); Stanford, CA, Aug. 3, 2015.

Corliss, Richard, 71, critic who edited *Film Comment* magazine (1970-90) and reviewed films for *Time* (1980-2015); New York, NY, Apr. 23, 2015.

Crane, Phil, 84, U.S. representative (R, IL, 1969-2005) who campaigned for president (1980); Jefferson, MD, Nov. 8, 2014.

Craven, Wes, 76, filmmaker known for horror films, notably the Nightmare on Elm Street and Scream franchises; Los Angeles, CA, Aug. 30, 2015.

Cuomo, Mario, 82, New York governor (D, 1983-94) known for liberal views and keynote speech at the 1984 Democratic convention; New York, NY, Jan. 1, 2015.

D

Dahl, Gary, 78, advertising copywriter who invented pet rocks (1975); Jacksonville, OR, Mar. 23, 2015.

Dark, Alvin, 92, All-Star MLB shortstop and manager who was dogged by controversy over racist comments he allegedly made; Easley, SC, Nov. 13, 2014.

Dawkins, Darryl, 58, basketball center known for dunking with backboard-smashing strength; Allentown, PA, Aug. 27, 2015.

DeFranco, Buddy, 91, jazz clarinetist whose style evolved from swing to bebop; Panama City, FL, Dec. 24, 2014.

DeLuca, Fred, 67, cofounder of fast-food franchise Subway, which he started at the age of 17; Lauderdale Lakes, FL, Sept. 14, 2015.

Demirel, Suleyman, 90, seven-time prime minister and president (1993-2000) of Turkey; Ankara, Turkey, June 17, 2015.

Dickens, "Little" Jimmy, 94, country singer known for novelty songs and diminutive size; Nashville, TN, Jan. 2, 2015.

Doctorow, E(dgar) L(awrence), 84, novelist who placed fictional characters in historic situations; best known for *Ragtime* (1975); New York, NY, July 21, 2015.

Doubleday, Nelson, Jr., 81, president of publishing business Doubleday & Co., which became majority owner of the NY Mets (1980); Locust Valley, NY, June 17, 2015.

Douglas, Donna, 82, actress known as Elly May Clampett on *The Beverly Hillbillies* (1962-71); Baton Rouge, LA, Jan. 1, 2015.

Dyer, Wayne, 75, self-help author whose *Your Erroneous Zones* (1976) sold over 35 mil copies; Maui, HI, Aug. 29, 2015.

E

Egan, Edward Cardinal, 82, Roman Catholic archbishop of New York whose tenure dealt with financial challenges and the clergy sexual abuse scandals; New York, NY, Mar. 5, 2015.

Ekberg, Anita, 83, Swedish-Italian actress and sex symbol of the 1960s known for Fellini's *La Dolce Vita* (1960); Rocca di Papa, Italy, Jan. 11, 2015.

F

Fairchild, John, 87, magazine publisher and editor who transformed *Women's Wear Daily* into industry standard; founder of *W*; New York, NY, Feb. 27, 2015.

Featherstone, Don, 79, artist who invented the plastic pink flamingo (1957); Fitchburg, MA, June 22, 2015.

Feinberg, Leslie, 65, transgender activist and writer known for *Stone Butch Blues* (1993); Syracuse, NY, Nov. 15, 2014.

Ferrero, Michele, 89, Italian owner of Ferrero SpA, the company that marketed Nutella, a hazelnut chocolate spread (1964); Monte Carlo, Monaco, Feb. 14, 2015.

Ford, Wendell H., 90, Kentucky governor (D, 1971-74) and U.S. senator (1974-99); Owensboro, KY, Jan. 22, 2015.

Fraser, Malcolm, 84, Australian prime minister (1975-83); Melbourne, Australia, Mar. 20, 2015.

Freberg, Stan, 88, humorist, voice artist, and advertising director who made hit comedy records; Santa Monica, CA, Apr. 7, 2015.

Friel, Brian, 86, Tony Award-winning Irish playwright best known for *Dancing at Lughnasa* (1990); Greencastle, Ireland, Oct. 2, 2015.

G

Gagne, Verne, 89, 16-time world heavyweight champion wrestler who founded the Amer. Wrestling Assn.; Bloomington, MN, Apr. 27, 2015.

Gay, Peter, 91, German-born American cultural historian best known for a biography of Sigmund Freud and a history of the Enlightenment; New York, NY, May 12, 2015.

George, Francis Cardinal, 78, Roman Catholic archbishop of Chicago who helped adopt zero-tolerance policy for priests who committed child sexual abuse; Chicago, IL, Apr. 17, 2015.

Gifford, Frank, 84, Hall of Fame running back for the NY Giants; sportscaster for *Monday Night Football* (1971-97); Greenwich, CT, Aug. 9, 2015.

Gilbert, Ronnie, 88, folk singer with the Weavers, a group blacklisted in 1952; Mill Valley, CA, June 6, 2015.

Gilroy, Frank D., 89, Pulitzer Prize- and Tony Award-winning playwright of *The Subject Was Roses* (1964); Monroe, NY, Sept. 12, 2015.

Gimble, Johnny, 88, Grammy Award-winning country fiddler; Marble Falls, TX, May 9, 2015.

Glatzer, Richard, 63, filmmaker who co-directed *Still Alice* (2014) while suffering from ALS; Los Angeles, CA, Mar. 10, 2015.

Gómez Bolaños, Roberto "Chespirito," 85, Mexican comic known for TV sitcom *El Chavo del Ocho* (*The Boy From Number 8*); Cancún, Mexico, Nov. 28, 2014.

Gordon, Bernice, 101, crossword puzzle constructor; Philadelphia, PA, Jan. 29, 2015.

Gore, Lesley, 68, pop singer and songwriter known for "It's My Party" (1963); New York, NY, Feb. 16, 2015.

Gotbaum, Victor, 93, New York City labor leader who helped the city avoid bankruptcy in 1975; New York, NY, Apr. 5, 2015.

Grass, Günter, 87, Nobel Prize-winning German writer whose work confronted his country's past; best known for first novel *The Tin Drum* (1959); admitted in 2006 that he was a member of the Waffen-SS in WWII; Lubeck, Germany, Apr. 13, 2015.

Graves, Michael, 80, architect of postmodern buildings and designer of household items; Princeton, NJ, Mar. 12, 2015.

Graziani, Bettina, 89, French fashion model; one of the world's first supermodels; Paris, France, Mar. 2, 2015.

Guillermin, John, 89, British film director known for action movies including *The Towering Inferno* (1974); Topanga, CA, Sept. 27, 2015.

H

Hart, Doris, 89, tennis player who won 35 Grand Slam titles (singles, doubles, and mixed doubles); Coral Gables, FL, May 29, 2015.

Haruf, Kent, 71, novelist whose tales, set in a fictional small Colorado town, included the best-seller *Plainsong* (1999); Salida, CO, Nov. 30, 2014.

Herrmann, Edward, 71, Tony and Emmy Award-winning actor known for portrayals of Franklin D. Roosevelt and TV's *Gilmore Girls* (2000-07); New York, NY, Dec. 31, 2014.

Hesburgh, Theodore, 97, Catholic priest who was Notre Dame Univ. (1952-87) president; member of the Civil Rights Commission (1957-72); Notre Dame, IN, Feb. 26, 2015.

Horner, James, 61, Academy Award-winning composer best known for *Titanic* (1997); Los Padres National Forest, CA, June 22, 2015.

J

James, P(hyllis) D(orothy), 94, British crime novelist whose works featured the fictional detective and poet Adam Dalgliesh; Oxford, Eng., UK, Nov. 27, 2014.

Jones, Dean, 84, actor known for boyish good looks and Disney films (1965-77) including the Love Bug franchise; Los Angeles, CA, Sept. 1, 2015.

Jones, Howard W., Jr., 104, surgeon who with wife Dr. Georgeanna Seegar Jones (1912-2005), pioneered in vitro fertilization; Norfolk, VA, July 31, 2015.

Jourdan, Louis, 93, French-born actor best remembered for *Gigi* (1958) and *Can-Can* (1960); Beverly Hills, CA, Feb. 14, 2015.

K

Kastenmeier, Robert, 91, U.S. representative (D, WI, 1959-91) who opposed the Vietnam War; Arlington, VA, Mar. 20, 2015.

Kelsey, Frances Oldham, 101, Canadian-born pharmacologist; prevented outbreak of birth defects in 1960 by denying FDA approval for a drug containing thalidomide; London, ON, Canada, Aug. 7, 2015.

Kerkorian, Kirk, 98, financier who helped build hotels and casinos in Las Vegas; bought and sold MGM studios three times; Los Angeles, CA, June 15, 2015.

King, (Riley) B. B., 89, Grammy Award-winning blues singer and guitarist; hits included "The Thrill Is Gone" (1970); Las Vegas, NV, May 14, 2015.

King, Ben E., 76, Hall of Fame singer and songwriter with the Drifters (1958-60); solo career included "Stand by Me" (1961); Hackensack, NJ, Apr. 30, 2015.

King, Michael, 67, media executive who syndicated *Jeopardy!* and *The Oprah Winfrey Show*; Los Angeles, CA, May 27, 2015.

L

Larson, Jack, 87, actor and playwright known for playing Jimmy Olsen on TV's *The Adventures of Superman* (1952-58); Brentwood, CA, Sept. 20, 2015.

LeBaron, Eddie, 85, NFL quarterback nicknamed "Little General"; Stockton, CA, Apr. 1, 2015.

Lee, Christopher, 93, British actor known for horror and villainous roles; London, Eng., UK, June 7, 2015.

Lee Kuan Yew, 91, Singapore prime minister who transformed the nation from a British colony into one of Asia's wealthiest countries; Singapore, Mar. 23, 2015.

Leslie, Joan, 90, actress whose biggest roles—including ones in *Sergeant York* (1941) and *Yankee Doodle Dandy* (1942)—came before she turned 18; Los Angeles, CA, Oct. 12, 2015.

Levine, Philip, 87, Pulitzer Prize-winning poet whose works reflected the hardship of manual labor; U.S. poet laureate (2011-12); Fresno, CA, Feb. 14, 2015.

Long, Thelma Coyne, 96, Australian tennis player with 19 Grand Slam victories; Narrabeen, Australia, Apr. 13, 2015.

Lynch, Peg, 98, writer and actress who created the radio and TV sitcom *Ethel and Albert*; Becket, MA, July 24, 2015.

M

Macnee, Patrick, 93, British actor best known for role on the TV series *The Avengers* (1966-69); Rancho Mirage, CA, June 25, 2015.

Magliozzi, Tom, 77, co-host of the Peabody Award-winning public radio show *Car Talk* (1977-2012); Belmont, MA, Nov. 3, 2014.

Malone, Moses, 60, Hall of Fame basketball center nicknamed "Chairman of the Boards" for his rebounding; three-time NBA MVP; Norfolk, VA, Sept. 13, 2015.

Marotta, Vincent, 91, businessman who was co-creator of Mr. Coffee coffeemakers; Pepper Pike, OH, Aug. 1, 2015.

Marshall, Anthony, 90, U.S. ambassador and theatrical producer convicted in 2009 of defrauding his mother, philanthropist Brooke Astor; New York, NY, Nov. 30, 2014.

Maynard, Brittany, 29, terminally ill death-with-dignity advocate; Portland, OR, Nov. 1, 2014.

Maysles, Albert, 88, documentary filmmaker who with brother David was best known for *Grey Gardens* (1975); New York, NY, Mar. 5, 2015.

McCullough, Colleen, 77, Australian-born writer known for best-selling novel *The Thorn Birds* (1977); Norfolk Island, Australia, Jan. 29, 2015.

McKuen, Rod, 81, poet and composer best known for *The Prime of Miss Jean Brodie* (1969); Beverly Hills, CA, Jan. 29, 2015.

Meadows, Jayne, 95, actress who costarred with husband Steve Allen; also a well-known panelist on *I've Got a Secret* (1952-59); Encino, CA, Apr. 26, 2015.

Meara, Anne, 85, actress and comedian, who was half of the comedy team Stiller and Meara with husband Jerry Stiller; New York, NY, May 23, 2015.

Milner, Martin, 83, actor best known for TV roles on *Route 66* (1960-64) and *Adam-12* (1968-75); Carlsbad, CA, Sept. 6, 2015.

Miñoso, Orestes "Minnie," 92?, Cuban-born All-Star outfielder who played in Negro Leagues and helped integrate baseball with the Chicago White Sox; Chicago, IL, Mar. 1, 2015.

Molinaro, Al, 96, actor best known for *Happy Days* (1974-84); Glendale, CA, Oct. 30, 2015.

Moore, Dickie, 89, child actor who appeared in *Our Gang* shorts; later became a public relations executive; CT, Sept. 7, 2015.

Mueller, George, 97, engineer who as head of NASA's Office of Manned Space Flight (1963-69) helped Americans land on the Moon; Irvine, CA, Oct. 12, 2015.

Musetto, Vincent, 74, *NY Post* editor credited with iconic headlines, including HEADLESS BODY IN TOPLESS BAR (1983); Bronx, NY, June 9, 2015.

Myerson, Bess, 90, first Jewish Miss America (1945) and TV personality who later held positions in New York City government; her political career ended in scandal; Santa Monica, CA, Dec. 14, 2014.

N

Nambu, Yoichiro, 94, Japan-born American Nobel Prize-winning physicist whose elementary atomic particle research provided a better understanding of matter; Osaka, Japan, July 5, 2015.

Nash, John Forbes, Jr., 86, Nobel Prize-winning economist and mathematician; life inspired the book and film *A Beautiful Mind* (1998, 2001); Monroe Township, NJ, May 23, 2015.

Nemtsov, Boris, 55, Russian physicist who became an adversary of Pres. Vladimir Putin; murdered in Moscow, Russia, Feb. 27, 2015.

Nichols, Mike, 83, German-born, EGOT-winning director, producer, and actor known for performing comedy with Elaine May and for directing the Broadway production of *The Odd Couple* (1965) and film *The Graduate* (1967); New York, NY, Nov. 19, 2014.

Nidetch, Jean, 91, cofounder of Weight Watchers (1963); Parkland, FL, Apr. 29, 2015.

Nimoy, Leonard, 83, actor and film director best known for playing Spock in the *Star Trek* TV series (1966-69) and seven subsequent films; Los Angeles, CA, Feb. 27, 2015.

O

Obraztsova, Elena, 75, Russian mezzo-soprano; Leipzig, Germany, Jan. 12. 2015.

O'Hara, Maureen, 95, Irish-American actress known for *How Green Is My Valley* (1941), *Miracle on 34th Street* (1947), and *The Quiet Man* (1952); Boise, ID, Oct. 24, 2015.

de Oliveira, Manoel, 106, Portuguese filmmaker whose career spanned nine decades; Porto, Portugal, Apr. 2, 2015.

Otto, Frei, 89, German architect and engineer best known for the tented roof for Munich's Olympic Stadium (1972); Germany, Mar. 9, 2015.

Owens, Gary, 80, performer best known as the announcer of *Rowan and Martin's Laugh-In* (1968-73); Encino, CA, Feb. 12, 2015.

P

Palmer, Betsy, 88, actress and panelist on *I've Got a Secret* (1957-67); also known as the killer in the slasher movie *Friday the 13th* (1980); Danbury, CT, May 29, 2015.

Peress, Irving, 97, dentist whose Army promotion made him a focus of anti-communist Army-McCarthy hearings (1954); Queens, NY, Nov. 13, 2014.

Petersen, Frank, 83, first African-American Marine general; flew over 350 combat missions; Stevensville, MD, Aug. 25, 2015.

Pierce, Billy, 88, left-handed pitcher, mostly for the Chicago White Sox (1949-61); Palos Heights, IL, July 31, 2015.

Piper, Roddy "Rowdy," 61, Canadian pro wrestler known for a feud with Hulk Hogan; Los Angeles, CA, July 30, 2015.

Plisetskaya, Maya, 89, Russian ballet dancer; Munich, Germany, May 2, 2015.

Pratchett, Terry, 66, British fantasy novelist best known for his Discworld series; Broad Chalke, Eng., UK, Mar. 12, 2015.

Prudhomme, Paul, 75, Louisiana chef who promoted Creole and Cajun cuisine; New Orleans, LA, Oct. 8, 2015.

R

Rainer, Luise, 104, German-born actress who won Oscars for *The Great Ziegfeld* (1936) and *The Good Earth* (1937); London, Eng., UK, Dec. 30, 2014.

Reagle, Merl, 65, crossword puzzle constructor; Tampa, FL, Aug. 22, 2015.

Rees, Roger, 71, Tony Award-winning Welsh actor and director famed for *The Life and Adventures of Nicholas Nickleby* (1980); New York, NY, July 10, 2015.

Rendell, Ruth, 85, British crime novelist whose works featured the fictional detective Reginald Wexford; London, Eng., UK, May 2, 2015.

Ritchie, Jean, 92, folk singer who performed traditional Appalachian songs; Berea, KY, June 1, 2015.

Roberts, Ralph J., 95, cofounder and CEO of Comcast, the largest U.S. cable TV provider; Philadelphia, PA, June 18, 2015.

Robinson, Amelia Boynton, 104, civil rights activist; beaten during the 1965 Selma-to-Montgomery march she helped organize; Montgomery, AL, Aug. 26, 2015.

Rocco, Alex, 79, Emmy Award-winning actor best known for playing Moe Greene in *The Godfather* (1972); Studio City, CA, July 18, 2015.

Rockefeller, Margaretta "Happy," 88, socialite and philanthropist wife of Vice Pres. Nelson Rockefeller; Tarrytown, NY, May 19, 2015.

Rose, Irwin, 88, Nobel Prize-winning biochemist whose work on proteins led to cancer drugs; Deerfield, MA, June 2, 2015.

Rosen, Al, 91, Cleveland MVP third baseman who later served as president of several teams; Goodyear, AZ, Mar. 13, 2015.

Roukema, Marge, 85, U.S. representative (R, NJ, 1981-2003) who helped win passage of the Family and Medical Leave Act (1993); Wyckoff, NJ, Nov. 12, 2014.

Ruffin, Jimmy, 78, soul singer known for "What Becomes of the Brokenhearted" (1966); Las Vegas, NV, Nov. 17, 2014.

Rule, Ann, 83, true crime writer who wrote *The Stranger Beside Me* (1980) about Ted Bundy; Burien, WA, July 26, 2015.

S

Sabol, Ed, 98, Emmy Award-winning filmmaker who helped found NFL Films; Scottsdale, AZ, Feb. 9, 2015.

Sacks, Oliver, 82, British neurologist and author best known for books based on patients, including *The Man Who Mistook His Wife for a Hat* (1985); New York, NY, Aug. 30, 2015.

Saks, Gene, 93, Tony Award-winning director known for Neil Simon's *Brighton Beach Memoirs* (1983) and *Biloxi Blues* (1985); East Hampton, NY, Mar. 28, 2015.

Salter, James, 90, novelist whose works received critical praise but never reached popular acclaim; Sag Harbor, NY, June 19, 2015.

Sanders, Marlene, 84, Emmy Award-winning TV journalist who was the first woman to anchor an evening newscast (ABC, 1964); New York, NY, July 14, 2015.

Sargent, Joseph, 89, Emmy Award-winning director known for *The Taking of Pelham One Two Three* (1974); Malibu, CA, Dec. 22, 2014.

Scaasi, Arnold, 85, Canadian-born fashion designer who designed formal wear for first ladies and Hollywood stars; New York, NY, Aug. 3, 2015.

Schiff, Irwin, 87, activist who argued federal income taxes were unconstitutional; repeatedly convicted for tax evasion; Fort Worth, TX, Oct. 16, 2015.

Schuller, Gunther, 89, Pulitzer Prize-winning composer, orchestral conductor, and jazz historian; Boston, MA, June 21, 2015.

Schuller, Robert H., 88, televangelist who hosted the weekly *Hour of Power* TV show (1970-2010); Artesia, CA, Apr. 2, 2015.

Schweiker, Richard, 89, U.S. senator (R, PA, 1969-81) and representative (1961-69); Pomona, NJ, July 31, 2015.

Scott, Lizabeth, 92, sultry actress known for film noir roles; Los Angeles, CA, Jan. 31, 2015.

Scott, Stuart, 49, sportscaster for ESPN's *SportsCenter* who created catchphrases that became part of the vernacular; Avon, CT, Jan. 4, 2015.

Shanks, Nelson, 77, painter best known for portraits of Diana, Princess of Wales (1994), and Pres. Bill Clinton (2006); Andalusia, PA, Aug. 28, 2015.

Sharif, Omar, 83, Golden Globe-winning Egyptian actor known for *Lawrence of Arabia* (1962), *Doctor Zhivago* (1965), and *Funny Girl* (1968); Cairo, Egypt, July 10, 2015.

Shavitz, Burt, 80, beekeeper who founded Burt's Bees, a personal care products company; Bangor, ME, July 5, 2015.

Sifford, Charlie, 92, Hall of Fame golfer who was the first African American to play on the PGA tour; Cleveland, OH, Feb. 3, 2015.

Simon, Bob, 73, Emmy Award-winning TV journalist and correspondent on *60 Minutes* (1996-2015); New York, NY, Feb. 11, 2015.

Simon, Sam, 59, Emmy Award-winning TV director and writer who co-created *The Simpsons* (1989-); later a noted philanthropist; Los Angeles, CA, Mar. 8, 2015.

Sischy, Ingrid, 63, South African-born cultural critic who served as the editor of *Interview* magazine (1989-2008); New York, NY, July 24, 2015.

Sitton, Claude, 89, Pulitzer Prize-winning newspaper writer and editor who covered the civil rights movement in the South; Atlanta, GA, Mar. 10, 2015.

Sledge, Percy, 74, R&B singer best known for "When a Man Loves a Woman" (1966); Baton Rouge, LA, Apr. 14, 2015.

Smith, Dean, 83, Hall of Fame college basketball coach who led North Carolina to 879 wins and two men's national championships; Chapel Hill, NC, Feb. 7, 2015.

Stabler, Ken, 69, quarterback nicknamed "The Snake" who helped lead the Oakland Raiders to their first Super Bowl win (1977); Gulfport, MS, July 8, 2015.

Starr, Blaze, 83, stripper known as the Queen of Burlesque; Wilsondale, WV, June 15, 2015.

Stemberg, Thomas, 66, cofounder of office supply company Staples; Chestnut Hill, MA, Oct. 23, 2015.

Stern, Phil, 95, photographer known for iconic images of Hollywood legends; Los Angeles, CA, Dec. 13, 2014.

Stern, Stewart, 92, screenwriter best known for *Rebel Without a Cause* (1955); Seattle, WA, Feb. 2, 2015

Stoddard, Brandon, 77, TV executive who developed epic miniseries, including *Roots* (1977) and *The Thorn Birds* (1983); Los Angeles, CA, Dec. 22, 2014.

Stokes, Louis, 90, U.S. representative (D, OH, 1969-99) who helped found the Congressional Black Caucus (1971); Cleveland, OH, Aug. 18, 2015.

Stone, Robert, 77, novelist whose works reflected the turbulence of the 1960s; best known for *Dog Soldiers* (1974); Key West, FL, Jan. 10, 2015.

Stookey, S(tanley) Donald, 99, chemist who created CorningWare, heat-resistant glass ceramic cookware; Pittsford, NY, Nov. 4, 2014.

Strand, Mark, 80, Canadian-born Pulitzer Prize-winning poet; U.S. poet laureate (1990-91); Brooklyn, NY, Nov. 29, 2014.

Suggs, Louise, 91, Hall of Fame golfer who cofounded the Ladies Professional Golf Association (1950); won 11 major titles; Sarasota, FL, Aug. 7, 2015.

Swingle, Ward, 87, singer and arranger who founded The Swingle Singers to perform jazzy versions of classical music; Eastbourne, Eng., UK; Jan. 19, 2015.

T

Tallmer, Jerry, 93, arts critic and *Village Voice* editor who created the Obie Awards for off-Broadway theater; New York, NY, Nov. 9, 2014.

Tarkanian, Jerry, 84, college basketball coach who led UNLV team to men's championship (1990); also known for battling the NCAA; Las Vegas, NV, Feb. 11, 2015.

Tate, James, 71, Pulitzer Prize-winning poet who used humor even in tragic poems; Amherst, MA, July 8, 2015.

Taylor, Rod, 84, Australian-born actor known for *The Time Machine* (1960) and *The Birds* (1963); Los Angeles, CA, Jan. 7, 2015.

Terry, Clark, 94, trumpeter and flugelhorn player who collaborated with Count Basie and Duke Ellington; Pine Bluff, AR, Feb. 21, 2015.

Townes, Charles H., 99, Nobel Prize-winning physicist whose work led to the laser; discovered black hole at center of Milky Way galaxy; Oakland, CA, Jan. 27, 2015.

Trimpe, Herb, 75, illustrator and Marvel Comics artist who co-created the X-Men character Wolverine; Hurley, NY, Apr. 13, 2015.

V

Van Patten, Dick, 86, actor best remembered for his role as the patriarch on TV series *Eight Is Enough* (1977-81); Santa Monica, CA, June 23, 2015.

Vergé, Roger, 85, French chef and restaurateur known for promoting nouvelle cuisine; Mougins, France, June 5, 2015.

Vickers, Jon, 88, Canadian heldentenor opera singer; Ontario, Canada, July 10, 2015.

Villanueva, Danny, 77, NFL football player (1960-67) who cofounded Univision (1962), a Spanish-language TV network; Ventura, CA, June 18, 2015.

W

Weintraub, Jerry, 77, talent agent turned film producer who produced *The Karate Kid* (1984, 2010) and *Ocean's Eleven* (2001); Santa Barbara, CA, July 6, 2015.

Wells, Cory, 74, singer best known as a founding member of Three Dog Night; Dunkirk, NY, Oct. 20, 2015.

Williams, C(harles) K(enneth), 78, Pulitzer Prize-winning poet whose work dealt with war and social injustices; Hopewell, NJ, Sept. 20, 2015.

Williams, Dell, 92, founder of Eve's Garden, the first sex boutique for women; New York, NY, Mar. 11, 2015.

Williams, John A., 89, writer on the black experience whose best known novel was *The Man Who Cried I Am* (1967); Paramus, NJ, July 3, 2015.

Wilson, Elizabeth, 94, Tony Award-winning actress best remembered for the film *9 to 5* (1980); New Haven, CT, May 9, 2015.

Wilson, Jane, 90, artist best known for Abstract Expressionist landscapes; New York, NY, Jan. 13, 2015.

Winton, Sir Nicholas, 106, British humanitarian who rescued 669 children after Nazis invaded Czechoslovakia in 1939; Slough, Eng., UK, July 1, 2015.

Wright, Franz, 62, Austrian-born American Pulitzer Prize-winning poet whose works reflected inner torment; Waltham, MA, May 14, 2015.

Wright, Jim, 92, U.S. representative (D, TX, 1955-89) and House speaker (1987-89) who resigned in an ethics scandal; Fort Worth, TX, May 6, 2015.

Y

Yepremian, Garo, 70, Cyprus-born NFL kicker (1966-81) whose famous fumble in Super Bowl VII sent the ball into the arms of the opposing team; Media, PA, May 15, 2015.

Z

Zapf, Hermann, 96, typeface designer and calligrapher who designed around 200 fonts including Palatino and Optima; Darmstadt, Germany, June 4, 2015.

STATE GOVERNMENT

Governors of the 50 States

Source: National Governors Association; Council of State Governments; World Almanac research

As of Oct. 2015, of the 50 state governors, 31 are Republicans, 18 are Democrats, and 1 is independent. Salary information is as of May 2015.

State	Capital, ZIP code	Governor	Party	Term years	Term expires	Annual salary
Alabama	Montgomery, 36130	Robert Bentley	Rep.	4	Jan. 2019	$120,395[1]
Alaska	Juneau, 99811	Bill Walker	Ind.	4	Dec. 2018	145,000
Arizona	Phoenix, 85007	Doug Ducey	Rep.	4	Jan. 2019	95,000
Arkansas	Little Rock, 72201	Asa Hutchinson	Rep.	4	Jan. 2019	87,759
California	Sacramento, 95814	Jerry Brown	Dem.	4	Jan. 2019	177,467
Colorado	Denver, 80203	John Hickenlooper	Dem.	4	Jan. 2019	90,000
Connecticut	Hartford, 06106	Dan Malloy	Dem.	4	Jan. 2019	150,000
Delaware	Dover, 19902	Jack Markell	Dem.	4	Jan. 2017	171,000
Florida	Tallahassee, 32399	Rick Scott	Rep.	4	Jan. 2019	130,273
Georgia	Atlanta, 30334	Nathan Deal	Rep.	4	Jan. 2019	139,339
Hawaii	Honolulu, 96813	David Ige	Dem.	4	Dec. 2018	146,628
Idaho	Boise, 83702	C.L. "Butch" Otter	Rep.	4	Jan. 2019	121,975
Illinois	Springfield, 62706	Bruce Rauner	Rep.	4	Jan. 2019	177,412
Indiana	Indianapolis, 46204	Mike Pence	Rep.	4	Jan. 2017	111,688
Iowa	Des Moines, 50319	Terry Branstad	Rep.	4	Jan. 2019	130,000
Kansas	Topeka, 66612	Sam Brownback	Rep.	4	Jan. 2019	99,636
Kentucky	Frankfort, 40601	Steven L. Beshear	Dem.	4	Dec. 2015	151,643[2]
Louisiana	Baton Rouge, 70804	Bobby Jindal	Rep.	4	Jan. 2016	130,000
Maine	Augusta, 04333	Paul LePage	Rep.	4	Jan. 2019	70,000
Maryland	Annapolis, 21401	Larry Hogan	Rep.	4	Jan. 2019	150,000
Massachusetts	Boston, 02133	Charlie Baker	Rep.	4	Jan. 2019	151,800
Michigan	Lansing, 48909	Rick Snyder	Rep.	4	Jan. 2019	159,300[3]
Minnesota	St. Paul, 55155	Mark Dayton	Dem.	4	Jan. 2019	123,427
Mississippi	Jackson, 39205	Phil Bryant	Rep.	4	Jan. 2016	122,160
Missouri	Jefferson City, 65102	Jay Nixon	Dem.	4	Jan. 2017	133,821
Montana	Helena, 59620	Steve Bullock	Dem.	4	Jan. 2017	108,167
Nebraska	Lincoln, 68509	Pete Ricketts	Rep.	4	Jan. 2019	105,000
Nevada	Carson City, 89701	Brian Sandoval	Rep.	4	Jan. 2019	149,730
New Hampshire	Concord, 03301	Maggie Hassan	Dem.	2	Jan. 2017	113,834
New Jersey	Trenton, 08625	Chris Christie	Rep.	4	Jan. 2018	175,000
New Mexico	Santa Fe, 87300	Susana Martinez	Rep.	4	Jan. 2019	110,000
New York	Albany, 12224	Andrew Cuomo	Dem.	4	Jan. 2019	179,000[2]
North Carolina	Raleigh, 27699	Pat McCrory	Rep.	4	Jan. 2017	142,265
North Dakota	Bismarck, 58505	Jack Dalrymple	Rep.	4	Dec. 2016	125,330
Ohio	Columbus, 43215	John Kasich	Rep.	4	Jan. 2019	148,886
Oklahoma	Oklahoma City, 73105	Mary Fallin	Rep.	4	Jan. 2019	147,000
Oregon	Salem, 97301	Kate Brown[4]	Dem.	4	Jan. 2019	98,600
Pennsylvania	Harrisburg, 17120	Tom Wolf	Dem.	4	Jan. 2019	190,823[5]
Rhode Island	Providence, 02903	Gina Raimondo	Dem.	4	Jan. 2019	129,210
South Carolina	Columbia, 29201	Nikki Haley	Rep.	4	Jan. 2019	106,078
South Dakota	Pierre, 57501	Dennis Daugaard	Rep.	4	Jan. 2019	107,121
Tennessee	Nashville, 37243	Bill Haslam	Rep.	4	Jan. 2019	184,632[1]
Texas	Austin, 78711	Greg Abbott	Rep.	4	Jan. 2019	150,000
Utah	Salt Lake City, 84114	Gary Herbert	Rep.	4	Jan. 2017	109,470
Vermont	Montpelier, 05609	Peter Shumlin	Dem.	2	Jan. 2017	145,538[2]
Virginia	Richmond, 23219	Terry McAuliffe	Dem.	4	Jan. 2018	175,000
Washington	Olympia, 98504	Jay Inslee	Dem.	4	Jan. 2017	166,891
West Virginia	Charleston, 25305	Earl Ray Tomblin	Dem.	4	Jan. 2017	150,000
Wisconsin	Madison, 53707	Scott Walker	Rep.	4	Jan. 2019	147,328
Wyoming	Cheyenne, 82002	Matt Mead	Rep.	4	Jan. 2019	105,000

Note: Kentucky, Massachusetts, Pennsylvania, and Virginia are self-designated commonwealths. (1) Does not accept salary. (2) Governor has voluntarily reduced his salary by 10% (KY), 5% (NY), or 3% (VT). (3) Accepts only $1. (4) Secretary of State Kate Brown became governor Feb. 18, 2015, following four-term Gov. John Kitzhaber's resignation. A special election is scheduled to be held in Nov. 2016 to fill the position for the term's final two years. (5) Donates salary to charity at the end of each quarter.

Governors of Commonwealths and Territories

State	Capital, ZIP code	Governor	Party	Term years	Term expires	Annual salary
American Samoa	Pago Pago, 96799	Lolo Matalasi Moliga	Ind.	4	Jan. 2017	$90,000
Guam	Hagåtña, 96932	Eddie Baza Calvo	Rep.	4	Jan. 2019	130,000
Northern Mariana Islands	Saipan, 96950	Eloy S. Inos	Cov.[1]	4	Jan. 2019	70,000
Puerto Rico	San Juan, 00902	Alejandro García Padilla	PDP[2]	4	Jan. 2017	70,000
Virgin Islands	Charlotte Amalie, 00802	Kenneth Mapp	Ind.	4	Jan. 2019	150,000

(1) Covenant Party. (2) Popular Democratic Party.

U.S. SUPREME COURT

The U.S. Supreme Court's 2014-15 term began Oct. 6, 2014, and concluded June 29, 2015, for its summer recess. The justices decided 74 cases (66 of which carried signed opinions) and issued 19 rulings (26%) by a 5-4 majority.

Chief Justice John G. Roberts Jr. presided over his 10th full term. The eight associate justices, by order of seniority, were Antonin Scalia, Anthony M. Kennedy, Clarence Thomas, Ruth Bader Ginsburg, Stephen G. Breyer, Samuel A. Alito Jr., Sonia Sotomayor, and Elena Kagan.

Roberts, Scalia, Thomas, and Alito tended to vote as a conservative bloc, while Ginsburg, Breyer, Sotomayor, and Kagan composed the court's liberal wing. Associate Justice Kennedy tended to be a swing vote in many 5-4 split decisions.

Notable Supreme Court Decisions, 2014-15

Note: The columns on the right provide information on how each justice voted. Gray shading indicates a justice who was part of the majority. MO = justice authored majority opinion; CO = justice authored concurring opinion; COJ = justice authored opinion concurring in judgment but not its reasoning; DO = justice authored dissenting opinion; CD in part = justice authored opinion containing both concurring and dissenting opinions.

	Kagan	Sotomayor	Breyer	Ginsburg	Kennedy	Scalia	Thomas	Roberts	Alito
Capital Punishment The U.S. Supreme Court June 29 ruled, 5-4, in *Glossip v. Gross*, that Oklahoma could continue to use the sedative midazolam as the first part of a three-drug cocktail used to carry out lethal injections. Lawyers for three condemned inmates had argued that midazolam was not effective at preventing an inmate from feeling pain induced by the other two drugs, thus subjecting him to severe pain in violation of the Eighth Amendment.		DO	DO			CO	CO		MO
Congressional Redistricting The court June 29 ruled, 5-4, to uphold an amendment to Arizona's state constitution—passed by voters in a 2000 ballot initiative—that had created an independent commission, intended to curb gerrymandering, to make decisions about redistricting in the state. Arizona's state legislature had argued that the U.S. Constitution required redistricting decisions to be made by state legislatures. The case was *Arizona State Legislature v. Arizona Independent Redistricting Commission*.				MO		DO	DO	DO	
Environment The court June 29 ruled, 5-4, against an Environmental Protection Agency (EPA) regulation that limited mercury emissions from power plants. The court said the EPA had failed to calculate, before making the decision to regulate emissions, whether the rule's benefits justified its significant costs to power companies. The regulation was sent back to a lower court. The case was *Michigan v. EPA*.	DO					MO	CO		
Free Speech The court June 18 ruled unanimously to strike down a town ordinance that regulated signs directing people to nonprofit events, such as church services, more strictly than other signs. The court was divided in its reasoning, with a six-justice majority saying that laws making content-based distinctions between signs were subject to the strictest judicial scrutiny. The case was *Reed v. Town of Gilbert, Arizona*.	COJ		COJ				MO		CO
The court June 18 ruled, 5-4, that Texas could reject a proposed specialty license plate design featuring the Confederate battle flag. A July 2014 decision from the 5th Circuit Court of Appeals had said the license plate design was private speech and protected under the First Amendment, but the Supreme Court ruled that specialty license plates constitute government speech. The case was *Walker v. Texas Division, Sons of Confederate Veterans*.			MO						DO
Health Care The court June 25 ruled, 6-3, in *King v. Burwell*, to uphold a system of subsidies for lower-income consumers buying health insurance under the Affordable Care Act (ACA) in states that lack their own exchanges. The plaintiffs in the case argued that Congress had intended the subsidies to be offered only to consumers using state insurance exchanges, not those on the federal insurance marketplace.						DO		MO	
Housing The court June 25 ruled, 5-4, that policies and actions that had not been designed with a discriminatory intent but that had a "disparate impact" on the housing opportunities of low-income minority groups could be challenged under the 1968 Fair Housing Act (FHA). The case was *Texas Dept. of Housing and Community Affairs v. the Inclusive Communities Project*.					MO		DO		DO
Religion The court June 1 ruled, 8-1, that a job applicant who was denied employment because her religious practice (the wearing of a headscarf) interfered with the company's dress policy had grounds to sue the company for discrimination even if she did not explicitly establish that she needed an exemption on religious grounds. The case was *Equal Employment Opportunity Commission v. Abercrombie & Fitch Stores*.						MO	CD in part		COJ
The court Jan. 20 unanimously ruled the Arkansas prison system was violating a Muslim inmate's religious rights by refusing to allow him to grow a ½-inch beard in accordance with his religious beliefs. State prison officials had argued that beards could create security concerns or facilitate prisoner escapes. The case was *Holt v. Hobbs*.		CO		CO					MO
Same-Sex Marriage The court June 26 ruled, 5-4, that state bans on same-sex marriage violated the rights of gay and lesbian couples under the due process and equal protection clauses of the U.S. Constitution's 14th Amendment. The decision had the effect of legalizing same-sex marriage across the U.S. and requiring every state to recognize same-sex marriages performed elsewhere. The ruling, known as *Obergefell v. Hodges*, was on four consolidated cases.					MO	DO	DO	DO	DO
Separation of Powers The court June 8 struck down, 6-3, a 2002 federal law requiring the State Dept. to allow U.S. citizens born in Jerusalem to have their birthplace listed as "Israel" on their U.S. passports if they requested such a designation. The ruling settled a dispute between the federal government's legislative and executive branches. (The executive branch has never recognized any country as having sovereignty over Jerusalem.) The case was *Zivotofsky v. Kerry*.			CO		MO	DO	CD in part	DO	

NOTABLE QUOTES, 2015

Around the World

"Je suis Charlie."
—Comment trending on Twitter, after the Jan. 7 attack by Islamic terrorists on the Paris office of the French satirical magazine *Charlie Hebdo*, in which 12 people were killed.
"This framework would cut off every pathway that Iran could take to develop a nuclear weapon."
—Pres. **Barack Obama**, Apr. 2, hailing a tentative agreement between world powers and Iran over its development of nuclear technology.
"Such a deal would not block Iran's path to the bomb. It would pave it."
—Israeli Prime Min. **Benjamin Netanyahu**, Apr. 3, in opposition to the framework deal with Iran.
"The creditors want to humiliate the Greek people."
—Greek Prime Min. **Alexis Tsipras**, June 16, as European leaders tried to reach a deal with chronically indebted Greece for fiscal reforms as conditions for providing additional bailout money.
"He seemed like he was ready to fight to the end, and so were we."
—**Spencer Stone**, one of three young Americans who helped thwart an attack on a Paris-bound train, Aug. 21, by a gunman linked to Islamist groups.
"We thought we would be freed. They knocked out Saddam and brought a hundred Saddams."
—**Yasir Abdulrahman**, an unemployed Iraqi, as quoted in a *New York Times* story Aug. 31, on weekly Friday protests against government failure to live up to hopes after the 2003 U.S. invasion.
"The only thing I could do was to make his scream heard."
—Turkish photographer **Nilufer Demir**, whose Sept. 2 photo of a drowned three-year-old Kurdish boy on a Turkish beach dramatized the plight of hundreds of thousands fleeing chaos, persecution, and poverty in Syria and other countries.
"We hope that the messages we have been sending migrants for a long time have reached them. Don't come."
—**Gyorgy Bakondi**, an aide to Prime Min. Viktor Orban of Hungary, after an intensified crackdown on the border took effect, Sept. 15.
"I too am a son of this great continent, from which we have all received so much and toward which we share a common responsibility."
—**Pope Francis**, speaking to a joint session of the U.S. Congress, Sept. 24.

U.S. Campaign Trail

"Just yesterday, a leader from yesterday began a campaign for president by promising to take us back to yesterday. Yesterday is over and we're never going back."
—Sen. **Marco Rubio** (R, FL) announcing his presidential bid, Apr. 13, referring to former Sec. of State Hillary Clinton, who had announced hers the day prior.
"When Mexico sends its people, they're not sending their best. … They're sending people that have lots of problems. … They're bringing drugs. They're bringing crime. They're rapists."
—Real estate mogul **Donald Trump**, announcing his Republican candidacy, June 26.
"I am my own man."
—Former Florida Gov. **Jeb Bush**, in the first Republican debate, Aug. 6.
"That was a mistake. I'm sorry about that."
—Democratic presidential contender **Hillary Clinton**, apologizing for her controversial use of a private email server as secretary of state, in an interview with ABC, Sept. 8.
"You've just got to get up. And I feel like I was letting down Beau, letting down my parents, letting down my family if I didn't just get up."
—Vice Pres. **Joe Biden**, on *The Late Show With Stephen Colbert*, Sept. 10, referring to his grief over his son's death, when he was still contemplating a campaign for president.
"Women all over this country heard very clearly what Mr. Trump said."
—Former Hewlett-Packard CEO **Carly Fiorina** on comments Donald Trump had made to a reporter about her looks, in the second Republican debate, Sept. 16.
"I'm not sending our sons and daughters back to Iraq. The war didn't work. … There will always be a Bush or Clinton for you if you want to go back to war in Iraq."
—Sen. **Rand Paul** (R, KY) in the second GOP debate, on putting "boots on the ground" in the Middle East.
"I encourage other Republican presidential candidates to consider doing the same so the voters can focus on a limited number of candidates who can offer a positive conservative alternative to the current front-runner."
—Gov. **Scott Walker** (WI), referencing the poll-leading Trump, as he bowed out of the crowded presidential race, Sept. 21.
"The American people are sick and tired of hearing about your damn emails."
—Sen. **Bernie Sanders** (I, VT) to Hillary Clinton in the first Democratic debate, Oct. 13.

National News

"We're in a new era. The idea of your nice little green grass getting lots of water every day, that's going to be a thing of the past."
—California Gov. **Jerry Brown** (D), as he imposed mandatory statewide restrictions on water use, Apr. 1.
"We decided to come together rather than pull apart. It's our choice. It's our choice not to raise hell and tear up the city or tear up the streets because something tragic happened."
—**Norvel Goff**, interim pastor of Emanuel African Methodist Episcopal Church in Charleston, SC, June 24, to those gathered at the sanctuary where nine people, including the former pastor, were slain one week before.
"Their hope is not to be condemned to live in loneliness, excluded from one of civilization's oldest institutions. They ask for equal dignity in the eyes of the law."
—Associate Justice **Anthony Kennedy**, referring to same-sex couples in his majority opinion June 26, for the U.S. Supreme Court, which ruled that same-sex marriages must be recognized as legal.
"The truth is that today's decision rests on nothing more than the majority's own conviction that same-sex couples should be allowed to marry because they want to."
—U.S. Supreme Court Chief Justice **John Roberts**, in his dissenting opinion on same-sex marriage.
"I have heard enough about heritage. … I am a descendant of Jefferson Davis, OK? But … [i]t's not about Jenny Horne. It's about the people of South Carolina who have demanded that this symbol of hate come off of the statehouse grounds."
—South Carolina state Rep. **Jenny Horne** (R), in a fiery speech, July 8, that influenced the passage of a bill that removed the Confederate flag from capitol grounds.
"We have a healthy spacecraft."
—**Alice Bowman**, mission operations manager, July 14, confirming that NASA's *New Horizons* spacecraft had successfully passed Pluto earlier that day.
"We only get one planet. There's no plan B."
—Pres. **Obama**, Aug. 3, unveiling a major climate-change plan requiring states to slash carbon dioxide emissions from power plants 32% from 2005 levels by 2030.
"Under God's authority."
—Kentucky county clerk **Kim Davis**, Sept. 1, when asked by a gay couple under whose authority she was acting in refusing to issue a marriage license to them.
"Last night I started thinking about this and this morning I woke up and I said my prayers—as I always do—and I decided today's the day I'm going to do this."
—Beleaguered House Speaker **John Boehner** (R, OH), announcing his resignation in a press conference, Sept. 25.

People

"I wasn't 100% sober."
—U.S. Supreme Court Justice **Ruth Bader Ginsburg**, who appeared to be asleep on camera during Obama's Jan. 20 State of the Union speech; she wryly admitted Feb. 12 to having had a glass of wine at dinner with the other justices before the speech.
"We're going to be fine. This isn't ISIS. You know, no one's dying."
—New England Patriots quarterback **Tom Brady**, at a press conference Jan. 22, attempting to tamp down controversy over his team's use of underinflated footballs in the AFC championship game.
"What the hell did I do? Killed them all, of course."
—**Robert Durst**, real estate heir and multiple murder suspect, in words picked up on the microphone he wore in filming the HBO documentary *The Jinx*; they were heard in broadcast, Mar. 15.
"When I screw up now, and Lord knows I'll be screwing up, I have to go on somebody else's show to apologize."
—*Late Show* host **David Letterman**, on his 6,028th and final show, May 20.
"I'm so happy after such a long struggle to be living my true self."
—Olympic gold medalist and reality TV figure **Caitlyn Jenner**, June 1 on Twitter, speaking of her transition from male to female.
"I don't think we'll go with another direction."
—**Kim Kardashian West**, talking to NPR, June 13, about naming the second child she and Kanye West were expecting; they had named their first child "North."
"Q. When you got the Quaaludes, was it in your mind that you were going to use these Quaaludes for young women that you wanted to have sex with?
"A. Yes."
—Testimony of comedian **Bill Cosby**, from a deposition in a 2005 civil suit by one of many women accusing him of sexual assault; unsealed July 6.
"I'm perfectly at ease with whatever comes."
—Pres. **Jimmy Carter**, after announcing he had terminal cancer, Aug, 20, at the Carter Center in Atlanta.
"You cannot win an Emmy for roles that are simply not there."
—**Viola Davis**, Sept. 20, accepting the first-ever Emmy awarded to a black actress for a leading role in a TV drama.

Sue the Bartman

Many children's birthday parties have crowd-pleasing themes, like superheroes or Disney princesses. But in Jan. 2015, L'erin Dobra of Prairieville, LA, decided to celebrate the second birthday of her son Grayson with a theme based on his favorite media personality: Morris Bart, a personal-injury attorney in New Orleans. Bart's television commercials—featuring the slogan "One call, that's all!"—have been airing in Louisiana for 35 years. Dobra told the *Advocate*, a Louisiana newspaper, "Before [Grayson] could walk or talk, every time the Morris Bart commercial would come on, he was just fixated ... when he started talking he would say 'One call' or 'Bart, Bart, Morris Bart, Morris Bart.' They were not his first words, but they were a close second and third." The party featured a cake with an edible picture of Bart (the bakery had been expecting Bart Simpson); a signed photo of Bart provided by his office, along with some other goodies; a Morris Bart T-shirt; and a life-sized cardboard cutout of Bart's upper body. Grayson was thrilled.

The *Advocate* wrote about the unusual party in July, and the story was picked up by media outlets around the world. This culminated in Dobra and Grayson's Aug. Skype interview with talk-show host Jimmy Kimmel on ABC, during which Morris Bart dropped by the Dobra home to meet his biggest fan.

Cutting a Rug

As of Jan. 2015, according to the *Wall Street Journal*, there were upwards of 31,000 Instagram photos of people's feet on a particular backdrop—specifically, the distinctive 28-year-old carpet at Portland Intl. Airport (PDX), which was being replaced throughout 2015. The PDX carpet pattern featured blue, purple, and red lines and X's—representing the airport's runways—over a teal background. In 2006, PDX officials had determined that it was getting worn out and decided to replace it. In 2013, when the airport began installing test patches of the new carpet, the public realized that the old one was on its way out. Suddenly carpet pre-nostalgia was all over social media, and the pattern appeared on T-shirts, socks, coffee mugs, and even bottles of beer. The valediction came too late to change the best-laid plans of the airport administrators, but four local companies were given large pieces of the removed carpet to repurpose, giving fans a permanent way to celebrate #PDXcarpet.

Dirty Laundry

A henley is a collarless shirt with a short row of buttons. To don an item of clothing is to put it on. And "take it easy" is an overused bit of advice reminding us that we could all stand to relax a bit. Combine these seemingly unrelated phrases and risk a lawsuit. In Apr. 2015, Duluth Trading Co. agreed to settle a lawsuit brought by musician Don Henley. The apparel company in Oct. 2014 had advertised several of its products, including short-sleeved and long-sleeved henleys, in an email with the headline "Don a Henley and Take It Easy." Don Henley, who played drums and sang backup on the 1972 Eagles song "Take It Easy," filed the lawsuit against the company two days later. The suit claimed that "large numbers of consumers who receive and see Duluth Trading Company's advertisements will unquestionably believe that Mr. Henley is associated with and/or has endorsed the company and its products."

In the settlement, Duluth Trading Co. agreed never to use the words "don" and "henley" in close proximity again; posted an apology on its website "not just to Mr. Henley, but to anyone else who took offense"; and donated an unspecified sum to the Walden Woods Project, a nonprofit founded by Henley in 1990.

What's 59,995,500 Years Between Friends?

In early 2015, Edgar Nernberg was digging out a basement in Calgary, AB, Canada, as part of his job at an excavation firm, when he noticed five nearly perfect fish fossils embedded in a block of sandstone. Nernberg's lifelong interest in fossils was piqued, and he consulted Darla Zelenitsky, a paleontologist at the Univ. of Calgary. In May 2015, when the fossils were unveiled to the press, she described the find as "a 10 out of 10 for significance. ... There's not many complete fossils known in rocks of this age in Alberta."

From the conventional scientific standpoint, "this age" is roughly 60 mil years old, shortly after the mass extinction that killed off the dinosaurs. But Nernberg's find attracted media attention mostly because he serves on the board of directors at the Big Valley Creation Science Museum in Alberta. He believes that the world was created about 6,000 years ago, and that the fossils he found date back to Noah's flood, about 4,500 years ago, explaining, "We all have the same evidence and it's just a matter of how you interpret it." Regardless, he is happy that the fossils will be going to Alberta's Royal Tyrrell Museum of Paleontology, where they will be studied by scientists and possibly displayed to the public.

Kittens All Over the World, Join Paws

Approximately 3,000 people attending the funeral of the stationmaster of a small train station in Japan would have been notable even if the deceased were a person. But Tama, stationmaster of Kishi station in Wakayama prefecture, was a cat who died at age 16 on June 22, 2015. Tama had been official stationmaster since Jan. 2007, after the last (human) employee of the station was laid off. The railway was in decline and losing about $4 mil a year, but Tama—a former stray who hung around the station—turned things around. Passenger numbers rose 10% in her first year on the job and continued to go up as tourists flocked to the rural station to visit Tama. In 2009, a cat-train was added, decorated with pictures of her, and in 2010, the station was redesigned to look like a cat. A themed café was opened, and knickknacks with her likeness went on sale. Her impact on the local economy has been estimated at $9 mil.

Thanks to seniority-based promotions, Tama had worked her way up to being a vice president of the railroad; she was posthumously given the title of honorable eternal stationmaster. She was buried in a Shinto shrine and is survived by her deputy, Nitama ("Tama the Second"), who took over the stationmaster position.

Repaint, Repaint, and Sin No More!

Selectman George Simolaris heard from one of his Billerica, MA, constituents in July 2015 that the town had failed to repaint some faded crosswalks despite having promised to do so several times. Perhaps the complainant hoped that Simolaris would bring the matter up at the next town meeting, but Simolaris—a painter by trade—got a bucket of green deck paint and repainted seven crosswalks himself. "We said we would have these crosswalks painted in May," he told the *Boston Globe*. "I used a good paint, and did it as a temporary measure. But mainly I did it for safety."

It turned out to be a costly approach. Simolaris was charged with defacing public property, and some called for his resignation. The town manager noted that the crosswalks had already been slated to be painted, using thermal plastic paint, and that the color Simolaris used was hard to see at night. The town had to pay for the paint to be stripped and replaced by temporary stripes. Simolaris refused to resign but ultimately acknowledged that he should have left the painting to others. He arranged to pay the $4,200 spent by the town to clean up his work, and all criminal charges were dropped.

Genius in France

Nigel Richards was widely recognized as the greatest Scrabble player in history even before the 48-year-old competed in the French-language World Scrabble Championships in July 2015. The New Zealand native, now a resident of Malaysia, had won the English-language world championships three times and racked up numerous wins in national championships in the U.S., the UK, Thailand, and Singapore. All of those wins had been in English-language games, but it turned out that Richards's skill translated just fine. He won the French contest, playing quickly, correctly challenging invalid words, and breezing his way to a 565-434 point win in his final match. French tiles have different point values and distribution than those in English-language games, but the most impressive aspect of Richards's achievement was that he doesn't speak or understand French. He'd spent nine weeks memorizing the 386,000 words in the French Scrabble dictionary.

HISTORICAL ANNIVERSARIES

1916 – 100 Years Ago

War rages in Europe: Germany and France fight the massive Battle of Verdun Feb.-Dec. and are joined by British troops in the futile Battle of the Somme, July-Nov.; hundreds of thousands are killed.

Mexican troops under revolutionary leader Francisco "Pancho" Villa Mar. 9 raid and loot Columbus, NM; U.S. sends troops across border to pursue Villa.

Irish republicans seek to secede from the UK in Dublin's Easter Rising Apr. 24-29 but are suppressed by British troops.

U.S. troops land in the Dominican Republic May 5, beginning an occupation that would last through 1924.

Louis Brandeis is sworn in June 5 as the first Jewish justice to sit on the U.S. Supreme Court.

A suitcase bomb explodes at San Francisco's Preparedness Day parade July 22, killing 10. (Labor organizers Thomas J. Mooney and Warren K. Billings, convicted of the crime in 1916-17, are both later pardoned.)

The U.S. reaches an agreement with Denmark to purchase the Virgin Islands Aug. 4.

Pres. Woodrow Wilson Aug. 25 signs legislation establishing the National Park Service.

Congress Aug. 29 passes the Jones Act, which declares U.S. intentions to grant independence to the Philippines.

Campaigning on an antiwar theme, Wilson is reelected president Nov. 7 over former New York Gov. and U.S. Supreme Court Justice Charles E. Hughes (R). Montana's Jeannette Rankin becomes the first woman to be elected to the House of Representatives.

The Liberal Party's Lloyd George replaces H.H. Asquith as prime minister of the UK's coalition government Dec. 6.

Art. Naum Gabo's *Head No. 2*, Christopher R. W. Nevinson's *A Taube*. *Saturday Evening Post* publishes its first Norman Rockwell cover.

Film. *Civilization*, *Hell's Hinges*, D. W. Griffith's *Intolerance*, Lois Weber's *Where Are My Children?*

Health and medicine. Margaret Sanger establishes the first U.S. birth control clinic in Brooklyn, NY, and is arrested 10 days later for disseminating information on contraception.

Literature. Charlotte Perkins Gilman's *With Her in Ourland*, Edgar Albert Guest's *A Heap o' Livin'*, James Joyce's *A Portrait of the Artist as a Young Man*, Carl Sandberg's *Chicago Poems*, Booth Tarkington's *Seventeen*.

Music. Gustav Holst finishes composing *The Planets*.

Nonfiction. John Dewey's *Democracy and Education*, Madison Grant's *The Passing of the Great Race*.

Pop music. Future pop standards "I Ain't Got Nobody" and "If You Were the Only Girl (In the World)" are first published.

Science and technology. Lewis Terman's *The Measurement of Intelligence* introduces the first of the Stanford-Binet IQ models.

Sports. Philadelphia Athletics establish record for worst baseball season in modern era with 36 wins, 117 losses. Chicago Cubs play their first games at Wrigley Field.

Theater. Anton Chekhov's *The Seagull* debuts on Broadway.

Miscellaneous. New York City passes the first comprehensive zoning laws in the nation.

1966 – 50 Years Ago

U.S. involvement in the Vietnam War escalates throughout the year, with 385,000 U.S. troops stationed in Vietnam, plus 60,000 offshore, by Dec. 31.

Robert C. Weaver becomes secretary of the newly created Dept. of Housing and Urban Development Jan. 18; he is the first black member of the presidential cabinet.

Indira Gandhi becomes prime minister of India Jan. 24.

Mao Zedong launches the Cultural Revolution in China in May, alleging that bourgeois elements had infiltrated Chinese culture. He shuts down schools and encourages former students to pursue purges of "revisionist" party leadership and intellectuals.

The U.S. Supreme Court June 13 announce their landmark decision in *Miranda v. Arizona*, holding that detained criminal suspects must be informed of their constitutional rights prior to questioning.

Federal health insurance program Medicare begins functioning July 1 with 19 mil enrollees by year-end.

Eight nursing students are murdered in their shared Chicago townhouse July 14.

A 25-year-old student killed 15 and wounded 32 Aug. 1, mostly by shooting from a tower on the Univ. of Texas's Austin campus.

South African Prime Min. Hendrik Verwoerd is assassinated in the House of Assembly in Cape Town Sept. 6.

Pres. Lyndon B. Johnson Sept. 9 signs landmark safety measures the National Traffic and Motor Vehicle Safety Act and the Highway Safety Act. The Dept. of Transportation is created, Oct. 15.

In Oakland, CA, civil-rights activists Bobby Seale and Huey Newton form the Black Panther Party for Self-Defense in Oct.

On Election Day, Nov. 8, former actor Ronald Reagan is elected governor of California and Edward Brooke (R, MA) is elected the first black U.S. senator in 85 years.

Art. David Hockney's *Peter Getting out of Nick's Pool*; Ellsworth Kelly's *Blue, Green, Yellow, Orange, Red*; Andy Warhol's *Chelsea Girls*.

Film. John Huston's *The Bible: In the Beginning...*; Michelangelo Antonioni's *Blow-Up*; *The Endless Summer*; *The Group*; *A Man for All Seasons*; Jean-Luc Godard's *Masculin Féminin*; Alfred Hitchcock's *Torn Curtain* starring Julie Andrews and Paul Newman; *Who's Afraid of Virginia Woolf?* starring Richard Burton and Elizabeth Taylor.

Health and medicine. First successful installation of an artificial heart pump by Michael DeBakey and Domingo Liotta.

Literature. Truman Capote publishes "nonfiction novel" *In Cold Blood*. Graham Greene's *The Comedians*, Bernard Malamud's *The Fixer*, Thomas Pynchon's *The Crying of Lot 49*, Jean Rhys's *Wide Sargasso Sea*, Jacqueline Susann's *Valley of the Dolls*.

Music. New York City's Metropolitan Opera House opens with debut performance of Samuel Barber's *Antony and Cleopatra*.

Nonfiction. Peter Berger and Thomas Luckmann's *The Social Construction of Reality*; Masters and Johnson's *Human Sexual Response*; Susan Sontag's *Against Interpretation*.

Pop music. The Beach Boys' "Good Vibrations" and *Pet Sounds*; The Beatles' *Revolver*; Bob Dylan's *Blonde on Blonde*; *Jefferson Airplane Takes Off*; The Mamas and the Papas' "Monday Monday"; The Rolling Stones' *Aftermath*; SSgt. Barry Sadler's "Ballad of the Green Berets"; Frank Sinatra's "Strangers in the Night."

Science and technology. Unmanned Soviet mission *Luna 9* makes first-ever controlled soft landing on the Moon; NASA ends the Gemini space program. Charles Kao and George Hockham propose fiber-optic cables for telecommunications.

Sports. The Milwaukee Braves baseball franchise relocates to Atlanta. Boston Celtics win an eighth consecutive NBA championship. The NFL and AFL agree to merge. Host nation England wins its first World Cup soccer tournament.

Television. *Star Trek* and *Batman* premiere. *Dr. Seuss' How the Grinch Stole Christmas!* animated special airs for the first time.

Theater. Broadway debuts include *Cabaret*, *Mame* starring Angela Lansbury, *Sweet Charity*, Edward Albee's *A Delicate Balance*, and Woody Allen's *Don't Drink the Water*.

Miscellaneous. Endangered Species Preservation Act is passed. The National Organization for Women is founded.

1991 – 25 Years Ago

"Keating Five" hearings—in which five U.S. senators were accused of corruption for work on behalf of Lincoln Savings and Loan chair Charles H. Keating Jr.—conclude Jan. 16.

The U.S. and allies fight Iraq in Persian Gulf War: air attacks begin Jan. 17, followed by ground war starting Feb. 24. U.S. Pres. George H.W. Bush orders cease-fire Feb. 28.

South African Pres. F. W. de Klerk Feb. 1 announces plan to repeal remaining apartheid laws and proposes multiparty conference to discuss a new constitution.

A Los Angeles grand jury begins an investigation into the Mar. 3 police beating of 25-year-old black motorist Rodney King, which was documented in a video publicized nationwide.

Cyclone Marian surges through southeastern Bangladesh Apr. 30, killing an estimated 139,000.

Former Indian Prime Min. Rajiv Gandhi is assassinated May 21 by a suicide bomber.

Slovenia and Croatia declare independence from Yugoslavia June 25; an independence referendum in Macedonia is supported by 95% of voters Sept. 8 and independence is declared.

Soviet Pres. Mikhail S. Gorbachev and Pres. Bush July 31 sign START treaty—first ever to mandate reductions in strategic nuclear arms by the two powers.

Senate narrowly confirms Clarence Thomas's appointment to U.S. Supreme Court Oct. 15 despite charges of sexual harassment during confirmation hearings.

In deadliest mass shooting to date, a gunman Oct. 16 kills 23 people and leaves at least 20 wounded at a Luby's Cafeteria in Killeen, TX, before committing suicide.

After nearly seven years of captivity in Beirut, Lebanon, journalist Terry Anderson is the last American hostage to be released Dec. 4.

The Soviet Union officially disbands Dec. 25 as Soviet Pres. Gorbachev steps down, and Russian Pres. Boris Yeltsin takes over the Kremlin.

Art. L.A. County Museum of Art recreates the Nazi-era "Degenerate Art" exhibition. Visual AIDS Artists Caucus begins to distribute red ribbons to create a visual symbol of solidarity with people living with AIDS and their caregivers. Christo and Jeanne-Claude's *The Umbrellas* is created simultaneously in the U.S. and Japan. Damien Hirst's *The Physical Impossibility of Death in the Mind of Someone Living*.

Film. *Beauty and the Beast*; John Singleton's *Boyz n the Hood*; *City Slickers*; *Daughters of the Dust*; *Father of the Bride* starring Steve Martin and Diane Keaton; *Fried Green Tomatoes*; Steven Spielberg's *Hook* starring Robin Williams and Dustin Hoffman; *My Girl*; *Robin Hood: Prince of Thieves*; *The Silence of the Lambs* starring Jodie Foster and Anthony Hopkins; Richard Linklater's *Slacker*; *Terminator 2*; *Thelma & Louise* starring Geena Davis and Susan Sarandon.

Health and medicine. U.S. Centers for Disease Control and Prevention reports that 1 mil Americans have been infected with HIV.

Literature. Second and final volume of Art Spiegelman's *Maus: A Survivor's Tale* is published. Alexandra Ripley's *Scarlett* is marketed as the sequel to Margaret Mitchell's *Gone With the Wind*. Martin Amis's *Time's Arrow*, Tom Clancy's *The Sum of All Fears*, John Grisham's *The Firm*, Jane Smiley's *A Thousand Acres*.

Music. John Adams's *The Death of Klinghoffer*; Harrison Birtwistle's *Gawain* premieres in London at the Royal Opera House.

Nonfiction. Katharine Hepburn's *Me: Stories of My Life*; Alex Kotlowitz's *There Are No Children Here*; Naomi Wolf's *The Beauty Myth*.

Pop music. Bryan Adams's "(Everything I Do) I Do It For You"; "Unforgettable" by Natalie Cole with Nat King Cole; Color Me Badd's "I Wanna Sex You Up"; Michael Jackson's "Black or White" and *Dangerous*; Massive Attack's *Blue Lines*; Metallica's *Metallica*; My Bloody Valentine's *Loveless*; Nirvana's *Nevermind* and "Smells Like Teen Spirit"; Pearl Jam's *Ten*; Red Hot Chili Peppers' *Blood Sugar Sex Magik*; R.E.M.'s "Losing My Religion"; A Tribe Called Quest's *The Low End Theory*; U2's *Achtung Baby*.

Science and technology. A 5,000-year-old body, later nicknamed Ötzi the Iceman, is discovered preserved in ice on the Austrian-Italian border. Linus Torvalds announces the creation of the Linux operating system kernel.

Sports. Minnesota Twins beat Atlanta Braves in the first worst-to-first World Series. Chicago Bulls win first NBA championship. First women's World Cup soccer tournament is won by U.S. national team.

Television. Charlie Rose's eponymous interview show and *The Jerry Springer Show* debut. Comedy Central adopts its brand and format.

Theater. *Lost in Yonkers*, *Miss Saigon*, and *The Will Rogers Follies* debut on Broadway.

Miscellaneous. First *Sonic the Hedgehog* video game is released. Jeffrey Dahmer is arrested in Milwaukee and charged with more than a dozen murders over a five-year period. L.A. Lakers star Magic Johnson announces he has been diagnosed with HIV and will retire from the NBA.

WORLD ALMANAC EDITORS' PICKS
2015 Time Capsule

The editors of *The World Almanac* have selected the following items as representative of the year 2015.

- A box of Cuban cigars, acknowledging the steps toward U.S.-Cuban rapprochement completed in 2015 and as a reminder of the trade embargo that is still in place.
- Pope Francis's cap, which was blown off by a gust of wind on arrival in the Philippines Jan. 15, at the beginning of his whirlwind year of travel.
- One of the underinflated footballs that ignited the "Deflategate" investigation and legal proceedings after the AFC championship game Jan. 18.
- An image of #TheDress, the exact colors of which somehow became a hotly debated topic (black and blue? white and gold?) on social media in Feb.
- A body camera like those worn with increasing frequency by law enforcement officers in the wake of numerous high-profile incidents of police appearing to misuse force against people of color.
- The year in sports from head to toe: video of Carli Lloyd's World Cup final hat trick, July 5; the $25,000 mouth guard that protected boxer Floyd Mayweather in his $200-million victory over Manny Pacquiao May 2; and a horseshoe worn by American Pharoah, the first Triple Crown winner since 1978.
- A shade ball—one of millions placed into diminishing California reservoirs to prevent further evaporation as the state entered its fourth year of historic drought in 2015.
- Iran's enriched uranium stockpile, of which it can keep only a limited amount under the terms of the nuclear agreement reached with six world powers July 14.
- The images of Pluto that vastly sharpened Earth's picture of the dwarf planet following the *New Horizons* flyby July 14, and a vial of water, which NASA's planetary scientists announced in Sept. flowed as a liquid on the surface of Mars.
- Seventeen red debate podiums, representing the declared Republican presidential candidates at the time of their first televised debates Aug. 5, and six blue debate podiums, for the five candidates in the first Democratic debate Oct. 13 and for Vice Pres. Joe Biden (then still contemplating a run).
- A same-sex marriage license issued in Rowan County, KY, after the county clerk was jailed in Sept. for her refusal to do so.
- The movie trailer for *Star Wars: The Force Awakens*, which was viewed more than 112 million times according to Disney in the first 24 hours after its release Oct. 19.

ECONOMICS

U.S. Gross Domestic Product, 1930-2014

Source: Bureau of Economic Analysis, U.S. Dept. of Commerce
(in billions of current dollars)

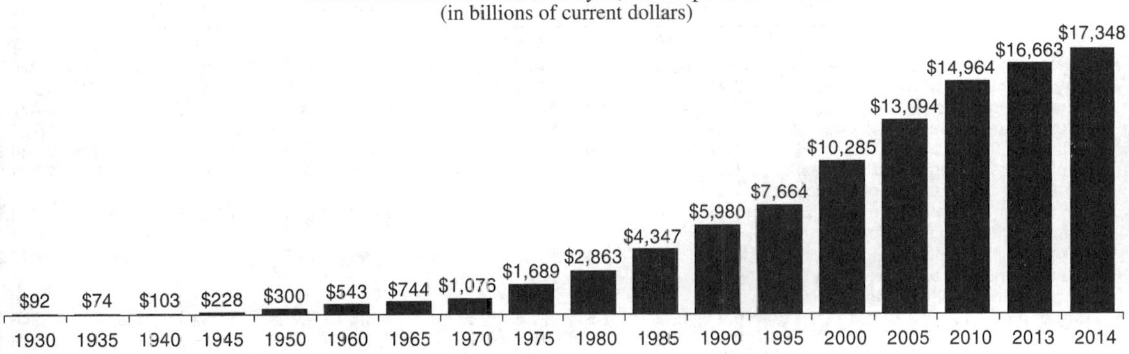

Tracking the U.S. Economy, 1960-2014

Source: Bureau of Economic Analysis, U.S. Dept. of Commerce
(in billions of current dollars, revised)

	1960	1970	1980	1990	2000	2010	2013	2014
Gross domestic product	**$543.3**	**$1,075.9**	**$2,862.5**	**$5,979.6**	**$10,284.8**	**$14,964.4**	**$16,663.2**	**$17,348.1**
Gross national product	**546.4**	**1,082.3**	**2,896.7**	**6,014.3**	**10,321.8**	**15,170.3**	**16,913.5**	**17,611.2**
Less: Consumption of fixed capital	67.9	136.8	426.0	886.8	1,514.2	2,381.6	2,632.8	2,746.7
Equals: Net national product	**478.5**	**945.5**	**2,470.7**	**5,127.5**	**8,807.5**	**12,788.8**	**14,280.7**	**14,864.5**
Less: Statistical discrepancy	–1.4	5.3	43.9	91.4	–99.5	49.2	–177.6	–212.0
Equals: National income	**479.9**	**940.1**	**2,426.8**	**5,036.1**	**8,907.0**	**12,739.5**	**14,458.3**	**15,076.5**
Less: Corporate profits with inventory valuation and capital consumption adjustments	54.7	86.2	223.6	417.2	781.2	1,746.4	2,037.4	2,072.9
Taxes on production and imports less subsidies[1]	43.4	86.6	190.5	398.0	662.7	1,001.2	1,118.6	1,155.8
Contributions for government social insurance	16.4	46.4	166.2	410.1	705.8	984.1	1,106.8	1,159.0
Net interest and miscellaneous payments on assets	10.7	40.5	186.2	450.1	565.0	489.4	513.5	532.3
Business current transfer payments (net)	1.7	4.4	14.0	39.2	85.3	128.5	119.4	127.3
Current surplus of government enterprises	0.5	–1.2	–5.1	3.2	10.7	–22.9	–18.8	–18.3
Plus: Personal income receipts on assets	44.3	112.7	386.0	991.2	1,453.5	1,739.6	2,060.4	2,117.5
Personal current transfer receipts	25.7	74.7	280.1	596.9	1,087.3	2,324.7	2,426.6	2,529.2
Equals: Personal income	**422.5**	**864.6**	**2,317.5**	**4,906.4**	**8,637.1**	**12,477.1**	**14,068.4**	**14,694.2**
Addenda:								
Gross domestic income	544.6	1,070.5	2,818.6	5,888.2	10,384.3	14,915.2	16,840.8	17,560.1
Gross national income	547.8	1,076.9	2,852.8	5,922.9	10,421.3	15,121.1	17,091.2	17,823.2

Note: Numbers may not add up to totals due to rounding. (1) Subsidies are included net of the current surplus of government enterprises.

U.S. Gross Domestic Product, 2000-14

Source: Bureau of Economic Analysis, U.S. Dept. of Commerce

	Billions of current dollars				Billions of constant (2009) dollars			
	2000	2005	2013	2014	2000	2005	2013	2014
Gross domestic product	**$10,284.8**	**$13,093.7**	**$16,663.2**	**$17,348.1**	**$12,559.7**	**$14,234.2**	**$15,583.3**	**$15,961.7**
Personal consumption expenditures	**6,792.4**	**8,794.1**	**11,392.3**	**11,865.9**	**8,170.7**	**9,531.8**	**10,590.4**	**10,875.7**
Goods	2,452.9	3,080.3	3,836.8	3,948.4	2,588.3	3,177.2	3,612.8	3,731.2
Durable goods	912.6	1,127.2	1,237.8	1,280.2	758.3	1,046.9	1,307.6	1,384.1
Nondurable goods	1,540.3	1,953.1	2,598.9	2,668.2	1,863.6	2,132.3	2,319.8	2,367.8
Services	4,339.5	5,713.8	7,555.5	7,917.5	5,599.3	6,353.4	6,977.0	7,144.6
Gross private domestic investment	**2,033.8**	**2,527.1**	**2,665.0**	**2,860.0**	**2,375.5**	**2,672.6**	**2,577.3**	**2,717.7**
Fixed investment	1,979.2	2,467.5	2,593.2	2,782.9	2,316.2	2,611.0	2,501.9	2,633.8
Nonresidential	1,493.8	1,611.5	2,084.3	2,233.7	1,647.7	1,717.4	2,023.7	2,148.3
Structures	318.1	345.6	462.1	507.0	533.5	421.2	429.7	464.6
Equipment	766.1	790.7	972.3	1,036.7	726.9	801.6	969.5	1,026.2
Intellectual property products	409.5	475.1	649.9	690.0	426.1	495.0	626.9	659.5
Residential	485.4	856.1	508.9	549.2	637.9	872.6	478.0	486.4
Change in inventories	54.5	59.6	71.8	77.1	66.2	64.3	61.4	68.0
Net exports of goods and services	**–375.8**	**–721.2**	**–508.4**	**–530.0**	**–477.8**	**–782.3**	**–417.5**	**–442.5**
Exports	1,096.8	1,308.9	2,263.3	2,341.9	1,258.4	1,381.9	2,018.1	2,086.4
Goods	797.3	926.6	1,560.9	1,618.0	902.2	970.6	1,382.3	1,443.0
Services	299.6	382.3	702.3	723.9	354.3	410.3	635.5	642.9
Imports	1,472.6	2,030.1	2,771.7	2,871.9	1,736.2	2,164.2	2,435.6	2,528.9
Goods	1,251.5	1,719.4	2,301.9	2,388.5	1,455.4	1,817.9	1,991.3	2,076.5
Services	221.2	310.7	469.8	483.4	276.4	341.1	443.5	450.8
Government consumption expenditures and gross investment	**1,834.4**	**2,493.7**	**3,114.2**	**3,152.1**	**2,498.2**	**2,826.2**	**2,854.9**	**2,838.3**
Federal	632.4	946.3	1,230.6	1,219.9	817.7	1,034.8	1,144.1	1,116.3
National defense	391.7	608.3	767.7	748.2	512.3	665.5	716.6	689.1
Nondefense	240.7	338.1	463.0	471.6	305.4	369.4	427.5	427.0
State and local	1,202.0	1,547.4	1,883.6	1,932.3	1,689.1	1,792.3	1,710.2	1,720.8

U.S. National Income by Type, 1930-2014

Source: Bureau of Economic Analysis, U.S. Dept. of Commerce
(in billions of current dollars)

	1930	1940	1950	1970	1980	1990	2000	2010	2013	2014
NATIONAL INCOME[1]	**$83.1**	**$91.6**	**$267.0**	**$940.1**	**$2,426.8**	**$5,036.1**	**$8,907.0**	**$12,739.5**	**$14,458.3**	**$15,076.5**
Employee compensation	**47.2**	**52.8**	**158.5**	**625.1**	**1,626.2**	**3,342.7**	**5,856.6**	**7,961.4**	**8,839.7**	**9,248.9**
Wages and salaries	46.2	49.9	147.3	551.6	1,373.4	2,741.2	4,825.9	6,377.5	7,114.4	7,477.8
Government	5.2	8.5	22.6	117.2	261.5	519.0	779.8	1,191.1	1,207.6	1,237.2
Other	41.0	41.4	124.6	434.3	1,112.0	2,222.2	4,046.1	5,186.4	5,906.8	6,240.5
Supplements to wages and salaries	1.0	2.9	11.2	73.6	252.8	601.5	1,030.7	1,583.9	1,725.3	1,771.2
Employer contributions for employee pension and insurance funds	1.0	1.6	7.8	49.7	163.9	395.0	685.5	1,114.6	1,197.8	1,224.0
Employer contributions for government social insurance	0.0	1.4	3.4	23.8	88.9	206.5	345.2	469.4	527.5	547.2
Proprietors' income with inventory valuation and capital consumption adjustments	**10.9**	**12.2**	**37.5**	**77.8**	**171.6**	**354.4**	**757.8**	**1,032.7**	**1,285.1**	**1,346.7**
Farm	3.9	4.1	12.9	12.9	11.7	32.2	31.5	46.0	88.8	78.1
Nonfarm	7.0	8.2	24.6	64.9	159.9	322.3	726.3	986.7	1,196.3	1,268.6
Rental income of persons with capital consumption adjustments	**5.4**	**3.8**	**8.8**	**20.7**	**19.7**	**31.4**	**187.7**	**402.8**	**563.4**	**610.8**
Corporate profits with inventory valuation and capital consumption adjustments	**7.5**	**9.9**	**36.1**	**86.2**	**223.6**	**417.2**	**781.2**	**1,746.4**	**2,037.4**	**2,072.9**
Taxes on corporate income	0.8	2.8	17.9	34.8	87.2	145.4	265.1	370.6	468.9	513.9
Profits after tax with inventory valuation and capital consumption adjustments	6.7	7.0	18.1	51.5	136.4	271.7	516.1	1,375.9	1,568.5	1,559.1
Net dividends	5.5	4.0	8.8	24.3	64.1	169.1	384.7	564.0	924.0	860.0
Undistributed profits with inventory valuation and capital consumption adjustments	1.2	3.0	9.3	27.2	72.3	102.7	131.4	811.9	644.5	699.0
Net interest and miscellaneous payments	**4.8**	**3.3**	**3.2**	**40.5**	**186.2**	**450.1**	**565.0**	**489.4**	**513.5**	**532.3**

Note: Numbers may not add up to totals because of rounding and incomplete enumeration. (1) National income is the aggregate of labor and property earnings that arise in the production of goods and services. It is the sum of employee compensation, proprietors' income, rental income, adjusted corporate profits, and net interest. It measures the total factor costs of goods and services produced by the economy. Income is measured before deduction of taxes. Total national income figures include adjustments not itemized.

U.S. National Income by Industry, 2000-14

Source: Bureau of Economic Analysis, U.S. Dept. of Commerce
(in billions of current dollars)

	2000	2005	2010	2011	2012	2013	2014
National income without capital consumption adjustment	**$8,817.5**	**$11,338.8**	**$12,662.6**	**$13,101.7**	**$14,043.0**	**$14,422.7**	**$15,036.1**
Domestic industries	**8,780.5**	**11,246.3**	**12,456.7**	**12,855.0**	**13,805.5**	**14,172.4**	**14,773.0**
Private industries	**7,729.4**	**9,865.5**	**10,776.9**	**11,165.1**	**12,104.0**	**12,454.0**	**13,015.2**
Agriculture, forestry, fishing, and hunting	73.8	94.0	123.1	153.0	154.3	183.1	175.8
Mining	90.7	175.0	184.7	222.8	241.6	253.6	254.6
Utilities	137.3	162.1	188.2	165.6	167.4	179.7	179.2
Construction	470.7	648.9	523.4	535.5	587.0	619.7	667.8
Manufacturing	1,243.1	1,326.7	1,350.2	1,411.3	1,552.1	1,589.5	1,635.2
Durable goods	758.2	753.2	752.8	785.4	885.0	905.0	937.8
Nondurable goods	485.0	573.5	597.5	626.0	667.2	684.4	697.5
Wholesale trade	570.6	685.2	737.3	770.0	848.5	878.5	909.3
Retail trade	666.7	857.0	872.2	893.4	964.1	998.2	1,027.4
Transportation and warehousing	268.5	333.4	368.4	375.3	417.2	426.3	450.1
Information	306.8	423.0	442.7	441.6	495.0	540.7	554.9
Finance, insurance, real estate, rental, and leasing	1,472.6	1,969.1	2,142.5	2,179.1	2,411.3	2,436.3	2,618.9
Professional and business services[1]	1,115.7	1,428.1	1,697.4	1,790.5	1,913.8	1,927.3	2,013.1
Educational services, health care, and social assistance	689.4	988.4	1,294.8	1,337.1	1,395.5	1,431.8	1,486.4
Arts, entertainment, recreation, accommodation, and food services	340.1	437.2	483.3	509.1	551.8	577.8	609.4
Other services, except government	283.3	337.4	368.4	380.8	404.4	411.6	433.1
Government	**1,051.0**	**1,380.8**	**1,679.8**	**1,689.9**	**1,701.5**	**1,718.3**	**1,757.8**
Rest of the world	**37.0**	**92.6**	**206.0**	**246.6**	**237.6**	**250.4**	**263.1**

Note: Estimates based on the 2002 North American Industry Classification System (NAICS). (1) Consists of professional, scientific, and technical services; management of companies and enterprises; and administrative and waste management services.

Consumer Price Index

The Consumer Price Index (CPI) is a measure of the change in prices over time of one or more kinds of basic consumer goods and services. The overall CPI is based on the price of food, clothing, shelter, and fuels; transportation fares; charges for doctors' and dentists' services; drug prices; and the cost of other goods and services bought for day-to-day living. Since Jan. 1988, the base period for comparison has been 1982-84, which equals 100.0. As the accompanying table shows, the price of apparel, entertainment and recreation, and education and communication have not risen significantly, while the cost of medical care has more than quadrupled since 1982-84. The table shows the Consumer Price Index for all urban consumers (CPI-U), which covers about 87% of the total U.S. population. The Bureau of Labor Statistics also publishes a separate Consumer Price Index for urban wage earners and clerical workers (CPI-W), which covers about 32% of the total U.S. population.

Distribution of U.S. Total Personal Income, 1930-2014

Source: Bureau of Economic Analysis, U.S. Dept. of Commerce
(in billions of current dollars, except for per capita figures)

Year	Personal income	Personal current taxes	Disposable personal income	Personal outlays	Personal savings	Savings as % of income[1]	Disposable personal income per capita: Current dollars	Disposable personal income per capita: Constant (2009) dollars
1930	$76.5	$1.6	$74.9	$71.6	$3.3	4.4%	$608	$6,411
1940	79.4	1.7	77.7	72.4	5.3	6.8	588	7,464
1950	233.9	18.9	215.0	195.0	20.0	9.3	1,417	10,033
1960	422.5	46.1	376.5	338.6	37.8	10.0	2,083	11,877
1970	864.6	103.1	761.5	665.5	96.1	12.6	3,713	16,643
1980	2,316.8	298.9	2,018.0	1,804.8	213.2	10.6	8,861	20,159
1990	4,904.5	592.7	4,311.8	3,976.3	335.4	7.8	17,235	25,556
2000	8,637.1	1,236.6	7,400.5	7,092.8	307.7	4.2	26,206	31,524
2005	10,614.0	1,213.2	9,400.8	9,157.7	243.1	2.6	31,760	34,424
2008	12,502.2	1,507.8	10,994.4	10,457.7	536.7	4.9	36,101	36,078
2009	12,094.8	1,152.3	10,942.5	10,275.1	667.4	6.1	35,616	35,616
2010	12,477.1	1,239.3	11,237.9	10,607.9	630.0	5.6	36,274	35,684
2011	13,254.5	1,453.2	11,801.4	11,091.2	710.1	6.0	37,804	36,298
2012	13,915.1	1,511.4	12,403.7	11,457.0	946.7	7.6	39,440	37,165
2013	14,068.4	1,672.8	12,395.6	11,805.7	589.9	4.8	39,123	36,369
2014	14,694.2	1,780.2	12,913.9	12,293.7	620.2	4.8	40,461	37,084

Note: Personal income minus current taxes equals disposable income; disposable income minus outlays equals savings. Figures may not add up to totals because of rounding. (1) Personal savings as a percentage of disposable personal income.

U.S. Consumer Price Index, 1915-2014

Source: Bureau of Labor Statistics, U.S. Dept. of Labor

Excluding 2009, prices as measured by the U.S. Consumer Price Index have risen steadily since World War II. What cost $1.00 in 1982-84 cost about $0.10 in 1913, $0.18 in 1945, and nearly $2.37 in 2014.

(Annual averages of monthly figures, for all urban consumers. **1982-84 = 100.**)

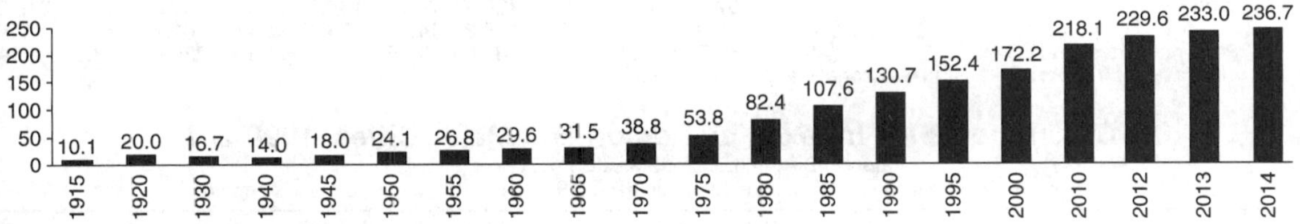

U.S. Consumer Price Index by Major Group, 1915-2014

Source: Bureau of Labor Statistics, U.S. Dept. of Labor
For all urban consumers. **1982-84 = 100**, unless otherwise noted.

Year	All items	Apparel	Food & beverages	Housing	Transportation	Medical care	Entertainment & recreation[1]	Educ. & communication[1]	Other goods & services
1915	10.1	15.3	—	—	—	—	—	—	—
1920	20.0	43.1	—	—	—	—	—	—	—
1930	16.7	24.2	—	—	—	—	—	—	—
1940	14.0	21.8	—	—	14.2	10.4	—	—	—
1945	18.0	31.4	—	—	15.9	11.9	—	—	—
1950	24.1	40.3	—	—	22.7	15.1	—	—	—
1955	26.8	42.9	—	—	25.8	18.2	—	—	—
1960	29.6	45.7	—	—	29.8	22.3	—	—	—
1965	31.5	47.8	—	—	31.9	25.2	—	—	—
1970	38.8	59.2	40.1	36.4	37.5	34.0	—	—	40.9
1975	53.8	72.5	60.2	50.7	50.1	47.5	—	—	53.9
1980	82.4	90.9	86.7	81.1	83.1	74.9	—	—	75.2
1985	107.6	105.0	105.6	107.7	106.4	113.5	—	—	114.5
1990	130.7	124.1	132.1	128.5	120.5	162.8	—	—	159.0
1995	152.4	132.0	148.9	148.5	139.1	220.5	94.5	92.2	206.9
2000	172.2	129.6	168.4	169.6	153.3	260.8	103.3	102.5	271.1
2005	195.3	119.5	191.2	195.7	173.9	323.2	109.4	113.7	313.4
2010	218.1	119.5	220.0	216.3	193.4	388.4	113.3	129.9	381.3
2011	224.9	122.1	227.9	219.1	212.4	400.3	113.4	131.5	387.2
2012	229.6	126.3	233.7	222.7	217.3	414.9	114.7	133.8	394.4
2013	233.0	127.4	237.0	227.4	217.4	425.1	115.3	135.9	401.0
2014	236.7	127.5	242.4	233.2	215.9	435.3	115.5	137.5	408.1

— = Comparable data not available. (1) Dec. 1997 = 100. Entertainment was reclassified as Recreation in 1997. Data is not seasonally adjusted.

U.S. Consumer Price Indexes for Selected Items and Groups, 1970-2014

Source: Bureau of Labor Statistics, U.S. Dept. of Labor

Annual averages of monthly figures, for all urban consumers. **1982-84 = 100**, unless otherwise noted.

	1970	1975	1980	1985	1990	1995	2000	2005	2010	2013	2014
ALL ITEMS	**38.8**	**53.8**	**82.4**	**107.6**	**130.7**	**152.4**	**172.2**	**195.3**	**218.1**	**233.0**	**236.7**
Food and beverages	**40.1**	**60.2**	**86.7**	**105.6**	**132.1**	**148.9**	**168.4**	**191.2**	**220.0**	**237.0**	**242.4**
Food	39.2	59.8	86.8	105.6	132.4	148.4	167.8	190.7	219.6	237.0	242.7
Food at home	39.9	61.8	88.4	104.3	132.3	148.8	167.9	189.8	215.8	233.9	239.5
Cereals and bakery products	37.1	62.9	83.9	107.9	140.0	167.5	188.3	209.0	250.4	270.4	271.1
Meats, poultry, fish, eggs	44.6	67.0	92.0	100.1	130.0	138.8	154.5	184.7	207.7	236.0	253.0
Dairy products	44.7	62.6	90.9	103.2	126.5	132.8	160.7	182.4	199.2	217.6	225.3
Fruits and vegetables	37.8	56.9	82.1	108.4	149.0	177.7	204.6	241.4	273.5	290.0	294.4
Nonalcoholic beverages	27.1	41.3	91.4	104.3	113.5	131.7	137.8	144.4	161.6	166.9	166.0
Sugar and sweets	30.5	65.3	90.5	105.8	124.7	137.5	154.0	165.2	201.2	211.0	209.3
Fats and oils	39.2	73.5	89.3	108.9	126.3	137.3	147.4	167.7	200.6	229.3	229.7
Other foods	39.6	58.9	83.6	106.4	131.2	151.1	172.2	182.5	204.6	217.7	219.9
Food away from home	37.5	54.5	83.4	108.3	133.4	149.0	169.0	193.4	226.1	243.1	249.0
Alcoholic beverages	52.1	65.9	86.4	106.4	129.3	153.9	174.7	195.9	223.3	234.6	237.3
Housing	**36.4**	**50.7**	**81.1**	**107.7**	**128.5**	**148.5**	**169.6**	**195.7**	**216.3**	**227.4**	**233.2**
Shelter	35.5	48.8	81.0	109.8	140.0	165.7	193.4	224.4	248.4	263.1	270.5
Rent of primary residence	46.5	58.0	80.9	111.8	138.4	157.8	183.9	217.3	249.4	267.7	276.2
Fuels and utilities	29.1	45.4	75.4	106.5	111.6	123.7	137.9	179.0	214.2	225.2	234.6
Household furnishings and operations	46.8	63.4	86.3	103.8	113.3	123.0	128.2	126.1	125.5	124.8	123.1
Apparel	**59.2**	**72.5**	**90.9**	**105.0**	**124.1**	**132.0**	**129.6**	**119.5**	**119.5**	**127.4**	**127.5**
Men's and boys'	62.2	75.5	89.4	105.0	120.4	126.2	129.7	116.1	111.9	121.6	120.6
Women's and girls'	71.8	85.5	96.0	104.9	122.6	126.9	121.5	110.8	107.1	113.3	114.4
Footwear	56.8	69.6	91.8	102.3	117.4	125.4	123.8	122.6	128.0	135.0	135.5
Transportation	**37.5**	**50.1**	**83.1**	**106.4**	**120.5**	**139.1**	**153.3**	**173.9**	**193.4**	**217.4**	**215.9**
Private transportation	37.5	50.6	84.2	106.2	118.8	136.3	149.1	170.2	188.7	212.4	211.0
New vehicles	53.1	63.0	88.5	106.1	121.4	141.0	142.8	137.9	138.0	145.8	146.3
Used cars and trucks	31.2	43.8	62.3	113.7	117.6	156.5	155.8	139.4	143.1	149.9	149.0
Gasoline	27.9	45.1	97.5	98.6	101.0	99.8	128.6	194.7	238.6	302.6	290.9
Public transportation	35.2	43.5	69.0	110.5	142.6	175.9	209.6	217.3	251.4	278.9	276.4
Medical care	**34.0**	**47.5**	**74.9**	**113.5**	**162.8**	**220.5**	**260.8**	**323.2**	**388.4**	**425.1**	**435.3**
Recreation[1]	**NA**	**NA**	**NA**	**NA**	**NA**	**94.5**	**103.3**	**109.4**	**113.3**	**115.3**	**115.5**
Other goods and services	**40.9**	**53.9**	**75.2**	**114.5**	**159.0**	**206.9**	**271.1**	**313.4**	**381.3**	**401.0**	**408.1**
Tobacco products	43.1	54.7	72.0	116.7	181.5	225.7	394.9	502.8	807.3	876.8	903.3
Personal care	43.5	57.9	81.9	108.3	130.4	147.1	165.6	185.6	206.6	215.0	218.0
Personal care products	42.7	58.0	79.6	107.6	128.2	143.1	153.7	154.4	161.1	161.8	NA
Personal care services	44.2	57.7	83.7	108.9	132.8	151.5	178.1	203.9	229.6	238.8	NA

NA = Not available. **Note:** Data is not seasonally adjusted. (1) Dec. 1997 = 100.

Consumer Price Indexes by Region and Major Cities, 1990-2014

Source: Bureau of Labor Statistics, U.S. Dept. of Labor

For all urban consumers; % change not annualized. **1982-84 = 100**, unless otherwise noted.

Region and city	**1990**	**1995**	**2000**	**2005**	**2010**	**2011**	**2012**	**2013**	**2014**
U.S. city average	**130.7**	**152.4**	**172.2**	**195.3**	**218.1**	**224.9**	**229.6**	**233.0**	**236.7**
Northeast urban	**136.3**	**159.1**	**179.4**	**207.5**	**233.9**	**241.0**	**245.7**	**249.0**	**252.5**
Boston-Brockton-Nashua, MA-NH-ME-CT	138.9	158.6	183.6	216.4	237.4	243.9	247.7	251.1	255.2
New York-Northern New Jersey-Long Island, NY-NJ-CT-PA	138.5	162.2	182.5	212.7	240.9	247.7	252.6	256.8	260.2
Philadelphia-Wilmington-Atlantic City, PA-NJ-DE-MD	135.8	158.7	176.5	204.2	227.7	233.8	238.1	240.9	244.1
Pittsburgh, PA	126.2	149.2	168.0	189.8	215.4	225.1	232.9	235.9	239.0
Midwest urban	**127.4**	**148.4**	**168.3**	**188.4**	**208.0**	**214.7**	**219.1**	**222.2**	**225.4**
Chicago-Gary-Kenosha, IL-IN-WI	131.7	153.3	173.8	194.3	212.9	218.7	222.0	224.5	228.5
Cincinnati-Hamilton, OH-KY-IN	126.5	146.2	164.8	181.6	204.7	211.1	216.3	220.0	224.1
Cleveland-Akron, OH	129.0	147.9	168.0	187.9	204.6	211.0	214.7	217.5	220.6
Detroit-Ann Arbor-Flint, MI	128.6	148.6	169.8	190.8	205.1	211.8	216.1	219.5	221.8
Kansas City, MO-KS	126.0	145.3	166.6	185.3	205.4	213.5	218.5	221.6	222.7
Milwaukee-Racine, WI	126.2	151.0	168.6	185.2	209.6	216.9	221.1	225.1	227.8
Minneapolis-St. Paul, MN-WI	127.0	147.0	170.1	193.1	211.7	219.3	224.5	228.8	232.0
St. Louis, MO-IL	128.1	145.2	163.1	186.2	203.2	209.8	214.8	218.0	220.2
South urban	**127.9**	**149.0**	**167.2**	**188.3**	**211.3**	**218.6**	**223.2**	**226.7**	**230.6**
Atlanta, GA	131.7	150.9	170.6	188.9	203.5	209.1	212.8	216.3	221.0
Dallas-Fort Worth, TX	125.1	144.9	164.7	184.7	201.6	207.9	212.2	216.0	218.4
Houston-Galveston-Brazoria, TX	120.6	139.8	154.2	175.6	194.2	200.5	204.2	207.6	213.4
Miami-Fort Lauderdale, FL	128.0	148.9	167.8	194.3	223.1	230.9	235.2	238.2	243.1
Tampa-St. Petersburg-Clearwater, FL[1]	111.7	129.7	145.7	168.5	193.5	198.9	203.6	206.8	210.8
Washington-Baltimore, DC-MD-VA-WV[2]	NA	NA	107.6	124.3	142.2	147.0	150.2	152.5	154.8
West urban	**131.5**	**153.5**	**174.8**	**198.9**	**221.2**	**227.5**	**232.4**	**235.8**	**240.2**
Anchorage, AK	118.6	138.9	150.9	171.8	195.1	201.4	205.9	212.4	215.8
Denver-Boulder-Greeley, CO	120.9	147.9	173.2	190.9	212.4	220.3	224.6	230.8	237.2
Honolulu, HI	138.1	168.1	176.3	197.8	234.9	243.6	249.5	253.9	257.6
Los Angeles-Riverside-Orange County, CA	135.9	154.6	171.6	201.8	225.9	231.9	236.6	239.2	242.4
Phoenix-Mesa, AZ[3]	NA	NA	NA	108.3	118.2	121.5	124.2	125.8	127.8
Portland-Salem, OR-WA	127.4	153.2	178.0	196.0	218.3	224.6	229.8	235.5	241.2
San Diego, CA	138.4	156.8	182.8	220.6	245.5	252.9	257.0	260.3	265.1
San Francisco-Oakland-San Jose, CA	132.1	151.6	180.2	202.7	227.5	233.4	239.6	245.0	252.0
Seattle-Tacoma-Bremerton, WA	126.8	152.3	179.2	200.2	226.7	232.8	238.7	241.6	246.0

NA = Not available. **Note:** Data is not seasonally adjusted. (1) 1987 = 100. (2) Nov. 1996 = 100. (3) Dec. 2001 = 100.

Median Income by Race, Hispanic Origin, and Sex, 1948-2014

Source: *Current Population Survey*, U.S. Census Bureau, U.S. Dept. of Commerce

Race, Hispanic origin, and year		Male			Female		
		Number with income (thous.)	Median income		Number with income (thous.)	Median income	
			Current dollars	2014 dollars		Current dollars	2014 dollars
All races	2014	110,372	$36,302	$36,302	112,599	$22,240	$22,240
	2013	109,937	35,630	36,213	112,066	22,126	22,488
	2010	105,191	32,205	34,970	107,220	20,775	22,559
	2000	98,504	28,343	38,963	101,704	16,063	22,082
	1990	88,220	20,293	35,664	92,245	10,070	17,698
	1980	78,661	12,530	34,287	80,826	4,920	13,463
	1970	65,008	6,670	36,304	51,647	2,237	12,176
	1960	55,172	4,080	28,552	36,526	1,261	8,824
	1950	47,585	2,570	22,070	24,651	953	8,184
	1948	47,370	2,396	20,576	22,725	1,009	8,665
White	2014	89,203	37,574	37,574	88,417	22,479	22,479
	2013	89,327	37,080	37,687	88,397	22,325	22,690
	2010	86,368	34,374	37,325	85,486	20,896	22,690
	2000	83,372	29,797	40,962	84,123	16,079	22,104
	1999	81,911	28,664	40,741	83,690	15,352	21,820
	1990	76,480	21,170	37,205	78,566	10,317	18,132
	1980	69,420	13,328	36,471	70,573	4,947	13,537
	1970	58,447	7,011	38,160	45,288	2,266	12,334
	1960	49,788	4,296	30,063	32,001	1,352	9,461
	1950	NA	2,709	23,264	NA	1,060	9,103
	1948	NA	2,510	21,555	NA	1,133	9,730
White, not Hispanic	2014	73,897	41,072	41,072	75,502	24,005	24,005
	2013	74,159	40,856	41,525	75,598	23,733	24,121
	2010	72,723	37,154	40,344	73,995	21,715	23,579
	2000	72,530	31,508	43,314	75,206	16,665	22,909
	1990	69,987	21,958	38,590	72,939	10,581	18,596
	1980	65,564	13,681	37,437	67,084	4,980	13,627
Black	2014	12,539	26,433	26,433	15,383	20,938	20,938
	2013	12,343	25,049	25,459	15,289	20,920	21,262
	2010	11,433	23,086	25,068	14,212	19,548	21,226
	2000	9,905	21,343	29,340	12,461	15,881	21,832
	1990	8,820	12,868	22,615	10,687	8,328	14,636
	1980	7,387	8,009	21,916	8,596	4,580	12,533
	1970	5,844	4,157	22,626	5,844	2,063	11,229
	1960	5,384	2,260	15,815	4,525	837	5,857
	1950	NA	1,471	12,632	NA	474	4,071
	1948	NA	1,363	11,705	NA	492	4,225
Asian	2014	6,411	40,457	40,457	6,564	25,231	25,231
	2013	6,057	42,077	42,766	6,481	25,497	25,914
	2010	5,406	35,121	38,136	5,604	23,552	25,574
	2000	4,303	30,833	42,386	4,192	17,356	23,859
	1990	2,235	19,394	34,084	2,333	11,086	19,483
Hispanic	2014	17,036	26,675	26,675	14,691	17,585	17,585
	2013	16,757	24,201	24,597	14,376	16,952	17,229
	2010	15,106	22,420	24,345	12,947	16,292	17,691
	2000	11,343	19,498	26,804	9,431	12,248	16,837
	1990	6,767	13,470	23,673	5,903	7,532	13,237
	1980	3,996	9,659	26,431	3,617	4,405	12,054

NA = Not available. **Note:** Income for persons 15 years of age and over beginning in Mar. 1980; 14 years of age and over as of Mar. of the following year for previous years. Beginning in 2010, totals for White, Black, and Asian include those who identified themselves as being that race in combination with some other race. Before 2010, Asian category includes Pacific Islanders. Hispanic persons may be of any race.

Consumer Credit Outstanding, 2010-14

Source: Federal Reserve System

(in billions of dollars as of Dec. of year shown, not seasonally adjusted)

	2010	2013	2014
TOTAL	**$2,646.9**	**$3,098.8**	**$3,317.2**
Major holders			
Depository institutions	1,185.5	1,271.6	1,343.1
Finance companies	705.0	679.1	684.1
Credit unions	226.5	265.6	302.8
Federal government[1]	356.2	729.8	840.9
Nonfinancial business	78.4	59.3	53.6
Pools of securitized assets[2]	45.0	44.3	43.0
Major types of credit, by holder			
Revolving	**839.5**	**858.2**	**890.0**
Depository institutions	664.7	693.5	731.6
Finance companies	81.5	67.1	60.3
Credit unions	36.3	43.4	46.8
Federal government[1]	—	—	—
Nonfinancial business	$25.5	$23.7	$22.4
Pools of securitized assets[2]	31.4	30.5	28.9
Nonrevolving[3]	**1,807.4**	**2,240.6**	**2,427.2**
Depository institutions	520.8	578.1	611.6
Finance companies	623.5	612.1	623.8
Credit unions	190.1	222.2	256.0
Federal government[1]	356.2	729.8	840.9
Nonprofit and educational institutions[4]	78.4	59.3	53.6
Nonfinancial business	19.4	20.5	20.5
Pools of securitized assets[2]	19.0	18.6	20.9

— = Not available. (1) Includes student loans originated by the Dept. of Education under the Federal Direct Loan Program and the Perkins Loan Program, as well as Federal Family Education Program loans that the government purchased under the Ensuring Continued Access to Student Loans Act. (2) Outstanding balances of pools upon which securities have been issued; these balances are no longer carried on the balance sheets of the loan originators. (3) Includes motor vehicle loans and all other loans not included in revolving credit, such as loans for mobile homes, education, boats, trailers, or vacations. These loans may be secured or unsecured. (4) Includes student loans originated under the Federal Family Education Loan Program and held by educational institutions and nonprofit organizations that are affiliated with state governments.

Financial Assets of U.S. Families, 1989-2013

Source: *Survey of Consumer Finances* (triennial), Federal Reserve System

Category	1989	1992	1995	1998	2001	2004	2007	2010	2013
Median net worth (thous.)	**$46.9**	**$49.5**	**$57.8**	**$71.7**	**$86.6**	**$93.1**	**$120.6**	**$77.3**	**$81.2**
Average net worth (thous.)	**185.9**	**186.6**	**212.1**	**282.9**	**397.4**	**449.4**	**557.8**	**498.8**	**534.6**
Financial assets			**Percent of families holding asset**						
Transaction accounts	19.0%	17.4%	13.9%	11.4%	11.4%	13.1%	10.9%	13.3%	13.3%
Certificates of deposit	10.2	8.0	5.6	4.3	3.1	3.7	4.0	3.9	2.0
Savings bonds	1.5	1.1	1.3	0.7	0.7	0.5	0.4	0.3	0.3
Bonds	10.2	8.4	6.3	4.3	4.5	5.3	4.1	4.4	3.2
Stocks	15.0	16.5	15.6	22.7	21.5	17.5	17.8	14.0	15.9
Pooled investment funds (excluding money market funds)	5.3	7.6	12.7	12.4	12.1	14.6	15.8	15.0	14.8
Retirement accounts	21.5	25.8	28.3	27.8	29.0	32.4	35.0	38.1	38.8
Cash value life insurance	6.0	5.9	7.2	6.3	5.3	2.9	3.2	2.5	2.7
Other managed assets	6.5	5.4	5.8	8.5	10.5	7.9	6.5	6.2	7.6
Other	4.8	3.8	3.3	1.7	1.9	2.1	2.1	2.3	1.5
Financial assets as % of total assets	**30.5**	**31.6**	**36.8**	**40.7**	**42.2**	**35.8**	**34.0**	**37.9**	**40.8**

World's Wealthiest Individuals, 2015

Source: *Forbes* magazine, Mar. 2, 2015

Rank	Name, country	Source of wealth	Net worth (bil)
1.	Bill Gates, U.S.	Microsoft	$79.2
2.	Carlos Slim Helú, Mexico	Telecom	77.1
3.	Warren Buffett, U.S.	Berkshire Hathaway	72.7
4.	Amancio Ortega, Spain	Zara	64.5
5.	Larry Ellison, U.S.	Oracle	54.3
6.	Charles Koch, U.S.	Manufacturing, energy	42.9
6.	David Koch, U.S.	Manufacturing, energy	42.9
8.	Christy Walton, U.S.	Wal-Mart	41.7
9.	Jim Walton, U.S.	Wal-Mart	40.6
10.	Liliane Bettencourt, France	L'Oreal	40.1
11.	Alice Walton, U.S.	Wal-Mart	39.4
12.	S. Robson Walton, U.S.	Wal-Mart	39.1
13.	Bernard Arnault, France	Louis Vuitton-Moët Hennessy	37.2
14.	Michael Bloomberg, U.S.	Bloomberg, LP	35.5
15.	Jeff Bezos, U.S.	Amazon.com	34.8
16.	Mark Zuckerberg, U.S.	Facebook	33.4
17.	Li Ka-shing, Hong Kong	Hutchison Whampoa	33.3
18.	Sheldon Adelson, U.S.	Sands casinos	31.4
19.	Larry Page, U.S.	Google	29.7
20.	Sergey Brin, U.S.	Google	29.2
21.	Georg Schaeffler, Germany	Schaeffler ball bearings	$26.9
22.	Forrest Mars Jr., U.S.	Candy	26.6
22.	Jacqueline Mars, U.S.	Candy	26.6
22.	John Mars, U.S.	Candy	26.6
25.	David Thomson, Canada	Media, publishing	25.5
26.	Jorge Paulo Lemann, Brazil	Beer	25.0
27.	Lee Shau Kee, Hong Kong	Real estate	24.8
28.	Stefan Persson, Sweden	H&M	24.5
29.	Wang Jianlin, China	Real estate	24.2
29.	George Soros, U.S.	Hedge funds	24.2
31.	Carl Icahn, U.S.	Investments	23.5
32.	Maria Franca Fissolo, Italy	Nutella, chocolates	23.4
33.	Jack Ma, China	Alibaba	22.7
34.	Al-Waleed bin Talal, Saudi Arabia	Investments	22.6
35.	Steve Ballmer, U.S.	Microsoft	21.5
35.	Phil Knight, U.S.	Nike	21.5
37.	Beate Heister and Karl Albrecht Jr, Germany	Aldi supermarkets	21.3
38.	Li Hejun, China	Solar power equipment	21.1
39.	Mukesh Ambani, India	Petrochemicals, oil, gas	21.0
40.	Leonardo Del Vecchio, Italy	Eyeglasses	20.4

Persons Below Poverty Level, 1960-2014

Source: U.S. Census Bureau, U.S. Dept. of Commerce

	Number below poverty level (mil)					% of subgroup below poverty level					Avg. income cut-off, family of 4 at poverty level[4]
Year	All races[1]	Asian[2]	White	Black[2]	Hispanic[3]	All races[1]	Asian[2]	White	Black[2]	Hispanic[3]	
1960	39.9	NA	28.3	NA	NA	22.2%	NA	17.8%	NA	NA	$3,022
1970	25.4	NA	17.5	7.5	NA	12.6	NA	9.9	33.5%	NA	3,968
1980	29.3	NA	19.7	8.6	3.5	13.0	NA	10.2	32.5	25.7%	8,414
1990	33.6	0.9	22.3	9.8	6.0	13.5	12.2%	10.7	31.9	28.1	13,359
1995	36.4	1.4	24.4	9.9	8.6	13.8	14.6	11.2	29.3	30.3	15,569
2000	31.6	1.3	21.6	8.0	7.7	11.3	9.9	9.5	22.5	21.5	17,604
2001	32.9	1.3	22.7	8.1	8.0	11.7	10.2	9.9	22.7	21.4	18,104
2002	34.6	1.2	23.5	8.9	8.6	12.1	10.0	10.2	23.9	21.8	18,392
2003	35.9	1.5	24.3	9.1	9.1	12.5	11.8	10.5	24.3	22.5	18,810
2004	37.0	1.3	25.3	9.4	9.1	12.7	9.7	10.8	24.7	21.9	19,307
2005	37.0	1.5	24.9	9.5	9.4	12.6	10.9	10.6	24.7	21.8	19,971
2006	36.5	1.4	24.4	9.5	9.2	12.3	10.1	10.3	24.2	20.6	20,614
2007	37.3	1.5	25.1	9.7	9.9	12.5	10.2	10.5	24.4	21.5	21,203
2008	39.8	1.7	27.0	9.9	11.0	13.2	11.6	11.2	24.6	23.2	22,025
2009	43.6	1.9	29.8	10.6	12.4	14.3	12.4	12.3	25.9	25.3	21,954
2010	46.3	2.1	31.1	11.6	13.5	15.1	12.0	13.0	27.4	26.5	22,315
2011	46.2	2.2	30.8	11.7	13.2	15.0	12.3	12.8	27.5	25.3	23,021
2012	46.5	2.1	30.8	11.8	13.6	15.0	11.4	12.7	27.1	25.6	23,492
2013	46.3	2.4	31.3	11.1	13.4	14.8	12.5	12.9	25.3	24.7	23,834
2014	46.7	2.3	31.1	11.6	13.1	14.8	11.5	12.7	26.0	23.6	24,230

NA = Not available. **Note:** Because of a change in the definition of poverty, data prior to 1980 are not directly comparable to data since 1980. (1) Includes other races not shown separately. (2) Beginning in 2002, numbers include those who identified themselves as being Asian or black in combination with some other race. For 1990-2000, Asian includes Pacific Islanders. (3) Persons of Hispanic origin may be of any race. (4) Figures for 1960-80 for nonfarm families only.

Poverty Thresholds by Family Size, 1980-2014

Source: U.S. Census Bureau, U.S. Dept. of Commerce

	1980	1990	2000	2010	2014
1 person	$4,190	$6,652	$8,791	$11,137	$12,071
Under age 65	4,290	6,800	8,959	11,344	12,316
Age 65 or older	3,949	6,268	8,259	10,458	11,354
2 people	5,363	8,509	11,235	14,216	15,379
Householder under age 65	5,537	8,794	11,589	14,676	15,934
Householder age 65 or older	4,983	7,905	10,418	13,194	14,326
3 people	$6,565	$10,419	$13,740	$17,373	$18,850
4 people	8,414	13,359	17,604	22,315	24,230
5 people	9,966	15,792	20,815	26,442	28,695
6 people	11,269	17,839	23,533	29,904	32,473
7 people	12,761	20,241	26,750	34,019	36,927
8 people	14,199	22,582	29,701	37,953	40,968
9 or more people	16,896	26,848	35,150	45,224	49,021

Note: Weighted averages; not used for computing poverty data.

Families Below Poverty Level by Status, Race, and Sex, 1980-2014

Source: U.S. Census Bureau, U.S. Dept. of Commerce
(numbers in thousands)

Year and race	All families			Married-couple families			Male householder, no wife present			Female householder, no husband present		
		Below poverty level			Below poverty level			Below poverty level			Below poverty level	
	Total	Number	Percent	Total	Number	Percent	Total	Number	Percent	Total	Number	Percent
All races												
1980	60,309	6,217	10.3%	49,294	3,032	6.2%	1,933	213	11.0%	9,082	2,972	32.7%
1990	66,322	7,098	10.7	52,147	2,981	5.7	2,907	349	12.0	11,268	3,768	33.4
2000	73,778	6,400	8.7	56,598	2,637	4.7	4,277	485	11.3	12,903	3,278	25.4
2010	79,559	9,400	11.8	58,667	3,681	6.3	5,649	892	15.8	15,243	4,827	31.7
2012	80,944	9,520	11.8	59,224	3,705	6.3	6,231	1,023	16.4	15,489	4,793	30.9
2013	82,316	9,645	11.7	59,643	3,394	5.7	6,497	1,048	16.1	16,176	5,203	32.2
2014	81,730	9,467	11.6	60,015	3,735	6.2	6,162	969	15.7	15,553	4,764	30.6
White(1)												
1980	52,710	4,195	8.0	44,860	2,437	5.4	1,584	149	9.4	6,266	1,609	25.7
1990	56,803	4,622	8.1	47,014	2,386	5.1	2,277	226	9.9	7,512	2,010	26.8
2000	61,330	4,333	7.1	49,473	2,181	4.4	3,283	332	10.1	8,574	1,820	21.2
2010	63,976	6,305	9.9	50,016	2,921	5.8	4,176	563	13.5	9,784	2,822	28.8
2012	64,735	6,299	9.7	50,171	2,875	5.7	4,592	651	14.2	9,972	2,774	27.8
2013	65,837	6,526	9.9	50,543	2,647	5.2	4,850	766	15.8	10,444	3,113	29.8
2014	64,945	6,310	9.7	50,489	2,944	5.8	4,448	595	13.4	10,008	2,771	27.7
Black(1)												
1980	6,317	1,826	28.9	3,392	474	14.0	291	52	17.7	2,634	1,301	49.4
1990	7,471	2,193	29.3	3,569	448	12.6	472	97	20.6	3,430	1,648	48.1
2000	8,731	1,686	19.3	4,214	266	6.3	732	120	16.3	3,785	1,300	34.3
2010	9,571	2,311	24.1	4,267	377	8.8	916	236	25.7	4,387	1,698	38.7
2012	9,823	2,327	23.7	4,483	440	9.8	1,040	262	25.2	4,300	1,624	37.8
2013	9,850	2,204	22.4	4,251	330	7.8	1,023	192	18.8	4,576	1,681	36.7
2014	9,909	2,265	22.9	4,488	399	8.9	1,133	270	23.9	4,289	1,596	37.2

(1) Data are for one race only. The Census Bureau revised race categories in 2002, so data after 2002 are not directly comparable with data for previous years.

Poverty Rates by State, 1990-2013

Source: U.S. Census Bureau, U.S. Dept. of Commerce

The poverty rate is the proportion of the population with income below the government's official poverty level, which is the same nationwide but is adjusted each year for inflation. More than 46 mil people in the U.S. were living in poverty in 2014, up from 33.6 mil in 1990. State-level poverty rates will not be updated again by the Census Bureau until 2016.

State	1990	2000	2005	2010	2013	State	1990	2000	2005	2010	2013
Alabama	19.2%	13.3%	16.7%	17.2%	16.7%	Montana	16.3%	14.1%	13.8%	14.5%	14.5%
Alaska	11.4	7.6	10.0	12.5	10.9	Nebraska	10.3	8.6	9.5	10.2	11.0
Arizona	13.7	11.7	15.2	18.8	20.2	Nevada	9.8	8.8	10.6	16.6	17.4
Arkansas	19.6	16.5	13.8	15.3	17.1	New Hampshire	6.3	4.5	5.6	6.5	9.0
California	13.9	12.7	13.2	16.3	14.9	New Jersey	9.2	7.3	6.8	11.1	11.1
Colorado	13.7	9.8	11.4	12.3	10.6	New Mexico	20.9	17.5	17.9	18.3	21.7
Connecticut	6.0	7.7	9.3	8.6	11.3	New York	14.3	13.9	14.5	16.0	14.5
Delaware	6.9	8.4	9.2	12.2	14.0	North Carolina	13.0	12.5	13.1	17.4	18.6
Dist. of Columbia	21.1	15.2	21.3	19.5	21.3	North Dakota	13.7	10.4	11.2	12.6	9.9
Florida	14.4	11.0	11.1	16.0	14.9	Ohio	11.5	10.0	12.3	15.4	13.7
Georgia	15.8	12.1	14.4	18.8	16.3	Oklahoma	15.6	14.9	15.6	16.3	14.0
Hawaii	11.0	8.9	8.6	12.4	11.1	Oregon	9.2	10.9	12.0	14.3	15.1
Idaho	14.9	12.5	9.9	13.8	12.9	Pennsylvania	11.0	8.6	11.2	12.2	12.4
Illinois	13.7	10.7	11.5	14.1	13.3	Rhode Island	7.5	10.2	12.1	14.0	13.5
Indiana	13.0	8.5	12.6	16.3	11.6	South Carolina	16.2	11.1	15.0	16.9	15.9
Iowa	10.4	8.3	11.3	10.3	10.8	South Dakota	13.3	10.7	11.8	13.6	10.3
Kansas	10.3	8.0	12.5	14.5	13.2	Tennessee	16.9	13.5	14.9	16.7	18.1
Kentucky	17.3	12.6	14.8	17.7	20.0	Texas	15.9	15.5	16.2	18.4	16.8
Louisiana	23.6	17.2	18.3	21.5	19.2	Utah	8.2	7.6	9.2	10.0	8.3
Maine	13.1	10.1	12.6	12.6	12.3	Vermont	10.9	10.0	7.6	10.8	8.7
Maryland	9.9	7.4	9.7	10.9	10.3	Virginia	11.1	8.3	9.2	10.7	10.4
Massachusetts	10.7	9.8	10.1	10.9	11.9	Washington	8.9	10.8	10.2	11.6	12.0
Michigan	14.3	9.9	12.0	15.7	14.5	West Virginia	18.1	14.7	15.4	16.8	17.3
Minnesota	12.0	5.7	8.1	10.8	12.0	Wisconsin	9.3	9.3	10.2	10.1	11.0
Mississippi	25.7	14.9	20.1	22.5	22.5	Wyoming	11.0	10.8	10.6	9.6	11.8
Missouri	13.4	9.2	11.6	15.0	13.7	**United States**	**13.5**	**11.3**	**12.6**	**15.1**	**14.5**

Temporary Assistance for Needy Families (TANF), 1997-2014

Source: Office of Family Assistance, Admin. for Children and Families, U.S. Dept of Health and Human Services

Category	Total federal and state TANF Expenditures	Average monthly cash benefit, 2014 Per family	Per recipient	Average number of monthly cash beneficiaries in 2014 Families	Recipients	Children
1997 U.S. total	**$19,010,190,000**	**$402**	**$145**	**3,936,610**	**10,935,125**	**NA**
2000 U.S. total	**24,780,711,000**	**926**	**354**	**2,229,315**	**5,833,043**	**4,303,943**
2005 U.S. total	**25,580,110,000**	**1,121**	**474**	**1,901,810**	**4,495,175**	**3,428,885**
2006 U.S. total	**25,593,809,000**	**1,192**	**510**	**1,789,460**	**4,179,295**	**3,207,216**
2007 U.S. total	**26,921,973,000**	**1,322**	**567**	**1,697,432**	**3,957,330**	**3,047,043**
2008 U.S. total	**28,129,745,000**	**1,439**	**621**	**1,629,344**	**3,780,543**	**2,911,078**
2009 U.S. total	**30,577,765,000**	**1,476**	**631**	**1,726,799**	**4,041,292**	**3,084,413**
2010 U.S. total	**33,255,476,000**	**1,500**	**635**	**1,847,152**	**4,364,979**	**3,280,150**
2011 U.S. total	**30,264,118,000**	**1,546**	**674**	**1,921,243**	**4,599,846**	**3,435,218**
2012 U.S. total	**28,867,300,000**	**1,472**	**645**	**1,876,426**	**4,476,476**	**3,351,971**
2013 U.S. total	**29,147,086,849**	**1,387**	**592**	**1,751,067**	**4,102,491**	**3,091,076**
2014 U.S. total	**29,350,927,096**	**1,480**	**628**	**1,652,996**	**3,894,213**	**2,934,582**
2014 by state						
Alabama	179,524,456	876	366	17,078	40,903	30,708
Alaska	75,949,483	1,797	669	3,523	9,466	6,370
Arizona	335,884,400	2,127	952	13,159	29,409	21,485
Arkansas	140,899,391	1,957	870	6,000	13,493	9,759
California	6,341,455,425	983	407	537,583	1,298,103	1,021,708
Colorado	315,459,854	1,538	584	17,098	45,018	31,865
Connecticut	470,463,547	2,711	1,361	14,458	28,806	20,264
Delaware	106,170,159	1,884	670	4,697	13,209	8,077
Dist. of Columbia	260,528,062	3,345	1,301	6,491	16,687	12,628
Florida	832,365,056	1,383	799	50,146	86,765	72,150
Georgia	507,253,732	2,747	1,411	15,390	29,948	26,608
Guam	NA	NA	NA	1,248	2,971	2,300
Hawaii	241,311,849	2,374	824	8,470	24,399	16,257
Idaho	37,201,871	1,660	1,106	1,867	2,803	2,662
Illinois	1,218,540,212	5,065	2,280	20,050	44,546	36,736
Indiana	205,405,563	1,617	804	10,587	21,296	19,050
Iowa	181,892,407	976	388	15,529	39,028	27,671
Kansas	134,610,746	1,583	660	7,087	16,990	12,461
Kentucky	258,520,710	754	373	28,587	57,766	46,304
Louisiana	202,629,993	2,926	1,310	5,770	12,889	11,314
Maine	78,061,646	254	122	25,608	53,208	29,445
Maryland	573,456,428	2,301	953	20,770	50,146	36,921
Massachusetts	962,114,661	1,169	494	68,598	162,239	109,643
Michigan	1,306,871,660	4,076	1,777	26,721	61,280	47,081
Minnesota	486,141,013	1,847	830	21,939	48,805	37,425
Mississippi	73,186,977	702	338	8,694	18,036	13,423
Missouri	373,488,423	1,018	422	30,582	73,733	50,569
Montana	41,390,227	1,127	464	3,060	7,418	5,519
Nebraska	99,332,753	1,378	574	6,009	14,410	11,737
Nevada	98,292,072	675	257	12,134	31,869	22,976
New Hampshire	60,180,011	847	347	5,924	14,442	9,820
New Jersey	1,200,433,479	3,566	1,512	28,052	66,125	48,050
New Mexico	186,703,641	1,182	430	13,161	36,143	27,366
New York	5,211,548,074	2,886	1,131	150,461	383,880	274,904
North Carolina	530,834,809	2,672	1,417	16,554	31,223	26,857
North Dakota	37,172,730	2,376	946	1,304	3,274	2,621
Ohio	1,052,489,369	1,152	536	76,140	163,521	129,732
Oklahoma	153,318,748	1,784	813	7,162	15,707	13,355
Oregon	341,235,427	613	238	46,333	119,618	80,457
Pennsylvania	874,691,237	1,052	425	69,295	171,544	123,382
Puerto Rico	NA	NA	NA	12,207	33,703	21,089
Rhode Island	156,878,162	2,336	974	5,597	13,423	9,314
South Carolina	271,161,678	2,008	891	11,252	25,356	20,118
South Dakota	27,492,637	734	367	3,122	6,237	5,460
Tennessee	241,414,710	422	177	47,692	113,749	83,459
Texas	854,536,254	1,951	889	36,500	80,118	70,588
Utah	78,604,277	1,516	620	4,320	10,562	7,684
Vermont	78,555,795	1,840	801	3,557	8,177	5,715
Virgin Islands	NA	NA	NA	423	1,245	890
Virginia	255,438,645	766	351	27,777	60,724	44,472
Washington	863,458,600	1,753	763	41,044	94,337	64,943
West Virginia	129,946,230	1,260	581	8,591	18,649	13,939
Wisconsin	579,048,807	1,771	730	27,240	66,071	48,656
Wyoming	27,381,000	6,391	3,071	357	743	598

Adults Receiving TANF Funds by Employment Status, 2013

Source: Office of Family Assistance, Admin. for Children and Families, U.S. Dept of Health and Human Services

State	Adults	Employed	State	Adults	Employed	State	Adults	Employed	State	Adults	Employed
AL	12,544	36.2%	IL	8,228	47.4%	NE	1,991	39.9%	SC	5,842	24.2%
AK	3,117	30.0	IN	3,183	24.9	NV	7,003	36.7	SD	909	17.5
AZ	9,548	15.8	IA	11,077	41.6	NH	2,226	27.8	TN	33,683	28.7
AR	4,496	29.3	KS	5,767	35.6	NJ	21,514	12.9	TX	11,195	26.6
CA	288,244	21.4	KY	12,788	28.3	NM	10,280	22.1	UT	1,725	22.2
CO	11,488	40.0	LA	2,333	20.7	NY	69,253	32.4	VT	2,059	18.8
CT	8,871	27.0	ME	4,939	18.1	NC	6,332	14.4	Virgin Isls.	354	3.1
DE	1,891	26.9	MD	12,839	16.9	ND	784	41.8	VA	17,228	27.4
DC	4,106	20.6	MA	30,973	11.3	OH	26,295	19.2	WA	35,293	13.3
FL	16,597	12.2	MI	20,118	35.5	OK	2,821	6.0	WV	4,174	19.7
GA	4,385	12.3	MN	10,809	30.8	OR	19,304	4.6	WI	15,663	24.7
Guam	785	3.2	MS	5,684	17.6	PA	50,613	21.3	WY	146	8.8
HI	9,175	39.2	MO	23,982	14.8	Puerto Rico	12,257	1.6	**U.S. total**	**893,735**	**22.6**
ID	178	4.7	MT	2,021	22.9	RI	4,620	14.9			

Selected Personal Consumption Expenditures in the U.S., 1990-2014

Source: Bureau of Economic Analysis, U.S. Dept. of Commerce
(in billions of dollars)

	1990	1995	2000	2005	2010	2013	2014
Personal consumption expenditures	**$3,825.6**	**$4,984.2**	**$6,792.4**	**$8,794.1**	**$10,202.2**	**$11,392.3**	**$11,865.9**
Goods	**1,491.3**	**1,815.5**	**2,452.9**	**3,080.3**	**3,362.8**	**3,836.8**	**3,948.4**
Durable goods	**497.1**	**635.7**	**912.6**	**1,127.2**	**1,070.7**	**1,237.8**	**1,280.2**
Motor vehicles and parts	**205.1**	**255.7**	**363.2**	**410.0**	**342.0**	**416.7**	**440.2**
New motor vehicles	134.7	147.5	210.7	248.9	182.3	250.0	265.5
Net purchases of used motor vehicles	42.2	72.9	110.7	110.5	104.2	102.9	109.2
Motor vehicle parts and accessories	28.3	35.4	41.8	50.6	55.5	63.8	65.5
Furnishings, durable household equip.	**120.9**	**146.7**	**208.1**	**271.3**	**250.4**	**280.2**	**287.9**
Furniture and furnishings	69.2	83.4	121.7	160.6	148.4	165.2	170.4
Household appliances	23.7	26.6	34.1	45.1	41.7	45.9	46.1
Glassware, tableware, and household utensils	18.4	23.7	35.3	44.6	42.7	49.1	50.4
Recreational goods and vehicles	**105.6**	**153.7**	**230.9**	**305.0**	**312.7**	**346.8**	**354.6**
Video, audio, photo equip.	56.1	84.7	127.7	172.7	194.1	208.8	210.8
Sporting equipment, guns, ammunition	19.9	27.2	39.1	50.9	51.3	61.6	63.5
Sports and recreational vehicles	16.6	22.5	34.9	49.1	35.6	44.1	47.4
Other durable goods	**65.5**	**79.6**	**110.4**	**141.0**	**165.6**	**194.1**	**197.5**
Jewelry and watches	30.3	37.8	49.1	59.8	62.6	73.9	74.7
Therapeutic appliances and equipment	18.4	21.0	32.2	43.2	55.6	62.5	64.6
Nondurable goods	**994.2**	**1,179.8**	**1,540.3**	**1,953.1**	**2,292.1**	**2,598.9**	**2,668.2**
Food and beverages purchased for off-premises consumption	**391.2**	**443.7**	**540.6**	**668.2**	**788.9**	**866.0**	**886.5**
Food and nonalcoholic beverages	341.2	388.3	463.1	575.3	675.9	742.2	759.9
Alcoholic beverages	49.3	55.0	77.1	92.6	112.6	123.1	125.9
Clothing and footwear	**195.2**	**231.2**	**230.8**	**310.7**	**320.6**	**362.5**	**368.9**
Women's and girls' clothing	94.5	108.9	132.7	149.6	152.8	171.9	175.5
Men's and boys' clothing	57.4	72.2	85.9	86.3	84.9	96.1	97.3
Children's and infants' clothing	8.1	9.0	11.4	15.4	17.7	19.0	19.1
Other clothing materials and footwear	35.3	41.2	50.8	59.3	65.2	75.6	77.0
Gasoline and other energy goods	**124.2**	**133.4**	**184.5**	**283.8**	**333.4**	**413.0**	**401.1**
Other nondurable goods	**283.6**	**371.4**	**534.4**	**690.4**	**849.2**	**957.5**	**1,011.7**
Pharmaceutical and other medical products	59.1	85.1	159.0	248.5	334.1	389.1	428.4
Recreational items	50.9	68.9	91.9	112.6	127.7	143.7	150.7
Household supplies	54.2	70.4	86.7	102.0	108.3	118.6	120.6
Personal care products	39.3	50.2	68.5	88.0	104.7	117.9	122.3
Tobacco	41.0	49.2	68.5	76.7	106.3	106.1	104.2
Magazines, newspapers, and stationery	36.5	46.1	56.6	58.0	62.8	76.2	79.8
Services	**2,334.3**	**3,168.6**	**4,339.5**	**5,713.8**	**6,839.4**	**7,555.5**	**7,917.5**
Housing and utilities	696.5	913.7	1,193.6	1,583.6	1,909.0	2,057.4	2,142.6
Housing	570.6	756.1	1,010.5	1,332.5	1,609.7	1,752.5	1,824.8
Rental of tenant-occupied nonfarm housing	150.8	186.6	227.9	268.3	372.6	424.3	448.7
Imputed rental of owner-occupied nonfarm housing	412.8	559.4	768.9	1,044.3	1,214.5	1,303.7	1,351.0
Household utilities	125.9	157.6	188.1	251.1	299.3	304.9	317.7
Water supply and sanitation	27.1	39.3	50.4	61.3	78.0	85.0	86.6
Electricity	71.8	87.6	98.4	128.5	166.8	169.1	175.4
Natural gas	27.0	30.7	39.3	61.3	54.6	50.8	55.7
Health care	**506.2**	**719.9**	**918.4**	**1,322.3**	**1,690.7**	**1,880.7**	**1,954.0**
Outpatient services	232.1	336.6	436.6	626.2	767.9	844.5	874.7
Physician services	134.8	177.8	229.2	333.9	402.8	437.0	451.1
Dental services	32.4	45.4	63.6	87.9	104.5	110.2	114.0
Paramedical services	64.9	113.4	143.8	204.4	260.6	297.3	309.6
Hospitals	228.8	318.4	393.9	577.2	770.5	872.4	908.9
Nursing homes	45.3	64.8	87.9	119.0	152.3	163.8	170.4
Transportation services	**126.4**	**177.9**	**263.5**	**289.4**	**292.9**	**333.9**	**354.5**
Motor vehicle services	87.2	129.1	189.3	211.8	211.9	239.4	254.8
Motor vehicle maintenance and repair	73.9	93.5	127.4	155.1	152.4	169.2	177.4
Public transportation	39.2	48.8	74.3	77.6	81.0	94.5	99.7
Recreation services	**121.8**	**181.1**	**254.4**	**328.9**	**385.1**	**434.7**	**455.5**
Membership clubs, sports centers, parks, theaters, museums	49.7	69.5	91.9	117.9	141.8	160.5	168.8
Gambling	23.7	45.4	67.6	96.5	105.6	118.1	123.3
Food services and accommodations	**262.7**	**316.1**	**408.8**	**530.6**	**617.7**	**710.2**	**750.9**
Purchased meals and beverages	228.3	271.8	344.9	446.0	516.9	590.7	623.8
Accommodations	27.6	36.6	55.0	72.5	85.5	102.1	109.2
Financial services and insurance	**247.4**	**366.4**	**566.3**	**689.6**	**763.2**	**837.7**	**882.7**
Financial services	135.7	212.9	360.0	417.4	473.3	530.9	565.1
Insurance	111.7	153.5	206.3	272.2	290.0	306.8	317.7
Other services	**297.5**	**391.2**	**571.5**	**759.1**	**905.4**	**997.0**	**1,055.0**
Telecommunication services	60.7	85.2	126.4	137.7	152.1	156.6	164.1
Postal and delivery services	7.5	9.2	9.9	10.4	11.7	10.3	10.6
Internet access	0.1	1.6	16.4	29.7	63.0	88.7	96.0
Higher education	34.7	51.9	76.8	110.9	158.3	175.1	179.4
Nursery, elementary, and secondary schools	14.8	19.2	24.1	29.6	35.3	38.5	39.3
Commercial and vocational schools	11.1	14.4	24.3	30.3	42.0	45.9	48.7
Professional and other services	67.7	82.8	113.0	148.4	163.3	173.4	179.5
Personal care and clothing services	44.5	57.1	80.4	103.3	114.9	132.4	142.1
Social services and religious activities	41.2	58.1	81.1	110.2	138.9	153.5	161.2
Household maintenance	25.4	34.5	48.6	57.9	58.6	68.2	73.0

Note: Subtotals may not add up to totals due to rounding or incomplete enumeration.

Leading U.S. Businesses, 2015

Source: *Financial Times 500*, based on data from Thomson ONE Banker, Thomson Reuters Datastream, and individual companies (ranked by market value, in millions of dollars; as of Mar. 31, 2015)

Company (rank)	Market value
Aerospace & defense	
United Technologies (41)	$106,470.3
Boeing (42)	105,032.2
Lockheed Martin (71)	64,192.5
General Dynamics (102)	44,815.8
Raytheon (143)	33,575.0
Northrop Grumman (153)	31,935.4
Precision Castparts (164)	29,771.2
Rockwell Collins (367)	12,772.3
Textron (378)	12,279.8
Transdigm (393)	11,528.6
L3 Communications (430)	10,415.0
Automobiles & parts	
Ford Motor (73)	$63,010.7
General Motors (78)	60,388.7
Johnson Controls (145)	33,153.9
Tesla Motors (215)	23,740.2
Delphi Automotive (223)	23,204.3
Genuine Parts (342)	14,230.1
Borgwarner (351)	13,727.3
Harley-Davidson (365)	12,816.0
TRW Automotive (382)	12,054.8
Autoliv (432)	10,399.7
Banks	
Wells Fargo (6)	$279,919.7
JP Morgan Chase (10)	225,861.1
Bank of America (22)	161,908.8
Citigroup (24)	156,359.8
US Bancorp (57)	77,784.5
PNC Financial Services (95)	48,549.1
BB&T (177)	28,106.1
Suntrust Banks (238)	21,563.9
M&T Bank (293)	16,879.9
Fifth Third Bancorp (315)	15,366.7
Citizens Financial (352)	13,693.9
Regions Financial (370)	12,689.5
Keycorp (381)	12,111.4
Credicorp (401)	11,216.7
Huntington Bancshares (492)	8,961.0
Beverages	
Coca-Cola (18)	$177,142.3
PepsiCo (29)	141,742.7
Monster Beverage (216)	23,529.4
Constellation Brands (255)	19,766.1
Brown-Forman (265)	19,062.1
Dr Pepper Snapple Group (323)	15,124.8
Molson Coors Brewing (383)	12,037.4
Coca Cola Entertainments (436)	10,297.3
Chemicals	
E. I. Du Pont de Nemours (70)	$64,709.9
Dow Chemical (86)	55,274.0
LyondellBasell Industries (111)	41,880.4
Praxair (136)	34,847.0
Ecolab (140)	34,010.9
Air Products & Chemicals (150)	32,415.4
PPG Industries (157)	30,763.1
Sigma Aldrich (296)	16,515.3
Mosaic (300)	16,059.6
CF Industries (353)	13,590.5
Eastman Chemical (435)	10,318.1
Westlake Chemical (460)	9,557.8
Intl. Flavors & Fragrance (463)	9,479.6
Ashland (498)	8,818.1
Construction & materials	
Sherwin-Williams (189)	$27,047.0
Vulcan Materials (405)	11,179.5
Martin Marietta Materials (467)	9,394.8
Masco (470)	9,332.8
Electricity	
NextEra Energy (99)	$46,211.0
Dominion Resources (112)	41,698.2
Southern (116)	40,289.4
Exelon (171)	28,937.8
American Electric Power (186)	27,541.2
PG&E (200)	25,370.9
PPL (229)	22,412.5
Public Service Enterprise (241)	21,226.7
Edison International (248)	$20,353.4
Consolidated Edison (283)	17,866.2
Xcel Energy (285)	17,613.3
Eversource Energy (301)	16,035.3
Firstenergy (327)	14,766.6
DTE Energy (336)	14,466.1
Entergy (344)	13,988.1
CMS Energy (457)	9,634.4
AES (487)	9,036.2
Electronic and electrical equipment	
Emerson Electric (120)	$38,796.1
TE Connectivity (169)	29,093.5
Amphenol (275)	18,279.8
Roper Industries (289)	17,261.3
Agilent Technologies (346)	13,952.9
Ametek (371)	12,684.7
Sensata Techs. Holding (453)	9,727.2
Mettler Toledo Intl. (475)	9,228.2
Financial services	
Visa (31)	$128,455.3
Mastercard (46)	96,001.8
Goldman Sachs (53)	81,883.6
American Express (56)	79,617.9
Morgan Stanley (63)	70,545.3
BlackRock (76)	60,511.8
Bank of New York Mellon (101)	44,853.0
Capital One Financial (106)	43,308.3
Charles Schwab (117)	39,967.8
CME Group (152)	31,949.5
Franklin Resources (154)	31,912.2
State Street (158)	30,315.0
McGraw Hill Financial (175)	28,340.3
Intercontinental Exchange (196)	26,128.3
Synchrony Financial (201)	25,304.8
Discover Financial Services (204)	25,139.7
Ameriprise Financial (213)	23,853.6
T. Rowe Price (242)	21,101.4
Moody's (245)	20,973.0
TD Ameritrade Holding (249)	20,252.0
Invesco (291)	17,029.5
Northern Trust (298)	16,271.6
Affiliated Managers (388)	11,790.4
Equifax (409)	11,098.3
Western Union (417)	10,851.3
Voya Financial (429)	10,427.9
Fidelity National Financial (437)	10,290.4
Ally Financial (442)	10,101.9
Fixed line telecommunications	
Verizon Communications (13)	$198,035.3
AT&T (20)	169,458.8
Centurylink (258)	19,572.0
Level 3 Communications (271)	18,603.6
Food & drug retailers	
CVS Caremark (34)	$117,170.8
Walgreens (50)	92,298.9
McKesson (90)	52,669.4
Kroger (123)	37,664.9
Cardinal Health (163)	29,800.9
AmerisourceBergen (207)	24,962.5
Sysco (231)	22,349.1
Whole Foods Market (267)	18,788.6
Food producers	
Mondelēz International (81)	$59,181.0
Monsanto (87)	54,389.0
Kraft Foods Group (92)	51,234.7
General Mills (141)	33,738.7
Archer Daniels Midland (162)	29,811.6
Kellogg (218)	23,490.7
Mead Johnson Nutrition (247)	20,361.0
Keurig Green Mountain (279)	18,064.0
The Hershey Company (302)	16,015.6
ConAgra Foods (314)	15,600.2
Hormel Foods (326)	15,012.2
Campbell Soup (332)	14,513.8
J.M. Smucker (348)	13,847.7
Bunge (385)	11,984.1
Tyson Foods (391)	$11,665.1
McCormick (491)	8,968.3
Forestry & paper	
International Paper (219)	$23,463.7
Gas, water, & multiutilities	
Duke Energy (88)	$54,361.5
Sempra Energy (190)	26,964.9
Nisource (345)	13,963.9
Wisconsin Energy (407)	11,162.1
Ameren (438)	10,239.2
Oneok (446)	10,053.2
American Water Works (452)	9,752.8
General industrials	
General Electric (9)	$249,774.4
3M (43)	104,795.4
Honeywell International (54)	81,427.3
Danaher (79)	60,034.1
Eaton (155)	31,763.0
Parker-Hannifin (292)	16,920.8
Ball (455)	9,713.4
Sealed Air (459)	9,574.5
Rock-Tenn (489)	9,024.9
General retailers	
Wal-Mart Stores (8)	$265,107.3
Amazon.com (19)	172,797.3
Home Depot (25)	148,533.1
Lowe's Companies (60)	71,414.3
eBay (65)	69,945.6
Costco Wholesale (69)	66,653.9
Target (91)	52,667.5
TJX Cos. (97)	48,257.4
L Brands (184)	27,569.8
Netflix (203)	25,208.9
Dollar General (226)	22,871.5
Macy's (233)	22,108.3
O'Reilly Automotive (234)	22,013.5
Ross Stores (235)	21,966.1
Autozone (237)	21,640.4
Gap (277)	18,145.4
Dollar Tree (294)	16,696.4
Kohl's (307)	15,869.3
Nordstrom (317)	15,293.4
Carmax (333)	14,492.9
Bed Bath & Beyond (341)	14,249.5
Best Buy (359)	13,282.0
Tractor Supply (392)	11,609.0
Tiffany & Co (397)	11,366.6
Signet Jewelers (408)	11,138.0
Advance Auto Participations (415)	10,948.4
Staples (428)	10,430.3
Ulta Salon Cosmetics & Fragrance (456)	9,709.6
Family Dollar Stores (485)	9,068.8
H&R Block (497)	8,827.2
Foot Locker (500)	8,797.9
Health care equipment & services	
UnitedHealth Group (37)	$112,812.6
Medtronic (38)	111,140.9
Express Scripts (72)	63,237.3
Thermo Fisher Scientific (89)	53,303.8
Wellpoint (114)	41,194.6
Baxter International (125)	37,231.9
Aetna (126)	37,147.0
Stryker (135)	34,960.6
Cigna (144)	33,462.6
HCA Holdings (156)	31,559.3
Becton Dickinson (160)	29,983.2
Humana (194)	26,636.8
Boston Scientific (214)	23,770.5
Zimmer (251)	19,979.0
Intuitive Surgical (272)	18,603.3
St. Jude Medical (274)	18,320.0
Davita Healthcare Partners (287)	17,540.2
Edwards Lifesciences (316)	15,317.9
Laboratory Corp. of America (373)	12,646.8

Company (rank)	Market value
C. R. Bard (376)	$12,438.4
Henry Schein (390)	11,700.4
Quest Diagnostics (410)	11,090.3
Universal Health Services (421)	10,788.9
Waters (434)	10,322.1
Resmed (444)	10,089.0
Varian Medical Systems (466)	9,415.8
Hologic (473)	9,245.4
Cooper Cos. (486)	9,050.3
Household goods & home construction	
Procter & Gamble (11)	$221,279.6
Whirlpool (308)	15,856.7
Stanley Black & Decker (331)	14,615.5
Clorox (334)	14,480.7
Mohawk Industries (354)	13,561.5
Church & Dwight (406)	11,165.6
Newell Rubbermaid (425)	10,490.3
D. R. Horton (431)	10,406.8
Jarden (440)	10,205.1
Lennar (490)	9,009.8
Industrial engineering	
Caterpillar (96)	$48,511.5
Illinois Tool Works (133)	36,264.6
Deere (165)	29,770.4
Cummins (205)	25,136.3
Paccar (230)	22,393.6
Ingersoll-Rand (282)	17,926.9
Rockwell Automation (312)	15,710.2
Pentair (398)	11,306.0
Dover (411)	11,083.3
Pall (423)	10,706.1
Wabtec (480)	9,153.6
Industrial metals & mining	
Southern Copper (220)	$23,463.7
Freeport-McMoran Copper & Gold (256)	19,705.4
Alcoa (310)	15,791.8
Nucor (320)	15,168.3
Industrial transportation	
Union Pacific (47)	$95,451.8
United Parcel Service (68)	68,085.1
Fedex (98)	46,947.5
Norfolk Southern (142)	33,618.3
CSX (146)	32,841.5
Kansas City Southern (400)	11,270.8
C.H. Robinson Worldwide (419)	10,826.0
J.B. Hunt Transport Services (447)	9,949.8
Aercap NV (472)	9,267.7
Expeditor International of Washington (474)	9,238.6
Leisure goods	
Electronic Arts (276)	$18,234.8
Activision Blizzard (297)	16,428.3
Polaris Industries (468)	9,385.6
Harman Intl. Industries (479)	9,170.8
Life insurance	
MetLife (84)	$56,577.5
Prudential Financial (132)	36,475.5
Aflac (178)	28,062.4
Principal Financial (324)	15,108.4
Lincoln National (329)	14,732.2
Media	
Walt Disney (17)	$178,267.1
Comcast (28)	142,798.5
Twenty-First Century Fox (61)	71,181.8
Time Warner (64)	70,129.3
Liberty Global (103)	44,101.9
DirecTV (107)	42,788.4
Time Warner Cable (110)	42,101.3
CBS (180)	27,856.2
Viacom (181)	27,734.8
Charter Communications (236)	21,646.7
Sirius XM Radio (240)	21,321.1
Liberty Interactive (254)	19,788.6
Omnicom (262)	19,239.3
Nielsen (295)	16,521.7
Dish Network (313)	15,651.0
Discovery Communications (362)	12,945.1
Liberty Media (368)	12,763.4
News (471)	9,269.5
Interpublic (481)	9,120.9

Company (rank)	Market value
Mining	
Newmont Mining (418)	$10,835.1
Mobile telecommunications	
T-Mobile US (199)	$25,598.5
Sprint (268)	18,760.2
SBA Communications (322)	15,126.5
Nonlife insurance	
Berkshire Hathaway (3)	$356,510.7
American International Group (59)	74,183.9
Ace (131)	36,495.4
Travelers Cos. (137)	34,749.6
Marsh & McLennan (159)	30,199.3
Allstate (166)	29,637.1
Aon (191)	26,937.7
Chubb (221)	23,305.8
Hartford Financial Services (286)	17,604.2
Progressive Ohio (303)	15,981.8
Loews (319)	15,196.3
CNA Financial (404)	11,189.3
Markel (424)	10,690.8
XL Group (464)	9,442.9
Oil & gas producers	
Exxon Mobil (2)	$356,548.7
Chevron (14)	197,381.3
ConocoPhillips (58)	76,670.7
Occidental Petroleum (85)	56,251.3
EOG Resources (94)	50,288.8
Anadarko Petroleum (108)	42,686.7
Phillips 66 (109)	42,626.9
Valero Energy (147)	32,702.5
Marathon Petroleum (179)	27,951.0
Devon Energy (209)	24,793.4
Pioneer Natural Resources (210)	24,357.1
Apache (227)	22,713.2
Hess (261)	19,399.6
Noble Energy (264)	19,066.4
Cheniere Energy (273)	18,321.4
Marathon Oil (284)	17,628.9
Continental Resources (299)	16,241.2
Concho Resources (350)	13,806.2
EQT (374)	12,587.3
Cabot Oil & Gas (380)	12,213.6
Tesoro (395)	11,479.3
Cimarex Energy (445)	10,081.6
Antero Resources (454)	9,719.1
Chesapeake Energy (465)	9,416.9
Southwestern Energy (495)	8,916.1
Oil equipment & services	
Schlumberger (40)	$106,628.4
Kinder Morgan (52)	90,622.5
Williams Cos. (122)	37,836.1
Halliburton (124)	37,283.6
Baker Hughes (183)	27,629.6
Spectra Energy (211)	24,281.7
National Oilwell Varco (246)	20,492.7
Buckeye Partners (458)	9,608.7
Weatherford International (461)	9,523.6
Personal goods	
Nike (67)	$68,620.7
Colgate-Palmolive (74)	62,880.0
Kimberly-Clark (119)	39,116.6
VF (151)	32,043.5
Estée Lauder (263)	19,137.2
Under Armour (335)	14,479.6
HanesBrands (356)	13,431.0
Michael Kors (360)	13,199.7
Coach (396)	11,427.7
Pharmaceuticals & biotechnology	
Johnson & Johnson (7)	$279,723.9
Pfizer (12)	213,621.9
Merck (21)	163,139.3
Gilead Sciences (27)	145,532.9
Amgen (32)	121,303.9
Actavis (33)	120,536.1
Bristol Myers Squibb (39)	107,500.1
Biogen Idec (44)	99,063.5
Abbvie (49)	93,204.1
Celgene (51)	92,292.0
Eli Lilly (55)	80,714.4
Abbott Laboratories (66)	69,910.9

Company (rank)	Market value
Regeneron Pharmaceuticals (100)	$45,008.9
Alexion Pharmaceuticals (134)	35,032.3
Mylan (170)	28,985.9
Vertex Pharmaceuticals (173)	28,559.2
Illumina (193)	26,695.0
Perrigo (222)	23,305.6
Zoetis (224)	23,175.8
Biomarin Pharmaceutical (253)	19,831.5
Pharmacyclics (259)	19,456.5
Endo International (304)	15,956.3
Incyte (311)	15,744.0
Hospira (321)	15,141.9
Mallinckrodt (328)	14,752.5
Jazz Pharmaceuticals (426)	10,481.0
Medivation (443)	10,097.5
Alkermes (488)	9,028.0
Real estate investment & services	
CBRE Group (364)	$12,891.4
Real estate investment trusts	
Simon Property Group (75)	$61,493.9
American Tower (118)	39,783.9
Public Storage (139)	34,058.1
Equity Residential Trust Properties (176)	28,325.3
Crown Castle International (185)	27,557.4
Health Care REIT (188)	27,084.0
General Growth Properties (195)	26,164.7
Ventas (212)	24,158.6
Avalonbay Communications (225)	23,009.7
Prologis (228)	22,702.4
Boston Properties (239)	21,519.8
Vornado Realty Trust (243)	21,026.3
HCP (252)	19,940.9
Weyerhaeuser (288)	17,403.7
Host Hotels & Resorts (318)	15,286.8
Essex Property Trust (330)	14,700.3
Macerich (357)	13,337.6
Equinix (361)	13,149.9
SL Green Realty (372)	12,661.6
Realty Income (389)	11,714.5
Kimco Realty (412)	11,078.9
Federal Realty Investment Trust (441)	10,110.1
Annaly Capital Management (449)	9,855.8
Digital Realty Trust (493)	8,949.5
American Real Cap Properties (494)	8,916.2
UDR (499)	8,805.8
Software & computer services	
Google (4)	$345,849.2
Microsoft (5)	333,524.8
Oracle (15)	188,438.8
Facebook (16)	183,860.1
IBM (23)	158,642.0
Salesforce.com (105)	43,466.6
Yahoo! (113)	41,596.5
Cognizant Technology Solutions (121)	38,034.0
Adobe Systems (128)	36,989.9
Twitter (149)	32,443.7
Intuit (192)	26,831.3
Cerner (206)	25,098.0
Workday (305)	15,953.5
Symantec (306)	15,943.8
Check Point Software Technologies (325)	15,066.1
CA (343)	14,218.0
Red Hat (347)	13,893.7
Autodesk (358)	13,323.3
Akamai Technologies (369)	12,705.2
Palo Alto Networks (384)	12,018.4
ServiceNow (387)	11,856.4
VMware (427)	10,465.8
Citrix System (439)	10,208.1
Computer Sciences (476)	9,207.5
Mobileye (483)	9,107.7
IMS Health (484)	9,078.1

Company (rank)	Market value
Support services	
Accenture (82)	$58,673.8
Automatic Data Processing (115)	40,692.0
LinkedIn (187)	27,299.2
Waste Management (208)	24,815.1
Fidelity National Information Services (260)	19,401.7
Fiserv (266)	18,952.2
Alliance Data Systems (270)	18,606.1
Tyco International (278)	18,087.2
Paychex (280)	18,021.6
WW Grainger (309)	15,835.2
Republic Services (339)	14,320.1
Xerox (340)	14,291.8
Fleetcor Technologies (349)	13,836.0
Fastenal (379)	12,243.7
Stericycle (386)	11,928.2
Verisk Analytics (399)	11,288.9
Cintas (469)	9,334.0
Towers Watson (477)	9,195.9
United Rentals (496)	8,829.6
Technology hardware & equipment	
Apple (1)	$724,773.1
Intel (26)	148,094.7
Cisco Systems (30)	140,507.8
Qualcomm (36)	114,380.5
Texas Instruments (80)	59,880.8
Hewlett-Packard (83)	56,635.1
EMC (93)	$50,527.6
Avago Technologies (148)	32,581.4
Micron Technology (168)	29,227.5
Corning (172)	28,776.4
Applied Materials (182)	27,719.4
Broadcom (197)	25,931.0
NXP Semiconductors (202)	25,265.7
Western Digital (244)	21,026.2
Analog Devices (257)	19,632.5
Skyworks Solutions (269)	18,755.6
Seagate Technology (290)	17,083.4
Motorola Solutions (337)	14,446.0
Sandisk (355)	13,551.9
Altera (363)	12,911.3
Freescale Semiconductor (375)	12,522.4
Nvidia (394)	11,505.4
Linear Technology (402)	11,194.3
Lam Research (403)	11,189.6
Xilinx (413)	11,058.8
NetApp (414)	11,054.9
Microchip Technology (450)	9,850.8
Maxim Integrated Products (451)	9,847.1
KLA Tencor (462)	9,481.7
Juniper Networks (478)	9,189.8
Garmin (482)	9,115.1
Tobacco	
Philip Morris International (35)	$116,693.1
Altria Group (45)	$98,505.2
Reynolds American (130)	36,661.0
Lorillard (217)	23,526.0
Travel & leisure	
McDonald's (48)	$93,651.4
Starbucks (62)	71,006.0
Priceline.com (77)	60,465.0
Las Vegas Sands (104)	43,950.0
Delta Air Lines (127)	37,059.3
American Airlines (129)	36,769.2
Yum! Brands (138)	34,116.8
Southwest Airlines (161)	29,946.5
Hilton Worldwide (167)	29,248.1
Carnival (174)	28,354.2
United Continental (198)	25,839.2
Marriott International (232)	22,211.9
Chipotle Mexican Grill (250)	20,198.5
Royal Caribbean Cruises (281)	17,976.0
Starwood Hotels & Restaurants Worldwide (338)	14,336.3
Wynn Resorts (366)	12,779.9
Norwegian Cruise Line (377)	12,342.8
Wyndham Worldwide (416)	10,906.9
Tripadvisor (420)	10,822.6
Expedia (422)	10,723.3
MGM Resorts International (433)	10,332.3
Hertz Global (448)	9,925.3

World's Largest Companies, 2015

Source: *FT Global 500*, based on data from Thomson ONE Banker, Thomson Reuters Datastream, and individual companies (ranked by market value, in millions of dollars; as of Mar. 31, 2015)

Rank	Company (2014 rank), country	Market value
1.	Apple (1), U.S.	$724,773.1
2.	Exxon Mobil (2), U.S.	356,548.7
3.	Berkshire Hathaway (5), U.S.	356,510.7
4.	Google (4), U.S.	345,849.2
5.	Microsoft (3), U.S.	333,524.8
6.	PetroChina (16), China	329,715.1
7.	Wells Fargo (7), U.S.	279,919.7
8.	Johnson & Johnson (6), U.S.	279,723.9
9.	Industrial & Commercial Bank of China (21), China	275,389.1
10.	Novartis (14), Switzerland	267,897.0
11.	China Mobile (25), Hong Kong	267,252.3
12.	Wal-Mart Stores (10), U.S.	265,107.3
13.	General Electric (8), U.S.	249,774.4
14.	Nestlé (11), Switzerland	243,701.8
15.	Toyota Motor (23), Japan	238,924.8
16.	Roche (9), Switzerland	237,747.6
17.	JP Morgan Chase (13), U.S.	225,861.1
18.	Procter & Gamble (17), U.S.	221,279.6
19.	Samsung Electronics (18), South Korea	214,039.7
20.	Pfizer (19), U.S.	213,621.9
21.	China Construction Bank (29), China	209,139.8
22.	Verizon Communications (22), U.S.	198,035.3
23.	Chevron (15), U.S.	197,381.3
24.	Bank of China (52), China	197,225.6
25.	Anheuser-Busch InBev (32), Belgium	196,554.3
26.	Royal Dutch Shell (12), UK	192,134.9
27.	Agricultural Bank of China (38), China	189,297.4
28.	Oracle (27), U.S.	188,438.8
29.	Facebook (49), U.S.	183,860.1
30.	Walt Disney (39), U.S.	178,267.1
31.	Tencent (42), Hong Kong	177,960.6
32.	Coca-Cola (31), U.S.	177,142.3
33.	Amazon.com (35), U.S.	172,797.3
34.	AT&T (26), U.S.	169,458.8
35.	HSBC (24), UK	164,249.6
36.	Merck (33), U.S.	163,139.3
37.	Bank of America (28), U.S.	161,908.8
38.	IBM (20), U.S.	158,642.0
39.	China Life Insurance (131), China	157,029.7
40.	Citigroup (37), U.S.	156,359.8
41.	Home Depot (59), U.S.	148,533.1
42.	Intel (46), U.S.	148,094.7
43.	Gilead Sciences (60), U.S.	145,532.9
44.	Comcast (44), U.S.	142,798.5
45.	PepsiCo (47), U.S.	141,742.7
46.	Cisco Systems (56), U.S.	140,507.8
47.	Sanofi (40), France	130,260.0
48.	Visa (61), U.S.	128,455.3
49.	Volkswagen (50), Germany	124,335.3
50.	Bayer (57), Germany	124,157.7
51.	BHP Billiton (30), Australia/UK	$122,335.4
52.	Amgen (80), U.S.	121,303.9
53.	Taiwan Semiconductor Manufacturing (67), Taiwan	120,577.1
54.	Actavis (285), U.S.	120,536.1
55.	Sinopec (74), China	119,104.8
56.	Unilever (51), Netherlands/UK	118,902.5
57.	Total (34), France	118,541.9
58.	BP (36), UK	118,345.6
59.	CVS Caremark (88), U.S.	117,170.8
60.	Philip Morris International (43), U.S.	116,693.1
61.	Commonwealth Bank of Australia (55), Australia	115,688.2
62.	Qualcomm (41), U.S.	114,380.5
63.	Ping An Insurance (172), China	113,119.0
64.	Novo Nordisk (68), Denmark	112,977.6
65.	UnitedHealth Group (100), U.S.	112,812.6
66.	GlaxoSmithKline (45), UK	111,649.6
67.	Medtronic (144), U.S.	111,140.9
68.	Bristol Myers Squibb (93), U.S.	107,500.1
69.	Schlumberger (48), U.S.	106,628.4
70.	United Technologies (62), U.S.	106,470.3
71.	Banco Santander (58), Spain	105,960.3
72.	Boeing (81), U.S.	105,032.2
73.	3M (87), U.S.	104,795.4
74.	Daimler (66), Germany	103,741.0
75.	L'Oreal (71), France	103,279.4
76.	Inditex (79), Spain	100,013.2
77.	Biogen Idec (115), U.S.	99,063.5
78.	Altria Group (109), U.S.	98,505.2
79.	British American Tobacco (63), UK	96,536.7
80.	Mastercard (95), U.S.	96,001.8
81.	Union Pacific (94), U.S.	95,451.8
82.	Westpac Banking (70), Australia	93,870.4
83.	McDonald's (73), U.S.	93,651.4
84.	Abbvie (97), U.S.	93,204.1
85.	Walgreens (138), U.S.	92,298.9
86.	Celgene (166), U.S.	92,292.0
87.	BASF (65), Germany	91,489.5
88.	Ambev (54), Brazil	90,732.6
89.	Kinder Morgan (314), U.S.	90,622.5
90.	Siemens (53), Germany	90,196.5
91.	LVMH (82), France	89,497.4
92.	SAP (69), Germany	88,793.3
93.	Mitsubishi UFJ Financial (104), Japan	87,866.4
94.	Royal Bank Canada (77), Canada	86,842.8
95.	AstraZeneca (98), UK	86,763.1
96.	Vodafone Group (72), UK	86,760.2
97.	SABMiller (101), UK	84,939.6
98.	Deutsche Telekom (116), Germany	83,314.0
99.	Lloyds Banking Group (89), UK	82,941.0
100.	Goldman Sachs (110), U.S.	81,883.6

Note: Revenue figures rounded at source.

Top U.S. Franchises, 2015

Source: *Entrepreneur* magazine

Rank	Company (2014 rank)	Type of business	Locations	Startup costs[1]
1.	Hampton by Hilton (2)	Mid-price hotels	2,054	$4 mil-14 mil
2.	Anytime Fitness (1)	Fitness center	2,869	$63,000-418,000
3.	Subway (3)	Submarine sandwiches, salads	43,916	$117,000-263,000
4.	Jack in the Box	Hamburgers	2,249	$1 mil-2 mil
5.	Supercuts (4)	Hair salon	2,486	$114,000-234,000
6.	Jimmy John's Gourmet Sandwiches (5)	Gourmet sandwiches	2,286	$323,000-544,000
7.	Servpro (7)	Insurance/disaster restoration and cleaning	1,694	$142,000-191,000
8.	Denny's Inc. (8)	Family restaurants	1,696	$1 mil-2 mil
9.	Pizza Hut Inc. (9)	Pizza, pasta, wings	15,605	$297,000-2 mil
10.	7-Eleven Inc. (6)	Convenience stores	56,439	$38,000-1 mil
11.	Dunkin' Donuts (10)	Coffee, doughnuts, baked goods	11,460	$276,000-2 mil
12.	Jan-Pro Franchising Intl. Inc. (12)	Commercial cleaning	7,849	$4,000-52,000
13.	Days Inn (13)	Hotels	1,782	$179,000-8 mil
14.	McDonald's (16)	Burgers, chicken, salads, beverages	36,368	$1 mil-2 mil
15.	Aaron's (17)	Furniture, electronics, computer, and appliance leasing and sales	2,081	$276,000-783,000
16.	KFC Corp. (14)	Chicken	19,420	$1 mil-3 mil
17.	Hardee's (11)	Burgers, chicken, biscuits	2,086	$1 mil-2 mil
18.	H&R Block (15)	Tax preparation, electronic filing	10,800	$32,000-149,000
19.	Taco Bell (20)	Mexican food	6,198	$1 mil-3 mil
20.	Kumon Math & Reading Centers (18)	Supplemental education	25,386	$64,000-134,000
21.	The UPS Store (22)	Postal, business, print, and communications services	4,862	$150,000-420,000
22.	Cruise Planners (19)	Travel agency	2,072	$2,000-23,000
23.	GNC Franchising (28)	Vitamins and nutrition products	6,734	$191,000-322,000
24.	Sonic (26)	Drive-in restaurants	3,518	$1 mil-2 mil
25.	Snap-on Tools (24)	Professional tools and equipment	4,804	$160,000-316,000

NA = Not available. **Note:** Franchises are ranked by a combination of factors, including financial strength and stability, growth rate, number of locations, startup costs, and whether the company provides financing. (1) Does not include franchise fees, which vary.

United States Mint

Source: United States Mint, U.S. Dept. of the Treasury

The United States Mint was created on Apr. 2, 1792, by an act of Congress, which established the U.S. national coinage system. In 1799, the mint became an independent agency reporting directly to the president. It was made a statutory bureau of the Treasury Department in 1873, with a director appointed by the president.

The mint manufactures and ships all U.S. coins for circulation to Federal Reserve banks and branches, which in turn issue coins to the public and business community through depository institutions. The mint also safeguards the Treasury Department's stored gold and silver, as well as other monetary assets.

The composition of dimes, quarters, and half dollars, traditionally produced from silver, was changed by the Coinage Act of 1965, which mandated that these coins from then on be minted from a cupronickel-clad alloy. In 1970, legislative action mandated that the half dollar and a dollar coin be minted from the same alloy.

Mint headquarters are in Washington, DC. Mint production facilities are in Philadelphia, Denver, San Francisco, and West Point, NY. In addition, the mint is responsible for the U.S. Bullion Depository at Fort Knox, KY.

Contact information: (800) USA-MINT

Website: www.usmint.gov

New Circulating and Commemorative Coins

Source: United States Mint, U.S. Dept. of the Treasury

Dollar coins. A large, unwieldy dollar coin featuring the likeness of Pres. Dwight D. Eisenhower was minted 1971-78. The smaller Susan B. Anthony dollar, minted 1979-81, marked the first time that a woman other than a mythical figure appeared on a generally circulated U.S. coin. A golden dollar coin was first minted in 2000. It depicts Sacagawea, a Shoshone woman who helped guide explorers Lewis and Clark, on the obverse. In 2007, the mint began issuing a series of golden dollar coins featuring U.S. presidents on the front and the Statue of Liberty on the back. Each includes the president's name, likeness, and years of service. Four are to be issued each year in the order in which the presidents served. The 2015 set featured Harry S. Truman, Dwight D. Eisenhower, John F. Kennedy, and Lyndon B. Johnson. Only presidents deceased more than two years will be honored, so the program is currently slated to end in 2016 with coins commemorating Richard Nixon, Gerald Ford, and Ronald Reagan. The mint also issues golden dollar coins whose reverse sides celebrate the important contributions made by American Indian tribes to the development of the U.S. The 2013 coin celebrated the treaty with the Delaware tribe of Native Americans; the 2014 coin commemorated the hospitality that ensured the success of the Lewis and Clark exhibition; and the 2015 coin celebrates the contribution of Mohawk iron workers.

America the Beautiful quarters. In 2010, the U.S. Mint began an initiative to honor 56 national parks and other sites of national importance. Five new reverse designs appear on the quarter-dollar each year in 2010-21; the order of issuance corresponds to the order in which the featured site was first established. The 2014 coins commemorated Great Smoky Mountains National Park, TN; Shenandoah National Park, VA; Arches National Park, UT; Great Sand Dunes National Park, CO, and Everglades National Park, FL. The 2015 coins celebrated Homestead National Monument of America, NE;, Kisatchie National Forest, LA; Blue Ridge Parkway, NC; Bombay Hook National Wildlife Refuge, DE; and Saratoga National Historical Park, NY. The 2016 coins commemorate Shawnee National Forest, IL; Cumberland Gap National Historical Park, KY; Harpers Ferry National Historical Park, VA; Theodore Roosevelt National Park, ND; and Fort Moultrie at Fort Sumter National Monument, SC.

Commemorative coins. From 1892 to 1954, and again since 1982, Congress has authorized the mint to produce more than 50 different commemorative coins. Recent issues include the 2009 Louis Braille Bicentennial-Braille Literacy silver dollar, the 2014 Civil Rights Act of 1964 silver dollar, and the 2014 National Baseball Hall of Fame Coins.

Bureau of Engraving and Printing

Source: Bureau of Engraving and Printing, U.S. Dept. of the Treasury

The Bureau of Engraving and Printing manufactures the financial and other securities of the U.S. It designs and prints a variety of products, including Federal Reserve notes (bills in various denominations), Treasury securities, identification cards, naturalization certificates, and other special security documents. The bureau produces printings in denominations ranging from a 1/5-cent wine stamp to a $100,000,000 Intl. Monetary Fund special note. It also produces all hand-engraved invitations issued by the White House.

The first general circulation of paper money by the federal government dates back to 1861, prior to the establishment of the bureau, when Congress authorized the U.S. Treasury to issue non-interest-bearing demand notes, nicknamed "greenbacks" because of their color, to finance the Civil War. A portrait of Pres. Abraham Lincoln appeared on the face of the first $10 notes. By 1862, the design of U.S. currency incorporated fine-line engraving, intricate geometric lathe work patterns, a Treasury seal, and engraved signatures to aid in counterfeit deterrence. All U.S. currency issued since 1861 remain valid and redeemable at full face value.

The Bureau of Engraving and Printing began operations by 1862, originally separating and sealing bank notes that were printed by private companies. In 1877, the bureau became the sole producer of U.S. currency. The Federal Reserve Act of 1913 created the Federal Reserve as the nation's central bank and provided for currency called Federal Reserve notes. The first notes, issued the following year, were $10 notes bearing a portrait of Pres. Andrew Jackson. In 1929, the look of U.S. currency was standardized. The national motto, "In God We Trust," was added to paper money in 1957.

On Oct. 9, 2003, the Treasury began a major currency redesign, beginning with the introduction of a new $20 note. The bills were the first since 1905 to use background colors other than green and black. Other security features include color-shifting ink in the number 20 in the lower right corner on the note's face. A new $50 note with similar security features was released Sept. 28, 2004, followed by a $10 note on Mar. 2, 2006, and a $5 note Mar. 13, 2008. The $100 bill was the last note to be redesigned. The new hundreds went into circulation Oct. 8, 2013. Their security and anti-counterfeiting features include a blue 3-D security ribbon and the image of a bell in an inkwell on the face. The bell changes color from copper to green when the note is tilted. All older notes remain legal tender, but will gradually be withdrawn from circulation. For more information, see uscurrency.gov.

The Bureau of Engraving and Printing currently operates two facilities, one in Washington, DC, opened in 1914, and one in Fort Worth, TX, which began operations in 1991.

Denominations of U.S. Currency

Since 1969 the largest denomination of U.S. currency that has been issued is the $100 bill. As larger-denomination bills reach the Federal Reserve Bank, they are removed from circulation. Because some discontinued currency is expected to be in the hands of holders for many years, the description of the various denominations below is continued.

Note	Portrait	Embellishment on back
$1	George Washington	Great Seal of U.S.
2	Thomas Jefferson	Signers of Declaration
5	Abraham Lincoln	Lincoln Memorial
10	Alexander Hamilton	U.S. Treasury
20	Andrew Jackson	White House
50	Ulysses S. Grant	U.S. Capitol
100	Benjamin Franklin	Independence Hall

Note	Portrait	Embellishment on back
$500	William McKinley	Ornate denominational marking
1,000	Grover Cleveland	Ornate denominational marking
5,000	James Madison	Washington resigning as Army commander
10,000	Salmon Chase	Embarkation of the Pilgrims
100,000*	Woodrow Wilson	Ornate denominational marking

* = For use only in transactions between Federal Reserve System and Treasury Department.

The U.S. $1 Bill

Plate position: Shows where on the 32-note plate this bill was printed.

Serial number: Each bill has its own.

Federal Reserve District number: Shows which district issued the bill.

Federal Reserve District seal: The name of the Federal Reserve Bank that issued the bill is printed in the seal. The letter tells you where the bill is from. Here are the letter codes for the 12 Federal Reserve Districts:

- **A:** Boston
- **B:** New York
- **C:** Philadelphia
- **D:** Cleveland
- **E:** Richmond
- **F:** Atlanta
- **G:** Chicago
- **H:** St. Louis
- **I:** Minneapolis
- **J:** Kansas City
- **K:** Dallas
- **L:** San Francisco

Treasury Department seal: The balancing scales represent justice. The pointed stripe across the middle has 13 stars for the original 13 colonies. The key represents authority.

Plate serial number: Shows which printing plate was used for the face of the bill.

Treasurer of the U.S. signature

Series indicator: Year note's design was first used.

Secretary of the Treasury signature

Plate serial number: Shows which plate was used for the back.

Front of the Great Seal of the United States: The bald eagle is the national bird. The shield has 13 stripes for the 13 original colonies. The eagle holds 13 arrows (symbol of war) and an olive branch with 13 olives and leaves (symbol of peace). Above the eagle is the motto "E Pluribus Unum," Latin for "out of many, one," and a constellation of 13 stars.

Reverse of the Great Seal of the United States: The pyramid symbolizes something that endures for ages. The eye, known as the Eye of Providence, probably comes from an ancient Egyptian symbol. The pyramid has 13 levels; at its base are the Roman numerals for 1776, the year of American independence. "Annuit Coeptis" is Latin for "God has favored our undertaking." "Novus Ordo Seclorum" is Latin for "a new order of the ages." Both phrases are from the works of the Roman poet Virgil.

U.S. Currency and Coin

Source: Bureau of the Fiscal Service, U.S. Dept. of the Treasury

Total Money in Circulation, 1955-2015

Date	Dollars (mil)	Per capita[1]	Date	Dollars (mil)	Per capita[1]	Date	Dollars (mil)	Per capita[1]
June 30, 1955	$30,229	$183	Sept. 30, 1985	$187,337	$782	June 30, 2010	$945,138	$3,051
June 30, 1960	32,064	177	Sept. 30, 1990	278,903	1,105	June 30, 2011	1,028,910	3,302
June 30, 1965	39,719	204	Sept. 30, 1995	409,272	1,553	June 30, 2012	1,111,901	3,540
June 30, 1970	54,351	265	Sept. 30, 2000	568,614	2,061	June 30, 2013	1,193,771	3,774
June 30, 1975	81,196	380	Sept. 30, 2005	766,487	2,578	June 30, 2014	1,282,431	4,027
Sept. 30, 1980	129,916	581	June 30, 2009	909,697	2,963	June 30, 2015	1,368,622	4,260

(1) Based on U.S. Census Bureau population estimates.

Money in Circulation by Denomination, 2015

(in millions of dollars)

Denomination	Amount in circulation	Denomination	Amount in circulation	Denomination	Amount in circulation
$1	$11,120,248,580	$50	$76,569,395,950	$10,000	$3,460,000
$2	2,190,068,864	$100	1,039,382,402,300	Fractional notes	600
$5	13,150,147,950	$500	142,013,000	**Total currency**	**1,324,065,239,764**
$10	18,437,091,000	$1,000	165,357,000	**Total coins**	**44,556,970,978**
$20	162,903,289,520	$5,000	1,765,000	**Total currency and coins**	**1,368,622,210,742**

Note: Totals include fractional notes and the value of partial denominations not presented for redemption.

Budget Receipts and Outlays, 1789-1940

Source: U.S. Dept. of the Treasury

(in thousands of dollars; annual statements for years ending June 30, unless otherwise noted)

Yearly average	Receipts	Outlays	Yearly average	Receipts	Outlays	Yearly average	Receipts	Outlays
1789-1800[1]	$5,717	$5,776	1866-1870	$447,301	$377,642	1906-1910	$628,507	$639,178
1801-1810[2]	13,056	9,086	1871-1875	336,830	287,460	1911-1915	710,227	720,252
1811-1820[2]	21,032	23,943	1876-1880	288,124	255,598	1916-1920	3,483,652	8,065,333
1821-1830[2]	21,928	16,162	1881-1885	366,961	257,691	1921-1925	4,306,673	3,578,989
1831-1840[2]	30,461	24,495	1886-1890	375,448	279,134	1926-1930	4,069,138	3,182,807
1841-1850[2]	28,545	34,097	1891-1895	352,891	363,599	1931-1935	2,770,973	5,214,874
1851-1860	60,237	60,163	1896-1900	434,877	457,451	1936-1940	4,960,614	10,192,367
1861-1865	160,907	683,785	1901-1905	559,481	535,559			

(1) Average for period Mar. 4, 1789, to Dec. 31, 1800. (2) Years 1801-42 end Dec. 31; average for 1841-50 is for the period Jan. 1, 1841, to June 30, 1850.

U.S. Budget Receipts and Outlays, Fiscal Years 2000-14

Source: Congressional Budget Office; *Budget of the U.S. Government*, Office of Mgmt. and Budget, Exec. Office of the President

A $236 bil surplus in 2000 turned into a $1.4 tril deficit by 2009. Since then, however, the deficit has been trimmed by nearly $1 tril. A nearly 50% increase in tax receipts over the past decade has helped the government keep pace with increased spending on national defense, Medicare, and other health and income security programs.

(in millions of current dollars; numbers may not add up to totals because of independent rounding or omitted subcategories, including some subcategories with negative values)

Function and subfunction	2000	2005	2010	2012	2013	2014
NET RECEIPTS	**$2,025,191**	**$2,153,611**	**$2,162,706**	**$2,450,164**	**$2,775,103**	**$3,021,487**
Individual income taxes	**1,004,462**	**927,222**	**898,549**	**1,132,206**	**1,316,405**	**1,394,568**
Corporation income taxes	**207,289**	**278,282**	**191,437**	**242,289**	**273,506**	**320,731**
Social insurance and retirement receipts	**652,852**	**794,125**	**864,814**	**845,314**	**947,820**	**1,023,458**
Employment and general retirement	**620,451**	**747,664**	**815,894**	**774,927**	**887,445**	**955,029**
Old-age and survivors insurance (off-budget)	411,677	493,646	539,996	486,783	575,555	628,792
Disability insurance (off-budget)	68,907	83,830	91,691	82,718	97,719	106,773
Hospital insurance	135,529	166,068	180,068	201,143	209,270	224,107
Railroad retirement/pension fund	2,688	2,284	2,285	2,519	2,791	3,032
Railroad social security equivalent account	1,650	1,836	1,854	1,764	2,110	2,325
Unemployment insurance	**27,640**	**42,002**	**44,823**	**66,647**	**56,811**	**54,957**
Other retirement	**4,761**	**4,459**	**4,097**	**3,740**	**3,564**	**3,472**
Excise taxes	**68,865**	**73,094**	**66,909**	**79,061**	**84,007**	**93,368**
Federal funds	**22,692**	**22,547**	**18,256**	**20,359**	**28,330**	**34,240**
Alcohol	8,140	8,111	9,229	9,765	9,253	9,815
Tobacco	7,221	7,920	17,160	16,351	15,083	15,562
Telephone	5,670	6,047	993	757	733	611
Transportation fuels	819	−770	−11,030	−5,751	−2,681	−3,509
Trust funds	**46,173**	**50,547**	**48,653**	**58,702**	**55,677**	**59,128**
Transportation	34,972	37,892	34,992	40,169	36,462	39,049
Airport and airway	9,739	10,314	10,612	12,532	12,854	13,513
Black lung disability	518	610	595	629	531	579
Inland waterway	101	91	74	90	75	82
Oil spill liability	182	—	476	497	410	436
Aquatic resources	342	429	580	614	539	569
Leaking underground storage tank	184	189	169	170	162	173
Tobacco assessments	—	899	937	939	947	1,140
Vaccine injury compensation	133	123	218	254	204	243
Other receipts	**91,723**	**80,888**	**140,997**	**151,294**	**153,365**	**189,362**

Function and subfunction	2000	2005	2010	2012	2013	2014
OUTLAYS	**$1,788,950**	**$2,471,957**	**$3,457,079**	**$3,537,127**	**$3,454,647**	**$3,506,089**
National defense	**294,363**	**495,294**	**693,485**	**677,852**	**633,446**	**603,457**
Department of Defense—Military	281,029	474,071	666,703	650,851	607,795	577,897
Military personnel	75,950	127,463	155,690	152,266	150,825	148,923
Operation and maintenance	105,812	188,118	275,988	282,297	259,662	244,481
Procurement	51,696	82,294	133,603	124,712	114,912	107,485
Research, development, test, and evaluation	37,602	65,694	76,990	70,396	66,892	64,928
Military construction	5,109	5,331	21,169	14,553	12,318	9,823
Family housing	3,413	3,720	3,173	2,331	1,829	1,354
Atomic energy defense activities	12,138	18,031	19,308	19,246	17,634	17,416
Defense-related activities	1,196	3,192	7,474	7,755	8,017	8,144
International affairs	**17,213**	**34,565**	**45,195**	**47,189**	**46,231**	**46,684**
International development and humanitarian assistance	6,516	17,696	19,014	21,882	22,551	23,532
International security assistance	6,387	7,895	11,363	11,464	9,954	11,381
Conduct of foreign affairs	4,708	9,148	13,557	13,553	13,038	12,859
Foreign information and exchange activities	817	1,129	1,485	1,556	1,519	1,464
International financial programs	–1,215	–1,303	–224	–1,266	–831	–2,552
General science, space, and technology	**18,594**	**23,597**	**30,100**	**29,060**	**28,908**	**28,570**
General science and basic research	6,167	8,819	11,730	12,458	12,479	12,011
Space flight, research, and supporting activities	12,427	14,778	18,370	16,602	16,429	16,559
Energy	**–761**	**440**	**11,618**	**14,858**	**11,042**	**5,270**
Energy supply	–1,818	–929	5,801	9,017	9,038	4,056
Energy conservation	666	883	4,997	4,941	1,240	910
Emergency energy preparedness	162	162	199	375	217	–140
Energy information, policy, and regulation	229	324	621	525	547	444
Natural resources and environment	**25,003**	**27,983**	**43,667**	**41,631**	**38,145**	**36,171**
Water resources	5,078	5,724	11,662	9,178	7,675	7,912
Conservation and land management	6,762	6,226	10,783	11,101	10,723	9,707
Recreational resources	2,540	2,990	3,911	3,752	3,506	3,362
Pollution control and abatement	7,395	8,065	10,841	10,813	9,624	8,634
Agriculture	**36,458**	**26,565**	**21,356**	**17,791**	**29,678**	**24,386**
Farm income stabilization	33,446	22,048	16,604	13,173	25,213	20,012
Agricultural research and services	3,012	4,517	4,752	4,618	4,465	4,374
Commerce and housing credit	**3,207**	**7,566**	**–82,316**	**40,823**	**–83,199**	**–94,861**
Mortgage credit	–3,335	–862	35,804	–8,143	–87,854	–84,300
Postal Service	2,129	–1,223	–682	2,744	–1,839	–2453
Deposit insurance	–3,053	–1,371	–32,033	6,666	4,292	–13,823
Transportation	**46,853**	**67,894**	**91,972**	**93,019**	**91,673**	**91,915**
Ground transportation	31,697	42,317	60,784	61,308	60,005	60,827
Air transportation	10,571	18,807	21,431	21,725	21,464	20,923
Water transportation	4,394	6,439	9,351	9,650	9,774	9,759
Community and regional development	**10,623**	**26,262**	**23,894**	**25,132**	**32,336**	**20,670**
Community development	5,480	5,861	9,901	8,769	7,814	7,896
Area and regional development	2,538	2,745	3,249	4,424	1,540	3,027
Disaster relief and insurance	2,605	17,656	10,744	11,939	22,982	9,747
Education, training, employment, and social services	**53,764**	**97,555**	**128,598**	**90,823**	**72,808**	**90,615**
Elementary, secondary, and vocational education	20,578	38,271	73,261	47,492	42,407	40,813
Higher education	10,115	31,442	20,908	12,113	–525	20,104
Research and general education aids	2,543	3,124	3,631	3,704	3,705	3,552
Training and employment	6,777	6,852	9,854	7,779	7,271	7,013
Social services	12,557	16,251	19,179	17,867	18,062	17,299
Health	**154,504**	**250,548**	**369,068**	**346,742**	**358,315**	**409,449**
Health care services	136,201	219,559	330,710	308,160	321,849	374,581
Health research and training	15,979	28,050	34,214	34,502	32,881	30,911
Consumer and occupational health and safety	2,324	2,939	4,144	4,080	3,585	3,957
Medicare	**197,113**	**298,638**	**451,636**	**471,793**	**497,826**	**511,688**
Income security	**253,724**	**345,847**	**622,210**	**541,344**	**536,511**	**513,644**
General retirement and disability insurance (excl. social security)	5,189	6,976	6,564	7,760	6,969	8,776
Federal employee retirement and disability	77,152	93,351	119,867	122,388	131,739	134,613
Unemployment compensation	23,012	35,435	160,145	93,771	70,729	45,717
Housing assistance	28,949	37,899	58,651	47,948	46,687	47,615
Food and nutrition assistance	32,483	50,833	95,110	106,871	109,706	102,936
Social security	**409,423**	**523,305**	**706,737**	**773,290**	**813,551**	**850,533**
Veterans benefits and services	**46,989**	**70,120**	**108,384**	**124,595**	**138,938**	**149,616**
Income security for veterans	24,907	35,767	49,163	55,899	65,890	70,906
Veterans education, training, and rehabilitation	1,285	2,790	8,089	10,402	12,893	13,506
Hospital and medical care for veterans	19,516	28,754	45,714	50,588	52,544	56,226
Veterans housing	364	860	540	1,413	1,328	2,143
Administration of justice	**28,499**	**40,019**	**54,383**	**56,277**	**52,601**	**50,457**
Federal law enforcement activities	12,121	19,912	28,713	28,977	27,295	26,106
Federal litigative and judicial activities	7,762	9,641	13,073	14,670	14,633	14,224
Federal correctional activities	3,707	5,862	7,748	8,294	6,892	6,751
Criminal justice assistance	4,909	4,604	4,849	4,336	3,781	3,376
General government	**13,013**	**16,997**	**23,014**	**28,036**	**27,737**	**26,913**
Legislative functions	2,227	3,460	4,100	3,908	3,729	3,568
Executive direction and management	456	569	528	628	478	484
Central fiscal operations	8,285	9,515	11,906	11,985	12,051	11,695
General property and records management	–32	472	1,194	2,247	–10	–386
Central personnel management	184	101	338	67	372	268
General purpose fiscal assistance	2,084	3,333	5,082	7,787	7,852	7,643
Deductions for offsetting receipts	–2,383	–2,841	–1,721	–2,011	–2,692	3,512
Net interest	**222,949**	**183,986**	**196,194**	**220,408**	**220,885**	**228,956**
Undistributed offsetting receipts	**–42,581**	**–65,224**	**–82,116**	**–103,536**	**–92,785**	**–88,044**
Employer share, employee retirement (on-budget)	–30,214	–47,977	–62,100	–68,347	–65,155	–63,612
TOTAL SURPLUS/DEFICIT	**236,241**	**–318,346**	**–1,294,373**	**–1,086,963**	**–679,544**	**–484,602**

Federal Receipts, Outlays, and Surpluses or Deficits, 1901-2015

Source: *Budget of the U.S. Government, Fiscal Year 2015*, Office of Management and Budget, Exec. Office of the President
(in millions of current dollars)

Fiscal year	Receipts	Outlays	Surplus or deficit (–)	Fiscal year	Receipts	Outlays	Surplus or deficit (–)	Fiscal year	Receipts	Outlays	Surplus or deficit (–)
1901	$588	$525	**$63**	1940	$6,548	$9,468	–2,920	1978	$399,561	$458,746	–59,185
1902	562	485	**77**	1941	8,712	13,653	–4,941	1979	463,302	504,028	–40,726
1903	562	517	**45**	1942	14,634	35,137	–20,503	1980	517,112	590,941	–73,830
1904	541	584	–43	1943	24,001	78,555	–54,554	1981	599,272	678,241	–78,968
1905	544	567	–23	1944	43,747	91,304	–47,557	1982	617,766	745,743	–127,977
1906	595	570	**25**	1945	45,159	92,712	–47,553	1983	600,562	808,364	–207,802
1907	666	579	**87**	1946	39,296	55,232	–15,936	1984	666,438	851,805	–185,367
1908	602	659	–57	1947	38,514	34,496	**4,018**	1985	734,037	946,344	–212,308
1909	604	694	–89	1948	41,560	29,764	**11,796**	1986	769,155	990,382	–221,227
1910	676	694	–18	1949	39,415	38,835	**580**	1987	854,288	1,004,017	–149,730
1911	702	691	**11**	1950	39,443	42,562	–3,119	1988	909,238	1,064,416	–155,178
1912	693	690	**3**	1951	51,616	45,514	**6,102**	1989	991,105	1,143,744	–152,639
1913	714	715	—	1952	66,167	67,686	–1,519	1990	1,031,958	1,252,994	–221,036
1914	725	726	—	1953	69,608	76,101	–6,493	1991	1,054,988	1,324,226	–269,238
1915	683	746	–63	1954	69,701	70,855	–1,154	1992	1,091,208	1,381,529	–290,321
1916	761	713	**48**	1955	65,451	68,444	–2,993	1993	1,154,335	1,409,386	–255,051
1917	1,101	1,954	–853	1956	74,587	70,640	**3,947**	1994	1,258,566	1,461,753	–203,186
1918	3,645	12,677	–9,032	1957	79,990	76,578	**3,412**	1995	1,351,790	1,515,742	–163,952
1919	5,130	18,493	–13,363	1958	79,636	82,405	–2,769	1996	1,453,053	1,560,484	–107,431
1920	6,649	6,358	**291**	1959	79,249	92,098	–12,849	1997	1,579,232	1,601,116	–21,884
1921	5,571	5,062	**509**	1960	92,492	92,191	**301**	1998	1,721,728	1,652,458	**69,270**
1922	4,026	3,289	**736**	1961	94,388	97,723	–3,335	1999	1,827,452	1,701,842	**125,610**
1923	3,853	3,140	**713**	1962	99,676	106,821	–7,146	2000	2,025,191	1,788,950	**236,241**
1924	3,871	2,908	**963**	1963	106,560	111,316	–4,756	2001	1,991,082	1,862,846	**128,236**
1925	3,641	2,924	**717**	1964	112,613	118,528	–5,915	2002	1,853,136	2,010,894	–157,758
1926	3,795	2,930	**865**	1965	116,817	118,228	–1,411	2003	1,782,314	2,159,899	–377,585
1927	4,013	2,857	**1,155**	1966	130,835	134,532	–3,698	2004	1,880,114	2,292,841	–412,727
1928	3,900	2,961	**939**	1967	148,822	157,464	–8,643	2005	2,153,611	2,471,957	–318,346
1929	3,862	3,127	**734**	1968	152,973	178,134	–25,161	2006	2,406,869	2,655,050	–248,181
1930	4,058	3,320	**738**	1969	186,882	183,640	**3,242**	2007	2,567,985	2,728,686	–160,701
1931	3,116	3,577	–462	1970	192,807	195,649	–2,842	2008	2,523,991	2,982,544	–458,553
1932	1,924	4,659	–2,735	1971	187,139	210,172	–23,033	2009	2,104,989	3,517,677	–1,412,688
1933	1,997	4,598	–2,602	1972	207,309	230,681	–23,373	2010	2,162,706	3,457,079	–1,294,373
1934	2,955	6,541	–3,586	1973	230,799	245,707	–14,908	2011	2,303,466	3,603,059	–1,299,593
1935	3,609	6,412	–2,803	1974	263,224	269,359	–6,135	2012	2,449,988	3,536,951	–1,086,963
1936	3,923	8,228	–4,304	1975	279,090	332,332	–53,242	2013	2,775,103	3,454,647	–679,544
1937	5,387	7,580	–2,193	1976	298,060	371,792	–73,732	2014	3,021,487	3,506,089	–484,602
1938	6,751	6,840	–89	1977	355,559	409,218	–53,659	2015[1]	3,176,072	3,758,577	–582,505
1939	6,295	9,141	–2,846								

— = $500,000 or less. Figures in **bold** denote annual surplus. **Note:** Budget figures prior to 1933 are based on administrative budget concepts rather than unified budget concepts. Through 1976, fiscal year ends June 30; after 1976, fiscal year ends Sept. 30. Surplus or deficit column may not equal difference between figures because of rounding. (1) Estimate as of Feb. 1, 2015.

Budget Deficits as Percent of GDP in Selected Countries, 1995-2015

Source: *OECD Economic Outlook*, Organization for Economic Cooperation and Development (OECD)

Country	1995	2000	2005	2009	2010	2011	2012	2013	2014	2015
Australia	–3.9%	0.4%	1.2%	–4.7%	–5.1%	–3.6%	–2.9%	–1.4%	–2.5%	–1.4%
Austria	–5.9	–1.9	–1.8	–4.1	–4.5	–2.4	–2.6	–1.5	–2.8	–1.3
Canada	–5.3	2.9	1.5	–4.5	–4.9	–3.7	–3.4	–3.0	–2.1	–1.2
Czech Republic	–13.4	–3.7	–3.6	–5.8	–4.7	–3.2	–4.2	–1.5	–2.1	–2.6
Denmark	–2.9	2.2	5.0	–2.8	–2.7	–2.0	–3.9	–0.9	–1.5	–3.0
Estonia	1.1	–0.2	1.6	–2.0	0.2	1.1	–0.2	–0.2	–0.2	–0.1
Finland	–6.2	6.8	2.5	–2.7	–2.8	–1.0	–2.2	–2.5	–2.2	–0.9
France	–5.5	–1.5	–3.0	–7.5	–7.0	–5.2	–4.9	–4.3	–3.8	–3.1
Germany	–9.7	1.3	–3.3	–3.1	–4.2	–0.8	0.1	0.0	–0.2	0.2
Greece	–9.1	–3.7	–5.3	–15.6	–11.0	–9.6	–8.9	–12.7	–2.5	–1.4
Hungary	–8.7	–3.0	–7.9	–4.5	–4.4	4.2	–2.2	–2.3	–2.9	–2.9
Iceland	–3.0	1.7	4.9	–9.9	–10.1	–5.6	–3.8	–2.1	–2.0	–2.1
Ireland	–2.1	4.8	1.6	–13.7	–30.6	–13.0	–8.1	–7.0	–4.7	–3.1
Israel	NA	–4.0	–4.9	–6.2	–4.6	–3.9	–5.1	–4.3	–3.9	–3.6
Italy	–7.4	–0.9	–4.4	–5.4	–4.4	–3.6	–2.9	–2.8	–2.7	–2.1
Japan	–4.7	–7.6	–6.7	–8.8	–8.3	–8.8	–8.7	–9.3	–8.4	–6.7
Korea, South	3.5	5.4	3.4	–1.0	1.0	1.0	1.0	–0.4	0.1	0.5
Luxembourg	2.4	6.0	0.0	–0.7	–0.8	0.2	0.0	0.1	0.3	–0.9
Netherlands	–9.2	2.0	–0.3	–5.6	–5.0	–4.3	–4.0	–2.4	–2.7	–2.0
New Zealand	2.5	1.8	4.7	–2.7	–7.4	–4.4	–2.1	–0.3	0.1	0.7
Norway	3.2	15.4	15.1	10.5	11.1	13.6	13.9	11.1	10.7	10.2
Poland	–4.4	–3.0	–4.1	–7.5	–7.8	–5.1	–3.9	–4.3	5.6	–2.9
Portugal	–5.0	–2.9	–5.9	–10.2	–9.9	–4.3	–6.5	–5.0	–4.0	–2.4
Slovakia	–3.4	–12.3	–2.8	–8.0	–7.5	–4.8	–4.5	–2.8	–2.7	–2.6
Slovenia	–8.4	–3.7	–1.5	–6.3	–5.9	–6.4	–4.0	–14.7	–4.1	–2.6
Spain	–6.5	–1.0	1.0	–11.1	–9.6	–9.6	–10.6	–7.1	–5.5	–4.5
Sweden	–7.3	3.6	1.9	–1.0	0.0	0.0	–0.7	–1.3	–1.5	–0.8
Switzerland	–2.0	0.1	–0.7	0.8	0.3	0.7	–0.2	0.1	0.1	0.3
United Kingdom	–5.8	3.7	–3.3	–11.2	–10.0	–7.9	–6.3	–5.9	–5.3	–4.1
United States	–3.3	1.5	–3.3	–12.8	–12.2	–10.7	–9.3	–6.4	–5.8	–4.6
Total OECD	**–4.8**	**0.1**	**–2.8**	**–8.4**	**–8.0**	**–6.5**	**–5.9**	**–4.6**	**–3.9**	**–3.2**
Brazil	NA	NA	NA	–3.3	–2.5	–2.6	–2.5	–3.3	–3.4	–3.1
China	NA	NA	NA	–1.1	–0.7	0.1	–0.3	–0.7	–1.2	–1.2
India	NA	NA	NA	–9.6	–7.4	–7.4	–7.5	–7.1	–6.5	–5.9
Indonesia	NA	NA	NA	–1.6	–0.7	–1.1	–1.9	–2.2	–2.2	–2.0
Russia	NA	NA	NA	–4.0	–1.2	4.2	0.5	–0.5	0.0	0.2
South Africa	NA	NA	NA	–5.2	–6.0	–5.6	6.2	–6.1	–5.8	–5.5

NA = Not available.

Public Debt of the U.S., 1946-2020

Source: *Budget of the U.S. Government*, Office of Management and Budget, Exec. Office of the President

Year	Debt held by public: Current dollars (bil)	Debt held by public: FY2014 dollars (bil)	Debt held by public: As % of GDP	Interest on public debt as % of—: Total federal outlays	Interest on public debt as % of—: GDP
1946	241.9	2,383.8	106.1%	7.4%	1.8%
1950	219.0	1,746.4	78.5	11.4	1.7
1955	226.6	1,588.0	55.7	7.6	1.3
1960	236.8	1,470.5	44.3	8.5	1.5
1965	260.8	1,516.5	36.7	8.1	1.3
1970	283.2	1,372.2	27.0	7.9	1.5
1975	394.7	1,409.5	24.5	7.5	1.6
1980	711.9	1,769.3	25.5	10.6	2.2
1985	1,507.3	2,859.0	35.3	16.2	3.6
1990	2,411.6	3,933.0	40.8	16.2	3.4
1995	3,604.4	5,187.5	47.5	15.8	3.2
2000	3,409.8	4,523.8	33.6	13.0	2.3
2005	4,592.2	5,435.5	35.6%	7.7%	1.5%
2010	9,018.9	9,663.0	60.9	6.6	1.5
2011	10,128.2	10,635.5	65.9	7.4	1.7
2012	11,281.1	11,634.8	70.4	6.6	1.4
2013	11,982.7	12,165.4	72.3	7.5	1.6
2014	12,779.9	12,779.9	74.1	7.7	1.6
2015[1]	13,506.3	13,326.4	75.1	7.5	1.6
2016[1]	14,108.5	13,702.9	75.0	8.5	1.8
2017[1]	14,704.9	14,030.7	74.6	9.7	2.1
2018[1]	15,315.0	14,335.7	74.3	10.7	2.3
2019[1]	15,959.2	14,645.1	74.1	11.6	2.5
2020[1]	16,634.7	14,965.4	74.0	12.4	2.7

Note: As of end of fiscal year. Through 1976, the fiscal year ended June 30. For 1977 on, the fiscal year ended Sept. 30. (1) Estimate.

State Finances: Revenues, Taxes, Expenditures, and Debt, 2013

Source: U.S. Census Bureau, U.S. Dept. of Commerce

(in thousands of dollars)

State	Revenues: Total revenue	Revenues: General revenues	Revenues: Intergovt. revenue	Revenues: Taxes	Total expenditures	Debt at end of fiscal year
Alabama	$29,092,950	$22,759,645	$8,338,033	$9,267,567	$28,203,758	$9,055,227
Alaska	14,018,474	12,280,315	2,754,412	5,132,811	12,214,598	6,218,363
Arizona	36,947,686	29,176,274	10,580,523	13,471,690	31,968,081	13,723,166
Arkansas	21,541,707	17,310,068	5,724,598	8,586,407	19,522,252	3,947,169
California	315,358,675	219,692,720	58,096,373	133,184,246	283,572,491	152,186,012
Colorado	30,986,766	23,129,280	6,508,932	11,245,662	28,743,913	16,309,217
Connecticut	31,851,296	25,446,414	5,962,699	16,189,525	29,302,715	32,356,807
Delaware	8,908,038	7,793,920	1,996,011	3,346,316	8,648,250	5,754,587
Florida	95,693,798	74,725,923	23,880,229	35,377,566	80,436,036	37,892,165
Georgia	53,486,765	38,391,794	14,619,221	17,794,152	45,483,779	13,292,965
Hawaii	12,944,952	10,825,114	2,331,449	6,092,893	11,477,711	8,318,403
Idaho	9,391,142	7,340,263	2,541,438	3,579,093	8,530,858	3,647,841
Illinois	84,493,376	65,561,519	17,312,790	38,729,322	75,324,720	63,660,340
Indiana	38,141,709	33,499,152	11,267,810	16,930,731	36,793,639	22,564,017
Iowa	23,102,534	18,533,679	5,991,401	8,374,376	20,517,934	6,647,699
Kansas	18,013,265	15,245,978	3,845,073	7,620,282	16,436,706	6,825,293
Kentucky	28,637,166	22,926,606	8,083,482	10,815,954	28,887,783	14,983,712
Louisiana	31,238,181	25,255,359	10,660,261	9,223,829	32,037,578	18,589,438
Maine	9,571,311	7,990,979	2,830,353	3,884,450	8,950,407	5,374,528
Maryland	41,802,233	34,779,321	10,325,181	18,118,191	39,556,993	26,066,617
Massachusetts	55,437,787	46,180,318	13,706,498	23,901,047	56,772,774	76,160,503
Michigan	66,400,989	54,343,294	18,007,780	24,936,087	62,945,494	30,377,220
Minnesota	45,593,764	34,651,478	9,315,259	21,031,809	39,943,492	13,572,769
Mississippi	21,865,219	17,510,532	7,649,292	7,402,725	20,101,926	7,112,560
Missouri	37,529,136	26,662,036	10,497,449	11,139,394	30,451,378	19,307,770
Montana	7,982,053	5,767,554	2,161,997	2,644,610	7,075,417	3,558,343
Nebraska	11,484,492	9,819,327	3,212,304	4,718,944	9,880,837	1,846,583
Nevada	17,040,569	11,402,396	3,080,240	7,026,626	13,273,807	3,609,752
New Hampshire	8,163,713	6,132,439	1,883,424	2,349,693	7,420,420	8,763,339
New Jersey	67,918,016	53,863,834	14,471,986	29,076,881	67,362,610	64,264,050
New Mexico	17,808,300	14,295,361	5,416,068	5,201,576	17,200,474	7,232,938
New York	212,858,793	165,200,561	71,682,137	73,667,171	184,040,200	136,014,460
North Carolina	60,004,493	47,574,530	15,769,950	23,768,578	53,625,862	19,054,585
North Dakota	8,830,465	8,059,929	1,572,480	5,298,770	6,410,161	1,834,319
Ohio	90,343,990	60,945,518	21,113,847	27,516,947	76,291,671	33,132,906
Oklahoma	26,344,587	20,799,702	7,159,511	8,892,503	22,920,374	9,514,281
Oregon	32,914,634	22,833,016	8,003,252	9,160,887	26,850,084	13,598,468
Pennsylvania	87,910,876	69,755,731	21,412,638	33,965,626	87,532,654	47,020,552
Rhode Island	8,681,540	6,933,496	2,369,822	2,940,433	8,189,015	9,568,297
South Carolina	29,638,637	22,160,859	7,202,824	8,721,305	28,245,704	14,723,546
South Dakota	5,759,268	4,035,680	1,605,537	1,533,663	4,476,725	3,425,424
Tennessee	32,356,348	27,401,810	10,900,626	12,366,891	30,586,320	6,191,955
Texas	136,486,968	112,935,910	37,580,061	51,714,295	124,929,538	39,624,672
Utah	18,442,207	14,810,655	4,304,061	6,325,126	16,822,502	7,049,552
Vermont	6,295,755	5,635,209	1,872,013	2,878,930	6,018,247	3,330,238
Virginia	50,851,769	41,140,409	9,959,041	19,186,853	47,614,065	28,022,656
Washington	47,862,480	35,669,826	10,030,961	18,667,044	45,725,863	30,474,333
West Virginia	14,581,453	12,390,766	4,325,052	5,378,122	13,234,155	7,355,630
Wisconsin	45,891,806	32,280,837	9,228,907	16,513,692	37,524,804	23,187,772
Wyoming	7,574,100	5,929,052	2,318,877	2,186,054	5,834,892	1,020,546
United States	**2,216,076,231**	**1,709,786,388**	**551,464,163**	**847,077,345**	**2,005,911,667**	**1,137,363,585**

Note: Figures may not add up to totals because of rounding.

State and Local Government Receipts and Current Expenditures, 1960-2014

Source: Bureau of Economic Analysis, U.S. Dept. of Commerce
(in billions of current dollars; as of Aug. 2015)

	1960	1970	1980	1990	2000	2010	2012	2013	2014
Receipts	**$44.2**	**$118.9**	**$335.3**	**$729.6**	**$1,303.1**	**$1,998.5**	**$2,057.2**	**$2,136.5**	**$2,225.0**
Current tax receipts	37.0	91.3	230.0	519.1	893.2	1,305.6	1,416.1	1,479.8	1,517.5
Personal current taxes	4.2	14.2	48.9	122.6	236.7	297.6	346.7	372.2	383.3
Income taxes	2.5	10.9	42.6	109.6	217.4	267.1	314.3	339.2	349.9
Other	1.7	3.3	6.3	13.0	19.4	30.5	32.4	32.9	33.4
Taxes on production and imports	31.5	73.3	166.7	374.1	621.3	960.4	1,016.9	1,052.2	1,075.9
Sales taxes	12.2	31.6	82.9	184.3	316.8	446.0	482.8	507.2	524.9
Property taxes	16.2	36.7	68.8	161.5	254.7	435.0	442.2	449.5	455.6
Other	3.1	5.0	15.0	28.3	49.8	79.4	92.0	95.4	95.4
Taxes on corporate income	1.2	3.7	14.5	22.5	35.2	47.7	52.5	55.5	58.3
Contributions for government social insurance	0.5	1.1	3.6	10.0	10.8	18.1	18.0	18.6	18.9
Income receipts on assets	1.3	5.2	26.3	68.5	93.9	82.6	75.4	74.3	75.7
Interest receipts	1.0	4.3	23.1	64.1	86.3	69.1	59.8	58.0	58.7
Dividends	—	—	0.1	0.2	1.4	2.3	3.3	3.7	3.8
Rents and royalties	0.3	0.8	3.1	4.2	6.3	11.2	12.3	12.6	13.2
Current transfer receipts	4.3	20.1	76.9	126.4	299.7	612.0	558.0	571.2	621.5
Federal grants-in-aid	3.8	18.3	69.7	104.4	233.1	505.3	444.0	450.1	494.8
From business (net)	0.2	0.6	2.5	7.1	28.6	43.4	44.0	49.6	48.7
From persons	0.3	1.2	4.7	14.9	38.0	63.2	70.1	71.5	72.8
Current surplus of government enterprises	1.2	1.3	–1.4	5.6	5.4	–19.8	–10.4	–7.5	–8.6
Expenditures	**41.6**	**115.9**	**329.9**	**736.0**	**1,293.2**	**2,235.8**	**2,277.9**	**2,323.6**	**2,392.7**
Consumption expenditures	34.1	92.1	252.8	546.2	969.1	1,518.3	1,536.3	1,560.7	1,601.0
Government social benefit payments to persons	4.6	16.1	51.2	127.7	271.4	523.8	540.0	562.3	609.9
Interest payments	3.0	7.7	25.6	61.8	52.1	192.1	201.2	200.1	181.4
Subsidies	0.0	0.0	0.4	0.4	0.5	1.6	0.5	0.5	0.5
Net state and local government saving	**2.6**	**3.0**	**5.4**	**–6.5**	**9.9**	**–237.3**	**–220.8**	**–187.1**	**–167.7**
Social insurance funds	0.0	0.2	1.3	2.0	2.0	3.2	4.2	4.1	4.2
Other	2.5	2.8	4.1	–8.4	7.9	–240.5	–225.0	–191.2	–171.9
Addenda:									
Total receipts	**47.2**	**125.1**	**353.9**	**754.6**	**1,347.3**	**2,075.2**	**2,131.3**	**2,207.9**	**2,296.0**
Current receipts	44.2	118.9	335.3	729.6	1,303.1	1,998.5	2,057.2	2,136.5	2,225.0
Capital transfer receipts	3.0	6.2	18.6	25.0	44.2	76.7	74.2	71.4	71.0
Total expenditures	**52.0**	**135.4**	**364.7**	**807.2**	**1,418.5**	**2,385.5**	**2,384.9**	**2,417.6**	**2,487.8**
Current expenditures	41.6	115.9	329.9	736	1,293.2	2,235.8	2,277.9	2,323.6	2,392.7
Gross government investment	14.1	29.3	65.7	132.2	232.9	351.9	329.7	322.9	331.3
Capital transfer payments	—	—	—	0.0	0.0	0.0	0.0	0.0	0.0
Net purchases of nonproduced assets	0.9	1.1	2.2	5.7	8.6	10.6	9.1	9.6	9.9
Less: Consumption of fixed capital	4.5	10.9	33.1	66.7	116.2	212.7	231.9	238.5	246.1
Net lending or net borrowing (–)	**–4.8**	**–10.3**	**–10.8**	**–52.7**	**–71.2**	**–310.3**	**–253.6**	**–209.7**	**–191.8**

Federal Deposit Insurance Corporation (FDIC)

The Federal Deposit Insurance Corporation (FDIC) was created by Congress during the height of the Depression to maintain stability and public confidence in the nation's banking system. It covered depositors for up to $2,500 in case of bank failure in 1934; the limit today is 100 times that much, or $250,000. In its unique role as deposit insurer of banks and savings associations, and in cooperation with other federal and state regulatory agencies, the FDIC seeks to promote the safety and soundness of insured depository institutions in the U.S. financial system.

The quarterly premiums on deposit insurance are paid by the banks rather than by consumers. The amount of the premium is based on the institution's balance of insured deposits for the preceding quarter and the institution's risk to the insurance fund. In 2009, Congress permanently increased the limit that the FDIC may borrow from the U.S. Treasury from $30 bil to $100 bil.

U.S. Banks, 1935-2015

Source: *Summary of Deposits*, Federal Deposit Insurance Corp.
Comprises all FDIC-insured commercial and savings banks, including savings and loan institutions (S&Ls).

	Number of banks					Deposits (in mil dollars)				
		Commercial banks[1]					Commercial banks[1]			
Year	All banks[2]	National charter	State charter	Non-members	Savings banks, total	All deposits[2]	National charter	State charter	Non-members	Savings banks, total
1935[3]	**15,295**	5,386	1,001	7,735	1,173	**$45,102**	$24,802	$13,653	$5,669	$978
1940	**15,772**	5,144	1,342	6,956	2,330	**67,494**	35,787	20,642	7,040	4,025
1950	**16,500**	4,958	1,912	6,576	3,054	**171,963**	84,941	41,602	19,726	25,694
1960	**17,549**	4,530	1,641	6,955	4,423	**310,262**	120,242	65,487	34,369	90,164
1970	**18,205**	4,621	1,147	7,743	4,694	**686,901**	285,436	101,512	95,566	204,367
1980	**18,763**	4,425	997	9,013	4,328	**1,832,716**	656,752	191,183	344,311	640,470
1990	**15,158**	3,979	1,009	7,355	2,815	**3,637,292**	1,558,915	397,797	693,438	987,142
1995	**12,289**	2,941	995	6,230	2,082	**3,214,678**	1,337,105	439,430	696,108	735,856
2000	**10,119**	2,302	996	5,180	1,622	**4,003,744**	1,792,773	707,562	793,275	706,461
2005	**8,855**	1,864	906	4,779	1,293	**5,933,742**	2,946,589	765,673	1,191,977	1,023,620
2007	**8,605**	1,676	888	4,786	1,244	**6,702,053**	3,273,531	831,116	1,425,412	1,165,119
2008	**8,441**	1,585	874	4,744	1,227	**7,025,791**	3,596,712	857,003	1,432,614	1,132,356
2009	**8,185**	1,505	858	4,632	1,180	**7,559,590**	4,141,792	962,232	1,512,677	936,101
2010	**7,821**	1,427	836	4,413	1,135	**7,676,878**	4,305,697	1,002,425	1,464,022	891,159
2011	**7,523**	1,349	824	4,240	1,100	**8,249,233**	4,708,210	1,120,747	1,491,112	909,912
2012	**7,255**	1,285	836	4,101	1,023	**8,947,239**	5,250,842	1,220,930	1,576,616	874,850
2013	**6,950**	1,194	849	3,937	960	**9,433,525**	5,667,790	1,281,662	1,648,153	806,933
2014	**6,669**	1,110	860	3,789	900	**10,112,716**	6,089,894	1,445,246	1,729,789	807,157
2015	**6,358**	1,027	816	3,629	876	**10,657,721**	6,393,433	1,573,880	1,823,558	823,906

Note: Figures are for the end of the year shown through 1990 and for June 30 thereafter. (1) Nonmembers are banks that are not members of the Federal Reserve System; national charter and state charter institutions are Federal Reserve members. (2) Includes U.S. branches of foreign banks not listed separately. (3) Figures for 1935 do not include S&Ls, the data for which are not available.

U.S. Bank Failures, 1934-2015

Source: Federal Deposit Insurance Corp.

Covers all FDIC-insured commercial and savings banks, including savings and loan institutions (S&Ls) 1980 and after. As of Oct. 1, 2015.

Year	Closed or assisted	Year	Closed or assisted	Year	Closed or assisted	Year	Closed or assisted	Year	Closed or assisted
1934	9	1960-69	44	1988	470	1998	3	2008	30
1935	25	1970-79	79	1989	534	1999	8	2009	148
1936	69	1980	22	1990	382	2000	7	2010	157
1937	75	1981	40	1991	271	2001	4	2011	92
1938	74	1982	119	1992	181	2002	11	2012	51
1939	60	1983	99	1993	50	2003	3	2013	24
1940	43	1984	106	1994	15	2004	4	2014	18
1941	15	1985	180	1995	8	2005	0	2015	8
1942	20	1986	204	1996	6	2006	0	**Total, 1934-2015**	**4,083**
1950-59	28	1987	262	1997	1	2007	3		

Largest U.S. Bank Holding Companies, 2015

Source: National Information Center, Federal Financial Institutions Examination Council

(ranked by total assets, in millions of dollars; as of Mar. 31, 2015)

Rank	Institution name, location	Assets
1.	JPMorgan Chase & Co., New York, NY	$2,577,148
2.	Bank of America Corp., Charlotte, NC	2,145,027
3.	Citigroup Inc., New York, NY	1,831,801
4.	Wells Fargo & Co., San Francisco, CA	1,737,737
5.	Goldman Sachs Group, Inc., New York, NY	865,512
6.	Morgan Stanley, New York, NY	829,099
7.	General Electric Capital Corp., Norwalk, CT	481,615
8.	U.S. Bancorp, Minneapolis, MN	410,233
9.	Bank of New York Mellon Corp., New York, NY	399,088
10.	PNC Financial Services Group, Inc., Pittsburgh, PA	351,162
11.	Capital One Financial Corp., McLean, VA	306,501
12.	HSBC North America Holdings Inc., New York, NY	301,957
13.	State Street Corp., Boston, MA	279,480
14.	Teachers Insurance & Annuity Assn. of America, New York, NY	264,300
15.	TD Bank US Holding Co., Cherry Hill, NJ	252,651
16.	SunTrust Banks, Inc., Atlanta, GA	190,223
17.	BB&T Corp., Winston-Salem, NC	189,228
18.	Charles Schwab Corp., San Francisco, CA	160,169
19.	American Express Co., New York, NY	154,674
20.	Ally Financial Inc., Detroit, MI	$153,524
21.	Fifth Third Bancorp, Cincinnati, OH	140,470
22.	State Farm Mutual Automobile Insurance Co., Bloomington, IL	139,397
23.	Citizens Financial Group, Inc., Providence, RI	136,906
24.	United Services Auto. Assn., San Antonio, TX	132,978
25.	Santander Holdings USA, Inc., Boston, MA	123,248
26.	Regions Financial Corp., Birmingham, AL	122,516
27.	BMO Financial Corp., Wilmington, DE	118,264
28.	MUFG Americas Holdings Corp., New York, NY	113,698
29.	Northern Trust Corp., Chicago, IL	106,952
30.	M&T Bank Corp., Buffalo, NY	98,379
31.	Keycorp, Cleveland, OH	94,296
32.	BancWest Corp., Honolulu, HI	89,670
33.	BBVA Compass Bancshares, Inc., Houston, TX	85,486
34.	Discover Financial Services, Riverwoods, IL	84,178
35.	Comerica Incorporated, Dallas, TX	69,420
36.	Huntington Bancshares Inc., Columbus, OH	68,003
37.	Zions Bancorp., Salt Lake City, UT	57,556
38.	Deutsche Bank Trust Corp., New York, NY	55,616

Note: Includes foreign-owned banks with a strong presence in the U.S.

Status of Top Recipients of Treasury Department "Bailout" Funds, 2015

Source: ProPublica

Since Oct. 2008, the federal government has spent more than $615 bil to bail out more than 900 institutions severely affected by the financial crisis. As of Oct. 1, 2015, the government had recouped $390 bil in loans and $283 bil in dividends, interest, and other returns, leading to an overall profit of more than $56 bil. Companies that have failed to repay the government, resulting in a loss to the taxpayers, are listed in bold italics.

(in billions of dollars, ranked by amount disbursed; as of Oct. 1, 2015)

Recipient	Disbursed	Repaid[1]	Net profit or amount outstanding[2]
Fannie Mae	$116.1	$138.2	$22.0
Freddie Mac	71.3	92.6	21.2
AIG	67.8	72.9	5.0
General Motors	***50.7***	***39.3***	***–11.4***
Bank of America	45.0	49.6	4.6
Citigroup	45.0	58.4	13.4
JPMorgan Chase	25.0	26.7	1.7
Wells Fargo	25.0	27.3	2.3
GMAC (now Ally Financial)	16.3	19.3	3.1
Chrysler	***10.7***	***9.4***	***–1.3***
Goldman Sachs	10.0	11.4	1.4
Morgan Stanley	10.0	11.3	1.3
PNC Financial Services	7.6	8.3	0.7
U.S. Bancorp	6.6	6.9	0.3
SunTrust	4.9	5.4	0.5
Capital One Financial Corp.	3.6	3.8	0.3
Regions Financial Corp.	3.5	4.1	0.6
Wellington Management Legacy Securities PPIF Master Fund, LP	3.4	4.2	0.7
Fifth Third Bancorp	3.4	4.0	0.6
Hartford Financial Services	3.4	4.2	0.8
American Express	3.4	3.8	0.4
AG GECC PPIF Master Fund, L.P.	3.4	4.3	0.9
AllianceBernstein Legacy Securities Master Fund, L.P.	3.2	3.8	0.6
BB&T	3.1	3.3	0.2
Bank of New York Mellon	$3.0	$3.2	$0.2
KeyCorp	2.5	2.9	0.4
CIT Group	***2.3***	—	***–2.3***
Comerica Incorporated	2.3	2.6	0.3
Ocwen Loan Servicing, LLC	***2.2***	***0.0***	***–2.2***
JPMorgan Chase subsidiaries	***2.1***	***0.0***	***–2.1***
State Street	2.0	2.1	0.1
Wells Fargo Bank, NA	***1.9***	***0.0***	***–1.9***
RLJ Western Asset Public/Private Master Fund, L.P.	1.9	2.3	0.5
Invesco Legacy Securities Master Fund, L.P.	1.7	2.3	0.6
Marshall & Ilsley	1.7	1.9	0.2
Bank of America subsids. (incl. Countrywide)	***1.7***	***0.0***	***–1.7***
Oaktree PPIP Fund, L.P.	1.7	2.0	0.3
Blackrock PPIF, L.P.	1.6	2.0	0.4
Northern Trust	1.6	1.7	0.1
Chrysler Financial Services	1.5	1.5	—
CalHFA Mortgage Assistance Corp.	***1.5***	***0.0***	***–1.5***
Marathon Legacy Securities Public-Private Investment Partnership, L.P.	1.4	1.8	0.4
Zions Bancorp	1.4	1.7	0.3
Huntington Bancshares	1.4	1.6	0.2
Discover Financial Services	1.2	1.5	0.2
Total	**617.0**	**673.0**	**56.2**

— = less than $0.1 bil. **Note:** Total includes other disbursements not shown. Figures may not add up to totals due to rounding. (1) Amounts repaid include principal, dividends, interest, warrants, and other proceeds. (2) Negative number represents outstanding debt.

Federal Reserve System

The Federal Reserve System is the central bank for the U.S. The system was established on Dec. 23, 1913, originally to give the country an elastic currency, provide facilities for discounting commercial paper, and improve the supervision of banking. Since then, the system's responsibilities have been broadened. Over the years, stability and growth of the economy, a high level of employment, stability in the purchasing power of the dollar, and reasonable balance in transactions with other countries have come to be recognized as primary objectives of governmental economic policy.

The Federal Reserve System consists of the Board of Governors, the 12 District Reserve Banks and their branch offices, and the Federal Open Market Committee. Several advisory councils help the board meet its varied responsibilities.

The hub of the system is the seven-member **Board of Governors** in Washington, DC. The members of the board are appointed by the president and confirmed by the Senate to 14-year terms. The president also appoints the chairman and vice chairman of the board from among the board members for four-year terms. As of Aug. 2015, the board members were Janet L. Yellen, chair; Stanley Fischer, vice chair; Daniel K. Tarullo; Jerome H. Powell; and Lael Brainard. There were two vacancies.

The 12 **District Reserve Banks** and their branch offices serve as the decentralized portion of the system, carrying out day-to-day operations such as circulating currency and coin and providing fiscal agency functions and payments mechanism services. The 12 are in Boston, New York, Philadelphia, Cleveland, Richmond, Atlanta, Chicago, St. Louis, Minneapolis, Kansas City, Dallas, and San Francisco.

The system's principal function is monetary policy, which it controls using three tools: reserve requirements, the discount rate, and open market operations.

Uniform **reserve requirements**, set by the board, are applied to the transaction accounts and nonpersonal time deposits of all depository institutions. Responsibility for setting the **discount rate** (the interest rate at which depository institutions can borrow money from the Reserve Banks) is shared by the Board of Governors and the Reserve Banks. Changes in the discount rate are recommended by the individual boards of directors of the Reserve Banks and are subject to approval by the Board of Governors.

The most important tool of monetary policy is **open market operations**, or the purchase and sale of government securities. Responsibility for influencing the cost and availability of money and credit through the purchase and sale of government securities lies with the **Federal Open Market Committee** (FOMC), which comprises the seven members of the Board of Governors, the president of the Federal Reserve Bank of New York, and four other Federal Reserve Bank presidents, who each serve one-year terms on a rotating basis. The committee bases its decisions on economic and financial developments and outlook, setting yearly growth objectives for key measures of money supply and credit. The decisions of the committee are carried out by the domestic trading desk of the Federal Reserve Bank of New York.

A Federal Advisory Council of banking industry representatives meets with the Federal Reserve Board four times a year to discuss business and financial conditions, as well as to make recommendations.

Website: www.federalreserve.gov

Federal Reserve Board Discount Rates, 1955-2015

The interest rate that the Federal Reserve charges its member banks to borrow money overnight is often referred to as the discount rate. On Jan. 9, 2003, the Fed divided the discount window into two categories: primary credit, for banks in sound financial condition, and secondary credit, for banks that do not qualify for primary credit. The secondary credit rate is ½ a percentage point higher than the primary credit rate. Banks typically raise or lower the rates they extend to their customers to track changes in the discount rate.

Effective date	Rate
1955:	
Jan. 3	1½
Apr. 15	1¾
Aug. 5	2
Sept. 9	2¼
Nov. 18	2½
1956:	
Apr. 13	2¾
Aug. 24	3
1957:	
Aug. 23	3½
Nov. 15	3
1958:	
Jan. 24	2¾
Mar. 7	2¼
Apr. 18	1¾
Sept. 12	2
Nov. 7	2½
1959:	
Mar. 6	3
May 29	3½
Sept. 11	4
1960:	
June 10	3½
Aug. 12	3
1963:	
July 17	3½
1964:	
Nov. 24	4
1965:	
Dec. 6	4½
1967:	
Apr. 7	4
Nov. 20	4½
1968:	
Mar. 22	5
Apr. 19	5½
Aug. 30	5¼
Dec. 18	5½
1969:	
Apr. 4	6

Effective date	Rate
1970:	
Nov. 13	5¾
Dec. 4	5½
1971:	
Jan. 8	5¼
Jan. 22	5
Feb. 19	4¾
July 16	5
Nov. 19	4¾
Dec. 17	4½
1973:	
Jan. 15	5
Feb. 26	5½
May 4	5¾
May 11	6
June 11	6½
July 2	7
Aug. 14	7½
1974:	
Apr. 25	8
Dec. 9	7¾
1975:	
Jan. 10	7¼
Feb. 5	6¾
Mar. 19	6¼
May 16	6
1976:	
Jan. 19	5½
Nov. 22	5¼
1977:	
Aug. 31	5¾
Oct. 26	6
1978:	
Jan. 9	6½
May 11	7
July 3	7¼
Aug. 21	7¾
Sept. 22	8
Oct. 16	8½
Nov. 1	9½

Effective date	Rate
1979:	
July 20	10
Aug. 17	10½
Sept. 19	11
Oct. 8	12
1980:	
Feb. 15	13
May 30	12
June 13	11
July 28	10
Sept. 26	11
Nov. 17	12
Dec. 5	13
1981:	
May 5	14
Nov. 2	13
Dec. 4	12
1982:	
July 20	11½
Aug. 2	11
Aug. 16	10
Aug. 27	10
Oct. 12	9½
Dec. 15	8½
1984:	
Apr. 9	9
Nov. 21	8½
Dec. 24	8
1985:	
May 20	7½
1986:	
Mar. 7	7
Apr. 21	6½
July 11	6
Aug. 21	5½
1987:	
Sept. 4	6
1988:	
Aug. 9	6½
1989:	
Feb. 24	7

Effective date	Rate
1990:	
Dec. 18	6½
1991:	
Apr. 30	5½
Sept. 13	5
Nov. 6	4½
Dec. 20	3½
1992:	
July 2	3
1994:	
May 17	3½
Aug. 16	4
Nov. 15	4¾
1995:	
Feb. 1	5
1996:	
Jan. 31	5
1998:	
Oct. 15	4¾
Nov. 17	4½
1999:	
Aug. 24	4¾
Nov. 16	5
2000:	
Feb. 2	5¼
Mar. 21	5½
May 16	6
2001:	
Jan. 3	5¾
Jan. 31	5
Mar. 20	4½
Apr. 18	4
May 15	3½
June 27	3¼
Aug. 21	3
Sept. 17	2½
Oct. 2	2
Dec. 11	1¼
2002:	
Nov. 6	¾

Effective date	Rate
2003:	
Jan. 9	2¼[1]
June 25	2
2004:	
June 30	2¼
Aug. 10	2½
Sept. 21	2¾
Nov. 10	3
Dec. 14	3¼
2005:	
Feb. 2	3½
Mar. 22	3¾
May 3	4
June 30	4¼
Aug. 9	4½
Sept. 20	4¾
Nov. 1	5
Dec. 13	5¼
2006:	
Jan. 31	5½
Mar. 28	5¾
May 10	6
June 29	6¼
2007:	
Aug. 17	5¾
Sept.18	5¼
Nov. 1	5
Dec. 12	4¾
2008:	
Jan. 22	4
Jan. 30	3½
Mar. 17	3¼
Mar. 18	2½
Apr. 30	2¼
Oct. 8	1¾
Oct. 29	1¼
Dec. 16	½
2010:	
Feb. 19	¾

Note: As of Oct. 15, 2015, rate effective Feb. 19, 2010, was unchanged. (1) Adjustment credit rate replaced with primary credit rate. See note above.

Standard & Poor's 500 Index, 1998-2015

Monthly closing levels beginning with Oct. 1998; record high daily closing was 2,130.82 on May 21, 2015.

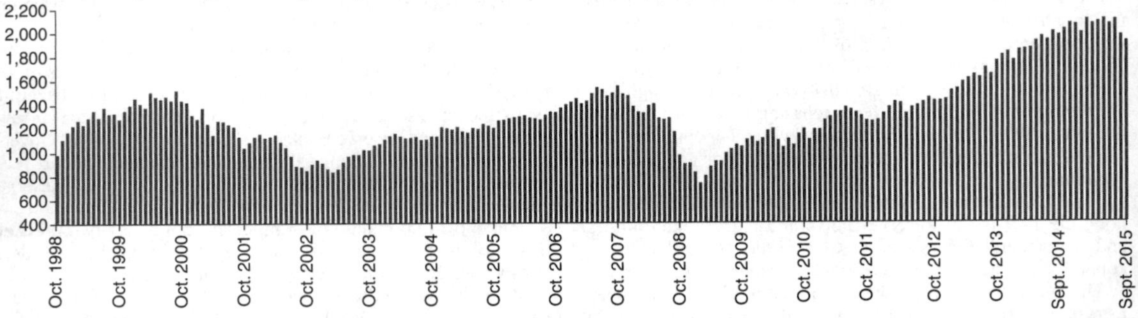

U.S. Holdings of Foreign Securities, 2006-13

Source: *U.S. Portfolio Holdings of Foreign Securities*, U.S. Dept. of the Treasury
(in billions of dollars; countries within a region ranked by 2013 figure)

	2006	2010	2011	2012	2013[1]
Europe	**$3,129**	**$3,154**	**$2,978**	**$3,562**	**$4,433**
UK	1,076	1,001	989	1,129	1,341
France	402	366	306	375	465
Switzerland	264	327	292	333	443
Germany	292	299	266	330	391
Netherlands	234	233	242	286	386
Ireland	121	132	149	181	281
Sweden	102	122	115	122	165
Spain	111	87	76	99	133
Luxembourg	60	100	93	105	125
Italy	106	66	62	110	124
Canada	**478**	**695**	**736**	**808**	**826**
Africa	**57**	**99**	**88**	**110**	**103**
South Africa	43	78	71	86	77
Australia	**173**	**323**	**334**	**351**	**337**

	2006	2010	2011	2012	2013[1]
Latin America and Caribbean	**$946**	**$1,064**	**$1,393**	**$1,598**	**$1,715**
Cayman Islands	376	366	709	797	902
Brazil	110	235	196	216	180
Bermuda	208	159	161	178	211
Mexico	108	109	108	157	153
Curaçao[2]	58	83	70	70	86
Asia	**1,166**	**1,342**	**1,232**	**1,426**	**1,640**
Japan	596	519	509	521	686
South Korea	124	148	146	175	183
Hong Kong	88	135	116	145	140
China (mainland)	75	102	77	120	135
Taiwan	74	95	72	88	98
India	49	91	59	79	86
Total holdings	**5,991**	**6,763**	**6,841**	**7,941**	**9,156**

(1) Preliminary. (2) Figures are for Netherlands Antilles prior to 2012.

Record One-Day Gains and Losses of the Dow Jones Industrial Average

Source: Dow Jones & Co., Inc.
(ranked by largest one-day losses and gains for two terms; as of Oct. 1, 2015)

Greatest % gains

Rank	Date	Close	Net chg.	% chg.
1.	3/15/1933	62.10	8.26	15.34%
2.	10/6/1931	99.34	12.86	14.87
3.	10/30/1929	258.47	28.40	12.34
4.	9/21/1932	75.16	7.67	11.36
5.	10/13/2008	9,387.61	936.42	11.08

Greatest point gains

Rank	Date	Close	Net chg.	% chg.
1.	10/13/2008	9,387.61	936.42	11.08%
2.	10/28/2008	9,065.12	889.35	10.88
3.	11/13/2008	8,835.25	552.60	6.67
4.	3/16/2000	10,630.61	499.19	4.93
5.	3/23/2009	7,775.86	497.48	6.84

Greatest % losses

Rank	Date	Close	Net chg.	% chg.
1.	10/19/1987	1,738.74	–508.00	–22.61%
2.	10/28/1929	260.64	–38.33	–12.82
3.	10/29/1929	230.07	–30.57	–11.73
4.	11/6/1929	232.13	–25.55	–9.92
5.	12/18/1899	58.27	–5.57	–8.72

Greatest point losses

Rank	Date	Close	Net chg.	% chg.
1.	9/29/2008	10,365.45	–777.68	–6.98%
2.	10/15/2008	8,577.91	–733.08	–7.87
3.	9/17/2001	8,920.70	–684.81	–7.13
4.	12/1/2008	8,149.09	–679.95	–7.70
5.	10/9/2008	8,579.19	–678.92	–7.33

Dow Jones Industrial Average, 1965-2015

Source: Dow Jones & Co., Inc.
(as of Oct. 1, 2015)

Year	Highest close		Lowest close	
1965	Dec. 31	969.26	June 28	840.59
1970	Dec. 29	842.00	May 6	631.16
1975	July 15	881.81	Jan. 2	632.04
1980	Nov. 20	1,000.17	Apr. 21	759.13
1985	Dec. 16	1,553.10	Jan. 4	1,184.96
1990	July 16	2,999.75	Oct. 11	2,365.10
1991	Dec. 31	3,168.83	Jan. 9	2,470.30
1992	June 1	3,413.21	Oct. 9	3,136.58
1993	Dec. 29	3,794.33	Jan. 20	3,241.95
1994	Jan. 31	3,978.36	Apr. 4	3,593.35
1995	Dec. 13	5,216.47	Jan. 30	3,832.08
1996	Dec. 27	6,560.91	Jan. 10	5,032.94
1997	Aug. 6	8,259.31	Apr. 11	6,391.69
1998	Nov. 23	9,374.27	Aug. 31	7,539.07
1999	Dec. 31	11,497.12	Jan. 22	9,120.67
2000	Jan. 14	11,722.98	Mar. 7	9,796.03

Year	Highest close		Lowest close	
2001	May 21	11,337.92	Sept. 21	8,235.81
2002	Mar. 19	10,635.25	Oct. 9	7,286.27
2003	Dec. 31	10,453.90	Mar. 11	7,524.06
2004	Dec. 28	10,854.54	Oct. 25	9,749.99
2005	Mar. 4	10,940.50	Apr. 20	10,012.36
2006	Dec. 27	12,510.57	Jan. 20	10,667.39
2007	Oct. 9	14,164.53	Mar. 5	12,050.41
2008	Jan. 3	13,056.72	Nov. 20	7,552.29
2009	Dec. 30	10,548.51	Mar. 9	6,547.05
2010	Dec. 29	11,585.38	July 2	9,686.48
2011	Apr. 29	12,810.54	Oct. 3	10,655.30
2012	Oct. 5	13,610.15	June 4	12,101.46
2013	Dec. 31	16,576.66	Jan. 8	13,328.85
2014	Dec. 26	18,053.71	Feb. 3	15,372.80
2015	May 19	18,312.39*	Aug. 25	15,666.44

* = Record high closing.

Milestones of the Dow Jones Industrial Average

(as of Oct. 1, 2015)

First close over—		First close over—		First close over—		First close over—		First close over—	
100	Jan. 12, 1906	3,500	May 19, 1993	6,500	Nov. 25, 1996	9,500	Jan. 6, 1999	13,000	Apr. 25, 2007
500	Mar. 12, 1956	4,000	Feb. 23, 1995	7,000	Feb. 13, 1997	10,000	Mar. 29, 1999	14,000	July 19, 2007
1,000	Nov. 14, 1972	4,500	June 16, 1995	7,500	June 10, 1997	10,500	Apr. 21, 1999	15,000	June 27, 2013
1,500	Dec. 11, 1985	5,000	Nov. 21, 1995	8,000	July 16, 1997	11,000	May 3, 1999	16,000	Nov. 21, 2013
2,000	Jan. 8, 1987	5,500	Feb. 8, 1996	8,500	Feb. 27, 1998	11,500	Jan. 7, 2000	17,000	July 3, 2014
2,500	July 17, 1987	6,000	Oct. 14, 1996	9,000	Apr. 6, 1998	12,000	Oct. 19, 2006	18,000	Dec. 23, 2014
3,000	Apr. 17, 1991								

Components of the Dow Jones Averages

(as of Oct. 1, 2015)

Dow Jones Industrial Average

Company name (ticker symbol)
American Express Co. (AXP)
Apple Inc. (AAPL)
Boeing Co. (BA)
Caterpillar Inc. (CAT)
Chevron Corp. (CVX)
Cisco Systems, Inc. (CSCO)
Coca-Cola Co. (KO)
E. I. DuPont de Nemours & Co. (DD)
Exxon Mobil Corp. (XOM)
General Electric Co. (GE)
Goldman Sachs Group, Inc. (GS)

Company name (ticker symbol)
Home Depot Inc. (HD)
Intel Corp. (INTC)
International Business Machines Corp. (IBM)
Johnson & Johnson (JNJ)
JPMorgan Chase & Co. (JPM)
McDonald's Corp. (MCD)
Merck & Co., Inc. (MRK)
Microsoft Corp. (MSFT)
Nike, Inc. (NKE)

Company name (ticker symbol)
Pfizer Inc. (PFE)
Procter & Gamble Co. (PG)
3M Co. (MMM)
Travelers Companies, Inc. (TRV)
United Technologies Corp. (UTX)
UnitedHealth Group Inc. (UNH)
Verizon Communications Inc. (VZ)
Visa Inc. (V)
Wal-Mart Stores Inc. (WMT)
Walt Disney Co. (DIS)

Dow Jones Utility Average

Company name (ticker symbol)
AES Corp. (AES)
American Electric Power Co. Inc. (AEP)
American Water Works Co. (AWK)
CenterPoint Energy (CNP)
Consolidated Edison Inc. (ED)

Company name (ticker symbol)
Dominion Resources Inc. (Virginia) (D)
Duke Energy Corp. (DUK)
Edison International (EIX)
Exelon Corp. (EXC)
FirstEnergy Corp. (FE)
NextEra Energy, Inc. (NEE)

Company name (ticker symbol)
NiSource Inc. (NI)
PG&E Corp. (PCG)
Public Service Enterprise Group Inc. (PEG)
Southern Co. (SO)

Dow Jones Transportation Average

Company name (ticker symbol)
Alaska Air Group, Inc. (ALK)
Avis Budget Group Inc. (CAR)
C.H. Robinson Worldwide Inc. (CHRW)
Con-way Inc. (CNW)
CSX Corp. (CSX)
Delta Air Lines, Inc. (DAL)
Expeditors Intl. of Washington Inc. (EXPD)

Company name (ticker symbol)
FedEx Corp. (FDX)
J.B. Hunt Transport Services Inc. (JBHT)
JetBlue Airways Corp. (JBLU)
Kansas City Southern (KSU)
Kirby Corp. (KEX)
Landstar System Inc. (LSTR)

Company name (ticker symbol)
Matson Inc. (MATX)
Norfolk Southern Corp. (NSC)
Ryder System Inc. (R)
Southwest Airlines Co. (LUV)
Union Pacific Corp. (UNP)
United Continental Holdings (UAL)
United Parcel Service Inc. (UPS)

Record One-Day Gains and Losses on the Nasdaq Stock Market

Source: Nasdaq Stock Market

(ranked by largest one-day losses and gains for two terms; as of Oct. 1, 2015)

Greatest point gains			Greatest % gains			Greatest point losses			Greatest % losses		
Rank	Date	Change	Rank	Date	% change	Rank	Date	Change	Rank	Date	% change
1.	1/3/2001	324.83	1.	1/3/2001	14.17%	1.	4/14/2000	−355.49	1.	10/19/1987	−11.35%
2.	12/5/2000	274.05	2.	10/13/2008	11.81	2.	4/3/2000	−349.15	2.	4/14/2000	−9.67
3.	4/18/2000	254.41	3.	12/5/2000	10.48	3.	4/12/2000	−286.27	3.	9/29/2008	−9.14
4.	5/30/2000	254.37	4.	10/28/2008	9.53	4.	4/10/2000	−258.25	4.	10/20/1987	−9.00
5.	10/19/2000	247.04	5.	4/5/2001	8.92	5.	1/4/2000	−229.46	5.	10/26/1987	−9.00
6.	10/13/2000	242.09	6.	4/18/2001	8.12	6.	3/14/2000	−200.61	6.	12/1/2008	−8.95
7.	6/2/2000	230.88	7.	5/30/2000	7.94	7.	5/10/2000	−200.28	7.	8/31/1998	−8.56
8.	4/25/2000	228.75	8.	10/13/2000	7.87	8.	5/23/2000	−199.66	8.	10/15/2008	−8.47
9.	4/17/2000	217.87	9.	10/19/2000	7.79	9.	9/29/2008	−199.61	9.	4/3/2000	−7.64
10.	10/13/2008	194.74	10.	5/8/2002	7.78	10.	10/25/2000	−190.22	10.	1/2/2001	−7.23

Nasdaq Stock Market Closing Prices, 1971-2015

Source: Nasdaq Stock Market; as of Oct. 1, 2015

Year	High	Low	Year	High	Low	Year	High	Low	Year	High	Low
1971	114.12	99.68	**1983**	329.11	229.88	**1994**	803.93	691.23	**2005**	2,273.37	1,904.18
1972	135.15	113.65	**1984**	288.41	223.91	**1995**	1,072.82	740.53	**2006**	2,465.98	2,020.39
1973	136.84	88.67	**1985**	325.53	245.82	**1996**	1,328.45	978.17	**2007**	2,811.61	2,340.68
1974	96.53	54.87	**1986**	411.21	322.14	**1997**	1,748.62	1,194.39	**2008**	2,609.63	1,505.90
1975	88.00	60.70	**1987**	456.27	288.49	**1998**	2,200.63	1,357.09	**2009**	2,167.70	1,265.52
1976	97.88	78.06	**1988**	397.54	329.00	**1999**	4,090.61	2,193.13	**2010**	2,671.48	2,091.79
1977	105.05	93.66	**1989**	487.60	376.87	**2000**	5,048.62	2,332.78	**2011**	2,873.54	2,335.83
1978	139.25	99.09	**1990**	470.30	322.93	**2001**	2,892.36	1,387.06	**2012**	3,183.95	2,648.36
1979	152.29	117.84	**1991**	586.35	352.85	**2002**	2,059.38	1,114.11	**2013**	4,176.59	3,091.81
1980	208.29	124.09	**1992**	676.95	545.85	**2003**	2,009.88	1,271.47	**2014**	4,806.91	3,996.96
1981	223.96	170.80	**1993**	790.56	645.02	**2004**	2,178.00	1,752.00	**2015**	5,218.86*	4,506.49
1982	241.63	158.92									

* = Record high closing, July 20, 2015.

Average Yields of Treasury, Corporate, and State and Local Bonds, 1986-2015

Source: Office of Market Finance, U.S. Dept. of the Treasury; Federal Reserve System

Period	Treasury 30-year bonds[1]	New Aa corporate bonds[2]	State and local bonds[3]	Period	Treasury 30-year bonds[1]	New Aa corporate bonds[2]	State and local bonds[3]	Period	Treasury 30-year bonds[1]	New Aa corporate bonds[2]	State and local bonds[3]
1986				**1996**				**2006**			
June	7.57%	9.39%	7.87%	June	7.06%	8.00%	6.02%	June	5.15%	5.89%	4.60%
Dec.	7.37	8.87	6.87	Dec.	6.55	7.45	5.64	Dec.	4.68	5.32	4.11
1987				**1997**				**2007**			
June	8.57	9.64	7.79	June	6.77	7.71	5.53	June	5.20	5.79	4.60
Dec.	9.12	10.22	7.96	Dec.	5.99	6.68	5.19	Dec.	4.53	5.49	4.42
1988				**1998**				**2008**			
June	9.00	10.08	7.78	June	5.70	6.43	5.12	June	4.69	5.68	4.69
Dec.	9.01	10.05	7.61	Dec.	5.06	6.13	4.98	Dec.	2.87	5.05	5.56
1989				**1999**				**2009**			
June	8.27	9.24	7.02	June	6.04	7.21	5.37	June	4.52	5.61	4.81
Dec.	7.90	9.23	6.98	Dec.	6.35	7.55	5.95	Dec.	4.49	5.26	4.21
1990				**2000**				**2010**			
June	8.46	9.69	7.24	June	5.93	7.75	5.80	June	4.13	4.88	4.36
Dec.	8.24	9.55	7.09	Dec.	5.49	7.21	5.22	Dec.	4.42	5.02	4.92
1991				**2001**				**2011**			
June	8.47	9.37	7.13	June	5.67	7.11	5.20	June	4.23	4.99	4.51
Dec.	7.70	8.55	6.69	Dec.	5.48	6.80	5.25	Dec.	2.98	3.93	3.95
1992				**2002**				**2012**			
June	7.84	8.45	6.49	June	5.65	6.57	5.09	June	2.70	3.64	3.94
Dec.	7.44	8.12	6.22	Dec.	5.01	5.93	4.85	Dec.	2.88	3.65	3.48
1993				**2003**				**2013**			
June	6.81	7.48	5.63	June	4.34	4.97	4.33	June	3.40	4.27	4.27
Dec.	6.25	7.22	5.35	Dec.	5.11	5.62	4.65	Dec.	3.89	3.79	4.73
1994				**2004**				**2014**			
June	7.40	8.16	6.11	June	5.45	6.01	5.05	June	3.42	4.19	4.35
Dec.	7.87	8.66	6.80	Dec.	4.88	5.47	4.49	Dec.	2.83	3.79	3.70
1995				**2005**				**2015**			
June	6.57	7.42	5.84	June	4.35	4.96	4.23	June	3.11	4.19	3.82
Dec.	6.06	7.02	5.45	Dec.	4.73	5.37	4.46				

(1) On Feb. 18, 2002, the U.S. Treasury discontinued the 30-year constant maturity yield and reintroduced it on Feb. 9, 2006; rates in the interim are for 20-year yields. (2) Treasury series based on 3-week moving average of reoffering yields of new corporate bonds rated Aa by Moody's Investors Service with an original maturity of at least 20 years. Treasury discontinued yield index after Jan. 31, 2003. Rates thereafter are for Moody's seasoned Aaa corporate bonds as listed by Federal Reserve. (3) Index of new reoffering yields on 20-year general obligations rated Aa by Moody's Investors Service; discontinued by Treasury Jan. 31, 2003; rates thereafter are from Bond Buyer Index of general obligation, 20 years to maturity, mixed quality state and local bonds.

Ownership of U.S. Treasury Securities, 2001-14

Source: *Treasury Bulletin, Sept. 2015*, Financial Management Service, U.S. Dept. of the Treasury

In 2001, just over 17% of U.S. treasury securities were held by foreign and international investors. By 2014, the total public debt had tripled, while the portion held by investors outside the U.S. had nearly doubled, to 33.9%.

(in billions of dollars)

	2001	2005	2007	2008	2009	2010	2011	2012	2013	2014
Total public debt	**$5,943**	**$8,170**	**$9,229**	**$10,700**	**$12,311**	**$14,025**	**$15,223**	**$16,433**	**$17,352**	**$18,141**
Federal Reserve and intra-governmental holdings	3,124	4,200	4,834	4,806	5,277	5,656	6,440	6,524	7,205	7,579
Total privately held	2,819	3,971	4,396	5,893	7,034	8,369	8,783	9,909	10,147	10,563
Depository institutions	181	129	130	105	202	319	280	348	321	514
U.S. savings bonds	190	205	196	194	191	188	185	182	179	176
Private pension funds[1]	146	184	229	260	296	337	387	444	493	530
Pension funds of state and local governments	155	154	144	130	151	159	166	179	194	204
Insurance companies	106	202	142	171	222	248	272	271	265	285
Mutual funds	262	254	344	758	669	721	895	1,030	1,116	1,160
State and local governments	328	512	648	601	586	596	561	606	592	661
Foreign and international	1,040	2,034	2,353	3,077	3,685	4,436	5,007	5,574	5,793	6,156
Other investors[2]	411	295	210	597	1,032	1,364	1,031	1,275	1,194	877

(1) Includes securities held by the Federal Employees Retirement System Thrift Savings Plan "G Fund." (2) Includes individuals, government-sponsored enterprises, brokers and dealers, bank personal trusts and estates, corporate and noncorporate businesses, and other investors.

Federal Corporate Tax Rates, 2015

Personal service corporations (used by incorporated professionals such as attorneys and doctors) pay a flat rate of 35%.

Taxable income amount	Tax rate	Taxable income amount	Tax rate
Not more than $50,000	15%	$335,001 to $10,000,000	34%
$50,001 to $75,000	25	$10,000,001 to $15,000,000	35
$75,001 to $100,000	34	$15,000,001 to $18,333,333	38
$100,001 to $335,000	39	More than $18,333,333	35

Characteristics of Mutual Fund Investors, 2014

Source: *The Investment Company Fact Book 2015*, Investment Company Institute

Median age	51	Married or living with a partner	73%
Median annual household income	$85,000	Four-year college degree or more	49%
Median household financial assets	$200,000	Own Individual Retirement Accounts (IRAs)	62%
Median mutual fund assets	$100,000	Hold more than half their financial assets in mutual funds	68%
Median number of funds owned	4		
Employed	77%		

Performance of Mutual Funds by Type, 2015

Source: *Kiplinger's Personal Finance* magazine analysis of Morningstar data (as of Aug. 31, 2015)

Fund type/fund objective	Average annual return 1-year	3-year	5-year
Large-Company			
Growth	2.70%	14.59%	15.72%
Blend	–1.35	13.34	14.32
Value	–3.88	12.45	13.29
Midsize-Company			
Growth	1.93	14.45	15.23
Blend	–2.19	14.12	14.39
Value	–3.40	14.43	14.46
Small-Company			
Growth	3.64	14.38	16.19
Blend	–2.37	13.06	14.41
Value	–5.09	12.61	13.39
Taxable Government Bond			
Short-Term	0.68	0.21	0.73
Intermediate-Term	1.59	0.80	2.10
Long-Term	3.57	0.64	4.57
Tax-Free Government Bond			
Short-Term	–0.15	0.56	1.27
Intermediate-Term	1.41	2.03	3.19
Long-Term Municipal	2.46	2.69	4.10
Sector			
Equity Precious Metals	–43.23%	–28.86%	–20.25%
Financial	0.18	14.66	11.93
Health	18.98	28.23	25.26
Natural Resources	–30.40	–5.02	0.40
Real Estate	0.27	7.22	11.62
Technology	0.39	14.25	14.46
Utilities	–6.78	8.67	10.26
Multialternative			
Multialternative Funds	–1.71	2.63	3.37
International			
Diversified Emerging Markets	–21.67	–1.74	–0.92
World Bond	–6.07	–0.37	1.80
World Stock	–4.88	10.29	10.20
Corporate Bond			
High Yield	–3.23	4.21	6.37
Short-Term	0.17	0.86	1.57
Intermediate-Term	0.44	1.68	3.19
Long-Term	0.34	2.59	5.80

Mutual Fund Ownership, 1940-2014

Source: *The Investment Company Fact Book 2015*, Investment Company Institute

Year	Mutual funds	Mutual fund accounts (thous.)	Households owning mutual funds: Number (thous.)	Percent of all households	Total net assets (bil)	Exchange-traded funds (ETFs): Number of funds	Total net assets (bil)
1940	68	296	NA	NA	$0.45	NA	NA
1950	98	939	NA	NA	2.53	NA	NA
1960	161	4,898	NA	NA	17.03	NA	NA
1970	361	10,690	NA	NA	47.62	NA	NA
1980	564	12,088	4,600	5.7%	134.76	NA	NA
1990	3,079	61,948	23,400	25.1	1,065.19	NA	NA
2000	8,155	244,705	48,600	45.7	6,964.63	80	$65.59
2005	7,977	275,479	50,300	44.4	8,891.38	204	300.82
2009	7,666	269,449	50,400	43.0	11,112.62	797	777.13
2010	7,554	291,299	53,200	45.3	11,832.99	923	991.99
2011	7,587	272,628	52,900	44.1	11,631.89	1,134	1,048.13
2012	7,588	257,074	53,800	44.4	13,052.23	1,194	1,337.11
2013	7,713	264,848	56,700	46.3	15,034.78	1,294	1,674.62
2014	7,923	NA	53,200	43.3	15,852.34	1,411	1,974.38

NA = Not available. **Note:** Does not include data for funds that invest primarily in other mutual funds. Mutual fund accounts data include both individual and omnibus accounts.

CME Average Daily Volume 2013-14

Source: CME Group, Inc.
(in thousands)

By Product	Average daily volume (thous.) 2013	2014	Percent change, 2013-14
Interest Rates	5,903	7,009	19%
Equity Indexes	2,642	2,764	5
Foreign Exchange (FX)	885	803	–9
Energy	1,676	1,630	–3
Agricultural Commodities	1,053	1,120	6
Metals	386	337	–13

By Venue	Average daily volume (thous.) 2013	2014	Percent change, 2013-14
Open outcry	1,040	1,176	13%
CME Globex	10,821	11,805	9
Privately negotiated	679	682	0
Total	**12,546**	**13,663**	**9**

CME = Chicago Mercantile Exchange.

Gold Owned by the U.S, 2015

Source: *Status Report of U.S. Treasury-Owned Gold*, Bureau of the Fiscal Service, U.S. Dept. of the Treasury
(as of July 31, 2015)

	Fine troy ounces	Book value
Total Treasury-owned gold	**261,498,926**	**$11,041,059,957**
Gold bullion	258,641,878	10,920,429,099
Gold coins, blanks, miscellaneous	2,857,048	120,630,859
Held by the U.S. Mint	**248,046,116**	**10,473,052,701**
Denver, CO, deep storage	43,853,707	1,851,599,996
Fort Knox, KY, deep storage	147,341,858	6,221,097,413
West Point, NY, deep storage	54,067,331	2,282,841,677
Gold coins, blanks, miscellaneous	2,783,219	117,513,615
Held by the Federal Reserve Bank	**13,452,811**	**$568,007,257**
Gold bullion	13,378,981	564,890,013
Federal Reserve Banks–NY vault	13,376,988	564,805,851
Federal Reserve Banks–display	1,993	84,162
Gold coins	73,830	3,117,244
Federal Reserve Banks–NY vault	73,452	3,101,308
Federal Reserve Banks–display	377	15,936

World's Leading Gold Producers, 1980-2014

Source: *Mineral Commodity Summaries 2015*, U.S. Geological Survey, U.S. Dept. of the Interior
(ranked by 2014 production; in thousands of troy ounces)

Country	1980	1990	2000	2005	2009	2010	2011	2012	2013	2014[1]
China	225	3,215	5,787	7,234	10,288	11,092	11,639	12,957	13,825	14,468
Australia	548	7,845	9,530	8,423	7,202	8,391	8,295	8,038	8,520	8,681
Russia[2]	8,300	9,710	4,598	5,279	6,200	6,173	6,430	7,009	7,395	7,877
United States	970	9,452	11,349	8,231	7,170	7,427	7,523	7,555	7,395	6,784
Canada	1,627	5,433	5,022	3,844	3,130	2,926	3,119	3,344	3,987	5,144
Peru[3]	134	293	4,263	6,682	5,864	5,273	5,272	5,176	4,855	4,823
South Africa	21,669	19,451	13,767	9,474	6,354	6,076	5,819	5,144	5,144	4,823
Uzbekistan	NA	NA	2,733	2,894	2,894	2,894	2,926	2,990	3,151	3,279
Mexico	196	311	848	976	1,652	2,347	2,701	3,119	3,151	2,958
Ghana	353	540	2,318	2,149	2,568	2,637	2,572	2,797	2,894	2,894
Brazil	NA	NA	NA	NA	1,929	1,865	1,993	2,090	2,283	2,251
Indonesia[4]	60	360	4,006	4,200	4,180	3,858	3,087	1,897	1,961	2,090
World	**39,197**	**70,089**	**82,949**	**79,412**	**79,091**	**82,306**	**85,520**	**86,485**	**90,022**	**91,951**

NA = Not available. **Note:** One kg is equal to 32.1507 troy oz. (1) Estimated. (2) Figures for 1980-90 refer to the former USSR. Includes gold recovered as a byproduct but excludes secondary production. (3) Includes documented production from placer artisanal production. (4) Excludes production from "people's mines" or unauthorized small-scale mines, which may add more than 600,000 troy oz. to the total.

Prices of Precious Metals, 1990-2014

Source: *Mineral Commodity Summaries 2015*, U.S. Geological Survey, U.S. Dept. of the Interior

	Dollars per troy ounce			Dollars per pound			
Year	Platinum[1]	Gold	Silver	Copper[2]	Lead	Tin[3]	Zinc[4]
1990	$467	$385	$4.82	$1.23	$0.46	$3.86	$0.75
1995	425	386	5.15	1.38	0.42	4.16	0.56
1999	379	280	5.25	0.76	0.44	3.66	0.53
2000	549	280	5.00	0.88	0.44	3.70	0.56
2001	533	272	4.39	0.77	0.44	3.15	0.44
2002	543	311	4.62	0.76	0.44	2.92	0.39
2003	694	365	4.91	0.85	0.44	3.40	0.41
2004	849	411	6.69	1.34	0.55	5.47	0.52
2005	900	446	7.34	1.74	0.61	4.83	0.67
2006	1,144	606	11.57	3.15	0.77	5.65	1.59
2007	1,308	699	13.41	3.28	1.24	8.99	1.54
2008	1,578	874	15.00	3.19	1.20	11.29	0.89
2009	1,208	975	14.69	2.41	0.87	8.37	0.78
2010	1,616	1,228	20.20	3.48	1.09	12.40	1.02
2011	1,725	1,572	35.26	4.06	1.22	15.75	1.06
2012	1,555	1,673	31.21	3.67	1.14	12.83	0.96
2013	1,490	1,415	23.80	3.40	1.15	13.52	0.96
2014[5]	1,440	1,270	19.03	3.22	NA	NA	1.08

NA = Not available. (1) Average annual dealer prices. (2) U.S. producer price for cathode copper. (3) Platt's Metals Week price. (4) Platt's Metals Week price for North American special high grade zinc except for 1990, which shows average price for high grade zinc. (5) Estimated.

Top Brands in Selected Categories, 2014-15

Source: Information Resources, Inc., a Chicago-based marketing research company
Figures for 52-week period ending Aug. 9, 2015. Percent change represents dollar sales change in 2014-15 over same period in 2013-14.

Product	Sales (mil)	% change	Market share
Baby food, total	**$1,048,725,570**	**2.7%**	
Gerber Second Foods	107,003,007	32.2	10.2%
Gerber Second Foods Nature Select	99,875,893	–25.0	9.5
Gerber	72,854,465	3.8	7.0
Gerber Graduates	57,637,815	–4.6	5.5
Plum Organics Yum	43,389,717	5.4	4.1
Batteries (alkaline), total	**$1,044,986,761**	**–2.2%**	
Duracell Coppertop	401,547,818	–0.8	38.4%
Energizer Max	315,686,450	–9.7	30.2
Private label	189,778,614	–8.7	18.2
Duracell Quantum	43,995,738	22.4	4.2
Duracell	21,245,768	10.6	2.0
Beer, domestic, total	**$8,845,886,525**	**1.9%**	
Bud Light	1,421,366,764	–2.0	16.1%
Coors Light	779,074,569	–2.0	8.8
Miller Lite	650,207,814	0.8	7.4
Budweiser	536,176,495	–3.6	6.1
Michelob Ultra	322,368,119	12.7	3.6
Beer, imported, total	**$2,256,202,489**	**4.1%**	
Corona Extra	479,590,368	3.6	21.3%
Heineken	270,545,279	–0.7	12.0
Modelo Especial	240,808,413	21.0	10.7
Stella Artois Lager	154,304,497	15.8	6.8
Corona Light	147,815,799	4.7	6.6

Product	Sales (mil)	% change	Market share
Bottled water, total	**$4,321,722,512**	**5.0%**	
Private label	1,222,142,472	7.6	28.3%
Dasani	402,373,245	7.0	9.3
Aquafina	298,451,970	2.3	6.9
Poland Spring	287,502,255	6.8	6.7
Nestle Pure Life	279,748,430	6.1	6.5
Cat food (dry), total	**$1,065,762,290**	**–2.4%**	
Iams Proactive Health	82,585,388	–13.2	7.8%
Meow Mix Original Choice	77,715,857	–3.1	7.3
Purina Kit & Kaboodle	70,302,459	–1.6	6.6
Purina Cat Chow Indoor	68,068,529	–8.8	6.4
Private label	63,180,179	–4.5	5.9
Cereal (ready-to-eat), total	**$5,838,693,045**	**–2.7%**	
Private label	548,590,097	–5.4	9.4%
General Mills Honey Nut Cheerios	304,034,939	–5.1	5.2
Post Honey Bunches of Oats	274,978,848	3.9	4.7
Kellogg's Frosted Flakes	240,293,523	–3.8	4.1
General Mills Cheerios	224,815,641	–2.0	3.9
Chocolate candy, total	**$2,668,683,989**	**5.7%**	
M&M's	326,126,396	4.8	12.2%
Hershey's	202,494,845	7.8	7.6
Reese's	123,353,651	–1.7	4.6
Private label	120,175,652	10.4	4.5
Dove Promises	110,791,727	1.4	4.2

Product	Sales (mil)	% change	Market share
Coffee (ground), total	**$2,652,480,291**	**2.0%**	
Folger's	657,488,324	–4.6	24.8%
Maxwell House	375,595,936	–1.9	14.2
Starbucks	277,427,968	3.8	10.5
Private label	277,258,820	5.5	10.5
Dunkin' Donuts	182,789,377	–1.8	6.9
Coffee (ground decaffeinated), total	**$220,837,511**	**–1.9%**	
Folger's	46,938,446	–5.8	21.3%
Private label	37,492,293	1.2	17.0
Starbucks	23,030,406	3.3	10.4
Dunkin' Donuts	19,909,884	–3.5	9.0
Maxwell House	16,745,283	–3.8	7.6
Cookies, total	**$4,626,482,840**	**0.2%**	
Private label	665,681,534	–1.6	14.4%
Nabisco Oreo	460,444,568	8.5	10.0
Nabisco Chips Ahoy	378,671,992	–5.1	8.2
Nabisco Oreo Double Stuf	177,583,424	–1.7	3.8
Nabisco BelVita	129,101,068	14.4	2.8
Dog food (dry), total	**$2,021,621,461**	**–3.0%**	
Purina One Smart Blend	160,051,037	4.8	7.9%
Iams Proactive Health	149,080,470	–9.9	7.4
Private label	145,294,560	–9.4	7.2
Purina Dog Chow	135,167,075	–5.4	6.7
Pedigree	134,682,319	–6.4	6.7
Ice cream, total	**$4,102,405,728**	**2.3%**	
Private label	958,269,646	–2.0	23.4%
Häagen-Dazs	348,562,333	5.6	8.5
Ben & Jerry's	329,435,507	13.9	8.0
Breyer's	288,067,458	6.8	7.0
Blue Bell	261,852,265	–33.7	6.4
Pizza (frozen), total	**$3,030,796,759**	**0.4%**	
DiGiorno	591,161,058	–4.5	19.5%
Red Baron	366,042,484	3.7	12.1
Private label	345,003,049	2.6	11.4
Totino's Party Pizza	194,929,268	1.9	6.4
Freschetta	183,023,494	6.7	6.0
Potato chips, total	**$3,911,357,335**	**0.6%**	
Lay's	1,095,406,662	–1.1	28.0%
Wavy Lay's	369,790,514	–0.3	9.5
Ruffles	315,707,653	2.6	8.1
Private label	302,460,338	2.1	7.7
Pringles	284,749,860	2.3	7.3
Salad dressing, total	**$1,324,247,459**	**–2.1%**	
Kraft	243,443,595	–4.9	18.4%
Hidden Valley Ranch	235,967,064	–0.7	17.8
Private label	190,417,935	–6.5	14.4
Ken's Steak House	165,598,645	1.3	12.5
Wishbone	160,683,034	–3.7	12.1
Soft drinks, total	**$8,085,640,329**	**0.7%**	
Coca-Cola	1,934,285,576	1.5	23.9%
Pepsi	1,183,225,307	0.3	14.6
Mountain Dew	765,897,622	–0.8	9.5
Dr Pepper	640,227,546	1.2	7.9
Sprite	592,214,946	2.2	7.3
Soft drinks (low-calorie), total	**$3,998,617,212**	**–4.2%**	
Diet Coke	1,010,221,254	–2.9	25.3%
Diet Pepsi	573,773,577	–0.9	14.4
Coca-Cola Zero	347,318,841	–1.9	8.7
Diet Mountain Dew	315,425,183	–1.9	7.9
Diet Dr Pepper	257,559,224	–2.2	6.4

Note: "Private label" represents the aggregated sales figures for store-branded products in that category. Total category sales include other brands not listed here.

Who Owns What: Familiar Consumer Products and Services

The following is a partial list of well-known consumer brands with their (U.S.) parent companies as of Sept. 2015. Among brands not listed are many whose parent companies have the same or a similar name (e.g., Colgate is owned by Colgate-Palmolive Co.).

ABC broadcasting: Walt Disney
Advil: Pfizer
Ajax cleanser: Colgate-Palmolive
Altoids mints: Mars
Amana appliances: Whirlpool
American Girl: Mattel
Aquafina water: PepsiCo
Arm & Hammer: Church & Dwight
Band-Aid bandages: Johnson & Johnson
Barbie dolls: Mattel
Bejeweled video game: PopCap
Ben & Jerry's ice cream: Unilever
Betty Crocker products: General Mills
Bounty paper towels: Procter & Gamble
Braun appliances: Procter & Gamble
Brita water systems: Clorox
Cadbury chocolates: Mondelēz International
Calphalon cookware: Newell Rubbermaid
Canada Dry ginger ale: Dr Pepper Snapple Group
ChapStick: Pfizer
Charmin toilet tissue: Procter & Gamble
Cheer detergent: Procter & Gamble
Cheez Whiz: Kraft Heinz
Chips Ahoy!: Mondelēz International
Claritin allergy products: Merck
Contadina tomatoes: Del Monte
Coppertone sunscreen: Merck
Crest toothpaste: Procter & Gamble
Crisco shortening: J.M. Smucker
Dasani water: Coca-Cola
Depends adult diapers: Kimberly-Clark
Doritos chips: PepsiCo
Dove soap: Unilever
Dreyer's ice cream: Nestlé
Duracell batteries: Procter & Gamble
ESPN networks: Walt Disney
Febreze: Procter & Gamble
Fisher-Price toys: Mattel
Folger's coffee: J.M. Smucker
Formula 409 spray cleaner: Clorox
Friskies cat food: Nestlé
Frito-Lay's snacks: PepsiCo
Fruit of the Loom apparel: Berkshire Hathaway
Gatorade: PepsiCo
GEICO auto insurance: Berkshire Hathaway
Gerber baby food: Nestlé
Gillette: Procter & Gamble
Glad products: Clorox
Glade air fresheners: S.C. Johnson
Green Giant vegetables: General Mills
Halls cough drops: Mondelēz International
Head & Shoulders shampoo: Procter & Gamble
Healthy Choice meals: ConAgra
Hebrew National meats: ConAgra
Hellmann's mayonnaise: Unilever
Hillshire Farm: Tyson
Hot Wheels/Matchbox cars: Mattel
Huggies diapers: Kimberly-Clark
Hunt's tomatoes: ConAgra
Iams pet food: Mars
Irish Spring soap: Colgate-Palmolive
Ivory soap: Procter & Gamble
Jell-O: Kraft Heinz
Jennie-O turkey: Hormel
Jif peanut butter: J.M. Smucker
Jimmy Dean sausages: Hillshire Brands
Keebler cookies: Kellogg Co.
KFC restaurants: Yum! Brands
Kibbles 'n Bits pet food: Big Heart Pet Brands
Kingsford charcoal: Clorox
Kit Kat candy: Hershey
KitchenAid appliances: Whirlpool
Kiwi shoe products: S.C. Johnson
Kleenex: Kimberly-Clark
Knorr soups: Unilever
Kool-Aid: Kraft Heinz
Lea & Perrins Worcestershire sauce: Kraft Heinz
Lipton tea: Unilever
Listerine mouthwash: Johnson & Johnson
Maxwell House coffee: Kraft Heinz
Maytag appliances: Whirlpool
Minute Maid juices: Coca-Cola
Mr. Clean: Procter & Gamble
Monopoly board game: Hasbro
Mountain Dew soda: PepsiCo
Neosporin: Johnson & Johnson
Neutrogena soap: Johnson & Johnson
9 Lives cat food: Big Heart Pet Brands
OFF! insect repellents: S.C. Johnson
Olay: Procter & Gamble
Old Navy clothing: Gap
Old Spice: Procter & Gamble
Oreo cookies: Mondelēz International
Oscar Mayer meats: Kraft Heinz
Pampers: Procter & Gamble

Pantene shampoo: Procter & Gamble
Paper Mate pens: Newell Rubbermaid
Pedigree pet food: Mars
Pepperidge Farm prods.: Campbell Soup
Pepto-Bismol: Procter & Gamble
Perrier water: Nestlé
Pillsbury: General Mills
Pine-Sol cleaner: Clorox
Pizza Hut restaurants: Yum! Brands
Planters nuts: Kraft Heinz
Post-it notes: 3M
Prego pasta sauce: Campbell Soup
Pringles snacks: Kellogg Co.
Promise spread: Unilever
Purina pet foods: Nestlé
Q-Tips: Unilever
Quaker Oats: PepsiCo
Raid insecticide: S.C. Johnson
Reese's candy: Hershey
Rice-A-Roni: PepsiCo
Right Guard deodorant: Henkel
Ritz crackers: Mondelēz International
Robitussin: Pfizer
Rogaine hair regrowth treatment: Johnson & Johnson
Saran wrap: S.C. Johnson
Schick razors: Edgewell Personal Care
Scope mouthwash: Procter & Gamble
Scotch tape: 3M
Skippy peanut butter: Hormel
Splenda sweetener: Johnson & Johnson
Sprite soda: Coca-Cola
Sudafed: Johnson & Johnson
Swanson broth: Campbell Soup
Taco Bell restaurants: Yum! Brands
Tampax tampons: Procter & Gamble
Tide detergent: Procter & Gamble
Timberland apparel: V.F. Corp.
Trident gum: Mondelēz International
Trojan condoms: Church & Dwight
Tropicana juice: PepsiCo
Twizzlers candy: Hershey
Tylenol: Johnson & Johnson
Uncle Ben's Rice: Mars
V8 vegetable juice: Campbell Soup
Vans apparel: V.F. Corp.
Vaseline: Unilever
Velveeta cheese products: Kraft Foods
Viagra: Pfizer
Vicks cold medicines: Procter & Gamble
Visine eye drops: Johnson & Johnson
Windex: S.C. Johnson
Wrigley's candy and gum: Mars
Xanax: Pfizer
Yoplait yogurt: General Mills
Ziploc storage bags: S.C. Johnson

U.S. Home Ownership Rates, by Selected Characteristics, 2005, 2015

Source: U.S. Census Bureau, U.S. Dept. of Commerce

Region	2005	2015
Northeast	64.7%	60.2%
Midwest	73.4	68.4
South	70.4	64.9
West	63.8	58.5

Age	2005	2015
Under 35	42.8%	34.8%
35-44	68.7	58.0
45-54	76.3	69.9
55-64	81.3	75.4
65+	80.3	78.5

Race/ethnicity[1]	2005	2015
White, non-Hispanic	75.6%	71.6%
Black	48.0	43.0
Hispanic	49.2	45.4
Other	58.0	52.6

Income	2005	2015
Median family income or more	84.0%	78.3%
Below median family income	52.7	48.6
Total U.S.	**68.6**	**63.4**

Note: Figures are for 2nd quarter of year shown. Not seasonally adjusted. (1) Hispanic householders may be of any race. "Other" includes householders self-identifying as Asian, Native Hawaiian/Pacific Islander, and Native American/Alaska Native, as well as combinations of two or more races/ethnicities.

U.S. Housing Affordability, 1990-2015

Source: National Association of REALTORS®

Year	Median-priced existing home	Avg. mortgage rate[1]	Monthly principal & interest payment	Payment as % of median monthly income
1990	$92,000	10.04%	$648	22.0%
1995	110,500	7.85	639	18.9
2000	139,000	8.03	818	19.3
2005	219,000	5.91	1,040	22.4
2006	221,900	6.58	1,131	23.2
2007	217,900	6.52	1,104	21.7
2008	196,600	6.15	958	18.1
2009	$172,100	5.14%	$751	14.8%
2010	173,100	4.89	734	14.5
2011	166,200	4.67	687	13.4
2012	177,200	3.83	663	12.7
2013	197,400	4.00	754	14.1
2014	208,900	4.31	828	15.2
2015[2]	230,500	3.90	870	15.7

(1) All figures assume a down payment of 20% of the home price. Based on effective rate on loans closed on existing homes for the period shown. (2) Figures are for May, the latest available. All other figures are annual averages.

S&P/Case-Shiller National Home Price Index, 1975-2015

Source: S&P Dow Jones Indices

This index compares the median price of existing U.S. homes over time. The baseline for comparison is Jan. 2000; all numbers before or after reflect home prices in relation to it. For example, the Jan. 2015 index of 166.5 means that home prices were 66.5% higher than they were 15 years earlier, while the Jan. 1975 index of 25.2 means prices then were 25.2% of what they were in 2000.

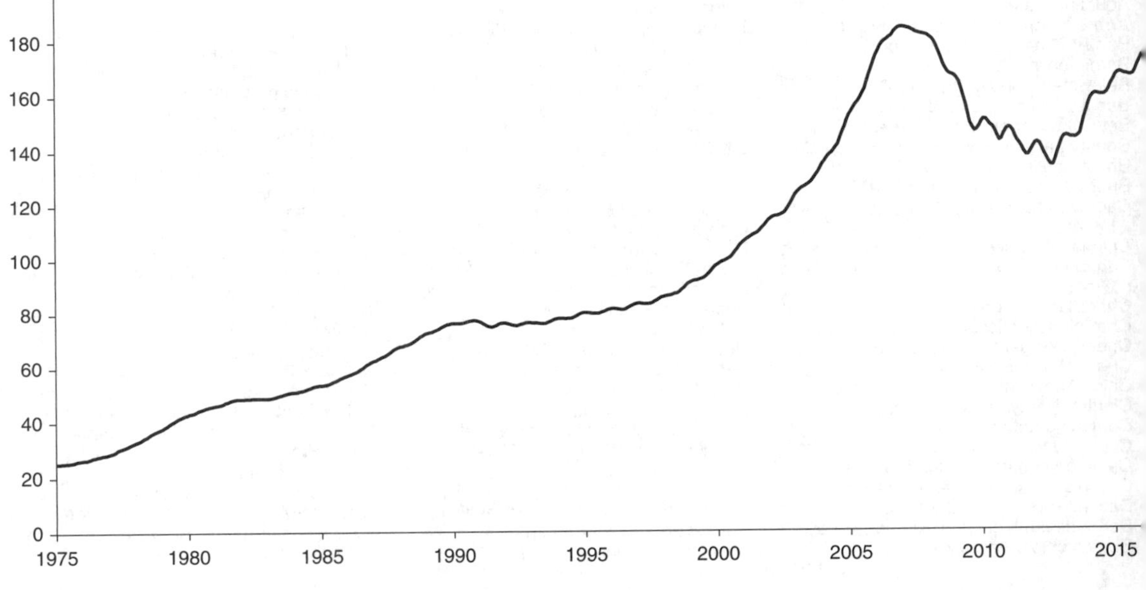

Median Price of Existing Single-Family Homes, by Metropolitan Area, 2010-15

Source: National Association of REALTORS®

Median prices are in thousands of dollars and based on all transactions within time period shown.

Metropolitan area	2010	2014	2015[1]
Akron, OH	$108.9	$115.7	$120.6
Albany-Schenectady-Troy, NY	195.7	202.0	206.6
Albuquerque, NM	178.7	177.6	184.0
Allentown-Bethlehem-Easton, PA-NJ	224.0	179.1	188.9
Amarillo, TX	124.7	144.5	153.3
Anaheim-Santa Ana-Irvine, CA	546.4	687.9	713.2
Atlanta-Sandy Springs-Marietta, GA	114.8	159.5	181.5
Atlantic City, NJ	226.4	207.6	214.6
Austin-Round Rock, TX	193.6	240.7	271.6
Baltimore-Towson, MD	246.1	244.1	254.5
Barnstable Town, MA	326.0	345.2	360.7
Baton Rouge, LA	169.6	171.3	184.8
Beaumont-Port Arthur, TX	125.1	135.6	140.5
Birmingham-Hoover, AL	143.0	167.9	190.4
Bismarck, ND	163.4	237.8	252.7
Bloomington-Normal, IL	157.9	156.0	158.9
Boise City-Nampa, ID	136.2	172.9	190.1
Boston-Cambridge-Quincy, MA-NH	357.3	389.8	414.6
Boulder, CO	358.1	390.7	463.7
Bridgeport-Stamford-Norwalk, CT	408.6	397.6	403.5
Buffalo-Niagara Falls, NY	121.2	129.0	129.8
Burlington-South Burlington, VT	261.2	283.3	293.3
Canton-Massillon, OH	90.9	112.9	120.6
Cape Coral-Fort Myers, FL	88.9	188.7	218.0
Cedar Rapids, IA	144.7	151.6	164.0
Champaign-Urbana, IL	141.9	136.1	145.2
Charleston-North Charleston, SC	200.5	228.2	244.5
Charleston, WV	129.1	132.6	139.2
Charlotte-Gastonia-Concord, NC-SC	143.3	193.8	211.4
Chattanooga, TN-GA	121.4	139.7	155.2
Chicago-Naperville-Joliet, IL	191.4	205.9	230.5
Cincinnati-Middletown, OH-KY-IN	128.0	140.6	151.9
Cleveland-Elyria-Mentor, OH	114.5	122.6	129.7
Colorado Springs, CO	195.5	222.3	244.8
Columbia, MO	146.3	161.2	176.6
Columbia, SC	142.6	150.4	157.3
Columbus, OH	136.4	156.3	172.0
Corpus Christi, TX	135.1	171.1	186.2
Cumberland, MD-WV	100.3	92.0	82.4
Dallas-Fort Worth-Arlington, TX	143.8	188.3	215.2
Davenport-Moline-Rock Island, IA-IL	112.2	116.0	123.6
Dayton, OH	103.6	114.9	125.1
Deltona-Daytona Beach-Ormond Beach, FL	115.6	135.1	147.0
Denver-Aurora, CO	232.4	310.2	362.9
Des Moines, IA	150.9	171.5	184.0
Detroit-Warren-Livonia, MI[2]	NA	NA	NA
Dover, DE	193.3	186.1	190.8
Durham, NC	158.3	199.1	233.7
El Paso, TX	134.3	140.8	142.2
Erie, PA	107.7	117.9	125.0
Eugene-Springfield, OR	196.3	200.9	222.6
Fargo, ND-MN	NA	173.0	190.3
Gainesville, FL	161.6	172.3	190.0
Gary-Hammond, IN	122.9	135.1	149.0
Grand Rapids, MI	91.5	138.3	155.2
Green Bay, WI	130.4	146.6	145.0
Greensboro-High Point, NC	129.8	136.6	159.8
Greenville, SC	145.3	165.4	179.5
Gulfport-Biloxi, MS	125.0	117.1	131.3
Hartford-West Hartford-East Hartford, CT	235.8	220.9	229.5
Honolulu, HI	607.6	682.8	698.6
Houston-Baytown-Sugar Land, TX	155.0	198.4	221.1
Indianapolis, IN	123.3	144.6	160.2
Jackson, MS	133.2	155.3	172.0
Jacksonville, FL	137.7	181.1	204.0
Kansas City, MO-KS	141.6	158.8	177.8
Knoxville, TN	140.9	149.7	159.8
Lansing-East Lansing, MI	84.4	120.1	135.2
Las Vegas-Paradise, NV	138.0	198.0	216.3
Lexington-Fayette, KY	143.2	144.0	149.3
Lincoln, NE	133.6	145.6	158.7
Little Rock-North Little Rock, AR	132.5	131.7	139.6
Los Angeles-Long Beach-Santa Ana, CA	$323.3	$449.5	$445.2
Louisville, KY-IN	134.6	142.8	159.2
Madison, WI	217.7	228.2	237.2
Manchester-Nashua, NH	232.0	234.8	253.5
Memphis, TN-MS-AR	120.2	138.6	153.6
Miami-Fort Lauderdale-Miami Beach, FL	201.9	266.0	289.9
Milwaukee-Waukesha-West Allis, WI	205.9	207.8	226.9
Minneapolis-St. Paul-Bloomington, MN-WI	170.6	210.1	229.2
Mobile, AL	121.0	115.5	127.7
Montgomery, AL	129.0	137.3	143.7
Nashville-Davidson–Murfreesboro, TN	153.8	183.0	208.5
New Haven-Milford, CT	231.0	233.3	218.1
New Orleans-Metairie-Kenner, LA	159.7	165.0	NA
New York-Northern New Jersey-Long Island, NY-NJ-PA	393.7	395.9	410.4
Norwich-New London, CT	204.7	180.2	187.3
Oklahoma City, OK	145.7	150.3	156.3
Omaha, NE-IA	137.3	149.0	163.5
Orlando, FL	134.7	180.0	198.0
Palm Bay-Melbourne-Titusville, FL	103.0	137.6	165.0
Pensacola-Ferry Pass-Brent, FL	141.0	150.8	160.7
Peoria, IL	116.9	118.9	127.3
Philadelphia-Camden-Wilmington, PA-NJ-DE-MD	214.9	220.7	231.7
Phoenix-Mesa-Scottsdale, AZ	139.2	198.5	217.9
Pittsfield, MA	195.5	186.2	199.4
Portland-Vancouver-Beaverton, OR-WA	237.3	286.0	314.8
Providence-New Bedford-Fall River, RI-MA	228.5	238.8	249.7
Raleigh-Cary, NC	190.4	208.6	247.9
Reading, PA	153.3	148.7	151.0
Reno-Sparks, NV	179.5	247.5	283.2
Richmond, VA	NA	220.2	231.9
Riverside-San Bernardino-Ontario, CA	179.3	273.9	291.7
Rochester, NY	118.9	125.3	135.0
Rockford, IL	NA	86.3	94.7
Sacramento–Arden-Arcade–Roseville, CA	184.2	268.7	291.0
Saint Louis, MO-IL	131.1	141.7	157.1
Salem, OR	173.5	187.7	216.2
Salt Lake City, UT	206.5	239.1	262.0
San Antonio, TX	151.0	182.1	199.4
San Diego-Carlsbad-San Marcos, CA	385.7	497.9	547.8
San Francisco-Oakland-Fremont, CA	525.6	737.6	841.6
San Jose-Sunnyvale-Santa Clara, CA	595.0	860.0	980.0
Sarasota-Bradenton-Venice, FL	164.6	220.2	246.8
Seattle-Tacoma-Bellevue, WA	295.7	356.6	385.3
Shreveport-Bossier City, LA	156.6	158.6	160.0
Sioux Falls, SD	143.3	162.3	177.0
Spartanburg, SC	118.2	129.9	139.5
Spokane, WA	172.2	178.3	191.3
Springfield, IL	124.0	122.4	122.2
Springfield, MA	190.0	193.3	196.9
Springfield, MO	109.1	121.2	128.0
Syracuse, NY	125.1	125.8	130.9
Tallahassee, FL	152.8	167.5	181.6
Tampa-St. Petersburg-Clearwater, FL	134.2	151.5	175.0
Toledo, OH	81.5	87.2	109.8
Topeka, KS	107.2	111.9	126.4
Trenton-Ewing, NJ	250.7	267.1	283.9
Tucson, AZ	156.6	175.8	183.2
Tulsa, OK	132.3	145.5	156.2
Virginia Beach-Norfolk-Newport News, VA-NC	205.0	196.0	213.0
Washington-Arlington-Alexandria, DC-VA-MD-WV	325.3	383.8	403.8
Wichita, KS	118.7	125.7	136.6
Wilmington, NC	NA	211.4	214.5
Winston-Salem, NC	NA	135.2	153.8
Worcester, MA	223.3	236.1	250.9

NA = Not available. (1) Second quarter figures for 2015 are preliminary. (2) $53,800 in 2011 and $63,400 in 2012.

Characteristics of American Housing Units, 2013

Source: *American Housing Survey, 2013*, U.S. Dept. of Housing and Urban Development

Characteristic	Number of homes (thous.)	% of all homes
Total housing units	**132,832**	**100.0%**
Units in structure		
1, detached	83,392	62.8
1, attached	7,581	5.7
2-4	10,724	8.1
5-9	6,604	5.0
10-19	6,135	4.6
20-49	4,579	3.4
50 or more	5,213	3.9
Manufactured/mobile home/trailer	8,603	6.5
Cooperatives	853	0.6
Condominiums	10,125	7.6
Year built		
2010-14	2,390	1.8
2005-09	7,890	5.9
2000-04	9,100	6.9
1995-99	8,967	6.8
1990-94	7,116	5.4
1985-89	8,927	6.7
1980-84	7,779	5.9
1975-79	13,760	10.4
1970-74	10,949	8.2
1960-69	15,145	11.4
1950-59	13,392	10.1
1940-49	7,836	5.9
1930-39	5,660	4.3
1920-29	5,201	3.9
1919 or earlier	8,720	6.6
Median year built	*1975*	—
Square footage of unit		
Less than 500	3,874	2.9
500-749	10,178	7.7
750-999	16,028	12.1
1,000-1,499	31,319	23.6
1,500-1,999	24,446	18.4
2,000-2,499	15,967	12.0
2,500-2,999	8,005	6.0
3,000-3,999	7,565	5.7
4,000 or more	4,989	3.8
Not reported	10,461	7.9
Median square footage	*1,480*	—
Number of bedrooms		
None	1,101	0.8%
1	15,151	11.4
2	34,731	26.1
3	54,731	41.2
4 or more	27,118	20.4
Number of complete bathrooms		
None	1,510	1.1
1	46,130	34.7
1-1/2	17,055	12.8
2 or more	68,136	51.3
Location[1]		
Inside metropolitan statistical areas	92,772	80.1
Outside metropolitan statistical areas	23,080	19.9
Northeast	21,110	18.2
Midwest	25,912	22.4
South	42,951	37.1
West	25,879	22.3
Lot size[2]		
Less than 1/8 acre	16,223	16.9
1/8-1/4 acre	25,008	26.0
1/4-1/2 acre	16,841	17.5
1/2-1 acre	10,199	10.6
1-5 acres	20,593	21.4
5-10 acres	3,117	3.2
10+ acres	4,177	4.3
Median lot size (acres)	*0.25*	—
Equipment		
Washing machine	104,458	78.6
Clothes dryer	101,905	76.7
Dishwasher	86,877	65.4
Central air conditioning	86,847	65.4
Kitchen sink disposal	66,901	50.4
Trash compactor	4,418	3.3
Lacking full kitchen facilities	5,579	4.2
Main heating source[3]		
Piped gas	64,041	48.5
Electricity	50,210	38.0
Fuel oil	7,861	6.0
Bottled gas	6,335	4.8
Wood	2,388	1.8

— = Not applicable. (1) Percentages based on 115,852 occupied homes. (2) Percentages based on 96,159 1-unit structures; does not include cooperatives or condominiums. (3) Percentages based on 131,972 homes with heat. Not all heating fuels are shown here.

Fair Market Rents for Select Metropolitan Areas, 2015

Source: *Fair Market Rents 2015*, U.S. Dept. of Housing and Urban Development

Metropolitan area	Number of bedrooms 0	1	2	3	4
Atlanta, GA	$755	$810	$938	$1,239	$1,514
Austin, TX	731	892	1,113	1,505	1,824
Baltimore-Towson, MD	778	945	1,187	1,520	1,769
Birmingham-Hoover, AL	605	717	830	1,121	1,235
Boston-Cambridge-Quincy, MA-NH	1,044	1,247	1,549	1,922	2,123
Buffalo-Niagara Falls, NY	582	618	746	948	1,085
Charlotte-Concord-Gastonia, NC-SC	645	737	854	1,159	1,452
Chicago-Joliet-Naperville, IL	850	989	1,162	1,476	1,758
Cincinnati, OH-KY-IN	502	591	775	1,085	1,277
Cleveland-Elyria, OH	493	606	764	1,005	1,061
Columbus, OH	525	630	821	1,052	1,228
Dallas, TX	650	787	974	1,314	1,655
Denver-Aurora-Lakewood, CO	766	954	1,213	1,768	2,059
Detroit-Warren-Livonia, MI	526	651	853	1,134	1,220
Hartford, CT	749	956	1,196	1,484	1,701
Honolulu, HI	1,318	1,489	1,961	2,858	3,102
Houston, TX	677	766	939	1,279	1,634
Indianapolis-Carmel, IN	546	644	800	1,072	1,217
Jacksonville, FL	608	778	948	1,254	1,558
Kansas City, MO-KS	555	712	882	1,204	1,368
Las Vegas-Henderson, NV	625	772	957	1,395	1,671
Los Angeles-Long Beach, CA	936	1,140	1,473	1,986	2,202
Louisville, KY-IN	545	637	808	1,111	1,261
Memphis, TN-MS-AR	595	692	817	1,114	1,293
Miami-Miami Beach, FL	765	963	1235	1,651	1,963
Milwaukee-Waukesha, WI	$589	$715	$897	$1,134	$1,252
Minneapolis-St. Paul, MN-WI	648	804	1,015	1,427	1,673
Nashville-Davidson, TN	653	747	914	1,213	1,416
New Orleans-Metairie, LA	662	778	952	1,205	1,448
New York, NY	1,276	1,342	1,553	1,997	2,199
Oklahoma City, OK	535	607	782	1,075	1,290
Orlando-Kissimmee, FL	739	825	991	1,316	1,588
Philadelphia-Camden-Wilmington, PA-NJ-DE-MD	820	992	1,196	1,484	1,639
Phoenix-Mesa-Scottsdale, AZ	589	726	903	1,316	1,540
Pittsburgh, PA	549	649	817	1,014	1,120
Portland-Vancouver, OR-WA	744	857	1,014	1,474	1,770
Providence-Fall River, RI-MA	647	791	960	1,191	1,434
Richmond, VA	784	825	955	1,261	1,539
Riverside-San Bernardino-Ontario, CA	788	934	1,173	1,653	2,032
Sacramento-Roseville, CA	699	806	1,014	1,478	1,770
St. Louis, MO-IL	551	637	830	1,096	1,269
Salt Lake City, UT	596	748	927	1,335	1,557
San Antonio, TX	590	730	918	1,208	1,413
San Diego-Carlsbad, CA	1,028	1,139	1,481	2,141	2,301
San Francisco, CA	1,395	1,793	2,262	2,952	3,515
San Jose-Santa Clara, CA	1,333	1,564	1,971	2,745	3,062
San Juan-Guaynabo, PR	418	467	562	755	918
Seattle-Bellevue, WA	1,025	1197	1,488	2,169	2,557
Tampa-St. Petersburg, FL	660	785	980	1,303	1,556
Washington-Arlington-Alexandria, DC-VA-MD	1,292	1,386	1,604	2,119	2,694

Note: Figures are projections made in the previous fiscal year. Metropolitan area may include individual cities not shown here.

TRADE

U.S. Trade With Selected Countries and Major Areas, 2014

Source: U.S. Census Bureau and U.S. Bureau of Economic Analysis, U.S. Dept. of Commerce
(in millions of dollars; top 25 countries as ranked by amount of total trade with U.S.)

Rank	Country	Total trade with U.S.	U.S. exports to	Rank[1]	U.S. imports from	Rank[1]	U.S. trade balance with	Rank[2]
1.	Canada	$660,219	$312,421	1	$347,798	2	–$35,377	5
2.	China[3]	590,431	123,676	3	466,755	1	–343,079	1
3.	Mexico	534,323	240,249	2	294,074	3	–53,825	4
4.	Japan	200,831	66,827	4	134,004	4	–67,176	3
5.	Germany	172,623	49,363	6	123,260	5	–73,896	2
6.	South Korea	113,989	44,471	7	69,518	6	–25,047	9
7.	United Kingdom	108,215	53,823	5	54,392	7	–569	50
8.	France	78,175	31,301	12	46,874	9	–15,573	14
9.	Brazil	72,966	42,429	9	30,537	16	11,893	228
10.	Taiwan	67,252	26,670	14	40,582	12	–13,911	16
11.	India	66,852	21,608	18	45,244	10	–23,637	11
12.	Saudi Arabia	65,746	18,705	20	47,041	8	–28,336	6
13.	Netherlands	63,893	43,075	8	20,818	23	22,257	233
14.	Italy	59,083	16,968	21	42,115	11	–25,147	8
15.	Belgium	55,675	34,790	11	20,885	22	13,904	230
16.	Switzerland	53,367	22,176	16	31,191	14	–9,015	20
17.	Hong Kong	46,727	40,858	10	5,869	42	34,989	234
18.	Singapore	46,663	30,237	13	16,426	26	13,811	229
19.	Malaysia	43,488	13,068	24	30,420	17	–17,352	13
20.	Ireland	41,762	7,806	37	33,956	13	–26,149	7
21.	Venezuela	41,357	11,138	27	30,219	18	–19,082	12
22.	Thailand	38,933	11,810	25	27,123	19	–15,313	15
23.	Colombia	38,407	20,107	19	18,300	25	1,807	214
24.	Israel	38,045	15,083	23	22,962	21	–7,879	21
25.	Australia	37,254	26,582	15	10,672	32	15,910	231
Major area/group								
	North America	$1,194,542	$552,670		$641,872		–$89,203	
	Europe	824,480	333,292		491,188		–157,896	
	Euro Area	532,450	205,456		326,994		–121,538	
	EU	694,344	276,143		418,201		–142,058	
	Africa	72,667	38,077		34,590		3,488	
	OECD	2,321,504	1,005,093		1,316,411		–311,318	
	Pacific Rim Countries	1,202,446	394,511		807,935		–413,424	
	Asia-Near East	177,040	73,744		103,296		–29,552	
	Asia-South	82,440	25,412		57,028		–31,616	
	Asia-NICs	274,632	142,237		132,395		9,842	
	ASEAN	215,653	78,586		137,067		–58,481	
	APEC	2,548,266	1,001,612		1,546,654		–545,042	
	South/Central America	334,710	184,019		150,691		33,328	
	Twenty Latin American Republics	843,466	407,379		436,087		–28,708	
	CAFTA-DR	59,503	31,124		28,379		2,745	
	Central American Common Market	47,060	23,201		23,859		–658	
	NATO Allies	1,303,770	585,465		718,305		–132,841	
	OPEC	214,695	82,346		132,349		–50,003	
	WORLD TOTAL	**3,968,217**	**1,620,532**		**2,347,685**		**–727,153**	

Note: Figures shown are on Census Bureau basis and are not seasonally adjusted. Figures may not equal totals due to rounding. Country grouping data reflect groups at the time of reporting. (1) Rank shown is for column to the left. Ranking includes territories as well as nations. (2) Rank by size of U.S. trade deficit. Ranking includes territories as well as nations. (3) Not incl. Hong Kong, Macao, and Taiwan. ***Definitions of major areas/groups used in table, as provided by source*: North America**—Canada, Mexico. **Europe**—Albania, Andorra, Armenia, Austria, Azerbaijan, Belarus, Belgium, Bosnia-Herzegovina, Bulgaria, Croatia, Cyprus, Czech Republic, Denmark, Estonia, Faroe Isls., Finland, France, Georgia, Germany, Gibraltar, Greece, Hungary, Iceland, Ireland, Italy, Kazakhstan, Kosovo, Kyrgyzstan, Latvia, Liechtenstein, Lithuania, Luxembourg, Macedonia, Malta, Moldova, Monaco, Montenegro, Netherlands, Norway, Poland, Portugal, Romania, Russia, San Marino, Serbia, Slovakia, Slovenia, Spain, Svalbard-Jan Mayen Isl., Sweden, Switzerland, Tajikistan, Turkey, Turkmenistan, Ukraine, United Kingdom, Uzbekistan, Vatican City. **Euro Area**—Austria, Belgium, Cyprus, Estonia, Finland, France, Germany, Greece, Ireland, Italy, Latvia, Lithuania, Luxembourg, Malta, Netherlands, Portugal, Slovakia, Slovenia, Spain. **EU (European Union)**—Euro Area plus Bulgaria, Croatia, Czech Republic, Denmark, Hungary, Latvia, Poland, Romania, Sweden, United Kingdom. **Africa**—Algeria, Angola, Benin, Botswana, British Indian Ocean Territories, Burkina Faso, Burundi, Cabo Verde, Cameroon, Central African Republic, Chad, Comoros, Congo (Brazzaville), Congo (Kinshasa), Côte d'Ivoire, Djibouti, Egypt, Equatorial Guinea, Eritrea, Ethiopia, French Southern and Antarctic Lands, Gabon, Gambia, Ghana, Guinea, Guinea-Bissau, Kenya, Lesotho, Liberia, Libya, Madagascar, Malawi, Mali, Mauritania, Mauritius, Mayotte, Morocco, Mozambique, Namibia, Niger, Nigeria, Réunion, Rwanda, St. Helena, São Tomé and Príncipe, Senegal, Seychelles, Sierra Leone, Somalia, South Africa, South Sudan, Sudan, Swaziland, Tanzania, Togo, Tunisia, Uganda, Western Sahara, Zambia, Zimbabwe. **OECD (Org. for Economic Cooperation and Development)**—Australia, Austria, Belgium, Canada, Chile, Czech Republic, Denmark, Estonia, Finland, France, Germany, Greece, Hungary, Iceland, Ireland, Israel, Italy, Japan, Korea (South), Luxembourg, Mexico, Netherlands, New Zealand, Norway, Poland, Portugal, Slovakia, Slovenia, Spain, Sweden, Switzerland, Turkey, United Kingdom. **Pacific Rim Countries**—Australia, Brunei, China, Hong Kong, Indonesia, Japan, Korea (South), Macao, Malaysia, New Zealand, Papua New Guinea, Philippines, Singapore, Taiwan. **Asia-Near East**—Bahrain, Gaza Strip Administered by Israel, Iran, Iraq, Israel, Jordan, Kuwait, Lebanon, Oman, Qatar, Saudi Arabia, Syria, United Arab Emirates, West Bank Administered by Israel, Yemen. **Asia-South**—Afghanistan, Bangladesh, India, Nepal, Pakistan, Sri Lanka. **Asia-NICs (Newly Industrialized Countries)**—Hong Kong, Korea (South), Singapore, Taiwan. **ASEAN (Assn. of South East Asia Nations)**—Brunei, Cambodia, Indonesia, Laos, Malaysia, Myanmar, Philippines, Singapore, Thailand, Vietnam. **APEC (Asia-Pacific Economic Cooperation)**—Australia, Brunei, Canada, Chile, China, Hong Kong, Indonesia, Japan, Korea (South), Malaysia, Mexico, New Zealand, Papua New Guinea, Peru, Philippines, Russia, Singapore, Taiwan, Thailand, Vietnam. **South/Central America**—Anguilla, Antigua and Barbuda, Argentina, Aruba, Bahamas, Barbados, Belize, Bermuda, Bolivia, Brazil, British Virgin Isls., Cayman Isls., Chile, Colombia, Costa Rica, Curaçao, Cuba, Dominica, Dominican Republic, Ecuador, El Salvador, Falkland Isls., French Guiana, Grenada, Guadeloupe, Guatemala, Guyana, Haiti, Honduras, Jamaica, Martinique, Montserrat, Netherlands Antilles, Nicaragua, Panama, Paraguay, Peru, Sint Marten, St. Kitts and Nevis, St. Lucia, St. Vincent and the Grenadines, Suriname, Trinidad and Tobago, Turks and Caicos Isls., Uruguay, Venezuela. **Twenty Latin American Republics**—Argentina, Bolivia, Brazil, Chile, Colombia, Costa Rica, Cuba, Dominican Republic, Ecuador, El Salvador, Guatemala, Haiti, Honduras, Mexico, Nicaragua, Panama, Paraguay, Peru, Uruguay, Venezuela. **CAFTA-DR (Dominican Republic-Central America-U.S. Free Trade Agreement)**—Costa Rica, Dominican Republic, El Salvador, Guatemala, Honduras, Nicaragua. **Central American Common Market**—Costa Rica, El Salvador, Guatemala, Honduras, Nicaragua. **NATO (North Atlantic Treaty Org.) Allies**—Albania, Belgium, Bulgaria, Canada, Croatia, Czech Republic, Denmark, Estonia, France, Germany, Greece, Hungary, Iceland, Italy, Latvia, Lithuania, Luxembourg, Netherlands, Norway, Poland, Portugal, Romania, Slovakia, Slovenia, Spain, Turkey, United Kingdom. **OPEC (Org. of Petroleum Exporting Countries)**—Algeria, Angola, Ecuador, Iran, Iraq, Kuwait, Libya, Nigeria, Qatar, Saudi Arabia, United Arab Emirates, Venezuela.

U.S. Exports and Imports by Principal Commodities, 2014

Source: U.S. Census Bureau and U.S. Bureau of Economic Analysis, U.S. Dept. of Commerce

(in millions of dollars)

Item	Exports	Imports
Total[1]	**$1,620,532**	**$2,347,685**
Manufactured goods	**1,192,583**	**1,927,026**
Agricultural commodities	**150,006**	**111,855**
Food and live animals	**108,494**	**97,055**
Live animals other than fish	927	3,542
Meat and preparations	19,332	8,914
Dairy products and birds	6,290	1,989
Fish and preparations	5,369	20,112
Cereals and preparations	26,892	9,235
Vegetables and fruits	22,245	28,193
Sugar, preparations, and honey	2,229	4,541
Coffee, tea, cocoa, and spices	3,147	13,021
Feeding stuff for animals	13,172	3,101
Miscellaneous edible products	8,891	4,407
Beverages and tobacco	**6,462**	**21,594**
Beverages	4,949	19,537
Tobacco and manufactures	1,513	2,056
Crude materials except fuels	**85,535**	**36,504**
Hides, skins, and furskins (raw)	2,927	307
Oil seeds and oleaginuos fruits	26,121	2,199
Crude rubber	3,148	3,772
Cork and wood	7,273	7,188
Pulp and waste paper	8,689	3,588
Textile fibers including waste	6,916	1,419
Crude fertilizers	2,813	2,934
Metalliferous ores and metal scrap	24,485	8,835
Crude animal and vegetable materials	3,164	6,261
Mineral fuels and lubricants	**153,697**	**347,477**
Coal, coke, and briquettes	8,718	1,196
Petroleum products and preparations	126,928	326,715
Gas, natural, and manufactured	17,487	16,896
Electric current	564	2,670
Animal and vegetable oils	**2,793**	**5,776**
Animal oil and fat	725	244
Fixed vegetable fats and oil, crude	1,682	5,379
Animal or vegetable fats, processed	385	153
Chemicals and related products	**203,076**	**207,714**
Organic chemicals	39,574	52,169
Inorganic chemicals	11,431	13,137
Dyeing, tanning, and coloring materials	7,697	3,967
Medicinal and pharmaceutical products	46,264	76,166

Item	Exports	Imports
Essential oil and reinoids	$15,377	$13,337
Fertilizers	3,725	8,104
Plastics in primary forms	35,137	15,754
Plastics in nonprimary forms	12,808	9,629
Chemical materials and products	31,064	15,450
Manufactured goods by material	**117,755**	**254,193**
Leather and leather manufactures	1,437	1,398
Rubber manufactures	10,177	21,821
Cork and wood manufactures	2,216	9,569
Paper and paperboard	16,034	16,698
Textile yarn, fabrics	13,261	26,996
Nonmetallic mineral manufactures	13,050	45,121
Iron and steel	18,427	46,828
Nonferrous metals	15,548	38,538
Manufactures of metals	27,606	47,223
Machinery and transport equipment	**534,213**	**939,287**
Power generating machinery	40,186	66,378
Specialized industrial machinery	48,744	47,298
Metalworking machinery	5,813	9,932
General industrial machinery	70,252	92,447
Office machinery	21,849	117,903
Telecommunications equipment	23,715	152,582
Electrical machinery	80,905	158,714
Road vehicles	121,548	256,882
Transport equipment	121,200	37,151
Miscellaneous manufactured articles	**122,935**	**348,643**
Prefabricated buildings	3,245	11,483
Furniture	6,476	41,462
Travel goods	568	10,995
Apparel and clothing accessories	3,424	90,157
Footwear	826	26,014
Scientific and controlling equipment	50,006	50,480
Photographic equipment	6,462	14,331
Miscellaneous manufactured articles	51,928	103,721
Miscellaneous commodities	**64,409**	**89,444**
Special transactions	8,033	61,708
Coin, including gold coin	303	1,645
Coin, other than gold	32	15
Gold, nonmonetary	21,260	14,434
Low value estimate	34,781	11,642
Re-exports	**221,163**	**NA**
Agricultural commodities	4,607	NA
Manufactured goods	209,703	NA

NA = Not applicable. (1) Total on Census Bureau basis; includes re-exports.

Trends in U.S. Foreign Trade, 1790-2014

Source: U.S. Census Bureau and U.S. Bureau of Economic Analysis, U.S. Dept. of Commerce

In 1790, U.S. exports and imports combined came to $43 mil, and there was a $3 mil trade deficit. The trade balance was positive for much of the 20th century, but the U.S. has had a trade deficit in every year since 1975.

(in millions of dollars)

Year	Exports	Imports	Trade balance	Year	Exports	Imports	Trade balance	Year	Exports	Imports	Trade balance
1790	$20	$23	–$3	1895	$808	$732	$76	1995	$794,387	$890,771	–$96,384
1795	48	70	–22	1900	1,394	850	545	1996	851,602	955,667	–104,065
1800	71	91	–20	1905	1,519	1,118	401	1997	934,453	1,042,726	–108,273
1805	96	121	–25	1910	1,745	1,557	188	1998	933,174	1,099,314	–166,140
1810	67	85	–19	1915	2,769	1,674	1,094	1999	969,867	1,228,485	–258,617
1815	53	113	–60	1920	8,228	5,278	2,950	2000	1,075,321	1,447,837	–372,517
1820	70	74	–5	1925	4,910	4,227	683	2001	1,005,654	1,367,165	–361,511
1825	91	90	1	1930	3,843	3,061	782	2002	978,706	1,397,660	–418,955
1830	72	63	9	1935	2,283	2,047	235	2003	1,020,418	1,514,308	–493,890
1835	115	137	–22	1940	4,021	2,625	1,396	2004	1,161,549	1,771,433	–609,883
1840	124	98	25	1945	9,806	4,159	5,646	2005	1,286,022	2,000,267	–714,245
1845	106	113	–7	1950	9,997	8,954	1,043	2006	1,457,642	2,219,358	–761,716
1850	144	174	–29	1955	14,298	11,566	2,732	2007	1,653,548	2,358,922	–705,375
1855	219	258	–39	1960	25,940	22,432	3,508	2008	1,841,612	2,550,339	–708,726
1860	334	354	–20	1965	35,285	30,621	4,664	2009	1,583,053	1,966,827	–383,774
1865	166	239	–73	1970	56,640	54,386	2,254	2010	1,853,606	2,348,263	–494,658
1870	393	436	–43	1975	132,585	120,181	12,404	2011	2,127,021	2,675,646	–548,625
1875	513	533	–20	1980	271,834	291,241	–19,407	2012	2,216,540	2,754,145	–537,605
1880	836	668	168	1985	289,070	410,950	–121,880	2013	2,280,194	2,756,586	–476,392
1885	742	578	165	1990	535,233	616,097	–80,864	2014	2,345,424	2,850,471	–505,047
1890	858	789	69								

Note: Figures shown using Balance of Payments basis.

World Trade Organization (WTO)

The World Trade Organization is an international body that seeks to promote free trade by eliminating barriers to trade. Founded in 1995, the WTO had grown to 161 member countries as of June 1, 2015, with 23 others, including Belarus and Iran, granted observer status. International intergovernmental organizations, such as the International Monetary Fund and the World Bank, may also be granted observer status. With the exception of Vatican City, observers must start accession negotiations within five years of becoming observers.

U.S. Trade in Goods and Services, 2014

Source: U.S. Census Bureau and U.S. Bureau of Economic Analysis, U.S. Dept. of Commerce
(top countries as ranked by amount of total trade with U.S.; in millions of dollars)

Country and category	Food and live animals	Beverages and tobacco	Crude materials, except fuels	Mineral fuels, lubricants	Chemicals	Manufactured goods	Machinery and transport equipment	Misc. manufactured	Commodities and transactions[1]	Total
Canada										
U.S. exports to	$22,476	$1,878	$7,758	$32,619	$33,853	$38,734	$133,056	$30,772	$10,463	**$312,125**
U.S. imports fr.	–22,212	–880	–14,249	–119,603	–28,229	–40,706	–93,812	–13,164	–18,623	**–353,229**
Trade balance	264	998	–6,491	–86,984	5,624	–1,972	39,245	17,608	–8,159	**–41,104**
China										
U.S. exports to	7,279	337	31,033	1,770	13,746	6,404	52,700	8,855	1,390	**123,676**
U.S. imports fr.	–6,144	–72	–2,307	–453	–16,933	–56,443	–249,532	–149,824	–4,595	**–486,355**
Trade balance	1,135	264	28,726	1,318	–3,187	–50,038	–196,832	–140,969	–3,205	**–362,679**
Mexico										
U.S. exports to	15,188	540	8,516	23,668	27,978	31,618	107,195	17,528	7,443	**240,326**
U.S. imports fr.	–17,206	–4,178	–1,797	–30,689	–6,261	–20,276	–173,676	–31,264	–11,508	**–296,953**
Trade balance	–2,017	–3,638	6,719	–7,020	21,717	11,342	–66,481	–13,736	–4,065	**–56,627**
Japan										
U.S. exports to	12,284	555	4,237	2,721	11,352	3,593	21,152	9,738	1,285	**66,964**
U.S. imports fr.	–654	–83	–662	–526	–9,524	–10,642	–101,672	–10,207	–3,425	**–137,438**
Trade balance	11,630	472	3,575	2,195	1,828	–7,049	–80,520	–469	–2,140	**–70,474**
Germany										
U.S. exports to	1,417	264	1,933	673	7,606	3,699	24,528	7,180	2,057	**49,443**
U.S. imports fr.	–1,239	–428	–969	–445	–24,087	–10,575	–72,468	–11,299	–3,938	**–125,464**
Trade balance	177	–164	963	227	–16,481	–6,876	–47,939	–4,120	–1,882	**–76,022**
South Korea										
U.S. exports to	6,052	100	3,269	1,830	7,229	2,915	18,148	4,178	702	**44,471**
U.S. imports fr.	–507	–159	–557	–3,101	–3,587	–11,295	–47,698	–3,828	–1,011	**–71,746**
Trade balance	5,545	–59	2,712	–1,271	3,642	–8,380	–29,550	349	–310	**–27,275**
United Kingdom										
U.S. exports to	1,254	444	1,901	2,432	6,840	4,242	22,233	8,814	5,618	**53,823**
U.S. imports fr.	–697	–1,973	–297	–5,885	–9,472	–4,457	–20,535	–6,976	–5,106	**–55,412**
Trade balance	558	–1,529	1,604	–3,453	–2,632	–215	1,697	1,837	512	**–1,589**

Note: Figures for exports are "free alongside ship" values; figures for imports are "cost, insurance, and freight" values. Neither is directly comparable with the Census Bureau basis shown in other tables in this section. Trade balance is with U.S. Total includes categories not shown here. (1) Not classified elsewhere.

Foreign Exchange Rates, 1970-2014

Source: Federal Reserve Board

One U.S. dollar was worth the following amounts in each country's national currency; exchange rates are annual averages.

Year	1970	1980	1990	2000	2005	2010	2011	2012	2013	2014
Australia (dollar)	0.898	0.877	1.280	1.720	1.311	1.087	0.968	0.965	1.033	1.107
Austria (schilling; euro)	25.880	12.945	11.370	1.083	0.803	0.754	0.718	0.778	0.753	0.752
Belgium (franc; euro)	49.680	29.237	33.418	1.083	0.803	0.754	0.718	0.778	0.753	0.752
Brazil (real)	NA	NA	NA	1.830	2.435	1.760	1.672	1.954	2.157	2.351
Canada (dollar)	1.010	1.169	1.167	1.485	1.211	1.030	0.989	1.000	1.030	1.104
China (yuan)	NA	NA	NA	8.278	8.194	6.770	6.463	6.309	6.148	6.162
Denmark (krone)	7.489	5.634	6.189	8.095	5.995	5.627	5.354	5.792	5.617	5.615
France (franc; euro)	5.520	4.225	5.445	1.083	0.803	0.754	0.718	0.778	0.753	0.752
Germany[1] (deutschemark; euro)	3.648	1.817	1.616	1.083	0.803	0.754	0.718	0.778	0.753	0.752
Greece (drachma; euro)	30.000	42.620	158.510	365.920	0.803	0.754	0.718	0.778	0.753	0.752
Hong Kong (dollar)	NA	NA	NA	7.793	7.778	7.769	7.784	7.757	7.757	7.755
India (rupee)	7.576	7.890	17.504	45.000	44.000	45.650	46.580	53.370	58.510	61.000
Ireland (pound; euro)	2.396	2.058	1.659	1.083	0.803	0.754	0.718	0.778	0.753	0.752
Italy (lira; euro)	623.000	856.000	1,198.000	1.083	0.803	0.754	0.718	0.778	0.753	0.752
Japan (yen)	357.600	226.630	144.790	107.800	110.110	87.780	79.700	79.820	97.600	105.740
Malaysia (ringgit)	3.090	2.177	2.705	3.800	3.787	3.218	3.056	3.086	3.149	3.270
Mexico (new peso)	NA	NA	2.812	9.459	10.894	12.623	12.427	13.154	12.758	13.302
Netherlands (guilder; euro)	3.597	1.988	1.821	1.083	0.803	0.754	0.718	0.778	0.753	0.752
Norway (krone)	7.140	4.938	6.260	8.813	6.441	6.045	5.602	5.818	5.877	6.297
Portugal (escudo; euro)	28.750	50.080	142.550	1.083	0.803	0.754	0.718	0.778	0.753	0.752
Singapore (dollar)	3.080	2.141	1.813	1.725	1.664	1.363	1.257	1.249	1.251	1.257
South Korea (won)	310.570	607.430	707.760	1,130.900	1,023.750	1,155.740	1,106.940	1,126.160	1,094.670	1,052.290
Spain (peseta; euro)	69.720	71.760	101.930	1.083	0.803	0.754	0.718	0.778	0.753	0.752
Sweden (krona)	5.170	4.231	5.919	9.174	7.471	7.205	6.488	6.772	6.512	6.858
Switzerland (franc)	4.316	1.677	1.389	1.690	1.246	1.043	0.886	0.938	0.927	0.915
Taiwan (dollar)	NA	NA	NA	31.260	32.131	31.498	29.382	29.558	29.680	30.299
Thailand (baht)	21.000	20.476	25.585	40.210	40.252	31.700	30.462	31.055	30.696	32.461
United Kingdom (pound)	0.417	0.430	0.560	0.660	0.549	0.647	0.623	0.634	0.639	0.607

NA = Not available. **Note:** The euro, the European Union's single currency, replaced the national currencies in the EU nations shown above. Since 1999 (or 2001 in the case of Greece), the euro has been fixed at the following conversion rates: 13.7603 Austrian schillings, 40.3399 Belgian francs, 6.55957 French francs, 1.95583 German marks, 340.750 Greek drachmas, 0.787564 Irish pounds, 1,936.27 Italian lire, 2.20371 Netherlands guilders, 200.482 Portuguese escudos, and 166.386 Spanish pesetas. (1) West Germany before 1991.

Top U.S. Trading Partners, 1995-2014

Source: U.S. Census Bureau, U.S. Dept. of Commerce
(in millions of dollars; top five countries as ranked by amount of total trade with U.S. in 2014)

Country/category	1995	2000	2005	2010	2011	2012	2013	2014
Canada								
U.S. exports	$127,226.0	$178,940.9	$211,898.7	$249,256.5	$281,291.5	$292,650.5	$301,609.6	$312,032.0
U.S. imports from	144,369.9	230,838.3	290,384.3	277,636.7	315,324.8	324,264.0	332,552.8	346,062.6
Trade balance	–17,143.9	–51,897.4	–78,485.6	–28,380.3	–34,033.2	–31,613.5	–30,943.2	–34,030.6
China								
U.S. exports to	11,753.7	16,185.2	41,192.0	91,911.1	104,121.5	110,515.6	121,736.4	124,024.0
U.S. imports from	45,543.2	100,018.2	243,470.1	364,952.6	–399,371.2	–425,626.2	440,447.7	466,656.5
Trade balance	–33,789.5	–83,833.0	–202,278.1	–273,041.6	–295,249.7	–315,110.6	–318,711.3	–342,632.5
Mexico								
U.S. exports to	46,292.1	111,349.0	120,247.6	163,664.6	198,288.7	215,907.1	226,079.1	240,326.2
U.S. imports from	62,100.4	135,926.3	170,108.6	229,985.6	–262,873.6	–277,593.6	280,528.8	294,157.5
Trade balance	–15,808.3	–24,577.3	–49,861.0	–66,321.0	–64,584.9	–61,686.5	–54,449.7	–53,831.3
Japan								
U.S. exports to	64,342.7	64,924.4	54,680.6	60,471.9	65,799.7	69,963.6	65,205.8	66,964.1
U.S. imports from	123,479.3	146,479.4	138,003.7	120,552.1	128,927.9	146,437.7	–138,573.3	133,938.7
Trade balance	–59,136.6	–81,555.0	–83,323.1	–60,080.3	–63,128.2	–76,474.1	–73,367.5	–66,974.6
Germany								
U.S. exports to	22,394.3	29,448.4	34,183.7	48,155.3	49,294.2	48,800.5	47,361.6	49,442.6
U.S. imports from	36,843.9	58,512.9	84,750.9	82,450.4	–98,684.3	–109,225.7	–114,344.5	–123,181.0
Trade balance	–14,449.6	–29,064.5	–50,567.2	–34,295.1	–49,390.1	–60,425.2	–66,982.9	–73,738.5

Note: Figures shown are on Census Bureau basis.

Busiest U.S. Ports, 2013

Source: U.S. Army Corps of Engineers, Dept. of the Army, U.S. Dept. of Defense
(figures in millions of tons; ranked by total tonnage handled)

Rank	Port	Domestic	Foreign	Total
1.	South Louisiana, LA	126.9	111.7	238.6
2.	Houston, TX	69.7	159.6	229.2
3.	New York, NY-NJ	46.7	76.6	123.3
4.	Beaumont, TX	33.4	61.0	94.4
5.	Long Beach, CA	10.8	73.7	84.5
6.	New Orleans, LA	43.2	34.0	77.2
7.	Corpus Christi, TX	31.9	44.2	76.2
8.	Baton Rouge, LA	38.7	25.1	63.9
9.	Los Angeles, CA	5.9	52.0	57.9
10.	Plaquemines, LA	33.8	23.1	56.9
11.	Lake Charles, LA	25.5	31.1	56.6
12.	Mobile, AL	23.3	30.7	54.0
13.	Texas City, TX	19.3	30.4	49.7
14.	Norfolk Harbor, VA	6.6	42.3	48.9
15.	Huntington-Tristate, WV	46.8	0.0	46.8
16.	Baltimore, MD	6.6	30.0	36.6
17.	Duluth-Superior, MN-WI	28.7	7.7	36.5
18.	Port Arthur, TX	9.5	25.2	34.7
19.	St. Louis, MO-IL	33.6	0.0	33.6
20.	Pittsburgh, PA	32.7	0.0	32.7
21.	Pascagoula, MS	8.3	24.1	32.4
22.	Tampa, FL	21.7	10.7	32.4
23.	Savannah, GA	1.8	30.2	32.0
24.	Newport News, VA	0.8	29.0	29.8
25.	Valdez, AK	28.2	0.0	28.2
26.	Philadelphia, PA	11.2	14.9	26.0
27.	Richmond, CA	9.4	14.1	23.5
28.	Portland, OR	8.4	15.0	23.4
29.	Tacoma, WA	4.5	18.4	22.9
30.	Port Everglades, FL	9.9	11.8	21.7
31.	Seattle, WA	5.7	14.8	20.6
32.	Freeport, TX	7.2	12.5	19.7
33.	Oakland, CA	2.8	16.5	19.3
34.	Paulsboro, NJ	7.1	12.0	19.1
35.	Charleston, SC	2.0	16.5	18.5
36.	Boston, MA	5.7	11.4	17.1
37.	Two Harbors, MN	16.6	0.1	16.7
38.	Jacksonville, FL	6.7	9.7	16.5
39.	Chicago, IL	13.9	1.6	15.4
40.	Honolulu, HI	12.9	1.4	14.3
41.	Memphis, TN	14.2	0.0	14.2
42.	Longview, WA	2.5	11.2	13.7
43.	Detroit, MI	10.7	2.3	13.0
44.	Indiana Harbor, IN	12.1	0.3	12.4
45.	Portland, ME	0.9	11.1	12.0
46.	Marcus Hook, PA	6.3	5.6	11.9
47.	Cincinnati, OH	11.7	0.0	11.7
48.	Cleveland, OH	9.9	1.5	11.5
49.	Galveston, TX	7.1	4.3	11.4
50.	Albany, NY	10.0	1.0	11.0

World's Busiest Ports, 2011-13

Source: United Nations Conference on Trade and Development
(ranked by throughput volume in 2013 as measured in twenty-ft equivalent units (TEUs))

Rank, port	Volume (TEUs)			Percent change	
	2011	2012	2013[1]	2011-12	2012-13
1. Shanghai, China	31,700,000	32,529,000	36,617,000	2.62%	12.57%
2. Singapore[2]	29,937,700	31,649,400	32,600,000	5.72	3.00
3. Shenzhen, China	22,569,800	22,940,130	23,279,000	1.64	1.48
4. Hong Kong, China	24,384,000	23,117,000	22,352,000	–5.20	–3.31
5. Busan, South Korea	16,184,706	17,046,177	17,686,000	5.32	3.75
6. Ningbo, China	14,686,200	15,670,000	17,351,000	6.70	10.73
7. Qingdao, China	13,020,000	14,503,000	15,520,000	11.39	7.01
8. Guangzhou, China	14,400,000	14,743,600	15,309,000	2.39	3.83
9. Dubai, United Arab Emirates	13,000,000	13,270,000	13,641,000	2.08	2.80
10. Tianjin, China	11,500,000	12,300,000	13,000,000	6.96	5.69
11. Rotterdam, Netherlands	11,876,921	11,865,916	11,621,000	–0.09	–2.06
12. Port Klang, Malaysia	9,603,926	10,001,495	10,350,000	4.14	3.48
13. Dalian, China	6,400,000	8,064,000	10,015,000	26.00	24.19
14. Kaohsiung, Taiwan	9,636,289	9,781,221	9,938,000	1.50	1.60
15. Hamburg, Germany	9,014,165	8,863,896	9,258,000	–1.67	4.45
16. Long Beach, CA, U.S.	6,061,099	6,045,662	8,730,000	–0.25	44.40
17. Antwerp, Belgium	8,664,243	8,635,169	8,578,000	–0.34	–0.66
18. Xiamen, China	6,460,700	7,201,700	8,008,000	11.47	11.20
19. Los Angeles, CA, U.S.	7,940,511	8,077,714	7,869,000	1.73	–2.58
20. Tanjung Pelepas, Malaysia	7,500,000	7,700,000	7,628,000	2.67	–0.94
Total top 20	**274,540,260**	**284,005,080**	**299,350,000**	**3.45**	**5.40**

Note: A TEU is the size of a typical shipping container. (1) Preliminary. (2) Port of Jurong not included.

U.S. Railroad Freight and Miles, 1890-2013

Source: Assn. of Amer. Railroads; Bureau of Transportation Statistics, Research and Innovative Tech. Admin., U.S. Dept. of Transportation

(freight figures in billion ton-miles)

Year	Class I freight[1]	All freight	Miles[2]	Year	Class I freight[1]	All freight	Miles[2]	Year	Class I freight[1]	All freight	Miles[2]
1890 . . .	NA	76	163,597	1950 . . .	589	592	223,779	2005 . . .	1,696	1,733	140,810
1900 . . .	NA	142	193,346	1960 . . .	572	575	217,552	2009 . . .	1,532	1,582	139,118
1910 . . .	NA	255	240,293	1970 . . .	765	771	205,782	2010 . . .	1,691	NA	138,623
1920 . . .	410	414	252,845	1980 . . .	919	932	178,056	2011 . . .	1,729	NA	138,565
1930 . . .	383	386	249,052	1990 . . .	1,034	1,064	145,979	2012 . . .	1,713	NA	138,524
1940 . . .	373	375	233,670	2000 . . .	1,466	1,546	144,473	2013 . . .	1,741	NA	NA

NA = Not available. **Note:** A ton-mile equals one ton of freight transported one statute mile. (1) Largest class of freight railroad companies, determined by annual operating revenue. (2) Aggregate length of operating roadway in U.S., excluding yard tracks, sidings, and parallel tracks.

Merchant Fleets of the World, 2014

Source: *Review of Maritime Transport, 2014*, United Nations Conference on Trade and Development.

(ranked by tonnage under flag of registration as of Jan. 31, 2014; figures in thousands of dead-weight tons)

Flag of registration	Number of ships	Tonnage	Percent of world total	Tonnage owned by nation of registration	Tonnage owned by another nation	Foreign ownership as % of total tonnage
Panama	7,068	355,700	21.21%	589	355,111	99.83%
Liberia	3,126	205,206	12.24	10	205,195	99.99
Marshall Islands	2,207	152,339	9.08	457	151,882	99.70
Hong Kong	2,065	138,134	8.24	18,637	119,497	86.51
Singapore	2,318	103,467	6.17	41,080	62,387	60.30
Greece	883	77,078	4.60	70,499	6,579	8.54
Bahamas	1,327	74,874	4.47	1,104	73,770	98.53
China	2,802	73,522	4.38	73,252	270	0.37
Malta	1,698	72,935	4.35	446	72,489	99.39
Cyprus	937	32,594	1.94	6,131	26,462	81.19
Isle of Man	409	23,711	1.41	0	23,711	100.00
Italy	719	20,022	1.19	18,790	1,232	6.15
United Kingdom	658	18,805	1.12	8,264	10,541	56.06
Norway (NIS)[1]	531	18,221	1.09	15,035	3,187	17.49
Japan	766	17,915	1.07	17,871	44	0.24
South Korea	777	16,881	1.01	16,266	615	3.64
Germany	381	16,380	0.98	15,987	393	2.40
India	702	15,245	0.91	14,636	608	3.99
Denmark (DIS)[2]	381	14,371	0.86	13,276	1,095	7.62
Indonesia	1,609	13,846	0.83	12,519	1,327	9.58
Antigua and Barbuda	1,207	13,391	0.80	1	13,390	100.00
United States	850	11,848	0.71	8,495	3,353	28.30
Tanzania	163	11,663	0.70	26	11,637	99.77
Bermuda	145	11,542	0.69	210	11,333	98.18
Malaysia	531	9,212	0.55	8,668	544	5.91
Turkey	632	8,891	0.53	8,600	291	3.27
Netherlands	926	8,789	0.52	6,572	2,217	25.22
France	226	7,577	0.45	4,096	3,480	45.93
Belgium	110	6,693	0.40	3,733	2,959	44.22
Vietnam	811	6,652	0.40	6,511	141	2.12

(1) Norwegian Intl. Shipping Register. (2) Danish Intl. Shipping Register.

U.S. International Transactions, 1970-2014

Source: U.S. Bureau of Economic Analysis, U.S. Dept. of Commerce

(in millions of dollars)

CURRENT ACCOUNT	1970	1980	1990	2000	2005	2010	2013	2014[1]
Exports of goods and services and income payments (credits)	**$68,388**	**$344,440**	**$712,128**	**$1,471,532**	**$1,895,983**	**$2,630,799**	**$3,178,744**	**$3,291,353**
Goods	42,469	224,250	387,401	784,940	913,016	1,290,273	1,592,784	1,635,133
Services	14,171	47,585	147,833	290,381	373,006	563,333	687,410	709,395
Primary income receipts	11,748	72,605	176,894	358,822	543,982	684,915	780,120	819,705
Imports of goods and services and income payments (debits)	**66,055**	**342,124**	**791,097**	**1,882,288**	**2,641,418**	**3,074,729**	**3,578,998**	**3,701,981**
Goods	39,866	249,750	498,438	1,231,722	1,695,820	1,938,950	2,294,453	2,370,920
Services	14,519	41,492	117,660	216,115	304,448	409,313	462,134	478,319
Primary income payments	5,514	42,533	148,345	339,643	476,349	507,254	580,466	601,801
Secondary income payments (current transfers)[2]	6,156	8,349	26,654	94,808	164,801	219,212	241,945	250,940
CAPITAL ACCOUNT								
Capital transfer receipts and other credits	NA	NA	0	35	15,462	0	0	0
Capital transfer payments and other debits	NA	NA	7,220	36	2,346	157	412	44
Net U.S. acquisition of financial assets[2]	9,336	86,968	103,985	589,315	572,317	963,449	644,763	820,488
Net U.S. incurrence of liabilities[3]	7,226	62,036	162,109	1,067,016	1,273,038	1,386,345	1,017,669	908,601
Balance on current account	**2,331**	**2,318**	**–78,969**	**–410,756**	**–745,434**	**–443,930**	**–400,254**	**–410,628**
Balance on capital account	**NA**	**NA**	**–7,221**	**–1**	**13,116**	**–157**	**–412**	**–44**
Net lending (+) or net borrowing (–) from financial-acct. transactions[4]	2,110	24,932	–58,124	–477,701	–700,721	–436,972	–370,658	–141,644

NA = Not available or applicable. (1) Preliminary. (2) Includes U.S. government and private transfers, such as U.S. government grants and pensions, fines and penalties, withholding taxes, personal transfers (remittances), insurance-related transfers, and other current transfers. (3) Excludes financial derivatives. (4) Net lending means that U.S. residents are net suppliers of funds to foreign residents, and net borrowing means the opposite. Net lending or net borrowing can be computed from current- and capital-account transactions or from financial-account transactions.

U.S. International Direct Investments, 1990-2014

Source: U.S. Bureau of Economic Analysis, U.S. Dept. of Commerce
(in millions of dollars)

	U.S. direct investment abroad					Foreign direct investment in U.S.				
	1990	2000	2010	2013	2014	1990	2000	2010	2013	2014
All countries[1]	**$430,521**	**$1,316,247**	**$3,741,910**	**$4,693,348**	**$4,920,653**	**$394,911**	**$1,256,867**	**$2,280,044**	**$2,754,704**	**$2,901,059**
Canada	69,508	132,472	295,206	**390,172**	386,121	29,544	114,309	192,463	235,247	261,247
Europe[1]	**214,739**	**687,320**	**2,034,559**	**2,650,757**	**2,781,666**	**247,320**	**887,014**	**1,659,774**	**1,894,777**	**1,977,215**
Austria	1,113	2,872	11,485	15,641	15,787	625	3,007	4,532	6,012	6,887
Belgium	9,464	17,973	43,975	51,702	48,128	3,900	14,787	69,565	92,197	89,097
Czech Rep.	NA	1,228	5,268	6,990	7,247	NA	NA	65	NA	NA
Denmark	1,726	5,270	11,802	13,605	14,108	819	4,025	7,772	10,084	12,912
Finland	544	1,342	1,597	1,919	1,784	1,504	8,875	4,943	7,251	9,100
France	19,164	42,628	78,320	77,690	76,823	18,650	125,740	189,763	208,793	223,164
Germany	27,609	55,508	103,319	123,322	115,533	28,232	122,412	203,077	207,131	224,114
Greece	282	795	1,775	–583	–447	NA	NA	–41	NA	NA
Hungary	NA	1,920	4,237	6,189	5,879	NA	NA	39,266	NA	NA
Ireland	5,894	35,903	158,851	247,755	310,598	1,340	25,523	24,097	17,067	16,195
Italy	14,063	23,484	27,137	28,018	26,733	1,524	6,576	20,142	24,843	21,824
Luxembourg	1,697	27,849	272,206	445,498	465,160	2,195	58,930	170,309	221,999	242,862
Netherlands	19,120	115,429	514,689	717,035	753,224	64,671	138,894	234,408	261,358	304,848
Norway	4,209	4,379	28,541	41,842	39,522	773	2,665	10,478	17,940	17,565
Poland	NA	3,884	13,152	12,540	11,516	NA	NA	4,386	NA	NA
Portugal	897	2,664	2,612	1,978	2,053	NA	NA	204	NA	NA
Russia	NA	1,147	10,040	13,140	9,263	NA	NA	5,689	NA	NA
Spain	7,868	21,236	52,390	34,146	36,363	792	5,068	43,095	48,438	58,138
Sweden	1,787	25,959	23,275	35,968	28,842	5,484	21,991	38,780	39,038	41,909
Switzerland	25,099	55,377	119,891	126,652	152,879	17,674	64,719	180,642	202,703	224,021
Turkey	522	1,826	4,155	4,366	4,384	NA	NA	749	NA	NA
UK	72,707	230,762	501,247	576,516	587,943	98,676	277,613	400,435	501,241	448,548
Latin America[1]	**71,413**	**266,576**	**752,788**	**849,777**	**897,679**	**20,168**	**53,691**	**62,130**	**116,031**	**127,032**
Argentina	2,531	17,488	11,747	13,447	13,418	NA	NA	464	NA	NA
Bahamas	NA	NA	28,501	NA	NA	1,535	1,254	1,753	510	597
Barbados	252	2,141	7,524	12,552	14,682	NA	NA	706	NA	NA
Bermuda	20,169	60,114	265,524	256,137	273,792	1,550	18,336	365	–9,586	–4,757
Brazil	14,384	36,717	66,963	69,335	70,457	377	882	1,357	1,104	616
Chile	1,896	10,052	30,747	28,617	27,560	NA	NA	391	NA	NA
Colombia	1,677	3,693	6,181	7,373	7,085	NA	NA	382	NA	NA
Costa Rica	251	1,716	1,827	998	955	NA	NA	–48	NA	NA
Curaçao[2]	NA	NA	NA	NA	NA	12,974	3,807	NA	5,162	2,779
Dominican Rep.	529	1,143	1,432	1,183	1,224	NA	NA	–142	NA	NA
Ecuador	280	832	1,283	581	650	NA	NA	77	NA	NA
Honduras	262	399	936	772	754	NA	NA	7	NA	NA
Mexico	10,313	39,352	85,751	102,418	107,825	575	7,462	10,970	17,036	17,710
Panama	9,289	30,758	5,156	4,636	4,687	4,188	3,819	952	1,346	1,185
Peru	599	3,130	7,196	5,364	6,486	NA	NA	182	NA	NA
UK isls. in Caribbean	5,929	33,451	191,680	263,096	287,546	–2,979	15,191	38,477	93,635	100,000
Venezuela	1,087	10,531	10,255	13,365	11,169	496	792	3,122	3,871	5,127
Africa[1]	**3,650**	**11,891**	**54,816**	**59,569**	**64,233**	**505**	**2,700**	**2,265**	**2,317**	**2,321**
Egypt	1,231	1,998	12,599	18,795	21,320	NA	NA	–277	NA	NA
Nigeria	–401	470	5,058	5,029	5,173	NA	NA	23	NA	NA
South Africa	775	3,562	6,017	6,377	6,181	10	704	699	880	765
Middle East[1]	**3,959**	**10,863**	**34,431**	**46,626**	**52,168**	**4,425**	**6,506**	**16,808**	**22,073**	**20,338**
Israel	746	3,735	9,464	9,758	10,801	640	3,012	8,714	10,052	8,982
Saudi Arabia	1,899	3,661	7,436	10,084	10,064	NA	NA	NA	NA	NA
UAE	409	683	4,935	11,717	15,035	99	64	747	2,253	2,700
Asia and Pacific[1]	**64,718**	**207,125**	**570,111**	**696,447**	**738,786**	**92,948**	**192,647**	**346,605**	**484,259**	**512,906**
Australia	15,110	34,838	125,421	169,917	180,315	6,542	18,775	35,632	47,616	47,340
China	354	11,140	58,996	59,886	65,767	NA	NA	3,300	8,451	9,465
Hong Kong	6,055	27,447	41,264	60,001	66,240	1,511	1,493	4,440	7,135	7,604
India	372	2,379	24,666	25,036	27,963	NA	NA	4,102	7,757	7,823
Indonesia	3,207	8,904	10,558	11,250	13,536	NA	NA	138	NA	NA
Japan	22,599	57,091	113,523	120,508	108,068	83,091	159,690	255,012	350,295	372,800
Korea, South	2,695	8,968	102,778	33,036	34,896	–1,009	3,110	15,746	31,800	36,056
Malaysia	1,466	7,910	26,233	12,959	14,357	56	310	338	636	809
New Zealand	3,156	4,271	11,791	7,646	7,760	157	395	584	1,011	1,011
Philippines	1,355	3,638	6,724	4,180	5,071	77	47	103	NA	NA
Singapore	3,975	24,133	5,399	159,759	179,764	1,289	5,087	21,517	19,283	20,609
Taiwan	2,226	7,836	22,188	16,809	17,073	836	3,174	4,642	6,563	5,676
Thailand	1,790	5,824	12,999	9,825	11,729	NA	NA	158	NA	NA
EU[1,3]	**180,491**	**609,674**	**2,036,631**	**2,402,905**	**2,514,771**	**220,874**	**814,033**	**1,457,842**	**1,661,393**	**1,723,599**
OPEC[4]	**7,145**	**28,545**	**53,114**	**60,221**	**63,545**	**4,216**	**4,330**	**11,282**	**15,660**	**16,204**

NA = Not available. **Note:** On a historical cost basis for comparison purposes. Direct investment in all industries. Book value of foreign direct investors' equity in, and net outstanding loans to, their U.S. affiliates. A U.S. affiliate is a U.S. business enterprise in which a single foreign direct investor owns at least 10% of the voting securities, or the equivalent. (1) Totals and subtotals include countries or territories not shown in table. (2) Curaçao figures before 2010 are for the entire Netherlands Antilles, a confederation that ended in 2010. (3) European Union members in 2014: Austria, Belgium, Bulgaria, Croatia, Cyprus, Czech Republic, Denmark, Estonia, Finland, France, Germany, Greece, Hungary, Ireland, Italy, Latvia, Lithuania, Luxembourg, Malta, Netherlands, Poland, Portugal, Romania, Slovakia, Slovenia, Spain, Sweden, and the United Kingdom. (4) Org. of Petroleum Exporting Countries in 2014: Algeria, Angola, Ecuador, Iran, Iraq, Kuwait, Libya, Nigeria, Qatar, Saudi Arabia, United Arab Emirates, and Venezuela.

TRANSPORTATION AND TRAVEL

Top Motor Vehicle Producing Nations, 2014

Source: International Organization of Motor Vehicle Manufacturers (OICA)
(in thousands of units; ranked by total production)

Nation	Total motor vehicles	Cars	Light commercial vehicles[1]	% change, 2013-14[2]
China[3]	23,723	19,920	3,803	7.3%
U.S.	11,661	4,253	7,408	5.4
Japan	9,775	8,277	1,497	1.5
Germany	5,908	5,604	304	3.3
South Korea	4,525	4,124	401	0.1
India	3,840	3,158	682	–1.5
Mexico	3,365	1,916	1,450	10.2
Brazil	3,146	2,315	831	–15.3
Spain	2,403	1,898	505	11.1
Canada	2,394	914	1,480	0.6
Russia	1,887	1,684	203	–13.6
Thailand	1,880	743	1,137	–23.5
France	1,817	1,495	322	4.4
UK	1,599	1,528	71	0.1
Indonesia	1,299	1,011	287	7.6
Czech Rep.	1,251	1,247	5	10.4
Turkey	1,170	733	437	4.0
Iran	1,091	926	165	46.7
Slovakia	993	993	0	1.8
Italy	698	401	297	6.0
Argentina	617	364	254	–22.0
Malaysia	597	547	49	–0.8
Poland	594	473	121	0.6%
South Africa	566	277	289	3.7
Belgium	517	482	35	2.6
Romania	391	391	0	–4.8
Taiwan	379	333	47	12.0
Uzbekistan	246	246	0	–0.4
Hungary	227	225	2	2.1
Australia	180	146	35	–16.5
Portugal	162	118	44	4.9
Austria	154	136	18	–7.3
Sweden	154	154	NA	–4.3
Slovenia	119	119	—	26.5
Finland	45	45	—	484.6
Netherlands	30	0	30	2.1
Ukraine	29	26	3	–43.0
Egypt	27	18	9	–30.8
Serbia	11	10	1	–2.1
Others	662	555	107	2.9
NAFTA	**17,420**	**7,082**	**10,338**	**5.6**
World total	**89,747**	**67,525**	**22,222**	**2.6**

NA = Not available. — = Less than 500 units. NAFTA = North American Free Trade Agreement. **Note:** Numbers may not add up to totals due to rounding. (1) Also includes heavy trucks, coaches, and buses. (2) Percent change in number of total motor vehicles. (3) Not including Taiwan.

World Motor Vehicle Production, 1950-2014

Source: For 1950-90, American Automobile Manufacturers Assn.; 2000-12, Automotive News Data Center and R.L. Polk; 2013-14, OICA
(in thousands of units)

Year	U.S.	Canada	Europe[1]	Japan	Other	World total	U.S. % of world total
1950	8,006	388	1,991	32	160	10,577	75.7%
1960	7,905	398	6,837	482	866	16,488	47.9
1970	8,284	1,160	13,049	5,289	1,637	29,419	28.2
1980	8,010	1,324	15,496	11,043	2,692	38,565	20.8
1990	9,783	1,928	18,866	13,487	4,496	48,554	20.1
2000	12,832	2,952	17,678	10,145	16,098	59,704	21.5
2002	12,328	2,624	17,419	10,240	16,975	59,587	20.7
2003	12,145	2,547	16,943	10,286	19,641	61,562	19.7
2004	12,021	2,698	20,850	10,512	16,573	65,654	18.3
2005	12,018	2,665	20,855	10,800	20,691	67,892	17.7
2006	11,351	2,545	21,490	11,486	23,180	70,992	16.0
2007	10,611	2,602	22,858	11,596	26,019	74,647	14.2
2008	8,503	2,046	21,608	10,969	31,224	67,602	12.6
2009	5,591	1,476	17,075	7,648	32,374	59,096	9.5
2010	7,632	2,074	19,371	9,197	35,036	73,311	10.4
2011	8,462	2,127	20,709	7,901	36,828	76,027	11.1
2012	10,142	2,454	22,324	9,448	36,714	81,082	12.5
2013	11,066	2,380	19,923	9,630	44,508	87,507	12.6
2014	11,661	2,394	20,382	9,775	45,536	89,747	13.0

Note: Data may not be fully comparable across all years because they are derived from different sources. Number of units may not add up to totals due to rounding. (1) Prior to 2004, numbers exclude Eastern European production.

New and Used Passenger Cars Imported Into the U.S. by Country of Origin, 1970-2014

Source: Foreign Trade Division, U.S. Census Bureau
(in number of units)

Year	Japan	Germany[1]	Italy	UK	Sweden	France	S. Korea	Mexico	Canada	Total[2]
1970	381,338	674,945	42,523	76,257	57,844	37,114	NA	NA	692,783	2,013,420
1975	695,573	370,012	102,344	67,106	51,993	15,647	NA	0	733,766	2,074,653
1980	1,991,502	338,711	46,899	32,517	61,496	47,386	NA	1	594,770	3,116,448
1985	2,527,467	473,110	8,689	24,474	142,640	42,882	NA	13,647	1,144,805	4,397,679
1990	1,867,794	245,286	11,045	27,271	93,084	1,976	201,475	215,986	1,220,221	3,944,602
1995	1,114,360	204,932	1,031	42,450	82,593	14	131,718	462,800	1,552,691	3,624,428
2000	1,839,093	488,323	3,125	81,196	86,707	134	568,121	934,000	2,138,811	6,324,284
2005	1,832,534	547,191	5,377	184,716	93,736	412	730,500	693,149	1,967,985	6,564,844
2006	2,347,532	532,022	5,469	148,014	81,008	567	697,061	947,824	1,963,922	7,380,077
2007	2,300,913	466,458	5,650	108,576	92,600	1,746	676,594	889,474	1,912,744	7,220,792
2008	2,190,013	502,971	5,783	110,737	59,638	28,198	612,300	928,273	1,609,005	6,525,836
2009	1,238,773	348,093	3,067	78,999	27,017	16,909	476,912	649,740	1,164,849	4,276,163
2010	1,569,220	506,053	4,298	96,689	38,749	4,153	515,601	902,565	1,741,493	5,668,111
2011	1,421,750	537,158	5,372	95,742	26,884	3,580	587,574	953,514	1,835,819	5,673,139
2012	1,723,014	629,579	11,767	114,073	24,653	10,949	705,089	1,052,212	2,094,793	6,590,863
2013	1,722,119	657,832	14,289	115,326	21,617	12,694	759,964	1,127,375	2,009,140	6,440,356
2014	1,530,386	624,892	21,587	105,113	26,443	25,292	895,141	1,290,183	2,021,986	6,541,023

NA = Not available. **Note:** Excludes cars assembled in U.S. foreign trade zones. (1) Figures prior to 1991 are for West Germany. (2) Includes units imported from countries not shown in table.

Passenger Car Production in U.S. Plants, 2012-14

Source: WardsAuto Group, a division of Penton
(in number of units)

	2014	2013	2012
FCA TOTAL[1]	**263,176**	**343,204**	**334,825**
Chrysler 200 Series	160,941	129,685	150,321
Chrysler Total	**160,941**	**129,685**	**150,321**
Dodge Avenger	18,533	121,944	113,541
Dodge Dart	83,099	88,973	69,645
Dodge Viper	549	1,501	—
Dodge Total	**102,181**	**212,418**	**183,186**
Lancia Flavia	54	1,101	1,318
FLAT ROCK ASSEMBLY[2] TOTAL	—	—	**133,004**
Ford Mustang	—	—	95,438
Mazda6	—	—	37,566
FORD TOTAL	**485,349**	**553,446**	**419,907**
Ford C-Max	27,094	38,532	19,890
Ford Focus	235,666	292,809	283,447
Ford Fusion	45,679	29,277	—
Ford Mustang	95,231	88,020	—
Ford Taurus	73,355	93,115	101,875
Ford Total	**477,025**	**541,753**	**405,212**
Lincoln MKS	8,324	11,693	14,695
GENERAL MOTORS TOTAL	**861,483**	**831,854**	**840,700**
Buick Lacrosse	51,473	53,484	56,561
Buick Verano	47,181	53,646	57,435
Buick Total	**98,654**	**107,130**	**113,996**
Cadillac ATS	38,254	47,650	26,278
Cadillac CTS	31,155	34,956	48,247
Cadillac ELR	2,468	271	—
Cadillac Total	**71,877**	**82,877**	**74,525**
Chevrolet Corvette	39,918	15,726	14,960
Chevrolet Cruze	290,028	282,946	279,382
Chevrolet Impala	17,971	36,210	—
Chevrolet Malibu	216,498	189,870	229,170
Chevrolet Sonic	105,499	94,038	97,840
Chevrolet Volt	20,699	22,507	24,196
Chevrolet Total	**690,613**	**641,297**	**645,548**
Opel Ampera	339	550	6,631
HYUNDAI TOTAL	**398,851**	**399,495**	**361,348**
Hyundai Elantra	162,943	194,059	138,997
Hyundai Sonata	235,908	205,436	222,351

	2014	2013	2012
HONDA TOTAL	**684,196**	**733,998**	**639,108**
Acura ILX	17,800	17,196	30,244
Acura TL	3,765	25,714	39,421
Acura TLX	36,947	—	—
Acura Total	**58,512**	**42,910**	**69,665**
Honda Accord	401,423	466,695	400,143
Honda Civic	224,261	224,393	169,300
Honda Total	**625,684**	**691,088**	**569,443**
KIA MOTORS TOTAL	**142,561**	**133,946**	**128,536**
Kia Optima	142,561	133,946	128,536
MERCEDES-BENZ TOTAL	**40,096**	—	—
Mercedes-Benz Mercedes C Class	40,096	—	—
MITSUBISHI TOTAL	—	—	**13,716**
Mitsubishi Galant	—	—	13,716
NISSAN TOTAL	**461,777**	**470,232**	**406,782**
Nissan Altima	366,472	383,818	334,710
Nissan Leaf	32,201	26,387	192
Nissan Maxima	58,156	48,247	71,877
Nissan Sentra	4,948	11,780	3
SUBARU TOTAL[3]	**148,481**	**137,803**	**143,529**
Subaru Legacy	55,005	40,800	50,403
Toyota Camry	93,476	97,003	93,126
TESLA TOTAL	**34,481**	**24,093**	**3,139**
Tesla Model S	34,481	24,093	3,139
TOYOTA TOTAL	**615,019**	**607,623**	**531,876**
Toyota Avalon	72,277	100,006	42,442
Toyota Camry	353,428	348,970	359,832
Toyota Corolla	189,314	158,647	129,602
VOLKSWAGEN TOTAL	**117,628**	**133,141**	**152,543**
Volkswagen Passat	117,628	133,141	152,543
TOTAL CARS	**4,253,098**	**4,368,835**	**4,109,013**

— = No production. (1) Fiat Chrysler Automobiles, or FCA, was formed in 2014 when Fiat acquired the remaining shares of Chrysler Group that it did not already own. (2) AutoAlliance Intl., a joint venture between Ford and Mazda, produced cars for both automakers (1992-2012). In 2012, Ford Motor Co. took full control of the plant and renamed it Flat Rock Assembly; it produces Ford Fusion and Mustang. (3) SIA (Subaru of Indiana Automotive) also builds the Toyota Camry in collaboration with Toyota.

Domestic and Imported Retail Car Sales in the U.S., 1980-2014

Source: WardsAuto Group, a division of Penton
(in number of units)

	Cars			Light trucks			All vehicles		
Year	Domestic[1]	Imports	Total cars	Domestic[1]	Imports	Total light trucks	Domestic[1]	Imports	Total vehicles
1980	6,579,778	2,369,457	8,949,235	1,750,735	478,887	2,229,622	8,330,513	2,848,344	11,178,857
1985	8,204,670	2,774,517	10,979,187	3,629,080	832,186	4,461,266	11,833,750	3,606,703	15,440,453
1990	6,918,869	2,384,346	9,303,215	3,956,756	611,941	4,568,697	10,875,625	2,996,287	13,871,912
1991	6,161,573	2,023,406	8,184,979	3,605,633	538,008	4,143,641	9,767,206	2,561,414	12,328,620
1992	6,285,916	1,927,197	8,213,113	4,247,097	408,003	4,655,100	10,533,013	2,335,200	12,868,213
1993	6,741,667	1,776,192	8,517,859	5,000,482	377,639	5,378,121	11,742,149	2,153,831	13,895,980
1994	7,255,303	1,735,214	8,990,517	5,658,302	409,759	6,068,061	12,913,605	2,144,973	15,058,578
1995	7,113,902	1,506,257	8,620,159	5,705,708	402,181	6,107,889	12,819,610	1,908,438	14,728,048
1996	7,206,349	1,272,196	8,478,545	6,179,881	438,757	6,618,638	13,386,230	1,710,953	15,097,183
1997	6,862,175	1,355,305	8,217,480	6,324,758	579,483	6,904,241	13,186,933	1,934,788	15,121,721
1998	6,705,208	1,379,781	8,084,989	6,802,016	656,002	7,458,018	13,507,224	2,035,783	15,543,007
1999	6,918,781	1,718,927	8,637,708	7,480,607	775,223	8,255,830	14,399,388	2,494,150	16,893,538
2000	6,761,603	2,016,120	8,777,723	7,719,707	852,325	8,572,032	14,481,310	2,868,445	17,349,755
2001	6,254,371	2,097,629	8,352,000	7,789,089	981,280	8,770,369	14,043,460	3,078,909	17,122,369
2002	5,816,671	2,225,584	8,042,255	7,707,738	1,066,375	8,774,113	13,524,409	3,291,959	16,816,368
2003	5,472,500	2,083,051	7,555,551	7,856,322	1,227,180	9,083,502	13,328,822	3,310,231	16,639,053
2004	5,333,496	2,149,059	7,482,555	8,138,107	1,246,258	9,384,365	13,471,603	3,395,317	16,866,920
2005	5,473,450	2,186,533	7,659,983	8,072,456	1,215,315	9,287,771	13,545,906	3,401,848	16,947,754
2006	5,416,828	2,344,764	7,761,592	7,396,058	1,346,750	8,742,808	12,812,886	3,691,514	16,504,400
2007	5,197,271	2,365,063	7,562,334	7,138,803	1,388,085	8,526,888	12,336,074	3,753,148	16,089,222
2008	4,490,863	2,278,271	6,769,134	5,329,165	1,096,469	6,425,634	9,820,028	3,374,740	13,194,768
2009	3,558,283	1,843,282	5,401,565	4,116,550	884,242	5,000,792	7,674,833	2,727,524	10,402,357
2010	3,791,499	1,844,240	5,635,739	5,020,441	898,644	5,919,085	8,811,940	2,742,884	11,554,824
2011	4,142,811	1,946,897	6,089,708	5,662,578	982,443	6,645,021	9,805,389	2,929,340	12,734,729
2012	5,119,114	2,125,325	7,244,439	6,137,440	1,060,720	7,198,160	11,256,554	3,186,045	14,442,599
2013	5,432,737	2,152,604	7,585,341	6,707,097	1,239,268	7,946,365	12,139,834	3,391,872	15,531,706
2014	5,589,374	2,098,245	7,687,619	7,387,697	1,359,910	8,747,607	12,977,071	3,458,155	16,435,226

Note: Vehicles are cars and light trucks belonging to gross vehicle weight (GWV) classes 1-3 (under 14,001 lbs). (1) Includes the U.S., Canada, and Mexico.

U.S. Vehicle Sales, 2000-14

Source: WardsAuto Group, a division of Penton

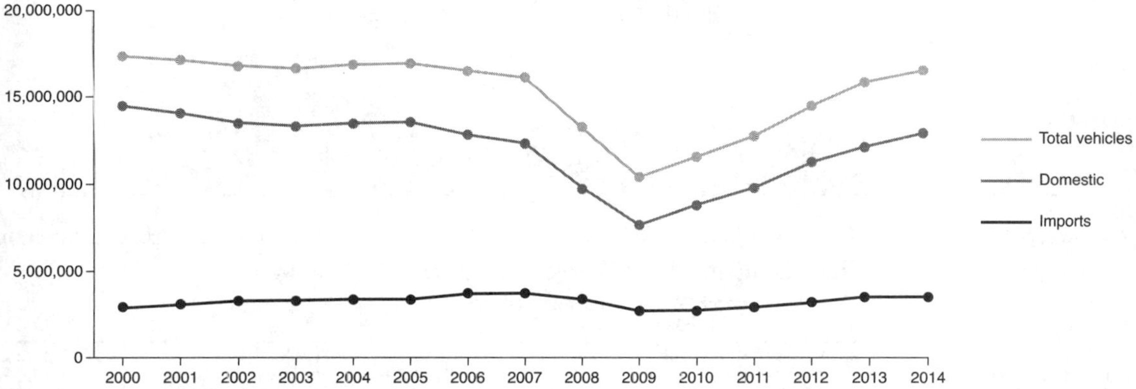

Note: Vehicles are cars and light trucks belonging to gross vehicle weight (GWV) classes 1-3 (under 14,001 lbs). Domestic sales include the U.S., Canada, and Mexico.

U.S. Sales of Hybrid and Electric Vehicles, 2000-14

Source: WardsAuto Group, a division of Penton; in number of units

Power type	2000	2005	2007	2008	2009	2010	2011	2012	2013	2014
Hybrid car	9,350	151,253	282,790	250,462	237,263	231,819	231,075	407,628	478,031	424,959
Hybrid light truck	0	54,575	70,072	65,226	53,477	42,286	30,432	24,170	20,023	26,872
Total hybrid	**9,350**	**205,828**	**352,862**	**315,688**	**290,740**	**274,105**	**261,507**	**431,798**	**498,054**	**451,831**
Electric car	463	0	0	27	675	326	10,447	14,534	47,424	64,163
Electric light truck	0	0	0	0	0	0	0	192	1,096	1,184
Total electric	**463**	**0**	**0**	**27**	**675**	**326**	**10,447**	**14,726**	**48,520**	**65,347**
Plug-in hybrid car	0	0	0	0	0	326	7,671	38,585	49,043	55,441
Plug-in hybrid light truck	0	0	0	0	0	0	0	0	0	100
Total plug-in hybrid	**0**	**0**	**0**	**0**	**0**	**326**	**7,671**	**38,585**	**49,043**	**55,441**

Top-Selling Passenger Cars in the U.S., 2011-14

Source: WardsAuto Group, a division of Penton
(ranked by number of vehicles sold)

Car	2014 sales	Car	2014 sales	Car	2014 sales
1. Toyota Camry	428,606	8. Hyundai Elantra	222,023	15. Kia Optima	159,020
2. Honda Accord	388,374	9. Ford Focus	219,634	16. Kia Soul	145,316
3. Toyota Corolla	339,498	10. Hyundai Sonata	216,936	17. Chevrolet Impala	140,280
4. Nissan Altima	335,644	11. Chevrolet Malibu	188,519	18. Nissan Versa	139,781
5. Honda Civic	325,981	12. Nissan Sentra	183,268	19. Chrysler 200 Series	117,363
6. Ford Fusion	306,860	13. Toyota Prius	166,802	20. Mazda3	104,985
7. Chevrolet Cruze	273,060	14. Volkswagen Jetta	160,873		

Car	2013 sales	Car	2012 sales	Car	2011 sales
1. Toyota Camry	408,484	1. Toyota Camry	404,886	1. Toyota Camry	308,510
2. Honda Accord	366,678	2. Honda Accord	331,872	2. Nissan Altima	268,981
3. Honda Civic	336,180	3. Honda Civic	317,909	3. Ford Fusion	248,067
4. Nissan Altima	320,723	4. Nissan Altima	302,934	4. Toyota Corolla	240,259
5. Toyota Corolla	302,180	5. Toyota Corolla	290,947	5. Honda Accord	235,625
6. Ford Fusion	295,280	6. Ford Focus	245,922	6. Chevrolet Cruze	231,732
7. Chevrolet Cruze	248,224	7. Ford Fusion	241,263	7. Hyundai Sonata	225,961
8. Hyundai Elantra	247,912	8. Chevrolet Cruze	237,758	8. Honda Civic	221,235
9. Ford Focus	234,570	9. Hyundai Sonata	230,605	9. Chevrolet Malibu	204,808
10. Hyundai Sonata	203,648	10. Chevrolet Malibu	210,951	10. Hyundai Elantra	186,361

U.S. Retail Car Sales by Vehicle Size, 1985-2014

Source: WardsAuto Group, a division of Penton
(as percent of total U.S. sales)

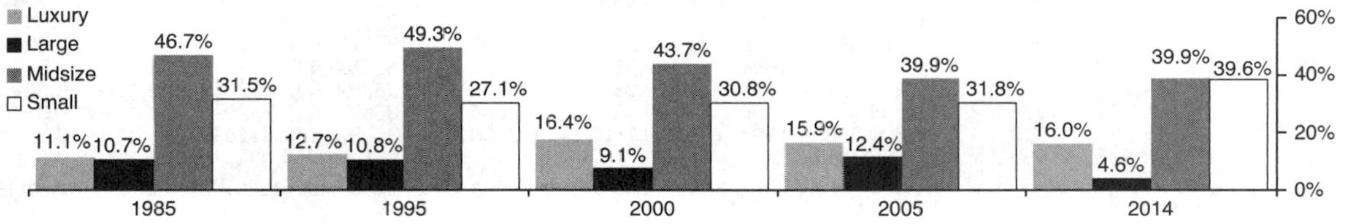

U.S. Light Truck Sales by Type, 1985-2014

Source: WardsAuto Group, a division of Penton
(as percent of total U.S. sales)

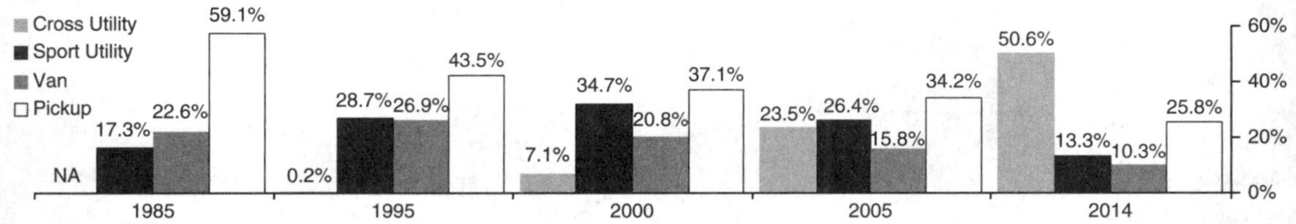

NA = Not applicable. **Note:** Comm. chassis sales (not shown) were 1.0% (for 1985), 0.7% (1995), 0.2% (2000), 0.1% (2005), 0.1% (2014).

Top-Selling Light Trucks in the U.S., 2012-14

Source: WardsAuto Group, a division of Penton
(ranked by number of vehicles sold)

Truck	2014 sales	Truck	2013 sales	Truck	2012 sales
1. Ford F-Series	701,102	1. Ford F-Series	713,960	1. Ford F-Series	607,854
2. Chevrolet Silverado	529,755	2. Chevrolet Silverado	480,414	2. Chevrolet Silverado	418,312
3. Ram Pickup	425,388	3. Ram Pickup	344,772	3. Ram Pickup	283,056
4. Honda CR-V	335,019	4. Honda CR-V	303,904	4. Honda CR-V	281,652
5. Ford Escape	306,212	5. Ford Escape	295,993	5. Ford Escape	261,008
6. Toyota RAV4	267,698	6. Chevrolet Equinox	238,192	6. Chevrolet Equinox	218,621
7. Chevrolet Equinox	242,242	7. Toyota RAV4	218,249	7. Toyota RAV4	171,877
8. GMC Sierra	211,833	8. Ford Explorer	192,397	8. Ford Explorer	164,207
9. Ford Explorer	209,994	9. GMC Sierra	184,389	9. GMC Sierra	157,185
10. Nissan Rogue	199,199	10. Jeep Grand Cherokee	174,275	10. Jeep Grand Cherokee	154,734

Most Popular Colors by Vehicle Type, 2014

Source: WardsAuto Group, a division of Penton; Axalta Coating Systems; for 2014 model year

Luxury cars/SUVs		Intermediate cars/CUVs		Compact/sports cars		Light trucks	
Color	**Percent**	**Color**	**Percent**	**Color**	**Percent**	**Color**	**Percent**
Black/black effect	32%	White/white pearl	22%	White/white pearl	20%	White/white pearl	31%
White/white pearl	22	Black/black effect	17	Black/black effect	19	Black/black effect	19
Gray	13	Gray	17	Silver	16	Silver	11
Silver	10	Silver	15	Gray	14	Red	11
Beige/brown	7	Red	12	Red	13	Gray	10
Red	6	Blue	7	Blue	7	Blue	8
Blue	4	Beige/brown	5	Beige/brown	6	Beige/brown	6
Yellow/gold	3	Green	2	Yellow/gold	1	Yellow/gold	1
Green	1	Yellow/gold	2	Green	1	Green	1
Other	2	Other	1	Other	3	Other	2

U.S. Light-Duty Vehicle Fuel Efficiency, 1975-2014

Source: Natl. Vehicle and Fuel Emissions Laboratory, Office of Transportation and Air Quality, U.S. Environmental Protection Agency

Cars and light-duty trucks (SUVs, minivans, passenger vans, and pickup trucks) showed significant fuel-efficiency improvements from 1975 through 1987, when the fuel economy for both reached a high of 22 miles per gallon (mpg). The fuel economy value mainly declined, 1988-2004, but since 2005, fuel economy has generally increased, reaching a new all-time high of 24.2 mpg in 2014.

Year[1]	Cars (mpg)	Light-duty trucks (mpg)	All light-duty vehicles (mpg)	Year[1]	Cars (mpg)	Light-duty trucks (mpg)	All light-duty vehicles (mpg)
1975	13.5	11.6	13.1	2004	22.9	16.5	19.3
1980	20.0	15.8	19.2	2005	23.1	16.9	19.9
1985	23.0	17.5	21.3	2006	23.0	17.2	20.1
1990	23.3	17.4	21.2	2007	23.7	17.4	20.6
1995	23.3	17.0	20.5	2008	23.9	17.8	21.0
1998	23.0	17.1	20.1	2009	25.0	18.5	22.4
1999	22.7	16.6	19.7	2010	25.7	18.8	22.6
2000	22.5	16.8	19.8	2011	25.6	19.1	22.4
2001	22.6	16.5	19.6	2012	27.0	19.3	23.6
2002	22.8	16.5	19.5	2013	27.6	19.8	24.1
2003	23.0	16.7	19.6	2014[2]	27.9	20.1	24.2

Note: Adjusted mpg composite values (city and highway fuel efficiency combined in a 55%/45% ratio) are used for all vehicles and are intended to reflect real-world use. (1) Because of changes in methodology, mpg figures prior to 1986 are not entirely comparable with later values. (2) Preliminary.

Registered Cars in the U.S., 1900-2013

Source: Office of Highway Policy Information, Federal Highway Administration, U.S. Dept. of Transportation

(number of automobiles for public and private use)

Year	Reg. cars	Year	Reg. cars	Year	Reg. cars	Year	Reg. cars	Year	Reg. cars
1900	8,000	1945	25,796,985	1990	133,700,497	1998	131,838,538	2006	135,399,945
1905	77,400	1950	40,339,077	1991	128,299,601	1999	132,432,044	2007	135,932,930
1910	458,377	1955	52,144,739	1992	126,581,148	2000	133,621,420	2008	137,079,843
1915	2,332,426	1960	61,671,390	1993	127,327,189	2001	137,633,467	2009	134,879,600
1920	8,131,522	1965	75,257,588	1994	127,883,469	2002	135,920,677	2010	130,892,240
1925	17,481,001	1970	89,243,557	1995	128,386,775	2003	135,669,897	2011	125,656,528
1930	23,034,753	1975	106,705,934	1996	129,728,311	2004	136,430,651	2012	111,289,906
1935	22,567,827	1980	121,600,843	1997	129,748,704	2005	136,568,083	2013	113,676,345
1940	27,465,826	1985	127,885,193						

Note: There were no publicly owned vehicles before 1925; statistics also exclude military vehicles for all years. Alaska and Hawaii data included since 1960.

Licensed Drivers by Age and Sex, 1980-2013

Source: Office of Highway Policy Information, Federal Highway Administration, U.S. Dept. of Transportation (numbers in thousands)

	1980	1990	2000	2010			2013			
Age (years)	Total	Total	Total	Male	Female	Total	Male	Female	Total	% total drivers
Under 16	**93**	**43**	**27**	**199**	**198**	**398**	**31**	**31**	**62**	**0.0%**
16	1,823	1,443	1,470	608	605	1,213	584	584	1,169	0.6
17	2,790	2,132	2,331	1,025	1,004	2,028	1,024	987	2,010	0.9
18	3,247	2,595	2,839	1,408	1,323	2,731	1,381	1,299	2,680	1.3
19	3,542	3,037	3,077	1,641	1,546	3,187	1,578	1,484	3,061	1.4
19 and under	**11,496**	**9,249**	**9,744**	**4,880**	**4,676**	**9,556**	**4,598**	**4,384**	**8,982**	**4.2**
20	3,636	3,229	3,140	1,744	1,682	3,426	1,690	1,605	3,294	1.6
21	3,733	3,249	3,172	1,756	1,717	3,474	1,747	1,687	3,435	1.6
22	3,811	3,262	3,182	1,757	1,725	3,483	1,807	1,769	3,576	1.7
23	3,938	3,398	3,247	1,767	1,748	3,515	1,858	1,831	3,689	1.7
24	3,915	3,758	3,225	1,792	1,779	3,571	1,843	1,832	3,675	1.7
20-24	**19,032**	**16,897**	**15,966**	**8,817**	**8,651**	**17,469**	**8,945**	**8,723**	**17,668**	**8.3**
25-29	18,925	19,895	17,586	9,179	9,253	18,431	9,129	9,213	18,341	8.6
30-34	17,369	20,578	19,155	8,934	8,915	17,849	9,083	9,273	18,357	8.7
35-39	13,696	19,055	21,059	9,079	9,082	18,161	8,567	8,707	17,274	8.1
40-44	11,134	16,905	21,093	9,613	9,565	19,178	9,333	9,412	18,745	8.8
45-49	10,076	13,020	19,154	10,381	10,433	20,814	9,621	9,678	19,299	9.1
50-54	10,090	10,484	16,868	10,241	10,388	20,628	10,207	10,401	20,608	9.7
55-59	9,770	9,438	12,760	9,127	9,313	18,440	9,564	9,835	19,399	9.1
60-64	8,232	9,235	9,915	7,847	8,011	15,858	8,179	8,478	16,657	7.9
65-69	6,580	8,375	8,386	5,652	5,816	11,468	6,494	6,733	13,227	6.2
70-74	NA	NA	7,468	4,029	4,202	8,231	4,533	4,775	9,307	4.4
75-79	NA	NA	5,911	2,966	3,192	6,158	3,091	3,329	6,420	3.0
80-84	NA	NA	3,511	2,090	2,373	4,464	2,076	2,323	4,399	2.1
85 and over	**NA**	**NA**	**2,050**	**1,541**	**1,870**	**3,411**	**1,588**	**1,888**	**3,477**	**1.6**
Total	**145,295**	**167,015**	**190,625**	**104,374**	**105,740**	**210,115**	**105,008**	**107,152**	**212,160**	**100.0**

NA = Not available. **Note:** Numbers may not add up to totals due to rounding.

Handheld Phone and Texting Device Laws for Drivers, 2015

Source: Insurance Institute for Highway Safety; as of Aug. 2015

State	Handheld ban	Texting ban	Enforcement	State	Handheld ban	Texting ban	Enforcement	State	Handheld ban	Texting ban	Enforcement
AL	No[1]	Yes	P[2]	KY	No[4]	Yes	P	ND	No[4]	Yes	P
AK	No	Yes	P	LA	No[4,5,7]	Yes	P[8]	OH	No[4]	Yes	P[12]
AZ	No	No	NA	ME	No[5]	Yes	P	OK	No[5]	Yes[13]	P
AR	No[3]	Yes	P[2]	MD	Yes	Yes	P	OR	Yes	Yes	P
CA	Yes	Yes	P[2]	MA	No[4]	Yes	P	PA	No	Yes	P
CO	No[4]	Yes	P	MI	No[5]	Yes	P	RI	No[4]	Yes	P
CT	Yes	Yes	P	MN	No[9]	Yes	P	SC	No	Yes	P
DE	Yes	Yes	P	MS	No	Yes	P	SD	No[5]	Yes	S
DC	Yes	Yes	P	MO	No	No[10]	P	TN	No[5]	Yes	P
FL	No	Yes	S	MT	No	No	NA	TX	No[4]	No[4]	P
GA	No[4]	Yes	P	NE	No[11]	Yes	S	UT	No[4]	Yes	P
HI	Yes	Yes	P	NV	Yes	Yes	P	VT	Yes	Yes	P
ID	No	Yes	P	NH	Yes	Yes	P	VA	No[4]	Yes	P[2]
IL	Yes	Yes	P	NJ	Yes	Yes	P	WA	Yes	Yes	P
IN	No[3]	Yes	P	NM	No[5]	Yes	P	WV	Yes	Yes	P
IA	No[5]	Yes	S[6]	NY	Yes	Yes	P	WI	No[5]	Yes	P
KS	No[5]	Yes	P	NC	No[4]	Yes	P	WY	No	Yes	P

NA = Not applicable. P = Officer may stop vehicle for violation (primary); S = Officer may issue citation only when vehicle is stopped for another moving violation (secondary). **Note:** Laws shown for licensed passenger car drivers. Different laws and regulations apply to school bus, municipal transit, and other mass transit operators. Different laws may apply in school zones, construction zones, or other such areas. (1) Yes for 16-year-old drivers and for 17-year-old drivers who have held an intermediate license for fewer than 6 months. (2) Secondary for cell phone use by young drivers. (3) Yes for drivers under 21 years of age. (4) Yes for drivers under 18. (5) Yes for learner's permit and intermediate license holders. (6) Primary for learner's permit and intermediate license holders. (7) Yes for drivers in the year after getting their first license. (8) Secondary for cell phone use by novice drivers. (9) Yes for learner's permit and provisional license holders in their first year after licensing. (10) Yes for drivers 21 and younger. (11) Yes for learner's permit and intermediate license holders under 18. (12) Primary for drivers younger than 18, and secondary for texting. (13) Ban for all drivers to go into effect 11/1/15.

Selected Motor Vehicle Statistics

Source: Federal Highway Admin., U.S. Dept. of Transportation; Insurance Inst. for Highway Safety; American Petroleum Inst.

Driver's license age requirements, state gas tax, and safety belt use laws (incl. laws passed, but not in effect) as of 2015. Other figures are for 2013.

	Driver's license age requirements				Licensed drivers				Annual miles driven		
STATE	Learner's permit	Regular[1]	Gas taxes (cents/ gal)[5]	Safety belt use law[6]	Per 1,000 resident pop.	Per reg. motor vehicle	Reg. motor vehicles per 1,000 pop.	Fuel use per reg. motor vehicle (gal)	Per gal used	Per reg. vehicle	Per lic. driver
Alabama	15	17	39.3	P	798	0.81	990	697	19.50	13,588	16,854
Alaska	14	16y, 6m	29.7	P	719	0.69	1,069	526	11.73	6,170	9,168
Arizona	15y, 6m	16y, 6m	37.4	S	723	0.90	812	635	17.74	11,259	12,645
Arkansas	14	18	40.2	P	709	0.89	817	831	16.67	13,852	15,970
California	15y, 6m	17[2]	66.0	P	636	0.89	732	620	18.92	11,738	13,511
Colorado	15	17	40.4	S	728	0.83	889	583	17.20	10,029	12,239
Connecticut	16	18[2,3,4]	59.3	P	705	0.90	794	598	18.11	10,836	12,210
Delaware	16	17[2]	41.4	P	782	0.77	1,023	523	18.78	9,824	12,862
Dist. of Columbia	16	18[4]	41.9	P	627	1.30	515	353	30.05	10,600	8,697
Florida	15	18	54.8	P	699	0.92	774	639	19.94	12,735	14,096
Georgia	15	18[2]	44.9	P	661	0.86	779	781	18.00	14,055	16,551
Hawaii	15y, 6m	17[2]	62.1	P	652	0.70	951	379	19.98	7,567	11,037
Idaho	14y, 6m	16[2]	43.4	S	689	0.66	1,050	575	16.41	9,442	14,377
Illinois	15	18[2]	52.5	P	641	0.82	791	602	17.17	10,330	12,745
Indiana	15	18	51.3	P	685	0.81	848	768	18.29	14,049	17,401
Iowa	14	17[2]	50.4	P	694	0.61	1,146	652	13.71	8,936	14,760
Kansas	14	16y, 6m	42.4	P(a)	697	0.78	908	680	16.91	11,495	14,971
Kentucky	16	17[2]	44.4	P	687	0.76	917	711	16.40	11,656	15,565
Louisiana	15	17[2]	38.4	P	709	0.85	856	754	16.02	12,069	14,569
Maine	15	16y, 9m[2]	48.4	P	761	0.85	903	799	14.75	11,783	13,970
Maryland	15y, 9m	18	48.7	P(a)	698	1.10	647	863	17.13	14,787	13,692
Massachusetts	16	18[2]	44.9	S	712	0.97	745	657	17.19	11,295	11,816
Michigan	14y, 9m	17[2]	51.5	P	706	0.86	828	672	17.29	11,612	13,616
Minnesota	15	17[2]	47.0	P	614	0.64	963	615	17.76	10,916	17,106
Mississippi	15	16y, 6m	37.2	P	658	0.96	693	1,051	17.79	18,692	19,685
Missouri	15	17y, 11m	35.7	S(b)	708	0.74	963	573	20.83	11,933	16,227
Montana	14y, 6m	16[2]	46.2	S	755	0.50	1,517	504	15.51	7,814	15,694
Nebraska	15	17	44.9	S	736	0.75	1,012	678	15.07	10,216	14,057
Nevada	15y, 6m	18[2]	51.6	S	629	0.81	790	642	17.43	11,189	14,036
New Hampshire	15y, 6m	18[2]	42.2	None	802	0.76	1,065	565	16.20	9,158	12,156
New Jersey	16	18[2]	32.9	P(a)	683	0.87	793	674	15.67	10,555	12,255
New Mexico	15	16y, 6m[2]	37.3	P	698	0.79	903	769	17.33	13,326	17,224
New York	16	17[2]	62.9	P	570	1.07	543	630	19.29	12,154	11,572
North Carolina	15	16y, 6m[2]	54.7	P(a)	693	0.88	793	682	19.73	13,465	15,420
North Dakota	14	16	41.4	S	710	0.62	1,168	1,001	11.93	11,951	19,655
Ohio	15y, 6m	18[2]	46.4	S	694	0.79	895	626	17.38	10,884	14,042
Oklahoma	15y, 6m	16y, 6m	35.4	P	628	0.71	899	792	17.51	13,872	19,848
Oregon	15	17[2,3]	49.5	P	706	0.78	917	554	16.87	9,353	12,153
Pennsylvania	16	17	70.0	S(b)	696	0.86	819	628	15.01	9,428	11,086
Rhode Island	16	17y, 6m[2]	51.4	P	713	0.90	811	505	18.04	9,113	10,377
South Carolina	15	16y, 6m	35.2	P	741	0.91	835	861	14.27	12,288	13,852
South Dakota	14	16	48.4	S	714	0.61	1,202	661	13.60	8,985	15,111
Tennessee	15	17	39.8	P	709	0.87	839	744	17.51	13,035	15,432
Texas	15	18	38.4	P	584	0.79	763	864	14.04	12,123	15,830
Utah	15	17[2]	42.9	P	573	0.81	710	769	17.04	13,106	16,256
Vermont	15	16y, 6m[2]	48.9	S	867	0.90	976	619	18.80	11,631	13,103
Virginia	15y, 6m	18[2]	40.8	S	678	0.81	854	695	16.47	11,455	14,416
Washington	15	17[2]	55.9	P	760	0.84	917	531	16.84	8,949	10,791
West Virginia	15	17	53.0	P	635	0.83	784	741	17.87	13,233	16,338
Wisconsin	15y, 6m	16y, 9m[2]	51.3	P	726	0.80	930	599	18.59	11,142	14,260
Wyoming	15	16y, 6m[2]	42.4	S	723	0.51	1,425	855	13.11	11,208	22,087
U.S. AVERAGE			**48.9**		**671**	**0.84**	**809**	**678**	**17.23**	**11,679**	**14,085**

Note: Most states have graduated licensing systems that phase in full driving privileges. During the learner's stage, driving generally is not permitted without adult supervision. In an intermediate stage, young licensees may be allowed to drive unsupervised under certain conditions. (1) Min. age at which all restrictions may be lifted on private passenger car operation. (2) Applicants under a specified age (typically between 17 and 19) must complete driver education. (3) Home training (CT) or more hours of supervised driving (OR) may be substituted for driver ed. (4) Learner's stage mandatory for all license applicants regardless of age. (5) Some values rounded. Includes 18.4 cents per gallon in federal excise taxes. (6) P = Officer may stop vehicle for violation (primary); S = Officer may issue seat belt citation only when vehicle is stopped for another moving violation (secondary). (a) Secondary enforcement for rear seat occupants; (b) Primary enforcement for children under a specified age.

International Tourism Receipts, 2000-14

Source: World Tourism Organization (UNWTO), © UNWTO
(in billions of U.S. dollars; ranked by most recent figures available)

Rank	Country	2000	2005	2010	2012	2013	2014*
1.	U.S.	$100.2	$101.5	$137.0	$161.2	$173.1	$177.0
2.	Spain	30.0	48.0	54.6	58.2	62.6	65.2
3.	China[1]	16.2	29.3	45.8	50.0	51.7	56.9
4.	France	33.0	44.0	47.0	53.7	56.7	55.4
5.	Macao	3.2	7.9	27.8	43.9	51.8	50.8
6.	Italy	27.5	35.4	38.8	41.2	43.9	45.5
7.	UK	21.9	30.7	32.4	36.6	41.0	45.3
8.	Germany	18.7	29.2	34.7	38.1	41.3	43.3
9.	Thailand	7.5	9.6	20.1	33.9	41.8	38.4
10.	Hong Kong	5.9	10.3	22.2	33.1	38.9	38.4
11.	Australia	9.4	16.7	28.6	31.9	31.3	32.0
12.	Turkey	7.6	19.2	22.6	25.3	28.0	29.6
13.	Malaysia	5.0	8.8	18.1	20.2	21.5	21.8
14.	Austria	9.8	16.1	18.6	18.9	20.2	20.6
15.	India	3.5	7.5	14.5	18.0	18.4	19.7
16.	Singapore	5.1	6.2	14.2	18.9	19.3	19.2
17.	Japan	3.4	6.6	13.2	14.6	15.1	18.9
18.	South Korea	6.8	5.8	10.3	13.4	14.6	18.1
19.	Greece	9.2	13.3	12.7	13.4	16.1	17.8
20.	Canada	10.8	13.7	15.8	17.4	17.7	17.4
21.	Switzerland	6.6	10.0	14.7	16.1	16.9	17.4
22.	Mexico	8.3	11.8	12.0	12.7	13.9	16.3
23.	Netherlands	7.2	10.5	11.7	12.3	13.8	14.7
24.	Taiwan	3.7	5.0	8.7	11.8	12.3	14.7
25.	Belgium	6.6	9.9	11.4	12.7	13.4	14.3
26.	Portugal	5.2	7.7	10.1	11.1	12.3	13.8
27.	Sweden	4.1	6.8	8.7	10.6	11.5	12.7
28.	Russia	$3.4	$5.9	$8.8	$10.8	$12.0	$11.8
29.	United Arab Emirates	1.1	3.2	8.6	10.4	11.6	NA
30.	Poland	5.7	6.3	9.5	10.9	11.3	10.9
31.	Croatia	2.8	7.4	8.1	8.7	9.5	9.9
32.	Indonesia	5.0	4.5	7.0	8.3	9.1	9.8
33.	South Africa	2.7	7.5	9.1	10.0	9.2	9.3
34.	New Zealand	2.9	6.5	6.5	7.1	7.5	8.5
35.	Saudi Arabia	NA	4.6	6.7	7.4	7.7	8.2
36.	Vietnam	NA	2.3	4.5	6.9	7.3	7.3
37.	Denmark	3.7	5.3	5.9	6.5	6.9	7.3
38.	Egypt	4.3	6.9	12.5	9.9	6.0	7.2
39.	Morocco	2.0	4.6	6.7	6.7	6.9	7.1
40.	Brazil	1.8	3.9	5.7	6.6	6.7	6.8
41.	Czech Republic	3.0	4.8	7.1	7.0	7.0	6.7
42.	Lebanon	NA	5.5	8.0	6.3	5.9	NA
43.	Hungary	3.8	4.1	5.6	5.1	5.4	5.9
44.	Israel	4.4	3.3	5.1	5.4	5.7	5.7
45.	Dominican Republic	2.9	3.5	4.2	4.7	5.1	5.6
46.	Norway	2.2	3.5	4.7	5.4	5.7	5.6
47.	Luxembourg	1.8	3.5	4.1	4.6	4.8	5.4
48.	Ireland	2.6	4.8	4.1	3.9	4.5	4.9
49.	Philippines	2.2	2.3	2.6	4.1	4.7	4.8
50.	Argentina	2.9	2.7	4.9	4.9	4.3	4.6
	World	**494**	**701**	**965**	**1,115**	**1,197**	**1,245**

NA = Not available. * = Preliminary. (1) Not including Hong Kong and Macao.

International Tourist Arrivals by Country of Destination, 2000-14

Source: World Tourism Organization (UNWTO), © UNWTO
(visitors in millions; ranked by most recent figures available)

Rank	Country	2000	2005	2010	2012	2013	2014*	% change, 2013-14
1.	France	77.2	75.0	77.6	82.0	83.6	83.7	0.1%
2.	U.S.	51.2	49.2	60.0	66.7	69.9	74.7	6.9
3.	Spain	46.4	55.9	52.7	57.5	60.7	65.0	7.1
4.	China[1]	31.2	46.8	55.7	57.7	55.7	55.6	–0.1
5.	Italy	41.2	36.5	43.6	46.4	47.7	48.6	1.8
6.	Turkey	9.6	24.2	31.4	35.7	37.8	39.8	5.3
7.	Germany	19.0	21.5	26.9	30.4	31.5	33.0	4.6
8.	UK	23.2	28.0	28.3	29.3	31.2	NA	NA
9.	Russia	19.2	19.9	20.3	25.7	28.4	29.8	5.3
10.	Mexico	20.6	21.9	23.3	23.4	24.2	29.1	20.5
11.	Hong Kong	8.8	14.8	20.1	23.8	25.7	27.8	8.2
12.	Malaysia	10.2	16.4	24.6	25.0	25.7	27.4	6.7
13.	Austria	18.0	20.0	22.0	24.2	24.8	25.3	1.9
14.	Thailand	9.6	11.6	15.9	22.4	26.5	24.8	–6.7
15.	Greece	13.1	14.8	15.0	15.5	17.9	22.0	23.0
16.	Canada	19.6	18.8	16.2	16.3	16.6	17.1	3.2
17.	Poland	17.4	15.2	12.5	14.8	15.8	NA	NA
18.	Saudi Arabia	6.6	8.0	10.9	14.3	13.4	15.1	12.8
19.	Macao	5.2	9.0	11.9	13.6	14.3	14.6	2.1
20.	South Korea	5.3	6.0	8.8	11.1	12.2	14.2	16.6
21.	Netherlands	10.0	10.0	10.9	12.2	12.8	13.9	9.0
22.	Japan	4.8	6.7	8.6	8.4	10.4	13.4	29.4
23.	Ukraine	6.4	17.6	21.2	23.0	24.7	12.7	–48.5
24.	Hungary	3.0	10.0	9.5	10.4	10.7	12.1	13.7
25.	Singapore	6.1	7.1	9.2	11.1	11.9	11.9	–0.3
26.	Sweden	3.8	4.9	5.0	12.2	11.6	NA	NA
27.	Croatia	5.3	7.7	9.1	10.4	10.9	11.6	6.2
28.	Czech Republic	4.8	9.4	8.6	10.1	10.3	10.6	3.1%
29.	Morocco	4.3	5.8	9.3	9.4	10.0	10.3	2.4
30.	Dubai	3.1	5.8	7.4	9.0	10.0	NA	NA
31.	Taiwan	2.6	3.4	5.6	7.3	8.0	9.9	23.6
32.	Egypt	5.1	8.2	14.1	11.2	9.2	9.6	5.0
33.	South Africa	5.9	7.4	8.1	9.2	9.5	9.5	0.1
34.	Indonesia	5.1	5.0	7.0	8.0	8.8	9.4	7.2
35.	Portugal	5.7	6.0	6.8	7.7	8.3	9.3	12.3
36.	Switzerland	7.8	7.2	8.6	8.6	9.0	9.2	2.1
37.	Denmark	3.5	9.2	8.7	8.4	8.6	NA	NA
38.	Ireland	6.6	7.3	7.1	7.6	8.3	NA	NA
39.	Belgium	6.5	6.7	7.2	7.6	7.7	8.0	4.6
40.	Vietnam	2.1	3.5	5.0	6.8	7.6	7.9	4.0
41.	India	2.6	3.9	5.8	6.6	7.0	7.5	7.1
42.	Bulgaria	2.8	4.8	6.0	6.5	6.9	7.3	6.0
43.	Australia	4.9	5.5	5.8	6.0	6.4	6.9	7.5
44.	Tunisia	5.1	6.4	6.9	6.0	6.3	6.1	–3.2
45.	Slovakia	1.1	6.2	5.4	6.2	NA	NA	NA
46.	Argentina	2.9	3.8	5.3	5.6	5.2	5.9	13.1
47.	Brazil	5.3	5.4	5.2	5.7	5.8	NA	NA
48.	Dominican Republic	3.0	3.7	4.1	4.6	4.7	5.1	9.6
49.	Philippines	NA	2.6	3.5	4.3	4.7	4.8	3.2
50.	Iran	1.3	1.9	2.9	3.8	4.8	NA	NA
	World	**674**	**809**	**949**	**1,038**	**1,087**	**1,135**	**4.4**

NA = Not available or not applicable. * = Preliminary. (1) Not including Hong Kong and Macao.

World Tourism Receipts, 1990-2014

Source: World Tourism Organization (UNWTO), © UNWTO
(in billions of U.S. dollars)

Year	Receipts[1]	Year	Receipts[1]	Year	Receipts[1]	Year	Receipts[1]	Year	Receipts[1]	Year	Receipts[1]
1990	$271	1998	$457	2002	$501	2006	$766	2009	$882	2012	$1,115
1995	415	1999	475	2003	549	2007	883	2010	965	2013	1,197
1996	449	2000	494	2004	652	2008	967	2011	1,080	2014	1,245*
1997	449	2001	481	2005	701						

* = Provisional. (1) Total of all transactions made by or on behalf of visitors for the duration of their visit. Does not include receipts from international passenger transport contracted from companies outside a traveler's country of residence.

International Travel to the U.S., 1990-2014

Source: Office of Travel and Tourism Industries, Intl. Trade Admin., U.S. Dept. of Commerce; World Tourism Organization
(number of visitors in millions)

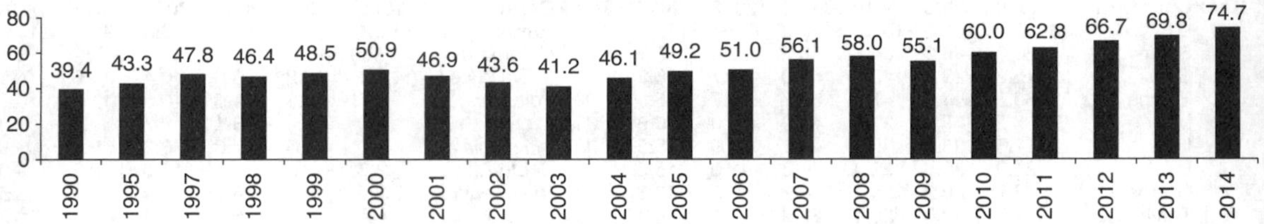

U.S. Domestic Leisure Travel Volume, 1995-2014

Source: U.S. Travel Assn.
(in billions of person-trips of 50 mi or more, one-way)

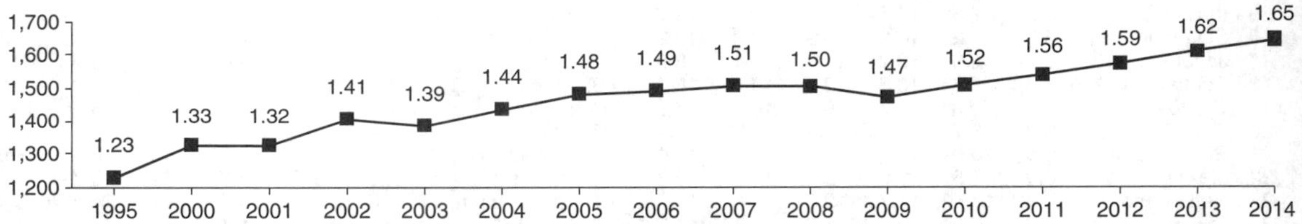

Note: Method of collecting travel data has been revised; data for earlier years have been adjusted to maintain comparability.

Top 10 U.S. States by Traveler Spending, 2013

Source: U.S. Travel Assn.
(domestic and international traveler spending within state, in billions of dollars)

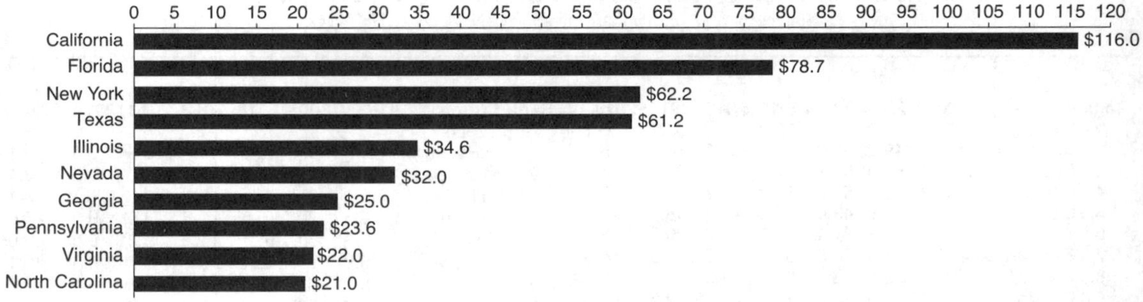

International Visitors to the U.S. by Top Countries of Origin, 2013

Source: Office of Travel and Tourism Industries, Intl. Trade Admin., U.S. Dept. of Commerce
(ranked by number of visitors)

Country of origin	Visitors	Expenditures (mil)	Expenditures per visitor
1. Canada	23,387,275	$27,033	$1,155.88
2. Mexico	14,342,722	10,509	732.71
3. United Kingdom	3,835,308	13,715	3,575.98
4. Japan	3,730,287	17,973	4,818.13
5. Brazil	2,060,291	10,476	5,084.72
6. Germany	1,916,471	7,538	3,933.27
7. China[1]	1,806,553	9,797	5,423.03
8. France	1,504,654	5,879	3,907.21
9. South Korea	1,359,924	4,617	3,395.04
10. Australia	1,205,060	6,070	5,037.09
11. India	859,156	5,550	6,459.83
12. Italy	838,883	$4,143	$4,938.71
13. Venezuela	788,069	3,567	4,526.25
14. Colombia	748,116	NA	NA
15. Argentina	686,098	3,503	5,105.68
16. Spain	619,860	NA	NA
17. Netherlands	589,296	2,467	4,186.35
18. Sweden	476,571	1,482	3,109.72
19. Switzerland	473,064	NA	NA
20. Taiwan	384,581	1,380	3,588.32
All countries	**69,768,455**	**180,700**	**2,590.00**

NA = Not available. **Note:** Expenditures include passenger fares. (1) Not including Hong Kong, Macao, and Taiwan.

Traveler Spending in the U.S., 1987-2014

Source: Office of Travel and Tourism Industries, Intl. Trade Admin., U.S. Dept. of Commerce; U.S. Travel Assn.
(in billions of dollars by origin of traveler)

Year	Domestic	International
1987	$235	$31
1990	291	43
1991	296	48
1992	306	55
1993	323	58
1994	340	58
1995	360	63
1996	385	70
1997	406	73
1998	$425	$71
1999	458	75
2000	503	82
2001	484	72
2002	478	67
2003	496	65
2004	532	75
2005	572	82
2006	610	86
2007	$641	$97
2008	662	110
2009	606	94
2010	644	104
2011	697	116
2012	728	126
2013	748	140
2014	778	148

Characteristics of U.S. Travelers Visiting Overseas Destinations, 2014

Source: Survey of Intl. Air Travelers, Office of Travel and Tourism Industries, Intl. Trade Admin., U.S. Dept. of Commerce

Total U.S. resident travelers	**30,780,000**
Males (adults)	50%
Females (adults)	50%
Avg. age of males (yrs.)	45.4
Avg. age of females (yrs.)	44.0
Median annual household income	$100,000
Avg. total trip expend. per visitor (incl. airfare)	$2,831
Avg. international airfare	$1,347
Avg. expend. outside the U.S. per visitor per day	$84
Purchased travel insurance	28%
Median number of nights	10

Region of residence	**% of travelers**
Middle Atlantic	24%
South Atlantic (incl. Florida, DC metro area)	20
Pacific (incl. California, Washington)	16
West South Central (incl. Texas)	10
East North Central (incl. Illinois, Ohio)	10
New England	7
West North Central	5
Mountain	5
East South Central	3

Main purpose of trip	**% of travelers**
Vacation/holiday	51%
Visit friends/relatives	27
Business	11
Education	5
Convention/conference/trade show	3
Religion/pilgrimages	2
Health treatment	<1

(1) Percentages based on multiple responses.

Occupation	**% of travelers**
Management, business, science, arts	42%
Retired	15
Service	11
Student	10
Sales and office	7
Homemaker	5
Military/government	3
Production, transportation, material moving	3
Natural resources, construction, maintenance	3

Leisure/recreational activities[1]	**% of travelers**
Sightseeing	80%
Shopping	75
Small towns/countryside	44
Historical locations	40
Fine dining	39
Guided tours	37
Art galleries/museums	32
Cultural/ethnic heritage sights	32
National parks/monuments	29
Nightclubbing/dancing	23
Water sports	21
Concert/play/musical	13
Amusement/theme parks	10
Casino/gamble	9
Camping/hiking	8
Environmental/ecological excursions	8
Sporting event	7
Golfing/tennis	4
Hunting/fishing	4
Snow sports	1

U.S. Resident Travel Abroad, 1997-2014

Source: Office of Travel and Tourism Industries, Intl. Trade Admin., U.S. Dept. of Commerce
(numbers in thousands)

Region/country[1]	2014	2000	1997
Total outbound[2]	**68,176**	**61,327**	**52,735**
Mexico	25,882	19,285	17,909
Canada	11,515	15,189	13,401
Overseas subtotal[3]	**30,780**	**26,853**	**21,634**
Europe	10,804	13,373	NA
United Kingdom	2,832	4,189	3,570
France	2,124	2,927	2,098
Italy	1,908	2,148	1,471
Germany	1,878	2,309	1,796
Spain	1,170	1,262	714
Caribbean	7,387	3,867	NA
Dominican Republic	2,709	779	195
Jamaica	1,385	886	1,341
Asia	5,694	4,914	NA
China[4]	1,139	644	476
India	1,077	457	368
Central America	2,370	886	NA
South America	2,278	2,095	NA
Middle East	1,724	1,370	NA
Africa	893	483	NA
Oceania	585	1,047	NA

NA = Not available. **Note:** Visits of one or more nights. Visitation estimates for Canada and Mexico include all modes of transportation used. Estimates for all other countries are available only for air travel to that country and are based upon data from the airlines that voluntarily provided it. (1) Only individual countries that received more than 1 mil visitors in 2014 are shown. Region figures include U.S. resident travelers to all countries in region. (2) To Canada, Mexico, and overseas. (3) To all countries except Canada and Mexico. (4) Not including Hong Kong, Macao, and Taiwan.

Airline Safety, U.S. Scheduled Commercial Carriers, 1985-2014

Source: National Transportation Safety Board; Federal Aviation Administration, U.S. Dept. of Transportation

Year	Departures (mil)	Fatal accidents	Fatalities[1]	Rate of fatal accidents[2]
1985	6.1	4	197	0.066
1990	7.8	4	11	0.051
1995	8.1	1	160	0.012
1996	7.9	3	342	0.038
1997	9.9	3	3	0.030
1998	10.5	1	1	0.009
1999	10.9	2	12	0.018
2000	11.1	2	89	0.018
2001[3]	10.6	6	531	0.019
2002	10.3	0	0	—
2003	10.2	2	22	0.020
2004	10.8	1	13	0.009
2005	10.9	3	22	0.027
2006	10.6	2	50	0.019
2007	10.7	0	0	—
2008	10.3	0	0	—
2009	9.6	1	50	0.010
2010	9.5	0	0	—
2011	9.4	0	0	—
2012	9.2	0	0	—
2013	9.1	0	0	—
2014	8.9	0	0	—

— = Not applicable. * = Preliminary. (1) Includes deaths that occurred on the ground as a result of an accident, except for fatalities resulting from the Sept. 11, 2001, terrorist attacks. (2) Per 100,000 departures. (3) The Sept. 11, 2001, terrorist attacks have been included among the number of fatal accidents but have been excluded when calculating the accident rate.

U.S. Airline Statistics, 1995-2014

Source: Airlines for America
(in millions, except where otherwise noted)

	1995	2000	2005	2009	2010	2011	2012	2013	2014
Passengers enplaned[1]	547.8	666.1	738.6	703.9	720.5	730.8	736.7	743.2	762.1
Revenue passenger miles[1,2]	540.7	692.8	779.0	769.5	798.0	814.4	823.2	840.4	862.1
Available seat miles[1,3]	807.1	957.0	1,003.3	957.2	972.6	992.7	994.5	1,011.2	1,033.8
Cargo revenue ton miles[1,2]	16,921	23,888	28,039	24,970	27,885	28,123	27,790	26,441	27,236
% of seating utilized[1]	67.0%	72.4%	77.6%	80.4%	82.1%	82.0%	82.8%	83.1%	83.4%
Passenger revenue[4]	$69,470	$93,639	$93,633	$91,443	$103,978	$114,299	$115,975	$120,642	$126,706
Net profit[4]	2,314	2,533	–27,220	–2,610	3,666	1,392	364	12,711	8,514
Total employment[5]	546.6	739.6	619.6	573.9	564.4	577.3	584.5	584	589.1

(1) Scheduled service only. (2) One fare-paying passenger or one ton of revenue cargo transported one mile. (3) One seat transported one mile. (4) Passenger carriers only. (5) Figures are of avg. full-time equivalents (FTE), i.e., the number of full-time employees that could have been employed if the reported number of hours worked by part-time employees had been worked by full-time employees. In this table, part-time employees are treated as 0.5 FTEs.

Top 25 U.S. Passenger Airlines, 2014

Source: Airlines for America
(in millions; ranked by number of passengers enplaned in scheduled service)

	Airline	Passengers
1.	American/US Airways	145.6
2.	Delta Air Lines	128.2
3.	Southwest/AirTran	135.8
4.	US Airways	57.6
5.	JetBlue Airways	32.1
6.	ExpressJet Airlines	31.0
7.	SkyWest Airlines	27.8
8.	Alaska Airlines	21.0
9.	Envoy Air	16.1
10.	Spirit Airlines	14.0
11.	Republic Airlines	13.3
12.	Frontier Airlines	12.2
13.	Endeavor Air	12.1
14.	Hawaiian Airlines	10.1
15.	Mesa Airlines	9.0
16.	Allegiant Air	8.2
17.	Horizon Air	7.5
18.	Virgin America	6.5
19.	Air Wisconsin Airlines	6.1
20.	Shuttle America	5.8
21.	PSA Airlines	5.6
22.	GoJet Airlines[1]	4.3
23.	Compass Airlines	4.0
24.	Chautauqua Airlines	3.3
25.	Piedmont Airlines	3.0

Note: Includes domestic and international passengers on U.S. airlines. (1) Doing business as United Express.

Top North American Airports by Passenger Traffic, 2014

Source: *2014 World Annual Traffic Report*, Airports Council Intl.

	City/airport name (airport code)	Total passengers[1]
1.	Hartsfield-Jackson Atlanta Intl. (ATL)	96,178,899
2.	Los Angeles Intl. (LAX)	70,663,265
3.	Chicago O'Hare Intl. (ORD)	69,999,010
4.	Dallas/Ft. Worth Intl. (DFW)	63,554,402
5.	Denver Intl. (DEN)	53,472,514
6.	New York John F. Kennedy Intl. (JFK)	53,254,533
7.	San Francisco Intl. (SFO)	47,114,631
8.	Charlotte Douglas Intl. (CLT)	44,279,504
9.	Las Vegas McCarran Intl. (LAS)	42,869,517
10.	Phoenix Sky Harbor Intl. (PHX)	42,134,662
11.	Houston George Bush Intercontinental (IAH)	41,239,700
12.	Miami Intl. (MIA)	40,941,879
13.	Toronto Pearson Intl. (YYZ)	38,572,416
14.	Seattle-Tacoma Intl. (SEA)	37,498,267
15.	Orlando Intl. (MCO)	35,714,091
16.	Newark Liberty Intl. (EWR)	35,610,759
17.	Minneapolis/St. Paul Intl. (MSP)	35,147,083
18.	Detroit Metro Wayne County (DTW)	32,513,555
19.	Boston Logan Intl. (BOS)	31,658,351
20.	Philadelphia Intl. (PHL)	30,740,180
21.	New York LaGuardia (LGA)	26,954,588
22.	Ft. Lauderdale-Hollywood Intl. (FLL)	24,648,306
23.	Baltimore/Wash. Intl. Thurgood Marshall (BWI)	22,312,676
24.	Washington Dulles Intl. (IAD)	21,420,385
25.	Salt Lake City Intl. (SLC)	21,141,610

Top World Airports by Passenger Traffic, 2014

Source: *2014 World Annual Traffic Report*, Airports Council Intl.

	City/airport name (country; airport code)	Total passengers[1]
1.	Beijing Capital Intl. (China; PEK)	86,128,270
2.	London Heathrow (UK; LHR)	73,408,489
3.	Tokyo Haneda Intl. (Japan; HND)	72,826,565
4.	Dubai Intl. (United Arab Emirates; DXB)	70,475,636
5.	Paris Charles de Gaulle (France; CDG)	63,813,756
6.	Hong Kong Intl. (China; HKG)	63,121,786
7.	Frankfurt Intl. (Germany; FRA)	59,566,132
8.	Jakarta Soekarno-Hatta Intl. (Indonesia; CGK)	57,221,169
9.	Istanbul Atatürk Intl. (Turkey; IST)	56,715,541
10.	Amsterdam Schipol (Netherlands; AMS)	54,978,023
11.	Guangzhou Baiyun Intl. (China; CAN)	54,780,346
12.	Singapore Changi (Singapore; SIN)	54,093,000
13.	Shanghai Pudong Intl. (China; PVG)	51,687,894
14.	Kuala Lumpur Intl. (Malaysia; KUL)	48,930,409
15.	Bangkok Suvarnabhumi (Thailand; BKK)	46,423,352
16.	Seoul Incheon Intl. (South Korea; ICN)	45,662,322
17.	Madrid-Barajas (Spain; MAD)	41,822,863
18.	São Paulo/Guarulhos Intl. (Brazil; GRU)	39,765,714
19.	Delhi Indira Gandhi Intl. (India; DEL)	39,752,819
20.	Munich (Germany; MUC)	39,700,515
21.	Sydney Intl. (Australia; SYD)	38,863,380
22.	Rome Leonardo da Vinci-Fiumicino (Italy; FCO)	38,506,467
23.	London Gatwick (UK; LGW)	38,117,322
24.	Shanghai Hongqiao Intl. (China; SHA)	37,971,135
25.	Chengdu Shuangliu Intl. (China; CTU)	37,712,357

Note: World list excludes North American airports and airports that do not participate in Airports Council Intl.'s Airport Traffic Statistics collection. (1) Arriving and departing passengers and direct transit passengers counted once.

Busiest Amtrak Stations, 2014

Source: Amtrak National Fact Sheet, Amtrak; ranked by total ridership

Station	Tickets from	Tickets to	Total ridership
New York, NY	5,032,941	4,991,533	10,024,474
Washington, DC	2,510,842	2,518,086	5,028,928
Philadelphia, PA	2,047,561	2,036,143	4,083,704
Chicago, IL	1,694,031	1,683,228	3,377,259
Los Angeles, CA	800,256	750,834	1,551,090
Boston South Station, MA	752,472	738,623	1,491,095
Baltimore, MD	518,776	513,751	1,032,527
Sacramento, CA	519,190	503,132	1,022,322
Albany-Rensselaer, NY	391,123	390,474	781,597
New Haven, CT	359,498	354,648	714,146
Wilmington, DE	352,479	352,044	704,523
San Diego, CA	356,998	343,109	700,107
BWI Airport, MD	342,356	349,912	692,268
Newark, NJ	339,501	337,674	677,175
Providence, RI	322,901	342,769	665,670
Seattle, WA	315,355	311,268	626,623
Milwaukee, WI	300,281	296,134	596,415
Portland, OR	290,848	294,980	585,828
Emeryville, CA	290,013	288,373	578,386
Boston Back Bay, MA	290,784	276,108	566,892
Lancaster, PA	265,886	263,523	529,409
Bakersfield, CA	260,856	260,567	521,423
Harrisburg, PA	245,536	253,459	498,995
Route 128, MA	222,004	214,355	436,359
Boston North Station, MA	217,831	215,229	433,060

Top Travel Websites, 2015

Source: comScore Media Metrix, Inc.; ranked by number of visitors

Rank	Website	Visitors (thous.)[1]	Rank	Website	Visitors (thous.)[1]
1.	TripAdvisor Inc.	68,996	12.	Hilton Worldwide	10,743
2.	Expedia Inc.	40,669	13.	Delta Airlines	10,207
3.	Priceline.com Inc.	27,552	14.	InterContinental Hotels Group	9,831
4.	Southwest Airlines Co.	20,047	15.	Fareportal Media Group	9,750
5.	HomeAway	15,853	16.	American Airlines	9,285
6.	Uber.com	14,457	17.	Disney Parks & Travel	9,222
7.	Marriott	12,719	18.	United Airlines	8,688
8.	Yahoo Travel	12,447	19.	MSN Travel	7,838
9.	USAToday Travel	12,311	20.	About.com Travel	7,728
10.	Orbitz Worldwide	12,091	**Total travel audience[2]**		**187,562**
11.	Kayak.com Network	10,964	**Total Internet audience[2]**		**255,681**

(1) Number of unique visitors, in thousands, who visited website at least once in June 2015. (2) Audience comprises all persons older than 2 years of age, at U.S. home/work locations.

Number of Paid Days Off Per Year in Selected Countries

Source: *No-Vacation Nation Revisited*, May 2013, Center for Economic and Policy Research

The figures are based on statutory entitlements for an employee working five days a week. Ranked by total paid days off.

Country	Paid vacation days	Paid holidays	Total paid days off	Country	Paid vacation days	Paid holidays	Total paid days off	Country	Paid vacation days	Paid holidays	Total paid days off
Austria	25	13	38	New Zealand	20	10	30	Finland	25	0	25
Portugal	22	13	35	Ireland	20	9	29	Sweden	25	0	25
Spain	22	12	34	Australia	20	8	28	Netherlands	20	0	20
France	30	1	31	UK	28	0	28	Switzerland	20	0	20
Italy	20	10	30	Norway	25	2	27	Canada	10	9	19
Belgium	20	10	30	Greece	20	6	26	Japan	10	0	10
Germany	20	10	30	Denmark	25	0	25	U.S.	0	0	0

Note: The U.S. has no nationwide statutory entitlement that mandates paid days off.

Record-Breaking Roller Coasters

Source: UltimateRollerCoaster.com; speed measured in mph, length and height in ft

Steel-Tracked Roller Coasters

Fastest	Roller coaster	Theme park, location
149.1 mph	Formula Rossa	Ferrari World Abu Dhabi, United Arab Emirates
128	Kingda Ka	Six Flags Great Adventure, Jackson, NJ
120	Top Thrill Dragster	Cedar Point, Sandusky, OH
106.8	Dodonpa	Fuji-Q High Land, Fujiyoshida-shi, Japan
100	Tower of Terror	Dreamworld, Gold Coast, Australia
100	Superman: Escape From Krypton	Six Flags Magic Mountain, Valencia, CA
Tallest		
456 ft	Kingda Ka	Six Flags Great Adventure, Jackson, NJ
420	Top Thrill Dragster	Cedar Point, Sandusky, OH
415	Superman: Escape From Krypton	Six Flags Magic Mountain, Valencia, CA
377	Tower of Terror	Dreamworld, Gold Coast, Australia
318	Steel Dragon 2000	Nagashima Spa Land, Mie, Japan
Largest drop		
418 ft	Kingda Ka	Six Flags Great Adventure, Jackson, NJ
400	Top Thrill Dragster	Cedar Point, Sandusky, OH
306.8	Steel Dragon 2000	Nagashima Spa Land, Mie, Japan
306	Leviathan	Canada's Wonderland, Vaughan, ON, Canada
Longest		
8,133 ft	Steel Dragon 2000	Nagashima Spa Land, Mie, Japan
7,450	The Ultimate	Lightwater Valley, UK
6,709	Fujiyama	Fuji-Q High Land, Fujiyoshida-shi, Japan
6,595	Millennium Force	Cedar Point, Sandusky, OH
6,562	Formula Rossa	Ferrari World Abu Dhabi, United Arab Emirates

Wood-Tracked Roller Coasters

Fastest	Roller coaster	Theme park, location
72 mph	Goliath	Six Flags Great America, Gurnee, IL
70	El Toro	Six Flags Great Adventure, Jackson, NJ
68.4	Colossos	Heide Park, Soltau, Germany
68	Outlaw Run	Silver Dollar City, Branson, MO
67.4	The Voyage	Holiday World & Splashin' Safari, Santa Claus, IN
Tallest		
197 ft	Colossos	Heide Park, Soltau, Germany
183	T Express	Everland, Yongin, S. Korea
181	El Toro	Six Flags Great Adventure, Jackson, NJ
165	Goliath	Six Flags Great America, Gurnee, IL
163	The Voyage	Holiday World & Splashin' Safari, Santa Claus, IN
Largest drop		
180 ft	Goliath	Six Flags Great America, Gurnee, IL
176	El Toro	Six Flags Great Adventure, Jackson, NJ
162	Outlaw Run	Silver Dollar City, Branson, MO
159	Colossos	Heide Park, Soltau, Germany
155	Mean Streak	Cedar Point, Sandusky, OH
Longest		
7,400 ft	The Beast	Kings Island, Cincinnati, OH
6,442	The Voyage	Holiday World & Splashin' Safari, Santa Claus, IN
5,578	White Cyclone	Nagashima Spa Land, Mie, Japan
5,427	Mean Streak	Cedar Point, Sandusky, OH
5,384	Shivering Timbers	Michigan's Adventure, Muskegon, MI

Passports, Health Regulations, and Travel Warnings for Foreign Travel

Source: Bureau of Consular Affairs, U.S. Dept. of State; Centers for Disease Control and Prevention (CDC), U.S. Dept. of Health and Human Services; World Health Organization (WHO); Transportation Security Administration (TSA), U.S. Dept. of Homeland Security

Passports, Visas

Passports are issued by the Dept. of State to U.S. citizens and nationals to provide documentation for foreign travel. As of Oct. 2015, the fees for a new passport book and passport card for persons ages 16 and over total $165; provided certain criteria are met, these can be renewed for $140. For a passport book alone, fees are $135 for a new passport and $110 for passport renewal.

In July 2008, the U.S. government began issuing passport cards. Travelers arriving by land or sea from Canada, Mexico, the Caribbean, and Bermuda may present a passport card to enter the U.S. Passport cards may not be used for air travel, however. The fees for a new passport card for persons ages 16 and over total $55.

A U.S. passport is often sufficient for U.S. citizens to gain admission for a limited stay in another country. Some countries also require an entry visa. Each country has its own specific guidelines concerning length and purpose of visit, among other considerations. Visitors may need to provide proof of sufficient funds for their intended stay, onward/return tickets, and/or at least six months remaining validity on their U.S. passports.

All persons traveling by air outside of the U.S. (excluding direct travel to and from a U.S. territory) are required to present a passport or other valid document upon reentering the U.S.

For up-to-date passport and international travel information, visit the Consular Affairs website (travel.state.gov) or call the National Passport Information Center at 1-877-4USA-PPT (1-877-487-2778).

Health Regulations

Under WHO regulations, first instituted in 1969, member countries agree to abide by resolutions meant to contain the spread of disease. For example, some countries require travelers to provide proof of vaccination against yellow fever before entering.

Detailed information can be found in *Health Information for International Travel*, or the "yellow book," published every two years by the CDC. The book is written primarily for health care providers but may be of use to other travelers. The CDC also issues travel notices on outbreaks, health precautions, and health warnings. For current notices and more on travelers' health, visit wwwnc.cdc.gov/travel/.

WHO publishes a more technical guide, *International Travel and Health*, which can be found online at www.who.int/ith/.

Travel Warnings and Alerts

The State Dept. issues travel warnings as recommendations that Americans avoid travel to certain countries. Long-term conditions in such countries may be dangerous or unstable; an embassy closure or limited personnel may reduce the U.S. government's ability to assist U.S. citizens. As of Oct. 2015, travel warnings were in effect for the following countries: Afghanistan, Algeria, Burkina Faso, Burundi, Cameroon, Central African Republic, Chad, Colombia, Dem. Rep. of the Congo, Djibouti, El Salvador, Eritrea, Haiti, Honduras, Iran, Iraq, Israel (incl. West Bank and Gaza), Kenya, Lebanon, Libya, Mali, Mauritania, Mexico, Nepal, Niger, Nigeria, North Korea, Pakistan, Philippines, Saudi Arabia, Sierra Leone, Somalia, South Sudan, Sudan, Syria, Turkey, Ukraine, Venezuela, and Yemen.

The department issues travel alerts when it has concerns about short-term conditions—natural disasters, terrorist attacks, anniversaries of attacks, election-related demonstrations, and regional sporting events, among others. For the latest travel warnings and alerts, see travel.state.gov.

Summary of TSA Regulations

Airplane carry-ons. TSA promotes the "3-1-1" rule regarding carry-on items. Containers with liquids, gels, aerosols, creams, or pastes must hold **3.4** oz or less; these containers should be packed inside a single **1**-quart, clear plastic, zip-top bag; and this **1** bag must be X-rayed when going through security. Exceptions to the 3-1-1 rule include medication, baby formula and food, and breast milk. Travelers must declare any exceptions at security.

Security checkpoint identification. Adult travelers (18 years of age and over) must present a photo ID. Acceptable documents include a U.S. passport or passport card; foreign government-issued passport; state-issued driver's license; permanent resident card; or U.S. military ID, among others.

Screening process. Travelers may wear loose fitting or religious garments (incl. head coverings) through security. They may be subject to additional screening if clothing could conceal prohibited items. Travelers may request a private area if selected for personal screening. Travelers will be screened by someone of the same gender.

Disability-related permitted carry-on items:

- Wheelchairs, scooters
- Crutches, canes, and walkers
- Portable oxygen concentrators (though not permitted by all airlines)
- Canes, Braille note-takers
- Medications and associated supplies
- Service animals

Permitted carry-on items:

- Disposable razors
- Eye drops and saline solution (amounts greater than 3.4 oz must be declared)
- Nail clippers, tweezers
- Scissors with pointed tips and blades shorter than 4 inches
- Mobile phones
- Strollers (must be inspected at security)
- Beverages (any size) purchased after security screening
- Musical instruments (must undergo screening; must fit into overhead bin or under seats; some airlines may allow purchase of seat for an instrument)

Prohibited carry-on items:

- Knives (except for plastic or round-bladed butter knives), incl. knives that are religious objects
- Baseball bats, golf clubs
- Flare guns
- Firearms or realistic firearm replicas, ammunition, firearm parts
- Hammers, screwdrivers, wrenches, pliers, and other tools more than 7 in. in length
- Brass knuckles
- Lighter fluid
- Liquid bleach, turpentine, paint thinner
- Spray paint
- Self-defense sprays

For complete travel information, visit www.tsa.gov/travel.

Air Distances Between Selected World Cities

Point-to-point measurements, in miles, are usually from City Hall or its equivalent.

	Bangkok	Beijing	Berlin	Cairo	Cape Town	Caracas	Chicago	Hong Kong	Honolulu	Lima
Bangkok	...	2,046	5,352	4,523	6,300	10,555	8,570	1,077	6,609	12,244
Beijing	2,046	...	4,584	4,698	8,044	8,950	6,604	1,217	5,077	10,349
Berlin	5,352	4,584	...	1,797	5,961	5,238	4,414	5,443	7,320	6,896
Cairo	4,523	4,698	1,797	...	4,480	6,342	6,141	5,066	8,848	7,726
Cape Town	6,300	8,044	5,961	4,480	...	6,366	8,491	7,376	11,535	6,072
Caracas	10,555	8,950	5,238	6,342	6,366	...	2,495	10,165	6,021	1,707
Chicago	8,570	6,604	4,414	6,141	8,491	2,495	...	7,797	4,256	3,775
Hong Kong	1,077	1,217	5,443	5,066	7,376	10,165	7,797	...	5,556	11,418
Honolulu	6,609	5,077	7,320	8,848	11,535	6,021	4,256	5,556	...	5,947
London	5,944	5,074	583	2,185	5,989	4,655	3,958	5,990	7,240	6,316
Los Angeles	7,637	6,250	5,782	7,520	9,969	3,632	1,745	7,240	2,557	4,171
Madrid	6,337	5,745	1,165	2,087	5,308	4,346	4,189	6,558	7,872	5,907
Melbourne	4,568	5,643	9,918	8,675	6,425	9,717	9,673	4,595	5,505	8,059
Mexico City	9,793	7,753	6,056	7,700	8,519	2,234	1,690	8,788	3,789	2,639
Montreal	8,338	6,519	3,740	5,427	7,922	2,438	745	7,736	4,918	3,970
Moscow	4,389	3,607	1,006	1,803	6,279	6,177	4,987	4,437	7,047	7,862
New York, NY	8,669	6,844	3,979	5,619	7,803	2,120	714	8,060	4,969	3,639
Paris	5,877	5,120	548	1,998	5,786	4,732	4,143	5,990	7,449	6,370
Rio de Janeiro	9,994	10,768	6,209	6,143	3,781	2,804	5,282	11,009	8,288	2,342
Rome	5,494	5,063	737	1,326	5,231	5,195	4,824	5,774	8,040	6,750
San Francisco	7,931	5,918	5,672	7,466	10,248	3,902	1,859	6,905	2,398	4,518
Singapore	883	2,771	6,164	5,137	6,008	11,402	9,372	1,605	6,726	11,689
Stockholm	5,089	4,133	528	2,096	6,423	5,471	4,331	5,063	6,875	7,166
Tokyo	2,865	1,307	5,557	5,958	9,154	8,808	6,314	1,791	3,859	9,631
Warsaw	5,033	4,325	322	1,619	5,935	5,559	4,679	5,147	7,366	7,215
Washington, DC	8,807	6,942	4,181	5,822	7,895	2,047	596	8,155	4,838	3,509

	London	Los Angeles	Madrid	Melbourne	Mexico City	Montreal	Moscow	New Delhi	New York, NY	Paris
Bangkok	5,944	7,637	6,337	4,568	9,793	8,338	4,389	1,813	8,669	5,877
Beijing	5,074	6,250	5,745	5,643	7,753	6,519	3,607	2,353	6,844	5,120
Berlin	583	5,782	1,165	9,918	6,056	3,740	1,006	3,598	3,979	548
Cairo	2,185	7,520	2,087	8,675	7,700	5,427	1,803	2,758	5,619	1,998
Cape Town	5,989	9,969	5,308	6,425	8,519	7,922	6,279	5,769	7,803	5,786
Caracas	4,655	3,632	4,346	9,717	2,234	2,438	6,177	8,833	2,120	4,732
Chicago	3,958	1,745	4,189	9,673	1,690	745	4,987	7,486	714	4,143
Hong Kong	5,990	7,240	6,558	4,595	8,788	7,736	4,437	2,339	8,060	5,990
Honolulu	7,240	2,557	7,872	5,505	3,789	4,918	7,047	7,412	4,969	7,449
London	...	5,439	785	10,500	5,558	3,254	1,564	4,181	3,469	214
Los Angeles	5,439	...	5,848	7,931	1,542	2,427	6,068	7,011	2,451	5,601
Madrid	785	5,848	...	10,758	5,643	3,448	2,147	4,530	3,593	655
Melbourne	10,500	7,931	10,758	...	8,426	10,395	8,950	6,329	10,359	10,430
Mexico City	5,558	1,542	5,643	8,426	...	2,317	6,676	9,120	2,090	5,725
Montreal	3,254	2,427	3,448	10,395	2,317	...	4,401	7,012	331	3,432
Moscow	1,564	6,068	2,147	8,950	6,676	4,401	...	2,698	4,683	1,554
New York, NY	3,469	2,451	3,593	10,359	2,090	331	4,683	7,318	...	3,636
Paris	214	5,601	655	10,430	5,725	3,432	1,554	4,102	3,636	...
Rio de Janeiro	5,750	6,330	5,045	8,226	4,764	5,078	7,170	8,753	4,801	5,684
Rome	895	6,326	851	9,929	6,377	4,104	1,483	3,684	4,293	690
San Francisco	5,367	347	5,803	7,856	1,887	2,543	5,885	7,691	2,572	5,577
Singapore	6,747	8,767	7,080	3,759	10,327	9,203	5,228	2,571	9,534	6,673
Stockholm	942	5,454	1,653	9,630	6,012	3,714	716	3,414	3,986	1,003
Tokyo	5,959	5,470	6,706	5,062	7,035	6,471	4,660	3,638	6,757	6,053
Warsaw	905	5,922	1,427	9,598	6,337	4,022	721	3,277	4,270	852
Washington, DC	3,674	2,300	3,792	10,180	1,885	489	4,876	7,500	205	3,840

	Rio de Janeiro	Rome	San Francisco	Singapore	Stockholm	Tehran	Tokyo	Vienna	Warsaw	Wash., DC
Bangkok	9,994	5,494	7,931	883	5,089	3,391	2,865	5,252	5,033	8,807
Beijing	10,768	5,063	5,918	2,771	4,133	3,490	1,307	4,648	4,325	6,942
Berlin	6,209	737	5,672	6,164	528	2,185	5,557	326	322	4,181
Cairo	6,143	1,326	7,466	5,137	2,096	1,234	5,958	1,481	1,619	5,822
Cape Town	3,781	5,231	10,248	6,008	6,423	5,241	9,154	5,656	5,935	7,895
Caracas	2,804	5,195	3,902	11,402	5,471	7,320	8,808	5,372	5,559	2,047
Chicago	5,282	4,824	1,859	9,372	4,331	6,502	6,314	4,698	4,679	596
Hong Kong	11,009	5,774	6,905	1,605	5,063	3,843	1,791	5,431	5,147	8,155
Honolulu	8,288	8,040	2,398	6,726	6,875	8,070	3,859	7,632	7,366	4,838
London	5,750	895	5,367	6,747	942	2,743	5,959	771	905	3,674
Los Angeles	6,330	6,326	347	8,767	5,454	7,682	5,470	6,108	5,922	2,300
Madrid	5,045	851	5,803	7,080	1,653	2,978	6,706	1,128	1,427	3,792
Melbourne	8,226	9,929	7,856	3,759	9,630	7,826	5,062	9,790	9,598	10,180
Mexico City	4,764	6,377	1,887	10,327	6,012	8,184	7,035	6,320	6,337	1,885
Montreal	5,078	4,104	2,543	9,203	3,714	5,880	6,471	4,009	4,022	489
Moscow	7,170	1,483	5,885	5,228	716	1,532	4,660	1,043	721	4,876
New York, NY	4,801	4,293	2,572	9,534	3,986	6,141	6,757	4,234	4,270	205
Paris	5,684	690	5,577	6,673	1,003	2,625	6,053	645	852	3,840
Rio de Janeiro	...	5,707	6,613	9,785	6,683	7,374	11,532	6,127	6,455	4,779
Rome	5,707	...	6,259	6,229	1,245	2,127	6,142	477	820	4,497
San Francisco	6,613	6,259	...	8,448	5,399	7,362	5,150	5,994	5,854	2,441
Singapore	9,785	6,229	8,448	...	5,936	4,103	3,300	6,035	5,843	9,662
Stockholm	6,683	1,245	5,399	5,936	...	2,173	5,053	780	494	4,183
Tokyo	11,532	6,142	5,150	3,300	5,053	4,775	...	5,689	5,347	6,791
Warsaw	6,455	820	5,854	5,843	494	1,879	5,689	347	...	4,472
Washington, DC	4,779	4,497	2,441	9,662	4,183	6,341	6,791	4,438	4,472	...

Number and Acreage of Farms by State, 2000, 2014

Source: National Agricultural Statistics Service, U.S. Dept. of Agriculture

State	No. of farms (thous.) 2014	No. of farms (thous.) 2000	Acreage in farms (mil) 2014	Acreage in farms (mil) 2000	Acreage per farm 2014	Acreage per farm 2000
AL	43.4	47.0	8.9	9.0	205	191
AK	0.8	0.6	0.8	0.9	1,092	1,569
AZ	19.6	10.7	26.0	26.9	1,327	2,518
AR	44.0	48.0	13.8	14.6	314	304
CA	76.4	83.1	25.5	28.0	334	337
CO	35.0	30.0	31.8	31.6	909	1,060
CT	6.0	4.2	0.4	0.4	73	86
DE	2.5	2.6	0.5	0.6	200	215
FL	47.6	44.0	9.5	10.4	200	238
GA	41.1	49.1	9.4	10.9	229	223
HI	7.0	5.5	1.1	1.4	160	251
ID	24.4	24.5	11.8	11.9	484	486
IL	74.5	77.0	26.9	27.5	361	357
IN	58.2	63.4	14.7	15.2	253	240
IA	88.0	94.0	30.5	32.5	347	346
KS	61.0	64.5	46.0	47.5	754	736
KY	76.4	90.0	13.0	13.7	170	152
LA	27.2	29.0	7.8	8.0	287	277
ME	8.2	7.1	1.5	1.4	177	190
MD	12.3	12.4	2.0	2.1	165	172
MA	7.8	6.1	0.5	0.5	67	89
MI	51.6	53.0	10.0	10.2	193	192
MN	74.0	81.0	25.9	27.9	350	344
MS	37.1	42.0	10.9	11.2	294	266
MO	97.7	109.0	28.3	30.2	290	277
MT	27.8	27.8	59.7	59.3	2,147	2,133
NE	49.1	46.1	45.2	46.1	921	887
NV	4.2	3.1	6.0	6.4	1,417	2,065
NH	4.4	3.3	0.5	0.4	107	133
NJ	9.1	9.7	0.7	0.8	79	86
NM	24.7	18.0	43.2	44.9	1,749	2,494
NY	35.5	37.5	7.2	7.7	202	205
NC	49.5	55.5	8.4	9.2	170	166
ND	30.3	30.8	39.3	39.4	1,297	1,279
OH	74.5	79.0	14.0	14.8	188	187
OK	79.6	84.5	34.3	33.8	431	401
OR	34.6	40.0	16.4	17.3	474	433
PA	58.8	59.0	7.7	7.7	131	130
RI	1.2	0.8	0.1	0.1	56	75
SC	24.4	24.2	5.0	4.9	205	203
SD	31.7	32.4	43.3	44.0	1,366	1,358
TN	67.3	88.0	10.9	11.8	162	134
TX	245.5	228.3	130.0	130.9	530	573
UT	18.1	15.5	11.0	11.6	608	747
VT	7.3	6.6	1.3	1.3	171	192
VA	45.9	48.5	8.2	8.7	179	180
WA	36.7	37.0	14.7	15.6	401	420
WV	21.3	20.8	3.6	3.6	169	173
WI	69.0	77.5	14.5	16.0	210	206
WY	11.7	9.2	30.4	34.5	2,598	3,750
U.S.	**2,084.0**	**2,166.8**	**913.0**	**945.1**	**438**	**436**

Supplemental Nutrition Assistance Program (SNAP), 1969-2014

Source: Food and Nutrition Service (FNS), U.S. Dept. of Agriculture

Fiscal year	Avg. participation (thous.)	Avg. monthly benefit per person	Total benefits (mil)	All other costs (mil)[1]	Total costs (mil)
1969	2,878	$6.63	$228.8	$21.7	$250.5
1970	4,340	10.55	549.7	27.2	576.9
1975	17,064	21.40	4,385.5	233.2	4,618.7
1980	21,082	34.47	8,720.9	485.6	9,206.5
1985	19,899	44.99	10,743.6	959.6	11,703.2
1990	20,049	58.78	14,142.8	1,304.5	15,447.3
1995	26,619	71.27	22,764.1	1,856.3	24,620.4
1996	25,543	73.21	22,440.1	1,890.9	24,331.0
1997	22,858	71.27	19,548.9	1,958.7	21,507.6
1998	19,791	71.12	16,890.5	2,097.8	18,988.3
1999	18,183	72.27	15,769.4	2,051.5	17,820.9
2000	17,194	72.62	14,983.3	2,070.7	17,054.0
2001	17,318	74.81	15,547.4	2,242.0	17,789.4
2002	19,096	$79.67	$18,256.2	$2,380.8	$20,637.0
2003	21,250	83.94	21,404.3	2,412.0	23,816.3
2004	23,811	86.16	24,618.9	2,480.1	27,099.0
2005	25,628	92.89	28,567.9	2,504.2	31,072.1
2006	26,549	94.75	30,187.4	2,715.7	32,903.1
2007	26,316	96.18	30,373.3	2,800.3	33,173.5
2008	28,223	102.19	34,608.4	3,031.3	37,639.6
2009	33,490	125.31	50,359.9	3,260.1	53,620.0
2010	40,302	133.79	64,702.2	3,581.8	68,283.9
2011	44,709	133.85	71,810.9	3,876.3	75,687.2
2012	46,609	133.41	74,619.3	3,791.7	78,411.1
2013	47,636	133.07	76,066.3	3,862.8	79,929.1
2014	46,536	125.35	69,999.8	4,137.4	74,137.2

(1) Includes the federal share of state administrative expenses, nutrition education, and employment and training programs, in addition to other federal costs (e.g., benefit and retailer redemption and monitoring, payment accuracy, EBT [electronic benefit transfer] systems, program evaluation and modernization, program access, health and nutrition pilot projects).

U.S. Federal Food Assistance Programs, 1990-2014

Source: Food and Nutrition Service (FNS), U.S. Dept. of Agriculture

(in millions of dollars; for fiscal years ending on Sept. 30)

Program	1990	1995	2000	2005	2010	2011	2012	2013	2014
Supplemental Nutrition Assistance Program (SNAP)[1]	$15,491	$24,620	$17,054	$31,073	$68,284	$75,687	$78,411	$79,933	$74,130
Puerto Rico nutrition assistance[2]	937	1,131	1,268	1,495	2,001	2,001	2,001	2,001	1,903
Natl. school lunch[3]	3,834	5,160	6,149	8,031	10,880	11,300	11,578	12,220	12,658
School breakfast[3,4]	596	1,048	1,393	1,927	2,859	3,034	3,277	3,514	3,686
WIC (Women, Infants, and Children)[5]	2,122	3,440	3,982	4,994	6,690	7,179	6,800	6,479	6,294
Summer food service[6]	164	237	267	267	359	373	398	428	466
Child and adult care[7]	813	1,464	1,683	2,111	2,638	2,724	2,855	2,994	3,133
Special milk[4]	19	17	15	16	12	12	12	11	11
Nutrition for the elderly (NSIP)[8]	142	148	137	4	3	2	3	3	2
Food distrib. to Indian reserv.[9]	66	65	76	76	95	94	97	100	110
Commodity supplemental food prog.[9]	85	99	98	156	165	198	209	203	198
Food distrib. to charitable insts.[10]	104	64	2	4	1	0	0	0	0
Emergency food assistance (TEFAP)[11]	334	135	225	373	631	532	444	693	629
Total	**24,707**	**37,628**	**32,349**	**50,527**	**94,618**	**103,136**	**106,085**	**108,579**	**103,220**

Note: 2014 data are preliminary. All data subject to revision by the FNS. (1) Formerly known as the Food Stamp Program. Includes benefits and admin. expenses. (2) Provides benefits analogous to SNAP. (3) Nine-month averages (summer months excluded). (4) Cash payments based on federal reimbursement rates to states. (5) Includes food benefits, nutrition services and admin. funds, Farmers' Market Nutrition Program, infrastructure, breastfeeding promotion and peer counseling, program evaluation, and technical assistance. (6) Includes cash payments, commodity costs, and admin. costs for services similar to natl. school lunch and breakfast programs. (7) Includes cash payments, entitlement and bonus commodities, cash-in-lieu of commodities, sponsor admin. costs, start-up costs, and audits. (8) For 2003 and on, program administered by the Agency on Aging; FNS costs limited to value of commodities distributed. (9) Includes cost of commodities and distrib. and admin. expenses. (10) Includes summer camps. (11) Includes cost of commodities to hunger relief orgs. (e.g., food banks, soup kitchens) and admin. expenses.

U.S. Cost of Food, 2015

Source: Center for Nutrition Policy and Promotion (CNPP), U.S. Dept. of Agriculture (USDA)

Age-gender group	Weekly cost[1] Thrifty plan	Low-cost plan	Mod.-cost plan	Liberal plan	Monthly cost[1] Thrifty plan	Low-cost plan	Mod.-cost plan	Liberal plan
Individual child[2]								
1 year	$21.80	$29.20	$33.00	$40.10	$94.40	$126.30	$142.80	$173.60
2-3 years	23.90	30.40	36.60	44.70	103.40	131.80	158.70	193.60
4-5 years	25.00	31.40	39.00	47.50	108.50	136.10	168.90	205.60
6-8 years	32.20	45.10	53.50	63.00	139.30	195.50	231.60	273.00
9-11 years	36.10	47.70	61.70	71.80	156.30	206.70	267.40	310.90
Individual male[2]								
12-13 years	39.00	55.10	69.10	80.90	168.80	238.80	299.30	350.70
14-18 years	40.00	55.80	71.40	82.00	173.30	241.90	309.50	355.20
19-50 years	43.10	55.60	70.00	86.20	186.80	240.90	303.30	373.30
51-70 years	39.30	52.40	65.60	78.70	170.30	227.00	284.20	341.10
71+ years	39.60	52.10	64.30	79.90	171.50	225.60	278.70	346.10
Individual female[2]								
12-13 years	38.90	47.30	56.90	70.10	168.70	205.00	246.40	303.90
14-18 years	38.10	47.50	57.80	71.10	165.10	205.90	250.60	308.10
19-50 years	38.10	48.20	59.70	75.90	165.20	208.80	258.70	328.80
51-70 years	37.70	47.00	58.50	70.30	163.50	203.50	253.40	304.70
71+ years	36.70	46.60	57.70	69.50	158.80	201.90	250.10	301.00
2-person family								
19-50 years	89.40	114.20	142.70	178.30	387.20	494.70	618.20	772.40
51-70 years	84.70	109.30	136.50	164.00	367.10	473.50	591.30	710.40
4-person family[3] with 2 children ages—								
2-3 and 4-5 years	130.10	165.60	205.30	254.20	563.80	717.70	889.60	1,101.40
6-8 and 9-11 years	149.50	196.60	244.90	296.80	647.60	852.00	1,061.00	1,286.10

Note: As of June 2015. The official USDA food plans represent a nutritious diet at four different cost levels. The nutritional bases are the 1997-2005 Dietary Reference Intakes, 2005 Dietary Guidelines for Americans, and 2005 MyPyramid food intake recommendations. In addition to cost, differences among plans are in specific foods and quantities of foods. Another basis of the food plans is that all meals and snacks are prepared at home. For specific foods and quantities, see *Thrifty Food Plan, 2006* and *The Low-Cost, Moderate-Cost, and Liberal Food Plans, 2007* from the CNPP. All four food plans are based on 2001-02 data and updated to current dollars using the consumer price index for specific food items. (1) All costs are rounded to nearest 10 cents. (2) The costs given are for individuals in 4-person families. (3) Defined as a couple, 19-50 years old, and two children.

Direct Government Payments to Farmers by State, 1950-2013

Source: Economic Research Service, U.S. Dept. of Agriculture

In Feb. 2014, Pres. Barack Obama signed the Agricultural Act of 2014 (known as the 2014 Farm Act), which eliminates direct payments to farmers. The data in this table applies to payments prior to passage of the 2014 law.

(in millions of dollars)

State	1950	1960	1970	1980	1990	2000	2010	2011	2012	2013
Alabama	$8.1	$13.0	$79.5	$23.0	$82.2	$171.0	$134.6	$115.8	$118.0	$90.6
Alaska	NA	0.1	0.1	0.2	1.1	1.7	9.6	11.3	12.4	12.2
Arizona	1.7	2.2	52.0	5.1	43.3	107.2	70.0	58.1	50.2	47.4
Arkansas	5.7	13.4	87.7	34.5	312.7	976.8	389.4	364.8	365.1	346.9
California	13.6	21.9	131.9	14.1	252.3	689.0	363.6	259.1	287.5	248.7
Colorado	11.9	24.8	68.0	18.0	236.7	351.4	271.6	235.4	215.7	239.0
Connecticut	0.5	0.6	0.8	0.9	2.1	18.1	15.5	10.5	8.9	7.0
Delaware	0.4	0.6	1.7	1.0	3.2	25.1	24.3	21.0	15.4	15.3
Florida	3.2	7.1	18.5	7.0	37.2	114.1	93.0	175.1	69.1	71.1
Georgia	10.6	22.9	83.6	28.9	130.6	385.1	262.3	222.3	256.7	247.6
Hawaii	NA	9.2	11.1	0.7	0.5	11.9	16.2	16.9	11.4	13.2
Idaho	3.5	13.3	48.0	7.9	133.4	264.1	163.6	113.4	126.7	129.1
Illinois	10.1	17.9	166.6	35.7	506.6	2,010.4	697.9	627.4	630.8	607.9
Indiana	5.7	16.8	111.0	15.0	244.2	939.9	372.5	300.5	323.0	329.8
Iowa	10.9	20.8	235.8	44.6	753.7	2,303.2	1,024.8	811.8	855.4	782.4
Kansas	9.1	28.5	227.6	93.3	834.7	1,233.9	631.8	542.8	518.6	697.6
Kentucky	7.4	15.8	45.8	10.0	81.6	449.5	319.6	273.8	303.4	290.1
Louisiana	11.4	15.1	55.1	20.0	154.6	471.0	209.7	209.8	219.1	215.2
Maine	1.0	2.7	1.7	3.4	7.0	13.9	48.8	17.4	21.9	17.5
Maryland	1.3	2.8	8.0	3.5	17.4	104.4	54.3	41.1	56.2	43.5
Massachusetts	0.6	0.7	0.6	0.7	3.0	11.0	20.1	20.9	17.0	10.1
Michigan	7.2	18.0	65.7	10.7	168.8	381.3	184.6	156.6	175.4	142.4
Minnesota	8.2	31.7	151.8	69.6	511.8	1,504.4	566.1	487.9	534.7	527.0
Mississippi	9.9	12.5	146.5	18.8	186.0	464.9	251.3	245.6	219.1	206.2
Missouri	10.4	23.7	153.9	78.9	299.1	872.3	435.5	367.1	396.0	428.5
Montana	6.1	15.6	85.4	58.5	299.6	490.4	327.1	298.6	239.3	250.4
Nebraska	8.8	22.1	203.0	82.9	624.6	1,407.8	509.4	470.3	480.3	599.7
Nevada	0.2	0.9	2.1	1.3	5.3	3.9	9.8	10.4	12.9	9.5
New Hampshire	0.6	0.7	0.5	0.7	1.9	4.8	20.1	12.9	14.9	12.4
New Jersey	0.9	1.8	4.3	0.9	15.7	22.5	22.0	17.1	11.9	9.7
New Mexico	2.4	11.2	43.1	20.9	63.8	79.8	91.5	88.1	97.7	115.6
New York	5.7	12.7	22.0	5.8	59.3	160.2	66.0	57.4	104.3	74.6
North Carolina	8.8	12.8	59.7	13.2	73.3	449.1	438.4	401.1	430.4	411.3
North Dakota	5.9	38.6	167.2	116.6	545.4	1,178.0	844.8	460.8	409.1	600.8

State	1950	1960	1970	1980	1990	2000	2010	2011	2012	2013
Ohio	$7.3	$19.2	$89.6	$9.4	$197.0	$678.3	$373.1	$256.7	$279.8	$258.3
Oklahoma	8.8	24.9	118.0	34.9	319.0	440.1	318.7	341.8	295.6	356.8
Oregon	3.4	8.7	23.1	5.9	89.1	137.6	150.4	110.8	118.0	116.1
Pennsylvania	6.3	11.8	25.2	8.3	41.4	147.9	81.3	73.8	119.3	94.2
Rhode Island	0.1	0.1	0.1	0.1	0.2	1.2	6.4	3.9	3.9	2.2
South Carolina	3.8	14.2	54.4	13.4	62.6	144.9	125.5	113.6	110.2	106.1
South Dakota	5.4	28.9	91.7	65.3	332.9	795.7	401.0	303.4	330.8	303.6
Tennessee	6.7	14.9	71.0	18.7	91.0	300.8	153.3	140.2	176.2	147.9
Texas	24.9	72.5	543.2	231.8	974.7	1,670.4	1,018.3	917.4	838.1	1,125.5
Utah	2.4	6.6	11.1	5.1	34.9	36.3	39.2	35.1	39.5	39.2
Vermont	1.3	1.6	1.4	1.3	5.8	26.1	21.1	17.8	22.2	16.0
Virginia	5.0	7.1	20.0	13.3	32.4	153.0	110.9	100.4	139.9	111.0
Washington	3.3	9.7	57.9	9.5	205.4	352.8	313.8	231.1	203.7	191.3
West Virginia	2.1	3.0	3.6	2.5	6.0	23.5	16.5	14.3	25.2	17.4
Wisconsin	7.7	16.9	51.7	12.4	181.2	603.8	259.3	196.0	281.8	221.8
Wyoming	3.0	9.9	15.2	7.3	31.3	37.3	42.7	41.3	42.6	46.0
U.S.	**283.5**	**702.4**	**3,717.4**	**1,285.7**	**9,298.0**	**23,221.6**	**12,391.3**	**10,420.5**	**10,635.1**	**11,003.8**

NA = Not available. **Note:** Direct federal government payments to farmers were for eligible historic production of wheat, corn, barley, grain sorghum, oats, upland cotton, long/medium grain rice, soybeans, other oilseeds, and peanuts. Producers enrolled annually to receive payments based on rates specified in the Farm Act and on their historic program payment acres and yields.

U.S. Annual Per Capita Consumption of Selected Foods, 1970-2013

Source: Economic Research Service, U.S. Dept. of Agriculture; Distilled Spirits Council of the U.S.; Beer Institute; Wine Institute

(fruits and vegetables in pounds, beverages in gallons)

	1970	1990	2013	% change, 1970-2013
Fresh fruit	**96.3**	**111.4**	**129.5**	**34.5%**
Apples	16.5	19.0	16.7	1.1
Avocados	0.4	1.3	5.2	1,134.9
Bananas	17.4	24.3	28.1	61.6
Grapes	2.7	7.2	7.1	167.5
Melons	19.4	22.3	23.0	18.2
Oranges	15.7	12.0	10.1	–35.7
Peaches/nectarines	5.5	5.3	2.9	–47.1
Pears	1.8	3.1	2.7	48.6
Pineapples	0.7	1.9	6.4	863.5
Strawberries	1.6	3.0	7.2	353.0
Canned vegetables	**93.0**	**110.3**	**91.7**	**–1.3**
Green peas	0.9	2.0	0.9	–7.0
Snap beans	1.1	3.7	2.9	157.6
Sweet corn	14.3	11.0	5.8	–59.6
Tomatoes	62.1	75.3	65.9	6.1
Frozen vegetables	**43.7**	**66.7**	**68.7**	**57.2**
Broccoli	1.0	2.2	2.5	157.2
Carrots	1.4	2.3	1.7	18.0
Green peas	1.9	2.2	1.5	–21.2
Potatoes	28.5	46.4	49.2	72.4
Sweet corn	5.7	8.6	7.0	22.0

	1970	1990	2013	% change, 1970-2013
Fresh vegetables	**144.4**	**163.9**	**170.6**	**18.2%**
Bell peppers	2.0	5.4	9.2	363.5
Broccoli	0.5	3.1	6.4	1,200.5
Cabbage	8.1	7.8	6.4	–20.1
Carrots	5.8	8.0	7.8	34.3
Celery	6.8	6.7	5.1	–24.6
Cucumbers	2.6	4.3	6.7	159.7
Garlic	0.4	1.1	1.6	353.6
Head lettuce	20.8	25.8	13.1	–37.0
Onions	9.5	14.2	17.5	83.4
Potatoes	59.3	44.9	33.3	–44.0
Sweet corn	7.2	6.2	8.2	14.0
Tomatoes	10.3	13.2	17.2	66.5
Beverages				
Bottled water	NA	8.8	NA	NA
Carbonated soft drinks	24.3	46.2	NA	NA
Regular	22.2	35.6	NA	NA
Diet	2.1	10.7	NA	NA
Coffee	33.4	26.8	25.3	–24.2
Fruit juice	5.5	7.0	6.9	25.0
Beer	18.5	23.9	20.2	9.0
Wine	1.3	2.1	2.8	113.3
Distilled spirits	1.8	1.5	1.6	–11.6

NA = Not available. **Note:** All figures are rounded; percent change is calculated based on unrounded original data. Per capita consumption based on total population. Alcoholic beverage consumption would be higher if based on legal drinking age population.

U.S. Meat Production and Consumption, 1940-2015

Source: Economic Research Service, U.S. Dept. of Agriculture

(in millions of pounds)

	Beef		Veal		Lamb and mutton		Pork		All red meats[1]		All poultry[2]	
Year	Prod.	Cons.	Prod.	Cons.	Prod.	Cons.	Prod.	Cons.	Prod.	Cons.	Prod.	Cons.
1940	7,175	7,257	981	981	876	873	10,044	9,701	19,076	18,812	NA	NA
1950	9,534	9,529	1,230	1,206	597	596	10,714	10,390	22,075	21,721	3,174	3,097
1960	14,728	15,465	1,109	1,118	769	857	13,905	14,057	30,511	31,497	6,310	6,168
1970	21,684	23,451	588	613	551	669	14,699	14,957	37,522	39,689	10,193	9,981
1980	21,643	23,560	400	420	318	351	16,617	16,838	38,978	41,170	14,173	13,525
1990	22,743	24,030	327	325	363	397	15,354	16,025	38,787	40,778	23,468	22,152
1995	25,222	25,534	319	319	285	346	17,849	17,768	43,675	43,967	30,393	25,944
2000	26,888	27,338	225	225	234	354	18,952	18,643	46,299	46,560	36,073	30,508
2009	25,965	26,904	147	147	177	339	22,999	19,839	49,274	47,227	41,673	34,116
2010	26,304	26,392	145	150	168	317	22,437	19,072	49,039	45,931	43,058	35,201
2011	26,195	25,545	136	137	153	295	22,758	18,384	49,232	44,363	43,513	35,548
2012	25,913	25,752	125	123	161	299	23,253	18,604	49,439	44,779	43,523	34,870
2013	25,720	25,483	117	119	161	324	23,187	19,095	49,174	45,020	44,159	35,630
2014	24,252	24,686	100	98	161	340	22,843	19,069	47,345	44,192	44,827	36,379
2015*	23,824	24,915	91	92	159	343	24,581	20,566	48,644	45,916	46,572	38,591

NA = Not available. * = Projected. (1) Includes beef, veal, lamb and mutton, and pork. May not add up to totals because of rounding. (2) Includes broilers, turkeys, and mature chicken.

U.S. Annual Per Capita Consumption of Meat and Dairy, 1910-2013

Source: Economic Research Service, U.S. Dept. of Agriculture
(in pounds per capita per year, unless otherwise noted)

Meat	1910	1930	1950	1970	1990	2000	2010	2012	2013	% change, 1910-2013
Beef	48.5	33.7	44.6	79.6	63.9	64.5	56.7	54.5	53.6	10.4%
Chicken	11.0	11.1	14.3	27.4	42.4	54.2	58.0	56.6	57.7	425.3
Fish/shellfish	11.2	10.2	11.9	11.7	14.9	15.2	15.8	14.2	14.3	27.9
Pork	38.2	41.1	43.0	48.1	46.4	47.8	44.4	42.6	43.4	13.6
Red meat	96.0	83.6	95.8	131.9	112.2	113.7	102.1	98.0	97.9	2.1
Dairy										
Butter	18.4	17.6	10.9	5.4	4.3	4.5	4.9	5.5	5.5	–70.3
Cheese, American	2.8	3.2	5.5	7.0	11.1	12.7	13.3	13.3	13.3	383.6
Cheese, other	1.5	1.5	2.2	4.4	13.5	16.9	19.4	20.0	20.1	1,225.3
Ice cream	1.9	9.3	16.4	16.7	14.8	15.6	13.5	12.8	12.8	558.3
Milk, skim/lower fat (gallons)	7.1	5.0	2.9	5.8	15.2	14.4	14.7	14.1	13.7	93.9
Milk, whole (gallons)	25.2	28.2	34.2	25.3	10.5	8.0	5.6	5.4	5.4	–78.7

U.S. Organic Farmland and Animals, 1995-2011

Source: Economic Research Service, U.S. Dept. of Agriculture

	Organic acreage[1]								
Crop	1995	2000	2004	2005	2008	2011	% change, 1995-2011	% change, 2005-11	Total U.S. farmland[2]
Total cropland	**638,500**	**1,218,905**	**1,452,353**	**1,723,271**	**2,655,382**	**3,084,989**	**383.2%**	**79.0%**	**370,653,755**
Grains									
Corn	32,650	77,912	99,111	130,672	194,637	234,470	618.1	79.4	93,600,000
Wheat	120,820	206,474	214,244	293,824	415,902	344,644	185.3	17.3	60,433,000
Oats	13,250	29,771	42,616	46,465	57,374	62,015	368.0	33.5	3,760,000
Barley	17,150	41,904	26,629	39,271	46,954	63,903	272.6	62.7	4,020,000
Rice	8,400	26,870	22,173	26,428	49,638	48,533	477.8	83.6	2,761,000
Beans									
Soybeans	47,200	136,071	114,239	122,217	125,621	132,411	180.5	8.3	63,631,000
Dry beans	NA	14,010	7,642	10,561	16,465	28,656	NA	171.3	1,526,900
Dry peas & lentils	5,900	10,144	15,893	17,757	16,987	17,887	203.2	0.7	571,000
Hay & silage	84,100	231,207	356,590	411,342	793,442	785,970	834.6	91.1	61,625,000
All vegetables	NA	62,342	86,822	98,525	177,049	147,446	NA	49.7	2,045,020
All fruits	NA	43,481	80,707	97,277	121,066	131,498	NA	35.2	3,839,300
Other crops									
Cotton	32,850	15,027	9,213	9,537	15,377	12,030	–63.4	26.1	10,830,300
Peanuts	NA	2,085	9,514	11,940	16,776	13,258	NA	11.0	1,230,000
Potatoes	NA	5,433	7,300	6,581	8,273	13,258	NA	101.5	1,148,800
Trees for maple syrup	10,200	11,965	13,357	12,247	31,340	43,831	329.7	257.9	NA
Fallow land	NA	57,688	116,582	198,650	194,428	271,644	NA	36.7	37,968,749
Total pasture & rangeland	**276,300**	**557,167**	**1,592,756**	**2,331,158**	**2,160,577**	**2,298,130**	**731.8**	**–1.4**	**473,212,960**
Total farmland	**914,800**	**1,776,073**	**3,045,109**	**4,054,429**	**4,815,959**	**5,383,119**	**488.4**	**32.8**	**843,866,715**

	Number of organic animals[1]								
Animal	1995	2000	2004	2005	2008	2011	% change, 2000-11	% change, 2005-11	Total U.S. animals
Total livestock	**NA**	**56,028**	**157,253**	**196,506**	**475,829**	**492,353**	**778.8%**	**150.6%**	**167,512,858**
Beef cows	NA	13,829	36,662	36,113	63,680	106,181	667.8	194.0	32,834,801
Milk cows	NA	38,196	74,840	87,082	249,766	254,771	567.0	192.6	9,266,574
Other cows[3]	NA	NA	36,598	58,822	144,817	113,114	NA	92.3	54,246,483
Hogs & pigs	NA	1,724	4,883	10,018	10,111	12,373	617.7	23.5	65,110,000
Sheep & lambs	NA	2,279	4,270	4,471	7,455	5,914	159.5	32.3	6,055,000
Total poultry	**NA**	**3,159,050**	**7,304,566**	**13,757,270**	**15,518,075**	**37,028,242**	**1,072.1**	**169.2**	**9,632,362,000**
Layer hens	NA	1,113,746	1,787,901	2,415,056	5,538,011	6,663,278	498.3	175.9	377,492,000
Broilers	NA	1,924,807	4,769,104	10,405,879	9,015,984	28,644,354	1,388.2	175.3	8,882,000,000
Turkeys	NA	9,138	164,292	144,086	398,531	504,315	5,418.9	250.0	262,460,000
Other/ unclassified	**NA**	**111,359**	**583,269**	**792,249**	**565,549**	**1,216,295**	**992.2**	**53.5**	**110,410,000**

NA = Not available. (1) Based on information from USDA-accredited state and private organic certifiers. (2) Total acreage of organic and nonorganic land used for agricultural purposes. (3) Includes breeding stock, replacement heifers, and unclassified cows.

Livestock on Farms in the U.S., 1900-2015

Source: National Agricultural Statistics Service, U.S. Dept. of Agriculture
(in thousands as of Jan. 1, unless otherwise noted)

Year	All cattle[1]	Milk cows	Sheep and lambs	Hogs and pigs[2]	Year	All cattle[1]	Milk cows	Sheep and lambs	Hogs and pigs[2]
1900	59,739	16,544	48,105	51,055	1995	102,755	9,487	8,886	57,150
1910	58,993	19,450	50,239	48,072	2000	98,199	9,183	7,036	59,335
1920	70,400	21,455	40,743	60,159	2005	95,838	9,005	6,135	60,975
1930	61,003	23,032	51,565	55,705	2006	96,702	9,063	6,230	61,449
1940	68,309	24,940	52,107	61,165	2007	97,003	9,132	6,165	62,490
1950	77,963	23,853	29,826	58,937	2008	96,035	9,257	5,950	66,963
1955	96,592	23,462	31,582	50,474	2009	94,521	9,333	5,747	66,768
1960	96,236	19,527	33,170	59,026	2010	93,881	9,086	5,620	65,327
1965	109,000	16,981	25,127	56,106	2011	100,000	9,200	5,480	64,625
1970	112,369	12,091	20,423	57,046	2012	90,769	9,230	5,365	66,361
1975	132,028	11,220	14,515	54,693	2013	89,300	9,218	5,335	66,373
1980	111,242	10,758	12,699	67,318	2014	88,526	9,208	5,245	64,775
1985	109,582	10,777	10,716	54,073	2015	89,800	9,307	5,280	66,145
1990	95,816	10,015	11,358	53,788					

(1) For 1970 and on, includes milk cows and heifers that have calved. (2) As of Dec. 1 of preceding year.

Production of Principal U.S. Crops, 1990-2014

Source: National Agricultural Statistics Service, U.S. Dept. of Agriculture

Year	Corn for grain (1,000 bu)	Oats (1,000 bu)	Barley (1,000 bu)	Sorghum for grain (1,000 bu)	All wheat (1,000 bu)	Rye (1,000 bu)	Flaxseed (1,000 bu)	Cotton (upland) (1,000 b)	Cottonseed (1,000 t)
1990	7,934,028	357,654	422,196	573,303	2,729,778	10,176	3,812	15,505.4	5,968.5
1995	7,373,876	162,027	359,562	460,373	2,182,591	10,064	2,211	17,532.2	6,848.7
2000	9,915,051	149,545	318,728	470,526	2,232,460	8,386	10,730	16,799.2	6,435.6
2003	10,089,222	144,383	278,283	411,237	2,344,760	8,634	10,516	17,822.9	6,664.6
2004	11,807,086	115,695	279,743	453,654	2,158,245	8,255	10,368	22,505.1	8,242.1
2005	11,114,082	114,878	211,896	392,933	2,104,690	7,537	19,695	23,259.7	8,172.1
2006	10,534,868	93,638	180,165	277,538	1,812,036	7,193	11,019	20,822.4	7,347.9
2007	13,037,875	90,430	210,110	497,445	2,051,088	6,311	5,896	18,355.1	6,588.7
2008	12,091,648	89,135	240,193	472,342	2,499,164	7,979	5,716	12,384.5	4,300.3
2009	13,091,862	93,081	227,323	382,983	2,218,061	6,993	7,423	11,787.6	4,148.8
2010	12,446,865	81,190	180,268	345,625	2,206,916	7,431	9,056	17,600.0	6,098.1
2011	12,359,612	53,649	155,780	214,443	1,999,347	6,326	2,791	14,722.0	5,370.0
2012	10,755,111	61,486	218,990	247,742	2,252,307	6,542	5,798	16,534.0	5,666.0
2013	13,828,964	64,642	216,745	392,331	2,134,979	7,626	3,356	12,275.0	4,203.0
2014	14,215,532	69,684	176,794	432,575	2,025,651	7,189	6,368	15,496.0	5,314.0

Year	Tobacco (1,000 lb)	All hay (1,000 t)	Beans, dry edible (1,000 cwt)	Peas, dry edible (1,000 cwt)	Peanuts[1] (1,000 lb)	Soybeans[2] (1,000 bu)	Potatoes (1,000 cwt)	Sweet potatoes (1,000 cwt)
1990	1,626,380	146,212	32,379	2,372	3,602,770	1,925,947	402,110	12,594
1995	1,268,538	154,166	30,812	4,765	4,247,455	2,176,814	443,606	12,906
2000	1,052,999	151,921	26,409	3,474	3,265,505	2,757,810	513,621	13,794
2003	802,560	157,585	22,492	5,202	4,144,150	2,453,665	457,814	15,891
2004	881,973	158,247	17,788	11,419	4,288,200	3,123,686	456,041	16,112
2005	645,015	151,017	26,772	14,003	4,869,860	3,063,237	423,926	15,730
2006	727,347	142,336	24,247	13,203	3,464,250	3,188,247	441,348	16,248
2007	787,653	146,901	25,586	16,287	3,672,250	2,667,117	444,875	18,070
2008	800,504	146,270	25,558	12,270	5,162,400	2,967,007	415,055	18,443
2009	822,581	147,700	25,427	17,137	3,691,650	3,359,011	432,601	19,469
2010	718,190	145,624	31,801	14,221	4,156,840	3,329,181	404,273	23,845
2011	598,252	131,216	19,890	5,625	3,658,590	3,093,524	429,647	26,964
2012	762,709	117,072	31,925	11,002	6,753,880	3,042,044	464,970	26,482
2013	723,579	135,002	24,576	15,620	4,173,170	3,357,984	434,652	24,785
2014	876,415	139,798	29,206	17,155	5,210,100	3,968,823	446,693	29,584

Year	Rice (1,000 cwt)	Sugarcane (1,000 t)	Sugar beets (1,000 t)	Pecans[3] (1,000 lb)	Apples (1,000 t)	Grapes (1,000 t)	Peaches (1,000 t)	Oranges[4] (1,000 bx)	Grapefruit[4] (1,000 bx)
1990	156,088	28,136	27,513	205,000	4,828	5,660	1,121	184,415	49,300
1995	173,871	30,944	27,954	268,000	5,293	5,922	1,150	263,605	71,050
2000	190,872	36,114	32,541	209,850	5,291	7,688	1,276	299,760	66,980
2003	199,897	33,858	30,710	282,100	4,397	6,664	1,260	267,040	50,080
2004	232,362	29,013	30,021	185,800	5,220	6,240	1,307	294,620	52,540
2005	223,235	26,606	27,433	280,250	4,853	7,814	1,185	216,500	25,640
2006	193,736	29,564	34,064	207,300	4,912	6,378	1,010	210,750	30,600
2007	198,388	29,969	31,834	387,305	4,545	7,057	1,127	177,280	39,900
2008	203,733	27,603	26,881	202,080	4,817	7,319	1,135	234,376	37,900
2009	219,850	30,432	29,783	302,020	4,853	7,307	1,104	210,709	32,025
2010	243,104	27,360	32,034	293,740	4,646	7,471	1,150	192,835	30,400
2011	184,941	29,224	28,896	269,700	4,713	7,448	1,072	204,949	30,360
2012	199,939	32,227	35,224	302,300	4,496	7,531	968	206,119	27,650
2013	189,953	30,761	32,789	266,330	5,216	8,632	904	189,888	28,950
2014	221,035	30,869	31,386	264,150	5,716	7,772	853	156,376	25,350

b = bale; bu = bushel; bx = box; cwt = hundred weight; lb = pound; t = ton. **Note:** Some 2014 figures are preliminary estimates. (1) Harvested for nuts. (2) Harvested for beans. (3) Utilized production only. (4) Crop year ending in year cited.

Animal Products: Average Prices Received by U.S. Farmers, 1940-2014

Source: National Agricultural Statistics Service, U.S. Dept. of Agriculture

Figures represent dollars per 100 lb for veal calves, beef cattle, hogs, lambs, milk (wholesale), and sheep; dollars per head for milk cows; cents per lb for broilers, chickens, turkeys, and wool; and cents per dozen for eggs. Weighted calendar year prices for livestock and livestock products other than wool. For 1943-63, wool prices were weighted on marketing year basis. The marketing year was changed in 1964 from a calendar year to a Dec.-Nov. basis for broilers, chickens, eggs, and hogs.

Year	Broilers	Calves (veal)	Cattle (beef)	Chickens (excl. broilers)	Eggs	Hogs	Lambs[1]	Milk	Milk cows	Sheep[1]	Turkeys	Wool
1940	17.3	8.83	7.56	13.0	18.0	5.39	8.10	1.82	61	3.95	15.2	28.4
1950	27.4	26.30	23.30	22.2	36.3	18.00	25.10	3.89	198	11.60	32.8	62.1
1960	16.9	22.90	20.40	12.2	36.1	15.30	17.90	4.21	223	5.61	25.4	42.0
1970	13.6	34.50	27.10	9.1	39.1	22.70	26.40	5.71	332	7.51	22.6	35.4
1980	27.7	76.80	62.40	11.0	56.3	38.00	63.60	13.05	1,190	21.30	41.3	88.1
1990	32.6	95.60	74.60	9.3	70.9	53.70	55.50	13.74	1,160	23.20	39.4	80.0
2000	33.6	104.00	68.60	5.7	61.8	42.30	79.80	12.40	1,340	34.30	40.7	33.0
2002	30.5	96.40	66.50	4.8	58.9	33.40	73.80	12.18	1,600	27.90	36.5	53.0
2003	34.6	102.00	79.70	4.9	73.2	37.20	94.40	12.55	1,340	34.90	36.1	73.0
2004	44.6	119.00	85.80	5.8	71.4	49.30	101.00	16.13	1,580	38.80	42.0	80.0
2005	43.6	135.00	89.70	6.5	54.0	50.20	110.00	15.19	1,770	45.10	44.9	71.0
2006	36.3	133.00	87.20	5.8	58.2	46.00	95.50	12.96	1,730	35.20	47.9	68.0
2007	43.6	119.00	89.90	5.6	88.5	46.60	98.50	19.21	1,830	31.00	52.3	87.0
2008	45.8	110.00	89.10	6.6	109.0	47.00	99.60	18.45	1,950	27.20	56.5	99.0

Year	Broilers	Calves (veal)	Cattle (beef)	Chickens (excl. broilers)	Eggs	Hogs	Lambs[1]	Milk	Milk cows	Sheep[1]	Turkeys	Wool
2009	45.7	105.00	80.30	7.2	81.7	41.60	99.60	12.93	1,390	32.50	50.0	79.0
2010	48.2	117.00	92.20	8.1	85.7	54.10	125.00	16.35	1,330	49.70	61.5	115.0
2011	46.6	142.00	113.00	8.7	95.6	65.30	NA	20.25	1,420	NA	68.2	167.0
2012	50.0	168.00	122.00	8.8	101.1	64.20	NA	18.56	1,430	NA	72.1	153.0
2013	60.6	181.00	125.00	9.5	107.2	67.20	NA	20.12	1,380	NA	66.5	145.0
2014	63.7	264.00	153.00	10.2	122.3	76.50	NA	24.07	1,830	NA	73.5	146.0

NA = Not available. (1) Prices not calculated after 2010.

Crops: Average Prices Received by U.S. Farmers, 1940-2014

Source: National Agricultural Statistics Service, U.S. Dept. of Agriculture

Figures represent cents per lb for apples, cotton, and peanuts; dollars per bushel for barley, corn, oats, soybeans, and wheat; dollars per 100 lb for potatoes, rice, and sorghum; and dollars per ton for cottonseed and baled hay. Weighted crop year prices. The marketing year is described as follows: apples, June-May; barley, hay, oats, potatoes, and wheat, July-June; cotton, cottonseed, peanuts, and rice, Aug.-July; soybeans, Sept.-Aug.; and corn and sorghum grain, Oct.-Sept.

Year	Apples	Barley	Corn	Cotton-seed	Cotton (upland)*	Hay	Oats	Peanuts	Pota-toes	Rice	Sor-ghum	Soy-beans	Wheat
1940	NA	0.39	0.62	21.70	9.8	9.78	0.30	3.7	0.85	1.80	0.87	0.89	0.67
1950	NA	1.19	1.52	86.60	39.9	21.10	0.79	10.9	1.50	5.09	1.88	2.47	2.00
1960	2.7	0.84	1.00	42.50	30.1	21.70	0.60	10.0	2.00	4.55	1.49	2.13	1.74
1970	6.5	0.97	1.33	56.40	21.9	26.10	0.62	12.8	2.21	5.17	2.04	2.85	1.33
1980	12.1	2.86	3.11	129.00	74.4	71.00	1.79	25.1	6.55	12.80	5.25	7.57	3.91
1990	20.9	2.14	2.28	121.00	67.1	80.60	1.14	34.7	6.08	6.68	3.79	5.74	2.61
2000	17.8	2.11	1.85	105.00	49.8	84.60	1.10	27.4	5.08	5.61	3.37	4.54	2.62
2002	25.6	2.72	2.32	101.00	44.5	92.40	1.81	18.2	6.69	4.49	4.14	5.53	3.56
2003	29.4	2.83	2.42	117.00	61.8	85.50	1.48	19.3	5.89	8.08	4.26	7.34	3.40
2004	21.8	2.48	2.06	107.00	41.6	92.00	1.48	18.9	5.67	7.33	3.19	5.74	3.40
2005	24.4	2.53	2.00	96.00	47.7	98.20	1.63	17.3	7.06	7.65	3.33	5.66	3.42
2006	31.7	2.85	3.04	111.00	46.5	110.00	1.87	17.7	7.33	9.96	5.88	6.43	4.26
2007	28.8	4.02	4.20	162.00	59.3	128.00	2.63	20.5	7.51	12.80	7.28	10.10	6.48
2008	23.2	5.37	4.06	223.00	47.8	152.00	3.15	23.0	9.09	16.80	5.72	9.97	6.78
2009	23.1	4.66	3.55	158.00	62.9	108.00	2.02	21.7	8.25	14.40	5.75	9.59	4.87
2010	25.1	3.86	5.18	161.00	81.5	114.00	2.52	22.5	9.20	12.70	8.96	11.30	5.70
2011	30.3	5.35	6.22	260.00	88.3	178.00	3.49	31.8	9.41	14.50	10.70	12.50	7.24
2012	37.1	6.43	6.89	252.00	72.5	191.00	3.89	30.1	8.63	15.10	11.30	14.40	7.77
2013	30.2	6.06	4.46	246.00	77.9	176.00	3.75	24.9	9.71	16.30	7.64	13.00	6.87
2014[1]	26.5	5.25	3.65	194.00	61.8	180.00	3.25	21.3	8.62	14.00	6.80	10.20	6.00

*Beginning in 1964, 480-lb net weight bales. NA = Not available. (1) Preliminary data.

World Meat Production, 2000, 2013

Source: UN Food and Agriculture Organization; in thousands of metric tons; ranked by top producers in 2013

Top beef producers

Rank	Country	2000	2013
1.	U.S.	12,298	11,698
2.	Brazil	6,579	9,675
3.	China[1]	4,988	6,730
4.	Argentina	2,718	2,822
5.	India	2,237	2,577
6.	Australia	1,988	2,318
7.	Mexico	1,409	1,807
8.	Pakistan	886	1,646
9.	Russia	1,894	1,633
10.	France	1,528	1,400
11.	Germany	1,304	1,106
12.	Canada	1,263	1,056
13.	Turkey	359	870
14.	Egypt	544	862
15.	Italy	1,153	854
16.	South Africa	625	851
17.	Colombia	745	848
18.	UK	705	847
19.	Uzbekistan	390	813
20.	Indonesia	386	586
21.	Spain	651	581
22.	New Zealand	572	564
23.	Ireland	577	518
24.	Venezuela	429	516
25.	Japan	530	508
	Africa	4,312	6,084
	Asia	12,858	17,694
	Central America	1,766	2,264
	Europe	11,768	10,152
	North America	13,561	12,754
	Oceania	2,581	2,901
	South America	11,846	15,618
	World total	**58,916**	**67,706**

Top pork producers

Rank	Country	2000	2013
1.	China[1]	35,694	52,733
2.	U.S.	8,597	10,510
3.	Germany	3,982	5,494
4.	Spain	2,905	3,431
5.	Brazil	2,600	3,280
6.	Vietnam	1,409	3,218
7.	Russia	1,569	2,816
8.	France	2,312	2,121
9.	Canada	1,640	1,977
10.	Poland	1,923	1,745
11.	Philippines	1,213	1,681
12.	Italy	1,479	1,625
13.	Denmark	1,625	1,589
14.	Japan	1,256	1,309
15.	Mexico	1,030	1,284
16.	Netherlands	1,623	1,282
17.	Belgium	1,042	1,131
18.	South Korea	916	1,007
19.	Thailand	693	967
20.	Taiwan	921	887
21.	UK	899	833
22.	Ukraine	676	748
23.	Indonesia	413	743
24.	Myanmar	123	621
25.	Chile	261	550
	Africa	769	1,304
	Asia	44,041	64,449
	Central America	1,140	1,464
	Europe	25,377	27,122
	North America	10,237	12,487
	Oceania	489	498
	South America	3,774	5,371
	World total	**86,036**	**113,035**

Top poultry producers

Rank	Country	2000	2013
1.	U.S.	16,416	20,085
2.	China[1]	11,890	18,265
3.	Brazil	6,125	12,915
4.	Russia	775	3,463
5.	Mexico	1,868	2,846
6.	India	904	2,358
7.	Iran	815	1,967
8.	Indonesia	818	1,872
9.	Argentina	1,000	1,826
10.	Turkey	661	1,771
11.	France	2,221	1,743
12.	UK	1,513	1,662
13.	Poland	589	1,652
14.	South Africa	821	1,504
15.	Thailand	1,149	1,470
16.	Germany	790	1,457
17.	Japan	1,195	1,450
18.	Malaysia	714	1,360
19.	Venezuela	693	1,276
20.	Colombia	504	1,276
21.	Canada	1,065	1,254
22.	Italy	1,092	1,233
23.	Peru	542	1,203
24.	Spain	987	1,200
25.	Myanmar	248	1,196
	Africa	2,955	5,030
	Asia	22,899	38,561
	Central America	2,371	3,703
	Europe	11,866	18,149
	North America	17,480	21,339
	Oceania	767	1,297
	South America	9,733	20,020
	World total	**68,562**	**108,669**

(1) Not including Hong Kong or Macao.

World Corn, Rice, and Wheat Production, 2000, 2013

Source: UN Food and Agriculture Organization; in millions of metric tons; ranked by top producers in 2013

Top corn producers			
Rank	**Country**	**2000**	**2013**
1.	U.S.	251.9	353.7
2.	China	106.2	217.8
3.	Brazil	31.9	80.5
4.	Argentina	16.8	32.1
5.	Ukraine	3.8	30.9
6.	India	12.0	23.3
7.	Mexico	17.6	22.7
8.	Indonesia	9.7	18.5
9.	France	16.0	15.1
10.	Canada	7.0	14.2
11.	South Africa	11.4	12.4
12.	Russia	1.5	11.6
13.	Romania	4.9	11.3
14.	Nigeria	4.1	10.4
15.	Philippines	4.5	7.4
16.	Hungary	5.0	6.7
17.	Ethiopia	2.7	6.7
18.	Italy	10.1	6.5
19.	Egypt	6.5	6.5
20.	Turkey	2.3	5.9
21.	Serbia	NA	5.9
22.	Vietnam	2.0	5.2
23.	Thailand	4.5	5.1
24.	Spain	4.0	4.9
25.	Pakistan	1.6	4.8
	Africa	44.3	71.0
	Asia	149.1	304.3
	Central America	20.3	26.6
	Europe	63.5	117.5
	North America	258.8	367.9
	Oceania	0.6	0.7
	South America	55.4	127.6
	World total	**592.5**	**1,016.4**

NA = Not available.

Top rice producers			
Rank	**Country**	**2000**	**2013**
1.	China	189.8	205.0
2.	India	127.5	159.2
3.	Indonesia	51.9	71.3
4.	Bangladesh	37.6	51.5
5.	Vietnam	32.5	44.1
6.	Thailand	25.8	38.8
7.	Myanmar	21.3	28.0
8.	Philippines	12.4	18.4
9.	Brazil	11.1	11.8
10.	Japan	9.4	10.8
11.	Pakistan	7.2	9.8
12.	Cambodia	4.0	9.3
13.	U.S.	8.7	8.6
14.	Egypt	6.0	6.8
15.	South Korea	7.2	5.6
16.	Nigeria	3.3	4.7
17.	Nepal	4.2	4.5
18.	Sri Lanka	2.9	4.5
19.	Madagascar	2.5	3.6
20.	Laos	2.2	3.3
21.	Peru	1.9	3.1
22.	North Korea	1.7	2.9
23.	Malaysia	2.1	2.6
24.	Iran	2.0	2.5
25.	Colombia	2.7	2.4
	Africa	17.5	29.0
	Asia	543.1	674.7
	Central America	1.2	1.2
	Europe	3.2	3.9
	North America	8.7	8.6
	Oceania	1.1	1.2
	South America	20.9	24.9
	World total	**596.9**	**745.2**

Top wheat producers			
Rank	**Country**	**2000**	**2013**
1.	China	99.6	121.7
2.	India	76.4	93.5
3.	U.S.	60.6	58.0
4.	Russia	34.5	52.1
5.	France	37.4	38.6
6.	Canada	26.5	37.5
7.	Germany	21.6	25.0
8.	Pakistan	21.1	24.2
9.	Australia	22.1	22.9
10.	Ukraine	10.2	22.8
11.	Turkey	21.0	22.1
12.	Iran	8.1	14.0
13.	Kazakhstan	9.1	13.9
14.	UK	16.7	11.9
15.	Poland	8.5	9.5
16.	Egypt	6.6	9.5
17.	Argentina	16.1	8.0
18.	Spain	7.3	7.6
19.	Romania	4.5	7.3
20.	Italy	7.5	7.0
21.	Morocco	1.4	6.9
22.	Uzbekistan	3.5	6.8
23.	Brazil	1.7	5.7
24.	Afghanistan	1.5	5.2
25.	Bulgaria	2.8	5.1
	Africa	14.3	28.1
	Asia	254.5	318.8
	Central America	3.5	3.4
	Europe	183.6	225.5
	North America	87.2	95.5
	Oceania	22.4	23.3
	South America	20.2	18.6
	World total	**585.7**	**713.2**

Value of U.S. Agricultural Exports and Imports, 1978-2014

Source: Economic Research Service, U.S. Dept. of Agriculture
(in billions of dollars, unless otherwise noted)

Year[1]	Agric. trade surplus	Agric. exports	% of all exports	Agric. imports	% of all imports	Year[1]	Agric. trade surplus	Agric. exports	% of all exports	Agric. imports	% of all imports
1978	$13.4	$27.3	21%	$13.9	8%	1998	$16.8	$53.7	8%	$36.8	4%
1980	23.2	40.5	19	17.3	7	1999	11.8	49.1	8	37.3	4
1983	18.5	34.8	18	16.3	7	2000	11.9	50.8	7	38.9	3
1984	19.1	38.0	18	18.9	6	2001	13.7	52.7	8	39.0	3
1985	11.5	31.2	15	19.7	6	2002	12.4	53.3	8	41.0	4
1986	5.4	26.3	13	20.9	6	2003	10.3	56.0	9	45.7	4
1987	7.2	27.9	12	20.7	5	2004	9.7	62.4	9	52.7	4
1988	14.3	35.3	12	21.0	5	2005	4.8	62.5	8	57.7	4
1989	18.1	39.7	12	21.6	5	2006	4.6	68.6	8	64.0	3
1990	16.6	39.5	11	22.9	5	2007	12.2	82.2	8	70.1	4
1991	16.4	39.3	10	22.9	5	2008	35.6	114.9	10	79.3	4
1992	18.3	43.1	10	24.8	5	2009	22.9	96.3	10	73.4	5
1993	17.7	42.9	10	25.1	4	2010	29.6	108.5	10	79.0	4
1994	19.2	46.2	10	27.0	4	2011	43.0	137.5	11	94.5	4
1995	26.0	56.3	10	30.3	4	2012	32.5	135.9	10	103.4	5
1996	26.8	60.3	10	33.5	4	2013	37.1	141.0	10	103.9	5
1997	21.7	57.3	9	35.7	4	2014	43.3	152.5	11	109.2	5

(1) Fiscal year (Oct.-Sept.).

Crop Consumption Per Capita in Selected Nations, 1980-2011

Source: UN Food and Agriculture Organization
(in kilograms per capita per year, unless otherwise noted)

	Corn				Rice				Wheat			
Country	**1980**	**1990**	**2011**	**% change, 1980-2011**	**1980**	**1990**	**2011**	**% change, 1980-2011**	**1980**	**1990**	**2011**	**% change, 1980-2011**
Afghanistan	33	24	3	−92.4%	20	17	16	−16.8%	162	140	162	0.2%
Argentina	6	5	10	65.0	3	6	8	212.0	115	114	103	−9.9
Australia	2	4	5	121.7	8	8	11	42.1	81	70	70	−13.4
Bangladesh	0	0	0	NA	144	159	173	19.7	29	21	17	−39.7
Brazil	22	22	24	9.5	39	41	34	−12.8	50	44	54	7.9
Canada	4	3	19	421.6	3	5	10	185.3	76	78	70	−8.8
China	5	4	7	51.0	76	81	79	4.6	59	77	63	7.7
Congo Republic	5	3	4	−23.4	2	5	20	1,064.7	33	33	40	20.8
Cuba	0	0	24	NA	51	47	64	25.1	78	74	52	−33.5
Egypt	49	57	63	30.2	26	31	40	49.6	129	151	146	13.0
France	2	13	11	533.3	4	4	6	62.9	96	92	106	11.4
Germany	3	6	10	212.9	2	2	3	57.9	69	67	85	24.5
India	8	8	7	−17.5	64	78	72	12.4	45	41	59	31.2
Indonesia	24	29	34	43.5	125	131	133	6.4	10	9	24	142.3
Iran	1	1	3	316.7	30	30	29	−1.7	154	164	152	−1.1
Iraq	0	3	0	NA	31	37	30	−2.9	144	185	140	−3.3
Israel	12	23	17	46.1	6	8	9	53.3	138	124	122	−11.6

Country	Corn 1980	Corn 1990	Corn 2011	Corn % change, 1980-2011	Rice 1980	Rice 1990	Rice 2011	Rice % change, 1980-2011	Wheat 1980	Wheat 1990	Wheat 2011	Wheat % change, 1980-2011
Italy	5	3	4	–16.0%	5	5	5	13.0%	174	149	146	–16.2%
Japan	15	19	11	–24.7	59	53	43	–26.7	44	44	49	11.0
Kenya	114	88	77	–32.4	2	1	10	329.2	20	23	34	70.5
Korea, North	43	56	45	6.3	71	70	75	4.9	32	22	23	–26.3
Korea, South	2	13	13	700.0	138	97	86	–37.8	49	48	52	5.3
Mexico	118	124	116	–1.8	5	4	6	21.3	42	42	34	–20.4
New Zealand	1	3	4	200.0	2	4	7	191.7	78	69	76	–3.2
Nigeria	6	33	31	409.8	15	21	30	104.8	16	3	25	57.1
Pakistan	7	6	14	113.4	23	14	12	–44.9	114	128	114	0.0
Philippines	22	19	31	40.5	97	94	119	22.7	17	20	15	–12.5
Russia	NA	NA	1	NA	NA	NA	5	NA	NA	NA	131	NA
Saudi Arabia	12	13	22	93.9	33	18	37	12.0	88	104	91	3.4
South Africa	120	108	100	–16.5	4	8	17	288.6	56	57	61	7.7
Thailand	5	5	10	117.4	137	114	112	–18.6	4	4	12	195.0
Turkey	9	21	18	110.6	4	7	10	182.9	210	223	174	–17.3
Ukraine	NA	NA	12	NA	NA	NA	4	NA	NA	NA	106	NA
United Arab Emirates	1	1	1	–22.2	43	34	50	16.5	63	65	96	52.5
UK	3	3	3	–9.4	2	3	7	263.2	82	82	97	17.7
U.S.	8	13	13	58.2	4	7	8	92.3	70	81	80	13.2
Venezuela	55	54	57	3.4	21	13	27	28.2	50	51	55	8.5
Vietnam	7	7	11	58.2	128	133	145	13.2	17	3	9	–47.6
Africa	37	41	43	16.7	15	17	23	57.4	48	48	49	3.8
Asia	8	9	10	26.3	76	82	78	2.0	54	61	63	17.0
Central America	107	113	103	–4.6	8	7	10	33.3	38	38	34	–10.6
Europe	4	5	7	94.6	5	4	5	–2.0	118	117	108	–8.5
North America	8	12	13	74.7	4	7	8	102.6	71	81	79	10.9
Oceania	2	4	5	136.8	9	10	13	50.6	79	69	70	–11.2
South America	22	23	26	19.0	30	32	30	0.0	58	53	58	0.2
World per capita consumption	**13**	**15**	**18**	**36.2**	**49**	**54**	**54**	**9.8**	**65**	**68**	**65**	**0.8**

NA = Not available or not applicable. **Note:** All figures are rounded. Percent change based on unrounded raw data.

Meat Consumption Per Capita in Selected Nations, 1980-2011

Source: UN Food and Agriculture Organization

(in kilograms per capita per year, unless otherwise noted)

Country	Beef 1980	Beef 1990	Beef 2011	Beef % change, 1980-2011	Pork 1980	Pork 1990	Pork 2011	Pork % change, 1980-2011	Poultry 1980	Poultry 1990	Poultry 2011	Poultry % change, 1980-2011
Afghanistan	5	7	5	–5.9%	NA	NA	NA	NA	1	1	3	188.9%
Argentina	85	64	55	–35.4	10	4	9	–5.3%	11	11	35	215.2
Australia	53	47	41	–22.8	15	18	23	58.2	21	24	45	116.8
Bangladesh	2	1	1	–13.3	0	0	0	NA	1	1	1	133.3
Brazil	23	28	39	73.8	8	7	13	57.5	10	14	41	302.0
Canada	40	36	30	–26.1	35	28	24	–29.5	22	28	37	67.9
China	0	1	5	1,100.0	12	20	36	200.8	2	3	13	652.9
Congo Republic	4	1	3	–25.0	1	2	3	257.1	2	5	22	1,015.0
Cuba	15	13	6	–58.4	5	10	19	306.4	9	12	17	81.9
Egypt	7	8	13	88.6	0	0	0	NA	4	5	12	205.3
France	33	33	25	–22.3	38	34	34	–10.7	16	21	23	44.4
Germany	23	22	13	–41.7	60	60	54	–11.0	10	11	18	85.6
India	2	2	1	–43.5	0	1	0	–25.0	0	1	2	800.0
Indonesia	2	2	3	38.9	1	3	3	150.0	1	3	7	483.3
Iran	6	6	6	–6.5	0	0	0	NA	6	7	26	346.6
Iraq	5	7	3	–43.5	0	0	0	NA	9	11	14	67.4
Israel	13	14	28	111.5	3	2	3	0.0	35	39	70	97.5
Italy	26	27	22	–17.9	25	32	40	61.0	18	20	18	0.0
Japan	5	8	9	80.0	14	15	21	51.9	10	14	19	89.1
Kenya	12	9	11	–7.6	0	0	0	NA	2	1	1	–75.0
Korea, North	2	2	1	–50.0	10	11	5	–51.6	2	3	2	–19.0
Korea, South	3	6	15	461.5	8	13	31	296.2	3	6	16	556.0
Mexico	11	14	16	50.9	18	9	14	–22.5	6	10	30	368.3
New Zealand	57	39	48	–17.1	12	14	19	68.7	10	17	36	269.8
Nigeria	5	2	2	–57.4	1	1	2	200.0	2	2	2	0.0
Pakistan	5	6	9	79.2	0	0	0	NA	1	2	4	633.3
Philippines	3	2	4	57.1	9	12	18	110.3	5	4	11	129.2
Russia	NA	NA	16	NA	NA	NA	23	NA	NA	NA	23	NA
Saudi Arabia	6	5	6	–1.6	NA	NA	NA	NA	24	29	48	100.8
South Africa	20	17	16	–19.8	3	4	5	50.0	8	15	35	346.2
Thailand	6	6	3	–55.2	6	6	13	128.6	7	9	12	78.3
Turkey	3	7	10	221.9	0	0	0	NA	6	8	19	233.3
Ukraine	NA	NA	9	NA	NA	NA	18	NA	NA	NA	22	NA
United Arab Emirates	14	13	5	–63.1	NA	NA	NA	NA	43	39	39	–9.2
UK	23	21	19	–17.2	26	25	27	1.1	14	19	31	126.5
U.S.	47	43	37	–21.8	33	28	28	–15.5	26	39	51	94.7
Venezuela	22	18	20	–8.6	6	5	7	18.3	17	13	45	159.8
Vietnam	2	2	7	278.9	5	10	34	549.1	2	3	16	766.7
Africa	7	6	6	–12.5	1	1	1	100.0	3	3	6	148.0
Asia	2	3	4	120.0	6	9	15	144.3	2	3	9	327.3
Central America	10	12	14	35.6	14	8	12	–17.6	6	9	27	365.5
Europe	23	25	15	–35.0	32	35	35	7.8	12	15	22	85.5
North America	47	43	36	–22.3	33	28	28	–16.6	26	38	50	92.3
Oceania	50	43	39	–22.1	14	17	22	58.1	18	22	42	135.2
South America	28	27	31	11.3	7	6	11	50.0	9	12	35	275.0
World per capita consumption	**11**	**10**	**9**	**–11.3**	**12**	**13**	**16**	**31.4**	**6**	**8**	**14**	**148.3**

NA = Not available or not applicable. **Note:** All figures are rounded. Percent change based on unrounded raw data.

World Capture of Fish, Crustaceans, and Mollusks, 2004-13

Source: UN Food and Agriculture Organization
(in thousands of metric tons; ranked by 2013 captures)

Country	2004	2005	2010	2012	2013
China	14,465	14,589	15,415	16,167	16,275
Indonesia	4,605	4,684	5,375	5,814	6,102
Peru	9,605	9,388	4,302	4,849	5,854
U.S.	4,960	4,893	4,426	5,128	5,231
India	3,391	3,691	4,689	4,872	4,645
Russia	2,942	3,198	4,070	4,331	4,346
Myanmar	1,587	1,732	3,063	3,579	3,787
Japan	4,337	4,334	4,066	3,651	3,657
Vietnam	1,940	1,988	2,414	2,705	2,804
Philippines	2,211	2,270	2,612	2,323	2,332
Norway	2,524	2,393	2,680	2,151	2,074
Thailand	2,840	2,814	1,811	1,720	1,844
Chile	4,927	4,328	2,680	2,573	1,771
Mexico	1,262	1,319	1,527	1,575	1,627
South Korea	1,581	1,647	1,734	1,670	1,598
Bangladesh	1,187	1,334	1,727	1,536	1,550
Malaysia	1,336	1,214	1,433	1,477	1,489
Iceland	1,734	1,665	1,061	1,359	1,367
Morocco	918	1,026	1,136	1,162	1,253
Spain	811	854	973	932	1,034
World total[1]	**92,763**	**92,485**	**89,154**	**91,306**	**92,573**

(1) Includes nations not shown.

World Aquaculture Production, 2004-13

Source: UN Food and Agriculture Organization; ranked by 2013 production volume

	Metric tons (thous.)					Value (mil)				
Country	2004	2005	2010	2012	2013	2004	2005	2010	2012	2013
China	26,567	28,121	36,734	41,108	43,550	$26,985	$30,204	$58,822	$66,213	$70,037
India	2,799	2,967	3,786	4,209	4,550	3,788	3,763	7,339	9,249	10,356
Indonesia	1,045	1,197	2,305	3,068	3,820	1,993	1,999	4,895	6,715	8,779
Vietnam	1,199	1,437	2,672	3,086	3,207	2,444	2,931	5,150	5,899	6,198
Bangladesh	915	882	1,309	1,726	1,860	1,363	1,246	2,840	3,911	4,414
Norway	637	662	1,020	1,321	1,248	1,681	2,136	5,087	5,167	6,897
Egypt	472	540	920	1,018	1,098	613	792	1,546	2,011	2,089
Thailand	1,260	1,304	1,286	1,272	1,057	1,705	1,741	2,817	3,484	3,166
Chile	676	724	701	1,071	1,033	2,803	3,229	3,753	5,993	7,525
Myanmar	400	485	851	885	929	1,025	959	956	1,501	1,715
Philippines	512	557	745	791	815	701	794	1,563	1,955	1,977
Japan	777	746	718	633	609	3,062	3,012	4,091	4,290	3,332
Brazil	270	258	478	480	473	470	445	1,465	1,451	1,310
U.S.	608	514	497	420	441	922	896	1,023	1,005	1,211
South Korea	406	437	476	487	402	980	1,195	1,482	1,414	1,455
Taiwan	318	305	310	344	344	943	969	1,116	1,238	1,326
Ecuador	109	139	273	322	332	469	610	1,250	1,513	1,763
Iran	104	112	220	297	325	317	320	638	867	957
Nigeria	44	56	201	254	279	124	159	576	712	799
Malaysia	171	176	373	303	261	324	339	839	863	706
World total[1]	**41,909**	**44,298**	**59,038**	**66,477**	**70,190**	**59,900**	**65,754**	**118,607**	**138,338**	**150,348**

Note: Does not include production of aquatic plants or marine mammals. (1) Includes nations not shown.

U.S. Commercial Landings of Fish and Shellfish, 1990-2013

Source: Natl. Marine Fisheries Service, Natl. Oceanic and Atmospheric Admin., U.S. Dept. of Commerce

	Landings for human food		Landings for industrial purposes[1]		Total	
Year	Weight (mil lbs)	Value (mil)	Weight (mil lbs)	Value (mil)	Weight (mil lbs)	Value (mil)
1990	7,041	$3,366	2,363	$156	9,404	$3,522
1995	7,667	3,625	2,121	145	9,788	3,770
2000	6,912	3,398	2,157	152	9,069	3,550
2002	7,205	2,940	2,192	152	9,397	3,092
2003	7,521	3,185	1,986	157	9,507	3,347
2004	7,794	3,611	1,889	145	9,683	3,756
2005	7,997	3,825	1,710	117	9,707	3,942
2006	7,842	3,911	1,641	113	9,483	4,024
2007	7,490	4,015	1,819	177	9,309	4,192
2008	6,633	4,231	1,692	152	8,325	4,383
2009	6,198	3,733	1,833	158	8,031	3,891
2010	6,526	4,356	1,705	164	8,231	4,520
2011	7,909	5,108	1,949	181	9,858	5,289
2012	7,477	4,923	2,157	180	9,634	5,103
2013[2]	8,053	5,292	1,827	198	9,880	5,490

Note: Does not include products of aquaculture, except oysters and clams. Landings reported in round (live) weight for all items except univalve and bivalve mollusks (e.g., clams, oysters, and scallops), which are reported in weight of meats (excluding the shell). (1) Processed into meal, oil, solubles, and shell products or used as bait or animal food. (2) Preliminary.

U.S. Domestic Landings by Region, 2005, 2013

Source: Natl. Marine Fisheries Service, Natl. Oceanic and Atmospheric Admin., U.S. Dept. of Commerce

	2005		2013[1]	
Region	Weight (thous. lbs)	Value (thous.)	Weight (thous. lbs)	Value (thous.)
New England	684,090	$971,663	635,885	$1,161,981
Middle Atlantic[2]	199,937	221,505	582,662	435,373
Chesapeake[2]	508,953	218,933	NA	NA
South Atlantic	122,422	125,117	91,514	160,281
Gulf	1,196,355	620,987	1,457,419	905,340
Pacific Coast (incl. Alaska)	6,950,647	1,700,927	7,060,900	2,696,521
Great Lakes[3]	16,732	12,434	18,725	23,023
Hawaii	28,139	70,811	32,447	107,979
Total	**9,707,275**	**3,942,376**	**9,879,552**	**5,490,498**

NA = Not available. **Note:** Landings reported in round (live) weight for all items except univalve and bivalve mollusks (e.g., clams, oysters, scallops), which are reported in weight of meats (excluding the shell). (1) Preliminary. (2) Chesapeake Region states (Maryland and Virginia) included with Middle Atlantic in 2013. (3) Data for the Great Lakes states lag by one year (i.e., figures are for 2004 and 2012).

EMPLOYMENT

Employment and Unemployment in the U.S., 1900-2014

Source: Bureau of Labor Statistics, U.S. Dept. of Labor

(civilian labor force, persons 16 years of age and older unless otherwise noted; annual averages, in thousands)

Year	Employed	Unemployed Number	Unemployed Rate	Year	Employed	Unemployed Number	Unemployed Rate	Year	Employed	Unemployed Number	Unemployed Rate
1900[1]	26,956	1,420	5.0%	1987	112,440	7,425	6.2%	2001	136,933	6,801	4.7%
1910[1]	34,599	2,150	5.9	1988	114,968	6,701	5.5	2002	136,485	8,378	5.8
1920[1]	39,208	2,132	5.2	1989	117,342	6,528	5.3	2003	137,736	8,774	6.0
1930[1]	44,183	4,340	8.9	1990	118,793	7,047	5.6	2004	139,252	8,149	5.5
1940[1]	47,520	8,120	14.6	1991	117,718	8,628	6.8	2005	141,730	7,591	5.1
1950	58,918	3,288	5.3	1992	118,492	9,613	7.5	2006	144,427	7,001	4.6
1955	62,170	2,852	4.4	1993	120,259	8,940	6.9	2007	146,047	7,078	4.6
1960	65,778	3,852	5.5	1994	123,060	7,996	6.1	2008	145,362	8,924	5.8
1965	71,088	3,366	4.5	1995	124,900	7,404	5.6	2009	139,877	14,265	9.3
1970	78,678	4,093	4.9	1996	126,708	7,236	5.4	2010	139,064	14,825	9.6
1975	85,846	7,929	8.5	1997	129,558	6,739	4.9	2011	139,869	13,747	8.9
1980	99,303	7,637	7.1	1998	131,463	6,210	4.5	2012	142,469	12,506	8.1
1985	107,150	8,312	7.2	1999	133,488	5,880	4.2	2013	143,929	11,460	7.4
1986	109,597	8,237	7.0	2000	136,891	5,692	4.0	2014	146,305	9,617	6.2

Note: Because of revisions in population controls, data for a given year may not be strictly comparable to other years. **Other unemployment rates (1905-45)**, persons 14 years of age and older: 1905, 4.3%; 1915, 8.5%; 1925, 3.2%; 1935, 20.3%; 1936, 16.9%; 1937, 14.3%; 1938, 19.0%; 1939, 17.2%; 1945, 1.9%. (1) Persons 14 years of age and older.

Unemployment Rate and Benefits Data by State, 2014

Source: Employment and Training Admin., U.S. Dept. of Labor; state programs only

State/ terr.	Unemployment rate	Monetarily eligible claimants	Number of first payments	Number of final payments	Initial claims	Benefits paid	Average weekly benefit	Employers subject to state law
AL	6.8%	117,504	74,968	31,245	207,978	$231,273,223	$211.64	85,577
AK	6.8	45,009	30,753	16,398	72,002	128,267,641	253.52	17,970
AZ	6.9	145,833	96,768	43,940	248,822	322,328,651	222.27	123,523
AR	6.1	96,850	63,181	23,868	159,334	211,909,540	290.89	68,217
CA	7.5	995,399	1,127,480	594,884	2,880,575	5,595,465,469	302.05	1,236,500
CO	5.0	121,538	93,969	46,995	148,384	493,142,851	366.84	154,902
CT	6.6	147,279	137,079	51,443	228,413	683,996,401	345.24	99,071
DE	5.7	28,986	16,707	8,260	45,455	78,592,785	246.72	27,059
DC	7.8	25,449	24,342	12,923	20,345	128,090,431	297.57	30,854
FL	6.3	363,165	198,172	139,696	651,071	766,609,470	237.01	492,313
GA	7.2	266,813	188,713	84,300	456,749	474,420,014	268.61	211,580
HI	4.4	36,147	26,958	9,465	82,769	172,617,322	430.25	30,857
ID	4.8	48,065	35,999	11,268	81,881	110,392,062	281.46	47,636
IL	7.1	355,085	351,737	142,969	630,594	1,871,385,190	327.47	308,324
IN	6.0	164,473	112,728	36,118	251,149	407,526,993	252.04	124,948
IA	4.4	111,826	93,158	26,559	164,981	386,045,809	348.46	75,917
KS	4.5	80,260	63,004	27,356	134,687	197,678,787	351.58	69,662
KY	6.5	121,542	63,394	26,579	211,186	334,229,768	291.55	90,559
LA	6.4	93,527	54,527	18,687	121,663	175,464,609	207.68	99,216
ME	5.7	45,366	35,401	12,726	70,147	135,406,507	289.93	41,265
MD	5.8	146,688	122,399	53,291	229,492	623,273,914	325.48	139,467
MA	5.8	242,494	220,516	83,548	352,642	1,500,424,543	433.17	200,608
MI	7.3	334,925	275,308	111,234	583,161	1,002,874,952	284.59	204,251
MN	4.1	172,910	127,596	49,902	243,496	695,209,793	390.00	130,735
MS	7.8	71,350	47,987	18,872	111,039	131,137,687	197.89	52,898
MO	6.1	177,386	118,063	53,692	333,393	374,133,109	243.63	145,488
MT	4.7	36,090	23,653	9,261	59,586	95,630,985	297.62	37,843
NE	3.3	44,484	28,595	11,056	71,806	92,820,442	287.90	57,428
NV	7.8	104,578	79,000	33,521	175,232	369,487,772	312.16	60,246
NH	4.3	33,104	21,157	5,061	52,058	79,244,667	289.22	40,926
NJ	6.6	360,446	322,654	154,386	548,646	2,087,137,720	405.61	229,480
NM	6.5	46,673	35,519	17,493	63,287	184,145,025	304.61	45,041
NY	6.3	678,357	494,864	200,083	1,094,347	2,356,333,626	307.21	514,611
NC	6.1	218,484	139,657	77,000	281,976	447,966,279	228.88	201,145
ND	2.8	23,895	17,731	7,461	24,148	95,035,885	427.90	25,912
OH	5.7	289,328	208,622	66,745	450,523	943,364,298	326.75	220,419
OK	4.5	73,258	43,981	21,431	95,186	218,680,818	316.95	85,454
OR	6.9	150,145	102,495	40,465	303,456	559,033,063	326.54	113,585
PA	5.8	425,790	413,685	139,418	1,077,330	2,115,444,468	363.77	309,750
PR	13.9	84,388	76,690	41,068	115,118	162,406,354	118.27	48,183
RI	7.7	43,542	34,847	13,803	76,357	179,068,358	338.78	33,264
SC	6.4	124,095	60,728	23,448	196,654	192,544,455	251.10	102,017
SD	3.4	10,868	6,432	1,067	15,083	26,461,835	290.80	26,378
TN	6.7	154,880	105,249	40,821	244,056	339,919,548	223.40	115,286
TX	5.1	592,292	408,789	194,815	805,533	2,024,982,854	354.55	495,981
UT	3.8	60,502	40,690	14,151	78,045	166,021,692	351.95	72,924
VT	4.1	23,850	19,507	3,619	37,420	71,397,959	320.45	21,624
VA	5.2	178,214	104,660	49,756	234,898	478,025,788	298.84	202,942
VI	NA	2,447	2,275	1,209	2,810	10,730,327	312.39	3,475
WA	6.2	234,767	178,030	56,829	420,751	958,841,551	396.61	216,641
WV	6.5	57,994	47,715	15,899	70,534	202,615,906	278.54	35,768
WI	5.5	235,507	175,853	54,575	496,994	646,019,554	285.28	134,874
WY	4.3	17,334	12,016	4,119	21,501	56,027,276	362.82	22,030
U.S.	**6.2**	**8,861,181**	**7,006,001**	**3,034,778**	**15,834,743**	**34,878,306,432**	**314.74**	**7,782,618**

NA = Not available.

U.S. Unemployment Duration by Industry and Occupation, 2014

Source: Bureau of Labor Statistics, U.S. Dept. of Labor

	Number of unemployed persons (thous.)					Weeks of unemployment	
Occupation	**Total**	**Less than 5 weeks**	**5 to 14 weeks**	**15 to 26 weeks**	**27 weeks and over**	**Average (mean) duration**	**Median duration**
Management, professional, and related	1,777	444	449	259	625	36.2	14.4
Management, business, and financial operations	704	141	170	110	282	40.3	18.8
Professional and related	1,073	303	278	149	343	33.5	12.5
Service	2,048	561	502	311	673	32.3	13.6
Sales and office	2,119	492	527	338	760	35.3	15.9
Sales and related	1,022	245	263	177	338	32.9	14.7
Office and administrative support	1,096	247	265	161	423	37.6	17.1
Natural resources, construction, and maintenance	1,171	340	297	188	346	31.2	12.4
Farming, fishing, and forestry	134	39	36	26	33	27.6	12.1
Construction and extraction	813	245	206	128	233	30.6	12.0
Installation, maintenance, and repair	224	56	55	34	79	35.8	14.9
Production, transportation, and material moving	1,385	350	352	222	461	32.6	14.2
Production	632	153	158	99	222	33.1	15.1
Transportation and material moving	754	197	194	123	239	32.3	13.6
Industry[1]							
Agriculture and related industries	154	46	42	29	37	27.6	11.2
Mining, quarrying, and oil and gas extraction	54	16	14	10	13	24.8	11.3
Construction	776	230	206	122	218	29.8	11.8
Manufacturing	766	165	190	120	291	37.0	17.3
Durable goods	465	103	117	73	172	36.0	16.7
Nondurable goods	301	63	74	46	118	38.7	18.3
Wholesale and retail trade	1,275	313	328	208	427	32.7	14.4
Transportation and utilities	391	93	87	71	141	35.8	17.3
Information	161	38	39	24	60	37.8	16.1
Financial activities	386	77	89	64	156	39.3	19.1
Professional and business services	1,114	276	296	172	369	33.5	13.9
Education and health services	1,222	330	304	171	417	33.5	13.5
Leisure and hospitality	1,209	330	317	183	379	30.7	12.9
Other services	371	107	85	53	126	35.4	13.7
Public administration	179	38	40	27	74	42.4	19.6
No previous work experience	1,086	277	296	172	340	33.3	13.3
Total unemployed	**9,617**	**2,471**	**2,432**	**1,497**	**3,218**	**33.7**	**14.0**

Note: Persons 16 years of age and older. (1) Includes wage and salary workers only.

Persons Not in the U.S. Labor Force, 2014

Source: Bureau of Labor Statistics, U.S. Dept. of Labor

The Labor Dept.'s unemployment rate, based on its household survey, shows the number of people out of work as a percentage of U.S. adults age 16 and older in the labor force. That rate excludes the millions of adults considered to be not in the labor force.

(in thousands)

		Age in years			Sex	
	Number	**16 to 24**	**25 to 54**	**55 and over**	**Men**	**Women**
Total not in the labor force	**92,025**	**17,418**	**23,744**	**50,863**	**36,865**	**55,159**
Do not want a job now[1]	85,702	15,377	21,075	49,250	33,932	51,770
Want a job[1]	6,323	2,041	2,669	1,614	2,934	3,389
Did not search for work in previous year	3,448	1,072	1,337	1,039	1,524	1,924
Searched in previous year but not previous 4 weeks[2]	2,875	969	1,332	574	1,409	1,465
Not available to work now	667	303	284	81	270	397
Available to work now	2,207	666	1,048	493	1,139	1,068
Reason not currently looking[3]						
Discouragement over job prospects[4]	739	184	350	205	443	296
Reasons other than discouragement	1,468	482	697	289	696	772
Family responsibilities	239	34	160	45	65	174
In school or training	267	208	54	4	149	118
Ill health or disability	161	16	84	61	82	80
Other[5]	801	224	398	179	400	401

(1) Includes some persons who are not asked if they want a job. (2) Persons who had a job in the prior 12 months must have searched since the end of that job to be considered unemployed. (3) Of those available to work now. (4) Includes believing no work is available, not being able to find work, lacking necessary schooling or training, thought of as too young or old by employers, and other types of discrimination. (5) Includes those who did not actively look for work in the prior four weeks for such reasons as child care and transportation problems, as well as a small number for which reason for nonparticipation was not ascertained.

U.S. Displaced Workers, 2014

Source: Bureau of Labor Statistics, U.S. Dept. of Labor

		Reason for job loss (% distrib.)		
	Number (thous.)	**Plant or company closed down or moved**	**Insufficient work**	**Position or shift abolished**
Total displaced workers	**4,292**	**35.3%**	**32.6%**	**32.1%**
Age: 20 to 24 years	91	45.6	33.1	21.3
25 to 54 years	2,897	35.1	34.6	30.3
55 to 64 years	1,004	34.2	28.8	37.0
65 years and over	301	37.1	25.8	37.1
Sex: Men	2,390	35.0	37.8	27.2
Women	1,902	35.5	26.1	38.4
Race: White	3,499	35.4	31.1	33.6
Black	465	40.1	38.0	21.8
Asian	192	36.2	28.4	35.4
Hispanic or Latino	685	41.5	40.0	18.4

Note: As of Jan. 2014. Displaced workers are persons age 20 or older who lost or left jobs they had held for at least three years. Workers in this table were displaced between Jan. 2011 and Dec. 2013. Hispanic or Latino persons may be of any race.

U.S. Unemployment Rates by Selected Characteristics, 1995-2015

Source: Bureau of Labor Statistics, U.S. Dept. of Labor

	1995	2000	2005	2010	2011	2012	2013	2014 Jan.	2014 June	2014 Yr.	2015 Jan.	2015 June
Total (all civilian workers)	**5.6%**	**4.0%**	**5.1%**	**9.6%**	**8.9%**	**8.1%**	**7.4%**	**7.0%**	**6.3%**	**6.2%**	**6.1%**	**5.5%**
Men, 20 years and older	4.8	3.3	4.4	9.8	8.7	7.5	7.0	7.0	5.5	5.7	6.0	4.6
Women, 20 years and older	4.9	3.6	4.6	8.0	7.9	7.3	6.5	6.0	5.5	5.6	5.2	4.9
Both sexes, 16 to 19 years	17.3	13.1	16.6	25.9	24.4	24.0	22.9	21.0	23.9	19.6	19.2	20.7
White	4.9	3.5	4.4	8.7	7.9	7.2	6.5	6.2	5.5	5.3	5.3	4.8
Black	10.4	7.6	10.0	16.0	15.8	13.8	13.1	12.6	11.1	11.3	10.7	9.8
Asian	—	3.6	4.0	7.5	7.0	5.9	5.2	4.8	5.1	5.0	4.1	4.1
Hispanic or Latino (any race)	9.3	5.7	6.0	12.5	11.5	10.3	9.1	9.1	7.8	7.4	7.5	6.8
Married men, spouse present	3.3	—	—	6.8	5.8	4.9	4.3	3.8	3.4	3.4	2.9	2.8
Married women, spouse present	3.9	—	—	5.9	5.6	5.3	4.6	3.9	3.8	3.8	3.3	3.2
Women who maintain families, spouse absent	8.0	5.9	7.8	12.3	12.4	11.4	10.2	9.1	8.1	8.6	8.1	7.8
Occupation												
Management, professional, and related	2.4	1.8	2.3	4.7	4.5	4.1	3.6	3.1	3.5	3.1	2.9	2.9
Service	7.5	5.2	6.4	10.3	9.9	9.1	8.6	8.5	6.9	7.3	7.6	6.3
Sales and office	5.0	3.8	4.8	9.0	8.7	7.7	7.2	7.1	5.8	6.0	5.5	5.0
Natural resources, constr., and maintenance	—	5.3	6.5	16.1	13.3	11.5	9.8	10.2	7.3	8.0	9.9	6.2
Production, transp., and material moving	—	5.1	6.5	12.8	11.3	9.8	9.1	9.0	6.9	7.4	7.2	6.0
Industry												
Nonagricultural, private wage, and salary workers	5.8	4.1	5.2	9.9	9.0	7.9	7.2	7.0	5.8	5.9	6.0	5.0
Mining	5.2	4.4	3.1	9.4	6.1	6.0	5.8	6.5	2.5	4.7	6.0	8.9
Construction	11.5	6.2	7.4	20.6	16.4	13.9	11.3	12.3	8.2	8.9	9.8	6.3
Manufacturing	4.9	3.5	4.9	10.6	9.0	7.3	6.6	5.6	4.4	4.9	5.2	3.9
Durable goods	4.4	3.2	4.6	11.2	9.2	7.2	6.3	5.1	4.0	4.7	4.9	3.6
Nondurable goods	5.7	4.0	5.3	9.6	8.5	7.5	7.1	6.4	5.1	5.2	5.8	4.4
Wholesale and retail trade	6.5	4.3	5.4	9.5	8.9	8.1	7.3	7.8	5.8	6.1	6.2	5.7
Transportation and utilities	4.5	3.4	4.1	8.4	8.2	6.9	6.6	6.8	5.4	5.7	5.2	4.5
Information	—	3.2	5.0	9.7	7.3	7.6	6.2	6.6	5.2	5.2	4.4	3.9
Financial activities	3.3	2.4	2.9	6.9	6.4	5.1	4.5	3.8	4.4	4.0	3.0	2.5
Professional and business services	—	4.8	6.2	10.8	9.7	8.9	8.3	8.4	6.6	6.9	6.8	5.2
Education and health services	—	2.5	3.4	5.8	5.6	5.5	4.9	4.1	4.5	4.2	4.0	4.2
Leisure and hospitality	—	6.6	7.8	12.2	11.6	10.4	10.0	9.5	8.6	8.6	9.4	7.5
Other services	8.4	3.9	4.8	8.5	8.8	7.2	6.9	7.4	5.9	5.7	6.1	4.3
Agriculture and related	11.1	9.0	8.3	13.9	12.5	12.4	10.1	13.0	4.7	9.4	13.3	7.6
Government	2.9	2.1	2.6	4.4	4.7	4.3	4.0	3.4	3.6	3.2	2.8	3.3
Self-employed and unpaid family workers	—	2.1	2.7	5.9	6.0	5.4	5.3	5.2	4.6	4.4	4.7	3.6

— = Not available. **Note:** All monthly rates are unadjusted, except for married men and women, which are seasonally adjusted.

Employed Persons in the U.S. by Occupation and Sex, 2013-14

Source: Bureau of Labor Statistics, U.S. Dept. of Labor
(persons 16 years of age and older; numbers in thousands)

	Total 2013	Total 2014	Men 2013	Men 2014	Women 2013	Women 2014
Total	**143,929**	**146,305**	**76,353**	**77,692**	**67,577**	**68,613**
Management, professional, and related occupations	**54,712**	**56,050**	**26,597**	**27,119**	**28,114**	**28,931**
Management, business, and financial operations	22,794	23,171	12,898	13,041	9,896	10,129
Management	16,037	16,199	9,906	9,953	6,131	6,246
Business and financial operations	6,757	6,972	2,992	3,088	3,765	3,884
Professional and related	31,917	32,879	13,699	14,078	18,218	18,801
Computer and mathematical	3,980	4,303	2,941	3,204	1,039	1,100
Architecture and engineering	2,806	2,798	2,410	2,369	396	430
Life, physical, and social science	1,307	1,355	705	737	602	618
Community and social services	2,332	2,495	879	890	1,453	1,605
Legal	1,809	1,814	891	893	918	921
Education, training, and library	8,623	8,686	2,261	2,252	6,362	6,434
Arts, design, entertainment, sports, and media	2,879	2,935	1,520	1,544	1,359	1,391
Health-care practitioner and technical	8,182	8,493	2,092	2,189	6,090	6,304
Service occupations	**25,929**	**25,854**	**11,260**	**11,203**	**14,669**	**14,651**
Healthcare support	3,537	3,461	393	430	3,145	3,031
Protective service	3,130	3,140	2,469	2,456	661	684
Food preparation and serving related	8,209	8,112	3,721	3,641	4,488	4,471
Building and grounds cleaning and maintenance	5,661	5,803	3,473	3,469	2,188	2,335
Personal care and service	5,392	5,337	1,205	1,207	4,187	4,130
Sales and office occupations	**33,246**	**33,416**	**12,680**	**12,761**	**20,566**	**20,655**
Sales and related	15,444	15,646	7,935	7,948	7,509	7,697
Office and administrative support	17,802	17,771	4,745	4,813	13,057	12,958
Natural resources, construction, and maintenance occupations	**13,058**	**13,537**	**12,461**	**12,939**	**598**	**598**
Farming, fishing, and forestry	964	1,022	755	792	209	229
Construction and extraction	7,130	7,637	6,948	7,440	182	197
Installation, maintenance, and repair	4,964	4,879	4,757	4,707	207	172
Production, transportation, and material moving occupations	**16,984**	**17,448**	**13,354**	**13,670**	**3,630**	**3,778**
Production	8,275	8,438	5,991	6,074	2,284	2,364
Transportation and material moving	8,709	9,010	7,363	7,596	1,346	1,414

Note: Numbers may not add up to totals because of independent rounding.

U.S. Occupations Projected to Grow Most, 2012-22

Source: Employment Projections Program, Bureau of Labor Statistics, U.S. Dept. of Labor
(numbers in thousands)

Occupation	Employment 2012	Employment 2022	Change, 2012-22 Number	Change, 2012-22 Percent	Median annual wage, 2012
Total, all occupations	**145,355.8**	**160,983.7**	**15,628.0**	**10.8%**	**$34,750**
Personal care aides	1,190.6	1,771.4	580.8	48.8	19,910
Registered nurses	2,711.5	3,238.4	526.8	19.4	65,470
Retail salespersons	4,447.0	4,881.7	434.7	9.8	21,110
Home health aides	875.1	1,299.3	424.2	48.5	20,820
Food prep. and serving workers, incl. fast food	2,969.3	3,391.2	421.9	14.2	18,260
Nursing assistants	1,479.8	1,792.0	312.2	21.1	24,420
Secretaries and administrative assistants, excl. legal, medical, and executive	2,324.4	2,632.3	307.8	13.2	32,410
Customer service representatives	2,362.8	2,661.4	298.7	12.6	30,580
Janitors and cleaners, excl. maids and housekeeping cleaners	2,324.0	2,604.0	280.0	12.1	22,320
Construction laborers	1,071.1	1,331.0	259.8	24.3	29,990
General and operations managers	1,972.7	2,216.8	244.1	12.4	95,440
Laborers and freight, stock, and material movers, hand	2,197.3	2,439.2	241.9	11.0	23,890
Carpenters	901.2	1,119.4	218.2	24.2	39,940
Bookkeeping, accounting, and auditing clerks	1,799.8	2,004.5	204.6	11.4	35,170
Heavy and tractor-trailer truck drivers	1,701.5	1,894.1	192.6	11.3	38,200
Medical secretaries	525.6	714.9	189.2	36.0	31,350
Childcare workers	1,312.7	1,496.8	184.1	14.0	19,510
Office clerks, general	2,983.5	3,167.6	184.1	6.2	27,470
Maids and housekeeping cleaners	1,434.6	1,618.0	183.4	12.8	19,570
Licensed practical and licensed vocational nurses	738.4	921.3	182.9	24.8	41,540

Projected Employment by Education and Training Characteristics, 2012-22

Source: Employment Projections Program, Bureau of Labor Statistics, U.S. Dept. of Labor
(numbers in thousands)

Characteristic	Employment Number 2012	Employment Number 2022	Percent distribution 2012	Percent distribution 2022	Change, 2012-22 Number	Change, 2012-22 Percent	Total job openings[1], 2012-22 Number	Total job openings[1], 2012-22 Percent distribution	Median annual wage, 2012
TOTAL, ALL OCCUPATIONS	**145,355.8**	**160,983.7**	**100.0%**	**100.0%**	**15,628.0**	**10.8%**	**50,557.3**	**100.0%**	**$34,750**
Typical entry-level education									
Doctoral or professional degree	4,002.4	4,640.8	2.8	2.9	638.4	16.0	1,426.8	2.8	96,420
Master's degree	2,432.2	2,880.7	1.7	1.8	448.5	18.4	950.8	1.9	63,400
Bachelor's degree	26,033.0	29,176.7	17.9	18.1	3,143.6	12.1	8,618.7	17.0	67,140
Associate's degree	5,954.9	7,000.9	4.1	4.3	1,046.0	17.6	2,269.5	4.5	57,590
Postsecondary non-degree	8,554.2	9,891.2	5.9	6.1	1,337.1	15.6	3,067.2	6.1	34,760
Some college, no degree	1,987.2	2,212.2	1.4	1.4	225.0	11.3	642.6	1.3	28,730
High school diploma or equivalent	58,264.4	62,895.2	40.1	39.1	4,630.8	7.9	17,667.4	34.9	35,170
Less than high school	38,127.6	42,286.0	26.2	26.3	4,158.4	10.9	15,914.3	31.5	20,110
Previous work experience in a related occupation									
5 years or more	4,831.9	5,091.8	3.3	3.2	259.9	5.4	1,330.9	2.6	90,760
Less than 5 years	16,167.7	17,663.5	11.1	11.0	1,495.9	9.3	4,863.4	9.6	52,270
None	124,356.2	138,228.4	85.6	85.9	13,872.2	11.2	44,363.0	87.7	32,260
Typical on-the-job training needed to attain competency									
Internship/residency	5,989.1	6,658.9	4.1	4.1	669.8	11.2	1,997.8	4.0	53,570
Apprenticeship	2,336.9	2,855.2	1.6	1.8	518.3	22.2	879.8	1.7	45,440
Long-term on-the-job training	6,876.5	7,448.7	4.7	4.6	572.2	8.3	2,163.7	4.3	41,810
Moderate-term on-the-job training	23,057.8	24,968.5	15.9	15.5	1,910.8	8.3	6,841.0	13.5	36,950
Short-term on-the-job training	58,928.4	64,673.7	40.5	40.2	5,745.3	9.7	22,273.7	44.1	22,960
None	48,167.2	54,378.8	33.1	33.8	6211.6	12.9	16,401.3	32.4	56,970

(1) Due to growth/replacement needs.

Highest Average Weekly Wages by County, 2014

Source: Bureau of Labor Statistics, U.S. Dept. of Labor

County	Avg. weekly wage	% change, 2013-14	County	Avg. weekly wage	% change, 2013-14
San Mateo, CA	$2,166	–20.4%	Fairfax, VA	$1,584	2.0%
New York, NY	2,138	4.4	Somerset, NJ	1,543	3.6
Santa Clara, CA	2,114	6.8	Morris, NJ	1,512	–2.9
Suffolk, MA	1,856	6.2	Middlesex, MA	1,482	3.6
San Francisco, CA	1,850	4.9	Alexandria City, VA	1,464	3.7
Washington, DC	1,696	3.0	Midland, TX	1,425	9.0
Fairfield, CT	1,674	1.1	Westchester, NY	1,407	4.5
Arlington, VA	1,613	1.5	**United States**	**1,035**	**3.5**

Note: Figures shown are for the 4th quarter, from among the 340 largest U.S. counties, which comprise 72.1% of total covered workers. Horry County, SC, recorded the lowest average weekly earnings among the largest counties, with an average weekly wage of $610 in the 4th quarter of 2014. It was followed by Cameron County, TX ($621); Hidalgo County, TX ($641); Osceola County, FL ($687); Lake County, TX ($691); and Webb County, TX ($696). Data include all workers covered by state and federal unemployment insurance programs.

Federal Minimum Hourly Wage Rates

Source: Bureau of Labor Statistics, U.S. Dept. of Labor; as of June 30, 2015

Effective date	Minimum wage	% avg. earnings[1]	In 2015 dollars	Effective date	Minimum wage	% avg. earnings[1]	In 2015 dollars
Oct. 24, 1938	$0.25	40%	$4.22	Jan. 1, 1978	$2.65	43%	$9.67
Oct. 24, 1939	0.30	48	5.13	Jan. 1, 1979	2.90	43	9.50
Oct. 24, 1945	0.40	39	5.28	Jan. 1, 1980	3.10	43	8.95
Jan. 25, 1950	0.75	52	7.40	Jan. 1, 1981	3.35	42	8.76
Mar. 1, 1956	1.00	51	8.74	Apr. 1, 1990	3.80	35	6.91
Sept. 3, 1961	1.15	50	9.15	Apr. 1, 1991	4.25	38	7.42
Sept. 3, 1963	1.25	51	9.71	Oct. 1, 1996	4.75	37	7.20
Feb. 1, 1967	1.40	49	9.97	Sept. 1, 1997	5.15	39	7.63
Feb. 1, 1968	1.60	53	10.93	July 24, 2007	5.85	34	6.71
May 1, 1974	2.00	45	9.65	July 24, 2008	6.55	37	7.23
Jan. 1, 1975	2.10	43	9.28	July 24, 2009	7.25	40	8.04
Jan. 1, 1976	2.30	44	9.61				

Note: Before 1961, the minimum wage applied primarily to employees engaged in, or producing goods for, interstate commerce. Coverage was added 1961-64 primarily to employees in large retail and service enterprises and to local transit, construction, and gas station employees. Coverage was added 1966-77 (at reduced rates) to farm workers; federal, state, and local government employees; workers in various retail and service trades; and certain domestic workers. Starting in 1978, the minimum wage applied equally to all covered, nonexempt workers. At present, exceptions apply under specific circumstances to workers with disabilities, full-time students, persons under age 20 in their first 90 consecutive calendar days of employment, tipped employees, and student-learners. (1) Percent of gross hourly earnings of production workers in manufacturing.

Fatal Occupational Injuries, 2014

Source: Census of Fatal Occupational Injuries, Bureau of Labor Statistics, U.S. Dept. of Labor, in cooperation with other agencies

Event or exposure	Fatalities Number	%
Total	**4,679**	**100%**
Transportation incidents	**1,891**	**40**
Roadway, involving motorized land vehicles	1,075	23
Collision with other vehicles	566	12
Collision with object other than vehicle	294	6
Noncollision	211	5
Jackknifed or overturned	178	4
Nonroadway	246	5
Jackknifed or overturned	127	3
Pedestrian vehicular incidents	313	7
Rail vehicle incidents	55	1
Water vehicle incidents	53	1
Aircraft incidents	135	3
Violence by persons or animals	**749**	**16**
Homicides	403	9
Shooting	307	7
Stabbing	39	1
Self-inflicted injury—intentional	271	6

Event or exposure	Fatalities Number	%
Contact with objects and equipment	**708**	**15%**
Struck by object or equipment	498	11
Struck by falling object or equipment	240	5
Struck by flying object	21	—
Caught in or compressed by equipment or objects	131	3
Caught in running equipment or machinery	104	2
Struck, caught, or crushed in collapsing structure, equipment, or material	74	2
Falls, slips, trips	**793**	**17**
Fall to lower level	647	14
Fall on same level	129	3
Exposure to harmful substances or environments	**390**	**8**
Exposure to electricity	156	3
Exposure to temperature extremes	26	1
Exposure to other harmful substances	180	4
Inhalation of harmful substance	59	1
Fires and explosions	**137**	**3**

— = Less than 0.5%. **Note:** Category totals may include subcategories not shown. Percentages show incidence rate per total fatalities.

U.S. Occupational Injuries and Illnesses Involving Days Away From Work, 2013

Source: Bureau of Labor Statistics, U.S. Dept. of Labor

		Percent of days-away-from-work cases[1] involving—							
Characteristic	Illnesses/ injuries[2]	1 day	2 days	3-5 days	6-10 days	11-20 days	21-30 days	31 days or more	Median days away from work
Total	**917,090**	**14.2%**	**11.1%**	**17.0%**	**12.0%**	**10.8%**	**6.4%**	**28.7%**	**8**
Male	562,790	13.5	10.4	16.6	11.9	10.9	6.7	30.0	10
Female	350,510	15.3	12.2	17.6	12.1	10.6	5.8	26.3	7
Occupation(s)									
Management	23,080	21.6	12.9	18.3	11.3	10.2	5.3	20.4	5
Business, financial operations	7,440	16.4	6.7	17.7	18.4	9.5	9.5	21.6	9
Computer and mathematical	1,860	21.0	11.3	17.2	7.5	7.5	7.0	28.0	6
Architecture, engineering	3,000	15.3	8.0	22.3	8.3	16.3	6.0	23.7	8
Life, physical, social science	1,600	18.1	12.5	18.8	13.1	10.0	10.0	17.5	6
Community, social services	7,780	16.2	14.3	21.6	13.2	10.4	5.5	18.6	5
Legal	650	41.5	10.8	12.3	6.2	—	3.1	26.2	2
Education, training, library	8,140	21.0	13.1	18.9	17.2	8.1	4.7	17.0	5
Arts, design, entertainment, sports, media	8,350	16.6	4.6	10.4	9.0	9.3	9.8	40.1	20
Health care practitioners	50,630	14.8	12.5	19.3	13.8	11.7	5.0	23.0	6
Health care support	58,020	15.5	12.3	19.6	13.9	11.4	5.3	22.1	6
Protective service	10,770	9.8	11.1	15.4	10.5	12.2	8.6	32.3	12
Food preparation, serving	73,310	16.6	14.9	19.7	11.3	10.2	6.0	21.3	5
Building and grounds cleaning, maintenance	56,020	14.4	10.6	19.1	12.7	9.9	6.3	27.0	8
Personal care, service	24,220	16.9	15.4	19.3	10.9	10.6	5.2	21.8	5
Sales	62,870	12.9	11.4	17.5	10.8	10.5	6.8	30.0	9
Office and administrative support	67,030	14.8	12.5	15.8	11.3	11.4	6.1	28.1	8
Farming, fishing, forestry	15,560	14.1	10.7	21.3	16.3	9.5	5.8	22.3	6
Construction, extraction	77,380	12.8	8.7	14.4	12.9	9.9	6.3	35.1	12
Installation, maintenance, repair	81,870	13.7	10.6	17.3	10.7	10.0	6.5	31.3	9
Production	104,590	15.5	11.5	15.5	11.6	11.8	6.3	27.8	8
Transportation, material moving	170,290	10.4	8.6	14.7	11.7	11.4	7.3	36.0	14

(1) Cases include those that resulted in days away from work. (2) Number of nonfatal occupational injuries and illnesses involving days away from work for private industry workers; excludes farms with fewer than 11 employees.

Civilian Employment of the Executive Branch, 1940-2013

Source: U.S. Office of Personnel Management
(numbers in thousands)

			Civilian agencies/depts.									
Year	Total executive branch	Dept. of Defense	Total employees	Agriculture	HHS, Education, Social Sec.[1]	Homeland Sec.	Interior	Justice	Transportation	Treasury	Veterans Affairs	Other
1940	699	256	443	98	9	18	46	11	NA	45	40	176
1945	3,370	2,635	736	82	11	20	45	19	NA	84	65	409
1950	1,439	753	686	84	13	20	66	20	NA	76	188	219
1955	1,860	1,187	673	86	40	21	54	24	NA	65	178	206
1960	1,808	1,047	761	99	62	21	56	24	NA	62	172	265
1965	1,901	1,034	867	113	87	21	71	27	NA	74	167	307
1970	2,203	1,219	983	118	112	23	75	33	62	84	169	308
1975	2,149	1,042	1,107	121	147	31	80	47	69	101	213	297
1980	2,161	960	1,201	129	163	40	77	48	66	102	228	346
1985	2,252	1,107	1,145	122	147	40	80	55	56	110	247	286
1990	2,250	1,034	1,216	123	129	49	78	71	61	132	248	326
1995	2,012	802	1,210	113	132	56	76	87	58	128	264	297
2000	1,778	651	1,127	104	126	70	74	98	58	113	220	265
2001	1,792	647	1,145	109	129	73	76	99	59	117	226	258
2002	1,818	645	1,173	98	130	76	77	96	96	118	223	258
2003	1,867	636	1,231	100	131	153	72	102	58	132	226	257
2004	1,882	644	1,238	111	130	153	77	104	57	111	236	257
2005	1,872	649	1,224	108	131	147	76	105	56	108	235	258
2006	1,880	653	1,227	105	129	154	72	107	54	107	239	260
2007	1,888	651	1,237	103	129	159	72	107	54	104	254	254
2008	1,960	670	1,289	104	132	172	76	109	55	106	274	261
2009	2,094	737	1,357	104	139	180	75	113	57	109	297	283
2010	2,133	773	1,360	107	144	183	70	118	58	110	305	265
2011	2,146	774	1,372	104	143	194	77	117	58	108	314	257
2012	2,104	730	1,374	99	143	191	77	117	57	112	323	255
2013	2,084	729	1,355	95	139	192	71	116	55	112	323	252

NA = Not available. HHS = Health and Human Services. **Note:** End-of-fiscal-year count; U.S. Postal Service excluded. (1) Estimated, 1940-50.

Median Earnings by Industry and Sex, 2014

Source: American Community Survey, U.S. Census Bureau, U.S. Dept. of Commerce

Industry	Number employed	Male (%)	Female (%)	Median earnings	Median earnings (male)	Median earnings (female)
Agriculture; forestry; fishing, hunting; mining	2,963,918	81.1%	18.9%	$32,250	$36,285	$20,529
Arts, entertainment, recreation; accommodation, food services	14,536,953	48.7	51.3	15,660	18,461	13,189
Construction	9,292,826	91.0	9.0	35,398	35,642	32,014
Educational services; health care, social assistance	34,091,965	25.6	74.4	34,870	43,727	31,798
Finance, insurance; real estate, rental, leasing	9,614,483	45.9	54.1	46,238	59,426	40,233
Information	3,222,160	59.0	41.0	49,770	56,948	39,474
Manufacturing	15,216,294	71.2	28.8	41,880	46,524	32,860
Other services, except public administration	7,289,277	46.8	53.2	22,450	30,697	17,470
Professional, scientific, management; administrative, waste management services	16,438,747	58.1	41.9	41,110	49,066	34,012
Public administration	6,897,327	56.4	43.6	51,249	58,349	43,275
Retail trade	17,065,344	50.9	49.1	21,386	26,108	17,412
Transportation, warehousing; utilities	7,327,146	76.2	23.8	42,198	45,812	35,254
Wholesale trade	4,063,468	70.1	29.9	41,428	45,374	34,786

Note: For the civilian employed population 16 years of age and over including workers not employed full-time.

Unemployment Rates and Earnings by Education, 2014

Source: Bureau of Labor Statistics, U.S. Dept. of Labor

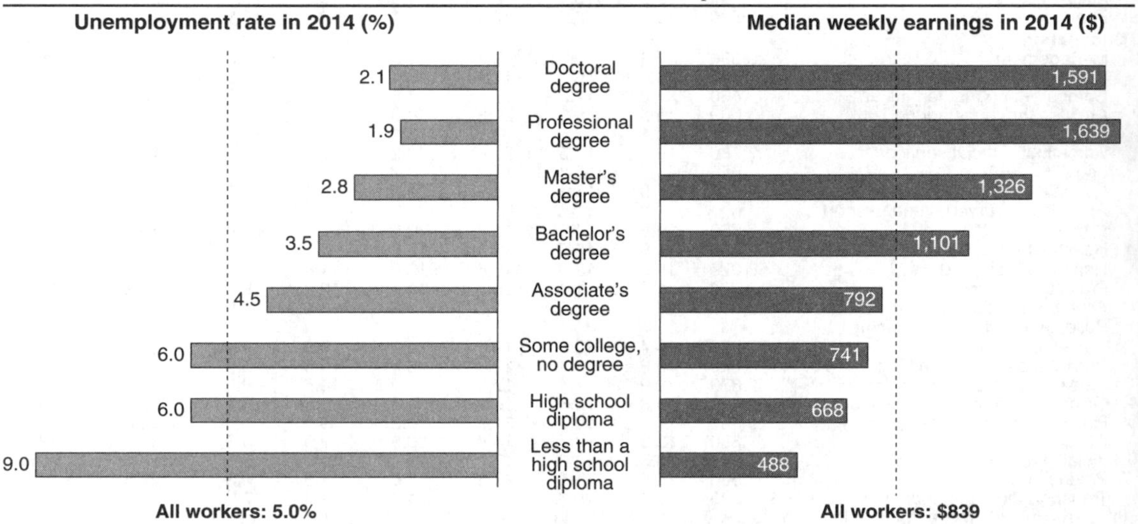

Note: Data are for persons age 25 and over. Earnings are for full-time wage and salary workers.

U.S. Median Weekly Earnings, 2015

Source: Bureau of Labor Statistics, U.S. Dept. of Labor

	Total		Men		Women	
AGE, RACE, AND ETHNICITY	Number of workers (thous.)	Median weekly earnings	Number of workers (thous.)	Median weekly earnings	Number of workers (thous.)	Median weekly earnings
All workers, by age						
16 years and over	108,769	$801	60,638	$886	48,131	$726
16 to 24 years	9,647	476	5,335	497	4,313	444
16 to 19 years	1,083	376	609	382	474	366
20 to 24 years	8,565	489	4,726	510	3,839	459
25 years and over	99,121	852	55,303	942	43,818	759
25 to 54 years	77,076	835	43,315	918	33,761	753
25 to 34 years	26,569	721	15,200	752	11,369	675
35 to 44 years	24,836	896	14,053	985	10,783	792
45 to 54 years	25,671	925	14,062	1,058	11,609	797
55 years and over	22,045	916	11,988	1,032	10,057	782
55 to 64 years	17,965	925	9,691	1,037	8,274	794
65 years and over	4,080	883	2,297	1,003	1,783	743
White						
16 years and over	85,383	829	48,785	914	36,598	742
16 to 24 years	7,552	488	4,295	507	3,256	457
25 years and over	77,831	878	44,490	969	33,341	774
25 to 54 years	59,685	858	34,332	943	25,352	768
55 years and over	18,146	953	10,157	1,080	7,989	811
Black						
16 years and over	13,566	647	6,442	696	7,124	615
16 to 24 years	1,290	407	580	417	710	399
25 years and over	12,276	691	5,862	732	6,414	654
25 to 54 years	9,905	683	4,754	726	5,151	647
55 years and over	2,371	725	1,108	756	1,263	680
Asian						
16 years and over	6,608	965	3,612	1,085	2,996	836
16 to 24 years	344	544	195	602	149	511
25 years and over	6,264	989	3,417	1,109	2,847	863
25 to 54 years	5,118	1,005	2,884	1,121	2,234	871
55 years and over	1,146	902	533	1,034	613	838
Hispanic[1]						
16 years and over	18,240	601	11,102	619	7,138	572
16 to 24 years	2,148	444	1,276	459	872	430
25 years and over	16,092	623	9,826	654	6,266	597
25 to 54 years	13,866	620	8,501	646	5,365	594
55 years and over	2,226	659	1,324	711	901	615
OCCUPATION						
Managerial, professional, and related	44,819	1,147	21,899	1,357	22,920	987
Management, business, and financial	18,400	1,243	10,126	1,401	8,274	1,064
Professional and related	26,420	1,097	11,773	1,319	14,647	953
Service	15,313	506	7,732	587	7,582	457
Sales and office	23,601	668	9,395	765	14,205	632
Sales and related	9,724	688	5,373	864	4,352	556
Office and administrative support	13,876	661	4,023	683	9,853	655
Natural resources, construction, and maintenance	10,604	750	10,194	761	410	507
Farming, fishing, and forestry	778	440	607	448	172	427
Construction and extraction	5,664	741	5,531	742	133	700
Installation, maintenance, and repair	4,162	835	4,056	838	106	603
Production, transportation, and material moving	14,431	653	11,418	702	3,013	524
Production	7,525	666	5,508	734	2,017	524
Transportation and material moving	6,906	634	5,909	663	996	524

Note: Not seasonally adjusted; figures are median usual weekly earnings of full-time wage and salary workers for second quarter 2015. Total includes races not shown here. (1) May be of any race.

Average Hours and Earnings of U.S. Production Workers, 1969-2014

Source: Bureau of Labor Statistics, U.S. Dept. of Labor
(annual averages)

Year	Weekly hours	Hourly earnings	Weekly earnings	Year	Weekly hours	Hourly earnings	Weekly earnings	Year	Weekly hours	Hourly earnings	Weekly earnings
1969	37.5	$3.22	$120.70	1985	34.9	$8.74	$304.62	2000	34.3	$14.02	$480.99
1970	37.0	3.40	125.79	1986	34.7	8.93	309.78	2001	34.0	14.54	493.74
1971	36.7	3.63	133.22	1987	34.7	9.14	317.39	2002	33.9	14.97	506.60
1972	36.9	3.90	143.87	1988	34.6	9.44	326.48	2003	33.7	15.37	517.82
1973	36.9	4.14	152.59	1989	34.5	9.80	338.34	2004	33.7	15.69	528.89
1974	36.4	4.43	161.61	1990	34.3	10.20	349.63	2005	33.8	16.12	544.05
1975	36.0	4.73	170.29	1991	34.1	10.51	358.46	2006	33.9	16.75	567.39
1976	36.1	5.06	182.65	1992	34.2	10.77	368.20	2007	33.8	17.42	589.27
1977	35.9	5.44	195.58	1993	34.3	11.05	378.89	2008	33.6	18.07	607.53
1978	35.8	5.88	210.29	1994	34.5	11.34	391.17	2009	33.1	18.61	616.01
1979	35.6	6.34	225.69	1995	34.3	11.65	400.04	2010	33.4	19.05	636.25
1980	35.2	6.85	241.07	1996	34.3	12.04	413.25	2011	33.6	19.44	653.19
1981	35.2	7.44	261.53	1997	34.5	12.51	431.86	2012	33.7	19.74	665.82
1982	34.7	7.87	273.10	1998	34.5	13.01	448.59	2013	33.7	20.13	677.67
1983	34.9	8.20	286.43	1999	34.3	13.49	463.15	2014	33.7	20.61	694.89
1984	35.1	8.49	298.26								

Note: Data refer to production workers in natural resources, mining, and manufacturing; construction workers; and nonsupervisory workers in the service industries.

Elderly in U.S. Labor Force, 1890-2014

Source: U.S. Census Bureau, U.S. Dept. of Commerce

(percent of persons age 65 and older who participated in the labor force; 1910 figures not available)

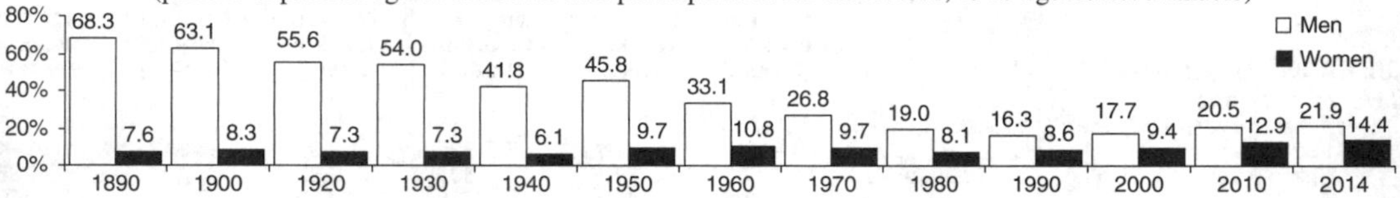

U.S. Union Membership, 1930-2014

Source: Bureau of Labor Statistics, U.S. Dept. of Labor
(numbers in thousands)

Year	Total employed[1]	% in union	Union members[2]	Year	Total employed[1]	% in union	Union members[2]	Year	Total employed[1]	% in union	Union members[2]
1930	29,424	11.6%	3,401	1975	76,945	25.5%	19,611	2007	129,767	12.1%	15,670
1935	27,053	13.2	3,584	1980	90,564	21.9	19,843	2008	129,377	12.4	16,098
1940	32,376	26.9	8,717	1985	94,521	18.0	16,996	2009	124,490	12.3	15,327
1945	40,394	35.5	14,322	1990	103,905	16.1	16,740	2010	124,073	11.9	14,715
1950	45,222	31.5	14,267	1995	110,038	14.9	16,360	2011	125,187	11.8	14,764
1955	50,675	33.2	16,802	2000	120,786	13.5	16,258	2012	127,577	11.3	14,366
1960	54,234	31.4	17,049	2005	125,889	12.5	15,685	2013	129,110	11.3	14,528
1965	60,815	28.4	17,299	2006	128,237	12.0	15,359	2014	131,431	11.1	14,576
1970	70,920	27.3	19,381								

(1) Prior to 1985, total labor force figure, which includes unemployed persons. From 1985 on, does not include self-employed workers. (2) From 1930 to 1980, includes dues-paying members of traditional trade unions, regardless of employment status; after 1980, includes employed only. From 1985 on, includes members of employee associations similar to a union.

Median Weekly Earnings of U.S. Workers by Union Affiliation, 2000, 2014

Source: Bureau of Labor Statistics, U.S. Dept. of Labor

	2000				2014			
Sex and age	Total	Union member[1]	Represented by unions[2]	Non-union	Total	Union member[1]	Represented by unions[2]	Non-union
Total, 16 years and older	**$576**	**$696**	**$691**	**$542**	**$791**	**$970**	**$965**	**$763**
16 to 24 years	361	437	436	355	477	602	605	470
25 years and older	611	709	705	592	839	987	985	810
25 to 34 years	550	627	624	529	726	874	867	705
35 to 44 years	631	716	712	614	881	1,034	1,029	848
45 to 54 years	671	755	752	639	899	1,025	1,022	872
55 to 64 years	617	727	723	592	911	1,014	1,017	885
65 years and older	442	577	565	422	824	908	920	813
Men, 16 years and older	**646**	**739**	**737**	**620**	**871**	**1,015**	**1,013**	**840**
16 to 24 years	376	458	457	370	493	644	643	485
25 years and older	700	753	752	682	922	1,036	1,035	899
25 to 34 years	603	678	675	591	755	896	889	740
35 to 44 years	731	776	774	718	964	1,102	1,097	933
45 to 54 years	777	801	799	769	1,011	1,083	1,088	994
55 to 64 years	738	755	757	729	1,021	1,068	1,076	1,007
65 years and older	537	613	613	514	942	921	936	943
Women, 16 years and older	**491**	**616**	**613**	**472**	**719**	**904**	**899**	**687**
16 to 24 years	342	406	405	339	451	557	562	445
25 years and older	515	627	623	497	752	921	917	728
25 to 34 years	493	579	578	483	679	848	843	655
35 to 44 years	520	605	604	506	781	962	956	751
45 to 54 years	565	697	692	522	780	951	945	754
55 to 64 years	505	659	647	481	780	931	935	757
65 years and older	378	485	484	365	740	879	887	719

Note: Data refer to the sole or principal job of full-time wage and salary workers. Excludes self-employed workers regardless of whether or not their businesses are incorporated. (1) Includes members of an employee association similar to a union. (2) Includes members of a labor union as well as those whose jobs are covered by a union or an employee-association contract.

Work Stoppages (Strikes and Lockouts) in the U.S., 1950-2014

Source: Bureau of Labor Statistics, U.S. Dept. of Labor; involving 1,000 workers or more

Year	No.	Workers (thous.)	Days idle (thous.)	Year	No.	Workers (thous.)	Days idle (thous.)	Year	No.	Workers (thous.)	Days idle (thous.)
1950	424	1,698	30,390	1985	54	324	7,079	2000	39	394	20,419
1955	363	2,055	21,180	1986	69	533	11,861	2001	29	99	1,151
1960	222	896	13,260	1987	46	174	4,481	2002	19	46	660
1965	268	999	15,140	1988	40	118	4,381	2003	14	129	4,091
1970	381	2,468	52,761	1989	51	452	16,996	2004	17	171	3,344
1975	235	965	17,563	1990	44	185	5,926	2005	22	100	1,736
1976	231	1,519	23,962	1991	40	392	4,584	2006	20	70	2,688
1977	298	1,212	21,258	1992	35	364	3,989	2007	21	189	1,265
1978	219	1,006	23,774	1993	35	182	3,981	2008	15	72	1,954
1979	235	1,021	20,409	1994	45	322	5,021	2009	5	13	124
1980	187	795	20,844	1995	31	192	5,771	2010	11	45	302
1981	145	729	16,908	1996	37	273	4,889	2011	19	113	1,020
1982	96	656	9,061	1997	29	339	4,497	2012	19	148	1,131
1983	81	909	17,461	1998	34	387	5,116	2013	15	55	290
1984	62	376	8,499	1999	17	73	1,996	2014	11	34	200

Note: Numbers cover stoppages that began in the year indicated. Workers are counted more than once if they are involved in more than one stoppage during the year. For work stoppages ongoing at the end of a calendar year, days idle include only the days for the calendar year.

ENERGY

U.S. Energy Overview, 1960-2014

Source: *Monthly Energy Review*, Aug. 2015, Energy Information Administration (EIA), U.S. Dept. of Energy; in quadrillion Btu

	1960	1970	1980	1985	1990	1995	2000	2005	2010	2013	2014
Production	**42.80**	**63.50**	**67.23**	**67.80**	**70.70**	**71.17**	**71.33**	**69.43**	**74.78**	**81.89**	**87.26**
Fossil fuels	39.87	59.19	59.01	57.54	58.56	57.54	57.37	55.04	58.23	64.31	69.28
Coal[1]	10.82	14.61	18.60	19.33	22.49	22.13	22.74	23.19	22.04	20.00	20.29
Natural gas (dry)	12.66	21.67	19.91	16.98	18.33	19.08	19.66	18.56	21.81	24.99	25.52*
Crude oil[2]	14.93	20.40	18.25	18.99	15.57	13.89	12.36	10.97	11.60	15.79	18.45*
Natural gas plant liquids (NGPL)	1.46	2.51	2.25	2.24	2.17	2.44	2.61	2.33	2.78	3.53	4.03
Nuclear electric power	0.01	0.24	2.74	4.08	6.10	7.08	7.86	8.16	8.43	8.24	8.33
Renewable energy	2.93	4.08	5.49	6.18	6.04	6.56	6.10	6.23	8.11	9.33	9.66
Conventional hydroelectric power[3]	1.61	2.63	2.90	2.97	3.05	3.21	2.81	2.70	2.54	2.56	2.47
Biomass[4]	1.32	1.43	2.48	3.02	2.74	3.10	3.01	3.10	4.32	4.65	4.80
Geothermal energy	—	0.01	0.11	0.20	0.17	0.15	0.16	0.18	0.21	0.21	0.22
Solar	NA	NA	NA	—	0.06	0.07	0.07	0.06	0.13	0.31	0.43
Wind	NA	NA	NA	—	0.03	0.03	0.06	0.18	0.92	1.60	1.73
Imports	**4.19**	**8.34**	**15.80**	**11.78**	**18.82**	**22.26**	**28.97**	**34.71**	**29.87**	**24.63**	**23.31**
Coal	0.01	—	0.03	0.05	0.07	0.24	0.31	0.76	0.48	0.20	0.24
Natural gas	0.16	0.85	1.01	0.95	1.55	2.90	3.87	4.45	3.83	2.96	2.76
All petroleum prods.[5]	4.00	7.47	14.66	10.61	17.12	18.88	24.53	29.25	25.36	21.13	20.04
Electricity[6]	0.02	0.02	0.09	0.16	0.06	0.15	0.17	0.15	0.15	0.24	0.21
Exports	**1.48**	**2.63**	**3.69**	**4.20**	**4.75**	**4.51**	**4.01**	**4.56**	**8.18**	**11.79**	**12.31**
Coal	1.02	1.94	2.42	2.44	2.77	2.32	1.53	1.27	2.10	2.90	2.47
Natural gas	0.01	0.07	0.05	0.06	0.09	0.16	0.25	0.74	1.15	1.59	1.53
All petroleum prods.[5]	0.43	0.55	1.16	1.66	1.82	1.99	2.15	2.44	4.78	7.17	8.16
Electricity[6]	—	0.01	0.01	0.02	0.06	0.01	0.05	0.07	0.06	0.08	0.08
Consumption	**45.09**	**67.84**	**78.12**	**76.49**	**84.49**	**91.03**	**98.81**	**100.28**	**97.48**	**97.26**	**98.46**
Fossil fuels	42.14	63.52	69.83	66.09	72.33	77.26	84.73	85.79	80.89	79.45	80.34
Coal	9.84	12.26	15.42	17.48	19.17	20.09	22.58	22.80	20.83	18.04	17.99
Natural gas[7]	12.39	21.80	20.24	17.70	19.60	22.67	23.82	22.57	24.58	26.82	27.59
Petroleum[8]	19.92	29.52	34.20	30.92	33.55	34.44	38.26	40.39	35.49	34.61	34.78
Nuclear electric power	0.01	0.24	2.74	4.08	6.10	7.08	7.86	8.16	8.43	8.24	8.33
Renewable energy	2.93	4.08	5.49	6.18	6.04	6.56	6.11	6.24	8.07	9.36	9.62
Conventional hydroelectric power[3]	1.61	2.63	2.90	2.97	3.05	3.21	2.81	2.70	0.21	0.21	0.22
Biomass[4]	1.32	1.43	2.48	3.02	2.74	3.10	3.01	3.12	4.27	4.67	4.77
Geothermal energy	—	0.01	0.11	0.20	0.17	0.15	0.16	0.18	0.21	0.21	0.22
Solar	NA	NA	NA	—	0.06	0.07	0.07	0.06	0.13	0.31	0.43
Wind	NA	NA	NA	—	0.03	0.03	0.06	0.02	0.92	1.60	1.73

* = Estimate. NA = Not available. — = Less than 0.005 quadrillion Btu. **Note:** Numbers may not add up to totals because of rounding. (1) Incl. waste coal supplied beginning in 1989 and refuse recovery beginning in 2001. (2) Incl. lease condensate. (3) Starting in 1990, pumped storage was removed and expanded coverage of industrial use of hydroelectric power was included. (4) Category known as "wood, waste, and alcohol" for years prior to 2000. Includes wood, waste, and alcohol fuels (ethanol blended into motor gasoline). Ethanol is included in both Petroleum and Biomass categories but is only counted once in totals. (5) Incl. imports of crude oil for the Strategic Petroleum Reserve, which began in 1977; excl. biofuels. (6) Small amts. transmitted across borders with Canada and Mexico. (7) Incl. supplemental gaseous fuels. (8) Petroleum products supplied, incl. natural gas plant liquids and crude oil burned as fuel.

World's Largest Energy Producers and Consumers, 1980-2012

Source: Energy Information Administration (EIA), U.S. Dept. of Energy
(primary energy in quadrillion Btu; ranked by top producers/consumers in 2011)

Production	1980	1985	1990	1995	2000	2005	2010	2011	2012
1. China	18.12	24.30	29.37	34.88	37.71	60.41	84.23	90.57	NA
2. United States	67.18	67.70	70.70	71.17	71.33	69.43	74.77	78.00	79.20
3. Russia	NA	NA	NA	41.42	41.70	51.05	53.74	54.63	NA
4. Saudi Arabia	22.43	8.64	15.92	20.66	21.59	25.44	24.93	26.40	NA
5. Canada	10.28	12.02	13.41	16.83	18.13	18.89	18.36	18.83	19.22
6. India	3.10	5.27	6.82	9.48	9.83	11.74	15.44	15.89	NA
7. Iran	3.94	5.59	7.67	9.35	10.40	13.12	14.61	14.86	NA
8. Indonesia	4.23	4.20	5.30	6.95	7.69	9.06	13.78	14.40	NA
9. Australia	3.24	5.00	6.16	7.43	9.66	10.97	12.91	12.35	12.85
10. Brazil	1.90	3.38	3.76	4.47	6.36	7.66	9.47	9.91	NA
Consumption	**1980**	**1985**	**1990**	**1995**	**2000**	**2005**	**2010**	**2011**	**2012**
1. China	17.29	22.01	26.99	34.59	39.76	64.20	95.74	103.72	NA
2. United States	78.07	76.39	84.49	91.03	98.81	100.28	98.02	97.46	94.95
3. Russia	NA	NA	NA	27.94	26.14	27.89	29.73	29.96	NA
4. India	4.04	5.91	7.88	11.54	13.33	16.33	22.71	23.47	NA
5. Japan	15.20	15.69	18.77	20.94	22.41	22.57	21.85	21.11	20.43
6. Canada	9.80	10.15	10.98	12.21	13.02	13.84	12.95	13.54	13.29
7. Germany[1]	14.86	14.83	14.86	14.39	14.26	14.10	14.03	13.45	13.51
8. Brazil	4.02	4.59	5.75	7.02	8.53	9.35	11.30	12.13	NA
9. Korea, South	1.76	2.31	3.84	6.36	7.84	9.21	10.82	11.32	11.45
10. France	8.39	8.35	9.13	10.05	10.86	11.38	11.02	10.80	10.67

NA = Not available. (1) Data for 1980-90 represent sum of figures for East and West Germany and may not be directly comparable with data for other years.

U.S. Energy Consumption by Source, 1949-2014

Source: *Monthly Energy Review*, Aug. 2015, Energy Information Administration (EIA), U.S. Dept. of Energy

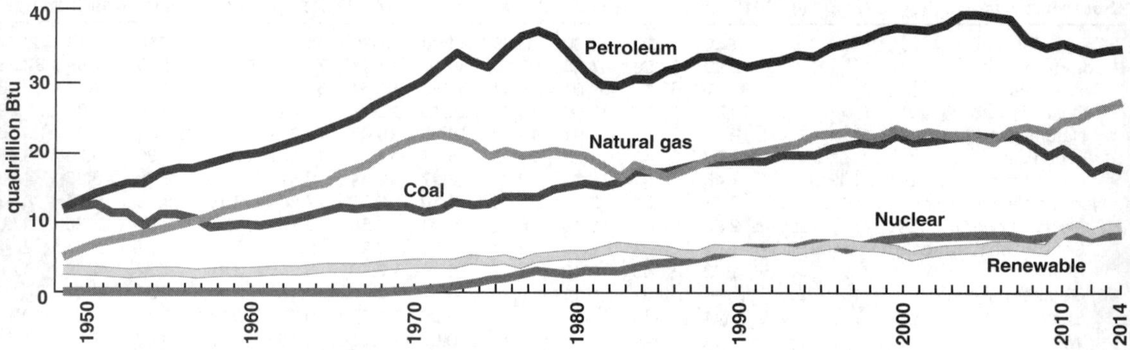

Gasoline Retail Prices in Selected Countries, 1990-2014

Source: *Energy Prices and Taxes*, International Energy Agency

(average price in dollars per gallon, including taxes)

	Regular unleaded														
Country	**1990**	**1995**	**2000**	**2003**	**2004**	**2005**	**2006**	**2007**	**2008**	**2009**	**2010**	**2011**	**2012**	**2013**	**2014**
Australia	NA	$1.93	$1.93	$2.20	$2.73	$3.22	$3.52	$3.86	$4.47	$3.79	$4.35	$5.60	$5.60	$5.30	$5.00
Canada	$1.85	1.51	1.85	2.01	2.35	2.88	3.26	3.60	4.09	3.14	3.79	4.77	4.81	4.69	4.39
China	NA	NA	NA	1.32	1.48	1.70	2.12	2.31	3.10	3.26	3.71	NA	NA	NA	NA
Germany	2.65	3.97	3.44	4.58	5.26	5.64	6.02	6.89	7.76	6.81	7.12	NA	NA	NA	NA
Japan	3.14	4.43	3.63	3.48	3.94	4.28	4.47	4.50	5.75	4.85	5.72	6.93	6.97	6.06	5.83
Korea, South	2.04	2.95	4.16	4.13	4.50	5.26	5.91	6.21	5.83	4.69	5.60	6.59	6.66	6.66	6.59
Mexico	1.02	1.10	2.01	2.04	2.04	2.23	2.31	2.42	2.46	2.12	2.46	2.80	2.95	3.37	3.60
Taiwan	2.46	2.23	2.16	2.16	2.46	2.76	3.07	3.22	3.52	3.03	3.56	4.05	NA	NA	NA
United States	1.17	1.10	1.48	1.55	1.85	2.27	2.57	2.80	3.26	2.35	2.76	3.52	3.63	3.52	3.37

	Premium unleaded														
Country	**1990**	**1995**	**2000**	**2003**	**2004**	**2005**	**2006**	**2007**	**2008**	**2009**	**2010**	**2011**	**2012**	**2013**	**2014**
France	$3.63	$4.28	$3.79	$4.35	$5.00	$5.45	$5.87	$6.59	$7.50	$6.36	$6.74	$7.91	$7.61	$7.72	$7.46
Germany	2.76	4.09	3.56	4.69	5.34	5.75	6.13	6.97	7.76	6.81	7.12	8.21	8.03	8.03	7.72
Italy	4.58	4.01	3.79	4.54	5.30	5.75	6.09	6.74	7.65	6.47	6.85	8.18	8.71	8.78	8.59
Mexico	NA	NA	2.23	2.31	2.38	2.57	2.73	2.95	3.03	2.65	2.95	3.14	3.14	3.56	3.79
South Africa	NA	NA	1.78	1.93	2.57	3.07	3.41	3.63	4.13	3.22	4.09	NA	NA	NA	NA
Spain	NA	3.26	2.84	3.48	4.09	4.50	4.85	5.38	6.13	5.26	5.83	6.97	6.93	7.19	6.97
Thailand	NA	1.25	1.36	1.51	1.78	2.23	2.76	3.22	4.01	4.13	4.85	NA	NA	NA	NA
United Kingdom	2.84	3.22	4.58	4.69	5.56	5.98	6.36	7.15	7.42	5.87	6.85	8.10	8.14	7.95	7.95
United States	NA	1.21	1.59	1.67	1.97	2.38	2.69	2.91	3.37	2.46	2.91	3.63	3.75	3.67	3.56

NA = Not available. **Note:** Premium unleaded refers to fuels with a research octane number of 95.

Average U.S. Gasoline Prices, 1950-2014

Source: *Monthly Energy Review*, Aug. 2015; *Short-Term Energy Outlook*, Aug. 2015; Energy Information Administration (EIA), U.S. Dept. of Energy

(in dollars per gallon, including taxes; constant dollars is price in Aug. 2015 dollars)

	Current dollars				Constant dollars,
Year	**Leaded regular**	**Unleaded regular**	**Unleaded premium**	**All types[1]**	**unleaded regular[2]**
1950	$0.27	NA	NA	NA	NA
1955	0.29	NA	NA	NA	NA
1960	0.31	NA	NA	NA	NA
1965	0.31	NA	NA	NA	NA
1970	0.36	NA	NA	NA	NA
1975	0.57	NA	NA	NA	NA
1980	1.19	$1.25	NA	$1.22	$3.60
1985	1.12	1.20	$1.34	1.20	2.58
1986	0.86	0.93	1.09	0.93	1.92
1987	0.90	0.95	1.09	0.96	1.91
1988	0.90	0.95	1.11	0.96	1.83
1989	1.00	1.02	1.20	1.06	1.89
1990	1.15	1.16	1.35	1.22	2.05
1991	NA	1.14	1.32	1.20	1.92
1992	NA	1.13	1.32	1.19	1.84
1993	NA	1.11	1.30	1.17	1.76
1994	NA	1.11	1.31	1.17	1.73
1995	NA	1.15	1.34	1.21	1.73
1996	NA	1.23	1.41	1.29	1.82
1997	NA	$1.23	$1.42	$1.29	$1.78
1998	NA	1.06	1.25	1.12	1.50
1999	NA	1.17	1.36	1.22	1.63
2000	NA	1.51	1.69	1.56	2.05
2001	NA	1.46	1.66	1.53	1.91
2002	NA	1.36	1.56	1.44	1.78
2003	NA	1.59	1.78	1.64	2.01
2004	NA	1.88	2.07	1.92	2.33
2005	NA	2.30	2.49	2.34	2.77
2006	NA	2.59	2.81	2.64	3.04
2007	NA	2.80	3.03	2.85	3.22
2008	NA	3.27	3.52	3.32	3.60
2009	NA	2.35	2.61	2.40	2.60
2010	NA	2.79	3.05	2.84	3.03
2011	NA	3.53	3.79	3.58	3.73
2012	NA	3.64	3.92	3.70	3.76
2013	NA	3.53	3.84	3.58	3.58
2014	NA	3.37	3.71	3.42	3.38

NA = Not applicable. **Note:** Until unleaded gas became available in 1976, leaded was the only type used in automobiles. (1) Includes types of motor gasoline not shown separately. Includes gasohol starting in 1985. (2) Base prices vary slightly from unleaded regular column at left.

Energy Consumption, Total and Per Capita, by State, 2013

Source: State Energy Data System, Energy Information Administration (EIA), U.S. Dept. of Energy

Total Consumption				Consumption per Capita			
Rank, state	**Btu (tril)**	**Rank, state**	**Btu (tril)**	**Rank, state**	**Btu (mil)**	**Rank, state**	**Btu (mil)**
1. Texas	12,944.1	27. Arizona	1,414.8	1. Wyoming	918.1	27. Maine	306.4
2. California	7,684.1	28. Maryland	1,403.8	2. Louisiana	828.4	28. Pennsylvania	296.9
3. Florida	4,077.9	29. Kansas	1,163.1	3. Alaska	826.0	29. Delaware	296.6
4. Illinois	4,011.5	30. Mississippi	1,141.8	4. North Dakota	813.1	30. Washington	292.4
5. Louisiana	3,835.0	31. Arkansas	1,093.0	5. Iowa	490.4	31. Virginia	291.5
6. Pennsylvania	3,795.0	32. Oregon	996.7	6. Texas	488.4	32. Michigan	287.2
7. Ohio	3,745.4	33. Nebraska	871.8	7. Nebraska	466.5	33. Utah	286.2
8. New York	3,625.3	34. Utah	830.6	8. South Dakota	461.7	34. Georgia	279.7
9. Indiana	2,900.0	35. Connecticut	748.1	9. Indiana	441.4	35. Colorado	279.2
10. Michigan	2,843.2	36. West Virginia	737.8	10. Oklahoma	421.2	36. Dist. of Columbia	263.3
11. Georgia	2,795.4	37. New Mexico	688.5	11. Kentucky	414.3	37. New Jersey	259.7
12. North Carolina	2,524.1	38. Nevada	657.1	12. Kansas	401.6	38. North Carolina	256.3
13. Virginia	2,410.7	39. Alaska	609.0	13. Alabama	399.5	39. Oregon	253.7
14. New Jersey	2,314.5	40. North Dakota	588.6	14. West Virginia	398.0	40. Maryland	236.4
15. Tennessee	2,135.9	41. Wyoming	535.5	15. Montana	395.3	41. Nevada	235.4
16. Washington	2,039.3	42. Idaho	529.5	16. Mississippi	381.6	42. New Hampshire	228.9
17. Alabama	1,931.4	43. Maine	407.1	17. Arkansas	369.4	43. Massachusetts	215.0
18. Minnesota	1,859.8	44. Montana	401.2	18. Minnesota	343.0	44. Arizona	213.2
19. Missouri	1,857.0	45. South Dakota	390.4	19. South Carolina	333.5	45. Vermont	213.2
20. Kentucky	1,822.7	46. New Hampshire	302.8	20. New Mexico	329.9	46. Florida	208.1
21. Wisconsin	1,804.0	47. Hawaii	277.1	21. Tennessee	328.7	47. Connecticut	207.8
22. Oklahoma	1,622.8	48. Delaware	274.5	22. Idaho	328.3	48. California	199.9
23. South Carolina	1,591.4	49. Rhode Island	193.6	23. Ohio	323.7	49. Hawaii	196.7
24. Iowa	1,516.5	50. Dist. of Columbia	170.9	24. Wisconsin	314.1	50. New York	184.1
25. Colorado	1,471.8	51. Vermont	133.6	25. Illinois	311.2	51. Rhode Island	183.8
26. Massachusetts	1,442.6	**United States**	**97,144.7**	26. Missouri	307.2	**United States**	**306.9**

Note: U.S. total includes 17.4 trillion Btu of net exports of coal coke that is not allocated to the states.

U.S. Production of Crude Oil by State, 2014

Source: *Petroleum Supply Annual 2014*, Energy Information Administration (EIA), U.S. Dept. of Energy

Oil production in North Dakota nearly tripled between 2010 and 2014 through the use of hydraulic fracturing, or fracking, a process by which water, sand, and chemicals are injected at high pressure to create fractures in shale rock, releasing the oil within.

(in thousands of barrels)

Rank, state	**Total**	**Rank, state**	**Total**	**Rank, state**	**Total**	**Rank, state**	**Total**
1. Texas	1,157,429	9. Louisiana	68,549	17. Illinois	9,540	25. South Dakota	1,786
2. North Dakota	396,749	10. Kansas	49,521	18. Michigan	7,247	26. New York	332
3. California	204,289	11. Utah	40,893	19. Arkansas	6,845	27. Tennessee	329
4. Alaska	181,425	12. Montana	29,346	20. Pennsylvania	6,439	28. Nevada	316
5. Oklahoma	124,253	13. Mississippi	24,466	21. Kentucky	3,376	29. Missouri	198
6. New Mexico	123,624	14. Ohio	18,996	22. Nebraska	3,038	30. Arizona	56
7. Colorado	95,320	15. West Virginia	9,872	23. Indiana	2,507	31. Virginia	12
8. Wyoming	76,071	16. Alabama	9,860	24. Florida	2,227	**U.S. total**	**3,183,013**

Note: One barrel is equal to 42 U.S. gallons. U.S. total includes 528,106 thousand barrels of federal offshore oil production.

Fracking in the U.S.

Hydraulic fracturing, more commonly known as fracking, is a process by which water, sand, and chemicals are injected at high pressure to create fractures in shale rock, releasing the oil and/or natural gas within. Enormous shale deposits in Pennsylvania, California, and other parts of North America have inspired predictions that the U.S. could some day be a net energy exporting nation. However, more recent estimates from the U.S. Dept. of Energy have significantly reduced the amount of oil that can realistically be derived from some of those shale deposits. Fracking also involves numerous environmental concerns, including pollution of groundwater, massive use of freshwater in drought-prone areas, and effects on seismicity in earthquake-prone areas. Vermont and New York have both banned fracking within their borders, while Connecticut has prohibited the storage or handling of fracking waste.

Shale Oil and Gas Resources in the U.S., 2013

Source: *Oil and Gas Module, Assumptions to the Annual Energy Outlook, 2014*, Energy Information Administration (EIA), U.S. Dept. of Energy

	Technically recoverable resources		
Region/basin	**Crude oil (bil barrels)**	**Dry natural gas (tril cu ft)**	**Natural gas plant liquids (bil barrels)**
East			
Appalachian	1.6	243.8	11.8
Illinois	—	29.1	2.3
Michigan	—	19.3	1.1
Gulf Coast			
Black Warrior	—	4.3	—
TX-LA-MS Salt	0.8	212.6	2.7
Western Gulf	21.9	116.2	2.2
Midcontinent			
Anadarko	1.0	24.9	1.2
Arkoma	—	29.8	0.6
Black Warrior	—	1.6	—
Southwest			
Fort Worth	0.1	17.5	0.7
Permian	21.2	71.0	5.5

	Technically recoverable resources		
Region/basin	**Crude oil (bil barrels)**	**Dry natural gas (tril cu ft)**	**Natural gas plant liquids (bil barrels)**
Rocky Mountain			
Denver	0.5	14.2	0.1
Greater Green R.	0.9	10.6	0.5
MT Thrust Belt	0.6	0.4	—
North Central MT	—	0.1	—
Paradox	1.0	0.8	—
Powder River	2.1	2.4	0.1
San Juan	—	20.5	—
SW Wyoming	1.1	50.1	5.0
Uinta-Piceance	0.7	42.4	—
Williston	22.7	16.3	1.2
Wind R.	0.1	6.4	0.3
West Coast			
Columbia	—	12.2	—
San Joaquin/L.A.	0.6	3.0	—
Total	**78.2**	**949.3**	**35.8**

— = Less than 500 mil barrels.

U.S. Petroleum Trade, 1955-2014

Source: *Monthly Energy Review*, Aug. 2015, Energy Information Administration (EIA), U.S. Dept. of Energy
(in thousands of barrels per day; average for the year)

Year	Imports from Persian Gulf[1]	Total imports	Total exports	Net imports[2]	Petroleum products supplied[3]	Year	Imports from Persian Gulf[1]	Total imports	Total exports	Net imports[2]	Petroleum products supplied[3]
1955	NA	1,248	368	880	8,455	2001	2,761	11,871	971	10,900	19,649
1960	326	1,815	202	1,613	9,797	2002	2,269	11,530	984	10,546	19,761
1965	359	2,468	187	2,281	11,512	2003	2,501	12,264	1,027	11,238	20,034
1970	184	3,419	259	3,161	14,697	2004	2,493	13,145	1,048	12,097	20,731
1975	1,165	6,056	209	5,846	16,322	2005	2,334	13,714	1,165	12,549	20,802
1980	1,519	6,909	544	6,365	17,056	2006	2,211	13,707	1,317	12,390	20,687
1985	311	5,067	781	4,286	15,726	2007	2,163	13,468	1,433	12,036	20,680
1990	1,966	8,018	857	7,161	16,988	2008	2,370	12,915	1,802	11,114	19,498
1995	1,573	8,835	949	7,886	17,725	2009	1,689	11,691	2,024	9,667	18,771
1996	1,604	9,478	981	8,498	18,309	2010	1,711	11,793	2,353	9,441	19,180
1997	1,755	10,162	1,003	9,158	18,620	2011	1,861	11,436	2,986	8,450	18,882
1998	2,136	10,708	945	9,764	18,917	2012	2,156	10,598	3,205	7,393	18,490
1999	2,464	10,852	940	9,912	19,519	2013	2,009	9,859	3,621	6,237	18,961
2000	2,488	11,459	1,040	10,419	19,701	2014	1,869	9,221	4,180	5,041	19,035

NA = Not available. **Note:** U.S. exports include shipments to U.S. territories; imports include receipts from U.S. territories. Numbers may not add up to totals because of rounding. (1) Bahrain, Iran, Iraq, Kuwait, Qatar, Saudi Arabia, United Arab Emirates, and the Neutral Zone between Kuwait and Saudi Arabia. (2) Total imports minus total exports. (3) Includes domestic production and imports minus change in stocks, refinery imports, and exports.

World Fossil Fuel Reserves

Source: International Energy Statistics Database, Energy Information Administration (EIA), U.S. Dept. of Energy

	Crude oil (bil barrels), 2015	Natural gas (tril cu ft), 2015	Coal (mil short tons), 2011
North America[1]	**219.8**	**422.1**	**267,411**
Canada	172.5	71.8	7,255
Greenland	0.0	0.0	202
Mexico	9.8	16.5	1,335
United States[1]	36.5	338.3	258,619
Central & South America	**329.4**	**274.3**	**16,139**
Argentina	2.4	11.1	606
Bolivia	0.2	9.9	1
Brazil	15.3	16.2	7,308
Chile	0.2	3.5	171
Colombia	2.4	6.4	7,436
Cuba	0.1	2.5	NA
Ecuador	8.8	0.2	26
Peru	0.7	15.0	49
Trinidad & Tobago	0.7	12.2	NA
Venezuela	298.4	197.1	528
Europe	**11.7**	**130.9**	**90,743**
Albania	0.2	0.0	875
Bosnia & Herz.	0.0	0.0	3,145
Bulgaria	0.0	0.2	2,608
Czech Republic	0.0	0.1	1,160
Germany	0.0	3.4	44,697
Greece	0.0	0.0	3,329
Hungary	0.0	0.3	1,830
Italy	0.5	2.0	55
Macedonia	0.0	0.0	366
Montenegro	0.0	0.0	157
Netherlands	0.1	31.7	NA
Norway	5.5	72.4	6
Poland	0.1	3.0	6,024
Romania	0.6	3.7	321
Serbia	0.1	1.7	14,783
Slovakia	0.0	0.5	289
Slovenia	0.0	0.0	246
Spain	0.2	0.1	584
Turkey	0.3	0.2	9,592
United Kingdom	3.0	8.5	251
Eurasia	**118.9**	**2,178.0**	**251,364**
Armenia	0.0	0.0	180
Azerbaijan	7.0	35.0	NA
Belarus	0.2	0.1	110
Georgia	0.0	0.3	222
Kazakhstan	30.0	85.0	37,038
Kyrgyzstan	0.0	0.2	895
Russia	80.0	1,688.2	173,074
Tajikistan	0.0	0.2	413
Turkmenistan	0.6	265.0	NA
Ukraine	0.4	39.0	37,339
Uzbekistan	0.6	65.0	2,094

	Crude oil (bil barrels), 2015	Natural gas (tril cu ft), 2015	Coal (mil short tons), 2011
Middle East	**808.1**	**2,818.2**	**1,237**
Bahrain	0.1	3.3	NA
Iran	157.8	1,201.4	1,237
Iraq	144.2	111.5	NA
Israel	0.0	7.0	NA
Kuwait	104.0	63.5	NA
Oman	5.2	24.9	NA
Qatar	25.2	871.6	NA
Saudi Arabia	268.3	294.3	NA
Syria	2.5	8.5	NA
UAE	97.8	215.1	NA
Yemen	3.0	16.9	NA
Africa	**126.5**	**604.1**	**35,069**
Algeria	12.2	159.1	65
Angola	9.0	9.7	NA
Congo, Dem. Rep.	0.2	0.0	97
Congo Rep.	1.6	3.2	NA
Egypt	4.4	77.2	18
Libya	48.4	53.2	NA
Mozambique	0.0	100.0	234
Namibia	0.0	2.2	NA
Niger	0.2	NA	77
Nigeria	37.1	180.5	209
South Africa	0.0	NA	33,241
Sudan[2]	5.0	3.0	NA
Swaziland	0.0	0.0	159
Tanzania	0.0	0.2	220
Zimbabwe	0.0	0.0	553
Asia & Oceania	**46.0**	**534.5**	**317,827**
Afghanistan	0.0	1.8	73
Australia	1.2	30.4	84,217
Bangladesh	0.0	8.5	323
Brunei	1.1	13.8	NA
China	24.6	164.0	126,215
India	5.7	50.4	66,800
Indonesia	3.7	103.4	30,883
Japan	0.0	0.7	383
Korea, North	0.0	0.0	661
Korea, South	NA	0.3	139
Laos	0.0	0.0	554
Malaysia	4.0	83.0	4
Mongolia	NA	0.0	2,778
Myanmar	0.1	10.0	2
New Zealand	0.1	1.4	629
Pakistan	0.4	24.7	2,282
Philippines	0.1	3.5	348
Thailand	0.5	8.4	1,366
Vietnam	4.4	24.7	165
World[1]	**1,655.6**	**6,927.5**	**979,791**

NA = Not reported separately but included in regional and world totals. **Note:** Regional and world totals may include countries not shown. Proved reserves only. Some countries omitted for lack of appreciable reserves. (1) Figures for crude oil and natural gas are from 2013, the latest year available. (2) Includes South Sudan.

U.S. Crude Oil Imports by Selected Countries, 1975-2014

Source: *Petroleum Supply Annual*, Energy Information Administration (EIA), U.S. Dept. of Energy

The United States' dependence on foreign oil continues to decline thanks to increased U.S. production of crude oil, natural gas, and domestic biofuels like ethanol and biodiesel. Imports fell to just 7.3 mil barrels a day in 2014, down from a peak of more than 10 mil barrels per day a decade ago. And imports from the Oil Producing and Exporting Countries (OPEC) declined to 3.0 mil barrels daily, an amount not seen in two decades. In 2014, approximately 27% of the petroleum consumed by the United States was imported from foreign countries, the lowest level since 1985. Since 2005, Canada has been the largest supplier of U.S. oil by far, responsible for nearly 40% of all U.S. oil imports. Sanctions do not permit the U.S. to import oil from Iran.

(in thousands of barrels per day; ranked by 2014 imports)

Country	1975	1980	1985	1990	1995	2000	2005	2010	2013	2014
Canada	600	199	468	643	1,040	1,348	1,633	1,970	2,579	2,885
Saudi Arabia#	701	1,250	132	1,195	1,260	1,523	1,445	1,082	1,325	1,159
Mexico	70	507	715	689	1,027	1,313	1,556	1,152	850	781
Venezuela#	395	156	306	666	1,151	1,223	1,241	912	755	733
Iraq#	2	28	46	514	0	620	527	415	341	364
Kuwait#	4	27	4	79	213	263	227	195	326	309
Colombia	0	0	0	140	207	318	156	338	367	294
Ecuador#[1]	0	0	0	0	96	125	276	210	232	210
Brazil	0	1	0	0	0	5	94	255	110	145
Angola#[2]	71	37	104	236	360	295	456	383	201	136
Chad	NA	NA	NA	NA	NA	NA	74	18	66	61
Nigeria#	746	841	280	784	621	875	1,077	983	239	59
Argentina	NA	NA	NA	NA	44	53	56	29	13	29
Azerbaijan	NA	NA	NA	NA	NA	NA	NA	55	29	23
Indonesia	379	314	292	98	64	36	19	33	18	20
Russia[3]	0	0	0	1	14	7	199	269	42	18
Gabon[4]	NA	NA	NA	NA	229	143	127	47	24	16
United Kingdom	0	173	278	155	341	291	224	120	21	10
Vietnam	NA	NA	NA	NA	1	9	31	12	13	10
Norway	12	144	31	96	258	302	119	25	17	9
Peru	NA	NA	NA	NA	21	4	4	14	11	9
Algeria#	264	456	84	63	27	1	228	328	29	6
Thailand	NA	NA	NA	NA	1	3	2	13	9	6
Libya#	223	548	0	0	0	0	44	43	43	5
Trinidad and Tobago	115	115	98	76	62	56	64	45	8	5
Congo Republic	NA	NA	NA	NA	20	42	25	70	18	4
Equatorial Guinea	NA	NA	NA	NA	NA	6	68	50	17	4
Non-OPEC countries[1,2,4]	**NA**	**NA**	**NA**	**NA**	**3,660**	**4,526**	**5,310**	**4,661**	**4,237**	**4,342**
OPEC countries[1,2,4]	**3,211**	**3,864**	**1,312**	**3,514**	**3,570**	**4,544**	**4,816**	**4,553**	**3,493**	**2,995**
Persian Gulf countries	**1,121**	**1,508**	**244**	**1,801**	**1,479**	**2,409**	**2,207**	**1,694**	**1,994**	**1,846**
TOTAL	**4,105**	**5,263**	**3,201**	**5,894**	**7,230**	**9,071**	**10,126**	**9,213**	**7,730**	**7,337**

= OPEC member. NA = Not available. (1) Ecuador suspended its OPEC membership Dec. 1992-Nov. 2007. Ecuador's imports in 1993-2007 appear in non-OPEC totals. (2) Angola became a member of OPEC as of Jan. 1, 2007, and is not included in OPEC totals from before that year. (3) May include oil from USSR states before 1992. (4) Gabon withdrew from OPEC Dec. 31, 1994. Imports from Jan. 1, 1995, on appear in non-OPEC totals.

U.S. Coal Production and Consumption, 1950-2014

Source: *Monthly Energy Review*, Aug. 2015; *Annual Coal Report, 2013*; Energy Information Administration (EIA), U.S. Dept. of Energy

(in thousand short tons)

	Coal production[1]			Coal consumption				
Year	Surface mining	Underground mining	Total production	Residential	Commercial	Industrial	Electric power[2]	Total consumption
1950	139,388	421,000	560,388	51,562	63,021	224,637	91,871	494,102
1960	141,745	292,584	434,329	24,159	16,789	177,402	176,685	398,081
1970	272,131	340,530	612,661	9,024	7,090	186,637	320,182	523,231
1975	361,174	293,467	654,641	2,823	6,587	147,244	405,962	562,640
1980	492,192	337,508	829,700	1,355	5,097	127,004	569,274	702,730
1985	532,838	350,800	883,638	1,711	6,068	116,429	693,841	818,049
1990	604,529	424,546	1,029,076	1,345	5,379	115,207	782,567	904,498
1995	636,725	396,249	1,032,974	755	5,052	106,067	850,230	962,104
2000	699,953	373,659	1,073,612	454	3,673	94,147	985,821	1,084,095
2005	762,887	368,612	1,131,498	378	4,342	83,774	1,037,485	1,125,978
2006	803,728	359,022	1,162,750	290	2,936	82,429	1,026,636	1,112,292
2007	794,845	351,790	1,146,635	353	3,173	79,331	1,045,141	1,127,998
2008	814,729	357,079	1,171,809	351	3,506	76,463	1,040,580	1,120,548
2009	742,862	332,062	1,074,923	353	3,210	60,641	933,627	997,478
2010	745,357	337,155	1,084,368	339	3,081	70,381	975,052	1,048,514
2011	748,372	345,606	1,095,628	307	2,793	67,671	932,484	1,002,948
2012	672,748	342,387	1,016,458	NA	2,045	63,589	823,551	889,185
2013	641,191	341,685	984,482	NA	1,951	64,529	857,962	924,442
2014	NA	NA	NA	NA	2,212	63,214	851,428	916,854

NA = Not available. (1) A small amount of refuse recovery has been included in coal production figures since 2001. (2) Electricity-only and combined-heat-and-power (CHP) plants whose primary business is to sell electricity or electricity and heat to the public. Through 1988, data are for electric utilities only; beginning in 1989, data are for electric utilities and independent power producers.

World Nuclear Power Summary, 2014

Source: *Nuclear Power Reactors in the World*, International Atomic Energy Agency; as of Dec. 31, 2014

Country	Reactors in operation		Reactors under construction		Nuclear electricity supplied in 2014		Total operating experience[2]	
	No. of units	Total MW(e)	No. of units	Total MW(e)	TW(e).h[1]	% of nation's total	Years	Months
Argentina	3	1,627	1	25	5.3	4.1%	73	2
Armenia	1	375	—	—	2.3	30.7	40	8
Belgium	7	5,927	—	—	32.1	47.5	268	7
Brazil	2	1,884	1	1,245	14.5	2.9	47	3
Bulgaria	2	1,926	—	—	15.0	31.8	157	3
Canada	19	13,500	—	—	98.6	16.8	674	6
China	23	19,007	26	25,756	123.8	2.4	181	7
Czech Republic	6	3,904	—	—	28.6	35.8	140	10
Finland	4	2,752	1	1,600	22.6	34.7	143	4
France	58	63,130	1	1,630	418.0	76.9	1,990	4
Germany	9	12,074	—	—	91.8	15.8	808	1
Hungary	4	1,889	—	—	14.8	53.6	118	2
India	21	5,308	6	3,907	33.2	3.5	418	6
Iran	1	915	—	—	3.7	1.5	3	4
Japan	48	42,388	2	2,650	0.0	0.0	1,694	4
Korea, South	23	20,717	5	6,370	149.2	30.4	450	1
Mexico	2	1,330	—	—	9.3	5.6	45	11
Netherlands	1	482	—	—	3.9	4.0	70	0
Pakistan	3	690	2	630	4.6	4.3	61	8
Romania	2	1,300	—	—	10.8	18.5	25	11
Russia	34	24,654	9	7,371	169.1	18.6	1,157	3
Slovakia	4	1,814	2	880	14.4	56.8	152	7
Slovenia	1	688	—	—	6.1	37.3	33	3
South Africa	2	1,860	—	—	14.8	6.2	60	3
Spain	7	7,121	—	—	54.9	20.4	308	1
Sweden	10	9,470	—	—	62.3	41.5	422	6
Switzerland	5	3,333	—	—	26.5	37.9	199	11
Taiwan	6	5,032	2	2,600	40.8	18.9	200	1
Ukraine	15	13,107	2	1,900	83.1	49.4	443	6
United Kingdom	16	9,373	—	—	57.9	17.2	1,543	7
United States	99	98,639	5	5,633	798.6	19.5	4,012	4
TOTAL	**438**	**376,216**	**70**	**68,450**	**2,410.4**	**NA**	**16,096**	**10**

— = Not applicable. MW(e) = Megawatt electricity. (1) 1 terawatt-hour [TW(e).h] = 106 megawatt-hour [MW(e).h]. For an average power plant, 1 TW(e).h = 0.39 megaton of coal equivalent (input) and 0.23 megaton of oil equivalent (input). (2) Total includes shutdown plants for countries not listed here: Italy (80 years, 8 months), Kazakhstan (25 years, 10 months), and Lithuania (43 years, 6 months).

Nations Most Reliant on Nuclear Energy, 2014

Source: *Nuclear Power Reactors in the World*, International Atomic Energy Agency (IAEA)
(nuclear electricity generation as % of total electricity generated within country)

Rank	Country	Nuclear share	Rank	Country	Nuclear share	Rank	Country	Nuclear share	Rank	Country	Nuclear share
1.	France	76.9%	9.	Czech Republic	35.8%	17.	Russia	18.6%	25.	Argentina	4.1%
2.	Slovakia	56.8	10.	Finland	34.7	18.	Romania	18.5	26.	Netherlands	4.0
3.	Hungary	53.6	11.	Bulgaria	31.8	19.	United Kingdom	17.2	27.	India	3.5
4.	Ukraine	49.4	12.	Armenia	30.7	20.	Canada	16.8	28.	Brazil	2.9
5.	Belgium	47.5	13.	Korea, South	30.4	21.	Germany	15.9	29.	China	2.4
6.	Sweden	41.5	14.	Spain	20.4	22.	South Africa	6.2	30.	Iran	1.5
7.	Switzerland	37.9	15.	United States	19.5	23.	Mexico	5.6	31.	Japan	0.0
8.	Slovenia	37.3	16.	Taiwan	18.9	24.	Pakistan	4.3			

U.S. Nuclear Reactors and Power Plant Operations, 1953-2014

Source: *Monthly Energy Review*, Aug. 2015, Energy Information Administration (EIA), U.S. Dept. of Energy

Years	Number of reactor units								Nuclear electricity generation (bil net kWh)[6]	Nuclear share of domestic electricity generation[6]
	Ordered[1]	Cancelled	Construction permits issued[2]	Low-power licenses issued[3]	Full-power licenses issued[4]	Shutdown[5]	Operable units[6]	Capacity factor[6,7]		
1953-59	14	0	8	2	2	0	2	NA	0.2	NA
1960-64	7	0	12	13	12	2	13	NA	3.3	0.3%
1965-69	81	0	50	8	9	4	17	NA	13.9	1.0
1970-74	143	16	59	41	41	5	55	47.8%	114.0	6.1
1975-79	13	43	48	17	17	3	69	58.4	255.2	11.3
1980-84	0	54	0	24	19	1	87	56.3	327.6	13.5
1985-89	0	7	0	24	28	4	111	62.2	529.4	17.8
1990-94	0	2	0	2	3	3	109	73.8	640.4	19.7
1995-99	0	2	0	1	1	6	104	85.3	728.3	19.7
2000-04	0	0	0	0	0	0	104	90.1	788.5	19.9
2005-09	0	0	0	0	0	0	104	90.3	798.9	20.2
2010-14	0	0	0	0	0	5	99	91.7	797.1	19.5
Total	**259**	**124**	**177**	**132**	**132**	**32**	**NA**	**NA**	**NA**	**NA**

NA = Not applicable. **Note:** The permit/license categories shown here are historic. The Nuclear Regulatory Commission anticipates 16 or more new combined license applications under current regulations over the next few years—the first of which was submitted in Sept. 2007—which may amount to 25 or more new reactor units. (1) Order placed by a utility or government agency for a nuclear steam supply system. (2) Permits issued in a given period, not extant permits. (3) Permission to conduct testing but not operate at full power. (4) Permission to operate at full power. (5) Permanently ceased operation. (6) As of the end of the designated period. (7) The ratio of electric energy produced to the amount that could be produced at continuous full-power operation.

U.S. Nuclear Reactors Generating the Most Electricity, 2014

Source: U.S. Nuclear Statistics Database, Energy Information Administration (EIA), U.S. Dept. of Energy
(in thousand net megawatt-hours)

Rank	Reactor, location	Electricity generated	Capacity[1]
1.	South Texas-2, Bay City, TX	11,605,094	104%
2.	Palo Verde-3, Wintersburg, AZ	11,579,129	101
3.	Braidwood-1, Braceville, IL	10,592,046	103
4.	Perry-1, Perry, OH	10,455,271	96
5.	Palo Verde-2, Wintersburg, AZ	10,391,477	90
6.	PSEG Hope Creek-1, Salem, NJ	10,373,816	102
7.	Palo Verde-1, Wintersburg, AZ	10,350,311	90
8.	Seabrook-1, Seabrook, NH	10,168,265	93
9.	Grand Gulf-1, Port Gibson, MS	10,151,268	82
10.	Peach Bottom-3, Delta, PA	10,119,906	103
11.	Catawba-2, York, SC	10,091,895	100
12.	Sequoyah-1 Soddy-Daisy, TN	10,051,759	100
13.	Limerick-2, Limerick, PA	9,985,562	99
14.	Byron-1, Byron, IL	9,879,902	97
15.	Nine Mile Point-2, Scriba, NY	9,797,055	87%
16.	Comanche Peak-2, Glen Rose, TX	9,692,330	93
17.	Braidwood-2, Braceville, IL	9,671,619	96
18.	PPL Susquehanna-2, Salem Township, PA	9,667,805	88
19.	Columbia-2, Richland, WA	9,497,321	96
20.	LaSalle-2, Marseilles, IL	9,487,267	95
21.	Browns Ferry-2, Athens, AL	9,481,426	98
22.	Byron-2, Byron, IL	9,372,479	94
23.	McGuire-2, Huntersville, NC	9,362,485	94
24.	Millstone-3, Waterford, CT	9,338,918	87
25.	Donald C. Cook-2, Bridgman, MI	9,333,992	101

(1) The ratio of power generated to the maximum potential generation expressed as a percentage.

Renewable Energy Sources

Source: U.S. Dept. of Energy

Concern over the environmental impact of burning fossil fuels has helped spur interest in alternative fuels that are less polluting. And because the supply of fossil fuels is finite and diminishing, there is interest in "renewable" sources that do not deplete existing supplies. However, renewable energy sources still make up only a small share of U.S. domestic energy production (about 11% in 2014). The main reason for this is their relatively higher cost (in some cases two to four times that of power obtained from traditional fuels). The following are the major renewable energy sources available.

Biomass is plant-derived material usable as an energy source. It includes wood energy crops such as hybrid poplars and willow trees, agricultural crops including soybeans and corn, and animal and other wastes. Biomass is one of the two most common renewable energy sources in the U.S. today, along with hydropower. Biomass such as wood can be burned to produce heat and generate electricity. Agricultural crops can be chemically converted into fuels such as ethanol and biodiesel; these are the only known renewable liquid energy sources and may one day replace petroleum and fossil-fuel-produced diesel. But bringing ethanol and biodiesel into wide use would require more energy-efficient methods of production and transportation. Overall, biomass fuels burn much cleaner than fossil fuels, though biomass fuels still produce carbon dioxide and other pollutants.

Geothermal energy is generated from heat inside of the Earth. This form of energy is both clean and renewable. The technology has caught on in countries with substantial geothermal activity such as Iceland, where it accounted for 66% of primary energy use in 2011. In the U.S., the best sources for geothermal power are in the West, where there are many heated underground lakes. Large-scale access would require drilling. A major goal in this field is to find a way to harness energy directly from magma (molten rock material), which has great potential because of its high temperatures.

Hydrogen is the third most abundant element on Earth. It does not naturally occur on Earth as a pure gas or liquid but is always combined with other elements (such as oxygen, to form water, or carbon, to form methane). If hydrogen is to be used for energy, it must be separated from these other elements. That can be achieved through methods involving heat, photosynthesis, sunlight, or electricity.

Hydrogen batteries, or fuel cells, were used by NASA's space shuttles. Within a fuel cell, a chemical reaction occurs in which electrons are released from hydrogen atoms. These electrons flow through an external circuit as electricity. The hydrogen atoms' protons combine with oxygen (and some of the electrons in the electric current) to produce heat and water suitable for drinking. Fuel cells do not run down but work as long as hydrogen is supplied. Some experts think hydrogen will be the power source of the future. An infrastructure would need to be created for safe and cost-effective transportation and storage of hydrogen.

Hydropower, or hydroelectric power, is generated by water flowing through turbines. Along with biomass fuels, it is one of the two most common renewable energy sources in the U.S. today. A dam on a river is a common hydropower producer. No harmful greenhouse gases are produced, but the dams needed to generate power can harm river ecosystems. Researchers are working on turbine technologies to maximize use of hydropower and reduce adverse environmental effects.

Ocean energy can be generated in two ways. Thermal ocean energy uses heat that the ocean absorbs from the sun to power generators, sometimes producing drinkable desalinated water as a byproduct. Mechanical ocean energy is generated by the movement of tides and waves through turbines. In both cases, power generation is not very efficient with current technology. Much more research is needed. Mechanical ocean energy requires the building of large dams or breakwater-type structures called tidal barrages, which could harm coastal ecosystems.

Solar energy is generated using heat and light from the sun. Solar energy is an increasingly common source of electricity. Photovoltaic (PV) solar cells are made of semiconducting materials that can directly convert sunlight to electricity without producing any harmful waste. Arrays of mirrors can concentrate the sun's rays onto PV panels, making solar collectors more efficient. Sunlight can also be used to heat water directly. According to the Dept. of Energy, homes incorporating solar heating designs can save as much as 50% on heating bills. The downside to solar energy is that it depends heavily on a range of factors including location, time of year, and weather.

Wind energy uses wind turbines to produce energy. They are perched on high towers, usually 100 ft tall or higher, and often placed in large groups ("farms"). Farmers and homeowners sometimes use stand-alone turbines to generate supplemental electricity. Tax credits for wind energy producers and government incentives for homeowners have significantly lowered the price of wind power. But some object to wind farms because of their appearance or the noise the turbines make. Wind power raises few other environmental problems, but the turbines can pose a danger to birds. In addition, because weather is involved, consistent energy generation can be a challenge.

CRIME

Crime in the U.S., 1990-2013

Source: *Crime in the United States, 2013*, Federal Bureau of Investigation (FBI), U.S. Dept. of Justice

Offenses are classified as **violent crimes** if they involve force or the threat of force: murder and nonnegligent manslaughter, forcible rape, robbery, and aggravated assault. The following offenses are considered **property crimes**: burglary, larceny-theft, motor vehicle theft, and arson (excluded from this table).

		Violent crime					Property crime			
Year	Population[1]	All violent crimes	Murder and nonnegligent manslaughter	Forcible rape[2]	Robbery	Aggravated assault[3]	All property crimes	Burglary	Larceny-theft[4]	Motor vehicle theft
NUMBER OF OFFENSES										
1990	249,464,396	1,820,127	23,438	102,555	639,271	1,054,863	12,655,486	3,073,909	7,945,670	1,635,907
1995	262,803,276	1,798,792	21,606	97,470	580,509	1,099,207	12,063,935	2,593,784	7,997,710	1,472,441
2000	281,421,906	1,425,486	15,586	90,178	408,016	911,706	10,182,584	2,050,992	6,971,590	1,160,002
2005	296,507,061	1,390,745	16,740	94,347	417,438	862,220	10,174,754	2,155,448	6,783,447	1,235,859
2006	299,398,484	1,435,123	17,309	94,472	449,246	874,096	10,019,601	2,194,993	6,626,363	1,198,245
2007	301,621,157	1,422,970	17,128	92,160	447,324	866,358	9,882,212	2,190,198	6,591,542	1,100,472
2008	304,059,724	1,394,461	16,465	90,750	443,563	843,683	9,774,152	2,228,887	6,586,206	959,059
2009	307,006,550	1,325,896	15,399	89,241	408,742	812,514	9,337,060	2,203,313	6,338,095	795,652
2010	309,330,219	1,251,248	14,722	85,593	369,089	781,844	9,112,625	2,168,459	6,204,601	739,565
2011	311,587,816	1,206,005	14,661	84,175	354,746	752,423	9,052,743	2,185,140	6,151,095	716,508
2012	313,873,685	1,217,057	14,856	85,141	355,051	762,009	9,001,992	2,109,932	6,168,874	723,186
2013	316,128,839	1,163,146	14,196	79,770	345,031	724,149	8,632,512	1,928,465	6,004,453	699,594
PERCENT CHANGE: NUMBER OF OFFENSES										
2012-13		–4.4%	–4.4%	–6.3%	–2.8%	–5.0%	–4.1%	–8.6%	–2.7%	–3.3%
2009-13		–12.3	–7.8	–10.6	–15.6	–10.9	–7.5	–12.5	–5.3	–12.1
2004-13		–14.5	–12.1	–16.1	–14.1	–14.5	–16.3	–10.1	–13.4	–43.5
RATE PER 100,000 RESIDENTS										
1990		729.6	9.4	41.1	256.3	422.9	5,073.1	1,232.2	3,185.1	655.8
1995		684.5	8.2	37.1	220.9	418.3	4,590.5	987.0	3,043.2	560.3
2000		506.5	5.5	32.0	145.0	324.0	3,618.3	728.8	2,477.3	412.2
2005		469.0	5.6	31.8	140.8	290.8	3,431.5	726.9	2,287.8	416.8
2006		479.3	5.8	31.6	150.0	292.0	3,346.6	733.1	2,213.2	400.2
2007		471.8	5.7	30.6	148.3	287.2	3,276.4	726.1	2,185.4	364.9
2008		458.6	5.4	29.8	145.9	277.5	3,214.6	733.0	2,166.1	315.4
2009		431.9	5.0	29.1	133.1	264.7	3,041.3	717.7	2,064.5	259.2
2010		404.5	4.8	27.7	119.3	252.8	2,945.9	701.0	2,005.8	239.1
2011		387.1	4.7	27.0	113.9	241.5	2,905.4	701.3	1,974.1	230.0
2012		387.8	4.7	27.1	113.1	242.8	2,868.0	672.2	1,965.4	230.4
2013		367.9	4.5	25.2	109.1	229.1	2,730.7	610.0	1,899.4	221.3
PERCENT CHANGE: RATE PER 100,000 RESIDENTS										
2012-13		–5.1%	–5.1%	–7.0%	–3.5%	–5.6%	–4.8%	–9.3%	–3.4%	–4.0%
2009-13		–14.8	–10.5	–13.2	–18.0	–13.4	–10.2	–15.0	–8.0	–14.6
2004-13		–20.6	–18.3	–22.1	–20.2	–20.6	–22.3	–16.5	–19.6	–47.5

— = Less than 0.1%. (1) U.S. Census Bureau estimates for July 1 of each year except for 1990, 2000, and 2010, which show Apr. 1 decennial census counts. (2) The FBI revised its definition of rape in 2012 for data collection from 2013 on. For comparison purposes, however, the 2013 figures for rape refer to the legacy definition of rape: "carnal knowledge of a female forcibly and against her will." That definition does not include statutory rape, other types of sexual offenses, or sexual attacks on males, which were considered aggravated assaults or sex offenses, depending on circumstances and extent of injuries. (3) Attack upon another with the intent of doing serious bodily harm; usually accompanied by the use of a weapon or other means likely to produce death or great bodily harm. (4) The unlawful taking of another's property not involving force or fraud (e.g., theft of motor vehicle parts, shoplifting). Excludes crimes such as embezzlement and check fraud.

Violent Crime Rates in the U.S., 1976-2013

Source: *Crime in the United States*, 1995, 2000, and 2013 editions, Federal Bureau of Investigation (FBI), U.S. Dept. of Justice

After rising during much of the 1980s, the violent crime rate dropped by more than 50% between 1991 and 2013. Between 1992 and 2013, rates for aggravated assault and rape fell by 48% and 41% respectively, and the 2013 murder rate was exactly half what it was in 1994. Crime rate is number of reported offenses per 100,000 residents.

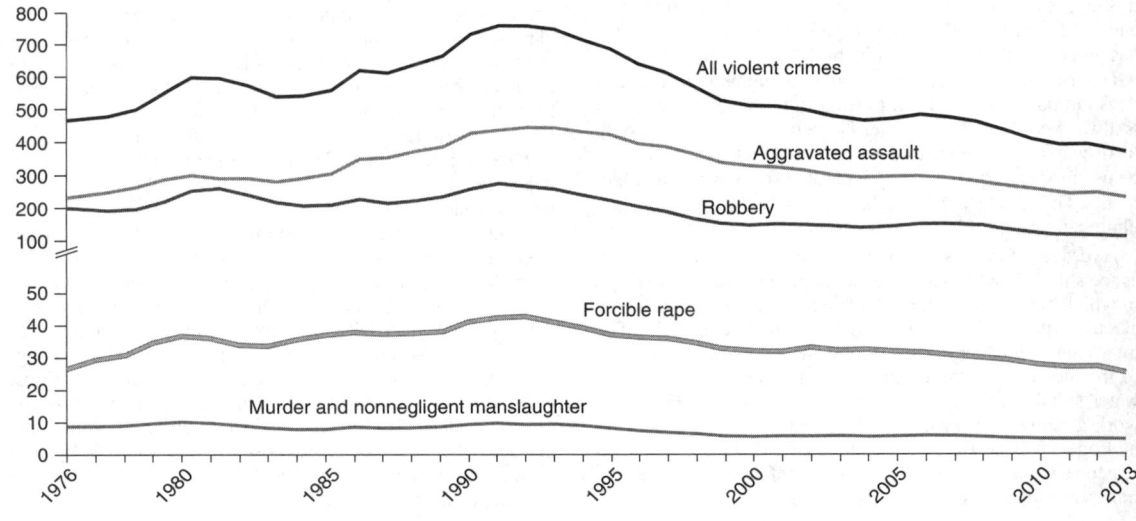

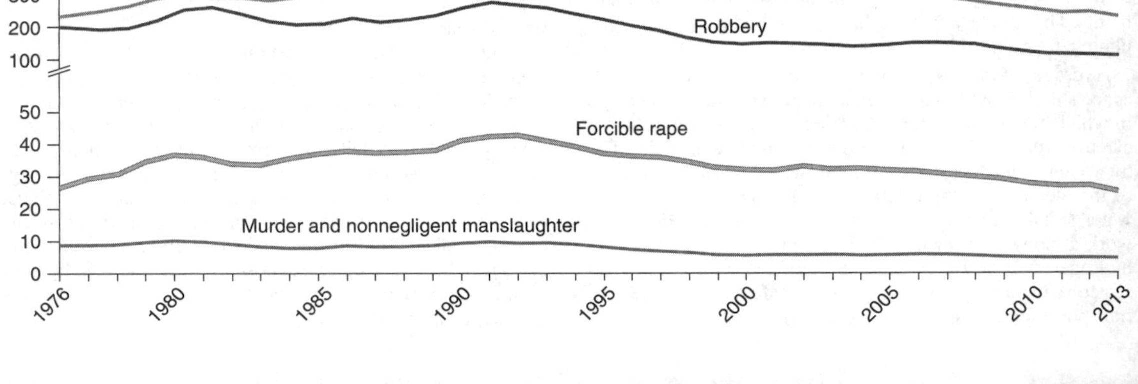

U.S. Crime Rates by Region, Geographic Division, and State, 2013

Source: *Crime in the United States, 2013*, Federal Bureau of Investigation (FBI), U.S. Dept. of Justice

(per 100,000 residents, as estimated by U.S. Census Bureau for July 1 of year)

	Violent crime					Property crime[1]			
	All violent crimes	Murder and nonnegligent manslaughter	Forcible rape[2]	Robbery	Aggravated assault[3]	All property crimes	Burglary	Larceny-theft[4]	Motor vehicle theft
Total U.S.[5]	**367.9**	**4.5**	**34.4**	**109.1**	**229.1**	**2,730.7**	**610.0**	**1,899.4**	**221.3**
Northeast	**335.1**	**3.5**	**24.4**	**118.1**	**195.5**	**1,960.4**	**372.4**	**1,475.8**	**112.2**
New England	**299.2**	**2.1**	**36.8**	**81.9**	**187.9**	**2,102.2**	**437.6**	**1,529.4**	**135.2**
Connecticut	254.5	2.4	26.6	98.2	135.4	1,974.1	358.5	1,442.6	173.0
Maine	121.6	1.8	33.7	25.2	68.7	2,292.2	488.1	1,735.3	68.8
Massachusetts	404.0	2.0	40.6	100.2	270.5	2,051.2	459.2	1,455.7	136.3
New Hampshire	199.6	1.7	51.8	49.0	112.7	2,194.3	373.0	1,750.3	71.0
Rhode Island	244.6	2.9	41.8	65.0	147.4	2,442.0	533.2	1,696.4	212.4
Vermont	114.9	1.6	20.7	11.6	87.1	2,214.2	528.7	1,632.2	53.3
Middle Atlantic	**347.8**	**4.0**	**20.0**	**130.9**	**198.2**	**1,910.2**	**349.3**	**1,456.9**	**104.1**
New Jersey	285.6	4.5	12.6	135.8	135.6	1,882.8	403.1	1,325.2	154.5
New York	389.8	3.3	17.1	138.6	234.7	1,824.8	287.2	1,458.8	78.8
Pennsylvania	326.6	4.7	29.5	115.6	185.7	2,060.8	407.3	1,545.6	107.8
Midwest	**333.4**	**4.5**	**39.9**	**99.1**	**201.0**	**2,560.4**	**567.4**	**1,802.5**	**190.4**
East North Central	**345.0**	**4.9**	**40.1**	**116.0**	**194.8**	**2,518.7**	**585.6**	**1,747.4**	**185.6**
Illinois	372.5	5.5	33.1	137.6	204.0	2,274.3	452.1	1,659.8	162.5
Indiana	349.9	5.4	32.6	108.2	211.3	2,854.0	653.0	1,984.9	216.2
Michigan	429.8	6.4	66.6	102.1	274.8	2,327.6	569.4	1,510.0	248.3
Ohio	275.7	3.9	34.9	124.2	123.2	2,927.5	790.2	1,968.5	168.8
Wisconsin	271.1	2.8	29.4	84.2	161.6	2,188.7	424.0	1,636.0	128.6
West North Central	**307.6**	**3.5**	**39.3**	**61.3**	**215.0**	**2,653.6**	**526.8**	**1,925.7**	**201.1**
Iowa	260.9	1.4	35.0	30.4	204.6	2,193.9	513.5	1,543.0	137.4
Kansas	327.5	3.9	41.3	46.6	248.1	2,946.8	600.4	2,117.0	229.5
Minnesota	223.2	2.1	37.0	67.8	127.5	2,420.4	419.0	1,854.4	147.0
Missouri	422.0	6.1	37.8	90.7	298.7	3,137.0	643.0	2,223.9	270.1
Nebraska	252.2	3.1	42.9	55.7	160.5	2,623.4	476.3	1,908.2	238.9
North Dakota	256.3	2.2	45.6	22.4	199.9	2,094.0	405.6	1,492.7	195.7
South Dakota	298.7	2.4	59.1	18.8	236.2	1,914.7	399.1	1,404.6	111.0
South[5]	**403.5**	**5.3**	**34.7**	**109.7**	**263.1**	**3,094.8**	**735.8**	**2,154.6**	**204.4**
South Atlantic[5]	**395.0**	**5.2**	**30.9**	**112.6**	**254.8**	**2,993.9**	**696.9**	**2,107.0**	**190.0**
Delaware	479.1	4.2	41.0	132.4	313.7	3,065.5	662.3	2,259.4	143.9
District of Columbia[5]	1,281.9	15.9	61.1	630.8	592.5	4,808.3	513.0	3,795.0	500.3
Florida	460.0	5.0	34.6	118.7	312.3	3,105.3	710.5	2,216.3	178.6
Georgia	359.7	5.6	25.8	125.0	209.3	3,346.6	823.2	2,254.9	268.5
Maryland	467.8	6.4	25.8	169.5	272.0	2,663.5	538.9	1,898.3	226.3
North Carolina	336.6	4.8	24.1	94.9	218.4	3,128.0	921.0	2,058.7	148.3
South Carolina	494.8	6.2	45.5	83.2	373.6	3,624.2	857.8	2,502.9	263.5
Virginia	187.9	3.8	27.4	55.3	109.7	2,065.9	322.5	1,640.1	103.3
West Virginia	289.7	3.3	35.2	35.1	226.7	2,103.9	521.7	1,478.9	103.3
East South Central	**398.6**	**5.5**	**37.1**	**94.1**	**272.7**	**2,959.9**	**772.8**	**2,011.8**	**175.4**
Alabama	418.1	7.2	42.3	96.2	285.2	3,351.3	877.8	2,254.8	218.7
Kentucky	198.8	3.8	36.7	73.9	95.5	2,362.9	596.4	1,629.3	137.2
Mississippi	267.4	6.5	31.1	80.5	156.5	2,724.7	835.6	1,742.3	146.7
Tennessee	579.7	5.0	36.2	112.5	436.9	3,180.9	785.1	2,213.7	182.1
West South Central	**419.8**	**5.3**	**39.6**	**112.6**	**271.8**	**3,326.2**	**781.1**	**2,302.8**	**242.3**
Arkansas	445.7	5.4	48.1	76.3	330.5	3,602.6	1,030.1	2,380.6	191.9
Louisiana	510.4	10.8	35.0	119.9	352.8	3,582.0	890.4	2,493.6	198.0
Oklahoma	428.1	5.1	56.6	78.7	300.8	3,273.7	866.1	2,116.4	291.2
Texas	399.8	4.3	36.9	120.2	246.9	3,258.2	721.8	2,287.8	248.6
West	**367.4**	**4.0**	**36.4**	**110.7**	**225.6**	**2,885.4**	**627.2**	**1,899.6**	**358.5**
Mountain	**367.7**	**4.1**	**50.4**	**81.2**	**245.3**	**2,955.0**	**629.9**	**2,074.6**	**250.4**
Arizona	405.8	5.4	46.0	101.1	263.9	3,399.1	732.4	2,403.5	263.2
Colorado	291.2	3.4	55.7	59.8	189.1	2,658.5	476.1	1,944.5	237.9
Idaho	204.7	1.7	40.6	13.6	161.0	1,864.3	411.9	1,357.1	95.3
Montana	240.7	2.2	40.4	20.1	190.2	2,556.5	400.3	1,974.0	182.2
Nevada	591.2	5.8	50.8	185.8	360.6	2,837.7	826.0	1,653.4	358.3
New Mexico	596.7	6.0	70.3	86.8	449.9	3,704.8	1,029.9	2,391.8	283.2
Utah	209.2	1.7	49.0	42.8	130.4	2,950.4	459.6	2,233.4	257.3
Wyoming	197.7	2.9	32.1	12.9	157.2	2,198.4	335.5	1,763.6	99.2
Pacific	**367.3**	**4.0**	**30.2**	**123.8**	**216.8**	**2,854.4**	**626.1**	**1,821.6**	**406.7**
Alaska	602.6	4.6	125.4	84.9	425.5	2,885.2	396.7	2,258.0	230.6
California	396.2	4.6	25.3	139.9	232.3	2,658.1	605.4	1,621.5	431.2
Hawaii	245.3	1.5	27.4	80.6	142.2	3,053.7	536.5	2,254.8	262.4
Oregon	242.9	2.0	48.3	61.0	142.7	3,173.9	528.5	2,394.5	250.9
Washington	277.9	2.3	36.9	83.5	166.4	3,710.3	837.0	2,465.9	407.4
Puerto Rico	**257.8**	**24.4**	**0.9**	**166.4**	**66.3**	**1,351.3**	**386.2**	**812.2**	**153.0**

Note: Offense totals are based on all reporting agencies and estimates for unreported areas. Figures may not add up to totals due to rounding. (1) Data for arson, considered a property crime, are not included in this table. (2) Beginning in 2013, the FBI expanded the definition of rape to include "penetration, no matter how slight, of the vagina or anus with any body part or object, or oral penetration by a sex organ of another person, without the consent of the victim." The new definition, which applies to people of any gender, updated the 80-year-old historical definition of rape which was "carnal knowledge of a female forcibly and against her will." (3) Attack upon another with the intent of doing serious bodily harm; usually accompanied by the use of a weapon or other means likely to produce death or great bodily harm. (4) The unlawful taking of another's property not involving force or fraud (e.g., theft of motor vehicle parts, shoplifting). Excludes crimes such as embezzlement and check fraud. (5) Includes offenses reported by National Zoological Park Police and Washington Metro Transit Police.

Crime Rates in the Largest U.S. Metropolitan Areas, 2013

Source: *Crime in the United States, 2013*, Federal Bureau of Investigation, U.S. Dept. of Justice
(per 100,000 population, as estimated by U.S. Census Bureau for July 1 of year)

Memphis was the U.S. metropolitan statistical area (MSA) with the highest rate of violent crime in 2013, with more than 1,000 violent crimes per 100,000 people. It is not shown in the table below, which includes only the 30 largest MSAs; among them, Las Vegas MSA had the highest violent crime rate. San Juan, PR, had the highest murder rate, with 29 homicides per 100,000 residents. Among MSAs with populations over 2 mil, Portland, OR, had the lowest murder rate (1.4) and the lowest overall violent crime rate (250.9).

Metropolitan statistical area (MSA)	MSA pop. (mil)	Violent crime: All violent crimes	Murder and nonnegligent manslaughter	Forcible rape	Robbery	Aggravated assault	Property crime: All property crimes	Burglary	Larceny-theft	Motor vehicle theft
Atlanta-Sandy Springs-Roswell, GA	5.5	389.1	5.9	19.5	158.1	205.6	3,330.8	809.1	2,184.4	337.4
Baltimore-Columbia-Towson, MD	2.8	633.4	10.0	23.3	227.4	372.5	3,012.1	601.2	2,155.2	255.7
Boston-Cambridge-Newton, MA-NH	4.7	354.5	1.8	28.0	95.4	229.3	1,890.3	349.9	1,411.5	129.0
Chicago-Naperville-Elgin, IL-IN-WI	9.5	NA	6.4	NA	167.7	NA	2,339.0	421.4	1,716.4	201.2
Cincinnati, OH-KY-IN	2.1	285.2	4.8	32.3	127.1	120.9	3,147.4	749.5	2,252.9	145.0
Dallas-Fort Worth-Arlington, TX	6.8	332.9	4.4	31.8	120.8	175.8	3,036.4	701.3	2,071.8	263.3
Denver-Aurora-Lakewood, CO	2.7	328.5	3.7	53.0	78.9	193.0	2,746.8	463.1	1,985.1	298.6
Detroit-Warren-Dearborn, MI	4.3	569.6	9.6	50.3	164.3	345.5	2,579.1	610.4	1,522.6	446.1
Houston-The Woodlands-Sugar Land, TX	6.3	559.0	5.9	22.9	233.3	296.8	3,488.8	790.3	2,327.6	370.9
Kansas City, MO-KS	2.0	468.5	7.4	42.1	116.2	302.8	3,254.4	675.5	2,169.2	409.7
Las Vegas-Henderson-Paradise, NV	2.0	678.0	5.7	42.2	232.8	397.3	3,016.8	916.5	1,693.2	407.0
Los Angeles-Long Beach-Anaheim, CA	13.1	353.3	4.5	16.6	142.9	189.3	2,207.3	445.8	1,410.2	351.3
Miami-Fort Lauderdale-West Palm Beach, FL	5.8	538.9	6.6	31.2	189.2	311.9	3,690.5	759.7	2,674.6	256.2
Minneapolis-St. Paul-Bloomington, MN-WI	3.5	273.9	2.5	35.5	96.7	139.2	2,594.9	435.5	1,986.2	173.3
New York-Newark-Jersey City, NY-NJ-PA	19.9	390.2	3.5	9.6	156.0	221.2	1,609.9	247.6	1,254.4	107.9
Orlando-Kissimmee-Sanford, FL	2.3	540.1	3.9	41.5	123.3	371.3	3,420.1	882.4	2,335.4	202.3
Philadelphia-Camden-Wilmington, PA-NJ-DE-MD	6.0	497.5	7.1	35.8	197.5	257.2	2,477.7	474.2	1,833.3	170.2
Phoenix-Mesa-Scottsdale, AZ	4.4	392.3	4.8	29.5	115.3	242.8	NA	731.0	2,219.4	NA
Pittsburgh, PA	2.4	292.8	4.1	15.5	83.7	189.5	1,856.5	367.2	1,412.4	76.9
Portland-Vancouver-Hillsboro, OR-WA	2.3	250.9	1.4	30.9	73.5	145.2	2,991.4	475.2	2,219.4	296.8
Riverside-San Bernardino-Ontario, CA	4.4	333.3	5.0	17.3	107.8	203.2	2,794.4	764.4	1,541.1	489.0
Sacramento–Roseville–Arden-Arcade, CA	2.2	415.9	4.1	21.2	128.7	262.0	2,766.6	663.2	1,723.2	380.2
St. Louis, MO-IL	2.8	431.7	7.2	35.0	102.0	287.4	2,670.2	538.4	1,912.9	218.9
San Antonio-New Braunfels, TX	2.3	459.7	4.6	39.1	107.0	308.9	4,415.2	849.6	3,226.3	339.3
San Diego-Carlsbad, CA	3.2	348.6	2.2	20.8	95.3	230.3	2,191.9	435.7	1,404.6	351.6
San Francisco-Oakland-Hayward, CA	4.5	558.6	4.8	19.0	294.6	240.2	3,571.5	667.0	2,271.0	633.5
San Juan-Carolina-Caguas, Puerto Rico	2.3	312.7	28.7	0.7	216.8	66.6	1,503.1	371.2	921.1	210.8
Seattle-Tacoma-Bellevue, WA	3.6	323.5	2.2	31.6	112.0	177.8	4,023.3	875.4	2,639.6	508.3
Tampa-St. Petersburg-Clearwater, FL	2.9	396.5	4.3	31.0	90.8	270.5	2,732.1	619.5	1,959.0	153.6
Washington-Arlington-Alexandria, DC-VA-MD-WV	5.9	331.1	3.7	22.2	141.3	163.8	2,169.1	291.8	1,692.1	185.2

NA = Not available.

Criminal Victimization, 2004-13

Source: *Criminal Victimization, 2013*, Bureau of Justice Statistics, U.S. Dept. of Justice

A crime committed against an individual or single household counts as one **victimization**. Because a personal crime may involve more than one victim, the number of victimizations may be greater than the number of personal crime incidents.

Victimization rates measure the frequency with which victimizations occured. Personal crime victimization rates are based on the number of victimizations per 1,000 persons in the total population age 12 and over.

Type of crime	Number of victimizations 2004	2012	2013	Rate per 1,000 persons 2004	2012	2013
Violent crime[1]	**6,726,060**	**6,842,590**	**6,126,420**	**27.8**	**26.1**	**23.2**
Rape/sexual assault	255,770	346,830	300,170	1.1	1.3	1.1
Robbery	616,420	741,760	645,650	2.6	2.8	2.4
Assault	5,853,870	5,754,010	5,180,610	24.2	22.0	19.6
Aggravated assault	1,418,660	996,110	994,220	5.9	3.8	3.8
Simple assault	4,435,220	4,757,900	4,186,390	18.3	18.2	15.8
Domestic violence[2]	1,434,190	1,259,390	1,116,090	5.9	4.8	4.2
Intimate partner violence[3]	1,031,720	810,790	748,800	4.3	3.1	2.8
Violent crime involving injury	1,984,920	1,573,460	1,603,960	8.2	6.0	6.1
Serious violent crime[4]	**2,290,850**	**2,084,690**	**1,940,030**	**9.5**	**8.0**	**7.3**
Serious domestic violence[2]	467,240	411,080	464,730	1.9	1.6	1.8
Serious intimate partner violence[3]	334,620	270,240	360,820	1.4	1.0	1.4
Serious violent crime involving weapons	1,650,430	1,415,120	1,174,370	6.8	5.4	4.4
Serious violent crime involving injury	828,620	762,170	739,210	3.4	2.9	2.8

Note: Details may not add up to totals due to rounding. (1) Includes rape or sexual assault, robbery, aggravated assault, and simple assault but excludes murder because victimization data are based on interviews with victims. (2) Victimization by intimate partners and family members. (3) Victimization by current or former spouses, boyfriends, or girlfriends. (4) Includes rape or sexual assault, robbery, and aggravated assault.

Prison Population and Death Penalty by State

Source: *Prisoners in 2013*; *Capital Punishment, 2013*; Bureau of Justice Statistics, U.S. Dept. of Justice

The prison population increased in 2013 for the first time in four years, resuming a four-decade-long trend. As of Dec. 31, 2013, 1,574,741 prisoners were under the jurisdiction, or legal authority, of state (86.3%) or federal (13.7%) correctional authorities. New Hampshire's prison population increased the most (8.2%), followed by Nebraska (6.8%), Wyoming (4.8%), and Washington (4.1%). Jails, which are locally operated, typically hold persons awaiting trial or sentencing as well as those sentenced to one year or less.

But while the total number of prisoners increased, the imprisonment rate, or number of prisoners per 100,000 U.S. residents, continued to decline from its all-time high of 506 in 2007. The imprisonment rate for black males (2,805 per 100,000 U.S. residents) was still six times higher than that for white males and more than twice as high as the rate for Hispanic males (1,134).

For the 13th straight year, the number of persons under sentence of death declined; there were 2,979 inmates on death row at year-end 2013, down from 3,033 the year prior. Nine states executed a total of 39 inmates; Texas executed 40% of the total. Since 2000, the death row population has decreased every year, but the composition has changed little: 98% were male, 56% were white, and 42% were black.

On May 27, 2015, the Nebraska legislature outlawed capital punishment, overriding the governor's veto. That lowered to 32 the number of states that authorize the death penalty (the federal government also authorizes capital sentences). Nebraska's decision followed on the heels of similar repeals in Maryland (for offenses committed after May 2, 2013), Connecticut (for crimes after Apr. 25, 2012), Illinois (on July 1, 2011), and New Mexico (for crimes after July 1, 2009). All death penalty states authorize lethal injection as a method of execution; eight also permit electrocution; three permit the gas chamber, three hanging, and two (Oklahoma and Utah) authorize firing squads.

	Prisoners				Death penalty[1]				
Jurisdiction	Year-end 2000	Year-end 2012	Year-end 2013	% change, 2012-13	Death penalty statute?	Under sentence of death, year-end 2013[3]	Executed in 2013	Executed, as of 2013[2]— Since 1930	Executed, as of 2013[2]— Since 1977
U.S. total	**1,391,261**	**1,570,397**	**1,574,741**	**0.3%**	—	**2,979**	**39**	**5,218[4]**	**1,359[4]**
Federal[5]	**145,416**	**217,815**	**215,866**	**–0.9**	**Y**	**56**	**0**	**36**	**3**
State	**1,245,845**	**1,352,582**	**1,358,875**	**0.5**	**32**	**2,923**	**39**	**5,182**	**1,356**
Alabama	26,332	32,431	32,381	–0.2	Y	190	1	191	56
Alaska[6]	4,173	5,633	5,081	–9.8	N	—	—	—	—
Arizona	26,510	40,080	41,104	2.6	Y	122	2	74	36
Arkansas	11,915	14,654	17,235	—	Y	37	0	145	27
California	163,001	134,534	135,981	1.1	Y	735	0	305	13
Colorado	16,833	20,462	20,371	–0.4	Y	3	0	48	1
Connecticut[6]	18,355	17,530	17,563	0.2	N	10	0	22	1
Delaware[6]	6,921	6,914	7,004	1.3	Y	17	0	28	16
Florida	71,319	101,930	103,028	1.1	Y	398	7	251	81
Georgia	44,232	55,457	54,004	–2.6	Y	82	1	419	53
Hawaii[6]	5,053	5,831	5,632	–3.4	N	—	—	—	—
Idaho	5,535	7,985	7,549	–5.5	Y	12	0	6	3
Illinois	45,281	49,348	48,653	—	N	—	—	102	12
Indiana	20,125	28,831	29,913	—	Y	14	0	61	20
Iowa	7,955	8,733	8,697	–0.4	N	—	—	18	—
Kansas	8,344	9,682	9,763	0.8	Y	9	0	15	0
Kentucky	14,919	22,110	21,030	–4.9	Y	33	0	106	3
Louisiana	35,207	40,172	39,299	–2.2	Y	84	0	161	28
Maine	1,679	2,108	2,173	3.1	N	—	—	—	—
Maryland	23,538	21,522	21,335	–0.9	N	5	0	73	5
Massachusetts	10,722	11,308	10,950	–3.2	N	—	—	27	—
Michigan	47,718	43,636	43,759	0.3	N	—	—	—	—
Minnesota	6,238	9,938	10,289	3.5	N	—	—	—	—
Mississippi	20,241	22,319	21,969	–1.6	Y	50	0	175	21
Missouri	27,543	31,247	31,537	0.9	Y	45	2	132	70
Montana	3,105	3,609	3,642	0.9	Y	2	0	9	3
Nebraska	3,895	4,705	5,026	6.8	N	11	0	7	3
Nevada	10,063	12,883	13,056	—	Y	81	0	41	12
New Hampshire	2,257	2,790	3,018	8.2	Y	1	0	1	0
New Jersey	29,784	23,225	22,452	–3.3	N	—	—	74	0
New Mexico	5,342	6,727	6,849	1.8	N	2	0	9	1
New York	70,199	54,210	53,550	–1.2	Y	0	0	329	0
North Carolina	31,266	37,136	36,922	–0.6	Y	151	0	306	43
North Dakota	1,076	1,512	1,513	0.1	N	—	—	—	—
Ohio	45,833	50,876	51,729	1.7	Y	136	3	224	52
Oklahoma	23,181	25,225	27,547	—	Y	48	6	168	108
Oregon	10,580	14,840	15,362	3.5	Y	34	0	21	2
Pennsylvania	36,847	51,125	50,312	–1.6	Y	190	0	155	3
Rhode Island[6]	3,286	3,318	3,361	1.3	N	—	—	—	—
South Carolina	21,778	22,388	22,060	–1.5	Y	45	0	205	43
South Dakota	2,616	3,650	3,651	0.0	Y	3	0	4	3
Tennessee	22,166	28,411	28,521	0.4	Y	75	0	99	6
Texas	166,719	166,372	168,280	1.1	Y	273	16	805	508
Utah	5,637	6,962	7,075	1.6	Y	8	0	20	7
Vermont[6]	1,697	2,034	2,078	2.2	N	—	—	4	—
Virginia	30,168	37,044	36,982	—	Y	7	1	202	110
Washington	14,915	17,271	17,984	4.1	Y	9	0	52	5
West Virginia	3,856	7,070	6,824	–3.5	N	—	—	40	0
Wisconsin	20,754	22,600	22,471	—	N	—	—	—	—
Wyoming	1,680	2,204	2,310	4.8	Y	1	0	8	1

— = Not available or applicable. (1) Figures do not include persons held under Armed Forces jurisdiction with a military death sentence for murder. (2) Data do not include 160 executions carried out by military authorities between 1930 and 1961. (3) As of mid-2015, Connecticut, Maryland, Nebraska, and New Mexico continue to hold prisoners on death row for crimes committed before each state repealed capital punishment. (4) Total includes 40 executions performed under the jurisdiction of the District of Columbia when capital punishment was legal there. (5) Prisoners sentenced under DC's criminal code are housed in federal facilities. (6) Prisons and jails form one integrated system. Data includes total jail and prison population.

U.S. Prison Population, 1925-2013

Source: *Prisoners* series, Bureau of Justice Statistics, U.S. Dept. of Justice

As recently as 1970, the U.S. had fewer than 200,000 people behind bars nationwide, or less than 1 in 1,000 residents. That number rose steadily throughout the 1970s, '80s, and '90s, reaching an all-time high of more than 1.6 mil prisoners (504 imprisonment rate) in 2009.

Year[1]	Prisoners	Imprisonment rate	Year[1]	Prisoners	Imprisonment rate	Year[1]	Prisoners	Imprisonment rate
1925	91,669	79	1970	196,429	96	2010	1,613,803	500
1930	129,453	104	1980	329,821	138	2011	1,598,968	492
1940	173,706	131	1990	773,919	295	2012	1,570,397	480
1950	166,123	109	2000	1,394,231	470	2013	1,575,434	478
1960	212,953	117	2005	1,525,910	492			

Note: Imprisonment rate is per 100,000 U.S. residents. (1) Data for 1940-70 include all adult felons serving sentences in state and federal institutions. In 1977, the Bureau of Justice Statistics began to include persons incarcerated in private prisons, local jails, and other facilities not in the state's physical custody. Figures may not be directly comparable.

Prison Situation Under Correctional Authorities' Jurisdiction, 2013

Source: *Prisoners in 2013*, Bureau of Justice Statistics, U.S. Dept. of Justice

Largest prison populations		Imprisonment rate of sentenced prisoners		% change in prison population, 2012-13		Prison population as % of maximum prison capacity	
Jurisdiction	Number	Jurisdiction	Rate[1]	Jurisdiction	% change	Jurisdiction	% max. capacity
U.S. total	**1,570,397**	**U.S. total**	**478**	**U.S. total**	**0.3%**	**U.S. total**	**NA**
Federal[2]	**217,815**	**Federal[2]**	**61**	**Federal[2]**	**–0.9**	**Federal[2]**	**133.1%**
State	**1,352,582**	**State**	**417**	**State**	**0.5**	**State**	**NA**
1. Texas	166,372	1. Louisiana	847	1. New Hampshire	8.2	1. Illinois	151.7
2. California	134,534	2. Mississippi	692	2. Nebraska	6.8	2. North Dakota[5]	150.5
3. Florida	101,930	3. Oklahoma	659	3. Wyoming	4.8	3. California[6]	142.7
4. Georgia	55,457	4. Alabama	647	4. Washington	4.1	4. Massachusetts	132.3
5. New York	54,210	5. Texas	602	5. Oregon	3.5	5. Nebraska[6]	126.3
6. Pennsylvania	51,125	6. Arizona	586	6. Minnesota	3.5	6. Ohio	119.8
7. Ohio	50,876	7. Arkansas	578	7. Maine	3.1	7. Delaware[6]	117.7
8. Illinois[3]	49,348	8. Georgia	533	8. Arizona	2.6	8. Colorado	115.3
9. Michigan	43,636	9. Florida	524	9. Vermont[4]	2.2	9. Iowa[7]	114.0
10. Louisiana	40,172	10. Missouri	521	10. New Mexico	1.8	10. Hawaii	112.8
11. Arizona	40,080	11. Idaho	466	11. Ohio	1.7	11. Washington	105.7
12. North Carolina	37,136	12. Kentucky	462	12. Utah	1.6	12. Pennsylvania[6]	104.1
13. Virginia	37,044	13. Indiana	454	13. Delaware[4]	1.3	13. Louisiana[8]	103.7
14. Alabama	32,431	14. South Carolina	447	14. Rhode Island[4]	1.3	14. Minnesota	103.2
15. Missouri	31,247	15. Ohio	446	15. Texas	1.1	15. Kansas	103.1
16. Indiana	28,831	16. Virginia	446	16. California	1.1	16. Idaho[6,7]	103.0
17. Tennessee	28,411	17. Delaware[4]	442	17. Florida	1.1	17. Oregon[5]	101.7
18. Oklahoma	25,225	18. Michigan	441	18. Missouri	0.9	18. Alabama[6]	100.5
19. New Jersey	23,225	19. Tennessee	438	19. Montana	0.9	19. New Hampshire[6]	100.0
20. Wisconsin	22,600	20. South Dakota	428	20. Kansas	0.8	20. New York	99.8

NA = Not applicable. **Note:** Excludes jail population unless otherwise noted. (1) Prisoners sentenced to more than one year. Rates are per 100,000 population, based upon U.S. Census Bureau population estimates. (2) Federal totals include prisoners sentenced under DC's criminal code. (3) Includes inmates held in nonsecure privately operated community corrections facilities and juveniles held in contract facilities. (4) Prisons and jails form one integrated system. Data includes total jail and prison population. (5) Data from 2012. (6) State defines capacity in a way that differs from standard definition. (7) Excludes inmates in community-based work release facilities. (8) Includes prisoners held in private facilities.

Imprisonment Rate by Gender, Race, Hispanic Origin, and Age, 2013

Source: *Prisoners in 2013*, Bureau of Justice Statistics, U.S. Dept. of Justice

(number of prisoners sentenced to more than one year per 100,000 of each group in the U.S. resident population)

	Male				Female			
Age	Total[1]	White	Black	Hispanic	Total[1]	White	Black	Hispanic
Total[2]	**904**	**466**	**2,805**	**1,134**	**65**	**51**	**113**	**66**
18-19	340	115	1,092	412	14	7	33	17
20-24	1,382	601	3,956	1,617	95	73	154	100
25-29	1,937	954	5,730	2,289	168	140	260	173
30-34	2,183	1,104	6,746	2,529	180	156	277	169
35-39	1,994	1,009	6,278	2,321	151	133	240	133
40-44	1,713	938	5,244	2,007	131	113	224	107
45-49	1,464	827	4,486	1,700	112	90	202	99
50-54	1,082	615	3,382	1,382	70	54	128	72
55-59	679	389	2,132	1,016	36	26	72	44
60-64	415	252	1,269	714	19	14	34	25
65 or older	153	108	406	301	5	4	7	8

Note: Rates are based on U.S. Census Bureau population estimates. Hispanics may be of any race but are not included in white and black populations here. (1) Includes racial categories not shown here. (2) Includes persons under age 18.

Prisoners and Incarceration Rates by Nation, 2005-13

Source: *Adults Held in Prisons, Penal Institutions or Correctional Institutions* (2015), United Nations Office on Drugs and Crime

The U.S. imprisons more residents than any other nation in the world, both in terms of total prisoners and in its imprisonment rate, or the number of prisoners per 100,000 residents. The following table lists the 25 countries with the highest incarceration rates in 2013. Numbers and rates include jail populations.

	Total number of prisoners					Incarceration rate				
Country	**2005**	**2010**	**2011**	**2012**	**2013**	**2005**	**2010**	**2011**	**2012**	**2013**
United States	2,179,600	2,259,800	2,232,900	2,221,600	2,211,200	973.1	953.1	931.6	917.3	904.1
El Salvador	12,525	24,662	25,367	27,033	26,848	359.1	652.9	659.8	689.8	671.7
Russia	804,489	812,281	751,209	698,013	673,930	699.3	692.1	641.0	597.6	579.7
Guyana	1,439	2,160	2,019	1,986	1,998	326.7	484.1	447.8	435.9	433.1
Mongolia	6,948	7,344	7,929	8,058	8,004	433.6	402.8	427.3	426.4	416.2
Barbados	—	910	1,060	1,045	908	—	424.9	490.7	479.7	413.5
Costa Rica	8,271	10,541	12,154	13,257	13,457	290.4	324.2	365.1	389.6	387.2
Uruguay	—	8,700	9,070	9,418	9,448	—	354.7	367.2	378.5	377.0
Lithuania	7,958	8,981	9,790	9,617	9,172	308.3	362.4	397.1	391.2	373.6
Colombia	66,829	84,444	100,451	113,884	120,032	244.3	277.4	323.4	359.4	371.5
Kazakhstan	43,572	54,688	49,156	45,175	41,936	418.8	489.9	436.1	396.8	364.8
Trinidad and Tobago	3,566	2,927	4,074	3,531	3,447	379.3	294.1	406.6	350.6	340.9
Peru	33,010	—	—	—	67,597	192.7	—	—	—	339.8
Mexico	205,621	219,027	230,943	224,969	246,334	300.7	289.9	299.5	285.7	306.4
Latvia	7,342	6,692	—	6,062	5,090	408.5	388.5	—	356.4	301.1
Azerbaijan	17,803	19,159	17,587	17,821	20,599	309.0	294.8	265.3	263.9	300.0
Singapore	14,453	12,782	12,405	12,361	12,805	418.9	320.8	302.8	293.6	296.3
Estonia	3,349	3,350	3,371	3,250	3,090	315.0	317.0	320.2	309.8	295.5
Botswana	4,679	6,678	4,466	—	3,573	436.7	574.8	379.4	—	295.2
Turkey	55,293	118,701	126,270	134,019	143,500	123.9	241.8	252.6	263.3	276.9
Poland	77,607	77,522	78,467	81,306	76,596	256.7	249.8	252.2	260.7	245.1
Liechtenstein	130	76	71	60	68	471.9	262.2	242.6	203.0	227.9
Algeria	39,544	48,506	49,582	49,567	59,744	181.8	195.1	195.6	191.6	226.4
Paraguay	6,281	6,197	7,161	7,916	9,233	184.9	159.5	179.8	194.0	220.9
Argentina	43,689	58,917	60,106	61,192	64,109	165.2	208.4	209.9	211.0	218.3

— = Not available. **Note:** Data is not available for all nations. Use caution when making comparisons between countries because of the differences in each country's legal definitions of offenses and the differences in methods of counting and reporting.

Law Enforcement Officers and Civilian Employees, 2013

Source: *Crime in the United States, 2013*; *Law Enforcement Officers Killed and Assaulted, 2013*; Federal Bureau of Investigation (FBI), U.S. Dept. of Justice

As of Oct. 31, 2013, 13,051 city, county, state, college and university, and tribal agencies around the country collectively employed 902,410 full-time law enforcement workers. About two-thirds of these employees were sworn officers. The FBI defines a sworn law enforcement officer as a person who ordinarily carries a firearm and badge, has full arrest powers, and is paid from government funds specifically dedicated to law enforcement. Civilians (e.g., clerks, radio dispatchers, correctional officers) made up the remainder.

Altogether, they provided service to an estimated 269 mil people around the country, meaning there were 3.4 full-time law enforcement employees and 2.3 sworn officers per 1,000 residents.

The great majority of sworn officers (88.4%) were male, but females made up 60.7% of civilian employees. Not surprisingly, the most populous state, California, employed the greatest number of full-time law enforcement workers (117,322). The nation's capital, Washington, DC, had the highest rate, with 7.8 full-time law enforcement employees for every 1,000 residents in its population.

Nationwide, 27 law enforcement officers were killed in the line of duty in 2013, down dramatically from 49 in 2012 and 72 in 2011. Of that number, six died while attempting to make arrests, five in ambush situations, five while investigating suspicious persons or circumstances, and four while answering disturbance calls. Almost all of the officers killed were white (two were black) and 26 of 27 were killed with firearms, even though 19 of those officers were wearing body armor. Handguns were responsible for a majority (18) of officer murders.

Sentenced Prisoners by Offense, Race, and Hispanic Origin, 2012

Source: *Prisoners in 2013*, Bureau of Justice Statistics, U.S. Dept. of Justice

	All inmates		White[1]		Black[1]		Hispanic	
Offense	**Number**	**% of total**	**Number**	**% of total**	**Number**	**% of total**	**Number**	**% of total**
Total	**1,314,900**	**100.0%**	**462,600**	**100.0%**	**498,100**	**100.0%**	**271,700**	**100.0%**
All violent crimes	**707,500**	**53.8**	**228,100**	**49.3**	**290,300**	**58.3**	**162,900**	**60.0**
Murder[2]	166,800	12.7	45,800	9.9	68,400	13.7	40,400	14.9
Manslaughter	17,700	1.3	7,500	1.6	5,200	1.0	3,300	1.2
Rape/sexual assault	160,900	12.2	78,500	17.0	40,100	8.1	35,900	13.2
Robbery	179,500	13.7	37,900	8.2	101,500	20.4	36,500	13.4
Aggravated or simple assault	140,100	10.7	43,200	9.3	57,100	11.5	36,800	13.5
Other violent crimes	42,500	3.2	15,300	3.3	18,000	3.6	9,900	3.6
All property crimes	**247,100**	**18.8**	**113,400**	**24.5**	**79,600**	**16.0**	**35,100**	**12.9**
Burglary	130,700	9.9	55,500	12.0	46,900	9.4	21,700	8.0
Larceny-theft	49,100	3.7	24,100	5.2	15,900	3.2	5,200	1.9
Motor vehicle theft	11,800	0.9	5,300	1.1	2,500	0.5	2,800	1.0
Fraud	26,300	2.0	13,500	2.9	7,200	1.4	2,200	0.8
Other property crimes	29,200	2.2	14,900	3.2	7,100	1.4	3,300	1.2
Drug offenses[3]	**210,200**	**16.0**	**64,800**	**14.0**	**79,300**	**15.9**	**41,100**	**15.1**
Public-order offenses[4]	**140,200**	**10.7**	**53,500**	**11.6**	**47,300**	**9.5**	**31,300**	**11.5**
Other/unspecified[5]	**10,000**	**0.8**	**2,800**	**0.6**	**1,500**	**0.3**	**1,300**	**0.5**

Note: Counts based on state prisoners with a sentence of more than one year. Details may not add up to totals due to rounding and missing offense data, and because "All inmates" includes race categories not shown here. (1) White and black totals exclude Hispanics and persons of two or more races. (2) Includes nonnegligent manslaughter. (3) Includes trafficking, possession, and other drug offenses. (4) Includes weapons, drunk driving, and court offenses; commercialized vice, morals, and decency offenses; liquor law violations; and other public-order offenses. (5) Includes juvenile offenses and other unspecified offense categories.

Arrests by Race, 2013

Source: *Crime in the United States, 2013*, Federal Bureau of Investigation, U.S. Dept. of Justice

Each instance in which a person is arrested, cited, or summoned for an offense is counted as one arrest. The figures below therefore do not represent the number of individuals arrested but the number of times persons were arrested, as an individual may be arrested multiple times in one year. Arrest estimates are based on statistics from law enforcement agencies that reported 12 months of arrest data.

		Number of arrests where arrestee was—				% distrib. for offense charged[1]			
Offense charged	**Total**	**White**	**Black**	**Amer. Indian/ Alaska Native**	**Asian/ Pacific Islander**	**White**	**Black**	**Amer. Indian/ Alaska Native**	**Asian/ Pacific Islander**
Total arrests	**9,014,635**	**6,214,197**	**2,549,655**	**140,290**	**110,493**	**68.9%**	**28.3%**	**1.6%**	**1.3%**
Violent crime	**391,467**	**228,782**	**151,627**	**5,193**	**5,865**	**58.4**	**38.7**	**1.3**	**1.5**
Murder and nonnegligent manslaughter	8,383	3,799	4,379	98	107	45.3	52.2	1.2	1.3
Forcible rape[2]	13,515	8,946	4,229	160	180	66.2	31.3	1.2	1.4
Robbery	78,538	32,945	44,271	579	743	41.9	56.4	0.7	0.9
Aggravated assault	291,031	183,092	98,748	4,356	4,835	62.9	33.9	1.5	1.6
Property crime	**1,254,696**	**855,225**	**363,952**	**19,183**	**16,336**	**68.2**	**29.0**	**1.5**	**1.3**
Burglary	203,089	136,990	61,709	1,966	2,424	67.5	30.4	1.0	1.2
Larceny-theft	990,936	677,173	284,358	16,402	13,003	68.3	28.7	1.7	1.3
Motor vehicle theft	52,307	34,864	15,960	685	798	66.7	30.5	1.3	1.5
Arson	8,364	6,198	1,925	130	111	74.1	23.0	1.6	1.3
Other assaults[3]	881,086	573,546	283,357	14,041	10,142	65.1	32.2	1.6	1.1
Forgery and counterfeiting	48,581	31,208	16,375	288	710	64.2	33.7	0.6	1.5
Fraud	112,920	74,682	35,958	1,145	1,135	66.1	31.8	1.0	1.0
Embezzlement	12,574	7,882	4,386	87	219	62.7	34.9	0.7	1.7
Stolen property: buying, receiving, possessing	74,541	50,237	22,687	684	933	67.4	30.4	0.9	1.3
Vandalism	161,078	113,842	42,566	2,951	1,719	70.7	26.4	1.8	1.1
Weapons: carrying, possessing, etc.	112,228	65,317	44,671	888	1,352	58.2	39.8	0.8	1.2
Prostitution and commercialized vice	41,946	22,666	17,378	386	1,516	54.0	41.4	0.9	3.7
Sex offenses (except forcible rape and prostitution)	46,553	33,695	11,462	622	774	72.4	24.6	1.3	1.7
Drug abuse violations	1,204,162	815,181	365,785	9,408	13,788	67.7	30.4	0.8	1.2
Gambling	5,055	1,433	3,362	27	233	28.3	66.5	0.5	4.6
Offenses against the family and children	78,465	51,017	25,519	1,414	515	65.0	32.5	1.8	0.7
Driving under the influence	910,470	766,440	113,928	12,575	17,527	84.2	12.5	1.4	1.9
Liquor laws	277,444	222,201	40,665	10,861	3,717	80.1	14.7	3.9	1.3
Drunkenness	356,427	288,146	56,885	7,399	3,997	80.8	16.0	2.1	1.1
Disorderly conduct	372,202	231,604	129,782	7,982	2,834	62.2	34.9	2.1	0.7
Vagrancy	21,354	13,732	6,802	581	239	64.3	31.9	2.7	1.1
All other offenses (except traffic violations)	2,602,939	1,741,855	790,854	43,953	26,277	66.9	30.4	1.7	1.0
Suspicion	825	499	303	12	11	60.5	36.7	1.5	1.3
Curfew and loitering law violations	47,622	25,007	21,351	610	654	52.5	44.8	1.3	1.4

(1) Percentages may not add up to 100 due to rounding. (2) The rape figures in this table are an aggregate total of the data submitted using both the revised and legacy Uniform Crime Reporting definitions. (3) Simple assaults, where no weapons were used and where the victim did not sustain serious injury (e.g., stalking).

Firearm Violence, 1993-2011

Source: *Firearm Violence, 1993-2011*, Bureau of Justice Statistics, U.S. Dept. of Justice

The number of homicides due to firearms has declined by nearly 40% since 1993, the year Congress passed the Brady Handgun Violence Prevention Act. The Brady Act required licensed dealers to conduct background checks on individuals seeking to purchase firearms. As of Dec. 31, 2012, federal, state, and local authorities had denied more than 2.4 mil of 148 mil applications to purchase firearms; the most common reason for denial was a previous felony conviction or indictment.

	Homicides				Nonfatal victimizations			
Year	**By handgun**	**By other type of firearm[1]**	**Total**	**Rate[2]**	**By handgun**	**By other type of firearm**	**Total**	**Rate[3]**
1993	NA	NA	18,253	7.0	NA	NA	1,529,700	730
1995	12,090	2,670	15,551	5.8	1,240,200	132,800	1,193,200	550
2000	8,020	2,190	10,801	3.8	555,800	65,300	610,200	270
2001	7,820	2,220	11,348	4.0	506,600	65,900	563,100	250
2002	8,230	2,620	11,829	4.1	471,600	63,200	540,000	230
2003	8,890	2,180	11,920	4.1	436,100	53,200	467,300	200
2004	8,330	2,350	11,624	4.0	391,700	53,400	456,500	190
2005	8,550	2,840	12,352	4.2	410,600	56,200	503,500	210
2006	9,060	2,700	12,791	4.3	497,400	47,600	614,400	250
2007	8,570	3,080	12,632	4.2	509,700	65,600	554,800	220
2008	7,930	3,120	12,179	4.0	400,700	57,400	371,300	150
2009	7,370	2,970	11,493	3.8	348,700	37,600	410,100	160
2010	6,920	3,030	11,078	3.6	382,100	26,700	415,000	160
2011	7,230	2,690	11,101	3.6	389,400	49,700	467,300	180

NA = Not available. **Note:** Numbers may not add up to totals because of small differences in sample sizes. (1) Includes shotguns and rifles. (2) Per 100,000 persons. (3) Per 100,000 persons age 12 or older.

Hate Crimes by Offense Type, Bias Motivation, 2013

Source: *Hate Crime Statistics, 2013*, Federal Bureau of Investigation (FBI), U.S. Dept. of Justice

Hate crimes are defined as crimes in which victims are chosen because of one or more personal characteristics, such as race, ethnicity, or religion. Congress enacted the Hate Crime Statistics Act of 1990, which led to the collection of hate crime data as part of the FBI's Uniform Crime Report (UCR) program beginning in 1992. Not all agencies that participate in the UCR program submit hate crime data, so the data presented is not representative of the nation as a whole.

		Crimes against persons					Crimes against property						
Bias motivation	**Incidents**	**Aggravated assault**	**Simple assault**	**Intimidation**	**Other[1]**	**Total crimes against persons[1]**	**Robbery**	**Burglary**	**Larceny-theft**	**Destruction/ damage/vandalism**	**Other[2]**	**Total crimes against property[2]**	**Total crimes against society[3]**
SINGLE-BIAS INCIDENTS	**6,921**	**733**	**1,717**	**1,922**	**45**	**4,417**	**125**	**174**	**225**	**1,779**	**116**	**2,419**	**79**
Race	**3,407**	**398**	**750**	**1,087**	**24**	**2,259**	**54**	**91**	**126**	**759**	**64**	**1,094**	**54**
Anti-white	728	79	194	155	16	444	24	32	75	98	27	256	28
Anti-black	2,263	288	478	829	3	1,598	23	36	16	557	19	651	14
Anti-American Indian/ Alaska Native	146	11	16	26	1	54	3	16	27	22	14	82	10
Anti-Asian/Pacific Islander	161	16	44	44	3	107	4	6	5	34	4	53	1
Anti-multiple races, group	109	4	18	33	1	56	0	1	3	48	0	52	1
Religion	**1,163**	**23**	**134**	**255**	**2**	**414**	**3**	**29**	**38**	**649**	**24**	**743**	**5**
Anti-Jewish	689	5	72	152	0	229	1	6	11	437	5	460	0
Anti-Catholic	74	0	6	11	0	17	0	6	9	36	4	55	2
Anti-Protestant	42	0	0	3	0	3	0	6	5	24	4	39	0
Anti-Islamic	165	17	41	53	0	111	2	2	2	43	3	52	1
Anti-other religion	135	1	11	26	2	40	0	5	4	78	7	94	1
Anti-multiple religions, group	51	0	3	10	0	13	0	3	6	27	1	37	1
Anti-atheism/ agnosticism/etc.	7	0	1	0	0	1	0	1	1	4	0	6	0
Sexual orientation	**1,402**	**193**	**547**	**318**	**6**	**1,064**	**47**	**30**	**17**	**223**	**13**	**330**	**4**
Anti-male homosexual	849	120	359	188	2	669	30	23	4	115	8	180	0
Anti-female homosexual	185	24	66	56	0	146	3	0	3	28	1	35	0
Anti-homosexual	317	47	111	58	1	217	13	3	4	76	3	99	1
Anti-heterosexual	24	0	6	6	2	14	0	3	2	2	0	7	3
Anti-bisexual	27	2	5	10	1	18	1	1	4	2	1	9	0
Ethnicity/national origin	**794**	**103**	**241**	**235**	**8**	**587**	**15**	**18**	**23**	**132**	**10**	**198**	**9**
Anti-Hispanic	418	79	118	128	2	327	11	9	7	55	5	87	4
Anti-other ethnicity/ national origin	376	24	123	107	6	260	4	9	16	77	5	111	5
Disability	**92**	**6**	**16**	**21**	**3**	**46**	**3**	**5**	**17**	**11**	**4**	**40**	**6**
Anti-physical	23	1	5	5	1	12	2	0	6	2	1	11	0
Anti-mental	69	5	11	16	2	34	1	5	11	9	3	29	6
MULTIPLE-BIAS INCIDENTS[4]	**12**	**1**	**3**	**3**	**0**	**7**	**1**	**0**	**0**	**4**	**0**	**5**	**0**
TOTAL OFFENSES	**6,933**	**734**	**1,720**	**1,925**	**45**	**4,424**	**126**	**174**	**225**	**1,783**	**116**	**2,424**	**79**

(1) Includes murder, nonnegligent manslaughter, forcible rape, and additional offenses not shown here in detail. (2) Includes arson, motor vehicle theft, and additional offenses not shown here in detail. (3) Includes drug or narcotic offenses, gambling and prostitution offenses, and weapon law violations where society as a whole is considered the victim. (4) More than one offense type must occur and at least two offense types must be motivated by different biases to count as a multiple-bias incident.

Notable Assassinations Since 1865

1865—Apr. 14: U.S. Pres. Abraham Lincoln shot by John Wilkes Booth, well-known actor with Confederate sympathies, at Ford's Theater in Washington, DC; died Apr. 15.

1881—Mar. 13: Alexander II of Russia. **July 2:** U.S. Pres. James A. Garfield shot by Charles J. Guiteau, disappointed office seeker, in Washington, DC; died Sept. 19.

1894—June 24: French Pres. Sadi Carnot by Sante Caserio, Italian anarchist, in Lyon.

1898—Sept. 10: Empress Elizabeth of Austria stabbed by Luigi Luccheni, Italian anarchist.

1900—July 29: Umberto I, king of Italy, by an anarchist.

1901—Sept. 6: U.S. Pres. William McKinley shot by Leon Czolgosz, anarchist, in Buffalo, NY; died Sept. 14.

1908—Feb. 1: King Carlos I of Portugal and his son Luís Filipe, in Lisbon.

1913—Feb. 23: Mexican Pres. Francisco I. Madero and Vice Pres. José María Pino Suárez. **Mar. 18:** King George of Greece.

1914—June 28: Archduke Franz Ferdinand of Austria-Hungary and his wife shot by Gavrilo Princip, Serb nationalist, in Sarajevo, Bosnia.

1916—Dec. 30: Grigory Rasputin, Russian mystic and court figure, by group of aristocrats.

1918—July 12: Grand Duke Michael of Russia, at Perm. **July 16:** Nicholas II, former (abdicated) czar of Russia; his wife, Czarina Alexandra; their son, Czarevitch Alexis; their daughters, Grand Duchesses Olga, Tatiana, Marie, Anastasia; and 4 members of household executed by Bolsheviks at Ekaterinburg.

1920—May 20: Mexican Pres. Gen. Venustiano Carranza, in Tlaxcalantongo.

1922—Aug. 22: Michael Collins, Irish revolutionary, in West Cork. **Dec. 16:** Polish Pres. Gabriel Narutowicz in Warsaw.

1923—July 20: Gen. Francisco "Pancho" Villa, ex-rebel leader, in Parral, Mexico.

1928—July 17: Gen. Alvaro Obregon, president-elect of Mexico, in San Angel.

1932—May 6: French Pres. Paul Doumer shot by Russian émigré, Pavel Gorgulov, in Paris.

1934—July 25: Austrian Chancellor Engelbert Dollfuss by Nazis, in Vienna.

1935—Sept. 8: Sen. Huey P. Long, former Louisiana governor, shot by Dr. Carl Austin Weiss, son-in-law of political opponent, in Baton Rouge; died Sept. 10.

1940—Aug. 20: Leon Trotsky (Lev Bronstein), exiled Soviet commissar of war, fatally wounded with ice ax by Soviet agent nr. Mexico City.

1948—Jan. 30: Leader of movement for Indian independence Mohandas K. Gandhi (Mahatma) shot by Hindu fanatic in New Delhi. **Sept. 17:** Count Folke Bernadotte, UN mediator for Palestine, by Jewish extremists in Jerusalem.

1951—July 20: Jordanian King Abdullah ibn Hussein. **Oct. 16:** Prime Min. Liaquat Ali Khan of Pakistan shot, in Rawalpindi.

1956—Sept. 21: Pres. Anastasio Somoza of Nicaragua shot in Leon by a young poet; died Sept. 29.

1957—July 26: Guatemalan Pres. Carlos Castillo Armas, in Guatemala City by one of his guards.

1958—July 14: King Faisal of Iraq, Crown Prince Abdullah, and **July 15**, Prem. Nuri as-Said, by rebels in Baghdad.

1959—Sept. 25: Prime Min. Solomon Bandaranaike of Ceylon (Sri Lanka), by Buddhist monk in Colombo.

1961—Jan. 17: First elected prime min. of the Congo, Patrice Lumumba, in Katanga Prov. by political rivals. **May 30:** Dominican dictator Rafael Leónidas Trujillo Molina, nr. Ciudad Trujillo.

1963—June 12: Medgar Evers, NAACP's Mississippi field secretary, shot by Byron De La Beckwith in Jackson, MS. **Nov. 2:** Pres. Ngo Dinh Diem of South Vietnam and his brother, Ngo Dinh Nhu, in military coup. **Nov. 22:** U.S. Pres. John F. Kennedy shot while riding in motorcade through downtown Dallas, TX; accused gunman Lee Harvey Oswald murdered by nightclub owner Jack Ruby while awaiting trial.

1965—Jan. 21: Iranian Prem. Hassan Ali Mansour, in Tehran. **Feb. 21:** Malcolm X, black nationalist leader, shot by 3 men linked to Nation of Islam at New York City rally.

1966—Sept. 6: Prime Min. Hendrik F. Verwoerd of South Africa stabbed to death in parliament at Cape Town.

1968—Apr. 4: Rev. Martin Luther King Jr. fatally shot in Memphis, TN; James Earl Ray convicted of crime. **June 5:** Sen. Robert F. Kennedy (D, NY) shot in Los Angeles; died June 6. Sirhan Sirhan convicted of crime.

1971—Nov. 28: Jordanian Prime Min. Wasfi Tal by Palestinian guerrillas, in Cairo, Egypt.

1973—Mar. 2: U.S. Amb. Cleo A. Noel Jr., U.S. Charge d'Affaires George C. Moore, and Belgian Charge d'Affaires Guy Eid by Palestinian guerrillas, in Khartoum, Sudan. **Dec. 20:** Spanish Prem. Luis Carrero Blanco in car bombing by Basque separatist group ETA, in Madrid.

1974—Aug. 19: U.S. Amb. to Cyprus, Rodger P. Davies, by sniper's bullet in Nicosia.

1975—Feb. 11: Pres. Richard Ratsimandrava of Madagascar shot in Antananarivo. **Mar. 25:** Saudi Arabian King Faisal shot by nephew Prince Musad Abdel Aziz, in Riyadh. **Aug. 15:** Bangladesh Pres. Sheik Mujibur Rahman killed in coup.

1976—Feb. 13: Nigerian head of state, Gen. Murtala Ramat Mohammed, by self-styled young revolutionaries.

1977—Mar. 16: Kamal Jumblat, Lebanese Druse chieftain, shot nr. Beirut. **Mar. 18:** Rep. of the Congo Pres. Marien Ngouabi shot in Brazzaville.

1978—May 9: Former Italian Prem. Aldo Moro killed by Red Brigades terrorists who had abducted him Mar. 16 in Rome and held him hostage. **July 9:** Former Iraqi Prem. Abdul Razak Al-Naif shot in London.

1979—Feb. 14: U.S. Amb. Adolph Dubs shot by Afghan Muslim extremists in Kabul. **Aug. 27:** Lord Mountbatten, WWII hero, and 2 others when a bomb exploded on his fishing boat off coast of Co. Sligo, Ireland. IRA claimed responsibility. **Oct. 26:** S. Korean Pres. Park Chung Hee and 6 bodyguards fatally shot by Kim Jae Kyu, head of S. Korean intelligence agency.

1980—Apr. 12: Liberian Pres. William R. Tolbert, in military coup. **Sept. 17:** Former Nicaraguan Pres. Anastasio Somoza Debayle shot in Paraguay.

1981—Oct. 6: Egyptian Pres. Anwar al-Sadat shot by commandos while reviewing military parade in Cairo; 7 others killed, 28 wounded.

1982—Sept. 14: Lebanese Pres.-elect Bashir Gemayel killed by bomb in east Beirut.

1983—Aug. 21: Philippine opposition leader Benigno Aquino Jr. shot at Manila Intl. Airport.

1984—Oct. 31: Indian Prime Min. Indira Gandhi shot by 2 Sikh bodyguards in New Delhi.

1986—Feb. 28: Swedish Prime Min. Olof Palme shot on Stockholm street; case still unsolved

1987—June 1: Lebanese Prem. Rashid Karami killed when bomb exploded aboard helicopter.

1988—Apr. 16: PLO military chief Khalil Wazir (Abu Jihad) gunned down by Israeli commandos in Tunisia.

1989—Aug. 18: Colombian pres. candidate Luis Carlos Galán killed by Medellín cartel drug traffickers at campaign rally in Bogotá. **Nov. 22:** Lebanese Pres. Rene Moawad killed when bomb exploded next to his motorcade.

1990—Mar. 22: Colombian pres. candidate Bernardo Jaramillo Ossa shot at airport in Bogotá.

1991—May 21: Former Indian Prime Min. Rajiv Gandhi killed by bomb during election rally in Madras.

1992—June 29: Algerian Pres. Mohammed Boudiaf shot in Annaba.

1993—May 1: Sri Lankan Pres. Ranasinghe Premadasa killed by bomb in Colombo.

1994—Apr. 6: Burundian Pres. Cyprien Ntaryamira and Rwandan Pres. Juvénal Habyarimana killed with 8 others when their plane was shot down, precipitating Rwandan genocide.

1995—Nov. 4: Israeli Prime Min. Yitzhak Rabin shot by Yigal Amir, Jewish extremist, at peace rally in Tel Aviv.

1996—Oct. 2: Andrei Lukanov, former Bulgarian prime min., shot outside home by unidentified assailant.

1998—Feb. 6: Prefect of Corsica, Claude Erignac, shot in back by 2 men while walking to concert. **Apr. 26:** Guatemalan Roman Catholic Bishop Juan Gerardi Conedera, human rights champion, found beaten to death in Guatemala City.

1999—Mar. 23: Paraguayan Vice Pres. Luis María Argaña ambushed and shot to death along with his driver by 4 unidentified assailants, in Asunción. **Apr. 9:** Niger Pres. Ibrahim Bare Mainassara ambushed and killed by dissident soldiers. **Oct. 27:** Armenian Prime Min. Vazgen Sarkissian, along with 7 others, shot during session of parliament.

2000—Jan. 15: Serbian paramilitary leader Zeljko Raznjatovic (Arkan), with 2 others, shot in Belgrade. **June 8:** Brig. Gen. Stephen Saunders, Britain's senior military rep. in Greece, fatally shot by 2 men on motorcycle while driving in Athens suburb.

2001—Jan. 16: Dem. Rep. of the Congo Pres. Laurent Kabila shot to death by bodyguard at pres. palace in Kinshasa. **June 1:** Nepal's King Birendra, Queen Aiswarya, and 7 other royals fatally shot by Crown Prince Dipendra, who also killed himself. **Oct. 14:** Abdel Rahman Hamad, a leader of Palestinian militant group Hamas, shot by Israeli military snipers. **Oct. 17:** Israeli tourism min. Rehavam Zeevifatally shot; Popular Front for the Liberation of Palestine claimed responsibility.

2002—Mar. 16: Colombian cleric Isaías Duarte Cancino, critic of Colombian guerrillas and drug traffickers, shot outside of church in Cali. **May 6:** Dutch right-wing politician Pim Fortuyn shot outside radio station in Hilversum. **July 6:** Afghan Vice Pres. Haji Abdul Qadir shot outside his office in Kabul.

2003—Mar. 12: Serbian Prime Min. Zoran Djindjic shot by paramilitary snipers outside govt. headquarters in Belgrade. **Apr. 10:** Shiite Muslim cleric Abdul Majid al-Khoei attacked by crowd, hacked to death at Imam Ali mosque, Najaf, Iraq. **Apr. 17:** Sergei Yushenkov, former Russian legislator and Liberal Party head, shot outside apartment in Moscow. **Sept. 10:** Swedish Foreign Min. Anna Lindh stabbed in Stockholm dept. store by mentally ill man; died Sept. 11.

2004—Feb. 13: Former Chechen Pres. Zelimkhan Yandarbiyev killed after car exploded in Qatar. **Mar. 22:** Sheik Ahmed Yassin, spiritual leader of Hamas, by Israeli missile attack in Gaza City. **Apr. 17:** Hamas leader Abdel Aziz Rantisi by Israeli missile strike, in Gaza City. **May 9:** Chechen Pres. Akhmad Kadyrov by bomb at WWII memorial service in Grozny. **Nov. 2:** Filmmaker Theo van Gogh, critic of Islam and great-grandnephew of painter Vincent van Gogh, shot and stabbed by Muslim militant in Amsterdam.

2005—Jan. 4: Baghdad Gov. Ali al-Haidari gunned down by insurgents in Baghdad, Iraq. **Feb. 14:** Former Lebanese Prime Min. Rafik al-Hariri killed when motorcade bombed in Beirut.

2006—Feb. 11: Leading Kazakhstan opposition politician Altynbek Sarsenbayev (Sarsenbaiuly) kidnapped, found murdered outside Almaty. **Sept. 14:** Andrei Kozlov, Russian central banker active in reforming industry, shot in Moscow. **Oct. 7:** Anna Politkovskaya, reporter critical of Kremlin's Chechnya policies, fatally shot in apartment building in Moscow.

2007—June 13: Walid Eido, Lebanese parliament member who was part of anti-Syria coalition, killed by car bomb in Beirut. **Aug. 2:** *Oakland Post* editor Chauncey Bailey, who was investigating financial status of black Muslim organization, shot in Oakland, CA. **Dec. 27:** Benazir Bhutto, former Pakistani prime min. and first female elected leader of a Muslim state, by bomb and gunman later linked to then-Pres. Pervez Musharraf.

2008—Feb. 12: Imad Mughniyeh, top Hezbollah commander and reputed mastermind of the 1983 bombing of U.S. embassy in Beirut, by car bomb in Damascus, Syria. Mughniyeh had been on FBI's Most Wanted Terrorist list. **May 8:** Edgar Eusebio Millán Gómez, Mexico's acting national police chief, by gunmen outside his Mexico City home. **Aug. 1:** Syrian brig. gen. and top aide Mohammed Suleiman reportedly shot by sniper nr. Tartus. **Oct. 23:** Ivo Pukanic, editor-in-chief of Croatian political newspaper *Nacional*, killed in Zagreb when bomb exploded nr. his car.

2009—Mar. 2: Guinea-Bissau's longtime Pres. João Bernardo Vieira shot by army troops outside his home in Bissau. **May 31:** Dr. George Tiller, one of the few doctors in the U.S. to perform abortions late in pregnancy, shot to death in his Wichita, KS, church by anti-abortion activist. **Sept. 27:** Two officials from the Russian republic of Dagestan, Alim-Sultan Alkhamatov and Alim-Sultan Atuyev, shot dead in separate incidents.

2010—Aug. 2: Raza Haider, member of Pakistan's parliament, shot by 4 gunmen in a mosque in Karachi.

2011—July 12: Ahmed Wali Karzai, power-wielding half-brother of Afghan Pres. Hamid Karzai, shot dead in his Kandahar home by a longtime confidant. Two other Karzai allies, including Kandahar mayor Ghulam Hamidi, assassinated over the next 2 weeks. **Sept. 20:** Burhanuddin Rabbani, leader of Afghanistan's High Peace Council and a former pres., killed in his Kabul home by assassin with explosives hidden in his turban.

2012—Jan. 11: Iranian nuclear scientist Mostafa Ahmadi Roshan killed by car bomb. **July 18:** Three senior Syrian officials, including Defense Min. Dawoud Rajiha and Assef Shawkat, brother-in-law to Pres. Bashar al-Assad, killed by bomb.
2013—May 3: Gunmen on motorbikes killed Sadiq Zaman Khattak, an anti-Taliban candidate for Pakistan's National Assembly, and his 4-year-old son in Karachi. **July 25:** Tunisian secular opposition lawmaker, Mohamed Brahmi, shot to death outside his home in Tunis; members of ISIS later claimed credit.
2014—Sept. 1: U.S. airstrikes killed Ahmed Abdi Godane, leader of Somalia-based Islamist militant group al-Shabab.
2015—Feb. 27: Boris Y. Nemtsov, Russian opposition leader and former first deputy prime minister, shot near Red Square.

Notable Assassination Attempts Since 1912

1912—Oct. 14: Former U.S. Pres. Theodore Roosevelt shot and wounded by mentally ill man in Milwaukee, WI.
1933—Feb. 15: In Miami, FL, anarchist Joseph Zangara shot at Pres.-elect Franklin D. Roosevelt, but a woman seized Zangara's arm; bullet fatally wounded Chicago Mayor Anton J. Cermak, who died Mar. 6.
1944—July 20: Adolf Hitler injured when bomb, planted by German officer, exploded in his headquarters; one aide killed,12 injured.
1950—Nov. 1: In attempt to assassinate Pres. Harry Truman, 2 members of Puerto Rican nationalist movement—Griselio Torresola and Oscar Collazo—tried to shoot their way into Blair House, across the street from White House. Torresola killed. Pvt. Leslie Coffelt, White House policeman, fatally shot.
1970—Nov. 27: Pope Paul VI unharmed by knife-wielding assailant who attempted to attack him in airport in Manila, Philippines.
1972—May 15: Alabama Gov. George Wallace seriously wounded when shot in Laurel, MD, by fame-seeking Arthur Bremer.
1975—Sept. 5: Pres. Gerald R. Ford unharmed when Secret Service agent grabbed pistol aimed at him by Lynette "Squeaky" Fromme, follower of cult leader Charles Manson, in Sacramento, CA. **Sept. 22:** Pres. Ford unharmed when bystander grabbed arm of Sara Jane Moore as she fired upon Ford in San Francisco.
1980—May 29: Civil rights leader Vernon E. Jordan Jr. shot and wounded in Ft. Wayne, IN.
1981—Mar. 30: Pres. Ronald Reagan, along with Press Sec. James Brady, Secret Service agent Timothy J. McCarthy, and Wash., DC, policeman Thomas Delahanty shot and seriously wounded by John W. Hinckley Jr. in DC. **May 13:** Pope John Paul II and 2 bystanders shot and wounded by Mehmet Ali Agca, escaped Turkish prisoner, in St. Peter's Square, Vatican City.
1982—May 12: Pope John Paul II wounded by ultra-conservative priest wielding bayonet, in Fatima, Portugal.
1984—Oct. 12: British Prime Min. Margaret Thatcher unharmed when a bomb, said to have been planted by the IRA, exploded at the Grand Hotel in Brighton, Eng., during a Party conference; 4 died, incl. a member of Parliament.
1986—Sept. 7: Chilean Pres. Gen. Augusto Pinochet Ugarte unharmed after motorcade was attacked by rebels.
1995—June 26: Egyptian Pres. Hosni Mubarak unharmed when shots fired on his motorcade in Addis Ababa, Ethiopia; 4 died, incl. 2 Ethiopian police officers.
1997—Feb. 12: Colombian Pres. Ernesto Samper Pizano unharmed when bomb exploded on runway in Barranquilla as his plane was preparing to land. **Apr. 30:** Tajik Pres. Imamali Rakhmanov injured when a grenade was thrown at him.
1998—Feb. 9: Georgian Pres. Eduard A. Shevardnadze unharmed when gunmen fired on his motorcade in Tbilisi.
2002—Apr. 14: Leading Colombian pres. candidate Álvaro Uribe Vélez unharmed after bomb exploded under parked bus as his motorcade passed in Barranquilla; 3 bystanders killed. **July 14:** French Pres. Jacques Chirac unharmed after Maxime Brunerie, gunman with ties to neo-Nazi groups, fired at his open-top vehicle during Bastille Day parade in Paris. **Sept. 5:** Afghan Pres. Hamid Karzai unharmed after militant shot at car in Kandahar. **Nov. 25:** Turkmenistan Pres. Saparmurat Niyazov unharmed after gunmen opened fire on his motorcade in Ashgabat.
2003—Dec. 14: Pakistani Pres. Pervez Musharraf unharmed after bomb detonated on bridge in Rawalpindi seconds after his motorcade crossed.
2004—Mar. 19: Taiwanese Pres. Chen Shui-bian shot while campaigning in motorcade; minor injuries. **July 13:** Separatists bombed motorcade of Sergei Abramov, Chechnya's acting pres. **Sept. 5:** Ukrainian opposition presidential candidate Viktor Yushchenko, who later won office, fell ill after meeting; diagnosed with dioxin poisoning. **Sept. 16:** Rocket fired at helicopter carrying Afghan Pres. Hamid Karzai, nr. Gardez.
2005—Mar. 15: Kosovo Pres. Ibrahim Rugova survived bombing of his motorcade as it traveled through Pristina.
2008—Feb. 11: Pres. José Ramos-Horta shot in attack led by fugitive former army official in Dili, Timor-Leste. Ambush of Prime Min. Xanana Gusmão's motorcade a short time later unsuccessful. **Apr. 27:** Afghan Pres. Hamid Karzai unharmed after Taliban fired on military parade in Kabul where Karzai was in attendance.
2009—June 22: Yunus-Bek Yevkurov, pres. of Ingushetia region of Russia, seriously wounded when suicide bomber in car packed with explosives crashed into his motorcade.
2010—Sept. 23: Alexander Ankvab, vice pres. of Georgian region of Ankhazia, survived 4th assassination attempt in 5 years, a grenade fired into his Gudauta home.
2011—Jan. 8: U.S. Rep. Gabrielle Giffords (D, AZ) severely wounded by lone gunman at public meeting nr. Arizona supermarket; 6 others killed, including a federal judge. **June 3:** Yemeni Pres. Ali Abdullah Saleh survived presidential palace bombing.
2012—May 18: Taliban killed 7 in assassination attempt on governor of the Afghanistan prov. of Farah. **Sept. 12:** Hassan Sheik Mohamud survived suicide bombing attack on his home 2 days after being elected Somalia's president.
2013—Apr. 29: Syrian Prime Min. Wael Nader al-Halqi survived car bombing of his motorcade in Damascus.

Notable U.S. Kidnappings Since 1924

Bobby Franks, 14, in Chicago, May 21, 1924, by 2 youths from wealthy families—Richard Loeb, 18, and Nathan Leopold, 19—who killed boy. Demand for $10,000 ignored. Loeb killed in prison; Leopold paroled 1958.
Charles A. Lindbergh Jr., 20 months old, nr. Hopewell, NJ, Mar. 1, 1932; found dead May 12. Ransom of $50,000 paid to man identified as Bruno Richard Hauptmann, 35, paroled German convict who entered U.S. illegally. Hauptmann convicted, electrocuted in Trenton, NJ, prison, Apr. 3, 1936.
William A. Hamm Jr., 39, brewing company pres. in St. Paul, MN, June 15, 1933, by Karpis-Barker gang. $100,000 paid. Alvin Karpis given life sentence, paroled in 1969.
Charles F. Urschel, in Oklahoma City, July 22, 1933. Released July 31 after $200,000 paid. George "Machine Gun" Kelly and 5 others sentenced to life.
Brooke L. Hart, 22, in San Jose, CA. Thomas Thurmond and John Holmes arrested after demanding $40,000. When Hart's body was found in San Francisco Bay, Nov. 26, 1933, a mob forced its way into jail and lynched the 2 kidnappers.
June Robles, 6, abducted in Tucson, AZ, Apr. 25, 1934. Missing for 19 days after ransom note sent to parents. Found alive in iron cage buried in desert. No arrests ever made.
George Weyerhaeuser, 9, of Weyerhaeuser lumber company, in Tacoma, WA, May 24, 1935. Returned home June 1 after $200,000 paid. Kidnappers given 20 to 60 years.
Robert C. Greenlease, 6, son of wealthy car dealer, taken from Kansas City, MO, school Sept. 28, 1953; held for $600,000. Body found Oct. 7. Bonnie Brown Heady and Carl A. Hall pleaded guilty, were executed.
Lee Crary, 8, in Everett, WA, Sept. 22, 1957; $10,000 ransom not paid. Crary escaped after 3 days and led police to George E. Collins, who was convicted.
Frank Sinatra Jr., 19, from hotel room in Lake Tahoe, CA, Dec. 8, 1963. Released Dec. 11 after his father paid $240,000 ransom. Three men sentenced to prison.
Barbara Jane Mackle, 20, abducted Dec. 17, 1968, from Atlanta, GA, motel; found unharmed 3 days later, buried in coffin-like box 18 in. underground, after her father paid $500,000 ransom. Gary Steven Krist sentenced to life, Ruth Eisenmann-Schier to 7 years.
Virginia Piper, 49, abducted July 27, 1972, from her home in suburban Minneapolis, MN; found unharmed nr. Duluth 2 days later after husband, retired banker, paid $1 mil ransom.
J. Paul Getty III, 17, grandson of the oil billionaire, disappeared July 10, 1973, in Rome, Italy. Ransom of $2.8 mil paid

after abductors sent one of Getty's ears to an Italian newspaper with a warning that other parts of his body would be mutilated. Released Dec. 15.

Patricia "Patty" Hearst, 19, taken from her Berkeley, CA, apartment Feb. 4, 1974; "Symbionese Liberation Army" captors demanded her father, publisher Randolph Hearst, give millions to area poor. Patty implicated in San Francisco bank holdup, Apr. 15. The FBI, Sept. 18, 1975, captured her and others. She was convicted of bank robbery, Mar. 20, 1976; released from prison under executive clemency, Feb. 1, 1979. In 1978, William and Emily Harris were sentenced to 10 years to life for the kidnapping; both were paroled in 1983.

J. Reginald Murphy, 40, an editor of *Atlanta Constitution* (GA), kidnapped Feb. 20, 1974; freed Feb. 22 after newspaper paid $700,000 ransom. William A. H. Williams later convicted.

Jack Teich, Kings Point, NY, steel executive, seized Nov. 12, 1974; released Nov. 19 after payment of $750,000.

Adam Walsh, 6, abducted from Hollywood, FL, dept. store, July 27, 1981. Severed head found 2 weeks later. John Walsh, Adam's father, became active in raising awareness about missing children. Case officially closed in 2008; drifter who had died in prison while serving life sentences for murder found responsible.

Terry Anderson, 37, Middle East bureau chief for Associated Press, in Beirut, Lebanon, by members of Islamic fundamentalist group Hezbollah on Mar. 16, 1985. Freed Dec. 4, 1991. Anderson had been held hostage with **William Buckley**, 55, CIA station chief in Beirut who was kidnapped Mar. 16, 1984, and died in captivity.

Jaycee Dugard, 11, kidnapped nr. her home in South Lake Tahoe, CA, June 10, 1991; held for 18 years by Nancy and Philip Garrido, who fathered 2 girls with Dugard during her captivity. Dugard, along with her 11- and 15-year-old daughters, was reunited with her family Aug. 27, 2009, after police arrested the Garridos.

Sidney J. Reso, oil company exec., seized Apr. 29, 1992; died May 3. Arthur D. Seale—former security official at oil company—and his wife, Irene, arrested June 19. Arthur sentenced to life in prison; Irene sentenced to 20-year prison term.

Polly Klaas, 12, Petaluma, CA, abducted at knife point, Oct. 1, 1993, during slumber party at her home. Police arrested Richard Allen Davis on Nov. 30; he led them to her body, found Dec. 4 in wooded area of Cloverdale, CA. Davis found guilty June 18, 1996, and sentenced to death Sept. 26.

Amber Hagerman, 9, abducted Jan. 13, 1996, while riding her bicycle in Arlington, TX, found dead five days later. Her murder, which has never been solved, led to the creation of the AMBER Alert (America's Missing: Broadcast Emergency Response), used to broadcast child abductions over the nation's Emergency Alert System.

Tionda Z. Bradley, 10, and sister **Diamond Yvette Bradley**, 3, went missing July 6, 2001, in Chicago. Note left by Tionda at home stated the 2 girls were going to the store and playground. Disappearance still unsolved.

Daniel Pearl, 38, reporter for *Wall Street Journal*, disappeared Jan. 23, 2002, while researching story in Karachi, Pakistan. British-born militant Ahmad Omar Saeed Sheikh Feb. 14 admitted to organizing the kidnapping and said Pearl was dead. Sheikh and 3 others convicted July 15 of kidnapping and murder by judge in Hyderabad.

Elizabeth Smart, 14, abducted from her home in Salt Lake City, UT, June 5, 2002, by Brian D. Mitchell, and forced to live with Mitchell and wife Wanda for 9 months in various U.S. cities; found walking down street with captors in Sandy, UT, 15 mi from Smart family home, Mar. 12, 2003.

Michelle Knight, 21, abducted Aug. 23, 2002; **Amanda Berry**, 17, seized Apr. 21, 2003; and **Gina DeJesus**, 14, kidnapped Apr. 2, 2004. All 3 women escaped from the Cleveland, OH, home of Ariel Castro, May 6, 2013, after a decade in captivity during which Berry gave birth to a daughter.

Jill Carroll, 28, freelance journalist on assignment for *Christian Science Monitor*, seized in Baghdad by group called the Revenge Brigade, Jan. 7, 2006. She was released Mar. 30; 4 Iraqis arrested in connection with her kidnapping.

Steve Centanni, 60, Fox News reporter released Aug. 26, 2006 (along with a colleague), after being held hostage for 13 days by Palestinian militant group Holy Jihad Brigades. The group had demanded U.S. release of all Muslims in its prisons.

Reigh Storrow Mills, 7, abducted July 27, 2008, by her father, Christian Gerhartsreiter (alias Clark Rockefeller); reunited with her mother Aug. 2, 2008, by FBI agents who took Gerhartsreiter into custody.

Felix Batista, 55, Cuban-American security expert who negotiated the release of numerous kidnapping victims in Latin America, abducted in Mexico Dec. 10, 2008.

Jessica Buchanan, 32, aid worker for Danish Refugee Council, taken hostage by Somali pirates Oct. 25, 2011; rescued by U.S. Navy SEALs Jan. 25, 2012.

James Foley, 39, freelance journalist, taken hostage during civil war in Syria's Idlib province, Nov. 22, 2012. ISIS militants released video Aug. 19, 2014, showing execution of Foley.

Richard Engel, 39, NBC News foreign correspondent in Syria and his crew held captive, Dec. 13, 2012; freed by rebel militia 5 days later.

Hannah Anderson, 16, abducted Aug. 3, 2013, by James DiMaggio, a family friend who killed her mother and brother at his California home before fleeing with her to Idaho; freed Aug. 10 when FBI agents shot and killed DiMaggio.

Madyson Middleton, 8, reported missing July 26, 2015; found dead July 27. A 15-year-old neighbor was charged with her rape and murder.

Notable Terrorist Incidents Worldwide Since 1971

Source: U.S. Dept. of State; *Facts On File World News Digest*; World Almanac research

Selected noteworthy incidents, excluding most assassinations, kidnappings, and military targets. Does not include all incidents in Iraq or Afghanistan, 2001-present; see also Chronology of the Year's Events.

1971—Mar. 1: Senate wing of U.S. Capitol Building in Wash., DC, bombed by Weather Underground; no deaths.

1972—July 21: "Bloody Friday." Provisional IRA exploded 20+ bombs across Belfast, N. Ireland; 9 killed, hundreds injured. **Sept. 5:** Palestinian group Black September killed 2 Israeli athletes and seized 9 others at Olympic Village in Munich, W. Germany, during Summer Olympics; 9 hostages, 5 militants, 1 Ger. officer died in botched rescue.

1973—Dec. 17: Palestinian gunmen attacked Rome airport and bombed plane on tarmac; hijacked Lufthansa plane with 5 Italian hostages to Athens, Greece, then to Kuwait; 31 killed in all.

1974—June 17: Houses of Parliament in London, England, bombed by Provisional IRA; 11 injured.

1975—Jan. 27: Puerto Rican FALN nationalists bombed Fraunces Tavern in New York City; 4 killed, 53 injured. **Jan. 29:** U.S. State Dept. building in Wash., DC, bombed by Weather Underground; no deaths.

1976—June 27: Palestinian and Baader-Meinhof militants forced Air France jet to land in Entebbe, Uganda. Israeli army rescued 103 hostages from airport terminal in battle with terrorists and Ugandan troops, July 3-4; 32 killed in all.

1978—Mar. 11: Palestinian militants shot civilians and hijacked bus with hostages from Haifa to Tel Aviv, Israel. Bus exploded during firefight with police at a roadblock; 38 killed.

1979—Nov. 4: Iranian radicals seized U.S. embassy in Tehran, taking 66 Americans hostage. 52 were held until Jan. 20, 1981. **Nov. 20:** 200 Islamic terrorists seized Grand Mosque in Mecca, Saudi Arabia, and held hundreds of pilgrims hostage. Saudi forces retook mosque Dec. 4; about 250 died.

1980—Feb. 27: Members of leftist guerrilla group April 19 Movement (M-19) seized Dominican Republic embassy in Bogota, Colombia; 80 hostages taken, 18 held until Apr. 27.

1983—Apr. 18: Hezbollah suicide truck bomb at U.S. embassy in Beirut, Lebanon, killed 63. **Oct. 9:** N. Korean agents ambushed a S. Korean govt. delegation in Rangoon, Burma, killing 21. **Oct. 23:** Hezbollah suicide truck bombings of U.S. and French military bases, Beirut, Lebanon; 242 Americans, 58 French killed.

1984—Sept. 20: U.S. embassy annex nr. Beirut, Lebanon, bombed, killing approx. 20. **Sept. 20:** In worst bioterrorism attack in U.S. history, members of Rajneesh cult poisoned an Oregon salsa bar with salmonella, sickening 751.

1985—Apr. 12: Bomb blast at restaurant nr. U.S. air base in Torrejon, Spain; 18 killed. **June 14:** Hezbollah members hijacked TWA Flight 847 with 153 passengers and crew to Beirut, Lebanon; 39 held for 17 days, 1 U.S. Navy sailor killed. **June 23:** Air India Flight 182 destroyed by bomb off coast of Ireland; 329 killed. Blamed on Sikh terrorists. **Oct. 7:** Four Palestinians hijacked Italian cruise ship *Achille Lauro*; 1 passenger killed. **Nov. 23:** EgyptAir Flight 648 from Athens, Greece, to Cairo hijacked to Malta by Palestinian group Abu Nidal; 60 killed in rescue. **Dec. 27:** Palestinian militants opened fire at El-Al airline counters at Rome and Vienna airports; 19 killed.

1986—Apr. 5: Nightclub in Berlin, W. Germany, bombed; 3 killed, incl. 2 U.S. service personnel, 200+ hurt. 3 Libyan embassy workers in Germany convicted.

1987—Apr. 17: Bomb in Sri Lankan capital killed 100+; blamed on Tamil rebels who, 4 days later, attacked Sinhalese travelers on highway, killing 127. **June 19:** Basque group ETA bombed supermarket garage in Barcelona, Spain; 21 killed, 45 injured. **Nov. 29:** Bomb planted by N. Korean agents exploded on Korean Air Lines Flight 858 over Indian Ocean; 115 killed.

1988—Dec. 21: Pan Am Flight 103 exploded over Lockerbie, Scotland, killing all 259 aboard and 11 on ground; Libya took responsibility for bombing in Aug. 2003.

1989—Sept. 19: French UTA Flight 722 from Congo Republic to Paris destroyed by bomb in midair over Niger; 170 killed.

1992—Mar. 17: Israeli embassy in Buenos Aires, Argentina, bombed; 28 killed, 200+ injured. Hezbollah suspected.

1993—Feb. 26: Truck bomb exploded in World Trade Center garage in New York City; 6 killed. Blast later linked to al- Qaeda. **Mar. 12-19:** At least 11 bombs ripped through Bombay and Calcutta, India; 300+ killed.

1994—Feb. 25: U.S.-born Israeli settler Baruch Goldstein opened fire in mosque in Hebron, West Bank; about 30 Muslim worshippers killed. **July 18:** Buenos Aires, Argentina, Jewish center bombed; 87 killed. Blamed on Hezbollah.

1995—Mar. 20: Twelve killed and over 5,000 injured when Japanese Aum Shinri-kyu cult members released sarin nerve gas in several Tokyo subway cars. **Apr. 19:** Murrah Federal Building in Oklahoma City bombed, killing 168 and injuring 500+. Timothy McVeigh and Terry Nichols convicted. McVeigh executed in 2001; Nichols sentenced to life in prison. **Nov. 13:** U.S. military compound in Riyadh, Saudi Arabia, bombed by Islamic Movement of Change; 7 killed.

1996—Jan. 31: Tamil Tigers drove explosives-laden truck into Central Bank in Colombo, Sri Lanka; 90 killed. **June 25:** Bomb-laden fuel truck exploded outside Khobar Towers, U.S. military complex in Dhahran, Saudi Arabia; killed 19. **July 27:** Bomb exploded at Centennial Olympic Park in Atlanta, GA, during Summer Games; killed 2, injured 100+. Extremist Eric Robert Rudolph sentenced to life in prison, 2005. **Dec. 3:** Bomb exploded on subway train in Paris; 4 killed, 86 injured. Algerian extremists suspected.

1997—Nov. 17: Gamaa al-Islamiya militants killed 58 tourists and 4 Egyptians in Valley of the Kings nr. Luxor, Egypt.

1998—Aug. 7: U.S. embassies in Nairobi, Kenya, and Dar-es-Salaam, Tanzania, bombed; 257 people killed. Al-Qaeda blamed. **Aug. 15:** IRA car bomb exploded outside courthouse in Omagh, N. Ireland; killed 29, injured 300+. **Oct. 18:** National Liberation Army of Colombia blew up Ocensa oil pipeline; about 71 killed, 100+ injured.

1999—Sept. 9-16: Three buildings bombed in Moscow and Volgodonsk, Russia; about 300 killed. Chechen rebels blamed.

2000—Oct. 12: Small boat assisting in docking of U.S.S. *Cole* exploded while alongside it in Aden, Yemen; 17 U.S. sailors killed, 39 injured. Blamed on al-Qaeda.

2001—Sept. 11: 19 al-Qaeda terrorists hijacked 4 U.S. domestic flights, including 2 planes that crashed into New York City's World Trade Center towers and 1 into Pentagon. Total dead minus hijackers: 2,973; deadliest terrorist attack yet on U.S. soil. **Sept.-Nov. 7:** Letters tainted with deadly anthrax bacteria mailed through U.S. postal system killed 5, sickened 17; investigation concluded in 2010 that microbiologist Bruce Ivins, who committed suicide in 2008, was responsible.

2002—Mar. 27: Suicide bombing at hotel in Netanya, Israel, during Passover celebration; 27 killed. **Oct. 12:** Resort in Bali, Indonesia, bombed; 202 dead. Jemaah Islamiah blamed. **Oct. 23:** Chechen guerrillas seized theater in Moscow, held 700+ hostages. Russian authorities gassed theater; most guerrillas and about 128 hostages killed. **Dec. 27:** Chechen rebels plowed truck bomb into pro-Russian govt. headquarters in Grozny, Chechnya; 80 killed, 152 injured.

2003—May 12-13: Al-Qaeda militants detonated car bombs at 3 residential complexes used by Westerners in Riyadh, Saudi Arabia; 34 killed. **May 16:** Five explosions in Casablanca, Morocco; 44 killed, 100+ wounded. Blamed on al-Qaeda. **Aug. 19:** UN headquarters in Baghdad bombed by truck; 22 killed, incl. UN envoy to Iraq. **Aug. 25:** 2 bombs exploded in taxis in Mumbai, India; 46 killed, 100+ injured. Islamic militants suspected. **Nov. 15:** Two synagogues in Istanbul, Turkey, bombed; 25 killed. **Nov. 20:** British consulate and offices of British bank HSBC bombed in Istanbul, Turkey; 27 killed. Blamed on al-Qaeda. **Dec. 5:** Suicide bombing on commuter train in Yessentuki, Russia; 44 killed, 150 injured. Blamed on Chechen rebels.

2004—Feb. 6: Bomb exploded in Moscow subway; 39 killed, 130 injured. Chechen rebels blamed. **Mar. 11:** Al-Qaeda cell bombed 4 commuter trains during morning rush hour in Madrid, Spain; 191 killed, about 1,200 injured. **May 29:** Al-Qaeda militants stormed foreigner compound in Khobar, Saudi Arabia, taking hostages; 22 killed. **Aug. 24:** Chechen suicide bombers caused near-simultaneous crash of two Russian passenger planes in diff. parts of Russia; 90 killed. **Sept. 1:** Chechen militants seized school in Beslan, in North Ossetia, Russia; held 1,000+ hostage for 3 days before Russian troops stormed school. About 330 killed, incl. 27 hostage-takers.

2005—July 7: Four bombs exploded on 3 separate subways and 1 bus in central London, Eng.; 52 killed, about 700 injured. **July 21:** Four bombs placed on 3 subways and 1 bus in London malfunction. No deaths reported. **July 23:** Three car bombs explode nr. resorts at Sharm el Sheik, Egypt; about 90 killed. **Nov. 9:** 3 suicide bombings targeted hotels in Amman, Jordan; killed 56+, injured about 100. Al-Qaeda in Iraq took responsibility.

2006—July 11: 8 explosions struck 7 different trains and 1 station of public commuter rail system in Mumbai, India; 207 killed, 700+ wounded. Lashkar-e-Qahhar (Army of Terror) claimed responsibility.

2007—Feb. 19: Train traveling between New Delhi and border with Pakistan caught fire, 68 killed; Indian ministers blamed Muslim militants for trying to disrupt peace talks between India and Pakistan. **Dec. 11:** Two coordinated car bombs went off outside govt. building and UN office building in Algiers, Algeria; 41 killed, incl. 17 UN employees, 170 wounded.

2008—Sept. 20: Suicide bomber in truck set off explosion outside of Marriott Hotel in Islamabad, Pakistan. Hotel was popular among foreigners, wealthy residents and was located nr. prime min.'s house and parliament building; 53 killed, 271 wounded. **Nov. 26-29:** Series of attacks and bombings on luxury hotels and high-profile targets in Mumbai, India; 171 killed, 300 injured.

2009—Feb. 20: Suicide bomber targeted Shiite funeral in Dera Ismail Khan, Pakistan; 30 killed, 50+ wounded. **Dec. 25:** Umar Farouk Abdulmutallab, 23-year-old Nigerian, failed to blow up a Northwest Airlines flight from Amsterdam to Detroit with bomb hidden in his underpants.

2010—Jan. 1: Taliban suicide bomber killed more than 100 on a playground in NW Pakistan. **Mar. 29:** Two female Chechen separatists detonated suicide bombs at two landmark subway stations in Moscow, killing at least 40. **July 9:** Suicide bombers targeted tribal elders in Mohmand, Pakistan, killing more than 100. **July 11:** Several bombs exploded simultaneously in Kampala, Uganda, killing more than 70 people who had gathered to watch the broadcast of the World Cup final.

2011—Jan. 24: Suicide bomber killed 35 in Moscow's Domodedovo Airport, location chosen to maximize deaths of foreigners. **July 22:** Anders Behring Breivik, a right-wing Norwegian extremist, set off a bomb in van outside govt. buildings in Oslo, then massacred dozens of young people at a summer camp on Tyrifjorden Lake, bringing death toll to 77.

2012—Jan. 21: Series of attacks by Islamist extremist group Boko Haram killed more than 185 in Kano, Nigeria. **May 21:** Suicide bomber claimed by al-Qaeda in the Arabian Peninsula killed more than 100 soldiers, wounded 200 during military parade rehearsal nr. Yemeni presidential palace. **Sept. 11:** Terrorists stormed U.S. embassy in Benghazi, Libya, killing 4 Americans, including U.S. Amb. J. Christopher Stevens.

2013—Apr. 15: Two bombs exploded nr. Boston Marathon finish line, killing 3 and injuring 264; 4-day search ended in death of 1 bomber, Tamerlan Tsarnaev, and capture of the other, his brother Dzhokhar, a naturalized Chechen immigrant. **Sept. 21:** Al-Shabab, a Somali militant group, killed at least 60 people and wounded at least 175 at a Nairobi, Kenya, shopping mall.

2014—Apr.-May: Islamist extremist group Boko Haram kidnapped more than 250 girls from schools in Nigeria; killed more than 150 villagers in town of Gamboru. **Dec. 15:** Nine Taliban gunmen attacked military-affiliated school in Peshawar, Pakistan, executing about 150 people including 132 children.

2015—Jan. 7: Gunmen stormed Paris offices of *Charlie Hebdo*, a satirical newspaper, killing 12. Two days later, French police killed suspects, brothers Cherif and Said Kouachi. **Mar. 18:** Gunmen killed 21 tourists and a police officer at Tunisia's National Bardo Museum. Several terrorist groups claimed credit. **Apr. 2:** Al-Shabab militants killed 147 students at Kenya's Garissa Univ. after separating Christian and Muslim students. **June 17:** Lone white-supremacist gunman killed 9, incl. a state senator, in a historically black church in Charleston, SC.

Chairmen of the Joint Chiefs of Staff, 1949-2015

Chairman	Service
Gen. of the Army Omar N. Bradley, USA	8/16/1949-8/15/1953
Adm. Arthur W. Radford, USN	8/15/1953-8/15/1957
Gen. Nathan F. Twining, USAF	8/15/1957-9/30/1960
Gen. Lyman L. Lemnitzer, USA	10/1/1960-9/30/1962
Gen. Maxwell D. Taylor, USA	10/1/1962-7/1/1964
Gen. Earle G. Wheeler, USA	7/3/1964-7/2/1970
Adm. Thomas H. Moorer, USN	7/2/1970-7/1/1974
Gen. George S. Brown, USAF	7/1/1974-6/20/1978
Gen. David C. Jones, USAF	6/21/1978-6/18/1982
Gen. John W. Vessey Jr., USA	6/18/1982-9/30/1985
Adm. William J. Crowe Jr., USN	10/1/1985-9/30/1989
Gen. Colin L. Powell, USA	10/1/1989-9/30/1993
Gen. John M. Shalikashvili, USA	10/25/1993-9/30/1997
Gen. Henry H. Shelton, USA	9/30/1997-9/30/2001
Gen. Richard B. Myers, USAF	10/1/2001-9/30/2005
Gen. Peter Pace, USMC	9/30/2005-9/30/2007
Adm. Michael G. Mullen, USN	10/1/2007-9/30/2011
Gen. Martin E. Dempsey, USA	10/1/2011-9/25/2015
Gen. Joseph F. Dunford Jr., USMC	9/25/2015-

Chief Commanding Officers of the U.S. Military

Chairman, Joint Chiefs of Staff: Gen. Joseph F. Dunford Jr. (USMC)
Vice Chairman: Gen. Paul J. Selva (USAF)

Date of rank is date when the individual achieved his or her current rank. While serving in any of these positions, or as commander of a unified or specified combatant command, basic pay is $21,147.30 per month. Officers hold positions listed as of Oct. 1, 2015.

Army

Chief of Staff (CSA)	Date of rank
Milley, Mark A.	Aug. 15, 2014
Other Generals	
Abrams, Robert B.	Aug. 10, 2015
Allyn, Daniel	Apr. 26, 2013
Austin, Lloyd J., III	Sept. 1, 2010
Brooks, Vincent K.	July 2, 2013
Campbell, John F.	Mar. 8, 2013
Grass, Frank J.	Sept. 7, 2012
Perkins, David G.	Mar. 14, 2014
Rodriguez, David M.	Aug. 15, 2011
Scaparrotti, Curtis M.	Oct. 2, 2013
Via, Dennis L.	Aug. 7, 2012
Votel, Joseph L., III	Aug. 28, 2014

Navy

Chief of Naval Operations (CNO)	Date of rank
Richardson, John M. (submariner)	July 26, 2012
Other Admirals	
Caldwell, James F. (submariner)	Aug. 14, 2015
Davidson, Philip S. (surface warfare)	Dec. 19, 2014
Ferguson, Mark E., III (surface warfare)	Aug. 2, 2011
Gortney, William E. (aviator)	May 24, 2012
Haney, Cecil D. (surface warfare)	Jan. 20, 2012
Harris, Harry B., Jr. (aviator)	Oct. 16, 2013
Howard, Michelle J. (surface warfare)	July 1, 2014
Rogers, Michael S. (information warfare)	Mar. 31, 2014
Swift, Scott H. (aviator)	May 27, 2015

Air Force

Chief of Staff (CSAF or AF/CC)	Date of rank
Welsh III, Mark A.	Dec. 13, 2010
Other Generals	
Breedlove, Philip M.	Jan. 14, 2011
Carlisle, Herbert J.	Aug. 3, 2012
Everhart, Carlton D.	Aug. 11, 2015
Goldfein, David L.	Aug. 17, 2015
Gorenc, Frank	Aug. 2, 2013
Hyten, John E.	Aug. 15, 2014
McDew, Darren W.	May 5, 2014
Pawlikowski, Ellen M.	June 8, 2015
Rand, Robin	Oct. 10, 2013
Robinson, Lori J.	Oct. 16, 2014
Selva, Paul J.	Nov. 30, 2012

Marine Corps

Commandant of the Marine Corps (CMC)	Date of rank
Neller, Robert B.	Sept. 24, 2015
Other Generals	
Kelly, John F.	July 26, 2012
Paxton, John M., Jr.	Dec. 15, 2012

Coast Guard

Commandant, with rank of Admiral	Date of rank
Zukunft, Paul F.	May 30, 2014
Vice Commandant, with rank of Vice Admiral	
Michel, Charles D.	May 1, 2014

Unified Combatant Commands Commanders-in-Chief

U.S. European Command, Stuttgart-Vaihingen, Germany: Gen. Philip M. Breedlove (USAF)
U.S. Pacific Command, Honolulu, Hawaii: Adm. Harry B. Harris Jr. (USN)
U.S. Special Operations Command, MacDill AFB, Florida: Gen. Joseph L. Votel III (U.S. Army)
U.S. Transportation Command, Scott AFB, Illinois: Gen. Darren W. McDew (USAF)
U.S. Central Command, MacDill AFB, Florida: Gen. Lloyd J. Austin III (U.S. Army)
U.S. Southern Command, Doral, Florida: Gen. John F. Kelly (USMC)
U.S. Northern Command, Peterson AFB, Colorado: Adm. William E. Gortney (USN)
U.S. Strategic Command, Offutt AFB, Nebraska: Adm. Cecil D. Haney (USN)
U.S. Africa Command, Kelley Barracks, Stuttgart, Germany: Gen. David M. Rodriguez (U.S. Army)

North Atlantic Treaty Organization (NATO) International Commands

NATO Headquarters: Chairman, NATO Military Committee: Gen. Petr Pavel (Czech Army)
- **ACO Subordinate Commands:**
  - Joint Force Command Brunssum (JFC Brunssum): Gen. Hans-Lothar Domröse (German Army), Commander
  - Joint Force Command Naples (JFC Naples): Adm. Mark Ferguson (USN), Commander

Strategic Commands:
- Allied Command Operations (ACO): Gen. Philip M. Breedlove (USAF), Supreme Allied Commander, Europe
- Allied Command Transformation (ACT): Gen. Jean-Paul Paloméros (French Air Force), Supreme Allied Commander Transformation

Directors of the Central Intelligence Agency, 1946-2015

In 1942, Pres. Franklin D. Roosevelt established the Office of Strategic Services (OSS); it was disbanded in 1945. In 1946, Pres. Harry Truman established the Central Intelligence Group (CIG) to operate under the National Intelligence Authority (NIA). A 1947 law replaced the NIA with the National Security Council (NSC) and the CIG with the Central Intelligence Agency (CIA).

Director	Served	Appointed by President
Adm. Sidney W. Souers	1946	Truman
Gen. Hoyt S. Vandenberg	1946-1947	Truman
Adm. Roscoe H. Hillenkoetter	1947-1950	Truman
Gen. Walter Bedell Smith	1950-1953	Truman
Allen W. Dulles	1953-1961	Eisenhower
John A. McCone	1961-1965	Kennedy
Adm. William F. Raborn Jr.	1965-1966	Johnson, L. B.
Richard Helms	1966-1973	Johnson, L. B.
James R. Schlesinger	1973	Nixon
William E. Colby	1973-1976	Nixon
George H. W. Bush	1976-1977	Ford
Adm. Stansfield Turner	1977-1981	Carter
William J. Casey	1981-1987	Reagan
William H. Webster	1987-1991	Reagan
Robert M. Gates	1991-1993	Bush, G. H. W.
R. James Woolsey	1993-1995	Clinton
John M. Deutch	1995-1997	Clinton
George J. Tenet	1997-2004	Clinton
Porter Goss	2004-2006	Bush, G. W.
Gen. Michael V. Hayden	2006-2009	Bush, G. W.
Leon E. Panetta	2009-2011	Obama
Gen. David H. Petraeus	2011-2012	Obama
John O. Brennan	2013-	Obama

U.S. Army and Air Force Units

Army Units. Squad: In infantry, usually 8-16 enlisted personnel under a sergeant or staff sergeant. **Platoon:** In infantry, 3 squads under a lieutenant. **Company:** Headquarters and 3-5 platoons under a captain. (Company-size unit in the artillery is a battery; in the cavalry, a troop.) **Battalion:** 3-6 companies under a lieutenant colonel. (Battalion-size unit in the cavalry is a squadron.) **Brigade:** Three or more battalions under a colonel. (Brigade-size unit in the cavalry and rangers is a regiment; in the special forces, a group.) **Division:** 3 brigades with combat support and combat service support units under a major general. **Corps:** 2-5 divisions with corps troops under a lieutenant general. **Army:** 2-5 corps with operational and support responsibilities under a general.

Air Force Units. Flight: Numerically designated flights are the lowest level unit. They are used primarily where there is a need for small mission elements to be incorporated into an organized unit. **Squadron:** The basic unit. Designates specific operational or support capability like mission units in operational commands. **Group:** Flexible unit composed of 2 or more squadrons whose functions may be operational, support, or administrative in nature. **Wing:** Primary group with supporting groups on a distinct mission with significant scope such as combat, flying training, or airlift. **Numbered Air Force (NAF):** Normally operationally oriented, the numbered air force is designed for the control of subordinate units with the same mission and/or geographical location. **Major Command (MAJCOM):** A major subdivision with full staff that manages a major segment of the USAF mission. Major command is composed of 3 or more numbered air forces.

U.S. Military Personnel Strength on Active Duty Worldwide, 2015

Source: U.S. Dept. of Defense
(as of Mar. 31, 2015)

Location	Personnel
TOTAL WORLDWIDE[1]	**1,305,292**
U.S. TERRITORIES AND SPEC. LOCATIONS	
U.S., 48 contiguous states	1,072,387
Alaska	19,406
Guam	5,499
Hawaii	51,078
Puerto Rico	155
Regional total[2]	**1,148,530**
OTHER WESTERN HEMISPHERE	
Canada	131
Colombia	50
Cuba (Guantánamo)	693
Haiti	5
Honduras	381
Regional total[2]	**1,586**
EUROPE	
Belgium	1,220
Germany	38,015
Greece	387
Greenland	144
Italy	11,425
Netherlands	373
Portugal	623
Spain	2,193
Turkey	1,529
United Kingdom	9,078
Regional total[2]	**65,356**
SUB-SAHARAN AFRICA	
South Africa	207
Regional total[2]	**371**
FORMER SOVIET UNION	
Total	**85**
EAST ASIA AND PACIFIC	
Australia	187
British Indian Ocean Territory (Diego Garcia)	511
Japan	49,430
South Korea	29,041
Philippines	28
Singapore	186
Thailand	282
Regional total[2]	**79,794**
NORTH AFRICA, NEAR EAST, AND SOUTH ASIA	
Afghanistan[3]	14,542
Bahrain	3,369
Egypt	264
Iraq[3]	2,679
Qatar	607
Saudi Arabia	319
United Arab Emirates	349
Regional total[2,4]	**5,074**

NA = Not available. (1) Includes undistributed personnel. (2) Most countries and areas with fewer than 100 assigned U.S. military members not listed; regional totals include personnel stationed in countries and areas not shown. (3) Includes troops in surrounding areas and deployed Reserve/National Guard. (4) Excludes troops deployed to Afghanistan/Iraq.

U.S. Army Personnel on Active Duty, 1940-2015

Source: Dept. of the Army, U.S. Dept. of Defense
(as of midyear, except where noted)

Date	Total strength[1]	Commissioned officers			Warrant officers[3]		Enlisted personnel		
		Total	Male	Female[2]	Male	Female	Total	Male	Female
1940	267,767	17,563	16,624	939	763	—	249,441	249,441	—
1942	3,074,184	203,137	190,662	12,475	3,285	—	2,867,762	2,867,762	—
1943	6,993,102	557,657	521,435	36,222	21,919	—	6,413,526	6,358,200	55,325
1944	7,992,868	740,077	692,351	47,726	36,893	10	7,215,888	7,144,601	71,287
1945	8,266,373	835,403	772,511	62,892	56,216	44	7,374,710	7,283,930	90,780
1946	1,889,690	257,300	240,658	16,642	9,826	18	1,622,546	1,605,847	16,699
1950	591,487	67,784	63,375	4,409	4,760	22	518,921	512,370	6,551
1955	1,107,606	111,347	106,196	5,151	10,552	48	985,659	977,943	7,716
1960	871,348	91,056	86,832	4,224	10,141	39	770,112	761,833	8,279
1965	967,049	101,812	98,029	3,783	10,285	23	854,929	846,409	8,520
1970	1,319,735	143,704	138,469	5,235	23,005	13	1,153,013	1,141,537	11,476
1975	781,316	89,756	85,184	4,572	13,214	22	678,324	640,621	37,703
1980 (Sept. 30)	772,661	85,339	77,843	7,496	13,265	113	673,944	612,593	61,351
1985 (Sept. 30)	776,244	94,103	83,563	10,540	15,296	288	666,557	598,639	67,918
1990 (Mar. 31)	746,220	91,330	79,520	11,810	15,177	470	639,713	567,015	72,698
1995	521,036	72,646	62,250	10,396	12,053	599	435,807	377,832	57,975
2000	471,633	66,344	56,391	9,953	10,608	781	393,900	333,947	59,953
2005 (Sept. 30)	492,728	69,174	57,675	11,499	11,506	976	406,923	346,194	57,354
2006 (Sept. 30)	505,402	68,742	57,318	11,424	11,931	1,035	419,353	361,528	57,825
2007 (Sept. 30)	522,017	70,657	58,854	11,803	13,844	1,160	433,109	374,989	58,120
2008 (Sept. 30)	539,170	72,650	60,357	12,293	13,428	1,246	451,846	392,163	59,683
2009 (Sept. 30)	553,044	75,337	63,146	12,191	13,815	1,348	457,980	398,579	59,401
2010 (Sept. 30)	566,045	78,588	64,952	13,636	14,106	1,434	467,248	406,871	60,377
2011 (Sept. 30)	565,463	81,395	67,140	14,255	14,373	1,472	463,605	403,381	60,224
2012 (Sept. 30)	550,064	82,538	68,021	14,517	14,401	1,484	447,075	389,646	57,429
2013 (Sept. 30)	532,043	82,916	68,219	14,697	14,229	1,489	428,923	373,263	55,660
2014 (Dec. 31)	498,642	81,184	66,615	14,569	13,965	1,455	397,690	344,897	52,793
2015	491,177	80,788	66,134	14,654	13,766	1,426	390,702	337,953	52,749

— = Not applicable. **Note:** Represents strength of active Army, including Philippine Scouts (1940-46), ret. Regular Army personnel on extended active duty, and National Guard and Reserve personnel on extended active duty; excl. U.S. Military Academy cadets, contract surgeons, and National Guard and Reserve personnel not on extended active duty. (1) Includes categories not listed, e.g., West Point cadets. Data for 1940-46 include personnel in the Army Air Forces and its predecessors (Air Service and Air Corps). (2) Includes Army Nurse Corps for all years, Women's Army Corps (1942-78), and Medical Specialists Corps (1949 and after). (3) Act of Congress approved Apr. 27, 1926, directed the appointment as warrant officers of field clerks still in active service. Includes flight officers as follows: 1943, 5,700; 1944, 13,615; 1945, 31,117; 1946, 2,580.

U.S. Navy Personnel on Active Duty, 1940-2015

Source: U.S. Dept. of Defense
(as of midyear, except where noted)

Year	Officers	Nurses[1]	Enlisted	Officer candidates[1]	Total[2]
1940	13,162	442	144,824	2,569	160,997
1945	320,293	11,086	2,988,207	61,231	3,380,817
1950	42,687	1,964	331,860	5,037	381,538
1960	67,456	2,103	544,040	4,385	617,984
1970	78,488	2,273	605,899	6,000	692,660
1980	63,100	—	464,100	—	527,200
1990 (Sept.)	74,429	—	530,133	—	604,562
1995 (May)	61,075	—	402,626	—	463,701
1996	60,013	—	376,595	—	436,608
1997	57,341	—	340,616	—	397,957
1998 (Sept.)	55,007	—	326,196	—	381,203
1999	55,726	—	322,372	—	378,098
2000 (Oct.)	53,698	—	320,212	—	373,910
2005	54,039	—	305,368	—	363,858
2006	53,209	—	295,773	—	353,496
2007 (Sept.)	51,385	—	281,772	—	337,547
2008	52,184	—	276,346	—	331,785
2009	52,233	—	274,858	—	331,637
2010	53,071	—	273,609	—	330,065
2011	53,620	—	270,425	—	328,648
2012 (Mar.)	52,558	—	263,928	—	320,961
2013 (Feb.)	52,450	—	260,581	—	317,464
2014	54,852	—	265,622	—	323,792
2015	54,770	—	268,408	—	326,504

— = Not applicable. (1) Starting in 1980, "Nurses" are included with "Officers," and "Officer candidates" are included with "Enlisted." (2) May include categories not shown, e.g., midshipmen.

U.S. Air Force Personnel on Active Duty, 1918-2015

Source: U.S. Dept. of Defense
(as of midyear, except where noted)

Year[1]	Strength
1918	195,023
1920	9,050
1930	13,531
1940	51,165
1941	152,125
1942	764,415
1943	2,197,114
1944	2,372,292
1945	2,282,259
1950	411,277
1960	814,213
1970	791,078
1980	557,969
1986	608,200
1990	535,233
1991	510,432
1992	470,315
1993	444,351
1994	426,327
1995	400,051
1996	389,400
1997	378,681
1998	363,479
1999	357,929
2000	357,777
2005	358,705
2006	352,620
2007	340,596
2008	328,771
2009	334,009
2010	337,505
2011	333,729
2012[2]	332,709
2013[3]	334,157
2014	328,791
2015	312,195

(1) Prior to 1950, data are for U.S. Army Air Corps and Air Service of the Signal Corps. (2) In Mar. (3) In Feb.

U.S. Marine Corps Personnel on Active Duty, 1940-2015

Source: U.S. Dept. of Defense
(as of midyear, except where noted)

Year	Officers	Enlisted	Total
1940	1,800	26,545	28,345
1945	37,067	437,613	474,680
1950	7,254	67,025	74,279
1960	16,203	154,418	170,621
1970	24,941	234,796	259,737
1980	18,198	170,271	188,469
1990	19,958	176,694	196,652
1993	18,878	161,205	180,083
1994	18,430	159,949	178,379
1995	18,017	153,929	171,946
1996	18,146	154,141	172,287
1997	18,089	154,240	172,329
1998	17,984	154,648	172,632
1999	17,892	155,250	173,142
2000	17,897	154,744	172,641
2005	19,118	159,113	178,231
2006	19,218	159,705	178,923
2007	19,456	162,085	181,541
2008	20,137	172,903	193,040
2009	21,031	183,243	204,274
2010	21,680	179,446	201,126
2011	22,281	178,546	200,827
2012 (Mar.)	22,253	176,174	198,427
2013 (Feb.)	21,907	173,222	195,129
2014	21,507	169,327	190,834
2015	21,144	163,144	184,587

U.S. Coast Guard Personnel on Active Duty, 1970-2015

Source: U.S. Dept. of Defense
(as of midyear, except where noted)

Year	Officers	Cadets	Enlisted	Total
1970	5,512	653	31,524	37,689
1980	6,463	877	32,041	39,381
1985	6,775	733	31,087	38,595
1990	6,475	820	29,860	37,308
1995	7,489	841	28,401	36,731
2000	7,154	863	27,695	35,712
2005	7,908	1,006	31,900	40,814
2006	8,032	1,004	32,001	40,639
2007	8,231	720	32,314	41,265
2008	8,282	1,005	33,137	42,424
2009	8,497	993	34,024	43,514
2010	8,678	744	33,713	43,135
2011	8,659	1,053	33,615	43,327
2012 (Mar.)	8,316	988	33,758	43,062
2013 (Jan.)	8,376	1,010	32,971	42,357
2014	8,572	676	31,233	40,481
2015	8,550	623	30,896	40,069

Women in the U.S. Armed Forces

Source: U.S. Dept. of Defense; U.S. Census Bureau, U.S. Dept. of Commerce; U.S. Coast Guard, U.S. Dept. of Homeland Security

Women in the Army, Navy, Air Force, Marines, and Coast Guard are fully integrated with male personnel. All enlisted jobs were opened to women when the draft ended June 30, 1973. Admission to service academies began in 1976. Under rules instituted in 1993, women were allowed to fly combat aircraft and serve aboard warships. By the mid-1990s, 80% of all jobs and more than 90% of all career fields had been opened to women. The first woman achieved the rank of four-star general in 2009. In Apr. 2010, the Navy announced that women would be placed on submarine crews by Jan. 2012. The Pentagon in 2013 lifted its ban on women serving in direct ground combat units. In Aug. 2015, the first two women graduated from the Army's Ranger School.

Women Active Duty Troops, 2015

Service	% women
Army	14.2%
Navy	18.1
Marines	7.7
Air Force	19.1
Coast Guard	14.8[1]

Women on Active Duty, All Services, 1973-2015

Year	% women
1973	2.5%
1975	4.6
1981	8.9
1987	10.2
1993	11.6
1997	13.6
2000	14.4%
2005	14.6
2012	14.6
2013	14.9
2014	15.2
2015	15.4

Women Veterans by Period of Service, 2015

Period of service[2]	% of women vets
Gulf War era[3]	57.5%
Vietnam era	12.5
Korean War	2.5
World War II	2.2
Peacetime only	25.3

Note: Numbers on active duty are as of Sept. 30 in previous years and June 30 in 2015. (1) As of May 31. (2) Includes women who served in multiple periods. (3) Includes women who served both pre- and post-9/11 but not in peacetime only.

Average Age and Length of Service of Active Enlisted Personnel, 1973-2013

Source: U.S. Dept. of Defense

Year	Avg. age	Avg. months of service	Year	Avg. age	Avg. months of service	Year	Avg. age	Avg. months of service
1973	25.0	69.8	1987	26.1	74.8	2000	27.1	85.5
1974	25.0	69.6	1988	26.3	76.7	2001	27.0	84.4
1975	24.9	68.2	1989	26.4	78.0	2002	27.1	84.1
1976	24.9	67.6	1990	26.7	81.8	2003	27.0	83.3
1977	24.9	66.5	1991	27.0	84.8	2004	27.0	82.6
1978	25.0	67.3	1992	27.1	86.4	2005	27.1	83.2
1979	25.1	67.7	1992	27.1	86.4	2006	27.1	82.0
1980	25.0	66.5	1993	27.2	87.7	2007	27.1	81.0
1981	25.1	67.1	1994	27.3	89.6	2008	27.1	80.3
1982	25.4	68.6	1995	27.4	89.3	2009	27.2	80.4
1983	25.6	70.0	1996	27.4	89.6	2010	27.3	80.9
1984	25.7	71.1	1997	27.4	89.2	2011	27.4	81.1
1985	25.8	72.3	1998	27.3	88.4	2012	27.4	NA
1986	25.9	73.1	1999	27.3	87.3	2013	27.3	NA

NA = Not available.

Monthly Military Pay Scale

Source: U.S. Dept. of Defense

(effective Jan. 1, 2015; salaries rounded to nearest dollar)

	Cumulative years of service														
	<2	2	3	4	6	8	10	12	14	16	18	20	22	24	26
Commissioned officers															
O-10	NA	NA	NA	NA	NA	NA	NA	NA	NA	NA	NA	15,125	15,125	15,125	15,125
O-9	NA	NA	NA	NA	NA	NA	NA	NA	NA	NA	NA	14,057	14,260	14,552	15,062
O-8	9,946	10,272	10,488	10,549	10,819	11,269	11,374	11,802	11,925	12,293	12,827	13,319	13,647	13,647	13,647
O-7	8,264	8,648	8,826	8,967	9,223	9,476	9,768	10,059	10,351	11,269	12,044	12,044	12,044	12,044	12,106
O-6	6,187	6,797	7,243	7,243	7,271	7,582	7,623	7,623	8,057	8,822	9,272	9,722	9,977	10,236	10,738
O-5	5,158	5,810	6,212	6,288	6,539	6,689	7,019	7,262	7,575	8,054	8,281	8,507	8,762	8,762	8,762
O-4	4,450	5,151	5,495	5,572	5,891	6,233	6,659	6,991	7,221	7,354	7,430	7,430	7,430	7,430	7,430
O-3	3,913	4,435	4,787	5,219	5,470	5,744	5,921	6,213	6,365	6,365	6,365	6,365	6,365	6,365	6,365
O-2	3,381	3,850	4,434	4,584	4,679	4,679	4,679	4,679	4,679	4,679	4,679	4,679	4,679	4,679	4,679
O-1	2,934	3,054	3,692	3,692	3,692	3,692	3,692	3,692	3,692	3,692	3,692	3,692	3,692	3,692	3,692
Commissioned officers with over 4 years of active duty service as enlisted member or warrant officer															
O-3E	NA	NA	NA	5,219	5,470	5,744	5,921	6,213	6,459	6,601	6,793	6,793	6,793	6,793	6,793
O-2E	NA	NA	NA	4,584	4,679	4,828	5,079	5,273	5,418	5,418	5,418	5,418	5,418	5,418	5,418
O-1E	NA	NA	NA	3,692	3,942	4,088	4,237	4,384	4,584	4,584	4,584	4,584	4,584	4,584	4,584
Warrant officers															
W-5	NA	NA	NA	NA	NA	NA	NA	NA	NA	NA	NA	7,190	7,554	7,826	8,127
W-4	4,043	4,350	4,474	4,597	4,809	5,018	5,230	5,549	5,828	6,094	6,312	6,524	6,836	7,092	7,384
W-3	3,692	3,846	4,004	4,056	4,221	4,547	4,886	5,045	5,230	5,420	5,762	5,993	6,131	6,278	6,477
W-2	3,267	3,576	3,672	3,737	3,949	4,278	4,442	4,602	4,799	4,952	5,091	5,258	5,367	5,454	5,454
W-1	2,868	3,177	3,260	3,435	3,643	3,948	4,091	4,290	4,487	4,641	4,783	4,956	4,956	4,956	4,956
Enlisted members															
E-9	NA	NA	NA	NA	NA	NA	4,885	4,996	5,135	5,299	5,465	5,730	5,955	6,191	6,552
E-8	NA	NA	NA	NA	NA	3,999	4,176	4,285	4,417	4,559	4,815	4,945	5,167	5,289	5,591
E-7	2,780	3,034	3,150	3,304	3,425	3,631	3,747	3,953	4,125	4,242	4,367	4,415	4,578	4,665	4,996
E-6	2,405	2,646	2,762	2,876	2,995	3,261	3,365	3,566	3,627	3,672	3,724	3,724	3,724	3,724	3,724
E-5	2,203	2,351	2,465	2,581	2,762	2,951	3,107	3,126	3,126	3,126	3,126	3,126	3,126	3,126	3,126
E-4	2,020	2,123	2,238	2,351	2,452	2,452	2,452	2,452	2,452	2,452	2,452	2,452	2,452	2,452	2,452
E-3	1,823	1,938	2,055	2,055	2,055	2,055	2,055	2,055	2,055	2,055	2,055	2,055	2,055	2,055	2,055
E-2	1,734	1,734	1,734	1,734	1,734	1,734	1,734	1,734	1,734	1,734	1,734	1,734	1,734	1,734	1,734
E-1[1]	1,547	1,547	1,547	1,547	1,547	1,547	1,547	1,547	1,547	1,547	1,547	1,547	1,547	1,547	1,547

NA = Not applicable. **Note:** Basic pay rate for Academy cadets/midshipmen and ROTC members/applicants is $1,027. See Dept. of Defense Financial Management Regulations for details on pay-scale limitations and eligibility requirements. **Over 30 years**—O-10: 15,125; O-9: 15,125; O-8: 13,989; O-7: 12,348; O-6: 10,952; W-5: 8,534; W-4: 7,532; E-9: 6,879; E-8: 5,704. **Over 34 years**—O-10: 15,125; O-9: 15,125; O-8: 14,339; W-5: 8,960; E-9: 7,223. **Over 38 years**—O-10: 15,125; O-9: 15,125; W-5: 9,408; E-9: 7,585. (1) Applicable to E-1 with 4 months or more of active duty. Basic pay for an E-1 with less than 4 months of active duty is $1,430.40.

U.S. Veteran Population, 2015

Source: U.S. Dept. of Veterans Affairs

(projected population, in thousands, as of Sept. 30)

Period of service	Vet. pop.
Total peacetime veterans[1]	**5,381.8**
Service between Vietnam War era and Gulf War era	3,359.3
Service between Korean War and Vietnam War era	1,930.0
Service between WWII and Korean War	83.6
Pre-WWII service	8.9
Total wartime veterans[2]	**16,298.7**
Total World War II[3]	847.4
WWII only	756.5
Total Korean War[3]	1,739.1
Korean War with no other wartime service	1,487.6
Korean War with service in WWII	63.3

Period of service	Vet. pop.
Total Vietnam War era[3]	7,102.8
Vietnam War era with no other wartime service	6,551.5
Vietnam War era with service in Korea	160.7
Vietnam War era with service in Korea and WWII	27.6
Total Gulf War era[3]	7,251.6
Gulf War era pre-9/11 with service in Vietnam era	308.2
Gulf War era pre-9/11, post-9/11, and with service in Vietnam War era	54.9
Gulf War era pre-9/11	2,778.5
Gulf War era pre-9/11 and post-9/11	1,315.0
Gulf War era post-9/11	2,794.9
TOTAL VETERANS IN CIVILIAN LIFE	**21,680.5**

Note: Figures are for U.S. veterans worldwide. Includes those who served on active duty in Army, Navy, Air Force, Marines, Coast Guard, uniformed Public Health Service and NOAA, and reservists called to federal active duty. Excludes those dishonorably discharged, those whose only active duty was training, and those currently on active duty. (1) Veterans with both wartime and peacetime service are counted only as "wartime veterans." (2) Veterans serving in more than one period are counted only once in total. (3) Total includes veterans who also served in other periods.

African American Service in U.S. Wars

Source: U.S. Dept. of Defense; U.S. Census Bureau, U.S. Dept. of Commerce

American Revolution. About 5,000 served in the Continental Army, mostly in integrated units, some in all-black combat units.

Civil War. Some 180,000 served in 163 units of the Union Army's U.S. Colored Troops, and 200,000 worked in service units—10% of the Union Army in all; about 37,000 died, 31,000 wounded.

World War I. 350,000-400,000 served in the armed forces, 100,000 in France. Some 40,000 fought.

World War II. Some 1 mil served in the armed forces—8% of all troops—mostly in Army service units; all-black fighter and bomber Army Air Force units and infantry divisions gave distinguished service.

Korean War. More than 600,000 served in the military; 3,075 lost their lives in combat. By 1954, armed forces were completely desegregated.

Vietnam War. 274,937 served in the armed forces (1965-74)—9.8% of all troops; 7,243 were killed in combat.

Persian Gulf War. About 104,000 served in the Kuwaiti theater—20% of all U.S. troops; 66 died in combat.

Operation Enduring Freedom. 193 military deaths and 1,407 wounded in Afghanistan and elsewhere.

Operation Iraqi Freedom/Operation New Dawn. 444 military deaths and 2,766 wounded.

Outlays for Individual Payments to Veterans, 1940-2016

Source: White House Office of Management and Budget
(in millions of dollars)

Year	Total	Compensation	Pensions	Hospital, medical	Education	Insurance & burial
1940	$574	$244	$185	$69	—	$76
1950	8,613	1,533	476	764	$2,739	3,101
1960	5,300	2,049	1,263	931	392	665
1970	8,883	2,980	2,255	1,798	1,002	848
1980	21,153	7,446	3,585	6,513	2,421	1,188
1990	28,801	10,735	3,594	12,281	791	1,400
2000	46,835	20,777	2,969	20,090	1,636	1,363
2001	46,187	18,587	2,760	21,730	1,763	1,347
2002	52,621	22,429	3,166	23,465	2,241	1,320
2003	57,407	24,705	3,229	25,568	2,574	1,331
2004	62,567	26,307	3,334	28,556	2,978	1,392
2005	69,824	30,888	3,663	30,650	3,254	1,369
2006	$71,139	$31,000	$3,547	$31,888	$3,354	$1,350
2007	73,726	31,064	3,376	34,485	3,456	1,345
2008	84,463	36,266	3,790	39,409	3,634	1,364
2009	94,985	40,490	4,161	44,637	4,328	1,369
2010	106,454	43,498	4,359	48,506	8,773	1,318
2011	122,524	52,780	4,664	52,681	11,112	1,287
2012	119,574	50,058	4,537	53,002	10,734	1,243
2013	136,120	59,393	5,173	55,091	13,220	1,230
2014	145,452	64,360	5,251	58,932	13,729	1,166
2015*	153,220	71,023	5,570	60,673	14,702	1,252
2016*	171,643	81,762	6,353	66,027	16,323	1,178

— = Not available. * = Estimate. **Note:** Compensation is service-connected; pension is not.

Veterans Health Administration Characteristics, 2002-13

Source: U.S. Dept. of Veterans Affairs

Fiscal year	Total enrollees[1] (mil)	Outpatient visits[2] (mil)	Inpatient admissions (thous.)
2002	6.8	46.5	564.7
2003	7.1	49.8	567.3
2004	7.3	54.0	589.8
2005	7.7	57.5	585.8
2006	7.9	59.1	568.9
2007	7.8	62.3	589.0
2008	7.8	67.7	641.4
2009	8.1	74.9	662.0
2010	8.3	80.2	682.3
2011	8.6	79.8	692.1
2012	8.8	83.6	703.5
2013	8.9	86.4	694.7
2014	9.1	92.4	707.4

(1) Includes non-enrolled veteran patients. (2) Includes fee visits.

Employment Status of Veterans With Service-Connected Disabilities, 2014

Source: Bureau of Labor Statistics, U.S. Dept. of Labor; as of Aug. 2014

Veteran status, presence of disability, and period of service	Employed (thous.)			Unemployed (thous.)			Unemployment rate (%)			Not in labor force (thous.)		
	Total	Men	Women	Total	Men	Women	Total	Men	Women	Total	Men	Women
Total veterans	**10,070**	**8,784**	**1,286**	**598**	**516**	**82**	**5.6%**	**5.5%**	**6.0%**	**10,457**	**9,570**	**886**
With service-connected disability	1,456	1,223	233	92	76	16	5.9	5.9	6.3	1,887	1,746	141
Without service-connected disability	6,441	5,689	752	407	351	55	5.9	5.8	6.8	6,845	6,328	517
Gulf War era, total	4,946	4,090	856	327	271	56	6.2	6.2	6.1	1,235	840	395
With service-connected disability	1,060	848	212	67	51	16	5.9	5.7	6.9	385	309	76
Without service-connected disability	2,808	2,359	449	199	159	40	6.6	6.3	8.2	469	299	170
Gulf War era II	2,282	1,843	439	201	165	36	8.1	8.2	7.6	670	455	215
With service-connected disability	633	497	136	64	48	16	9.1	8.8	10.3	231	183	48
Without service-connected disability	1,178	977	201	100	80	20	7.8	7.5	9.2	215	133	82
Gulf War era I	2,663	2,247	417	125	105	20	4.5	4.5	4.6	565	385	180
With service-connected disability	427	351	76	3	3	NA	0.7	0.9	NA	154	126	28
Without service-connected disability	1,630	1,382	248	100	79	20	5.8	5.4	7.5	254	166	88
WWII, Korean War, and Vietnam era	2,507	2,411	96	144	144	NA	5.4	5.6	NA	6,670	6,416	254
With service-connected disability	186	179	7	12	12	NA	6.0	6.2	NA	1,218	1,188	30
Without service-connected disability	1,751	1,690	60	107	107	NA	5.8	6.0	NA	4,515	4,320	196
Other service periods	2,617	2,282	335	127	101	26	4.6	4.3	7.1	2,552	2,314	237
With service-connected disability	210	196	15	13	13	NA	6.0	6.4	NA	284	249	35
Without service-connected disability	1,882	1,640	243	100	85	15	5.0	4.9	5.8	1,860	1,709	151

NA = Not available. **Note:** Veterans in survey were on active duty in the U.S. Armed Forces during these periods of service: Gulf War era II (Sept. 2001-present), Gulf War era I (Aug. 1990-Aug. 2001), Vietnam era (Aug.1964-Apr. 1975), Korean War (July 1950-Jan. 1955), World War II (Dec. 1941-Dec. 1946), and other service periods. Veterans who served in more than one wartime period are classified in the most recent period only. A service-connected disability is a health condition or impairment caused or made worse by military service.

Nations With Largest Armed Forces

Source: *The Military Balance 2015*, International Institute for Strategic Studies, published by Routledge Journals, Taylor & Francis, UK
(ranked by active-duty troop strength as of 2015; all other data as of Nov. 2014)

		Troop strength				Navy		Combat aircraft (air force only)	
Rank	Country	Active troops (thous.)	Reserve troops (thous.)	Defense expend. (mil)	Tanks (MBT) (army only)	Cruisers/ frigates/ destroyers	Sub-marines	FGA	FTR
1.	China	2,333	510	$129,408	6,540	54F/17D*	70	573+	842
2.	United States	1,433	855	581,000	5,838	22C/11F/62D*	73	838	275
3.	India	1,346	1,155	45,212	2,874+	13F/12D*	14	753	62
4.	North Korea	1,190	600	—	3,500+	3F	72	48	401+
5.	Russia	771	2,000	70,048	2,600	6C/10F/18D*	59	345	420
6.	South Korea	655	4,500	34,438	2,414	3C/14F/6D	23	314	174
7.	Pakistan	644	0	6,006	2,531+	10F	8	190	211
8.	Iran	523	350	15,705	1,663+	0	29	110	184+
9.	Turkey	511	379	10,047	2,504	18F	14	282	53
10.	Vietnam	482	5,000	4,248	1,270	2F	4	97	0
11.	Egypt	439	479	5,449	2,540	8F	4	310	62
12.	Myanmar	406	0	2,433	185+	4F	0	0	88
13.	Indonesia	396	400	7,076	26	11F	2	21	22
14.	Thailand	361	200	5,685	288	10F*	0	12	79
15.	Brazil	318	1,340	31,930	393	11F/3D*	5	49	57
16.	Colombia	297	35	13,444	0	4F	4	20	0
17.	Taiwan	290	1,657	10,126	565	4C/22F	4	128	288
18.	Mexico	267	87	6,548	0	6F	0	0	8
19.	Japan	247	56	47,685	688	2C/9F/34D*	18	152	201
20.	Sudan	244	0	1,892[2]	465	0	0	0	22
21.	Saudi Arabia	227	0	80,762	600	4F/3D	0	180	81
22.	France	215	28	53,080	200	11F/11D*	10	171	40
23.	Eritrea	202	120	78[1]	270	0	0	10	6
24.	Morocco	196	150	3,859	434	5F/1D	0	51	22
25.	South Sudan	185	0	1,044	80+	0	0	0	0
26.	Germany	182	45	43,934	410	9F/7D	5	114	101
27.	Afghanistan	179	0	3,286	20	0	0	0	0
28.	Iraq	178	0	18,868	270+	0	0	1	0
29.	Syria	178	0	—	—	0	0	185	75
30.	Israel	177	465	20,139	500	0	3	251	143

— = Not available. * = Navy with aircraft carrier(s), as follows: Brazil 1, China 1, France 1, India 2, Japan 2, Russia 1, Thailand 1, U.S. 10. FGA = Fighter, ground attack. FTR = Fighter. MBT = Main battle tank. (1) As of 2012. (2) As of 2013.

Budget for Global War on Terror Operations, 2001-14

Source: Congressional Research Service, Library of Congress
(in billions of dollars)

	2001/02[1]	2003	2004	2005	2007	2008	2010	2012	2013	2014	Total 2001-14
Total: war designated funding	**$35.8**	**$74.4**	**96.0**	**$108.4**	**$169.7**	**$195.2**	**$165.4**	**$129.7**	**$99.9**	**$95.2**	**$1,608.9**
Dept. of Defense.	35.0	70.7	74.3	103.6	164.0	188.7	154.6	115.3	87.5	85.4	1,498.7
Foreign aid and diplomacy[2]	0.8	3.8	21.7	4.8	5.0	5.4	8.9	11.5	9.2	6.0	92.7
Veterans Affairs medical. . . .	0.0	0.0	0.0	0.0	0.7	1.0	1.9	2.9	3.2	3.7	17.6
Total: war designated funding not war-related	**0.0**	**0.0**	**0.0**	**6.6**	**7.3**	**12.1**	**6.4**	**8.6**	**6.6**	**12.8**	**81.3**
Dept. of Defense.	0.0	0.0	0.0	6.6	7.3	12.1	6.4	5.4	1.9	10.2	70.9
Foreign aid and diplomacy[2]	0.0	0.0	0.0	0.0	0.0	0.0	0.0	3.2	4.6	2.6	10.4
Op. Iraqi Freedom/New Dawn	**0.0**	**51.0**	**76.7**	**79.1**	**130.8**	**143.9**	**64.8**	**20.3**	**7.7**	**4.8**	**814.6**
Dept. of Defense.	0.0	48.0	57.1	77.1	127.1	140.3	59.9	13.5	4.9	1.1	753.1
Foreign aid and diplomacy[2]	0.0	3.0	19.5	2.0	3.2	2.7	3.3	4.7	0.7	1.4	48.6
Veterans Affairs medical. . . .	0.0	0.0	0.0	0.0	0.6	0.9	1.6	2.1	2.1	2.3	12.9
Op. Enduring Freedom[3]	**22.8**	**17.4**	**15.4**	**20.7**	**31.1**	**39.0**	**94.1**	**100.6**	**85.6**	**77.4**	**685.6**
Dept. of Defense.	22.0	16.7	13.2	17.9	29.2	36.1	88.2	96.3	80.6	74.0	647.3
Foreign aid and diplomacy[2]	0.8	0.7	2.2	2.8	1.9	2.7	5.6	3.5	3.9	2.0	33.6
Veterans Affairs medical. . . .	0.0	0.0	0.0	0.0	0.1	0.1	0.3	0.8	1.1	1.4	4.7
Op. Noble Eagle[4].	**13.0**	**6.0**	**4.0**	**2.0**	**0.5**	**0.2**	**0.1**	**0.2**	**0.1**	**0.1**	**27.4**

(1) Fiscal year (FY) 2001 and FY2002 funds combined because most were obligated in FY2002 after the Sept. 11, 2001, attacks at the end of FY2001, on Sept. 30, 2001. (2) Includes monies for reconstruction, development and humanitarian aid, embassy operations, counternarcotics, initial training of the Afghan and Iraqi armies, foreign military sales credits, and Economic Support Funds. (3) Covers Afghanistan (officially ended Dec. 2014) and other Global War on Terror operations, ranging from the Philippines to Djibouti, that began immediately after the Sept. 11, 2001, attacks. (4) Dept. of Defense funds that rebuilt the Pentagon and provided higher security at U.S. military bases and other homeland security, including combat air patrol.

Leading Purchasers of U.S. Defense Articles and Services

Source: Congressional Research Service, Library of Congress

Worldwide deliveries, 2004-07						Worldwide deliveries, 2008-11					
Rank	Country	Value	Rank	Country	Value	Rank	Country	Value	Rank	Country	Value
1.	Israel.	$5.7 bil	6.	South Korea . . .	$2.5 bil	1.	Saudi Arabia. . .	$5.9 bil	6.	Iraq	$2.6 bil
2.	Egypt	5.2 bil	7.	Japan	2.4 bil	2.	Egypt	3.9 bil	7.	Japan	2.5 bil
3.	Saudi Arabia. . .	4.3 bil	8.	Poland	1.9 bil	3.	Israel.	3.8 bil	8.	South Korea	2.5 bil
4.	Taiwan	4.3 bil	9.	Australia	1.7 bil	4.	Australia	2.9 bil	9.	Greece	2.1 bil
5.	Greece	2.8 bil	10.	UK.	1.6 bil	5.	Taiwan	2.9 bil	10.	Turkey.	2.0 bil

Note: Total dollar value of all U.S. defense articles and services actually delivered to top 10 purchasers worldwide. Figures include government-to-government sales through the Foreign Military Sales system (which accounts for the overwhelming majority of U.S. conventional arms deliveries) concluded in calendar years listed, as well as commercially licensed exports concluded in pertinent fiscal years.

U.S. Foreign Military Financing, 2005-13

Source: Defense Security Cooperation Agency, U.S. Dept. of Defense

Listed are grants extended to foreign governments in a fiscal year to pay for military equipment and services. May be from the U.S. Dept. of Defense (DOD) or, for specific countries, negotiated directly with U.S. commercial suppliers with DOD approval.

(in thousands of U.S. dollars)

	2005	2010	2013
Western Hemisphere	**$108,155**	**$89,720**	**$54,442**
Colombia	99,200	55,000	28,862
El Salvador	1,488	1,000	1,709
Mexico	0	5,250	6,646
Near East and South Asia	**4,541,843**	**4,666,797**	**4,616,855**
Afghanistan	396,800	0	0
Bahrain	18,847	19,000	12,575
Egypt	1,289,600	1,300,000	1,234,259
Israel	2,202,240	2,775,000	2,943,234
Jordan	304,352	300,000	284,829
Lebanon	0	0	71,207
Oman	19,840	8,847	7,595
Pakistan	298,000	248,000	0
Yemen	10,420	12,500	18,989
East Asia and Pacific	**36,537**	**59,100**	**53,316**
Indonesia	0	20,000	13,292
Mongolia	2,778	4,500	3,048
Philippines	29,760	29,000	25,483
Europe	**$220,274**	**$151,696**	**$100,824**
Bosnia and Herzegovina	8,480	4,000	4,272
Bulgaria	6,944	9,000	7,406
Czech Republic	5,952	6,000	4,747
Georgia	11,904	16,000	13,672
Macedonia	5,208	4,000	3,418
Poland	76,470	47,000	18,989
Romania	13,412	12,999	11,391
Turkey	33,728	0	0
Ukraine	2,976	11,000	6,646
Africa	**49,453**	**45,370**	**43,924**
Djibouti	4,468	2,000	949
Liberia	2,976	6,000	4,421
Morocco	15,128	9,000	7,595
Tunisia	10,407	18,000	20,554
World total	**4,956,262**	**5,015,952**	**4,874,146**

Note: Regional subtotals include countries not listed.

Defense Contracts, 2014

Source: U.S. Dept. of Defense

Listed are the 50 companies or organizations receiving the largest dollar volume of prime contract awards from the U.S. Dept. of Defense during fiscal year 2013 (Oct. 1, 2013-Sept. 30, 2014).

(in millions of U.S. dollars)

Rank	Contractor	Contracts awarded[1]	% of total
1.	Lockheed Martin Corp.	$21,450.7	7.39%
2.	The Boeing Co.	15,983.1	5.51
3.	General Dynamics Corp.	13,506.4	4.66
4.	Raytheon Co.	10,892.7	3.75
5.	Northrop Grumman Corp.	6,254.3	2.16
6.	BAE Systems PLC	4,712.2	1.62
7.	L-3 Communications Holdings Inc.	4,526.3	1.56
8.	United Technologies Corp.	4,008.7	1.38
9.	Huntington Ingalls Industries Inc.	3,908.5	1.35
10.	Humana Inc.	3,526.1	1.22
11.	UnitedHealth Group Inc.	3,203.3	1.10
12.	Health Net Inc.	3,097.0	1.07
13.	Bechtel Group Inc.	2,471.0	0.85
14.	General Electric Co.	2,186.5	0.75
15.	Booz Allen Hamilton Holding Corp.	2,108.9	0.73
16.	SAIC Inc.	2,107.8	0.73
17.	Exelis Inc.	2,075.0	0.72
18.	Bell Boeing Joint Project Office	2,019.0	0.70
19.	Northrop Grumman Systems Corp.	1,935.1	0.67
20.	McKesson Corp.	1,659.3	0.57
21.	Royal Dutch Shell PLC	1,573.1	0.54
22.	Textron Inc.	1,511.5	0.52
23.	General Atomic Technologies Corp.	1,482.5	0.51
24.	United Launch Alliance LLC	1,468.9	0.51
25.	AmerisourceBergen Corp.	1,468.7	0.51
26.	Lockheed Martin Corp.	1,460.5	0.50
27.	Computer Sciences Corp.	$1,454.4	0.50%
28.	CACI International Inc.	1,359.4	0.47
29.	Sikorsky Aircraft Corp.	1,318.6	0.45
30.	URS Corp.	1,185.4	0.41
31.	Alliant Techsystems Inc.	1,088.5	0.38
32.	United Launch Services, LLC	1,050.3	0.36
33.	Cardinal Health Inc.	988.0	0.34
34.	Anham FZCO	985.9	0.34
35.	Lockheed Martin Corp.	935.5	0.32
36.	Honeywell International Inc.	923.7	0.32
37.	Fluor Corp.	918.9	0.32
38.	Massachusetts Institute of Tech.	916.3	0.32
39.	Hewlett-Packard Co.	896.9	0.31
40.	Harris Corp.	892.1	0.31
41.	Atlantic Diving Supply Inc.	889.0	0.31
42.	Exxon Mobil Corp.	878.3	0.30
43.	Foster Fuels Inc.	858.4	0.30
44.	Alion Science and Tech. Corp.	823.6	0.28
45.	Rockwell Collins Inc.	783.1	0.27
46.	The MITRE Corp.	782.0	0.27
47.	Jacobs Engineering Group Inc.	740.3	0.26
48.	Austal Ltd.	736.7	0.25
49.	The Aerospace Corp.	729.2	0.25
50.	Valero Marketing and Supply Co.	727.7	0.25
	Other	146,631.8	50.55
	Total	**290,091.1**	

Note: Contractors listed more than once represent different company locations or facilities. (1) Amounts include contracts awarded to subsidiaries of each company.

Arms Transfer Agreements With the World by Supplier, 2004-11

Source: Congressional Research Service, Library of Congress

(in millions of current U.S. dollars)

Supplier	2004	2005	2006	2007	2008	2009	2010	2011	2004-11
United States	$12,368	$12,099	$15,435	$23,691	$36,323	$22,002	$21,103	$66,274	$209,295
Russia	8,800	8,400	15,400	10,400	6,600	13,300	8,800	4,800	76,500
France	2,900	6,300	7,700	2,200	3,800	9,600	1,800	4,400	38,700
United Kingdom	4,200	2,900	4,100	9,500	300	1,400	1,500	400	24,300
China	1,000	2,700	2,000	2,500	2,100	2,500	1,600	2,100	16,500
Germany	4,100	2,000	2,800	1,800	5,500	3,600	100	100	20,000
Italy	400	1,500	1,200	1,400	4,100	1,600	1,900	1,200	13,300
All other European	5,200	7,400	5,600	6,700	5,300	6,500	4,200	3,300	44,200
All others	3,300	1,900	3,400	2,800	3,100	5,000	2,900	2,700	25,100
Total	**42,268**	**45,199**	**57,635**	**60,991**	**67,123**	**65,502**	**43,903**	**85,274**	**467,895**

Note: All data are for the calendar year given except for U.S. MAP (Military Assistance Program), IMET (International Military Education, and Training), and Excess Defense Article data, which are included with the particular fiscal year. All amounts given include the values of all categories of weapons, spare parts, construction, all associated services, military assistance, excess defense articles, and training programs. Statistics for foreign countries are based upon estimated selling prices. All foreign data are rounded to the nearest $100 mil.

Personal Salutes and Honors

The U.S. **national salute**, 21 guns, is also the salute to a national flag. U.S. independence is commemorated by the salute to the Union—one gun for each state—fired at noon July 4, at all military posts provided with suitable artillery.

A 21-gun salute on arrival and departure, with 4 ruffles and flourishes, is rendered to the **president**, to a former president, and to a president-elect. The national anthem or "Hail to the Chief," as appropriate, is played for the president, and the national anthem for the others. A 21-gun salute on arrival and departure, with 4 ruffles and flourishes, also is rendered to the **sovereign or chief of state of a foreign country** or a member of a reigning royal family, and the national anthem of his or her country is played. The music is considered an inseparable part of the salute and immediately follows the ruffles and flourishes without pause. For the Honors March, generals receive the "General's March," admirals receive the "Flag Officer's March," and all others receive the 32-bar medley of "The Stars and Stripes Forever."

GRADE, TITLE, OR OFFICE	SALUTE (IN GUNS) Arriving	Leaving	Ruffles and flourishes	Music
Vice President of U.S.	19	—	4	Hail, Columbia
Speaker of the House	19	—	4	Honors March
U.S. or foreign ambassador in country to which accredited	19	—	4	Natl. anthem of official
Premier or prime minister	19	—	4	Natl. anthem of official
Secretary of Defense, Army, Navy, or Air Force	19	19	4	Honors March
Other cabinet members, Senate president pro tempore, governor, or chief justice of U.S.	19	—	4	Honors March
Chairman, Joint Chiefs of Staff	19	19	4	Honors March
Army chief of staff, chief of naval operations, Air Force chief of staff, Marine commandant	19	19	4	Honors March
General of the Army, general of the Air Force, fleet admiral	19	19	4	Honors March
Generals, admirals	17	17	4	Honors March
Assistant secretaries of Defense, Army, Navy, or Air Force	17	17	4	Honors March
Chair of a committee of Congress	17	—	4	Honors March

Medal of Honor

Source: Congressional Medal of Honor Society; U.S. Army, U.S. Dept. of Defense
(as of Aug. 25, 2015)

The Medal of Honor is the highest military award for bravery that can be given to any individual in the U.S. The first Army Medals of Honor were awarded on Mar. 25, 1863; the first Navy medals went to sailors and Marines on Apr. 3, 1863.

On Dec. 21, 1861, Pres. Abraham Lincoln signed a bill to create the Navy Medal of Honor. Lincoln, on July 14, 1862, approved a resolution providing for the presentation of Medals of Honor to enlisted men of the Army and Voluntary Forces. The law was amended on Mar. 3, 1863, so that officers as well as enlisted men were eligible.

The Medal of Honor is awarded in the name of Congress to a person who, while a member of the armed forces, distinguishes himself or herself conspicuously by gallantry and intrepidity at the risk of life above and beyond the call of duty while engaged in an action against any enemy of the U.S.; while engaged in military operations involving conflict with an opposing foreign force; or while serving with friendly foreign forces engaged in an armed conflict against an opposing armed force in which the U.S. is not a belligerent party.

The deed performed must have been one of personal bravery or self-sacrifice so conspicuous as to clearly distinguish the individual above his or her comrades and must have involved risk of life. Incontestable proof of the performance of service is required, and each recommendation for award of this decoration is considered on the standard of extraordinary merit.

Prior to World War I, the 2,625 Army Medal of Honor awards up to that time were reviewed to determine which met new stringent criteria. The Army removed 911 names from the list, most of them former members of a Civil War volunteer infantry group who had been induced to extend their enlistments when they were promised the medal. However, the medal was restored to Dr. Mary Walker in 1977 and to Buffalo Bill Cody and seven other Indian scouts in 1989.

Seven African American soldiers were awarded Medals of Honor for service in World War II (six of them posthumously) in Jan. 1997. Previously, no black soldier had received the medal for World War II service; an Army inquiry begun in 1993 concluded that the prevailing political climate and Army practices of the time had prevented proper recognition of heroism on the part of black soldiers in that war. In 1996, Congress authorized a review of Asian American and Pacific Islander recipients of the Distinguished Service Cross whose award should be upgraded. Twenty-two Asian Americans received the Medal of Honor for World War II service in June 2000.

In one of the largest Medal of Honor ceremonies in U.S. history, Pres. Barack Obama Mar. 18, 2014, awarded 24 mostly Hispanic, Jewish, and African-American veterans with the nation's highest military decoration for valor displayed in World War II, the Korean War, and Vietnam. The recipients, three of whom were alive to receive the award, had been found deserving following a congressionally mandated review of the records of service members who may have been overlooked due to discrimination.

Medal of Honor Recipients From Recent Conflicts

Honoree; rank (branch of service)	Date of action	Date of award
Somalia Campaign		
Gordon, Gary I.; Master Sgt. (U.S. Army)*	10/3/1993	5/23/1994
Shughart, Randall D.; Sgt. First Class (U.S. Army)*	10/3/1993	5/23/1994
War in Iraq		
Dunham, Jason L.; Cpl. (USMC)*	4/14/2004	1/11/2007
McGinnis, Ross A.; Pvt. First Class (U.S. Army)*	12/4/2006	6/5/2008
Monsoor, Michael A.; Petty Officer Second Class (U.S. Navy)*	9/29/2006	4/8/2008
Smith, Paul R.; Sgt. First Class (U.S. Army)*	4/4/2003	4/5/2005
War in Afghanistan		
Carpenter, William Kyle; Lance Cpl. (USMC)	11/21/2010	6/19/2014
Carter, Ty M.; Specialist (U.S. Army)	10/3/2009	8/26/2013
Giunta, Salvatore A.; Specialist (U.S. Army)	10/25/2007	11/16/2010
Meyer, Dakota; Sgt. (USMC)	9/8/2009	9/15/2011
Miller, Robert J.; Staff Sgt. (U.S. Army)*	1/25/2008	10/6/2010
Monti, Jared C.; Sgt. First Class (U.S. Army)*	6/21/2006	9/17/2009
Murphy, Michael P.; Lt. (U.S. Navy)*	6/28/2005	10/22/2007
Petry, Leroy A.; Staff Sgt. (U.S. Army)	5/26/2008	7/12/2011
Pitts, Ryan M.; Sgt. (U.S. Army)	7/13/2008	7/21/2014
Romesha, Clinton L.; Staff Sgt. (U.S. Army)	10/3/2009	2/11/2013
Swenson, William D.; Capt. (U.S. Army)	9/8/2009	10/15/2013
White, Kyle J.; Sgt. (U.S. Army)	11/9/2007	5/13/2014

* = Awarded posthumously.

Other Selected Awards

Source: The Institute of Heraldry, U.S. Army; Navy Department Awards Web Service; Air Force Personnel Center

Distinguished Service Cross

Established by Congress July 9, 1918, on recommendation of Gen. John J. "Black Jack" Pershing, and awarded for extraordinary heroism not justifying the award of a Medal of Honor. The act or acts of heroism must have been so notable and have involved risk of life so extraordinary as to set the individual apart from his or her comrades.

Silver Star

Third-highest military combat honor. An earlier version of this award, the Citation Star, was established by Congress on July 19, 1918, and retroactively awarded to soldiers for "gallantry in action," back to the Spanish-American War. The Silver Star medal replaced the Citation Star in 1932 and is awarded for gallantry in action which, while of a lesser degree than that required for award of the Distinguished Service Cross, must nevertheless have been performed with marked distinction.

Legion of Merit

Established by Congress on July 20, 1942, and awarded to individuals who have distinguished themselves by exceptionally meritorious conduct in the performance of outstanding services. There are different designs depending on the level of command of the award recipient.

Distinguished Flying Cross

Established by Congress July 2, 1926, and awarded for heroism or extraordinary achievement while participating in aerial flight. Awards are made only to recognize single acts of heroism or extraordinary achievement, not sustained operational activities against an armed enemy. Initial awards were given to persons who made record-breaking long-distance and endurance flights or who set altitude records. The first DFC was awarded to Cpt. Charles A. Lindbergh on May 31, 1927. DFCs were awarded retroactively to Orville and Wilbur Wright.

Soldier's Medal

Established by Congress July 2, 1926, to recognize acts of heroism not involving actual conflict with an enemy. The same degree of heroism is required as for the award of the Distinguished Flying Cross. The performance must have involved personal hazard or danger and the voluntary risk of life under conditions not involving conflict with an armed enemy. Awards are not made solely on the basis of having saved a life.

Bronze Star

Established by executive order Feb. 4, 1944, largely to raise the morale of ground troops in WWII, on the recommendation of Gen. George C. Marshall. It is awarded to any person who, while serving in any capacity in or with the U.S. military, distinguishes himself or herself by heroic or meritorious achievement or service not involving participation in aerial flight.

Purple Heart

The original Purple Heart, designated as the Badge of Military Merit, was established by Gen. George Washington on Aug. 7, 1782. Following the American Revolution, the badge fell into disuse until 1932, the 200th anniversary of Washington's birth. During WWII, the Order of the Purple Heart was awarded for both wounds received in action and for meritorious service. Following the introduction of the Legion of Merit, the Purple Heart was awarded only for combat wounds. Today, it is awarded to any armed forces member who, while serving with the U.S. Armed Services, has been wounded or killed, or who has died or may hereafter die after being wounded in action against an enemy of the U.S. or in an armed conflict in which the U.S. or friendly foreign forces are engaged; as the result of an act of any hostile foreign force; as a result of an international terrorist attack against the U.S. or a friendly foreign nation; or as a result of military operations outside the U.S. as part of a peacekeeping force. Wounds must be inflicted directly by enemy action, including while held as a prisoner of war or while being taken captive.

Air Medal

Authorized by Pres. Franklin D. Roosevelt on May 11, 1942, and awarded for heroism or meritorious achievement while participating in aerial flight. Awards may be made to recognize single acts of merit or heroism or for meritorious service. Awards are not made to individuals who use air transportation solely for the purpose of moving between points in a combat zone.

Army Commendation

Established Dec. 18, 1945, and awarded for heroism, meritorious achievement, or meritorious service. It may also be awarded to a member of the armed forces of a friendly foreign nation who distinguishes him- or herself by an act of heroism, extraordinary achievement, or meritorious service.

U.S. Military Awards in Selected Wars and Conflicts

Source: U.S. Army Human Resources Command, U.S. Dept. of Defense; Congressional Medal of Honor Society

Award	Civil War	WWI	WWII	Korea	Vietnam	Gulf War	OEF[1]	Iraq[2]
Medal of Honor	1,523	122	473	146	259	0	12	4
Distinguished Service Cross	NA	6,428	4,427	715	840	0	16	15
Silver Star	NA	NA	73,654	10,061	21,634	75	377	355
Legion of Merit	NA	NA	20,273	NA	10,356	158	219	133
Distinguished Flying Cross	NA	NA	126,318	NA	21,697	108	207	118
Soldier's Medal	NA	NA	12,485	581	5,402	43	61	111
Bronze Star (total)[3]	NA	NA	395,380	30,359	719,968	27,967	68,043	111,475
Purple Heart	NA	NA	NA	NA	220,516	504	9,143	22,432
Air Medal (total)[3]	NA	NA	1,166,471	0	1,039,124	6,399	16,608	21,887
Army Commendation (total)[3]	NA	NA	0	0	837,037	81,979	177,535	388,208

NA = Not available or applicable. **Note:** Numbers for the individual decorations shown here represent only those awards that were properly processed and reported to Dept. of the Army Headquarters. The actual number of individual decorations awarded under combat conditions, when award approval authority is delegated to field commanders, cannot be stated with absolute certainty. Numbers here reflect the current statistics recorded by the Military Awards Branch, as of Apr. 30, 2015, except for MOH, which is as reported by the Congressional Medal of Honor Society as of Aug. 25, 2015. (1) Operation Enduring Freedom (primarily Afghanistan). (2) Operation Iraqi Freedom and Operation New Dawn. (3) Includes awards for valor/heroism and for meritorious service or achievement.

Federal Service Academies

U.S. Military Academy, West Point, NY. Founded 1802. Awards BS degree and Army commission for a 5-year service obligation. **Website:** www.usma.edu

U.S. Naval Academy, Annapolis, MD. Founded 1845. Awards BS degree and Navy or Marine Corps commission for a 5-year service obligation. **Website:** www.usna.edu

U.S. Air Force Academy, Colorado Springs, CO. Founded 1954. Awards BS degree and Air Force commission for a 6-year service obligation. **Website:** www.usafa.edu

U.S. Coast Guard Academy, New London, CT. Founded 1876. Awards BS degree and Coast Guard commission for a 5-year service obligation. **Website:** www.cga.edu

U.S. Merchant Marine Academy, Kings Point, NY. Founded 1943. Awards BS degree; a license as a deck, engineer, or dual officer; and a U.S. Naval Reserve commission. Service obligations vary according to options taken by the graduate. **Website:** www.usmma.edu

U.S. Army, Navy, Air Force, Marine Corps, and Coast Guard Insignia

Source: Dept. of the Army, Dept. of the Navy, Dept. of the Air Force, U.S. Dept. of Defense; U.S. Coast Guard, U.S. Dept. of Homeland Security

Army

General of the Armies—Gen. John J. Pershing (1860-1948), the only person to have held this rank while living, was authorized to prescribe his own insignia but never wore in excess of four stars. Congress established the rank in 1799 to be bestowed on George Washington; Washington was finally promoted to the rank by joint resolution of Congress, approved by Pres. Gerald Ford, Oct. 19, 1976.

General of the Army—Five silver stars fastened together in a circle and the coat of arms of the U.S. in gold color metal with shield and crest enameled. Reserved for wartime use only.

Rank	Insignia
General of the Army*	Five silver stars
General	Four silver stars
Lieutenant General	Three silver stars
Major General	Two silver stars
Brigadier General	One silver star
Colonel	Silver eagle
Lieutenant Colonel	Silver oak leaf
Major	Gold oak leaf
Captain	Two silver bars
First Lieutenant	One silver bar
Second Lieutenant	One gold bar

Warrant Officers

Grade Five—Silver bar with enamel black line.
Grade Four—Silver bar with 4 enamel black squares.
Grade Three—Silver bar with 3 enamel black squares.
Grade Two—Silver bar with 2 enamel black squares.
Grade One—Silver bar with 1 enamel black square.

Noncommissioned Officers

Sergeant Major of the Army (E-9)—Three chevrons above 3 arcs, with a U.S. coat of arms centered on the chevrons, flanked by 2 stars—1 star on each side of the eagle. Also distinctive red-and-white shield collar insignia.

Command Sergeant Major (E-9)—Three chevrons above 3 arcs with a 5-pointed star with a wreath around the star between the chevrons and arcs.

Sergeant Major (E-9)—Three chevrons above 3 arcs with a 5-pointed star between the chevrons and arcs.

First Sergeant (E-8)—Three chevrons above 3 arcs with a lozenge between the chevrons and arcs.

Master Sergeant (E-8)—Three chevrons above 3 arcs.
Sergeant First Class (E-7)—Three chevrons above 2 arcs.
Staff Sergeant (E-6)—Three chevrons above 1 arc.
Sergeant (E-5)—Three chevrons.
Corporal (E-4)—Two chevrons.

Specialists

Specialist (E-4)—Eagle device only.

Other Enlisted

Private First Class (E-3)—One chevron above 1 arc.
Private (E-2)—One chevron.
Private (E-1)—None.

*Rank reserved for wartime use only.

Air Force

Insignia for Air Force officers are identical to those of the Army. Insignia for enlisted personnel are worn on both sleeves and consist of 1 star and an appropriate number of rockers. Chevrons appear above 5 rockers for the top three noncommissioned officer ranks, as follows (in ascending order): Master Sergeant, 1 chevron; Senior Master Sergeant, 2 chevrons; Chief Master Sergeant, 3 chevrons. The insignia of the Chief Master Sergeant of the Air Force has 3 chevrons and a wreath around the star design. General of the Air Force is reserved for wartime use only.

Navy

The following stripes are worn on the lower sleeves of the Service Dress Blue uniform. They are of gold embroidery.

Rank	Insignia
Fleet Admiral*	1 two inch with 4 one-half inch
Admiral	1 two inch with 3 one-half inch
Vice Admiral	1 two inch with 2 one-half inch
Rear Admiral (upper half)	1 two inch with 1 one-half inch
Rear Admiral (lower half)	1 two inch
Captain	4 one-half inch
Commander	3 one-half inch
Lieutenant Commander	2 one-half inch with 1 one-quarter inch between
Lieutenant	2 one-half inch
Lieutenant (jr. grade)	1 one-half inch with 1 one-quarter inch above
Ensign	1 one-half inch
Warrant Officer W-5	½" stripe under ⅛" bluestrip with 1 break
Warrant Officer W-4	½" stripe with 1 break
Warrant Officer W-3	½" stripe with 2 breaks, 2" apart
Warrant Officer W-2	½" stripe with 3 breaks, 2" apart

Enlisted personnel (noncommissioned petty officers)—Rating badge worn on the upper left sleeve consisting of a spread eagle, appropriate number of chevrons, and centered specialty mark.

*Rank reserved for wartime use only.

Marine Corps

Marine Corps' distinctive cap and collar ornament is the Marine Corps emblem—a combination of the American eagle, a globe, and an anchor. Marine Corps and Army officer insignia are similar. Marine Corps enlisted insignia, although basically similar to the Army's, feature crossed rifles beneath the chevrons. Marine Corps enlisted rank insignia are as follows:

Sergeant Major of the Marine Corps (E-9)—Same as Sergeant Major (below) but with Marine Corps emblem in the center with a 5-pointed star on both sides of the emblem.

Sergeant Major (E-9)—Three chevrons above 4 rockers with a 5-pointed star in the center.

Master Gunnery Sergeant (E-9)—Three chevrons above 4 rockers with a bursting bomb insignia in the center.

First Sergeant (E-8)—Three chevrons above 3 rockers with a diamond in the middle.

Master Sergeant (E-8)—Three chevrons above 3 rockers with crossed rifles in the middle.

Gunnery Sergeant (E-7)—Three chevrons above 2 rockers with crossed rifles in the middle.

Staff Sergeant (E-6)—Three chevrons above 1 rocker with crossed rifles in the middle.

Sergeant (E-5)—Three chevrons above crossed rifles.

Corporal (E-4)—Two chevrons above crossed rifles.

Lance Corporal (E-3)—One chevron above crossed rifles.

Private First Class (E-2)—One chevron.

Private (E-1)—None.

Coast Guard

Coast Guard insignia follow Navy custom, with certain minor changes such as the officer cap insignia. The Coast Guard shield is worn on both sleeves of officers and on the right sleeve of all enlisted personnel.

U.S. Armed Forces Contact Information

Additional information on all the U.S. Armed Forces branches, as well as many other related organizations, can be accessed through the official website of the Dept. of Defense: www.defense.gov.

Army—Office of the Chief of Public Affairs, Media Relations Division—MRD, 1500 Army Pentagon, Washington, DC 20310-1500. **Website:** www.army.mil

Navy—Chief of Information, 1200 Navy Pentagon, Washington, DC 20350-1200. **Website:** www.navy.mil

Air Force—Office of Public Affairs, 1690 Air Force Pentagon, Washington, DC 20330-1690. **Website:** www.af.mil

Marine Corps—Marine Corps Headquarters, Division of Public Affairs, 3000 Marine Corps, Pentagon, Washington, DC 20350-3000. **Website:** www.usmc.mil

Coast Guard—Commandant (CG-09222), Attn: Chief of Media Relations, U.S. Coast Guard, 2100 2nd St. SW, Stop 7362, Washington, DC 20593-7362. **Website:** www.uscg.mil

Casualties in Principal Wars of the U.S.

Source: U.S. Dept. of Defense; U.S. Coast Guard, U.S. Dept. of Homeland Security

Data prior to World War I are based on incomplete records in many cases. Casualty data are confined to dead and wounded personnel and, therefore, exclude personnel captured or missing in action who were subsequently returned to military control.

	Branch of service	Number serving	CASUALTIES Battle deaths	Other deaths	Wounds not mortal[1]	Total[2]
Revolutionary War	**Total**	—	**4,435**	—	**6,188**	**10,623**
1775-83	Army	184,000	4,044	—	6,004	10,048
	Navy	to	342	—	114	456
	Marines	250,000[13]	49	—	70	119
War of 1812	**Total**	**286,730[14]**	**2,260**	—	**4,505**	**6,765**
1812-15	Army	—	1,950	—	4,000	5,950
	Navy	—	265	—	439	704
	Marines	—	45	—	66	111
Mexican War	**Total**	**78,718[14]**	**1,733**	**11,550**	**4,152**	**17,435**
1846-48	Army	—	1,721	11,550	4,102	17,373
	Navy	—	1	—	3	4
	Marines	—	11	—	47	58
	Coast Guard[8]	71 off.	—	—	—	—
Civil War						
1861-65						
Union forces[3]	**Total**	**2,213,363**	**140,414**	**224,097**	**281,881**	**646,392**
	Army	2,128,948[14]	138,154	221,374	280,040	639,568
	Navy	84,415	2,112	2,411	1,710	6,233
	Marines	(in Navy total)	148	312	131	591
	Coast Guard[8]	219 off.	1	—	—	1
Confederate forces (estimate)[3]	**Total**	—	**74,524**	**59,297**	—	**133,821**
	Army	600,000	—	—	—	—
	Navy	to	—	—	—	—
	Marines	1,500,000	—	—	—	—
Spanish-American War	**Total**	**306,760**	**385**	**2,061**	**1,662**	**4,108**
1898	Army[9]	280,564	369	2,061	1,594	4,024
	Navy	22,875	10	—	47	57
	Marines	3,321	6	—	21	27
	Coast Guard[8]	660	0	—	—	—
World War I	**Total**	**4,734,991**	**53,402**	**63,114**	**204,002**	**320,518**
Apr. 6, 1917-Nov. 11, 1918	Army[10]	4,057,101	50,510	55,868	193,663	300,041
	Navy	599,051	431	6,856	819	8,106
	Marines	78,839	2,461	390	9,520	12,371
	Coast Guard	8,835	111	81	—	192
World War II[4]	**Total**	**16,112,566**	**291,557**	**113,842**	**670,846**	**1,076,245**
Dec. 7, 1941-Dec. 31, 1946	Army[11]	11,260,000	234,874	83,400	565,861	884,135
	Navy[12]	4,183,466	36,950	25,664	37,778	100,392
	Marines	669,100	19,733	4,778	67,207	91,718
	Coast Guard	241,093	574	1,343	—	1,917
Korean War[5]	**Total**	**5,720,000**	**33,739**	**2,835**	**103,284**	**139,858**
June 25, 1950-July 27, 1953	Army	2,834,000	27,731	2,125	77,596	107,452
	Navy	1,177,000	503	154	1,576	2,233
	Marines	424,000	4,267	242	23,744	28,253
	Air Force	1,285,000	1,238	314	368	1,920
	Coast Guard	44,143	—	—	—	—
Vietnam War[6]	**Total**	**8,744,000**	**47,434**	**10,786**	**153,303**	**211,523**
Aug. 4, 1964-Jan. 27, 1973	Army	4,368,000	30,963	7,261	96,802	135,026
	Navy	1,842,000	1,631	935	4,178	6,744
	Marines	794,000	13,095	1,749	51,392	66,236
	Air Force	1,740,000	1,745	841	931	3,517
	Coast Guard	8,000	7	2	60	69
Persian Gulf War	**Total**	**2,225,000**	**148**	**235**	**467**	**850**
1991	Army	782,000	98	126	354	578
	Navy	669,000	6	50	12	68
	Marines	213,000	24	44	92	160
	Air Force	561,000	20	15	9	44
	Coast Guard	400	—	—	—	—
Iraq War[7]	**Total**	**269,363[15]**	**3,519**	**958**	**32,246**	**36,724**
Mar. 19, 2003-Dec. 15, 2011	Army	99,664[15]	2,574	719	22,522	25,815
	Navy	61,018[15]	64	41	646	751
	Marines	66,166[15]	852	171	8,626	9,649
	Air Force	42,515[15]	29	27	452	508
	Coast Guard	1,250[15]	1	—	1	2

— = Not available. Off. = Officers. **Note:** As of Sept. 2015, there were 1,843 battle deaths, 508 non-hostile deaths, and 20,071 wounded in Op. Enduring Freedom (Oct. 7, 2001-Dec. 28, 2014), mostly in Afghanistan and the Persian Gulf area. (1) Marine Corps data for Iraq War, World War II, the Spanish-American War, and prior wars represent the number of individuals wounded, whereas all other data in this column represent the total number (incidence) of wounds. (2) Totals for all branches do not include categories for which no data are listed. (3) From the final report of the Provost Marshal General, 1863-66. Authoritative statistics for the Confederate forces are not available. In addition, an estimated 26,000-31,000 Confederate personnel died in Union prisons. New estimates published in *Civil War History* in 2012 recalculated the death toll for both sides and determined that it was 20% higher than previously thought, at 750,000. (4) Data are for Dec. 1, 1941, through Dec. 31, 1946, when hostilities were officially terminated by presidential proclamation; few battle deaths or wounds not mortal were incurred after Japanese acceptance of Allied peace terms on Aug. 14, 1945. Numbers serving Dec. 1, 1941-Aug. 31, 1945: Total—14,903,213; Army—10,420,000; Navy—3,883,520; Marine Corps—599,693. (5) As a result of an ongoing Dept. of Defense review of available Korean War casualty record information, updates have been made to previously reported figures for battle deaths and other deaths. (6) Number serving Aug. 5, 1964-Jan. 27, 1973 (date of cease-fire). Includes casualties incurred in Mayaguez incident. Wounds not mortal exclude 150,341 persons not requiring hospital care. (7) Military deaths during the invasion phase, which ended Apr. 30, 2003, totaled 115 combat-related and 23 other. (8) Then known as the U.S. Revenue Cutter Services, predecessor to the U.S. Coast Guard. (9) Number serving Apr. 21-Aug. 13, 1898, while dead and wounded data are for May 1-Aug. 31, 1898. Active hostilities ceased on Aug. 13, 1898, but the U.S. and Spain did not exchange ratifications of the treaty of peace until Apr. 11, 1899. (10) Includes Army Air Forces battle deaths and wounds not mortal, as well as casualties suffered by American forces in northern Russia to Aug. 25, 1919, and in Siberia to Apr. 1, 1920. Other deaths cover Apr. 1, 1917-Dec. 31, 1918. (11) Includes Army Air Forces. (12) Battle deaths and wounds not mortal include casualties incurred in Oct. 1941 due to hostile action. (13) Estimated. (14) As reported by Commissioner of Pensions in his Annual Report for Fiscal Year 1903. (15) Number serving as of Mar. 31, 2003, i.e., does not include numbers of troops deployed since then.

Timeline of Major Wars Since 1066

Norman Conquest 1066-71	William I, duke of Normandy, landed on the English coast near Hastings on Sept. 28, 1066, and defeated Harold II, Saxon king of England, at Battle of Hastings Oct. 14. William crowned king Dec. 25 in Westminster Abbey. Most revolts were suppressed by 1071. **Conquest linked England's interests with those of the continent and led to its rise as a powerful monarchy.**
Crusades 1095-1270/1291	Military expeditions undertaken by **Western European Christians**, usually at the behest of the **papacy**, to recover **Jerusalem** and other Biblical places of pilgrimage from **Muslim** control. In the long term, stimulated trade and flow of ideas between East and West. Pope Urban II called Nov. 27, 1095, for the **First Crusade**; Crusaders took Jerusalem on July 15, 1099, massacred inhabitants, and founded four temporary states: Antioch, Edessa, Jerusalem, and Tripoli. The failed **Second Crusade** was prompted by Muslims' capture of Edessa in 1144. Jerusalem was captured by Ayyubid sultan Saladin on Oct. 2, 1187, leading to the **Third Crusade**, which involved the Holy Roman emperor, Frederick I (Barbarossa); the French king, Philip II (Augustus); and the English king, Richard I (Lion-Heart) but did not lead to a Crusader victory. The **Fourth Crusade** sacked Constantinople on Apr. 13, 1204. The **Fifth Crusade** began with capture of Damietta in Egypt (1219) but failed at Cairo. A **Sixth Crusade** led to the Treaty of Jaffa in 1229, giving Jerusalem to the Crusaders until 1244, when its seizure by the Khwarezmians led to the launch of a **Seventh Crusade**. The last crusade abruptly ended when its leader, French King Louis IX, died in 1270. The last major Crusader stronghold, Acre, was lost on May 18, 1291.
Hundred Years War 1337-1453	Series of armed conflicts over rival claims to the French throne, broken by a number of truces and peace treaties. Edward III declared self king of France in 1338 and invaded, with victories at Crécy (1346) and Poitiers (1356). **Treaty of Brétigny** signed May 8, 1360, but French king Charles V renewed fighting in 1369. Truce from 1396 until **Henry V** of England invaded in 1415 and **defeated French army at Agincourt**, capturing land north of Loire River, including Paris. **Treaty of Troyes** in 1420 made Henry VI heir of both thrones. The siege of French stronghold Orléans, lifted in 1429 with help from **Joan of Arc**, turned tide in favor of French, who won last battle (1453). **War ended English claims to France, paved way for French absolute monarchy.**
Wars of the Roses 1455-85	Series of dynastic civil wars for the throne in England fought by the **rival houses of Lancaster and York**. Richard, third duke of York, in conflict with the Lancastrian King **Henry VI**, won victories at St. Albans (1455) and Northampton (1460); Richard died at battle of Wakefield on Dec. 30, 1460, before coronation, leaving his son to become King Edward IV. Henry VI imprisoned in Tower of London, 1465. Edward died in 1483; his brother became **Richard III** after usurping throne from Edward V, nephew. Henry Tudor defeated Richard III at the Battle of Bosworth Field (1485). As Henry VII, he married Edward IV's daughter Elizabeth, 1486, **uniting the houses**.
Thirty Years' War 1618-48	A series of religious and political conflicts involving **most countries of Western Europe**; majority of fighting in Germany, devastating it. Protestants stormed Hapsburg palace in the "Defenestration of Prague" (May 23, 1618). Major conflicts included defeat of King Christian IV of Denmark and Norway by Catholic League (1626); victories by Lutheran King Gustav II Adolph of Sweden at Breitenfeld (1631) and Lützen (1632). France, under cardinal and statesman **Richelieu**, chief minister of King Louis XIII, declared war on the Hapsburgs in May 1635; defeated Austro-Bavarian army (Aug. 3, 1645), leading to Truce of Ulm. **Peace of Westphalia** signed at Münster on Oct. 24, 1648, bringing peace by recognizing the rulers' sovereignty within their lands and their right to determine the religious beliefs of their subjects.
English Civil Wars 1638-60	Series of conflicts between followers of King Charles (Cavaliers) and of Parliament (Roundheads), over divine right of king versus Parliament's right to control national finances. Presbyterian Scots, allied with Parliament, rioted and in 1640 occupied the northern counties of England. **Oliver Cromwell**, second in command of Parliament's New Model Army, destroyed the king's army at Battle of Naseby (June 14, 1645); first civil war ended May 1646 when Charles surrendered to the Scots. Charles later allied with Scots but was defeated by Cromwell at Preston Aug. 17-19, 1648, and executed Jan. 30, 1649. Parliament abolished monarchy and House of Lords. Cromwell suppressed Irish and Scottish rebellions, was briefly succeeded by son Richard after death (1658). **Charles II restored to the throne** by the "Long Parliament," May 1660.
War of the Spanish Succession 1701-14	War fought by the Grand Alliance (originally England, Netherlands, Denmark, and Austria; later also Portugal), against coalition of France, Spain, and a number of small Italian and German principalities to preserve balance of power after death of Spanish king Charles II. Opened with invasion of Italy, via Venice, by an Austrian army under Prince Eugène of Savoy in May 1701. French forced to withdraw from Netherlands and Italy in 1706 and were finally defeated in 1709 in bloodiest battle of the war at French village of Malplaquet. Treaty of Rastatt and Baden signed in 1714; **Austria given control of Spanish Netherlands, and peace settled between Austria and France.**
War of the Austrian Succession 1740-48	Conflict over rival claims for the **hereditary dominions of the Habsburg family**, following death (1740) of Charles VI, Holy Roman emperor and archduke of Austria. An alliance of Bavaria, France, Spain, Sardinia, Prussia, and Saxony fought against Austria, allied with Holland and Great Britain. King Frederick the Great of Prussia captured Silesia from Austria in the First (1740-42) and Second (1744-45) Silesian Wars. British king George II defeated French army at Battle of Dettingen am Main (June 27, 1743). French conquered Austrian Netherlands (1745-46). Treaty of Aix-la-Chapelle Oct. 18, 1748, **restored most original borders; Prussia became significant force.**
Seven Years' War 1756-63	Worldwide conflicts fought for **control of Germany** and for **supremacy in colonial N America and India**. French defeated British Gen. Edward Braddock in Battle of Monongahela in 1754, leading to formal declaration of **French-Indian War**, May 1756. Frederick II of Prussia invaded Saxony on Aug. 29, 1756; defeated French at Rossbach (1757), Austrians at Leuthen (1757), Russians at Zorndorf (1758). By 1760, British conquered French Canada. Peter III of Russia signed armistice with Prussia, 1762. Treaty of Paris signed Feb. 10, 1763; Peace of Hubertusburg Feb. 15, 1763, between Prussia and Austria. **England emerged as leading world naval power.**
American Revolution 1775-83	Conflict between Great Britain and 13 British colonies in eastern N America. George Washington took command of the Continental Army, July 2, 1775, and King George III declared colonies traitors on Aug. 23. **Declaration of Independence of colonies adopted July 4, 1776.** France recognized the colonies' independence Feb. 6, 1778, followed by Spain on June 21, 1779; both pledged support. French fleet drove British fleet under Adm. Thomas Graves from Chesapeake Bay on Sept. 5, 1781. French and Americans laid siege to Yorktown, VA, Sept. 28-Oct. 19, forcing British Gen. Cornwallis to surrender. **Treaty of Paris** (Sept. 3, 1783) recognized U.S. independence.
Wars of French Revolution and Napoleonic Wars 1792-1815	Large-scale wars fought between France and two multinational coalitions. France declared war on the Austrian part of the Holy Roman Empire, Apr. 20, 1792. Newly created French Republic declared war on monarchs of Britain and Holland, Feb. 1, 1793, and of Spain, Mar. 7. **Napoleon Bonaparte** defeated Austria in N Italy (1796-97), captured Egypt from Britain (1798-99; Battle of the Pyramids, July 21, 1798), and became First Consul after coup d'état of Nov. 9-10, 1799. French Grande Armée later swept through Europe using innovative and aggressive tactics. French navy defeated by British under Adm. Horatio Nelson at **Trafalgar** (Oct. 21, 1805), but Napoleon defeated Austro-Russian forces at Austerlitz (Dec. 2) and controlled most of Europe except Russia and Great Britain by 1808. France suffered its first major defeat by Austria at Aspern-Essling, May 21-22, 1809. **Napoleon invaded Russia**, captured Moscow Sept. 14, 1812, but fled the bitter Russian winter and abandoned Germany after defeat at Leipzig, Oct. 16-19, 1813. Paris captured by Allied armies Mar. 30-31, 1814. Napoleon exiled to Elba May 4 but returned for "Hundred Days" reign, Mar. 20-June 28, 1815; **final defeat at Waterloo** by British and Prussian troops (June 18). The **Bourbon monarchy was restored under Louis XVIII**, and Britain, Prussia, Russia, and Austria maintained European peace.

Crimean War 1853-56	Conflict between **Russia** and coalition of **Great Britain, France, Sardinia, and Turkey for influence over Balkans** and the straits between the Black Sea and Mediterranean. Russia destroyed Turkish fleet at Sinope on Nov. 30, 1853. Britain and France declared war in Mar. 1854 and with Turkish troops defeated Russians at Battle of Alma River, Sept. 20. Lord Lucan of Britain prevented Russia from capturing Balaklava on Oct. 25 ("Charge of the Light Brigade" led by Lord Cardigan). Siege of Sevastopol ended when Russia evacuated Sept. 8, 1855. Treaty of Paris signed Mar. 30, 1856; **curbed Russian expansion and loosened European power alignments**.
American Civil War 1861-65	Conflict between the U.S. (the Union) and 11 secessionist Southern states, organized as the Confederate States of America. Union garrison at Fort Sumter in harbor of Charleston, SC, surrendered to Brig. Gen. Pierre Beauregard (Apr. 12-13, 1861). 22,000 Confederates under Beauregard repelled 35,000 Union troops under Gen. Irvin McDowell along Bull Run stream near Manassas, VA (July 21). The *Merrimack* (renamed the *Virginia*) battled the *Monitor* Mar. 9, 1862. In **Battle of Antietam** (Sept. 17), some 12,000 Northerners and 12,700 Southerners were killed or wounded. Pres. Abraham Lincoln announced **Emancipation Proclamation** on Sept. 22. Confederate Gen. Robert E. Lee's forces numbering 75,000 battled 88,000 Union troops under Gen. George Meade at **Gettysburg** July 1-3, 1863; Lee's army forced back across the Potomac River. Lee surrendered to Ulysses S. Grant at **Appomattox Court House** (Apr. 9, 1865). **The Union was preserved and slavery abolished.**
Franco-Prussian War 1870-71	German states led by Prussia defeated France, seizing Alsace and part of Lorraine. French defeated in several major battles, culminating at **Sedan** Sept. 1, 1870, when Prussian forces decisively defeated the French army and captured emperor Napoleon III. Prussian king crowned William I, emperor of unified Germany, Jan 18, 1871. **France surrendered** Jan. 28. Final treaty signed May 10; set the stage for later **German imperialistic expansion**.
Spanish-American War 1898	War waged by the U.S. to **liberate Cuba from Spanish rule**. A mysterious explosion, blamed on Spain by American newspapers, sank the U.S. battleship *Maine* in Havana's harbor (Feb. 15, 1898), killing 260. The U.S. called for Spain's withdrawal from Cuba, and Spain declared war (Apr. 24). Rufus Shafter led 17,000 U.S. troops from Daiquirí to Santiago de Cuba, taking **San Juan Hill** with help of the Rough Riders under Teddy Roosevelt. Santiago de Cuba surrendered July 17. The Treaty of Paris (Dec. 10, 1898) provided for the **independence of Cuba** and the cession by Spain to the U.S. of **Puerto Rico, Guam, and for a $20 mil payment, the Philippine Islands**.
World War I 1914-18	Local European war that grew into a global war involving 32 nations: the Allies and the Associated Powers—28 nations including Great Britain, France, Russia, Italy, and the U.S.—versus the Central Powers of Germany, Austria-Hungary, Turkey, and Bulgaria. Archduke Francis Ferdinand of Austria assassinated in Sarajevo, Bosnia (June 28, 1914). Germany invaded France through Belgium; advance on Paris halted by the French under Gen. Joseph Jacques Césaire Joffre at the **First Battle of the Marne**, Sept. 5-12. Germany checked the Russian army at the Battle of Tannenberg, Aug. 26-30. The British suffered 57,470 casualties (19,240 dead) in the opening day of the **First Battle of the Somme** (July 1-Nov. 18, 1916), first of 12 battles that forced Germany back to Hindenburg Line. **U.S. declared war on Germany Apr. 6, 1917.** Russian involvement ended when Bolshevik party seized power on Nov. 7; signed armistice Dec. 15. German offensive halted by U.S. and French troops at **Second Battle of the Marne** (July 15-Aug. 5, 1918), turning point of the war. Allied counteroffensive broke the Hindenburg Line, and an armistice was signed Nov. 11.
World War II 1939-45	Global military conflict stemming from European unrest after World War I and Japan's aggressive expansion into Asia and the Pacific. **War in Europe:** Nazi-Soviet nonaggression pact (Aug. 23, 1939) freed Germany and the Soviet Union to attack Poland in Sept. **Britain and France declared war on Germany** Sept. 3. German forces raced through Europe (Apr.-June 1940), captured Paris June 14. **Italy declared war on France and Britain** June 10. German-Italian campaigns won the Balkans and N Africa by June 1941. U.S. entered war Dec. 1941. Three million Axis troops invaded Russia June 22, 1941, but Russian counterthrusts stopped the German advance (**Stalingrad**, Aug. 20, 1942-Feb. 2, 1943), and Allies took N Africa (Nov. 8, 1942-May 13, 1943), Italy (July 10, 1943-May 2, 1945). Normandy invaded on **D-Day**, June 6, 1944; Paris liberated Aug. 25. Leaders at Yalta Conference (Feb. 4-11, 1945) discussed defeat and division of Germany into four. Adolf Hitler committed suicide Apr. 30. **Germany surrendered unconditionally** May 7. **War in the Pacific:** Japan invaded China (July 7, 1937), joined alliance with Germany and Italy (Sept. 27, 1940), and signed nonaggression pact with Russia (Apr. 13, 1941); attacked Hawaii's Pearl Harbor, Dec. 7, 1941; U.S. declared war on Japan Dec. 8. **Battle of Midway** (June 4-7, 1942) repulsed Japanese advance. Marines landed on Guadalcanal Aug. 7. Navy defeated Japanese fleet at **Leyte Gulf**, Oct. 23-26, 1944. B-29 bombing raids on Japan began in Nov. Marines invaded Iwo Jima (Feb. 19-Mar. 16, 1945) with heavy casualties, then Okinawa (Apr. 1-June 21). **U.S. atom bombs dropped** on Hiroshima (Aug. 6) and Nagasaki (Aug. 9) and Soviet invasion of Manchuria (Aug. 8) **forced Japan to agree, on Aug. 14, to surrender**; formal surrender on Sept. 2.
Korean War 1950-53	Military struggle fought on the Korean Peninsula between the Democratic Peoples' Republic of Korea (N Korea) and the Republic of Korea (S Korea) that developed into an international war involving China allied with N Korea against the U.S. and other nations under the UN flag. DPRK army crossed the 38th parallel and invaded S Korea (June 25, 1950), entering Seoul (June 26). Amphibious assault launched at **Inchon** by Gen. Douglas MacArthur (Sept. 15) helped U.S. forces rout DPRK close to Yalu River by Nov. 24. Chinese counterattack retook Seoul (Jan. 4, 1951) but were forced back to the 38th parallel by Apr. 22. Armistice was signed (July 27, 1953) by the UN, DPRK, and China, but not ROK, **leaving the peninsula partitioned at about the 38th parallel**.
Vietnam War 1959-75	Struggle primarily in S Vietnam that widened into a war between S Vietnam supported mainly by the U.S. and N Vietnam supported by the USSR and China. Viet Minh, led by Communist leader Ho Chi Minh, formed the Democratic Republic of Vietnam (Sept. 2, 1945). Colonial power France withdrew after fortress at Dien Bien Phu fell (May 8, 1954). Pres. John F. Kennedy pledged U.S. commitment to S Vietnamese independence Dec. 14, 1961. USS *Maddox* destroyer damaged in **Gulf of Tonkin** (Aug. 2, 1964), prompting Congress to increase involvement. Regular bombing of N Vietnam began (Feb. 24, 1965), and the first U.S. combat ground forces arrived (Mar. 6). N Vietnamese Army siege of **Khe Sanh** (Jan. 21-Apr. 7, 1968) and the **"Tet" offensive** (Jan. 30) aimed to cause insurrection in the S. **My Lai Massacre** by U.S. soldiers of civilians (Mar. 16, 1968) created scandal, fueled U.S. disaffection with war. U.S. forces peaked at 543,400 in Apr. 1969. NVA **"Easter Offensive"** (Mar. 30, 1972) rebuffed, and U.S. responded with aerial bombings in May and Dec. U.S. withdrew after ceasefire, Jan. 1973. **NVA offensive captured Saigon, Apr. 30, 1975, and unified Vietnam under Communist rule.**
Persian Gulf Wars 1991, 2003-10	Conflicts fought principally between Iraq and the U.S. concerning Iraq's influence in the Middle East and its development of weapons of mass destruction. **First Gulf War:** Iraq under dictator Saddam Hussein invaded Kuwait Aug 2, 1990, and annexed it; UN Security Council ordered Iraqi forces to withdraw by Jan. 15, 1991. Beginning Jan. 17, a U.S.-led multinational force (**Operation Desert Storm**) bombed military targets in Iraq and Kuwait. A coordinated air-land offensive (**Operation Desert Sabre**, begun Feb. 24) retook Kuwait City Feb. 26, and permanent cease-fire was signed on Apr. 6. Iraq was ordered to pay reparations to Kuwait, reveal locations of biological and chemical weapons, and eliminate weapons of mass destruction. **Second Gulf War:** The U.S. and UK mistakenly asserted that Iraq was still producing WMDs and posed an imminent threat. The UN passed Resolution 1441, Nov. 8, 2002, warning Iraq of "serious consequences" if it failed to cooperate fully and unconditionally with UN weapons inspectors. Iraq rejected a Mar. 17, 2003, U.S. ultimatum demanding Hussein and his sons leave Iraq. U.S. launched **Operation Iraqi Freedom** Mar. 19, 2003, with support from UK and other allies, but without full UN Security Council support. Baghdad fell Apr. 9, and major combat operations declared over May 1. Hussein was captured Dec. 13, 2003, but guerrilla opposition to U.S. troops and insurgent violence continued. U.S. combat operations in Iraq formally ended Aug. 31, 2010.

HEALTH

U.S. Health Expenditures, 1960-2013

Source: *Health, United States, 2014*, National Center for Health Statistics, Centers for Disease Control and Prevention

	1960	1970	1980	1990	2000	2009	2012	2013
				Amount in billions				
National health expenditures	**$27.4**	**$74.9**	**$255.8**	**$724.3**	**$1,378.0**	**$2,505.8**	**$2,817.3**	**$2,919.1**
				Percent distribution				
Health consumption expenditures	**90.6%**	**89.6%**	**92.1%**	**93.3%**	**93.6%**	**94.2%**	**94.2%**	**94.4%**
Personal health care	85.4	84.3	84.9	85.2	84.6	84.5	84.5	84.6
Hospital care	32.8	36.3	39.3	34.6	30.2	31.0	31.9	32.1
Professional services	29.3	26.4	25.3	28.7	28.3	26.8	26.7	26.6
Physician and clinical services	20.6	19.1	18.7	21.9	21.1	20.1	20.1	20.1
Other professional services	1.4	1.0	1.4	2.4	2.7	2.7	2.7	2.7
Dental services	7.3	6.3	5.2	4.4	4.5	4.1	3.9	3.8
Other personal care	1.6	1.8	3.3	3.4	4.7	4.9	5.0	5.1
Home health care[1]	0.2	0.3	0.9	1.7	2.4	2.7	2.7	2.7
Nursing care facilities and retirement communities[1]	3.0	5.4	6.0	6.2	6.2	5.5	5.4	5.3
Retail outlet sales of medical products	18.4	14.1	10.1	10.6	12.9	13.6	12.8	12.7
Prescription drugs	9.8	7.3	4.7	5.6	8.8	10.2	9.4	9.3
Durable medical equipment	2.7	2.3	1.6	1.9	1.8	1.4	1.5	1.5
Nondurable medical products	5.9	4.4	3.8	3.1	2.3	2.0	1.9	1.9
Government administration	0.2	1.0	1.1	1.0	1.2	1.2	1.2	1.3
Net cost of health insurance	3.7	2.5	3.6	4.4	4.7	5.5	5.9	5.9
Government public health activities[2]	1.4	1.8	2.5	2.8	3.1	3.0	2.7	2.6
Investment	**9.4**	**10.4**	**7.9**	**6.7**	**6.4**	**5.8**	**5.8**	**5.6**
Research[3]	2.4	2.6	2.1	1.8	1.8	1.8	1.7	1.6
Structures and equipment	6.8	7.8	5.7	5.0	4.5	4.0	4.1	4.0
			Average annual percent change from previous year shown					
National health expenditures	—	**10.6%**	**13.1%**	**11.0%**	**6.6%**	**6.9%**	**4.0%**	**3.6%**
Health consumption expenditures	—	**10.5**	**13.4**	**11.1**	**6.7**	**6.9**	**4.0**	**3.8**
Personal health care	—	10.4	13.2	11.0	6.6	6.9	4.0	3.8
Hospital care	—	11.7	14.0	9.6	5.2	7.2	5.0	4.3
Professional services	—	9.5	12.6	12.4	6.5	6.2	3.8	3.4
Physician and clinical services	—	9.8	12.8	12.8	6.2	6.2	4.0	3.8
Other professional services	—	6.4	17.0	17.5	7.8	6.8	4.7	4.5
Dental services	—	9.0	11.0	9.0	7.0	5.7	2.4	0.9
Other personal care	—	11.4	20.4	11.1	10.2	7.4	4.6	5.8
Home health care[1]	—	14.5	26.9	18.1	9.9	8.4	4.7	3.4
Nursing care facilities and retirement communities[1]	—	17.4	14.2	11.4	6.6	5.6	3.2	2.4
Retail outlet sales of medical products	—	7.7	9.4	11.4	8.8	7.5	1.8	2.9
Prescription drugs	—	7.5	8.2	12.8	11.6	8.6	1.2	2.5
Durable medical equipment	—	9.0	8.8	13.0	6.2	3.7	5.6	4.2
Nondurable medical products	—	7.4	11.4	8.6	3.5	5.3	2.2	4.0
Government administration	—	29.9	14.1	10.0	9.1	6.4	4.7	8.2
Net cost of health insurance	—	6.4	17.3	13.1	7.3	8.9	6.3	5.0
Government public health activities[2]	—	13.8	16.9	12.0	8.0	6.2	0.3	0.8
Investment	—	**11.7**	**10.0**	**9.2**	**6.1**	**5.8**	**3.8**	**0.5**
Research[3]	—	10.9	10.8	8.9	7.2	6.6	2.1	−2.6
Structures and equipment	—	12.0	9.7	9.4	5.7	5.5	4.6	1.9

— = Not applicable. **Note:** Numbers may not add up to totals because of rounding. (1) In freestanding facilities only. Additional services of this type provided in hospital-based facilities are counted as hospital care. (2) Includes health care services delivered by government public health agencies. (3) Excludes research and development expenditures of drug companies and other mfrs. and providers of medical equipment and supplies. They are included in the expenditure class in which a product falls.

Health Coverage for Persons Under 65, 1984-2013

Source: *Health, United States, 2014*, National Center for Health Statistics, Centers for Disease Control and Prevention

	Private insurance				Medicaid[1]				Not covered[2]			
	1984[3]	2000	2010	2013	1984[3]	2000	2010	2013	1984[3]	2000	2010	2013
					Percent of each population group							
Total	**76.8%**	**71.5%**	**61.7%**	**61.8%**	**6.8%**	**9.5%**	**16.9%**	**18.1%**	**14.5%**	**17.0%**	**18.2%**	**16.7%**
Age												
Under 18 years	72.6	66.6	54.1	53.2	11.9	19.6	36.4	38.9	13.9	12.6	7.8	6.6
18-44 years	76.5	70.5	60.0	61.8	5.1	5.6	10.9	11.6	17.1	22.4	27.1	24.2
45-64 years	83.3	78.7	71.3	69.5	3.4	4.5	6.8	8.4	9.6	12.6	15.7	15.4
Race and Hispanic origin[4]												
White only, non-Hispanic	79.9	75.7	64.9	64.7	4.6	7.1	14.5	15.6	13.6	15.4	17.6	16.3
Black only, non-Hispanic	58.1	55.9	44.8	45.4	20.5	21.2	30.4	31.6	19.9	19.5	20.6	18.9
Hispanic, any race	55.7	47.8	36.8	37.3	13.3	15.5	28.6	29.5	29.5	35.6	32.0	30.7
Percent of poverty level												
Below 100%	32.2	25.2	16.0	15.5	33.0	38.4	50.8	53.7	33.9	34.2	30.3	28.0
100%-199%	70.3	50.1	34.8	35.1	5.3	16.2	28.5	38.8	21.8	31.0	32.4	29.3
200%-399%	89.3	78.1	70.7	71.3	0.8	4.0	8.4	9.0	7.6	15.4	17.4	16.1
400% or more	95.4	91.9	89.9	90.4	0.2	0.9	2.0	1.9	3.2	5.9	5.6	4.8
Geographic region												
Northeast	80.5	76.3	68.2	66.1	8.6	10.6	17.9	20.8	10.2	12.2	12.4	11.2
Midwest	80.6	78.8	66.7	68.0	7.4	8.0	17.3	16.9	11.3	12.3	14.1	13.1
South	74.3	66.8	57.5	57.4	5.1	9.4	16.0	17.8	17.7	20.5	21.9	19.9
West	71.9	66.5	58.9	59.6	7.0	10.4	17.1	18.0	18.2	20.7	20.6	18.9

Note: Data based on household interviews of a sample of the civilian noninstitutionalized population. Percents may not add up to 100 because other types of health insurance (e.g., Medicare, military) are not shown, and persons with both private insurance and Medicaid appear in both sections. (1) Includes Medicaid and other public assistance. (2) Includes persons not covered by private insurance, Medicaid or other public assistance, Medicare, or military plans. (3) A change in the questionnaire in 1997 prevents direct comparison with later years. (4) Changed reporting methods make race data before 1999 not strictly comparable with those from 1999 on.

Spending on Health in the 50 Most Populous Countries, 2012

Source: *World Health Statistics 2015*, World Health Organization

Country	As % of GDP	Per capita[1]	Country	As % of GDP	Per capita[1]	Country	As % of GDP	Per capita[1]	Country	As % of GDP	Per capita[1]
Afghanistan	8.5%	$58	Germany	11.3%	$4,717	Mozambique	5.8%	$33	Sudan	6.7%	$113
Algeria	6.0	319	Ghana	5.2	86	Myanmar (Burma)	1.8	20	Tanzania	7.1	42
Argentina	6.8	994	India	3.8	58	Nepal	5.5	36	Thailand	4.5	247
Australia	8.9	6,097	Indonesia	3.0	108	Nigeria	3.4	93	Turkey	5.4	569
Bangladesh	3.5	26	Iran	6.6	485	Pakistan	2.8	34	Uganda	9.8	57
Brazil	9.5	1,078	Iraq[2]	4.8	282	Peru	5.2	333	Ukraine	7.5	290
Canada	10.9	5,763	Italy	9.2	3,114	Philippines	4.4	115	UK	9.3	3,595
China	5.4	322	Japan	10.3	4,787	Poland	6.8	859	U.S.	17.0	8,845
Colombia	6.8	530	Kenya	4.5	42	Russia	6.5	913	Uzbekistan	6.1	110
Congo, Dem. Rep. of the	3.6	15	Korea, South	7.6	1,724	Saudi Arabia	3.8	992	Venezuela	4.7	592
Egypt	4.9	158	Malaysia	4.0	418	South Africa	8.9	651	Vietnam	6.0	102
Ethiopia	4.9	22	Mexico	6.1	618	Spain	9.3	2,626	Yemen	5.6	76
France	11.6	4,644	Morocco	6.1	181				**World[3]**	**8.6**	**1,025**

(1) At average exchange rate. (2) Not including expenditures for Northern Iraq. (3) Includes other nations not shown.

Population Not Covered by Health Insurance by State, 1990-2014

Source: American Community Survey, U.S. Census Bureau, U.S. Dept. of Commerce
(numbers in thousands)

	1990		2000		2014			1990		2000		2014	
	No. not covered	% pop. not covered	No. not covered	% pop. not covered	No. not covered	% pop. not covered		No. not covered	% pop. not covered	No. not covered	% pop. not covered	No. not covered	% pop. not covered
AL	710	17.4%	557	12.7%	579	12.1%	MT	115	14.0%	146	16.4%	143	14.2%
AK	77	15.4	114	18.3	122	17.2	NE	138	8.5	140	8.3	179	9.7
AZ	547	15.5	834	16.0	903	13.6	NV	201	16.5	336	16.4	427	15.2
AR	421	17.4	367	13.8	343	11.8	NH	107	9.9	99	8.0	120	9.2
CA	5,683	19.1	6,154	18.1	4,767	12.4	NJ	773	10.0	985	11.7	965	10.9
CO	495	14.7	598	13.8	543	10.3	NM	339	22.2	426	23.7	298	14.5
CT	226	6.9	313	9.3	245	6.9	NY	2,176	12.1	3,001	16.0	1,697	8.7
DE	96	13.9	69	8.9	72	7.8	NC	883	13.8	1,046	13.1	1,276	13.1
DC	109	19.2	75	13.6	34	5.3	ND	40	6.3	66	10.7	57	7.9
FL	2,376	18.0	2,727	17.0	3,245	16.6	OH	1,123	10.3	1,191	10.7	955	8.4
GA	971	15.3	1,145	14.1	1,568	15.8	OK	574	18.6	624	18.4	584	15.4
HI	81	7.3	110	9.1	72	5.3	OR	360	12.4	417	12.2	383	9.7
ID	159	15.2	194	15.0	219	13.6	PA	1,218	10.1	963	8.0	1,065	8.5
IL	1,272	10.9	1,632	13.3	1,238	9.7	RI	105	11.1	74	7.1	77	7.4
IN	587	10.7	650	10.8	776	11.9	SC	550	16.2	473	11.9	642	13.6
IA	225	8.1	239	8.4	189	6.2	SD	81	11.6	77	10.5	82	9.8
KS	272	10.8	274	10.3	291	10.2	TN	673	13.7	585	10.4	776	12.0
KY	480	13.2	521	13.0	366	8.5	TX	3,569	21.1	4,650	22.4	5,047	19.1
LA	797	19.7	755	17.3	672	14.8	UT	156	9.0	259	11.5	366	12.5
ME	139	11.2	135	10.6	134	10.1	VT	54	9.5	50	8.3	31	5.0
MD	601	12.7	511	9.7	463	7.9	VA	996	15.7	747	10.7	884	10.9
MA	530	9.1	527	8.4	219	3.3	WA	557	11.4	772	13.2	643	9.2
MI	865	9.4	838	8.5	837	8.5	WV	249	13.8	247	13.9	156	8.6
MN	389	8.9	368	7.5	317	5.9	WI	321	6.7	398	7.5	418	7.3
MS	531	19.9	361	12.9	424	14.5	WY	58	12.5	74	15.3	69	12.0
MO	665	12.7	511	9.3	694	11.7	**U.S.**	**34,719**	**13.9**	**38,426**	**13.7**	**36,670**	**11.7**

Persons Not Covered by Health Insurance by Selected Characteristics, 2014

Source: Annual Social and Economic Supplement, Current Population Survey, U.S. Census Bureau, U.S. Dept. of Commerce
(numbers in thousands)

Race and Hispanic origin	Number not covered	% of pop. specified at left
White	24,083	10.4%
White, not Hispanic	15,686	8.1
Black	5,307	13.6
American Indian or Alaska Native	585	23.1
Asian	1,757	10.6
Native Hawaiian and Other Pacific Islander	74	13.5
Hispanic (any race)	12,801	23.5
Age		
Under 65 years	32,339	12.0
Under 18 years	4,472	6.0
Under 6 years	1,579	6.6
6 to 11 years	1,316	5.3
12 to 17 years	1,577	6.2
18 to 24 years	4,712	15.6
25 to 34 years	7,877	18.3
35 to 44 years	6,163	15.4
45 to 54 years	5,054	11.8
55 to 64 years	4,061	10.0
65 years and older	629	1.4

(1) Persons aged 18 to 64 only.

Nativity	Number not covered	% of pop. specified at left
Native	23,955	8.7%
Foreign-born	9,012	21.4
Naturalized citizen	2,008	10.2
Not a citizen	7,004	31.2
Marital status[1]		
Married	10,462	10.3
Widowed	528	15.6
Divorced	3,453	17.1
Separated	1,205	24.8
Never married	12,256	18.5
Household income		
Less than $25,000	9,147	16.6
$25,000 to $49,999	9,481	14.1
$50,000 to $74,999	5,962	10.7
$75,000 or more	8,378	6.1
Work experience[1]		
Worked during the year	19,473	13.2
Full-time	14,956	12.4
Part-time	4,518	16.8
Did not work	8,394	17.3
Total	**32,968**	**10.4**

Health Insurance Marketplace Plan Enrollment by Selected Characteristics

Source: Office of the Asst. Sec. for Planning and Evaluation, U.S. Dept. of Health and Human Services (cumulative enrollment-related activity for Nov. 15, 2014-Feb. 15, 2015, incl. additional special enrollment period activity through Feb. 22, 2015; as of June 1, 2015)

	Marketplace total		State marketplaces[1]		Federal marketplace[2]	
	Number[3]	Percent	Number[3]	Percent	Number[3]	Percent
Number who have selected a plan	**11,688,074**	**NA**	**2,849,783**	**100.0%**	**8,838,291**	**NA**
By known age	**11,664,361**	**100%**	**2,846,782**	**100.0**	**8,817,579**	**100%**
0 to 34 years of age	4,142,286	36	946,139	33.2	3,196,147	36
18 years of age and younger	890,017	8	163,712	5.8	726,305	8
18 to 25 years of age	1,269,792	11	279,041	9.8	990,751	11
18 to 34 years of age	3,252,269	28	782,427	27.5	2,469,842	28
26 to 34 years of age	1,982,477	17	503,386	17.7	1,479,091	17
35 to 44 years of age	1,940,164	17	465,650	16.4	1,474,514	17
45 to 54 years of age	2,559,338	22	647,288	22.7	1,912,050	22
55 to 64 years of age	2,947,749	25	765,369	26.9	2,182,380	25
65 years of age and older	74,824	1	22,336	0.8	52,488	1
Age unknown	3,001	NA	3,001	NA	NA	NA
By known financial assistance status[4]	**11,623,965**	**100**	**2,785,674**	**100.0**	**8,838,291**	**100**
With financial assistance	9,941,820	86	2,250,909	80.8	7,690,911	87
Without financial assistance	1,682,145	14	534,765	19.2	1,147,380	13
Financial assistance status unknown	0	NA	64,109	NA	NA	NA

NA = Not applicable. **Note:** Numbers and percentages may not add up to totals due to rounding. (1) For states implementing their own marketplaces, known as state-based marketplaces. Not all states reported data by selected characteristics. (2) For states with marketplaces supported or fully run by the Dept. of Health and Human Services, or the federally facilitated marketplace. (3) Includes individuals whether or not a first premium payment has been made. (4) Advance premium tax credit with or without cost-sharing reduction.

Federal Health Insurance Marketplace Average Monthly Premiums, 2015

Source: Office of the Asst. Sec. for Planning and Evaluation, U.S. Dept. of Health and Human Services

(based on enrollment-related activity for Nov. 15, 2014-Feb. 15, 2015, incl. additional special enrollment period activity through Feb. 22, 2015; as of June 1, 2015)

In states with health insurance marketplaces supported or fully run by the federal government, 87% of those who selected a plan chose one with tax credits based on projected income. Comparable data for states that implemented their own marketplaces are not available.

State	Avg. premium after tax credits	Avg. % reduction in premium after tax credits	Avg. premium before tax credits	Avg. tax credit
Alabama	$88	75%	$354	$266
Alaska	105	84	639	534
Arizona	123	56	278	155
Arkansas	109	72	389	280
Delaware	140	65	404	264
Florida	82	78	376	294
Georgia	73	79	346	273
Illinois	128	62	336	208
Indiana	120	73	438	319
Iowa	111	70	371	260
Kansas	90	70	301	211
Louisiana	97	77	416	319
Maine	93	78	425	332
Michigan	130	64	366	236
Mississippi	52	87	405	353
Missouri	82	77	363	281
Montana	116	66	346	230
Nebraska	104	70	354	250
New Hampshire	$141	63%	$385	$244
New Jersey	164	65	470	306
North Carolina	95	77	410	315
North Dakota	141	62	369	228
Ohio	145	63	389	244
Oklahoma	89	70	295	206
Pennsylvania	129	64	355	226
South Carolina	86	76	365	278
South Dakota	130	64	358	228
Tennessee	102	68	316	213
Texas	89	73	328	239
Utah	89	64	248	159
Virginia	89	74	348	259
West Virginia	137	69	448	311
Wisconsin	125	72	440	315
Wyoming	130	76	550	420
Federal total	**101**	**72**	**364**	**263**

Health Care Visits by Selected Characteristics, 1997-2013

Source: National Health Interview Survey; *Health, United States*; National Center for Health Statistics; Centers for Disease Control and Prevention; U.S. Dept. of Health and Human Services

Characteristic	Zero visits 1997	2010	2013	1-3 visits 1997	2010	2013	4-9 visits 1997	2010	2013	10 or more visits 1997	2010	2013
	Percent distribution											
All persons	**16.5%**	**15.6%**	**16.1%**	**46.2%**	**45.4%**	**47.6%**	**23.6%**	**25.8%**	**24.0%**	**13.7%**	**13.2%**	**12.3%**
Age												
Under 6 years	5.0	3.7	4.7	44.9	48.9	49.6	37.0	36.8	37.1	13.0	10.6	8.6
6-17 years	15.3	10.4	9.9	58.7	59.1	64.5	19.3	23.6	19.3	6.8	6.9	6.3
18-44 years	21.7	24.2	24.8	46.7	43.9	45.9	19.0	20.6	18.5	12.6	11.3	10.7
45-64 years	16.9	14.8	15.2	42.9	42.8	43.0	24.7	26.1	26.7	15.5	16.4	15.0
65-74 years	9.8	6.3	7.8	36.9	36.1	37.4	31.6	35.7	33.7	21.6	21.9	21.0
75 years and over	7.7	4.1	4.5	31.8	31.0	33.7	33.8	38.0	35.4	26.6	27.0	26.3
Sex												
Male	21.3	20.4	21.0	47.1	46.4	47.7	20.6	22.7	21.2	11.0	10.5	10.1
Female	11.8	10.9	11.4	45.4	44.4	47.5	26.5	28.8	26.7	16.3	15.9	14.4
Race and Hispanic origin												
White, not Hispanic	16.0	15.3	16.1	46.1	44.9	47.3	23.9	26.1	24.0	14.0	13.7	12.7
Black, not Hispanic	16.8	15.7	15.2	46.1	47.2	47.6	23.2	24.7	25.7	13.9	12.4	11.5
Hispanic[1]	24.9	23.5	24.0	42.3	43.2	45.8	20.3	22.6	20.5	12.5	10.7	9.7
Health insurance status[2]												
Insured continuously	14.1	12.1	12.6	49.2	48.6	51.5	23.6	26.2	24.2	13.0	13.0	11.7
Uninsured for any period	18.9	18.5	20.0	46.0	47.8	46.4	20.8	22.0	21.9	14.4	11.6	11.7
Uninsured	39.0	43.8	45.1	41.4	39.7	39.9	13.2	12.6	11.1	6.4	3.9	3.8

Note: Totals include persons of races not shown separately and of unknown health insurance status. (1) Persons of Hispanic origin may be of any race. (2) In 12 months prior to interview, for persons under age 65 only.

Reasons Given by Patients for Outpatient Visits, 2011

Source: National Hospital Ambulatory Medical Care Survey, National Center for Health Statistics, Centers for Disease Control and Prevention, U.S. Dept. of Health and Human Services

Rank	Reason	Number of visits (thous.)	% of all visits
1.	Progress visit, not otherwise specified	16,695	13.3%
2.	General medical examination	7,736	6.2
3.	Postoperative visit	3,337	2.7
4.	Medication, other and unspecified kinds	2,711	2.2
5.	Counseling, not otherwise specified	2,698	2.1
6.	Cough	2,631	2.1
7.	Prenatal examination, routine	2,398	1.9
8.	Diabetes mellitus	2,339	1.9
9.	Symptoms referable to throat	2,106	1.7
10.	Well-baby examination	1,915	1.5
11.	Preoperative visit for surgery	1,689	1.3%
12.	Earache or ear infection	1,658	1.3
13.	Stomach pain, cramps, and spasms	1,559	1.2
14.	Fever	1,532	1.2
15.	Psychotherapy	1,525*	1.2*
16.	Knee symptoms	1,508	1.2
17.	Gynecological examination	1,489	1.2
18.	Skin rash	1,381	1.1
19.	Hypertension	1,369	1.1
20.	Back symptoms	1,332	1.1
All other reasons		**66,115**	**52.6**
All visits		**125,721**	**100.0**

* = Figure does not meet standards of reliability or precision. **Note:** Numbers may not add to totals due to rounding.

Emergency Room Visits by Diagnosis, 2011

Source: National Hospital Ambulatory Medical Care Survey, National Center for Health Statistics, Centers for Disease Control and Prevention, U.S. Dept. of Health and Human Services

Rank	Principal diagnosis group	Number of visits (thous.)	% of all visits
1.	Heart disease, excluding ischemic	969	6.0%
2.	Chest pain	937	5.8
3.	Pneumonia	701	4.3
4.	Psychoses, excluding major depressive disorder	459	2.8
5.	Cerebrovascular disease	452	2.8
6.	Ischemic heart disease	403	2.5
7.	Fracture of the lower limb	389	2.4
8.	Syncope and collapse	312	1.9
9.	Cellulitis and abscess	310	1.9
10.	Diabetes mellitus	301	1.9
11.	Chronic and unspecified bronchitis	285	1.8
12.	Urinary tract infection, site not specified	282	1.7%
13.	Gastrointestinal hemorrhage	273	1.7
14.	Abdominal pain	268	1.7
15.	Anemias	237	1.5
16.	Fractures, excluding lower limb	236	1.5
17.	Disorder of gallbladder and biliary tract	228	1.4
18.	Asthma	185	1.1
19.	Malignant neoplasms	184	1.1
20.	Essential hypertension	184	1.1
All other diagnoses[1]		**8,634**	**53.2**
All visits		**16,229**	**100.0**

Note: Numbers may not add to totals due to rounding. (1) Includes blanks and discharges in which diagnosis was unknown.

Most Frequently Mentioned Drugs at Outpatient Department Visits, 2011

Source: National Hospital Ambulatory Medical Care Survey, National Center for Health Statistics, Centers for Disease Control and Prevention, U.S. Dept. of Health and Human Services

Rank	Therapeutic drug category[1]	No. of mentions (thous.)	% of total[2]
1.	Analgesics	41,130	12.5%
2.	Antidiabetic agents	15,610	4.7
3.	Antihyperlipidemic agents	14,547	4.4
4.	Antidepressants	14,286	4.3
5.	Immunostimulants	12,923	3.9
6.	Anxiolytics, sedatives, and hypnotics	12,337	3.7
7.	Bronchodilators	10,937	3.3
8.	Anticonvulsants	10,412	3.2
9.	Dermatological agents	10,287	3.1
10.	Antiplatelet agents	10,128	3.1
11.	Beta-adrenergic blocking agents	10,124	3.1%
12.	Vitamins	9,206	2.8
13.	Diuretics	9,161	2.8
14.	ACE[3] inhibitors	9,140	2.8
15.	Proton pump inhibitors	8,247	2.5
16.	Antiemetic or antivertigo agents	8,063	2.4
17.	Antihistamines	7,898	2.4
18.	Calcium channel blocking agents	6,251	1.9
19.	Vitamin and mineral combinations	5,996	1.8
20.	Minerals and electrolytes	5,564	1.7

Note: A mention is a documentation in a patient's record of a drug provided, prescribed, or continued. (1) Based on the Multum Lexicon second-level therapeutic drug category. (2) Based on an estimated 329,191,000 drugs provided, prescribed, or continued at outpatient department visits in 2011. (3) Angiotensin-converting enzyme.

U.S. Organ Transplants

Source: Organ Procurement and Transplantation Network (OPTN), United Network for Organ Sharing (UNOS)

Waiting List, June 2015

Type of transplant	Patients waiting	% of total
Any organ	**134,519**	—
Kidney	109,533	81.4%
Liver	15,743	11.7
Heart	4,232	3.1
Kidney-pancreas	2,056	1.5
Lung	1,598	1.2
Pancreas	1,069	0.8
Intestine	246	0.2
Heart-lung	42	0.0

Note: Waiting list as of June 5, 2015.

Transplants Performed, 2014

Type of transplant	Number	% of total
Any organ	**29,532**	—
Kidney	17,106	57.9%
Liver	6,729	22.8
Heart	2,655	9.0
Lung	1,925	6.5
Kidney-pancreas	709	2.4
Pancreas	245	0.8
Intestine	139	0.5
Heart-lung	24	0.1

Drug Use in the General U.S. Population, 2013

Source: Substance Abuse and Mental Health Services Administration (SAMHSA), U.S. Dept. of Health and Human Services

According to the 2013 results of SAMHSA's annual survey, an estimated 127.5 mil Americans 12 years of age and older (or 48.6% of that population) had used an illicit drug at least once in their lifetimes. Of that number, an estimated 78.1 mil (29.8% of persons 12 or older) had used an illicit drug other than marijuana at least once in their lives. About 15.9% of the 12-and-older population had used an illicit drug in the previous year; 9.4% had used one in the month prior to their participation in the survey. The rate of current illicit drug use (i.e., within the past month) in 2012 was 11.5% for men and 7.3% for women.

SAMHSA's Drug Abuse Warning Network (DAWN) reported 2.5 mil drug abuse or misuse-related visits to hospital emergency departments in 2011. Just over half (51%) of all visits involved illicit drugs, with the highest rates for cocaine and marijuana. About 25% of all visits associated with drug misuse or abuse also involved alcohol.

Illicit Drug Use Among Persons Age 12 or Older, 2005-13

Source: National Survey on Drug Use and Health, Substance Abuse and Mental Health Services Admin. (SAMHSA), U.S. Dept. of Health and Human Services

(numbers in thousands)

	2005		2009		2010		2011		2012		2013	
Used in lifetime	No.	%	No.	%	No.	%	No.	%	No.	%	No.	%
Illicit drugs[1]	112,085	46.1	118,705	47.1	119,508	47.1	121,078	47.0	124,808	48.0	127,458	48.6
Illicit drugs other than marijuana[1]	71,822	29.5	75,780	30.1	76,203	30.0	75,447	29.3	78,034	30.0	78,076	29.8
Used in past month												
Illicit drugs[1]	19,720	8.1	21,813	8.7	22,622	8.9	22,454	8.7	23,863	9.2	24,573	9.4
Illicit drugs other than marijuana[1]	8,963	3.7	9,157	3.6	9,017	3.6	8,020	3.1	8,883	3.4	8,665	3.3
Used in past year												
Illicit drugs[1]	35,041	14.4	37,954	15.1	38,806	15.3	38,287	14.9	41,479	16.0	41,591	15.9
Marijuana and hashish	25,375	10.4	28,521	11.3	29,206	11.5	29,739	11.5	31,513	12.1	32,952	12.6
Illicit drugs other than marijuana[1]	20,109	8.3	21,000	8.3	20,576	8.1	18,959	7.4	21,267	8.2	19,868	7.6
Cocaine	5,523	2.3	4,797	1.9	4,499	1.8	3,857	1.5	4,671	1.8	4,182	1.6
Crack	1,381	0.6	1,016	0.4	871	0.3	625	0.2	921	0.4	632	0.2
Heroin	379	0.2	605	0.2	618	0.2	620	0.2	669	0.3	681	0.3
Hallucinogens	3,809	1.6	4,509	1.8	4,517	1.8	4,069	1.6	4,306	1.7	4,430	1.7
LSD	563	0.2	779	0.3	874	0.3	880	0.3	1,057	0.4	1,111	0.4
PCP	164	0.1	122	0.0	95	0.0	119	0.0	172	0.1	90	0.0
Ecstasy	1,960	0.8	2,799	1.1	2,645	1.0	2,422	0.9	2,610	1.0	2,588	1.0
Inhalants	2,187	0.9	2,090	0.8	2,030	0.8	1,861	0.7	1,693	0.7	1,533	0.6
Nonmedical use of psychotherapeutics[2]	15,346	6.3	16,006	6.4	16,031	6.3	14,657	5.7	16,666	6.4	15,348	5.8
Pain relievers	11,815	4.9	12,405	4.9	12,213	4.8	11,143	4.3	12,489	4.8	11,082	4.2
OxyContin®	1,226	0.5	1,677	0.7	1,869	0.7	1,623	0.6	1,477	0.6	1,442	0.5
Tranquilizers	5,249	2.2	5,460	2.2	5,581	2.2	5,109	2.0	6,073	2.3	5,269	2.0
Stimulants	3,088	1.3	3,060	1.2	2,887	1.1	2,700	1.0	3,317	1.3	3,492	1.3
Methamphetamine	NA	NA	1,165	0.5	959	0.4	1,033	0.4	1,155	0.4	1,186	0.5
Sedatives	750	0.3	811	0.3	907	0.4	526	0.2	590	0.2	639	0.2

NA = Not available. (1) Illicit drugs include marijuana/hashish, cocaine (including crack), heroin, hallucinogens, inhalants, or prescription-type psychotherapeutics used nonmedically. (2) Includes the nonmedical use of pain relievers, tranquilizers, stimulants, or sedatives but not over-the-counter drugs.

Lifetime Prevalence of Drug Use in 12th Graders, 1975-2014

Source: Monitoring the Future study, Univ. of Michigan Inst. for Social Research; National Institute on Drug Abuse

(percent who have ever used)

Drug	1975	1980	1985	1990	1995	2000	2005	2010	2011	2012	2013	2014	2013-14 change
Any illicit drug[1]	55.2%	65.4%	60.6%	47.9%	48.4%	54.0%	50.4%	48.2%	49.9%	49.1%	49.8%	49.1%	–0.8%
Marijuana/hashish	47.3	60.3	54.2	40.7	41.7	48.8	44.8	43.8	45.5	45.2	45.5	44.4	–1.1
Inhalants[2]	—	17.3	18.1	18.5	17.8	14.6	11.9	9.0	8.1	7.9	6.9	6.5	–0.4
Nitrites	—	11.1	7.9	2.1	1.5	0.8	1.1	—	—	—	—	—	—
Hallucinogens[3]	—	15.6	12.1	9.7	13.1	13.6	9.3	8.6	8.3	7.5	7.6	6.3	–1.3
LSD	11.3	9.3	7.5	8.7	11.7	11.1	3.5	4.0	4.0	3.8	3.9	3.7	–0.2
PCP	—	9.6	4.9	2.8	2.7	3.4	2.4	1.8	2.3	1.6	1.3	—	—
Ecstasy (MDMA)	—	—	—	—	—	11.0	5.4	7.3	8.0	7.2	7.1	5.6	–1.5
Cocaine	9.0	15.7	17.3	9.4	6.0	8.6	8.0	5.5	5.2	4.9	4.5	4.6	0.0
Crack	—	—	—	3.5	3.0	3.9	3.5	2.4	1.9	2.1	1.8	1.8	–0.1
Heroin (with and without a needle)	2.2	1.1	1.2	1.3	1.6	2.4	1.5	1.6	1.4	1.1	1.0	1.0	–0.1
Narcotics other than heroin[4]	9.0	9.8	10.2	8.3	7.2	10.6	12.8	13.0	13.0	12.2	11.1	9.5	–1.6
Amphetamines[4]	22.3	26.4	26.2	17.5	15.3	15.6	13.1	11.1	12.2	12.0	13.8	12.1	–1.7
Methamphetamine	—	—	—	—	—	7.9	4.5	2.3	2.1	1.7	1.5	1.9	0.4
Crystal meth. (ice)	—	—	—	2.7	3.9	4.0	4.0	1.8	2.1	1.7	2.0	1.3	–0.6
Sedatives (barbiturates)[4]	18.2	14.9	11.8	7.5	7.6	9.3	11.0	7.5	7.0	6.9	7.5	6.8	–0.6
Methaqualone[4]	8.1	9.5	6.7	2.3	1.2	0.8	1.3	0.4	0.6	0.8	—	—	—
Tranquilizers[4]	17.0	15.2	11.9	7.2	7.1	8.9	9.9	8.5	8.7	8.5	7.7	7.4	–0.3
Alcohol	90.4	93.2	92.2	89.5	80.7	80.3	75.1	71.0	70.0	69.4	68.2	66.0	–2.2
Cigarettes	73.6	71.0	68.8	64.4	64.2	62.5	50.0	42.2	40.0	39.5	38.1	34.4	–3.7
Smokeless tobacco	—	—	—	—	30.9	23.1	17.5	17.6	16.9	17.4	17.2	15.1	–2.1
Steroids[4]	—	—	—	2.9	2.3	2.5	2.6	2.0	1.8	1.8	2.1	1.9	–0.2

— = Not available. **Note:** Because of changes to question wording, some data may not be directly comparable to data from previous years. (1) Includes marijuana, LSD, other hallucinogens, crack, other cocaine, or heroin; or any use of narcotics other than heroin, amphetamines, sedatives (barbiturates), or tranquilizers not under a doctor's orders. (2) Not adjusted for underreporting of amyl and butyl nitrites. (3) Not adjusted for underreporting of PCP. (4) Includes only drug use not under a doctor's orders.

Cigarette Use in the U.S., 1985-2013

Source: National Survey on Drug Use and Health, Substance Abuse and Mental Health Services Admin. (SAMHSA), U.S. Dept. of Health and Human Services

(percentage reporting use in the month prior to the survey)

	1985	2000	2005	2010	2012	2013
Total[1]	**38.7**	**24.9**	**24.9**	**23.0**	**22.1**	**21.3**
Sex						
Male	43.4	26.9	27.4	25.4	24.6	23.6
Female	34.5	23.1	22.5	20.7	19.8	19.0
Age group						
12-17 years	29.4	13.4	10.8	8.3	6.6	5.6
18-25 years	47.4	38.3	39.0	34.2	31.8	30.6
26 years and older	45.7[3]	24.2	24.3	22.8	22.4	21.6
Race/ethnicity						
White, not Hispanic	38.9	25.9	26.0	24.3	23.7	22.7
Black, not Hispanic	38.0	23.3	24.5	22.6	23.0	23.0
Hispanic	40.0	20.7	22.1	20.1	16.8	16.8
Education[2]						
Non-high school graduate	37.3	32.4	34.8	34.3	33.7	33.6
High school graduate	37.0	31.1	31.8	29.6	29.4	27.7
Some college	32.6	27.7	28.1	25.8	25.5	25.5
College graduate	23.0	13.9	13.8	12.8	11.5	11.2

(1) Persons 12 years of age and older. (2) Persons aged 18 and older. (3) Persons aged 26 to 34 only.

Daily Use of Cigarettes by 8th, 10th, and 12th Graders, 1995-2014

Source: Monitoring the Future study, Univ. of Michigan Inst. for Social Research; National Institute on Drug Abuse

(percent who smoked daily in last 30 days)

	8th grade						10th grade						12th grade					
	1995	2000	2005	2010	2014	% change, 2010-14	1995	2000	2005	2010	2014	% change, 2010-14	1995	2000	2005	2010	2014	% change, 2010-14
Total	**9.3**	**7.4**	**4.0**	**2.9**	**1.4**	**–51.7%**	**16.3**	**14.0**	**7.5**	**6.6**	**3.2**	**–51.5%**	**21.6**	**20.6**	**13.6**	**10.7**	**6.7**	**–37.4%**
Sex																		
Male	9.2	7.0	3.9	3.5	1.2	–65.7	16.3	13.7	7.2	7.2	3.5	–51.4	21.7	20.9	14.6	12.3	7.9	–35.8
Female	9.2	7.5	4.0	2.3	1.3	–43.5	16.1	14.1	7.7	5.9	2.8	–52.5	20.8	19.7	11.9	8.7	5.4	–37.9
College plans																		
None or under 4 yrs.	22.5	21.7	14.4	12.8	4.7	–63.3	32.7	28.8	19.2	19.1	10.5	–45.0	33.7	31.7	24.9	21.6	14.0	–35.2
Complete 4 yrs.	7.5	5.6	2.9	2.0	1.0	–50.0	13.3	11.6	5.9	5.0	2.3	–54.0	17.4	16.6	10.5	8.2	5.0	–39.0
Region																		
Northeast	9.2	6.9	3.2	2.4	1.2	–50.0	15.8	14.1	7.6	5.7	2.8	–50.9	22.5	22.8	13.3	10.3	6.8	–34.0
Midwest	11.0	9.0	4.8	3.3	0.9	–72.7	17.6	16.3	8.6	7.3	3.9	–46.6	25.7	23.6	16.3	12.5	6.6	–47.2
South	9.4	7.8	5.0	3.8	1.9	–50.0	19.3	15.7	8.8	7.9	3.4	–57.0	21.7	19.4	15.4	12.3	8.2	–33.3
West	7.0	4.9	2.4	1.4	1.1	–21.4	9.4	7.8	4.0	4.4	2.4	–45.5	14.5	16.9	7.6	6.7	4.5	–32.8
Race/ethnicity[1]																		
White	10.5	9.0	4.6	3.2	1.7	–46.9	23.9	25.7	17.1	7.4	4.8	–35.1	23.9	25.7	17.1	13.5	9.3	–31.1
Black	2.8	3.2	2.1	1.9	1.2	–36.8	6.1	8.0	5.6	3.5	2.3	–34.3	6.1	8.0	5.6	5.3	5.1	–3.8
Hispanic	9.2	7.1	3.1	2.3	1.3	–43.5	11.6	15.7	7.7	4.4	2.3	–47.7	11.6	15.7	7.7	5.7	4.1	–28.1

Note: Figures may not add up to totals because of rounding. (1) For each of these groups, data for the specified year and previous year have been combined to increase sample size and thus provide a more reliable estimate.

Tobacco Use by High School and Middle School Students, 2014

Source: Centers for Disease Control and Prevention (CDC), U.S. Dept. of Health and Human Services

Between 2011 and 2014, high school and middle school students increased their current use (defined as use on 1 or more days in the past 30 days) of both e-cigarettes and hookahs, while decreasing use of more traditional products, such as cigarettes and cigars, resulting in no change in overall tobacco use.

	High school students using tobacco				Middle school students using tobacco			
Tobacco product	**Female**	**Male**	**All students**	**Estimated no. of users[3]**	**Female**	**Male**	**All students**	**Estimated no. of users[3]**
Electronic cigarettes	11.9%	15.0%	13.4%	2,010,000	3.3%	4.5%	3.9%	450,000
Hookah	9.8	8.9	9.4	1,380,000	2.6	2.4	2.5	280,000
Cigarettes	7.9	10.6	9.2	1,370,000	2.0	3.0	2.5	290,000
Cigars	5.5	10.8	8.2	1,200,000	1.4	2.4	1.9	220,000
Smokeless tobacco	1.2	9.9	5.5	830,000	—	2.1	1.6	180,000
Snus	0.8	3.0	1.9	280,000	—	0.7	0.5	50,000
Pipes	0.9	2.1	1.5	220,000	—	0.6	0.6	60,000
Bidis	0.6	1.2	0.9	130,000	0.3	—	0.5	60,000
Dissolvable tobacco	0.4	0.8	0.6	80,000	—	0.4	0.3	30,000
Any tobacco product use[1]	20.9	28.3	24.6	3,720,000	6.6	8.8	7.7	910,000
2+ tobacco product use[2]	10.0	15.3	12.7	1,910,000	2.4	3.8	3.1	360,000

— = Not available. (1) Defined as preceding 30-day use of any tobacco product on at least one day in the past 30 days. (2) Defined as preceding 30-day use of two or more of the tobacco products here on at least one day in the past 30 days. (3) Rounded down to nearest 10,000.

Alcohol Use by 8th and 12th Graders, 1980-2014

Source: Monitoring the Future study, Univ. of Michigan Inst. for Social Research; National Inst. on Drug Abuse

	1980	1990	1995	2000	2005	2010	2011	2012	2013	2014	% change, 2013-14
Alcohol use[1]					Percent using in the month before the survey						
All 8th graders	—	—	**24.6%**	**22.4%**	**17.1%**	**13.8%**	**12.7%**	**11.0%**	**10.2%**	**9.0%**	**–1.3%**
Male	—	—	25.0	22.5	16.2	13.2	12.1	10.3	9.3	8.2	–1.0
Female	—	—	24.0	22.0	17.9	14.3	12.8	11.6	11.2	9.5	–1.7
White.	—	—	25.4	24.7	17.9	13.9	12.3	10.7	9.5	9.0	–0.4
Black.	—	—	18.7	16.0	14.9	11.8	11.6	10.0	9.7	8.8	–0.9
Hispanic	—	—	32.4	26.7	20.6	18.1	18.0	17.5	14.3	11.2	–3.1
All 12th graders . . .	**72.0%**	**57.1%**	**51.3**	**50.0**	**47.0**	**41.2**	**40.0**	**41.5**	**39.2**	**37.4**	**–1.8**
Male	77.4	61.3	55.7	54.0	50.7	44.2	42.1	43.8	41.8	37.4	–4.4
Female	66.8	52.3	47.0	46.1	43.3	37.9	37.5	38.8	36.3	37.1	0.8
White.	75.4	63.8	54.5	55.1	52.3	45.4	43.8	43.8	43.6	42.5	–1.1
Black.	47.6	35.8	35.2	30.0	29.0	31.4	30.1	29.6	28.4	25.9	–2.6
Hispanic	63.6	49.1	48.7	51.2	43.3	40.1	39.7	39.8	39.0	37.0	–2.1
Heavy alcohol use[2]					Percent heavily using in the two weeks before the survey						
All 8th graders	—	—	**12.3%**	**11.7%**	**8.4%**	**7.2%**	**6.4%**	**5.1%**	**5.1%**	**4.1%**	**–1.0%**
Male	—	—	12.5	11.7	8.2	6.5	6.1	4.6	4.5	3.5	–1.1
Female	—	—	12.1	11.3	8.6	7.8	6.5	5.5	5.7	4.6	–1.1
White.	—	—	12.1	13.0	9.0	7.1	6.2	4.9	4.2	4.2	–0.1
Black.	—	—	8.3	7.3	6.1	5.3	5.1	4.3	4.5	4.4	–0.1
Hispanic	—	—	18.4	16.0	12.1	10.8	10.4	9.9	7.8	5.7	–2.1
All 12th graders . . .	**41.2%**	**32.2%**	**29.8**	**30.0**	**27.1**	**23.2**	**21.6**	**23.7**	**22.1**	**19.4**	**–2.7**
Male	52.1	39.1	36.9	36.7	32.6	28.0	25.5	27.2	26.1	22.3	–3.8
Female	30.5	24.4	23.0	23.5	21.6	18.4	17.6	19.7	18.1	16.6	–1.4
White.	44.3	36.6	32.3	34.6	32.5	27.6	25.9	25.7	25.6	23.8	–1.8
Black.	17.7	14.4	14.9	11.5	11.3	13.1	11.3	11.3	12.5	11.3	–1.2
Hispanic	33.1	25.6	26.6	31.0	23.9	22.1	20.8	21.8	22.4	20.4	–2.1

— = Not available. (1) Since 1993 the alcohol question has indicated that a "drink" is defined as "more than a few sips." (2) Five or more drinks in a row.

Acquired Immune Deficiency Syndrome (AIDS)

Source: Centers for Disease Control and Prevention (CDC), U.S. Dept. of Health and Human Services

AIDS (Acquired Immune Deficiency Syndrome) is caused by the human immunodeficiency virus (HIV). HIV kills or disables crucial immune cells, progressively destroying the body's ability to fight disease.

HIV is commonly spread through unprotected sexual contact with an infected partner's semen or vaginal fluids. It is also spread through contact with infected blood. Where modern screening techniques are used, it is rare to contract HIV from transfusion or organ/tissue transplants. But it can be contracted when intravenous drug users share syringes and similar equipment with others. A woman can also transmit HIV to her child during pregnancy or delivery or through breastfeeding. With treatment, a woman can reduce her transmission rate from about 20% to 1%-2%. There is no evidence HIV can spread through saliva or casual contact such as in the sharing of food utensils, towels and bedding, telephones, or toilet seats.

Some people experience flu-like symptoms within a few weeks of being infected with HIV. Even when symptoms are not present, HIV is active in the body, multiplying, infecting, and killing crucial CD4+ T cells, also known as T-lymphocytes or T-helper cells, which signal other immune cells to perform their functions.

The term AIDS applies to the most advanced stages of HIV infection. According to the official case definition issued by the CDC, an HIV-infected person with fewer than 200 CD4+ T cells per cubic millimeter of blood can be said to have AIDS. (Healthy adults usually have 500-1,600 per cubic millimeter.) An HIV-infected person, regardless of T cell count, is diagnosed with AIDS if he or she develops one of 20+ conditions that typically affect people with advanced HIV. Most of these conditions are opportunistic infections that occur when the immune system is so ravaged by HIV that the body cannot fight off certain bacteria, viruses, and microbes.

Months or years prior to the onset of AIDS, people may experience such symptoms as swollen glands, lack of energy, fevers and sweats, and skin rashes. People diagnosed with AIDS may develop infections of the intestinal tract, lungs, brain, eyes, and other organs and become severely debilitated. They also are prone to developing certain cancers, such as Kaposi's sarcoma, cervical cancer, and lymphoma. Children with AIDS may have delayed development or fail to thrive.

HIV is primarily detected by testing a person's blood for the presence of antibodies (disease-fighting proteins of the immune system) to HIV. In very rare cases, HIV antibodies may take more than six months after exposure to reach detectable levels. But in 97% of infected individuals, the antibodies are detectable in the first three months. Rapid HIV tests can provide preliminary results in 30 minutes or less. There are also two home HIV tests available.

Patients receiving antiretroviral therapy typically take a combination of drugs. Taking more than one drug reduces the chance of the virus becoming resistant to any single one. While these drugs extend the period between HIV infection and the development of serious illness, they do not prevent the spread of the disease to others and can have severe side effects.

In 1987, a drug called zidovudine (commonly known as AZT) became the first approved treatment for HIV disease. Since then, the U.S. Food and Drug Administration has approved approximately 35 drugs to treat people living with HIV/AIDS. These drugs belong in different classes: Nucleoside/Nuclectide Reverse Transcriptase Inhibitors (NRTIs), Non-Nucleoside Reverse Transcriptase Inhibitors (NNRTIs), Protease Inhibitors (PIs), Entry Inhibitors, Fusion Inhibitors, and Integrase Inhibitors. Each class of drug attacks the virus at a different point in its life cycle. Patients generally take three different antiretrovirals (ARVs) from two different classes.

There are also fixed-dose combinations of drugs. These are not a separate class of HIV medications but combinations of two or more medications, with specific fixed doses from one or more different classes, combined into a single pill.

Since there is no vaccine or cure for AIDS, the best way to prevent HIV is to avoid activities that carry a risk. The CDC recommends abstinence, mutual monogamy with an uninfected partner, limiting the number of sexual partners, never sharing needles, and using condoms correctly and consistently. Pre-exposure prophylaxis, or PrEP, is a prevention option for people who do not have HIV but are at high risk of getting HIV. It is meant to be used consistently, as a pill taken every day, and to be used with other prevention options. PrEP has been shown to greatly reduce the risk of HIV infection. PEP, or post-exposure prophylaxis, is the use of ARVs after a single high-risk event to stop HIV from making copies of itself and spreading throughout the body. PEP must be started no more than 72 hours after the exposure to HIV, and it is not always effective.

New AIDS Diagnoses in the U.S., by Transmission Category, 1985-2013

Source: *HIV Surveillance Report, 2013*; National Center for HIV/AIDS, Viral Hepatitis, STD, and TB Prevention; CDC

Transmission category	All years[1]	1985	1990	2000	2005	2010	2011	2012	2013
All males 13 years of age and older	**942,440**	**7,504**	**36,193**	**30,251**	**27,436**	**21,387**	**20,055**	**19,546**	**20,256**
Male-to-male sexual contact	577,403	5,348	23,658	13,648	16,824	14,575	13,958	13,821	14,611
Injection drug use	187,218	1,103	6,923	5,554	4,350	2,152	1,825	1,705	1,610
Male-to-male sexual contact and injection drug use	83,828	661	2,943	1,587	2,085	1,389	1,232	1,115	1,026
Heterosexual contact[2]	82,447	32	715	2,537	3,920	3,155	2,918	2,790	2,865
Other[3]	11,545	—	—	—	256	116	122	115	144
All females 13 years of age and older	**242,178**	**524**	**4,547**	**9,979**	**9,799**	**7,206**	**6,684**	**6,417**	**6,424**
Injection drug use	89,790	287	2,347	2,545	2,724	1,472	1,313	1,225	1,143
Heterosexual contact[2]	146,521	119	1,538	4,025	6,856	5,599	5,240	5,077	5,109
Other[3]	5,868	—	—	—	219	136	132	114	172
All children, under 13 years of age	**9,421**	—	—	—	**55**	**24**	**16**	**10**	**8**
Perinatal	8,553	—	—	—	50	18	13	9	7
Other[4]	869	—	—	—	5	6	3	1	1

— = Not available. **Note:** The definition of AIDS cases for reporting purposes was expanded in 1985, 1987, and 1993, as more was learned about the spectrum of human immunodeficiency virus-associated diseases. (1) Includes number of diagnoses for years not shown, from the beginning of the epidemic (1981) through 2013. (2) Heterosexual contact with a person known to have or be at high risk for HIV infection. (3) Includes hemophilia, blood transfusion, perinatal exposure, and risk factor not reported or not identified. (4) Includes hemophilia, blood transfusion, and risk factor not reported or not identified.

New HIV Diagnoses in the U.S., 2008-11

Source: *Health, United States*; National Center for Health Statistics, Centers for Disease Control and Prevention

	Male				Female			
Characteristic	**2008**	**2009**	**2010**	**2011**	**2008**	**2009**	**2010**	**2011**
Total diagnoses, age 13 and over	**38,104**	**36,392**	**35,918**	**38,825**	**12,146**	**10,804**	**10,125**	**10,257**
Race/Hispanic origin								
White	12,206	11,583	11,355	12,041	2,046	1,772	1,680	1,776
Black or African American	16,277	15,491	15,293	16,447	7,967	6,977	6,592	6,595
Asian	685	612	646	821	123	134	132	153
Native Hawaiian or other Pacific Islander	68	62	53	70	10	18	9	8
American Indian or Alaska Native	179	151	161	161	44	53	61	51
Hispanic or Latino[1]	7,979	7,825	7,725	8,605	1,681	1,635	1,463	1,530
Multiple race	710	667	686	679	274	214	188	144
Age diagnosed								
13-14 years	13	11	20	27	30	20	25	26
15-24 years	7,113	7,480	8,093	8,680	1,835	1,704	1,563	1,615
25-34 years	10,127	9,990	9,933	11,107	3,206	2,687	2,581	2,586
35-44 years	10,319	9,146	8,371	8,527	3,242	2,898	2,562	2,511
45-54 years	7,352	6,787	6,547	7,220	2,618	2,388	2,229	2,295
55-64 years	2,503	2,363	2,357	2,551	966	874	944	990
65 years and over	677	616	597	713	249	234	221	235

Note: Data are based on reporting by 50 states and DC. Subpopulations were calculated independent of total and may not equal totals. Children under age 13 made up fewer than 300 cases per year and are not shown. (1) May be of any race.

U.S. Deaths of Persons With HIV Ever Classified as AIDS, 1981-2012

Source: *HIV Surveillance Report, 2013*; National Center for HIV/AIDS, Viral Hepatitis, STD, and TB Prevention; CDC

Age at death	Deaths	% of total
Under 13 years old	4,951	0.8%
13-14	295	0.0
15-19	1,302	0.2
20-24	9,796	1.5
25-29	46,950	7.1
30-34	101,897	15.5
35-39	128,057	19.4
40-44	121,596	18.5
45-49	94,089	14.3
50-54	63,752	9.7
55-59	39,477	6.0
60-64	23,020	3.5
65 years and over	23,323	3.5
Race/ethnicity		
Black/African American	270,726	41.1
White	269,653	40.9
Hispanic/Latino (any race)	100,888	15.3
Asian[1]	3,441	0.5
American Indian/Alaska Native	1,867	0.3
Native Hawaiian/Other Pacific Islander	356	0.1
Multiple races	11,577	1.8

Transmission category	Deaths	% of total
Male adult or adolescent	**535,758**	**81.4%**
Male-to-male sexual contact	311,087	47.2
Injection drug use	130,406	19.8
Male-to-male sexual contact and injection drug use	50,001	7.6
Heterosexual contact[2]	35,230	5.3
Perinatal	376	0.1
Other[3]	8,658	1.3
Female adult or adolescent	**117,797**	**17.9**
Injection drug use	56,322	8.6
Heterosexual contact[2]	57,383	8.7
Perinatal	490	0.1
Other[3]	3,603	0.5
Child (under 13 years old at death)	**4,951**	**0.8**
Perinatal	4,491	0.7
Other[3]	461	0.1
Region of residence		
Northeast	208,570	31.7
Midwest	66,856	10.2
South	253,080	38.4
West	130,001	19.7
Total[4]	**658,507**	

Note: Deaths of persons with diagnosed HIV infection may be due to any cause. (1) Includes "Asian/Pacific Islander" legacy cases. (2) Heterosexual contact with a person known to have or to be at high risk for HIV infection. (3) Includes hemophilia, blood transfusion, and risk factor not reported or not identified. (4) Because estimated totals were calculated independently, subpopulation values may not add up to the total.

Allergies and Asthma

Source: Asthma and Allergy Foundation of America

An estimated one in five Americans suffers from allergies. People with allergies have immune systems that overreact to a foreign protein substance ("allergen") that is eaten, breathed into the lungs, injected, or touched. Common allergens include plant pollens, dust mites, or animal dander; plants such as poison ivy; certain drugs, such as penicillin; and foods such as eggs, milk, wheat, nuts, or seafood.

The tendency to develop allergies is usually inherited. While allergies typically manifest in childhood, they can show up at any age. Food allergies and eczema (patches of dry skin) are common allergies among infants. Older children and adults may develop allergic rhinitis, or hay fever, in reaction to an inhaled allergen. Allergic rhinitis symptoms include nasal congestion, runny nose, and sneezing.

People with allergies should avoid contact with an allergen, if feasible. Medications, such as antihistamines and nasal steroids, may be used to decrease an allergic reaction. Other effective allergy treatments include decongestants, eye drops, and ointments. There are also treatments aimed at gradually desensitizing a patient to an allergen.

Some allergy sufferers also have asthma. Asthma, which can develop at any age, is a chronic inflammation disease affecting the passageways that carry air into and out of the lungs. About 26 mil Americans have asthma. During an asthma attack, these symptoms are exacerbated. The airways narrow even more and fill with mucus. A person may experience wheezing, difficulty breathing, tightening of the chest, and coughing. Exposure to an allergen can set off an attack. Asthma can become life-threatening if not controlled in its early stages. The following symptoms may be indicative of an emergency: the patient shows no improvement minutes after initial treatment; struggles to breathe while hunched over with chest and neck pulled in; has trouble walking or talking; and develops gray or blue lips or fingernails.

Tobacco smoke, cold air, and expressing strong emotion can also trigger an asthma attack, as can respiratory infections or physical exercise. An accurate diagnosis by a physician is important. Although there is no cure for asthma or allergies, they can be controlled through lifestyle changes and medications (including quick-relief and long-term control).

Website: www.aafa.org

Persons With Asthma, 2013

Source: Centers for Disease Control and Prevention, U.S. Dept. of Health and Human Services

	Number (thous.)	Percent
Total	**22,648**	**7.3%**
Child (under age 18)	6,109	8.3
Adult	16,540	7.0
Age		
0-4 years	826	4.2
5-14 years	4,080	9.9
15-19 years	1,761	8.6
20-24 years	1,585	7.2
25-34 years	2,764	6.6
35-64 years	8,914	7.3
65+ years	2,719	6.3
Sex		
Males	9,430	6.2
Under age 18	3,489	9.3
Over age 18	5,940	5.2
Females	13,218	8.3
Under age 18	2,619	7.3
Over age 18	10,599	8.6
Race/ethnicity		
White, non-Hispanic	14,383	7.4
Black, non-Hispanic	3,712	9.9
Other non-Hispanic	1,397	5.8
Hispanic (any race)	3,157	5.9
Puerto Rican	686	14.6
Mexican/Mexican American	1,612	4.7

Note: Includes only those with a current diagnosis of asthma. Numbers may not add to totals due to rounding.

Alzheimer's Disease

Source: Alzheimer's Association

Alzheimer's disease, the most common form of dementia, is a progressive, degenerative brain disease in which nerve cells deteriorate and die. The most common early symptom is forgetting newly learned information. As the disease advances, it leads to disorientation and mood/behavior changes; confusion about events, time, and place; suspicions about family, friends, and caregivers; more serious memory loss; and difficulty speaking, swallowing, and walking.

The rate of progression of Alzheimer's varies, ranging from 4 to 20 years. The average length of time from onset of symptoms until death is eight years. As they become progressively debilitated, affected individuals grow increasingly susceptible to infections of the lungs, urinary tract, and other organs.

Alzheimer's disease affects an estimated 5.3 mil Americans, striking men and women of all races and ethnicities. Almost two-thirds of all Americans living with Alzheimer's are women. Although most people are older than age 65 when diagnosed with Alzheimer's, younger-onset, or early-onset, cases occur in people in their 40s and 50s. An estimated 11% of the U.S. population over age 65 and 32% over age 85 have Alzheimer's.

Diagnosis involves a comprehensive evaluation that may include a complete health history, physical examination, neurological and mental status assessments, and other tests. Skilled health care professionals can generally diagnose Alzheimer's with more than 90% accuracy. Depression, drug interactions, nutritional imbalances, and infections such as AIDS, meningitis, and syphilis can cause similar symptoms. Other forms of dementia, such as those associated with Huntington's disease, Parkinson's disease, frontotemporal dementia, and vascular disease, can also appear to be Alzheimer's. Absolute confirmation of a diagnosis requires a brain biopsy or autopsy.

Treatments for cognitive and behavioral symptoms are available, but no intervention has yet been developed to prevent Alzheimer's or reverse its course. The U.S. Food and Drug Administration has approved six drugs that temporarily slow worsening of symptoms for about six to twelve months. They are effective for only about half of the individuals who take them. Some research suggests that risk factors for heart disease, such as high blood pressure, elevated cholesterol, diabetes, and excess body weight, may increase a person's risk of developing Alzheimer's. Staying physically and mentally active and socially connected may be associated with a lower risk for the disease.

Providing care for people with Alzheimer's is physically and psychologically demanding. About 60%-70% of affected individuals live at home, where family or friends tend to them without pay. In the disease's advanced stages, many individuals require long-term residential care. Nearly half of all nursing home residents in the U.S. have Alzheimer's.

The U.S. cost of diagnosing, treating, and providing long-term care for Alzheimer's patients is estimated to be $226 bil in 2015. People with Alzheimer's need a safe, stable environment and a regular daily schedule offering appropriate stimulation. Physical exercise and social interaction are important, as are proper nutrition and adequate pain management. Security is also a consideration, because many people with Alzheimer's tend to wander. An identification bracelet with the person's name, address, and condition can help ensure the safe return of an individual who wanders.

Website: www.alz.org

Warning Signs of Alzheimer's Disease

- Memory loss that disrupts daily life
- Challenges in planning or solving problems
- Difficulty completing familiar tasks at home, at work, or at leisure
- Confusion with time or place
- Trouble understanding visual images and spatial relationships
- New problems with words in speaking or writing
- Misplacing things and losing the ability to retrace steps
- Decreased or poor judgment
- Withdrawal from work or social activities
- Changes in mood and personality

Arthritis

Source: Arthritis Foundation; Centers for Disease Control and Prevention (CDC), U.S. Dept. of Health and Human Services

The term arthritis refers to more than 100 different diseases that cause pain, aching, stiffness, and swelling in or around the joints. The condition is usually chronic. The CDC estimates that nearly 53 mil adults in the United States report being told by a doctor that they have arthritis. Arthritis annually results in 44.2 mil ambulatory care visits and an estimated 992,000 hospitalizations. The cause for most types of arthritis is unknown; scientists are studying the roles played by genetics, lifestyle, and environment.

Symptoms may develop gradually or suddenly. A visit to the doctor is indicated when pain, stiffness, swelling in a joint, or difficulty in moving a joint persists for three days or more. To diagnose arthritis, the doctor records the patient's symptoms and examines his or her joints, looking for any swelling or limited movement. In addition, the doctor checks for other signs often seen with arthritis, such as rashes, mouth sores, or eye involvement. The doctor may test blood, urine, or joint fluid, or take X-rays of the joints.

Of the three most prevalent forms of arthritis, **osteoarthritis** is the most common, affecting approximately 27 mil Americans. It usually occurs after age 40. In patients with osteoarthritis, also called degenerative arthritis, the protective cartilage of joints is lost and changes occur in the bone, leading to pain and stiffness. The joints most commonly affected are the lower back, hips, knees, hands, and feet.

Fibromyalgia, another common arthritis condition, affects about 5 mil Americans. People suffering from fibromyalgia experience widespread pain, abnormal pain processing, sleep disturbance, fatigue, and psychological distress. Other symptoms include morning stiffness, tingling or numbness in hands and feet, headaches, or problems with thinking and memory. More women than men are afflicted with this type of arthritis.

Rheumatoid arthritis, which affects an estimated 1.5 mil in the U.S., is one of the most serious and disabling forms of the disease. In this type—which is also more common and more degenerative in women—inflammation of the joints leads to cartilage and bone damage. The hands, wrists, feet, knees, ankles, and elbows can be affected.

Other forms of arthritis and related conditions include lupus, gout, psoriatic arthritis, and Sjögren's syndrome. Bursitis and tendinitis, which may result from injuring or overusing a joint, are also related.

Medications that relieve pain and swelling, such as analgesics, anti-inflammatory drugs, biologic response modifiers, glucocorticoids, and antirheumatic drugs, can be used to treat arthritis. They also tend to slow the disease process. Most treatment programs call for exercise, use of heat or cold, and joint-protection techniques, such as avoidance of excess stress on the joints, the use of assistive devices, and weight loss and control. In some cases, surgery may help.

Website: www.arthritis.org

Attention Deficit Hyperactivity Disorder (ADHD)

Source: Centers for Disease Control and Prevention; Natl. Institute of Mental Health

Attention deficit hyperactivity disorder, or ADHD, is one of the most common neurodevelopmental disorders of childhood. It is usually first diagnosed in childhood and often lasts into adulthood. Children with ADHD may have trouble paying attention, controlling impulsive behaviors, or be overly active.

Signs and Symptoms of ADHD

- Daydreaming a lot
- Forgetting or losing things a lot
- Squirming or fidgeting
- Talking too much
- Making careless mistakes or taking unnecessary risks
- Having a hard time resisting temptation or taking turns
- Having difficulty getting along with others

There are three different types of ADHD, depending on which types of symptoms are strongest in the individual. A person who is **predominantly inattentive** is easily distracted or forgets details of daily routines. Someone who is **predominantly hyperactive-impulsive** may fidget and talk a lot and find it hard to sit still for long. In the third type, **combined presentation**, the individual displays symptoms of the first two types equally. The cause of ADHD is unknown, but current research shows that genetics plays an important role.

The average age of onset is 7 years old. ADHD affects about 4.1% of American adults age 18 years and older in a given year. The disorder affects 9.0% of American children age 13 to 18 years. Boys are four times more at risk than girls. Studies show that the number of children being diagnosed with ADHD is increasing, but it is unclear why. Rates of ADHD diagnosis increased an average of 3% per year from 1997 to 2006 and an average of 5% per year from 2003 to 2011. In addition, a 2013 survey found that in 2011, 11% of children aged 4-17 years had ever received an ADHD diagnosis and that 8.8% currently had ADHD.

In most cases, ADHD is treated with a combination of medication and behavior therapy. Stimulants are the most widely used medication. Nonstimulants, approved for treating ADHD in 2003, have fewer side effects than stimulants and can last up to 24 hours.

Breast Cancer

Source: American Cancer Society, Inc.

In 2015, an estimated 231,840 women and 2,350 men in the U.S. will be newly diagnosed with breast cancer, and about 40,290 women and 440 men will die from it. Currently, nearly 3.0 mil women are living with a history of breast cancer, the second biggest cause of cancer death for women in the U.S. (lung cancer ranks first). But mortality rates have been declining, especially among younger women, probably because of earlier detection and improved treatment.

The risk for breast cancer increases with age. It is higher for women with a personal or family history of cancer (particularly breast cancer), a long menstrual history (menstrual periods that started early and ended later in life), physical inactivity, recent use of birth control pills, use of menopausal hormone therapy containing estrogen and progestin, and in those who have no children or had no live birth until age 30 or older. Other risk factors include alcohol consumption and being overweight or obese. Inherited mutations such as in the BRCA1 and BRCA2 genes greatly increase risk, but these probably account for 5% to 10% of all breast cancers. By far the majority of women who develop breast cancer have no family history of it.

Breast cancer often manifests first as an abnormality on a mammogram X-ray. Physical symptoms that show up later, which may be detectable by a woman or her doctor, include a breast lump and, less commonly, persistent changes to the breast, such as thickening, swelling, distortion, tenderness, skin irritation, redness, scaliness, or nipple abnormalities, such as ulceration, retraction, or spontaneous discharge. Breast pain is more likely to be caused by benign conditions and is not a common early symptom of breast cancer.

Studies show that early detection increases survival and treatment options. Although most detected breast lumps are noncancerous, any suspicious lump should be biopsied.

Treatment for breast cancer may involve breast-conserving surgery (removal of the tumor and surrounding tissue), mastectomy (surgical removal of the breast), radiation therapy, chemotherapy, hormone therapy, and/or targeted therapy. The five-year survival rate for female invasive breast cancer patients has improved from 75% in the mid-1970s to 85% today. The five-year survival for women diagnosed with localized breast cancer (cancer that has not spread to lymph nodes or other locations outside the breast) is 99%.

Website: www.cancer.org

Prostate Cancer

Source: Prostate Cancer Foundation; American Cancer Society, Inc.

The prostate is a male gland located between the bladder and scrotum that secretes seminal fluid. Prostate cancer is the most common non-skin cancer in the U.S., and the second-most common cause, after lung cancer, of cancer deaths in American men. In 2015, an estimated 220,800 men will be diagnosed with prostate cancer, and about 27,540 will die from the disease. Currently, nearly 3.0 mil men in the U.S. are living with a history of prostate cancer.

The exact cause of prostate cancer is unknown. The most identifiable risk factors are age, family history, and race. About 56% of all prostate cancers are diagnosed in men 65 years of age and older, and the chances of developing the disease rise dramatically with age. Having a single first-degree relative with a history of prostate cancer more than doubles a man's risk of developing the disease, and those with several affected relatives have a much higher risk. African-American men are much more likely to develop prostate cancer than non-Hispanic white men and are more than twice as likely to die from it. The cause for this disparity remains unclear.

Usually, the disease has no symptoms in its early stages. As the disease advances, a man may experience weak or interrupted urine flow; inability to urinate or difficulty starting or stopping the urine flow; the need to urinate frequently, especially at night; blood in the urine; or pain or burning with urination. Advanced prostate cancer commonly spreads to the bones, which can cause pain in the hips, spine, ribs, or other areas.

The American Cancer Society recommends that once they reach 50, men at average risk of prostate cancer should speak with their health care provider about the benefits and limitations of prostate-specific antigen (PSA) testing. African-American men or those with a family history of the disease should be aware of their screening options beginning at age 40 or 45. Men under 40 seldom get prostate cancer.

Prostate cancer treatment may include surgery, radiation, hormonal therapy, chemotherapy, or some combination. If caught early on, while tumor cells are localized within the prostate, the five-year relative survival rate approaches 100%.

Websites: www.pcf.org; www.cancer.org

Skin Cancer

Source: American Cancer Society, Inc.

Skin cancer is generally divided into two main classes, **nonmelanomas** and **melanomas**, affecting different types of skin cells. Melanoma is the most dangerous type of skin cancer because it can easily spread to other parts of the body. Although skin cancer is the most common type of cancer diagnosed in the U.S., melanoma accounts for less than 2% of all skin cancers. The exact causes of melanoma are unclear, but risk factors include overexposure to UV light, multiple or unusual moles, fair skin, family or personal history of skin cancers, history of severe sunburns, and occupational exposure to certain compounds.

Melanomas generally look like abnormal moles on the surface of the skin. Abnormal moles differ from regular skin cells and may be a sign of skin cancer. An irregular mole should be examined by a doctor as soon as possible.

If caught early, melanoma is highly curable. The overall five-year survival rate for melanoma is 91%. For localized melanoma, the five-year survival rate is 98%; survival rates for regional and distant stage diseases are 62% and 16%, respectively. About 84% of melanomas are diagnosed at a localized stage.

Treatment may include simple removal of the melanoma; amputation if the cancer is found on a finger or toe; or chemotherapy, immunotherapy, and/or radiation if the melanoma has spread to other parts of the body.

Warning Signs of Abnormal Moles

- Asymmetry: one half does not match the other half
- Border: edges are irregular, ragged, notched, or blurred
- Color: not uniform; may be shades of brown or black, and patches of pink, red, blue, or white
- Diameter: moles wider than ¼ inch are abnormal (however, melanomas can be smaller)
- Evolving: mole changes size, shape, or color

Website: www.cancer.org

Cancer Risk Factors

Source: American Cancer Society, Inc., www.cancer.org

Alcohol: Alcohol consumption increases the risk of cancers of the mouth, pharynx, larynx, esophagus, liver, colorectum, breast, and possibly pancreas. Alcohol consumption combined with tobacco use increases the risk of cancers of the mouth, pharynx, larynx, and esophagus far more than either drinking or smoking alone.

Diet and physical activity: Overweight and obesity are associated with increased risk for developing many cancers, including cancers of the breast in postmenopausal women, colon and rectum, endometrium, kidney, pancreas, and esophagus. Overweight and obesity may also be associated with increased risk of aggressive prostate cancer, non-Hodgkin lymphoma, multiple myeloma, and cancers of the liver, cervix, ovary, and gallbladder. It's not yet known for certain how diet, nutrition intake, and the amount and distribution of body fat factor into the development of certain cancers.

Environmental hazards: Exposure to various chemicals (including benzene, asbestos, vinyl chloride, arsenic, and aflatoxin) increases risk of various cancers. Risk of lung cancer from asbestos is greatly increased among smokers.

Estrogen: Menopausal hormone therapy (MHT, formerly called hormone replacement therapy) without the use of progestin can increase the risk of endometrial and ovarian cancer. Combining progestin with estrogen MHT may help minimize that risk. Studies, however, suggest that use of MHT increases the risk of breast cancer. The benefits and risks of the use of estrogen should be discussed carefully with one's doctor.

HPV infection: There are three vaccines (Gardasil, Gardasil 9, and Cervarix) approved for use in females ages 9-26 for the prevention of the most common types of HPV infection that cause cervical cancer. Gardasil is also approved for use in males ages 9-26 for the prevention of anal and penile cancers, and the prevention of anal, vaginal, and vulvar cancers (and precancers) in women. Gardasil 9 is approved for use in males ages 9-15 for the prevention of anal cancer.

Radiation: Excessive exposure to ionizing radiation can increase cancer risk. Medical and dental X-rays are adjusted to snus, deliver the lowest dose possible without sacrificing image quality. Excessive radon exposure in the home may increase lung cancer risk, especially in cigarette smokers.

Smokeless tobacco: Use of chewing tobacco, snuff, snus, and other tobacco products that are not smoked causes oral, esophageal, stomach, and pancreatic cancers. The excess risk of cancer of the cheek and gum is especially high among long-term snuff users.

Smoking: The risk of developing lung cancer is about 25 times higher for current male smokers and nearly 26 times higher for current female smokers than for those who have never smoked. Smoking accounts for about 27% of all U.S. cancer deaths. Tobacco use is responsible for nearly 1 in 5 deaths in the U.S. Smoking increases the risk of the following types of cancer: lung, larynx, oral cavity, nose and sinuses, pharynx, esophagus, stomach, pancreas, cervix, kidney, bladder, ovary, colorectum, and acute myeloid leukemia.

Sunlight: Many of the 3.5 mil skin cancers diagnosed annually in the U.S. could have been prevented by protection from the sun's rays and avoiding indoor tanning. Epidemiological evidence shows that sun exposure is a major factor in the development of melanoma and that incidence rates are increasing worldwide.

Screening Guidelines for Early Detection of Cancer

Cancer site	Population	Test or procedure	Frequency
Breast	Women, age 20+	Breast self-examination (BSE)	Beginning in their early 20s: women should be told about BSE. Reporting any new breast symptoms to a health professional should be emphasized. Women should receive instruction and have their technique reviewed at a periodic health exam.
		Clinical breast examination (CBE)	Women in their 20s and 30s: CBE should be part of a periodic health exam, preferably at least every 3 years. Asymptomatic women aged 40+ should continue to receive a CBE as part of a periodic health exam, preferably annually.
		Mammography	At age 40: begin annual mammography. A CBE should be performed prior to mammography.
Cervix	Women, ages 21-65	Pap test, HPV DNA test	All women should begin screening by age 21. Women ages 21-29 should have a Pap test every 3 years. From ages 30-65, the preferred way to screen is with a Pap test combined with an HPV test every 5 years. Another option is to get tested every 3 years with just the Pap test. Some women age 65 or over who have had a certain number of negative consecutive tests in the previous 10 years should consult a physician; health history may allow them to stop cervical cancer screening. Women who have had a total hysterectomy may stop screening. Women should not be screened annually by any method at any age.
Colorectal	Men and women, age 50+	Fecal occult blood test (FOBT) with at least 50% test sensitivity for cancer, or fecal immunochemical test (FIT) with at least 50% test sensitivity for cancer, **or**	Annual, starting at age 50. Testing at home with adherence to manufacturer's recommendation for collection techniques and number of samples is recommended. FOBT with the single stool sample collected on the clinician's fingertip during a digital rectal examination in a health care setting is not recommended. Guaiac-based toilet bowl FOBT tests also are not recommended. In comparison with guaiac-based tests for the detection of occult blood, immunochemical tests are more patient-friendly and are likely to be equal or better in sensitivity and specificity. There is no need to repeat an FOBT in response to an initial positive finding.
		Stool DNA test, **or**	Every 3 years, starting at age 50
		Flexible sigmoidoscopy (FSIG), **or**	Every 5 years, starting at age 50. FSIG can be performed alone, or consideration can be given to combining FSIG performed every 5 years with a highly sensitive guaiac FOBT or FIT performed annually.
		Double contrast barium enema (DCBE), **or**	Every 5 years, starting at age 50
		Colonoscopy	Every 10 years, starting at age 50
		CT colonography	Every 5 years, starting at age 50
Endometrial	Women, at menopause	Women at average risk should be informed about risks and symptoms of endometrial cancer and strongly encouraged to report any unexpected bleeding or spotting to their physicians.	
Lung	Current or former smokers, ages 55-74	Low dose helical CT (LDCT)	Apparently healthy patients who currently smoke or have quit within the past 15 years should discuss lung-cancer screening with a clinician. Informed and shared decision making related to the potential benefits, limitations, and harms associated with screening for lung cancer with LDCT should occur before any decision is made.
Prostate	Men, age 50+	Digital rectal examination (DRE) and prostate-specific antigen test (PSA)	Men who have at least a 10-year life expectancy should make an informed decision with their health care provider about whether to be screened for prostate cancer after receiving information about the potential benefits, risks, and uncertainties associated with prostate cancer screening.

New U.S. Cancer Cases and Deaths for Leading Sites, 2015

Source: *Cancer Facts & Figures 2015*, American Cancer Society, Inc.

The following estimates exclude basal cell and squamous cell skin cancers and in situ carcinomas (i.e., noninvasive cancers), except of the urinary bladder. In 2015, an estimated 60,290 new cases of carcinoma in situ of the female breast and 63,440 cases of melanoma in situ are expected to be diagnosed. More than 3 mil cases of basal cell and squamous cell skin cancer are diagnosed yearly; most cases are highly curable.

Estimated New Cases

Both sexes		Male		Female	
Breast	234,190	Prostate	220,800	Breast	231,840
Lung and bronchus	221,200	Lung and bronchus	115,610	Lung and bronchus	105,590
Prostate	220,800	Urinary bladder	56,320	Uterine corpus	54,870
Colon and rectum	93,090	Colon and rectum	45,890	Thyroid	47,230
Urinary bladder	74,000	Melanoma—skin	42,670	Colon and rectum	47,200
Melanoma—skin	73,870	Non-Hodgkin lymphoma	39,850	Non-Hodgkin lymphoma	32,000
Non-Hodgkin lymphoma	71,850	Kidney and renal pelvis	38,270	Melanoma—skin	31,200
Thyroid	62,450	Liver and intrahepatic bile duct	25,510	Pancreas	24,120
Kidney and renal pelvis	61,560	Pancreas	24,840	Kidney and renal pelvis	23,290
Uterine corpus	54,870	Rectum	23,200	Ovary	21,290
All sites	**1,658,370**	**All sites**	**848,200**	**All sites**	**810,170**

Estimated Deaths

Both sexes		Male		Female	
Lung and bronchus	158,040	Lung and bronchus	86,380	Lung and bronchus	71,660
Colon and rectum	49,700	Prostate	27,540	Breast	40,290
Breast	40,730	Colon and rectum	26,100	Colon and rectum	23,600
Pancreas	40,560	Pancreas	20,710	Pancreas	19,850
Prostate	27,540	Liver and intrahepatic bile duct	17,030	Ovary	14,180
Liver and intrahepatic bile duct	24,550	Esophagus	12,600	Uterine corpus	10,170
Non-Hodgkin lymphoma	19,790	Urinary bladder	11,510	Non-Hodgkin lymphoma	8,310
Urinary bladder	16,000	Non-Hodgkin lymphoma	11,480	Liver and intrahepatic bile duct	7,520
Esophagus	15,590	Kidney and renal pelvis	9,070	Brain and other nervous system	6,380
Brain and other nervous system	15,320	Brain and other nervous system	8,940	Kidney and renal pelvis	5,010
All sites	**589,430**	**All sites**	**312,150**	**All sites**	**277,280**

U.S. Cancer Survival Rates by Year of Diagnosis, 1960-2011

Source: SEER (Surveillance, Epidemiology, and End Results) Cancer Statistics Review, 1975-2012, National Cancer Institute, National Institutes of Health

	All races			White			Black		
Year of diagnosis	% total	% male	% female	% total	% male	% female	% total	% male	% female
1960-63	—	—	—	39%	—	—	27%	—	—
1970-73	—	—	—	43	—	—	31	—	—
1975-77	48.9%	41.7%	55.8%	49.8	42.7%	56.5%	39.1	32.7%	46.2%
1978-80	49.0	43.1	54.9	50.0	44.3	55.6	39.0	33.3	45.6
1981-83	50.1	45.2	55.1	51.3	46.5	55.9	38.8	34.2	44.4
1984-86	52.4	47.1	57.6	53.6	48.5	58.5	40.2	35.5	45.5
1987-89	55.3	51.1	59.6	56.6	52.8	60.6	43.0	38.9	47.7
1990-92	59.9	59.1	60.9	61.4	60.8	62.0	47.8	47.6	48.2
1993-95	61.3	60.8	61.8	62.4	62.0	62.8	52.7	54.4	50.6
1996-98	63.3	62.9	63.6	64.3	64.0	64.6	55.2	57.9	52.0
1999-2001	65.9	66.2	65.7	67.1	67.5	66.8	57.9	61.0	54.2
2002-04	67.0	67.6	66.4	68.3	68.9	67.6	59.4	63.1	55.2
2005-11	68.7	69.3	68.1	69.7	70.2	69.2	62.2	65.4	58.5

— = Statistic could not be calculated. **Note:** The geographic areas of surveillance may vary for different years. Rates are five-year relative (estimated) survival rates for all invasive cancer sites; based on follow-up of patients into 2012.

U.S. Cancer Survival Rates by Age at Diagnosis, 2005-11

Source: SEER (Surveillance, Epidemiology, and End Results) Cancer Statistics Review, 1975-2012, National Cancer Institute, National Institutes of Health

	All races			White			Black		
Age at diagnosis	% total	% male	% female	% total	% male	% female	% total	% male	% female
Under age 45	81.6%	77.0%	84.5%	83.1%	78.9%	86.0%	70.3%	64.6%	73.6%
Ages 45-54	73.4	68.0	77.8	74.8	69.1	79.4	63.6	62.2	65.1
Ages 55-64	70.2	69.9	70.4	71.0	70.6	71.6	63.3	66.0	59.0
Under age 65	73.5	70.5	76.4	74.6	71.5	77.7	64.7	64.7	64.8
Ages 65-74	66.2	69.2	61.9	66.8	69.5	62.9	61.0	66.8	52.5
Ages 65 and older	59.1	63.2	54.2	59.6	63.3	55.2	54.2	61.8	45.5
Ages 75 and older	51.6	55.6	47.7	52.2	55.7	48.8	44.2	52.0	37.8

Note: Rates are five-year relative (estimated) survival rates for all invasive cancer sites; based on follow-up of patients into 2012.

Depression

Source: National Institute of Mental Health (NIMH), National Institutes of Health, U.S. Dept. of Health and Human Services

Depression is a serious illness that affects thoughts, feelings, and the ability to function in everyday life. It strikes all age groups and often goes unrecognized or is inadequately treated. The NIMH estimates that about 20.9 mil American adults age 18 and older suffer from depression or some other mood or depressive disorder in any given year; more than 16% of all Americans will have had depression at some point in life. Young people are at particular risk; in a one-year period, persons aged 18 to 29 years were 200% more likely to have experienced depression than those who were 60 or older. Women are 70% more likely than men to experience depression during their lifetime.

Available treatments can alleviate symptoms, and with awareness growing, more people with depression are seeking help. But many depressed people—and those around them—still fail to realize that they have an illness or could benefit from medical help.

Symptoms and Types of Depression

- Persistent sad, anxious, or "empty" feelings
- Feelings of hopelessness or pessimism
- Feelings of guilt, worthlessness, or helplessness
- Irritability, restlessness
- Loss of interest in activities or hobbies once pleasurable, including sex
- Fatigue and decreased energy
- Difficulty concentrating, remembering details, and making decisions
- Insomnia, early-morning wakefulness, or excessive sleeping
- Overeating or appetite loss
- Thoughts of suicide, suicide attempts
- Aches or pains, headaches, cramps, or digestive problems that do not ease even with treatment

A diagnosis of **major depressive disorder** (or **major depression**) is made if an individual reports experiencing five or more of these symptoms in the same two-week period.

Bipolar disorder (or **manic-depressive illness**) is characterized by episodes of major depression alternating with periods of mania, when a person experiences a persistent, abnormally elevated mood or irritability, accompanied by feelings of inflated self-esteem, less need for sleep, increased talkativeness, racing thoughts, distractibility, agitation, and excessive involvement in pleasurable activities that have a high potential for painful consequences. While it shares some of the features of major depression, bipolar disorder is a distinct illness.

Treatments for Depression

A variety of medicines are used to treat depression. These drugs influence the functioning of certain neurotransmitters in the brain, primarily serotonin and norepinephrine. Older drugs—tricyclic antidepressants (TCAs) and monoamine oxidase inhibitors (MAOIs)—affect the functioning of both of these neurotransmitters. But they can have strong side effects or, in the case of MAOIs, require dietary restrictions. Newer medications, such as selective serotonin reuptake inhibitors (SSRIs), have fewer side effects.

NIMH research has shown that certain types of psychotherapy, particularly cognitive-behavioral therapy (CBT) and interpersonal therapy (IPT), can help relieve depression. CBT helps patients change the negative thinking and behaving patterns often associated with depression. IPT focuses patients on working through personal relationships that may contribute to depression. Studies of adults have shown that a combination of psychotherapy and antidepressant medication is most effective in treating moderate-to-severe depression.

Electroconvulsive therapy (ECT) has been found effective in treating some cases of severe depression, particularly those that have not responded to other forms of treatment. ECT involves producing a seizure in the brain of a patient under general anesthesia by applying electrical stimulation through electrodes placed on the scalp. Memory loss and other cognitive problems, though common side effects, are typically short-lived.

Website: www.nimh.nih.gov

Diabetes

Source: American Diabetes Association; Centers for Disease Control and Prevention, U.S. Dept. of Health and Human Services

Diabetes is a chronic disease in which the body does not produce or properly use the hormone **insulin**. Insulin is needed to convert sugar, starches, and other foods into energy. Both genetics and environment appear to play roles in the onset of diabetes. This disease, which has no cure, is the seventh leading cause of death by disease in the U.S. According to death certificate data, 75,578 people in the U.S. died as a result of diabetes in 2013. In 2012, an estimated 29.1 mil Americans had diabetes, 8.1 mil of whom were undiagnosed.

The American Diabetes Association supports studies proving that detection at an earlier stage and modest lifestyle changes, such as eating better and exercising more, will help prevent or delay complications.

There are two major types of diabetes:

Type 1 (formerly known as insulin-dependent or juvenile diabetes). The body does not produce insulin; the disease is usually diagnosed in children and young adults. People with type 1 diabetes must take daily insulin to stay alive.

Type 2 (formerly known as non-insulin dependent or adult-onset diabetes). The body does not produce enough or cannot properly use insulin. It is the most common form of the disease (90%-95% of diabetes cases in people over age 20) and often begins later in life.

Prediabetes

In 2012, 86 mil Americans age 20 and older had prediabetes, the state that occurs when a person's blood glucose levels are higher than normal but not high enough for a diagnosis of diabetes. According to the Centers for Disease Control and Prevention, 15%-30% of people with prediabetes will develop type 2 diabetes within five years unless lifestyle changes are made.

Complications From Diabetes

People often have diabetes for many years before it is diagnosed. During that time, serious complications may develop. Potential complications include the following:

Blindness. Diabetes is the leading cause of new cases of blindness in people ages 20-74. Each year, 12,000 to 24,000 people lose their eyesight because of diabetes.

Kidney disease. About 30% of patients with type 1 diabetes and 10%-40% of those with type 2 diabetes eventually suffer from kidney failure. In 2011, a total of 49,677 people in the U.S. initiated treatment for kidney failure due to diabetes.

Amputations. Diabetes is the most frequent cause for nontraumatic lower-limb amputations. The risk of a leg amputation is 15-40 times greater for a person with diabetes than for the average American. In 2010, approximately 73,000 lower-limb amputations were performed as a result of complications brought on by diabetes.

Heart disease and stroke. People with diabetes are about 1.7 times more likely to die of heart disease. They are 1.5 times more likely to suffer a stroke.

Common Diabetes Symptoms

- Frequent urination
- Thirst
- Hunger
- Extreme fatigue
- Blurry vision
- Cuts/bruises that are slow to heal
- Weight loss, even with increased caloric intake (type 1)
- Tingling, pain, or numbness in the hands/feet (type 2)

Gestational Diabetes

Gestational diabetes is a form of diabetes that affects about 18% of pregnant women. Usually there are no symptoms, or the symptoms are mild. Because the condition usually appears around the 24th week, it is recommended that all pregnant women receive a glucose tolerance test between the 24th and 28th week. Pregnancy hormones can cause insulin resistance, making blood glucose levels rise. The goal of treatment is to keep blood glucose levels within normal limits, mainly through diet and exercise; treatment may also include daily blood glucose testing and insulin injections. Women with gestational diabetes tend to have larger babies at birth, which can increase the chance of problems at the time of delivery. Glucose levels usually return to normal after delivery, but odds of recurrence in future pregnancies and development of type 2 diabetes later in life increase.

Website: www.diabetes.org

Eating Disorders

Source: National Institute of Mental Health, National Institutes of Health, U.S. Dept. of Health and Human Services

Eating disorders involve serious disturbances in eating behavior, usually in the forms of extreme and unhealthy reduction of food intake or severe overeating. They are not due to a failure of will; rather, they are real and treatable medical illnesses in which certain behavior patterns get out of control. The main types are anorexia nervosa, bulimia nervosa, and binge-eating disorder (technically categorized with "eating disorders not otherwise specified"). These disorders usually develop in adolescence or early adulthood and often occur with other illnesses such as depression, substance abuse, and anxiety disorders. They are much more common among females; about 5%-10% of anorexia patients, 20% of bulimia patients, and 40% of binge eaters are male.

If not treated, eating disorders can lead to serious complications, including heart conditions and kidney failure, which may result in death.

Anorexia nervosa affects an estimated 0.9% of all females. Symptoms include resistance to maintaining weight at minimally healthy levels, intense fear of gaining weight, exaggerated importance of body weight or shape in one's self image, and infrequent or absent menstrual periods. Anorexics see themselves as overweight even when they are dangerously thin. In response, they avoid food and take other extreme measures to lose weight, such as exercising compulsively or purging by means of vomiting or laxatives and enemas. While some anorexics fully recover after a single episode, others may relapse frequently or experience chronic deterioration.

Bulimia nervosa affects an estimated 0.5% of females. It is characterized by recurrent uncontrolled binge-eating episodes followed by what is believed to be compensatory behavior to prevent weight gain, such as self-induced vomiting, use of laxatives or diuretics, exercising excessively, or fasting. Persons with bulimia can weigh within the normal range for their age and height, but they still fear gaining weight and are intensely dissatisfied with their bodies. They often perform their behaviors in secret, feeling shame when they binge and relief when they purge.

Binge-eating disorder affects an estimated 2%-3.5% of males and females in the U.S. As with bulimia, a binge-eating disorder involves episodes of excessive eating during which the sufferer may feel a complete lack of control. But individuals with this disorder do not compensate by purging, exercising, or fasting. Many are thus overweight or obese, and the shame they feel can lead to further binge-eating.

Eating disorder sufferers may not admit they are ill. Early diagnosis and a comprehensive treatment program are essential to recovery. Some patients may need immediate hospitalization. For anorexia, treatment usually follows three established steps: weight restoration, usually in an inpatient hospital setting; treatment of any accompanying psychological disturbances, including the use of medications; and achieving long-term remission or recovery by reducing or eliminating negative thoughts and behaviors.

Heart and Blood Vessel Disease

Source: American Heart Association; National Center for Chronic Disease Prevention and Health Promotion, Centers for Disease Control and Prevention; National Heart, Blood, and Lung Institute, National Institutes of Health, U.S. Dept. of Health and Human Services

Warning Signs of Heart Attack

- Chest discomfort. Most heart attacks involve discomfort in the center of the chest that lasts more than a few minutes or that goes away and then returns. It can feel like uncomfortable pressure, squeezing, fullness, or pain.
- Discomfort in other areas of the upper body. Symptoms can include pain or discomfort in one or both arms, the back, neck, jaw, or stomach.
- Shortness of breath. This feeling may occur with or without chest discomfort.
- Other signs may include breaking out in a cold sweat, nausea, or lightheadedness.

The American Heart Association advises immediate action at onset of symptoms, as more than half of heart attack victims die within an hour of symptoms first manifesting. Call 9-1-1. Get to a hospital right away.

Warning Signs of Stroke

- Sudden numbness or weakness of the face, arm, or leg, especially on one side of the body.
- Sudden confusion, trouble speaking, or understanding.
- Sudden trouble seeing in one or both eyes.
- Sudden trouble walking, dizziness, loss of balance or coordination.
- Sudden severe headache with no known cause.

Prompt treatment of a stroke can be a major factor in controlling the effects. If you have one or more stroke symptoms that last more than a few minutes, call 9-1-1 or the emergency medical service number immediately so an ambulance, ideally one with advanced life support, can be sent for you quickly.

Major Modifiable Risk Factors

High blood pressure. High blood pressure, or hypertension, increases the risk of stroke, heart attack, kidney failure, and congestive heart failure. It affects men and women of all races, ethnic origins, and ages. Obesity, physical inactivity, and an unhealthy diet can contribute to this often symptomless disease. Individuals should have a blood pressure reading at least once every two years or more often if advised by a physician.

A blood pressure reading consists of two measurements, with one value written above the other, such as 122/78 mmHg (millimeters of mercury). The upper number (systolic pressure) represents the amount of pressure in the arteries when the heart contracts (beats) and pushes blood through the circulatory system. The lower number (diastolic pressure) represents the pressure in the arteries between beats, when the heart is resting. According to National Institutes of Health (NIH) guidelines, a blood pressure reading below 120/80 is considered normal, while readings from 120/80 to 139/89 are considered prehypertension.

There are two stages of high blood pressure:
Stage 1 is 140-159 (systolic) over 90-99 (diastolic);
Stage 2 is 160+ (systolic) over 100+ (diastolic).

The diagnosis can be based on either the systolic or the diastolic reading.

High blood pressure usually cannot be cured, but it can be controlled in a variety of ways, including lifestyle modifications and medication. Treatment always should be at the direction and under the supervision of a physician. The treatment goal for patients with hypertension is blood pressure below 140/90. Individuals with hypertension and diabetes or chronic kidney disease should aim for blood pressure lower than 130/80.

High blood cholesterol. Cholesterol is a waxy fat-like substance found in all cells of the body. It is produced by the body and also comes in some foods. The body needs some cholesterol, but excess levels increase the risk of heart disease. High cholesterol in itself usually does not cause symptoms, so many people are unaware that they have a problem.

There are two major kinds of cholesterol: LDL (low-density lipoprotein), often called "bad" cholesterol, leads to narrowing of the arteries. HDL (high-density lipoprotein), known as "good" cholesterol, helps reduce that risk.

NIH guidelines classify total cholesterol levels (determined by a blood test) of less than 200 mg/dl as desirable, 200-239 as borderline high, and 240 and higher as high. About 13% of Americans have a cholesterol level of 240 mg/dl or higher. LDL levels of less than 100 mg/dl are considered optimal, 130-159 as borderline high, 160-189 as high, and 190 and higher as very high. For HDL, levels of 60 mg/dl and higher are considered protective against heart disease, while levels under 40 mg/dl are considered a risk factor.

As with high blood pressure, high blood cholesterol can be controlled by lifestyle changes and medication and should be treated by a physician.

Triglycerides, another form of fat in the blood, can also raise the risk of heart disease. Levels that are borderline high (150-199 mg/dl) or high (200 or more) may need treatment.

Diabetes. Diabetes is a major risk factor for heart disease; at least 65% of people with diabetes mellitus die of some form of heart disease or stroke.

Smoking. Cigarette smokers are two to four times more likely to develop coronary heart disease (CHD). Smoking is also associated with the risk of sudden cardiac death.

Obesity. Using a body mass index (BMI) of 25 and higher for overweight and 30 and higher for obesity, about 69% of Americans aged 20 and over are either overweight or obese, and 35% are obese.

Physical inactivity. A sedentary lifestyle is a risk factor for CHD. The risk increase is comparable to that observed for high blood cholesterol, high blood pressure, or cigarette smoking.

Women and Cardiovascular Disease

The American Heart Association reports that heart disease, stroke, and other cardiovascular diseases are the number one cause of death in American women. (Cancer is the second leading cause.) Nearly one in three women died of some form of cardiovascular disease in 2011. Because heart disease was long viewed as a "man's" disease, many of the major cardiovascular studies were conducted only on men. Recent attention has been directed toward understanding the influence of gender on cardiovascular disease risk and prevention, but important gaps in knowledge remain.

Women often present some of the same classic symptoms of heart attack as men, such as chest pain that spreads to the shoulders and arms. But women may more often report atypical chest pain, abdominal pain, difficulty breathing (dyspnea), nausea/vomiting, and back or jaw pain. Another problem in **diagnosis** is that women tend to have heart attacks later in life than men, so symptoms may be masked by other age-related diseases such as arthritis or osteoporosis. Even certain diagnostic tests and procedures such as the exercise stress test may not be as accurate in women, with the result that the disease process leading to heart attack or stroke may not be detected early on, with potentially serious consequences.

Website: www.heart.org

Common Infectious Diseases

Source: National Institutes of Health, Centers for Disease Control and Prevention, U.S. Dept. of Health and Human Services; World Health Organization

The following is a list of major infectious diseases. It is meant to be used for reference purposes only and not as a tool for diagnosis. Statistics may appear uneven because of the different reporting methods used by the various agencies and because not all diseases are surveyed in the same year.

Chicken pox

(*Varicella simplex*) Usually nonthreatening viral disease commonly associated with children. In adults, the disease can be serious. **Transmission:** highly contagious. Transmitted by direct contact with rash, coughing, or sneezing of infected persons. **Symptoms:** blister-like rash, discomfort, high fever. Infected people may develop shingles later in life. **Vaccine:** available since 1995. **Treatment:** none; antibiotics in some severe cases. **Annual U.S. cases:** before 1995, about 4 mil, mostly children; 13,447 reported in 2012.

Chlamydia

(*Chlamydia trachomatis*) One of the most widely spread sexually transmitted diseases (STDs). **Transmission:** sexually transmitted. **Symptoms:** about 70% of those infected show no symptoms. In women, vaginal discharge, infection of the cervix and urinary tract; can cause pelvic inflammatory disease. In men, infection of urinary tract and epididymitis (inflammation of testicular duct); can also infect the throat, rectum, and eyes. **Treatment:** curable with antibiotics. **Annual U.S. cases:** 1,422,976 in 2012.

Common cold

(More than 200 different viruses) An upper respiratory viral infection. **Transmission:** touching one's nose, eyes, or mouth after touching something contaminated by the virus; inhalation of airborne virus. **Symptoms:** irritated nose or scratchy throat, sneezing and watery green or yellow nasal discharge, coughing, muscle aches, headaches, postnasal drip, decreased appetite. **Treatment:** no cure. Over-the-counter remedies can relieve symptoms; effectiveness of antiviral drugs uncertain. **Est. annual U.S. cases:** about 1 bil.

Gonorrhea

(*Neisseria gonorrhoeae*) Common bacterial STD. **Transmission:** sexually transmitted. **Symptoms:** in men, discomfort in urethra, yellow or green discharge, burning during urination. In women, pelvic pain, bleeding associated with intercourse, burning during urination, yellow or bloody discharge. **Treatment:** highly curable with antibiotics. **Annual U.S. cases:** 334,826 in 2012.

Hepatitis

A viral disease that causes inflammation of the liver. In the U.S., five forms are endemic: A, B, C, D, and E. Forms A, B, and C are the most common. **Symptoms:** all forms have generally similar symptoms including jaundice, fatigue, abdominal pain, loss of appetite, nausea, mild flu-like symptoms. Many cases cause no symptoms. In extreme cases, liver transplants may be necessary.

Hepatitis A (*Hepatovirus picornaviridae*). **Transmission:** consuming food or water contaminated with feces from infected persons. **Vaccine:** effective; travelers are advised to not drink tap water in countries where disease is common. **Treatment:** disease usually resolves on its own; alcohol consumption should be avoided. **Est. annual U.S. cases:** 2,700 infections in 2011; 1,562 acute lab-confirmed cases reported in 2012.

Hepatitis B (*Orthohepadnavirus hepadnaviridae*). **Transmission:** unsterilized needle sharing; contaminated blood transfusions; sexual contact. **Vaccine:** highly effective. **Treatment:** for chronic cases, drug treatment is necessary. For acute cases, disease usually resolves itself. Severe cases treated with lamivudine. **Est. annual U.S. cases:** 18,800 infections in 2011; 2,895 acute lab-confirmed cases reported in 2012.

Hepatitis C (*Hepacivirus flavinviridae*). **Transmission:** unsterilized needle sharing; contaminated blood transfusions; sexual contact. **Vaccine:** none. **Treatment:** chronic cases treated with drugs, which eliminates virus in about 50% of patients. For acute cases, treatment recommended if disease present after two to three months. **Est. annual U.S. cases:** 16,500 infections in 2011; 1,782 acute lab-confirmed cases reported in 2012.

HPV

(More than 100 strains of human papillomavirus) Common viral infection; leading cause of cervical cancer. **Transmission:** sexually transmitted. **Symptoms:** most of those infected have no symptoms but can still transmit virus. In some cases, genital warts and precancerous bumps on anus, cervix or vulva, or penis. **Vaccine:** Gardasil and Cervarix. **Treatment:** while there is no cure, a healthy immune system can usually fight off HPV on its own. Women with HPV should have a Pap smear and pelvic exam every six months. **Est. annual U.S. cases:** 14 mil new cases; approximately 79 mil currently infected with HPV.

Influenza

(Various influenza viruses) Highly contagious viral respiratory infection. **Transmission:** airborne; contact with face after touching infected surface. **Symptoms:** chills, fatigue, fever, headaches, sore throat, sinus congestion, coughing. ("Stomach flu" is not influenza.) **Vaccine:** yearly vaccinations recommended; available as injection or nasal spray. **Treatment:** antiviral drugs; disease normally runs its course in a matter of days. **Est. annual U.S. cases:** 5%-20% of population; more than 200,000 flu-related hospitalizations, 3,000-49,000 flu-related deaths.

Lyme disease

(*Borrelia burgdorferi*) Bacterial inflammatory disease, first identified 1975 in Old Lyme, CT. Found across the U.S., usually in areas with large deer populations. **Transmission:** bite from infected deer tick. Mice and deer are most common tick hosts. **Symptoms:** mimic those of other diseases. Flu-like symptoms: fatigue, stiff neck, joints. Skin rash may appear at site of tick bite. **Treatment:** antibiotics in early stages; anti-inflammatory drugs to relieve symptoms. Without treatment, long-term complications (some fatal) involving joints, heart, and nervous system. **Annual U.S. cases:** from 9,895 reported cases in 1992 to 30,831 confirmed and probable cases in 2012.

Malaria

(*Plasmodium* parasite) Infectious disease known from as early as 2700 BCE. Virtually eradicated in developed countries; still a major killer in tropical regions. **Transmission:** bite from infected mosquito. **Symptoms:** high fever, shaking chills, heavy sweating, headaches, fatigue, enlarged spleen. If left untreated, organ damage and death. **Treatment:** antimalarial drugs, including chloroquine, for treatment and prevention. **Annual cases:** 1,503 in the U.S. in 2012; worldwide, an estimated 207 mil cases and 627,000 deaths, mostly young children in sub-Saharan Africa, in 2012.

Measles

(*Rubeola* virus) Once-common viral infection; occurs sporadically in U.S. **Transmission:** airborne transmission by infected persons. **Symptoms:** itchy and raised rash, sore throat, cough, pink eye, high fever. In rare cases, encephalitis, seizures, permanent deafness, death. **Vaccine:** highly effective. **Treatment:** no specific treatment; symptoms relieved with bed rest, acetaminophen, humidified air. **Annual U.S. cases:** 55 in 2012.

Mumps

(Mumps virus) Acute and contagious viral infection. **Transmission:** direct contact with mucus or saliva of infected persons. **Symptoms:** painful, visible swelling of the salivary or parotid glands in the face. Chills, headaches, fever, painful swallowing. In some cases, inflammation of testes, pancreas, ovaries. In severe cases, brain swelling and symptoms ranging from nausea and drowsiness to seizures and permanent deafness. **Vaccine:** MMR (measles, mumps, and rubella) vaccine is effective. **Treatment:** no specific treatment; symptoms may be relieved by applying ice or heat to swollen glands. **Annual U.S. cases:** 229 in 2012.

Peptic ulcer

(Most from *Helicobacter pylori* [*H. pylori*] bacteria; also overuse of aspirin or other anti-inflammatory drugs) Weakening of the stomach's protective mucous coating, allowing stomach acid and bacteria to irritate stomach lining. **Transmission:** *H. pylori* may be transmitted through food and water. **Symptoms:** indigestion; bloating; dull, transient abdominal pain or discomfort; nausea; vomiting. **Treatment:** antibiotics, acid-suppressing drugs. **Est. annual U.S. cases:** about 20% of the population under 40 years of age and half of those over 60 may be infected with *H. pylori*. An estimated 500,000 to 850,000 develop peptic ulcers each year.

Pertussis or Whooping cough

(*Bordetella pertussis* or *B. parepertussis*) Upper respiratory bacterial infection. **Transmission:** airborne transmission by infected persons; highly contagious. **Symptoms:** initially, mild cold-like symptoms, fever, diarrhea, difficulty breathing; later, violent coughing with characteristic "whooping" sound when patient tries to breathe between coughs, vomiting. In severe cases, apnea, pneumonia, seizures, encephalopathy. **Vaccine:** available as part of Tdap (tetanus, diphtheria, pertussis) combination vaccine. **Treatment:** antibiotics in early cases; otherwise, disease must run its course. **Annual U.S. cases:** 48,277 in 2012.

Salmonella or Salmonellosis

(*Salmonella enteritidis*) Bacterial infection. **Transmission:** eating foods contaminated by feces carrying the bacteria or eating undercooked meats or raw eggs contaminated by bacteria. Contact with feces of infected animal or pet. **Symptoms:** fever, diarrhea, abdominal cramps 12 to 72 hours after infection. **Treatment:** no standard treatment. Runs its course in four to seven days. Antibiotics in severe cases. **Annual U.S. cases:** 53,800 in 2012.

Shigellosis

(Four species of *Shigella*: *boydii*, *dysenteriae*, *flexneri*, and *sonnei*) Bacterial infection and a form of dysentery, an intestinal disease. **Transmission:** consuming food contaminated by infected feces or eating vegetables grown in fields containing contaminated sewage. Swimming in contaminated water. **Symptoms:** watery or bloody diarrhea one to four days after infection, high fever, vomiting, painful bowel movements. In extreme cases, seizures in children, intestinal perforation. **Treatment:** mild infection allowed to run its course; replacement of fluids and salts lost through excessive diarrhea. Antibiotics in severe cases. Although severe diarrhea is symptomatic, antidiarrheal medicines may make illness worse. **Annual U.S. cases:** 15,283 in 2012.

Syphilis

(*Treponema pallidum*) Bacterial infection known since ancient times that spread rampantly throughout Europe in the Middle Ages. **Transmission:** sexually transmitted. **Symptoms:** primary stage: painless sore, called a chancre, where bacteria enters the body; usually heals in 3 to 12 weeks with or without treatment. Without treatment, disease enters secondary stage: skin rash as chancre is healing or weeks after it is healed. Without treatment, enters tertiary stage: mouth sores, fever, fatigue, loss of appetite, weight loss, hair loss, jaundice, syphilitic meningitis, aortal aneurysms, lesions, damage to nervous system, heart, and eyes. Most infected do not progress beyond primary or secondary stage. **Treatment:** curable with antibiotics (mostly penicillin). **Annual U.S. cases:** 49,903 in 2012; 15,667 primary and secondary.

Tetanus or Lockjaw

(*Clostridium tetani*) Bacterial infection. **Transmission:** bacteria, found in soil, entering body through broken skin. **Symptoms:** muscle stiffness and spasms or "locking" of muscles of the jaw, neck, and limbs. **Vaccine:** four forms of immunization. **Treatment:** tetanus immune globulin to fight infection. With treatment, less than 10% of cases are fatal. **Annual U.S. cases:** 37 in 2012.

Tuberculosis

(*Mycobacterium tuberculosis*) Bacterial infection that primarily affects the lungs. **Transmission:** airborne transmission by persons with active TB infection. **Symptoms:** weight loss, fever, cough with discharge (sometimes with bloody sputum), night sweats, growing shortness of breath over time, chest pains. **Vaccine/treatment:** BCG (Bacille Calmette Guerin) vaccine only effective in protecting young children and used where TB is prevalent. Not recommended by health experts for use in the U.S. because of the low risk of infection and its variable effectiveness. **Annual U.S. cases:** 9,945 in 2012.

Yellow fever

(Yellow fever virus, in *flavivirus* group) Viral infection that has caused large epidemics in South America, the Caribbean, and Africa. **Transmission:** bite from mosquito carrying the virus. **Symptoms:** headaches, muscle aches, fever, jaundice (yellowing skin), nausea and vomiting, kidney failure, severe generalized pain. In severe cases, shock, coma, and death. **Vaccine:** available, safe, and effective. **Treatment:** symptoms treated until disease runs its course. **Annual cases:** none in the U.S.; an estimated 200,000 new cases and 30,000 deaths worldwide.

U.S. Reported Cases and Deaths From Vaccine-Preventable Diseases, 1950-2013

Source: Centers for Disease Control and Prevention, U.S. Dept. of Health and Human Services

	Diphtheria		Tetanus		Pertussis		Polio (paralytic)		Measles		Mumps		Rubella	
Year	Cases	Deaths	Cases	Deaths	Cases	Deaths	Cases	Deaths	Cases	Deaths	Cases	Deaths	Cases	Deaths
1950	5,796	410	486	336	120,718	1,118	33,300	1,904	319,124	468	NR		NR	
1960	918	69	368	231	14,809	118	3,190	230	441,703	380	NR	42	NR	12
1970	435	30	148	79	4,249	12	33	7	47,351	89	104,953	16	56,552	31
1980	3	1	95	28	1,730	11	9	2	13,506	11	8,576	2	3,904	1
1990	4	1	64	11	4,570	12	6	0	27,786	64	5,292	1	1,125	8
2000	1	0	35	5	7,867	12	0	0	86	1	338	2	176	0
2001	2	0	37	5	7,580	17	0	0	116	1	266	0	23	2
2002	1	0	25	5	9,771	18	0	0	44	0	270	1	18	0
2003	1	1	20	4	11,647	11	0	0	56	1	231	0	7	0
2004	0	0	34	4	25,827	16	0	0	37	0	258	0	10	1
2005	0	0	27	1	25,616	31	1[1]	0	66	NA	314	0	11	0
2006	0	0	41	4	15,632	9	0	0	55	0	6,584	1	11	0
2007	0	0	28	5	10,454	9	0	0	43	0	800	0	11	1
2008	0	0	19	3	13,278	20	0	0	140	0	454	2	16	0
2009	0	0	18	6	16,858	15	1[1]	0	71	NA	1,991	2	3	2
2010	0	0	26	3	27,550	26	0	0	63	NA	2,612	2	5	2
2011	0	NA	36	NA	18,719	NA	0	NA	220	NA	404	NA	4	NA
2012	1	NA	37	NA	48,277	NA	0	NA	55	NA	229	NA	9	NA
2013	0	NA	26	NA	28,639	NA	1[1]	NA	187	NA	584	NA	9	NA

NA = Not available. NR = Not nationally reportable. (1) Vaccine-associated/derived paralytic polio.

Dietary Guidelines for Americans, 2010: Key Recommendations

Source: *Dietary Guidelines for Americans, 2010,* U.S. Dept. of Agriculture; U.S. Dept. of Health and Human Services

Balancing Calories to Manage Weight

- Prevent and/or reduce overweight and obesity through improved eating and physical activity behaviors.
- Control total calorie intake to manage body weight.
- Increase physical activity and reduce time spent in sedentary behaviors.
- Maintain appropriate calorie balance during each stage of life.

Foods and Food Components to Reduce

- Reduce daily sodium intake to less than 2,300 mg. Further reduce intake to 1,500 mg among persons who are 51 and older and those of any age who are African American or have hypertension, diabetes, or chronic kidney disease.
- Consume less than 10% of calories from saturated fatty acids by replacing them with monounsaturated and polyunsaturated fatty acids.
- Consume less than 300 mg per day of dietary cholesterol.
- Keep trans fatty acid consumption as low as possible by limiting foods that contain synthetic sources of trans fats, such as partially hydrogenated oils.
- Reduce the intake of calories from solid fats and added sugars.
- Limit the consumption of foods that contain refined grains, especially refined grain foods that contain solid fats, added sugars, and sodium.
- If alcohol is consumed, it should be consumed in moderation—up to one drink per day for women and two drinks per day for men.

Foods and Nutrients to Increase

- Increase vegetable and fruit intake.
- Eat a variety of vegetables (especially dark-green, red, and orange vegetables), beans, and peas.
- Consume at least half of all grains as whole grains. Replace refined grains with whole grains.
- Increase intake of fat-free or low-fat milk and milk products, such as milk, yogurt, cheese, or fortified soy beverages.
- Choose a variety of protein foods, which include seafood, lean meat/poultry, eggs, beans and peas, soy products, and unsalted nuts and seeds.
- Increase seafood consumed by choosing seafood in place of some meat and poultry.
- Replace protein foods that are higher in solid fats with choices that are lower in solid fats and calories and/or are sources of oils.
- Use oils to replace solid fats where possible.
- Choose foods that provide more potassium, dietary fiber, calcium, and vitamin D, which are nutrients of concern in American diets. These foods include vegetables, fruits, whole grains, and milk and milk products.

Building Healthy Eating Patterns

- Select an eating pattern that meets nutrient needs over time at an appropriate calorie level.
- Account for all foods and beverages consumed and assess how they fit within a total healthy eating pattern.
- Follow food safety recommendations when preparing and eating foods to reduce the risk of foodborne illnesses.

Website: www.health.gov/dietaryguidelines/

Dietary Requirements

The Food and Nutrition Board of the National Academy of Sciences' Institute of Medicine, in reports published between 1997 and 2010, established **Dietary Reference Intakes (DRIs)**. DRIs establish daily consumption values for vitamins and elements (often called minerals) that aim to optimize health, not just guard against nutritional deficiencies, at all stages of life.

There are four DRI categories. The **Recommended Dietary Allowance (RDA)** gives intake values that meet the nutrient requirements of almost all (97%-98%) healthy individuals in a specified group. The **Estimated Average Requirement (EAR)** specifies the average daily nutrient intake level estimated to meet the requirement of half the healthy individuals in a specified group. **Adequate Intake (AI)** values are given when there is inadequate scientific evidence to calculate an RDA. For healthy breastfed infants, the AI is the mean intake; for other life stage groups, the AI is thought to cover the needs of all group individuals, but lack of data or uncertainty in the data prevents the percentage of individuals covered from being specified with confidence. The **Tolerable Upper Intake Level (UL)** designates the maximum intake amount that is unlikely to pose a risk of adverse health effects in almost all healthy individuals in a group. RDAs and AIs may both be used as individual intake goals.

Estimated Calorie Requirements

Source: *Dietary Guidelines for Americans, 2010,* U.S. Dept. of Agriculture; U.S. Dept. of Health and Human Services

Estimated amount of calories, rounded to the nearest 200, needed to maintain energy balance by sex, for various age groups and levels of physical activity.

	Age (years)	Sedentary[1]	Moderately active[2]	Active[3]
Child	2-3	1,000-1,200	1,000-1,400	1,000-1,400
Female[4]	4-8	1,200-1,400	1,400-1,600	1,400-1,800
	9-13	1,400-1,600	1,600-2,000	1,800-2,200
	14-18	1,800	2,000	2,400
	19-30	1,800-2,000	2,000-2,200	2,400
	31-50	1,800	2,000	2,200
	51+	1,600	1,800	2,000-2,200

	Age (years)	Sedentary[1]	Moderately active[2]	Active[3]
Male	4-8	1,200-1,400	1,400-1,600	1,600-2,000
	9-13	1,600-2,000	1,800-2,200	2,000-2,600
	14-18	2,000-2,400	2,400-2,800	2,800-3,200
	19-30	2,400-2,600	2,600-2,800	3,000
	31-50	2,200-2,400	2,400-2,600	2,800-3,000
	51+	2,000-2,200	2,200-2,400	2,400-2,800

Note: Based on Estimated Energy Requirements (EER) equations, using reference heights (average) and reference weights (healthy) for each age/gender group. For children and adolescents, reference height and weight vary. For adults, the reference man is 5 ft 10 in. tall and weighs 154 lbs. The reference woman is 5 ft 4 in. tall and weighs 126 lbs. (1) Engaging only in the light activities associated with ordinary day-to-day life. (2) Includes physical activity equivalent to walking 1.5 to 3 miles per day at 3-4 mph. (3) Includes physical activity equivalent to walking more than 3 miles per day at 3-4 mph. (4) Excludes women who are pregnant or breastfeeding.

Understanding Food Components

Proteins, composed of amino acids, are essential to good nutrition. They build, maintain, and repair the body. Best sources: eggs, milk, fish, meat, poultry, soybeans, nuts. High-quality proteins such as eggs, meat, or fish supply all eight amino acids needed in a diet. Plant-sourced foods can be combined to meet protein needs as well.

Fats provide energy by furnishing calories to the body. They also help the body absorb vitamins A, D, E, and K. Best sources of polyunsaturated and monounsaturated fats: vegetable/plant oils, nuts. Concentrated sources of saturated fats: meats, cheeses, butter, cream, egg yolks, lard.

Carbohydrates are the most important source of energy for the body. The digestive system changes carbohydrates into glucose, which the body uses for energy for cells, tissues, and organs. The body stores extra sugar in the liver and muscles. Best sources: grains, legumes, potatoes, vegetables, fruits.

Fiber is the portion of plant foods that our bodies cannot digest. There are two basic types: insoluble and soluble. Insoluble fibers help move food materials through the digestive tract; soluble fibers tend to slow them down. Both types absorb water, thus preventing and treating constipation. Soluble fibers may also be helpful in reducing blood cholesterol levels. Best sources: beans, bran, fruits, whole grains, vegetables.

Water dissolves and transports other nutrients throughout the body, aiding in the processes of digestion, absorption, circulation, and excretion. It helps regulate body temperature.

Vitamins

Vitamin A promotes good eyesight; helps keep skin and mucous membranes resistant to infection. Best sources: liver, sweet potatoes, carrots, kale, cantaloupe, turnip greens, collard greens, broccoli, fortified milk.

Vitamin B_1 (thiamine) prevents beriberi. Essential to carbohydrate metabolism and nervous system health. Best sources: eggs, enriched bread and flour, nuts, seeds, organ meats, whole grains.

Vitamin B_2 (riboflavin) protects the skin, mouth, eyes, and mucous membranes. Essential to growth, red blood cell production, and energy metabolism. Best sources: dairy products, meat, poultry, broccoli, spinach, eggs, nuts.

Vitamin B_6 (pyridoxine) is important in the regulation of the central nervous system and in protein metabolism. Best sources: whole grains, meat, fish, nuts, avocado, bananas.

Vitamin B_{12} (cobalamin) is needed to form red blood cells. Best sources: meat, shellfish, poultry, eggs, dairy products.

Niacin maintains health of skin, nerves, and the digestive system. Best sources: poultry, nuts, fish, eggs.

Folic acid (folacin) is required for new cell formation, growth, and reproduction and for important chemical reactions in body cells. Best sources: leafy green vegetables, fruits, dried beans, peas, nuts, enriched bread, cereals.

Other B vitamins include biotin and pantothenic acid.

Vitamin C (ascorbic acid) maintains collagen, a protein necessary for the formation of skin, ligaments, and bones. Helps heal wounds and mend fractures. Best sources: citrus fruits and juices, cantaloupe, broccoli, Brussels sprouts, potatoes and sweet potatoes, tomatoes, cabbage.

Vitamin D is important for bone development. Best sources: sunlight, milk products, tuna, salmon, oysters.

Vitamin E (tocopherol) helps protect red blood cells. Best sources: vegetable oils, wheat germ, whole grains, eggs, peanuts, margarine, green leafy vegetables.

Vitamin K is necessary for formation of prothrombin, which helps blood to clot. Also made by intestinal bacteria. Best dietary sources: green leafy vegetables, tomatoes.

Minerals

Calcium works with phosphorus to build and maintain bones and teeth. Best sources: dairy, leafy green vegetables.

Phosphorus's main function is in the formation of bones and teeth, but it performs more functions than any other mineral and plays a part in nearly every chemical reaction in the body. Best sources: cheese, milk, meats, poultry, fish, tofu.

Iron is necessary for the formation of myoglobin, a reservoir of oxygen for muscle tissue, and hemoglobin, which transports oxygen within blood. Best sources: lean meats, beans, green leafy vegetables, shellfish, whole grains.

Other minerals include chloride, chromium, cobalt, copper, fluoride, iodine, magnesium, manganese, molybdenum, potassium, selenium, sodium, sulfur, zinc.

Understanding Food Label Claims

Source: Center for Food Safety and Applied Nutrition, U.S. Food and Drug Admin. (FDA), U.S. Dept. of Health and Human Services; Food Safety and Inspection Service, Agricultural Marketing Service, U.S. Dept. of Agriculture (USDA)

Nutrition Packaging Terms

Manufacturers can make certain claims on processed food labels only if they meet the definitions specified here.

SUGAR. Sugar free: less than 0.5 g per serving; **No added sugars; Without added sugars:** no sugars or sugar-containing ingredients added during processing; must state if food is not "low calorie" or "reduced calorie"; **Unsweetened; No added sweeteners:** remain as factual statements; **Reduced sugar:** at least 25% less sugar than reference food.

FAT. Fat free: less than 0.5 g of fat per serving; **Saturated fat free:** less than 0.5 g of saturated fat and less than 0.5 g of trans fatty acids per serving; **Low fat:** 3 g or less per serving and, if the serving is 30 g or less or 2 tbs or less, per 50 g of the food; **Low saturated fat:** 1 g or less per serving and not more than 15% of calories from saturated fat; **Reduced fat; Less fat:** at least 25% less per serving than reference food.

FIBER. High fiber: 5 g or more per serving (must also meet low-fat definition or state level of total fat); **Good source of fiber:** 2.5 g to 4.9 g per serving; **More fiber; Added fiber:** at least 2.5 g more per serving than reference food.

SODIUM. Sodium free: less than 5 mg per serving; **Low sodium:** 140 mg or less per serving and, if the serving is 30 g or less or 2 tbs or less, per 50 g of the food; **Very low sodium:** 35 mg or less per serving and, if the serving is 30 g or less or 2 tbs or less, per 50 g of the food; **Reduced sodium; Less sodium:** at least 25% less per serving than reference food.

CALORIES. Calorie free: less than 5 calories per serving; **Low calorie:** 40 calories or less per serving; if the serving is 30 g or less or 2 tbs or less, 40 calories or less per 50 g of the food; **Reduced calories; Fewer calories:** at least 25% fewer calories than reference food.

CHOLESTEROL. Cholesterol free: less than 2 mg of cholesterol and 2 g or less of saturated fat per serving; **Low cholesterol:** 20 mg or less of cholesterol and 2 g or less of saturated fat per serving and, if the serving is 30 g or less or 2 tbs or less, per 50 g of the food; **Reduced cholesterol; Less cholesterol:** at least 25% less than reference food.

Other Packaging Terms

The FDA allows food producers and marketers to use language on their packaging that advertises the health benefits and production methods of their products. Products marked "certified" have been formally evaluated for class, grade, or other quality characteristics by the USDA's Food Safety and Inspection Service. Below are some common packaging terms and their meanings.

Organic: Produced by farmers who use environmentally friendly methods to raise their crops or animals. Before a product can be labeled organic, the farm where the food is grown must pass a special inspection by a USDA official. Organic foods must be produced without irradiation, sewage sludge, synthetic fertilizers, prohibited pesticides, and genetically modified organisms.

Foods that contain 100% organic ingredients may advertise "100 percent certified organic" on the front of the packaging along with the USDA organic seal. Foods with at least 95% organic ingredients may be called "organic" and may place the official seal on their packaging. Products with at least 70% organic ingredients may advertise "made with organic" prominently on the front of the package that the item contains organic ingredients. Products with less than 70% organic ingredients may not make any organic claims on the front of the package but may list organic ingredients on the side panel.

Natural: The FDA has not developed a definition for use of the term *natural* or its derivatives. However, the agency has not objected to the use of the term if the food does not contain added color, artificial flavors, or synthetic substances.

Free range or **free roaming:** Producers must demonstrate to the USDA that the poultry has been allowed access to the outside.

Fresh poultry: Whole poultry and cuts that have never been below 26°F.

Frozen poultry: Temperature of raw, frozen poultry is 0°F or below.

Gluten free: Products with a gluten limit of 20 parts per million.

Halal and **Zabiah Halal:** Produced in federally inspected meat packing plants and handled in accordance with Islamic law and under Islamic authority.

Kosher: Meat and poultry products prepared under rabbinical supervision.

No hormones added: Hormones are not allowed in the raising of hogs or poultry, so those products may not make this claim. If sufficient documentation is provided to the USDA, this term may appear on packages of beef.

No antibiotics added: Claim may be made on a package (red meat and poultry) if sufficient documentation is provided to the USDA showing that the animals were raised without antibiotics.

Recommended Levels for Elements (Minerals)

Source: Food and Nutrition Board, Institute of Medicine, National Academy of Sciences, 2010

(in milligrams per day (mg/d) or micrograms per day (µg/d); asterisk denotes level defined as "adequate intake" (AI))

Life stage group		Calcium (mg/d)	Chromium (µg/d)	Copper (µg/d)	Fluoride (mg/d)	Iodine (µg/d)	Iron (mg/d)	Magnesium (mg/d)	Manganese (mg/d)	Molybdenum (µg/d)	Phosphorus (mg/d)	Selenium (µg/d)	Zinc (mg/d)
Infants	0-6 mos.	200*	0.2*	200*	0.01*	110*	0.27*	30*	0.003*	2*	100*	15*	2*
	6-12 mos.	260*	5.5*	220*	0.5*	130*	11	75*	0.6*	3*	275*	20*	3
Children	1-3 yrs.	700	11*	340	0.7*	90	7	80	1.2*	17	460	20	3
	4-8 yrs.	1,000	15*	440	1*	90	10	130	1.5*	22	500	30	5
Males	9-13 yrs.	1,300	25*	700	2*	120	8	240	1.9*	34	1,250	40	8
	14-18 yrs.	1,300	35*	890	3*	150	11	410	2.2*	43	1,250	55	11
	19-30 yrs.	1,000	35*	900	4*	150	8	400	2.3*	45	700	55	11
	31-50 yrs.	1,000	35*	900	4*	150	8	420	2.3*	45	700	55	11
	51-70 yrs.	1,000	30*	900	4*	150	8	420	2.3*	45	700	55	11
	over 70 yrs.	1,200	30*	900	4*	150	8	420	2.3*	45	700	55	11
Females	9-13 yrs.	1,300	21*	700	2*	120	8	240	1.6*	34	1,250	40	8
	14-18 yrs.	1,300	24*	890	3*	150	15	360	1.6*	43	1,250	55	9
	19-30 yrs.	1,000	25*	900	3*	150	18	310	1.8*	45	700	55	8
	31-50 yrs.	1,000	25*	900	3*	150	18	320	1.8*	45	700	55	8
	51-70 yrs.	1,200	20*	900	3*	150	8	320	1.8*	45	700	55	8
	over 70 yrs.	1,200	20*	900	3*	150	8	320	1.8*	45	700	55	8
Pregnancy	14-18 yrs.	1,300	29*	1,000	3*	220	27	400	2.0*	50	1,250	60	12
	19-30 yrs.	1,000	30*	1,000	3*	220	27	350	2.0*	50	700	60	11
	31-50 yrs.	1,000	30*	1,000	3*	220	27	360	2.0*	50	700	60	11
Lactation	14-18 yrs.	1,300	44*	1,300	3*	290	10	360	2.6*	50	1,250	70	13
	19-30 yrs.	1,000	45*	1,300	3*	290	9	310	2.6*	50	700	70	12
	31-50 yrs.	1,000	45*	1,300	3*	290	9	320	2.6*	50	700	70	12

Note: For healthy breastfed infants, the AI is the mean intake. The AI for other life stage and gender groups is believed to cover the needs of all healthy individuals in the group, but lack of data or uncertainty in the data prevents the percentage of individuals covered by this intake from being specified with confidence.

Recommended Levels for Vitamins

Source: Food and Nutrition Board, Institute of Medicine, National Academy of Sciences, 2010

(in milligrams per day (mg/d) or micrograms per day (µg/d); asterisk denotes level defined as "adequate intake" (AI))

Life stage group		Vitamin A (µg/d)	Vitamin C (mg/d)	Vitamin D (µg/d)	Vitamin E (mg/d)	Vitamin K (µg/d)	Thiamin (mg/d)	Riboflavin (mg/d)	Niacin (mg/d)	Vitamin B_6 (mg/d)	Folate (µg/d)	Vitamin B_{12} (µg/d)	Pantothenic acid (mg/d)	Biotin (µg/d)	Choline (mg/d)
Infants	0-6 mos.	400*	40*	10	4*	2.0*	0.2*	0.3*	2*	0.1*	65*	0.4*	1.7*	5*	125*
	6-12 mos.	500*	50*	10	5*	2.5*	0.3*	0.4*	4*	0.3*	80*	0.5*	1.8*	6*	150*
Children	1-3 yrs.	300	15	15	6	30*	0.5	0.5	6	0.5	150	0.9	2*	8*	200*
	4-8 yrs.	400	25	15	7	55*	0.6	0.6	8	0.6	200	1.2	3*	12*	250*
Males	9-13 yrs.	600	45	15	11	60*	0.9	0.9	12	1.0	300	1.8	4*	20*	375*
	14-18 yrs.	900	75	15	15	75*	1.2	1.3	16	1.3	400	2.4	5*	25*	550*
	19-30 yrs.	900	90	15	15	120*	1.2	1.3	16	1.3	400	2.4	5*	30*	550*
	31-50 yrs.	900	90	15	15	120*	1.2	1.3	16	1.3	400	2.4	5*	30*	550*
	51-70 yrs.	900	90	15	15	120*	1.2	1.3	16	1.7	400	2.4	5*	30*	550*
	over 70 yrs.	900	90	20	15	120*	1.2	1.3	16	1.7	400	2.4	5*	30*	550*
Females	9-13 yrs.	600	45	15	11	60*	0.9	0.9	12	1.0	300	1.8	4*	20*	375*
	14-18 yrs.	700	65	15	15	75*	1.0	1.0	14	1.2	400	2.4	5*	25*	400*
	19-30 yrs.	700	75	15	15	90*	1.1	1.1	14	1.3	400	2.4	5*	30*	425*
	31-50 yrs.	700	75	15	15	90*	1.1	1.1	14	1.3	400	2.4	5*	30*	425*
	51-70 yrs.	700	75	15	15	90*	1.1	1.1	14	1.5	400	2.4	5*	30*	425*
	over 70 yrs.	700	75	20	15	90*	1.1	1.1	14	1.5	400	2.4	5*	30*	425*
Pregnancy	14-18 yrs.	750	80	15	15	75*	1.4	1.4	18	1.9	600	2.6	6*	30*	450*
	19-30 yrs.	770	85	15	15	90*	1.4	1.4	18	1.9	600	2.6	6*	30*	450*
	31-50 yrs.	770	85	15	15	90*	1.4	1.4	18	1.9	600	2.6	6*	30*	450*
Lactation	14-18 yrs.	1,200	115	15	19	75*	1.4	1.6	17	2.0	500	2.8	7*	35*	550*
	19-30 yrs.	1,300	120	15	19	90*	1.4	1.6	17	2.0	500	2.8	7*	35*	550*
	31-50 yrs.	1,300	120	15	19	90*	1.4	1.6	17	2.0	500	2.8	7*	35*	550*

Note: For healthy breastfed infants, the AI is the mean intake. The AI for other life stage and gender groups is believed to cover the needs of all healthy individuals in the group, but lack of data or uncertainty in the data prevents the percentage of individuals covered by this intake from being specified with confidence.

Top 10 Calorie Sources in American Diets

Source: *Dietary Guidelines for Americans, 2010*, U.S. Dept. of Agriculture

Rank	All Americans (ages 2+)	Children and adolescents (ages 2-18)	All adults (ages 19+)
1.	Grain-based desserts	Grain-based desserts	Grain-based desserts
2.	Yeast breads	Pizza	Yeast breads
3.	Chicken dishes	Soda/energy/sports drinks	Chicken dishes
4.	Soda/energy/sports drinks	Yeast breads	Soda/energy/sports drinks
5.	Pizza	Chicken dishes	Alcoholic beverages
6.	Alcoholic beverages	Pasta dishes	Pizza
7.	Pasta dishes	Reduced-fat milk	Tortillas, burritos, tacos
8.	Tortillas, burritos, tacos	Dairy desserts	Pasta dishes
9.	Beef dishes	Potato/corn/other chips	Beef dishes
10.	Dairy desserts	Ready-to-eat cereals	Dairy desserts

Note: Data are drawn from analyses of usual dietary intakes conducted by the Natl. Cancer Institute. Foods and beverages consumed were divided into 97 categories and ranked according to calorie contribution to the diet. Average total daily calorie intake was 2,157 overall, 2,027 for children and adolescents (ages 2-18), and 2,199 for adults (ages 19+).

Weight Guidelines for Adults

Source: *Dietary Guidelines for Americans, 2010*, U.S. Dept. of Agriculture; National Center for Health Statistics, CDC

Guidelines on identification, evaluation, and treatment of overweight and obesity in adults were released in June 1998 by the National Heart, Lung, and Blood Institute (NHLBI), in cooperation with the National Institute of Diabetes and Digestive and Kidney Diseases (NIDDK). The guidelines, based on research into risk factors contributing to heart disease, stroke, and other conditions, define overweight and obesity in terms of **body mass index (BMI)**. BMI is based on a person's weight and height and is strongly correlated with total body fat content. A BMI of 25-29 is said to indicate **overweight**; a BMI of 30 or higher indicates **obesity**. Weight reduction is advised for persons with a BMI of 25 or higher. Factors such as a large waist circumference, high blood pressure or cholesterol, and family medical history may increase a person's risk of developing an obesity-related disease. Calculate your BMI at www.nhlbi.nih.gov/health/educational/lose_wt/BMI/bmicalc.htm.

The National Center for Health Statistics notes that in 2011-12, 34.9% of American adults were obese. Over the past four decades, childhood obesity rates in America have more than tripled, and in 2011-12, 16.9% of children and adolescents (ages 2-19) were obese. Based on directly measured weight and height, between 1988-94 and 2011-12, the proportion of adults ages 20 years and over who were obese rose by 52.4%, from 22.9%. During the same period, obesity increased by 56.6% in children ages 6-11, from 11.3% to 17.7%, and by 95.2% in adolescents ages 12-19, from 10.5% to 20.5%.

A high prevalence of overweight and obesity is a public health concern because excess body fat has been associated with type 2 diabetes, hypertension, dyslipidemia, cardiovascular disease, stroke, gallbladder disease, respiratory dysfunction, gout, osteoarthritis, and certain kinds of cancers.

Adults Meeting U.S. Fitness Guidelines, 1998-2013

Source: *Health, United States*, National Center for Health Statistics, Centers for Disease Control and Prevention

	% meeting aerobic exercise guidelines					% meeting muscle-strengthening guidelines				
Characteristic	**1998**	**2000**	**2005**	**2010**	**2013**	**1998**	**2000**	**2005**	**2010**	**2013**
Sex and age										
Men, ages 18-44	51.5%	53.6%	50.0%	59.0%	61.8%	27.2%	26.3%	28.7%	35.6%	35.2%
Men, ages 45-54	44.3	45.2	42.6	50.7	50.4	18.8	18.0	19.2	24.8	25.5
Men, ages 55-64	38.3	38.9	38.4	46.0	46.7	12.9	13.8	15.7	22.9	21.1
Men, ages 65-74	38.5	41.8	38.3	40.7	46.5	12.0	12.2	14.5	20.6	20.0
Men, age 75+	26.1	30.7	28.6	32.3	33.2	9.5	10.1	12.4	14.5	14.3
Women, ages 18-44	40.0	42.0	43.1	48.5	52.0	17.9	17.9	19.8	22.1	22.0
Women, ages 45-54	36.1	39.1	38.1	44.7	46.4	13.7	16.1	19.8	20.4	21.2
Women, ages 55-64	32.5	33.5	34.1	38.6	41.7	10.3	12.4	15.9	17.5	17.1
Women, ages 65-74	26.2	32.6	30.2	31.8	37.7	7.8	10.5	13.3	15.6	18.5
Women, age 75+	14.0	16.8	18.8	18.3	23.7	5.7	6.7	6.7	10.8	12.7
Race or Hispanic origin[1]										
White	41.5	44.1	42.9	48.9	51.5	18.0	18.5	20.9	24.8	25.0
Black or African American	30.4	31.7	29.2	37.3	41.4	15.6	16.0	15.8	21.4	21.7
American Indian or Alaska Native	39.7	29.7	41.6	42.0	47.4	18.2	13.9	20.5	16.7	20.0
Asian	37.1	41.7	37.5	44.2	49.5	17.2	17.2	16.9	21.9	21.0
Two or more races	—	43.9	41.1	50.2	51.6	—	22.2	23.6	30.4	26.7
Hispanic or Latino	29.1	30.8	28.5	36.2	42.9	12.7	11.9	12.9	18.1	19.8
Geographic region										
Northeast	39.6	45.3	43.3	46.9	49.2	17.5	20.0	21.6	24.3	26.0
Midwest	42.0	43.5	43.5	46.1	50.0	18.2	19.3	21.9	24.7	25.3
South	35.3	37.3	36.5	45.0	47.3	15.0	15.1	17.6	22.0	21.5
West	46.7	46.9	44.4	52.0	55.4	22.3	19.7	21.3	27.5	26.9

— = Data not available or estimates considered unreliable due to small sample size. **Note:** Fitness guidelines reflect the federal 2008 Physical Activity Guidelines for Americans, which recommend that for substantial health benefits, adults perform at least 150 minutes a week of moderate-intensity aerobic physical activity, 75 minutes a week of vigorous-intensity activity, or an equivalent combination of moderate- and vigorous-intensity activity. Adults who performed muscle-strengthening activities that are moderate or high intensity and involve all major muscle groups on two or more days a week met the muscle strengthening guidelines. (1) Reflects persons reporting only one race. Persons of Hispanic origin may be of any race.

Obesity Among Adults in the U.S., 2014

Source: National Health Interview Survey, National Center for Health Statistics, CDC

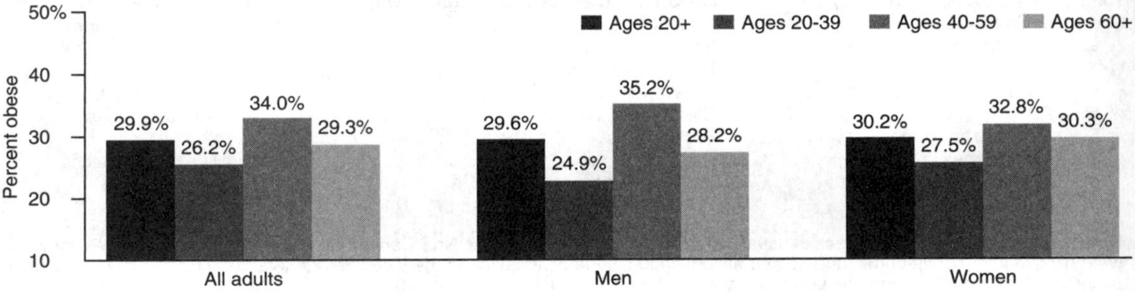

Percent of Adults Who Meet U.S. Fitness Guidelines for Aerobic Activity, 2014

Source: National Health Interview Survey, National Center for Health Statistics, CDC

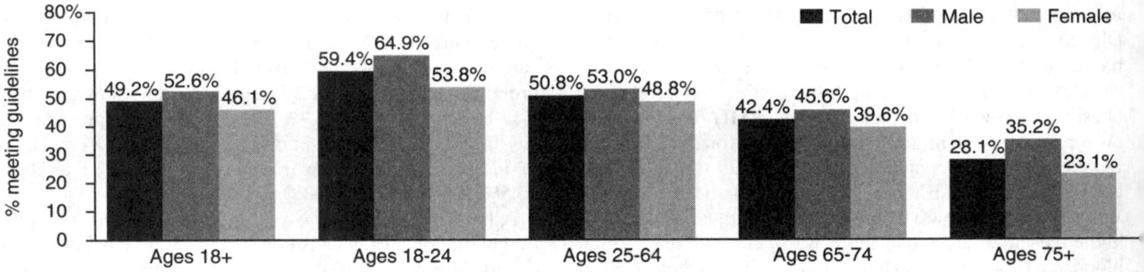

Note: Fitness guidelines reflect the federal 2008 Physical Activity Guidelines for Americans, which recommend that for substantial health benefits, adults perform at least 150 minutes a week of moderate-intensity aerobic physical activity, 75 minutes a week of vigorous-intensity activity, or an equivalent combination of moderate- and vigorous-intensity activity.

Obesity Among Children and Adolescents in the U.S., 1988-2012

Source: *Health, United States*, National Center for Health Statistics, Centers for Disease Control and Prevention

	1988-94	1999-2002	2001-04	2003-06	2005-08	2007-10	2009-12
				Percent of population			
2-5 years							
Both sexes	7.2%	10.3%	12.4%	12.5%	10.5%	11.1%	10.2%
Boys	6.1	10.0	13.1	12.8	9.8	11.9	12.0
Girls	8.2	10.6	11.7	12.2	11.2	10.2	8.4
Percent of poverty level[1]							
Below 100%	9.7	10.9	14.4	14.3	12.3	13.2	12.3
100%-199%	7.2	13.8*	13.3	12.7	10.0	11.8	11.6
200%-399%	5.6	7.6*	13.6	11.9	11.6	13.9	11.0
400% or more	*	*	*	10.0*	*	5.8*	5.0*
6-11 years							
Both sexes	11.3	15.9	17.5	17.0	17.4	18.8	17.9
Boys	11.6	16.9	18.7	18.0	18.7	20.7	18.3
Girls	11.0	14.7	16.3	15.8	16.0	16.9	17.4
Percent of poverty level[1]							
Below 100%	11.4	19.1	20.0	22.0	21.5	22.2	24.6
100%-199%	11.1	16.4	18.4	19.2	22.2	20.7	18.5
200%-399%	11.7	15.3	18.2	16.7	16.8	18.9	15.8
400% or more	*	12.9	11.4	9.2	9.5*	12.5*	12.2*
12-19 years							
Both sexes	10.5	16.0	17.0	17.6	17.9	18.2	19.4
Boys	11.3	16.7	17.9	18.2	18.7	19.4	20.0
Girls	9.7	15.3	16.0	16.8	17.0	16.9	18.9
Percent of poverty level[1]							
Below 100%	15.8	19.8	18.2	19.3	23.1	24.3	23.2
100%-199%	11.2	15.1	17.0	18.4	19.8	20.1	22.5
200%-399%	9.4	15.7	19.0	19.3	17.2	16.3	17.9
400% or more	*	13.9	13.2	12.6	14.0	14.0	13.8

* = Estimates are considered unreliable. (1) Ratio of family's household income to contemporary federal poverty guidelines.

Basic First Aid

Source: Courtesy of the American National Red Cross, www.redcross.org.

Note: This information is not intended to be a substitute for formal training. It is recommended that you contact your local American Red Cross chapter to sign up for a First Aid/CPR/AED (automated external defibrillator) course.

In an emergency, it is important to get medical assistance as soon as possible, but knowing what to do until a doctor or other trained person gets to the scene can save a life, especially in cases of severe bleeding, choking, poisoning, and shock.

People with special medical problems, such as diabetes, cardiovascular disease, epilepsy, or allergies, are urged to wear some sort of emblem identifying the problem as a safeguard against receiving medication that might be harmful or even fatal. Emblems can be obtained from MedicAlert Foundation, 2323 Colorado Ave., Turlock, CA 95382; (800) 432-5378; www.medicalert.org.

Animal bite: Call 9-1-1 or the local emergency number if the wound is bleeding seriously or if you suspect the animal might have rabies. Control any bleeding. Wash minor wounds with soap under running water and apply antibiotic ointment and a dressing. When possible, proper authorities should test the animal for rabies.

Asphyxiation: Call 9-1-1 or the local emergency number.

Bleeding: Use a barrier between your hand and the wound to help prevent infection. Cover wound with a sterile dressing. Apply direct pressure until bleeding stops. Cover compress with a bandage. Call 9-1-1 or the local emergency number if bleeding is severe.

Burn: Check for life-threatening conditions. If the burn is mild, with skin unbroken and no blisters, flush with cold running water for at least 20 minutes. Gently wash with soap and water and pat dry. Apply a thin layer of antibiotic ointment. Apply a loose, sterile dry dressing to prevent infection. If the burn is severe, call 9-1-1 or the local emergency number. Care for shock (see separate entry). Keep the person from getting chilled or overheated until advanced medical assistance arrives. Do not try to clean a severe burn or break blisters.

Chemical in eye: Call 9-1-1 or the local emergency number. Turn the person's head to the side so that the affected eye is lower than the unaffected eye. Flush the affected eye with large amounts of water for at least 20 minutes.

Choking: See **First Aid for Choking** below.

Convulsions (seizures): Remove nearby objects that might cause injury. Protect the person's head by placing a thin folded towel or item of clothing under it. Roll him or her on one side to drain fluids from the mouth. Do not place anything between the person's teeth. Stay with the person until he or she is fully conscious. If convulsions do not stop, get medical attention immediately.

Cut (minor): Use a clean barrier between your hand and the wound to prevent infection. Apply direct pressure for a few minutes to control any bleeding. Wash the wound thoroughly with soap and water and apply a thin layer of antibiotic ointment or a microthin film dressing. Cover the wound with a sterile dressing and a bandage.

Foreign object in eye: If an object is impaled in someone's eye, do not remove it. If not impaled, try to remove the object by having the person blink several times. If the object doesn't come out, gently flush the eye with saline solution or water. Do not rub the eye. If the object still doesn't come out, the person should receive professional medical attention.

Frostbite: Handle the frostbitten area gently. Do not rub. If there is no danger of the affected area refreezing, soak it in warm water (not warmer than 105°F). Do not allow the frostbitten area to touch the side of the water container. Keep the frostbitten part in the water until normal color returns and it feels warm. Loosely bandage the area with dry, sterile dressings. If fingers or toes are frostbitten, put cotton or gauze between them. Do not break any blisters. Call 9-1-1 or seek emergency help as soon as possible.

Heart attack and stroke: See **Heart and Blood Vessel Disease** earlier in chapter.

Heat stroke: Remove the person from the heat. Loosen any tight clothing. Immerse person in cold water until he or she becomes alert. If a large enough source of water is not available, drench the person with cold water and fan constantly. If the person is conscious, have him or her slowly drink some cool water. Call 9-1-1 if the person's condition does not improve.

Hypothermia: Call 9-1-1 or the local emergency number. For mild hypothermia, cover all exposed skin. Replace wet clothes with something dry. If the person is alert, give him or her simple carbohydrates to eat and warm, nonalcoholic and decaffeinated liquids to drink. Apply heat pads or other heat sources if available but do not place against bare skin.

Loss of limb: Call 9-1-1 or the local emergency number and care for any life-threatening conditions. If a limb is severed, it is important to properly protect the limb so that it can possibly be reattached. After the victim is cared for, the limb should be wrapped in sterile gauze and placed in a plastic bag. Place bag in a larger bag or container of an ice and water slurry, not ice alone. Be sure the limb is taken to the hospital with the person.

Poisoning: Care for any life-threatening conditions. Call the National Capital Poison Center (800-222-1222), 9-1-1, or the local emergency number and follow their directions. Do not give the person any food or drink or induce vomiting unless specified to do so by medical professionals.

Shock (injury-related): Monitor breathing and consciousness. Have the person lie down and keep him or her as comfortable as possible. Maintain an open airway. Give sips of cool water if he or she can tolerate fluids. Elevate his or her legs about 12 inches unless you suspect injuries to the head or lower extremities. Maintain normal body temperature. If the weather is cold or damp, place blankets or extra clothing over and under the person; if the weather is hot, provide shade.

Snakebite: Call 9-1-1 or the local emergency number. Gently wash the injury. Splint bitten extremities, and keep the area at approximately the level of the heart. Keep the person calm. Do not cut, suck, apply a constricting band, or apply cold to a bite from a pit viper (such as a rattlesnake, copperhead, or cottonmouth). For a bite from an elapid snake, such as a coral snake, apply an elastic roller bandage after washing the wound.

Sprains and strains: Splint any injured bone or joint that the person cannot use.

Sting from bee or wasp: If possible, remove the stinger by scraping it away with your finger or a plastic card (like a credit card) or using tweezers. If you use tweezers, grasp the stinger, not the venom sac. Wash the area with soap and water. Cover it to keep it clean. Apply cold to the area. Call 9-1-1 or the local emergency number immediately if the wound does not stop swelling, the person collapses, or he or she is known to be allergic to the sting.

Unconsciousness: Call 9-1-1 or the local emergency number immediately. Do not move the person if a spinal injury is suspected.

First Aid for Choking

The recommended first aid for a conscious choking victim who is unable to speak, cough, or breathe is to deliver a series of five blows to the back and five thrusts to the abdomen. Have another person call 9-1-1 or the local emergency number. Obtain consent from the victim to treat him or her. Lean the victim forward and apply five blows to his or her back with the heel of your hand. If the victim is still choking, stand or kneel behind the victim and wrap your arms around his or her waist. Make a fist with one hand and place the thumb side against the middle of the person's abdomen, just above the navel and well below the lower tip of the breastbone. Grasp your fist in your other hand and quickly thrust upwards into the abdomen five times. Continue back blows and abdominal thrusts until the object is dislodged, and the person can breathe or cough forcefully, or the person loses consciousness.

VITAL STATISTICS

Births and Deaths in the U.S., 1960-2014

Source: National Center for Health Statistics (NCHS), CDC, U.S. Dept. of Health and Human Services

	BIRTHS		DEATHS	
Year	Total number	Rate	Total number	Rate
1960	4,257,850	23.7	1,711,982	9.5
1970	3,731,386	18.4	1,921,031	9.5
1980	3,612,258	15.9	1,989,841	8.8
1990	4,092,994	16.7	2,148,463	8.6
1995	3,899,589	14.6	2,312,132	8.7
1996	3,891,494	14.4	2,314,690	8.6
1997	3,880,894	14.2	2,314,245	8.5
1998	3,941,553	14.3	2,337,256	8.5
1999	3,959,417	14.2	2,391,399	8.6
2000	4,058,814	14.4	2,403,351	8.5
2001	4,025,933	14.1	2,416,425	8.5
2002	4,021,726	13.9	2,443,387	8.5
2003	4,089,950	14.1	2,448,288	8.4
2004	4,112,052	14.0	2,397,615	8.2
2005	4,138,349	14.0	2,448,017	8.3
2006	4,265,555	14.2	2,426,264	8.1
2007	4,316,233	14.3	2,423,712	8.0
2008	4,247,694	14.0	2,471,984	8.1
2009	4,130,665	13.5	2,437,163	7.9
2010	3,999,386	13.0	2,468,435	8.0
2011	3,953,590	12.7	2,515,458	8.1
2012	3,952,841	12.6	2,543,279	8.1
2013	3,932,181	12.4	2,596,993	8.2
2014[1]	3,997,000	12.6	2,625,000	8.2

Note: Statistics cover only events occurring within the U.S. and exclude fetal deaths. Rates per 1,000 population; enumerated as of Apr. 1 for decennial census years; estimated as of July 1 for all other years. Beginning in 1970, statistics exclude births and deaths among nonresidents of the U.S. (1) Provisional.

Marriage and Divorce Rates in the U.S., 1920-2012

Source: National Center for Health Statistics (NCHS), CDC, U.S. Dept. of Health and Human Services

(Per 1,000 total population. Divorce rates for 2005-12 were calculated excluding data and populations from the nonreporting states California, Georgia, Hawaii, Indiana, Louisiana, and Minnesota. Some data are provisional.)

The U.S. marriage rate dipped during the Depression and peaked sharply just after World War II; the trend after that has been more gradual. The divorce rate generally rose from the 1920s through 1981, when it peaked at 5.3 per 1,000 population, before declining somewhat. The graph below shows marriage and divorce rates since 1920.

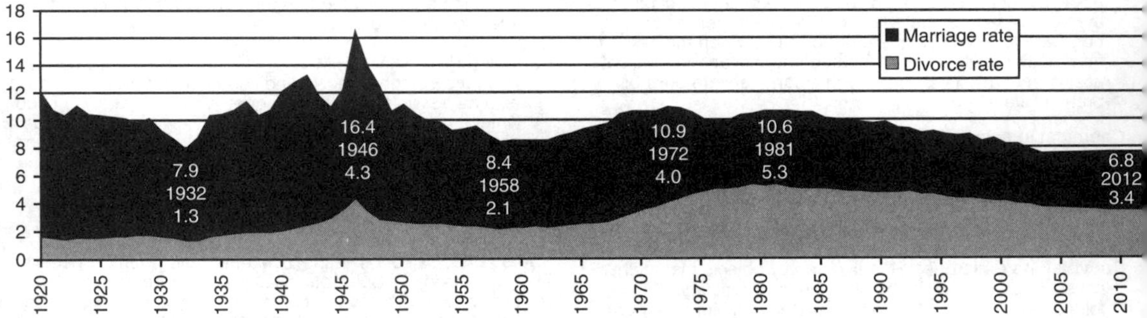

U.S. Median Age at First Marriage, 1890-2014

Source: U.S. Census Bureau, U.S. Dept. of Commerce

Year[1]	Men	Women	Year[1]	Men	Women	Year[1]	Men	Women	Year[1]	Men	Women	Year[1]	Men	Women
1890	26.1	22.0	1950	22.8	20.3	1985	25.5	23.3	2003	27.1	25.3	2009	28.1	25.9
1900	25.9	21.9	1960	22.8	20.3	1990	26.1	23.9	2004	27.4	25.3	2010	28.2	26.1
1910	25.1	21.6	1965	22.8	20.6	1995	26.9	24.5	2005	27.1	25.3	2011	28.4	26.4
1920	24.6	21.2	1970	23.2	20.8	2000	26.8	25.1	2006	27.5	25.5	2012	28.6	26.6
1930	24.3	21.3	1975	23.5	21.1	2001	26.9	25.1	2007	27.5	25.6	2013	29.0	26.6
1940	24.3	21.5	1980	24.7	22.0	2002	26.9	25.3	2008	27.6	25.9	2014	29.3	27.0

(1) Figures after 1947 based on Current Population Survey data; earlier figures based on decennial censuses.

Divorce Rates by State, 2012

Source: National Center for Health Statistics (NCHS), CDC, U.S. Dept. of Health and Human Services

State	Divorce rate
Alabama	3.6
Alaska	4.5
Arizona	4.3
Arkansas	5.3
California	NA
Colorado	4.3
Connecticut	2.7
Delaware	3.5
District of Columbia	2.9
Florida	4.2
Georgia	NA
Hawaii	NA
Idaho	4.7
Illinois	2.4
Indiana	NA
Iowa	2.2
Kansas	3.4
Kentucky	4.1
Louisiana	NA
Maine	3.9
Maryland	2.8
Massachusetts	2.7
Michigan	3.3
Minnesota	NA
Mississippi	4.0
Missouri	3.7
Montana	3.9
Nebraska	3.4
Nevada	5.5
New Hampshire	3.6
New Jersey	2.8
New Mexico	3.0
New York	2.9
North Carolina	3.7
North Dakota	3.1
Ohio	3.4
Oklahoma	4.8
Oregon	3.8
Pennsylvania	2.8
Rhode Island	3.2
South Carolina	3.2
South Dakota	3.0
Tennessee	4.2
Texas	3.0
Utah	3.3
Vermont	3.5
Virginia	3.7
Washington	3.9
West Virginia	4.7
Wisconsin	2.9
Wyoming	4.4
United States	**3.4**

NA = Not available. **Note:** Rate per 1,000 population; estimated as of July 1. Rate includes annulments and may also include divorce petitions filed and legal separations in some counties and states.

Birth Rates and Fertility Rates by Age of Mother, 1950-2014

Source: National Center for Health Statistics (NCHS), CDC, U.S. Dept. of Health and Human Services

Year	Birth rate[1]	Fertility rate[2]	Live births per 1,000 women by age of mother: 10-14 years	15-19 years	15-17 years	18-19 years	20-24 years	25-29 years	30-34 years	35-39 years	40-44 years	45-49 years
1950	24.1	106.2	1.0	81.6	40.7	132.7	196.6	166.1	103.7	52.9	15.1	1.2
1960	23.7	118.0	0.8	89.1	43.9	166.7	258.1	197.4	112.7	56.2	15.5	0.9
1970	18.4	87.9	1.2	68.3	38.8	114.7	167.8	145.1	73.3	31.7	8.1	0.5
1980	15.9	68.4	1.1	53.0	32.5	82.1	115.1	112.9	61.9	19.8	3.9	0.2
1990	16.7	70.9	1.4	59.9	37.5	88.6	116.5	120.2	80.8	31.7	5.5	0.2
1995	14.6	64.6	1.3	56.0	35.5	87.7	107.5	108.8	81.1	34.0	6.6	0.3
1996	14.4	64.1	1.2	53.5	33.3	84.7	107.8	108.6	82.1	34.9	6.8	0.3
1997	14.2	63.6	1.1	51.3	31.4	82.1	107.3	108.3	83.0	35.7	7.1	0.4
1998	14.3	64.3	1.0	50.3	29.9	80.9	108.4	110.2	85.2	36.9	7.4	0.4
1999	14.2	64.4	0.9	48.8	28.2	79.1	107.9	111.2	87.1	37.8	7.4	0.4
2000	14.4	65.9	0.9	47.7	26.9	78.1	109.7	113.5	91.2	39.7	8.0	0.5
2001	14.1	65.3	0.8	45.3	24.7	76.1	106.2	113.4	91.9	40.6	8.1	0.5
2002	13.9	64.8	0.7	43.0	23.2	72.8	103.6	113.6	91.5	41.4	8.3	0.5
2003	14.1	66.1	0.6	41.6	22.4	70.7	102.6	115.6	95.1	43.8	8.7	0.5
2004	14.0	66.3	0.7	41.1	22.1	70.0	101.7	115.5	95.3	45.4	8.9	0.5
2005	14.0	66.7	0.7	40.5	21.4	69.9	102.2	115.5	95.8	46.3	9.1	0.6
2006	14.2	68.5	0.6	41.9	22.0	73.0	105.9	116.7	97.7	47.3	9.4	0.6
2007	14.3	69.5	0.6	42.5	22.1	73.9	106.3	117.5	99.9	47.5	9.5	0.6
2008	14.0	68.6	0.6	41.5	21.7	70.6	103.0	115.1	99.3	46.9	9.8	0.7
2009	13.5	66.2	0.5	37.9	19.6	64.0	96.2	111.5	97.5	46.1	10.0	0.7[4]
2010	13.0	64.1	0.4	34.2	17.3	58.2	90.0	108.3	96.5	45.9	10.2	0.7[4]
2011	12.7	63.2	0.4	31.3	15.4	54.1	85.3	107.2	96.5	47.2	10.3	0.7
2012	12.6	63.0	0.4	29.4	14.1	51.4	83.1	106.5	97.3	48.3	10.4	0.7
2013	12.4	62.5	0.3	26.5	12.3	47.1	80.7	105.5	98.0	49.3	10.4	0.8
2014[3]	12.5	62.9	0.3	24.2	10.9	43.8	79.0	105.7	100.8	50.9	10.6	0.8

(1) Live births per 1,000 population. (2) Live births per 1,000 women 15-44 years of age. (3) Preliminary. (4) Women 45-54 years of age.

Cesarean Delivery Rates by State, 2000-2014

Source: National Center for Health Statistics (NCHS), CDC, U.S. Dept. of Health and Human Services

State	2000	2010	2013	2014[1]	Percent change, 2000-14
Alabama	26.3%	35.3%	35.8%	35.4%	34.6%
Alaska	17.0	21.5	24.0	23.7	39.4
Arizona	18.6	27.0	27.4	27.8	49.5
Arkansas	26.3	34.8	34.4	32.1	22.1
California	23.4	33.0	33.2	32.7	39.7
Colorado	18.3	25.9	26.0	25.6	39.9
Connecticut	21.6	35.1	34.8	34.2	58.3
Delaware	24.8	33.9	31.5	31.5	27.0
District of Columbia	22.6	33.0	34.2	32.7	44.7
Florida	24.9	37.8	37.7	37.2	49.4
Georgia	22.5	33.8	34.2	33.9	50.7
Hawaii	14.6	27.2	25.2	24.6	68.5
Idaho	18.3	24.8	24.9	24.2	32.2
Illinois	20.9	31.1	31.7	31.3	49.8
Indiana	21.5	30.3	30.5	30.3	40.9
Iowa	20.8	30.3	30.8	30.0	44.2
Kansas	22.2	30.5	30.2	29.8	34.2
Kentucky	23.6	35.4	36.6	35.1	48.7
Louisiana	26.6	39.6	38.9	38.3	44.0
Maine	22.8	29.8	30.0	29.8	30.7
Maryland	24.1	34.5	35.1	34.9	44.8
Massachusetts	23.3	33.0	31.5	31.7	36.1
Michigan	21.9	32.6	32.6	32.8	49.8
Minnesota	19.4	27.1	26.9	26.5	36.6
Mississippi	28.2	37.0	38.5	37.7	33.7
Missouri	22.3%	31.9%	31.1%	30.2%	35.4%
Montana	19.0	30.3	29.7	31.4	65.3
Nebraska	22.5	31.1	30.3	30.8	36.9
Nevada	21.7	34.8	34.9	34.5	59.0
New Hampshire	21.0	30.4	30.1	29.9	42.4
New Jersey	27.3	38.4	38.4	37.4	37.0
New Mexico	17.1	22.8	24.3	23.8	39.2
New York	24.6	34.5	34.3	33.9	37.8
North Carolina	23.0	30.8	30.4	29.5	28.3
North Dakota	20.6	27.7	28.6	27.7	34.5
Ohio	20.0	30.7	31.1	30.6	53.0
Oklahoma	21.0	34.7	33.8	33.1	57.6
Oregon	19.4	29.4	28.0	27.5	41.8
Pennsylvania	21.7	31.3	31.3	30.5	40.6
Rhode Island	21.9	33.0	31.3	30.7	40.2
South Carolina	25.2	35.0	35.0	34.3	36.1
South Dakota	22.8	26.6	25.5	24.8	8.8
Tennessee	24.8	34.2	33.4	33.7	35.9
Texas	24.7	35.1	35.2	34.9	41.3
Utah	16.8	23.1	22.4	22.3	32.7
Vermont	17.3	27.5	27.3	25.8	49.1
Virginia	23.1	34.3	33.7	33.1	43.3
Washington	20.6	29.5	28.3	27.6	34.0
West Virginia	25.4	36.0	35.9	35.4	39.4
Wisconsin	17.5	26.0	26.2	26.1	49.1
Wyoming	19.4	27.9	28.9	27.8	43.3
United States	**22.8**	**32.7**	**32.7**	**32.2**	**41.2**

Note: The cesarean rate is the percentage of all live births by cesarean delivery. (1) Preliminary.

Use of Infertility Services by Selected Characteristics, 2006-10

Source: National Center for Health Statistics (NCHS), CDC, U.S. Dept. of Health and Human Services

		Age in years				Prior live births		Current fertility problems[2]	
Characteristic	**Total[1]**	**25-29**	**30-34**	**35-39**	**40-44**	**None**	**One or more**	**Yes**	**No**
Number of women (thous.)	40,912	10,535	9,188	10,538	10,652	10,340	30,572	5,791	35,121
					Percent				
Any infertility service	16.8%	12.5%	14.4%	20.7%	19.3%	14.4%	17.6%	41.0%	12.8%
Any medical help to get pregnant	12.5	7.7	11.1	16.4	14.5	13.6	12.1	36.3	8.6
Advice	9.4	6.2	7.8	13.3	9.9	11.4	8.7	28.9	6.1
Tests on either partner	7.3	3.3	6.3	10.4	9.0	8.5	6.9	27.4	4.0
Ovulation drugs	5.8	2.4	5.5	8.6	6.5	5.6	5.8	19.5	3.5
Surgery or treatment of blocked tubes	1.3	0.3	0.5	2.0	2.3	1.8	1.1	3.2	1.0
Artificial insemination	1.7	0.3	0.9	2.9	2.8	2.3	1.5	7.4	0.8
Assisted reproductive technology	0.7	NA	0.2	1.5	0.9	0.9	0.6	3.1	0.3
Any medical help to prevent miscarriage	6.8	6.1	5.7	8.1	7.3	2.7	8.2	12.8	5.8

NA = Not available. **Note:** Data is for women or their partners who have ever used service shown. Respondents could report one or more types of medical help, so sum of figures will not equal totals. From interviews conducted 2006-10. (1) Women aged 25-44. (2) Impaired fecundity (physical difficulty in either getting pregnant or carrying a pregnancy to live birth) or 12-month infertility at time of interview.

Numbers of Multiple Births in the U.S., 1990-2013

Source: National Center for Health Statistics (NCHS), CDC, U.S. Dept. of Health and Human Services

The general upward trend in multiple births reflects greater numbers of births to older women and increased use of fertility therapies.

Year	Twins	Triplets	Quadruplets	Quintuplets[1]	Year	Twins	Triplets	Quadruplets	Quintuplets[1]
1990	93,865	2,830	185	13	2006	137,085	6,118	355	67
1995	96,736	4,551	365	57	2007	138,961	5,967	369	91
2000	118,916	6,742	506	77	2008	138,660	5,877	345	46
2001	121,246	6,885	501	85	2009	137,217	5,905	355	80
2002	125,134	6,898	434	69	2010	132,562	5,153	313	37
2003	128,665	7,110	468	85	2011	131,269	5,137	239	41
2004	132,219	6,750	439	86	2012	131,024	4,598	276	45
2005	133,122	6,208	418	68	2013	132,324	4,364	270	66

(1) Quintuplets and other multiple births of five or more.

Origin Countries for U.S. Foreign Adoptions, 2000-14

Source: Office of Immigration Statistics, U.S. Dept. of Homeland Security
(ranked by 2014 adoptions)

Country	2014	2013	2012	2011	2010	2009	2008	2007	2006	2005	2000
China	2,040	2,306	2,697	2,589	3,401	2,990	3,852	5,453	6,493	7,906	5,053
Ethiopia	716	993	1,568	1,727	2,513	2,221	1,666	1,255	732	441	95
Ukraine	521	438	395	632	445	605	487	606	460	821	659
Haiti	464	388	154	33	133[1]	336	300	190	309	234	131
South Korea	370	138	627	736	863	1,106	1,038	939	1,376	1,630	1,794
Congo, Dem. Rep. of the	230	313	240	133	41	21	9	10	4	11	1
Uganda	201	276	238	207	62	69	55	54	12	17	1
Bulgaria	183	160	125	75	40	15	5	20	28	30	214
Colombia	172	159	195	216	235	237	308	310	344	291	246
Philippines	172	178	125	230	214	292	279	265	245	271	173
Total[2]	**6,441**	**7,094**	**8,668**	**9,320**	**11,059[1]**	**12,782**	**17,229**	**19,741**	**20,705**	**22,710**	**18,120**

(1) Does not reflect approximately 1,090 Haitian children admitted as part of the Special Humanitarian Parole following the 2010 earthquake in Haiti. (2) Includes countries not shown.

Leading Causes of Infant Death in the U.S., 2013

Source: National Center for Health Statistics (NCHS), CDC, U.S. Dept. of Health and Human Services

Cause	Number	Percent of total deaths	Mortality rate[1]
Congenital malformations, deformations, and chromosomal abnormalities	4,758	20.3%	121.0
Disorders related to short gestation and low birth weight, not elsewhere classified	4,202	17.9	106.9
Newborn affected by maternal complications of pregnancy	1,595	6.8	40.6
Sudden infant death syndrome	1,563	6.7	39.7
Accidents (unintentional injuries)	1,156	4.9	29.4
Newborn affected by complications of placenta, cord, and membranes	953	4.1	24.2
Bacterial sepsis[2] of newborn	578	2.5	14.7
Respiratory distress of newborn	522	2.2	13.3
Diseases of the circulatory system	458	2.0	11.6
Neonatal hemorrhage	389	1.7	9.9
All other causes	7,266	31.0	—
All causes	**23,440**	**100.0**	**596.1**

— = Not available. (1) Infant deaths during the first year of life per 100,000 live births. (2) Toxic condition resulting from the spread of bacteria.

Nonmarital Childbearing in the U.S., 1970-2013

Source: National Center for Health Statistics (NCHS), CDC, U.S. Dept. of Health and Human Services

	1970	1975	1980	1985	1990	1995	2000	2005	2010	2011	2012	2013
Births to unmarried mothers (thous.)	**399**	**448**	**666**	**828**	**1,165**	**1,254**	**1,347**	**1,527**	**1,633**	**1,608**	**1,610**	**1,596**
Race/Hispanic origin of mother	**Percent of live births to unmarried mothers**											
All races and origins	10.7%	14.3%	18.4%	22.0%	28.0%	32.2%	33.2%	36.9%	40.8%	40.7%	40.7%	40.6%
White	5.5	7.1	11.2	14.7	20.4	25.3	27.1	31.7	35.9	35.7	35.9	35.8
Black	37.5	49.5	56.1	61.2	66.5	69.9	68.5	69.3	72.1	71.8	71.6	71.0
American Indian or Alaska Native	22.4	32.7	39.2	46.8	53.6	57.2	58.4	63.5	65.6	66.2	66.9	66.4
Asian or Pacific Islander	—	—	7.3	9.5	13.2	16.3	14.8	16.2	17.0	17.2	17.0	17.0
Hispanic origin (selected states)[1,2]	—	—	23.6	29.5	36.7	40.8	42.7	48.0	53.4	53.3	53.5	53.2
Maternal age	**Percent distribution of live births to unmarried mothers**											
Under 20 years	50.1%	52.1%	40.8%	33.8%	30.9%	30.9%	28.0%	23.1%	20.1%	18.4%	17.1%	15.4%
20-24 years	31.8	29.9	35.6	36.3	34.7	34.5	37.4	38.3	36.8	36.9	36.9	36.8
25 years and over	18.1	18.0	23.5	29.9	34.4	34.7	34.6	38.6	43.1	44.8	46.1	47.9
Race/Hispanic origin of mother	**Rate of live births per 1,000 unmarried women 15-44 years of age[3]**											
All races and origins	26.4	24.5	29.4	32.8	43.8	44.3	44.0	47.5	47.6	46.0	45.3	44.3
White[4]	13.9	12.4	18.1	22.5	32.9	37.0	38.2	43.0	44.5	42.7	42.1	40.8
Black[4]	95.5	84.2	81.1	77.0	90.5	74.5	70.5	67.8	65.3	63.7	62.6	61.7
Hispanic origin (selected states)[1,2]	—	—	—	—	89.6	88.7	87.2	100.3	80.6	75.1	72.6	69.9

— = Not available. (1) Hispanic origin data prior to 1995 is not directly comparable with data for more recent years due to differences in reporting area. (2) Hispanics may be of any race. (3) Rates computed by relating total births to unmarried mothers, regardless of mother's age, to unmarried women 15-44 years of age. (4) For 1970 and 1975, birth rates are by race of child.

Number, Ratio, and Rate of Legal Abortions in U.S., 1970-2011

Source: *Abortion Surveillance—United States, 2011*, Centers for Disease Control and Prevention, U.S. Dept. of Health and Human Services

Year	Legal abortions	Ratio[1]	Rate[2]	Year	Legal abortions	Ratio[1]	Rate[2]	Year	Legal abortions	Ratio[1]	Rate[2]
1970	193,491	52	5	1993	1,330,414	333	23	2003	848,163	245	16
1971	485,816	137	11	1994	1,267,415	321	21	2004	839,226	241	16
1972	586,760	180	13	1995	1,210,883	311	20	2005	820,151	236	16
1973	615,831	196	14	1996	1,225,937	315	21	2006	852,385	237	16
1974	763,476	242	17	1997	1,186,039	306	20	2007	827,609	230	16
1975	854,853	272	18	1998	884,273	270	17	2008	825,564	232	16
1980	1,297,606	359	25	1999	861,789	261	17	2009	789,217	227	15
1990	1,429,247	344	24	2000	857,475	251	16	2010	765,651	228	15
1991	1,388,937	338	24	2001	853,485	249	16	2011	730,322	219	14
1992	1,359,146	334	23	2002	854,122	250	16				

Note: After 1998, reporting area varies. (1) Number of abortions per 1,000 live births. (2) Number of abortions per 1,000 women aged 15-44 years.

Reported U.S. Abortions by Age, Race, and Marital Status, 2011

Source: *Abortion Surveillance—United States, 2011*, Centers for Disease Control and Prevention, U.S. Dept. of Health and Human Services

Characteristic	White No.	White %	Black No.	Black %	Other No.	Other %	Total, all races No.	Total, all races %
Age[1]								
Under 15 years	542	0.4%	654	0.6%	59	0.3%	1,255	0.5%
15-19 years	20,780	13.8	14,860	14.6	2,525	11.5	38,165	13.9
20-24 years	51,350	34.1	35,723	35.1	6,452	29.4	93,525	34.1
25-29 years	36,560	24.3	25,499	25.0	5,376	24.5	67,435	24.6
30-34 years	22,347	14.8	15,559	15.3	3,886	17.7	41,792	15.2
35-39 years	13,169	8.7	7,333	7.2	2,565	11.7	23,067	8.4
40 years and over	5,793	3.8	2,213	2.2	1,084	4.9	9,090	3.3
Total	**150,541**	**100.0**	**101,841**	**100.0**	**21,947**	**100.0**	**274,329**	**100.0**
Marital status[2]								
Married	21,593	16.6	7,166	7.7	6,069	28.8	34,828	14.3
Unmarried	108,615	83.4	85,401	92.3	15,006	71.2	209,022	85.7
Total	**130,208**	**100.0**	**92,567**	**100.0**	**21,075**	**100.0**	**243,850**	**100.0**

Note: The CDC requests data annually from the central health agencies of 52 reporting areas (all states, DC, and NYC). Reporting is voluntary. (1) Data from 30 reporting areas; excludes 22 (AZ, CA, CT, FL, GA, HI, IL, KY, ME, MD, MA, NE, NV, NH, NM, NYC, PA, TX, VT, WA, WI, WY) that did not report, did not report by race/age, or did not meet reporting standards. (2) Data from 29 reporting areas; excludes 23 (AZ, CA, CT, FL, GA, HI, IL, KY, ME, MD, MA, NE, NV, NH, NM, NYC, NY state, PA, TX, VT, WA, WI, WY) that did not report, did not report by race/marital status, or did not meet reporting standards.

Number of Sexual Partners for U.S. Adults by Age and Race, 2008

Source: *Sexual Behavior, Sexual Attraction, and Sexual Identity in the United States*, National Center for Health Statistics (NCHS), U.S. Dept. of Health and Human Services

	No. of opposite-sex partners in lifetime, % distrib. 0	1	2	3-6	7-14	15+	Median no.[2]
Male, 15-44 years[1]	**11.4**	**15.0**	**7.6**	**26.5**	**18.1**	**21.4**	**5.1**
Age							
15-19 years	43.3	21.2	9.4	17.6	5.4	3.1	1.8
20-24 years	14.4	19.1	8.0	26.1	18.1	14.2	4.1
25-44 years	2.4	12.3	7.0	28.9	21.5	27.9	6.1
Race/ethnicity[3]							
White	11.6	16.1	7.3	25.7	18.4	20.9	5.1
Black	9.6	8.3	5.0	25.6	21.6	30.0	6.9
Hispanic	7.9	12.5	10.2	32.6	17.8	19.1	4.6

	No. of opposite-sex partners in lifetime, % distrib. 0	1	2	3-6	7-14	15+	Median no.[2]
Female, 15-44 years[1]	**11.3**	**22.2**	**10.7**	**31.6**	**16.0**	**8.3**	**3.2**
Age							
15-19 years	48.1	22.7	8.2	15.7	4.1	1.1	1.4
20-24 years	12.6	24.5	12.5	31.6	11.7	7.2	2.6
25-44 years	1.6	21.4	10.9	35.6	20.1	10.4	3.6
Race/ethnicity[3]							
White	11.7	19.2	9.7	31.4	18.9	8.9	3.7
Black	10.5	12.3	8.3	40.9	16.7	11.3	4.4
Hispanic	10.7	35.0	16.7	26.6	6.6	4.4	1.6

(1) Includes people of other or multiple races and origin groups, not shown separately. (2) Excludes people who have never had sex with a partner. (3) Figures are for whites and blacks who are not Hispanic. Hispanics may be of any race.

Sexual Orientation Among U.S. Adults, 2013

Source: *National Health Interview Survey, 2013*, National Center for Health Statistics (NCHS), U.S. Dept. of Health and Human Services

Sexual orientation	Gay or lesbian[1] Number (thous.)	Gay or lesbian[1] % of group	Straight[2] Number (thous.)	Straight[2] % of group	Bisexual Number (thous.)	Bisexual % of group
Overall	3,729	1.6%	224,163	97.7%	1,514	0.7%
Sex						
Men	2,000	1.8	108,093	97.8	481	0.4
Women	1,729	1.5	116,071	97.7	1,033	0.9
Age						
18-44 years	2,028	1.9	104,947	97.1	1,153	1.1
45-64 years	1,422	1.8	77,686	97.8	289	0.4
65 years and older	278	0.7	41,531	99.2	73	0.2

Note: Percent distributions may not total 100 because of rounding. (1) Response option provided was "gay" for men and "gay or lesbian" for women. (2) Response option provided was "straight, that is, not gay" for men and "straight, that is, not gay or lesbian" for women.

Number of Opposite-Sex Partners in Past Year, 2008

Source: *Sexual Behavior, Sexual Attraction, and Sexual Identity in the United States*, National Center for Health Statistics, USDHHS (U.S. males and females 15-44 years of age)

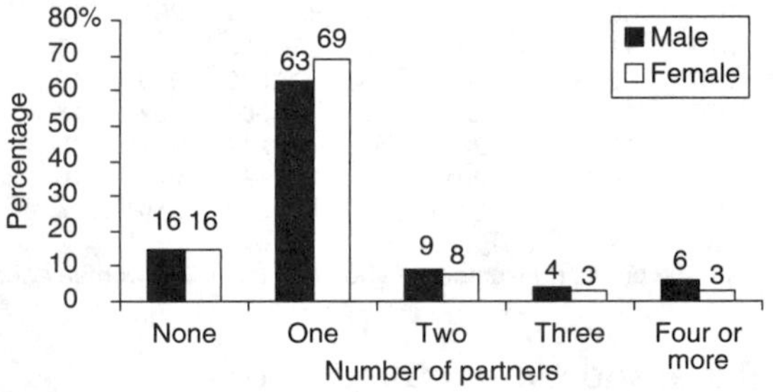

Number of Opposite-Sex Partners in Lifetime by Age, 2008

Source: *Sexual Behavior, Sexual Attraction, and Sexual Identity in the United States*, National Center for Health Statistics, USDHSS (U.S. males and females 15-44 years of age)

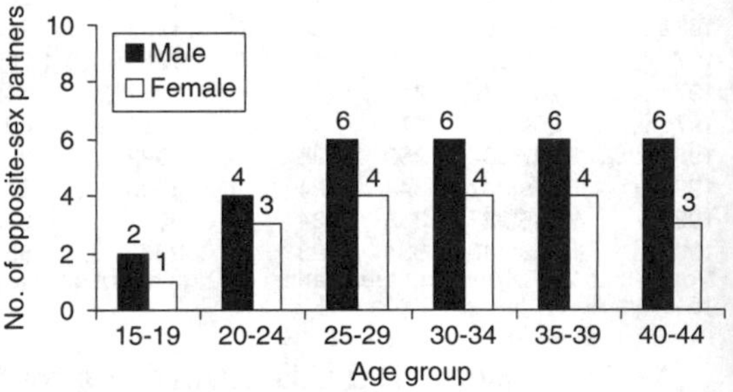

Contraceptive Use in the U.S. by Age and Race, 2006-10

Source: National Survey of Family Growth, National Center for Health Statistics (NCHS), U.S. Dept. of Health and Human Services

	All women	Age in years						Race and ethnicity[1]			
		15-19	20-24	25-29	30-34	35-39	40-44	White	Black	Asian	Hispanic
All women (thous.)	**61,755**	**10,478**	**10,365**	**10,535**	**9,188**	**10,538**	**10,652**	**37,384**	**8,451**	**2,456**	**10,474**
Contraceptive status and method		Percent distribution									
Using contraception	**62.2%**	**30.5%**	**58.3%**	**65.3%**	**69.7%**	**74.6%**	**75.3%**	**65.6%**	**54.2%**	**58.5%**	**59.7%**
Female sterilization	16.5	—	1.5	10.7	20.9	27.9	38.1	15.5	20.2	6.6	18.9
Male sterilization	6.2	—	0.5	2.7	6.6	12.4	15.1	8.7	0.9	4.0	3.3
Pill	17.1	16.2	27.4	21.5	17.7	12.7	7.4	21.0	9.9	12.3	11.8
Other hormonal methods	4.5	4.9	7.1	7.4	3.9	2.0	1.4	3.5	7.2	2.2	5.5
Implant, Lunelle™, or patch	0.9	0.7	1.1	1.5	0.9	0.5	—	0.5	1.0	—	1.5
3-month injectable (Depo-Provera™)	2.3	3.5	3.3	3.4	1.7	1.0	0.6	1.6	4.6	—	2.9
Contraceptive ring	1.3	0.7	2.7	2.4	1.4	0.5	0.4	1.4	1.6	—	1.0
Intrauterine device (IUD)	3.5	0.8	3.3	4.7	4.9	4.8	2.4	3.6	2.6	2.7	4.0
Condom	10.2	6.1	14.9	13.6	10.8	9.0	6.8	9.2	10.5	23.6	10.8
Periodic abstinence, calendar rhythm	0.6	—	0.2	0.5	0.8	1.0	1.1	0.6	0.2	1.8	0.8
Periodic abstinence, natural family planning	0.1	0.0	0.0	0.0	0.4	—	—	0.1	—	—	—
Withdrawal	3.2	2.1	3.3	4.1	3.2	4.1	2.6	3.1	2.4	4.9	3.4
Other methods[2]	0.3	0.2	—	0.3	0.5	0.6	0.4	0.3	0.1	—	0.7
Not using contraception[3]	**37.8**	**69.5**	**41.7**	**34.7**	**30.3**	**25.4**	**24.7**	**34.4**	**45.8**	**41.6**	**40.3**
Surgically sterile, female (noncontraceptive)	0.4	—	—	0.2	—	0.4	1.5	0.3	0.4	0.0	0.7
Nonsurgically sterile, female or male	1.7	0.5	1.4	1.4	1.8	2.0	3.1	1.5	2.3	1.5	1.6
Pregnant or postpartum	5.0	3.2	8.1	8.4	7.2	2.3	1.4	4.5	6.1	3.6	6.7
Seeking pregnancy	4.0	0.6	4.0	6.3	6.0	4.8	2.4	3.6	4.7	3.4	4.5
Never had intercourse	11.8	51.4	11.6	3.1	1.9	1.1	0.6	11.3	11.8	17.6	12.4
No intercourse in 3 months before interview	7.3	7.1	7.9	7.0	6.6	6.5	8.6	6.4	9.2	8.8	7.5
Had intercourse in 3 months before interview	7.7	6.7	8.7	8.4	6.7	8.4	7.1	6.9	11.2	6.7	7.0

— = Figure does not meet standards of reliability or precision. **Note:** Data was collected in interviews with women aged 15-44, in 2006-10. For all methods shown, the reported standard error was less than 3.9%. (1) Hispanics may be of any race. Other columns show data for non-Hispanic persons. (2) Includes diaphragm (with or without jelly or cream), emergency contraception, female condom or vaginal pouch, foam, cervical cap, Today™ sponge, suppository or insert, jelly or cream (without diaphragm), and other methods. (3) Includes male sterilization unknown reason and male surgical sterilization for noncontraceptive reasons, not shown separately.

Child Care Arrangements of Young Children, 1991-2012

Source: National Center for Education Statistics, U.S. Dept. of Education

	1991	1995	1999	2001	2005	2012
	Number in thousands					
All 3- to 5-year-olds[1]	8,402	9,222	8,518	8,551	9,066	8,244
	Percent of total					
Nonparental arrangements[2]	69.0%	74.1%	76.9%	73.9%	73.7%	77.9%
Relative care	16.9	19.4	22.8	22.8	22.6	26.2
Nonrelative care	14.8	16.9	16.1	14.0	11.6	13.3
Center-based programs[3]	52.8	55.1	59.7	56.4	57.2	60.6
Parental care only	31.0	25.9	23.1	26.1	26.3	22.1

(1) 3- to 5-year-old children not yet enrolled in kindergarten. (2) Total percentage of children who participated in nonparental arrangements. Each child is counted only once, even if he or she participated in more than one type of nonparental care; percentages may not add up to 100. (3) Includes day care centers, nursery schools, prekindergartens, preschools, and Head Start programs.

Sexual Activity of U.S. High School Students, 2013

Source: *Youth Risk Behavior Surveillance—United States, 2013*, Centers for Disease Control and Prevention, U.S. Dept. of Health and Human Services

Race/ethnicity	Ever had sexual intercourse			First sexual intercourse before age 13			Currently sexually active[1]			Condom use during last sexual intercourse[2]		
	Female	Male	Total	Female	Male	Total	Female	Male	Total	Female	Male	Total
White[3]	45.3%	42.2%	43.7%	2.1%	4.4%	3.3%	35.9%	29.7%	32.8%	53.2%	61.8%	57.1%
Black[3]	53.4	68.4	60.6	4.9	24.0	14.0	37.6	47.0	42.1	55.3	73.0	64.7
Hispanic	46.9	51.7	49.2	3.8	9.2	6.4	34.7	34.7	34.7	50.7	66.5	58.3
Grade												
9	28.1	32.0	30.0	2.9	8.7	5.8	19.8	19.3	19.6	56.5	69.5	62.7
10	41.7	41.1	41.4	3.2	8.7	6.0	31.8	27.0	29.4	55.5	69.3	61.7
11	53.9	54.3	54.1	3.3	8.0	5.6	40.7	39.6	40.2	54.8	70.6	62.3
12	62.8	65.4	64.1	2.5	7.4	4.9	50.7	47.8	49.3	48.4	58.0	53.0
Total	**46.0**	**47.5**	**46.8**	**3.1**	**8.3**	**5.6**	**35.2**	**32.7**	**34.0**	**53.1**	**65.8**	**59.1**

(1) Sexual intercourse during the 3 months preceding the survey. (2) Among the 34.0% who were sexually active. (3) Non-Hispanic.

Risk Behaviors in U.S. High School Students, 2013

Source: *Youth Risk Behavior Surveillance—United States, 2013*, Centers for Disease Control and Prevention, U.S. Dept. of Health and Human Services

		Percent rarely or never wore seat belts[1]			Percent rarely or never wore bicycle helmets[2]			Percent who rode with a driver who had been drinking alcohol[3]		
		Female	Male	Total	Female	Male	Total	Female	Male	Total
Race/ethnicity	White, non-Hispanic	4.7%	8.5%	6.6%	85.7%	85.8%	85.7%	19.9%	19.6%	19.7%
	Black, non-Hispanic	7.1	11.8	9.5	90.6	96.2	93.9	24.8	18.9	21.9
	Hispanic, any race	8.7	8.9	8.8	90.9	93.7	92.4	29.2	28.9	29.1
Grade	9	7.1	9.8	8.5	85.4	87.4	86.5	20.8	18.1	19.4
	10	5.7	8.4	7.1	87.6	89.3	88.5	23.8	19.9	21.8
	11	6.3	9.7	8.0	87.2	90.2	88.9	21.8	23.4	22.6
	12	5.1	8.3	6.7	88.2	87.8	88.0	23.2	25.3	24.2
Total		**6.1**	**9.1**	**7.6**	**87.0**	**88.6**	**87.9**	**22.4**	**21.4**	**21.9**

(1) When riding in a car driven by someone else. (2) Among the 67.0% of students who rode a bicycle during the 12 months preceding the survey. (3) In a car or other vehicle one or more times in the 30 days preceding the survey.

Risky Driving Behaviors by U.S. High School Students, 2013

Source: *Youth Risk Behavior Surveillance–United States, 2013*, Centers for Disease Control and Prevention, U.S. Dept. of Health and Human Services

		Percent who drove when drinking alcohol[1]			Percent who texted or emailed while driving[2]		
		Female	Male	Total	Female	Male	Total
Race/ethnicity	White, non-Hispanic	8.2%	12.4%	10.4%	46.7%	45.1%	45.8%
	Black, non-Hispanic	5.4	6.9	6.2	26.5	31.5	29.1
	Hispanic, any race	8.4	14.5	11.6	32.1	39.5	36.0
Grade	9	6.1	9.6	8.0	15.1	18.3	16.9
	10	4.6	7.4	6.2	25.0	27.8	26.5
	11	8.0	14.0	11.0	48.7	49.6	49.0
	12	10.5	15.7	13.1	59.5	61.0	60.3
Total		**7.8**	**12.0**	**10.0**	**40.9**	**41.8**	**41.4**

(1) Among the 64.3% of students who had driven a car or other vehicle one or more times during the 30 days before the survey. (2) Among the 64.7% of students who drove a car or other vehicle on at least one day during the 30 days before the survey.

U.S. Motor Vehicle Crashes, 2013

Source: National Safety Council (NSC); Natl. Highway Traffic Safety Admin. (NHTSA)

An estimated 35,500 people in the U.S. were killed in motor vehicle crashes in 2013, down 2% from the total for 2012. Both the number of drivers (212.6 mil) and the vehicle miles driven (3.0 tril) increased in 2013; the death rate per 100 mil vehicle miles decreased (11%) to 1.20.

Motor vehicle deaths per 10,000 registered vehicles decreased 3% from 1.44 in 2012 to 1.40 in 2013, and they were down from 1.85 in 2004, a decrease of 24% over nine years. The rate of fatalities per 100,000 population declined 27% between 2004 and 2013 but only decreased 3% between 2012 and 2013.

Male drivers were involved in about 5.6 mil crashes, whereas female drivers were in 4.4 mil. Male drivers were also involved in 74% of fatal crashes, or about 32,442, compared with 11,364 incidents involving female drivers.

In 2013, 10,076 traffic fatalities, or 31%, involved an intoxicated (blood alcohol concentration of 0.08 or greater) driver or motorcycle operator, a decrease of 2.5% from 2012.

Seat belt use was 87% in 2014. In 2013, safety belts and child restraints saved an estimated 12,847 lives. Another 2,388 lives were saved by frontal air bags. Women used safety belts (89%) more often than men (85%). In 2014, the least likely safety belt users were in pickup trucks (77%) or traveling in light traffic (74%).

Crashes	Deaths	Injuries
All motor vehicle crashes	35,500	4,300,000
Collision between motor vehicles	13,700	3,260,000
Collision with fixed object	11,100	590,000
Collision with pedestrian	6,100	160,000
Noncollision accidents (e.g., rollovers)	3,400	150,000
Collision with pedalcycle	1,000	120,000
Collision with railroad train	100	1,000
Other (mostly collisions with animals)	100	19,000

Note: NSC numbers are rounded and preliminary.

Improper Driving Reported in U.S. Crashes, 2000-13

Source: National Safety Council

Type	Percent of fatal crashes 2013	2005	2000	Percent of injury crashes 2013	2005	2000	Percent of all crashes 2013	2005	2000
Improper driving	**55.9%**	**62.7%**	**61.6%**	**62.5%**	**62.7%**	**60.3%**	**55.7%**	**58.5%**	**57.8%**
Speed too fast or unsafe	16.1	18.1	23.7	14.6	15.0	16.3	11.7	12.7	13.6
Right of way	11.9	12.2	18.6	18.4	17.5	19.9	14.1	14.3	20.1
Failed to yield	8.1	8.0	10.1	13.2	12.5	12.5	10.6	10.8	12.7
Disregarded signal	1.5	1.4	4.6	3.0	2.5	3.6	1.9	1.7	5.3
Passed stop sign	2.4	2.8	3.8	2.2	2.5	1.3	1.5	1.8	2.2
Drove left of center	6.2	8.0	8.2	1.2	2.2	1.1	1.0	1.6	1.0
Made improper turn	3.8	4.5	0.7	3.9	4.2	2.0	3.0	4.5	2.4
Improper overtaking	1.4	1.4	0.9	1.1	0.6	0.6	1.3	0.8	0.9
Followed too closely	0.8	1.0	0.5	6.8	6.8	4.3	7.6	8.7	5.7
Other improper driving	15.7	17.5	9.0	15.5	16.4	16.1	17.0	15.9	14.1
No improper driving stated	**44.1**	**37.3**	**38.4**	**38.5**	**37.3**	**39.7**	**44.3**	**41.5**	**42.2**

Note: Based on reports from state traffic authorities. When a driver was under the influence of alcohol or drugs, the crash was considered a result of the driver's physical condition, not a driving error. Percents may not add up to totals due to rounding.

U.S. Passenger Deaths and Death Rates, 1999-2012

Source: National Safety Council

Year	Light duty vehicles[1] Deaths	Rate[4]	Vans, SUVs, pickup trucks[1] Deaths	Rate[4]	Buses[2] Deaths	Rate[4]	Railroad passenger trains Deaths	Rate[4]	Scheduled airlines[3] Deaths	Rate[4]
1999	20,851	0.84	11,295	0.76	40	0.07	14	0.10	24	0.005
2000	20,689	0.81	11,545	0.76	3	0.01	4	0.03	94	0.02
2001	20,310	0.78	11,736	0.76	11	0.02	3	0.02	279	0.06
2002	20,564	0.78	12,278	0.78	36	0.06	7	0.05	0	0.00
2003	19,723	0.74	12,551	0.78	30	0.05	3	0.02	24	0.005
2004	19,183	0.71	12,678	0.75	27	0.05	3	0.02	13	0.002
2005	18,509	0.68	13,043	0.76	43	0.07	16	0.10	22	0.004
2006	17,792	0.66	12,723	0.72	15	0.02	2	0.01	52	0.01
2007	29,075	0.66	NA	NA	18	0.03	5	0.03	0	0.00
2008	25,457	0.59	NA	NA	50	0.08	24	0.13	0	0.00
2009	23,441	0.53	NA	NA	21	0.04	3	0.02	49	0.01
2010	22,271	0.50	NA	NA	28	0.05	3	0.02	0	0.00
2011	21,221	0.48	NA	NA	35	0.06	6	0.03	0	0.00
2012	21,669	0.49	NA	NA	25	0.04	5	0.02	0	0.00

NA = Not available. (1) From 2007 on, light duty vehicles includes passenger cars, light trucks, vans, and SUVs, which are shown separately in previous years. Drivers of light duty vehicles are considered passengers. Includes taxi passengers. (2) Excludes school buses. (3) Excludes charter, cargo, and on-demand service and deaths due to suicide/sabotage. (4) Deaths per 100 mil passenger miles.

U.S. Death Rates for Suicide at Selected Ages, 1960-2013

Source: *Health, United States, 2014*, National Center for Health Statistics (NCHS), CDC, U.S. Dept. of Health and Human Services

Age	2013 Both sexes	Male	Female	2000 Both sexes	Male	Female	1980 Both sexes	Male	Female	1960 Both sexes	Male	Female
15-24 years	11.1	17.3	4.5	10.2	17.1	3.0	12.3	20.2	4.3	5.2	8.2	2.2
25-44 years	15.5	24.1	6.8	13.4	21.3	5.4	15.6	24.0	7.7	12.2	17.9	6.6
45-64 years	19.0	29.0	9.4	13.5	21.3	6.2	15.9	23.7	8.9	22.0	34.4	10.2
65 years and older	16.1	30.9	4.6	15.2	31.1	4.0	17.6	35.0	6.1	24.5	44.0	8.4
All ages	**12.6**	**20.3**	**5.5**	**10.4**	**17.7**	**4.0**	**12.2**	**19.9**	**5.7**	**12.5**	**20.0**	**5.6**

Note: Rate is per 100,000 population. Rates for all ages include ages not shown here.

U.S. Fires, 2014

Source: National Fire Protection Association

Fires

- Public fire departments responded to 1,298,000 fires in 2014, an increase of 4.7% from 2013.
- Every 24 seconds, a fire department responds to a fire somewhere in the United States.
- There were 494,000 structure fires in 2014, a slight increase of 1.3% from 2013. Of those fires, 74% (367,500 fires) occurred in homes.
- Fires in highway vehicles increased 2.1% from the previous year, totaling 167,500 in 2014.
- There were 610,500 fires in outside properties, a significant increase of 8.1% from 2013.

Intentionally set fires

- There were an estimated 19,000 intentionally set structure fires in 2014, a decrease of 15.6% from 2013.
- Intentionally set structure fires are believed to have resulted in 157 civilian deaths in 2014, an increase of 4.7% from the year before. Property damage from intentionally set structure fires totaled $613 mil, an increase of 6.2% from the 2013 figure.

Civilian deaths

- There were an estimated 3,275 civilian fire deaths in 2014. This was a 1.1% increase from the year before.
- The number of civilian fire deaths that occurred in home structure fires remained virtually unchanged (a decrease of 0.4%) to 2,745, and fires in the home caused 84% of all fire deaths.
- Fires caused an average of one civilian death every 161 minutes.

Civilian injuries

- There were an estimated 15,775 civilian fire injuries reported in 2014, a 0.9% decrease from 2013. Nationwide, a civilian was injured in a fire every 33 minutes; a civilian fire injury occurred in a home fire every 44 minutes.
- Home structure fires were the site of 11,825 civilian fire injuries in 2014. Non-home structure fires accounted for 1,600 civilian injuries.

Property damage

- Direct property damage from fires amounted to an estimated $11.6 bil in 2014, an increase of 0.7% from 2013. Structure fires accounted for $9.8 bil of property damage.
- Property loss associated with home fires came to $6.8 bil for 2014.

Leading Causes of Death in the U.S., 2013

Source: National Center for Health Statistics (NCHS), CDC, U.S. Dept. of Health and Human Services

	Number	% of total deaths	Death rate[1]
All causes	**2,596,993**	**100.0%**	**731.9**
1. Diseases of the heart	611,105	23.5	169.8
2. Cancer	584,881	22.5	163.2
3. Chronic lower respiratory diseases	149,205	5.7	42.1
4. Accidents (unintentional injuries)	130,557	5.0	39.4
5. Stroke	128,978	5.0	36.2
6. Alzheimer's disease	84,767	3.3	23.5
7. Diabetes	75,578	2.9	21.2
8. Influenza and pneumonia	56,979	2.2	15.9
9. Kidney disease	47,112	1.8	13.2
10. Suicide	41,149	1.6	12.6
All other causes (residual)	686,682	26.4	—

(1) Per 100,000 population.

Principal Types of Accidental Deaths in the U.S., 1970-2013

Source: National Safety Council; National Center for Health Statistics, U.S. Dept. of Health and Human Services

Year[1]	Total	Motor vehicle	Falls	Poisoning	Drowning	Fires, flames, smoke	Choking: inhalation of food, object	Firearms	Mechanical suffocation
1970	NA	54,633	16,926	5,299	7,860	6,718	2,753	2,406	NA
1980	105,718	53,172	13,294	4,331	7,257	5,822	3,249	1,955	NA
1985	93,457	45,901	12,001	5,170	5,316	4,938	3,551	1,649	NA
1990	91,983	46,814	12,313	5,803	4,685	4,175	3,303	1,416	NA
1995	93,320	43,363	13,986	9,072	4,350	3,761	3,185	1,225	NA
2000	97,900	43,354	13,322	12,757	3,482	3,377	4,313	776	1,335
2005	117,809	45,343	19,656	23,617	3,582	3,197	4,386	789	1,514
2006	121,599	45,316	20,823	27,531	3,579	3,109	4,332	642	1,580
2007	123,706	43,945	22,631	29,846	3,443	3,286	4,344	613	1,653
2008	121,902	39,790	24,013	31,116	3,548	2,912	4,366	592	1,759
2009	118,046	36,216	24,792	31,758	3,517	2,756	4,370	554	1,569
2010	120,859	35,332	26,009	33,041	3,782	2,782	4,570	606	1,595
2011	126,438	35,303	27,483	36,280	3,556	2,746	4,708	591	1,534
2012	127,792	36,415	28,753	36,332	3,551	2,464	4,634	548	1,604
2013[2]	130,800	35,500	30,300	38,800	3,700	2,400	4,800	530	1,800
Death rates per 100,000 population									
1970	NA	26.8	8.3	2.6	3.9	3.3	1.4	1.2	NA
1980	46.5	23.4	5.9	1.9	3.2	2.6	1.4	0.9	NA
1985	39.3	19.3	5.0	2.2	2.2	2.1	1.5	0.7	NA
1990	36.9	18.8	4.9	2.3	1.9	1.7	1.3	0.6	NA
1995	35.5	16.5	5.3	3.4	1.7	1.4	1.2	0.5	NA
2000	35.6	15.7	4.8	4.6	1.3	1.2	1.6	0.3	0.5
2005	39.7	15.3	6.6	8.0	1.2	1.1	1.5	0.3	0.5
2006	40.8	15.2	7.0	9.2	1.2	1.0	1.5	0.2	0.5
2007	41.1	14.6	7.5	9.9	1.1	1.1	1.4	0.2	0.5
2008	40.0	13.1	7.9	10.2	1.2	1.0	1.4	0.2	0.6
2009	38.5	11.8	8.1	10.3	1.1	0.9	1.4	0.2	0.5
2010	39.0	11.4	8.4	10.7	1.2	0.9	1.5	0.9	0.5
2011	40.6	11.3	8.8	11.6	1.1	0.9	1.5	0.2	0.5
2012	40.7	11.6	9.2	11.6	1.1	0.8	1.5	0.2	0.5
2013[2]	41.4	11.2	9.6	12.3	1.2	0.8	1.5	0.2	0.6

NA = Not available. **Note:** All figures include on-the-job deaths. (1) Data after 1999 are not comparable with earlier data because of classification changes. (2) Preliminary. Total includes 12,970 other accidental deaths (4.2 death rate).

Deaths in the U.S. Involving Firearms by Age and Sex, 2011

Source: National Safety Council

Type and sex	All ages	Under 5	5-14	15-19	20-24	25-44	45-64	65-74	75 & older
Total firearms deaths	**32,351**	**86**	**311**	**2,306**	**3,979**	**11,015**	**9,650**	**2,444**	**2,560**
Male	27,738	56	232	2,041	3,568	9,383	8,003	2,122	2,333
Female	4,613	30	79	265	411	1,632	1,647	322	227
Unintentional	**591**	**29**	**45**	**66**	**64**	**152**	**151**	**46**	**38**
Male	511	22	32	59	55	134	131	44	34
Female	80	7	13	7	9	18	20	2	4
Suicide	**19,990**	—	**92**	**758**	**1,410**	**5,577**	**7,622**	**2,159**	**2,372**
Male	17,320	—	81	674	1,262	4,722	6,435	1,916	2,230
Female	2,670	—	11	84	148	855	1,187	243	142
Homicide	**11,068**	**55**	**162**	**1,434**	**2,391**	**4,989**	**1,693**	**210**	**134**
Male	9,270	32	109	1,264	2,142	4,257	1,274	136	56
Female	1,798	23	53	170	249	732	419	74	78
Legal intervention	**454**	**0**	**1**	**28**	**72**	**214**	**121**	**15**	**3**
Male	438	0	0	27	71	208	114	15	3
Female	16	0	1	1	1	6	7	0	0
Undetermined[1]	**248**	**2**	**11**	**20**	**42**	**83**	**63**	**14**	**13**
Male	199	2	10	17	38	62	49	11	10
Female	49	0	1	3	4	21	14	3	3

— = Not applicable. (1) The intention involved (whether accident, suicide, or homicide) could not be determined.

U.S. Infant Mortality Rates by Race and Sex, 1960-2013

Source: National Center for Health Statistics (NCHS), CDC, U.S. Dept. of Health and Human Services

	All races[1]			White			Black		
Year	**Both sexes**	**Male**	**Female**	**Both sexes**	**Male**	**Female**	**Both sexes**	**Male**	**Female**
1960	26.0	29.3	22.6	22.9	26.0	19.6	44.3	49.1	39.4
1970	20.0	22.4	17.5	17.8	20.0	15.4	32.6	36.2	29.0
1980	12.6	13.9	11.2	11.0	12.3	9.6	21.4	23.3	19.4
1990	9.2	10.3	8.1	7.6	8.5	6.6	18.0	19.6	16.2
1995	7.6	8.3	6.8	6.3	7.0	5.6	15.1	16.3	13.9
1996	7.3	8.0	6.6	6.1	6.7	5.4	14.7	16.0	13.3
1997	7.2	8.0	6.5	6.0	6.7	5.4	14.2	15.5	12.8
1998	7.2	7.8	6.5	6.0	6.5	5.4	14.3	15.7	12.8
1999	7.1	7.7	6.4	5.8	6.4	5.2	14.6	15.9	13.2
2000	6.9	7.6	6.2	5.7	6.2	5.1	14.1	15.5	12.6
2001	6.8	7.5	6.1	5.7	6.2	5.1	14.0	15.5	12.5
2002	7.0	7.6	6.3	5.8	6.4	5.1	14.4	15.4	13.3
2003	6.9	7.6	6.1	5.7	6.3	5.0	14.0	15.5	12.4
2004	6.8	7.5	6.1	5.7	6.2	5.1	13.8	15.2	12.3
2005	6.9	7.6	6.2	5.7	6.3	5.1	13.7	15.2	12.3
2006	6.7	7.3	6.0	5.6	6.1	5.0	13.3	14.4	12.2
2007	6.8	7.4	6.1	5.6	6.2	5.1	13.2	14.5	11.9
2008	6.6	7.2	6.0	5.6	6.1	5.0	12.7	13.9	11.5
2009	6.4	7.0	5.8	5.3	5.8	4.8	12.6	14.1	11.2
2010	6.2	6.7	5.6	5.2	5.7	4.7	11.6	12.7	10.5
2011	6.1	6.6	5.5	5.1	5.5	4.7	11.5	12.6	10.4
2012	6.0	6.5	5.4	5.1	5.5	4.7	11.2	12.3	10.0
2013	6.0	6.5	5.4	5.1	5.6	4.5	11.2	12.0	10.4

Note: Rates of infant deaths (under 1 year of age) per 1,000 live births in specified group. (1) Includes races other than white and black.

Years of Life Expected at Birth in U.S., 1900-2013

Source: National Center for Health Statistics (NCHS), CDC, U.S. Dept. of Health and Human Services

	All races[1]			White			Black		
Year[2]	**Both sexes**	**Male**	**Female**	**Both sexes**	**Male**	**Female**	**Both sexes**	**Male**	**Female**
1900	47.3	46.3	48.3	47.6	46.6	48.7	33.0	32.5	33.5
1950	68.2	65.6	71.1	69.1	66.5	72.2	60.8	59.1	62.9
1960	69.7	66.6	73.1	70.6	67.4	74.1	63.6	61.1	66.3
1970	70.8	67.1	74.7	71.7	68.0	75.6	64.1	60.0	68.3
1980	73.7	70.0	77.4	74.4	70.7	78.1	68.1	63.8	72.5
1990	75.4	71.8	78.8	76.1	72.7	79.4	69.1	64.5	73.6
1995	75.8	72.5	78.9	76.5	73.4	79.6	69.6	65.2	73.9
2000	76.8	74.1	79.3	77.3	74.7	79.9	71.8	68.2	75.1
2001	77.0	74.3	79.5	77.5	74.9	80.0	72.0	68.5	75.3
2002	77.0	74.4	79.6	77.5	74.9	80.1	72.2	68.7	75.4
2005	77.6	75.0	80.1	78.0	75.5	80.5	73.0	69.5	76.2
2006	77.8	75.2	80.3	78.3	75.8	80.7	73.4	69.9	76.7
2007	78.1	75.5	80.6	78.5	76.0	80.9	73.8	70.3	77.0
2008	78.2	75.6	80.6	78.5	76.1	80.9	74.3	70.9	77.3
2009	78.5	76.0	80.9	78.8	76.4	81.2	74.7	71.4	77.7
2010	78.7	76.2	81.0	78.9	76.5	81.3	75.1	71.8	78.0
2011	78.7	76.3	81.1	79.0	76.6	81.3	75.3	72.2	78.2
2012	78.8	76.4	81.2	79.1	76.7	81.4	75.5	72.3	78.4
2013	78.8	76.4	81.2	79.1	76.7	81.4	75.5	72.3	78.4

(1) Includes races other than white and black. (2) Data prior to 1940 does not include all states.

U.S. Life Expectancy at Selected Ages, 2013

Source: National Center for Health Statistics (NCHS), CDC, U.S. Dept. of Health and Human Services

Exact age	All races[1]			White			Black		
in years	**Both sexes**	**Male**	**Female**	**Both sexes**	**Male**	**Female**	**Both sexes**	**Male**	**Female**
0	78.8	76.4	81.2	79.1	76.7	81.4	75.5	72.3	78.4
1	78.3	75.9	80.6	78.5	76.1	80.7	75.4	72.2	78.2
5	74.4	72.0	76.7	74.5	72.2	76.8	71.5	68.3	74.3
10	69.4	67.1	71.7	69.6	67.3	71.8	66.5	63.4	69.4
15	64.5	62.1	66.8	64.6	62.3	66.9	61.6	58.5	64.4
20	59.6	57.3	61.8	59.7	57.5	62.0	56.8	53.7	59.5
25	54.8	52.6	57.0	55.0	52.8	57.1	52.1	49.2	54.7
30	50.1	48.0	52.1	50.2	48.1	52.2	47.4	44.6	49.9
35	45.4	43.3	47.3	45.5	43.5	47.4	42.8	40.1	45.1
40	40.7	38.7	42.6	40.8	38.8	42.6	38.2	35.7	40.4
45	36.1	34.1	37.9	36.2	34.3	37.9	33.7	31.2	35.9
50	31.6	29.7	33.3	31.7	29.9	33.4	29.4	27.0	31.5
55	27.3	25.6	28.9	27.4	25.7	28.9	25.3	23.0	27.3
60	23.2	21.7	24.6	23.3	21.7	24.6	21.6	19.5	23.3
65	19.3	17.9	20.5	19.3	18.0	20.5	18.1	16.3	19.5
70	15.6	14.4	16.6	15.6	14.4	16.5	14.8	13.2	15.9
75	12.2	11.2	12.9	12.1	11.1	12.9	11.8	10.4	12.7
80	9.1	8.3	9.7	9.1	8.3	9.7	9.1	8.0	9.7
85	6.6	5.9	7.0	6.5	5.9	6.9	6.8	6.0	7.2
90	4.6	4.1	4.8	4.5	4.0	4.8	5.1	4.5	5.3
95	3.2	2.8	3.3	3.1	2.8	3.2	3.8	3.4	3.8
100	2.3	2.0	2.3	2.2	2.0	2.3	2.8	2.6	2.8

(1) Includes races other than white and black.

NOTED PERSONALITIES

Widely Known Americans of the Present 173
Widely Known World Personalities of the Present 176
Other Noted Personalities (excluding Performing Arts)
Architects 177
Artists, Photographers, and Sculptors of the Past 178
Business Leaders and Philanthropists of the Past 181
Cartoonists, American 182
Economists, Educators, Historians, and Social Scientists of the Past 183
Journalists of the Past, American 184
Military and Naval Leaders of the Past 186
Philosophers and Religious Figures of the Past 187
Political Leaders of the Past 188
Scientists of the Past 192
Social Reformers, Activists, and Humanitarians of the Past 201
Sports Personalities of the Past and Present 202
Writers of the Present 208
Writers of the Past 209
Poets Laureate 214
Noted Personalities in the Performing Arts
Composers of Classical and Avant Garde Music 214
Composers of Operettas, Musicals, and Popular Music 215
Lyricists 216
Performers, by Type
Blues and Jazz Artists of the Past 216
Country Music Artists of the Past and Present 218
Dance Figures of the Past 219
Opera Singers of the Past 219
Rock and Roll, Rhythm and Blues, and Rap Artists 220
Personalities in Entertainment
Entertainment Personalities of the Present 222
Entertainment Personalities of the Past 235
Original Names of Selected Entertainers 241

Widely Known Americans of the Present

Political leaders, journalists, other prominent living persons. As of Oct. 2015. Excludes most who fall in categories listed elsewhere in Noted Personalities, such as Writers of the Present and Entertainment Personalities of the Present. Includes some figures who are active in American life but are not U.S. citizens.

Roger Ailes, b 5/15/1940 (Warren, OH), TV exec.
Madeleine K. Albright, b 5/15/1937 (Prague, Czech.), former sec. of state.
Edwin "Buzz" Aldrin, b 1/20/1930 (Montclair, NJ), former astronaut, second person to walk on the Moon.
Samuel A. Alito Jr., b 4/1/1950 (Trenton, NJ), Supreme Court justice.
Paul Allen, b 1/21/1953 (Seattle, WA), cofounder of Microsoft.
Christiane Amanpour, b 1/12/1958 (London, Eng., UK), TV journalist.
Marc Andreessen, b 7/9/1971 (New Lisbon, IA), co-author of web browser Mosaic, cofounder of Netscape.
David Axelrod, b 2/22/1955 (New York, NY), political strategist; former sr. adviser to Pres. Obama.
Michele Bachmann, b 4/6/1956 (Waterloo, IA), U.S. rep. (R, MN), 2012 pres. contender.
F. Lee Bailey, b 6/10/1933 (Waltham, MA), attorney.
Russell Baker, b 8/14/1925 (Morrisonville, VA), columnist.
Mary Barra, b 12/24/1961 (Waterford, MI), General Motors CEO.
Dave Barry, b 7/3/1947 (Armonk, NY), humorist.
Max Baucus, b 12/11/1941 (Helena, MT), U.S. amb. to China, former senator (D, MT).
Gary Bauer, b 5/4/1946 (Covington, KY), domestic policy adviser to Pres. Reagan; founder, Campaign for Working Families.
Glenn Beck, b 2/10/1964 (Mount Vernon, WA), political commentator.
Chris Berman, b 5/10/1955 (Greenwich, CT), sportscaster.
Ben Bernanke, b 12/13/1953 (Augusta, GA), former Federal Reserve chair.
Carl Bernstein, b 2/14/1944 (Washington, DC), journalist; with Bob Woodward cracked Watergate scandal.
Jeff Bezos, b 1/12/1964 (Albuquerque, NM), founder and CEO of Amazon.com.
Jill Biden, b 6/5/1951 (Hammonton, NJ), English college professor, wife of U.S. vice pres. Joe Biden.
Joseph R. Biden Jr., b 11/20/1942 (Scranton, PA), U.S. vice pres.; former sen. (D, DE).
James H. Billington, b 6/1/1929 (Bryn Mawr, PA), librarian of U.S. Congress.
Lloyd Blankfein, b 9/20/1954 (Bronx, NY), CEO and chairman of Goldman Sachs.
Wolf Blitzer, b 3/22/1948 (Augsburg, Germany), TV journalist.
Harold Bloom, b 7/11/1930 (New York, NY), literary critic.
Michael R. Bloomberg, b 2/14/1942 (Brighton, MA), former NYC mayor, financial information/media entrepreneur.
John Boehner, b 11/17/1949 (Cincinnati, OH), former U.S. rep. (R, OH) and speaker of the House.
Charles F. Bolden, b 8/19/1946 (Columbia, SC), NASA head.
Cory Booker, b 4/27/1969 (Washington, DC), U.S. sen. (D, NJ), former Newark mayor.
Barbara Boxer, b 11/11/1940 (Brooklyn, NY), U.S. senator (D, CA).
L. Paul Bremer III, b 9/30/1941 (Hartford, CT), diplomat, former top U.S. civilian administrator in Iraq.
John O. Brennan, b 9/22/1955 (North Bergen, NJ), CIA director.
Jimmy Breslin, b 10/17/1930 (Jamaica, Queens, NY), columnist, author.
Stephen Breyer, b 8/15/1938 (San Francisco, CA), U.S. Supreme Court justice.
Sergey Brin, b 8/21/1973 (Moscow, Russia), cofounder of Google.
Roslyn M. Brock, b 5/30/1965 (Fort Pierce, FL), NAACP chair.
Tom Brokaw, b 2/6/1940 (Webster, SD), TV journalist, retired anchor.
David Brooks, b 8/11/1961 (Toronto, ON, Can.), columnist, political commentator.
Aaron Brown, b 11/10/1948 (Hopkins, MN), broadcast journalist.
Jerry (Edmund G.) Brown Jr., b 4/7/1938 (San Francisco, CA), CA gov. (D, 1975-83, 2011-), former pres. candidate.
Pat Buchanan, b 11/2/1938 (Washington, DC), journalist, former pres. candidate (R).
Warren Buffett, b 8/30/1930 (Omaha, NE), investor, leading philanthropist.
Sylvia Mathews Burwell, b 6/1/1965 (Hinton, WV), health and human services sec.
Barbara Bush, b 6/8/1925 (Flushing, NY), former first lady.
Barbara Bush, b 11/25/1981 (Dallas, TX), daughter of former Pres. George W. Bush.
George H. W. Bush, b 6/12/1924 (Milton, MA), former U.S. president.
George W. Bush, b 7/6/1946 (New Haven, CT), former U.S. president.
Jeb Bush, b 2/11/1953 (Midland, TX), FL gov. (R); 2016 pres. contender.
Laura Bush, b 11/4/1946 (Midland, TX), former first lady.
Eric Cantor, b 6/6/1963 (Richmond, VA), former U.S. rep. (R, VA), former House majority leader.
Tucker Carlson, b 5/16/1969 (San Francisco, CA), journalist, TV commentator.
Jay Carney, b 5/22/1965 (Washington, DC), political commentator, former White House press secretary.
Ben Carson, b 9/18/1951 (Detroit, MI), neurosurgeon; 2016 pres. contender (R).
Jimmy Carter, b 10/1/1924 (Plains, GA), former U.S. president; 2002 Nobel Peace Prize winner.
Rosalynn Carter, b 8/18/1927 (Plains, GA), former first lady.
James Carville Jr., b 10/25/1944 (Fort Benning, GA), TV political commentator.
Steve Case, b 8/21/1958 (Honolulu, HI), former AOL Time Warner chairman.
Joaquin Castro, b 9/16/1974 (San Antonio, TX), U.S. rep. (D, TX).
Julian Castro, b 9/16/1974 (San Antonio, TX), housing and urban development sec., former San Antonio mayor.
Dick Cheney, b 1/30/1941 (Lincoln, NE), former U.S. vice president.
Lynne Cheney, b 8/14/1941 (Casper, WY), political commentator, wife of former U.S. vice pres. Dick Cheney.
Noam Chomsky, b 12/7/1928 (Philadelphia, PA), linguist, activist.
Chris Christie, b 9/6/1962 (Newark, NJ), NJ gov. (R); 2016 pres. contender.
Connie Chung, b 8/20/1946 (Washington, DC), TV journalist.
James R. Clapper Jr., b 1941, director of national intelligence.
Bill Clinton, b 8/19/1946 (Hope, AR), former U.S. president.
Chelsea Clinton, b 2/27/1980 (Little Rock, AR), daughter of former pres. Bill Clinton and Hillary Rodham Clinton.
Hillary Rodham Clinton, b 10/26/1947 (Chicago, IL), former sec. of state, U.S. sen. (D, NY), first lady; pres. contender (2008, '16).
Kate Clinton, b 11/9/1947 (Buffalo, NY), political humorist.
Kenneth Cole, b 3/23/1954 (Brooklyn, NY), fashion designer.
Gail Collins, b 11/25/1945 (Cincinnati, OH), newspaper columnist, writer.
Jason Collins, b 12/2/1978 (Northridge, CA), first openly gay active NBA player.
James Comey, b 12/14/1960 (Yonkers, NY), FBI director.
Tim Cook, b 11/1/1960 (Robertdale, AZ), CEO of Apple, Inc.
Anderson Cooper, b 6/3/1967 (New York, NY), TV news anchor.
Misty Copeland, b 9/10/82 (Kansas City, MO), ballet dancer; first African-American principal dancer at American Ballet Theater.
Bob Corker, b 8/24/52 (Orangeburg, SC), U.S. sen. (R, TN).
John Cornyn, b 2/2/1952 (Houston, TX), U.S. sen. (R, TX), majority whip.
Jon Corzine, b 1/1/1947 (Willey's Station, IL), former U.S. sen. (D, NJ) and NJ gov.
Bob Costas, b 3/22/1952 (Astoria, Queens, NY), TV sports journalist.
Ann Coulter, b 12/8/1961 (New Canaan, CT), political commentator, author.
Katie Couric, b 1/7/1957 (Arlington, VA), TV and online journalist.
Candy Crowley, b 12/12/1948 (Kalamazoo, MI), TV journalist.
Ted Cruz, b 12/22/1970 (Calgary, AB, Can.), U.S. sen. (R, TX); 2016 pres. contender.
Mark Cuban, b 7/31/1958 (Pittsburgh, PA), entrepreneur, Dallas Mavericks (NBA) owner.
Andrew Cuomo, b 12/6/1957 (New York, NY), NY gov. (D), former state atty. gen.
Ann Curry, b 11/19/1956 (Guam), former *Today* show news anchor.
Bill de Blasio, b 5/8/1961 (New York, NY), NYC mayor (D).

Michael Dell, b 2/23/1965 (Houston, TX), founder, chairman, and CEO of Dell computers.
Martin Dempsey, b 3/14/1952 (Bayonne, NJ) former chair, Joint Chiefs of Staff.
Alan Dershowitz, b 9/1/1938 (Brooklyn, NY), attorney, political commentator.
Barry Diller, b 2/2/1942 (San Francisco, CA), media exec.
Jamie Dimon, b 3/13/1956 (New York, NY), chairman, CEO of JPMorgan Chase.
Lou Dobbs, b 9/24/1945 (Childress, TX), TV journalist.
James Dobson, b 4/21/1936 (Shreveport, LA), evangelical Christian leader, founder of Focus on the Family.
Christopher Dodd, b 5/27/1944 (Willimantic, CT), Motion Picture Assn. of America chair/CEO; former U.S. sen. (D, CT).
Timothy Dolan, b 2/6/1950 (St. Louis, MO), Rom. Cath. cardinal, archbishop of NY.
Elizabeth Hanford Dole, b 7/29/1936 (Salisbury, NC), former U.S. sen. (R, NC), Red Cross pres., cabinet member.
Robert Dole, b 7/22/1923 (Russell, KS), former U.S. Senate majority leader (R, KS), 1996 pres. nominee.
Sam Donaldson, b 3/11/1934 (El Paso, TX), TV journalist.
Jack Dorsey, b 11/19/1976 (St. Louis, MO), Twitter cofounder.
Elizabeth Drew, b 11/16/1935 (Cincinnati, OH), journalist.
Matt Drudge, b 10/27/1966 (Takoma Park, MD), Internet journalist.
Michael S. Dukakis, b 11/3/1933 (Brookline, MA), former MA gov. (D), 1988 pres. nominee.
Arne Duncan, b 11/6/1964 (Chicago, IL), outgoing education secretary.
Dick Durbin, b 11/21/1944 (East St. Louis, IL), U.S. Senate minority whip (D, IL).
Josh Earnest, b 5/2/1977 (Kansas City, MO), White House press secretary.
Bernard Ebbers, b 8/27/1941 (Edmonton, AB, Can.), former WorldCom CEO; jailed for fraud.
Marian Wright Edelman, b 6/6/1939 (Bennettsville, SC), pres. and founder of Children's Defense Fund.
John Edwards, b 6/10/1953 (Seneca, SC), former U.S. sen. (D, NC), 2004 vice-pres. nominee, 2008 pres. contender.
Michael Eisner, b 3/7/1942 (Mt. Kisco, NY), former Disney Co. CEO.
Lawrence J. Ellison, b 8/17/1944 (New York, NY), Oracle Corp. founder, CEO.
Rahm Emanuel, b 11/29/1959 (Chicago, IL), Chicago mayor; former White House chief of staff, U.S. rep. (D, IL).
Myrlie Evers-Williams, b 3/17/1933 (Vicksburg, MS), civil rights activist.
Louis Farrakhan, b 5/11/1933 (Roxbury, MA), Nation of Islam leader.
Dianne Feinstein, b 6/22/1933 (San Francisco, CA), U.S. sen. (D, CA).
Carly (Carleton) S. Fiorina, b 9/6/1954 (Austin, TX), former Hewlett-Packard CEO, 2016 pres. contender (R).
Larry Flynt, b 11/1/1942 (Lakeville, KY), publisher.
Steve (Malcolm) Forbes Jr., b 7/18/1947 (Morristown, NJ), publisher, former pres. contender.
Tom Ford, b 8/27/1961 (Austin, TX), fashion designer.
Barney Frank, b 3/31/1940 (Bayonne, NJ), attorney, former U.S. rep. (D, MA).
Al Franken, b 5/21/1951 (New York, NY), U.S. sen. (D, MN); humorist.
Thomas Friedman, b 7/20/1953 (Minneapolis, MN), columnist, author.
Bill Gates, b 10/28/1955 (Seattle, WA), software pioneer; Microsoft exec.
Henry Louis Gates Jr., b 9/16/1950 (Keyser, WV), African American studies scholar.
Robert M. Gates, b 9/25/1943 (Wichita, KS), former sec. of defense; Boy Scouts of America pres.
David Geffen, b 2/21/1943 (Brooklyn, NY), entertainment exec.
Timothy Geithner, b 8/18/1961 (New York, NY), former Treasury secretary.
Charles Gibson, b 3/4/1943 (Evanston, IL), TV journalist, former host of ABC's *World News*.
Gabrielle Giffords, b 6/8/1970 (Tucson, AZ), former U.S. rep. (D, AZ); shot in 2011 assassination attempt.
Kirsten Gillibrand, b 12/9/1966 (Albany, NY), U.S. sen. (D, NY), attorney.
Jim Gilmore, b 10/6/1949 (Richmond, VA), former VA gov. (R); 2016 pres. contender.
Newt Gingrich, b 6/17/1943 (Harrisburg, PA), former House speaker (R, GA), 2012 pres. contender.
Ruth Bader Ginsburg, b 3/15/1933 (Brooklyn, NY), U.S. Supreme Court justice.
Rudolph Giuliani, b 5/28/1944 (Brooklyn, NY), former NYC mayor (R).
Ira Glass, b 3/3/1959 (Baltimore, MD), radio host.
John Glenn, b 7/18/1921 (Cambridge, OH), former U.S. sen. (D, OH), astronaut.
Alberto Gonzales, b 8/4/1955 (San Antonio, TX), former U.S. attorney general.
Roger Goodell, b 2/19/1959 (Jamestown, NY), NFL commissioner.
Ellen Goodman, b 4/11/1941 (Newton, MA), columnist.
Doris Kearns Goodwin, b 1/4/1943 (Brooklyn, NY), historian, TV commentator.
Berry Gordy, b 11/28/1929 (Detroit, MI), Motown record label founder.
Al Gore Jr., b 3/31/1948 (Washington, DC), former U.S. sen. (D, TN), vice pres., 2000 pres. nominee; 2007 Nobel Peace Prize winner.
Billy Graham, b 11/7/1918 (Charlotte, NC), evangelist.
(William) Franklin Graham III, b 7/14/1952 (Asheville, NC), evangelist, son of Billy Graham.
Lindsey Graham, b 7/9/1955 (Central, SC), U.S. sen. (R, SC); 2016 pres. contender.
Temple Grandin, b 8/29/1947 (Boston, MA), animal behavioral scientist, autism activist.
Jeff Greenfield, b 6/10/1943 (New York, NY), TV journalist.
Alan Greenspan, b 3/6/1926 (New York, NY), former Federal Reserve chairman.
Chuck Hagel, b 10/4/1946 (North Platte, NE), defense sec., former U.S. sen. (R, NE).
Jenna Bush Hager, b 11/25/1981 (Dallas, TX), daughter of former Pres. George W. Bush.
Pete Hamill, b 6/24/1935 (Brooklyn, NY), journalist, author.
Sean Hannity, b 12/30/1961 (New York, NY), radio and TV host, author, political commentator.
Kamala Harris, b 10/20/1964 (Oakland, CA), atty. gen. (CA).
Reed Hastings, b 10/8/1960 (Boston, MA), founder, pres., CEO and board chair, Netflix, Inc.
Orrin Hatch, b 3/22/1934 (Homestead Park, PA), U.S. sen. (R, UT) and Senate pres. pro tempore.
Hugh Hefner, b 4/9/1926 (Chicago, IL), publisher.
Tommy Hilfiger, b 3/24/1951 (Elmira, NY), fashion designer.
Anita Hill, b 7/30/1956 (Morris, OK), legal scholar; complainant against Supreme Court justice Clarence Thomas.
Paris Hilton, b 2/17/1981 (New York, NY), heiress, actress.
Perez Hilton, b 3/23/1978 (Miami, FL), gossip columnist.
James P. Hoffa, b 5/19/1941 (Detroit, MI), Teamsters Union head.
Eric Holder Jr., b 1/21/1951 (Bronx, NY), former U.S. atty. gen.
David Horowitz, b 1/10/1939 (New York, NY), consumer advocate, columnist, author.
Steny H. Hoyer, b 6/14/1939 (New York, NY), House minority whip (D, MD).
Mike Huckabee, b 8/24/1955 (Hope, AR), former AR gov. (R), minister, TV host; pres. contender (2008, '16).
Arianna Huffington, b 7/15/1950 (Athens, Greece), political commentator.
H. Wayne Huizenga, b 12/29/1939 (Evergreen Park, IL), entrepreneur, sports exec.
Brit Hume, b 6/22/1943 (Washington, DC), TV journalist on FOX.
Jon Huntsman Jr., b 3/26/1960 (Palo Alto, CA), former UT gov. (R), ambassador to China, 2012 pres. contender.
Lee Iacocca, b 10/15/1924 (Allentown, PA), former auto exec. (Ford, Chrysler).
Carl Icahn, b 2/16/1936 (Queens, NY), financier.
Gwen Ifill, b 9/29/1955 (Queens, NY), TV journalist, moderator on PBS.
Bob Iger, b 2/10/1951 (Oceanside, NY), Walt Disney Co. CEO.
Don Imus, b 7/23/1940 (Riverside, CA), talk-show host.
Patricia Ireland, b 10/19/1945 (Oak Park, IL), feminist leader.
Jesse Jackson, b 10/8/1941 (Greenville, SC), civil rights leader, former pres. contender (D).
Marc Jacobs, b 4/9/1964 (New York, NY), fashion designer.
Valerie Jarrett, b 11/14/1956 (Shiraz, Iran), sr. adviser to Pres. Obama.
Bobby Jindal, b 6/10/1971 (Baton Rouge, LA), LA gov. (R); 2016 pres. contender.
Jasper Johns, b 5/15/1930 (Augusta, GA), artist.
Robert L. Johnson, b 4/8/1946 (Hickory, MS), Black Entertainment Television founder.
Vernon E. Jordan Jr., b 8/15/1935 (Atlanta, GA), attorney, former pres. adviser, civil rights leader.
Elena Kagan, b 4/28/1960 (New York, NY), U.S. Supreme Court justice.
Donna Karan, b 10/2/1948 (Forest Hills, Queens, NY), fashion designer.
John Kasich, b 5/13/1952 (McKees Rocks, PA), OH gov. (R); 2016 pres. contender.
Jeffrey Katzenberg, b 12/21/1950 (New York, NY), entertainment exec.
Garrison Keillor, b 8/7/1942 (Anoka, MN), author, broadcaster.
Mark Kelly, b 2/21/1964 (Orange, NJ), U.S. Navy capt., former NASA shuttle commander.
Megyn Kelly, b 11/18/1970 (Syracuse, NY), TV commentator, host.
Anthony M. Kennedy, b 7/23/1936 (Sacramento, CA), U.S. Supreme Court justice.
John Kerry, b 12/11/1943 (Aurora, CO), sec. of state, former U.S. sen. (D, MA), 2004 pres. nominee.
Larry King, b 11/19/1933 (Brooklyn, NY), TV talk-show host.
Michael Kinsley, b 3/9/1951 (Detroit, MI), editor, political commentator.
Henry Kissinger, b 5/27/1923 (Furth, Germany), former sec. of state.
Calvin Klein, b 11/19/1942 (Bronx, NY), fashion designer.
Philip H. Knight, b 2/24/1938 (Portland, OR), founder and chairman of the board of Nike.
Charles G. Koch, b 5/3/1940 (Wichita, KS), Koch Industries exec., philanthropist.
David H. Koch, b 11/1/1935 (Wichita, KS), Koch Industries exec., philanthropist.
Sarah Koenig, b 7/9/1969 (New York, NY), radio journalist.
Ted Koppel, b 2/8/1940 (Lancashire, Eng., UK), former TV journalist.
Michael Kors, b 8/9/1959 (Merrick, NY), fashion designer.
Larry Kramer, b 6/25/1935 (Bridgeport, CT), AIDS activist, writer.
Nicholas D. Kristof, b 4/27/1959 (Chicago, IL), columnist, author.
William Kristol, b 12/23/1952 (New York, NY), editor, columnist.
Steve Kroft, b 8/22/1945 (Kokomo, IN), TV journalist.
Paul Krugman, b 2/28/1953 (Albany, NY), economist, columnist.
Brian Lamb, b 10/9/1941 (Lafayette, IN), cable TV exec., journalist.
Wayne LaPierre Jr., b 11/8/1949 (Schenectady, NY), National Rifle Assn. exec. VP.
Matt Lauer, b 12/30/1957 (New York, NY), TV journalist.

Ralph Lauren, b 10/14/1939 (Bronx, NY), fashion designer.
Bernard F. Law, b 11/4/1931 (Torreon, Mexico), cardinal archbishop emeritus of Boston.
Patrick Leahy, b 3/31/1940 (Montpelier, VT), U.S. sen. (D, VT).
Norman Lear, b 7/27/1922 (New Haven, CT), TV producer, political activist.
Jim Lehrer, b 5/19/1934 (Wichita, KS), TV journalist, author.
Jacob Lew, b 8/29/1955 (New York, NY), sec. of treasury, former White House chief of staff.
Monica Lewinsky, b 7/23/1973 (San Francisco, CA), former White House intern.
Joseph Lieberman, b 2/24/1942 (Stamford, CT), former U.S. sen. (I, CT), 2000 vice-pres. nominee (D).
Rush Limbaugh, b 1/12/1951 (Cape Girardeau, MO), radio talk-show host.
Trent Lott, b 10/9/1941 (Grenada, MS), former U.S. sen. (R, MS) and majority leader.
Shannon Lucid, b 1/14/1943 (Shanghai, China), NASA scientist, astronaut.
Loretta Lynch, b 5/21/1959 (Greensboro, NC), U.S. atty. gen.
Rachel Maddow, b 4/1/1973 (Castro Valley, CA), TV/radio host, political commentator.
Bernie Madoff, b 4/29/1938 (Queens, NY), financier who swindled investors; sentenced to 150 years in prison.
Rob Manfred, b 9/28/1958 (Rome, NY), MLB commissioner.
Chelsea (fmr. Bradley) Manning, b 12/17/1987 (Crescent, OK), Army pvt. convicted on espionage charges for providing classified information to WikiLeaks.
Susana Martinez, b 7/14/1959 (El Paso, TX), NM gov. (R).
Mary Matalin, b 8/19/1953 (Chicago, IL), political commentator.
Chris Matthews, b 12/17/1945 (Philadelphia, PA), TV journalist.
Marissa Mayer, b 5/30/1975 (Wausau, WI), Yahoo! CEO.
John McCain, b 8/29/1936 (Panama Canal Zone), U.S. sen. (R, AZ), 2008 Republican pres. candidate.
Kevin McCarthy, b 1/26/1965 (Bakersfield, CA), U.S. rep. (R, CA), House majority leader.
Mitch McConnell, b 2/20/1942 (Tuscumbia, AL), U.S. sen. (R, KY) majority leader.
David McCullough, b 7/7/1933 (Pittsburgh, PA), historian, biographer.
Denis McDonough, b 12/2/1969 (Stillwater, MN), White House chief of staff.
Dr. Phil McGraw, b 9/1/1950 (Vinita, OK), talk-show host, motivational speaker, author.
John McLaughlin, b 3/29/1927 (Providence, RI), TV journalist.
Lorne Michaels, b 11/17/44 (Toronto, ON, Canada), creator and producer of *Saturday Night Live*.
Kate Michelman, b 8/4/1942 (NJ), abortion-rights activist.
Kate Millett, b 9/14/1934 (St. Paul, MN), author, feminist.
George Mitchell, b 8/20/1933, (Waterville, ME), former spec. envoy for Middle East peace, U.S. Sen. majority leader (D, ME), diplomat, Disney Co. chair.
Walter Mondale, b 1/5/1928 (Ceylon, MN), former vice pres., U.S. sen. (D, MN), 1984 pres. nominee.
Ernest Moniz, b 12/22/1944 (Fall River, MA), energy sec., nuclear physicist.
Michael Moore, b 4/23/1954 (Davison, MI), activist, documentary filmmaker, author.
Bill Moyers, b 6/5/1934 (Hugo, OK), TV journalist, author.
Robert S. Mueller III, b 8/7/1944 (New York, NY), former FBI director.
David Muir, b 11/8/1973 (Syracuse, NY), TV news anchor.
Rupert Murdoch, b 3/11/1931 (Melbourne, Vic., Austral.), media exec.
Vivek Murthy, b 7/10/1977 (Huddersfield, Eng., UK), U.S. surgeon gen.
Ralph Nader, b 2/27/1934 (Winsted, CT), consumer advocate, independent pres. cand. (1996, 2000, '04, '08).
Janet Napolitano, b 11/29/1957 (New York, NY), Univ. of Calif. pres.; former homeland security sec., AZ gov. (D).
Craig Newmark, b 12/6/1952 (Morristown, NJ), founder of Craigslist.com.
Peggy Noonan, b 9/7/1950 (Brooklyn, NY), columnist, speechwriter.
Oliver North, b 10/7/1943 (San Antonio, TX), talk-show host, former Natl. Sec. Council aide, figure in Iran-contra scandal.
Eleanor Holmes Norton, b 6/13/1937 (Washington, DC), U.S. House delegate for Washington, DC (D).
Barack Obama, b 8/4/1961 (Honolulu, HI), U.S. president, former U.S. sen. (D, IL).
Michelle Obama, b 1/17/1964 (Chicago, IL), first lady, lawyer.
Soledad O'Brien, b 9/19/1966 (Smithtown, NY), TV journalist.
Sandra Day O'Connor, b 3/26/1930 (El Paso, TX), former Supreme Court justice.
Keith Olbermann, b 1/27/1959 (New York, NY), political commentator, former ESPN/MSNBC host.
Todd Oldham, b 11/22/1961 (Corpus Christi, TX), fashion designer.
Martin O'Malley, b 1/18/63 (Bethesda, MD), former MD gov. (D); 2016 pres. contender.
Bill O'Reilly, b 9/10/1949 (New York, NY), TV commentator, host.
Joel Osteen, b 3/5/1963 (Houston, TX), televangelist, author.
Michael Ovitz, b 12/14/1946 (Encino, CA), entertainment exec.
Clarence Page, b 6/2/1947 (Dayton, OH), journalist, TV commentator.
Lawrence Page, b 3/26/1973 (East Lansing, MI), cofounder of Google.
Camille Paglia, b 4/2/1947 (Endicott, NY), scholar, author.
Sarah Palin, b 2/11/1964 (Sandpoint, ID), former AK gov. (R), 2008 vice-pres. nominee.
Leon E. Panetta, b 6/28/1938 (Monterey, CA), former sec. of defense, CIA director, White House chief of staff, U.S. rep. (D, CA).
Sean Parker, b 12/3/1979 (Herndon, VA), cofounder of Napster, Facebook.
George Pataki, b 6/24/1945 (Peekskill, NY), former NY gov. (R); 2016 pres. contender.
David Paterson, b 5/20/1954 (Brooklyn, NY), attorney, former NY gov. (D).
Rand Paul, b 1/7/1963 (Pittsburgh, PA), U.S. sen. (R, KY); 2016 pres. contender.
Ron Paul, b 8/20/1935 (Pittsburgh, PA), physician, former U.S. rep. (R, TX), pres. contender (2008, '12).
Jane Pauley, b 10/31/1950 (Indianapolis, IN), TV journalist.
Nancy Pelosi, b 3/26/1940 (Baltimore, MD), U.S. rep. (D, CA), House minority leader, former House speaker.
Ross Perot, b 6/27/1930 (Texarkana, TX), entrepreneur, independent and Reform pres. contender (1992, '96).
Rick Perry, b 3/4/1950 (Paint Creek, TX), TX gov. (R), pres. contender (2012, '16).
David Petraeus, b 11/7/1952 (Cornwall-on-Hudson, NY), former CIA director, U.S. Forces Afghanistan cmdr., CENTCOM cmdr.
Colin Powell, b 4/5/1937 (New York, NY), former sec. of state, natl. security adviser, Joint Chiefs of Staff chairman.
Samantha Power, b 9/21/1970 (Dublin, Ire.), U.S. ambassador to UN.
Reince Priebus, b 3/18/1972 (Kenosha, WI), Rep. Natl. Committee chair.
Dan Quayle, b 2/4/1947 (Indianapolis, IN), former U.S. vice pres., U.S. sen. (R, IN).
Anna Quindlen, b 7/8/1953 (Philadelphia, PA), author, columnist.
Martha Raddatz, b 1953 (Idaho Falls, ID), TV journalist.
Dan Rather, b 10/31/1931 (Wharton, TX), TV journalist, retired anchor.
Nancy Reagan, b 7/6/1921 (Flushing, Queens, NY), former first lady.
Sumner Redstone, b 5/27/1923 (Boston, MA), media executive.
Ralph Reed Jr., b 6/24/1961 (Portsmouth, VA), political adviser.
Robert B. Reich, b 6/24/1946 (Scranton, PA), economist, author, former labor sec.
Harry Reid, b 12/2/1939 (Searchlight, NV), U.S. Sen. minority leader (D, NV).
Janet Reno, b 7/21/1938 (Miami, FL), former U.S. attorney gen.
Condoleezza Rice, b 11/14/1954 (Birmingham, AL), former sec. of state, former natl. security adviser.
Susan Rice, b 11/17/1964 (Washington, DC), national security adviser, former U.S. ambassador to UN.
Frank Rich, b 6/2/1949 (Washington, DC), essayist, columnist.
Cecile Richards, b 1957 (Waco, TX), pres. of Planned Parenthood.
Bill Richardson, b 11/15/1947 (Pasadena, CA), former energy sec., UN rep., U.S. rep. (D, NM), NM gov. (D); 2008 pres. contender.
Tom Ridge, b 8/26/1945 (Munhall, PA), former homeland security sec., PA gov. (R).
Geraldo Rivera, b 7/4/1943 (New York, NY), TV journalist.
Cokie Roberts, b 12/27/1943 (New Orleans, LA), TV journalist.
John G. Roberts, b 1/27/1955 (Buffalo, NY), Supreme Court chief justice.
Robin Roberts, b 11/23/1960 (Tuskeegee, AL), *Good Morning America* co-host.
Pat Robertson, b 3/22/1930 (Lexington, VA), religious broadcasting exec., former pres. contender (R).
V. Gene Robinson, b 5/29/1947 (Lexington, KY), first openly gay Episcopal bishop (retired).
David Rockefeller, b 6/12/1915 (New York, NY), banker.
Al Roker, b 8/20/1954 (Queens, NY), TV weather person.
Mitt Romney, b 3/12/1947 (Detroit, MI), 2012 pres. nominee, former MA gov. (R).
Charlie Rose, b 1/5/1942 (Henderson, NC), TV journalist.
Karl Rove, b 12/25/1950 (Denver, CO), former adviser to Pres. G. W. Bush, political commentator.
Marco Rubio, b 5/28/1971 (Miami, FL), U.S. sen. (R, FL), 2016 pres. contender.
Donald Rumsfeld, b 7/9/1932 (Chicago, IL), former sec. of defense.
Edward Ruscha, b 12/16/1937 (Omaha, NE), artist.
Paul Ryan, b 1/29/1970 (Janesville, WI), 2012 vice-pres. nominee, U.S. rep. (R, WI).
Morley Safer, b 11/8/1931 (Toronto, ON, Can.), TV journalist.
Bernie Sanders, b 9/8/1941 (New York, NY), U.S. sen. (I, VT); 2016 Dem. pres. contender.
Rick Santorum, b 5/10/1958 (Winchester, VA), former U.S. sen. (R, PA); pres. contender (2012, '16).
Diane Sawyer, b 12/22/1945 (Glasgow, KY), TV journalist.
Antonin Scalia, b 3/11/1936 (Trenton, NJ), U.S. Supreme Court justice.
Stephen Scalise, b 10/6/1965 (New Orleans, LA), U.S. rep. (R, LA), House majority whip.
Bob Schieffer, b 2/25/1937 (Austin, TX), TV journalist.
Phyllis Schlafly, b 8/15/1924 (St. Louis, MO), political activist.
Caroline Kennedy Schlossberg, b 11/27/1957 (New York, NY), ambassador to Japan, author, daughter of Pres. Kennedy.
Eric Schmidt, b 4/27/1955 (Washington, DC), former Google CEO.
Charles Schumer, b 11/23/1950 (Brooklyn, NY), U.S. sen. (D, NY).
Arnold Schwarzenegger, b 7/30/1947 (Thal, Styria, Austria), actor, former CA gov. (R).
Willard Scott, b 3/7/1934 (Alexandria, VA), former TV weather person.
Kathleen Sebelius, b 5/15/1958 (Cincinnati, OH), former health and human services sec., KS gov. (D).

Richard Serra, b 11/2/1939 (San Francisco, CA), sculptor.
Al Sharpton, b 10/3/1954 (Brooklyn, NY), activist, civil rights leader, TV personality.
Will Shortz, b 8/26/1952 (Crawfordsville, IN), puzzle editor.
Maria Shriver, b 11/6/1955 (Chicago, IL), TV journalist, former CA first lady.
George P. Shultz, b 12/13/1920 (New York, NY), former sec. of state, other cabinet posts.
Michelangelo Signorile, b 12/19/1960 (Brooklyn, NY), journalist, author.
Adam Silver, b 4/25/1962 (Rye, NY), NBA commissioner.
Nate Silver, b 1/13/1978 (E. Lansing, MI), statistician.
Russell Simmons, b 10/4/1957 (Queens, NY), music producer.
O. J. Simpson, b 7/9/1947 (San Francisco, CA), former football star, murder defendant.
Harry Smith, b 8/21/1951 (Lansing, IL), TV journalist.
Liz Smith, b 2/2/1923 (Ft. Worth, TX), gossip columnist.
Edward Snowden, b 6/21/1983 (Elizabeth City, NC), computer specialist accused of leaking classified information about U.S. and UK govt. surveillance.
George Soros, b 8/12/1930 (Budapest, Hung.), financier, philanthropist.
Sonia Sotomayor, b 6/25/1954 (Bronx, NY), U.S. Supreme Court justice.
David H. Souter, b 9/17/1939 (Melrose, MA), former Supreme Court justice.
Kate Spade, b 1962 (Kansas City, MO), fashion designer.
Steven Spielberg, b 12/18/1946 (Cincinnati, OH), movie director, producer.
Eliot Spitzer, b 6/10/1959 (Bronx, NY), former NY gov. (D); resigned after involvement with prostitutes exposed.
Lesley Stahl, b 12/16/1941 (Swampscott, MA), TV journalist.
Shelby Steele, b 1/1/1946 (Chicago, IL), scholar, critic.
Ben Stein, b 11/25/1944 (Washington, DC), attorney, columnist, TV personality.
Gloria Steinem, b 3/25/1934 (Toledo, OH), author, feminist.
Frank Stella, b 5/12/1936 (Malden, MA), painter.
George Stephanopoulos, b 2/10/1961 (Fall River, MA), TV journalist, *Good Morning America* co-host; former pres. adviser.
Howard Stern, b 1/12/1954 (Roosevelt, NY), radio talk-show host.
John Paul Stevens, b 4/20/1920 (Chicago, IL), former Supreme Court justice.
Martha Stewart, b 8/3/1941 (Nutley, NJ), homemaking adviser, entrepreneur, TV personality.
Biz Stone, b 3/10/1974 (Boston, MA), cofounder of Twitter.
Chesley Sullenberger III, b 1/23/1951 (Denison, TX), pilot who safely landed a passenger jet in the Hudson River.
Andrew Sullivan, b 8/10/1963 (Eng., UK), political commentator and blogger.
Arthur Ochs Sulzberger Jr., b 9/22/1951 (Mt. Kisco, NY), newspaper publisher.
Lawrence H. Summers, b 11/30/1954 (New Haven, CT), economist; former Natl. Economic Council dir., Harvard Univ. pres., sec. of treasury.
George Tenet, b 1/5/1953 (Flushing, Queens, NY), former CIA director.
Clarence Thomas, b 6/23/1948 (Savannah, GA), U.S. Supreme Court justice.
Chuck Todd, b 4/8/1972 (Miami, FL), TV journalist, *Meet the Press* moderator.
Richard Trumka, b 7/24/1949 (Waynesburg, PA), pres. of AFL-CIO.
Donald Trump, b 6/14/1946 (Jamaica, Queens, NY), real estate exec., TV personality; 2016 pres. contender (R).
Ted Turner, b 11/19/1938 (Cincinnati, OH), TV exec., philanthropist.
Neil deGrasse Tyson, b 10/5/1958 (New York, NY), astrophysicist, director of NYC's Hayden Planetarium, author, TV host.
Urvashi Vaid, b 10/8/1958 (New Delhi, India), LGBT rights activist.
Gloria Vanderbilt, b 2/20/1924 (New York, NY), fashion designer, heiress.
Greta Van Susteren, b 6/11/1954 (Appleton, WI), attorney, TV journalist.
Jesse Ventura, b 7/15/1951 (Minneapolis, MN), former wrestler, MN gov. (I).
Meredith Vieira, b 12/30/1953 (Providence, RI), TV personality.
Paul Volcker, b 9/5/1927 (Cape May, NJ), economist, former Federal Reserve chairman.
Diane von Fürstenberg, b 12/31/1946 (Brussels, Belgium), fashion designer.
Jimmy Wales, b 8/8/1966 (Huntsville, AL), cofounder of Wikipedia.
Scott Walker, b 11/2/1967 (Colorado Springs, CO), WI gov. (R), 2016 pres. contender.
Barbara Walters, b 9/25/1929 (Boston, MA), TV journalist.
Vera Wang, b 6/27/1949 (New York, NY), fashion designer.
Elizabeth Warren, b 6/22/1949 (Oklahoma City, OK), U.S. sen. (D, MA).
Rick Warren, b 1/28/1954 (San Jose, CA), evangelical Christian pastor, founder of Saddleback Church, author.
Debbie Wasserman Schultz, b 9/27/1966 (Forest Hills, NY), U.S. rep. (D, FL), Dem. Natl. Committee chair.
James Watson, b 4/6/1928 (Chicago, IL), biochemist, DNA pioneer, co-winner of the 1962 Nobel Prize in Physiology/Medicine.
Jim Webb, b 2/9/1946 (St. Joseph, MO), U.S. sen. (D, VA); 2016 pres. contender.
Andrew Weil, b 6/8/1942 (Philadelphia, PA), health adviser.
Harvey Weinstein, b 3/19/1952 (Flushing, Queens, NY), movie exec.
Jack Welch, b 11/19/1935 (Peabody, MA), former General Electric CEO.
Jann Wenner, b 1/7/1946 (New York, NY), publisher, founder of *Rolling Stone*.
Cornel West, b 6/23/1953 (Tulsa, OK), African American scholar, critic.
Ruth Westheimer, b 6/4/1928 (Frankfurt am Main, Germany), human sexuality expert.
Mary Jo White, b 12/27/1947 (Kansas City, MO), Securities and Exchange Commission chair.
Meg Whitman, b 8/4/1956 (Cold Spring Harbor, NY), 2010 CA gubernatorial candidate (R), former eBay CEO; HP CEO.
Elie Wiesel, b 9/30/1928 (Sighet, Romania), scholar, author, 1986 Nobel Peace Prize winner.
George Will, b 5/4/1941 (Champaign, IL), journalist, author.
Brian Williams, b 5/5/1959 (Ridgewood, NJ), TV journalist.
Evan Williams, b 3/31/1972 (Clarks, NE), Twitter cofounder.
Jody Williams, b 10/9/1950 (Brattleboro, VT), peace activist, 1997 Nobel Peace Prize winner.
Edie (Edith) Windsor, b 6/20/1929 (Philadelphia, PA), LGBT activist.
Oprah Winfrey, b 1/29/1954 (Kosciusko, MS), TV and media personality, entrepreneur, actress.
Susan Wojcicki, b 7/5/1968 (CA), CEO of YouTube.
Bob Woodward, b 3/26/1943 (Geneva, IL), journalist; with Carl Bernstein cracked Watergate scandal.
Steve Wozniak, b 8/11/1950 (Sunnyvale, CA), inventor, cofounder of Apple.
Steve Wynn, b 1/27/1942 (New Haven, CT), casino developer.
Chuck Yeager, b 2/13/1923 (Myra, WV), test pilot, first to break sound barrier.
Janet Yellen, b 8/13/1946 (New York, NY), Federal Reserve chair.
Paula Zahn, b 2/24/1956 (Omaha, NE), TV journalist.
Mark Zuckerberg, b 5/14/1984 (Dobbs Ferry, NY), founder of Facebook.
Mortimer Zuckerman, b 6/4/1937 (Montréal, QC, Can.), publisher, columnist.

Widely Known World Personalities of the Present

Living non-Americans only. Generally excludes current heads of state or government (see Nations of the World) and excludes most others covered elsewhere, such as in Widely Known Americans, Writers, and Entertainment or Sports Personalities.

Mahmoud Abbas (Abu Mazen), b 3/26/1935 (Safed, Palestine [now Israel]), president of the Palestinian National Authority.
Gerry Adams, b 10/6/1948 (Belfast, N. Ireland, UK), Sinn Fein leader.
Mahmoud Ahmadinejad, b 10/28/1956 (Garmsar, Iran), former Iranian pres.
Albert II, b 6/6/1934 (Brussels, Belgium), former king (1993-2013).
Prince Andrew (Duke of York), b 2/19/1960 (London, Eng., UK), second son of Queen Elizabeth II.
Kofi Annan, b 4/8/1938 (Kumasi, Ghana), former UN sec.-gen.; 2001 Nobel laureate.
Princess Anne (Princess Royal), b 8/15/1950 (London, Eng., UK), daughter of Queen Elizabeth II.
Michael Arad, b 1969 (London, Eng., UK), designer of the Natl. 9/11 Memorial in NYC.
Oscar Arias Sánchez, b 9/13/1941 (Heredia, Costa Rica), former Costa Rican pres., peace negotiator, 1987 Nobel Peace Prize laureate.
Giorgio Armani, b 7/30/1934 (Piacenza, Italy), fashion designer.
Hanan Ashrawi, b 10/8/1946 (Nablus, Israel), Palestinian activist.
Julian Assange, b 7/3/1971 (Townsville, Qld., Austral.), founder of WikiLeaks media org.
Ban Ki-moon, b 6/13/1944 (Umsong, [now] South Korea), UN sec.-gen.
Ehud Barak, b 2/12/1942 (Mishmar Ha-Sharon Kibbutz, Israel), former Israeli min. of defense, prime min.
Beatrix, b 1/31/1938 (Baarn, Netherlands), former Dutch queen (1980-2013).
Benedict XVI (Joseph Ratzinger), b 4/16/1927 (Marktl am Inn, Germany), pope emeritus of Rom. Cath. Church, elected 2005, resigned 2013.
Boris Berezovsky, b 1/23/1946 (Moscow, USSR), businessman, politician.
Tim Berners-Lee, b 6/8/1955 (London, Eng., UK), World Wide Web inventor.
Tony Blair, b 5/6/1953 (Edinburgh, Scot., UK), former British prime min.
Hans Blix, b 6/28/1928 (Uppsala, Swed.), former UN weapons inspector.
Bono (Paul David Hewson), b 5/20/1960 (Glasnevin, Dublin, Ire.), musician, social activist, philanthropist.
Fernando Botero, b 4/19/1932 (Medellín, Colombia), artist.
Boutros Boutros-Ghali, b 11/14/1922 (Cairo, Egypt), former UN sec.-gen.
Richard Branson, b 7/18/1950 (S. London, Eng., UK), British Virgin Records and Airways founder.
Gordon Brown, b 2/20/1951 (Glasgow, Scot., UK), former British prime min.
Tina Brown, b 11/21/1953 (Maidenhead, Eng., UK), journalist, author.
Carla Bruni, b 12/23/1967 (Turin, Italy), former first lady of France; musician, actress, model.
Mark Burnett, b 7/17/1960 (Myland, Eng., UK), reality TV producer.
Rhonda Byrne, b 3/12/1951 (Australia), author, TV writer and producer.
Kim Campbell, b 3/10/1947 (Port Alberni, BC, Can.), former Canadian prime min.
Pierre Cardin, b 7/7/1922 (San Biaggio di Callalta, Italy), fashion designer.
Magnus Carlsen, b 11/30/1990 (Tonsberg, Norway), world chess champion.
Princess Caroline, b 1/23/1957 (Monte Carlo, Monaco), Monaco royal (eldest

daughter of Prince Rainier and Princess Grace).
Fidel Castro, b 8/13/1926 (Birán, Cuba), former prime min., pres. of Cuba.
Catherine (Kate) Middleton (Duchess of Cambridge), b 1/9/1982 (Reading, Eng., UK), wife of Prince William.
Prince Charles (of Wales), b 11/14/1948 (London, Eng., UK), eldest son of Queen Elizabeth II; heir to British throne.
Princess Charlotte Elizabeth Diana (of Cambridge), b 5/2/2015 (London, Eng., UK), daughter of Prince William and Catherine.
Chen Guangcheng, b 11/12/1971 (Dongshigu, China), civil rights activist.
Yao Chen, b 10/5/1979 (Nanping, Fujian, China), actress, microblogger.
Jacques Chirac, b 11/29/1932 (Paris, France), former French pres.
Deepak Chopra, b 1946 (New Delhi, India), writer, alternative medicine advocate.
Jean Chrétien, b 1/11/1934 (Shawinigan, QC, Can.), former Canadian prime min.
Christo (Javacheff), b 6/13/1935 (Gabrovo, Bulg.), artist.
Joe (Charles Joseph) Clark, b 6/5/1939 (High River, AB, Can.), former Canadian prime min.
King Constantine II, b 6/2/1940 (Psychiko, Greece), former king of Greece.
Simon Cowell, b 10/7/1959 (Brighton, East Sussex, Eng., UK), music exec., TV producer, former *American Idol* host.
Dalai Lama, 14th (Tenzin Gyatso), b 7/6/1935 (Taktser, Amdo, Tibet), Buddhist leader; 1989 Nobel Peace Prize laureate.
Richard Dawkins, b 3/26/1941 (Nairobi, Kenya), ethologist, evolutionary biologist, author.
F. W. (Frederik Willem) de Klerk, b 3/18/1936 (Johannesburg, S. Afr.), former S. African pres.; 1993 Nobel Peace Prize winner.
Mario Draghi, b 9/3/1947 (Rome, Italy), European Central Bank pres.
Shirin Ebadi, b 6/21/1947 (Hamadan, Iran), human rights activist, 2003 Nobel Peace Prize winner.
Prince Edward (Earl of Essex), b 3/10/1964 (London, Eng., UK), third son of Queen Elizabeth II.
Mohamed ElBaradei, b 6/17/1942 (Cairo, Egypt), former director general of the International Atomic Energy Agency (IAEA); 2005 Nobel Peace Prize winner.
Sarah Ferguson, b 10/15/1958 (London, Eng., UK), Duchess of York, ex-wife of Prince Andrew.
Francis (Jorge Mario Bergoglio), b 12/17/1936 (Buenos Aires, Argentina), pope of Rom. Cath. Church.
John Galliano, b 11/28/1960 (Gibraltar, UK), fashion designer.
Prince George Alexander Louis (of Cambridge), b 7/22/2013 (London, Eng., UK), son of Prince William and Catherine.
Wael Ghonim, b 12/23/1980 (Cairo, Egypt), computer engineer and Internet activist.
Valery Giscard d'Estaing, b 2/2/1926 (Koblenz, Ger.), former French pres.
Jane Goodall, b 4/3/1934 (London, Eng., UK), anthropologist, primatologist.
Mikhail Gorbachev, b 3/2/1931 (Privolnoye, USSR), former Soviet pres.; 1990 Nobel Peace Prize winner.
Jürgen Habermas, b 6/18/1929 (Dusseldorf, Ger.), philosopher.
Stephen Hawking, b 1/8/1942 (Oxford, Eng., UK), physicist, author.
Prince Henry (Harry) (of Wales), b 9/15/1984 (London, Eng., UK), son of Prince Charles and Diana.
Damien Hirst, b 6/7/1965 (Bristol, Eng., UK), artist.
David Hockney, b 7/9/1937 (Bradford, Eng., UK), artist.
Hu Jintao, b 12/21/1942 (Shanghai, China), former pres. of China.
Jiang Zemin, b 8/17/1926 (Yangzhou, Jiangsu Prov., China), former pres. of China.
Juan Carlos I, b 1/5/1938 (Rome, Italy), former king of Spain (1975-2014).
Hamid Karzai, b 12/24/1957 (Kandahar, Afghanistan), former pres. of Afghanistan.
Garry Kasparov, b 4/13/1963 (Baku Azerbaijan, USSR), former world chess champion; Russian pro-democracy leader.
Ayatollah Ali Khamenei, b 7/17/1939 (Mashhad, Iran), Supreme Leader, cleric; former president of Iran.
Helmut Kohl, b 4/3/1930 (Ludwigshafen, Ger.), former German chancellor.
Hans Küng, b 3/19/1928 (Sursee, Switz.), Rom. Cath. theologian.
Christine Lagarde, b 1/1/1956 (Paris, Fr.), Intl. Monetary Fund managing dir.
Karl Lagerfeld, b 9/10/1938 (Hamburg, Ger.), fashion designer.
Richard Leakey, b 12/19/1944 (Nairobi, Kenya), anthropologist, paleontologist, conservationist.
Jean-Marie Le Pen, b 6/20/1928 (La Trinité-sur-Mer, Fr.), French right-wing politician.
Marine Le Pen, b 8/5/1968 (Neuilly-sur-Seine, Fr.), head of France's Nationa Front.
Tzipi Livni, b 7/5/1958 (Tel Aviv, Isr.), attorney, Israeli justice minister.
John Major, b 3/29/1943 (Wimbledon, Eng., UK), former British prime min.
Nouri al-Malaki, b 7/1/1950 (Iraq), former prime min. of Iraq.
Imelda Marcos, b 7/2/1929 (Manila, Philip.), former first lady of the Philippines.
Paul Martin, b 8/28/1938 (Windsor, ON, Can.), former prime min. of Canada.
Peter Max, b 10/19/1937 (Berlin, Ger.), artist, designer.
Stella McCartney, b 9/13/1971 (London, Eng., UK), fashion designer.
Angela Merkel, b 7/17/1954 (Hamburg, Ger.), first woman chancellor of Germany.
Jean-Marie Messier, b 12/13/1956 (Grenoble, Fr.), former CEO of Vivendi Universal.
Empress Michiko, b 10/20/1934 (Tokyo, Japan), empress of Japan.
Maryam Mirzakhani, b 5/1977 (Tehran, Iran), mathematician.
Mohammed Morsi, b 8/8/1951 (Edwa, Egypt), first democratically elected pres. of Egypt; deposed July 2013.
Kate Moss, b 1/16/1974 (Addiscombe, Surrey, Eng., UK), model.
Hosni Mubarak, b 5/4/1928 (Kafre al-Musailha, Egypt), deposed Egyptian president.
Brian Mulroney, b 3/20/1939 (Baie-Corneau, QC, Can.), former Canadian prime min.
Prince Naruhito, b 2/23/1960 (Tokyo, Japan), crown prince of Japan.
Hassan Nasrallah, b 8/31/1960 (Qarantina, Lebanon), sec.-gen. of Hezbollah.
Queen Noor (Lisa Halaby), b 8/23/1951 (Washington, DC), American-born widow of Jordan's King Hussein.
Ehud Olmert, b 9/30/1945 (Binyamina, Palestine), former prime min. of Israel.
Daniel Ortega Saavedra, b 11/11/1945 (La Libertad, Nicar.), Nicaraguan pres., Sandinista leader.
Camilla Parker-Bowles (Duchess of Cornwall), b 7/17/1947 (London, Eng., UK), wife of Prince Charles.
Javier Perez de Cuellar, b 1/19/1920 (Lima, Peru), former UN sec.-gen.
Prince Philip (Duke of Edinburgh), b 6/10/1921 (Corfu, Greece), husband of Queen Elizabeth II.
Gerhard Richter, b 2/9/1932 (Dresden, Ger.), artist.
Mary Robinson, b 5/21/1944 (Ballina, Co. Mayo, Ire.), former Irish pres., former UN High Commissioner for Human Rights.
Arundhati Roy, b 11/24/1961 (Shillong, Meghalaya, India), author, political activist.
Ségolène Royal, b 9/22/1953 (Dakar, Senegal), French socialist politician.
Muqtada al-Sadr, b 8/12/1973? (Najaf, Iraq), extremist Shiite cleric.
Nicolas Sarkozy, b 1/28/1955 (Paris, France), former French pres.
Helmut Schmidt, b 12/23/1918 (Hamburg, Ger.), former German chancellor.
Gerhard Schröder, b 4/7/1944 (Mossenburg, Ger.), former German chancellor.
Ayatollah Ali al-Sistani, b 8/4/1930 (Mashhad, Iran), major Iraqi Shiite religious leader.
Carlos Slim Helú, b 1/28/1940 (Mexico City, Mex.), founder Grupo Carso; former chairman of Telmex, América Móvil.
Princess Stephanie, b 2/1/1965 (Monte Carlo, Monaco), youngest child of Prince Rainier and Princess Grace.
Dominique Strauss-Kahn, b 4/25/1949 (Neuilly-sur-Seine, France), former Intl. Monetary Fund managing dir.
Aung San Suu Kyi, b 6/19/1945 (Rangoon, Myanmar), member of parliament, pro-democracy political activist, 1991 Nobel Peace Prize winner.
Valentina Tereshkova, b 3/6/1937 (Maslennikovo, Russia, USSR), first woman in space.
John Napier Turner, b 6/7/1929 (Richmond, Surrey, Eng., UK), former Canadian prime min.
Desmond Tutu, b 10/7/1931 (Klerksdorp, Transvaal, S. Afr.), former S. African archbishop; 1984 Nobel Peace Prize winner.
Lech Walesa, b 9/29/1943 (Popowo, Pol.), Solidarity leader, former pres. of Poland; 1983 Nobel Peace Prize winner.
Justin Welby, b 1/6/1956 (London, Eng., UK), archbishop of Canterbury.
Prince William (Duke of Cambridge), b 6/21/1982 (London, Eng., UK), eldest son of Prince Charles and Diana; 2nd in line to British throne.
Rowan Williams, b 6/14/1950 (Ystradgynlais, Wales, UK), former archbishop of Canterbury.
Malala Yousafzai, b 7/12/1997 (Mingora, Pakistan), education activist, 2014 Nobel Peace Prize winner.
Muhammad Yunus, b 6/28/1940 (Chittagong, Bangladesh), economist, 2006 Nobel Peace Prize winner.
Mohammad Javad Zarif, b 1/8/1960 (Tehran, Iran), Irani minister of foreign affairs.
Ayman al-Zawahiri, b 6/19/1951 (Cairo, Egypt), reputed high-ranking al-Qaeda leader.

Architects

Alvar Aalto, 1898-1976, Säynätsalo, Jyväskylä, Finland; Vuoksenniska Church, Vuoksenniska, Finland.
Max Abramovitz, 1908-2004, Avery Fisher Hall, New York, NY; U.S. Steel Bldg., Pittsburgh, PA.
Tadao Ando, b 1941, Modern Art Museum, Ft. Worth, TX; Stone Hill Center, MA.
Michael Arad, b 1969, World Trade Center Memorial, New York, NY.
Henry Bacon, 1866-1924, Lincoln Memorial, Washington, DC.
Benjamin Banneker, 1731-1806, African American inventor, astronomer, mathematician; helped design and lay out Washington, DC.
Pietro Belluschi, 1899-1994, Juilliard School, Lincoln Center, Pan Am Bldg. (now MetLife Bldg.) with Walter Gropius, New York, NY.
Marcel Breuer, 1902-81, Whitney Museum of American Art (with Hamilton Smith), New York, NY.
Charles Bulfinch, 1763-1844, State House, Boston, MA; Capitol (part), Wash., DC.
Gordon Bunshaft, 1909-90, Lever House, New York, NY; Hirshhorn Museum, Washington, DC.
Daniel H. Burnham, 1846-1912, Union Station, Washington, DC; Flatiron Bldg., New York, NY.
Irwin Chanin, 1892-1988, theaters, skyscrapers, New York, NY.
David Childs, b 1941, Washington Mall Master Plan/Constitution Gardens, Washington, DC; One World Trade Center, New York, NY.
Lucio Costa, 1902-98, master plan for city of Brasilia, Brazil (with Oscar Niemeyer).
Ralph Adams Cram, 1863-1942, Cath. of St. John the Divine, New York, NY; U.S. Military Acad. (part), West Point, NY.

Norman Foster, b 1935, Commerzbank Headquarters, Frankfurt-am-Main, Ger.; London Millennium Bridge, 30 St. Mary Axe ("The Gherkin"), London, Eng., UK.
James Ingo Freed, 1930-2005, Holocaust Memorial Museum, Washington, DC; Jacob K. Javits Center, New York, NY.
R. Buckminster Fuller, 1895-1983, U.S. Pavilion (geodesic domes), Expo 67, Montreal, QC, Can.
Frank O. Gehry, b 1929, Guggenheim Museum, Bilbao, Spain; Experience Music Project, Seattle, WA; Walt Disney Concert Hall, Los Angeles, CA.
Cass Gilbert, 1859-1934, Custom House, Woolworth Bldg., New York, NY; Supreme Court Bldg., Washington, DC.
Bertram G. Goodhue, 1869-1924, Capitol, Lincoln, NE; St. Thomas's Church, St. Bartholomew's Church, New York, NY.
Michael Graves, 1934-2015, Portland Bldg., Portland, OR; Humana Bldg., Louisville, KY.
Walter Gropius, 1883-1969, Pan Am Bldg. (now MetLife Bldg.) (with Pietro Belluschi), New York, NY.
Zaha Hadid, b 1950, Rosenthal Center for Contemporary Art, Cincinnati, OH; London Aquatics Centre, Eng., UK.
Lawrence Halprin, 1916-2009, Ghirardelli Sq., San Francisco, CA; Nicollet Mall, Minneapolis, MN; FDR Memorial, Wash., DC.
Peter Harrison, 1716-75, Touro Synagogue, Redwood Library, Newport, RI.
Wallace K. Harrison, 1895-1981, Metropolitan Opera House, Lincoln Center, New York, NY.
Thomas Hastings, 1860-1929, NY Public Library (with John Carrère), Frick Mansion, New York, NY.
James Hoban, 1762-1831, White House, Washington, DC.
Raymond Hood, 1881-1934, Rockefeller Center (part), Daily News Bldg., New York, NY; Tribune Tower, Chicago, IL.
Richard M. Hunt, 1827-95, Metropolitan Museum (part), New York, NY; Biltmore Estate, Asheville, NC.
Helmut Jahn, b 1940, United Airlines Terminal, O'Hare Airport, Chicago, IL.
William Le Baron Jenney, 1832-1907, Home Insurance Bldg. (demolished 1931), Chicago, IL.
Philip C. Johnson, 1906-2005, AT&T Bldg. (now 550 Madison Ave.), New York, NY; Transco (now Williams) Tower, Houston, TX.
Albert Kahn, 1869-1942, General Motors Bldg., Detroit, MI.
Louis Kahn, 1901-74, Salk Laboratory, La Jolla, CA; Yale Art Gallery, New Haven, CT.
Rem Koolhaus, b 1944, Seattle Central Library, Seattle, WA.
Christopher Grant LaFarge, 1862-1938, Roman Catholic Chapel, West Point, NY.
Benjamin H. Latrobe, 1764-1820, Capitol (part), Washington, DC; State Capitol Bldg., Richmond, VA.
Le Corbusier (Charles-Edouard Jeanneret), 1887-1965, Salvation Army Hostel, Swiss Dormitory, Paris, France; master plan for cities of Algiers and Buenos Aires.
William Lescaze, 1896-1969, Philadelphia Savings Fund Society, PA; Borg-Warner Bldg., Chicago, IL.
Daniel Libeskind, b 1946, primary architect for the rebuilding of World Trade Center site, New York, NY.
Maya Lin, b 1959, Vietnam Veterans Mem., Washington, DC.
Charles Rennie Mackintosh, 1868-1928, Glasgow School of Art; Hill House, Helensburgh, Scot., UK.
Bernard R. Maybeck, 1862-1957, Hearst Hall, Univ. of CA, Berkeley; First Church of Christ Scientist, Berkeley, CA.
Charles F. McKim, 1847-1909, Boston Public Library; Columbia Univ. (part), New York, NY.
Charles M. McKim, b 1920, KUHT-TV Transmitter Bldg., Lutheran Church of the Redeemer, Houston, TX.
Richard Meier, b 1934, Getty Center Museum, Los Angeles, CA; High Museum of Art, Atlanta, GA.
Ludwig Mies van der Rohe, 1886-1969, Seagram Bldg. (with Philip C. Johnson), New York, NY; National Gallery, Berlin, Ger.
Robert Mills, 1781-1855, Washington Monument, Washington, DC.
Charles Moore, 1925-93, Sea Ranch, nr. San Francisco, CA; Piazza d'Italia, New Orleans, LA.
Julia Morgan, 1872-1957, San Simeon, CA.
John Nash, 1752-1835, Buckingham Palace, London, Eng., UK.
Richard J. Neutra, 1892-1970, Mathematics Park, Princeton, NJ; Orange Co. Courthouse, Santa Ana, CA.
Oscar Niemeyer, 1907-2012, government buildings, Brasilia Palace Hotel, Brasilia, Braz.
Gyo Obata, b 1923, Natl. Air and Space Museum, Smithsonian Inst., Washington, DC; Dallas-Ft. Worth Airport, TX.
Frederick L. Olmsted, 1822-1903, Central Park, New York, NY; Fairmount Park, Philadelphia, PA.
I(eoh) M(ing) Pei, b 1917, East Wing, Natl. Gallery of Art, Washington, DC; Pyramid, The Louvre, Paris, Fr.; Rock & Roll Hall of Fame and Museum, Cleveland, OH.
Cesar Pelli, b 1926, World Financial Center, Carnegie Hall Tower, New York, NY; Petronas Twin Towers, Malaysia.
William Pereira, 1909-85, Cape Canaveral, FL; Transamerica Pyramid, San Francisco, CA.
Renzo Piano, b 1937, Pompidou Centre, Paris, Fr.; New York Times Bldg., New York, NY; The Shard, London.
John Russell Pope, 1874-1937, National Gallery, Jefferson Memorial, Wash., DC.
John Portman, b 1924, Peachtree Center, Atlanta, GA.
George Browne Post, 1837-1913, NY Stock Exchange, New York, NY; Capitol, Madison, WI.
James Renwick Jr., 1818-95, Grace Church, St. Patrick's Cathedral, New York, NY; Smithsonian Institution (Castle), Washington, DC.
Henry H. Richardson, 1838-86, Trinity Church, Boston, MA.
Kevin Roche, b 1922, Oakland Museum, Oakland, CA; Fine Arts Center, Univ. of Massachusetts, Amherst, MA.
James Gamble Rogers, 1867-1947, Columbia-Presbyterian Medical Ctr., New York, NY; Northwestern Univ., Evanston, IL.
John Wellborn Root, 1887-1963, Palmolive Bldg., Chicago, IL; Hotel Statler, Wash., DC.
Paul Rudolph, 1918-97, Jewitt Art Center, Wellesley College, MA; Art & Architecture Bldg., Yale Univ., New Haven, CT.
Eero Saarinen, 1910-61, Gateway to the West Arch, St. Louis, MO; TWA Flight Center, JFK Airport, New York, NY.
Kazuyo Sejima, b 1956, 21st Century Museum of Contemporary Art (with Ryue Nishizawa), Kanazawa, Japan.
Louis Skidmore, 1897-1962, Atomic Energy Commission town site, Oak Ridge, TN; Terrace Plaza Hotel, Cincinnati, OH.
Norma Merrick Sklarek, 1928-2012, Terminal One, Los Angeles International Airport, CA.
Clarence S. Stein, 1882-1975, Temple Emanu-El, New York, NY.
Edward Durell Stone, 1902-78, interior of Radio City Music Hall, Museum of Modern Art, New York, NY.
Louis H. Sullivan, 1856-1924, Auditorium Bldg., Chicago, IL.
Kenzo Tange, 1913-2005, Hiroshima Peace Park, 1964 Tokyo Olympic stadiums, Japan.
Richard Upjohn, 1802-78, Trinity Church, New York, NY.
Max O. Urbahn, 1912-95, Vehicle Assembly Bldg., Cape Canaveral, FL.
Joern Utzon, 1918-2008, Sydney Opera House, NSW, Australia.
William Van Alen, 1883-1954, Chrysler Building, New York, NY.
Robert Venturi, b 1925, Gordon Wu Hall, Princeton, NJ; Mielparque Nikko Kirifuri Resort, Japan.
Ralph T. Walker, 1889-1973, NY Telephone Bldg. (now Verizon Bldg.), New York, NY; IBM Research Lab, Poughkeepsie, NY.
Wang Shu, 1963, Ningbo Museum, China.
Roland A. Wank, 1898-1970, Cincinnati Union Terminal, OH; head architect, 1933-44, Tennessee Valley Authority.
Stanford White, 1853-1906, Washington Arch in Washington Square Park, first Madison Square Garden, New York, NY.
Christopher Wren, 1632-1723, St. Paul's Cathedral, London, Eng., UK.
Frank Lloyd Wright, 1867-1959, Imperial Hotel, Tokyo, Jpn.; Guggenheim Museum, New York, NY; Kaufmann "Fallingwater" house, Mill Run, PA; Taliesin West, Scottsdale, AZ.
Thomas Wright, b 1957, Burj Al Arab hotel, Dubai, UAE.
William Wurster, 1895-1973, Ghirardelli Sq., San Francisco, CA.
Minoru Yamasaki, 1912-86, World Trade Center (destroyed 2001), New York, NY.

Artists, Photographers, and Sculptors of the Past

Artists are painters unless otherwise indicated.

Berenice Abbott, 1898-1991, (U.S.) photographer. Documentary of New York City, *Changing New York* (1939).
Ansel Easton Adams, 1902-84, (U.S.) photographer. Landscapes of the American Southwest.
Washington Allston, 1779-1843, (U.S.) landscapist. *Belshazzar's Feast*.
Albrecht Altdorfer, 1480-1538, (Ger.) landscapist.
Fra Angelico, c. 1400-55, (It.) Renaissance muralist. *Madonna of the Linen Drapers' Guild*.
Diane Arbus, 1923-71, (U.S.) photographer. Disturbing images.
Alexsandr Archipenko, 1887-1964, (U.S.) sculptor. *Boxing Match*, *Medranos*.
Jean Arp, 1887-1966, (Fr.) sculptor and painter. Founder of Dada movement.
Richard Artschwager, 1923-2013, (U.S.) painter and sculptor. *Table With Pink Tablecloth*.
Eugène Atget, 1856-1927, (Fr.) photographer. Paris life.
John James Audubon, 1785-1851, (U.S.) *Birds of America*.
Richard Avedon, 1923-2004, (U.S.) fashion and celebrity photographer.
Hans Baldung-Grien, 1484-1545, (Ger.) *Todentanz*.
Ernst Barlach, 1870-1938, (Ger.) Expressionist sculptor. *Man Drawing a Sword*.
Frédéric-Auguste Bartholdi, 1834-1904, (Fr.) sculptor. *Liberty Enlightening the World* (Statue of Liberty).
Fra Bartolommeo, 1472-1517, (It.) *Vision of St. Bernard*.
Romare Bearden, 1911-88, (U.S.) collage and other media. *The Visitation*.
Aubrey Beardsley, 1872-98, (Br.) illustrator. *Salome*, *Lysistrata*, *Morte d'Arthur*, *Volpone*.
Cecil Beaton, 1904-80, (Br.) fashion and celebrity photographer.
Max Beckmann, 1884-1950, (Ger.) Expressionist. *The Descent From the Cross*.
Gentile Bellini, 1426-1507, (It.) Renaissance. *Procession in St. Mark's Square*.
Giovanni Bellini, 1428-1516, (It.) Renaissance. *St. Francis in Ecstasy*.
Jacopo Bellini, 1400-70, (It.) Renaissance. *Crucifixion*.

George Wesley Bellows, 1882-1925, (U.S.) sports artist, portraitist, landscapist. *Stag at Sharkey's*, *Edith Clavell*.
Thomas Hart Benton, 1889-1975, (U.S.) American regionalist. *Threshing Wheat*, *Arts of the West*.
Ruth Bernhard, 1905-2006, (Ger.-U.S.) photographer. Black-and-white studies of female nudes.
Gianlorenzo Bernini, 1598-1680, (It.) Baroque sculptor. *The Assumption*.
Albert Bierstadt, 1830-1902, (U.S.) landscapist. *The Rocky Mountains*, *Mount Corcoran*.
George Caleb Bingham, 1811-79, (U.S.) American frontier. *Fur Traders Descending the Missouri*.
William Blake, 1757-1827, (Br.) engraver. *Book of Job*, *Songs of Innocence*, *Songs of Experience*.
Rosa Bonheur, 1822-99, (Fr.) Realist. *The Horse Fair*.
Pierre Bonnard, 1867-1947, (Fr.) Intimist. *The Breakfast Room*, *Girl in a Straw Hat*.
Gutzon Borglum, 1867-1941, (U.S.) sculptor. Mt. Rushmore Memorial.
Hieronymus Bosch, 1450-1516, (Flem.) religious allegories. *The Crowning With Thorns*.
Sandro Botticelli, 1444-1510, (It.) Renaissance. *Birth of Venus*, *Adoration of the Magi*, *Guiliano de'Medici*.
Louise Bourgeois, 1911-2010, (Fr.) sculptor. *Maman*.
Margaret Bourke-White, 1904-71, (U.S.) photographer, photojournalist. WWII, USSR, rural South during the Depression.
Mathew Brady, c. 1823-96, (U.S.) photographer. Civil War.
Constantin Brancusi, 1876-1957, (Romania-Fr.) Nonobjective sculptor. *Flying Turtle*, *The Kiss*.
Georges Braque, 1882-1963, (Fr.) Cubist. *Violin and Palette*.
Pieter Bruegel the Elder, c. 1525-69, (Flem.) Renaissance. *The Peasant Dance*, *Hunters in the Snow*, *Magpie on the Gallows*.
Pieter Bruegel the Younger, 1564-1638, (Flem.) Baroque. *Village Fair*, *The Crucifixion*.
Edward Burne-Jones, 1833-98, (Br.) Pre-Raphaelite artist-craftsman. *The Mirror of Venus*.
Alexander Calder, 1898-1976, (U.S.) sculptor. *Lobster Trap and Fish Tail*.
Julia Margaret Cameron, 1815-79, (Br.) photographer, prominent portraitist.
Robert Capa (Endre Friedmann), 1913-54, (Hung.-U.S.) photographer, war photojournalist. Invasion of Normandy.
Michelangelo Merisi da Caravaggio, 1573-1610, (It.) Baroque. *The Supper at Emmaus*.
Emily Carr, 1871-1945, (Can.) landscapist. *Blunden Harbour*, *Big Raven*, *Rushing Sea of Undergrowth*.
Carlo Carrà, 1881-1966, (It.) Metaphysical school. *Lot's Daughters*, *The Enchanted Room*.
Leonora Carrington, 1917-2011, (Br.) Surrealist. *The Inn of the Dawn Horse (Self-Portrait)*.
Henri Cartier-Bresson, 1908-2004, (Fr.) photographer. *Imagenes à la sauvette*.
Mary Cassatt, 1844-1926, (U.S.) Impressionist. *The Cup of Tea*, *Woman Bathing*, *The Boating Party*.
George Catlin, 1796-1872, (U.S.) American Indian life. *Gallery of Indians*, *Buffalo Dance*.
Benvenuto Cellini, 1500-71, (It.) Mannerist sculptor, goldsmith. *Perseus and Medusa*.
Paul Cézanne, 1839-1906, (Fr.) Post-Impressionist. *Card Players*, *Mont-Sainte-Victoire With Large Pine Trees*.
Marc Chagall, 1887-1985, (Russ.) Jewish life and folklore. *I and the Village*, *The Praying Jew*.
John Chamberlain, 1927-2011, (U.S.) sculptor of automobile metal.
Jean Simeon Chardin, 1699-1779, (Fr.) still lifes. *The Kiss*, *The Grace*.
Giorgio de Chirico, 1888-1978, (It.) founded the Metaphysical school. *Enigma of an Autumn Night*.
Frederick Church, 1826-1900, (U.S.) Hudson River school. *Niagara*, *Andes of Ecuador*.
Giovanni Cimabue, 1240-1302, (It.) Byzantine mosaicist. *Madonna Enthroned With St. Francis*.
Claude (Lorrain) (Claude Gellée), 1600-82, (Fr.) Ideal-landscapist. *The Enchanted Castle*.
Thomas Cole, 1801-48, (U.S.) Hudson River school. *The Ox-Bow*, *In the Catskills*.
John Constable, 1776-1837, (Br.) landscapist. *Salisbury Cathedral From the Bishop's Grounds*.
John Singleton Copley, 1738-1815, (U.S.) portraitist. *Samuel Adams*, *Watson and the Shark*.
Lovis Corinth, 1858-1925, (Ger.) Expressionist. *Apocalypse*.
Jean-Baptiste-Camille Corot, 1796-1875, (Fr.) landscapist. *Souvenir de Mortefontaine*, *Pastorale*.
Correggio, 1494-1534, (It.) Renaissance muralist. *Mystic Marriages of St. Catherine*.
Gustave Courbet, 1819-77, (Fr.) Realist. *The Artist's Studio*.
Lucas Cranach the Elder, 1472-1553, (Ger.) Protestant Reformation portraitist. *Luther*.
Imogen Cunningham, 1883-1976, (U.S.) photographer, portraitist. Plants.
Nathaniel Currier, 1813-88, and **James M. Ives**, 1824-95, (both U.S.) lithographers. *A Midnight Race on the Mississippi*, *American Forest Scene—Maple Sugaring*.
John Steuart Curry, 1897-1946, (U.S.) Americana, murals. *Baptism in Kansas*.
Edward S. Curtis, 1868-1952, (U.S.) photographer. *The North American Indian*.
Salvador Dalí, 1904-89, (Sp.) Surrealist. *Persistence of Memory*, *The Crucifixion*.
Honoré Daumier, 1808-79, (Fr.) caricaturist. *The Third-Class Carriage*.
Jacques-Louis David, 1748-1825, (Fr.) Neoclassicist. *The Oath of the Horatii*.
Arthur Davies, 1862-1928, (U.S.) Romantic landscapist. *Unicorns*, *Leda and the Dioscuri*.
Edgar Degas, 1834-1917, (Fr.) Realist/Impressionist. *The Ballet Class*.
Willem de Kooning, 1904-97, (Neth.-U.S.) Abstract Expressionist. *Excavation*, *Woman I*, *Door to the River*.
Eugène Delacroix, 1798-1863, (Fr.) Romantic. *Massacre at Chios*, *Liberty Leading the People*.
Paul Delaroche, 1797-1856, (Fr.) historical themes. *Children of Edward IV*.
Luca Della Robbia, 1400-82, (It.) Renaissance terra-cotta. *Cantoria* (singing gallery), Florence cathedral.
Donatello, 1386-1466, (It.) Renaissance sculptor. *David*, *Gattamelata*.
Aaron Douglas, 1899-79, (U.S.) Harlem Renaissance illustrator and muralist.
Jean Dubuffet, 1902-85, (Fr.) painter, sculptor, printmaker. *Group of Four Trees*.
Marcel Duchamp, 1887-1968, (Fr.) Dadaist. *Nude Descending a Staircase, No. 2*.
Raoul Dufy, 1877-1953, (Fr.) Fauvist. *Chateau and Horses*.
Asher Brown Durand, 1796-1886, (U.S.) Hudson River school. *Kindred Spirits*.
Albrecht Dürer, 1471-1528, (Ger.) Renaissance painter, engraver, woodcuts. *St. Jerome in His Study*, *Melencolia I*.
Anthony van Dyck, 1599-1641, (Flem.) Baroque portraitist. *Portrait of Charles I Hunting*.
Thomas Eakins, 1844-1916, (U.S.) Realist. *The Gross Clinic*.
Alfred Eisenstaedt, 1898-1995, (Ger.-U.S.) photographer, photojournalist. Famous photo, V-J Day, Aug. 14, 1945.
Peter Henry Emerson, 1856-1936, (Br.) photographer. Promoted photography as an independent art form.
Jacob Epstein, 1880-1959, (Br.) religious and allegorical sculptor. *Genesis*, *Ecce Homo*.
Erté (Romain de Tiertoff), 1892-1990, (Fr.) painter, fashion and stage designer.
Walker Evans, 1903-75, (U.S.) photographer. Documented Great Depression.
Jan van Eyck, c. 1390-1441, (Flem.) naturalistic panels. *Adoration of the Lamb*.
Horst Faas, 1933-2012, (Ger.) Vietnam War photographer.
Roger Fenton, 1819-69, (Br.) photographer. Crimean War.
Anselm Feuerbach, 1829-80, (Ger.) Romantic Classicist. *Judgment of Paris*, *Iphigenia*.
John Bernard Flannagan, 1895-1942, (U.S.) animal sculptor. *Triumph of the Egg*.
Jean-Honoré Fragonard, 1732-1806, (Fr.) Rococo. *The Swing*.
Helen Frankenthaler, 1928-2011, (U.S.) Abstract Expressionist. *Mountains and Sea*.
Daniel Chester French, 1850-1931, (U.S.) sculptor. *The Minute Man of Concord*; seated *Lincoln*, Lincoln Memorial, Washington, DC.
Lucian Freud, 1922-2011, (Ger.-Br.) portraitist. *Girl With Roses*.
Caspar David Friedrich, 1774-1840, (Ger.) Romantic landscapist. *Man and Woman Gazing at the Moon*.
Thomas Gainsborough, 1727-88, (Br.) portraitist. *The Blue Boy*, *The Watering Place*, *The Parish Clerk*.
Alexander Gardner, 1821-82, (U.S.) photographer. Civil War, railroad construction, Great Plains Indians.
Paul Gauguin, 1848-1903, (Fr.) Post-Impressionist. *The Tahitians*, *Spirit of the Dead Watching*.
Lorenzo Ghiberti, 1378-1455, (It.) Renaissance sculptor. "Gates of Paradise" baptistery doors, Florence, It.
Alberto Giacometti, 1901-66, (Switz.) attenuated sculptures of solitary figures. *Man Pointing*.
Giorgione, c. 1477-1510, (It.) Renaissance. *The Tempest*.
Giotto di Bondone, 1267-1337, (It.) Renaissance. *Presentation of Christ in the Temple*.
François Girardon, 1628-1715, (Fr.) Baroque sculptor of classical themes. *Apollo Tended by the Nymphs*.
Edward Gorey, 1925-2000, (U.S.) illustrator. *The Doubtful Guest*.
Arshile Gorky, 1905-48, (U.S.) Surrealist. *The Liver Is the Cock's Comb*.
Francisco de Goya y Lucientes, 1746-1828, (Sp.) painter, printmaker. *The Naked Maja*, *The Disasters of War* (etchings).
El Greco (Domenikos Theotokopoulos), 1541-1614, (Gr.-Sp.) painter, sculptor. *View of Toledo*, *Assumption of the Virgin*.
Horatio Greenough, 1805-52, (U.S.) Neoclassical sculptor.
Matthias Grünewald, 1480-1528, (Ger.) mystical religious themes. *The Resurrection*.
Frans Hals, c. 1580-1666, (Neth.) portraitist. *Laughing Cavalier*, *Gypsy Girl*.
Richard Hamilton, 1922-2011, (Br.) Pop Art. *Just What Is It That Makes Today's Homes So Different, So Appealing?*
Austin Hansen, 1910-96, (U.S.) photographer. Harlem, NY, life.
Childe Hassam, 1859-1935, (U.S.) Impressionist. *Southwest Wind*, *July 14 Rue Daunon*.
Edward Hicks, 1780-1849, (U.S.) folk. *The Peaceable Kingdom*.
Lewis Wickes Hine, 1874-1940, (U.S.) photographer. Studies of immigrants, children in industry.
Hans Hofmann, 1880-1966, (U.S.) early Abstract Expressionist. *Spring*, *The Gate*.
William Hogarth, 1697-1764, (Br.) caricaturist. *The Rake's Progress*.
Katsushika Hokusai, 1760-1849, (Jpn.) printmaker. *Crabs*.
Hans Holbein the Elder, 1460-1524, (Ger.) late Gothic. *Presentation of Christ in the Temple*.
Hans Holbein the Younger, 1497-1543, (Ger.) portraitist. *Henry VIII*, *The French Ambassadors*.
Winslow Homer, 1836-1910, (U.S.) naturalist, marine themes. *Marine Coast*, *High Cliff*.
Edward Hopper, 1882-1967, (U.S.) realistic urban scenes. *Nighthawks*, *House by the Railroad*.
Horst P. Horst, 1906-99, (Ger.) fashion, celebrity photographer.
Jean-Auguste-Dominique Ingres, 1780-1867, (Fr.) Classicist. *Valpincon Bather*.

George Inness, 1825-94, (U.S.) luminous landscapist. *Delaware Water Gap.*

William Henry Jackson, 1843-1942, (U.S.) photographer. American West, building of Union Pacific Railroad.

Jeanne-Claude (Javacheff), 1935-2009, (Moroc.), created large-scale, temporary installations in public places with her husband, Christo.

Donald Judd, 1928-94, (U.S.) sculptor, major Minimalist.

Frida Kahlo, 1907-54, (Mex.) folkloric stylist. *Self-Portrait With Monkey.*

Wassily Kandinsky, 1866-1944, (Russ.) Abstractionist. *Capricious Forms, Improvisation 28 (second version).*

Paul Klee, 1879-1940, (Switz.) Abstractionist. *Twittering Machine, Pastoral, Death and Fire.*

Gustav Klimt, 1862-1918, (Austria) cofounder of Vienna Secession Movement. *The Kiss.*

Oscar Kokoschka, 1886-1980, (Austria) Expressionist. *View of Prague, Harbor of Marseilles.*

Kathe Kollwitz, 1867-1945, (Ger.) printmaker, social justice themes. *The Peasant War.*

Gaston Lachaise, 1882-1935, (U.S.) figurative sculptor. *Standing Woman.*

John La Farge, 1835-1910, (U.S.) muralist. *Red and White Peonies, The Ascension.*

Sir Edwin (Henry) Landseer, 1802-73, (Br.) painter, sculptor. *Shoeing, Rout of Comus.*

Dorothea Lange, 1895-1965, (U.S.) photographer. Great Depression, migrant farm workers.

Fernand Léger, 1881-1955, (Fr.) Machine art. *The Cyclists.*

Saul Leiter, 1923-2013, (U.S) photographer.

Leonardo da Vinci, 1452-1519, (It.) Renaissance. *Mona Lisa, Last Supper, The Annunciation.*

Emanuel Leutze, 1816-68, (U.S.) historical themes. *Washington Crossing the Delaware.*

Roy Lichtenstein, 1923-97, (U.S.) Pop Art.

Jacques Lipchitz, 1891-1973, (Fr.) Cubist sculptor. *Harpist.*

Filippino Lippi, 1457-1504, (It.) Renaissance. *Adoration of the Magi.*

Fra Filippo Lippi, 1406-69, (It.) Renaissance. *Coronation of the Virgin, Madonna and Child With Angels.*

Morris Louis, 1912-62, (U.S.) Abstract Expressionist. *Signa, Stripes, Alpha-Phi.*

René Magritte, 1898-1967, (Belg.) Surrealist. *The Descent of Man, The Betrayal of Images.*

Aristide Maillol, 1861-1944, (Fr.) sculptor. *L'Harmonie.*

Édouard Manet, 1832-83, (Fr.) forerunner of Impressionism. *Luncheon on the Grass, Olympia.*

Andrea Mantegna, 1431-1506, (It.) Renaissance frescoes. *Triumph of Caesar.*

Robert Mapplethorpe, 1946-89, (U.S.) photographer.

Franz Marc, 1880-1916, (Ger.) Expressionist. *Blue Horses.*

John Marin, 1870-1953, (U.S.) Expressionist seascapes. *Maine Island.*

Reginald Marsh, 1898-1954, (U.S.) satire. *Tattoo and Haircut.*

Agnes Martin, 1912-2004, (U.S.) abstract artist. *Night Sea.*

Masaccio, 1401-28, (It.) Renaissance. *The Tribute Money.*

Henri Matisse, 1869-1954, (Fr.) Fauvist. *Woman With the Hat.*

John McCracken, 1934-2011, (U.S.) Minimalist sculptor.

Michelangelo Buonarroti, 1475-1564, (It.) Renaissance. *Pietà, David, Moses, The Last Judgment*, Sistine Chapel ceiling.

Jean-Francois Millet, 1814-75, (Fr.) peasants. *The Gleaners, The Man With a Hoe.*

Joan Miró, 1893-1983, (Sp.) exuberant colors, playful images. Catalan landscape, *Dutch Interior.*

Amedeo Modigliani, 1884-1920, (It.) figurative paintings, sculptures. *Reclining Nude.*

Piet Mondrian, 1872-1944, (Neth.) Abstractionist. *Composition With Red, Yellow and Blue.*

Claude Monet, 1840-1926, (Fr.) Impressionist. *The Bridge at Argenteuil, Haystacks, Bridge Over a Pond of Water Lillies.*

Henry Moore, 1898-1986, (Br.) sculptor of large-scale, abstract works. *Reclining Figure* (several).

Gustave Moreau, 1826-98, (Fr.) Symbolist. *The Apparition, Dance of Salome.*

James Wilson Morrice, 1865-1924, (Can.) landscapist. *The Ferry, Quebec, Venice, Looking Over the Lagoon.*

William Morris, 1834-96, (Br.) decorative artist, leader of Arts and Crafts movement.

Grandma Moses (Anna Mary Robertson Moses), 1860-1961, (U.S.) folk. *Out for the Christmas Tree, Catching the Thanksgiving Turkey.*

Edvard Munch, 1863-1944, (Nor.) Expressionist. *The Cry.*

Bartolome Murillo, 1618-82, (Sp.) Baroque religious artist. *Vision of St. Anthony, The Two Trinities.*

Elizabeth Murray, 1940-2007, (U.S.) abstract colors. *Kitchen Party.*

Eadweard Muybridge, 1830-1904, (Br.-U.S.) photographer. Studies of motion, *Animal Locomotion.*

Nadar (Gaspar-Félix Tournachon), 1820-1910, (Fr.) photographer, caricaturist, portraitist. Invented photo-essay.

LeRoy Neiman, 1921-2012, (U.S.) sports expressionist painter.

Arnold Newman, 1918-2006, (U.S.) portrait photographer.

Barnett Newman, 1905-70, (U.S.) Abstract Expressionist. *Stations of the Cross.*

Isamu Noguchi, 1904-88, (U.S.) abstract sculptor, designer. *Kouros, BirdC(MU)*, sculptural gardens.

Kenneth Noland, 1924-2010, (U.S.) Color Field, abstract.

Georgia O'Keeffe, 1887-1986, (U.S.) Southwest motifs. *Cow's Skull: Red, White, and Blue; The Shelton With Sunspots.*

José Clemente Orozco, 1883-1949, (Mex.) frescoes. *House of Tears, Pre-Columbian Golden Age.*

Timothy H. O'Sullivan, 1840-82, (U.S.) Civil War photographer.

Gordon Parks, 1912-2006, (U.S.) African American photographer, filmmaker. *Life* photographer, 1948-68.

Charles Willson Peale, 1741-1827, (U.S.) Amer. Revolutionary portraitist. *The Staircase Group*, U.S. presidents.

Rembrandt Peale, 1778-1860, (U.S.) portraitist. *Thomas Jefferson.*

Irving Penn, 1917-2009, (U.S.) portraitist, fashion photographer.

Pietro Perugino, 1446-1523, (It.) Renaissance. *Delivery of the Keys to St. Peter.*

Pablo Picasso, 1881-1973, (Sp.) painter, sculptor. *Guernica, Dove, Head of a Woman, Head of a Bull, Metamorphosis.*

Piero della Francesca, c. 1415-92, (It.) Renaissance. *Duke of Urbino, Flagellation of Christ.*

Camille Pissarro, 1830-1903, (Fr.) Impressionist. *Boulevard des Italiens, Morning, Sunlight; Bather in the Woods.*

Jackson Pollock, 1912-56, (U.S.) Abstract Expressionist. *Autumn Rhythm.*

Nicolas Poussin, 1594-1665, (Fr.) Baroque pictorial classicism. *St. John on Patmos.*

Maurice B. Prendergast, c. 1860-1924, (U.S.) Postimpressionist watercolorist. *Umbrellas in the Rain.*

Pierre-Paul Prud'hon, 1758-1823, (Fr.) Romanticist. *Crime Pursued by Vengeance and Justice.*

Pierre Cecile Puvis de Chavannes, 1824-98, (Fr.) muralist. *The Poor Fisherman.*

Raphael Sanzio, 1483-1520, (It.) Renaissance. *Disputa, School of Athens, Sistine Madonna.*

Robert Rauschenberg, 1925-2008, (U.S.) printmaker. *Combine, Bed, Revolvers, Outpost.*

Man Ray (Emmanuel Radnitsky), 1890-1976, (U.S.) Dadaist and Surrealist. *Observing Time, The Lovers, Marquis de Sade.*

Odilon Redon, 1840-1916, (Fr.) Symbolist painter, lithographer. *In the Dream, Vase of Flowers.*

Rembrandt van Rijn, 1606-69, (Neth.) painter, printmaker. *The Bridal Couple, The Night Watch.*

Frederic Remington, 1861-1909, (U.S.) painter, sculptor. Portrayer of the American West, *Bronco Buster.*

Pierre-Auguste Renoir, 1841-1919, (Fr.) Impressionist. *The Luncheon of the Boating Party, Dance in the Country.*

Joshua Reynolds, 1723-92, (Br.) portraitist. *Mrs. Siddons as the Tragic Muse.*

Herb Ritts, 1952-2002, (U.S.) photographer. Nudes, celebrities.

Diego Rivera, 1886-1957, (Mex.) frescoes. *The Fecund Earth.*

Larry Rivers, 1923-2002, (U.S.) painter, sculptor, often realistic. Dutch Masters series.

Henry Peach Robinson, 1830-1901, (Br.) a leader of "high art" photography.

Norman Rockwell, 1894-1978, (U.S.) painter, illustrator. *Saturday Evening Post* covers.

Auguste Rodin, 1840-1917, (Fr.) sculptor. *The Thinker.*

Milton Rogovin, 1909-2011, (U.S.) documentary photographer.

Willy Ronis, 1910-2009, (Fr.) photographer. Postwar Paris.

Joe Rosenthal, 1911-2006, (U.S.) photojournalist; photographed six Marines raising the U.S. flag over Iwo Jima in WWII.

Mark Rothko, 1903-70, (U.S.) Abstract Expressionist. *Light, Earth and Blue.*

Georges Rouault, 1871-1958, (Fr.) Expressionist. *Three Judges.*

Henri Rousseau, 1844-1910, (Fr.) primitive exotic themes. *The Snake Charmer.*

Theodore Rousseau, 1812-67, (Switz.-Fr.) landscapist. *Under the Birches, Evening.*

Peter Paul Rubens, 1577-1640, (Flem.) Baroque. *Mystic Marriage of St. Catherine.*

Jacob van Ruisdael, c. 1628-82, (Neth.) landscapist. *Jewish Cemetery.*

Charles M. Russell, 1866-1926, (U.S.) Western life.

Salomon van Ruysdael, c. 1600-70, (Neth.) landscapist. *River With Ferry-Boat.*

Albert Pinkham Ryder, 1847-1917, (U.S.) seascapes, allegories. *Toilers of the Sea.*

Augustus Saint-Gaudens, 1848-1907, (U.S.) memorial statues. *Farragut, Mrs. Henry Adams (Grief).*

Niki de Saint Phalle,1930-2002, (Fr.) paintings, sculptures, prints, large public installations.

Andrea Sansovino, 1460-1529, (It.) Renaissance sculptor. *Baptism of Christ.*

Jacopo Sansovino, 1486-1570, (It.) Renaissance sculptor. *St. John the Baptist.*

John Singer Sargent, 1856-1925, (U.S.) Edwardian society portraitist. *The Wyndham Sisters, Madame X.*

Andrea del Sarto, 1486-1530, (It.) frescoes. *Madonna of the Harpies.*

George Segal, 1924-2000, (U.S.) sculptor. Life-sized figures realistically depicting daily life.

Georges Seurat, 1859-91, (Fr.) Pointillist. *Sunday Afternoon on the Island of La Grande Jatte.*

Gino Severini, 1883-1966, (It.) Futurist and Cubist. *Dynamic Hieroglyph of the Bal Tabarin.*

Ben Shahn, 1898-1969, (U.S.) social and political themes. Sacco and Vanzetti series, *Seurat's Lunch, Handball.*

Charles Sheeler, 1883-1965, (U.S.) abstractionist.

David Alfaro Siqueiros, 1896-1974, (Mex.) political muralist. *March of Humanity.*

David Smith, 1906-65, (U.S.) welded metal sculpture. *Hudson River Landscape, Zig, Cubi* series.

Edward Steichen, 1879-1973, (U.S.) photographer. Credited with transforming photography into an art form.

Alfred Stieglitz, 1864-1946, (U.S.) photographer, editor. Helped create acceptance of photography as art.

Paul Strand, 1890-1976, (U.S.) photographer. People, nature, landscapes.

Gilbert Stuart, 1755-1828, (U.S.) portraitist. George Washington, Thomas Jefferson, James Madison.

Thomas Sully, 1783-1872, (U.S.) portraitist. *Col. Thomas Handasyd Perkins*, *The Passage of the Delaware*.
William Henry Fox Talbot, 1800-77, (Br.) photographer. *Pencil of Nature*, early photographically illustrated book.
George Tames, 1919-94, (U.S.) photographer. Presidents, political leaders.
Yves Tanguy, 1900-55, (Fr.) Surrealist. *Rose of the Four Winds*; *Mama, Papa Is Wounded!*
Giovanni Battista Tiepolo, 1696-1770, (It.) Rococo frescoes. *The Crucifixion*.
Jacopo Tintoretto, 1518-94, (It.) Mannerist. *The Last Supper*.
Titian (Tiziano Vecellio), c. 1488-1576, (It.) Renaissance. *Venus and the Lute Player*, *The Bacchanal*.
Jose Rey Toledo, 1916-94, (U.S.) Native American life. Tribal dances.
George Tooker, 1920-2011, (U.S.) Magic Realist. *Subway*.
Henri de Toulouse-Lautrec, 1864-1901, (Fr.) Postimpressionist. *At the Moulin Rouge*.
John Trumbull, 1756-1843, (U.S.) historical themes. *The Declaration of Independence*.
Deborah Turbeville, 1937-2013, (U.S.) fashion photographer.
J(oseph) M(allord) W(illiam) Turner, 1775-1851, (Br.) Romantic landscapist. *Snow Storm*.
Cy Twombly, 1928-2011, (U.S.) painter and sculptor. *Leda and the Swan*.
Paolo Uccello, 1397-1475, (It.) Gothic-Renaissance. *The Rout of San Romano*.
Maurice Utrillo, 1883-1955, (Fr.) Impressionist. *Sacre-Coeur de Montmartre*.
Vincent van Gogh, 1853-90, (Neth.) *The Starry Night*, *L'Arlesienne*, *Bedroom at Arles*, *Self-Portrait*.
John Vanderlyn, 1775-1852, (U.S.) Neo-classicist. *Ariadne Asleep on the Island of Naxos*.
Diego Velázquez, 1599-1660, (Sp.) Baroque. *Las Meninas*, *Portrait of Juan de Pareja*.
Jan Vermeer, 1632-75, (Neth.) interior genre subjects. *Young Woman With a Water Jug*.
Paolo Veronese, 1528-88, (It.) devotional themes, vastly peopled canvases. *The Temptation of St. Anthony*.
Andrea del Verrocchio, 1435-88, (It.) sculptor. *Colleoni*.
Maurice de Vlaminck, 1876-1958, (Fr.) Fauvist landscapist. *Red Trees*.
Andy Warhol, 1928-87, (U.S.) Pop Art. *Campbell's Soup Cans*, *Marilyn Diptych*.
Antoine Watteau, 1684-1721, (Fr.) Rococo "scenes of gallantry." *The Embarkation for Cythera*.
George Frederic Watts, 1817-1904, (Br.) painter and sculptor. Grandiose allegorical themes. *Hope*.
Benjamin West, 1738-1820, (U.S.) realistic historical themes. *Death of General Wolfe*.
Edward Weston, 1886-1958, (U.S.) photographer. Landscapes of American West.
James Abbott McNeill Whistler, 1834-1903, (U.S.) *Arrangement in Grey and Black No. 1* (*Portrait of the Artist's Mother*).
Archibald M. Willard, 1836-1918, (U.S.) murals. *The Spirit of '76*.
Grant Wood, 1891-1942, (U.S.) Midwestern regionalist. *American Gothic*, *Daughters of Revolution*.
Andrew Wyeth, 1917-2009, (U.S.), regionalist. *Christina's World*.
Ossip Zadkine, 1890-1967, (Russ.) School of Paris sculptor. *The Destroyed City*, *Musicians*, *Christ*.

Business Leaders and Philanthropists of the Past

Giovanni Agnelli, 1921-2003, (It.) industrialist; principal shareholder of Fiat.
Karl Albrecht, 1920-2014, and **Theo Albrecht**, 1922-2010, (both Ger.) cofounders of Aldi supermarkets.
Walter Annenberg, 1908-2002, (U.S.) publisher, founder of *TV Guide*, philanthropist.
Elizabeth Arden (F. N. Graham), 1884-1966, (U.S.) Canadian-born founder of cosmetics empire.
Philip D. Armour, 1832-1901, (U.S.) industrialist; streamlined meatpacking.
Brooke Astor, 1902-2007, (U.S.) philanthropist; pres. of Vincent Astor Foundation.
John Jacob Astor, 1763-1848, (U.S.) German-born fur trader, banker, real estate magnate; at death, richest in U.S.
Francis W. Ayer, 1848-1923, (U.S.) ad industry pioneer.
August Belmont, 1816-90, (U.S.) German-born financier.
James B. (Diamond Jim) Brady, 1856-1917, (U.S.) financier, philanthropist, legendary bon vivant.
Adolphus Busch, 1839-1913, (U.S.) German-born businessman; established brewery empire.
Asa Candler, 1851-1929, (U.S.) founded Coca-Cola Co.
Andrew Carnegie, 1835-1919, (U.S.) Scottish-born industrialist, philanthropist; founded Carnegie Steel Co.
Tom Carvel, 1908-89, (Gr.-U.S.) founded ice cream chain.
William Colgate, 1783-1857, (Br.-U.S.) businessman, philanthropist; founded soap-making empire.
Jay Cooke, 1821-1905, (U.S.) financier.
Peter Cooper, 1791-1883, (U.S.) industrialist, inventor, philanthropist; founded Cooper Union college (1859).
Ezra Cornell, 1807-74, (U.S.) businessman, philanthropist; headed Western Union.
Erastus Corning, 1794-1872, (U.S.) financier; headed New York Central Railroad.
Charles Crocker, 1822-88, (U.S.) railroad builder, financier.
Samuel Cunard, 1787-1865, (Can.) pioneered transatlantic steam navigation.
Marcus Daly, 1841-1900, (U.S.) Irish-born copper magnate.
W. Edwards Deming, 1900-93, (U.S.) quality-control expert who revolutionized Japanese manufacturing.
Walt Disney, 1901-66, (U.S.) pioneer in cinema animation; built entertainment empire.
Herbert H. Dow, 1866-1930, (U.S.) founder of chemical co.
Anthony Drexel, 1826-93, (U.S.) banker, philanthropist, university founder.
James Duke, 1856-1925, (U.S.) founded American Tobacco, Duke Univ.
Eleuthere I. du Pont, 1771-1834, (Fr.-U.S.) gunpowder manufacturer; founded one of the largest business empires.
Thomas C. Durant, 1820-85, (U.S.) railroad official, financier.
William C. Durant, 1861-1947, (U.S.) industrialist; formed General Motors.
George Eastman, 1854-1932, (U.S.) inventor; manufacturer of photographic equipment.
Marshall Field, 1834-1906, (U.S.) merchant; founded Chicago's largest department store.
Harvey Firestone, 1868-1938, (U.S.) founded tire company.
Avery Fisher, 1906-94, (U.S.) industrialist, philanthropist; founded Fisher Electronics.
Henry M. Flagler, 1830-1913, (U.S.) financier; helped form Standard Oil, developed FL as resort state.
Malcolm Forbes, 1919-90, (U.S.) magazine publisher.
Henry Ford, 1863-1947, (U.S.) automaker; developed first popular low-priced car.
Henry Ford II, 1917-87, (U.S.) headed auto company founded by grandfather.
Henry C. Frick, 1849-1919, (U.S.) steel and coke magnate; had prominent role in development of U.S. Steel.
Jakob Fugger (Jakob the Rich), 1459-1525, (Ger.) headed leading banking, trading house in 16th-cent. Europe.
Alfred C. Fuller, 1885-1973, (U.S.) Canadian-born businessman; founded brush company.
Elbert H. Gary, 1846-1927, (U.S.) chaired board of U.S. Steel, 1903-27.
Jean Paul Getty, 1892-1976, (U.S.) founded oil empire.
Amadeo Giannini, 1870-1949, (U.S.) founded Bank of America.
Stephen Girard, 1750-1831, (U.S.) French-born financier, philanthropist; richest man in U.S. at time of death.
Leonard H. Goldenson, 1905-99, (U.S.) turned ABC into major TV network.
Jay Gould, 1836-92, (U.S.) railroad magnate, financier.
Hetty Green, 1834-1916, (U.S.) financier, the "witch of Wall St."; richest woman in U.S. in her day.
William Gregg, 1800-67, (U.S.) launched textile industry in the South.
Meyer Guggenheim, 1828-1905, (U.S.) Swiss-born merchant, philanthropist; built merchandising, mining empires.
Armand Hammer, 1898-1990, (U.S.) headed Occidental Petroleum, promoted U.S.-Soviet ties.
Elliot Handler, 1916-2011, (U.S.) cofounder of Mattel; introduced the Barbie doll.
Edward H. Harriman, 1848-1909, (U.S.) railroad financier; headed Union Pacific.
Henry J. Heinz, 1844-1919, (U.S.) founded food empire.
Harry (1909-97) and **Leona Helmsley**, 1920-2007, (U.S.) real estate magnates, philanthropists.
Milton Snavely Hershey, 1857-1945, (U.S.) chocolate co. founder, philanthropist.
James J. Hill, 1838-1916, (U.S.) Canadian-born railroad magnate, financier; founded Great Northern Railway.
Conrad N. Hilton, 1888-1979, (U.S.) hotel chain founder.
Howard Hughes, 1905-76, (U.S.) industrialist, aviator, filmmaker.
H. L. Hunt, 1889-1974, (U.S.) oil magnate.
Collis P. Huntington, 1821-1900, (U.S.) railroad magnate.
Henry E. Huntington, 1850-1927, (U.S.) railroad builder, philanthropist.
Walter L. Jacobs, 1898-1985, (U.S.) founder of the first rental car agency.
Steve Jobs, 1955-2011, (U.S.) Apple cofounder and exec.; Pixar exec.
Howard Johnson, 1896-1972, (U.S.) founded restaurants.
John H. Johnson, 1918-2005, (U.S.) built publishing empire based on *Ebony* and *Jet*.
Samuel Curtis Johnson, 1928-2004, (U.S.) headed S.C. Johnson & Sons.
Henry J. Kaiser, 1882-1967, (U.S.) industrialist; built empire in steel, aluminum.
Minor C. Keith, 1848-1929, (U.S.) railroad magnate; founded United Fruit Co.
Will K. Kellogg, 1860-1951, (U.S.) businessman, philanthropist; founded breakfast food co.
Kirk Kerkorian, 1917-2015, (U.S.) private equity magnate; real estate developer.
Richard King, 1825-85, (U.S.) cattle farmer; founded King Ranch in Texas.
John W. Kluge, 1914-2010, (Ger.-U.S.) Metromedia chair; philanthropist.
William S. Knudsen, 1879-1948, (U.S.) Danish-born auto industry executive.
Samuel H. Kress, 1863-1955, (U.S.) businessman, art collector, philanthropist; founded "dime store" chain.
Ray A. Kroc, 1902-84, (U.S.) original CEO of McDonald's Corp.; oversaw company's vast expansion.
Alfred Krupp, 1812-87, (Ger.) armaments magnate.
Estée Lauder, 1908-2004, (U.S.) cofounder of Estée Lauder companies.
Kenneth L. Lay, 1942-2006, (U.S.), former CEO of Enron; indicted on fraud charges.
William Levitt, 1907-94, (U.S.) industrialist; "suburb maker."
Thomas Lipton, 1850-1931, (Scot.) merchant; tea empire.
James McGill, 1744-1813, (Scot.-Can.) funded Montréal's McGill Univ.
Andrew W. Mellon, 1855-1937, (U.S.) financier, industrialist, philanthropist.
Charles E. Merrill, 1885-1956, (U.S.) financier; developed firm of Merrill Lynch.
J(ohn) P(ierpont) Morgan, 1837-1913, (U.S.) most powerful figure in finance and industry at turn of 20th cent.
Akio Morita, 1921-99, (Jpn.) cofounded Sony Corp.
Malcolm Muir, 1885-1979, (U.S.) created *Business Week* magazine; headed *Newsweek*, 1937-61.

Roy Neuberger, 1903-2010, (U.S.) financier, art patron.
Samuel Newhouse, 1895-1979, (U.S.) publishing and broadcasting magnate.
Jean Nidetch, 1923-2015, (U.S.) Weight Watchers cofounder.
Aristotle Onassis, 1906-75, (Gr.) shipping magnate.
William S. Paley, 1901-90, (U.S.) built CBS communications empire.
Frederick D. Patterson, 1901-88, (U.S.) founder of United Negro College Fund, 1944.
George Peabody, 1795-1869, (U.S.) merchant, financier, philanthropist.
James C. Penney, 1875-1971, (U.S.) businessman; developed department store.
Frank Perdue, 1920-2005, (U.S.) founder of Perdue Farms, chicken-processing co.
William C. Procter, 1862-1934, (U.S.) headed soap co.
John D. Rockefeller, 1839-1937, (U.S.) industrialist; established Standard Oil.
John D. Rockefeller Jr., 1874-1960, (U.S.) philanthropist; provided land for UN.
Laurance S. Rockefeller, 1910-2004, (U.S.) philanthropist, conservationist.
Meyer A. Rothschild, 1743-1812, (Ger.) founded international banking house.
Thomas Fortune Ryan, 1851-1928, (U.S.) financier; a founder of American Tobacco.
Edmond J. Safra, 1932-99, (U.S.) banker.
David Sarnoff, 1891-1971, (U.S.) broadcasting pioneer; established first radio network, NBC.
Richard Sears, 1863-1914, (U.S.) founded mail-order co.
Werner von Siemens, 1816-92, (Ger.) industrialist, inventor.
Alfred P. Sloan, 1875-1966, (U.S.) industrialist, philanthropist; headed General Motors.
A. Leland Stanford, 1824-93, (U.S.) railroad official, philanthropist; founded university.
Frank Stanton, 1908-2006, (U.S.) president of CBS network, 1946-71.
Nathan Straus, 1848-1931, (U.S.) German-born merchant, philanthropist; headed Macy's dept. stores.
Levi Strauss, c. 1829-1902, (U.S.) pants manufacturer.
Clement Studebaker, 1831-1901, (U.S.) wagon, carriage maker.
Gustavus Swift, 1839-1903, (U.S.) pioneer meatpacker.
Gerard Swope, 1872-1957, (U.S.) industrialist, economist; headed General Electric.
Dave Thomas, 1932-2002, (U.S.) Wendy's restaurant chain founder.
James Walter Thompson, 1847-1928, (U.S.) ad exec., founder of ad agency.
Alice Tully, 1902-93, (U.S.) philanthropist, arts patron.
Theodore N. Vail, 1845-1920, (U.S.) organized Bell Telephone system, headed AT&T.
Cornelius Vanderbilt, 1794-1877, (U.S.) financier; established steamship, railroad empires.
Henry Villard, 1835-1900, (U.S.) German-born railroad executive, financier.
Charles R. Walgreen, 1873-1939, (U.S.) founded drugstore chain.
Madame C. J. Walker, 1867-1919, (U.S.) African-American hair care entrepreneur, philanthropist.
DeWitt Wallace, 1889-1981, and **Lila Wallace**, 1889-1984, (both U.S.) cofounders of *Reader's Digest* magazine.
Sam Walton, 1918-92, (U.S.) founder of Wal-Mart stores.
John Wanamaker, 1838-1922, (U.S.) department-store merchandising pioneer.
Aaron Montgomery Ward, 1843-1913, (U.S.) established first mail-order firm.
Thomas J. Watson, 1874-1956, (U.S.) IBM head, 1914-56.
George Westinghouse, 1846-1914, (U.S) inventor, manufacturer; organized Westinghouse Electric Co., 1886.
John Hay Whitney, 1905-82, (U.S.) publisher, sportsman, philanthropist.
Charles E. Wilson, 1890-1961, (U.S.) auto exec., public official.
Frank W. Woolworth, 1852-1919, (U.S.) created five-and-dime chain.
William Wrigley Jr., 1861-1932, (U.S.) founded Wrigley chewing gum co.

American Cartoonists

Reviewed by Lucy Shelton Caswell, Professor and Curator, Cartoon Research Library, Ohio State University.

Scott Adams, b 1957, Dilbert.
Charles Addams, 1912-88, macabre cartoons.
Brad Anderson, 1924-2015, Marmaduke.
Sergio Aragonés, b 1937, (Span.-Mex.) *Mad* magazine.
Peter Arno, 1904-68, *The New Yorker*.
Tex Avery, 1908-80, animator; Bugs Bunny, Porky Pig.
George Baker, 1915-75, The Sad Sack.
Carl Barks, 1901-2000, Donald Duck comic books.
C. C. Beck, 1910-89, Captain Marvel.
Dave Berg, 1920-2002, *Mad* magazine.
Jim Berry, 1932-2015, Berry's World.
Herb Block (Herblock), 1909-2001, political cartoonist.
George Booth, b 1926, *The New Yorker*.
Berkeley Breathed, b 1957, Bloom County.
Dik Browne, 1917-89, Hi & Lois, Hagar the Horrible.
Marjorie Buell, 1904-93, Little Lulu.
Ernie Bushmiller, 1905-82, Nancy.
Milton Caniff, 1907-88, Terry & the Pirates, Steve Canyon.
Al Capp, 1909-79, Li'l Abner.
Roz Chast, b 1954, *The New Yorker*.
Gene Colan, 1926-2011, *Daredevil*.
Paul Conrad, 1924-2010, political cartoonist.
Roy Crane, 1901-77, Captain Easy, Buz Sawyer.
R(obert) Crumb, b 1943, underground cartoonist.
Shamus Culhane, 1908-96, animator.
Jay N. "Ding" Darling, 1876-1962, political cartoonist.
Jack Davis, b 1924, *Mad* magazine.
Jim Davis, b 1945, Garfield.
Billy DeBeck, 1890-1942, Barney Google.
Rudolph Dirks, 1877-1968, The Katzenjammer Kids.
Walt Disney, 1901-66, produced animated cartoons; created Mickey Mouse, Donald Duck.
Steve Ditko, b 1927, Spider-Man.
Mort Drucker, b 1929, *Mad* magazine.
Will Eisner, 1917-2005, The Spirit.
Jules Feiffer, b 1929, political cartoonist.
Bud Fisher, 1884?-1954, Mutt & Jeff.
Ham Fisher, 1900-55, Joe Palooka.
Max Fleischer, 1883-1972, Betty Boop.
Hal Foster, 1892-1982, Tarzan, Prince Valiant.
Fontaine Fox, 1884-1964, Toonerville Folks.
Isadore "Friz" Freleng, 1905-95, animator; Yosemite Sam, Porky Pig, Sylvester and Tweety Bird.
Rube Goldberg, 1883-1970, Boob McNutt.
Chester Gould, 1900-85, Dick Tracy.
Harold Gray, 1894-1968, Little Orphan Annie.
Matt Groening, b 1954, Life in Hell, The Simpsons.
Cathy Guisewite, b 1950, Cathy.
Bill Hanna, 1910-2001, and **Joe Barbera**, 1911-2006, animators; Tom & Jerry, Yogi Bear, Flintstones.
Oliver Harrington, 1912-95, Bootsie.
Johnny Hart, 1931-2007, B.C., Wizard of Id.
Alfred Harvey, 1913-94, created Casper the Friendly Ghost.
Jimmy Hatlo, 1898-1963, Little Iodine.
John Held Jr., 1889-1958, Jazz Age.
George Herriman, 1881-1944, Krazy Kat.
Harry Hershfield, 1885-1974, Abie the Agent.
Stephen Hillenburg, b 1961, SpongeBob SquarePants.
Al Hirschfeld, 1903-2003, *NY Times* theater caricaturist.
Burne Hogarth, 1911-96, Tarzan.
Helen Hokinson, 1900-49, *The New Yorker*.
Nicole Hollander, b 1939, Sylvia.
Lynn Johnston, b 1947, (Can.) For Better or For Worse.
Oliver Johnston, 1912-2008, Disney animator.
Chuck Jones, 1912-2002, animator; Bugs Bunny, Porky Pig; created Road Runner, Wile E. Coyote.
Mike Judge, b 1962, Beavis and Butt-Head, King of the Hill.
Bob Kane, 1916-98, Batman.
Bil Keane, 1922-2011, The Family Circus.
Walt Kelly, 1913-73, Pogo.
Hank Ketcham, 1920-2001, Dennis the Menace.
Ted Key, 1912-2008, Hazel.
Frank King, 1883-1969, Gasoline Alley.
Jack Kirby, 1917-94, Fantastic Four, The Incredible Hulk.
Rollin Kirby, 1875-1952, political cartoonist.
B(ernard) Kliban, 1935-90, cat books.
Edward Koren, b 1935, *The New Yorker*.
John Kricfalusi, b 1955, Ren & Stimpy.
Joe Kubert, 1926-2012, Sgt. Rock.
Harvey Kurtzman, 1921-93, *Mad* magazine.
Walter Lantz, 1900-94, Woody Woodpecker.
Gary Larson, b 1950, The Far Side.
Mell Lazarus, b 1927, Momma, Miss Peach.
Stan Lee, b 1922, Marvel Comics.
David Levine, 1926-2009, *NY Review of Books* caricatures.
Seth MacFarlane, b 1973, Family Guy.
Jeff MacNelly, 1947-2000, political cartoonist; Shoe.
Doug Marlette, 1949-2007, political cartoonist; Kudzu.
Don Martin, 1931-2000, *Mad* magazine.
Bill Mauldin, 1921-2003, political cartoonist.
Winsor McCay, 1872-1934, Little Nemo.
John T. McCutcheon, 1870-1949, political cartoonist.
Dwayne McDuffie, 1962-2011, *Justice League*.
Aaron McGruder, b 1974, The Boondocks.
George McManus, 1884-1954, Bringing Up Father.
Dale Messick, 1906-2005, Brenda Starr.
Norman Mingo, 1896-1980, Alfred E. Neuman.
Bob Montana, 1920-75, Archie.
Dick Moores, 1909-86, Gasoline Alley.
Willard Mullin, 1902-78, sports cartoonist; Dodgers' "Brooklyn Bum," "Mets Kid."
Russell Myers, b 1938, Broom Hilda.
Thomas Nast, 1840-1902, political cartoonist; Republican elephant, Democratic donkey.
Pat Oliphant, b 1935, political cartoonist.
Frederick Burr Opper, 1857-1937, Happy Hooligan.
Richard Outcault, 1863-1928, Yellow Kid, Buster Brown.
Brant Parker, 1920-2007, Wizard of Id.
Trey Parker, b 1969, animator, co-creator of South Park.
Harvey Pekar, 1939-2010, American Splendor.
Mike Peters, b 1943, Mother Goose & Grimm.
George Price, 1901-95, *The New Yorker*.
Antonio Prohias, 1921-98, Spy vs. Spy.
Alex Raymond, 1909-56, Flash Gordon, Jungle Jim.
Forrest (Bud) Sagendorf, 1915-94, Popeye.
Art Sansom, 1920-91, The Born Loser.
Charles Schulz, 1922-2000, Peanuts.
Elzie C. Segar, 1894-1938, Popeye.
Joe Shuster, 1914-92, and **Jerry Siegel**, 1914-96, Superman.
Sidney Smith, 1887-1935, The Gumps.
Otto Soglow, 1900-75, Little King.
Art Spiegelman, b 1948, Raw, Maus.
William Steig, 1907-2003, *The New Yorker*.
Matt Stone, b 1971, animator, co-creator of South Park.
James Swinnerton, 1875-1974, Little Jimmy, Canyon Kiddies.
Paul Szep, b 1941, political cartoonist.
Paul Terry, 1887-1971, animator of Mighty Mouse.
Bob Thaves, 1924-2006, Frank and Ernest.
James Thurber, 1894-61, *The New Yorker*.
Garry Trudeau, b 1948, Doonesbury.
Jim Unger, 1937-2012, Herman.
Mort Walker, b 1923, Beetle Bailey.
Bill Watterson, b 1958, Calvin and Hobbes.
Russ Westover, 1887-1966, Tillie the Toiler.
Signe Wilkinson, b 1950, political cartoonist.
Frank Willard, 1893-1958, Moon Mullins.
J. R. Williams, 1888-1957, The Willets Family, Out Our Way.
Gahan Wilson, b 1930, *The New Yorker*.
Tom Wilson, 1931-2011, Ziggy.
Art Young, 1866-1943, political cartoonist.
Chic Young, 1901-73, Blondie.

Economists, Educators, Historians, and Social Scientists of the Past

For psychologists, see Scientists of the Past.

Brooks Adams, 1848-1927, (U.S.) historian, political theoretician; *The Law of Civilization and Decay*.
Henry Adams, 1838-1918, (U.S.) historian, autobiographer; *The Education of Henry Adams*.
Stephen Ambrose, 1936-2002, (U.S.) historian; *Eisenhower*.
Francis Bacon, 1561-1626, (Eng.) philosopher, essayist, statesman; championed observation and induction.
George Bancroft, 1800-91, (U.S.) historian; 10-volume *History of the United States*.
Jack Barbash, 1910-94, (U.S.) labor economist; helped create the AFL-CIO.
Henry Barnard, 1811-1900, (U.S.) public school reformer.
Charles A. Beard, 1874-1948, (U.S.) historian; *The Economic Basis of Politics*.
(St.) Bede (the Venerable), c. 673-735, (Br.) scholar, historian; *Ecclesiastical History of the English People*.
Daniel Bell, 1919-2011, (U.S.) sociologist; *The End of Ideology*.
Ruth Benedict, 1887-1948, (U.S.) anthropologist; studied Indian tribes of the Southwest.
Sir Isaiah Berlin, 1909-97, (Br.) philosopher, historian; *The Age of Enlightenment*.
Leonard Bloomfield, 1887-1949, (U.S.) linguist; *Language*.
Franz Boas, 1858-1942, (U.S.) German-born anthropologist; studied American Indians.
Van Wyck Brooks, 1886-1963, (U.S.) historian; critic of New England culture, especially literature.
Edmund Burke, 1729-97, (Ire.) British parliamentarian and political philosopher; *Reflections on the Revolution in France*.
James MacGregor Burns, 1918-2014, (U.S.) historian, political scientist.
Nicholas Murray Butler, 1862-1947, (U.S.) educator; headed Columbia Univ., 1902-45; Nobel Peace Prize, 1931.
Joseph Campbell, 1904-87, (U.S.) author, editor, teacher; wrote books on mythology, folklore.
Thomas Carlyle, 1795-1881, (Scot.) historian, critic; *Sartor Resartus*, *Past and Present*, *The French Revolution*.
(Charles) Bruce Catton, 1899-1978, (U.S.) historian; *A Stillness at Appomattox*.
Edward Channing, 1856-1931, (U.S.) historian; 6-volume *History of the United States*.
Henry Steele Commager, 1902-98, (U.S.) historian, educator; *The Growth of the American Republic*.
John R. Commons, 1862-1945, (U.S.) economist, labor historian; *Legal Foundations of Capitalism*.
James B. Conant, 1893-1978, (U.S.) educator, diplomat; *The American High School Today*.
Benedetto Croce, 1866-1952, (It.) philosopher, statesman, historian; *Philosophy of the Spirit*.
Bernard A. De Voto, 1897-1955, (U.S.) historian; wrote trilogy on American West, edited Mark Twain manuscripts.
Melvil Dewey, 1851-1931, (U.S.) devised decimal system of library-book classification.
Donald Herbert Donald, 1920-2009, (U.S.) Pulitzer Prize-winning Civil War and Lincoln historian.
St. Clair Drake, 1911-90, (U.S.) sociologist, black studies pioneer; *Black Metropolis* (1945), with Horace R. Cayton.
W(illiam) E(dward) B(urghardt) Du Bois, 1868-1963, (U.S.) historian, sociologist; NAACP founder, 1909.
Will(iam), 1885-1981, (U.S.) and **Ariel Durant**, 1898-1981, (Ukraine) historians; *The Story of Civilization*.
Emile Durkheim, 1858-1917, (Fr.) a founder of modern sociology; *The Rules of Sociological Method*.
Jean Baptiste Point du Sable, c. 1750-1818, (U.S.) pioneer trader and first settler of Chicago, 1779.
Charles Eliot, 1834-1926, (U.S.) educator, Harvard president.
Friedrich Engels, 1820-95, (Ger.) political writer; with Marx wrote the *Communist Manifesto*.
Irving Fisher, 1867-1947, (U.S.) economist; contributed to the development of modern monetary theory.
John Fiske, 1842-1901, (U.S.) historian and lecturer; popularized Darwinian theory of evolution.
Charles Fourier, 1772-1837, (Fr.) utopian socialist.
John Hope Franklin, 1915-2009, (U.S.) historian; *From Slavery to Freedom: A History of African Americans*.
Sir James George Frazer, 1854-1941, (Br.) anthropologist; studied myth in religion; *The Golden Bough*.
Milton Friedman, 1912-2006, (U.S.) economist.
Paul Fussell, 1924-2012, (U.S.) literary historian; *The Great War and Modern Memory*.
John Kenneth Galbraith, 1908-2006, (Can.-U.S.) economist, author, professor, former amb. to India.
Peter Gay, 1923-2015, (Ger.-U.S.) cultural historian; *The Enlightenment: An Interpretation*.
Giovanni Gentile, 1875-1944, (It.) philosopher, educator; reformed Italian educational system.
Henry George, 1839-97, (U.S.) economist, reformer; led single-tax movement.
Edward Gibbon, 1737-94, (Br.) historian; *The History of the Decline and Fall of the Roman Empire*.
Andrew Greeley, 1928-2013, (U.S.) Rom. Cath. priest; sociologist.
Francesco Guicciardini, 1483-1540, (It.) historian; *Storia d'Italia*, principal historical work of the 16th cent.
Thomas Hobbes, 1588-1679, (Eng.) philosopher, political theorist; *Leviathan*.
Richard Hofstadter, 1916-70, (U.S.) historian; *The Age of Reform*.
Charles Hamilton Houston, 1895-1950, (U.S.) African American lawyer, Howard University instructor; champion of minority rights.
Samuel Huntington, 1927-2008, (U.S.), political scientist, Harvard University professor; *The Clash of Civilizations*.
Alfred Kahn, 1917-2010, (U.S.) economist; deregulated the U.S. airline industry.
John Keegan, 1934-2012, (Br.) war historian; *The Face of Battle*.
George F. Kennan, 1904-2005, (U.S.) diplomat, historian; main architect of U.S. Cold War "containment" strategy.
John Maynard Keynes, 1883-1946, (Br.) economist; principal advocate of deficit spending.
Alfred Kinsey, 1894-1956, (U.S.) zoologist; pioneering human sex researcher.
Russell Kirk, 1918-94, (U.S.), social philosopher; *The Conservative Mind*.
Alfred L. Kroeber, 1876-1960, (U.S.) cultural anthropologist; studied Indians of North and South America.
Elisabeth Kubler-Ross, 1926-2004, (Switz.) psychiatrist, author; *On Death and Dying*.
Christopher Lasch, 1932-94, (U.S.) social critic, historian; *The Culture of Narcissism*.
James L. Laughlin, 1850-1933, (U.S.) economist; helped establish Federal Reserve System.
Margaret Leech, 1893-1974, (U.S.) historian; *Reveille in Washington, 1860-1865*.
Lucien Lévy-Bruhl, 1857-1939, (Fr.) philosopher; studied the psychology of primitive societies; *Primitive Mentality*.
John Locke, 1632-1704, (Eng.) philosopher, political theorist; *Two Treatises of Government*.
Thomas B. Macaulay, 1800-59, (Br.) historian, statesman.
Niccolò Machiavelli, 1469-1527, (It.) writer, statesman; *The Prince*.
Bronislaw Malinowski, 1884-1942, (Pol.) considered the father of social anthropology.
Thomas R. Malthus, 1766-1834, (Br.) economist; *Essay on the Principle of Population*.
Horace Mann, 1796-1859, (U.S.) pioneered modern public school system.
Karl Mannheim, 1893-1947, (Hung.) sociologist, historian; *Ideology and Utopia*.
Harriet Martineau, 1802-76, (Eng.) writer, feminist; *Society in America*.
Karl Marx, 1818-83, (Ger.) political theorist, proponent of Communism; *Communist Manifesto*, *Das Kapital*.
Benjamin Mays, 1895-1984, (U.S.) minister, educator, civil rights leader; headed Morehouse College, 1940-67.
Giuseppe Mazzini, 1805-72, (It.) political philosopher.
William H. McGuffey, 1800-73, (U.S.) his *Reader* was a mainstay of 19th-cent. U.S. public education.
George H. Mead, 1863-1931, (U.S.) philosopher, social psychologist.
Margaret Mead, 1901-78, (U.S.) cultural anthropologist; popularized field; *Coming of Age in Samoa*.
Alexander Meiklejohn, 1872-1964, (U.S.) Br.-born educator; championed academic freedom and experimental curricula.
James Mill, 1773-1836, (Scot.) philosopher, historian, economist; a proponent of utilitarianism.
John Stuart Mill, 1806-73, (Eng.) philosopher, economist; *Utilitarianism*. Eldest son of James Mill.
Perry G. Miller, 1905-63, (U.S.) historian; interpreted 17th-cent. New England.
Theodor Mommsen, 1817-1903, (Ger.) historian; *The History of Rome*.
Ashley Montagu, 1905-99, (Eng.) anthropologist; *The Natural Superiority of Women*.
Charles-Louis Montesquieu, 1689-1755, (Fr.) social philosopher; *The Spirit of Laws*.
Maria Montessori, 1870-1952, (It.) educator, physician; started Montessori method of student self-motivation.
Samuel Eliot Morison, 1887-1976, (U.S.) historian; chronicled voyages of early explorers.
Lewis Mumford, 1895-1990, (U.S.) sociologist, critic; *The Culture of Cities*.
Gunnar Myrdal, 1898-1987, (Swed.) economist, social scientist; *Asian Drama: An Inquiry Into the Poverty of Nations*.
Allan Nevins, 1890-1971, (U.S.) historian, biographer; *The Ordeal of the Union*.
José Ortega y Gasset, 1883-1955, (Sp.) philosopher; advocated control by elite; *The Revolt of the Masses*.
Elinor Ostrom, 1933-2012, (U.S.) political economist.
Robert Owen, 1771-1858, (Br.) political philosopher, reformer; pioneer in cooperative movement.
Thomas Paine, 1737-1809, (Br.-U.S.) political theorist, writer; *Common Sense*.
Vilfredo Pareto, 1848-1923, (It.) economist, sociologist.
Francis Parkman, 1823-93, (U.S.) historian; *France and England in North America*.
Elizabeth P. Peabody, 1804-94, (U.S.) education pioneer; founded first kindergarten in U.S., 1860.
William Prescott, 1796-1859, (U.S.) early American historian; *The Conquest of Peru*.
Pierre Joseph Proudhon, 1809-65, (Fr.) social theorist; father of anarchism; *The Philosophy of Property*.
François Quesnay, 1694-1774, (Fr.) economic theorist.

Robert V. Remini, 1921-2013, (U.S.) historian; *The Life of Andrew Jackson*.
David Ricardo, 1772-1823, (Br.) economic theorist; advocated free international trade.
David Riesman, 1909-2002, (U.S.) sociologist; co-author, *The Lonely Crowd*.
Jacqueline de Romilly, 1913-2010, (Fr.) scholar of Greek civilization and language.
Theodore Roszak, 1933-2011, (U.S.) historian; *The Making of a Counter Culture*.
Jean-Jacques Rousseau, 1712-78, (Fr.) social philosopher; the father of romantic sensibility; *Confessions*.
Paul Samuelson, 1915-2009, (U.S.) economist, famed for modern mathematical approach to economics.
Edward Sapir, 1884-1939, (Ger.-U.S.) anthropologist; studied ethnology and linguistics of American Indian groups.
Ferdinand de Saussure, 1857-1913, (Switz.) a founder of modern linguistics.
Arthur Schlesinger Jr., 1917-2007, (U.S.) historian, author; *The Imperial Presidency*.
Joseph Schumpeter, 1883-1950, (Czech.-U.S.) economist, sociologist.
Elizabeth Seton, 1774-1821, (U.S.) nun; est. parochial school education in U.S., first native-born American saint.
Georg Simmel, 1858-1918, (Ger.) sociologist, philosopher; helped establish German sociology.
Robert Sklar, 1936-2011, (U.S.) film scholar.
Adam Smith, 1723-90, (Br.) economist; advocated laissez-faire economy, free trade; *The Wealth of Nations*.
Jared Sparks, 1789-1866, (U.S.) historian, educator, editor; *The Library of American Biography*.
Oswald Spengler, 1880-1936, (Ger.) philosopher, historian; *The Decline of the West*.
Leo Steinberg, 1920-2011, (Russ.-U.S.) art historian.
William G. Sumner, 1840-1910, (U.S.) social scientist, economist; laissez-faire economy, Social Darwinism.
Hippolyte Taine, 1828-93, (Fr.) historian, basis of naturalistic school; *The Origins of Contemporary France*.
A(lan) J(ohn) P(ercivale) Taylor, 1906-90, (Br.) historian; *The Origins of the Second World War*.
Nikolaas Tinbergen, 1907-88, (Neth.-Br.) ethologist; pioneer in study of animal behavior.
Alexis de Tocqueville, 1805-59, (Fr.) political scientist, historian; *Democracy in America*.
Francis E. Townsend, 1867-1960, (U.S.) led old-age pension movement, 1933.
Arnold Toynbee, 1889-1975, (Br.) historian; *A Study of History*, sweeping analysis of hist. of civilizations.
George Trevelyan, 1876-1962, (Br.) historian, statesman. Favored "literary" over "scientific" history; *History of England*.
Henri Troyat, 1911-2007, (Russ.-Fr.), biographies of major figures in Russian history.
Frederick J. Turner, 1861-1932, (U.S.) historian, educator; *The Frontier in American History*.
Thorstein B. Veblen, 1857-1929, (U.S.) economist, social philosopher; *The Theory of the Leisure Class*.
Giovanni Vico, 1668-1744, (It.) historian, biographer; regarded by many as first modern historian; *New Science*.
Izaak Walton, 1593-1683, (Eng.) biographer; political-philosophical study of fishing, *The Compleat Angler*.
Booker T. Washington, 1856-1915, (U.S.) founder, 1881, and first pres. of Tuskegee Institute; *Up From Slavery*.
Sidney J., 1859-1947, and **Beatrice Webb**, 1858-1943, (both Br.) leading figures in Fabian Society and Labor Party.
Max Weber, 1864-1920, (Ger.) sociologist; *The Protestant Ethic and the Spirit of Capitalism*.
Walter White, 1893-1955, (U.S.) exec. sec., NAACP, 1931-55.
Roy Wilkins, 1901-81, (U.S.) exec. director, NAACP, 1955-77.
Emma Hart Willard, 1787-1870, (U.S.) pioneered higher education for women.
James Q. Wilson, 1931-2012, (U.S.) political scientist; co-authored broken windows theory.
Carter G. Woodson, 1875-1950, (U.S.) historian; founded Assn. for the Study of Negro Life and History.
C. Vann Woodward, 1908-99, (U.S.) historian; *The Strange Career of Jim Crow*.
Howard Zinn, 1922-2010, (U.S.) historian; *A People's History of the United States*.

American Journalists of the Past

Reviewed by Dean Mills, Dean, Missouri School of Journalism.

See also Business Leaders and Philanthropists, American Cartoonists, and Writers of the Past.

Franklin P. Adams (F.P.A.), 1881-1960, humorist; wrote column "The Conning Tower."
Joseph W. Alsop, 1910-89, and **Stewart Alsop**, 1914-74, Washington-based political analysts, columnists.
Jack Anderson, 1922-2006, muckraking Washington, DC, syndicated columnist.
Brooks Atkinson, 1894-1984, theater critic.
Robert L. Bartley, 1937-2003, editorial-page editor for *Wall Street Journal*.
James Gordon Bennett, 1795-1872, editor and publisher; founded *NY Herald*.
James Gordon Bennett, 1841-1918, succeeded father, financed expeditions, founded afternoon paper.
Nellie Bly (Elizabeth Cochrane), 1867-1922, pioneer woman journalist, investigative reporter; noted for series on trip around the world.
Elias Boudinot, c. 1803-39, founding editor of first Native American newspaper in U.S., *Cherokee Phoenix* (1828-34).
Benjamin Bradlee, 1921-2014, (U.S.) *Washington Post* exec. editor.
Ed Bradley, 1941-2006, TV journalist (*60 Minutes*).
Andrew Breitbart, 1969-2012, conservative commentator and blogger.
David Brinkley, 1920-2003, co-anchor of NBC's *Huntley-Brinkley Report*, host of ABC's *This Week With David Brinkley*.
Arthur Brisbane, 1864-1936, editor; helped introduce "yellow journalism" with sensational, simply written articles.
David Broder, 1929-2011, political journalist for *The Washington Post*.
Joyce Brothers, 1927-2013, psychologist, columnist.
Heywood Broun, 1888-1939, author, columnist; founded American Newspaper Guild.
Helen Gurley Brown, 1922-2012, author; editor-in-chief of *Cosmopolitan* magazine (1965-97).
Art Buchwald, 1925-2007, journalist, humorist, syndicated columnist.
William F. Buckley Jr., 1925-2008, columnist and commentator; founder of *National Review*.
Herb Caen, 1916-97, longtime columnist for *San Francisco Chronicle* and *Examiner*.
John Campbell, 1653-1728, published *Boston News-Letter*, first continuing newspaper in the American colonies.
Jimmy Cannon, 1909-73, syndicated sports columnist.
John Chancellor, 1927-96, NBC reporter, anchor.
Harry Chandler, 1864-1944, *Los Angeles Times* publisher (1917-41); made it a dominant force.
Otis Chandler, 1928-2006, *Los Angeles Times* publisher (1960-80).
Marquis Childs, 1903-90, reporter and columnist for *St. Louis Post-Dispatch* and United Feature syndicate.
Craig Claiborne, 1920-2000, *NY Times* food editor and critic; key in internationalizing American tastes.
Alexander Cockburn, 1941-2012, left-wing journalist.
Charles Collingwood, 1917-85, CBS news correspondent.
Alistair Cooke, 1908-2004, Brit. journalist, TV narrator; naturalized American citizen, "Letter From America" series.
Howard Cosell, 1920-95, TV and radio sportscaster.
Gardner Cowles, 1861-1946, founded newspaper chain.
Judith Crist, 1922-2012, film critic.
Walter Cronkite, 1916-2009, CBS evening news anchor, TV journalist.
Evelyn Cunningham, 1916-2010, African American civil rights reporter.
Cyrus Curtis, 1850-1933, publisher of *Saturday Evening Post*, *Ladies' Home Journal*, *Country Gentleman*.
John Charles Daly, 1914-91, war correspondent, TV journalist; Voice of America head.
Charles Anderson Dana, 1819-97, editor, publisher; made *NY Sun* famous for its news reporting.
Elmer (Holmes) Davis, 1890-1958, *NY Times* editorial writer, radio commentator.
Richard Harding Davis, 1864-1916, war correspondent, travel writer, fiction writer.
Benjamin Day, 1810-89, published *NY Sun* beginning in 1833, introducing penny press to the U.S.
Dorothy Dix (Elizabeth Meriwether Gilmer), 1861-1951, reporter; pioneer of the advice column genre.
Finley Peter Dunne, 1867-1936, humorist, social critic; wrote "Mr. Dooley" columns.
Roger Ebert, 1942-2013, film critic.
Mary Baker Eddy, 1821-1910, founded Christian Science movement and *Christian Science Monitor*.
Rowland Evans Jr., 1921-2001, Washington columnist.
Fanny Fern (Sara Willis Parton), 1811-72, newspaper columnist, author.
Marshall Field III, 1893-1956, retail magnate, *Chicago Sun* founder.
Doris Fleeson, 1901-70, war correspondent, columnist.
Benjamin Franklin, 1706-90, publisher of *Poor Richard's Almanack*.
James Franklin, 1697-1735, printer, pioneer journalist; publisher of *New England Courant* and *Rhode Island Gazette*.
Fred W. Friendly, 1915-98, radio, TV reporter, producer, executive; collaborator with Edward R. Murrow.
Margaret Fuller, 1810-50, social reformer, transcendentalist, critic and foreign correspondent for *NY Tribune*.
Frank E. Gannett, 1876-1957, founded newspaper chain.
Mary Ellen Garber, 1916-2008, sports journalist.
William Lloyd Garrison, 1805-79, abolitionist; publisher of *The Liberator*.
Jack Germond, 1928-2013, political reporter.
Edwin Lawrence Godkin, 1831-1902, founder of *The Nation*, editor of *NY Evening Post*.
Katharine Graham,1917-2001, *Washington Post* publisher.
Sheilah Graham, 1904-89, Hollywood gossip columnist.
Horace Greeley, 1811-72, editor, politician; founded *NY Tribune*.
Meg Greenfield, 1930-99, *Newsweek* columnist, *Washington Post* editorial page editor.
Gilbert Hovey Grosvenor, 1875-1966, longtime editor of *National Geographic* magazine.
John Gunther, 1901-70, *Chicago Daily News* foreign correspondent, author.
David Halberstam, 1934-2007, journalist, sports reporter, author; *The Best and the Brightest*, *Summer of '49*.

Sarah Josepha Buell Hale, 1788-1879, first female magazine editor; *Ladies' Magazine*, later *Godey's Lady's Book*.
Paul Harvey, 1918-2009, radio broadcaster and commentator.
William Randolph Hearst, 1863-1951, founder of Hearst newspaper chain, one of the pioneers of yellow journalism.
Gabriel Heatter, 1890-1972, radio commentator.
John Hersey, 1914-98, foreign correspondent for *Time*, *Life*, and *The New Yorker*; author.
Marguerite Higgins, 1920-66, reporter, war correspondent.
Christopher Hitchens, 1949-2011, columnist and literary critic.
Hedda Hopper, 1885-1966, Hollywood gossip columnist.
Roy Howard, 1883-1964, editor, executive; Scripps-Howard papers and United Press (later United Press International).
Chet (Chester Robert) Huntley, 1911-74, co-anchor of NBC's *Huntley-Brinkley Report*.
Ada Louise Huxtable, 1921-2013, architecture critic.
Ralph Ingersoll, 1900-85, editor; *Fortune*, *Time*, *Life* exec.
Molly Ivins, 1944-2007, author, syndicated political columnist.
Peter Jennings, 1938-2005, ABC correspondent, anchor.
Pauline Kael, 1919-2001, film critic.
H. V. (Hans von) Kaltenborn, 1878-1965, radio commentator, reporter.
Murray Kempton, 1917-97, reporter, columnist for magazines and newspapers, including *NY Post*.
Dorothy Kilgallen, 1913-65, crime reporter, columnist.
James J. Kilpatrick, 1920-2010, political columnist, author and television personality.
John S. Knight, 1894-1981, editor, publisher; founded Knight newspaper group, which merged into Knight-Ridder.
Joseph Kraft, 1942-86, foreign policy columnist.
Irving Kristol, 1920-2009, columnist, commentator.
Arthur Krock, 1886-1974, *NY Times* political writer, Washington bureau chief.
Charles Kuralt, 1934-97, TV anchor; host of CBS "On the Road" featuring stories about life in the U.S.
Ann Landers (Eppie Lederer), 1918-2002, advice columnist.
David Lawrence, 1888-1973, reporter, columnist, publisher; founded *U.S. News & World Report*.
Frank Leslie, 1821-80, engraver, publisher of newspapers and magazines, notably *Leslie's Illustrated Newspaper*.
Anthony Lewis, 1927-2013, legal journalist.
Alexander Liberman, 1912-99, editorial director for Condé Nast magazines.
A(bbott) J(oseph) Liebling, 1904-63, foreign correspondent, critic; principally with *The New Yorker*.
Walter Lippmann, 1889-1974, political analyst, social critic, columnist, author.
Peter Lisagor, 1915-76, Washington bureau chief, *Chicago Daily News*; broadcast commentator.
David Ross Locke, 1833-88, humorist, satirist under pseudonym P.V. Nasby; owned *Toledo (Ohio) Blade*.
Elijah Parish Lovejoy, 1802-37, abolitionist editor in St. Louis and in Alton, IL; killed by proslavery mob.
Clare Booth Luce, 1903-87, war correspondent for *Life*, diplomat, playwright.
Henry R. Luce, 1898-1967, founded *Time*, *Fortune*, *Life*, *Sports Illustrated*.
Dwight Macdonald, 1906-82, reporter, social critic.
Don Marquis, 1878-1937, humor columnist for *NY Sun* and *NY Tribune*; wrote "Archy and Mehitabel" stories.
Nancy Hicks Maynard, 1946-2008, African American publisher, journalist.
Robert Maynard, 1937-97, first African American editor and then owner of major U.S. paper, the *Oakland Tribune*.
C(harles) K(enny) McClatchy, 1858-1936, founder of McClatchy newspaper chain.
Sarah McClendon, 1910-2003, veteran White House correspondent.
Samuel McClure, 1857-1949, founder (1893) of *McClure's Magazine*, famous for its investigative reporting.
Anne O'Hare McCormick, 1889-1954, foreign correspondent; first woman on *NY Times* editorial board.
Robert R. McCormick, 1880-1955, editor, publisher, executive of *Chicago Tribune* and *NY Daily News*.
Ralph McGill, 1893-1969, crusading editor, publisher of *Atlanta Constitution*.
Mary McGrory, 1918-2004, Washington columnist.
O(scar) O(dd) McIntyre, 1884-1938, feature writer, syndicated columnist on everyday life in New York City.
Joseph Medill, 1823-99, longtime editor of the *Chicago Tribune*.
H(enry) L(ouis) Mencken, 1880-1956, reporter, editor, columnist with *Baltimore Sun* papers; anti-establishment viewpoint.
Edwin Meredith, 1876-1928, founder of magazine company.
Frank A. Munsey, 1854-1925, owner, editor, and publisher of newspapers and magazines, including *Munsey's Magazine*.
Edward R. Murrow, 1908-65, broadcast reporter, exec.; reported from Britain in WWII; hosted *See It Now*, *Person to Person*.
Allen Neuharth, 1924-2013, *USA Today* founder.
Edwin Newman, 1919-2010, NBC news correspondent.
Louella Parsons, 1881-1972, Hollywood gossip columnist.
Ethel L. Payne, 1911-91, African American civil rights reporter.
Daniel Pearl, 1963-2002, American journalist; kidnapped and murdered in Pakistan.
Drew (Andrew Russell) Pearson, 1897-1969, investigative reporter, columnist.
(James) Westbrook Pegler, 1894-1969, reporter, columnist.
Shirley Povich, 1905-98, sports columnist.
Joseph Pulitzer, 1847-1911, *NY World* publisher; founded Columbia Journalism School, Pulitzer Prizes.
Joseph Pulitzer II, 1885-1955, longtime *St. Louis Post-Dispatch* editor, publisher; built it into major paper.
Ernie Pyle, 1900-45, reporter, war correspondent; killed in WWII.
William Raspberry, 1935-2012, public affairs columnist.
Henry Raymond, 1820-69, cofounder, editor, *NY Times*.
Harry Reasoner, 1923-91, ABC and CBS news reporter, anchor.
John Reed, 1887-1920, reporter; foreign correspondent famous for coverage of Bolshevik Revolution; buried at the Kremlin.
Whitelaw Reid, 1837-1912, longtime editor, *NY Tribune*.
James Reston, 1909-95, *NY Times* political reporter, columnist.
Frank Reynolds, 1923-83, ABC reporter, anchor.
(Henry) Grantland Rice, 1880-1954, sportswriter.
Jacob Riis, 1849-1914, reporter, photographer; exposed slum conditions in *How the Other Half Lives*.
Max Robinson, 1939-88, first African American to anchor network news (ABC), 1978.
Andy Rooney, 1919-2011, radio and TV commentator (*60 Minutes*).
A. M. Rosenthal, 1922-2006, reporter, editor for *NY Times* (1943-99).
Harold Ross, 1892-1951, founder, editor, *The New Yorker*.
Carl T. Rowan, 1925-2000, reporter, columnist, author.
Mike Royko, 1932-97, Chicago newspaper columnist; wrote *Boss*, biography of Mayor Richard J. Daley (1902-76).
Louis Rukeyser, 1933-2006, TV journalist, financial analyst; hosted *Wall Street Week* on public television.
(Alfred) Damon Runyon, 1884-1946, sportswriter, columnist; stories collected in *Guys and Dolls*.
Tim Russert, 1950-2008, TV journalist; moderator of *Meet the Press* (NBC).
John B. Russwurm, 1799-1851, cofounded (1827) nation's first black newspaper, *Freedom's Journal*, in New York, NY.
William Safire, 1929-2009, Pulitzer Prize-winning columnist, *NY Times*.
Adela Rogers St. Johns, 1894-1988, reporter, sportswriter for Hearst newspapers.
Pierre Salinger, 1925-2004, press sec. under Pres. Kennedy and Johnson, foreign correspondent.
Harrison Salisbury, 1908-93, reporter, foreign correspondent; Soviet specialist.
Andrew Sarris, 1928-2012, film critic, *Village Voice*.
Daniel Schorr, 1916-2010, broadcast and print journalist.
E(dward) W(illis) Scripps, 1854-1926, founded first large U.S. newspaper chain, pioneered syndication.
Eric Sevareid, 1912-92, war correspondent, radio newscaster, CBS commentator.
Anthony Shadid, 1968-2012, foreign correspondent.
Randy Shilts, 1951-94, journalist; author of *And the Band Played On*.
William L. Shirer, 1904-93, broadcaster, foreign correspondent; wrote *The Rise and Fall of the Third Reich*.
Howard K. Smith, 1914-2002, ABC news reporter, anchor.
Red (Walter) Smith, 1905-82, sportswriter.
Edgar P. Snow, 1905-71, correspondent; expert on Chinese Communist movement.
Tony Snow, 1955-2008, columnist, radio/TV journalist, White House press sec.
Tom Snyder, 1936-2007, television journalist.
Lawrence Spivak, 1900-94, co-creator, moderator, producer of *Meet the Press*.
(Joseph) Lincoln Steffens, 1866-1936, muckraking journalist.
I(sidor) F(einstein) Stone, 1907-89, one-man editor of *I. F. Stone's Weekly*.
Arthur Hays Sulzberger, 1891-1968, long-time publisher of *NY Times* (1935-61).
Arthur Ochs "Punch" Sulzberger, 1926-2012, long-time publisher of *NY Times* (1963-92).
C(yrus) L(eo) Sulzberger, 1912-93, *NY Times* foreign correspondent, columnist.
David Susskind, 1920-87, TV producer, public affairs talk-show host (*Open End*).
John Cameron Swayze, 1906-95, early TV newscaster (NBC).
Herbert Bayard Swope, 1882-1958, war correspondent, editor of *NY World*.
Ida Tarbell, 1857-1944, muckraking journalist.
Helen Thomas, 1920-2013, White House correspondent, 1959-2010.
Isaiah Thomas, 1750-1831, printer, publisher; cofounder of revolutionary journal, *Massachusetts Spy*.
Lowell Thomas, 1892-1981, radio newscaster, world traveler.
Dorothy Thompson, 1894-1961, foreign correspondent, columnist, radio commentator.
Hunter S. Thompson, 1937-2005, political journalist, author; *Fear and Loathing on the Campaign Trail* (1972).
Kenneth Thompson, 1923-2006, Canadian media magnate; owned Toronto *Globe and Mail* newspaper.
Abigail Van Buren (Pauline Phllips), 1918-2013, advice columnist.
Mike Wallace, 1918-2012, TV journalist (*60 Minutes*).
Ida Bell Wells-Barnett, 1862-1931, African American reporter, editor, anti-lynching crusader.
William Allen White, 1868-1944, newspaper editor, publisher.
Tom Wicker, 1926-2011, *NY Times* political reporter, columnist.
Walter Winchell, 1897-1972, reporter, columnist, broadcaster of celebrity news.
John Peter Zenger, 1697-1746, printer, journalist; acquitted in precedent-setting libel suit (1735).

Military and Naval Leaders of the Past

Reviewed by Alan C. Aimone, U.S. Military Academy Library.

Alexander the Great, 356-323 BCE, (Maced.) conquered Persia and much of the world known to Europeans.
Harold Alexander, 1891-1969, (Br.) led Allied invasion of Italy, 1943, WWII.
Ethan Allen, 1738-89, (U.S.) headed Green Mountain Boys; captured Ft. Ticonderoga, 1775, Amer. Rev.
Edmund Allenby, 1861-1936, (Br.) in Boer War, WWI; led Egyptian expeditionary force, 1917-18.
Benedict Arnold, 1741-1801, (U.S.) victorious at Saratoga; tried to betray West Point to British, Amer. Rev.
Henry "Hap" Arnold, 1886-1950, (U.S.) commanded Army Air Force in WWII.
Ashurnasirpal II, 884-859 BCE, (Assyria) king; began Assyrian conquest of Middle East.
John Barry, 1745-1803, (U.S.) won numerous sea battles during Amer. Rev.
Pierre Beauregard, 1818-93, (U.S.) Confed. general; ordered bombardment of Ft. Sumter that began Civil War.
Belisarius, c. 505-565, (Byzant.) won remarkable victories for Byzantine emperor Justinian I.
Gebhard von Blücher, 1742-1819, (Ger.) helped defeat Napoleon at Waterloo.
Simón Bolívar, 1783-1830, (Venez.) S. Amer. revolutionary who liberated much of the continent from Spanish rule.
Napoleon Bonaparte, 1769-1821, (Fr.) defeated Russia and Austria at Austerlitz, 1805; invaded Russia, 1812; defeated at Waterloo, 1815.
Edward Braddock, 1695-1755, (Br.) commanded forces in French and Indian War.
Omar N. Bradley, 1893-1981, (U.S.) headed U.S. ground troops in Normandy invasion, 1944, WWII.
John Burgoyne, 1722-92, (Br.) general; defeated at Saratoga, Amer. Rev.
Julius Caesar, 100-44 BCE, (Rom.) general and politician; conquered northern Gaul, overthrew Roman Republic.
Charlemagne, 742-814, (Fr.) king of the Franks, Holy Roman Emperor; conquered most of Western Europe.
Claire Lee Chennault, 1893-1958, (U.S.) headed Flying Tigers in WWII.
El Cid (Rodrigo Diaz de Vivar), 1040-99, (Sp.) renowned knight; captured Valencia (1094), hero of "Song of Cid" epic.
Mark W. Clark, 1896-1984, (U.S.) helped plan N African invasion in WWII; commander of UN forces, Korean War.
Karl von Clausewitz, 1780-1831, (Prus.) military theorist.
Lucius D. Clay, 1897-1978, (U.S.) led Berlin airlift, 1948-49.
Henry Clinton, 1738-95, (Br.) commander of forces in Amer. Rev., 1778-81.
Cochise, c. 1815-74, (Amer. Ind.) chief of Chiricahua band of Apache Indians in Southwest U.S.
Charles Cornwallis, 1738-1805, (Br.) victorious at Brandywine, 1777; surrendered at Yorktown, Amer. Rev.
Hernán Cortés, 1485-1547, (Sp.) led Spanish conquistadors in the defeat of the Aztec empire, 1519-28.
Crazy Horse, 1849-77, (Amer. Ind.) Sioux war chief victorious at Battle of Little Bighorn.
George Armstrong Custer, 1839-76, (U.S.) army officer defeated and killed at Battle of Little Bighorn.
Benjamin O. Davis Jr., 1912-2002, (U.S.) leader of WWII black aviators; first African American general in U.S. Air Force.
Benjamin O. Davis Sr., 1877-1970, (U.S.) first African American general in U.S. Army, 1940.
Moshe Dayan, 1915-81, (Isr.) directed campaigns in the 1967, 1973 Arab-Israeli wars.
Stephen Decatur, 1779-1820, (U.S.) naval hero of Barbary wars, War of 1812.
Anton Denikin, 1872-1947, (Russ.) led White forces in Russian civil war.
George Dewey, 1837-1917, (U.S.) destroyed Spanish fleet at Manila, 1898, Span.-Amer. War.
Karl Doenitz, 1891-1980, (Ger.) submarine cmdr. in chief and naval cmdr., WWII; last pres. of Third Reich.
Jimmy Doolittle, 1896-1993, (U.S.) led 1942 air raid on Tokyo and other Japanese cities in WWII.
Hugh Dowding, 1882-1970, (Br.) headed RAF Fighter Command, 1936-40, WWII.
Jubal Early, 1816-94, (U.S.) Confed. general; led raid on Washington, DC, 1864, Civil War.
Dwight D. Eisenhower, 1890-1969, (U.S.) commanded Allied forces in Europe, WWII.
Erich von Falkenhayn, 1861-1922, (Ger.) minister of war, general, commander at Verdun in WWI.
David Farragut, 1801-70, (U.S.) Union admiral; captured New Orleans, Mobile Bay, Civil War.
John Arbuthnot Fisher, 1841-1920, (Br.) WWI admiral; naval reformer.
Ferdinand Foch, 1851-1929, (Fr.) headed victorious Allied armies, 1918, WWI.
Nathan Bedford Forrest, 1821-77, (U.S.) Confed. general; led raids against Union supply lines, Civil War.
Frederick the Great, 1712-86, (Prus.) led Prussia in Seven Years War.
Horatio Gates, 1728-1806, (U.S.) commanded army at Saratoga, Amer. Rev.
Genghis Khan, 1162-1227, (Mongol) unified Mongol tribes, subjugated much of Asia, 1206-21.
Geronimo, 1829-1909, (Amer. Ind.) leader of Chiricahua band of Apache Indians.
Vo Nguyen Giap, 1911?-2013, (Viet.) commanded People's Army of Vietnam against U.S.
Charles G. Gordon, 1833-85, (Br.) led forces in China, Crimean War; killed at Khartoum.
Ulysses S. Grant, 1822-85, (U.S.) headed Union army, Civil War, 1864-65; forced Robert E. Lee's surrender, 1865.
Nathanael Greene, 1742-86, (U.S.) defeated British in Southern campaign, 1780-81, Amer. Rev.
Heinz Guderian, 1888-1954, (Ger.) tank theorist; led panzer tank forces in Poland, France, Russia, WWII.
Gustavus Adolphus, 1594-1632, (Swed.) king, military tactician, reformer; led forces in Thirty Years' War.
Douglas Haig, 1861-1928, (Br.) led British armies in France, 1915-18, WWI.
William F. Halsey, 1882-1959, (U.S.) defeated Japanese fleet at Leyte Gulf, 1944, WWII.
Hannibal, 247-183 BCE, (Carthage) invaded Rome, crossing Alps, in Second Punic War, 218-201 BCE.
Sir Arthur Travers Harris, 1895-1984, (Br.) led Britain's WWII bomber command.
Paul von Hindenburg, 1847-1934, (Ger.) chief of general staff, WWI; second pres. of Weimar Republic.
Richard Howe, 1726-99, (Br.) commanded navy in Amer. Rev., 1776-78; June 1 victory against French, 1794.
William Howe, 1729-1814, (Br.) commanded forces in Amer. Rev., 1776-78.
Isaac Hull, 1773-1843, (U.S.) sunk British frigate *Guerriere*, War of 1812.
Thomas "Stonewall" Jackson, 1824-63, (U.S.) Confed. general; led Shenandoah Valley campaign, Civil War.
Daniel James Jr., 1920-78, (U.S.) first black 4-star general, 1975; commander, N. American Air Defense Command.
Joseph Joffre, 1852-1931, (Fr.) headed Allied armies; won Battle of the Marne, 1914, WWI.
John Paul Jones, 1747-92, (U.S.) commanded *Bonhomme Richard* in victory over *Serapis*, Amer. Rev., 1779.
Chief Joseph, c. 1840-1904, (Amer. Ind.) chief of the Nez Percé; forced by U.S. army to retreat and surrender.
Stephen Kearny, 1794-1848, (U.S.) headed Army of the West in Mexican War.
Albert Kesselring, 1885-1960, (Ger.) field marshal who led the defense of Italy in WWII.
Ernest J. King, 1878-1956, (U.S.) key WWII naval strategist.
Horatio H. Kitchener, 1850-1916, (Br.) led forces in Boer War, victorious at Khartoum, organized army in WWI.
Henry Knox, 1750-1806, (U.S.) general in Amer. Rev.; first sec. of war under U.S. Constitution.
Lavrenti Kornilov, 1870-1918, (Russ.) commander-in-chief, 1917; led counter-revolutionary march on Petrograd.
Thaddeus Kosciusko, 1746-1817, (Pol.) aided Amer. Rev.
Walter Krueger, 1881-1967, (U.S.) led Sixth Army in WWII in Southwest Pacific.
Mikhail Kutuzov, 1745-1813, (Russ.) fought at Borodino, Napol. Wars, 1812; abandoned Moscow, forced French retreat.
Marquis de Lafayette, 1757-1834, (Fr.) fought in, secured French aid for Amer. Rev.
T(homas) E. Lawrence (of Arabia), 1888-1935, (Br.) organized revolt of Arabs against Turks in WWI.
William Daniel Leahy, 1875-1959, (U.S.) chief of staff to Pres. Roosevelt in WWII, Fleet Admiral.
Henry (Light-Horse Harry) Lee, 1756-1818, (U.S.) cavalry officer in Amer. Rev.
Robert E. Lee, 1807-70, (U.S.) Confed. general; defeated at Gettysburg, Civil War; surrendered to Grant, 1865.
Curtis LeMay, 1906-90, (U.S.) Air Force cmdr. in WWII, Korean War, Vietnam War.
Lyman Lemnitzer, 1899-1988, (U.S.) WWII hero; later general, chairman of Joint Chiefs of Staff.
James Longstreet, 1821-1904, (U.S.) aided Lee at Gettysburg, Civil War.
Erich Ludendorff, 1865-1937, (Ger.) general; victor at Tannenberg, WWI.
Douglas MacArthur, 1880-1964, (U.S.) commanded forces in SW Pacific in WWII; headed occupation forces in Japan, 1945-51; UN commander in Korean War.
Carl Gustaf Mannerheim, 1867-1951, (Fin.) army officer and pres. of Finland, 1944-46.
Erich von Manstein, 1887-1973, (Ger.) served WWI, WWII; planned invasion of France (1940); convicted of war crimes.
Francis Marion, 1733-95, (U.S.) led guerrilla actions in South Carolina during Amer. Rev.
Duke of Marlborough, 1650-1722, (Br.) led forces against Louis XIV in War of the Spanish Succession.
George C. Marshall, 1880-1959, (U.S.) chief of staff in WWII; authored Marshall Plan.
Maurice, Count of Nassau, 1567-1625, (Neth.) military innovator; led forces in Thirty Years' War.
George B. McClellan, 1826-85, (U.S.) Union general; commanded Army of the Potomac, 1861-62, Civil War.
George Meade, 1815-72, (U.S.) commanded Union forces at Gettysburg, Civil War.
Doris "Dorie" Miller, 1919-43, (U.S.) Navy hero of Pearl Harbor attack; first African American awarded Navy Cross.
Billy Mitchell, 1879-1936, (U.S.) WWI air-power advocate; court-martialed for insubordination, later vindicated.
Helmuth von Moltke, 1800-91, (Ger.) victorious in Austro-Prussian, Franco-Prussian wars.
Louis de Montcalm, 1712-59, (Fr.) headed troops in Canada, French and Indian War; defeated at Quebec, 1759.
Bernard Law Montgomery, 1887-1976, (Br.) stopped German offensive at Alamein, 1942, WWII; helped plan Normandy invasion.

Daniel Morgan, 1736-1802, (U.S.) victorious at Cowpens, 1781, Amer. Rev.
Louis Mountbatten, 1900-79, (Br.) Supreme Allied Commander of SE Asia, 1943-46, WWII.
Joachim Murat, 1767-1815, (Fr.) led cavalry at Marengo, Austerlitz, and Jena, Napoleonic Wars.
Horatio Nelson, 1758-1805, (Br.) naval cmdr.; destroyed French fleet at Trafalgar.
Michel Ney, 1769-1815, (Fr.) commanded forces in Switz., Austria, Russ., Napoleonic Wars; defeated at Waterloo.
Chester Nimitz, 1885-1966, (U.S.) cmdr. of naval forces in Pacific in WWII.
George S. Patton, 1885-1945, (U.S.) led assault on Sicily, 1943, Third Army invasion of Europe, WWII.
Oliver Perry, 1785-1819, (U.S.) won Battle of Lake Erie in War of 1812.
John Pershing, 1860-1948, (U.S.) commanded Mexican border campaign, 1916; Amer. Expeditionary Force, WWI.
Henri Philippe Pétain, 1856-1951, (Fr.) defended Verdun, 1916; headed Vichy government in WWII.
George E. Pickett, 1825-75, (U.S.) Confed. general famed for "charge" at Gettysburg, Civil War.
Charles Portal, 1893-1971, (Br.) chief of staff, Royal Air Force, 1940-45; led in Battle of Britain.
Manfred Freiherr von Richthofen (Red Baron), 1892-1918, (Ger.) WWI flying ace, led elite fighter squadron.
Hyman Rickover, 1900-86, (U.S.) father of nuclear navy.
Matthew Bunker Ridgway, 1895-1993, (U.S.) commanded Allied ground forces in Korean War.
Erwin Rommel, 1891-1944, (Ger.) headed Afrika Korps, WWII.
Gerd von Rundstedt, 1875-1953, (Ger.) supreme cmdr. in West, 1942-45, WWII.
Saladin, 1138-93, (Kurdish Muslim) recaptured Jerusalem from Crusaders.
Aleksandr Samsonov, 1859-1914, (Russ.) led invasion of E Prussia, WWI; defeated at Tannenberg, 1914.
Antonio Lopez de Santa Anna, 1794-1876, (Mex.) defeated Texans at the Alamo; defeated in Mexican War.
Maurice, Count of Saxe, 1696-1750, (Fr.) general, noted tactician; War of Austrian Succession, War of Pol. Succession.
H. Norman Schwarzkopf, 1934-2012, (U.S.) army general; led Persian Gulf War, 1991.
Scipio Africanus the Elder, 234?-183 BCE, (Rom.) hero of Second Punic War; defeated Hannibal, invaded N Africa.
Winfield Scott, 1786-1866, (U.S.) hero of War of 1812; headed forces in Mexican War, took Mexico City.
Philip Sheridan, 1831-88, (U.S.) Union cavalry officer; headed Army of the Shenandoah, 1864-65, Civil War.
William T. Sherman, 1820-91, (U.S.) Union general; sacked Atlanta during "march to the sea," 1864, Civil War.
Sitting Bull, c. 1831-90, (Amer. Ind.) Hunkpapa Sioux chief; victorious at Battle of the Little Big Horn.
Carl Spaatz, 1891-1974, (U.S.) directed strategic bombing against Germany, later Japan, in WWII.
Raymond Spruance, 1886-1969, (U.S.) victorious at Midway Island, 1942, WWII.
Joseph W. Stilwell, 1883-1946, (U.S.) headed forces in the China, Burma, India theater in WWII.
J.E.B. Stuart, 1833-64, (U.S.) Confed. cavalry commander, Civil War.
Sun Tzu, 6th? cent. BCE, (China) general; author of *The Art of War*.
Aleksandr Suvorov, 1729-1800, (Russ.) commanded Allied Russian and Austrian armies, Russo-Turkish War.
Tamerlane, 1336-1405, (Turkoman Mongol) conqueror; established empire from India to Mediterranean Sea.
Tecumseh, 1768-1813, (Amer. Ind.) Shawnee chief; led Indian confederation opposing colonists.
George H. Thomas, 1816-70, (U.S.) saved Union army at Chattanooga, 1863; won at Nashville, 1864, Civil War.
Semyon Timoshenko, 1895-1970, (USSR) defended Moscow, Stalingrad, WWII; led winter offensive, 1942-43.
Alfred von Tirpitz, 1849-1930, (Ger.) responsible for submarine blockade in WWI.
Henri de la Tour d'Auvergne, Viscount of Turenne, 1611-75, (Fr.) marshal; Thirty Years' War, Fronde, War of Devolution.
Sebastien Le Prestre de Vauban, 1633-1707, (Fr.) innovative military engineer, theorist.
Jonathan M. Wainwright, 1883-1953, (U.S.) forced to surrender on Corregidor, Philippines, 1942, WWII.
George Washington, 1732-99, (U.S.) led Continental army, 1775-83, Amer. Rev.
Archibald Wavell, 1883-1950, (Br.) commanded forces in N and E Africa, SE Asia in WWII.
Anthony Wayne, 1745-96, (U.S.) captured Stony Point, NY, 1779, Amer. Rev.
Duke of Wellington, 1769-1852, (Br.) defeated Napoleon at Waterloo, 1815.
William Westmoreland, 1914-2005, (U.S.) commanded forces in Vietnam, 1964-68.
William I (The Conqueror), 1027-87, (Br.) victor, Battle of Hastings, 1066; became first Norman king of England.
James Wolfe, 1727-59, (Br.) captured Quebec from French, 1759, French and Indian War.
Isoroku Yamamoto, 1884-1943, (Jpn.) cmdr. in chief of Japanese fleet, naval planner before and during WWII.
Georgi Zhukov, 1895-1974, (Russ.) defended Moscow, 1941; led assault on Berlin, 1945, WWII.

Philosophers and Religious Figures of the Past

Excludes biblical figures and popes (see Religion chapter). For Greeks and Romans, see also Historical Figures chapter.

Lyman Abbott, 1835-1922, (U.S.) clergyman, reformer; advocate of Christian Socialism.
Pierre Abelard, 1079-1142, (Fr.) philosopher, theologian, teacher; used dialectic method to support Christian beliefs.
Felix Adler, 1851-1933, (U.S.) German-born founder of the Ethical Culture Soc.
Mortimer Adler, 1902-2001, (U.S.) philosopher; helped create "Great Books" program.
(St.) Anselm, c. 1033-1109, (It.) philosopher-theologian, church leader; "ontological argument" for God's existence.
(St.) Thomas Aquinas, 1225-74, (It.) preeminent medieval philosopher-theologian; *Summa Theologica*.
Aristotle, 384-322 BCE, (Gr.) pioneering wide-ranging philosopher, logician, ethician, naturalist.
(St.) Augustine, 354-430, (N Africa) philosopher, theologian, bishop; *Confessions, City of God, On the Trinity*.
J. L. Austin, 1911-60, (Br.) ordinary-language philosopher.
Averroes (Ibn Rushd), 1126-98, (Sp.) Islamic philosopher, physician.
Avicenna (Ibn Sina), 980-1037, (Iran) Islamic philosopher, scientist.
A(lfred) J(ules) Ayer, 1910-89, (Br.) philosopher, logical positivist; *Language, Truth, and Logic*.
Roger Bacon, c. 1214-94, (Eng.) philosopher, scientist.
Bahá'u'lláh (Mirza Husayn Ali), 1817-92, (Pers.) founder of Bahá'í faith.
Karl Barth, 1886-1968, (Switz.) theologian; a leading force in 20th-cent. Protestantism.
Thomas à Becket, 1118-70, (Eng.) archbishop of Canterbury; opposed Henry II, murdered by king's men.
(St.) Benedict, c. 480-547, (It.) founded the Benedictines.
Jeremy Bentham, 1748-1832, (Br.) philosopher, reformer; enunciated utilitarianism.
Henri Bergson, 1859-1941, (Fr.) philosopher of evolution.
George Berkeley, 1685-1753, (Ire.) idealist philosopher, bishop.
John Biddle, 1615-62, (Eng.) founder of English Unitarianism.
Jakob Boehme, 1575-1624, (Ger.) theosophist, mystic.
Dietrich Bonhoeffer, 1906-45, (Ger.) Lutheran theologian, pastor; executed as opponent of Nazis.
William Brewster, 1567-1644, (Eng.) *Mayflower* passenger, Plymouth Colony leader.
Emil Brunner, 1889-1966, (Switz.) Protestant theologian.
Giordano Bruno, 1548-1600, (It.) philosopher, pantheist.
Martin Buber, 1878-1965, (Ger.) Jewish philosopher, theologian; *I and Thou*.
Buddha (Siddhartha Gautama), c. 563-c. 483 BCE, (India) philosopher; founded Buddhism.
John Calvin, 1509-64, (Fr.) theologian; a key figure in the Protestant Reformation.
Rudolph Carnap, 1891-1970, (U.S.) German-born analytic philosopher; a founder of logical positivism.
William Ellery Channing, 1780-1842, (U.S.) clergyman; early spokesman for Unitarianism.
Auguste Comte, 1798-1857, (Fr.) philosopher; originated positivism.
Confucius, 551-479 BCE, (China) founder of Confucianism.
John Cotton, 1584-1652, (Eng.) Puritan theologian.
Thomas Cranmer, 1489-1556, (Eng.) Anglican churchman; wrote much of *Book of Common Prayer*.
Jacques Derrida, 1930-2004, (Fr.) deconstructionist philosopher.
René Descartes, 1596-1650, (Fr.) philosopher, mathematician; "father of modern philosophy"; *Discourse on Method, Meditations on First Philosophy*.
John Dewey, 1859-1952, (U.S.) philosopher, educator; instrumentalist theory of knowledge, progressive education.
Denis Diderot, 1713-84, (Fr.) philosopher, encyclopedist.
John Duns Scotus, c. 1266-1308, (Scot.) Franciscan philosopher, theologian.
Mary Baker Eddy, 1821-1910, (U.S.) founder of Christian Science; *Science and Health*.
Jonathan Edwards, 1703-58, (U.S.) preacher, theologian; "Sinners in the Hands of an Angry God."
(Desiderius) Erasmus, c. 1466-1536, (Neth.) Renaissance humanist; *On the Freedom of the Will*.
Jerry Falwell, 1933-2007, (U.S.) TV evangelist, religious commentator.
Johann Fichte, 1762-1814, (Ger.) idealist philosopher.
Michel Foucault, 1926-84, (Fr.) structuralist philosopher, historian.
George Fox, 1624-91, (Br.) founder of Society of Friends (Quakers).
(St.) Francis of Assisi, 1182-1226, (It.) espoused voluntary poverty, founded Franciscans.
al-Ghazali, 1058-1111, (Iran) Islamic philosopher.
Billy James Hargis, 1925-2004, (U.S.) anti-Communist televangelist; founder of the Church of the Christian Crusade.
Georg W. F. Hegel, 1770-1831, (Ger.) idealist philosopher; *Phenomenology of Mind*.
Martin Heidegger, 1889-1976, (Ger.) existentialist philosopher; affected many fields; *Being and Time*.
Johann G. Herder, 1744-1803, (Ger.) philosopher, cultural historian; a founder of German Romanticism.

Thomas Hobbes, 1588-1679, (Eng.) philosopher, political theorist; *Leviathan*.
David Hume, 1711-76, (Scot.) empiricist philosopher; *Enquiry Concerning Human Understanding*.
Jan Hus, 1369-1415, (Czech.) religious reformer.
Edmund Husserl, 1859-1938, (Ger.) philosopher; founded the phenomenological movement.
Thomas Huxley, 1825-95, (Br.) philosopher, educator.
William Ralph Inge, 1860-1954, (Br.) theologian; explored mystic aspects of Christianity.
William James, 1842-1910, (U.S.) philosopher, psychologist, pragmatist; studied religious experience.
Karl Jaspers, 1883-1969, (Ger.) existentialist philosopher.
Joan of Arc, 1412-31, (Fr.) national heroine, a patron saint of France; key figure in the Hundred Years' War.
Immanuel Kant, 1724-1804, (Ger.) philosopher; founder of modern critical philosophy; *Critique of Pure Reason*.
Thomas à Kempis, c. 1380-1471, (Ger.) monk, devotional writer; *Imitation of Christ* attributed to him.
Soren Kierkegaard, 1813-55, (Den.) religious philosopher, pre-existentialist; *Either/Or*, *The Sickness Unto Death*.
John Knox, 1505-72, (Scot.) leader of Protestant Reformation in Scotland.
Lao-Tzu, 604-531 BCE, (China) philosopher; considered the founder of the Taoist religion.
Gottfried von Leibniz, 1646-1716, (Ger.) rationalistic philosopher, logician, mathematician.
John Locke, 1632-1704, (Eng.) political theorist, empiricist philosopher; *Essay Concerning Human Understanding*.
(St.) Ignatius Loyola, 1491-1556, (Sp.) founder of the Jesuits; *Spiritual Exercises*.
Martin Luther, 1483-1546, (Ger.) leader of the Protestant Reformation; founded Lutheran church.
Jean-Francois Lyotard, 1924-98, (Fr.) postmodern philosopher, lecturer; *The Post-Modern Condition*.
Maimonides, 1135-1204, (Sp.) major Jewish philosopher.
Gabriel Marcel, 1889-1973, (Fr.) Rom. Cath. existentialist philosopher, dramatist.
Jacques Maritain, 1882-1973, (Fr.) neo-Thomist philosopher.
Cotton Mather, 1663-1728, (U.S.) defender of orthodox Puritanism; founded Yale, 1701.
Aimee Semple McPherson, 1890-1944, (Can.) Pentecostal evangelist.
Philipp Melanchthon, 1497-1560, (Ger.) theologian, humanist; an important voice in the Reformation.
Maurice Merleau-Ponty, 1908-61, (Fr.) existentialist philosopher; *Phenomenology of Perception*.
Thomas Merton, 1915-68, (U.S.) Trappist monk, spiritual writer; *The Seven Storey Mountain*.
Dwight Moody, 1837-99, (U.S.) evangelist.
Rev. Sun Myung Moon, 1920-2012, (N. Kor.) Unification Church founder.
G(eorge) E(dward) Moore, 1873-1958, (Br.) philosopher; *Principia Ethica*, "A Defense of Common Sense."
Muhammad, c. 570-632, (Arab.) prophet of Islam.
Elijah Muhammad, 1897-1975, (U.S.) founder of Black Muslim group, Nation of Islam.
Heinrich Muhlenberg, 1711-87, (Ger.) organized the Lutheran Church in America.
John H. Newman, 1801-90, (Br.) Rom. Cath. convert, cardinal; led Oxford Movement; *Apologia pro Vita Sua*.
Reinhold Niebuhr, 1892-1971, (U.S.) Protestant theologian.
Richard Niebuhr, 1894-1962, (U.S.) Protestant theologian.
Friedrich Nietzsche, 1844-1900, (Ger.) philosopher; *The Birth of Tragedy*, *Beyond Good and Evil*, *Thus Spake Zarathustra*.
Robert Nozick, 1938-2002, (U.S.) political philosopher; *Anarchy, State, and Utopia*.
Blaise Pascal, 1623-62, (Fr.) philosopher, mathematician; *Pensées*.
(St.) Patrick, c. 389-c. 461, (Br.) brought Christianity to Ireland.
Norman Vincent Peale, 1898-1993, (U.S.) minister, author; *The Power of Positive Thinking*.
C(harles) S. Peirce, 1839-1914, (U.S.) philosopher, logician; originated concept of pragmatism, 1878.
Plato, c. 428-347 BCE, (Gr.) philosopher; wrote Socratic dialogues; argued for immortality of soul, indep. reality of ideas or forms; *Republic*, *Meno*, *Phaedo*, *Apology*.
Plotinus, 205-70, (Rom.) a founder of neo-Platonism; *Enneads*.
W(illard) V(an) O(rman) Quine, 1908-2001, (U.S.) philosopher, logician; "On What There Is."
John Rawls, 1922-2002, (U.S.) political philosopher; *A Theory of Justice*.
Oral Roberts, 1918-2009, (U.S.) televangelist, university founder.
Moishe Rosen, 1932-2010, (U.S.) Jews for Jesus founder.
Josiah Royce, 1855-1916, (U.S.) idealist philosopher.
Bertrand Russell, 1872-1970, (Br.) philosopher, logician; one of the founders of modern logic; prolific popular writer.
Charles T. Russell, 1852-1916, (U.S.) founder of Jehovah's Witnesses.
Gilbert Ryle, 1900-76, (Br.) analytic philosopher; *The Concept of Mind*.
George Santayana, 1863-1952, (U.S.) philosopher, writer, critic; *The Sense of Beauty*, *The Realms of Being*.
Jean-Paul Sartre, 1905-80, (Fr.) philosopher, novelist, playwright; *Nausea*, *No Exit*, *Being and Nothingness*.
Friedrich von Schelling, 1775-1854, (Ger.) philosopher of romantic movement.
Friedrich Schleiermacher, 1768-1834, (Ger.) theologian; a founder of modern Protestant theology.
Arthur Schopenhauer, 1788-1860, (Ger.) philosopher; *The World as Will and Idea*.
Robert Schuller, 1926-2015, (U.S.) evangelist; Crystal Cathedral founder.
Albert Schweitzer, 1875-1965, (Ger.) theologian, social philosopher, medical missionary.
Joseph Smith, 1805-44, (U.S.) founded Latter-Day Saints (Mormon) movement, 1830.
Socrates, 469-399 BCE, (Gr.) philosopher immortalized by Plato.
Herbert Spencer, 1820-1903, (Br.) philosopher of evolution.
Herbert Spiegel, 1914-2009, (U.S.) psychiatrist who popularized hypnosis.
Baruch de Spinoza, 1632-77, (Neth.) rationalist philosopher; *Ethics*.
John Stott, 1921-2011, (Br.) evangelical Anglican cleric.
Billy Sunday, 1862-1935, (U.S.) evangelist.
Daisetz Teitaro Suzuki, 1870-1966, (Jpn.) Buddhist scholar.
Emanuel Swedenborg, 1688-1772, (Swed.) philosopher, mystic; *Principia*.
Pierre Teilhard de Chardin, 1881-1955, (Fr.) Jesuit priest, paleontologist, philosopher-theologian; *The Divine Milieu*.
(St.) Therese of Lisieux, 1873-97, (Fr.) Carmelite nun ("Little Flower"), revered for everyday sanctity; *The Story of a Soul*.
Paul Tillich, 1886-1965, (U.S.) German-born philosopher, theologian; brought depth psychology to Protestantism.
John Wesley, 1703-91, (Br.) theologian, evangelist; founded Methodism.
Alfred North Whitehead, 1861-1947, (Br.) philosopher, mathematician; *Process and Reality*.
William of Occam, c. 1285-c. 1349, (Eng.) medieval scholastic philosopher, nominalist.
Roger Williams, c. 1603-83, (U.S.) clergyman; championed religious freedom and separation of church and state.
Ludwig Wittgenstein, 1889-1951, (Austria) philosopher; major influence on contemporary language philosophy; *Tractatus Logico-Philosophicus*, *Philosophical Investigations*.
John Woolman, 1720-72, (U.S.) Quaker social reformer, abolitionist, writer; *The Journal*.
John Wycliffe, 1320-84, (Eng.) theologian, reformer.
(St.) Francis Xavier, 1506-52, (Sp.) Jesuit missionary; "Apostle of the Indies."
Brigham Young, 1801-77, (U.S.) Mormon leader after Joseph Smith's assassination; colonized Utah.
Huldrych Zwingli, 1484-1531, (Switz.) theologian; led Swiss Protestant Reformation.

Political Leaders of the Past

U.S. presidents, vice presidents, Supreme Court justices, and signers of the Declaration of Independence listed elsewhere.

Abu Bakr, 573-634, (Arab.) Muslim leader, first caliph, chosen successor to Muhammad.
Dean Acheson, 1893-1971, (U.S.) sec. of state; architect of Cold War foreign policy.
Samuel Adams, 1722-1803, (U.S.) patriot; Boston Tea Party firebrand.
Konrad Adenauer, 1876-1967, (Ger.) first West German chancellor.
Emilio Aguinaldo, 1869-1964, (Philip.) revolutionary; fought against Spain and the U.S.
Corazon Aquino, 1933-2009, (Philip.) pres. of the Philippines, 1986-92.
Akbar, 1542-1605, Mogul emperor of India.
Carl Albert, 1908-2000, (U.S.) House rep. (D, OK), Speaker, 1971-76.
Salvador Allende Gossens, 1908-73, (Chile) Marxist pres., 1970-73; ousted and died in coup.
Idi Amin, 1925-2003, (Uganda) Ugandan ruler, 1971-79; blamed for hundreds of thousands of deaths.
Yasir Arafat, 1929-2004, (Egypt) leader of the Palestine Liberation Organization (PLO).
Herbert H. Asquith, 1852-1928, (Br.) Liberal prime min.; instituted major social reforms.
Hafez al Assad, 1930-2000, (Syr.) pres. of Syria, 1970-2000.
Atahualpa, 1500?-33, (Inca) ruling chief of Peru.
Kemal Ataturk, 1881-1938, (Turk.) founded modern Turkey.
Clement Attlee, 1883-1967, (Br.) Labour party leader, prime min.; enacted natl. health care system, nationalized many industries.
Stephen F. Austin, 1793-1836, (U.S.) led Texas colonization.
Mikhail Bakunin, 1814-76, (Russ.) revolutionary; leading exponent of anarchism.
Arthur J. Balfour, 1848-1930, (Br.) foreign sec. under Lloyd George; issued Balfour Declaration backing Zionism.
Bernard M. Baruch, 1870-1965, (U.S.) financier, govt. adviser.
Fulgencio Batista y Zaldívar, 1901-73, (Cub.) Cuban pres., 1940-44, 1952-59; overthrown by Castro.
Lord Beaverbrook, 1879-1964, (Br.) financier, statesman, newspaper owner.
Menachem Begin, 1913-92, (Isr.) Israeli prime min.; shared 1978 Nobel Peace Prize.

Ahmed Ben Bella, 1918-2012, (Alg.) first Algerian pres., 1963-65.
Eduard Benes, 1884-1948, (Czech.) pres. during interwar and post-WWII eras.
David Ben-Gurion, 1886-1973, (Isr.) first prime min. of Israel, 1948-53, 1955-63.
Thomas Hart Benton, 1782-1858, (U.S.) MO senator; championed agrarian interests and westward expansion.
Aneurin Bevan, 1897-1960, (Br.) Labour party leader.
Ernest Bevin, 1881-1951, (Br.) Labour party leader, foreign minister; helped lay foundation for NATO.
Benazir Bhutto, 1953-2007, (Pak.) prime min. of Pakistan.
Otto von Bismarck, 1815-98, (Ger.) statesman known as the Iron Chancellor; uniter of Germany, 1870.
James G. Blaine, 1830-93, (U.S.) Republican politician, diplomat; influential in Pan-American movement.
Léon Blum, 1872-1950, (Fr.) socialist leader, writer; headed first Popular Front government.
William E. Borah, 1865-1940, (U.S.) isolationist senator (R, ID); helped block U.S. membership in League of Nations.
Cesare Borgia, 1476-1507, (It.) soldier, politician; an outstanding figure of the Italian Renaissance.
P. W. Botha, 1916-2006, (S. Afr.) S. African president, prime min.
Tom Bradley, 1917-98, (U.S.) first African American mayor of L.A.
Willy Brandt, 1913-92, (Ger.) statesman, chancellor of West Germany, 1969-74; promoted East/West peace, *Ostpolitik*.
Leonid Brezhnev, 1906-82, (USSR) Soviet leader, 1964-82.
Aristide Briand, 1862-1932, (Fr.) foreign min.; chief architect of Locarno Pact and anti-war Kellogg-Briand Pact.
William Jennings Bryan, 1860-1925, (U.S.) Democratic, populist leader, orator; three times lost race for presidency.
Ralph Bunche, 1904-71, (U.S.) first black person to win the Nobel Peace Prize, 1950; undersecretary of the UN, 1950.
Robert Byrd, 1917-2010, (U.S.) longest serving U.S. senator (D, WV).
John C. Calhoun, 1782-1850, (U.S.) political leader; champion of states' rights and a symbol of the Old South.
James Callaghan (Baron Callaghan), 1912-2005, (Br.) Labour party politician, prime min., 1976-79.
Robert Castlereagh, 1769-1822, (Br.) foreign sec.; guided Grand Alliance against Napoleon.
Camillo Benso Cavour, 1810-61, (It.) statesman; largely responsible for uniting Italy under the House of Savoy.
Nicolae Ceausescu, 1918-89, (Roman.) Communist leader, head of state, 1967-89; executed.
Austen Chamberlain, 1863-1937, (Br.) statesman; helped finalize Locarno Treaties, both 1925.
Neville Chamberlain, 1869-1940, (Br.) Conservative prime min. whose appeasement of Hitler led to Munich Pact.
Hugo Chávez, 1954-2013, (Venez.) socialist Venezuelan pres., 1999-2013.
Chiang Kai-shek, 1887-1975, (China) Nationalist Chinese pres. whose government was driven from mainland to Taiwan.
Madame Chiang Kai-shek (Mayling Soong), 1898-2003, (China) highly influential wife of Nationalist Chinese leader Chiang Kai-shek.
Shirley Chisholm, 1924-2005, (U.S.) first black woman elected to U.S. House (1968, D, NY); pres. contender, 1972.
Warren Christopher, 1925-2011, (U.S.) secretary of state, diplomat.
Winston Churchill, 1874-1965, (Br.) prime min., soldier, author; guided Britain through WWII.
Galeazzo Ciano, 1903-44, (It.) Fascist foreign minister; helped create Rome-Berlin Axis; executed by Benito Mussolini.
Henry Clay, 1777-1852, (U.S.) "The Great Compromiser"; one of the most influential pre-Civil War political leaders.
Georges Clemenceau, 1841-1929, (Fr.) twice prem.; Woodrow Wilson's antagonist at Paris Peace Conference after WWI.
DeWitt Clinton, 1769-1828, (U.S.) political leader; responsible for promoting the Erie Canal.
Robert Clive, 1725-74, (Br.) first administrator of Bengal; laid foundation for British Empire in India.
Jean Baptiste Colbert, 1619-83, (Fr.) statesman; influential under Louis XIV; created the French navy.
Bettino Craxi, 1934-2000, (It.) Italy's first post-WWII Socialist prem.
David Crockett, 1786-1836, (U.S.) frontiersman, congressman; died defending the Alamo.
Oliver Cromwell, 1599-1658, (Br.) Lord Protector of England; led parliamentary forces during Civil War.
Mario Cuomo, 1932-2015, NY governor (D), 1983-94.
Curzon of Kedleston, 1859-1925, (Br.) viceroy of India, foreign sec.; major force in post-WWI world.
Édouard Daladier, 1884-1970, (Fr.) Radical Socialist politician, arrested by Vichy, interned by Germans until 1945.
Richard J. Daley, 1902-76, (U.S.) Chicago mayor.
Georges Danton, 1759-94, (Fr.) leading French Rev. figure.
Jefferson Davis, 1808-89, (U.S.) pres. of the Confederacy.
Charles G. Dawes, 1865-1951, (U.S.) statesman, banker; advanced plan to stabilize post-WWI German finances.
William L. Dawson, 1886-1970, (U.S.) U.S. rep. (D, IL); first black chairman of a major U.S. House committee.
Alcide De Gasperi, 1881-1954, (It.) prime min.; founder of Christian Democratic party.
Charles De Gaulle, 1890-1970, (Fr.) general, statesman; first pres. of the Fifth Republic.
Deng Xiaoping, 1904-97, (China) "paramount leader" of China; backed economic modernization.
Eamon De Valera, 1882-1975, (Ire.-U.S.) statesman; led fight for Irish independence.
Thomas E. Dewey, 1902-71, (U.S.) NY governor (R); twice lost in try for presidency.
Ngo Dinh Diem, 1901-63, (Viet.) South Vietnamese pres.; assassinated in government takeover.
Everett M. Dirksen, 1896-1969, (U.S.) Senate Republican minority leader, orator.
Benjamin Disraeli, 1804-81, (Br.) prime min.; considered founder of modern Conservative party.
Anatoly Dobrynin, 1919-2010, (Russ.) diplomat and Soviet amb. to U.S. (1962-86).
Engelbert Dollfuss, 1892-1934, (Austria) chancellor; assassinated by Austrian Nazis.
Andrea Doria, 1466-1560, (It.) Genoese admiral, statesman; called "Father of Peace" and "Liberator of Genoa."
Stephen A. Douglas, 1813-61, (U.S.) Democratic leader, orator; ran against Lincoln for IL sen. seat, presidency.
Alexander Dubcek, 1921-92, (Czech.) statesman whose attempted liberalization was crushed, 1968.
John Foster Dulles, 1888-1959, (U.S.) sec. of state under Eisenhower; Cold War policy maker.
Lawrence Eagleburger, 1930-2011, (U.S.) diplomat and foreign policy advisor.
Abba Eban, 1915-2002, (Isr.) diplomat; foreign min., 1966-74.
Friedrich Ebert, 1871-1925, (Ger.) Social Democratic movement leader; first pres., Weimar Republic, 1919-25.
Sir Anthony Eden, 1897-1977, (Br.) foreign sec., prime min. during Suez invasion of 1956.
Ludwig Erhard, 1897-1977, (Ger.) economist, West German chancellor; led nation's economic rise after WWII.
King Fahd, 1923-2005, (Saudi Arabia) monarch from 1982 but inactive after 1995 stroke; encouraged U.S. relations.
Geraldine Ferraro, 1935-2011, (U.S.) U.S. rep. (D, NY), vice-pres. nominee.
Joao Baptista de Figueiredo, 1918-99, (Braz.) president of Brazil; restored the nation's democracy.
Hamilton Fish, 1808-93, (U.S.) sec. of state; successfully mediated disputes with Great Britain, Latin America.
James V. Forrestal, 1892-1949, (U.S.) sec. of navy, first sec. of defense.
Francisco Franco, 1892-1975, (Sp.) leader of rebel forces during Spanish Civil War, longtime ruler of Spain.
Benjamin Franklin, 1706-90, (U.S.) printer, publisher, author, inventor, scientist, diplomat.
Louis de Frontenac, 1620-98, (Fr.) governor of New France (Canada); encouraged explorations, fought Iroquois.
J. William Fulbright, 1905-95, (U.S.) U.S. senator (D, AR); leading figure in U.S. foreign policy during Cold War years.
Hugh Gaitskell, 1906-63, (Br.) Labour party leader; major force in reversing its stand for unilateral disarmament.
Albert Gallatin, 1761-1849, (U.S.) sec. of treasury; instrumental in negotiating end of War of 1812.
Léon Gambetta, 1838-82, (Fr.) statesman, politician; one of the founders of the Third Republic.
Indira Gandhi, 1917-84, (India) daughter of Jawaharlal Nehru; prime min. of India, 1966-77, 1980-84; assassinated.
Mohandas K. Gandhi, 1869-1948, (India) political leader, ascetic; led movement against British rule; assassinated.
Giuseppe Garibaldi, 1807-82, (It.) patriot, soldier; a leader in the Risorgimento, Italian unification movement.
William E. Gladstone, 1809-98, (Br.) prime min.; dominant force of Liberal party 1868-94.
Paul Joseph Goebbels, 1897-1945, (Ger.) Nazi propagandist; master of mass psychology.
Barry Goldwater, 1909-98, (U.S.) conservative U.S. senator (R, AZ), 1964 pres. nominee.
Klement Gottwald, 1896-1953, (Czech.) Communist leader; ushered Communism into his country.
Alexander Hamilton, 1755-1804, (U.S.) first treasury sec.; champion of strong central government.
Dag Hammarskjold, 1905-61, (Swed.) statesman; UN sec.-general.
King Hassan II, 1929-99, (Moroc.) ruler of Morocco, 1962-99.
Vaclav Havel, 1936-2011, (Czech.) first president of Czech Republic, 1989-92.
John Hay, 1838-1905, (U.S.) sec. of state; primarily associated with Open Door Policy toward China.
Sir Edward Heath, 1916-2005, (Br.) Conservative prime min., 1970-74; promoted European unity.
Jesse Helms, 1921-2008, (U.S.) conservative U.S. senator (R, NC).
Patrick Henry, 1736-99, (U.S.) major Revolutionary War figure, orator.
Édouard Herriot, 1872-1957, (Fr.) Radical Socialist leader; twice prem., pres. of National Assembly.
Theodor Herzl, 1860-1904, (Hung.) founded modern Zionism.
Heinrich Himmler, 1900-45, (Ger.) head of Nazi SS and Gestapo.

Paul von Hindenburg, 1847-1934, (Ger.) field marshal, WWI; second pres. of Weimar Republic, 1925-34.
Adolf Hitler, 1889-1945, (Ger.) dictator; built Nazism, launched WWII, presided over the Holocaust.
Ho Chi Minh, 1890-1969, (Viet.) N. Vietnamese pres., Vietnamese Communist leader.
Harry L. Hopkins, 1890-1946, (U.S.) New Deal administrator; closest adviser to Franklin D. Roosevelt during WWII.
Edward M. House, 1858-1938, (U.S.) diplomat; confidential adviser to Woodrow Wilson.
Samuel Houston, 1793-1863, (U.S.) leader of struggle for Texas independence.
Cordell Hull, 1871-1955, (U.S.) sec. of state, 1933-44; initiated reciprocal trade to lower tariffs, helped organize UN.
Hubert H. Humphrey, 1911-78, (U.S.) U.S. senator (D, MN), vice pres., pres. candidate.
King Hussein, 1935-99, (Jordan) peacemaker; ruler of Jordan, 1952-99.
Saddam Hussein, 1937-2006, (Iraq) Iraqi ruler; put to death for crimes against humanity.
Muhammad Ali Jinnah, 1876-1948, (Pak.) founder, first gov.-gen. of Pakistan.
Barbara Jordan, 1936-96, (U.S.) U.S. rep. (D, TX), orator, educator; first black woman to win a seat in the TX state senate, 1966.
Benito Juarez, 1806-72, (Mex.) rallied his country against foreign threats; sought to create democratic, federal republic.
Constantine Karamanlis, 1907-98, (Gr.) Greek prime min.; restored democracy, later president.
Frank B. Kellogg, 1856-1937, (U.S.) sec. of state; negotiated Kellogg-Briand Pact to outlaw war.
Jack Kemp, 1935-2009, (U.S.) sec. of HUD, U.S. rep. (R, NY), football player.
Edward M. Kennedy, 1932-2009, (U.S.) senator (D, MA); championed progressive causes.
Robert F. Kennedy, 1925-68, (U.S.) attorney general, U.S. sen. (D, NY); assassinated while seeking presidency.
Aleksandr Kerensky, 1881-1970, (Russ.) headed provisional government after Feb. 1917 revolution.
Ayatollah Ruhollah Khomeini, 1900-89, (Iran), religious-political leader; spearheaded overthrow of Shah, 1979.
Nikita Khrushchev, 1894-1971, (USSR) prem., first sec. of Communist party; initiated de-Stalinization.
Kim Dae Jung, 1925-2009, (Korea) S. Korean dissident, opposition leader, pres.; 2000 Nobel Peace Prize winner.
Kim Il Sung, 1912-94, (Korea) N. Korean dictator, 1948-94.
Kim Jong Il, 1942-2011, (Korea) N. Korean dictator, 1994-2011.
Edward I. Koch, 1924-2013, (U.S.) New York City mayor, 1978-89.
Lajos Kossuth, 1802-94, (Hung.) principal figure in 1848 Hungarian revolution.
Pyotr Kropotkin, 1842-1921, (Russ.) anarchist; championed the peasants but opposed Bolshevism.
Kublai Khan, c. 1215-94, (Mongol) emperor; founder of Yüan dynasty in China.
Béla Kun, 1886-c. 1939, (Hung.) member of Third Communist International; tried to foment worldwide revolution.
Robert M. LaFollette, 1855-1925, (U.S.) WI public official; leader of progressive movement.
Fiorello La Guardia, 1882-1947, (U.S.) New York City reform mayor, 1933-45.
Pierre Laval, 1883-1945, (Fr.) politician, Vichy foreign min.; executed for treason.
Andrew Bonar Law, 1858-1923, (Can.) Conservative party politician, British prime min.; led opposition to Irish home rule.
Vladimir Ilyich Lenin (Ulyanov), 1870-1924, (Russ.) revolutionary; founded Bolshevism; Soviet leader, 1917-24.
Ferdinand de Lesseps, 1805-94, (Fr.) diplomat, engineer; conceived idea of Suez Canal.
Rene Levesque, 1922-87, (Can.) prem. of Quebec, 1976-85; led unsuccessful separatist campaign.
Trygve Lie, 1896-1968, (Nor.) first UN sec.-gen.
Maxim Litvinov, 1876-1951, (Pol.-Russ.) revolutionary, commissar of foreign affairs; favored cooperation with West.
Liu Shaoqi, c. 1898-1969, (China) Communist leader; fell from grace during Cultural Revolution.
David Lloyd George, 1863-1945, (Br.) Liberal party prime min.; laid foundations for modern welfare state.
Henry Cabot Lodge, 1850-1924, (U.S.) U.S. senator (R, MA); led opposition to participation in League of Nations.
Huey P. Long, 1893-1935, (U.S.) Louisiana political demagogue, governor, U.S. senator (D); assassinated.
Rosa Luxemburg, 1871-1919, (Ger.) revolutionary; leader of the German Social Democratic party and Spartacus party.
J. Ramsay MacDonald, 1866-1937, (Br.) first Labour party prime min. of Great Britain.
Harold Macmillan, 1895-1986, (Br.) prime min. of Great Britain, 1957-63.
Makarios III, 1913-77, (Cyprus) Greek Orthodox archbishop; first pres. of Cyprus.
Nelson Mandela, 1918-2013, (S. Afr.) anti-apartheid leader; 1st black pres. of S. Africa, 1994-99.
Wilma Mankiller, 1945-2010, (U.S.) first female chief of the Cherokee Nation.
Mao Zedong, 1893-1976, (China) chief Chinese Marxist theorist, revolutionary, political leader; led revolution establishing his nation as Communist state.
Jean Paul Marat, 1743-93, (Fr.) revolutionary, politician; identified with radical Jacobins; assassinated.
Thurgood Marshall, 1908-93, (U.S.) first black U.S. solicitor general, 1965; first black justice of U.S. Supreme Court, 1967-91.
José Martí, 1853-95, (Cub.) patriot, poet; independence leader.
Jan Masaryk, 1886-1948, (Czech.) foreign min.; died under mysterious circumstances, allegedly committed suicide following Communist coup.
Thomas G. Masaryk, 1850-1937, (Czech.) statesman, philosopher; first pres. of Czechoslovakia.
Jules Mazarin, 1602-61, (Fr.) cardinal, statesman; prime min. under Louis XIII and queen regent Anne of Austria.
Giuseppe Mazzini, 1805-72, (It.) reformer dedicated to Risorgimento movement for renewal of Italy.
Tom Mboya, 1930-69, (Kenya) political leader; instrumental in securing independence for Kenya.
Eugene McCarthy, 1916-2005, (U.S.) political leader, author; 1968 Dem. presidential contender.
Joseph R. McCarthy, 1908-57, (U.S.) senator (R, WI); extremist in searching out alleged Communists and pro-Communists.
George McGovern, 1922-2012, (U.S.) liberal senator (D, SD), 1972 pres. nominee.
Cosimo I de' Medici, 1519-74, (It.) Duke of Florence, grand duke of Tuscany.
Lorenzo de' Medici (the Magnificent), 1449-92, (It.) merchant prince; a towering figure in Italian Renaissance.
Catherine de Médicis, 1519-89, (Fr.) queen consort of Henry II, regent of France; influential in Catholic-Huguenot wars.
Golda Meir, 1898-1978, (Isr.) a founder of the state of Israel; prime min., 1969-74.
Klemens W. N. L. Metternich, 1773-1859, (Austria) statesman; arbiter of post-Napoleonic Europe.
Slobodan Milosevic, 1941-2006, (Serb./Yugo.) former Yugoslav pres.; tried for war crimes.
François Mitterrand, 1916-96, (Fr.) pres. of France, 1981-95.
Mobutu Sese Seko, 1930-97, (Zaire) longtime ruler of Zaire (now Dem. Rep. of Congo), 1965-97; exiled after rebellion.
Guy Mollet, 1905-75, (Fr.) socialist politician, resistance leader.
Henry Morgenthau Jr., 1891-1967, (U.S.) sec. of treasury; fundraiser for New Deal and U.S. WWII activities.
Gouverneur Morris, 1752-1816, (U.S.) statesman, diplomat, financial expert; helped plan decimal coinage.
Daniel Patrick Moynihan, 1927-2003, (U.S.) senator (D, NY), diplomat, social scientist, author.
Benito Mussolini, 1883-1945, (It.) leader of the Italian fascist state; assassinated.
Imre Nagy, c. 1896-1958, (Hung.) Communist prem.; assassinated after Soviets crushed 1956 uprising.
Gamal Abdel Nasser, 1918-70, (Egypt) leader of Arab unification, second Egyptian pres.
Jawaharlal Nehru, 1889-1964, (India) prime min.; guided India through its early years of independence.
Kwame Nkrumah, 1909-72, (Ghana) first prime min., 1957-60; pres., 1960-66, of Ghana.
Frederick North, 1732-92, (Br.) prime min.; his policies led to loss of American colonies.
Julius K. Nyerere, 1922-99, (Tanz.) founding father; first pres., 1962-85, of Tanzania.
Daniel O'Connell, 1775-1847, (Ire.) nationalist political leader; known as The Liberator.
Omar, c. 581-644, (Arab.) Muslim leader; second caliph, led Islam to become an imperial power.
Thomas P. (Tip) O'Neill Jr., 1912-94, (U.S.) U.S. rep. (D, MA), speaker of the House, 1977-86.
Ignace Paderewski, 1860-1941, (Pol.) statesman, pianist, composer, briefly prime min.; ardent patriot.
Ian Paisley, 1926-2014, (Ire.) Unionist Party leader who agreed to power sharing in N. Ireland.
Viscount Palmerston, 1784-1865, (Br.) Whig-Liberal prime min., foreign min.; embodied British nationalism.
Andreas George Papandreou, 1919-96, (Gr.) leftist politician; served as prem., 1981-89, 1993-96.
Georgios Papandreou, 1888-1968, (Gr.) Republican politician; served 3 times as prime min.
Franz von Papen, 1879-1969, (Ger.) politician; major role in overthrow of Weimar Republic and rise of Hitler.
Charles Stewart Parnell, 1846-1891, (Ire.) nationalist leader; "uncrowned king of Ireland."
Lester Pearson, 1897-1972, (Can.) diplomat, Liberal party leader, prime min.
Robert Peel, 1788-1850, (Br.) reformist prime min.; founder of Conservative party.
Frances Perkins, 1882-1965, (U.S.) first female cabinet member (sec. of labor).
Eva (Evita) Perón, 1919-52, (Arg.) highly influential second wife of Juan Perón.
Juan Perón, 1895-1974, (Arg.) dynamic pres. of Argentina, 1946-55, 1973-74.
Joseph Pilsudski, 1867-1935, (Pol.) statesman; instrumental in reestablishing Polish state in the 20th cent.

Charles Pinckney, 1757-1824, (U.S.) founding father; his Pinckney plan largely incorporated into Constitution.
Christian Pineau, 1905-95, (Fr.) leader of French Resistance during WWII; French foreign min., 1956-58.
Augusto Pinochet (Ugarte), 1915-2006, (Chile) former Chilean ruler; indicted for human rights abuses while in office.
William Pitt the Elder, 1708-78, (Br.) statesman; the "Great Commoner," transformed Britain into imperial power.
William Pitt the Younger, 1759-1806, (Br.) prime min. during French Revolutionary wars.
Georgi Plekhanov, 1857-1918, (Russ.) revolutionary, social philosopher; called "father of Russian Marxism."
Raymond Poincaré, 1860-1934, (Fr.) French pres.; advocated harsh punishment of Germany after WWI.
Pol Pot, 1925-98, (Camb.) leader of Khmer Rouge; ruled Cambodia, 1975-79; responsible for mass deaths.
Georges Pompidou, 1911-74, (Fr.) Gaullist political leader; pres., 1969-74.
Grigori Potemkin, 1739-91, (Russ.) field marshal; favorite of empress Catherine II.
Adam Clayton Powell Jr., 1908-72, (U.S.) civil rights leader; U.S. rep. (D, NY), 1945-69.
Muammar al-Qaddafi, 1942-2011, (Libya) Libyan ruler, 1969-2011.
Yitzhak Rabin, 1922-95, (Isr.) military, political leader; prime min. of Israel, 1974-77, 1992-95; assassinated.
Joseph H. Rainey, 1832-87, (U.S.) first black person elected to U.S. House (1869), from SC.
Edmund Randolph, 1753-1813, (U.S.) attorney; prominent in drafting, ratification of Constitution.
John Randolph, 1773-1833, (U.S.) Southern planter; strong advocate of states' rights.
Jeannette Rankin, 1880-1973, (U.S.) pacifist; first woman member of U.S. Congress (R, MT).
Walter Rathenau, 1867-1922, (Ger.) industrialist, statesman.
Sam Rayburn, 1882-1961, (U.S.) U.S. rep. (D, TX) for 47 years, House speaker for 17.
Hiram R. Revels, 1822-1901, (U.S.) first African-American U.S. senator (R); elected in MS, served 1870-71.
Paul Reynaud, 1878-1966, (Fr.) statesman; prem. in 1940 at time of France's defeat by Germany.
Syngman Rhee, 1875-1965, (Korea) first pres. of S. Korea.
Cecil Rhodes, 1853-1902, (Br.) imperialist, industrial magnate; established Rhodes scholarships in his will.
Ann Richards, 1933-2006, (U.S.) former TX gov.
Cardinal de Richelieu, 1585-1642, (Fr.) statesman, known as "red eminence"; chief minister to Louis XIII.
Maximilien Robespierre, 1758-94, (Fr.) leading figure in French Revolution and Reign of Terror.
Nelson Rockefeller, 1908-79, (U.S.) Republican governor of NY, 1959-73; U.S. vice pres., 1974-77.
Eleanor Roosevelt, 1884-1962, (U.S.) influential first lady, humanitarian, UN diplomat.
Elihu Root, 1845-1937, (U.S.) lawyer, statesman, diplomat; leading Republican supporter of the League of Nations.
Dean Rusk, 1909-95, (U.S.) statesman; sec. of state, 1961-69.
John Russell, 1792-1878, (Br.) Liberal prime min. during the Irish potato famine.
Anwar al-Sadat, 1918-81, (Egypt) pres., 1970-81; promoted peace with Israel; Nobel laureate; assassinated.
António de Oliveira Salazar, 1889-1970, (Port.) longtime dictator.
José de San Martin, 1778-1850, S. Amer. revolutionary; protector of Peru.
Eisaku Sato, 1901-75, (Jpn.) prime min.; presided over Japan's post-WWII emergence as major world power.
Abdul Aziz Ibn Saud, c. 1880-1953, (Saudi Arabia) king of Saudi Arabia, 1932-53.
Robert Schuman, 1886-1963, (Fr.) statesman; founded European Coal and Steel Community.
Carl Schurz, 1829-1906, (U.S.) German-American political leader, journalist, orator, dedicated reformer.
Kurt Schuschnigg, 1897-1977, (Austria) chancellor; unsuccessful in stopping Austria's annexation by Germany.
William H. Seward, 1801-72, (U.S.) anti-slavery activist; as U.S. sec. of state purchased Alaska.
Carlo Sforza, 1872-1952, (It.) foreign min., anti-Fascist.
Yitzhak Shamir, 1915-2012, (Isr.) prime min. of Israel, 1983-84, 1986-92.
Ariel Sharon, 1928-2014, (Isr.) prime min. of Israel, 2001-06.
Eduard Shevardnadze, 1928-2014, (Geo.) Georgian pres., 1995-2003.
Norodom Sihanouk, 1922-2012, (Camb.) king of Cambodia (1941-55, 1993-2004).
Sitting Bull, c. 1831-90, (Amer. Ind.) Sioux leader in Battle of Little Bighorn against George A. Custer, 1876.
Alfred E. Smith, 1873-1944, (U.S.) NY Democratic governor; first Roman Catholic to run for president.
Margaret Chase Smith, 1897-1995, (U.S.) U.S. rep., senator (R, ME); first woman elected to both houses of Congress.
Jan C. Smuts, 1870-1950, (S. Afr.) statesman, philosopher, soldier, prime min.
Paul Henri Spaak, 1899-1972, (Belg.) statesman, socialist leader.
Joseph Stalin, 1879-1953, (USSR) Soviet dictator, 1924-53; instituted forced collectivization, massive purges, and labor camps, causing millions of deaths.
Edwin M. Stanton, 1814-69, (U.S.) sec. of war, 1862-68.
Alexander Stephens, 1812-83, (U.S.) vice pres. of the Confederacy.
Edward R. Stettinius Jr., 1900-49, (U.S.) industrialist; sec. of state who coordinated aid to WWII allies.
Adlai E. Stevenson, 1900-65, (U.S.) Democratic leader, diplomat, governor (IL), presidential candidate.
Henry L. Stimson, 1867-1950, (U.S.) statesman; served in 5 administrations, foreign policy adviser in 1930s and 1940s.
Carl Stokes, 1927-96, (U.S.) first black mayor of a major American city (Cleveland, 1967-72).
Suharto, 1921-2008, (Indon.) former longtime Indonesian ruler.
Sukarno, 1901-70, (Indon.) dictatorial first pres. of the Indonesian republic.
Sun Yat-sen, 1866-1925, (China) revolutionary; leader of Kuomintang political party, regarded as father of modern China.
Robert A. Taft, 1889-1953, (U.S.) conservative Senate leader (OH); called "Mr. Republican."
Charles de Talleyrand, 1754-1838, (Fr.) statesman, diplomat; the major force of the Congress of Vienna of 1814-15.
U Thant, 1909-74, (Burma) statesman, UN sec.-general.
Margaret Thatcher, 1925-2013, (Br.) conservative British prime min., 1979-90; first woman UK prime min.
Norman M. Thomas, 1884-1968, (U.S.) social reformer; six times Socialist party presidential candidate.
Josip Broz Tito, 1892-1980, (Yugo.) pres. of Yugoslavia from 1953; WWII guerrilla chief, postwar rival of Stalin.
Palmiro Togliatti, 1893-1964, (It.) major Italian Communist leader.
Hideki Tojo, 1885-1948, (Jpn.) statesman, soldier; prime min. during most of WWII.
François Toussaint L'Ouverture, c. 1744-1803, (Haiti) patriot, martyr; thwarted French colonial aims.
Leon Trotsky, 1879-1940, (Russ.) revolutionary; founded Red Army, expelled from party in conflict with Stalin; assassinated.
Pierre Elliott Trudeau, 1919-2000, (Can.) longtime liberal prime min. of Canada, 1968-79, 1980-84; achieved native Canadian constitution.
Rafael L. Trujillo Molina, 1891-1961, (Dom. Rep.) dictator of Dominican Republic, 1930-61; assassinated.
Moise K. Tshombe, 1919-69, (Congo) pres. of secessionist Katanga prov., prem. of Congo (now Dem. Rep. of the Congo).
William M. Tweed, 1823-78, (U.S.) political boss of Tammany Hall, New York City's Democratic political machine.
Walter Ulbricht, 1893-1973, (Ger.) Communist leader of German Democratic Republic.
Arthur H. Vandenberg, 1884-1951, (U.S.) senator (R, MI); proponent of bipartisan anti-Communist foreign policy.
Eleutherios Venizelos, 1864-1936, (Gr.) most prominent Greek statesman of early 20th cent.
Hendrik F. Verwoerd, 1901-66, (S. Afr.) prime min.; rigorously applied apartheid policy despite protest.
Kurt Waldheim, 1918-2007, (Austria) UN sec.-gen., Austrian pres.
George Wallace, 1919-98, (U.S.) former segregationist governor of Alabama, pres. candidate.
Robert Walpole, 1676-1745, (Br.) statesman; generally considered Britain's first prime min.
Harold Washington, 1922-87, (U.S.) first black mayor of Chicago.
Robert C. Weaver, 1907-97, (U.S.) first African American appointed to cabinet; sec. of Housing and Urban Development.
Daniel Webster, 1782-1852, (U.S.) orator, politician; advocate of business interests during Jacksonian agrarianism.
Caspar Weinberger, 1917-2006, (U.S.) business exec., former defense sec., other cabinet posts.
Chaim Weizmann, 1874-1952, (Russ.-Isr.) Zionist leader, scientist; first Israeli pres.
Kevin White, 1929-2012, (U.S.) Boston mayor, 1967-84.
Wendell L. Willkie, 1892-1944, (U.S.) Republican who tried to unseat Franklin D. Roosevelt when he ran for his third term.
Harold Wilson, 1916-95, (Br.) Labour party leader; prime min., 1964-70, 1974-76.
Boris Yeltsin, 1931-2007, (Russ.) first freely elected pres. of post-Soviet Russia.
Coleman A. Young, 1918-97, (U.S.) first African-American mayor of Detroit, 1974-93.
Emiliano Zapata, c. 1879-1919, (Mex.) revolutionary; major influence on modern Mexico.
Todor Zhivkov, 1911-98, (Bulg.) Communist ruler of Bulgaria from 1954 until ousted in a 1989 coup.
Zhou Enlai, 1898-1976, (China) diplomat, prime min.; a leading figure of the Chinese Communist party.

Scientists of the Past

Revised by Peter Barker, Prof. and Chair, Dept. of the History of Science, Univ. of Oklahoma.

For pre-modern scientists, see also Philosophers and Religious Figures of the Past and the Historical Figures chapter.

Albertus Magnus, c. 1200-80, (Ger.) theologian, philosopher; helped found medieval study of natural science.
Alhazen (Ibn al-Haytham), c. 965-c. 1040, mathematician, astronomer, optical theorist.
Andre-Marie Ampère, 1775-1836, (Fr.) mathematician, chemist; founder of electrodynamics.
Neil Armstrong, 1930-2012, (U.S.) astronaut, first man to walk on the Moon.
John V. Atanasoff, 1903-95, (U.S.) physicist; co-invented Atanasoff-Berry electronic digital computer (1939-41).
Amedeo Avogadro, 1776-1856, (It.) chemist, physicist; proposed that equal volumes of gas contain equal numbers of molecules, permitting determination of molecular weights.
John Bardeen, 1908-91, (U.S.) double Nobel laureate in physics (transistor, 1956; superconductivity, 1972).
A. H. Becquerel, 1852-1908, (Fr.) physicist; discovered radioactivity in uranium (1896).
Alexander Graham Bell, 1847-1922, (U.S.) inventor; first to patent and commercially exploit the telephone (1876).
Daniel Bernoulli, 1700-82, (Switz.) mathematician; developed fluid dynamics and kinetic theory of gases.
Clifford Berry, 1918-63, (U.S.) collaborated with John V. Atanasoff on the ABC electronic digital computer (1939-41).
Jöns Jakob Berzelius, 1779-1848, (Swed.) chemist; developed modern chemical symbols and formulas.
Henry Bessemer, 1813-98, (Br.) engineer; invented Bessemer steel-making process.
Hans Bethe, 1906-2005, (Ger.-U.S.) physicist; won Nobel Prize in 1967 for describing how stars generate energy.
Bruno Bettelheim, 1903-90, (Austria-U.S.) psychoanalyst; studied disturbed children; *Uses of Enchantment* (1976).
Louis Blériot, 1872-1936, (Fr.) engineer; monoplane pioneer, first English Channel flight (1909).
Franz Boas, 1858-1942, (Ger.-U.S.) founded modern anthropology; studied Pacific Coast tribes.
Niels Bohr, 1885-1962, (Den.) atomic and nuclear physicist; founded quantum mechanics.
Norman Borlaug, 1914-2009, (U.S.) plant pathologist and geneticist; father of "green" (agricultural) revolution.
Max Born, 1882-1970, (Ger.) atomic and nuclear physicist; helped develop quantum mechanics.
Satyendranath Bose, 1894-1974, (India) physicist; forerunner of modern quantum theory for integral-spin particles.
Louis de Broglie, 1892-1987, (Fr.) physicist; proposed quantum wave-particle duality.
Robert Bunsen, 1811-99, (Ger.) chemist; pioneered spectroscopic analysis; discovered rubidium, caesium.
Luther Burbank, 1849-1926, (U.S.) naturalist; developed plant breeding into a modern science.
Vannevar Bush, 1890-1974, (U.S.) electrical engineer; developed differential analyzer, an early analogue computer; headed WWII Office of Scientific Res. and Dev.
Marvin Camras, 1916-95, (U.S.) inventor, electrical engineer; invented magnetic tape recording.
Alexis Carrel, 1873-1944, (Fr.) surgeon, biologist; developed methods of suturing blood vessels, transplanting organs.
Rachel Carson, 1907-64, (U.S.) marine biologist, environmentalist; *Silent Spring* (1962).
George Washington Carver, 1864-1943, (U.S.) chemist and botanist; promoted alternative crops.
James Chadwick, 1891-1974, (Br.) physicist; discovered the neutron (1932); led Brit. team on Manhattan Project in U.S.
Eugenie Clark, 1922-2015, (U.S.) ichthyologist and oceanographer.
Albert Claude, 1898-1983, (Belg.-U.S.) a founder of modern cell biology; determined role of mitochondria.
Samuel Cohen, 1921-2010, (U.S.) physicist who invented the neutron bomb.
Barry Commoner, 1917-2012, biologist; noted environmentalist.
Nicolaus Copernicus, 1473-1543, (Pol.) first modern astronomer to propose Sun as center of the planets' motions.
Jacques Yves Cousteau, 1910-97, (Fr.) oceanographer; co-inventor, with Emile Gagnan (Fr.), of the Aqualung (1943).
Seymour Cray, 1925-96, (U.S.) computer industry pioneer; developed supercomputers.
Francis Crick, 1916-2004, (Br.) biophysicist; co-discoverer of genetic code; shared 1962 Nobel Prize.
Marie, 1867-1934, (Pol.-Fr.) and **Pierre Curie**, 1859-1906, (Fr.) physical chemists; pioneer investigators of radioactivity; discovered radium and polonium (1898).
Gottlieb Daimler, 1834-1900, (Ger.) engineer, inventor; pioneer automobile manufacturer.
John Dalton, 1766-1844, (Br.) chemist, physicist; formulated atomic theory, made first table of atomic weights.
Charles Darwin, 1809-82, (Br.) naturalist; established theory of organic evolution; *Origin of Species* (1859).
Lee De Forest, 1873-1961, (U.S.) inventor of triode; pioneer in wireless telegraphy, sound pictures, television.
Pierre-Gilles de Gennes, 1932-2007, (Fr.) physicist whose research aided development of liquid-crystal display (LCD); awarded 1991 Nobel Prize for Physics.
Max Delbrück, 1906-81, (Fr.-Ger.-U.S.) founded molecular biology.
Rudolf Diesel, 1858-1913, (Ger.) mechanical engineer; patented Diesel engine (1892).
Theodosius Dobzhansky, 1900-75, (Russ.-U.S.) biologist; reconciled genetics and natural selection.
Christian Doppler, 1803-53, (Austria) physicist; showed change in wave frequency caused by motion of source, now known as Doppler effect.
J. Presper Eckert Jr., 1919-95, (U.S.) co-inventor, with John W. Mauchly, of the ENIAC computer (1943-45).
Thomas A. Edison, 1847-1931, (U.S.) inventor; held more than 1,000 patents, including incandescent electric lamp.
Robert Edwards, 1925-2013, (Br.) physiologist; pioneered in vitro fertilization.
Paul Ehrlich, 1854-1915, (Ger.) medical researcher in immunology and bacteriology; pioneered antitoxin production.
Albert Einstein, 1879-1955, (Ger.-U.S.) theoretical physicist; founded relativity theory.
John F. Enders, 1897-1985, (U.S.) virologist; helped discover vaccines against polio, measles, mumps, and chicken pox.
Erik Erikson, 1902-94, (U.S.) psychoanalyst, author; theory of developmental stages of life; *Childhood and Society* (1950).
Leonhard Euler, 1707-83, (Switz.) mathematician, physicist; pioneer of calculus, revived ideas of Fermat.
Gabriel Fahrenheit, 1686-1736, (Ger.) physicist; improved thermometers and introduced Fahrenheit temperature scale.
Michael Faraday, 1791-1867, (Br.) chemist, physicist; discovered electrical induction and invented dynamo (1831).
Philo T. Farnsworth, 1906-71, (U.S.) inventor; built first television system (San Francisco, 1928).
Pierre de Fermat, 1601-65, (Fr.) mathematician; founded modern theory of numbers.
Enrico Fermi, 1901-54, (It.-U.S.) nuclear physicist; demonstrated first controlled chain reaction (Chicago, 1942).
Richard Feynman, 1918-88, (U.S.) theoretical physicist, author; founder of Quantum Electrodynamics (QED).
Alexander Fleming, 1881-1955, (Br.) bacteriologist; discovered penicillin (1928).
Jean B. J. Fourier, 1768-1830, (Fr.) introduced Fourier Series, method of analysis in math and physics.
Sigmund Freud, 1856-1939, (Austria) psychiatrist; founder of psychoanalysis; *Interpretation of Dreams* (1901).
Erich Fromm, 1900-80, (U.S.) psychoanalyst; *Man for Himself* (1947).
Galileo Galilei, 1564-1642, (It.) physicist; used telescope to vindicate Copernicus, founded modern science of motion.
Carl Friedrich Gauss, 1777-1855, (Ger.) mathematician; completed work of Fermat and Euler in number theory.
Josiah W. Gibbs, 1839-1903, (U.S.) theoretical physicist, chemist; founded chemical thermodynamics.
Robert H. Goddard, 1882-1945, (U.S.) physicist; invented liquid fuel rocket (1926).
George W. Goethals, 1858-1928, (U.S.) chief engineer who completed Panama Canal (1907-14).
William C. Gorgas, 1854-1920, (U.S.) physician; pioneer in prevention of yellow fever and malaria.
Stephen Jay Gould, 1941-2002, (U.S.) paleontologist, evolutionary biologist, writer.
Ernest Haeckel, 1834-1919, (Ger.) zoologist, evolutionist; early Darwinist, introduced concept of "ecology."
Otto Hahn, 1879-1968, (Ger.) chemist; with Lise Meitner discovered nuclear fission (1938).
Edmund Halley, 1656-1742, (Br.) astronomer; predicted return of 1682 comet (Halley's Comet) in 1759.
William Harvey, 1578-1657, (Br.) physician, anatomist; discovered circulation of the blood (1628).
Werner Heisenberg, 1901-76, (Ger.) physicist; developed matrix mechanics and uncertainty principle (1927).
Hermann von Helmholtz, 1821-94, (Ger.) physicist, physiologist; formulated principle of conservation of energy.
William Herschel, 1738-1822, (Ger.-Br.) astronomer; discovered Uranus (1781).
Heinrich Hertz, 1857-94, (Ger.) physicist; discovered radio waves and photo-electric effect (1886-87).
David Hilbert, 1862-1943, (Ger.) mathematician; contributed to algebra, calculus, and foundational studies (formalism).
Albert Hofmann, 1906-2008, (Switz.) chemist; inventor of LSD.
Edwin P. Hubble, 1889-1953, (U.S.) astronomer; discovered observational evidence of expanding universe.
Alexander von Humboldt, 1769-1859, (Ger.) naturalist; explored Central, S. America, ideated ecology.
Edward Jenner, 1749-1823, (Br.) physician; pioneered vaccination, introduced term "virus."
James Joule, 1818-89, (Br.) physicist; found relation between heat and mechanical energy (conservation of energy).
Carl Jung, 1875-1961, (Switz.) psychiatrist; founder of analytical psychology.
Ernest Everett Just, 1883-1941, (U.S.) marine biologist; studied egg development; *Biology of Cell Surfaces* (1941).
Johannes Kepler, 1571-1630, (Ger.) astronomer; discovered laws of planetary motion.
Al-Khwarizmi, early 9th cent., (Arab.) mathematician; regarded as founder of algebra.
Robert Koch, 1843-1910, (Ger.) bacteriologist; isolated bacterial causes of tuberculosis and other diseases.

2015 YEAR IN PICTURES

WORLD

SEEKING REFUGE Fleeing strife, overcrowded refugee camps, or poverty in Northern Africa, the Middle East, and Afghanistan, tens of thousands of refugees and migrants sought refuge in sometimes unwelcoming European countries in 2015.

PERILOUS VOYAGE Water rescues of boats overloaded with migrants and refugees were a frequent occurrence on the Mediterranean Sea in 2015, but many boats also capsized or sank during the crossing, killing thousands.

ISIS PROPAGANDA Graphic videos periodicall released in 2015 by the Sunni extremist group Islamic State in [illegible] Syria (ISIS) showed violen deaths of their captives.

YEMEN AIRSTRIKES A Saudi Arabia-led coalition of Sunni nations continued airstrikes against Houthi Shiite-held targets in Sanaa, Yemen, in June 2015.

GREECE IN CRISIS In danger of running out of money, Greece's banks were closed June 29-July 20 as the nation sought a way out of its financial crisis in negotiation with austerity champion and German Chancellor Angela Merkel, the Intl. Monetary Fund, and the eurozone.

SEEKING JUSTICE After Russian opposition leader Boris Nemtsov was shot dead near the Kremlin Feb. 27, 2015, tens of thousands of his supporters marched near the site of his death.

RAN NUCLEAR NEGOTIATIONS After a 17-day final round of negotiations, ran and six major world powers, led by U.S. Sec. of State John Kerry, reached a nistoric deal on the future of Iran's nuclear program July 14, 2015.

NETANYAHU SPEAKS Israeli Prime Min. 3enjamin Netanyahu, campaigning both for eelection and against the ongoing Iran nuclear alks, spoke before a joint session of the U.S. Congress Mar. 3, 2015.

JE SUIS CHARLIE Three days of terrorism in France, beginning with a deadly attack Jan. 7, 2015, on the Paris staff of satirical magazine *Charlie Hebdo*, elicited solidarity throughout Europe.

WORLD

NEPAL QUAKES A magnitude-7.8 earthquake near Kathmandu, Nepal, on Apr. 25, 2015, killed more than 8,000 people and displaced 2.8 million.

TERROR IN KENYA Somali Islamist group al-Shabab attacked Garissa Univ. College in Kenya, Apr. 2, 2015, killing 148 and continuing the group's campaign against civilian targets.

TIANJIN EXPLOSION At least 170 were killed when a hazardous chemical storage facility in Tianjin, China, exploded Aug. 12, 2015.

INTENTIONAL TRAGEDY The copilot of a Germanwings Airbus jet deliberately crashed the plane into the French Alps Mar. 24, 2015, killing all 150 people aboard.

OVERHEATED Heat waves in India and Pakistan killed thousands in May-June 2015 as residents sought escape from the oppressive heat by any means, including sleeping on rooftops.

CUBA REVISITED Retired Marines who had removed the American flag when the U.S. left Cuba in 1961 were present for the symbolic reopening of the U.S. embassy there Aug. 14, 2015.

TRAVELING MAN Pope Francis, leader of the Roman Catholic Church, was greeted by crowds of millions during a five-day trip to the Philippines in Jan. 2015 and in trips to Cuba and the U.S. in Sept.

NIGERIAN LEADERSHIP TRANSITION Former Nigerian Gen. Muhammadu Buhari, who had led the country as military ruler (1984-85), defeated sitting Pres. Goodluck Jonathan in historic voting Mar. 28-29, 2015.

FIRST DEBATE The crowded stage Aug. 6, 2015, at the first debate for Republican 2016 presidential contenders—New Jersey Gov. Chris Christie, Sen. Marco Rubio (FL), Dr. Ben Carson, Wisconsin Gov. Scott Walker, Donald Trump, former Florida Gov. Jeb Bush, former Arkansas Gov. Mike Huckabee, Sen. Ted Cruz (TX), Sen. Rand Paul (KY), and Ohio Gov. John Kasich—did not even reflect the full breadth of the Republican field; seven lower-polling candidates participated in a separate debate.

HITTING THE ROAD Democratic 2016 presidential contenders Sen. Bernie Sanders (I, VT) and former Sec. of State Hillary Clinton launched their campaigns with events large and small in 2015.

SPEAK NO MORE House Speaker John Boehner (R, OH) announced Sept. 25, 2015, that he would resign his post and his seat after an embattled five-year tenure as House leader.

HIGH AND DRY In its fourth year, the California drought forced extreme measures in 2015, including statewide limits on water usage; Los Angeles covered its reservoirs with floating "shade balls" to protect the diminishing reserves.

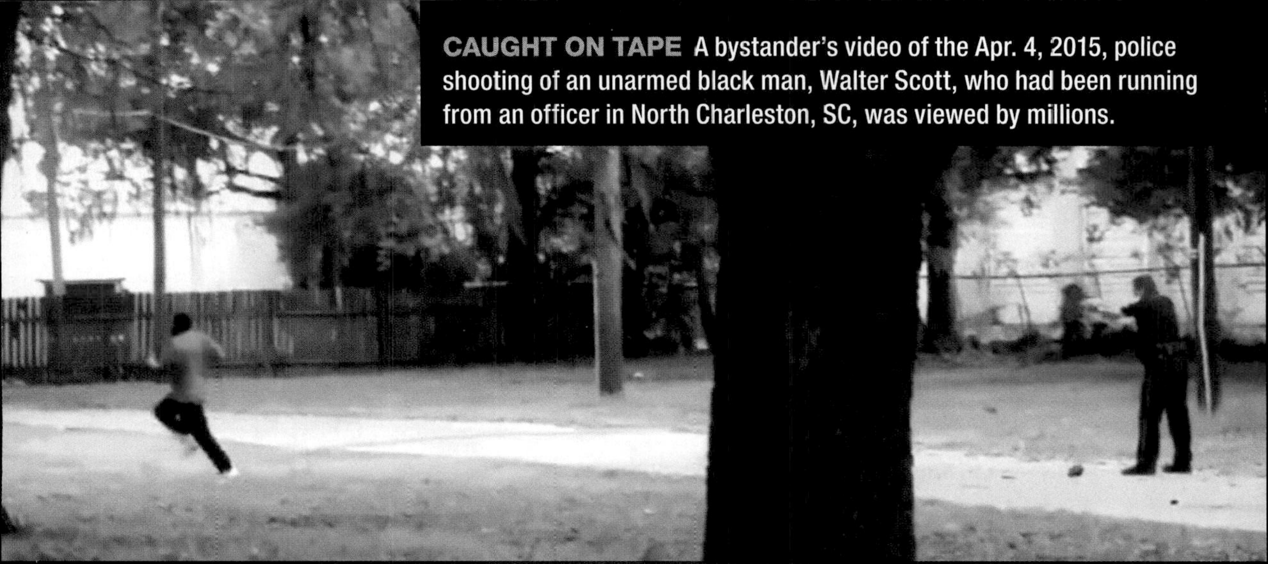

CAUGHT ON TAPE A bystander's video of the Apr. 4, 2015, police shooting of an unarmed black man, Walter Scott, who had been running from an officer in North Charleston, SC, was viewed by millions.

FLAG LOWERED In a formal ceremony July 10, 2015, South Carolina removed the Confederate battle flag from its Capitol grounds, where it had flown for more than 50 years.

BALTIMORE PROTESTS The Apr. 19, 2015, death of 25-year-old Freddie Gray, who had sustained fatal injuries while he was in police custody, elicited sometimes-violent protests in Baltimore.

CHARLESTON MOURNS The Emanuel African Methodist Episcopal Church in Charleston, SC, was the site of a shooting June 17, 2015, in which a white supremacist killed nine black parishoners; the historic church was also the site of victims' viewings and funerals.

NATIONAL

HOOSIER HOSPITALITY Critics of Indiana's Religious Freedom Restoration Act, signed into law Mar. 26, 2015, said it would promote discrimination based on sexual orientation; Indiana amended the law Apr. 2.

RIGHT TO MARRY Same-sex marriage supporters celebrated in Washington, DC, after the U.S. Supreme Court ruled that state laws against marriage between same-sex couples were unconstitutional June 26, 2015.

OUNCE OF PREVENTION In the wake of a measles outbreak linked to Disneyland that infected more than 100, California Gov. Jerry Brown signed a hotly debated bill June 30, 2015, that required vaccinations for nearly all children who attend the state's public schools.

LAST RESORT Kentucky county clerk Kim Davis went to jail Aug. 3, 2015, after refusing, on what she said were religious grounds, to issue marriage licenses to same-sex couples.

Georges Köhler, 1946-95, (Ger.) immunologist; with César Milstein, developed monoclonal antibody technique.
Willem Kolff, 1911-2009, (Neth.-U.S.) physician, biomedical engineer; developed first practical kidney dialysis machine; considered the "father of artificial organs."
Jacques Lacan, 1901-81, (Fr.) influential psychoanalyst.
Joseph Lagrange, 1736-1813, (Fr.) geometer, astronomer; showed that gravity of Earth and Moon cancel, creating stable points in space around them.
Jean B. Lamarck, 1744-1829, (Fr.) naturalist; forerunner of Darwin in evolutionary theory.
Pierre Simon de Laplace, 1749-1827, (Fr.) astronomer, physicist; proposed nebular origin for solar system.
Lewis H. Latimer, 1848-1928, (U.S.) African American scientist; associate of Edison; supervised installation of first electric street lighting in New York City.
Antoine Lavoisier, 1743-94, (Fr.) a founder of modern chemistry.
Ernest O. Lawrence, 1901-58, (U.S.) physicist; invented the cyclotron.
Louis, 1903-72, and **Mary Leakey**, 1913-96, (both Br.) early hominid paleoanthropologists; discovered remains in Africa.
Anton van Leeuwenhoek, 1632-1723, (Neth.) founder of microscopy.
Jerome Lejeune, 1927-94, (Fr.) geneticist; discovered chromosomal cause of Down syndrome (1959).
Claude Levi-Strauss, 1908-2009, (Belg.-Fr.) cultural anthropologist, sociologist, philosopher.
Kurt Lewin, 1890-1947, (Ger.-U.S.) social psychologist; studied human motivation and group dynamics.
Justus von Liebig, 1803-73, (Ger.) founded quantitative organic chemistry.
Joseph Lister, 1827-1912, (Br.) physician; pioneered antiseptic surgery.
Hendrik Lorentz, 1853-1928, (Neth.) physicist; developed electron theory of matter, contributed to relativity theory.
Konrad Lorenz, 1903-89, (Austria) ethologist; pioneer in study of animal behavior.
Bernard Lovell, 1913-2012, (Br.) physicist and radio astronomer.
Percival Lowell, 1855-1916, (U.S.) astronomer; predicted the existence of Pluto.
Louis, 1864-1948, and **Auguste Lumière**, 1862-1954, (both Fr.) invented cinematograph, made first motion picture (1895).
Theodore H. Maiman, 1927-2007, (U.S.) physicist; invented the first workable laser, which he displayed in 1960.
Guglielmo Marconi, 1874-1937, (It.) physicist; developed wireless telegraphy.
John W. Mauchly, 1907-80, (U.S.) co-inventor, with J. Presper Eckert Jr., of computer ENIAC (1943-45).
James Clerk Maxwell, 1831-79, (Br.) physicist; unified electricity and magnetism, electromagnetic theory of light.
Maria Goeppert Mayer, 1906-72, (Ger.-U.S.) physicist; developed shell model of atomic nuclei.
Barbara McClintock, 1902-92, (U.S.) geneticist; showed that some genetic elements are mobile.
Lise Meitner, 1878-1968, (Austria) co-discoverer, with Otto Hahn, of nuclear fission (1938).
Gregor J. Mendel, 1822-84, (Austria) botanist, monk; his experiments became the foundation of modern genetics.
Dmitri Mendeleyev, 1834-1907, (Russ.) chemist; established Periodic Table of the Elements.
Bruce R. Merrifield, 1921-2006, (U.S.) chemist; discovered how to synthesize proteins quickly and efficiently.
Franz Mesmer, 1734-1815, (Ger.) physician; introduced hypnotherapy.
Albert A. Michelson, 1852-1931, (U.S.) physicist; invented interferometer.
Robert A. Millikan, 1868-1953, (U.S.) physicist; measured electronic charge.
Thomas Hunt Morgan, 1866-1945, (U.S.) geneticist, embryologist; established role of chromosomes in heredity.
John F. Nash Jr., 1928-2015, (U.S.) mathematician; Nobel Prize winner (1994) for work on game theory.
Isaac Newton, 1642-1727, (Br.) natural philosopher; discovered laws of gravitation, motion; with Gottfried Wilhelm von Leibniz, founded calculus.
Robert N. Noyce, 1927-90, (U.S.) invented microchip.
J. Robert Oppenheimer, 1904-67, (U.S.) physicist; scientific director of Manhattan Project.
Wilhelm Ostwald, 1853-1932, (Ger.) chemist, philosopher; main founder of modern physical chemistry.
Louis Pasteur, 1822-95, (Fr.) chemist; showed that germs cause disease and fermentation; originated pasteurization.
Linus C. Pauling, 1901-94, (U.S.) chemist; studied chemical bonds; campaigned for nuclear disarmament.
Jean Piaget, 1896-1980, (Switz.) psychologist; four-stage theory of intellectual development in children.
Max Planck, 1858-1947, (Ger.) physicist; introduced quantum hypothesis (1900).
Jules Henri Poincaré, 1854-1912, (Fr.) mathematician; founded algebraic topology, many other discoveries.
Walter S. Reed, 1851-1902, (U.S.) Army physician; proved mosquitoes transmit yellow fever.
Theodor Reik, 1888-1969, (Austria-U.S.) psychoanalyst; major Freudian disciple.
Sally Ride, 1951-2012, (U.S.) astronaut, 1st U.S. woman in space.
Bernhard Riemann, 1826-66, (Ger.) mathematician; developed non-Euclidean geometry used by Einstein.
Norbert Rillieux, 1806-94, (U.S.) African American inventor of a vacuum pan evaporator (1846); revolutionized sugar-refining industry.
Wilhelm Roentgen, 1845-1923, (Ger.) physicist; discovered X-rays (1895).
Carl Rogers, 1902-87, (U.S.) psychotherapist, author; originated nondirective therapy.
Ernest Rutherford, 1871-1937, (Br.) physicist; pioneer investigator of radioactivity, identified the atomic nucleus.
Albert B. Sabin, 1906-93, (Russ.-U.S.) developed oral polio live-virus vaccine.
Carl Sagan, 1934-96, (U.S.) astronomer, author.
Jonas Salk, 1914-95, (U.S.) developed first successful polio vaccine, widely used in U.S. after 1955.
Allan Sandage, 1926-2010, (U.S.) astronomer; refined the Hubble Constant, a measure of the universe's expansion.
Frederick Sanger, 1918-2013, (Br.) biochemist, detailed molecular structure of insulin.
Giovanni Schiaparelli, 1835-1910, (It.) astronomer; reported canals on Mars.
Erwin Schrödinger, 1887-1961, (Austria) physicist; developed wave equation for quantum systems.
Glenn T. Seaborg, 1912-99, (U.S.) chemist; Nobel Prize winner (1951); co-discoverer of plutonium.
Harlow Shapley, 1885-1972, (U.S.) astronomer; mapped galactic clusters and position of Sun in our galaxy.
Norman E. Shumway, 1923-2006, (U.S.) surgeon; performed world's first successful heart-lung transplant.
B. F. Skinner, 1904-90, (U.S.) psychologist; leading advocate of behaviorism.
Richard E. Smalley, 1943-2005, (U.S.) chemist; with three other scientists, discovered buckminsterfullerenes, a previously unknown class of carbon molecules.
Roger W. Sperry, 1913-94, (U.S.) neurobiologist; established different functions of right and left sides of brain.
Benjamin Spock, 1903-98, (U.S.) pediatrician, child care expert; *Common Sense Book of Baby and Child Care*.
Charles P. Steinmetz, 1865-1923, (Ger.-U.S.) electrical engineer; developed basic ideas on alternating current.
Ernst Stuhlinger, 1913-2008, (Ger.) rocket scientist; electric propulsion for NASA in early space age.
Leo Szilard, 1898-1964, (Hung.-U.S.) physicist; helped on Manhattan Project, later opposed nuclear weapons.
Edward Teller, 1908-2003, (Hung.-U.S.) physicist; aided on Manhattan Project, had key role in development of H-bomb.
Nikola Tesla, 1856-1943, (Serb.-U.S.) invented electrical devices including AC dynamos, transformers, and motors.
William Thomson (Lord Kelvin), 1824-1907, (Br.) physicist; aided in success of transatlantic telegraph cable (1865); proposed Kelvin absolute temperature scale.
Alan Turing, 1912-54, (Br.) mathematician; helped develop basis for computers.
James Van Allen, 1914-2006, (U.S.) physicist; discovered the presence of radiation belts around Earth (Van Allen belts).
Rudolf Virchow, 1821-1902, (Ger.) pathologist; pioneered the modern theory that diseases affect the body through cells.
Alessandro Volta, 1745-1827, (It.) physicist; electricity pioneer.
Wernher von Braun, 1912-77, (Ger.-U.S.) developed rockets for warfare and space exploration.
John von Neumann, 1903-57, (Hung.-U.S.) mathematician; originated game theory; basic design for modern computers.
Alfred Russell Wallace, 1823-1913, (Br.) naturalist; proposed concept of evolution independently of Darwin.
John B. Watson, 1878-1958, (U.S.) psychologist; a founder of behaviorism.
James E. Watt, 1736-1819, (Br.) mechanical engineer, inventor; invented modern steam engine (1765).
Alfred L. Wegener, 1880-1930, (Ger.) meteorologist, geophysicist; postulated continental drift.
Norbert Wiener, 1894-1964, (U.S.) mathematician; founder of cybernetics.
Daniel Hale Williams, 1858-1931, (U.S.) African American surgeon; performed one of first two open-heart operations (1893).
Sewall Wright, 1889-1988, (U.S.) evolutionary theorist; helped found population genetics.
Wilhelm Wundt, 1832-1920, (Ger.) founder of experimental psychology.
Qian Xuesen, 1911-2009, (China) rocket scientist; helped found Jet Propulsion Lab, father of China's space program.
Rosalyn Yalow, 1921-2011, (U.S.), physicist; co-developer of radioimmunoassay.
Ferdinand von Zeppelin, 1838-1917, (Ger.) soldier, aeronaut, airship designer.

Social Reformers, Activists, and Humanitarians of the Past

Ralph David Abernathy, 1926-90, (U.S.) black civil rights activist; pres., 1968, Southern Christian Leadership Conf.
Jane Addams, 1860-1935, (U.S.) cofounder of Hull House; won Nobel Peace Prize, 1931.
Susan B. Anthony, 1820-1906, (U.S.) a leader in temperance, antislavery, and woman suffrage movements.
Thomas Barnardo, 1845-1905, (Br.) social reformer; pioneer in care of destitute children.
Clara Barton, 1821-1912, (U.S.) organized American Red Cross.
Daisy Bates, 1914-99, (U.S.) black civil rights leader who fought for integration; advocate for the "Little Rock 9" during Arkansas desegregation crisis in 1957.
Henry Ward Beecher, 1813-87, (U.S.) clergyman, abolitionist.
Peter Benenson, 1921-2005, (Br.) activist; founded Amnesty International, 1961.
Mary McLeod Bethune, 1875-1955, (U.S.) black educator, civil rights activist; adviser to FDR and Truman; founder, pres., Bethune-Cookman College.

Amelia Bloomer, 1818-94, (U.S.) suffragette, social reformer.
Julian Bond, 1940-2015, (U.S.) civil rights leader, NAACP chair, 1998-2015.
Yelena Bonner, 1923-2011, (Russ.) human rights activist in former Soviet Union.
William Booth, 1829-1912, (Br.) founded Salvation Army.
James Brady, 1940-2014, (U.S.) gun control advocate; Reagan press sec.
John Brown, 1800-59, (U.S.) abolitionist who led murder of five pro-slavery men; hanged.
Frances Xavier (Mother) Cabrini, 1850-1917, (It.-U.S.) nun; founded charitable institutions; first American canonized as a saint, 1946.
Stokely Carmichael (Kwame Toure), 1941-98, (Trinidad-U.S.) black power activist; major proponent of Pan-Africanism; prime min. of Black Panthers.
Carrie Chapman Catt, 1859-1947, (U.S.) suffragette.
Cesar Chavez, 1927-93, (U.S.) labor leader; helped establish United Farm Workers of America.
Eldridge Cleaver, 1935-98, (U.S.) revolutionary social critic; former minister of information for Black Panthers; *Soul on Ice*.
Clarence Darrow, 1857-1938, (U.S.) lawyer; defender of underdog, opponent of capital punishment.
Ossie Davis, 1917-2005, (U.S.) black civil rights activist, actor, director.
Dorothy Day, 1897-1980, (U.S.) founder of Catholic Worker movement.
Eugene V. Debs, 1855-1926, (U.S.) labor leader; led Pullman strike, 1894; 4-time Socialist presidential candidate.
Vine Deloria Jr., 1933-2005, (U.S.) Native American activist, author; *Custer Died for Your Sins*.
Dorothea Dix, 1802-87, (U.S.) crusader for mentally ill.
Thomas Dooley, 1927-61, (U.S.) "jungle doctor"; noted for efforts to supply medical aid to developing countries.
Marjory Stoneman Douglas, 1890-1998, (U.S.) writer, environmentalist; campaigned to save Florida Everglades.
Frederick Douglass, 1817-95, (U.S.) slave, author, editor, orator, diplomat; edited abolitionist weekly *The North Star*.
Andrea Dworkin, 1946-2005, (U.S.) radical feminist, antipornography crusader.
Medgar Evers, 1925-63, (U.S.) black civil rights leader; campaigned to register black voters; assassinated.
James Farmer, 1920-99, (U.S.) black civil rights leader; founded Congress of Racial Equality (CORE).
Betty Friedan, 1921-2006, (U.S.) author, feminist; *The Feminine Mystique*.
Millard Fuller, 1935-2009, (U.S.) founder of Habitat for Humanity.
William Lloyd Garrison, 1805-79, (U.S.) abolitionist.
Miep Gies, 1909-2010, (Neth.) protector of Anne Frank and her family during WWII.
Emma Goldman, 1869-1940, (Russ.-U.S.) published anarchist *Mother Earth*; birth-control advocate.
Samuel Gompers, 1850-1924, (U.S.) labor leader; first pres. of the American Federation of Labor (AFL).
Prince Hall, 1735-1807, (U.S.) activist; founded black Freemasonry; served in American Revolutionary War.
Michael Harrington, 1928-89, (U.S.) exposed poverty in affluent U.S. in *The Other America*, 1963.
Dorothy Height, 1912-2010, (U.S.) civil rights activist; pres. of the National Council of Negro Women, 1957-97.
Sidney Hillman, 1887-1946, (U.S.) labor leader; helped organize CIO.
Benjamin Hooks, 1925-2010, (U.S.) civil rights activist; exec. dir. NAACP, 1977-92.
Samuel G. Howe, 1801-76, (U.S.) social reformer; changed public attitudes toward the blind, deaf, mentally challenged.
Franklin Kameny, 1925-2011, (U.S.) gay rights activist.
Helen Keller, 1880-1968, (U.S.) crusader for better treatment for the disabled; deaf and blind herself.
Jack Kevorkian 1928-2011, (U.S.) pathologist; assisted-suicide activist.
Coretta Scott King, 1927-2006, (U.S.) black civil rights leader; wife of Rev. Martin Luther King Jr.
Rev. Martin Luther King Jr., 1929-68, (U.S.) civil rights leader; led 1955-56 Montgomery, AL, boycott; founder, pres., Southern Christian Leadership Conference, 1957; Nobel peace laureate, 1964; assassinated.
Maggie Kuhn, 1905-95, (U.S.) founded Gray Panthers, 1970.
William Kunstler, 1919-95, (U.S.) civil liberties attorney.
John L. Lewis, 1880-1969, (U.S.) labor leader; headed United Mine Workers, 1920-60.
Almena Lomax, 1915-2011, (U.S.) civil rights activist; journalist who founded *The Los Angeles Tribune*.
Clara Luper, 1923-2011, (U.S.) civil rights activist.
Wangari Maathai, 1940-2011, (Kenya), environmental activist; 2004 Nobel Peace Prize winner.
Robert Macauley, 1923-2010, (U.S.) founder of AmeriCares.
Malcolm X (Little), 1925-65, (U.S.) Black Muslim, black nationalist leader; promoted black pride; assassinated.
Russell Means, 1939-2012, (U.S.) American Indian activist.
Karl Menninger, 1893-1990, (U.S.) with brother William, founded Menninger Clinic and Menninger Foundation.
Lucretia Mott, 1793-1880, (U.S.) reformer, pioneer feminist.
Philip Murray, 1886-1952, (U.S.) Scottish-born labor leader.
Huey P. Newton, 1942-89, (U.S.) cofounded Black Panther Party, 1966.
Florence Nightingale, 1820-1910, (Br.) founder of modern nursing.
Emmeline Pankhurst, 1858-1928, (Br.) suffragette.
Rosa Parks,1913-2005, (U.S.) black civil rights activist; her actions sparked 1955-56 Montgomery, AL, bus boycott.
A. Philip Randolph, 1889-1979, (U.S.) organized Brotherhood of Sleeping Car Porters, 1925; an organizer of 1941 and 1963 March on Washington movements.
Walter Reuther, 1907-70, (U.S.) labor leader; headed United Auto Workers.
Jacob Riis, 1849-1914, (U.S.) crusader for urban reforms.
Paul Robeson, 1898-1976, (U.S.) actor, singer, black civil rights activist.
Bayard Rustin, 1910-87, (U.S.) an organizer of the 1963 March on Washington; exec. dir., A. Philip Randolph Institute.
Margaret Sanger, 1883-1966, (U.S.) social reformer; pioneered the birth-control movement.
Earl of Shaftesbury (A. A. Cooper), 1801-85, (Br.) social reformer.
Eunice Kennedy Shriver, 1921-2009, (U.S.) cofounder of Special Olympics for mentally challenged athletes.
Sargent Shriver, 1915-2011, (U.S.) founding director of Peace Corps; founder of Job Corps, Head Start.
Fred Shuttlesworth, 1922-2011, (U.S.) civil rights activist.
Albertina Sisulu, 1918-2011, (S. Africa), anti-apartheid activist.
Elizabeth Cady Stanton, 1815-1902, (U.S.) woman suffrage pioneer.
Lucy Stone, 1818-93, (U.S.) feminist, abolitionist.
Mother Teresa of Calcutta, 1910-97, (Alban.) nun; founded order to care for sick, dying poor; 1979 Nobel Peace Prize.
Willard Townsend, 1895-1957, (U.S.) organized the United Transport Service Employees (Red Caps), 1935.
Sojourner Truth (Isabella Baumfree), 1797-1883, (U.S.) preacher, abolitionist; worked for black educ. opportunity.
Harriet Tubman, 1823-1913, (U.S.) prominent figure in the Underground Railroad, which helped runaway slaves in the South reach safety in the North; nurse, spy for Union Army in the Civil War.
Nat Turner, 1800-31, (U.S.) slave who led the most significant of more than 200 slave revolts in U.S., in Southampton, VA; hanged.
Philip Vera Cruz, 1905-94, (Philip.-U.S.) helped found the United Farm Workers Union.
Edgar Wayburn, 1906-2010, (U.S.) conservationist; Sierra Club pres.
William Wilberforce, 1759-1833, (Br.) social reformer; prominent in struggle to abolish slave trade.
Frances E. Willard, 1839-98, (U.S.) temperance, women's rights leader.
Mary Wollstonecraft, 1759-97, (Br.) *Vindication of the Rights of Women*.

Sports Personalities of the Past and Present

Henry (Hank) Aaron, b 1934, Milwaukee-Atlanta outfielder; hit record 755 home runs, led NL 4 times; record 2,297 RBI.
Kareem Abdul-Jabbar, b 1947, Milwaukee, L.A. Lakers center; MVP 6 times; all-time leading NBA scorer, 38,387 pts.
Andre Agassi, b 1970, tennis player; won Wimbledon (1992); U.S. Open ('94, '99), Austral. Open ('95, 2000-01, '03), French Open ('99).
Troy Aikman, b 1966, quarterback; led Dallas Cowboys to Super Bowl wins in 1993-94, '96; Super Bowl MVP, 1993.
Ben Ainslie, b 1977, (Br.) most decorated Olympic sailor; gold, 2000, '04, '08, '12. silver, 1996.
Amy Alcott, b 1956, golfer; 33 career wins (5 majors); inducted into Hall of Fame, 1999.
Grover Cleveland "Pete" Alexander, 1887-1950, pitcher; won 373 NL games; pitched 16 shutouts, 1916.
Muhammad Ali, b 1942, 3-time heavyweight champion.
Fernando Alonso, b 1981, (Sp.) Formula 1 racer; youngest ever to win a World Grand Prix championship, 2005; defended title, 2006.
Morten Andersen, b 1960, (Den.) kicker; NFL's career points leader, with 2,544 (1982-2007).
Gary Anderson, b 1959, (S. Afr.) kicker; NFL's 2nd in career points, with 2,434.
Sparky Anderson, 1934-2010, first manager to win World Series in the NL (Cincinnati, 1975-76) and AL (Detroit, 1984).
Mario Andretti, b 1940, (It.) race-car driver; won Daytona 500 (1967), Indy 500 (1969); Formula 1 world title (1978).
Earl Anthony, 1938-2001, bowler; won record 6 PBA Championships (1973-75, '81-'83), 43 career PBA tournaments.
Eddie Arcaro, 1916-97, only jockey to win racing's Triple Crown twice, 1941, '48; rode to 4,779 wins in his career.
Lance Armstrong, b 1971, cyclist; record 7-time winner of Tour de France (1999-2005); stripped of victories in 2012 for use of performance-enhancing drugs.
Arthur Ashe, 1943-93, tennis player; won U.S. Open (1968); Wimbledon (1975).
Evelyn Ashford, b 1957, sprinter; won 100m gold (1984) and silver (1988); member of 5 U.S. Olympic teams.
Red Auerbach, 1917-2006, coached Boston to 9 NBA titles.
Tracy Austin, b 1962, youngest player to win U.S. Open tennis title (age 16 in 1979).
Victoria Azarenka, b 1989, (Belarus) tennis player; won Austral. Open (2012-13).
Ernie Banks, 1931-2015, Chicago Cubs slugger; hit 512 NL homers; twice MVP.

Roger Bannister, b 1929, (Br.) physician; ran 1st sub-4-min. mile, May 6, 1954 (3 min. 59.4 sec.).

Charles Barkley, b 1963, NBA MVP, 1993; 4th player ever to surpass 20,000 pts., 10,000 rebounds, 4,000 assists.

Rick Barry, b 1944, NBA scoring leader, 1967; ABA scoring leader, 1969.

Sammy Baugh, 1914-2008, Washington Redskins quarterback; held numerous records upon retirement after 16 seasons.

Elgin Baylor, b 1934, L.A. Lakers forward; 11-time all-star.

Bob Beamon, b 1946, Olympic long jump gold medalist, 1968; world record jump of 29 ft 2½ in. stood until 1991.

Boris Becker, b 1967, (Ger.) tennis star; won U.S. Open 1989; Wimbledon champ 1985-86, '89.

David Beckham, b 1975, (Br.) soccer star; joined L.A. Galaxy, 2007-12, with record-breaking $250-mil contract.

Bill Belichick, b 1952, NFL coach; led New England Patriots to 4 Super Bowl wins (2001, '03-'04, '14); best all-time post-season coaching record.

Jean Béliveau, 1931-2014, (Can.) Montréal Canadiens center; scored 507 goals; twice MVP.

Johnny Bench, b 1947, Cincinnati Reds catcher; twice MVP; led league in home runs twice, RBIs 3 times.

Patty Berg, 1918-2006, 80+ golf tournament wins; AP Woman Athlete of the Year 3 times.

Chris Berman, b 1955, sportscaster, anchor for ESPN and ABC Sports.

Yogi Berra, 1925-2015, Yankee catcher (1946-63); 3-time MVP.

Abebe Bikila, 1932-73, (Eth.) runner; won consecutive Olympic marathon gold medals in 1960 (barefoot), '64.

Matt Biondi, b 1965, swimmer; won 5 golds, 1988 Olympics.

Larry Bird, b 1956, Boston Celtics forward (1979-92); NBA MVP, 1984-86; 1998 coach of the year with Indiana Pacers.

Bonnie Blair, b 1964, speed skater; won 5 individual gold medals in 3 Olympics (1988, '92, '94).

George Blanda, 1927-2010, quarterback, kicker; 26 years as active player, scored 2,002 career points.

Fanny Blankers-Koen, 1918-2004, (Neth.) track star; won 4 golds in 1948 Olympics.

Wade Boggs, b 1958, AL batting champ, 1983, '85-'88; reached 3,000 career hits, 1999 (3,010).

Usain Bolt, b 1986, (Jam.) Olympic sprinter, gold medalist, 2008, '12; world record for men's 100m, 200m runs.

Barry Bonds, b 1964, outfielder; hit record 73 homers, 2001; NL MVP, 1990, '92-'93, 2001-04; 1st all-time in HRs (762); indicted in steroid scandal, 2007; convicted of obstruction of justice, 2011.

Björn Borg, b 1956, (Swed.) led Sweden to first Davis Cup, 1975; 6-time French Open, 5-time Wimbledon champion.

Ray Bourque, b 1960, (Can.) Boston defenseman,1979-2000; 5-time Norris Trophy winner; won Stanley Cup with Colorado, 2001.

Bill Bradley, b 1943, All-American at Princeton; led NY Knicks to 2 NBA titles (1970, '73); U.S. senator, 1979-97.

Donald Bradman, 1908-2001, (Austral.) widely regarded as greatest cricketer ever; set several batting records.

Terry Bradshaw, b 1948, quarterback; led Pittsburgh to 4 Super Bowl wins, 1975-76, '79-'80; NFL MVP, 1978.

Tom Brady, b 1977, quarterback; led New England to 4 Super Bowl titles, 2002, '04-'05, '15; Super Bowl MVP, 2002, '04, '15; NFL MVP, 2007, '11.

Ryan Braun, b 1983, Milwaukee Brewers left fielder; NL MVP, 2011.

Drew Brees, b 1979, New Orleans Saints quarterback; Super Bowl MVP, 2010.

Christine Brennan, b 1958, sports journalist for *USA Today*, radio and TV commentator specializing in figure skating.

George Brett, b 1953, Kansas City Royals infielder; led AL in batting, 1976, '80, '90; MVP, 1980.

Lou Brock, b 1939, St. Louis Cardinals outfielder; stole NL single-season record 118 bases, 1974; led NL 8 times.

Jim Brown, b 1936, Cleveland fullback; 12,312 career yds; NFL MVP 1957-58, '65.

Paul Brown, 1908-91, football team owner, coach; led eponymous Cleveland Browns to 3 NFL championships.

Bob Bryan and **Mike Bryan**, b 1978, doubles tennis players; won 16 Grand Slam doubles titles (2003-14); Olympic gold, 2012.

Kobe Bryant, b 1978, NBA guard; won 3 straight titles with Lakers (2000-02); leading NBA scorer, 2006 and '07; NBA MVP, 2008; NBA Finals MVP, 2010; member of U.S. Olympic gold medal teams (2008, '12).

Paul "Bear" Bryant, 1913-83, college football coach with 323 wins; led Alabama to 6 national titles (1961, '64-'65, '73, '78-'79).

Sergei Bubka, b 1963, (Ukr.) pole vaulter; first to clear 20 ft; gold medal, 1988 Olympics.

Don Budge, 1915-2000, won numerous amateur and pro tennis titles; Grand Slam, 1938.

Reggie Bush, b 1985, NFL running back; helped USC to 2 national titles (2003-04; '04 vacated).

Dick Butkus, b 1942, Chicago Bears linebacker; NFL defensive player of the year (1969-70).

Dick Button, b 1929, figure skater; won 1948, '52 Olympic gold medals; world titleholder, 1948-52.

Miguel Cabrera, b 1983, (Venez.) 9-time All-Star; won AL triple crown (2012); AL MVP 2013.

Walter Camp, 1859-1925, Yale football player, coach, athletic director; established many rules for modern football.

Roy Campanella, 1921-93, Hall of Fame catcher for the Brooklyn Dodgers (1948-57); 3-time NL MVP.

Earl Campbell, b 1955, NFL running back; MVP 1978-79.

Jose Canseco, b 1964, outfielder; led Oakland A's to the World Series, 1988; wrote book about steroids in baseball, 2005.

Eric Cantona, b 1966, (Fr.) soccer star; Manchester United (1992-97).

Rod Carew, b 1945, AL infielder; 7 batting titles, 1977 MVP.

Steve Carlton, b 1944, NL pitcher; won 20 games 6 times, Cy Young award 4 times; 4,136 career strikeouts.

Pete Carroll, b 1951, college and pro football coach; coached the USC Trojans to 2 championships (2003-04).

Billy Casper, 1931-2015, PGA Player of the Year 2 times; U.S. Open champ twice.

Tamika Catchings, b 1979, Indiana Fever forward; 3-time Olympic gold medalist (2004, '08, '12); WNBA MVP, 2011.

Wilt Chamberlain, 1936-99, center; NBA leading scorer 7 times, MVP 4 times; scored 100 pts. in a game, 1962.

Bobby Clarke, b 1949, (Can.) Philadelphia Flyers center; led team to 2 Stanley Cup championships; MVP 3 times.

Roger Clemens, b 1962, pitcher; 1986 AL MVP; only 7-time Cy Young winner (1986-87, '91, '97-'98, 2001, '04); twice recorded record 20 Ks in a game; 354 wins, 4,672 Ks (3rd all-time); accused of lying to Congress about steroids, 2010.

Roberto Clemente, 1934-72, Pittsburgh Pirates outfielder; won 4 batting titles; MVP, 1966; 3,000 career hits; killed in plane crash.

Kim Clijsters, b 1983, (Belg.) tennis player; U.S. Open winner (2005, '09-'10); Austral. Open (2011).

Ty Cobb, 1886-1961, Detroit Tigers outfielder; record .367 lifetime batting average, 12 batting titles.

Sebastian Coe, b 1956, (Br.) runner; won Olympic 1,500m gold medal and 800m silver medal in both 1980, '84.

Nadia Comaneci, b 1961, (Rom.) gymnast; won 3 gold medals, achieved 7 perfect scores, 1976 Olympics; 9 Olympic medals overall.

Maureen Connolly, 1934-69, won tennis Grand Slam, 1953; AP Woman Athlete of the Year 3 times.

Jimmy Connors, b 1952, tennis player; 8 Grand Slam singles titles.

Alberto Contador, b 1982, (Sp.) cyclist; won Tour de France 2007, '09; stripped of 2010 title because of doping offense.

Cynthia Cooper, b 1963, basketball; 4-time MVP of WNBA finals; 2-time league MVP for the Houston Comets.

James J. Corbett, 1866-1933, heavyweight champion, 1892-97; credited with being the first "scientific" boxer.

Angel Cordero Jr., b 1942, jockey; leading money winner, 1976, '82-'83; rode 3 Kentucky Derby winners.

Margaret Smith Court, b 1942, (Austral.) tennis great; won 24 Grand Slam events.

Bob Cousy, b 1928, Boston guard; 6 NBA titles, 1957 MVP.

Sidney Crosby, b 1987, (Can.) hockey player; Art Ross Trophy (2007, '14), Olympic gold medal (2010).

Mark Cuban, b 1958, Dallas Mavericks owner; known for outspokenness.

Stephen Curry, b 1988, NBA point guard; NBA MVP, 2015.

Bjoern Daehlie, b 1967, (Nor.) cross-country skier; won record 8 Winter Olympic gold medals.

Lindsay Davenport, b 1976, tennis player; won Olympic gold, 1996; U.S. Open, 1998; Wimbledon, 1999; Austral. Open, 2000.

Al Davis, 1929-2011, Oakland Raiders owner, former coach.

Oscar De La Hoya, b 1973, won IBF lightweight (1995); WBC super lightweight (1996); welterweight (1997-99, 2000) titles.

Donna de Varona, b 1947, swimmer; won 2 Olympic golds, 1964; 1st female sportscaster at a major network, 1965.

Dizzy Dean, 1910-74, pitcher; St. Louis Cardinals' "Gashouse Gang" in the '30s.

Mary Decker Slaney, b 1958, runner; has held 6 separate American records from the 800m to 10,000m.

Frank Deford, b 1938, sr. contributing writer for *Sports Illustrated*; author, commentator.

Jack Dempsey, 1895-1983, heavyweight champ, 1919-26.

Gail Devers, b 1966, Olympic 100m gold medalist (1992, '96).

Joe DiMaggio, 1914-99, NY Yankees outfielder; hit safely in record 56 consecutive games, 1941; AL MVP 3 times.

Novak Djokovic, b 1987, (Serb.) tennis player; 10 Grand Slam singles titles.

Landon Donovan, b 1982, soccer forward; all-time leading U.S. men's intl. goal scorer with 57; MLS MVP, 2009.

Tony Dorsett, b 1954, Heisman winner who led the Dallas Cowboys to an NFL title in his rookie year, 1977.

Gabrielle Douglas, b 1995, first African-American gymnast to win Olympic gold in all-around (2012).

Tim Duncan, b 1976, San Antonio center; 3-time NBA Finals MVP, 1999, 2003, '05; NBA MVP, 2003.

Roberto Duran, b 1951, (Pan.) boxer; held titles at 3 weights; lost 1980 "no mas" fight to Sugar Ray Leonard.

Kevin Durant, b 1988, NBA forward; NBA MVP, 2014.

Leo Durocher, 1905-91, manager; won 3 NL pennants (Brooklyn, 1941; NY Giants, 1951, '54), 1954 World Series.
Dale Earnhardt Jr., b 1974, stock car racer; Daytona 500 winner (2004, '14).
Dale Earnhardt Sr., 1951-2001, 7-time NASCAR Winston Cup champ; died in a last-lap crash at 2001 Daytona 500.
Stefan Edberg, b 1966, (Swed.) tennis player; U.S. Open (1991-92), Wimbledon (1988, '90), Austral. Open (1985, '87).
Gertrude Ederle, 1905-2003, first woman to swim English Channel; broke existing men's record, 1926.
Teresa Edwards, b 1964, 5-time basketball Olympian; gold medalist, 1984, '88, '96, 2000; bronze medalist, 1992.
Hicham El Guerrouj, b 1974, (Morocco) runner; holds world records in mile (3:43.13) and 1,500m (3:26); won gold medals in 1,500m and 5,000m, 2004 Olympics.
John Elway, b 1960, quarterback; led Denver Broncos to 2 Super Bowl wins, 1998-99; NFL MVP, 1987; Super Bowl MVP, 1999.
Julius "Dr. J" Erving, b 1950, 3-time ABA MVP, 1981 NBA MVP.
Phil Esposito, b 1942, (Can.) NHL scoring leader 5 times.
Janet Evans, b 1971, 4 Olympic swimming golds, 1988, '92.
Lee Evans, b 1947, Olympic 400m gold medalist in 1968 with 43.86-sec. world record not broken until 1988.
Chris Evert, b 1954, 6-time U.S. Open tennis champ, 3-time Wimbledon champ.
Ray Ewry, 1873-1937, track-and-field star; won 8 Olympics gold medals (1900, '04, '08).
Nick Faldo, b 1957, (Br.) golfer; won Masters, British Open 3 times each.
Juan Manuel Fangio, 1911-95 (Arg.), 5-time World Grand Prix driving champ (1951, '54-'57).
Marshall Faulk, b 1973, 2000 NFL MVP; scored then-record 26 TDs, 2001; 3-time Off. Player of the Year (1999-2001).
Brett Favre, b 1969, quarterback; led Green Bay to Super Bowl win, 1997; NFL MVP, 1995-96; co-MVP, 1997.
Roger Federer, b 1981, (Switz.) tennis player; 17 Grand Slam singles titles (1st all-time).
Bob Feller, 1918-2010, Cleveland Indians pitcher; won 266 games; pitched 3 no-hitters, 12 one-hitters.
Rollie Fingers, b 1946, pitcher; 341 career saves; AL MVP, Cy Young Award, 1981; World Series MVP, 1974.
Peggy Fleming, b 1948, world figure skating champion, 1966-68; gold medalist, 1968 Olympics.
Whitey Ford, b 1928, NY Yankees pitcher; won record 10 World Series games.
George Foreman, b 1949, heavyweight champion, 1973-74, '94-'95; at 45, oldest to win a heavyweight title; gold medalist, 1968 Olympics.
Dick Fosbury, b 1947, high jumper; won 1968 Olympic gold medal; developed the "Fosbury Flop."
Jimmie Foxx, 1907-67, Red Sox, Athletics slugger; MVP 3 times; triple crown, 1933.
A. J. Foyt, b 1935, won Indy 500 4 times; U.S. Auto Club champ 7 times.
Dario Franchitti, b 1973, (Scot.) 3-time Indy 500 winner, 2007, '10, '12.
Missy Franklin, b 1995, won 4 Olympic swimming golds, 2012.
Joe Frazier, 1944-2011, heavyweight champion, 1970-73; gold medalist, 1964 Olympics.
Walt Frazier, b 1945, Hall of Fame guard for NY Knicks' NBA championship teams (1970, '73).
Peter Gammons, b 1945, sportswriter, broadcaster; named to Baseball Hall of Fame.
Lou Gehrig, 1903-41, NY Yankees 1st baseman; MVP, 1927, '36; triple crown, 1934; AL record 184 RBIs, 1931; played in 2,130 straight games (1925-39), a record that stood until 1995.
Althea Gibson, 1927-2003, 2-time U.S. Nationals and Wimbledon champ.
Bob Gibson, b 1935, St. Louis Cardinals pitcher; won Cy Young award twice; struck out 3,117 batters.
Josh Gibson, 1911-47, Hall of Fame catcher; known as "Babe Ruth of the Negro Leagues"; credited with as many as 84 homers in 1 season, about 800 in his career.
Marc Girardelli, b 1963, (Lux.) skier; won 5 World Cup titles.
Raúl González, b 1977, (Sp.) soccer player; led Real Madrid to 3 Champions League titles (1998, 2000, '02); all-time top UEFA goal scorer (71).
Jeff Gordon, b 1971, race-car driver; youngest to win NASCAR title 4 times (1995, '97-'98, 2001).
Steffi Graf, b 1969, (Ger.) tennis player; 22 Grand Slam singles titles (2nd all-time).
Otto Graham, 1921-2003, Cleveland quarterback; 4-time all-pro.
Red Grange, 1903-91, All-American at Univ. of Illinois, 1923-25; played for Chicago Bears, 1925-35.
"Mean" Joe Greene, b 1946, Pittsburgh Steelers lineman; twice NFL outstanding defensive player.
Wayne Gretzky, b 1961, (Can.) top scorer in NHL history with record 894 goals, 1,963 assists, 2,857 pts.; MVP, 1980-87, '89.
Bob Griese, b 1945, All-Pro quarterback; led Miami Dolphins to 17-0 season, 1972, 2 Super Bowl titles, 1973-74.
Ken Griffey Jr., b 1969, outfielder; led AL in homers 1994, '97-'99; 1997 AL MVP; 10 gold gloves.
Archie Griffin, b 1954, Ohio State running back; only 2-time winner of the Heisman Trophy (1974-75).
Florence Griffith Joyner, 1959-98, sprinter; won 3 gold medals at 1988 Olympics; world and Olympic record for 100m.
Lefty Grove, 1900-75, pitcher; won 300 AL games.
Vladimir Guerrero, b 1975, (Dom. Rep.) right fielder; 2004 AL MVP award.
Janet Guthrie, b 1938, 1st woman driver in Indy 500 (1977).
Tony Gwynn, 1960-2014, 8-time NL batting champ (1984, '87-'89, '94-'97); 3,141 career hits.
Walter Hagen, 1892-1969, golfer; 5 PGA, 4 British Open titles.
Mika Hakkinen, b 1968, (Fin.) Formula One racing driver; Formula One champion, 1998-99.
George Halas, 1895-1983, founder/player/coach of Chicago Bears; won 6 NFL championships as coach.
Roy Halladay, b 1977, pitcher; Cy Young Award, 2003, '10; pitched perfect game, 2010.
Dorothy Hamill, b 1956, figure skater; gold medalist at the Olympics and World championships, 1976.
Josh Hamilton, b 1981, Texas Rangers outfielder; AL MVP, 2010.
Scott Hamilton, b 1958, U.S. and world figure skating champion, 1981-84; Olympic gold medalist, 1984.
Mia Hamm, b 1972, soccer player; led U.S. teams to World Cup victories (1991, '99) and Olympic gold (1996, 2004).
Franco Harris, b 1950, running back; 4 Super Bowls with Steelers (1975-76, '79-'80); 1,000+ yds in a season 8 times.
Marvin Harrison, b 1972, Indianapolis Colts wide receiver; NFL record for single-season receptions (143), 2002.
Bill Hartack, 1932-2007, jockey; rode 5 Kentucky Derby winners.
Dominik Hasek, b 1965, (Czech.) NHL goaltender; won Vezina Trophy, 1994-95, '97-'99, 2001; NHL MVP, 1997-98.
John Havlicek, b 1940, Boston Celtics forward; scored 26,395 career pts.
Eric Heiden, b 1958, speed skater; won 5 Olympic golds, 1980.
Rickey Henderson, b 1958, outfielder; 1990 AL MVP; record 130 stolen bases, 1982; all-time leader in steals, runs.
Sonja Henie, 1912-69, (Nor.) world champion figure skater, 1927-36; Olympic gold medalist, 1928, '32, '36.
Martina Hingis, b 1980, (Switz.) won Austral. and U.S. Opens, Wimbledon; youngest number one player (16 yrs., 6 mos.), 1997.
Ben Hogan, 1912-97, golfer; won 4 U.S. Open titles, 2 PGA Championships, 2 Masters.
Santonio Holmes, b 1984, wide receiver; Super Bowl MVP, 2009.
Evander Holyfield, b 1962, 4-time heavyweight champion.
Rogers Hornsby, 1896-1963, NL 2nd baseman; batted record .424, 1924; twice won triple crown.
Paul Hornung, b 1935, Green Bay Packers running back, placekicker; scored record 176 pts., 1960.
Ryan Howard, b 1979, first baseman for Philadelphia Phillies; known for his hitting; 2006 NL MVP.
Gordie Howe, b 1928, (Can.) hockey forward; NHL MVP 6 times; scored 801 goals in 26 NHL seasons.
Carl Hubbell, 1903-88, NY Giants pitcher; 20-game winner 5 consecutive seasons, 1933-37.
Bobby Hull, b 1939, (Can.) NHL all-star 10 times; MVP, 1965-66.
Brett Hull, b 1964, (Can.) St. Louis Blues forward; led NHL in goals, 1990-92; MVP, 1991.
Catfish Hunter, 1946-99, pitched perfect game, 1968; 20-game winner 5 times.
Don Hutson, 1913-97, Packers receiver; caught 99 TD passes; 2-time NFL MVP.
Juli Inkster, b 1960, Hall of Fame golfer; won 7 career major titles.
Bo Jackson, b 1962, NFL running back (1987-90) and MLB outfielder (1986-91, '93-'94); 1985 Heisman Trophy winner.
Phil Jackson, b 1945, won 11 NBA titles as coach of Bulls and Lakers; 1970, '73 title as player with NY Knicks.
Reggie Jackson, b 1946, slugger; led AL in home runs 4 times; MVP, 1973; hit 5 World Series home runs, 1977.
"Shoeless" Joe Jackson, 1889-1951, outfielder; 3rd highest career batting average (.356); one of the "Black Sox" banned for allegedly throwing 1919 World Series.
Jaromir Jagr, b 1972, (Czech.) hockey player; NHL MVP, 1999; Art Ross Trophy (leading scorer), 1995, 1998-2001.
LeBron James, b 1984, NBA forward; Olympic gold medalist (2008, '12); NBA MVP, 2009, '10, '12, '13.
Ron Jaworski, b 1951, former NFL quarterback (1974-89); NFL analyst on ESPN.
Sally Jenkins, b 1960, sports journalist and writer for *Washington Post*.
Caitlyn (fmr. Bruce) Jenner, b 1949, Olympic decathlon gold medalist, 1976; came out as a transgender woman in 2015.
Lynn Jennings, b 1960, runner; 3-time World, 9-time U.S. cross country champ; bronze (10,000m), 1992 Olympics.
Derek Jeter, b 1974, shortstop; led NY Yankees to 5 World Series titles; World Series MVP, 2000.
Earvin "Magic" Johnson, b 1959, NBA MVP, 1987, '89, '90; playoff MVP, 1980, '82, '87; 4th in career assists.

Jack Johnson, 1878-1946, heavyweight champion, 1908-15.
Jimmie Johnson, b 1975, 5-time NASCAR Sprint Cup Series champ, 2006-10, '13; Daytona 500 winner, 2006.
Michael Johnson, b 1967, 4-time Olympic gold medalist (1992, '96, 2000); world and Olympic record, 400m and 4 × 400m.
Randy Johnson, b 1963, 5-time Cy Young winner; strikeout leader, 1992-95, 1999-2002, '04; 4,875 strikeouts (2nd all-time); pitched perfect game, 2004.
Walter Johnson, 1887-1946, Washington Senators pitcher; won 417 games; record 110 shutouts.
Bobby Jones, 1902-71, won golf's Grand Slam, 1930; U.S. amateur champ 5 times, U.S. Open champ 4 times.
Cobi Jones, b 1970, soccer player; most U.S. national team appearances with 164.
David "Deacon" Jones, 1938-2013, 5-time All-Pro with L.A. Rams (1965-69); "sack" specialist credited with inventing the term.
Marion Jones, b 1975, multi-event Olympic medalist; stripped of medals in 2007 after admitting use of PEDs.
Roy Jones Jr., b 1969, light heavyweight champ, 1999-2004.
Michael Jordan, b 1963, guard; leading NBA scorer, 1987-93, '96-'98; MVP, 1988, '91-'92, '96, '98; playoff MVP, 1991-93, '96-'98; ESPN Athlete of the Century.
Dorothy Kamenshek, 1925-2010, led Rockford (IL) Peaches to 4 All-American Girls Baseball League titles in the 1940s.
Jackie Joyner-Kersee, b 1962, Olympic gold medalist in heptathlon (1988, '92), long jump (1988).
Clayton Kershaw, b 1988, pitcher; NL Cy Young Award (2011, '13, '14).
Harmon Killebrew, 1936-2011, Minnesota Twins slugger; led AL in home runs 6 times; 573 lifetime.
Jean Claude Killy, b 1943, (Fr.) skier; 3 Olympic golds, 1968.
Kim Yu-Na, b 1990, (S. Kor.) figure skater; Olympic gold medal winner, 2010; world champion, 2009.
Ralph Kiner, 1922-2014, Pittsburgh Pirates slugger; led NL in home runs 7 consecutive years, 1946-52.
Billie Jean King, b 1943, U.S. singles champ 4 times; Wimbledon champ 6 times; beat Bobby Riggs, 1973.
Peter King, b 1957, senior writer for *Sports Illustrated*.
Bob Knight, b 1940, ESPN studio analyst, ret. basketball coach; led Indiana U. to NCAA title in 1976, '81, '87; winningest men's college basketball coach (902).
Olga Korbut, b 1955, (Belarus) gymnast; 3 Olympic golds, 1972.
Sandy Koufax, b 1935, 3-time Cy Young winner; lowest ERA in NL, 1962-66; pitched 4 no-hitters, 1 perfect game.
Jack Kramer, 1921-2009, world's number one tennis player, 1946-53; first at Wimbledon to compete in shorts.
Ingrid Kristiansen, b 1956, (Nor.) only runner to have held world records in 5,000m, 10,000m, and marathon.
Julie Krone, b 1963, winningest female jockey; first woman to ride a winner in a Triple Crown race (Belmont, 1993).
Petra Kvitová, b 1990, (Czech.) tennis player; won Wimbledon, 2011, '14.
Michelle Kwan, b 1980, figure skater; 9 U.S., 5 World titles; silver medalist at 1998 Olympics, bronze in 2002.
Guy Lafleur, b 1951, (Can.) 3-time NHL scoring leader; 1977-78 MVP.
Alexi Lalas, b 1970, soccer player; first modern-era American to play in Italian League Serie A.
Kenesaw Mountain Landis, 1866-1944, 1st commissioner of baseball (1920-44); banned the 8 "Black Sox" involved in fixing 1919 World Series.
Tom Landry, 1924-2000, Dallas Cowboys head coach, 1960-88; won 2 Super Bowls (1972, '78); 3rd in career wins (270).
Dick "Night Train" Lane, 1928-2002, Hall of Fame defensive back; intercepted an NFL season record 14 passes (1952).
Don Larsen, b 1929, as NY Yankee, pitched only World Series perfect game, Oct. 8, 1956—2-0 win over Brooklyn.
Rod Laver, b 1938, (Austral.) won tennis Grand Slam, 1962, '69; Wimbledon champ 4 times.
Katie Ledecky, b 1997, swimmer; Olympic gold medalist (2012).
Mario Lemieux, b 1965, (Can.) 6-time NHL leading scorer; MVP, 1988, '93, '96; playoff MVP, 1991-92.
Greg Lemond, b 1961, cyclist; 3-time Tour de France winner (1986, '89-'90); first American to win the event.
Ivan Lendl, b 1960, (Czech.) 8 Grand Slam tennis titles, including U.S. Open, 1985-87.
Sugar Ray Leonard, b 1956, boxer; held titles in 5 different weight classes.
Lisa Leslie, b 1972, L.A. Sparks center; 3-time WNBA MVP (2001, '04, '06).
Carl Lewis, b 1961, track-and-field star; won 9 Olympic gold medals in sprinting and long jump.
Lennox Lewis, b 1965, (Br.) heavyweight champ, 1994, 1997-2004; Olympic gold medalist, 1998.
Ray Lewis, b 1975, linebacker for the Baltimore Ravens; Super Bowl MVP, 2001.
Li Na, b 1982, (China) tennis player; won French Open, 2011, Austral. Open 2014.
Tim Lincecum, b 1984, S.F. Giants pitcher; NL Cy Young Award, 2008-09.
Tara Lipinski, b 1982, youngest figure skater to win U.S., world championships, 1997, and Winter Olympic gold, 1998.
Carli Lloyd, b 1982, soccer midfielder; Olympic gold medalist (2008, '12); World Cup champion (2015).
Ryan Lochte, b 1984, swimmer; 11-time Olympic medalist, incl. 5 gold (2004, '08, '12).
Vince Lombardi, 1913-70, Green Bay Packers coach; led team to 5 NFL championships, 2 Super Bowl victories.
Nancy Lopez, b 1957, Hall of Fame golfer; 4-time LPGA Player of the Year, 3-time winner of the LPGA Championship.
Greg Louganis, b 1960, won Olympic gold medals in both springboard and platform diving, 1984, '88.
Joe Louis, 1914-81, heavyweight champion, 1937-49.
Sid Luckman, 1916-98, Chicago Bears quarterback; led team to 4 NFL championships; MVP, 1943.
Evan Lysacek, b 1985, figure skater; world champion, 2009; Olympic gold winner, 2010.
Connie Mack, 1862-1956, Philadelphia Athletics manager, 1901-50; won 9 pennants, 5 championships.
John Madden, b 1936, won Super Bowl as coach of Oakland Raiders (1977); former NFL TV analyst.
Greg Maddux, b 1966, NL pitcher; won 4 consecutive Cy Young awards, 1992-95; 355 career wins.
Karl Malone, b 1963, Utah Jazz, L.A. Lakers forward; MVP, 1997, '99; 14-time All-Star; 36,928 career pts. (2nd all-time).
Moses Malone, 1955-2015, NBA center; MVP, 1979, '82, '83.
Eli Manning, b 1981, NY Giants quarterback; Super Bowl MVP, 2008, '12.
Peyton Manning, b 1976, quarterback; most NFL MVP awards, 2003-04, '08-'09, '13; Super Bowl MVP, 2007; single-season passing yards record (5,477), 2013.
Mickey Mantle, 1931-95, NY Yankees outfielder; triple crown, 1956; 18 World Series home runs; MVP 3 times.
Diego Maradona, b 1960, (Arg.) soccer player; led Argentina to World Cup, 1986.
"Pistol" Pete Maravich, 1947-88, guard; scored NCAA record 44.2 ppg during collegiate career; led NBA in scoring, 1977.
Rocky Marciano, 1923-69, heavyweight champion, 1952-56; retired undefeated.
Dan Marino, b 1961, Miami quarterback; NFL record single-season yards passing (5,084), 1984.
Roger Maris, 1934-85, NY Yankees outfielder; hit AL record 61 home runs, 1961, record held 37 years; MVP, 1960-61.
Marta (Marta Vieira da Silva), b 1986, (Braz.) soccer forward; FIFA World Player of the Year, 2006-10.
Curtis Martin, b 1973, Jets running back; 5-time Pro-Bowler; 4th in all-time rushing yards with 14,101.
Eddie Mathews, 1931-2001, Milwaukee-Atlanta Braves 3rd baseman; hit 512 career home runs.
Christy Mathewson, 1880-1925, pitcher; won 373 games.
Bob Mathias, 1930-2006, decathlon gold, 1948, '52 Olympics.
Misty May-Treanor, b 1977, beach volleyball player; 3-time Olympic gold medalist with Kerri Walsh Jennings (2004, '08, '12).
Willie Mays, b 1931, NY-S.F. Giants center fielder; hit 660 home runs, led NL 4 times; had 3,283 hits; twice MVP.
Willie McCovey, b 1938, S.F. Giants slugger; hit 521 home runs; led NL 3 times; MVP, 1969.
John McEnroe, b 1959, U.S. Open tennis champ (1979-81, '84); Wimbledon champ (1981, '83-'84).
John McGraw, 1873-1934, NY Giants manager; led team to 10 pennants, 3 championships.
Mark McGwire, b 1963, hit then-record 70 home runs in 1998; 583 career home runs (10th); admitted career steroid use, 2010.
Rory McIlroy, b 1989, (N. Ire.) golfer; won U.S. Open, 2011; won PGA Championship, 2012, '14; British Open, 2014.
Tamara McKinney, b 1962, 1st U.S. skier to win overall Alpine World Cup championship (1983).
Andrea Mead Lawrence, 1932-2009, skier; first woman to win 2 gold medals in alpine skiing at one Olympics (1952).
Lionel Messi, b 1987, (Arg.) forward for FC Barcelona; FIFA World Player of the Year, 2009-10.
Mark Messier, b 1961, (Can.) center; NHL MVP, 1990, '92; Conn Smythe Trophy, 1984.
Debbie Meyer, b 1952, 1st swimmer to win 3 individual Olympic golds (1968).
Al Michaels, b 1944, *NBC Sunday Night Football* announcer; 5-time Outstanding Sports Personality Emmy winner.
Phil Mickelson, b 1970, golfer; 5 career major titles.
George Mikan, 1924-2005, Minn. Lakers center; considered the best basketball player of first half of 20th cent.
Stan Mikita, b 1940, (Czech.) Chicago Blackhawks center; led NHL in scoring 4 times; MVP twice.
Billy Mills, b 1938, runner; upset winner of the 1964 Olympic 10,000m; only American man ever to win the event.
Joe Montana, b 1956, S.F. 49ers quarterback; Super Bowl MVP, 1982, '85, '90.
Archie Moore, 1913-98, light-heavyweight champ, 1952-62.
Howie Morenz, 1902-37, (Can.) Montréal Canadiens forward; considered best hockey player of first half of 20th cent.
Edwin Moses, b 1955, undefeated in 122 consecutive 400m hurdles races, 1977-87; Olympic gold medalist, 1976, '84.
Shirley Muldowney, b 1940, 1st woman to race Natl. Hot Rod Assn. Top Fuel dragsters; 3-time NHRA points champ.
Eddie Murray, b 1956, 3rd player with both 3,000+ hits and 500+ home runs.
Stan Musial, 1920-2013, St. Louis Cardinals star; won 7 NL batting titles; MVP 3 times.
Rafael Nadal, b 1986, (Sp.) tennis player; 14-time Grand Slam singles champion; Olympic gold medal in men's singles (2008).

Bronko Nagurski, 1908-90, (Can.) Chicago Bears fullback and tackle; gained more than 4,000 yds rushing.
Joe Namath, b 1943, Jets quarterback; 1969 Super Bowl MVP.
Rosie Napravnik, b 1988, jockey.
Steve Nash, b 1974, (Can.) Phoenix Suns point guard; NBA MVP, 2005, '06.
Martina Navratilova, b 1956, (Czech.) tennis player; won 18 Grand Slam singles titles.
Byron Nelson, 1912-2006, won 11 consecutive golf tournaments in 1945; twice Masters and PGA titlist.
Ernie Nevers, 1903-76, Stanford football star; selected as best college fullback to play between 1919 and 1969.
Paula Newby-Fraser, b 1962, ([now] Zimbabwe) 8-time Ironman Triathlon world champ; holds women's course record.
John Newcombe, b 1944, (Austral.) twice U.S. Open tennis champ; Wimbledon champ 3 times.
Jack Nicklaus, b 1940, PGA Player of the Year, 1967, '72; leading money winner 8 times; won 18 majors (6 Masters).
Chuck Noll, 1932-2014, Pittsburgh Steelers coach; won 4 Super Bowls.
Dirk Nowitzki, b 1978, (Ger.) NBA forward; led Mavericks to NBA title, 2011; NBA MVP, 2007.
Paavo Nurmi, 1897-1973, (Fin.) distance runner; won 9 Olympic gold medals, 1920, '24, '28.
Lorena Ochoa, b 1981, (Mex.) LPGA Player of the Year, 2006-09, money leader 2006-08.
Al Oerter, 1936-2007, discus thrower; won gold medal at 4 consecutive Olympics, 1956, '60, '64, '68.
Apolo Ohno, b 1982, speed skater; most decorated American Winter Olympic athlete with 2 gold, 2 silver, 4 bronze (2002, '06, '10).
Hakeem Olajuwon, b 1963, (Nigeria) Houston center; NBA MVP, 1994, playoff MVP, 1994-95; career blocked shots leader (3,830).
Barney Oldfield, 1878-1946, pioneer auto racer; was first to drive a car 60 mph, 1903.
Shaquille O'Neal, b 1972, center; led L.A. Lakers to NBA titles, 2000-02, and Miami Heat to NBA title, 2006; Finals MVP 2000-02; NBA MVP 2000.
Bobby Orr, b 1948, (Can.) Boston Bruins defenseman; 8-time Norris Trophy winner; led NHL in scoring twice, assists 5 times.
Mel Ott, 1909-58, NY Giants right fielder; hit 511 home runs; led NL 6 times.
Jesse Owens, 1913-80, track-and-field athlete; 4 1936 Olympic golds.
Terrell Owens, b 1973, wide receiver.
Satchel Paige, 1906-82, pitcher; starred in Negro leagues, 1924-48; entered major leagues at age 42.
Arnold Palmer, b 1929, golf's first $1 mil winner; won 4 Masters, 2 British Opens.
Jim Palmer, b 1945, Baltimore Orioles pitcher; won Cy Young award 3 times; 20-game winner 8 times.
Inbee Park, b 1988, (S. Kor.) golfer; 2nd ever to win first 3 majors.
Candace Parker, b 1986, L.A. Sparks forward; first woman to dunk in an NCAA tournament game; WNBA MVP (2008, '13).
Joe Paterno, 1926-2012, Penn St. football coach; national title-winner, 1982, '86; most wins in NCAA Div. I coaching history (409); legacy complicated by child sex abuse scandal at Penn St.
Danica Patrick, b 1982, race car driver; 1st woman to lead Indy 500 and to win NASCAR Sprint Cup series pole.
Floyd Patterson, 1935-2006, 2-time heavyweight champion; first to ever regain the title after losing it.
Walter Payton, 1954-99, Chicago Bears running back; 2nd most rushing yards in NFL history; top NFC rusher, 1976-80.
Pelé (Edson Arantes do Nascimento), b 1940, (Braz.) soccer player; led Brazil to 3 World Cups (1958, '62, '70); scored 1,281 goals.
Bob Pettit, b 1932, first NBA player to score 20,000 pts.; twice NBA scoring leader.
Richard Petty, b 1937, NASCAR national champ 7 times; 7-time Daytona 500 winner.
Michael Phelps, b 1985, swimmer; holds record for most Olympic medals (22) and gold medals (18) won by single athlete; won 8 medals at 2004 Olympics; 8 gold in 2008; 6 medals in 2012.
Oscar Pistorius, b 1986, (S. Afr.) sprinter, 1st double-leg amputee to compete in Olympics, 2012; convicted of culpable homicide in girlfriend's death, 2014.
Jacques Plante, 1929-86, (Can.) NHL goaltender; 7 Vezina trophies; first goalie to wear mask in a game.
Gary Player, b 1935, (S. Afr.) golfer; won 3 Masters, 3 British Opens, 2 PGA Championships, and U.S. Open.
Mike Powell, b 1963, track-and-field athlete; holds world record for long jump (29 ft 4.5 in.).
Steve Prefontaine, 1951-75, runner; 1st to win 4 NCAA titles in same event (5,000m, 1970-73).
Kirby Puckett, 1960-2006, Minnesota Twins center fielder (1984-95); led team to World Series titles in 1987, '91.
Albert Pujols, b 1980, St. Louis first baseman; NL MVP, 2005, '08-'09.
Paula Radcliffe, b 1973, British runner; set marathon world record of 2:15:25 in London, 2003.
Manny Ramirez, b 1972, (Dom. Rep.) outfielder; 2004 World Series MVP; suspended for violating MLB performance-enhancing drug policy, 2009, '11.
Willis Reed, b 1942, NY Knicks center; MVP, 1970; playoff MVP, 1970, '73.
Mary Lou Retton, b 1968, gymnast; won all-around gold medal at 1984 Olympics; also won 2 silvers, 2 bronzes.
Claudio Reyna, b 1973, midfielder; U.S. National Team; named to the FIFA World Cup All-Star team, 2002.
Jerry Rice, b 1962, receiver; 1989 Super Bowl MVP; NFL record for career touchdowns (208), receptions (1,549).
Maurice Richard, 1921-2000, (Can.) Montréal Canadiens forward; scored 544 regular season goals, 82 playoff goals.
Branch Rickey, 1881-1965, MLB exec. helped break baseball's color barrier, 1947; initiated farm system, 1919.
Cal Ripken Jr., b 1960, Baltimore shortstop; AL MVP, 1983, '91; most consecutive games played (2,632).
Mariano Rivera, b 1969, (Pan.) relief pitcher; helped NY Yankees to 5 World Series titles; World Series MVP, 1999; all-time MLB leader in regular season and postseason saves.
Oscar Robertson, b 1938, NBA guard; averaged career 25.7 pts. per game; 5th in career assists (9,887); MVP, 1964.
Brooks Robinson, b 1937, Baltimore Orioles 3rd baseman; played in 4 World Series; MVP, 1964; 16 gold gloves.
Frank Robinson, b 1935, MVP in both NL and AL; triple crown, 1966; 586 career home runs; first black manager in majors.
Jackie Robinson, 1919-72, broke baseball's color barrier with Brooklyn Dodgers, 1947; NL MVP, 1949.
Sugar Ray Robinson, 1921-89, boxer; middleweight champion 5 times; welterweight champion, 1946-51.
Knute Rockne, 1888-1931, Notre Dame football coach, 1918-31; revolutionized game by stressing forward pass.
Aaron Rodgers, b 1983, Green Bay quarterback; led Packers to victory in Super Bowl XLV; Super Bowl MVP, 2011; NFL MVP, 2011, '15.
Bill Rodgers, b 1947, runner; won Boston and New York City marathons 4 times each between 1975 and 1980.
Alex Rodriguez, b 1975, MLB infielder; AL MVP in 2003, '05, '07; 14-time All Star; admitted steroid use 2001-03; suspended 162 games for PED use, 2013-14.
Juan "Chi Chi" Rodriguez, b 1935, champion golfer; 8 PGA tour wins, 22 Champions tour wins.
Ben Roethlisberger, b 1982, Pittsburgh Steelers quarterback; youngest QB to win Super Bowl, 2005.
Ronaldinho (Ronaldo de Assis Moreira), b 1980, (Braz.) soccer midfielder; led Brazil to World Cup Finals in 2006; FIFA World Player of the Year, 2004, '05.
Ronaldo (Ronaldo Luiz Nazario de Lima), b 1976, (Braz.) soccer forward; led Brazil to 2002 World Cup title; 3-time FIFA world player of the year, 1996-97, 2002; most World Cup goals, 15.
Cristiano Ronaldo, b 1985, (Port.) soccer forward; FIFA player of the year, 2008.
Art Rooney, 1901-88, NFL owner; bought Pittsburgh Pirates in 1933, renamed Steelers, 1940.
Pete Rose, b 1941, won 3 NL batting titles; hit in 44 consecutive games, 1978; most career hits, 4,256; banned for gambling, 1989; admitted betting on his team, 2004.
Ken Rosewall, b 1934, (Austral.) tennis player; 8 Grand Slam singles titles.
Ronda Rousey, b 1987, judoka and mixed martial arts fighter.
Patrick Roy, b 1965, (Can.) Montréal-Colorado goalie; only 3-time NHL playoffs MVP, 1986, '93, 2001.
Wilma Rudolph, 1940-94, sprinter; won 3 1960 Olympic golds.
Adolph Rupp, 1901-77, NCAA basketball coach; led Kentucky to 4 national titles, 1948-49, '51, '58.
Bill Russell, b 1934, Boston Celtics center; led team to 11 NBA titles; MVP 5 times; first black coach of major pro sports team.
Babe Ruth, 1895-1948, NY Yankees outfielder; hit 60 home runs, 1927, 714 lifetime (3rd all-time); led AL 12 times.
Johnny Rutherford, b 1938, auto racer; won 3 Indy 500s.
Nolan Ryan, b 1947, pitcher; holds season (383), career (5,714) strikeout records; won 324 games (7 no-hitters).
Pete Sampras, b 1971, tennis player; 14 Grand Slam singles wins (2nd-most all-time).
Joan Benoit Samuelson, b 1957, won 1st Olympic women's marathon (1984), Boston Marathon (1979, '83).
Barry Sanders, b 1968, rushed for 2,053 yds in 1997; led NFL in rushing, 1990, '94, '96-'97.
Deion Sanders, b 1967, NFL cornerback (1989-2000, '04-'05) and MLB outfielder (1989-95, '97, 2005).
Gale Sayers, b 1943, Chicago running back; twice led NFL in rushing.
Mike Schmidt, b 1949, Phillies 3rd baseman; led NL in home runs 8 times; 548 lifetime; NL MVP, 1980-81, '86.
Michael Schumacher, b 1969, (Ger.) race-car driver; 7-time Formula 1 world champ (1994-95, 2000-04).
Tom Seaver, b 1944, pitcher; won NL Cy Young award 3 times; won 311 major league games.
Monica Seles, b 1973, (Yugo.) tennis player; won 9 Grand Slam singles titles; stabbed on court by spectator, 1993.
Maria Sharapova, b 1987, (Russ.) tennis player; won Wimbledon (2004), U.S. Open (2006), Austral. Open (2008), French Open (2012, '14); Olympic silver, 2012.
Patty Sheehan, b 1956, Hall of Fame golfer; 3 LPGA Championships (1983-84, '93).
Willie Shoemaker, 1931-2003, jockey; rode 4 Kentucky Derby, 5 Belmont Stakes winners.
Frank Shorter, b 1947, runner; only American to win men's Olympic marathon (1972) since 1908; silver medalist (1976).
Don Shula, b 1930, all-time winningest NFL coach (347 games).
Bill Simmons, b 1969, columnist, podcast host; Grantland.com founding editor.

O. J. Simpson, b 1947, running back; rushed for 2,003 yds, 1973; AFC leading rusher 4 times; acquitted of murder, 1995; jailed after being found guilty of robbery and kidnapping, 2008.
Webb Simpson, b 1985, golfer; won U.S. Open, 2012.
Dean Smith, 1931-2015, retired basketball coach; 879 Division I wins; led North Carolina to 2 NCAA titles (1982, '93).
Emmitt Smith, b 1969, running back; NFL and Super Bowl MVP, 1993; rushed for career record 18,355 yds.
Conn Smythe, 1895-1980, (Can.) won 7 Stanley Cups as Toronto GM (1929-61); playoff MVP award named in his honor.
Sam Snead, 1912-2002, PGA and Masters champ 3 times each; record 82 PGA tournament victories.
Annika Sorenstam, b 1970, (Swed.) golfer; set LPGA 18-hole record of 59 (–13), 72-hole record of 27-under-par, 2001; won 10 LPGA majors, including career Grand Slam.
Sammy Sosa, b 1968, (Dom. Rep.) right fielder; 66 homers, NL MVP, 1998; 1st to hit 60+ homers 3 times (1998-99, 2001).
Warren Spahn, 1921-2003, pitcher; won 363 NL games; 20-game winner 13 times; Cy Young award, 1957.
Tris Speaker, 1888-1958, AL outfielder; batted .345 over 22 seasons; hit record 792 career doubles.
Jordan Spieth, b 1993, golfer; won Masters, 2015; U.S. Open, 2015.
Mark Spitz, b 1950, swimmer; won 7 golds at 1972 Olympics.
Amos Alonzo Stagg, 1862-1965, football innovator; Univ. of Chicago football coach for 41 years, 5 undefeated seasons.
Bart Starr, b 1934, Green Bay Packers quarterback; led team to 5 NFL titles, 2 Super Bowl victories.
Roger Staubach, b 1942, Dallas Cowboys quarterback; leading NFC passer 5 times.
George Steinbrenner, 1930-2010, NY Yankees owner.
Casey Stengel, 1890-1975, managed Yankees to 10 pennants, 7 World Series wins between 1949 and 1960.
Jackie Stewart, b 1939, (Scot.) auto racer; 27 Grand Prix wins.
John Stockton, b 1962, Utah Jazz guard; NBA career leader in assists, steals; NBA assists leader, 1988-96.
Samantha Stosur, b 1984, (Austral.) tennis player.
Picabo Street, b 1971, skier; 2-time World Cup downhill champion (1995-96); Olympic super G gold medalist, 1998.
Louise Suggs, 1923-2015, golfer; U.S. Women's Open champ, 1949, '52; 11 major victories.
John L. Sullivan, 1858-1918, last bare-knuckle heavyweight champion, 1882-92.
Pat Summerall, 1930-2013, NFL kicker, radio and TV sportscaster who announced 26 Super Bowls.
Pat Summit, b 1952, women's basketball coach; led Tennessee Lady Vols to 8 NCAA titles (1987, '89, '91, '96-'98, 2007-08); all-time winningest NCAA coach.
Ichiro Suzuki, b 1973, (Jpn.) center fielder; AL MVP, 2001; single-season hits record (262), 2004; 4,000th career (Japan/U.S.) hit (2013).
Sheryl Swoopes, b 1971, guard/forward; 1st player named WNBA MVP 3 times (2000, '02, '05).
Fran Tarkenton, b 1940, Minnesota, NY Giants quarterback; 4th in career TD passes (342); 1975 Player of the Year.
Diana Taurasi, b 1982, WNBA shooting guard, Phoenix Mercury; Olympic gold medalist, 2008, '12; WNBA MVP, 2009.
Lawrence Taylor, b 1959, linebacker; led NY Giants to 2 Super Bowl titles; played in 10 Pro Bowls.
Daley Thompson, b 1958, (Br.) decathlete; Olympic gold medalist in 1980, '84.
Jenny Thompson, b 1973, swimmer; most decorated U.S. female Olympian; 12 medals (8 gold) in 1992, '96, 2000, '04.
Bobby Thomson, 1923-2010, MLB utility player known for pennant-clinching "Shot Heard 'Round the World" for the NY Giants, 1951.
Jim Thorpe, 1888-1953, football All-American, 1911-12; won pentathlon and decathlon, 1912 Olympics.
Bill Tilden, 1893-1953, won 7 U.S. tennis titles, 3 Wimbledon.
Y. A. Tittle, b 1926, NY Giants quarterback; MVP, 1961, '63.
Alberto Tomba "La Bomba," b 1966, (It.) skier; 5 Olympic alpine medals (3 golds, 2 silver) in 1988, '92, '94.
LaDainian "L.T." Tomlinson, b 1979, running back; NFL records for single season touchdowns (31), rushing touchdowns (28), most points scored in a single season (186).
Joe Torre, b 1940, former MLB player; managed L.A. Dodgers, NY Yankees, St. Louis Cardinals, Atlanta Braves, and NY Mets.
Lee Trevino, b 1939, golfer; won U.S., British Open twice.
Bryan Trottier, b 1956, (Can.) Islanders, Penguins center for 6 Stanley Cup champs.
Mike Trout, b 1991, MLB player; AL MVP, 2014.
Gene Tunney, 1897-1978, heavyweight champion, 1926-28.
Mike Tyson, b 1966, undisputed heavyweight champ, 1987-90; at 20, youngest to win a heavyweight title (WBC, 1986).
Wyomia Tyus, b 1945, Olympic 100m gold medalist, 1964, '68.
Johnny Unitas, 1933-2002, Baltimore Colts quarterback; passed for more than 40,000 yds; MVP, 1957, '67.
Al Unser, b 1939, Indy 500 winner 4 times.
Bobby Unser, b 1934, Indy 500 winner 3 times.
Brian Urlacher, b 1978, Chicago Bears linebacker; Defensive Rookie of the Year, 2000; 7-time Pro Bowler.
Norm Van Brocklin, 1926-83, quarterback; passed for game record 554 yds, 1951; MVP, 1960.
Amy Van Dyken, b 1973, swimmer; first American woman to win 4 gold medals in one Olympics (1996).
Justin Verlander, b 1983, pitcher; won AL MVP and Cy Young, 2011.
Michael Vick, b 1980, quarterback; suspended and convicted (2007) of illegal dog fighting, gambling activities.
Lasse Viren, b 1949, (Fin.) runner; Olympic 5,000m and 10,000m gold medalist in 1972, '76.
Lindsey Vonn, b 1984; 1st U.S. woman to win the world super-G championship, gold medal in downhill, 2010 Olympics; 4 World Cup titles 2008-10, '12.
Joey Votto, b 1983, (Can.) Cincinnati Reds 1st baseman; NL MVP, 2010.
Dwyane Wade, b 1982, guard; led Miami Heat to NBA title, 2006, '12-'13; finals MVP, 2006; NBA scoring title, 2009.
Honus Wagner, 1874-1955, Pittsburgh Pirates shortstop; 8 NL batting titles.
Grete Waitz, 1953-2011, (Nor.) 9-time winner of the New York City Marathon (1978-80, '82-'86, '88).
"Jersey" Joe Walcott, 1914-94, boxer; became heavyweight champion at age 37, 1951-52.
Kerri Walsh Jennings, b 1978, beach volleyball player; 3-time Olympic gold medalist with Misty May-Treanor (2004, '08, '12).
Bill Walton, b 1952, center; led Portland Trail Blazers to 1977 NBA title; MVP, 1978; NBA TV commentator.
Abby Wambach, b 1980, soccer; 2 gold medals in Olympics (2004, '12); all-time intl.-competition goal scorer.
Kurt Warner, b 1971, Rams, Giants, Cardinals quarterback; NFL MVP, 1999, 2001; Super Bowl MVP, 2000.
Gerry "Bubba" Watson, b 1978, golfer; won Masters, 2012, '14.
Tom Watson, b 1949, golfer; 6-time PGA Player of the Year; won 5 British Opens, 2 Masters, U.S. Open.
Stan Wawrinka, b 1985, (Switz.) tennis player.
Karrie Webb, b 1974, (Austral.) golfer; youngest woman (26 yrs., 6 mos.) to win career Grand Slam, 1999-2001.
Johnny Weissmuller, 1903-84, swimmer; won 52 national championships, 5 Olympic gold medals; set 67 world records.
Jerry West, b 1938, L.A. Lakers guard; had career average 27 pts. per game; first team all-star 10 times.
Dan Wheldon, 1978-2011, (Br.) race-car driver; 2-time Indy 500 winner (2005, '11).
Byron "Whizzer" White, 1917-2002, running back; led NCAA in scoring and rushing at Colorado, 1937; led NFL in rushing twice, 1938, '40; Supreme Court justice, 1962-93.
Shaun White, b 1986, snowboarder/skateboarder, Olympic gold medalist in halfpipe (2006, '10).
Kathy Whitworth, b 1939, 7-time LPGA Player of the Year (1966-69, '71-'73); 88 tour wins, most on LPGA or PGA tour.
Michelle Wie, b 1989, golfer; in 2002 became youngest-ever qualifier for LPGA event; turned pro at age 15.
Bradley Wiggins, b 1980, (Br.) cyclist; Tour de France winner, 2012; 4-time Olympic gold medalist (2004, '08, '12).
Michael Wilbon, b 1958, commentator/analyst for ESPN and ABC.
Lenny Wilkens, b 1937, 2nd winningest coach in NBA history; Hall of Fame player and coach.
Serena Williams, b 1981, tennis player; 21-time Grand Slam singles champion (3rd all-time); Olympic gold medals in singles (2012) and doubles (2000, '08, '12) with sister Venus.
Ted Williams, 1918-2002, Boston Red Sox outfielder; won 6 batting titles, 2 triple crowns; hit .406 in 1941.
Venus Williams, b 1980, tennis player; 7-time Grand Slam singles winner; Olympic gold medals in singles (2000) and doubles with sister Serena (2000, '08, '12).
Helen Wills Moody, 1905-98, tennis star; won U.S. Open 7 times, Wimbledon 8 times.
Katarina Witt, b 1965, (Ger.) figure skater; won Olympic gold medal, 1984, '88; world champ, 1984-85, '87-'88.
John Wooden, 1910-2010, UCLA basketball coach; 10 NCAA titles.
Tiger Woods, b 1975, golfer; youngest to win career Grand Slam, at age 24 (1997-2000); 14 career major titles.
Mickey Wright, b 1935, golfer; won LPGA and U.S. Open championship 4 times; 82 career wins, including 13 majors.
Eric Wynalda, b 1969, soccer; scored 1st goal in major league soccer history (1996).
Kristi Yamaguchi, b 1971, figure skater; won national, world, Olympic titles, in 1992.
Yao Ming, b 1980, (China) center for Houston Rockets; 8-time NBA All-Star.
Carl Yastrzemski, b 1939, Boston Red Sox slugger; won 3 batting titles; triple crown, 1967.
Cy Young, 1867-1955, pitcher; won record 511 games.
Steve Young, b 1961, 49ers quarterback; led NFL in passing, 1991-94, '96-'97; NFL MVP, 1992, '94; Super Bowl MVP, 1995.
Babe Didrikson Zaharias, 1911-56, all-around athlete; 3 track-and-field medals (2 golds), 1932 Olympics; won 10 golf majors; also played baseball; 6-time AP Female Athlete of the Year.
Emil Zátopek, 1922-2000, (Czech.) runner; won 3 gold medals at 1952 Olympics (5,000m, 10,000m, marathon).
Zinedine Zidane, b 1972, (Fr.) soccer midfielder; led France to 1998 World Cup title; named top player in 2006; 3-time FIFA world player of the year (1998, 2000, '03).

Writers of the Present

Name	Birthplace	Birthdate
Richard Adams	Newbury, England, UK	5/9/1920
Chimamanda Ngozi Adichie	Enugu, Nigeria	9/15/1977
Edward Albee	Washington, DC	3/12/1928
Mitch Albom	Passaic, NJ	5/23/1958
Elizabeth Alexander	New York, NY	5/30/1962
Sherman Alexie	Wellpinit, WA	10/7/1966
Isabel Allende	Lima, Peru	8/2/1942
Dorothy Allison	Greenville, SC	4/11/1949
Martin Amis	Oxford, England, UK	8/25/1949
Piers Anthony	Oxford, England, UK	8/6/1934
Jeffrey Archer	Somerset, England, UK	4/15/1940
John Ashbery	Rochester, NY	7/28/1927
Margaret Atwood	Ottawa, ON, Canada	11/18/1939
David Auburn	Chicago, IL	11/30/1969
Jean Auel	Chicago, IL	2/18/1936
Paul Auster	Newark, NJ	2/3/1947
Alan Ayckbourn	Hampstead, England, UK	4/12/1939
Nicholson Baker	New York, NY	1/7/1957
David Baldacci	Richmond, VA	8/5/1960
Russell Banks	Newton, MA	3/28/1940
John Barth	Cambridge, MD	5/27/1930
Ann Beattie	Washington, DC	9/8/1947
Alan Bennett	Leeds, England, UK	5/9/1934
John Berendt	Syracuse, NY	12/5/1939
Elizabeth Berg	St. Paul, MN	12/2/1948
Judy Blume	Elizabeth, NJ	2/12/1938
T. Coraghessan Boyle	Peekskill, NY	12/2/1948
Barbara Taylor Bradford	Leeds, England, UK	5/10/1933
Christopher Bram	Buffalo, NY	2/22/1952
Geraldine Brooks	Sydney, NSW, Australia	9/14/1955
Dan Brown	Exeter, NH	6/22/1964
Rita Mae Brown	Hanover, PA	11/28/1944
Christopher Buckley	New York, NY	9/28/1952
James Lee Burke	Houston, TX	12/5/1936
Augusten Burroughs	Pittsburgh, PA	10/23/1965
Robert Olen Butler	Granite City, IL	1/20/1945
A. S. Byatt	Sheffield, England, UK	8/24/1936
Ethan Canin	Ann Arbor, MI	7/19/1960
Peter Carey	Bacchus-Marsh, Victoria, Australia	5/7/1943
Robert A. Caro	New York, NY	10/30/1935
Caleb Carr	New York, NY	8/2/1955
Michael Chabon	Washington, DC	5/24/1963
Tracy Chevalier	Washington, DC	10/19/1962
Sandra Cisneros	Chicago, IL	12/20/1954
Mary Higgins Clark	Bronx, NY	12/24/1927
Beverly Cleary	McMinnville, OR	4/12/1916
Harlan Coben	Newark, NJ	1/4/1962
Paulo Coelho	Rio de Janeiro, Brazil	8/24/1947
J(ohn) M(axwell) Coetzee	Capetown, South Africa	2/9/1940
Billy Collins	New York, NY	3/22/1941
Suzanne Collins	Hartford, CT	8/10/1962
Pat Conroy	Atlanta, GA	10/26/1945
Robin Cook	New York, NY	5/4/1940
Patricia Cornwell	Miami, FL	6/9/1956
Michael Cunningham	Cincinnati, OH	11/6/1952
Clive Cussler	Aurora, IL	7/15/1931
Don DeLillo	Bronx, NY	11/20/1936
Nelson DeMille	New York, NY	8/23/1943
Junot Díaz	Santo Domingo, Dominican Republic	12/31/1968
Joan Didion	Sacramento, CA	12/5/1934
Annie Dillard	Pittsburgh, PA	4/30/1945
Anthony Doerr	Cleveland, OH	10/27/1973
Emma Donoghue	Dublin, Ireland	10/24/1969
Rita Dove	Akron, OH	8/28/1952
Roddy Doyle	Dublin, Ireland	5/8/1958
Carol Ann Duffy	Glasgow, Scotland, UK	12/23/1955
Umberto Eco	Alessandria, Italy	1/5/1932
Jennifer Egan	Chicago, IL	9/7/1962
Dave Eggers	Boston, MA	3/12/1970
Bret Easton Ellis	Los Angeles, CA	3/7/1964
James Ellroy	Los Angeles, CA	3/4/1948
Louise Erdrich	Little Falls, MN	6/7/1954
Laura Esquivel	Mexico City, Mexico	9/30/1950
Jeffrey Eugenides	Detroit, MI	3/8/1960
Janet Evanovich	South River, NJ	4/22/1943
Lawrence Ferlinghetti	Yonkers, NY	3/24/1919
Helen Fielding	Morley, Yorkshire, Eng., UK	2/19/1958
Fannie Flagg	Birmingham, AL	9/21/1944
Gillian Flynn	Kansas City, MO	2/24/1971
Dario Fo	San Giano, Italy	3/26/1926
Ken Follett	Cardiff, Wales, UK	6/5/1949
Richard Ford	Jackson, MS	2/16/1944
Frederick Forsyth	Ashford, England, UK	8/25/1938
Paula Fox	New York, NY	4/22/1923
Jonathan Franzen	Western Springs, IL	8/17/1959
Michael Frayn	London, England, UK	9/8/1933
Charles Frazier	Asheville, NC	11/4/1950
Brian Friel	Killyclogher, N. Ireland, UK	1/9/1929
Neil Gaiman	Portchester, England, UK	11/10/1960
Ernest J. Gaines	Oscar, LA	1/15/1933
Malcolm Gladwell	Fareham, Hampshire, Eng., UK	9/3/1963
Robert Goddard	Fareham, Hampshire, Eng., UK	11/13/1954
Gail Godwin	Birmingham, AL	6/18/1937
William Goldman	Highland Park, IL	8/12/1931
Mary Gordon	Far Rockaway, NY	12/8/1949
Sue Grafton	Louisville, KY	4/24/1940
Shirley Ann Grau	New Orleans, LA	7/8/1929
John Green	Indianapolis, IN	8/24/1977
John Grisham	Jonesboro, AR	2/8/1955
John Guare	New York, NY	2/5/1938
Pete Hamill	Brooklyn, NY	6/24/1935
David Handler	Los Angeles, CA	9/14/1952
Paul Harding	Wenham, MA	12/19/1967
David Hare	St. Leonards, Sussex, Eng., UK	6/5/1947
Jim Harrison	Grayling, MI	12/11/1937
Robert Hass	San Francisco, CA	3/1/1941
Mark Helprin	New York, NY	6/28/1947
Carl Hiaasen	Plantation, FL	3/12/1953
Laura Hillenbrand	Fairfax, VA	5/15/1967
S. E. Hinton	Tulsa, OK	7/22/1948
Alice Hoffman	New York, NY	3/16/1952
Alan Hollinghurst	Stroud, Gloucestershire, England, UK	5/26/1954
Khaled Hosseini	Kabul, Afghanistan	3/4/1965
John Irving	Exeter, NH	3/2/1942
Walter Isaacson	New Orleans, LA	5/20/1952
Kazuo Ishiguro	Nagasaki, Japan	11/8/1954
John Jakes	Chicago, IL	3/31/1932
E. L. James	London, England, UK	7/3/1963
Elfriede Jelinek	Müzzuschlag, Austria	10/20/1946
Ha Jin	Liaoning, China	2/21/1956
Edward P. Jones	Washington, DC	10/5/1950
Erica Jong	New York, NY	3/26/1942
Sebastian Junger	Boston, MA	1/17/1962
Jan Karon	Lenoir, NC	3/14/1937
Garrison Keillor	Anoka, MN	8/7/1942
Thomas Keneally	Sydney, NSW, Australia	10/7/1935
William Kennedy	Albany, NY	1/16/1928
Sue Monk Kidd	Sylvester, GA	8/12/1948
Jamaica Kincaid	St. John's, Antigua and Barbuda	5/25/1949
Stephen King	Portland, ME	9/21/1947
Barbara Kingsolver	Annapolis, MD	4/8/1955
Maxine Hong Kingston	Stockton, CA	10/27/1940
Dean Koontz	Everett, PA	7/9/1945
Ted Kooser	Ames, IA	4/25/1939
Jon Krakauer	Brookline, MA	4/12/1954
Larry Kramer	Bridgeport, CT	6/25/1935
Judith Krantz	New York, NY	1/9/1928
Milan Kundera	Brno, Czechoslovakia	4/1/1929
Tony Kushner	New York, NY	7/16/1956
Jhumpa Lahiri	London, England, UK	7/11/1967
Erik Larson	Brooklyn, NY	1/3/1954
John Le Carré	Poole, England, UK	10/19/1931
Jean Marie Gustave Le Clézio	Nice, France	4/13/1940
Ursula K. Le Guin	Berkeley, CA	10/21/1929
David Leavitt	Pittsburgh, PA	6/23/1961
Harper Lee	Monroeville, AL	4/28/1926
Jonathan Lethem	Brooklyn, NY	2/19/1964
David Lodge	South London, England, UK	1/28/1935
Alison Lurie	Chicago, IL	9/3/1926
Gregory Maguire	Albany, NY	6/9/1954
David Malouf	Brisbane, Qld., Australia	3/20/1934
Thomas Mallon	Glen Cove, NY	11/2/1951
David Mamet	Chicago, IL	11/30/1947
Hilary Mantel	Derbyshire, England, UK	7/6/1952
Yann Martel	Salamanca, Spain	6/25/1963
George R. R. Martin	Bayonne, NJ	9/20/1948
Bobbie Ann Mason	nr. Mayfield, KY	5/1/1940
Armistead Maupin	Washington, DC	4/13/1944
Cormac McCarthy	Providence, RI	7/20/1933
David McCullough	Pittsburgh, PA	7/7/1933
Alice McDermott	Brooklyn, NY	6/27/1953
Ian McEwan	Aldershot, England, UK	6/21/1948
Thomas McGuane	Wyandotte, MI	12/11/1939
Jay McInerney	Hartford, CT	1/13/1955
Terry McMillan	Port Huron, MI	10/18/1951
Larry McMurtry	Wichita Falls, TX	6/3/1936
Terrence McNally	St. Petersburg, FL	11/3/1939
John McPhee	Princeton, NJ	3/8/1931
W(illiam) S(tanley) Merwin	New York, NY	9/30/1927
Stephenie Meyer	Hartford, CT	12/24/1973
Steven Millhauser	New York, NY	8/3/1943
Toni Morrison	Lorain, OH	2/18/1931

Name	Birthplace	Birthdate
Walter Mosley	Los Angeles, CA	1/12/1952
Andrew Motion	London, England, UK	10/26/1952
Bharati Mukherjee	Calcutta, India	7/27/1940
Herta Müller	Nitzkydorf, Banat, Romania	8/17/1953
Alice Munro	Wingham, ON, Canada	7/10/1931
Haruki Murakami	Kyoto, Japan	1/12/1949
V. S. Naipaul	Chaguanas, Trinidad and Tobago	8/17/1932
Joyce Carol Oates	Lockport, NY	6/16/1938
Edna O'Brien	Tuamgraney, Ireland	12/15/1932
Tim O'Brien	Austin, MN	10/1/1946
Kenzaburo Oe	Uchiko, Japan	1/31/1935
Michael Ondaatje	Colombo, Sri Lanka	9/12/1943
Cynthia Ozick	New York, NY	4/17/1928
Orhan Pamuk	Istanbul, Turkey	6/7/1952
Suzan-Lori Parks	Fort Knox, KY	5/10/1963
Ann Patchett	Los Angeles, CA	12/2/1963
James Patterson	Newburgh, NY	3/22/1947
Jodi Picoult	New York, NY	5/19/1966
Marge Piercy	Detroit, MI	3/31/1936
Robert Pinsky	Long Branch, NJ	10/20/1940
Michael Pollan	New York, NY	2/6/1955
Richard Powers	Evanston, IL	6/18/1957
Richard Price	Bronx, NY	10/12/1949
E. Annie Proulx	Norwich, CT	8/22/1935
Philip Pullman	Norwich, England, UK	10/19/1946
Thomas Pynchon	Glen Cove, NY	5/8/1937
David Rabe	Dubuque, IA	3/10/1940
Ishmael Reed	Chattanooga, TN	2/22/1938
Anne Rice	New Orleans, LA	10/4/1941
Mary Roach	Etna, NH	3/20/1959
Nora Roberts	Silver Spring, MD	10/10/1950
Marilynne Robinson	Sandpoint, IL	11/26/1943
Philip Roth	Newark, NJ	3/19/1933
Veronica Roth	New York, NY	8/19/1988
J. K. Rowling	Chipping Sodbury, Eng., UK	7/31/1965
Norman Rush	Oakland, CA	10/24/1933
Salman Rushdie	Bombay, India	6/19/1947
Richard Russo	Johnstown, NY	7/15/1949
Alice Sebold	Madison, WI	9/6/1963
David Sedaris	Johnson City, NY	12/26/1956
Vikram Seth	Calcutta, India	6/20/1952
John Patrick Shanley	New York, NY	10/13/1950
Sam Shepard	Ft. Sheridan, IL	11/5/1943
Lionel Shriver	Gastonia, NC	5/18/1957
Anne Rivers Siddons	Atlanta, GA	1/9/1936
Neil Simon	Bronx, NY	7/4/1927
Jane Smiley	Los Angeles, CA	9/26/1949
Wole Soyinka	Abeokuta, Nigeria	7/13/1934
Nicholas Sparks	Omaha, NE	12/31/1965
Danielle Steel	New York, NY	8/14/1947
R(obert) L(awrence) Stine	Columbus, OH	10/8/1943
Kathryn Stockett	Jackson, MS	1969
Tom Stoppard	Zlin, Czechoslovakia	7/3/1937
Elizabeth Strout	Portland, ME	1/6/1956
Amy Tan	Oakland, CA	2/19/1952
Donna Tartt	Greenwood, MS	12/23/1963
Paul Theroux	Medford, MA	4/10/1941
Calvin Trillin	Kansas City, MO	12/5/1935
Scott F. Turow	Chicago, IL	4/12/1949
Anne Tyler	Minneapolis, MN	10/25/1941
Mario Vargas Llosa	Arequipa, Peru	3/28/1936
Paula Vogel	Washington, DC	11/16/1951
Sarah Vowell	Muskogee, OK	12/27/1969
Derek Walcott	Castries, Saint Lucia	1/23/1930
Alice Walker	Eatonton, GA	2/9/1944
Joseph Wambaugh	East Pittsburgh, PA	1/22/1937
Edmund White	Cincinnati, OH	1/13/1940
Elie Wiesel	Sighet, Romania	9/30/1928
Tom Wolfe	Richmond, VA	3/2/1931
Tobias Wolff	Birmingham, AL	6/19/1945
Herman Wouk	New York, NY	5/27/1915
Yevgeny Yevtushenko	Zima, Russia	7/18/1933

Writers of the Past

See also Journalists, and Greeks and Romans in Historical Figures chapter.

Chinua Achebe, 1930-2013, (Nigeria) novelist. *Things Fall Apart.*

Alice Adams, 1926-99, (U.S.) novelist, short-story writer. *Superior Woman.*

James Agee, 1909-55, (U.S.) novelist. *A Death in the Family.*

S(hmuel) Y(osef) Agnon, 1888-1970, (Isr.) Hebrew novelist. *Only Yesterday.*

Conrad Aiken, 1889-1973, (U.S.) poet, critic. *Ushant.*

Anna Akhmatova, 1889-1966, (Russ.) poet. *Requiem.*

Louisa May Alcott, 1832-88, (U.S.) novelist. *Little Women.*

Sholom Aleichem, 1859-1916, (Russ.) Yiddish writer. *Tevye's Daughters, The Old Country.*

Vicente Aleixandre, 1898-1984, (Sp.) poet. *La destrucción o el amor, Dialogolos del conocimiento.*

Horatio Alger, 1832-99, (U.S.) "rags-to-riches" books.

Jorge Amado, 1912-2001, (Brazil) novelist. *Dona Flor and Her Two Husbands, The Violent Land.*

Eric Ambler, 1909-98, (Br.) suspense novelist. *A Coffin for Dimitrios.*

Kingsley Amis, 1922-95, (Br.) novelist, critic. *Lucky Jim.*

Hans Christian Andersen, 1805-75, (Den.) author of fairy tales. *The Ugly Duckling.*

Maxwell Anderson, 1888-1959, (U.S.) playwright. *What Price Glory?, High Tor, Winterset, Key Largo.*

Sherwood Anderson, 1876-1941, (U.S.) short-story writer. "Death in the Woods," *Winesburg, Ohio.*

Maya Angelou, 1928-2014, (U.S.) poet, memoirist. *I Know Why the Caged Bird Sings.*

Reinaldo Arenas, 1943-90, (Cuba) short-story writer, novelist. *Before Night Falls.*

Ludovico Ariosto, 1474-1533, (It.) poet. *Orlando Furioso.*

Matthew Arnold, 1822-88, (Br.) poet, critic. "Thrysis," "Dover Beach," "Culture and Anarchy."

Isaac Asimov, 1920-92, (U.S.) versatile writer, espec. of science fiction. *I Robot.*

Miguel Angel Asturias, 1899-1974, (Guat.) novelist. *El Señor Presidente.*

Louis Auchincloss, 1917-2010, (U.S.) novelist, memoirist, short-story writer. *The Rector of Justin.*

W(ystan) H(ugh) Auden, 1907-73, (Br.) poet, playwright, literary critic. "The Age of Anxiety."

Jane Austen, 1775-1817, (Br.) novelist. *Pride and Prejudice, Sense and Sensibility, Emma, Mansfield Park.*

Ba Jin (Li Yaotang), 1904-2005, (China) novelist of pre-revolutionary China.

Isaac Babel, 1894-1941, (Russ.) short-story writer, playwright. *Odessa Tales, Red Cavalry.*

James Baldwin, 1924-87, (U.S.) author, playwright. *The Fire Next Time, Blues for Mister Charlie.*

Honoré de Balzac, 1799-1850, (Fr.) novelist. *Le Père Goriot, Cousine Bette, Eugénie Grandet.*

James M. Barrie, 1860-1937, (Br.) playwright, novelist. *Peter Pan, Dear Brutus, What Every Woman Knows.*

Charles Baudelaire, 1821-67, (Fr.) poet. *Les Fleurs du Mal.*

L(yman) Frank Baum, 1856-1919, (U.S.) Wizard of Oz series.

Simone de Beauvoir, 1908-86, (Fr.) novelist, essayist. *The Second Sex, Memoirs of a Dutiful Daughter.*

Samuel Beckett, 1906-89, (Ire.) novelist, playwright. *Waiting for Godot, Endgame* (plays); *Murphy, Watt, Molloy* (novels).

Brendan Behan, 1923-64, (Ire.) playwright. *The Quare Fellow, The Hostage, Borstal Boy.*

Saul Bellow, 1915-2005, (U.S.) novelist. *The Adventures of Augie March, Humboldt's Gift.*

Robert Benchley, 1889-1945, (U.S.) humorist.

Stephen Vincent Benét, 1898-1943, (U.S.) poet, novelist. *John Brown's Body.*

Jan Berenstain, 1923-2012, and **Stan Berenstain**, 1923-2005, (both U.S.) co-writers and illustrators of Berenstain Bears series of children's books.

Thomas Berger, 1924-2014, (U.S.) novelist. *Little Big Man.*

John Berryman, 1914-72, (U.S.) poet. *Homage to Mistress Bradstreet.*

Ambrose Bierce, 1842-1914, (U.S.) short-story writer, journalist. *In the Midst of Life, The Devil's Dictionary.*

Maeve Binchy, 1940-2012, (Ire.) novelist, short-story writer, *Circle of Friends, Tara Road.*

Elizabeth Bishop, 1911-79, (U.S.) poet. *North and South—A Cold Spring.*

William Blake, 1757-1827, (Br.) poet, artist. *Songs of Innocence, Songs of Experience.*

Aleksandr Blok, 1880-1921, (Russ.) poet. "The Twelve," "The Scythians."

Enid Blyton, 1897-1968, (Br.) children's writer. Famous Five series.

Giovanni Boccaccio, 1313-75, (It.) poet. *Decameron.*

Heinrich Böll, 1917-85, (Ger.) novelist, short-story writer. *Group Portrait With Lady.*

Jorge Luis Borges, 1900-86, (Arg.) short-story writer, poet, essayist. *Labyrinths.*

James Boswell, 1740-95, (Scot.) biographer. *The Life of Samuel Johnson.*

Pierre Boulle, 1913-94, (Fr.) novelist. *The Bridge Over the River Kwai, Planet of the Apes.*

Paul Bowles, 1910-99, (U.S.) novelist, short-story writer. *The Sheltering Sky.*

Ray Bradbury, 1920-2012, (U.S.) novelist, short-story writer. *Fahrenheit 451, The Martian Chronicles.*

Anne Bradstreet, c. 1612-72, (U.S.) poet. *The Tenth Muse Lately Sprung Up in America.*

Bertolt Brecht, 1898-1956, (Ger.) dramatist, poet. *The Threepenny Opera, Mother Courage and Her Children.*

Joseph Brodsky, 1940-96, (Russ.-U.S.) poet. *A Part of Speech*, *Less Than One*, *To Urania*.
Charlotte Brontë, 1816-55, (Br.) novelist. *Jane Eyre*.
Emily Brontë, 1818-48, (Br.) novelist. *Wuthering Heights*.
Sterling A. Brown, 1901-89, (U.S.) poet, literature professor. *Southern Road*.
William Wells Brown, 1815-84, (U.S.) writer, memoirist; first novel by an African American, *Clotel*, 1853.
Elizabeth Barrett Browning, 1806-61, (Br.) poet. *Sonnets From the Portuguese*, *Aurora Leigh*.
Robert Browning, 1812-89, (Br.) poet. "My Last Duchess," "Fra Lippo Lippi," *The Ring and the Book*.
Pearl S. Buck, 1892-1973, (U.S.) novelist. *The Good Earth*.
Charles Bukowski, 1920-94, (U.S.) novelist, poet. *Ham on Rye*, *Women*.
Mikhail Bulgakov, 1891-1940, (Russ.) novelist, playwright. *The Heart of a Dog*, *The Master and Margarita*.
John Bunyan, 1628-88, (Br.) writer. *Pilgrim's Progress*.
Anthony Burgess, 1917-93, (Br.) author. *A Clockwork Orange*.
Frances Hodgson Burnett, 1849-1924, (Br.-U.S.) novelist. *The Secret Garden*.
Robert Burns, 1759-96, (Scot.) poet. "Flow Gently, Sweet Afton," "My Heart's in the Highlands," "Auld Lang Syne."
Edgar Rice Burroughs, 1875-1950, (U.S.) writer; created Tarzan, John Carter.
William S. Burroughs, 1914-97, (U.S.) novelist. *Naked Lunch*.
George Gordon, Lord Byron, 1788-1824, (Br.) poet. *Don Juan*, *Childe Harold*, *Manfred*, *Cain*.
Pedro Calderon de la Barca, 1600-81, (Sp.) playwright. *Life Is a Dream*.
Hortense Calisher, 1911-2009, (U.S.) novelist, short-story writer. *False Entry*.
Italo Calvino, 1923-85, (It.) novelist, short-story writer. *If on a Winter's Night a Traveler*.
Luis Vaz de Camoes, 1524?-80 (Port.) poet. *The Lusiads*.
Albert Camus, 1913-60, (Fr.) writer. *The Stranger*, *The Fall*.
Elias Canetti, 1905-94, (Bulg.) novelist, essayist. *Auto-Da-Fe*.
Karel Capek, 1890-1938, (Czech.) playwright, novelist, essayist. *R.U.R. (Rossum's Universal Robots)*.
Truman Capote, 1924-84, (U.S.) author. *Other Voices, Other Rooms*; *Breakfast at Tiffany's*; *In Cold Blood*.
Lewis Carroll (Charles Dodgson), 1832-98, (Br.) writer, mathematician. *Alice's Adventures in Wonderland*.
Barbara Cartland 1901-2000, (Br.) romance novelist.
Giacomo Casanova, 1725-98, (It.) adventurer, memoirist.
Willa Cather, 1873-1947, (U.S.) novelist. *O Pioneers!*, *My Ántonia*, *Death Comes for the Archbishop*.
Constantine Cavafy, 1863-1933, (Gr.) poet. "Ithaka," "Sensual Pleasures."
Camilo Jose Cela, 1916-2001, (Sp.) novelist. *The Family of Pascual Duarte*, *The Hive*.
Miguel de Cervantes Saavedra, 1547-1616, (Sp.) novelist, dramatist, poet. *Don Quixote*.
Raymond Chandler, 1888-1959, (U.S.) writer of detective fiction. Philip Marlowe series.
Geoffrey Chaucer, c. 1340-1400, (Br.) poet. *The Canterbury Tales*, *Troilus and Criseyde*.
John Cheever, 1912-82, (U.S.) novelist, short-story writer. *The Wapshot Scandal*, "The Country Husband."
Anton Chekhov, 1860-1904, (Russ.) short-story writer, dramatist. *Uncle Vanya*, *The Cherry Orchard*, *The Three Sisters*.
Charles Waddell Chesnutt, 1858-1932, (U.S.) author known for his short stories. *The Conjure Woman*.
G(ilbert) K(eith) Chesterton, 1874-1936, (Br.) critic, novelist, relig. apologist. Father Brown series of mysteries.
Kate Chopin, 1851-1904, (U.S.) writer. *The Awakening*.
Agatha Christie, 1890-1976, (Br.) mystery writer; created Miss Marple, Hercule Poirot. *And Then There Were None*, *Murder on the Orient Express*, *Murder of Roger Ackroyd*.
Tom Clancy, 1947-2013, novelist. *The Hunt for Red October*.
Arthur C. Clarke, 1917-2008, (Br.) science-fiction writer. *2001: A Space Odyssey*.
James Clavell, 1924-94, (Br.-U.S.) novelist. *Shogun*, *King Rat*.
Jean Cocteau, 1889-1963, (Fr.) writer, visual artist, filmmaker. *The Beauty and the Beast*, *Les Enfants Terribles*.
Samuel Taylor Coleridge, 1772-1834, (Br.) poet, critic. "Kubla Khan," "The Rime of the Ancient Mariner."
(Sidonie) Colette, 1873-1954, (Fr.) novelist. *Claudine*, *Gigi*.
Wilkie Collins, 1824-89, (Br.) novelist. *The Moonstone*.
Evan S. Connell, 1924-2013, (Br.) novelist, short-story writer. *Mrs. Bridge*.
Joseph Conrad, 1857-1924, (Br.) novelist. *Lord Jim*, *Heart of Darkness*, *The Secret Agent*.
James Fenimore Cooper, 1789-1851, (U.S.) novelist. *Leatherstocking Tales*, *The Last of the Mohicans*.
Pierre Corneille, 1606-84, (Fr.) dramatist. *Medeé*, *Le Cid*.
Hart Crane, 1899-1932, (U.S.) poet. "The Bridge."
Stephen Crane, 1871-1900, (U.S.) novelist, short-story writer. *The Red Badge of Courage*, "The Open Boat."
Harry Crews, 1935-2012, (U.S.) novelist. *A Feast of Snakes*.
Michael Crichton, 1942-2008, (U.S.) writer. *The Andromeda Strain*, *Jurassic Park*.
Countee Cullen, 1903-46, (U.S.) poet, prominent in the Harlem Renaissance of the 1920s. *The Black Christ*.
E. E. Cummings, 1894-1962, (U.S.) poet. *Tulips and Chimneys*.
Roald Dahl, 1916-90, (Br.-U.S.) writer. *Charlie and the Chocolate Factory*, *James and the Giant Peach*.
Gabriele D'Annunzio, 1863-1938, (It.) poet, novelist, dramatist. *The Child of Pleasure*, *The Intruder*, *The Victim*.
Dante Alighieri, 1265-1321, (It.) poet. *The Divine Comedy*.
Robertson Davies, 1913-95, (Can.) novelist, playwright, essayist. Salterton, Deptford, and Cornish trilogies.
Daniel Defoe, 1660-1731, (Br.) writer. *Robinson Crusoe*, *Moll Flanders*, *Journal of the Plague Year*.
Philip K. Dick, 1928-82, (U.S.) science-fiction writer. *Do Androids Dream of Electric Sheep?*
Charles Dickens, 1812-70, (Br.) novelist. *David Copperfield*, *Oliver Twist*, *Great Expectations*, *A Tale of Two Cities*.
James Dickey, 1923-97, (U.S.) poet, novelist. *Deliverance*.
Emily Dickinson, 1830-86, (U.S.) poet. "Because I could not stop for Death ...," "Success is counted sweetest ..."
Isak Dinesen (Karen Blixen), 1885-1962, (Den.) author. *Out of Africa*, *Seven Gothic Tales*, *Winter's Tales*.
E(dgar) L(awrence) Doctorow, 1931-2015, (U.S.) novelist. *Ragtime*, *Billy Bathgate*.
John Donne, 1573-1631, (Br.) poet. *Songs and Sonnets*.
José Donoso, 1924-96, (Chile) surreal novelist and short-story writer. *The Obscene Bird of Night*.
John Dos Passos, 1896-1970, (U.S.) novelist. *U.S.A.*
Fyodor Dostoyevsky, 1821-81, (Russ.) novelist. *Crime and Punishment*, *The Brothers Karamazov*, *The Possessed*.
Arthur Conan Doyle, 1859-1930, (Br.) novelist. Sherlock Holmes mystery stories.
Theodore Dreiser, 1871-1945, (U.S.) novelist. *An American Tragedy*, *Sister Carrie*.
John Dryden, 1631-1700, (Br.) poet, dramatist, critic. *All for Love*, *Mac Flecknoe*, *Absalom and Achitophel*.
Alexandre Dumas (père), 1802-70, (Fr.) novelist, dramatist. *The Three Musketeers*, *The Count of Monte Cristo*.
Alexandre Dumas (fils), 1824-95, (Fr.) dramatist, novelist. *La Dame aux Camélias*, *Le Demi-Monde*.
Paul Laurence Dunbar, 1872-1906, (U.S.) poet, novelist. *Lyrics of Lowly Life*.
Lawrence Durrell, 1912-90, (Br.) novelist, poet. *Alexandria Quartet*.
Ilya G. Ehrenburg, 1891-1967, (Russ.) writer. *The Thaw*.
George Eliot (Mary Ann or Marian Evans), 1819-80, (Br.) novelist. *Silas Marner*, *Middlemarch*.
T(homas) S(tearns) Eliot, 1888-1965, (Br.) poet, critic. *The Waste Land*, "The Love Song of J. Alfred Prufrock."
Stanley Elkin, 1930-95, (U.S.) novelist, short-story writer. *George Mills*.
Ralph Ellison, 1914-94, (U.S.) writer. *Invisible Man*.
Ralph Waldo Emerson, 1803-82, (U.S.) poet, essayist. "Brahma," "Nature," "The Over-Soul," "Self-Reliance."
James T. Farrell, 1904-79, (U.S.) novelist. *Studs Lonigan*.
Howard Fast, 1914-2003, (U.S.) novelist. *Spartacus*, *The Immigrants*.
William Faulkner, 1897-1962, (U.S.) novelist. *Sanctuary*; *Light in August*; *The Sound and the Fury*; *Absalom, Absalom!*
Edna Ferber, 1887-1968, (U.S.) novelist, short-story writer, playwright. *So Big*, *Cimarron*, *Show Boat*.
Henry Fielding, 1707-54, (Br.) novelist. *Tom Jones*.
F(rancis) Scott Fitzgerald, 1896-1940, (U.S.) short-story writer, novelist. *The Great Gatsby*, *Tender Is the Night*.
Gustave Flaubert, 1821-80, (Fr.) novelist. *Madame Bovary*.
Ian Fleming, 1908-64, (Br.) novelist. James Bond spy thrillers: *Dr. No*, *Goldfinger*.
Horton Foote, 1916-2009, (U.S.) playwright, screenwriter. *The Trip to Bountiful*.
Ford Madox Ford, 1873-1939, (Br.) novelist, critic, poet. *The Good Soldier*.
C(ecil) S(cott) Forester, 1899-1966, (Br.) writer. Horatio Hornblower books.
E(dward) M(organ) Forster, 1879-1970, (Br.) novelist. *A Passage to India*, *Howards End*.
Anatole France, 1844-1924, (Fr.) writer. *Penguin Island*, *My Friend's Book*, *The Crime of Sylvestre Bonnard*.
Dick Francis, 1920-2010, (Br.) crime novelist.
Marilyn French, 1929-2009, (U.S.) novelist. *The Women's Room*.
Robert Frost, 1874-1963, (U.S.) poet. "Birches," "Fire and Ice," "Stopping by Woods on a Snowy Evening."
Carlos Fuentes, 1928-2012, (Pan.) novelist, essayist. *The Old Gringo*.
William Gaddis, 1922-98, (U.S.) novelist. *The Recognitions*.
John Galsworthy, 1867-1933, (Br.) novelist, dramatist. *The Forsyte Saga*.
Federico García Lorca, 1898-1936, (Sp.) poet, dramatist. *Blood Wedding*.
Gabriel García Márquez, 1927-2014, (Col.) novelist. *One Hundred Years of Solitude*.
Erle Stanley Gardner, 1889-1970, (U.S.) mystery writer; created Perry Mason.
Jean Genet, 1911-86, (Fr.) playwright, novelist. *The Maids*.

Kahlil Gibran, 1883-1931, (Leban.-U.S.) mystical novelist, essayist, poet. *The Prophet*.
André Gide, 1869-1951, (Fr.) writer. *The Immoralist, The Pastoral Symphony, Strait Is the Gate*.
Allen Ginsberg, 1926-97, (U.S.) Beat poet. "Howl."
Jean Giraudoux, 1882-1944, (Fr.) novelist, dramatist. *Electra, The Madwoman of Chaillot, Ondine, Tiger at the Gate*.
Johann Wolfgang von Goethe, 1749-1832, (Ger.) poet, dramatist, novelist. *Faust, Sorrows of Young Werther*.
Nikolai Gogol, 1809-52, (Russ.) short-story writer, dramatist, novelist. *Dead Souls, The Inspector General*.
William Golding, 1911-93, (Br.) novelist. *Lord of the Flies*.
Oliver Goldsmith, 1728-74, (Br.-Ire.) dramatist, novelist. *The Vicar of Wakefield, She Stoops to Conquer*.
Nadine Gordimer, 1923-2014, (S. Afr.) novelist. *Burger's Daughter*.
Maxim Gorky, 1868-1936, (Russ.) dramatist, novelist. *The Lower Depths*.
Günter Grass, 1927-2015, (Ger.) novelist, poet. *The Tin Drum*.
Robert Graves, 1895-1985, (Br.) poet, classical scholar, novelist. *I, Claudius; The White Goddess*.
Thomas Gray, 1716-71, (Br.) poet. "Elegy Written in a Country Churchyard," "The Progress of Poesy."
Julien Green, 1900-98, (U.S.-Fr.) expatriate American novelist. *Moira, Each Man in His Darkness*.
Graham Greene, 1904-91, (Br.) novelist. *The Power and the Glory, The Heart of the Matter, The Ministry of Fear*.
Zane Grey, 1872-1939, (U.S.) writer of Western stories.
Jakob Grimm, 1785-1863, philologist, folklorist; with brother **Wilhelm Grimm**, 1786-1859, (both Ger.) collected *Grimm's Fairy Tales*.
Alex Haley, 1921-92, (U.S.) author. *Roots*.
Dashiell Hammett, 1894-1961, (U.S.) detective-story writer; created Sam Spade. *The Maltese Falcon*.
Jupiter Hammon, c. 1720-1800, (U.S.) poet; first African American to have his works published, 1761.
Knut Hamsun, 1859-1952, (Nor.) novelist. *Hunger*.
Lorraine Hansberry, 1930-65, (U.S.) playwright. *A Raisin in the Sun*.
Thomas Hardy, 1840-1928, (Br.) novelist, poet. *The Return of the Native, Tess of the D'Urbervilles, Jude the Obscure*.
E. Lynn Harris, 1955-2009, (U.S.) novelist. *Invisible Life, Basketball Jones*.
Joel Chandler Harris, 1848-1908, (U.S.) writer. Uncle Remus stories.
Moss Hart, 1904-61, (U.S.) playwright. *Once in a Lifetime, You Can't Take It With You, The Man Who Came to Dinner*.
Bret Harte, 1836-1902, (U.S.) short-story writer, poet. *The Luck of Roaring Camp*.
Jaroslav Hasek, 1883-1923, (Czech.) writer, playwright. *The Good Soldier Schweik*.
Vaclav Havel, 1936-2011, (Czech.) essayist, poet, playwright. *The Power of the Powerless*.
John Hawkes, 1925-98, (U.S.) experimental fiction writer. *The Goose on the Grave, Blood Oranges*.
Nathaniel Hawthorne, 1804-64, (U.S.) novelist, short-story writer. *The Scarlet Letter*, "Young Goodman Brown."
Seamus Heaney, 1939-2013, (Ire.) poet. *Death of a Naturalist*.
Heinrich Heine, 1797-1856, (Ger.) poet. *Book of Songs*.
Robert Heinlein, 1907-88, (U.S.) science-fiction writer. *Stranger in a Strange Land*.
Joseph Heller, 1923-99, (U.S.) novelist. *Catch-22*.
Lillian Hellman, 1905-84, (U.S.) playwright, memoirist. *The Little Foxes, An Unfinished Woman, Pentimento*.
Ernest Hemingway, 1899-1961, (U.S.) novelist, short-story writer. *A Farewell to Arms, For Whom the Bell Tolls*.
O. Henry (W. S. Porter), 1862-1910, (U.S.) short-story writer. "The Gift of the Magi."
George Herbert, 1593-1633, (Br.) poet. "The Altar," "Easter Wings."
Zbigniew Herbert, 1924-98, (Pol.) poet. "Apollo and Marsyas."
Robert Herrick, 1591-1674, (Br.) poet. "To the Virgins to Make Much of Time."
John Hersey, 1914-93, (U.S.) novelist, journalist. *Hiroshima, A Bell for Adano*.
Hermann Hesse, 1877-1962, (Ger.) novelist, poet. *Death and the Lover, Steppenwolf, Siddhartha*.
Oscar Hijuelos, 1951-2013, (U.S.) novelist. *The Mambo Kings Play Songs of Love*.
Tony Hillerman, 1925-2008, (U.S.) novelist. *Dance Hall of the Dead*.
James Hilton, 1900-54, (Br.) novelist. *Lost Horizon*.
Chester Himes, 1909-84, (U.S.) novelist. *Cotton Comes to Harlem*.
Oliver Wendell Holmes, 1809-94, (U.S.) poet, novelist. *The Autocrat of the Breakfast-Table*.
Gerard Manley Hopkins, 1844-89, (Br.) poet. "Pied Beauty," "God's Grandeur."
A(lfred) E. Housman, 1859-1936, (Br.) poet. *A Shropshire Lad*.
William Dean Howells, 1837-1920, (U.S.) novelist, critic. *The Rise of Silas Lapham*.
Langston Hughes, 1902-67, (U.S.) poet, lyric writer, author; a major influence in 1920s Harlem Renaissance.
Ted Hughes, 1930-98, (Br.) British poet laureate, 1984-98. *Crow, The Hawk in the Rain*.
Victor Hugo, 1802-85, (Fr.) poet, dramatist, novelist. *Notre Dame de Paris, Les Misérables*.
Zora Neale Hurston, 1903-60, (U.S.) novelist, folklorist. *Their Eyes Were Watching God, Mules and Men*.
Aldous Huxley, 1894-1963, (Br.) writer. *Brave New World*.
Henrik Ibsen, 1828-1906, (Nor.) dramatist, poet. *A Doll's House, Ghosts, The Wild Duck, Hedda Gabler*.
William Inge, 1913-73, (U.S.) playwright. *Picnic; Come Back, Little Sheba; Bus Stop*.
Eugene Ionesco, 1910-94, (Fr.) surrealist dramatist. *The Bald Soprano, The Chairs*.
Washington Irving, 1783-1859, (U.S.) writer. "Rip Van Winkle," "The Legend of Sleepy Hollow."
Christopher Isherwood, 1904-86, (Br.) novelist, playwright. *The Berlin Stories*.
Shirley Jackson, 1919-65, (U.S.) short-story writer. "The Lottery."
Henry James, 1843-1916, (U.S.) novelist, short-story writer, critic. *The Portrait of a Lady, The Ambassadors, Daisy Miller*.
P(hyllis) D(orothy) James, 1920-2014, (Br.) novelist. *Death Comes to Pemberley*.
Robinson Jeffers, 1887-1962, (U.S.) poet, dramatist. *Tamar and Other Poems, Medea*.
James Weldon Johnson, 1871-1938, (U.S.) poet, novelist, diplomat; lyricist for *Lift Every Voice and Sing*.
Samuel Johnson, 1709-84, (Br.) author, scholar, critic. *Dictionary of the English Language, Vanity of Human Wishes*.
Ben Jonson, 1572-1637, (Br.) dramatist, poet. *Volpone*.
James Joyce, 1882-1941, (Ire.) writer. *Ulysses, Dubliners, A Portrait of the Artist as a Young Man, Finnegans Wake*.
Ernst Junger, 1895-1998, (Ger.) novelist, essayist. *The Peace, On the Marble Cliff*.
Franz Kafka, 1883-1924, (Austria-Hung./Czech.) novelist, short-story writer. *The Trial, The Castle*, "The Metamorphosis."
George S. Kaufman, 1889-1961, (U.S.) playwright. *The Man Who Came to Dinner, You Can't Take It With You*.
Yasunari Kawabata, 1899-1972, (Jpn.) novelist. *The Sound of the Mountains*.
Nikos Kazantzakis, 1883-1957, (Gr.) novelist. *Zorba the Greek, A Greek Passion*.
Alfred Kazin, 1915-98 (U.S.) author, critic, teacher. *On Native Grounds*.
John Keats, 1795-1821, (Br.) poet. "Ode on a Grecian Urn," "Ode to a Nightingale," "La Belle Dame Sans Merci."
Jack Kerouac, 1922-69, (U.S.) author, Beat poet. *On the Road, The Dharma Bums*, "Mexico City Blues."
Joyce Kilmer, 1886-1918, (U.S.) poet. "Trees."
Galway Kinnell, 1927-2014, (U.S.) poet.
Rudyard Kipling, 1865-1936, (Br.) author, poet. "The White Man's Burden," "Gunga Din," *The Jungle Book*.
Maxine Kumin, 1925-2014, (U.S.) poet, author. *Up Country: Poems of New England*.
Jean de la Fontaine, 1621-95, (Fr.) poet. *Fables choisies* (Selected Fables).
Pär Lagerkvist, 1891-1974, (Swed.) poet, dramatist, novelist. *Barabbas, The Sybil*.
Selma Lagerlöf, 1858-1940, (Swed.) novelist. *Jerusalem, The Ring of the Lowenskolds*.
Alphonse de Lamartine, 1790-1869, (Fr.) poet, novelist, statesman. *Méditations poétiques*.
Charles Lamb, 1775-1834, (Br.) essayist. *Specimens of English Dramatic Poets, Essays of Elia*.
Louis L'Amour, 1908-88, (U.S.) Western author, screenwriter. *Hondo, The Cherokee Trail*.
Giuseppe di Lampedusa, 1896-1957, (It.) novelist. *The Leopard*.
William Langland, c. 1332-1400, (Br.) poet. *Piers Plowman*.
Ring Lardner, 1885-1933, (U.S.) short-story writer, humorist.
Steig Larsson, 1954-2004, (Swed.) novelist. *The Girl With the Dragon Tattoo*.
Arthur Laurents, 1917-2011, (U.S.) playwright and director. *West Side Story*.
D(avid) H(erbert) Lawrence, 1885-1930, (Br.) novelist. *Sons and Lovers, Women in Love, Lady Chatterley's Lover*.
Halldór Laxness, 1902-98, (Iceland) novelist. *Iceland's Bell*.
Madeleine L'Engle, 1918-2007, (U.S.) novelist of young adult fiction. *A Wrinkle in Time*.
Elmore Leonard, 1925-2013, (U.S.) novelist. *Get Shorty*.
Mikhail Lermontov, 1814-41, (Russ.) novelist, poet. "Demon," *Hero of Our Time*.
Alain-René Lesage, 1668-1747, (Fr.) novelist. *Gil Blas de Santillane*.
Doris Lessing, 1919-2013, (Br.) writer. *The Golden Notebook*.
Gotthold Lessing, 1729-81, (Ger.) dramatist, philosopher, critic. *Miss Sara Sampson, Minna von Barnhelm*.
Ira Levin, 1929-2007, (U.S.) novelist, playwright. *Deathtrap*.
C(live) S(taples) Lewis, 1898-1963, (Br.) critic, novelist, religious writer. *Allegory of Love; The Lion, the Witch and the Wardrobe; Out of the Silent Planet*.
Sinclair Lewis, 1885-1951, (U.S.) novelist. *Babbitt, Main Street, Arrowsmith, Dodsworth*.
Li Po, 701-762, (China) poet. "Song Before Drinking," "She Spins Silk."
Vachel Lindsay, 1879-1931, (U.S.) poet. *General William Booth Enters Into Heaven, The Congo*.
Hugh Lofting, 1886-1947, (Br.) writer. Dr. Doolittle series.
Jack London, 1876-1916, (U.S.) novelist, journalist. *Call of the Wild, The Sea-Wolf, White Fang*.
Henry Wadsworth Longfellow, 1807-82, (U.S.) poet. *Evangeline, The Song of Hiawatha*.
Lope de Vega, 1562-1635, (Sp.) playwright. *Noche de San Juan, Maestro de Danzar*.
H(oward) P(hillips) Lovecraft, 1890-1937, (U.S.) novelist, short-story writer. "At the Mountains of Madness."

Amy Lowell, 1874-1925, (U.S.) poet, critic. "Lilacs."
James Russell Lowell, 1819-91, (U.S.) poet, editor. *Poems, The Biglow Papers.*
Robert Lowell, 1917-77, (U.S.) poet. "Lord Weary's Castle."
Joaquim Maria Machado de Assis, 1839-1908, (Brazil) novelist, poet. *The Posthumous Memoirs of Bras Cubas.*
Archibald MacLeish, 1892-1982, (U.S.) poet. *Conquistador.*
Naguib Mahfouz, 1911-2006, (Egypt) novelist; first Arabic-language writer to win the Nobel Prize for Literature. *Cairo Trilogy.*
Norman Mailer, 1923-2007, (U.S.) novelist, essayist, journalist. *The Naked and the Dead.*
Bernard Malamud, 1914-86, (U.S.) short-story writer, novelist. "The Magic Barrel," *The Assistant, The Fixer.*
Stéphane Mallarmé, 1842-98, (Fr.) poet. *Poésies.*
Sir Thomas Malory, c. 1410-71, (Br.) writer. *Morte d'Arthur.*
Andre Malraux, 1901-76, (Fr.) novelist. *Man's Fate.*
Osip Mandelstam, 1891-1938, (Russ.) poet. *Stone, Tristia.*
Thomas Mann, 1875-1955, (Ger.) novelist, essayist. *Buddenbrooks, The Magic Mountain,* "Death in Venice."
Katherine Mansfield, 1888-1923, (Br.) short-story writer. "Bliss."
Christopher Marlowe, 1564-93, (Br.) dramatist, poet. *Tamburlaine the Great, Dr. Faustus, The Jew of Malta.*
Andrew Marvell, 1621-78, (Br.) poet. "To His Coy Mistress."
John Masefield, 1878-1967, (Br.) poet. "Sea Fever," "Cargoes," *Salt Water Ballads.*
Edgar Lee Masters, 1869-1950, (U.S.) poet, biographer. *Spoon River Anthology.*
Peter Matthiessen, 1927-2014, (U.S.) novelist. *The Snow Leopard.*
W(illiam) Somerset Maugham, 1874-1965, (Br.) author. *Of Human Bondage, The Moon and Sixpence.*
Guy de Maupassant, 1850-93, (Fr.) novelist, short-story writer. "A Life," "Bel-Ami," "The Necklace."
François Mauriac, 1885-1970, (Fr.) novelist, dramatist. *Viper's Tangle, The Kiss to the Leper.*
Vladimir Mayakovsky, 1893-1930, (Russ.) poet, dramatist. *The Cloud in Trousers.*
Mary McCarthy, 1912-89, (U.S.) critic, novelist, memoirist. *Memories of a Catholic Girlhood.*
Frank McCourt, 1930-2009, (U.S.) memorist. *Angela's Ashes, 'Tis, Teacher Man.*
Carson McCullers, 1917-67, (U.S.) novelist. *The Heart Is a Lonely Hunter, Member of the Wedding.*
Colleen McCullough, 1937-2015, (Austral.) novelist. *The Thorn Birds.*
Herman Melville, 1819-91, (U.S.) novelist, poet. *Moby-Dick, Typee, Billy Budd, Omoo.*
George Meredith, 1828-1909, (Br.) novelist, poet. *The Ordeal of Richard Feverel, The Egoist.*
Prosper Mérimée, 1803-70, (Fr.) author. *Carmen.*
James Merrill, 1926-95, (U.S.) poet. *Divine Comedies.*
James Michener, 1907-97, (U.S.) novelist. *Tales of the South Pacific.*
Edna St. Vincent Millay, 1892-1950, (U.S.) poet. *The Harp Weaver and Other Poems.*
Arthur Miller,1915-2005, (U.S.) playwright. *The Crucible, After the Fall, Death of a Salesman.*
Henry Miller, 1891-1980, (U.S.) erotic novelist. *Tropic of Cancer.*
A(lan) A(lexander) Milne, 1882-1956, (Br.) author. *Winnie-the-Pooh.*
Czeslaw Milosz, 1911-2004, (Pol.) essayist, poet. "Esse," "Encounter."
John Milton, 1608-74, (Br.) poet, writer. *Paradise Lost, Comus, Lycidas, Areopagitica.*
Mishima Yukio (Hiraoka Kimitake) 1925-70, (Jpn.) writer. *Confessions of a Mask.*
Gabriela Mistral, 1889-1957, (Chile) poet. *Sonnets of Death.*
Margaret Mitchell, 1900-49, (U.S.) novelist. *Gone With the Wind.*
Jean Baptiste Molière, 1622-73, (Fr.) dramatist. *Tartuffe, Le Misanthrope, Le Bourgeois Gentilhomme.*
Ferenc Molnár, 1878-1952, (Hung.) dramatist, novelist. *Liliom, The Guardsman, The Swan.*
Michel de Montaigne, 1533-92, (Fr.) essayist. *Essais.*
Eugenio Montale, 1896-1981, (It.) poet.
Brian Moore, 1921-99, (Ire.-U.S.) novelist. *The Lonely Passion of Judith Hearne.*
Clement C. Moore, 1779-1863, (U.S.) poet, educator. "A Visit From Saint Nicholas."
Marianne Moore, 1887-1972, (U.S.) poet.
Alberto Moravia, 1907-90, (It.) novelist, short-story writer. *The Time of Indifference.*
Sir Thomas More, 1478-1535, (Br.) writer, statesman, saint. *Utopia.*
Wright Morris, 1910-98, (U.S.) novelist. *My Uncle Dudley.*
Murasaki Shikibu, c. 978-1026, (Jpn.) novelist. *The Tale of Genji.*
Iris Murdoch, 1919-99, (Br.) novelist, philosopher. *The Sea, the Sea.*
Alfred de Musset, 1810-57, (Fr.) poet, dramatist. *La Confession d'un Enfant du Siècle.*
Vladimir Nabokov, 1899-1977, (Russ.-U.S.) novelist. *Lolita, Pale Fire.*
R. K. Narayan, 1906-2001, (India) novelist. *The Guide.*
Ogden Nash, 1902-71, (U.S.) poet of light verse.
Irène Némirovsky, 1903-42, (Ukraine) novelist. *David Golder, Suite Française.*
Pablo Neruda, 1904-73, (Chile) poet. *Twenty Love Poems and One Song of Despair, Toward the Splendid City.*
Patrick O'Brian, 1914-2000, (Br.) historical novelist. *Master and Commander, Blue at the Mizzen.*
Sean O'Casey, 1884-1964, (Ire.) dramatist. *Juno and the Paycock, The Plough and the Stars.*
Flannery O'Connor, 1925-64, (U.S.) novelist, short-story writer. *Wise Blood,* "A Good Man Is Hard to Find."
Frank O'Connor (Michael Donovan), 1903-66, (Ire.) short-story writer. "Guests of a Nation."
Clifford Odets, 1906-63, (U.S.) playwright. *Waiting for Lefty, Awake and Sing, Golden Boy, The Country Girl.*
John O'Hara, 1905-70, (U.S.) novelist, short-story writer. *From the Terrace, Appointment in Samarra, Pal Joey.*
Omar Khayyam, c. 1028-1122, (Per.) poet. *Rubaiyat.*
Eugene O'Neill, 1888-1953, (U.S.) playwright. *Emperor Jones, Anna Christie, Long Day's Journey Into Night.*
George Orwell (Eric Arthur Blair), 1903-50, (Br.) novelist, essayist. *Animal Farm, Nineteen Eighty-Four.*
John Osborne, 1929-95, (Br.) dramatist, novelist. *Look Back in Anger, The Entertainer.*
Wilfred Owen, 1893-1918, (Br.) poet. "Dulce et Décorum Est."
Grace Paley, 1922-2007, (U.S.) short-story writer, poet. *The Little Disturbances of Man.*
Dorothy Parker, 1893-1967, (U.S.) poet, short-story writer. *Enough Rope, Laments for the Living.*
Robert B. Parker, 1932-2010, (U.S.) crime novelist. "Spenser" novels.
Boris Pasternak, 1890-1960, (Russ.) poet, novelist. *Doctor Zhivago.*
Alan Paton, 1903-88, (S. Africa) novelist. *Cry, the Beloved Country.*
Octavio Paz, 1914-98, (Mex.) poet, essayist. *The Labyrinth of Solitude, They Shall Not Pass!, The Sun Stone.*
Samuel Pepys, 1633-1703, (Br.) public official, diarist.
S(idney) J(oseph) Perelman, 1904-79, (U.S.) humorist. *The Road to Miltown, Under the Spreading Atrophy.*
Charles Perrault, 1628-1703, (Fr.) writer. *Tales From Mother Goose (Sleeping Beauty, Cinderella).*
Petrarch (Francesco Petrarca), 1304-74, (It.) poet. *Africa, Trionfi, Canzoniere.*
Harold Pinter, 1930-2008, (Br.) playwright. *The Birthday Party, The Caretaker, The Homecoming.*
Luigi Pirandello, 1867-1936, (It.) novelist, dramatist. *Six Characters in Search of an Author.*
Sylvia Plath, 1932-63, (U.S.) author, poet. *The Bell Jar.*
Edgar Allan Poe, 1809-49, (U.S.) poet, short-story writer, critic. "Annabel Lee," "The Raven," "The Purloined Letter."
Alexander Pope, 1688-1744, (Br.) poet. *The Rape of the Lock, The Dunciad, An Essay on Man.*
Katherine Anne Porter, 1890-1980, (U.S.) novelist, short-story writer. *Ship of Fools.*
Chaim Potok, 1929-2002, (U.S.) novelist. *The Chosen.*
Ezra Pound, 1885-1972, (U.S.) poet. *Cantos.*
Anthony Powell, 1905-2000, (Br.) novelist. A Dance to the Music of Time series.
Terry Pratchett, 1948-2015 (Br.) fantasy novelist. Discworld series.
Reynolds Price, 1933-2011, (U.S.) novelist, short-story writer, poet. *A Long and Happy Life.*
J(ohn) B(oynton) Priestley, 1894-1984, (Br.) novelist, dramatist. *The Good Companions.*
Marcel Proust, 1871-1922, (Fr.) novelist. *Remembrance of Things Past.*
Aleksandr Pushkin, 1799-1837, (Russ.) poet, novelist. *Boris Godunov, Eugene Onegin.*
Mario Puzo, 1920-99, (U.S.) novelist. *The Godfather.*
François Rabelais, 1495-1553, (Fr.) writer. *Gargantua.*
Jean Racine, 1639-99, (Fr.) dramatist. *Andromaque, Phèdre, Bérénice, Britannicus.*
David Rakoff, 1964-2012, (Can.-U.S.) essayist. *Fraud, Don't Get Too Comfortable.*
Ayn Rand, 1905-82, (Russ.-U.S.) novelist, moral theorist. *The Fountainhead, Atlas Shrugged.*
Terence Rattigan, 1911-77, (Br.) playwright. *Separate Tables, The Browning Version.*
Erich Maria Remarque, 1898-1970, (Ger.-U.S.) novelist. *All Quiet on the Western Front.*
Mary Renault, 1905-83, (Br.) novelist. *The Last of the Wine.*
Ruth Rendell, 1930-2015, (Br.) novelist. Chief Inspector Reginald Wexford mysteries.
Adrienne Rich, 1929-2012, (U.S.) poet. *Diving Into the Wreck: Poems, 1971-1972.*
Samuel Richardson, 1689-1761, (Br.) novelist. *Pamela; or Virtue Rewarded.*
Rainer Maria Rilke, 1875-1926, (Ger.) poet. *Life and Songs, Duino Elegies, Poems From the Book of Hours.*
Arthur Rimbaud, 1854-91, (Fr.) poet. *A Season in Hell.*
Harold Robbins, 1916-97, (U.S.) novelist, *The Carpetbaggers.*
Edwin Arlington Robinson, 1869-1935, (U.S.) poet. "Richard Cory," "Miniver Cheevy," *Merlin.*
Theodore Roethke, 1908-63, (U.S.) poet. *Open House, The Waking, The Far Field.*
Romain Rolland, 1866-1944, (Fr.) novelist, biographer. *Jean-Christophe.*

Pierre de Ronsard, 1524-85, (Fr.) poet. *Sonnets pour Hélène, La Franciade.*
Christina Rossetti, 1830-94, (Br.) poet. "When I Am Dead, My Dearest."
Dante Gabriel Rossetti, 1828-82, (Br.) poet, painter. "The Blessed Damozel."
Edmond Rostand, 1868-1918, (Fr.) poet, dramatist. *Cyrano de Bergerac.*
Damon Runyon, 1880-1946, (U.S.) short-story writer, journalist. *Guys and Dolls, Blue Plate Special.*
John Ruskin, 1819-1900, (Br.) critic, social theorist. *Modern Painters, The Seven Lamps of Architecture.*
Oliver Sacks, 1933-2015, (Br.) neurologist, writer. *The Man Who Mistook His Wife for a Hat.*
François Sagan (Françoise Quoirez), 1935-2004, (Fr.) novelist. *Bonjour Tristesse.*
Antoine de Saint-Exupéry, 1900-44, (Fr.) writer. *Wind, Sand and Stars; The Little Prince.*
Saki (or H[ector] H[ugh] Munro), 1870-1916, (Br.) writer. *The Chronicles of Clovis.*
J. D. Salinger, 1919-2010, (U.S.) novelist. *The Catcher in the Rye.*
George Sand (Amandine Lucie Aurore Dupin), 1804-76, (Fr.) novelist. *Indiana, Consuelo.*
Carl Sandburg, 1878-1967, (U.S.) poet. *The People, Yes; Chicago Poems; Smoke and Steel; Harvest Poems.*
Jose Saramago, 1922-2010, (Port.) novelist. *Blindness.*
William Saroyan, 1908-81, (U.S.) playwright, novelist. *The Time of Your Life, The Human Comedy.*
Nathalie Sarraute, 1900-99, (Fr.) Nouveau Roman novelist. *Tropismes.*
May Sarton, 1914-95, (Belg.-U.S.) poet, novelist. *Encounter in April, Anger.*
Dorothy L. Sayers, 1893-1957, (Br.) mystery writer; created Lord Peter Wimsey.
Richard Scarry, 1920-94, (U.S.) author of children's books. *Richard Scarry's Best Story Book Ever.*
Friedrich von Schiller, 1759-1805, (Ger.) dramatist, poet, historian. *Don Carlos, Maria Stuart, Wilhelm Tell.*
Sir Walter Scott, 1771-1832, (Scot.) novelist, poet. *Ivanhoe.*
Gil Scott-Heron, 1949-2011, (U.S.) poet. "The Revolution Will Not Be Televised."
Jaroslav Seifert, 1902-86, (Czech.) poet.
Maurice Sendak, 1928-2012, (U.S.) children's book author and illustrator. *Where the Wild Things Are.*
Dr. Seuss (Theodor Seuss Geisel), 1904-91, (U.S.) children's book author and illustrator. *The Cat in the Hat.*
William Shakespeare, 1564-1616, (Br.) dramatist, poet. *Romeo and Juliet, Hamlet, King Lear, Julius Caesar*, sonnets.
Karl Shapiro, 1913-2000, (U.S.) poet. "Elegy for a Dead Soldier."
George Bernard Shaw, 1856-1950, (Ire.-Br.) playwright, critic. *St. Joan, Pygmalion, Major Barbara, Man and Superman.*
Sidney Sheldon, 1917-2007, (U.S.) screenwriter, novelist. *Rage of Angels, Memories of Midnight.*
Mary Wollstonecraft Shelley, 1797-1851, (Br.) novelist, feminist. *Frankenstein, The Last Man.*
Percy Bysshe Shelley, 1792-1822, (Br.) poet. *Prometheus Unbound, Adonais*, "Ode to the West Wind," "To a Skylark."
Richard B. Sheridan, 1751-1816, (Br.) dramatist. *The Rivals, School for Scandal.*
Robert Sherwood, 1896-1955, (U.S.) playwright, biographer. *The Petrified Forest, Abe Lincoln in Illinois.*
Mikhail Sholokhov, 1906-84, (Russ.) writer. *The Silent Don.*
Shel Silverstein, 1932-99, (U.S.) poet, writer. *The Giving Tree, Where the Sidewalk Ends.*
Georges Simenon (Georges Sims), 1903-89, (Belg.-Fr.) mystery writer; created Inspector Maigret.
Upton Sinclair, 1878-1968, (U.S.) novelist. *The Jungle.*
Isaac Bashevis Singer, 1904-91, (Pol.-U.S.) novelist, short-story writer, in Yiddish. *The Magician of Lublin.*
C(harles) P(ercy) Snow, 1905-80, (Br.) novelist, scientist. *Strangers and Brothers, Corridors of Power.*
Aleksandr Solzhenitsyn, 1918-2008, (Russ.) novelist, dramatist. *One Day in the Life of Ivan Denisovich.*
Susan Sontag, 1933-2004, (U.S.) critic, essayist, novelist. *Notes on Camp, The Volcano Lover, In America.*
Stephen Spender, 1909-95, (Br.) poet, critic, novelist. *Twenty Poems*, "Elegy for Margaret."
Edmund Spenser, 1552-99, (Br.) poet. *The Faerie Queene.*
Mickey Spillane, 1918-2006, (U.S.) novelist; Mike Hammer detective novels. *The Killing Man.*
Johanna Spyri, 1827-1901, (Switz.) children's author. *Heidi.*
Christina Stead, 1903-83, (Austral.) novelist, short-story writer. *The Man Who Loved Children.*
Richard Steele, 1672-1729, (Br.) essayist, playwright; began the *Tatler* and *Spectator. The Conscious Lovers.*
Gertrude Stein, 1874-1946, (U.S.) writer. *Three Lives.*
John Steinbeck, 1902-68, (U.S.) novelist. *The Grapes of Wrath, Of Mice and Men, The Winter of Our Discontent.*
Stendhal (Marie Henri Beyle), 1783-1842, (Fr.) novelist. *The Red and the Black, The Charterhouse of Parma.*
Laurence Sterne, 1713-68, (Br.) novelist. *Tristram Shandy.*
Wallace Stevens, 1879-1955, (U.S.) poet. *Harmonium, The Man With the Blue Guitar, Notes Toward a Supreme Fiction.*
Robert Louis Stevenson, 1850-94, (Br.) novelist, poet, essayist. *Treasure Island, A Child's Garden of Verses.*
Mary Stewart, 1916-2014, (Br.) fantasy novelist. Merlin series.
Bram Stoker, 1847-1912, (Br.) writer. *Dracula.*
Rex Stout, 1886-1975, (U.S.) mystery writer; created Nero Wolfe.
Harriet Beecher Stowe, 1811-96, (U.S.) novelist. *Uncle Tom's Cabin.*
Lytton Strachey, 1880-1932, (Br.) biographer, critic. *Eminent Victorians, Queen Victoria, Elizabeth and Essex.*
Mark Strand, 1934-2014, (Can.-U.S.) poet. *Blizzard of One.*
August Strindberg, 1849-1912, (Swed.) dramatist, novelist. *The Father, Miss Julie, The Creditors.*
William Styron, 1925-2006, (U.S.) novelist, essayist. *The Confessions of Nat Turner, Sophie's Choice, Darkness Visible: A Memoir of Madness.*
Jonathan Swift, 1667-1745, (Br.) satirist, poet. *Gulliver's Travels*, "A Modest Proposal."
Algernon C. Swinburne, 1837-1909, (Br.) poet, dramatist. *Atalanta in Calydon.*
John M. Synge, 1871-1909, (Ire.) poet, dramatist. *Riders to the Sea, The Playboy of the Western World.*
Wislawa Szymborska, 1923-2012, (Pol.) poet. "Cat in an Empty Apartment."
Rabindranath Tagore, 1861-1941, (India) author, poet. *Sadhana, The Realization of Life, Gitanjali.*
Booth Tarkington, 1869-1946, (U.S.) novelist. *The Magnificent Ambersons.*
Peter Taylor, 1917-94, (U.S.) novelist. *A Summons to Memphis.*
Sara Teasdale, 1884-1933, (U.S.) poet. *Helen of Troy and Other Poems, Rivers to the Sea.*
Alfred, Lord Tennyson, 1809-92, (Br.) poet. *Idylls of the King, In Memoriam*, "The Charge of the Light Brigade."
William Makepeace Thackeray, 1811-63, (Br.) novelist. *Vanity Fair, Henry Esmond, Pendennis.*
Dylan Thomas, 1914-53, (Wales) poet. *Under Milk Wood, A Child's Christmas in Wales.*
Hunter S. Thompson, 1937-2005, (U.S.) author, journalist. *Hell's Angels, Fear and Loathing in Las Vegas.*
Henry David Thoreau, 1817-62, (U.S.) writer, philosopher, naturalist. *Walden*, "Civil Disobedience."
James Thurber, 1894-1961, (U.S.) humorist. "The Secret Life of Walter Mitty," *My Life and Hard Times.*
J(ohn) R(onald) R(euel) Tolkien, 1892-1973, (Br.) writer. *The Hobbit*, Lord of the Rings trilogy.
Leo Tolstoy, 1828-1910, (Russ.) novelist, short-story writer. *War and Peace, Anna Karenina*, "The Death of Ivan Ilyich."
Lionel Trilling, 1905-75, (U.S.) critic, author, teacher. *The Liberal Imagination.*
Anthony Trollope, 1815-82, (Br.) novelist. *The Warden, Barchester Towers*, the Palliser novels.
Ivan Turgenev, 1818-83, (Russ.) novelist, short-story writer. *Fathers and Sons, First Love, A Month in the Country.*
Amos Tutuola, 1920-97, (Nigeria) novelist. *The Palm-Wine Drunkard, My Life in the Bush of Ghosts.*
Mark Twain (Samuel Clemens), 1835-1910, (U.S.) novelist, humorist. *The Adventures of Huckleberry Finn.*
Sigrid Undset, 1881-1949, (Nor.) novelist. *Kristin Lavransdatter.*
John Updike, 1932-2009, (U.S.) novelist, literary critic. *Rabbit is Rich, The Witches of Eastwick.*
Paul Valéry, 1871-1945, (Fr.) poet, critic. *La Jeune Parque, The Graveyard by the Sea.*
Paul Verlaine, 1844-96, (Fr.) Symbolist poet. *Songs Without Words.*
Jules Verne, 1828-1905, (Fr.) novelist. *Twenty Thousand Leagues Under the Sea.*
Gore Vidal, 1925-2012, (U.S.) novelist. *The City and the Pillar.*
François Villon, 1431-c. 1463, (Fr.) poet. *The Lays, The Grand Testament.*
Voltaire (F. M. Arouet), 1694-1778, (Fr.) writer of "philosophical romances"; philosopher, historian. *Candide.*
Kurt Vonnegut Jr., 1922-2007, (U.S.) novelist, essayist. *Cat's Cradle, Slaughterhouse-Five, Breakfast of Champions.*
David Foster Wallace, 1962-2008, (U.S.) novelist, essayist. *Infinite Jest, A Supposedly Fun Thing I'll Never Do Again.*
Robert Penn Warren, 1905-89, (U.S.) novelist, poet, critic. *All the King's Men.*
Wendy Wasserstein, 1950-2006, (U.S.) playwright. *The Heidi Chronicles.*
Evelyn Waugh, 1903-66, (Br.) novelist. *The Loved One, Brideshead Revisited, A Handful of Dust.*
H(erbert) G(eorge) Wells, 1866-1946, (Br.) novelist. *The Time Machine, The Invisible Man, The War of the Worlds.*
Eudora Welty, 1909-2001, (U.S.) Southern short-story writer, novelist. "Why I Live at the P.O.," "The Ponder Heart."
Rebecca West, 1893-1983, (Br.) novelist, critic, journalist. *Black Lamb and Grey Falcon.*
Edith Wharton, 1862-1937, (U.S.) novelist. *The Age of Innocence, The House of Mirth, Ethan Frome.*
Phillis Wheatley, c. 1753-84, (U.S.) poet; 2nd American woman and first black woman to be published, 1770.
E(lwyn) B(rooks) White, 1899-1985, (U.S.) essayist, novelist. *Charlotte's Web, Stuart Little.*
Patrick White, 1912-90, (Austral.) novelist. *The Tree of Man.*
T(erence) H(anbury) White, 1906-64, (Br.) author. *The Once and Future King, A Book of Beasts.*
Walt Whitman, 1819-92, (U.S.) poet. *Leaves of Grass.*
John Greenleaf Whittier, 1807-92, (U.S.) poet, journalist. *Snow-Bound.*
Oscar Wilde, 1854-1900, (Ire.) novelist, playwright. *The Picture of Dorian Gray, The Importance of Being Earnest.*
Laura Ingalls Wilder, 1867-1957, (U.S.) novelist. Little House on the Prairie series of children's books.

Thornton Wilder, 1897-1975, (U.S.) playwright. *Our Town, The Skin of Our Teeth, The Matchmaker.*
Tennessee Williams, 1911-83, (U.S.) playwright. *A Streetcar Named Desire, Cat on a Hot Tin Roof, The Glass Menagerie.*
William Carlos Williams, 1883-1963, (U.S.) poet, physician. *The Tempers, Al Que Quiere! Paterson,* "This Is Just to Say."
Edmund Wilson, 1895-1972, (U.S.) critic, novelist. *Axel's Castle, To the Finland Station.*
Lanford Wilson, 1937-2011, (U.S.) playwright. *Talley's Folly, Fifth of July.*
P(elham) G(renville) Wodehouse, 1881-1975, (Br.-U.S.) humorist. "Jeeves" novels, *Anything Goes.*
Thomas Wolfe, 1900-38, (U.S.) novelist. *Look Homeward, Angel; You Can't Go Home Again.*
Virginia Woolf, 1882-1941, (Br.) novelist, essayist. *Mrs. Dalloway, To the Lighthouse, A Room of One's Own.*
William Wordsworth, 1770-1850, (Br.) poet. "Tintern Abbey," "Ode: Intimations of Immortality," *The Prelude.*
Richard Wright, 1908-60, (U.S.) novelist, short-story writer. *Native Son, Black Boy, Uncle Tom's Children.*
Elinor Wylie, 1885-1928, (U.S.) poet. *Nets to Catch the Wind.*
William Butler Yeats, 1865-1939, (Ire.) poet, playwright. "The Second Coming," *The Wild Swans at Coole.*
Frank Yerby, 1916-91, (U.S.) first best-selling African American novelist. *The Foxes of Harrow.*
Émile Zola, 1840-1902, (Fr.) novelist. *Nana, Théresè Raquin.*

Poets Laureate

There is no record of the origin of the office of Poet Laureate of England. Henry III (1216-72) reportedly had a Versificator Regis, or King's Poet, paid 100 shillings per year. Other poets said to have filled the role include Geoffrey Chaucer (d 1400), Edmund Spenser (d 1599), Ben Jonson (d 1637), and Sir William d'Avenant (d 1668). The first official English poet laureate was John Dryden, appointed 1668, for life (as was customary). Then came Thomas Shadwell, in 1689; Nahum Tate, 1692; Nicholas Rowe, 1715; Rev. Laurence Eusden, 1718; Colley Cibber, 1730; William Whitehead, 1757; Rev. Thomas Warton, 1785; Henry James Pye, 1790; Robert Southey, 1813; William Wordsworth, 1843; Alfred, Lord Tennyson, 1850; Alfred Austin, 1896; Robert Bridges, 1913; John Masefield, 1930; C. Day Lewis, 1968; Sir John Betjeman, 1972; Ted Hughes, 1984; Andrew Motion, 1999; and Carol Ann Duffy, 2009.

In the U.S., appointment is by the Librarian of Congress to a term of one year, which may be renewed: Robert Penn Warren, appointed 1986; Richard Wilbur, 1987; Howard Nemerov, 1988; Mark Strand, 1990; Joseph Brodsky, 1991; Mona Van Duyn, 1992; Rita Dove, 1993; Robert Hass, 1995; Robert Pinsky, 1997; Stanley Kunitz, 2000; Billy Collins, 2001; Louise Gluck, 2003; Ted Kooser, 2004; Donald Hall, 2006; Charles Simic, 2007; Kay Ryan, 2008; W. S. Merwin, 2010; Philip Levine, 2011; Natasha Trethewey, 2012; Charles Wright, 2014; Juan Felipe Herrera, 2015.

Composers of Classical and Avant Garde Music

John Adams, b 1947, (U.S.) *Nixon in China, The Death of Klinghoffer.*
Milton Babbitt, 1916-2011, (U.S.) serial and electronic music.
Carl Philipp Emanuel Bach, 1714-88, (Ger.) cantatas, passions, numerous keyboard and instrumental works.
Johann Christian Bach, 1735-82, (Ger.) concertos, operas, sonatas. Known as the "English" Bach.
Johann Sebastian Bach, 1685-1750, (Ger.) *St. Matthew Passion, The Well-Tempered Clavier.*
Samuel Barber, 1910-81, (U.S.) *Adagio for Strings, Vanessa.*
Béla Bartók, 1881-1945, (Hung.) *Concerto for Orchestra, The Miraculous Mandarin.*
Amy Beach (Mrs. H. H. A. Beach), 1867-1944, (U.S.) *The Year's at the Spring, Fireflies, The Chambered Nautilus.*
Ludwig van Beethoven, 1770-1827, (Ger.) concertos (*Emperor*), sonatas (*Moonlight, Pathétique*), 9 symphonies.
Vincenzo Bellini, 1801-35, (It.) *I Puritani, La Sonnambula, Norma.*
Alban Berg, 1885-1935, (Austria) *Wozzeck, Lulu.*
Hector Berlioz, 1803-69, (Fr.) *Damnation of Faust, Symphonie Fantastique, Requiem.*
Leonard Bernstein, 1918-90, (U.S.) *Chichester Psalms, Jeremiah Symphony, Mass.*
Georges Bizet, 1838-75, (Fr.) *Carmen, Pearl Fishers.*
Ernest Bloch, 1880-1959, (Switz.-U.S.) *Macbeth* (opera), *Schelomo, Voice in the Wilderness.*
Luigi Boccherini, 1743-1805, (It.) chamber music and guitar pieces.
Alexander Borodin, 1833-87, (Russ.) *Prince Igor, In the Steppes of Central Asia, Polovtzian Dances.*
Pierre Boulez, b 1925, (Fr.) *Le Visage* nuptial, *Edats/Multiple, Domaines.*
Johannes Brahms, 1833-97, (Ger.) Liebeslieder Waltzes, *Acad. Festival Overture,* chamber music, 4 symphonies.
Henry Brant, 1913-2008, (Can.) spatial music.
Benjamin Britten, 1913-76, (Br.) *Peter Grimes, Turn of the Screw, A Ceremony of Carols, War Requiem.*
Anton Bruckner, 1824-96, (Austria) 9 symphonies.
Dietrich Buxtehude, 1637-1707, (Den.) organ works, vocal music.
William Byrd, 1543-1623, (Br.) masses, motets.
John Cage, 1912-92, (U.S.) *Winter Music, Fontana Mix.*
Elliott Carter, 1908-2012, (U.S.) *Second String Quartet, Third String Quartet.*
Emmanuel Chabrier, 1841-94, (Fr.) *Le Roi Malgré Lui, España.*
Gustave Charpentier, 1860-1956, (Fr.) *Louise.*
Frédéric Chopin, 1810-49, (Pol.) mazurkas, waltzes, etudes, nocturnes, polonaises, sonatas.
Aaron Copland, 1900-90, (U.S.) *Appalachian Spring, Fanfare for the Common Man, Lincoln Portrait.*
John Corigliano, b 1938, (U.S.) *Symphony No. 2.*
Paul Creston, 1906-85, (U.S.) *Walt Whitman.*
Claude Debussy, 1862-1918, (Fr.) *Pelleas et Melisande, La Mer, Prelude to the Afternoon of a Faun.*
David Del Tredici, b 1937, (U.S.) *Child Alice, In Memory of a Summer Day.*
Gaetano Donizetti, 1797-1848, (It.) *Elixir of Love, Lucia di Lammermoor, Daughter of the Regiment.*
Paul Dukas, 1865-1935, (Fr.) *Sorcerer's Apprentice.*
Antonín Dvořák, 1841-1904, (Czech.) *Songs My Mother Taught Me, Symphony in E Minor (From the New World).*
Edward Elgar, 1857-1934, (Br.) *Enigma Variations, Pomp and Circumstance.*
Manuel de Falla, 1876-1946, (Sp.) *El Amor Brujo, La Vida Breve, The Three-Cornered Hat.*
Gabriel Faurè, 1845-1924, (Fr.) *Requiem,* Elègie for Cello and Piano.
Cesar Franck, 1822-90, (Belg.) Symphony in D minor, Violin Sonata.
George Gershwin, 1898-1937, (U.S.) *Rhapsody in Blue, An American in Paris, Porgy and Bess.*
Philip Glass, b 1937, (U.S.) *Einstein on the Beach, The Voyage.*
Mikhail Glinka, 1804-57, (Russ.) *A Life for the Tsar, Ruslan and Ludmilla.*
Christoph W. Gluck, 1714-87, (Ger.) *Alceste, Iphigènie en Tauride.*
Henryk Gorecki, 1933-2010, (Pol.) Symphony no. 3 (*Symphony of Sorrowing Songs*).
Charles Gounod, 1818-93, (Fr.) *Faust, Romeo and Juliet.*
Percy Grainger, 1882-1961, (Austral.) *Country Gardens.*
Edvard Grieg, 1843-1907, (Nor.) *Peer Gynt Suite,* Concerto in A minor for piano.
George Frideric Handel, 1685-1759, (Ger.-Br.) *Messiah, Water Music.*
Howard Hanson, 1896-1981, (U.S.) Symphonies No. 1 (Nordic) and No. 2 (Romantic).
Roy Harris, 1898-1979, (U.S.) symphonies.
(Franz) Joseph Haydn, 1732-1809, (Austria) symphonies (*Clock, London, Toy*), chamber music, oratorios.
Hildegard von Bingen, 1098-1179, (Ger.) *Ordo virtutum.*
Paul Hindemith, 1895-1963, (U.S.) *Mathis der Maler.*
Gustav Holst, 1874-1934, (Br.) *The Planets.*
Arthur Honegger, 1892-1955, (Fr.) *Judith, Le Roi David, Pacific 231.*
Alan Hovhaness, 1911-2000, (U.S.) symphonies, *Magnificat.*
Engelbert Humperdinck, 1854-1921, (Ger.) *Hansel and Gretel.*
Charles Ives, 1874-1954, (U.S.) *Concord Sonata,* symphonies.
Aram Khachaturian, 1903-78, (Russ.) ballets, piano pieces, *Sabre Dance.*
Zoltán Kodaly, 1882-1967, (Hung.) *Háry János, Psalmus Hungaricus.*
Fritz Kreisler, 1875-1962, (Austria) *Caprice Viennois, Tambourin Chinois.*
Edouard Lalo, 1823-92, (Fr.) *Symphonie Espagnole.*
David Lang, b 1957, (U.S.) *The Little Match Girl Passion.*
Morten Lauridsen, b 1943, (U.S.) *Lux Aeterna.*
Ruggero Leoncavallo, 1857-1919, (It.) *Pagliacci.*
György Ligeti, 1923-2006, (Rom.) *Atmosphères, Requiem.*
Franz Liszt, 1811-86, (Hung.) 20 Hungarian rhapsodies, symphonic poems.
Edward MacDowell, 1861-1908, (U.S.) *To a Wild Rose.*
Gustav Mahler, 1860-1911, (Austria) *Das Lied von der Erde*; 9 complete symphonies.
Pietro Mascagni, 1863-1945, (It.) *Cavalleria Rusticana.*

Jules Massenet, 1842-1912, (Fr.) *Manon, Le Cid, Thaïs*.
Felix Mendelssohn, 1809-47, (Ger.) *A Midsummer Night's Dream, Songs Without Words*, violin concerto.
Gian Carlo Menotti, 1911-2007, (It.-U.S.) *The Medium, The Consul, Amahl and the Night Visitors*.
Olivier Messiaen, 1908-1992, (Fr.) *Apparition de l'Église Éternelle*.
Claudio Monteverdi, 1567-1643, (It.) opera, masses, madrigals.
Wolfgang Amadeus Mozart, 1756-91, (Austria) chamber music, concertos, operas (*Magic Flute, Marriage of Figaro*), 41 symphonies.
Modest Mussorgsky, 1839-81, (Russ.) *Boris Godunov, Pictures at an Exhibition*.
Carl Nielsen, 1865-1931, (Den.) *Saul og David*.
Jacques Offenbach, 1819-80, (Fr.) *Tales of Hoffmann*.
Carl Orff, 1895-1982, (Ger.) *Carmina Burana*.
Johann Pachelbel, 1653-1706, (Ger.) Canon and Fugue in D major.
Ignacy Paderewski, 1860-1941, (Pol.) Minuet in G.
Niccolò Paganini, 1782-1840, (It.) Caprices for violin solo.
Giovanni Palestrina, c. 1525-94, (It.) masses, madrigals.
Arvo Pärt, b 1935, (Eston.) sacred music. *Fratres, Cantus in memoriam Benjamin Britten, Tabula Rasa*.
Krzysztof Penderecki, b 1933, (Pol.) *Psalmus, Polymorphia, De natura sonoris*.
Francis Poulenc, 1899-1963, (Fr.) *Dialogues des Carmélites*.
Mel Powell, 1923-98, (U.S.) *Duplicates: A Concerto for Two Pianos and Orchestra, Cantilena Concertante*.
Sergei Prokofiev, 1891-1953, (Russ.) Classical Symphony, *Love for Three Oranges, Peter and the Wolf*.
Giacomo Puccini, 1858-1924, (It.) *La Boheme, Manon Lescaut, Tosca, Madama Butterfly*.
Henry Purcell, 1659-95, (Br.) *Dido and Aeneas*.
Sergei Rachmaninoff, 1873-1943, (Russ.) concertos, preludes (Prelude in C sharp minor), symphonies.
Maurice Ravel, 1875-1937, (Fr.) *Bolèro, Daphnis et Chloè*, Piano Concerto in D for Left Hand Alone.
Steve Reich, b 1936, (U.S.) *Double Sextet, Three Tales*.
Nikolai Rimsky-Korsakov, 1844-1908, (Russ.) *Golden Cockerel, Scheherazade, Flight of the Bumblebee*.
Gioacchino Rossini, 1792-1868, (It.) *Barber of Seville, Otello, William Tell*.
John Rutter, b 1945, (Br.) *Magnificat, Requiem*.
Camille Saint-Saëns, 1835-1921, (Fr.) *Carnival of Animals (The Swan), Samson and Delilah, Danse Macabre*.
Alessandro Scarlatti, 1660-1725, (It.) cantatas, oratorios, operas.
Domenico Scarlatti, 1685-1757, (It.) harpsichord works.
Alfred Schnittke, 1934-98 (Russ.-Ger.) *Life With an Idiot*.
Arnold Schoenberg, 1874-1951, (Austria) *Pelleas and Melisande, Pierrot Lunaire, Verklärte Nacht*.
Franz Schubert, 1797-1828, (Austria) chamber music (*Trout Quintet*), lieder, symphonies ("Unfinished").
Robert Schumann, 1810-56, (Ger.) *Die Frauenliebe und Leben, Träumerei*.
Dmitri Shostakovich, 1906-75, (Russ.) symphonies, *Lady Macbeth of the District Mzensk*.
Jean Sibelius, 1865-1957, (Fin.) *Finlandia*.
Bedrich Smetana, 1824-84, (Czech.) *The Bartered Bride*.
Karlheinz Stockhausen, 1928-2008, (Ger.) *Kontra-Punkte, Kontakte for Electronic Instruments*.
Richard Strauss, 1864-1949, (Ger.) *Salome, Elektra, Der Rosenkavalier, Thus Spake Zarathustra*.
Igor Stravinsky, 1882-1971, (Russ.) *Noah and the Flood, The Rake's Progress, The Rite of Spring*.
Toru Takemitsu, 1930-96, (Jpn.) *Requiem for Strings, Dorian Horizon*.
Thomas Tallis, c. 1505-85, (Br.) anthems, motets.
Peter I. Tchaikovsky, 1840-93, (Russ.) *Nutcracker, Swan Lake, The Sleeping Beauty*.
Georg Philipp Telemann, 1681-1767, (Ger.) church music, orchestral suites, chamber music.
Virgil Thomson, 1896-1989, (U.S.) opera, film music, *Four Saints in Three Acts*.
Dmitri Tiomkin, 1894-1979, (Russ.-U.S.) film scores, including *High Noon*.
Sir Michael Tippett, 1905-98, (Br.) *A Child of Our Time, The Midsummer Marriage, The Knot Garden*.
Michael Torke, b 1961, (U.S.) *Bright Blue Music, Ecstatic Orange*.
Eric Whitacre, b 1970, (U.S.) *Cloudburst*.
Ralph Vaughan Williams, 1872-1958, (Br.) *Fantasia on a Theme by Thomas Tallis*, symphonies, vocal music.
Giuseppe Verdi, 1813-1901, (It.) *Aida, Rigoletto, Don Carlo, Il Trovatore, La Traviata, Falstaff, Macbeth*.
Heitor Villa-Lobos, 1887-1959, (Braz.) *Bachianas Brasileiras*.
Antonio Vivaldi, 1678-1741, (It.) Concerto grossos (*The Four Seasons*).
Richard Wagner, 1813-83, (Ger.) *Rienzi, Tannhäuser, Lohengrin, Tristan und Isolde*.
William Walton, 1902-83, (Br.) *Façade, Belshazzar's Feast*.
Carl Maria von Weber, 1786-1826, (Ger.) *Der Freischutz*.

Composers of Operettas, Musicals, and Popular Music

Richard Adler, 1921-2012, (U.S.) *Pajama Game; Damn Yankees*.
Milton Ager, 1893-1979, (U.S.) "I Wonder What's Become of Sally"; "Hard-Hearted Hannah"; "Ain't She Sweet?"
Leroy Anderson, 1908-75, (U.S.) "Sleigh Ride"; "Blue Tango"; "Syncopated Clock."
Paul Anka, b 1941, (Can.) "My Way"; *Tonight Show* theme.
Harold Arlen, 1905-86, (U.S.) "Stormy Weather"; "Over the Rainbow"; "Blues in the Night"; "That Old Black Magic."
Burt Bacharach, b 1928, (U.S.) "Raindrops Keep Fallin' on My Head"; "Walk on By"; "What the World Needs Now Is Love."
Ernest Ball, 1878-1927, (U.S.) "Mother Machree"; "When Irish Eyes Are Smiling."
John Barry, 1933-2011, (U.S.) *Born Free; Lion in Winter; Out of Africa*.
Irving Berlin, 1888-1989, (U.S.) *Annie Get Your Gun; Call Me Madam*; "God Bless America"; "White Christmas."
Leonard Bernstein, 1918-90, (U.S.) *On the Town; Wonderful Town; Candide; West Side Story*.
Eubie Blake, 1883-1983, (U.S.) *Shuffle Along*; "I'm Just Wild About Harry."
Jerry Bock, 1928-2010, (U.S.) *Mr. Wonderful; Fiorello; Fiddler on the Roof; The Rothschilds*.
Carrie Jacobs Bond, 1862-1946, (U.S.) "I Love You Truly."
Nacio Herb Brown, 1896-1964, (U.S.) "Singing in the Rain"; "You Were Meant for Me"; "All I Do Is Dream of You."
Hoagy Carmichael, 1899-1981, (U.S.) "Stardust"; "Georgia on My Mind"; "Old Buttermilk Sky."
James Cleveland, 1931-91, (U.S.) composer, musician, singer; first black gospel artist to appear at Carnegie Hall.
George M. Cohan, 1878-1942, (U.S.) "Give My Regards to Broadway"; "You're a Grand Old Flag"; "Over There."
Cy Coleman, 1929-2004, (U.S.) *Sweet Charity*; "Witchcraft."
John Frederick Coots, 1895-1985, (U.S.) "Santa Claus Is Coming to Town"; "You Go to My Head"; "For All We Know."
Noël Coward, 1899-1973, (Br.) *Bitter Sweet*; "Mad Dogs and Englishmen"; "Mad About the Boy."
Neil Diamond, b 1941, (U.S.) "I'm a Believer"; "Sweet Caroline."
Walter Donaldson, 1893-1947, (U.S.) "My Buddy"; "Carolina in the Morning"; "Makin' Whoopee."
Vernon Duke, 1903-69, (U.S.) "April in Paris."
Bob Dylan, b 1941, (U.S.) "Blowin' in the Wind"; "Like a Rolling Stone."
Gus Edwards, 1879-1945, (U.S.) "School Days"; "By the Light of the Silvery Moon"; "In My Merry Oldsmobile."
Sherman Edwards, 1919-81, (U.S.) "See You in September"; "Wonderful! Wonderful!"
Duke Ellington, 1899-1974, (U.S.) "Sophisticated Lady"; "Satin Doll"; "It Don't Mean a Thing"; "Solitude."
Sammy Fain, 1902-89, (U.S.) "I'll Be Seeing You"; "Love Is a Many-Splendored Thing."
Fred Fisher, 1875-1942, (U.S.) "Peg O' My Heart"; "Chicago."
Stephen Collins Foster, 1826-64, (U.S.) "My Old Kentucky Home"; "Old Folks at Home"; "Beautiful Dreamer."
Rudolf Friml, 1879-1972, (Czech.-U.S.) *The Firefly; Rose Marie; Vagabond King; Bird of Paradise*.
John Gay, 1685-1732, (Br.) *The Beggar's Opera*.
George Gershwin, 1898-1937, (U.S.) "Someone to Watch Over Me"; "I've Got a Crush on You"; "Embraceable You."
Morton Gould, 1913-96, (U.S.) "Fall River Suite"; "Holocaust Suite"; "Spirituals for Orchestra"; "Stringmusic."
Ferde Grofe, 1892-1972, (U.S.) "Grand Canyon Suite."
Marvin Hamlisch, 1944-2012, (U.S.) "The Way We Were"; "Nobody Does It Better"; *A Chorus Line*.
Ray Henderson, 1896-1970, (U.S.) *George White's Scandals*; "That Old Gang of Mine"; "Five Foot Two, Eyes of Blue."
Victor Herbert, 1859-1924, (Ire.-U.S.) *Mlle. Modiste; Babes in Toyland; The Red Mill; Naughty Marietta; Sweethearts*.
Jerry Herman, b 1931, (U.S.) *Hello Dolly; Mame*.
Brian Holland, b 1941, **Lamont Dozier**, b 1941, **Eddie Holland**, b 1939, (all U.S.) "Heat Wave"; "Stop! In the Name of Love"; "Baby, I Need Your Loving."
Rupert Holmes, b 1947, (Br.-U.S.) *The Mystery of Edwin Drood; Curtains*.
James Horner, 1953-2015, (U.S.) *Titanic*; "Somewhere Out There"; "My Heart Will Go On."
Antonio Carlos Jobim, 1927-94, (Brazil) "The Girl From Ipanema"; "Desafinado"; "One Note Samba."
Billy Joel (William Martin), b 1949, (U.S.) "Just the Way You Are"; "Honesty"; "Piano Man."
Elton John, b 1947, (Br.) *The Lion King*; "Candle in the Wind"; "Your Song."
Scott Joplin, 1868-1917, (U.S.) Maple Leaf Rag; *Treemonisha*.
John Kander, b 1927, (U.S.) *Cabaret; Chicago; Funny Lady*.
Jerome Kern, 1885-1945, (U.S.) *Sally; Sunny; Show Boat*.
Carole King, b 1942, (U.S.) "Will You Love Me Tomorrow?"; "Natural Woman"; "One Fine Day"; "Up on the Roof."
Burton Lane, 1912-97, (U.S.) *Finian's Rainbow*.
Jonathan Larson, 1960-96, (U.S.) *tick, tick... BOOM!; Rent*.

Franz Lehar, 1870-1948, (Hung.) *Merry Widow*.
Jerry Leiber, 1933-2011, and **Mike Stoller**, b 1933, (both U.S.) "Hound Dog"; "Searchin'"; "Yakety Yak"; "Love Me Tender."
Mitch Leigh, 1928-2014, (U.S.) *Man of La Mancha*.
John Lennon, 1940-80, and **Paul McCartney**, b 1942, (both Br.) "I Want to Hold Your Hand"; "She Loves You."
Jay Livingston, 1915-2001, (U.S.) "Mona Lisa"; "Que Sera, Sera."
Andrew Lloyd Webber, b 1948, (Br.) *Jesus Christ Superstar*; *Evita*; *Cats*; *The Phantom of the Opera*.
Frank Loesser, 1910-69, (U.S.) *Guys and Dolls*; *Where's Charley?*; *The Most Happy Fella*; *How to Succeed in Business....*
Frederick Loewe, 1901-88, (Austria-U.S.) *Brigadoon*; *Paint Your Wagon*; *My Fair Lady*; *Camelot*.
Robert Lopez, b 1975, (U.S.) *Avenue Q*; *The Book of Mormon*; *Frozen*.
Henry Mancini, 1924-94, (U.S.) "Moon River"; "Days of Wine and Roses"; "Pink Panther Theme."
Barry Mann, b 1939, and **Cynthia Weil**, b 1937, (both U.S.) "You've Lost That Loving Feeling."
Hugh Martin, 1914-2011, (U.S.) "Have Yourself a Merry Little Christmas"; "The Trolley Song."
Jimmy McHugh, 1894-1969, (U.S.) "Don't Blame Me"; "I'm in the Mood for Love"; "I Feel a Song Coming On."
Alan Menken, b 1949, (U.S.) *Little Shop of Horrors*; *Beauty and the Beast*.
Joseph Meyer, 1894-1987, (U.S.) "If You Knew Susie"; "California, Here I Come"; "Crazy Rhythm."
Lin-Manuel Miranda, b 1980, (U.S.) *In the Heights*; *Hamilton*.
Chauncey Olcott, 1858-1932, (U.S.) "Mother Machree."
Jerome "Doc" Pomus, 1925-91, (U.S.) "Save the Last Dance for Me"; "A Teenager in Love."
Cole Porter, 1891-1964, (U.S.) *Anything Goes*; *Kiss Me Kate*; *Can Can*; *Silk Stockings*.
Smokey Robinson, b 1940, (U.S.) "Shop Around"; "My Guy"; "My Girl"; "Get Ready."
Richard Rodgers, 1902-79, (U.S.) *Oklahoma!*; *Carousel*; *South Pacific*; *The King and I*; *The Sound of Music*.
Sigmund Romberg, 1887-1951, (Hung.) *Maytime*; *The Student Prince*; *Desert Song*; *Blossom Time*.
Harold Rome, 1908-93, (U.S.) *Pins and Needles*; *Call Me Mister*; *Wish You Were Here*; *Fanny*; *Destry Rides Again*.
Vincent Rose, 1880-1944, (U.S.) "Avalon"; "Whispering"; "Blueberry Hill."
Harry Ruby, 1895-1974, (U.S.) "Three Little Words"; "Who's Sorry Now?"
Arthur Schwartz, 1900-84, (U.S.) *The Band Wagon*; "Dancing in the Dark"; "By Myself"; "That's Entertainment."
Steven Schwartz, b 1948, (U.S.) *Godspell*; *Pippin*; *Wicked*.
Neil Sedaka, b 1939, (U.S.) "Breaking Up Is Hard to Do."
Marc Shaiman, b 1959, (U.S.) *Hairspray*.
Paul Simon, b 1942, (U.S.) "Sounds of Silence"; "I Am a Rock"; "Mrs. Robinson"; "Bridge Over Troubled Waters."
Stephen Sondheim, b 1930, (U.S.) *A Little Night Music*; *Company*; *Sweeney Todd*; *Sunday in the Park With George*.
John Philip Sousa, 1854-1932, (U.S.) *El Capitan*; "Stars and Stripes Forever."
Oskar Straus, 1870-1954, (Austrian) *Chocolate Soldier*.
Johann Strauss, 1825-99, (Austrian) *Gypsy Baron*; *Die Fledermaus*; waltzes: Blue Danube; Artist's Life.
Charles Strouse, b 1928, (U.S.) *Bye Bye, Birdie*; *Annie*.
Jule Styne, 1905-94, (Br.-U.S.) *Gentlemen Prefer Blondes*; *Bells Are Ringing*; *Gypsy*; *Funny Girl*.
Arthur S. Sullivan, 1842-1900, (Br.) *H.M.S. Pinafore*; *Pirates of Penzance*; *The Mikado*.
Deems Taylor, 1885-1966, (U.S.) *Peter Ibbetson*.
Harry Tobias, 1905-94, (U.S.) *I'll Keep the Lovelight Burning*.
Egbert van Alstyne, 1882-1951, (U.S.) "In the Shade of the Old Apple Tree"; "Memories"; "Pretty Baby."
Jimmy Van Heusen, 1913-90, (U.S.) "Moonlight Becomes You"; "Swinging on a Star"; "All the Way"; "Love and Marriage."
Albert von Tilzer, 1878-1956, (U.S.) "I'll Be With You in Apple Blossom Time"; "Take Me Out to the Ball Game."
Harry von Tilzer, 1872-1946, (U.S.) "Only a Bird in a Gilded Cage"; "Wait 'til the Sun Shines, Nellie."
Fats Waller, 1904-43, (U.S.) "Honeysuckle Rose"; "Ain't Misbehavin."
Harry Warren, 1893-1981, (U.S.) "You're My Everything"; "We're in the Money"; "I Only Have Eyes for You."
Jimmy Webb, b 1946, (U.S.) "Up, Up and Away"; "By the Time I Get to Phoenix"; "Didn't We?"; "Wichita Lineman."
Kurt Weill, 1900-50, (Ger.-U.S.) *Threepenny Opera*; *Lady in the Dark*; *Knickerbocker Holiday*; *One Touch of Venus*.
Percy Wenrich, 1887-1952, (U.S.) "When You Wore a Tulip"; "Moonlight Bay"; "Put On Your Old Gray Bonnet."
Richard A. Whiting, 1891-1938, (U.S.) "Till We Meet Again"; "Sleepytime Gal"; "Beyond the Blue Horizon"; "My Ideal."
Fred Wildhorn, b 1959, (U.S.) *Jekyll and Hyde*; *Victor/Victoria*; *The Civil War*.
John Williams, b 1932, (U.S.) *Jaws*; *E.T.*; *Star Wars* series; *Raiders of the Lost Ark* series.
Meredith Willson, 1902-84, (U.S.) *The Music Man*.
Stevie Wonder, b 1950, (U.S.) "You Are the Sunshine of My Life"; "Signed, Sealed, Delivered, I'm Yours."
Vincent Youmans, 1898-1946, (U.S.) *Two Little Girls in Blue*; *Wildflower*; *No, No, Nanette*; *Hit the Deck*; *Rainbow*; *Smiles*.

Lyricists

Howard Ashman, 1950-91, (U.S.) *Little Shop of Horrors*; *The Little Mermaid*.
Johnny Burke, 1908-84, (U.S.) "Misty"; "Imagination."
Irving Caesar, 1895-1996, (U.S.) "Swanee"; "Tea for Two"; "Just a Gigolo."
Sammy Cahn, 1913-93, (U.S.) "High Hopes"; "Love and Marriage"; "The Second Time Around"; "It's Magic."
Leonard Cohen, b 1934, (Can.) "Suzanne"; "Stranger Song."
Betty Comden, 1917-2006, and **Adolph Green**, 1915-2002, (both U.S.) "The Party's Over"; "New York, New York."
Hal David, 1921-2012, (U.S.) "What the World Needs Now Is Love."
Buddy De Sylva, 1895-1950, (U.S.) "When Day Is Done"; "Look for the Silver Lining"; "April Showers."
Howard Dietz, 1896-1983, (U.S.) "Dancing in the Dark"; "That's Entertainment."
Al Dubin, 1891-1945, (U.S.) "Tiptoe Through the Tulips"; "Lullaby of Broadway."
Fred Ebb, 1936-2004, (U.S.) *Cabaret*; *Zorba*; *Woman of the Year*; *Chicago*.
Ray Evans, 1915-2007, (U.S.) "Mona Lisa"; "Que Sera, Sera."
Dorothy Fields, 1905-74, (U.S.) "On the Sunny Side of the Street"; "Don't Blame Me"; "The Way You Look Tonight."
Ira Gershwin, 1896-1983, (U.S.) "The Man I Love"; "S'Wonderful"; "Embraceable You."
William S. Gilbert, 1836-1911, (Br.) *H.M.S. Pinafore*; *Pirates of Penzance*.
Gerry Goffin, 1939-2014, (U.S.) "Will You Love Me Tomorrow"; "Take Good Care of My Baby"; "Up on the Roof."
Mack Gordon, 1905-59, (Pol.-U.S.) "You'll Never Know"; "The More I See You"; "Chattanooga Choo-Choo."
Oscar Hammerstein II, 1895-1960, (U.S.) *Ol' Man River*; *Oklahoma!*; *Carousel*.
E. Y. (Yip) Harburg, 1898-1981, (U.S.) "Brother, Can You Spare a Dime"; "April in Paris"; "Over the Rainbow."
Sheldon Harnick, b 1924, (U.S.) *Fiddler on the Roof*; *She Loves Me*.
Lorenz Hart, 1895-1943, (U.S.) "Isn't It Romantic"; "Blue Moon"; "Lover"; "Manhattan"; "My Funny Valentine."
DuBose Heyward, 1885-1940, (U.S.) "Summertime."
Gus Kahn, 1886-1941, (U.S.) "Memories"; "Ain't We Got Fun."
Alan J. Lerner, 1918-86, (U.S.) *Brigadoon*; *My Fair Lady*; *Camelot*; *Gigi*; *On a Clear Day You Can See Forever*.
Johnny Mercer, 1909-76, (U.S.) "Blues in the Night"; "Come Rain or Come Shine"; "Laura"; "That Old Black Magic."
Bob Merrill, 1921-98, (U.S.) "People"; "(How Much Is That) Doggie in the Window."
Jack Norworth, 1879-1959, (U.S.) "Take Me Out to the Ball Game"; "Shine On Harvest Moon."
Mitchell Parish, 1901-93, (U.S.) "Stardust"; "Stairway to the Stars."
Andy Razaf, 1895-1973, (U.S.) "Honeysuckle Rose"; "Ain't Misbehavin."
Leo Robin, 1900-84, (U.S.) "Thanks for the Memory"; "Diamonds Are a Girl's Best Friend."
Robert Sherman, 1925-2012, (U.S.) *Mary Poppins*, *The Jungle Book*.
Bernie Taupin, b 1947 (Br.) "Rocket Man"; "Your Song."
Paul Francis Webster, 1907-84, (U.S.) "Secret Love"; "The Shadow of Your Smile"; "Love Is a Many-Splendored Thing."
Jack Yellen, 1892-1991, (U.S.) "Ain't She Sweet"; "Happy Days Are Here Again."

Blues and Jazz Artists of the Past

Julian "Cannonball" Adderley, 1928-75, alto sax.
Nat Adderley, 1931-2000, cornet.
Henry "Red" Allen, 1908-67, trumpet.
Louis "Satchmo" Armstrong, 1901-71, trumpet, singer, bandleader.
Albert Ayler, 1936-70, tenor sax, alto sax.
Mildred Bailey, 1907-51, singer.
Chet Baker, 1929-88, trumpet, singer.
Ray Barretto, 1930-2006, conga drummer.
William "Count" Basie, 1904-84, bandleader, piano, composer.
Sidney Bechet, 1897-1959, soprano sax, clarinet.
Bix Beiderbecke, 1903-31, cornet, composer, piano.
Rowland "Bunny" Berigan, 1908-42, trumpet.
Barney Bigard, 1906-80, clarinet.
Eubie Blake, 1883-1983, composer, piano.
Art Blakey, 1919-90, drums, bandleader.
Jimmy Blanton, 1921-42, bass.
Charles "Buddy" Bolden, 1877-1931, cornet, pioneer bandleader.
Lester Bowie, 1941-99, trumpet, composer, bandleader.
Michael Brecker, 1949-2007, saxophone.
Big Bill Broonzy, 1893-1958, blues singer, guitar.
Clarence "Gatemouth" Brown, 1924-2005, guitar, singer.
Clifford Brown, 1930-56, trumpet.
Ray Brown, 1926-2002, bass.
Dave Brubeck, 1920-2012, piano, bandleader.
Don Byas, 1912-72, tenor sax.
Charlie Byrd, 1925-99, guitar; popularized bossa nova.
Cab Calloway, 1907-94, bandleader, singer.

Harry Carney, 1910-74, baritone sax, clarinet.
Benny Carter, 1907-2003, alto sax.
Betty Carter, 1930-98, jazz singer.
Sidney "Big Sid" Catlett, 1910-51, drums.
Adolphus Anthony "Doc" Cheatham, 1905-97, trumpet.
Don Cherry, 1936-95, trumpet.
Charlie Christian, 1916-42, guitar.
Terry Clark, 1920-2015, trumpet.
Kenny "Klook" Clarke, 1914-85, drums.
Buck Clayton, 1911-91, trumpet.
Al Cohn, 1925-88, tenor sax.
Nat "King" Cole, 1919-65, piano, singer.
William "Cozy" Cole, 1909-81, drums.
Alice Coltrane, 1937-2007, piano, composer.
John Coltrane, 1926-67, tenor sax, soprano sax, composer.
Eddie Condon, 1905-73, guitar, bandleader.
Tadd Dameron, 1917-65, piano, composer.
Eddie "Lockjaw" Davis, 1921-86, tenor sax.
Miles Davis, 1926-91, trumpet, composer.
Wild Bill Davison, 1906-89, cornet.
Blossom Dearie, 1924-2009, singer.
Paul Desmond, 1924-77, alto sax.
Vic Dickenson, 1906-84, trombone.
Willie Dixon, 1915-92, composer, bass.
Johnny Dodds, 1892-1940, clarinet.
Warren "Baby" Dodds, 1898-1959, drums.
Eric Dolphy, 1928-64, alto sax, bass clarinet, flute.
Jimmy Dorsey, 1904-57, alto sax, bandleader.
Tommy Dorsey, 1905-56, trombone, bandleader.
Billy Eckstine, 1914-93, singer, bandleader.
Harry "Sweets" Edison, 1915-99, trumpet.
David "Honeyboy" Edwards, 1915-2011, guitar, singer.
Roy Eldridge, 1911-89, trumpet, singer.
Duke Ellington, 1899-1974, piano, bandleader, composer.
Bill Evans, 1929-80, piano.
Gil Evans, 1912-88, composer, arranger, piano.
Art Farmer, 1928-99, trumpet, flugelhorn.
Maynard Ferguson, 1926-2006, trumpet, bandleader.
Ella Fitzgerald, 1917-96, singer.
Tommy Flanagan, 1930-2001, piano.
Erroll Garner, 1921-77, piano, composer.
Stan Getz, 1927-91, tenor sax.
Dizzy Gillespie, 1917-93, trumpet, composer, singer.
Benny Goodman, 1909-86, clarinet, bandleader.
Dexter Gordon, 1923-90, tenor sax.
Stéphane Grappelli, 1908-97, violin.
Bobby Hackett, 1915-76, trumpet, cornet.
Lionel Hampton, 1908-2002, vibraphone, bandleader.
W. C. Handy, 1873-1958, composer.
Jimmy Harrison, 1900-31, trombone.
Coleman Hawkins, 1904-69, tenor sax.
Percy Heath, 1923-2005, bass.
Fletcher Henderson, 1898-1952, bandleader, arranger.
Woody Herman, 1913-87, clarinet, alto sax, bandleader.
Jay C. Higginbotham, 1906-73, trombone.
Ruiz Hilton, 1952-2006, piano, composer.
Earl "Fatha" Hines, 1903-83, piano.
Milt Hinton, 1910-2000, bass.
Al Hirt, 1922-99, trumpet.
Johnny Hodges, 1906-70, alto sax.
Billie Holiday, 1915-59, singer.
John Lee Hooker, 1917-2001, blues guitar, singer.
Sam "Lightnin'" Hopkins, 1912-82, blues singer, guitar.
Shirley Horn, 1934-2005, piano, singer.
Howlin' Wolf (Chester Burnett), 1910-76, blues singer, harmonica, guitar.
Alberta Hunter, 1895-1984, singer.
Mahalia Jackson, 1911-72, gospel singer.
Milt Jackson, 1923-99, vibraphone.
Elmore James, 1918-63, blues singer, guitar.
Etta James, 1938-2012, blues singer.
"Blind" Lemon Jefferson, 1897-1929, blues singer, guitar.
J. J. Johnson, 1924-2001, trombone.
James P. Johnson, 1891-1955, piano, composer.
Robert Johnson, 1912-38, blues singer, guitar.
William "Bunk" Johnson, 1879-1949, trumpet.
Elvin Jones, 1927-2004, drums.
Jo Jones, 1911-85, drums.
Philly Joe Jones, 1923-85, drums.
Thad Jones, 1923-86, cornet, bandleader, composer.
Scott Joplin, 1868-1917, ragtime composer.
Louis Jordan, 1908-75, singer, alto sax.
Stan Kenton, 1911-79, bandleader, composer, piano.
Barney Kessel, 1923-2004, guitar.
Albert King, 1923-92, blues guitar.
B. B. King, 1925-2015, blues guitar, singer.
John Kirby, 1908-52, bandleader, bass.
Rahsaan Roland Kirk, 1936-77, saxophone, composer.
Gene Krupa, 1909-73, drums, bandleader.
Scott LaFaro, 1936-61, bass.
Lead Belly (Huddie Ledbetter), 1888-1949, folk and blues singer, guitar.
Peggy Lee, 1920-2002, singer.
John Lewis, 1920-2001, piano, Modern Jazz Quartet founder.
Mel Lewis, 1929-90, drums, bandleader.
Jimmie Lunceford, 1902-47, bandleader.
Machito (Frank Grillo), 1908-84, Latin percussion, singer, bandleader.
Shelly Manne, 1920-84, drums, bandleader.
Jackie McLean, 1931-2006, saxophone, composer.
Jimmy McPartland, 1907-91, trumpet.
Marian McPartland, 1918-2013, jazz pianist.
Carmen McRae, 1920-94, singer.
Glenn Miller, 1904-44, trombone, bandleader.
Charles Mingus, 1922-79, bass, composer, bandleader.
Thelonious Monk, 1917-82, piano, composer.
Wes Montgomery, 1925-68, guitar.
James Moody, 1925-2010, saxophone.
Ferdinand "Jelly Roll" Morton, 1885-1941, composer, piano.
Bennie Moten, 1894-1935, piano, bandleader.
Gerry Mulligan, 1927-96, baritone sax, composer.
Theodore "Fats" Navarro, 1923-50, trumpet.
Red Nichols, 1905-65, cornet, bandleader.
Red Norvo, 1908-99, vibraphone, xylophone, bandleader.
Anita O'Day, 1919-2006, singer.
Arturo "Chico" O'Farrill, 1921-2001, Latin composer, arranger.
King Oliver, 1885-1938, cornet, bandleader.
Sy Oliver, 1910-88, arranger, composer.
Edward "Kid" Ory, 1886-1973, trombone, bandleader.
Johnny Otis, 1921-2012, blues singer.
Oran "Hot Lips" Page, 1908-54, trumpet, singer.
Charlie "Bird" Parker, 1920-55, alto sax, composer.
Joe Pass, 1929-94, guitar.
Art Pepper, 1925-82, alto sax.
Pinetop Perkins, 1913-2011, piano.
Oscar Peterson, 1925-2007, piano.
Oscar Pettiford, 1922-60, bass.
Earl "Bud" Powell, 1924-66, piano.
Chano Pozo, 1915-48, percussionist, singer.
Louis Prima, 1911-78, singer, bandleader.
Tito Puente, 1923-2000, Latin percussion, bandleader.
Gertrude "Ma" Rainey, 1886-1939, blues singer.
Lou Rawls, 1933-2006, singer.
Dewey Redman, 1931-2006, tenor sax.
Don Redman (Robert Rodney Chudnick), 1900-64, composer, arranger.
Django Reinhardt, 1910-53, guitar.
Buddy Rich, 1917-87, drums.
Max Roach, 1924-2007, drums, composer.
Red Rodney (Robert Chudnick), 1927-94, trumpet.
Jimmy Rowles, 1918-96, piano.
Jimmy Rushing, 1903-72, blues and jazz singer.
Charles "Pee Wee" Russell, 1906-69, clarinet.
Artie Shaw, 1910-2004, swing-era bandleader, clarinet.
George Shearing, 1919-2011, piano.
Nina Simone (Eunice Waymon), 1933-2003, singer.
John "Zoot" Sims, 1925-85, tenor sax.
Zutty Singleton, 1898-1975, drums.
Bessie Smith, 1894-1937, blues singer.
Clarence "Pinetop" Smith, 1904-29, piano, singer, boogie woogie pioneer.
Willie "The Lion" Smith, 1897-1973, piano, composer.
Francis "Muggsy" Spanier, 1906-67, cornet.
Edward "Sonny" Stitt, 1924-82, tenor sax, alto sax.
Billy Strayhorn, 1915-67, composer, piano, Duke Ellington collaborator.
Sun Ra (Herman Blount), 1915?-93, bandleader, piano, composer.
Art Tatum, 1910-56, piano.
Art Taylor, 1929-95, drums.
Billy Taylor, 1921-2010, piano.
Jack Teagarden, 1905-64, trombone, singer.
Mel Tormé, 1925-99, singer ("The Velvet Fog").
Dave Tough, 1908-48, drums.
Lennie Tristano, 1919-78, piano, composer.
Joe Turner, 1911-85, blues singer.
Sarah Vaughan, 1924-90, singer.
Joe Venuti, 1903-78, violin.
Aaron "T-Bone" Walker, 1910-75, blues guitar.
Thomas "Fats" Waller, 1904-43, piano, singer, composer.
Dinah Washington (Ruth Jones), 1924-63, singer.
Grover Washington Jr., 1943-99, pop-jazz sax, composer.
Ethel Waters, 1896-1977, jazz and blues singer.
Muddy Waters (McKinley Morganfield), 1915-83, blues singer, songwriter.
Julius Watkins, 1921-77, French horn.
William "Chick" Webb, 1902-39, bandleader, drums.
Ben Webster, 1909-73, tenor sax.
Junior Wells (Amos Blackmore), 1934-98, blues singer, harmonica.
Paul Whiteman, 1890-1967, bandleader.
Margaret Whiting, 1924-2011, singer.
Charles "Cootie" Williams, 1910-85, trumpet, bandleader.
Joe Williams, 1918-99, singer.
Mary Lou Williams, 1910-81, piano, composer.
Tony Williams, 1945-97, drums.
John Lee "Sonny Boy" Williamson, 1914-48, blues singer, harmonica.
Sonny Boy Williamson (Aleck "Rice" Miller), 1900?-65, blues singer, harmonica.
Teddy Wilson, 1912-86, piano.
Kai Winding, 1922-83, trombone.
Jimmy Yancey, 1894-1951, piano.
Lester "Pres" Young, 1909-59, tenor sax.

Country Music Artists of the Past and Present

Roy Acuff, 1903-92, fiddler, singer, songwriter; "Wabash Cannon Ball."
Alabama (Jeff Cook, b 1949; Teddy Gentry, b 1952; Mark Herndon, b 1955; Randy Owen, b 1949); "Feels So Right."
Jason Aldean, b 1977, singer; "Don't You Wanna Stay."
James "Whispering Bill" Anderson, b 1937, singer, songwriter; "Make Mine Night Time."
Eddy Arnold, 1918-2008, singer, guitarist, known as the "Tennessee Plowboy."
Chet Atkins, 1924-2001, guitarist, composer, producer; helped create the "Nashville sound."
Gene Autry, 1907-98, first great singing movie cowboy; "Back in the Saddle Again."
Clint Black, b 1962, singer, songwriter; "Killin' Time."
Garth Brooks, b 1962, singer, songwriter; "Friends in Low Places."
Brooks & Dunn (Kix Brooks, b 1955; Ronnie Dunn, b 1953); "Hard Workin' Man."
Luke Bryan, b 1976, singer, songwriter; "Someone Else Calling You Baby."
Boudleaux, 1920-87, and **Felice Bryant**, 1925-2003, songwriting team; "Hey Joe."
Glen Campbell, b 1936, singer, guitarist; "Gentle on My Mind."
Mary Chapin Carpenter, b 1958, singer, songwriter; "I Feel Lucky."
Carter Family (original members A. P., 1891-1960; "Mother" Maybelle, 1909-78; Sara, 1898-1979); "Wildwood Flower."
Johnny Cash, 1932-2003, singer, songwriter; "I Walk the Line," "Ring of Fire," "Folsom Prison Blues."
Kenny Chesney, b 1968, guitarist, singer, songwriter; "You Had Me From Hello."
Roy Clark, b 1933, guitarist, banjoist, singer, co-host of *Hee Haw*; "Yesterday, When I Was Young."
Patsy Cline, 1932-63, singer; "Walkin' After Midnight," "Crazy," "Sweet Dreams."
Billy Ray Cyrus, b 1961, singer, songwriter; "Achy Breaky Heart."
Charlie Daniels, b 1936, guitarist, fiddler; "The Devil Went Down to Georgia."
Jimmy Dean, 1928-2010, singer; "Big Bad John."
John Denver, 1943-97, singer, songwriter; "Rocky Mountain High."
Dixie Chicks (Natalie Maines, b 1974; Emily Erwin Robison, b 1972; Martie Seidel, b 1969); "Wide Open Spaces."
Dale Evans, 1912-2001, singer, actress, married Roy Rogers.
Sara Evans, b 1971, singer, songwriter; "Born to Fly."
Flatt & Scruggs (Lester Flatt, 1914-79; Earl Scruggs, 1924-2012), guitar-banjo duo and soloists; "Foggy Mountain Breakdown."
Red Foley, 1910-68, singer; "Chattanoogie Shoe Shine Boy."
Tennessee Ernie Ford, 1919-91, singer, TV host; "Sixteen Tons."
William "Lefty" Frizzell, 1928-75, singer, guitarist; "Long Black Veil."
Vince Gill, b 1957, singer, songwriter; "When I Call Your Name."
Merle Haggard, b 1937, singer, songwriter; "Okie From Muskogee."
Emmylou Harris, b 1947, singer, songwriter, folk-country crossover artist; "If I Could Only Win Your Love."
Hunter Hayes, b 1991, singer; "Wanted."
Faith Hill, b 1967, singer, songwriter; "Breathe."
Alan Jackson, b 1958, singer, songwriter; "Where Were You (When the World Stopped Turning)."
Waylon Jennings, 1937-2002, singer, songwriter, "outlaw country" pioneer; "Luckenbach, Texas."
George Jones, 1931-2013, singer; "He Stopped Loving Her Today."
The Judds (Naomi, b 1946; Wynonna, b 1964), mother-daughter duo; Wynonna also a solo act.
Toby Keith, b 1961, singer, songwriter, guitarist; "Should've Been a Cowboy."
Alison Krauss, b 1971, bluegrass fiddler, singer, bandleader; "When You Say Nothing at All."
Kris Kristofferson, b 1936, singer, songwriter, actor; "Me and Bobby McGee."
Lady Antebellum (Dave Haywood, b 1982; Charles Kelley, b 1981; Hillary Scott, b 1984); "I Run to You."
Miranda Lambert, b 1983, singer, guitarist; "The House That Built Me."
Louvin Brothers (Charlie, 1927-2011; Ira, 1924-65), singers; "If I Could Only Win Your Love."
Patty Loveless, b 1957, singer, songwriter; "How Can I Help You Say Goodbye."
Lyle Lovett, b 1957, singer, songwriter, bandleader, actor; "Cowboy Man."
Loretta Lynn, b 1935?, singer; "Coal Miner's Daughter."
Barbara Mandrell, b 1948, singer; "I Was Country When Country Wasn't Cool."
Kathy Mattea, b 1959, singer, songwriter; "Eighteen Wheels and a Dozen Roses."
Martina McBride, b 1966, singer, songwriter; "Independence Day."
Reba McEntire, b 1955, singer, songwriter, actress; "Whoever's in New England."
Tim McGraw, b 1967, singer; "It's Your Love," "I Like It, I Love It."
Roger Miller, 1936-92, singer, songwriter; "King of the Road."
Ronnie Milsap, b 1944, singer, songwriter; "There's No Gettin' Over Me."
Bill Monroe, 1911-96, singer, songwriter, mandolin player, "father of bluegrass music"; "Mule Skinner Blues."
Anne Murray, b 1945, singer; "You Needed Me."
Willie Nelson, b 1933, singer, songwriter, actor; "On the Road Again."
Mark O'Connor, b 1961, fiddler, country-classical crossover composer.
Buck Owens, 1929-2006, singer, guitarist; "Act Naturally."
Brad Paisley, b 1972, singer, songwriter; "Whiskey Lullaby," "When I Get Where I'm Going."
Dolly Parton, b 1946, singer, songwriter, actress; "Here You Come Again," "9 to 5."
Johnny Paycheck (Don Lytle), 1938-2003, singer, guitarist; "Take This Job and Shove It."
Minnie Pearl, 1912-96, comedienne, Grand Ole Opry star.
Kellie Pickler, b 1986, singer, songwriter.
Ray Price, 1926-2013, country singer, guitarist, songwriter; "Crazy Arms."
Charley Pride, b 1938, singer, 1st African American country star; "Kiss an Angel Good Mornin'."
Eddie Rabbit, 1941-98, singer, songwriter; "I Love a Rainy Night."
Rascal Flatts (Jay DeMarcus, b 1971; Gary LeVox, b 1970; Joe Don Rooney, b 1975); "Life Is a Highway."
Jim Reeves, 1923-64, singer, songwriter; "Four Walls."
Charlie Rich, 1932-95, singer, songwriter called the "Silver Fox"; "The Most Beautiful Girl."
LeAnn Rimes, b 1982, singer; "Blue."
Tex Ritter, 1905-74, singer, songwriter; "Jingle, Jangle, Jingle."
Marty Robbins, 1925-82, singer, songwriter; "A White Sport Coat and a Pink Carnation."
Jimmie Rodgers, 1897-1933, singer, songwriter; "T for Texas."
Kenny Rogers, b 1938, singer, songwriter; "The Gambler."
Roy Rogers (Leonard Slye), 1911-98, singer, actor, "King of the Cowboys," sang with Sons of the Pioneers.
Fred Rose, 1898-1954, songwriter, singer, producer; "Blue Eyes Cryin' in the Rain."
Blake Shelton, b 1976, singer; "Home."
Ricky Skaggs, b 1954, singer, songwriter, bandleader; "Don't Cheat in Our Hometown."
Ralph Stanley, b 1927, singer, banjo player; "Man of Constant Sorrow."
George Strait, b 1952, singer, bandleader; "Ace in the Hole."
Sugarland (Kristian Bush, b 1970; Jennifer Nettles, b 1974); "Stay."
Taylor Swift, b 1989, singer, songwriter; "You Belong With Me."
Lonnie "Mel" Tillis, b 1932, singer, songwriter, bandleader; "I Ain't Never."
Merle Travis, 1917-83, singer, guitarist, songwriter; "Divorce Me C.O.D."
Randy Travis, b 1959, singer, songwriter; "Forever and Ever, Amen."
Ernest Tubb, 1914-84, singer, songwriter, guitarist; "Walking the Floor Over You."
Josh Turner, b 1977, singer; "Why Don't We Just Dance."
Shania Twain, b 1965, singer, songwriter; "You're Still the One."
Conway Twitty, 1933-93, singer, songwriter; "Hello Darlin'."
Carrie Underwood, b 1983, singer, songwriter; *American Idol* winner.
Keith Urban, b 1967, guitarist, singer, songwriter; "It's a Love Thing."
Porter Wagoner, 1927-2007, singer, songwriter, guitarist; "Soul of a Convict."
Kitty Wells (Ellen Deason), 1919-2012, singer, songwriter; "It Wasn't God Who Made Honky-Tonk Angels."
Dottie West, 1932-91, singer, songwriter; "Here Comes My Baby."
Hank Williams Jr., b 1949, singer, songwriter; "Bocephus"; "All My Rowdy Friends (Have Settled Down)."
Hank Williams Sr., 1923-53, singer, songwriter; "Your Cheatin' Heart."
Bob Wills, 1905-75, Western Swing fiddler, singer, bandleader, songwriter; "New San Antonio Rose."
Lee Ann Womack, b 1966, singer, songwriter; "I Hope You Dance."
Tammy Wynette, 1942-98, singer; "Stand By Your Man."
Trisha Yearwood, b 1964, singer, songwriter; "How Do I Live."
Dwight Yoakam, b 1957, singer, songwriter, actor; "Ain't That Lonely Yet."
Zac Brown Band (Coy Bowles, b 1979; Zac Brown, b 1978; Clay Cook, Jimmy De Martini, Chris Fryar, b 1970; John Driskell Hopkins, b 1971); "Chicken Fried."

Dance Figures of the Past

Alvin Ailey, 1931-89, (U.S.) modern dancer, choreographer; melded modern dance and Afro-Caribbean techniques.
Frederick Ashton, 1904-88, (Br.) ballet choreographer; director of Great Britain's Royal Ballet, 1963-70.
Fred Astaire, 1899-1987, dancer, actor; teamed with dancer/actress **Ginger Rogers**, 1911-95, (both U.S.) in movie musicals.
George Balanchine, 1904-83, (Russ.-U.S.) ballet choreographer, teacher; most influential exponent of neoclassical style; founded, with Lincoln Kirstein, School of American Ballet and New York City Ballet.
Pina Bausch, 1940-2009, (Ger.) modern dance choreographer influencing the Tanztheater style of dance.
Carlo Blasis, 1795-1878, (It.) ballet dancer, choreographer, writer; his teaching methods are standards of classical dance.
August Bournonville, 1805-79, (Den.) ballet dancer, choreographer, teacher; exuberant, light style.
Fernando Bujones, 1955-2005, (Cuba-U.S.) ballet dancer.
Gisella Caccialanza, 1914-98, (U.S.) ballerina; charter member of Balanchine's American Ballet.
Irene, 1893-1969, (U.S.) and **Vernon Castle**, 1887-1918, (Br.) husband-and-wife ballroom dancers.
Enrico Cecchetti, 1850-1928, (It.) ballet dancer, leading dancer of Russia's Imperial Ballet; his technique was basis for Britain's Imperial Soc. of Teachers of Dancing.
Gower, 1921-80, dancer, choreographer, director; with wife **Marge Champion**, b 1923, (both U.S.) choreographed, danced in Broadway musicals and films.
John Cranko, 1927-73, (S. Afr.) choreographer; created narrative ballets based on literary works.
Merce Cunningham, 1919-2009, (U.S.) dancer, choreographer of avant-garde dance.
Alexandra Danilova, 1903-97, (Russ.) ballerina; noted teacher at the School of American Ballet.
Agnes de Mille, 1905-93, (U.S.) ballerina, choreographer; known for using American themes, she choreographed the ballet *Rodeo* and the musical *Oklahoma!*
Dame Ninette De Valois, 1898-2001, (Br.) choreographer, founding director of London's Royal Ballet; *The Rake's Progress*.
Sergei Diaghilev, 1872-1929, (Russ.) impresario; founded Les Ballet Russes; saw ballet as art unifying dance, drama, music, and decor.
Isadora Duncan, 1877-1927, (U.S.) expressive dancer who united free movement with serious music; one of the founders of modern dance.
Katherine Dunham, 1910-2006, (U.S.) dancer, choreographer; internationally known for African, Caribbean, and African American dance forms.
Fanny Elssler, 1810-84, (Austria) ballerina of the Romantic era; known for dramatic skill, sensual style.
Michel Fokine, 1880-1942, (Russ.) ballet dancer, choreographer, teacher; rejected strict classicism in favor of dramatically expressive style.
Margot Fonteyn, 1919-91, (Br.) prima ballerina, Royal Ballet of Great Britain; famed performance partner of Rudolf Nureyev.
Bob Fosse, 1927-87, (U.S.) jazz dancer, choreographer, director; Broadway musicals and film.
Serge Golovine, 1924-98, (Fr.) ballet dancer with Grand Ballet du Marquis de Cuevas, choreographer.
Martha Graham, 1894-1991, (U.S.) modern dancer, choreographer; created and codified her own dramatic technique.
Melissa Hayden, 1923-2006, (Can.) ballet dancer.
Martha Hill, 1900-95, (U.S.) educator; leading figure in modern dance. Founded American Dance Festival.
Gregory Hines, 1946-2003, (U.S.) tap-dance innovator; master of improvisation.
Doris Humphrey, 1895-1958, (U.S.) modern dancer, choreographer, writer, teacher.
Michael Jackson, 1958-2009, (U.S.) singer and dancer who perfected the "moonwalk."
Robert Joffrey, 1930-88, ballet dancer, choreographer; cofounded with **Gerald Arpino**, 1928-2008, (both U.S.) the Joffrey Ballet.
Kurt Jooss, 1901-79, (Ger.) choreographer, teacher; created expressionist works using modern and classical techniques.
Tamara Karsavina, 1885-1978, (Russ.) prima ballerina of Russia's Imperial Ballet and Diaghilev's Ballets Russes; partner of Nijinsky.
Nora Kaye, 1920-87, (U.S.) ballerina with Metropolitan Opera Ballet and Ballet Theater (now American Ballet Theatre).
Gene Kelly, 1912-96, (U.S.) dancer, actor in movie musicals.
Michael Kidd, 1915-2003, (U.S.) dancer, film and theater choreographer.
Lincoln Kirstein, 1907-96 (U.S.) brought ballet as an art form to U.S.; founded, with George Balanchine, School of American Ballet and New York City Ballet.
Serge Lifar, 1905-86, (Russ.-Fr.) prem. danseur, choreographer; director of dance at Paris Opera, 1930-45, 1947-58.
José Limón, 1908-72, (Mex.-U.S.) modern dancer, choreographer, teacher; developed technique based on Humphrey.
Catherine Littlefield, 1908-51, (U.S.) ballerina, choreographer, teacher; pioneer of American ballet.
Kenneth MacMillan, 1929-92, (Br.) dancer, choreographer; directed Royal Ballet of Great Britain, 1970-77.
Dame Alicia Markova, 1910-2004, (Br.) ballerina known for title role in *Giselle*; helped popularize ballet in U.S. and Britain.
Léonide Massine, 1896-1979, (Russ.-U.S.) ballet dancer, choreographer; known for his "symphonic ballet."
Fayard Nicholas, 1914-2006, tap dancer, choreographer, actor; together with brother **Harold Nicholas**, 1921-2000, (both U.S.) formed the "Nicholas Brothers."
Vaslav Nijinsky, 1890-50, (Russ.) prem. danseur, choreographer; leading member of Diaghilev's Ballets Russes. His ballets were revolutionary for their time.
Alwin Nikolais, 1910-93, (U.S.) modern choreographer; created dance theater utilizing mixed media effects.
Jean-George Noverre, 1727-1810, (Fr.) ballet choreographer, teacher, writer; "Shakespeare of the Dance."
Rudolf Nureyev, 1938-93, (Russ.) prem. danseur, choreographer; leading male dancer of his generation; director of dance at Paris Opera, 1983-89.
Ruth Page, 1899-1991, (U.S.) ballerina, choreographer; danced, directed ballet at Chicago Lyric Opera.
Anna Pavlova, 1881-1931, (Russ.) prima ballerina; toured with her own company to world acclaim.
Marius Petipa, 1818-1910, (Fr.) ballet dancer, choreographer; ballet master of the Imperial Ballet; established Russian classicism as leading style of late 19th cent.
Roland Petit, 1924-2011, (Fr.) dancer, choreographer; founder of Les Ballets de Paris.
Pearl Primus, 1919-95, (Trinidad-U.S.) modern dancer, choreographer, scholar; combined African, Caribbean, and African American styles.
Jerome Robbins, 1918-98, (U.S.) choreographer, director, dancer; *The King and I*, *West Side Story*, *Fiddler on the Roof*.
Bill "Bojangles" Robinson, 1878-1949, (U.S.) famed tap dancer; called "King of Tapology" on stage and screen.
Ruth St. Denis, 1877-1968, (U.S.) influential interpretive dancer, choreographer, teacher.
Ted Shawn, 1891-1972, (U.S.) modern dancer, choreographer; formed dance company and school with Ruth St. Denis; established Jacob's Pillow Dance Festival.
Marie Taglioni, 1804-84, (It.) ballerina, teacher; in title role of *La Sylphide* established image of the ethereal ballerina.
Maria Tallchief, 1925-2013, (U.S.) prima ballerina, 1st of Amer. Indian descent.
Glen Tetley, 1926-2007, (U.S.) dancer, choreographer, ballet director; fused elements of modern dance with ballet.
Antony Tudor, 1908-87, (Br.) choreographer, teacher; exponent of the "psychological ballet."
Galina Ulanova, 1910-98, (Russ.) revered ballerina with Bolshoi Ballet.
Agrippina Vaganova, 1879-1951, (Russ.) ballet teacher, director called "queen of variations"; codified Soviet ballet technique.
Mary Wigman, 1886-1973, (Ger.) modern dancer, choreographer, teacher; influenced European expressionist dance.

Opera Singers of the Past

Licia Albanese, 1909-2014, (It.) soprano.
Frances Alda, 1879-1952, (N.Z.) soprano.
Pasquale Amato, 1878-1942, (It.) baritone.
Marian Anderson, 1897-1993, (U.S.) contralto.
Charles Anthony, 1929-2012, (U.S.) tenor.
Jussi Björling, 1911-60, (Swed.) tenor.
Lucrezia Bori, 1887-1960, (It.) soprano.
Maria Callas, 1923-77, (U.S.) soprano.
Emma Calvé, 1858-1942, (Fr.) soprano.
Enrico Caruso, 1873-1921, (It.) tenor.
Feodor Chaliapin, 1873-1938, (Russ.) bass.
Lili Chookasian, 1921-2012, (U.S.) contralto.
Boris Christoff, 1914-93, (Bulg.) bass.
Franco Corelli, 1921-2003, (It.) tenor.
Hughes Cuenod, 1902-2010, (Switz.) tenor.
Victoria De Los Angeles, 1923-2005, (Sp.) soprano.
Giuseppe De Luca, 1876-1950, (It.) baritone.
Fernando De Lucia, 1860-1925, (It.) tenor.
Edouard De Reszke, 1853-1917, (Pol.) bass.
Jean De Reszke, 1850-1925, (Pol.) tenor.
Emmy Destinn, 1878-1930, (Czech.) soprano.
Emma Eames, 1865-1952, (U.S.) soprano.
(Carlo Broschi) Farinelli, 1705-82, (It.) castrato.
Geraldine Farrar, 1882-1967, (U.S.) soprano.
Eileen Farrell, 1920-2002, (U.S.) soprano.
Kathleen Ferrier, 1912-53, (Eng.) contralto.
Dietrich Fischer-Dieskau, 1925-2012, (Ger.) baritone.

Kirsten Flagstad, 1895-1962, (Nor.) soprano.
Olive Fremstad, 1871-1951, (Swed.-U.S.) soprano.
Amelita Galli-Curci, 1882-1963, (It.) soprano.
Mary Garden, 1874-1967, (Br.) soprano.
Nicolai Ghiaurov, 1929-2004, (Bulg.) bass.
Beniamino Gigli, 1890-1957, (It.) tenor.
Tito Gobbi, 1913-84, (It.) baritone.
Giulia Grisi, 1811-69, (It.) soprano.
Frieda Hempel, 1885-1955, (Ger.) soprano.
Jerome Hines, 1921-2003, (U.S.) bass.
Hans Hotter, 1909-2003, (Ger.) bass-baritone.
Maria Jeritza, 1887-1982, (Czech.) soprano.
Sena Jurinac, 1921-2011, (Yugo.) soprano.
Alexander Kipnis, 1891-1978, (Russ.-U.S.) bass.
Dorothy Kirsten, 1910-92, (U.S.) soprano.
Alfredo Kraus, 1927-99, (Sp.) tenor.
Luigi Lablache, 1794-1858, (It.) bass.
Lilli Lehmann, 1848-1929, (Ger.) soprano.
Lotte Lehmann, 1888-1976, (Ger.-U.S.) soprano.
Jenny Lind, 1820-87, (Swed.) soprano.
Cornell MacNeil, 1922-2011, (U.S.) baritone.
Maria Malibran, 1808-36, (Sp.) mezzo-soprano.
Giovanni Martinelli, 1885-1969, (It.) tenor.
John McCormack, 1884-1945, (Ire.) tenor.
Nellie Melba, 1861-1931, (Austral.) soprano.
Lauritz Melchior, 1890-1973, (Den.) tenor.
Robert Merrill, 1919-2004, (U.S.) baritone.
Zinka Milanov, 1906-89, (Yugo.) soprano.
Patricia Neway, 1919-2012, (U.S.) soprano.
Birgit Nilsson, 1918-2005, (Swed.) soprano.
Lillian Nordica, 1857-1914, (U.S.) soprano.
Magda Olivero, 1910-2014, (It.) soprano.
Giuditta Pasta, 1797-1865, (It.) soprano.
Adelina Patti, 1843-1919, (It.) soprano.
Luciano Pavarotti, 1935-2007, (It.) tenor.
Peter Pears, 1910-86, (Eng.) tenor.
Jan Peerce, 1904-84, (U.S.) tenor.
Ezio Pinza, 1892-1957, (It.) bass.
Lily Pons, 1898-1976, (Fr.) soprano.
Rosa Ponselle, 1897-1981, (U.S.) soprano.
Hermann Prey, 1929-98, (Ger.) baritone.
Margaret Price, 1941-2011, (U.K.) soprano.
Regina Resnik, 1922-2013, (U.S.) soprano turned mezzo-soprano.
Elisabeth Rethberg, 1894-1976, (Ger.) soprano.
Giovanni Battista Rubini, 1794-1854, (It.) tenor.
Leonie Rysanek, 1926-98, (Austria) soprano.
Dorothy Sarnoff, 1914-2008, (U.S.) soprano.
Bidú Sayão, 1902-99, (Braz.) soprano.
Friedrich Schorr, 1888-1953, (Hung.) bass-baritone.
Elisabeth Schwarzkopf, 1915-2006, (Ger.) soprano.
Marcella Sembrich, 1858-1935, (Pol.) soprano.
Cesare Siepi, 1923-2010, (It.) bass.
Beverly Sills, 1929-2007, (U.S.) soprano.
Elisabeth Söderström, 1927-2009, (Swed.) soprano.
Eleanor Steber, 1914-90, (U.S.) soprano.
Risë Stevens, 1913-2013, (U.S.) mezzo-soprano.
Joan Sutherland, 1926-2010, (Austral.) soprano.
Ferrucio Tagliavini, 1913-95, (It.) tenor.
Renata Tebaldi, 1922-2004 (It.) soprano.
Luisa Tetrazzini, 1871-1940, (It.) soprano.
Lawrence Tibbett, 1896-1960, (U.S.) baritone.
Giorgio Tozzi, 1923-2011, (U.S.) bass-baritone.
Tatiana Troyanos, 1938-93, (U.S.) mezzo-soprano.
Richard Tucker, 1913-75, (U.S.) tenor.
Shirley Verrett, 1931-2010, (U.S.) mezzo-soprano.
Pauline Viardot, 1821-1910, (Fr.) mezzo-soprano.
Jon Vickers, 1926-2015, (Can.) tenor.
William Warfield, 1920-2002, (U.S.) bass-baritone.
Leonard Warren, 1911-60, (U.S.) baritone.
Ljuba Welitsch, 1913-96, (Bulg.) soprano.
Camilla Williams, 1919-2012, (U.S.) soprano.
Wolfgang Windgassen, 1914-74, (Ger.) tenor.

Rock and Roll, Rhythm and Blues, and Rap Artists

Titles in quotation marks are singles; others are albums. * = Inducted into Rock and Roll Hall of Fame as performer between 1986 and 2015; year is in parentheses.

***ABBA (2010):** "Dancing Queen"
Paula Abdul: "Straight Up"
***AC/DC (2003):** "Back in Black"
Bryan Adams: "Cuts Like a Knife"
Adele: "Rolling in the Deep"
***Aerosmith (2001):** "Sweet Emotion"
Christina Aguilera: "What a Girl Wants"
Alice in Chains: "Heaven Beside You"
***The Allman Brothers Band (1995):** "Ramblin' Man"
***The Animals (1994):** "House of the Rising Sun"
Paul Anka: "Lonely Boy"
Fiona Apple: "Criminal"
Frankie Avalon: "Venus"
Iggy Azalea: "Fancy"
The B-52s: "Love Shack"
Bachman Turner Overdrive: "Takin' Care of Business"
Backstreet Boys: "I Want It That Way"
Bad Company: "Can't Get Enough"
Erykah Badu: "On and On"
***La Vern Baker (1991):** "I Cried a Tear"
***Hank Ballard[1] and the Midnighters (1990):** "Work With Me, Annie"
***The Band (1994):** "The Weight"
Barenaked Ladies: "One Week"
***The Beach Boys (1988):** "Good Vibrations"
***Beastie Boys (2012):** "(You Gotta) Fight for Your Right (to Party)"
***The Beatles (1988):** *Sgt. Pepper's Lonely Hearts Club Band*
Beck: "Loser"
***Jeff Beck (2009):** "Escape"
***The Bee Gees (1997):** "Stayin' Alive"
Pat Benatar: "Hit Me With Your Best Shot"
***Chuck Berry (1986):** "Johnny B. Goode"
Beyoncé: "Crazy in Love"
The Big Bopper: "Chantilly Lace"
Björk: "Human Behavior"
The Black Crowes: "Hard to Handle"
Black Eyed Peas: *Elephunk*
***Black Sabbath (2006):** "Paranoid"
***Bobby "Blue" Bland (1992):** "Turn On Your Love Light"
Mary J. Blige: *My Life*
Blind Faith: "Can't Find My Way Home"
Blink-182: "All the Small Things"
***Blondie (2006):** "Heart of Glass"
Blood, Sweat, and Tears: "Spinning Wheel"
Blues Traveler: "Run-Around"
Gary "U.S." Bonds: "Quarter to Three"
Bon Jovi: "Livin' on a Prayer"
***Booker T. and the M.G.'s (1992):** "Green Onions"
Boston: "More Than a Feeling"
***David Bowie (1996):** "Space Oddity"
Boyz II Men: "I'll Make Love to You"
Toni Braxton: "Un-Break My Heart"
Chris Brown: "Kiss Kiss"
***James Brown (1986):** "Papa's Got a Brand New Bag"
***Ruth Brown (1993):** "Lucky Lips"
***Jackson Browne (2004):** "Doctor My Eyes"
***Buffalo Springfield (1997):** "For What It's Worth"
Jimmy Buffett: "Margaritaville"
***Solomon Burke (2001):** "Over and Over (Huggin' and Lovin')"
***The Paul Butterfield Blues Band (2015):** "Born in Chicago"
***The Byrds (1991):** "Turn! Turn! Turn!"
Mariah Carey: "Vision of Love"
The Carpenters: "(They Long to Be) Close to You"
The Cars: "Shake It Up"
***Johnny Cash (1992):** "I Walk the Line"
***Ray Charles (1986):** "Georgia on My Mind"
Cheap Trick: "Surrender"
Chubby Checker: "The Twist"
Chicago: "Saturday in the Park"
***Eric Clapton (2000):** "Layla"
Kelly Clarkson: "Since U Been Gone"
***The Clash (2003):** "Rock the Casbah"
***Jimmy Cliff (2010):** "I Can See Clearly Now"
***The Coasters (1987):** "Yakety Yak"
***Eddie Cochran (1987):** "Summertime Blues"
Joe Cocker: "With a Little Help From My Friends"
***Leonard Cohen (2008):** "Suzanne"
Coldplay: "Clocks"
Collective Soul: "The World I Know"
Phil Collins: "Against All Odds"
***Sam Cooke (1986):** "You Send Me"
Coolio: "Gangsta's Paradise"
***Alice Cooper (2011):** "School's Out"
***Elvis Costello and the Attractions (2003):** "Alison"
Counting Crows: "Mr. Jones"
***Cream (1993):** "Sunshine of Your Love"
Creed: "Arms Wide Open"
***Creedence Clearwater Revival (1993):** "Proud Mary"
***Crosby, Stills, and Nash (1997):** "Suite: Judy Blue Eyes"
Sheryl Crow: "All I Want to Do"
The Crystals: "Da Doo Ron Ron"
The Cure: "Boys Don't Cry"
Daft Punk: "Get Lucky"
Danny and the Juniors: "At the Hop"
***Bobby Darin (1990):** "Splish Splash"
Daughtry: "It's Not Over"
***The Dave Clark Five (2008):** "Glad All Over"
Dave Matthews Band: "Don't Drink the Water"
***Miles Davis (2006):** *Bitches Brew*
Spencer Davis Group: "Gimme Some Lovin'"
Deep Purple: "Smoke on the Water"
Def Leppard: "Photograph"
***The Dells (2004):** "Oh, What a Night"
Depeche Mode: "Strange Love"
Destiny's Child: "Survivor"
***Neil Diamond (2011):** "Cracklin' Rosie"
***Bo Diddley (1987):** "Who Do You Love?
***Dion[1] and the Belmonts (1989):** "A Teenager in Love"
Celine Dion: "Because You Loved Me"
Dire Straits: "Money for Nothing"
DMX: "What's My Name"
***Fats Domino (1986):** "Blueberry Hill"
***Donovan (2012):** "Mellow Yellow"
The Doobie Brothers: "What a Fool Believes"
***The Doors (1993):** "Light My Fire"
Drake: "Over"
Dr. Dre: "Nothin' But a 'G' Thang"
***Dr. John (2011):** "Right Place, Wrong Time"
***The Drifters (1988):** "Save the Last Dance for Me"
Duran Duran: "Hungry Like the Wolf"
***Bob Dylan (1988):** "Like a Rolling Stone"
***The Eagles (1998):** "Hotel California"
***Earth, Wind, and Fire (2000):** "Shining Star"
***Duane Eddy (1994):** "Rebel-Rouser"
Missy Elliott: "Sock It 2 Me"
Eminem: "The Real Slim Shady"
En Vogue: "Hold On"
The Eurythmics: "Sweet Dreams (Are Made of This)"
Everclear: "Father Of Mine"
***The Everly Brothers (1986):** "Wake Up, Little Susie"
50 Cent (Curtis Jackson): *Get Rich or Die Tryin'*
The Five Satins: "In the Still of the Night"
Roberta Flack: "The First Time Ever I Saw Your Face"
***The Flamingos (2001):** "I Only Have Eyes for You"
***Fleetwood Mac (1998):** *Rumours*
The Foo Fighters: "I'll Stick Around"
Foreigner: "Double Vision"
***The Four Seasons (1990):** "Sherry"
***The Four Tops (1990):** "I Can't Help Myself (Sugar Pie, Honey Bunch)"
***Aretha Franklin (1987):** "Respect"
fun.: "We Are Young"

Nelly Furtado: "I'm Like a Bird"
***Peter Gabriel (2014):** "Shock the Monkey"
***Gamble (Kenny) and Huff (Leon) (2008):** "If You Don't Know Me By Now"
***Marvin Gaye (1987):** "I Heard It Through the Grapevine"
***Genesis (2010):** "No Reply at All"
Goo Goo Dolls: "Iris"
Grand Funk Railroad: "We're an American Band"
***Grandmaster Flash and the Furious Five (2007):** "The Message"
***The Grateful Dead (1994):** "Uncle John's Band"
***Al Green (1995):** "Let's Stay Together"
***Green Day (2015):** "Boulevard of Broken Dreams"
The Guess Who: "American Woman"
***Guns N' Roses (2012):** "Sweet Child o' Mine"
***Buddy Guy (2005):** *A Man and His Blues*
***Bill Haley[1] and His Comets (1987):** "Rock Around the Clock"
***Hall and Oates (2014):** "Kiss on My List"
***George Harrison (2004):** "My Sweet Lord"
***Isaac Hayes (2002):** "Theme From 'Shaft'"
***Heart (2013):** "Barracuda"
***Jimi Hendrix (1992):** "Purple Haze"
Lauryn Hill: "Doo-Wop (That Thing)"
***The Hollies (2010):** "Long Cool Woman (In a Black Dress)"
***Buddy Holly (1986):** "Peggy Sue"
***John Lee Hooker (1991):** "Boogie Chillen"
Hootie and the Blowfish: *Cracked Rear View*
Whitney Houston: "I Will Always Love You"
***The Impressions (1991):** "For Your Precious Love"
Indigo Girls: "Closer to Fine"
INXS: "Need You Tonight"
***The Isley Brothers (1992):** "It's Your Thing"
Ja Rule: *Venni, Vetti, Vecci*
***The Jackson Five (1997):** "ABC"
Janet Jackson: *Rhythm Nation*
***Michael Jackson (2001):** *Thriller*
***Etta James (1993):** "At Last"
Tommy James and the Shondells: "Crimson and Clover"
Jane's Addiction: "Jane Says"
Jay and the Americans: "This Magic Moment"
Jay Z: "99 Problems"
***Jefferson Airplane (1996):** "White Rabbit"
Jethro Tull: *Aqualung*
***Joan Jett and the Blackhearts (2015):** "I Love Rock 'n' Roll"
Jewel: "You Were Meant For Me"
***Billy Joel (1999):** "Piano Man"
***Elton John (1994):** "Candle in the Wind"
***Little Willie John (1996):** "Sleep"
Norah Jones: *Come Away With Me*
***Janis Joplin (1995):** "Me and Bobby McGee"
Journey: "Don't Stop Believin' "
K.C. and the Sunshine Band: "Get Down Tonight"
R. Kelly: "I Can't Sleep Baby (If I)"
Alicia Keys: "Fallin'"
Kid Rock: "Cowboy"
***B.B. King (1987):** "The Thrill Is Gone"
Carole King: *Tapestry*
***The Kinks (1990):** "You Really Got Me"
***Kiss (2014):** "Rock 'n' Roll All Night"
***Gladys Knight and the Pips (1996):** "Midnight Train to Georgia"
Korn: "Blind"
Lenny Kravitz: "Are You Gonna Go My Way?"
Lady Gaga: "Poker Face"
***Led Zeppelin (1995):** "Stairway to Heaven"
***Brenda Lee (2002):** "I'm Sorry"
John Legend: "Ordinary People"
***John Lennon (1994):** "Imagine"
***Jerry Lee Lewis (1986):** "Whole Lotta Shakin' Going On"
Lil' Kim: "No Matter What They Say"
Lil Wayne: *The Block Is Hot.*
Limp Bizkit: "Break Stuff"
Linkin Park: "One Step Closer"
***Little Anthony and the Imperials (2009):** "Tears on My Pillow"
***Little Richard (1986):** "Tutti Frutti"
***Little Walter (2008):** "Juke"
LL Cool J: "Mama Said Knock You Out"
Jennifer Lopez: "Love Don't Cost a Thing"
***Darlene Love (2011):** "He's a Rebel"
***The Lovin' Spoonful (2000):** "Summer in the City"
Ludacris: "Money Maker"
***Frankie Lymon and the Teenagers (1993):** "Why Do Fools Fall in Love?"
***Lynyrd Skynyrd (2006):** "Free Bird"
***Madonna (2008):** "Material Girl"
***The Mamas and the Papas (1998):** "Monday, Monday"
Marilyn Manson: "Beautiful People"
***Bob Marley (1994):** *Exodus*
Maroon 5: *Songs About Jane*
Bruno Mars: "Just the Way You Are"
***Martha and the Vandellas (1995):** "Dancin' in the Streets"
The Marvelettes: "Please, Mr. Postman"
Matchbox 20: "Push"
John Mayer: "Daughters"
***Curtis Mayfield (1999):** "Superfly"
***Paul McCartney (1999):** "Band on the Run"
Don McLean: "American Pie"
***Clyde McPhatter (1987):** "A Lover's Question"
Meat Loaf: "Paradise by the Dashboard Light"
***John (Cougar) Mellencamp (2008):** "Jack and Diane"
Men at Work: "Who Can It Be Now?"
***Metallica (2009):** "Enter Sandman"
George Michael: "Faith"
Nicki Minaj: *Pink Friday.*
***Joni Mitchell (1997):** "Both Sides Now"
Moby: "Bodyrock"
The Monkees: "I'm a Believer"
Moody Blues: "Nights in White Satin"
***The Moonglows (2000):** "Blue Velvet"
Alanis Morissette: "Ironic"
***Van Morrison (1993):** "Brown-Eyed Girl"
Mötley Crüe: "Live Wire"
Motörhead: "Ace of Spades"
Jason Mraz: "I'm Yours"
Mumford & Sons: "Little Lion Man"
Nelly: *Country Grammar*
***Ricky Nelson (1987):** "Hello, Mary Lou"
Nine Inch Nails: "Closer"
***Nirvana (2014):** *Nevermind*
No Doubt: *Rock Steady*
The Notorious B.I.G.: "Mo Money Mo Problems"
'N Sync: "Bye, Bye, Bye"
Ted Nugent: "Stranglehold"
***The O'Jays (2005):** "Back Stabbers"
One Direction: "What Makes You Beautiful"
***Roy Orbison (1987):** "Oh, Pretty Woman"
Ozzy Osbourne: "Crazy Train"
OutKast: *Speakerboxxx/The Love Below*
***Parliament/Funkadelic (1997):** "One Nation Under a Groove"
Pearl Jam: "Jeremy"
***Carl Perkins (1987):** "Blue Suede Shoes"
Katy Perry: "Firework"
Peter, Paul, and Mary: "Leaving on a Jet Plane"
***Tom Petty and the Heartbreakers (2002):** "Refugee"
Liz Phair: *Exile in Guyville*
Phish: "Sample in a Jar"
***Wilson Pickett (1991):** "Land of 1,000 Dances"
Pink: *Missundaztood*
***Pink Floyd (1996):** *The Wall*
***Gene Pitney (2002):** "Only Love Can Break a Heart"
***The Platters (1990):** "The Great Pretender"
The Pointer Sisters: "I'm So Excited"
***The Police (2003):** "Every Breath You Take"
Iggy Pop: "Lust for Life"
***Elvis Presley (1986):** "Love Me Tender"
***The Pretenders (2005):** "Back on the Chain Gang"
***Lloyd Price (1998):** "Stagger Lee"
***Prince (The Artist) (2004):** "Purple Rain"
***Public Enemy (2013):** "Fight the Power"
Puff Daddy and the Family: *No Way Out*
***Queen (2001):** "Bohemian Rhapsody"
Radiohead: *OK Computer*
Rage Against the Machine: "Bulls on Parade"
***Bonnie Raitt (2000):** "Something to Talk About"
***The Ramones (2002):** "I Wanna Be Sedated"
***Red Hot Chili Peppers (2012):** "Under the Bridge"
***Otis Redding (1989):** "(Sittin' on) The Dock of the Bay"
***Jimmy Reed (1991):** "Ain't That Loving You, Baby?"
***Lou Reed (2015):** "Walk on the Wild Side"
***R.E.M. (2007):** "Losing My Religion"
REO Speedwagon: "Can't Fight This Feeling"
Busta Rhymes: "What's It Gonna Be?"
***The Righteous Brothers (2003):** "You've Lost That Lovin' Feelin' "
Rihanna: "Umbrella"
Johnny Rivers: "Poor Side of Town"
***Smokey Robinson[1] and the Miracles (1987):** "Shop Around"
***The Rolling Stones (1989):** "Satisfaction"
***The Ronettes (2007):** "Be My Baby"
***Linda Ronstadt (2014):** "You're No Good"
Diana Ross: "I'm Coming Out"
***Run-D.M.C. (2009):** "Raisin' Hell"
***Rush (2013):** "Tom Sawyer"
Sade: "Smooth Operator"
Salt-N-Pepa: "Shoop"
***Sam and Dave (1992):** "Soul Man"
***Santana (1998):** "Black Magic Woman"
Seal: "Kiss From a Rose"
Neil Sedaka: "Breaking Up Is Hard to Do"
***Bob Seger (2004):** "Old Time Rock & Roll"
***Sex Pistols (2006):** "Anarchy in the UK"
Shakira: "Whenever, Wherever"
Tupac Shakur: "How Do U Want It"
***Del Shannon (1999):** "Runaway"
Ed Sheeran: "Thinking Out Loud"
***The Shirelles (1996):** "Soldier Boy"
Carly Simon: "You're So Vain"
***Paul Simon (2001):** "50 Ways to Leave Your Lover"
***Simon and Garfunkel (1990):** "Bridge Over Troubled Water"
***Percy Sledge (2005):** "When a Man Loves a Woman"
***Sly and the Family Stone (1993):** "Everyday People"
Smashing Pumpkins: "Today"
***Patti Smith (2007):** "Because the Night"
Sam Smith: "Stay With Me"
Will Smith: "Gettin' Jiggy With It"
The Smiths: "This Charming Man"
Snoop Dogg (a.k.a. Snoop Lion, Snoopzilla): "Gin and Juice"
Sonic Youth: "Bull in the Heather"
Soundgarden: "Black Hole Sun"
Britney Spears: "Hit Me Baby One More Time"
Spice Girls: "Wannabe"
***Dusty Springfield (1999):** "I Only Want to Be With You"
***Bruce Springsteen (1999):** "Born to Run"
***Staple Singers (1999):** "I'll Take You There"
***Steely Dan (2001):** "Rikki Don't Lose That Number"
Gwen Stefani: "Hollaback Girl"
Steppenwolf: "Born to Be Wild"
***Cat Stevens (2014):** "Wild World"
***Rod Stewart (1994):** "Maggie Mae"
Sting: "If You Love Somebody, Set Them Free"
Stone Temple Pilots: "Plush"
***The Stooges (2010):** "I Wanna Be Your Dog"
Styx: "Come Sail Away"
The Sugar Hill Gang: "Rapper's Delight"
***Donna Summer (2013):** "Bad Girls"
***The Supremes (1988):** "Stop! In the Name of Love"
***Talking Heads (2002):** "Once in a Lifetime"
***James Taylor (2001):** "You've Got a Friend"
***The Temptations (1989):** "My Girl"
Robin Thicke: "Blurred Lines"
Three Dog Night: "Joy to the World"
Justin Timberlake: "SexyBack"
TLC: "Waterfalls"
***Traffic (2004):** *Traffic*
***Big Joe Turner (1987):** "Shake, Rattle & Roll"
***Ike and Tina Turner (1991):** "Proud Mary"
***Tina Turner (1991):** "What's Love Got to Do With It?"
The Turtles: "Happy Together"
***U2 (2005):** "With or Without You"
Usher: "You Make Me Wanna"
***Ritchie Valens (2001):** "La Bamba"
***Van Halen (2007):** "Running With the Devil"
***Stevie Ray Vaughan & Double Trouble (2015):** "Change It"
***The Velvet Underground (1996):** "Sweet Jane"
***The Ventures (2008):** "Walk, Don't Run"

***Gene Vincent (1998):** "Be-Bop-A-Lula"
***Tom Waits (2011):** "Downtown Train"
The Wallflowers: "One Headlight"
Dionne Warwick: "I Say a Little Prayer"
***Muddy Waters (1987):** "I Can't Be Satisfied"
Mary Wells: "My Guy"
Kanye West: "Gold Digger"
The White Stripes: "Seven Nation Army"
Whitesnake: "Here I Go Again"
***The Who (1990):** *Tommy*
Pharrell Williams: "Happy"
***Jackie Wilson (1987):** "That's Why"
***Bill Withers (2015):** "Lean on Me"
***Bobby Womack (2009):** "Lookin' for a Love"
***Stevie Wonder (1989):** "You Are the Sunshine of My Life"
Wu-Tang Clan: "Protect Ya Neck"
***The Yardbirds (1992):** "For Your Love"
Yes: "Roundabout"
***Neil Young (1995):** "Down by the River"
***The Young Rascals/The Rascals (1997):** "Good Lovin' "
***Frank Zappa[1]/Mothers of Invention (1995):** *Hot Rats*
***ZZ Top (2004):** "Legs"

(1) Only individual performer is in Rock and Roll Hall of Fame.

Entertainment Personalities of the Present

Living actors, musicians, dancers, singers, producers, directors, and radio-TV performers.

Name	Birthplace	Birthdate
Abdul, Paula	San Fernando, CA	6/19/1962
Abraham, F. Murray	Pittsburgh, PA	10/24/1939
Abrams, J(effrey) J(acob)	New York, NY	6/27/1966
Adams, Amy	Vicenza, Italy	8/20/1974
Adams, Bryan	Kingston, ON, Canada	11/5/1959
Adams, Yolanda	Houston, TX	8/27/1961
Adele	London, England, UK	5/5/1988
Adjani, Isabelle	Paris, France	6/27/1955
Ad-Rock	South Orange, NJ	10/31/1966
Aduba, Uzo	Boston, MA	2/10/1981
Affleck, Ben	Berkeley, CA	8/15/1972
Affleck, Casey	Falmouth, MA	8/12/1975
Aghdashloo, Shohreh	Tehran, Iran	5/11/1952
Aguilera, Christina	Staten Island, NY	12/18/1980
Aiello, Danny	New York, NY	6/20/1933
Aiken, Clay	Raleigh, NC	11/30/1978
Aimée, Anouk	Paris, France	4/27/1932
Alba, Jessica	Pomona, CA	4/28/1981
Alberghetti, Anna Maria	Pesaro, Italy	5/15/1936
Albert, Marv	Brooklyn, NY	6/12/1941
Alda, Alan	New York, NY	1/28/1936
Alexander, Jane	Boston, MA	10/28/1939
Alexander, Jason	Newark, NJ	9/23/1959
Allen, Debbie	Houston, TX	1/16/1950
Allen, Joan	Rochelle, IL	8/20/1956
Allen, Karen	Carrollton, IL	10/5/1951
Allen, Kris	Jacksonville, AR	6/21/1985
Allen, Marty	Pittsburgh, PA	3/23/1922
Allen, Tim	Denver, CO	6/13/1953
Allen, Woody	Bronx, NY	12/1/1935
Alley, Kirstie	Wichita, KS	1/12/1951
Allman, Gregg	Nashville, TN	12/8/1947
Alpert, Herb	Los Angeles, CA	3/31/1935
Almodóvar, Pedro	Calzada de Calatrava, Spain	9/24/1949
Ambrose, Lauren	New Haven, CT	2/20/1978
Ames, Ed	Malden, MA	7/9/1927
Amos, John	Newark, NJ	12/27/1939
Amos, Tori	Newton, NC	8/22/1963
Anderson, Anthony	Los Angeles, CA	8/15/1970
Anderson, Gillian	Chicago, IL	8/9/1968
Anderson, Harry	Newport, RI	10/14/1952
Anderson, Ian	Dunfermline, Scotland, UK	8/10/1947
Anderson, Loni	St. Paul, MN	8/5/1946?
Anderson, Melissa Sue	Berkeley, CA	9/26/1962
Anderson, Pamela	Ladysmith, BC, Canada	7/1/1967
Anderson, Richard	Long Branch, NJ	8/8/1926
Anderson, Richard Dean	Minneapolis, MN	1/23/1950
Anderson, Wes	Houston, TX	5/1/1969
Andersson, Bibi	Stockholm, Sweden	11/11/1935
André 3000	Atlanta, GA	5/27/1975
Andress, Ursula	Bern, Switzerland	3/19/1936
Andrews, Julie	Walton-on-Thames, Surrey, England, UK	10/1/1935
Andrews, Naveen	London, England, UK	1/17/1969
Aniston, Jennifer	Sherman Oaks, CA	2/11/1969
Anka, Paul	Ottawa, ON, Canada	7/30/1941
Ann-Margret	Stockholm, Sweden	4/28/1941
Ansari, Aziz	Columbia, SC	2/23/1983
Anthony, Marc	New York, NY	9/16/1968
Apatow, Judd	Syosset, NY	12/6/1967
Apple, Fiona	New York, NY	9/13/1977
Applegate, Christina	Los Angeles, CA	11/25/1971
Archer, Anne	Los Angeles, CA	8/24/1947
Arkin, Adam	Brooklyn, NY	8/19/1956
Arkin, Alan	New York, NY	3/26/1934
Armisen, Fred	Hattiesburg, MS	12/4/1966
Arnaz, Desi, Jr.	Hollywood, CA	1/19/1953
Arnaz, Lucie	Hollywood, CA	7/17/1951
Arnett, Will	Toronto, ON, Canada	5/4/1970
Arnold, Tom	Ottumwa, IA	3/6/1959
Arquette, David	Winchester, VA	9/8/1971
Arquette, Patricia	Chicago, IL	4/8/1968
Arquette, Rosanna	New York, NY	8/10/1959
Arroyo, Martina	New York, NY	2/2/1937
Ashanti (Douglas)	Glen Cove, NY	10/13/1980
Ashley, Elizabeth	Ocala, FL	8/30/1939
Asner, Ed	Kansas City, KS	11/15/1929
Assante, Armand	New York, NY	10/4/1949
Astin, John	Baltimore, MD	3/30/1930
Astin, Sean	Santa Monica, CA	2/25/1971
Atkins, Eileen	London, England, UK	6/16/1934
Atkins, Sharif	Pittsburgh, PA	1/29/1975
Atkinson, Rowan	Newcastle upon Tyne, Eng., UK	1/6/1955
Auberjonois, Rene	New York, NY	6/1/1940
Austin, Patti	New York, NY	8/10/1948
Avalon, Frankie	Philadelphia, PA	9/18/1940
Aykroyd, Dan	Ottawa, ON, Canada	7/1/1952
Azalea, Iggy	Sydney, NSW, Australia	6/7/1990
Azaria, Hank	Forest Hills, Queens, NY	4/25/1964
Aznavour, Charles	Paris, France	5/22/1924
Babyface	Indianapolis, IN	4/10/1959
Baccarin, Morena	Rio de Janeiro, Brazil	6/2/1979
Bacon, Kevin	Philadelphia, PA	7/8/1958
Badalucco, Michael	Brooklyn, NY	12/20/1954
Bader, Diedrich	Alexandria, VA	12/24/1966
Badu, Erykah	Dallas, TX	2/26/1971
Baez, Joan	Staten Island, NY	1/9/1941
Baio, Scott	Brooklyn, NY	9/22/1960
Baker, Anita	Toledo, OH	1/26/1958
Baker, Carroll	Johnstown, PA	5/28/1931
Baker, Diane	Hollywood, CA	2/25/1938
Baker, Joe Don	Groesbeck, TX	2/12/1936
Baker, Kathy	Midland, TX	6/8/1950
Baker, Simon	Launceston, Tas., Australia	7/30/1969
Bakula, Scott	St. Louis, MO	10/9/1954
Baldwin, Alec	Massapequa, NY	4/3/1958
Baldwin, Daniel	Massapequa, NY	10/5/1960
Baldwin, Stephen	Massapequa, NY	5/12/1966
Baldwin, William	Massapequa, NY	2/21/1963
Bale, Christian	Pembrokeshire, Wales, UK	1/30/1974
Ballard, Kaye	Cleveland, OH	11/20/1926
Ballas, Mark	Houston, TX	5/24/1986
Bana, Eric	Melbourne, Vic., Australia	8/9/1968
Banderas, Antonio	Málaga, Spain	8/10/1960
Banks, Elizabeth	Pittsfield, MA	2/10/1974
Banks, Jonathan	Washington, DC	1/31/1947
Banks, Tyra	Los Angeles, CA	12/4/1973
Baranski, Christine	Buffalo, NY	5/2/1952
Barbeau, Adrienne	Sacramento, CA	6/11/1945
Bardem, Javier	Las Palmas, Canary Islands, Spain	3/1/1969
Bardot, Brigitte	Paris, France	9/28/1934
Barker, Bob	Darrington, WA	12/12/1923
Barkin, Ellen	Bronx, NY	4/16/1955
Barrie, Barbara	Chicago, IL	5/23/1931
Barrino, Fantasia	High Point, NC	6/30/1984
Barrymore, Drew	Los Angeles, CA	2/22/1975
Bartoli, Cecilia	Rome, Italy	6/4/1966
Barton, Misha	London, England, UK	1/24/1986
Baryshnikov, Mikhail	Riga, Latvia	1/28/1948
Basinger, Kim	Athens, GA	12/8/1953
Bass, Lance	Laurel, MS	5/4/1979
Bassett, Angela	New York, NY	8/16/1958
Bassey, Shirley	Cardiff, Wales, UK	1/8/1937
Batali, Mario	Yakima, WA	9/9/1960
Bateman, Jason	Rye, NY	1/14/1969
Bateman, Justine	Rye, NY	2/19/1966
Bates, Kathy	Memphis, TN	6/28/1948
Batt, Bryan	New Orleans, LA	3/1/1963
Battle, Kathleen	Portsmouth, OH	8/13/1948
Baxter, Meredith	South Pasadena, CA	6/21/1947
Bean, Orson	Burlington, VT	7/22/1928
Bean, Sean	Sheffield, England, UK	4/17/1959
Beatty, Ned	Louisville, KY	7/6/1937
Beatty, Warren	Richmond, VA	3/30/1937
Beauvais, Garcelle	St. Marc, Haiti	11/26/1966
Beck	Los Angeles, CA	7/8/1970
Beck, Jeff	Wallington, Surrey, Eng., UK	6/24/1944
Beckham, Victoria	Hertfordshire, England, UK	4/17/1974
Beckinsale, Kate	London, England, UK	7/26/1973
Bedelia, Bonnie	New York, NY	3/25/1948
Begley, Ed, Jr.	Los Angeles, CA	9/16/1949
Behar, Joy	Brooklyn, NY	10/7/1942
Belafonte, Harry	New York, NY	3/1/1927
Bell, Art	Camp Lejeune, NC	6/17/1945
Bell, Kristen	Huntington Woods, MI	7/18/1980
Bello, Maria	Norristown, PA	4/18/1967
Belmondo, Jean-Paul	Neuilly-sur-Seine, France	4/9/1933
Belushi, Jim	Chicago, IL	6/15/1954
Belzer, Richard	Bridgeport, CT	8/4/1944
Benanti, Laura	Kinnelon, NJ	7/15/1979
Benatar, Pat	Brooklyn, NY	1/10/1953

Name	Birthplace	Birthdate
Benedict, Dirk	Helena, MT	3/1/1945
Benigni, Roberto	Misericordia, Italy	10/27/1952
Bening, Annette	Topeka, KS	5/29/1958
Benjamin, Richard	New York, NY	5/22/1938
Bennett, Alan	Leeds, England, UK	5/9/1934
Bennett, Tony	Astoria, Queens, NY	8/3/1926
Benson, George	Pittsburgh, PA	3/22/1943
Benson, Robby	Dallas, TX	1/21/1956
Berenger, Tom	Chicago, IL	5/31/1950
Bergen, Candice	Beverly Hills, CA	5/9/1946
Bergeron, Tom	Haverhill, MA	5/6/1955
Berman, Shelley	Chicago, IL	2/3/1925
Bernard, Crystal	Garland, TX	9/30/1961
Bernhard, Sandra	Flint, MI	6/6/1955
Bernsen, Corbin	North Hollywood, CA	9/7/1954
Berry, Chuck	St. Louis, MO	10/18/1926
Berry, Halle	Cleveland, OH	8/14/1966
Berry, Ken	Moline, IL	11/3/1933
Bertinelli, Valerie	Wilmington, DE	4/23/1960
Bertolucci, Bernardo	Parma, Italy	3/16/1940
Best, Eve	London, England, UK	7/31/1971
Bettany, Paul	London, England, UK	5/27/1971
Bialik, Mayim	San Diego, CA	12/12/1975
Bichir, Demián	Mexico City, Mexico	8/1/1963
Bieber, Justin	Stratford, ON, Canada	3/1/1994
Biel, Jessica	Ely, MN	3/3/1982
Big Boi	Savannah, GA	2/1/1975
Bigelow, Kathryn	San Carlos, CA	11/27/1951
Biggs, Jason	Pompton Plains, NJ	5/12/1978
Bilson, Rachel	Los Angeles, CA	8/25/1981
Binoche, Juliette	Paris, France	3/9/1964
Birch, Thora	Beverly Hills, CA	3/11/1982
Birney, David	Washington, DC	4/23/1939
Bisset, Jacqueline	Weybridge, England, UK	9/13/1944
Björk (Gudmundsdottir)	Reykjavik, Iceland	11/21/1965
Black, Clint	Long Branch, NJ	2/4/1962
Black, Jack	Santa Monica, CA	4/7/1969
Black, Lewis	Washington, DC	8/30/1948
Blades, Ruben	Panama City, Panama	7/16/1948
Blair, Linda	St. Louis, MO	1/22/1959
Blake, Robert	Nutley, NJ	9/18/1933
Blanchett, Cate	Melbourne, Vic., Australia	5/14/1969
Bledsoe, Tempestt	Chicago, IL	8/1/1973
Bleeth, Yasmine	New York, NY	6/14/1968
Blethyn, Brenda	Ramsgate, Kent, Eng., UK	2/20/1946
Blige, Mary J.	Bronx, NY	1/11/1971
Bloom, Claire	London, England, UK	2/15/1931
Bloom, Orlando	Canterbury, England, UK	1/13/1977
Blyth, Ann	Mt. Kisco, NY	8/16/1928
Bochco, Steven	New York, NY	12/16/1943
Bocelli, Andrea	Lajatico, Italy	9/22/1958
Bogdanovich, Peter	Kingston, NY	7/30/1939
Bogosian, Eric	Woburn, MA	4/24/1953
Bologna, Joseph	Brooklyn, NY	12/30/1934?
Bolton, Michael	New Haven, CT	2/26/1953
Bomer, Matt	Spring, TX	10/11/1977
Bon Jovi, Jon	Sayreville, NJ	3/2/1962
Bonet, Lisa	San Francisco, CA	11/16/1967
Bonham Carter, Helena	London, England, UK	5/26/1966
Bonneville, Hugh	London, England, UK	11/10/1963
Bono	Dublin, Ireland	5/10/1960
Boone, Debby	Hackensack, NJ	9/22/1956
Boone, Pat	Jacksonville, FL	6/1/1934
Boreanaz, David	Buffalo, NY	5/16/1969
Bosco, Philip	Jersey City, NJ	9/26/1930
Bostwick, Barry	San Mateo, CA	2/24/1945
Bosworth, Kate	Los Angeles, CA	1/2/1983
Bottoms, Timothy	Santa Barbara, CA	8/30/1951
Bourdain, Anthony	Leonia, NJ	6/25/1956
Bow Wow	Columbus, OH	3/9/1987
Bowen, Julie	Baltimore, MD	3/3/1970
Bowie, David	London, England, UK	1/8/1947
Bowles, Peter	London, England, UK	10/16/1936
Boxleitner, Bruce	Elgin, IL	5/12/1950
Boy George	Bexleyheath, England, UK	6/14/1961
Boyle, Danny	Manchester, England, UK	10/20/1956
Boyle, Lara Flynn	Davenport, IA	3/24/1970
Boyle, Susan	Blackburn, Scotland, UK	4/1/1961
Bracco, Lorraine	Brooklyn, NY	10/2/1955
Brady, Wayne	Orlando, FL	6/2/1972
Braff, Zach	South Orange, NJ	4/6/1975
Branagh, Kenneth	Belfast, N. Ireland, UK	12/10/1960
Brand, Russell	Grays, Essex, UK	6/4/1975
Brandauer, Klaus Maria	Steiermark, Austria	6/22/1944
Brandy (Norwood)	McComb, MS	2/11/1979
Bratt, Benjamin	San Francisco, CA	12/16/1963
Braugher, Andre	Chicago, IL	7/1/1962
Braxton, Toni	Severn, MD	10/7/1966
Bremner, Ewen	Edinburgh, Scotland, UK	1/23/1972
Brendon, Nicholas	Los Angeles, CA	4/12/1971
Brenneman, Amy	Glastonbury, CT	6/22/1964
Bridges, Beau	Los Angeles, CA	12/9/1941
Bridges, Jeff	Los Angeles, CA	12/4/1949
Brightman, Sarah	Berkhamsted, England, UK	8/14/1960
Brimley, Wilford	Salt Lake City, UT	9/27/1934
Brinkley, Christie	Monroe, MI	2/2/1954
Britton, Connie	Boston, MA	3/6/1967
Broadbent, Jim	Lincolnshire, England, UK	5/24/1949
Broderick, Matthew	New York, NY	3/21/1962
Brody, Adam	San Diego, CA	12/15/1979
Brody, Adrien	New York, NY	4/14/1973
Brolin, James	Los Angeles, CA	7/18/1940
Brolin, Josh	Los Angeles, CA	2/12/1968
Brooks, Albert	Beverly Hills, CA	7/22/1947
Brooks, Garth	Tulsa, OK	2/7/1962
Brooks, James L.	North Bergen, NJ	5/9/1940
Brooks, Mel	Brooklyn, NY	6/28/1926
Brosnan, Pierce	Navan, Co. Meath, Ireland	5/16/1953
Brown, Blair	Washington, DC	4/23/1946
Brown, Bobby	Roxbury, MA	2/5/1969
Brown, Bryan	Panania, NSW, Australia	6/23/1947
Brown, Chris	Tappahannock, VA	5/5/1989
Brown, Foxy	Brooklyn, NY	9/6/1979
Browne, Jackson	Heidelberg, Germany	10/9/1948
Bryan, Luke	Leesburg, GA	7/17/1976
Bryson, Peabo	Greenville, SC	4/13/1951
Bublé, Michael	Burnaby, BC, Canada	9/9/1975
Buckley, Betty	Big Spring, TX	7/3/1947
Buffett, Jimmy	Pascagoula, MS	12/25/1946
Bujold, Genevieve	Montreal, QC, Canada	7/1/1942
Bullock, Sandra	Arlington, VA	7/26/1964
Bumbry, Grace	St. Louis, MO	1/4/1937
Bündchen, Gisele	Horizontina, Brazil	7/20/1980
Burghoff, Gary	Bristol, CT	5/24/1943
Burke, Cheryl	San Francisco, CA	5/3/1984
Burke, Delta	Orlando, FL	7/30/1956
Burnett, Carol	San Antonio, TX	4/26/1933
Burns, Edward	Woodside, Queens, NY	1/29/1968
Burrell, Ty	Grants Pass, OR	8/22/1967
Burstyn, Ellen	Detroit, MI	12/7/1932
Burton, LeVar	Landstuhl, Germany	2/16/1957
Burton, Tim	Burbank, CA	8/25/1958
Buscemi, Steve	Brooklyn, NY	12/13/1957
Busey, Gary	Goose Creek, TX	6/29/1944
Busfield, Timothy	Lansing, MI	6/12/1957
Butler, Brett	Montgomery, AL	1/30/1958
Butler, Dan	Fort Wayne, IN	12/2/1954
Butler, Gerard	Glasgow, Scotland, UK	11/13/1969
Butz, Norbert Leo	St. Louis, MO	1/30/1967
Buzzi, Ruth	Westerly, RI	7/24/1936
Bynes, Amanda	Thousand Oaks, CA	4/3/1986
Byrne, David	Dumbarton, Scotland, UK	5/14/1952
Byrne, Gabriel	Dublin, Ireland	5/12/1950
Byrne, Rose	Sydney, NSW, Australia	7/24/1979
Caan, James	Bronx, NY	3/26/1940
Caballe, Montserrat	Barcelona, Spain	4/12/1933
Cage, Nicolas	Long Beach, CA	1/7/1964
Cain, Dean	Mt. Clemens, MI	7/31/1966
Caine, Michael	London, England, UK	3/14/1933
Caldwell, Zoe	Hawthorn, Vic., Australia	9/14/1933
Callies, Sarah Wayne	LaGrange, IL	6/1/1977
Callow, Simon	London, England, UK	6/15/1949
Cameron, James	Kapuskasing, ON, Canada	8/16/1954
Cameron, Kirk	Panorama City, CA	10/12/1970
Campanella, Joseph	New York, NY	11/21/1927
Campbell, Bruce	Royal Oak, MI	6/22/1958
Campbell, Glen	Delight, AR	4/22/1936
Campbell, Naomi	South London, Eng., UK	5/22/1970
Campbell, Neve	Guelph, ON, Canada	10/3/1973
Campion, Jane	Waikanae, New Zealand	4/30/1954
Cannavale, Bobby	Union City, NJ	5/3/1971
Cannon, Dyan	Tacoma, WA	1/4/1937
Cannon, Nick	San Diego, CA	10/8/1980
Caplan, Lizzy	Los Angeles, CA	6/30/1982
Capshaw, Kate	Ft. Worth, TX	11/3/1953
Cara, Irene	New York, NY	3/18/1959
Cardellini, Linda	Redwood City, CA	6/25/1975
Cardinale, Claudia	Tunis, Tunisia	4/15/1938
Carell, Steve	Concord, MA	8/16/1962
Carey, Drew	Cleveland, OH	5/23/1958
Carey, Mariah	Huntington, NY	3/27/1970
Cariou, Len	St. Boniface, MB, Canada	9/30/1939
Carlton, Vanessa	Milford, PA	8/16/1980
Carlyle, Robert	Glasgow, Scotland, UK	4/14/1961
Carmen, Eric	Cleveland, OH	8/11/1949
Caron, Leslie	Boulogne, France	7/1/1931
Carpenter, John	Carthage, NY	1/16/1948
Carpenter, Mary Chapin	Princeton, NJ	2/21/1958
Carr, Vikki	El Paso, TX	7/19/1941
Carreras, Jose	Barcelona, Spain	12/5/1946
Carrere, Tia	Honolulu, HI	1/2/1967
Carrey, Jim	Newmarket, ON, Canada	1/17/1962
Carroll, Diahann	Bronx, NY	7/17/1935
Carroll, Pat	Shreveport, LA	5/5/1927
Carter, Jack	Brooklyn, NY	6/24/1923
Carter, Jim	Harrogate, Yorkshire, England, UK	8/19/1948
Carter, Lynda	Phoenix, AZ	7/24/1951
Carter, Nick	Jamestown, NY	1/28/1980
Carter, Ron	Ferndale, MI	5/4/1937
Cartwright, Nancy	Kettering, OH	10/25/1957
Caruso, David	Forest Hills, Queens, NY	1/17/1956

Name	Birthplace	Birthdate
Carvey, Dana	Missoula, MT	6/2/1955
Cash, Rosanne	Memphis, TN	5/24/1955
Cassidy, David	New York, NY	4/12/1950
Castellaneta, Dan	Chicago, IL	10/29/1957
Castle-Hughes, Keisha	Donnybrook, WA, Australia	3/24/1990
Cates, Phoebe	New York, NY	7/16/1963
Cattrall, Kim	Liverpool, England, UK	8/21/1956
Cavanagh, Tom	Ottawa, ON, Canada	10/26/1963
Cavett, Dick	Gibbon, NE	11/19/1936
Caviezel, Jim	Mount Vernon, WA	9/26/1968
Cavill, Henry	Jersey, Channel Islands, UK	5/5/1983
Cedric the Entertainer	Jefferson City, MO	4/24/1964
Cera, Michael	Brampton, ON, Canada	6/7/1988
Chalke, Sarah	Ottawa, ON, Canada	8/27/1976
Chamberlain, Richard	Beverly Hills, CA	3/31/1934
Chambers, Justin	Springfield, OH	7/11/1970
Chan, Jackie	Hong Kong	4/7/1954
Chandler, Kyle	Buffalo, NY	9/17/1965
Channing, Carol	Seattle, WA	1/31/1921
Channing, Stockard	New York, NY	2/13/1944
Chaplin, Geraldine	Santa Monica, CA	7/31/1944
Chapman, Tracy	Cleveland, OH	3/30/1964
Chappelle, Dave	Washington, DC	8/24/1973
Charles, Josh	Baltimore, MD	9/15/1971
Charo	Murcia, Spain	1/15/1951?
Chase, Chevy	New York, NY	10/8/1943
Chasez, JC (Joshua)	Washington, DC	8/8/1976
Chastain, Jessica	Sacramento, CA	3/29/1977
Cheadle, Don	Kansas City, MO	11/29/1964
Checker, Chubby	Spring Gulley, SC	10/3/1941
Chen, Julie	New York, NY	1/6/1970
Chenoweth, Kristin	Broken Arrow, OK	7/24/1968
Cher	El Centro, CA	5/20/1946
Chesney, Kenny	Lutrelle, TN	3/26/1968
Chianese, Dominic	Bronx, NY	2/24/1931
Chiba, Sonny	Fukuoka, Kyushu, Japan	1/23/1939
Chiklis, Michael	Lowell, MA	8/30/1963
Chlumsky, Anna	Chicago, IL	12/3/1980
Chmerkovskiy, Maksim	Odessa, Ukraine	1/17/1980
Cho, Margaret	San Francisco, CA	12/5/1968
Chong, Thomas	Edmonton, AB, Canada	5/24/1938
Chow Yun-Fat	Lamma Island, Hong Kong	5/18/1955
Christensen, Hayden	Vancouver, BC, Canada	4/19/1981
Christie, Julie	Chukua, Assam, India	4/14/1941
Christopher, William	Evanston, IL	10/20/1932
Chuck D	Roosevelt, NY	8/1/1960
Church, Charlotte	Llandaff, Cardiff, Wales, UK	2/21/1986
Church, Thomas Haden	El Paso, TX	6/17/1960
Clapp, Gordon	North Conway, NH	9/24/1948
Clapton, Eric	Ripley, Surrey, England, UK	3/30/1945
Clark, Petula	Epson, Surrey, England, UK	11/15/1932
Clark, Roy	Meherrin, VA	4/15/1933
Clarkson, Kelly	Burleson, TX	4/24/1982
Clarkson, Patricia	New Orleans, LA	12/29/1959
Clay, Andrew Dice	Brooklyn, NY	9/29/1957
Cleese, John	Weston-super-Mare, Eng., UK	10/27/1939
Clooney, George	Lexington, KY	5/6/1961
Close, Glenn	Greenwich, CT	3/19/1947
Coen, Ethan	St. Louis Park, MN	9/21/1957
Coen, Joel	St. Louis Park, MN	11/29/1954
Cohen, Andy	St. Louis, MO	6/2/1968
Cohen, Leonard	Montreal, QC, Canada	9/21/1934
Cohen, Sacha Baron	London, England, UK	10/13/1971
Colbert, Stephen	Washington, DC	5/13/1964
Cole, Gary	Park Ridge, IL	9/20/1956
Cole, Natalie	Los Angeles, CA	2/6/1950
Coleman, Dabney	Austin, TX	1/3/1932
Colfer, Chris	Fresno, CA	5/27/1990
Collette, Toni	Blacktown, NSW, Australia	11/1/1972
Collins, Joan	London, England, UK	5/23/1933
Collins, Judy	Seattle, WA	5/1/1939
Collins, Pauline	Exmouth, England, UK	9/3/1940
Collins, Phil	London, England, UK	1/30/1951
Collins, Stephen	Des Moines, IA	10/1/1947
Columbus, Chris	Spangler, PA	9/10/1958?
Colvin, Shawn	Vermillion, SD	1/10/1956
Combs, Sean	New York, NY	11/4/1969
Connelly, Jennifer	Round Top, NY	12/12/1970
Connery, Sean	Edinburgh, Scotland, UK	8/25/1930
Connick, Harry, Jr.	New Orleans, LA	9/11/1967
Connolly, Kevin	Patchogue, NY	3/5/1974
Connors, Mike	Fresno, CA	8/15/1925
Conrad, Robert	Chicago, IL	3/1/1935
Conroy, Frances	Monroe, GA	11/13/1953
Constantine, Michael	Reading, PA	5/22/1927
Conti, Tom	Paisley, Scotland, UK	11/22/1941
Conway, Tim	Willoughby, OH	12/15/1933
Cook, Barbara	Atlanta, GA	10/25/1927
Cook, David	Houston, TX	12/20/1982
Coolidge, Rita	Nashville, TN	5/1/1945
Coolio	Compton, CA	8/1/1963
Cooper, Alice	Detroit, MI	2/4/1948
Cooper, Bradley	Philadelphia, PA	1/5/1975
Cooper, Chris	Kansas City, MO	7/9/1951
Copperfield, David	Metuchen, NJ	9/16/1956
Coppola, Francis Ford	Detroit, MI	4/7/1939
Coppola, Sofia	New York, NY	5/14/1971
Corbett, John	Wheeling, WV	5/9/1961
Corbin, Barry	Lamesa, TX	10/16/1940
Corden, James	Hillingdon, England, UK	8/22/1978
Corea, Chick	Chelsea, MA	6/12/1941
Corgan, Billy	Elk Grove, IL	3/17/1967
Cornell, Chris	Seattle, WA	7/20/1964
Corwin, Jeff	Norwell, MA	7/11/1967
Cosby, Bill	Philadelphia, PA	7/12/1937
Cosgrove, Miranda	Los Angeles, CA	5/14/1993
Costas, Bob	Astoria, Queens, NY	3/22/1952
Costello, Elvis	London, England, UK	8/25/1954
Costner, Kevin	Compton, CA	1/18/1955
Cotillard, Marion	Paris, France	9/30/1975
Cowell, Simon	London, England, UK	10/7/1959
Cox, Brian	Dundee, Scotland, UK	6/1/1946
Cox, Courteney	Birmingham, AL	6/15/1964
Cox, Laverne	Mobile, AL	5/29/1984?
Cox, Ronny	Cloudcroft, NM	7/23/1938
Coyote, Peter	New York, NY	10/10/1941
Craig, Daniel	Chester, England, UK	3/2/1968
Cranston, Bryan	San Fernando Valley, CA	3/7/1956
Crawford, Cindy	DeKalb, IL	2/20/1966
Crawford, Michael	Salisbury, England, UK	1/19/1942
Criss, Darren	San Francisco, CA	2/5/1987
Cromwell, James	Los Angeles, CA	1/27/1940
Crosby, David	Los Angeles, CA	8/14/1941
Cross, Ben	London, England, UK	12/16/1947
Cross, Marcia	Marlborough, MA	3/25/1962
Crouse, Lindsay	New York, NY	5/12/1948
Crow, Sheryl	Kennett, MO	2/11/1962
Crowe, Cameron	Palm Springs, CA	7/13/1957
Crowe, Russell	Wellington, New Zealand	4/7/1964
Crudup, Billy	Manhasset, NY	7/8/1948
Cruise, Tom	Syracuse, NY	7/3/1962
Cruz, Penelope	Madrid, Spain	4/28/1974
Cryer, Jon	New York, NY	4/16/1965
Crystal, Billy	Long Beach, NY	3/14/1948
Cuarón, Alfonso	Mexico City, Mexico	11/28/1961
Culkin, Macaulay	New York, NY	8/26/1980
Cullum, John	Knoxville, TN	3/2/1930
Cumberbatch, Benedict	London, England, UK	7/19/1976
Cumming, Alan	Aberfeldy, Perthshire, Scotland, UK	1/27/1965
Cuoco, Kaley	Camarillo, CA	11/30/1985
Curry, Tim	Grappenhall, Cheshire, England, UK	4/19/1946
Curtin, Jane	Cambridge, MA	9/6/1947
Curtis, Jamie Lee	Los Angeles, CA	11/22/1958
Cusack, Joan	New York, NY	10/11/1962
Cusack, John	Evanston, IL	6/28/1966
Cyrus, Billy Ray	Flatwoods, KY	8/25/1961
Cyrus, Miley	Nashville, TN	11/23/1992
Dafoe, Willem	Appleton, WI	7/22/1955
Dahl, Arlene	Minneapolis, MN	8/11/1925
Dale, Jim	Rothwell, England, UK	8/15/1935
Dalton, Timothy	Colwyn Bay, Wales, UK	3/21/1946
Daltrey, Roger	London, England, UK	3/1/1944
Daly, Carson	Santa Monica, CA	6/22/1973
Daly, Timothy	New York, NY	3/1/1956
Daly, Tyne	Madison, WI	2/21/1946
Damon, Matt	Cambridge, MA	10/8/1970
Damone, Vic	Brooklyn, NY	6/12/1928
Dane, Eric	San Francisco, CA	11/9/1972
Danes, Claire	New York, NY	4/12/1979
D'Angelo	Richmond, VA	2/11/1974
D'Angelo, Beverly	Columbus, OH	11/15/1954
Daniels, Anthony	Salisbury, England, UK	2/21/1946
Daniels, Charlie	Wilmington, NC	10/28/1936
Daniels, Jeff	Athens, GA	2/19/1955
Daniels, William	Brooklyn, NY	3/31/1927
Danner, Blythe	Rosemont, PA	2/3/1943
Danson, Ted	San Diego, CA	12/29/1947
Danza, Tony	Brooklyn, NY	4/21/1951
Darby, Kim	Hollywood, CA	7/8/1948
Daughtry, Chris	Roanoke Rapids, NC	12/26/1979
David, Larry	Brooklyn, NY	7/2/1947
Davidson, John	Pittsburgh, PA	12/13/1941
Davis, Clifton	Chicago, IL	10/4/1945
Davis, Geena	Wareham, MA	1/21/1956
Davis, Hope	Englewood, NJ	3/23/1964
Davis, Judy	Perth, WA, Australia	4/23/1955
Davis, Kristin	Boulder, CO	2/24/1965
Davis, Mac	Lubbock, TX	1/21/1942
Davis, Viola	Saint Matthews, SC	8/11/1965
Dawber, Pam	Farmington Hills, MI	10/18/1951
Dawson, Rosario	New York, NY	5/9/1979
Day, Doris	Cincinnati, OH	4/3/1924
Day-Lewis, Daniel	London, England, UK	4/29/1957
De Havilland, Olivia	Tokyo, Japan	7/1/1916
De Mornay, Rebecca	Santa Rosa, CA	8/29/1962
De Niro, Robert	New York, NY	8/17/1943
De Rossi, Portia	Melbourne, Vic., Australia	1/31/1973
DeGeneres, Ellen	Metairie, LA	1/26/1958
DeGraw, Gavin	Middletown, NY	2/4/1977
DeHaven, Gloria	Los Angeles, CA	7/23/1925

Name	Birthplace	Birthdate
Del Toro, Benicio	Santurce, Puerto Rico	2/19/1967
Delaney, Kim	Philadelphia, PA	11/29/1961
Delany, Dana	New York, NY	3/13/1956
Delon, Alain	Sceaux, France	11/8/1935
Demme, Jonathan	Baldwin, NY	2/22/1944
Dempsey, Patrick	Lewiston, ME	1/13/1966
Dench, Judi	York, England, UK	12/9/1934
Deneuve, Catherine	Paris, France	10/22/1943
Dennehy, Brian	Bridgeport, CT	7/9/1938
DePalma, Brian	Newark, NJ	9/11/1940
Depardieu, Gerard	Chateauroux, France	12/27/1948
Depp, Johnny	Owensboro, KY	6/9/1963
Derek, Bo	Long Beach, CA	11/20/1956
Dern, Bruce	Winnetka, IL	6/4/1936
Dern, Laura	Santa Monica, CA	2/10/1967
Deschanel, Zooey	Los Angeles, CA	1/17/1980
Devine, Loretta	Houston, TX	8/21/1949
DeVito, Danny	Neptune, NJ	11/17/1944
DeWitt, Joyce	Wheeling, WV	4/23/1949
Dey, Susan	Pekin, IL	12/10/1952
Diamond, Neil	Brooklyn, NY	1/24/1941
Diaz, Cameron	San Diego, CA	8/30/1972
DiCaprio, Leonardo	Hollywood, CA	11/11/1974
Dick, Andy	Charleston, SC	12/21/1965
Dickinson, Angie	Kulm, ND	9/30/1931
Diesel, Vin	New York, NY	7/18/1967
Diggs, Taye	Newark, NJ	1/2/1972
Dillahunt, Garret	Castro Valley, CA	11/24/1964
Dillman, Bradford	San Francisco, CA	4/14/1930
Dillon, Kevin	Mamaroneck, NY	8/19/1965
Dillon, Matt	New Rochelle, NY	2/18/1964
Dinklage, Peter	Morristown, NJ	6/11/1969
DioGuardi, Kara	Scarsdale, NY	12/9/1970
Dion, Celine	Charlemagne, QC, Canada	3/30/1968
Djalili, Omid	London, England, UK	9/30/1965
Dobrev, Nina	Sofia, Bulgaria	1/9/1989
Dobson, Kevin	Jackson Heights, Queens, NY	3/18/1943
Dockery, Michelle	Barking, Essex, England, UK	12/15/1981
Doherty, Shannen	Memphis, TN	4/12/1971
Dolenz, Mickey	Los Angeles, CA	3/8/1945
Domingo, Placido	Madrid, Spain	1/21/1941
Domino, Fats	New Orleans, LA	2/26/1928
Donahue, Phil	Cleveland, OH	12/21/1935
Donen, Stanley	Columbia, SC	4/13/1924
D'Onofrio, Vincent	Brooklyn, NY	6/30/1959
Donovan (Leitch)	Glasgow, Scotland, UK	5/10/1946
Donovan, Tate	New York, NY	9/25/1963
Dorn, Michael	Luling, TX	12/9/1952
Dotrice, Roy	Guernsey, Channel Isls., UK	5/26/1923
Douglas, Kirk	Amsterdam, NY	12/9/1916
Douglas, Michael	New Brunswick, NJ	9/25/1944
Dourdan, Gary	Philadelphia, PA	12/11/1966
Dovolani, Tony	Pristina, Kosovo	7/17/1973
Dow, Tony	Hollywood, CA	4/13/1945
Down, Lesley-Anne	London, England, UK	3/17/1954
Downey, Robert, Jr.	New York, NY	4/4/1965
Downey, Roma	Derry, N. Ireland, UK	5/6/1960
Downs, Hugh	Akron, OH	2/14/1921
Drake	Toronto, ON, Canada	10/24/1986
Drescher, Fran	Flushing, Queens, NY	9/30/1957
Dreyfuss, Richard	Brooklyn, NY	10/29/1947
Driver, Adam	San Bernardino, CA	11/19/1983
Driver, Minnie	London, England, UK	1/31/1970
Dryer, Fred	Hawthorne, CA	7/6/1946
Duchovny, David	New York, NY	8/7/1960
Duff, Hilary	Houston, TX	9/28/1987
Duffy (Aimee Anne)	Bangor, Gwynedd, Wales, UK	6/23/1984
Duffy, Julia	Minneapolis, MN	6/27/1951
Duffy, Patrick	Townsend, MT	3/17/1949
Duhamel, Josh	Minot, ND	11/14/1972
Dujardin, Jean	Rueil-Malmaison, France	6/19/1972
Dukakis, Olympia	Lowell, MA	6/20/1931
Duke, Patty	Elmhurst, Queens, NY	12/14/1946
Dullea, Keir	Cleveland, OH	5/30/1936
Dunaway, Faye	Bascom, FL	1/14/1941
Duncan, Lindsay	Edinburgh, Scotland, UK	11/7/1950
Duncan, Sandy	Henderson, TX	2/20/1946
Dunham, Lena	New York, NY	5/13/1986
Dunne, Griffin	New York, NY	6/8/1955
Dunst, Kirsten	Point Pleasant, NJ	4/30/1982
Dussault, Nancy	Pensacola, FL	6/30/1936
Dutton, Charles S.	Baltimore, MD	1/30/1951
Duvall, Robert	San Diego, CA	1/5/1931
Duvall, Shelley	Houston, TX	7/7/1949
Dylan, Bob	Duluth, MN	5/24/1941
Dylan, Jakob	New York, NY	12/9/1969
Dzundza, George	Rosenheim, Germany	7/19/1945
Eads, George	Fort Worth, TX	3/1/1967
Easton, Sheena	Bellshill, Scotland, UK	4/27/1959
Eastwood, Clint	San Francisco, CA	5/31/1930
Ebersole, Christine	Chicago, IL	2/21/1953
Eckhart, Aaron	Cupertino, CA	3/12/1968
Eden, Barbara	Tucson, AZ	8/23/1931

Name	Birthplace	Birthdate
Edwards, Anthony	Santa Barbara, CA	7/19/1962
Efron, Zac	San Luis Obispo, CA	10/18/1987
Ehle, Jennifer	Winston-Salem, NC	12/29/1969
Eikenberry, Jill	New Haven, CT	1/21/1947
Eisenberg, Jesse	Bayside, NY	10/5/1983
Ejiofor, Chiwetel	London, England, UK	7/10/1974
Ekland, Britt	Stockholm, Sweden	10/6/1942
Elba, Idris	London, England, UK	9/6/1972
Electra, Carmen	Cincinnati, OH	4/20/1972
Elfman, Jenna	Los Angeles, CA	9/30/1971
Elizondo, Hector	New York, NY	12/22/1936
Elliott, Bob	Boston, MA	3/26/1923
Elliott, Chris	New York, NY	5/31/1960
Elliott, Missy	Portsmouth, VA	7/1/1971
Elliott, Sam	Sacramento, CA	8/9/1944
Elvira	Manhattan, KS	9/17/1951
Emerson, Michael	Cedar Rapids, IA	9/7/1954
Eminem	St. Joseph, MO	10/17/1972
Enberg, Dick	Mt. Clemens, MI	1/9/1935
Englund, Robert	Glendale, CA	6/6/1949
Enya	Gweedore, Ireland	5/17/1961
Epps, Omar	Brooklyn, NY	7/23/1973
Estefan, Gloria	Havana, Cuba	9/1/1957
Estevez, Emilio	New York, NY	5/12/1962
Estrada, Erik	New York, NY	3/16/1949
Etheridge, Melissa	Leavenworth, KS	5/29/1961
Evans, Chris	Framingham, MA	6/13/1981
Evans, Linda	Hartford, CT	11/18/1942
Evans, Robert	New York, NY	6/29/1930
Everett, Rupert	Norfolk, England, UK	5/29/1959
Everly, Don	Brownie, KY	2/1/1937
Evigan, Greg	South Amboy, NJ	10/14/1953
Fabares, Shelley	Santa Monica, CA	1/19/1944
Fabian	Philadelphia, PA	2/6/1943
Fabio (Lanzoni)	Milan, Italy	3/15/1959
Fabolous	Brooklyn, NY	11/18/1977
Facinelli, Peter	Queens, NY	11/26/1973
Fairchild, Morgan	Dallas, TX	2/3/1950
Faison, Donald	New York, NY	6/22/1974
Falana, Lola	Philadelphia, PA	9/11/1942
Falco, Edie	Brooklyn, NY	7/5/1963
Fallon, Jimmy	Brooklyn, NY	9/19/1974
Fanning, Dakota	Conyers, GA	2/23/1994
Fargo, Donna	Mt. Airy, NC	11/10/1949
Farmiga, Vera	Clifton, NJ	8/6/1973
Farr, Jamie	Toledo, OH	7/1/1934
Farrell, Colin	Dublin, Ireland	5/31/1976
Farrell, Mike	St. Paul, MN	2/6/1939
Farrell, Perry	Bayside, Queens, NY	3/29/1959
Farrell, Suzanne	Cincinnati, OH	8/16/1945?
Farrelly, Bobby	Cumberland, RI	6/17/1958
Farrelly, Peter	Phoenixville, PA	12/17/1956
Farrow, Mia	Los Angeles, CA	2/9/1945
Fassbender, Michael	Heidelberg, Germany	4/2/1977
Fatone, Joey	Brooklyn, NY	1/28/1977
Feinstein, Michael	Columbus, OH	9/7/1956
Feldon, Barbara	Bethel Park, PA	3/12/1933
Feldshuh, Tovah	New York, NY	12/27/1952
Feliciano, Jose	Lares, Puerto Rico	9/10/1945
Fenn, Sherilyn	Detroit, MI	2/1/1965
Fergie	Hacienda Heights, CA	3/27/1975
Ferguson, Craig	Glasgow, Scotland, UK	5/17/1962
Ferguson, Jesse Tyler	Missoula, MT	10/22/1975
Ferrara, Jerry	Brooklyn, NY	11/29/1979
Ferrell, Conchata	Charleston, WV	3/28/1943
Ferrell, Will	Irvine, CA	7/16/1967
Ferrera, America	Los Angeles, CA	4/18/1984
Feuerstein, Mark	New York, NY	6/8/1971
Fey, Tina	Upper Darby, PA	5/18/1970
Field, Sally	Pasadena, CA	11/6/1946
Fiennes, Joseph	Salisbury, England, UK	5/27/1970
Fiennes, Ralph	Suffolk, England, UK	12/22/1962
Fierstein, Harvey	Brooklyn, NY	6/6/1954
50 Cent	Jamaica, Queens, NY	7/6/1976
Fillion, Nathan	Edmonton, AB, Canada	3/27/1971
Fincher, David	Denver, CO	8/28/1962
Finney, Albert	Salford, England, UK	5/9/1936
Fiorentino, Linda	Philadelphia, PA	3/9/1960
Firth, Colin	Grayshott, England, UK	9/10/1960
Firth, Peter	Bradford, Yorkshire, Eng., UK	10/27/1953
Fischer, Jenna	Ft. Wayne, IN	3/7/1974
Fishburne, Laurence	Augusta, GA	7/30/1961
Fisher, Carrie	Beverly Hills, CA	10/21/1956
Flack, Roberta	Black Mountain, NC	2/10/1939
Flanagan, Fionnula	Dublin, Ireland	12/10/1941
Flavor Flav	Roosevelt, NY	3/16/1959
Fleetwood, Mick	Redruth, Cornwall, Eng., UK	6/24/1942
Fleming, Rhonda	Hollywood, CA	8/10/1923
Fletcher, Louise	Birmingham, AL	7/22/1934
Flockhart, Calista	Freeport, IL	11/11/1964
Florek, Dann	Flat Rock, MI	5/1/1950
Fogerty, John	Berkeley, CA	5/28/1945
Foley, Dave	Etobicoke, ON, Canada	1/4/1963
Fonda, Bridget	Los Angeles, CA	1/27/1964
Fonda, Jane	New York, NY	12/21/1937
Fonda, Peter	New York, NY	2/23/1940

Name	Birthplace	Birthdate
Ford, Faith	Alexandria, LA	9/14/1964
Ford, Harrison	Chicago, IL	7/13/1942
Forman, Milos	Caslav, Czechoslovakia	2/18/1932
Forte, Will	Alameda Co., CA	6/17/1970
Foster, Jodie	Los Angeles, CA	11/19/1962
Foster, Sutton	Statesboro, GA	3/18/1975
Fox, James	London, England, UK	5/19/1939
Fox, Jorja	New York, NY	7/7/1968
Fox, Matthew	Abington, PA	7/14/1966
Fox, Megan	Rockwood, TN	5/16/1986
Fox, Michael J.	Edmonton, AB, Canada	6/9/1961
Fox, Vivica A.	South Bend, IN	7/30/1964
Foxworth, Robert	Houston, TX	11/1/1941
Foxworthy, Jeff	Atlanta, GA	9/6/1958
Foxx, Jamie	Terrell, TX	12/13/1967
Frampton, Peter	Kent, England, UK	4/22/1950
Francis, Connie	Newark, NJ	12/12/1938
Franco, Dave	Palo Alto, CA	6/12/1985
Franco, James	Palo Alto, CA	4/19/1978
Franken, Al	New York, NY	5/21/1951
Franklin, Aretha	Memphis, TN	3/25/1942
Franz, Dennis	Maywood, IL	10/28/1944
Fraser, Brendan	Indianapolis, IN	12/3/1968
Freeman, Martin	Aldershot, Hampshire, Eng., UK	9/8/1971
Freeman, Morgan	Memphis, TN	6/1/1937
French, Dawn	Holyhead, Wales, UK	10/11/1957
Fricker, Brenda	Dublin, Ireland	2/17/1945
Friedkin, William	Chicago, IL	8/29/1939
Froggatt, Joanne	Littlebeck, North Yorkshire, England, UK	8/21/1980
Fry, Stephen	London, England, UK	8/24/1957
Fuentes, Daisy	Havana, Cuba	11/17/1966
Fuller, Robert	Troy, NY	7/29/1934
Furlong, Edward	Pasadena, CA	8/2/1977
Furtado, Nelly	Victoria, BC, Canada	12/2/1978
Gabor, Zsa Zsa	Budapest, Hungary	2/6/1917
Gabriel, Peter	Surrey, England, UK	2/13/1950
Gaines, Boyd	Atlanta, GA	5/11/1953
Galecki, Johnny	Bree, Belgium	4/30/1975
Galifianakis, Zach	Wilkesboro, NC	10/1/1969
Gallagher, Peter	Armonk, NY	8/19/1955
Gallo, Vincent	Buffalo, NY	4/11/1961
Galway, James	Belfast, N. Ireland, UK	12/8/1939
Garagiola, Joe	St. Louis, MO	2/12/1926
Garber, Victor	London, ON, Canada	3/16/1949
Garcia, Andy	Havana, Cuba	4/12/1956
Garfield, Andrew	Los Angeles, CA	8/20/1983
Garfunkel, Art	Forest Hills, Queens, NY	11/5/1941
Garlin, Jeff	Chicago, IL	6/5/1962
Garner, Jennifer	Houston, TX	4/17/1972
Garofalo, Janeane	Newton, NJ	9/28/1964
Garr, Teri	Lakewood, OH	12/11/1944
Garrett, Brad	Woodland Hills, CA	4/14/1960
Garth, Jennie	Urbana, IL	4/3/1972
Gatlin, Larry	Seminole, TX	5/2/1948
Gavin, John	Los Angeles, CA	4/8/1931
Gayle, Crystal	Paintsville, KY	1/9/1951
Gaynor, Mitzi	Chicago, IL	9/4/1931
Geary, Anthony	Coalville, UT	5/29/1947
Gedda, Nicolai	Stockholm, Sweden	7/11/1925
Gellar, Sarah Michelle	New York, NY	4/14/1977
Gere, Richard	Philadelphia, PA	8/31/1949
Gervais, Ricky	Reading, England, UK	6/25/1961
Giannini, Giancarlo	La Spezia, Italy	8/1/1942
Gibb, Barry	Isle of Man, England, UK	9/1/1946
Gibbons, Leeza	Hartsville, SC	3/26/1957
Gibbs, Marla	Chicago, IL	6/14/1931
Gibson, Debbie	Brooklyn, NY	8/31/1970
Gibson, Mel	Peekskill, NY	1/3/1956
Gibson, Thomas	Charleston, SC	7/3/1962
Gifford, Kathie Lee	Neuilly-sur-Seine, France	8/16/1953
Gilbert, Melissa	Los Angeles, CA	5/8/1964
Gilbert, Sara	Santa Monica, CA	1/29/1975
Gilberto, Astrud	Salvador, Brazil	3/30/1940
Gill, Vince	Norman, OK	4/12/1957
Gillette, Anita	Baltimore, MD	8/16/1936
Gilley, Mickey	Natchez, MS	3/9/1936
Gilliam, Terry	Minneapolis, MN	11/22/1940
Gilmour, David	Cambridge, England, UK	3/6/1946
Gilpin, Peri	Waco, TX	5/27/1961
Gilsig, Jessalyn	Montreal, QC, Canada	11/30/1971
Givens, Robin	New York, NY	11/27/1964
Glaser, Paul Michael	Cambridge, MA	3/25/1943
Gleeson, Brendan	Belfast, N. Ireland, UK	11/29/1955?
Glenn, Scott	Pittsburgh, PA	1/26/1941
Gless, Sharon	Los Angeles, CA	5/31/1943
Glover, Crispin	New York, NY	4/20/1964
Glover, Danny	San Francisco, CA	7/22/1947
Glover, John	Kingston, NY	8/7/1944
Glover, Julian	London, England, UK	3/27/1935
Glover, Savion	Newark, NJ	11/19/1973
Godard, Jean-Luc	Paris, France	12/3/1930
Goldberg, Whoopi	New York, NY	11/13/1955
Goldblum, Jeff	Pittsburgh, PA	10/22/1952
Goldthwait, Bobcat	Syracuse, NY	5/26/1962

Name	Birthplace	Birthdate
Goldwyn, Tony	Los Angeles, CA	5/20/1960
Gomez, Selena	Grand Prairie, TX	7/22/1992
Gooding, Cuba, Jr.	Bronx, NY	1/2/1968
Goodman, John	Affton, MO	6/20/1952
Goodman, Len	London, England, UK	4/25/1944
Gordon-Levitt, Joseph	Los Angeles, CA	2/17/1981
Gosling, Ryan	London, ON, Canada	11/12/1980
Gosselaar, Mark-Paul	Panorama City, CA	3/1/1974
Gossett, Louis, Jr.	Brooklyn, NY	5/27/1936
Gould, Elliott	Brooklyn, NY	8/29/1938
Grace, Topher	New York, NY	7/12/1978
Graham, Heather	Milwaukee, WI	1/29/1970
Grammer, Kelsey	St. Thomas, U.S. Virgin Isls.	2/21/1955
Grant, Amy	Augusta, GA	11/25/1960
Grant, Hugh	London, England, UK	9/9/1960
Grant, Lee	New York, NY	10/31/1927?
Gray, Linda	Santa Monica, CA	9/12/1940
Gray, Macy	Canton, OH	9/6/1969
Green, Al	Forrest City, AR	4/13/1946
Green, Cee Lo	Atlanta, GA	5/30/1974
Green, Seth	Philadelphia, PA	2/8/1974
Green, Tom	Pembroke, ON, Canada	7/30/1971
Greene, Shecky	Chicago, IL	4/8/1926
Greenfield, Max	Dobbs Ferry, NY	9/4/1980
Greenwood, Bruce	Noranda, QC, Canada	8/12/1956
Gregory, Cynthia	Los Angeles, CA	7/8/1946
Gregory, Dick	St. Louis, MO	10/12/1932
Grenier, Adrian	Santa Fe, NM	7/10/1976
Grey, Jennifer	New York, NY	3/26/1960
Grey, Joel	Cleveland, OH	4/11/1932
Grier, David Alan	Detroit, MI	6/30/1955
Grier, Pam	Winston-Salem, NC	5/26/1949
Gries, Jon	Glendale, CA	6/17/1957
Griffin, Kathy	Oak Park, IL	11/4/1961
Griffith, Melanie	New York, NY	8/9/1957
Griffiths, Rachel	Melbourne, Vic., Australia	12/18/1968
Grimes, Tammy	Lynn, MA	1/30/1934
Grint, Rupert	Walton-at-Stone, Hertfordshire, Eng., UK	8/24/1988
Groban, Josh	Los Angeles, CA	2/27/1981
Grodin, Charles	Pittsburgh, PA	4/21/1935
Groff, Jonathan	Lancaster, PA	3/26/1985
Grohl, David	Warren, OH	1/14/1969
Gross, Michael	Chicago, IL	6/21/1947
Guest, Christopher	New York, NY	2/5/1948
Guillaume, Robert	St. Louis, MO	11/30/1927
Gumbel, Greg	New Orleans, LA	5/3/1946
Gunn, Anna	Santa Fe, NM	8/11/1968
Gunn, Tim	Washington, DC	7/29/1953
Guthrie, Arlo	Brooklyn, NY	7/10/1947
Guttenberg, Steve	Brooklyn, NY	8/24/1958
Guy, Buddy	Lettsworth, LA	7/30/1936
Guy, Jasmine	Boston, MA	3/10/1964
Gyllenhaal, Jake	Los Angeles, CA	12/19/1980
Gyllenhaal, Maggie	New York, NY	11/16/1977
Hackman, Gene	San Bernardino, CA	1/30/1930
Hader, Bill	Tulsa, OK	6/7/1978
Hagerty, Julie	Cincinnati, OH	6/15/1955
Haggard, Merle	Bakersfield, CA	4/6/1937
Haid, Charles	San Francisco, CA	6/2/1943
Hale, Barbara	DeKalb, IL	4/18/1922
Hale, Tony	West Point, NY	9/30/1970
Hall, Anthony Michael	West Roxbury, MA	4/14/1968
Hall, Arsenio	Cleveland, OH	2/12/1955
Hall, Daryl	Pottstown, PA	10/11/1946
Hall, Deidre	Milwaukee, WI	10/31/1947
Hall, Michael C.	Raleigh, NC	2/1/1971
Hall, Monty	Winnipeg, MB, Canada	8/25/1921
Hall, Tom T.	Olive Hill, KY	5/25/1936
Halliwell, Geri	Watford, England, UK	8/6/1972
Hamill, Mark	Oakland, CA	9/25/1951
Hamilton, George	Memphis, TN	8/12/1939
Hamilton, Linda	Salisbury, MD	9/26/1956
Hamlin, Harry	Pasadena, CA	10/30/1951
Hamm, Jon	St. Louis, MO	3/10/1971
Hammer, Armie	Los Angeles, CA	8/28/1986
Hammer (M.C.)	Oakland, CA	3/30/1963
Hammond, Darrell	Melbourne, FL	10/8/1955
Hancock, Herbie	Chicago, IL	4/12/1940
Handler, Chelsea	Livingston, NJ	2/25/1975
Hanks, Colin	Sacramento, CA	11/24/1977
Hanks, Tom	Concord, CA	7/9/1956
Hannah, Daryl	Chicago, IL	12/3/1960
Hannigan, Alyson	Washington, DC	3/24/1974
Hanson, Curtis	Reno, NV	3/24/1945
Hanson, Isaac	Tulsa, OK	11/17/1980
Hanson, Taylor	Tulsa, OK	3/14/1983
Hanson, Zac	Tulsa, OK	10/22/1985
Harden, Marcia Gay	La Jolla, CA	8/14/1959
Harewood, Dorian	Dayton, OH	8/6/1950
Hargitay, Mariska	Los Angeles, CA	1/23/1964
Harmon, Angie	Highland Park, TX	8/10/1972
Harmon, Mark	Burbank, CA	9/2/1951
Harper, Ben	Claremont, CA	10/28/1969
Harper, Tess	Mammoth Spring, AR	8/15/1950
Harper, Valerie	Suffern, NY	8/22/1939

Name	Birthplace	Birthdate
Harrelson, Woody	Midland, TX	7/23/1961
Harrington, Pat	New York, NY	8/13/1929
Harris, Barbara	Evanston, IL	7/25/1935
Harris, Ed	Tenafly, NJ	11/28/1950
Harris, Emmylou	Birmingham, AL	4/2/1947
Harris, Neil Patrick	Albuquerque, NM	6/15/1973
Harris, Rosemary	Ashby, England, UK	9/19/1927?
Harris, Steve	Chicago, IL	12/3/1965
Harrison, Gregory	Avalon, CA	5/31/1950
Harry, Deborah	Miami, FL	7/1/1945
Hart, Kevin	Philadelphia, PA	7/3/1980
Hart, Mary	Madison, SD	11/8/1950
Hart, Melissa Joan	Smithtown, NY	4/18/1976
Hartley, Mariette	New York, NY	6/21/1940
Hartman, David	Pawtucket, RI	5/19/1935
Hartman Black, Lisa	Houston, TX	6/1/1956
Hartnett, Josh	San Francisco, CA	7/21/1978
Harvey, P. J.	Yeovil, Somerset, Eng., UK	10/9/1969
Harvey, Steve	Welch, WV	11/23/1956
Hasselbeck, Elisabeth	Cranston, RI	5/28/1977
Hasselhoff, David	Baltimore, MD	7/17/1952
Hatcher, Teri	Sunnyvale, CA	12/8/1964
Hatfield, Juliana	Wiscasset, ME	7/27/1967
Hathaway, Anne	Brooklyn, NY	11/12/1982
Hauer, Rutger	Breukelen, Netherlands	1/23/1944
Hawke, Ethan	Austin, TX	11/6/1970
Hawn, Goldie	Washington, DC	11/21/1945
Hayek, Salma	Coatzacoalcos, Mexico	9/2/1966
Hayes, Hunter	Breaux Bridge, LA	9/9/1991
Hayes, Sean	Glen Ellyn, IL	6/26/1970
Haynes, Roy	Roxbury, MA	3/13/1925
Hays, Robert	Bethesda, MD	7/24/1947
Haysbert, Dennis	San Mateo, CA	6/2/1955
Head, Anthony	Camden Town, Eng., UK	2/20/1954
Heard, John	Washington, DC	3/7/1945
Hearn, George	St. Louis, MO	6/18/1934
Heaton, Patricia	Bay Village, OH	3/4/1958
Heche, Anne	Aurora, OH	5/25/1969
Heder, Jon	Fort Collins, CO	10/26/1977
Hedren, Tippi	New Ulm, MN	1/19/1930?
Heigl, Katherine	Washington, DC	11/24/1978
Helberg, Simon	Los Angeles, CA	12/9/1980
Helfgott, David	Melbourne, Vic., Australia	5/19/1947
Helgenberger, Marg	Fremont, NE	11/16/1958
Helmond, Katherine	Galveston, TX	7/5/1928?
Helms, Ed	Atlanta, GA	1/24/1974
Hemingway, Mariel	Mill Valley, CA	11/22/1961
Hemsworth, Chris	Melbourne, Vic., Australia	8/11/1983
Hemsworth, Liam	Melbourne, Vic., Australia	1/13/1990
Henderson, Florence	Dale, IN	2/14/1934
Hendricks, Christina	Knoxville, TN	5/3/1975
Henley, Don	Gilmer, TX	7/22/1947
Henner, Marilu	Chicago, IL	4/6/1952
Hennessy, Jill	Edmonton, AB, Canada	11/25/1968
Henry, Buck	New York, NY	12/9/1930
Henson, Taraji P.	Washington, DC	9/11/1970
Herman, Pee-Wee	Peekskill, NY	8/27/1952
Hershey, Barbara	Hollywood, CA	2/5/1948
Hesseman, Howard	Lebanon, OR	2/27/1940
Hetfield, James	Downey, CA	8/3/1963
Hewitt, Jennifer Love	Waco, TX	2/21/1979
Hicks, Catherine	Scottsdale, AZ	8/6/1951
Higgins, John Michael	Boston, MA	2/12/1963
Hightower, Chelsie	Las Vegas, NV	7/21/1989
Hill, Dulé	Orange, NJ	5/3/1975
Hill, Faith	Jackson, MS	9/21/1967
Hill, Jonah	Los Angeles, CA	12/20/1983
Hill, Lauryn	South Orange, NJ	5/26/1975
Hill, Steven	Seattle, WA	2/24/1922
Hillerman, John	Denison, TX	12/20/1932
Hilton, Paris	New York, NY	2/17/1981
Hines, Cheryl	Miami Beach, FL	9/21/1965
Hirsch, Emile	Palms, CA	3/13/1985
Hirsch, Judd	Bronx, NY	3/15/1935
Hodgman, John	Cambridge, MA	6/3/1971
Hoffman, Dustin	Los Angeles, CA	8/8/1937
Hogan, Hulk	Augusta, GA	8/11/1953
Hogan, Paul	Lightning Ridge, NSW, Australia	10/8/1939
Holbrook, Hal	Cleveland, OH	2/17/1925
Holliday, Polly	Jasper, AL	7/2/1937
Holliman, Earl	Delhi, LA	9/11/1928
Holloway, Josh	San Jose, CA	7/20/1969
Holly, Lauren	Bristol, PA	10/28/1963
Holm, Ian	Ilford, England, UK	9/12/1931
Holmes, Katie	Toledo, OH	12/18/1978
Hopkins, Anthony	Port Talbot, South Wales, UK	12/31/1937
Hopkins, Bo	Greenville, SC	2/2/1942
Hopkins, Telma	Louisville, KY	10/28/1948
Horne, Marilyn	Bradford, PA	1/16/1934
Hornsby, Bruce	Williamsburg, VA	11/23/1954
Horsley, Lee	Muleshoe, TX	5/15/1955
Hough, Derek	Salt Lake City, UT	5/17/1985
Hough, Julianne	Salt Lake City, UT	7/20/1988
Hounsou, Djimon	Cotonou, Benin	4/24/1964
Howard, Clint	Burbank, CA	4/20/1959
Howard, Ken	El Centro, CA	3/28/1944
Howard, Ron	Duncan, OK	3/1/1954
Howard, Terrence	Chicago, IL	3/11/1969
Howell, C. Thomas	Van Nuys, CA	12/7/1966
Howes, Sally Ann	St. John's Wood, London, England, UK	7/20/1930
Hudgens, Vanessa	Salinas, CA	12/14/1988
Hudson, Jennifer	Chicago, IL	9/12/1981
Hudson, Kate	Los Angeles, CA	4/19/1979
Huffman, Felicity	Bedford, NY	12/9/1962
Hughley, D. L.	Los Angeles, CA	3/6/1963
Hulce, Tom	Detroit, MI	12/6/1953
Humperdinck, Engelbert	Madras, India	5/2/1936
Humphries, Barry	Melbourne, Vic., Australia	2/17/1934
Hunt, Bonnie	Chicago, IL	9/22/1964
Hunt, Helen	Culver City, CA	6/15/1963
Hunt, Linda	Morristown, NJ	4/2/1945
Hunter, Holly	Conyers, GA	3/20/1958
Hunter, Tab	New York, NY	7/11/1931
Hurley, Elizabeth	Hampshire, England, UK	6/10/1965
Hurt, John	Chesterfield, England, UK	1/22/1940
Hurt, Mary Beth	Marshalltown, IA	9/26/1948
Hurt, William	Washington, DC	3/20/1950
Huston, Anjelica	Santa Monica, CA	7/8/1951
Hutcherson, Josh	Union, KY	10/12/1992
Hutton, Lauren	Charleston, SC	11/17/1943
Hutton, Timothy	Malibu, CA	8/16/1960
Hyman, Earle	Rocky Mount, NC	10/11/1926
Ian, Janis	Bronx, NY	4/7/1951
Ice Cube	Los Angeles, CA	6/15/1969
Ice-T	Newark, NJ	2/16/1958
Idle, Eric	S. Shields, England, UK	3/29/1943
Idol, Billy	Middlesex, England, UK	11/30/1955
Iglesias, Enrique	Madrid, Spain	5/8/1975
Iglesias, Julio	Madrid, Spain	9/23/1943
Iler, Robert	New York, NY	3/2/1985
Iman	Mogadishu, Somalia	7/25/1955
Imbruglia, Natalie	Sydney, NSW, Australia	2/4/1975
Imperioli, Michael	Mount Vernon, NY	3/26/1966
Imus, Don	Riverside, CA	7/23/1940
Ingram, James	Akron, OH	2/16/1952
Innes, Laura	Pontiac, MI	8/16/1957?
Ireland, Kathy	Glendale, CA	3/20/1963
Irons, Jeremy	Cowes, Isle of Wight, Eng., UK	9/19/1948
Irving, Amy	Palo Alto, CA	9/10/1953
Irving, George S.	Springfield, MA	11/1/1922
Irwin, Bill	Santa Monica, CA	4/11/1950
Ivanek, Željko	Ljubljana, Yugoslavia	8/15/1957
Ivey, Judith	El Paso, TX	9/4/1951
Ivory, James	Berkeley, CA	6/7/1928
Izzard, Eddie	Aden, Yemen	2/7/1962
Ja Rule	Hollis, Queens, NY	2/29/1976
Jackée (Harry)	Winston-Salem, NC	8/14/1956
Jackman, Hugh	Sydney, NSW, Australia	10/12/1968
Jackson, Anne	Allegheny, PA	9/3/1926
Jackson, Cheyenne	Newport, WA	7/12/1975
Jackson, Glenda	Birkenhead, England, UK	5/9/1936
Jackson, Janet	Gary, IN	5/16/1966
Jackson, Jermaine	Gary, IN	12/11/1954
Jackson, Jonathan	Orlando, FL	5/11/1982
Jackson, Joshua	Vancouver, BC, Canada	6/11/1978
Jackson, Kate	Birmingham, AL	10/29/1948
Jackson, La Toya	Gary, IN	5/29/1956
Jackson, Peter	Wellington, New Zealand	10/31/1961
Jackson, Samuel L.	Washington, DC	12/21/1948
Jacobi, Derek	London, England, UK	10/22/1938
Jagger, Mick	Dartford, England, UK	7/26/1943
James, Kevin	Mineola, NY	4/26/1965
Jamison, Judith	Philadelphia, PA	5/10/1943
Janis, Conrad	New York, NY	2/11/1928
Janney, Allison	Dayton, OH	11/19/1959
Janssen, Famke	Amsterdam, Netherlands	11/5/1965
Jardine, Al	Lima, OH	9/3/1942
Jarmusch, Jim	Akron, OH	1/22/1953
Jarreau, Al	Milwaukee, WI	3/12/1940
Jarrett, Keith	Allentown, PA	5/8/1945
Jay Z	Brooklyn, NY	12/4/1969
Jeffreys, Anne	Goldsboro, NC	1/26/1923
Jenkins, Richard	DeKalb, IL	5/4/1947
Jenner, Caitlyn	Mount Kisco, NY	10/28/1949
Jenner, Kris	San Diego, CA	11/5/1955
Jepsen, Carly Rae	Mission, BC, Canada	11/21/1985
Jett, Joan	Philadelphia, PA	9/22/1958
Jewel (Kilcher)	Payson, UT	5/23/1974
Jewison, Norman	Toronto, ON, Canada	7/21/1926
Jillette, Penn	Greenfield, MA	3/5/1955
Jillian, Ann	Cambridge, MA	1/29/1950
Joel, Billy	Bronx, NY	5/9/1949
Johansson, Scarlett	New York, NY	11/22/1984
John, Elton	Pinner, Middlesex, Eng., UK	3/25/1947
Johns, Glynis	Durban, South Africa	10/5/1923

Name	Birthplace	Birthdate
Johnson, Arte	Benton Harbor, MI	1/20/1929
Johnson, Beverly	Buffalo, NY	10/13/1952
Johnson, Don	Flatt Creek, MO	12/15/1949
Johnson, Dwayne "The Rock"	Hayward, CA	5/2/1972
Johnston, Bruce	Los Angeles, CA	6/24/1942
Johnston, Kristen	Washington, DC	9/20/1967
Jolie, Angelina	Los Angeles, CA	6/4/1975
Jonas, Joe	Casa Grande, AZ	8/15/1989
Jonas, Kevin	Teaneck, NJ	11/5/1987
Jonas, Nick	Dallas, TX	9/16/1992
Jones, Angus T.	Austin, TX	10/8/1993
Jones, Bill T.	Bunnell, FL	2/15/1952
Jones, Cherry	Paris, TN	11/21/1956
Jones, Gemma	London, England, UK	12/4/1942
Jones, Grace	Spanish Town, Jamaica	5/19/1948
Jones, Jack	Hollywood, CA	1/14/1938
Jones, James Earl	Arkabutla, MS	1/17/1931
Jones, John Paul	Sidcup, England, UK	1/3/1946
Jones, January	Sioux Falls, SD	1/5/1978
Jones, Mick	London, England, UK	6/26/1955
Jones, Norah	New York, NY	3/30/1979
Jones, Quincy	Chicago, IL	3/14/1933
Jones, Shirley	Charleroi, PA	3/31/1934
Jones, Star	Badin, NC	3/24/1962
Jones, Tom	Pontypridd, Wales, UK	6/7/1940
Jones, Tommy Lee	San Saba, TX	9/15/1946
Jonze, Spike	Rockville, MD	10/22/1969
Jovovich, Milla	Kiev, Ukraine	12/17/1975
Judd, Ashley	Granada Hills, CA	4/19/1968
Judd, Naomi	Ashland, KY	1/11/1946
Judd, Wynonna	Ashland, KY	5/30/1964
Kaczmarek, Jane	Milwaukee, WI	12/21/1955
Kaling, Mindy	Cambridge, MA	6/24/1979
Kanaly, Steve	Burbank, CA	3/14/1946
Kane, Carol	Cleveland, OH	6/18/1952
Kaplan, Gabe	Brooklyn, NY	3/31/1945
Kardashian, Khloe	Los Angeles, CA	6/27/1984
Kardashian, Kim	Los Angeles, CA	10/21/1980
Kardashian, Kourtney	Los Angeles, CA	4/18/1979
Karlen, John	New York, NY	5/28/1940
Karn, Richard	Seattle, WA	2/17/1956
Katic, Stana	Hamilton, ON, Canada	4/26/1978
Kattan, Chris	Sherman Oaks, CA	10/19/1970
Kavner, Julie	Burbank, CA	9/7/1951
Kaye, Judy	Phoenix, AZ	12/11/1948
Kazan, Lainie	New York, NY	5/15/1940
Keach, Stacy	Savannah, GA	6/2/1941
Keaton, Diane	Santa Ana, CA	1/5/1946
Keaton, Michael	Coraopolis, PA	9/5/1951
Keener, Catherine	Miami, FL	3/23/1959
Keillor, Garrison	Anoka, MN	8/7/1942
Keitel, Harvey	Brooklyn, NY	5/13/1939
Keith, David	Knoxville, TN	5/8/1954
Keith, Penelope	Sutton, Surrey, Eng., UK	4/2/1940
Kellerman, Sally	Long Beach, CA	6/2/1937
Kelly, Minka	Los Angeles, CA	6/24/1980
Kelly, R(obert)	Chicago, IL	1/8/1967
Kennedy, George	New York, NY	2/18/1925
Kennedy, Jamie	Upper Darby, PA	5/25/1970
Kenny G	Seattle, WA	6/5/1956
Kent, Allegra	Santa Monica, CA	8/11/1937
Keoghan, Phil	Christchurch, New Zealand	5/31/1967
Kercheval, Ken	Wolcottville, IN	7/15/1935
Kerns, Joanna	San Francisco, CA	2/12/1953
Kesha	Los Angeles, CA	3/1/1987
Keys, Alicia	New York, NY	1/25/1981
Khan, Chaka	Great Lakes, IL	3/23/1953
Kid Rock	Romeo, MI	1/17/1971
Kidder, Margot	Yellowknife, NT, Canada	10/17/1948
Kidman, Nicole	Honolulu, HI	6/20/1967
Kilborn, Craig	Kansas City, KS	8/24/1962
Kilmer, Val	Los Angeles, CA	12/31/1959
Kim, Daniel Dae	Pusan, South Korea	8/4/1968
Kimmel, Jimmy	Brooklyn, NY	11/13/1967
King, Carole	Brooklyn, NY	2/9/1942
King, Gayle	Chevy Chase, MD	12/28/1954?
King, Larry	Brooklyn, NY	11/19/1933
King, Perry	Alliance, OH	4/30/1948
King, Regina	Los Angeles, CA	1/15/1971
Kingsley, Ben	Scarborough, England, UK	12/31/1943
Kingston, Alex	London, England, UK	3/11/1963
Kinnear, Greg	Logansport, IN	6/17/1963
Kinney, Kathy	Stevens Point, WI	11/3/1954
Kinski, Nastassja	Berlin, W. Germany	1/24/1960
Kirkland, Gelsey	Bethlehem, PA	12/29/1952
Kirkpatrick, Chris	Clarion, PA	10/17/1971
Kirshner, Mia	Toronto, ON, Canada	1/25/1975
Kitsch, Taylor	Kelowna, BC, Canada	4/8/1981
Klein, Robert	Bronx, NY	2/8/1942
Kline, Kevin	St. Louis, MO	10/24/1947
Klum, Heidi	Bergish-Gladbach, Germany	6/1/1973
Knight, Gladys	Atlanta, GA	5/28/1944
Knight, Shirley	Goessel, KS	7/5/1936
Knight, T. R.	Minneapolis, MN	3/26/1973
Knight, Wayne	New York, NY	8/7/1955

Name	Birthplace	Birthdate
Knightley, Keira	Teddington, England, UK	3/26/1985
Knopfler, Mark	Glasgow, Scotland, UK	8/12/1949
Knowles, Beyoncé	Houston, TX	9/4/1981
Knoxville, Johnny	Knoxville, TN	3/11/1971
Konitz, Lee	Chicago, IL	10/13/1927
Kopell, Bernie	Brooklyn, NY	6/21/1933
Kotto, Yaphet	New York, NY	11/15/1937
Krakowski, Jane	Parsippany, NJ	10/11/1968
Krasinski, John	Newton, MA	10/20/1979
Krause, Peter	Alexandria, MN	8/12/1965
Kressley, Carson	Allentown, PA	11/11/1969
Kretschmann, Thomas	Dessau, E. Germany	9/8/1962
Kristofferson, Kris	Brownsville, TX	6/22/1936
Kudrow, Lisa	Encino, CA	7/30/1963
Kunis, Mila	Kiev, Ukraine	8/14/1983
Kuriyama, Chiaki	Tsuchiura, Ibaraki, Japan	10/10/1984
Kurtz, Swoosie	Omaha, NE	9/6/1944
Kutcher, Ashton	Cedar Rapids, IA	2/7/1978
Kwan, Nancy	Hong Kong	5/19/1939
LaBelle, Patti	Philadelphia, PA	5/24/1944
LaBeouf, Shia	Los Angeles, CA	6/11/1986
Lachey, Nick	Harlan, KY	11/9/1973
Ladd, Cheryl	Huron, SD	7/12/1951
Ladd, Diane	Meridian, MS	11/29/1932
Lady Gaga	New York, NY	3/28/1986
Lagasse, Emeril	Fall River, MA	10/15/1959
Lahti, Christine	Birmingham, MI	4/4/1950
Laine, Cleo	Southall, England, UK	10/28/1927
Lake, Ricki	Hastings-on-Hudson, NY	9/21/1968
Lamas, Lorenzo	Santa Monica, CA	1/20/1958
Lambert, Adam	Indianapolis, IN	1/29/1982
Lambert, Christopher	Great Neck, NY	3/29/1957
Lambert, Miranda	Longview, TX	11/10/1983
Landau, Martin	Brooklyn, NY	6/20/1928
Landis, John	Chicago, IL	8/3/1950
Lane, Diane	New York, NY	1/22/1965
Lane, Nathan	Jersey City, NJ	2/3/1956
lang, k.d.	Consort, AB, Canada	11/2/1961
Lang, Stephen	Jamaica Estates, Queens, NY	7/11/1952
Lange, Jessica	Cloquet, MN	4/20/1949
Langella, Frank	Bayonne, NJ	1/1/1938
Lansbury, Angela	London, England, UK	10/16/1925
LaPaglia, Anthony	Adelaide, SA, Australia	1/31/1959
Larroquette, John	New Orleans, LA	11/25/1947
LaSalle, Eriq	Hartford, CT	6/23/1962
Lauper, Cyndi	Ozone Park, Queens, NY	6/22/1953
Laurie, Hugh	Oxford, England, UK	6/11/1959
Laurie, Piper	Detroit, MI	1/22/1932
Lautner, Taylor	Grand Rapids, MI	2/11/1992
Lavigne, Avril	Belleville, ON, Canada	9/27/1984
Lavin, Linda	Portland, ME	10/15/1937
Law, Jude	London, England, UK	12/29/1972
Lawless, Lucy	Mount Albert, New Zealand	3/29/1968
Lawrence, Carol	Melrose Park, IL	9/5/1934
Lawrence, Jennifer	Louisville, KY	8/15/1990
Lawrence, Joey	Montgomery, PA	4/20/1976
Lawrence, Martin	Frankfurt, Germany	4/16/1965
Lawrence, Steve	Brooklyn, NY	7/8/1935
Lawrence, Vicki	Inglewood, CA	3/26/1949
Leach, Robin	London, England, UK	8/29/1941
Leachman, Cloris	Des Moines, IA	4/30/1926
Lear, Norman	New Haven, CT	7/27/1922
Learned, Michael	Washington, DC	4/9/1939
Leary, Denis	Worcester, MA	8/18/1957
LeBlanc, Matt	Newton, MA	7/25/1967
LeBon, Simon	Bushey, England, UK	10/27/1958
Lee, Ang	Pingtung, Taiwan	10/23/1954
Lee, Brenda	Lithonia, GA	12/11/1944
Lee, Jason	Huntington Beach, CA	4/25/1970
Lee, Michele	Los Angeles, CA	6/24/1942
Lee, Spike	Atlanta, GA	3/20/1957
Leeves, Jane	Ilford, England, UK	4/18/1961
Legrand, Michel	Paris, France	2/24/1932
Leguizamo, John	Bogotá, Colombia	7/22/1964
Leibman, Ron	New York, NY	10/11/1937
Leigh, Jennifer Jason	Hollywood, CA	2/5/1962
Leighton, Laura	Iowa City, IA	7/24/1968
Lennox, Annie	Aberdeen, Scotland, UK	12/25/1954
Leno, Jay	New Rochelle, NY	4/28/1950
Leo, Melissa	New York, NY	9/14/1960
Leonard, Robert Sean	Westwood, NJ	2/28/1969
Leoni, Tea	New York, NY	2/25/1966
Leslie, Joan	Detroit, MI	1/26/1925
Leto, Jared	Bossier City, LA	12/26/1971
Letterman, David	Indianapolis, IN	4/12/1947
Levin, Harvey	Los Angeles, CA	9/2/1960
Levine, Adam	Los Angeles, CA	3/18/1979
Levine, James	Cincinnati, OH	6/23/1943
Levine, Ted	Bellaire, OH	5/29/1957
Levinson, Barry	Baltimore, MD	4/6/1942
Levy, Eugene	Hamilton, ON, Canada	12/17/1946
Lewis, Damian	London, Eng., UK	2/11/1971
Lewis, Huey	New York, NY	7/5/1950
Lewis, Jason	Newport Beach, CA	6/25/1971
Lewis, Jerry	Newark, NJ	3/16/1926

Name	Birthplace	Birthdate
Lewis, Jerry Lee	Ferriday, LA	9/29/1935
Lewis, Juliette	Los Angeles, CA	6/21/1973
Lewis, Leona	London, England, UK	4/3/1985
Lewis, Richard	Brooklyn, NY	6/29/1947
Li, Jet	Beijing, China	4/26/1963
Light, Judith	Trenton, NJ	2/9/1949
Lightfoot, Gordon	Orillia, ON, Canada	11/17/1938
Lil' Kim	Brooklyn, NY	7/11/1975
Lil' Romeo	New Orleans, LA	8/19/1989
Lil Wayne	New Orleans, LA	9/27/1982
Lilly, Evangeline	Fort Saskatchewan, AB, Can.	8/3/1979
Lincoln, Andrew	London, England, UK	9/14/1973
Linden, Hal	Bronx, NY	3/20/1931
Ling, Lisa	Sacramento, CA	8/30/1973
Linn-Baker, Mark	St. Louis, MO	6/17/1954
Linney, Laura	New York, NY	2/5/1964
Liotta, Ray	Newark, NJ	12/18/1954
Lithgow, John	Rochester, NY	10/19/1945
Little, Rich	Ottawa, ON, Canada	11/26/1938
Little Richard	Macon, GA	12/5/1932
Littrell, Brian	Lexington, KY	2/20/1975
Liu, Lucy	Jackson Heights, Queens, NY	12/2/1968
Lively, Blake	Tarzana, CA	8/25/1987
LL Cool J	St. Albans, Queens, NY	1/14/1968
Lloyd, Christopher	Stamford, CT	10/22/1938
Lloyd Webber, Andrew	London, England, UK	3/22/1948
Locke, Sondra	Shelbyville, TN	5/28/1947
Lockhart, June	New York, NY	6/25/1925
Locklear, Heather	Westwood, CA	9/25/1961
Loggia, Robert	Staten Island, NY	1/3/1930
Loggins, Kenny	Everett, WA	1/7/1948
Lohan, Lindsay	New York, NY	7/2/1986
Lollobrigida, Gina	Subiaco, Italy	7/4/1927
Lonergan, Kenneth	New York, NY	10/16/1962
Long, Nia	Brooklyn, NY	10/30/1970
Long, Shelley	Ft. Wayne, IN	8/23/1949
Longoria, Eva	Corpus Christi, TX	3/15/1975
Lopez, George	Mission Hills, CA	4/23/1961
Lopez, Jennifer	Bronx, NY	7/24/1969
Lopez, Mario	San Diego, CA	10/10/1973
Lorde	Takapuna, New Zealand	11/7/1996
Loren, Sophia	Rome, Italy	9/20/1934
Loring, Gloria	New York, NY	12/10/1946
Louis C.K.	Washington, DC	9/12/1967
Louis-Dreyfus, Julia	New York, NY	1/13/1961
Lovato, Demi	Dallas, TX	8/20/1992
Love, Courtney	San Francisco, CA	7/9/1964
Love, Mike	Baldwin Hills, CA	3/15/1941
Loveless, Patty	Pikeville, KY	1/4/1957
Lovett, Lyle	Klein, TX	11/1/1957
Lovitz, Jon	Tarzana, CA	7/21/1957
Lowe, Rob	Charlottesville, VA	3/17/1964
Lucas, George	Modesto, CA	5/14/1944
Lucci, Susan	Scarsdale, NY	12/23/1946
Luckinbill, Laurence	Ft. Smith, AR	11/21/1934
Ludacris	Champaign, IL	9/11/1977
Ludwig, Christa	Berlin, Germany	3/16/1924
Luhrmann, Baz	Sydney, NSW, Australia	9/17/1962
LuPone, Patti	Northport, NY	4/21/1949
Lynch, David	Missoula, MT	1/20/1946
Lynch, Jane	Dolton, IL	7/14/1960
Lynley, Carol	New York, NY	2/13/1942
Lynn, Loretta	Butcher Hollow, KY	4/14/1932
Lynn, Vera	London, England, UK	3/20/1917
Lynne, Shelby	Quantico, VA	10/22/1968
Ma, Yo-Yo	Paris, France	10/7/1955
Macchio, Ralph	Huntington, NY	11/4/1961
MacDonald, Kelly	Glasgow, Scotland, UK	2/23/1976
MacDowell, Andie	Gaffney, SC	4/21/1958
MacFarlane, Seth	Kent, CT	10/26/1973
MacGowan, Shane	Tunbridge, Kent, Eng., UK	12/25/1957
MacGraw, Ali	Pound Ridge, NY	4/1/1939
Macklemore	Seattle, WA	6/19/1983
MacLachlan, Kyle	Yakima, WA	2/22/1959
MacLaine, Shirley	Richmond, VA	4/24/1934
MacLeod, Gavin	Mt. Kisco, NY	2/28/1931
MacNicol, Peter	Dallas, TX	4/10/1954
MacPherson, Elle	Sydney, NSW, Australia	3/29/1964
Macy, Bill	Revere, MA	5/18/1922
Macy, William H.	Miami, FL	3/13/1950
Madden, John	Austin, MN	4/10/1936
Madigan, Amy	Chicago, IL	9/11/1950
Madonna (Ciccone)	Bay City, MI	8/16/1958
Madsen, Michael	Chicago, IL	9/25/1959
Maguire, Tobey	Santa Monica, CA	6/27/1975
Maher, Bill	New York, NY	1/20/1956
Mahoney, John	Blackpool, Lancashire, England, UK	6/20/1940
Majors, Lee	Wyandotte, MI	4/23/1939
Makarova, Natalia	Leningrad, Russia	11/21/1940
Malick, Terrence	Ottawa, IL	11/30/1943
Malick, Wendie	Buffalo, NY	12/13/1950
Malina, Joshua	New York, NY	1/17/1966
Malkovich, John	Christopher, IL	12/9/1953
Malone, Dorothy	Chicago, IL	1/30/1925
Mamet, David	Chicago, IL	11/30/1947
Manchester, Melissa	Bronx, NY	2/15/1951
Mandel, Howie	Toronto, ON, Canada	11/29/1955
Mandrell, Barbara	Houston, TX	12/25/1948
Mangione, Chuck	Rochester, NY	11/29/1940
Manheim, Camryn	Caldwell, NJ	3/8/1961
Manilow, Barry	Brooklyn, NY	6/17/1943
Mann, Aimee	Richmond, VA	8/9/1960
Manoff, Dinah	New York, NY	1/25/1958
Manson, Marilyn	Canton, OH	1/5/1969
Mantegna, Joe	Chicago, IL	11/13/1947
Mantello, Joe	Rockford, IL	12/27/1962
Mara, Kate	Bedford, NY	2/27/1983
Mara, Rooney	Bedford, NY	4/17/1985
Marcil, Vanessa	Indio, CA	10/15/1969
Margulies, Julianna	Spring Valley, NY	6/8/1966
Marie, Constance	Hollywood, CA	9/9/1965
Marin, Cheech	Los Angeles, CA	7/13/1946
Marinaro, Ed	New York, NY	3/31/1950
Marriner, Neville	Lincoln, England, UK	4/15/1924
Mars, Bruno	Honolulu, HI	10/8/1985
Marsalis, Branford	Breaux Bridge, LA	8/26/1960
Marsalis, Wynton	New Orleans, LA	10/18/1961
Marsh, Jean	London, England, UK	7/1/1934
Marshall, Garry	Bronx, NY	11/13/1934
Marshall, Penny	Bronx, NY	10/15/1942
Marshall, Peter	Huntington, WV	3/30/1926
Martin, Chris	Devon, England, UK	3/22/1977
Martin, Jesse L.	Rocky Mount, VA	1/18/1969
Martin, Kellie	Riverside, CA	10/16/1975
Martin, Ricky	San Juan, Puerto Rico	12/24/1971
Martin, Steve	Waco, TX	8/14/1945
Martindale, Margo	Jacksonville, TX	7/18/1951
Martins, Peter	Copenhagen, Denmark	10/27/1946
Maslany, Tatiana	Regina, SK, Canada	9/22/1985
Mason, Jackie	Sheboygan, WI	6/9/1931
Mason, Marsha	St. Louis, MO	4/3/1942
Masterson, Christopher	Long Island, NY	1/22/1980
Masterson, Mary Stuart	New York, NY	6/28/1966
Mastrantonio, Mary Elizabeth	Lombard, IL	11/17/1958
Masur, Kurt	Brieg, Germany	7/18/1927
Masur, Richard	New York, NY	11/20/1948
Mathers, Jerry	Sioux City, IA	6/2/1948
Matheson, Tim	Glendale, CA	12/31/1947
Mathis, Johnny	Gilmer, TX	9/30/1935
Matlin, Marlee	Morton Grove, IL	8/24/1965
Matthews, Dave	Johannesburg, South Africa	1/9/1967
May, Elaine	Philadelphia, PA	4/21/1932
Mayer, John	Bridgeport, CT	10/16/1977
Mays, Jayma	Bristol, TN	7/16/1979
Mazar, Debi	Jamaica, Queens, NY	8/13/1964
McAdams, Rachel	London, ON, Canada	11/17/1978
McArdle, Andrea	Abington, PA	11/5/1963
McAvoy, James	Glasgow, Scotland, UK	4/21/1979
McBride, Patricia	Teaneck, NJ	8/23/1942
McCallum, David	Glasgow, Scotland, UK	9/19/1933
McCarthy, Andrew	Westfield, NJ	11/29/1962
McCarthy, Jenny	Chicago, IL	11/1/1972
McCarthy, Melissa	Plainfield, IL	8/26/1970
McCartney, Paul	Liverpool, England, UK	6/18/1942
McCarver, Tim	Memphis, TN	10/16/1941
McConaughey, Matthew	Uvalde, TX	11/4/1969
McCoo, Marilyn	Jersey City, NJ	9/30/1943
McCormack, Eric	Toronto, ON, Canada	4/18/1963
McCormack, Mary	Plainsfield, NJ	2/8/1969
McCrane, Paul	Philadelphia, PA	1/19/1961
McCreery, Scotty	Garner, NC	10/9/1993
McDaniel, James	Washington, DC	3/25/1958
McDermott, Dylan	Waterbury, CT	10/26/1961
McDiarmid, Ian	Carnoustie, Tayside, Scot., UK	4/17/1944?
McDonald, Audra	Berlin, Germany	7/3/1970
McDonnell, Mary	Wilkes-Barre, PA	4/28/1952
McDormand, Frances	Chicago, IL	6/23/1957
McDowell, Malcolm	Leeds, England, UK	6/13/1943
McEntire, Reba	McAlester, OK	3/28/1955
McFerrin, Bobby	New York, NY	3/11/1950
McGillis, Kelly	Newport Beach, CA	7/9/1957
McGovern, Elizabeth	Evanston, IL	7/18/1961
McGovern, Maureen	Youngstown, OH	7/27/1949
McGraw, Tim	Delhi, LA	5/1/1967
McGregor, Ewan	Crieff, Scotland, UK	3/31/1971
McHale, Joel	Rome, Italy	11/20/1971
McHale, Kevin	Plano, TX	6/14/1988
McKean, Michael	New York, NY	10/17/1947
McKechnie, Donna	Pontiac, MI	11/16/1942
McKellen, Ian	Burnley, England, UK	5/25/1939
McKenzie, Ben	Austin, TX	9/12/1978
McKidd, Kevin	Elgin, Scotland, UK	8/9/1973
McLachlan, Sarah	Halifax, NS, Canada	1/28/1968
McLean, A. J.	West Palm Beach, FL	1/9/1978
McNichol, Kristy	Los Angeles, CA	9/11/1962
McRaney, Gerald	Collins, MS	8/19/1947
McQueen, Steve	London, England, UK	10/9/1969

Name	Birthplace	Birthdate
McQueen, Steven R.	Los Angeles, CA	7/13/1988
McShane, Ian	Blackburn, England, UK	9/29/1942
Meat Loaf	Dallas, TX	9/27/1947
Meester, Leighton	Marco Island, FL	4/9/1986
Mehta, Zubin	Bombay, India	4/29/1936
Mellencamp, John	Seymour, IN	10/7/1951
Meloni, Christopher	Washington, DC	4/2/1961
Mendes, Sam	Redding, England, UK	8/1/1965
Mendes, Sergio	Niteroi, Brazil	2/11/1941
Menzel, Idina	Syosset, NY	5/30/1971
Merchant, Natalie	Jamestown, NY	10/26/1963
Merkerson, S. Epatha	Saginaw, MI	11/28/1952
Merrill, Dina	New York, NY	12/9/1925
Messing, Debra	Brooklyn, NY	8/15/1968
Metcalf, Laurie	Carbondale, IL	6/16/1955
Meyers, Seth	Bedford, NH	12/28/1973
Michael, George	London, England, UK	6/25/1963
Michaels, Al	Brooklyn, NY	11/12/1944
Michaels, Bret	Butler, PA	3/15/1963
Michaels, Lorne	Toronto, ON, Canada	11/17/1944
Michele, Lea	Bronx, NY	8/29/1986
Midler, Bette	Honolulu, HI	12/1/1945
Midori (Goto)	Osaka, Japan	10/25/1971
Mike D	Brooklyn, NY	11/20/1965
Milano, Alyssa	Brooklyn, NY	12/19/1972
Miles, Sarah	Ingatestone, England, UK	12/31/1941
Miles, Vera	nr. Boise City, OK	8/23/1930
Miller, Dennis	Pittsburgh, PA	11/3/1953
Miller, Jonny Lee	Kingston Upon Thames, England, UK	11/15/1972
Miller, Penelope Ann	Santa Monica, CA	1/13/1964
Mills, Donna	Chicago, IL	12/11/1943
Mills, Hayley	London, England, UK	4/18/1946
Milnes, Sherrill	Downers Grove, IL	1/10/1935
Milsap, Ronnie	Robinsville, NC	1/16/1944
Mimieux, Yvette	Hollywood, CA	1/8/1942
Minaj, Nicki	St. James, Trinidad and Tobago	12/8/1982
Ming-Na (Wen)	Coloane Island, Macao	11/20/1963
Minnelli, Liza	Los Angeles, CA	3/12/1946
Minogue, Kylie	Melbourne, Vic., Australia	5/28/1968
Mirren, Helen	London, England, UK	7/26/1945
Mitchell, Brian Stokes	Seattle, WA	10/31/1957
Mitchell, Elizabeth	Los Angeles, CA	3/27/1970
Mitchell, Jerry	Paw Paw, MI	1/15/1960
Mitchell, Joni	Fort McLeod, AB, Canada	11/7/1943
Moby	New York, NY	9/11/1965
Modine, Matthew	Loma Linda, CA	3/22/1959
Moffat, Donald	Plymouth, England, UK	12/26/1930
Molina, Alfred	London, England, UK	5/24/1953
Molinaro, Al	Kenosha, WI	6/24/1919
Moll, Richard	Pasadena, CA	1/13/1943
Moloney, Janel	Woodland Hills, CA	10/3/1969
Monaghan, Dominic	Berlin, Germany	12/8/1976
Monica (Arnold)	College Park, GA	10/24/1980
Mo'Nique	Woodlawn, MD	12/11/1967
Moore, Demi	Roswell, NM	11/11/1962
Moore, Julianne	Fort Bragg, NC	12/3/1960
Moore, Mandy	Nashua, NH	4/10/1984
Moore, Mary Tyler	Brooklyn, NY	12/29/1936
Moore, Melba	New York, NY	10/29/1945
Moore, Michael	Flint, MI	4/23/1954
Moore, Roger	London, England, UK	10/14/1927
Moore, Terry	Los Angeles, CA	1/7/1929
Morales, Esai	Brooklyn, NY	10/1/1962
Moranis, Rick	Toronto, ON, Canada	4/18/1953
Moreau, Jeanne	Paris, France	1/23/1928
Moreno, Rita	Humacao, Puerto Rico	12/11/1931
Morgan, Jeffrey Dean	Seattle, WA	4/22/1966
Morgan, Piers	Guildford, Surrey, UK	3/30/1965
Morgan, Tracy	Bronx, NY	11/10/1968
Moriarty, Michael	Detroit, MI	4/5/1941
Morris, Garrett	New Orleans, LA	2/1/1937
Morissette, Alanis	Ottawa, ON, Canada	6/1/1974
Morrison, Matthew	Fort Ord, CA	10/30/1978
Morrison, Van	Belfast, N. Ireland, UK	8/31/1945
Morrissey (Steven Patrick)	Manchester, England, UK	5/22/1959
Morrow, Rob	New Rochelle, NY	9/21/1962
Morse, David	Beverly, MA	10/11/1953
Morse, Robert	Newton, MA	5/18/1931
Mortensen, Viggo	New York, NY	10/20/1958
Mortimer, Emily	London, England, UK	12/1/1971
Morton, Joe	New York, NY	10/18/1947
Morton, Samantha	Nottingham, England, UK	5/13/1977
Moses, William	Los Angeles, CA	11/17/1959
Moss, Carrie-Anne	Vancouver, BC, Canada	8/21/1967
Moss, Elisabeth	Los Angeles, CA	7/24/1982
Moss, Kate	Croydon, Surrey, Eng., UK	1/16/1974
Moyer, Stephen	Brentwood, UK	10/11/1969
Moynahan, Bridget	Binghamton, NY	4/28/1971
Mueller-Stahl, Armin	Tilsit, E. Prussia	12/17/1930
Muldaur, Diana	Brooklyn, NY	8/19/1938
Mulgrew, Kate	Dubuque, IA	4/29/1955
Mull, Martin	Chicago, IL	8/18/1943
Mullally, Megan	Los Angeles, CA	11/12/1958
Mullan, Peter	Peterhead, Scotland, UK	11/2/1959
Mulroney, Dermot	Alexandria, VA	10/31/1963
Muniz, Frankie	Wood-Ridge, NJ	12/5/1985
Munsel, Patrice	Spokane, WA	5/14/1925
Murphy, Ben	Jonesboro, AR	3/6/1942
Murphy, Donna	Corona, Queens, NY	3/7/1958
Murphy, Eddie	Brooklyn, NY	4/3/1961
Murphy, Michael	Los Angeles, CA	5/5/1938
Murray, Anne	Springhill, NS, Canada	6/20/1945
Murray, Bill	Wilmette, IL	9/21/1950
Murray, Don	Hollywood, CA	7/31/1929
Musburger, Brent	Portland, OR	5/26/1939
Muti, Riccardo	Naples, Italy	7/28/1941
Myers, Mike	Scarborough, ON, Canada	5/25/1963
Nabors, Jim	Sylacauga, AL	6/12/1930
Nagra, Parminder	Leicester, England, UK	10/5/1975
Nash, Graham	Blackpool, England, UK	2/2/1942
Naughton, James	Middletown, CT	12/6/1945
Navarro, Dave	Santa Monica, CA	6/7/1967
Nealon, Kevin	St. Louis, MO	11/18/1953
Neeson, Liam	Ballymena, N. Ireland, UK	6/7/1952
Neff, Lucas	Chicago, IL	11/7/1985
Neill, Sam	Ulster, N. Ireland, UK	9/14/1947
Nelligan, Kate	London, ON, Canada	3/16/1951
Nelly	Austin, TX	11/2/1974
Nelson, Craig T.	Spokane, WA	4/4/1944
Nelson, Judd	Portland, ME	11/28/1959
Nelson, Tracy	Santa Monica, CA	10/25/1963
Nelson, Willie	Abbott, TX	4/30/1933
Nero, Peter	Brooklyn, NY	5/22/1934
Nesmith, Mike	Houston, TX	12/30/1942
Neuwirth, Bebe	Newark, NJ	12/31/1958
Neville, Aaron	New Orleans, LA	1/24/1941
Newhart, Bob	Oak Park, IL	9/5/1929
Newman, Randy	New Orleans, LA	11/28/1943
Newton, Wayne	Norfolk, VA	4/3/1942
Newton-John, Olivia	Cambridge, England, UK	9/26/1948
Nicholas, Denise	Detroit, MI	7/12/1944
Nicholson, Jack	Neptune, NJ	4/22/1937
Nicks, Stevie	Phoenix, AZ	5/26/1948
Nighy, Bill	Caterham, Surrey, Eng., UK	12/12/1949
Nixon, Cynthia	New York, NY	4/9/1966
Noah, Trevor	Soweto, South Africa	2/20/1984
Nolan, Christopher	London, England, UK	7/30/1970
Nolte, Nick	Omaha, NE	2/8/1941
Noone, Peter	Manchester, England, UK	11/5/1947
Norman, Jessye	Augusta, GA	9/15/1945
Norris, Chuck	Ryan, OK	3/10/1940
Northam, Jeremy	Cambridge, England, UK	12/1/1961
Norton, Edward	Boston, MA	8/18/1969
Noth, Christopher	Madison, WI	11/13/1954
Novak, Kim	Chicago, IL	2/13/1933
Nuyen, France	Marseilles, France	7/31/1939
Nyong'o, Lupita	Mexico City, Mexico	3/1/1983
Oates, John	New York, NY	4/7/1949
O'Brian, Hugh	Rochester, NY	4/19/1925
O'Brien, Conan	Brookline, MA	4/18/1963
O'Brien, Margaret	San Diego, CA	1/15/1937
Ocean, Billy	Fyzabad, Trinidad and Tobago	1/21/1950
Ocean, Frank	Long Beach, CA	10/28/1987
O'Connor, Sinead	Glenageary, Ireland	12/8/1966
Odenkirk, Bob	Berwyn, IL	10/22/1962
O'Donnell, Chris	Winnetka, IL	6/26/1970
O'Donnell, Rosie	Commack, NY	3/21/1962
O'Grady, Gail	Detroit, MI	1/23/1963
Oh, Sandra	Nepean, ON, Canada	7/20/1971
O'Hara, Catherine	Toronto, ON, Canada	3/4/1954
O'Hara, Maureen	Dublin, Ireland	8/17/1920
O'Hare, Denis	Kansas City, MO	1/17/1962
Oka, Masi	Tokyo, Japan	12/27/1974
Oldman, Gary	South London, Eng., UK	3/21/1958
Olin, Ken	Chicago, IL	7/30/1954
Olin, Lena	Stockholm, Sweden	3/22/1955
Oliver, Jamie	Clavering, England, UK	5/27/1975
Oliver, John	Birmingham, England, UK	4/23/1977
Olmos, Edward James	E. Los Angeles, CA	2/24/1947
Olsen, Ashley	Sherman Oaks, CA	6/13/1986
Olsen, Mary-Kate	Sherman Oaks, CA	6/13/1986
Olson, Nancy	Milwaukee, WI	7/14/1928
Olyphant, Timothy	Honolulu, HI	5/20/1968
O'Malley, Mike	Boston, MA	10/31/1966
O'Neal, Ryan	Los Angeles, CA	4/20/1941
O'Neal, Tatum	Los Angeles, CA	11/5/1963
O'Neill, Ed	Youngstown, OH	4/12/1946
Ontkean, Michael	Vancouver, BC, Canada	1/24/1946
O'Quinn, Terry	Newbury, MI	7/15/1952
Orlando, Tony	New York, NY	4/3/1944
Ormond, Julia	Epsom, England, UK	1/4/1965
Osbourne, Jack	London, England, UK	11/8/1985
Osbourne, Kelly	London, England, UK	10/27/1984
Osbourne, Ozzy	Birmingham, England, UK	12/3/1948
Osbourne, Sharon	London, England, UK	10/9/1952
Osment, Haley Joel	Los Angeles, CA	4/10/1988
Osmond, Donny	Ogden, UT	12/9/1957
Osmond, Marie	Ogden, UT	10/13/1959
O'Toole, Annette	Houston, TX	4/1/1951

Name	Birthplace	Birthdate
Owen, Clive	Keresley, England, UK	10/3/1964
Oyelowo, David	Oxford, England, UK	4/1/1976
Oz, Frank	Herford, England, UK	5/25/1944
Ozawa, Seiji	Shenyang, China	9/1/1935
Pacino, Al	New York, NY	4/25/1940
Packer, Billy	Wellsville, NY	2/25/1940
Page, Ellen	Halifax, NS, Canada	2/21/1987
Page, Jimmy	Heston, England, UK	1/9/1944
Paget, Debra	Denver, CO	8/19/1933
Paige, Janis	Tacoma, WA	9/16/1922
Paisley, Brad	Glen Dale, WV	10/28/1972
Palin, Michael	Sheffield, England, UK	5/5/1943
Palmer, Geoffrey	London, England, UK	6/4/1927
Palminteri, Chazz	Bronx, NY	5/15/1951
Paltrow, Gwyneth	Los Angeles, CA	9/27/1972
Panettiere, Hayden	Palisades, NY	8/21/1989
Panjabi, Archie	Edgware, England, UK	5/31/1972
Pantoliano, Joe	Hoboken, NJ	9/12/1951
Papas, Irene	Chiliomodi, Greece	9/3/1926
Paquin, Anna	Winnipeg, MB, Canada	7/24/1982
Parker, Alan	Islington, England, UK	2/14/1944
Parker, Jameson	Baltimore, MD	11/18/1947
Parker, Mary-Louise	Fort Jackson, SC	8/2/1964
Parker, Sarah Jessica	Nelsonville, OH	3/25/1965
Parsons, Estelle	Marblehead, MA	11/20/1927
Parsons, Jim	Houston, TX	3/24/1973
Parton, Dolly	Sevierville, TN	1/19/1946
Pasdar, Adrian	Pittsfield, MA	4/30/1965
Patinkin, Mandy	Chicago, IL	11/30/1952
Patric, Jason	Queens, NY	6/17/1966
Pattinson, Robert	London, England, UK	5/13/1986
Patton, Will	Charleston, SC	6/14/1954
Paul, Aaron	Emmett, ID	8/27/1979
Paul, Adrian	London, England, UK	5/29/1959
Paulson, Sarah	Tampa, FL	12/17/1975
Paxton, Bill	Fort Worth, TX	5/17/1955
Pearce, Guy	Ely, England, UK	10/5/1967
Peet, Amanda	New York, NY	1/11/1972
Penn, Kal	Montclair, NJ	4/23/1977
Penn, Sean	Burbank, CA	8/17/1960
Pepper, Barry	Campbell River, BC, Can.	4/4/1970
Perez, Rosie	Brooklyn, NY	9/6/1964
Perkins, Elizabeth	Queens, NY	11/18/1960
Perlman, Itzhak	Tel Aviv, Israel	8/31/1945
Perlman, Rhea	Brooklyn, NY	3/31/1948
Perlman, Ron	New York, NY	4/13/1950
Perrine, Valerie	Galveston, TX	9/3/1943
Perry, Katy	Santa Barbara, CA	10/25/1984
Perry, Luke	Mansfield, OH	10/11/1965
Perry, Matthew	Williamstown, MA	8/19/1969
Perry, Tyler	New Orleans, LA	9/13/1969
Persoff, Nehemiah	Jerusalem, Israel	8/2/1919
Pesci, Joe	Newark, NJ	2/9/1943
Peters, Bernadette	Ozone Park, Queens, NY	2/28/1948
Peters, Roberta	Bronx, NY	5/4/1930
Petersen, Wolfgang	Emden, Germany	3/14/1941
Petty, Lori	Chattanooga, TN	3/23/1963
Petty, Tom	Gainesville, FL	10/20/1950
Pfeiffer, Michelle	Santa Ana, CA	4/29/1958
Phair, Liz	New Haven, CT	4/17/1967
Philbin, Regis	New York, NY	8/25/1931
Phillippe, Ryan	New Castle, DE	9/10/1974
Phillips, Lou Diamond	Subic Bay, Philippines	2/17/1962
Phillips, Mackenzie	Alexandria, VA	11/10/1959
Phillips, Michelle	Long Beach, CA	6/4/1944
Phillips, Phillip	Leesburg, GA	9/20/1990
Phillips, Sian	Bettws, Wales, UK	5/14/1934
Phoenix, Joaquin	San Juan, Puerto Rico	10/28/1974
Pierce, David Hyde	Albany, NY	4/3/1959
Pinchot, Bronson	New York, NY	5/20/1959
Pink	Doylestown, PA	9/8/1979
Pinkett Smith, Jada	Baltimore, MD	9/18/1971
Pirner, David	Green Bay, WI	4/16/1964
Piscopo, Joe	Passaic, NJ	6/17/1951
Pitt, Brad	Shawnee, OK	12/18/1963
Piven, Jeremy	New York, NY	7/26/1965
Plant, Robert	W. Bromwich, England, UK	8/20/1948
Plimpton, Martha	New York ,NY	11/16/1970
Plowright, Joan	Brigg, England, UK	10/28/1929
Plummer, Amanda	New York, NY	3/23/1957
Plummer, Christopher	Toronto, ON, Canada	12/13/1927
Poehler, Amy	Newton, MA	9/16/1971
Poitier, Sidney	Miami, FL	2/20/1927
Polanski, Roman	Paris, France	8/18/1933
Pompeo, Ellen	Everett, MA	11/10/1969
Pop, Iggy	Muskegon, MI	4/21/1947
Portman, Natalie	Jerusalem, Israel	6/9/1981
Posey, Parker	Baltimore, MD	11/8/1968
Post, Markie	Palo Alto, CA	11/4/1950
Potente, Franka	Dulmen bei Munster, Germany	7/22/1974
Potts, Annie	Nashville, TN	10/28/1952
Povich, Maury	Washington, DC	1/17/1939
Powell, Jane	Portland, OR	4/1/1929
Powers, Stefanie	Hollywood, CA	11/2/1942
Pratt, Chris	Virginia, MN	6/21/1979
Prentiss, Paula	San Antonio, TX	3/4/1939
Prepon, Laura	Watchung, NJ	3/7/1980
Presley, Priscilla	Brooklyn, NY	5/24/1945
Pressly, Jaime	Kinston, NC	7/30/1977
Previn, Andre	Berlin, Germany	4/6/1929
Price, Leontyne	Laurel, MS	2/10/1927
Price, Molly	North Plainfield, NJ	12/15/1966
Pride, Charley	Sledge, MS	3/18/1938
Priestley, Jason	Vancouver, BC, Canada	8/28/1969
Prince (The Artist)	Minneapolis, MN	6/7/1958
Prince, Faith	Augusta, GA	8/5/1957
Principal, Victoria	Fukuoka, Japan	1/3/1950
Probst, Jeff	Wichita, KS	11/4/1962
Proctor, Emily	Raleigh, NC	10/8/1968
Pryce, Jonathan	Holywell, N. Wales, UK	6/1/1947
Puck, Wolfgang	St. Veit, Austria	1/8/1949
Pulliam, Keshia Knight	Newark, NJ	4/9/1979
Pullman, Bill	Hornell, NY	12/17/1953
Purcell, Sarah	Richmond, IN	10/8/1948
Purefoy, James	Taunton, England, UK	6/3/1964
Quaid, Dennis	Houston, TX	4/9/1954
Quaid, Randy	Houston, TX	10/1/1950
Queen Latifah	Newark, NJ	3/18/1970
Quinn, Aidan	Chicago, IL	3/8/1959
Quinn, Colin	Brooklyn, NY	6/6/1959
Quinn, Martha	Albany, NY	5/11/1959
Quinto, Zachary	Pittsburgh, PA	6/2/1977
Rachins, Alan	Cambridge, MA	10/3/1942
Radcliffe, Daniel	London, England, UK	7/23/1989
Radnor, Josh	Columbus, OH	7/29/1974
Rae, Charlotte	Milwaukee, WI	4/22/1926
Raffi (Cavoukian)	Cairo, Egypt	7/8/1948
Raitt, Bonnie	Burbank, CA	11/8/1949
Ramey, Samuel	Colby, KS	3/28/1942
Ramirez, Efren	Los Angeles, CA	10/2/1973
Ramirez, Sara	Mazatlan, Mexico	8/31/1975
Rampling, Charlotte	Sturmer, MA	2/5/1946
Rancic, Giuliana	Naples, Italy	8/17/1975
Randolph, Joyce	Detroit, MI	10/21/1924
Raphael, Sally Jessy	Easton, PA	2/25/1935
Rashad, Phylicia	Houston, TX	6/19/1948
Ratzenberger, John	Bridgeport, CT	4/6/1947
Raver, Kim	New York, NY	3/15/1969
Ray, Rachael	Glen Falls, NY	8/25/1968
Reddy, Helen	Melbourne, Vic., Australia	10/25/1941
Redford, Robert	Santa Monica, CA	8/18/1936
Redgrave, Vanessa	London, England, UK	1/30/1937
Reed, Rex	Ft. Worth, TX	10/2/1938
Reese, Della	Detroit, MI	7/6/1931
Reeves, Keanu	Beirut, Lebanon	9/2/1964
Reeves, Martha	Eufaula, AL	7/18/1941
Regalbuto, Joe	New York, NY	8/24/1949
Reid, Tara	Wyckoff, NJ	11/8/1975
Reid, Tim	Norfolk, VA	12/19/1944
Reid, Vernon	London, England, UK	8/22/1958
Reilly, John C.	Chicago, IL	5/24/1965
Reiner, Carl	Bronx, NY	3/20/1922
Reiner, Rob	Bronx, NY	3/6/1947
Reinhold, Judge	Wilmington, DE	5/21/1957
Reinking, Ann	Seattle, WA	11/10/1949
Reiser, Paul	New York, NY	3/30/1957
Reitman, Ivan	Komarno, Czechoslovakia	10/26/1946
Remini, Leah	Brooklyn, NY	6/15/1970
Renner, Jeremy	Modesto, CA	1/7/1971
Reynolds, Burt	Waycross, GA	2/11/1936
Reynolds, Debbie	El Paso, TX	4/1/1932
Reynolds, Ryan	Vancouver, BC, Canada	10/23/1976
Reznor, Trent	Mercer, PA	5/17/1965
Rhames, Ving	New York, NY	5/12/1959
Rhimes, Shonda	Chicago, IL	1/13/1970
Rhymes, Busta	Brooklyn, NY	5/20/1972
Rhys, Matthew	Cardiff, Wales, UK	11/4/1974
Rhys Meyers, Jonathan	Dublin, Ireland	7/27/1977
Ribisi, Giovanni	Los Angeles, CA	12/17/1974
Ricci, Christina	Santa Monica, CA	2/12/1980
Richards, Denise	Downers Grove, IL	2/17/1971
Richards, Keith	Dartford, Kent, Eng., UK	12/18/1943
Richards, Michael	Culver City, CA	7/24/1949
Richardson, Kevin	Lexington, KY	10/3/1971
Richardson, Miranda	Lancashire, England, UK	3/3/1958
Richardson, Patricia	Bethesda, MD	2/23/1951
Richie, Lionel	Tuskegee, AL	6/20/1949
Richie, Nicole	Berkeley, CA	9/21/1981
Richter, Andy	Grand Rapids, MI	10/28/1966
Rickles, Don	Jackson Heights, Queens, NY	5/8/1926
Rickman, Alan	Hammersmith, Eng., UK	2/21/1946
Riegert, Peter	New York, NY	4/11/1947
Rigg, Diana	Doncaster, England, UK	7/20/1938
Rihanna	St. Michael, Barbados	2/20/1988
Riley, Amber	Long Beach, CA	2/15/1986
Rimes, LeAnn	Jackson, MS	8/28/1982
Ringwald, Molly	Roseville, CA	2/18/1968
Ripa, Kelly	Stratford, NJ	10/2/1970
Rivera, Chita	Washington, DC	1/23/1933
Rivera, Geraldo	New York, NY	7/4/1943

Name	Birthplace	Birthdate
Robbins, Tim	W. Covina, CA	10/16/1958
Roberts, Doris	St. Louis, MO	11/4/1925
Roberts, Eric	Biloxi, MS	4/18/1956
Roberts, Julia	Smyrna, GA	10/28/1967
Roberts, Tony	New York, NY	10/22/1939
Robinson, Smokey	Detroit, MI	2/19/1940
Rock, Chris	Andrews, SC	2/7/1965
Rodgers, Jimmy	Camas, WA	9/18/1933
Rodriguez, Johnny	Sabinal, TX	12/10/1951
Rodriguez, Michelle	Bexar County, TX	7/12/1978
Rogan, Joe	Newark, NJ	8/11/1967
Rogen, Seth	Vancouver, BC, Canada	4/15/1982
Rogers, Kenny	Houston, TX	8/21/1938
Rogers, Mimi	Coral Gables, FL	1/27/1956
Rogers, Wayne	Birmingham, AL	4/7/1933
Rohm, Elisabeth	Dusseldorf, Germany	4/28/1973
Rollins, Henry	Washington, DC	2/13/1961
Rollins, Sonny	New York, NY	9/7/1930
Romano, Ray	Forest Hills, Queens, NY	12/21/1957
Romijn, Rebecca	Berkeley, CA	11/6/1972
Ronstadt, Linda	Tucson, AZ	7/15/1946
Root, Stephen	Sarasota, FL	11/17/1951
Rose, Axl	Lafayette, IN	2/6/1962
Rose Marie	New York, NY	8/15/1923
Roseanne	Salt Lake City, UT	11/3/1952
Ross, Charlotte	Winnetka, IL	1/21/1968
Ross, Diana	Detroit, MI	3/26/1944
Ross, Katharine	Hollywood, CA	1/29/1940
Ross, Marion	Albert Lea, MN	10/25/1928
Rossdale, Gavin	London, England, UK	10/30/1965
Rossellini, Isabella	Rome, Italy	6/18/1952
Rossum, Emmy	New York, NY	9/12/1986
Roth, David Lee	Bloomington, IN	10/10/1955
Roth, Tim	London, England, UK	5/14/1961
Rotten, Johnny	London, England, UK	1/31/1956
Roundtree, Richard	New Rochelle, NY	7/9/1942
Rourke, Mickey	Schenectady, NY	9/16/1952
Routh, Brandon	Des Moines, IA	10/9/1979
Routledge, Patricia	Birkenhead, England, UK	2/17/1929
Rowan, Kelly	Ottawa, ON, Canada	10/26/1965
Rowlands, Gena	Cambria, WI	6/19/1930
Rubinstein, John	Beverly Hills, CA	12/8/1946
Rudd, Paul	Passaic, NJ	4/6/191969
Rudner, Rita	Miami, FL	9/17/1955?
Rudolph, Maya	Gainesville, FL	7/27/1972
Ruehl, Mercedes	Jackson Heights, Queens, NY	2/28/1948
Ruffalo, Mark	Kenosha, WI	11/22/1967
Rupp, Debra Jo	Glendale, CA	2/24/1951
Rush, Barbara	Denver, CO	1/4/1927
Rush, Geoffrey	Toowoomba, Qld., Australia	7/6/1951
Russell, Keri	Fountain Valley, CA	3/23/1976
Russell, Kurt	Springfield, MA	3/17/1951
Russell, Leon	Lawton, OK	4/2/1941
Russell, Mark	Buffalo, NY	8/23/1932
Russell, Theresa	San Diego, CA	3/20/1957
Russo, Rene	Burbank, CA	2/17/1954
Ruttan, Susan	Oregon City, OR	9/16/1950
Ryan, Meg	Fairfield, CT	11/19/1961
Ryan, Roz	Detroit, MI	7/7/1951
Rydell, Bobby	Philadelphia, PA	4/26/1942
Ryder, Winona	Winona, MN	10/29/1971
Rylance, Mark	Ashford, England, UK	1/18/1960
Sabato, Antonio, Jr.	Rome, Italy	2/29/1972
Sade (Adu)	Ibadan, Nigeria	1/16/1959
Sagal, Katey	Hollywood, CA	1/19/1954
Saget, Bob	Philadelphia, PA	5/17/1956
Sagnier, Ludivine	La Celle-St.-Cloud, France	7/3/1979
Sahl, Mort	Montreal, QC, Canada	5/11/1927
Saint, Eva Marie	Newark, NJ	7/4/1924
St. James, Susan	Hollywood, CA	8/14/1946
St. John, Jill	Los Angeles, CA	8/19/1940
St. Patrick, Mathew	Philadelphia, PA	3/17/1968
Sajak, Pat	Chicago, IL	10/26/1946
Saldana, Zoë	Passaic, NJ	6/19/1978
Salling, Mark	Dallas, TX	8/17/1982
Salonga, Lea	Manila, Philippines	2/22/1971
Samberg, Andy	Berkeley, CA	8/18/1978
Samms, Emma	London, England, UK	8/28/1960
San Giacomo, Laura	Hoboken, NJ	11/14/1962
Sandler, Adam	Brooklyn, NY	9/9/1966
Sands, Julian	West Yorkshire, Eng., UK	1/15/1958
Santana, Carlos	Autlan, Mexico	7/20/1947
Sara, Mia	Brooklyn, NY	6/19/1967
Sarandon, Susan	New York, NY	10/4/1946
Sartain, Gailard	Tulsa, OK	9/18/1946
Savage, Ben	Highland Park, IL	9/13/1980
Savage, Fred	Highland Park, IL	7/9/1976
Sawa, Devon	Vancouver, BC, Canada	9/7/1978
Saxon, John	Brooklyn, NY	8/5/1936
Sayles, John	Schenectady, NY	9/28/1950
Scacchi, Greta	Milan, Italy	2/18/1960
Scaggs, Boz	Canton, OH	6/8/1944
Scales, Prunella	Sutton Abinger, Eng., UK	6/22/1932
Scalia, Jack	Brooklyn, NY	11/10/1951
Schallert, William	Los Angeles, CA	7/6/1922
Schiff, Richard	Bethesda, MD	5/27/1955
Schiffer, Claudia	Rheinbach, Germany	8/25/1970
Schneider, John	Mt. Kisco, NY	4/8/1960
Schneider, Rob	San Francisco, CA	10/31/1963
Schreiber, Liev	San Francisco, CA	10/4/1967
Schroder, Rick	Staten Island, NY	4/13/1970
Schumer, Amy	New York, NY	6/1/1981
Schwarzenegger, Arnold	Thal, Austria	7/30/1947
Schwimmer, David	Astoria, Queens, NY	11/2/1966
Sciorra, Annabella	Wethersfield, CT	3/24/1964
Scolari, Peter	New Rochelle, NY	9/12/1954
Scorsese, Martin	Flushing, Queens, NY	11/17/1942
Scott, Ridley	South Shields, England, UK	11/30/1937
Scott, Seann William	Cottage Grove, MN	10/3/1976
Scott Thomas, Kristin	Redruth, England, UK	5/24/1960
Scotto, Renata	Savona, Italy	2/24/1934
Scully, Vin	Bronx, NY	11/29/1927
Seacrest, Ryan	Atlanta, GA	12/24/1974
Seagal, Steven	Lansing, MI	4/10/1951
Secor, Kyle	Tacoma, WA	5/31/1957
Sedaka, Neil	Brooklyn, NY	3/13/1939
Sedgwick, Kyra	New York, NY	8/19/1965
Segal, George	Great Neck, NY	2/13/1934
Segel, Jason	Los Angeles, CA	1/18/1980
Seidelman, Susan	Abington, PA	12/11/1952
Seinfeld, Jerry	Brooklyn, NY	4/29/1954
Sellecca, Connie	Bronx, NY	5/25/1955
Selleck, Tom	Detroit, MI	1/29/1945
Severinsen, Doc	Arlington, OR	7/7/1927
Sevigny, Chloë	Springfield, MA	11/18/1974
Sewell, Rufus	Twickenham, Middlesex, England, UK	10/29/1967
Seyfried, Amanda	Allentown, PA	12/3/1985
Seymour, Jane	Hillingdon, England, UK	2/15/1951
Shackelford, Ted	Oklahoma City, OK	6/23/1946
Shaffer, Paul	Thunder Bay, ON, Canada	11/28/1949
Shakira (Mebarak Ripoll)	Barranquilla, Colombia	2/2/1977
Shalhoub, Tony	Green Bay, WI	10/9/1953
Shandling, Garry	Chicago, IL	11/29/1949
Shannon, Molly	Shaker Heights, OH	9/16/1964
Shatner, William	Montreal, QC, Canada	3/22/1931
Shaughnessy, Charles	London, England, UK	2/9/1955
Shaver, Helen	St. Thomas, ON, Canada	2/24/1951
Shawkat, Alia	Riverside, CA	4/18/1989
Shea, John	North Conway, NH	4/14/1949
Shearer, Harry	Los Angeles, CA	12/23/1943
Sheedy, Ally	New York, NY	6/13/1962
Sheen, Charlie	Los Angeles, CA	9/3/1965
Sheen, Martin	Dayton, OH	8/3/1940
Sheen, Michael	Newport, Wales, UK	2/5/1969
Sheeran, Ed	Hebden Bridge, West Yorkshire, Eng., UK	2/17/1991
Sheindlin, Judy	Brooklyn, NY	10/21/1942
Shelley, Carole	London, England, UK	8/16/1939
Shelton, Blake	Ada, OK	6/18/1976
Shepard, Sam	Ft. Sheridan, IL	11/5/1943
Shepherd, Cybill	Memphis, TN	2/18/1950
Shepherd, Sherri	Chicago, IL	4/22/1967
Sheridan, Nicollette	Worthing, England, UK	11/21/1963
Shields, Brooke	New York, NY	5/31/1965
Shire, Talia	Lake Success, NY	4/25/1946
Short, Martin	Hamilton, ON, Canada	3/26/1950
Shortz, Will	Crawfordsville, IN	8/26/1952
Show, Grant	Detroit, MI	2/27/1962
Shue, Andrew	South Orange, NJ	2/20/1967
Shue, Elisabeth	Wilmington, DE	10/6/1963
Shyamalan, M. Night	Pondicherry, India	8/6/1970
Sidibe, Gabourey	Brooklyn, NY	5/6/1983
Sigler, Jamie-Lynn	Jericho, NY	5/15/1981
Sikking, James B.	Los Angeles, CA	3/5/1934
Silverman, Jonathan	Beverly Hills, CA	8/5/1966
Silverman, Sarah	Bedford, NH	12/1/1970
Silverstone, Alicia	San Francisco, CA	10/4/1976
Simmons, Gene	Haifa, Israel	8/25/1949
Simmons, Henry	Stamford, CT	7/1/1970
Simmons, Richard	New Orleans, LA	7/12/1948
Simon, Carly	New York, NY	6/25/1945
Simon, Paul	Newark, NJ	10/13/1941
Simpson, Ashlee	Waco, TX	10/3/1984
Simpson, Jessica	Abilene, TX	7/10/1980
Sinatra, Nancy	Jersey City, NJ	6/8/1940
Sinbad	Benton Harbor, MI	11/10/1956
Singleton, John	Los Angeles, CA	1/6/1968
Sinise, Gary	Blue Island, IL	3/17/1955
Sirico, Tony	Brooklyn, NY	7/29/1942
Sisto, Jeremy	Grass Valley, CA	10/6/1974
Sizemore, Tom	Detroit, MI	9/29/1961
Skerritt, Tom	Detroit, MI	8/25/1933
Slater, Christian	New York, NY	8/18/1969
Slater, Helen	Massapequa, NY	12/15/1963
Slattery, John	Boston, MA	8/13/1962
Slezak, Erika	Hollywood, CA	8/5/1946
Slick, Grace	Evanston, IL	10/30/1939
Smirnoff, Karina	Kharkiv, Ukraine	1/2/1978
Smirnoff, Yakov	Odessa, Ukraine	1/24/1951

Name	Birthplace	Birthdate
Smith, Allison	New York, NY	12/9/1969
Smith, Jaclyn	Houston, TX	10/26/1945
Smith, Jaden	Malibu, CA	7/8/1998
Smith, Keely	Norfolk, VA	3/9/1928
Smith, Kevin	Red Bank, NJ	8/2/1970
Smith, Maggie	Ilford, England, UK	12/28/1934
Smith, Patti	Chicago, IL	12/30/1946
Smith, Robert	Blackpool, England, UK	4/21/1959
Smith, Sam	London, England, UK	5/19/1992
Smith, Will	Philadelphia, PA	9/25/1968
Smith, Willow	Los Angeles, CA	10/31/2000
Smits, Jimmy	Brooklyn, NY	7/9/1955
Smothers, Dick	Governor's Island, NY	11/20/1938
Smothers, Tom	Governor's Island, NY	2/2/1937
Smulders, Cobie	Vancouver, BC, Canada	4/3/1982
Snipes, Wesley	Orlando, FL	7/31/1962
Snooki (Nicole Polizzi)	Santiago, Chile	11/23/1987
Snoop Dogg (aka Snoop Lion, Snoopzilla)	Long Beach, CA	10/20/1971
Soderbergh, Steven	Atlanta, GA	1/14/1963
Soloway, Jill	Chicago, IL	9/26/1965
Somerhalder, Ian	Covington, LA	12/8/1978
Somers, Suzanne	San Bruno, CA	10/16/1946
Sommer, Elke	Berlin, Germany	11/5/1940
Sorbo, Kevin	Mound, MN	9/24/1958
Sorvino, Mira	Tenafly, NJ	9/28/1967
Sorvino, Paul	Brooklyn, NY	4/13/1939
Soul, David	Chicago, IL	8/28/1943
Spacek, Sissy	Quitman, TX	12/25/1949
Spacey, Kevin	South Orange, NJ	7/26/1959
Spade, David	Birmingham, MI	7/22/1964
Spader, James	Boston, MA	2/7/1960
Spalding, Esperanza	Portland, OR	10/18/1984
Spano, Joe	San Francisco, CA	7/7/1946
Sparks, Jordin	Phoenix, AZ	12/22/1989
Spears, Britney	Kentwood, LA	12/2/1981
Spears, Jamie-Lynn	McComb, MS	4/4/1991
Spector, Phil	Bronx, NY	12/26/1940
Spelling, Tori	Los Angeles, CA	5/16/1973
Spencer, Octavia	Montgomery, AL	5/25/1972
Spielberg, Steven	Cincinnati, OH	12/18/1946
Spiner, Brent	Houston, TX	2/2/1949
Springer, Jerry	London, England, UK	2/13/1944
Springfield, Rick	Sydney, NSW, Australia	8/23/1949
Springsteen, Bruce	Long Branch, NJ	9/23/1949
Spurlock, Morgan	Parksburg, WV	11/7/1970
Stahl, Nick	Harlingen, TX	12/5/1979
Stallone, Sylvester	New York, NY	7/6/1946
Stamos, John	Cypress, CA	8/19/1963
Stamp, Terence	Stepney, England, UK	7/22/1938
Stanton, Harry Dean	West Irvine, KY	7/14/1926
Starr, Ringo	Liverpool, England, UK	7/7/1940
Steenburgen, Mary	Newport, AR	2/8/1953
Stefani, Gwen	Fullterton, CA	10/3/1969
Stein, Ben	Washington, DC	11/25/1944
Stern, Daniel	Bethesda, MD	8/28/1957
Stern, Howard	Roosevelt, NY	1/12/1954
Sternhagen, Frances	Washington, DC	1/13/1930
Stevens, Andrew	Memphis, TN	6/10/1955
Stevens, Cat (Yusef Islam)	London, England, UK	7/21/1948
Stevens, Connie	Brooklyn, NY	8/8/1938
Stevens, Stella	Yazoo City, MS	10/1/1936
Stevenson, Parker	Philadelphia, PA	6/4/1952
Stewart, French	Albuquerque, NM	2/20/1964
Stewart, Jon	New York, NY	11/28/1962
Stewart, Kristen	Los Angeles, CA	4/9/1990
Stewart, Patrick	Mirfield, England, UK	7/13/1940
Stewart, Rod	London, England, UK	1/10/1945
Stiers, David Ogden	Peoria, IL	10/31/1942
Stiles, Julia	New York, NY	3/28/1981
Stiller, Ben	New York, NY	11/30/1965
Stiller, Jerry	Brooklyn, NY	6/8/1927
Stills, Stephen	Dallas, TX	1/3/1945
Sting	Newcastle upon Tyne, England, UK	10/2/1951
Stipe, Michael	Decatur, GA	1/4/1960
Stockwell, Dean	North Hollywood, CA	3/5/1936
Stoltz, Eric	Whittier, CA	9/30/1961
Stone, Dee Wallace	Kansas City, KS	12/14/1948
Stone, Emma	Scottsdale, AZ	11/6/1988
Stone, Oliver	New York, NY	9/15/1946
Stone, Sharon	Meadville, PA	3/10/1958
Stonestreet, Eric	Kansas City, KS	9/9/1971
Stookey, Paul	Baltimore, MD	12/30/1937
Storch, Larry	New York, NY	1/8/1923
Stowe, Madeleine	Eagle Rock, CA	8/18/1958
Strahan, Michael	Houston, TX	11/21/1971
Strait, George	Pearsall, TX	5/18/1952
Strasser, Robin	New York, NY	5/7/1945
Stratas, Teresa	Toronto, ON, Canada	5/26/1938
Strathairn, David	San Francisco, CA	1/26/1949
Strauss, Peter	Croton-on-Hudson, NY	2/20/1947
Streep, Meryl	Summit, NJ	6/22/1949
Streisand, Barbra	Brooklyn, NY	4/24/1942
Stringfield, Sherry	Colorado Springs, CO	6/24/1967

Name	Birthplace	Birthdate
Stroman, Susan	Wilmington, DE	10/17/1954
Struthers, Sally	Portland, OR	7/28/1948
Studdard, Ruben	Frankfurt, Germany	9/12/1978
Styles, Harry	Holmes Chapel, Cheshire, Eng., UK	2/1/1994
Suchet, David	London, England, UK	5/2/1946
Sudeikis, Jason	Fairfax, VA	9/18/1975
Sullivan, Erik Per	Worcester, MA	7/12/1991
Sullivan, Susan	New York, NY	11/18/1942
Sunjata, Daniel	Evanston, IL	12/30/1971
Sutherland, Donald	St. John, NB, Canada	7/17/1934
Sutherland, Kiefer	London, England, UK	12/21/1966
Suvari, Mena	Newport, RI	2/9/1979
Swank, Hilary	Lincoln, NE	7/30/1974
Swift, Taylor	Wyomissing, PA	12/13/1989
Swinton, Tilda	London, England, UK	11/5/1960
Swit, Loretta	Passaic, NJ	11/4/1937
Sykes, Wanda	Portsmouth, VA	3/7/1964
Szmanda, Eric	Milwaukee, WI	7/24/1975
T, Mr.	Chicago, IL	5/21/1952
Takei, George	Los Angeles, CA	4/20/1937
Tamblyn, Amber	Santa Monica, CA	5/14/1983
Tamblyn, Russ	Los Angeles, CA	12/30/1934
Tambor, Jeffrey	San Francisco, CA	7/8/1944
Tarantino, Quentin	Knoxville, TN	3/27/1963
Tatum, Channing	Cullman, AL	4/26/1980
Tautou, Audrey	Beaumont, France	8/9/1976?
Taylor, Buck	Hollywood, CA	5/13/1938
Taylor, James	Boston, MA	3/12/1948
Taylor, Paul	Englewood, PA	7/29/1930
Taylor, Rip	Washington, DC	1/13/1934
Taymor, Julie	Newton, MA	12/15/1952
Te Kanawa, Kiri	Gisborne, New Zealand	3/6/1944
Teller	Philadelphia, PA	2/14/1948
Tennant, David	Bathgate, West Lothian, Scotland, UK	4/18/1971
Tennant, Victoria	London, England, UK	9/30/1950
Tennille, Toni	Montgomery, AL	5/8/1940
Tesh, John	Garden City, NY	7/9/1952
Tharp, Twyla	Portland, IN	7/1/1941
Theron, Charlize	Benoni, South Africa	8/7/1975
Thicke, Alan	Kirkland Lake, ON, Canada	3/1/1947
Thicke, Robin	Los Angeles, CA	3/10/1977
Thiessen, Tiffani	Long Beach, CA	1/23/1974
Thomas, Jay	Kermit, TX	7/12/1948
Thomas, Jonathan Taylor	Bethlehem, PA	9/8/1981
Thomas, Marlo	Deerfield, MI	11/21/1937
Thomas, Michael Tilson	Hollywood, CA	12/21/1944
Thomas, Philip Michael	Columbus, OH	5/26/1949
Thomas, Richard	New York, NY	6/13/1951
Thomas, Sean Patrick	Wilmington, DE	12/17/1970
Thompson, Emma	London, England, UK	4/15/1959
Thompson, Jack	Sydney, NSW, Australia	8/31/1940
Thompson, Kenan	Atlanta, GA	5/10/1978
Thompson, Lea	Rochester, MN	5/31/1961
Thorne-Smith, Courtney	San Francisco, CA	11/8/1967
Thornton, Billy Bob	Hot Springs, AR	8/4/1955
Thurman, Uma	Boston, MA	4/29/1970
Tiegs, Cheryl	Breckenridge, MN	9/25/1947
Tierney, Maura	Boston, MA	2/3/1965
Tillis, Mel	Tampa, FL	8/8/1932
Tilly, Jennifer	Harbor City, CA	9/16/1958
Tilly, Meg	Long Beach, CA	2/14/1960
Timberlake, Justin	Memphis, TN	1/31/1981
Tisdale, Ashley	West Deal, NJ	7/2/1985
Tomei, Marisa	Brooklyn, NY	12/4/1964
Tomlin, Lily	Detroit, MI	9/1/1939
Tonioli, Bruno	Ferrara, Italy	11/25/1955
Tork, Peter	Washington, DC	2/13/1942
Torn, Rip	Temple, TX	2/6/1931
Townsend, Robert	Chicago, IL	2/6/1957
Townshend, Peter	Chiswick, England, UK	5/19/1945
Travanti, Daniel J.	Kenosha, WI	3/7/1940
Travis, Nancy	Astoria, Queens, NY	9/21/1961
Travis, Randy	Marshville, NC	5/4/1959
Travolta, John	Englewood, NJ	2/18/1954
Trebek, Alex	Sudbury, ON, Canada	7/22/1940
Tripplehorn, Jean	Tulsa, OK	6/10/1963
Tritt, Travis	Marietta, GA	2/9/1963
Tucci, Stanley	Peekskill, NY	1/11/1960
Tucker, Chris	Decatur, GA	8/31/1972
Tucker, Michael	Baltimore, MD	2/6/1944
Tucker, Tanya	Seminole, TX	10/10/1958
Tune, Tommy	Wichita Falls, TX	2/28/1939
Turlington, Christy	Walnut Creek, CA	1/2/1969
Turner, Janine	Lincoln, NE	12/6/1962
Turner, Kathleen	Springfield, MO	6/19/1954
Turner, Tina	Nutbush, TN	11/26/1939
Turturro, John	Brooklyn, NY	2/28/1957
Tveit, Aaron	Middletown, NY	10/21/1983
Twain, Shania	Windsor, ON, Canada	8/28/1965
Twiggy (Lawson)	London, England, UK	9/19/1949
Tyler, Liv	New York, NY	7/1/1977
Tyler, Steven	Yonkers, NY	3/26/1948

Name	Birthplace	Birthdate
Tyson, Cicely	New York, NY	12/19/1933
Uecker, Bob	Milwaukee, WI	1/26/1934
Uggams, Leslie	New York, NY	5/25/1943
Ullman, Tracey	Slough, England, UK	12/30/1959
Ullmann, Liv	Tokyo, Japan	12/16/1938
Ulrich, Skeet	Lynchburg, VA	1/20/1970
Underwood, Blair	Tacoma, WA	8/25/1964
Underwood, Carrie	Muskogee, OK	3/10/1983
Urban, Keith	Whangarei, North Island, New Zealand	10/26/1967
Urie, Michael	Dallas, TX	8/8/1980
Usher (Raymond IV)	Dallas, TX	10/14/1978
Vaccaro, Brenda	Brooklyn, NY	11/18/1939
Valley, Mark	Ogdensburg, NY	12/24/1964
Valli, Frankie	Newark, NJ	5/3/1934
Van Ark, Joan	New York, NY	6/16/1943
Van Damme, Jean-Claude	Brussels, Belgium	10/18/1960
Van Der Beek, James	Cheshire, CT	3/8/1977
Van Doren, Mamie	Rowena, SD	2/6/1931
Van Dyke, Dick	West Plains, MO	12/13/1925
Van Dyke, Jerry	Danville, IL	7/27/1931
Van Halen, Eddie	Nijmegen, Netherlands	1/26/1955
Van Peebles, Mario	Mexico City, Mexico	1/15/1957
Van Sant, Gus	Louisville, KY	7/24/1952
Van Zandt, Steven	Winthrop, MA	11/22/1950
VanCamp, Emily	Port Perry, ON, Canada	5/12/1986
Vance, Courtney B.	Detroit, MI	3/12/1960
Vardalos, Nia	Winnipeg, MB, Canada	9/24/1962
Vaughn, Robert	New York, NY	11/22/1932
Vaughn, Vince	Minneapolis, MN	3/28/1970
Vedder, Eddie	Evanston, IL	12/23/1964
Vega, Alexa	Miami, FL	8/27/1988
Ventimiglia, Milo	Anaheim, CA	7/8/1977
Vereen, Ben	Miami, FL	10/10/1946
Vergara, Sofia	Barranquilla, Colombia	7/10/1972
Vieira, Meredith	Providence, RI	12/30/1953
Vigoda, Abe	New York, NY	2/24/1921
Villella, Edward	Long Island, NY	10/1/1936
Vincent, Jan-Michael	Denver, CO	7/15/1944
Vinton, Bobby	Canonsburg, PA	4/16/1935
Visnjic, Goran	Sibenik, Yugo. (Croatia)	9/9/1972
Vitale, Dick	East Rutherford, NJ	6/9/1939
Voight, Jon	Yonkers, NY	12/29/1938
Von Stade, Frederica	Somerville, NJ	6/1/1945
Von Sydow, Max	Lund, Sweden	4/10/1929
Von Trier, Lars	Copenhagen, Denmark	4/30/1956
Wagner, Jack	Washington, MO	10/3/1959
Wagner, Lindsay	Los Angeles, CA	6/22/1949
Wagner, Robert	Detroit, MI	2/10/1930
Wahl, Ken	Chicago, IL	10/31/1954
Wahlberg, Donnie	Dorchester, MA	8/17/1969
Wahlberg, Mark	Dorchester, MA	6/5/1971
Wain, Bea	Bronx, NY	4/30/1917
Waits, Tom	Pomona, CA	12/7/1949
Walden, Robert	New York, NY	9/25/1943
Walken, Christopher	Astoria, Queens, NY	3/31/1943
Walker, Clint	Hartford, IL	5/30/1927
Wallis, Quvenzhané	Houma, LA	8/23/2008
Walsh, Kate	San Jose, CA	10/13/1967
Walter, Jessica	Brooklyn, NY	1/31/1941
Waltz, Christoph	Vienna, Austria	10/4/1956
Warburton, Patrick	Paterson, NJ	11/14/1964
Ward, Fred	San Diego, CA	12/30/1942
Ward, Sela	Meridian, MS	7/11/1956
Warfield, Marsha	Chicago, IL	3/5/1954
Warner, Malcolm-Jamal	Jersey City, NJ	8/18/1970
Warren, Lesley Ann	New York, NY	8/16/1946
Warwick, Dionne	East Orange, NJ	12/12/1940
Washington, Denzel	Mt. Vernon, NY	12/28/1954
Washington, Isaiah	Houston, TX	8/3/1963
Washington, Kerry	Bronx, NY	1/31/1977
Wasikowska, Mia	Canberra, Australia	10/14/1989
Watanabe, Ken	Koide, Niigata, Japan	10/21/1959
Waters, John	Baltimore, MD	4/22/1946
Waters, Roger	Great Bookham, Eng., UK	9/6/1943
Waterston, Sam	Cambridge, MA	11/15/1940
Watson, Emily	London, England, UK	1/14/1967
Watson, Emma	Paris, France	4/15/1990
Watts, Naomi	Shoreham, England, UK	9/28/1968
Wayans, Damon	New York, NY	9/4/1960
Wayans, Keenen Ivory	Brooklyn, NY	6/8/1958
Wayans, Marlon	New York, NY	7/23/1972
Wayans, Shawn	New York, NY	1/19/1971
Weathers, Carl	New Orleans, LA	1/14/1948
Weaver, Fritz	Pittsburgh, PA	1/19/1926
Weaver, Sigourney	New York, NY	10/8/1949
Weiland, Scott	Santa Cruz, CA	10/27/1967
Weir, Peter	Sydney, NSW, Australia	8/21/1944
Weisz, Rachel	London, England, UK	3/7/1971
Weitz, Bruce	Norwalk, CT	5/27/1943
Welch, Raquel	Chicago, IL	9/5/1940
Weld, Tuesday	New York, NY	8/27/1943
Weller, Peter	Stevens Point, WI	6/24/1947
Welling, Tom	Putnam Valley, NY	4/26/1977
Wendt, George	Chicago, IL	10/17/1948
Wentz, Pete	Wilmette, IL	6/5/1979
West, Adam	Walla Walla, WA	9/19/1928
West, Kanye	Atlanta, GA	6/8/1977
West, Shane	Baton Rouge, LA	6/10/1978
Wettig, Patricia	Cincinnati, OH	12/4/1951
Whalley, Joanne	Manchester, England, UK	8/25/1964
Wheaton, Wil	Burbank, CA	7/29/1972
Whitaker, Forest	Longview, TX	7/15/1961
White, Betty	Oak Park, IL	1/17/1922
White, Jack	Detroit, MI	7/9/1975
White, Jaleel	Pasadena, CA	11/27/1976
White, Vanna	N. Myrtle Beach, SC	2/18/1957
Whitford, Bradley	Madison, WI	10/10/1959
Wiest, Dianne	Kansas City, MO	3/28/1948
Wiig, Kristen	Canandaigua, NY	8/22/1973
Wilde, Olivia	New York, NY	3/10/1984
Wilder, Gene	Milwaukee, WI	6/11/1933
Wilkinson, Tom	Leeds, England, UK	12/12/1948
Williams, Armstrong	Marion, SC	2/5/1959
Williams, Barry	Santa Monica, CA	9/30/1954
Williams, Billy Dee	New York, NY	4/6/1937
Williams, Cindy	Van Nuys, CA	8/22/1947
Williams, Hal	Columbus, OH	12/14/1938
Williams, Hank, Jr.	Shreveport, LA	5/26/1949
Williams, JoBeth	Houston, TX	12/6/1948
Williams, Kimberly	Rye, NY	9/14/1971
Williams, Lucinda	Lake Charles, LA	1/26/1953
Williams, Michelle	Kalispell, MT	9/9/1980
Williams, Montel	Baltimore, MD	7/3/1956
Williams, Paul	Omaha, NE	9/19/1940
Williams, Pharrell	Virginia Beach, VA	4/5/1973
Williams, Treat	Rowayton, CT	12/1/1951
Williams, Vanessa	Millwood, NY	3/18/1963
Williamson, Kevin	New Bern, NC	3/14/1965
Willis, Bruce	Idar-Oberstein, W. Germany	3/19/1955
Wilmore, Larry	Los Angeles, CA	10/30/1961
Wilson, Brian	Ingelwood, CA	6/20/1942
Wilson, Cassandra	Jackson, MS	12/4/1955
Wilson, Chandra	Houston, TX	8/27/1969
Wilson, Demond	Valdosta, GA	10/13/1946
Wilson, Luke	Dallas, TX	9/21/1971
Wilson, Nancy	Chillicothe, OH	2/20/1937
Wilson, Owen	Dallas, TX	11/18/1968
Wilson, Rainn	Seattle, WA	1/20/1966
Wilson, Rebel	Sydney, NSW, Australia	2/3/1980
Winfrey, Oprah	Kosciusko, MS	1/29/1954
Winger, Debra	Cleveland, OH	5/16/1955
Winkler, Henry	New York, NY	10/30/1945
Winningham, Mare	Phoenix, AZ	5/16/1959
Winokur, Marissa Jaret	New York, NY	2/2/1973
Winslet, Kate	Reading, England, UK	10/5/1975
Winwood, Steve	Birmingham, England, UK	5/12/1948
Withers, Jane	Atlanta, GA	4/12/1926
Witherspoon, Reese	New Orleans, LA	3/22/1976
Witt, Alicia	Worcester, MA	8/21/1975
Wolf, Scott	Boston, MA	6/4/1968
Wonder, Stevie	Saginaw, MI	5/13/1950
Wong, Faye	Beijing, China	8/8/1969
Woo, John	Guangzhou, China	5/1/1946
Wood, Elijah	Cedar Rapids, IA	1/28/1981
Woodard, Alfre	Tulsa, OK	11/8/1952
Woodley, Shailene	Simi Valley, CA	11/15/1991
Woods, James	Vernal, UT	4/18/1947
Woodward, Joanne	Thomasville, GA	2/27/1930
Wopat, Tom	Lodi, WI	9/9/1951
Worthington Sam	Godalming, Surrey, Eng., UK	8/2/1976
Wright, Jeffrey	Washington, DC	12/7/1965
Wright, Max	Detroit, MI	8/2/1943
Wright, Robin	Dallas, TX	4/8/1966
Wright, Steven	New York, NY	12/6/1955
Wyle, Noah	Hollywood, CA	6/4/1971
Wyman, Bill	London, England, UK	10/24/1936
Yankovic, Weird Al	Lynwood, CA	10/23/1959
Yanni (Chrysomallis)	Kalamata, Greece	11/14/1954
Yarrow, Peter	New York, NY	5/31/1938
Yearwood, Trisha	Monticello, GA	9/19/1964
Yoakam, Dwight	Pikesville, KY	10/23/1956
York, Michael	Fulmer, England, UK	3/27/1942
Young, Alan	North Shields, England, UK	11/19/1919
Young, Burt	New York, NY	4/30/1940
Young, Neil	Toronto, ON, Canada	11/12/1945
Young, Sean	Louisville, KY	11/20/1959
Zane, Billy	Chicago, IL	2/24/1966
Zeffirelli, Franco	Florence, Italy	2/12/1923
Zellweger, Renée	Katy, TX	4/25/1969
Zemeckis, Robert	Chicago, IL	5/14/1952
Zerbe, Anthony	Long Beach, CA	5/20/1936
Zeta-Jones, Catherine	Swansea, Wales, UK	9/25/1969
Zimbalist, Stephanie	New York, NY	10/8/1956
Zimmer, Kim	Grand Rapids, MI	2/2/1955
Zhang, Ziyi	Beijing, China	2/9/1979
Zukerman, Pinchas	Tel Aviv, Israel	7/16/1948
Zuniga, Daphne	Berkeley, CA	10/28/1962

Entertainment Personalities of the Past

See also other lists for some deceased entertainers not included here.

Name	Born	Died
Aaliyah (Haughton)	1979	2001
Abbado, Claudio	1933	2014
Abbott, Bud	1895	1974
Abbott, George	1887	1995
Acuff, Roy	1903	1992
Adams, Don	1923	2005
Adams, Edie	1927	2008
Adams, Joey	1911	1999
Adams, Maude	1872	1953
Adler, Jacob P.	1855	1926
Adoree, Renee	1898	1933
Agar, John	1921	2002
Aherne, Brian	1902	1986
Ailey, Alvin	1931	1989
Akins, Claude	1918	1994
Albert, Eddie	1906	2005
Albertson, Frank	1909	1964
Albertson, Jack	1907	1981
Alda, Robert	1914	1986
Allen, Fred	1894	1956
Allen, Gracie	1906	1964
Allen, Mel	1913	1996
Allen, Peter	1944	1992
Allen, Steve	1921	2000
Allgood, Sara	1883	1950
Allyson, June	1917	2006
Altman, Robert	1925	2006
Ameche, Don	1908	1993
Ames, Leon	1903	1993
Amsterdam, Morey	1908	1996
Anderson, G. M. "Bronco Billy"	1882	1971
Anderson, Judith	1897	1992
Anderson, Lynn	1947	2015
Anderson, Marian	1897	1993
Andre the Giant	1946	1993
Andrews, Dana	1909	1992
Andrews, Laverne	1913	1967
Andrews, Maxene	1916	1995
Andrews, Patty	1918	2013
Angeli, Pier	1932	1971
Antonioni, Michelangelo	1912	2007
Arbuckle, Fatty (Roscoe)	1887	1933
Archerd, Army	1922	2009
Arden, Eve	1908	1990
Arlen, Richard	1900	1976
Arliss, George	1868	1946
Armstrong, Louis	1901	1971
Arnaz, Desi	1917	1986
Arness, James	1923	2011
Arnold, Eddy	1918	2008
Arnold, Edward	1890	1956
Arquette, Cliff	1905	1974
Arthur, Beatrice	1922	2009
Arthur, Jean	1900	1991
Arzner, Dorothy	1897	1979
Ashcroft, Peggy	1907	1991
Astaire, Fred	1899	1987
Astor, Mary	1906	1987
Atkins, Chet	1924	2001
Attenborough, Richard	1923	2014
Atwill, Lionel	1885	1946
Auer, Mischa	1905	1967
Aumont, Jean-Pierre	1911	2001
Austin, Gene	1900	1972
Autry, Gene	1907	1998
Axton, Hoyt	1938	1999
Ayres, Lew	1908	1996
Bacall, Lauren	1924	2014
Backus, Jim	1913	1989
Bailey, Pearl	1918	1990
Bain, Conrad	1923	2013
Bainter, Fay	1892	1968
Baker, Josephine	1906	1975
Balanchine, George	1904	1983
Ball, Lucille	1911	1989
Balsam, Martin	1919	1996
Bancroft, Anne	1931	2005
Bankhead, Tallulah	1902	1968
Bara, Theda	1885?	1955
Barnett, Etta Moten	1902	2004
Barnum, Phineas T.	1810	1891
Barrett, Syd	1946	2006
Barry, Gene	1919	2009
Barrymore, Ethel	1879	1959
Barrymore, John	1882	1942
Barrymore, Lionel	1878	1954
Barrymore, Maurice	1848	1905
Barthelmess, Richard	1895	1963
Bartholomew, Freddie	1924	1992
Barty, Billy	1924	2000
Basehart, Richard	1914	1984
Basie, Count	1904	1984
Bates, Alan	1934	2003
Bavier, Frances	1902	1989
Baxter, Anne	1923	1985
Baxter, Warner	1889	1951
Beaumont, Hugh	1909	1982
Beavers, Louise	1902	1962
Beery, Noah, Jr.	1913	1994
Beery, Noah, Sr.	1884	1946
Beery, Wallace	1885	1949
Begley, Ed	1901	1970
Bel Geddes, Barbara	1922	2005
Bellamy, Ralph	1904	1991
Belushi, John	1949	1982
Benaderet, Bea	1906	1968
Bendix, William	1906	1964
Bennett, Constance	1904	1965
Bennett, Joan	1910	1990
Bennett, Michael	1943	1987
Benny, Jack	1894	1974
Berg, Gertrude	1899	1966
Bergen, Edgar	1903	1978
Bergen, Polly	1930	2014
Bergman, Ingmar	1918	2007
Bergman, Ingrid	1915	1982
Berkeley, Busby	1895	1976
Berle, Milton	1908	2002
Berlin, Irving	1888	1989
Bernardi, Herschel	1923	1986
Bernhardt, Sarah	1844	1923
Bernstein, Leonard	1918	1990
Berry, Jan	1941	2004
Bessell, Ted	1939	1996
Bickford, Charles	1889	1967
Big Bopper, The	1930	1959
Bikel, Theodore	1924	2015
Billingsley, Barbara	1915	2010
Bing, Rudolf	1902	1997
Bishop, Joey	1918	2007
Bitzer, Billy	1872	1944
Bixby, Bill	1934	1993
Black, Karen	1939	2013
Blackstone, Harry, Jr.	1934	1997
Blackstone, Harry, Sr.	1885	1965
Blaine, Vivian	1921	1995
Blake, Amanda	1931	1989
Blake, Eubie	1883	1983
Blanc, Mel	1908	1989
Blocker, Dan	1928	1972
Blondell, Joan	1909	1979
Blondin, Charles	1824	1897
Blore, Eric	1887	1959
Blue, Ben	1901	1975
Blyden, Larry	1925	1975
Bogarde, Dirk	1921	1999
Bogart, Humphrey	1899	1957
Boland, Mary	1880	1965
Boles, John	1895	1969
Bolger, Ray	1904	1987
Bond, Ward	1903	1960
Bondi, Beulah	1888	1981
Bono, Sonny	1935	1998
Boone, Richard	1917	1981
Booth, Edwin	1833	1893
Booth, John Wilkes	1838	1865
Booth, Junius Brutus	1796	1852
Booth, Shirley	1898	1992
Borge, Victor	1909	2000
Borgnine, Ernest	1917	2012
Borzage, Frank	1893	1962
Bosley, Tom	1927	2010
Bow, Clara	1905	1965
Bowes, Maj. Edward	1874	1946
Bowman, Lee	1914	1979
Boxcar Willie	1931	1999
Boyd, Stephen	1928	1977
Boyd, William	1898	1972
Boyer, Charles	1899	1978
Boyle, Peter	1935	2006
Bracken, Eddie	1915	2002
Brady, Alice	1892	1939
Brando, Marlon	1924	2004
Branigan, Laura	1957	2004
Brazzi, Rossano	1916	1994
Brennan, Eileen	1932	2013
Brennan, Walter	1894	1974
Brenner, David	1936	2014
Brent, George	1904	1979
Brett, Jeremy	1935	1995
Brewer, Teresa	1931	2007
Brice, Fanny	1891	1951
Bridges, Lloyd	1913	1998
Broderick, Helen	1891	1959
Bronson, Charles	1921	2003
Brooks, Foster	1912	2001
Brooks, Louise	1906	1985
Brown, Clarence	1890	1987
Brown, James	1933	2006
Brown, Joe E.	1892	1973
Brown, Johnny Mack	1904	1974
Brown, Les	1912	2001
Browne, Roscoe Lee	1925	2007
Browning, Tod	1882	1962
Brubeck, Dave	1920	2012
Bruce, Lenny	1925	1966
Bruce, Nigel	1895	1953
Bruce, Virginia	1910	1982
Brynner, Yul	1915	1985
Buchanan, Edgar	1903	1979
Buchholz, Horst	1933	2003
Buñuel, Luis	1900	1983
Buono, Victor	1938	1982
Burke, Billie	1885	1970
Burnette, Smiley	1911	1967
Burns, George	1896	1996
Burr, Raymond	1917	1993
Burton, Richard	1925	1984
Busch, Mae	1897	1946
Bushman, Francis X.	1883	1966
Buttons, Red	1919	2006
Byington, Spring	1893	1971
Cabot, Bruce	1904	1972
Cabot, Sebastian	1918	1977
Caesar, Sid	1922	2014
Cagney, James	1899	1986
Caldwell, Sarah	1924	2006
Calhern, Louis	1895	1956
Calhoun, Rory	1922	1999
Callas, Charlie	1927	2011
Callas, Maria	1923	1977
Calloway, Cab	1907	1994
Cambridge, Godfrey	1933	1976
Campbell, Mrs. Patrick	1865	1940
Candy, John	1950	1994
Cantinflas	1911	1993
Cantor, Eddie	1892	1964
Capra, Frank	1897	1991
Carey, Harry	1878	1947
Carey, Harry, Jr.	1921	2012
Carey, Macdonald	1913	1994
Carle, Frankie	1903	2001
Carlin, George	1937	2008
Carlisle Hart, Kitty	1910	2007
Carney, Art	1918	2003
Carpenter, Karen	1950	1983
Carradine, David	1936	2009
Carradine, John	1906	1988
Carrillo, Leo	1880	1961
Carroll, Leo G.	1892	1972
Carroll, Madeleine	1906	1987
Carson, Jack	1910	1963
Carson, Johnny	1925	2005
Carter, Benny	1907	2003
Carter, Dixie	1939	2010
Carter, Nell	1948	2003
Caruso, Enrico	1873	1921
Casals, Pablo	1876	1973
Cash, Johnny	1932	2003
Cash, June Carter	1929	2003
Cass, Peggy	1924	1999
Cassavetes, John	1929	1989
Cassidy, Jack	1927	1976
Castle, Irene	1893	1969
Castle, Vernon	1887	1918
Chaliapin, Feodor	1873	1938
Champion, Gower	1919	1980
Chandler, Jeff	1918	1961

Name	Born	Died
Chaney, Lon	1883	1930
Chaney, Lon, Jr.	1905	1973
Chapin, Harry	1942	1981
Chaplin, Charles	1889	1977
Chapman, Graham	1941	1989
Charisse, Cyd	1921	2008
Charles, Ray	1930	2004
Chase, Ilka	1905	1978
Chatterton, Ruth	1893	1961
Cherrill, Virginia	1908	1996
Chevalier, Maurice	1888	1972
Child, Julia	1912	2004
Clair, René	1898	1981
Clark, Dick	1929	2012
Clayburgh, Jill	1944	2010
Clayton, Jan	1917	1983
Clemons, Clarence	1942	2011
Cliburn, Van	1934	2013
Clift, Montgomery	1920	1966
Cline, Patsy	1932	1963
Clooney, Rosemary	1928	2002
Clyde, Andy	1892	1967
Cobain, Kurt	1967	1994
Cobb, Lee J.	1911	1976
Coburn, Charles	1877	1961
Coburn, James	1928	2002
Coca, Imogene	1908	2001
Cocker, Joe	1944	2014
Coco, James	1930	1987
Cody, Buffalo Bill	1846	1917
Cody, Iron Eyes	1907	1999
Cohan, George M.	1878	1942
Cohen, Myron	1902	1986
Colbert, Claudette	1903	1996
Cole, Nat "King"	1919	1965
Coleman, Gary	1968	2010
Coleman, Ornette	1930	2015
Collins, Gary	1938	2012
Collins, Ray	1890	1965
Colman, Ronald	1891	1958
Columbo, Russ	1908	1934
Comden, Betty	1917	2006
Como, Perry	1912	2001
Conniff, Ray	1916	2002
Connors, Chuck	1921	1992
Conrad, William	1920	1994
Conried, Hans	1917	1982
Conte, Richard	1911	1975
Convy, Bert	1933	1991
Conway, Tom	1904	1967
Coogan, Jackie	1914	1984
Cook, Elisha, Jr.	1904	1995
Cooke, Alistair	1908	2004
Cooke, Sam	1931	1964
Cooper, Gary	1901	1961
Cooper, Gladys	1888	1971
Cooper, Jackie	1922	2011
Copland, Aaron	1900	1990
Corby, Ellen	1913	1999
Corelli, Franco	1921	2003
Corey, Jeff	1914	2002
Corio, Ann	1914	1999
Corley, Pat	1930	2006
Cornelius, Don	1936	2012
Cornell, Katharine	1893	1974
Correll, Charles	1890	1972
Costello, Dolores	1905	1979
Costello, Lou	1906	1959
Cotten, Joseph	1905	1994
Coward, Noel	1899	1973
Cox, Wally	1924	1973
Crabbe, Buster	1908	1983
Crain, Jeanne	1925	2003
Crane, Bob	1928	1978
Craven, Wes	1939	2015
Crawford, Broderick	1911	1986
Crawford, Joan	1904	1977
Crenna, Richard	1926	2003
Crews, Laura Hope	1880	1942
Crisp, Donald	1880	1974
Crisp, Quentin	1908	1999
Croce, Jim	1942	1973
Cronyn, Hume	1911	2003
Crosby, Bing	1903	1977
Crothers, Scatman	1910	1986
Cruz, Celia	1925	2003
Cugat, Xavier	1900	1990

Name	Born	Died
Cukor, George	1899	1983
Cullen, Bill	1920	1990
Culp, Robert	1930	2010
Cummings, Constance	1910	2005
Cummings, Robert	1908	1990
Curtis, Ken	1916	1991
Curtis, Tony	1925	2010
Curtiz, Michael	1888	1962
Cushing, Peter	1913	1994
Da Silva, Howard	1909	1986
Dailey, Dan	1915	1978
Dandridge, Dorothy	1923	1965
Dangerfield, Rodney	1921	2004
Daniell, Henry	1894	1963
Daniels, Bebe	1901	1971
Darin, Bobby	1936	1973
Darnell, Linda	1923	1965
Darwell, Jane	1879	1967
Davenport, Harry	1866	1949
Davies, Marion	1897	1961
Davis, Ann B.	1926	2014
Davis, Bette	1908	1989
Davis, Joan	1907	1961
Davis, Ossie	1917	2005
Davis, Sammy, Jr.	1925	1990
Dawson, Richard	1932	2012
Day, Dennis	1917	1988
Day, Laraine	1920	2007
De Carlo, Yvonne	1922	2007
De Laurentiis, Dino	1919	2010
de Mille, Agnes	1905	1993
De Mille, Cecil B.	1881	1959
De Wilde, Brandon	1942	1972
De Wolfe, Billy	1907	1974
Dean, James	1931	1955
Dean, Jimmy	1928	2010
Dearie, Blossom	1924	2009
Dee, Frances	1907	2004
Dee, Ruby	1924	2014
Dee, Sandra	1942	2005
Defore, Don	1917	1993
DeFranco, Buddy	1923	2014
Dekker, Albert	1905	1968
Del Rio, Dolores	1905	1983
DeLuise, Dom	1933	2009
Demarest, William	1892	1983
Dennis, Sandy	1937	1992
Denny, Reginald	1891	1967
Denver, Bob	1935	2005
Denver, John	1943	1997
Derek, John	1926	1998
DeSica, Vittorio	1901	1974
Devine, Andy	1905	1977
Dewhurst, Colleen	1924	1991
Diamond, Selma	1920	1985
Diddley, Bo	1928	2008
Dietrich, Marlene	1901	1992
Diller, Phyllis	1917	2012
Disney, Walt	1901	1966
Dix, Richard	1894	1949
Dmytryk, Edward	1908	1999
Donahue, Troy	1936	2001
Donat, Robert	1905	1958
Donlevy, Brian	1901	1972
Dors, Diana	1931	1984
Dorsey, Jimmy	1904	1957
Dorsey, Tommy	1905	1956
Douglas, Melvyn	1901	1981
Douglas, Paul	1907	1959
Dove, Billie	1900	1998
Downey, Morton, Jr.	1933	2001
Doyle, David	1929	1997
Drake, Alfred	1914	1992
Draper, Ruth	1884	1956
Dressler, Marie	1869	1934
Drew, Ellen	1915	2003
Drew, Mrs. John	1820	1897
Dru, Joanne	1923	1996
Duchin, Eddy	1909	1951
Duff, Howard	1917	1990
Duggan, Andrew	1923	1988
Dumbrille, Douglass	1890	1974
Dumont, Margaret	1889	1965
Duncan, Isadora	1878	1927
Duncan, Michael Clarke	1957	2012
Dunham, Katherine	1910	2006

Name	Born	Died
Dunn, James	1905	1967
Dunne, Irene	1898	1990
Dunnock, Mildred	1901	1991
Durante, Jimmy	1893	1980
Durbin, Deanna	1921	2013
Durning, Charles	1923	2012
Duryea, Dan	1907	1968
Duse, Eleanora	1858	1924
Dvorak, Ann	1912	1979
Dysart, Richard	1929	2015
Eagels, Jeanne	1894	1929
Ebert, Roger	1942	2013
Ebsen, Buddy	1908	2003
Eckstine, Billy	1914	1993
Eddy, Nelson	1901	1967
Edelman, Herb	1933	1996
Edwards, Blake	1922	2010
Edwards, Cliff	1895	1971
Edwards, Ralph	1913	2005
Edwards, Vince	1928	1996
Egan, Richard	1923	1987
Eisenstein, Sergei	1898	1948
Ekberg, Anita	1931	2015
Elam, Jack	1916	2003
Ellington, Duke	1899	1974
Elliot, Cass	1941	1974
Elliott, Denholm	1922	1992
Ellis, Mary	1897	2003
Elman, Mischa	1891	1967
Ephron, Nora	1941	2012
Errol, Leon	1881	1951
Evans, Dale	1912	2001
Evans, Edith	1888	1976
Evans, Maurice	1901	1989
Everett, Chad	1936?	2012
Everly, Phil	1939	2014
Ewell, Tom	1909	1994
Fadiman, Clifton	1904	1999
Fairbanks, Douglas	1883	1939
Fairbanks, Douglas, Jr.	1909	2000
Falk, Peter	1927	2011
Farentino, James	1938	2012
Farina, Dennis	1944	2013
Farley, Chris	1964	1997
Farmer, Frances	1913	1970
Farnsworth, Richard	1920	2000
Farnum, Dustin	1874	1929
Farnum, William	1876	1953
Farrar, Geraldine	1882	1967
Farrell, Charles	1901	1990
Farrell, Eileen	1920	2002
Fassbinder, Rainer Werner	1946	1982
Fawcett, Farrah	1947	2009
Faye, Alice	1915	1998
Fazenda, Louise	1895	1962
Feld, Fritz	1900	1993
Feldman, Marty	1933	1982
Fell, Norman	1924	1998
Fellini, Federico	1920	1993
Fenneman, George	1919	1997
Ferrer, Jose	1912	1992
Ferrer, Mel	1917	2008
Fetchit, Stepin	1898	1985
Fiedler, Arthur	1894	1979
Fiedler, John	1925	2005
Fields, Gracie	1898	1979
Fields, Totie	1930	1978
Fields, W. C.	1879	1946
Finch, Peter	1916	1977
Fine, Larry	1902	1975
Fisher, Eddie	1928	2010
Fiske, Minnie Maddern	1865	1932
Fitzgerald, Barry	1888	1961
Fitzgerald, Ella	1917	1996
Fitzgerald, Geraldine	1913	2005
Fleischer, Richard	1916	2006
Fleming, Art	1924	1995
Fleming, Victor	1889	1949
Flynn, Errol	1909	1959
Flynn, Joe	1925	1974
Foch, Nina	1924	2008
Fogelberg, Dan	1951	2007
Foley, Red	1910	1968
Fonda, Henry	1905	1982
Fontaine, Frank	1920	1978
Fontaine, Joan	1917	2013
Fontanne, Lynn	1887	1983

Name	Born	Died
Fonteyn, Margot	1919	1991
Ford, Glenn	1916	2006
Ford, John	1895	1973
Ford, Paul	1901	1976
Ford, Tennessee Ernie	1919	1991
Forrest, Helen	1917	1999
Forsythe, John	1918	2010
Fosse, Bob	1927	1987
Foster, Phil	1914	1985
Foster, Preston	1901	1970
Foxx, Redd	1922	1991
Foy, Eddie	1856	1928
Franchi, Sergio	1926	1990
Franciosa, Anthony	1928	2006
Francis, Anne	1930	2011
Francis, Arlene	1907	2001
Francis, Kay	1905	1968
Franciscus, James	1934	1991
Frankenheimer, John	1930	2002
Franklin, Bonnie	1944	2013
Frann, Mary	1943	1998
Frawley, William	1887	1966
Frederick, Pauline	1885	1938
Freed, Alan	1921	1965
Freeman, Al, Jr.	1934	2012
Freeman, Mona	1926	2014
French, Victor	1934	1989
Friganza, Trixie	1870	1955
Froman, Jane	1907	1980
Frost, David	1939	2013
Funicello, Annette	1942	2013
Funt, Allen	1914	1999
Furness, Betty	1916	1994
Gabin, Jean	1904	1976
Gable, Clark	1901	1960
Gabor, Eva	1920	1995
Gandolfini, James	1961	2013
Garbo, Greta	1905	1990
Garcia, Jerry	1942	1995
Gardenia, Vincent	1922	1992
Gardner, Ava	1922	1990
Garfield, John	1913	1952
Garland, Beverly	1926	2008
Garland, Judy	1922	1969
Garner, James	1928	2014
Garrett, Betty	1919	2011
Garson, Greer	1904	1996
Gassman, Vittorio	1922	2000
Gaye, Marvin	1939	1984
Gaynor, Janet	1906	1984
Gazzara, Ben	1930	2012
Gebel-Williams, Gunther	1934	2001
Geer, Will	1902	1978
George, Gladys	1904	1954
Gershwin, George	1898	1937
Getty, Estelle	1923	2008
Ghostley, Alice	1926	2007
Gibb, Andy	1958	1988
Gibb, Maurice	1949	2003
Gibb, Robin	1949	2012
Gibson, Henry	1935	2009
Gibson, Hoot	1892	1962
Gielgud, John	1904	2000
Gifford, Frank	1930	2015
Gilbert, Billy	1894	1971
Gilbert, John	1895	1936
Gilford, Jack	1907	1990
Gillespie, Dizzy	1917	1993
Gillette, William	1853	1937
Gingold, Hermione	1897	1987
Gish, Dorothy	1898	1968
Gish, Lillian	1893	1993
Giulini, Carlo Maria	1914	2005
Gleason, Jackie	1916	1987
Gleason, James	1886	1959
Gluck, Alma	1884	1938
Gobel, George	1919	1991
Goddard, Paulette	1905?	1990
Godfrey, Arthur	1903	1983
Godunov, Alexander	1949	1995
Goldwyn, Samuel	1882	1974
Goodman, Benny	1909	1986
Gorcey, Leo	1917	1969
Gordon, Gale	1906	1995
Gordon, Ruth	1896	1985
Gorme, Eydie	1932	2013
Gorshin, Frank	1934	2005
Gosden, Freeman	1899	1982
Gottschalk, Louis	1829	1869
Gould, Glenn	1932	1982
Gould, Harold	1923	2010
Gould, Morton	1913	1996
Goulet, Robert	1933	2007
Grable, Betty	1916	1973
Graham, Martha	1894	1991
Graham, Virginia	1912	1998
Grahame, Gloria	1925	1981
Granger, Farley	1925	2011
Granger, Stewart	1913	1993
Grant, Cary	1904	1986
Granville, Bonita	1923	1988
Grapewin, Charley	1869	1956
Graves, Peter	1926	2010
Gray, Dolores	1924	2002
Gray, Spalding	1941	2004
Grayson, Kathryn	1922	2010
Greco, Jose	1918	2000
Green, Adolph	1915	2002
Greene, Lorne	1915	1987
Greenstreet, Sydney	1879	1954
Greenwood, Charlotte	1890	1978
Gregory, James	1911	2002
Griffin, Merv	1925	2007
Griffith, Andy	1926	2012
Griffith, David Wark	1874	1948
Griffith, Hugh	1912	1980
Griffiths, Richard	1947	2013
Grizzard, George	1928	2007
Guardino, Harry	1925	1995
Guinness, Sir Alec	1914	2000
Guthrie, Woody	1912	1967
Gwenn, Edmund	1875	1959
Gwynne, Fred	1926	1993
Hackett, Buddy	1924	2003
Hackett, Joan	1934	1983
Hagen, Uta	1919	2004
Hagman, Larry	1931	2012
Haines, William	1900	1973
Hale, Alan, Jr.	1918	1990
Hale, Alan, Sr.	1892	1950
Haley, Bill	1925	1981
Haley, Jack	1899	1979
Hall, Huntz	1919	1999
Hall, Jon	1915	1979
Hamilton, Margaret	1902	1985
Hammerstein, Oscar	1847	1919
Hammerstein, Oscar, II	1895	1960
Hampton, Lionel	1908	2002
Hardwicke, Cedric	1893	1964
Hardy, Oliver	1892	1957
Harlow, Jean	1911	1937
Harris, Julie	1925	2013
Harris, Phil	1904	1995
Harris, Richard	1930	2002
Harrison, George	1943	2001
Harrison, Rex	1908	1990
Hart, William S.	1864	1946
Hartman, Phil	1948	1998
Harvey, Laurence	1928	1973
Harvey, Paul	1918	2009
Harwell, Ernie	1918	2010
Hatfield, Bobby	1940	2003
Havens, Richie	1941	2013
Havoc, June	1912	2010
Hawkins, Jack	1910	1973
Hawkins, Screamin' Jay	1929	2000
Hawks, Howard	1896	1977
Hawthorne, Nigel	1929	2001
Hayakawa, Sessue	1890	1973
Hayden, Sterling	1916	1986
Hayes, Gabby	1885	1969
Hayes, Helen	1900	1993
Hayes, Isaac	1942	2008
Hayward, Leland	1902	1971
Hayward, Louis	1909	1985
Hayward, Susan	1917	1975
Hayworth, Rita	1918	1987
Head, Edith	1897	1981
Healy, Ted	1896	1937
Heckart, Eileen	1919	2001
Heflin, Van	1910	1971
Heifetz, Jascha	1901	1987
Held, Anna	1873	1918
Helm, Levon	1940	2012
Hemingway, Margaux	1955	1996
Hemmings, David	1941	2003
Hemsley, Sherman	1938	2012
Henderson, Skitch	1918	2005
Hendrix, Jimi	1942	1970
Henie, Sonja	1912	1969
Henreid, Paul	1908	1992
Henson, Jim	1936	1990
Hepburn, Audrey	1929	1993
Hepburn, Katharine	1907	2003
Herrmann, Edward	1943	2014
Hersholt, Jean	1886	1956
Heston, Charlton	1923	2008
Hewett, Christopher	1922	2001
Hickey, William	1928	1997
Hickson, Joan	1906	1998
Hildegarde	1906	2005
Hill, Arthur	1922	2006
Hill, Benny	1925	1992
Hill, George Roy	1921	2002
Hiller, Wendy	1912	2003
Hines, Gregory	1946	2003
Hines, Jerome	1921	2003
Hingle, Pat	1924	2009
Hirt, Al	1922	1999
Hitchcock, Alfred	1899	1980
Ho, Don	1930	2007
Hodiak, John	1914	1955
Hoffman, Philip Seymour	1967	2014
Holden, William	1918	1981
Holder, Geoffrey	1930	2014
Holiday, Billie	1915	1959
Holliday, Judy	1921	1965
Holloway, Sterling	1905	1992
Holly, Buddy	1936	1959
Holm, Celeste	1919	2012
Holt, Jack	1888	1951
Holt, Tim	1918	1973
Homolka, Oscar	1898	1978
Hooker, John Lee	1917	2001
Hoon, Shannon	1967	1995
Hope, Bob	1903	2003
Hopkins, Miriam	1902	1972
Hopper, Dennis	1936	2010
Hopper, DeWolf	1858	1935
Hopper, Hedda	1885	1966
Hopper, William	1915	1970
Horowitz, Vladimir	1904	1989
Horne, Lena	1917	2010
Horton, Edward Everett	1886	1970
Hoskins, Bob	1942	2014
Houdini, Harry	1874	1926
Houseman, John	1902	1988
Houston, Whitney	1963	2012
Howard (Horwitz), Curly	1903	1952
Howard, Leslie	1890	1943
Howard (Horwitz), Moe	1897	1975
Howard (Horwitz), Shemp	1895	1955
Howard, Trevor	1916	1988
Hudson, Rock	1925	1985
Hughes, Bernard	1915	2006
Hughes, John	1950	2009
Hull, Henry	1890	1977
Hull, Josephine	1886	1957
Hunter, Jeffrey	1926	1969
Hunter, Kim	1922	2002
Hunter, Ross	1920	1996
Hussey, Ruth	1911	2005
Huston, John	1906	1987
Huston, Walter	1884	1950
Hutchence, Michael	1960	1997
Hutton, Betty	1921	2007
Hutton, Jim	1934	1979
Hyde-White, Wilfrid	1903	1991
Ingram, Rex	1895	1969
Ireland, Jill	1936	1990
Ireland, John	1915	1992
Irving, Henry	1838	1905
Ives, Burl	1909	1995
Irwin, Steve	1962	2006
Iturbi, Jose	1895	1980
Jack, Wolfman	1938	1995
Jackson, Joe	1875	1942
Jackson, Mahalia	1911	1972
Jackson, Michael	1958	2009
Jackson, Milt	1923	1999
Jaeckel, Richard	1926	1997

Name	Born	Died
Jaffe, Sam	1891	1984
Jagger, Dean	1903	1991
Jam Master Jay	1965	2002
James, Dennis	1917	1997
James, Etta	1938	2012
James, Harry	1916	1983
James, Rick	1948	2004
Janis, Elsie	1889	1956
Jannings, Emil	1886	1950
Janssen, David	1930	1980
Jenkins, Allen	1900	1974
Jennings, Waylon	1937	2002
Jessel, George	1898	1981
Jeter, Michael	1952	2003
Johnson, Ben	1918	1996
Johnson, Celia	1908	1982
Johnson, Chic	1892	1962
Johnson, J.J.	1924	2001
Johnson, Robert	1911	1938
Johnson, Van	1916	2008
Jolson, Al	1886	1950
Jones, Brian	1942	1969
Jones, Buck	1889	1942
Jones, Carolyn	1933	1983
Jones, Charlie	1930	2008
Jones, Davy	1945	2012
Jones, Dean	1931	2015
Jones, Elvin	1927	2004
Jones, George	1931	2013
Jones, Henry	1912	1999
Jones, Jennifer	1919	2009
Jones, Spike	1911	1965
Joplin, Janis	1943	1970
Joplin, Scott	1868	1917
Jordan, Richard	1937	1993
Jory, Victor	1902	1982
Joslyn, Allyn	1905	1981
Jourdan, Louis	1921	2015
Julia, Raul	1940	1994
Jump, Gordon	1932	2003
Jurado, Katy	1924	2002
Jurgens, Curt	1915	1982
Kahn, Madeline	1942	1999
Kane, Helen	1904	1966
Kanin, Garson	1912	1999
Karloff, Boris	1887	1969
Karns, Roscoe	1893	1970
Karras, Alex	1935	2012
Kasem, Casey	1932	2014
Kaufman, Andy	1949	1984
Kaye, Danny	1913	1987
Kaye, Stubby	1918	1997
Kazan, Elia	1909	2003
Kean, Charles	1811	1868
Kean, Mrs. Charles	1806	1880
Kean, Edmund	1787	1833
Keaton, Buster	1895	1966
Keel, Howard	1919	2004
Keeler, Ruby	1910	1993
Keeshan, Bob (Captain Kangaroo)	1927	2004
Keith, Brian	1921	1997
Kellaway, Cecil	1893	1973
Kelley, DeForest	1920	1999
Kelly, Emmett	1898	1979
Kelly, Gene	1912	1996
Kelly, Grace	1929	1982
Kelly, Jack	1927	1992
Kelly, Patsy	1910	1981
Kennedy, Arthur	1914	1990
Kennedy, Edgar	1890	1948
Kerr, Deborah	1921	2007
Kibbee, Guy	1886	1956
Kiel, Richard	1939	2014
Kilbride, Percy	1888	1964
Kiley, Richard	1922	1999
King, Alan	1927	2004
King, B. B.	1925	2015
King, Henry	1896	1982
Kinski, Klaus	1926	1991
Kirby, Bruno	1949	2006
Kirby, George	1923	1995
Kirby, Durward	1912	2000
Kitt, Eartha	1927	2008
Klemperer, Werner	1920	2000
Klugman, Jack	1922	2012
Knight, Ted	1923	1986
Knotts, Don	1924	2006
Korman, Harvey	1927	2008
Kostelanetz, Andre	1901	1980
Kovacs, Ernie	1919	1962
Kramer, Stanley	1913	2001
Kruger, Otto	1885	1974
Kubrick, Stanley	1928	1999
Kulp, Nancy	1921	1991
Kurosawa, Akira	1910	1998
Kyser, Kay	1906	1985
Ladd, Alan	1913	1964
Lahr, Bert	1895	1967
Laine, Frankie	1913	2007
Lake, Arthur	1905	1987
Lake, Veronica	1919	1973
LaLanne, Jack	1914	2011
Lamarr, Hedy	1913	2000
Lamas, Fernando	1915	1982
Lamour, Dorothy	1914	1996
Lancaster, Burt	1913	1994
Lanchester, Elsa	1902	1986
Landis, Carole	1919	1948
Landon, Michael	1936	1991
Lane, Priscilla	1917	1995
Lang, Fritz	1890	1976
Langdon, Harry	1884	1944
Lange, Hope	1931	2003
Langford, Frances	1914	2005
Langtry, Lillie	1853	1929
Lanza, Mario	1921	1959
LaRue, Lash (Alfred)	1917	1996
Lauder, Harry	1870	1950
Laughton, Charles	1899	1962
Laurel, Stan	1890	1965
Lawford, Peter	1923	1984
Lawrence, Florence	1886	1938
Lawrence, Gertrude	1898	1952
Lean, David	1908	1991
Ledger, Heath	1979	2008
Lee, Anna	1913	2004
Lee, Bernard	1908	1981
Lee, Bruce	1940	1973
Lee, Canada	1907	1952
Lee, Christopher	1922	2015
Lee, Gypsy Rose	1914	1970
Lee, Peggy	1920	2002
LeGallienne, Eva	1899	1991
Leigh, Janet	1927	2004
Leigh, Vivien	1913	1967
Leighton, Margaret	1922	1976
Lemmon, Jack	1925	2001
Lennon, John	1940	1980
Lenya, Lotte	1898	1981
Leonard, Eddie	1870	1941
Leonard, Sheldon	1907	1997
Leone, Sergio	1929	1989
LeRoy, Mervyn	1900	1987
Levant, Oscar	1906	1972
Levene, Sam	1905	1980
Levenson, Sam	1911	1980
Lewis, Al	1923	2006
Lewis, Joe E.	1902	1971
Lewis, Shari	1934	1998
Lewis, Ted	1892	1971
Liberace	1919	1987
Lillie, Beatrice	1894	1989
Lincoln, Elmo	1889	1952
Lind, Jenny	1820	1887
Lindfors, Viveca	1920	1995
Lindley, Audra	1918	1997
Linkletter, Art	1912	2010
Linville, Larry	1939	2000
Little, Cleavon	1939	1992
Llewelyn, Desmond	1914	1999
Lloyd, Harold	1893	1971
Lloyd, Marie	1870	1922
Lockhart, Gene	1891	1957
Lom, Herbert	1917	2012
Lombard, Carole	1908	1942
Lombardo, Guy	1902	1977
Long, Richard	1927	1974
Lopes, Lisa	1971	2002
Lopez, Vincent	1895	1975
Lord, Jack	1920	1998
Lorne, Marion	1888	1968
Lorre, Peter	1904	1964
Loudon, Dorothy	1933	2003
Lowe, Edmund	1890	1971
Loy, Myrna	1905	1993
Lubitsch, Ernst	1892	1947
Ludden, Allen	1918	1981
Lugosi, Bela	1882	1956
Lukas, Paul	1894	1971
Lumet, Sidney	1924	2011
Lunt, Alfred	1892	1977
Lupino, Ida	1918	1995
Lymon, Frankie	1942	1968
Lynde, Paul	1926	1982
Maazel, Lorin	1930	2014
Mac, Bernie	1957	2008
MacArthur, James	1937	2010
MacCorkindale, Simon	1952	2010
MacDonald, Jeanette	1903	1965
Mack, Ted	1904	1976
MacKenzie, Gisele	1927	2003
MacLane, Barton	1902	1969
MacMurray, Fred	1908	1991
MacNee, Patrick	1922	2015
MacRae, Gordon	1921	1986
Macready, George	1909	1973
Madison, Guy	1922	1996
Magnani, Anna	1908	1973
Mancini, Henry	1924	1994
Main, Marjorie	1890	1975
Malden, Karl	1912	2009
Malle, Louis	1932	1995
Mamoulian, Rouben	1897	1987
Mankiewicz, Joseph	1909	1993
Mann, Herbie	1930	2003
Mansfield, Jayne	1932	1967
Mantovani, Annunzio	1905	1980
Marais, Jean	1913	1998
March, Fredric	1897	1975
March, Hal	1920	1970
Marchand, Nancy	1928	2000
Markova, Alicia	1910	2004
Marley, Bob	1945	1981
Marshall, E.G.	1910	1998
Marshall, Herbert	1890	1966
Martin, Barney	1923	2005
Martin, Dean	1917	1995
Martin, Dick	1922	2008
Martin, Mary	1913	1990
Martin, Ross	1920	1981
Martin, Tony	1913	2012
Marvin, Lee	1924	1987
Marx, Harpo (Arthur)	1888	1964
Marx, Zeppo (Herbert)	1901	1979
Marx, Groucho (Julius)	1890	1977
Marx, Chico (Leonard)	1887	1961
Marx, Gummo (Milton)	1893	1977
Mason, James	1909	1984
Massey, Raymond	1896	1983
Mastroianni, Marcello	1924	1996
Matthau, Walter	1920	2000
Mature, Victor	1913	1999
Maxwell, Marilyn	1921	1972
Mayer, Louis B.	1885	1957
Mayfield, Curtis	1942	1999
Mayo, Virginia	1920	2005
Mazurki, Mike	1909	1990
Mazursky, Paul	1930	2014
MCA (Adam Yauch)	1964	2012
McCambridge, Mercedes	1916	2004
McCarey, Leo	1898	1969
McCarthy, Kevin	1914	2010
McCartney, Linda	1941	1998
McClanahan, Rue	1934	2010
McClure, Doug	1935	1995
McCormack, John	1884	1945
McCrary, Tex	1910	2003
McCrea, Joel	1905	1990
McDaniel, Hattie	1895	1952
McDowall, Roddy	1928	1998
McFarland, Spanky (George)	1928	1993
McGoohan, Patrick	1928	2009
McGuire, Al	1931	2001
McGuire, Dorothy	1916	2001
McHugh, Frank	1898	1981
McIntire, John	1907	1991
McLaglen, Victor	1886	1959
McMahon, Ed	1923	2009
McNeill, Don	1907	1996
McPartland, Marian	1918	2013

Name	Born	Died
McQueen, Butterfly	1911	1995
McQueen, Steve	1930	1980
Meader, Vaughn	1936	2004
Meadows, Audrey	1924	1996
Meadows, Jayne	1919	2015
Meara, Anne	1929	2015
Meek, Donald	1880	1946
Meeker, Ralph	1920	1988
Melba, Nellie	1861	1931
Méliès, Georges	1861	1938
Menjou, Adolphe	1890	1963
Menken, Helen	1902	1966
Menuhin, Yehudi	1916	1999
Mercer, Marian	1935	2011
Mercouri, Melina	1925	1994
Mercury, Freddie	1946	1991
Meredith, Burgess	1909	1997
Merman, Ethel	1908	1984
Merrick, David	1911	2000
Merrill, Gary	1915	1990
Milestone, Lewis	1895	1980
Mifune, Toshiro	1920	1997
Milland, Ray	1905	1986
Miller, Ann	1923	2004
Miller, Glenn	1904	1944
Miller, Marilyn	1898	1936
Miller, Mitch	1911	2010
Miller, Roger	1936	1992
Mills, Donald	1915	1999
Mills, Harry	1913	1982
Mills, Herbert	1912	1989
Mills, John	1889	1967
Mills, Sir John	1908	2005
Milner, Martin	1931	2015
Mineo, Sal	1939	1976
Miner, Jan	1917	2004
Minghella, Anthony	1954	2008
Mingus, Charles	1922	1979
Minnelli, Vincente	1903	1986
Miranda, Carmen	1909	1955
Mitchell, Thomas	1892	1962
Mitchum, Robert	1917	1997
Mix, Tom	1880	1940
Moffo, Anna	1932	2006
Monroe, Marilyn	1926	1962
Monroe, Vaughn	1911	1973
Montalban, Ricardo	1920	2009
Montand, Yves	1921	1991
Monteith, Cory	1982	2013
Montez, Maria	1917	1951
Montgomery, Elizabeth	1933	1995
Montgomery, George	1916	2000
Montgomery, Robert	1904	1981
Moody, Ron	1924	2015
Moore, Clayton	1914	1999
Moore, Colleen	1900	1988
Moore, Dudley	1935	2002
Moore, Garry	1915	1993
Moore, Grace	1898	1947
Moorehead, Agnes	1906	1974
Moreland, Mantan	1902	1973
Morgan, Dennis	1910	1994
Morgan, Frank	1890	1949
Morgan, Harry	1915	2011
Morgan, Helen	1900	1941
Morgan, Henry	1915	1994
Morita, Pat	1932	2005
Morley, Robert	1908	1992
Morris, Chester	1901	1970
Morris, Greg	1934	1996
Morris, Howard	1919	2005
Morris, Wayne	1914	1959
Morrison, Jim	1943	1971
Morrow, Vic	1929	1982
Morton, Jelly Roll	1885	1941
Mostel, Zero	1915	1977
Mowbray, Alan	1897	1969
Mulhare, Edward	1923	1997
Mulligan, Gerry	1927	1996
Mulligan, Richard	1932	2000
Muni, Paul	1895	1967
Munshin, Jules	1915	1970
Murnau, F. W.	1888	1931
Murphy, Audie	1924	1971
Murphy, Brittany	1977	2009
Murphy, George	1902	1992
Murray, Arthur	1895	1991
Murray, Kathryn	1906	1999
Murray, Mae	1889	1965
Nagel, Conrad	1897	1970
Naish, J. Carroll	1900	1973
Naldi, Nita	1898	1961
Nance, Jack	1943	1996
Natwick, Mildred	1908	1994
Nazimova, Alla	1879	1945
Neal, Patricia	1926	2010
Negri, Pola	1897	1987
Nelson, David	1936	2011
Nelson, Ed	1928	2014
Nelson, Harriet (Hilliard)	1909	1994
Nelson, Ozzie	1906	1975
Nelson, Rick	1940	1985
Nesbit, Evelyn	1884	1967
Nettleton, Lois	1927	2008
Newley, Anthony	1931	1999
Newman, Edwin	1919	2010
Newman, Paul	1925	2008
Nicholas, Fayard	1914	2006
Nicholas, Harold	1924	2000
Nichols, Mike	1931	2014
Nielsen, Leslie	1926	2010
Nijinsky, Vaslav	1890	1950
Nilsson, Anna Q.	1888	1974
Nimoy, Leonard	1931	2015
Niven, David	1910	1983
Nolan, Lloyd	1902	1985
Normand, Mabel	1894	1930
North, Sheree	1933	2005
Notorious B.I.G.	1972	1997
Novarro, Ramon	1899	1968
Nureyev, Rudolf	1938	1993
Oakie, Jack	1903	1978
Oakley, Annie	1860	1926
Oates, Warren	1928	1982
Oberon, Merle	1911	1979
O'Brien, Edmond	1915	1985
O'Brien, Pat	1899	1983
O'Connell, Arthur	1908	1981
O'Connell, Helen	1921	1993
O'Connor, Carroll	1924	2001
O'Connor, Donald	1925	2003
O'Connor, Una	1880	1959
Odetta (Holmes)	1930	2008
O'Herlihy, Daniel	1919	2005
O'Keefe, Dennis	1908	1968
Oland, Warner	1880	1938
Olcott, Chauncey	1860	1932
Oliveira, Manoel de	1908	2015
Oliver, Edna May	1883	1942
Olivier, Laurence	1907	1989
Olsen, Merlin	1940	2010
Olsen, Ole	1892	1963
O'Neal, Ron	1937	2004
O'Neill, James	1849	1920
Ophüls, Max	1902	1957
Orbach, Jerry	1935	2004
Orbison, Roy	1936	1988
Ormandy, Eugene	1899	1985
O'Shea, Milo	1926	2013
O'Sullivan, Maureen	1911	1998
O'Toole, Peter	1932	2013
Ouspenskaya, Maria	1876	1949
Owen, Reginald	1887	1972
Owens, Buck	1929	2006
Paar, Jack	1918	2004
Paderewski, Ignace	1860	1941
Page, Bettie	1923	2008
Page, Geraldine	1924	1987
Page, Patti	1927	2013
Pakula, Alan	1928	1998
Palance, Jack	1919	2006
Pallette, Eugene	1889	1954
Palmer, Betsy	1926	2015
Palmer, Lilli	1914	1986
Palmer, Robert	1949	2003
Pangborn, Franklin	1894	1958
Pardo, Don	1918	2014
Parker, Eleanor	1922	2013
Parker, Fess	1925	2010
Parker, Jean	1915	2005
Parks, Bert	1914	1992
Parks, Larry	1914	1975
Pasternack, Josef A.	1881	1940
Pastor, Tony (vaudevillian)	1837	1908
Pastor, Tony (bandleader)	1907	1969
Patrick, Gail	1911	1980
Patti, Adelina	1843	1919
Patti, Carlotta	1840	1889
Paul, Les	1915	2009
Pavarotti, Luciano	1935	2007
Pavlova, Anna	1885	1931
Paycheck, Johnny	1938	2003
Payne, John	1912	1989
Pearl, Minnie	1912	1996
Peck, Gregory	1916	2003
Peckinpah, Sam	1925	1984
Peerce, Jan	1904	1984
Pendergrass, Teddy	1950	2010
Penn, Arthur	1922	2010
Penn, Chris	1965	2006
Penner, Joe	1905	1941
Peppard, George	1928	1994
Perkins, Anthony	1932	1992
Perkins, Carl	1932	1998
Perkins, Marlin	1905	1986
Peters, Brock	1927	2005
Peters, Jean	1926	2000
Peters, Susan	1921	1952
Peterson, Oscar	1925	2007
Phillips, John	1935	2001
Phoenix, River	1970	1993
Piaf, Edith	1915	1963
Pickens, Slim	1919	1983
Pickett, Wilson	1941	2006
Pickford, Mary	1893	1979
Picon, Molly	1898	1992
Pidgeon, Walter	1897	1984
Pinza, Ezio	1892	1957
Pitney, Gene	1941	2006
Pitts, Zasu	1898	1963
Plato, Dana	1964	1999
Pleasence, Donald	1919	1995
Pleshette, Suzanne	1937	2008
Pollack, Sydney	1934	2008
Pons, Lily	1904	1976
Ponselle, Rosa	1897	1981
Ponti, Carlo	1912	2007
Porter, Edwin S.	1870	1941
Postlethwaite, Pete	1946	2011
Poston, Tom	1921	2007
Powell, Dick	1904	1963
Powell, Eleanor	1912	1982
Powell, William	1892	1984
Power, Tyrone	1914	1958
Preminger, Otto	1905	1986
Presley, Elvis	1935	1977
Preston, Billy	1946	2006
Preston, Robert	1918	1987
Price, Ray	1926	2013
Price, Vincent	1911	1993
Prima, Louis	1911	1978
Prinze, Freddie	1954	1977
Prosky, Robert	1930	2008
Provine, Dorothy	1937	2010
Prowse, Juliet	1936	1996
Pryor, Richard	1940	2005
Puente, Tito	1923	2000
Pyle, Denver	1920	1997
Quayle, Anthony	1913	1989
Questel, Mae	1908	1998
Quinn, Anthony	1915	2001
Quintero, José	1924	1999
Rabb, Ellis	1930	1998
Rabbit, Eddie	1941	1998
Radner, Gilda	1946	1989
Rafferty, Gerry	1947	2011
Raft, George	1895	1980
Rainer, Luise	1910	2014
Rains, Claude	1889	1967
Raitt, John	1917	2005
Ralston, Esther	1902	1994
Ramis, Harold	1944	2014
Ramone, Dee Dee	1952	2002
Ramone, Joey	1951	2001
Ramone, Johnny	1948	2004

Name	Born	Died
Ramone, Tommy	1949	2014
Rampal, Jean-Pierre	1922	2000
Randall, Tony	1920	2004
Randolph, John	1915	2004
Rathbone, Basil	1892	1967
Ratoff, Gregory	1897	1960
Rawls, Lou	1933	2006
Ray, Aldo	1926	1991
Ray, Johnnie	1927	1990
Ray, Nicholas	1911	1979
Rayburn, Gene	1917	1999
Raye, Martha	1916	1994
Raymond, Gene	1908	1998
Reagan, Ronald	1911	2004
Redding, Otis	1941	1967
Redgrave, Corin	1939	2010
Redgrave, Lynn	1943	2010
Redgrave, Michael	1908	1985
Reed, Donna	1921	1986
Reed, Jerry	1937	2008
Reed, Lou	1942	2013
Reed, Oliver	1938	1999
Reed, Robert	1932	1992
Rees, Roger	1944	2015
Reeve, Christopher	1952	2004
Reeves, George	1914	1959
Reeves, Steve	1926	2000
Reid, Wallace	1891	1923
Reilly, Charles Nelson	1931	2007
Reinhardt, Max	1873	1943
Remick, Lee	1935	1991
Renaldo, Duncan	1904	1980
Rennie, Michael	1909	1971
Renoir, Jean	1894	1979
Rettig, Tommy	1941	1996
Reynolds, Marjorie	1921	1997
Rich, Charlie	1932	1995
Richardson, Ian	1934	2007
Richardson, Natasha	1963	2009
Richardson, Ralph	1902	1983
Riddle, Nelson	1921	1985
Riefenstahl, Leni	1902	2003
Ripperton, Minnie	1947	1979
Ritchard, Cyril	1898	1977
Ritter, John	1948	2003
Ritter, Tex	1905	1974
Ritter, Thelma	1905	1969
Ritz, Al	1901	1965
Ritz, Harry	1906	1986
Ritz, Jimmy	1903	1985
Rivers, Joan	1933	2014
Roach, Hal	1892	1992
Roach, Max	1924	2007
Robards, Jason	1922	2000
Robbins, Jerome	1918	1998
Robbins, Marty	1925	1982
Roberts, Pernell	1928	2010
Roberts, Rachel	1927	1980
Robertson, Cliff	1925	2011
Robertson, Dale	1923	2013
Robeson, Paul	1898	1976
Robinson, Bill	1878	1949
Robinson, Edward G.	1893	1973
Robson, Flora	1902	1984
Roche, Eugene	1928	2004
Rochester (Eddie Anderson)	1905	1977
Roddenberry, Gene	1921	1991
Rodgers, Jimmie	1897	1933
Rogers, Buddy	1904	1999
Rogers, Fred	1928	2003
Rogers, Ginger	1911	1995
Rogers, Roy	1911	1998
Rogers, Will	1879	1935
Rohmer, Éric	1920	2010
Roland, Gilbert	1905	1994
Rolle, Esther	1920?	1998
Rollins, Howard	1950	1996
Roman, Ruth	1924	1999
Romero, Cesar	1907	1994
Rooney, Mickey	1920	2014
Rose, Billy	1899	1966
Rossellini, Roberto	1906	1977
Rostropovich, Mstislav	1927	2007
Rowan, Dan	1922	1987
Rubinstein, Artur	1887	1982

Name	Born	Died
Rubenstein, Zelda	1933	2010
Ruggles, Charles	1886	1970
Russell, Harold	1914	2002
Russell, Jane	1921	2011
Russell, Ken	1927	2011
Russell, Lillian	1861	1922
Russell, Nipsey	1923	2005
Russell, Rosalind	1911	1976
Rutherford, Ann	1917	2012
Rutherford, Margaret	1892	1972
Ryan, Irene	1903	1973
Ryan, Robert	1909	1973
Sabu (Dastagir)	1924	1963
St. Cyr, Lili	1917	1999
St. Denis, Ruth	1877	1968
Sakall, S. Z.	1883	1955
Saks, Gene	1921	2015
Sale (Chic), Charles	1885	1936
Sales, Soupy	1926	2009
Sanders, George	1906	1972
Sanford, Isabel	1917	2004
Sargent, Dick	1933	1994
Sarrazin, Michael	1940	2011
Savalas, Telly	1924	1994
Scheider, Roy	1935	2008
Schell, Maria	1926	2005
Schell, Maximilian	1930	2014
Schenkel, Chris	1923	2005
Schiavelli, Vincent	1948	2005
Schildkraut, Joseph	1896	1964
Schipa, Tito	1888	1965
Schlesinger, John	1926	2003
Schnabel, Artur	1882	1951
Schneider, Maria	1952	2011
Schneider, Romy	1938	1982
Schwartzkopf, Elizabeth	1915	2006
Scofield, Paul	1922	2008
Scott, George C.	1927	1999
Scott, Gordon	1926	2007
Scott, Hazel	1920	1981
Scott, Lizabeth	1922	2015
Scott, Martha	1914	2003
Scott, Randolph	1898	1987
Scott, Stuart	1965	2015
Scott, Zachary	1914	1965
Scott-Heron, Gil	1949	2011
Scott-Siddons, Mrs.	1843	1896
Seberg, Jean	1938	1979
Seeger, Pete	1919	2014
Seeley, Blossom	1892	1974
Segovia, Andres	1893	1987
Seldes, Marian	1928	2014
Selena (Quintanilla)	1971	1995
Sellers, Peter	1925	1980
Selznick, David O.	1902	1965
Sennett, Mack	1880	1960
Señor Wences	1896	1999
Serling, Rod	1924	1975
Shakur, Tupac	1971	1996
Shankar, Ravi	1920	2012
Sharif, Omar	1932	2015
Shaw, Artie	1910	2004
Shaw, Robert (actor)	1927	1978
Shaw, Robert (conductor)	1916	1999
Shawn, Ted	1891	1972
Shean, Al	1868	1949
Shearer, Moira	1926	2006
Shearer, Norma	1902	1983
Shearing, George	1919	2011
Sheppard, Bob	1910	2010
Sheridan, Ann	1915	1967
Shore, Dinah	1917	1994
Short, Bobby	1924	2005
Shubert, Lee	1875	1953
Shull, Richard B.	1929	1999
Siddons, Sarah	1755	1831
Sidney, Sylvia	1910	1999
Siegel, Don	1912	1991
Signoret, Simone	1921	1985
Sills, Beverly	1929	2007
Silver, Ron	1946	2009
Silverheels, Jay	1912	1980
Silvers, Phil	1912	1985
Sim, Alastair	1900	1976
Simmons, Jean	1929	2010

Name	Born	Died
Simone, Nina	1933	2003
Sinatra, Frank	1915	1998
Sinclair, Madge	1938	1995
Singleton, Penny	1908	2003
Sirk, Douglas	1900	1987
Siskel, Gene	1946	1999
Sjostrom, Victor	1879	1960
Skelton, Red	1913	1997
Skinner, Otis	1858	1942
Sledge, Percy	1940	2015
Smith, Alexis	1921	1993
Smith, Bessie	1894?	1937
Smith, Buffalo Bob	1917	1998
Smith, C. Aubrey	1863	1948
Smith, Elliott	1969	2003
Smith, Kate	1907	1986
Snodgress, Carrie	1946	2004
Snow, Hank	1914	1999
Snyder, Tom	1936	2007
Solti, George	1912	1997
Sondergaard, Gale	1899	1985
Sothern, Ann	1909	2001
Sousa, John Philip	1854	1932
Sparks, Ned	1884	1957
Spelling, Aaron	1923	2006
Spencer, John	1946	2005
Sperber, Wendie Jo	1958	2005
Springfield, Dusty	1939	1999
Stack, Robert	1919	2003
Stafford, Jo	1917	2008
Stander, Lionel	1908	1994
Stang, Arnold	1918	2009
Stanley, Kim	1925	2001
Stanwyck, Barbara	1907	1990
Stapleton, Jean	1923	2013
Stapleton, Maureen	1925	2006
Steiger, Rod	1925	2002
Sterling, Jan	1921	2004
Stern, Isaac	1920	2001
Stevens, Craig	1918	2000
Stevens, George	1904	1975
Stevens, Inger	1934	1970
Stevens, Mark	1916	1994
Stevens, Risë	1913	2013
Stevenson, McLean	1929	1996
Stewart, James	1908	1997
Stickney, Dorothy	1896	1998
Stokowski, Leopold	1882	1977
Stone, Fred	1873	1959
Stone, Lewis	1879	1953
Stone, Milburn	1904	1980
Storm, Gale	1922	2009
Straight, Beatrice	1918	2001
Strasberg, Lee	1901	1982
Strasberg, Susan	1938	1999
Stritch, Elaine	1925	2014
Strode, Woody	1914	1994
Strummer, Joe	1952	2002
Stuart, Gloria	1910	2010
Stuarti, Enzo	1919	2005
Sturges, Preston	1898	1959
Sullavan, Margaret	1911	1960
Sullivan, Barry	1912	1994
Sullivan, Ed	1902	1974
Sullivan, Francis L.	1903	1956
Sumac, Yma	1922	2008
Summer, Donna	1948	2012
Summerville, Slim	1892	1946
Sutherland, Joan	1926	2010
Swanson, Gloria	1899	1983
Swarthout, Gladys	1904	1969
Swayze, Patrick	1952	2009
Sweet, Blanche	1896	1986
Switzer, Carl "Alfalfa"	1927	1959
Talbot, Lyle	1902	1996
Tallchief, Maria	1925	2013
Talmadge, Constance	1900	1973
Talmadge, Norma	1893	1957
Tamiroff, Akim	1899	1972
Tandy, Jessica	1909	1994
Tanguay, Eva	1878	1947
Tati, Jacques	1908	1982
Taylor, Billy	1921	2010
Taylor, Deems	1885	1966
Taylor, Dub	1907	1994

Name	Born	Died
Taylor, Elizabeth	1932	2011
Taylor, Estelle	1899	1958
Taylor, Laurette	1887	1946
Taylor, Robert	1911	1969
Taylor, Rod	1930	2015
Temple Black, Shirley	1928	2014
Terry, Ellen	1847	1928
Thalberg, Irving	1899	1936
Thaw, John	1942	2002
Thaxter, Phyllis	1919	2012
Thigpen, Lynne	1948	2003
Thomas, Danny	1912	1991
Thompson, Sada	1927	2011
Thorndike, Sybil	1882	1976
Thulin, Ingrid	1926	2004
Tierney, Gene	1920	1991
Tiny Tim	1932	1996
Todd, Michael	1909	1958
Todd, Richard	1919	2009
Tomlinson, David	1917	2000
Tone, Franchot	1905	1968
Torme, Mel	1925	1999
Toscanini, Arturo	1867	1957
Tracy, Lee	1898	1968
Tracy, Spencer	1900	1967
Travers, Henry	1874	1965
Travers, Mary	1936	2009
Treacher, Arthur	1894	1975
Tree, Herbert Beerbohm	1853	1917
Trevor, Claire	1909	2000
Truex, Ernest	1890	1973
Truffaut, Francois	1932	1984
Tucker, Forrest	1919	1986
Tucker, Richard	1913	1975
Tucker, Sophie	1884	1966
Turner, Big Joe	1911	1985
Turner, Ike	1931	2008
Turner, Lana	1920	1995
Turpin, Ben	1869	1940
Twitty, Conway	1933	1993
Urich, Robert	1946	2002
Ustinov, Peter	1921	2004
Valens, Ritchie	1941	1959
Valentino, Rudolph	1895	1926
Vallee, Rudy	1901	1986
Van, Bobby	1928	1980
Van Cleef, Lee	1925	1989
Van Fleet, Jo	1922	1996
Van Patten, Dick	1928	2015
Vance, Vivian	1912	1979
Vandross, Luther	1951	2005
Varney, Jim	1949	2000
Vaughan, Sarah	1924	1990
Veidt, Conrad	1893	1943
Velez, Lupe	1908	1944
Vera-Ellen (Rohe)	1926	1981
Verdon, Gwen	1925	2000

Name	Born	Died
Verrett, Shirley	1931	2010
Vickers, Jon	1926	2015
Vidor, King	1894	1982
Villechaize, Herve	1943	1993
Vincent, Gene	1935	1971
Vicious, Sid	1957	1979
Von Stroheim, Erich	1885	1957
Von Zell, Harry	1906	1981
Waite, Ralph	1928	2014
Walker, Junior	1942	1995
Walker, Nancy	1922	1992
Walker, Robert	1918	1951
Wallace, Marcia	1942	2013
Wallach, Eli	1915	2014
Wallenda, Karl	1905	1978
Walsh, J. T.	1943	1998
Walsh, Raoul	1887	1980
Walston, Ray	1914	2001
Walter, Bruno	1876	1962
Ward, Simon	1941	2012
Warden, Jack	1920	2006
Waring, Fred	1900	1984
Warner, H. B.	1876	1958
Warrick, Ruth	1915	2005
Washington, Dinah	1924	1963
Waters, Ethel	1896	1977
Waters, Muddy	1915	1983
Waxman, Al	1935	2001
Wayne, David	1914	1995
Wayne, John	1907	1979
Weaver, Dennis	1924	2006
Webb, Clifton	1891	1966
Webb, Jack	1920	1982
Weems, Ted	1901	1963
Weissmuller, Johnny	1904	1984
Welk, Lawrence	1903	1992
Welles, Orson	1915	1985
Wellman, William	1896	1975
Wells, Kitty	1919	2012
Werner, Oskar	1922	1984
West, Mae	1893	1980
Weston, Jack	1924	1996
Whale, James	1889	1957
White, Barry	1944	2003
White, Jesse	1919	1997
White, Pearl	1889	1938
Whiteman, Paul	1891	1967
Whiting, Margaret	1924	2011
Whitmore, James	1921	2009
Whitty, May	1865	1948
Wickes, Mary	1910	1995
Widmark, Richard	1914	2008
Wilde, Cornel	1915	1989
Wilder, Billy	1906	2002
Wilding, Michael	1912	1979
Williams, Andy	1927	2012

Name	Born	Died
Williams, Bert	1874	1922
Williams, Esther	1921	2013
Williams, Guy	1924	1989
Williams, Hank, Sr.	1923	1953
Williams, Robin	1951	2014
Williamson, Nicol	1936	2011
Wills, Bob	1905	1975
Wills, Chill	1902	1978
Wilson, Carl	1946	1998
Wilson, Dennis	1944	1983
Wilson, Dooley	1894	1953
Wilson, Elizabeth	1921	2015
Wilson, Flip	1933	1998
Wilson, Jackie	1934	1984
Wilson, Marie	1917	1972
Windom, William	1923	2012
Windsor, Marie	1919	2000
Winehouse, Amy	1983	2011
Winfield, Paul	1941	2004
Winter, Johnny	1944	2014
Winters, Jonathan	1925	2013
Winters, Shelley	1920	2006
Wise, Robert	1914	2005
Wiseman, Joseph	1918	2009
Wong, Anna May	1907	1961
Wood, Ed	1924	1978
Wood, Natalie	1938	1981
Wood, Peggy	1892	1978
Wood, Sam	1884	1949
Woodard, Edward	1930	2009
Wooley, Sheb	1921	2003
Woolley, Monty	1888	1963
Worth, Irene	1916	2002
Wray, Fay	1907	2004
Wright, Teresa	1918	2005
Wyatt, Jane	1910	2006
Wyler, William	1902	1981
Wyman, Jane	1914?	2007
Wynette, Tammy	1942	1998
Wynn, Ed	1886	1966
Wynn, Keenan	1916	1986
York, Dick	1928	1992
York, Susannah	1939	2011
Young, Clara Kimball	1890	1960
Young, Gig	1913	1978
Young, Loretta	1913	2000
Young, Robert	1907	1998
Young, Roland	1887	1953
Youngman, Henny	1906	1998
Zanuck, Darryl F.	1902	1979
Zappa, Frank	1940	1993
Zevon, Warren	1947	2003
Ziegfeld, Florenz	1869	1932
Zimbalist, Efrem, Jr.	1918	2014
Zinneman, Fred	1907	1997
Zukor, Adolph	1873	1976

Original Names of Selected Entertainers

Adele: Adele Laurie Blue Adkins
Ad-Rock: Adam Horovitz
Clay Aiken: Clayton Grissom
Alan Alda: Alphonso D'Abruzzo
Jason Alexander: Jay Greenspan
Woody Allen: Allen Konigsberg
André 3000: Andre Benjamin
Julie Andrews: Julia Wells
Criss Angel: Christopher Sarantakos
Beatrice Arthur: Bernice Frankel
Fred Astaire: Frederick Austerlitz
Babyface: Kenneth Edmonds
Lauren Bacall: Betty Joan Perske
Erykah Badu: Erica Wright
Eric Bana: Eric Banadinovich
Anne Bancroft: Anna Maria Italiano
Theda Bara: Theodosia Goodman
Beck: Bek David Campbell
Pat Benatar: Patricia Andrejewski
Tony Bennett: Anthony Benedetto
Jack Benny: Benjamin Kubelsky
Milton Berle: Mendel Berlinger
Irving Berlin: Israel Baline
Sarah Bernhardt: Henriette-Rosine Bernard
Jello Biafra: Eric Reed Boucher
Big Boi: Antwan Patton
The Big Bopper: Jiles Perry "J.P." Richardson
Robert Blake: Michael James Vijencio Gubitosi
Jon Bon Jovi: John Francis Bongiovi
Bono: Paul Hewson
David Bowie: David Robert Jones
Boy George: George Alan O'Dowd
Fanny Brice: Fanny Borach
Charles Bronson: Charles Buchinski
Albert Brooks: Albert Einstein
Mel Brooks: Melvin Kaminsky
Foxy Brown: Inga Marchand
George Burns: Nathan Birnbaum
Ellen Burstyn: Edna Gilhooley
Richard Burton: Richard Jenkins
Red Buttons: Aaron Chwatt
Nicolas Cage: Nicholas Coppola
Michael Caine: Maurice Micklewhite
Maria Callas: Maria Kalogeropoulos
Jackie Chan: Chan Kwong-Sung
Cyd Charisse: Tula Finklea
Ray Charles: Ray Charles Robinson
Charo: María Rosario Pilar Martínez Molina Baeza
Chubby Checker: Ernest Evans
Cher: Cherilyn Sarkisian
Chuck D: Carlton Ridenhour
Patsy Cline: Virginia Patterson Hensley
Claudette Colbert: Lily Chauchoin
Coolio: Artis Leon Ivey Jr.
Alice Cooper: Vincent Furnier
David Copperfield: David Kotkin
Howard Cosell: Howard Cohen
Elvis Costello: Declan McManus
Lou Costello: Louis Cristillo
Peter Coyote: Peter Cohon
Quentin Crisp: Denis Pratt
Tom Cruise: Thomas Cruise Mapother IV
Tony Curtis: Bernard Schwartz
Miley Cyrus: Destiny Hope Cyrus
D'Angelo: Michael D'Angelo Archer
Rodney Dangerfield: Jacob Cohen
Bobby Darin: Walden Robert Cassotto
Doris Day: Doris von Kappelhoff
Yvonne De Carlo: Peggy Middleton

Portia de Rossi: Amanda Lee Rogers
Sandra Dee: Alexandra Zuck
John Denver: Henry John Deutschendorf Jr.
Bo Derek: Mary Cathleen Collins
Danny DeVito: Daniel Michaeli
Angie Dickinson: Angeline Brown
Bo Diddley: Elias Bates
Vin Diesel: Mark Vincent
Phyllis Diller: Phyllis Driver
Divine: Harris Glenn Milstead
DMX: Earl Simmons
Troy Donahue: Merle Johnson Jr.
Kirk Douglas: Issur Danielovitch
Drake: Aubrey Drake Graham
Bob Dylan: Robert Zimmerman
Barbara Eden: Barbara Huffman
Elvira: Cassandra Peterson
Eminem: Marshall Mathers
Enya: Eithne Ni Bhraonian
Dale Evans: Frances Smith
Chad Everett: Raymon Cramton
Fabian: Fabian Anthony Forte
Fabolous: John David Jackson
Douglas Fairbanks: Douglas Ullman
Morgan Fairchild: Patsy McClenny
Jamie Farr: Jameel Farah
Fergie: Stacy Ferguson
Stepin Fetchit: Lincoln Perry
W. C. Fields: William Claude Dukenfield
50 Cent: Curtis Jackson
Flavor Flav: William Drayton
Joan Fontaine: Joan de Havilland
Jodie Foster: Alicia Christian Foster
Jamie Foxx: Eric Bishop
Redd Foxx: John Sanford
Arlene Francis: Arlene Kazanjian
Connie Francis: Concetta Franconero
Greta Garbo: Greta Gustafsson
Judy Garland: Frances Gumm
James Garner: James Bumgarner
Crystal Gayle: Brenda Gail Webb
George Gershwin: Jacob Gershowitz
Kathie Lee Gifford: Kathie Epstein
Whoopi Goldberg: Caryn Johnson
Cary Grant: Archibald Leach
Lee Grant: Lyova Rosenthal
Robert Guillaume: Robert Williams
Buddy Hackett: Leonard Hacker
Hammer: Stanley Kirk Burrell
Jean Harlow: Harlean Carpenter
Helen Hayes: Helen Brown
Susan Hayward: Edythe Marrener
Rita Hayworth: Margarita Cansino
Pee-Wee Herman: Paul Reubenfeld
Charlton Heston: John Charles Carter
Perez Hilton: Mario Armando Lavandeira Jr.
Hulk Hogan: Terry Gene Bollea
Billie Holiday: Eleanora Fagan
Judy Holliday: Judith Tuvim
Bob Hope: Leslie Townes Hope
Harry Houdini: Erik Weisz
Howlin' Wolf: Chester Burnett
Rock Hudson: Roy Scherer Jr. (later Fitzgerald)
Engelbert Humperdinck: Arnold Dorsey
Kim Hunter: Janet Cole
Ice Cube: O'Shea Jackson
Ice-T: Tracy Morrow
Billy Idol: William Broad
Etta James: Jamesetta Hawkins
Ja Rule: Jeffrey Atkins
Jay-Z: Shawn Carter
Elton John: Reginald Dwight
Al Jolson: Asa Yoelson
Jennifer Jones: Phylis Isley
Tom Jones: Thomas Woodward
Spike Jonze: Adam Spiegel
Wynonna Judd: Christina Ciminella
Boris Karloff: William Henry Pratt
Diane Keaton: Diane Hall
Michael Keaton: Michael Douglas
Kesha: Kesha Rose Sebert
Alicia Keys: Alicia Augello Cook
Chaka Khan: Yvette Stevens
Kid Rock: Robert Ritchie
Carole King: Carole Klein
Larry King: Larry Zeiger
Ben Kingsley: Krishna Banji
Ted Knight: Tadewurz Wladziu Konopka
Cheryl Ladd: Cheryl Stoppelmoor
Lady Gaga: Stefani Germanotta
Veronica Lake: Constance Ockleman
Hedy Lamarr: Hedwig Kiesler
Dorothy Lamour: Mary Leta Dorothy Slaton
Michael Landon: Eugene Orowitz
Mario Lanza: Alfredo Cocozza
Queen Latifah: Dana Owens
Stan Laurel: Arthur Jefferson
Brenda Lee: Brenda Mae Tarpley
Gypsy Rose Lee: Rose Louise Hovick
Peggy Lee: Norma Egstrom
Janet Leigh: Jeanette Morrison
Vivien Leigh: Vivian Hartley
Huey Lewis: Hugh Cregg
Jerry Lewis: Joseph Levitch
Lil' Kim: Kimberly Denise Jones
Little Richard: Richard Penniman
LL Cool J: James Todd Smith
Carole Lombard: Jane Peters
Lorde: Ella Yelich-O'Connor
Sophia Loren: Sophia Scicolone
Peter Lorre: Laszlo Lowenstein
Louis C.K.: Louis Szekely
Myrna Loy: Myrna Williams
Bela Lugosi: Bela Ferenc Blasko
Moms Mabley: Loretta Mary Aiken
Macklemore: Ben Haggerty
Shirley MacLaine: Shirley Beaty
Elle Macpherson: Eleanor Gow
Madonna: Madonna Louise Veronica Ciccone
Lee Majors: Harvey Lee Yeary
Karl Malden: Mladen Sekulovich
Barry Manilow: Barry Alan Pincus
Jayne Mansfield: Vera Jane Palmer
Marilyn Manson: Brian Warner
Bruno Mars: Peter Gene Hernandez
Dean Martin: Dino Crocetti
Ricky Martin: Enrique Jose Martin Morales
MCA: Adam Yauch
Meat Loaf: Marvin Lee Aday
Freddie Mercury: Farrokh Bulsara
Ethel Merman: Ethel Zimmermann
George Michael: Georgios Panayiotou
Mike D: Michael Diamond
Nicki Minaj: Onika Tanya Maraj
Helen Mirren: Ilynea Lydia Mironoff
Joni Mitchell: Roberta Joan Anderson
Moby: Richard Melville Hall
Mo'Nique: Monique Imes
Marilyn Monroe: Norma Jean Mortenson (later Baker)
Yves Montand: Ivo Livi
Demi Moore: Demetria Guynes
Rita Moreno: Rosita Alverio
Harry Morgan: Harry Bratsburg
Morrissey: Steven Patrick Morrissey
Mr. T: Lawrence Tureaud
Paul Muni: Mehilem Weisenfreund
Nelly: Cornell Haynes Jr.
Mike Nichols: Michael Igor Peschowsky
Chuck Norris: Carlos Ray Norris
Notorious B.I.G.: Christopher Wallace
Hugh O'Brian: Hugh Krampke
Maureen O'Hara: Maureen FitzSimons
Jack Palance: Vladimir Palanuik
Minnie Pearl: Sarah Ophelia Cannon
Katy Perry: Kathryn Hudson
Bernadette Peters: Bernadette Lazzara
Joaquin Phoenix: Joaquin Bottom
Edith Piaf: Edith Gassion
Slim Pickens: Louis Lindley
Mary Pickford: Gladys Smith
Pink: Alecia Moore
Iggy Pop: James Newell Osterberg
Natalie Portman: Natalie Hershlag
Prince: Prince Rogers Nelson
Dee Dee Ramone: Douglas Colvin
Joey Ramone: Jeffrey Hyman
Johnny Ramone: John Cummings
Tommy Ramone: Tom Erdelyi
Tony Randall: Leonard Rosenberg
Della Reese: Delloreese Patricia Early
Busta Rhymes: Trevor Smith Jr.
Joan Rivers: Joan Sandra Molinsky
Edward G. Robinson: Emmanuel Goldenberg
The Rock: Dwayne Johnson
Ginger Rogers: Virginia McMath
Roy Rogers: Leonard Franklin Slye
Mickey Rooney: Joe Yule Jr.
Johnny Rotten: John Lydon
Lillian Russell: Helen Leonard
Meg Ryan: Margaret Hyra
Winona Ryder: Winona Horowitz
Sade: Helen Folsade Abu
Soupy Sales: Milton Supman
Susan Sarandon: Susan Tomaling
Seal: Seal Henry Olusegun Olumide Adeola Samuel
Jane Seymour: Joyce Frankenberg
Omar Sharif: Michael Shalhoub
Charlie Sheen: Carlos Irwin Estevez
Martin Sheen: Ramon Estevez
Talia Shire: Talia Coppola
Beverly Sills: Belle Silverman
Phil Silvers: Philip Silversmith
Gene Simmons: Chaim Witz
Sinbad: David Adkins
Anna Nicole Smith: Vickie Lynn Hogan
Snoop Dogg (a.k.a Snoop Lion, Snoopzilla): Calvin Broadus
Barbara Stanwyck: Ruby Stevens
Jean Stapleton: Jeanne Murray
Ringo Starr: Richard Starkey
Cat Stevens: Stephen Demetre Georgiou
Connie Stevens: Concetta Ingolia
Jon Stewart: Jonathan Stuart Leibowitz
Sting: Gordon Sumner
Joe Strummer: John Graham Mellor
Donna Summer: La Donna Gaines
Rip Taylor: Charles Elmer Taylor Jr.
Robert Taylor: Spangler Brugh
Danny Thomas: Muzyad Yakhoob (later Amos Jacobs)
Tiny Tim: Herbert Khaury
Rip Torn: Elmore Rual Torn Jr.
Randy Travis: Randy Traywick
Tina Turner: Annie Mae Bullock
Shania Twain: Eilleen Regina Edwards
Twiggy: Lesley Hornby
Conway Twitty: Harold Lloyd Jenkins
Steven Tyler: Stephen Tallarico
Rudolph Valentino: Rudolpho D'Antonguolla
Frankie Valli: Frank Castelluccio
Eddie Vedder: Edward Louis Seversen III
Sid Vicious: John Simon Ritchie
John Wayne: Marion Morrison
Raquel Welch: Raquel Tejada
Gene Wilder: Jerome Silberman
Shelley Winters: Shirley Schrift
Stevie Wonder: Stevland Morris
Jane Wyman: Sarah Jane Mayfield
Loretta Young: Gretchen Michaels Young
Buckwheat Zydeco: Stanley Dural Jr.

Some Notable Movies, Sept. 2014-Aug. 2015

Film (rating)	Stars	Director(s)
Alexander and the Terrible, Horrible, No Good, Very Bad Day (PG)	Steve Carell, Jennifer Garner	Miguel Arteta
American Sniper (R)	Bradley Cooper, Kyle Gallner, Jake McDorman, Sienna Miller	Clint Eastwood
Annie (PG)	Quvenzhané Wallis, Cameron Diaz, Jamie Foxx, Rose Byrne	Will Gluck
Ant-Man (PG-13)	Paul Rudd, Michael Douglas, Evangeline Lilly	Peyton Reed
Avengers: Age of Ultron (PG-13)	Robert Downey Jr., Chris Evans, Chris Hemsworth, Mark Ruffalo	Joss Whedon
Big Hero 6 (PG)	Animated. Jamie Chung, Genesis Rodriguez, Damon Wayans Jr.	Don Hall
Birdman (R)	Michael Keaton, Edward Norton, Emma Stone, Naomi Watts	Alejandro G. Iñárritu
The Book of Life (PG)	Animated. Diego Luna, Zoe Saldana, Channing Tatum	Jorge R. Gutierrez
The Boxtrolls (PG)	Animated. Toni Collette, Elle Fanning, Ben Kingsley	Graham Annable, Anthony Stacchi
Cinderella (PG)	Lily James, Cate Blanchett, Richard Madden	Kenneth Branagh
CitizenFour (NR)	Documentary. Edward Snowden	Laura Poitras
Dracula Untold (PG-13)	Dominic Cooper, Luke Evans	Gary Shore
Dumb and Dumber To (PG-13)	Jim Carrey, Jeff Daniels	Bobby Farrelly
Entourage (R)	Adrian Grenier, Jeremy Piven, Kevin Connolly, Kevin Dillon	Doug Ellin
The Equalizer (R)	Melissa Leo, Chloë Grace Moretz, Denzel Washington	Antoine Fuqua
Exodus: Gods and Kings (PG-13)	Christian Bale, Joel Edgerton, Ben Kingsley	Ridley Scott
Fantastic Four (PG-13)	Miles Teller, Kate Mara, Michael B. Jordan, Jamie Bell	Josh Trank
Fifty Shades of Grey (R)	Dakota Johnson, Jamie Dornan	Sam Taylor-Johnson
Focus (R)	Will Smith, Margot Robbie, Rodrigo Santoro	Glenn Ficarra, John Requa
Foxcatcher (R)	Steve Carell, Channing Tatum, Mark Ruffalo, Sienna Miller	Bennett Miller
Furious 7 (PG-13)	Paul Walker, Vin Diesel, Dwayne Johnson, Michelle Rodriguez, Jason Statham, Kurt Russell	James Wan
Fury (R)	Brad Pitt, Shia LaBeouf, Logan Lerman, Michael Peña	David Ayer
Get Hard (R)	Will Ferrell, Kevin Hart, Alison Brie	Etan Cohen
The Gift (R)	Jason Bateman, Rebecca Hall, Joel Edgerton	Joel Edgerton
Gone Girl (R)	Ben Affleck, Rosamund Pike, Neil Patrick Harris, Tyler Perry	David Fincher
The Hobbit: The Battle of the Five Armies (PG-13)	Richard Armitage, Martin Freeman, Ian McKellen	Peter Jackson
Home (PG)	Animated. Jim Parsons, Rihanna, Steve Martin	Tim Johnson
The Hunger Games: Mockingjay Part 1 (PG-13)	Jennifer Lawrence, Liam Hemsworth, Josh Hutcherson	Francis Lawrence
The Imitation Game (PG-13)	Benedict Cumberbatch, Keira Knightley, Matthew Goode	Morten Tyldum
Inside Out (PG)	Animated. Amy Poehler, Bill Hader, Mindy Kaling, Phyllis Smith	Pete Docter
Insurgent (PG-13)	Shailene Woodley, Theo James, Ansel Elgort	Robert Schwentke
Interstellar (PG-13)	Matthew McConaughey, Anne Hathaway, Jessica Chastain	Christopher Nolan
The Interview (R)	James Franco, Seth Rogen, Randall Park	Evan Goldberg, Seth Rogen
Into the Woods (PG)	Anna Kendrick, Meryl Streep, Chris Pine, Johnny Depp, Emily Blunt	Rob Marshall
Irrational Man (R)	Joaquin Phoenix, Emma Stone, Parker Posey	Woody Allen
John Wick (R)	Keanu Reeves, Willem Dafoe, Adrianne Palicki	David Leitch, Chad Stahelski
The Judge (R)	Robert Downey Jr., Robert Duvall, Vera Farmiga	David Dobkin
Jurassic World (PG-13)	Chris Pratt, Bryce Dallas Howard, Ty Simpkins	Colin Trevorrow
Kingsman: The Secret Service (R)	Colin Firth, Samuel L. Jackson, Taron Egerton	Matthew Vaughn
The Longest Ride (PG-13)	Scott Eastwood, Britt Robertson, Alan Alda	George Tillman Jr.
Mad Max: Fury Road (R)	Tom Hardy, Charlize Theron, Nicholas Hoult	George Miller
Magic Mike XXL (R)	Channing Tatum, Matt Bomer, Joe Manganiello	Gregory Jacobs
The Man From U.N.C.L.E. (PG-13)	Henry Cavill, Armie Hammer, Alicia Vikander	Guy Ritchie
The Maze Runner (PG-13)	Dylan O'Brien, Will Poulter, Kaya Scodelario, Patricia Clarkson	Wes Ball
McFarland, USA (PG)	Kevin Costner, Maria Bello, Ramiro Rodriguez	Christopher Cleveland
Minions (PG)	Animated. Sandra Bullock, Jon Hamm, Michael Keaton	Brian Lynch
Mission: Impossible–Rogue Nation (PG-13)	Tom Cruise, Rebecca Ferguson, Jeremy Renner, Simon Pegg	Christopher McQuarrie
Night at the Museum: Secret of the Tomb (PG)	Ben Stiller, Robin Williams, Owen Wilson	Shawn Levy
Nightcrawler (R)	Jake Gyllenhaal, Bill Paxton, Rene Russo	Dan Gilroy
Paddington (PG)	Hugh Bonneville, Colin Firth, Nicole Kidman	Paul King
Penguins of Madagascar (PG)	Animated. Benedict Cumberbatch, John Malkovich, Tom McGrath	Eric Darnell, Simon Smith
Pitch Perfect 2 (PG-13)	Anna Kendrick, Rebel Wilson, Hailee Steinfeld	Elizabeth Banks
Poltergeist (PG-13)	Sam Rockwell, Rosemarie DeWitt, Jane Adams, Jared Harris	Gil Kenan
Ricki and the Flash (PG-13)	Meryl Streep, Kevin Kline, Rick Springfield	Jonathan Demme
St. Vincent (PG-13)	Melissa McCarthy, Bill Murray, Naomi Watts	Theodore Melfi
San Andreas (PG-13)	Dwayne Johnson, Carla Gugino, Alexandra Daddario	Brad Peyton
The Second Best Exotic Marigold Hotel (PG)	Judi Dench, Maggie Smith, Bill Nighy	John Madden
Selma (PG-13)	Lorraine Toussaint, David Oyelowo	Ava DuVernay
Shaun the Sheep Movie (PG)	Animated. Justin Fletcher, John Sparkes, Omid Djalili	Mark Burton, Richard Starzak
The Skeleton Twins (R)	Bill Hader, Kristen Wiig, Luke Wilson, Ty Burrell	Craig Johnson
Southpaw (R)	Jake Gyllenhaal, Forest Whitaker, Rachel McAdams	Antoine Fuqua
The SpongeBob Movie: Sponge Out of Water (PG)	Animated/live action. Tom Kenny, Antonio Banderas, Bill Fagerbakke	Paul Tibbitt
Spy (R)	Melissa McCarthy, Rose Byrne, Jason Statham, Jude Law	Paul Feig
Still Alice (PG-13)	Julianne Moore, Kristen Stewart, Kate Bosworth, Alec Baldwin	Richard Glatzer, Wash Westmoreland
Straight Outta Compton (R)	O'Shea Jackson Jr., Corey Hawkins, Jason Mitchell	F. Gary Gray
Taken 3 (PG-13)	Liam Neeson, Forest Whitaker, Maggie Grace	Olivier Megaton
Ted 2 (R)	Mark Wahlberg, Seth MacFarlane, Amanda Seyfried	Seth MacFarlane
Terminator: Genisys (PG-13)	Arnold Schwarzenegger, Jason Clarke, Emilia Clarke	Alan Taylor
The Theory of Everything (PG-13)	Eddie Redmayne, Felicity Jones, David Thewlis, Emily Watson	James Marsh
Timbuktu (PG-13)	Ibrahim Ahmed, Abel Jafri, Toulou Kiki	Abderrahmane Sissako
Tomorrowland (PG)	George Clooney, Britt Robertson, Hugh Laurie	Brad Bird
Trainwreck (R)	Amy Schumer, Bill Hader, Brie Larson	Judd Apatow
Unbroken (PG-13)	Jack O'Connell, Miyavi, Domhnall Gleeson	Angelina Jolie
Vacation (R)	Ed Helms, Christina Applegate	John Francis Daley, Jonathan M. Goldstein
The Wedding Ringer (R)	Kevin Hart, Josh Gad, Kaley Cuoco-Sweeting	Jeremy Garelick
Whiplash (R)	Paul Reiser, J. K. Simmons, Miles Teller	Damien Chazelle
Wild (R)	Reese Witherspoon, Laura Dern, Gaby Hoffmann	Jean-Marc Vallée

50 Top-Grossing Movies, 2014

Source: Rentrak Corporation

Rank	Title	Gross (mil)
1.	Guardians of the Galaxy	$333.0
2.	The Hunger Games: Mockingjay Part 1	316.2
3.	Captain America: The Winter Soldier	259.8
4.	The Lego Movie	257.8
5.	Transformers: Age of Extinction	245.4
6.	Maleficent	241.4
7.	X-Men: Days of Future Past	233.9
8.	Dawn of the Planet of the Apes	208.5
9.	Big Hero 6	206.5
10.	The Amazing Spider-Man 2	202.9
11.	Godzilla	200.7
12.	The Hobbit: The Battle of the Five Armies	198.9
13.	22 Jump Street	191.7
14.	Teenage Mutant Ninja Turtles	191.2
15.	Interstellar	180.3
16.	How to Train Your Dragon 2	177.0
17.	Gone Girl	166.3
18.	Divergent	150.9
19.	Neighbors	150.1
20.	Ride Along	134.2
21.	Rio 2	131.5
22.	Lucy	126.6
23.	The Fault in Our Stars	124.9
24.	Lone Survivor	124.9
25.	Frozen	123.6
26.	Mr. Peabody and Sherman	111.5
27.	300: Rise of an Empire	$106.6
28.	The Maze Runner	102.1
29.	Noah	101.2
30.	The Equalizer	100.8
31.	Edge of Tomorrow	100.2
32.	Non-Stop	91.7
33.	Heaven Is for Real	91.4
34.	Fury	85.3
35.	Dumb and Dumber To	85.1
36.	Tammy	84.5
37.	Annabelle	84.3
38.	The Other Woman	83.9
39.	Let's Be Cops	82.4
40.	Monuments Men	77.5
41.	Night at the Museum: Secret of the Tomb	75.3
42.	Penguins of Madagascar	75.2
43.	American Hustle	74.6
44.	Hercules	72.7
45.	Into the Woods	72.1
46.	The Purge: Anarchy	71.6
47.	Unbroken	69.5
48.	The Wolf of Wall Street	67.0
49.	Alexander and the Terrible, Horrible, No Good, Very Bad Day	65.7
50.	Think Like a Man Too	65.2

Note: Box-office grosses in the U.S. and Canada Jan. 3, 2014-Jan. 1, 2015; some films had 2013 release dates.

All-Time Top-Grossing American Movies

Source: Rentrak Corporation

Rank	Title (original release date)	Gross (mil)
1.	Avatar (2009)	$760.5
2.	Jurassic World (2015)	643.3
3.	The Avengers (2012)	623.4
4.	Titanic (1997)	600.8
5.	The Dark Knight (2008)	533.3
6.	Star Wars: Episode I—The Phantom Menace (1999)	474.5
7.	Star Wars (1977)	461.0
8.	Avengers: Age of Ultron (2015)	457.8
9.	The Dark Knight Rises (2012)	448.1
10.	Shrek 2 (2004)	436.7
11.	E.T. the Extra-Terrestrial (1982)	435.0
12.	The Hunger Games: Catching Fire (2013)	424.7
13.	Pirates of the Caribbean: Dead Man's Chest (2006)	423.3
14.	Toy Story 3 (2010)	415.0
15.	Iron Man 3 (2013)	409.0
16.	The Hunger Games (2012)	408.0
17.	Spider-Man (2002)	403.7
18.	Transformers: Revenge of the Fallen (2009)	402.1
19.	Frozen (2013)	400.7
20.	Harry Potter and the Deathly Hallows: Part 2 (2011)	381.0
21.	Star Wars: Episode III—Revenge of the Sith (2005)	380.3
22.	The Lord of the Rings: The Return of the King (2003)	377.0
23.	Spider-Man 2 (2004)	373.4
24.	The Passion of Christ (2004)	370.3
25.	Despicable Me 2 (2013)	368.1
26.	Jurassic Park (1993)	357.1
27.	Furious 7 (2015)	$352.8
28.	Transformers: Dark of the Moon (2011)	352.4
29.	American Sniper (2014)	350.1
30.	Inside Out (2015)	344.7
31.	The Lord of the Rings: The Two Towers (2002)	341.7
32.	Finding Nemo (2003)	339.7
33.	The Hunger Games: Mockingjay Part 1 (2014)	337.1
34.	Spider-Man 3 (2007)	336.5
35.	Alice in Wonderland (2010)	334.2
36.	Guardians of the Galaxy (2014)	333.2
37.	Forrest Gump (1994)	330.3
38.	Shrek the Third (2007)	322.7
39.	Transformers (2007)	319.2
40.	Iron Man (2008)	318.6
41.	Harry Potter and the Sorcerer's Stone (2001)	317.6
42.	Indiana Jones and the Kingdom of the Crystal Skull (2008)	317.1
43.	The Lord of the Rings: The Fellowship of the Ring (2001)	314.2
44.	The Lion King (1994)	312.9
45.	Iron Man 2 (2010)	312.4
46.	Star Wars: Episode II—Attack of the Clones (2002)	310.7
47.	Pirates of the Caribbean: At World's End (2007)	309.4
48.	Star Wars: Episode VI—Return of the Jedi (1983)	309.2
49.	Independence Day (1996)	306.2
50.	Pirates of the Caribbean: The Curse of the Black Pearl (2003)	305.4

Note: Box-office grosses in the U.S. and Canada through Aug. 31, 2015, in absolute dollars. Rising ticket prices favor newer films. Revenues from re-releases are included.

Most Pirated Movies

Source: Excipio

(ranked by number of torrent downloads worldwide)

2014

Rank	Film (release date)	Downloads
1.	The Wolf of Wall Street (2013)	30,035,000
2.	Frozen (2013)	29,919,000
3.	RoboCop (2014 and 1987)[1]	29,879,000
4.	Gravity (2013)	29,357,000
5.	The Hobbit: The Desolation of Smaug (2013)	27,627,000
6.	Thor: The Dark World (2013)	25,749,000
7.	Captain America: The Winter Soldier (2014)	25,628,000
8.	The Legend of Hercules (2014)	25,137,000
9.	X-Men: Days of Future Past (2014)	24,380,000
10.	12 Years a Slave (2013)	23,653,000

2015

Rank	Film (release date)	Downloads
1.	Interstellar (2014)	35,343,370
2.	Furious 7 (2015)	27,061,111
3.	American Sniper (2014)	25,637,985
4.	The Hobbit: The Battle of the Five Armies (2014)	24,576,790
5.	Fifty Shades of Grey (2015)	23,845,250
6.	Big Hero 6 (2014)	21,875,233
7.	Exodus: Gods and Kings (2014)	20,452,562
8.	Taken 3 (2014)	20,381,472
9.	Fury (2014)	19,676,628
10.	John Wick (2014)	19,255,597

Note: 2015 data is for Jan.-June. (1) Number of downloads are for the original and remake combined as they share the same name.

Best American Movies of All Time

Source: American Film Institute

First unveiled in 1998 based on ballots sent to 1,500 individuals, mostly from the film world, in 1997. Updated in 2007 (the version shown here) to include newly eligible films and reflect shifting cultural perspectives. Criteria for judging included historical significance, cultural impact, critical recognition and awards, and popularity. The year each film was first released is in parentheses.

1. Citizen Kane (1941)
2. The Godfather (1972)
3. Casablanca (1942)
4. Raging Bull (1980)
5. Singin' in the Rain (1952)
6. Gone With the Wind (1939)
7. Lawrence of Arabia (1962)
8. Schindler's List (1993)
9. Vertigo (1958)
10. The Wizard of Oz (1939)
11. City Lights (1931)
12. The Searchers (1956)
13. Star Wars (1977)
14. Psycho (1960)
15. 2001: A Space Odyssey (1968)
16. Sunset Boulevard (1950)
17. The Graduate (1967)
18. The General (1927)
19. On the Waterfront (1954)
20. It's a Wonderful Life (1946)
21. Chinatown (1974)
22. Some Like It Hot (1959)
23. The Grapes of Wrath (1940)
24. E.T. the Extra-Terrestrial (1982)
25. To Kill a Mockingbird (1962)
26. Mr. Smith Goes to Washington (1939)
27. High Noon (1952)
28. All About Eve (1950)
29. Double Indemnity (1944)
30. Apocalypse Now (1979)
31. The Maltese Falcon (1941)
32. The Godfather Part II (1974)
33. One Flew Over the Cuckoo's Nest (1975)
34. Snow White and the Seven Dwarfs (1937)
35. Annie Hall (1977)
36. The Bridge on the River Kwai (1957)
37. The Best Years of Our Lives (1946)
38. The Treasure of the Sierra Madre (1948)
39. Dr. Strangelove (1964)
40. The Sound of Music (1965)
41. King Kong (1933)
42. Bonnie and Clyde (1967)
43. Midnight Cowboy (1969)
44. The Philadelphia Story (1940)
45. Shane (1953)
46. It Happened One Night (1934)
47. A Streetcar Named Desire (1951)
48. Rear Window (1954)
49. Intolerance (1916)
50. The Lord of the Rings: The Fellowship of the Ring (2001)

National Film Registry, 2014

Source: National Film Registry, Library of Congress

The National Film Registry adds 25 "culturally, historically, or aesthetically significant" American films annually.

13 Lakes (2004)
Bert Williams Lime Kiln Club Field Day (1913)
The Big Lebowski (1998)
Down Argentine Way (1940)
The Dragon Painter (1919)
Felicia (1965)
Ferris Bueller's Day Off (1986)
The Gang's All Here (1943)
House of Wax (1953)
Into the Arms of Strangers: Stories of the Kindertransport (2000)
Little Big Man (1970)
Luxo Jr. (1986)
Moon Breath Beat (1980)
Please Don't Bury Me Alive! (1976)
The Power and the Glory (1933)
Rio Bravo (1959)
Rosemary's Baby (1968)
Ruggles of Red Gap (1935)
Saving Private Ryan (1998)
Shoes (1916)
State Fair (1933)
Unmasked (1917)
V-E +1 (1945)
The Way of Peace (1947)
Willy Wonka and the Chocolate Factory (1971)

Movie Theaters, 1946-2014

Source: Motion Picture Association of America (MPAA); Rentrak Corporation

Year	Box office (mil)	Admissions (mil)	Admissions per week (mil)	Screens	Avg. ticket price	Films produced	Films released
1946	$1,692.0	4,067.3	78.2	NA	$0.42	NA	400
1950	1,379.0	3,017.5	58.0	NA	0.46	NA	483
1955	1,204.0	2,072.3	39.9	NA	0.58	NA	319
1960	984.4	1,304.5	25.1	NA	0.76	NA	248
1965	1,041.8	1,031.5	19.8	NA	1.01	NA	279
1970	1,429.2	920.6	17.7	NA	1.55	279	306
1975	2,114.8	1,032.8	19.9	15,030	2.03	258	233
1980	2,748.5	1,021.5	19.6	17,590	2.69	214	233
1985	3,749.4	1,056.1	20.3	21,147	3.55	264	470
1990	5,021.8	1,188.6	22.9	23,689	4.22	346	410
1995	5,269.0	1,211.0	23.3	27,805	4.35	631	411
2000	7,468.0	1,383.0	26.6	37,396	5.39	683	475
2001	8,125.0	1,438.0	27.7	36,764	5.65	611	454
2002	9,272.0	1,599.0	30.8	35,280	5.80	546	475
2003	9,165.0	1,521.0	29.3	35,786	6.03	593	455
2004	9,215.0	1,484.0	28.5	36,594	6.21	611	489
2005	8,832.0	1,376.0	26.5	38,852	6.41	920	507
2006	9,138.0	1,395.0	26.8	38,415	6.55	928	594
2007	9,629.0	1,400.0	26.9	38,974	6.88	789	611
2008	9,791.0	1,364.0	26.2	38,834	7.18	773	638
2009	10,543.6	1,415.0	27.2	39,233	7.50	751	558
2010	10,741.0	1,341.0	25.8	39,547	7.89	795	563
2011	10,186.1	1,285.0	24.7	39,641	7.93	818	609
2012	10,774.5	1,358.0	26.0	39,918	7.96	476[1]	677
2013	10,919.7	1,340.0	25.8	42,814	8.13	455[1]	659
2014	10,357.4	1,267.6	24.4	43,265	8.17	481[1]	707

NA = Not available. (1) Non-MPAA members with est. budget under $1 mil were not tracked.

Top Film Websites, 2015

Source: comScore Media Metrix, Inc.; ranked by number of visitors

Rank	Website	Visitors[1]	Rank	Website	Visitors[1]
1.	IMDb	71,906	11.	Disney Movies	7,486
2.	Fandango sites	42,527	12.	Putlocker.is	6,930
3.	Now Playing Entertainment	25,849	13.	AMC Entertainment Inc.	6,736
4.	Viewster Media	20,018	14.	MovieGoer Network	6,274
5.	Flixster	17,296	15.	ComplexMovies	5,612
6.	Yahoo Movies	13,524	16.	StarWars.com	5,599
7.	Moviepilot.com	12,193	17.	Paramount Online	5,278
8.	Moviefone	10,110	18.	Cinemark.com	4,555
9.	MSN Movies	8,911	19.	Regal Entertainment	4,294
10.	Hollywood.com sites	7,714	20.	HollywoodReporter.com Movies	3,875

(1) Number of persons age 2 and older, in thousands, who visited the media property (including website/apps) at least once from any U.S. location in June 2015. Mobile users under age 18 are not measured.

Most Popular Movie DVDs, 2014

Source: Rentrak Corporation

Top Rentals, 2014

Rank	Movie	Rank	Movie
1.	Captain Phillips (2013)	11.	Last Vegas (2013)
2.	The Hunger Games: Catching Fire (2013)	12.	Jack Ryan: Shadow Recruit
3.	The Wolf of Wall Street (2013)	13.	Dallas Buyers Club (2013)
4.	Jackass Presents: Bad Grandpa (2013)	14.	Despicable Me 2 (2013)
5.	Ride Along	15.	The Monuments Men
6.	Frozen (2013)	16.	Neighbors
7.	Gravity (2013)	17.	Anchorman 2: The Legend Continues (2013)
8.	Escape Plan (2013)	18.	Heaven Is for Real
9.	Divergent	19.	Lone Survivor (2013)
10.	American Hustle (2013)	20.	Non-Stop

Top-Selling DVDs, 2014

Rank	Movie	Rank	Movie
1.	Frozen (2013)	11.	Captain America: The Winter Soldier
2.	The Lego Movie	12.	X-Men: Days of Future Past
3.	The Hunger Games: Catching Fire (2013)	13.	Despicable Me 2 (2013)
4.	The Hobbit: The Desolation of Smaug (2013)	14.	Thor: The Dark World (2013)
5.	Guardians of the Galaxy	15.	Divergent
6.	How to Train Your Dragon 2	16.	Gravity (2013)
7.	Maleficent	17.	Godzilla
8.	Transformers: Age of Extinction	18.	Rio 2
9.	Lone Survivor (2013)	19.	The Fault in Our Stars
10.	Teenage Mutant Ninja Turtles	20.	Dawn of the Planet of the Apes

Note: Includes Blu-ray format titles. Top rentals exclude kiosk and subscription-by-mail channels. Top-selling DVDs exclude units sold into the rental channel, online, and in Canada. Movies released in 2014 unless otherwise noted.

Top-Selling Video Games, 2014

Source: The NPD Group/Retail Tracking Service

U.S. consumers spent $15.4 bil on video game content in 2014: $7.3 bil on physical software, $8.1 bil on content in digital formats, and $1.9 bil on other physical formats (including rental/used content). Spending decreased 10% on physical content, but digital content spending grew 12%.

Rank	Game (console)
1.	Call of Duty: Advanced Warfare (360, XBO, PC, PS3, PS4)*
2.	Madden NFL 15 (360, XBO, PS3, PS4)*
3.	Destiny (XBO, 360, PS3, PS4)*
4.	Grand Theft Auto V (360, XBO, PS3, PS4)*
5.	Minecraft (360, XBO, PS3, PS4)
6.	Super Smash Bros. (3DS, Wii U)*
7.	NBA 2K15 (360, XBO, PC, PS3, PS4)
8.	Watch Dogs (360, XBO, PS3, PS4, PC, Wii U)*
9.	FIFA 15 (360, XBO, PS3, PS4, PSV, Wii, 3DS)*
10.	Call of Duty: Ghosts (360, XBO, PC, PS3, PS4, Wii U)*

* = Includes bundled, collector's, or game-of-the-year editions, except those bundled with hardware. 3DS = Nintendo 3DS; 360 = Microsoft Xbox 360; PC = personal computer; PS3 = PlayStation 3; PS4 = PlayStation 4; PSV = PlayStation Vita; Wii/Wii U = Nintendo Wii or Wii U; XBO = Microsoft Xbox One.

Film and TV Content Ratings

The Motion Picture Association of America (MPAA) began rating movies in 1968. The system was revised in 1984 and in 1990. The MPAA, Natl. Cable Television Assn., and Natl. Assn. of Broadcasters developed the TV ratings system in 1997, in accordance with the Telecommunications Act of 1996; it was implemented in Oct. 1997.

Film Ratings

G: General Audience. All ages admitted. Does not contain themes, language, nudity, sex, or violence that the MPAA ratings board believes would offend parents whose younger children see the film. Does not necessarily denote a certificate of approval nor children's movie. No nudity, sex scenes, or drug use depicted.

PG: Parental Guidance Suggested. Some material may not be suited for children. The MPAA ratings board recommends that parents determine whether the content of the film is appropriate for their children. The film may contain more mature themes, some profanity, violence, or brief nudity. No drug use depicted.

PG-13: Parents Strongly Cautioned. Some material may be inappropriate for children under 13. The MPAA urges more strongly that parents vet the movie to see if its content is appropriate for their children. Any movie depicting drug use or more than brief nudity is automatically rated at least PG-13. Violence is permitted, though it is generally not both realistic or extreme and persistent violence. The single use of one sexually-derived expletive rates a PG-13; more than one use requires at least an R rating.

R: Restricted. Under 17 requires accompanying parent or adult guardian. Movies given R ratings contain some adult material, defined as adult themes or activity, hard language, intense or persistent violence, sexually-oriented nudity, or drug abuse.

NC-17: No One 17 and Under Admitted. The ratings board considers NC-17 films those that most parents would consider too adult for children under 17. An NC-17 rating does not mean the film is obscene or pornographic. The rating can be based on violence, sex, aberrational behavior, drug abuse, or any other element that most parents would consider too adult for children.

TV Ratings

TV-Y: All Children. Program designed to be acceptable for children of all ages. Its themes and elements are designed for a very young audience.

TV-Y7: Directed to Older Children. Program designed for children ages 7 and older, and more appropriate for those who have the skills to distinguish between make-believe and reality. May include mild fantasy/comedic violence. Programs with more than mild fantasy violence are denoted with FV.

TV-G: General Audience. Program not necessarily designed for children, but most parents would find it suitable for all ages. Little or no violence, no strong language, and little or no sexual dialogue or situations.

TV-PG: Parental Guidance Suggested. Program might contain material that parents would consider inappropriate for children, such as an adult theme or one or more of the following: suggestive dialogue (D), infrequent coarse language (L), some sexual situations (S), or moderate violence (V).

TV-14: Parents Strongly Cautioned. Program contains material that many parents would consider inappropriate for children under 14, such as one or more of the following: intensely suggestive dialogue (D), strong coarse language (L), intense sexual situations (S), or intense violence (V).

TV-MA: Mature Audience Only. Program specifically designed for adults and may be unsuitable for children under 17. Contains one or more of the following: crude indecent language (L), explicit sexual activity (S), or graphic violence (V).

Opera: Most Produced Works, 2014-15

Source: OPERA America

Work, composer	Productions
La bohème, Giacomo Puccini	11
Don Giovanni, Wolfgang Amadeus Mozart	10
The Barber of Seville, Gioachino Rossini	9
The Marriage of Figaro, Wolfgang Amadeus Mozart	9
Rigoletto, Giuseppe Verdi	9
La traviata, Giuseppe Verdi	8
Carmen, Georges Bizet	8
Madama Butterfly, Giacomo Puccini	8
The Magic Flute, Wolfgang Amadeus Mozart	7
Tosca, Giacomo Puccini	7

Note: Scheduled productions of a given work (not individual performances) during the 2014-15 season (generally Oct.-Sept.) by members of OPERA America and Opera.ca.

Longest-Running Broadway Shows

Source: The Broadway League, New York, NY

Rank	Title (run)[1]	Performances[2]
1.	*The Phantom of the Opera (1988-)	11,367
2.	*Chicago (revival) (1996-)	7,693
3.	Cats (1982-2000)	7,485
4.	*The Lion King (1997-)	7,288
5.	Les Misérables (1987-2003)	6,680
6.	A Chorus Line (1975-90)	6,137
7.	Oh! Calcutta! (revival) (1976-89)	5,959
8.	*Mamma Mia! (2001-)	5,630
9.	Beauty and the Beast (1994-2007)	5,461
10.	Rent (1996-2008)	5,123
11.	*Wicked (2003-)	4,819
12.	Miss Saigon (1991-2001)	4,092
13.	*Jersey Boys (2005-)	3,956
14.	42nd Street (1980-89)	3,486
15.	Grease (1972-80)	3,388
16.	Fiddler on the Roof (1964-72)	3,242
17.	Life With Father (1939-47)	3,224
18.	Tobacco Road (1933-41)	3,182
19.	Hello, Dolly! (1964-70)	2,844
20.	My Fair Lady (1956-62)	2,717
21.	Hairspray (2002-09)	2,642
22.	Mary Poppins (2006-13)	2,619
23.	Avenue Q (2003-09)	2,534
24.	The Producers (2001-07)	2,502
25.	Cabaret (revival) (1998-2004)	2,377
	Annie (1977-83)	2,377
27.	Rock of Ages (2009-15)	2,328
	Man of La Mancha (1965-71)	2,328
29.	Abie's Irish Rose (1922-27)	2,327
30.	Oklahoma! (1943-48)	2,212
31.	Smokey Joe's Cafe (1995-2000)	2,036
32.	Pippin (1972-77)	1,944
33.	South Pacific (1949-54)	1,925
34.	The Magic Show (1974-78)	1,920
35.	Aida (2000-04)	1,852
36.	Gemini (1977-81)	1,819
37.	Deathtrap (1978-82)	1,793
38.	Harvey (1944-49)	1,775
39.	Dancin' (1978-82)	1,774
40.	La Cage aux Folles (1983-87)	1,761
41.	Hair (1968-72)	1,750
42.	*The Book of Mormon (2011-)	1,742
43.	The Wiz (1975-79)	1,672
44.	Born Yesterday (1946-49)	1,642
45.	Crazy For You (1992-96)	1,622
46.	Ain't Misbehavin' (1978-82)	1,604
47.	The Best Little Whorehouse in Texas (1978-82)	1,584
48.	Spamalot (2005-09)	1,575
49.	Mary, Mary (1961-64)	1,572
50.	Evita (1979-83)	1,567

* = Still running as of Sept. 1, 2015. (1) Unless noted, listings reflect a play's first run on Broadway. (2) Number of performances through May 24, 2015.

Broadway Season Statistics, 1959-2015

Source: The Broadway League, New York, NY

Season	Gross (mil $)	Attendance (mil)	Playing weeks	New productions	Avg. ticket price
1959-1960	$46	7.9	1,156	58	$5.82
1964-1965	51	8.2	1,250	67	6.20
1969-1970	53	7.1	1,047	62	7.46
1974-1975	57	6.6	1,101	54	8.64
1979-1980	146	9.6	1,540	61	15.21
1984-1985	209	7.3	1,078	33	28.47
1989-1990	282	8.0	1,070	39	35.07
1994-1995	406	9.0	1,120	33	44.91
1999-2000	603	11.4	1,460	37	52.99
2004-2005	769	11.5	1,494	39	66.70
2005-2006	$862	12.0	1,501	39	$71.83
2006-2007	939	12.3	1,509	35	76.28
2007-2008	938	12.3	1,560	36	76.45
2008-2009	943	12.2	1,548	43	77.61
2009-2010	1,020	11.9	1,464	39	85.79
2010-2011	1,081	12.5	1,588	42	86.27
2011-2012	1,139	12.3	1,522	41	92.38
2012-2013	1,139	11.6	1,430	46	98.44
2013-2014	1,269	12.2	1,496	44*	103.93
2014-2015	1,365	13.1	1,626	37	104.20

* = Includes one return engagement.

Notable U.S. Museums

This unofficial list of some of the largest museums in the U.S., by budget, was compiled with the assistance of the American Association of Museums, a national association representing the concerns of the museum community. Association members also include zoos, aquariums, arboretums, botanical gardens, and planetariums, but these are not included in *The World Almanac* listings.

Museum	City	State
American Museum of Natural History	New York	NY
Amon Carter Museum of Western Art	Ft. Worth	TX
The Art Institute of Chicago	Chicago	IL
Boston Children's Museum	Boston	MA
Brooklyn Museum of Art	Brooklyn	NY
Busch-Reisinger Museum	Cambridge	MA
California Academy of Sciences	San Francisco	CA
California Science Center	Los Angeles	CA
Carnegie Museums of Pittsburgh	Pittsburgh	PA
Children's Museum of Indianapolis	Indianapolis	IN
Cincinnati Art Museum	Cincinnati	OH
Cincinnati Museum Center	Cincinnati	OH
Cleveland Museum of Art	Cleveland	OH
Colonial Williamsburg	Williamsburg	VA
Corning Museum of Glass	Corning	NY
Crystal Bridges Museum of American Art	Bentonville	AR
Dallas Museum of Art	Dallas	TX
Denver Art Museum	Denver	CO
Denver Museum of Nature and Science	Denver	CO
Detroit Institute of Arts	Detroit	MI
Exploratorium	San Francisco	CA
The Field Museum	Chicago	IL
Fine Arts Museums of San Francisco	San Francisco	CA
Franklin Institute	Philadelphia	PA
The Frick Collection	New York	NY
J. Paul Getty Museum	Los Angeles	CA
Solomon R. Guggenheim Museum of Art	New York	NY
Harvard University Art Museums	Cambridge	MA
Henry F. DuPont Winterthur Museum	Winterthur	DE
Henry Ford Museum/Greenfield Village	Dearborn	MI
High Museum of Art	Atlanta	GA
Houston Museum of Natural Science	Houston	TX
Jamestown-Yorktown Foundation	Williamsburg	VA
Jewish Museum	New York	NY
L.A. County Museum of Art	Los Angeles	CA
Liberty Science Center, Liberty State Park	Jersey City	NJ
Maryland Science Center	Baltimore	MD
Mashantucket Pequot Museum and Research Center	Mashantucket	CT
Metropolitan Museum of Art	New York	NY
Milwaukee Public Museum	Milwaukee	WI
Minneapolis Institute of Arts	Minneapolis	MN
Museum of African American History	Detroit	MI
Museum of the American West	Los Angeles	CA
Museum of Contemporary Art	Los Angeles	CA
Museum of Fine Arts	Boston	MA

Museum	City	State
Museum of Fine Arts	Houston	TX
Museum of Modern Art	New York	NY
Museum of New Mexico	Santa Fe	NM
Museum of Science	Boston	MA
Museum of Science and Industry	Chicago	IL
Musical Instrument Museum	Phoenix	AZ
Mystic Seaport Museum	Mystic	CT
National Air and Space Museum	Washington	DC
National Baseball Hall of Fame and Museum, Inc.	Cooperstown	NY
National Constitution Center	Philadelphia	PA
National Gallery of Art	Washington	DC
National Museum of American History	Washington	DC
National Museum of the American Indian	Washington	DC
National Museum of Natural History	Washington	DC
Nelson-Atkins Museum of Art	Kansas City	MO
New-York Historical Society	New York	NY
New York State Museum	Albany	NY
Peabody Essex Museum	Salem	MA
Philadelphia Museum of Art	Philadelphia	PA
Rock and Roll Hall of Fame and Museum, Inc.	Cleveland	OH
St. Louis Science Center	St. Louis	MO
San Diego Museum of Art	San Diego	CA
San Francisco Museum of Modern Art	San Francisco	CA
Science Museum of Minnesota	St. Paul	MN
Toledo Museum of Art	Toledo	OH
U.S. Holocaust Memorial Museum	Washington	DC
Univ. of Pennsylvania Museum of Archaeology and Anthropology	Philadelphia	PA
Virginia Museum of Fine Arts	Richmond	VA
Wadsworth Atheneum	Hartford	CT
Walker Art Center	Minneapolis	MN
Whitney Museum of American Art	New York	NY

Best-Selling U.S. Magazines, 2015

Source: Audit Bureau of Circulations (ABC)

General magazines, exclusive of comics; also excludes magazines that failed to file reports to ABC. Based on total average paid and verified circulation during the six months ending June 30, 2015; ranked by paid circulation size.

	Publication	Paid circ.
1.	AARP The Magazine	23,064,378
2.	AARP Bulletin	22,197,918
3.	Better Homes and Gardens	7,623,163
4.	Game Informer Magazine	6,878,530
5.	AAA Living	4,962,367
6.	Good Housekeeping	4,348,965
7.	Family Circle	4,066,378
8.	People	3,469,098
9.	National Geographic	3,404,745
10.	Woman's Day	3,272,720
11.	Sports Illustrated	3,044,430
12.	Time	3,038,254
13.	Cosmopolitan	3,003,601
14.	Southern Living	2,827,407
15.	Reader's Digest	2,744,725
16.	Shape	2,575,900
17.	O, The Oprah Magazine	2,381,900
18.	Glamour	2,348,000
19.	Taste of Home	2,263,546
20.	Redbook	2,224,953
21.	ESPN The Magazine	2,139,323
22.	FamilyFun Magazine	2,118,655
23.	American Rifleman	2,077,683
24.	Parents	2,063,402
25.	American Legion Magazine	2,061,984
26.	Martha Stewart Living	2,061,598
27.	Seventeen	2,014,246
28.	Maxim	2,012,632
29.	Real Simple	2,012,139
30.	Us Weekly	1,963,995
31.	Prevention	1,874,613
32.	Smithsonian	1,865,086
33.	TV Guide Magazine	1,817,030
34.	Men's Health	1,812,571
35.	Cooking Light	1,799,156
36.	Entertainment Weekly	1,742,412
37.	InStyle	1,741,043
38.	Food Network Magazine	1,733,904
39.	Money	1,717,473
40.	Every Day With Rachael Ray	1,714,834
41.	Golf Digest	1,630,264
42.	Country Living	1,628,724
43.	All You	1,555,519
44.	Guideposts	1,546,966
45.	Bon Appetit	1,521,651
46.	Women's Health	1,517,906
47.	Fitness	1,510,866
48.	Self	1,495,537
49.	Rolling Stone	1,459,154
50.	Golf Magazine	1,410,817

Best-Selling Digital Replica U.S. Magazines, 2015

Source: Audit Bureau of Circulations (ABC)

General magazines, exclusive of comics; also excludes magazines that failed to file reports to ABC. Based on total average paid and verified circulation during the six months ending June 30, 2015; ranked by paid circulation size.

	Publication	Paid circ.
1.	Game Informer Magazine	2,796,398
2.	Maxim	266,642
3.	National Geographic	174,073
4.	Star Magazine	149,209
5.	Better Homes and Gardens	149,003
6.	Men's Health	139,075
7.	Cosmopolitan	132,655
8.	Women's Health	129,802
9.	Food Network Magazine	118,552
10.	Popular Science	118,204
11.	ESPN The Magazine	118,091
12.	O, The Oprah Magazine	114,579
13.	Backpacker	109,490
14.	OK! Weekly	107,272
15.	HGTV Magazine	106,169
16.	Motor Trend	101,296
17.	Nylon	100,676
18.	New Yorker	96,178
19.	Prevention	95,692
20.	Yoga Journal	89,190
21.	Us Weekly	87,155
22.	People	86,370
23.	Shape	85,539
24.	EatingWell	83,802
25.	Bloomberg BusinessWeek	82,054
26.	Real Simple	81,963
27.	Men's Fitness	81,244
28.	Vanidades	80,830
29.	Vanity Fair	79,576
30.	Wired	77,738
31.	GQ	76,739
32.	Martha Stewart Living	75,826
33.	Hot Rod Magazine	74,963
34.	Reader's Digest	74,318
35.	Every Day With Rachael Ray	73,610
36.	Taste of Home	72,324
37.	Family Circle	72,132
38.	Weight Watchers	71,601
39.	Fitness	71,175
40.	Time	70,559
41.	Runner's World	69,777
42.	New York	68,911
43.	Esquire	68,171
44.	Popular Mechanics	67,417
45.	Good Housekeeping	66,596
46.	Popular Photography	65,818
47.	Fast Company	64,975
48.	AllRecipes	61,878
49.	Rolling Stone	61,142
50.	The Knot	59,587

Most Challenged Books, 2014

Source: Office for Intellectual Freedom, American Library Association (ALA)

A challenge is a formal, written complaint filed with a library or school requesting that materials be removed because of content or appropriateness.

Rank	Title, author	Common reasons given for challenge
1.	*The Absolutely True Diary of a Part-Time Indian*, Sherman Alexie	Anti-family, cultural insensitivity, drugs/alcohol/smoking, gambling, offensive language, sex education, sexually explicit, unsuited for age group, violence, "depictions of bullying"
2.	*Persepolis*, Marjane Satrapi	Gambling, offensive language, political viewpoint, "politically, racially, and socially offensive," "graphic depictions"
3.	*And Tango Makes Three*, Justin Richardson and Peter Parnell	Anti-family, homosexuality, political viewpoint, religious viewpoint, unsuited for age group, "promotes the homosexual agenda"
4.	*The Bluest Eye*, Toni Morrison	Sexually explicit, unsuited for age group, "contains controversial issues"
5.	*It's Perfectly Normal*, Robie Harris	Nudity, sex education, sexually explicit, unsuited to age group, "alleges it child pornography"
6.	*Saga*, Brian Vaughan and Fiona Staples	Anti-family, nudity, offensive language, sexually explicit, unsuited for age group
7.	*The Kite Runner*, Khaled Hosseini	Offensive language, unsuited to age group, violence
8.	*The Perks of Being a Wallflower*, Stephen Chbosky	Drugs/alcohol/smoking, homosexuality, offensive language, sexually explicit, unsuited for age group, "date rape and masturbation"
9.	*A Stolen Life*, Jaycee Dugard	Drugs/alcohol/smoking, offensive language, sexually explicit, unsuited for age group
10.	*Drama*, Raina Telgemeier	Sexually explicit

Some Notable New Books, 2015

Source: Reference and User Services Association, American Library Association (ALA)

Fiction

All My Puny Sorrows, Miriam Toews
All the Light We Cannot See, Anthony Doerr
The Bone Clocks: A Novel, David Mitchell
The Children Act, Ian McEwan
The Crane Wife, Patrick Ness
The Enchanted: A Novel, Rene Denfeld
Narrow Road to the Deep North: A Novel, Richard Flanagan
On Such a Full Sea, Chang-Rae Lee
Orfeo: A Novel, Richard Powers
Something Rich and Strange: Selected Stories, Ron Rash
Station Eleven: A Novel, Emily St. John Mandel
Tigerman, Nick Harkaway

Poetry

The Blue Buick: New and Selected Poems, B. H. Fairchild
Gabriel: A Poem, Edward Hirsch

Nonfiction

The Birth of the Pill: How Four Crusaders Reinvented Sex and Launched a Revolution, Jonathan Eig
Blood Royal: A True Tale of Crime and Detection in Medieval Paris, Eric Jager
Dark Invasion: 1915 Germany's Secret War and the Hunt for the First Terrorist Cell in America, Howard Blum
Factory Man, Beth Macy
In the Kingdom of Ice: The Grand and Terrible Polar Voyage of the USS Jeannette, Hampton Sides
Jerry Lee Lewis: His Own Story, Rick Bragg
Just Mercy: A Story of Justice and Redemption, Bryan Stevenson
The Most Dangerous Book: The Battle for James Joyce's Ulysses, Kevin Birmingham
No Place to Hide: Edward Snowden, the NSA, and the U.S. Surveillance State, Glenn Greenwald
Pandora's DNA: Tracing the Breast Cancer Genes Through History, Science, and One Family Tree, Lizzie Stark
The Secret History of Wonder Woman, Jill Lepore
The Sixth Extinction: An Unnatural History, Elizabeth Kolbert

Some Notable New Books for Children, 2015

Source: Association for Library Service to Children, American Library Association (ALA)

Younger Readers

The Adventures of Beekle: The Unimaginary Friend, Dan Santat
The Baby Tree, Sophie Blackall
Beautiful Moon: A Child's Prayer, Tonya Bolden, Eric Velasquez (illus.)
Blizzard, John Rocco
A Boy and a Jaguar, Alan Rabinowitz, Catia Chien (illus.)
The Chicken Squad: The First Misadventure, Doreen Cronin, Kevin Cornell (illus.)
A Dance Like Starlight: One Ballerina's Dream, Kristy Dempsey, Floyd Cooper (illus.)
Dory Fantasmagory, Abby Hanlon
Draw! Raúl Colón
Early Bird, Toni Yuly
The Farmer and the Clown, Marla Frazee
The Farmer's Away! Baa! Neigh! Anne Vittur Kennedy
Feathers: Not Just for Flying, Melissa Stewart, Sarah S. Brannen (illus.)
Firebird, Misty Copeland, Christopher Myers (illus.)
Firefly July: A Year of Very Short Poems, selected by Paul B. Janeczko, Melissa Sweet (illus.)
Flashlight, Lizi Boyd
Fox's Garden, Princesse Camcam
Froodle, Antoinette Portis
Gaston, Kelly DiPucchio, Christian Robinson (illus.)
Green Is a Chile Pepper, Roseanne Greenfield Thong, John Parra (illus.)
Handle With Care: An Unusual Butterfly Journey, Loree Griffin Burns, photos by Ellen Harasimowicz
Have You Seen My Dragon? Steve Light
Hi, Koo!: A Year of Seasons, Jon J. Muth
The Iridescence of Birds: A Book about Henri Matisse, Patricia MacLachlan, Hadley Hooper (illus.)
Little Melba and Her Big Trombone, Katheryn Russell-Brown, Frank Morrison (illus.)
Little Roja Riding Hood, Susan Middleton Elya, Susan Guevara (illus.)
Mama Built a Little Nest, Jennifer Ward, Steve Jenkins (illus.)
The Most Magnificent Thing, Ashley Spires
Mr. Putter & Tabby Turn the Page, Cynthia Rylant, Arthur Howard (illus.)
My Teacher Is a Monster! (No, I Am Not), Peter Brown
Nana in the City, Lauren Castillo
Naptime, Iris de Moüy, trans. by Shelley Tanaka
The Noisy Paint Box: The Colors and Sounds of Kandinsky's Abstract Art, Barb Rosenstock, Mary Grandpré (illus.)
The Pigeon Needs a Bath! Mo Willems
Queen Victoria's Bathing Machine, Gloria Whelan, Nancy Carpenter (illus.)
Sam and Dave Dig a Hole, Mac Barnett, Jon Klassen (illus.)
Shh! We Have a Plan, Chris Haughton
Star Stuff: Carl Sagan and the Mysteries of the Cosmos, Stephanie Roth Sisson
Tap Tap Boom Boom, Elizabeth Bluemle, G. Brian Karas (illus.)
Telephone, Mac Barnett, Jen Corace (illus.)
Tiny Creatures: The World of Microbes, Nicola Davies, Emily Sutton (illus.)
Viva Frida, Yuyi Morales
Waiting Is Not Easy! Mo Willems
Water Rolls, Water Rises: El agua rueda, el agua sube, Pat Mora, Meilo So (illus.), trans. by Adriana Domínguez and Pat Mora
Weeds Find a Way, Cindy Jenson-Elliott, Carolyn Fisher (illus.)
Winter Bees & Other Poems of the Cold, Joyce Sidman, Rick Allen (illus.)
Work, An Occupational ABC, Kellen Hatanaka
You Are (Not) Small, Anna Kang, Christopher Weyant (illus.)

Middle Readers

Absolutely Almost, Lisa Graff
Angel Island: Gateway to Gold Mountain, Russell Freedman; Chinese trans. by Evans Chan
Arcady's Goal, Eugene Yelchin
Before After, Anne-Margot Ramstein & Matthias Arégui
The Boundless, Kenneth Oppel
Brown Girl Dreaming, Jacqueline Woodson
The Case of the Vanishing Little Brown Bats: A Scientific Mystery, Sandra Markle
Chasing Cheetahs: The Race to Save Africa's Fastest Cats, Sy Montgomery, photos by Nic Bishop
Dare the Wind: The Record-Breaking Voyage of Eleanor Prentiss and the Flying Cloud, Tracey Fern, Emily Arnold McCully (illus.)
El Deafo, Cece Bell, David Lasky (colorist)
Eye to Eye: How Animals See the World, Steve Jenkins
The Fourteenth Goldfish, Jennifer L. Holm
Freedom Summer: The 1964 Struggle for Civil Rights in Mississippi, Susan Goldman Rubin
The Great Greene Heist, Varian Johnson
Half a Chance, Cynthia Lord
Harlem Hellfighters, J. Patrick Lewis, Gary Kelley (illus.)
Hello, I'm Johnny Cash, G. Neri, A. G. Ford (illus.)
Hidden: A Child's Story of the Holocaust, Loïc Dauvillier, Marc Lizano (illus.), Greg Salsedo (colorist)
Hope Is a Ferris Wheel, Robin Herrera
I Lived on Butterfly Hill, Marjorie Agosín, Lee White (illus.)
Josephine: The Dazzling Life of Josephine Baker, Patricia Hruby Powell, Christian Robinson (illus.)
Kinda Like Brothers, Coe Booth
Lowriders in Space, Cathy Camper, Raúl the Third (illus.)
The Luck Uglies, Paul Durham, Pétur Antonsson (illus.)
Mikis and the Donkey, Bibi Dumon Tak, Philip Hopman (illus.), trans. by Laura Watkinson
The Misadventures of the Family Fletcher, Dana Alison Levy
A Moose Boosh: A Few Choice Words About Food, Eric-Shabazz Larkin
Mysterious Patterns: Finding Fractals in Nature, Sarah C. Campbell, photos by author and Richard P. Campbell
Neighborhood Sharks: Hunting With the Great Whites of California's Farallon Islands, Katherine Roy
Nest, Esther Ehrlich
Once Upon an Alphabet, Oliver Jeffers
Rain Reign, Ann M. Martin
The Red Pencil, Andrea Davis Pinkney, Shane W. Evans (illus.)
Separate Is Never Equal: Sylvia Mendez & Her Family's Fight for Desegregation, Duncan Tonatiuh
Sisters, Raina Telgemeier
A Snicker of Magic, Natalie Lloyd
Three Bird Summer, Sara St. Antoine
The Turtle of Oman, Naomi Shihab Nye
Under the Egg, Laura Marx Fitzgerald
West of the Moon, Margi Preus
The Whispering Town, Jennifer Elvgren, Fabio Santomauro (illus.)
The Witch's Boy, Kelly Barnhill

Older Readers

Because They Marched: The People's Campaign for Voting Rights That Changed America, Russell Freedman
Caminar, Skila Brown
The Crossover, Kwame Alexander
The Family Romanov: Murder, Rebellion & the Fall of Imperial Russia, Candace Fleming
How I Discovered Poetry, Marilyn Nelson, Hadley Hooper (illus.)
The Night Gardener, Jonathan Auxier
Nine Open Arms, Benny Lindelauf, Dasha Tolstikova (illus.), trans. by John Nieuwenhuizen
The Port Chicago 50: Disaster, Mutiny, and the Fight for Civil Rights, Steve Sheinkin
Portraits of Hispanic American Heroes, Juan Felipe Herrera, Raúl Colón (illus.)
Revolution: The Sixties Trilogy, Book Two, Deborah Wiles
This One Summer, Mariko Tamaki, Jillian Tamaki (illus.)
A Time to Dance, Padma Venkatraman

All Ages

The Right Word: Roget and His Thesaurus, Jen Bryant, Melissa Sweet (illus.)
The Scraps Book: Notes From a Colorful Life, Lois Ehlert
Take Away the A: An Alphabeast of a Book! Michaël Escoffier, Kris DiGiacomo (illus.)

Best-Selling Books, 2014

Source: Publishers Weekly; Nielsen BookScan

Hardcover Fiction

1. *Gray Mountain*, John Grisham
2. *The Goldfinch*, Donna Tartt
3. *Revival*, Stephen King
4. *The Invention of Wings*, Sue Monk Kidd
5. *Mr. Mercedes*, Stephen King
6. *Edge of Eternity*, Ken Follett
7. *Hope to Die*, James Patterson
8. *All the Light We Cannot See*, Anthony Doerr
9. *Top Secret Twenty-One*, Janet Evanovich
10. *The Escape*, David Baldacci

Hardcover Nonfiction

1. *Killing Patton: The Strange Death of World War II's Most Audacious General*, Bill O'Reilly
2. *Jesus Calling: Enjoying Peace in His Presence*, Sarah Young
3. *Strengths Finder 2.0*, Tom Rath
4. *Make It Ahead*, Ina Garten
5. *41: A Portrait of My Father*, George W. Bush
6. *Guinness World Records 2015*
7. *Killing Jesus: A History*, Bill O'Reilly
8. *Yes Please*, Amy Poehler
9. *What If?: Serious Scientific Answers to Absurd Hypothetical Questions*, Randall Munroe
10. *Unbroken: A World War II Story of Survival, Resilience, and Redemption*, Laura Hillenbrand

Trade Paperback

1. *Gone Girl*, Gillian Flynn
2. *Unbroken: A World War II Story of Survival, Resilience, and Redemption*, Laura Hillenbrand
3. *Orphan Train*, Christina Baker Kline
4. *Heaven Is for Real: A Little Boy's Astounding Story of His Trip to Heaven and Back*, Todd Burpo
5. *Heaven Is for Real* (movie edition), Todd Burpo
6. *Gone Girl* (movie edition), Gillian Flynn
7. *The Boys in the Boat: Nine Americans and Their Epic Quest for Gold at the 1936 Berlin Olympics*, Daniel James Brown
8. *The 5 Love Languages: The Secret to Love That Lasts*, Gary Chapman
9. *Wild: From Lost to Found on the Pacific Crest Trail*, Cheryl Strayed
10. *Fifty Shades of Grey*, E. L. James

Mass Market Fiction

1. *Gone Girl*, Gillian Flynn
2. *To Kill a Mockingbird*, Harper Lee
3. *Sycamore Row*, John Grisham
4. *The Best of Me*, Nicholas Sparks
5. *1984*, George Orwell
6. *A Game of Thrones*, George R. R. Martin
7. *Dust*, Patricia Cornwell
8. *Winners*, Danielle Steel
9. *Starry Night*, Debbie Macomber
10. *Outlander*, Diana Gabaldon

E-books

1. *The Fault in Our Stars*, John Green
2. *Gone Girl*, Gillian Flynn
3. *Divergent (Divergent #1)*, Veronica Roth
4. *Insurgent (Divergent #2)*, Veronica Roth
5. *Allegiant (Divergent #3)*, Veronica Roth
6. *The Goldfinch*, Donna Tartt
7. *Unbroken: A World War II Story of Survival, Resilience, and Redemption*, Laura Hillenbrand
8. *The Husband's Secret*, Liane Moriarty
9. *If I Stay*, Gayle Forman
10. *Orphan Train*, Christina Baker Kline

Children's and Young Adult Hardcover

1. *The Long Haul (Diary of a Wimpy Kid Series #9)*, Jeff Kinney
2. *Insurgent (Divergent #2)*, Veronica Roth
3. *Allegiant (Divergent #3)*, Veronica Roth
4. *Frozen*, Victoria Saxon
5. *Four: A Divergent Collection*, Veronica Roth
6. *Hard Luck (Diary of a Wimpy Kid Series #8)*, Jeff Kinney
7. *Wonder*, R. J. Palacio
8. *The Blood of Olympus* (*Heroes of Olympus* #5), Rick Riordan
9. *Disney Frozen*, Bill Scollon
10. *The Day the Crayons Quit*, Drew Daywalt, Oliver Jeffers (illus.)

U.S. Daily Newspapers, 2014

Source: *Editor & Publisher International Data Book*
(ranked by circulation as of Sept. 30, 2014)

Rank	Newspaper	Circulation
1.	McLean (VA) *USA Today*	3,255,157
2.	New York (NY) *Wall Street Journal*	2,294,093
3.	New York (NY) *Times*	2,149,012
4.	Santa Ana (CA) *The Orange County Register*	793,582
5.	Los Angeles (CA) *Times*	717,432
6.	Fort Myers (FL) *The News-Press*	601,697
7.	San Jose (CA) *Mercury News*	581,546
8.	New York (NY) *Post*	477,314
9.	Melville (NY) *Newsday*	460,149
10.	New York (NY) *Daily News*	456,360
11.	Woodland Hills (CA) *Los Angeles Daily News*	448,234
12.	Chicago (IL) *Tribune*	438,935
13.	Washington (DC) *Post*	436,601
14.	Dallas (TX) *Morning News*	413,481
15.	Denver (CO) *Post*	391,096
16.	Philadelphia (PA) *Inquirer*	373,479
17.	Houston (TX) *Chronicle*	370,961
18.	Chicago (IL) *Sun-Times*	370,449
19.	Las Vegas (NV) *Review-Journal*	322,556
20.	St. Petersburg (FL) *Tampa Bay Times*	317,270
21.	Minneapolis (MN) *Star Tribune*	301,494
22.	Newark (NJ) *Star-Ledger*	296,466
23.	Brooklyn (OH) *Plain Dealer*	284,850
24.	Boston (MA) *Globe*	274,538
25.	Honolulu (HI) *Star-Advertiser*	272,856
26.	Portland (OR) *Oregonian*	263,726
27.	Seattle (WA) *Times*	261,441
28.	Phoenix (AZ) *Republic*	261,174
29.	Atlanta (GA) *Journal-Constitution*	257,135
30.	San Diego (CA) *Union-Tribune*	254,238
31.	St. Paul (MN) *Pioneer Press*	239,968
32.	Albuquerque (NM) *Daily Lobo*	230,687
33.	Silver City (NM) *Sun-News*	230,687
34.	Detroit (MI) *Free Press*	216,269
35.	San Francisco (CA) *Chronicle*	211,777
36.	Springfield (MA) *Republican*	210,159
37.	Greensburg (PA) *Tribune-Review*	199,182
38.	Milwaukee (WI) *Journal Sentinel*	192,667
39.	Sacramento (CA) *Bee*	191,608
40.	St. Louis (MO) *Post-Dispatch*	186,820
41.	Tampa (FL) *Tribune*	181,589
42.	Kansas City (MO) *Star*	175,833
43.	Fort Worth (TX) *Star-Telegram*	173,833
44.	Orlando (FL) *Sentinel*	173,542
45.	Ogden (UT) *Standard-Examiner*	167,823
46.	Ft. Lauderdale (FL) *South Florida Sun-Sentinel*	162,721
47.	Woodland Park (NJ) *Record*	160,571
48.	San Antonio (TX) *Express-News*	160,545
49.	Pittsburgh (PA) *Post-Gazette*	155,700
50.	Woodland Park (NJ) *Herald News*	152,167

Note: Excludes newspapers for which no average weekday circulation number was available.

Paid U.S. Newspaper Circulation, 1940-2014

Source: *Editor & Publisher International Data Book*
(circulation figures in thousands as of Sept. 30, 2014)

Year	Number of daily newspapers			Circulation of daily newspapers			Sunday newspapers	
	Morning	Evening	Total	Morning	Evening	Total	Number	Circulation
1940	380	1,498	1,878	16,114	25,018	41,132	525	32,371
1950	322	1,450	1,772	21,266	32,563	53,829	549	46,582
1960	312	1,459	1,763	24,029	34,853	58,882	563	47,699
1970	334	1,429	1,748	25,934	36,174	62,108	586	49,217
1980	387	1,388	1,745	29,414	32,787	62,202	736	54,676
1990	559	1,084	1,611	41,311	21,017	62,328	863	62,635
2000	766	727	1,480	46,772	9,000	55,773	917	59,421
2005	817	645	1,452	46,122	7,222	53,345	914	55,270
2006	833	614	1,437	45,441	6,888	52,329	907	53,179
2007	867	565	1,422	44,548	6,194	50,742	907	51,246
2008	872	546	1,408	42,758	5,840	48,598	902	49,115
2009	869	528	1,397	40,796	5,482	46,278	919	46,850
2011	931	451	1,382	40,321	4,100	44,421	900	48,510
2012	985	442	1,427	38,723	4,709	43,432	981	48,821
2013	980	444	1,395	36,795	3,737	40,712	934	43,292
2014	953	402	1,331	36,765	3,655	40,420	923	42,751

Newspaper Advertising Revenues, 1950-2013

Source: Research Dept., Newspaper Association of America

Year	National ad revenue (mil)	Retail ad revenue (mil)	Classified ad revenue (mil)	Print advertising total revenue		Online advertising total revenue		Total advertising revenue	
				(mil)	% change[1]	(mil)	% change	(mil)	% change
1950	$518	$1,175	$377	$2,070	—	—	—	—	—
1955	712	1,755	610	3,077	48.7%	—	—	—	—
1960	778	2,100	803	3,681	19.6	—	—	—	—
1965	783	2,429	1,214	4,426	20.2	—	—	—	—
1970	891	3,292	1,521	5,704	28.9	—	—	—	—
1975	1,109	4,966	2,159	8,234	44.4	—	—	—	—
1980	1,963	8,609	4,222	14,794	79.7	—	—	—	—
1985	3,352	13,443	8,375	25,170	70.1	—	—	—	—
1990	4,122	16,652	11,506	32,280	28.3	—	—	—	—
1995	4,251	18,099	13,742	36,092	11.8	—	—	—	—
2000	7,653	21,409	19,608	48,670	5.1	—	—	—	—
2005	7,910	22,187	17,312	47,408	1.5	$2,027	31.5%	$49,435	2.5%
2006	7,505	22,121	16,986	46,611	−1.7	2,664	31.4	49,275	−0.3
2007	7,005	21,018	14,186	42,209	−9.4	3,166	18.8	45,375	−7.9
2008	5,996	18,769	9,975	34,740	−17.7	3,109	−1.8	37,848	−16.6
2009	4,424	14,218	6,179	24,821	−28.6	2,743	−11.8	27,564	−27.2
2010	4,221	12,926	5,648	22,795	−8.2	3,042	10.9	25,838	−6.3
2011[2]	3,777	11,887	5,028	20,692	−9.2	3,249	6.8	23,941	−7.3
2012[2]	3,335	10,894	4,626	18,931	−8.5	3,370	3.7	22,314	−6.8
2013[2]	3,068	10,105	4,140	17,300	−8.6	3,420	1.5	20,720	−7.1

— = Not applicable/available. (1) Percent change for years 1950-2000 refers to the rate of change over the preceding five-year period; for 2005 and on, it represents the rate of change over the past year. (2) Revenue from niche publications, direct marketing, and non-daily publication advertising ($3.0 bil in 2011, $2.9 bil in 2012, and $2.85 bil in 2013) is excluded from total revenue.

Canadian Daily Newspapers, 2014

Source: *Editor & Publisher International Data Book*
(ranked by circulation as of Sept. 30, 2014)

Rank	Newspaper	Circulation
1.	Toronto (ON) *Globe and Mail*	360,658
2.	Montréal (QC) *La Presse*	267,603
3.	Toronto (ON) *Star*	220,231
4.	Montréal (QC) *Le Journal de Montréal*	192,192
5.	Toronto (ON) *National Post*	159,483
6.	Vancouver (BC) *Sun*	154,058
7.	Vancouver (BC) *Province*	137,061
8.	Calgary (AB) *Herald*	114,919
9.	Toronto (ON) *Sun*	114,247
10.	Ottawa (ON) *Citizen*	111,272

Top Newspaper Websites, 2015

Source: comScore Media Metrix, Inc.; ranked by number of visitors

Rank	Website	Visitors[1]
1.	Mail Online	64,753
2.	The New York Times Brand	59,763
3.	WashingtonPost.com	54,353
4.	T365-Tribune Newspapers	40,789
5.	Hearst Newspapers	38,717
6.	The Guardian	30,956
7.	NY Post Network	20,178
8.	Telegraph Media Group	17,539
9.	MediaNews Group	17,448
10.	Topix	13,383
11.	Lee Enterprises, Inc.	12,631
12.	Independent.co.uk	12,405
13.	Sun-Times Media/Chicago Region-Wide Network (CRWN)	10,881
14.	Mirror Online	10,620
15.	Cox Media Group-Newspaper	10,110
16.	ConservativeTribune.com	8,186
17.	Michigan.com sites	8,029
18.	BostonGlobe.com sites	7,518
19.	A. H. Belo	7,230
20.	Postmedia Network Canada Corp.	6,185

NA = Not available. (1) Number of persons age 2 and older, in thousands, who visited the media property (including website/apps) at least once from any U.S. location in June 2015. Mobile users under age 18 are not measured.

Top News/Information Websites, 2015

Source: comScore Media Metrix, Inc.; ranked by number of visitors

Rank	Website	Visitors[1]
1.	Yahoo-ABC News Network	117,400
2.	HPMG News	116,511
3.	Gannett sites	109,060
4.	The Weather Company	106,144
5.	CNN Network	105,945
6.	NBC News Digital	94,021
7.	Buzzfeed.com	79,557
8.	About.com	73,784
9.	CBS News	73,694
10.	Mail Online	64,753
11.	New York Times Digital	59,920
12.	WashingtonPost.com	54,353
13.	Fox News Digital Network	52,894
14.	AccuWeather sites	51,765
15.	WorldNow sites	46,948
16.	Advance Digital	42,960
17.	T365-Tribune Newspapers	40,789
18.	Time.com sites	39,726
19.	Hearst Newspapers	38,717
20.	The Guardian	30,956

NA = Not available. (1) Number of persons age 2 and older, in thousands, who visited the media property (including website/apps) at least once from any U.S. location in June 2015. Mobile users under age 18 are not measured.

Top-Selling Albums of All-Time

Source: Recording Industry Assn. of America (RIAA)
(Sales figures represent RIAA multi-platinum certifications; albums ranked by latest sales certification. As of Aug. 20, 2015.)

Rank	Title, artist	Unit sales (mil)
1.	*Thriller*, Michael Jackson	29.0
2.	*Eagles/Their Greatest Hits 1971-1975*, Eagles	29.0
3.	*The Wall*, Pink Floyd	23.0
4.	*Led Zeppelin IV*, Led Zeppelin	23.0
5.	*Greatest Hits Volume I & Volume II*, Billy Joel	23.0
6.	*Back in Black*, AC/DC	22.0
7.	*Double Live*, Garth Brooks	21.0
8.	*Rumours*, Fleetwood Mac	20.0
9.	*Come on Over*, Shania Twain	20.0
10.	*The Beatles*, The Beatles	19.0
11.	*Appetite for Destruction*, Guns N' Roses	18.0
12.	*The Beatles 1967-1970*, The Beatles	17.0
13.	*No Fences*, Garth Brooks	17.0
14.	*Boston*, Boston	17.0
15.	*The Bodyguard* (soundtrack), Whitney Houston	17.0
16.	*Cracked Rear View*, Hootie & the Blowfish	16.0
17.	*Physical Graffiti*, Led Zeppelin	16.0
18.	*Hotel California*, Eagles	16.0
19.	*Greatest Hits*, Elton John	16.0
20.	*Jagged Little Pill*, Alanis Morissette	16.0
21.	*Metallica*, Metallica	16.0
22.	*Supernatural*, Santana	15.0
23.	*The Beatles 1962-1966*, The Beatles	15.0
24.	*Greatest Hits*, Journey	15.0
25.	*Born in the U.S.A.*, Bruce Springsteen	15.0
26.	*Legend*, Bob Marley and the Wailers	15.0
27.	*Dark Side of the Moon*, Pink Floyd	15.0
28.	*Saturday Night Fever* (soundtrack), Bee Gees	15.0

Top-Selling Artists by Digital Sales

Source: Recording Industry Assn. of America (RIAA)
(Sales figures represent RIAA-confirmed digital units sold. As of Aug. 20, 2015.)

Artist	Unit sales (mil)
Rihanna	100.0
Taylor Swift	89.5
Katy Perry	80.5
Kanye West	47.5
Lady Gaga	39.5
Justin Bieber	35.0
Eminem	34.0
Lil Wayne	33.0
Flo Rida	32.5
Bruno Mars	29.0
Drake	29.0
Carrie Underwood	28.0
Beyoncé	24.0
Nicki Minaj	24.0
Jason Aldean	23.5
The Black Eyed Peas	22.0
Adele	22.0
Jason Derulo	21.5
Blake Shelton	21.5
Florida Georgia Line	20.0
Fall Out Boy	19.5
LMFAO	18.0
Luke Bryan	16.5
Tim McGraw	16.5
Imagine Dragons	16.0
Selena Gomez & the Scene	15.0
Kenny Chesney	15.0
Maroon 5	15.0
Lady Antebellum	14.5
Ariana Grande	14.5
Brad Paisley	14.5
Wiz Khalifa	13.5
One Direction	13.5
Akon	13.5
Macklemore and Ryan Lewis	13.0
Jay Z	13.0
Fun.	13.0
Train	12.5
Ed Sheeran	12.0
David Guetta	12.0
Nelly	11.5
Jason Mraz	11.5
Miranda Lambert	11.5
The Band Perry	11.5
Justin Timberlake	11.0
The Fray	11.0
Miley Cyrus	11.0
Toby Keith	11.0
OneRepublic	11.0
Linkin Park	11.0
John Legend	10.5
Christina Perri	10.5
Kelly Clarkson	10.0
T.I.	10.0
Demi Lovato	10.0
Timbaland	10.0
Paramore	10.0

U.S. Commercial Radio Stations by Format, 2005-15

Source: The Radio Book by Inside Radio © 2015
(as of July 2015; ranked by 2015 numbers)

Primary format	2015	2014	2013	2012	2011	2010	2009	2008	2007	2006	2005
1. Country	2,112	2,053	2,042	2,020	1,987	1,997	1,995	2,018	2,027	2,038	2,022
2. News/Talk	1,360	1,409	1,453	1,503	1,455	1,437	1,416	1,365	1,368	1,338	1,326
3. Spanish	862	844	835	816	818	806	803	799	786	706	696
4. Classic Hits	805	754	678	657	657	637	582	524	477	429	271
5. Sports	788	788	740	692	670	665	634	595	564	535	508
6. Adult Contemporary	609	597	605	597	607	634	626	670	665	660	683
7. Top 40	579	577	573	559	523	495	484	472	472	484	503
8. Classic Rock	486	486	486	477	477	481	477	474	456	456	461
9. Hot Adult Contemporary	462	465	428	420	435	417	409	373	373	378	374
10. Oldies	413	476	566	597	628	637	649	708	709	725	762
11. Religion (Teaching, Variety)	318	324	336	342	332	322	324	299	287	311	319
12. Rock	304	302	299	295	301	294	298	287	281	276	269
13. Black Gospel	218	211	212	214	225	235	242	244	253	267	286
14. Adult Standards	192	221	227	240	251	265	327	358	369	368	404
15. Contemporary Christian	168	157	172	171	166	166	162	136	153	150	172
Total stations	**11,104**	**11,099**	**11,107**	**11,078**	**11,034**	**11,024**	**10,977**	**10,853**	**10,760**	**10,711**	**10,674**

Note: Totals include stations that are changing or did not report format, as well as formats not listed here.

Multi-Platinum and Platinum Awards for Recorded Music, 2014-15

Source: Recording Industry Assn. of America

To be certified platinum, an **album** must sell 1 mil units (LPs, CDs, or digital) with a manufacturer's dollar volume of at least $2 mil based on one-third of the suggested retail list price for each copy sold. To achieve multi-platinum status, an album must reach minimum total sales of at least 2 mil units with a manufacturer's dollar volume of at least $4 mil based on one-third of the list price. **Digital singles** must sell 1 mil units to achieve a platinum award and 2 mil to achieve a multi-platinum award.

Awards listed here are for albums and digital singles (released Sept. 2013-Aug. 2015) that were certified Sept. 2014-Aug. 2015. Number in parentheses represents millions sold. Alphabetized by artist name.

Albums, Multi-Platinum

Sex and Love, Enrique Iglesias (2)
Pure Heroine, Lorde (2)
Prism, Katy Perry (2)
In the Lonely Hour, Sam Smith (2)
1989, Taylor Swift (5)
Frozen soundtrack, various artists (4)

Albums, Platinum

Old Boots, New Dirt, Jason Aldean
Man Against Machine, Garth Brooks
The Outsiders, Eric Church
If You're Reading This It's Too Late, Drake
Nothing Was the Same, Drake
Los Duo, Juan Gabriel
My Everything, Ariana Grande
Cama Incendiada, Mana
A Quien Quiera Escuchar, Ricky Martin
Four, One Direction
That's Christmas to Me, Pentatonix
X, Ed Sheeran
Partners, Barbra Streisand
Guardians of the Galaxy soundtrack, various artists

Digital Singles, Platinum and Multi-Platinum

"The Worst," Jhené Aiko
"Burnin' It Down," Jason Aldean
"Heroes (We Could Be)," Alesso
"Beg for It," "Black Widow" (3), "Fancy" (5), Iggy Azalea
"Shower" (2), Becky G
"Drunk on a Plane," Dierks Bentley
"Drunk in Love" (3), "Partition," "7/11," "XO," Beyoncé
"Blessings," "I Don't F**k With You" (2), Big Sean
"I Don't Dance," Lee Brice
"Try," Colbie Caillat
"Boom Clap," Charli XCX
"American Kids," Kenny Chesney
"Give Me Back My Hometown," Eric Church
"Heartbeat Song," Kelly Clarkson
"Rather Be" (2), Clean Bandit feat. Jess Glynne
"Marry Me," "Trumpets" (2), "Want to Want Me," Jason Derulo
"Wiggle" (2), Jason Derulo feat. Snoop Dogg
"Latch" (3), Disclosure
"Turn Down for What?" (5), DJ Snake feat. Lil Jon
"0 to 100 / The Catch Up," Drake
"Rap God" (3), Eminem
"Budapest," George Ezra
"Centuries" (3), "Uma Thurman," Fall Out Boy
"Trap Queen," Fetty Wap
"Bo$$," "Sledgehammer," Fifth Harmony
"Worth It" (2), Fifth Harmony feat. Kid Ink
"Amnesia," "She Looks So Perfect" (2), 5 Seconds of Summer
"Gdfr" (2), Flo Rida
"Dirt" (2), Florida Georgia Line
"Bottoms Up" (2), Brantley Gilbert
"The Heart Wants What It Wants," Selena Gomez
"Good for You," Selena Gomez feat. A$AP Rocky
"Love Me Like You Do" (2), Ellie Goulding
"Honey, I'm Good" (2), Andy Grammer
"Break Free" (3), "Love Me Harder," "One Last Time," "Problem" (6), Ariana Grande
"Hey Mama," David Guetta feat. Nicki Minaj, Bebe Rexha, Afrojack
"Outside," "Summer" (3), Calvin Harris
"Blame," Calvin Harris feat. John Newman
"Ghost," Ella Henderson
"Oceans (Where Feet May Fail)," Hillsong United
"The Hanging Tree," James Newton Howard feat. Jennifer Lawrence
"Take Me to Church" (5), Hozier
"House Party," "Leave the Night On," "Take Your Time" (2), Sam Hunt
"Bailando" (3), Enrique Iglesias
"Tuesday," ILoveMakonnen feat. Drake
"Don't Tell 'Em" (2), Jeremih
"Bang Bang" (5), Jessie J, Ariana Grande, Nicki Minaj
"Chains," "Jealous" (3), Nick Jonas
"Cut Her Off," K Camp
"Somebody" (2), Natalie La Rose
"Bartender," Lady Antebellum
"Do What U Want," Lady Gaga
"Somethin' Bad," Miranda Lambert & Carrie Underwood
"All of Me" (8), John Legend
"Believe Me," Lil Wayne
"Girl Crush," Little Big Town
"Where It's At," Dustin Lynch
"Girl in a Country Song," Maddie & Tae
"Lean On," Major Lazer feat. Mo & DJ Snake
"Meanwhile Back at Mama's," "Shotgun Rider," Tim McGraw
"Life of the Party," Shawn Mendes
"Let It Go" (8), Idina Menzel
"Stolen Dance," Milky Chance
"Anaconda" (2), "Only" (3), Nicki Minaj
"Waves (Robin Schulz Radio Edit)," Mr. Probz
"She Knows," Ne-Yo
"Am I Wrong" (2), Nico & Vinz
"Post to Be," Omarion
"Cheerleader," OMI
"Night Changes," "Story of My Life" (3), One Direction
"Birthday," "Dark Horse" (9), "This Is How We Do," Katy Perry
"Timber" (6), Pitbull feat. Ke$ha
"Fight Song," Rachel Platten
"Rewind," Rascal Flatts
"Get Me Some of That," Thomas Rhett
"Ready Set Roll," Chase Rice
"Lifestyle," Rich Gang
"Bitch Better Have My Money," "FourFiveSeconds (2), Rihanna
"Uptown Funk" (9), Mark Ronson feat. Bruno Mars
"Red Nose," Sage the Gemini
"Empire," Shakira
"Don't" (2), "Sing," "Thinking out Loud" (5), Ed Sheeran
"Geronimo," Sheppard
"Hot Boy aka Hot N****," Bobby Shmurda
"Where Are U Now," Skrillex & Diplo
"I'm Not the Only One" (4), "Stay With Me" (6), Sam Smith
"No Flex Zone," "No Type," Rae Sremmurd
"Bad Blood" (3), "Blank Space" (7), "Shake It Off" (7), "Style" (2), Taylor Swift
"No Mediocre," T.I. feat. Iggy Azalea
"Wasted," Tiesto
"2 On," Tinashe
"Habits (Stay High)" (3), "Talking Body" (2), Tove Lo
"All About That Bass" (9), "Dear Future Husband" (2), "Lips Are Movin" (2), Meghan Trainor
"Na Na," Trey Songz
"Something in the Water," Carrie Underwood
"I Don't Mind" (2), Usher feat. Juicy J
"Shut Up and Dance" (3), Walk the Moon
"Can't Feel My Face" (2), "Earned It (Fifty Shades of Grey)" (4), "The Hills" (2), "Often," The Weeknd
"Happy" (7), Pharrell Williams
"See You Again" (3), Wiz Khalifa feat. Charlie Puth
"Who Do You Love," YG feat. Drake
"Homegrown," Zac Brown Band

Top-Grossing North American Concert Tours, 1985-2014

Source: Pollstar

Rank	Artist (year)	Total gross[1]	Cities/ shows
1.	The Rolling Stones (2005)	$162.0	38/42
2.	U2 (2011)	156.0	21/25
3.	U2 (2005)	138.9	43/78
4.	The Rolling Stones (2006)	138.5	35/39
5.	Madonna (2012)	133.7	31/45
6.	The Police (2007)	133.2	41/54
7.	One Direction (2014)	127.2	21/31
8.	U2 (2009)	123.0	16/20
9.	The Rolling Stones (1994)	121.2	43/60
10.	Bruce Springsteen & The E Street Band (2003)	115.9	30/47
11.	Taylor Swift (2013)	112.7	47/66
12.	U2 (2001)	109.7	56/80
13.	Bon Jovi (2010)	108.2	38/51
14.	Bon Jovi (2013)	107.3	58/62
15.	Madonna (2008)	$105.3	19/30
16.	Bruce Springsteen & The E Street Band (2012)	104.7	42/52
17.	Pink Floyd (1994)	103.5	39/59
18.	Paul McCartney (2002)	103.3	43/53
19.	The Rolling Stones (1989)	98.0	33/60
20.	Taylor Swift (2011)	97.7	59/80
21.	Kenny Chesney and Tim McGraw (2012)	96.5	22/23
22.	Beyoncé/Jay Z	96.0	16/19
23.	Bruce Springsteen & The E Street Band (2009)	94.5	44/58
24.	Katy Perry	94.3	50/66
25.	Céline Dion (2008)	94.0	31/47

(1) In millions. Not adjusted for inflation.

Sales of Recorded Music and Music Videos, by Units Shipped and Value, 2000-14

Source: Recording Industry Assn. of America

(in millions, net after returns)

	2000	2005	2008	2009	2010	2011	2012	2013	2014	% change, 2013-14
Physical units shipped	**1,079.2**	**748.7**	**385.5**	**309.2**	**233.0**	**222.0**	**182.9**	**187.2**	**163.0**	**–13.0%**
Dollar value	**$14,323.7**	**11,195.0**	**5,758.5**	**4,555.9**	**3,438.7**	**3,170.9**	**2,584.3**	**2,444.8**	**2,272.2**	**–7.1**
Compact discs (CDs)	942.5	705.4	368.4	292.9	253.0	240.8	198.2	172.2	144.1	–16.3
Dollar value	$13,214.5	10,520.2	5,471.3	4,274.1	3,389.4	3,100.7	2,485.6	2,123.5	1,854.1	–12.7
Cassettes	76.0	2.5	0.1	—	—	—	—	—	—	—
Dollar value	$626.0	13.1	0.9	—	—	—	—	—	—	—
LPs/EPs	2.2	1.0	2.9	3.2	4.2	5.5	6.9	9.4	13.2	41.0
Dollar value	$27.7	14.2	56.7	60.2	88.9	119.4	160.7	210.7	314.9	49.4
CD singles	34.2	2.8	0.7	0.9	1.0	1.3	1.1	0.6	1.0	60.1
Dollar value	$142.7	10.9	3.5	3.1	2.9	3.5	3.2	2.4	3.8	57.3
Vinyl singles	4.8	2.3	0.4	0.3	0.3	0.4	0.4	0.3	0.5	61.4
Dollar value	$26.3	13.2	2.9	2.5	2.3	4.6	4.7	3.0	5.9	99.2
Music videos[1]	18.2	33.8	12.8	11.8	9.1	7.7	6.0	4.7	4.1	–13.4
Dollar value	$281.9	602.2	218.9	212.0	177.6	151.0	116.6	104.7	90.5	–13.6
Digital formats[2]	—	**383.1**	**1,128.6**	**1,236.8**	**1,283.4**	**1,454.7**	**1,521.4**	**1,458.0**	**1,326.4**	**–9.0**
Dollar value	—	**$503.6**	**1,711.5**	**2,030.7**	**2,232.9**	**2,628.3**	**2,852.9**	**2,822.6**	**2,576.6**	**–8.7**
Download albums	—	13.6	63.6	76.4	85.8	103.9	116.7	118.0	117.6	–0.3
Dollar value	—	$135.7	635.3	763.4	872.4	1,070.8	1,204.8	1,232.1	1,150.8	–6.6
Download singles	—	366.9	1,042.7	1,138.3	1,177.4	1,332.3	1,392.2	1,327.9	1,200.4	–9.6
Dollar value	—	$363.3	1,032.2	1,220.3	1,317.4	1,522.4	1,623.6	1,567.6	1,409.6	–10.1
Music videos	—	1.9	20.8	20.4	18.4	16.3	10.5	8.4	6.8	–18.9
Dollar value	—	$3.7	41.3	40.6	36.6	32.4	20.8	16.7	13.6	–18.9
Mobile formats[3]	—	170.0	405.1	305.8	188.5	115.4	69.3	39.4	26.7	–32.2
Dollar value	—	$421.6	977.1	728.8	448.0	276.2	166.9	98.0	66.5	–32.2
Subscription formats[4]	—	1.3	1.6	1.2	1.5	1.8	3.4	6.2	7.7	25.6
Dollar value	—	$149.2	221.4	213.1	212.4	359.2	570.8	639.2	799.1	25.0
Digital performances & streaming[5]	—	27.4	100.0	155.5	249.2	292.0	462.0	590.4	773.4	31.0
On-demand streaming (ad supported)	—	—	—	—	—	—	170.9	220.0	294.8	34.0
Total units[6]	**1,079.2**	**1,301.8**	**1,919.2**	**1,851.8**	**1,739.6**	**1,824.9**	**1,803.3**	**1,684.6**	**1,516.1**	**–10.0**
Total value	**$14,323.7**	**12,296.9**	**8,768.4**	**7,683.9**	**6,995.0**	**7,133.1**	**7,015.7**	**7,004.8**	**6,972.2**	**–0.5**

— = Not available or not applicable. (1) Includes DVD videos. (2) Includes kiosk singles and albums. (3) Includes master ringtones, ringbacks, music videos, full-length downloads, and other mobile music. (4) Weighted annual average. (5) Estimated payments in dollars to performers and copyright holders for digital radio services under statutory licenses. (6) Includes albums and singles; excludes subscriptions and royalties.

Top Basic Cable TV Networks, 2014

Source: SNL Kagan

Rank	Network (year began)	Subscribers (mil)
1.	C-SPAN (1979)	99.9
2.	The Weather Channel (1982)	97.3
3.	Food Network (1993)	97.0
4.	TBS (1976)	96.6
5.	Discovery Channel (1985)	96.6
6.	USA Network (1980)	96.5
7.	Disney Channel (1983)	96.2
8.	Cartoon Network (1992)	96.2
9.	History Channel (1995)	96.1
10.	A&E (1994)	96.1
11.	Lifetime Television (1984)	96.0
12.	HGTV (1994)	95.8
13.	TNT (1988)	95.5
14.	FX (1994)	95.2
15.	TLC (1980)	95.1
16.	AMC (1984)	95.0
17.	Syfy (1992)	94.9
18.	Nickelodeon/Nick At Nite (1979)	94.9
19.	Fox News (1996)	94.7
20.	Comedy Central (1991)	94.7

U.S. Television Set Owners, 2015

Source: Nielsen Media Research, July 2015

Of the 116.4 mil U.S. households that owned at least one TV set in 2015:

83.7% had 2 or more TV sets
31.7% had 4 or more TV sets
12.7% had a VCR
78.4% had a DVD player
48.4% had a DVR
86.0% received basic cable
50.7% received premium cable

U.S. Households With Cable Television, 1980-2015

Source: Nielsen Media Research

Year[1]	Subscribers[2] (mil)	As % of households with TVs	Year[1]	Subscribers[2] (mil)	As % of households with TVs	Year[1]	Subscribers[2] (mil)	As % of households with TVs
1980	17.7	22.6%	2000	78.6	77.9%	2008	99.7	88.2%
1985	38.7	45.3	2001	81.5	79.8	2009	103.0	89.7
1990	53.9	58.6	2002	87.8	83.8	2010	104.1	90.6
1995	62.1	65.1	2003	88.4	82.9	2011	104.8	90.4
1996	63.6	66.3	2004	92.4	85.3	2012	103.6	90.3
1997	65.1	67.2	2005	94.0	85.7	2013	103.3	90.5
1998	65.9	67.2	2006	95.0	86.2	2014	103.7	89.6
1999	76.4	76.9	2007	94.5	83.8	2015	100.2	86.0

(1) After 1998, figures include wired-cable households as well as households that receive TV programming via alternate delivery systems (including satellite receivers, SMATV, MMDS). (2) Households that subscribe to basic cable service.

Selected Reality TV Show Winners, 2000-15

Numbers in parentheses represent the season, edition, or cycle of the show. As of Sept. 2015.

The Amazing Race. Debuted Aug. 2001 on CBS. Rob Frisbee & Brennan Swain (1); Chris Luca & Alex Boylan (2); Flo Pesenti & Zach Behr (3); Reichen Lehmkuhl & Chip Arndt (4); Chip & Kim McAllister (5); Freddy Holliday & Kendra Bentley (6); Uchenna & Joyce Agu (7); The Linz Family (8); B. J. Averell & Tyler MacNiven (9); Tyler Denk & James Branaman (10); All-Stars: Eric Sanchez & Danielle Turner (11); TK Erwin & Rachel Morales (12); Nick & Starr Spangler (13); Tammy & Victor Jih (14); Meghan Rickey & Cheyne Whitney (15); Dan & Jordan Pious (16); Natalie Strand & Katherine Chang (17); LaKisha & Jennifer Hoffman (18); Ernie Halvorsen & Cindy Chiang (19); Rachel Brown & Dave Brown Jr. (20); Josh Kilmer-Purcell & Brent Ridge (21); Bates & Anthony Battaglia (22); Jason Case & Amy Diaz (23); David & Connor O'Leary (24); Amy DeJong & Maya Warren (25); Laura Pierson & Tyler Adams (26).

American Idol. Debuted July 2002 on FOX. Kelly Clarkson (1); Ruben Studdard (2); Fantasia Barrino (3); Carrie Underwood (4); Taylor Hicks (5); Jordin Sparks (6); David Cook (7); Kris Allen (8); Lee DeWyze (9); Scotty McCreery (10); Phillip Phillips (11); Candice Glover (12); Caleb Johnson (13); Nick Fradiani (14).

America's Got Talent. Debuted June 2006 on NBC. Bianca Ryan (1); Terry Fator (2); Neil E. Boyd (3); Kevin Skinner (4); Michael Grimm (5); Landau Eugene Murphy Jr. (6); Olate Dogs (7); Kenichi Ebina (8); Mat Franco (9); Paul Zerdin (10).

America's Next Top Model. Debuted May 2003 on UPN. Adrianne Curry (1); Yoanna House (2); Eva Pigford (3); Naima Mora (4); Nicole Linkletter (5); Danielle Evans (6); CariDee English (7); Jaslene Gonzalez (8); Saleisha Stowers (9); Whitney Thompson (10); McKey Sullivan (11); Teyona Anderson (12); Nicole Fox (13); Krista White (14); Ann Ward (15); Brittani Kline (16); Lisa D'Amato (17); Sophie Sumner (18); Laura James (19); Jourdan Miller (20); Keith Carlos (21).

The Apprentice. Debuted Jan. 2004 on NBC. Bill Rancic (1); Kelly Perdew (2); Kendra Todd (3); Randal Pinkett (4); Sean Yazbeck (5); Stefani Schaeffer (6); Brandy Kuentzel (7). *Celebrity Apprentice*: Piers Morgan (1); Joan Rivers (2); Bret Michaels (3); John Rich (4); Arsenio Hall (5); Trace Adkins (6); Leeza Gibbons (7).

The Bachelor. Debuted Mar. 2002 on ABC. Alex Michel chose Amanda Marsh (1); Aaron Buerge chose Helene Eksterowicz (2); Andrew Firestone chose Jen Schefft (3); Bob Guiney chose Estella Gardinier (4); Jesse Palmer chose Jessica Bowlin (5); Byron Velvick chose Mary Delgado (6); Charlie O'Connell chose Sarah Brice (7); Travis Stork chose Sarah Stone (8); Lorenzo Borghese chose Jennifer Wilson (9); Andy Baldwin chose Tessa Horst (10); Brad Womack chose no one (11); Matt Grant chose Shayne Lamas (12); Jason Mesnick chose Melissa Rycroft (13); Jake Pavelka chose Vienna Girardi (14); Brad Womack chose Emily Maynard (15); Ben Flajnik chose Courtney Robertson (16); Sean Lowe chose Catherine Giudici (17); Juan Pablo Galavis chose Nikki Ferrell (18); Chris Soules chose Whitney Bischoff (19).

The Bachelorette. Debuted Jan. 2003 on ABC. Trista Rehn chose Ryan Sutter (1); Meredith Phillips chose Ian McKee (2); Jen Schefft chose Jerry Ferris (3); DeAnna Pappas chose Jesse Csincsak (4); Jillian Harris chose Ed Swiderski (5); Ali Fedotowsky chose Roberto Martinez (6); Ashley Hebert chose J. P. Rosenbaum (7); Emily Maynard chose Jef Holm (8); Desiree Hartsock chose Chris Siegfried (9); Andi Dorfman chose Josh Murray (10); Kaitlyn Bristowe chose Shawn Booth (11).

Big Brother. Debuted July 2000 on CBS. Eddie McGee (1); Will Kirby (2); Lisa Donahue (3); Jun Song (4); Drew Daniel (5); Maggie Ausburn (6); Mike Malinto (7); Dick Donato (8); Adam Jasinski (9); Dan Gheesling (10); Jordan Lloyd (11); Hayden Moss (12); Rachel Reilly (13); Ian Terry (14); Andy Herren (15); Derrick Levasseur (16); Steve Moses (17).

The Biggest Loser. Debuted Oct. 2004 on NBC. Ryan Benson (1); Matt Hoover (2); Erik Chopin (3); Bill Germanakos (4); Ali Vincent (5); Michelle Aguilar (6); Helen Phillips (7); Danny Cahill (8); Michael Ventrella (9); Patrick House (10); Olivia Ward (11); John Rhode (12); Jeremy Britt (13); Danni Allen (14); Rachel Frederickson (15); Toma Dobrosavljevic (16).

Dancing With the Stars. Debuted June 2005 on ABC. Kelly Monaco & Alex Mazo (1); Drew Lachey & Cheryl Burke (2); Emmitt Smith & Cheryl Burke (3); Apolo Anton Ohno & Julianne Hough (4); Helio Castroneves & Julianne Hough (5); Kristi Yamaguchi & Mark Ballas (6); Brooke Burke & Derek Hough (7); Shawn Johnson & Mark Ballas (8); Donny Osmond & Kym Johnson (9); Nicole Scherzinger & Derek Hough (10); Jennifer Grey & Derek Hough (11); Hines Ward & Kym Johnson (12); J.R. Martinez & Karina Smirnoff (13); Donald Driver & Peta Murgatroyd (14). All-Stars: Melissa Rycroft & Tony Dovolani (15); Kellie Pickler & Derek Hough (16); Amber Riley & Derek Hough (17); Meryl Davis & Maksim Chmerkovskiy (18); Alfonso Ribeiro & Witney Carson (19); Rumer Willis & Val Chmerkovskiy (20).

Food Network Star. Debuted June 2005 on Food Network. Steve McDonagh & Dan Smith (1); Guy Fieri (2); Amy Finley (3); Aaron McCargo Jr. (4); Melissa d'Arabian (5); Aarti Sequeria (6); Jeff Mauro (7); Justin Warner (8); Damaris Phillips (9); Lenny McNab (10); Eddie Jackson (11).

Hell's Kitchen. Debuted Mar. 2005 on FOX. Michael Wray (1); Heather West (2); Rock Harper (3); Christina Machamer (4); Danny Veltri (5); Dave Levey (6); Holli Ugalde (7); Nona Sivley (8); Paul Niedermann (9); Christina Wilson (10); Ja'Nel Witt (11); Scott Commings (12); La Tasha McCutchen (13); Meghan Gill (14).

Project Runway. Debuted Dec. 2004 on Bravo. Jay McCarroll (1); Chloe Dao (2); Jeffrey Sebelia (3); Christian Siriano (4); Leanne Marshall (5); Irina Shabayeva (6); Seth Aaron Henderson (7); Gretchen Jones (8); Anya Ayoung-Chee (9); Dmitry Sholokhov (10); Michelle Lesniak Franklin (11); Dom Streater (12); Sean Kelly (13). *All-Stars*: Mondo Guerra (1); Anthony Ryan Auld (2); Seth Aaron Henderson (3); Dmitry Sholokhov (4).

So You Think You Can Dance. Debuted July 2005 on FOX. Nick Lazzarini (1); Benji Schwimmer (2); Sabra Johnson (3); Joshua Allen (4); Jeanine Mason (5); Russell Ferguson (6); Lauren Froderman (7); Melanie Moore (8); Eliana Girard & Chehon Wespi-Tschopp (9); DuShaunt "Fik-Shun" Stegall & Amy Yakima (10); Ricky Ubeda (11); Gaby Diaz (12).

Survivor. Debuted May 2000 on CBS. Borneo: Richard Hatch (1); Outback: Tina Wesson (2); Africa: Ethan Zohn (3); Marquesas: Vecepia Towery (4); Thailand: Brian Heidik (5); The Amazon: Jenna Morasca (6); Pearl Islands: Sandra Diaz-Twine (7); All-Stars, Panama: Amber Brkich (8); Vanuatu: Chris Daugherty (9); Palau: Tom Westman (10); Guatemala: Danni Boatwright (11); Panama: Aras Baskauskas (12); Cook Islands: Yul Kwon (13); Fiji: Earl Cole (14); China: Todd Herzog (15); Micronesia: Parvati Shallow (16); Gabon: Robert Crowley (17); Tocantins: James "JT" Thomas (18); Samoa: Natalie White (19); Heroes vs. Villains: Sandra Diaz-Twine (20); Nicaragua: Jud Birza (21); Redemption Island: Rob Mariano (22); South Pacific: Sophie Clarke (23); One World: Kim Spradlin (24); Philippines: Denise Stapley (25); Caramoan—Fans vs. Favorites: John Cochran (26); Blood vs. Water: Tyson Apostol (27); Cagayan: Tony Vlachos (28); San Juan del Sur: Natalie Anderson (29); Worlds Apart: Mike Holloway (30).

Top Chef. Debuted Mar. 2006 on Bravo. Harold Dieterle (1); Ilan Hall (2); Hung Huynh (3); Stephanie Izard (4); Hosea Rosenberg (5); Michael Voltaggio (6); Kevin Sbraga (7); Richard Blais (8); Paul Qui (9); Kristen Kish (10); Nicholas Elmi (11); Mei Lin (12). *Top Chef Masters*: Rick Bayless (1); Marcus Samuelsson (2); Floyd Cardoz (3); Chris Cosentino (4); Douglas Keane (5).

The Voice. Debuted Apr. 2011 on NBC. Javier Colon (1); Jermaine Paul (2); Cassadee Pope (3); Danielle Bradbery (4); Tessanne Chin (5); Josh Kaufman (6); Craig Wayne Boyd (7); Sawyer Fredericks (8).

Average U.S. Television Viewing Time, 2014-15

Source: Nielsen Media Research; viewing time given in hours:minutes

Group	Age	Total per week	M-F 7-10 AM	M-F 10 AM-4 PM	M-Sun. 8-11 PM	M-F 11:30 PM-1 AM	Sat. 7 AM-1 PM	Sun. 1-7 PM
Men	18+	33:05	1:58	4:28	7:53	1:37	0:60	1:49
	18-24	17:16	0:47	2:28	3:45	1:02	0:26	0:56
	25-54	29:04	1:34	3:26	7:05	1:36	0:54	1:38
	55+	45:09	3:02	6:47	10:40	1:51	1:22	2:25
Women	18+	37:27	2:27	5:47	8:42	1:48	1:05	1:45
	18-24	19:54	0:59	3:14	4:19	1:07	0:30	0:54
	25-54	32:41	2:06	4:41	7:39	1:43	0:58	1:33
	55+	49:20	3:23	8:03	11:27	2:07	1:26	2:16
Children	2-11	22:37	1:36	3:41	4:31	0:47	1:01	1:10
Teens	12-17	18:03	0:48	2:07	4:12	0:53	0:35	0:58
All viewers[1]		**32:13**	**2:01**	**4:42**	**7:28**	**1:31**	**1:00**	**1:38**

Note: For viewing period Sept. 22, 2014-Aug. 9, 2015. Includes DVR playback. (1) Ages 2+.

Highest-Rated Prime-Time Television Programs, 2014-15

Source: Nielsen Media Research

Data are for regularly scheduled network programs Sept. 22, 2014-May 20, 2015 (unless otherwise noted). Ranked by average audience percentages, or ratings, which are estimates of the percentage of all TV-owning households watching a particular program live or on DVR within seven days of broadcast. Audience share percentages are estimates of the percentage of those watching TV at a certain time that are tuned in to a particular program.

Rank	Program, network	Avg. audience	Audience share
1.	The Big Bang Theory, CBS	11.6%	20%
2.	NCIS, CBS	11.6	19
3.	NCIS: New Orleans, CBS	11.3	18
4.	Empire, FOX	10.9	18
5.	Dancing With the Stars, ABC	9.7	15
6.	Madam Secretary, CBS	9.1	14
7.	Criminal Minds, CBS	9.0	15
8.	Scandal, ABC	9.0	15
9.	Blue Bloods, CBS	8.8	16
10.	Blacklist, NBC	8.7	15
11.	The Voice, NBC	8.5	13
12.	Scorpion, CBS	8.4	13
13.	The Voice-Tuesday, NBC	8.3	14
14.	The Good Wife, CBS	8.1	13
15.	60 Minutes, CBS	7.9	13
16.	Grey's Anatomy, ABC	7.8	13
17.	Hawaii Five-0, CBS	7.8	14
18.	Person of Interest, CBS	7.7	14
19.	How to Get Away With Murder, ABC	7.7	14
20.	NCIS: Los Angeles, CBS	7.6	13
21.	Two and a Half Men, CBS	7.5	12
22.	Modern Family, ABC	7.5	12
23.	America's Got Talent-Tuesday[1], NBC	7.5	13
24.	Mom, CBS	7.3	12
25.	The Mentalist, CBS	7.3	12
26.	Elementary, CBS	7.3%	13%
27.	CSI: Cyber, CBS	7.2	13
28.	Castle, ABC	7.2	12
29.	CSI, CBS	7.2	13
30.	The Odd Couple, CBS	7.1	12
31.	American Idol-Thursday, FOX	6.9	11
32.	Survivor, CBS	6.8	11
33.	Stalker, CBS	6.8	12
34.	Chicago Fire, NBC	6.4	11
35.	American Idol-Wednesday, FOX	6.4	11
36.	The Bachelor, ABC	6.4	10
37.	Mike & Molly, CBS	6.3	10
38.	Law and Order: SVU, NBC	5.9	10
39.	Chicago P.D., NBC	5.9	10
40.	2 Broke Girls, CBS	5.9	10
41.	Undercover Boss, CBS	5.7	10
42.	Celebrity Family Feud[2], ABC	5.7	11
43.	The Bachelorette[3], ABC	5.5	10
44.	Mysteries of Laura, NBC	5.5	9
45.	Black-ish, ABC	5.5	9
46.	The Middle, ABC	5.4	9
47.	Once Upon a Time, ABC	5.4	9
48.	Battle Creek, CBS	5.4	10
49.	Nashville, ABC	5.3	9
50.	Shark Tank, ABC	5.3	10

(1) May 26-Aug. 23, 2015. (2) June 21-July 26, 2015. (3) May 18-July 27, 2015.

Highest-Rated Syndicated Programs, 2014-15

Source: Nielsen Media Research

Average audience percentages, or ratings, are estimates of the percentage of all TV-owning households watching a program live or on DVR within seven days of broadcast, Sept. 22, 2014-Aug. 23, 2015.

Rank	Program	Avg. audience
1.	Judge Judy	7.0%
2.	Litton's Weekend Adventure	7.0
3.	Wheel of Fortune	6.7
4.	Jeopardy	6.7
5.	Family Feud	6.3
6.	The Big Bang Theory	5.8
7.	Law & Order: Criminal Intent (weekend)	5.5
8.	The Big Bang Theory (weekend)	4.3
9.	Law & Order: SVU (weekend)	3.8
10.	Modern Family	3.8
11.	Entertainment Tonight	3.3
12.	Dr. Phil Show	3.2
13.	Inside Edition	3.1
14.	Two and a Half Men	3.0%
15.	Live With Kelly & Michael	3.0
16.	Modern Family (weekend)	2.9
17.	Wheel of Fortune (weekend)	2.8
18.	Family Guy (weekend)	2.7
19.	The Ellen DeGeneres Show	2.6
20.	Blue Bloods	2.6
21.	Family Guy	2.5
22.	Mike & Molly	2.3
23.	How I Met Your Mother	2.3
24.	Castle (weekend)	2.1
25.	Seinfeld	2.0

Highest-Rated Basic Cable Programs, 2014-15

Source: Nielsen Media Research

Data are for regularly scheduled basic cable programs Sept. 22, 2014-Aug. 23, 2015; excludes children's series, miniseries, movies, and news events. Average audience percentages, or ratings, are estimates of the percentage of all TV-owning households watching a program live or on DVR within seven days of broadcast.

Rank	Program, channel	Avg. audience
1.	Walking Dead, AMC	10.7%
2.	Sons of Anarchy, FX	5.0
3.	American Horror Story, FX	4.7
4.	Rizzoli & Isles, TNT	4.2
5.	Better Call Saul, AMC	4.0
6.	Major Crimes, TNT	4.0
7.	Gold Rush, Discovery	3.5
8.	The Librarians, TNT	3.4
9.	The Last Ship, TNT	3.2
10.	Vikings, History	3.0
11.	Alaskan Bush People, Discovery	3.0
12.	Real Housewives of Atlanta, Bravo	2.8
13.	The Haves and the Have Nots, Oprah Winfrey Network	2.6
14.	Justified, FX	2.5
15.	Proof, TNT	2.5
16.	Keeping up With the Kardashians, E! Network	2.4%
17.	Deadliest Catch, Discovery	2.4
18.	Suits, USA	2.4
19.	Mad Men, AMC	2.4
20.	Murder in the First, TNT	2.4
21.	Love & Hip Hop Atlanta, VH1	2.4
22.	Duck Dynasty, A&E	2.4
23.	Naked and Afraid XL, Discovery	2.4
24.	Falling Skies, TNT	2.3
25.	Anarchy Afterword, FX	2.3
26.	19 Kids and Counting, TLC	2.3
27.	Project Runway, Lifetime	2.3
28.	Real Housewives of New Jersey, Bravo	2.2
29.	Perception, TNT	2.2
30.	Bates Motel, A&E	2.2

Highest-Rated Premium Cable Programs, 2014-15

Source: Nielsen Media Research

Average audience percentages, or ratings, are estimates of the percentage of all TV-owning households watching a program live or on DVR within seven days of broadcast, Sept. 22, 2014-Aug. 23, 2015.

Highest-Rated Series

Rank	Program, channel	Avg. audience
1.	Game of Thrones, HBO	5.6%
2.	True Detective, HBO	2.4
3.	Boardwalk Empire, HBO	1.9
4.	Ballers, HBO	1.8
5.	Homeland, Showtime	1.7
6.	Shameless, Showtime	1.5
7.	Power, Starz	1.5
8.	Ray Donovan, Showtime	1.4
9.	Outlander, Starz	1.3
10.	Silicon Valley, HBO	1.3
11.	The Newsroom, HBO	1.3
12.	Last Week Tonight With John Oliver, HBO	1.2
13.	The Brink, HBO	1.2
14.	Real Time With Bill Maher, HBO	1.1
15.	Black Sails, Starz	0.9

Highest-Rated Movies

Rank	Movie, channel	Avg. audience
1.	The Hobbit: The Battle of the Five Armies, HBO	0.6%
2.	John Wick, HBO	0.5
3.	Gone Girl, HBO	0.4
4.	X-Men: Days of Future Past, HBO	0.4
5.	The Judge, HBO	0.4
6.	Horrible Bosses 2, HBO	0.4
7.	Let's Be Cops, HBO	0.4
8.	Divergent, HBO	0.3
9.	Blended, HBO	0.3
10.	A Million Ways to Die in the West, HBO	0.3
11.	The Other Woman, HBO	0.3
12.	Lone Survivor, HBO	0.3
13.	The Drop, HBO	0.3
14.	The Maze Runner, HBO	0.3
15.	Ride Along, HBO	0.3

All-Time Most Watched Television Programs

Source: Nielsen Media Research, Jan. 1961-Aug. 2015

Estimates exclude unsponsored or joint network telecasts (e.g., presidential addresses) and programs under 30 minutes long. Ranked by number of TV-owning households tuned in to the program. (Rating is percentage of all TV-owning households tuned in.)

Rank	Program	Telecast date	Network	Rating	Avg. audience (thous.)
1.	Super Bowl XLIX	2/1/2015	NBC	48.1%	55,948
2.	Super Bowl XLVIII	2/2/2014	FOX	47.1	54,585
3.	Super Bowl XLVI	2/5/2012	NBC	47.0	53,910
4.	Super Bowl XLV	2/6/2011	FOX	46.1	53,435
5.	Super Bowl XLVII	2/3/2013	CBS	46.7	53,363
6.	Super Bowl XLIV	2/7/2010	CBS	45.2	51,873
7.	Super Bowl XLVII Delay	2/3/2013	CBS	44.5	50,861
8.	M*A*S*H (last episode)	2/28/1983	CBS	60.2	50,150
9.	Super Bowl XLII	2/3/2008	FOX	43.2	48,721
10.	Super Bowl XLIII	2/1/2009	NBC	42.0	48,139
11.	Super Bowl XLI	2/4/2007	CBS	42.7	47,535
12.	Super Bowl XL	2/5/2006	ABC	41.6	45,869
13.	XVII Winter Olympics (Women's figure skating)	2/23/1994	CBS	48.5	45,690
14.	Super Bowl XXXIX	2/6/2005	FOX	41.1	45,080
15.	Super Bowl XXXVIII	2/1/2004	CBS	41.4	44,910
16.	Super Bowl XXX	1/28/1996	NBC	46.0	44,150
17.	Super Bowl XXXII	1/25/1998	NBC	44.5	43,630
18.	Super Bowl XXXIV	1/30/2000	ABC	43.3	43,620
19.	Super Bowl XXXVII	1/26/2003	ABC	40.7	43,430
20.	Super Bowl XXVIII	1/30/1994	NBC	45.5	42,860
21.	Super Bowl XXXVI	2/3/2002	FOX	40.4	42,660
22.	Cheers (last episode)	5/20/1993	NBC	45.5	42,360
23.	Super Bowl XXXI	1/26/1997	FOX	43.3	42,000

Highest-Rated Television Programs by Season, 1950-2015

Source: Nielsen Media Research; regular series programs, Sept.-May season

Rating is percentage of all TV-owning households tuned in to the program. Data prior to 1988-89 exclude Alaska and Hawaii.

Season	Program	Rating	TV-owning households (thous.)
1950-51	Texaco Star Theatre	61.6%	10,320
1951-52	Godfrey's Talent Scouts	53.8	15,300
1952-53	I Love Lucy	67.3	20,400
1953-54	I Love Lucy	58.8	26,000
1954-55	I Love Lucy	49.3	30,700
1955-56	$64,000 Question	47.5	34,900
1956-57	I Love Lucy	43.7	38,900
1957-58	Gunsmoke	43.1	41,920
1958-59	Gunsmoke	39.6	43,950
1959-60	Gunsmoke	40.3	45,750
1960-61	Gunsmoke	37.3	47,200
1961-62	Wagon Train	32.1	48,555
1962-63	Beverly Hillbillies	36.0	50,300
1963-64	Beverly Hillbillies	39.1	51,600
1964-65	Bonanza	36.3	52,700
1965-66	Bonanza	31.8	53,850
1966-67	Bonanza	29.1	55,130
1967-68	Andy Griffith	27.6	56,670
1968-69	Rowan & Martin's Laugh-In	31.8	58,250
1969-70	Rowan & Martin's Laugh-In	26.3	58,500
1970-71	Marcus Welby, M.D.	29.6	60,100
1971-72	All in the Family	34.0	62,100
1972-73	All in the Family	33.3	64,800
1973-74	All in the Family	31.2	66,200
1974-75	All in the Family	30.2	68,500
1975-76	All in the Family	30.1	69,600
1976-77	Happy Days	31.5	71,200
1977-78	Laverne & Shirley	31.6	72,900
1978-79	Laverne & Shirley	30.5	74,500
1979-80	60 Minutes	28.2	76,300
1980-81	Dallas	31.2	79,900
1981-82	Dallas	28.4	81,500
1982-83	60 Minutes	25.5%	83,300
1983-84	Dallas	25.7	83,800
1984-85	Dynasty	25.0	84,900
1985-86	Cosby Show	33.8	85,900
1986-87	Cosby Show	34.9	87,400
1987-88	Cosby Show	27.8	88,600
1988-89	Roseanne	25.5	90,400
1989-90	Roseanne	23.4	92,100
1990-91	Cheers	21.6	93,100
1991-92	60 Minutes	21.7	92,100
1992-93	60 Minutes	21.6	93,100
1993-94	Home Improvement	21.9	94,200
1994-95	Seinfeld	20.5	95,400
1995-96	E.R.	22.0	95,900
1996-97	E.R.	21.2	97,000
1997-98	Seinfeld	22.0	98,000
1998-99	E.R.	17.8	99,400
1999-2000	Who Wants to Be a Millionaire	18.6	100,800
2000-01	Survivor II	17.4	102,200
2001-02	Friends	15.3	105,500
2002-03	CSI	16.3	106,700
2003-04	CSI	15.9	108,400
2004-05	CSI	16.5	106,900
2005-06	American Idol-Tuesday	17.6	110,200
2006-07	American Idol-Wednesday	17.3	112,800
2007-08	American Idol-Tuesday	15.5	113,050
2008-09	American Idol-Wednesday	14.4	114,900
2009-10	American Idol-Tuesday	13.7	114,900
2010-11	American Idol-Wednesday	14.5	115,900
2011-12	NCIS	12.3	114,700
2012-13	NCIS	13.5	114,200
2013-14	NCIS	12.6	115,800
2014-15	The Big Bang Theory	11.6	116,400

All-Time Highest-Rated Television Programs

Source: Nielsen Media Research, Jan. 1961-Aug. 2015

Estimates exclude unsponsored or joint network telecasts (e.g., presidential addresses) and programs under 30 minutes long. Ranked by rating (percentage of all TV-owning households tuned in to the program). Average audience is number of TV-owning households tuned in.

Rank	Program	Telecast date	Network	Rating	Avg. audience (thous.)
1.	M*A*S*H (last episode)	2/28/1983	CBS	60.2%	50,150
2.	Dallas ("Who Shot J.R.?" episode)	11/21/1980	CBS	53.3	41,470
3.	Roots-Pt. 8	1/30/1977	ABC	51.1	36,380
4.	Super Bowl XVI	1/24/1982	CBS	49.1	40,020
5.	Super Bowl XVII	1/30/1983	NBC	48.6	40,480
6.	XVII Winter Olympics (Women's figure skating)	2/23/1994	CBS	48.5	45,690
7.	Super Bowl XX	1/26/1986	NBC	48.3	41,490
8.	Super Bowl XLIX	2/1/2015	NBC	48.1	55,948
9.	Gone With the Wind-Pt. 1	11/7/1976	NBC	47.7	33,960
10.	Gone With the Wind-Pt. 2	11/8/1976	NBC	47.4	33,750
11.	Super Bowl XII	1/15/1978	CBS	47.2	34,410
12.	Super Bowl XLVIII	2/2/2014	FOX	47.1	54,585
13.	Super Bowl XIII	1/21/1979	NBC	47.1	35,090
14.	Super Bowl XLVI	2/5/2012	NBC	47.0	53,910
15.	Super Bowl XLVII	2/3/2013	CBS	46.7	53,363
16.	Bob Hope Christmas Show	1/15/1970	NBC	46.6	27,260
17.	Super Bowl XIX	1/20/1985	ABC	46.4	39,390
18.	Super Bowl XVIII	1/22/1984	CBS	46.4	38,880
19.	Super Bowl XIV	1/20/1980	CBS	46.3	35,330
20.	Super Bowl XLV	2/6/2011	FOX	46.1	53,435
21.	Super Bowl XXX	1/28/1996	NBC	46.0	44,150
22.	ABC Sunday Night Movie ("The Day After")	11/20/1983	ABC	46.0	38,550
23.	Roots-Pt. 6	1/28/1977	ABC	45.9	32,680
24.	The Fugitive (last episode)	8/29/1967	ABC	45.9	25,700
25.	Super Bowl XXI	1/25/1987	CBS	45.8	40,030
26.	Roots-Pt. 5	1/27/1977	ABC	45.7	32,540
27.	Super Bowl XXVIII	1/30/1994	NBC	45.5	42,860
28.	Cheers (last episode)	5/20/1993	NBC	45.5	42,360
29.	The Ed Sullivan Show (first live U.S. TV appearance of The Beatles)	2/9/1964	CBS	45.3	23,240

AWARDS — MEDALS — PRIZES

Alfred B. Nobel Prizes, 1901-2015

Alfred B. Nobel (1833-96) bequeathed $9 mil, the interest on which was to be distributed yearly to those judged to have most benefited humankind in chemistry, literature, promotion of peace, physics, and physiology or medicine. Prizes were first awarded in 1901. The prize in economics, funded by Sweden's central bank, was first awarded in 1969. Each prize is now worth 8 mil Swedish kronor (about $1.1 mil). If year is omitted, no award was given. The Royal Swedish Academy selects prize winners for chemistry, economics, and physics; the Nobel Assembly at Karolinska Institutet, physiology or medicine; the Swedish Academy, literature; and the Norwegian Nobel Committee, the peace prize. The 2015 Nobel Prizes were announced Oct. 5-12. Winners sharing a prize are generally listed in alphabetical order, except when the awarding body has given a larger proportion of a shared prize to one or more recipients.

Nobel Prizes, 2015

Chemistry: Tomas Lindahl, Sweden-UK; Paul Modrich, U.S.; and Aziz Sancar, Turkey-U.S., shared the prize for work showing how damaged DNA is repaired at the molecular level.

Economics: Angus Deaton, UK-U.S., was given the prize "for his analysis of consumption, poverty, and welfare."

Literature: Belarussian journalist and author Svetlana Alexievich was awarded the prize for works creating "a monument to suffering and courage in our time."

Medicine: William C. Campbell, Ireland-U.S.; Satoshi Omura, Japan; and Youyou Tu, China, were recognized for their work developing therapies for parasitic diseases.

Peace: The National Dialogue Quartet of Tunisia was awarded the prize for the coalition's contributions to democracy following the country's 2011 revolution.

Physics: Japan's Takaaki Kajita and Canada's Arthur B. McDonald shared the prize for discovering that neutrinos—the second most common particles in the universe—have mass.

Physics

1901 Wilhelm C. Röntgen, Ger.
1902 Hendrik A. Lorentz, Pieter Zeeman, Neth.
1903 Antoine Henri Becquerel, Pierre Curie, Fr.; Marie Curie, Pol.-Fr.
1904 Lord Rayleigh (John W. Strutt), UK
1905 Philipp E. A. von Lenard, Ger.
1906 Sir Joseph J. Thomson, UK
1907 Albert A. Michelson, U.S.
1908 Gabriel Lippmann, Fr.
1909 Carl F. Braun, Ger.; Guglielmo Marconi, Ital.
1910 Johannes D. van der Waals, Neth.
1911 Wilhelm Wien, Ger.
1912 Nils G. Dalén, Swed.
1913 Heike Kamerlingh Onnes, Neth.
1914 Max von Laue, Ger.
1915 Sir William H. Bragg, William L. Bragg, UK
1917 Charles G. Barkla, UK
1918 Max K. E. L. Planck, Ger.
1919 Johannes Stark, Ger.
1920 Charles E. Guillaume, Fr.-Switz.
1921 Albert Einstein, Ger.-U.S.
1922 Niels Bohr, Den.
1923 Robert A. Millikan, U.S.
1924 Karl M. G. Siegbahn, Swed.
1925 James Franck, Gustav Hertz, Ger.
1926 Jean B. Perrin, Fr.
1927 Arthur H. Compton, U.S.; Charles T. R. Wilson, UK
1928 Owen W. Richardson, UK
1929 Prince Louis-Victor de Broglie, Fr.
1930 Sir Chandrasekhara V. Raman, India
1932 Werner Heisenberg, Ger.
1933 Paul A. M. Dirac, UK; Erwin Schrödinger, Austria
1935 Sir James Chadwick, UK
1936 Carl D. Anderson, U.S.; Victor F. Hess, Austria
1937 Clinton J. Davisson, U.S.; Sir George P. Thomson, UK
1938 Enrico Fermi, Ital.-U.S.
1939 Ernest O. Lawrence, U.S.
1943 Otto Stern, U.S.
1944 Isidor Isaac Rabi, U.S.
1945 Wolfgang Pauli, U.S.-Austria
1946 Percy W. Bridgman, U.S.
1947 Sir Edward V. Appleton, UK
1948 Patrick M. S. Blackett, UK
1949 Hideki Yukawa, Jpn.
1950 Cecil F. Powell, UK
1951 Sir John D. Cockcroft, UK; Ernest T. S. Walton, Ire.
1952 Felix Bloch, Edward M. Purcell, U.S.
1953 Frits Zernike, Neth.
1954 Max Born, UK; Walter Bothe, Ger.
1955 Polykarp Kusch, Willis E. Lamb, U.S.
1956 John Bardeen, Walter H. Brattain, William Shockley, U.S.
1957 Tsung-Dao Lee, Chen Ning Yang, U.S.-China
1958 Pavel Cherenkov, Il'ja Frank, Igor Y. Tamm, USSR
1959 Owen Chamberlain, Emilio G. Segre, U.S.
1960 Donald A. Glaser, U.S.
1961 Robert Hofstadter, U.S.; Rudolf L. Mossbauer, Ger.
1962 Lev D. Landau, USSR
1963 Maria Goeppert-Mayer, Eugene P. Wigner, U.S.; J. Hans D. Jensen, Ger.
1964 Nicolay G. Basov, Aleksandr M. Prokhorov, USSR; Charles H. Townes, U.S.
1965 Sin-Itiro Tomonaga, Jpn.; Julian S. Schwinger, Richard P. Feynman, U.S.
1966 Alfred Kastler, Fr.
1967 Hans A. Bethe, U.S.
1968 Luis W. Alvarez, U.S.
1969 Murray Gell-Mann, U.S.
1970 Hannes Alfvén, Swed.; Louis Néel, Fr.
1971 Dennis Gabor, UK
1972 John Bardeen, Leon N. Cooper, John R. Schrieffer, U.S.
1973 Brian D. Josephson, UK; Leo Esaki, Jpn.; Ivar Giaever, U.S.
1974 Antony Hewish, Sir Martin Ryle, UK
1975 Aage Bohr, Den.; Ben Mottelson, U.S.-Den.; Leo James Rainwater, U.S.
1976 Burton Richter, Samuel C. C. Ting, U.S.
1977 Philip W. Anderson, John H. van Vleck, U.S.; Sir Nevill F. Mott, UK
1978 Pyotr Kapitsa, USSR; Arno Penzias, Robert Wilson, U.S.
1979 Sheldon L. Glashow, Steven Weinberg, U.S.; Abdus Salam, Pakistan
1980 James W. Cronin, Val L. Fitch, U.S.
1981 Nicolaas Bloembergen, Arthur Schawlow, U.S.; Kai M. Siegbahn, Swed.
1982 Kenneth G. Wilson, U.S.
1983 Subramanyan Chandrasekhar, William A. Fowler, U.S.
1984 Carlo Rubbia, Ital.; Simon van der Meer, Neth.
1985 Klaus von Klitzing, Ger.
1986 Ernest Ruska, Gerd Binnig, Ger.; Heinrich Rohrer, Switz.
1987 J. Georg Bednorz, Ger.; K. Alex Müller, Switz.
1988 Leon M. Lederman, Melvin Schwartz, Jack Steinberger, U.S.
1989 Norman F. Ramsey, U.S.; Hans G. Dehmelt, Ger.-U.S.; Wolfgang Paul, Ger.
1990 Jerome I. Friedman, Henry W. Kendall, U.S.; Richard E. Taylor, Can.
1991 Pierre-Gilles de Gennes, Fr.
1992 Georges Charpak, Pol.-Fr.
1993 Russell A. Hulse, Joseph H. Taylor, U.S.
1994 Bertram N. Brockhouse, Can.; Clifford G. Shull, U.S.
1995 Martin Perl, Frederick Reines, U.S.
1996 David M. Lee, Douglas D. Osheroff, Robert C. Richardson, U.S.
1997 Steven Chu, William D. Phillips, U.S.; Claude Cohen-Tannoudji, Fr.
1998 Robert B. Laughlin, U.S.; Horst L. Störmer, Ger.-U.S; Daniel C. Tsui, China-U.S.
1999 Gerardus 't Hooft, Martinus J. G. Veltman, Neth.
2000 Jack S. Kilby, U.S.; Herbert Kroemer, Ger.-U.S.; Zhores I. Alferov, Russ.
2001 Eric A. Cornell, Carl E. Wieman, U.S.; Wolfgang Ketterle, Ger.
2002 Raymond Davis Jr., Riccardo Giacconi, U.S.; Masatoshi Koshiba, Jpn.
2003 Alexei A. Abrikosov, Vitaly L. Ginzburg, Russ.; Anthony J. Leggett, UK
2004 David J. Gross, H. David Politzer, Frank Wilczek, U.S.
2005 Roy J. Glauber, John L. Hall, U.S.; Theodor W. Hänsch, Ger.
2006 John C. Mather, George F. Smoot, U.S.
2007 Albert Fert, Fr.; Peter Grünberg, Ger.
2008 Yoichiro Nambu, U.S.; Makoto Kobayashi, Toshihide Maskawa, Jpn.
2009 Charles K. Kao, U.S.-UK; Willard S. Boyle, U.S.-Can.; George E. Smith, U.S.
2010 Andre Geim, Russ.-Neth.; Konstantin Novoselov, Russ.-UK
2011 Saul Perlmutter, Adam G. Riess, U.S.; Brian P. Schmidt, Austral.-U.S.
2012 Serge Haroche, Fr.; David J. Wineland, U.S.
2013 François Englert, Belg.; Peter W. Higgs, UK
2014 Isamu Akasaki, Hiroshi Amano, Jpn.; Shuji Nakamura, Jpn.-U.S.
2015 Takaaki Kajita, Jpn.; Arthur B. McDonald, Can.

Chemistry

1901 Jacobus H. van 't Hoff, Neth.
1902 Emil Fischer, Ger.
1903 Svante A. Arrhenius, Swed.
1904 Sir William Ramsay, UK
1905 Adolf von Baeyer, Ger.
1906 Henri Moissan, Fr.
1907 Eduard Buchner, Ger.
1908 Ernest Rutherford, UK
1909 Wilhelm Ostwald, Ger.
1910 Otto Wallach, Ger.
1911 Marie Curie, Pol.-Fr.
1912 Victor Grignard, Paul Sabatier, Fr.
1913 Alfred Werner, Switz.
1914 Theodore W. Richards, U.S.
1915 Richard M. Willstätter, Ger.
1918 Fritz Haber, Ger.
1920 Walther H. Nernst, Ger.
1921 Frederick Soddy, UK
1922 Francis W. Aston, UK
1923 Fritz Pregl, Austria
1925 Richard A. Zsigmondy, Ger.
1926 Theodor Svedberg, Swed.
1927 Heinrich O. Wieland, Ger.
1928 Adolf O. R. Windaus, Ger.
1929 Sir Arthur Harden, UK; Hans von Euler-Chelpin, Swed.
1930 Hans Fischer, Ger.
1931 Friedrich Bergius, Carl Bosch, Ger.
1932 Irving Langmuir, U.S.
1934 Harold C. Urey, U.S.
1935 Frédéric Joliot, Irène Joliot-Curie, Fr.
1936 Peter J. W. Debye, Neth.
1937 Walter N. Haworth, UK; Paul Karrer, Switz.
1938 Richard Kuhn, Ger.
1939 Adolf F. J. Butenandt, Ger.; Leopold Ruzicka, Switz.
1943 George de Hevesy, Hung.
1944 Otto Hahn, Ger.
1945 Artturi I. Virtanen, Fin.
1946 James B. Sumner, John H. Northrop, Wendell M. Stanley, U.S.
1947 Sir Robert Robinson, UK
1948 Arne W. K. Tiselius, Swed.
1949 William F. Giauque, U.S.
1950 Kurt Alder, Otto P. H. Diels, Ger.
1951 Edwin M. McMillan, Glenn T. Seaborg, U.S.
1952 Archer J. P. Martin, Richard L. M. Synge, UK
1953 Hermann Staudinger, Ger.
1954 Linus C. Pauling, U.S.
1955 Vincent du Vigneaud, U.S.
1956 Sir Cyril N. Hinshelwood, UK; Nikolay N. Semenov, USSR
1957 Lord (Alexander R.) Todd, UK
1958 Frederick Sanger, UK
1959 Jaroslav Heyrovsky, Czech.
1960 Willard F. Libby, U.S.
1961 Melvin Calvin, U.S.
1962 John C. Kendrew, Max F. Perutz, UK
1963 Giulio Natta, Ital.; Karl Ziegler, Ger.
1964 Dorothy C. Hodgkin, UK
1965 Robert B. Woodward, U.S.
1966 Robert S. Mulliken, U.S.
1967 Manfred Eigen, Ger.; Ronald G. W. Norrish, George Porter, UK
1968 Lars Onsager, U.S.
1969 Derek H. R. Barton, UK; Odd Hassel, Nor.
1970 Luis F. Leloir, Arg.
1971 Gerhard Herzberg, Can.
1972 Christian B. Anfinsen, Stanford Moore, William H. Stein, U.S.
1973 Ernst Otto Fischer, Ger.; Geoffrey Wilkinson, UK
1974 Paul J. Flory, U.S.
1975 John Cornforth, Austral.-UK; Vladimir Prelog, Bosnia-Switz.
1976 William N. Lipscomb, U.S.
1977 Ilya Prigogine, Belg.
1978 Peter Mitchell, UK
1979 Herbert C. Brown, U.S.; Georg Wittig, Ger.
1980 Paul Berg, Walter Gilbert, U.S.; Frederick Sanger, UK
1981 Kenichi Fukui, Jpn.; Roald Hoffmann, U.S.
1982 Aaron Klug, UK-Lith.
1983 Henry Taube, Can.
1984 Robert Bruce Merrifield, U.S.
1985 Herbert A. Hauptman, Jerome Karle, U.S.
1986 Dudley Herschbach, Yuan T. Lee, U.S.; John C. Polanyi, Can.
1987 Donald J. Cram, Charles J. Pedersen, U.S.; Jean-Marie Lehn, Fr.
1988 Johann Deisenhofer, Robert Huber, Hartmut Michel, Ger.
1989 Sidney Altman, Thomas R. Cech, U.S.
1990 Elias James Corey, U.S.
1991 Richard R. Ernst, Switz.
1992 Rudolph A. Marcus, Can.-U.S.
1993 Kary B. Mullis, U.S.; Michael Smith, UK-Can.
1994 George A. Olah, U.S.
1995 Paul Crutzen, Neth.; Mario Molina, Mex.-U.S.; Sherwood Rowland, U.S.
1996 Robert F. Curl Jr., Richard E. Smalley, U.S.; Sir Harold W. Kroto, UK
1997 Paul D. Boyer, U.S.; John E. Walker, UK; Jens C. Skou, Den.
1998 Walter Kohn, U.S.; John A. Pople, UK
1999 Ahmed H. Zewail, U.S.
2000 Alan J. Heeger, U.S.; Alan G. MacDiarmid, N.Z.-U.S.; Hideki Shirakawa, Jpn.
2001 K. Barry Sharpless, William S. Knowles, U.S.; Ryoji Noyori, Jpn.
2002 John B. Fenn, U.S.; Koichi Tanaka, Jpn.; Kurt Wüthrich, Switz.
2003 Peter Agre, Roderick MacKinnon, U.S.
2004 Aaron Ciechanover, Avram Hershko, Isr.; Irwin Rose, U.S.
2005 Yves Chauvin, Fr.; Robert H. Grubbs, Richard R. Schrock, U.S.
2006 Roger D. Kornberg, U.S.
2007 Gerhard Ertl, Ger.
2008 Martin Chalfie, Osamu Shimomura, Roger Y. Tsien, U.S.
2009 Venkatraman Ramakrishnan, UK; Thomas A. Steitz, U.S.; Ada E. Yonath, Isr.
2010 Richard F. Heck, U.S.; Ei-ichi Negishi, Jpn.-U.S.; Akira Suzuki, Jpn.
2011 Dan Shechtman, Isr.
2012 Brian K. Kobilka, Robert J. Lefkowitz, U.S.
2013 Martin Karplus, Austria-U.S.; Michael Levitt, S. Afr.-U.S.; Arieh Warshel, Isr.-U.S.
2014 Eric Betzig, William E. Moerner, U.S.; Stefan W. Hell, Ger.
2015 Tomas Lindahl, Swed.-UK; Paul Modrich, U.S.; Aziz Sancar, Turk.-U.S.

Physiology or Medicine

1901 Emil A. von Behring, Ger.
1902 Sir Ronald Ross, UK
1903 Niels R. Finsen, Den.
1904 Ivan P. Pavlov, Russ.
1905 Robert Koch, Ger.
1906 Camillo Golgi, Ital.; Santiago Ramón y Cajal, Spain
1907 Charles L. A. Laveran, Fr.
1908 Paul Ehrlich, Ger.; Ilya Mechnikov, Fr.
1909 Emil T. Kocher, Switz.
1910 Albrecht Kossel, Ger.
1911 Allvar Gullstrand, Swed.
1912 Alexis Carrel, Fr.
1913 Charles R. Richet, Fr.
1914 Robert Bárány, Austria
1919 Jules Bordet, Belg.
1920 Schack A. S. Krogh, Den.
1922 Archibald V. Hill, UK; Otto F. Meyerhof, Ger.
1923 Frederick G. Banting, Can.; John J. R. Macleod, UK
1924 Willem Einthoven, Neth.
1926 Johannes A. G. Fibiger, Den.
1927 Julius Wagner-Jauregg, Austria
1928 Charles J. H. Nicolle, Fr.
1929 Christiaan Eijkman, Neth.; Sir Frederick G. Hopkins, UK
1930 Karl Landsteiner, U.S.
1931 Otto H. Warburg, Ger.
1932 Edgar D. Adrian, Sir Charles S. Sherrington, UK
1933 Thomas H. Morgan, U.S.
1934 George R. Minot, William P. Murphy, G. H. Whipple, U.S.
1935 Hans Spemann, Ger.
1936 Sir Henry H. Dale, UK; Otto Loewi, U.S.
1937 Albert Szent-Gyorgyi, Hung.-U.S.
1938 Corneille J. F. Heymans, Belg.
1939 Gerhard Domagk, Ger.
1943 Henrik C. P. Dam, Den.; Edward A. Doisy, U.S.
1944 Joseph Erlanger, Herbert S. Gasser, U.S.
1945 Ernst B. Chain, Sir Alexander Fleming, Sir Howard W. Florey, UK
1946 Hermann J. Muller, U.S.
1947 Carl F. Cori, Gerty T. Cori, U.S.; Bernardo A. Houssay, Arg.
1948 Paul H. Müller, Switz.
1949 Walter R. Hess, Switz.; Antonio Egas Moniz, Port.
1950 Philip S. Hench, Edward C. Kendall, U.S.; Tadeus Reichstein, Switz.
1951 Max Theiler, U.S.
1952 Selman A. Waksman, U.S.
1953 Hans A. Krebs, UK; Fritz A. Lipmann, U.S.
1954 John F. Enders, Frederick C. Robbins, Thomas H. Weller, U.S.
1955 Alex H. T. Theorell, Swed.
1956 André F. Cournand, Dickinson W. Richards, U.S.; Werner Forssmann, Ger.
1957 Daniel Bovet, Ital.
1958 George W. Beadle, Edward L. Tatum, Joshua Lederberg, U.S.
1959 Arthur Kornberg, Severo Ochoa, U.S.
1960 Sir Frank Macfarlane Burnet, Austral.; Peter B. Medawar, UK
1961 Georg von Békésy, U.S.
1962 Francis H. C. Crick, Maurice H. F. Wilkins, UK; James D. Watson, U.S.
1963 Sir John C. Eccles, Austral.; Alan L. Hodgkin, Andrew F. Huxley, UK
1964 Konrad E. Bloch, U.S.; Feodor Lynen, Ger.
1965 François Jacob, André Lwoff, Jacques Monod, Fr.
1966 Charles B. Huggins, Peyton Rous, U.S.
1967 Ragnar Granit, Swed.; Haldan Keffer Hartline, George Wald, U.S.
1968 Robert W. Holley, H. Gobind Khorana, Marshall W. Nirenberg, U.S.
1969 Max Delbrück, Alfred D. Hershey, Salvador Luria, U.S.
1970 Julius Axelrod, U.S.; Sir Bernard Katz, UK; Ulf von Euler, Swed.
1971 Earl W. Sutherland Jr., U.S.
1972 Gerald M. Edelman, U.S.; Rodney R. Porter, UK

1973 Konrad Lorenz, Austria; Nikolaas Tinbergen, UK; Karl von Frisch, Ger.
1974 Albert Claude, Lux.-U.S.; Christian de Duve, Belg.; George Emil Palade, Rom.-U.S.
1975 David Baltimore, Howard Temin, U.S.; Renato Dulbecco, Ital.-U.S.
1976 Baruch S. Blumberg, Daniel Carleton Gajdusek, U.S.
1977 Rosalyn S. Yalow, Roger C.L. Guillemin, Andrew V. Schally, U.S.
1978 Werner Arber, Switz.; Daniel Nathans, Hamilton O. Smith, U.S.
1979 Allan M. Cormack, U.S.; Godfrey N. Hounsfield, UK
1980 Baruj Benacerraf, George Snell, U.S.; Jean Dausset, Fr.
1981 Roger W. Sperry, David H. Hubel, Torsten N. Wiesel, U.S.
1982 Sune K. Bergström, Bengt I. Samuelsson, Swed.; John R. Vane, UK
1983 Barbara McClintock, U.S.
1984 Niels K. Jerne, UK-Den.; Georges J. F. Köhler, Ger.; César Milstein, UK-Arg.
1985 Michael S. Brown, Joseph L. Goldstein, U.S.
1986 Stanley Cohen, U.S.; Rita Levi-Montalcini, Ital.-U.S.
1987 Susumu Tonegawa, Jpn.
1988 Sir James W. Black, UK; Gertrude B. Elion, George H. Hitchings, U.S.
1989 J. Michael Bishop, Harold E. Varmus, U.S.
1990 Joseph E. Murray, E. Donnall Thomas, U.S.
1991 Edwin Neher, Bert Sakmann, Ger.
1992 Edmond H. Fisher, Edwin G. Krebs, U.S.
1993 Richard J. Roberts, UK; Phillip A. Sharp, U.S.
1994 Alfred G. Gilman, Martin Rodbell, U.S.
1995 Edward B. Lewis, Eric F. Wieschaus, U.S.; Christiane Nüsslein-Volhard, Ger.
1996 Peter C. Doherty, Austral.; Rolf M. Zinkernagel, Switz.
1997 Stanley B. Prusiner, U.S.
1998 Robert F. Furchgott, Louis J. Ignarro, Ferid Murad, U.S.
1999 Günter Blobel, U.S.
2000 Arvid Carlsson, Swed.; Paul Greengard, U.S.; Eric R. Kandel, Austria-U.S.
2001 Leland H. Hartwell, U.S.; R. Timothy (Tim) Hunt, Sir Paul M. Nurse, UK
2002 Sydney Brenner, John E. Sulston, UK; H. Robert Horvitz, U.S.
2003 Paul C. Lauterbur, U.S.; Sir Peter Mansfield, UK
2004 Richard Axel, Linda B. Buck, U.S.
2005 Barry J. Marshall, J. Robin Warren, Austral.
2006 Andrew Z. Fire, Craig C. Mello, U.S.
2007 Mario R. Capecchi, Oliver Smithies, U.S.; Sir Martin J. Evans, UK
2008 Harald zur Hausen, Ger.; Françoise Barré-Sinoussi, Luc Montagnier, Fr.
2009 Elizabeth H. Blackburn, Carol W. Greider, Jack W. Szostak, U.S.
2010 Robert G. Edwards, UK
2011 Bruce A. Beutler, U.S.; Jules A. Hoffmann, Fr.; Ralph M. Steinman, Can.-U.S.
2012 John B. Gurdon, UK; Shinya Yamanaka, Jpn.-U.S.
2013 James E. Rothman, Randy W. Schekman, U.S.; Thomas C. Südhof, Ger.-U.S.
2014 John O'Keefe, U.S.-UK; May-Britt Moser, Edvard I. Moser, Nor.
2015 William C. Campbell, Ire.; Satoshi Omura, Jpn.; Youyou Tu, China

Literature

1901 Rene F. A. Sully Prudhomme, Fr.
1902 Theodor Mommsen, Ger.
1903 Bjørnstjerne Bjørnson, Nor.
1904 José Echegaray y Eizaguirre, Spain; Fréderic Mistral, Fr.
1905 Henryk Sienkiewicz, Pol.
1906 Giosuè Carducci, Ital.
1907 Rudyard Kipling, UK
1908 Rudolf C. Eucken, Ger.
1909 Selma Lagerlöf, Swed.
1910 Paul J. L. Heyse, Ger.
1911 Maurice Maeterlinck, Belg.
1912 Gerhart Hauptmann, Ger.
1913 Rabindranath Tagore, India
1915 Romain Rolland, Fr.
1916 Verner von Heidenstam, Swed.
1917 Karl A. Gjellerup, Henrik Pontoppidan, Den.
1919 Carl F. G. Spitteler, Switz.
1920 Knut Hamsun, Nor.
1921 Anatole France, Fr.
1922 Jacinto Benavente, Spain
1923 William Butler Yeats, Ire.
1924 Wladyslaw S. Reymont, Pol.
1925 George Bernard Shaw, Ire.-UK
1926 Grazia Deledda, Ital.
1927 Henri Bergson, Fr.
1928 Sigrid Undset, Nor.
1929 Thomas Mann, Ger.
1930 Sinclair Lewis, U.S.
1931 Erik A. Karlfeldt, Swed.
1932 John Galsworthy, UK
1933 Ivan A. Bunin, USSR
1934 Luigi Pirandello, Ital.
1936 Eugene O'Neill, U.S.
1937 Roger Martin du Gard, Fr.
1938 Pearl S. Buck, U.S.
1939 Frans E. Sillanpää, Fin.
1944 Johannes V. Jensen, Den.
1945 Gabriela Mistral, Chile
1946 Hermann Hesse, Ger.-Switz.
1947 André Gide, Fr.
1948 T. S. Eliot, UK
1949 William Faulkner, U.S.
1950 Bertrand Russell, UK
1951 Pär F. Lagerkvist, Swed.
1952 François Mauriac, Fr.
1953 Sir Winston Churchill, UK
1954 Ernest Hemingway, U.S.
1955 Halldór K. Laxness, Ice.
1956 Juan Ramón Jiménez, Spain
1957 Albert Camus, Fr.
1958 Boris L. Pasternak, USSR (declined)
1959 Salvatore Quasimodo, Ital.
1960 Saint-John Perse, Fr.
1961 Ivo Andric, Yugo.
1962 John Steinbeck, U.S.
1963 Giorgos Seferis, Greece
1964 Jean-Paul Sartre, Fr. (declined)
1965 Mikhail Sholokhov, USSR
1966 Shmuel Yosef Agnon, Isr.; Nelly Sachs, Swed.
1967 Miguel Angel Asturias, Guat.
1968 Yasunari Kawabata, Jpn.
1969 Samuel Beckett, Ire.
1970 Aleksandr I. Solzhenitsyn, USSR
1971 Pablo Neruda, Chile
1972 Heinrich Böll, Ger.
1973 Patrick White, Austral.
1974 Eyvind Johnson, Harry Edmund Martinson, Swed.
1975 Eugenio Montale, Ital.
1976 Saul Bellow, U.S.
1977 Vicente Aleixandre, Spain
1978 Isaac Bashevis Singer, U.S.
1979 Odysseus Elytis, Greece
1980 Czeslaw Milosz, Pol.-U.S.
1981 Elias Canetti, Bulg.-UK
1982 Gabriel García Márquez, Colombia
1983 William Golding, UK
1984 Jaroslav Siefert, Czech.
1985 Claude Simon, Fr.
1986 Wole Soyinka, Nigeria
1987 Joseph Brodsky, USSR-U.S.
1988 Naguib Mahfouz, Egypt
1989 Camilo José Cela, Spain
1990 Octavio Paz, Mex.
1991 Nadine Gordimer, S. Afr.
1992 Derek Walcott, St. Lucia
1993 Toni Morrison, U.S.
1994 Kenzaburo Oe, Jpn.
1995 Seamus Heaney, Ire.
1996 Wislawa Szymborska, Pol.
1997 Dario Fo, Ital.
1998 Jose Saramago, Por.
1999 Günter Grass, Ger.
2000 Gao Xingjian, China-Fr.
2001 Sir V. S. Naipaul, UK
2002 Imre Kertész, Hung.
2003 J. M. Coetzee, S. Afr.
2004 Elfriede Jelinek, Austria
2005 Harold Pinter, UK
2006 Orhan Pamuk, Turk.
2007 Doris Lessing, UK
2008 Jean-Marie Gustave Le Clézio, Fr.
2009 Herta Müller, Ger.
2010 Mario Vargas Llosa, Peru
2011 Tomas Tranströmer, Swed.
2012 Mo Yan, China
2013 Alice Munro, Can.
2014 Patrick Modiano, Fr.
2015 Svetlana Alexievich, Belarus

Peace

1901 Jean H. Dunant, Switz.; Frédéric Passy, Fr.
1902 Élie Ducommun, Charles A. Gobat, Switz.
1903 Sir William R. Cremer, UK
1904 Institute of International Law
1905 Baroness Bertha von Suttner, Austria
1906 Theodore Roosevelt, U.S.
1907 Ernesto T. Moneta, Ital.; Louis Renault, Fr.
1908 Klas P. Arnoldson, Swed.; Fredrik Bajer, Den.
1909 Auguste M. F. Beernaert, Belg.; Paul H. B. B. d'Estournelles de Constant, Fr.
1910 Permanent Intl. Peace Bureau
1911 Tobias M. C. Asser, Neth.; Alfred H. Fried, Austria
1912 Elihu Root, U.S.
1913 Henri La Fontaine, Belg.
1917 Intl. Committee of the Red Cross
1919 Woodrow Wilson, U.S.
1920 Léon V. A. Bourgeois, Fr.
1921 Karl H. Branting, Swed.; Christian L. Lange, Nor.
1922 Fridtjof Nansen, Nor.
1925 Sir Austen Chamberlain, UK; Charles G. Dawes, U.S.
1926 Aristide Briand, Fr.; Gustav Stresemann, Ger.
1927 Ferdinand E. Buisson, Fr.; Ludwig Quidde, Ger.

1929 Frank B. Kellogg, U.S.
1930 Nathan Söderblom, Swed.
1931 Jane Addams, Nicholas Murray Butler, U.S.
1933 Sir Norman Angell, UK
1934 Arthur Henderson, UK
1935 Carl von Ossietzky, Ger.
1936 Carlos Saavedra Lamas, Arg.
1937 Lord Robert Cecil, UK
1938 Nansen Intl. Office for Refugees
1944 Intl. Committee of the Red Cross
1945 Cordell Hull, U.S.
1946 Emily G. Balch, John R. Mott, U.S.
1947 Friends Service Council, UK; Amer. Friends Service Committee, U.S.
1949 Lord John Boyd Orr of Brechin, UK
1950 Ralph J. Bunche, U.S.
1951 Léon Jouhaux, Fr.
1952 Albert Schweitzer, Fr.
1953 George C. Marshall, U.S.
1954 Office of UN High Commissioner for Refugees
1957 Lester B. Pearson, Can.
1958 Georges Pire, Belg.
1959 Philip J. Noel-Baker, UK
1960 Albert J. Lutuli, S. Afr.
1961 Dag Hammarskjöld, Swed.
1962 Linus C. Pauling, U.S.
1963 Intl. Committee of the Red Cross, League of Red Cross Societies
1964 Martin Luther King Jr., U.S.
1965 UN Children's Fund (UNICEF)
1968 René Cassin, Fr.
1969 Intl. Labor Organization
1970 Norman E. Borlaug, U.S.
1971 Willy Brandt, Ger.
1973 Henry Kissinger, U.S.; Le Duc Tho, N. Viet. (Tho declined)
1974 Seán MacBride, Ire.; Eisaku Sato, Jpn.
1975 Andrei Sakharov, USSR
1976 Mairead Corrigan, Betty Williams, N. Ire.
1977 Amnesty International
1978 Anwar al-Sadat, Egypt; Menachem Begin, Isr.
1979 Mother Teresa of Calcutta, Alb.-India
1980 Adolfo Pérez Esquivel, Arg.
1981 Office of UN High Commissioner for Refugees
1982 Alfonso García Robles, Mex.; Alva Myrdal, Swed.
1983 Lech Walesa, Pol.
1984 Bishop Desmond Tutu, S. Afr.
1985 Intl. Physicians for the Prevention of Nuclear War, U.S.
1986 Elie Wiesel, Rom.-U.S.
1987 Oscar Arias Sánchez, Costa Rica
1988 UN Peacekeeping Forces
1989 Dalai Lama (Tenzin Gyatso), Tibet
1990 Mikhail S. Gorbachev, USSR
1991 Aung San Suu Kyi, Burma
1992 Rigoberta Menchú Tum, Guat.
1993 Frederik W. de Klerk, Nelson Mandela, S. Afr.
1994 Yasser Arafat, Pal.; Shimon Peres, Yitzhak Rabin, Isr.
1995 Joseph Rotblat, Pol.-UK; Pugwash Conferences
1996 Bishop Carlos Ximenes Belo, José Ramos-Horta, Timor-Leste
1997 Jody Williams, U.S.; Intl. Campaign to Ban Landmines
1998 John Hume, David Trimble, N. Ire.
1999 Médecins Sans Frontières (Doctors Without Borders), Fr.
2000 Kim Dae Jung, S. Kor.
2001 UN; Kofi Annan, Ghana
2002 Jimmy Carter, U.S.
2003 Shirin Ebadi, Iran
2004 Wangari Maathai, Kenya
2005 Mohamed ElBaradei, Egypt; Intl. Atomic Energy Agency, Austria
2006 Muhammad Yunus, Grameen Bank, Bangl.
2007 Intergovernmental Panel on Climate Change, Switz.; Albert Arnold Gore Jr., U.S.
2008 Martti Ahtisaari, Fin.
2009 Barack H. Obama, U.S.
2010 Liu Xiaobo, China
2011 Leymah Gbowee, Ellen Johnson Sirleaf, Liberia; Tawakkol Karman, Yemen
2012 European Union
2013 Organization for the Prohibition of Chemical Weapons
2014 Kailash Satyarthi, India; Malala Yousafzai, Pakistan
2015 National Dialogue Quartet, Tunisia

Nobel Memorial Prize in Economic Sciences

1969 Ragnar Frisch, Nor.; Jan Tinbergen, Neth.
1970 Paul A. Samuelson, U.S.
1971 Simon Kuznets, U.S.
1972 Kenneth J. Arrow, U.S.; John R. Hicks, UK
1973 Wassily Leontief, U.S.
1974 Gunnar Myrdal, Swed.; Friedrich A. von Hayek, Austria
1975 Leonid Kantorovich, USSR; Tjalling C. Koopmans, Neth.-U.S.
1976 Milton Friedman, U.S.
1977 James E. Meade, UK; Bertil Ohlin, Swed.
1978 Herbert A. Simon, U.S.
1979 Sir Arthur Lewis, UK; Theodore W. Schultz, U.S.
1980 Lawrence R. Klein, U.S.
1981 James Tobin, U.S.
1982 George J. Stigler, U.S.
1983 Gerard Debreu, Fr.-U.S.
1984 Richard Stone, UK
1985 Franco Modigliani, Ital.-U.S.
1986 James M. Buchanan, U.S.
1987 Robert M. Solow, U.S.
1988 Maurice Allais, Fr.
1989 Trygve Haavelmo, Nor.
1990 Harry M. Markowitz, Merton H. Miller, William F. Sharpe, U.S.
1991 Ronald H. Coase, UK-U.S.
1992 Gary S. Becker, U.S.
1993 Robert W. Fogel, Douglass C. North, U.S.
1994 John C. Harsanyi, John F. Nash, U.S.; Reinhard Selten, Ger.
1995 Robert E. Lucas Jr., U.S.
1996 James A. Mirrlees, UK; William Vickrey, Can.-U.S.
1997 Robert C. Merton, U.S.; Myron S. Scholes, Can.-U.S.
1998 Amartya Sen, India
1999 Robert A. Mundell, Can.
2000 James J. Heckman, Daniel L. McFadden, U.S.
2001 George A. Akerlof, A. Michael Spence, Joseph E. Stiglitz, U.S.
2002 Daniel Kahneman, U.S.-Isr.; Vernon L. Smith, U.S.
2003 Robert F. Engle, U.S.; Clive W. J. Granger, UK
2004 Finn E. Kydland, Nor.; Edward C. Prescott, U.S.
2005 Robert J. Aumann, Isr.-U.S.; Thomas C. Schelling, U.S.
2006 Edmund S. Phelps, U.S.
2007 Leonid Hurwicz, Eric S. Maskin, Roger B. Myerson, U.S.
2008 Paul Krugman, U.S.
2009 Elinor Ostrom, Oliver E. Williamson, U.S.
2010 Peter A. Diamond, Dale T. Mortensen, U.S.; Christopher A. Pissarides, Cyprus-UK
2011 Thomas J. Sargent, Christopher A. Sims, U.S.
2012 Alvin E. Roth, Lloyd S. Shapley, U.S.
2013 Eugene F. Fama, Lars Peter Hansen, Robert J. Shiller, U.S.
2014 Jean Tirole, Fr.
2015 Angus Deaton, UK-U.S.

Pulitzer Prizes in Journalism, Letters, and Music, 1917-2015

Endowed by Joseph Pulitzer (1847-1911), publisher of the *New York World*, in a bequest to Columbia Univ. and awarded annually, in years shown, for work published the previous year. Prizes are currently $10,000 in each category except Public Service (in Journalism), for which a gold medal is given. The prize board began considering submissions from online-only publications in 2009. For letters and music, prizes in past years are listed; if a year is omitted, no award was given that year.

Pulitzer Prizes in Journalism, 2015

Public Service: *The Post and Courier* (Charleston, SC), for series on why South Carolina is one of the deadliest states for women involved in domestic violence.

Breaking News Reporting: *Seattle Times* staff, for digital coverage and follow-up reporting on a landslide that killed 43 people.

Investigative Reporting: Eric Lipton, *NY Times*, on the influence of lobbyists on congressional leaders and state attorneys general; and *Wall Street Journal* (New York, NY) staff, for "Medicare Unmasked," data on the practices of health care providers.

Explanatory Reporting: Zachary R. Mider, Bloomberg News (New York, NY), on how U.S. corporations avoid paying taxes.

Local Reporting: Rob Kuznia, Rebecca Kimitch, and Frank Suraci, *Daily Breeze* (Torrance, CA), for investigating widespread corruption in a small school district.

National Reporting: Carol D. Leonnig, *Washington Post*, for examining the Secret Service and its security lapses.

International Reporting: *NY Times* staff, for stories on the Ebola outbreak in Africa.

Feature Writing: Diana Marcum, *L.A. Times*, for features on drought-affected lives in California's Central Valley.

Commentary: Lisa Falkenberg, *Houston Chronicle*, on grand jury abuses that led to problems in the legal and immigration systems.

Criticism: Mary McNamara, *L.A. Times*, for cultural criticism.

Editorial Writing: Kathleen Kingsbury, *Boston Globe*, for exploring the real cost of cheap food and income inequality.

Editorial Cartooning: Adam Zyglis, *Buffalo News* (NY), for strong images and layers of meaning.

Breaking News Photography: *St. Louis Post-Dispatch* staff, for images of despair and anger in Ferguson, MO.

Feature Photography: Daniel Berehulak, freelance for *NY Times*, on Ebola epidemic in West Africa.

Pulitzer Prizes in Letters, 1917-2015

Fiction

1918 Ernest Poole, *His Family*
1919 Booth Tarkington, *The Magnificent Ambersons*
1921 Edith Wharton, *The Age of Innocence*
1922 Booth Tarkington, *Alice Adams*
1923 Willa Cather, *One of Ours*
1924 Margaret Wilson, *The Able McLaughlins*
1925 Edna Ferber, *So Big*
1926 Sinclair Lewis, *Arrowsmith* (refused)
1927 Louis Bromfield, *Early Autumn*
1928 Thornton Wilder, *The Bridge of San Luis Rey*
1929 Julia Peterkin, *Scarlet Sister Mary*
1930 Oliver La Farge, *Laughing Boy*
1931 Margaret Ayer Barnes, *Years of Grace*
1932 Pearl S. Buck, *The Good Earth*
1933 T. S. Stribling, *The Store*
1934 Caroline Miller, *Lamb in His Bosom*
1935 Josephine W. Johnson, *Now in November*
1936 Harold L. Davis, *Honey in the Horn*
1937 Margaret Mitchell, *Gone With the Wind*
1938 John P. Marquand, *The Late George Apley*
1939 Marjorie Kinnan Rawlings, *The Yearling*
1940 John Steinbeck, *The Grapes of Wrath*
1942 Ellen Glasgow, *In This Our Life*
1943 Upton Sinclair, *Dragon's Teeth*
1944 Martin Flavin, *Journey in the Dark*
1945 John Hersey, *A Bell for Adano*
1947 Robert Penn Warren, *All the King's Men*
1948 James A. Michener, *Tales of the South Pacific*
1949 James Gould Cozzens, *Guard of Honor*
1950 A. B. Guthrie Jr., *The Way West*
1951 Conrad Richter, *The Town*
1952 Herman Wouk, *The Caine Mutiny*
1953 Ernest Hemingway, *The Old Man and the Sea*
1955 William Faulkner, *A Fable*
1956 MacKinlay Kantor, *Andersonville*
1958 James Agee, *A Death in the Family*
1959 Robert Lewis Taylor, *The Travels of Jaimie McPheeters*
1960 Allen Drury, *Advise and Consent*
1961 Harper Lee, *To Kill a Mockingbird*
1962 Edwin O'Connor, *The Edge of Sadness*
1963 William Faulkner, *The Reivers*
1965 Shirley Ann Grau, *The Keepers of the House*
1966 Katherine Anne Porter, *Collected Stories*
1967 Bernard Malamud, *The Fixer*
1968 William Styron, *The Confessions of Nat Turner*
1969 N. Scott Momaday, *House Made of Dawn*
1970 Jean Stafford, *Collected Stories*
1972 Wallace Stegner, *Angle of Repose*
1973 Eudora Welty, *The Optimist's Daughter*
1975 Michael Shaara, *The Killer Angels*
1976 Saul Bellow, *Humboldt's Gift*
1978 James Alan McPherson, *Elbow Room*
1979 John Cheever, *The Stories of John Cheever*
1980 Norman Mailer, *The Executioner's Song*
1981 John Kennedy Toole, *A Confederacy of Dunces*
1982 John Updike, *Rabbit Is Rich*
1983 Alice Walker, *The Color Purple*
1984 William Kennedy, *Ironweed*
1985 Alison Lurie, *Foreign Affairs*
1986 Larry McMurtry, *Lonesome Dove*
1987 Peter Taylor, *A Summons to Memphis*
1988 Toni Morrison, *Beloved*
1989 Anne Tyler, *Breathing Lessons*
1990 Oscar Hijuelos, *The Mambo Kings Play Songs of Love*
1991 John Updike, *Rabbit at Rest*
1992 Jane Smiley, *A Thousand Acres*
1993 Robert Olen Butler, *A Good Scent From a Strange Mountain*
1994 E. Annie Proulx, *The Shipping News*
1995 Carol Shields, *The Stone Diaries*
1996 Richard Ford, *Independence Day*
1997 Steven Millhauser, *Martin Dressler: The Tale of an American Dreamer*
1998 Philip Roth, *American Pastoral*
1999 Michael Cunningham, *The Hours*
2000 Jhumpa Lahiri, *Interpreter of Maladies*
2001 Michael Chabon, *The Amazing Adventures of Kavalier & Clay*
2002 Richard Russo, *Empire Falls*
2003 Jeffrey Eugenides, *Middlesex*
2004 Edward P. Jones, *The Known World*
2005 Marilynne Robinson, *Gilead*
2006 Geraldine Brooks, *March*
2007 Cormac McCarthy, *The Road*
2008 Junot Díaz, *The Brief Wondrous Life of Oscar Wao*
2009 Elizabeth Strout, *Olive Kitteridge*
2010 Paul Harding, *Tinkers*
2011 Jennifer Egan, *A Visit From the Goon Squad*
2013 Adam Johnson, *The Orphan Master's Son*
2014 Donna Tartt, *The Goldfinch*
2015 Anthony Doerr, *All the Light We Cannot See*

Drama

1918 Jesse Lynch Williams, *Why Marry?*
1920 Eugene O'Neill, *Beyond the Horizon*
1921 Zona Gale, *Miss Lulu Bett*
1922 Eugene O'Neill, *Anna Christie*
1923 Owen Davis, *Icebound*
1924 Hatcher Hughes, *Hell-Bent Fer Heaven*
1925 Sidney Howard, *They Knew What They Wanted*
1926 George Kelly, *Craig's Wife*
1927 Paul Green, *In Abraham's Bosom*
1928 Eugene O'Neill, *Strange Interlude*
1929 Elmer Rice, *Street Scene*
1930 Marc Connelly, *The Green Pastures*
1931 Susan Glaspell, *Alison's House*
1932 George S. Kaufman, Morrie Ryskind, and Ira Gershwin, *Of Thee I Sing*
1933 Maxwell Anderson, *Both Your Houses*
1934 Sidney Kingsley, *Men in White*
1935 Zoe Akins, *The Old Maid*
1936 Robert E. Sherwood, *Idiot's Delight*
1937 George S. Kaufman and Moss Hart, *You Can't Take It With You*
1938 Thornton Wilder, *Our Town*
1939 Robert E. Sherwood, *Abe Lincoln in Illinois*
1940 William Saroyan, *The Time of Your Life*
1941 Robert E. Sherwood, *There Shall Be No Night*
1943 Thornton Wilder, *The Skin of Our Teeth*
1945 Mary Chase, *Harvey*
1946 Russel Crouse and Howard Lindsay, *State of the Union*
1948 Tennessee Williams, *A Streetcar Named Desire*
1949 Arthur Miller, *Death of a Salesman*
1950 Richard Rodgers, Oscar Hammerstein II, and Joshua Logan, *South Pacific*
1952 Joseph Kramm, *The Shrike*
1953 William Inge, *Picnic*
1954 John Patrick, *The Teahouse of the August Moon*
1955 Tennessee Williams, *Cat on a Hot Tin Roof*
1956 Frances Goodrich and Albert Hackett, *The Diary of Anne Frank*
1957 Eugene O'Neill, *Long Day's Journey Into Night*
1958 Ketti Frings, *Look Homeward, Angel*
1959 Archibald MacLeish, *J. B.*
1960 George Abbott, Jerome Weidman, Sheldon Harnick, and Jerry Bock, *Fiorello!*
1961 Tad Mosel, *All the Way Home*
1962 Frank Loesser and Abe Burrows, *How to Succeed in Business Without Really Trying*
1965 Frank D. Gilroy, *The Subject Was Roses*
1967 Edward Albee, *A Delicate Balance*
1969 Howard Sackler, *The Great White Hope*
1970 Charles Gordone, *No Place to Be Somebody*
1971 Paul Zindel, *The Effect of Gamma Rays on Man-in-the-Moon Marigolds*
1973 Jason Miller, *That Championship Season*
1975 Edward Albee, *Seascape*
1976 Michael Bennett, James Kirkwood, Nicholas Dante, Marvin Hamlisch, and Edward Kleban, *A Chorus Line*
1977 Michael Cristofer, *The Shadow Box*
1978 Donald L. Coburn, *The Gin Game*
1979 Sam Shepard, *Buried Child*
1980 Lanford Wilson, *Talley's Folly*
1981 Beth Henley, *Crimes of the Heart*
1982 Charles Fuller, *A Soldier's Play*
1983 Marsha Norman, *'night, Mother*
1984 David Mamet, *Glengarry Glen Ross*
1985 Stephen Sondheim and James Lapine, *Sunday in the Park With George*
1987 August Wilson, *Fences*
1988 Alfred Uhry, *Driving Miss Daisy*
1989 Wendy Wasserstein, *The Heidi Chronicles*
1990 August Wilson, *The Piano Lesson*
1991 Neil Simon, *Lost in Yonkers*
1992 Robert Schenkkan, *The Kentucky Cycle*
1993 Tony Kushner, *Angels in America: Millennium Approaches*
1994 Edward Albee, *Three Tall Women*
1995 Horton Foote, *The Young Man From Atlanta*

1996 Jonathan Larson, *Rent*
1998 Paula Vogel, *How I Learned to Drive*
1999 Margaret Edson, *Wit*
2000 Donald Margulies, *Dinner With Friends*
2001 David Auburn, *Proof*
2002 Suzan-Lori Parks, *Topdog/Underdog*
2003 Nilo Cruz, *Anna in the Tropics*
2004 Doug Wright, *I Am My Own Wife*
2005 John Patrick Shanley, *Doubt, a parable*
2007 David Lindsay-Abaire, *Rabbit Hole*
2008 Tracy Letts, *August: Osage County*
2009 Lynn Nottage, *Ruined*
2010 Tom Kitt and Brian Yorkey, *Next to Normal*
2011 Bruce Norris, *Clybourne Park*
2012 Quiara Alegría Hudes, *Water by the Spoonful*
2013 Ayad Akhtar, *Disgraced*
2014 Annie Baker, *The Flick*
2015 Stephen Adly Guirgis, *Between Riverside and Crazy*

History (U.S.)

1917 J. J. Jusserand, *With Americans of Past and Present Days*
1918 James Ford Rhodes, *History of the Civil War, 1861-1865*
1920 Justin H. Smith, *The War With Mexico*
1921 William Sowden Sims in collab. with Burton J. Hendrick, *The Victory at Sea*
1922 James Truslow Adams, *The Founding of New England*
1923 Charles Warren, *The Supreme Court in United States History*
1924 Charles Howard McIlwain, *The American Revolution: A Constitutional Interpretation*
1925 Frederick L. Paxton, *A History of the American Frontier*
1926 Edward Channing, *A History of the United States*
1927 Samuel Flagg Bemis, *Pinckney's Treaty*
1928 V. L. Parrington, *Main Currents in American Thought*
1929 Fred A. Shannon, *The Organization and Administration of the Union Army, 1861-1865*
1930 Claude H. Van Tyne, *The War of Independence*
1931 Bernadotte E. Schmitt, *The Coming of the War, 1914*
1932 John J. Pershing, *My Experiences in the World War*
1933 Frederick J. Turner, *The Significance of Sections in American History*
1934 Herbert Agar, *The People's Choice*
1935 Charles McLean Andrews, *The Colonial Period of American History*
1936 Andrew C. McLaughlin, *The Constitutional History of the United States*
1937 Van Wyck Brooks, *The Flowering of New England*
1938 Paul Herman Buck, *The Road to Reunion, 1865-1900*
1939 Frank Luther Mott, *A History of American Magazines*
1940 Carl Sandburg, *Abraham Lincoln: The War Years*
1941 Marcus Lee Hansen, *The Atlantic Migration, 1607-1860*
1942 Margaret Leech, *Reveille in Washington, 1860-1865*
1943 Esther Forbes, *Paul Revere and the World He Lived In*
1944 Merle Curti, *The Growth of American Thought*
1945 Stephen Bonsal, *Unfinished Business*
1946 Arthur M. Schlesinger Jr., *The Age of Jackson*
1947 James Phinney Baxter III, *Scientists Against Time*
1948 Bernard DeVoto, *Across the Wide Missouri*
1949 Roy F. Nichols, *The Disruption of American Democracy*
1950 Oliver W. Larkin, *Art and Life in America*
1951 R. Carlyle Buley, *The Old Northwest: Pioneer Period 1815-1840*
1952 Oscar Handlin, *The Uprooted*
1953 George Dangerfield, *The Era of Good Feelings*
1954 Bruce Catton, *A Stillness at Appomattox*
1955 Paul Horgan, *Great River: The Rio Grande in North American History*
1956 Richard Hofstadter, *The Age of Reform*
1957 George F. Kennan, *Russia Leaves the War*
1958 Bray Hammond, *Banks and Politics in America From the Revolution to the Civil War*
1959 Leonard D. White with Jean Schneider, *The Republican Era, 1869-1901*
1960 Margaret Leech, *In the Days of McKinley*
1961 Herbert Feis, *Between War and Peace: The Potsdam Conference*
1962 Lawrence H. Gipson, *The Triumphant Empire: Thunder-Clouds Gather in the West, 1763-1766*
1963 Constance McLaughlin Green, *Washington: Village and Capital, 1800-1878*
1964 Sumner Chilton Powell, *Puritan Village: The Formation of a New England Town*
1965 Irwin Unger, *The Greenback Era*
1966 Perry Miller, *The Life of the Mind in America*
1967 William H. Goetzmann, *Exploration and Empire*
1968 Bernard Bailyn, *The Ideological Origins of the American Revolution*
1969 Leonard W. Levy, *Origins of the Fifth Amendment*
1970 Dean Acheson, *Present at the Creation: My Years in the State Department*
1971 James MacGregor Burns, *Roosevelt: The Soldier of Freedom*
1972 Carl N. Degler, *Neither Black nor White*
1973 Michael Kammen, *People of Paradox: An Inquiry Concerning the Origins of American Civilization*
1974 Daniel J. Boorstin, *The Americans: The Democratic Experience*
1975 Dumas Malone, *Jefferson and His Time*
1976 Paul Horgan, *Lamy of Santa Fe*
1977 David M. Potter, *The Impending Crisis, 1841-1867*
1978 Alfred D. Chandler Jr., *The Visible Hand: The Managerial Revolution in American Business*
1979 Don E. Fehrenbacher, *The Dred Scott Case: Its Significance in American Law and Politics*
1980 Leon F. Litwack, *Been in the Storm So Long*
1981 Lawrence A. Cremin, *American Education: The National Experience, 1783-1876*
1982 C. Vann Woodward, ed., *Mary Chesnut's Civil War*
1983 Rhys L. Issac, *The Transformation of Virginia, 1740-179(*
1985 Thomas K. McCraw, *Prophets of Regulation*
1986 Walter A. McDougall, *The Heavens and the Earth*
1987 Bernard Bailyn, *Voyagers to the West*
1988 Robert V. Bruce, *The Launching of Modern American Science, 1846-1876*
1989 Taylor Branch, *Parting the Waters: America in the King Years, 1954-63*; James M. McPherson, *Battle Cry of Freedom: The Civil War Era*
1990 Stanley Karnow, *In Our Image: America's Empire in the Philippines*
1991 Laurel Thatcher Ulrich, *A Midwife's Tale: The Life of Martha Ballard, Based on Her Diary, 1785-1812*
1992 Mark E. Neely Jr., *The Fate of Liberty: Abraham Lincoln and Civil Liberties*
1993 Gordon S. Wood, *The Radicalism of the American Revolutio*
1995 Doris Kearns Goodwin, *No Ordinary Time: Franklin and Eleanor Roosevelt: The Home Front in World War II*
1996 Alan Taylor, *William Cooper's Town: Power and Persuasion on the Frontier of the Early American Republic*
1997 Jack N. Rakove, *Original Meanings: Politics and Ideas in the Making of the Constitution*
1998 Edward J. Larson, *Summer for the Gods: The Scopes Trial and America's Continuing Debate Over Science and Religion*
1999 Edwin G. Burrows and Mike Wallace, *Gotham: A History o New York City to 1898*
2000 David M. Kennedy, *Freedom From Fear: The American People in Depression and War, 1929-1945*
2001 Joseph J. Ellis, *Founding Brothers: The Revolutionary Generation*
2002 Louis Menand, *The Metaphysical Club: A Story of Ideas ir America*
2003 Rick Atkinson, *An Army at Dawn: The War in North Africa, 1942-1943*
2004 Steven Hahn, *A Nation Under Our Feet: Black Political Struggles in the Rural South From Slavery to the Great Migration*
2005 David Hackett Fischer, *Washington's Crossing*
2006 David M. Oshinsky, *Polio: An American Story*
2007 Gene Roberts and Hank Klibanoff, *The Race Beat: The Press, the Civil Rights Struggle, and the Awakening of a Nation*
2008 Daniel Walker Howe, *What Hath God Wrought: The Transformation of America, 1815-1848*
2009 Annette Gordon-Reed, *The Hemingses of Monticello: An American Family*
2010 Liaquat Ahamed, *Lords of Finance: The Bankers Who Broke the World*
2011 Eric Foner, *The Fiery Trial: Abraham Lincoln and America Slavery*
2012 Manning Marable, *Malcolm X: A Life of Reinvention*
2013 Fredrik Logevall, *Embers of War: The Fall of an Empire anc the Making of America's Vietnam*
2014 Alan Taylor, *The Internal Enemy: Slavery and War in Virgin 1772-1832*
2015 Elizabeth A. Fenn, *Encounters at the Heart of the World: A History of the Mandan People*

Biography or Autobiography

1917 Laura E. Richards and Maude Howe Elliott, assisted by Florence Howe Hall, *Julia Ward Howe*
1918 William Cabell Bruce, *Benjamin Franklin, Self-Revealed*
1919 Henry Adams, *The Education of Henry Adams*
1920 Albert J. Beveridge, *The Life of John Marshall*
1921 Edward Bok, *The Americanization of Edward Bok*

1922 Hamlin Garland, *A Daughter of the Middle Border*
1923 Burton J. Hendrick, *The Life and Letters of Walter H. Page*
1924 Michael Pupin, *From Immigrant to Inventor*
1925 M. A. DeWolfe Howe, *Barrett Wendell and His Letters*
1926 Harvey Cushing, *The Life of Sir William Osler*
1927 Emory Holloway, *Whitman: An Interpretation in Narrative*
1928 Charles Edward Russell, *The American Orchestra and Theodore Thomas*
1929 Burton J. Hendrick, *The Training of an American: The Earlier Life and Letters of Walter H. Page*
1930 Marquis James, *The Raven* (Sam Houston)
1931 Henry James, *Charles W. Eliot*
1932 Henry F. Pringle, *Theodore Roosevelt*
1933 Allan Nevins, *Grover Cleveland*
1934 Tyler Dennett, *John Hay*
1935 Douglas Southall Freeman, *R. E. Lee*
1936 Ralph Barton Perry, *The Thought and Character of William James*
1937 Allan Nevins, *Hamilton Fish: The Inner History of the Grant Administration*
1938 Odell Shepard, *Pedlar's Progress*;
Marquis James, *Andrew Jackson, 2 vols.*
1939 Carl Van Doren, *Benjamin Franklin*
1940 Ray Stannard Baker, *Woodrow Wilson, Life and Letters*
1941 Ola Elizabeth Winslow, *Jonathan Edwards*
1942 Forrest Wilson, *Crusader in Crinoline* (Harriet Beecher Stowe)
1943 Samuel Eliot Morison, *Admiral of the Ocean Sea* (Christopher Columbus)
1944 Carleton Mabee, *The American Leonardo: The Life of Samuel F. B. Morse*
1945 Russell Blaine Nye, *George Bancroft: Brahmin Rebel*
1946 Linnie Marsh Wolfe, *Son of the Wilderness* (John Muir)
1947 William Allen White, *Autobiography of William Allen White*
1948 Margaret Clapp, *Forgotten First Citizen: John Bigelow*
1949 Robert E. Sherwood, *Roosevelt and Hopkins*
1950 Samuel Flagg Bemis, *John Quincy Adams and the Foundations of American Foreign Policy*
1951 Margaret Louise Coit, *John C. Calhoun: American Portrait*
1952 Merlo J. Pusey, *Charles Evans Hughes*
1953 David J. Mays, *Edmund Pendleton, 1721-1803*
1954 Charles A. Lindbergh, *The Spirit of St. Louis*
1955 William S. White, *The Taft Story*
1956 Talbot F. Hamlin, *Benjamin Henry Latrobe*
1957 John F. Kennedy, *Profiles in Courage*
1958 Douglas Southall Freeman, *George Washington, Vols. I-VI*
1959 Arthur Walworth, *Woodrow Wilson: American Prophet*
1960 Samuel Eliot Morison, *John Paul Jones*
1961 David Donald, *Charles Sumner and the Coming of the Civil War*
1963 Leon Edel, *Henry James: Vols. 2-3*
1964 Walter Jackson Bate, *John Keats*
1965 Ernest Samuels, *Henry Adams*
1966 Arthur M. Schlesinger Jr., *A Thousand Days* (JFK)
1967 Justin Kaplan, *Mr. Clemens and Mark Twain*
1968 George F. Kennan, *Memoirs (1925-1950)*
1969 Benjamin L. Reid, *The Man From New York: John Quinn and His Friends*
1970 T. Harry Williams, *Huey Long*
1971 Lawrence Thompson, *Robert Frost: The Years of Triumph, 1915-1938*
1972 Joseph P. Lash, *Eleanor and Franklin*
1973 W. A. Swanberg, *Luce and His Empire*
1974 Louis Sheaffer, *O'Neill, Son and Artist*
1975 Robert A. Caro, *The Power Broker: Robert Moses and the Fall of New York*
1976 R. W. B. Lewis, *Edith Wharton: A Biography*
1977 John E. Mack, *A Prince of Our Disorder: The Life of T. E. Lawrence*
1978 Walter Jackson Bate, *Samuel Johnson*
1979 Leonard Baker, *Days of Sorrow and Pain: Leo Baeck and the Berlin Jews*
1980 Edmund Morris, *The Rise of Theodore Roosevelt*
1981 Robert K. Massie, *Peter the Great: His Life and World*
1982 William S. McFeely, *Grant: A Biography*
1983 Russell Baker, *Growing Up*
1984 Louis R. Harlan, *Booker T. Washington*
1985 Kenneth Silverman, *The Life and Times of Cotton Mather*
1986 Elizabeth Frank, *Louise Bogan: A Portrait*
1987 David J. Garrow, *Bearing the Cross: Martin Luther King Jr. and the Southern Christian Leadership Conference*
1988 David Herbert Donald, *Look Homeward: A Life of Thomas Wolfe*
1989 Richard Ellmann, *Oscar Wilde*
1990 Sebastian de Grazia, *Machiavelli in Hell*
1991 Steven Naifeh and Gregory White Smith, *Jackson Pollock: An American Saga*
1992 Lewis B. Puller Jr., *Fortunate Son: The Healing of a Vietnam Vet*
1993 David McCullough, *Truman*
1994 David Levering Lewis, *W.E.B. Du Bois: Biography of a Race, 1868-1919*
1995 Joan D. Hedrick, *Harriet Beecher Stowe: A Life*
1996 Jack Miles, *God: A Biography*
1997 Frank McCourt, *Angela's Ashes: A Memoir*
1998 Katharine Graham, *Personal History*
1999 A. Scott Berg, *Lindbergh*
2000 Stacy Schiff, *Véra (Mrs. Vladimir Nabokov)*
2001 David Levering Lewis, *W.E.B. Du Bois: The Fight for Equality and the American Century, 1919-1963*
2002 David McCullough, *John Adams*
2003 Robert A. Caro, *The Years of Lyndon Johnson: Master of the Senate*
2004 William Taubman, *Khrushchev: The Man and His Era*
2005 Mark Stevens and Annalyn Swan, *de Kooning: An American Master*
2006 Kai Bird and Martin J. Sherwin, *American Prometheus: The Triumph and Tragedy of J. Robert Oppenheimer*
2007 Debby Applegate, *The Most Famous Man in America: The Biography of Henry Ward Beecher*
2008 John Matteson, *Eden's Outcasts: The Story of Louisa May Alcott and Her Father*
2009 Jon Meacham, *American Lion: Andrew Jackson in the White House*
2010 T. J. Stiles, *The First Tycoon: The Epic Life of Cornelius Vanderbilt*
2011 Ron Chernow, *Washington: A Life*
2012 John Lewis Gaddis, *George F. Kennan: An American Life*
2013 Tom Reiss, *The Black Count: Glory, Revolution, Betrayal, and the Real Count of Monte Cristo* (Alex Dumas)
2014 Megan Marshall, *Margaret Fuller: A New American Life*
2015 David I. Kertzer, *The Pope and Mussolini: The Secret History of Pius XI and the Rise of Fascism in Europe*

Poetry

1922 Edwin Arlington Robinson, *Collected Poems*
1923 Edna St. Vincent Millay, *The Ballad of the Harp-Weaver*; *A Few Figs From Thistles*; and other works
1924 Robert Frost, *New Hampshire: A Poem With Notes and Grace Notes*
1925 Edwin Arlington Robinson, *The Man Who Died Twice*
1926 Amy Lowell, *What's O'Clock*
1927 Leonora Speyer, *Fiddler's Farewell*
1928 Edwin Arlington Robinson, *Tristram*
1929 Stephen Vincent Benet, *John Brown's Body*
1930 Conrad Aiken, *Selected Poems*
1931 Robert Frost, *Collected Poems*
1932 George Dillon, *The Flowering Stone*
1933 Archibald MacLeish, *Conquistador*
1934 Robert Hillyer, *Collected Verse*
1935 Audrey Wurdemann, *Bright Ambush*
1936 Robert P. Tristram Coffin, *Strange Holiness*
1937 Robert Frost, *A Further Range*
1938 Marya Zaturenska, *Cold Morning Sky*
1939 John Gould Fletcher, *Selected Poems*
1940 Mark Van Doren, *Collected Poems*
1941 Leonard Bacon, *Sunderland Capture*
1942 William Rose Benet, *The Dust Which Is God*
1943 Robert Frost, *A Witness Tree*
1944 Stephen Vincent Benet, *Western Star*
1945 Karl Shapiro, *V-Letter and Other Poems*
1947 Robert Lowell, *Lord Weary's Castle*
1948 W. H. Auden, *The Age of Anxiety*
1949 Peter Viereck, *Terror and Decorum*
1950 Gwendolyn Brooks, *Annie Allen*
1951 Carl Sandburg, *Complete Poems*
1952 Marianne Moore, *Collected Poems*
1953 Archibald MacLeish, *Collected Poems, 1917-1952*
1954 Theodore Roethke, *The Waking*
1955 Wallace Stevens, *Collected Poems*
1956 Elizabeth Bishop, *Poems: North and South*
1957 Richard Wilbur, *Things of This World*
1958 Robert Penn Warren, *Promises: Poems 1954-1956*
1959 Stanley Kunitz, *Selected Poems 1928-1958*
1960 W. D. Snodgrass, *Heart's Needle*
1961 Phyllis McGinley, *Times Three: Selected Verse From Three Decades*
1962 Alan Dugan, *Poems*
1963 William Carlos Williams, *Pictures From Brueghel*
1964 Louis Simpson, *At the End of the Open Road*
1965 John Berryman, *77 Dream Songs*
1966 Richard Eberhart, *Selected Poems*
1967 Anne Sexton, *Live or Die*

1968 Anthony Hecht, *The Hard Hours*
1969 George Oppen, *Of Being Numerous*
1970 Richard Howard, *Untitled Subjects*
1971 William S. Merwin, *The Carrier of Ladders*
1972 James Wright, *Collected Poems*
1973 Maxine Kumin, *Up Country*
1974 Robert Lowell, *The Dolphin*
1975 Gary Snyder, *Turtle Island*
1976 John Ashbery, *Self-Portrait in a Convex Mirror*
1977 James Merrill, *Divine Comedies*
1978 Howard Nemerov, *Collected Poems*
1979 Robert Penn Warren, *Now and Then: Poems 1976-1978*
1980 Donald Justice, *Selected Poems*
1981 James Schuyler, *The Morning of the Poem*
1982 Sylvia Plath, *The Collected Poems*
1983 Galway Kinnell, *Selected Poems*
1984 Mary Oliver, *American Primitive*
1985 Carolyn Kizer, *Yin*
1986 Henry Taylor, *The Flying Change*
1987 Rita Dove, *Thomas and Beulah*
1988 William Meredith, *Partial Accounts*
1989 Richard Wilbur, *New and Collected Poems*
1990 Charles Simic, *The World Doesn't End*
1991 Mona Van Duyn, *Near Changes*
1992 James Tate, *Selected Poems*
1993 Louise Glück, *The Wild Iris*
1994 Yusef Komunyakaa, *Neon Vernacular*
1995 Philip Levine, *The Simple Truth*
1996 Jorie Graham, *The Dream of the Unified Field*
1997 Lisel Mueller, *Alive Together: New and Selected Poems*
1998 Charles Wright, *Black Zodiac*
1999 Mark Strand, *Blizzard of One*
2000 C. K. Williams, *Repair*
2001 Stephen Dunn, *Different Hours*
2002 Carl Dennis, *Practical Gods*
2003 Paul Muldoon, *Moy Sand and Gravel*
2004 Franz Wright, *Walking to Martha's Vineyard*
2005 Ted Kooser, *Delights & Shadows*
2006 Claudia Emerson, *Late Wife*
2007 Natasha Trethewey, *Native Guard*
2008 Robert Hass, *Time and Materials*; Philip Schultz, *Failure*
2009 W. S. Merwin, *The Shadow of Sirius*
2010 Rae Armantrout, *Versed*
2011 Kay Ryan, *The Best of It: New and Selected Poems*
2012 Tracy K. Smith, *Life on Mars*
2013 Sharon Olds, *Stag's Leap*
2014 Vijay Seshadri, *3 Sections*
2015 Gregory Pardlo, *Digest*

General Nonfiction

1962 Theodore H. White, *The Making of the President 1960*
1963 Barbara W. Tuchman, *The Guns of August*
1964 Richard Hofstadter, *Anti-Intellectualism in American Life*
1965 Howard Mumford Jones, *O Strange New World*
1966 Edwin Way Teale, *Wandering Through Winter*
1967 David Brion Davis, *The Problem of Slavery in Western Culture*
1968 Will and Ariel Durant, *Rousseau and Revolution*
1969 Norman Mailer, *The Armies of the Night*; Rene Jules Dubos, *So Human an Animal: How We Are Shaped by Surroundings and Events*
1970 Eric H. Erikson, *Gandhi's Truth*
1971 John Toland, *The Rising Sun*
1972 Barbara W. Tuchman, *Stilwell and the American Experience in China, 1911-1945*
1973 Frances FitzGerald, *Fire in the Lake: The Vietnamese and the Americans in Vietnam*; Robert Coles, *Children of Crisis, Vols. II and III*
1974 Ernest Becker, *The Denial of Death*
1975 Annie Dillard, *Pilgrim at Tinker Creek*
1976 Robert N. Butler, *Why Survive? Being Old in America*
1977 William W. Warner, *Beautiful Swimmers*
1978 Carl Sagan, *The Dragons of Eden*
1979 Edward O. Wilson, *On Human Nature*
1980 Douglas R. Hofstadter, *Gödel, Escher, Bach: An Eternal Golden Braid*
1981 Carl E. Schorske, *Fin-de-Siecle Vienna: Politics and Culture*
1982 Tracy Kidder, *The Soul of a New Machine*
1983 Susan Sheehan, *Is There No Place on Earth for Me?*
1984 Paul Starr, *Social Transformation of American Medicine*
1985 Studs Terkel, *The Good War*
1986 Joseph Lelyveld, *Move Your Shadow*; J. Anthony Lukas, *Common Ground*
1987 David K. Shipler, *Arab and Jew: Wounded Spirits in a Promised Land*
1988 Richard Rhodes, *The Making of the Atomic Bomb*
1989 Neil Sheehan, *A Bright Shining Lie: John Paul Vann and America in Vietnam*
1990 Dale Maharidge and Michael Williamson, *And Their Children After Them*
1991 Bert Holldobler and Edward O. Wilson, *The Ants*
1992 Daniel Yergin, *The Prize: The Epic Quest for Oil, Money, and Power*
1993 Garry Wills, *Lincoln at Gettysburg*
1994 David Remnick, *Lenin's Tomb: The Last Days of the Soviet Empire*
1995 Jonathan Weiner, *The Beak of the Finch: A Story of Evolution in Our Time*
1996 Tina Rosenberg, *The Haunted Land: Facing Europe's Ghosts After Communism*
1997 Richard Kluger, *Ashes to Ashes: America's Hundred-Year Cigarette War, the Public Health, and the Unabashed Triumph of Philip Morris*
1998 Jared Diamond, *Guns, Germs, and Steel: The Fates of Human Societies*
1999 John McPhee, *Annals of the Former World*
2000 John W. Dower, *Embracing Defeat: Japan in the Wake of World War II*
2001 Herbert P. Bix, *Hirohito and the Making of Modern Japan*
2002 Diane McWhorter, *Carry Me Home: Birmingham, Alabama, the Climactic Battle of the Civil Rights Revolution*
2003 Samantha Power, *A Problem From Hell: America and the Age of Genocide*
2004 Anne Applebaum, *Gulag: A History*
2005 Steve Coll, *Ghost Wars*
2006 Caroline Elkins, *Imperial Reckoning: The Untold Story of Britain's Gulag in Kenya*
2007 Lawrence Wright, *The Looming Tower: Al-Qaeda and the Road to 9/11*
2008 Saul Friedländer, *The Years of Extermination: Nazi Germany and the Jews, 1939-1945*
2009 Douglas A. Blackmon, *Slavery by Another Name: The Re-Enslavement of Black Americans From the Civil War to World War II*
2010 David E. Hoffman, *The Dead Hand: The Untold Story of the Cold War Arms Race and Its Dangerous Legacy*
2011 Siddhartha Mukherjee, *The Emperor of All Maladies: A Biography of Cancer*
2012 Stephen Greenblatt, *The Swerve: How the World Became Modern*
2013 Gilbert King, *Devil in the Grove: Thurgood Marshall, the Groveland Boys, and the Dawn of a New America*
2014 Dan Fagin, *Toms River: A Story of Science and Salvation*
2015 Elizabeth Kolbert, *The Sixth Extinction: An Unnatural History*

Special Citation in Letters

1944 Richard Rodgers and Oscar Hammerstein II, for *Oklahoma!*
1957 Kenneth Roberts, for his historical novels
1960 *The Armada*, by Garrett Mattingly
1961 *American Heritage Picture History of the Civil War*
1973 *George Washington, Vols. I-IV*, by James Thomas Flexner
1977 Alex Haley, for *Roots*
1978 E. B. White
1984 Theodor Seuss Geisel (Dr. Seuss)
1992 Art Spiegelman, for *Maus*
2006 Edmund S. Morgan
2007 Ray Bradbury

Pulitzer Prizes in Music, 1943-2015

1943 William Schuman, *Secular Cantata No. 2, A Free Song*
1944 Howard Hanson, *Symphony No. 4, Op. 34*
1945 Aaron Copland, *Appalachian Spring*
1946 Leo Sowerby, *The Canticle of the Sun*
1947 Charles Ives, *Symphony No. 3*
1948 Walter Piston, *Symphony No. 3*
1949 Virgil Thomson, *Louisiana Story*
1950 Gian-Carlo Menotti, *The Consul*
1951 Douglas Moore, *Giants in the Earth*
1952 Gail Kubik, *Symphony Concertante*
1954 Quincy Porter, *Concerto for Two Pianos and Orchestra*
1955 Gian-Carlo Menotti, *The Saint of Bleecker Street*
1956 Ernest Toch, *Symphony No. 3*
1957 Norman Dello Joio, *Meditations on Ecclesiastes*
1958 Samuel Barber, *Vanessa*
1959 John LaMontaine, *Concerto for Piano and Orchestra*

1960 Elliott Carter, *Second String Quartet*
1961 Walter Piston, *Symphony No. 7*
1962 Robert Ward, *The Crucible*
1963 Samuel Barber, *Piano Concerto No. 1*
1966 Leslie Bassett, *Variations for Orchestra*
1967 Leon Kirchner, *Quartet No. 3*
1968 George Crumb, *Echoes of Time and the River*
1969 Karel Husa, *String Quartet No. 3*
1970 Charles Wuorinen, *Time's Encomium*
1971 Mario Davidovsky, *Synchronisms No. 6*
1972 Jacob Druckman, *Windows*
1973 Elliott Carter, *String Quartet No. 3*
1974 Donald Martino, *Notturno*
1975 Dominick Argento, *From the Diary of Virginia Woolf*
1976 Ned Rorem, *Air Music*
1977 Richard Wernick, *Visions of Terror and Wonder*
1978 Michael Colgrass, *Deja Vu for Percussion and Orchestra*
1979 Joseph Schwantner, *Aftertones of Infinity*
1980 David Del Tredici, *In Memory of a Summer Day*
1982 Roger Sessions, *Concerto for Orchestra*
1983 Ellen Taaffe Zwilich, *Symphony No. 1*
1984 Bernard Rands, *Canti del Sole*
1985 Stephen Albert, *Symphony, RiverRun*
1986 George Perle, *Wind Quintet IV*
1987 John Harbison, *The Flight Into Egypt*
1988 William Bolcom, *12 New Etudes for Piano*
1989 Roger Reynolds, *Whispers Out of Time*
1990 Mel Powell, *Duplicates: A Concerto for Two Pianos and Orchestra*
1991 Shulamit Ran, *Symphony*
1992 Wayne Peterson, *The Face of the Night, The Heart of the Dark*
1993 Christopher Rouse, *Trombone Concerto*
1994 Gunther Schuller, *Of Reminiscences and Reflections*
1995 Morton Gould, *Stringmusic*
1996 George Walker, *Lilacs for Voice and Orchestra*
1997 Wynton Marsalis, *Blood on the Fields*
1998 Aaron Jay Kernis, *String Quartet No. 2 (musica instrumentalis)*
1999 Melinda Wagner, *Concerto for Flute, Strings, and Percussion*
2000 Lewis Spratlan, *Life is a Dream, Opera in Three Acts: Act II, Concert Version*
2001 John Corigliano, *Symphony No. 2 for String Orchestra*
2002 Henry Brant, *Ice Field*
2003 John Adams, *On the Transmigration of Souls*
2004 Paul Moravec, *Tempest Fantasy*
2005 Steven Stucky, *Second Concerto for Orchestra*
2006 Yehudi Wyner, *Piano Concerto: "Chiavi in Mano"*
2007 Ornette Coleman, *Sound Grammar*
2008 David Lang, *The Little Match Girl Passion*
2009 Steve Reich, *Double Sextet*
2010 Jennifer Higdon, *Violin Concerto*
2011 Zhou Long, *Madame White Snake*
2012 Kevin Puts, *Silent Night: Opera in Two Acts*
2013 Caroline Shaw, *Partita for 8 Voices*
2014 John Luther Adams, *Become Ocean*
2015 Julia Wolfe, *Anthracite Fields*

Special Citation in Music

1974 Roger Sessions
1976 Scott Joplin
1982 Milton Babbitt
1985 William Schuman
1998 George Gershwin
1999 Edward Kennedy "Duke" Ellington
2006 Thelonious Monk
2007 John Coltrane
2008 Bob Dylan
2010 Hank Williams

Man Booker Prize for Fiction, 1969-2015

The Booker Prize for fiction, established in 1968 and renamed the Man Booker Prize in 2002, is £50,000, awarded annually to the author of the best new full-length novel written in English. Award-winning authors were required to be a citizen of the UK, the Commonwealth, or Ireland until 2014, the first year in which all English-language novels published in Britain were considered.

Year	Author, book
1969	P. H. Newby, *Something to Answer For*
1970	Bernice Rubens, *The Elected Member*
1971	V. S. Naipaul, *In a Free State*
1972	John Berger, *G*
1973	J. G. Farrell, *The Siege of Krishnapur*
1974	Nadine Gordimer, *The Conservationist*; Stanley Middleton, *Holiday*
1975	Ruth Prawer Jhabvala, *Heat and Dust*
1976	David Storey, *Saville*
1977	Paul Scott, *Staying On*
1978	Iris Murdoch, *The Sea, the Sea*
1979	Penelope Fitzgerald, *Offshore*
1980	William Golding, *Rites of Passage*
1981	Salman Rushdie, *Midnight's Children*[1]
1982	Thomas Keneally, *Schindler's Ark*
1983	J. M. Coetzee, *Life and Times of Michael K*
1984	Anita Brookner, *Hotel du Lac*
1985	Keri Hulme, *The Bone People*
1986	Kingsley Amis, *The Old Devils*
1987	Penelope Lively, *Moon Tiger*
1988	Peter Carey, *Oscar and Lucinda*
1989	Kazuo Ishiguro, *The Remains of the Day*
1990	A. S. Byatt, *Possession*
1991	Ben Okri, *The Famished Road*
1992	Michael Ondaatje, *The English Patient*; Barry Unsworth, *Sacred Hunger*
1993	Roddy Doyle, *Paddy Clarke Ha Ha Ha*
1994	James Kelman, *How Late It Was, How Late*
1995	Pat Barker, *The Ghost Road*
1996	Graham Swift, *Last Orders*
1997	Arundhati Roy, *The God of Small Things*
1998	Ian McEwan, *Amsterdam*
1999	J. M. Coetzee, *Disgrace*
2000	Margaret Atwood, *The Blind Assassin*
2001	Peter Carey, *True History of the Kelly Gang*
2002	Yann Martel, *Life of Pi*
2003	DBC Pierre, *Vernon God Little*
2004	Alan Hollinghurst, *The Line of Beauty*
2005	John Banville, *The Sea*
2006	Kiran Desai, *The Inheritance of Loss*
2007	Anne Enright, *The Gathering*
2008	Aravind Adiga, *The White Tiger*
2009	Hilary Mantel, *Wolf Hall*
2010	Howard Jacobson, *The Finkler Question*
2011	Julian Barnes, *The Sense of an Ending*
2012	Hilary Mantel, *Bring up the Bodies*
2013	Eleanor Catton, *The Luminaries*
2014	Richard Flanagan, *The Narrow Road to the Deep North*
2015	Marlon James, *A Brief History of Seven Killings*

(1) Rushdie's *Midnight's Children* also won the Booker of Bookers prize in 1993 and the Best of the Booker prize in 2008.

Newbery Medal, 1922-2015

The Newbery Medal is awarded annually by the Association for Library Service to Children, a division of the American Library Association, to the most distinguished contribution to American children's literature published in the previous year.

Year	Book, author
1922	*The Story of Mankind*, Hendrik Willem van Loon
1923	*The Voyages of Dr. Dolittle*, Hugh Lofting
1924	*The Dark Frigate*, Charles Boardman Hawes
1925	*Tales From Silver Lands*, Charles J. Finger
1926	*Shen of the Sea*, Arthur Bowie Chrisman
1927	*Smoky, the Cowhorse*, Will James
1928	*Gay-Neck: The Story of a Pigeon*, Dhan Gopal Mukerji
1929	*The Trumpeter of Krakow*, Eric P. Kelly
1930	*Hitty, Her First Hundred Years*, Rachel Field
1931	*The Cat Who Went to Heaven*, Elizabeth Coatsworth
1932	*Waterless Mountain*, Laura Adams Armer
1933	*Young Fu of the Upper Yangtze*, Elizabeth Foreman Lewis
1934	*Invincible Louisa*, Cornelia Meigs
1935	*Dobry*, Monica Shannon
1936	*Caddie Woodlawn*, Carol Ryrie Brink
1937	*Roller Skates*, Ruth Sawyer
1938	*The White Stag*, Kate Seredy
1939	*Thimble Summer*, Elizabeth Enright
1940	*Daniel Boone*, James Daugherty
1941	*Call It Courage*, Armstrong Sperry
1942	*The Matchlock Gun*, Walter D. Edmonds
1943	*Adam of the Road*, Elizabeth Janet Gray
1944	*Johnny Tremain*, Esther Forbes
1945	*Rabbit Hill*, Robert Lawson

Year	Book, author
1946	*Strawberry Girl*, Lois Lenski
1947	*Miss Hickory*, Carolyn Sherwin Bailey
1948	*The Twenty-One Balloons*, William Pène du Bois
1949	*King of the Wind*, Marguerite Henry
1950	*The Door in the Wall*, Marguerite de Angeli
1951	*Amos Fortune, Free Man*, Elizabeth Yates
1952	*Ginger Pye*, Eleanor Estes
1953	*Secret of the Andes*, Ann Nolan Clark
1954	*... And Now Miguel*, Joseph Krumgold
1955	*The Wheel on the School*, Meindert DeJong
1956	*Carry On, Mr. Bowditch*, Jean Lee Latham
1957	*Miracles on Maple Hill*, Virginia Sorensen
1958	*Rifles for Watie*, Harold Keith
1959	*The Witch of Blackbird Pond*, Elizabeth George Speare
1960	*Onion John*, Joseph Krumgold
1961	*Island of the Blue Dolphins*, Scott O'Dell
1962	*The Bronze Bow*, Elizabeth George Speare
1963	*A Wrinkle in Time*, Madeleine L'Engle
1964	*It's Like This, Cat*, Emily Cheney Neville
1965	*Shadow of a Bull*, Maia Wojciechowska
1966	*I, Juan de Pareja*, Elizabeth Borton de Trevino
1967	*Up a Road Slowly*, Irene Hunt
1968	*From the Mixed-Up Files of Mrs. Basil E. Frankweiler*, E. L. Konigsburg
1969	*The High King*, Lloyd Alexander
1970	*Sounder*, William H. Armstrong
1971	*The Summer of the Swans*, Betsy Byars
1972	*Mrs. Frisby and the Rats of NIMH*, Robert C. O'Brien
1973	*Julie of the Wolves*, Jean Craighead George
1974	*The Slave Dancer*, Paula Fox
1975	*M. C. Higgins, the Great*, Virginia Hamilton
1976	*The Grey King*, Susan Cooper
1977	*Roll of Thunder, Hear My Cry*, Mildred D. Taylor
1978	*Bridge to Terabithia*, Katherine Paterson
1979	*The Westing Game*, Ellen Raskin
1980	*A Gathering of Days*, Joan Blos
1981	*Jacob Have I Loved*, Katherine Paterson
1982	*A Visit to William Blake's Inn: Poems for Innocent and Experienced Travelers*, Nancy Willard
1983	*Dicey's Song*, Cynthia Voigt
1984	*Dear Mr. Henshaw*, Beverly Cleary
1985	*The Hero and the Crown*, Robin McKinley
1986	*Sarah, Plain and Tall*, Patricia MacLachlan
1987	*The Whipping Boy*, Sid Fleischman
1988	*Lincoln: A Photobiography*, Russell Freedman
1989	*Joyful Noise: Poems for Two Voices*, Paul Fleischman
1990	*Number the Stars*, Lois Lowry
1991	*Maniac Magee*, Jerry Spinelli
1992	*Shiloh*, Phyllis Reynolds Naylor
1993	*Missing May*, Cynthia Rylant
1994	*The Giver*, Lois Lowry
1995	*Walk Two Moons*, Sharon Creech
1996	*The Midwife's Apprentice*, Karen Cushman
1997	*The View From Saturday*, E. L. Konigsburg
1998	*Out of the Dust*, Karen Hesse
1999	*Holes*, Louis Sachar
2000	*Bud, Not Buddy*, Christopher Paul Curtis
2001	*A Year Down Yonder*, Richard Peck
2002	*A Single Shard*, Linda Sue Park
2003	*Crispin: The Cross of Lead*, Avi
2004	*The Tale of Despereaux*, Kate DiCamillo
2005	*Kira-Kira*, Cynthia Kadohata
2006	*Criss Cross*, Lynne Rae Perkins
2007	*The Higher Power of Lucky*, Susan Patron
2008	*Good Masters! Sweet Ladies! Voices From a Medieval Village*, Laura Amy Schlitz
2009	*The Graveyard Book*, Neil Gaiman
2010	*When You Reach Me*, Rebecca Stead
2011	*Moon Over Manifest*, Clare Vanderpool
2012	*Dead End in Norvelt*, Jack Gantos
2013	*The One and Only Ivan*, Katherine Applegate
2014	*Flora & Ulysses: The Illuminated Adventures*, Kate DiCamillo
2015	*The Crossover*, Kwame Alexander

Caldecott Medal, 1938-2015

The Caldecott Medal is awarded annually by the Association for Library Service to Children, a division of the American Library Association, to the illustrator of the most distinguished American picture book for children.

Year	Book, illustrator
1938	*Animals of the Bible*, Dorothy P. Lathrop
1939	*Mei Li*, Thomas Handforth
1940	*Abraham Lincoln*, Ingri and Edgar Parin d'Aulaire
1941	*They Were Strong and Good*, Robert Lawson
1942	*Make Way for Ducklings*, Robert McCloskey
1943	*The Little House*, Virginia Lee Burton
1944	*Many Moons*, Louis Slobodkin
1945	*Prayer for a Child*, Elizabeth Orton Jones
1946	*The Rooster Crows*, Maude and Miska Petersham
1947	*The Little Island*, Leonard Weisgard
1948	*White Snow, Bright Snow*, Roger Duvoisin
1949	*The Big Snow*, Berta and Elmer Hader
1950	*Song of the Swallows*, Leo Politi
1951	*The Egg Tree*, Katherine Milhous
1952	*Finders Keepers*, Nicolas, pseud. (Nicholas Mordvinoff)
1953	*The Biggest Bear*, Lynd Ward
1954	*Madeline's Rescue*, Ludwig Bemelmans
1955	*Cinderella, or the Little Glass Slipper*, Marcia Brown
1956	*Frog Went A-Courtin'*, Feodor Rojankovsky
1957	*A Tree Is Nice*, Marc Simont
1958	*Time of Wonder*, Robert McCloskey
1959	*Chanticleer and the Fox*, Barbara Cooney
1960	*Nine Days to Christmas*, Marie Hall Ets
1961	*Baboushka and the Three Kings*, Nicolas Sidjakov
1962	*Once a Mouse*, Marcia Brown
1963	*The Snowy Day*, Ezra Jack Keats
1964	*Where the Wild Things Are*, Maurice Sendak
1965	*May I Bring a Friend?*, Beni Montresor
1966	*Always Room for One More*, Nonny Hogrogian
1967	*Sam, Bangs, and Moonshine*, Evaline Ness
1968	*Drummer Hoff*, Ed Emberley
1969	*The Fool of the World and the Flying Ship*, Uri Shulevitz
1970	*Sylvester and the Magic Pebble*, William Steig
1971	*A Story A Story*, Gail E. Haley
1972	*One Fine Day*, Nonny Hogrogian
1973	*The Funny Little Woman*, Blair Lent
1974	*Duffy and the Devil*, Margot Zemach
1975	*Arrow to the Sun*, Gerald McDermott
1976	*Why Mosquitoes Buzz in People's Ears*, Leo and Diane Dillon
1977	*Ashanti to Zulu: African Traditions*, Leo and Diane Dillon
1978	*Noah's Ark*, Peter Spier
1979	*The Girl Who Loved Wild Horses*, Paul Goble
1980	*Ox-Cart Man*, Barbara Cooney
1981	*Fables*, Arnold Lobel
1982	*Jumanji*, Chris Van Allsburg
1983	*Shadow*, Marcia Brown
1984	*The Glorious Flight: Across the Channel With Louis Bleriot*, Alice and Martin Provensen
1985	*Saint George and the Dragon*, Trina Schart Hyman
1986	*The Polar Express*, Chris Van Allsburg
1987	*Hey, Al*, Richard Egielski
1988	*Owl Moon*, John Schoenherr
1989	*Song and Dance Man*, Stephen Grammell
1990	*Lon Po Po: A Red-Riding Hood Story From China*, Ed Young
1991	*Black and White*, David Macaulay
1992	*Tuesday*, David Wiesner
1993	*Mirette on the High Wire*, Emily Arnold McCully
1994	*Grandfather's Journey*, Allen Say
1995	*Smoky Night*, David Diaz
1996	*Officer Buckle and Gloria*, Peggy Rathmann
1997	*Golem*, David Wisniewski
1998	*Rapunzel*, Paul O. Zelinsky
1999	*Snowflake Bentley*, Mary Azarian
2000	*Joseph Had a Little Overcoat*, Simms Taback
2001	*So You Want to be President?*, David Small
2002	*The Three Pigs*, David Wiesner
2003	*My Friend Rabbit*, Eric Rohmann
2004	*The Man Who Walked Between the Towers*, Mordicai Gerstein
2005	*Kitten's First Full Moon*, Kevin Henkes
2006	*The Hello, Goodbye Window*, Chris Raschka
2007	*Flotsam*, David Wiesner
2008	*The Invention of Hugo Cabret*, Brian Selznick
2009	*The House in the Night*, Beth Krommes
2010	*The Lion & the Mouse*, Jerry Pinkney
2011	*A Sick Day for Amos McGee*, Erin E. Stead
2012	*A Ball for Daisy*, Chris Raschka
2013	*This Is Not My Hat*, Jon Klassen
2014	*Locomotive*, Brian Floca
2015	*The Adventures of Beekle: The Unimaginary Friend*, Dan Santat

National Book Awards, 1950-2014

The National Book Awards (known as American Book Awards 1980-86) are administered by the National Book Foundation and have been given annually since 1950. The prizes, each valued at $10,000, are awarded to U.S. citizens for works published in the U.S. In some years, multiple awards were given for nonfiction in various categories; in such cases, the history and biography (if any) or biography winner is listed. Selected additional awards in nonfiction are listed in footnotes.

Other National Book Awards, 2014: Poetry: Louise Glück, *Faithful and Virtuous Night*. Young People's Literature: Jacqueline Woodson, *Brown Girl Dreaming*. Distinguished Contribution to American Letters: Ursula K. Le Guin. Literarian Award: Kyle Zimmer.

Fiction

Year	Author, book
1950	Nelson Algren, *The Man With the Golden Arm*
1951	William Faulkner, *The Collected Stories*
1952	James Jones, *From Here to Eternity*
1953	Ralph Ellison, *Invisible Man*
1954	Saul Bellow, *The Adventures of Augie March*
1955	William Faulkner, *A Fable*
1956	John O'Hara, *Ten North Frederick*
1957	Wright Morris, *The Field of Vision*
1958	John Cheever, *The Wapshot Chronicle*
1959	Bernard Malamud, *The Magic Barrel*
1960	Philip Roth, *Goodbye, Columbus*
1961	Conrad Richter, *The Waters of Kronos*
1962	Walker Percy, *The Moviegoer*
1963	J. F. Powers, *Morte d'Urban*
1964	John Updike, *The Centaur*
1965	Saul Bellow, *Herzog*
1966	Katherine Anne Porter, *The Collected Stories*
1967	Bernard Malamud, *The Fixer*
1968	Thornton Wilder, *The Eighth Day*
1969	Jerzy Kosinski, *Steps*
1970	Joyce Carol Oates, *Them*
1971	Saul Bellow, *Mr. Sammler's Planet*
1972	Flannery O'Connor, *The Complete Stories*
1973	John Barth, *Chimera*
1974	Thomas Pynchon, *Gravity's Rainbow*
1974	Isaac Bashevis Singer, *A Crown of Feathers*
1975	Robert Stone, *Dog Soldiers*
1976	William Gaddis, *JR*
1977	Wallace Stegner, *The Spectator Bird*
1978	Mary Lee Settle, *Blood Ties*
1979	Tim O'Brien, *Going After Cacciato*
1980	William Styron, *Sophie's Choice*
1981	Wright Morris, *Plains Song*
1982	John Updike, *Rabbit Is Rich*
1983	Alice Walker, *The Color Purple*
1984	Ellen Gilchrist, *Victory Over Japan*
1985	Don DeLillo, *White Noise*
1986	E. L. Doctorow, *World's Fair*
1987	Larry Heinemann, *Paco's Story*
1988	Pete Dexter, *Paris Trout*
1989	John Casey, *Spartina*
1990	Charles Johnson, *Middle Passage*
1991	Norman Rush, *Mating*
1992	Cormac McCarthy, *All the Pretty Horses*
1993	E. Annie Proulx, *The Shipping News*
1994	William Gaddis, *A Frolic of His Own*
1995	Philip Roth, *Sabbath's Theater*
1996	Andrea Barrett, *Ship Fever and Other Stories*
1997	Charles Frazier, *Cold Mountain*
1998	Alice McDermott, *Charming Billy*
1999	Ha Jin, *Waiting*
2000	Susan Sontag, *In America*
2001	Jonathan Franzen, *The Corrections*
2002	Julia Glass, *Three Junes*
2003	Shirley Hazzard, *The Great Fire*
2004	Lily Tuck, *The News From Paraguay*
2005	William T. Vollmann, *Europe Central*
2006	Richard Powers, *The Echo Maker*
2007	Denis Johnson, *Tree of Smoke*
2008	Peter Matthiessen, *Shadow Country*
2009	Colum McCann, *Let the Great World Spin*
2010	Jaimy Gordon, *Lord of Misrule*
2011	Jesmyn Ward, *Salvage the Bones*
2012	Louise Erdrich, *The Round House*
2013	James McBride, *The Good Lord Bird*
2014	Phil Klay, *Redeployment*

Nonfiction

Year	Author, book
1950	Ralph L. Rusk, *Ralph Waldo Emerson*
1951	Newton Arvin, *Herman Melville*
1952	Rachel Carson, *The Sea Around Us*
1953	Bernard A. De Voto, *The Course of an Empire*
1954	Bruce Catton, *A Stillness at Appomattox*
1955	Joseph Wood Krutch, *The Measure of Man*
1956	Herbert Kubly, *An American in Italy*
1957	George F. Kennan, *Russia Leaves the War*
1958	Catherine Drinker Bowen, *The Lion and the Throne*
1959	J. Christopher Herold, *Mistress to an Age: A Life of Madame De Stael*
1960	Richard Ellman, *James Joyce*
1961	William L. Shirer, *The Rise and Fall of the Third Reich*
1962	Lewis Mumford, *The City in History: Its Origins, Its Transformations, and Its Prospects*
1963	Leon Edel, *Henry James, Vol. II: The Conquest of London* and *Vol. III: The Middle Years*
1964	William H. McNeill, *The Rise of the West: A History of the Human Community*
1965	Louis Fisher, *The Life of Lenin*
1966	Arthur M. Schlesinger Jr., *A Thousand Days: John F. Kennedy in the White House*
1967	Peter Gay, *The Enlightenment, An Interpretation, Vol. I: The Rise of Modern Paganism*
1968	George F. Kennan, *Memoirs: 1925-1950*[1]
1969	Winthrop D. Jordan, *White Over Black: American Attitudes Toward the Negro, 1550-1812*[2]
1970	T. Harry Williams, *Huey Long*[3]
1971	James MacGregor Burns, *Roosevelt: The Soldier of Freedom*
1972	Joseph P. Lash, *Eleanor and Franklin: The Story of Their Relationship, Based on Eleanor Roosevelt's Private Papers*
1973	James Thomas Flexner, *George Washington, Vol. IV: Anguish and Farewell, 1793-1799*[4]
1974	John Clive, *Macaulay, The Shaping of the Historian*; Douglas Day, *Malcolm Lowry: A Biography*[5]
1975	Richard B. Sewall, *The Life of Emily Dickinson*[6]
1976	David Brion Davis, *The Problem of Slavery in the Age of Revolution, 1770-1823*
1977	W. A. Swanberg, *Norman Thomas: The Last Idealist*[7]
1978	W. Jackson Bate, *Samuel Johnson*
1979	Arthur M. Schlesinger Jr., *Robert Kennedy and His Times*
1980	Tom Wolfe, *The Right Stuff*
1981	Maxine Hong Kingston, *China Men*
1982	Tracy Kidder, *The Soul of a New Machine*
1983	Fox Butterfield, *China: Alive in the Bitter Sea*
1984	Robert V. Remini, *Andrew Jackson and the Course of American Democracy, 1833-1845*
1985	J. Anthony Lukas, *Common Ground: A Turbulent Decade in the Lives of Three American Families*
1986	Barry Lopez, *Arctic Dreams*
1987	Richard Rhodes, *The Making of the Atom Bomb*
1988	Neil Sheehan, *A Bright Shining Lie: John Paul Vann and America in Vietnam*
1989	Thomas L. Friedman, *From Beirut to Jerusalem*
1990	Ron Chernow, *The House of Morgan: An American Banking Dynasty and the Rise of Modern Finance*
1991	Orlando Patterson, *Freedom*
1992	Paul Monette, *Becoming a Man: Half a Life Story*
1993	Gore Vidal, *United States: Essays 1952-1992*
1994	Sherwin B. Nuland, *How We Die: Reflections on Life's Final Chapter*
1995	Tina Rosenberg, *The Haunted Land: Facing Europe's Ghosts After Communism*
1996	James Carroll, *An American Requiem: God, My Father, and the War That Came Between Us*
1997	Joseph J. Ellis, *American Sphinx: The Character of Thomas Jefferson*
1998	Edward Ball, *Slaves in the Family*
1999	John W. Dower, *Embracing Defeat: Japan in the Wake of World War II*
2000	Nathaniel Philbrick, *In the Heart of the Sea: The Tragedy of the Whaleship Essex*

Year	Author, book
2001	Andrew Solomon, *The Noonday Demon: An Atlas of Depression*
2002	Robert A. Caro, *Master of the Senate: The Years of Lyndon Johnson*
2003	Carlos Eire, *Waiting for Snow in Havana: Confessions of a Cuban Boy*
2004	Kevin Boyle, *Arc of Justice: A Saga of Race, Civil Rights, and Murder in the Jazz Age*
2005	Joan Didion, *The Year of Magical Thinking*
2006	Timothy Egan, *The Worst Hard Time: The Untold Story of Those Who Survived the Great American Dust Bowl*
2007	Tim Weiner, *Legacy of Ashes: The History of the CIA*
2008	Annette Gordon-Reed, *The Hemingses of Monticello: An American Family*
2009	T. J. Stiles, *The First Tycoon: The Epic Life of Cornelius Vanderbilt*
2010	Patti Smith, *Just Kids*
2011	Stephen Greenblatt, *The Swerve: How the World Became Modern*
2012	Katherine Boo, *Behind the Beautiful Forevers: Life, Death, and Hope in a Mumbai Undercity*
2013	George Packer, *The Unwinding: An Inner History of the New America*
2014	Evan Osnos, *Age of Ambition: Chasing Fortune, Truth, and Faith in the New China*

(1) Science, Philosophy, & Religion: Jonathan Kozol, *Death at an Early Age*. (2) Arts & Letters: Norman Mailer, *The Armies of the Night: History as a Novel, the Novel as History*. (3) Arts & Letters: Lillian Hellman, *An Unfinished Woman: A Memoir*. (4) Contemp. Affairs: Frances FitzGerald, *Fire in the Lake: The Vietnamese and the Americans in Vietnam*. (5) Arts & Letters: Pauline Kael, *Deeper Into the Movies*. (6) Arts & Letters: Roger Shattuck, *Marcel Proust*; Lewis Thomas, *The Lives of a Cell: Notes of a Biology Watcher*. (7) Contemp. Thought: Bruno Bettelheim, *The Uses of Enchantment: The Meaning and Importance of Fairy Tales*.

Journalism Awards, 2015

National Magazine Awards, by American Society of Magazine Editors and Columbia Univ. Graduate School of Journalism. Magazine of the Year: *Vogue*. General Excellence: Active Interest, *Men's Health*; General Interest, *The New Yorker*; Literature/Science/Politics, *Nautilus*; Service/Lifestyle, *Glamour*; Special Interest, *The Hollywood Reporter*; Style/Design, *Garden & Gun*. Columns and Commentary: *New York*. Design: *New York*. Essays and Criticism: *The New Yorker*. Feature Photography: *Time*. Feature Writing: *The Atavist*. Fiction: *The New Yorker*. Leisure Interests: *Backpacker*. Magazine Section: *New York*. Multimedia: *The Texas Observer* in partnership with *Guardian US*. Personal Service: *O, The Oprah Magazine*. Photography: *National Geographic*. Public Interest: *Pacific Standard*. Reporting: *GQ*. Single-Topic Issue: *San Francisco*. Tablet Magazine: *National Geographic*. Video: *Vice News*. Website: *Nautilus*.

George Foster Peabody Awards, by Univ. of Georgia, awarded to the best in electronic media. Afropop Worldwide. David Attenborough. *Ebola*, BBC World Service. *Adventure Time*, Cartoon Network. *Black Mirror*, *Children on the Frontline*, Channel 4. *The Knick*, Cinemax. *CNN Investigative Reports: Crisis at the VA*, *Coverage of Kidnapped Nigerian Schoolgirls*, CNN. *Inside Amy Schumer*, Comedy Central. *Jane the Virgin*, The CW. *Doc McStuffins*, Disney Junior. *The Americans*, *Fargo*, FX. *Last Week Tonight With John Oliver*, *Mr. Dynamite: The Rise of James Brown*, *The Newburgh Sting*, HBO. *Human Harvest: China's Illegal Organ Trade*, International Syndication. *The Cost of Troubled Minds*, KVUE-TV. *Betrayed by Silence*, MPR News. *Cosmos: A SpaceTime Odyssey*, National Geographic Channel and Fox. *ISIS—Continuing Coverage*, NBC/MSNBC. *Virunga*, Netflix. "Gangs, Murder, and Migration in Honduras," *Latino USA*; *Reporting From the Frontlines: The Ebola Outbreak*; NPR. *State of the Re:Union*, NPR, PRX. "Freedom Summer," *American Experience*; "United States of Secrets," *Frontline*; "Brakeless," *Independent Lens*; "American Revolutionary: The Evolution of Grace Lee Boggs," *POV*; PBS. *Soft Vengeance: Albie Sachs and the New South Africa*, SABC 2, DSTV/GOTV. *Under the Radar*, Scripps Washington Bureau. *Serial*, SerialPodcast.org. *The Honorable Woman*, *Rectify*, SundanceTV. *Entre el Abandono y el Rechazo* (*Between Abandonment and Rejection*), Univision. *The Islamic State*, *Last Chance High*, Vice News. *Chris Christie, White House Ambitions, and the Abuse of Power*, WNYC Radio. "60 Words," *Radiolab*, WNYC, and Gregory Johnsen, Buzzfeed.

Scripps Howard Awards, by Scripps Howard Foundation. Breaking News: *St. Louis Post-Dispatch*. Business/Economics Reporting: Rita Price and Ben Sutherly, *Columbus Dispatch*. Commentary: Stephen Henderson, *Detroit Free Press*. Community Journalism: Rob Kuznia, Rebecca Kimitch, and Frank Suraci, *Daily Breeze* (Torrance, CA). Distinguished Service to the First Amendment: Carol Rosenberg, *Miami Herald*. Editorial Writing: Kathleen Kingsbury, *Boston Globe*. Environmental Reporting: Paul Rogers and Lisa M. Krieger, *San Jose Mercury News*. Human Interest Storytelling: David Abel, *Boston Globe*. Investigative Reporting: *Arizona Republic*. Digital Innovation: *Wall Street Journal*. Photojournalism: Daniel Berehulak, *NY Times*. Public Service Reporting: *NY Times*. Radio In-Depth Coverage: Chicago Public Media. TV/Cable In-Depth Local Coverage: Vicky Nguyen, Kevin Nious, David Paredes, Felipe Escamilla, Jeremy Carroll, Mark Villarreal, and Julie Putnam, KNTV-TV (San Jose, CA). TV/Cable In-Depth Natl. and Intl. Coverage: Holly Williams, *CBS Evening News*.

Miscellaneous Book Awards, 2015

Bollingen Prize for American Poetry, by the Yale Univ. Library, $150,000 (biennial): Nathaniel Mackey.

Coretta Scott King Awards, by American Library Assn., for African American authors and illustrators of outstanding books for children and young adults. Author: Jacqueline Woodson, *Brown Girl Dreaming*. Illustrator: Christopher Myers, *Firebird*. New talent: Jason Reynolds, *When I Was the Greatest*.

Costa Book Awards. Book of the Year (formerly Whitbread Award): *H is for Hawk*, Helen Macdonald.

Edgar Awards, by the Mystery Writers of America. Novel: *Mr. Mercedes*, Stephen King. First Novel: *Dry Bones in the Valley*, Tom Bouman. Paperback Original: *The Secret History of Las Vegas*, Chris Abani. Fact Crime: *Tinseltown: Murder, Morphine, and Madness at the Dawn of Hollywood*, William J. Mann. Critical/Biographical: *Poe-Land: The Hallowed Haunts of Edgar Allan Poe*, J. W. Ocker. Short Story: "What Do You Do?" Gillian Flynn, *Rogues*. Juvenile: *Greenglass House*, Kate Milford. Young Adult: *The Art of Secrets*, James Klise. TV Episode: "Episode 1," *Happy Valley* (Netflix), Sally Wainwright. Robert L. Fish Award: "Getaway Girl," Zoë Z. Dean, *Ellery Queen Mystery Magazine*. Grand Master: Lois Duncan, James Ellroy. Raven Award: Ruth and Jon Jordan, *Crimespree Magazine*; Kathryn Kennison, Magna Cum Murder. Ellery Queen Award: Charles Ardai, *Hard Case Crime*. Simon & Schuster-Mary Higgins Clark Award: *The Stranger You Know*, Jane Casey.

Golden Kite Awards, by the Society of Children's Book Writers and Illustrators. Fiction: *Revolution*, Deborah Wiles. Nonfiction: *The Family Romanov*, Candace Fleming. Picture Book Text: *A Dance Like Starlight: One Ballerina's Dream*, Kristy Dempsey. Picture Book Illustration: *The Right Word: Roget and His Thesaurus*, Melissa Sweet.

Hugo Awards, by the World Science Fiction Society (WSFS). Novel: *The Three Body Problem*, Cixin Liu (trans. by Ken Liu). Novelette: "The Day the World Turned Upside Down," Thomas Olde Heuvelt (trans. by Lia Belt). Graphic Story: *Ms. Marvel Volume 1: No Normal*, G. Willow Wilson, illus. by Adrian Alphona and Jake Wyatt. Dramatic Presentation, long form: *Guardians of the Galaxy*. Dramatic Presentation, short form: "By Means Which Have Never Yet Been Tried," *Orphan Black*, BBC America. (No award given in five standard categories.)

Lincoln Prize, by Gettysburg College and the Gilder Lehrman Inst. of American History, $50,000: Harold Holzer, *Lincoln and the Power of the Press: The War for Public Opinion*.

National Book Critics Circle Awards. Fiction: Marilynne Robinson, *Lila*. Nonfiction: David Brion Davis, *The Problem of Slavery in the Age of Emancipation*. Autobiography: Roz Chast, *Can't We Talk About Something More Pleasant?* Biography: John Lahr, *Tennessee Williams: Mad Pilgrimage of the Flesh*. Criticism: Ellen Willis, *The Essential Ellen Willis*. Poetry: Claudia Rankine, *Citizen: An American Lyric*. John Leonard Prize: Phil Klay, *Redeployment*. Ivan Sandrof Lifetime Achievement Award: Toni Morrison. Nona Balakian Citation for Excellence in Reviewing: Alexandra Schwartz.

Nebula Awards, by the Science Fiction and Fantasy Writers of America. Novel: *Annihilation*, Jeff VanderMeer. Novella: *Yesterday's Kin*, Nancy Kress. Novelette: "A Guide to the Fruits of Hawai'i," Alaya Dawn Johnson. Short Story: "Jackalope Wives," Ursula Vernon. Ray Bradbury Award: *Guardians of the Galaxy*. Andre Norton Award: *Love Is the Drug*, Alaya Dawn Johnson. Damon Knight Grand Master Award: Larry Niven.

PEN/Faulkner Award, for fiction, $15,000: Atticus Lish, *Preparation for the Next Life*.

Spingarn Medal, 1915-2015

The Spingarn Medal has been awarded annually in most years since 1915 by the National Assn. for the Advancement of Colored People for outstanding achievement by an African American.

1915	Ernest E. Just
1916	Charles Young
1917	Harry T. Burleigh
1918	William S. Braithwaite
1919	Archibald H. Grimké
1920	W. E. B. Du Bois
1921	Charles S. Gilpin
1922	Mary B. Talbert
1923	George W. Carver
1924	Roland Hayes
1925	James W. Johnson
1926	Carter G. Woodson
1927	Anthony Overton
1928	Charles W. Chesnutt
1929	Mordecai W. Johnson
1930	Henry A. Hunt
1931	Richard B. Harrison
1932	Robert R. Moton
1933	Max Yergan
1934	William T. B. Williams
1935	Mary McLeod Bethune
1936	John Hope
1937	Walter White
1939	Marian Anderson
1940	Louis T. Wright
1941	Richard Wright
1942	A. Philip Randolph
1943	William H. Hastie
1944	Charles Drew
1945	Paul Robeson
1946	Thurgood Marshall
1947	Dr. Percy L. Julian
1948	Channing H. Tobias
1949	Ralph J. Bunche
1950	Charles H. Houston
1951	Mabel K. Staupers
1952	Harry T. Moore
1953	Paul R. Williams
1954	Theodore K. Lawless
1955	Carl Murphy
1956	Jack R. Robinson
1957	Martin Luther King Jr.
1958	Daisy Bates and the Little Rock Nine
1959	Duke Ellington
1960	Langston Hughes
1961	Kenneth B. Clark
1962	Robert C. Weaver
1963	Medgar W. Evers
1964	Roy Wilkins
1965	Leontyne Price
1966	John H. Johnson
1967	Edward W. Brooke
1968	Sammy Davis Jr.
1969	Clarence M. Mitchell Jr.
1970	Jacob Lawrence
1971	Leon H. Sullivan
1972	Gordon Parks
1973	Wilson C. Riles
1974	Damon Keith
1976	Henry (Hank) Aaron
1977	Alvin Ailey
1977	Alex Haley
1979	Andrew Young
1979	Rosa L. Parks
1980	Dr. Rayford W. Logan
1981	Coleman Young
1982	Dr. Benjamin E. Mays
1983	Lena Horne
1985	Thomas Bradley
1985	Bill Cosby
1986	Dr. Benjamin L. Hooks
1987	Percy E. Sutton
1988	Frederick D. Patterson
1989	Jesse Jackson
1990	L. Douglas Wilder
1991	Gen. Colin L. Powell
1992	Barbara Jordan
1993	Dorothy I. Height
1994	Maya Angelou
1995	John Hope Franklin
1996	A. Leon Higginbotham Jr.
1997	Carl T. Rowan
1998	Myrlie Evers-Williams
1999	Earl G. Graves Sr.
2000	Oprah Winfrey
2001	Vernon E. Jordan Jr.
2002	John Lewis
2003	Constance Baker Motley
2004	Robert L. Carter
2005	Oliver W. Hill
2006	Dr. Benjamin S. Carson
2007	John Conyers Jr.
2008	Ruby Dee
2009	Julian Bond
2010	Cicely Tyson
2011	Frankie Muse Freeman
2012	Harry Belafonte
2013	Jessye Norman
2014	Quincy Jones
2015	Sidney Poitier

Miss America Winners, 1921-2016

Year	Winner, hometown
1921	Margaret Gorman, Washington, DC
1922-23	Mary Campbell, Columbus, Ohio
1924	Ruth Malcolmson, Philadelphia, Pennsylvania
1925	Fay Lamphier, Oakland, California
1926	Norma Smallwood, Tulsa, Oklahoma
1927	Lois Delander, Joliet, Illinois
1933	Marion Bergeron, West Haven, Connecticut
1935	Henrietta Leaver, Pittsburgh, Pennsylvania
1936	Rose Coyle, Philadelphia, Pennsylvania
1937	Bette Cooper, Bertrand Island, New Jersey
1938	Marilyn Meseke, Marion, Ohio
1939	Patricia Donnelly, Detroit, Michigan
1940	Frances Marie Burke, Philadelphia, Pennsylvania
1941	Rosemary LaPlanche, Los Angeles, California
1942	Jo-Caroll Dennison, Tyler, Texas
1943	Jean Bartel, Los Angeles, California
1944	Venus Ramey, Washington, DC
1945	Bess Myerson, New York, New York
1946	Marilyn Buferd, Los Angeles, California
1947	Barbara Walker, Memphis, Tennessee
1948	BeBe Shopp, Hopkins, Minnesota
1949	Jacque Mercer, Litchfield, Arizona
1951	Yolande Betbeze, Mobile, Alabama
1952	Coleen Kay Hutchins, Salt Lake City, Utah
1953	Neva Jane Langley, Macon, Georgia
1954	Evelyn Margaret Ay, Ephrata, Pennsylvania
1955	Lee Meriwether, San Francisco, California
1956	Sharon Ritchie, Denver, Colorado
1957	Marian McKnight, Manning, South Carolina
1958	Marilyn Van Derbur, Denver, Colorado
1959	Mary Ann Mobley, Brandon, Mississippi
1960	Lynda Lee Mead, Natchez, Mississippi
1961	Nancy Fleming, Montague, Michigan
1962	Maria Fletcher, Asheville, North Carolina
1963	Jacquelyn Mayer, Sandusky, Ohio
1964	Donna Axum, El Dorado, Arkansas
1965	Vonda Kay Van Dyke, Phoenix, Arizona
1966	Deborah Irene Bryant, Overland Park, Kansas
1967	Jane Anne Jayroe, Laverne, Oklahoma
1968	Debra Dene Barnes, Moran, Kansas
1969	Judith Anne Ford, Belvidere, Illinois
1970	Pamela Anne Eldred, Birmingham, Michigan
1971	Phyllis Ann George, Denton, Texas
1972	Laurie Lea Schaefer, Bexley, Ohio
1973	Terry Anne Meeuwsen, DePere, Wisconsin
1974	Rebecca Ann King, Denver, Colorado
1975	Shirley Cothran, Denton, Texas
1976	Tawney Elaine Godin, Saratoga Springs, New York
1977	Dorothy Kathleen Benham, Edina, Minnesota
1978	Susan Perkins, Columbus, Ohio
1979	Kylene Barker, Roanoke, Virginia
1980	Cheryl Prewitt, Ackerman, Mississippi
1981	Susan Powell, Elk City, Oklahoma
1982	Elizabeth Ward, Russellville, Arkansas
1983	Debra Maffett, Anaheim, California
1984[1]	Suzette Charles, Mays Landing, New Jersey
1985	Sharlene Wells, Salt Lake City, Utah
1986	Susan Akin, Meridian, Mississippi
1987	Kellye Cash, Memphis, Tennessee
1988	Kaye Lani Rae Rafko, Monroe, Michigan
1989	Gretchen Carlson, Anoka, Minnesota
1990	Debbye Turner, Columbia, Missouri
1991	Marjorie Vincent, Oak Park, Illinois
1992	Carolyn Suzanne Sapp, Honolulu, Hawaii
1993	Leanza Cornett, Jacksonville, Florida
1994	Kimberly Aiken, Columbia, South Carolina
1995	Heather Whitestone, Birmingham, Alabama
1996	Shawntel Smith, Muldrow, Oklahoma
1997	Tara Dawn Holland, Overland Park, Kansas
1998	Kate Shindle, Evanston, Illinois
1999	Nicole Johnson, Roanoke, Virginia
2000	Heather Renee French, Maysville, Kentucky
2001	Angela Perez Baraquio, Honolulu, Hawaii
2002	Katie Harman, Gresham, Oregon
2003	Erika Harold, Urbana, Illinois
2004	Ericka Dunlap, Orlando, Florida
2005	Deidre Downs, Birmingham, Alabama
2006	Jennifer Berry, Tulsa, Oklahoma
2007	Lauren Nelson, Lawton, Oklahoma
2008	Kirsten Haglund, Farmington Hills, Michigan
2009	Katie Stam, Seymour, Indiana
2010	Caressa Cameron, Fredricksburg, Virginia
2011	Teresa Scanlan, Gering, Nebraska
2012	Laura Kaeppeler, Kenosha, Wisconsin
2013	Mallory Hytes Hagen, Brooklyn, New York
2014	Nina Davuluri, Syracuse, New York
2015	Kira Kazantsev, New York, New York
2016	Betty Cantrell, Warner Robins, Georgia

Note: Since the 1950 pageant, winners have been crowned Miss America of the following year (e.g., Miss America 1951 competed in 1950). (1) Miss New York, Vanessa Williams, resigned July 23, 1984.

Entertainment Awards

Selected Tony (Antoinette Perry) Awards, 2015

Play: *The Curious Incident of the Dog in the Night-Time*, Simon Stephens
Musical: *Fun Home*
Book of a musical: *Fun Home*, Lisa Kron
Original score: *Fun Home*, Jeanine Tesori and Lisa Kron
Play revival: *Skylight*
Musical revival: *The King and I*
Actor, play: Alex Sharp, *The Curious Incident of the Dog in the Night-Time*
Actress, play: Helen Mirren, *The Audience*
Actor, musical: Michael Cerveris, *Fun Home*
Actress, musical: Kelli O'Hara, *The King and I*
Featured actor, play: Richard McCabe, *The Audience*
Featured actress, play: Annaleigh Ashford, *You Can't Take It With You*
Featured actor, musical: Christian Borle, *Something Rotten!*
Featured actress, musical: Ruthie Ann Miles, *The King and I*
Direction, play: Marianne Elliott, *The Curious Incident of the Dog in the Night-Time*
Direction, musical: Sam Gold, *Fun Home*
Choreography: Christopher Wheeldon, *An American in Paris*
Orchestrations: Christopher Austin, Don Sebesky, Bill Elliott, *An American in Paris*
Scenic design, play: Bunny Christie and Finn Ross, *The Curious Incident of the Dog in the Night-Time*
Scenic design, musical: Bob Crowley and 59 Productions, *An American in Paris*
Costume design, play: Christopher Oram, *Wolf Hall Parts One & Two*
Costume design, musical: Catherine Zuber, *The King and I*
Regional theatre: Cleveland Play House, Cleveland, OH
Special Tony Award: John Cameron Mitchell
Special Tony Award, lifetime achievement: Tommy Tune
Isabelle Stevenson Award: Stephen Schwartz
Tony Honors for Excellence in the Theatre: Arnold Abramson, Adrian Bryan-Brown, Gene O'Donovan

Tony Awards, 1948-2015

Year	Play	Musical
1948	*Mister Roberts*	No award
1949	*Death of a Salesman*	*Kiss Me Kate*
1950	*The Cocktail Party*	*South Pacific*
1951	*The Rose Tattoo*	*Guys and Dolls*
1952	*The Fourposter*	*The King and I*
1953	*The Crucible*	*Wonderful Town*
1954	*The Teahouse of the August Moon*	*Kismet*
1955	*The Desperate Hours*	*The Pajama Game*
1956	*The Diary of Anne Frank*	*Damn Yankees*
1957	*Long Day's Journey Into Night*	*My Fair Lady*
1958	*Sunrise at Campobello*	*The Music Man*
1959	*J.B.*	*Redhead*
1960	*The Miracle Worker*	*Fiorello!* and *The Sound of Music*
1961	*Becket*	*Bye, Bye Birdie*
1962	*A Man for All Seasons*	*How to Succeed in Business Without Really Trying*
1963	*Who's Afraid of Virginia Woolf?*	*A Funny Thing Happened on the Way to the Forum*
1964	*Luther*	*Hello, Dolly!*
1965	*The Subject Was Roses*	*Fiddler on the Roof*
1966	*Marat/Sade*	*Man of La Mancha*
1967	*The Homecoming*	*Cabaret*
1968	*Rosencrantz and Guildenstern Are Dead*	*Hallelujah, Baby!*
1969	*The Great White Hope*	*1776*
1970	*Borstal Boy*	*Applause*
1971	*Sleuth*	*Company*
1972	*Sticks and Bones*	*Two Gentlemen of Verona*
1973	*That Championship Season*	*A Little Night Music*
1974	*The River Niger*	*Raisin*
1975	*Equus*	*The Wiz*
1976	*Travesties*	*A Chorus Line*
1977	*The Shadow Box*	*Annie*
1978	*Da*	*Ain't Misbehavin'*
1979	*The Elephant Man*	*Sweeney Todd*
1980	*Children of a Lesser God*	*Evita*
1981	*Amadeus*	*42nd Street*
1982	*The Life and Adventures of Nicholas Nickelby*	*Nine*
1983	*Torch Song Trilogy*	*Cats*
1984	*The Real Thing*	*La Cage aux Folles*
1985	*Biloxi Blues*	*Big River*
1986	*I'm Not Rappaport*	*The Mystery of Edwin Drood*
1987	*Fences*	*Les Miserables*
1988	*M. Butterfly*	*Phantom of the Opera*
1989	*The Heidi Chronicles*	*Jerome Robbins' Broadway*
1990	*The Grapes of Wrath*	*City of Angels*
1991	*Lost in Yonkers*	*The Will Rogers Follies*
1992	*Dancing at Lughnasa*	*Crazy for You*
1993	*Angels in America: Millennium Approaches*	*Kiss of the Spider Woman*
1994	*Angels in America: Perestroika*	*Passion*
1995	*Love! Valour! Compassion!*	*Sunset Boulevard*
1996	*Master Class*	*Rent*
1997	*The Last Night of Ballyhoo*	*Titanic*
1998	*Art*	*The Lion King*
1999	*Side Man*	*Fosse*
2000	*Copenhagen*	*Contact*
2001	*Proof*	*The Producers*
2002	*Edward Albee's The Goat or Who Is Sylvia?*	*Thoroughly Modern Millie*
2003	*Take Me Out*	*Hairspray*
2004	*I Am My Own Wife*	*Avenue Q*
2005	*Doubt*	*Monty Python's Spamalot*
2006	*The History Boys*	*Jersey Boys*
2007	*The Coast of Utopia*	*Spring Awakening*
2008	*August: Osage County*	*In the Heights*
2009	*God of Carnage*	*Billy Elliot, The Musical*
2010	*Red*	*Memphis*
2011	*War Horse*	*The Book of Mormon*
2012	*Clybourne Park*	*Once*
2013	*Vanya and Sonia and Masha and Spike*	*Kinky Boots*
2014	*All the Way*	*A Gentleman's Guide to Love & Murder*
2015	*The Curious Incident of the Dog in the Night-Time*	*Fun Home*

Selected Daytime Emmy Awards, 2015

Drama: *Days of Our Lives*, NBC, and *The Young and the Restless*, CBS
Game show: *Jeopardy!*, synd.
Culinary show: *Barefoot Contessa: Back to Basics*, Food Network
Entertainment news show: *Entertainment Tonight*, CBS
Morning show: *CBS Sunday Morning*, CBS
Morning show, Spanish language: *Un Nuevo Día*, Telemundo
Talk show, entertainment: *The Ellen DeGeneres Show*, synd.
Talk show, informative: *Steve Harvey*, synd.
Lead actress: Maura West, *General Hospital*, ABC
Lead actor: Anthony Geary, *General Hospital*, ABC
Game show host: Craig Ferguson, *Celebrity Name Game*, synd.
Talk show host, informative: Mario Batali, Carla Hall, Clinton Kelly, Daphne Oz, Michael Symon, *The Chew*, ABC

Selected Prime-Time Emmy Awards, 2015

Drama series: *Game of Thrones*, HBO
Comedy series: *Veep*, HBO
Limited series: *Olive Kitteridge*, HBO
Variety series: *The Daily Show With Jon Stewart*, Comedy Central
Variety sketch series: *Inside Amy Schumer*, Comedy Central
Lead actor, drama: John Hamm, *Mad Men*, AMC
Lead actress, drama: Viola Davis, *How to Get Away With Murder*, ABC
Lead actor, comedy: Jeffrey Tambor, *Transparent*, Amazon
Lead actress, comedy: Julia Louis-Dreyfus, *Veep*, HBO
Lead actor, limited series: Richard Jenkins, *Olive Kitteridge*, HBO
Lead actress, limited series: Frances McDormand, *Olive Kitteridge*, HBO
Sup. actor, drama: Peter Dinklage, *Game of Thrones*, HBO
Sup. actress, drama: Uzo Aduba, *Orange Is the New Black*, Netflix
Sup. actor, comedy: Tony Hale, *Veep*, HBO
Sup. actress, comedy: Allison Janney, *Mom*, CBS
Sup. actor, limited series: Bill Murray, *Olive Kitteridge*, HBO
Sup. actress, limited series: Regina King, *American Crime*, ABC
Reality-competition program: *The Voice*, NBC

Prime-Time Emmy Awards, 1952-2015

The Academy of Television Arts and Sciences presented the first Emmy Awards in 1949. Through the years, award categories have changed, but since 1952, the Academy has given out an outstanding comedy and drama award annually.

Year	Comedy	Drama
1952	*Red Skelton Show*, NBC	*Studio One*, CBS
1953	*I Love Lucy*, CBS	*Robert Montgomery Presents*, NBC
1954	*I Love Lucy*, CBS	*The U.S. Steel Hour*, ABC
1955	*Make Room for Daddy*, ABC	*The U.S. Steel Hour*, ABC
1956	*Phil Silvers Show*, CBS	*Producers' Showcase*, NBC
1957	*Phil Silvers Show*, CBS	"Requiem for a Heavyweight," CBS[1]
1958	*Phil Silvers Show*, CBS	*Gunsmoke*, CBS
1959[2]	*Jack Benny Show*, CBS	2 awards[3]
1960	*Art Carney Special*, NBC	*Playhouse 90*, CBS
1961	*Jack Benny Show*, CBS	*Hallmark Hall of Fame: Macbeth*, NBC
1962	*Bob Newhart Show*, CBS	*The Defenders*, CBS
1963	*Dick Van Dyke Show*, CBS	*The Defenders*, CBS
1964	*Dick Van Dyke Show*, CBS	*The Defenders*, CBS
1965	*Dick Van Dyke Show*, CBS	*Hallmark Hall of Fame: The Magnificent Yankee*, NBC
1966	*Dick Van Dyke Show*, CBS	*The Fugitive*, ABC
1967	*The Monkees*, NBC	*Mission: Impossible*, CBS
1968	*Get Smart*, NBC	*Mission: Impossible*, CBS
1969	*Get Smart*, NBC	*NET Playhouse*, NET
1970	*My World and Welcome to It*, NBC	*Marcus Welby, M.D.*, ABC
1971	*All in the Family*, CBS	*The Bold Ones: The Senator*, NBC
1972	*All in the Family*, CBS	*Masterpiece Theatre: Elizabeth R*, PBS
1973	*All in the Family*, CBS	*The Waltons*, CBS
1974	*M*A*S*H*, CBS	*Masterpiece Theatre: Upstairs, Downstairs*; PBS
1975	*Mary Tyler Moore Show*, CBS	*Masterpiece Theatre: Upstairs, Downstairs*; PBS
1976	*Mary Tyler Moore Show*, CBS	*Police Story*, NBC
1977	*Mary Tyler Moore Show*, CBS	*Masterpiece Theatre: Upstairs, Downstairs*; PBS
1978	*All in the Family*, CBS	*The Rockford Files*, NBC
1979	*Taxi*, ABC	*Lou Grant*, CBS
1980	*Taxi*, ABC	*Lou Grant*, CBS
1981	*Taxi*, ABC	*Hill Street Blues*, NBC
1982	*Barney Miller*, ABC	*Hill Street Blues*, NBC
1983	*Cheers*, NBC	*Hill Street Blues*, NBC
1984	*Cheers*, NBC	*Hill Street Blues*, NBC
1985	*The Cosby Show*, NBC	*Cagney & Lacey*, CBS
1986	*Golden Girls*, NBC	*Cagney & Lacey*, CBS
1987	*Golden Girls*, NBC	*L.A. Law*, NBC
1988	*The Wonder Years*, ABC	*thirtysomething*, ABC
1989	*Cheers*, NBC	*L.A. Law*, NBC
1990	*Murphy Brown*, CBS	*L.A. Law*, NBC
1991	*Cheers*, NBC	*L.A. Law*, NBC
1992	*Murphy Brown*, CBS	*Northern Exposure*, CBS
1993	*Seinfeld*, NBC	*Picket Fences*, CBS
1994	*Frasier*, NBC	*Picket Fences*, CBS
1995	*Frasier*, NBC	*NYPD Blue*, ABC
1996	*Frasier*, NBC	*ER*, NBC
1997	*Frasier*, NBC	*Law & Order*, NBC
1998	*Frasier*, NBC	*The Practice*, ABC
1999	*Ally McBeal*, FOX	*The Practice*, ABC
2000	*Will & Grace*, NBC	*The West Wing*, NBC
2001	*Sex and the City*, HBO	*The West Wing*, NBC
2002	*Friends*, NBC	*The West Wing*, NBC
2003	*Everybody Loves Raymond*, CBS	*The West Wing*, NBC
2004	*Arrested Development*, FOX	*The Sopranos*, HBO
2005	*Everybody Loves Raymond*, CBS	*Lost*, ABC
2006	*The Office*, NBC	*24*, FOX
2007	*30 Rock*, NBC	*The Sopranos*, HBO
2008	*30 Rock*, NBC	*Mad Men*, AMC
2009	*30 Rock*, NBC	*Mad Men*, AMC
2010	*Modern Family*, ABC	*Mad Men*, AMC
2011	*Modern Family*, ABC	*Mad Men*, AMC
2012	*Modern Family*, ABC	*Homeland*, Showtime
2013	*Modern Family*, ABC	*Breaking Bad*, AMC
2014	*Modern Family*, ABC	*Breaking Bad*, AMC
2015	*Veep*, HBO	*Game of Thrones*, HBO

(1) Best single program of the year; shown on *Playhouse 90*, which was named best new series. (2) Beginning in 1959, Emmys were awarded for work in the season encompassing the previous and current year. (3) *Playhouse 90* (CBS) was best dramatic series of one hour or longer, *Alcoa-Goodyear Theatre* (NBC) of less than one hour.

Golden Globe Awards, 2015

The Hollywood Foreign Press Association (then the Hollywood Foreign Correspondents Association) presented its first awards for achievement in film in 1944; television was considered for the first time in 1955.

Film

Drama: *Boyhood*
Comedy/musical: *The Grand Budapest Hotel*
Actress, drama: Julianne Moore, *Still Alice*
Actor, drama: Eddie Redmayne, *The Theory of Everything*
Actress, comedy/musical: Amy Adams, *Big Eyes*
Actor, comedy/musical: Michael Keaton, *Birdman*
Supporting actress: Patricia Arquette, *Boyhood*
Supporting actor: J. K. Simmons, *Whiplash*
Director: Richard Linklater, *Boyhood*
Screenplay: Alejandro G. Iñárritu, Nicolás Giacobone, Alexander Dinelaris, and Armando Bo, *Birdman*
Animated film: *How to Train Your Dragon 2*
Foreign-language film: *Leviathan*, Russia
Original score: Jóhann Jóhannsson, *The Theory of Everything*
Original song: "Glory," *Selma*, words and music by John Legend and Common
Cecil B. DeMille Award: George Clooney

Television

Series, drama: *The Affair*, Showtime
Series, comedy/musical: *Transparent*, Amazon
Actress, drama: Ruth Wilson, *The Affair*, Showtime
Actor, drama: Kevin Spacey, *House of Cards*, Netflix
Actress, comedy/musical: Gina Rodriguez, *Jane the Virgin*, The CW
Actor, comedy/musical: Jeffrey Tambor, *Transparent*, Amazon
Miniseries or made-for-TV movie: *Fargo*, FX
Actress, miniseries/TV movie: Maggie Gyllenhaal, *The Honorable Woman*, Sundance
Actor, miniseries/TV movie: Billy Bob Thornton, *Fargo*, FX
Supporting actress: Joanne Froggatt, *Downton Abbey*, PBS
Supporting actor: Matt Bomer, *The Normal Heart*, HBO

Selected People's Choice Awards, 2015

The People's Choice Awards, sponsored by Procter & Gamble, were first presented in 1975. The nominees and awards were initially selected by a Gallup Poll. Since 2005, winners have been selected by Internet voting.

Film

Movie: *Maleficent*
Actor: Robert Downey Jr.
Actress: Jennifer Lawrence
Duo: Shailene Woodley and Theo James, *Divergent*
Comedy: *22 Jump Street*
Comedic actor: Adam Sandler
Comedic actress: Melissa McCarthy
Drama: *The Fault in Our Stars*
Dramatic actor: Robert Downey Jr.
Dramatic actress: Chloë Grace Moretz

Music

Album: *X*, Ed Sheeran
Song: "Shake It Off," Taylor Swift
Male artist: Ed Sheeran
Female artist: Taylor Swift
Group: Maroon 5

Television

Network comedy: *The Big Bang Theory*
Network drama: *Grey's Anatomy*
Cable comedy: *Melissa & Joey*
Cable drama: *Pretty Little Liars*
New comedy: *Jane the Virgin*
New drama: *The Flash*
Comedic actor: Chris Colfer, *Glee*
Comedic actress: Kaley Cuoco-Sweeting, *The Big Bang Theory*
Dramatic actor: Patrick Dempsey, *Grey's Anatomy*
Dramatic actress: Ellen Pompeo, *Grey's Anatomy*
Cable actor: Matt Bomer, *White Collar*
Cable actress: Angie Harmon, *Rizzoli & Isles*
Daytime host: Ellen DeGeneres
Late-night talk show host: Jimmy Fallon

Academy Awards (Oscars), 1927-2014

Year	Picture	Actor	Actress	Supporting actor[1]	Supporting actress[1]	Director
1927-28	*Wings*	Emil Jannings *The Way of All Flesh*	Janet Gaynor *Seventh Heaven*	NA	NA	Frank Borzage *Seventh Heaven*; Lewis Milestone *Two Arabian Knights*
1928-29	*Broadway Melody*	Warner Baxter *In Old Arizona*	Mary Pickford *Coquette*	NA	NA	Frank Lloyd *The Divine Lady*
1929-30	*All Quiet on the Western Front*	George Arliss *Disraeli*	Norma Shearer *The Divorcee*	NA	NA	Lewis Milestone *All Quiet on the Western Front*
1930-31	*Cimarron*	Lionel Barrymore *Free Soul*	Marie Dressler *Min and Bill*	NA	NA	Norman Taurog *Skippy*
1931-32	*Grand Hotel*	Fredric March *Dr. Jekyll and Mr. Hyde*; Wallace Beery *The Champ*	Helen Hayes *The Sin of Madelon Claudet*	NA	NA	Frank Borzage *Bad Girl*
1932-33	*Cavalcade*	Charles Laughton *The Private Life of Henry VIII*	Katharine Hepburn *Morning Glory*	NA	NA	Frank Lloyd *Cavalcade*
1934	*It Happened One Night*	Clark Gable *It Happened One Night*	Claudette Colbert *It Happened One Night*	NA	NA	Frank Capra *It Happened One Night*
1935	*Mutiny on the Bounty*	Victor McLaglen *The Informer*	Bette Davis *Dangerous*	NA	NA	John Ford *The Informer*
1936	*The Great Ziegfeld*	Paul Muni *Story of Louis Pasteur*	Luise Rainer *The Great Ziegfeld*	Walter Brennan *Come and Get It*	Gale Sondergaard *Anthony Adverse*	Frank Capra *Mr. Deeds Goes to Town*
1937	*Life of Emile Zola*	Spencer Tracy *Captains Courageous*	Luise Rainer *The Good Earth*	Joseph Schildkraut *Life of Emile Zola*	Alice Brady *In Old Chicago*	Leo McCarey *The Awful Truth*
1938	*You Can't Take It With You*	Spencer Tracy *Boys Town*	Bette Davis *Jezebel*	Walter Brennan *Kentucky*	Fay Bainter *Jezebel*	Frank Capra *You Can't Take It With You*
1939	*Gone With the Wind*	Robert Donat *Goodbye, Mr. Chips*	Vivien Leigh *Gone With the Wind*	Thomas Mitchell *Stage Coach*	Hattie McDaniel *Gone With the Wind*	Victor Fleming *Gone With the Wind*
1940	*Rebecca*	James Stewart *The Philadelphia Story*	Ginger Rogers *Kitty Foyle*	Walter Brennan *The Westerner*	Jane Darwell *The Grapes of Wrath*	John Ford *The Grapes of Wrath*
1941	*How Green Was My Valley*	Gary Cooper *Sergeant York*	Joan Fontaine *Suspicion*	Donald Crisp *How Green Was My Valley*	Mary Astor *The Great Lie*	John Ford *How Green Was My Valley*
1942	*Mrs. Miniver*	James Cagney *Yankee Doodle Dandy*	Greer Garson *Mrs. Miniver*	Van Heflin *Johnny Eager*	Teresa Wright *Mrs. Miniver*	William Wyler *Mrs. Miniver*
1943	*Casablanca*	Paul Lukas *Watch on the Rhine*	Jennifer Jones *The Song of Bernadette*	Charles Coburn *The More the Merrier*	Katina Paxinou *For Whom the Bell Tolls*	Michael Curtiz *Casablanca*
1944	*Going My Way*	Bing Crosby *Going My Way*	Ingrid Bergman *Gaslight*	Barry Fitzgerald *Going My Way*	Ethel Barrymore *None But the Lonely Heart*	Leo McCarey *Going My Way*
1945	*The Lost Weekend*	Ray Milland *The Lost Weekend*	Joan Crawford *Mildred Pierce*	James Dunn *A Tree Grows in Brooklyn*	Anne Revere *National Velvet*	Billy Wilder *The Lost Weekend*
1946	*The Best Years of Our Lives*	Fredric March *The Best Years of Our Lives*	Olivia de Havilland *To Each His Own*	Harold Russell *The Best Years of Our Lives*	Anne Baxter *The Razor's Edge*	William Wyler *The Best Years of Our Lives*
1947	*Gentleman's Agreement*	Ronald Colman *A Double Life*	Loretta Young *The Farmer's Daughter*	Edmund Gwenn *Miracle on 34th Street*	Celeste Holm *Gentleman's Agreement*	Elia Kazan *Gentleman's Agreement*
1948	*Hamlet*	Laurence Olivier *Hamlet*	Jane Wyman *Johnny Belinda*	Walter Huston *Treasure of Sierra Madre*	Claire Trevor *Key Largo*	John Huston *Treasure of Sierra Madre*
1949	*All the King's Men*	Broderick Crawford *All the King's Men*	Olivia de Havilland *The Heiress*	Dean Jagger *Twelve O'Clock High*	Mercedes McCambridge *All the King's Men*	Joseph L. Mankiewicz *Letter to Three Wives*
1950	*All About Eve*	Jose Ferrer *Cyrano de Bergerac*	Judy Holliday *Born Yesterday*	George Sanders *All About Eve*	Josephine Hull *Harvey*	Joseph L. Mankiewicz *All About Eve*
1951	*An American in Paris*	Humphrey Bogart *The African Queen*	Vivien Leigh *A Streetcar Named Desire*	Karl Malden *A Streetcar Named Desire*	Kim Hunter *A Streetcar Named Desire*	George Stevens *A Place in the Sun*
1952	*The Greatest Show on Earth*	Gary Cooper *High Noon*	Shirley Booth *Come Back Little Sheba*	Anthony Quinn *Viva Zapata!*	Gloria Grahame *The Bad and the Beautiful*	John Ford *The Quiet Man*
1953	*From Here to Eternity*	William Holden *Stalag 17*	Audrey Hepburn *Roman Holiday*	Frank Sinatra *From Here to Eternity*	Donna Reed *From Here to Eternity*	Fred Zinnemann *From Here to Eternity*

Year	Picture	Actor	Actress	Supporting actor[1]	Supporting actress[1]	Director
1954	*On the Waterfront*	Marlon Brando *On the Waterfront*	Grace Kelly *The Country Girl*	Edmond O'Brien *The Barefoot Contessa*	Eva Marie Saint *On the Waterfront*	Elia Kazan *On the Waterfront*
1955	*Marty*	Ernest Borgnine *Marty*	Anna Magnani *The Rose Tattoo*	Jack Lemmon *Mister Roberts*	Jo Van Fleet *East of Eden*	Delbert Mann *Marty*
1956	*Around the World in 80 Days*	Yul Brynner *The King and I*	Ingrid Bergman *Anastasia*	Anthony Quinn *Lust for Life*	Dorothy Malone *Written on the Wind*	George Stevens *Giant*
1957	*The Bridge on the River Kwai*	Alec Guinness *The Bridge on the River Kwai*	Joanne Woodward *The Three Faces of Eve*	Red Buttons *Sayonara*	Miyoshi Umeki *Sayonara*	David Lean *The Bridge on the River Kwai*
1958	*Gigi*	David Niven *Separate Tables*	Susan Hayward *I Want to Live*	Burl Ives *The Big Country*	Wendy Hiller *Separate Tables*	Vincente Minnelli *Gigi*
1959	*Ben-Hur*	Charlton Heston *Ben-Hur*	Simone Signoret *Room at the Top*	Hugh Griffith *Ben-Hur*	Shelley Winters *Diary of Anne Frank*	William Wyler *Ben-Hur*
1960	*The Apartment*	Burt Lancaster *Elmer Gantry*	Elizabeth Taylor *Butterfield 8*	Peter Ustinov *Spartacus*	Shirley Jones *Elmer Gantry*	Billy Wilder *The Apartment*
1961	*West Side Story*	Maximilian Schell *Judgment at Nuremberg*	Sophia Loren *Two Women*	George Chakiris *West Side Story*	Rita Moreno *West Side Story*	Jerome Robbins and Robert Wise *West Side Story*
1962	*Lawrence of Arabia*	Gregory Peck *To Kill a Mockingbird*	Anne Bancroft *The Miracle Worker*	Ed Begley *Sweet Bird of Youth*	Patty Duke *The Miracle Worker*	David Lean *Lawrence of Arabia*
1963	*Tom Jones*	Sidney Poitier *Lilies of the Field*	Patricia Neal *Hud*	Melvyn Douglas *Hud*	Margaret Rutherford *The V.I.P.s*	Tony Richardson *Tom Jones*
1964	*My Fair Lady*	Rex Harrison *My Fair Lady*	Julie Andrews *Mary Poppins*	Peter Ustinov *Topkapi*	Lila Kedrova *Zorba the Greek*	George Cukor *My Fair Lady*
1965	*The Sound of Music*	Lee Marvin *Cat Ballou*	Julie Christie *Darling*	Martin Balsam *A Thousand Clowns*	Shelley Winters *A Patch of Blue*	Robert Wise *The Sound of Music*
1966	*A Man for All Seasons*	Paul Scofield *A Man for All Seasons*	Elizabeth Taylor *Who's Afraid of Virginia Woolf?*	Walter Matthau *The Fortune Cookie*	Sandy Dennis *Who's Afraid of Virginia Woolf?*	Fred Zinnemann *A Man for All Seasons*
1967	*In the Heat of the Night*	Rod Steiger *In the Heat of the Night*	Katharine Hepburn *Guess Who's Coming to Dinner*	George Kennedy *Cool Hand Luke*	Estelle Parsons *Bonnie and Clyde*	Mike Nichols *The Graduate*
1968	*Oliver!*	Cliff Robertson *Charly*	Katharine Hepburn *The Lion in Winter*; Barbra Streisand *Funny Girl*	Jack Albertson *The Subject Was Roses*	Ruth Gordon *Rosemary's Baby*	Sir Carol Reed *Oliver!*
1969	*Midnight Cowboy*	John Wayne *True Grit*	Maggie Smith *The Prime of Miss Jean Brodie*	Gig Young *They Shoot Horses Don't They?*	Goldie Hawn *Cactus Flower*	John Schlesinger *Midnight Cowboy*
1970	*Patton*	George C. Scott *Patton* (refused)	Glenda Jackson *Women in Love*	John Mills *Ryan's Daughter*	Helen Hayes *Airport*	Franklin Schaffner *Patton*
1971	*The French Connection*	Gene Hackman *The French Connection*	Jane Fonda *Klute*	Ben Johnson *The Last Picture Show*	Cloris Leachman *The Last Picture Show*	William Friedkin *The French Connection*
1972	*The Godfather*	Marlon Brando *The Godfather* (refused)	Liza Minnelli *Cabaret*	Joel Grey *Cabaret*	Eileen Heckart *Butterflies Are Free*	Bob Fosse *Cabaret*
1973	*The Sting*	Jack Lemmon *Save the Tiger*	Glenda Jackson *A Touch of Class*	John Houseman *The Paper Chase*	Tatum O'Neal *Paper Moon*	George Roy Hill *The Sting*
1974	*The Godfather Part II*	Art Carney *Harry and Tonto*	Ellen Burstyn *Alice Doesn't Live Here Anymore*	Robert DeNiro *The Godfather Part II*	Ingrid Bergman *Murder on the Orient Express*	Francis Ford Coppola *The Godfather Part II*
1975	*One Flew Over the Cuckoo's Nest*	Jack Nicholson *One Flew Over the Cuckoo's Nest*	Louise Fletcher *One Flew Over the Cuckoo's Nest*	George Burns *The Sunshine Boys*	Lee Grant *Shampoo*	Milos Forman *One Flew Over the Cuckoo's Nest*
1976	*Rocky*	Peter Finch *Network*	Faye Dunaway *Network*	Jason Robards *All the President's Men*	Beatrice Straight *Network*	John G. Avildsen *Rocky*
1977	*Annie Hall*	Richard Dreyfuss *The Goodbye Girl*	Diane Keaton *Annie Hall*	Jason Robards *Julia*	Vanessa Redgrave *Julia*	Woody Allen *Annie Hall*
1978	*The Deer Hunter*	Jon Voight *Coming Home*	Jane Fonda *Coming Home*	Christopher Walken *The Deer Hunter*	Maggie Smith *California Suite*	Michael Cimino *The Deer Hunter*
1979	*Kramer vs. Kramer*	Dustin Hoffman *Kramer vs. Kramer*	Sally Field *Norma Rae*	Melvyn Douglas *Being There*	Meryl Streep *Kramer vs. Kramer*	Robert Benton *Kramer vs. Kramer*
1980	*Ordinary People*	Robert DeNiro *Raging Bull*	Sissy Spacek *Coal Miner's Daughter*	Timothy Hutton *Ordinary People*	Mary Steenburgen *Melvin and Howard*	Robert Redford *Ordinary People*
1981	*Chariots of Fire*	Henry Fonda *On Golden Pond*	Katharine Hepburn *On Golden Pond*	John Gielgud *Arthur*	Maureen Stapleton *Reds*	Warren Beatty *Reds*
1982	*Gandhi*	Ben Kingsley *Gandhi*	Meryl Streep *Sophie's Choice*	Louis Gossett Jr. *An Officer and a Gentleman*	Jessica Lange *Tootsie*	Richard Attenborough *Gandhi*
1983	*Terms of Endearment*	Robert Duvall *Tender Mercies*	Shirley MacLaine *Terms of Endearment*	Jack Nicholson *Terms of Endearment*	Linda Hunt *The Year of Living Dangerously*	James L. Brooks *Terms of Endearment*

Year	Picture	Actor	Actress	Supporting actor[1]	Supporting actress[1]	Director
1984	*Amadeus*	F. Murray Abraham *Amadeus*	Sally Field *Places in the Heart*	Haing S. Ngor *The Killing Fields*	Peggy Ashcroft *A Passage to India*	Milos Forman *Amadeus*
1985	*Out of Africa*	William Hurt *Kiss of the Spider Woman*	Geraldine Page *The Trip to Bountiful*	Don Ameche *Cocoon*	Anjelica Huston *Prizzi's Honor*	Sydney Pollack *Out of Africa*
1986	*Platoon*	Paul Newman *The Color of Money*	Marlee Matlin *Children of a Lesser God*	Michael Caine *Hannah and Her Sisters*	Dianne Wiest *Hannah and Her Sisters*	Oliver Stone *Platoon*
1987	*The Last Emperor*	Michael Douglas *Wall Street*	Cher *Moonstruck*	Sean Connery *The Untouchables*	Olympia Dukakis *Moonstruck*	Bernardo Bertolucci *The Last Emperor*
1988	*Rain Man*	Dustin Hoffman *Rain Man*	Jodie Foster *The Accused*	Kevin Kline *A Fish Called Wanda*	Geena Davis *The Accidental Tourist*	Barry Levinson *Rain Man*
1989	*Driving Miss Daisy*	Daniel Day-Lewis *My Left Foot*	Jessica Tandy *Driving Miss Daisy*	Denzel Washington *Glory*	Brenda Fricker *My Left Foot*	Oliver Stone *Born on the Fourth of July*
1990	*Dances With Wolves*	Jeremy Irons *Reversal of Fortune*	Kathy Bates *Misery*	Joe Pesci *Goodfellas*	Whoopi Goldberg *Ghost*	Kevin Costner *Dances With Wolves*
1991	*The Silence of the Lambs*	Anthony Hopkins *The Silence of the Lambs*	Jodie Foster *The Silence of the Lambs*	Jack Palance *City Slickers*	Mercedes Ruehl *The Fisher King*	Jonathan Demme *The Silence of the Lambs*
1992	*Unforgiven*	Al Pacino *Scent of a Woman*	Emma Thompson *Howards End*	Gene Hackman *Unforgiven*	Marisa Tomei *My Cousin Vinny*	Clint Eastwood *Unforgiven*
1993	*Schindler's List*	Tom Hanks *Philadelphia*	Holly Hunter *The Piano*	Tommy Lee Jones *The Fugitive*	Anna Paquin *The Piano*	Steven Spielberg *Schindler's List*
1994	*Forrest Gump*	Tom Hanks *Forrest Gump*	Jessica Lange *Blue Sky*	Martin Landau *Ed Wood*	Dianne Wiest, *Bullets Over Broadway*	Robert Zemeckis *Forrest Gump*
1995	*Braveheart*	Nicolas Cage *Leaving Las Vegas*	Susan Sarandon *Dead Man Walking*	Kevin Spacey *The Usual Suspects*	Mira Sorvino *Mighty Aphrodite*	Mel Gibson *Braveheart*
1996	*The English Patient*	Geoffrey Rush *Shine*	Frances McDormand *Fargo*	Cuba Gooding Jr. *Jerry Maguire*	Juliette Binoche *The English Patient*	Anthony Minghella *The English Patient*
1997	*Titanic*	Jack Nicholson *As Good As It Gets*	Helen Hunt *As Good As It Gets*	Robin Williams *Good Will Hunting*	Kim Basinger *L.A. Confidential*	James Cameron *Titanic*
1998	*Shakespeare in Love*	Roberto Benigni *Life Is Beautiful*	Gwyneth Paltrow *Shakespeare in Love*	James Coburn *Affliction*	Judi Dench *Shakespeare in Love*	Steven Spielberg *Saving Private Ryan*
1999	*American Beauty*	Kevin Spacey *American Beauty*	Hilary Swank *Boys Don't Cry*	Michael Caine, *The Cider House Rules*	Angelina Jolie *Girl, Interrupted*	Sam Mendes *American Beauty*
2000	*Gladiator*	Russell Crowe *Gladiator*	Julia Roberts *Erin Brockovich*	Benicio Del Toro *Traffic*	Marcia Gay Harden *Pollock*	Steven Soderbergh *Traffic*
2001	*A Beautiful Mind*	Denzel Washington *Training Day*	Halle Berry *Monster's Ball*	Jim Broadbent *Iris*	Jennifer Connelly *A Beautiful Mind*	Ron Howard *A Beautiful Mind*
2002	*Chicago*	Adrien Brody *The Pianist*	Nicole Kidman *The Hours*	Chris Cooper *Adaptation*	Catherine Zeta-Jones, *Chicago*	Roman Polanski *The Pianist*
2003	*The Lord of the Rings: The Return of the King*	Sean Penn *Mystic River*	Charlize Theron *Monster*	Tim Robbins *Mystic River*	Renée Zellweger *Cold Mountain*	Peter Jackson *The Lord of the Rings: The Return of the King*
2004	*Million Dollar Baby*	Jamie Foxx *Ray*	Hilary Swank *Million Dollar Baby*	Morgan Freeman *Million Dollar Baby*	Cate Blanchett *The Aviator*	Clint Eastwood *Million Dollar Baby*
2005	*Crash*	Philip Seymour Hoffman *Capote*	Reese Witherspoon *Walk the Line*	George Clooney *Syriana*	Rachel Weisz *The Constant Gardener*	Ang Lee *Brokeback Mountain*
2006	*The Departed*	Forest Whitaker, *The Last King of Scotland*	Helen Mirren *The Queen*	Alan Arkin *Little Miss Sunshine*	Jennifer Hudson *Dreamgirls*	Martin Scorsese *The Departed*
2007	*No Country for Old Men*	Daniel Day-Lewis *There Will Be Blood*	Marion Cotillard *La Vie en Rose*	Javier Bardem *No Country for Old Men*	Tilda Swinton *Michael Clayton*	Joel Coen and Ethan Coen, *No Country for Old Men*
2008	*Slumdog Millionaire*	Sean Penn *Milk*	Kate Winslet *The Reader*	Heath Ledger *The Dark Knight*	Penelope Cruz, *Vicky Cristina Barcelona*	Danny Boyle *Slumdog Millionaire*
2009	*The Hurt Locker*	Jeff Bridges *Crazy Heart*	Sandra Bullock *The Blind Side*	Christoph Waltz *Inglourious Basterds*	Mo'Nique *Precious*	Kathryn Bigelow *The Hurt Locker*
2010	*The King's Speech*	Colin Firth *The King's Speech*	Natalie Portman *Black Swan*	Christian Bale *The Fighter*	Melissa Leo *The Fighter*	Tom Hooper *The King's Speech*
2011	*The Artist*	Jean Dujardin *The Artist*	Meryl Streep *The Iron Lady*	Christopher Plummer, *Beginners*	Octavia Spencer *The Help*	Michel Hazanavicius *The Artist*
2012	*Argo*	Daniel Day-Lewis *Lincoln*	Jennifer Lawrence *Silver Linings Playbook*	Christoph Waltz *Django Unchained*	Anne Hathaway *Les Misérables*	Ang Lee *Life of Pi*
2013	*12 Years a Slave*	Matthew McConaughey *Dallas Buyers Club*	Cate Blanchett *Blue Jasmine*	Jared Leto *Dallas Buyers Club*	Lupita Nyong'o *12 Years a Slave*	Alfonso Cuarón *Gravity*
2014	*Birdman*	Eddie Redmayne *The Theory of Everything*	Julianne Moore *Still Alice*	J. K. Simmons *Whiplash*	Patricia Arquette *Boyhood*	Alejandro G. Iñárritu *Birdman*

(1) Award not given until 1936.

Other Academy Award Winners, 2014

Animated film: *Big Hero 6*
Cinematography: *Birdman*
Costume design: *The Grand Budapest Hotel*
Documentary feature: *Citizenfour*
Film editing: *Whiplash*
Foreign language film: *Ida*, Poland
Makeup and hairstyling: *The Grand Budapest Hotel*
Original score: *The Grand Budapest Hotel*, Alexandre Desplat
Original song: "Glory," *Selma*, John Legend and Common
Production design: *The Grand Budapest Hotel*
Screenplay, adapted: *The Imitation Game*, Graham Moore
Screenplay, original: *Birdman*, Alejandro G. Iñárritu, Nicolás Giacobone, Alexander Dinelaris Jr., and Armando Bo

Other Film Awards, 2015

(Awarded in 2014, unless otherwise noted.)

British Academy of Film and Television Awards (BAFTAs)

Awarded in 2015 to films released in the UK in 2014.
Best film: *Boyhood*
British film: *The Theory of Everything*
Director: Richard Linklater, *Boyhood*
Original screenplay: Wes Anderson, *The Grand Budapest Hotel*
Adapted screenplay: Anthony McCarten, *The Theory of Everything*
Foreign language film: *Ida*, Poland
Animated film: *The Lego Movie*
Actor: Eddie Redmayne, *The Theory of Everything*
Actress: Julianne Moore, *Still Alice*
Supporting actor: J. K. Simmons, *Whiplash*
Supporting actress: Patricia Arquette, *Boyhood*

Canadian Screen Awards

Motion picture: *Mommy*
Actor: Antoine Olivier Pilon, *Mommy*
Actress: Anne Dorval, *Mommy*
Supporting actor: John Cusack, *Maps to the Stars*
Supporting actress: Suzanne Clément, *Mommy*
Director: Xavier Dolan, *Mommy*

Cannes International Film Festival Awards

Palme d'Or: *Dheepan*, France
Grand Prix: *Saul Fia* [*Son of Saul*], Hungary
Best Director: Hou Hsiao-Hsien, *Nie Yinniang* [*The Assassin*], Taiwan/China/Hong Kong/France
Best Screenplay: Michel Franco, *Chronic*, Mexico/France
Best Actress: Rooney Mara, *Carol*, UK-U.S., and Emmanuelle Bercot, *Mon Roi*, France
Best Actor: Vincent Lindon, *La Loi du Marché* [*The Measure of a Man*], France
Jury Prize: *The Lobster*, Ireland/UK/Greece/France/Netherlands
Palme d'Or, short film: *Waves '98*, Lebanon/Qatar

Director's Guild of America Awards

Feature film: Alejandro G. Iñárritu, *Birdman*
Documentary: Laura Poitras, *Citizenfour*
TV movie/miniseries: Lisa Cholodenko, *Olive Kitteridge*
TV series (drama): Lesli Linka Glatter, *Homeland*, "From A to B and Back Again"
TV series (comedy): Jill Soloway, *Transparent*, "Best New Girl"

Sundance Film Festival Awards

U.S. Grand Jury Prize: *Me and Earl and the Dying Girl* (drama); *The Wolfpack* (doc.)
World Cinema Jury Prize: *Slow West*, UK/New Zealand (drama); *The Russian Woodpecker*, Ukraine/UK/U.S. (doc.)
U.S. Audience Award: *Me and Earl and the Dying Girl* (drama); *Meru* (doc.)
World Cinema Audience Award: *Umrika*, India (drama); *Dark Horse*, UK (doc.)
NEXT Audience Award: *James White*
U.S. Directing: Robert Eggers, *The Witch* (drama); Matthew Heineman, *Cartel Land* (doc.)
World Cinema Directing: Alanté Kavaïté, *The Summer of Sangaile*, Lithuania/France/Netherlands (drama); Kim Longinotto, *Dreamcatcher*, Ukraine/UK/U.S. (doc.)
Waldo Salt Screenwriting Award: Tim Talbott, *The Stanford Prison Experiment*
Alfred P. Sloan Feature Film Prize: *The Stanford Prison Experiment*

Toronto International Film Festival

People's Choice Award: *Room*
People's Choice Documentary Award: *Winter on Fire: Ukraine's Fight for Freedom*
People's Choice Midnight Madness Award: *Hardcore*
Canadian Feature Film: *Closet Monster*
Canadian Short Film: *Overpass*
Canadian First Feature Film: *Sleeping Giant*
International Critics' Prize (FIPRESCI Prize) for Discovery: *Eva Nová*
FIPRESCI Prize for Special Presentations: *Desierto*
NETPAC Award: *The Whispering Star*

Academy of Country Music Awards, 2015

Entertainer of the year: Luke Bryan
Male vocalist: Jason Aldean
Female vocalist: Miranda Lambert
Vocal duo: Florida Georgia Line
Vocal group: Little Big Town
New artist: Cole Swindell
Album: *Platinum*, Miranda Lambert
Record (single): "I Don't Dance," Lee Brice
Song: "Automatic," Miranda Lambert
Vocal event: "This Is How We Roll," Florida Georgia Line
Video: "Drunk on a Plane," Dierks Bentley

Selected Grammy Awards, 2014

Source: National Academy of Recording Arts and Sciences
For albums released Oct. 1, 2013-Sept. 30, 2014, awarded in Feb. 2015.

Record of the year (single): "Stay With Me," Sam Smith
Album of the year: *Morning Phase*, Beck
Song of the year: "Stay With Me," Sam Smith
New artist: Sam Smith
Pop performance, solo: "Happy," Pharrell Williams
Pop performance, duo/group: "Say Something," A Great Big World and Christina Aguilera
Pop album, traditional vocal: *Cheek to Cheek*, Tony Bennett and Lady Gaga
Pop album, vocal: *In the Lonely Hour*, Sam Smith
Dance recording: "Rather Be," Clean Bandit feat. Jess Glynne
Dance/electronic album: *Syro*, Aphex Twin
Contemporary instrumental album: *Bass & Mandolin*, Chris Thile and Edgar Meyer
Rock performance: "Lazaretto," Jack White
Metal performance: "The Last in Line," Tenacious D
Rock song: "Ain't It Fun," Paramore
Rock album: *Morning Phase*, Beck
Alternative album: *St. Vincent*, St. Vincent
R&B performance: "Drunk in Love," Beyoncé feat. Jay Z
R&B performance, traditional: "Jesus Children," Robert Glasper Experiment feat. Lalah Hathaway and Malcolm-Jamal Warner
R&B song: "Drunk in Love," Beyoncé feat. Jay Z
R&B album: *Love, Marriage & Divorce*, Toni Braxton and Babyface
Urban contemporary album: *Girl*, Pharrell Williams
Rap performance: "I," Kendrick Lamar
Rap/sung collaboration: "The Monster," Eminem feat. Rihanna
Rap song: "I," Kendrick Lamar
Rap album: *The Marshall Mathers LP2*, Eminem
Country performance, solo: "Something in the Water," Carrie Underwood
Country performance, duo/group: "Gentle on My Mind," The Band Perry
Country song: "I'm Not Gonna Miss You," Glen Campbell
Country album: *Platinum*, Miranda Lambert
Jazz album, instrumental: *Trilogy*, Chick Corea Trio
Jazz album, vocal: *Beautiful Life*, Dianne Reeves
New age album: *Winds of Samsara*, Ricky Kej and Wouter Kellerman
Comedy album: *Mandatory Fun*, "Weird Al" Yankovic
Spoken word album: *Diary of a Mad Diva*, Joan Rivers
Soundtrack album, compilation: *Frozen*, Kristen Anderson-Lopez, Robert Lopez, Tom MacDougall, and Chris Montan, compilation producers
Soundtrack album, score: *The Grand Budapest Hotel*, Alexandre Desplat
Song, visual media: "Let It Go," *Frozen*, Idina Menzel
Music video: "Happy," Pharrell Williams
Music film: *20 Feet From Stardom*, Darlene Love, Merry Clayton, Lisa Fischer, and Judith Hill

Grammy Awards, 1958-2014

Record of the Year (single)	Year	Album of the Year
Domenico Modugno, "Nel Blu Dipinto Di Blu (Volare)"	**1958**	Henry Mancini, *The Music From Peter Gunn*
Bobby Darin, "Mack the Knife"	**1959**	Frank Sinatra, *Come Dance With Me*
Percy Faith, "Theme From a Summer Place"	**1960**	Bob Newhart, *Button Down Mind*
Henry Mancini, "Moon River"	**1961**	Judy Garland, *Judy at Carnegie Hall*
Tony Bennett, "I Left My Heart in San Francisco"	**1962**	Vaughn Meader, *The First Family*
Henry Mancini, "The Days of Wine and Roses"	**1963**	Barbra Streisand, *The Barbra Streisand Album*
Stan Getz and Astrud Gilberto, "The Girl From Ipanema"	**1964**	Stan Getz and João Gilberto, *Getz/Gilberto*
Herb Alpert, "A Taste of Honey"	**1965**	Frank Sinatra, *September of My Years*
Frank Sinatra, "Strangers in the Night"	**1966**	Frank Sinatra, *A Man and His Music*
5th Dimension, "Up, Up and Away"	**1967**	The Beatles, *Sgt. Pepper's Lonely Hearts Club Band*
Simon and Garfunkel, "Mrs. Robinson"	**1968**	Glen Campbell, *By the Time I Get to Phoenix*
5th Dimension, "Aquarius/Let the Sunshine In"	**1969**	Blood, Sweat & Tears, *Blood, Sweat & Tears*
Simon and Garfunkel, "Bridge Over Troubled Water"	**1970**	Simon and Garfunkel, *Bridge Over Troubled Water*
Carole King, "It's Too Late"	**1971**	Carole King, *Tapestry*
Roberta Flack, "The First Time Ever I Saw Your Face"	**1972**	George Harrison and Friends, *The Concert for Bangla Desh*
Roberta Flack, "Killing Me Softly With His Song"	**1973**	Stevie Wonder, *Innervisions*
Olivia Newton-John, "I Honestly Love You"	**1974**	Stevie Wonder, *Fulfillingness' First Finale*
Captain & Tennille, "Love Will Keep Us Together"	**1975**	Paul Simon, *Still Crazy After All These Years*
George Benson, "This Masquerade"	**1976**	Stevie Wonder, *Songs in the Key of Life*
Eagles, "Hotel California"	**1977**	Fleetwood Mac, *Rumours*
Billy Joel, "Just the Way You Are"	**1978**	Bee Gees, *Saturday Night Fever*
The Doobie Brothers, "What a Fool Believes"	**1979**	Billy Joel, *52nd Street*
Christopher Cross, "Sailing"	**1980**	Christopher Cross, *Christopher Cross*
Kim Carnes, "Bette Davis Eyes"	**1981**	John Lennon and Yoko Ono, *Double Fantasy*
Toto, "Rosanna"	**1982**	Toto, *Toto IV*
Michael Jackson, "Beat It"	**1983**	Michael Jackson, *Thriller*
Tina Turner, "What's Love Got to Do With It"	**1984**	Lionel Richie, *Can't Slow Down*
USA for Africa, "We Are the World"	**1985**	Phil Collins, *No Jacket Required*
Steve Winwood, "Higher Love"	**1986**	Paul Simon, *Graceland*
Paul Simon, "Graceland"	**1987**	U2, *The Joshua Tree*
Bobby McFerrin, "Don't Worry, Be Happy"	**1988**	George Michael, *Faith*
Bette Midler, "Wind Beneath My Wings"	**1989**	Bonnie Raitt, *Nick of Time*
Phil Collins, "Another Day in Paradise"	**1990**	Quincy Jones, *Back on the Block*
Natalie Cole, with Nat "King" Cole, "Unforgettable"	**1991**	Natalie Cole, with Nat "King" Cole, *Unforgettable*
Eric Clapton, "Tears in Heaven"	**1992**	Eric Clapton, *Unplugged*
Whitney Houston, "I Will Always Love You"	**1993**	Whitney Houston, *The Bodyguard*
Sheryl Crow, "All I Wanna Do"	**1994**	Tony Bennett, *MTV Unplugged*
Seal, "Kiss From a Rose"	**1995**	Alanis Morissette, *Jagged Little Pill*
Eric Clapton, "Change the World"	**1996**	Celine Dion, *Falling Into You*
Shawn Colvin, "Sunny Came Home"	**1997**	Bob Dylan, *Time Out of Mind*
Celine Dion, "My Heart Will Go On"	**1998**	Lauryn Hill, *The Miseducation of Lauryn Hill*
Santana feat. Rob Thomas, "Smooth"	**1999**	Santana, *Supernatural*
U2, "Beautiful Day"	**2000**	Steely Dan, *Two Against Nature*
U2, "Walk On"	**2001**	Various artists, *O Brother, Where Art Thou?*
Norah Jones, "Don't Know Why"	**2002**	Norah Jones, *Come Away With Me*
Coldplay, "Clocks"	**2003**	OutKast, *Speakerboxxx/The Love Below*
Ray Charles and Norah Jones, "Here We Go Again"	**2004**	Ray Charles and various artists, *Genius Loves Company*
Green Day, "Boulevard of Broken Dreams"	**2005**	U2, *How to Dismantle an Atomic Bomb*
Dixie Chicks, "Not Ready to Make Nice"	**2006**	Dixie Chicks, *Taking the Long Way*
Amy Winehouse, "Rehab"	**2007**	Herbie Hancock, *River: The Joni Letters*
Robert Plant and Alison Krauss, "Please Read the Letter"	**2008**	Robert Plant and Alison Krauss, *Raising Sand*
Kings of Leon, "Use Somebody"	**2009**	Taylor Swift, *Fearless*
Lady Antebellum, "Need You Now"	**2010**	Arcade Fire, *The Suburbs*
Adele, "Rolling in the Deep"	**2011**	Adele, *21*
Gotye, "Somebody That I Used to Know"	**2012**	Mumford & Sons, *Babel*
Daft Punk feat. Pharrell Williams and Nile Rodgers, "Get Lucky"	**2013**	Daft Punk, *Random Access Memories*
Sam Smith, "Stay With Me"	**2014**	Beck, *Morning Phase*

MTV Video Music Awards, 2015

Video of the year: "Bad Blood," Taylor Swift feat. Kendrick Lamar
Artist to watch: Fetty Wap
Female video: "Blank Space," Taylor Swift
Male video: "Uptown Funk," Mark Ronson feat. Bruno Mars
Hip-hop video: "Anaconda," Nicki Minaj
Pop video: "Blank Space," Taylor Swift
Rock video: "Uma Thurman," Fall Out Boy
Video with a social message: "One Man Can Change the World," Big Sean feat. Kanye West and John Legend
Song of the summer: "She's Kinda Hot," 5 Seconds of Summer
Collaboration: "Bad Blood," Taylor Swift feat. Kendrick Lamar
Art direction: "So Many Pros," Snoop Dogg
Choreography: "I Won't Let You Down," OK Go
Cinematography: "Never Catch Me," Flying Lotus feat. Kendrick Lamar
Direction: "Alright," Kendrick Lamar
Editing: "7/11," Beyoncé
Visual effects: "Where Are U Now," Skrillex and Diplo feat. Justin Bieber

Science and Technology News, 2015

The following were some of the more newsworthy developments in science and technology in the past year.

Dwarf Planets Visited

Unmanned spacecraft in 2015 paid the first-ever visits to two of the solar system's five recognized dwarf planets: Ceres and Pluto. Ceres is located in the asteroid belt between Mars and Jupiter, and Pluto lies in the Kuiper Belt beyond Neptune, the outermost planet. Both probes, *Dawn* and *New Horizons*, were on NASA exploratory missions, and both produced remarkable images along with scientific data. Launched in 2007, *Dawn* spent more than a year studying the asteroid Vesta before proceeding to Ceres, which it began orbiting in Mar. 2015. It revealed the presence on Ceres of enigmatic bright spots and an isolated conical mountain estimated to be about 4 mi high. *New Horizons*'s primary objective was to study Pluto and its moons. Launched in 2006, *New Horizons* made its closest approach to Pluto July 14, 2015. Its preliminary discoveries about the dwarf planet included the existence of mountain ranges and flowing ices, along with the presence of sizable atmospheric hazes. More data from the flyby would be sent back to Earth through late 2016.

New Finds on Early Humans

Two discoveries in East Africa pushed back key dates regarding early human ancestors. One, a partial lower jawbone, was found in the Afar region of Ethiopia and was dated to 2.8 mil years ago—some 400,000 years before the oldest-known fossil specimens from any species of *Homo*. Features of the new find, such as relatively small back molar teeth, seemed to tie it more closely to *Homo* than to any known species of the protohuman genus *Australopithecus* in the same period. The environment in the Afar area at the time may have been drier and more open than has been thought, conceivably helping to prompt primitive humans' transition from tree dwellers to ground dwellers. The jawbone and its environmental context were analyzed in two reports in the Mar. 20 issue of *Science*. The other find, stone tools analyzed in the May 21 issue of *Nature* by U.S., French, and Kenyan researchers, was made near Lake Turkana in Kenya. It included stone flakes, hammer stones, and anvils dating to about 3.3 mil years ago—roughly 700,000 years earlier than the previously oldest-known tools. Apparently, primitive human ancestors, perhaps belonging to *Australopithecus*, began using this technology even before the advent of *Homo*.

An international team of researchers described a massive South African find in two online papers in the Sept. 10 issue of *eLife*. The roughly 1,500 bones from at least 15 individuals represented the largest assemblage of a single early human species ever discovered in Africa. The fossils reflected both *Australopithecus* and *Homo* traits and belonged, researchers claimed, to a new species that they dubbed *Homo naledi*. Evidence suggested that members of the species had deliberately placed its dead in a cave, shaking up the belief that modern humans were the first to have death rituals. However, a dating analysis had yet to be carried out.

First Warm-Blooded Fish

Humans and other mammals are warm-blooded animals, or endotherms, who can generate heat within their body to keep warm. Fish, by contrast, tend to be cold-blooded ectotherms, drawing heat from their environment. A few species are "regionally endothermic," able to keep specific organs or tissues warmer than the surrounding water. The opah (*Lampris guttatus*) is the first fish found to be a whole-body endotherm. A roundish silvery fish with red fins, it grows to an average of 100 pounds, with a diameter of 3 feet, and is native to oceans around the world. Researchers at the U.S. National Oceanic and Atmospheric Administration's Southwest Fisheries Science Center described their findings in the May 15 issue of *Science*. The opah can spend prolonged periods in cold deep water. It produces heat mainly by constantly flapping its pectoral fins. Blood vessels in the gills are arrayed as heat exchangers, helping to preserve warmth. The fish's warm temperature gives it a big advantage over slower, cold-blooded prey. The study's lead author, Nicholas Wegner, noted, "The muscles can contract faster, the temporal resolution of the eye is increased, and neurological transmissions are sped up."

Yellowstone's Supervolcano

Colossal volcanic eruptions hit the Yellowstone National Park area in the remote past. The most recent major eruption, 640,000 years ago, ejected some 240 cu mi of material and left a caldera, or crater, measuring roughly 25 by 37 mi. Today, the park experiences frequent earthquakes and has dozens of geysers and hot springs. Scientists knew that a chamber of hot rock and molten magma lay within the Earth's crust 6 mi or so below the surface. But it seemed too small, and its distance from the mantle too great, for it to account for all the surface activity.

In the May 15, 2015, issue of *Science*, U.S. researchers used seismic waves like an ultrasound scan to create the first three-dimensional picture of the park's underlying structure. This showed that subsurface reserves of hot rock and magma were vastly larger than had been thought. It also revealed the presence of an additional massive reserve roughly 20 mi below the surface, which provides a link between the upper chamber and a plume of hot material believed to be welling up in the mantle. With an estimated size of 11,000 cu mi, the new reserve greatly exceeds the upper chamber, estimated at 2,400 cu mi. The discovery did not shed light on when, or even whether, a new cataclysmic eruption might occur.

An Alloy That Remembers Its Shape

Scientists have known about the shape-memory effect in certain alloy metals for decades. If an object made of certain alloys is deformed—say, by bending—the application of heat can make it regain its original shape. For example, if you stretched out a spring made of such an alloy and then put it in a cup of hot liquid, it might pop back into shape. Up to now, alloys based on a titanium-nickel combination have been used most widely, in applications ranging from surgical stents to frames for eyeglasses. Their drawback has been that they wear out after repeated changes, eventually breaking apart. But in the May 29 issue of *Science* a team of German and U.S. scientists reported that embedding titanium-copper particles in a titanium-nickel alloy resulted in a material capable of regaining its original shape even after being bent 10 mil times—hundreds of times better than the previous record. The discovery may lead to the development of additional alloys that can repeatedly and reliably recover from deformation. Such metals could find use in actuators, sensors, artificial heart valves, and other devices in a broad range of industries.

Mass Extinctions—Now and in the Past

On several occasions in Earth's history, large numbers of living species have died off in a relatively short time. Among them, the "Big Five" mass extinctions are recognized among scientists as having been particularly devastating, each involving the death of at least half the species on Earth. Some experts contend that humans are currently causing a sixth major extinction. Support for this position came in a paper published by a U.S.-Mexican team in the online journal *Science Advances* on June 19. Focusing on vertebrates, for which the best modern and fossil data exist, and using conservative estimates, the researchers found that species over the past century have been vanishing up to 100 times faster than the normal rate between mass extinctions. They contended that a true mass extinction could still be averted, but that "the window of opportunity is rapidly closing."

Yet another mass extinction, about 260 mil years ago in the mid-Permian period, was the subject of a study by a U.S.-South African group published online on July 8 in the journal *Proceedings of the Royal Society B*. Previous evidence had indicated the disappearance of more than half of land plant species and marine invertebrate genera in that extinction, but this has been debated. The new study focused on South Africa's fossil-rich Karoo Basin. It suggested that 74 to 80 percent of its land vertebrates died off at about the same time.

Science Glossary

This glossary covers some concepts that come up frequently in the news, in biology, chemistry, geology, and physics.

Biology

Amino acid: one of about 20 similar small molecules that are the building blocks of proteins.

Antibiotic: a substance produced by or derived from a bacterium, fungus, or other organism that battles infections and diseases caused by microorganisms, especially bacteria; it works by killing the microorganism or halting its growth.

Archaeon (plural, archaea): one of a group of single-celled microorganisms; archaea are prokaryotes, like bacteria, but they share some similarities with eukaryotes.

Autoimmunity: a condition in which an individual's immune system reacts against his or her own tissues; leads to diseases such as lupus, some forms of diabetes, inflammatory bowel disease, and rheumatoid arthritis.

Bacterium (plural, bacteria): one of a large, varied class of microscopic and simple, single-celled organisms; bacteria live almost everywhere—some forms cause disease, while others are useful in digestion and other natural processes.

Biodiversity: richness of variety of life-forms—both plant and animal—in a given environment.

Cell: the smallest unit of life capable of living independently, or with other cells; usually bounded by a membrane. May include a nucleus and other specialized parts.

Cholesterol: a fatty substance in animal tissues. It is produced by the liver in humans; is found in foods such as butter, eggs, and meat; and is an essential body constituent.

Chromosome: one of the rod-like structures in cell nuclei that carry genetic material (DNA).

Cloning: the process of copying a particular piece of DNA to allow it to be sequenced, studied, or used in some other way; can also refer to producing a genetic copy of an organism.

DNA (deoxyribonucleic acid): the usually double-stranded molecule that carries genetic information, which determines the form and functioning of all living things.

Ecosystem: an interdependent community of living organisms and their climatic and geographical habitat.

Enzyme: a protein that promotes a particular chemical reaction in the body.

Estrogen: one of a group of hormones that promote development of female secondary sex characteristics and the growth and health of the female reproductive system; males also produce small amounts of estrogen.

Eukaryote: any of the group of single- or multi-celled organisms whose cells have distinct nuclei.

Evolution: the process of gradual change that can occur in a species as it adapts to its environment; natural selection is the process by which evolution occurs.

Gene: a portion of a DNA molecule that provides the blueprint for the assembly of a protein.

Gene pool: the collection and total diversity of genes in an interbreeding population.

Gene therapy: a treatment in which scientists try to implant functioning genes into a person's cells so the genes can produce proteins that the person lacks or that help the person fight disease.

Genetic sequencing: the process of finding the order of subunits in a gene or the order of all an organism's genes.

Genome: the complete set of an organism's genetic material.

Hormone: a substance secreted in one part of an organism that regulates the functioning of other tissues or organs.

Meiosis: the process of cell division that results in gametes (sperm or egg cells), all of which contain half the number of chromosomes as their precursor.

Metabolism: the sum total of the body's chemical processes providing energy for vital functions and enabling new material to be synthesized.

Mitosis: the process by which a cell divides its nucleus and other cell materials into two duplicate daughter cells with the same DNA.

Neuron or **nerve cell:** any of the cells in the nervous system that send electrical and chemical messages to other cells.

Nucleus (plural, nuclei): the center of an atom; or the portion of a eukaryotic cell that contains most of the cell's genetic material.

Organism: a living entity, capable of growth, metabolism, and usually reproduction.

Phenotype: the observable properties and characteristics of an organism arising at least in part from its genetic makeup.

Pheromone: a chemical secreted by an animal or plant to influence the behavior of other members of its species.

Placebo effect: a phenomenon in which patients show improvements even though they have taken a medically inactive substance, called a placebo.

Prokaryote: a single-celled organism that does not have a distinct nucleus, such as a bacterium or archaeon.

Protein: a complex molecule made up of one or more chains of amino acids; essential to the structure and function of all cells.

RNA (ribonucleic acid): a complex molecule similar to the genetic material DNA but usually single-stranded; several forms of RNA translate the genetic code of DNA and use that code to assemble proteins for structural and biological functions in the body. RNA also serves as the genetic material of some viruses.

Species: a population of organisms that breed with each other in nature and produce fertile offspring; other definitions of species exist to accommodate the diversity of life on Earth.

Stem cell: a cell that can give rise to other types of cells; for instance, bone marrow stem cells can divide and produce different types of blood cells.

Steroid: a type of chemical substance with a certain molecular structure. Some steroids are hormones that can suppress immune response or influence stress reaction, blood pressure, or sexual development.

Testosterone: a steroid hormone that stimulates the development and maintenance of male sexual characteristics and the production of sperm; women also produce small amounts of testosterone.

Virus: a microscopic, often disease-causing, agent made of genetic material surrounded by a protein shell; can only reproduce inside a living cell.

Chemistry

Acid: a class of compounds that contrasts with bases. Acids taste sour, turn litmus red/pink, and often produce hydrogen gas in contact with some metals. Acids donate protons (hydrogen atoms minus the electron) in chemical reactions.

Base: a substance that yields hydroxyl ions (OH-) when dissolved in water; any of a class of compounds whose aqueous solutions taste bitter, feel slippery, turn litmus blue, and react with acids to form salts; also known as **alkaline**.

Carbon fiber: an extremely strong, thin fiber made by pyrolyzing (decomposing by heat) synthetic fibers, such as rayon, until charred; used to make high-strength composites.

Chlorofluorocarbon (CFC): one of a group of industrial chemicals that contain chlorine, fluorine, and carbon and can damage Earth's ozone layer.

Element: a substance that cannot be chemically decomposed into simpler substances; all the atoms of an element have the same number of protons.

Isotope: an atom of a chemical element with the same number of protons in its nucleus as other atoms of that element, but with a different number of neutrons.

Molecule: the basic unit of a chemical compound, composed of two or more atoms bound together.

Noble gases or **inert gases:** a group of gases including helium, neon, argon, krypton, xenon, and radon that are not reactive except in rare and limited instances.

Osmosis: the transfer of a fluid across a semipermeable membrane, usually from an area of higher concentration to one of lower concentration.

Phase: any of the possible states of matter—solid, liquid, gas, or plasma—that change according to temperature and pressure.

Polymer: a huge molecule containing hundreds or thousands of smaller molecules arranged in repeating units.

Salt: a neutral compound produced by the reaction of an acid and a base.

Geology

Fault, tectonic: a crack or break in Earth's crust, often due to the slippage of tectonic plates past or over one another; usually geologically unstable.

Igneous: a type of rock formed by solidification from a molten state, especially from molten magma.

Magma: hot liquid rock material under Earth's surface, from which igneous rock is formed by cooling.

Metamorphic: in geology, the name given to rocks or minerals that have recrystallized under the influence of heat and pressure since their original formation.

Pangaea: a single supercontinent that scientists believe began to break apart at least 200 mil years ago to form the current continents.

Plate tectonics: theory that Earth's lithosphere—the uppermost layer that includes the crust—is made up of many separate rigid plates of rock that float on top of hot semi-liquid rock.

Sedimentary: a type of rock formed by the buildup of material at the bottoms of bodies of water.

Physics

Absolute zero: the theoretical temperature at which all motion within a molecule stops, corresponding to –273.15°C (–459.67°F).

Antimatter: matter that consists of antiparticles, such as antiprotons, that have an opposite charge from normal particles; when matter meets antimatter, both are destroyed, and their combined mass is converted to energy. Antimatter is created in certain radioactive decay processes but appears to be present in only small amounts in the universe.

Atom: the basic unit of a chemical element.

Atomic mass: the total mass of an atom of a given element; atoms of the same element with different atomic masses (different numbers of neutrons, not protons) are called **isotopes**.

Atomic number: the number of protons in an atom of a given element of the periodic table; the characteristic that sets atoms of different elements apart.

Axion: a hypothetical subatomic particle with low mass and energy that is thought to exist because of the properties of the strong nuclear force.

Bose-Einstein condensate (BEC): a "super-atom" comprising thousands of atoms super-cooled to within a few hundred millionths of a degree of absolute zero and thus condensed into the lowest energy state. Atoms bound in the BEC behave synchronously, giving the BEC wavelike properties.

Boson: one of the two primary categories of particles in the Standard Model; bosons include the Higgs boson and force-carrying particles such as photons, gluons, and the W and Z particles.

Dark energy: a mysterious, undefined energy leading to a repulsive force pervading all of space-time; proposed by cosmologists as counteracting gravity and accelerating the expansion of the universe; predicted to make up 68.3% of the universe's composition.

Dark matter: hypothetical, invisible matter that some scientists believe makes up 26.8% of the universe (dark matter and ordinary matter together make up 31.7% of the universe). Its existence was proposed to account for otherwise inexplicable gravitational forces observed in space.

Doppler effect: a change in the frequency of sound, light, or radio waves caused by the motion of the source emitting the waves or the motion of the person or instrument perceiving the waves.

Electron: negatively charged particle that is the least massive electrically charged fundamental particle.

Energy: capacity to perform work. Energy can take various forms, such as potential energy, kinetic energy, and chemical energy.

Entropy: a measure of disorder in a system.

Fermion: any one of a number of matter particles including electrons, protons, neutrons, neutrinos, and quarks; one of the two primary categories of particles in the Standard Model, the other being bosons.

Field: the existence of physical effects such as forces (gravitational, electric, etc.) is visualized and described mathematically by physicists in terms of fields, which show the strength and direction of a force at a given position.

Fission: a nuclear reaction that occurs when the nuclei of large, unstable atoms break apart, releasing large amounts of energy.

Fluorescence: luminescence that is caused by the absorption of radiation at one wavelength followed by an almost immediate re-radiation, usually at a different wavelength, that stops almost immediately when the causative radiation stops.

Force: in classical physics, something that causes acceleration in a body; can be thought of as a push or pull.

Fusion: a nuclear reaction occurring when atomic nuclei collide at high temperatures and combine to form one heavier atomic nucleus, releasing enormous energy in the process.

Gravity: an attractive force between any two objects or particles, proportional to the mass (or energy) of the objects; strength of the force decreases with greater distance; the only fundamental force still unaccounted for by the Standard Model.

Half-life: the time it takes for half of a given amount of a radioactive element to decay.

Hertz (Hz): a measure of frequency, or how many times a given event occurs per second; applied to sound waves, electrical current, and microchip clock speeds.

Higgs boson: a boson associated with a field accounting for the existence of mass in many particles.

Laser: light consisting of a cascade of photons all having the same wavelength; stands for Light Amplification by Stimulated Emission of Radiation.

Light-emitting diode (LED): a semiconductor that emits light when an electrical current is passed through it. The color of the light depends on the material used in making the diode.

Neutrino: a tiny fundamental particle with no electrical charge and very small mass that moves very quickly through the universe; comes in three varieties, or flavors, called electron, muon, and tau.

Neutron: a neutral particle found in the nuclei of atoms.

Particle accelerator: a large machine with a circular or long, straight tunnel in which charged particles are accelerated to extremely high speeds.

Phosphorescence: luminescence that is caused by the absorption of radiation at one wavelength followed by a delayed re-radiation, usually at a different wavelength, that continues for a time after the causative radiation stops.

Photon: the elementary unit, or quantum, of electromagnetic radiation, such as light. It has no mass or electrical charge and is one of the fundamental force-carrying particles described by the Standard Model.

Plasma: a high-energy state of matter different from solid, liquid, or gas in which atomic nuclei and the electrons orbiting them separate from each other.

Proton: a positively charged subatomic particle found in the nuclei of atoms.

Quantum: a natural unit of some physically measurable property, such as energy or electrical charge.

Quark: a fermion and a fundamental matter particle that makes up neutrons and protons, forming atomic nuclei; there are six different varieties, or flavors, of quarks grouped in pairs: up and down, charm and strange, top and bottom.

Radiation: energy emitted as rays or particles. Radiation includes heat, light, ultraviolet rays, gamma rays, X-rays, cosmic rays, alpha particles, and beta particles.

Relativity, general theory of: a theory of space-time proposed by Albert Einstein in 1915; it links gravity to the curvature of space-time.

Relativity, special theory of: Einstein's theory of space and time: all laws of physics are valid in all uniformly moving frames of reference, and the speed of light in a vacuum is always the same, so long as the source and the observer are moving uniformly (not accelerating).

Standard Model: prevailing theory of the interaction of subatomic particles. Particles are either fermions, such as electrons, neutrinos, and quarks, or bosons, such as Higgs bosons, gluons, W or Z bosons, and photons; successfully explains three of the four elementary forces acting on particles (strong, weak, electromagnetic) but thus far has not incorporated gravity.

String theory: a theory that seeks to unify quantum mechanics and general relativity, positing that the basic constituents of matter can best be understood not as point objects but as tiny oscillating "strings."

Subatomic particle: one of the small particles, such as electrons, neutrons, and protons, which make up an atom.

Superconductivity: the property of certain materials, usually metals and chemically complex ceramics, to conduct electricity without resistance, generally at very cold temperatures.

Thermodynamics: the branch of physics that describes how energy, heat, and temperature flow in physical systems.

Ultraviolet radiation: a form of light, invisible to the human eye, that has a shorter wavelength and greater energy than visible light but a longer wavelength and less energy than X-rays.

Virtual particle: subatomic particles that rapidly pop into and out of existence and can exert real forces; usually occur in particle-antiparticle pairs and are rapidly annihilated.

Mohs Scale of Hardness

Hardness is the ability of a solid substance to resist abrasion or deformation on its surface. Soft minerals scratch more easily than hard ones. For example, a diamond will scratch graphite because graphite is softer. In 1812, German mineralogist Frederich Mohs (1773-1839) created the arbitrary scale shown below to measure relative hardness using 10 minerals that were readily available at that time. The numbers in the Mohs scale are arranged in order of increasing hardness. An item's hardness is obtained by determining which mineral in the Mohs scale can scratch it.

Mohs scale

1	Talc	6	Orthoclase feldspar
2	Gypsum	7	Quartz
3	Calcite	8	Topaz
4	Fluorite	9	Corundum
5	Apatite	10	Diamond

Selected items and their relative hardness

2.5	Fingernail	5.5	Knife blade
2.5-3	Gold, silver	6-7	Glass
3	Copper penny	6.5	Iron pyrite
4-4.5	Platinum	7+	Hardened steel file
4-5	Iron		

Chemical Elements, Atomic Numbers, Year Discovered

See Periodic Table of the Elements on the following page for atomic weights.

Element	Symbol	Atomic number	Year discov.
Actinium	Ac	89	1899
Aluminum	Al	13	1825
Americium	Am	95	1944
Antimony	Sb	51	1450
Argon	Ar	18	1894
Arsenic	As	33	13th cent.
Astatine	At	85	1940
Barium	Ba	56	1808
Berkelium	Bk	97	1949
Beryllium	Be	4	1798
Bismuth	Bi	83	15th cent.
Bohrium	Bh	107	1981
Boron	B	5	1808
Bromine	Br	35	1826
Cadmium	Cd	48	1817
Calcium	Ca	20	1808
Californium	Cf	98	1950
Carbon	C	6	BCE
Cerium	Ce	58	1803
Cesium	Cs	55	1860
Chlorine	Cl	17	1774
Chromium	Cr	24	1797
Cobalt	Co	27	1735
Copernicium	Cn	112	1996
Copper	Cu	29	BCE
Curium	Cm	96	1944
Darmstadtium	Ds	110	1995
Dubnium (Hahnium)[1]	Db (Ha)	105	1970
Dysprosium	Dy	66	1886
Einsteinium	Es	99	1952
Erbium	Er	68	1843
Europium	Eu	63	1901
Fermium	Fm	100	1953
Flerovium	Fl	114	1999
Fluorine	F	9	1771
Francium	Fr	87	1939
Gadolinium	Gd	64	1886
Gallium	Ga	31	1875
Germanium	Ge	32	1886
Gold	Au	79	BCE
Hafnium	Hf	72	1923
Hassium	Hs	108	1984
Helium	He	2	1868
Holmium	Ho	67	1878
Hydrogen	H	1	1766
Indium	In	49	1863
Iodine	I	53	1811
Iridium	Ir	77	1804
Iron	Fe	26	BCE
Krypton	Kr	36	1898
Lanthanum	La	57	1839
Lawrencium	Lr	103	1961
Lead	Pb	82	BCE
Lithium	Li	3	1817
Livermorium	Lv	116	2000
Lutetium	Lu	71	1907
Magnesium	Mg	12	1829
Manganese	Mn	25	1774
Meitnerium	Mt	109	1982
Mendelevium	Md	101	1955
Mercury	Hg	80	BCE
Molybdenum	Mo	42	1782
Neodymium	Nd	60	1885
Neon	Ne	10	1898
Neptunium	Np	93	1940
Nickel	Ni	28	1751
Niobium[2]	Nb	41	1801
Nitrogen	N	7	1772
Nobelium	No	102	1958
Osmium	Os	76	1804
Oxygen	O	8	1774
Palladium	Pd	46	1803
Phosphorus	P	15	1669
Platinum	Pt	78	1735
Plutonium	Pu	94	1941
Polonium	Po	84	1898
Potassium	K	19	1807
Praseodymium	Pr	59	1885
Promethium	Pm	61	1945
Protactinium	Pa	91	1917
Radium	Ra	88	1898
Radon	Rn	86	1900
Rhenium	Re	75	1925
Rhodium	Rh	45	1803
Roentgenium	Rg	111	1995
Rubidium	Rb	37	1861
Ruthenium	Ru	44	1845
Rutherfordium	Rf	104	1969
Samarium	Sm	62	1879
Scandium	Sc	21	1879
Seaborgium	Sg	106	1974
Selenium	Se	34	1817
Silicon	Si	14	1823
Silver	Ag	47	BCE
Sodium	Na	11	1807
Strontium	Sr	38	1790
Sulfur	S	16	BCE
Tantalum	Ta	73	1802
Technetium	Tc	43	1937
Tellurium	Te	52	1782
Terbium	Tb	65	1843
Thallium	Tl	81	1861
Thorium	Th	90	1828
Thulium	Tm	69	1879
Tin	Sn	50	BCE
Titanium	Ti	22	1791
Tungsten (Wolfram)	W	74	1783
*Ununoctium	Uuo	118	2006
*Ununpentium	Uup	115	2004
*Ununseptium	Uus	117	2010
*Ununtrium	Uut	113	2004
Uranium	U	92	1789
Vanadium	V	23	1830
Xenon	Xe	54	1898
Ytterbium	Yb	70	1878
Yttrium	Y	39	1794
Zinc	Zn	30	BCE
Zirconium	Zr	40	1789

Note: 118 elements are listed here. Of those, 4 have not yet been accepted by the IUPAC and are indicated by an asterisk (*). Between 2004 and 2010, observations of isotopes of these four elements—113, 115, 117, and 118—were reported in refereed journals. Their numbers are shown in italics in the periodic table. (1) The name Dubnium (Db) has been approved by IUPAC for element 105, but the name Hahnium (Ha) was used in most of the scientific literature before 1998 and is still sometimes used in the U.S. (2) Formerly Columbium.

Periodic Table of the Elements

Source: Los Alamos National Laboratory Chemistry Division; International Union of Pure and Applied Chemistry (IUPAC)

Shaded elements are commonly regarded as metals.

Key: 14 (atomic number) 28.09 (atomic weight[1]) Si (symbol) Silicon (name)

1 1.007-1.009 **H** Hydrogen																	2 4.003 **He** Helium
3 6.938-6.997 **Li** Lithium	4 9.012 **Be** Beryllium											5 10.80-10.83 **B** Boron	6 12.00-12.02 **C** Carbon	7 14.00-14.01 **N** Nitrogen	8 15.99-16.00 **O** Oxygen	9 19.00 **F** Fluorine	10 20.18 **Ne** Neon
11 22.99 **Na** Sodium	12 24.30-24.31 **Mg** Magnesium											13 26.98 **Al** Aluminum	14 28.08-28.09 **Si** Silicon	15 30.97 **P** Phosphorus	16 32.05-32.08 **S** Sulfur	17 35.44-35.46 **Cl** Chlorine	18 39.95 **Ar** Argon
19 39.10 **K** Potassium	20 40.08 **Ca** Calcium	21 44.96 **Sc** Scandium	22 47.87 **Ti** Titanium	23 50.94 **V** Vanadium	24 52.00 **Cr** Chromium	25 54.94 **Mn** Manganese	26 55.85 **Fe** Iron	27 58.93 **Co** Cobalt	28 58.69 **Ni** Nickel	29 63.55 **Cu** Copper	30 65.38 **Zn** Zinc	31 69.72 **Ga** Gallium	32 72.63 **Ge** Germanium	33 74.92 **As** Arsenic	34 78.96 **Se** Selenium	35 79.90-79.91 **Br** Bromine	36 83.80 **Kr** Krypton
37 85.47 **Rb** Rubidium	38 87.62 **Sr** Strontium	39 88.91 **Y** Yttrium	40 91.22 **Zr** Zirconium	41 92.91 **Nb** Niobium	42 95.96 **Mo** Molybdenum	43 [98]* **Tc** Technetium	44 101.1 **Ru** Ruthenium	45 102.9 **Rh** Rhodium	46 106.4 **Pd** Palladium	47 107.9 **Ag** Silver	48 112.4 **Cd** Cadmium	49 114.8 **In** Indium	50 118.7 **Sn** Tin	51 121.8 **Sb** Antimony	52 127.6 **Te** Tellurium	53 126.9 **I** Iodine	54 131.3 **Xe** Xenon
55 132.9 **Cs** Cesium	56 137.3 **Ba** Barium	57-71 Lanthanoids	72 178.5 **Hf** Hafnium	73 180.9 **Ta** Tantalum	74 183.8 **W** Tungsten	75 186.2 **Re** Rhenium	76 190.2 **Os** Osmium	77 192.2 **Ir** Iridium	78 195.1 **Pt** Platinum	79 197.0 **Au** Gold	80 200.6 **Hg** Mercury	81 204.3-204.4 **Tl** Thallium	82 207.2 **Pb** Lead	83 209.0 **Bi** Bismuth	84 [209]* **Po** Polonium	85 [210]* **At** Astatine	86 [222]* **Rn** Radon
87 [223]* **Fr** Francium	88 [226]* **Ra** Radium	89-103 Actinoids	104 [265]* **Rf** Rutherfordium	105 [268]* **Db** Dubnium	106 [271]* **Sg** Seaborgium	107 [270]* **Bh** Bohrium	108 [277]* **Hs** Hassium	109 [276]* **Mt** Meitnerium	110 [281]* **Ds** Darmstadtium	111 [280]* **Rg** Roentgenium	112 [285]* **Cn** Copernicium	[284]* ***113***	114 [289]* **Fl** Flerovium	[288]* ***115***	116 [293]* **Lv** Livermorium	[294]* ***117***	[294]* ***118***

Lanthanide series	57 138.9 **La** Lanthanum	58 140.1 **Ce** Cerium	59 140.9 **Pr** Praseodymium	60 144.2 **Nd** Neodymium	61 [145]* **Pm** Promethium	62 150.4 **Sm** Samarium	63 152.0 **Eu** Europium	64 157.3 **Gd** Gadolinium	65 158.9 **Tb** Terbium	66 162.5 **Dy** Dysprosium	67 164.9 **Ho** Holmium	68 167.3 **Er** Erbium	69 168.9 **Tm** Thulium	70 173.1 **Yb** Ytterbium	71 175.0 **Lu** Lutetium
Actinide series	89 [227]* **Ac** Actinium	90 232.0 **Th** Thorium	91 231.0 **Pa** Protactinium	92 238.0 **U** Uranium	93 [237]* **Np** Neptunium	94 [244]* **Pu** Plutonium	95 [243]* **Am** Americium	96 [247]* **Cm** Curium	97 [247]* **Bk** Berkelium	98 [251]* **Cf** Californium	99 [252]* **Es** Einsteinium	100 [257]* **Fm** Fermium	101 [258]* **Md** Mendelevium	102 [259]* **No** Nobelium	103 [262]* **Lr** Lawrencium

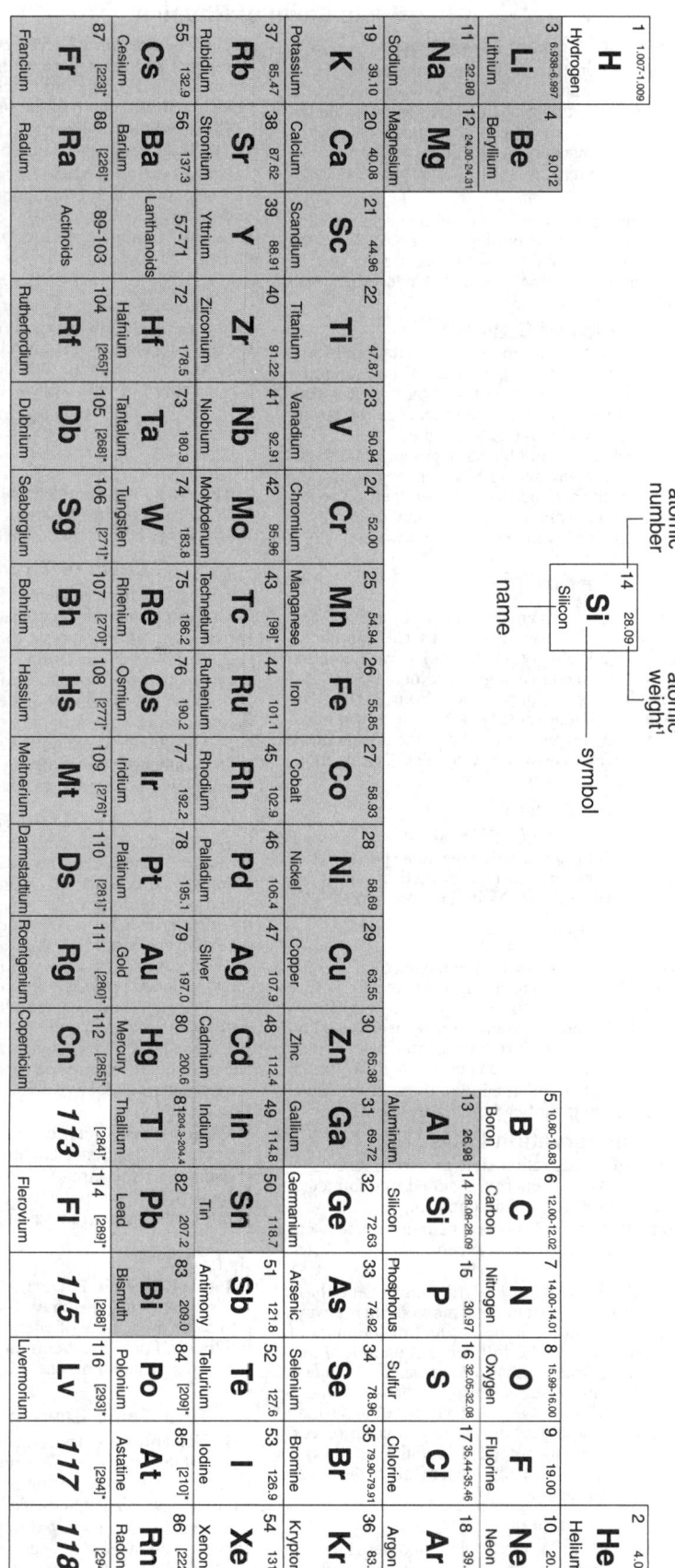

*Element has no stable nuclides. The value enclosed in brackets, e.g. [209], indicates the mass number of the longest-lived isotope of the element. However, three such elements (Th, Pa, and U) do have a characteristic terrestrial isotopic composition, and for these an atomic weight is tabulated. (1) For elements whose atomic weight varies, a range is shown.

Basic Laws of Physics

Newton's Laws of Motion

1. An object in motion moves at a constant velocity in a straight line unless acted upon by a force. Likewise, an object at rest will stay at rest. These two properties are known as inertia.

2. The acceleration of an object is proportional to the force acting on it and inversely proportional to the mass of an object. Force (*F*) equals mass (*m*) times acceleration (*a*):

$$F = ma$$

3. For every action, there is an equal and opposite reaction. For example, if a force of one ton pushes down on an object, the object pushes up with an equal force. As per the second law, the amount of movement (acceleration) produced in the object will depend on the object's mass.

Law of Gravity

In common usage, gravity refers to the gravitational force between planets and objects on or near them. But in scientific parlance, gravitation represents one of four basic forces controlling the interactions of matter. The others are the strong and weak nuclear forces and electromagnetic force. The gravitational force (*F*) between objects is proportional to the product of their masses (m_1 and m_2) and inversely proportional to the square of the distance (*d*) between them. *G* represents the gravitational constant in Newton's law of gravity, a fixed ratio of approximately 6.67384×10^{-11} newton m^2/kg^2.

The basic law of gravity is:

$$F = G\frac{m_1 m_2}{d^2}$$

Near Earth's surface, Earth's gravitational force pulls objects downward at a constant acceleration of 9.8 m/s^2 (*g*). This allows calculation of the vertical velocity (*v*) of an object with an initial vertical velocity of v_0 in free fall at a given point in time (*t*) and calculation of the distance (*d*) of an object from Earth at any given time with a given initial velocity (v_0) and a known initial height (*a*) via the following equations (here, the effects of air resistance are ignored, and downward velocities and directions are negative):

$$v = v_0 - gt$$

$$d = -\tfrac{1}{2}g(t^2) + v_0 t + a$$

Assuming that height is measured in feet and speeds in feet per second, the maximum height (*H*) reached by an object with a positive (upward) initial velocity is expressed as:

$$H = a + \frac{v_0^2}{64}$$

For motion not near Earth's surface, more complicated equations are required. Also, if the object's upward velocity is very great, the object may escape Earth's gravity. Even near Earth's surface, there are slight complications. Gravity is lessened by the centrifugal force of the Earth's rotation. At the poles, where centrifugal force is absent, acceleration due to gravity is greater.

Gravity is weaker on a mountaintop than at sea level because the mountaintop is farther from Earth's center.

Conservation Laws

In physics, laws of conservation state that in a closed system, where neither mass nor energy is added or subtracted, certain measurable quantities remain constant.

Conservation of Mass: Mass is neither created nor destroyed within a closed system except when converted from or to energy.

Conservation of Momentum: All moving objects have momentum, and in a closed system, total momentum is always conserved. Linear momentum is the product of the mass of an object and its velocity. In the following equation, *M* and *V* represent the initial total mass and velocity of objects within a closed system. After a collision between those objects, the mass and velocity of individual objects may change (for example, one object breaks into smaller pieces, each traveling at a different velocity), but the product of the total mass and velocity in the system after the collision (*mv*) will remain the same.

$$MV = mv$$

Any object moving in a circle has another kind of momentum—angular momentum. This is because circular motion requires acceleration toward the center of the circle. The amount of acceleration depends on the speed of the object and the square of the radius of the circle. (Angular momentum is the product of this speed, the mass of the object, and the square of the radius.)

Conservation of Energy: The total amount of energy in a closed system will not change except when converted to mass.

Conservation of Mass-Energy: Although mass and energy can be converted into one another, the total amount of mass and energy together must be conserved. This is reflected in Einstein's famous equation, where *m* is mass, *E* is energy, and *c* is the speed of light in a vacuum (which is constant):

$$E = mc^2$$

Relativistic mass can describe how mass increases with velocity. The following equation—where *m* is the mass of a moving object, m_0 is the object's mass when not moving, *v* is the object's velocity in relation to a stationary observer, and *c* is the speed of light—shows the relationship:

$$m = \frac{m_0}{\sqrt{1 - \frac{v^2}{c^2}}}$$

The theory that no object can travel faster than the speed of light is based in this equation. As an object approaches *c*, so much energy is converted to mass that it no longer accelerates.

Laws of Thermodynamics

1. Heat is a form of energy. Within a closed system energy must be conserved except in nuclear reactions or other extreme conditions. It is neither created nor destroyed.

2. Within a self-sustaining system, heat can never go from an area of low temperature to an area of high temperature, for this would require added energy. Without added energy, disorder, or entropy, can only increase.

3. Absolute zero cannot be attained by any procedure in a finite number of steps. Although it can be approached asymptotically, it can never be reached.

Laws of Current Electricity

Electric current generally represents the flow of electrons through a conductor. The rate at which electrons flow can be measured in amperes, defined as the number of electrons (measured in a unit called the coulomb, equal to about 6.24 quintillion or 6.24×10^{18} electrons) moving past a particular point every second. One ampere is equal to 1 coulomb of charge passing each second. Like water, electrons tend to move from areas of high pressure to low pressure. The difference between these two pressures, known as potential difference, is measured in volts.

Certain substances, such as copper and carbon, allow electric currents to pass more readily than others—that is, they have greater conductivity. Resistance to conductivity is measured in ohms.

Ohm's Law: Electric current is directly proportional to the potential difference and inversely proportional to the total resistance of the circuit. *I* is electric current (measured in amperes), *V* is the potential difference (measured in volts), and *R* is resistance (measured in ohms):

$$I = \frac{V}{R}$$

Law of Electric Power: Electric power (*P*), measured in watts, represents the rate at which electricity is converted into some other form of energy (such as light, in the case of a lightbulb). For a direct-current circuit, *P* is the product of current and potential difference:

$$P = IV$$

Two Basic Laws of Quantum Physics

1. Heisenberg's uncertainty principle: Certain pairs of observable quantities like energy and time or position and momentum cannot be measured with complete accuracy simultaneously. Also known as the indeterminacy principle.

2. Pauli's exclusion principle: Two electrons in an atom cannot simultaneously occupy the same quantum or energy state. This has since been shown to be true for many subatomic particles.

Breaking the Sound Barrier; Speed of Sound

The prefix **Mach** is used to describe supersonic speed. It was named for Ernst Mach (1838-1916), a Czech-born Austrian physicist. Mach may be defined as the ratio of the velocity of an object to the velocity of sound in a particular medium. A plane moving at the speed of sound moves at Mach 1. At twice the speed of sound, it moves at Mach 2.

When a plane passes the sound barrier—that is, flies faster than the speed at which sound travels—people in the area, though not the people on the plane, hear what seem to be thunderclaps. These sounds are sometimes called sonic booms.

Sound is produced by vibrations of an object. It is transmitted by the alternating increase and decrease in pressure that radiates outward from a source through a material medium of molecules, like waves spreading out on a pond after a rock has been tossed in.

The **frequency of sound** is determined by the number of times the vibrating waves undulate per second. It is measured in cycles per second. The slower the cycle of waves, the lower the frequency. As the frequency increases, the sound becomes higher in pitch. The human ear is sensitive to frequencies between 20 and 20,000 vibrations per second, although this range varies among individuals.

Intensity, or loudness, is the strength of the pressure of these radiating waves and is measured in decibels.

The **speed of sound** varies depending on temperature and altitude. It moves faster in water than in air, for example. At sea level and a temperature of 59°F (15°C), the speed of sound is approximately 761 mph, or 1,100 ft per sec.

Light; Colors of the Spectrum

Light, a form of electromagnetic radiation similar to radiant heat, radio waves, and X-rays, is emitted from a source in straight lines and spreads in area as it travels. For emission from a point source, light per unit area diminishes in proportion to the square of the distance.

The English mathematician and physicist Isaac Newton (1642-1727) described light as an **emission of particles**; the Dutch astronomer, mathematician, and physicist Christiaan Huygens (1629-95) and others developed the theory that light travels in a **wave motion**. It is now believed that these two theories are essentially complementary. The development of quantum theory has led to results where light acts like a series of particles in some experiments and like a wave in others.

The first relatively accurate measurement of the **speed of light** was made by French physicist Armand Hippolyte Louis Fizeau (1819-96). Today the speed of light is known precisely as 299,792.458 km per sec (or 186,282.397 mi/sec) in a vacuum. In water the speed of light is about 25% less, and in glass, 33% less.

Color sensations are produced through the excitation of the retina of the eye by light vibrating at different frequencies. The different colors of the visible spectrum may be seen by viewing light refracted by passage through a prism, which separates light into its component wavelengths.

Customarily, the basic colors are taken to be the six monochromatic (single) colors that occupy relatively large areas of the spectrum: red, orange, yellow, green, blue, and violet. So-called primary colors can be combined to produce the sensation of other colors. However, scientists disagree about how many and what primary colors to recognize. The color sensation of **black** is due to complete lack of stimulation of the retina, that of **white** to complete stimulation.

Infrared and **ultraviolet rays**, which are below the red (long) end and above the violet (short) end of the visible spectrum, respectively, are invisible to the naked eye. Heat is the principal effect of infrared rays, and chemical action that of ultraviolet rays.

Discoveries and Innovations: Biology, Chemistry, Medicine, Physics

Discovery	Date	Discoverer(s)	Nationality
Acetylene gas	**1862**	Berthelot	French
ACTH	**1927**	Evans, Long	U.S.
Adrenaline	**1901**	Takamine	Japanese
Aluminum, electrolytic process	**1886**	Hall	U.S.
Aluminum, isolated	**1825**	Oersted	Danish
Anesthesia, ether	**1842**	Long	U.S.
Anesthesia, local	**1885**	Koller	Austrian
Anesthesia, spinal	**1898**	Bier	German
Aniline dye	**1856**	Perkin	English
Anti-rabies	**1885**	Pasteur	French
Antiseptic surgery	**1867**	Lister	English
Antitoxin, diphtheria	**1891**	Von Behring	German
Argyrol	**1897**	Bayer	German
Arsphenamine	**1910**	Ehrlich	German
Aspirin	**1853**	Gerhardt	French
Atabrine	**1932**	Mietzsch, et al.	German
Atomic numbers	**1913**	Moseley	English
Atomic theory	**1803**	Dalton	English
Atomic time clock	**1948**	Lyons	U.S.
Atom-smashing theory	**1919**	Rutherford	English
Bacitracin	**1943**	Johnson, Meleneyl	U.S.
Bacteria, description	**1676**	Leeuwenhoek	Dutch
Bleaching powder	**1798**	Tennant	English
Blood, circulation	**1628**	Harvey	English
Bordeaux mixture	**1885**	Millardet	French
Bromine from the sea	**1826**	Balard	French
Calcium carbide	**1888**	Wilson	U.S.
Calculus	**1670**	Newton	English
Camphor synthetic	**1896**	Haller	French
Canning (food)	**1804**	Appert	French
Carbon oxides	**1925**	Fisher	German
Chemotherapy	**1909**	Ehrlich	German
Chloamphenicol	**1947**	Burkholder	U.S.
Chlorine	**1774**	Scheele	Swedish
Chloroform	**1831**	Guthrie	U.S.
Chlortetracycline	**1948**	Duggen	U.S.
Classification of plants and animals	**1735**	Linnaeus	Swedish
Cloning, DNA	**1973**	Boyer, Cohen	U.S.
Cloning, mammal	**1996**	Wilmut, et al.	Scottish
Cocaine	**1860**	Niermann	German
Combustion explained	**1777**	Lavoisier	French

Discovery	Date	Discoverer(s)	Nationality
Conditioned reflex	**1914**	Pavlov	Russian
Cortisone	**1936**	Kendall	U.S.
Cortisone, synthesis	**1946**	Sarett	U.S.
Cosmic rays	**1910**	Gockel	Swiss
Cyclotron	**1930**	Lawrence	U.S.
DDT (not applied as insecticide until 1939)	**1874**	Zeidler	German
Denisovan humans (DNA analysis)	**2010**	Krause, et al.	German
		Pääbo	Swedish
Deuterium	**1932**	Urey, Brickwedde, Murphy	U.S.
DNA (structure)	**1953**	Crick, Wilkins	English
		Watson	U.S.
Electric resistance, law of	**1827**	Ohm	German
Electric waves	**1888**	Hertz	German
Electrolysis	**1852**	Faraday	English
Electromagnetism	**1819**	Oersted	Danish
Electron	**1897**	Thomson, J.	English
Electron diffraction	**1936**	Thomson, G.	English
		Davisson	U.S.
Electroshock treatment	**1938**	Cerletti, Bini	Italian
Erythromycin	**1952**	McGuire	U.S.
Evolution, natural selection	**1858**	Darwin	English
Falling bodies, law of	**1590**	Galileo	Italian
Gases, law of combining volumes	**1808**	Gay-Lussac	French
Geometry, analytic	**1619**	Descartes	French
Gold, cyanide process for extraction	**1887**	MacArthur, R. Forrest, W. Forrest	British
Gravitation, law	**1687**	Newton	English
Higgs boson	**2012**	CERN	International
HIV (human immuno-deficiency virus)	**1984**	Montagnier	French
		Gallo	U.S.
Holograph	**1948**	Gabor	Hung.-British
Homo floresiensis ("hobbit" humans)	**2003**	Morwood, et al.	New Zea.
Human heart transplant	**1967**	Barnard	S. African
Indigo, synthesis of	**1880**	Baeyer	German
Induction, electric	**1830**	Henry	U.S.

Discovery	Date	Discoverer(s)	Nationality
Insulin	**1922**	Banting, Best	Canadian
		Macleod	Scottish
Intelligence testing	**1905**	Binet, Simon	French
In vitro fertilization	**1978**	Steptoe, Edwards	English
Isotopes, theory	**1912**	Soddy	English
Laser	**1957**	Gould	U.S.
Light, velocity	**1675**	Roemer	Danish
Light, wave theory	**1690**	Huygens	Dutch
Lithography	**1796**	Senefelder	Bohemian
Logarithms	**1614**	Napier	Scottish
LSD-25	**1943**	Hoffman	Swiss
Mendelian laws	**1866**	Mendel	Austrian
Mercator projection (map)	**1568**	Mercator (Kremer)	Flemish
Methanol	**1661**	Boyle	Irish
Milk condensation	**1853**	Borden	U.S.
Molecular hypothesis	**1811**	Avogadro	Italian
Motion, laws of	**1687**	Newton	English
Neomycin	**1949**	Waksman, Lechevalier	U.S.
Neutrino	**1956**	Reines, Cowan	U.S.
Neutron	**1932**	Chadwick	English
Nitric acid	**1648**	Glauber	German
Nitric oxide	**1772**	Priestley	English
Nitroglycerin	**1846**	Sobrero	Italian
Oil cracking process	**1891**	Dewar	U.S.
Oxygen	**1774**	Priestley	English
Oxytetracycline	**1950**	Finlay, et al.	U.S.
Ozone	**1840**	Schonbein	German
Paper, sulfite process	**1867**	Tilghman	U.S.
Paper, wood pulp, sulfate process	**1884**	Dahl	German
Penicillin	**1928**	Fleming	Scottish
Penicillin, practical use	**1941**	Florey, Chain	English
Periodic law and table of elements	**1869**	Mendeleyev	Russian
Physostigmine synthesis	**1935**	Julian	U.S.
Pill, birth-control	**1954**	Pincus, Rock	U.S.
Planetary motion, laws	**1609**	Kepler	German
Plutonium fission	**1940**	Kennedy, Wahl, Seaborg, Segre	U.S.
Polymyxin	**1947**	Ainsworth	English
Positron	**1932**	Anderson	U.S.
Proton	**1919**	Rutherford	New Zea.
Psychoanalysis	**1900**	Freud	Austrian
Pulsars	**1967**	Bell	English
Quantum theory	**1900**	Planck	German
Quasars	**1963**	Matthews, Sandage	U.S.
Quinine synthetic	**1946**	Woodward, Doering	U.S.
Radioactivity	**1896**	Becquerel	French
Radiocarbon dating	**1947**	Libby	U.S.
Radium	**1898**	Curie, Pierre	French
		Curie, Marie	Pol.-Fr.
Relativity theory	**1905**	Einstein	German
Reserpine	**1949**	Jal Vakil	Indian
Schick test	**1913**	Schick	U.S.
Silicon	**1823**	Berzelius	Swedish
Smallpox eradication	**1979**	World Health Org.	UN
Streptomycin	**1944**	Waksman, et al.	U.S.
Sulfanilamide	**1935**	Bovet, Trefouel	French
Sulfanilamide theory	**1908**	Gelmo	German
Sulfapyridine	**1938**	Ewins, Phelps	English
Sulfathiazole	**1939**	Fosbinder, Walter	U.S.
Sulfuric acid	**1831**	Phillips	English
Sulfuric acid, lead	**1746**	Roebuck	English
Superconductivity	**1911**	Onnes	Dutch
Superconductivity theory	**1957**	Bardeen, Cooper, Schreiffer	U.S.
Superconductors, high-temp.	**1986**	Bednorz, Muller	Ger., Swiss
Syphilis test	**1906**	Wassermann	German
Transplant, heart	**1967**	Barnard	S. African
Tuberculin	**1890**	Koch	German
Uranium fission, atomic reactor	**1942**	Fermi, Szilard	U.S.
Uranium fission theory	**1939**	Hahn, Meitner, Strassmann	German
		Bohr	Danish
		Fermi	Italian
		Einstein, Pegram, Wheeler	U.S.
Vaccine, measles	**1963**	Enders	U.S.
Vaccine, MMR	**1971**	Hilleman	U.S.
Vaccine, meningitis (first conjugate)	**1987**	Gordon, et al., Connaught Labs	U.S.
Vaccine, polio	**1954**	Salk	U.S.
Vaccine, polio, oral	**1960**	Sabin	U.S.
Vaccine, rabies	**1885**	Pasteur	French
Vaccine, smallpox	**1796**	Jenner	English
Vaccine, typhus	**1909**	Nicolle	French
Vaccine, varicella	**1974**	Takahashi	Japanese
Van Allen belts, radiation	**1958**	Van Allen	U.S.
Vitamin A	**1913**	McCollum, Davis	U.S.
Vitamin B	**1916**	McCollum	U.S.
Vitamin C	**1928**	Szent-Gyorgyi	Hungarian
		King	U.S.
Vitamin D	**1922**	McCollum	U.S.
Xerography	**1938**	Carlson	U.S.
X-ray	**1895**	Roentgen	German

Inventions

Invention	Date	Inventor(s)	Nationality
Adding machine	**1642**	Pascal	French
Adding machine	**1885**	Burroughs	U.S.
Aerosol spray	**1926**	Rotheim	Norwegian
Air brake	**1868**	Westinghouse	U.S.
Air conditioning	**1902**	Carrier	U.S.
Air pump	**1654**	Guericke	German
Airbag	**1952**	Hetrick	U.S.
Airplane, automatic pilot	**1912**	Sperry	U.S.
Airplane, experimental	**1896**	Langley	U.S.
Airplane, hydro	**1911**	Curtiss	U.S.
Airplane jet engine	**1939**	Ohain	German
Airplane with motor	**1903**	Wright Bros.	U.S.
Airship	**1852**	Giffard	French
Aqua-Lung	**1943**	Cousteau, Gagnan	French
Arc welder	**1919**	Thomson	U.S.
Aspartame	**1965**	Schlatter	U.S.
Autogyro	**1920**	de la Cierva	Spanish
Automobile, diff. gear	**1885**	Benz	German
Automobile, electric	**1892**	Morrison	U.S.
Automobile, exp'mtl	**1864**	Marcus	Austrian
Automobile, gasoline	**1889**	Daimler	German
Automobile, gasoline	**1892**	Duryea	U.S.
Automobile magneto	**1897**	Bosch	German
Automobile muffler	**1904**	Pope	U.S.
Automobile self-starter	**1911**	Kettering	U.S.
Bakelite	**1907**	Baekeland	Belg., U.S.
Bar code	**1952**	Woodland, Silver	U.S.
Barometer	**1643**	Torricelli	Italian
Bicycle, modern	**1885**	Starley	English
Bifocal lens	**1780**	Franklin	U.S.
Bottle machine	**1895**	Owens	U.S.
Braille printing	**1829**	Braille	French
Brassiere, modern	**1913**	Jacob	U.S
Bubble gum	**1928**	Diemer	U.S.
Burner, gas	**1855**	Bunsen	German
Calculating machine	**1833**	Babbage	English
Calculator, electronic pocket	**1972**	Merryman, Van Tassel	U.S.
Camera, digital	**1977**	Lloyd, Sasson	U.S.
Camera, Kodak	**1888**	Eastman, Walker	U.S.
Camera, Polaroid Land	**1948**	Land	U.S.
Can, pop-top	**1959**	Fraze	U.S.
Car coupler	**1873**	Janney	U.S.
Carburetor, gasoline	**1893**	Maybach	German
Carding machine	**1797**	Whittemore	U.S.
Carpet sweeper	**1876**	Bissell	U.S.
Cash register	**1879**	Ritty	U.S.
Cassette, audio	**1963**	Philips Co.	Dutch
Cassette, videotape	**1969**	Sony	Japanese
CAT, or CT, scan	**1973**	Hounsfield	English
Cathode-ray tube	**1897**	Braun	German
Cellophane	**1908**	Brandenberger	Swiss
Celluloid	**1870**	Hyatt	U.S.
Cement, Portland	**1824**	Aspdin	English
Chronometer	**1735**	Harrison	English
Circuit breaker	**1925**	Hilliard	U.S.
Circuit, integrated	**1959**	Kilby, Noyce, Texas Instr.	U.S.
Clock, pendulum	**1657**	Huygens	Dutch
Coaxial cable system	**1929**	Affel, Espensched	U.S.
Coca-Cola	**1885**	Pemberton	U.S.
Coffeemaker, auto. drip	**1963**	Bunn Corp.	U.S.
Compressed air rock drill	**1871**	Ingersoll	U.S.
Comptometer	**1887**	Felt	U.S.
Computer, automatic sequence	**1944**	Aiken, et al.	U.S.
Computer, electronic	**1942**	Atanasoff, Berry	U.S.
Computer, laptop	**1987**	Sinclair	English
Computer, mini	**1960**	Digital Corp.	U.S.
Condenser microphone (telephone)	**1916**	Wente	U.S.
Contact lens, corneal	**1948**	Tuohy	U.S.
Contraceptive, oral	**1954**	Pincus, Rock	U.S.
Corn, hybrid	**1917**	Jones	U.S.
Cotton gin	**1793**	Whitney	U.S.
Cream separator	**1878**	DeLaval	Swedish

Invention	Date	Inventor(s)	Nationality
Cultivator, disc	**1878**	Mallon	U.S.
Cyclotron	**1931**	Lawrence	U.S.
Cystoscope	**1878**	Nitze	German
Diapers, disposable	**1950**	Donovan	U.S.
Diesel engine	**1895**	Diesel	German
Disc, compact	**1972**	RCA	U.S.
Disc player, compact	**1979**	Sony, Philips Co.	Japanese, Dutch
Dishwasher	**1893**	Cochrane	U.S.
Disk, floppy	**1970**	IBM	U.S.
Disk, video	**1972**	Philips Co.	Dutch
Dynamite	**1866**	Nobel	Swedish
Dynamo, contin. current	**1871**	Gramme	Belgian
Electric battery	**1800**	Volta	Italian
Electric fan	**1882**	Wheeler	U.S.
Electrocardiograph	**1903**	Einthoven	Dutch
Electroencephalograph	**1929**	Berger	German
Electromagnet	**1824**	Sturgeon	English
Electron microscope	**1931**	Ruska, Knoll	German
Electron spectrometer	**1944**	Deutsch, Elliott, Evans	U.S.
Electron tube multigrid	**1913**	Langmuir	U.S.
Electronic paper (e-ink)	**1974**	Sheridon	U.S.
Electroplating	**1805**	Brugnatelli	Italian
Electrostatic generator	**1929**	Van de Graaff	U.S.
Elevator brake	**1852**	Otis	U.S.
Elevator, push button	**1922**	Larson	U.S.
Engine, automatic transmission	**1910**	Fottinger	German
Engine, coal-gas 4-cycle	**1876**	Otto	German
Engine, compression ignition	**1883**	Daimler	German
Engine, electric ignition	**1883**	Benz	German
Engine, gas, compound	**1926**	Eickemeyer	U.S.
Engine, gasoline	**1872**	Brayton	U.S.
Engine, gasoline	**1889**	Daimler	German
Engine, jet	**1930**	Whittle	English
Engine, steam, piston	**1705**	Newcomen	English
Engine, steam, piston	**1769**	Watt	Scottish
Engraving, half-tone	**1852**	Talbot	U.S.
Ferris wheel	**1893**	Ferris	U.S.
Fiber optic wire	**1970**	Keck, Maurer, Schultz	U.S.
Fiber optics	**1955**	Kapany	English
Fiberglass	**1938**	Owens-Corning	U.S.
Filament, tungsten	**1913**	Coolidge	U.S.
Flanged rail	**1831**	Stevens	U.S.
Flatiron, electric	**1882**	Seely	U.S.
Food, frozen	**1923**	Birdseye	U.S.
Freon	**1930**	Midgley, et al.	U.S.
Furnace (for steel)	**1858**	Siemens	German
Galvanometer	**1820**	Sweigger	German
Garbage bag, polyethylene	**1950**	Wasylyk	Canadian
Gas discharge tube	**1922**	Hull	U.S.
Gas lighting	**1792**	Murdoch	Scottish
Gas mantle	**1885**	Welsbach	Austrian
Gasoline, cracked	**1913**	Burton	U.S.
Gasoline, high octane	**1930**	Ipatieff	Russian
Gasoline (lead ethyl)	**1922**	Midgley	U.S.
Geiger counter	**1913**	Geiger	German
Geodesic dome	**1948**	Fuller	U.S.
Glass, laminated safety	**1909**	Benedictus	French
Glider	**1853**	Cayley	English
Google search software	**1996**	Brin, Page	U.S.
Gun, breechloader	**1811**	Thornton	U.S.
Gun, Browning	**1897**	Browning	U.S.
Gun, magazine	**1875**	Hotchkiss	U.S.
Gun, silencer	**1908**	Maxim, H. P.	U.S.
Guncotton	**1847**	Schoenbein	German
Gyrocompass	**1911**	Sperry	U.S.
Gyroscope	**1852**	Foucault	French
Hard drive, computer	**1955**	Johnson	U.S.
Harvester-thresher	**1818**	Lane	U.S.
Heart, artificial	**1982**	Jarvik	U.S.
Helicopter	**1939**	Sikorsky	U.S.
Hovercraft	**1955**	Cockerell	English
Hydrometer	**1768**	Baume	French
Ice resurfacing machine	**1949**	Zamboni	U.S.
Iron lung	**1928**	Drinker, Slaw	U.S.
Jet Ski	**1973**	Jacobsen	U.S.
Kaleidoscope	**1817**	Brewster	Scottish
Kevlar	**1965**	Kwolek, Blades	U.S.
Kidney dialysis machine	**1941**	Kolff	Dutch
Kinetoscope	**1889**	Edison	U.S.
Lamp, arc	**1847**	Staite	English
Lamp, fluorescent	**1938**	General Electric, Westinghouse	U.S.
Lamp, incandescent	**1879**	Edison	U.S.
Lamp, incand., gas	**1913**	Langmuir	U.S.
Lamp, klieg	**1911**	Kliegl, A. and J.	U.S.
Lamp, mercury vapor	**1912**	Hewitt	U.S.
Lamp, miner's safety	**1816**	Davy	English
Lamp, neon	**1909**	Claude	French
Lathe, turret	**1845**	Fitch	U.S.
Launderette	**1934**	Cantrell	U.S.
Lens, achromatic	**1758**	Dollond	English
Lens, fused bifocal	**1908**	Borsch	U.S.
Leyden jar (condenser)	**1745**	von Kleist	German
Lightning rod	**1752**	Franklin	U.S.
Linoleum	**1860**	Walton	English
Linotype	**1884**	Mergenthaler	U.S.
Linux	**1991**	Torvalds	Finnish
Liquid Paper	**c.1951**	Graham	U.S.
Lock, cylinder	**1851**	Yale	U.S.
Locomotive, electric	**1851**	Vail	U.S.
Locomotive, exp'mtl	**1802**	Trevithick	English
Locomotive, exp'mtl	**1812**	Fenton, et al.	English
Locomotive, exp'mtl	**1814**	Stephenson	English
Locomotive, 1st U.S.	**1830**	Cooper	U.S.
Locomotive, practical	**1829**	Stephenson	English
Loom, power	**1785**	Cartwright	English
Loudspeaker, dynamic	**1924**	Rice, Kellogg	U.S.
Machine gun	**1862**	Gatling	U.S.
Machine gun, improved	**1872**	Hotchkiss	U.S.
Machine gun (Maxim)	**1883**	Maxim, H. S.	U.S.-Eng.
Magnet, electro	**1828**	Henry	U.S.
Magnetic Resonance Imaging (MRI)	**1971**	Damadian	U.S.
Maser	**1953**	Townes	U.S.
Mason jar	**1858**	Mason	U.S.
Match, friction	**1827**	Walker	English
Mercerized textiles	**1843**	Mercer	English
Meter, induction	**1888**	Shallenberger	U.S.
Metronome	**1816**	Malezel	German
Microcomputer	**1973**	Truong, et al.	French
Micrometer	**1636**	Gascoigne	English
Microphone	**1877**	Berliner	U.S.
Microprocessor	**1971**	Intel Corp.	U.S.
Microscope, compound	**1590**	Janssen	Dutch
Microscope, electronic	**1931**	Knoll, Ruska	German
Microscope, field ion	**1951**	Mueller	German
Microwave oven	**1947**	Spencer	U.S.
Monitor, warship	**1861**	Ericsson	U.S.
Monotype	**1887**	Lanston	U.S.
Motor, AC	**1892**	Tesla	U.S.
Motor, DC	**1837**	Davenport	U.S.
Motor, induction	**1887**	Tesla	U.S.
Motorcycle	**1885**	Daimler	German
Mouse, computer	**1968**	Engelbart	U.S.
Movie machine	**1894**	Jenkins	U.S.
Movie, panoramic	**1952**	Waller	U.S.
Movie, talking	**1927**	Warner Bros.	U.S.
Mower, lawn	**1831**	Budding, Ferrabee	English
Mowing machine	**1822**	Bailey	U.S.
Neoprene	**1930**	Carothers	U.S.
Nylon	**1937**	Carothers, DuPont	U.S.
Oil cracking furnace	**1891**	Gavrilov	Russian
Oil filled power cable	**1921**	Emanueli	Italian
Oleomargarine	**1869**	Mege-Mouries	French
Ophthalmoscope	**1851**	Helmholtz	German
Pacemaker	**1952**	Zoll	U.S.
Pacemaker, implantable cardiac	**1958**	Greatbatch	U.S.
Paper	**105**	Ts'ai	Chinese
Paper clip	**1900**	Waaler	Norwegian
Paper machine	**1809**	Dickinson	U.S.
Parachute	**1785**	Blanchard	French
Pen, ballpoint	**1888**	Loud	U.S.
Pen, fountain	**1884**	Waterman	U.S.
Pen, steel	**1780**	Harrison	English
Pendulum	**1583**	Galileo	Italian
Percussion cap	**1807**	Forsythe	Scottish
Phonograph	**1877**	Edison	U.S.
Photo, color	**1892**	Ives	U.S.
Photo film, celluloid	**1893**	Reichenbach	U.S.
Photo film, transparent	**1884**	Eastman, Goodwin	U.S.
Photocopier	**1938**	Carlson	U.S.
Photoelectric cell	**1895**	Elster	German
Photographic paper	**1835**	Talbot	English
Photography	**1816**	Niepce	French
Photography	**1835**	Daguerre	French
Photography	**1835**	Talbot	English

Invention	Date	Inventor(s)	Nationality
Photophone	1880	Bell	U.S.-Scot.
Phototelegraphy	1925	Bell Labs	U.S.
Piano	1709	Cristofori	Italian
Piano, player	1863	Fourneaux	French
Pin, safety	1849	Hunt	U.S.
Pistol (revolver)	1836	Colt	U.S.
Plow, cast iron	1785	Ransome	English
Plow, disc	1896	Hardy	U.S.
Pneumatic hammer	1890	King	U.S.
Post-it note	1980	Fry, Silver	U.S.
Potato chip	1853	Crum	U.S.
Powder, smokeless	1884	Vieille	French
Printing press, rotary	1845	Hoe	U.S.
Printing press, web	1865	Bullock	U.S.
Propeller, screw	1804	Stevens	U.S.
Propeller, screw	1837	Ericsson	Swedish
Punch card accounting	1889	Hollerith	U.S.
Radar	1940	Watson-Watt	Scottish
Radio amplifier	1906	De Forest	U.S.
Radio beacon	1928	Donovan	U.S.
Radio crystal oscillator	1918	Nicolson	U.S.
Radio FM, 2-path	1933	Armstrong	U.S.
Radio, magnetic detector	1902	Marconi	Italian
Radio receiver, cascade tuning	1913	Alexanderson	U.S.
Radio receiver, heterodyne	1913	Fessenden	Canadian
Radio, signals	1895	Marconi	Italian
Radio transmitter triode modulation	1914	Alexanderson	U.S.
Radio tube diode	1904	Fleming	English
Radio tube oscillator	1915	De Forest	U.S.
Radio tube triode	1906	De Forest	U.S.
Rayon (acetate)	1895	Cross	English
Rayon (cuprammonium)	1890	Despeissis	French
Rayon (nitrocellulose)	1884	Chardonnet	French
Razor, electric	1917	Schick	U.S.
Razor, safety	1895	Gillette	U.S.
Reaper	1834	McCormick	U.S.
Record, cylinder	1887	Bell, Tainter	U.S.
Record, disc	1887	Berliner	U.S.
Record, long playing	1947	Goldmark	U.S.
Record, wax cylinder	1888	Edison	U.S.
Refrigerator car	1868	David	U.S.
Remote control	1898	Tesla	U.S.
Resin, synthetic	1931	Hill	English
Richter scale	1935	Richter	U.S.
Rifle, repeating	1860	Henry	U.S.
Rocket, liquid fuel	1926	Goddard	U.S.
Rollerblades	1980	Olson	U.S.
Rubber, vulcanized	1839	Goodyear	U.S.
Saccharin	1879	Remsen, Fahlberg	U.S.
Saw, circular	1777	Miller	English
Scotch tape	1930	Drew	U.S.
Seat belt	1959	Volvo	Swedish
Segway human transporter	2001	Kamen	U.S.
Seismograph	1880	Milne, Ewing, Gray	Eng.-Scot.
Sewing machine	1846	Howe	U.S.
Shoe-lasting machine	1883	Matzeliger	U.S.
Shoe-sewing machine	1860	McKay	U.S.
Shrapnel shell	1784	Shrapnel	English
Shuttle, flying	1733	Kay	English
Skates, in-line	1759	Merlin	Belgian
Sleeping-car	1865	Pullman	U.S.
Slide rule	1620	Oughtred	English
Slinky	1943	James	U.S.
Smoke detector	1969	Smith, House	U.S.
Soap, hardwater	1928	Bertsch	German
Spectroscope	1859	Kirchoff, Bunsen	German
Spectroscope (mass)	1918	Dempster	U.S.
Spinning jenny	c.1764	Hargreaves	English
Spinning mule	1779	Crompton	English
Steam car	1770	Cugnot	French
Steam turbine	1884	Parsons	English
Steamboat, exp'mtl	1778	Jouffroy	French
Steamboat, exp'mtl	1785	Fitch	U.S.
Steamboat, exp'mtl	1787	Rumsey	U.S.
Steamboat, exp'mtl	1803	Fulton	U.S.
Steamboat, exp'mtl	1804	Stevens	U.S.
Steamboat, practical	1802	Symington	Scottish
Steamboat, practical	1807	Fulton	U.S.
Steel alloy, high-speed	1901	Taylor, White	U.S.
Steel (converter)	1856	Bessemer	English
Steel, manganese	1884	Hadfield	English
Steel, stainless	1916	Brearley	English
Stereoscope	1838	Wheatstone	English
Stethoscope	1819	Laennec	French
Stethoscope, binaural	1840	Cammann	U.S.
Stock ticker	1870	Edison	U.S.
Storage battery, rechargeable	1859	Plante	French
Stove, electric	1896	Hadaway	U.S.
Submarine	1891	Holland	U.S.
Submarine, even keel	1894	Lake	U.S.
Submarine, torpedo	1776	Bushnell	U.S.
Synthesizer	1964	Moog	U.S.
Tank, military	1914	Swinton	English
Tape recorder, magnetic	1899	Poulsen	Danish
Taser	1974	Cover	U.S.
Teflon	1938	Du Pont	U.S.
Telegraph, magnetic	1837	Morse	U.S.
Telegraph, quadruplex	1864	Edison	U.S.
Telegraph, railroad	1887	Woods	U.S.
Telegraph, wireless high frequency	1895	Marconi	Italian
Telephone[1]	1871	Meucci	U.S.-Italian
Telephone[1]	1876	Bell	U.S.-Scot.
Telephone amplifier	1912	De Forest	U.S.
Telephone answering machine (1st practical)	1954	Hashimoto	Japanese
Telephone, automatic	1891	Strowger	U.S.
Telephone, cellular	1947	Bell Labs	U.S.
Telephone, cordless[2]	1950	Gross	U.S.
Telephone, radio	1900	Poulsen Fessenden	Danish Canadian
Telephone, radio	1906	De Forest	U.S.
Telephone, radio, long dist.	1915	AT&T	U.S.
Telephone, recording	1898	Poulsen	Danish
Telescope	1608	Lippershey	Dutch
Telescope	1609	Galileo	Italian
Telescope, astronomical	1611	Kepler	German
Telescope, reflecting	1668	Newton	English
Teletype	1928	Morkrum, Kleinschmidt	U.S.
Television, color	1928	Baird	Scottish
Television, electronic	1927	Farnsworth	U.S.
Television, iconoscope	1923	Zworykin	U.S.
Television, mech. scanner	1923	Baird	Scottish
Tesla Coil	1891	Tesla	U.S.
Thermometer	1593	Galileo	Italian
Thermometer	1730	Reaumur	French
Thermometer, mercury	1714	Fahrenheit	German
3D printing (stereolithography)	1984	Hull	U.S.
Time recorder	1890	Bundy	U.S.
Tire, double-tube	1845	Thomson	Scottish
Tire, pneumatic	1888	Dunlop	Scottish
Toaster, automatic	1918	Strite	U.S.
Toilet, flush	1589	Harington	English
Torpedo, marine	1804	Fulton	U.S.
Tractor, crawler	1904	Holt	U.S.
Transformer, AC	1885	Stanley	U.S.
Transistor	1947	Shockley, Brattain, Bardeen	U.S.
Trolley car, electric	1884-87	Van DePoele, Sprague	U.S.
Tungsten, ductile	1912	Coolidge	U.S.
Tupperware®	1945	Tupper	U.S.
Turbine, gas	1849	Bourdin	French
Turbine, hydraulic	1849	Francis	U.S.
Turbine, steam	1884	Parsons	English
Type, movable	1447	Gutenberg	German
Typewriter	1867	Sholes, Soule, Glidden	U.S.
Universal Serial Bus (USB)	1994	Bhatt, et al.	U.S.
Vacuum cleaner, electric	1907	Spangler	U.S.
Vacuum evaporating pan	1846	Rillieux	U.S.
Velcro	1948	de Mestral	Swiss
Video game ("Pong")	1972	Bushnell	U.S.

Invention	Date	Inventor(s)	Nationality
Video home system (VHS)	1975	Matsushita, JVC	Japanese
Vinyl	1926	Semon	U.S.
Washer, electric	1901	Fisher	U.S.
Welding, atomic hydrogen	1924	Langmuir, Palmer	U.S.
Welding, electric	1877	Thomson	U.S.
Wheelchair, multiterrain	1986	Twitchell	U.S.
Wheelchair, stair-climbing	1962	Blanco	U.S.
Wiki software	1995	Cunningham	U.S.
Wind tunnel	1912	Eiffel	French
Windshield wiper	1903	Anderson	U.S.
Wire, barbed	1874	Glidden	U.S.
World Wide Web	1989	Berners-Lee	English
Wrench, double-acting	1913	Owen	U.S.
X-ray tube	1913	Coolidge	U.S.
Zeppelin	1900	Zeppelin	German
Zipper, early model	1893	Judson	U.S.
Zipper, improved	1913	Sundback	Canadian

(1) While Alexander Graham Bell has traditionally been credited with invention of the telephone, which he patented, Antonio Meucci developed a working model before Bell. (2) Al Gross held a number of important early patents in the field of wireless communication; other people were also involved in the development of practical cordless telephones.

Corporations Receiving U.S. Patents, 2014

Source: U.S. Patent and Trademark Office, U.S. Dept. of Commerce

(ranked by number of U.S. utility patents, or patents for inventions, granted)

Rank	Company	No. of patents
1.	International Business Machines Corp.	7,481
2.	Samsung Electronics Co., Ltd.	4,936
3.	Canon Kabushiki Kaisha	4,048
4.	Sony Corp.	3,214
5.	Microsoft Corp.	2,829
6.	Qualcomm, Inc.	2,586
7.	Google, Inc.	2,566
8.	Toshiba Corp.	2,537
9.	LG Electronics Inc.	2,119
10.	Panasonic Corp.	2,079
11.	Apple, Inc.	2,003
12.	General Electric Co.	1,858
13.	Fujitsu Limited	1,812
14.	Seiko Epson Corp.	1,660
15.	Ricoh Co., Ltd.	1,634
16.	Hewlett-Packard Development Co., L.P.	1,573
17.	Intel Corp.	1,573
18.	Telefonaktiebolaget LM Ericsson (Publ.)	1,537
19.	Samsung Display Co., Ltd.	1,500
20.	GM Global Technology Operations L.L.C.	1,470

Note: Reflects patent ownership at time of patent granting. Changes may occur after patent is granted. Where more than one assignee exists, patents are attributed to first-named assignee.

U.S. Patents by Country, 2014

Source: U.S. Patent and Trademark Office, U.S. Dept. of Commerce

(ranked by number of U.S. utility patents, or patents for inventions, granted)

Rank	Country	Patents	% change, 2012-13	% share of total issued
1.	Japan	53,849	3.7%	17.9%
2.	Germany	16,550	6.8	5.5
3.	South Korea	16,469	13.2	5.5
4.	Taiwan	11,332	2.4	3.8
5.	China	7,236	22.1	2.4
6.	Canada	7,043	7.6	2.3
7.	France	6,691	10.0%	2.2%
8.	UK	6,487	11.7	2.2
9.	Israel	3,471	15.2	1.2
10.	India	2,987	23.2	1.0
	United States	**144,621**	**8.3**	**48.1**
	All countries	**300,678**	**8.2**	**100.0**

Note: Country of origin is determined by residence of first-named inventor in patent.

U.S. Patents by Category, 1977-2014

Source: U.S. Patent and Trademark Office, U.S. Dept. of Commerce

(ranked by number of utility patents or patents for inventions, issued in 2014)

Rank	Category	1977-93	1994	2003	2013	2014	% change, 1994-2014
1.	Multiplex communications	4,715	744	2,576	9,288	11,411	1,433.7%
2.	Active solid-state devices (e.g., transistors, solid-state diodes)	8,946	1,390	4,300	8,528	9,991	618.8
3.	Telecommunications	3,815	464	1,780	8,260	8,294	1,687.5
4.	Electrical computers and digital processing systems: multicomputer data transferring	554	129	1,173	5,381	7,040	5,357.4
5.	Computer graphics processing and selective visual display systems	4,430	703	1,885	5,858	6,683	850.6
6.	Drug, bio-affecting and body treating compositions (class 514)	31,305	2,130	3,863	6,333	6,556	207.8
7.	Semiconductor device manufacturing: process	8,309	1,233	5,119	5,572	6,221	404.5
8.	Data processing: database and file management or data structures	559	170	1,329	5,085	5,728	3,269.4
9.	Drug, bio-affecting and body treating compositions (class 424)	11,387	1,268	3,088	4,668	5,550	337.7
10.	Television	9,643	962	1,069	4,281	5,192	439.7
11.	Image analysis	3,303	419	1,630	5,149	4,980	1,088.5
12.	Data processing: financial, business practice, management, or cost/price determination	1,074	171	443	5,901	4,851	2,736.8
13.	Data processing: vehicles, navigation, and relative location	3,003	328	1,192	4,177	4,735	1,343.6
14.	Pulse or digital communications	4,396	610	1,572	4,501	4,647	661.8
15.	Chemistry: molecular biology and microbiology	11,054	1,424	3,078	3,908	4,338	204.6
16.	Information security	91	23	137	3,094	4,004	17,308.7
17.	Surgery (class 600)	8,618	1,093	2,123	3,534	3,764	244.4
18.	Surgery (class 606)	5,054	836	1,625	3,321	3,414	308.4
19.	Electrical computers and digital processing systems: support	764	174	679	3,030	3,355	1,828.2
20.	Facsimile and static presentation processing	4,070	630	791	3,152	3,104	392.7

Geologic Time Scale

Our understanding of Earth's ancient history is largely a result of geoscientists' study of climate, rock strata, ice samples, mineral deposits, and fossils from around the world; clues to the planet's origin have also been found through the study of extraterrestrial bodies. Geologists divide Earth's history into the following units (MYA = million years ago):

PRECAMBRIAN TIME (4,600-541 MYA)

HADEAN EON (4,600-4,000 MYA) Earth has no continents, oceans, or life; surface conditions are defined by intense volcanic activity and widespread meteorite impact. Oldest known minerals and rocks, many of meteoric origin, date to this era.

ARCHEAN EON (4,000-2,500 MYA) Earth's surface cools and water vapor in atmosphere condenses to form early oceans, which define small protocontinents; the first single-celled organisms, bacteria and archaea, appear in these oceans.

PROTEROZOIC EON (2,500-541 MYA) Protocontinents merge into larger landmasses as Earth's crust continues to shift. Atmospheric oxygen levels increase, and first known multicellular life appears. Later, soft-bodied marine animals emerge.

PHANEROZOIC EON (541 MYA-present)

Paleozoic Era (541-252 MYA)

Cambrian Period (541-485 MYA). The supercontinent known as Gondwana, or Gondwanaland, dominates the Southern Hemisphere. Seas experience an explosion of invertebrate animal life, including thousands of species of trilobites; the first known vertebrates appear. There is no life on land.

Ordovician Period (485-444 MYA). Gondwanaland extends from South Pole to tropic regions; Northern Hemisphere is mostly open ocean. Average global temperatures are warmer than in the current era. First primitive land plants, early ancestors of starfish and mollusks, and first armored, jawless fishes appear. The period ends in mass extinction of a majority of species, possibly a result of a global drop in sea level due to glaciation.

Silurian Period (444-419 MYA). South Pole remains covered by supercontinent, but precursors of present-day N America, Europe, and Asia coalesce around the equator and middle latitudes. Appearance of first known vascular land plants, first freshwater fish, first jawed fish, first coral reefs, and first air-breathing animals (certain eurypterids, a scorpion-like creature).

Devonian Period (419-359 MYA). Collisions between Gondwanaland and ancestral landmasses of N America and Eurasia produce mountains visible today as northern Appalachians. Newly-formed ozone layer offers protection from sun's rays, allowing first air-breathing spiders and mites to appear on dry land. Fish with fins and scales and first amphibians emerge. Late Devonian mass extinction.

Carboniferous Period (359-299 MYA). Precursors of modern N America and Northern Europe lie in tropical latitudes N of the equator; warm and humid conditions there facilitate spread of lush forests and peat swamps that later form most of the world's coal and limestone. Later period sees emergence of first true conifers, Lepidodendrales ("scale trees") as tall as 100 ft, and first true reptiles.

Permian Period (299-252 MYA). All major landmasses collide to form the supercontinent Pangaea, surrounded by the world ocean Panthalassa. Gradual warming through much of the Permian allows for initial flourishing of species—including dinosaur precursors (up to 10 ft in length) and marine species in shallow inland seas. The period ended with a mass extinction—the largest of Earth's five mass extinctions. As much as 95% of all marine species and most land species went extinct.

Mesozoic Era (252-66 MYA)

Triassic Period (252-201 MYA). Pangaea separates into supercontinents of Laurasia and Gondwana; subtropical conditions extend as far N as present-day Wyoming and New England. Emergence of icthyosaurs and plesiosaurs (large marine reptiles), several species of dinosaurs (up to 15 ft long), first true mammals, and first insects to undergo metamorphosis from larva to pupa to adult. Triassic-Jurassic mass extinction.

Jurassic Period (201-145 MYA). N American continent drifts westward, opening Gulf of Mexico; rift forms between S America and Africa. Warm, moist climate contributes to flourishing of coral reefs and temperate and subtropical forests. Appearance of first angiosperms (flowering plants), pterosaurs (winged reptiles), the earliest known birds (offshoots of a dinosaur group), and huge dinosaurs such as the carnivorous *Allosaurus* and herbivorous *Apatosaurus*.

Cretaceous Period (145-66 MYA). African continental plate drifts N, creating roots of European Alps; gap between S America and Africa broadens; western movement of N America drives formation of Sierra Nevada and Rocky Mountains, turning the western interior of continent into a vast swamp. Later, sea levels rise and cover about one-third of Earth's present land area. The global climate is warm and mild. The period ends in a mass extinction of plant and animal species (including dinosaurs). Likely causes include an asteroid impact and increased volcanic activity.

Cenozoic Era (66 MYA-present)

Paleogene Period (66-23 MYA)
- Paleocene Epoch (66-56 MYA). Australia begins to separate from Antarctica; N America and Greenland begin to spread apart. Mammalian life predominates, including early marsupials, insectivores, creodonts (carnivorous relatives of cats and dogs), and primitive hoofed mammals.
- Eocene Epoch (56-33.9 MYA). Australia drifts farther from Antarctica; the Indian subcontinent becomes welded to Asia, and tectonic forces drive the upheaval of the Alpine-Himalayan system. Climate in N America and Europe is subtropical and moist, with temperate forests as far N as Greenland and Siberia. Ancestors of modern horses, elephants, rhinoceroses, camels, bats, primates, and squirrel-like rodents emerge; earliest known marine mammals appear in later Eocene.
- Oligocene Epoch (33.9-23 MYA). San Andreas fault develops between N American and Pacific plates. Mammalian species continue to diversify, producing modern horse and multiple rodent, camel, and rhinoceros-like species, as well as first known species of great ape. Long-term cooling trend begins that would later cause Pleistocene ice ages.

Neogene Period (23 MYA-2.6 MYA)
- Miocene Epoch (23-5.3 MYA). Crustal plate collisions continue to drive uplift of Alps, Himalayas, and Cordilleran Ranges in Americas; eroded sediment is deposited in shallow marine basins, forming reservoirs for oil fields of California, Romania, and Caspian Sea. Ocean currents prevent Antarctica from receiving warmer waters, fostering growth of Antarctic ice sheet. Northern forests become grassy prairies. Large apes related to the orangutan live in Asia and southern Europe. Oldest hominin fossils from Africa date to this epoch.
- Pliocene Epoch (5.3-2.6 MYA). Alps continue to rise in Europe, and subduction of the Pacific tectonic plate elevates the Sierra Nevada and volcanic Cascade Range. Climate becomes cooler and drier, driving formation of permanent Arctic ice cap. Rapid primate evolution produces *Ardipithecus* and *Australopithecus*, two of the earliest known direct ancestors of *Homo sapiens*.

Quarternary Period (2.6 MYA-present)
- Pleistocene Epoch (2.6 MYA-11,700 years ago). Glacier ice covers as much as 25% or more of Earth's land surface, carving numerous present-day features including the Great Lakes; increased rainfall in lower latitudes allows plant and animal life to flourish in northern and eastern Africa. Late Pleistocene brings worldwide extinction of many large mammals, including the mastodon, saber-toothed tiger, and ground sloth. Evidence of Neanderthals and Denisovans dates from the latter part of the Pleistocene.
- Holocene Epoch (11,700 years ago-present). Melting ice caused sea levels to rise 100 ft or more in early Holocene, covering large areas of land and extending continental shelf of N America. Humans proliferate, and civilization begins.

Biological Classification

In biology, classification is the identification, naming, and grouping of organisms into a formal system. The two fields that are most directly concerned with classification are taxonomy and systematics. Although they overlap, taxonomy is more concerned with nomenclature (naming) and with constructing hierarchical systems, and systematics with uncovering evolutionary relationships. Two kingdoms of living forms, Plantae and Animalia, have been recognized since Aristotle established the first taxonomy in the 4th century BCE. Plants and animals are examples of eukaryotes; their cells have nuclei bound by membranes. Two other kingdoms of eukaryotes that have been identified are Protista (one-celled organisms) and Fungi. The single-celled bacteria and archaea lack such nuclei. They are referred to as prokaryotes (or procaryotes) and are commonly placed in separate kingdoms. The seven basic categories of classification (from most general to most specific) are kingdom, phylum (or division), class, order, family, genus, and species. (In addition, many scientists group all eukaryotes in a single "domain." Bacteria and archaea are also often treated as separate domains.) Below are two examples of classification:

ZOOLOGICAL HIERARCHY

Kingdom	Phylum	Class	Order	Family	Genus	Species name	Common name
Animalia	Chordata	Mammalia	Primates	Hominidae	*Homo*	*Homo sapiens*	Human

BOTANICAL HIERARCHY

Kingdom	Division*	Class	Order	Family	Genus	Species name	Common name
Plantae	Magnoliophyta	Magnoliopsida	Magnoliales	Magnoliaceae	*Magnolia*	*M. virginiana*	Sweet bay

*In botany, the division is generally used in place of the phylum.

Gestation, Longevity, and Incubation of Selected Animals

Information reviewed by Ronald M. Nowak, author of *Walker's Mammals of the World* (6th ed., Johns Hopkins University Press, 1999). Average longevity figures supplied by Ronald T. Reuther. These apply to animals in captivity; the potential life span of animals is rarely attained in nature. Figures on gestation and incubation are averages based on estimates.

Animal	Gestation (days)	Average longevity (yrs.)	Maximum longevity (yrs.-mos.)
Ass	365	12	47
Baboon	187	20	45
Bear (black)	219	18	36-10
Bear (grizzly)	225	25	50
Bear (polar)	240	20	45
Beaver	105	5	50
Bison	285	15	40
Camel	406	12	50
Cat (domestic)	63	12	38
Chimpanzee	230	20	60
Chipmunk	31	6	10
Cow	284	15	30
Deer (white-tailed)	201	8	20
Dog (domestic)	61	12	21
Elephant (African)	660	35	70
Elephant (Asian)	645	40	77
Elk	250	15	26-8
Fox (red)	52	7	14
Giraffe	457	10	36-2
Goat (domestic)	151	8	18
Gorilla	258	20	54
Guinea pig	68	4	8
Hippopotamus	238	41	61
Horse	330	20	50
Kangaroo (gray)	36	7	24
Leopard	98	12	23
Lion	100	15	30
Monkey (rhesus)	166	15	37
Moose	240	12	27
Mouse (domestic white)	19	3	6
Mouse (meadow)	21	3	4
Opossum (American)	13	1	5
Pig (domestic)	112	10	27
Puma	90	12	20
Rabbit (domestic)	31	5	18-10
Rhinoceros (black)	450	15	45-10
Rhinoceros (white)	480	20	50
Sea lion (California)	350	12	34
Sheep (domestic)	154	12	23
Squirrel (gray)	44	10	23-6
Tiger	105	16	26-3
Wolf (maned)	63	5	15-8
Zebra (Grant's)	365	15	50

Animal	Incubation time (days)
Chicken	21
Duck	30
Goose	30
Pigeon	18
Turkey	26

Major Venomous Animals

Snakes

Asian pit viper—2 ft to 5 ft long; throughout Asia; reactions and mortality vary, but most bites cause tissue damage; mortality generally low.

Australian brown snake—4 ft to 7 ft long; very slow onset of cardiac or respiratory distress; moderate mortality, but because death can be sudden and unexpected, it is the most dangerous of the Australian snakes; antivenom.

Barba amarilla or fer-de-lance—up to 7 ft long; from tropical Mexico to Brazil; severe tissue damage common; moderate mortality; antivenom.

Black mamba—up to 14 ft long; southern and central Africa; rapid onset of dizziness, difficulty breathing, erratic heartbeat; mortality high, nears 100% without antivenom.

Boomslang—less than 6 ft long; African savannahs; rapid onset of nausea and dizziness, often followed by slight recovery and then sudden death from internal hemorrhaging; bites rare, mortality high; antivenom.

Bushmaster—up to 12 ft long; tropical forests of Central and S America; few bites occur, but mortality high.

Common, or Asian, cobra—4 ft to 8 ft long; throughout S Asia; considerable tissue damage, sometimes paralysis; mortality probably not more than 10%; antivenom.

Copperhead—less than 4 ft long; New England to Texas; pain and swelling; very seldom fatal; antivenom seldom needed.

Coral snake—2 ft to 5 ft long; in Americas S of Canada; bite may be painless; slow onset of paralysis, impaired breathing; mortalities rare but high without antivenom and mechanical respiration.

Cottonmouth water moccasin—up to 5 ft long; wetlands of southern U.S. from Virginia to Texas; rapid onset of severe pain, swelling, tissue destruction can be extensive; mortality low; antivenom.

Death adder—less than 3 ft long; Australia; rapid onset of faintness, cardiac and respiratory distress; at least 50% mortality without antivenom.

Desert horned viper—up to 2 ft long; dry areas of Africa and western Asia; swelling and tissue damage; mortality low; antivenom.

European viper—1 ft to 3 ft long; throughout Europe; bleeding and tissue damage; mortality low; antivenom.

Gaboon viper—more than 6 ft long; S of the Sahara; massive tissue damage, internal bleeding; few recorded bites.

King cobra—up to 16 ft long; throughout S Asia; rapid swelling, dizziness, loss of consciousness, difficulty breathing, erratic heartbeat; mortality varies with amount of venom involved, but most bites involve nonfatal amounts; antivenom.

Krait—up to 5 ft long; SE Asia; rapid onset of sleepiness, numbness; up to 50% mortality even with use of antivenom.

Puff adder—up to 5 ft long, fat; S of the Sahara, throughout the Middle East; rapid large swelling, great pain, dizziness; moderate mortality, often from internal bleeding; antivenom.

Rattlesnake—2 ft to 6 ft long; throughout Western Hemisphere; rapid onset of severe pain, swelling; mortality low, but amputation of affected digits is sometimes necessary; antivenom. Mojave rattler may produce temporary paralysis.

Ringhals, or spitting, cobra—5 ft to 7 ft long; southern Africa; squirts venom through holes in front of fangs as a defense; venom severely irritating and can cause blindness.

Russell's viper or tic-polonga—more than 5 ft long; throughout Asia; internal bleeding; bite reports common; moderate mortality rate; antivenom.

Saw-scaled, or carpet, viper—up to 2 ft long; dry areas from India to Africa; severe bleeding, fever; high mortality, causes more human fatalities than any other snake; antivenom.

Sea snake—3 ft to 10 ft long; throughout Pacific, Indian Oceans except NE Pacific; almost painless bite; variety of muscle pain, paralysis; mortality low, many bites not envenomed; some antivenoms.

Sharp-nosed pit viper or hundred-pace snake—up to 5 ft long; S Vietnam, Taiwan, and China; the most toxic of Asian pit vipers; very rapid onset of swelling and tissue damage, internal bleeding; moderate mortality; antivenom.

Taipan—up to 11 ft long; Australia and New Guinea; rapid paralysis with severe breathing difficulty; mortality nears 100% without antivenom.

Tiger snake—2 ft to 6 ft long; southern Australia; pain, numbness, mental disturbances with rapid paralysis; may be deadliest of all land snakes, but antivenom is quite effective.

Yellow, or cape, cobra—7 ft long; southern Africa; most toxic venom of any cobra; rapid onset of swelling, breathing and cardiac difficulties; mortality is high without treatment; antivenom.

Note: Not all bites by venomous snakes are actually envenomed. Any animal bite, however, carries the danger of tetanus, and anyone suffering a venomous snake bite should seek medical attention. Antivenoms do not cure; they are only an aid in the treatment of bites. Mortality rates above are for envenomed bites: low mortality, c. 2% or less; moderate, 2%-5%; high, 5%-15%.

Lizards

Gila monster—up to 24 in. long, with heavy body and tail; high desert in SW U.S. and northern Mexico; immediate severe pain, transient low blood pressure; no recent mortality.

Mexican beaded lizard—similar to Gila monster; W coast of Mexico; reaction and mortality similar to Gila monster.

Insects

Ants, bees, hornets, wasps—global distribution; usual reaction is piercing pain in area of sting, though many people suffer allergic reactions (swelling, rashes); not directly fatal, except in cases of massive multiple stings, and a few may die within minutes from severe sensitivity to the venom (anaphylactic shock).

Spiders, scorpions

Black widow—small, round-bodied with red hourglass marking; the widow and its relatives are found in tropical and temperate zones; severe musculoskeletal pain, weakness, breathing difficulty, convulsions, which may be more serious in small children; low mortality; antivenom. The **redback** spider of Australia has the hourglass marking on its back, rather than on its front, but is otherwise identical to the black widow.

Brown recluse, or fiddleback, spider—small, oblong body; throughout U.S.; pain with later ulceration, which may last months, at place of bite; fever, nausea, and stomach cramps in severe cases; very low mortality.

Funnel web spider—several varieties, often large; Australia; slow onset of breathing, circulation difficulties; low mortality; antivenom.

Scorpion—crablike body with stinger in tail, various sizes; many varieties throughout tropical and subtropical areas; severe pain spreading from the wound, numbness, severe agitation, cramps, and even respiratory failure; low mortality, usually in children; antivenoms.

Tarantula—large, hairy spider; worldwide; the American tarantula, and probably all other tarantulas, are harmless to humans, though their bite may cause some pain and swelling.

Sea life

Cone-shell—mollusk in small shell; S Pacific and Indian Oceans; shoots barbs into victims; paralysis; low mortality.

Octopus—global distribution, usually in warm waters; rapid onset of paralysis with breathing difficulty; all varieties produce venom, but only a few can cause death.

Portuguese man-of-war—jellyfish-like siphonophore with tentacles up to 100 ft long; in most warm water areas; immediate severe pain; not directly fatal, though shock may cause death in rare cases.

Sea wasp—jellyfish, with tentacles up to 30 ft long; S Pacific; very rapid onset of circulatory problems; high mortality because of speed of toxic reaction; antivenom.

Stingray—several varieties of differing sizes; tropical and temperate seas and some freshwater; severe pain, rapid onset of nausea, vomiting, breathing difficulties; wound area may ulcerate, gangrene may occur; seldom fatal.

Stonefish—brownish fish that lies motionless on bottom of shallow waters; throughout S Pacific and Indian Oceans; extraordinary pain, rapid paralysis; low mortality; antivenom, warm water relieves pain.

Speeds of Selected Animals

Source: *Natural History* magazine. © American Museum of Natural History

Animal	Speed (mph)	Animal	Speed (mph)	Animal	Speed (mph)
Cheetah	70	Mongolian wild ass	40	Human	27.89
Pronghorn antelope	61	Greyhound	39.35	Elephant	25
Wildebeest	50	Whippet	35.50	Black mamba snake	20
Lion	50	Rabbit (domestic)	35	Six-lined race runner (lizard)	18
Thomson's gazelle	50	Mule deer	35	Wild turkey	15
Quarterhorse	47.5	Jackal	35	Squirrel	12
Elk	45	Reindeer	32	Pig (domestic)	11
Cape hunting dog	45	Giraffe	32	Chicken	9
Coyote	43	White-tailed deer	30	Spider (*Tegenaria atrica*)	1.17
Gray fox	42	Warthog	30	Giant tortoise	0.17
Hyena	40	Grizzly bear	30	Three-toed sloth	0.15
Zebra	40	Cat (domestic)	30	Garden snail	0.03

Note: Most of these measurements are for maximum speeds over approximate quarter-mile distances. Exceptions are the lion and elephant, whose speeds were clocked in the act of charging; the whippet, which was timed over a 200-yd course; the cheetah, timed over a 100-yd distance; a human, timed over a 15-yd segment of a 100-yd run; and the black mamba, six-lined race runner, spider, giant tortoise, three-toed sloth, and garden snail, which were measured over various small distances.

Top American Kennel Club Breed Registrations, 2009-14

Source: American Kennel Club (AKC)

Breed	Rank 2014	Rank 2013	Rank 2009
Labrador Retrievers	1	1	1
German Shepherds	2	2	2
Golden Retrievers	3	3	4
Bulldogs	4	5	7
Beagles	5	4	5
Yorkshire Terriers	6	6	3
Poodles	7	8	9
Boxers	8	7	6
French Bulldogs	9	11	24
Rottweilers	10	9	13
Dachshunds	11	10	8
German Shorthaired Pointers	12	13	16
Siberian Huskies	13	14	22
Doberman Pinschers	14	12	15
Great Danes	15	16	21
Miniature Schnauzers	16	17	11
Shih Tzu	17	15	10
Australian Shepherds	18	20	28
Cavalier King Charles Spaniels	19	18	25
Pomeranians	20	19	14
Shetland Sheepdogs	21	21	18
Pembroke Welsh Corgis	22	24	26
Boston Terriers	23	23	19
Chihuahuas	24	22	12
Havanese	25	25	32
Mastiffs	26	26	27
Brittanys	27	30	30
English Springer Spaniels	28	28	29
Maltese	29	27	20
Cocker Spaniels	30	29	23
Bernese Mountain Dogs	31	32	39
Pugs	32	31	17
Vizslas	33	34	42
Weimaraners	34	33	31
Collies	35	35	38
Newfoundlands	36	37	46
West Highland White Terriers	37	36	36
Rhodesian Ridgebacks	38	39	48
Border Collies	39	44	52
Chesapeake Bay Retrievers	40	43	49
Basset Hounds	41	41	34
Papillons	42	38	37
Bichon Frises	43	40	35
Bullmastiffs	44	40	42
Akitas	45	45	50
Shiba Inu	46	46	65
Cane Corso	47	50	NA
Soft Coated Wheaten Terriers	48	51	62
Bloodhounds	49	48	43
Saint Bernards	50	47	45

NA = Not available.

Dog Breeds by Type

Source: American Kennel Club (AKC)

As of mid-2015, the AKC recognized more than 180 breeds and used the following seven groups to classify breeds, according to functions and other distinctive traits.

Herding Group: Australian Cattle Dog, Australian Shepherd, Bearded Collie, Beauceron, Belgian Malinois, Belgian Sheepdog, Belgian Tervuren, Bergamasco, Border Collie, Bouvier des Flandres, Briard, Canaan Dog, Cardigan Welsh Corgi, Collie, Entlebucher Mountain Dog, Finnish Lapphund, German Shepherd Dog, Icelandic Sheepdog, Norwegian Buhund, Old English Sheepdog, Pembroke Welsh Corgi, Polish Lowland Sheepdog, Puli, Pyrenean Shepherd, Shetland Sheepdog, Spanish Water Dog, Swedish Vallhund.

Hound Group: Afghan Hound, American English Coonhound, American Foxhound, Basenji, Basset Hound, Beagle, Black and Tan Coonhound, Bloodhound, Bluetick Coonhound, Borzoi, Cirneco dell'Etna, Dachshund, English Foxhound, Greyhound, Harrier, Ibizan Hound, Irish Wolfhound, Norwegian Elkhound, Otterhound, Petit Basset Griffon Vendéen, Pharaoh Hound, Plott, Portuguese Podengo Pequeno, Redbone Coonhound, Rhodesian Ridgeback, Saluki, Scottish Deerhound, Treeing Walker Coonhound, Whippet.

Non-Sporting Group: American Eskimo Dog, Bichon Frise, Boston Terrier, Bulldog, Chinese Shar-Pei, Chow Chow, Coton de Tulear, Dalmatian, Finnish Spitz, French Bulldog, Keeshond, Lhasa Apso, Löwchen, Norwegian Lundehund, Poodle (standard and miniature), Schipperke, Shiba Inu, Tibetan Spaniel, Tibetan Terrier, Xoloitzcuintli.

Sporting Group: American Water Spaniel, Boykin Spaniel, Brittany, Chesapeake Bay Retriever, Clumber Spaniel, Cocker Spaniel, Curly-Coated Retriever, English Cocker Spaniel, English Setter, English Springer Spaniel, Field Spaniel, Flat-Coated Retriever, German Shorthaired Pointer, German Wirehaired Pointer, Golden Retriever, Gordon Setter, Irish Red and White Setter, Irish Setter, Irish Water Spaniel, Labrador Retriever, Nova Scotia Duck Tolling Retriever, Pointer, Spinone Italiano, Sussex Spaniel, Vizsla, Weimaraner, Welsh Springer Spaniel, Wirehaired Pointing Griffon, Wirehaired Vizsla.

Terrier Group: Airedale Terrier, American Staffordshire Terrier, Australian Terrier, Bedlington Terrier, Border Terrier, Bull Terrier, Cairn Terrier, Cesky Terrier, Dandie Dinmont Terrier, Glen of Imaal Terrier, Irish Terrier, Kerry Blue Terrier, Lakeland Terrier, Manchester Terrier, Miniature Bull Terrier, Miniature Schnauzer, Norfolk Terrier, Norwich Terrier, Parson Russell Terrier, Rat Terrier, Russell Terrier, Scottish Terrier, Sealyham Terrier, Skye Terrier, Smooth Fox Terrier, Soft Coated Wheaten Terrier, Staffordshire Bull Terrier, Welsh Terrier, West Highland White Terrier, Wire Fox Terrier.

Toy Group: Affenpinscher, Brussels Griffon, Cavalier King Charles Spaniel, Chihuahua, Chinese Crested, English Toy Spaniel, Havanese, Italian Greyhound, Japanese Chin, Maltese, Manchester Terrier (toy), Miniature Pinscher, Papillon, Pekingese, Pomeranian, Poodle (toy), Pug, Shih Tzu, Silky Terrier, Toy Fox Terrier, Yorkshire Terrier.

Working Group: Akita, Alaskan Malamute, Anatolian Shepherd Dog, Bernese Mountain Dog, Black Russian Terrier, Boerboel, Boxer, Bullmastiff, Cane Corso, Chinook, Doberman Pinscher, Dogue de Bordeaux, German Pinscher, Giant Schnauzer, Great Dane, Great Pyrenees, Greater Swiss Mountain Dog, Komondor, Kuvasz, Leonberger, Mastiff, Neapolitan Mastiff, Newfoundland, Portuguese Water Dog, Rottweiler, Saint Bernard, Samoyed, Siberian Husky, Standard Schnauzer, Tibetan Mastiff.

Registrations for Pedigreed Cats, 2014

Source: The Cat Fanciers' Association
(ranked by total registrations)

Rank	Breed
1.	Exotic
2.	Persian
3.	Maine Coon Cat
4.	Ragdoll
5.	British Shorthair
6.	American Shorthair
7.	Abyssinian
8.	Sphynx
9.	Siamese
10.	Scottish Fold
11.	Cornish Rex
12.	Devon Rex
13.	Oriental
14.	Norwegian Forest Cat
15.	Birman
16.	Burmese
17.	Siberian
18.	Tonkinese
19.	Russian Blue
20.	Egyptian Mau
21.	Ocicat
22.	Singapura
23.	Manx
24.	Japanese Bobtail
25.	Selkirk Rex

Computer Milestones

1623: German mathematician Wilhelm Schickard developed the first mechanical calculator, capable of adding, subtracting, multiplying, and dividing.

1642: French mathematician Blaise Pascal built the first of more than four dozen copies of an adding and subtracting machine that he invented.

1801: French inventor Joseph Marie Jacquard demonstrated a new control system for looms. He "programmed" the loom, communicating desired weaving operations to the machine via patterns of holes in paper cards.

1833-71: British mathematician and scientist Charles Babbage used the Jacquard punch-card system in his design for a sophisticated, programmable "Analytical Engine" that foreshadowed basic features of today's computers. Babbage's concept was beyond the capabilities of the technology of his time, and the machine remained unfinished at his death in 1871.

1889: American engineer Herman Hollerith patented an electromechanical punch-card tabulating system that facilitated the handling of large amounts of statistical data and quickly found use in censuses in the U.S. and other countries.

1911: Hollerith's Tabulating Machine Company merged with two other enterprises to form the Computing-Tabulating-Recording Company, which was renamed the International Business Machines Corporation (IBM) in 1924.

1941: German engineer Konrad Züse completed the Z3, the first fully functional digital computer to be controlled by a program; the Z3 was not electronic—it was based on electrical switches called relays.

1942: Iowa State Coll. physicist John Vincent Atanasoff and his assistant Clifford Berry completed a working model of the first fully electronic computer using vacuum tubes, which could operate much more quickly than relays; the rudimentary machine was not programmable.

1943: IBM and Harvard professor Howard Aiken completed the first large-scale automatic digital computer, the Mark I, a relay-based machine 55 ft long and 8 ft high. British scientists built the Colossus, an electronic computer for breaking German codes during World War II.

1946: ENIAC (Electronic Numerical Integrator and Computer), a 30-ton room-sized electronic computer with more than 18,000 vacuum tubes, was completed by physicist John Mauchly and engineer J. Presper Eckert at the Univ. of Pennsylvania for the U.S. Army. ENIAC could be programmed to do different tasks, but cables had to be plugged in, and switches had to be set by hand.

1951: Eckert and Mauchly's UNIVAC (Universal Automatic Computer) became the first commercially available computer in the U.S. The first customer was the Census Bureau. CBS-TV used a UNIVAC in 1952 to predict presidential election results.

1959: COBOL, a computer programming language designed for business use, first appeared, based on programming language innovations of Grace Hopper.

1967: Computer pioneer Doug Engelbart applied for a patent on the mouse.

1969-71: The powerful Unix operating system was developed at Bell Laboratories; later versions became widely used on large computers and formed the basis for the Macintosh OS X operating system.

1971: Intel released the 4004, the first commercial microprocessor (an entire computer processing unit on a chip).

1973: The Alto computer, developed at Xerox's Palo Alto Research Center, became operational, implementing many features of modern commercial personal computers, including a graphical user interface (GUI) featuring windows, icons, and pointers that could be manipulated by a mouse.

1975: The first widely marketed personal computer (PC), the MITS Altair 8800, was introduced in kit form, with no keyboard, video display, or printer, for under $400. Microsoft was founded by Bill Gates and Paul Allen.

1976: The first word-processing program for personal computers, Electric Pencil, was written. Apple Computer Company was founded by Steven Jobs and Stephen Wozniak.

1977: Apple introduced the Apple II; capable of displaying text and graphics in color, the machine enjoyed phenomenal success.

1981: IBM unveiled its Personal Computer (IBM 5150), which used an operating system from Microsoft known as MS-DOS (Disk Operating System).

1984: Apple introduced the first Macintosh. The easy-to-use Macintosh came with a proprietary operating system and was the first popular computer to have a GUI and a mouse.

1990: Microsoft released Windows 3.0, the first workable version of its own GUI.

1991: The Unix-like Linux operating system was invented by Helsinki Univ. student Linus Torvalds and made available for free.

1996: The Palm Pilot, the first widely successful handheld computer and personal information manager, arrived.

1997: The IBM computer Deep Blue beat world chess champion Garry Kasparov in a 6-game match, 2-1, with 3 draws.

2001: Apple introduced the Unix-based operating system OS X for the Macintosh.

2002: The total number of personal computers, including desktop and laptop machines of all types, shipped by manufacturers since 1975 reached 1 bil.

2006: Apple began using Intel microprocessors instead of the IBM PowerPC in its Macintosh computers.

2007: Amazon launched the Kindle, a hardware/software system for displaying books electronically; the product line later included tablet computers.

2008: Google released the Linux-based Android operating system for mobile devices.

2010: Apple released the iPad tablet computer and sold more than 3 mil devices in the first 80 days.

2012: Microsoft released Windows 8, featuring enhanced support for touchscreens and an interface with a grid of tiles displaying actively updated content and apps.

2015: Microsoft released Windows 10, promising faster startup and improved security, along with features like a personal digital assistant and a new web browser, Microsoft Edge.

Nations With the Most Personal Computers in Use, 2014

Source: Computer Industry Almanac, year-end 2014

Rank	Nation	PCs in use (mil)	% of world total
1.	U.S.	354.5	16.99%
2.	China	314.4	15.06
3.	Japan	110.5	5.30
4.	India	98.8	4.73
5.	Germany	80.4	3.85
6.	Russia	75.9	3.64
7.	Brazil	62.8	3.01
8.	United Kingdom	61.8	2.96
9.	France	61.8	2.96
10.	Italy	52.8	2.53%
11.	South Korea	46.6	2.23
12.	Mexico	38.1	1.83
13.	Canada	34.9	1.67
14.	Spain	32.2	1.54
15.	Australia	22.0	1.06
	Top 15 countries	**1,448**	**69.36**
	World	**2,087**	**100.00**

World's Fastest Supercomputers, 2015

Source: Top500.org, as of midyear 2015

Rank	Name	Location	Manufacturer/ vendor	Processors (cores)	Top speed[1]
1.	Tianhe-2 (Milky Way-2)	National Supercomputing Center, Guangzhou, China	NUDT[2]	3,120,000	33.86
2.	Titan	Oak Ridge National Laboratory, TN, U.S.	Cray	560,640	17.59
3.	Sequoia	Lawrence Livermore National Laboratory, CA, U.S.	IBM	1,572,864	17.17
4.	K Computer	RIKEN Advanced Institute for Computational Science, Japan	Fujitsu	705,024	10.51
5.	Mira	Argonne National Laboratory, IL, U.S.	IBM	786,432	8.59
6.	Piz Daint	Swiss National Supercomputing Centre, Switzerland	Cray	115,984	6.27
7.	Shaheen II	King Abdullah Univ. of Science and Technology, Saudi Arabia	Cray	196,608	5.54
8.	Stampede	Texas Advanced Computing Center/Univ. of Texas, TX, U.S.	Dell	462,462	5.17
9.	JUQUEEN	Forschungszentrum Juelich, Germany	IBM	458,752	5.01
10.	Vulcan	Lawrence Livermore National Laboratory, CA, U.S.	IBM	393,216	4.29

Note: The 10 fastest supercomputers, and almost all of the 500 fastest supercomputers, use a version of the Linux operating system. (1) Top speed, in petaflops, achieved as measured according to the Linpack Benchmark. 1 petaflop = 1 quadrillion floating-point operations per sec. (2) NUDT = National University of Defense Technology.

U.S. Sales of Selected Hardware, 2011-14

Source: Consumer Electronics Association
(factory sales to dealers in thousands of units and millions of dollars)

Hardware	2011 Units	2011 Sales	2013 Units	2013 Sales	2014 Units	2014 Sales
Desktop computers[1]	10,655	$7,204	9,791	$6,539	9,705	$6,635
Notebooks and netbooks	27,383	15,417	24,619	15,202	25,573	16,403
Tablet PCs	31,900	15,937	77,405	26,476	76,457	24,551
E-readers	21,060	2,472	9,061	716	8,071	606
Smartphones	87,431	27,541	151,000	42,958	160,221	48,868
Electronic gaming hardware	NA	4,684	NA	3,091	NA	4,159
Digital video recorders (DVRs)	16,573	2,652	13,750	2,200	15,950	2,009
Digital cameras	37,697	7,007	15,341	4,798	11,532	3,785
Digital camcorders	5,459	616	1,633	162	1,195	290
Portable media/MP3 players	35,263	5,891	19,503	2,933	15,272	1,966
Smart watches	NA	NA	600	95	2,355	542
Wearable fitness technology[2]	3,200	240	10,267	921	16,800	1,508

NA = Not available. (1) Includes all-in-one computers. (2) Includes devices containing one or more of the following sensors: pedometer, accelerometer, altimeter/barometric pressure sensor, heart-rate monitor.

U.S. Household Penetration of Selected Technologies, 2009-15

Source: Consumer Electronics Association (CEA)
(% of all households for Jan. of year shown)

Product	2009	2010	2011	2012	2013	2014	2015
Smartphones	23%	33%	39%	46%	58%	64%	72%
Digital cameras	77	80	79	74	73	66	64
Multifunction printers	62	66	66	68	65	63	63
Home network[1]	34	40	48	54	61	62	64
Home Internet access	78	78	78	78	78	78	78

Note: Based on sales data tracking and consumer surveys conducted by CEA. (1) Wired or wireless.

About the Internet

The Internet is not owned or funded by any one institution, organization, or government. It has no CEO and is not a commercial service. Its development is guided by the Internet Society (ISOC), which is composed of volunteers. The ISOC appoints the Internet Architecture Board (IAB), which oversees issues of standards and network resources, among others.

Major Historical Highlights

1969: ARPANET, an experimental four-computer network, was established by the Advanced Research Projects Agency (ARPA) of the U.S. Defense Dept. Two years later, ARPANET linked about 23 computers ("hosts") at 15 sites, including MIT and Harvard.

1978: The first spam, or junk email, was sent over ARPANET.

1983: The set of communications rules (protocol) known as TCP/IP became the main networking protocol of ARPANET. Its adoption was tantamount to the birth of the Internet. The military portion of ARPANET was moved onto MILNET.

1986: The U.S. National Science Foundation (NSF) launched NSFNET, the first large-scale network using Internet technology.

1988: Internet Relay Chat (IRC) was developed by Finnish student Jarkko Oikarinen, enabling people to communicate via the Internet in "real time."

1988: A "worm" crafted by Cornell Univ. computer science graduate student Robert Morris Jr. infected thousands of computers, shutting many down and causing millions of dollars of damage—the first known case of large-scale damage caused by a computer virus spread via the Internet.

1989: The World—the first commercial Internet service provider supplying dial-up access—debuted.

1989-90: Tim Berners-Lee invented the World Wide Web. Created as an environment in which scientists at the European Center for Nuclear Research in Switzerland could share information, it gradually evolved into a medium with text, graphics, audio, animation, and video.

1990: ARPANET was disbanded.

1991: NSFNET was opened to commercial traffic. Berners-Lee introduced the first browser, or software for accessing the Web.

1993: The National Center for Supercomputing Applications released versions of Mosaic, the first Web browser able to present both text and images on a single page.

1994: Netscape Communications released the Netscape Navigator browser.

1995: Microsoft released its Internet Explorer browser. It initially failed to make a dent in Netscape's dominance of the browser market but surpassed it by 1999.

1996: A group of universities launched Internet2, an advanced, high-performance network for the research community and a test bed for development of new capabilities that might find use in the commercial Internet.

1998: Under a contract with the U.S. Dept. of Commerce, the nonprofit Internet Corporation for Assigned Numbers and Names (ICANN) took over the management of assigning domain names and Internet Protocol (IP) addresses.

1999: Release of the free Napster file-sharing service enabled users to easily exchange files containing music or other content without regard to copyright restrictions.

2000: Estonia became the first country to pass a law declaring Internet access a fundamental human right of its citizens.

2003: Niue, a self-governing Pacific island associated with New Zealand, became the first country to offer free nationwide wireless access to the Internet, using Wi-Fi technology.

2004: The Mozilla Foundation released the first official version of the open-source browser Mozilla Firefox.

2008: Google introduced its Chrome browser. By 2012, Chrome ranked as the most widely used browser in the world, according to StatCounter.com.

2009: The U.S. relinquished direct control over ICANN.

2011: ICANN decided to allow the use of almost any characters in any language for the names of generic top-level domains.

2012: The number of Facebook users surpassed 1 bil.

2014: The number of Internet hosts (websites) passed 1 bil.

Safety and Security on the Internet

Common sense dictates some basic security rules:

- Pick passwords that are difficult to guess, preferably consisting of letters, numbers, and symbols, if permitted. Avoid using the same password for multiple websites. A password manager can generate passwords and then save them.
- Do not give out your phone number, address, credit card number, or other personal information unless needed for a transaction at a site you trust.
- If you feel someone is being threatening or dangerous, inform your Internet service provider.
- Use protective "firewall," antivirus, and antispyware software to guard your system against attacks by hackers.
- Be careful about opening email and file attachments from unknown correspondents.
- To avoid falling victim to the scam known as **phishing**—which uses a forged email message, purportedly from a respectable organization, to elicit personal data—do not click on hyperlinks in emails from companies with which you do business. Phishing emails typically contain a link leading to a fabricated website resembling the site of the ostensible sender. If you want to visit a company's website, open your browser and manually enter the site's address.
- Users of so-called **peer-to-peer** (P2P) file-sharing networks or protocols should open up only part of their computer system to sharing, not the entire hard drive.
- When manufacturers provide **patches** to solve security flaws or other problems with operating systems, Web browsers, or other software, it is usually advisable to install these fixes. If a fix is not available for a serious security problem, consider switching to an alternative program.

Internet Addresses

The fundamental part of an address on the Internet is called the domain. The final part of a domain name, known as the **top-level domain (TLD)**, is its most basic part. For example, .com is the top-level domain of *The World Almanac*'s web address (www.worldalmanac.com).

So-called generic top-level domains (gTLDs), consisting of three or more letters, include the following:

Domain	What it is (usually)
.biz	a business
.cat	a site associated with Catalan language and culture
.com	generally a commercial organization, business, or company
.edu	an educational institution
.gov	a nonmilitary governmental entity in the U.S.
.info	an informational site for an individual or organization
.int	an international organization
.mil	a U.S. military organization
.mobi	a site providing content for mobile devices
.net	suggested for a network administration but actually used by a wide variety of sites
.org	suggested for a nonprofit organization but actually used by a wide variety of sites
.xxx	adult entertainment community

Domain names with two letters are generally for countries or regions. Country-code TLDs (ccTLDs) are usually managed by an organization within a certain country.

Data Breaches and Information Exposure, 2012-14

Source: Symantec Global Intelligence Network

	2011	2012	2013	2014
Total data breaches	211	156	253	312
Average number of identities exposed per breach (mil)	1.1	0.6	2.2	1.1
Total identities exposed (mil)	232	93	552	348

Information type exposed in breach	Percentage of breaches 2013	Percentage of breaches 2014
Real names	72%	69%
Government ID numbers (e.g., Social Security)	40	45
Home addresses	38	43
Financial information	18	36
Birth dates	43	35
Medical records	34	34
Phone numbers	19	21
Email addresses	15	20
User names and passwords	12	13
Insurance	6	11

Note: Numbers are self-reported and are not necessarily inclusive of all data breaches.

Nations With Highest Percentage of Population Using the Internet, 2000-14

Source: © International Telecommunication Union; ranked by 2014 figures

Rank	Nation	2000	2005	2008	2009	2010	2011	2012	2013	2014
1.	Iceland	44.47%	87.00%	91.00%	93.00%	93.39%	94.82%	96.21%	96.55%	98.16%
2.	Norway	52.00	81.99	90.57	92.08	93.39	93.49	94.65	95.05	96.30
3.	Denmark	39.17	82.74	85.02	86.84	88.72	89.81	92.26	94.63	95.99
4.	Andorra	10.54	37.61	70.04	78.53	81.00	81.00	86.43	94.00	95.90
5.	Liechtenstein	36.52	63.37	70.00	75.00	80.00	85.00	89.41	93.80	95.21
6.	Luxembourg	22.89	70.00	82.23	87.31	90.62	90.03	91.95	93.78	94.67
7.	Netherlands	43.98	81.00	87.42	89.63	90.72	91.42	92.86	93.96	93.17
8.	Sweden	45.69	84.83	90.00	91.00	90.00	92.77	93.18	94.78	92.52
9.	Monaco	42.18	55.46	67.25	70.10	75.00	80.30	87.00	90.70	92.40
10.	Finland	37.25	74.48	83.67	82.49	86.89	88.71	89.88	91.51	92.38
11.	United Kingdom	26.82	70.00	78.39	83.56	85.00	85.38	87.48	89.84	91.61
12.	Qatar	4.86	24.73	44.30	53.10	69.00	69.00	69.30	85.30	91.49
13.	Bahrain	6.15	21.30	51.95	53.00	55.00	77.00	88.00	90.00	91.00
14.	Japan	29.99	66.92	75.40	78.00	78.21	79.05	79.50	89.71	90.58
15.	United Arab Emirates	23.63	40.00	63.00	64.00	68.00	78.00	85.00	88.00	90.40
16.	United States	43.08	67.97	74.00	71.00	71.69	69.73	79.30	84.20	87.36
17.	Canada	51.30	71.66	76.70	80.30	80.30	83.00	83.00	85.80	87.12
18.	Switzerland	47.10	70.10	79.20	81.30	83.90	85.19	85.20	86.34	87.00
19.	Germany	30.22	68.71	78.00	79.00	82.00	81.27	82.35	84.17	86.19
20.	New Zealand	47.38	62.72	72.03	79.70	80.46	81.23	82.00	82.78	85.50

Nations With the Most Internet Users, 2014

Source: Computer Industry Almanac, year-end 2014

Rank	Nation	Internet users (mil)	% of worldwide users
1.	China	581.0	20.08%
2.	U.S.	281.6	9.73
3.	India	250.0	8.64
4.	Japan	110.4	3.81
5.	Brazil	100.7	3.48
6.	Germany	69.7	2.41
7.	Russia	74.8	2.59
8.	Indonesia	70.1	2.42
9.	United Kingdom	53.5	1.85
10.	France	53.0	1.83%
11.	Italy	49.1	1.70
12.	Mexico	42.8	1.48
13.	South Korea	42.5	1.47
14.	Turkey	37.1	1.28
15.	Spain	36.7	1.27
Top 15 countries		**1,853**	**64.03**
World		**2,894**	**100.00**

Most-Visited World Websites, 2015

Source: comScore Media Metrix

Some websites represent an aggregation of commonly owned domain names; examples of popular domains within a group added in parentheses by World Almanac editors.

Rank	Website	Visitors[1]
1.	Google sites (YouTube, Blogger)	1,229,937
2.	Microsoft sites (Bing, Xbox Live)	919,432
3.	Facebook (Instagram)	843,403
4.	Yahoo! sites (Flickr, Tumblr)	612,664
5.	Baidu.com Inc.	441,890
6.	Alibaba.com Corp.	430,308
7.	Sohu.com Inc.	422,274
8.	Tencent Inc. (QQ)	409,456
9.	Qihoo.com sites	387,147
10.	Wikimedia Foundation sites (Wikipedia)	374,819
11.	Amazon sites (Zappos, Audible, IMDb)	363,941
12.	Iqiyi & PPS	263,142
13.	Youku & Tudou	254,940
14.	CBS Interactive (CNET, ZDNet)	251,605
15.	SINA Corp.	245,432
16.	Apple Inc. (iTunes)	237,183
17.	BitTorrent Network	232,742
18.	eBay (PayPal[2], Half.com, StubHub)	232,592
19.	Mode Media (Glam, Brash)	226,973
20.	NetEase.com Inc.	210,133

(1) Number of persons age 15 or older, in thousands, who visited a website from a desktop computer in any location, at least once in June 2015. (2) PayPal was spun off by eBay in July 2015.

Top Web Browsers Worldwide, 2008-15

Source: StatCounter Global Stats, gs.statcounter.com

Browser	% of browser market 2008	2010	2012	2014	2015
Chrome	—	9.88%	33.81%	45.28%	51.74%
Internet Explorer	68.57	52.68	32.04	21.38	17.19
Firefox	26.14	30.69	23.73	17.52	15.68
Safari	3.30	4.09	7.12	10.60	9.79
Opera	1.78	1.91	1.72	1.39	1.83
Android	—	—	0.36	1.36	1.51

— = Not available. **Note:** Percent of World Wide Web users accessing the Web via a particular browser, for July of year shown.

Top Operating Systems Worldwide, 2009-15

Source: StatCounter Global Stats, gs.statcounter.com

Operating system	% of OS market 2009	2010	2012	2014	2015
Windows 7	0.97%	17.34%	45.50%	36.39%	31.12%
Android	0.02	0.23	3.29	16.38	25.62
Apple iOS	0.36	0.88	5.16	11.62	11.37
Windows 8.1	—	—	—	4.90	9.59
Windows XP	69.21	54.70	25.89	9.96	5.70
Mac OS X	4.07	5.38	6.16	5.65	4.90
Windows 8	—	—	0.17	4.94	2.10

— = Not available. **Note:** Percent of World Wide Web users accessing Web with a particular operating system (OS), for July of year shown. Includes mobile devices' operating systems.

U.S. Internet Use by Selected Characteristics, 2013-15

Source: Pew Research Center

	% who are users 2013	% who are users 2015
All adults	84%	84%
Gender		
Male	84	85
Female	84	84
Age		
18-29	97	96
30-49	92	93
50-64	81	81
65+	56	58
Race/ethnicity		
White, non-Hispanic	85%	85%
Black, non-Hispanic	79	78
Hispanic	81	81
Education		
No high school diploma	60	66
High school graduate	76	76
Some college	92	90
College graduate	96	95
Annual household income		
Less than $30,000	72%	74%
$30,000-$49,999	86	85
$50,000-$74,999	93	95
$75,000 or more	97	97
Geography		
Urban	86	85
Suburban	85	85
Rural	78	78

Note: Percent of U.S. adults, age 18 and over, who use the Internet, email, or access the Internet via a mobile device. Six surveys and 13,282 interviews were conducted in 2013; two surveys and 3,004 interviews in 2015.

Most-Visited U.S. Websites, 2015

Source: comScore Media Metrix; comScore qSearch

Some websites represent an aggregation of commonly owned domain names; examples of popular domains within a group as of June 2015 added in parentheses by World Almanac editors.

All U.S. Sites

Rank	Website	Visitors[1]
1.	Google sites (YouTube, Blogger)	241,833
2.	Facebook (Instagram)	213,865
3.	Yahoo! sites (Flickr, Rivals.com, Tumblr)	208,746
4.	Amazon sites (Zappos, Audible, IMDb)	181,575
5.	Microsoft sites (Bing, Xbox Live)	174,550
6.	AOL, Inc. (Moviefone, Huffington Post)	170,578
7.	Mode Media (Glam, Brash)	141,855
8.	Apple Inc. (iTunes)	140,721
9.	Comcast NBCUniversal	135,734
10.	CBS Interactive (CNET, ZDNet)	127,459

Blog Sites

Rank	Website	Visitors[1]
1.	WordPress.com	80,566
2.	Blogger	69,010
3.	Gawker Media (Gizmodo, Lifehacker)	55,367
4.	Federated Media Publishing (Fark)	32,620
5.	Reddit	31,523

Search and Navigation

Rank	Website	Searches (mil)	% of searches
1.	Google sites	11,184	64.0%
2.	Microsoft sites (Bing)	3,553	20.3
3.	Yahoo! sites	2,225	12.7
4.	Ask Network	301	1.7
5.	AOL Inc.	202	1.2

Email

Rank	Website	Visitors[1]
1.	Google Gmail	129,811
2.	Yahoo! Mail	68,855
3.	Outlook	33,887
4.	AOL Email	14,819

Social Networking Sites

Rank	Website	Visitors[1]
1.	Facebook and Messenger	211,313
2.	Twitter	115,733
3.	LinkedIn	110,619
4.	Google+	98,824
5.	Instagram	98,541
6.	Pinterest	75,788
7.	Tumblr	74,368

Video Sites

Rank	Website[2]	Visitors[3]
1.	Google sites (YouTube)	172,652
2.	Facebook	85,683
3.	Yahoo! sites (Flickr)	57,527
4.	Vevo	43,046
5.	Maker Studios Inc.	40,280
6.	Vimeo	37,909
7.	AnyClip Media	33,379
8.	Fullscreen	32,719
9.	Comcast NBCUniversal	32,554
10.	Microsoft sites (Xbox Live)	31,011

Note: Search and navigation data are for desktop computer users. (1) Number of persons age 2 and older, in thousands, who visited the media property (including website/apps) at least once from any U.S. location in June 2015. Mobile users under age 18 are not measured. (2) Excludes advertisement videos. (3) Number of persons age 2 and older, in thousands, who visited website from a desktop computer in any U.S. location at least once in June 2015.

Fixed Broadband Penetration in Selected Countries, 2002-14

Source: Organisation for Economic Co-operation and Development (OECD)
(nonmobile broadband subscriptions per 100 inhabitants, for fourth quarter of given year; ranked by 2014 figures)

Country	2002	2005	2010	2011	2012	2013	2014
France	2.7	15.0	32.7	34.8	36.6	37.9	39.2
United Kingdom	2.3	16.3	31.3	32.8	34.3	35.6	36.8
Germany	3.9	13.0	32.0	33.3	34.1	34.9	35.9
Canada	12.1	20.8	31.8	32.8	33.6	34.4	35.4
United States	6.7	16.4	27.3	28.3	29.4	30.3	31.4
Japan	6.2	18.1	26.6	27.3	27.7	28.1	28.5
Italy	1.7	11.8	21.8	22.5	22.7	22.9	23.6

Note: Includes Internet connections with speeds greater than 256 kilobits per second (256 kbps).

U.S. Broadband Residential Internet Connections by Technology, 2009-13

Source: Federal Communications Commission
(Internet connections in thousands, as of June of given year)

Connection type	2009	2010	2011	2012	2013
DSL	4,897	5,559	7,913	11,575	14,366
Cable modem	23,025	29,398	32,321	36,583	43,061
Fiber optic (FTTP)	3,177	3,982	4,894	5,632	6,512
Total nonmobile[1]	**31,161**	**39,037**	**45,263**	**53,070**	**65,041**
Mobile wireless	196	3,206	6,520	25,539	72,014
Total[1,2]	**31,356**	**42,243**	**51,783**	**78,609**	**137,056**

Note: Includes connections with transmission speeds of at least 3 megabits per second (3 mbps) downstream (Internet to user) and 768 kilobits per second (768 kbps) upstream (user to Internet). (1) Includes categories not listed individually. (2) Numbers may not add up to totals due to rounding.

Internet Use in the U.S., 2000-13

Source: 2014 Digital Future Report, USC Annenberg School Center for the Digital Future

	2000	2002	2003	2005	2006	2007	2008	2009	2010	2012	2013
Weekly time online[1]	9	11	13	13	14	15	17	19	18	20	21
Weekly time online, at home[1]	3.3	6.8	6.9	7.8	8.9	10.0	10.1	10.6	12.3	14.1	14.1
Weekly time online, at work[2]	NA	5.5	4.9	5.6	7.8	7.4	8.3	9.0	9.2	9.4	10.4
% of Internet users aged 18 and above who make purchases online	45%	40%	43%	46%	51%	67%	65%	65%	68%	76%	79%
Average monthly spending by Internet purchasers aged 18 and above	NA	NA	NA	NA	NA	$64	$83	$84	$71	$88	$101

NA = Not available. (1) Average number of active-use hours per week among Internet users. (2) Average number of active-use hours per week among Internet users who access the Internet at work.

U.S. Internet Use by Race and Ethnicity, 2000-13

Source: Current Population Survey, 2000-12; American Community Survey, 2013; U.S. Census Bureau, U.S. Dept. of Commerce

	White, non-Hispanic		Black[1]		Asian[1]		Hispanic[2]	
Year	Households (thous.)	% with Internet use	Households (thous.)	% with Internet use	Households (thous.)	% with Internet use	Households (thous.)	% with Internet use
2000	78,719	46.1%	13,171	23.6%	3,457	56.2%	9,565	23.6%
2003	81,857	59.9	13,746	36.0	4,009	66.7	12,023	36.0
2007	83,294	66.9	14,730	45.3	4,576	75.2	13,619	43.4
2009	83,810	73.3	15,254	54.5	4,625	80.5	13,799	52.8
2010	83,613	74.9	15,357	58.1	4,744	82.6	14,142	59.1
2011	83,148	76.2	15,369	56.9	4,795	82.7	14,222	58.3
2012	83,512	78.6	15,843	61.9	5,384	85.0	15,632	64.3
2013	80,699	77.4	13,816	61.3	4,941	86.6	14,209	66.7

Note: Numbers by race/ethnicity of householder. Data for 2013 was obtained using different methodology and is not directly comparable to preceding years. (1) Non-Hispanic only in 2013. (2) Hispanic persons may be of any race.

U.S. Internet Use by Educational Attainment, 2000-13

Source: Current Population Survey, 2000-12; American Community Survey, 2013; U.S. Census Bureau, U.S. Dept. of Commerce

	Less than high school		High school degree[1]		Some college		Bachelor's degree or more	
Year	Households (thous.)	% with Internet use	Households (thous.)	% with Internet use	Households (thous.)	% with Internet use	Households (thous.)	% with Internet use
2000	17,402	11.7%	32,278	29.9%	27,883	49.0%	27,684	66.0%
2003	16,972	20.2	34,377	43.1	30,320	62.6	31,457	78.3
2007	13,978	24.0	33,099	49.5	30,434	68.9	33,302	84.0
2009	13,711	32.2	32,990	57.5	31,050	74.7	34,910	88.5
2010	13,257	35.5	33,008	60.4	31,549	77.2	35,156	89.2
2011	13,183	36.9	33,060	61.2	31,586	77.3	35,301	89.9
2012	12,951	39.3	32,687	64.8	32,517	79.5	37,239	91.7
2013	12,855	43.8	28,277	62.9	34,218	79.2	36,349	90.1

Note: Numbers by educational attainment of householders 25 years and older. Data for 2013 was obtained using different methodology and is not directly comparable to preceding years. (1) Includes high school degree equivalent.

Popular U.S. Online Purchases, 2002-13

Source: The 2014 Digital Future Report, USC Annenberg School Center for the Digital Future
(percent of Internet users who buy item(s) online; ranked by 2013 figures)

Item	2002	2006	2008	2010	2012	2013
Clothes	39%	42%	61%	59%	66%	68%
Gifts	10	12	61	63	60	64
Books	29	34	60	63	66	61
Travel	16	17	57	57	66	58
Electronic goods/ appliances	14	11	47	50	51	54
Software/ games	12%	11%	43%	44%	37%	43%
Videos/DVDs	6	13	48	47	42	43
Computers/ peripherals	10	11	43	44	40	38

Frequency of Selected Internet Activities in the U.S., 2013

Source: The 2014 Digital Future Report, USC Annenberg School Center for the Digital Future
(as % of all Internet users age 12 and older)

Online activity	Several times a day	Daily	Weekly	Monthly	Less than monthly	Never
Check email	51%	34%	8%	4%	2%	3%
Browse the Web	30	33	16	8	5	8
Visit social networking sites	24	28	13	4	6	24
Look for news	14	36	18	11	9	12
Instant message	12	18	13	8	15	35
Download or listen to music	12	16	19	10	13	30
Find or check a fact	11	22	32	14	10	10
Play games	11	17	16	8	14	35
Download or watch videos	8	14	21	13	12	33
Listen to online radio	6	14	11	8	19	41
Look up a definition	5	15	33	15	15	17
Online banking	2	13	35	20	7	23

Telecommunications Milestones

1753: Scottish surgeon Charles Morrison proposed using 26 electric lines, one for each letter of the alphabet, to make an electric telegraph. A letter would be indicated by charging the corresponding line, causing movement of a light object at the receiving end. Swiss scientist Georges-Louis Lesage built such a 26-line "electrostatic" system in 1774.

1837: In England, Charles Wheatstone and William Fothergill Cooke patented an electromagnetic telegraph. To indicate letters, their system used the magnetic field generated by a current to deflect compass needles. In 1839, they built the first commercial electric telegraph along a 13-mi (21-km) route.

1837: American inventor Samuel Morse filed a provisional patent application for a different type of electric telegraph that indicated letters by making marks of various lengths on paper. In 1844, he completed a 30-mi telegraph line from Washington, DC, to Baltimore, MD.

1866: The first successful transatlantic telegraph cable was laid.

1876: Alexander Graham Bell applied for a U.S. patent on the telephone. In his first successful experiment, on Mar. 10, he used the device to call his assistant.

1901: Italian inventor Guglielmo Marconi successfully transmitted the first transatlantic radio signal—from Cornwall, England, to Newfoundland, Canada.

1927: Commercial transatlantic telephone service (via radio) began between New York and London.

1946: The first commercial mobile phone service was launched, in St. Louis, MO.

1947: U.S. scientists invented the transistor, thereby giving birth to a revolution in telecommunications and electronics.

1948: U.S. mathematician/engineer Claude Shannon's epochal paper "A Mathematical Theory of Communication" laid the foundation for modern information theory. Its treatment of such crucial concepts as data compression and error detection and correction opened the way to digital communication.

1951: The mayors of Englewood, NJ, and Alameda, CA, made the first customer-dialed long-distance telephone call, facilitated by the introduction of area codes.

1956: The first transoceanic telephone cable went into service.

1962: NASA launched the world's first active communications satellite, AT&T's *Telstar 1*.

1978: Trials were conducted in Chicago and Newark, NJ, on a cellular approach to mobile telephony. This divided a region into a multitude of small overlapping areas, or cells, and made possible a significant increase in quality of calls and quantity of callers. Callers could be switched from one cell to another as they moved about.

1983: The first commercial cellular system in the U.S. went into operation in Chicago. A similar system was also launched in the Baltimore, MD-Washington, DC, area.

1984: As a result of a 1982 antitrust settlement with the U.S. government, AT&T, which handled most telephone service in the U.S., was broken up into several separate entities.

1994: The first smartphone, IBM's Simon Personal Communicator, went on the market. A bricklike touchscreen device, it combined a cellular phone with such features as an address book, calendar, calculator, email and faxing capability, and games.

2007: Apple released the iPhone, inaugurating a new era in multifunctional smartphones.

2012: By late in the year more than 1 bil smartphones of all types were in use worldwide.

Global Communications Technology Developments, 2001-15

Source: ITU World Telecommunication/Information and Communication Technology (ICT) Indicators Database
(per 100 inhabitants; 2015 data is estimated)

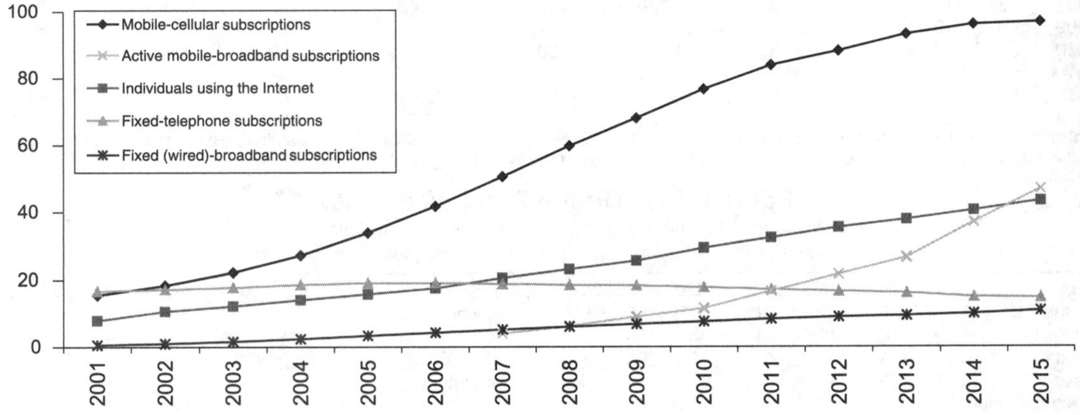

Nations With the Most Cell Phone Use, 2014

Source: © International Telecommunication Union, estimated; ranked by countries with most cell phone subscriptions

Rank	Country	Subscriptions (thous.)	Per 100 pop.	Rank	Country	Subscriptions (thous.)	Per 100 pop.
1.	China	1,286,093	92.27	14.	Germany	99,529	120.42
2.	India	944,009	74.48	15.	Thailand	97,096	144.44
3.	Indonesia	319,000	126.18	16.	Egypt	95,316	114.31
4.	United States	317,444	98.41	17.	Italy	94,200	154.25
5.	Brazil	280,729	138.95	18.	South Africa	79,540	149.68
6.	Russia	221,030	155.14	19.	United Kingdom	78,461	123.58
7.	Japan	152,696	120.23	20.	Turkey	71,888	94.79
8.	Nigeria	138,960	77.84	21.	Iran	68,891	87.79
9.	Vietnam	136,148	147.11	22.	Argentina	66,357	158.74
10.	Pakistan	135,762	73.33	23.	France	64,875	100.36
11.	Bangladesh	120,350	75.92	24.	Ukraine	61,170	144.08
12.	Philippines	111,326	111.22	25.	Poland	59,796	156.45
13.	Mexico	102,188	82.54		**World**	**6,954,110**	**96.07**

U.S. Wireless Industry, 1985-2014

Source: CTIA Semi-Annual[1] Industry Survey, used with permission of CTIA. As of Dec. of year shown.

Year	Est. total subscribers	Total service revenues (thous.)	Cell phone antennas	Avg. monthly revenue per subscriber unit	Avg. local call length (min.)
1985	340,213	$482,428	913	NA	NA
1987	1,230,855	1,151,519	2,305	NA	2.33
1989	3,508,944	3,340,595	4,169	NA	2.48
1991	7,557,148	5,708,522	7,847	NA	2.38
1993	16,009,461	10,892,175	12,824	$76.55	2.41
1995	33,785,661	19,081,239	22,663	59.43	2.15
1997	55,312,293	27,485,633	51,600	49.39	2.31
1999	86,047,003	40,018,489	81,698	46.39	2.38
2000	109,478,031	52,466,020	104,288	48.55	2.56
2001	128,374,512	65,316,235	127,540	49.79	2.74
2002	140,766,842	76,508,187	139,338	51.00	2.73
2003	158,721,981	87,624,093	162,986	51.55	3.07
2004	182,140,362	102,121,210	175,725	52.54	3.05
2005	207,896,198	113,538,221	183,689	50.65	3.00
2006	233,040,781	125,456,825	195,613	49.07	3.03
2007	255,395,599	138,869,304	213,299	49.26	NA
2008	270,333,881	148,084,170	242,130	48.87	2.27
2009	285,646,191	152,551,854	247,081	47.97	1.81
2010	296,285,629	159,929,648	253,086	47.53	1.79
2011	315,963,848	169,767,314	283,385	46.11	1.78
2012	326,475,248	185,013,936	301,779	48.99	1.80
2013	335,652,171	189,192,812	304,360	48.79	NA
2014	355,445,472	187,848,447	298,055	46.64	NA

NA = Not available. (1) Annual survey beginning 2013.

U.S. Use of Selected Cell Phone Functions, 2007-13

Source: The 2014 Digital Future Report, USC Annenberg School Center for the Digital Future (as % of cell phone users age 12 and older)

Function	2007	2008	2009	2010	2012	2013
Text message	31%	45%	54%	62%	82%	77%
Take pictures	33	47	52	60	79	70
Access the Internet	8	13	18	23	59	59
Play games	17	22	20	23	43	43

U.S. Use of Selected Cell Phone Functions, 2013

Source: The 2014 Digital Future Report, USC Annenberg School Center for the Digital Future (% of cell phone users age 12 and older who used function)

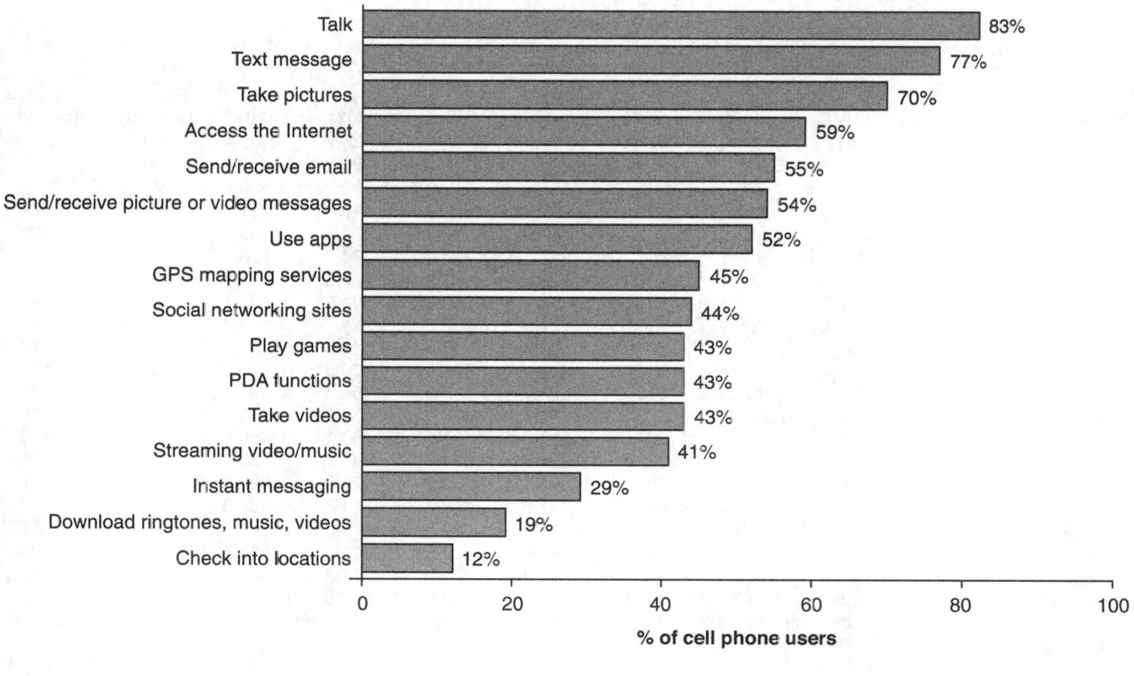

ENVIRONMENT

U.S. Greenhouse Gas Emissions From Human Activities, 1990-2013

Source: U.S. Environmental Protection Agency

Gas and major source(s)	1990	2005	2009	2010	2011	2012	2013	% change, 1990-2013
Carbon dioxide (CO_2)	5,123.7	6,134.0	5,500.6	5,704.5	5,568.9	5,358.3	5,505.2	7.4%
Fossil fuel combustion	4,740.7	5,747.7	5,197.1	5,367.1	5,231.3	5,026.0	5,157.7	8.8
Methane (CH_4)	745.5	707.8	709.5	667.2	660.9	647.6	636.3	−14.6
Enteric fermentation[1]	164.2	168.9	172.7	171.1	168.7	166.3	164.5	0.2
Natural gas systems	179.1	176.3	168.0	159.6	159.3	154.4	157.4	−12.1
Landfills	186.2	165.5	158.1	121.8	121.3	115.3	114.6	−38.5
Coal mining	96.5	64.1	79.9	82.3	71.2	66.5	64.6	−33.1
Nitrous oxide (N_2O)	329.9	355.9	356.1	360.1	371.9	365.6	355.2	7.7
Agricultural soil management	224.0	243.6	264.1	264.3	265.8	266.0	263.7	17.7
Hydrofluorocarbons (HFCs), etc.[2]	102.0	152.5	156.5	167.0	175.0	173.5	176.3	72.8
Total U.S. emissions	**6,301.1**	**7,350.2**	**6,722.7**	**6,898.8**	**6,776.6**	**6,545.1**	**6,673.0**	**5.9**
Net U.S. emissions[3]	**5,525.2**	**6,438.3**	**5,851.9**	**6,027.2**	**5,895.6**	**5,664.7**	**5,791.2**	**4.8**

Note: Emissions given in terms of equivalent emissions of carbon dioxide (CO_2), using units of million metric tons of carbon dioxide equivalent (MMT CO_2 eq.). (1) Digestive process of ruminant animals, such as cattle and sheep, producing methane as a by-product. (2) Includes HFCs, PFCs (perfluorocarbons), SF_6 (sulfur hexafluoride), and NF_3 (nitrogen trifluoride). (3) Total emissions minus carbon dioxide absorbed by forests or other means.

U.S. Greenhouse Gas Emissions, 2013

Source: U.S. Environmental Protection Agency

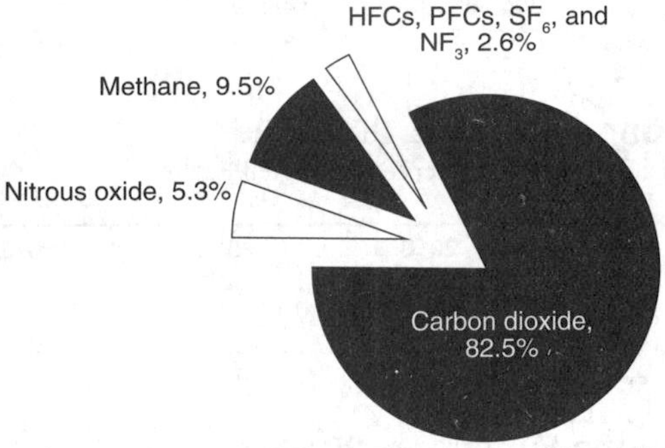

World Carbon Dioxide Emissions From the Use of Fossil Fuels, 2012

Source: U.S. Energy Information Administration

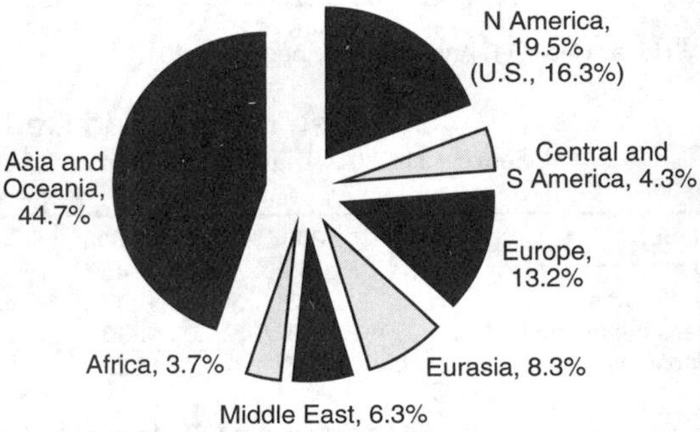

HFC = hydrofluorocarbon; PFC = perfluorocarbon; SF_6 = sulfur hexafluoride; NF_3 = nitrogen trifluoride. **Note:** Emissions sources are independently rounded; percentages may not add up to 100.

Top 20 Nations Producing Carbon Dioxide Emissions, 1980-2012

Source: U.S. Dept. of Energy

(in million metric tons of carbon dioxide emitted from the consumption of energy; ranked by 2012 totals)

Country	1980	1990	2000	2005	2010	2011	2012	% change, 1980-2012	% change, 1990-2012
China	1,448.5	2,268.9	3,165.3	5,116.3	7,388.5	8,126.7	8,106.4	460%	257%
United States	4,775.6	5,040.8	5,863.8	5,999.1	5,580.0	5,483.2	5,270.4	10	5
India	291.2	578.6	991.0	1,181.4	1,714.9	1,752.7	1,830.9	529	216
Russia[1]	3,081.9	3,817.6	1,498.8	1,587.5	1,685.1	1,710.0	1,781.7	NA	NA
Japan	947.0	1,047.0	1,201.4	1,241.3	1,177.3	1,200.3	1,259.1	33	20
Germany[2]	761.1	698.1	854.7	833.6	797.0	784.4	788.3	NA	NA
Korea, South	131.7	242.1	438.8	493.8	584.0	650.5	657.1	399	171
Iran	116.8	202.1	321.5	451.1	566.6	594.5	603.6	417	199
Saudi Arabia	176.9	208.0	290.5	401.9	506.6	551.4	582.7	229	180
Canada	457.4	470.6	573.3	609.6	547.9	551.6	550.8	20	17
Brazil	185.7	237.3	344.4	370.8	461.4	476.6	500.2	169	111
United Kingdom	613.6	601.8	560.3	583.1	529.5	488.3	498.9	−19	−17
South Africa	235.0	298.0	386.0	432.4	478.8	471.5	473.2	101	59
Indonesia	85.8	156.0	267.6	326.1	431.1	450.1	456.2	432	192
Mexico	240.3	302.2	382.9	397.8	434.0	446.2	453.8	89	50
Australia	198.8	267.6	356.3	409.2	431.1	426.5	420.6	112	57
Italy	371.8	415.4	447.7	471.9	419.8	411.6	385.8	4	−7
France	488.9	367.7	401.7	414.0	385.6	374.3	364.5	−25	−1
Spain	195.0	224.1	315.6	382.9	312.6	318.2	312.4	60	39
Taiwan	70.6	118.3	256.1	288.8	292.9	311.3	307.1	335	160
World total[3]	**18,434.7**	**21,610.4**	**24,041.0**	**27,876.4**	**31,154.8**	**32,155.0**	**32,310.3**	**75**	**50**

NA = Not applicable. (1) Numbers for 1980-90 are for the former Soviet Union. (2) Numbers for 1980-90 are for former West Germany. (3) Includes nations not listed.

Atmospheric Concentration of Carbon Dioxide, 1744-2014

Source: Carbon Dioxide Information Analysis Center, U.S. Dept. of Energy; Earth System Research Laboratory, Natl. Oceanic and Atmospheric Admin., U.S. Dept. of Commerce

Year[1]	CO_2 in ppm	Year[1]	CO_2 in ppm	Year[1]	CO_2 in ppm	Year[1]	CO_2 in ppm	Year[1]	CO_2 in ppm
1744	277	1878	290	1960	317	2005	380	2010	390
1791	280	1903	295	1970	326	2006	382	2011	392
1816	284	1915	301	1980	339	2007	384	2012	394
1843	287	1927	306	1990	354	2008	386	2013	396
1869	289	1943	308	2000	369	2009	387	2014	399

ppm = Parts per million. (1) Measurements for the years 1744-1943 were derived from a 200-m-deep ice core sample drilled near Siple Station in Antarctica in 1983-84. Measurements for 1960-2014 were taken directly from the atmosphere at Mauna Loa Observatory in Hawaii.

Emissions of Principal Air Pollutants in the U.S., 1970-2014

Source: Office of Air Quality Planning and Standards, U.S. Environmental Protection Agency; in million tons

Pollutant	1970	1975	1980	1985	1990	1995	2000	2005	2010	2014
Carbon monoxide	204.0	188.4	185.4	176.8	154.2	126.8	114.5	88.5	73.8	67.8
Nitrogen oxides[1]	26.9	26.4	27.1	25.8	25.5	25.0	22.6	20.4	14.8	12.4
Particulate matter[2]										
PM10	13.0	7.6	7.0	41.3	27.8	25.8	23.7	21.3	20.8	20.6
PM2.5	NA	NA	NA	NA	7.6	6.9	7.3	5.6	6.0	6.0
Sulfur dioxide	31.2	28.0	25.9	23.3	23.1	18.6	16.3	14.5	7.7	5.0
Volatile org. compounds[1]	34.7	30.8	31.1	27.4	24.1	22.0	17.5	17.8	17.8	17.1
Ammonia	NA	NA	NA	NA	4.3	4.7	4.9	3.9	4.3	4.2
Total[3]	**309.8**	**281.2**	**276.5**	**294.6**	**266.6**	**229.8**	**206.8**	**172.0**	**145.2**	**133.1**

NA = Not available. (1) Ozone, a major air pollutant and the primary constituent of smog, is not emitted directly to the air but is formed by sunlight acting on emissions of nitrogen oxides and volatile organic compounds. (2) PM10 = particulates 10 microns or smaller in diameter. PM2.5 = particulates 2.5 microns or smaller in diameter. (3) Totals are rounded, as are components of totals.

Sources of Air Pollutants in the U.S., 1970-2014

Source: Office of Air Quality Planning and Standards, U.S. Environmental Protection Agency; in thousand tons

Carbon monoxide sources	1970	1975	1980	1985	1990	1995	2000	2005	2010	2014
Fuel combustion, elec. util.	237	276	322	291	363	372	484	643	766	784
Industrial processes[1]	10,610	8,304	7,700	5,894	5,572	5,631	3,628	3,074	2,807	2,903
Transportation[2]	174,602	167,884	160,512	153,216	131,702	107,755	92,239	64,729	43,595	36,298
Total carbon monoxide[3]	**204,042**	**188,398**	**185,408**	**176,845**	**154,188**	**126,778**	**114,467**	**88,546**	**73,771**	**67,756**
Nitrogen oxide sources										
Fuel combustion, elec. util.	4,900	5,694	7,024	6,127	6,663	6,384	5,330	3,792	2,458	1,776
Industrial processes[1]	5,100	4,546	4,110	4,009	3,831	3,909	3,518	2,783	2,406	2,418
Transportation[2]	15,276	15,029	14,846	14,508	13,373	12,989	12,560	12,612	9,017	7,158
Total nitrogen oxide[3]	**26,882**	**26,378**	**27,080**	**25,757**	**25,527**	**24,955**	**22,598**	**20,355**	**14,846**	**12,412**
Sulfur dioxide sources										
Fuel combustion, elec. util.	17,398	18,268	17,469	16,272	15,909	12,080	11,396	10,404	5,696	3,195
Industrial processes[1]	11,661	7,993	6,725	5,597	5,402	4,945	3,516	2,721	1,447	1,254
Transportation[2]	551	635	717	809	874	741	697	682	158	100
Total sulfur dioxide[3]	**31,218**	**28,044**	**25,926**	**23,307**	**23,077**	**18,619**	**16,347**	**14,546**	**7,732**	**4,991**

(1) Industrial fuel combustion, chemical and allied manufacturing, metals processing, and petroleum and other industrial sectors. (2) Highway and off-highway vehicles. (3) Numbers may not add up to totals because not all categories are listed.

Average Global Temperature and Atmospheric Carbon Dioxide, 1880-2014

Source: Goddard Institute for Space Studies, National Aeronautics and Space Administration, via Earth Policy Institute

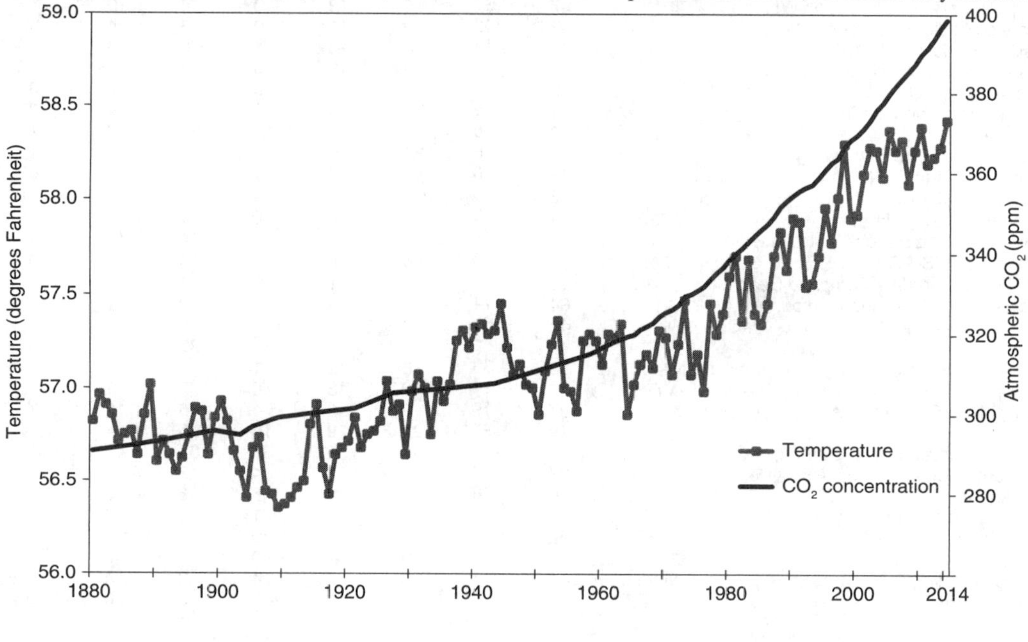

Air Pollution in Selected World Cities

Source: World Health Organization (WHO); *World Development Indicators 2015*, The World Bank

Particulate matter in the following table refers to smoke, soot, dust, and liquid droplets from combustion that are in the air—specifically, to particulates less than 10 microns in diameter (PM10) capable of reaching deep into the respiratory tract. The level of particulates, an important indicator of air quality, is significantly affected by the state of technology and pollution controls. WHO estimated that outdoor air pollution caused 3.7 mil premature deaths worldwide in 2012, due to exposure to PM10. **Sulfur dioxide** is a pollutant formed when fossil fuels containing sulfur are burned. **Nitrogen dioxide** is a poisonous, pungent gas formed when nitric oxide combines with hydrocarbons in sunlight, producing photochemical smog. Nitrogen oxides are emitted by bacteria, nitrogenous fertilizers, aerobic decomposition of organic matter, biomass combustion, and, especially, burning fuel for vehicles and industrial activities. Emissions of sulfur dioxide and nitrogen oxides lead to acid rain.

Data in the table represent the annual average of outdoor particulates, in micrograms per cubic meter (mpcm), that a resident of a city is exposed to. They are based on reports from urban monitoring sites. The figures give a general indication of air quality, but results should be interpreted with caution. World Health Organization standards for acceptable air quality are annual mean concentrations of 20 mpcm for particulate matter less than 10 microns in diameter and 40 mpcm for nitrogen dioxide and daily mean concentrations of 20 mpcm for sulfur dioxide.

City, country	Particulate matter[1]	Sulfur dioxide[2]	Nitrogen dioxide[2]
Accra, Ghana	98	NA	NA
Amsterdam, Netherlands	25	10	58
Bangkok, Thailand	38	11	23
Barcelona, Spain	25	11	43
Beijing, China	121	90	122
Berlin, Germany	24	18	26
Cairo, Egypt	135	69	NA
Cape Town, South Africa	30	21	72
Caracas, Venezuela	45	33	57
Chicago, IL, U.S.	22	14	57
Delhi, India	286	24	41
Jakarta, Indonesia	48	NA	NA
Kolkata, India	97	49	34
London, England, UK	22	25	77
Los Angeles, CA, U.S.	33	9	74
Manila, Philippines	49	33	NA
Mexico City, Mexico	93	74	130
Milan, Italy	37	31	248
Montréal, QC, Canada	34	10	42
Moscow, Russia	33	109	NA
Mumbai, India	136	33	39
New York, NY, U.S.	23	26	79
Oslo, Norway	23	8	43
Paris, France	24	14	57
Prague, Czech Republic	26	14	33
Quito, Ecuador	38	22	NA
Rio de Janeiro, Brazil	67	129	NA
Rome, Italy	32	NA	NA
São Paulo, Brazil	35	43	83
Seoul, South Korea	49	44	60
Shanghai, China	79	53	73
Sofia, Bulgaria	65	39	122
Sydney, Australia	9	28	81
Tehran, Iran	91	209	NA
Tokyo, Japan	22	18	68
Toronto, ON, Canada	24	17	43
Warsaw, Poland	35	16	32

NA = Not available. (1) WHO data is most recent available, as of 2008-12. (2) World Bank data as of 2001.

Air Quality of Selected U.S. Urban Areas, 1980-2014

Source: Office of Air Quality Planning and Standards, U.S. Environmental Protection Agency

Data indicate the number of days metropolitan statistical areas or corresponding core-based statistical areas failed to meet acceptable air-quality standards.

Urban area	1980	1990	2000	2005	2010	2011	2012	2013	2014
Atlanta-Sandy Springs-Marietta, GA	19	33	28	6	2	0	3	1	1
Bakersfield, CA	47	59	68	39	17	18	17	22	25
Baltimore-Towson, MD	51	14	8	6	6	5	2	0	0
Baton Rouge, LA	21	15	20	11	2	1	0	0	0
Boston-Cambridge-Quincy, MA-NH	14	4	2	3	1	0	1	0	0
Chicago-Naperville-Joliet, IL-IN-WI	87	31	5	12	0	4	10	1	1
Cincinnati-Middletown, OH-KY-IN	63	42	9	11	0	3	4	0	0
Cleveland-Elyria-Mentor, OH	34	14	6	10	1	0	5	0	2
Dallas-Fort Worth-Arlington, TX	30	10	18	16	0	6	4	1	0
Denver-Aurora, CO	28	1	0	0	0	2	4	0	1
Detroit-Warren-Livonia, MI	41	9	3	9	0	0	4	0	0
Fresno, CA	68	26	73	25	13	25	17	17	23
Houston-Sugar Land-Baytown, TX	68	48	31	19	1	7	4	1	0
Indianapolis-Carmel, IN	43	6	18	4	1	0	2	0	1
Kansas City, MO-KS	43	5	6	6	0	2	4	1	0
Las Vegas-Paradise, NV	24	8	1	3	0	0	2	1	1
Los Angeles-Long Beach-Santa Ana, CA	189	124	46	34	5	14	11	4	13
Memphis, TN-MS-AR	58	8	6	6	0	0	1	0	0
Miami-Fort Lauderdale-Pompano Beach, FL	16	0	0	1	0	1	0	0	0
Minneapolis-St. Paul-Bloomington, MN-WI	64	14	1	3	0	0	1	0	0
Nashville-Davidson–Murfreesboro–Franklin, TN	42	52	6	2	0	0	1	0	0
New Orleans-Metairie-Kenner, LA	4	1	5	1	17	29	7	3	0
New York-Northern New Jersey-Long Island, NY-NJ-PA	83	33	8	12	1	3	0	0	1
Philadelphia-Camden-Wilmington, PA-NJ-DE-MD	73	24	9	13	4	5	2	0	2
Phoenix-Mesa-Scottsdale, AZ	107	19	2	2	4	46	16	27	33
Pittsburgh, PA	119	92	29	29	16	5	4	1	1
Riverside-San Bernardino-Ontario, CA	160	132	76	56	33	35	42	37	34
Sacramento–Arden-Arcade–Roseville, CA	38	26	26	23	4	7	6	4	3
Salt Lake City, UT	70	46	13	3	6	3	0	9	2
San Francisco-Oakland-Fremont, CA	8	2	2	1	1	0	0	0	0
Seattle-Tacoma-Bellevue, WA	32	3	4	1	0	1	1	0	0
Tucson, AZ	49	0	0	1	0	0	0	3	0
Washington-Arlington-Alexandria, DC-VA-MD-WV	42	11	5	4	4	3	3	0	0
Winston-Salem, NC	0	3	4	0	0	0	0	0	0

Municipal Solid Waste, 2013

Source: U.S. Environmental Protection Agency

In 2013, Americans generated about 254 mil tons of refuse collected as municipal solid waste (MSW). Of that MSW, paper represented 27.0%; food 14.6%; yard trimmings 13.5%; plastics 12.8%; metals 9.1%; rubber, leather, and textiles 9.0%; wood 6.2%; glass 4.5%; and other material 3.3%. About 34.3%, or 87 mil tons, was recycled or composted; nearly half of recycled/composted materials consisted of paper and paperboard.

Municipal Solid Waste Generation, 1960-2013

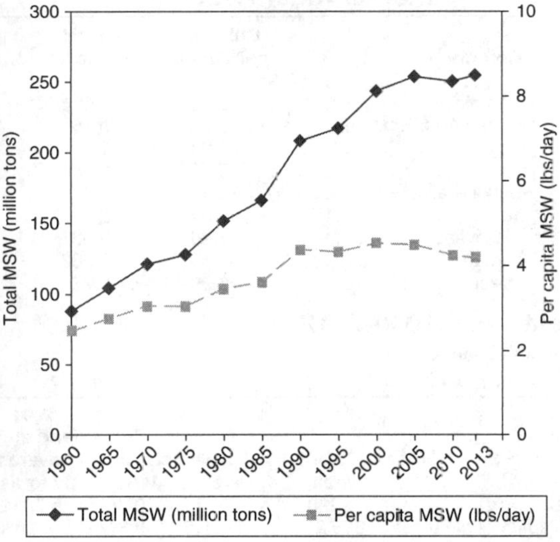

Municipal Solid Waste Recycling, 1960-2013

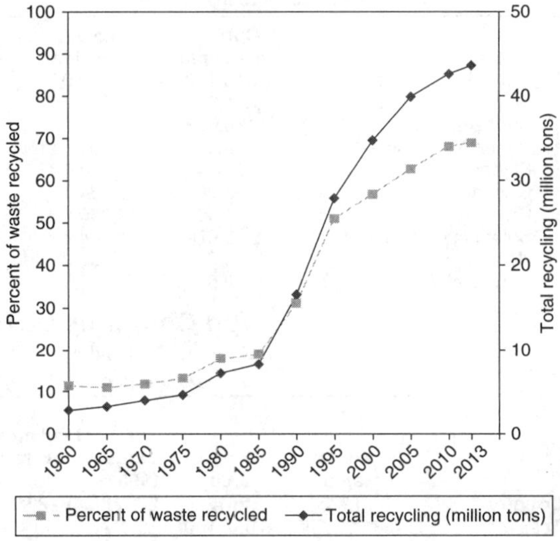

Hazardous Waste Sites in the U.S., 2015

Source: *National Priorities List*, U.S. Environmental Protection Agency; as of May 2015

State/territory	Proposed		Final		Total
	Gen.	Fed.	Gen.	Fed.	
Alabama	2	0	11	3	16
Alaska	0	0	1	5	6
Arizona	0	0	7	2	9
Arkansas	0	0	9	0	9
California	1	0	73	24	98
Colorado	1	0	16	3	20
Connecticut	1	0	13	1	15
Delaware	1	0	12	1	14
District of Columbia	0	0	0	1	1
Florida	1	0	47	6	54
Georgia	1	0	14	2	17
Guam	0	0	1	1	2
Hawaii	0	0	1	2	3
Idaho	3	0	4	2	9
Illinois	4	1	39	4	48
Indiana	0	0	38	0	38
Iowa	1	0	10	1	12
Kansas	1	0	11	1	13
Kentucky	0	0	13	1	14
Louisiana	4	0	9	1	14
Maine	0	0	10	3	13
Maryland	1	0	10	10	21
Massachusetts	2	0	25	6	33
Michigan	1	1	66	0	68
Minnesota	0	0	23	2	25
Mississippi	1	0	8	0	9
Missouri	0	0	30	3	33
Montana	3	0	16	0	19
Nebraska	0	0	14	1	15
Nevada	0	0	1	0	1
New Hampshire	1	0	19	1	21
New Jersey	1	0	108	6	115
New Mexico	0	0	14	1	15
New York	1	0	81	4	86
North Carolina	0	0	37	2	39
North Dakota	0	0	0	0	0
Ohio	4	2	34	3	43
Oklahoma	1	0	6	1	8
Oregon	1	0	11	2	14
Pennsylvania	2	0	89	6	97
Puerto Rico	0	0	15	1	16
Rhode Island	0	0	10	2	12
South Carolina	0	0	23	2	25
South Dakota	0	0	1	1	2
Tennessee	0	0	14	3	17
Texas	2	0	46	4	52
Utah	3	0	10	5	18
Vermont	0	0	12	0	12
Virgin Islands	0	0	1	0	1
Virginia	0	0	20	11	31
Washington	1	0	37	13	51
West Virginia	0	0	7	2	9
Wisconsin	1	0	37	0	38
Wyoming	0	0	1	1	2
Total	**47**	**4**	**1,165**	**157**	**1,373**

Note: Fed. = Hazardous waste produced by federal agency; Gen. = Non-fed. sites. Sites that have been proposed for federal Superfund financing are listed under Proposed; sites that have qualified for Superfund financing are under Final.

Renewable Water Resources, 2014

Source: Food and Agriculture Organization (FAO), United Nations

Globally, water supplies are abundant, but they are unevenly distributed among and within countries. In some areas, water withdrawals are so high, relative to supply, that surface water supplies are shrinking, and groundwater reserves are being depleted faster than they can be replenished by precipitation. According to the FAO, the U.S. (including Alaska and Hawaii) has 8,805 cubic meters per capita and 2,818 cubic kilometers of internal renewable water resources total.

The tables below take into account only countries for which data are available, draw upon studies done over a number of years, and use 2013 population data. Numbers represent each country's internal resources. Countries ranked by per capita figures.

Countries With Greatest Internal Water Resources

Country	Cubic m per capita	Total cubic km
Iceland	515,152	170.0
Guyana	301,250	241.0
Suriname	183,673	99.0
Papua New Guinea	109,411	801.0
Bhutan	103,448	78.0
Gabon	98,086	164.0
Canada	81,007	2,850.0
Solomon Islands	79,679	44.7
Norway	75,749	382.0
New Zealand	72,570	327.0

Countries With Lowest Internal Water Resources

Country	Cubic m per capita	Total cubic km
Kuwait	0.0	0.0
Bahrain	3.003	0.004
United Arab Emirates	16.05	0.15
Egypt	21.94	1.8
Qatar	25.82	0.056
Saudi Arabia	83.25	2.4
Yemen	86.04	2.1
Maldives	86.96	0.03
Jordan	93.76	0.682
Israel	96.99	0.75

Top Countries by Forest Area, 1990-2012

Source: Food and Agriculture Organization, United Nations
(in square kilometers; ranked by 2012 area)

Country	Forest area, 1990	Forest area, 2012	% change, 1990-2012	% of land area covered by forest in 2012
Russia	8,089,500	8,092,100	0.0%	49.4%
Brazil	5,748,390	5,151,332	−10.4	68.8
Canada	3,101,340	3,101,340	0.0	34.1
United States	2,963,350	3,047,876	2.9	32.4
China	1,571,410	2,123,873	35.2	16.7
Congo, Dem. Rep. of	1,603,630	1,535,122	−4.3	70.7
Australia	1,545,000	1,474,520	−4.6	20.1
Indonesia	1,185,450	930,620	−21.5	65.4
India	639,390	687,240	7.5	21.5
Peru	701,560	676,920	−3.5	54.8
Mexico	702,910	644,916	−8.3	36.2
Colombia	625,190	602,970	−3.6	56.3
Angola	609,760	582,304	−4.5	48.9
Bolivia	627,950	565,808	−9.9	58.0
Zambia	528,000	491,348	−6.9	71.0
Venezuela	520,260	456,998	−12.2	59.0
Mozambique	433,780	385,992	−11.0	55.2
Tanzania	414,950	326,212	−21.4	46.8
Myanmar	392,180	311,538	−20.6	60.0
Argentina	347,930	289,204	−16.9	12.7
Papua New Guinea	315,230	284,416	−9.8%	69.6%
Sweden	272,810	282,030	3.4	67.0
Japan	249,500	249,966	0.2	68.4
Central African Rep.	232,030	225,450	−2.8	37.2
Congo Rep.	227,260	223,870	−1.5	66.5
Finland	218,890	221,570	1.2	72.0
Gabon	220,000	220,000	0.0	85.4
Malaysia	223,760	202,824	−9.4	68.1
Cameroon	243,160	194,760	−19.9	51.4
Thailand	195,490	190,016	−2.8	38.3
Spain	138,180	185,253	34.1	27.7
Paraguay	211,570	172,248	−18.6	53.3
Chile	152,630	163,062	6.8	20.5
France	145,370	160,500	10.4	26.5
Laos	173,140	155,946	−9.9	75.0
Guyana	152,050	152,050	0.0	77.2
Zimbabwe	221,640	149,700	−32.5	57.3
Suriname	147,760	147,508	−0.2	94.7
Vietnam	93,630	140,850	50.4	30.2
Madagascar	136,920	124,390	−9.2	23.5
World	**40,330,620**	**40,219,108**	**−0.3**	**31.0**

NA = Not available.

Trees of the U.S.

Source: American Forests

More than 870 native and naturalized species of trees grow in the U.S. The trunk of the world's largest known living tree, the General Sherman giant sequoia in California, weighs almost 1,400 tons—about as much as 15 adult blue whales. To determine the country's largest trees (or "national champions"), American Forests uses a point system whereby trunk circumference, or girth (in inches) + height (in feet) + ¼ average crown spread (in feet) = total points. As of May 5, 2015.

10 Largest National Champion Trees

Tree type	Girth at 4.5 ft (in.)	Height (ft)	Crown spread (ft)	Total points	Location
Giant sequoia (Gen. Sherman tree)	1,020	274	107	1,321	Sequoia National Park, CA
Coast redwood	950	321	75	1,290	Jedediah Smith Redwoods State Park, CA
Coast redwood	895	307	83	1,223	Jedediah Smith Redwoods State Park, CA
Coast redwood	845	349	89	1,216	Redwood National Park, CA
Coast redwood	867	299	101	1,191	Prairie Creek Redwoods State Park, CA
Western redcedar	761	159	45	931	Olympic National Park, WA
Sitka spruce	668	191	96	883	Olympic National Park, WA
Coast Douglas-fir	599	200	37	808	Olympic National Park, WA
Coast Douglas-fir	505	281	71	804	Olympic National Forest, WA
Port-Orford-cedar	522	242	35	773	Coos, OR

Selected Endangered Animal Species

Source: Fish and Wildlife Service, U.S. Dept. of the Interior

Common name	Scientific name	Range
Albatross, Amsterdam	Diomedia amsterdamensis	Amsterdam Island, Indian Ocean
Antelope, giant sable	Hippotragus niger variani	Angola
Armadillo, giant	Priodontes maximus	Venezuela, Guyana, Argentina
Bandicoot, desert	Perameles eremiana	Australia
Bat, gray	Myotis grisescens	Central, southeastern U.S.
Bear, Mexican grizzly	Ursus arctos	Mexico
Bobcat, Mexican	Lynx rufus escuinapae	Central Mexico
Camel, Bactrian	Camelus bactrianus	Mongolia, China
Caribou, woodland	Rangifer tarandus caribou	Canada, U.S. (ID, WA)
Cheetah	Acinonyx jubatus	India
Chimpanzee, pygmy	Pan paniscus	Dem. Rep. of the Congo
Condor, California	Gymnogyps californianus	U.S. (AZ, CA)
Crane, whooping	Grus americana	Canada, U.S. (Rocky Mts. to Carolinas)
Crocodile, American	Crocodylus acutus	U.S. (FL)
Deer, Columbian white-tailed	Odocoileus virginianus leucurus	U.S. (OR, WA)
Dolphin, Chinese river	Lipotes vexillifer	China
Elephant, Asian	Elephas maximus	South-central and southeastern Asia
Fox, northern swift	Vulpes velox hebes	Canada
Frog, mountain yellow-legged	Rana muscosa	U.S. (CA, NV)
Gorilla	Gorilla gorilla	Central and West Africa
Hawk, Hawaiian	Buteo solitarius	U.S. (HI)
Hyena, brown	Parahyaena brunnea	Southern Africa
Impala, black-faced	Aepyceros melampus petersi	Angola, Namibia
Kangaroo, Tasmanian forester	Macropus giganteus tasmaniensis	Australia (Tasmania)
Leopard	Panthera pardus	Africa
Lion, Asiatic	Panthera leo persica	Turkey, India
Manatee, West Indian	Trichechus manatus	Southeastern U.S., Caribbean Sea, Mexico
Monkey, spider	Ateles geoffroyi frontatus	Costa Rica, Nicaragua
Ocelot	Leopardus pardalis	U.S. (AZ, TX), Mexico to Central and S America
Orangutan	Pongo pygmaeus	Borneo, Sumatra
Ostrich, West African	Struthio camelus spatzi	Western Sahara
Otter, marine	Lontra felina	Peru south to Straits of Magellan
Panda, giant	Ailuropoda melanoleuca	China
Panther, Florida	Puma concolor coryi	U.S. (FL)
Parakeet, golden	Aratinga guarouba	Brazil
Parrot, imperial	Amazona imperialis	West Indies (Dominica)
Penguin, Galapagos	Spheniscus mendiculus	Ecuador (Galapagos Islands)
Puma, eastern	Puma concolor couguar	Eastern N America (presumed extinct in wild)
Rhinoceros, black	Diceros bicornis	Sub-Saharan Africa
Salamander, Chinese giant	Andrias davidianus	China
Sea-lion, Steller	Eumetopias jubatus	U.S. (AK), Russia
Squirrel, Carolina northern flying	Glaucomys sabrinus coloratus	U.S. (NC, TN, VA)
Tiger	Panthera tigris	Asia
Tortoise, Galapagos	Geochelone nigra	Ecuador (Galapagos Islands)
Whale, gray	Eschrichtius robustus	N Pacific Ocean
Whale, humpback	Megaptera novaeangliae	All major oceans
Wolf, red	Canis rufus	Southeastern U.S.
Woodpecker, ivory-billed	Campephilus principalis	South-central and southeastern U.S., Cuba
Yak, wild	Bos mutus	China (Tibet), India
Zebra, mountain	Equus zebra zebra	South Africa

Status of Endangered and Threatened Species, 2015

Source: Fish and Wildlife Service, U.S. Dept. of the Interior; as of June 2015

	Endangered		Threatened			
Group	U.S.	Foreign	U.S.	Foreign	Total species[1]	U.S. species with recovery plans
Mammals	74	253	27	20	374	63
Birds	79	214	21	17	331	86
Reptiles	14	69	23	20	126	36
Amphibians	20	8	15	1	44	20
Fishes	93	19	70	3	185	104
Clams	75	2	13	0	90	71
Snails	34	1	12	0	47	29
Insects	61	4	11	0	76	40
Arachnids	12	0	0	0	12	12
Crustaceans	22	0	3	0	25	18
Corals	0	0	6	16	22	0
Animal subtotal	**484**	**570**	**201**	**77**	**1,332**	**479**
Flowering plants	693	1	155	0	849	645
Conifers and cycads	2	0	1	2	5	3
Ferns and allies	28	0	2	0	30	26
Lichens	2	0	0	0	2	2
Plant subtotal	**725**	**1**	**158**	**2**	**886**	**676**
Grand total	**1,209**	**571**	**359**	**79**	**2,218**	**1,155**

(1) 14 animal species are counted more than once in this table, primarily because these animals have distinct population segments, each with its own individual listing status. The dual status species, all tallied as endangered, are (U.S.) Atlantic sturgeon, California tiger salamander, Chinook salmon, chum salmon, coho salmon, gray wolf, grizzly bear, loggerhead sea turtle, mountain yellow-legged frog, sockeye salmon, steelhead and (foreign) broad-snouted caiman, loggerhead sea turtle, scalloped hammerhead shark.

METEOROLOGY

National Weather Service Watches and Warnings

Source: National Weather Service, National Oceanic and Atmospheric Admin. (NOAA), U.S. Dept. of Commerce; *Glossary of Meteorology*, American Meteorological Society

The National Weather Service issues watches, warnings, and advisories for specific geographic areas to alert people to the possibility or imminent arrival of severe weather or of flooding. Often the weather hazard is a convective storm (a storm involving upward and downward movement of heat and moisture). A severe thunderstorm or tornado watch is issued when a severe convective storm, covering a relatively small geographic area or moving in a narrow path, is sufficiently intense to threaten life and property. Excessive localized convective rains are not classified as severe storms but are often the product of severe local storms. Such rainfall may result in phenomena, such as flash floods, that threaten life and property. Lightning occurs with all thunderstorms and, along with flash floods, is a leading cause of storm deaths and injuries.

Cyclone: Atmospheric circulation of winds rotating counterclockwise in the Northern Hemisphere and clockwise in the Southern Hemisphere. Tornadoes, hurricanes/typhoons, and the lows shown on weather maps are all examples of cyclones. Cyclones are usually accompanied by precipitation or stormy weather.

Severe thunderstorm: Thunderstorm (any local atmospheric disturbance) that produces a tornado, winds of at least 50 knots (58 mph), and/or hail at least 1 in. in diameter. A severe thunderstorm watch indicates conditions are favorable for the development of a severe thunderstorm within 4 to 8 hours. A severe thunderstorm warning indicates a severe thunderstorm has been sighted by radar or reported by a spotter.

Tornado: Violently rotating column of air that extends from the base of a thunderstorm to the ground. On a local scale, it is the most destructive of all atmospheric phenomena. Tornado paths range from a few feet to more than 100 mi long (avg. 5 mi) and from a few feet to more than 1 mi in diameter (avg. 220 yds). The average forward speed is 30 mph, and wind speeds can exceed 200 mph. A rotating column of air over water, whether or not linked to a thunderstorm, is called a **waterspout**.

Tropical storm: Cyclone that develops over tropical or subtropical waters with 1-min. sustained surface winds between 34 and 63 knots (39-73 mph). A tropical storm watch is issued when tropical storm conditions pose a threat to specified coastal areas within 48 hours. A tropical storm warning is issued when such conditions are expected in a specified coastal area within 36 hours.

Hurricane: Tropical cyclone having 1-min. sustained surface winds of 64 knots (74 mph) or more. (In the western North Pacific Ocean, west of the International Date Line, such storms are known as **typhoons**.) The hurricane-force winds form a circle or oval, sometimes as wide as 300 mi in diameter. In the lower latitudes, hurricanes usually move W or NW at 10-15 mph. When the center approaches 25° to 30° N, the direction of motion often changes to the NE, with increased forward speed. In the Atlantic, hurricane season is June 1-Nov. 30. Hurricane season is May 15-Nov. 30 in the eastern Pacific. A hurricane warning is issued when a hurricane is forecast for an area within 36 hours.

Winter storm and **blizzard:** A winter storm watch is issued when there is a potential for heavy snow or significant ice accumulations, usually at least 24-36 hours in advance. A winter storm warning is issued when a winter storm is producing or is forecast to produce heavy snow or significant ice accumulations. A blizzard warning is issued for winter storm conditions where winds are 35 mph or more, there is sufficient falling and/or blowing snow to frequently reduce visibility to less than ¼ mi, and the conditions are expected to prevail for at least 3 hours.

River flooding: Occurs when rains, sometimes coupled with melting snow, quickly fill river basins with an excess of water. Torrential rains from decaying hurricanes or tropical systems are also a major cause. **Coastal flooding:** Tropical storm and hurricane winds or intense offshore low-pressure systems can drive ocean water inland. Coastal floods can also be produced by sea waves called **tsunamis**, produced by earthquakes or underwater volcanic eruptions or landslides. **Flash flooding:** Usually due to copious amounts of rain falling in a short time. Ice can also cause flash flooding. When ice accumulates at natural or artificial obstructions, it can stop the flow of water. The resulting buildup of water can lead to flooding upstream. If the jam suddenly gives way, a flash flood can happen downstream. Flash flooding typically occurs within 6 hours of the causative event.

Flash floods account for the majority of flood deaths in the U.S. and are the leading cause of deaths associated with thunderstorms. Urbanization significantly increases runoff because less rain is absorbed by the terrain, making flash flooding in urban areas extremely dangerous. Streets can become swift-moving rivers, and basements can fill with water.

A (flash) flood watch indicates flooding or flash flooding is possible within a designated area. A (flash) flood warning indicates flooding is in progress, imminent, or highly likely.

National Weather Service Marine Warnings and Advisories

Primary sources of dissemination are commercial radio, TV, U.S. Coast Guard radio stations, and NOAA VHF radio broadcasts. The NOAA Weather Radio All Hazards (NWR) network broadcasts on seven frequencies between 162.40 and 162.55 MHz. These broadcasts can usually be received within about 40 mi of the transmission site using a special radio receiver. The following are examples of the warnings and advisories that may be addressed to mariners.

Small craft advisory: Alerts mariners to sustained weather and/or sea conditions, present or forecast, potentially hazardous to small boats, including winds 20-33 knots (23-38 mph) and/or dangerous wave conditions. The advisory is also issued when sea or lake ice exists that could be hazardous to small boats. Criteria vary depending on region and type of marine environment.

Special marine warning: Indicates potentially hazardous weather conditions not covered by existing marine warnings. The conditions are usually of short duration (2 hours or less) and involve wind speeds of 34 knots (39 mph) or more, and/or hail at least ¾ in. in diameter or waterspouts.

Gale warning: Indicates winds of 34-47 knots (39-54 mph) not directly associated with a tropical storm are forecast for the area.

Storm warning: Indicates winds 48-63 knots (55-73 mph) not directly associated with a tropical storm are forecast for the area.

Hurricane and Tornado Classifications

Source: National Weather Service, NOAA, U.S. Dept. of Commerce

The Saffir-Simpson Hurricane Wind Scale, created by Herbert Saffir and expanded upon by Robert Simpson, rates a hurricane's intensity from 1 to 5. The scale, updated in 2012, provides examples of the type of damage and impacts associated with winds of the indicated intensity. The Fujita (or F) Scale was created by T. Theodore Fujita in 1971 to classify tornadoes. The Enhanced Fujita Scale, an update, was implemented in the U.S. in 2007. It uses 3-sec. gusts estimated at the point of damage based on a judgment of eight levels of damage to 28 indicators.

Saffir-Simpson Wind Scale (Hurricanes)

Category	Wind speed[1]	Summary of damage
1	74-95 mph	Very dangerous winds will produce some damage.
2	96-110 mph	Extremely dangerous winds will cause extensive damage.
3	111-129 mph	Devastating damage will occur.
4	130-156 mph	Catastrophic damage will occur.
5	Over 156 mph	Catastrophic damage will occur.

(1) 1-min. sustained winds.

Enhanced Fujita Scale (Tornadoes)

Rank	3-sec. gust
EF-0	65-85 mph
EF-1	86-110 mph
EF-2	111-135 mph
EF-3	136-165 mph
EF-4	166-200 mph
EF-5	Over 200 mph

Monthly Normal Mean Temperatures, Precipitation in U.S. Cities

Source: National Climatic Data Center, NESDIS, NOAA, U.S. Dept. of Commerce

Normals are averages covering a 30-year period. The temperature and precipitation normals given here are based on records for 1981-2010. Temperatures listed below represent means of the normal daily maximum and normal daily minimum temperatures for each month. For stations that did not have continuous records from the same site for the entire 30 years, the means have been adjusted to the record at the present site. (*) = City station. Other figures are for airport stations. T = Temperature in Fahrenheit; P = Precipitation in inches.

	Jan.		Feb.		Mar.		Apr.		May		June		July		Aug.		Sept.		Oct.		Nov.		Dec.	
Station	**T**	**P**	**T**	**P**	**T**	**P**	**T**	**P**	**T**	**P**	**T**	**P**	**T**	**P**	**T**	**P**	**T**	**P**	**T**	**P**	**T**	**P**	**T**	**P**
Albany, NY	23	2.6	26	2.2	35	3.2	48	3.2	58	3.6	67	3.8	72	4.1	70	3.5	62	3.3	50	3.7	40	3.3	29	2.9
Albuquerque, NM	36	0.4	41	0.5	48	0.5	56	0.6	66	0.5	75	0.7	78	1.5	76	1.6	69	1.1	58	1.0	45	0.6	36	0.5
Anchorage, AK	17	0.7	20	0.7	27	0.6	37	0.5	48	0.7	55	1.0	59	1.8	57	3.3	49	3.0	35	2.0	22	1.2	19	1.1
Asheville, NC	37	3.7	40	3.8	47	3.8	55	3.3	63	3.7	71	4.7	74	4.3	73	4.4	66	3.8	56	2.9	47	3.7	39	3.6
Atlanta, GA	43	4.2	47	4.7	54	4.8	62	3.4	70	3.7	77	4.0	80	5.3	79	3.9	74	4.5	63	3.4	54	4.1	45	3.9
Atlantic City, NJ	33	3.2	35	2.9	42	4.2	52	3.6	61	3.4	71	3.1	76	3.7	74	4.1	67	3.2	56	3.4	47	3.3	37	3.7
Baltimore, MD	33	3.1	36	2.9	44	3.9	54	3.2	54	4.0	72	3.5	77	4.1	75	3.3	68	4.0	56	3.3	47	3.3	37	3.4
Barrow, AK	–13	0.1	–14	0.1	–13	0.1	2	0.2	21	0.2	36	0.3	41	1.0	39	1.1	32	0.1	17	0.4	–2	0.2	–8	0.1
Birmingham, AL	44	4.8	48	4.5	55	5.2	63	4.4	71	5.0	78	4.4	81	4.8	81	3.9	75	3.9	64	3.4	54	4.9	46	4.5
Bismarck, ND	13	0.4	18	0.5	30	0.9	44	1.3	56	2.4	65	3.2	71	2.9	70	2.3	59	1.6	45	1.3	29	0.7	16	0.5
Boise, ID	31	1.2	37	1.0	45	1.4	51	1.2	59	1.4	68	0.7	76	0.3	75	0.2	65	0.6	53	0.8	40	1.4	31	1.6
Boston, MA	29	3.4	32	3.3	38	4.3	48	3.7	58	3.5	68	3.7	73	3.4	72	3.4	65	3.4	54	3.9	45	4.0	35	3.8
Buffalo, NY	25	3.2	26	2.5	34	2.9	46	3.0	57	3.5	66	3.7	71	3.2	70	3.3	62	3.9	51	3.5	41	4.0	30	3.9
Burlington, VT	19	2.1	22	1.8	31	2.2	45	2.8	56	3.5	66	3.7	71	4.2	69	3.9	61	3.6	48	3.6	38	3.1	26	2.4
Caribou, ME	10	2.7	14	2.2	25	2.5	39	2.7	52	3.3	61	3.5	66	4.1	64	3.8	55	3.3	43	3.5	32	3.6	18	3.3
Charleston, SC	48	3.7	52	3.0	58	3.7	65	2.9	73	3.0	79	5.7	82	6.5	81	7.2	76	6.1	67	3.8	59	2.4	51	3.1
Charleston, WV	34	3.0	38	3.2	46	3.9	56	3.2	64	4.8	72	4.3	75	4.9	74	3.7	67	3.3	57	2.7	47	3.7	37	3.3
Chicago, IL	24	1.7	28	1.8	38	2.5	49	3.4	59	3.7	69	3.5	74	3.7	72	4.9	65	3.2	53	3.2	40	3.2	28	2.3
Cleveland, OH	28	2.7	31	2.3	38	2.9	50	3.5	60	3.7	69	3.4	74	3.5	72	3.5	65	3.8	54	3.1	44	3.6	32	3.1
Columbus, OH	30	2.7	33	2.3	42	3.0	53	3.4	63	4.2	72	4.0	75	4.8	74	3.3	67	2.8	55	2.6	44	3.2	34	3.0
Dallas-Ft. Worth, TX	46	2.1	50	2.7	58	3.5	66	3.1	74	4.9	81	3.8	85	2.2	86	1.9	78	2.6	68	4.2	57	2.7	47	2.6
Denver, CO	31	0.4	33	0.3	40	0.9	47	1.7	57	2.2	67	2.0	74	3.0	73	1.6	63	1.0	51	1.0	38	0.6	30	0.3
Des Moines, IA	23	1.0	27	1.3	39	2.3	52	3.9	62	4.7	72	4.9	76	4.5	74	4.1	66	3.1	53	2.6	39	2.2	26	1.4
Detroit, MI	26	2.0	28	2.0	37	2.3	49	2.9	60	3.4	69	3.5	74	3.4	72	3.0	64	3.3	52	2.5	42	2.8	30	2.4
Dodge City, KS	32	0.6	36	0.7	44	1.6	54	1.8	64	2.9	74	3.2	80	3.1	78	2.8	69	1.7	57	1.7	43	0.8	33	0.8
Duluth, MN	10	1.0	15	0.8	26	1.5	40	2.4	51	3.2	60	4.2	66	3.9	64	3.7	56	4.1	43	2.9	29	2.1	15	1.2
Fairbanks, AK	–8	0.6	–1	0.4	11	0.3	33	0.3	49	0.6	60	1.4	63	2.2	56	1.9	45	1.1	24	0.8	3	0.7	–4	0.6
Fresno, CA	47	2.2	52	2.0	57	2.0	62	1.0	70	0.4	77	0.2	83	0.0	82	0.0	76	0.2	66	0.6	54	1.1	47	1.8
Galveston, TX*	53	3.7	55	3.0	61	2.9	68	2.2	76	3.0	82	4.8	84	3.9	84	3.4	80	5.4	73	4.2	64	3.4	56	3.4
Grand Rapids, MI	24	2.1	27	1.8	36	2.4	48	3.4	59	4.0	68	3.8	73	3.8	71	3.6	63	4.3	51	3.3	40	3.5	29	2.5
Helena, MT	23	0.4	28	0.3	36	0.6	45	1.0	54	1.9	62	2.1	70	1.2	68	1.2	58	1.1	46	0.7	33	0.5	22	0.4
Honolulu, HI	73	2.3	73	2.0	75	2.0	76	0.6	78	0.6	80	0.3	81	0.5	82	0.6	82	0.7	80	1.8	78	2.4	75	3.2
Houston, TX	53	3.4	56	3.2	63	3.4	70	3.3	77	5.1	82	5.9	84	3.8	85	3.8	80	4.1	72	5.7	62	4.3	54	3.7
Huron, SD	17	0.5	22	0.6	33	1.5	47	2.3	58	3.1	68	3.9	74	2.9	72	2.4	62	2.5	48	1.8	33	0.9	19	0.5
Indianapolis, IN	28	2.7	32	2.3	42	3.6	53	3.8	63	5.1	72	4.3	75	4.6	74	3.1	67	3.1	55	3.1	44	3.7	32	3.2
Jackson, MS	46	5.0	50	4.8	57	5.0	64	5.0	72	4.4	79	4.1	82	4.8	81	4.2	76	3.0	65	3.9	56	4.8	48	5.2
Jacksonville, FL	53	3.3	56	3.2	62	4.0	67	2.6	74	2.5	80	6.5	82	6.6	82	6.8	78	8.2	70	3.9	62	2.1	55	2.8
Juneau, AK	28	5.4	30	4.1	34	3.8	41	2.9	49	3.4	55	3.2	57	4.6	56	5.7	50	8.6	42	8.6	33	6.0	30	5.8
Kansas City, MO	29	1.1	34	1.5	44	2.4	55	3.7	65	5.2	74	5.2	78	4.5	77	3.9	68	4.6	56	3.2	44	2.2	32	1.5
Knoxville, TN	38	4.3	42	4.3	50	4.3	59	4.0	67	4.5	75	3.8	78	5.1	78	3.3	71	3.2	60	2.5	50	4.0	41	4.5
Lander, WY	22	0.4	25	0.6	36	1.2	44	1.9	53	2.2	63	1.3	71	0.8	70	0.6	59	1.1	46	1.3	31	0.9	21	0.6
Lexington, KY	33	3.2	37	3.2	46	4.1	55	3.6	64	5.3	73	4.4	76	4.7	75	3.3	68	2.9	57	3.1	46	3.5	36	3.9
Little Rock, AR	41	3.6	45	3.7	53	4.7	62	5.1	71	4.9	79	3.7	83	3.3	83	2.6	75	3.2	64	4.9	53	5.3	43	5.0
Los Angeles, CA*	58	3.1	59	3.8	61	2.4	63	0.9	66	0.3	69	0.1	73	0.0	74	0.0	73	0.2	69	0.7	62	1.0	58	2.3
Louisville, KY	35	3.2	39	3.2	48	4.2	58	4.0	67	5.3	76	3.8	79	4.2	78	3.3	71	3.1	60	3.2	49	3.6	38	3.8
Marquette, MI*	19	1.8	21	1.3	29	2.0	40	2.5	51	2.5	60	2.7	67	2.8	67	2.6	59	3.2	47	3.1	35	2.6	24	2.0
Memphis, TN	41	4.0	46	4.4	54	5.2	63	5.5	72	5.3	80	3.6	83	4.6	82	2.9	75	3.1	64	4.0	53	5.5	44	5.7
Miami, FL	68	1.6	70	2.3	73	3.0	76	3.1	80	5.3	83	9.7	84	6.5	84	8.9	83	9.9	80	6.3	75	3.3	71	2.0
Milwaukee, WI	22	1.8	26	1.7	35	2.3	46	3.6	56	3.4	66	3.9	72	3.7	71	4.0	63	3.2	51	2.7	39	2.7	27	2.0
Minneapolis, MN	16	0.9	21	0.8	33	1.9	48	2.7	59	3.4	69	4.2	74	4.0	71	4.3	62	3.1	49	2.4	34	1.8	20	1.2
Mobile, AL	50	5.7	54	5.1	60	6.1	66	4.8	74	5.1	80	6.1	82	7.2	82	7.0	78	5.1	68	3.7	60	5.1	52	5.1
Moline, IL	23	1.5	27	1.6	39	2.9	51	3.6	62	4.3	72	4.5	75	4.3	74	4.5	65	3.1	53	3.0	40	2.6	27	2.2
Nashua, NH	24	3.7	27	3.2	35	4.3	46	4.0	57	2.9	66	4.3	71	3.7	70	4.5	62	3.4	50	4.7	40	4.1	30	3.7
Nashville, TN	38	3.8	42	3.9	50	4.1	59	4.0	68	5.5	76	4.1	79	3.6	79	3.2	72	3.4	60	3.0	50	4.3	40	4.2
New Orleans, LA	53	5.2	57	5.3	63	4.6	69	4.6	77	4.6	82	8.1	83	5.9	83	6.0	80	5.1	71	3.6	63	4.5	56	5.3
New York, NY*	33	3.7	35	3.1	43	4.4	53	4.5	62	4.2	71	4.4	77	4.6	75	4.4	68	4.3	57	4.4	48	4.0	38	4.0
Newark, NJ	32	3.5	35	2.9	42	4.2	53	4.2	63	4.1	72	4.0	77	4.8	76	3.7	68	3.8	57	3.6	47	3.7	37	3.8
Norfolk, VA	40	3.4	43	3.1	49	3.7	58	3.4	67	3.4	75	4.3	80	5.1	78	5.5	72	4.8	62	3.4	53	3.2	44	3.3
Oklahoma City, OK	39	1.4	44	1.6	52	3.1	61	3.1	70	4.7	78	4.9	83	2.9	82	3.3	74	4.1	63	3.7	51	2.0	41	1.9
Omaha, NE	24	0.7	28	0.9	40	2.0	52	3.0	62	4.8	72	4.2	77	3.8	75	3.8	66	2.7	53	2.2	39	1.6	26	1.0
Philadelphia, PA	33	3.0	36	2.7	44	3.8	54	3.6	64	3.7	73	3.4	78	4.4	77	3.5	69	3.8	58	3.2	48	3.0	38	3.6
Phoenix, AZ	56	0.9	60	0.9	65	1.0	73	0.3	82	0.1	91	0.0	95	1.1	94	1.0	88	0.6	77	0.6	64	0.7	55	0.9
Pittsburgh, PA	29	2.7	32	2.7	40	3.1	52	3.2	61	4.2	69	4.0	73	3.8	72	3.5	65	3.4	53	2.5	43	3.4	33	2.9
Portland, ME	22	3.4	26	3.3	34	4.2	44	4.3	54	4.0	63	3.8	69	3.6	68	3.1	60	3.7	49	4.9	39	4.9	29	4.0
Portland, OR	41	4.9	44	3.7	48	3.7	52	2.7	58	2.5	64	1.7	69	0.7	70	0.7	65	1.5	55	3.0	47	5.6	40	5.5
Providence, RI	29	3.9	32	3.3	39	5.0	49	4.4	59	3.6	68	3.6	74	3.3	72	3.6	65	3.9	54	3.9	45	4.5	34	4.2
Raleigh, NC	41	3.5	45	3.2	52	4.1	60	2.9	68	3.3	76	3.5	80	4.7	79	4.3	72	4.4	61	3.3	52	3.1	44	3.1
Rapid City, SD	25	0.3	27	0.4	35	0.9	45	1.8	55	3.2	65	2.5	73	1.9	72	1.6	61	1.3	48	1.4	35	0.5	25	0.4
Reno, NV	36	1.0	40	1.0	46	0.8	51	0.5	60	0.5	68	0.5	75	0.2	73	0.2	65	0.4	54	0.5	43	0.8	35	1.0
Richmond, VA	38	3.0	41	2.8	49	4.0	58	3.3	66	3.8	75	3.9	79	4.5	78	4.7	71	4.1	60	3.0	50	3.2	41	3.3
St. Louis, MO	32	2.4	36	2.2	46	3.3	57	3.7	67	4.7	76	4.3	80	4.1	79	3.0	70	3.1	59	3.3	47	3.9	35	2.8
Salt Lake City, UT	30	1.3	34	1.3	44	1.8	51	2.0	60	2.0	70	1.0	79	0.6	77	0.7	66	1.2	53	1.5	40	1.5	30	1.4
San Antonio, TX	52	1.8	56	1.8	62	2.3	69	2.1	77	4.0	82	4.1	85	2.7	85	2.1	80	3.0	71	4.1	61	2.3	53	1.9
San Diego, CA	57	2.0	58	2.3	59	1.8	62	0.8	64	0.1	66	0.1	70	0.0	72	0.0	71	0.2	67	0.6	61	1.0	57	1.5
San Francisco, CA	50	4.2	53	4.1	55	3.0	57	1.3	60	0.5	62	0.1	64	0.0	65	0.0	65	0.2	62	1.0	56	2.4	51	4.0
San Juan, PR	78	3.8	78	2.4	79	2.0	80	4.7	82	5.9	83	4.4	83	5.1	84	5.5	84	5.8	83	5.6	81	6.4	79	5.0
Santa Fe, NM	32	0.6	36	0.5	43	0.8	50	0.7	60	0.9	69	1.1	73	1.8	71	2.6	64	1.6	53	1.4	40	0.7	31	0.8
Savannah, GA	50	3.7	53	2.8	59	3.7	66	3.1	73	3.0	80	6.0	83	5.6	82	6.6	77	4.6	68	3.7	59	2.4	52	3.0
Seattle, WA	42	5.6	43	3.5	47	3.7	50	2.7	56	1.9	61	1.6	66	0.7	66	0.9	61	1.5	53	3.5	45	6.6	41	5.4
Spokane, WA	30	1.8	33	1.3	40	1.6	47	1.3	55	1.6	62	1.3	70	0.6	69	0.6	60	0.7	48	1.2	36	2.3	27	2.3
Springfield, MO	33	2.5	37	2.5	46	3.6	56	4.3	65	5.1	73	4.9	78	3.7	78	3.6	69	4.6	58	3.6	46	4.2	35	3.0
Tampa, FL	61	2.2	63	2.8	67	3.0	72	2.0	78	2.1	82	6.7	83	7.1	83	7.8	82	6.3	76	2.3	69	1.6	63	2.5
Washington, DC	36	2.8	39	2.6	47	3.5	57	3.1	66	4.0	75	3.8	80	3.7	78	2.9	71	3.7	60	3.4	50	3.2	40	3.1
Wilmington, DE	32	3.0	35	2.7	43	3.9	53	3.5	63	4.0	72	3.9	77	4.6	75	3.2	68	4.3	56	3.4	47	3.1	37	3.5
Windsor Locks, CT	26	3.2	30	2.9	38	3.6	49	3.7	60	4.4	69	4.4	74	4.2	72	3.9	64	3.9	52	4.4	42	3.9	32	3.4

Normal High and Low Temperatures, Precipitation in U.S. Cities

Source: National Climatic Data Center, NESDIS, NOAA, U.S. Dept. of Commerce

The normal temperatures and precipitation data given here are based on records for the period 1981-2010. The extreme temperatures are based on records from the time of each station's installation. (*) = City station. Other figures are for airport stations.

		NORMAL TEMPERATURE (°F)				EXTREME TEMPERATURE (°F)		AVG. ANNUAL PRECIPITATION
		January		July				
State	Station	Max.	Min.	Max.	Min.	Highest	Lowest	(in.)
Alabama	Mobile	61	40	91	73	105	3	66.15
Alaska	Anchorage	23	11	65	52	85	–34	16.58
Alaska	Barrow	–7	–20	47	35	79	–56	4.53
Alaska	Juneau	33	24	64	50	90	–22	62.27
Arizona	Phoenix	67	46	106	78	122	17	8.03
Arkansas	North Little Rock	50	33	92	73	111	–6	50.03
California	Los Angeles	65	49	74	64	110	23	12.82
California	San Francisco	56	44	72	55	106	20	20.65
Colorado	Denver	44	17	89	59	105	–19	14.92
Connecticut	Windsor Locks	35	18	85	63	102	–26	45.85
Delaware	Wilmington	40	25	86	68	103	11	43.08
District of Columbia	Washington–Reagan	43	29	88	71	105	–5	39.74
Florida	Jacksonville	65	41	92	73	105	7	52.39
Florida	Miami	76	60	91	77	98	30	61.90
Georgia	Atlanta	52	34	89	71	105	–8	49.71
Georgia	Savannah	60	39	92	73	105	3	47.96
Hawaii	Honolulu	80	66	88	75	95	53	17.10
Idaho	Boise	38	25	91	60	111	–25	11.73
Illinois	Chicago	31	17	84	64	104	–27	36.89
Indiana	Indianapolis	36	21	85	66	104	–27	42.44
Iowa	Des Moines	31	14	86	67	108	–26	36.01
Kansas	Dodge City	44	20	93	66	110	–21	21.60
Kentucky	Lexington	41	25	86	66	103	–21	45.17
Kentucky	Louisville	43	27	89	70	106	–22	44.91
Louisiana	New Orleans	62	45	91	75	102	11	62.66
Maine	Caribou	20	1	76	55	96	–41	38.49
Maine	Portland	31	13	79	59	103	–39	47.25
Maryland	Baltimore	41	24	87	67	105	–7	41.88
Massachusetts	Boston	36	22	81	65	102	–12	43.77
Michigan	Detroit	32	19	83	64	104	–21	33.47
Michigan	Grand Rapids	31	18	83	62	100	–22	38.27
Michigan	Sault Ste. Marie	23	8	76	54	98	–36	32.95
Minnesota	Duluth	19	2	76	55	97	–39	30.96
Minnesota	Minneapolis	24	8	83	64	105	–34	30.61
Mississippi	Jackson	56	35	92	72	107	2	54.14
Missouri	Kansas City	38	20	88	68	109	–23	38.86
Missouri	St. Louis	40	24	89	71	107	–18	40.96
Montana	Helena	33	13	86	54	105	–42	11.22
Nebraska	Omaha	33	14	87	66	114	–23	30.62
Nevada	Reno	46	25	92	58	108	–16	7.40
New Hampshire	Concord	31	10	82	58	102	–37	40.61
New Jersey	Atlantic City	42	25	86	67	106	–11	41.75
New Mexico	Albuquerque	47	26	90	66	107	–17	9.45
New York	Albany	31	15	82	61	100	–28	39.35
New York	Buffalo	31	19	80	62	99	–20	40.48
New York	New York–Central Park*	38	27	84	69	106	–15	49.94
North Carolina	Raleigh	51	31	90	70	105	–9	43.34
North Dakota	Bismarck	23	2	85	57	112	–44	17.85
Ohio	Cleveland	34	22	83	64	104	–20	39.14
Ohio	Columbus	37	23	85	66	102	–22	39.31
Oklahoma	Oklahoma City	50	29	94	72	110	–8	36.52
Oregon	Portland	47	36	81	58	107	–3	36.03
Pennsylvania	Philadelphia	40	26	87	69	104	–7	41.53
Pennsylvania	Pittsburgh	36	21	83	63	103	–22	38.19
Puerto Rico	San Juan	83	72	89	78	98	60	56.35
Rhode Island	Providence	37	21	83	64	104	–13	47.18
South Carolina	Charleston	59	38	91	73	105	6	51.03
South Dakota	Huron	27	7	86	61	112	–41	22.90
South Dakota	Rapid City	37	13	87	58	111	–31	16.29
Tennessee	Memphis	50	33	92	74	108	–13	53.68
Tennessee	Nashville	47	28	89	68	107	–17	47.25
Texas	Dallas-Fort Worth	56	36	96	75	113	–1	36.14
Texas	Houston	63	43	94	75	109	7	49.77
Utah	Salt Lake City	37	22	93	65	107	–30	16.10
Vermont	Burlington	27	10	81	60	101	–30	36.82
Virginia	Norfolk	48	33	87	72	105	–3	46.53
Virginia	Richmond	47	28	90	69	105	–12	43.60
Washington	Seattle-Tacoma	47	37	76	56	103	0	37.49
Washington	Spokane	34	25	83	56	108	–25	16.56
West Virginia	Charleston	43	26	85	66	104	–16	44.03
Wisconsin	Milwaukee	29	16	80	64	103	–26	34.76
Wyoming	Lander	33	10	87	56	101	–37	12.66

Mean annual snowfall (in.), selected cities: Based on climate normals 1981-2010: Albany, NY, 59.1; Anchorage, AK, 74.5; Boston, MA, 43.8; Burlington, VT, 81.2; Lander, WY, 91.4; Sault Ste. Marie, MI, 123.4.

Wettest spot: Mt. Waialeale in Kauai, HI, may be the rainiest place in the U.S. It has a recorded average annual rainfall of 460 in.

Temperature extremes: The highest temperature ever recorded under standard conditions in the U.S. was 134°F in Death Valley, CA, on July 10, 1913. The record low in the U.S. was –80°F at Prospect Creek, AK, Jan. 23, 1971.

Annual Climatological Data for U.S. Cities, 2014

Source: National Climatic Data Center, NESDIS, NOAA, U.S. Dept. of Commerce

		TEMPERATURE (°F)				PRECIPITATION						FASTEST WIND[2]		NO. OF DAYS	
									Snowfall[1]						
Station	Elev. (ft)	Highest	Date	Lowest	Date	Total (in.)	Greatest in 24 hrs. (in.)	Date	Total snowfall (in.)	Greatest in 24 hrs. (in.)	Date	MPH	Date	Prec. 0.01 in. or more	Snow, sleet 1 in. or more
Albany, NY	281	91	7/23+	−12	1/4	39.70	2.22	7/27-28	75.9	10.4	2/5	38	8/5	137	16
Albuquerque, NM	5,308	100	7/26	13	12/31+	8.81	1.06	7/29	2.9	0.9	2/5	49	10/12	58	0
Anchorage, AK	222	76	7/3	0	2/11	18.37	1.44	7/24-25	43.9	5.7	3/14	33	2/7	111	13
Asheville, NC	2,174	90	8/22	−1	1/7	46.91	2.82	9/7-8	12.8	7.1	2/12	48	3/30	125	3
Atlanta, GA	974	95	8/7	6	1/7	47.62	2.87	4/6-7	4.6	2.6	1/28	45	6/5	118	2
Atlantic City, NJ	117	95	6/18	−3	1/30+	54.36	7.30	1/29	40.9	7.3	1/29	39	3/13	130	12
Baltimore, MD	196	96	6/18	3	1/23+	52.58	6.31	8/11-12	36.6	9.6	2/13	44	9/6	127	7
Barrow, AK	38	58	7/16	−38	1/16	7.41	0.50	6/22-23	51.3	4.4	9/2	41	10/20	118	12
Birmingham, AL	630	99	8/7	7	1/7	49.77	4.37	4/6-7	5.0	3.0	2/12	39	8/18	110	2
Bismarck, ND	1,654	96	7/5	−23	1/2	13.92	1.16	8/1	33.7	8.1	3/31	47	1/16	94	12
Boise, ID	2,861	104	7/13	1	11/15	15.47	1.21	11/1-2	19.5	4.3	11/14	41	3/17	100	6
Boston, MA	180	93	9/2	2	1/4+	45.25	2.93	10/22-23	50.1	10.7	2/5	45	4/15	127	11
Buffalo, NY	717	89	6/28	−5	1/7	42.40	1.78	2/20-21	123.2	13.8	3/12	46	1/6	173	30
Burlington, VT	348	92	7/1	−15	1/23+	36.33	1.67	4/15	97.3	15.2	3/12	33	3/14	155	25
Caribou, ME	626	91	7/2	−28	1/2	46.29	2.65	7/4-5	151.7	10.2	3/20	36	7/5	165	36
Charleston, SC	48	99	8/23+	17	1/25+	52.99	4.04	8/9-10	T	T	6/21	33	6/21	108	0
Chicago, IL	658	91	6/17	−16	1/6	39.47	2.76	8/4	69.8	8.7	1/5	49	5/12	131	20
Cleveland, OH	805	91	9/5	−11	1/7+	44.05	4.05	6/24-25	84.2	7.0	11/27	48	11/24	178	26
Columbus, OH	812	94	6/18	−11	1/28	38.09	1.84	8/30-31	43.1	7.1	2/4	43	11/24	140	12
Dallas-Ft. Worth, TX	562	104	8/8	15	1/6	21.32	2.85	8/16-17	0.8	0.7	2/6	41	10/10	68	0
Denver, CO	5,382	100	7/7	−19	12/30	18.77	2.85	7/29-30	46.3	5.4	12/29	51	7/11	98	17
Des Moines, IA	971	93	9/4	−12	1/6	42.00	3.60	8/28-29	41.0	4.7	2/4	44	8/31	116	16
Detroit, MI	631	94	7/22	−14	1/7+	37.57	4.59	8/11-12	82.3	10.2	1/5	46	11/24	144	22
Duluth, MN	1,429	88	7/21	−28	1/6	30.63	1.60	8/10-11	111.2	10.9	2/20	40	4/28	137	31
Fairbanks, AK	464	87	7/6	−41	1/13+	17.16	2.83	7/1-2	40.6	4.7	12/2	32	3/31	88	12
Fresno, CA	375	110	6/9	31	12/31	7.46	1.38	12/11-12	0.0	0.0	—	30	10/31	33	0
Grand Rapids, MI	788	89	7/22	−12	2/28	40.24	2.54	10/2-3	111.1	9.6	11/18	44	2/21	168	34
Helena, MT	3,867	96	8/11	−26	2/6	12.24	1.26	8/22-23	52.3	6.3	2/24	47	1/10	111	17
Honolulu, HI	18	93	9/7	60	12/29	20.82	4.40	10/18-19	—	—	—	36	1/22	104	—
Houston, TX	107	99	8/25	21	1/7	43.72	4.15	5/26-27	T	T	2/6	35	8/11	112	0
Huron, SD	1,284	94	7/11	−19	1/6+	16.38	3.35	7/12	26.5	4.4	11/15	47	1/16	89	10
Indianapolis, IN	797	93	8/26	−15	1/6	41.57	2.04	11/23-24	49.6	11.4	1/5	49	7/1	137	11
Jackson, MS	296	97	8/24+	14	1/30+	56.19	5.97	4/6	—	—	—	38	3/2	99	—
Jacksonville, FL	34	99	8/22	22	1/7	55.46	3.30	12/22-23	—	—	—	48	5/11	107	—
Kansas City, MO	1,008	97	8/23	−11	1/6	40.04	3.47	8/6	23.5	7.5	2/4	47	6/5	106	8
Knoxville, TN	982	93	7/14	−1	1/29	41.67	2.25	7/18-19	11.6	5.5	2/12	46	2/21	129	3
Lander, WY	5,560	99	7/23	−27	12/31	11.72	1.57	9/27-28	63.1	9.6	12/25	51	11/1	86	17
Lexington, KY	984	93	7/13	−6	1/22	54.21	5.56	8/9-10	26.7	4.6	3/3	43	8/20	137	7
Los Angeles, CA	326	97	5/15	40	12/27	8.30	1.62	2/27-28	—	—	—	37	5/6	23	—
Louisville, KY	484	97	7/13	−3	1/6	43.27	2.94	9/10-11	23.9	3.3	11/17	41	1/25	127	7
Marquette, MI	1,415	87	5/31	−28	2/28	44.73	2.51	11/10-11	224.9	21.1	11/10-11	—	—	187	71
Memphis, TN	286	100	8/24	8	1/7	57.63	7.02	6/28-29	1.0	0.5	3/3	43	10/2	113	0
Miami, FL	29	95	7/28+	46	1/19+	63.60	4.39	6/19-20	—	—	—	43	7/15	146	—
Milwaukee, WI	680	89	7/22	−14	1/7	32.11	1.54	4/13-14	47.4	6.7	2/17	37	2/21	130	13
Minneapolis, MN	874	92	7/21	−23	1/6	35.40	4.13	6/19	67.8	8.4	2/20	55	6/14	124	18
Mobile, AL	212	98	8/24	14	1/7	72.71	11.24	4/29	1.3	1.3	1/28	40	4/29	119	1
Moline, IL	607	94	8/25	−22	2/11+	39.29	5.10	6/30	54.9	5.9	2/17	39	1/26	123	18
Nashville, TN	574	97	8/6	2	1/29+	50.59	3.19	4/28	0.9	0.2	11/17	32	2/20	120	0
New Orleans, LA	7	96	8/23	24	1/7	54.74	3.95	3/28-29	—	—	—	37	12/23	110	—
New York, NY	161	92	9/2	4	1/7	53.79	4.97	4/30	50.0	11.0	1/21	25	12/7	129	12
Newark, NJ	28	96	7/2	3	1/7	49.33	5.24	4/30	53.4	10.0	1/21	38	1/6	118	12
Norfolk, VA	69	99	9/2	6	1/30	50.29	4.75	9/8-9	15.5	5.6	1/28	37	1/21	114	6
North Little Rock, AR	565	97	8/24	9	1/7	47.15	3.25	4/13-14	4.7	2.4	2/7-8	—	—	118	2
Oklahoma City, OK	1,284	101	8/25+	4	1/24	28.38	3.03	6/23	12.1	3.5	12/27	51	6/7	69	5
Philadelphia, PA	62	96	7/2	4	1/22+	47.37	4.54	4/29-30	56.9	13.5	1/21	48	7/8	121	12
Phoenix, AZ	1,106	116	7/24	35	12/27	8.37	3.30	9/8	—	—	—	54	9/27	22	—
Pittsburgh, PA	1,175	89	6/17	−9	1/7	36.84	1.80	8/20	43.3	5.2	1/25	41	6/18	148	15
Portland, ME	72	88	8/27	−14	1/4	55.87	6.44	8/13-14	70.6	9.2	2/13	37	11/2	136	17
Portland, OR	223	99	8/11	19	2/6	40.11	2.13	10/22-23	—	—	—	47	12/11	158	—
Providence, RI	53	91	9/2	−3	1/4	46.94	4.40	3/29-30	39.0	4.6	2/15	44	3/26	118	11
Raleigh-Durham, NC	430	98	7/14+	7	1/30	55.25	4.21	7/15	5.8	3.3	2/12	60	1/11	116	2
Rapid City, SD	3,153	96	7/21	−19	2/7+	21.52	2.28	9/29-30	55.0	5.0	11/10	53	1/26	108	21
Reno, NV	4,407	105	7/14	8	12/31	4.99	0.88	8/4-5	3.7	1.8	12/30	53	12/11	41	1
Richmond, VA	167	101	9/2	4	1/30	35.74	1.99	7/24	14.5	3.7	2/12	44	5/9	119	6
St. Louis, MO	710	100	8/25	−8	1/6	43.43	2.92	8/6-7	27.2	10.8	1/5	48	2/20	111	7
Salt Lake City, UT	4,224	103	7/23+	1	12/31	14.46	1.26	9/26-27	19.3	3.0	1/8	45	8/12	92	7
San Antonio, TX	821	102	8/21+	22	1/7	28.20	3.94	11/4-5	0.4	0.3	2/6	38	11/22	72	0
San Diego, CA	81	97	5/15	43	12/31+	7.77	1.95	12/3-4	—	—	—	37	2/28	29	—
San Francisco, CA	89	95	10/3	41	12/31	20.69	3.54	12/11-12	—	—	—	43	12/30	54	—
San Juan, PR	10	95	10/11	69	3/29	59.07	4.01	12/15-16	0.0	0.0	—	33	7/3	213	0
Sault Ste. Marie, MI	727	85	8/9	−21	2/28	40.52	2.51	10/13-14	182.2	18.2	11/13	32	3/22	181	52
Savannah, GA	143	100	8/23+	19	1/7	50.56	6.72	6/22-23	T	T	1/29	47	5/28	113	0
Scottsbluff, NE	3,949	105	7/24	−28	12/31	19.27	3.47	9/29-30	73.3	9.3	12/25	51	4/29	108	23
Seattle, WA	434	96	8/11	21	2/6	48.50	1.84	3/5	3.7	2.9	2/8	41	1/11	150	1
Spokane, WA	2,384	100	7/29	−5	2/6	14.99	1.01	6/17-18	35.0	5.2	2/24	54	7/23	111	12
Springfield, MO	1,280	101	8/25	−10	1/6	38.59	3.56	10/9-10	20.9	7.0	1/5	47	2/20	108	9
Tampa, FL	40	96	6/30+	33	1/7	57.87	4.49	7/8	0.0	0.0	—	35	5/28	121	0
Washington, DC	3	99	7/2	6	1/7	44.41	3.31	4/29-30	30.5	5.9	2/13	39	3/12	124	10
Wilmington, DE	77	93	7/8	3	1/30	50.91	4.26	4/29-30	44.7	10.5	1/21	43	7/8	128	14
Windsor Locks, CT	165	95	7/2	−9	1/4	45.83	2.35	3/29-30	44.2	10.2	2/5	46	7/28	143	10

(+) = Indicates value for extreme also occurred on an earlier date(s). (T) = Trace amount. — = Data not available or unreported. (1) Comprises all forms of frozen precipitation, including hail and sleet. (2) Sustained for at least 2 min., not peak gust.

Record Temperatures by State

Source: National Climatic Data Center, NESDIS, NOAA, U.S. Dept. of Commerce
(as of Apr. 29, 2015)

	LOWEST TEMPERATURE				HIGHEST TEMPERATURE			
State	°F	Date	Station	Approx. elevation (ft)	°F	Date	Station	Approx. elevation (ft)
Alabama	–27	Jan. 30, 1966	New Market	732	112	Sept. 6, 1925	Centerville	220
Alaska	–80	Jan. 23, 1971	Prospect Creek Camp	955	100	June 27, 1915	Fort Yukon	445
Arizona	–40	Jan. 7, 1971	Hawley Lake	8,180	128	June 29, 1994	Lake Havasu City	505
Arkansas	–29	Feb. 13, 1905	Gravette	1,260	120	Aug. 10, 1936	Ozark	390
California	–45	Jan. 20, 1937	Boca	5,575	134	July 10, 1913	Greenland Ranch	–194
Colorado	–61	Feb. 1, 1985	Maybell	5,944	114	July 11, 1954[1]	Sedgwick	3,584
Connecticut	–32	Jan. 22, 1961[1]	Coventry	480	106	July 15, 1995[1]	Danbury	405
Delaware	–17	Jan. 17, 1893	Millsboro	20	110	July 21, 1930	Millsboro	20
Florida	–2	Feb. 13, 1899	Tallahassee	192	109	June 29, 1931	Monticello	98
Georgia	–17	Jan. 27, 1940	CCC Fire Camp F-16	1,000	112	Aug. 20, 1983[1]	Greenville	960
Hawaii	12	May 17, 1979	Mauna Kea Observ.	13,773	100	Apr. 27, 1931	Pahala	840
Idaho	–60	Jan. 18, 1943	Island Park	6,290	118	July 28, 1934	Orofino	1,320
Illinois	–36	Jan. 5, 1999	Congerville	635	117	July 14, 1954	East St. Louis	410
Indiana	–36	Jan. 19, 1994	New Whiteland	785	116	July 14, 1936	Collegeville	650
Iowa	–47	Feb. 3, 1996[1]	Elkader	788	118	July 20, 1934	Keokuk	651
Kansas	–40	Feb. 13, 1905	Lebanon	1,874	121	July 24, 1936[1]	Alton	1,591
Kentucky	–37	Jan. 19, 1994	Shelbyville	730	114	July 28, 1930	Greensburg	590
Louisiana	–16	Feb. 13, 1899	Minden	200	114	Aug. 10, 1936	Plain Dealing	290
Maine	–50	Jan. 16, 2009	Big Black River	885	105	July 10, 1911[1]	North Bridgton	449
Maryland	–40	Jan. 13, 1912	Oakland	2,420	109	July 10, 1936[1]	Cumberland Frederick	899 380
Massachusetts	–35	Jan. 12, 1981[1]	Chester	640	107	Aug. 2, 1975	Chester New Bedford	640 70
Michigan	–51	Feb. 9, 1934	Vanderbilt	905	112	July 13, 1936	Mio Stanwood	960 830
Minnesota	–60	Feb. 2, 1996	Tower	1,485	115	July 29, 1917	Beardsley	1,089
Mississippi	–19	Jan. 30, 1966	Corinth	420	115	July 29, 1930	Holly Springs	502
Missouri	–40	Feb. 13, 1905	Warsaw	705	118	July 14, 1954	Warsaw Union	705 540
Montana	–70	Jan. 20, 1954	Rogers Pass	5,545	117	July 5, 1937[1]	Medicine Lake	1,942
Nebraska	–47	Dec. 22, 1989[1]	Oshkosh	3,390	118	July 24, 1936[1]	Minden	2,160
Nevada	–50	Jan. 8, 1937	San Jacinto	5,203	125	June 29, 1994	Laughlin	605
New Hampshire	–50	Jan. 22, 1885	Mt. Washington	6,267	106	July 4, 1911	Nashua	140
New Jersey	–34	Jan. 5, 1904	River Vale	70	110	July 10, 1936	Runyon	20
New Mexico	–50	Feb. 1, 1951	Gavilan	7,425	122	June 27, 1994	Waste Isolat. Pilot Plant	3,411
New York	–52	Feb. 18, 1979	Old Forge	1,748	108	July 22, 1926	Troy	35
North Carolina	–34	Jan. 21, 1985	Mt. Mitchell	6,240	110	Aug. 21, 1983	Fayetteville	186
North Dakota	–60	Feb. 15, 1936	Parshall	1,952	121	July 6, 1936	Steele	1,885
Ohio	–39	Feb. 10, 1899	Milligan	875	113	July 21, 1934	Gallipolis	669
Oklahoma	–31	Feb. 10, 2011	Nowata	NA	120	Aug. 12, 1936[1]	Altus Irrigation Res. Sta.	1,380
Oregon	–54	Feb. 10, 1933[1]	Seneca	4,660	119	Aug. 10, 1898[1]	Pendleton	1,040
Pennsylvania	–42	Jan. 5, 1904	Smethport	1,469	111	July 10, 1936[1]	Phoenixville	105
Rhode Island	–28	Jan. 11, 1942	Wood River Junction	49	104	Aug. 2, 1975	Providence	60
South Carolina	–19	Jan. 21, 1985	Caesars Head	3,200	113	June 29, 2012	Columbia	242
South Dakota	–58	Feb. 17, 1936	McIntosh	2,175	120	July 15, 2006[1]	Fort Pierre	1,590
Tennessee	–32	Dec. 30, 1917	Mountain City	2,503	113	Aug. 9, 1930[1]	Perryville	371
Texas	–23	Feb. 8, 1933	Seminole	3,336	120	June 28, 1994[1]	Monahans	2,547
Utah	–50	Jan. 5, 1913	East Portal	7,615	117	July 5, 1985	Saint George	2,770
Vermont	–50	Dec. 30, 1933	Bloomfield	1,040	107	July 7, 1912	Vernon	226
Virginia	–30	Jan. 21, 1985	Mountain Lake Bio. Station	3,870	110	July 15, 1954[1]	Balcony Falls	732
Washington	–48	Dec. 30, 1968	Mazama Winthrop	2,106 1,749	118	Aug. 5, 1961[1]	Ice Harbor Dam	368
West Virginia	–37	Dec. 30, 1917	Lewisburg	2,251	112	July 10, 1936[1]	Martinsburg	534
Wisconsin	–55	Feb. 4, 1996[1]	Couderay	1,300	114	July 13, 1936	Wisconsin Dells	835
Wyoming	–66	Feb. 9, 1933	Riverside Ranger Sta.	6,500	115	July 15, 1988[1]	Diversion Dam	5,575

NA = Not available. (1) Also on earlier dates at the same or other places.

Tropical Cyclone Names in 2016

Source: National Weather Service, NOAA, U.S. Dept. of Commerce

If there are more than 21 named Atlantic storms in one season, remaining storms take names from the Greek alphabet, starting with Alpha. (This has only been necessary in one year to date: 2005.)

Atlantic: Alex, Bonnie, Colin, Danielle, Earl, Fiona, Gaston, Hermine, Ian, Julia, Karl, Lisa, Matthew, Nicole, Otto, Paula, Richard, Shary, Tobias, Virginie, Walter.

Eastern North Pacific: Agatha, Blas, Celia, Darby, Estelle, Frank, Georgette, Howard, Ivette, Javier, Kay, Lester, Madeline, Newton, Orlene, Paine, Roslyn, Seymour, Tina, Virgil, Winifred, Xavier, Yolanda, Zeke.

World Temperature and Precipitation

Source: World Meteorological Organization (WMO)

Average daily maximum and minimum temperatures and annual precipitation based on records for the period 1961-90. Records of extreme temperatures include all available years of data for a given location and are usually for a longer period. Surface elevations are supplied by the WMO and may differ from figures in other sections of *The World Almanac*.

		Temperature (°F)						
		AVERAGE DAILY				EXTREME		Avg. annual precipitation (in.)
		January		July				
Station	Surface elevation (ft)	Max.	Min.	Max.	Min.	Max.	Min.	
Algiers, Algeria	82	61.7	42.6	87.1	65.3	NA	NA	27.0
Athens, Greece	49	56.1	44.6	88.9	73.0	NA	NA	14.6
Auckland, New Zealand	20	74.8	61.2	58.5	46.4	NA	NA	49.4
Bangkok, Thailand	66	89.6	69.8	90.9	77.0	104	51	59.0
Beijing, China	177	34.9	15.1	87.4	70.9	105	–17	22.7
Berlin, Germany	190	35.2	26.8	73.6	55.2	107	–4	23.3
Bogotá, Colombia	8,357	67.3	41.7	64.6	45.5	75	21	32.4
Bucharest, Romania	298	34.7	22.1	83.8	60.1	105	–18	23.4
Budapest, Hungary	456	34.2	24.8	79.7	59.7	103	–10	20.3
Buenos Aires, Argentina	82	85.8	67.3	59.7	45.7	104	22	45.2
Cairo, Egypt	243	65.8	48.2	93.9	71.1	118	34	1.0
Cape Town, South Africa	138	79.0	60.3	63.3	44.6	105	28	20.5
Caracas, Venezuela	2,739	79.9	60.8	81.3	66.0	96	45	36.1
Casablanca, Morocco	203	62.8	47.1	77.7	66.7	NA	NA	16.8
Copenhagen, Denmark	16	35.6	28.4	68.9	55.0	NA	NA	NA
Damascus, Syria	2,004	54.3	32.9	97.2	61.9	NA	NA	5.6
Dubai, United Arab Emirates[1]	16	75.2	56.7	105.1	84.0	117	45	3.7
Dublin, Ireland	279	45.7	36.5	66.0	52.5	86	8	28.8
Geneva, Switzerland	1,364	38.3	27.9	76.3	53.2	101	–3	35.6
Havana, Cuba	164	78.4	65.5	88.3	74.8	NA	NA	46.9
Hong Kong, China	203	65.5	56.5	88.7	79.9	97	32	87.2
Istanbul, Turkey	108	47.8	37.2	82.8	65.3	105	7	27.4
Jerusalem, Israel	2,483	53.4	39.4	83.8	63.0	107	26	23.2
Karachi, Pakistan	69	78.4	50.7	91.6	81.3	117	34	8.6
Lagos, Nigeria	125	90.0	72.3	82.8	72.1	NA	NA	59.3
Lima, Peru	43	79.0	66.9	66.4	59.4	NA	NA	0.2
London, England	203	44.1	32.7	71.1	52.3	99	2	29.7
Manila, Philippines	79	85.8	74.8	89.1	76.8	NA	NA	49.6
Mexico City, Mexico	7,570	70.3	43.7	73.8	53.2	NA	NA	33.4
Montreal, Canada	118	21.6	5.2	79.2	59.7	100	–36	37.0
Mumbai (Bombay), India	36	85.3	66.7	86.2	77.5	110	46	85.4
Nairobi, Kenya	5,897	77.9	50.9	71.6	48.6	NA	NA	41.9
New Delhi, India[2]	709	69.8	45.7	94.5	80.2	113	34	31.3
Paris, France	213	42.8	33.6	75.2	55.2	105	–1	25.6
Prague, Czech Republic	1,197	32.7	22.5	73.9	53.2	98	–16	20.7
Reykjavik, Iceland	200	35.4	26.6	55.9	46.9	76	–3	31.5
Riyadh, Saudi Arabia	2,034	68.4	46.8	109.0	81.3	120	28	NA
Rome, Italy	79	53.8	35.4	88.2	62.1	NA	NA	33.0
San Salvador, El Salvador	2,037	86.5	61.3	86.2	66.4	105	45	68.3
São Paulo, Brazil	2,598	81.1	65.7	71.2	53.1	NA	NA	57.4
Seoul, South Korea	285	33.4	19.2	83.3	70.9	NA	NA	NA
Shanghai, China	23	45.9	32.9	88.9	76.6	104	10	43.8
Singapore	52	85.8	73.6	87.4	75.6	NA	NA	84.6
Stockholm, Sweden	171	30.7	23.0	71.4	56.1	97	–26	21.2
Sydney, Australia	10	79.5	65.5	62.4	43.9	114	32	46.4
Tehran, Iran	3,906	45.0	30.0	98.2	75.2	109	–5	9.1
Tokyo, Japan	118	49.1	34.2	83.8	72.1	NA	NA	55.4
Toronto, Canada	567	27.5	12.0	80.2	57.6	105	–26	30.8

NA = Not available. (1) Records are for 1974-91. (2) Records are for 1971-90.

Speed of Winds in the U.S.

Source: National Climatic Data Center, NESDIS, NOAA, U.S. Dept. of Commerce

Based on available records through 2014. Maximum speeds are highest 3-sec. wind speeds.

Station	Avg. mph	Max. mph
Albuquerque, NM	8.2	89
Anchorage, AK	7.0	71
Atlanta, GA	8.3	71
Baltimore, MD	7.3	72
Birmingham, AL	6.2	72
Bismarck, ND	9.5	78
Boise, ID	7.6	68
Boston, MA	11.6	76
Buffalo, NY	10.3	75
Burlington, VT	8.3	63
Charleston, SC	7.9	67
Chicago, IL	9.9	70
Cleveland, OH	9.6	68
Dallas-Ft. Worth, TX	10.5	78
Denver, CO	10.0	72
Des Moines, IA	9.9	77
Detroit, MI	9.5	78
Fairbanks, AK	4.4	59
Helena, MT	6.9	64
Honolulu, HI	10.4	48
Houston, TX	7.5	70
Indianapolis, IN	9.5	85
Jackson, MS	6.1	72
Jacksonville, FL	6.6	77
Little Rock, AR	7.0	87
Los Angeles, CA	7.5	53
Louisville, KY	7.8	75
Miami, FL	8.4	104
Milwaukee, WI	10.2	70
Minneapolis, MN	9.7	71
Mobile, AL	7.6	83
Mount Washington, NH	35.1	231
Nashville, TN	7.1	67
New Orleans, LA	8.0	77
New York, NY	6.6	62
Newark, NJ	9.9	78
Oklahoma City, OK	11.4	87
Omaha, NE	10.0	92
Philadelphia, PA	9.3	75
Phoenix, AZ	6.1	77
Pittsburgh, PA	7.9	62
Portland, ME	8.0	72
Portland, OR	7.5	67
Providence, RI	9.3	64
Richmond, VA	7.7	72
St. Louis, MO	9.1	70
Salt Lake City, UT	8.4	75
San Francisco, CA	10.6	71
San Juan, PR	7.8	93
Seattle, WA	7.9	69
Sioux Falls, SD	10.3	87
Washington, DC	9.0	74
Wichita, KS	11.5	101
Wilmington, DE	8.5	76

Wind Chill Temperature

Source: National Weather Service, NOAA, U.S. Dept. of Commerce

Temperature and wind combine to cause heat loss from body surfaces. For example, when the air temperature is 5°F, a 10-mph wind can cause body heat loss equal to that which could occur when the air temperature is –10°F with no wind. In other words, a 10-mph wind can make 5°F feel like –10°F. Wind speeds greater than 45 mph have little additional chilling effect. Direct sunlight can increase the wind chill temperature 10°F to 15°F. When the wind chill temperature falls within the shaded areas, frostbite can occur on exposed skin in the times indicated or less.

	Air temperature (°F)																	
Calm	40	35	30	25	20	15	10	5	0	–5	–10	–15	–20	–25	–30	–35	–40	–45
Wind speed (mph)	Wind chill temperature (°F)																	
5	36	31	25	19	13	7	1	–5	–11	–16	–22	–28	–34	–40	–46	–52	–57	–63
10	34	27	21	15	9	3	–4	–10	–16	–22	–28	–35	–41	–47	–53	–59	–66	–72
15	32	25	19	13	6	0	–7	–13	–19	–26	–32	–39	–45	–51	–58	–64	–71	–77
20	30	24	17	11	4	–2	–9	–15	–22	–29	–35	–42	–48	–55	–61	–68	–74	–81
25	29	23	16	9	3	–4	–11	–17	–24	–31	–37	–44	–51	–58	–64	–71	–78	–84
30	28	22	15	8	1	–5	–12	–19	–26	–33	–39	–46	–53	–60	–67	–73	–80	–87
35	28	21	14	7	0	–7	–14	–21	–27	–34	–41	–48	–55	–62	–69	–76	–82	–89
40	27	20	13	6	–1	–8	–15	–22	–29	–36	–43	–50	–57	–64	–71	–78	–84	–91
45	26	19	12	5	–2	–9	–16	–23	–30	–37	–44	–51	–58	–65	–72	–79	–86	–93

30 minutes   10 minutes   5 minutes

Heat Index

Source: National Weather Service, NOAA, U.S. Dept. of Commerce

The heat index, or apparent temperature, is a measure of how hot it feels when the relative humidity is factored in with the actual air temperature. For example, when air temperature is 100°F, and relative humidity is 50%, it feels as if it's 118°F with no humidity. Full sunlight can make one feel even hotter. On the chart, the shaded areas indicate the likelihood of heat disorders with prolonged exposure or strenuous activity.

	Air temperature (°F)															
	80	82	84	86	88	90	92	94	96	98	100	102	104	106	108	110
Relative humidity (%)	Apparent temperature (°F)															
40	80	81	83	85	88	91	94	97	101	105	109	114	119	124	130	136
45	80	82	84	87	89	93	96	100	104	109	114	119	124	130	137	
50	81	83	85	88	91	95	99	103	108	113	118	124	131	137		
55	81	84	86	89	93	97	101	106	112	117	124	130	137			
60	82	84	88	91	95	100	105	110	116	123	129	137				
65	82	85	89	93	98	103	108	114	121	128	136					
70	83	86	90	95	100	105	112	119	126	134						
75	84	88	92	97	103	109	116	124	132							
80	84	89	94	100	106	113	121	129								
85	85	90	96	102	110	117	126	135								
90	86	91	98	105	113	122	131									
95	86	93	100	108	117	127										
100	87	95	103	112	121	132										

Caution   Extreme caution   Danger   Extreme danger

Ultraviolet (UV) Index Forecast

Source: National Weather Service (NWS), NOAA, U.S. Dept. of Commerce; U.S. Environmental Protection Agency (EPA); U.S. Food and Drug Administration, U.S. Dept. of Health and Human Services

The NWS and EPA developed and began offering a UV index in 1994 in response to increasing incidences of skin cancer, cataracts, and other effects from exposure to the sun's harmful rays. In 2004, they adapted their index to the Global Solar UV Index sponsored by the World Health Organization. The UV index is now a regular element of NWS atmospheric forecasts.

The UV index, ranging from 0 to 11+, is an indication of the expected intensity of UV radiation reaching the Earth's surface during the solar noon hour (the time of day, dependent on location and time of year, when the sun appears to have reached its highest point in the sky). The lower the UV index value, the less the expected radiation. The UV index forecast is produced daily for 58 cities by the NWS Climate Prediction Center and uses the following scale.

UV index	Exposure	Minimum precautions
0-2	Low	Sunscreen with an SPF of at least 15
3-5	Moderate	Sunscreen, covering up
6-7	High	Sunscreen, hat, UV-blocking sunglasses, avoid sun 10 AM-4 PM
8-10	Very high	Same as above
11+	Extreme	Same as above

UV levels are influenced by:

Ozone. Ozone, a form of oxygen, the molecules of which consist of three atoms rather than two, absorbs UV radiation. The more ozone, the lower the UV radiation at the surface.

Sun height. The higher the sun is in the sky, the higher the UV radiation level.

Cloudiness. UV radiation levels are highest under cloudless skies. Even with cloud cover, UV radiation levels can be high due to the scattering of UV radiation by water molecules and fine particles in the atmosphere.

Reflectivity. Reflective surfaces intensify UV exposure. White sand reflects about 15% of UV radiation that reaches it; sea foam, 25%; snow, as much as 80%; water, up to 100% depending on reflection angle.

Altitude. At higher altitudes, UV radiation travels a shorter distance to reach Earth's surface so there is less atmosphere to absorb the rays. For every 1,000 m (3,281 ft) one travels above sea level, UV levels increase by 10%-12%. Snow and lack of pollutants intensify UV exposure at higher altitudes.

Latitude. The closer a location is to the equator, the higher the UV radiation level.

Further information. For precautions to take after learning the UV index value, call the EPA's Stratospheric Ozone Protection Hotline at (800) 296-1996. For questions on scientific aspects, visit the NWS Climate Prediction Center online at www.cpc.ncep.noaa.gov.

Lightning

Source: National Weather Service, NOAA, U.S. Dept. of Commerce

Lightning is a powerful electric discharge, or spark, that can occur in the atmosphere when an imbalance of positive and negative charges develops. It can travel within a cloud, between clouds, between a cloud and clear sky, or between a cloud and the ground. Lightning generally accompanies rainstorms but it can also be seen with snowstorms, volcano eruption clouds, and violent forest fires. In a common form of cloud-to-ground lightning, a negatively charged area in a thunderstorm sends charges down toward positively charged objects. Lightning can travel miles away from the area of a storm.

The transfer of charges in lightning generates a huge amount of heat, sending the temperature in the channel to 50,000°F or more and causing the air within it to expand rapidly. The sound of that expansion is thunder. Sound travels more slowly than light, so lightning is usually observed before thunder is heard.

An estimated 25 mil cloud-to-ground lightning bolts happen in the U.S. each year. They killed an annual average of 49 people in 1985-2014. This is a small number compared to U.S. deaths from fire (about 3,000 a year) and motor vehicle crashes (more than 30,000 annually in recent years), but it is still significant. In comparison, tornadoes caused an average of 72 deaths a year and hurricanes an average of 47 over the same 30-year time period. According to preliminary figures from the National Weather Service, 26 people were struck and killed by lightning in 2014; 154 more were injured.

Most lightning deaths and injuries occur in summer when people are outdoors. If outdoors, one should run to a safe building or vehicle when thunder is first heard, lightning is seen, or dark threatening clouds are observed developing overhead. Even while indoors, one is advised to stay away from windows and doors and to avoid contact with anything conducting electricity, including corded phones, computers and other electrical equipment, and tubs, showers, and other plumbing. One should stay inside until 30 min. after the last occurrence of lightning or thunder.

More information about lightning can be found online at www.lightningsafety.noaa.gov.

Global Temperature Extremes and Precipitation Records

Source: World Weather/Climate Extremes Archive, World Meteorological Organization (WMO) Commission for Climatology

(records in each category ranked from most to least extreme)

Highest Temperature Extremes

Continent/area	Highest temp. (°F)	Place	Elevation (ft)	Date
North America	134	Death Valley, CA, U.S. (Greenland Ranch/Furnace Creek)	–179	July 10, 1913
Africa	131[1]	Kebili, Tunisia	125	July 7, 1931
Europe/Middle East/ Greenland	129	Tirat Tsvi, Israel	–722	June 21, 1942
Southwest Pacific	123	Oodnadatta, Australia	367	Jan. 2, 1960
South America	120	Rivadavia, Argentina	2,192	Dec. 11, 1905
Continental Europe	118.4	Athens, Greece (and Elefsina, Greece)	774	July 10, 1977
Antarctica	59	Vanda Station (New Zealand), Wright Valley	49	May 1, 1974
Asia	NA[2]			

(1) Previous record of 136.4°F set on Sept. 13, 1922, in El Azizia, Libya, was invalidated in Sept. 2012 after the WMO determined that an error had been made in recording the temperature. (2) Under investigation as of Aug. 2015.

Lowest Temperature Extremes

Continent/area	Lowest temp. (°F)	Place	Elevation (ft)	Date
Antarctica	–129	Vostok Station (Soviet Union/Russia)	11,220	July 21, 1983
Asia	–90	Verkhoyansk, Russia	350	Feb. 5 and 7, 1892
	–90	Oimekon, Russia	2,625	Feb. 6, 1933
Europe/Middle East/ Greenland	–87	Northice, Greenland	7,680	Jan. 9, 1954
North America	–81.4	Snag, Yukon, Canada	2,120	Feb. 3, 1947
Continental Europe	–72.6	Ust'-Shchugor, Russia	279	Dec. 31, 1978
South America	–27	Sarmiento, Argentina	879	June 1, 1907
Southwest Pacific	–14	Eweburn (now Ranfurly), New Zealand	1,388	July 17, 1903
Africa	–11	Ifrane, Morocco	5,364	Feb. 11, 1935
Australia	–9.4	Charlotte Pass, New South Wales	5,758	June 29, 1994

Highest Measured Average Annual Precipitation Extremes

Continent/area	Highest avg. (in.)[1]	Place	Elevation (ft)	Years in averaging period
Asia	467.4	Mawsynram, India	4,695	38
Southwest Pacific	460	Mt. Waialeale, Kauai, HI, U.S.	5,148	30
Africa	405	Debundscha, Cameroon	30	32
South America	354	Quibdo, Colombia	230	29
Australia	316.3	Bellenden Ker, Queensland	5,102	34
North America	276	Henderson Lake, British Columbia, Canada	12	15
Europe	180.8	Crkvice, Montenegro	3,461	30
Antarctica	>31.5[2]	Along coast of E and W and over the Antarctic Peninsula		3[3]

(1) Official greatest average annual precipitation. The frequently cited record of 523.6 in. in Lloro, Colombia (14 mi SE and at a higher elevation than Quibdo) is an estimate. (2) Water equivalent. (3) July 1996-June 1999.

Lowest Measured Average Annual Precipitation Extremes

Continent/area	Lowest avg. (in.)	Place	Elevation (ft)	Years in averaging period
South America	0.03	Arica, Chile	213	59
Antarctica	0.08	Amundsen-Scott South Pole Station (U.S.)	9,301	10
Africa	<0.1	Wadi Halfa, Sudan	590	39
North America	1.2	Batagues, Mexico	69	14
Asia	1.8	Aden, Yemen	63	50
Southwest Pacific	4.05	Troudaninna, Australia	46	42
Continental Europe	6.4	Astrakhan, Russia	66	25

OCEANOGRAPHY

Tides and Their Causes

Source: National Ocean Service, NOAA, U.S. Dept. of Commerce

The tides are natural phenomena involving the movement of waves in the Earth's large fluid bodies as a result of the gravitational attraction of the sun and moon. These two variable influences combined produce the complex recurrent cycle of the tides. Tides may occur in both oceans and seas; to a limited extent in large lakes and in the atmosphere; and, to a very minute degree, in the Earth itself. The length of time between succeeding tides can vary.

The tide-generating force represents the difference between (1) the centrifugal force produced by Earth's revolution around the common center-of-gravity of the Earth-moon system and (2) the gravitational attraction of the moon acting upon the Earth's overlying waters. The moon is about 390 times closer to Earth than is the sun. So despite its smaller mass, the moon's tide-raising force is two times greater.

The tide-generating forces of the moon and sun acting tangentially to the Earth's surface tend to cause a maximum accumulation of waters at two diametrically opposite points on the Earth's surface and to withdraw compensating amounts of water from all points 90° removed from these tidal bulges. As the Earth rotates beneath the maxima and minima of these tide-generating forces, a sequence of two high tides, separated by two low tides, is produced each lunar day (24 hrs. and 50 min., the time it takes for a specific site on the Earth to rotate from an exact point under the moon to the same point under the moon) in what is called a **semidiurnal tide**. Each ocean basin reacts differently to tidal forces.

Twice each month, when the sun, moon, and Earth are directly aligned—the moon between the Earth and sun (at new moon) or on the opposite side of Earth from the sun (at full moon)—the sun and moon exert gravitational forces in a mutual or additive fashion. The highest high tides and lowest low tides, called **spring tides**, are produced at these times. At two positions 90° in between, the moon and sun's gravitational forces—imposed at right angles—counteract each other to the greatest extent, and the range between high and low tides is reduced, resulting in **neap tides**.

The inclination of the moon's monthly orbit and of the sun to the equator during Earth's yearly passage through its orbit produce a difference in the height of succeeding high and low tides, known as the diurnal inequality. In most cases, this produces a so-called **mixed tide**. In extreme cases, these phenomena may result in a **diurnal tide**, with only one high tide and one low tide each day. There are other monthly and yearly variations in the tides because of the elliptical shape of the orbits.

The range of tides in the open ocean is generally less than in the coastal regions, where the incoming tide can be augmented by the continental shelves, as well as by bays and estuaries. The largest tidal ranges in the world occur in the Bay of Fundy, Canada, where the range of tide reaches 53.5 ft. In New Orleans, the periodic rise and fall of the diurnal tide is affected by the seasonal stages of the Mississippi River, being about 10 in. at low stage and 0 at high.

In every case, actual high or low tide can vary considerably from the average as a result of weather conditions such as strong winds, abrupt barometric pressure changes, or prolonged periods of extreme high or low pressure.

Mean Ranges of Tide

Place	Ft	In.	Place	Ft	In.	Place	Ft	In.
Baltimore, MD	1	2	Key West, FL	1	3	Provincetown, MA	9	3
Biloxi, MS	1	6	Los Angeles, CA	3	10	St. Petersburg, FL	1	7
Boston, MA	9	6	Miami Beach, FL	2	6	San Diego, CA	4	1
Charleston, SC	5	3	New London, CT	2	7	San Francisco, CA	4	1
Eastport, ME	18	4	New York, NY	4	6	San Juan, PR	1	1
Ft. Pulaski, GA	6	11	Newport, RI	3	6	Sandy Hook, NJ	4	8
Galveston, TX	1	0	Philadelphia, PA	6	1	Seattle, WA	7	8
Honolulu, HI	1	3	Portland, ME	9	1	Washington, DC	2	9

Note: Mean range is the difference in height between mean high water and mean low water.

El Niño and La Niña

Source: National Weather Service, NOAA, U.S. Dept. of Commerce

El Niño is a climatically significant disruption of the ocean-atmosphere system characterized by large-scale weakening of trade winds and warming of surface layer waters in the central and eastern equatorial Pacific. The term *El Niño*, Spanish for "the little boy" or "the Christ Child," was originally used by fishing crews to refer to a warm ocean current that appeared around Christmas off the west coast of Ecuador and Peru lasting several months. The term has come to be reserved for exceptionally strong, warm currents that bring heavy rains.

El Niño events generally occur at irregular intervals of two to seven years, at an average of once every three to four years. They typically last 12 to 18 months. The intensity of El Niño events varies depending on the area encompassed by the abnormally warm ocean temperatures. Some are strong, such as in 1982-83 and 1997-98. Others are considerably weaker, such as the 2009-10 event. The eastward extent of warmer-than-normal water varies from episode to episode.

El Niño influences weather around the globe, and its impacts are most clearly seen in the winter. During El Niño years, winter temperatures in the continental U.S. tend to be warmer than normal in the northern states and on the West Coast and cooler than normal in the Southeast. Conditions tend to be wetter than normal over central and southern California, the Southwest, and across much of the South, and drier than normal over the northern portions of the Rocky Mountains and in the Ohio Valley. Globally, El Niño brings wetter than normal conditions to Peru and Chile and dry conditions to Australia and Indonesia. It should be noted that El Niño is only one of a number of factors influencing seasonal variations of climate.

La Niña ("the little girl") is characterized by colder than normal sea surface temperatures in the equatorial Pacific. La Niña typically brings wetter, cooler conditions to the Pacific Northwest and drier, warmer conditions to much of the southern U.S. El Niño and La Niña are opposite phases of the El Niño-Southern Oscillation (ENSO) cycle, which involves a shift in tropical sea-level pressure between the Eastern and Western Hemispheres.

NOAA and other agencies monitor these events using satellites, weather balloons, and buoys in the Pacific Ocean. Numerical computer models of the ocean and atmosphere use these data to predict the onset and evolution of El Niño and La Niña. Following weak El Niño conditions in the Northern Hemisphere in early 2015, in Aug. 2015, NOAA put the chance of an El Niño occurrence during the Northern Hemisphere winter at greater than 90%, and an 85% chance it would last into early spring 2016.

DISASTERS

Some Notable Aircraft Disasters Since 1937

Source: National Transportation Safety Board; World Almanac research

Particularly notable disasters are in bold. Asterisk (*) indicates number of deaths includes people on ground. As of Aug. 2015.

Date	Aircraft	Site of accident	Deaths
1937, May 6	**German zeppelin Hindenburg**	**Burned at mooring, Lakehurst, NJ**	**36***
1944, Aug. 23	U.S. Air Force B-24 Liberator bomber	Hit school, Freckleton, England, UK	61*
1945, July 28	U.S. Army B-25	Hit Empire State Building after getting lost in fog, New York, NY	14*
1952, Dec. 20	U.S. Air Force C-124	Crashed at Moses Lake, WA	87
1953, Mar. 3	**Canadian Pacific DH-106 Comet**	**Crashed on takeoff from Karachi, Pakistan; world's first fatal commercial passenger jet crash**	**11**
1953, June 18	U.S. Air Force C-124	Crashed, burned near Tokyo, Japan	129
1955, Oct. 6	United Airlines DC-4	Crashed in Medicine Bow Peak, WY	66
1955, Nov. 1	United Airlines DC-6	Bomb on board exploded near Longmont, CO	44[1]
1956, June 20	Venezuelan Super Constellation	Crashed into Atlantic off Asbury Park, NJ	74
1956, June 30	TWA Super Const., United DC-7	Collided over Grand Canyon, AZ	128
1960, Dec. 16	United DC-8, TWA Super Const.	Collided over New York, NY, killing all 128 on planes, 6 on ground	134*
1962, Mar. 16	Flying Tiger Super Constellation	Vanished in W Pacific en route to Philippines from Guam	107
1962, June 3	Air France Boeing 707	Crashed on takeoff from Paris, France	130
1962, June 22	Air France Boeing 707	Crashed in storm, Guadeloupe, French W Indies	113
1963, Feb. 1	Lebanese Middle East Airlines Vickers Viscount 754, Turkish Mil. Douglas C-47	Collided over Ankara, Turkey, killing all 17 on planes, 87 on ground	104*
1963, Nov. 29	Trans-Canada Air Lines DC-8	Crashed after takeoff from Montreal, QC, Canada	118
1965, May 20	Pakistani Boeing 720	Crashed at airport in Cairo, Egypt	121
1966, Jan. 24	Air India Boeing 707	Crashed on Mont Blanc, France-Italy	117
1966, Feb. 4	All-Nippon Boeing 727	Plunged into Tokyo Bay, Japan	133
1966, Mar. 5	BOAC (British Overseas Airways Corp.) Boeing 707	Crashed into Mt. Fuji, Japan, after encountering severe turbulence	124
1966, Dec. 24	U.S. military-chartered CL-44	Crashed into village in S Vietnam	129*
1967, Apr. 20	Globe Air Bristol Britannia	Crashed on approach to airport, Nicosia, Cyprus	126
1967, July 19	Piedmont Boeing 727, Cessna 310	Collided over Hendersonville, NC	82
1968, Apr. 20	S. African Airways Boeing 707	Crashed on takeoff from Windhoek, Namibia	122
1968, May 3	Braniff International Electra	Crashed in storm near Dawson, TX	85
1968, May 12	U.S. Air Force Lockheed C-130B	Hit by enemy mortar while evacuating Kham Duc Camp, S Vietnam	155
1969, Mar. 16	Venezuelan DC-9	Crashed after takeoff from Maracaibo, Venezuela	155[2]
1970, July 3	British-chartered DH-106 Comet	Crashed near Barcelona, Spain	112
1970, July 5	Air Canada DC-8	Crashed near Toronto Intl. Airport, ON, Canada	108
1970, Nov. 14	Southern Airways DC-9	Crashed into mountains near Huntington, WV	75[3]
1971, July 30	All-Nippon Boeing 727, Japan Air Force F-86 fighter	Collided over Morioka, Japan	162[4]
1971, Sept. 4	Alaska Airlines Boeing 727	Crashed into mountain near Juneau, AK	111
1972, May 18	Aeroflot Antonov 10A	Wings separated from fuselage; crashed on approach to Kharkov, USSR	122
1972, June 18	British European Airways Trident-1C	Crashed near Staines after takeoff from London, Eng., UK	118
1972, Aug. 14	East German Ilyushin 62	Crashed on takeoff from East Berlin, E Germany	156
1972, Aug. 31	Aeroflot Ilyushin 18V	Crashed in field near Magnitogorsk, USSR	101
1972, Oct. 1	Aeroflot Ilyushin 18V	Crashed into Black Sea, USSR	109
1972, Oct. 13	Aeroflot Ilyushin 62	Crashed near Moscow, USSR	174
1972, Dec. 3	Spanish-chartered Convair CV-990	Crashed on takeoff from Canary Islands, Spain	155
1972, Dec. 29	Eastern Airlines Lockheed Tristar	Crashed on approach to Miami Intl. Airport, FL	99
1973, Jan. 22	Nigerian-chartered Boeing 707	Burst into flames upon landing at Kano Airport, Nigeria	176
1973, Feb. 21	**Libyan Arab Boeing 727**	**Flew off course, shot down by Israeli fighter planes over Sinai Desert**	**108**
1973, Apr. 10	Invicta Airways Vickers Vanguard	Crashed during snowstorm on approach to Basel, Switzerland	108
1973, June 3	Soviet Supersonic Tu-144	Crashed near Goussainville, France	14[5]
1973, July 11	Varig Airlines (Brazil) Boeing 707	Crashed on approach to Orly Airport, Paris, France	123
1973, July 31	Delta Airlines DC-9	Crashed while attempting landing in fog, Logan Airport, Boston, MA	89
1973, Sept. 30	Aeroflot Tupolev 104B	Crashed after takeoff from Sverdlovsk, USSR	108
1973, Oct. 13	Aeroflot Tupolev 104B	Crashed on approach to Moscow, USSR	122
1973, Dec. 22	Royal Air Maroc SE 210 Caravelle VIN	Flew into side of a mountain near Tangier, Morocco	106
1974, Mar. 3	Turkish DC-10	Crashed in Ermenonville, near Paris, France	346
1974, Apr. 22	Pan American Boeing 707	Crashed in Bali, Indonesia	107
1974, Apr. 27	Aeroflot Ilyushin 18V	Crashed after takeoff from Leningrad, USSR	109
1974, Dec. 1	TWA Boeing 727	Crashed on approach in storm, Upperville, VA	92
1974, Dec. 4	Dutch-chartered DC-8	Crashed in storm near Colombo, Sri Lanka	191
1975, Apr. 4	U.S. Air Force Galaxy C-5A	Crashed on takeoff nr. Saigon, S Vietnam; carried orphans	155
1975, June 24	Eastern Airlines 727	Crashed in storm, JFK Airport, New York, NY	113
1975, Aug. 3	Alia Royal Jordanian Boeing 707	Hit mountainside in heavy fog near Agadir, Morocco	188
1975, Aug. 20	Czechoslovakian Air Ilyushin 62	Crashed on approach to Damascus, Syria	126
1976, Mar. 6	Aeroflot Ilyushin 18E	Crashed between Moscow, USSR, and Yerevan, Armenia	111
1976, Sept. 10	British Airways Trident, Yugoslavian DC-9	Collided near Zagreb, Yugoslavia	176
1976, Sept. 19	Turkish Boeing 727	Hit mountain in southern Turkey	154
1976, Oct. 13	Lloyd Aero Boliviano Boeing 707	Crashed into soccer field after takeoff from Santa Cruz, Bolivia	91[6]
1977, Mar. 27	**KLM 747, Pan American 747**	**Collided on foggy runway, Tenerife, Canary Islands, Spain; world's worst airline disaster**	**583**
1977, Nov. 19	TAP Portugal Boeing 727	Crashed in Madeira, Portugal	131
1977, Dec. 4	Malaysian Airlines Boeing 737	Hijacked and forced to fly to Singapore, crashed near Johor Strait	100
1978, Jan. 1	Air India 747	Crashed into sea after takeoff from Bombay, India	213
1978, Sept. 25	Pacific SW Air Boeing 727, Cessna 172	Collided over San Diego, CA	144*
1978, Nov. 15	Indonesian-chartered DC-8	Crashed on approach to airport, Colombo, Sri Lanka	183
1979, May 25	**American Airlines DC-10**	**Crashed after takeoff from O'Hare Airport, Chicago, IL; highest death toll in U.S. aviation history**	**275***
1979, Aug. 11	Aeroflot/Moldova Tu-134, Aeroflot Tu-134	Collided over Ukraine	178
1979, Nov. 26	Pakistani Boeing 707	Crashed near Jidda, Saudi Arabia	156
1979, Nov. 28	Air New Zealand DC-10	Crashed into Mt. Erebus during Antarctica flyover	257
1980, Mar. 14	PLL LOT Ilyushin 62	Crashed making emergency landing, Warsaw, Poland	87[7]
1980, Apr. 25	Dan-Air Services (UK) Boeing 727	Crashed into mountain, Tenerife, Canary Islands, Spain	146

Date	Aircraft	Site of accident	Deaths
1980, July 8	Aeroflot Tupolev 154B	Crashed after takeoff from Alma-Ata, USSR	166
1980, Aug. 19	Saudi Arabian Tristar	Burned after emergency landing in Riyadh, Saudi Arabia	301
1981, Dec. 1	Inex Adria (Yugoslavia) DC-9	Crashed into mountain on island of Corsica, France	180
1982, Jan. 13	Air Florida Boeing 737	Crashed into Potomac R. after takeoff from Washington, DC	78
1982, June 8	VASP (Brazil) Boeing 727	Crashed into mountain near Fortaleza, Brazil	137
1982, June 28	Aeroflot Yokovlev 42	Crashed near Mozyr, USSR	132
1982, July 9	Pan Am Boeing 727	Crashed after takeoff from Kenner, LA, near New Orleans	153*
1983, July 11	Ecuadorean Boeing 737	Inexperienced pilot crashed into hill near Cuenca, Ecuador	119
1983, Sept. 1	**S. Korean Boeing 747**	**Shot down after violating Soviet airspace near Sakhalin; plane apparently misidentified**	**269**
1983, Sept. 23	Gulf Air Boeing 737	Bomb exploded in cargo hold over Mina Jebel Ali, UAE	112
1983, Nov. 27	Avianca Boeing 747	Crashed near Barajas Airport, Madrid, Spain	181
1984, Oct. 11	Aeroflot/East Siberia Tu-154	Crashed into vehicles on runway while landing in poor weather, Omsk, Russia	178*
1985, Feb. 19	Spanish Boeing 727	Crashed into Mt. Oiz, Spain	148
1985, June 23	Air India Boeing 747	Crashed into Atlantic off Ireland after bomb detonated on board	329
1985, July 10	Aeroflot Tupolev 154B	Crashed after takeoff from Uzbekistan, USSR	200
1985, Aug. 2	Delta Air Lines L-1011	Crashed at Dallas-Ft. Worth Airport, TX	135
1985, Aug. 12	**Japan Air Lines Boeing 747**	**Crashed into Mt. Ogura, Japan; world's worst single-plane disaster**	**520**
1985, Dec. 12	Arrow Air DC-8	Crashed after takeoff from Gander, NL, Canada	256[8]
1986, Mar. 31	Mexican Boeing 727	Crashed NW of Mexico City, Mexico	167
1986, Aug. 31	Aeromexico DC-9, Piper PA-28	Collided over Cerritos, CA	82*
1987, May 9	Polish IL-62M	Crashed after takeoff from Warsaw, Poland	183
1987, Aug. 16	Northwest Airlines MD-82	Crashed after takeoff from Romulus, MI	156
1987, Nov. 28	S. African Boeing 747	Crashed into Indian Ocean near Mauritius	159
1987, Nov. 29	Korean Air Boeing 707	Bomb planted by 2 N. Korean agents exploded while plane over Andaman Sea off Burma	115
1988, Mar. 17	Colombian Boeing 707	Crashed into mountainside near Venezuela border	143
1988, July 3	**Iran Air Airbus A300**	**Misidentified as hostile aircraft, shot down by U.S. Navy warship *Vincennes* over Persian Gulf**	**290**
1988, Oct. 19	Indian Airlines Boeing 737	Exploded after striking trees near runway, Ahmedabad, India	131
1988, Dec. 21	**Pan Am Boeing 747**	**Libyan agent planted bomb on board; exploded over Lockerbie, Scotland**	**270[9]**
1989, Feb. 8	U.S.-chartered Boeing 707	Crashed into mountain on Azores Isls., off Portugual	144
1989, June 7	Suriname DC-8	Crashed near Paramaribo Airport, Suriname	176
1989, July 19	United Airlines DC-10	Crashed on landing in Sioux City, IA	111
1989, Sept. 3	Cubana Aviacion Ilyushin 62M	Crashed on takeoff from Havana, Cuba	171*
1989, Sept. 19	**UTA DC-10**	**Bomb exploded on board flight from Chad to France while over desert in Niger**	**170**
1989, Oct. 21	Honduran Boeing 727	Crashed into mountain near Tegucigalpa, Honduras	131
1989, Nov. 27	Avianca (Colombia) Boeing 727	Bomb exploded on flight from Bogotá, Colombia	107
1990, Jan. 25	Avianca Boeing 707	Crashed on landing at JFK Airport, New York, NY	73
1990, Oct. 2	Xiamen Airlines Boeing 737	Hijacked after takeoff from Xiamen; collided with China Southern Airlines 757 on runway, Guangzhou, China	128
1991, May 26	Lauda-Air (Austria) Boeing 767-300	Exploded over rural Thailand	223
1991, July 11	Nigerian DC-8	Crashed on landing at Jidda, Saudi Arabia	261
1991, Oct. 5	U.S. Air Force Lockheed C-130 Hercules	Crashed after takeoff from Jakarta, Indonesia	135*
1992, July 31	Thai Airbus A300-310	Crashed into mountain N of Kathmandu, Nepal	113
1992, Sept. 26	Nigerian Air Force Lockheed C-130 Hercules	Transport full of military officers crashed near Lagos, Nigeria	158
1992, Sept. 28	Pakistan Intl. Air Airbus A300	Crashed into hillside near Kathmandu, Nepal	167
1992, Oct. 4	**El Al (Israel) Boeing 747-200F**	**Crashed into 2 apartment bldgs., Amsterdam, Netherlands**	**120***
1992, Nov. 24	China Southern Airlines Boeing 737	Crashed on approach to Giulin, China	141
1992, Dec. 22	Libyan Arab Air Boeing 727	Collided with Libyan Air Force MiG-23 on approach to Tripoli, Libya	159
1993, Feb. 8	Iran Air Tu-154, Iranian Air Force jet	Collided after military jet took off from Tehran, Iran	131
1993, May 19	SAM Colombia Boeing 727	Crashed into mountain near Medellin, Colombia	132
1993, Nov. 20	Macedonian Yakovlev 42D	Crashed into mountain near Skopje, Macedonia	116
1994, Jan. 3	Aeroflot Tu-154	Crashed and exploded after takeoff from Irkutsk, Russia	125*
1994, Apr. 26	China Airlines Airbus A300	Crashed on approach to Nagoya Airport, Japan	264
1994, June 6	China Northwest Airlines Tu-154	Crashed near Xian, China	160
1994, Sept. 8	USAir Boeing 737-300	Crashed near Pittsburgh Intl. Airport, Aliquippa, PA	132
1994, Oct. 31	American Eagle ATR-72-210	Crashed in field near Roselawn, IN	68
1995, Dec. 18	Zairean Lockheed L-188C Electra	Overloaded charter crashed in Lunda Norte, Angola	141
1995, Dec. 20	American Airlines Boeing 757	Crashed into mountain N of Cali, Colombia	159
1996, Jan. 8	African Air Antonov-32 cargo plane	Crashed into a market in Kinshasa, Zaire; all deaths on ground	237*
1996, Feb. 6	Dominican Boeing 757	Crashed into Atlantic off Dominican Republic	189
1996, Feb. 29	Peruvian Boeing 737	Crashed into hillside near Arequipa, Peru	123
1996, Apr. 3	U.S. Air Force Boeing T-43A	Crashed into mountain near Dubrovnik, Croatia	35[10]
1996, May 11	ValuJet DC-9	Crashed into Florida Everglades after improper cargo started fire	110
1996, July 17	Trans World Airlines Boeing 747	Exploded and crashed into Atlantic off Long Island, NY	230
1996, Aug. 29	Vnukovo Airlines (Russia) Tu-154	Crashed into mountain on Arctic island of Spitsbergen	141
1996, Nov. 7	Nigerian Boeing 727	Crashed into lagoon SE of Lagos, Nigeria	144
1996, Nov. 12	**Saudi Arabian Boeing 747, Kazakh Ilyushin 76 cargo plane**	**Collided near New Delhi, India; world's worst midair collision**	**349**
1996, Nov. 23	Ethiopian Airlines Boeing 767	Hijacked, then crashed into Indian Ocean off the Comoros	127
1997, Aug. 6	Korean Air Boeing 747-300	Crashed into jungle on Guam on approach to airport	228
1997, Sept. 26	Indonesian Airbus A300	Crashed near airport, Medan, Indonesia	234
1998, Feb. 16	China Airlines Airbus A300	Crashed on approach to airport in Taipei, Taiwan	203*
1998, Sept. 2	Swissair MD-11	Crashed into Atlantic off Nova Scotia, Canada	229
1999, Oct. 31	EgyptAir Boeing 767	Crashed off Nantucket, MA; result of deliberate actions by copilot, motives unknown	217
2000, Jan. 30	Kenya Airways Airbus A310	Crashed into Atlantic after takeoff from Abidjan, Côte d'Ivoire	169
2000, Jan. 31	Alaska Airlines MD-83	Crashed into Pacific off coast of Southern CA	88
2000, Apr. 19	Air Philippines Boeing 737-200	Crashed on approach to airport, Davao, Philippines	131

Date	Aircraft	Site of accident	Deaths
2000, July 25	**Air France Concorde**	**Crashed into hotel after takeoff from Paris; world's first Concorde crash**	**113***
2000, Aug. 23	Gulf Air Airbus A320	Crashed into Persian Gulf on approach to airport in Bahrain	143
2001, July 3	Vladivostokavia Tu-154	Crashed on approach to airport, Irkutsk, Russia	145
2001, Sept. 11	**2 Boeing 767s, 2 Boeing 757s**	**September 11 terrorist attacks**	**265**[11]
2001, Oct. 8	Cessna 525A Citation, Scandinavian Airlines System (SAS) MD-87	Collided in heavy fog on takeoff from Milan, Italy	118*
2001, Nov. 12	**American Airlines Airbus A300**	**Crashed after takeoff from JFK Airport, New York, NY**	**265***
2002, Feb. 12	Iran Air Tours Tu-154	Crashed into mountain on approach to airport, Khorramabad, Iran	119
2002, Apr. 15	Air China Boeing 767	Crashed into mountainside in rain and fog on approach to airport, Pusan, S. Korea	129
2002, May 4	EAS Airlines BAC 1-11	Crashed shortly after takeoff from Kano, Nigeria	149
2002, May 7	China Northern Airlines MD-82	Plunged into sea, apparently after a passenger started fire in cabin, NE China	112
2002, May 25	China Airlines Boeing 747	Broke apart in midair, plunged into Taiwan Strait en route to Hong Kong airport	225
2002, July 27	**Ukraine Air Force Sukhoi Su-27**	**Crashed while performing, Lviv, Ukraine; world's worst air-show crash**	**77**[12]
2002, Aug. 19	Russian Mi-26 transport helicopter	Hit by Chechen missile near Grozny, Chechnya	127
2003, Jan. 8	Turkish Airlines British Aerospace RJ-100	Crashed on approach to airport in Diyarbakir, Turkey	75
2003, Feb. 19	Iranian Revolutionary Guard Ilyushin 76	Crashed into mountain near Kerman, Iran; passengers were Revolutionary Guard members	275
2003, May 26	Ukrain.-Medit. Airlines Yak-42	Crashed into mountain in fog approaching Trabzon, Turkey; passengers incl. Spanish peacekeepers returning from Afghan.	75
2003, July 8	Sudan Airways Boeing 737-200	Mechanical problems reported shortly after takeoff; crashed upon return to Port Sudan Airport	115
2003, Dec. 25	Union Transp. Africains Boeing 727	Overloading caused crash on takeoff from Cotonou, Benin	141
2004, Jan. 3	Flash Airlines Boeing 737-300	Crashed into Red Sea after takeoff from Sharm el-Sheik, Egypt	148
2004, Aug. 24	Volga-Aviaexpress Tu-134, Sibir Airlines Tu-154	2 planes that took off from Moscow crashed within minutes of each other; brought down by Chechen suicide bombers	90
2005, Aug. 14	Helios Airways Boeing 737-300	Crashed after air pressure failure on board, near Athens, Greece	121
2005, Aug. 16	West Caribbean Airways MD-82	Crashed after engine failure, near Machiques, Venezuela	160
2005, Sept. 5	Mandala Airlines Boeing 737-200	Crashed shortly after takeoff from Medan, Sumatra, Indonesia	145*
2005, Oct. 22	Bellview Airlines Boeing 737-200	Crashed during heavy electrical storm near Lagos, Nigeria	117
2005, Dec. 6	Islamic Rep. of Iran Air Force Lockheed C-130	Crashed into apartment building after reportedly attempting emergency landing back at airport, Tehran, Iran	116*
2005, Dec. 10	Sosoliso Airlines DC-9-30	Crashed during storm on approach to Port Harcourt, Nigeria	107
2006, May 3	Armavia Airbus A320	Crashed into Black Sea on approach to airport, Sochi, Russia	113
2006, July 9	S7 Airlines Airbus A310	Skidded off runway, crashed into concrete barrier after landing, Irkutsk, Russia	125
2006, Aug. 22	Pulkovo Aviation Tu-154	Crashed after encountering storm, near Donetsk, Ukraine	170
2006, Sept. 29	Gol Airlines Boeing 737	Crashed into Amazon jungle after midair collision with Embraer Legacy jet, Brazil	154
2007, May 5	Kenya Airways Boeing 737-800	Crashed shortly after takeoff from Douala, Cameroon	114
2007, July 17	TAM Airlines Airbus 320	Crashed into cargo depot, gas station after skidding off airport runway, São Paulo, Brazil	199*
2008, Aug. 20	Spanair Boeing-MD-82	Swerved off runway, caught fire on takeoff attempt, Madrid, Spain	154
2009, Feb. 12	Colgan Air Bombardier Dash 8 Q400	Crashed into house near airport, Buffalo, NY	50*
2009, June 1	**Air France Airbus A330**	**Plunged into Atlantic Ocean en route from Rio de Janeiro, Brazil, to Paris, France**	**228**
2009, June 29	Yemenia Airbus A310-300	Fell into Indian Ocean on approach to Moroni, Comoros	152
2009, July 15	Caspian Airlines Tupolev 154	Crashed after takeoff from Tehran, Iran	168
2010, Apr. 10	Polish Air Force Tupolev 154M	Crashed on approach to Smolensk Air Base, killing Polish Pres. Lech Kaczynski, his wife, and several members of parliament	96
2010, May 12	Afriqiyah Airways Airbus A330-200	Crashed short of runway in Tripoli, Libya	103
2010, May 22	Air India Express Boeing 737-800	Overran runway on landing at Mangalore, India	158
2010, July 28	Airblue Airbus 321-231	Crashed into Margalla Hills near Islamabad, Pakistan	152
2012, Apr. 20	Bhoja Airlines Boeing 737-236	Crashed on approach to airport in Islamabad, Pakistan	127
2012, June 3	Dana Air MD-83	Crashed into residential area of Lagos, Nigeria	163*
2014, Mar. 8	Malaysia Airlines Boeing 777	All communication ceased shortly after takeoff from Kuala Lumpur	239
2014, July 17	Malaysia Airlines Boeing 777	Shot down in missile attack in Russian-occupied Donetsk, Ukraine	298
2014, July 24	Air Algérie Boeing-MD-83	Crashed in desert near Gossi, Mali	116
2014, Dec. 28	Indonesia AirAsia Airbus A320-216	Disappeared over Java Sea between Surabaya and Singapore	162
2015, Mar. 24	Germanwings Airbus A320-211	Copilot deliberately crashed aircraft into French Alps	150
2015, June 30	Indonesian Air Force Lockheed C-130B	Transport plane crashed near Medan Soewondo Air Force Base	139*

(1) Bomb was planted by Jack G. Graham in insurance plot to kill his mother, Daisie E. King, a passenger. (2) 84 on plane, 71 on ground killed. (3) Incl. 43 Marshall Univ. (WV) football players and coaches. (4) Fighter pilot parachuted to safety. (5) First supersonic plane crash; killed 8 on ground. (6) Crew of 3, 88 on ground killed. (7) Incl. 22 members of U.S. amateur boxing team. (8) Incl. 248 members of U.S. 101st Airborne Division. (9) Incl. 11 on ground. (10) Incl. U.S. Sec. of Commerce Ron Brown. (11) 4 planes were hijacked and crashed, with all on board killed (265, incl. 19 hijackers). American Airlines Flight 11, a Boeing 767-200, with 81 passengers, 11 crew, crashed into Tower 1 of World Trade Center (WTC); United Airlines Flight 175, a Boeing 767-200, with 56 passengers, 9 crew, crashed into Tower 2 of WTC; American Airlines Flight 77, a Boeing 757-200, with 58 passengers, 6 crew, crashed into Pentagon outside Washington, DC; United Airlines Flight 93, a Boeing 757-200, with 37 passengers, 7 crew, crashed near Shanksville, PA. The official death toll of 2,977 includes all those who perished on the ground at the Pentagon and the WTC, as well as those who died as many as 10 years later from pulmonary sarcoidosis, a lung disease caused by exposure to toxic dust created by the disaster. (12) The two pilots ejected to safety. All spectator deaths.

Plane Crash Murder-Suicide

Date: Mar. 24, 2015. **Location:** French Alps. **Fatalities:** 150.

Half an hour after takeoff from Barcelona, Spain, the Germanwings Flight 4U9525 copilot locked the pilot out of the cockpit and changed the plane's course from a selected altitude of 38,000 ft to 100 ft. The pilot could be heard banging on the door trying to gain re-entrance, according to the cockpit voice recorder, but the plane descended rapidly until crashing into the Alps near Digne, France, killing everyone aboard. Investigators later revealed Lubitz had been treated for depression, had researched suicide methods, and had practiced rapid descents on previous flights.

Some Notable Shipwrecks Since 1854

Does not include most wartime disasters.

Date—vessel(s)	Incident	Est. deaths
1854, Mar. 1—City of Glasgow	British steamer left Liverpool for Philadelphia, never heard from again	480
1854, Sept. 27—Arctic and Vesta	U.S. Collins Line steamer sunk in collision with French steamer nr. Cape Race, Canada	285-351
1856, Jan. 23—Pacific	U.S. Collins Line steamer went missing in N Atlantic	186-286
1857, Sept. 12—Central America	U.S. mail steamship sank off Florida coast with $1.5 mil in gold	427
1858, Sept. 23—Austria	German steamer destroyed by fire in N Atlantic	471
1863, Apr. 27—Anglo-Saxon	British steamer wrecked at Cape Race, Canada	238
1865, Apr. 27—Sultana	Mississippi R. steamer carrying 2,300 released Civil War prisoners exploded nr. Memphis, TN. Worst maritime disaster in U.S. history	1,700+
1869, Feb. 20—Radetzky	Austrian steam frigate exploded in Adriatic Sea	345
1869, Oct. 27—Stonewall	U.S. steamer burned, Mississippi R. below Cairo, IL	200
1872, Nov. 7—Mary Celeste	U.S. half-brig sailing from New York to Genoa, Italy, found abandoned	Unknown
1873, Jan. 22—Northfleet	British steamer rammed by Spanish steamer *Murillo* off Dungeness, England, UK	300
1873, Apr. 1—Atlantic	British White Star steamer off Halifax, Nova Scotia, Canada	585
1873, Nov. 23—Ville du Havre and Loch Earn	French steamer sank after collision with British sailing ship	226
1874, Nov. 17—Cospatrick	Burned off Auckland, New Zealand	468
1875, May 7—Schiller	German steamer off Isles of Scilly, UK	312
1875, Nov. 4—Pacific	U.S. steamer sank after collision off Cape Flattery, WA	236
1878, Mar. 24—Eurydice	British frigate sank off Isle of Wight, England, UK	398
1878, Sept. 3—Princess Alice	British steamer sank after collision with *Bywell Castle* in Thames R.	700
1878, Dec. 18—Byzantin and Rinaldo	French and British steamers collided in Dardanelles, off Turkey	210
1883, Jan. 19—Cimbria and Sultan	German steamer sank in collision with British steamer in North Sea	389
1887, Nov. 15—Wah Yeung	Chinese steamer burned in Canton R., Hong Kong	400
1890, Feb. 17—Duburg	British steamer wrecked, China Sea	400
1890, Sept. 19—Ertogrul	Turkish frigate off Japan	540
1891, Mar. 17—Utopia and Anson	British steamer sank in collision with British ironclad off Gibraltar	562
1893, June 22—Victoria	British battleship sank after collision with warship *Camperdown*, off Syrian coast	358
1895, Jan. 30—Elbe and Craithie	German steamer sank in collision with British steamer in North Sea	332
1895, Mar. 11—Reina Regenta	Spanish cruiser foundered nr. Gibraltar	400
1898, Feb. 15—USS Maine	Explosion caused battleship to sink in Havana Harbor, Cuba	260
1898, July 4—La Bourgogne and Cromartyshire	French steamer sank in collision with British sailing ship off Nova Scotia, Canada	549
1904, May 15—Yoshino	Japanese cruiser sank after collision with cruiser *Kasuga* in fog off Liao-Tung Peninsula, China	329
1904, June 15—General Slocum	Excursion steamer burned off N. Brother Isl., New York, NY	1,021
1904, June 28—Norge	Danish steamer wrecked on Rockall Isl., Scotland, UK	620
1906, Aug. 4—Sirio	Italian steamer wrecked off Cape Palos, Spain	350
1907, Feb. 11—Larchmont	U.S. steamer sank after collision with U.S. schooner *Harry Knowlton* nr. Block Island, RI	131
1908, Mar. 23—Mutsu Maru	Japanese steamer sank in collision with another steamer nr. Hakodate, Japan	300
1909, Aug. 1—Waratah	British steamer vanished en route from Sydney to London	300
1911, Sept. 25—Liberté	French battleship exploded at Toulon	285
1912, Apr. 14-15—Titanic	British White Star steamer hit iceberg in N Atlantic	1,503
1912, Sept. 28—Kichemaru	Japanese steamer sank off Japan coast	1,000
1914, May 29—Empress of Ireland	Canadian Pacific steamer collided with Norwegian coal transporter *Storstad* in St. Lawrence R., Canada	1,014
1914, Nov. 26—Bulwark	British battleship exploded in Sheerness Harbor, England, UK	788
1915, May 7—Lusitania	British Cunard Line steamer torpedoed and sunk by German submarine off Ireland	1,198
1915, July 24—Eastland	Steamer capsized, Chicago R., IL	844
1916, Feb. 26—Provence	French cruiser sank in Mediterranean; then-worst disaster in maritime history	3,100
1916, Mar. 5—Principe de Asturias	Spanish steamer wrecked nr. Santos, Brazil	558
1917, Dec. 6—Mont Blanc and Imo	French ammunition ship and Belgian steamer collided in Halifax Harbor, Canada	1,600
1918, Apr. 25—Kiang-Kwan	Chinese steamer sank after collision with Chinese gunboat *Chutai* off Hankow, China	500
1918, July 12—Kawachi	Japanese battleship blew up in Tokayama Bay	500
1918, Oct. 25—Princess Sophia	Canadian-Pacific steamer sank off Vanderbilt Reef, Alaska	398
1919, Jan. 17—Chaonia	French steamer lost in Straits of Messina, Italy	460
1919, Sept. 9—Valbanera	Spanish steamer lost off FL coast	500
1920, Jan. 11—Afrique	French liner sank nr. La Rochelle, France	553
1921, Mar. 18—Hong Kong	Chinese steamer wrecked, S China Sea	1,000
1922, Aug. 26—Niitaka	Japanese cruiser sank in storm off Kamchatka, USSR	300
1927, Sept. 20—Gentoku Maru	Japanese steamer capsized in Tsingtao Bay, China	278
1927, Oct. 25—Principessa Mafalda	Italian steamer blew up, sank off Porto Seguro, Brazil	314
1934, Sept. 8—Morro Castle	U.S. steamer en route from Havana to New York, burned off Asbury Park, NJ	134
1940, June 17—Lancastria	Nazi forces sank Cunard liner evacuating British troops from France	2,500-6,000
1940, July 24—Meknes	French liner torpedoed by Nazis in English Channel	350
1942, Feb. 18—USS Truxtun and USS Pollux	Destroyer and cargo ship ran aground, sank off Newfoundland, Canada	204
1942, Oct. 2—Curacao and Queen Mary	British cruiser sank off Ireland after collision with liner carrying U.S. troops	338
1944, Dec. 17-18—Spence, Monaghan, Hull	3 U.S. destroyers sank during typhoon, Philippine Sea	790
1945, Jan. 30—Wilhelm Gustloff	Liner with German refugees, soldiers sunk by Soviet submarine in Baltic	5,000-9,000
1945, Apr. 16—Goya	Cargo ship carrying German refugees, soldiers sunk by Soviet submarine in Baltic	6,000-7,000
1945, May 3—Cap Arcona and Thielbeck	German ocean liner and freighter carrying concentration camp inmates sunk by British warplanes in Lubeck Bay, Germany	7,000-8,000

Date—vessel(s)	Incident	Est. deaths
1947, Jan. 19—Himera	Greek steamer hit mine off Athens, Greece	392
1947, Apr. 16—Grandcamp	Ammonium nitrate explosion aboard French freighter caused fires throughout port, Texas City, TX	576+
1948, Dec. 3—Kiangya	Chinese refugee ship wrecked in explosion S of Shanghai	1,100+
1954, Sept. 26—Toya Maru	Japanese ferry sank, Tsugaru Strait, Japan	1,172
1956, July 26—Andrea Doria and Stockholm	Italian liner and Swedish liner collided off Nantucket Isl., MA	51
1957, July 14—Eshghabad	Soviet fishing boat ran aground in Caspian Sea	270
1961, Apr. 8—Dara	British liner exploded in Persian Gulf	236
1961, July 8—Save	Portuguese ship ran aground off Mozambique	259
1965, Nov. 13—Yarmouth Castle	Cruise ship burned and sank off Nassau, The Bahamas	89
1970, Dec. 15—Namyong-Ho	S. Korean ferry sank in Korea Strait	308
1975, Nov. 10—Edmund Fitzgerald	U.S. cargo ship sank during storm on Lake Superior	29
1980, Apr. 22—Don Juan	Sank off Mindoro Isl., Philippines, after colliding with barge	1,000+
1981, Jan. 27—Tamponas II	Indonesian car ferry caught fire and sank in Java Sea	580
1983, May 25—10th of Ramadan	Nile steamer caught fire and sank in Lake Nasser, Egypt	357
1986, May 25—Shamia	Ferry capsized in storm, Meghna R., Bangladesh	500+
1986, Sept. 1—Admiral Nakhimov and Pyotr Vasev	Soviet cruise ship collided with Soviet freighter in Black Sea	425
1987, Dec. 20—Doña Paz and Victor	Philippine ferry and oil tanker collided in Tablas Strait, Philippines	4,341
1988, Aug. 6	Indian ferry capsized on Ganges R.	400+
1988, Oct. 24—Doña Marilyn	Philippine ferry sank by typhoon near Leyte Isl.	350+
1991, Dec. 14—Salem Express	Ferry rammed coral reef nr. Safaga, Egypt	462
1993, Feb. 17—Neptune	Ferry capsized off Port-au-Prince, Haiti	500+
1993, Oct. 10—Seohae	S. Korean ferry capsized in Yellow Sea during storm	292
1994, Sept. 28—Estonia	Ferry sank in Baltic Sea off Finland	850+
1996, May 21—Bukoba	Overcrowded Tanzanian ferry sank in Lake Victoria	500+
1997, Sept. 8—Pride of la Gonâve	Haitian ferry sank off Montrouis, Haiti	200+
1999, Feb. 6—Harta Rimba	Cargo ship sank off Indonesia	280+
1999, May 1—Miss Majestic	"Duck" boat on tour sank, Lake Hamilton, AR	13
1999, Nov. 24—Dashun	Passenger ferry capsized nr. Yantai, China	280
2000, June 29—Cahaya Bahari	Overloaded ferry carrying refugees from religious strife capsized in storm off Sulawesi Isl., Indonesia	500+
2001, Oct. 19	Fishing boat overloaded with refugees, mainly from Middle East, sank off Indonesia	350+
2002, May 4—Salahuddin-2	Overloaded Bangladesh ferry sank in Meghna R.	300+
2002, Sept. 26—Joola	Overloaded Senegalese ferry capsized in ocean off The Gambia	1,863
2003, July 8—MV-Nasrin 1	Overcrowded ferry sank nr. Chandpur in Bangladesh R.	400
2003, Oct. 15—Andrew J. Barberi	NYC ferry crashed into dock on approach to Staten Island	11
2006, Feb. 3—Al-Salam Boccaccio 98	Ferry caught fire, sank in Red Sea off Egypt	1,000+
2006, Dec. 30—Senopati Nusantara	High waves capsized ferry en route to Java, Indonesia	400+
2007, Nov. 23—Explorer	Canadian cruise ship hit Antarctic iceberg; first commercial passenger ship to sink in region	0
2008, June 23—Princess of the Stars	Philippine ferry capsized during Typhoon *Fengshen* nr. Manila	800
2011, Sept. 10—MV Spice Islander	Overloaded ferry sank off coast of Tanzania	240+
2012, Jan 17—Costa Concordia	Cruise ship ran aground off Italian coast; captain abandoned ship before passengers	32
2013, Oct. 3	Boat carrying migrants fleeing Eritrea sank near Lampedusa Isl., Italy	366
2014, Apr. 16—Sewol	Ferry carrying 476 people sank off Korea's SW coast	304
2015, Feb. 8	Boat carrying migrants from N Africa sank in Mediterranean	329
2015, Apr. 19	Fishing boat overloaded with African migrants capsized off Libyan coast.	800
2015, June 1	Chinese cruise ship sank in Yangtze R. during torrential rains	442
2015, Aug. 6	Vessel carrying migrants capsized in Mediterranean	200+

Some Notable Railroad Disasters Since 1925

Date	Location	Deaths
1925, June 16	Hackettstown, NJ	50
1933, Dec. 23	Lagny-Pomponne, France	230
1937, July 16	Near Patna, India	107
1938, Dec. 25	Near Kishinev, Romania	150
1939, Dec. 22	Near Magdeburg, Germany	132
1943, Sept. 6	Frankford Junction, Philadelphia, PA	79
1943, Dec. 16	Between Rennert and Buie, NC	72
1944, Jan. 16	León Province, Spain	500
1944, Mar. 2	Salerno, Italy	521
1944, Dec. 31	Bagley, UT	50
1945, July 16	Munich, Germany	102
1946, Mar. 20	Aracaju, Mexico	185
1949, Oct. 22	Near Dwor, Poland	200+
1950, Nov. 22	Richmond Hill, NY	79
1951, Feb. 6	Woodbridge, NJ	84
1952, Mar. 4	Near Rio de Janeiro, Brazil	119
1952, July 9	Rzepin, Poland	160
1952, Oct. 8	Harrow, England, UK	112
1953, Dec. 24	Tangiwai, New Zealand	151
1953, Dec. 24	Sakvice, Czechoslovakia	103
1955, Apr. 3	Guadalajara, Mexico	300
1957, Sept. 1	Kendal, Jamaica	178
1957, Sept. 29	Montgomery, W Pakistan	300
1957, Dec. 4	London, England, UK	90
1958, May 8	Rio de Janeiro, Brazil	128
1960, Nov. 14	Pardubice, Czechoslovakia	117
1962, May 3	Tokyo, Japan	163
1963, Nov. 9	Yokohama, Japan	162
1965, Feb. 27	Near Port Sudan, Sudan	124
1970, Feb. 1	Buenos Aires, Argentina	236
1972, June 16	Near Soissons, France	108
1972, Oct. 6	Near Saltillo, Mexico	204

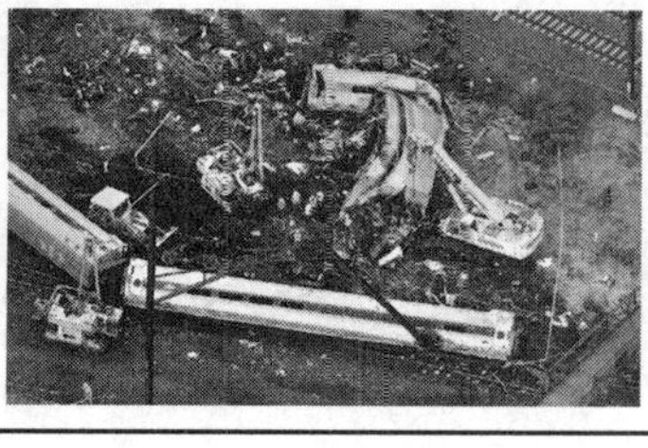

Runaway Train

Date: May 12, 2015. **Location:** Near Philadelphia, PA. **Fatalities:** 8.

Amtrak's Northeast Regional Train No. 188 from Washington to Boston derailed around 9:30 P.M., shortly after departing Philadelphia May 12, 2015. Records show the train was traveling at 106 mph, more than twice the speed limit for the curved section of track. More than 200 people were injured, including the train's engineer, who suffered a concussion and had no memory of the accident. The accident occurred in approximately the same site as a Sept. 6, 1943, derailment that killed 79 people.

Date	Location	Deaths
1974, Aug. 30	Zagreb, Yugoslavia	153
1981, June 6	Near Mansi, India	268
1982, Jan. 27	El Asnam, Algeria	120
1982, July 11	Tepic, Mexico	120
1983, Feb. 19	Empalme, Mexico	100
1985, Jan. 13	Awash, Ethiopia	392
1985, Sept. 12	Viseu, Portugal	118
1986, Aug. 6	Bihar, India	202
1987, July 2	Kasumbalesha Shaba, Zaire	125
1987, Aug. 7	Between Moscow and Rostov, USSR	106
1987, Oct. 19	Jakarta, Indonesia	153
1988, June 4	Arzamas, USSR	100
1988, July 8	Kerala, India	108
1989, Jan. 15	Maizdi Khan, Bangladesh	135
1989, June 4	Ufa, USSR	645
1989, Aug. 11	Sinaloa, Mexico	112
1990, Jan. 4	Sindh Province, Pakistan	307
1991, Mar. 5	Nacala, Mozambique	109
1991, June 8	Ghotki, Pakistan	100
1991, Sept. 5	Pointe-Noire, Congo Republic	110
1993, Jan. 30	Rural Kenya	340
1993, Apr. 25	Near Karachi, Pakistan	150
1994, Sept. 22	Lubango, Angola	300
1994, Dec. 30	Near Namkham, Myanmar	102
1995, Jan. 13	Dinajpur, Bangladesh	150
1995, Aug. 20	Firozabad, India	350
1995, Nov. 28	Baku, Azerbaijan	337
1997, Mar. 3	Punjab Province, Pakistan	128
1997, May 4	Kisangani, Zaire	100+
1998, Feb. 19	Yaounde, Cameroon	120
1998, June 3	Eschede, Germany	102
1998, Nov. 26	Khanna, India	108
1999, Aug. 2	Gauhati, India	285
2002, Feb. 20	S of Cairo, Egypt	377
2002, May 25	Muamba, Mozambique	195
2002, June 24	Igandu, Tanzania	281
2002, Sept. 10	Bihar, India	112
2004, Feb. 18	Neyshabur, NE Iran	300
2004, Apr. 22	Ryongchon, North Korea	161
2005, Apr. 25	Near Amagasaki, Japan	107
2005, July 13	Ghotki, Pakistan	132
2005, Oct. 29	Andra Pradesh, India	110
2007, Aug. 2	Nr. Benaleka, Dem. Rep. of Congo	100
2010, May 28	W. Bengal, India	148
2011, July 23	Wenzhou, China	140

Principal U.S. Mine Disasters Since 1867

Source: Bureau of Mines, U.S. Dept. of the Interior; Office of Mine Safety Health Research, Centers for Disease Control

All are bituminous coal mines unless otherwise noted.

Date	Location	Deaths
1867, Apr. 3	Winterpock, VA	69
1869, Sept. 6	Plymouth, PA	110
1883, Feb. 16	Braidwood, IL	69
1884, Mar. 13	Pocahontas, VA	112
1891, Jan. 27	Mt. Pleasant, PA	109
1892, Jan. 7	Krebs, OK	100
1895, Mar. 20	Red Canyon, WY	62
1900, May 1	Scofield, UT	200
1902, May 19	Coal Creek, TN	184
1902, July 10	Johnstown, PA	112
1903, June 30	Hanna, WY	169
1904, Jan. 25	Cheswick, PA	179
1905, Feb. 20	Virginia City, AL	112
1907, Jan. 29	Stuart, WV	84
1907, Dec. 6	Monongah, WV	362
1907, Dec. 19	Van Meter, PA	239
1908, Nov. 28	Marianna, PA	154
1909, Jan. 12	Switchback, WV	67
1909, Nov. 13	Cherry, IL	259
1910, Jan. 31	Primero, CO	75
1910, May 5	Palos, AL	84
1910, Nov. 8	Delagua, CO	79
1911, Apr. 7	Troop, PA	73
1911, Apr. 8	Littleton, AL	128
1911, Dec. 9	Briceville, TN	84
1912, Mar. 20	McCurtain, OK	73
1912, Mar. 26	Jed, WV	81
1913, Apr. 23	Finleyville, PA	98
1913, Oct. 22	Dawson, NM	263
1914, Apr. 28	Eccles, WV	181
1915, Mar. 2	Layland, WV	115
1917, Apr. 27	Hastings, CO	121
1917, June 8	Butte, MT[1]	163
1917, Aug. 4	Clay, KY	62
1919, June 5	Wilkes-Barre, PA	92
1922, Nov. 6	Spangler, PA	79
1922, Nov. 22	Dolomite, AL	90
1923, Feb. 8	Dawson, NM	120
1923, Aug. 14	Kemmerer, WY	99
1924, Mar. 8	Castle Gate, UT	172
1924, Apr. 28	Benwood, WV	119
1926, Jan. 13	Wilburton, OK	91
1927, Apr. 30	Everettville, WV	97
1928, May 19	Mather, PA	195
1929, Dec. 17	McAlester, OK	61
1930, Nov. 5	Millfield, OH	82
1940, Jan. 10	Bartley, WV	91
1940, Mar. 16	St. Clairsville, OH	72
1940, July 15	Portage, PA	63
1943, Feb. 27	Washoe, MT	74
1944, July 5	Powhatan Pt., OH	66
1947, Mar. 25	Centralia, IL	111
1951, Dec. 21	West Frankfort, IL	119
1968, Nov. 20	Farmington, WV	78
1970, Dec. 30	Hyden, KY	38
1972, Feb. 26	Saunders, WV	114
1972, May 2	Kellogg, ID[2]	91

Note: The world's worst mine disaster killed 1,549 workers in Manchuria, China, Apr. 25, 1942. (1) Copper mine. (2) Silver mine.

Some Notable U.S. Tornadoes Since 1925

Date	Location	Deaths
1925, Mar. 18	MO, IL, IN	747
1927, Apr. 12	Rocksprings, TX	74
1927, May 9	AR; Poplar Bluff, MO	92
1927, Sept. 29	St. Louis, MO	90
1930, May 6	Hill, Navarro, Ellis Cos., TX	41
1932, Mar. 21	Alabama	268
1936, Apr. 5-6	Tupelo, MS; Gainesville, GA	454
1938, Sept. 29	Charleston, SC	32
1942, Mar. 16	Central to NE Mississippi	75
1942, Apr. 27	Rogers and Mayes Cos., OK	52
1944, June 23	OH, PA, WV, MD	150
1945, Apr. 12	OK, AR	102
1947, Apr. 9	TX; Woodward, OK; KS	181
1948, Mar. 19	Bunker Hill and Gillespie, IL	33
1949, Jan. 3	LA, AR	58
1952, Mar. 21-22	AR, MO, TN	208
1953, May 11	Waco, TX	114
1953, June 8	Flint-Beecher, MI; OH	142
1953, June 9	Worcester and vicinity, MA	90
1953, Dec. 5	Vicksburg, MS	38
1955, May 25	Udall, KS; MO; Blackwell, OK; TX	115
1957, May 20	KS, MO	48
1958, June, 4	NW Wisconsin	30
1959, Feb. 10	St. Louis, MO	21
1960, May 5-6	Southeastern OK, AR	30
1962, Mar. 31	Milton, FL	17
1965, Apr. 11	IA, IN, IL, OH, MI, WI	271
1966, Mar. 3	Jackson, MS; AL	57
1967, Apr. 21	IL, MO, IA, MI	33
1968, May 15	Midwest	71
1969, Jan. 23	Mississippi	32
1970, May 11	Lubbock, TX	23
1971, Feb. 21	Mississippi Delta: MS, LA, AR, TN	110
1973, May 26-27	South, Midwest	47
1974, Apr. 3-4	AL; GA; KY; Xenia, OH; other states	315
1977, Apr. 4	AL, MS, GA	22
1979, Apr. 10	TX, OK	60
1984, Mar. 28	NC, SC	57
1985, May 31	NY; PA; OH; Ontario, Can.	75
1987, May 22	Saragosa, TX	30
1989, Nov. 15	Huntsville, AL	18
1990, Aug. 28	Northern IL	25
1991, Apr. 26	KS, OK	23
1992, Nov. 21-23	South, Midwest	26
1994, Mar. 27-28	AL, TN, GA, NC, SC	52
1995, May 6-7	Southern Oklahoma, northern Texas	23
1997, Mar. 1	Central AR	26
1997, May 27	Jarrell, TX	27
1998, Feb. 22-23	Central FL	42
1998, Apr. 8	AL, GA, MS	39
1999, May 3	OK, KS	54
2000, Feb. 14	SW Georgia	22+
2002, Nov. 10-11	AL, MS, TN, IN, OH, PA	36
2003, May 4-11	TN, MO, KS, IL, OK, WV, AL	48
2005, Nov. 6	KY, IN	22
2007, Mar. 1	AL, GA, MO, Midwest	20
2008, Feb. 25	"Super Tuesday"—TN, AR, KY, AL, MO	57
2008, May 10	MS, OK, GA	23
2011, Apr. 14-16	Southeast, Midwest, OK to VA	38
2011, Apr. 25-28	305 funnels from TX to NY	321
2011, May 22	Joplin, MO	161
2012, Mar. 2-3	IL, IN, KY, OH, AL	42
2013, May 20	Moore, OK	24
2013, May 31	El Reno, OK	21

Some Notable Hurricanes, Typhoons, Blizzards, Other Storms

C. = cyclone; H. = hurricane; TS. = tropical storm; T. = typhoon[1].

Date	Location	Est. deaths
1881, Aug. 24-29	H., GA, SC	700
1888, Mar. 11-14	Blizzard, Eastern U.S.	400
1893, Aug. 15-Sept. 2	H., GA, SC	1,000+
1893, Oct. 1	H., LA	1,100+
1900, Sept. 8	H., Galveston, TX	8,000+
1906, Sept. 18	T., Hong Kong	10,000+
1906, Sept. 19-24	H., LA, MS	350
1909, Sept. 20	H., LA	350+
1915, Aug. 16	H., Galveston, TX	275
1915, Sept. 29	H., LA	275
1919, Sept. 6-14	H., Carib., FL Keys, Gulf, TX	600+[2]
1922, July 27	T., Swatow, China	100,000
1926, Sept. 11-22	H., FL, AL, MS	370+
1926, Oct. 20	H., Cuba	600
1928, Sept. 6-20	H., southern FL	2,500+
1930, Sept. 3	H., Dominican Republic	2,000
1935, Aug. 29-Sept. 10	H., "Labor Day Hurricane," Caribbean, SE U.S.	400+
1937, Sept. 2	T., "The Great Typhoon," Hong Kong	10,000+
1938, Sept. 21	H., "Long Isl. Express," NY, New England	682
1940, Nov. 11-12	"Armistice Day Blizzard," NE, Midwest U.S.	154
1942, Oct.	T., W. Sundarbans, Bangladesh	61,000
1942, Oct. 15-16	H., Bengal, India	40,000
1947, Dec. 26	Blizzard, NYC, N Atl. states	55
1952, Oct. 22	T., Philippines	440
1954, Aug. 30	H. Carol, NE U.S.	68
1954, Oct. 5-18	H. Hazel, E Canada, U.S., Haiti	347
1955, Aug. 7-21	H. Diane, Eastern U.S.	400
1955, Sept. 19	H. Hilda, Mexico	200
1956, Feb. 1-29	Blizzard, W Europe	1,000
1957, June 25-30	H. Audrey, TX to AL	390
1958, Feb. 15-16	Blizzard, NE U.S.	171
1959, Sept. 17-19	T. Sarah, Japan, S. Korea	2,000
1959, Sept. 26-27	T. Vera, Honshu, Japan	4,466
1960, Sept. 4-12	H. Donna, Caribbean, E U.S.	148
1961, Oct. 31	H. Hattie, Brit. Honduras	400
1962, Sept. 1	T. Wanda, Hong Kong	130-200
1963, May 28-29	Windstorm, Bangladesh	22,000
1963, Oct. 4-8	H. Flora, Caribbean	6,000
1964, June 30	T. Winnie, N Philippines	107
1964, Sept. 5	T. Ruby, Hong Kong, China	735
1965, May 11-12	Windstorm, Bangladesh	17,000
1965, June 1-2	Windstorm, Bangladesh	30,000
1965, Sept. 7-12	H. Betsy, FL, MS, LA	74
1965, Dec. 15	Windstorm, Bangladesh	10,000
1966, June 4-10	H. Alma, Honduras, SE U.S.	51
1966, Sept. 24-30	H. Inez, Carib., FL, Mexico	293
1967, July 9	T. Billie, SW Japan	347
1967, Sept. 5-23	H. Beulah, Carib., Mex., TX	54
1967, Dec. 12-20	Blizzard, SW U.S.	51
1969, Aug. 17-18	H. Camille, MS, LA	256
1970, Sept. 15	T. Pitang (Georgia), Philippines	300
1970, Oct. 14	T. Sening (Joan), Philippines	583
1970, Oct. 15	T. Titang (Kate), Philippines	526
1970, Nov. 13	C., Bay of Bengal, Bangladesh	300,000
1971, Aug. 1	T. Rose, Hong Kong	130
1972, June 19-29	H. Agnes, FL to NY	118
1972, Dec. 3	T. Theresa, Philippines	169
1973, June-Aug.	Monsoon rains, India	1,217
1974, July 11	T. Gilda, Japan, S. Korea	108
1974, Sept. 19-20	H. Fifi, Honduras	2,000
1975, Sept. 13-27	H. Eloise, Caribbean, NE U.S.	71
1976, May 20	T. Olga, floods, Philippines	215
1976, Sept. 25-Oct. 2	H. Liza, western Mexico	630
1978, Oct. 27	T. Rita, Philippines	400
1979, Aug. 30-Sept. 7	H. David, Caribbean, E U.S.	1,100
1980, Aug. 4-11	H. Allen, Caribbean, TX	272
1981, Nov. 25	T. Irma, Luzon Isl., Philippines	176
1983, June	Monsoon, India	900
1984, Sept. 2	T. Ike, southern Philippines	1,363
1985, May 25	C., Bangladesh	15,000
1985, Oct. 26-Nov. 6	H. Juan, SE U.S.	97
1987, Nov. 25	T. Nina, Philippines	650
1988, Sept. 10-17	H. Gilbert, Carib., Gulf of Mex.	260
1989, Sept. 16-22	H. Hugo, Caribbean, SE U.S.	86
1990, May 6-11	C. (mult.), SE India	450
1991, Apr. 30	C., Bangladesh	139,000
1991, Nov. 5	TS. Thelma, flash floods, central Philippines	7,000+
1992, Aug. 24-26	H. Andrew, Southern FL, LA	65
1993, Mar. 12-14	Blizzard, Eastern U.S.	270+
1993, June	Monsoon, Bangladesh	2,000
1994, Nov. 8-18	TS. Gordon, Caribbean, FL	830
1995, Oct. 2-4	H. Opal, S Mexico, FL, AL	59
1995, Nov. 2-3	T. Angela, Philippines	600+
1996, Jan. 7-8	Blizzard, NE U.S.	100
1996, Aug. 22	Blizzard, Himalayas, N India	239
1996, Aug. 29-Sept. 6	H. Fran, Carib., NC, VA, WV	30
1996, Sept. 9	T. Sally, S China	114
1996, Nov. 6	C., Andhra Pradesh, India	1,000+
1996, Dec. 25	TS. Greg, eastern Malaysia	100+
1997, May 19	C., Bangladesh	108
1997, Aug. 18-21	T. Winnie, Taiwan, E China	140+
1997, Oct. 8-10	H. Pauline, SW Mexico	230
1998, June 9	C., Gujarat, India	1,320
1998, Aug.	Monsoon, Bangladesh	326
1998, Sept. 21-23	H. Georges, Carib., FL, U.S. Gulf	600+
1998, Oct. 27-29	H. Mitch, Honduras, Nicaragua, Guatemala, El Salvador	14,600
1999, Sept. 4-17	H. Floyd, The Bahamas, E seaboard U.S.	56
1999, Oct. 29	C., E India	9,392
1999, Dec. 26-29	Gales, France, Switz., Germany	120
2000, Dec. 27	Winter storm, TX, OK, AR	40+
2001, July 30	T. Toraji, Taiwan	200
2001, Nov. 6-12	T. Lingling, S Philip., Vietnam	220+
2002, Aug.-Sept.	T. Rusa, N. and S. Korea	115+
2003, Feb. 16-17	Blizzard, E seaboard U.S.	59
2003, Sept. 7-19	H. Isabel, NC, VA, E seaboard	40+
2003, Sept. 12	T. Maemi, S. Korea	130
2004, Mar. 7-19	C. Gafilo, Madagascar	198
2004, May 19	C., Myanmar	220
2004, Aug. 12-15	T. Rananim, eastern China	164
2004, Aug. 13-14	H. Charley, FL, SC	36
2004, Sept. 5-6	H. Frances, The Bahamas, FL	35
2004, Sept. 7-16	H. Ivan, Barbados, Grenada, U.S. Gulf Coast	115
2004, Sept. 16-26	H. Jeanne, Dom. Rep., Haiti, FL	1,500+
2005, July 7-11	H. Dennis, Jamaica, Haiti, Cuba, FL	50
2005, Aug. 25-29	H. Katrina, LA, MS, FL, AL, GA	1,833+[3]
2005, Aug. 31-Sept. 1	T. Talim, Taiwan, E China	129+
2005, Sept. 21-24	H. Rita, TX, LA	62[4]
2005, Sept. 21-28	T. Damrey, SE Asia; Philippines; Hainan, China	145
2005, Oct. 4	H. Stan, Central Amer., Mex.	1,000+[5]
2006, Jul. 14	TS. Bilis, SE China	612
2006, Aug. 10	T. Saomai, SE China	295
2006, Nov. 30	T. Durian, Philippines	450-1,000+
2007, June 6-7	C. Gonu, Oman, Iran	54[6]
2007, Nov. 15	C. Sidr, southern Bangladesh	3,363
2008, May 2-3	C. Nargis, southern Myanmar	138,366
2008, June 20-25	T. Fengshen, Philippines, China	233
2008, Aug. 26-Sept. 1	H. Gustav, Haiti, Dom. Rep., U.S.	138
2008, Sept. 1-4	TS. Hanna, Haiti	529
2008, Sept. 7-13	H. Ike, Haiti; Cuba; Galveston, TX	164
2009, May 23-26	C. Alia, India, Bangladesh	260
2009, Aug. 7-9	T. Morakot, mudslides, Taiwan	700+
2009, Sept. 23-30	T. Ketsana, Philippines, Vietnam, Cambodia, Laos	498+
2009, Oct. 3-10	T. Parma, Philippines	375
2009, Oct. 30-Nov. 3	T. Mirinae, Philippines, Vietnam	159+
2010, May 29	TS. Agatha, Guatemala, El Salvador, Honduras	184
2010, July 13-17	T. Conson, Luzon Isl., Philippines	105+
2011, Dec. 16	TS. Washi, Philippines	1,257
2012, Jan. 24-Feb. 14	Blizzard/cold snap, E Europe	650+
2012, Oct. 22-31	H. Sandy, Cuba, Haiti, Jamaica, Eastern U.S.	245[7]
2012, Dec. 4	T. Bopha, Philippines	1,146
2013, Nov. 8	T. Haiyan, Philippines	7,986
2013, Nov. 10	C., Puntland, Somalia	162
2014, July 15	T. Rammasun, Philippines, China, Vietnam	173

(1) What hurricanes are called W of Intl. Date Line and N of equator. (2) Incl. about 500 lost on ships at sea. (3) Official toll as of Aug. 2006 was 1,577 in LA, 238 in MS, 14 in FL, and 2 each in AL and GA. (4) Incl. 55 indirect deaths, among them 20 people, mostly elderly evacuees from a nursing home, whose bus exploded and caught fire outside Dallas. (5) Incl. deaths from floods and landslides generated by heavy rainstorms. (6) First documented super cyclone in Arabian Sea. (7) Includes 87 indirect deaths in the U.S.

Some Notable Floods, Tidal Waves

Source: EM-DAT: The OFDA/CRED Intl. Disaster Database, Université catholique de Louvain, Brussels, Belgium, www.emdat.be; World Almanac research

Date	Location	Est. deaths
1703	Awa, Japan	100,000+
1889, May 31	Johnstown, PA	2,200+
1903, June 15	Heppner, OR	325
1911	Chang Jiang R., China	100,000
1913, Mar. 25-27	OH, IN	732
1915, Aug. 17	Galveston, TX	275
1927, Jan.-July	Mississippi Valley	246+
1927, Nov. 1	Mostagenem, Algeria	3,000
1928, Mar. 13	Dam collapse, Saugus, CA	450
1928, Sept. 16	Lake Okeechobee, FL	1,770+
1931, Aug.	Huang He R., China	3,700,000
1933	Shandong, China	18,000
1937, Jan. 22	OH, MS valleys	250
1939, July	Hunan province, China	500,000
1946, Apr. 1	HI, AK	159
1947, Sept. 20	Honshu Isl., Japan	2,000
1949, July	China	57,000
1949, Oct.	Guatemala	40,000
1950	Pakistan	2,900
1951, Aug. 28	Manchuria	4,800
1953, Jan. 31	Storm surge, Zuiderzee, Netherlands	2,000
1953, June 23	Japan	2,566
1954, Aug.	China	30,000
1954, Aug. 17	Farahzad, Iran	2,000
1955, Oct. 7-12	India, Pakistan	1,700
1959, Nov. 1	Western Mexico	2,000
1959, Dec. 2	Frejus, France	412
1959-61	China	2,000,000
1960, Oct. 10	Bangladesh	6,000
1960, Oct. 31	Bangladesh	4,000
1961, July	N India	2,000
1962, Sept. 27	Barcelona, Spain	445
1963, Oct. 9	Dam collapse, Vaiont, Italy	1,800
1967, Jan. 18-24	Eastern Brazil	894
1967, Mar. 19	Rio de Janeiro, Brazil	436
1967, Nov. 26	Lisbon, Portugal	464
1968, July	Rajasthan, Gujarat states, India	4,892
1968, Oct. 7	NE India	780
1969, Jan. 18-26	Southern CA	100
1969, Aug. 20-22	Western VA	189
1969, Oct. 1-8	Tunisia	500
1970, July 22	Himalayas, India	500
1972, Feb. 26	Buffalo Creek, WV	118
1972, June 9	Rapid City, SD	238
1972, Aug. 7	Luzon Isl., Philippines	454
1972, Aug. 19-31	Pakistan	1,500
1974, Mar. 29	Tubaro, Brazil	1,000
1974, July	Bangladesh	28,700
1974, Aug. 12	Monty-Long, Bangladesh	2,500
1976, July 31	Big Thompson Canyon, CO	140
1978, July	N, NE India	3,800
1979, July 17	Lomblem Isl., Indonesia	539
1979, Aug. 11	Morvi, India	15,000
1980, June	Sichuan, China	6,200
1981, Apr.	N China	550
1981, July	Sichuan, Hubei Prov., China	1,300
1982, Jan. 23	Near Lima, Peru	600
1982, May 12	Guangdong, China	430
1982, Sept. 17-21	El Salvador, Guatemala	1,300+
1984, Aug.-Sept.	South Korea	200+
1987, July 22	Bangladesh	2,055
1987, Aug.-Sept.	Northern Bangladesh	1,000+
1988, June-Sept.	Bangladesh	2,379
1988, Sept.	N India	1,000+
1989, July 14	China	2,000
1994, May-Oct.	Assam, India	2,001
1995, July	NE China	1,200
1995, Sept. 1-20	India	1,479
1996, June-July	Guizhou, Hebei, China	2,775
1997, Oct.-Nov.	Somalia	2,311
1998, July 17	Papua New Guinea	3,000
1998, July-Aug.	Hunan, Sichuan, China	3,656
1998, July-Sept.	Bangladesh	1,441
1998, Aug.	India	1,811
1999, Oct.-Dec.	Central Vietnam	700+
1999, Dec. 15-20	NW Venezuela	30,000
2000, Feb.-Mar.	Mozambique	700
2000, Sept. 19-30	India, Bangladesh	1,000+
2001, Aug. 1-6	Taiwan	100+
2001, Nov. 9-10	Northern Algeria	711+
2002, Apr.-Aug.	China	800+
2002, July-Aug.	India, Nepal, Bangladesh	1,100+
2004, May 23-Jun. 1	Dom. Republic, Haiti	2,665
2004, June-Sept.	Bangladesh, India, Myanmar, Nepal	2,000+
2004, June-Sept.	China	500
2004, Nov.-Dec.	Philippines	1,060+
2004, Dec. 26	Indian Ocean nations	227,898
2005, July 26-Aug. 5	Western Maharashtra state, India	1,200
2006, Feb. 17	Leyte Isl., Philippines	1,000
2006, July 17	S of Java, Indonesia	530+
2007, July 21-Aug. 3	Bangladesh	1,110
2007, July-Sept.	India	1,103
2008, June-July	India	1,063
2009, July-Sept.	India	992
2010, May-Aug.	China	1,691
2010, June 13-24	Cenxi, China	377+
2010, July-Aug.	Pakistan	1,985
2010, Aug. 1-4	Zhouqu County, China	1,500+
2011, Jan. 11-12	SE Brazil	900
2011, Mar. 11	NE Japan	20,896
2011, Apr.-May	Northern Colombia	425+
2011, July-Dec.	Thailand	708+
2011, July-Dec.	Philippines, Cambodia, Myanmar	2,000+
2012, July-Oct.	Nigeria	363
2012, Aug.-Oct.	Pakistan	480
2012, Sept.-Oct.	Nigeria	431
2013, June	Uttarakhand, India	6,054

Shaken Nepal

Date: Apr. 25 and May 12, 2015. **Location:** Nepal. **Fatalities:** 8,669+.

Two major earthquakes, registering 7.8 and 7.3 on the Richter scale, devastated Nepal in the spring of 2015, killing nearly 9,000 people and destroying more than a half-million homes, leaving millions without shelter. Hundreds of aftershocks in the remote, mountainous terrain of the first epicenter of Gorkha hampered rescue and relief efforts. The Gorkha quake set off avalanches, with one in the Langtang Valley killing as many as 250 and another on Mt. Everest that killed at least 19 people. The quakes also damaged hundreds of historic monuments, including some UNESCO World Heritage sites.

Some Major Earthquakes

Source: Global Volcanism Network, Smithsonian Institution; U.S. Geological Survey, U.S. Dept. of the Interior; World Almanac research
Magnitude of earthquakes (mag.) is a relative measurement of an earthquake's energy. Deaths include those in aftershocks or related events.

Date	Location	Deaths	Mag.
526, May 20	Antioch, Syria	250,000	NA
856	Corinth, Greece	45,000	NA
856, Dec. 22	Damghan, Iran	200,000	NA
893, Mar. 23	Ardabil, Iran	150,000	NA
1057	Chihli, China	25,000	NA
1138, Aug. 9	Aleppo, Syria	230,000	NA
1169, Feb. 11	Nr. Mt. Etna, Sicily	15,000	NA[1]
1268	Silicia, Asia Minor	60,000	NA
1290, Sept. 27	Chihli, China	100,000	NA
1293, May 20	Kamakura, Japan	30,000	NA
1531, Jan. 26	Lisbon, Portugal	30,000	NA
1556, Jan. 24	Shaanxi, China	830,000	NA
1667, Nov.	Shemakha, Caucasia (now Azerbaijan)	80,000	NA
1693, Jan. 11	Catania, Italy	60,000	NA
1737, Oct. 11	India, Calcutta	300,000	NA
1755, June 7	N Persia (current-day Iran)	40,000	NA
1755, Nov. 1	Lisbon, Portugal	60,000	8.75[2]
1783, Feb. 4	Calabria, Italy	30,000	NA
1797, Feb. 4	Quito, Ecuador	41,000	NA
1822, Sept. 5	Asia Minor, Aleppo	22,000	NA
1828, Dec. 28	Echigo, Japan	30,000	NA
1868, Aug. 13-15	Peru, Ecuador	40,000	NA
1875, May 16	Venezuela, Colombia	16,000	NA
1886, Aug. 31	Charleston, SC	60	6.6
1896, June 15	Sanriku, Japan (tsunami)	27,120	8.5
1902, Apr. 19	Quezaltenango and San Marcos, Guatemala	2,000	7.5
1902, Dec. 16	Uzbekistan, Russia	4,700	6.4
1903, Apr. 28	Malazgirt, Turkey	3,500	7.0
1905, Apr. 4	Kangra, India	19,000	7.5
1906, Jan. 31	Off coast of Esmeraldas, Ecuador	1,000	8.8
1906, Mar. 16	Chia-i, Taiwan	1,250	6.8
1906, Apr. 18-19	San Francisco, CA	3,000+	7.7[3]
1906, Aug. 17	Valparaiso, Chile	3,882	8.6
1907, Oct. 21	Central Asia	12,000	8.1
1908, Dec. 28	Messina, Italy	72,000	7.2
1909, Jan. 23	Silakhor, Iran	5,000-6,000	7.3
1912, Aug. 9	Murefte, Turkey	2,800	7.4
1914, Oct. 3	Burdur, Turkey	4,000	7.0
1915, Jan. 13	Avezzano, Italy	32,610	7.0
1917, July 30	Yunnan prov., China	1,800	7.5
1920, Dec. 16	Gansu, China	200,000	7.8[4]
1923, Mar. 24	Sichuan, China	3,500	7.3
1923, Mar. 25	Torbat-e Heydariyeh, Iran	2,200	5.7
1923, Sept. 1	Yokohama, Japan	142,800	7.9
1925, Mar. 16	Yunnan prov., China	5,800	7.0
1927, Mar. 7	Tango, Japan	3,020	7.6
1927, May 22	Gansu, China	40,900	7.6
1929, May 1	Koppeh Dagh, Iran	3,800	7.2
1930, May 6	Salmas, Iran	2,500	7.2
1930, July 23	Irpinia, Italy	1,404	6.5
1931, Mar. 31	Managua, Nicaragua	2,500	6.0
1931, Apr. 27	Armenia-Azerbaijan border	2,800	5.7
1931, Aug. 10	Xinjiang, China	10,000	8.0
1933, Mar. 2	Sanriku, Japan (tsunami)	2,990	8.4
1933, Mar. 10	Long Beach, CA	115	6.2
1933, Aug. 25	Sichuan, China	9,300	7.5
1934, Jan. 15	Bihar, India-Nepal	10,700	8.1
1935, Apr. 21	Miao-li, Taiwan	3,270	7.1
1935, May 30	Quetta, Pakistan	30,000	7.6
1939, Jan. 25	Chillan, Chile	28,000	7.8
1939, Dec. 26	Erzincan, Turkey	32,700	7.8
1943, Sept. 10	Tottori, Japan	1,190	7.4
1943, Nov. 26	Ladik, Turkey	4,000	7.6
1944, Jan. 15	San Juan, Argentina	8,000	7.4
1944, Feb. 1	Gerede, Turkey	2,790	7.4
1945, Jan. 12	Mikawa, Japan	1,961	7.1
1945, Nov. 27	Makran Coast, Pakistan	4,000	8.0
1946, May 31	Ustukran, Turkey	1,300	5.9
1946, Nov. 10	Ancash, Peru	1,400	7.3
1946, Dec. 20	Honshu, Japan	1,362	8.1
1948, June 28	Fukui, Japan	3,769	7.3
1948, Oct. 5	Ashgabat, Turkmenistan	110,000	7.3
1949, July 10	Khait, Tajikistan	12,000	7.5
1949, Aug. 5	Pelileo, Ecuador	5,050	6.8
1950, Aug. 15	Assam, India	1,526	8.6
1954, Sept. 9	Orleansville, Algeria	1,250	6.8
1956, June 10-17	Northern Afghanistan	2,000	7.7
1957, July 2	Northern Iran	1,200	7.1
1960, Feb. 29	Agadir, Morocco	12,000	5.7
1960, May 21-30	Southern Chile	1,655	9.5[5]
1962, Sept. 1	NW Iran	12,255	7.1
1964, Mar. 27	Prince Wm. Sound, AK.	131	9.2[6]
1966, Aug. 19	Eastern Turkey	2,529	6.8
1968, Aug. 31	NE Iran	12,000	7.3
1969, July 25	Guangdong, China	3,000	5.9
1970, Jan. 5	Yunnan Prov., China	10,000	7.5
1970, May 31	Chimbote, Peru	70,000	7.9
1971, Feb. 9	San Fernando Valley, CA	65	6.6
1972, Apr. 10	Southern Iran	5,054	7.1
1972, Dec. 23	Managua, Nicaragua	5,000	6.2
1974, May 10	China	20,000	6.8
1974, Dec. 28	Northern Pakistan	5,300	6.2
1975, Feb. 4	Haicheng, China	2,000	7.0
1975, Sept. 6	Eastern Turkey	2,300	6.7
1976, Feb. 4	Guatemala	23,000	7.5
1976, May 6	NE Italy	1,000	6.5
1976, June 25	Irian Jaya, New Guinea	422	7.1
1976, July 28	Tangshan, China	242,769	7.5
1976, Aug. 16	Mindanao, Philippines	8,000	7.9
1976, Nov. 24	NW Iran-Turkey border	5,000	7.3
1977, Mar. 4	Romania	1,500	7.2
1978, Sept. 16	NE Iran	15,000	7.8
1980, Oct. 10	NW Algeria	5,000	7.7
1980, Nov. 23	Southern Italy	2,735	6.5
1981, June 11	Southern Iran	3,000	6.9
1981, July 28	Southern Iran	1,500	7.3
1982, Dec. 13	W Arabian Peninsula	2,800	6.0
1983, Oct. 30	Eastern Turkey	1,342	6.9
1985, Sept. 19	Michoacan, Mexico	9,500	8.0
1986, Oct. 10	El Salvador	1,000+	5.5
1987, Mar. 6	Colombia-Ecuador	1,000	7.0
1988, Aug. 20	India-Nepal border	1,000	6.8
1988, Dec. 7	Spitak, Armenia	25,000	6.8
1989, Oct. 17	San Francisco Bay area, CA	63	6.9
1990, June 20	Western Iran	40,000+	7.4
1990, July 16	Luzon, Philippines	1,621	7.7
1991, Feb. 1	Pakistan-Afgh. border	1,200	6.8
1991, Oct. 19	Northern India	2,000	7.0
1992, Dec. 12	Flores Isl., Indonesia	2,500	7.5
1993, Sept. 30	Maharashtra, S India	9,748	6.2
1994, Jan. 17	Northridge, CA	61	6.8
1994, June 6	Cauca, SW Colombia	1,000	6.8
1995, Jan. 16	Kobe, Japan	5,502	6.9
1995, May 27	Sakhalin Isl., Russia	1,989	7.5
1997, Feb. 28	NW Iran	1,000+	6.1
1997, May 10	Northern Iran	1,567	7.3
1998, Feb. 4, 8	Hindu Kush, Afghanistan	2,323	5.9
1998, May 30	Afghanistan-Tajikistan border	4,000+	6.6
1998, July 17	Papua New Guinea	2,183	7.0
1999, Jan. 25	Armenia, Colombia	1,185+	6.1
1999, Aug. 17	Izmit, western Turkey	17,118+	7.6
1999, Sept. 20	Taichung, Taiwan	2,400	7.6
2001, Jan. 26	Gujarat, India	20,085	7.6
2002, Mar. 25-26	Hindu Kush, Afghanistan	1,000+	6.1
2003, May 21	Northern Algeria	2,266	6.8
2003, Dec. 26	Bam, SE Iran	31,000	6.6
2004, Dec. 26	Sumatra-Andaman Isls., Indonesia	227,898	9.1[7]
2005, Mar. 28	N Sumatra, Indonesia	1,313	8.6
2005, Oct. 8	Kashmir, Pakistan, India	86,000	7.6
2006, May 26	Java, Indonesia	5,749	6.3
2008, May 12	E Sichuan Prov., China	87,857	7.9
2009, Sept. 30	Sumatra, Indonesia	1,117	7.5
2010, Jan. 12	Haiti	316,000	7.0
2010, Apr. 13	Southern Qinghai, China	2,698+	6.9
2011, Mar. 11	NE Japan	20,896	9.0[8]
2015, Apr. 25	Nepal	8,669+	7.8

NA = Not available. (1) Once thought to have been a volcanic eruption; evidence indicates a destructive earthquake and tsunami occurred on this date. (2) This earthquake caused the most deadly tsunami to date in the Atlantic Ocean. (3) Incl. deaths from resulting fires; revised estimates of magnitude range from 7.7 to 7.9. (4) Commonly referred to as the Gansu quake; actually located within the Ningxia autonomous region. (5) The largest recorded earthquake; caused a deadly tsunami that spread across the Pacific Ocean as far as Japan. (6) The "Good Friday" earthquake sent a tsunami that hit British Columbia, Canada, and the U.S. Pacific coast. (7) This undersea earthquake triggered devastating Indian Ocean tsunamis. (8) The most powerful earthquake in Japan's history set off a tsunami that inundated much of the coast and caused a partial meltdown of the Fukushima nuclear power plant.

Some Notable Fires Since 1918

See also Some Notable Explosions Since 1920.

Date	Location	Deaths
1918, Oct. 12	Cloquet-Moose Lake, MN	453
1922, Oct. 4-5	Wind-blown fire, Haileybury, ON, Canada	43
1929, May 10	Forest fire, Xochilapa, Mexico	60
1930, Apr. 21	Penitentiary, Columbus, OH	320
1931, July 24	Home for aged, Pittsburgh, PA	48
1934, Dec. 11	Hotel Kerns, Lansing, MI	34
1938, May 16	Terminal Hotel, Atlanta, GA	35
1940, Apr. 23	Nightclub, Natchez, MS	198
1942, Nov. 28	Cocoanut Grove Nightclub, Boston, MA	492
1942, Dec. 12	Hostel, St. John's, NL, Canada	100
1943, Sept. 7	Gulf Hotel, Houston, TX	55
1944, July 6	Ringling Circus, Hartford, CT	168
1946, June 5	LaSalle Hotel, Chicago, IL	61
1946, Dec. 7	Winecoff Hotel, Atlanta, GA	119
1946, Dec. 12	Ice plant, tenement, New York, NY	37
1949, Apr. 5	Hospital, Effingham, IL	77
1949, Aug.	Forest fire, Landes, France	80
1950, Jan. 7	Mercy Hospital, Davenport, IA	41
1953, Mar. 29	Nursing home, Largo, FL	35
1953, Apr. 16	Metalworking plant, Chicago, IL	35
1957, Feb. 17	Home for aged, Warrenton, MO	72
1958, Mar. 19	Loft building, New York, NY	24
1958, Dec. 1	Parochial school, Chicago, IL	95
1958, Dec. 16	Store, Bogotá, Colombia	83
1960, Mar. 12	Chemical plant, Pusan, Korea	68
1960, July 14	Mental hospital, Guatemala City	225
1960, Nov. 13	Movie theater, Amude, Syria	152
1960, Dec. 19	USS *Constellation*, Brooklyn, NY	49
1961, Jan. 6	Thomas Hotel, San Francisco, CA	20
1961, Dec. 17	Circus, Niteroi, Brazil	323
1963, May 4	Theater, Diourbel, Senegal	64
1963, Nov. 18	Surfside Hotel, Atlantic City, NJ	25
1963, Nov. 23	Nursing home, Fitchville, OH	63
1963, Dec. 29	Roosevelt Hotel, Jacksonville, FL	22
1964, Dec. 18	Nursing home, Fountaintown, IN	20
1965, Aug. 11-16	Watts riot fires, Los Angeles, CA	30+
1966, Dec. 7	Barracks, Erzurum, Turkey	68
1967, Feb. 7	Restaurant, Montgomery, AL	25
1967, Feb. 7	Scrub fire, Hobart, Tasmania, Australia	62
1967, May 22	Dept. store, Brussels, Belgium	322
1967, July 16	State prison, Jay, FL	37
1967, July 29	USS *Forrestal*, off N Vietnam	134
1968, May 11	Wedding hall, Vijayawada, India	58
1969, Dec. 2	Nursing home, Notre Dame, QC, Canada	54
1970, Jan. 9	Nursing home, Marietta, OH	27
1970, Nov. 1	Dance hall, Grenoble, France	145
1970, Dec. 20	Hotel, Tucson, AZ	28
1971, Dec. 25	Hotel, Seoul, S. Korea	162
1972, May 13	Nightclub, Osaka, Japan	116
1972, July 5	Hospital, Sherborne, England, UK	30
1973, June 24	Bar, New Orleans, LA	32
1973, Aug. 3	Amusement park, Isle of Man, UK	51
1973, Nov. 29	Dept. store, Kumamoto, Japan	107
1973, Dec. 2	Theater, Seoul, S. Korea	50
1974, Feb. 1	Bank building, São Paulo, Brazil	189
1974, June 30	Discotheque, Port Chester, NY	24
1974, Nov. 3	Hotel, disco, Seoul, S. Korea	88
1975, Dec. 12	Tent city, Mina, Saudi Arabia	138
1976, Oct. 24	Social club, Bronx, NY	25
1977, Feb. 25	Rossiya Hotel, Moscow, Russia	45
1977, May 28	Nightclub, Southgate, KY	164
1977, June 9	Nightclub, Abidjan, Ivory Coast	41
1977, June 26	Jail, Columbia, TN	42
1977, Nov. 14	Hotel, Manila, Philippines	47
1978, Aug. 19	Movie theater, Abadan, Iran	425+
1979, July 14	Hotel, Saragossa, Spain	80
1979, Dec. 31	Social club, Chapais, QC, Can.	42
1980, May 20	Nursing home, Kingston, Jamaica	157
1980, Nov. 21	MGM Grand Hotel, Las Vegas, NV	84
1980, Dec. 4	Stouffer Inn, Harrison, NY	26
1981, Jan. 9	Boarding home, Keansburg, NJ	30
1981, Feb. 14	Discotheque, Dublin, Ireland	44
1982, Nov. 8	County jail, Biloxi, MS	29
1983, Feb. 13	Movie theater, Turin, Italy	64
1983, Feb. 16	"Ash Wednesday" bushfires, S Australia	75
1983, Dec. 17	Discotheque, Madrid, Spain	83
1984, May 11	Great Adventure Amusement Park, Jackson Twp., NJ	8
1985, Apr. 21	Movie theaters, Tabaco, Philippines	44
1985, Apr. 26	Hospital, Buenos Aires, Argentina	79
1985, May 11	Soccer stadium, Bradford, Eng., UK	53
1985, May 13	MOVE headquarters, row houses, Philadelphia, PA	11
1986, Dec. 31	Dupont Plaza Hotel, Puerto Rico	96
1987, May 6-June 2	Forest fire, Mohe, China	191
1987, Nov. 17	Subway, London, England	30
1988, Mar. 20	About 2,000 buildings, Lashio, Myan.	134
1990, Mar. 25	Social club, Bronx, NY	87
1991, Mar. 3	Munitions dump, Addis Ababa, Ethiopia	260+
1991, Aug-Oct.	Wildfires, Sumatra, Borneo, Indonesia	57
1991, Sept. 3	Processing plant, Hamlet, NC	25
1991, Oct. 20-21	Wildfire, Oakland, Berkeley, CA	24
1992, Mar.	Forest fire, Terai, Nepal	56
1993, Apr. 19	Cult compound, Waco, TX	72
1994, May 10	Toy factory, Bangkok, Thailand	213
1994, July 4-10	South Canyon fire, Glenwood Springs, CO	14
1994, Nov. 2	Burning fuel flood, Durunka, Egypt	500
1994, Dec. 10	Theater, Karamay, China	300
1995, Oct. 28	Subway train, Baku, Azerbaijan	300
1995, Dec. 23	School, Mandi Dabwali, India	500+
1996, Mar. 19	Nightclub, Quezon City, Philippines	150+
1996, Mar. 28	Shopping mall, Bogor, Indonesia	78
1996, Nov. 20	Garley Building, Hong Kong	39
1997, Feb. 23	Worship site, Baripada, India	164
1997, Apr. 15	Encampment, Mina, Saudi Arabia	343
1997, June 7	Temple, Thanjavur, India	60+
1997, June 13	Movie theater, New Delhi, India	60
1997, July 11	Hotel, Pattaya, Thailand	90
1997, Sept.-Nov.	Drought-fueled fire, Sumatra, Indonesia	240
1998, Apr.-June	Wildfire, Oaxaca, Mexico	50
1998, Dec. 3	Orphanage, Manila, Philippines	28
1999, Mar. 24	Mt. Blanc Tunnel, France, Italy	40
1999, Oct. 30	Karaoke salon, Inchon, S. Korea	55+
2000, Mar. 17	Church, Kanungu, Uganda	530
2000, Nov. 11	Cable car, Kaprun, Austria	155
2000, Dec. 25	Shopping center, Luoyang, China	309
2001, Mar. 26	School, Machakos, Kenya	64
2001, Aug. 18	Hotel, Quezon City, Philippines	73
2001, Sept. 1	Nightclub, Tokyo, Japan	44
2001, Dec. 29	Fireworks accident, Lima, Peru	291
2003, Feb. 18	Subway train, Taegu, S. Korea	198
2003, Feb. 20	Pyrotechnics in nightclub, Warwick, RI	100
2003, Sept. 15	Prison, Riyadh, Saudi Arabia	94
2003, Nov. 24	Students' hostel, Moscow, Russia	36
2004, May 17	Prison, San Pedro Sula, Honduras	104
2004, July 16	Pvt. school, Kumbakonam, India	80+
2004, Aug. 1	Market, Asunción, Paraguay	400+
2004, Dec. 30	Club, Buenos Aires, Argentina	194
2005, Feb. 14	Mosque, Tehran, Iran	59
2005, Mar. 7	Prison, Higuey, Dom. Republic	159
2005, Sept. 5	Theater, Beni Suef, Egypt	32
2006, Dec. 9	Drug treatment center, Moscow, Russ.	45
2007, Mar. 20	Nursing home Kamyshevatskaya, Russia	62
2007, Aug. 24-Sept. 2	Wildfires (arson), Greece	67
2008, Apr. 26	Factory fire, Casablanca, Morocco	55
2008, Sept.	Wildfires, Mozambique, S. Africa, Swaziland	89
2009, Jan. 1	Nightclub fire, Bangkok, Thailand	67
2009, Jan.-Feb.	Wildfires (arson), Victoria, Australia	173
2010, July	Bushfires, Nizhiny Novgorod, Russia	53
2010, Dec. 2-5	Grassland fire, Israel	44
2012, Feb. 14	Prison fire, Comayagua, Honduras	360+
2013, Jan. 27	Pyrotechnics in nightclub, Santa Maria, Brazil	241
2013, June 30	Wildfire, Prescott, AZ	19
2014, May 2	Trade union building, Odessa, Ukraine	40+
2015, Apr. 12	Forest fires, Siberia, Russia	30

Some Notable Explosions Since 1920

See also Principal U.S. Mine Disasters Since 1867. Some bombings related to political conflicts and terrorism are not included.

Date	Location	Deaths
1920, Sept. 16	Wall Street, New York, NY	30
1921, Sept. 21	Chem. storage facility, Oppau, Ger.	561
1924, Jan. 3	Food plant, Pekin, IL	42
1927, May 18	School bombing, Bath, MI	45
1928, Apr. 13	Dance hall, West Plains, MO	40
1937, Mar. 18	School, New London, TX	311
1940, Sept. 12	Hercules Powder factory, Kenvil, NJ	55
1942, June 5	Ordnance plant, Elwood, IL	49
1944, Apr. 14	Harbor, Bombay, India	700
1944, July 17	Munitions ships, depot, Port Chicago, CA	322
1944, Oct. 20	Liquid natural gas tanks, Cleveland, OH	130
1947, Apr. 16	Freighter, chemical co. plant, Texas City, TX	576
1948, July 28	Farben works, Ludwigshafen, Ger.	184
1950, May 19	Munitions barges, S. Amboy, NJ	30
1954, May 26	USS *Bennington*, off RI	103
1956, Aug. 7	Dynamite trucks, Cali, Colombia	1,100
1958, Apr. 18	Sunken munitions ship, Okinawa, Japan	40
1959, Apr. 10	WWII bomb, Philippines	38
1959, June 28	Rail tank cars, Meldrim, GA	25
1959, Aug. 7	Truck filled with explosives, Roseburg, OR	14
1959, Nov. 2	Explosives, Jamuri Bazar, India	46
1959, Dec. 13	2 apt. bldgs., Dortmund, Ger.	26
1960, Mar. 4	Belgian munitions ship, Havana, Cuba	100
1962, Oct. 3	New York Telephone Co. office, New York, NY	23
1963, Jan. 2	Packing plant, Terre Haute, IN	17
1963, Mar. 9	Dynamite plant, S. Africa	45
1963, Aug. 13	Explosives dump, Gauhaiti, India	32
1963, Oct. 31	State Fair Coliseum, Indianapolis, IN	73
1964, July 23	Harbor munitions, Bone, Algeria	100
1965, Aug. 9	Missile silo, Searcy, AR	53
1965, Oct. 21	Bridge, Tila Bund, Pakistan	80
1965, Nov. 24	Armory, Keokuk, IA	20
1967, Dec. 25	Apartment bldg., Moscow, USSR	20
1968, Apr. 6	Sports store, Richmond, IN	43
1969, Mar. 31	Coal mine, nr. Barroteran, Mexico	180
1970, Apr. 8	Subway construction, Osaka, Japan	73
1971, June 24	Tunnel under construction, Sylmar, CA	17
1973, Feb., 10	Liquid gas tank, Staten Island, NY	40
1975, Dec. 27	Coal mine, Chasnala, India	431
1976, Apr. 13	Munitions works, Lapua, Finland	40
1977, Nov. 11	Freight train, Iri, S. Korea	57
1977, Dec. 22	Grain elevator, Westwego, LA	35
1978, July 11	Propylene tank truck, Tarragona, Spain	150
1980, Oct. 23	School, Ortuella, Spain	64
1982, Apr. 25	Antiques exhibition, Todi, Italy	33
1982, Nov. 2	Salang Tunnel, Afghanistan	1,000+
1984, Feb. 25	Oil pipeline, Cubatao, Brazil	508
1984, June 21	Naval supply depot, Severomorsk, USSR	200+
1984, Nov. 19	Gas storage area, NE Mexico City	334
1984, Dec. 3	Chemical plant, Bhopal, India	3,849
1984, Dec. 5	Coal mine, Taipei, Taiwan	94
1985, June 25	Fireworks factory, Hallett, OK	21
1988, Apr. 10	Army ammunitions dump nr. Rawalpindi and Islamabad, Pakistan	100
1988, July 6	Oil rig, North Sea off NE Scotland, UK	167
1989, June 3	Gas pipeline, between Ufa, Asha, USSR	650+
1992, Mar. 3	Coal mine, Kozlu, Turkey	270+
1992, Apr. 22	Gas leak in sewers, Guadalajara, Mexico	200+
1992, May 9	Coal mine, Plymouth, Nova Scotia, Can.	26
1993, Feb. 26	World Trade Center, New York, NY	6
1994, July 18	Jewish community center, Buenos Aires, Argentina	100
1995, Apr. 19	Fed. office building, Oklahoma City, OK	168
1995, Apr. 29	Subway construction, S. Korea	110
1996, Jan. 31	Bank, Colombo, Sri Lanka	53
1996, Mar. 3-4	Jerusalem and Tel Aviv, Israel	33
1996, June 25	U.S. military housing complex, nr. Dhahran, Saudi Arabia	19
1996, July 24	Train, Colombo, Sri Lanka	86
1996, Nov. 16	Military apt., Dagestan region, Russia	68
1996, Nov. 21	Propane gas leak in building, San Juan, Puerto Rico	33
1996, Nov. 27	Coal mine, Shanxi Prov., China	91+
1996, Dec. 30	Train, Assam, India	59+
1997, Dec. 2	Coal mine, Novokuznetsk, Russia	68
1998, Feb. 14	2 oil tankers, Yaounde, Cameroon	120
1998, Feb. 14	17 bombs, Coimbatore, India	50
1998, Apr. 4	Coal mine, Donetsk, Ukraine	63
1998, Aug. 7	Bomb, U.S. emb., Nairobi, Kenya	213
1998, Aug. 7	Bomb, U.S. emb., Dar-es-Salaam, Tanzania	11
1998, Sept. 8	2 buses, São Paulo, Brazil	59
1998, Oct. 17	Oil pipeline, Jesse, Nigeria	700+
1999, May 16	Fuel truck, Punjab Prov., Pakistan	75
1999, Sept. 10	Apartment building, Moscow, Russia	94
1999, Sept. 13	Apartment building, Moscow, Russia	118
1999, Sept. 16	Apartment building, Moscow, Russia	18
1999, Sept. 26	Fireworks factory, Celaya, Mexico	56
2000, Feb. 25	Bombs on 2 buses, Ozamis, Philippines	41
2000, Mar. 11	Coal mine, Krasnodon, Ukraine	80
2000, Apr. 16	Airport hangar, Dem. Rep. of Congo	100+
2000, July 16	Oil pipeline, Warri, Nigeria	30
2000, Sept. 9	Truck explosion, Urumqi, China	60
2000, Oct. 12	USS *Cole*, Yemen	17
2001, Mar. 6	School, Jianxi Prov., China	41
2001, Apr. 21	Coal mine, Shaanxi, China	51
2001, June 1	Dance club, Tel Aviv, Israel	21
2001, July 17	Coal mine, Guanxi, China	76+
2001, Aug. 19	Coal mine, Donetsk region, Ukraine	52
2001, Sept. 21	Chem. plant, Toulouse, France	29
2002, Jan. 21	Volcanic lava caused gas station blast, Goma, Dem. Rep. of Congo	50+
2002, Jan. 27	Munitions dump, Lagos, Nigeria	1,000+
2002, May 9	Land mine at parade, Kaspiisk, Russia	34+
2002, June 14	Car bomb outside U.S. consulate, Karachi, Pakistan	12
2002, June 18	Bomb on bus, Jerusalem, Israel	20
2002, July 5	Bomb in market, Larba, Algeria	35+
2002, Aug. 9	Explosion, Jalalabad, Afghanistan	25+
2002, Sept. 5	Car bomb, Kabul, Afghanistan	30
2002, Oct. 12	Nightclub bombings, Bali, Indonesia	202
2003, Aug. 25	Bombs in 2 taxis, Mumbai, India	52
2003, Dec. 5	Bomb on train, Yessentuki, Russia	45
2003, Dec. 23	Gas well explosion, Chongqing, China	233
2004, Jan. 19	Natural gas facility, Skikda, Algeria	27
2004, Feb. 6	Bomb on subway car, Moscow, Russia	39
2004, Mar. 11	Bombs on commuter trains, Madrid, Spain	191
2005, Feb. 14	Coal mine, NE China	214
2005, Mar. 23	Oil refinery, Texas City, TX	15
2005, May 2	Arms cache, Baghlan Prov., Afghan.	34+
2005, July 7	Bombs in mass transit, London, Eng., UK	56
2005, Oct. 1	Bombings of restaurants, Bali, Indonesia	26
2005, Nov. 27	Coal mine, NE China	161+
2006, May 12	Oil pipeline, nr. Lagos, Nigeria	200
2006, July 1	Bombings of trains, station, Mumbai, India	207
2007, Mar. 19	Coal mine, Siberia, Russia	108
2007, Mar. 22	Natl. weapons depot, Maputo, Mozambique	117
2007, June 9	Oil pipeline, Pyongan Prov., N. Korea	110
2007, Nov. 18	Methane gas buildup in coal mine, E Ukraine	90
2008, May 15	Pipeline explosion in Lagos, Nigeria	100+
2008, Sept. 20	Truck bomb outside hotel, Islamabad, Pakistan	40+
2009, Feb. 22	Coal mine, N China	74
2010, Apr. 5	Coal mine, Montcoal, WV	29
2010, May 8-9	Coal mine, Siberia, Russia	91
2010, June 17	Coal mine, Amaga, Colombia	73
2010, Nov. 19	Coal mine, Ataru, New Zealand	29
2011, Mar. 28	Munitions factory, Abyan, Yemen	150+
2011, July 13	Bombs in three locations in Mumbai, India	27
2012, Mar. 4	Arms depot, Brazzaville, Congo Rep.	250+
2013, Apr. 17	Fire at fertilizer plant, West, TX	14
2013, June 3	Poultry plant, Mishzai, China	119+
2013, June 30	Fuel tanker, Kampala, Uganda	30+
2013, July 6	Derailed oil train, Lac-Megantic, QC, Canada	47
2013, Aug. 1	Weapons cache, Homs, Syria	40
2014, May 13	Coal mine, Soma, Turkey	301
2014, May 19	Bus fire near Barranquilla, Colombia	32
2015, Aug. 13	Chemical warehouse, Tianjin, China	170+

Notable Nuclear Accidents

Oct. 7, 1957: Fire in the Windscale plutonium production reactor N of Liverpool, England, UK, released radioactive material; later blamed for 39 cancer deaths.

Jan. 3, 1961: Reactor explosion at a federal installation near Idaho Falls, ID, killed 3 workers. Radiation contained.

Oct. 5, 1966: Sodium cooling system malfunction caused a partial core meltdown at the Enrico Fermi demonstration breeder reactor, near Detroit, MI. Radiation contained.

Jan. 21, 1969: Coolant malfunction from an experimental underground reactor at Lucens Vad, Switzerland, released radiation into a cavern, which was then sealed.

Mar. 22, 1975: Fire at the Brown's Ferry reactor in Decatur, AL, caused dangerous lowering of cooling water levels.

Mar. 28, 1979: Worst commercial nuclear accident in the U.S. occurred as equipment failures and human mistakes led to a loss of coolant and a partial core meltdown at the Three Mile Island reactor in Middletown, PA.

Feb. 11, 1981: Eight workers were contaminated when 100,000 gallons of radioactive coolant leaked into the containment building of TVA's Sequoyah 1 plant near Chattanooga, TN.

Apr. 25, 1981: Some 100 workers were exposed to radiation during repairs of a nuclear plant at Tsuruga, Japan.

Jan. 6, 1986: Cylinder of nuclear material burst after being improperly heated at a Kerr-McGee plant in Gore, OK. One worker died; 100 were hospitalized.

Apr. 26, 1986: Fires and resulting explosions at the Chernobyl nuclear power plant near Kiev, USSR (now in Ukraine), left at least 31 dead in the immediate aftermath and spread radioactive material over much of Europe. An estimated 135,000 people were evacuated. Tens of thousands of excess cancer deaths (as well as increased birth defects) were expected.

Sept. 1987: Cesium chloride from an improperly discarded hospital irradiation machine contaminated more than 200 people and killed at least 4 in Goiânia, Brazil. The event focused international attention on improving security and safety standards for radioactive waste.

Mar. 11, 2011: A 9.0-magnitude earthquake caused a devastating tsunami that inundated the Fukushima Daiichi nuclear power plant on Japan's NE coast. Three of the plant's reactors suffered partial meltdowns, and more than 12,000 tons of radioactive water was released into the sea. More than two years later, the plant's owners reported that 300 tons of radioactive water was still leaking into the ocean every day.

Record Oil Spills

The exact number of barrels in a ton varies with the type of oil, but a good approximation is 7 barrels per ton. Each barrel contains 42 gallons.

Name, location	Date	Cause	Est. tons
BP *Deepwater Horizon* rig, Gulf of Mexico, U.S.	Apr. 20-July 15, 2010	Explosion	700,000[1]
Ixtoc I oil well, S Gulf of Mexico	June 3, 1979	Blowout	600,000
Nowruz oil field, Persian Gulf	Feb. 1983	Blowout	600,000
Atlantic Empress and *Aegean Captain*, off Trinidad and Tobago	July 19, 1979	Collision	300,000
ABT Summer, off Angola	May 28, 1991	Explosion	260,000
Castillo de Bellver, off Cape Town, South Africa	Aug. 6, 1983	Fire	250,000
Amoco Cadiz, near Portsall, France	Mar. 16, 1978	Grounding	223,000
Torrey Canyon, off Land's End, England, UK	Mar. 18, 1967	Grounding	119,000
Sea Star, Gulf of Oman	Dec. 19, 1972	Collision	115,000
Urquiola, La Coruna, Spain	May 12, 1976	Grounding	100,000

(1) The Dept. of Energy estimated the spill at 4.9 mil barrels, or more than 200 mil gallons.

Other Notable Oil Spills

Name, location	Date	Cause	Gallons
Persian Gulf	Jan. 21, 1991	Intentional spillage by Iraq	130,000,000[1]
Braer, off Shetland Islands, UK	Jan. 5, 1993	Grounding	26,000,000
Prestige, off N Spain	Nov. 13-19, 2002	Ship broke in half	22,600,000
Aegean Sea, off N Spain	Dec. 3, 1992	Grounding	21,500,000
Sea Empress, off SW Wales, UK	Feb. 15, 1996	Grounding	18,000,000
Newtown Creek, Greenpoint, Brooklyn, NY	Oct. 5, 1950-present	Industrial explosion[2]	17,000,000
World Glory, off South Africa	June 13, 1968	Hull failure	13,524,000
Exxon Valdez, Prince William Sound, AK	Mar. 24, 1989	Grounding	10,080,000
Ashland Oil facility, Floreffe, PA; Monongahela R.	Jan. 2, 1988	Storage tank collapse	3,850,000

(1) Est. by Saudi Arabia. Some estimates as low as 25 mil gal. (2) Preceded by leaks in 1940s-50s.

Notable Droughts

Source: EM-DAT: The OFDA/CRED Intl. Disaster Database, Université catholique de Louvain, Brussels, Belgium, www.emdat.be; World Almanac research

Date	Location	Est. deaths
1900	Bengal, India	1,250,000
1900	Cape Verde islands	11,000
1910-14	Zinder Dept., Niger	85,000
1920	China	500,000
1920	Cape Verde islands	24,000
1921	S Ukraine, Volga, USSR	1,200,000
1928-30	Shaanxi, Henan, Gansu, China	3,000,000
1940-44	Cape Verde islands	20,000
1942	Calcutta, Bengal, India	1,500,000
1943	Bangladesh	1,900,000
1946	Cape Verde islands	30,000
1965	Ethiopia	2,000
1965-67	India	1,500,000
1966	Lombok, Indonesia	8,000
1973-78	Ethiopia	100,000
1974-76	Somalia	19,000
1981-85	Mozambique	100,000
1981-85	Chad	3,000
1983	Swaziland	500
1983-84	Eritrea, Ethiopia	300,000
1983-85	N Sudan	150,000
1987	Somalia, Eritrea, Ethiopia	967
1987	NW India	300
1988	Central China	1,400
1991	Jiangxi, Hunan Provinces, China	2,000
1997	Irian Jaya, Indonesia	672
1999-2003	Pakistan	143
2002	Malawi	500
2006	SW China	134
2014	Tharparkar, Pakistan	166

Some Notable Miscellaneous Disasters Since 1950

Date	Event	Location	Details	Est. deaths
1952, Dec.	Pollution	London, England, UK	Heavy smog blanketed city; impeded breathing	4,000
1980, summer	Heat wave	United States	June through Sept.	1,265
1984, Dec. 3	Industrial accident	Bhopal, India	Toxic gas leaked from a Union Carbide factory	16,000
1986, Aug. 21	Gas	Nr. Lake Nyos, Cameroon	Volcanic lake released cloud of carbon dioxide gas	1,700
1990, July 2	Stampede	Mecca, Saudi Arabia	Pilgrims panicked in tunnel leading to the holy city	1,426
2003, summer	Heat wave	Europe	Abnormally high temperatures from Russia to Britain; France suffered most, with 14,800 dead	35,000
2013, Apr. 24	Building collapse	Savar, Bangladesh	Garment factory found to have substandard foundation collapsed	1,100+

AEROSPACE

Notable Human Spaceflight Missions

Source: National Aeronautics and Space Administration (NASA); Congressional Research Service; World Almanac research

The spaceflights listed are a selection of notable U.S. missions by NASA, unless otherwise noted, plus non-U.S. missions (shown with an asterisk). The non-U.S missions were sponsored by the USSR—later, the Commonwealth of Independent States (CIS) and, from 1997, Russia—or by China. Launch dates are Eastern standard time. **EVA** = extravehicular activity. **ASTP** = Apollo-Soyuz Test Project. **STS** = Space Transportation System, NASA's name for the overall shuttle program.

For shuttle flights, mission name is in parentheses following name of orbiter. Duration of flight is listed in hours:minutes for 1961-Apr. 1970; days (d.), hours (hr.), and minutes (min.) thereafter. Number of total flights taken by each crew member is given in parentheses when flight listed is not the person's first.

4/12/1961: ***Vostok 1**; 1:48; Yuri A. Gagarin. **1st human orbital flight.**

5/5/1961: ***Mercury-Redstone 3***; 0:15; Alan B. Shepard Jr. **1st American in space.**

7/21/1961: ***Mercury-Redstone 4***; 0:15; Virgil I. Grissom. Flight successful but spacecraft sank shortly after splashdown; Grissom rescued.

8/6/1961: ***Vostok 2**; 25:18; Gherman S. Titov. 1st spaceflight of more than 24 hours.

2/20/1962: ***Mercury-Atlas 6***; 4:55; John H. Glenn Jr. **1st American in orbit**; three orbits.

5/24/1962: ***Mercury-Atlas 7***; 4:56; M. Scott Carpenter. Manual retrofire error caused 250-mi landing overshoot.

8/11/1962: ***Vostok 3**; 94:22; Andrian G. Nikolayev. *Vostok 3* and *4* made 1st group flight.

8/12/1962: ***Vostok 4**; 70:57; Pavel R. Popovich. On 1st orbit, it came within 3 mi of *Vostok 3*.

10/3/1962: ***Mercury-Atlas 8***; 9:13; Walter M. Schirra Jr. Landed 5 mi from target; six orbits.

5/15/1963: ***Mercury-Atlas 9***; 34:19; L. Gordon Cooper. 1st U.S. evaluation of effects of one day in space on a person; 22 orbits.

6/14/1963: ***Vostok 5**; 119:06; Valery F. Bykovsky. *Vostok 5* and *6* made 2nd group flight.

6/16/1963: ***Vostok 6**; 70:50; Valentina V. Tereshkova. **1st woman in space**; passed within 3 mi of *Vostok 5*.

10/12/1964: ***Voskhod 1**; 24:17; Vladimir M. Komarov, Konstantin P. Feoktistov, Boris B. Yegorov. 1st three-person orbital flight; 1st without space suits.

3/18/1965: ***Voskhod 2**; 26:02; Pavel I. Belyayev, Aleksei A. Leonov. Leonov made **1st spacewalk** (10 min.).

3/23/1965: ***Gemini-Titan 3***; 4:53; Virgil I. Grissom (2), John W. Young. 1st piloted spacecraft to change its orbital path.

6/3/1965: ***Gemini-Titan 4***; 97:56; James A. McDivitt, Edward H. White II. White was **1st American to "walk in space"** (23 min.).

8/21/1965: ***Gemini-Titan 5***; 190:55; L. Gordon Cooper (2), Charles Conrad Jr. Longest-duration human flight to date.

12/4/1965: ***Gemini-Titan 7***; 330:35; Frank Borman, James A. Lovell Jr. Longest-duration *Gemini* flight.

12/15/1965: ***Gemini-Titan 6A***; 25:51; Walter M. Schirra Jr. (2), Thomas P. Stafford. Completed 1st U.S. space rendezvous, with *Gemini 7*.

3/16/1966: ***Gemini-Titan 8***; 10:41; Neil A. Armstrong, David R. Scott. **1st docking of one space vehicle with another**; mission aborted, control malfunction; 1st Pacific landing.

6/3/1966: ***Gemini-Titan 9A***; 72:21; Thomas P. Stafford (2), Eugene A. Cernan. Performed simulation of lunar module rendezvous.

7/18/1966: ***Gemini-Titan 10***; 70:47; John W. Young (2), Michael Collins. 1st use of Agena target vehicle's propulsion systems; 1st orbital docking.

9/12/1966: ***Gemini-Titan 11***; 71:17; Charles Conrad Jr. (2), Richard F. Gordon Jr. 1st tethered flight; highest Earth-orbit altitude (850 mi).

11/11/1966: ***Gemini-Titan 12***; 94:34; James A. Lovell Jr. (2), Edwin E. "Buzz" Aldrin Jr. Final *Gemini* mission; 5-hr. EVA.

1/27/1967: ***Apollo 1***; Virgil I. Grissom, Edward H. White II, and Roger B. Chaffee died in a fire on the ground at Cape Canaveral, FL.

4/23/1967: ***Soyuz 1**; 26:40; Vladimir M. Komarov (2). Crashed on reentry, killing Komarov; **1st space fatality**.

10/11/1968: ***Apollo-Saturn 7***; 260:09; Walter M. Schirra Jr. (3), Donn F. Eisele, R. Walter Cunningham. **1st piloted flight of *Apollo*** spacecraft command-service module only; live TV footage of crew.

12/21/1968: ***Apollo-Saturn 8***; 147:00; Frank Borman (2), James A. Lovell Jr. (3), William A. Anders. **1st lunar orbit** and piloted lunar return reentry (command-service module only); views of lunar surface televised to Earth.

1/14/1969: ***Soyuz 4**; 71:21; Vladimir A. Shatalov. Docked with *Soyuz 5*.

1/15/1969: ***Soyuz 5**; 72:54; Boris V. Volyanov, Aleksei S. Yeliseyev, Yevgeny V. Khrunov. Docked with *Soyuz 4*; Yeliseyev and Khrunov transferred to *Soyuz 4* via a spacewalk.

3/3/1969: ***Apollo-Saturn 9***; 241:00; James A. McDivitt (2), David R. Scott (2), Russell L. Schweickart. 1st piloted flight of lunar module.

5/18/1969: ***Apollo-Saturn 10***; 192:03; Thomas P. Stafford (3), John W. Young (3), Eugene A. Cernan (2). 1st lunar module orbit of Moon, 50,000 ft from Moon's surface.

7/16/1969: ***Apollo-Saturn 11***; 195:18; Neil A. Armstrong (2), Michael Collins (2), Edwin E. "Buzz" Aldrin Jr. (2). **1st Moon landing** made by Armstrong and Aldrin (7/20); collected 48.5 lbs of soil, rock samples; lunar stay time 21:36.

10/11/1969: ***Soyuz 6**; 118:43; Georgi S. Shonin, Valery N. Kubasov. 1st welding of metals in space.

10/12/1969: ***Soyuz 7**; 118:40; Anatoly V. Flipchenko, Vladislav N. Volkov, Viktor V. Gorbatko. Space lab construction test made; *Soyuz 6*, *7*, and *8*: 1st time three spacecraft, seven crew members orbited the Earth at once.

10/13/1969: ***Soyuz 8**; 118:51; Vladimir A. Shatalov (2), Aleksei S. Yeliseyev (2). Part of space lab construction team.

11/14/1969: ***Apollo-Saturn 12***; 244:36; Charles Conrad Jr. (3), Richard F. Gordon Jr. (2), Alan L. Bean. Conrad and Bean made **2nd Moon landing** (11/18); collected 74.7 lbs of samples; lunar stay time 31:31.

4/11/1970: ***Apollo-Saturn 13***; 142:54; James A. Lovell Jr. (4), Fred W. Haise Jr., John L. Swigert Jr. Aborted after service module oxygen tank ruptured; crew returned in lunar module.

6/1/1970: ***Soyuz 9**; 17 d., 16 hr., 59 min.; Andrian G. Nikolayev (2), Vitaly I. Sevastyanov. Longest human spaceflight to date.

1/31/1971: ***Apollo-Saturn 14***; 9 d., 2 min.; Alan B. Shepard Jr. (2), Stuart A. Roosa, Edgar D. Mitchell. Shepard and Mitchell made **3rd Moon landing** (2/3); collected 96 lbs of lunar samples; lunar stay 33:31.

4/19/1971: ***Salyut 1**; launched without crew. **1st space station.**

4/22/1971: ***Soyuz 10**; 1 d., 23 hr., 46 min.; Vladimir A. Shatalov (3), Aleksei S. Yeliseyev (3), Nikolay N. Rukavishnikov. **1st successful docking with a space station**; failed to enter space station.

6/6/1971: ***Soyuz 11**; 23 d., 28 hr., 22 min.; Georgi T. Dobrovolskiy, Vladislav N. Volkov (2), Viktor I. Patsayev. Docked and entered *Salyut 1* space station; **crew died** during reentry from loss of pressurization.

7/26/1971: ***Apollo-Saturn 15***; 12 d., 17 hr., 12 min.; David R. Scott (3), James B. Irwin, Alfred M. Worden. Scott and Irwin made **4th Moon landing** (7/30). 1st lunar rover use; 1st deep spacewalk; 170 lbs of samples; 66:55 stay.

4/16/1972: ***Apollo-Saturn 16***; 11 d., 1 hr., 51 min.; John W. Young (4), Charles M. Duke Jr., Thomas K. Mattingly II.

Young and Duke made **5th Moon landing** (4/20); collected 213 lbs of lunar samples; lunar stay 71:02.

12/7/1972: *Apollo-Saturn 17*; 12 d., 13 hr., 52 min.; Eugene A. Cernan (3), Ronald E. Evans, Harrison H. Schmitt. Cernan and Schmitt made 6th and **last crewed lunar landing** (12/11); collected 243 lbs of samples; record lunar stay over 75 hr.

5/14/1973: *Skylab 1*; launched without crew. **1st U.S. space station**; fell out of orbit 7/11/1979.

5/25/1973: *Skylab 2*; 28 d., 49 min.; Charles Conrad Jr. (4), Joseph P. Kerwin, Paul J. Weitz. 1st U.S.-piloted orbiting space station; crew repaired damage caused in boost.

7/28/1973: *Skylab 3*; 59 d., 11 hr., 1 min.; Alan L. Bean (2), Owen K. Garriott, Jack R. Lousma. Crew systems and operational tests; scientific activities; three EVAs, 13:44.

11/16/1973: *Skylab 4*; 84 d., 1 hr., 16 min.; Gerald P. Carr, Edward G. Gibson, William R. Pogue. Final *Skylab* mission.

7/15/1975: **Soyuz 19 (ASTP)*; 6 d., 11 hr., 31 min.; Aleksei A. Leonov (2), Valery N. Kubasov (2). U.S.-USSR joint flight; crews linked up in space (7/17), conducted experiments, shared meals, held a joint news conference.

7/15/1975: *Apollo (ASTP)*; 9 d., 7 hr., 28 min.; Vance D. Brand, Thomas P. Stafford (4), Donald K. Slayton. Joint flight with *Soyuz 19*.

12/10/1977: **Soyuz 26*; 96 d., 10 hr.; Yuri V. Romanenko, Georgiy M. Grechko (2). 1st multiple docking at a space station (*Soyuz 26* and *27* docked at *Salyut 6*).

1/10/1978: **Soyuz 27*; 5 d., 22 hr., 59 min.; Vladimir A. Dzhanibekov. See *Soyuz 26*.

3/2/1978: **Soyuz 28*; 7 d., 22 hr., 16 min.; Aleksei A. Gubarev (2), Vladimir Remek. 1st international crew launch; Remek was 1st Czech in space.

4/12/1981: *Columbia (STS-1)*; 2 d., 6 hr., 21 min.; John W. Young (5), Robert L. Crippen. **1st reusable space shuttle** to fly into Earth's orbit.

11/12/1981: *Columbia (STS-2)*; 3 days; Joe H. Engle, Richard H. Truly. 1st scientific payload; 1st reuse of space shuttle.

11/11/1982: *Columbia (STS-5)*; 6 days; Vance D. Brand (2), Robert F. Overmyer, Joseph P. Allen, William B. Lenoir. 1st four-person crew.

6/18/1983: *Challenger (STS-7)*; 7 days; Robert L. Crippen (2), Frederick H. Hauck, John M. Fabian, Sally K. Ride, Norman E. Thagard. Ride was **1st U.S. woman in space**; 1st 5-person crew.

6/27/1983: **Soyuz T-9*; 150 days; Vladimir A. Lyakhov (2), Aleksandr Pavlovich. Docked at *Salyut 7*. 1st construction in space.

8/30/1983: *Challenger (STS-8)*; 7 days; Richard H. Truly (2), Daniel C. Brandenstein, Dale A. Gardner, Guion S. Bluford Jr., William E. Thornton. Bluford was **1st African-American in space**; **1st night launch**.

11/28/1983: *Columbia (STS-9)*; 11 days; John W. Young (6), Brewster H. Shaw Jr., Owen K. Garriott (2), Robert A.R. Parker, Byron K. Lichtenberg, Ulf Merbold. 1st six-person crew; 1st Spacelab mission.

2/3/1984: *Challenger (41-B)*; 8 days; Vance Brand (3), Robert L. Gibson, Ronald E. McNair, Bruce McCandless II, Robert L. Stewart. 1st untethered EVA.

2/8/1984: **Soyuz T-10B*; 63 days; Leonid Kizim, Vladimir Solovyov, Oleg Atkov. Docked with *Salyut 7*; crew set space duration record of 237 days (since eclipsed).

4/3/1984: **Soyuz T-11*; 182 days; Yury Malyshev (2), Gennady Strekalov (3), Rakesh Sharma. Docked with *Salyut 7*; Sharma was 1st Indian in space.

4/6/1984: *Challenger (41-C)*; 7 days; Robert L. Crippen (3), Francis R. Scobee, George D. Nelson, Terry J. Hart, James D. van Hoften. 1st in-orbit satellite repair.

7/17/1984: **Soyuz T-12*; 12 days; Vladimir A. Dzhanibekov (4), Svetlana Y. Savitskaya (2), Igor P. Volk. Docked at *Salyut 7*; Savitskaya was 1st woman to perform EVA.

8/30/1984: *Discovery (41-D)*; 7 days; Henry W. Hartsfield Jr. (2), Michael L. Coats, Richard M. Mullane, Steven A. Hawley, Judith A. Resnik, Charles D. Walker. 1st flight of non-astronaut (payload specialist Walker).

10/5/1984: *Challenger (41-G)*; 9 days; Robert L. Crippen (4), Jon A. McBride, Kathryn D. Sullivan, Sally K. Ride (2), David C. Leestma, Marc Garneau, Paul D. Scully-Power. 1st seven-person crew.

11/8/1984: *Discovery (51-A)*; 8 days; Frederick H. Hauck (2), David M. Walker, Anna L. Fisher, Dale A. Gardner (2), Joseph P. Allen (2). 1st satellite retrieval/repair.

4/12/1985: *Discovery (51-D)*; 7 days; Karol J. Bobko, Donald E. Williams, Charles D. Walker (2), M. Rhea Seddon, Jeffrey A. Hoffman, S. David Griggs, E. Jake Garn. Garn (R, UT) was **1st U.S. senator in space.**

6/17/1985: *Discovery (51-G)*; 8 days; Daniel C. Brandenstein (2), John O. Creighton, Shannon W. Lucid, John M. Fabian (2), Steven R. Nagel, Prince Sultan Salman al-Saud, Patrick Baudry. Launched three satellites; Salman al-Saud was 1st Arab in space; Baudry was 1st French person on U.S. mission.

10/3/1985: *Atlantis (51-J)*; 5 days; Karol J. Bobko (3), Ronald J. Grabe, David C. Hilmers, Robert L. Stewart (2), William A. Pailes. 1st *Atlantis* flight.

10/30/1985: *Challenger (61-A)*; 8 days; Henry W. Hartsfield Jr. (3), Steven R. Nagel (2), James F. Buchli (2), Guion S. Bluford (2), Bonnie J. Dunbar, Wubbo J. Ockels, Richard Furrer, Ernst Messerschmid. 1st eight-person crew; 1st German Spacelab mission.

1/12/1986: *Columbia (61-C)*; 7 days; Robert L. Gibson (2), Charles F. Bolden Jr., Franklin R. Chang Díaz, Steven A. Hawley (2), George D. Nelson (2), Robert J. Cenker, Bill Nelson. B. Nelson (D, FL) was **1st U.S. representative in space**.

1/28/1986: *Challenger (51-L)*; 73 seconds; Francis R. Scobee (2), Michael J. Smith, Judith A. Resnik (2), Ellison S. Onizuka (2), Ronald E. McNair, Gregory B. Jarvis, Christa McAuliffe. **Exploded 73 seconds after liftoff; all aboard were killed**, including McAuliffe, a New Hampshire schoolteacher who had won a national competition to become 1st private citizen in space.

2/20/1986: **Mir*[1]; launched without crew. **Space station** with six docking ports launched.

3/13/1986: **Soyuz T-15*; 125 days; Leonid Kizim (3), Vladimir Solovyov (2). Ferry between stations; docked at *Mir*.

2/5/1987: **Soyuz TM-2*; 327 days; Yuri V. Romanenko (3), Aleksandr I. Laveikin. Romanenko set then-endurance record.

7/22/1987: **Soyuz TM-3*; 161 days; Aleksandr Viktorenko, Aleksandr Pavlovich Aleksandrov (2), Mohammed Faris. Docked with *Mir*; Faris was 1st Syrian in space.

9/29/1988: *Discovery (STS-26)*; 4 days; Frederick H. Hauck (3), Richard O. Covey (2), George D. Nelson (3), John M. Lounge (2), David C. Hilmers (2). **1st shuttle flight since *Challenger* explosion** 1/28/1986.

5/4/1989: *Atlantis (STS-30)*; 4 days; David M. Walker (2), Ronald J. Grabe (2), Norman E. Thagard (3), Mary L. Cleave (2), Mark C. Lee. Launched Venus orbiter *Magellan*.

10/18/1989: *Atlantis (STS-34)*; 5 days; Donald E. Williams (2), Michael J. McCulley, Shannon W. Lucid (2), Franklin R. Chang Díaz (2), Ellen S. Baker. Launched Jupiter probe and orbiter *Galileo*.

4/24/1990: *Discovery (STS-31)*; 6 days; Loren J. Shriver (2), Charles F. Bolden Jr. (2), Steven A. Hawley (3), Bruce McCandless (2), Kathryn D. Sullivan (2). **Launched Hubble Space Telescope.**

10/6/1990: *Discovery (STS-41)*; 5 days; Richard N. Richards (2), Robert D. Cabana, Bruce E. Melnick, William M. Shepherd (2), Thomas D. Akers. Launched *Ulysses* spacecraft to investigate interstellar space and the Sun.

5/18/1991: **Soyuz TM-12*; 145 days; Anatoly Artsebarsky, Sergei Krikalev (2) (to *Mir*), Helen Sharman. Docked with *Mir*; Sharman was 1st Briton in space.

3/17/1992: **Soyuz TM-14*; 146 days; Aleksandr Viktorenko (3) (to *Mir*), Alexandr Kaleri (to *Mir*), Klaus-Dietrich Flade, Aleksandr Volkov (3) (from *Mir*), Sergei Krikalev (2) (from *Mir*). 1st human CIS space mission; docked with *Mir* 3/19; Krikalev was in space 313 days.

5/7/1992: *Endeavour (STS-49)*; 9 days; Daniel C. Brandenstein (4), Kevin P. Chilton, Pierre J. Thuot (2), Kathryn Thornton (2), Richard J. Hieb (2), Thomas D. Akers (2), Bruce E. Melnick (2). 1st 3-person EVA; satellite recovery and redeployment.

9/12/1992: *Endeavour (STS-47)*; 8 days; Robert L. Gibson (4), Curtis L. Brown Jr., Mark C. Lee (2), N. Jan Davis, Jay Apt (2), Mae Carol Jemison, Mamoru Mohri. Jemison was **1st black woman in space**; Lee and Davis were **1st married couple to travel together in space**; 1st Japanese Spacelab.

6/21/1993: *Endeavour (STS-57)*; 10 days; Ronald J. Grabe (4), Brian J. Duffy (2), G. David Low (3), Nancy J. Sherlock, Janice E. Voss, Peter J. K. Wisoff. Carried Spacelab commercial payload module.

12/2/1993: *Endeavour (STS-61)*; 11 days; Richard O. Covey (3), Kenneth D. Bowersox (2), F. Story Musgrave (5), Kathryn Thornton (3), Claude Nicollier (2), Jeffrey A. Hoffman (4), Thomas D. Akers (3). Hubble Space Telescope repaired; Akers set new U.S. EVA duration record (29 hr., 40 min.).

2/3/1994: *Discovery (STS-60)*; 9 days; Charles F. Bolden Jr. (3), Kenneth S. Reightler Jr. (2), N. Jan Davis (2), Franklin R. Chang Díaz (3), Ronald M. Sega, Sergei Krikalev (3). Krikalev was 1st Russian on U.S. shuttle.

7/1/1994: **Soyuz TM-19*; 126 days; Yuri I. Malenchenko, Talgat A. Musabayev, Ulf Merbold (2) (from *Mir*). Docked with *Mir*.

9/9/1994: *Discovery (STS-64)*; 11 days; Richard N. Richards (4), L. Blaine Hammond Jr. (2), Jerry M. Linenger, Susan J. Helms (2), Carl J. Meade (3), Mark C. Lee (3). Performed atmospheric research; 1st untethered EVA in more than 10 years.

2/3/1995: *Discovery (STS-63)*; 9 days; James D. Wetherbee (3), Eileen M. Collins, Bernard A. Harris (2), C. Michael Foale (3), Janice E. Voss (2), Vladimir Titov (4). *Discovery* and Russian space station rendezvous.

3/2/1995: *Endeavour (STS-67)*; 17 days; Stephen S. Oswald (3), William G. Gregory, Tamara E. Jernigan (3), John M. Grunsfeld, Wendy B. Lawrence, Ronald Parise (2), Samuel T. Durrance (2). Shuttle data made available on the Internet.

3/14/1995: **Soyuz TM-21*; 112 days; Norman E. Thagard (5), Vladimir Dezhurov, Gennady Strekalov (5). Docked with *Mir* 3/16. Thagard was 1st American onboard Russian spacecraft; Valery Polyakov returned to Earth, 3/22/1995, after record stay in space (439 days).

6/27/1995: *Atlantis (STS-71)*; 10 days; Robert L. Gibson (5), Charles J. Precourt (2), Ellen S. Baker (3), Bonnie J. Dunbar (4), Gregory J. Harbaugh (3), Anatoly Solovyev (4) (to *Mir*), Nikolai M. Budarin (to *Mir*), Norman E. Thagard (5) (from *Mir*), Gennady Strekalov (from *Mir*), Vladimir Dezhurov (from *Mir*). **1st shuttle-*Mir* docking**; exchanged crew members with *Mir*.

11/12/1995: *Atlantis (STS-74)*; 9 days; Kenneth D. Cameron (3), James D. Halsell Jr. (2), Jerry L. Ross (5), William S. McArthur Jr. (2), Chris A. Hadfield. 2nd shuttle-*Mir* docking (11/15-11/18); erected a 15-ft permanent docking tunnel to *Mir* for future use by U.S. orbiters.

2/22/1996: *Columbia (STS-75)*; 16 days; Andrew M. Allen (3), Scott J. Horowitz, Franklin R. Chang Díaz (5), Umberto Guidoni, Jeffrey A. Hoffman (5), Maurizio Cheli, Claude Nicollier (3). Lost an Italian satellite when its tether was severed; microgravity experiments performed.

3/22/1996: *Atlantis (STS-76)*; 10 days; Kevin P. Chilton (3), Richard A. Searfoss (2), Shannon W. Lucid (5) (to *Mir*), Linda M. Godwin (3), Michael R. Clifford (3), Ronald M. Sega (2). 3rd shuttle-*Mir* docking (5 days); two-person EVA.

9/16/1996: *Atlantis (STS-79)*; 11 days; William F. Readdy (3), Terry W. Wilcutt (2), Thomas D. Akers (4), John E. Blaha (5) (to *Mir*), Jay Apt (4), Carl E. Walz (3), Shannon W. Lucid (5) (from *Mir*). Docked with *Mir* 9/18; exchanged crew members; Lucid set **U.S. and women's duration in space record** (188 days).

11/19/1996: *Columbia (STS-80)*; 18 days; Kenneth D. Cockrell (3), Kent V. Rominger (2), Tamara E. Jernigan (4), Thomas D. Jones (3), F. Story Musgrave (6). Longest-duration shuttle flight; Musgrave, 61, oldest thus far to fly in space; two science satellites deployed, retrieved.

1/12/1997: *Atlantis (STS-81)*; 11 days; Michael A. Baker (4), Brent W. Jett (2), John M. Grunsfeld (2), Marsha S. Ivins (4), Peter J. K. Wisoff (3), Jerry M. Linenger (2) (to *Mir*), John E. Blaha (5) (from *Mir*). Docked with *Mir* 1/14-1/19; Blaha spent 128 days in space.

2/11/1997: *Discovery (STS-82)*; 10 days; Kenneth D. Bowersox (4), Scott J. Horowitz (2), Mark C. Lee (4), Steven A. Hawley (4), Gregory J. Harbaugh (4), Steven L. Smith (2), Joseph R. Tanner (2). Increased capabilities of Hubble Space Telescope; five EVAs conducted to service it.

5/15/1997: *Atlantis (STS-84)*; 10 days; Charles J. Precourt (3), Eileen M. Collins (2), C. Michael Foale (4) (to *Mir*), Carlos I. Noriega, Edward T. Lu, Jean-François Clervoy (2), Elena Kondakova, Jerry M. Linenger (2) (from *Mir*). Docked with *Mir* 5/16-5/21. Foale's stay on *Mir* marked by major collision with cargo ship 6/25/1997.

8/5/1997: **Soyuz TM-26*; 198 days; Anatoly Solovyev (5), Pavel Vinogradov. Docked with *Mir* 8/7; repaired damaged space station.

8/7/1997: *Discovery (STS-85)*; 12 days; Curtis L. Brown Jr. (4), Kent V. Rominger (3), N. Jan Davis (3), Robert L. Curbeam Jr., Stephen K. Robinson, Bjarni V. Tryggvason. Deployed and retrieved satellite designed to study Earth's middle atmosphere; demonstrated robotic arm.

9/25/1997: *Atlantis (STS-86)*; 11 days; James D. Wetherbee (4), Michael J. Bloomfield, Vladimir Titov (4), Scott E. Parazynski (2), Jean-Loup J. Chrétien (3), Wendy B. Lawrence (2), David A. Wolf (2) (to *Mir*), C. Michael Foale (4) (from *Mir*). Docked with *Mir* 9/27-10/3; delivered new computer to *Mir*.

4/17/1998: *Columbia (STS-90)*; 16 days; Richard A. Searfoss (3), Scott D. Altman, Richard M. Linnehan (2), Dave R. Williams, Kathryn P. Hire, Jay C. Buckey, James A. Pawelczyk. Studied effects of microgravity on the nervous systems of the crew and more than 2,000 live animals; 1st surgery in space on animals meant to survive.

6/2/1998: *Discovery (STS-91)*; 10 days; Charles J. Precourt (4), Dominic L. Gorie, Wendy B. Lawrence (3), Franklin R. Chang Díaz (6), Janet L. Kavandi, Valery V. Ryumin (4), Andrew S. W. Thomas (2) (from *Mir*). Final docking mission with *Mir*; Thomas from *Mir*, 141 days in space.

10/29/1998: *Discovery (STS-95)*; 10 days; Curtis L. Brown Jr. (5), Steven W. Lindsey (2), Scott E. Parazynski (3), Stephen K. Robinson (2), Pedro Duque, Chiaki Mukai (2), John H. Glenn Jr. (2). The 77-year-old Glenn, one of the original *Mercury* astronauts, and at that point a senator (D, OH), became **oldest person to fly in space**; Duque was 1st Spaniard in space; experiments to study aging performed on Glenn.

12/4/1998: *Endeavour (STS-88)*; 12 days; Robert D. Cabana (4), Frederick W. Sturckow, Nancy J. Currie (3), Jerry L. Ross (6), James H. Newman (3), Sergei K. Krikalev (4). **1st assembly of International Space Station (ISS)**; attached U.S.-built *Unity* connecting module to Russian-built *Zarya* control module; 1st crew to enter ISS.

7/23/1999: *Columbia (STS-93)*; 5 days; Eileen M. Collins (3), Jeffrey S. Ashby, Steven A. Hawley (5), Catherine G. Coleman (2), Michel Tognini (2). Collins was **1st woman space shuttle commander**; deployed Chandra X-ray Observatory telescope.

2/11/2000: *Endeavour (STS-99)*; 12 days; Kevin R. Kregel (4), Dominic L. Gorie (2), Janet L. Kavandi (2), Janice E. Voss (5), Mamoru Mohri (2), Gerhard P.J. Thiele. Used radar to make most complete topographic map of Earth's surface ever produced.

9/8/2000: *Atlantis (STS-106)*; 12 days; Terry W. Wilcutt (4), Scott D. Altman (2), Edward T. Lu (2), Richard A. Mastracchio, Daniel C. Burbank, Yuri I. Malenchenko (2), Boris V. Morukov. Prepared ISS for 1st permanent crew; one EVA by all seven crew members.

10/31/2000: *Soyuz TM-31*; William M. Shepherd (4), Yuri Gidzenko (2), Sergei Krikalev (5). Established **1st permanent manning of ISS** with three-person crew for a 4-month stay.

3/8/2001: *Discovery (STS-102)*; 13 days; James D. Wetherbee (5), James M. Kelly, Andrew S.W. Thomas (2), Paul Richards, Susan J. Helms (4) (to ISS), James S. Voss (5) (to ISS), Yuri V. Usachev (4) (to ISS), William M. Shepherd (4) (from ISS), Sergei K. Krikalev (5) (from ISS), Yuri P. Gidzenko (2) (from ISS). Transported 2nd permanent crew to ISS and returned 1st crew to Earth; two EVAs.

7/12/2001: *Atlantis (STS-104)*; 13 days; Steven W. Lindsey (3), Charles O. Hobaugh, Michael L. Gernhardt (4), Janet L. Kavandi (3), James F. Reilly II (2). Installed the Joint Airlock, with nitrogen and oxygen tanks to permit future spacewalks from the ISS; three EVAs.

3/1/2002: *Columbia (STS-109)*; 11 days; Scott D. Altman (3), Duane G. Carey, John M. Grunsfeld (4), Nancy J. Currie (4), Richard M. Linnehan (3), James H. Newman (4), Michael J. Massimino. Installed powerful new camera and upgraded other equipment on Hubble Space Telescope; five EVAs.

4/8/2002: *Atlantis (STS-110)*; 11 days; Michael J. Bloomfield (3), Stephen N. Frick, Jerry L. Ross (7), Steven L. Smith (4) Ellen Ochoa (4), Lee M.E. Morin, Rex J. Walheim. Installed S0 Truss, backbone for expansion of ISS; Ross set records with 7th spaceflight, 9th spacewalk.

10/30/2002: *Soyuz TMA-1*[1]; Sergei Zalyotin (2), Frank De Winne, Yuri Lonchakov (2). 1st launch of *Soyuz TMA* (crew returned 11/10/2002 on *Soyuz TM-34* already docked at ISS).

1/16/2003: *Columbia (STS 107)*; 16 days; Rick D. Husband (2), William C. McCool, Michael P. Anderson (2), David M. Brown, Kalpana Chawla (2), Laurel B. Clark, Ilan Ramon. **Entire crew lost when *Columbia* broke apart** upon reentry, 2/1, due to heat shield damage; Ramon was 1st Israeli astronaut.

10/15/2003: *Shenzhou 5*; 21 hr.; Yang Liwei. **1st Chinese manned spacecraft.**

6/21/2004: *SpaceShipOne*[2]; 90 min.; Mike Melvill. **1st privately funded manned spaceflight.**

7/26/2005: *Discovery (STS-114)*; 14 days; Eileen M. Collins (4), James M. Kelly (2), Charles J. Camarda, Wendy B. Lawrence (4), Soichi Noguchi, Stephen K. Robinson (3), Andrew S.W. Thomas (3). **1st space shuttle flight since *Columbia* disaster**; tested new safety modifications to craft.

7/4/2006: *Discovery (STS-121)*; 13 days; Steven W. Lindsey (4), Mark E. Kelly, Michael E. Fossum, Piers J. Sellers (2), Lisa M. Nowak, Thomas Reiter (to ISS), Stephanie D. Wilson. 1st shuttle to launch on Independence Day; conducted more safety tests to craft; brought supplies to and performed maintenance on ISS.

4/7/2007: *Soyuz TMA-10*[1]; Oleg Kotov (to ISS), Sheikh Muszaphar Shukor (from ISS), Charles Simonyi (U.S.), Fyodor Yurchikhin (to ISS). Kotov and Yurchikhin joined ISS expedition 15; Simonyi became **5th space tourist** (returned on *TMA-9*); Shukor was 1st Malaysian in space (arrived on *TMA-11*).

6/8/2007: *Atlantis (STS-117)*; 14 days; Frederick W. Sturckow (3), Lee J. Archambault, Patrick G. Forrester (2), John "Danny" Olivas, James F. Reilly (3), Steven R. Swanson, Clayton C. Anderson (to ISS), Sunita L. Williams (from ISS). Delivered truss segments and solar arrays to ISS; Williams set record for **longest spaceflight by a woman**.

8/8/2007: *Endeavour (STS-118)*; 13 days; Scott J. Kelly (2), Charles O. Hobaugh (2), Alvin B. Drew, Barbara R. Morgan, Tracy Caldwell Dyson, Rick A. Mastracchio (2), Dave R. Williams (2). Brought **Teacher in Space** project participant Morgan to ISS; attached new truss segment; repaired faulty gyroscope.

10/10/2007: *Soyuz TMA-11*[1]; Yuri I. Malenchenko (3), Sheikh Muszaphar Shukor (to ISS), Peggy A. Whitson (2) (from ISS), Yi So-yeon (from ISS). Delivered and installed components of ISS; malfunctioned on return to Earth, landing short of its touchdown area but causing no fatalities.

10/23/2007: *Discovery (STS-120)*; 16 days; Pamela A. Melroy (3), George D. Zamka, Scott E. Parazynski (5), Douglas H. Wheelock, Stephanie D. Wilson (2), Paolo Nespoli, Daniel M. Tani (2) (to ISS), Clayton C. Anderson (from ISS). Installed living space (Harmony Node 2) on ISS.

2/7/2008: *Atlantis (STS-122)*; 13 days; Stephen N. Frick (2), Stanley G. Love, Leland D. Melvin, Alan G. Poindexter, Hans Schlegel (2), Léopold Eyharts (to ISS), Daniel M. Tani (from ISS), Rex J. Walheim (2). Installed European Space Agency's Columbus laboratory on the ISS; minor damage to a thermal plate caused concern about the shuttle's safety during reentry, but *Atlantis* landed safely.

3/11/2008: *Endeavour (STS-123)*; 16 days; Dominic L. Gorie (4), Gregory H. Johnson, Richard M. Linnehan (4), Robert L. Behnken, Michael J. Foreman, Takao Doi (2), Garrett E. Reisman (to ISS), Léopold Eyharts (from ISS). Delivered and installed components of the Japanese Kibo science laboratory.

4/8/2008: *Soyuz TMA-12*[1]; Oleg Kononenko, Sergei Volkov, Yi So-yeon (to ISS), Richard Garriott (from ISS). Yi became 1st S. Korean in space.

5/31/2008: *Discovery (STS-124)*; 14 days; Mark E. Kelly (3), Kenneth T. Ham, Karen L. Nyberg, Ronald J. Garan Jr., Michael E. Fossum (2), Akihiko Hoshide, Gregory E. Chamitoff (to ISS), Garrett E. Reisman (from ISS). Delivered and installed pressurized and experimental modules of Kibo.

9/25/2008: *Shenzhou 7*; 68 hr.; Jing Haipeng, Liu Boming, Zhai Zhigang. Zhai completed 1st Chinese spacewalk.

10/12/2008: *Soyuz TMA-13*[1]; Richard Garriott (to ISS), Yuri V. Lonchakov (3), Michael Fincke. Garriott became 6th space tourist.

3/15/2009: *Discovery (STS-119)*; 13 days; Lee J. Archambault (2), Dominic A. Antonelli, Joseph M. Acaba, John L. Phillips, Steven R. Swanson (2), Richard R. Arnold, Koichi Wakata (to ISS), Sandra H. Magnus (from ISS). Delivered final solar panels and last U.S.-made truss segment.

5/11/2009: *Atlantis (STS-125)*; 13 days; Scott D. Altman (4), Gregory C. Johnson, Andrew J. Feustel, Michael T. Good, John M. Grunsfeld (5), Michael J. Massimino (2), K. Megan McArthur. Final Hubble Space Telescope servicing mission.

11/16/2009: *Atlantis (STS-129)*; 11 days; Charles O. Hobaugh (3), Barry E. Wilmore, Leland D. Melvin (2), Michael J. Foreman (2), Randolph J. Bresnik, Robert L. Satcher Jr., Nicole P. Stott (from ISS). Final space shuttle crew rotation flight.

6/15/2010: *Soyuz TMA-19*[1]; Fyodor Yurchikhin (3), Shannon Walker, Douglas H. Wheelock (2). 100th mission since launching of the International Space Station.

7/8/2011: *Atlantis (STS-135)*; 13 days; Christopher Ferguson (3), Doug Hurley (2), Sandy H. Magnus (3), Rex J. Walheim (3). **Final Space Shuttle mission.**

Note: Four Soviet cosmonauts have died during spaceflight: one person was killed on *Soyuz 1* (1967) when parachute lines tangled during descent; the three-person *Soyuz 11* crew (1971) was asphyxiated. Three Americans died in the *Apollo 1* (1967) fire on the ground at Cape Canaveral, FL; seven Americans died in the *Challenger* (1986) explosion; and six Americans and an Israeli astronaut died aboard *Columbia* (2003). (1) *Soyuz* crew often return from the ISS on spacecraft that launched and were docked at the station before their arrival. (2) Date of first successful flight; later, *SpaceShipOne* flew at least 100 km (62 mi) into space, 9/29/2004, piloted by Mike Melvill, and 10/4/2004, piloted by Brian Binnie, winning the $10-mil Ansari Prize for first private venture to accomplish this feat twice within two weeks.

U.S. Manned Space Exploration and the International Space Station

Source: National Aeronautics and Space Administration (NASA); SpaceX

After 50 years of sending men and women into space, the United States ended its manned space program with the safe landing of the *Atlantis* space shuttle on July 21, 2011, at Florida's Kennedy Space Center. The surviving space shuttles are now on display at museums around the country. *Discovery* was placed at the Smithsonian National Air and Space Museum's Udvar-Hazy Center in Chantilly, VA. It replaced *Enterprise*, which performed test runs but never went into space. *Enterprise* was moved to New York City's Intrepid Air, Sea, and Space Museum. *Endeavour* took up residence at the California Science Center in Los Angeles. *Atlantis* remained on permanent display at the Kennedy Space Center.

With the end of the U.S. shuttle program, all U.S. astronauts must find alternative transport to visit the International Space Station (ISS). As of 2015, U.S. astronauts rented space on Russian *Soyuz* spacecraft. But private U.S. company SpaceX sent the first privately developed spacecraft to the ISS May 22, 2012; it returned to Earth nine days later. In Oct. 2012, as part of a $1.6-bil deal with NASA, the company launched the first of 12 ISS cargo resupply missions. The seventh of those missions failed June 28, 2015, as the SpaceX Falcon 9 rocket burst into flames three minutes into flight.

On May 29, 2014, SpaceX unveiled *Dragon2*, a reusable spacecraft designed to carry up to seven passengers. Its propulsive landing system will enable it to touch down almost anywhere with the precision of a helicopter. The company has not announced a date for its first manned flight.

The ISS is considered the largest cooperative scientific project in history. Construction began in 1998 and was completed in 2011. It has been inhabited by more than 200 international crew members since 2000.

About the ISS

- 15 cooperating nations: Belgium, Canada, Denmark, France, Germany, Italy, Japan, Netherlands, Norway, Russia, Spain, Sweden, Switzerland, United Kingdom, and the U.S.
- It has a mass of 924,739 lbs and is about as long as a football field at 357.5 ft.
- It is entirely powered by an acre of solar panels.
- It requires three people to keep it running but has room for up to 10 people to live aboard.
- Astronauts typically spend 4-6 months aboard.

ISS Research

- Studying the effects of long-term exposure to reduced gravity on plants, crystals, plant and animal cells, and pathogens
- Studying the effects on humans of long-term exposure to reduced gravity
- Recording large-scale long-term changes in Earth's environment by observing the planet from orbit
- Testing recycling technologies for human life support

Summary of Worldwide Successful Launches, 1957-2015

Source: National Aeronautics and Space Administration (NASA); Space Launch Report

Year	1957-59	1960-69	1970-79	1980-89	1990-99	2000-09	2010-15[1]	Total[1]
Russia[2]	6	399	1,028	1,132	542	246	166	**3,519**
U.S.	18	614	247	191	300	206	94	**1,670**
China	—	—	8	16	33	52	84	**193**
ESA[3]	—	2	5	14	55	63	35	**174**
Ukraine	—	—	—	—	59	57	21	**137**
Japan	—	—	18	26	23	18	16	**101**
India	—	—	1	9	11	13	15	**49**
France	—	4	14	5	16	0	(3)	**39**
UK	—	1	6	4	7	0	(3)	**18**
Germany	—	—	3	7	6	0	(3)	**16**
Canada	—	—	4	5	4	0	0	**13**
Israel	—	—	—	—	—	3	2	**5**
Iran	—	—	—	—	—	1	3	**4**
S. Korea	—	—	—	—	—	1	0	**1**
N. Korea	—	—	—	—	—	—	1	**1**
Total	**24**	**1,020**	**1,334**	**1,409**	**1,056**	**660**	**437**	**5,940**

— = Not applicable. (1) As of July 16, 2015. (2) Data for 1957-91 apply to the Soviet Union, for 1992-96 to the Commonwealth of Independent States, after 1996 to Russia. (3) European Space Agency. Member states are Austria, Belgium, Denmark, Finland, France, Germany, Greece, Ireland, Italy, Luxembourg, Netherlands, Norway, Portugal, Spain, Sweden, Switzerland, and United Kingdom. Canada, Czech Republic, and Hungary participate in some projects under cooperation agreements.

Notable Lunar and Planetary Science Missions

Source: National Aeronautics and Space Administration (NASA)

Spacecraft	Launch date[1]	Mission	Remarks
Mariner 2	Aug. 27, 1962	Venus	Passed within 22,000 mi of Venus 12/14/1962; confirmed high surface temperature on planet; contact lost 1/3/1963 at 54 mil mi.
Ranger 7	July 28, 1964	Moon	Yielded over 4,000 photos of lunar surface.
Mariner 4	Nov. 28, 1964	Mars	1st probe to fly by Mars; passed behind planet 7/14/1965.
Ranger 8	Feb. 17, 1965	Moon	Yielded over 7,000 photos of lunar surface.
Venera 3	Nov. 16, 1965	Venus	Soviet probe; 1st artificial probe to impact on the surface of another planet, 3/1/1966; probe failed to send back data.
Surveyor 3	Apr. 17, 1967	Moon	Scooped and tested lunar soil.
Mariner 5	June 14, 1967	Venus	In solar orbit; closest Venus flyby 10/19/1967; allowed scientists to obtain accurate readings on the composition of the Venusian atmosphere.
Mariner 6	Feb. 24, 1969	Mars	Came within 2,000 mi of Mars 7/31/1969; collected data, photos.
Mariner 7	Mar. 27, 1969	Mars	Came within 2,000 mi of Mars 8/5/1969.
Venera 7	Aug. 17, 1970	Venus	Soviet probe; 1st probe to land safely on the surface of another planet.
Mariner 9	May 30, 1971	Mars	1st craft to orbit Mars 11/13/1971; sent back over 7,000 photos.
Pioneer 10	Mar. 2, 1972	Jupiter	Passed Jupiter 12/4/1973; took readings on Jupiter's composition. Exited planetary system 6/13/1983; last signal received 1/23/2003 from 7.6 bil mi.
Pioneer 11	Apr. 5, 1973	Jupiter, Saturn	Passed Jupiter 12/3/1974, Saturn 9/1/1979; discovered an additional ring and 2 moons around Saturn. Transmission ended 9/30/1995.
Mariner 10	Nov. 3, 1973	Venus, Mercury	Passed Venus 2/5/1974, arrived at Mercury 3/29/1974. 1st time gravity of 1 planet (Venus) used to whip spacecraft toward another (Mercury); 1st probe to visit 2 planets; took cloud and wind pattern readings in Venusian atmosphere.
Viking 1	Aug. 20, 1975	Mars	Landed on Mars 7/20/1976; 1st probe to land safely on Mars; performed chemical analysis of soil; functioned 6 years.
Viking 2	Sept. 9, 1975	Mars	Sister probe of *Viking 1*; landed on Mars 9/3/1976; functioned 3 years.
Voyager 2	Aug. 20, 1977	Jupiter, Saturn, Uranus, Neptune	Encountered Jupiter 7/9/1979, Saturn 8/25/1981, Uranus 1/24/1986, Neptune 8/25/1989. Confirmed existence of rings around Neptune. As of 8/2015, it was 10.1 bil mi from Sun and still returning data to Earth.

Spacecraft	Launch date[1]	Mission	Remarks
Voyager 1	Sept. 5, 1977	Jupiter, Saturn	Encountered Jupiter 3/5/1979; provided evidence of rings around Jupiter; passed near Saturn 11/12/1980; passed *Pioneer 10* to become most distant human-made object 2/17/1998. As of 8/2015, it was 12.3 bil mi (19.2 bil km) from Sun and still returning data to Earth.
Pioneer Venus 1	May 20, 1978	Venus	Entered Venus orbit 12/4/1978; studied atmosphere, magnetic field, weather, and surface; fuel ran out; probe was destroyed in atmospheric entry, 8/1992.
Pioneer Venus 2 (multiprobe)	Aug. 8, 1978	Venus	Consisted of a "bus" carrying 1 large and 3 small atmospheric probes. All 4 probes entered the Venus atmosphere 12/9/1978, followed by the bus; took readings of atmosphere; probes impacted surface.
Magellan	May 4, 1989	Venus	Landed on Venus 8/10/1990; monitored geological activity; mapped more than 99% of planet surface, showed that about 85% is covered by volcanic flows; ceased operating 10/11/1994.
Galileo	Oct. 18, 1989	Jupiter	Used Earth's gravity to propel itself towards Jupiter; encountered Venus 2/10/1990, Jupiter 12/7/1995; encountered moons. Released probe into Jovian atmosphere; intentionally flown into Jupiter 9/21/2003 to prevent accidental contamination of Jupiter's moon Europa.
Mars Global Surveyor	Nov. 7, 1996	Mars	Began orbiting Mars 9/11/1997; began mapping entire surface 3/9/1999; discovered a weak magnetic field on planet; observed Martian moon Phobos; found evidence of liquid water in past 6/22/2000.
Mars Pathfinder	Dec. 4, 1996	Mars	Landed on Mars 7/4/1997; rover *Sojourner* made measurements of climate and soil composition, sending thousands of surface images; ceased operating 9/27/1997.
Cassini-Huygens	Oct. 15, 1997	Saturn	Began orbiting Saturn 6/30/2004; spotted evidence of a subterranean ocean and 300-mi-wide hot spots region on moon Titan; detected an atmosphere on moon Enceladus. *Huygens* probe landed on Titan 1/14/2005; found a muddy surface, possible water ice, channels carved by liquid methane springs.
Lunar Prospector	Jan. 6, 1998	Moon	Began orbiting Moon 1/11/1998; mapped abundance of 11 elements on Moon's surface; discovered evidence of water ice at both lunar poles; crashed into crater near Moon's south pole 7/31/1999 to end mission.
Deep Space 1	Oct. 24, 1998	Comet Borrelly	Flew within 1,500 mi of comet; sent back photos showing 6-mi-long nucleus.
Stardust	Feb. 7, 1999	Comet Wild 2	Reached comet 1/2/2004; gathered dust samples, capsule returned to Earth 1/15/2006. Spacecraft, on new mission Stardust-NExT (follow up for Deep Impact), reached comet Tempel 1, 2/14/2011.
2001 Mars Odyssey	Apr. 7, 2001	Mars	Reached Mars 10/24/2001; detected evidence of water ice near south pole; primary mission to study climate and geologic history completed 8/2004; began extended mission, aiming to identify minerals on Mars.
Genesis	Aug. 8, 2001	Sun	Orbited Sun, collected particles from solar wind; capsule containing specimens crashed to Earth 9/8/2004; some samples survived.
Mars Express/ Beagle 2 lander	June 3, 2003	Mars	1st European Space Agency probe to another planet; arrived at Mars 12/2003; performed remote sensing including photography in search of subsurface water; *Beagle 2* lander was deployed 12/19/2003, but contact was lost.
Mars Exploration Rovers	June 7 and July 10, 2003	Mars	Rovers *Spirit* and *Opportunity* landed on Mars 1/2004, found further evidence that water existed on surface; *Spirit* took 1st photo of a Martian meteor; survived severe dust storms in 2007. *Opportunity* explored massive Victoria Crater 2007-08, set record for most distance driven off-Earth (25 mi) 7/2014.
MESSENGER	Mar. 2, 2004	Mercury	Began returning images of Mercury during initial flyby 1/14/2008; entered orbit 3/17/2011; delivered 100,000th image 5/3/2012; impacted Mercury 4/30/2015.
Deep Impact	Jan. 12, 2005	Comet Tempel 1	Reached Tempel 1; deployed impact probe that slammed into comet 7/4/2005 with force roughly equivalent to 5 tons of TNT. Flyby spacecraft, on supplemental mission EPOXI, reached comet Hartley 2, 11/4/2010.
Mars Reconnaissance Orbiter	Aug. 12, 2005	Mars	Reached Mars 3/10/2006 and began taking detailed images of Martian surface; in 3/2008, found salt deposits suggesting ancient water supplies; in 6/2008, found largest known crater in solar system.
New Horizons (Pluto)	Jan. 19, 2006	Pluto, Charon	Flew past Jupiter 7/2007 on its way to Pluto and its largest moon, Charon. Returned first-ever photographs of Pluto 7/14/2015. Will examine other objects in the Kuiper Belt.
Phoenix Mars Lander	Aug. 4, 2007	Mars	Landed on Mars 5/25/2008; examined northern polar region, monitored weather and analyzed minerals; evidence of water ice verified 7/31/2008; lost contact 11/2/2008.
Dawn	Sept. 27, 2007	Asteroid Belt (bet. Jupiter and Mars)	Will compare evolution of dwarf planet Ceres with Vesta, an asteroid, in an effort to shed light on formation of the solar system. Departed Vesta 8/2012; reached Ceres 3/6/2015.
Kepler	Mar. 9, 2009	Extrasolar planets	Detect potentially habitable Earth-size planets around other Milky Way stars. As of 7/23/2015, Kepler had discovered more than 1,000 planets, including Kepler-452b, considered extremely similar to Earth in composition and orbit.
Lunar Crater Observation and Sensing Satellite (LCROSS)	June 18, 2009	Moon	Impacted the Cabeus crater; detected presence of water ice in Moon's surface 10/9/2009. Lunar Reconnaissance Orbiter (LRO), launched with LCROSS, mapped Moon's surface.
Mars Science Laboratory	Nov. 26, 2011	Mars	*Curiosity* rover landed on Mars 8/6/2012 and began assessing Mars's past and present ability to support life.
Lunar Atmosphere and Dust Environment Explorer (LADEE)	Sept. 6, 2013	Moon	Studied the fragile lunar atmosphere from orbit for 100 days; impacted with lunar surface 4/17/2014.
Mars Atmosphere and Volatile Evolution (MAVEN)	Nov. 18, 2013	Mars	Entered orbit 9/21/2014; exploring Mars's upper atmosphere to determine how loss of atmospheric gas has changed its climate over time.
InSight	Mar. 2016	Mars	Landing craft will study deep interior of Mars to investigate how rocky planets form and develop.
Osiris	Sept. 2016	Bennu, an asteroid	Will attempt to bring back a small sample of the asteroid by 2023 to help scientists understand the source of Earth's organic materials and water and improve understanding of potential asteroid-Earth impacts.
Transiting Exoplanet Survey Satellite (TESS)	Aug. 2017	Solar neighbor-hood	Two-year survey will monitor more than 500,000 stars for temporary changes in brightness caused by planetary transits.
Mars 2020	2020	Mars	Rover to investigate potential for human habitation.
Europa	2020s	Europa	Spacecraft will perform multiple flybys of Jupiter's ocean-bearing moon, Europa, to determine if it is suitable for life.

Note: U.S./NASA missions unless otherwise noted. (1) In Coordinated Universal Time.

General Aviation and Air Taxi Active Aircraft, 2013

Source: Federal Aviation Administration; aircraft not associated with major airlines or the military

Aircraft Type	Total active	Personal	Business	Instructional	Aerial apps.	Aerial observation	Other work	Sight-seeing	Air medical	Other	On-demand Operations
Fixed Wing	**158,911**	**105,054**	**25,265**	**10,934**	**2,971**	**2,737**	**765**	**375**	**156**	**3,258**	**6,912**
Piston	137,655	102,379	14,859	10,776	1,178	2,076	610	375	128	2,697	2,329
Turboprop	9,619	1,309	3,227	84	1,793	643	147	0	19	366	1,808
Turbojet	11,637	1,365	7,179	73	0	18	8	0	9	195	2,775
Rotorcraft	**9,765**	**1,205**	**669**	**1,373**	**620**	**1,876**	**76**	**131**	**208**	**466**	**2,362**
Piston	3,137	865	190	1,251	279	267	20	95	0	44	79
Turbine	6,628	340	479	122	342	1,610	56	36	208	422	2,284
Other Aircraft	**4,277**	**3,388**	**9**	**257**	**0**	**0**	**3**	**564**	**0**	**34**	**23**
Gliders	1,594	1,414	3	139	0	0	0	22	0	16	0
Lighter-than-air	2,684	1,974	6	118	0	0	3	542	0	18	23
Experimental	**24,918**	**22,581**	**570**	**563**	**40**	**174**	**130**	**13**	**10**	**716**	**100**
Amateur	17,503	16,577	339	242	0	76	57	5	0	202	5
Exhibition	1,908	1,632	20	42	0	5	25	2	0	182	0
Experimental Light-sport	4,157	3,874	16	150	0	31	30	0	0	56	0
Other	1,350	499	196	129	40	62	18	6	10	277	95
Special Light-sport	**2,056**	**1,647**	**56**	**274**	**3**	**18**	**0**	**0**	**0**	**45**	**12**
TOTAL ALL AIRCRAFT	**199,927**	**133,875**	**26,571**	**13,401**	**3,634**	**4,806**	**973**	**1,083**	**375**	**4,519**	**9,398**

Note: Columns may not add to totals due to rounding. **Personal**—Flying for personal reasons; **Business**—Individual or group use for business transportation without a paid, professional crew; **Corporate**—Individual or group business transportation with a paid, professional crew (includes fractional ownership); **Instructional**—Flying under the supervision of a flight instructor; **Aerial applications**—Includes agriculture, forestry, public health, fire fighting, and other applications; **Aerial observation**—Includes aerial mapping/photography, patrol, search and rescue, hunting, traffic advisory, ranching, surveillance, oil and mineral exploration, etc.; **Other work use**—Construction work, parachuting, aerial advertising, towing gliders, etc.; **Sight-seeing**—Commercial sight-seeing; **Air medical services**—Air ambulance services, rescue, human organ transportation, emergency medical services; **Other**—Positioning flights, proficiency flights, training, ferrying, sales demos; **On-demand operations**—On-demand air taxi, air tours, commuter, and air medical services.

Estimated Active Airmen Certificates Held, 2014

Source: Federal Aviation Administration, U.S. Dept. of Transportation

Category	Certificates	Category	Certificates	Category	Certificates
Pilot total	**593,499**	Rotorcraft (helicopters) (only)	15,511	Repairmen	39,566
Student	120,546	Glider (only)	19,927	Parachute Rigger	8,702
Recreational (only)	220	**Flight Instructor Certificates**	**100,993**	Ground Instructor	71,755
Sport (only)	5,157	**Instrument Ratings**	**306,066**	Dispatcher	23,113
Airplane[1]		**Nonpilot total**	**717,399**	Flight Navigator	115
Private	174,883	Mechanic	341,409	Flight Attendant	188,936
Commercial	104,322			Flight Engineer	43,803
Airline Transport	152,933				

Note: The term airmen includes men and women certified as pilots, mechanics, or other aviation technicians. (1) Includes pilots with an airplane-only certificate as well as those with an airplane and a helicopter and/or glider certificate.

Aircraft Operating Statistics

Source: Airbus S.A.S.; The Boeing Company; Embraer S.A.; as of July 30, 2014

Manufacturer and model	Max. # of seats	Typical # of seats	Fuel capacity (gal)	Typical cruising speed (mph)[1]	Max. range (naut. mi)	Max. thrust (thous. lbs)
Airbus						
A318	132	107	6,400	630	3,200	24.0
A319	156	124	6,400	630	3,700	27.0
A320	180	150	6,400	630	3,300	27.0
A321	220	185	6,350	630	6,200	33.0
A330-200	380	253	36,750	660	7,250	72.0
A330-300	440	295	26,765	660	5,850	72.0
A340-300	440	295	37,150	660	7,400	34.0
A340-500	375	313	56,870	660	9,000	56.0
A340-600	475	380	51,750	660	7,900	60.0
A380	853	525	84,600	684	8,300	70.0
Boeing						
727-200*	189	148	9,806	605	2,500	17.4
737-600	132	110	6,875	602	3,225	22.7
737-700	149	126	6,875	602	3,440	26.3
737-700C	140	126	6,875	599	3,285	27.3
737-800	189	162	6,875	602	3,115	27.3
737-900	215	180	7,837	599	3,265	27.3
747-100*	452	366	48,445	645	6,100	50.1
747-200/300*	452	366	52,410	645	7,900	54.8
747-400	524	416	57,285	653	7,260	63.3
747-8	467	467	64,055	653	8,000	66.5
757-200*	228	200	11,489	614	3,900	43.5
757-300*	280	243	11,466	614	3,395	43.5
767-200ER	255	181	23,980	614	6,385	62.1
767-300ER	350	218	23,980	614	5,990	63.3
767-400ER	375	245	23,980	614	5,625	63.5
777-200	440	305	31,000	645	5,420	77.0
777-200ER	440	301	45,220	645	7,725	93.7
777-200LR	314	301	47,890	645	9,395	115.3
777-300	550	368	45,220	645	6,005	98.0
777-300ER	386	386	47,890	645	7,390	115.3
787-8 Dreamliner	242	210	NA	652	8,200	NA
787-9 Dreamliner	280	250	NA	652	8,500	NA
Embraer						
190	114	98	NA	630	2,400	20.0
195	122	108	NA	630	2,200	20.0
McDonnell-Douglas						
DC-10 series*	380	250	36,650	600	6,220	24.0
MD-11*	410	285	NA	NA	7,360	NA
MD-80 series*	172	155	5,840	584	2,504	21.0
MD-90 series*	172	153	7,620	584	3,205	28.0

* = Aircraft no longer in production. NA = Not available. **Note:** Figures are for most commonly flown passenger models. When models within a series vary, maximums are shown. McDonnell-Douglas merged with Boeing in 1997. (1) Figures shown are converted from Mach speed (speed of sound), which varies depending on altitude and temperature. For comparison purposes, this table uses 768 mph as equivalent to Mach 1.

Milestones in Aviation History

Source: National Aeronautics and Space Administration (NASA); Smithsonian National Air and Space Museum; Air Transport Association of America; National Museum of the U.S. Air Force (USAF); National Park Service, U.S. Dept. of the Interior

1903, Dec. 17: Brothers Wilbur and Orville Wright (U.S.) made the first human-carrying, powered flight near Kitty Hawk, NC. Each brother made two flights; the longest, about 852 ft, lasted 59 sec.

1908, May 14: Charles Furnas (U.S.), worker for Wright brothers, became first American airplane passenger.

1911, Feb.: The Burgess Company and Curtiss, Inc. receive authorization to build Wright planes, becoming the first licensed airplane manufacturer in the U.S.

1911, Sept. 23: First transportation of mail by airplane officially approved by the U.S. Postal Service.

1914, Jan. 1: First scheduled passenger airline service began. A seaplane that landed on water operated between St. Petersburg and Tampa, FL.

1914, June 18: Lawrence Burst Sperry (U.S.) released the controls and stood in his airborne plane, successfully demonstrating his gyrostabilizer, the first autopilot system.

1918, Mar. 6: The Curtiss-Sperry "Flying Bomb" (U.S.) made its first successful flight. The first radio-controlled plane led to the development of cruise missiles.

1918, May 14: First scheduled airmail service began, between New York and Washington, DC, with intermediate stop in Philadelphia. In 1921, scheduled transcontinental airmail service began between New York City and San Francisco.

1919, June 14-15: Capt. John Alcock (UK) and Lt. Arthur W. Brown (U.S.) completed the first nonstop flight across the Atlantic Ocean. They traveled from Newfoundland, Canada, to Ireland in 16 hr., 12 min.

1923, Aug.: Rotating beacons enabled the first U.S. night flights.

1924, Apr. 6-Sept. 28: Two U.S. Army planes landed in Seattle, completing the first circumnavigation of the globe. They completed the 26,000-mi journey in 371 hours of flying time.

1926, May 12-13: Roald Amundsen (Norway), Umberto Nobile (Italy), Lincoln Ellsworth (U.S.), and Oscar Wisting (Norway) made the first flight over the North Pole, in a dirigible that flew between Spitsbergen, Norway, and Teller, AK. Two weeks earlier, Adm. Richard E. Byrd and Floyd Bennett (both U.S.) claimed to have made the first flight over the Pole (May 9, 1926) in a Fokker F-VII. But when Byrd's diary was released to the public in 1996, some historians began to question whether his plane had reached the Pole.

1927, May 20-21: Charles Lindbergh (U.S.) completed the first solo transatlantic flight in the *Spirit of St. Louis*. "Lucky Lindy" traveled 3,610 mi from New York to Paris in 33 hr., 29 min., 30 sec.

1929, Aug. 8-29: Hugo Eckener (Germany) piloted the *Graf Zeppelin* around the world in record time: 20,373 mi in 21 days, 5 hr., 31 min.

1929, Nov. 28: Adm. Richard E. Byrd (U.S.) and Bernt Balchen (Norway) became the first to fly to the South Pole and back, in 18 hr., 41 min.

1930, May 15: Ellen Church (U.S.) became first flight attendant.

1931, June 23-July 1: Wiley Post and Harold Gatty (both U.S.) broke the speed record for around-the-world flight, traveling 15,474 mi in 8 days, 15 hr., 51 min., in the monoplane *Winnie Mae*.

1931, Oct. 3-5: Clyde Pangborn and Hugh Herndon (both U.S.) completed the first nonstop transpacific flight. They traveled 4,558 mi from Misawa, Japan, to East Wenatchee, WA, in 41 hr., 34 min.

1932, May 20-21: Amelia Earhart (U.S.) completed first solo transoceanic flight by a woman, making the 2,026-mi journey from Newfoundland, Canada, to Ireland in 14 hr., 56 min.

1933, July 15-22: Wiley Post (U.S.) completed the first solo circumnavigation of the globe. His 15,596-mi trip took 7 days, 18 hr., 49 min.

1936, June 25: American Airlines began scheduled passenger service of the first Douglas DC-3 aircraft. The DC-3 was the first aircraft with a kitchen onboard and hence offered the first in-flight hot meal service.

1937, May 6: German *Hindenburg* zeppelin exploded in Lakehurst, NJ, killing 35 of the 97 people aboard (and one on the ground). The airship had made 34 transatlantic flights in 1936.

1938, July 10-13: Howard Hughes (U.S.) and four assistants established a new speed record for circumnavigating the globe: 14,824 mi in 3 days, 9 hr., 17 min.

1939, Aug. 27: The German-made Heinkel He 178 made the first successful flight powered by a jet engine.

1947, June 17-30: Pan American Airways began the first scheduled around-the-world passenger flights, from New York or San Francisco.

1947, Oct. 14: Chuck Yeager (U.S.) broke the sound barrier, reaching Mach 1 speed in a Bell X-1 rocket-powered aircraft.

1947, Nov. 2: Howard Hughes (U.S.) piloted the *Spruce Goose* on its maiden and only flight. The largest airplane ever built, it could carry 750 troops or two Sherman tanks.

1949, Mar. 2: James Gallagher (U.S.) piloted the first round-the-world flight to be refueled in midair. The *Lucky Lady* USAF B-50 covered 23,452 mi in 94 hr., 1 min. and was refueled four times.

1950, Sept. 22: Col. David Schilling (USAF) made the first nonstop transatlantic jet flight, covering 3,300 mi in 10 hr., 1 min.

1952, Aug. 26: The UK bomber Canberra made the first round-trip transatlantic crossing on the same day, from Northern Ireland to Newfoundland, Canada, and back in 7 hr., 59 min.

1953, May 18: Jacqueline Cochran (U.S.) became the first woman to fly faster than the speed of sound.

1956, Mar. 10: Britain's Fairey FD-2 aircraft set a world speed record of 1,132 mph.

1956, Nov. 11: Convair B-58 (USAF), the first supersonic bomber, was introduced.

1957, Jan. 15-18: Three USAF B-52 Stratofortresses made the first nonstop global flight by jet planes. They were refueled in flight by KC-97 aerial tankers.

1958, Oct. 24: A Mirage III-A achieved Mach 2 (twice the speed of sound) in level flight, first European plane to do so.

1962, Nov. 29: Britain and France signed an agreement to jointly develop the Concorde, a supersonic plane that could fly twice as fast as most U.S. jets.

1969, June 5: The Soviet Tupolev Tu-144 became the first passenger airliner to reach Mach 2.

1970, May 26: The Tupolev Tu-144 reached a top speed of about 1,335 mph at 53,475 ft.

1976, Aug. 23: The Concorde began the first scheduled supersonic commercial service.

1977, Aug. 23: The *Gossamer Condor*, built by aeronautical engineer Paul MacCready (U.S.), successfully demonstrated human-powered flight through pedalling, completing a figure-8 course of 1.15 mi.

1979, June 12: MacCready's human-powered *Gossamer Albatross* crossed the English Channel in 2 hr., 49 min.

1981, July 7: MacCready-developed *Solar Challenger* became first solar-powered airplane to cross the English Channel.

1995, Aug. 15-16: The Concorde set a new around-the-world speed record of 31 hr., 27 min., 49 sec.

1999, Mar. 1-21: Bertrand Piccard (Switz.) and Brian Jones (UK) completed the first around-the-world flight in a hot-air balloon. Their 29,055-mi journey began in Chateau-d'Oex, Switzerland, and ended 19 days, 21 hr., 55 min. later in the Egyptian desert.

2001, Aug. 13: Solar-powered, propeller-driven plane *Helios* (NASA) reached 96,863 ft, breaking altitude record for non-rocket-powered aircraft.

2002, June 19-July 4: Steve Fossett (U.S.) completed the first nonstop solo circumnavigation of globe in a balloon.

2003, Nov. 26: The Concorde flew its final flight.

2005, Mar. 1-3: Steve Fossett (U.S.) achieved the first nonstop solo circumnavigation in an airplane without refueling.

2006, Feb. 8-11: Steve Fossett (U.S.) flew the longest nonstop, non-refueled solo flight (25,766 mi).

2009, Dec. 15: Boeing's 787 Dreamliner, the company's most fuel-efficient plane and the first to be constructed primarily from composite materials, made its maiden voyage.

2011, Feb. 4: Northrop Grumman and the U.S. Navy reported the first successful flight for the unmanned X-47B fighter jet.

2012, May 22-31: SpaceX became the first private company to successfully launch (and later recover) a spacecraft to the International Space Station.

2013, July 6: *Solar Impulse* became first solar-powered airplane to fly across the U.S. without fuel. Flying both day and night, it traveled from San Francisco to New York, NY, with stops in Phoenix, Dallas, St. Louis, and Washington, DC, in 62 days.

2015, July 3: *Solar Impulse* 2 set record for longest nonstop solo flight and longest flight in a solar-powered plane (118 hr.), traveling from Japan to Hawaii.

ASTRONOMY

Edited by Michael J. Kaufman, Dept. of Physics and Astronomy, San Jose State University

Celestial Events Summary, 2016

There are four eclipses in 2016: one total solar eclipse, one annular solar eclipse, and two penumbral lunar eclipses. The Mar. total solar eclipse will only make landfall over limited areas of Indonesia, though the path of totality will extend from the Indian Ocean across a large portion of the Pacific; a partial eclipse may be observed over a much wider area from central Asia through the Hawaiian Islands. The Sept. annular solar eclipse will be visible across central Africa, with a partial phase observable over much of the African continent. Neither of the lunar eclipses is notable; penumbral lunar eclipses produce so little dimming of moonlight that they are hardly noticeable.

The best meteor shower viewing will be the Eta Aquarids in May, the Perseids in Aug., and the Taurids in Nov. Other major meteor showers will be hampered by unfavorably bright Moon phases in 2016. At the start of the year, Jupiter, Mars, Saturn, and Venus will be visible in the predawn sky. Venus is a "morning star" until May when it disappears into the glare of the Sun. Venus reemerges in the evening sky by late July and remains visible in the evening for the rest of the year. Mars and Saturn are in the morning sky into May, then become more prominent in the evening sky from June through the end of the year. Jupiter is an evening object late Mar. into Sept. before moving into the morning sky again in late Oct. Mercury begins the year as an evening object, setting soon after the Sun, before moving to the morning sky by mid-Jan. The best opportunities for seeing Mercury in the morning sky occur in early Feb., and early June, while the best opportunity to see it in the evening sky occurs in late Aug.

The crescent Moon, with its subdued light, regularly pairs with the two brightest planets, Venus and Jupiter. Waxing crescent pairings are visible in the early evening soon after sunset, while waning crescent pairings are visible in the early morning before sunrise. The waxing crescent Moon pairs with Venus in each of the months from Sept. to Dec., while the waning crescent pairs with Venus in the early morning sky each month from Jan. through Mar. The waxing crescent Moon pairs with Jupiter in the evening in June-Sept. and the waning crescent pairs with Jupiter in Oct. and Nov. Jupiter and Venus will have an exceptionally close encounter on the evening of Aug. 27. The waning crescent Moon joins Venus and Saturn Jan. 9.

A rare transit of Mercury, in which the planet Mercury is seen in silhouette crossing in front of the Sun, takes place May 8, 2016. The event will last more than 7 hr., and observers in the eastern U.S. and Canada, much of South America, western Europe, and NW Africa will be in position to see the entire transit. Use of a telescope or binoculars is generally necessary to observe the transit. Appropriate solar filters must be used to avoid permanent eye damage.

Astronomical Positions and Constants

Two celestial bodies are in **conjunction** when they are due north and south of each other, either in **right ascension** (with respect to the north celestial pole) or in **celestial longitude** (with respect to the north ecliptic pole). Celestial bodies in conjunction will rise and set at nearly the same time. For the inner planets—Mercury and Venus—**inferior conjunction** occurs when either planet passes between Earth and the Sun, while **superior conjunction** occurs when either Mercury or Venus is on the far side of the Sun. Celestial bodies are in **opposition** when their right ascensions differ by exactly 12 hours, or when their celestial longitudes differ by 180°. In this case one of the two objects in opposition will rise while the other is setting. **Quadrature** refers to the arrangement where the coordinates of two bodies differ by exactly 90°. These terms may refer to the relative positions of any two bodies as seen from Earth, but one of the bodies is so frequently the Sun that mention of the Sun is omitted in that case.

When objects are in conjunction, the alignment is not perfect, and one usually passes above or below the other. The geocentric angular separation between the Sun and an object is termed **elongation**. Elongation is limited only for Mercury and Venus; the greatest elongation for each of these bodies is approximately the time for longest observation. **Perihelion** is the point in an object's orbit when it is nearest to the Sun, and **aphelion** is the point when it is farthest from the Sun. **Perigee** is the point in an orbit where an object is nearest Earth, **apogee** the point when it is farthest from Earth. An **occultation** of a planet or a star is an eclipse of it by some other body, usually the Moon. A **transit** of the Sun occurs when Mercury or Venus passes directly between Earth and the Sun, appearing to cross the Sun's disk.

The following were adopted as part of the International Astronomical Union System of Astronomical Constants (1976/2009): **Speed of light**, 299,792.458 km per sec., or about 186,282 statute mi per sec.; **solar parallax**, 8".794143; **astronomical unit** (AU, mean distance between the Earth and Sun), 149,597,870 km, or 92,955,807 mi; **constant of nutation**, 9".2025; and **constant of aberration**, 20".49552.

Celestial Events Highlights, 2016

(In Coordinated Universal Time, or UTC, the standard time of the prime meridian.)

January

Mercury is low in the SW after sunset at beginning of month and low in the SE before sunrise at end of month.

Venus and **Saturn** are in the SE before sunrise all month.

Mars and **Jupiter** rise in the middle of the night and are high in the S before sunrise.

Uranus and **Neptune** are in the SW after sunset and set several hours later.

Jan. 1: Sun in Sagittarius, Mercury in Capricorn, Venus in Libra, Mars in Virgo, Jupiter in Leo, Saturn in Ophiuchus all year, Uranus in Pisces all year, Neptune in Aquarius all year

Jan. 2: Last Quarter Moon, Moon at apogee, Earth at perihelion, Venus enters Scorpius

Jan. 3: Spica 4.73° S of Moon, Mars 1.49° S of Moon, Quadrantid meteor shower

Jan. 5: Venus enters Ophiuchus

Jan. 6: Antares 6.46° S of Venus, Antares 9.54° S of Moon

Jan. 7: Venus 3.10° S of Moon, Saturn 3.31° S of Moon

Jan. 9: Saturn 0.09° S of Venus, Mercury enters Sagittarius

Jan. 10: New Moon, Mercury 2.13° S of Moon

Jan. 13: Neptune 2.26° S of Moon

Jan. 14: Mercury in inferior conjunction 3.03° N of Sun

Jan. 15: Moon at perigee

Jan. 16: Uranus 1.46° N of Moon, First Quarter Moon

Jan. 17: Mars enters Libra

Jan. 20: Aldebaran 0.50° S of Moon, Sun enters Capricorn, Venus enters Sagittarius

Jan. 23: Pollux 11.18° N of Moon

Jan. 24: Full Moon

Jan. 26: Regulus 2.53° N of Moon

Jan. 28: Jupiter 1.42° N of Moon

Jan. 30: Moon at apogee, Spica 4.98° S of Moon

February

Mercury and **Venus** are in the SE before sunrise all month.
Mars and **Saturn** rise after midnight and are high in the S before sunrise.
Jupiter rises late in the evening and is high in the SW at sunrise.
Uranus is high in the S at sunset and sets several hours later.
Neptune is low in the S at sunset at start of month, then lost in the Sun's glare by end of the month.

Feb. 1: Last Quarter Moon, Mars 2.73° S of Moon
Feb. 3: Antares 9.72° S of Moon, Saturn 3.49° S of Moon
Feb. 6: Venus 4.32° S of Moon, Mercury 3.78° S of Moon
Feb. 7: Mercury at greatest elongation 25.6° W of Sun
Feb. 8: New Moon
Feb. 10: Neptune 2.07° S of Moon
Feb. 11: Moon at perigee
Feb. 12: Uranus 1.73° N of Moon
Feb. 14: Mercury enters Capricorn
Feb. 15: First Quarter Moon
Feb. 16: Aldebaran 0.34° S of Moon, Sun enters Aquarius, Venus enters Capricorn
Feb. 19: Pollux 11.24° N of Moon
Feb. 22: Regulus 2.50° N of Moon, Full Moon
Feb. 24: Jupiter 1.69° N of Moon
Feb. 26: Spica 5.10° S of Moon
Feb. 27: Moon at apogee
Feb. 28: Neptune 0.79° S of Sun
Feb. 29: Mars 3.58° S of Moon

March

Mercury is in the SE before sunrise at beginning of month but lost in the Sun's glare by end of month.
Venus is in the SE before sunrise all month.
Mars and **Saturn** rise around midnight and are high in the S at sunrise.
Jupiter rises around sunset and is up all night.
Uranus is low in the W at sunset.
Nepture is low in the E at sunrise.

Mar. 1: Antares 9.84° S of Moon, Last Quarter Moon
Mar. 2: Saturn 3.57° S of Moon
Mar. 3: Mercury enters Aquarius
Mar. 7: Venus 3.50° S of Moon
Mar. 8: Mercury 3.90° S of Moon, Jupiter at opposition, Neptune 1.97° S of Moon
Mar. 9: New Moon, Total Solar Eclipse
Mar. 10: Moon at perigee, Neptune 1.49° N of Mercury, Venus enters Aquarius
Mar. 11: Uranus 1.90° N of Moon, Sun enters Pisces
Mar. 13: Mars enters Scorpius
Mar. 14: Aldebaran 0.28° S of Moon
Mar. 15: First Quarter Moon
Mar. 17: Pollux 11.28° N of Moon
Mar. 19: Mercury enters Pisces
Mar. 20: Equinox, Neptune 0.53° N of Venus, Regulus 2.52° N of Moon
Mar. 22: Jupiter 2.05° N of Moon
Mar. 23: Full Moon, Mercury in superior conjunction 1.29° S of Sun, Penumbral Lunar Eclipse
Mar. 25: Spica 5.09° S of Moon, Moon at apogee, Mercury enters Cetus
Mar. 26: Mercury enters Pisces
Mar. 28: Mars 4.19° S of Moon
Mar. 29: Antares 9.81° S of Moon, Saturn 3.50° S of Moon
Mar. 31: Last Quarter Moon

April

Mercury is low in the W at sunset all month.
Venus is low in the E at sunrise all month.
Mars and **Saturn** rise before midnight and are low in the SW at sunrise.
Jupiter is high in the W at sunset and sets several hours before sunrise.
Uranus is low in the SE at sunrise by the end of month.
Neptune is in the SE at sunrise all month.

Apr. 1: Uranus 0.63° S of Mercury, Venus enters Pisces
Apr. 2: Mars enters Ophiuchus
Apr. 5: Neptune 1.87° S of Moon, Mercury enters Aries
Apr. 6: Venus 0.69° S of Moon
Apr. 7: New Moon, Uranus 2.01° N of Moon, Moon at perigee
Apr. 8: Mercury 5.16° N of Moon
Apr. 9: Uranus 0.59° S of Sun
Apr. 10: Aldebaran 0.35° S of Moon, Venus enters Cetus
Apr. 14: First Quarter Moon, Pollux 11.19° N of Moon, Venus enters Pisces
Apr. 17: Regulus 2.45° N of Moon, Sun enters Aries
Apr. 18: Jupiter 2.20° N of Moon, Mercury at greatest elongation 19.9° E of Sun
Apr. 21: Spica 5.07° S of Moon, Moon at apogee
Apr. 22: Full Moon, Uranus 0.88° N of Venus
Apr. 23: Lyrid meteor shower
Apr. 25: Mars 4.92° S of Moon, Antares 9.71° S of Moon, Saturn 3.33° S of Moon
Apr. 30: Last Quarter Moon, Venus enters Aries, Mars enters Scorpius

May

Mercury is low in the W after sunset at beginning of month and low in the E before sunrise at end of month.
Venus is low in the E before sunrise at beginning of month before disappearing into the Sun's glare by the end of the month.
Mars and **Saturn** rise mid-evening and are low in the SW at sunrise.
Jupiter is high in the S at sunset and sets after midnight.
Uranus and **Neptune** rise after midnight and are in the SE before sunrise.

May 2: Neptune 1.69° S of Moon
May 5: Uranus 2.17° N of Moon
May 6: Venus 2.72° N of Moon, Moon at perigee, New Moon, Eta Aquarid meteor shower
May 7: Mercury 5.23° N of Moon
May 8: Aldebaran 0.46° S of Moon
May 9: Transit of Mercury
May 11: Pollux 11.00° N of Moon
May 13: First Quarter Moon, Venus 0.43° N of Mercury, Sun enters Taurus
May 14: Regulus 2.25° N of Moon
May 15: Jupiter 1.99° N of Moon
May 18: Spica 5.16° S of Moon, Moon at apogee, Venus enters Taurus
May 21: Mars 6.02° S of Moon, Full Moon
May 22: Mars at opposition, Antares 9.62° S of Moon, Saturn 3.21° S of Moon
May 28: Mars enters Libra
May 29: Last Quarter Moon, Neptune 1.43° S of Moon

June

Mercury is low in the E before sunrise all month.
Venus is low in the W after sunset late in the month.
Mars and **Saturn** are low in the SE at sunset and remain up most of the night.
Jupiter is high in the SSW at sunset and sets several hours later.
Uranus and **Neptune** rise after midnight and are high in the SSW before sunrise.

June 1: Uranus 2.42° N of Moon
June 2: Aldebaran 5.33° S of Venus
June 3: Saturn at opposition, Mercury 0.74° N of Moon, Moon at perigee
June 4: Aldebaran 0.50° S of Moon
June 5: Venus 4.95° N of Moon, New Moon, Mercury at greatest elongation 24.2° W of Sun
June 6: Venus in superior conjunction 0.01° S of Sun, Mercury enters Taurus
June 7: Pollux 10.80° N of Moon
June 10: Regulus 1.99° N of Moon
June 11: Jupiter 1.49° N of Moon
June 12: First Quarter Moon
June 14: Spica 5.36° S of Moon
June 15: Moon at apogee
June 17: Mars 7.10° S of Moon, Venus enters Gemini
June 18: Antares 9.65° S of Moon
June 19: Saturn 3.25° S of Moon, Aldebaran 3.94° S of Mercury
June 20: Full Moon, Solstice
June 21: Sun enters Gemini
June 26: Neptune 1.19° S of Moon
June 27: Last Quarter Moon
June 28: Uranus 2.70° N of Moon, Mercury enters Gemini

July

Mercury is low in the W at sunset late in the month.
Venus is low in the W at sunset all month.
Mars and **Saturn** are high in the SE at sunset and set before sunrise.
Uranus rises before midnight and high in the S at sunrise.
Neptune rises before midnight and is in the SW at sunrise.

July 1: Moon at perigee
July 2: Aldebaran 0.43° S of Moon
July 4: Mercury 5.64° N of Moon, New Moon, Earth at aphelion
July 5: Venus 5.10° N of Moon, Pollux 10.70° N of Moon
July 7: Mercury in superior conjunction 1.39° N of Sun, Pollux 5.69° N of Venus
July 8: Regulus 1.78° N of Moon
July 9: Jupiter 0.85° N of Moon
July 10: Venus enters Cancer
July 11: Pollux 5.05° N of Mercury
July 12: First Quarter Moon, Spica 5.60° S of Moon, Mercury enters Cancer
July 13: Moon at apogee
July 14: Mars 7.81° S of Moon
July 16: Antares 9.78° S of Moon, Saturn 3.43° S of Moon, Venus 0.53° S of Mercury
July 19: Full Moon
July 20: Sun enters Cancer
July 23: Neptune 1.06° S of Moon, Mercury enters Leo
July 26: Uranus 2.93° N of Moon, Last Quarter Moon, Venus enters Leo
July 27: Moon at perigee
July 28: Delta Aquarid meteor shower
July 29: Aldebaran 0.29° S of Moon
July 30: Regulus 0.33° S of Mercury

August

Mercury, **Venus**, and **Jupiter** are low in the W at sunset.
Mars and **Saturn** are in the S at sunset and set several hours later.
Uranus and **Neptune** rise mid-evening and are in the W at sunrise.

Aug. 1: Pollux 10.70° N of Moon
Aug. 2: New Moon, Mars enters Scorpius
Aug. 4: Venus 2.90° N of Moon, Regulus 1.68° N of Moon, Mercury 0.56° N of Moon
Aug. 5: Regulus 1.09° S of Venus
Aug. 6: Jupiter 0.21° N of Moon
Aug. 8: Spica 5.77° S of Moon, Jupiter enters Virgo
Aug. 10: Moon at apogee, First Quarter Moon, Sun enters Leo
Aug. 11: Mars 8.16° S of Moon
Aug. 12: Antares 9.92° S of Moon, Saturn 3.66° S of Moon, Perseid meteor shower
Aug. 16: Mercury at greatest elongation 27.4° E of Sun
Aug. 18: Full Moon
Aug. 19: Neptune 1.07° S of Moon
Aug. 20: Mercury enters Virgo
Aug. 21: Mars enters Ophiuchus
Aug. 22: Moon at perigee, Uranus 3.01° N of Moon
Aug. 24: Antares 1.81° S of Mars, Venus enters Virgo
Aug. 25: Last Quarter Moon, Aldebaran 0.19° S of Moon, Saturn 4.39° N of Mars
Aug. 27: Venus 5.26° N of Mercury, Jupiter 0.07° S of Venus, Mars enters Scorpius
Aug. 29: Pollux 10.75° N of Moon
Aug. 31: Regulus 1.68° N of Moon

September

Mercury is low in the W at sunset at beginning of month and low in the E at sunrise at end of month.
Venus is in the W at sunset all month.
Mars and **Saturn** are in the SSW at sunset and set several hours later.
Uranus rises after sunset and is up all night.
Neptune rises before sunset and is up most of the night.

Sept. 1: New Moon, Annular Solar Eclipse
Sept. 2: Mercury 6.05° S of Moon, Neptune at opposition, Jupiter 0.37° S of Moon, Mars enters Ophiuchus
Sept. 3: Venus 1.12° S of Moon
Sept. 4: Spica 5.82° S of Moon
Sept. 6: Moon at apogee
Sept. 7: Mercury enters Leo
Sept. 8: Antares 9.96° S of Moon, Saturn 3.81° S of Moon
Sept. 9: First Quarter Moon, Mars 7.94° S of Moon
Sept. 13: Mercury in inferior conjunction 3.39° S of Sun
Sept. 15: Neptune 1.15° S of Moon, Sun enters Virgo
Sept. 16: Full Moon, Penumbral Lunar Eclipse
Sept. 17: Spica 2.65° S of Venus
Sept. 18: Uranus 2.95° N of Moon, Moon at perigee
Sept. 21: Aldebaran 0.21° S of Moon, Mars enters Sagittarius
Sept. 22: Equinox
Sept. 23: Last Quarter Moon
Sept. 25: Pollux 10.73° N of Moon
Sept. 26: Jupiter 1.09° N of Sun
Sept. 27: Regulus 1.67° N of Moon
Sept. 28: Mercury at greatest elongation 17.9° W of Sun
Sept. 29: Mercury 0.71° N of Moon
Sept. 30: Jupiter 0.90° S of Moon, Venus enters Libra

October

Mercury is low in the E at sunrise the first half of the month.
Venus is in the SW at sunset all month.
Mars is in the S at sunset and sets several hours later.
Jupiter is low in the E at sunrise late in the month.
Saturn is in the W at sunset.
Uranus and **Neptune** are in the ESE at sunset and remain up most of the night.

Oct. 1: New Moon
Oct. 2: Spica 5.78° S of Moon, Mercury enters Virgo
Oct. 3: Venus 5.03° S of Moon
Oct. 4: Moon at apogee
Oct. 6: Antares 9.88° S of Moon, Saturn 3.81° S of Moon
Oct. 8: Mars 7.00° S of Moon
Oct. 9: First Quarter Moon
Oct. 11: Jupiter 0.87° S of Mercury
Oct. 13: Neptune 1.16° S of Moon

Oct. 15: Uranus at opposition
Oct. 16: Uranus 2.84° N of Moon, Full Moon
Oct. 17: Moon at perigee, Venus enters Scorpius
Oct. 19: Aldebaran 0.33° S of Moon
Oct. 20: Spica 3.56° S of Mercury
Oct. 21: Orionid meteor shower
Oct. 22: Pollux 10.58° N of Moon, Last Quarter Moon
Oct. 24: Venus enters Ophiuchus
Oct. 25: Regulus 1.55° N of Moon
Oct. 26: Antares 3.14° S of Venus
Oct. 27: Mercury in superior conjunction 0.51° N of Sun
Oct. 28: Jupiter 1.42° S of Moon
Oct. 29: Spica 5.77° S of Moon, Mercury enters Libra
Oct. 30: Saturn 3.03° N of Venus, New Moon, Mercury 4.32° S of Moon, Sun enters Libra
Oct. 31: Moon at apogee

November

Mercury is low in the W at sunset late in the month.
Venus, **Mars**, and **Saturn** are in the SSW at sunset all month.
Jupiter is in the W at sunrise all month.
Uranus and **Neptune** are in the SSE at sunset and up much of the night.

Nov. 2: Antares 9.74° S of Moon, Saturn 3.72° S of Moon
Nov. 3: Venus 6.84° S of Moon
Nov. 4: Taurid meteor shower
Nov. 6: Mars 5.30° S of Moon
Nov. 7: First Quarter Moon
Nov. 8: Mars enters Capricorn
Nov. 9: Neptune 1.00° S of Moon, Venus enters Sagittarius
Nov. 12: Uranus 2.84° N of Moon, Mercury enters Scorpius
Nov. 14: Moon at perigee, Full Moon
Nov. 15: Aldebaran 0.45° S of Moon
Nov. 17: Mercury enters Ophiuchus, Leonid meteor shower
Nov. 18: Pollux 10.35° N of Moon, Antares 2.82° S of Mercury
Nov. 21: Last Quarter Moon, Regulus 1.30° N of Moon
Nov. 23: Sun enters Scorpius
Nov. 24: Saturn 3.47° N of Mercury
Nov. 25: Jupiter 1.94° S of Moon, Spica 5.90° S of Moon
Nov. 27: Moon at apogee
Nov. 29: New Moon, Antares 9.67° S of Moon, Sun enters Ophiuchus
Nov. 30: Saturn 3.63° S of Moon, Mercury enters Sagittarius

December

Mercury is low in the W after sunset the first half of the month.
Venus, **Mars**, and **Neptune** are in the SSW at sunset all month.
Jupiter is in the E at sunrise all month.
Uranus is high in the SE at sunset and up most of the night.

Dec. 1: Mercury 7.09° S of Moon
Dec. 3: Venus 5.81° S of Moon
Dec. 5: Mars 2.95° S of Moon
Dec. 6: Neptune 0.70° S of Moon, Venus enters Capricorn
Dec. 7: First Quarter Moon
Dec. 9: Uranus 3.01° N of Moon
Dec. 10: Saturn 1.30° N of Sun
Dec. 11: Mercury at greatest elongation 20.8° E of Sun
Dec. 12: Moon at perigee
Dec. 13: Aldebaran 0.46° S of Moon, Geminid meteor shower
Dec. 14: Full Moon
Dec. 15: Mars enters Aquarius
Dec. 16: Pollux 10.15° N of Moon
Dec. 17: Sun enters Sagittarius
Dec. 18: Regulus 1.02° N of Moon
Dec. 21: Last Quarter Moon, Solstice
Dec. 22: Jupiter 2.41° S of Moon, Spica 6.14° S of Moon
Dec. 25: Moon at apogee
Dec. 26: Antares 9.73° S of Moon
Dec. 27: Saturn 3.60° S of Moon
Dec. 28: Mercury in inferior conjunction 2.44° N of Sun
Dec. 29: Mercury 1.76° S of Moon, New Moon
Dec. 31: Venus enters Aquarius

Meteorites and Meteor Showers

When a chunk of material, ice or rock, plunges into Earth's atmosphere and burns up in a fiery display, the event is a **meteor**. While the chunk of material is still in space, it is a **meteoroid**. If a portion of the material survives passage through the atmosphere and reaches the ground, the remnant on the ground is a **meteorite**.

Meteorites found on Earth are classified into types, depending on their composition: **irons**, those composed chiefly of iron, a small percentage of nickel, and traces of other metals such as cobalt; **stones**, stony meteors consisting of silicates; and **stony irons**, containing varying proportions of both iron and stone.

Serious study of meteorites as non-Earth objects began in the 20th century. Scientists use sophisticated chemical analysis, X-rays, and mass spectrography in determining their origin and composition. Although most meteorites are now believed to be fragments of asteroids or comets, geochemical studies have shown that a few Antarctic stones came from the Moon or from Mars, presumably ejected by the explosive impact of asteroids.

The largest known meteorite, estimated to weigh about 55 metric tons, is the Hoba meteorite near Grootfontein, Namibia. The Manicouagan impact crater in Quebec, Canada, with an estimated diameter of 60 mi, is one of the largest crater structures still visible on the surface of the Earth. Not obvious to the eye because of erosion, larger impact craters identified include the Vredefort crater in South Africa at 185 mi across and the Sudbury crater in Ontario, Canada, estimated at 125 mi across. The Bedout impact site off the NW coast of Australia gained attention in 2004 when scientists identified further evidence in support of the idea that it may be linked to the Permian extinction event 250 mil years ago.

Meteor showers vary in strength, but usually the three most visible meteor showers of the year are the **Perseids**, around Aug. 13, the **Orionids**, around Oct. 21, and the **Geminids**, around Dec. 14. These showers feature meteors at the rate of about 60 per hour. Best observing conditions occur in the absence of moonlight, usually when the Moon's phase is between waning crescent and waxing quarter. Bright Moons can adversely affect viewing of some of the best showers of the year.

For most meteor showers the cometary debris is relatively uniformly scattered along the comet's orbit. However, in the case of the **Leonid** meteor shower, which occurs every year around Nov. 17-18, the debris from Comet Temple-Tuttle seems to be bunched up in one stretch. Hence, the meteor shower produced in most years is relatively weak. However, about every 33 years, Earth encounters the bunched-up debris when it crosses the comet's orbit. Sometimes the expected shower is a disappointment, as in 1899 and 1933; at other times, the dense debris provides a spectacular show, as in 1833 and 1866. The Leonids stormed again more recently, producing rates of 1,000-3,000 meteors per hour in 2001.

Morning and Evening "Stars," 2016

(In Coordinated Universal Time, or UTC, the standard time of the prime meridian.)

	Morning	Evening
Jan.	Mercury from Jan. 15 Venus Mars Jupiter Saturn	Mercury to Jan. 14 Uranus Neptune
Feb.	Mercury Venus Mars Jupiter Saturn	Uranus Neptune
Mar.	Mercury to Mar. 23 Venus Mars Jupiter to Mar. 8 Saturn Neptune from Mar. 9	Mercury from Mar. 24 Jupiter from Mar. 9 Uranus Neptune to Mar. 8
Apr.	Venus Mars Saturn Uranus from Apr. 10 Neptune	Mercury Jupiter
May	Mercury from May 10 Venus Mars to May 22 Saturn Uranus Neptune	Mercury to May 9 Mars from May 23 Jupiter
June	Mercury Venus to June 6 Saturn to June 3 Uranus Neptune	Venus from June 7 Mars Jupiter Saturn from June 4
July	Mercury to July 7 Uranus Neptune	Mercury from July 8 Venus Mars Jupiter Saturn
Aug.	Uranus Neptune	Mercury Venus Mars Jupiter Saturn
Sept.	Mercury from Sept. 14 Jupiter from Sept. 27 Uranus Neptune to Sept. 2	Mercury to Sept. 13 Venus Mars Jupiter to Sept. 26 Neptune from Sept. 3
Oct.	Mercury to Oct. 27 Jupiter Uranus to Oct. 15	Mercury from Oct. 28 Venus Mars Saturn Uranus from Oct. 16 Neptune
Nov.	Jupiter	Mercury Venus Mars Saturn Uranus Neptune
Dec.	Mercury from Dec. 29 Jupiter Saturn from Dec. 11	Mercury to Dec. 28 Venus Mars Saturn to Dec. 10 Uranus Neptune

Greenwich Sidereal Time for 0h UTC, 2016

UTC = Coordinated Universal Time. Add 12 hours to obtain right ascension of mean sun.

Date	Hr.	Min.	Date	Hr.	Min.	Date	Hr.	Min.	Date	Hr.	Min.
Jan. 1	6	40.4	Apr. 10	13	14.6	July 9	19	9.5	Oct. 7	1	4.3
Jan. 11	7	19.8	Apr. 20	13	54.0	July 19	19	48.9	Oct. 17	1	43.7
Jan. 21	7	59.2	Apr. 30	14	33.5	July 29	20	28.3	Oct. 27	2	23.1
Jan. 31	8	38.6	May 10	15	12.9	Aug. 8	21	7.7	Nov. 6	3	2.6
Feb. 10	9	18.1	May 20	15	52.3	Aug. 18	21	47.2	Nov. 16	3	42.0
Feb. 20	9	57.5	May 30	16	31.8	Aug. 28	22	26.6	Nov. 26	4	21.4
Mar. 1	10	36.9	June 9	17	11.2	Sept. 7	23	6.0	Dec. 6	5	0.8
Mar. 11	11	16.3	June 19	17	50.6	Sept. 17	23	45.4	Dec. 16	5	40.3
Mar. 21	11	55.8	June 29	18	30.0	Sept. 27	0	24.9	Dec. 26	6	19.7
Mar. 31	12	35.2									

Largest Telescopes

Astronomers indicate the size of telescopes not by length or magnification but by the diameter of the primary light-gathering component, such as the lens or mirror. The larger the diameter of the mirror or lens, the fainter the objects that can be detected. In principle, larger telescopes also have better resolving power—the ability to discern small details—than smaller telescopes. However, the Earth's atmosphere limits the details that can be seen using ground-based telescopes. That is why the Hubble Space Telescope, which orbits the Earth outside of its atmosphere, can achieve higher resolutions with its 2.4-m (7.9-ft) mirror than much larger telescopes on Earth. Adaptive optics systems can compensate for the blurring effects of the Earth's atmosphere, allowing ground-based telescopes to achieve higher levels of detail. Telescopes to detect ultraviolet, X-ray, and gamma radiation must be placed in space or high-altitude balloons because the atmosphere absorbs most of these types of radiation; as a result, such telescopes are generally much smaller than optical, infrared, and radio telescopes.

Refracting (lens) telescopes are currently not made with lens diameters of more than 40 in. Because **reflecting telescopes** can be made less expensively and with more precision than refracting telescopes, all modern large optical telescopes are made with mirrors. **Radio telescopes** are larger than optical telescopes because larger diameters are required to obtain equivalent resolution of radio's longer wavelengths. A technique called interferometry, originally developed for radio telescopes, uses arrays of telescopes to achieve better resolution.

Largest refracting (lens) optical telescope: Yerkes Observatory, 1 m (40 in.), at Williams Bay, WI

Largest reflecting (mirror) optical/infrared telescope: Gran Telescopio Canarias, 10.4 m (34 ft), on La Palma, Canary Islands (segmented mirror)

Largest infrared interferometer: Four 8.2-m (27-ft) telescopes of the Very Large Telescope Interferometer (VLTI) with a 200-m (656-ft) baseline on Cerro Paranal in Chile

Largest fully steerable radio dish: Robert Byrd Green Bank Telescope (GBT), 100 m (328 ft), in Green Bank, WV

Largest single radio dish: Arecibo Observatory, 305 m (1,000 ft), in Puerto Rico

Largest baseline radio interferometer: 10 25-m (82-ft) diameter telescopes of the Very Long Baseline Array (VLBA), dispersed from Hawaii to the Virgin Islands with a resolution equal to a radio dish of 8,600 km (5,000 mi), making it the highest resolution telescope in the solar system

Largest submillimeter interferometer: 54 12-m (39-ft) and 12 7-m (23-ft) antennas of the Atacama Large Millimeter Array (ALMA), located at a site above 5,000-m (16,400-ft) in the Atacama Desert in Chile. The antennas can be spread out over a 16-km (10-mi) distance to increase the resolving power of the array.

Largest airborne telescope: Stratospheric Observatory for Infrared Astronomy (SOFIA), 2.5-m (8.2-ft) infrared telescope aboard a NASA 747

Constellations

Culturally, constellations are imagined patterns among the stars that, in some cases, have been recognized through millennia. Knowledge of constellations was once necessary in order to function as an astronomer. For today's astronomers, constellations are simply areas of the sky in which objects await observation and interpretation.

Because Western culture has dominated much of modern scientific discourse, constellations and celestial traditions of other cultures are not well known outside their regions of origin. Even the patterns with which we are most familiar today have undergone considerable change over the centuries.

Today, **88 constellations** are officially recognized. Although many have ancient origins, some are modern, devised out of unclaimed stars by astronomers a few centuries ago. Unclaimed stars were those too faint or inconveniently placed to be included in the more prominent constellations. Stars in a constellation are not necessarily near each other; they are just located in the same direction on the celestial sphere.

When Western astronomers began to travel to South Africa in the 16th and 17th centuries, they found an unfamiliar sky that showed numerous brilliant stars. Thus, constellations in the Southern Hemisphere are named after technological marvels of the time, as well as some arguably traditional forms, such as Musca, the fly.

Many of the commonly recognized constellations have their origins in ancient Asia Minor. These were adopted by the Greeks and Romans, who translated their names and stories into their own languages, modifying some details in the process. After the decline of those cultures, most such knowledge entered oral tradition or remained hidden in monastic libraries. In the 8th century, Muslims began to spread through the Mediterranean world. Wherever possible, everything was translated into Arabic to be taught in the universities the Muslims established throughout their newfound world.

In the 13th century, King Alfonso X of Castile, an avid student of astronomy, had Ptolemy's astronomical treatise *Almagest* translated into Latin. It thus became widely available to European scholars. In the process, the constellation names were translated, but the star names were retained in their Arabic forms. Thus the names of many stars—Altair, Alnitak, and Mirfak, among others—have Arabic roots, although linguistic adaptation and the inaccuracies of transliteration have wrought changes.

Until the 1920s, astronomers used curved boundaries for the constellation areas. As these were rather arbitrary, the International Astronomical Union adopted new constellation boundaries that run due N-S and E-W. These boundaries divide the sky into the 88 constellations, much as the contiguous U.S. is made up of the lower 48 states.

Common names of stars often referred to parts of the traditional figures they represented, such as Deneb, the tail of the swan, and Betelgeuse, the armpit of the giant. Astronomers may avoid traditional names by labeling stars with Greek letters, generally to denote order of brightness. Thus, the "alpha star" would typically be the brightest star in a constellation. The "of" implies possession, so the genitive (possessive) form of the constellation name is used as in Alpha Orionis, the first star of Orion (Betelgeuse). Astronomers usually use a three-letter abbreviation for the constellation name, as indicated below.

Asterisms are widely recognized patterns of stars. The so-called Big Dipper is a small part of the constellation Ursa Major, the big bear; the Sickle is the traditional head and mane of Leo, the lion; the three stars of the Summer Triangle are each in a different constellation, with Vega in Lyra the lyre, Deneb in Cygnus the swan, and Altair in Aquila the eagle. The northeast star of the asterism Great Square of Pegasus is Alpha Andromedae.

Name	Genitive case	Abbr.	Meaning
Andromeda	Andromedae	And	Chained Maiden
Antlia	Antliae	Ant	Air Pump
Apus	Apodis	Aps	Bird of Paradise
Aquarius	Aquarii	Aqr	Water Bearer
Aquila	Aquilae	Aql	Eagle
Ara	Arae	Ara	Altar
Aries	Arietis	Ari	Ram
Auriga	Aurigae	Aur	Charioteer
Boötes	Boötis	Boo	Herder
Caelum	Caeli	Cae	Chisel
Camelopardalis	Camelopardalis	Cam	Giraffe
Cancer	Cancri	Cnc	Crab
Canes Venatici	Canum Venaticorum	CVn	Hunting Dogs
Canis Major	Canis Majoris	CMa	Greater Dog
Canis Minor	Canis Minoris	CMi	Littler Dog
Capricornus	Capricorni	Cap	Sea-Goat
Carina	Carinae	Car	Keel
Cassiopeia	Cassiopeiae	Cas	Queen
Centaurus	Centauri	Cen	Centaur
Cepheus	Cephei	Cep	King
Cetus	Ceti	Cet	Whale
Chamaeleon	Chamaeleontis	Cha	Chameleon
Circinus	Circini	Cir	Compass (drawing)
Columba	Columbae	Col	Dove
Coma Berenices	Comae Berenices	Com	Berenice's Hair
Corona Australis	Coronae Australis	CrA	Southern Crown
Corona Borealis	Coronae Borealis	CrB	Northern Crown
Corvus	Corvi	Crv	Crow
Crater	Crateris	Crt	Cup
Crux	Crucis	Cru	Cross (southern)
Cygnus	Cygni	Cyg	Swan
Delphinus	Delphini	Del	Dolphin
Dorado	Doradus	Dor	Dolphinfish
Draco	Draconis	Dra	Dragon
Equuleus	Equulei	Equ	Little Horse
Eridanus	Eridani	Eri	River
Fornax	Fornacis	For	Furnace
Gemini	Geminorum	Gem	Twins
Grus	Gruis	Gru	Crane (bird)
Hercules	Herculis	Her	Hercules
Horologium	Horologii	Hor	Clock
Hydra	Hydrae	Hya	Water Snake (female)
Hydrus	Hydri	Hyi	Water Snake (male)
Indus	Indi	Ind	Indian
Lacerta	Lacertae	Lac	Lizard
Leo	Leonis	Leo	Lion
Leo Minor	Leonis Minoris	LMi	Littler Lion
Lepus	Leporis	Lep	Hare
Libra	Librae	Lib	Balance
Lupus	Lupi	Lup	Wolf
Lynx	Lyncis	Lyn	Lynx
Lyra	Lyrae	Lyr	Lyre
Mensa	Mensae	Men	Table Mountain
Microscopium	Microscopii	Mic	Microscope
Monoceros	Monocerotis	Mon	Unicorn
Musca	Muscae	Mus	Fly
Norma	Normae	Nor	Square (rule)
Octans	Octantis	Oct	Octant
Ophiuchus	Ophiuchi	Oph	Serpent Bearer
Orion	Orionis	Ori	Hunter
Pavo	Pavonis	Pav	Peacock
Pegasus	Pegasi	Peg	Flying Horse
Perseus	Persei	Per	Hero
Phoenix	Phoenicis	Phe	Phoenix
Pictor	Pictoris	Pic	Painter
Pisces	Piscium	Psc	Fishes
Piscis Austrinus	Piscis Austrini	PsA	Southern Fish
Puppis	Puppis	Pup	Stern (deck)
Pyxis	Pyxidis	Pyx	Compass (sea)
Reticulum	Reticuli	Ret	Reticle
Sagitta	Sagittae	Sge	Arrow
Sagittarius	Sagittarii	Sgr	Archer
Scorpius	Scorpii	Sco	Scorpion
Sculptor	Sculptoris	Scl	Sculptor
Scutum	Scuti	Sct	Shield
Serpens	Serpentis	Ser	Serpent
Sextans	Sextantis	Sex	Sextant
Taurus	Tauri	Tau	Bull
Telescopium	Telescopii	Tel	Telescope
Triangulum	Trianguli	Tri	Triangle
Triangulum Australe	Trianguli Australis	TrA	Southern Triangle
Tucana	Tucanae	Tuc	Toucan
Ursa Major	Ursae Majoris	UMa	Greater Bear
Ursa Minor	Ursae Minoris	UMi	Littler Bear
Vela	Velorum	Vel	Sail
Virgo	Virginis	Vir	Maiden
Volans	Volantis	Vol	Flying Fish
Vulpecula	Vulpeculae	Vul	Fox

Eclipses, 2016

(In Coordinated Universal Time, or UTC, the standard time of the prime meridian.)

There will be four eclipses in 2016: a total solar eclipse, an annular solar eclipse, and two penumbral lunar eclipses. Penumbral lunar eclipses are unremarkable since no part of the Moon enters into the dark central shadow of the Earth.

During an annular eclipse of the Sun, the Moon's angular diameter is not large enough to block the entire disk of the Sun, and the Sun appears as a bright ring about the dark disk of the Moon. The tables below give the times in UTC of when the Moon or Sun will reach certain phases of eclipse. In the case of the lunar eclipses, the times are relevant for any observer who can see the Moon. In the case of solar eclipses, the tabulated times refer to when the given event begins or ends from specific points along the eclipse path; as the Moon's shadow sweeps quickly across the Earth, the observed duration and degree of eclipse depends on the observer's precise location.

I. Total Eclipse of the Sun: Mar. 9

This total eclipse will be visible to observers within a roughly 100-mi wide path extending from the Indian Ocean, across parts of Indonesia and across much of the Pacific Ocean. A partial eclipse will be visible to observers across much of India, China and SE Asia, most of Australia, Papua New Guinea, and the Hawaiian Islands. Totality lasts just over 4 min.

Event	Date	Hr.	Min.
Partial eclipse begins	Mar. 8	23	19.3
Total eclipse begins	9	0	15.9
Greatest eclipse	9	1	58.3
Total eclipse ends	9	3	38.3
Partial eclipse ends	9	4	34.9

II. Penumbral Eclipse of the Moon: Mar. 23

This eclipse is potentially visible to observers from across the U.S., Pacific Ocean, and much of Asia. However, penumbral eclipses are unremarkable and difficult to distinguish from a normal full moon, as the Moon never passes into the dark umbra of the Earth.

Event	Date	Hr.	Min.
Penumbral eclipse begins	Mar. 23	9	39.5
Greatest eclipse	23	11	48.3
Penumbral eclipse ends	23	13	54.8

III. Annular Eclipse of the Sun: Sept. 1

Observers along a roughly 60-mi wide path extending from the S Atlantic, through Gabon, Congo Republic, the Dem. Rep. of the Congo, Tanzania, Mozambique, Madagascar, and across the Indian Ocean will be able to see the annular eclipse, where the Sun appears as a bright ring surrounding the Moon. Observers across most of Africa, parts of Saudi Arabia, and small regions of Indonesia, Australia, and the Antarctic will see a partial eclipse. The annular eclipse phase lasts just over 3 min.

Event	Date	Hr.	Min.
Penumbral eclipse begins	Sept. 1	6	13.1
Annular eclipse begins	1	7	17.8
Greatest eclipse	1	9	8.0
Annular eclipse ends	1	10	55.9
Penumbral eclipse ends	1	12	0.7

IV. Penumbral Eclipse of the Moon: Sept. 16

Like the Mar. 23 penumbral eclipse, this one will be difficult to distinguish from a full moon. The eclipse is potentially visible across a wide area including Africa, Europe and Asia.

Event	Date	Hr.	Min.
Penumbral eclipse begins	Sept. 16	16	54.7
Greatest eclipse	16	18	55.4
Penumbral eclipse ends	16	20	53.9

Total Solar Eclipses, 2016-35

Total solar eclipses actually take place nearly as often as total lunar eclipses. Total lunar eclipses are visible over at least half of the Earth, while total solar eclipses can be seen only along a very narrow path up to a few hundred miles wide and a few thousand miles long. Observing a total solar eclipse is thus a rarity for most people.

Solar eclipses can be dangerous to observe. This is not because the Sun emits more potent rays, but because the Sun is always dangerous to observe directly, and people are particularly likely to stare at it during a solar eclipse.

Date	Duration[1] min.	sec.	Width (mi)	Path of totality
2016, Mar. 9	4	10	96	Indonesia, Pacific Ocean
2017, Aug. 21	2	40	71	Pacific Ocean, U.S., Atlantic Ocean
2019, July 2	4	33	125	S Pacific Ocean, S America
2020, Dec. 14	2	10	56	S Pacific Ocean, S America, S Atlantic Ocean
2021, Dec. 4	1	54	260	Antarctica
2024, Apr. 8	4	27	123	Mexico, midwestern U.S., E Canada
2026, Aug. 12	2	18	183	Greenland, Iceland, Spain
2027, Aug. 2	6	24	160	Spain, N Africa, Arabian peninsula
2028, July 22	5	10	140	Indian Ocean, Australia, New Zealand
2030, Nov. 25	3	45	105	Namibia, Botswana, South Africa, Indian Ocean, E Australia
2033, Mar. 30	2	37	485	Alaska, E Russia, Arctic
2034, Mar. 20	4	9	100	Central and NE Africa, Arabian Peninsula, Central and E Asia
2035, Sept. 2	2	54	72	China, Korea, Japan, Pacific Ocean

(1) Length of time at optimal viewing area.

Total Solar Eclipses in the U.S. in the 21st Century

During the 21st century there will be eight total solar eclipses visible somewhere in the continental U.S. The first comes after a long gap. The last total solar eclipse was on Feb. 26, 1979, in the northwestern U.S.

Date	Path of totality	Date	Path of totality
Aug. 21, 2017	Oregon to South Carolina	Mar. 30, 2052	Florida to Georgia
Apr. 8, 2024	Mexico to Texas and N through Maine	May 11, 2078	Louisiana to North Carolina
Aug. 23, 2044	Montana to North Dakota	May 1, 2079	New Jersey to the lower edge of New England
Aug. 12, 2045	Northern California to Florida	Sept. 14, 2099	North Dakota to Virginia

Beginnings of the Universe

One of the dominating astronomical discoveries of the 20th century was that the galaxies of the universe all seem to be moving away from Earth. Doppler redshifts were observed for spiral nebulae around 1920 even though they were not yet known to be galaxies. By the early 1930s, Edwin Hubble and M. L. Humason had established that the more distant a galaxy, the faster it was receding. It turned out that they were moving away not just from the Earth but from one another—that is, the **universe is expanding**. Scientists conclude that the universe must once, very long ago, have been extremely compact and dense, until an explosion or a similar event caused the matter to spread out. The explosion that gave birth to the universe is called the **Big Bang**.

On the subatomic level, according to this theory, there were vast changes of energy and matter and the way physical laws operated during the first few minutes. After those early minutes the percentages of the basic matter of the universe—hydrogen, helium, and lithium—were set. Everything was so compact and hot that radiation dominated the early universe and there were no stable, un-ionized atoms. The universe was opaque, in the sense that any energy emitted was quickly absorbed and then re-emitted. As the universe expanded, density and temperature continued to drop. A few hundred thousand years after the Big Bang, the temperature dropped far enough that electrons and nuclei could combine to form stable atoms as the universe became transparent. Once that occurred, the radiation that had been trapped was free to escape.

In the 1940s, George Gamov and others predicted remnants of this escaped radiation should be observable. They had started to search for this background radiation when physicists Arno Penzias and Robert Wilson, using a radio telescope, inadvertently found it.

In 2003, NASA's Wilkinson Microwave Anisotropy Probe made measurements of the temperature of this **cosmic microwave background radiation** to within millionths of a degree. From these measurements, scientists were able to deduce that our universe is 13.7 bil years old and that first-generation stars began to form a mere 200 mil years after the Big Bang.

In 2014, scientists operating a telescope in Antarctica claimed to have found direct evidence for cosmic inflation, the rapid expansion of the Universe during the first 10^{-32} seconds after the Big Bang that helps explain why variations of the cosmic background radiation are so small. Follow-up observations have cast doubt on this result, and higher precision measurements are planned.

A related mystery is evidence suggesting hidden matter and hidden energy that cannot be directly observed. This **dark matter** may be composed of gas; large numbers of cool, small objects; or even subatomic particles. The presence of dark matter is indicated by the rotation curves of galaxies and the dynamics of clusters of galaxies. Evidence for **dark energy** is derived from studies of distant Type Ia supernovae indicating that the expansion of the universe is accelerating rather than slowing. Dark energy seems to work on the very fabric of the universe, spreading it apart. Visible matter seems to constitute only about 4% of the total mass of the universe while the rest of the universe's mass is in the form of dark matter (27%) and dark energy (68%).

Galaxies

The 20th century might be called the century of the galaxy. By the start of the century, more than 10,000 **nebulae**—cloud-like luminous objects in the sky—had been discovered. Some were correctly identified as star clusters and others as clouds of gas and dust. Those nebulae which were spiral or elliptical in shape were found in regions of the sky far from the glowing band that is our own Milky Way galaxy. Immanuel Kant had written in 1775 that some of these fuzzy objects might be **"island universes"** apart from our own. But the idea remained speculative until 1923-24, when Edwin Hubble discovered the existence of variable stars in some of these nebulae. This provided conclusive evidence that these systems were outside our own island universe, the Milky Way galaxy.

Galaxies range in size from small dwarf elliptical ones, with perhaps 1 mil stars, to spiral galaxies containing 300 bil stars, to giant elliptical galaxies that may be home to more than 10 tril stars. The diameters of galaxies range from 3,000 light-years in dwarf elliptical galaxies to over 500,000 light-years in giant elliptical galaxies. It is estimated that the Milky Way galaxy is about 100,000 light-years in diameter with about 400 bil stars.

Galaxies also congregate into **clusters**. The smallest are poor clusters of only a few dozen galaxies, while the largest rich clusters may contain thousands. The Milky Way is part of a poor cluster of about three dozen galaxies called the **Local Group**. The largest galaxy of the Local Group is Andromeda, a spiral galaxy visible to the unaided eye in the constellation of Andromeda on a very dark night. The Milky Way is the second largest galaxy in this group; most of the others are small.

The Solar System

The major planets of the solar system, in order of mean distance from the Sun, are **Mercury**, **Venus**, **Earth**, **Mars**, **Jupiter**, **Saturn**, **Uranus**, and **Neptune**. The dwarf planets in order of average distance from the Sun are **Ceres** (located between Mars and Jupiter), **Pluto**, **Haumea**, **Makemake**, and **Eris**. All planets orbit counterclockwise around the Sun as viewed from above the Earth's North Pole.

Because Mercury and Venus are nearer to the Sun than is Earth, their motions about the Sun appear from Earth as wide swings first to one side of the Sun then to the other, though both planets move around the Sun in almost circular orbits. When their passage takes them between Earth and the Sun or beyond the Sun in relation to Earth, they cannot be seen.

The planets that lie farther from the Sun than does Earth may be seen for longer periods. They are invisible only when so located in the sky that they rise and set at about the same time as the Sun and are thus overwhelmed by the Sun's light.

Mercury and Venus, because they are between Earth and the Sun, show phases much as the Moon does. The planets farther from the Sun are always seen as full, although Mars does occasionally present a slightly gibbous phase, like the Moon when it is not quite full.

The planets appear to move rapidly among the stars because they are relatively closer to Earth. The stars are also in motion, some at tremendous speeds, but they are so far away that their motion does not change their apparent positions in the heavens enough to be perceived. The nearest star is about 9,000 times farther away than Neptune. The count for identified **moons** in the solar system orbiting planets and dwarf planets stood at 181 as of mid-2015. Several dwarf planet candidates are also known to have moons.

Planet Superlatives

Largest, most massive planet	Jupiter	Smallest, least massive planet	Mercury
Fastest orbiting planet	Mercury	Slowest orbiting planet	Neptune
Fastest sidereal rotation	Jupiter	Slowest sidereal rotation	Venus
Longest (synodic) day	Mercury	Shortest (synodic) day	Jupiter
Rotational pole closest to ecliptic	Uranus	Hottest planet	Venus
Most moons	Jupiter	No moons	Mercury, Venus
Planet with largest moon	Jupiter	Planet with moon with most eccentric orbit	Neptune
Greatest average density	Earth	Lowest average density	Saturn
Tallest mountain	Mars	Deepest oceans	Jupiter
Strongest magnetic fields	Jupiter	Greatest amount of liquid, surface water	Earth
Most circular orbit	Venus		

Selected Characteristics of the Sun and Planets

Object	Radius— at unit distance[1] "	Radius— at mean least distance[2] "	Radius— in mi mean radius	Volume[3]	Mass[3]	Density[3]	Sidereal period d.	hr.	min.	sec.	Gravity at surface[3]	Reflecting power[4]	Daytime surface temp. (°F)
Sun	959.50	976.0	432,500	1,304,000	333,000	0.26	25	9	7		28.00	—	9,941
Mercury	3.36	6.5	1,516	0.0562	0.0553	0.98	58	15	36		0.38	0.11	845
Venus	8.34	33.0	3,760	0.857	0.815	0.95	243		30R		0.91	0.65	867
Earth	8.78	—	3,959	1.000	1.000	1.00		23	56	4.2	1.00	0.37	59
Moon	2.40	986.2	1,079	0.0203	0.0123	0.61	27	7	43	40	0.16	0.12	260
Mars	4.67	12.8	2,106	0.151	0.107	0.71		24	37	22	0.38	0.15	–24
Jupiter	96.40	24.5	43,441	1,321.3	317.83	0.24		9	55	30	2.53	0.52	–162
Saturn	80.29	10.05	36,184	763.6	95.16	0.12		10	39	20	1.06	0.47	–218
Uranus	34.97	2.05	15,759	63.1	14.54	0.23		17	14	20R	0.90	0.51	–323
Neptune	33.95	1.2	15,301	57.7	17.15	0.30		16	6	40	1.14	0.41	–330

R = Retrograde rotation. (1) Angular radius, in seconds of arc, if object were seen at a distance of 1 astronomical unit. (2) Angular radius, in seconds of arc, when object is closest to Earth. (3) Earth = 1. (4) A value of 1 would indicate a perfect reflector.

Planets of the Solar System

The International Astronomical Union (IAU) on Aug. 24, 2006, at their General Assembly in Prague, Czech Republic, agreed on a new definition for planet, and in the process effectively removed Pluto's planet status. The ruling came after years of debate as to whether Pluto, discovered in 1930, should still be considered the ninth planet in our solar system because of its size, orbit, and other characteristics. New discoveries of other Pluto-like objects in the solar system, such as the 2003 discovery of Eris, a **Kuiper Belt object** (KBO) bigger than Pluto, also contributed to the debate.

Under the IAU's new definition, Mercury, Venus, Earth, Mars, Jupiter, Saturn, Uranus, and Neptune are regarded as "classical" planets. A **planet** is now defined as a celestial body that (a) is in orbit around the Sun, (b) has sufficient mass for its self-gravity to overcome rigid body forces so that it assumes a hydrostatic equilibrium (nearly round) shape, and (c) has cleared the neighborhood around its orbit.

Pluto, Eris, Ceres, Makemake, and Haumea are regarded as dwarf planets, with the status of Pluto's largest moon, Charon, still to be determined. A **dwarf planet** is a celestial body that (a) is in orbit around the Sun, (b) has sufficient mass for its self-gravity to overcome rigid body forces so that it assumes a hydrostatic equilibrium (nearly round) shape, (c) has not cleared the neighborhood around its orbit, and (d) is not a satellite.

The IAU also created a new category, **small solar system bodies**, for all other objects orbiting the Sun, including comets, asteroids, KBOs, and other small objects. It has not yet established a process by which other solar system objects will be classified.

Note: AU = astronomical unit (92.96 mil mi, mean distance of Earth from the Sun); **d.** = 1 Earth synodic (solar) day (24 hours); **synodic day** = rotation period of a planet measured with respect to the Sun (the "true" day, i.e., the time from midday to midday, or from sunrise to sunrise); **sidereal day** = rotation period of a planet with respect to the stars.

Mercury

Distance from the Sun	
Perihelion	28.6 mil mi
Semi-major axis (mean distance)	36 mil mi (0.387 AU)
Aphelion	43.4 mil mi
Period of revolution around Sun	87.97 d.
Orbital eccentricity	0.2056
Orbital inclination	7.00°
Synodic day (midday to midday)	175.94 d.
Sidereal day	58.65 d.
Rotational inclination	0.01°
Mass (Earth = 1)	0.0553
Mean radius	1,516 mi
Mean density (Earth = 1)	0.984
Natural satellites	0
Average surface temperature	333°F

Mercury, named for the Roman gods' messenger, is the closest planet to the Sun and the smallest in the solar system. Mercury is too much in line with the Sun to be observed against a dark sky; therefore it is always seen during morning or twilight. In 2008, the *MESSENGER* spacecraft made the first flybys of Mercury since the 1970s. *Messenger* went into orbit about Mercury in Mar. 2011 for a reconnaissance mission; the original one-year science program was extended in 2012. The goals of the mission included mapping, imaging, and measuring the surface composition of Mercury, as well as probing the planet's interior structure and interactions with the Sun. Among the discoveries were that at least part of Mercury's metallic core is liquid, that there may be water ice in shadowed craters near the poles, and that the planet's magnetic field is offset from the planet's center.

Orbit and rotation. Mercury moves with great speed around the Sun, averaging about 30 mi per second to complete its orbit, which takes about 88 Earth days. Mercury takes nearly 59 days to rotate on its axis. Because its orbital period is only about 50% longer than its sidereal rotation, the time from one sunrise to the next on Mercury is about 176 days—twice as long as a Mercurial year. Oddly, Mercury has a magnetic field, albeit a very weak one. It has been held that both a fluid core and rapid rotation—neither of which Mercury was believed to have—are necessary for the generation of a planetary magnetic field. Mercury may demonstrate the contrary.

Atmosphere. Mercury's atmosphere is almost nonexistent. What very little it has is composed of 42% oxygen, 29% sodium, 22% hydrogen, 6% helium, 0.5% potassium, and 0.5% other particles. Because of Mercury's lack of atmosphere, the surface during the day may reach a temperature of about 845°F, while the temperature at night may fall as low as –300°F. Earth-based observation has provided evidence of water ice near the poles.

Surface and composition. Mercury's surface is rocky and cratered similar to that of the Earth's moon. The most imposing feature on Mercury, the Caloris Basin, is a huge impact crater more than 800 mi in diameter. Mercury has a huge iron core that takes up about 75% of the planet's radius; it has a higher percentage of iron than any other planet in the solar system.

Venus

Distance from the Sun	
Perihelion	66.8 mil mi
Semi-major axis (mean distance)	67.2 mil mi (0.723 AU)
Aphelion	67.7 mil mi
Period of revolution around Sun	224.7 d.
Orbital eccentricity	0.0067
Orbital inclination	3.39°
Synodic day (midday to midday)	116.75 d. (retrograde)
Sidereal day	243.02 d. (retrograde)
Rotational inclination	177.4°
Mass (Earth = 1)	0.815
Mean radius	3,760 mi
Mean density (Earth = 1)	0.951
Natural satellites	0
Average surface temperature	867°F

Venus, named for the Roman goddess of love, is the second planet out from the Sun. Because Venus is almost the same size as Earth, it is believed that the two planets were formed at the same time by the same general process and from the same mixture of chemical elements. Venus can easily be seen from Earth with the naked eye; it is the third-brightest object in the sky, exceeded only by the Sun and the Moon.

Orbit and rotation. It takes Venus 225 Earth days to complete its orbit around the Sun. Its synodic revolution—the amount of time it takes for Venus to return to the same position relative to Earth and the Sun, which is a result of the combination of its own motion with that of Earth—is 584 days. Because of this, every 19 months Venus is closer to Earth than to any other planet. The rotation period of Venus appears to be 243 days clockwise. In other words, its rotation is contrary to the rotation of the other planets and contrary to its own motion around the Sun. This rate and sense of rotation makes for a solar day (sunrise to sunrise) on Venus of 116.8 Earth days. Night lasts 58 days, and day lasts 58 days. Venus has no detectable magnetic field.

Atmosphere. The Venusian atmosphere is very thick and toxic. It is composed primarily of 96.5% carbon dioxide, 3.5% nitrogen, and trace concentrations of sulfur dioxide, argon, water, carbon monoxide, helium, and neon. In addition, it exerts an atmospheric pressure at the surface more than 90 times Earth's normal sea-level pressure. The planet is covered with a dense, white, cloudy atmosphere that conceals whatever is below. These clouds are believed to contain sulfuric acid, meaning that it rains sulfuric acid on Venus. Due to the thickness of the atmosphere and resulting extreme greenhouse effect, the temperature is essentially the same day and night; the planet has an average surface temperature of about 867°F, making it the hottest planet in the solar system. Winds of about 200 mph in the clouds may account for the transfer of heat into the night side despite the low rotation speed of the planet. However, at the surface, the winds are very slow.

Surface and composition. Radar-produced maps of the planet show large craters, continent-sized highlands, and extensive dry lowlands. No tectonic activity has been found similar to Earth's moving tectonic plates, but a system of global rift zones and numerous broad, low, dome-like structures, called coronae, may have been produced by the upwelling and subsidence of magma from the mantle. Volcanic surface features, such as vast lava plains, fields of small lava domes, and large shield volcanoes, are common. About 1,600 volcanoes and volcanic features appear on the Venusian surface; more than 85% of the surface is covered by volcanic flows. Theia Mons, a huge shield volcano, has a diameter of over 600 mi and a height of over 3.5 mi. (The largest Hawaiian volcano is only about 125 mi in diameter but rises nearly 5.5 mi from the ocean floor.) Aside from volcanoes, there are highly deformed mountain belts across Venus along with a few meteor-impact craters more than 20 mi wide. Erosion is a very slow process on Venus due to the lack of water. There are indications of some wind movement of dust and sand. The few impact craters on Venus suggest that the surface is generally geologically young—less than 800 mil years old. Despite the fact that probes have landed on Venus, there are very few pictures because the probes couldn't survive the high temperature and atmospheric pressure.

Mars

Distance from the Sun	
Perihelion	128.4 mil mi
Semi-major axis (mean distance)	141.6 mil mi (1.524 AU)
Aphelion	154.9 mil mi
Period of revolution around Sun	686.98 d. (1.88 yr.)
Orbital eccentricity	0.0935
Orbital inclination	1.85°
Synodic day (midday to midday)	24 hr., 39 min., 35 sec.
Sidereal day	24 hr., 37 min., 22 sec.
Rotational inclination	25.19°
Mass (Earth = 1)	0.107
Mean radius	2,106 mi
Mean density (Earth = 1)	0.713
Natural satellites	2
Average surface temperature	–81°F

Named for the Roman god of war, the Red Planet has some features much like Earth. Mars has climate, seasons, volcanoes, and possibly once had liquid water flowing across its surface. Mars can easily be seen with the naked eye on most clear nights, which is why it was one of the first planets to be studied by ancient astronomers. Later, when telescopes came into use, many observers claimed that canals made by Martians existed on the planet's surface, which led to speculation as to whether there was intelligent life there. Unmanned probes have since put all those theories to rest; the canals turned out to be topographic patterns and dust storms.

Mars is currently being explored by a number of robotic craft, both on the surface and in orbit. The *Curiosity*/Mars Science Laboratory, an SUV-sized robot, landed on the surface in Aug. 2012. Its mission was to understand the history of the Martian geology and climate, search for the presence of organic matter, and to assess the planet's past suitability for life.

Orbit and rotation. Although Mars's orbital path is nearly circular, it is somewhat more eccentric than that of most other planets. Mars is more than 26 mil mi farther from the Sun at its most distant point compared to its closest approach. Its orbit and speed in relation to Earth's bring it fairly close to Earth about every two years. Every 15-17 years the close approaches are especially favorable for observation.

Mars rotates in 24 hr. hours and 37 min., almost the same period of time as Earth. Mars's mean distance from the Sun is 142 mil mi. Because Mars's axis of rotation is inclined by about 25° from the vertical to the plane of its solar orbit about the Sun, the planet has seasons.

Unlike Earth's global magnetic field, the Martian magnetic field is small, weak, and localized and may be the remnant of a stronger field from the planet's past.

Atmosphere. The Martian atmosphere is composed primarily of 95.32% carbon dioxide, 2.7% nitrogen, 1.6% argon, 0.13% oxygen, 0.08% carbon monoxide, and in very minor quantities, water, hydrogen oxide, and neon. The atmosphere on Mars is very thin. It has an atmospheric pressure between 1% and 2% of Earth's (if Earth's atmosphere were that thin, there would not be enough oxygen to breathe). Because the Martian atmosphere is so thin and because of the planet's weak magnetic field, its surface is bombarded by cosmic radiation about 100 times as intense as on Earth.

Martian weather systems consist mainly of huge dust storms. On the poles, white caps (believed to be both water ice and carbon dioxide ice) grow in winter and shrink in summer. It is mainly the carbon dioxide that comes and goes with the seasons. The water ice is apparently in many layers with dust between them, indicating climatic cycles.

Surface and composition. Mars is an alien world with rust-red sand and pink skies. In the planet's beginning stages when it was much hotter, Mars's surface melted to a sufficient extent to separate into dense and lighter layers. Mars later cooled enough to allow liquid water to possibly flow across its surface. NASA scientists announced in Sept. 2015 the most convincing evidence to-date that liquid water flows on the present-day Martian surface. Using imaging and spectroscopy instruments on the Mars Reconnaissance Orbiter, they showed that seasonal flows on Martian slopes contain hydrated minerals that can only form in the presence of liquid water.

Natural satellites. Mars has two satellites called Phobos and Deimos, each discovered in 1877 by Asaph Hall. (Phobos measures about 11 by 17 mi and Deimos about 7 by 9 mi.) Deimos, the outer satellite, revolves around the planet in about 31 hours. Phobos, the inner satellite, whips around Mars in a little more than 7 hours, making three trips each Martian day. Since it orbits Mars faster than the planet rotates, Phobos rises in the west and sets in the east, opposite to what other bodies appear to do in the Martian sky. Both moons are irregularly shaped and pitted with numerous craters. Their origins are not known; however, some astronomers consider them to be asteroid-like objects that were captured by Mars very early in its history.

Jupiter

Distance from the Sun	
Perihelion	460.1 mil mi
Semi-major axis (mean distance)	483.8 mil mi (5.204 AU)
Aphelion	507.4 mil mi
Period of revolution around Sun	11.862 yr.
Orbital eccentricity	0.0489
Orbital inclination	1.304°
Synodic day (midday to midday)	9 hr., 55 min., 33 sec.
Sidereal day	9 hr., 55 min., 30 sec.
Rotational inclination	3.13°
Mass (Earth = 1)	317.8
Mean radius	43,441 mi
Mean density (Earth = 1)	0.24
Natural satellites	67
Average temperature*	–162°F

*i.e., temperature where atmospheric pressure equals 1 Earth atmosphere.

Jupiter, named for the Roman ruler of the gods, is the largest planet in the solar system (11 times the diameter of Earth). Its mass is more than twice the mass of all the other planets, moons, and asteroids put together. Visible to the naked eye and known to the ancients, it was a focus of the Italian scientist Galileo Galilei, who viewed the planet and its four largest moons through a homemade telescope.

Orbit and rotation. Jupiter is at an average distance of 484 mil mi from the Sun and takes almost 12 Earth years to make a complete revolution. The largest of the planets, Jupiter has an equatorial diameter of 88,846 mi; its polar diameter is more than 5,700 mi shorter. This noticeable oblateness is a result of the liquidity of the planet and its extremely rapid rotation rate—a Jupiter day is less than 10 Earth hours long. A point on Jupiter's equator moves at a speed of 22,000 mph, as compared with 1,000 mph for a point on Earth's equator. Jupiter's magnetic field is by far the strongest of any planet. Electrical activity caused by this field is so strong that it discharges billions of watts into Earth's magnetic field daily.

Atmosphere. Jupiter's atmosphere is primarily composed of 90% molecular hydrogen and 10% helium. Minor constituents include methane, ammonia, hydrogen deuteride, ethane, and water. Jupiter has a turbulent atmosphere characterized by thick clouds, high winds, and huge lightning storms many times larger than those on Earth. The atmospheric temperature varies, but the temperature at the tops of clouds may be about –280°F. The Great Red Spot seen prominently on Jupiter is a huge hurricane-like storm that is three times the diameter of Earth. In 2006, the Hubble Space Telescope detected the appearance of a second, smaller red spot.

Surface and composition. Gas giant planets like Jupiter, Saturn, and Neptune do not have a surface like Earth or any of the other rocky planets. The gases become denser with depth, until they may turn into a slush or slurry. Jupiter has a liquid hydrogen ocean more than 35,000 mi deep. It likely has a rocky core about the size of Earth, but 13 times more massive. There is no sharp interface between the gaseous atmosphere and the hydrogen ocean that accounts for most of Jupiter's volume. At lower depths, under enormous pressure, the liquid hydrogen takes on the properties of a metal. It is likely that this liquid metallic hydrogen is the source for both Jupiter's persistent radio noise and for its improbably strong magnetic field.

Natural satellites. Jupiter has 67 known satellites. Four of the moons (in order of distance from Jupiter), Io, Europa, Ganymede, and Callisto—all discovered by Galileo in 1610—are large and bright and are close in diameter to Earth's moon and Mercury. Because they move so rapidly around Jupiter, their change in position from night to night can be seen from Earth using binoculars.

Io is one of the most volcanically active bodies in the solar system. A gaseous, doughnut-shaped ring, or torus, enveloping Io's orbit around Jupiter may have been formed by material ejected from Io's active volcanoes. (This is not to be confused with Jupiter's rings.) These volcanoes, hotter than Earth's volcanoes, erupt mainly molten sulfur.

Europa may have a 30-mi-deep salty, liquid ocean beneath its icy crust, perhaps a small metallic core, and a very tenuous atmosphere. Ganymede is the biggest moon in the solar system. With a diameter of 3,120 mi, it is bigger than both Mercury and Pluto. Ganymede also has it own magnetic field produced by a molten core perhaps of iron sulfide. Callisto has the oldest, most heavily cratered surface in the solar system, a very thin atmosphere of carbon dioxide, and possibly a subsurface liquid ocean.

The other satellites are much smaller, with four closer to Jupiter than Io, five between Ganymede and Callisto, and the rest farther out. Most of Jupiter's moons revolve around Jupiter clockwise as seen from the north, contrary to the motions of most satellites in the solar system and to the direction of revolution of planets around the Sun. These moons may be captured asteroids.

Rings. Jupiter has a set of rings that cannot be seen from Earth without powerful telescopes. They are composed of small dust grains possibly blasted off the four innermost moons by meteoroid impacts.

Saturn

Saturn, named for the Roman ruler of the Titans, is the sixth planet from the Sun and most distant of the planets visible to the unaided eye. Saturn is second in size to Jupiter, but its mass is much smaller. Saturn is the only planet less dense than water, meaning that Saturn would float if there were a pool of water gigantic enough to hold it.

Orbit and rotation. Saturn's diameter is almost 74,900 mi at the equator, while its polar diameter is more than 7,300 mi shorter. Like Jupiter, its noticeable oblateness is a result of the liquidity of the planet and its extremely rapid rate of rotation; a day is little more than 10 Earth hours long.

Distance from the Sun	
Perihelion	840.44 mil mi
Semi-major axis (mean distance)	890.8 mil mi (9.582 AU)
Aphelion	941.07 mil mi
Period of revolution around Sun	29.458 yr.
Orbital eccentricity	0.0565
Orbital inclination	2.485°
Synodic day (midday to midday)	10 hr., 39 min., 23 sec.
Sidereal day	10 hr., 39 min., 22 sec.
Rotational inclination	26.73°
Mass (Earth = 1)	95.159
Mean radius	36,184 mi
Mean density (Earth = 1)	0.125
Natural satellites	62
Average temperature*	–218°F

*i.e., temperature where atmospheric pressure equals 1 Earth atmosphere.

Atmosphere. Saturn's atmosphere is composed primarily of 96.3% hydrogen, 3.3% helium, and traces of methane, ammonia, hydrogen deuteride, ethane, and water. Saturn's atmosphere is much like that of Jupiter, except that the temperature at the top of its cloud layer is at least 50°F colder.

Surface and composition. Saturn's atmosphere resembles Jupiter's; it likely has a small dense center surrounded by a deep ocean of hydrogen.

Natural satellites. Saturn has 62 known natural satellites, most of which were not discovered until space probes reached the planet. Saturn's moon Mimas has an impact crater 81 mi across (the moon itself is only 249 mi across). Enceladus has an atmosphere and shows evidence of geysers that spit water ice and vapor. Two tiny moons orbit within the rings, plowing through and making gaps in the rings along their orbits. Pan, the innermost satellite, creates the Encke Gap of Saturn's A-ring. Daphnis creates the Keeler Gap. The most intriguing Saturnian moon is Titan. The second-biggest moon in the solar system, Titan is bigger than Mercury. Its atmosphere is similar to Earth's atmosphere of long ago; it is made up of approximately 95% nitrogen with traces of methane. Titan's atmosphere extends about 360 mi into space whereas Earth's atmosphere extends about 37 mi. Photographs from its surface show a muddy terrain, with possible deposits of water ice, channels carved by liquid methane springs, and an interesting boundary between light and dark material on the surface. In 2006, scientists found sand dunes on Titan's surface. The "sand" is believed to be tiny water ice crystals or organic compounds. Surface phenomena such as sand dunes are signs of erosion and wind. Unlike winds on Earth or Mars, Titan's winds are not the result of uneven solar heating on the moon's surface but rather Saturn's gravitational pull (similar to how the Moon acts on the Earth's oceans).

Rings. Saturn's ring system is the planet's most recognizable feature. It begins about 4,000 mi above the visible disk of Saturn lying above its equator and extends about 260,000 mi into space. The diameter of the ring system visible from Earth is about 170,000 mi; the rings are estimated to be about 700 ft thick. The rings are composed of rock and ice and range in size from tiny particles to large chunks of material the size of a bus. There are several divisions in the rings. The 2,920-mi Cassini division, the gap between the A and B rings, is the largest division.

Uranus

Uranus, discovered by Sir William Herschel in 1781, was the first planet discovered using a telescope. It was named for the father of the Titans in Roman mythology.

Orbit and rotation. Uranus has a diameter of over 31,000 mi and spins once in approximately 17.23 hours, according to flyby magnetic data. One of the most fascinating features of Uranus is how far over it is tipped. Its north pole lies 98° from its orbital plane. Thus, its seasons are extreme. Over its 84-year orbit, when the Sun rises at the north pole, it shines there for about 42 Earth years; then it sets, and the north pole is in darkness for 42 Earth years. In addition to its rotational tilt, Uranus's magnetic field axis is tipped 58.6° from its rotational axis and is displaced about 30% of its radius away from the planet's center.

Distance from the Sun	
Perihelion	1,703.4 mil mi
Semi-major axis (mean distance)	1,784.8 mil mi (19.201 AU)
Aphelion	1,866.4 mil mi
Period of revolution around Sun	84.01 yr.
Orbital eccentricity	0.0457
Orbital inclination	0.772°
Synodic day (midday to midday)	17 hr., 14 min., 23 sec. (retrograde)
Sidereal day	17 hr., 14 min., 24 sec. (retrograde)
Rotational inclination	97.77°
Mass (Earth = 1)	14.536
Mean radius	15,759 mi
Mean density (Earth = 1)	0.23
Natural satellites	27
Average temperature*	–323°F

*i.e., temperature where atmospheric pressure equals 1 Earth atmosphere.

Atmosphere. The atmosphere is composed primarily of 82.5% hydrogen, 15.2% helium, and 2.3% methane, with small amounts of hydrogen deuteride, ammonia ice, water ice, ammonia hydrosulfide, and methane ice.

Surface and composition. Uranus has no solid surface, and likely no rocky core but rather a mixture of rocks and assorted ices with about 15% hydrogen and some helium.

Natural satellites. Uranus has 27 known moons, which have orbits lying in the plane of the planet's equator. Five moons are relatively large, while 22 are very small and were only discovered with the *Voyager 2* mission or in later observations. Miranda has grooved markings, reminiscent of Jupiter's Ganymede, but often arranged in a chevron pattern. Rifts and channels on Ariel provide evidence of liquid flowing over its surface in the past. Umbriel is extremely dark, prompting some observers to regard its surface as among the oldest in the system. Titania has rifts and fractures, but not the evidence of flow found on Ariel. Oberon's main feature is its surface saturated with craters, unrelieved by other formations.

Rings. In the equatorial plane there is also a complex of 11 rings, 9 of which were discovered in 1978 by observers watching Uranus pass before a star.

Neptune

Distance from the Sun	
Perihelion	2,761.7 mil mi
Semi-major axis (mean distance)	2,793.1 mil mi (30.047 AU)
Aphelion	2,824.5 mil mi
Period of revolution around Sun	164.79 yr.
Orbital eccentricity	0.0113
Orbital inclination	1.769°
Synodic day (midday to midday)	16 hr., 6 min., 37 sec.
Sidereal day	16 hr., 6 min., 36 sec.
Rotational inclination	28.32°
Mass (Earth = 1)	17.147
Mean radius	15,301 mi
Mean density (Earth = 1)	0.297
Natural satellites	14
Average temperature*	–330°F

*i.e., temperature where atmospheric pressure equals 1 Earth atmosphere.

Named for the Roman god of the sea, Neptune was the first planet discovered through mathematical calculations and not observation. Its approximate orbit and position were first calculated independently by British astronomer John Couch Adams and French astronomer Urbain Le Verrier in 1845. In 1846, German astronomer Johann Galle first observed Neptune through a telescope.

Orbit and rotation. Neptune orbits the Sun in 164.8 Earth years in a nearly circular orbit. Its magnetic field is considerably asymmetric to the planet's structure, similar to, but not so extreme as, Uranus's magnetic field. Neptune's magnetic field axis is tipped 46.9° from its rotational axis and is displaced more than 55% of its radius away from the planet's center.

Atmosphere. The Neptunian atmosphere is composed primarily of 80% hydrogen, 19% helium, 1.5% methane, and small amounts of hydrogen deuteride, ethane, ammonia ice, water ice, ammonia hydrosulfide, and methane ice. Neptune's atmosphere is quite blue, with quickly changing white clouds often suspended high above an apparent surface. A Great Dark Spot, reminiscent of Jupiter's Great Red Spot, was discovered in 1989 when *Voyager 2* visited the planet. Observations with the Hubble Space Telescope have shown that the Great Dark Spot originally seen by *Voyager* has apparently dissipated, but a new dark spot has since appeared. Lightning and auroras have been found on other giant planets, but only the aurora phenomenon has been seen on Neptune. As with the other giant planets, Neptune emits more energy than it receives from the Sun. The excess has been found to be 2.7 times the solar contribution.

Surface and composition. As with the other giant planets, Neptune may have no solid surface or exact diameter. However, a mean value of 30,600 mi may be assigned to a diameter between atmosphere levels where the pressure is about the same as sea level on Earth.

Natural satellites. Largest of Neptune's 14 satellites is Triton. It is the only large moon in a retrograde orbit, which suggests that it was captured rather than having been there from the beginning. Triton's large size, sufficient to raise significant tides on the planet, may one day, billions of years from now, bring Triton close enough to Neptune for Triton to be torn apart. Triton has a tenuous atmosphere of nitrogen with a trace of hydrocarbons and evidence of active geysers injecting material into it. Triton is the coldest object yet measured in the solar system with a surface temperature of –391°F. Only about half of Triton has been observed, but its terrain shows cratering and a strange regional feature described as resembling the skin of a cantaloupe. Nereid has the highest orbital eccentricity (0.75) of any moon. Its long looping orbit suggests that it was also captured. In 2003, two more moons, which orbit farther from their parent planet than any other moons in the solar system, were discovered. In July 2013, archival Hubble Space Telescope images were used to discover the existence of a 14th natural satellite of Neptune. At less than 20 km diameter, it is the smallest of Neptune's known moons. The *Voyager 2* probe in 1989 confirmed the existence of six rings around Neptune composed of very fine particles. There may be some clumps in the rings' structure. It is not known whether Neptune's satellites influence the formation or maintenance of the rings.

Dwarf Planets

Ceres

Distance from the Sun	
Perihelion	237 mil mi (2.55 AU)
Semi-major axis (mean distance)	257 mil mi (2.77 AU)
Period of revolution around Sun	4.6 yr.
Orbital eccentricity	0.0789
Orbital inclination	10.58°
Sidereal day	9.075 hr.
Mass (Earth = 1)	0.00015
Mean radius	294 mi

Ceres was the first asteroid discovered; it was found by Italian astronomer Guiseppe Piazzi on Jan. 1, 1801. In the 1800s, it was considered a planet but lost that designation. Ceres is the largest object in the asteroid belt, comprising nearly one third of all the mass of asteroids. In Aug. 2006, it was designated a dwarf planet by the Intl. Astronomical Union (IAU).

After a journey of over seven years, the *Dawn* spacecraft entered into orbit around Ceres in Mar. 2015, thus making Dawn the first spacecraft to visit a dwarf planet. Astronomers are particularly interested in asteroids since they are thought to be the rocky *protoplanets*, examples of the building blocks from which planets formed early in the history of the solar system. *Dawn*'s scientific instrumentation consists of cameras for surface imaging, a spectrometer for measuring surface mineralogy, and a neutron detector for measuring elemental composition of Ceres. *Dawn* has already produced high-resolution maps of the entire surface and more accurate measurements of Ceres's size and mass. The images show a heavily cratered surface with features such as extremely reflective spots within a crater—thought to be freshly exposed water ice—and at least one mountain several miles high.

Orbit and rotation. Ceres orbits the Sun in the asteroid belt region between Mars and Jupiter.

Surface and composition. Ceres is in a class of stony meteorites known as carbonaceous chondrites. These are considered to be the oldest materials in the solar system, with a composition reflecting that of the primitive solar nebula. Extremely dark in color, probably because of their hydrocarbon content, they show evidence of having absorbed water of hydration. Thus, unlike the Earth and the Moon, they have never melted nor been reheated since they first formed. *Dawn* observations suggest that the surface of Ceres consists largely of water ice, though its interior is mostly rock. Further study using *Dawn* will try to confirm observations suggesting that water evaporates from the surface and produces a diffuse atmosphere.

Pluto

Distance from the Sun	
Perihelion	2,756.9 mil mi
Semi-major axis (mean distance)	3,670.1 mil mi (39.482 AU)
Aphelion	4,583.2 mil mi
Period of revolution around Sun	248.09 yr.
Orbital eccentricity	0.2488
Orbital inclination	17.14°
Synodic day (midday to midday)	6 d., 9 hr., 17 min. (retrograde)
Sidereal day	6 d., 9 hr., 18 min. (retrograde)
Rotational inclination	119.59°
Mass (Earth = 1)	0.0022
Mean radius	736.5 mi
Mean density (Earth = 1)	0.339
Natural satellites	5
Average surface temperature	–369°F

Pluto, named for the Roman god of the underworld, is the largest Kuiper Belt object (KBO) by radius, and the second largest by mass. It was first discovered in 1930 by American astronomer Clyde Tombaugh and classified as a planet until 2006, when the IAU changed its designation to dwarf planet. In 2008, Pluto was designated by the IAU as the prototype for a class of objects called **plutoids**, bodies that (a) have an average distance from the Sun greater than Neptune's; (b) are large enough that gravity determines their shape; and (c) have not cleared their orbit of other objects. Haumea, Makemake, and Eris are also plutoids. Some 46 additional plutoid candidates have been identified through mid-2015. The *New Horizons* spacecraft, launched on a voyage to Pluto and beyond in 2006, made the first flyby of Pluto on July 14, 2015.

Orbit and rotation. Pluto's orbit is highly eccentric; although its average distance from the Sun is 3.6 bil mi, it may get as close as 2.76 bil mi. and as far as 4.58 bil mi. For about 20 years of its 248 year orbit, it is closer to the Sun than Neptune. Currently, it is beyond Neptune's orbit.

Atmosphere and surface. Before the *New Horizons* flyby, all observations of Pluto had been made with telescopes nearly 3 bil mi away, so the mission brought new data to light, some of which requires further analysis. The mass and density of Pluto suggests that it is composed of a rocky core with an overlying water-ice mantle. *New Horizons*'s close-up observations of Pluto revealed a mixed surface, with some ancient, heavily cratered terrain and other younger, smoother plains with no craters. The smooth terrain, estimated to be no more than 100 mil years old, is much younger than scientists expected and may indicate that geologic processes continue to modify Pluto. Nitrogen ice on the smooth plains appears to be flowing, like glaciers on Earth, onto the more heavily cratered surface. Compositional evidence shows that the smooth areas contain nitrogen, methane, and carbon monoxide ices. Scientists also found several mountain ranges rising more than 2 mi above the smooth plains; they speculated that the mountains are made of water ice thrust up from below Pluto's nitrogen-rich icy surface.

New Horizons also provided the first close-up measurements of Pluto's atmosphere, confirming earlier measurements of methane, nitrogen, and carbon monoxide, the same molecules that form ices on Pluto's surface. Scientists speculate that the atmosphere forms from evaporation of surface ices when the dwarf planet is closer to the Sun. The new measurements also revealed hydrocarbon hazes as much as 50 mi above Pluto's surface. The hazes are thought to form when Pluto's tenuous atmosphere is exposed to the Sun's ultraviolet rays. Dark regions on Pluto's surface likely result from these hydrocarbons settling. As of July 31, 2015, only a small fraction of the *New Horizons* Pluto-flyby data had been transmitted back to Earth; knowledge of Pluto will continue to improve as more data is downloaded and analyzed through 2016.

Natural satellites. Pluto has five known natural satellites. Charon, the biggest, has a diameter of 750 mi—about half of Pluto's diameter of 1,474 mi. No other object in the solar system has a moon so close to its size. Discovered in 1978, Charon orbits Pluto at a distance of 12,200 mi and takes 6.39 days to move around the dwarf planet. In this same length of time, Pluto and Charon both rotate once on their axes, meaning that the Pluto-Charon system appears to rotate as virtually a rigid body. Both worlds are roughly spherical and have comparable densities. Because of these similarities and their peculiar relationship, there is debate as to whether Charon should one day be designated a dwarf planet. *New Horizons* provided the first detailed look at Charon, revealing a surface with less color and likely dominated by water ice. Much of Charon's surface is smoother than expected, with few craters, implying that Charon has an active geology capable of resurfacing. The images also reveal fractures extending hundreds of miles and a canyon around 5 mi deep.

Two other moons, discovered in 2005 and 2006, were officially named Nix and Hydra. Two additional moons, discovered in 2011 and 2012, were officially named Kerberos and Styx by the IAU in 2013. As of mid-2015, NASA had released *New Horizons* images of Nix and Hydra, revealing irregularly-shaped objects about 25 and 35 mi across, respectively. Astronomers will be examining *New Horizons* data over the next year to look for additional moons.

Haumea

Distance from the Sun	
Semi-major axis (mean distance)	43.335 AU
Period of revolution around Sun	285 yr.
Orbital eccentricity	0.189
Orbital inclination	28.19°
Mass (Earth = 1)	0.0007
Mean radius	420 mi
Natural satellites	2

Haumea was discovered in 2004 and was accepted as a dwarf planet by the IAU in 2008.

Orbit and rotation. Haumea has a moderately eccentric orbit and takes about 285 years to go around the Sun.

Surface and composition. Spectra of Haumea indicate the presence of almost pure crystalline water ice. The surface reflects about 60% of the sunlight that reaches it. Haumea has a very oblong shape, twice as long as it is wide.

Natural satellites. Haumea has two natural satellites.

Makemake

Distance from the Sun	
Semi-major axis (mean distance)	45.791 AU
Period of revolution around Sun	310 yr.
Orbital eccentricity	0.159
Orbital inclination	28.96°
Mass (Earth = 1)	0.0007
Mean radius	450 mi

Makemake was discovered in 2005 and was accepted as a dwarf planet by the IAU in 2008.

Orbit and rotation. Makemake has a moderately eccentric orbit and takes about 310 years to go around the Sun.

Surface and composition. Spectra of Makemake indicate the presence of frozen methane, as well as several organic compounds. The surface is highly reflective and appears similar to that of Pluto.

Eris

Distance from the Sun	
Semi-major axis (mean distance)	67.6681 AU
Period of revolution around Sun	560 yr.
Orbital eccentricity	0.44177
Orbital inclination	44.177°
Mass (Earth = 1)	0.0027
Mean radius	925 mi
Natural satellites	1

By mass, Eris is the largest known dwarf planet. Discovered in 2003 by astronomers at the California Institute of Technology, it is the most distant object ever seen in orbit around the Sun.

Orbit and rotation. Eris has a highly elliptical orbit and takes about 560 years to go around the Sun—more than twice the time it takes Pluto. Its inclination is steep, tilted at 44° to the planetary plane. It also has an extremely eccentric orbit. It will be at its closest to the Sun, actually coming inside part of Pluto's orbit, in about 280 years.

Surface and composition. Eris, with a surface covered in frozen methane, may be similar to Pluto and the Neptunian moon Triton. Observations made by the Hubble Space Telescope show that Eris's surface is almost white and uniform, reflecting 86% of the light that hits it. This makes it the most reflective body in the solar system. The dwarf planet's interior is likely a mixture of rock and ice.

Natural satellites. Eris has one moon, Dysnomia.

Small Solar System Bodies

Asteroids

Besides planets and moons, many smaller objects orbit the Sun. In 2006, the International Astronomical Union (IAU) officially designated these objects "small solar system bodies." Asteroids or minor planets are found mainly in a belt between the orbits of Mars and Jupiter. Within this belt there may be millions of asteroids of varying sizes. Most asteroids are very small. Ceres, which can be classified both as an asteroid and a dwarf planet, is 588 mi in diameter, about one-quarter the diameter of our Moon.

Some of these objects, or asteroids, are gravitationally locked with Jupiter and the Sun so that they have roughly the same orbit as Jupiter but are either 60° ahead or behind the planet. These are the **Trojan asteroids**. Many of the smaller moons of the solar system, especially those in retrograde orbits, may be captured asteroids. Asteroids whose orbits either cross or come close to the Earth's orbit are labeled **Near Earth asteroids** or NEAs. A handful of asteroids have actually been imaged by the Arecibo and Goldstone radio telescopes and by the NEAR Shoemaker space probe. The *Galileo* spacecraft imaged the asteroids Gaspra and Ida (including its moon Dactyl) on its way to Jupiter.

Comets

Comets are small icy bodies that orbit the Sun. When one approaches the Sun, the energy from the Sun boils off material from the comet's icy nucleus, producing an enlarged head (or **coma**), and in many cases an extended tail. Because of that, comets are brighter when near the Sun. For large comets, the head may be 100,000 mi across and the tail more than a million mi long, though both are mainly empty space.

Comets have been known since ancient times. British astronomer Edmund Halley (1656-1742) ultimately realized that a group of historical reports were just repeated visits of the same object. Comets are the only astronomical objects named after their discoverers. In 1986, the European spacecraft *Giotto* took the first close-up images of a comet's nucleus, specifically of Comet Halley, showing it had a peanut-shaped nucleus and whose longest dimension was about 10 mi.

In 1995, U.S. observers Alan Hale (1958-) and Thomas Bopp (1949-) independently discovered a comet that was then beyond the orbit of Jupiter. It is one of the brightest comets of all time. It also holds the record for length of time visible to the naked eye—19 months—and is the most photographed comet in history. In July 2009, an amateur astronomer discovered a large impact scar in the upper atmosphere of Jupiter, likely the result of another cometary impact.

Kuiper Belt

The Kuiper Belt is a doughnut-shaped region that extends to about 50 AU (astronomical units) from the Sun and is thought to be the source of short-period comets such as Comets Halley or Swift-Tuttle. It is filled with icy bodies that are in solar orbit. The more than 1,000 objects found in this region in recent years are called Kuiper Belt objects (KBOs). It is estimated that there are more than 70,000 objects 60 mi in diameter or larger within the Kuiper Belt. Dwarf planets Pluto and Eris are considered KBO. There are at least six KBOs larger than 300 mi in diameter.

Oort Cloud

The Oort Cloud is a vast spherical shell hypothesized to exist around the Sun. Dutch astronomer Jan Oort (1900-92) proposed its existence as the origin for long-period comets that enter the inner part of the solar system where the planets orbit. Current technology is not sufficient to detect any members of the Oort Cloud other than observed comets whose orbits may reach out as far as 50,000 AU. Recent examples of such long-period comets are Comets Hale-Bopp and Hyakutake.

The Sun

Distance from Earth, mean	92.96 mil mi (1 AU)
Sidereal day (rotation period)	25.38 d.
Mass (Earth=1)	332,900
Mean radius	432,200 mi
Mean density (Earth=1)	0.255
Average surface temperature	9,941°F

The Sun is the Earth's primary source of light and heat and its closest star. The biggest object in the solar system, the Sun is 332,900 times more massive than Earth and contains 99.86% of the mass of the entire solar system. On the whole, the Sun is made up of about 92.1% hydrogen and 7.8% helium, with trace amounts of other elements. It has a mass and luminosity greater than that of 90% of the stars in the Milky Way galaxy. Although most of the stars that can be easily seen on a clear night are bigger and brighter than the Sun, its proximity to Earth makes it appear tremendously large and bright. The Sun is 400,000 times as bright as the full moon, and it gives Earth 6 mil times as much light as do all the other stars put together. Because of the great distance between the Sun and Earth, it takes about 499 sec., or slightly more than 8 min., for light from the Sun to reach Earth.

Composition. The Sun has six regions. The first three from the inside out are the core, the radiative zone, and the convective zone. Together they form the interior. The others, which comprise the visible surface, are the photosphere, the chromosphere, and the outermost region, the corona.

The Sun's heat and energy are produced in its core. Through a series of nuclear fusion reactions, hydrogen nuclei are converted to helium nuclei. Temperatures in the core are theorized to be 28 mil °F. From the core, photons transport the energy outward through the radiative zone. It can take photons several million years to pass through this area. In the convective zone, gases move energy outward at a faster rate. Like a boiling pot, bubbles of gas bring energy to the surface.

The photosphere is the visible surface of the Sun, that is, the light that we see as sunlight. When sunlight is analyzed with a spectroscope, it is found to consist of a continuous spectrum composed of all the colors of the rainbow, crossed by many dark lines. The dark "absorption lines" are produced by gaseous materials in the outer layers of the Sun. More than 60 of the natural terrestrial elements have been identified in the Sun, all in gaseous form because of the Sun's intense heat.

Just above the photosphere is the chromosphere, which is visible to the naked eye only in total solar eclipses, during which it appears to be a pinkish-violet layer with occasional great prominences projecting above its general level. With proper instruments, the chromosphere can be seen or photographed whenever the Sun is visible. Above the chromosphere is the corona, also visible to the naked eye only at times of total eclipse or with instruments that permit the brighter portions of the corona to be seen. The light of the corona surges millions of miles from the Sun; its atoms are all in a state of extreme attenuation and high ionization that indicates temperatures nearly 2 mil °F.

Sunspots. These dark, irregularly shaped regions may reach diameters of thousands of miles. There is an intimate connection between sunspots and the corona. At times of low sunspot activity, the fine streamers of the corona are longer above the Sun's equator than over the polar regions of the Sun; during periods of high sunspot activity, the corona extends fairly evenly outward from all regions of the Sun but to a much greater distance in space. The average life of a sunspot group is two months, but some have lasted for more than a year. Sunspots reach a low point, on average, every 11.3 years, with a peak of activity occurring irregularly between two successive periods of minimal activity. Currently, the number of sunspots is declining. Solar minimum occurred late in 2006.

Solar wind and magnetic field. Magnetic arches, called prominences, may extend tens of thousands of miles into the corona and may release enormous amounts of energy heating the corona. Coronal mass ejections are enormous releases of solar energy. Coronal holes are regions where the corona appears dark in X-rays, and are associated with open magnetic field lines, where the magnetic field lines project out into space instead of back toward the Sun. It is in these regions where the high-speed solar wind originates.

The solar wind carries the Sun's magnetic field, which extends beyond the planets. This is called the interplanetary magnetic field (IMF). Far past Pluto and the Kuiper Belt, the solar wind and the IMF lose their influence. The boundary between them and interstellar space is called the heliopause. In 2013, NASA announced that the *Voyager 1* spacecraft, launched in 1977, seemed at last to have reached the heliopause, at a distance 18 bil km (11 bil mi) from the Sun.

Searching for Extrasolar Planets

The Sun is a typical star in many respects and—with over 400 bil stars in the Milky Way—it is plausible that many other stars might have planets. During the last 10 years of the 20th century, astronomers began to note evidence of planets orbiting stars other than the Sun. Astronomers have not directly observed most of these objects but merely inferred their existence from observations of their parent stars.

Astronomers have used two main techniques to detect planets. The first, called the radial-velocity method, uses the Doppler effect to detect periodic changes in the motion of a star caused by the gravitational tug of an unseen planet. The magnitude of the star's motion and the time it takes to repeat can be used to infer the planet's mass and distance from its host star. This technique is most sensitive to high-mass planets orbiting close to their stars because that situation produces more noticeable changes in a star's motion. The first planets discovered using this technique were as massive as the planet Jupiter and orbiting stars at distances closer than Mercury orbits the Sun.

The second technique, the transit method, relies on the dimming of a star's light as an unseen planet repeatedly passes in front of it. Astronomers are able to infer the diameter of the planet and the distance at which the planet orbits the star. When combined with the mass determined from the radial-velocity method, astronomers can determine the density of the unseen planet and begin to infer its similarity to planets in our solar system.

Astronomers have also used optical gravitational lensing to detect extrasolar planets. This technique, which detects the observed brightening of a distant background star as a planet passes in front of it, has allowed Southern Hemisphere astronomers to find the most distant planet yet detected, about halfway to the center of our own Milky Way galaxy.

In 2005, astronomers obtained the first direct image of an extrasolar planet around a normal star called GQ Lupi, which is like our Sun but younger. The planet is about 100 AU (astronomical units) away from the star and estimated to be about twice as massive as Jupiter.

In 2006, astronomers discovered what they call a "super Earth" orbiting a red dwarf 9,000 light-years away. The planet appears to have about 13 times Earth's mass and may be composed of rock and ice, but it is believed not to have liquid on its surface. In 2007, astronomers detected water in the atmosphere of an extrasolar planet for the first time.

In 2009, NASA launched Kepler, the first telescope sensitive enough to detect Earth-sized planets around other stars. Kepler's first released data in 2010 indicated that small planets are more common than large planets. Kepler has now detected a large number of planets with diameters similar to that of Earth. Some of the planets are known to orbit within the host star's habitable zone, meaning that the conditions are such that liquid water could exist on the planetary surface. As of July 2015, astronomers had confirmed nearly than 1,900 planets orbiting more than 1,100 stars. Of those, more than 600 were at least as massive as Jupiter. Planets with masses less than Jupiter are now regularly discovered. Kepler 186f was the first Earth-size planet to be confirmed in the habitable zone of a star. In July 2015, the Kepler team announced the discovery of Kepler-452b, an Earth-size planet in the habitable zone of a star like the Sun, making this the most Earth-like of Kepler's discoveries to date.

NASA approved the Transiting Exoplanet Survey Satellite (TESS) mission in 2013. The mission, scheduled for launch in 2017, would conduct an all-sky survey of extrasolar planets.

Earth: Size, Computation of Time, Seasons

Distance from the Sun	
Perihelion	91.4 mil mi
Semi-major axis (mean distance)	93 mil mi (1.0000 AU)
Aphelion	94.5 mil mi
Period of revolution	365.256 d.
Orbital eccentricity	0.0167
Orbital inclination	0°
Synodic day (midday to midday)	24 hr., 0 min., 0 sec.
Sidereal day (rotation period)	23 hr., 56 min., 4.2 sec.
Rotational inclination	23.45°
Mass (Earth = 1)	1
Mean radius	3,958.8 mi
Mean density (Earth = 1)	1
Natural satellites	1
Average surface temperature	59°F

Earth is the fifth-largest planet and the third from the Sun. Its mass is 5.9736×10^{24} kg. Earth's equatorial diameter is 7,926 mi while its polar diameter is only 7,900 mi.

Size and dimensions. Earth is considered a solid mass, yet it has a large, liquid iron, **magnetic core** with a radius of about 2,160 mi. Surprisingly, it has a solid **inner core** that may be a large iron crystal, with a radius of 760 mi. Around the core is a thick shell, or **mantle**, of dense rock. This mantle is composed of materials rich in iron and magnesium. It is somewhat plastic-like, and under slow steady pressure, it can flow like a liquid. The mantle, in turn, is covered by a thin **crust** forming the solid granite and basalt base of the continents and ocean basins. Over broad areas of Earth's surface, the crust has a thin cover of sedimentary rock such as sandstone, shale, and limestone formed by weathering and by deposits of sands, clays, and plant and animal remains.

The temperature inside the Earth increases about 1°F with every 100 to 200 ft in depth, in the upper 100 km of Earth. It reaches nearly 8,000°F-9,000°F at the center. The heat is believed to come from radioactivity in rocks, pressures within Earth, and the original heat of formation.

Atmosphere. Earth's atmosphere is a blanket composed of 78% nitrogen, 21% oxygen, and 1% argon. Present in minute quantities are carbon dioxide, hydrogen, neon, helium, krypton, and xenon. Water vapor displaces other gases and varies from nearly zero to about 4% by volume. The atmosphere rests on Earth's surface with a weight equivalent to a layer of water 34 ft deep. For about 300,000 ft upward, the gases remain in the proportions stated. Gravity holds the gases to Earth. The weight of the air compresses it at the bottom so that the greatest density is at Earth's surface. Pressure and density decrease as height increases.

The lowest layer of the atmosphere extending up from the Earth's surface about 7.5 mi is the **troposphere**, which contains 90% of the air. This is also where most weather phenomena occur. The temperature drops with increasing height through this layer. The **stratosphere** extends about 23 mi above the troposphere; the the temperature generally increases with height within this layer. The stratosphere contains **ozone**, which prevents ultraviolet rays from reaching Earth's surface. Since there is very little convection in the stratosphere, jets regularly cruise in the lower parts to provide a smoother ride for passengers.

Above the stratosphere is the **mesosphere**, where the temperature again decreases with height for another 19 mi. Extending above the mesosphere to the outer fringes of the atmosphere is the **thermosphere**, a region where temperature once more increases with height to a value measured in thousands of degrees Fahrenheit. The lower portion of this region, extending from 50 to about 400 mi in altitude, is characterized by high ion density and is thus called the **ionosphere**. Most meteors are in the lower thermosphere or the mesosphere at the time they are observed.

Longitude and latitude. Position on the globe is measured by meridians and parallels. Meridians, which are imaginary lines drawn around Earth through the poles, determine **longitude**. The meridian running through Greenwich, England, is the **prime meridian** of longitude; all others are either E or W. Parallels, which are imaginary circles parallel with the equator, determine **latitude**. The length of a degree of longitude varies as the cosine of the latitude. At the equator a degree of longitude is 69.171 statute mi; this is gradually reduced toward the poles. Value of a longitude degree at the poles is zero.

Latitude is reckoned by the number of degrees N or S of the **equator**, an imaginary circle on Earth's surface everywhere equidistant between the two poles. According to the International Astronomical Union, the length of a degree of latitude is 68.708 statute mi at the equator and varies slightly N and S because of the oblate form of the globe. At the poles, it is 69.403 statute mi.

Definitions of time. Earth rotates on its axis and follows an elliptical orbit around the Sun. The rotation makes the Sun appear to move across the sky from E to W. This rotation determines day and night, and the complete rotation, in relation to the Sun, is called the **apparent or true solar day**. A sundial thus measures **apparent solar time**. This length of time varies, but an average determines a mean solar day of 24 hours.

The mean solar day and **mean solar time** are in universal use for civil purposes. Mean solar time may be obtained from apparent solar time by correcting observations of the Sun for the **equation of time**. Mean solar time may be up to 16 min. different from apparent solar time.

Sidereal time is the measure of time defined by the diurnal motion of the vernal equinox and is determined from observation of the meridian transits of stars. One complete rotation of Earth relative to the equinox is called the **sidereal day**. The **mean sidereal day** is 23 hr., 56 min., 4.2 sec. of mean solar time.

The interval required for Earth to make one absolute revolution around the Sun is a **sidereal year**; it consisted of 365 days, 6 hr., 9 min., and 9.5 sec. of mean solar time (approximately 24 hr. per day) in 1900 and has been increasing at the rate of 0.0001 second annually.

The **tropical year**, upon which our calendar is based, is the interval between two consecutive returns of the Sun to the vernal equinox. The tropical year consisted of 365 days, 5 hr., 48 min., and 46 sec. in 1900. It has been decreasing at the rate of 0.53 sec. per century. The **calendar year** begins at midnight precisely, local clock time, on the night of Dec. 31-Jan. 1. The day and the calendar month also begin at midnight by the clock.

On Jan. 1, 1972, the Bureau International des Poids et Mesures in Paris introduced **International Atomic Time** (TAI) as the most precisely determined time scale for astronomical usage. The fundamental unit of TAI in the international system of units is the second, defined as the duration of 9,192,631,770 periods of the radiation corresponding to the transition between two hyperfine levels of the ground state of the cesium-133 atom. **Coordinated Universal Time** (UTC), which serves as the basis for civil timekeeping and is the standard time of the prime meridian, is officially defined by a formula which relates UTC to mean sidereal time in Greenwich, England. (UTC replaced Greenwich Mean Time as the basis for standard time for the world.)

Zones and seasons. The five zones of Earth's surface are the Torrid, lying between the Tropics of Cancer and Capricorn; the N Temperate, between Cancer and the Arctic Circle; the S Temperate, between Capricorn and the Antarctic Circle; and the two Frigid Zones, between the Polar Circles and the Poles.

The inclination, or tilt, of Earth's axis, 23°45′ away from a perpendicular to Earth's orbit of the Sun, determines the seasons. These are commonly marked in the N Temperate Zone, where spring begins at the vernal equinox, summer at the summer solstice, autumn at the autumnal equinox, and winter at the winter solstice. In the S Temperate Zone, the seasons are reversed. Spring begins at the autumnal equinox, summer at the winter solstice and so on.

The points at which the Sun crosses the equator are the **equinoxes**, when day and night are most nearly equal. The points at which the Sun is at a maximum distance from the equator are the **solstices**. Days and nights are then most unequal. However, at the equator, day and night are equal throughout the year.

In June, the North Pole is tilted 23°27′ toward the Sun, and the days in the Northern Hemisphere are longer than the nights, while the days in the Southern Hemisphere are shorter than the nights. In Dec., the North Pole is tilted 23°27′ away from the Sun, and the situation is reversed.

Seasons in 2016. In 2016, the four seasons begin in the Northern Hemisphere as shown. (Add 1 hour to Eastern Standard Time for Atlantic Time; subtract 1 hour for Central, 2 for Mountain, 3 for Pacific, 4 for Alaska, 5 for Hawaii-Aleutian. Also shown is Coordinated Universal Time.)

Season	Date	UTC	EST/EDT
Vernal Equinox (spring)	Mar. 20	4:30	0:30 EDT
Northern Solstice (summer)	June 20	22:34	18:34 EDT
Autumnal Equinox (fall)	Sept. 22	14:21	10:21 EDT
Southern Solstice (winter)	Dec. 21	10:44	5:44 EST

Poles. The geographic (rotation) poles, or points where Earth's axis of rotation cuts the surface, are not absolutely fixed in the body of Earth. The pole of rotation describes an irregular curve about its mean position.

Two periods have been detected in this motion: (1) an annual period due to seasonal changes in barometric pressure, to load of ice and snow on the surface, and to other seasonal phenomena; (2) a period of about 14 months due to the shape and constitution of Earth. In addition, there are small but as yet unpredictable irregularities. The whole motion is so small that the actual pole at any time remains within a circle of 30 or 40 ft in radius centered at the mean position of the pole.

The pole of rotation for the time being is of course the pole having a latitude of 90° and an indeterminate longitude.

Magnetic poles. Although Earth's magnetic field resembles that of an ordinary bar magnet, this magnetic field is probably produced by electric currents in the liquid currents of the Earth's outer core. The **north magnetic pole** of Earth is that region where the magnetic force is downward, and the **south magnetic pole** is that region where the magnetic force is upward. A compass placed at the magnetic poles experiences no directive force in azimuth (i.e., direction).

There are slow changes in the distribution of Earth's magnetic field. This slow temporal change is referred to as the secular change of the main magnetic field, and the magnetic poles shift due to this. The location of the N magnetic pole was first measured in 1831 at Cape Adelaide on the W coast of Boothia Peninsula in Canada's Northwest Territories (about latitude 70° N and longitude 96° W). Since then it has moved over 500 mi. It is now estimated to be at 82.7° N and 114.4° W, NW of Ellef Ringnes Island in northern Canada. Measurement for several decades by Canadian scientists indicates the motion of the pole has accelerated, now averaging about 25 mi per year.

The direction of the horizontal components of the magnetic field at any point is known as magnetic N at that point, and the angle by which it deviates E or W of true N is known as the magnetic declination.

A compass without error points in the direction of magnetic north. (In general, this is not the direction of the true rotational north pole.) If you follow the direction indicated by the N end of the compass, you will go along an irregular curve that eventually reaches the north magnetic pole (though not usually by a great-circle route). However, the action of the compass should not be thought of as due to any influence of the distant pole, but simply as an indication of the distribution of Earth's magnetism at the place of observation.

Rotation. The speed of Earth's rotation about its axis is slightly variable. The variations may be classified as:

(A) **Secular.** Tidal friction acts as a brake on the rotation and causes a slow secular increase in the length of the day, about 1 millisecond per century.

(B) **Irregular.** The speed of rotation may increase for a number of years (about 5 to 10) and then start decreasing. The maximum difference from the mean in the length of the day during a century is about 5 milliseconds. The accumulated difference in time has amounted to approximately 44 seconds since 1900. The cause is probably motion in the interior of Earth.

(C) **Periodic.** Seasonal variations exist with periods of 1 year and 6 months. The cumulative effect is such that each year, Earth is late about 30 milliseconds near June 1 and is ahead about 30 milliseconds near Oct. 1. The maximum seasonal variation in the length of the day is about 0.5 millisecond. It is believed that the principal cause of the annual variation is the seasonal change in the wind patterns of the Northern and Southern Hemispheres. The semiannual variation is due chiefly to tidal action of the Sun, which distorts the shape of Earth slightly.

The Moon

Distance from Earth	
Perigee	225,744 mi
Semi-major axis (mean distance)	238,855 mi
Apogee	251,966 mi
Period of revolution	27.322 d.
Orbital eccentricity	0.0549
Orbital inclination	5.145°
Synodic orbital period (period of phases)	29.53 d.
Sidereal day (rotation period)	27.322 d.
Rotational inclination	6.68°
Mass (Earth = 1)	0.0123
Mean radius	1,079 mi
Mean density (Earth = 1)	0.607
Average surface temperature	–100°F

The Moon is the second-brightest object in the sky (the Sun is the first). Earth's only natural satellite, the Moon is the force behind the rising and falling of tides, and it helps to regulate Earth's orbit around the Sun. Many probes have been sent to the Moon, and between 1969 and 1972, 12 U.S. astronauts walked on its surface. The Moon is the subject of renewed international interest. In 2007, Japan and China orbited satellites around the Moon, India orbited a spacecraft in fall 2008, and the U.S. sent an orbiter and impactor in 2009. In Sept. 2009, American scientists announced the discovery of a thin layer of water ice near the lunar poles. The *LCROSS* impactor mission impacted the lunar south polar region in Oct. 2009. The plume of material thrown up in the impact included water plus a variety of other chemical species, indicating that the lunar regolith harbors a rich and active chemistry. In Sept. 2013, NASA launched *LADEE*, a mission to study the ephemeral lunar atmosphere and lunar dust from a low orbit. In Dec. 2013, China became the third nation to land a spacecraft on the Moon when *Chang'e 3* set down on Mare Imbrium. *Chang'e 3* released the *Yutu* rover to study the lunar surface.

Orbit and rotation. The Moon completes a circuit around Earth in a period that averages 27 days, 7 hr., 43.2 min. This is the Moon's sidereal period. Because of the motion of the Moon in common with Earth around the Sun, the mean duration of the lunar month—the period from one new moon to the next new moon—is 29 days, 12 hr., 44.05 min. This is the Moon's synodic period.

The mean distance of the Moon from Earth is 238,855 mi, but its orbit about Earth is elliptical, and thus the actual distance varies considerably. The maximum distance from Earth that the Moon may reach is 251,966 mi and the least distance is 225,744 mi.

The Moon rotates on its axis in a period of time that is exactly equal to its sidereal revolution about Earth—27.322 days. Thus the backside, or farside, of the Moon always faces away from Earth. But this does not mean that the backside is always dark. The farside of the Moon gets as much direct sunlight as the nearside; at new moon phase, the farside of the Moon is fully lit but not visible from Earth.

The Moon's revolution about Earth is irregular because of its elliptical orbit. The Moon's rotation, however, is regular, and this, together with the irregular revolution, produces what is called libration in longitude, which permits an observer on Earth to see first farther around the eastern side and then farther around the western side of the Moon. The Moon's variation north or south of the ecliptic permits one to see farther over first one pole of the Moon and then the other; this is called libration in latitude. These two libration effects permit observers on Earth to see a total of about 60% of the Moon's surface over a period of time.

Atmosphere and surface. The Moon, like the planet Mercury, has no real atmosphere to speak of. What little exists is variable and tenuous. With its long day and night, the daytime temperature can reach 260°F. The coldest nighttime temperature is –280°F. This day-to-night contrast is exceeded only by that on Mercury. The lunar surface has not changed much since humans began observing it. The side visible from Earth has large craters and vast dark areas called *maria* that were once lava. The farside has almost no maria but is pockmarked with craters; it was first photographed in 1959 by the Soviet space probe *Lunik III*.

Recent findings show that up to 300 mil metric tons of water ice may exist in craters at the lunar poles. In its interior, the Moon may have a small core, which supports the idea that most of the Moon's mass was ripped away from the early Earth when a Mars-size object collided with Earth.

Harvest moon and hunter's moon. The harvest moon, the full moon nearest the autumnal equinox, ushers in a period of several days when the Moon rises soon after sunset. This phenomenon gives farmers in temperate latitudes extra hours of light in which to harvest their crops. The 2016 harvest moon falls on Sept. 16. Harvest moon in the Southern Hemisphere temperate latitudes falls on Mar. 23.

The next full moon after harvest moon is called the hunter's moon; it is accompanied by a similar but less marked phenomenon. In 2016, the hunter's moon occurs on Oct. 16 in the Northern Hemisphere and on Apr. 22 in the Southern Hemisphere.

Moon Phases, 2016

(In Coordinated Universal Time, or UTC, the standard time of the prime meridian.)

New Moon			Waxing Quarter			Full Moon			Waning Quarter		
Date	Hr.	Min.	Date	Hr.	Min.	Date	Hr.	Min.	Date	Hr.	Min.
Jan. 10	1	31	Jan. 16	23	26	Jan. 24	1	46	Jan. 2	5	30
Feb. 8	14	39	Feb. 15	7	46	Feb. 22	18	20	Feb. 1	3	28
Mar. 9	1	54	Mar. 15	17	3	Mar. 23	12	1	Mar. 1	23	11
Apr. 7	11	24	Apr. 14	3	59	Apr. 22	5	24	Mar. 31	15	17
May 6	19	30	May 13	17	2	May 21	21	14	Apr. 30	3	29
June 5	3	0	June 12	8	10	June 20	11	2	May 29	12	12
July 4	11	1	July 12	0	52	July 19	22	57	June 27	18	19
Aug. 2	20	45	Aug. 10	18	21	Aug. 18	9	27	July 26	23	0
Sept. 1	9	3	Sept. 9	11	49	Sept. 16	19	5	Aug. 25	3	41
Oct. 1	0	11	Oct. 9	4	33	Oct. 16	4	23	Sept. 23	9	56
Oct. 30	17	38	Nov. 7	19	51	Nov. 14	13	52	Oct. 22	19	14
Nov. 29	12	18	Dec. 7	9	3	Dec. 14	0	6	Nov. 21	8	33
Dec. 29	6	53							Dec. 21	1	56

CALENDAR

Western Calendars

The **Julian calendar**, under which all Western nations measured time until 1582 CE, was authorized by Julius Caesar in 46 BCE. It called for a year of 365¼ days, starting in Jan., with every fourth year being a **leap year** of 366 days. St. Bede, an Anglo-Saxon monk also known as the Venerable Bede, announced in 730 CE that the Julian year was 11 min., 14 sec. too long, a cumulative error of about a day every 128 years, but nothing was done about this for centuries.

By 1582 the accumulated error was estimated at 10 days. In that year, Pope Gregory XIII decreed that the day following Oct. 4, 1582, should be called Oct. 15, thus dropping 10 days and initiating the **Gregorian calendar**.

The Gregorian calendar perpetuated a chronological system devised by the monk Dionysius Exiguus (fl. 6th cent.). His chronology started with the first year following the birth of Jesus Christ, which he inaccurately took to be year 753 in the Roman calendar. Leap years were continued but, to prevent further displacements, centesimal years (years ending in 00) were made common years, not leap years, unless divisible by 400. Under this plan, 1600 and 2000 were leap years; 1700, 1800, and 1900 were not.

The Gregorian calendar was adopted at once by France, Italy, Spain, Portugal, and Luxembourg. Within two years, most German Catholic states, Belgium, and parts of Switzerland and the Netherlands were brought under the new calendar, and Hungary followed in 1587. The rest of the Netherlands, along with Denmark and the German Protestant states, made the change in 1699-1700.

The British government adopted the Gregorian calendar and imposed it on all its possessions, including the American colonies, in 1752, decreeing that the day following Sept. 2, 1752, should be called Sept. 14, a loss of 11 days. All dates preceding were marked OS, for Old Style. In addition, New Year's Day was moved to Jan. 1 from Mar. 25. (Under the old reckoning, for example, Mar. 24, 1700, was followed by Mar. 25, 1701.) Thus George Washington's birth date, which was Feb. 11, 1731, OS, became Feb. 22, 1732, NS (New Style). In 1753, Sweden also went Gregorian.

In 1793, the French revolutionary government adopted a calendar of 12 months of 30 days each with five extra days in Sept. of each common year and six extra days every fourth year. Napoleon reinstated the Gregorian calendar in 1806.

The Gregorian system later spread to non-European regions, replacing traditional calendars at least for official purposes. Japan in 1873, Egypt in 1875, China in 1912, and Turkey in 1925 made the change, usually in conjunction with political upheaval. In China, the republican government began reckoning years from its 1911 founding. After 1949, the People's Republic adopted the Common, or Christian Era, year count, even for the traditional lunar calendar, which it retained. In 1918, the Soviet Union decreed that the day after Jan. 31, 1918, OS, would be Feb. 14, 1918, NS. Greece changed over in 1923. For the first time in history, all major nations had one calendar. The Russian Orthodox church and some other Christian sects retained the Julian calendar.

To convert from the Julian to the Gregorian calendar, add 10 days to dates Oct. 5, 1582, through Feb. 28, 1700; after that date, add 11 days through Feb. 28, 1800; 12 days through Feb. 28, 1900; and 13 days through Feb. 28, 2100.

A **century** consists of 100 consecutive years. The 1st century CE may be said to have run from the years 1 through 100. The 20th century by this reckoning consisted of the years 1901 through 2000 and ended Dec. 31, 2000, as did the 2nd millennium CE. The 21st century thus technically began on Jan. 1, 2001.

For a **perpetual calendar**, see pages 356-57.

Gregorian Calendar

Choose the desired year from the table below or from the perpetual calendar (for years 1803 to 2080). The number after each year designates which calendar to use for that year, as shown in the perpetual calendar. (The Gregorian calendar was inaugurated Oct. 15, 1582. From that date through Dec. 31, 1582, use calendar 6.)

1583-1802

1583	7	1603	4	1623	1	1643	5	1663	2	1683	6	1703	2	1723	6	1743	3	1763	7	1783	4
1584	8	1604	12	1624	9	1644	13	1664	10	1684	14	1704	10	1724	14	1744	11	1764	8	1784	12
1585	3	1605	7	1625	4	1645	1	1665	5	1685	2	1705	5	1725	2	1745	6	1765	3	1785	7
1586	4	1606	1	1626	5	1646	2	1666	6	1686	3	1706	6	1726	3	1746	7	1766	4	1786	1
1587	5	1607	2	1627	6	1647	3	1667	7	1687	4	1707	7	1727	4	1747	1	1767	5	1787	2
1588	13	1608	10	1628	14	1648	11	1668	8	1688	12	1708	8	1728	12	1748	9	1768	13	1788	10
1589	1	1609	5	1629	2	1649	6	1669	3	1689	7	1709	3	1729	7	1749	4	1769	1	1789	5
1590	2	1610	6	1630	3	1650	7	1670	4	1690	1	1710	4	1730	1	1750	5	1770	2	1790	6
1591	3	1611	7	1631	4	1651	1	1671	5	1691	2	1711	5	1731	2	1751	6	1771	3	1791	7
1592	11	1612	8	1632	12	1652	9	1672	13	1692	10	1712	13	1732	10	1752	14	1772	11	1792	8
1593	6	1613	3	1633	7	1653	4	1673	1	1693	5	1713	1	1733	5	1753	2	1773	6	1793	3
1594	7	1614	4	1634	1	1654	5	1674	2	1694	6	1714	2	1734	6	1754	3	1774	7	1794	4
1595	1	1615	5	1635	2	1655	6	1675	3	1695	7	1715	3	1735	7	1755	4	1775	1	1795	5
1596	9	1616	13	1636	10	1656	14	1676	11	1696	8	1716	11	1736	8	1756	12	1776	9	1796	13
1597	4	1617	1	1637	5	1657	2	1677	6	1697	3	1717	6	1737	3	1757	7	1777	4	1797	1
1598	5	1618	2	1638	6	1658	3	1678	7	1698	4	1718	7	1738	4	1758	1	1778	5	1798	2
1599	6	1619	3	1639	7	1659	4	1679	1	1699	5	1719	1	1739	5	1759	2	1779	6	1799	3
1600	14	1620	11	1640	8	1660	12	1680	9	1700	6	1720	9	1740	13	1760	10	1780	14	1800	4
1601	2	1621	6	1641	3	1661	7	1681	4	1701	7	1721	4	1741	1	1761	5	1781	2	1801	5
1602	3	1622	7	1642	4	1662	1	1682	5	1702	1	1722	5	1742	2	1762	6	1782	3	1802	6

The Julian Period

How many days have you lived? To determine this, multiply your age by 365, add the number of days since your last birthday, and account for all leap years. Chances are your calculations will go wrong somewhere. Astronomers, however, find it convenient to express dates and time intervals in days rather than in years, months, and days. This is done by placing events within the Julian period.

The Julian period was devised in 1582 by the French classical scholar Joseph Scaliger (1540-1609), who named it after his father, Julius Caesar Scaliger, not after the Julian calendar as might be supposed.

Scaliger began with a zero hour, or starting time, of noon on Jan. 1, 4713 BCE (on the Julian calendar). This was the most recent time that three major chronological cycles began on the same day: (1) the 28-year solar cycle, after which dates in the Julian calendar (e.g., Feb. 11) return to the same days of the week (e.g., Monday); (2) the 19-year lunar cycle, after which the phases of the moon return to the same dates of the year; and (3) the 15-year indiction cycle, used in ancient Rome to regulate taxes.

It will take 7,980 years to complete the period, the product of the numbers 28, 19, and 15.

Noon (Universal Time) of Jan. 1, 2016, will be Julian date (JD) 2,457,389; that many days will have passed since the start of the Julian period. The JD at noon of any date in 2016 may be found by adding to that number the day of the year for that date and subtracting one.

Julian Calendar

To find which of the 14 calendars of the perpetual calendar (pages 356-57) applies to any year under the Julian system, find the century for the desired year in the three leftmost columns below. Locate the desired year from among the four top rows. The number at the intersection of that row and column is the calendar designation for that year. For some years and countries, the Julian new year did not start Jan. 1; to find the correct perpetual calendar for Britain and its possessions, you can generally add one year for dates from Jan. 1 to Mar. 24. For example, to look up Feb. 2, 1705, Old Style, use the year 1706.

Year (last 2 digits of desired year)

Century	00	01 29 57 85	02 30 58 86	03 31 59 87	04 32 60 88	05 33 61 89	06 34 62 90	07 35 63 91	08 36 64 92	09 37 65 93	10 38 66 94	11 39 67 95	12 40 68 96	13 41 69 97	14 42 70 98	15 43 71 99	16 44 72	17 45 73	18 46 74	19 47 75	20 48 76	21 49 77	22 50 78	23 51 79	24 52 80	25 53 81	26 54 82	27 55 83	28 56 84
0 700 1400	12	7	1	2	10	5	6	7	8	3	4	5	13	1	2	3	11	6	7	1	9	4	5	6	14	2	3	4	12
100 800 1500	11	6	7	1	9	4	5	6	14	2	3	4	12	7	1	2	10	5	6	7	8	3	4	5	13	1	2	3	11
200 900 1600	10	5	6	7	8	3	4	5	13	1	2	3	11	6	7	1	9	4	5	6	14	2	3	4	12	7	1	2	10
300 1000 1700	9	4	5	6	14	2	3	4	12	7	1	2	10	5	6	7	8	3	4	5	13	1	2	3	11	6	7	1	9
400 1100 1800	8	3	4	5	13	1	2	3	11	6	7	1	9	4	5	6	14	2	3	4	12	7	1	2	10	5	6	7	8
500 1200 1900	14	2	3	4	12	7	1	2	10	5	6	7	8	3	4	5	13	1	2	3	11	6	7	1	9	4	5	6	14
600 1300 2000	13	1	2	3	11	6	7	1	9	4	5	6	14	2	3	4	12	7	1	2	10	5	6	7	8	3	4	5	13

Signs of the Zodiac

The zodiac is the apparent yearly path of the sun among the stars as viewed from Earth and was divided by the ancients into 12 equal sections or signs, each named for the constellation situated within its limits in ancient times. Astrologers claim that the temperament and destiny of each individual depend on the zodiac sign under which the person was born and the relationships between the planets at that time and throughout the person's life.

Below are the 12 traditional signs and the traditional range of dates pertaining to each:

- ♈ **Aries** (Ram), March 21-April 19
- ♉ **Taurus** (Bull), April 20-May 20
- ♊ **Gemini** (Twins), May 21-June 21
- ♋ **Cancer** (Crab), June 22-July 22
- ♌ **Leo** (Lion), July 23-August 22
- ♍ **Virgo** (Virgin), August 23-September 22
- ♎ **Libra** (Scales), September 23-October 23
- ♏ **Scorpio** (Scorpion), October 24-November 21
- ♐ **Sagittarius** (Archer), November 22-December 21
- ♑ **Capricorn** (Goat), December 22-January 19
- ♒ **Aquarius** (Water Bearer), January 20-February 18
- ♓ **Pisces** (Fishes), February 19-March 20

Chinese Calendar and Asian Festivals

The Chinese calendar, like the Jewish and Islamic calendars (see the Religion chapter), is a lunar calendar. It is divided into 12 months of 29 or 30 days (compensating for the lunar month's mean duration of 29 days, 12 hr., 44.05 min.). This calendar is synchronized with the solar year by the addition of extra months at fixed intervals.

The Chinese calendar runs on a 60-year cycle. The cycles 1876-1935 and 1936-95, along with the first 36 years of the current cycle, are shown below grouped by their association with 1 of 12 animals in the Chinese zodiac. This cycle began in 1996 and will last until 2055. Feb. 8, 2016, marks the beginning of the year 4714 in the Chinese calendar and is designated the Year of the Monkey. (Note: The first 3-7 weeks of each Western year belong to the previous Chinese year.)

Both the Western (Gregorian) and traditional lunar calendars are used publicly in China and in North and South Korea, and two New Year's celebrations are held. In Taiwan and Vietnam and in overseas Chinese communities, the lunar calendar is used only to set the dates for traditional festivals, with the Gregorian system in general use.

The 4-day Chinese New Year; the 3-day Vietnamese New Year festival, Tet; and the 3-to-4-day Korean festival, Suhl, begin at the second new moon after the winter solstice. The new moon in East Asia, which is west of the International Date Line, may be a day later than the new moon in the U.S. The festivals may start, therefore, anywhere between Jan. 21 and Feb. 19 of the Gregorian calendar.

Rat	Ox	Tiger	Hare (Rabbit)	Dragon	Snake	Horse	Sheep (Goat)	Monkey	Rooster	Dog	Pig (Boar)
1876	1877	1878	1879	1880	1881	1882	1883	1884	1885	1886	1887
1888	1889	1890	1891	1892	1893	1894	1895	1896	1897	1898	1899
1900	1901	1902	1903	1904	1905	1906	1907	1908	1909	1910	1911
1912	1913	1914	1915	1916	1917	1918	1919	1920	1921	1922	1923
1924	1925	1926	1927	1928	1929	1930	1931	1932	1933	1934	1935
1936	1937	1938	1939	1940	1941	1942	1943	1944	1945	1946	1947
1948	1949	1950	1951	1952	1953	1954	1955	1956	1957	1958	1959
1960	1961	1962	1963	1964	1965	1966	1967	1968	1969	1970	1971
1972	1973	1974	1975	1976	1977	1978	1979	1980	1981	1982	1983
1984	1985	1986	1987	1988	1989	1990	1991	1992	1993	1994	1995
1996	1997	1998	1999	2000	2001	2002	2003	2004	2005	2006	2007
2008	2009	2010	2011	2012	2013	2014	2015	2016	2017	2018	2019
2020	2021	2022	2023	2024	2025	2026	2027	2028	2029	2030	2031

Perpetual Calendar

The number shown for each year indicates which Gregorian calendar to use. For 1583-1802, see “Gregorian Calendar” on page 354. For 1803-20, use numbers for 1983-2000, respectively. The years in the calendar labels are the last and next occurrences of each calendar.

1821 . . . 2	1847 . . . 6	1873 . . . 4	1899 . . . 1	1925 . . . 5	1951 . . . 2	1977 . . . 7	2003 . . . 4	2029 . . . 2	2055 . . . 6
1822 . . . 3	1848 . . . 14	1874 . . . 5	1900 . . . 2	1926 . . . 6	1952 . . . 10	1978 . . . 1	2004 . . . 12	2030 . . . 3	2056 . . . 14
1823 . . . 4	1849 . . . 2	1875 . . . 6	1901 . . . 3	1927 . . . 7	1953 . . . 5	1979 . . . 2	2005 . . . 7	2031 . . . 4	2057 . . . 2
1824 . . . 12	1850 . . . 3	1876 . . . 14	1902 . . . 4	1928 . . . 8	1954 . . . 6	1980 . . . 10	2006 . . . 1	2032 . . . 12	2058 . . . 3
1825 . . . 7	1851 . . . 4	1877 . . . 2	1903 . . . 5	1929 . . . 3	1955 . . . 7	1981 . . . 5	2007 . . . 2	2033 . . . 7	2059 . . . 4
1826 . . . 1	1852 . . . 12	1878 . . . 3	1904 . . . 13	1930 . . . 4	1956 . . . 8	1982 . . . 6	2008 . . . 10	2034 . . . 1	2060 . . . 12
1827 . . . 2	1853 . . . 7	1879 . . . 4	1905 . . . 1	1931 . . . 5	1957 . . . 3	1983 . . . 7	2009 . . . 5	2035 . . . 2	2061 . . . 7
1828 . . . 10	1854 . . . 1	1880 . . . 12	1906 . . . 2	1932 . . . 13	1958 . . . 4	1984 . . . 8	2010 . . . 6	2036 . . . 10	2062 . . . 1
1829 . . . 5	1855 . . . 2	1881 . . . 7	1907 . . . 3	1933 . . . 1	1959 . . . 5	1985 . . . 3	2011 . . . 7	2037 . . . 5	2063 . . . 2
1830 . . . 6	1856 . . . 10	1882 . . . 1	1908 . . . 11	1934 . . . 2	1960 . . . 13	1986 . . . 4	2012 . . . 8	2038 . . . 6	2064 . . . 10
1831 . . . 7	1857 . . . 5	1883 . . . 2	1909 . . . 6	1935 . . . 3	1961 . . . 1	1987 . . . 5	2013 . . . 3	2039 . . . 7	2065 . . . 5
1832 . . . 8	1858 . . . 6	1884 . . . 10	1910 . . . 7	1936 . . . 11	1962 . . . 2	1988 . . . 13	2014 . . . 4	2040 . . . 8	2066 . . . 6
1833 . . . 3	1859 . . . 7	1885 . . . 5	1911 . . . 1	1937 . . . 6	1963 . . . 3	1989 . . . 1	2015 . . . 5	2041 . . . 3	2067 . . . 7
1834 . . . 4	1860 . . . 8	1886 . . . 6	1912 . . . 9	1938 . . . 7	1964 . . . 11	1990 . . . 2	2016 . . . 13	2042 . . . 4	2068 . . . 8
1835 . . . 5	1861 . . . 3	1887 . . . 7	1913 . . . 4	1939 . . . 1	1965 . . . 6	1991 . . . 3	2017 . . . 1	2043 . . . 5	2069 . . . 3
1836 . . . 13	1862 . . . 4	1888 . . . 8	1914 . . . 5	1940 . . . 9	1966 . . . 7	1992 . . . 11	2018 . . . 2	2044 . . . 13	2070 . . . 4
1837 . . . 1	1863 . . . 5	1889 . . . 3	1915 . . . 6	1941 . . . 4	1967 . . . 1	1993 . . . 6	2019 . . . 3	2045 . . . 1	2071 . . . 5
1838 . . . 2	1864 . . . 13	1890 . . . 4	1916 . . . 14	1942 . . . 5	1968 . . . 9	1994 . . . 7	2020 . . . 11	2046 . . . 2	2072 . . . 13
1839 . . . 3	1865 . . . 1	1891 . . . 5	1917 . . . 2	1943 . . . 6	1969 . . . 4	1995 . . . 1	2021 . . . 6	2047 . . . 3	2073 . . . 1
1840 . . . 11	1866 . . . 2	1892 . . . 13	1918 . . . 3	1944 . . . 14	1970 . . . 5	1996 . . . 9	2022 . . . 7	2048 . . . 11	2074 . . . 2
1841 . . . 6	1867 . . . 3	1893 . . . 1	1919 . . . 4	1945 . . . 2	1971 . . . 6	1997 . . . 4	2023 . . . 1	2049 . . . 6	2075 . . . 3
1842 . . . 7	1868 . . . 11	1894 . . . 2	1920 . . . 12	1946 . . . 3	1972 . . . 14	1998 . . . 5	2024 . . . 9	2050 . . . 7	2076 . . . 11
1843 . . . 1	1869 . . . 6	1895 . . . 3	1921 . . . 7	1947 . . . 4	1973 . . . 2	1999 . . . 6	2025 . . . 4	2051 . . . 1	2077 . . . 6
1844 . . . 9	1870 . . . 7	1896 . . . 11	1922 . . . 1	1948 . . . 12	1974 . . . 3	2000 . . . 14	2026 . . . 5	2052 . . . 9	2078 . . . 7
1845 . . . 4	1871 . . . 1	1897 . . . 6	1923 . . . 2	1949 . . . 7	1975 . . . 4	2001 . . . 2	2027 . . . 6	2053 . . . 4	2079 . . . 1
1846 . . . 5	1872 . . . 9	1898 . . . 7	1924 . . . 10	1950 . . . 1	1976 . . . 12	2002 . . . 3	2028 . . . 14	2054 . . . 5	2080 . . . 9

1 2006/2017

JANUARY

S	M	T	W	T	F	S
1	2	3	4	5	6	7
8	9	10	11	12	13	14
15	16	17	18	19	20	21
22	23	24	25	26	27	28
29	30	31				

FEBRUARY

S	M	T	W	T	F	S
			1	2	3	4
5	6	7	8	9	10	11
12	13	14	15	16	17	18
19	20	21	22	23	24	25
26	27	28				

MARCH

S	M	T	W	T	F	S
			1	2	3	4
5	6	7	8	9	10	11
12	13	14	15	16	17	18
19	20	21	22	23	24	25
26	27	28	29	30	31	

APRIL

S	M	T	W	T	F	S
						1
2	3	4	5	6	7	8
9	10	11	12	13	14	15
16	17	18	19	20	21	22
23	24	25	26	27	28	29
30						

MAY

S	M	T	W	T	F	S
	1	2	3	4	5	6
7	8	9	10	11	12	13
14	15	16	17	18	19	20
21	22	23	24	25	26	27
28	29	30	31			

JUNE

S	M	T	W	T	F	S
				1	2	3
4	5	6	7	8	9	10
11	12	13	14	15	16	17
18	19	20	21	22	23	24
25	26	27	28	29	30	

JULY

S	M	T	W	T	F	S
						1
2	3	4	5	6	7	8
9	10	11	12	13	14	15
16	17	18	19	20	21	22
23	24	25	26	27	28	29
30	31					

AUGUST

S	M	T	W	T	F	S
		1	2	3	4	5
6	7	8	9	10	11	12
13	14	15	16	17	18	19
20	21	22	23	24	25	26
27	28	29	30	31		

SEPTEMBER

S	M	T	W	T	F	S
					1	2
3	4	5	6	7	8	9
10	11	12	13	14	15	16
17	18	19	20	21	22	23
24	25	26	27	28	29	30

OCTOBER

S	M	T	W	T	F	S
1	2	3	4	5	6	7
8	9	10	11	12	13	14
15	16	17	18	19	20	21
22	23	24	25	26	27	28
29	30	31				

NOVEMBER

S	M	T	W	T	F	S
			1	2	3	4
5	6	7	8	9	10	11
12	13	14	15	16	17	18
19	20	21	22	23	24	25
26	27	28	29	30		

DECEMBER

S	M	T	W	T	F	S
					1	2
3	4	5	6	7	8	9
10	11	12	13	14	15	16
17	18	19	20	21	22	23
24	25	26	27	28	29	30
31						

2 2007/2018

JANUARY

S	M	T	W	T	F	S
	1	2	3	4	5	6
7	8	9	10	11	12	13
14	15	16	17	18	19	20
21	22	23	24	25	26	27
28	29	30	31			

FEBRUARY

S	M	T	W	T	F	S
				1	2	3
4	5	6	7	8	9	10
11	12	13	14	15	16	17
18	19	20	21	22	23	24
25	26	27	28			

MARCH

S	M	T	W	T	F	S
				1	2	3
4	5	6	7	8	9	10
11	12	13	14	15	16	17
18	19	20	21	22	23	24
25	26	27	28	29	30	31

APRIL

S	M	T	W	T	F	S
1	2	3	4	5	6	7
8	9	10	11	12	13	14
15	16	17	18	19	20	21
22	23	24	25	26	27	28
29	30					

MAY

S	M	T	W	T	F	S
		1	2	3	4	5
6	7	8	9	10	11	12
13	14	15	16	17	18	19
20	21	22	23	24	25	26
27	28	29	30	31		

JUNE

S	M	T	W	T	F	S
					1	2
3	4	5	6	7	8	9
10	11	12	13	14	15	16
17	18	19	20	21	22	23
24	25	26	27	28	29	30

JULY

S	M	T	W	T	F	S
1	2	3	4	5	6	7
8	9	10	11	12	13	14
15	16	17	18	19	20	21
22	23	24	25	26	27	28
29	30	31				

AUGUST

S	M	T	W	T	F	S
			1	2	3	4
5	6	7	8	9	10	11
12	13	14	15	16	17	18
19	20	21	22	23	24	25
26	27	28	29	30	31	

SEPTEMBER

S	M	T	W	T	F	S
						1
2	3	4	5	6	7	8
9	10	11	12	13	14	15
16	17	18	19	20	21	22
23	24	25	26	27	28	29
30						

OCTOBER

S	M	T	W	T	F	S
	1	2	3	4	5	6
7	8	9	10	11	12	13
14	15	16	17	18	19	20
21	22	23	24	25	26	27
28	29	30	31			

NOVEMBER

S	M	T	W	T	F	S
				1	2	3
4	5	6	7	8	9	10
11	12	13	14	15	16	17
18	19	20	21	22	23	24
25	26	27	28	29	30	

DECEMBER

S	M	T	W	T	F	S
						1
2	3	4	5	6	7	8
9	10	11	12	13	14	15
16	17	18	19	20	21	22
23	24	25	26	27	28	29
30	31					

3 2013/2019

JANUARY

S	M	T	W	T	F	S
		1	2	3	4	5
6	7	8	9	10	11	12
13	14	15	16	17	18	19
20	21	22	23	24	25	26
27	28	29	30	31		

FEBRUARY

S	M	T	W	T	F	S
					1	2
3	4	5	6	7	8	9
10	11	12	13	14	15	16
17	18	19	20	21	22	23
24	25	26	27	28		

MARCH

S	M	T	W	T	F	S
					1	2
3	4	5	6	7	8	9
10	11	12	13	14	15	16
17	18	19	20	21	22	23
24	25	26	27	28	29	30
31						

APRIL

S	M	T	W	T	F	S
	1	2	3	4	5	6
7	8	9	10	11	12	13
14	15	16	17	18	19	20
21	22	23	24	25	26	27
28	29	30				

MAY

S	M	T	W	T	F	S
			1	2	3	4
5	6	7	8	9	10	11
12	13	14	15	16	17	18
19	20	21	22	23	24	25
26	27	28	29	30	31	

JUNE

S	M	T	W	T	F	S
						1
2	3	4	5	6	7	8
9	10	11	12	13	14	15
16	17	18	19	20	21	22
23	24	25	26	27	28	29
30						

JULY

S	M	T	W	T	F	S
	1	2	3	4	5	6
7	8	9	10	11	12	13
14	15	16	17	18	19	20
21	22	23	24	25	26	27
28	29	30	31			

AUGUST

S	M	T	W	T	F	S
				1	2	3
4	5	6	7	8	9	10
11	12	13	14	15	16	17
18	19	20	21	22	23	24
25	26	27	28	29	30	31

SEPTEMBER

S	M	T	W	T	F	S
1	2	3	4	5	6	7
8	9	10	11	12	13	14
15	16	17	18	19	20	21
22	23	24	25	26	27	28
29	30					

OCTOBER

S	M	T	W	T	F	S
		1	2	3	4	5
6	7	8	9	10	11	12
13	14	15	16	17	18	19
20	21	22	23	24	25	26
27	28	29	30	31		

NOVEMBER

S	M	T	W	T	F	S
					1	2
3	4	5	6	7	8	9
10	11	12	13	14	15	16
17	18	19	20	21	22	23
24	25	26	27	28	29	30

DECEMBER

S	M	T	W	T	F	S
1	2	3	4	5	6	7
8	9	10	11	12	13	14
15	16	17	18	19	20	21
22	23	24	25	26	27	28
29	30	31				

4 2014/2025

JANUARY

S	M	T	W	T	F	S
			1	2	3	4
5	6	7	8	9	10	11
12	13	14	15	16	17	18
19	20	21	22	23	24	25
26	27	28	29	30	31	

FEBRUARY

S	M	T	W	T	F	S
						1
2	3	4	5	6	7	8
9	10	11	12	13	14	15
16	17	18	19	20	21	22
23	24	25	26	27	28	

MARCH

S	M	T	W	T	F	S
						1
2	3	4	5	6	7	8
9	10	11	12	13	14	15
16	17	18	19	20	21	22
23	24	25	26	27	28	29
30	31					

APRIL

S	M	T	W	T	F	S
		1	2	3	4	5
6	7	8	9	10	11	12
13	14	15	16	17	18	19
20	21	22	23	24	25	26
27	28	29	30			

MAY

S	M	T	W	T	F	S
				1	2	3
4	5	6	7	8	9	10
11	12	13	14	15	16	17
18	19	20	21	22	23	24
25	26	27	28	29	30	31

JUNE

S	M	T	W	T	F	S
1	2	3	4	5	6	7
8	9	10	11	12	13	14
15	16	17	18	19	20	21
22	23	24	25	26	27	28
29	30					

JULY

S	M	T	W	T	F	S
		1	2	3	4	5
6	7	8	9	10	11	12
13	14	15	16	17	18	19
20	21	22	23	24	25	26
27	28	29	30	31		

AUGUST

S	M	T	W	T	F	S
					1	2
3	4	5	6	7	8	9
10	11	12	13	14	15	16
17	18	19	20	21	22	23
24	25	26	27	28	29	30
31						

SEPTEMBER

S	M	T	W	T	F	S
	1	2	3	4	5	6
7	8	9	10	11	12	13
14	15	16	17	18	19	20
21	22	23	24	25	26	27
28	29	30				

OCTOBER

S	M	T	W	T	F	S
			1	2	3	4
5	6	7	8	9	10	11
12	13	14	15	16	17	18
19	20	21	22	23	24	25
26	27	28	29	30	31	

NOVEMBER

S	M	T	W	T	F	S
						1
2	3	4	5	6	7	8
9	10	11	12	13	14	15
16	17	18	19	20	21	22
23	24	25	26	27	28	29
30						

DECEMBER

S	M	T	W	T	F	S
	1	2	3	4	5	6
7	8	9	10	11	12	13
14	15	16	17	18	19	20
21	22	23	24	25	26	27
28	29	30	31			

5 2009/2015

JANUARY

S	M	T	W	T	F	S
				1	2	3
4	5	6	7	8	9	10
11	12	13	14	15	16	17
18	19	20	21	22	23	24
25	26	27	28	29	30	31

FEBRUARY

S	M	T	W	T	F	S
1	2	3	4	5	6	7
8	9	10	11	12	13	14
15	16	17	18	19	20	21
22	23	24	25	26	27	28

MARCH

S	M	T	W	T	F	S
1	2	3	4	5	6	7
8	9	10	11	12	13	14
15	16	17	18	19	20	21
22	23	24	25	26	27	28
29	30	31				

APRIL

S	M	T	W	T	F	S
			1	2	3	4
5	6	7	8	9	10	11
12	13	14	15	16	17	18
19	20	21	22	23	24	25
26	27	28	29	30		

MAY

S	M	T	W	T	F	S
					1	2
3	4	5	6	7	8	9
10	11	12	13	14	15	16
17	18	19	20	21	22	23
24	25	26	27	28	29	30
31						

JUNE

S	M	T	W	T	F	S
	1	2	3	4	5	6
7	8	9	10	11	12	13
14	15	16	17	18	19	20
21	22	23	24	25	26	27
28	29	30				

JULY

S	M	T	W	T	F	S
			1	2	3	4
5	6	7	8	9	10	11
12	13	14	15	16	17	18
19	20	21	22	23	24	25
26	27	28	29	30	31	

AUGUST

S	M	T	W	T	F	S
						1
2	3	4	5	6	7	8
9	10	11	12	13	14	15
16	17	18	19	20	21	22
23	24	25	26	27	28	29
30	31					

SEPTEMBER

S	M	T	W	T	F	S
		1	2	3	4	5
6	7	8	9	10	11	12
13	14	15	16	17	18	19
20	21	22	23	24	25	26
27	28	29	30			

OCTOBER

S	M	T	W	T	F	S
				1	2	3
4	5	6	7	8	9	10
11	12	13	14	15	16	17
18	19	20	21	22	23	24
25	26	27	28	29	30	31

NOVEMBER

S	M	T	W	T	F	S
1	2	3	4	5	6	7
8	9	10	11	12	13	14
15	16	17	18	19	20	21
22	23	24	25	26	27	28
29	30					

DECEMBER

S	M	T	W	T	F	S
		1	2	3	4	5
6	7	8	9	10	11	12
13	14	15	16	17	18	19
20	21	22	23	24	25	26
27	28	29	30	31		

6 2010/2021

JANUARY

S	M	T	W	T	F	S
					1	2
3	4	5	6	7	8	9
10	11	12	13	14	15	16
17	18	19	20	21	22	23
24	25	26	27	28	29	30
31						

FEBRUARY

S	M	T	W	T	F	S
	1	2	3	4	5	6
7	8	9	10	11	12	13
14	15	16	17	18	19	20
21	22	23	24	25	26	27
28						

MARCH

S	M	T	W	T	F	S
	1	2	3	4	5	6
7	8	9	10	11	12	13
14	15	16	17	18	19	20
21	22	23	24	25	26	27
28	29	30	31			

APRIL

S	M	T	W	T	F	S
				1	2	3
4	5	6	7	8	9	10
11	12	13	14	15	16	17
18	19	20	21	22	23	24
25	26	27	28	29	30	

MAY

S	M	T	W	T	F	S
						1
2	3	4	5	6	7	8
9	10	11	12	13	14	15
16	17	18	19	20	21	22
23	24	25	26	27	28	29
30	31					

JUNE

S	M	T	W	T	F	S
		1	2	3	4	5
6	7	8	9	10	11	12
13	14	15	16	17	18	19
20	21	22	23	24	25	26
27	28	29	30			

JULY

S	M	T	W	T	F	S
				1	2	3
4	5	6	7	8	9	10
11	12	13	14	15	16	17
18	19	20	21	22	23	24
25	26	27	28	29	30	31

AUGUST

S	M	T	W	T	F	S
1	2	3	4	5	6	7
8	9	10	11	12	13	14
15	16	17	18	19	20	21
22	23	24	25	26	27	28
29	30	31				

SEPTEMBER

S	M	T	W	T	F	S
			1	2	3	4
5	6	7	8	9	10	11
12	13	14	15	16	17	18
19	20	21	22	23	24	25
26	27	28	29	30		

OCTOBER

S	M	T	W	T	F	S
					1	2
3	4	5	6	7	8	9
10	11	12	13	14	15	16
17	18	19	20	21	22	23
24	25	26	27	28	29	30
31						

NOVEMBER

S	M	T	W	T	F	S
	1	2	3	4	5	6
7	8	9	10	11	12	13
14	15	16	17	18	19	20
21	22	23	24	25	26	27
28	29	30				

DECEMBER

S	M	T	W	T	F	S
			1	2	3	4
5	6	7	8	9	10	11
12	13	14	15	16	17	18
19	20	21	22	23	24	25
26	27	28	29	30	31	

7 2011/2022

JANUARY

S	M	T	W	T	F	S
						1
2	3	4	5	6	7	8
9	10	11	12	13	14	15
16	17	18	19	20	21	22
23	24	25	26	27	28	29
30	31					

FEBRUARY

S	M	T	W	T	F	S
		1	2	3	4	5
6	7	8	9	10	11	12
13	14	15	16	17	18	19
20	21	22	23	24	25	26
27	28					

MARCH

S	M	T	W	T	F	S
		1	2	3	4	5
6	7	8	9	10	11	12
13	14	15	16	17	18	19
20	21	22	23	24	25	26
27	28	29	30	31		

APRIL

S	M	T	W	T	F	S
					1	2
3	4	5	6	7	8	9
10	11	12	13	14	15	16
17	18	19	20	21	22	23
24	25	26	27	28	29	30

MAY

S	M	T	W	T	F	S
1	2	3	4	5	6	7
8	9	10	11	12	13	14
15	16	17	18	19	20	21
22	23	24	25	26	27	28
29	30	31				

JUNE

S	M	T	W	T	F	S
			1	2	3	4
5	6	7	8	9	10	11
12	13	14	15	16	17	18
19	20	21	22	23	24	25
26	27	28	29	30		

JULY

S	M	T	W	T	F	S
					1	2
3	4	5	6	7	8	9
10	11	12	13	14	15	16
17	18	19	20	21	22	23
24	25	26	27	28	29	30
31						

AUGUST

S	M	T	W	T	F	S
	1	2	3	4	5	6
7	8	9	10	11	12	13
14	15	16	17	18	19	20
21	22	23	24	25	26	27
28	29	30	31			

SEPTEMBER

S	M	T	W	T	F	S
				1	2	3
4	5	6	7	8	9	10
11	12	13	14	15	16	17
18	19	20	21	22	23	24
25	26	27	28	29	30	

OCTOBER

S	M	T	W	T	F	S
						1
2	3	4	5	6	7	8
9	10	11	12	13	14	15
16	17	18	19	20	21	22
23	24	25	26	27	28	29
30	31					

NOVEMBER

S	M	T	W	T	F	S
		1	2	3	4	5
6	7	8	9	10	11	12
13	14	15	16	17	18	19
20	21	22	23	24	25	26
27	28	29	30			

DECEMBER

S	M	T	W	T	F	S
				1	2	3
4	5	6	7	8	9	10
11	12	13	14	15	16	17
18	19	20	21	22	23	24
25	26	27	28	29	30	31

8 2012/2040

JANUARY

S	M	T	W	T	F	S
1	2	3	4	5	6	7
8	9	10	11	12	13	14
15	16	17	18	19	20	21
22	23	24	25	26	27	28
29	30	31				

FEBRUARY

S	M	T	W	T	F	S
			1	2	3	4
5	6	7	8	9	10	11
12	13	14	15	16	17	18
19	20	21	22	23	24	25
26	27	28	29			

MARCH

S	M	T	W	T	F	S
				1	2	3
4	5	6	7	8	9	10
11	12	13	14	15	16	17
18	19	20	21	22	23	24
25	26	27	28	29	30	31

APRIL

S	M	T	W	T	F	S
1	2	3	4	5	6	7
8	9	10	11	12	13	14
15	16	17	18	19	20	21
22	23	24	25	26	27	28
29	30					

MAY

S	M	T	W	T	F	S
		1	2	3	4	5
6	7	8	9	10	11	12
13	14	15	16	17	18	19
20	21	22	23	24	25	26
27	28	29	30	31		

JUNE

S	M	T	W	T	F	S
					1	2
3	4	5	6	7	8	9
10	11	12	13	14	15	16
17	18	19	20	21	22	23
24	25	26	27	28	29	30

JULY

S	M	T	W	T	F	S
1	2	3	4	5	6	7
8	9	10	11	12	13	14
15	16	17	18	19	20	21
22	23	24	25	26	27	28
29	30	31				

AUGUST

S	M	T	W	T	F	S
			1	2	3	4
5	6	7	8	9	10	11
12	13	14	15	16	17	18
19	20	21	22	23	24	25
26	27	28	29	30	31	

SEPTEMBER

S	M	T	W	T	F	S
						1
2	3	4	5	6	7	8
9	10	11	12	13	14	15
16	17	18	19	20	21	22
23	24	25	26	27	28	29
30						

OCTOBER

S	M	T	W	T	F	S
	1	2	3	4	5	6
7	8	9	10	11	12	13
14	15	16	17	18	19	20
21	22	23	24	25	26	27
28	29	30	31			

NOVEMBER

S	M	T	W	T	F	S
				1	2	3
4	5	6	7	8	9	10
11	12	13	14	15	16	17
18	19	20	21	22	23	24
25	26	27	28	29	30	

DECEMBER

S	M	T	W	T	F	S
						1
2	3	4	5	6	7	8
9	10	11	12	13	14	15
16	17	18	19	20	21	22
23	24	25	26	27	28	29
30	31					

9 1996/2024

JANUARY

S	M	T	W	T	F	S
	1	2	3	4	5	6
7	8	9	10	11	12	13
14	15	16	17	18	19	20
21	22	23	24	25	26	27
28	29	30	31			

FEBRUARY

S	M	T	W	T	F	S
				1	2	3
4	5	6	7	8	9	10
11	12	13	14	15	16	17
18	19	20	21	22	23	24
25	26	27	28	29		

MARCH

S	M	T	W	T	F	S
					1	2
3	4	5	6	7	8	9
10	11	12	13	14	15	16
17	18	19	20	21	22	23
24	25	26	27	28	29	30
31						

APRIL

S	M	T	W	T	F	S
	1	2	3	4	5	6
7	8	9	10	11	12	13
14	15	16	17	18	19	20
21	22	23	24	25	26	27
28	29	30				

MAY

S	M	T	W	T	F	S
			1	2	3	4
5	6	7	8	9	10	11
12	13	14	15	16	17	18
19	20	21	22	23	24	25
26	27	28	29	30	31	

JUNE

S	M	T	W	T	F	S
						1
2	3	4	5	6	7	8
9	10	11	12	13	14	15
16	17	18	19	20	21	22
23	24	25	26	27	28	29
30						

JULY

S	M	T	W	T	F	S
	1	2	3	4	5	6
7	8	9	10	11	12	13
14	15	16	17	18	19	20
21	22	23	24	25	26	27
28	29	30	31			

AUGUST

S	M	T	W	T	F	S
				1	2	3
4	5	6	7	8	9	10
11	12	13	14	15	16	17
18	19	20	21	22	23	24
25	26	27	28	29	30	31

SEPTEMBER

S	M	T	W	T	F	S
1	2	3	4	5	6	7
8	9	10	11	12	13	14
15	16	17	18	19	20	21
22	23	24	25	26	27	28
29	30					

OCTOBER

S	M	T	W	T	F	S
		1	2	3	4	5
6	7	8	9	10	11	12
13	14	15	16	17	18	19
20	21	22	23	24	25	26
27	28	29	30	31		

NOVEMBER

S	M	T	W	T	F	S
					1	2
3	4	5	6	7	8	9
10	11	12	13	14	15	16
17	18	19	20	21	22	23
24	25	26	27	28	29	30

DECEMBER

S	M	T	W	T	F	S
1	2	3	4	5	6	7
8	9	10	11	12	13	14
15	16	17	18	19	20	21
22	23	24	25	26	27	28
29	30	31				

10 2008/2036

JANUARY

S	M	T	W	T	F	S
		1	2	3	4	5
6	7	8	9	10	11	12
13	14	15	16	17	18	19
20	21	22	23	24	25	26
27	28	29	30	31		

FEBRUARY

S	M	T	W	T	F	S
					1	2
3	4	5	6	7	8	9
10	11	12	13	14	15	16
17	18	19	20	21	22	23
24	25	26	27	28	29	

MARCH

S	M	T	W	T	F	S
						1
2	3	4	5	6	7	8
9	10	11	12	13	14	15
16	17	18	19	20	21	22
23	24	25	26	27	28	29
30	31					

APRIL

S	M	T	W	T	F	S
		1	2	3	4	5
6	7	8	9	10	11	12
13	14	15	16	17	18	19
20	21	22	23	24	25	26
27	28	29	30			

MAY

S	M	T	W	T	F	S
				1	2	3
4	5	6	7	8	9	10
11	12	13	14	15	16	17
18	19	20	21	22	23	24
25	26	27	28	29	30	31

JUNE

S	M	T	W	T	F	S
1	2	3	4	5	6	7
8	9	10	11	12	13	14
15	16	17	18	19	20	21
22	23	24	25	26	27	28
29	30					

JULY

S	M	T	W	T	F	S
		1	2	3	4	5
6	7	8	9	10	11	12
13	14	15	16	17	18	19
20	21	22	23	24	25	26
27	28	29	30	31		

AUGUST

S	M	T	W	T	F	S
					1	2
3	4	5	6	7	8	9
10	11	12	13	14	15	16
17	18	19	20	21	22	23
24	25	26	27	28	29	30
31						

SEPTEMBER

S	M	T	W	T	F	S
	1	2	3	4	5	6
7	8	9	10	11	12	13
14	15	16	17	18	19	20
21	22	23	24	25	26	27
28	29	30				

OCTOBER

S	M	T	W	T	F	S
			1	2	3	4
5	6	7	8	9	10	11
12	13	14	15	16	17	18
19	20	21	22	23	24	25
26	27	28	29	30	31	

NOVEMBER

S	M	T	W	T	F	S
						1
2	3	4	5	6	7	8
9	10	11	12	13	14	15
16	17	18	19	20	21	22
23	24	25	26	27	28	29
30						

DECEMBER

S	M	T	W	T	F	S
	1	2	3	4	5	6
7	8	9	10	11	12	13
14	15	16	17	18	19	20
21	22	23	24	25	26	27
28	29	30	31			

11 1992/2020

JANUARY

S	M	T	W	T	F	S
			1	2	3	4
5	6	7	8	9	10	11
12	13	14	15	16	17	18
19	20	21	22	23	24	25
26	27	28	29	30	31	

FEBRUARY

S	M	T	W	T	F	S
						1
2	3	4	5	6	7	8
9	10	11	12	13	14	15
16	17	18	19	20	21	22
23	24	25	26	27	28	29

MARCH

S	M	T	W	T	F	S
1	2	3	4	5	6	7
8	9	10	11	12	13	14
15	16	17	18	19	20	21
22	23	24	25	26	27	28
29	30	31				

APRIL

S	M	T	W	T	F	S
			1	2	3	4
5	6	7	8	9	10	11
12	13	14	15	16	17	18
19	20	21	22	23	24	25
26	27	28	29	30		

MAY

S	M	T	W	T	F	S
					1	2
3	4	5	6	7	8	9
10	11	12	13	14	15	16
17	18	19	20	21	22	23
24	25	26	27	28	29	30
31						

JUNE

S	M	T	W	T	F	S
	1	2	3	4	5	6
7	8	9	10	11	12	13
14	15	16	17	18	19	20
21	22	23	24	25	26	27
28	29	30				

JULY

S	M	T	W	T	F	S
			1	2	3	4
5	6	7	8	9	10	11
12	13	14	15	16	17	18
19	20	21	22	23	24	25
26	27	28	29	30	31	

AUGUST

S	M	T	W	T	F	S
						1
2	3	4	5	6	7	8
9	10	11	12	13	14	15
16	17	18	19	20	21	22
23	24	25	26	27	28	29
30	31					

SEPTEMBER

S	M	T	W	T	F	S
		1	2	3	4	5
6	7	8	9	10	11	12
13	14	15	16	17	18	19
20	21	22	23	24	25	26
27	28	29	30			

OCTOBER

S	M	T	W	T	F	S
				1	2	3
4	5	6	7	8	9	10
11	12	13	14	15	16	17
18	19	20	21	22	23	24
25	26	27	28	29	30	31

NOVEMBER

S	M	T	W	T	F	S
1	2	3	4	5	6	7
8	9	10	11	12	13	14
15	16	17	18	19	20	21
22	23	24	25	26	27	28
29	30					

DECEMBER

S	M	T	W	T	F	S
		1	2	3	4	5
6	7	8	9	10	11	12
13	14	15	16	17	18	19
20	21	22	23	24	25	26
27	28	29	30	31		

12 2004/2032

JANUARY

S	M	T	W	T	F	S
				1	2	3
4	5	6	7	8	9	10
11	12	13	14	15	16	17
18	19	20	21	22	23	24
25	26	27	28	29	30	31

FEBRUARY

S	M	T	W	T	F	S
1	2	3	4	5	6	7
8	9	10	11	12	13	14
15	16	17	18	19	20	21
22	23	24	25	26	27	28
29						

MARCH

S	M	T	W	T	F	S
	1	2	3	4	5	6
7	8	9	10	11	12	13
14	15	16	17	18	19	20
21	22	23	24	25	26	27
28	29	30	31			

APRIL

S	M	T	W	T	F	S
				1	2	3
4	5	6	7	8	9	10
11	12	13	14	15	16	17
18	19	20	21	22	23	24
25	26	27	28	29	30	

MAY

S	M	T	W	T	F	S
						1
2	3	4	5	6	7	8
9	10	11	12	13	14	15
16	17	18	19	20	21	22
23	24	25	26	27	28	29
30	31					

JUNE

S	M	T	W	T	F	S
		1	2	3	4	5
6	7	8	9	10	11	12
13	14	15	16	17	18	19
20	21	22	23	24	25	26
27	28	29	30			

JULY

S	M	T	W	T	F	S
				1	2	3
4	5	6	7	8	9	10
11	12	13	14	15	16	17
18	19	20	21	22	23	24
25	26	27	28	29	30	31

AUGUST

S	M	T	W	T	F	S
1	2	3	4	5	6	7
8	9	10	11	12	13	14
15	16	17	18	19	20	21
22	23	24	25	26	27	28
29	30	31				

SEPTEMBER

S	M	T	W	T	F	S
			1	2	3	4
5	6	7	8	9	10	11
12	13	14	15	16	17	18
19	20	21	22	23	24	25
26	27	28	29	30		

OCTOBER

S	M	T	W	T	F	S
					1	2
3	4	5	6	7	8	9
10	11	12	13	14	15	16
17	18	19	20	21	22	23
24	25	26	27	28	29	30
31						

NOVEMBER

S	M	T	W	T	F	S
	1	2	3	4	5	6
7	8	9	10	11	12	13
14	15	16	17	18	19	20
21	22	23	24	25	26	27
28	29	30				

DECEMBER

S	M	T	W	T	F	S
			1	2	3	4
5	6	7	8	9	10	11
12	13	14	15	16	17	18
19	20	21	22	23	24	25
26	27	28	29	30	31	

13 1988/2016

JANUARY

S	M	T	W	T	F	S
					1	2
3	4	5	6	7	8	9
10	11	12	13	14	15	16
17	18	19	20	21	22	23
24	25	26	27	28	29	30
31						

FEBRUARY

S	M	T	W	T	F	S
	1	2	3	4	5	6
7	8	9	10	11	12	13
14	15	16	17	18	19	20
21	22	23	24	25	26	27
28	29					

MARCH

S	M	T	W	T	F	S
		1	2	3	4	5
6	7	8	9	10	11	12
13	14	15	16	17	18	19
20	21	22	23	24	25	26
27	28	29	30	31		

APRIL

S	M	T	W	T	F	S
					1	2
3	4	5	6	7	8	9
10	11	12	13	14	15	16
17	18	19	20	21	22	23
24	25	26	27	28	29	30

MAY

S	M	T	W	T	F	S
1	2	3	4	5	6	7
8	9	10	11	12	13	14
15	16	17	18	19	20	21
22	23	24	25	26	27	28
29	30	31				

JUNE

S	M	T	W	T	F	S
			1	2	3	4
5	6	7	8	9	10	11
12	13	14	15	16	17	18
19	20	21	22	23	24	25
26	27	28	29	30		

JULY

S	M	T	W	T	F	S
					1	2
3	4	5	6	7	8	9
10	11	12	13	14	15	16
17	18	19	20	21	22	23
24	25	26	27	28	29	30
31						

AUGUST

S	M	T	W	T	F	S
	1	2	3	4	5	6
7	8	9	10	11	12	13
14	15	16	17	18	19	20
21	22	23	24	25	26	27
28	29	30	31			

SEPTEMBER

S	M	T	W	T	F	S
				1	2	3
4	5	6	7	8	9	10
11	12	13	14	15	16	17
18	19	20	21	22	23	24
25	26	27	28	29	30	

OCTOBER

S	M	T	W	T	F	S
						1
2	3	4	5	6	7	8
9	10	11	12	13	14	15
16	17	18	19	20	21	22
23	24	25	26	27	28	29
30	31					

NOVEMBER

S	M	T	W	T	F	S
		1	2	3	4	5
6	7	8	9	10	11	12
13	14	15	16	17	18	19
20	21	22	23	24	25	26
27	28	29	30			

DECEMBER

S	M	T	W	T	F	S
				1	2	3
4	5	6	7	8	9	10
11	12	13	14	15	16	17
18	19	20	21	22	23	24
25	26	27	28	29	30	31

14 2000/2028

JANUARY

S	M	T	W	T	F	S
						1
2	3	4	5	6	7	8
9	10	11	12	13	14	15
16	17	18	19	20	21	22
23	24	25	26	27	28	29
30	31					

FEBRUARY

S	M	T	W	T	F	S
		1	2	3	4	5
6	7	8	9	10	11	12
13	14	15	16	17	18	19
20	21	22	23	24	25	26
27	28	29				

MARCH

S	M	T	W	T	F	S
			1	2	3	4
5	6	7	8	9	10	11
12	13	14	15	16	17	18
19	20	21	22	23	24	25
26	27	28	29	30	31	

APRIL

S	M	T	W	T	F	S
						1
2	3	4	5	6	7	8
9	10	11	12	13	14	15
16	17	18	19	20	21	22
23	24	25	26	27	28	29
30						

MAY

S	M	T	W	T	F	S
	1	2	3	4	5	6
7	8	9	10	11	12	13
14	15	16	17	18	19	20
21	22	23	24	25	26	27
28	29	30	31			

JUNE

S	M	T	W	T	F	S
				1	2	3
4	5	6	7	8	9	10
11	12	13	14	15	16	17
18	19	20	21	22	23	24
25	26	27	28	29	30	

JULY

S	M	T	W	T	F	S
						1
2	3	4	5	6	7	8
9	10	11	12	13	14	15
16	17	18	19	20	21	22
23	24	25	26	27	28	29
30	31					

AUGUST

S	M	T	W	T	F	S
		1	2	3	4	5
6	7	8	9	10	11	12
13	14	15	16	17	18	19
20	21	22	23	24	25	26
27	28	29	30	31		

SEPTEMBER

S	M	T	W	T	F	S
					1	2
3	4	5	6	7	8	9
10	11	12	13	14	15	16
17	18	19	20	21	22	23
24	25	26	27	28	29	30

OCTOBER

S	M	T	W	T	F	S
1	2	3	4	5	6	7
8	9	10	11	12	13	14
15	16	17	18	19	20	21
22	23	24	25	26	27	28
29	30	31				

NOVEMBER

S	M	T	W	T	F	S
			1	2	3	4
5	6	7	8	9	10	11
12	13	14	15	16	17	18
19	20	21	22	23	24	25
26	27	28	29	30		

DECEMBER

S	M	T	W	T	F	S
					1	2
3	4	5	6	7	8	9
10	11	12	13	14	15	16
17	18	19	20	21	22	23
24	25	26	27	28	29	30
31						

Calendar for the Year 2016

January

S	M	T	W	T	F	S
					1	2
3	4	5	6	7	8	9
10	11	12	13	14	15	16
17	**18**	19	20	21	22	23
24	25	26	27	28	29	30
31						

February

S	M	T	W	T	F	S
	1	2	3	4	5	6
7	8	9	10	11	12	13
14	**15**	16	17	18	19	20
21	22	23	24	25	26	27
28	29					

March

S	M	T	W	T	F	S
		1	2	3	4	5
6	7	8	9	10	11	12
13	14	15	16	17	18	19
20	21	22	23	24	25	26
27	28	29	30	31		

April

S	M	T	W	T	F	S
					1	2
3	4	5	6	7	8	9
10	11	12	13	14	15	16
17	18	19	20	21	22	23
24	25	26	27	28	29	30

May

S	M	T	W	T	F	S
1	2	3	4	5	6	7
8	9	10	11	12	13	14
15	16	17	18	19	20	21
22	23	24	25	26	27	28
29	**30**	31				

June

S	M	T	W	T	F	S
			1	2	3	4
5	6	7	8	9	10	11
12	13	14	15	16	17	18
19	20	21	22	23	24	25
26	27	28	29	30		

July

S	M	T	W	T	F	S
					1	2
3	**4**	5	6	7	8	9
10	11	12	13	14	15	16
17	18	19	20	21	22	23
24	25	26	27	28	29	30
31						

August

S	M	T	W	T	F	S
	1	2	3	4	5	6
7	8	9	10	11	12	13
14	15	16	17	18	19	20
21	22	23	24	25	26	27
28	29	30	31			

September

S	M	T	W	T	F	S
				1	2	3
4	**5**	6	7	8	9	10
11	12	13	14	15	16	17
18	19	20	21	22	23	24
25	26	27	28	29	30	

October

S	M	T	W	T	F	S
						1
2	3	4	5	6	7	8
9	**10**	11	12	13	14	15
16	17	18	19	20	21	22
23	24	25	26	27	28	29
30	31					

November

S	M	T	W	T	F	S
		1	2	3	4	5
6	7	8	9	10	**11**	12
13	14	15	16	17	18	19
20	21	22	23	**24**	25	26
27	28	29	30			

December

S	M	T	W	T	F	S
				1	2	3
4	5	6	7	8	9	10
11	12	13	14	15	16	17
18	19	20	21	22	23	24
25	**26**	27	28	29	30	31

Federal Holidays and Other Notable Dates, 2016

Some dates may be subject to change.

The dates in bold in the calendar above and named below in italics are U.S. federal holidays, designated by the president or Congress and applicable to federal employees and in the District of Columbia. Most U.S. states also observe these holidays, and many states observe others; practices vary by state. In most states the secretary of state's office can provide details.

January

1 *New Year's Day*; Sugar Bowl; Rose Bowl; Fiesta Bowl
11 College Football Playoff national championship game (Glendale, AZ)
18 *Martin Luther King Jr. Day*
18-31 Australian Open tennis tournament
26 Australia Day
31 NFL Pro Bowl (Honolulu, HI)

February

2 Groundhog Day
5-10 Carnival, Brazil
7 Super Bowl 50 (Santa Clara, CA)
9 Mardi Gras
10 Ash Wednesday
12 Lincoln's Birthday
14 Valentine's Day; NBA All-Star Game (Toronto, Canada)
15 *Washington's Birthday* (observed); Presidents' Day, or Washington-Lincoln Day (3rd Mon. in Feb.)
15-16 Westminster Dog Show
21 Daytona 500
28 Academy Awards

March

5 Iditarod Trail Sled Dog Race begins
13 Daylight-saving time begins in U.S.
17 St. Patrick's Day
20 First day of spring (Northern Hemisphere)
21 Benito Juárez's Birthday, Mexico
24 Purim (Feast of Lots) begins previous night
25 Good Friday
27 Easter

April

1 April Fools' Day
2, 4 NCAA Men's Basketball Final Four (Houston, TX)
3, 5 NCAA Women's Basketball Final Four (Indianapolis, IN)
4-10 Master's golf tournament
18 Tax Day (IRS filing deadline); Patriots' Day; Boston Marathon (3rd Mon. in April)
22 Earth Day
23 Passover, 1st full day
28 Take Our Daughters and Sons to Work Day
29 Arbor Day

May

1 Easter (Orthodox); May Day (International Workers' Day)
5 Cinco de Mayo (Battle of Puebla Day), Mexico
7 Kentucky Derby
8 Mother's Day
14 Buddha's Birthday, Hong Kong, Korea
21 Armed Forces Day; Preakness Stakes
22-June 5 French Open tennis tournament
23 Victoria Day, Canada
30 *Memorial Day*, or Decoration Day (last Mon. in May)

June

6 Ramadan (Islamic month of fasting), 1st full day
9 Dragon Boat Festival, China
11 Belmont Stakes
14 Flag Day
16-19 U.S. Open golf tournament (Oakmont, PA)
19 Father's Day
20 First day of summer (Northern Hemisphere)
27-July 10 Wimbledon tennis tournament

July

1 Canada Day
4 *Independence Day*
6-14 Running of the Bulls (Pamplona, Spain)
7-10 U.S. Women's Open golf tournament (San Martin, CA)
14 Bastille Day, France
21-24 British Open golf tournament (Ayrshire, Scotland, UK)
25-31 PGA Championship (Springfield, NJ)

August

5-21 Summer Olympic Games (Rio de Janeiro, Brazil)

September

5 *Labor Day*, U.S., Canada (1st Mon. in Sept.)
11 Grandparents' Day, U.S.
16 Independence Day, Mexico (celebration begins previous night)
17 Constitution Day and Citizenship Day, U.S.
22 First day of autumn (Northern Hemisphere)

October

2 Islamic New Year (Muharram 1) begins previous night
3 Rosh Hashanah (New Year), 1st full day; U.S. Supreme Court session begins; German Unity Day, Germany
10 *Columbus Day* (2nd Mon. in Oct.); Thanksgiving Day, Canada
12 Yom Kippur (Day of Atonement) begins previous night; Día de la Raza, Spain, Mexico
31 Halloween

November

6 Daylight-saving time ends in U.S.; New York City Marathon
8 Election Day (1st Tues. after 1st Mon. in Nov.)
11 *Veterans Day*; Remembrance Day, Canada
13 Remembrance Sunday, UK
24 *Thanksgiving Day* (4th Thurs. in Nov.)

December

12 Día de la Virgen de Guadalupe, Mexico
21 First day of winter (Northern Hemisphere)
25 *Christmas Day*
25-Jan. 1 Hanukkah (Festival of Lights) begins previous night
26 Christmas Day (federal holiday observed); Boxing Day, Australia, Canada, New Zealand, UK
26-Jan. 1 Kwanzaa
31 Orange Bowl; Chik-fil-A Peach Bowl; Fiesta Bowl

Other Calendars: Year and New Year's Day, 2016

Era	Year	Begins in 2016	Era	Year	Begins in 2016
Byzantine	7525	Sept. 14	Islamic/Muslim (Hijra)	1438	Oct. 2[1]
Chinese (Year of the Monkey)	4714	Feb. 8	Japanese	28	Jan. 1
Diocletian	1733	Sept. 11	Jewish	5777	Oct. 3[1]
Grecian (Seleucidae)	2328	Sept. 14 or Oct. 14	Nabonassar (Babylonian)	2765	Apr. 23
Indian (Saka)	1938	Mar. 22	Roman (Ab Urbe Condita)	2769	Jan. 14

(1) Year begins the previous night. (2) Era starts at 0 with new emperor.

Chronological Cycles, 2016

Dominical Letter	CB	Roman Indiction	9	Solar Cycle	9
Golden Number (lunar cycle)	III	Epact	21	Julian Period (year of)	6729

Special Months

There are many thousands of special months, days, and weeks because of anniversaries, official proclamations, and promotional events, both trivial and serious. Here are a few of the special months:

January: Get Organized Month, National Mentoring Month, National Poverty in America Awareness Month

February: African American History Month, American Heart Month, Library Lovers' Month, Youth Leadership Month, Return Shopping Carts to the Supermarket Month

March: Irish-American Heritage Month, National Women's History Month, Red Cross Month, National Frozen Food Month, National Talk With Your Teen About Sex Month, National Colorectal Cancer Awareness Month

April: National Child Abuse Prevention Month, National Humor Month, Stress Awareness Month, Grange Month

May: Clean Air Month, Get Caught Reading Month, National Barbecue Month, Asian American and Pacific Islander Heritage Month, National Inventors Month, National Mental Health Awareness Month

June: National Candy Month; Lesbian, Gay, Bisexual, and Transgender Pride Month; Great Outdoors Month; National Safety Month

July: Cell Phone Courtesy Month, National Make a Difference to Children Month, National Hot Dog Month, Women's Motorcycle Month

August: National Black Business Month, Happiness Happens Month, National Immunization Awareness Month, National Toddler Month

September: Library Card Sign-Up Month, National Hispanic Heritage Month (Sept. 15-Oct. 15), National Biscuit Month

October: National Domestic Violence Awareness Month, National Breast Cancer Awareness Month, Diversity Awareness Month, National Popcorn Poppin' Month

November: National American Indian Heritage Month, National Adoption Month, American Diabetes Month, National Peanut Butter Lovers' Month

December: Safe Toys and Gifts Month, National Impaired Driving Prevention Month, National Tie Month

Standard Time Differences: World Cities

The time indicated in the table is fixed by law and is called the legal time or, more generally, standard time. Use of daylight-saving time varies widely. An asterisk (*) indicates morning of the following day. At 12:00 noon, Eastern Standard Time, the standard time (in 24-hour time) in selected cities is as shown.

Addis Ababa	20 00	Denver	10 00	London	17 00	Santiago	13 00
Amsterdam	18 00	Dhaka	23 00	Los Angeles	9 00	São Paulo	14 00
Ankara	19 00	Dublin	17 00	Madrid	18 00	Sarajevo	18 00
Athens	19 00	Edinburgh	17 00	Manila	1 00*	Seoul	2 00*
Auckland	5 00*	Geneva	18 00	Mecca	20 00	Shanghai	1 00*
Baghdad	20 00	Helsinki	19 00	Melbourne	3 00*	Singapore	1 00*
Bangkok	0 00*	Ho Chi Minh City	0 00*	Montevideo	14 00	Stockholm	18 00
Beijing	1 00*	Hong Kong	1 00*	Moscow	21 00	Sydney	3 00*
Belfast	17 00	Houston	11 00	Mumbai (Bombay)	22 30	Taipei	1 00*
Belgrade	18 00	Islamabad	22 00	Munich	18 00	Tashkent	22 00
Berlin	18 00	Istanbul	19 00	Nagasaki	2 00*	Tehran	20 30
Bogotá	12 00	Jakarta	0 00*	Nairobi	20 00	Tel Aviv	19 00
Brussels	18 00	Jerusalem	19 00	New Delhi	22 30	Tokyo	2 00*
Bucharest	19 00	Johannesburg	19 00	New York	12 00	Toronto	12 00
Budapest	18 00	Kabul	21 30	Oslo	18 00	Vancouver	9 00
Buenos Aires	14 00	Karachi	22 00	Paris	18 00	Vienna	18 00
Cairo	19 00	Kathmandu	22 45	Prague	18 00	Vladivostok	4 00*
Cape Town	19 00	Kiev	19 00	Quito	12 00	Warsaw	18 00
Caracas	12 30	Kolkata (Calcutta)	22 30	Rio de Janeiro	14 00	Wellington	5 00*
Casablanca	17 00	Lagos	18 00	Riyadh	20 00	Yangon (Rangoon)	23 30
Chicago	11 00	Lima	12 00	Rome	18 00	Yokohama	2 00*
Copenhagen	18 00	Lisbon	17 00	St. Petersburg	21 00	Zurich	18 00

Wedding Anniversary Gifts

The traditional names for wedding anniversaries go back many years in social usage and have been used to suggest types of appropriate anniversary gifts. Traditional products for gifts are listed here in capital letters, with allowable revisions in parentheses, followed by common modern gifts in each category.

Anniversary	Gift	Anniversary	Gift	Anniversary	Gift
1st	PAPER, clocks	**9th**	POTTERY (CHINA), leather goods	**25th**	SILVER, sterling silver
2nd	COTTON, china	**10th**	TIN, ALUMINUM, diamond	**30th**	PEARL, diamond
3rd	LEATHER, crystal, glass	**11th**	STEEL, fashion jewelry	**35th**	CORAL (JADE), jade
4th	LINEN (SILK), appliances	**12th**	SILK, pearls, colored gems	**40th**	RUBY, ruby
5th	WOOD, silverware	**13th**	LACE, textiles, furs	**45th**	SAPPHIRE, sapphire
6th	IRON, wood objects	**14th**	IVORY, gold jewelry	**50th**	GOLD, gold
7th	WOOL (COPPER), desk sets	**15th**	CRYSTAL, watches	**55th**	EMERALD, emerald
8th	BRONZE, linens, lace	**20th**	CHINA, platinum	**60th**	DIAMOND, diamond

Birthstones

Source: American Gem Society

Birth month	Ancient[1] birthstone	Modern birthstone
January	Garnet	Garnet
February	Amethyst	Amethyst
March	Jasper	Bloodstone or Aquamarine
April	Sapphire	Diamond
May	Chalcedony, Carnelian, or Agate	Emerald
June	Emerald	Pearl, Moonstone, or Alexandrite
July	Onyx	Ruby
August	Carnelian	Sardonyx or Peridot
September	Chrysolite	Sapphire
October	Aquamarine	Opal or Tourmaline
November	Topaz	Topaz
December	Ruby	Turquoise, Tanzanite, or Zircon

(1) Varied by region and culture. Birthstones listed here are those of ancient Hebrew tradition.

Standard Time and Daylight-Saving Time

Source: National Institute of Standards and Technology, U.S. Dept. of Commerce

See also Time Zone map, page 476.

Standard Time

Standard Time is reckoned from the prime meridian of longitude in Greenwich, England. The world is divided into 24 zones, each 15 deg of arc, or one hour in time apart. The Greenwich meridian (0 deg) extends through the center of the initial zone. Zones to the east are numbered from 1 to 12, with the prefix "minus" indicating the number of hours to be subtracted to obtain Greenwich Time. Each zone extends 7.5 deg on either side of its central meridian.

Westward zones are similarly numbered, but prefixed "plus," showing the number of hours that must be added to get Greenwich Time. Although these zones apply generally to ocean areas, the standard time maintained in many countries does not coincide with zone time.

The U.S. and possessions are divided into nine standard time zones. All places in each zone use, instead of their local time, the time counted from the transit of the mean sun across the standard time meridian that passes near the middle of that zone. These time zones are designated as Atlantic, Eastern, Central, Mountain, Pacific, Alaska, Hawaii-Aleutian, Samoa, and Chamorro (Guam and Northern Mariana Isls.); the time in these zones is reckoned from the 60th, 75th, 90th, 105th, 120th, 135th, 150th, and 165th meridians west of Greenwich and the 150th meridian east of Greenwich. The time zone line wanders to conform to local geography. The time in the various zones in the U.S. and U.S. territories west of Greenwich is earlier than Greenwich Time by 4, 5, 6, 7, 8, 9, 10, and 11 hours, respectively. However, Chamorro crosses the International Date Line and is 10 hours later than Greenwich Time.

24-Hour Time

With the 24-hour system, the day begins at midnight, and times are designated 00:00 through 23:59. Twenty-four-hour time is widely used in scientific work throughout the world. In the U.S., it is also used in operations of the armed forces. In Europe, it is frequently used by the transportation networks in preference to the 12-hour AM and PM system.

International Date Line

The Date Line, approximately coinciding with the 180th meridian, separates the calendar dates. The date must be advanced one day when crossing in a westerly direction and set back one day when crossing in an easterly direction. The Date Line frequently deviates from the 180th meridian because of decisions made by individual nations affected. The line is deflected eastward through the Bering Strait and westward of the Aleutians to prevent separating these areas by date. The line is deflected eastward of the Tonga and New Zealand islands in the South Pacific. In 1995, Kiribati announced that all of its islands east of the Date Line would observe the same date as islands to the west, though most maps and atlases do not depict this as a deviation in the Date Line. The line is established by international custom; there is no international authority prescribing its exact course.

Daylight-Saving Time

Daylight-saving time is achieved by advancing the clock one hour. Since 2007, daylight-saving time has begun at 2 AM on the 2nd Sunday in Mar. and has ended at 2 AM on the first Sunday in Nov. **In 2016, daylight-saving time begins at 2 AM on Mar. 13 and ends at 2 AM on Nov. 6.** Prior to 2007, daylight-saving time traditionally ran from the first Sunday in Apr. to the last Sunday in Oct.

Daylight-saving time was first observed in the U.S. during World War I and again during World War II. In the intervening years, some states and communities observed daylight-saving time, using whatever beginning and ending dates they chose. In 1966, Congress passed the Uniform Time Act, which provided that any state or territory choosing to observe daylight-saving time must begin and end on the federal dates. Any state could, by law, exempt itself; a 1972 amendment to the act authorized states in more than one time zone to exempt the entire state or one time zone only. Currently, most of Arizona, Hawaii, Puerto Rico, the U.S. Virgin Islands, Guam, American Samoa, and Northern Mariana Isls. do not observe daylight-saving time. All of Indiana, which is in two time zones, observed daylight-saving time for the first time in 2006.

Congress and the secretary of transportation both have authority to change time zone boundaries, which they have done on a number of occasions since 1966. In addition, efforts to conserve energy have prompted various changes in the times that daylight-saving time is observed.

Daylight-Saving Time: International Usage

Adjusting clock time so as to gain daylight on summer evenings is common throughout the world.

Canada, which extends over six time zones, generally observes daylight-saving time during the same period as the U.S. Most provincial governments observe the four-week extension to daylight-saving time that went into effect in 2007 although most of Saskatchewan remains on standard time year-round. Communities elsewhere in Canada also may exempt themselves from daylight-saving time. Except for the state of Sonora, which shares a border with Arizona, most of Mexico observes daylight-saving time.

Member nations of the European Union observe a "summer-time period," a version of daylight-saving time, from the last Sunday of Mar. until the last Sunday in Oct.

Russia, which extends geographically over 11 time zones and uses 9, historically has maintained its standard time one hour ahead of its zone designation. Additionally, Russian observation of daylight-saving time ended in 2011. Though an hour of time was added in Mar. 2011, clocks were not set back an hour in the fall, meaning that standard time in most of Russia is effectively 2 hours ahead of the zone designation.

China, which extends across five time zones, has decreed that the entire country be placed on Greenwich time plus 8 hours. Daylight-saving time is not observed. Japan, which lies within one time zone, also does not modify its legal time during the summer months.

Many countries in the Southern Hemisphere maintain daylight-saving time generally from Oct. to Mar. However, most countries near the equator do not deviate from standard time.

WEIGHTS AND MEASURES

Source: National Institute of Standards and Technology (NIST), U.S. Dept. of Commerce

International System of Units (SI)

Two systems of weights and measures coexist in the U.S. today: the **U.S. Customary System** and the **International System of Units** (SI, for Système International d'Unités). The SI is a more complete, coherent version of the **metric system**. Throughout U.S. history, the Customary System—parts of which were inherited but are now different from the British Imperial System—has been generally used. Federal and state legislation gave it, through implication, standing as the primary weights and measures system. The metric system, however, is the only system that Congress has ever specifically sanctioned, dating back to an 1866 law. The U.S. was one of the original 17 countries to sign the International Metric Convention (or Treaty of the Meter) May 20, 1875, which established several intergovernmental organizations to oversee and refine the SI. The U.S. is represented at these organizations by the Natl. Institute of Standards and Technology (NIST).

Since that time, use of the metric system in the U.S. has slowly increased, particularly in the scientific community, the pharmaceutical industry, and the manufacturing sector—the last motivated by the predominant use of the metric system in international commerce.

On Dec. 23, 1975, Pres. Gerald R. Ford signed the Metric Conversion Act of 1975. It defined the "metric system of measurement" as the SI, as established in 1960 by the General Conference on Weights and Measures and interpreted in the U.S. by the secretary of commerce, who delegated that authority to the director of the NIST. The Trade and Competitiveness Act of 1988 declared the metric system the preferred system of weights and measures for U.S. trade and commerce, but explicitly permitted "the continued use of traditional systems of weights and measures in nonbusiness activities." The Code of Federal Regulations made the use of metric units mandatory for federal agencies in 1991. However, the metric system has still not become the system of choice for most Americans' daily use.

The following are the seven base SI units: **length**—meter; **mass**—kilogram; **time**—second; **electric current**—ampere; **thermodynamic temperature**—kelvin; **amount of substance**—mole; and **luminous intensity**—candela.

Frequently Used Conversions

Boldface indicates exact values. For greater accuracy, use the "multiply by" number in parentheses. For weights, avoirdupois (avdp) weight is the system applied to all goods except medicines, precious metals, and precious stones.

U.S. Customary to Metric

	If you have:	Multiply by:		To get:
Length	inches	**25.4**		millimeters
	inches	**2.54**		centimeters
	inches	**0.0254**		meters
	feet	0.3	(**0.3048**)	meters
	yards	0.9	(**0.9144**)	meters
	miles[1]	1.6	(**1.609344**)	kilometers
Area	sq inches	6.5	(**6.4516**)	sq cm
	sq feet	0.09	(**0.09290304**)	sq meters
	sq yards	0.84	(**0.83612736**)	sq meters
	acres	0.4	(0.4046873)	hectares
	sq miles[1]	2.6	(2.58998811)	sq kilometers
Weight	ounces (avdp)	28	(28.34952)	grams
	pounds (avdp)	454	(**453.59237**)	grams
	pounds (avdp)	0.45	(**0.45359237**)	kilograms
	short tons[2]	0.91	(**0.90718474**)	metric tons
	long tons[3]	1	(1.016047)	metric tons
Liquid	ounces	0.03	(0.02957353)	liters
	cups	0.24	(0.23658824)	liters
	pints	0.47	(0.473176473)	liters
	quarts	0.95	(0.946352946)	liters
	gallons	3.79	(3.785412)	liters

Metric to U.S. Customary

	If you have:	Multiply by:		To get:
Length	millimeters	0.04	(0.03937)	inches
	centimeters	0.4	(0.3937)	inches
	meters	39	(39.37)	inches
	meters	3.3	(3.280840)	feet
	meters	1.1	(1.093613)	yards
	kilometers	0.6	(0.621371)	miles[1]
Area	sq cm	0.16	(0.15500)	sq inches
	sq meters	10.8	(10.76391)	sq feet
	sq meters	1.2	(1.195990)	sq yards
	hectares	2.5	(2.471044)	acres
	sq kilometers	0.39	(0.386102)	sq miles[1]
Weight	grams	0.035	(0.03527396)	ounces (avdp)
	grams	0.002	(0.00220462)	pounds (avdp)
	kilograms	2.2	(2.204623)	pounds (avdp)
	metric tons	1.1	(1.102311)	short tons[2]
	metric tons	0.98	(0.9842065)	long tons[3]
Liquid	liters	33.8	(33.81402)	ounces
	liters	4.2	(4.226752)	cups
	liters	2.1	(2.113376)	pints
	liters	1.1	(1.056688)	quarts
	liters	0.26	(0.264172)	gallons

(1) Survey mile. (2) A short ton is 2,000 pounds. (3) A long ton is 2,240 pounds.

Temperature Conversions

The left-hand column below gives a temperature according to the **Celsius** scale, and the right-hand gives the same temperature according to the **Fahrenheit** scale. The lowest number on each scale is equivalent to absolute zero, the theoretical temperature at which all molecular motion would stop.

For temperatures not shown: To convert Fahrenheit to Celsius, subtract 32 degrees and divide by 1.8; to convert Celsius to Fahrenheit, multiply by 1.8 and add 32 degrees.

Celsius	Fahrenheit	Celsius	Fahrenheit	Celsius	Fahrenheit	Celsius	Fahrenheit	Celsius	Fahrenheit
–273.15	–459.67	–45.6	–50	–1.1	30	30	86	65.6	150
–250	–418	**–40**	**–40**	**0**	**32**	32.2	90	70	158
–200	–328	–34.4	–30	4.4	40	35	95	80	176
–184.4	–300	–30	–22	10	50	**37**	**98.6**	90	194
–156.7	–250	–28.9	–20	15.6	60	37.8	100	93.3	200
–150	–238	–23.3	–10	**20**	**68**	40	104	**100**	**212**
–128.9	–200	–20	–4	21.1	70	43.3	110	121.1	250
–101.1	–150	–17.8	0	23.9	75	48.9	120	148.9	300
–100	–148	–12.2	10	25	77	50	122	150	302
–73.3	–100	–10	14	26.7	80	54.4	130	200	392
–50	–58	–6.7	20	29.4	85	60	140	300	572

Note: Although the term *centigrade* is still frequently used, the International Committee on Weights and Measures and the National Institute of Standards and Technology have recommended since 1948 that this scale be called *Celsius*.

Boiling and Freezing Points

Water boils at 212°F (100°C) at sea level. For every 550 feet above sea level, the boiling point of water is lower by about 1°F. Methyl alcohol boils at 148.5°F. Average human oral temperature is 98.6°F. **Water freezes** at 32°F (0°C).

Mathematical Formulas

The value of π (the Greek letter pi) is approximately 3.14159265 (equal to the ratio of the circumference of a circle to its diameter). The equivalence is typically rounded further to 3.1416 or 3.14.

Calculating Circumference

Circle: Multiply the diameter by π.

Calculating Area

Circle: Multiply the square of the radius (equal to ½ the diameter) by π.
Rectangle: Multiply the length of the base by the height.
Sphere (surface): Multiply the square of the radius by π and multiply by 4.
Square: Square the length of one side.
Trapezoid: Add the length of the two parallel sides, multiply by the height, and divide by 2.
Triangle: Multiply the base by the height and divide by 2.

Calculating Volume

Cone: Multiply the square of the radius of the base by π, multiply by the height, and divide by 3.
Cube: Cube the length of one edge.
Cylinder: Multiply the square of the radius of the base by π and multiply by the height.
Pyramid: Multiply the area of the base by the height and divide by 3.
Rectangular prism: Multiply the length by the width by the height.
Sphere: Multiply the cube of the radius by π, multiply by 4, and divide by 3.

Playing Cards and Dice Chances

5-Card Poker Hands

Hand	Number possible	Odds against
Royal flush	4	649,739 to 1
Other straight flush	36	72,192 to 1
Four of a kind	624	4,164 to 1
Full house	3,744	693 to 1
Flush	5,108	508 to 1
Straight	10,200	254 to 1
Three of a kind	54,912	46 to 1
Two pairs	123,552	20 to 1
One pair	1,098,240	4 to 3 (1.37 to 1)
Nothing	1,302,540	1 to 1
Total	**2,598,960**	

Bridge

The odds—against suit distribution in a hand of 4-4-3-2 are about 4 to 1; against 5-4-2-2 about 8 to 1; against 6-4-2-1 about 20 to 1; against 7-4-1-1 about 254 to 1; against 8-4-1-0 about 2,211 to 1; and against 13-0-0-0 about 158,753,389,899 to 1.

Dice

(probabilities on 2 dice)

Total	Odds against (single toss)	Total	Odds against (single toss)
2	35 to 1	8	31 to 5
3	17 to 1	9	8 to 1
4	11 to 1	10	11 to 1
5	8 to 1	11	17 to 1
6	31 to 5	12	35 to 1
7	5 to 1		

Large Numbers

No. of zeros	U.S.	British[1], French, German	No. of zeros	U.S.	British[1], French, German
6	million	million	42	tredecillion	septillion
9	billion	milliard	45	quattuordecillion	1,000 septillion
12	trillion	billion	48	quindecillion	octillion
15	quadrillion	1,000 billion	51	sexdecillion	1,000 octillion
18	quintillion	trillion	54	septendecillion	nonillion
21	sextillion	1,000 trillion	57	octodecillion	1,000 nonillion
24	septillion	quadrillion	60	novemdecillion	decillion
27	octillion	1,000 quadrillion	63	vigintillion	1,000 decillion
30	nonillion	quintillion	100	googol	googol
33	decillion	1,000 quintillion	303	centillion	NA
36	undecillion	sextillion	600	NA	centillion
39	duodecillion	1,000 sextillion	googol	googolplex	googolplex

NA = Not available. (1) In recent years, it has become more common in Britain to use U.S. terminology for large numbers.

Prime Numbers to 1,009

A prime number is any positive integer greater than 1 that is divisible only by two positive integers—1 and itself.

	2	3	5	7	11	13	17	19	23
29	31	37	41	43	47	53	59	61	67
71	73	79	83	89	97	101	103	107	109
113	127	131	137	139	149	151	157	163	167
173	179	181	191	193	197	199	211	223	227
229	233	239	241	251	257	263	269	271	277
281	283	293	307	311	313	317	331	337	347
349	353	359	367	373	379	383	389	397	401
409	419	421	431	433	439	443	449	457	461
463	467	479	487	491	499	503	509	521	523
541	547	557	563	569	571	577	587	593	599
601	607	613	617	619	631	641	643	647	653
659	661	673	677	683	691	701	709	719	727
733	739	743	751	757	761	769	773	787	797
809	811	821	823	827	829	839	853	857	859
863	877	881	883	887	907	911	919	929	937
941	947	953	967	971	977	983	991	997	1,009

Common Fractions Converted to Decimals

8ths	16ths	32nds	64ths
			1 = 0.015625
		1	2 = 0.03125
			3 = 0.046875
	1	2	4 = 0.0625
			5 = 0.078125
		3	6 = 0.09375
			7 = 0.109375
1	2	4	8 = 0.125
			9 = 0.140625
		5	10 = 0.15625
			11 = 0.171875
	3	6	12 = 0.1875
			13 = 0.203125
		7	14 = 0.21875
			15 = 0.234375
2	4	8	16 = 0.25

8ths	16ths	32nds	64ths
			17 = 0.265625
		9	18 = 0.28125
			19 = 0.296875
	5	10	20 = 0.3125
			21 = 0.328125
		11	22 = 0.34375
			23 = 0.359375
3	6	12	24 = 0.375
			25 = 0.390625
		13	26 = 0.40625
			27 = 0.421875
	7	14	28 = 0.4375
			29 = 0.453125
		15	30 = 0.46875
			31 = 0.484375
4	8	16	32 = 0.5

8ths	16ths	32nds	64ths
			33 = 0.515625
		17	34 = 0.53125
			35 = 0.546875
	9	18	36 = 0.5625
			37 = 0.578125
		19	38 = 0.59375
			39 = 0.609375
5	10	20	40 = 0.625
			41 = 0.640625
		21	42 = 0.65625
			43 = 0.671875
	11	22	44 = 0.6875
			45 = 0.703125
		23	46 = 0.71875
			47 = 0.734375
6	12	24	48 = 0.75

8ths	16ths	32nds	64ths
			49 = 0.765625
		25	50 = 0.78125
			51 = 0.796875
	13	26	52 = 0.8125
			53 = 0.828125
		27	54 = 0.84375
			55 = 0.859375
7	14	28	56 = 0.875
			57 = 0.890625
		29	58 = 0.90625
			59 = 0.921875
	15	30	60 = 0.9375
			61 = 0.953125
		31	62 = 0.96875
			63 = 0.984375
8	16	32	64 = 1.0

Roman Numerals

I — 1	IV — 4	VII — 7	X — 10	XX — 20	L — 50	C — 100	D — 500
II — 2	V — 5	VIII — 8	XI — 11	XXX — 30	LX — 60	CC — 200	CM — 900
III — 3	VI — 6	IX — 9	XIX — 19	XL — 40	XC — 90	CD — 400	M — 1,000

Note: The numerals V, X, L, C, D, or M shown with a horizontal line on top denote 1,000 times the original value.

Ancient Measures

Biblical		**Greek**		**Roman**	
Cubit	= 21.8 inches	Cubit	= 18.3 inches	Cubit	= 17.5 inches
Omer	= 0.45 peck	Stadion	= 607.2 or 622 feet	Stadium	= 202 yards
	= 3.964 liters	Obolos	= 715.38 milligrams	As, libra, pondus	= 325.971 grams
Ephah	= 10 omers	Drachma	= 4.2923 grams		= 0.71864 pound
Shekel	= 0.497 ounce	Mina	= 0.9463 pound		
	= 14.1 grams	Talent	= 60 mina		

Metric System Prefixes

The following prefixes, in combination with the basic unit names, provide the multiples and submultiples in the metric system. For example, the unit name *meter*, with the prefix *kilo* added, produces *kilometer*, meaning "1,000 meters."

Prefix	Symbol	Multiples	Equivalent
yotta	Y	10^{24}	septillionfold
zetta	Z	10^{21}	sextillionfold
exa	E	10^{18}	quintillionfold
peta	P	10^{15}	quadrillionfold
tera	T	10^{12}	trillionfold
giga	G	10^{9}	billionfold
mega	M	10^{6}	millionfold
kilo	k	10^{3}	thousandfold
hecto	h	10^{2}	hundredfold
deka	da	10^{1}	tenfold

Prefix	Symbol	Multiples	Equivalent
deci	d	10^{-1}	tenth part
centi	c	10^{-2}	hundredth part
milli	m	10^{-3}	thousandth part
micro	μ	10^{-6}	millionth part
nano	n	10^{-9}	billionth part
pico	p	10^{-12}	trillionth part
femto	f	10^{-15}	quadrillionth part
atto	a	10^{-18}	quintillionth part
zepto	z	10^{-21}	sextillionth part
yocto	y	10^{-24}	septillionth part

Weight and Measurement Equivalents

In this table, there is a distinction between the international foot and the survey foot. The international foot, defined in 1959 as exactly equal to 0.3048 meter, is shorter than the survey foot by exactly 2 parts in 1 million. This means that an international mile is about ⅛ inch shorter than the survey mile. The survey foot is still used in the publication of some geodetic surveys within the U.S. In this table, the survey foot is indicated with capital letters, as FEET.

When the name of a unit is enclosed in brackets, e.g., [1 hand], either (1) the unit is not in general current use in the U.S. or (2) the unit is believed to be based on custom and usage rather than on formal definition.

Equivalents involving decimals are, in most instances, rounded to the third decimal place; exact equivalents are so designated.

Lengths

1 angstrom (Å)	= 0.1 nanometer (exactly)
	= 0.0001 micrometer (exactly)
	= 0.0000001 millimeter (exactly)
	= 0.000000004 inch
1 cable's length	= 120 fathoms (exactly)
	= 720 FEET (exactly)
	= 219 meters
1 centimeter (cm)	= 0.3937 inch
1 chain (ch) (engineer's)	= 30.48 meters (exactly)
	= 100 feet
1 chain (Gunter's or surveyor's)	= 66 FEET (exactly)
	= 20.1168 meters
1 decimeter (dm)	= 3.937 inches
1 degree (geographical)	= 364,566.929 feet
	= 69.047 miles (avg.)
	= 111.123 kilometers (avg.)
of latitude	= 68.708 miles at equator
	= 69.403 miles at poles
of longitude	= 69.171 miles at equator
1 dekameter (dam)	= 32.808 feet
1 fathom (fath)	= 6 FEET (exactly)
	= 1.8288 meters
1 foot (ft)	= 12 inches (exactly)
	= 0.3048 meters (exactly)
	= 0.015 chains (surveyor's)
1 furlong (fur)	= 660 FEET (exactly)
	= ⅛ survey mile (exactly)
	= 201.168 meters
[1 hand (height measure for horses, from ground to top of their shoulders)]	= 4 inches
1 inch (in.)	= 2.54 centimeters (exactly)
1 kilometer (km)	= 0.621371 mile
	= 3,280.8 feet
1 league (land)	= 3 survey miles (exactly)
	= 4.828 kilometers
1 link (engineer's)	= 1 foot
	= 0.305 meter
1 link (Gunter's or surveyor's)	= 7.92 inches (exactly)
	= 0.201 meter

1 meter (m)	= 39.37 inches
	= 1.09361 yards
1 micrometer (µm)	= 0.001 millimeter (exactly)
	= 0.00003937 inch
1 mil	= 0.001 inch (exactly)
	= 0.0254 millimeter (exactly)
1 mile (mi) (statute or land)	= 5,280 FEET (exactly)
	= 1.609344 kilometers (exactly)
1 mile (nmi) (international nautical)	= 1.852 kilometers (exactly)
	= 1.151 miles
	= 6,076.1 feet
1 millimeter (mm)	= 0.03937 inch
1 nanometer (nm)	= 0.001 micrometer (exactly)
	= 0.00000003937 inch
1 pica (typography)	= 12 points
1 point (pt) (typography)	= 0.013837 inch (exactly)
	= 0.351 millimeter
1 rod (rd), pole, or perch	= 16½ FEET (exactly)
	= 5.029 meters
1 yard (yd)	= 3 feet (exactly)
	= 0.9144 meter (exactly)

Areas or Surfaces

1 acre (A)	= 43,560 square FEET (exactly)
	= 4,840 square yards
	= 0.405 hectare
1 are (a)	= 119.599 square yards
	= 0.025 acre
1 bolt (cloth measure):	
length	= 100 yards
width	= 45 or 60 inches
1 hectare (ha)	= 2.471 acres
[1 square (building)]	= 100 square feet
1 square centimeter (cm^2)	= 0.155 square inch
1 square decimeter (dm^2)	= 15.500 square inches
1 square foot (ft^2)	= 929.030 square centimeters
1 square inch ($in.^2$)	= 6.4516 square centimeters (exactly)
1 square kilometer (km^2)	= 247.104 acres
	= 0.386102 square mile
1 square meter (m^2)	= 1.196 square yards
	= 10.764 square feet
1 square mile (mi^2)	= 640 acres (exactly)
	= 258.999 hectares
1 square millimeter (mm^2)	= 0.002 square inch
1 square rod (rd^2), square pole, or square perch	= 25.293 square meters
1 square yard (yd^2)	= 0.836127 square meter

Capacities or Volumes

1 barrel (bbl), liquid	= 31 to 42 gallons*

*There are a variety of "barrels" established by law or usage. For example, federal taxes on fermented liquors are based on a barrel of 31 gallons. Many state laws fix the "barrel for liquids" as 31½ gallons; one state fixes a 36-gallon barrel for cistern measurement. Federal law recognizes a 40-gallon barrel for "proof spirits." By custom, 42 gallons constitute a barrel of crude oil or petroleum products for statistical purposes, and this equivalent is recognized "for liquids" by some states.

1 barrel (bbl), standard for fruits, vegetables, and other dry commodities except dry cranberries	= 7,056 cubic inches
	= 105 dry quarts
	= 3.281 bushels, struck measure
1 barrel, standard, cranberry	= $86\frac{45}{64}$ dry quarts
	= 2.709 bushels, struck measure
	= 5,826 cubic inches
1 board foot (lumber measure)	= a foot-square board 1 inch thick
1 bushel (U.S.) (struck measure)	= 2,150.42 cu in. (exactly)
	= 35.239 liters
[1 bushel, heaped (U.S.)]	= 2,747.715 cubic inches
	= 1.278 bushels, struck measure**

**Frequently recognized as 1¼ bushels, struck measure.

[1 bushel (bu) (British Imperial) (struck measure)]	= 1.032 U.S. bushels, struck measure
	= 2,219.36 cubic inches
1 cord (cd) (firewood)	= 128 cubic feet (exactly)
1 cubic centimeter (cm^3)	= 0.061 cubic inch
1 cubic decimeter (dm^3)	= 61.024 cubic inches
1 cubic inch (in^3)	= 0.554 fluid ounce
	= 4.433 fluid drams
	= 16.387 cubic centimeters
1 cubic foot (ft^3)	= 7.481 gallons
	= 28.317 cubic decimeters
1 cubic meter (m^3)	= 1.308 cubic yards
1 cubic yard (yd^3)	= 0.765 cubic meter
1 cup, measuring	= 8 fluid ounces (exactly)
	= ½ liquid pint (exactly)
1 dekaliter (daL)	= 2.642 gallons
	= 1.135 pecks
[1 dram, fluid (fl dr) (British)]	= 0.961 U.S. fluid dram
	= 0.217 cubic inch
	= 3.552 milliliters
1 gallon (gal) (U.S.)	= 4 quarts, liquid (exactly)
	= 231 cubic inches (exactly)
	= 3.785 liters
	= 0.833 British gallon
	= 128 U.S. fluid ounces (exactly)
[1 gallon (British Imperial)]	= 277.42 cubic inches
	= 1.201 U.S. gallons
	= 4.546 liters
	= 160 British fluid ounces (exactly)
1 gill (gi)	= 7.219 cubic inches
	= 4 fluid ounces (exactly)
	= 0.118 liter
1 hectoliter (hL)	= 26.418 gallons
	= 2.838 bushels
1 liter (L) (1 cubic decimeter exactly)	= 1.057 liquid quarts
	= 0.908 dry quart
	= 61.025 cubic inches
1 milliliter (mL) (1 cu cm exactly)	= 0.271 fluid dram
	= 16.231 minims
	= 0.061 cubic inch
1 ounce, liquid (U.S.)	= 1.805 cubic inches
	= 29.573 milliliters
	= 1.041 British fluid ounces
[1 ounce, fluid (fl oz) (British)]	= 0.961 U.S. fluid ounce
	= 1.734 cubic inches
	= 28.412 milliliters
1 peck (pk)	= 8.810 liters
1 pint (pt), dry	= 33.600 cubic inches
	= 0.551 liter
1 pint, liquid	= 28.875 cubic inches (exactly)
	= 0.473 liter
1 quart (qt), dry (U.S.)	= 67.201 cubic inches
	= 1.101 liters
	= 0.969 British quart
1 quart, liquid (U.S.)	= 2 pints, liquid (exactly)
	= 4 cups (exactly)
	= 57.75 cubic inches (exactly)
	= 0.946 liter
	= 0.833 British quart
[1 quart (British)]	= 69.354 cubic inches
	= 1.032 U.S. dry quarts
	= 1.201 U.S. liquid quarts
1 tablespoon (T., Tbs, tbsp.)	= 3 teaspoons (exactly)
	= 4 fluid drams
	= ½ fluid ounce (exactly)
1 teaspoon (t., tsp.)	= $\frac{1}{3}$ tablespoon (exactly)
	= $1\frac{1}{3}$ fluid drams***

***The equivalent "1 teaspoon = $1\frac{1}{3}$ fluid drams" has been found to correspond more closely with the actual capacities of teaspoons in use than the equivalent "1 teaspoon = 1 fluid dram" given by many dictionaries.

Weights or Masses

1 assay ton* (AT)	= 29.167 grams

*Used in assaying. The assay ton bears the same relation to the milligram that a ton of 2,000 pounds avoirdupois bears to the ounce troy; hence, the weight in milligrams of precious metal obtained from one assay ton of ore gives directly the number of troy ounces to the net ton.

1 carat (c)	= 200 milligrams (exactly)
	= 3.086 grains
1 dram avoirdupois (dr avdp)	= $27\frac{11}{32}$ (= 27.344) grains
	= 1.772 grams
1 gamma (γ)	= 1 microgram (exactly)
1 grain (gr)	= 64.79891 milligrams (exactly)

1 gram (g)	= 15.432 grains
	= 0.035 ounce, avoirdupois
1 hundredweight, gross or long** (gross cwt)	= 112 pounds (exactly)
	= 50.802 kilograms

**The gross, or long, ton and hundredweight are used commercially in the U.S. to only a limited extent, usually in restricted industrial fields. These units are the same as the British ton and hundredweight.

1 hundredweight, gross or short (cwt or net cwt)	= 100 pounds (exactly)
	= 45.359 kilograms
1 kilogram (kg)	= 2.20462 pounds
1 microgram (μg)	= 0.000001 gram (exactly)
1 milligram (mg)	= 0.015 grain
1 ounce, avoirdupois (oz avdp)	= 437.5 grains (exactly)
	= 0.911 troy ounce
	= 28.3495 grams
1 ounce, troy (oz t)	= 480 grains (exactly)
	= 1.097 avoirdupois ounces
	= 31.103 grams
1 pennyweight (dwt)	= 1.555 grams
1 pound, avoirdupois (lb avdp)	= 7,000 grains (exactly)
	= 1.215 troy pounds
	= 453.59237 grams (exactly)
1 pound, troy (lb t)	= 5,760 grains (exactly)
	= 0.823 avoirdupois pound
	= 373.242 grams
1 stone (st)	= 14 pounds avdp (exactly)
	= 6.350 kilograms
1 ton, gross or long	= 2,240 pounds (exactly)
	= 1.12 net tons (exactly)
	= 1.016 metric tons
1 ton, metric (t)	= 2,204.623 pounds
	= 0.984 gross ton
	= 1.102 net tons
1 ton, net or short (tn)	= 2,000 pounds (exactly)
	= 0.893 gross ton
	= 0.907 metric ton

Electrical Units

The **watt** (W) is the unit of power (electrical, mechanical, thermal). Electrical power is given by the product of the voltage and the current.

Energy is sold by the **joule** (J), but in common practice the billing of electrical energy is expressed in terms of the **kilowatt-hour** (kWh), which is 3,600,000 joules, or 3.6 megajoules.

The **horsepower** (hp) is a nonmetric unit sometimes used in mechanics. It is equal to 746 watts.

The **ohm** (Ω) is the unit of electrical resistance and represents the physical property of a conductor that offers a resistance to the flow of electricity, permitting just 1 ampere to flow at 1 volt of pressure.

Measures of Force and Pressure

Dyne (dyn) = force necessary to accelerate a 1-gram mass 1 centimeter per second squared = 0.000072 poundal

Poundal (pdl) = force necessary to accelerate a 1-pound mass 1 foot per second squared = 13,825.5 dynes = 0.138255 newton

Newton (N) = force needed to accelerate a 1-kilogram mass 1 meter per second squared = 100,000 dynes (exactly)

Pascal (pressure) (Pa) = 1 newton per square meter = 0.020885 pound per square foot

Atmosphere (air pressure at sea level) (atm) = 2,116.217 pounds per square foot = 14.6959 pounds per square inch = 1.0332 kilograms per square centimeter = 101,325 newtons per square meter

Measures of Alcohol

Pony	= 1.0 fluid ounce
Shot	= varies, usu. 1.0-1.5 fluid ounces
Jigger	= 1.5 fluid ounces
Pint (pt)	= 16 fluid ounces
	= 0.625 fifth
Fifth	= 25.6 fluid ounces
	= 1.6 pints
	= 0.8 quart
	= 0.757 liter
Quart (qt)	= 32 fluid ounces
	= 1.25 fifths
Wine bottle (standard)	= 0.75 liter
	= 25.4 fluid ounces
Magnum	= 1.5 liters

For champagne and brandy:

Jeroboam	= 2 magnums
	= 3 liters
	= 101 fluid ounces

For champagne:

Rehoboam	= 3 magnums
Methuselah	= 4 magnums
Salmanazar	= 6 magnums
Balthazar	= 8 magnums
Nebuchadnezzar	= 10 magnums

Miscellaneous Measures

Caliber (cal)—the diameter of a gun bore. In the U.S., caliber is traditionally expressed in hundredths of inches, e.g., .22. In Britain, caliber is often expressed in thousandths of inches, e.g., .270. Now it is commonly expressed in millimeters, e.g., the 5.56 mm M16 rifle. The caliber of heavier weapons has long been expressed in millimeters, e.g., the 155 mm howitzer.

Naval guns' caliber refers to the barrel length as a multiple of the bore diameter. For example, a 5-inch, 50-caliber naval gun has a 5-inch bore and a barrel length of 250 inches.

Decibel (dB)—a measure of the relative intensity of sound. The threshold of hearing is given as 0 decibels. A 20-decibel sound is 10 times more intense than a 10-decibel sound; 30 decibels is 100 times more intense. (A 10-decibel increase corresponds generally to the perception of a sound being twice as loud.)

One decibel is the smallest difference between sounds detectable by the human ear. A 125-decibel sound is painful.

10 decibels	breathing
20	rustling leaves
30	whisper
40	refrigerator humming
50	quiet conversation
60	conversation, laughter
70	vacuum cleaner
80	city traffic
90	subway, lawn mower
100	chainsaw

Em—a printer's measure designating the width of any given type size. For example, an em of 10-point type is 10 points. An en is half an em.

Gauge (ga)—the diameter of a shotgun bore. Gauge numbers originally referred to the number of lead balls—of equal diameter as the gun barrel—required to make a pound. Thus, a 16-gauge shotgun's bore was smaller than a 12-gauge shotgun's. Today, an international agreement assigns millimeter measures to each gauge.

Gauge	Bore diameter (mm)	Gauge	Bore diameter (mm)
6	23.34	14	17.60
10	19.67	16	16.81
12	18.52	20	15.90

Horsepower (hp)—the power needed to lift 550 pounds 1 foot in 1 second or to lift 33,000 pounds 1 foot in 1 minute. Equivalent to 746 watts or 2,546 British thermal units per hour.

Karat or carat (k or c)—a measure of fineness for gold equal to 1/24 part of pure gold in an alloy. Thus 24-karat gold is pure; 18-karat gold is ¼ alloy. The carat is also used as a unit of weight for precious stones; it is equal to 200 milligrams or 3.086 grains.

Knot (kn or kt)—a measure of the speed of ships. A knot equals 1 nautical mile (about 1.151 statute miles) per hour.

Quire (qr)—25 sheets of paper of the same size and quality.

Ream (rm)—500 sheets of paper of the same size and quality.

POSTAL INFORMATION

Administration of the U.S. Postal Service

The Postal Reorganization Act, creating a government-owned postal service under the executive branch and replacing the old executive Post Office Department, was signed into law Aug. 12, 1970. The service officially came into being on July 1, 1971. The U.S. Postal Service is governed by an 11-person board. Nine members are appointed by the president, with Senate approval. These nine choose a postmaster general. The board and the postmaster general choose the 11th member, who serves as deputy postmaster general.

Congress passed the Postal Accountability and Enhancement Act, which overhauled postal service operations for the first time since 1971, on Dec. 8, 2006. New operating provisions included the ability to adjust rates annually, negotiate for contracts, and invest profits in internal improvements. (The Postal Service last received a public service subsidy, i.e., taxpayer dollars, in 1982.)

Historical Postage Rates, 1851-2015

Postage cost for a prepaid, 1-oz. letter (the first-class standard after July 1, 1885).

Effective date	Rate	2015 dollars	Effective date	Rate	2015 dollars	Effective date	Rate	2015 dollars
July 1, 1851	$0.06[1]	NA	May 16, 1971	$0.08	$0.47	Jan. 10, 1999	$0.33	$0.47
July 1, 1863	0.06	NA	Mar. 2, 1974	0.10	0.48	Jan. 7, 2001	0.34	0.46
Oct. 1, 1883	0.04	NA	Dec. 31, 1975	0.13	0.57	June 30, 2002	0.37	0.49
July 1, 1885	0.02	NA	May 29, 1978	0.15	0.55	Jan. 8, 2006	0.39	0.46
Nov. 2, 1917	0.03[2]	$0.56	Mar. 22, 1981	0.18	0.47	May 14, 2007	0.41	0.47
July 1, 1919	0.02[2]	0.27	Nov. 1, 1981	0.20	0.52	May 12, 2008	0.42	0.46
July 6, 1932	0.03	0.52	Feb. 17, 1985	0.22	0.49	May 11, 2009	0.44	0.49
Aug. 1, 1958	0.04	0.33	Apr. 3, 1988	0.25	0.50	Jan. 22, 2012	0.45	0.47
Jan. 7, 1963	0.05	0.39	Feb. 3, 1991	0.29	0.51	Jan. 27, 2013	0.46	0.47
Jan. 7, 1968	0.06	0.41	Jan. 1, 1995	0.32	0.50	Jan. 26, 2014	0.49[3]	0.49

NA = Not available. (1) For prepaid domestic letters traveling under 3,000 miles. (2) The price increased one cent during World War I; Congress restored its prewar rate in 1919. (3) The Postal Regulatory Commission approved a 6% total price increase: a 1.7% increase for inflation and an additional 4.3% temporary increase to compensate for USPS losses during the 2008-09 recession.

Status of the U.S. Postal Service, 2001-14

Source: *Postal Facts 2015*, U.S. Postal Service

	2001	2005	2007	2008	2009	2010	2011	2012	2013	2014
Total mail items (bil)	207.5	211.7	212.2	202.7	177.0	170.9	168.3	159.9	158.4	155.4
First-class mail items (bil)	103.7	98.1	95.9	91.7	83.8	77.6	72.5	68.7	65.8	63.6
Stamped mail items (bil)	53.6	45.9	42.3	35.4	31.6	28.9	25.8	23.2	22.6	21.5
Advertising mail items (bil)	89.9	100.9	103.5	99.1	82.7	81.8	84.0	79.5	80.9	NA
Annual revenue (bil)	$65.8	$69.9	$74.7	$74.9	$68.0	$67.1	$65.7	$65.2	$67.3	$67.8
Total retail revenue (bil)	$14.8	$17.3	$18.5	$18.7	$17.7	$17.5	$16.9	$17.5	$18.3	$19.0
Total customer visits (bil)	1.4	1.3	1.2	1.2	1.1	1.1	1.0	1.0	1.0	NA
Delivery points (mil)	137.7	144.3	148.0	149.2	150.0	150.9	151.5	152.1	152.9	153.9
Total delivery routes	242,600	243,000	246,500	244,800	232,900	230,600	228,160	227,000	225,152	244,365
Total retail offices	38,123	37,142	36,451	36,723	36,496	36,222	35,756	35,369	35,074	35,641
Career employees	775,903	704,716	684,762	663,238	623,128	583,908	551,570	522,144	489,727	486,822

NA = Not available.

U.S. Domestic Mail Rates

Source: *Price List (Notice 123)*, U.S. Postal Service. Effective May 31, 2015; updated July 13, 2015. Rates are for retail customers unless noted. Domestic rates apply to the U.S., its territories and possessions, APOs, FPOs, and Freely Associated States.

First-Class Mail

Includes written matter such as letters, postcards, bills, account statements, and any matter sealed or closed against inspection up to 13 oz. In most cases, **delivery is within 2-3 business days**.

Letters measuring up to 6⅛ by 11½ in. cost **49¢** for the first oz., 21¢ for each additional oz. or fraction thereof, up to 3.5 oz. Postcard postage is **35¢**. Large envelopes up to 12 by 15 in. (or letters over 3.5 oz.) cost **98¢** for the first oz. and 21¢ for each additional oz. or fraction thereof. Presort- and automation-compatible mail can qualify for lower rates if certain piece minimums, mailing permits, and other requirements are met.

Forever Stamps. The USPS introduced the "Forever" stamp Apr. 12, 2007, at an initial cost of 41¢. The Forever stamp can be purchased at the current First-Class standard rate and will always be valid as First-Class postage on standard envelopes weighing 1 oz. or less, even after rates increase.

Priority Mail

Due to expeditious handling and transportation, Priority Mail is **delivered within 1-3 business days** in most cases. Can be any mailable article up to 70 lbs and not over 108 in. in length and girth combined.

Priority Mail Flat Rate: $5.75, **$5.90**, or **$6.10**, regardless of weight, if matter fits into designated USPS flat-rate envelope. **$5.95**, **$12.65**, or **$17.90** if matter fits into flat-rate box.

Priority Mail Forever Prepaid Flat Rate packaging can be purchased online at the current priority mail flat rate and remains valid for use after future price increases.

Priority Mail Express

Provides guaranteed expedited service for any mailable article up to 70 lbs and not over 108 in. in combined length and girth. Offers **next-day delivery** to most destinations; $12.50 additional charge for Sunday or holiday delivery. Prices start at $16.95 for items weighing up to 8 oz., dependent on distance. Includes insurance up to $100, mailing receipt, proof of delivery signature record, and tracking.

Priority Mail Express Flat Rate: $19.99, regardless of weight, if matter fits into designated USPS flat-rate envelope. **$44.95**, regardless of weight, if matter fits into designated flat-rate box.

Domestic Mail Services and Fees

Adult signature required: $5.50 per piece; person 21 years of age or older must sign for shipment.

Adult signature restricted delivery: $5.75 per piece; specific addressee or agent 21 years of age or older must sign for shipment.

Certificate of mailing: $1.35 per piece.

Collect on delivery (COD): $7.25 for amount to be collected/insurance desired up to $50; $9.05 for $50.01-$100; $1.80 for each additional $100.

Domestic money order: $1.25 for money orders $0.01 to $500; $1.65 for $500.01 to $1,000.

Pickup on demand: $20.00 per pickup.

Restricted delivery: $5.15 per item. Item is delivered to addressee only or to an agent authorized to receive mail on behalf of addressee.

Return receipt: If requested at time of mailing, $2.80 for a receipt by mail, $1.40 for email receipt.

Signature confirmation: $2.45 online, $3.00 at post office.

Sunday/holiday delivery: Available for Priority Mail Express only. Fee: $12.50.

Tracking

Formerly known as Delivery Confirmation, tracking can be used with First-Class Mail parcels, Priority Mail, Standard Post, Standard Mail parcels, and Package Services (Bound Printed Matter, Media Mail, and Library Mail). Available free of charge at time of mailing, except Standard Mail parcels (fee: $0.36). Provides mailer with location and progress of item and date and time of delivery or attempted deliveries.

Change of Address

The USPS will forward mail to another address provided a Change of Address (COA) form has been filed in person (free) or online at www.usps.com ($1.05 fee). The form, which can be picked up at any post office, printed off the Internet, or requested by phone at (800) ASK-USPS, can also be dropped in any mailbox for free filing.

Special Handling

Provides preferential handling, but not preferential delivery, to a practical extent. Available for First-Class Mail, Priority Mail, Standard Post, and Media Mail for the following surcharge: $10.35.

Registered Mail

The most secure service provided by the USPS. USPS maintains a delivery record and provides sender with a mailing receipt. May be used with First-Class Mail or Priority Mail. Full value of item must be declared at time of registration and mailing. Insurance is included in fee for articles with a declared value of $0.01 up to $50,000. Fee: $12.20 for a declared value of $0, up to $23.15 for articles with a declared value of $4,000.01 to $5,000. For each additional $1,000.00 or fraction thereof above $5,000.00, add $1.60.

International Mail Rates

Source: *Price List (Notice 123)*, U.S. Postal Service. Effective May 31, 2015; updated July 13, 2015. Refer to www.usps.com for USPS price groups not shown here and weight limits by country.

First-Class Mail International

Letter-post items weighing up to 1 oz. and single postcards can be sent airmail for **$1.20** to all countries.

Priority Mail International

Delivery is in 6-10 business days in many markets. Items must not be more than 108 in. in length and girth combined; max. weight is 70 lbs, though the limit varies by country.

Priority Mail International Flat Rate: $21.95 to Canada, **$26.50** to all other countries if matter fits into designated USPS flat-rate envelope or small box. Medium and large flat-rate boxes are $45.25 (to Canada)/$66.25 (all other countries) and $59.75/$86.25, respectively.

Global Express Guaranteed

Provides international expedited delivery, in partnership with FedEx, to certain countries. Item to be mailed must not weigh more than 70 lbs nor measure more than 108 in. in combined length and girth. Rate: Starts at $55.85 to countries in price group 1 up to $95.95 to countries in price group 8, for items not over 0.5 lb in weight.

Priority Mail Express International

Priority Mail Express International Flat Rate: $38.50 to Canada, **$49.95** to all other countries if matter fits into designated USPS legal flat-rate envelope (max. weight 4 lbs). **$71.50** to Canada, **$90.95** to all other countries if matter fits into flat-rate envelope or box (max. weight 20 lbs).

International Mail Services and Fees

Business reply: Card: $1.35; envelope (up to 2 oz.): $1.85.

Customs clearance and delivery: $6.00 per piece.

Insurance: Available to many countries for loss of or damage to items. Consult USPS for each country's indemnity limits.

Registered mail: Available for letter-post items only to most countries. Fee: $13.95.

Return receipt: Shows to whom and when item is delivered. Fee: $3.85 per piece (must be purchased at time of mailing).

Postal money order: $4.50 per money order; maximum amount for a single money order is $700. Only accepted in certain countries.

U.S. Postal Abbreviations

The abbreviations below are approved by the U.S. Postal Service for use in addresses.

Alabama	AL	Illinois	IL	Missouri	MO	Pennsylvania	PA
Alaska	AK	Indiana	IN	Montana	MT	Puerto Rico	PR
American Samoa	AS	Iowa	IA	Nebraska	NE	Rhode Island	RI
Arizona	AZ	Kansas	KS	Nevada	NV	South Carolina	SC
Arkansas	AR	Kentucky	KY	New Hampshire	NH	South Dakota	SD
California	CA	Louisiana	LA	New Jersey	NJ	Tennessee	TN
Colorado	CO	Maine	ME	New Mexico	NM	Texas	TX
Connecticut	CT	Marshall Islands[1]	MH	New York	NY	Utah	UT
Delaware	DE	Maryland	MD	North Carolina	NC	Vermont	VT
District of Columbia	DC	Massachusetts	MA	North Dakota	ND	Virgin Islands	VI
Florida	FL	Michigan	MI	Northern Mariana Isls.	MP	Virginia	VA
Georgia	GA	Micronesia, Federated States of[1]	FM	Ohio	OH	Washington	WA
Guam	GU	Minnesota	MN	Oklahoma	OK	West Virginia	WV
Hawaii	HI	Mississippi	MS	Oregon	OR	Wisconsin	WI
Idaho	ID			Palau[1]	PW	Wyoming	WY

(1) Although an independent nation, this country is subject to domestic rates and fees.

Canadian Province and Territory Postal Abbreviations

Source: Canada Post

Alberta	AB	Newfoundland and Labrador	NL	Nunavut	NU	Quebec	QC
British Columbia	BC	Northwest Territories	NT	Ontario	ON	Saskatchewan	SK
Manitoba	MB	Nova Scotia	NS	Prince Edward Island	PE	Yukon	YT
New Brunswick	NB						

SOCIAL SECURITY AND MEDICARE

Social Security Coverage

Source: Social Security Administration; World Almanac research; provisions shown are as under current law, Aug. 2015

Social Security Benefits

Social Security's **Old-Age, Survivors, and Disability Insurance (OASDI)** program benefits are based on a worker's **primary insurance amount (PIA)**, which is related by law to the average indexed monthly earnings (AIME) on which Social Security contributions have been paid. The full PIA is payable to a worker who retires at full retirement age (FRA), which is 65-67 depending on birth year, and to an entitled disabled worker at any age. Spouses and children of retired or disabled workers and survivors of deceased workers receive set proportions of the PIA subject to a family maximum amount.

The PIA is calculated by applying varying percentages to succeeding parts of the AIME. The formula is adjusted annually to reflect changes in average annual wages.

Increases in Social Security benefits are initiated for Dec. of each year, assuming the Consumer Price Index (CPI) for the third calendar quarter of the year increased relative to the base quarter, which is the third calendar quarter of the year in which an increase last took effect. The size of the benefit increase is determined by the percentage rise of the CPI between the quarters measured.

The **average monthly benefit** payable to all retired workers amounted to $1,329 in Dec. 2014. The average benefit for disabled workers in that month was $1,165.

Maximum Monthly Retired-Worker Benefits Payable to Individuals who Retired at Age 65[1]

Year attaining age 65	Maximum benefit— Payable at retirement	Payable effective Dec. 2014
1990	$975	$1,850
1995	1,199	1,917
2000	1,435	2,050
2001	1,538	2,123
2002	1,660	2,234
2003	1,721	2,284
2004	1,784	2,319
2005	1,874	2,372
2006	1,961	2.385
2007	1,998	2,352
2008	2,030	2,336
2009	2,172	2,362
2010	2,191	2,383
2011	2,249	2,446
2012	2,310	2,425
2013	2,414	2,492
2014	2,431	2,473
2015	2,446	2,446

(1) Assumes retirement at beginning of year.

Amount of Work Required

To qualify for benefits, a worker generally must have worked a certain length of time in covered employment. Just how long depends on when the worker reaches age 62 or, if earlier, when he or she dies or becomes disabled. A person born after 1929 who dies, becomes disabled, or reaches 62 after 1991 must generally have had at least 10 years of work credit to qualify for benefits.

Contribution and Benefit Base

(annual limit on the amount of earnings subject to taxation under OASDI)

Calendar year	OASDI[1]	Calendar year	OASDI[1]	Calendar year	OASDI[1]
1995	$61,200	2002	$84,900	2009	$106,800
1996	62,700	2003	87,000	2010	106,800
1997	65,400	2004	87,900	2011	106,800
1998	68,400	2005	90,000	2012	110,100
1999	72,600	2006	94,200	2013	113,700
2000	76,200	2007	97,500	2014	117,000
2001	80,400	2008	102,000	2015	118,500

(1) Old-Age, Survivors, and Disability Insurance.

A person is **fully insured** when he or she has one quarter of coverage for every year after age 21 is reached (or 1950, if later) up to but not including the year the worker reaches 62, dies, or becomes disabled. In 2015, a person earns one quarter of coverage for each $1,220 of annual earnings in covered employment, up to four quarters per year.

To receive **disability benefits**, the worker, in addition to being fully insured, must generally have credit for 20 quarters of coverage out of the 40 calendar quarters before he or she became disabled. A disabled blind worker need meet only the fully insured requirement. Persons disabled before age 31 can qualify with a briefer period of coverage. Certain survivor benefits are payable if the deceased worker had 6 quarters of coverage in the 13 quarters preceding death.

Tax Rate Schedule

(percentage of covered earnings)

Year	Total	OASDI[1]	HI[2]
	(for employees and employers, each)		
1979-80	6.13%	5.08%	1.05%
1981	6.65	5.35	1.30
1982-83	6.70	5.40	1.30
1984	7.00	5.70	1.30
1985	7.05	5.70	1.35
1986-87	7.15	5.70	1.45
1988-89	7.51	6.06	1.45
1990 and after[3]	7.65	6.20	1.45
Year	(for self-employed)		
1979-80	8.10%	7.05%	1.05%
1981	9.30	8.00	1.30
1982-83	9.35	8.05	1.30
1984	14.00	11.40	2.60
1985	14.10	11.40	2.70
1986-87	14.30	11.40	2.90
1988-89	15.02	12.12	2.90
1990 and after[3]	15.30	12.40	2.90

(1) Old-Age, Survivors, and Disability Ins. (2) Hospital Ins. (Medicare). (3) Public Law 111-147 exempted most employers from paying the employer share of OASDI payroll tax on wages paid Mar. 19-Dec. 31, 2010, to certain qualified individuals hired after Feb. 3, 2010. PL 111-312 reduced the OASDI payroll tax rate for 2011 by 2 percentage points for employees and for self-employed workers. PL 112-96 extended the 2011 rate reduction through 2012. The laws require that the general fund of the Treasury reimburses the OASI and DI Trust Funds for these temporary reductions.

What Aged Workers Receive

A person may receive monthly old-age benefits when he or she has enough work in covered employment and has reached retirement age—age 62 for reduced benefits or the age below for full benefits.

Full Retirement Age (FRA) by Birth Year

Year of birth	FRA	Year of birth	FRA
1937 or earlier	65	1955	66 and 2 mos.
1938	65 and 2 mos.	1956	66 and 4 mos.
1939	65 and 4 mos.	1957	66 and 6 mos.
1940	65 and 6 mos.	1958	66 and 8 mos.
1941	65 and 8 mos.	1959	66 and 10 mos.
1942	65 and 10 mos.	1960 or later	67
1943-54	66		

Note: If born on Jan. 1, refer to the previous birth year.

In 2000, the retirement earnings test was eliminated beginning with the month when the beneficiary reaches **full retirement age (FRA)**. A person at or above FRA no longer receives reduced benefits because of current earnings. However, a person's benefits are reduced $1 for every $3 of earnings above the limit allowed by law ($41,880 for 2015) if he or she retires in the same calendar year but months prior to FRA. For retirees who have not yet attained FRA, the reduction is $1 for every $2 of earnings over the exempt amount ($15,720 for 2015).

For workers who reached age 65 between 1982 and 1989, Social Security benefits are raised by 3% for each year in which the worker did not receive benefits between FRA and 70 (72 before 1984), whether because of earnings from work, because the worker did not apply for benefits, or because the worker declined benefits after entitlement. The **delayed retirement credit** is 1% per year for workers who reached age 65 before 1982. The rate for workers who reached age 65 in 1998-99 is 5.5%; 2000-01, 6.0%; 2002-03, 6.5%; 2004-05, 7.0%. For 2006-07, it is 7.5%. The delayed retirement credit rose to 8% per year for 2008 and years after.

For workers retiring early, benefits are permanently reduced 5/9 of 1% for each month before the FRA, up to 36 months. If the number of months exceeds 36, then the benefit is further reduced 5/12 of 1% per month.

For example, if a person's FRA is 67, but the person retires at exactly age 62, there are a total of 60 months of reduction. The reduction for the first 36 months is 5/9 of 36%, or 20%. The reduction for the remaining 24 months is 5/12 of 24%, or 10%. Thus, this person's benefits will be reduced by 30%. The nearer to FRA a person is when he or she begins collecting a benefit, the larger the monthly benefit will be.

Benefits for Worker's Spouse

The spouse of a worker who is getting Social Security retirement or disability payments may become entitled to an insurance benefit of **one-half of the worker's PIA** if claiming benefits at full retirement age. Reduced spouse's benefits are available at age 62 and are permanently reduced 25/36 of 1% for each month before FRA, up to 36 months. If the number of months exceeds 36, then the benefit is further reduced 5/12 of 1% per month. Benefits are also payable to the aged divorced spouse of an insured worker if he or she was married to the worker for at least 10 years. To qualify for divorced spouse benefits, the insured worker does not have to be receiving benefits if the divorce occurred at least two years earlier. Benefits received as a spouse are reduced by the amount of one's PIA.

Benefits for Children of Workers

If a retired or disabled worker has a child under age 18, the child will usually get a benefit equal to **one-half of the worker's unreduced benefit**. So will the worker's spouse, regardless of age, if he or she is caring for an entitled child of the worker, and the child is under 16 or became disabled before age 22. However, total benefits paid on a worker's earnings record are subject to a family maximum. Total monthly benefits paid to the family of a worker who retired in 2015 at age 66 and always had the maximum earnings creditable under Social Security cannot exceed $4,673.

Entitled children generally stop receiving benefits at age 18, though they can continue receiving benefits until age 19 if they attend elementary or secondary school full-time. A child disabled before age 22 may get a benefit as long as the disability meets the definition in the law.

Benefits may also be paid to a grandchild or step-grandchild of a worker or of his or her spouse, in special circumstances.

OASDI Beneficiaries

Beneficiaries	May 2005	May 2010	May 2012	May 2015
Total (in thous.)[1]	**48,068**	**53,349**	**56,158**	**59,530**
Age 65 and over, total. .	33,811	36,914	38,905	42,536
Retired workers.	27,413	30,734	32,714	36,419
Disabled workers . . .	112	339	453	465
Survivors/ dependents.	6,286	5,841	5,738	5,652
Under age 65, total. . . .	14,257	16,435	17,253	16,994
Retired workers.	2,809	3,314	3,407	3,086
Disabled workers . . .	6,239	7,628	8,254	8,474
Survivors/ dependents.	5,209	5,492	5,592	5,434
Total monthly benefits (in mil)	**$42,074**	**$56,966**	**$63,243**	**$72,613**

OASDI = Old-Age, Survivors, and Disability Ins. (1) Numbers may not add up to totals due to rounding or incomplete enumeration.

What Disabled Workers Receive

A worker who becomes unable to work may be eligible for a monthly disability benefit. Benefits continue until it is determined that the individual is no longer disabled. When a disabled-worker beneficiary reaches FRA (66 years for workers born 1943-54), the disability benefit becomes a retired-worker benefit.

Benefits—like those for dependents of retired-worker beneficiaries generally—may be paid to dependents of disabled beneficiaries. However, the maximum family benefit in disability cases is generally lower than in retirement cases.

Survivor Benefits

If an insured worker should die, one or more types of benefits may be payable to survivors, again subject to a maximum family benefit described above.

1. If the **surviving spouse** claims benefits at FRA, he or she will receive a benefit equal to 100% of the deceased worker's benefit. Benefits claimed before FRA are reduced, with a maximum reduction of 28.5% at age 60. However, if the deceased worker claimed benefits before FRA, the surviving spouse's benefits are limited to the reduced amount the worker would be getting if alive, but not less than 82.5% of the worker's PIA. Remarriage after the worker's death ends the surviving spouse's benefit rights. However, if the widow(er) marries, and the marriage later ends, he or she regains benefit rights. (A marriage after age 60, age 50 if disabled, is deemed not to have occurred for benefit purposes.) Survivor benefits may also be paid to a divorced spouse if the marriage lasted for at least 10 years.

Disabled widows and widowers may under certain circumstances qualify for benefits after attaining age 50 at the rate of 71.5% of the deceased worker's PIA. The widow or widower must have become totally disabled before or within seven years after the spouse's death or the last month in which he or she received mother's or father's insurance benefits.

2. There is a benefit for each **child under age 18**. The monthly benefit for a child of a deceased worker is 3/4 of the PIA, subject to the family maximum. A child who became disabled before age 22 may also receive benefits. Also, a child can receive benefits until age 19 if he or she is in full-time attendance at an elementary or secondary school.

3. There is a **mother's or father's benefit** for the widow(er) if he or she is caring for the worker's children. The benefit is 75% of the PIA (subject to the family maximum), and it continues until the youngest child reaches age 16, at which time payments stop even if the child's benefit continues. Benefits may continue if the widow(er) has a disabled child beneficiary age 16 or over in his or her care.

4. Dependent parents may be eligible for benefits if they have been receiving at least half their support from the worker before his or her death, have reached age 62, and (except in certain circumstances) have not remarried since the worker's death. Each parent gets 75% of the worker's PIA; if only one parent survives, the benefit is 82% (could be reduced for the family maximum).

5. A lump sum cash payment of **$255** is made if the worker was living with a spouse or has a child who is eligible for immediate monthly survivor benefits.

Self-Employed Workers

A self-employed person who has **net earnings of $400 or more** in a year must report such earnings for Social Security tax and credit purposes. Income from real estate, savings, dividends, loans, pensions, or insurance policies are not included unless it is part of a person's business.

A self-employed person receives one quarter of coverage for each $1,220 for 2015, up to a maximum of four quarters per year.

The nonfarm self-employed have the option of reporting their earnings as 2/3 of their gross income from self-employment. This option can be used only if actual net earnings from self-employment income are less than $1,600 and less than 2/3 of their gross income. The option may be used only five times. Also, the self-employed person must have actual net earnings of $400 or more in two of the three taxable years immediately preceding the year in which he or she uses the option.

When a person has both taxable wages and earnings from self-employment, wages are credited for Social Security purposes first; only as much self-employment income as brings total earnings up to the current taxable maximum becomes subject to the self-employment tax.

Farm Owners and Workers

Self-employed farmers whose gross annual earnings from farming are from **$600 to $2,400** may report 2/3 of their gross earnings instead of net earnings for Social Security purposes. (Farmers whose gross annual earnings are under $600 cannot use the optional method.) Farmers whose gross income is over $2,400 and whose net earnings are less than $1,600 can report $1,600. Cash or crop shares received from a tenant or share farmer count if the owner participated materially in production or management. The self-employed farmer pays contributions at the same rate as other self-employed persons.

Agricultural employees. A worker's earnings from farm work count toward benefits if (1) the employer pays the worker $150 or more in cash during the year or (2) the employer spends $2,500 or more in the year for agricultural labor. Under these rules, a person gets credit for one calendar quarter for each $1,220 in cash pay in 2015.

Foreign farm workers admitted to the U.S. on a temporary basis are not covered.

Household Workers

If an employer pays a household worker (e.g., maid, cook, laundry worker, nurse, babysitter, chauffeur, gardener) who is age 18 or older $1,900 or more in wages in 2015, the wages are covered under Social Security. This includes transportation costs paid for in cash. The job need not be regular or full-time.

The employee should get a Social Security card at the Social Security office and show it to the employer. The employer deducts the amount of the employee's Social Security tax from the worker's pay, adds an identical amount as the employer's Social Security tax, and sends the total amount to the federal government.

Medicare Coverage

Source: Centers for Medicare & Medicaid Services, U.S. Dept. of Health and Human Services

The Medicare health insurance program provides acute-care coverage for Social Security and Railroad Retirement beneficiaries age 65 and over; workers and spouses age 65 and over with sufficient Medicare-only coverage in federal, state, or local government employment; certain persons entitled to receive Social Security or Railroad Retirement disability benefits; certain disabled persons with Medicare-only coverage through government employment; certain persons with end-stage kidney disease; and certain persons in the vicinity of Libby, MT, with asbestos-related conditions. What follows is a basic description that may not cover all circumstances.

The **basic Medicare plan**, available nationwide, is a fee-for-service arrangement where the beneficiary may use any provider accepting Medicare. Some services are not covered, and there are some out-of-pocket costs.

Hospital insurance (Part A). The basic hospital insurance program pays covered services for hospital and post-hospital care, including:

- All necessary inpatient hospital care for the first 60 days of each benefit period, except for a deductible ($1,260 in 2015). For days 61-90, Medicare pays for services over and above the coinsurance ($315 per day in 2015). After 90 days, the beneficiary has 60 lifetime reserve days for which Medicare helps pay. The coinsurance amount for reserve days was $630 in 2015.
- Up to 100 days of care in a skilled-nursing facility in each benefit period. Hospital insurance pays for all covered services for the first 20 days; for days 21-100, the beneficiary pays coinsurance ($157.50 per day in 2015).
- Part-time home health care provided by nurses or other health workers.
- Limited coverage of hospice care for the terminally ill.

There is a premium for this insurance in certain—but not most—cases.

Medical insurance (Part B). Eligible elderly and disabled persons can receive benefits under this supplementary program only if they sign up and agree to a monthly premium. As of 2007, the monthly premium is tied to annual income. Individuals with an income of $85,000 or less and couples with an income of $170,000 or less pay $104.90 per person if they sign up upon becoming eligible in 2015. Part B covers certain medical services and supplies, including:

- Physicians' and surgeons' services, as well as some services furnished by other medical professionals.
- Services in an emergency room, outpatient clinic, or ambulatory surgical center.
- Home health care not covered under Part A.
- Laboratory tests, X-rays, and other diagnostic radiology services.
- Certain preventative care services and screening tests.
- Most physical and occupational therapy and speech pathology services.
- Comprehensive outpatient rehabilitation facility services and mental health care in a partial hospitalization psychiatric program, if inpatient care would otherwise be required.
- Radiation therapy, renal (kidney) dialysis and transplants, heart, lung, heart-lung, liver, pancreas, bone marrow, and intestinal transplants.
- Approved durable medical equipment for home use.
- Drugs that are not usually self-administered. Certain services for diabetes.
- Ambulance services when other transportation methods are contraindicated.
- Rural health clinic and health center services, including some telemedicine.

Part B services are generally subject to a deductible ($147 in 2015), coinsurance (generally 20% of the remaining allowed charges with certain exceptions), a deductible for blood, and amounts above the allowed charge if a doctor or supplier does not accept the Medicare-approved rate as payment in full. For outpatient hospital services, coinsurance varies by service, usually falling between 20% and 50% of allowed charges. There are no deductibles or coinsurance for certain services, such as clinical lab tests, home health agency services (except some durable medical equipment, which is subject to 20% coinsurance), and some preventative care services. Payments for certain physical, speech, and occupational therapy services are subject to certain limits. Dental care, hearing aids, and routine eye care are generally not covered under the basic plan.

To get medical insurance (Part B), persons approaching age 65 may enroll during the seven-month initial enrollment period, which includes the month of their 65th birthday as well as the three months before and after. Persons desiring coverage to begin in the month they reach age 65 must enroll in the three months before their birthday. Persons who enroll after their initial enrollment period may be subject to late-enrollment premiums.

The monthly premium is deducted from the cash benefit for persons receiving Social Security, Railroad Retirement, or Civil Service Retirement benefits. Income from the medical premiums and the federal matching payments are put in a Supplementary Medical Insurance Trust Fund, from which benefits and administrative expenses are paid.

Medicare Advantage (Part C) (formerly Medicare+ Choice). Persons eligible for Medicare may have the option of getting services through a Medicare-certified local coordinated care plan, such as a health maintenance organization (HMO), local preferred provider organization (PPO), provider-sponsored organization (PSO), or other local Medicare-certified **managed care** plan; a regional preferred provider organization (RPPO); a private fee-for-service plan; or, in certain cases, a special-needs plan. Any such plan must provide at least the same benefits as Parts A and B, except for hospice services. They may provide added benefits (such as vision or hearing coverage) or reduce cost sharing or premiums. Enrollees may be required to use the plan's network of participating providers or pay higher out-of-pocket costs to go outside the network. Also available as options in some areas are Medicare-approved private fee-for-service plans and, for certain beneficiaries, special plans.

Prescription Drug Coverage (Part D). Effective Jan. 1, 2006, an optional Medicare prescription drug plan provides insurance coverage for prescription drugs. Medicare recipients pay a monthly premium (averaging about $32 in 2015, depending on the provider) and a portion of drug costs. The open enrollment period is Oct. 15-Dec. 7. Coverage varies depending on the drug plan selected.

Further details are available on the Internet at www.medicare.gov or by calling 1-800-MEDICARE (1-800-633-4227).

Medicare card. Persons qualifying for hospital insurance under Social Security receive a health insurance card. The card indicates whether the individual has taken out medical insurance protection. It is to be shown to the hospital, skilled-nursing facility, home health agency, doctor, or other provider of covered services.

Payments are generally made only in the 50 states, Puerto Rico, U.S. Virgin Isls., Guam, American Samoa, and Northern Mariana Isls.

Social Security Financing

Social Security is paid for by a tax on certain earnings (for 2015, on earnings up to $118,500) for **Old-Age, Survivors, and Disability Insurance (OASDI)** and on all earnings (no upper limit) for hospital insurance with the **Medicare** program; the taxable earnings base for OASDI is adjusted annually to reflect changes in average wages. The employed worker and his or her employer share Social Security taxes equally.

Employers remit amounts withheld from employee wages for Social Security and income taxes to the Internal Revenue Service; employer Social Security taxes are also payable at the same time. (Self-employed workers pay Social Security taxes when filing their regular income tax forms.) The Social Security taxes (along with revenues arising from partial taxation of the Social Security benefits of certain high-income people) are transferred to the Social Security Trust Funds; they can be used only to pay benefits, the cost of rehabilitation services, and administrative expenses. By law, money not immediately needed for those purposes is invested in obligations of the federal government, which must pay interest on the money borrowed and must repay the principal when the obligations are redeemed or mature.

On Jan. 1, 1974, the **Supplemental Security Income (SSI)** program, established by the Social Security Amendments of 1972, replaced federal grants to states for aid to the needy aged, blind, and disabled in the 50 states and the District of Columbia. The program provides for federal payments, based on uniform national standards and eligibility requirements, and for state supplementary payments, which vary by state. The Social Security Administration administers the federal payments—financed by general funds of the Treasury—as well as the state supplement for those states that choose to have it federally administered. States may supplement the federal payment of all recipients and must supplement it for persons otherwise adversely affected by the transition from the former public assistance programs. In May 2015, the number of persons receiving federally administered SSI payments was 8,330,371; the payments totaled about $4.7 bil.

The **maximum monthly federal SSI payment** for individuals without an eligible spouse and with no other countable income, living in their own household, was $733 in 2015. For couples where both members were eligible, the maximum payment was $1,100.

For further information, contact the Social Security Administration toll-free at 1-800-772-1213 or visit its website at www.socialsecurity.gov.

Examples of Monthly Social Security Benefits Available, 2015

Benefit or beneficiary	For low earnings ($20,830)[1]	For med. earnings ($46,289)[1]	For max. earnings ($112,085)[1,2]
Primary insurance amount (worker retiring at 66 years, 0 months)	$1,004.70	$1,655.90	$2,663.80
Maximum family benefit (worker retiring at 66 years, 0 months)	1,507.20	3,023.30	4,662.10
Maximum family disability benefit (worker disabled at 55)	1,450.90	2,539.20	4,062.40
Disabled worker (worker disabled at 55):			
Worker alone	1,025.30	1,692.80	2,708.30
Worker, spouse, and 1 child	1,450.90	2,539.20	4,062.30
Retired worker claiming benefits at age 62:			
Worker alone[3]	762.90	1,256.60	2,014.10
Worker with spouse claiming benefits at—			
NRA or over	1,271.50	2,094.30	3,356.80
Age 62[3]	1,118.90	1,843.00	2,954.00
Widow or widower claiming benefits at—			
Age 66 or over[4]	1,004.70	1,655.90	2,663.80
Age 60[4]	722.30	1,190.50	1,915.10
Disabled widow or widower claiming benefits at age 50-59[5]	718.30	1,183.90	1,904.60
1 surviving child[4]	753.50	1,241.90	1,997.80
Widow or widower at NRA or over and 1 child[4]	1,507.20	2,897.80	4,661.60
Widowed mother or father and 1 child[4]	1,507.00	2,483.80	3,995.70
Widowed mother or father and 2 children[4]	1,507.20	3,023.10	4,662.00

NRA = Normal retirement age. **Note:** Effective Jan. 2015. (1) Career average earnings: an average of lifetime earnings indexed to the year prior to entitlement (2014 in this case). (2) Assumes work beginning at age 22. (3) Assumes maximum reduction. (4) Assumes worker lived and worked until NRA without receiving reduced benefits. (5) Effective Jan. 1984, disabled widow or widower claiming a benefit at age 50-59 receives a benefit equal to 71.5% of the primary insurance amount.

Social Security Recipients by Age, Sex, Race, and Hispanic Origin, 2014

Source: Social Security Administration

Characteristic/benefit	Total	White	Black	American Indian, Alaska Native	Asian	Native Hawaiian/ other Pacific Isl.	Hispanic
Social Security beneficiaries (thous.)[1]	**48,370**	**41,164**	**5,355**	**753**	**1,565**	**108**	**3,587**
Sex							
Male	21,450	18,350	2,294	334	685	42	1549
Female	26,920	22,814	3,061	419	879	66	2038
Age							
15-54 years	5,209	3,852	1,101	184	196	30	537
55-64 years	6,517	5,230	1,049	120	187	12	587
65-74 years	19,995	17,360	1,778	278	735	46	1,363
75 years or older	16,650	14,723	1,426	171	447	20	1,100
Supplemental Security Income recipients (thous.)[1]	**6,053**	**4,036**	**1,650**	**212**	**280**	**20**	**1,064**
Sex							
Male	2,667	1,792	713	95	117	15	452
Female	3,386	2,244	937	117	163	5	612
Age							
15-54 years	3,265	2,213	957	132	48	15	550
55-64 years	1,521	996	449	55	44	5	232
65-74 years	711	526	124	14	55	0	169
75 years or older	556	301	121	11	133	0	113
Average annual benefit in 2013 (dollars)							
Social Security	$13,979	$14,196	$12,611	$12,655	$13,116	$13,921	$12,108
Supplemental Security Income	7,782	7,825	7,572	7,901	8,248	NA	7,470

NA = Not available. **Note:** Race categories include people who reported being of that race, alone or in combination with another race. Persons of Hispanic origin may be of any race. The sum of the individual categories may not add up to totals because of rounding and because the totals include persons who reported being of more than one race. (1) Persons 15 or older receiving Social Security benefits or Supplemental Security Income in Mar. 2014.

Old-Age, Survivors, and Disability Insurance Beneficiaries, 2014

Source: Social Security Administration

			Old-Age			Survivors		Disability		
State or area	**Total benefits (thous.)**	**Total beneficia-ries**	**Retired workers**	**Spouses**	**Children**	**Widow(er)s and parents**	**Children**	**Disabled workers**	**Spouses**	**Children**
Alabama	$1,276,223	1,095,925	631,443	33,748	11,553	84,463	42,968	236,857	3,922	50,971
Alaska	103,133	89,047	59,221	2,696	1,803	5,246	4,584	12,641	184	2,672
Arizona	1,517,597	1,207,102	849,142	44,447	12,490	76,677	35,016	156,217	2,478	30,635
Arkansas	761,036	673,193	399,334	18,584	6,818	48,324	25,326	140,453	2,276	32,078
California	6,701,027	5,538,810	3,804,073	273,455	73,857	376,501	160,382	709,509	12,586	128,447
Colorado	977,802	794,937	552,118	31,802	7,435	52,182	23,121	107,158	1,316	19,805
Connecticut	885,983	654,533	469,331	20,805	7,095	39,769	18,641	81,799	793	16,300
Delaware	254,374	192,187	134,871	5,513	1,526	11,903	5,773	27,404	261	4,936
Dist. of Columbia	89,987	79,716	52,477	1,902	770	4,640	3,345	14,732	31	1,819
Florida	5,190,945	4,223,274	2,977,966	149,451	42,864	271,000	108,169	560,856	8,352	104,616
Georgia	2,006,085	1,676,778	1,079,189	47,566	18,365	116,028	65,650	285,394	4,397	60,189
Hawaii	310,833	251,591	189,864	8,390	3,797	15,197	6,219	23,174	431	4,519
Idaho	365,258	306,264	208,370	11,520	3,281	19,779	9,015	43,820	842	9,637
Illinois	2,707,116	2,155,290	1,463,959	81,702	23,918	160,955	72,434	289,730	4,508	58,084
Indiana	1,626,829	1,286,099	837,039	41,380	12,286	93,791	45,513	208,645	3,211	44,234
Iowa	758,169	616,301	431,181	21,503	5,799	46,080	18,064	78,016	925	14,733
Kansas	653,569	521,955	353,737	17,085	5,156	36,920	17,330	75,123	931	15,673
Kentucky	1,081,642	954,284	536,540	35,385	8,867	79,977	36,327	208,016	4,880	44,292
Louisiana	944,524	854,211	471,272	43,671	10,183	88,547	42,963	157,558	3,977	36,040
Maine	368,682	325,496	209,810	10,459	3,013	20,954	8,350	59,093	788	13,029
Maryland	1,203,106	936,372	647,917	30,566	8,930	61,429	31,971	130,696	1,021	23,842
Massachusetts	1,517,385	1,224,469	806,825	40,721	12,736	75,031	34,201	205,642	1,854	47,459
Michigan	2,736,513	2,121,776	1,363,480	77,257	22,748	152,275	69,268	353,522	6,337	76,889
Minnesota	1,220,801	965,018	680,724	32,364	9,200	61,904	25,765	127,364	1,273	26,424
Mississippi	714,962	640,772	371,473	16,814	8,182	48,758	30,460	132,596	2,346	30,143
Missouri	1,487,510	1,246,269	796,376	37,599	11,613	87,551	43,428	222,218	3,060	44,424
Montana	248,665	212,535	148,405	7,671	2,341	14,672	6,470	27,807	490	4,679
Nebraska	397,847	326,078	226,858	11,409	2,947	23,707	9,821	42,347	431	8,558
Nevada	588,318	475,811	338,621	14,540	4,912	27,804	13,490	64,243	801	11,400
New Hampshire	363,341	283,983	190,433	7,719	2,401	15,256	6,815	48,091	426	12,842
New Jersey	2,134,807	1,568,016	1,100,899	54,459	17,514	101,724	44,822	203,208	2,868	42,522
New Mexico	453,482	399,987	257,667	16,593	4,285	27,724	14,942	64,694	1,211	12,871
New York	4,421,858	3,482,978	2,345,599	133,868	43,068	226,428	98,764	516,900	8,251	110,100
North Carolina	2,375,750	1,948,531	1,299,071	47,298	17,887	120,801	62,953	332,173	4,527	63,821
North Dakota	144,728	124,372	85,385	5,611	1,040	11,372	4,227	14,048	167	2,522
Ohio	2,725,919	2,267,508	1,446,106	97,288	20,290	195,124	77,729	356,270	5,980	68,721
Oklahoma	877,523	749,794	472,916	25,142	7,653	58,457	29,452	127,712	2,264	26,198
Oregon	990,560	798,156	561,330	28,450	8,569	51,823	19,104	109,329	1,885	17,666
Pennsylvania	3,432,758	2,722,892	1,814,793	98,167	23,867	206,941	79,732	409,608	6,356	83,428
Rhode Island	266,541	216,029	145,063	5,095	2,296	12,256	5,772	37,422	272	7,853
South Carolina	1,272,517	1,040,971	683,006	26,563	9,988	68,220	35,599	179,872	2,653	35,070
South Dakota	192,240	165,499	117,284	5,860	1,401	12,460	5,280	19,250	187	3,777
Tennessee	1,633,490	1,371,562	860,375	42,186	13,221	99,456	49,700	252,231	4,255	50,138
Texas	4,502,644	3,842,249	2,424,311	192,408	43,722	319,026	146,986	574,012	12,073	129,711
Utah	449,903	365,730	244,753	17,661	4,659	22,946	15,341	47,947	796	11,627
Vermont	170,863	140,634	94,631	4,587	1,441	8,640	3,569	22,600	248	4,918
Virginia	1,758,795	1,415,661	950,681	49,977	13,707	97,874	44,186	212,945	3,297	42,994
Washington	1,572,324	1,230,039	844,816	48,667	13,052	78,141	31,697	179,192	2,526	31,948
West Virginia	544,609	464,823	258,928	23,636	4,709	45,053	17,128	93,837	3,355	18,177
Wisconsin	1,454,566	1,153,149	802,537	33,824	11,176	74,661	32,790	161,894	2,095	34,172
Wyoming	126,060	101,296	71,052	3,423	877	6,764	3,469	13,170	188	2,353
American Samoa	4,276	6,169	2,223	208	301	598	816	1,318	54	651
Guam	12,954	16,136	9,435	1,035	615	1,447	1,348	1,618	66	572
N. Mariana Isls.	1,651	2,650	1,389	123	189	301	307	254	13	74
Puerto Rico	696,181	845,860	435,569	61,400	11,975	77,656	29,765	179,266	7,647	42,582
Virgin Isls. (U.S.)	23,078	21,366	15,570	973	442	1,343	800	1,710	51	477
Foreign countries	391,758	613,101	379,998	101,170	10,650	91,413	14,905	11,151	540	3,274
Unknown	2,255	1,924	1,335	84	16	251	37	166	2	33
U.S. total	**71,693,353**	**59,007,158**	**39,008,771**	**2,303,480**	**635,496**	**4,236,220**	**1,892,099**	**8,954,518**	**148,955**	**1,827,619**

Outcomes of Applications for Disability Benefits, 1999-2012

Source: Social Security Administration

				Medical denials		Medical allowances			
Year of application	**Total**	**Pending final decision**	**Technical denial[1]**	**Medical**	**Subsequent nonmedical[2]**	**Awards**	**Subsequent denials[2]**	**Award rate[3]**	**Allowance rate[4]**
1999	1,265,037	0	104,332	445,995	4,056	708,797	1,857	56.0%	61.3%
2000	1,364,323	0	136,054	456,467	3,817	766,047	1,938	56.1	62.6
2001	1,513,411	0	170,520	496,835	3,579	840,542	1,935	55.5	62.8
2002	1,715,710	0	231,067	580,430	4,067	898,047	2,099	52.3	60.7
2003	1,941,894	0	374,305	632,284	4,485	928,747	2,073	47.8	59.5
2004	2,262,119	0	616,830	680,941	5,680	957,023	1,645	42.3	58.3
2005	2,087,733	0	529,704	645,884	7,023	903,132	1,990	43.3	58.2
2006	2,164,393	934	612,227	657,574	7,341	884,369	1,948	40.9	57.2
2007	2,216,565	2,793	652,797	643,682	7,986	907,465	1,842	41.0	58.3
2008	2,358,630	6,227	718,009	658,497	9,085	965,001	1,811	41.0	59.2
2009	2,753,012	14,723	845,892	781,826	10,750	1,097,953	1,868	40.1	58.2
2010	2,981,613	53,508	979,242	822,375	19,289	1,105,097	2,102	37.7	56.9
2011	2,944,980	182,211	981,954	762,563	21,778	994,344	2,130	36.0	56.0
2012	2,847,503	463,463	963,158	646,291	23,484	749,005	2,102	31.4	52.9

Note: Data as of mid-2013. Applications for more recent years may still be pending; award and allowance rates will change. Does not include SSI-only applications. (1) Application denied for non-medical reason. (2) Denied for non-medical reasons after medical criteria were adjudicated. (3) Percent of all applications, minus pending claims, in which benefits were awarded. (4) Percent of all medical decisions that resulted in an allowance.

OASDI Recipients and Monthly Payments, 1940-2014

Source: Social Security Administration

Year	Total recipients	Monthly benefits: Total (thous.)	Avg.[1]	Avg. (2014 dollars)[2]	Year	Total recipients	Monthly benefits: Total (thous.)	Avg.[1]	Avg. (2014 dollars)[2]
1940	222,488	$4,070	$18.29	$301.77	1995	43,387,259	$28,148,078	$648.76	$1,007.84
1945	1,288,107	23,801	18.48	237.65	2000	45,414,794	34,848,920	767.35	1,057.02
1950	3,477,243	126,857	36.48	350.83	2005	48,434,445	44,351,772	915.71	1,115.53
1955	7,960,616	411,613	51.71	446.40	2007	49,864,982	49,218,232	987.03	1,133.08
1960	14,844,589	936,321	63.07	493.21	2008	50,898,396	53,666,202	1,054.38	1,162.88
1965	20,866,767	1,516,802	72.69	533.34	2009	52,522,819	55,905,731	1,064.41	1,181.91
1970	26,228,629	2,628,326	100.21	597.41	2010	54,032,097	58,048,364	1,074.33	1,168.74
1975	32,085,372	5,727,903	178.52	767.22	2011	55,404,480	62,213,382	1,122.89	1,179.62
1980	35,618,840	10,694,022	300.23	842.29	2012	56,758,185	65,430,104	1,152.79	1,186.12
1985	37,058,353	15,901,643	429.10	933.72	2013	57,978,510	68,544,382	1,182.24	1,200.01
1990	39,832,125	21,686,763	544.45	981.58	2014	59,007,158	71,693,353	1,214.99	1,214.99

OASDI = Old-Age, Survivors, and Disability Insurance. **Note:** Disability insurance payments began in 1957. (1) Avg. monthly benefit does not necessarily reflect individual payments to OASDI recipients. (2) Adjusted for inflation.

Social Security Trust Funds

Source: Social Security Administration

Old-Age and Survivors Insurance (OASI) Trust Fund, 1940-2014

(in millions)

Fiscal year[1]	INCOME: Total	Net payroll tax contribs.	Income from taxing benefits	General fund reimburse-ments[2]	Net interest[3]	DISBURSEMENTS: Total	Benefit pymts.[4]	Admin. expenses	Transfers to Railroad Retirement program	Net increase in fund[5]	Year-end balance
1940	$592	$550	—	—	$42	$28	$16	$12	—	$564	$1,745
1950	2,367	2,106	—	$4	257	784	727	57	—	1,583	12,893
1960	10,360	9,843	—	—	517	11,073	10,270	202	$600	–713	20,829
1970	31,746	29,955	—	442	1,350	27,321	26,268	474	579	4,425	32,616
1980	100,051	97,608	—	557	1,886	103,228	100,626	1,160	1,442	–3,177	24,566
1990	278,607	260,069	$2,924	1,471	14,143	223,481	218,948	1,564	2,969	55,126	203,445
2000	484,228	418,219	12,476	1	53,532	353,396	347,868	1,990	3,538	130,832	893,003
2005	599,992	502,998	15,332	—	81,662	436,919	430,439	2,900	3,579	163,073	1,615,623
2007	663,376	553,414	16,661	—	93,300	488,553	481,828	3,151	3,575	174,822	1,967,042
2008	692,873	573,750	16,396	—	102,727	509,864	502,973	3,259	3,632	183,009	2,150,052
2009	697,326	571,228	18,967	—	107,131	551,542	544,484	3,369	3,690	145,784	2,295,835
2010	682,448	552,037	21,068	737	108,606	579,907	572,515	3,462	3,930	102,541	2,398,377
2011	692,510	495,031	21,174	68,886	107,419	599,232	591,477	3,645	4,110	93,278	2,491,654
2012	728,981	500,661	27,150	95,927	105,243	634,700	627,208	3,352	4,139	94,281	2,585,936
2013	739,668	589,976	23,144	26,433	100,115	670,554	663,195	3,410	3,948	69,114	2,655,049
2014	763,295	642,256	24,641	126	96,271	705,645	698,235	3,153	4,257	57,650	2,712,699

Note: Numbers may not add up to totals due to rounding. (1) Fiscal years 1977 and later consist of the 12 months ending on Sept. 30 of each year. Fiscal years prior to 1977 consisted of the 12 months ending on June 30 of each year. (2) Includes reimbursements from the general fund of the Treasury to the OASI Trust Fund for certain legislated measures since 1957. (3) Includes net profits or losses on marketable investments. Beginning in 1967, the trust fund paid administrative expenses on an estimated basis, with a final adjustment including interest made in the following fiscal year. Net interest includes these interest adjustments. Beginning in Oct. 1973, figures include relatively small gifts to the fund. (4) Beginning in 1967, includes payments for vocational rehabilitation services furnished to disabled persons receiving benefits because of their disabilities; beginning in 1983, includes reimbursements paid from the general fund to the trust fund for unnegotiated benefit checks. (5) Net change in assets during fiscal year, including amounts borrowed or repaid by other funds.

Disability Insurance (DI) Trust Fund, 1960-2014

(in millions)

Fiscal year[1]	INCOME: Total	Net payroll tax contribs.	Income from taxing benefits	General fund reimburse-ments[2]	Net interest[3]	DISBURSEMENTS: Total	Benefit pymts.[4]	Admin. expenses	Transfers to Railroad Retirement program	Net increase in fund[5]	Year-end balance
1960	$1,034	$987	—	—	$47	$533	$528	$32	–$27	$501	$2,167
1970	4,380	4,141	—	$16	223	2,954	2,795	149	10	1,426	5,104
1980	17,376	16,805	—	118	453	15,320	14,998	334	–12	2,056	7,680
1990	28,215	27,154	$158	138	766	25,124	24,327	717	80	3,091	11,455
2000	77,023	70,001	756	—	6,266	56,008	54,244	1,608	159	21,014	113,752
2005	96,765	85,418	1,164	—	10,183	86,360	83,721	2,301	338	10,405	193,298
2007	108,396	93,973	1,351	—	13,072	96,758	93,955	2,357	445	11,638	213,577
2008	109,816	97,432	1,373	8	11,003	107,153	104,222	2,513	418	2,663	216,239
2009	109,681	97,008	1,841	—	10,832	118,144	115,073	2,623	448	–8,462	207,777
2010	105,513	93,739	1,745	125	9,904	126,344	122,935	2,947	462	–20,831	186,946
2011	106,225	84,031	1,878	11,745	8,571	131,489	127,990	3,034	465	–25,264	161,682
2012	108,845	85,072	383	16,234	7,156	138,546	135,114	2,920	512	–29,701	131,981
2013	111,262	100,169	1,051	4,504	5,538	142,757	139,446	2,760	551	–31,494	100,486
2014	114,105	109,060	1,022	27	3,997	144,667	141,327	2,897	444	–30,562	69,925

Note: Numbers may not add up to totals due to rounding. (1) Fiscal years 1977 and later consist of the 12 months ending on Sept. 30 of each year. Fiscal years prior to 1977 consisted of the 12 months ending on June 30 of each year. (2) Includes reimbursements from the general fund of the Treasury to the DI Trust Fund for certain legislated measures since 1957. (3) Includes net profits or losses on marketable investments. Beginning in 1967, the trust fund paid administrative expenses on an estimated basis, with a final adjustment including interest made in the following fiscal year. Net interest includes these interest adjustments. The 1970 report describes the accounting for administrative expenses for years prior to 1967. Beginning in July 1974, figures include relatively small gifts to the fund. (4) Beginning in 1967, includes payments for vocational rehabilitation services furnished to persons receiving benefits because of a disability; beginning in 1983, includes reimbursements paid from the general fund to the trust fund for unnegotiated benefit checks. (5) Net change in assets during fiscal year, including amounts borrowed or repaid by other funds.

Supplementary Medical Insurance Trust Fund (Medicare SMI), 1975-2014

Source: Centers for Medicare & Medicaid Services, U.S. Dept. of Health and Human Services
(in millions)

	INCOME					DISBURSEMENTS				
Fiscal year[1]	Total	Premium from participants[2]	Govt. contribs.[3]	Transfers from states[4]	Interest and other income[5,6]	Total	Benefit pymts.[6,7,8]	Admin. expenses	Net change	Year-end balance[9]
1975	$4,322	$1,887	$2,330	—	$106	$4,170	$3,765	$404	$152	$1,424
1980	10,275	2,928	6,932	—	416	10,737	10,144	593	–462	4,532
1990	46,138[10]	11,494[10]	33,210	—	1,434[10]	43,022[10]	41,498	1,524[10]	3,115[10]	14,527[10]
2000	89,239	20,515	65,561	—	3,164	88,992	87,212[11]	1,780	247	45,896
2005	152,505	35,939	115,200	—	1,366	152,735	149,820[12]	2,914	–230	16,885
2006	211,951	44,241[13]	162,601	$3,630	1,478	195,557	192,083[12,13]	3,474	16,394	33,279
2007	237,890	49,666[13]	179,181	6,977	2,065	232,022	228,596[12,13]	3,426	5,867	39,146
2008	244,872	54,158[13]	180,434	7,042	3,238	224,869	221,445[13,14]	3,423	20,003	59,149
2009	262,573	57,709[13]	194,267	7,504	3,093	260,257	256,938[13]	3,318	2,317	61,466
2010	282,734	61,364[13]	213,709	4,493	3,168	272,224	268,710[13]	3,514	10,510	71,976
2011	301,523	64,502[13]	225,178	6,536	5,307	300,672	296,842[13]	3,830	851	72,827
2012	290,864	66,067[13]	210,508	8,324	5,965	291,907	287,777[13]	4,130	–1,043	71,783
2013	313,158	71,300[13]	227,208	8,666	5,985	315,123	311,367[13]	3,756	–1,965	69,818
2014	334,945	75,889[13]	244,351	8,727	5,978	333,441	329,144[13]	4,297	1,504	71,323

Note: Numbers may not add up to totals because of rounding. (1) Fiscal year 1975 consists of the 12 months ending on June 30, 1975; fiscal years 1980 and later consist of the 12 months ending on Sept. 30 of each year. (2) For Part D, premiums include both amounts withheld from Social Security benefit checks (and certain other federal benefit payments) and amounts paid directly to Part D plans (estimated). (3) For Part B, includes matching payments from the general fund, plus certain interest-adjustment items. For Part D, includes all federal govt. transfers. (4) As of 2006, Medicaid is no longer the primary payer for full-benefit dual eligibles; states pay 90% of estimated costs. (5) Other income includes recoveries of amounts reimbursed from the trust fund that are not trust fund obligations and other miscellaneous income. In 2008, includes an adjustment of $812 mil for interest inadvertently unearned as a result of Hospital Insurance (HI) hospice costs misallocated to, and paid from, the Part B account of the SMI trust fund May 2005-Sept. 2007. (6) Values after 2005 include additional premiums for Medicare Advantage (MA) plans that are deducted from beneficiaries' Social Security checks, transferred to HI and SMI trust funds, and then transferred to the plans. (7) Includes costs of Peer Review Organizations in 1983-2001 and costs of Quality Review Organizations beginning in 2002. (8) For Part D, includes payments to plans, subsidies to employer-sponsored retiree drug plans, payments to states for low-income eligibility determinations, and Part D drug premiums (the amount collected from beneficiaries and transferred to plans and an estimated amount for premiums paid directly by enrollees to plans). Includes amounts for transitional assistance benefits in 2004-06. (9) The financial status of SMI depends on the trust fund's assets and liabilities. (10) Includes the impact of the Medicare Catastrophic Coverage Act of 1988. (11) Benefit payments less monies transferred from the HI trust fund for home health agency costs. (12) Certain HI hospice costs were misallocated to, and paid from, the Part B account of the SMI trust fund. See also footnote 14. (13) Includes an estimated $1.804 bil (2006), $2.295 bil (2007), $2.970 bil (2008), $3.699 bil (2009), $4.221 bil (2010), $4.843 bil (2011), $5.222 bil (2012), $6.306 bil (2013), and $7.453 bil (2014) for premiums paid directly to Part D plans. (14) Benefit payments were $229.9 bil; amount shown does not include transfer of $8.5 bil from the general fund of the Treasury for HI hospice costs that were misallocated to, and paid from, the Part B account of the SMI trust fund from May 2005 to Sept. 2007. (The HI trust fund, in turn, transferred $8.5 bil to the general fund.)

Hospital Insurance Trust Fund (Medicare HI), 1975-2014

Source: Centers for Medicare & Medicaid Services, U.S. Dept. of Health and Human Services
(in millions)

	INCOME								DISBURSEMENTS				
Fiscal year[1]	Total	Payroll taxes	Taxation of benefits	Transfers from Railroad Retire-ment acct.	Reimb. for uninsured persons	Premiums from voluntary enrollees	Pymts. for military wage credits	Interest and other income[2,3]	Total	Benefit pymts.[3,4]	Admin. expenses[5]	Net change	Year-end balance
1975	$12,568	$11,291	—	$132	$481	$6	$48	$609	$10,612	$10,353	$259	$1,956	$9,870
1980	25,415	23,244	—	244	697	17	141	1,072	24,288	23,790	497	1,127	14,490
1990	79,563	70,655	—	367	413	113	107	7,908	66,687	65,912	774	12,876	95,631
2000	159,681	137,738	$8,787	465	470	1,392	2	10,827	130,284	127,934[6]	2,350	29,397	168,084
2005	196,921	168,954	8,765	445	286	2,303	0	16,168	184,142	181,292[7]	2,850	12,779	277,723
2006	210,309	180,392	10,319	471	408	2,632	0	16,086	184,901	181,815[7]	3,086	25,408	303,130
2007	219,207	187,992	10,593	483	468	2,761	0	16,910	202,827	200,191[7]	2,636	16,380	319,510
2008	229,729	197,195	11,733	526	506	2,913	0	16,856	230,240	227,008[8]	3,231	–511	319,000
2009	228,915	194,102	12,376	524	614	2,817	968[9]	17,514	238,001	234,659	3,343	–9,086	309,914
2010	218,004	183,603	13,760	535	–142	3,314	0	16,933	248,978	245,650	3,328	–30,975	278,939
2011	226,486	192,063	15,143	477	275	3,273	0	15,255	259,628	255,717	3,911	–33,142	245,797
2012	241,730	204,752	18,643	511	262	3,400	0	14,162	258,155	254,459	3,696	–16,425	229,372
2013	243,560	212,901	14,310	577	0	3,397	0	12,375	266,546	262,411	4,135	–22,986	206,386
2014	262,753	227,579	18,066	612	432	3,259	0	12,805	266,853	262,520	4,332	–4,100	202,286

Note: Numbers may not add up to totals because of rounding. (1) Fiscal year 1975 consists of the 12 months ending on June 30, 1975; fiscal years 1980 and later consist of the 12 months ending on Sept. 30 of each year. (2) Other income includes recoveries of amounts reimbursed from the trust fund that are not trust fund obligations, receipts from the fraud and abuse control program, and other small amounts of miscellaneous income. In 2008, includes an adjustment of –$853 mil for interest inadvertently earned as a result of HI hospice costs that were misallocated to, and paid from, the Part B account of the Supplementary Medical Insurance (SMI) trust fund from May 2005 to Sept. 2007. (3) Values after 2005 include additional premiums for Medicare Advantage (MA) plans that are deducted from beneficiaries' Social Security checks, transferred to the HI and SMI trust funds, and then transferred to the plans. (4) Includes costs of Peer Review Organizations from 1983 through 2001 (beginning with implementation of the Prospective Payment System on Oct. 1, 1983), and costs of Quality Improvement Organizations beginning in 2002. (5) Includes costs of experiments and demonstration projects. Beginning in 1997, includes fraud and abuse control expenses. (6) Includes monies transferred to the SMI trust fund for home health agency costs. (7) Certain HI hospice costs were misallocated to, and paid from, the Part B account of the SMI trust fund. (8) Benefit payments were $218.5 bil. Amount shown includes transfer of $8.484 bil to the general fund of the Treasury for HI hospice costs that were misallocated to, and paid from, the Part B account of the SMI trust fund from May 2005 to Sept. 2007. (The general fund, in turn, transferred $8.484 bil to the Part B account of the SMI trust fund.) (9) Includes the lump-sum general revenue adjustment of –$968 mil.

Federal Personal Income Tax Return Facts, 2015

Source: George W. Smith III, CPA, Managing Partner, George W. Smith & Company, P.C.

Deadlines. The deadline for filing a 2015 U.S. individual income tax return (1040, 1040A, or 1040EZ) is Apr. 18, 2016.

Extensions. Taxpayers who cannot file a 2015 individual income tax return by Apr. 18, 2016, can apply for a six-month extension to Oct. 17, 2016. To qualify for an extension, Form 4868 must be filed no later than Apr. 18, 2016. Approximately 9 mil extensions were filed in 2015.

E-Filing. On June 10, 2011, the IRS announced that 1 bil individual tax returns had been processed since the electronic filing program began as a pilot program in 1986. By May 15, 2015, 120.6 mil returns for income tax year 2014 had been e-filed, compared to 117.8 mil by mid-May in 2014.

Penalties. The IRS can levy two potential penalties after the filing due date when there is a balance owed. One penalty is for failing to file a timely tax return; the other is for failure to pay the tax when due. In addition, interest can be charged on any unpaid tax balance.

Refunds. The average refund was $2,698 for 2015 filing season returns, up from $2,689 in the previous tax year. The IRS refunded $273.5 bil through May 15, 2015. Of those, $238.3 bil were refunded with direct deposit.

Statute of limitations. Taxpayers who have not yet filed their 2012 federal tax return have until Apr. 18, 2016, to file and claim their refund. After that date, any refunds for 2012 income tax or withholding tax, including the earned income tax credit, will be lost.

Federal Income Tax Rates for Taxable-Income Brackets, 2015

Tax rate	Single	Married filing jointly or qualifying widow(er)	Married filing separately	Head of household other than surviving spouses
10%	$1 to $9,225	$1 to $18,450	$1 to $9,225	$1 to $13,150
15%	$9,226 to $37,450	$18,451 to $74,900	$9,226 to $37,450	$13,151 to $50,200
25%	$37,451 to $90,750	$74 901 to $151,200	$37,451 to $75,600	$50,201 to $129,600
28%	$90,751 to $189,300	$151,201 to $230,450	$75,601 to $115,225	$129,601 to $209,850
33%	$189,301 to $411,500	$230,451 to $411,500	$115,226 to $205,750	$209,851 to $411,500
35%	$411,501 to $413,200	$411,501 to $464,850	$205,751 to $232,425	$411,501 to $439,000
39.6%	Over $413,200	Over $464,850	Over $232,425	Over $439,000

Standard Deduction, 2015

The standard deduction is a flat amount subtracted from the adjusted gross income of taxpayers who do not itemize deductions.

Single	$6,300
Married filing jointly or qualifying widow(er)	$12,600
Married filing separately	$6,300
Head of household	$9,250

Additional standard deduction. Elderly and blind, single: $1,550. Elderly and blind, married: $1,250.

Dependents. An individual reported as a dependent on another person's tax return generally may claim the greater of (1) $1,050 or (2) the sum of $350 plus the individual's earned income, not to exceed the standard deduction.

Personal exemption. Unless another person can claim the individual as a dependent in 2015, the personal exemption is $4,000 (phased out at higher income levels).

Common Income Tax Errors

Periodically, the IRS issues a list of the most commonly made income tax errors.

1. Wrong or missing Social Security numbers.
2. Wrong names.
3. Filing status errors, such as Head of Household instead of Single.
4. Math mistakes, for example, when adding or subtracting items on a form or worksheet.
5. Errors in credits or deductions, like the Earned Income Tax Credit, Child and Dependent Care Credit, and standard deductions.
6. Wrong bank and/or account numbers for direct deposit of any tax refund.
7. Forms not signed or dated. An unsigned tax return is not valid. Both spouses must sign a joint return.
8. E-file PIN errors. E-filed returns can be signed electronically with a personal identification number (PIN). Usually, last year's PIN can be used, but if it is unknown, adjusted gross income information from last year's original return needs to be entered for verification.

Retirement Savings Plans and Income Tax

401(k) plan. The maximum amount that an individual can contribute to a 401(k) plan for 2015 is $18,000. Individuals born before 1966 can put away an additional $6,000, for a total of $24,000.

IRAs. The 2015 limits for IRAs and Roth IRAs remain $5,500. Anyone who was born before 1966 can contribute an extra $1,000. Funds may be deposited into a traditional IRA for 2015 until Apr. 18, 2016. Contributions after Apr. 18 will automatically be considered funds deposited for 2016.

Roth IRA. Contributions paid into a Roth IRA are not tax deductible. Distributions of funds including investment earnings held in the account for five years or longer and distributed after age 59½ are both free of income tax and the 10% early-withdrawal penalty. Withdrawals from the account in less than five years can be subject to tax and a 10% withdrawal penalty regardless of age. There are income limitations on contributions.

Distributions. There is a 10% penalty for IRA distributions before age 59½. Distributions paid to a beneficiary due to disability/death of the owner are not subject to this penalty, nor are payments used for certain unreimbursed medical expenses, higher-education expenses, or first-time homebuyer acquisition costs (up to $10,000).

The owner of a traditional IRA (or a SIMPLE plan, pension, or profit-sharing plan account) must begin receiving distributions by Apr. 1 of the calendar year following the year in which he or she reaches age 70½. Any employee who works beyond 70½ and is not a 5% or more owner of the business can continue to defer profit-sharing and pension plan distributions.

Tax Credits

A tax deduction reduces a taxpayer's taxable income whereas tax credits reduce the amount of tax owed.

Adoption credit. The adoption credit in 2015 for qualified expenses is $13,400. The credit limit is per person, not per year, and is adjusted annually for inflation. The credit is not refundable and phases out for taxpayers at higher income levels.

American Opportunity Tax Credit. This education credit provides up to $2,500 per student per year in the first four years of a student's postsecondary education.

Child and dependent care credit. This credit is for expenses for the care of taxpayers' qualifying children under age 13 or care of a disabled spouse or dependent, while the taxpayer works or looks for work.

Child tax credit. The maximum child tax credit is $1,000 for each qualifying child.

Earned Income Credit. Lower-income workers who maintain a household may be eligible for an Earned Income Credit. This credit is based on total earned income such as wages, commissions, and tips. Military personnel can include tax-free combat pay in income to compute the credit.

Energy credits. There are many energy-related credits—from the purchase of an alternative fuel vehicle and the installation of solar/fuel cell property in a residence, to the production of biodiesel or ethanol.

Alternative Minimum Tax

The Alternative Minimum Tax (AMT) was established in 1969 to prevent individuals with very high incomes from using special tax breaks to pay little or no tax. The AMT exemption for a single taxpayer is $53,600 and $83,400 for married filing jointly.

Estate and Gift Taxes

Estate tax. The Tax Relief Act of 2010 reinstated the estate tax with a 35% flat rate and increased the exemptions to $5 mil in 2011 and $5.12 mil in 2012. The rate was increased to 40% for 2013 and 2014, and the 2015 exemption was set at $5.43 mil.

Gifting. U.S. citizens, residents, and nonresident aliens have an annual gift tax exclusion of up to $14,000 per individual to as many individuals as he or she chooses. For married couples the exclusion is $28,000, even if only one spouse does all the gifting.

International property. All property owned worldwide by American citizens is subject to U.S. estate tax rules and regulations.

Resident aliens. Aliens residing in the U.S. are subject to the same rules as American citizens.

Tax Rates for Estates and Trusts

If taxable income is—	The tax is—
Not over $2,500	15% of the taxable income
Over $2,500 but not over $5,900	$375 plus 25% of the excess over $2,500
Over $5,900 but not over $9,050	$1,225 plus 28% of the excess over $5,900
Over $9,050 but not over $12,300	$2,107 plus 33% of the excess over $9,050
Over $12,300	$3,179.59 plus 39.6% of the excess over $12,300

Taxable Social Security Benefits

Earnings limitations. Social Security recipients who have not reached the full retirement age of 66 in 2015 will lose $1 of their benefits for every $2 of earned income over $15,720. Recipients who reached full retirement age in 2015 will not lose any benefits if they earned $41,880 or less. Recipients will have to pay back some benefits if their income exceeded that amount.

Taxable benefits. Up to 50% of Social Security benefits may be taxable if the person's total income is more than $25,000 but less than $34,000 for a single individual, head of household, qualifying widow(er), or a married person who is filing separately if spouses lived apart all year; or more than $32,000 but less than $44,000 for married individuals filing jointly. For higher incomes, 85% of Social Security benefits may be taxable.

If the only income received during the year was Social Security, these benefits are not taxable, and the recipient probably does not have to file a tax return.

Retention of Income Tax Records

Federal tax returns generally can be audited for up to three years after filing or six years if the IRS suspects underreported income, so it's wise to keep copies of an income tax return and records for at least seven years after filing a return.

Tax Audits

Audit odds. The IRS audit rate for fiscal year 2014 was 0.86%. The odds of an audit increase with higher taxpayer income, especially certain types of income. For taxpayers with incomes of $200,000 or higher, the audit rate was 2.71%. For taxpayers with gross income of $1 mil or more, the rate was 7.50%. If income was lower than $200,000, the audit rate dropped below one in 100 (0.78%). Most taxpayers have no reason to be concerned about being audited.

The audit selection process is not random. It is based on a set of formulas that are designed to spot questionable returns. If the IRS concludes that a person owes more tax, and he or she disagrees with the findings, the taxpayer can meet with a supervisor.

If the taxpayer still does not agree, he or she can appeal to a separate Appeals Office or take it to the U.S. Tax Court, Federal District Court, or the U.S. Court of Federal Claims.

Tax Court. The U.S. Tax Court is a federal court where taxpayers can dispute tax deficiencies as determined by the Commissioner of Internal Revenue before payment of the disputed amounts. The Tax Court is composed of presidentially appointed members. Many taxpayers choose the Tax Court because they are not required to pay the contested tax up front.

Appeals. For more information about audits, call the IRS at (800) TAX-FORM (829-3676) for its free Publication 556, *Examination of Returns, Appeal Rights, and Claims for Refund* or visit www.irs.gov.

IRS Contact Information

Website: www.irs.gov

Tax questions: (800) 829-1040

Forms/publications: (800) TAX-FORM (829-3676)

Spanish forms/publications: Taxpayers can view and download tax forms and publications in Spanish directly from www.irs.gov/Spanish/.

Hearing impaired: (800) 829-4059 (TTY/TDD)

Additional services: Request Publication 910, *IRS Guide to Free Tax Services*. This guide contains a list of free tax publications and other information including tax education and assistance programs.

Report wrongdoing: Report misconduct, waste, fraud, or abuse by an IRS employee to the Treasury Inspector General for Tax Administration at (800) 366-4484.

Working With a Tax Preparer

The following are some suggestions when using a tax preparer:

- **Choose** wisely. Regulations require all paid tax return preparers including attorneys, certified public accountants, and IRS-enrolled agents to have a Preparer Tax Identification Number. Check the preparer's qualifications and history. Ask about service fees in advance.
- **Review** last year's tax return. Make note of any changes since then such as marriage, divorce, number of dependents, retirement, job changes, additional income, or new deductions.
- **Organize** your records with income items first, followed by itemized deductions (medical, taxes, interest, and charitable and other miscellaneous deductions), followed by gains, losses, rentals, or other items.
- **Time** spent with your preparer may affect your bill. If you provide disorganized records and deductions, there may be an additional cost to have your tax preparer organize your information.
- **Prepare** a list of questions in advance. Ask about any invoices or bills that you are not sure apply.
- **Alert** your preparer if you're waiting to receive additional information. He or she can begin preparing your tax return and include the missing data later to finalize your return. Amending a return after it is completed may incur additional fees.
- **Review** your tax return before signing it. Ask questions about any item you don't understand. Even though your preparer is required to sign the return, you are responsible for its contents.

Total U.S. Tax Collections by Type of Tax, 1960-2014

Source: *Internal Revenue Service Data Book, 2014*, Internal Revenue Service, U.S. Dept. of the Treasury
(as percent of total gross collection or total income taxes)

Fiscal year	Total IRS collections (bil)[1]	Income taxes: Total	Business[2]	Individual[3]	Estate and trust[3]	Employment taxes[4]	Estate taxes	Gift taxes	Excise taxes[5]
1960	$92	73.1%	33.0%	67.0%	—	12.2%	1.6%	0.20%	12.9%
1965	114	69.7	32.7	67.3	—	14.9	2.1	0.25	12.9
1970	196	70.9	25.3	74.7	—	19.1	1.7	0.22	8.1
1975	294	68.8	22.6	77.4	—	23.9	1.5	0.13	5.7
1980	519	69.3	20.1	79.9	—	24.7	1.2	0.04	4.7
1985	743	63.8	16.3	83.7	—	30.3	0.8	0.04	5.0
1990	1,056	61.6	16.9	83.1	—	34.8	0.9	0.20	2.6
1995	1,376	61.8	20.5	79.5	—	33.8	1.0	0.13	3.3
2000	2,097	65.5	17.2	82.8	—	30.5	1.2	0.20	2.6
2005	2,269	62.3	21.7	78.3	—	34.0	1.0	0.09	2.5
2010	2,345	62.0	19.1	80.0	0.5%	35.1	0.7	0.12	2.0
2011	2,415	65.8	15.3	83.8	0.6	31.8	0.1	0.27	2.0
2012	2,524	66.1	16.9	82.2	0.7	31.1	0.5	0.08	2.2
2013	2,855	65.7	16.6	82.1	0.9	31.4	0.5	0.20	2.1
2014	3,064	65.2	17.7	80.8	1.5	31.9	0.6	0.08	2.3

Note: Numbers may not add up to totals because of rounding. (1) Credits to taxpayer accounts excluded beginning with fiscal year 2009. (2) Incl. taxes on corporation income and unrelated business income from tax-exempt organizations. (3) Income tax reported for estates and trusts is included in individual income tax in FY1960-2007. Estate and trust income tax is reported separately from FY2008 on. (4) Incl. taxes for Old-Age, Survivors, Disability, and Hospital Insurance; federal unemployment insurance; and Railroad Retirement. (5) Excl. excise taxes collected by the U.S. Customs and Border Protection and the Alcohol and Tobacco Tax and Trade Bureau. The IRS collected taxes on alcohol and tobacco until FY1988 and taxes on firearms until FY1991.

Taxes Collected by State Governments, 2014

Source: Annual Survey of State Government Tax Collections, U.S. Census Bureau, U.S. Dept. of Commerce
(as percent of total taxes collected or total sales and gross receipts)

State	Total taxes collected in dollars (mil)[1]	Property taxes	Sales and gross receipts taxes: Total	General	Selective[2]	License taxes[3]	Individual income taxes	Corporation net income taxes	Other taxes[4]
Alabama	$9,294	3.5%	51.8%	49.7%	50.3%	4.2%	34.5%	4.4%	1.6%
Alaska	3,393	3.8	7.6	—	100.0	4.2	—	12.1	72.4
Arizona	13,084	6.3	59.3	77.2	22.8	3.3	26.5	4.4	0.2
Arkansas	8,937	12.1	48.4	72.4	27.6	4.1	29.1	4.5	1.9
California	138,070	1.6	36.2	74.4	25.6	6.5	49.2	6.4	0.1
Colorado	11,755	—	38.1	58.5	41.5	5.6	48.1	6.1	2.1
Connecticut	15,938	—	42.6	58.7	41.3	2.7	48.8	3.9	2.0
Delaware	3,176	—	15.1	—	100.0	41.0	32.8	8.8	2.4
Florida	35,384	<0.1	82.1	74.0	26.0	6.0	—	5.8	6.1
Georgia	18,629	4.2	39.2	70.1	29.9	3.3	48.1	5.1	0.1
Hawaii	6,033	—	63.8	73.4	26.6	3.7	28.9	2.1	1.5
Idaho	3,672	—	49.6	75.4	24.6	8.6	36.4	5.2	0.2
Illinois	39,183	0.1	40.2	54.0	46.0	6.8	41.0	10.9	0.9
Indiana	16,847	<0.1	61.7	67.4	32.6	3.5	29.1	5.1	0.5
Iowa	8,272	—	45.6	70.5	29.5	9.8	38.7	4.7	1.3
Kansas	7,334	1.1	53.0	76.7	23.3	5.4	34.2	4.5	1.7
Kentucky	11,104	5.1	48.2	58.5	41.5	4.3	33.8	6.1	2.6
Louisiana	9,695	0.6	52.8	57.1	42.9	4.4	28.4	5.0	8.9
Maine	3,847	0.9	49.7	62.3	37.7	6.6	36.8	4.8	1.3
Maryland	18,929	3.8	42.4	52.3	47.7	4.5	41.1	5.2	3.0
Massachusetts	25,236	<0.1	31.4	69.6	30.4	4.0	52.5	8.7	3.4
Michigan	24,804	7.7	49.6	68.4	31.6	6.1	31.7	3.6	1.2
Minnesota	23,129	3.6	42.2	55.8	44.2	5.7	41.2	5.7	1.6
Mississippi	7,575	0.3	62.1	70.2	29.8	7.4	22.0	6.9	1.2
Missouri	11,241	0.3	43.7	66.8	33.2	5.0	47.7	3.2	0.1
Montana	2,656	10.1	20.7	—	100.0	11.8	40.0	5.7	11.6
Nebraska	4,877	<0.1	47.2	76.6	23.4	2.6	43.6	6.3	0.3
Nevada	7,143	3.6	80.0	67.0	33.0	8.5	—	—	7.9
New Hampshire	2,283	16.8	38.4	—	100.0	12.3	4.1	23.8	4.7
New Jersey	29,679	<0.1	43.0	69.7	30.3	5.1	40.3	8.0	3.6
New Mexico	5,757	1.8	48.6	75.0	25.0	4.9	22.5	3.6	18.5
New York	76,979	—	30.6	53.8	46.2	2.4	55.8	6.3	4.8
North Carolina	23,397	—	42.6	58.5	41.5	6.8	44.4	5.8	0.3
North Dakota	6,120	<0.1	30.2	71.4	28.6	3.7	8.1	4.1	53.8
Ohio	27,021	—	57.8	65.4	34.6	10.8	31.2	0.0	0.2
Oklahoma	9,103	—	43.8	65.2	34.8	11.6	32.5	4.4	7.7
Oregon	9,684	0.2	14.9	—	100.0	9.9	68.7	5.1	1.2
Pennsylvania	34,193	0.1	50.9	54.5	45.5	6.7	31.6	6.7	3.8
Rhode Island	2,966	0.1	52.8	58.5	41.5	4.5	36.7	4.0	1.9
South Carolina	8,933	0.2	51.8	72.8	27.2	5.3	38.3	3.7	0.7
South Dakota	1,608	—	80.6	70.6	29.4	17.3	—	1.5	0.6
Tennessee	11,806	—	74.2	70.7	29.3	11.3	2.0	10.0	2.5
Texas	55,261	—	82.8	70.7	29.3	6.3	—	—	10.9
Utah	6,312	—	42.5	68.0	32.0	4.4	45.8	4.9	2.5
Vermont	2,963	33.3	34.3	34.9	65.1	3.7	22.8	3.6	2.4
Virginia	18,949	0.2	32.0	58.6	41.4	4.2	57.4	3.9	2.3
Washington	19,448	10.2	78.2	77.4	22.6	7.3	—	—	4.4
West Virginia	5,380	NA	47.6	47.7	52.3	2.8	32.9	3.8	12.9
Wisconsin	16,411	1.0	44.8	62.9	37.1	6.3	41.4	6.0	0.4
Wyoming	2,263	13.3	40.9	82.7	17.3	6.5	—	—	39.3
U.S. total	**865,752**	**1.6**	**47.5**	**65.9**	**34.1**	**5.9**	**35.9**	**5.3**	**3.7**

— = Tax not collected by state. NA = Not available. **Note:** For fiscal year 2014 (July 1, 2013-June 30, 2014) for all states except AL and MI (ends Sept. 30), NY (Mar. 31), and TX (Aug. 31). (1) Incl. taxes not shown separately. (2) Incl. taxes on sale of alcoholic beverages, insurance premiums, motor fuels, public utilities, and tobacco products. (3) Incl. taxes on licenses for motor vehicles and corporations among others. (4) Incl. death and gift taxes and severance taxes (on extraction or harvest of natural resources).

State Government Personal Income Tax Rates, 2015

Source: Reproduced with permission from *CCH State Tax Guide*, published and copyrighted by CCH Inc., a Wolters Kluwer business

Alaska, Florida, Nevada, South Dakota, Texas, Washington, and Wyoming did not have state income taxes and are thus not listed. Tax rates apply in stages—for example, a single person in Arizona making $60,000 in taxable income would pay 2.59% on the first $10,000 of income, 2.88% on the next $15,000, and so on. For further details, see notes at end of table.

Alabama

Single, Head of household, or Married filing separately
- $0 to $500 ... 2%
- $501 to $3,000 ... 4%
- $3,001 and over ... 5%

Married filing jointly
- $0 to $1,000 ... 2%
- $1,001 to $6,000 ... 4%
- $6,001 and over ... 5%

Arizona[1,2,3]

Single or Married filing separately
- $0 to $10,000 ... 2.59%
- $10,001 to $25,000 ... 2.88%
- $25,001 to $50,000 ... 3.36%
- $50,001 to $150,000 ... 4.24%
- $150,001 and over ... 4.54%

Married filing jointly or Head of household
- $0 to $20,000 ... 2.59%
- $20,001 to $50,000 ... 2.88%
- $50,001 to $100,000 ... 3.36%
- $100,001 to $300,000 ... 4.24%
- $300,001 and over ... 4.54%

Arkansas[2,3]

Single, Head of household, Married filing jointly, or Married filing separately
- $0 to $4,299 ... 0.9%
- $4,300 to $8,399 ... 2.5%
- $8,400 to $12,599 ... 3.5%
- $12,600 to $20,999 ... 4.5%
- $21,000 to $35,099 ... 6%
- $35,100 and over ... 7%

California[1,2]

Single, Married filing separately, or Registered domestic partner filing separately
- $0 to $7,850 ... 1%
- $7,851 to $18,610 ... 2%
- $18,611 to $29,372 ... 4%
- $29,373 to $40,773 ... 6%
- $40,774 to $51,530 ... 8%
- $51,531 to $263,222 ... 9.3%
- $263,223 to $315,866 ... 10.3%
- $315,867 to $526,443 ... 11.3%
- $526,444 and over ... 12.3%

Head of household
- $0 to $15,710 ... 1%
- $15,711 to $37,221 ... 2%
- $37,222 to $47,982 ... 4%
- $47,983 to $59,383 ... 6%
- $59,384 to $70,142 ... 8%
- $70,143 to $357,981 ... 9.3%
- $357,982 to $429,578 ... 10.3%
- $429,579 to $715,962 ... 11.3%
- $715,963 and over ... 12.3%

Married filing jointly, Registered domestic partner filing jointly, or Qualifying widow(er)
- $0 to $15,700 ... 1%
- $15,701 to $37,220 ... 2%
- $37,221 to $58,744 ... 4%
- $58,745 to $81,546 ... 6%
- $81,547 to $103,060 ... 8%
- $103,061 to $526,444 ... 9.3%
- $526,445 to $631,732 ... 10.3%
- $631,733 to $1,052,886 ... 11.3%
- $1,052,887 and over ... 12.3%

Colorado

4.63% of federal taxable income

Connecticut

Single or Married filing separately
- $0 to $10,000 ... 3%
- $10,001 to $50,000 ... 5%
- $50,001 to $100,000 ... 5.5%
- $100,001 to $200,000 ... 6%
- $200,001 to $250,000 ... 6.5%
- $250,001 to $500,000 ... 6.9%
- $500,001 and over ... 6.99%

Head of household
- $0 to $16,000 ... 3%
- $16,001 to $80,000 ... 5%
- $80,001 to $160,000 ... 5.5%
- $160,001 to $320,000 ... 6%
- $320,001 to $400,000 ... 6.5%
- $400,001 to $800,000 ... 6.9%
- $800,001 and over ... 6.99%

Married filing jointly or Qualifying widow(er)
- $0 to $20,000 ... 3%
- $20,001 to $100,000 ... 5%
- $100,001 to $200,000 ... 5.5%
- $200,001 to $400,000 ... 6%
- $400,001 to $500,000 ... 6.5%
- $500,001 to $1,000,000 ... 6.9%
- $1,000,001 and over ... 6.99%

Delaware

Single, Head of household, Married filing jointly, or Married filing separately
- $0 to $2,000 ... 0%
- $2,001 to $5,000 ... 2.2%
- $5,001 to $10,000 ... 3.9%
- $10,001 to $20,000 ... 4.8%
- $20,001 to $25,000 ... 5.2%
- $25,001 to $60,000 ... 5.55%
- $60,001 and over ... 6.6%

District of Columbia
- $0 to $10,000 ... 4%
- $10,001 to $40,000 ... 6%
- $40,001 to $60,000 ... 7%
- $60,001 to $350,000 ... 8.5%
- $350,001 and over ... 8.95%

Georgia

Single
- $0 to $750 ... 1%
- $751 to $2,250 ... 2%
- $2,251 to $3,750 ... 3%
- $3,751 to $5,250 ... 4%
- $5,251 to $7,000 ... 5%
- $7,001 and over ... 6%

Head of household, Married filing jointly, or Qualifying widow(er)
- $0 to $1,000 ... 1%
- $1,001 to $3,000 ... 2%
- $3,001 to $5,000 ... 3%
- $5,001 to $7,000 ... 4%
- $7,001 to $10,000 ... 5%
- $10,001 and over ... 6%

Married filing separately
- $0 to $500 ... 1%
- $501 to $1,500 ... 2%
- $1,501 to $2,500 ... 3%
- $2,501 to $3,500 ... 4%
- $3,501 to $5,000 ... 5%
- $5,001 and over ... 6%

Hawaii

Single or Married filing separately
- $0 to $2,400 ... 1.4%
- $2,401 to $4,800 ... 3.2%
- $4,801 to $9,600 ... 5.5%
- $9,601 to $14,400 ... 6.4%
- $14,401 to $19,200 ... 6.8%
- $19,201 to $24,000 ... 7.2%
- $24,001 to $36,000 ... 7.6%
- $36,001 to $48,000 ... 7.9%
- $48,001 to $150,000 ... 8.25%
- $150,001 to $175,000 ... 9%
- $175,001 to $200,000 ... 10%
- $200,001 and over ... 11%

Head of household
- $0 to $3,600 ... 1.4%
- $3,601 to $7,200 ... 3.2%
- $7,201 to $14,400 ... 5.5%
- $14,401 to $21,600 ... 6.4%
- $21,601 to $28,800 ... 6.8%
- $28,801 to $36,000 ... 7.2%
- $36,001 to $54,000 ... 7.6%
- $54,001 to $72,000 ... 7.9%
- $72,001 to $225,000 ... 8.25%
- $225,001 to $262,500 ... 9%
- $262,501 to $300,000 ... 10%
- $300,001 and over ... 11%

Married filing jointly or Surviving spouse
- $0 to $4,800 ... 1.4%
- $4,801 to $9,600 ... 3.2%
- $9,601 to $19,200 ... 5.5%
- $19,201 to $28,800 ... 6.4%
- $28,801 to $38,400 ... 6.8%
- $38,401 to $48,000 ... 7.2%
- $48,001 to $72,000 ... 7.6%
- $72,001 to $96,000 ... 7.9%
- $96,001 to $300,000 ... 8.25%
- $300,001 to $350,000 ... 9%
- $350,001 to $400,000 ... 10%
- $400,001 and over ... 11%

Idaho[1,2]

Single or Married filing separately
- $0 to $1,451 ... 1.6%
- $1,452 to $2,903 ... 3.6%
- $2,904 to $4,355 ... 4.1%
- $4,356 to $5,807 ... 5.1%
- $5,808 to $7,259 ... 6.1%
- $7,260 to $10,889 ... 7.1%
- $10,890 and over ... 7.4%

Head of household, Married filing jointly, or Surviving spouse
- $0 to $2,903 ... 1.6%
- $2,904 to $5,807 ... 3.6%
- $5,808 to $8,711 ... 4.1%
- $8,712 to $11,615 ... 5.1%
- $11,616 to $14,519 ... 6.1%
- $14,520 to $21,779 ... 7.1%
- $21,780 and over ... 7.4%

Illinois

3.75% of federal AGI with modifications

Indiana

3.3% of AGI

Iowa[2]
- $0 to $1,539 ... 0.36%
- $1,540 to $3,078 ... 0.72%
- $3,079 to $6,156 ... 2.43%
- $6,157 to $13,851 ... 4.5%
- $13,852 to $23,085 ... 6.12%
- $23,086 to $30,780 ... 6.48%
- $30,781 to $46,170 ... 6.8%
- $46,171 to $69,255 ... 7.92%
- $69,256 and over ... 8.98%

Kansas

Single, Head of household, or Married filing separately
- $0 to $15,000 ... 2.7%
- $15,001 and over ... 4.6%

Married filing jointly
- $0 to $30,000 ... 2.7%
- $30,001 and over ... 4.6%

Kentucky

Single, Head of household, Married filing jointly, or Married filing separately
- $0 to $3,000 ... 2%
- $3,001 to $4,000 ... 3%
- $4,001 to $5,000 ... 4%
- $5,001 to $8,000 ... 5%
- $8,001 to $75,000 ... 5.8%
- $75,001 and over ... 6%

Louisiana[1]

Single, Head of household, or Married filing separately
- $0 to $12,500 ... 2%
- $12,501 to $50,000 ... 4%
- $50,001 and over ... 6%

Married filing jointly
- $0 to $25,000 ... 2%
- $25,001 to $100,000 ... 4%
- $100,001 and over ... 6%

Maine[2]

Single or Married filing separately
- $0 to $5,199 ... 0%
- $5,200 to $20,899 ... 6.5%
- $20,900 and over ... 7.95%

Head of household
- $0 to $7,849 ... 0%
- $7,850 to $31,349 ... 6.5%
- $31,350 and over ... 7.95%

Married filing jointly or Qualifying widow(er)
- $0 to $10,449 ... 0%
- $10,450 to $41,849 ... 6.5%
- $41,850 and over ... 7.95%

Maryland

Single, Married filing separately, or Dependent taxpayers
- $0 to $1,000 ... 2%
- $1,001 to $2,000 ... 3%
- $2,001 to $3,000 ... 4%
- $3,001 to $100,000 ... 4.75%
- $100,001 to $125,000 ... 5%
- $125,001 to $150,000 ... 5.25%
- $150,001 to $250,000 ... 5.5%
- $250,001 and over ... 5.75%

Head of household, Married filing jointly, or Qualifying widow(er)
- $0 to $1,000 ... 2%
- $1,001 to $2,000 ... 3%
- $2,001 to $3,000 ... 4%
- $3,001 to $150,000 ... 4.75%
- $150,001 to $175,000 ... 5%
- $175,001 to $225,000 ... 5.25%
- $225,001 to $300,000 ... 5.5%
- $300,001 and over ... 5.75%

Massachusetts
- Part A income (short-term capital gains) 12%
- Part A income (interest and dividends) 5.15%
- Part B income ... 5.15%
- Part C income ... 5.15%

Michigan

4.25% of taxable income

Minnesota[2]

Single
- $0 to $25,070 ... 5.35%
- $25,071 to $82,360 ... 7.05%
- $82,361 to $154,950 ... 7.85%
- $154,951 and over ... 9.85%

Head of household
- $0 to $30,870 ... 5.35%
- $30,871 to $124,040 ... 7.05%
- $124,041 to $206,610 ... 7.85%
- $206,611 and over ... 9.85%

Married filing jointly
- $0 to $36,650 ... 5.35%
- $36,651 to $145,620 ... 7.05%
- $145,621 to $258,260 ... 7.85%
- $258,261 and over ... 9.85%

Married filing separately
- $0 to $18,330 ... 5.35%
- $18,331 to $72,810 ... 7.05%
- $72,811 to $129,130 ... 7.85%
- $129,131 and over ... 9.85%

Mississippi
- $0 to $5,000 ... 3%
- $5,001 to $10,000 ... 4%
- $10,001 and over ... 5%

Missouri
- $0 to $1,000 ... 1.5%
- $1,001 to $2,000 ... 2%
- $2,001 to $3,000 ... 2.5%
- $3,001 to $4,000 ... 3%
- $4,001 to $5,000 ... 3.5%
- $5,001 to $6,000 ... 4%
- $6,001 to $7,000 ... 4.5%
- $7,001 to $8,000 ... 5%
- $8,001 to $9,000 ... 5.5%
- $9,001 and over ... 6%

Montana[2]

$0 to $2,800 . . . . 1%
$2,801 to $5,000. . . . . 2%
$5,001 to $7,600. . . . . 3%
$7,601 to $10,300. . . . . 4%
$10,301 to $13,300. . . . . . . 5%
$13,301 to $17,100. . . . . . . 6%
$17,101 and over 6.9%

Nebraska[2]

Single
$0 to $3,050 . . . . 2.46%
$3,051 to $18,280. . . . . 3.51%
$18,281 to $29,460. . . . 5.01%
$29,461 and over 6.84%
Head of household
$0 to $5,690 . . . . 2.46%
$5,691 to $29,260. . . . . 3.51%
$29,261 to $43,680. . . . 5.01%
$43,681 and over 6.84%
Married filing jointly or Surviving spouse
$0 to $6,090 . . . . 2.46%
$6,091 to $36,570. . . . . 3.51%
$36,571 to $58,920. . . . 5.01%
$58,921 and over 6.84%
Married filing separately
$0 to $3,050 . . . . 2.46%
$3,051 to $18,280. . . . . 3.51%
$18,281 to $29,460. . . . 5.01%
$29,461 and over 6.84%

New Hampshire

5% on interest and dividends only

New Jersey

Single or Married/civil-union partner filing separately
$0 to $20,000 . . . . 1.4%
$20,001 to $35,000. . . . 1.75%
$35,001 to $40,000. . . . . 3.5%
$40,001 to $75,000. . . 5.525%
$75,001 to $500,000. . . 6.37%
$500,001 and over 8.97%
Head of household, Married/civil-union couple filing jointly, or Qualifying widow(er)/Surviving civil-union partner
$0 to $20,000 . . . . 1.4%
$20,001 to $50,000. . . . 1.75%
$50,001 to $70,000. . . . 2.45%
$70,001 to $80,000. . . . . 3.5%
$80,001 to $150,000. . 5.525%
$150,001 to $500,000. . 6.37%
$500,001 and over 8.97%

New Mexico[1]

Single
$0 to $5,500 . . . . 1.7%
$5,501 to $11,000. . . . . 3.2%
$11,001 to $16,000. . . . . 4.7%
$16,001 and over 4.9%
Head of household
$0 to $8,000 . . . . 1.7%
$8,001 to $16,000. . . . . 3.2%
$16,001 to $24,000. . . . . 4.7%
$24,001 and over 4.9%
Married filing jointly or Qualifying widow(er)
$0 to $8,000 . . . . 1.7%
$8,001 to $16,000. . . . . 3.2%
$16,001 to $24,000. . . . . 4.7%
$24,001 and over 4.9%
Married filing separately
$0 to $4,000. . . . . 1.7%
$4,001 to $8,000 . . . . . . 3.2%
$8,001 to $12,000 . . . . . 4.7%
$12,001 and over. 4.9%

New York[2]

Single or Married filing separately
$0 to $8,400 . . . . 4%
$8,401 to $11,600. . . . . . 4.5%
$11,601 to $13,750. . . . 5.25%
$13,751 to $21,150. . . . . 5.9%
$21,151 to $79,600. . . . 6.45%
$79,601 to $212,500. . . 6.65%
$212,501 to $1,062,650 6.85%
$1,062,651 and over. . . 8.82%
Head of household
$0 to $12,700 . . . . 4%
$12,701 to $17,450. . . . . 4.5%
$17,451 to $20,650. . . . 5.25%
$20,651 to $31,800. . . . . 5.9%
$31,801 to $106,200. . . 6.45%
$106,201 to $265,600. . 6.65%
$265,601 to $1,594,050 6.85%
$1,594,051 and over. . . 8.82%
Married filing jointly or Qualifying widow(er)
$0 to $16,950 . . . . 4%
$16,951 to $23,300. . . . . 4.5%
$23,301 to $27,550. . . . 5.25%
$27,551 to $42,450. . . . . 5.9%
$42,451 to $159,350. . . 6.45%
$159,351 to $318,750. . 6.65%
$318,751 to $2,125,450 6.85%
$2,125,451 and over. . . 8.82%

North Carolina

5.75% on state taxable income

North Dakota[2]

Single
$0 to $37,450 . . . . 1.1%
$37,451 to $90,750. . . . 2.04%
$90,751 to $189,300. . . 2.27%
$189,301 to $411,500. . 2.64%
$411,501 and over 2.9%
Head of household
$0 to $50,200 . . . . 1.1%
$50,201 to $129,600. . . 2.04%
$129,601 to $209,850. . 2.27%
$209,851 to $411,500. . 2.64%
$411,501 and over 2.9%
Married filing jointly or Surviving spouse
$0 to $62,600 . . . . 1.1%
$62,601 to $151,200. . . 2.04%
$151,201 to $230,450. . 2.27%
$230,451 to $411,500. . 2.64%
$411,501 and over 2.9%
Married filing separately
$0 to $31,300 . . . . 1.1%
$31,301 to $75,600. . . . 2.04%
$75,601 to $115,225. . . 2.27%
$115,226 to $205,750. . 2.64%
$205,751 and over 2.9%

Ohio[2]

$0 to $5,000 . . . . 0.495%
$5,001 to $10,000. . . . . 0.99%
$10,001 to $15,000. . . . 1.98%
$15,001 to $20,000. . . 2.476%
$20,001 to $40,000. . . . 2.969%
$40,001 to $80,000. . . . 3.465%
$80,001 to $100,000. . . . 3.96%
$100,001 to $200,000. . 4.597%
$200,001 and over 4.997%

Oklahoma

Single or Married filing separately
$0 to $1,000 . . . . 0.5%
$1,001 to $2,500. . . . . 1%
$2,501 to $3,750. . . . . 2%
$3,751 to $4,900. . . . . 3%
$4,901 to $7,200. . . . . 4%
$7,201 to $8,700. . . . . 5%
$8,701 and over 5.25%
Head of household, Married filing jointly, or Qualifying widow(er)
$0 to $2,000 . . . . 0.5%
$2,001 to $5,000. . . . . 1%
$5,001 to $7,500. . . . . 2%
$7,501 to $9,800. . . . . 3%
$9,801 to $12,200. . . . . 4%
$12,201 to $15,000. . . . . . . 5%
$15,001 and over 5.25%

Oregon[2]

Single or Married filing separately
$0 to $3,350 . . . . 5%
$3,351 to $8,400. . . . . 7%
$8,401 to $125,000. . . . . . . 9%
$125,001 and over 9.9%
Married filing jointly, Head of household, or Qualifying widow(er)
$0 to $6,700 . . . . 5%
$6,701 to $16,800. . . . . 7%
$16,801 to $250,000. . . . . . 9%
$250,001 and over 9.9%

Pennsylvania

3.07% of taxable compensation, net profits, net gains from the sale of property, rent, royalties, patents or copyrights, income from estates or trusts, dividends, interest, and winnings

Rhode Island[2]

Single, Head of household, Married filing jointly, Qualifying widow(er), or Married filing separately
$0 to $60,500 . . . . 3.75%
$60,501 to $137,650. . . 4.75%
$137,651 and over 5.99%

South Carolina[2]

$0 to $2,910 . . . . 0%
$2,911 to $5,820. . . . . 3%
$5,821 to $8,730. . . . . 4%
$8,731 to $11,640. . . . . 5%
$11,641 to $14,550. . . . . . . 6%
$14,551 and over 7%

Tennessee

6% on interest and dividend income

Utah

5% on state taxable income

Vermont[2]

Single
$0 to $37,450 . . . . 3.55%
$37,451 to $90,750 . . . . . 6.8%
$90,751 to $189,300 . . . . 7.8%
$189,301 to $411,500 . . . 8.8%
$411,501 and over. 8.95%
Head of household
$0 to $50,200 . . . . 3.55%
$50,201 to $129,600. . . . . 6.8%
$129,601 to $209,850. . . . 7.8%
$209,851 to $411,500. . . . 8.8%
$411,501 and over 8.95%
Married or Civil union filing jointly
$0 to $62,600 . . . . 3.55%
$62,601 to $151,200. . . . . 6.8%
$151,201 to $230,450. . . . 7.8%
$230,451 to $411,500. . . . 8.8%
$411,501 and over 8.95%
Married or Civil union filing separately
$0 to $31,300 . . . . 3.55%
$31,301 to $75,600. . . . . . 6.8%
$75,601 to $115,225. . . . . 7.8%
$115,226 to $205,750. . . . 8.8%
$205,751 and over 8.95%

Virginia

Single, Head of household, Married filing jointly, or Married filing separately
$0 to $3,000 . . . . 2%
$3,001 to $5,000. . . . . 3%
$5,001 to $17,000. . . . . 5%
$17,001 and over 5.75%

West Virginia

Single, Head of household, Married filing jointly, or Widow(er) with dependent child
$0 to $10,000 . . . . 3%
$10,001 to $25,000. . . . . . . 4%
$25,001 to $40,000. . . . . 4.5%
$40,001 to $60,000. . . . . . . 6%
$60,001 and over 6.5%
Married filing separately
$0 to $5,000 . . . . 3%
$5,001 to $12,500. . . . . 4%
$12,501 to $20,000. . . . . 4.5%
$20,001 to $30,000. . . . . . . 6%
$30,001 and over 6.5%

Wisconsin[1,2]

Single or Head of household
$0 to $11,090 . . . . 4%
$11,091 to $22,190. . . . . 5.84%
$22,191 to $244,270. . . . 6.27%
$244,271 and over 7.65%
Married filing jointly
$0 to $14,790 . . . . 4%
$14,791 to $29,580. . . . . 5.84%
$29,581 to $325,700. . . . 6.27%
$325,701 and over 7.65%
Married filing separately
$0 to $7,400 . . . . 4%
$7,401 to $14,790. . . . . . 5.84%
$14,791 to $162,850. . . . 6.27%
$162,851 and over 7.65%

AGI = Adjusted gross income; AMT = Alternative minimum tax. (1) Community property state in which, in general, one-half of the community income is taxable to each spouse. (2) Brackets indexed for inflation annually. (3) 2015 adjusted brackets were not available. Bracketed rates listed are for 2014. **California:** An additional 1% tax is imposed on taxable income in excess of $1 mil. **Colorado:** Individual taxpayers are subject to an AMT equal to the amount by which 3.47% of their Colorado alternative minimum taxable income exceeds their Colorado normal tax. **Connecticut:** Resident estates and trusts are subject to a 6.9% rate on all income. **Illinois:** Surcharge is imposed on certain types of sales income. **Indiana:** Counties may impose an AGI tax on residents or on nonresidents, or a county option income tax. **Iowa:** An AMT of 6.7% of alternative minimum income is imposed if the minimum tax exceeds the taxpayer's regular income tax liability. **Maine:** Inflation adjustment suspended for 2015 tax year. **Massachusetts:** Part A income represents either interest and dividends or short-term capital gains, long-term capital gains from collectibles, and long-term capital gains from pre-1996 installment sales. Part B income represents wages, salaries, tips, pensions, business income, rents, etc. Part C income represents gains from the sale of capital assets held for more than one year. 5.85% optional rate may be elected for Part A interest and dividend income, Part B income after exemptions, and Part C income. **Minnesota:** A 6.75% AMT is imposed. **Montana:** Minimum tax, $1. **Nebraska:** There is an additional tax on taxpayers with federal AGI of more than a certain amount, which is $309,900 for married filing jointly ($154,950 for married filing separately) in 2015. **New Mexico:** Qualified nonresident taxpayers may pay an alternative tax of 0.75% of gross receipts from sales in New Mexico. **New York:** A supplemental tax is imposed to recapture the tax table benefit. **Vermont:** The tax amount is increased by 24% for certain items.

U.S. Public Schools: Students, Staff, Spending, 1899-2013

Source: National Center for Education Statistics, U.S. Dept. of Education

	1899-1900	1919-20	1939-40	1959-60	1969-70	1979-80	1989-90	1999-2000	2012-13[1]
Population (thous.)									
Total U.S. population[2]	75,995	104,514	131,028	177,830	201,385	225,055	246,819	279,040	313,914
Population 5-17 years of age	21,573	27,571	30,151	43,881	52,386	48,043	44,947	52,811	53,728
Percentage 5-17 years of age	28.4%	26.4%	23.0%	24.7%	26.0%	21.3%	18.2%	18.9%	17.1%
Enrollment (thous.)									
Elementary and secondary[3]	15,503	21,578	25,434	36,087	45,550	41,651	40,543	46,857	49,771
Pre-kindergarten and grades 1-8	14,984	19,378	18,833	27,602	32,513	28,034	29,152	33,486	35,018
Grades 9-12	519	2,200	6,601	8,485	13,037	13,616	11,390	13,371	14,753
Percentage pop. ages 5-17 enrolled	71.9%	78.3%	84.4%	82.2%	87.0%	86.7%	90.2%	88.7%	92.6%
Percentage high school of all enrolled	3.3%	10.2%	26.0%	23.5%	28.6%	32.7%	28.1%	28.5%	29.6%
High school graduates	62	231	1,143	1,627	2,589	2,748	2,320	2,554	3,110
Instructional staff (thous.)									
Total instructional staff	*	678	912	1,457	2,286	2,406	2,986	3,819	4,158
Teachers, librarians, and other nonsupervisory instructional staff	423	657	875	1,393	2,195	2,300	2,860	3,682	3,989
Revenue and expenditures (mil)									
Total revenue	$220	$970	$2,261	$14,747	$40,267	$96,881	$208,548	$372,944	$600,489
Total expenditures	215	1,036	2,344	15,613	40,683	95,962	212,770	381,838	601,767
Current expenditures[4,5]	180	861	1,942	12,329	34,218	86,984	188,229	323,889	527,096
Capital outlay	35	154	258	2,662	4,659	6,506	17,781	43,357	48,773
Interest on school debt	*	18	131	490	1,171	1,874	3,776	9,135	17,701
Others	*	3	13	133	636	598	2,983	5,457	8,196
Salaries and pupil cost									
Avg. annual salary of instruct. staff[6]	$325	$871	$1,441	$4,995	$8,626	$15,970	$31,367	$41,807	$56,383
Expenditure per capita total pop.	3	10	18	88	202	426	862	1,368	1,917
Current expenditure per pupil ADA[5,7]	17	53	88	375	816	2,272	4,980	7,394	11,680

* = Data not collected. **Note:** Because of rounding, details may not add up to totals. Prior to 1959-60, data do not include Alaska and Hawaii. (1) Revenues and expenditures are fiscal year 2012 (2011-12 school year) provisional data; high school graduates and expenditure per pupil ADA are projected. (2) Data for 1899-1900 are based on total population from the decennial census. From 1919-20 to 1959-60, total population includes armed forces overseas, as of July 1 preceding the school year. Data for later years are for resident population excluding armed forces overseas. (3) Data for 1899-1960 are school year enrollment; data for later years are fall enrollment. (4) In 1899-1900, includes interest on school debt. (5) Because of changes in the definition of "current expenditures," data for 1959-60 and later years are not entirely comparable with prior years. (6) Data prior to 1959-60 include supervisors, principals, teachers, and nonsupervisory instructional staff. (7) ADA = average daily attendance.

U.S. Public High School Graduation Rates, 2012-13

Source: National Center for Education Statistics, U.S. Dept. of Education

State	Rate	Rank	State	Rate	Rank	State	Rate	Rank	State	Rate	Rank
Alabama	80.0%	32	Illinois	83.2%	23	Montana	84.4%	22	Rhode Island	79.7%	34
Alaska	71.8	45	Indiana	87.0	8	Nebraska	88.5	2	South Carolina	77.6	35
Arizona	75.1	43	Iowa	89.7	1	Nevada	70.7	47	South Dakota	82.7	25
Arkansas	84.9	19	Kansas	85.7	13	New Hampshire	87.3	7	Tennessee	86.3	11
California	80.4	30	Kentucky	86.1	12	New Jersey	87.5	5	Texas	88.0	3
Colorado	76.9	38	Louisiana	73.5	44	New Mexico	70.3	48	Utah	83.0	24
Connecticut	85.5	15	Maine	86.4	10	New York	76.8	39	Vermont	86.6	9
Delaware	80.4	30	Maryland	85.0	17	North Carolina	82.5	26	Virginia	84.5	21
Dist. of Columbia	62.3	50	Massachusetts	85.0	17	North Dakota	87.5	5	Washington	76.4	40
Florida	75.6	41	Michigan	77.0	36	Ohio	82.2	28	West Virginia	81.4	29
Georgia	71.7	46	Minnesota	79.8	33	Oklahoma	84.8	20	Wisconsin	88.0	3
Hawaii	82.4	27	Mississippi	75.5	42	Oregon	68.7	49	Wyoming	77.0	36
Idaho	NA	NA	Missouri	85.7	13	Pennsylvania	85.5	15	**Total U.S.**	**81.4**	

NA = Not available. **Note:** The 4-year adjusted cohort graduation rate (ACGR) is the number of students who graduate in 4 years with a regular high school diploma divided by the number of students who form the adjusted cohort for the graduating class. From the beginning of 9th grade (or the earliest high school grade), students who are entering that grade for the first time form a cohort that is "adjusted" by adding any students who subsequently transfer into the cohort and subtracting any students who subsequently transfer out, emigrate to another country, or die.

High School Dropouts by Sex, Race, and Ethnicity, 1960-2013

Source: Current Population Survey, U.S. Census Bureau, U.S. Dept. of Commerce

(data for Oct. of year shown unless otherwise noted)

	Total dropout rate				Male dropout rate				Female dropout rate			
Year[1]	All races[2]	White	Black	Hispanic	All races[2]	White	Black	Hispanic	All races[2]	White	Black	Hispanic
1960[3]	27.2%	NA	NA	NA	27.8%	NA	NA	NA	26.7%	NA	NA	NA
1970[4]	15.0	13.2%	27.9%	NA	14.2	12.2%	29.4%	NA	15.7	14.1%	26.6%	NA
1980	14.1	11.4	19.1	35.2%	15.1	12.3	20.8	37.2%	13.1	10.5	17.7	33.2%
1990	12.1	9.0	13.2	32.4	12.3	9.3	11.9	34.3	11.8	8.7	14.4	30.3
2000	10.9	6.9	13.1	27.8	12.0	7.0	15.3	31.8	9.9	6.9	11.1	23.5
2005[5]	9.4	6.0	10.4	22.4	10.8	6.6	12.0	26.4	8.0	5.3	9.0	18.1
2006[5]	9.3	5.8	10.7	22.1	10.3	6.4	9.7	25.7	8.3	5.3	11.7	18.1
2007[5]	8.7	5.3	8.4	21.4	9.8	6.0	8.0	24.7	7.7	4.5	8.8	18.0
2008[5]	8.0	4.8	9.9	18.3	8.5	5.4	8.7	19.9	7.5	4.2	11.1	16.7
2009[5]	8.1	5.2	9.3	17.6	9.1	6.3	10.6	19.0	7.0	4.1	8.1	16.1
2010[5]	7.4	5.1	8.0	15.1	8.5	5.9	9.5	17.3	6.3	4.2	6.7	12.8
2011[5]	7.1	5.0	7.3	13.6	7.7	5.4	8.3	14.6	6.5	4.6	6.4	12.4
2012[5]	6.6	4.3	7.5	12.7	7.3	4.8	8.1	13.9	5.9	3.8	7.0	11.3
2013[5]	6.8	5.1	7.3	11.7	7.2	5.5	8.2	12.6	6.3	4.7	6.6	10.8

NA = Not available. **Note:** Table shows "status" dropouts, defined as 16- to 24-year-olds who are not enrolled in school and who have not completed a high school program, regardless of when they left school. People who have received GED credentials are not shown. Excludes persons in prison or in the military, and other persons not living in households. Race categories exclude persons of Hispanic ethnicity unless otherwise noted. (1) Because of changes in data collection procedures, data for years prior to 1992 may not be comparable to later years. (2) Includes other racial/ethnic categories not separately shown. (3) Based on the Apr. 1960 decennial census. (4) White and black data include persons of Hispanic ethnicity. (5) White and black data exclude persons identifying themselves as being of two or more races.

Overview of U.S. Public Schools, 2013-14

Source: National Center for Education Statistics, U.S. Dept. of Education; National Education Association (NEA)

State	Local school districts	Elementary schools[1,2]	Secondary schools[2,3]	Classroom teachers	Total enrollment	Pupils per teacher	Teachers' avg. pay	Expend. per pupil
Alabama	135	721	420	46,433	736,789	15.9	$48,720	$8,821*
Alaska	54*	199	83	7,898	127,599*	16.2*	65,891	19,244*
Arizona	627*	1,342	741	59,308*	1,078,033*	18.2*	45,335*	7,143*
Arkansas	255	720	371	31,301	474,706	15.2	47,319	9,523
California	1,028	6,953	2,648	292,505	6,236,672	21.3	71,396	10,329
Colorado	178	1,294	393	56,916	876,999	15.4	49,615	10,723
Connecticut	196*	808	284	42,013	545,569*	13.0*	70,583	17,039*
Delaware	37*	161	39	9,022	132,664*	14.7*	59,305	15,362*
Dist. of Columbia	41*	169	35	6,233*	76,744*	12.3*	73,162*	14,527*
Florida	67	2,804	703	169,674	2,708,062	16.0	47,780	8,982
Georgia	198	1,784	469	108,842	1,723,439	15.8	52,924	9,392*
Hawaii	1	205	52	11,081	185,273	16.7	56,291	11,537
Idaho	137*	444	216	15,132	298,921*	19.8*	44,465	8,722*
Illinois	865*	3,154	954	129,150*	2,075,209*	16.1*	60,124*	13,372*
Indiana	369	1,367	451	60,425	1,034,285	17.1	50,289	8,135
Iowa	346	970	381	35,175	503,805	14.3	52,032	10,240
Kansas	286*	944	360	34,744*	488,671*	14.1*	48,221*	9,783 *
Kentucky	173	997	439	41,090	678,392	16.5	50,560	9,553
Louisiana	126*	952	270	44,553*	714,583*	16.0*	49,067	10,472*
Maine	198	452	151	15,179	183,545	12.1	49,232	8,829*
Maryland	24*	1,132	254	59,315	866,169	14.6	64,546	14,080*
Massachusetts	408	1,429	373	70,581	954,609	13.5	73,195	15,990
Michigan	773*	2,237	959	65,777	1,484,612*	22.6*	62,166	14,621*
Minnesota	519*	1,264	851	54,253	844,006*	15.6*	54,752	11,929*
Mississippi	151	623	324	32,389*	492,082*	15.2*	42,187*	8,649*
Missouri	524*	1,584	646	67,333	908,072*	13.5*	46,750	10,419*
Montana	410*	482	342	10,750*	142,564*	13.3*	49,893*	10,635*
Nebraska	249	718	307	23,706	307,398	13.0	49,539	9,891*
Nevada	17*	476	130	27,351	489,448*	17.9*	55,813	8,693*
New Hampshire	161*	377	104	15,659*	186,574*	11.9*	57,057*	16,225*
New Jersey	590*	1,951	549	114,877	1,352,000*	11.8*	68,238	20,117*
New Mexico	89	611	239	22,226	334,841	15.1	45,727	10,089
New York	695*	3,286	1,123	200,503	2,564,711*	12.8*	76,409	20,428*
North Carolina	115	1,876	533	95,116	1,441,447	15.2	44,990	8,632
North Dakota	177	298	187	8,235*	99,498*	12.1*	48,666*	8,733*
Ohio	1,016*	2,500	1,018	107,764	1,854,881	17.2	55,913	11,145*
Oklahoma	517	1,218	559	41,949	681,578	16.2	44,549	7,925*
Oregon	196	885	282	26,418	567,100	21.5	58,638	10,471
Pennsylvania	499*	2,199	817	118,135	1,725,820*	14.6*	63,701	15,061*
Rhode Island	49*	226	73	9,809	131,093*	13.4*	64,696*	18,627*
South Carolina	82	917	284	48,634	746,015	15.3	48,430	9,445
South Dakota	151	434	239	9,328	128,294	13.8	40,023	8,962*
Tennessee	135	1,343	376	64,596	970,035	15.0	47,742	8,797
Texas	1,227	5,951	2,084	334,612	5,135,880	15.3	49,690	8,681
Utah	131	634	266	27,249	612,395	22.5	45,695	7,476*
Vermont	286*	234	68	7,971	79,646	10.0	55,958	21,263*
Virginia	132	1,503	408	102,031*	1,279,544*	12.5*	49,826*	10,866*
Washington	295	1,521	631	54,725	1,060,298	19.4	52,969	9,929*
West Virginia	55	566	125	19,670	281,013	14.3	45,086	12,519*
Wisconsin	424	1,560	572	56,835	874,414	15.4	53,679	11,337*
Wyoming	48*	243	97	7,454	92,218	12.4	56,583	16,008
Total U.S.	**15,462***	**66,718**	**24,280**	**3,121,926***	**49,568,215***	**15.9***	**56,610***	**11,355***

* = NEA estimate. (1) Includes primary and middle schools (schools with no grade higher than 8th). (2) 2012-13 estimates. (3) Includes schools with no grade lower than 7th.

Programs for Students With Disabilities, 1995-2013

Source: Office of Special Education and Rehabilitative Services, U.S. Dept. of Education

Number of children and young adults 3-21 years old served annually in federally funded educational programs for the disabled. (in thousands)

Type of disability	1995-96	2000-01	2003-04	2004-05	2005-06	2006-07	2007-08	2008-09	2009-10	2010-11	2011-12	2012-13
Learning disabilities	2,578	2,868	2,831	2,798	2,735	2,665	2,577	2,537	2,498	2,423	2,364	2,347
Speech impairments	1,022	1,409	1,441	1,463	1,468	1,475	1,458	1,451	1,449	1,429	1,413	1,397
Intellectual disabilities[1]	571	624	593	578	556	534	500	488	473	457	443	439
Emotional disturbance	437	481	489	489	477	464	442	421	409	391	375	364
Multiple disabilities	93	133	140	140	141	142	138	132	132	131	133	135
Hearing impairments	67	78	79	79	79	80	79	79	79	79	79	78
Orthopedic impairments	63	83	77	73	71	69	67	70	66	63	62	60
Other health impairments[2]	133	303	464	521	570	611	641	666	698	724	755	792
Visual impairments	25	29	28	29	29	29	29	29	29	29	29	29
Autism	28	94	163	191	223	258	296	338	380	419	458	502
Deaf-blindness	1	1	2	2	2	2	2	2	2	2	2	2
Traumatic brain injury	9	16	23	24	24	25	25	26	25	26	26	26
Developmental delay	—	178	305	332	339	333	358	354	368	381	393	403
All disabilities	**5,572**	**6,296**	**6,634**	**6,719**	**6,713**	**6,686**	**6,613**	**6,593**	**6,608**	**6,553**	**6,531**	**6,574**

— = Not available or not reliable data. **Note:** Counts based on reports from states and District of Columbia. Details may not add up to totals because of rounding and/or incomplete enumeration. (1) Referred to in some prior years as "mental retardation." (2) Includes limited strength, vitality, or alertness due to chronic or acute health problems such as a heart condition, tuberculosis, rheumatic fever, nephritis, asthma, sickle cell anemia, hemophilia, epilepsy, lead poisoning, leukemia, or diabetes.

Revenues for Public Elementary and Secondary Schools by State, 2011-12

Source: National Center for Education Statistics, U.S. Dept. of Education; amounts in thousands

		Federal		State		Local and intermediate	
State/territory	Total	Amount	% of tot. rev.	Amount	% of tot. rev.	Amount	% of tot. rev.
Alabama	$7,099,553	$838,285	11.8%	$3,934,577	55.4%	$2,326,690	32.8%
Alaska	2,496,679	353,993	14.2	1,618,975	64.8	523,711	21.0
American Samoa	99,334	88,536	89.1	10,528[1]	10.6	271	0.3
Arizona	9,305,199	1,374,629	14.8	3,804,900	40.9	4,125,669	44.3
Arkansas	5,284,555	698,938	13.2	2,723,740	51.5	1,861,878	35.2
California	65,808,329	8,260,861	12.6	37,079,384	56.3	20,468,083	31.1
Colorado	8,698,810	722,810	8.3	3,765,940	43.3	4,210,060	48.4
Connecticut	10,274,602	535,208	5.2	3,978,525	38.7	5,760,869	56.1
Delaware	1,871,464	235,905	12.6	1,096,243	58.6	539,316	28.8
District of Columbia	2,073,564	208,249	10.0	NA	NA	1,865,315	90.0
Florida	23,988,519	3,122,488	13.0	8,702,310	36.3	12,163,720	50.7
Georgia	17,620,300	1,920,092	10.9	7,533,980	42.8	8,166,229	46.3
Guam	307,591	74,850	24.3	NA	NA	232,741	75.7
Hawaii	2,535,039	318,728	12.6	2,161,254	85.3	55,057	2.2
Idaho	2,062,254	278,914	13.5	1,302,949	63.2	480,391	23.3
Illinois	29,165,373	2,406,643	8.3	9,385,630	32.2	17,373,101	59.6
Indiana	11,940,988	1,149,521	9.6	6,510,737	54.5	4,280,730	35.8
Iowa	6,038,962	526,409	8.7	2,681,029	44.4	2,831,524	46.9
Kansas	5,796,537	485,235	8.4	3,209,527	55.4	2,101,775	36.3
Kentucky	7,086,717	971,266	13.7	3,841,443	54.2	2,274,008	32.1
Louisiana	8,412,167	1,458,572	17.3	3,602,717	42.8	3,350,878	39.8
Maine	2,556,186	233,761	9.1	1,022,269	40.0	1,300,156	50.9
Maryland	13,744,621	859,635	6.3	5,980,909	43.5	6,904,078	50.2
Massachusetts	15,835,037	1,059,639	6.7	6,206,699	39.2	8,568,699	54.1
Michigan	18,751,262	2,031,233	10.8	10,700,372	57.1	6,019,657	32.1
Minnesota	10,989,685	797,917	7.3	7,044,954	64.1	3,146,814	28.6
Mississippi	4,441,163	795,121	17.9	2,195,730	49.4	1,450,312	32.7
Missouri	10,221,689	1,034,047	10.1	3,275,438	32.0	5,912,203	57.8
Montana	1,622,721	218,297	13.5	770,180	47.5	634,244	39.1
Nebraska	3,778,749	358,930	9.5	1,167,743	30.9	2,252,076	59.6
Nevada	4,137,704	413,861	10.0	1,366,314	33.0	2,357,529	57.0
New Hampshire	2,864,747	188,927	6.6	1,031,778	36.0	1,644,043	57.4
New Jersey	26,590,517	1,425,761	5.4	10,507,939	39.5	14,656,818	55.1
New Mexico	3,611,545	540,071	15.0	2,455,787	68.0	615,688	17.0
New York	58,645,470	3,956,260	6.7	23,131,272	39.4	31,557,937	53.8
North Carolina	13,113,012	1,878,905	14.3	7,877,949	60.1	3,356,157	25.6
North Dakota	1,296,813	170,085	13.1	653,842	50.4	472,886	36.5
Northern Mariana Islands	65,214	33,334	51.1	31,880[1]	48.9	NA	NA
Ohio	22,886,511	2,186,000	9.6	10,132,936	44.3	10,567,575	46.2
Oklahoma	5,862,837	794,080	13.5	2,882,879	49.2	2,185,878	37.3
Oregon	6,172,422	618,981	10.0	3,038,044	49.2	2,515,397	40.8
Pennsylvania	26,807,485	2,201,593	8.2	9,594,823	35.8	15,011,068	56.0
Puerto Rico	3,374,611	1,153,166	34.2	2,221,384[1]	65.8	62	0.0
Rhode Island	2,278,095	217,363	9.5	846,435	37.2	1,214,297	53.3
South Carolina	8,041,045	871,480	10.8	3,670,717	45.6	3,498,848	43.5
South Dakota	1,303,055	215,937	16.6	400,362	30.7	686,756	52.7
Tennessee	8,979,871	1,263,157	14.1	4,059,869	45.2	3,656,845	40.7
Texas	49,533,579	6,311,758	12.7	20,341,491	41.1	22,880,330	46.2
Utah	4,619,102	461,333	10.0	2,418,166	52.4	1,739,603	37.7
Vermont	1,644,282	127,644	7.8	1,451,850	88.3	64,787	3.9
Virgin Islands (U.S.)	221,673	37,899	17.1	NA	NA	183,774	82.9
Virginia	14,659,153	1,356,037	9.3	5,564,497	38.0	7,738,618	52.8
Washington	11,844,779	1,057,047	8.9	7,001,099	59.1	3,786,633	32.0
West Virginia	3,556,656	433,205	12.2	2,069,942	58.2	1,053,510	29.6
Wisconsin	10,879,541	953,230	8.8	4,806,328	44.2	5,119,983	47.1
Wyoming	1,659,641	145,148	8.7	850,339	51.2	664,154	40.0

NA = Not applicable. (1) Reported state revenue data are revenues received from the central government of the jurisdiction.

Fighting, Bullying, and Safety Concerns of High School Students, 2013

Source: *Youth Risk Behavior Surveillance–United States, 2013*, Centers for Disease Control and Prevention

	In a physical fight on school property[1]			Bullied on school property[2]			Electronically bullied[2,3]			Did not go to school because of safety concerns[4]		
	Female	Male	Total	Female	Male	Total	Female	Male	Total	Female	Male	Total
Race/ethnicity[5]												
White	3.8%	8.9%	6.4%	27.3%	16.2%	21.8%	25.2%	8.7%	16.9%	7.4%	3.8%	5.6%
Black	11.2	14.5	12.8	15.1	10.2	12.7	10.5	6.9	8.7	8.0	7.8	7.9
Hispanic	6.7	12.1	9.4	20.7	14.8	17.8	17.1	8.3	12.8	12.6	6.9	9.8
Grade												
9	8.6	13.0	10.9	29.2	20.8	25.0	22.8	9.4	16.1	9.9	5.5	7.7
10	6.3	10.2	8.3	28.8	15.8	22.2	21.9	7.2	14.5	10.7	5.3	8.0
11	4.1	10.9	7.5	20.3	13.1	16.8	20.6	8.9	14.9	8.1	5.8	7.0
12	2.6	7.3	4.9	15.5	11.2	13.3	18.3	8.6	13.5	5.9	5.0	5.5
Total	5.6	10.7	8.1	23.7	15.6	19.6	21.0	8.5	14.8	8.7	5.4	7.1

(1) One or more times during the 12 months before the survey. (2) During the 12 months before the survey. (3) Including being bullied through email, chat rooms, instant messaging, websites, or texting. (4) On at least one day during the 30 days before the survey. (5) Race categories include non-Hispanics only. Hispanics may be of any race.

Program for International Student Assessment (PISA) Scores, 2003-12

Source: National Center for Education Statistics, U.S. Dept. of Education

Scores are reported on a scale from 0 to 1,000. The PISA test is administered to 15-year-old students.

Education system	Mathematics 2003	Mathematics 2012	Mathematics % change, 2003-12	Science 2006	Science 2012	Science % change, 2006-12
Albania	—	394	—	—	397	—
Argentina	—	388	—	391	406	3.68%
Australia*	524	504	−3.84%	527	521	−1.02
Austria*	506	506	−0.01	511	506	−0.99
Belgium*	529	515	−2.75	510	505	−0.96
Brazil	356	391	9.96	390	405	3.68
Bulgaria	—	439	—	434	446	2.85
Canada*	532	518	−2.71	534	525	−1.69
Chile*	—	423	—	438	445	1.54
Colombia	—	376	—	388	399	2.74
Costa Rica	—	407	—	—	429	—
Croatia	—	471	—	493	491	−0.37
Cyprus	—	440	—	—	438	—
Czech Rep.*	516	499	−3.39	513	508	−0.89
Denmark*	514	500	−2.77	496	498	0.52
Estonia*	—	521	—	531	541	1.88
Finland*	544	519	−4.69	563	545	−3.17
France*	511	495	−3.10	495	499	0.76
Germany*	503	514	2.10	516	524	1.64
Greece*	445	453	1.81	473	467	−1.41
Hong Kong	550	561	1.97	542	555	2.35
Hungary*	490	477	−2.65	504	494	−1.91
Iceland*	515	493	−4.33	491	478	−2.58
Indonesia	360	375	4.15	393	382	−2.94
Ireland*	503	501	−0.27	508	522	2.69
Israel*	—	466	—	454	470	3.56
Italy*	466	485	4.22	475	494	3.82
Japan*	534	536	0.43	531	547	2.89
Jordan	—	386	—	422	409	−2.99
Kazakhstan	—	432	—	—	425	—
Korea, South*	542	554	2.13	522	538	3.00
Latvia	483	491	1.49	490	502	2.58
Liechtenstein	536	535	−0.15	522	525	0.49
Lithuania	—	479	—	488	496	1.59
Luxembourg*	493	490	−0.68	486	491	1.01
Macao	527	538	2.06%	511	521	1.90%
Malaysia	—	421	—	—	420	—
Mexico*	385	413	7.28	410	415	1.29
Montenegro[1]	—	410	—	412	410	−0.41
Netherlands*	538	523	−2.76	525	522	−0.53
New Zealand*	523	500	−4.53	530	516	−2.78
Norway*	495	489	−1.17	487	495	1.64
Peru	—	368	—	—	373	—
Poland*	490	518	5.56	498	526	5.63
Portugal*	466	487	4.52	474	489	3.16
Qatar	—	376	—	349	384	9.83
Romania	—	445	—	418	439	4.87
Russia	468	482	2.94	479	486	1.42
Serbia[1]	—	449	—	436	445	2.10
Shanghai, China	—	613	—	—	580	—
Singapore	—	573	—	—	551	—
Slovakia*	498	482	−3.32	488	471	−3.53
Slovenia*	—	501	—	519	514	−0.90
Spain*	485	484	−0.16	488	496	1.64
Sweden*	509	478	−6.05	503	485	−3.68
Switzerland*	527	531	0.83	512	515	0.74
Taiwan	—	560	—	532	523	−1.72
Thailand	417	427	2.34	421	444	5.46
Tunisia	359	388	8.11	386	398	3.25
Turkey*	423	448	5.80	424	463	9.34
United Arab Emirates	—	434	—	—	448	—
UK*	—	494	—	515	514	−0.13
U.S.*	483	481	−0.31	489	497	1.74
Uruguay	422	409	−3.06	428	416	−2.87
Vietnam	—	511	—	—	528	—
OECD trend score[2]	**500**	**496**	**−0.68**	**498**	**501**	**0.57**

— = Not available. * = Organization for Economic Cooperation and Development (OECD) nation. (1) Montenegro and Serbia were a united country under the 2003 assessment. (2) The OECD trend scores are based on the averages of OECD countries with each country weighted equally.

Mathematics, Reading, and Science Achievement of U.S. Students, 1998-2013

Source: National Assessment of Educational Progress, National Center for Education Statistics, U.S. Dept. of Education

Percent of public school students in a grade who scored at or above basic levels in national tests. Basic level denotes a partial mastery of prerequisite knowledge and skills fundamental for proficient work at each grade.

	4th grade				8th grade					
	Math		Reading		Math		Reading		Science	
State	2000	2013	1998	2013	2000	2013	1998	2013	2000	2011
AL	55	75	56	65	52	60	67	68	53	54
AK	NA	77	NA	58	NA	72	NA	71	NA	68
AZ	57	82	51	60	62	69	72	72	55	57
AR	55	83	54	66	52	69	68	73	53	62
CA	50	74	48	58	52	65	63	72	38	52
CO	NA	87	69	74	NA	77	77	81	NA	74
CT	76	83	76	76	72	74	81	83	64	69
DE	NA	86	53	73	NA	71	64	77	NA	63
DC	24	66	27	50	23	54	44	57	NA	24
FL	NA	84	53	75	NA	70	67	77	NA	62
GA	57	81	54	67	55	68	68	75	52	63
HI	55	83	45	62	52	72	59	71	40	55
ID	68	83	NA	68	71	78	NA	82	71	75
IL	63	79	NA	64	68	74	NA	77	59	60
IN	77	90	NA	73	76	77	NA	79	66	68
IA	75	87	67	72	NA	76	NA	81	NA	73
KS	76	89	70	71	77	79	81	78	NA	70
KY	59	84	62	71	63	71	74	80	60	71
LA	57	75	44	56	48	64	63	68	44	56
ME	73	88	72	71	76	78	83	79	72	78
MD	60	82	58	77	65	74	70	82	57	64
MA	77	90	70	79	76	86	79	84	70	76
MI	71	77	62	64	70	70	NA	77	68	72
MN	76	90	69	74	80	83	78	82	72	76
MS	45	74	47	53	41	61	62	64	41	47
MO	71	83	61	70	67	74	75	78	66	72
MT	72	86	72	70	80	80	83	84	79	80
NE	65	84	NA	71	74	76	NA	81	52	72
NV	60	80	51	61	58	68	70	72	NA	58
NH	NA	93	75	80	NA	84	NA	84	NA	79
NJ	NA	87	NA	75	NA	82	NA	85	NA	69
NM	50	74	51	52	50	63	71	67	48	58
NY	66	82	62	70	68	72	76	76	NA	62
NC	73	87	58	69	70	75	74	76	54	61
ND	73	89	NA	73	77	82	NA	81	72	82
OH	73	86	NA	71	75	79	NA	79	72	73
OK	67	83	66	65	64	68	80	75	60	63
OR	65	81	58	66	71	73	78	79	68	71
PA	NA	85	NA	73	NA	78	NA	81	NA	66
RI	65	83	64	70	64	74	76	77	58	63
SC	59	79	53	60	55	69	66	73	48	61
SD	NA	84	NA	66	NA	79	NA	81	NA	79
TN	59	80	57	67	53	69	71	77	55	64
TX	76	84	59	63	68	80	74	76	52	67
UT	69	83	62	71	68	75	77	81	67	77
VT	73	87	NA	75	75	84	NA	84	71	80
VA	71	88	62	74	67	77	78	78	61	73
WA	NA	86	64	72	NA	79	76	81	NA	72
WV	65	81	60	62	62	65	75	70	57	64
WI	NA	85	72	68	NA	78	78	78	NA	75
WY	71	90	64	75	70	81	76	84	69	77
U.S.	**64**	**83**	**58**	**68**	**65**	**74**	**71**	**78**	**57**	**65**

NA = Not administered.

Enrollment in U.S. Public and Private Schools, 1889-2025

Source: National Center for Education Statistics, U.S. Dept. of Education

Of all students enrolled in private schools in 2011-12, 70% attended religious schools, and 30% attended nonsectarian schools.

School year[1]	Public school[2]	Private school[2]	% private[3]
1889-90	12,723	1,611	11.2%
1899-1900	15,503	1,352	8.0
1909-10	17,814	1,558	8.0
1919-20	21,578	1,699	7.3
1929-30	25,678	2,651	9.4
1939-40	25,434	2,611	9.3
1949-50	25,111	3,380	11.9
1959-60	35,182	5,675	13.9
1969-70	45,550	5,500[4]	10.8%
1979-80	41,651	5,000[4]	10.7
1989-90	40,543	5,599	12.1
1999-2000	46,857	6,018	11.4
2009-10	49,361	5,488	10.0
2011-12	49,522	5,268	9.6
2012-13	49,771	5,181[5]	9.4
2024-25[5]	52,920	4,952	8.6

Note: "Private" includes all nonpublic schools. (1) Fall enrollment. (2) In thousands. Data from fall 1980 onward covers an expanded universe of private schools; comparisons with earlier years should be avoided. (3) Percent of U.S. students enrolled in private schools. (4) Estimated. (5) Projected.

Characteristics of Public Charter Schools and Students, 1999-2013

Source: National Center for Education Statistics, U.S. Dept. of Education

	1999-2000	2001-02	2003-04	2005-06	2007-08	2009-10	2011-12	2012-13
Number of charter school students	**339,678**	**571,029**	**789,479**	**1,012,906**	**1,276,731**	**1,610,285**	**2,057,599**	**2,267,814**
	Percentage of charter school students who were—							
Sex								
Male	51.0%	50.8%	50.3%	49.9%	49.5%	49.5%	49.6%	49.6%
Female	49.0	49.2	49.7	50.1	50.5	50.5	50.4	50.4
Race/ethnicity								
White	42.5	42.6	41.8	40.5	38.8	37.3	35.6	35.4
Black	33.5	32.5	31.9	32.1	31.8	30.3	28.7	27.6
Asian/Pacific Islander	2.8	3.1	3.2	3.6	3.8	3.9	4.0	4.2
American Indian/Alaska Native	1.5	1.7	1.5	1.4	1.2	1.0	0.9	0.8
Two or more races	NA	NA	NA	NA	NA	1.4	2.8	2.9
Hispanic	19.6	20.1	21.5	22.4	24.5	26.0	28.0	29.1
Number of charter schools	**1,524**	**2,348**	**2,977**	**3,780**	**4,388**	**4,952**	**5,696**	**6,079**
	Percentage of charter schools that were—							
School level								
Elementary	54.6%	50.6%	52.0%	52.1%	53.3%	54.1%	54.9%	55.8%
Secondary	25.9	24.2	26.2	28.0	27.8	26.8	24.9	24.1
Combined	18.6	21.6	21.0	18.6	18.3	18.8	19.5	19.8
Enrollment size								
Under 300	77.1	73.6	71.1	69.6	65.6	61.5	55.8	54.1
300-499	12.0	13.6	15.6	16.5	19.3	20.8	23.1	23.5
500-999	8.6	9.9	10.1	10.9	12.0	14.0	17.0	18.0
1,000 or more	2.4	2.8	3.2	3.0	3.1	3.7	4.2	4.4
Locale								
City	NA	NA	52.7	52.5	54.3	54.8	55.4	56.7
Suburban	NA	NA	22.0	22.2	22.0	21.1	21.2	25.5
Town	NA	NA	9.6	9.4	8.5	8.0	7.4	7.0
Rural	NA	NA	15.8	16.0	15.2	16.1	16.0	10.8

NA = Not available. **Note:** Race categories exclude persons of Hispanic ethnicity, who may be of any race.

Homeschooled Students, 2011-12

Source: National Center for Education Statistics, U.S. Dept. of Education

A total of 1,770,000 U.S. students in grades K-12 were homeschooled in 2011-12, up from 1.5 mil in 2007 and 850,000 in 1999. In a 2012 U.S. Dept. of Education survey of parents who homeschool their children, the reasons they gave as most important in their decision to homeschool included concern over the school environment, with such factors as safety, drugs, or negative peer pressure (25%); dissatisfaction with academic instruction in schools (19%); desire to provide religious instruction (16%); desire to provide moral instruction (5%); desire to provide a nontraditional approach to education (5%); and the child having a physical or mental health problem (5%). In all, 91% cited concern over school environment as one of their reasons, 77% cited moral instruction, 74% cited dissatisfaction with academic instruction, and 64% cited religious instruction.

Characteristic	No. of students (thous.)	% distrib.	Home-schooling rate[1]
Total	**1,770**	**NA**	**3.4%**
Household locale			
City	489	28%	3.2
Suburban	601	34	3.1
Town	132	7	2.7
Rural	548	31	4.5
Race/ethnicity[2]			
White	1,201	68	4.5
Black	139	8	1.9
Asian/Pacific Islander	73	4	2.6
Other race(s)	90	5	3.2
Hispanic (any race)	267	15	2.3
Poverty status			
Poor	348	20	3.5
Nonpoor	1,422	80	3.4
Grade equivalent			
Kindergarten-2nd grade	415	23%	3.1%
3rd-5th grade	416	23	3.4
6th-8th grade	425	24	3.5
9th-12th grade	514	29	3.7
Parents' education			
Less than high school	203	11	3.4
High school	355	20	3.4
Vocational/technical or some college	525	30	3.4
Bachelor's degree	436	25	3.7
Graduate/professional school	252	14	3.3

NA = Not applicable. **Note:** Numbers may not add up to totals because of rounding. Homeschooled students are school-age children in a grade equivalent to K-12 who receive instruction at home all or most of the time. Excludes students enrolled in public or private school more than 25 hours per week or homeschooled because of temporary illness only. (1) Percentage of total subgroup (e.g., all "City" students) that is homeschooled. (2) Race categories exclude persons of Hispanic ethnicity, who may be of any race.

Common Core State Standards

Source: Common Core State Standards Initiative

In 2009, members of the Council of Chief State School Officers and the National Governors Association Center for Best Practices met to develop the Common Core State Standards, a set of college- and career-readiness standards for kindergarten through 12th grade in English language arts/literacy and mathematics. The Common Core State Standards were released in June 2010. As of Aug. 2015, 42 states; Washington, DC; American Samoa; Guam; Northern Mariana Islands; and the U.S. Virgin Islands had adopted and were working to implement the standards, which are designed to ensure that students graduating from high school are prepared to take credit-bearing introductory courses in two- or four-year college programs or to enter the workforce.

Assessment took place starting in the 2014-15 school year. Most states used tests developed by the Partnership for Assessment of Readiness for College and Careers (PARCC) or the Smarter Balanced Assessment Consortium.

The Common Core standards have received both support and criticism. Proponents claimed that the Common Core standards would better prepare students for college or the workforce and make them more competitive in the world. Critics claimed that teachers and parents did not have enough input in developing the standards, that the federal government would be too involved in education (in spite of the state-level adoption of Common Core), and that implementing the standards would be too costly.

Top 25 Public Libraries in the U.S. by Holdings, 2012

Source: *ALA Library Fact Sheet Number 13*, American Library Association (ALA)

Rank	Library name	Print materials	Electronic books	Audio and video	Total holdings
1.	New York Public Library, The Branch Libraries, NY	20,889,337	262,444	2,080,901	23,232,682
2.	Boston Public Library, MA	8,947,271	20,198	168,144	9,135,613
3.	Detroit Public Library, MI	6,870,782	982	245,137	7,116,901
4.	Los Angeles Public Library, CA	6,301,338	37,077	582,658	6,921,073
5.	County of Los Angeles Public Library, CA	5,367,967	16,593	948,541	6,333,101
6.	Public Library of Cincinnati and Hamilton County, OH	4,772,281	125,076	930,374	5,827,731
7.	Chicago Public Library, IL	5,032,111	11,016	365,282	5,408,409
8.	San Diego Public Library, CA	4,883,416	56,052	439,889	5,379,357
9.	Queens Borough Public Library, NY	4,481,261	27,192	497,674	5,006,127
10.	Hennepin County Library, MN	4,274,219	78,062	301,126	4,653,407
11.	King County Library System, WA	3,623,876	98,948	712,035	4,434,859
12.	Dallas Public Library, TX	4,131,672	10,153	249,993	4,391,818
13.	Hawaii State Public Library System, HI	3,393,557	11,688	415,035	3,820,280
14.	Cleveland Public Library, OH	3,283,319	79,089	358,892	3,721,300
15.	Broward County Libraries Division, FL	2,764,321	115,810	783,553	3,663,684
16.	Miami-Dade Public Library System, FL	3,294,232	30,002	253,858	3,578,092
17.	Brooklyn Public Library, NY	3,179,126	43,994	275,428	3,498,548
18.	Free Library of Philadelphia, PA	2,811,962	146,656	489,465	3,448,083
19.	Allen County Public Library, IN	2,996,595	28,220	230,980	3,255,795
20.	San Francisco Public Library, CA	2,723,178	19,170	360,927	3,103,275
21.	Las Vegas-Clark County Library District, NV	2,222,341	79,921	646,349	2,948,611
22.	Houston Public Library, TX	2,682,526	19,736	225,749	2,928,011
23.	Jacksonville Public Library, FL	2,342,818	31,502	498,316	2,872,636
24.	Cuyahoga County Public Library, OH	1,756,053	109,887	900,195	2,766,135
25.	Mid-Continent Public Library, MO	2,367,164	7,805	382,825	2,757,794

Number of Public Libraries and Operating Revenue by State, 2012

Source: Public Libraries Survey, Institute of Museum and Library Services

State	No.[1]	Revenue[2] (thous.)	State	No.[1]	Revenue[2] (thous.)	State	No.[1]	Revenue[2] (thous.)	State	No.[1]	Revenue[2] (thous.)
AL	219	$96,740	IL	622	$774,170	MT	82	$24,434	RI	48	$46,367
AK	77	33,478	IN	237	315,841	NE	265	52,475	SC	42	120,190
AZ	91	178,555	IA	533	115,079	NV	22	92,344	SD	112	23,365
AR	56	70,360	KS	321	113,098	NH	218	54,456	TN	185	107,833
CA	183	1,225,692	KY	119	174,540	NJ	297	477,711	TX	551	452,587
CO	115	264,006	LA	68	220,835	NM	85	46,829	UT	72	92,800
CT	183	184,194	ME	229	41,213	NY	756	1,228,769	VT	163	20,691
DE	21	23,827	MD	24	259,916	NC	77	200,122	VA	91	263,525
DC	1	37,049	MA	359	262,385	ND	75	16,390	WA	61	379,226
FL	79	497,802	MI	389	392,296	OH	251	848,093	WV	97	36,974
GA	61	195,289	MN	138	206,289	OK	118	108,054	WI	382	222,115
HI	1	31,324	MS	51	50,334	OR	128	184,435	WY	23	29,620
ID	101	47,749	MO	147	225,560	PA	456	327,277	**Total U.S.**	**9,082**	**$11,494,300**

(1) Includes central libraries only. (2) Some totals may be estimated because of nonresponse.

Population With Upper Secondary Education in Selected Countries, 2013

Source: Organization for Economic Cooperation and Development

Ranked by percentage of the population ages 25-64 that have received at least an upper secondary (senior high school) education.

Country	%	Country	%	Country	%	Country	%	Country	%
Czech Republic	93%	Switzerland	87%	Hungary	82%	Australia	76%	Greece	70%
Slovakia	92	Finland	86	Norway	82	Netherlands	76	Italy	58
Estonia	91	Germany	86	Luxembourg	80	France	75	Spain	56
Canada	90	Slovenia	85	United Kingdom	79	Belgium	73	Portugal	40
Poland	90	Israel	85	Denmark	78	Iceland	72	Mexico	38
United States	90	Austria	83	Ireland	77	New Zealand	71	Turkey	35
Sweden	88	South Korea	84						

Financial Aid to U.S. Undergraduate Students, 2000-13

Source: National Center for Education Statistics, U.S. Dept. of Education

Control and level of institution/ year	Number enrolled	Number receiving financial aid	Percent receiving aid	Percent of enrolled students in student aid programs				Average award[1]			
				Federal grants	State/ local grants	Institu-tional grants	Student loans[2]	Federal grants	State/ local grants	Institu-tional grants	Student loans[2]
All institutions											
2000-01	1,976,600	1,390,527	70.3%	31.6%	31.2%	31.1%	40.1%	$3,337	$2,736	$6,360	$5,051
2012-13	2,511,146	2,077,316	82.7	45.5	31.2	39.8	49.4	4,522	3,100	9,364	7,007
Public											
2000-01	1,333,236	872,109	65.4	30.0	33.5	22.7	30.7	3,231	2,290	3,052	4,093
2012-13	1,736,952	1,390,827	80.1	45.0	36.2	31.1	41.4	4,496	2,962	4,766	6,223
4-year											
2000-01	804,793	573,430	71.3	26.6	36.5	29.6	40.7	3,448	2,775	3,511	4,310
2012-13	1,056,185	872,769	82.6	37.8	37.3	43.8	50.9	4,579	3,727	5,245	6,682
2-year											
2000-01	528,443	298,679	56.5	35.2	28.8	12.1	15.3	2,982	1,355	1,347	3,215
2012-13	680,767	518,058	76.1	56.3	34.4	11.4	26.8	4,410	1,674	1,921	4,872
Private nonprofit											
2000-01	439,369	363,044	82.6	28.4	31.8	68.1	57.7	3,863	4,023	9,887	5,394
2012-13	515,423	459,216	89.1	33.8	26.1	79.9	62.0	4,741	3,729	16,197	8,009
4-year											
2000-01	419,499	347,638	82.9	27.4	32.2	70.1	58.1	3,933	4,028	10,008	5,367
2012-13	505,099	449,905	89.1	33.1	26.0	80.8	62.0	4,771	3,736	16,309	8,028
2-year											
2000-01	19,870	15,406	77.5	49.2	23.9	25.7	49.5	3,045	3,881	2,909	6,051
2012-13	10,324	9,311	90.2	67.1	30.3	37.6	60.6	4,001	3,427	4,415	7,080
Private for-profit											
2000-01	203,995	155,374	76.2	49.3	15.2	6.2	63.5	3,103	3,346	2,066	7,404
2012-13	258,771	227,273	87.8	71.9	7.8	18.2	77.4	4,425	3,207	2,387	8,224
4-year											
2000-01	81,075	51,739	63.8	36.1	11.9	8.3	57.7	3,080	3,877	2,168	7,714
2012-13	100,541	89,411	88.9	73.5	9.7	26.9	79.1	4,737	2,987	3,087	8,430
2-year											
2000-01	122,920	103,635	84.3	58.0	17.3	4.8	67.3	3,112	3,105	1,949	7,229
2012-13	158,230	137,862	87.1	70.9	6.6	12.7	76.2	4,220	3,412	1,443	8,088

Note: Data for full-time, first-time, degree-seeking undergraduate students. (1) Average amounts for students participating in indicated programs, in constant 2013-14 dollars. (2) Includes only loans made directly to students. Does not include Parent Loans for Undergraduate Students (PLUS) and other loans made directly to parents.

College Enrollment by Selected Characteristics, 1947-2013

Source: National Center for Education Statistics, U.S. Dept. of Education

Year	Total enrollment[1]	Attendance status			Sex of student		Control of institution			
		Full-time	Part-time	% part-time	Male	Female	Public	Private Total	Private Nonprofit	Private For-profit
1947[2]	2,338,226	NA	NA	NA	1,659,249	678,977	1,152,377	1,185,849	NA	NA
1950[2]	2,281,298	NA	NA	NA	1,560,392	720,906	1,139,699	1,141,599	NA	NA
1955[2]	2,653,034	NA	NA	NA	1,733,184	919,850	1,476,282	1,176,752	NA	NA
1965	5,920,864	4,095,728	1,825,136[3]	30.8%	3,630,020	2,290,844	3,969,596	1,951,268	NA	NA
1970	8,580,887	5,816,290	2,764,597	32.2	5,043,642	3,537,245	6,428,134	2,152,753	2,134,420	18,333
1975	11,184,859	6,841,334	4,343,525	38.8	6,148,997	5,035,862	8,834,508	2,350,351	2,311,448	38,903
1980	12,096,895	7,097,958	4,998,937	41.3	5,874,374	6,222,521	9,457,394	2,639,501	2,527,787	111,714[4]
1985	12,247,055	7,075,221	5,171,834	42.2	5,818,450	6,428,605	9,479,273	2,767,782	2,571,791	195,991
1990	13,818,637	7,820,985	5,997,652	43.4	6,283,909	7,534,728	10,844,717	2,973,920	2,760,227	213,693
1995	14,261,781	8,128,802	6,132,979	43.0	6,342,539	7,919,242	11,092,374	3,169,407	2,929,044	240,363
2000	15,312,289	9,009,600	6,302,689	41.2	6,721,769	8,590,520	11,752,786	3,559,503	3,109,419	450,084
2001	15,927,987	9,447,502	6,480,485	40.7	6,960,815	8,967,172	12,233,156	3,694,831	3,167,330	527,501
2002	16,611,711	9,946,359	6,665,352	40.1	7,202,116	9,409,595	12,751,993	3,859,718	3,265,476	594,242
2003	16,911,481	10,326,133	6,585,348	38.9	7,260,264	9,651,217	12,858,698	4,052,783	3,341,048	711,735
2004	17,272,044	10,610,177	6,661,867	38.6	7,387,262	9,884,782	12,980,112	4,291,932	3,411,685	880,247
2005	17,487,475	10,797,011	6,690,464	38.3	7,455,925	10,031,550	13,021,834	4,465,641	3,454,692	1,010,949
2006	17,758,870	10,957,305	6,801,565	38.3	7,574,815	10,184,055	13,180,133	4,578,737	3,512,866	1,065,871
2007	18,248,128	11,269,892	6,978,236	38.2	7,815,914	10,432,214	13,490,780	4,757,348	3,571,150	1,186,198
2008	19,102,814	11,747,743	7,355,071	38.5	8,188,895	10,913,919	13,972,153	5,130,661	3,661,519	1,469,142
2009	20,313,594	12,605,355	7,708,239	37.9	8,732,953	11,580,641	14,810,768	5,502,826	3,767,672	1,735,154
2010	21,019,438	13,087,182	7,932,256	37.7	9,045,759	11,973,679	15,142,171	5,877,267	3,854,482	2,022,785
2011	21,010,590	13,002,531	8,008,059	38.1	9,034,256	11,976,334	15,116,303	5,894,287	3,926,819	1,967,468
2012	20,642,819	12,737,013	7,905,806	38.3	8,919,087	11,723,732	14,880,343	5,762,476	3,953,578	1,808,898
2013	20,375,789	12,597,112	7,778,677	38.1	8,860,786	11,515,003	14,745,558	5,630,231	3,974,004	1,656,227

NA = Not available. **Note:** Data for 1947-95 are for institutions of higher education, while later data are for degree-granting institutions. Degree-granting institutions grant associate's or higher degrees and participate in Title IV federal financial aid programs. The degree-granting classification is very similar to the earlier higher education classification, but it includes more two-year colleges and excludes a few higher education institutions that do not grant degrees. (1) Fall enrollment. (2) Degree-credit enrollment only. (3) Includes part-time resident students and all extension students (students attending courses at sites separate from the primary reporting campus). In later years, part-time student enrollment was collected as a distinct category. (4) Large increases are due to the addition of schools accredited by the Accrediting Commission of Career Schools and Colleges of Technology.

Charges at U.S. Institutions of Higher Education, 1969-2014

Source: National Center for Education Statistics, U.S. Dept. of Education

Data are for the entire academic year and are average charges for full-time students at degree-granting postsecondary institutions. Room and board based on full-time students. For 1989-90 on, board is based on 20 meals per week.

	Tuition and fees			Board rates			Dormitory charges		
Public (in-state)	**All institutions**	**2-yr**	**4-yr**	**All institutions**	**2-yr**	**4-yr**	**All institutions**	**2-yr**	**4-yr**
1969-70	$323	$178	$358	$508	$465	$510	$366	$308	$369
1979-80	583	355	738	867	893	865	715	574	725
1989-90	1,356	756	1,780	1,635	1,581	1,638	1,513	962	1,557
1999-2000	2,504	1,348	3,349	2,364	1,834	2,406	2,440	1,549	2,519
2001-02	2,700	1,380	3,735	2,598	2,036	2,645	2,723	1,722	2,816
2002-03	2,903	1,483	4,046	2,669	2,164	2,712	2,930	1,954	3,029
2003-04	3,319	1,702	4,587	2,822	2,221	2,876	3,106	2,089	3,212
2004-05	3,629	1,849	5,027	2,931	2,353	2,981	3,304	2,174	3,418
2005-06	3,874	1,935	5,351	3,035	2,306	3,093	3,545	2,251	3,664
2006-07	4,102	2,018	5,666	3,191	2,390	3,253	3,757	2,407	3,878
2007-08	4,291	2,061	5,943	3,331	2,409	3,404	3,952	2,506	4,082
2008-09	4,512	2,136	6,312	3,554	2,769	3,619	4,190	2,664	4,331
2009-10	4,763	2,283	6,717	3,655	2,571	3,755	4,401	2,854	4,564
2010-11	5,075	2,441	7,132	3,846	2,683	3,956	4,646	2,955	4,832
2011-12	5,563	2,651	7,713	3,946	2,866	4,042	4,849	3,100	5,031
2012-13	5,899	2,792	8,070	4,061	2,889	4,163	5,062	3,247	5,241
2013-14	6,122	2,882	8,312	4,214	2,953	4,319	5,304	3,447	5,479
Private (nonprofit and for-profit)									
1969-70	$1,533	$1,034	$1,562	$560	$546	$561	$434	$413	$436
1979-80	3,130	2,062	3,225	955	923	957	827	766	831
1989-90	8,147	5,196	8,396	1,948	1,811	1,953	1,923	1,663	1,935
1999-2000	14,100	8,225	14,616	2,877	2,753	2,879	3,236	3,067	3,242
2001-02	15,742	10,076	16,211	3,104	2,633	3,109	3,567	3,116	3,576
2002-03	16,383	10,651	16,826	3,206	3,870	3,197	3,752	3,232	3,764
2003-04	17,315	11,545	17,763	3,364	4,432	3,354	3,945	3,581	3,952
2004-05	18,154	12,122	18,604	3,485	3,700	3,483	4,178	4,475	4,173
2005-06	18,862	12,450	19,292	3,645	4,781	3,637	4,400	4,173	4,404
2006-07	20,048	12,708	20,517	3,785	3,429	3,788	4,606	4,147	4,613
2007-08	20,972	13,126	21,427	3,992	4,074	3,991	4,804	4,484	4,808
2008-09	21,570	13,562	22,036	4,209	4,627	4,206	5,025	4,537	5,032
2009-10	21,764	14,862	22,269	4,329	4,390	4,329	5,248	5,211	5,248
2010-11	22,042	13,687	22,677	4,431	4,475	4,431	5,403	4,939	5,410
2011-12	22,850	13,961	23,464	4,586	4,475	4,586	5,622	5,169	5,627
2012-13	23,943	14,129	24,525	4,709	3,977	4,712	5,831	5,222	5,837
2013-14	25,101	14,168	25,696	4,865	4,199	4,867	6,021	5,493	6,026

Endowment Assets of Colleges and Universities, 2014

Source: *2014 NACUBO-Commonfund Study of Endowments*, National Association of College and University Business Officers (NACUBO)

Rank	College/university	Endowment assets[1]	% change, 2013-14
1.	Harvard University	$35,883,691	11.0%
2.	University of Texas System	25,425,922	24.3
3.	Yale University	23,900,000	15.0
4.	Stanford University	21,446,006	14.8
5.	Princeton University	20,995,518	15.4
6.	Massachusetts Institute of Technology	12,425,131	14.4
7.	The Texas A&M University System and Foundations	11,103,880	27.2
8.	Northwestern University	9,778,112	24.0
9.	University of Michigan	9,731,460	16.1
10.	University of Pennsylvania	9,582,335	23.8
11.	Columbia University	9,223,047	12.5
12.	University of Notre Dame	8,039,756	17.3
13.	University of Chicago	7,545,544	13.1
14.	University of California	7,384,410	15.8
15.	Duke University	7,036,776	16.5
16.	Emory University	6,681,479	14.9
17.	Washington University in St. Louis	6,643,379	17.5
18.	University of Virginia	5,945,952	15.1
19.	Cornell University	5,889,948	11.7
20.	Rice University	5,527,693	14.3
21.	University of Southern California	4,593,014	18.7
22.	Dartmouth College	$4,468,219	19.7%
23.	Vanderbilt University	4,086,040	11.2
24.	Ohio State University	3,547,566	12.7
25.	University of Pittsburgh	3,492,839	17.4
26.	Johns Hopkins University	3,451,947	15.6
27.	Pennsylvania State University	3,445.965	16.5
28.	New York University	3,424,000	16.1
29.	University of Minnesota and Foundations	3,164,792	14.8
30.	Brown University	2,999,749	11.1
31.	University of Washington	2,832,753	20.7
32.	University of North Carolina at Chapel Hill and Foundations	2,695,663	13.2
33.	Purdue University	2,443,494	12.0
34.	University of Wisconsin Foundation	2,332,185	15.5
35.	University of Richmond	2,313,305	14.3
36.	University of Illinois and Foundation	2,277,932	18.3
37.	Williams College	2,253,330	12.9
38.	Amherst College	2,149,203	17.8
39.	Michigan State University	2,145,424	31.0
40.	Boston College	2,131,400	17.8

Note: Market value of endowment assets in the fiscal year. (1) In thousands.

U.S. Higher Education Trends: Bachelor's Degrees Conferred, 1899-2025

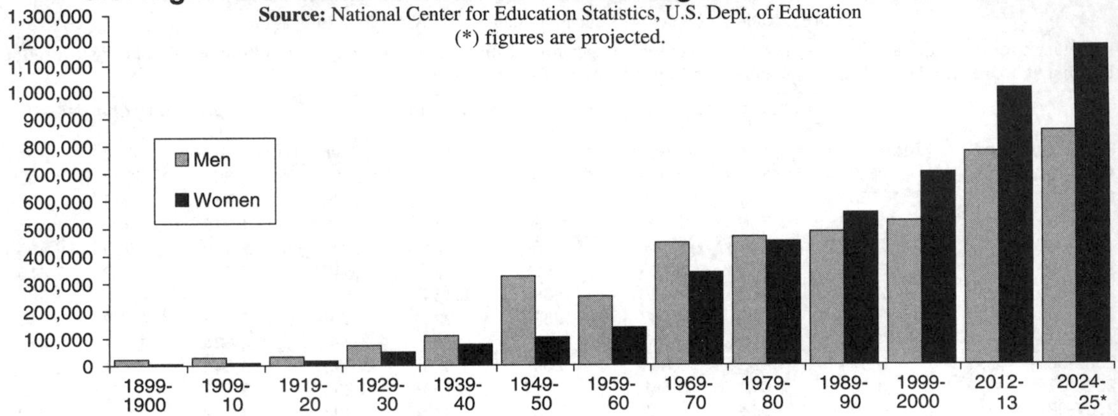

Financial Aid for College and Other Postsecondary Education

Reviewed by National Association of Student Financial Aid Administrators; as of Aug. 2015

The cost of postsecondary education in the U.S. continues to increase, but financial aid—in the form of **grants** (no repayment needed), **loans**, and/or **work-study** programs—is widely available to help families meet these expenses. Most federal aid is limited to families that demonstrate financial need as determined by standard formulas and is designed to help students attend the college of their choice regardless of their ability to pay. Financial aid personnel at each school can provide information about all aid programs (federal, state, institutional, and private) available to students, how to apply, and deadlines.

All applicants for federal aid must file a Free Application for Federal Student Aid (**FAFSA**), generally as soon as possible after Jan. 1 for the academic year starting the following Aug. or Sept. Figures provided should match federal income tax forms filed for the previous year. This is made easier by the availability of the IRS Data Retrieval Tool, which allows online applicants to access and transfer IRS tax return information directly into their FAFSA. Many other sources of aid—state governments, employers and unions, civic organizations, and the institutions themselves—also use the FAFSA to determine eligibility for aid. Some federal programs pay for postsecondary education in return for service: AmeriCorps (1-800-942-2677), Reserve Officers' Training Corps (1-800-USA-ROTC [Army], 1-800-USA-NAVY [Navy], and 1-800-522-0033 [Air Force]), the G.I. Bill (1-888-442-4551), and the National Health Service Corps (1-800-221-9393). A student must reapply for aid annually.

A **federal formula**, based on information provided on the FAFSA, takes into account such factors as family income in the preceding calendar year, parental and student assets (excluding the parents' home, farm, or certain small businesses), and length of time to parents' retirement. Financial aid personnel have the authority to consider unusual expenses, such as very high medical expenses, which are not reported on the FAFSA. Outside scholarships are also taken into account in determining eligibility for federal, institutional, and state financial aid programs.

The formula determines a family's **expected family contribution** (EFC), which is divided among the number of family members—excluding parents—in college. The EFC is subtracted from the total cost of attending college for each person. The difference determines financial need and the maximum federal aid for which the family may be eligible. (Some institutions use a separate formula for need-based institutional aid.) Some schools guarantee to meet the full financial need of each admitted student. Schools might try to cover a student's financial need using various forms of financial aid but be unable to because of a lack of funds.

The **aid package** offered by each school may include one or more of the following resources: Federal Pell Grants, for those who demonstrate sufficient financial need; Federal Supplemental Educational Opportunity Grants, for those who still have significant need after receiving Federal Pell Grants; grants from the school; Federal Work-Study or other work programs; low-interest Federal Perkins Loans; and federal Direct Subsidized and Unsubsidized Loans (often referred to as Stafford loans). Parents of undergraduates and students in graduate or professional school may apply for a PLUS loan. Direct Unsubsidized Loans and PLUS loans are available regardless of financial need, but students and parents must still complete the FAFSA to get these loans.

Loans have varying interest rates and other requirements. Repayment of Federal Perkins Loans, Direct Subsidized Loans, and Direct Unsubsidized Loans generally does not begin until after graduation; deferments, income-based repayment plans, and loan forgiveness are available on federal loans for students who meet certain requirements. For PLUS loans, parents and graduate-level students must pass a credit check and may need to begin repayment of both principal and interest while the student is still in school.

Terms may vary, but federal student loans must be repaid, even if financial circumstances change, education is incomplete or not as expected, or post-graduation income is less than expected. The loan servicer or lender is required to provide a loan repayment schedule that states the first payment due date, the number and frequency of payments, and the amount due. Some loans have a grace period, a set period of time (in most cases six months) after graduation before repayment begins. Some loan servicers have a number of repayment plan options—including graduated repayments, extended repayment, income-based repayment—or offer loan consolidation.

Certain federal income **tax credits and refunds** are available to families who meet requirements.

Rules for financial aid are complex and changeable. *Funding Your Education: The Guide to Federal Student Aid*, a comprehensive resource on financial aid from the U.S. Dept. of Education, is available online in English and Spanish at studentaid.ed.gov/sa/resources/. A Braille version is also available.

Further information and FAFSA forms are available from schools or from the Federal Student Aid Information Center: 1-800-4-FED-AID, Mon.-Fri., 8 AM-10 PM ET; www.fafsa.ed.gov.

Average Salaries of U.S. College Professors, 2014-15

Source: American Association of University Professors

Teaching level		Men			Women		
		Public institution	Private/ independent institution	Religiously affiliated institution	Public institution	Private/ independent institution	Religiously affiliated institution
Doctoral level	Professor	$133,468	$181,269	$147,834	$119,761	$166,084	$134,258
	Associate	91,354	112,937	100,108	84,997	104,852	93,936
	Assistant	80,858	99,160	87,086	73,741	90,328	79,328
Master's level	Professor	92,967	109,707	98,757	88,509	101,598	90,843
	Associate	75,192	82,399	77,787	72,465	78,260	73,114
	Assistant	65,124	70,952	65,467	62,928	67,363	62,538
Baccalaureate level	Professor	88,856	110,809	83,067	84,290	105,158	79,832
	Associate	73,860	81,166	66,814	70,860	79,097	65,262
	Assistant	62,282	66,097	56,882	59,706	64,503	56,327
2-year	Professor	79,432	NA	NA	79,029	NA	NA
	Associate	64,314	NA	NA	62,488	NA	NA
	Assistant	55,036	NA	NA	54,612	NA	NA

NA = Not available. **Note:** Salaries are for full-time faculty members only.

Average ACT Scores and Characteristics of College-Bound Students, 1990-2015

Source: ACT, Inc. (formerly American College Testing)

SCORES	Unit	1990	1995	2000	2005	2009	2010	2011	2012	2013	2014	2015
Composite score	**Points**	**20.6**	**20.8**	**21.0**	**20.9**	**21.1**	**21.0**	**21.1**	**21.1**	**20.9**	**21.0**	**21.0**
Male	Points	21.0	21.0	21.2	21.1	21.3	21.2	21.2	21.2	20.9	21.1	21.1
Female	Points	20.3	20.7	20.9	20.9	20.9	20.9	21.0	21.0	20.9	20.9	21.0
English score	**Points**	**20.5**	**20.2**	**20.5**	**20.4**	**20.6**	**20.5**	**20.6**	**20.5**	**20.2**	**20.3**	**20.4**
Male	Points	20.1	19.8	20.0	20.0	20.2	20.1	20.2	20.0	19.8	20.0	20.0
Female	Points	20.9	20.6	20.9	20.8	20.9	20.8	20.9	20.9	20.6	20.7	20.8
Math score	**Points**	**19.9**	**20.2**	**20.7**	**20.7**	**21.0**	**21.0**	**21.1**	**21.1**	**20.9**	**20.9**	**20.8**
Male	Points	20.7	20.9	21.4	21.3	21.6	21.6	21.6	21.7	21.4	21.4	21.3
Female	Points	19.3	19.7	20.2	20.2	20.4	20.5	20.6	20.6	20.5	20.5	20.4
PARTICIPANTS												
Total number	**(Thous.)**	**817**	**945**	**1,065**	**1,186**	**1,480**	**1,569**	**1,623**	**1,666**	**1,799**	**1,846**	**1,924**
Male	Percent	46%	44%	43%	44%	45%	45%	46%	46%	46%	46%	47%
White	Percent	79	80	72	66	64	62	60	59	58	56	55
Black	Percent	9	9	10	12	13	14	14	13	13	13	13
Hispanic[1]	Percent	4	5	5	7	9	10	12	14	14	15	16
Composite score												
27 or above	Percent	12	13	14	14	12	16	17	17	13	17	18
18 or below	Percent	35	34	32	34	34	35	34	34	36	36	37

Note: Minimum score, 1; maximum score, 36. Test scores and characteristics of college-bound students are based on the performance of all ACT-tested students who graduated in the spring of a given school year and took the ACT assessment during junior or senior year of high school. (1) Persons of Hispanic origin may be of any race.

Average ACT Composite Scores by State, 2015

Source: ACT, Inc. (formerly American College Testing)

State	Avg. comp. score	% grads taking ACT	State	Avg. comp. score	% grads taking ACT	State	Avg. comp. score	% grads taking ACT
Alabama	19.1	100%*	Louisiana	19.4	100%*	Ohio	22.0	73%
Alaska	21.1	39	Maine	24.2	10	Oklahoma	20.7	80
Arizona	19.9	56	Maryland	22.7	25	Oregon	21.5	38
Arkansas	20.4	93	Massachusetts	24.4	28	Pennsylvania	22.9	22
California	22.5	30	Michigan	20.1	100*	Rhode Island	23.1	19
Colorado	20.7	100*	Minnesota	22.7	78	South Carolina	20.4	62
Connecticut	24.4	32	Mississippi	19.0	100*	South Dakota	21.9	76
Delaware	23.5	21	Missouri	21.7	77	Tennessee	19.8	100*
District of Columbia	21.1	42	Montana	20.4	100*	Texas	20.9	41
Florida	19.9	79	Nebraska	21.5	88	Utah	20.2	100*
Georgia	21.0	58	Nevada	21.0	40	Vermont	23.5	29
Hawaii	18.5	93	New Hampshire	24.3	23	Virginia	23.1	30
Idaho	22.7	42	New Jersey	23.2	29	Washington	22.4	25
Illinois	20.7	100*	New Mexico	20.1	71	West Virginia	20.8	66
Indiana	22.1	41	New York	23.7	28	Wisconsin	22.2	73
Iowa	22.2	67	North Carolina	19.0	100*	Wyoming	20.2	100*
Kansas	21.9	74	North Dakota	20.6	100*	**U.S. average**	**21.0**	**59**
Kentucky	20.0	100*						

* = ACT administered as a required statewide achievement test.

Mean SAT Scores of College-Bound Seniors, 1975-2015

Source: The College Board

(recentered scale; for school year ending in year shown)

	1975	1980	1985	1990	1995	2000	2005	2007	2008	2009	2010	2011	2012	2013	2014	2015
Critical reading score[1]	**512**	**502**	**509**	**500**	**504**	**505**	**508**	**501**	**500**	**499**	**500**	**497**	**496**	**496**	**497**	**495**
Male	515	506	514	505	505	507	513	503	502	502	502	500	498	499	499	497
Female	509	498	503	496	502	504	505	500	499	497	498	495	493	494	495	493
Math score	**498**	**492**	**500**	**501**	**506**	**514**	**520**	**514**	**514**	**514**	**515**	**514**	**514**	**514**	**513**	**511**
Male	518	515	522	521	525	533	538	532	532	533	533	531	532	531	530	527
Female	479	473	480	483	490	498	504	499	499	498	499	500	499	499	499	496
Writing score	**NA**	**NA**	**NA**	**NA**	**NA**	**NA**	**NA**	**493**	**493**	**492**	**491**	**489**	**488**	**488**	**487**	**484**
Male	NA	NA	NA	NA	NA	NA	NA	487	486	485	485	482	481	482	481	478
Female	NA	NA	NA	NA	NA	NA	NA	499	499	498	497	496	494	493	492	490

NA = Not applicable. **Note:** In 1995, the College Board recentered the scoring scale for the SAT by reestablishing the original mean score of 500 on the 200-800 scale. Earlier scores have been adjusted to account for this recentering. The writing test was first given in Mar. 2005; only the scores of the first graduating class to take the revised test are given. (1) Pre-2006 scores are for the Verbal section.

Mean SAT Scores by State, 1990-2015

Source: The College Board

(for school year ending in year shown; V = Verbal, M = Math, CR = Critical reading, W = Writing)

	1990		2000		2010			2014			2015			% grads
State	**V**	**M**	**V**	**M**	**CR**	**M**	**W**	**CR**	**M**	**W**	**CR**	**M**	**W**	**taking SAT[1]**
Alabama	545	534	559	555	556	550	544	547	538	532	545	538	533	7%
Alaska	514	501	519	515	518	515	491	507	503	475	509	503	482	54
Arizona	521	520	521	523	519	525	500	522	525	500	523	527	502	36
Arkansas	545	532	563	554	566	566	552	573	571	554	568	569	551	4
California	494	508	497	518	501	516	500	498	510	496	495	506	491	60
Colorado	533	534	534	537	568	572	555	582	586	567	582	587	567	14
Connecticut	506	496	508	509	509	514	513	507	510	508	504	506	504	88
Delaware	510	496	502	496	493	495	481	456	459	444	462	461	445	100
District of Columbia	483	467	494	486	474	464	466	440	438	431	441	440	432	100
Florida	495	493	498	500	496	498	479	491	485	472	486	480	468	72
Georgia	478	473	488	486	488	490	475	488	485	472	490	485	475	77
Hawaii	480	505	488	519	483	505	470	484	504	472	487	508	477	63
Idaho	542	524	540	541	543	541	517	458	456	450	467	463	442	100
Illinois	542	547	568	586	585	600	577	599	616	587	599	616	587	5
Indiana	486	486	498	501	494	505	477	497	500	477	496	499	478	71
Iowa	584	588	589	600	603	613	582	605	611	578	589	600	566	3
Kansas	566	563	574	580	590	595	567	591	596	566	588	592	568	5
Kentucky	548	541	548	550	575	575	563	589	585	572	588	587	574	5
Louisiana	551	537	562	558	555	550	547	561	556	550	563	559	553	5
Maine	501	490	504	500	468	467	454	467	471	449	468	473	451	96
Maryland	506	502	507	509	501	506	495	492	495	481	491	493	478	79
Massachusetts	503	498	511	513	512	526	509	516	531	509	516	529	507	84
Michigan	529	534	557	569	585	605	576	593	610	581	594	609	585	4
Minnesota	552	558	581	594	594	607	580	598	610	578	595	607	576	6
Mississippi	552	538	562	549	566	548	552	583	566	565	580	563	570	3
Missouri	548	541	572	577	593	595	580	595	597	579	596	599	582	4
Montana	540	542	543	546	538	538	517	555	552	530	561	556	538	18
Nebraska	559	562	560	571	585	593	568	589	587	569	589	590	576	4
Nevada	511	511	510	517	496	501	473	495	494	469	494	494	470	54
New Hampshire	518	510	520	519	520	524	510	524	530	512	525	530	511	70
New Jersey	495	498	498	513	495	514	497	501	523	502	500	521	499	79
New Mexico	554	546	549	543	553	549	534	548	543	526	551	544	528	12
New York	489	496	494	506	484	499	478	488	502	478	489	502	478	76
North Carolina	478	470	492	496	497	511	477	499	507	477	498	504	476	64
North Dakota	579	578	588	609	580	594	559	612	620	584	597	608	586	2
Ohio	526	522	533	539	538	548	522	555	562	535	557	563	537	15
Oklahoma	553	542	563	560	569	568	547	576	571	550	576	569	548	5
Oregon	515	509	527	527	523	524	499	523	522	499	523	521	502	48
Pennsylvania	497	490	498	497	492	501	480	497	504	480	499	504	482	71
Rhode Island	498	488	505	500	494	495	488	497	496	487	494	494	484	73
South Carolina	475	467	484	482	484	495	468	488	490	465	488	487	467	65
South Dakota	580	570	587	588	592	603	571	604	609	579	592	597	564	3
Tennessee	558	544	563	553	576	571	565	578	570	566	581	574	568	8
Texas	490	489	493	500	484	505	473	476	495	461	470	486	454	62
Utah	566	555	570	569	568	559	547	571	568	551	579	575	554	5
Vermont	507	493	513	508	519	521	506	522	525	507	523	524	507	63
Virginia	501	496	509	500	512	512	497	518	515	497	518	516	499	73
Washington	513	511	526	528	524	532	508	510	518	491	502	510	484	63
West Virginia	520	514	526	511	515	507	500	517	505	500	509	497	495	15
Wisconsin	552	559	584	597	595	604	579	596	608	578	591	605	575	4
Wyoming	534	538	545	545	570	567	546	590	599	573	589	586	562	3
National average	**500**	**501**	**505**	**514**	**501**	**516**	**492**	**497**	**513**	**487**	**495**	**511**	**484**	

Note: In 1995, the College Board recentered the scoring scale for the SAT by reestablishing the original mean score of 500 on the 200-800 scale. In 2005, the SAT was changed. The Verbal portion became Critical reading, and a writing test was added. The 2006 graduating class was the first to take the new test. (1) Percentage of students from the class of 2014 who took the SAT in each state.

Four-Year Colleges and Universities

Source: Peterson's College Database © 2015 Peterson's Nelnet, LLC. All rights reserved.

Note: These listings **include only accredited degree-granting institutions** in the U.S. and U.S. territories with a total enrollment of 1,000 or more. Only four-year colleges and universities that award a bachelor's degree as their highest undergraduate degree are included. Data reported **only for institutions that provided updated information** on Peterson's Annual Survey of Undergraduate Institutions for the 2014-15 academic year, with some exceptions.

All institutions are coeducational except those where the ZIP code is followed directly by a number in parentheses: (1) = men only, (2) = primarily men, (3) = women only, (4) = primarily women.

The **Tuition & fees** column shows the annual tuition and required fees for full-time students or, where indicated, the tuition and standard fees per unit for part-time students. Where tuition varies according to residence, the figure is given for the most local resident and is coded as follows: (A) = area residents, (S) = state residents; all other figures apply to all students regardless of residence. Where annual expenses are expressed as a lump sum (including full-time tuition, mandatory fees, and room and board), the figure is entered under Tuition & fees and coded (C) = comprehensive fee. **Room & board** is the typical cost for one academic year.

Control: 1 = independent (nonprofit), 2 = independent-religious, 3 = proprietary (profit-making), 4 = federal, 5 = state, 6 = commonwealth (Puerto Rico), 7 = territory (U.S. territories), 8 = county, 9 = district, 10 = city, 11 = state and local, 12 = state-related, 13 = private (unspecified). **Degree** means the highest degree offered: B = bachelor's, M = master's, D = doctorate.

Enrollment is the total number of matriculated undergraduate and (if applicable) graduate students.

Faculty is the total number of full-time and part-time faculty members teaching courses.

Grad. rate is the percentage of full-time, first-time bachelor's (or equivalent) degree-seeking undergraduate students entering school in 2008 (or most recent available year prior) who obtained their degrees within six years.

NA indicates category is inapplicable, or data is not available from a consistent source.

Name, address	Year founded	Tuition & fees	Room & board	Control, degree	Enroll-ment	Faculty	Grad. rate
Abilene Christian Univ., Abilene, TX 79699-9100	1906	$29,450	$9,000	2-D	4,427	382	62%
Abraham Baldwin Agr. Coll., Tifton, GA 31793	1933	$3,920(S)	$4,630	5-B	3,327	162	NA
Acad. of Art Univ., San Francisco, CA 94105-3410	1929	$25,350	$14,160	3-M	15,212	1,484	31
Adams State Univ., Alamosa, CO 81101	1921	$7,951(S)	$8,400	5-D	3,152	182	24
Adelphi Univ., Garden City, NY 11530-0701	1896	$32,340	$13,620	1-D	7,610	1,017	64
Adrian Coll., Adrian, MI 49221-2575	1859	$32,660	$9,740	2-M	1,656	195	54
Adventist Univ. of Health Sciences, Orlando, FL 32803	1913	$13,030	$4,000	1-D	2,090	246	NA
Alabama Agr. & Mech. Univ., Huntsville, AL 35811	1875	$9,090(S)	$5,440	5-D	5,814	290	100
Alabama State Univ., Montgomery, AL 36101-0271	1867	$6,936(S)	$5,422	5-D	5,510	NA	26
Albany Coll. of Pharm. & Health Sciences, Albany, NY 12208	1881	$30,131	$10,240	1-D	1,559	132	77
Albany State Univ., Albany, GA 31705-2717	1903	$5,192(S)	$7,522	5-M	3,910	220	40
Albertus Magnus Coll., New Haven, CT 06511-1189	1925	$28,930	$12,960	2-M	1,550	134	44
Albion Coll., Albion, MI 49224-1831	1835	$37,300	$10,550	2-B	1,268	144	72
Albright Coll., Reading, PA 19612-5234	1856	$38,220	$10,400	2-M	1,808	180	52
Alcorn State Univ., Lorman, MS 39096-7500	1871	$6,192(S)	$8,650	5-M	3,639	218	40
Alderson Broaddus Univ., Philippi, WV 26416	1871	$22,740	$7,236	2-M	1,117	100	46
Alfred Univ., Alfred, NY 14802-1205	1836	$29,610	$11,790	1-D	2,362	190	64
Allegheny Coll., Meadville, PA 16335	1815	$42,470	$10,740	1-B	2,023	206	78
Alliant Intl. Univ.–San Diego, San Diego, CA 92131-1799	1952	$15,812	$11,268	1-D	3,523	626	NA
Alma Coll., Alma, MI 48801-1599	1886	$34,585	$9,490	2-B	1,396	154	61
Alvernia Univ., Reading, PA 19607-1799	1958	$31,100	$10,820	2-D	2,917	328	53
Alverno Coll., Milwaukee, WI 53234-3922	1887	$24,434	$7,500	2-M	2,389	269	36
Amberton Univ., Garland, TX 75041-5595	1971	$7,260	NA	2-M	1,461	40	NA
Amer. InterContinental Univ. Online, Schaumburg, IL 60173	1970	NA	NA	3-M	22,424	396	NA
Amer. Intl. Coll., Springfield, MA 01109-3189	1885	$31,870	$12,900	1-D	3,629	404	38
Amer. Public Univ. System, Charles Town, WV 25414	1991	$6,400	NA	3-M	57,539	2,290	NA
Amer. Univ., Washington, DC 20016-8001	1893	$42,556	$14,354	2-D	13,061	1,386	82
Amer. Univ. of Puerto Rico, Bayamón, PR 00960-2037	1963	$5,347	NA	1-M	2,468	162	NA
Amherst Coll., Amherst, MA 01002-5000	1821	$48,526	$12,680	1-B	1,792	271	94
Anderson Univ., Anderson, IN 46012-3495	1917	$26,850	$9,250	2-D	2,399	264	63
Anderson Univ., Anderson, SC 29621-4035	1911	$23,750	$8,674	2-D	2,922	259	41
Andrews Univ., Berrien Springs, MI 49104	1874	$26,262	$8,302	2-D	3,418	346	60
Angelo State Univ., San Angelo, TX 76909	1928	$7,642(S)	$7,602	5-D	6,494	351	31
Anna Maria Coll., Paxton, MA 01612	1946	$34,060	$12,730	2-D	1,455	NA	39
Antioch Univ. Seattle, Seattle, WA 98121-1814	1975	$20,595	NA	1-D	1,080	NA	NA
Appalachian State Univ., Boone, NC 28608	1899	$6,553(S)	$7,675	5-D	18,026	1,277	70
Aquinas Coll., Grand Rapids, MI 49506-1799	1886	$28,820	$8,558	2-M	1,933	232	52
Arcadia Univ., Glenside, PA 19038-3295	1853	$39,560	$13,200	2-D	3,939	475	60
Arizona State Univ. at the Downtown Phoenix campus, Phoenix, AZ 85004	2006	$10,127(S)	$11,974	5-D	11,217	479	58
Arizona State Univ. at the Polytechnic campus, Mesa, AZ 85212	1995	$9,811(S)	$10,720	5-D	4,094	202	60
Arizona State Univ. at the Tempe campus, Tempe, AZ 85287	1885	$10,127(S)	$10,010	5-D	50,358	2,277	63
Arizona State Univ. at the West campus, Glendale, AZ 85306	1984	$9,811(S)	$9,440	5-D	3,693	260	59
Arkansas State Univ., State University, AR 72467	1909	$7,720(S)	$7,750	5-D	13,144	700	37
Arkansas Tech. Univ., Russellville, AR 72801	1909	$7,248(S)	$6,734	5-M	12,002	561	45
Armstrong State Univ., Savannah, GA 31419-1997	1935	$6,214(S)	$10,266	5-D	7,094	421	30
Art Ctr. Coll. of Design, Pasadena, CA 91103	1930	$36,480	NA	1-M	2,045	NA	67
Asbury Univ., Wilmore, KY 40390-1198	1890	$27,736	$6,336	2-M	1,854	183	66
Ashford Univ., San Diego, CA 92123	1918	NA	NA	3-M	10,568	748	NA
Ashland Univ., Ashland, OH 44805-3702	1878	$19,852	$9,502	2-D	5,979	627	NA
Ashworth Coll., Norcross, GA 30092	1987	NA	NA	3-M	57,650	NA	NA
Aspen Univ., Denver, CO 80246-1930	1987	NA	NA	1-D	2,000	NA	NA
Assumption Coll., Worcester, MA 01609-1296	1904	$36,160	$10,962	2-M	2,502	226	71
Athens State Univ., Athens, AL 35611	1822	$6,120(S)	NA	5-B	3,128	207	NA
Atlantic Univ. Coll., Guaynabo, PR 00970	1983	NA	NA	1-M	1,236	NA	NA
Auburn Univ., Auburn University, AL 36849	1856	$10,200(S)	$12,178	5-D	25,912	1,384	70
Auburn Univ. at Montgomery, Montgomery, AL 36124-4023	1967	$9,080(S)	$5,390	5-D	5,057	360	25
Augsburg Coll., Minneapolis, MN 55454-1351	1869	$35,465	$9,380	2-D	3,580	371	63
Augustana Coll., Rock Island, IL 61201-2296	1860	$38,466	$9,746	2-B	2,500	267	74
Augustana Coll., Sioux Falls, SD 57197	1860	$29,214	$7,028	2-M	1,823	171	66
Aurora Univ., Aurora, IL 60506-4892	1893	$21,340	$9,542	1-D	4,946	405	52
Austin Coll., Sherman, TX 75090-4400	1849	$34,840	$11,503	2-M	1,301	107	77
Austin Peay State Univ., Clarksville, TN 37044	1927	$246/cr. hr.(S)	NA	5-M	10,111	604	39
Ave Maria Univ., Ave Maria, FL 34142	2002	$18,479	$10,137	2-D	1,081	84	45
Avila Univ., Kansas City, MO 64145-1698	1916	$688/cr. hr.	NA	2-M	1,907	246	47
Azusa Pacific Univ., Azusa, CA 91702-7000	1899	$33,096	$5,290	2-D	10,325	1,219	67
Babson Coll., Babson Park, MA 02457-0310	1919	$46,784	$14,928	1-M	3,049	254	91
Baker Coll., Flint, MI 48507-5508	1911	$8,460	$3,000	1-D	28,379	NA	NA
Baker Univ., Baldwin City, KS 66006-0065	1858	$26,290	$8,040	2-D	1,010	106	58
Baldwin Wallace Univ., Berea, OH 44017-2088	1845	$28,814	$8,048	2-M	3,979	441	68

Name, address	Year founded	Tuition & fees	Room & board	Control, degree	Enroll-ment	Faculty	Grad. rate
Ball State Univ., Muncie, IN 47306-1099	1918	$9,384(S)	$9,537	5-D	20,655	1,230	60%
Baptist Coll. of Health Sciences, Memphis, TN 38104 (4)	1994	$11,870	$2,200	2-B	1,043	107	60
Bard Coll., Annandale-on-Hudson, NY 12504	1860	$48,240	$13,772	1-D	2,306	278	75
Barnard Coll., New York, NY 10027-6598 (3)	1889	$46,040	$14,660	1-B	2,577	334	89
Barry Univ., Miami Shores, FL 33161-6695	1940	$28,160	$10,400	2-D	8,518	NA	36
Barton Coll., Wilson, NC 27893-7000	1902	$26,664	$8,906	2-M	1,065	110	48
Baruch Coll. of the City Univ. of New York, New York, NY 10010-5585	1919	$6,861(S)	NA	11-M	18,090	1,173	66
Bastyr Univ., Kenmore, WA 98028-4966	1978	$23,355	$6,975	1-D	1,195	299	NA
Bates Coll., Lewiston, ME 04240-6028	1855	$60,720(C)	NA	1-B	1,773	187	88
Bayamón Central Univ., Bayamón, PR 00960-1725	1970	NA	NA	2-M	1,202	153	NA
Baylor Univ., Waco, TX 76798	1845	$40,198	$11,360	2-D	16,263	1,185	72
Bay Path Univ., Longmeadow, MA 01106-2292	1897	$30,859	$12,240	1-M	2,593	335	60
Becker Coll., Worcester, MA 01609	1784	$32,870	$12,000	1-B	2,021	177	28
Belhaven Univ., Jackson, MS 39202-1789	1883	$21,626	$8,000	2-M	4,120	356	50
Bellarmine Univ., Louisville, KY 40205-0671	1950	$37,650	$11,360	2-D	3,609	413	67
Bellevue Univ., Bellevue, NE 68005-3098	1965	NA	NA	1-D	10,304	411	37
Belmont Abbey Coll., Belmont, NC 28012-1802	1876	$18,500	$10,094	2-B	1,560	132	38
Belmont Univ., Nashville, TN 37212-3757	1951	$28,660	$10,530	2-D	7,244	745	70
Beloit Coll., Beloit, WI 53511-5596	1846	$42,500	$7,470	1-B	1,303	147	80
Bemidji State Univ., Bemidji, MN 56601-2699	1919	$8,134(S)	$7,470	5-M	4,906	253	46
Benedict Coll., Columbia, SC 29204	1870	$18,286	$8,104	2-B	2,641	NA	NA
Benedictine Coll., Atchison, KS 66002-1499	1859	$25,590	$9,050	2-M	2,138	181	60
Benedictine Univ., Lisle, IL 60532-0900	1887	$28,240	$8,526	2-D	6,307	719	51
Bentley Univ., Waltham, MA 02452-4705	1917	$42,511	$13,949	1-D	5,568	465	88
Berea Coll., Berea, KY 40404	1855	$870	$6,322	1-B	1,621	185	62
Berkeley Coll., Woodland Park, NJ 07424-3353	1931	$24,300	NA	3-M	3,659	429	NA
Berkeley Coll.–New York City campus, New York, NY 10017-4604	1936	$24,300	NA	3-B	4,029	NA	NA
Berklee Coll. of Music, Boston, MA 02215-3693	1945	NA	NA	1-M	4,521	569	52
Berry Coll., Mount Berry, GA 30149-0159	1902	$30,530	$10,660	2-M	2,177	225	62
Bethel Coll., Mishawaka, IN 46545-5591	1947	$26,590	$8,340	2-M	1,792	197	68
Bethel Univ., McKenzie, TN 38201	1842	$32,990	$9,440	2-M	5,553	420	34
Bethel Univ., St. Paul, MN 55112-6999	1871	$32,990	$9,440	2-D	4,884	285	73
Beth Medrash Govoha, Lakewood, NJ 08701-2797 (1)	1943	NA	NA	2-M	5,639	NA	NA
Bethune-Cookman Univ., Daytona Beach, FL 32114-3099	1904	$14,410	$8,548	2-M	4,045	278	50
Binghamton Univ., State Univ. of New York, Vestal, NY 13850	1946	$8,620(S)	$13,028	5-D	16,695	944	81
Biola Univ., La Mirada, CA 90639-0001	1908	$34,498	NA	2-D	6,358	527	71
Birmingham-Southern Coll., Birmingham, AL 35254	1856	$33,128	$11,350	2-B	1,231	114	65
Black Hills State Univ., Spearfish, SD 57799	1883	$7,617(S)	$6,330	5-M	4,489	235	30
Bloomfield Coll., Bloomfield, NJ 07003-9981	1868	$27,800	$11,300	2-M	2,012	217	32
Bloomsburg Univ. of Pennsylvania, Bloomsburg, PA 17815-1301	1839	$8,914(S)	$8,168	5-D	9,998	516	65
Bluefield State Coll., Bluefield, WV 24701-2198	1895	$5,832(S)	NA	5-B	1,563	130	33
Bluffton Univ., Bluffton, OH 45817	1899	$29,316	$9,832	2-M	1,094	100	67
Bob Jones Univ., Greenville, SC 29614	1927	$14,220	$6,090	2-D	3,108	220	64
Boise State Univ., Boise, ID 83725-0399	1932	$6,640(S)	$6,829	5-D	21,981	1,175	38
Boricua Coll., New York, NY 10032-1560	1974	$11,750	NA	1-M	1,058	133	49
Boston Coll., Chestnut Hill, MA 02467-3800	1863	$47,436	$13,186	2-D	13,575	1,477	91
Boston Univ., Boston, MA 02215	1839	$46,664	$14,030	1-D	32,112	2,650	84
Bowdoin Coll., Brunswick, ME 04011	1794	$46,808	$12,760	1-B	1,805	235	93
Bowie State Univ., Bowie, MD 20715-9465	1865	$7,299(S)	$10,432	5-D	5,561	408	40
Bowling Green State Univ., Bowling Green, OH 43403	1910	$10,726(S)	$8,244	5-D	16,554	1,015	54
Bradley Univ., Peoria, IL 61625-0002	1897	$30,844	$9,420	1-D	5,300	583	74
Brandeis Univ., Waltham, MA 02454-9110	1948	$47,558	$13,192	1-D	5,945	535	91
Brenau Univ., Gainesville, GA 30501 (3)	1878	$25,478	$11,998	1-M	2,789	326	49
Briarcliffe Coll., Bethpage, NY 11714	1966	NA	NA	3-B	1,779	NA	NA
Briar Cliff Univ., Sioux City, IA 51104-0100	1930	$27,212	$7,888	2-M	1,174	93	46
Bridgewater Coll., Bridgewater, VA 22812-1599	1880	$31,480	$11,520	2-B	1,785	145	67
Bridgewater State Univ., Bridgewater, MA 02325-0001	1840	$8,353(S)	$11,400	5-M	11,187	810	59
Brigham Young Univ., Provo, UT 84602-1001	1875	$5,000	$7,330	2-D	30,484	1,741	79
Brigham Young Univ.–Hawaii, Laie, HI 96762-1294	1955	$4,940	$5,746	2-B	2,555	228	52
Brigham Young Univ.–Idaho, Rexburg, ID 83460	1888	$3,650	$4,000	2-B	14,944	NA	NA
Brookline Coll., Phoenix, AZ 85021	1979	NA	NA	3-B	1,072	43	NA
Brooklyn Coll. of the City Univ. of New York, Brooklyn, NY 11210-2889	1930	$6,283(S)	$8,990	11-D	17,094	1,401	43
Brooks Inst., Ventura, CA 93001	1945	NA	NA	3-M	1,240	NA	NA
Brown Univ., Providence, RI 02912	1764	$47,434	$11,994	1-D	9,181	NA	94
Bryan Coll., Dayton, TN 37321	1930	$23,300	$6,690	2-M	1,627	121	54
Bryant & Stratton Coll.–Wauwatosa campus, Wauwatosa, WI 53226	1854	NA	NA	3-B	1,264	NA	NA
Bryant Univ., Smithfield, RI 02917	1863	$39,808	$14,553	1-M	3,462	275	78
Bryn Mawr Coll., Bryn Mawr, PA 19010-2899	1885	$47,140	$14,850	1-D	1,709	212	82
Bucknell Univ., Lewisburg, PA 17837	1846	$50,152	$12,216	1-M	3,624	419	89
Buffalo State Coll., State Univ. of New York, Buffalo, NY 14222-1095	1867	$7,347(S)	$11,964	5-M	11,083	839	46
Butler Univ., Indianapolis, IN 46208-3485	1855	$35,652	$11,620	1-D	4,848	557	78
Cabrini Coll., Radnor, PA 19087-3698	1957	$29,842	$12,226	2-M	2,203	277	46
Cairn Univ., Langhorne, PA 19047-2990	1913	$23,920	$9,350	2-M	1,062	106	64
Caldwell Univ., Caldwell, NJ 07006-6195	1939	$30,050	NA	2-D	2,183	278	62
California Baptist Univ., Riverside, CA 92504-3206	1950	$29,422	$9,370	2-M	7,957	623	55
California Coll. of the Arts, San Francisco, CA 94107	1907	$1,733/cr.	NA	1-M	1,998	484	61
California Coll. San Diego, San Diego, CA 92111	1978	NA	NA	3-B	1,299	NA	NA
California Inst. of Integral Studies, San Francisco, CA 94103	1968	$25,095	NA	1-D	1,256	179	NA
California Inst. of Tech., Pasadena, CA 91125-0001	1891	$43,362	$12,918	1-D	2,209	354	92
California Inst. of the Arts, Valencia, CA 91355-2340	1961	$43,976	$6,100	1-D	1,454	314	60
California Lutheran Univ., Thousand Oaks, CA 91360-2787	1959	$37,590	$12,400	2-D	4,160	443	66
California Polytechnic State Univ., San Luis Obispo, San Luis Obispo, CA 93407	1901	$8,919(S)	$11,447	5-M	20,186	1,345	78
California State Polytechnic Univ., Pomona, Pomona, CA 91768-2557	1938	$6,872(S)	$13,284	5-D	23,966	1,155	57
California State Univ., Bakersfield, Bakersfield, CA 93311	1970	NA	$10,926	5-M	8,720	NA	NA
California State Univ., Channel Islands, Camarillo, CA 93012	2002	NA	NA	5-D	3,599	294	NA
California State Univ., Chico, Chico, CA 95929-0722	1887	$8,532(S)	$11,626	5-M	17,462	968	56
California State Univ., Dominguez Hills, Carson, CA 90747-0001	1960	$6,134(S)	$10,956	5-M	14,687	793	33
California State Univ., East Bay, Hayward, CA 94542-3000	1957	$1,422/term(S)	$12,246	5-D	14,526	761	38
California State Univ., Fresno, Fresno, CA 93740-8027	1911	NA	$10,604	5-D	23,179	1,291	52
California State Univ., Fullerton, Fullerton, CA 92834-9480	1957	$6,316(S)	$13,510	5-D	38,128	2,044	56
California State Univ., Long Beach, Long Beach, CA 90840	1949	$6,420(S)	$11,688	5-D	36,809	2,149	65
California State Univ., Los Angeles, Los Angeles, CA 90032-8530	1947	$6,340(S)	$12,833	5-D	24,488	1,120	41
California State Univ., Monterey Bay, Seaside, CA 93955-8001	1994	$5,963(S)	$10,112	5-M	6,631	422	45
California State Univ., Northridge, Northridge, CA 91330	1958	$6,544(S)	$10,980	5-M	40,131	2,025	47

Name, address	Year founded	Tuition & fees	Room & board	Control, degree	Enroll-ment	Faculty	Grad. rate
California State Univ., Sacramento, Sacramento, CA 95819	1947	$6,602(S)	$6,538	5-D	29,349	1,491	44%
California State Univ., San Bernardino, San Bernardino, CA 92407-2397	1965	$6,558(S)	$9,933	5-D	18,952	923	41
California State Univ., San Marcos, San Marcos, CA 92096-0001	1990	$7,164(S)	NA	5-D	12,150	687	47
California State Univ., Stanislaus, Turlock, CA 95382	1957	$6,491(S)	$11,900	5-D	9,045	521	54
California Univ. of Pennsylvania, California, PA 15419-1394	1852	$9,556(S)	$10,086	5-M	7,978	391	53
Calumet Coll. of St. Joseph, Whiting, IN 46394-2195	1951	$16,440	NA	2-M	1,072	125	22
Calvin Coll., Grand Rapids, MI 49546-4388	1876	$29,635	$9,485	2-M	3,993	345	74
Cambridge Coll., Cambridge, MA 02138-5304	1971	NA	NA	1-D	3,757	453	NA
Cameron Univ., Lawton, OK 73505-6377	1908	$5,340(S)	$4,664	5-M	5,538	312	23
Campbellsville Univ., Campbellsville, KY 42718-2799	1906	$23,828	$7,770	2-M	3,484	310	39
Campbell Univ., Buies Creek, NC 27506	1887	$27,530	$9,860	2-D	4,743	305	52
Canisius Coll., Buffalo, NY 14208-1098	1870	$34,000	$12,516	2-M	4,181	406	68
Capella Univ., Minneapolis, MN 55402	1993	NA	NA	3-D	36,375	NA	NA
Capital Univ., Columbus, OH 43209-2394	1830	$31,990	$9,060	2-D	3,494	414	59
Cardinal Stritch Univ., Milwaukee, WI 53217-3985	1937	$26,570	$7,470	2-D	3,811	461	49
Caribbean Univ., Bayamón, PR 00960-0493	1969	$4,970	NA	1-D	4,486	466	29
Carleton Coll., Northfield, MN 55057-4001	1866	$47,736	$12,366	1-B	2,057	242	93
Carlos Albizu Univ., Miami campus, Miami, FL 33172-2209	1980	$12,384	NA	1-D	1,000	55	50
Carlow Univ., Pittsburgh, PA 15213-3165 (4)	1929	$26,178	$10,314	2-D	2,327	254	60
Carnegie Mellon Univ., Pittsburgh, PA 15213-3891	1900	$49,022	$12,400	1-D	12,991	1,017	88
Carroll Coll., Helena, MT 59625-0002	1909	$29,280	$8,950	2-B	1,430	165	63
Carroll Univ., Waukesha, WI 53186-5593	1846	$28,550	$8,550	2-D	3,385	330	57
Carson-Newman Univ., Jefferson City, TN 37760	1851	$25,360	$8,270	2-D	2,362	209	48
Carthage Coll., Kenosha, WI 53140	1847	$36,570	$9,970	2-M	2,778	NA	54
Case Western Reserve Univ., Cleveland, OH 44106	1826	$43,158	$13,376	1-D	10,771	940	81
Castleton State Coll., Castleton, VT 05735	1787	$10,772(S)	$9,414	5-M	2,184	228	50
Catawba Coll., Salisbury, NC 28144-2488	1851	$28,730	$10,360	2-M	1,316	143	53
The Catholic Univ. of America, Washington, DC 20064	1887	$39,726	$14,518	2-D	6,699	808	67
Cazenovia Coll., Cazenovia, NY 13035-1084	1824	$30,560	$12,344	1-B	1,091	129	58
Cedar Crest Coll., Allentown, PA 18104-6196 (4)	1867	$34,504	$10,549	2-M	1,531	159	73
Cedarville Univ., Cedarville, OH 45314-0601	1887	$27,206	$6,542	2-D	3,585	345	70
Centenary Coll., Hackettstown, NJ 07840-2100	1867	$30,942	$10,420	2-M	2,400	226	57
Central Coll., Pella, IA 50219	1853	$33,345	$9,980	2-B	1,411	101	68
Central Connecticut State Univ., New Britain, CT 06050-4010	1849	$8,877(S)	$10,872	5-D	12,037	952	52
Central Methodist Univ., Fayette, MO 65248-1198	1854	$22,360	$7,340	2-M	1,185	98	52
Central Michigan Univ., Mount Pleasant, MI 48859	1892	$11,550(S)	$8,780	5-D	27,002	1,136	55
Central Penn Coll., Summerdale, PA 17093-0309	1881	$16,659	$7,170	3-M	1,334	141	45
Central State Univ., Wilberforce, OH 45384	1887	$6,246(S)	$9,318	5-B	1,751	214	22
Central Washington Univ., Ellensburg, WA 98926	1891	$8,321(S)	$9,316	5-M	11,794	687	53
Centre Coll., Danville, KY 40422-1394	1819	$38,200	$9,620	2-B	1,387	146	82
Chadron State Coll., Chadron, NE 69337	1911	NA	NA	5-M	2,649	NA	NA
Chamberlain Coll. of Nursing, Addison, IL 60101-6106	2005	$17,760	NA	3-D	17,374	388	NA
Chaminade Univ. of Honolulu, Honolulu, HI 96816-1578	1955	$20,940	$11,640	2-M	1,976	148	48
Champlain Coll., Burlington, VT 05402-0670	1878	$32,900	$13,750	1-M	3,585	408	57
Chapman Univ., Orange, CA 92866	1861	$47,260	$13,830	2-D	8,132	914	74
Charleston Southern Univ., Charleston, SC 29423-8087	1964	$22,840	$9,000	2-M	3,367	275	34
Charter Oak State Coll., New Britain, CT 06053-2142	1973	$8,592(S)	NA	5-B	1,929	173	NA
Chatham Univ., Pittsburgh, PA 15232-2826 (4)	1869	$34,440	$10,720	1-D	2,134	319	56
Chestnut Hill Coll., Philadelphia, PA 19118-2693	1924	$33,120	$10,200	2-D	2,063	341	47
Cheyney Univ. of Pennsylvania, Cheyney, PA 19319	1837	$9,090(S)	$8,660	5-M	1,022	90	25
Chicago State Univ., Chicago, IL 60628	1867	$9,846(S)	$8,724	5-D	5,211	366	19
Chowan Univ., Murfreesboro, NC 27855	1848	$23,400	$8,680	2-M	1,484	105	25
Christian Brothers Univ., Memphis, TN 38104-5581	1871	$30,106	$7,000	2-M	1,670	179	55
Christopher Newport Univ., Newport News, VA 23606-3072	1960	$11,646(S)	$10,314	5-M	5,221	448	68
The Citadel, The Military Coll. of South Carolina, Charleston, SC 29409 (2)	1842	$12,568(S)	$6,381	5-M	3,592	289	69
City Coll. of the City Univ. of New York, New York, NY 10031-9198	1847	$6,330(S)	NA	11-D	15,620	1,611	42
City Univ. of Seattle, Seattle, WA 98121	1973	$15,090	NA	1-D	2,065	332	28
Claflin Univ., Orangeburg, SC 29115	1869	$15,010	$8,420	2-M	1,886	162	44
Claremont McKenna Coll., Claremont, CA 91711	1946	$47,395	$14,820	1-M	1,324	165	90
Clarion Univ. of Pennsylvania, Clarion, PA 16214	1867	$9,788(S)	$8,152	5-D	5,712	294	49
Clark Atlanta Univ., Atlanta, GA 30314	1865	$21,334	$10,262	2-D	3,485	281	41
Clarke Univ., Dubuque, IA 52001-3198	1843	$29,940	$9,000	2-D	1,200	156	68
Clarkson Univ., Potsdam, NY 13699	1896	$44,630	$13,844	1-D	3,873	300	73
Clark Univ., Worcester, MA 01610-1477	1887	$41,940	$8,200	1-D	3,423	300	78
Clayton State Univ., Morrow, GA 30260-0285	1969	$6,194(S)	$9,240	5-M	7,022	369	35
Clemson Univ., Clemson, SC 29634	1889	$13,808(S)	$8,358	5-D	21,303	1,199	83
Cleveland State Univ., Cleveland, OH 44115	1964	$9,686(S)	$11,858	5-D	17,301	1,070	32
Coastal Carolina Univ., Conway, SC 29528-6054	1954	$10,140(S)	$8,440	5-D	9,976	704	45
Coe Coll., Cedar Rapids, IA 52402-5092	1851	$37,320	$8,230	2-B	1,436	171	71
Coker Coll., Hartsville, SC 29550	1908	$25,536	$7,830	1-M	1,219	105	49
Colby Coll., Waterville, ME 04901-8840	1813	$47,350	$12,150	1-B	1,847	205	90
Colby-Sawyer Coll., New London, NH 03257	1837	$38,610	NA	1-B	1,369	137	54
Colegio Universitario de San Juan, San Juan, PR 00918	1971	NA	NA	10-B	1,785	NA	NA
Colgate Univ., Hamilton, NY 13346-1386	1819	$48,175	$11,970	1-M	2,898	344	91
The Coll. at Brockport, State Univ. of New York, Brockport, NY 14420-2997	1867	$7,562(S)	$11,440	5-M	8,106	596	68
Coll. for Creative Studies, Detroit, MI 48202-4034	1926	$38,950	$8,450	1-M	1,459	289	62
Coll. of Charleston, Charleston, SC 29424-0001	1770	$10,670(S)	$11,043	5-M	11,456	979	67
Coll. of Coastal Georgia, Brunswick, GA 31520	1961	$4,360(S)	$8,404	5-B	3,008	195	NA
The Coll. of Idaho, Caldwell, ID 83605	1891	$26,165	$8,990	1-M	1,144	131	59
Coll. of Mount St. Vincent, Riverdale, NY 10471-1093	1911	$30,290	$12,060	1-M	1,918	NA	52
The Coll. of New Jersey, Ewing, NJ 08628	1855	$15,024(S)	$11,677	5-M	7,409	820	86
The Coll. of New Rochelle, New Rochelle, NY 10805-2308 (4)	1904	$32,300	$12,200	1-M	1,478	202	36
Coll. of St. Benedict, Saint Joseph, MN 56374 (3)	1887	$39,402	$9,956	2-B	2,020	168	81
Coll. of St. Elizabeth, Morristown, NJ 07960-6989 (4)	1899	$31,095	$12,744	2-D	1,411	158	50
Coll. of St. Mary, Omaha, NE 68106 (3)	1923	$28,964	$7,400	2-D	1,018	167	49
The Coll. of St. Rose, Albany, NY 12203-1419	1920	$29,016	$11,532	1-M	4,509	355	66
The Coll. of St. Scholastica, Duluth, MN 55811-4199	1912	$33,994	$8,932	2-D	4,237	389	61
Coll. of Staten Island of the City Univ. of New York, Staten Island, NY 10314-6600	1955	$6,509(S)	$12,364	11-D	14,344	1,251	41
Coll. of the Holy Cross, Worcester, MA 01610-2395	1843	$47,176	$12,748	2-B	2,937	332	92
Coll. of the Ozarks, Point Lookout, MO 65726	1906	$310/cr. hr.	NA	2-B	1,433	136	63
The Coll. of William & Mary, Williamsburg, VA 23187-8795	1693	$17,656(S)	$10,344	5-D	8,437	NA	90
The Coll. of Wooster, Wooster, OH 44691-2363	1866	$43,350	$10,250	2-B	2,066	215	75
Colorado Christian Univ., Lakewood, CO 80226	1914	$25,046	$9,640	2-M	2,511	NA	NA
The Colorado Coll., Colorado Springs, CO 80903-3294	1874	$46,410	$10,752	1-M	2,067	202	86

Name, address	Year founded	Tuition & fees	Room & board	Control, degree	Enroll-ment	Faculty	Grad. rate
Colorado Mesa Univ., Grand Junction, CO 81501-3122	1925	$7,115(S)	$8,706	5-D	9,116	NA	32%
Colorado Mountain Coll., Glenwood Springs, CO 81601	1965	$1,860(A)	$8,164	9-B	2,465	NA	NA
Colorado Mountain Coll., Leadville, CO 80461	1965	$1,860(A)	$8,164	9-B	1,209	NA	NA
Colorado Mountain Coll., Steamboat Springs, CO 80487	1965	$1,860(A)	$8,164	9-B	1,550	NA	NA
Colorado Sch. of Mines, Golden, CO 80401-1887	1874	$16,918(S)	$10,484	5-D	5,795	504	76
Colorado State Univ., Fort Collins, CO 80523-0015	1870	$9,897(S)	$10,488	5-D	31,449	1,029	67
Colorado State Univ.–Pueblo, Pueblo, CO 81001-4901	1933	$7,834(S)	$9,016	5-M	7,256	372	32
Colorado Tech. Univ. Colorado Springs, Colorado Springs, CO 80907-3896	1965	NA	NA	3-D	2,359	343	NA
Colorado Tech. Univ. Online, Colorado Springs, CO 80907	NA	NA	NA	3-M	25,797	613	NA
Columbia Centro Universitario, Caguas, PR 00726	1966	$9,730	NA	3-M	1,864	145	32
Columbia Coll., Columbia, MO 65216-0002	1851	$20,936	$8,240	2-M	1,199	121	41
Columbia Coll., Columbia, SC 29203-5998 (4)	1854	$28,100	$7,400	2-D	1,227	151	66
Columbia Coll. Chicago, Chicago, IL 60605-1996	1890	$23,629	$12,450	1-M	9,442	1,460	43
Columbia Intl. Univ., Columbia, SC 29230-3122	1923	$20,430	$7,530	2-D	1,104	92	66
Columbia Southern Univ., Orange Beach, AL 36561	1993	$5,040	NA	3-M	20,305	548	NA
Columbia Univ., New York, NY 10027	1754	$51,008	$12,432	1-D	6,170	NA	96
Columbia Univ., Sch. of General Studies, New York, NY 10027-6939	1754	$49,476	$11,430	1-B	1,898	NA	NA
Columbus Coll. of Art & Design, Columbus, OH 43215-1758	1879	$29,892	$7,980	1-M	1,347	196	55
Columbus State Univ., Columbus, GA 31907-5645	1958	$6,898(S)	$8,880	5-D	8,164	500	31
Concord Univ., Athens, WV 24712-1000	1872	$6,580(S)	$7,818	5-M	2,563	212	34
Concordia Coll., Moorhead, MN 56562	1891	$35,464	$7,600	2-M	2,398	257	72
Concordia Univ., Irvine, CA 92612-3299	1972	$31,690	$9,890	2-D	4,311	409	56
Concordia Univ., Portland, OR 97211-6099	1905	$27,420	$8,030	2-M	3,111	259	45
Concordia Univ. Chicago, River Forest, IL 60305-1499	1864	$29,450	$8,992	2-D	5,038	426	59
Concordia Univ. Nebraska, Seward, NE 68434-1556	1894	$27,110	$7,260	2-M	2,332	250	66
Concordia Univ. St. Paul, St. Paul, MN 55104-5494	1893	$20,750	$8,300	2-D	4,057	419	46
Concordia Univ. Texas, Austin, TX 78726	1926	$28,160	$9,284	2-M	2,504	302	35
Concordia Univ. Wisconsin, Mequon, WI 53097-2402	1881	$26,160	$9,780	2-D	8,161	565	61
Connecticut Coll., New London, CT 06320-4196	1911	$47,740	$13,155	1-M	1,900	254	83
Converse Coll., Spartanburg, SC 29302-0006	1889	$16,500	$9,500	1-M	1,335	84	62
Coppin State Univ., Baltimore, MD 21216-3698	1900	$4,889(S)	$9,236	5-M	3,800	312	15
Corban Univ., Salem, OR 97301-9392	1935	$28,640	$8,892	2-D	1,212	104	56
Cornell Coll., Mount Vernon, IA 52314-1098	1853	$37,725	$8,500	2-B	1,075	118	68
Cornell Univ., Ithaca, NY 14853-0001	1865	$47,286	$13,678	1-D	21,850	2,086	93
Cornerstone Univ., Grand Rapids, MI 49525-5897	1941	$25,112	$8,226	2-M	2,770	121	47
Covenant Coll., Lookout Mountain, GA 30750	1955	$30,160	$8,830	2-M	1,173	95	57
Creighton Univ., Omaha, NE 68178-0001	1878	$35,360	$9,996	2-D	8,236	827	78
Crown Coll., St. Bonifacius, MN 55375-9001	1916	$22,430	$7,480	2-M	1,269	160	50
The Culinary Inst. of America, Hyde Park, NY 12538-1499	1946	$28,240	$9,652	1-B	2,778	222	NA
Cumberland Univ., Lebanon, TN 37087	1842	$21,210	$7,550	1-M	1,481	159	37
Curry Coll., Milton, MA 02186-9984	1879	$36,445	$13,900	1-M	3,141	484	45
Daemen Coll., Amherst, NY 14226-3592	1947	$25,995	$12,050	1-D	2,800	289	48
Dakota State Univ., Madison, SD 57042-1799	1881	$8,286(S)	$5,941	5-D	3,047	133	41
Dallas Baptist Univ., Dallas, TX 75211-9299	1965	$23,650	$6,930	2-D	5,445	618	55
Dalton State Coll., Dalton, GA 30720	1963	$3,355(S)	$6,720	5-B	5,047	215	15
Dartmouth Coll., Hanover, NH 03755	1769	$48,108	$13,839	1-D	6,298	748	95
Davenport Univ., Grand Rapids, MI 49512	1866	$15,072	$9,840	1-M	10,221	874	37
Davidson Coll., Davidson, NC 28035	1837	$45,377	$12,769	2-B	1,770	186	93
Delaware State Univ., Dover, DE 19901-2277	1891	$7,336(S)	$10,708	5-D	4,397	NA	43
Delaware Valley Univ., Doylestown, PA 18901-2697	1896	$32,890	$11,977	1-M	2,253	195	55
Delta State Univ., Cleveland, MS 38733-0001	1924	$6,562(S)	$7,200	5-D	3,614	256	35
Denison Univ., Granville, OH 43023	1831	$47,290	$11,570	1-B	2,280	236	81
DePaul Univ., Chicago, IL 60604-2287	1898	$35,071	$12,552	2-D	23,799	1,872	71
DePauw Univ., Greencastle, IN 46135	1837	$42,746	$11,200	2-B	2,216	239	80
DeSales Univ., Center Valley, PA 18034-9568	1964	$32,350	$11,760	2-D	3,198	349	70
DeVry Coll. of New York, New York, NY 10016-5267	1998	$17,132	NA	3-M	1,526	98	NA
DeVry Univ., Chicago, IL 60618-5994	1931	$17,132	NA	3-M	1,294	164	NA
DeVry Univ., Columbus, OH 43209-2705	1952	$17,132	NA	3-M	1,971	65	NA
DeVry Univ., Decatur, GA 30030-2556	1969	$17,132	NA	3-M	1,921	148	NA
DeVry Univ., North Brunswick, NJ 08902-3362	1969	$17,132	NA	3-M	1,076	146	NA
DeVry Univ., Orlando, FL 32839	2000	$17,132	NA	3-M	1,205	48	NA
DeVry Univ., Pomona, CA 91768-2642	1983	$17,132	NA	3-M	1,729	96	NA
DeVry Univ. Online, Addison, IL 60101-6106	2000	$17,132	NA	3-M	20,432	2,500	NA
Dickinson Coll., Carlisle, PA 17013-2896	1773	$47,692	$11,972	1-B	2,364	247	84
Dickinson State Univ., Dickinson, ND 58601-4896	1918	$6,050(S)	$5,850	5-B	1,479	161	38
Dillard Univ., New Orleans, LA 70122-3097	1869	$16,094	$9,314	2-B	1,183	137	46
Dixie State Univ., St. George, UT 84770-3876	1911	$4,454(S)	$5,918	5-B	8,570	550	22
Doane Coll., Crete, NE 68333-2430	1872	$27,200	$8,030	2-M	1,067	125	59
Dominican Coll., Orangeburg, NY 10962-1210	1952	$26,450	$12,200	1-D	1,971	236	36
Dominican Univ., River Forest, IL 60305-1099	1901	$30,670	$9,380	2-D	3,498	431	63
Dominican Univ. of California, San Rafael, CA 94901-2298	1890	$42,550	$13,380	2-M	2,001	326	62
Dordt Coll., Sioux Center, IA 51250-1697	1955	$26,540	$7,620	2-M	1,405	105	62
Dowling Coll., Oakdale, NY 11769-1999	1955	$29,100	$10,770	1-D	2,453	241	34
Drake Univ., Des Moines, IA 50311-4516	1881	$32,246	$9,270	1-D	5,062	430	78
Drew Univ., Madison, NJ 07940-1493	1867	$45,214	$12,302	2-D	2,113	268	62
Drexel Univ., Philadelphia, PA 19104-2875	1891	$47,051	$14,367	1-D	26,359	2,168	67
Drury Univ., Springfield, MO 65802	1873	$23,885	$7,394	1-M	1,751	174	71
Duke Univ., Durham, NC 27708-0586	1838	$48,562	$12,576	2-D	15,386	1,335	94
Duquesne Univ., Pittsburgh, PA 15282-0001	1878	$32,636	$11,084	2-D	9,648	993	76
D'Youville Coll., Buffalo, NY 14201-1084	1908	$23,462	$10,800	1-D	3,067	310	44
Earlham Coll., Richmond, IN 47374-4095	1847	$42,870	$8,600	2-M	1,074	120	72
East Carolina Univ., Greenville, NC 27858-4353	1907	$6,143(S)	$8,833	5-D	27,511	1,484	59
East Central Univ., Ada, OK 74820	1909	$5,599(S)	$5,158	5-M	4,428	285	34
East Stroudsburg Univ. of Pennsylvania, East Stroudsburg, PA 18301-2999	1893	$9,376(S)	$7,980	5-M	6,778	316	56
East Tennessee State Univ., Johnson City, TN 37614	1911	$7,985(S)	$7,822	5-D	14,434	897	43
East Texas Baptist Univ., Marshall, TX 75670-1498	1912	$23,280	$8,297	2-M	1,299	118	38
Eastern Connecticut State Univ., Willimantic, CT 06226-2295	1889	$9,560(S)	$11,650	5-M	5,287	470	56
Eastern Illinois Univ., Charleston, IL 61920	1895	$11,108(S)	$9,358	5-M	8,913	665	59
Eastern Kentucky Univ., Richmond, KY 40475-3102	1906	$8,150(S)	$4,562	5-D	16,305	1,178	42
Eastern Mennonite Univ., Harrisonburg, VA 22802-2462	1917	$30,800	$9,860	2-M	1,640	204	63
Eastern Michigan Univ., Ypsilanti, MI 48197	1849	$9,663(S)	$8,940	5-D	22,261	1,342	37
Eastern Nazarene Coll., Quincy, MA 02170	1918	$27,922	$8,700	2-M	1,036	122	52
Eastern New Mexico Univ., Portales, NM 88130	1934	$4,856(S)	$6,452	5-M	5,887	330	27
Eastern Oregon Univ., La Grande, OR 97850-2899	1929	$7,440(S)	$9,642	5-M	3,653	112	23
Eastern Univ., St. Davids, PA 19087-3696	1952	$30,590	$10,188	2-D	3,762	564	62

Name, address	Year founded	Tuition & fees	Room & board	Control, degree	Enroll-ment	Faculty	Grad. rate
Eastern Washington Univ., Cheney, WA 99004-2431	1882	$7,982(S)	$9,628	5-D	12,791	687	45%
Eckerd Coll., St. Petersburg, FL 33711	1958	$38,668	$10,550	2-B	1,802	171	65
ECPI Univ., Virginia Beach, VA 23462	1966	NA	NA	3-B	13,717	1,371	NA
Edgewood Coll., Madison, WI 53711-1997	1927	$25,590	$8,973	2-D	2,980	307	62
Edinboro Univ. of Pennsylvania, Edinboro, PA 16444	1857	$9,197(S)	$8,612	5-D	6,837	371	49
EDP Univ. of Puerto Rico, Hato Rey, PR 00918	1968	$5,940	NA	3-M	1,568	156	18
EDP Univ. of Puerto Rico–San Sebastian, San Sebastian, PR 00685	1976	$5,940	NA	3-M	1,204	99	NA
Elizabeth City State Univ., Elizabeth City, NC 27909-7806	1891	$4,428(S)	$7,213	5-M	2,421	211	NA
Elizabethtown Coll., Elizabethtown, PA 17022-2298	1899	$41,710	$10,140	2-M	1,822	195	69
Elmhurst Coll., Elmhurst, IL 60126-3296	1871	$34,450	$9,666	2-M	3,257	360	74
Elmira Coll., Elmira, NY 14901	1855	$39,950	$12,000	1-M	1,482	156	59
Elms Coll., Chicopee, MA 01013-2839	1928	$32,335	$11,708	2-D	1,717	181	70
Elon Univ., Elon, NC 27244-2010	1889	$31,247	$10,667	2-D	6,483	558	81
Embry-Riddle Aeron Univ.–Daytona, Daytona Beach, FL 32114-3900	1926	$33,218	$10,382	1-D	5,538	NA	52
Embry-Riddle Aeron Univ.–Prescott, Prescott, AZ 86301-3720	1978	$33,144	$9,900	1-M	2,035	NA	58
Embry-Riddle Aeron Univ.–Worldwide, Daytona Beach, FL 32114-3900	1970	$8,040	$5,244	1-D	15,173	NA	NA
Emerson Coll., Boston, MA 02116-4624	1880	$39,036	$15,700	1-D	4,533	456	80
Emmanuel Coll., Boston, MA 02115	1919	$35,532	$13,580	2-M	2,311	231	64
Emory & Henry Coll., Emory, VA 24327-0947	1836	$30,900	$10,510	2-M	1,038	130	48
Emory Univ., Atlanta, GA 30322-1100	1836	$46,314	$13,130	2-D	14,769	1,526	91
Emporia State Univ., Emporia, KS 66801-5415	1863	$5,746(S)	$7,582	5-D	6,114	276	39
Endicott Coll., Beverly, MA 01915-2096	1939	$29,494	$13,734	1-D	4,655	429	73
Eugene Lang Coll. The New Sch. for Liberal Arts, New York, NY 10011-8601	1978	$38,570	$17,300	1-B	1,487	147	57
Evangel Univ., Springfield, MO 65802	1955	$20,796	$7,200	2-D	2,000	NA	47
Everest Univ., Pompano Beach, FL 33062	1940	NA	NA	1-M	1,633	NA	NA
Everest Univ., Tampa, FL 33614-5899	1890	NA	NA	1-M	3,430	61	NA
Everglades Univ., Boca Raton, FL 33431	1989	NA	NA	1-M	1,039	NA	NA
Everglades Univ., Sarasota, FL 34240	2003	$16,000	NA	1-M	1,451	229	58
The Evergreen State Coll., Olympia, WA 98505	1967	$8,523(S)	$9,492	5-M	4,219	224	56
Excelsior Coll., Albany, NY 12203-5159	1970	$465/cr. hr.	NA	1-M	38,825	NA	NA
Fairfield Univ., Fairfield, CT 06824	1942	$44,875	$13,520	2-D	5,123	611	80
Fairleigh Dickinson Univ., Coll. at Florham, Madison, NJ 07940-1099	1942	$37,344	$12,294	1-D	3,233	NA	56
Fairleigh Dickinson Univ., Metropolitan campus, Teaneck, NJ 07666-1914	1942	$35,740	$12,630	1-D	8,774	NA	49
Fairmont State Univ., Fairmont, WV 26554	1865	$6,306(S)	$7,800	5-M	4,035	325	34
Farmingdale State Coll., Farmingdale, NY 11735	1912	$7,483(S)	$12,190	5-B	8,394	658	43
Fashion Inst. of Tech., New York, NY 10001-5992 (4)	1944	$5,200(S)	$13,162	11-M	9,764	944	NA
Faulkner Univ., Montgomery, AL 36109-3398	1942	$18,750	$6,970	2-D	3,335	247	30
Fayetteville State Univ., Fayetteville, NC 28301-4298	1867	$2,743(S)	$6,445	5-D	5,899	320	35
Felician Coll., Lodi, NJ 07644-2117	1942	$30,605	$11,650	2-D	1,933	223	46
Ferris State Univ., Big Rapids, MI 49307	1884	$11,190(S)	$9,208	5-D	14,600	798	51
Ferrum Coll., Ferrum, VA 24088	1913	$29,795	$9,970	2-B	1,451	116	25
Fisher Coll., Boston, MA 02116-1500	1903	$29,937	$15,082	1-M	1,875	183	35
Fitchburg State Univ., Fitchburg, MA 01420-2697	1894	$9,260(S)	$8,840	5-M	6,818	304	50
Flagler Coll., St. Augustine, FL 32085-1027	1968	$16,900	$9,350	1-B	2,774	228	58
Florida Agr. & Mech. Univ., Tallahassee, FL 32307-3200	1887	$5,784(S)	$9,576	5-D	10,241	791	41
Florida Atlantic Univ., Boca Raton, FL 33431-0991	1961	$6,039(S)	$11,924	5-D	30,364	1,248	46
Florida Gulf Coast Univ., Fort Myers, FL 33965-6565	1991	$6,118(S)	$8,359	5-D	14,492	709	49
Florida Inst. of Tech., Melbourne, FL 32901-6975	1958	$37,990	$12,826	1-D	6,393	517	55
Florida Intl. Univ., Miami, FL 33199	1965	$6,497(S)	$10,702	5-D	49,703	2,255	54
Florida Memorial Univ., Miami-Dade, FL 33054	1879	$14,776	$6,112	2-M	1,750	173	33
Florida Natl Univ., Hialeah, FL 33012	1982	$525/cr.	NA	3-M	2,401	139	64
Florida Southern Coll., Lakeland, FL 33801-5698	1885	$29,990	$10,000	2-D	2,439	239	65
Florida State Univ., Tallahassee, FL 32306	1851	$6,507(S)	$10,208	5-D	41,226	1,670	77
Fontbonne Univ., St. Louis, MO 63105-3098	1917	$23,790	$8,811	2-M	1,819	250	48
Fordham Univ., New York, NY 10458	1841	$47,317	$16,350	2-D	15,231	1,598	80
Fort Hays State Univ., Hays, KS 67601-4099	1902	$3,314(S)	$7,130	5-M	13,825	522	42
Fort Lewis Coll., Durango, CO 81301-3999	1911	$7,601(S)	$9,130	5-M	3,776	239	38
Fort Valley State Univ., Fort Valley, GA 31030	1895	$6,448(S)	$7,920	5-M	2,594	142	31
Framingham State Univ., Framingham, MA 01701-9101	1839	$8,320(S)	$10,543	5-M	6,499	359	51
Franciscan Univ. of Steubenville, Steubenville, OH 43952-1763	1946	$24,780	$8,300	2-M	2,714	232	75
Francis Marion Univ., Florence, SC 29502-0547	1970	$9,738(S)	$7,256	5-M	3,944	292	41
Franklin & Marshall Coll., Lancaster, PA 17604-3003	1787	$48,514	$12,285	1-B	2,209	276	87
Franklin Coll., Franklin, IN 46131	1834	$29,025	$8,650	2-M	1,075	109	61
Franklin Pierce Univ., Rindge, NH 03461-0060	1962	$31,782	$12,060	1-D	2,204	334	45
Franklin Univ., Columbus, OH 43215-5399	1902	$13,920	NA	1-M	5,734	814	13
Freed-Hardeman Univ., Henderson, TN 38340-2399	1869	$20,468	$7,390	2-D	1,811	150	54
Fresno Pacific Univ., Fresno, CA 93702-4709	1944	$26,638	$7,360	2-M	3,483	427	54
Friends Univ., Wichita, KS 67213	1898	$24,630	$7,320	2-M	1,882	231	38
Frostburg State Univ., Frostburg, MD 21532-1099	1898	$8,488(S)	$8,574	5-D	5,645	386	49
Full Sail Univ., Winter Park, FL 32792-7437 (2)	1979	NA	NA	3-M	8,921	702	NA
Furman Univ., Greenville, SC 29613	1826	$44,668	$11,204	1-M	2,973	259	84
Gallaudet Univ., Washington, DC 20002-3625	1864	$15,604	$12,630	1-D	1,488	308	46
Gannon Univ., Erie, PA 16541-0001	1925	$28,368	$11,240	2-D	4,410	377	65
Gardner-Webb Univ., Boiling Springs, NC 28017	1905	$26,885	$8,780	2-D	4,636	300	56
Geneva Coll., Beaver Falls, PA 15010-3599	1848	$25,450	$9,630	2-M	1,568	191	65
George Fox Univ., Newberg, OR 97132-2697	1891	$31,866	$9,864	2-D	3,712	415	62
George Mason Univ., Fairfax, VA 22030	1957	$10,382(S)	$10,100	5-D	33,723	2,546	67
The George Washington Univ., Washington, DC 20052	1821	$50,435	$12,050	1-D	25,613	NA	80
Georgetown Coll., Georgetown, KY 40324-1696	1829	$32,960	$8,480	2-M	1,262	155	55
Georgetown Univ., Washington, DC 20057	1789	$46,744	$14,024	2-D	17,858	1,975	95
Georgia Coll. & State Univ., Milledgeville, GA 31061	1889	$8,960(S)	$9,940	5-D	6,772	411	61
Georgia Gwinnett Coll., Lawrenceville, GA 30043	2006	$5,262(S)	$11,494	5-B	10,828	602	27
Georgia Inst. of Tech., Atlanta, GA 30332-0001	1885	$11,394(S)	$12,840	5-D	23,109	1,153	82
Georgia Regents Univ., Augusta, GA 30912	1828	NA	NA	5-D	7,957	1,483	NA
Georgia Southern Univ., Statesboro, GA 30460	1906	$7,190(S)	$9,752	5-D	20,517	889	51
Georgia Southwestern State Univ., Americus, GA 31709-4693	1906	$6,070(S)	$8,350	5-M	2,666	154	32
Georgia State Univ., Atlanta, GA 30302-3083	1913	$10,240(S)	$13,342	5-D	32,542	1,711	54
Georgian Court Univ., Lakewood, NJ 08701-2697	1908	$30,998	$10,596	2-M	2,308	236	48
Gettysburg Coll., Gettysburg, PA 17325-1483	1832	$47,480	$11,340	2-B	2,451	312	84
Glenville State Coll., Glenville, WV 26351-1200	1872	$6,384(S)	$8,810	5-B	1,850	111	30
Global Univ., Springfield, MO 65804	1948	$3,870	NA	2-D	4,551	633	NA
Golden Gate Univ., San Francisco, CA 94105-2968	1901	NA	NA	1-D	3,528	489	NA
Goldey-Beacom Coll., Wilmington, DE 19808-1999	1886	$22,140	$5,353	1-M	1,352	56	49
Gonzaga Univ., Spokane, WA 99258	1887	$37,990	$10,835	2-D	7,352	728	83
Gordon Coll., Wenham, MA 01984-1899	1889	$34,390	$9,930	2-M	2,079	196	71
Goucher Coll., Baltimore, MD 21204-2794	1885	$40,558	$11,482	1-M	2,114	179	63

Name, address	Year founded	Tuition & fees	Room & board	Control, degree	Enroll-ment	Faculty	Grad. rate
Governors State Univ., University Park, IL 60484	1969	$9,386(S)	$9,000	5-D	5,776	443	NA
Grace Coll., Winona Lake, IN 46590-1294	1948	$24,670	$7,930	2-D	2,185	164	65%
Graceland Univ., Lamoni, IA 50140	1895	$25,890	$8,100	2-D	2,407	192	54
Grambling State Univ., Grambling, LA 71245	1901	$6,644(S)	$9,372	5-D	4,504	225	31
Grand Valley State Univ., Allendale, MI 49401-9403	1960	$10,752(S)	$8,200	5-D	25,094	1,726	70
Grand View Univ., Des Moines, IA 50316-1599	1896	$24,454	$7,866	2-M	2,064	216	47
Granite State Coll., Concord, NH 03301	1972	$7,065(S)	NA	11-M	2,208	202	50
Grantham Univ., Lenexa, KS 66219	1951	NA	NA	3-M	9,463	10	NA
Greensboro Coll., Greensboro, NC 27401-1875	1838	$26,900	$10,100	2-M	1,264	96	43
Greenville Coll., Greenville, IL 62246-0159	1892	$25,088	$8,288	2-M	1,307	182	50
Grinnell Coll., Grinnell, IA 50112-1690	1846	$46,023	$10,997	1-B	1,734	199	89
Grove City Coll., Grove City, PA 16127-2104	1876	$15,550	$8,472	2-B	2,509	215	83
Guilford Coll., Greensboro, NC 27410-4173	1837	$33,430	$9,370	2-B	2,137	181	61
Gustavus Adolphus Coll., St. Peter, MN 56082-1498	1862	$40,080	$9,250	2-B	2,456	255	82
Gwynedd Mercy Univ., Gwynedd Valley, PA 19437-0901	1948	$31,360	$11,010	2-D	2,477	316	67
Hamilton Coll., Clinton, NY 13323-1296	1812	$47,820	$12,150	1-B	1,900	230	91
Hamline Univ., St. Paul, MN 55104-1284	1854	$36,270	$9,392	2-D	4,469	426	65
Hampden-Sydney Coll., Hampden-Sydney, VA 23943 (1)	1776	$39,604	$12,312	2-B	1,105	105	67
Hampshire Coll., Amherst, MA 01002	1965	$49,360	$12,950	1-B	1,376	158	74
Hampton Univ., Hampton, VA 23668	1868	$21,760	$9,692	1-D	4,397	NA	66
Hannibal-LaGrange Univ., Hannibal, MO 63401-1999	1858	$20,710	$7,608	2-M	1,252	138	48
Hanover Coll., Hanover, IN 47243-0108	1827	$34,514	$10,452	2-B	1,145	104	69
Harding Univ., Searcy, AR 72149-0001	1924	$17,040	$6,516	2-D	6,238	499	64
Hardin-Simmons Univ., Abilene, TX 79698-0001	1891	$24,500	$7,740	2-D	2,084	201	53
Harrison Coll., Indianapolis, IN 46204	1902	NA	NA	3-B	3,756	290	33
Harris-Stowe State Univ., St. Louis, MO 63103-2136	1857	$5,220(S)	$9,250	5-B	1,280	166	8
Hartwick Coll., Oneonta, NY 13820-4020	1797	$40,070	$10,800	1-B	1,540	200	61
Harvard Univ., Cambridge, MA 02138	1636	$43,938	$14,669	1-D	10,803	1,164	98
Hastings Coll., Hastings, NE 68901	1882	$27,300	$8,080	2-M	1,212	119	59
Haverford Coll., Haverford, PA 19041-1392	1833	$49,098	$14,888	1-B	1,194	158	94
Hawai`i Pacific Univ., Honolulu, HI 96813	1965	$22,360	$13,610	1-M	5,827	515	42
Heidelberg Univ., Tiffin, OH 44883-2462	1850	$27,480	$9,226	2-M	1,337	153	47
Henderson State Univ., Arkadelphia, AR 71999-0001	1890	$7,561(S)	$6,350	5-M	3,583	240	29
Hendrix Coll., Conway, AR 72032-3080	1876	$40,870	$11,244	2-M	1,358	147	71
Heritage Univ., Toppenish, WA 98948-9599	1982	$18,566	NA	1-M	1,241	185	16
High Point Univ., High Point, NC 27268	1924	$32,430	$12,000	2-D	4,399	381	63
Hilbert Coll., Hamburg, NY 14075-1597	1957	$20,650	$9,160	1-M	1,012	124	45
Hillsdale Coll., Hillsdale, MI 49242-1298	1844	$24,591	$9,760	1-D	1,504	173	82
Hiram Coll., Hiram, OH 44234-0067	1850	$31,530	$10,190	1-M	1,259	149	63
Hobart & William Smith Colls., Geneva, NY 14456-3397	1822	$47,908	$12,126	1-M	2,425	234	79
Hodges Univ., Naples, FL 34119	1990	$13,220	NA	1-M	1,882	127	NA
Hofstra Univ., Hempstead, NY 11549	1935	$38,900	$13,510	1-D	10,953	1,157	60
Holy Family Univ., Philadelphia, PA 19114	1954	$29,168	$13,576	2-D	2,623	356	52
Holy Names Univ., Oakland, CA 94619-1699	1868	$34,488	$10,914	2-M	1,343	207	35
Hood Coll., Frederick, MD 21701-8575	1893	$35,150	$11,840	1-M	2,365	265	71
Hope Coll., Holland, MI 49422-9000	1866	$30,550	$9,390	2-B	3,455	382	79
Hope Intl. Univ., Fullerton, CA 92831-3138	1928	$28,550	$9,050	2-M	1,276	254	49
Houghton Coll., Houghton, NY 14744	1883	$28,556	$8,252	2-M	1,078	128	76
Houston Baptist Univ., Houston, TX 77074-3298	1960	$29,800	$7,715	2-M	3,128	240	44
Howard Payne Univ., Brownwood, TX 76801-2715	1889	$25,600	$7,489	2-M	1,137	147	45
Howard Univ., Washington, DC 20059-0002	1867	$23,970	$13,646	1-D	10,265	1,520	60
Humboldt State Univ., Arcata, CA 95521-8299	1913	$372/cr.(S)	$12,114	5-M	8,485	570	44
Hunter Coll. of the City Univ. of New York, New York, NY 10065-5085	1870	$275/cr.(S)	NA	11-D	23,112	2,218	52
Huntingdon Coll., Montgomery, AL 36106-2148	1854	$24,550	$8,550	2-B	1,160	109	45
Huntington Univ., Huntington, IN 46750-1299	1897	$24,771	$8,306	2-M	1,134	106	62
Husson Univ., Bangor, ME 04401-2999	1898	$16,060	$8,922	1-D	3,414	355	41
Huston-Tillotson Univ., Austin, TX 78702-2795	1875	$13,544	$7,568	2-M	1,031	87	31
Idaho State Univ., Pocatello, ID 83209	1901	$6,566(S)	$5,963	5-D	13,804	794	30
Illinois Inst. of Tech., Chicago, IL 60616-3793	1890	$42,000	NA	1-D	7,898	824	65
Illinois State Univ., Normal, IL 61790-2200	1857	$13,296(S)	$9,816	5-D	20,615	1,247	72
Illinois Wesleyan Univ., Bloomington, IL 61702-2900	1850	$40,844	$9,446	1-B	1,893	214	81
Immaculata Univ., Immaculata, PA 19345	1920	$32,000	$12,880	2-D	3,299	398	61
Indian River State Coll., Fort Pierce, FL 34981-5596	1960	$2,492(S)	$5,700	5-B	17,665	859	NA
Indiana State Univ., Terre Haute, IN 47809	1865	$8,416(S)	$9,182	5-D	13,183	703	40
Indiana Tech., Fort Wayne, IN 46803-1297	1930	$24,860	$9,521	1-D	6,355	510	35
Indiana Univ. Bloomington, Bloomington, IN 47405-7000	1820	$10,388(S)	$9,493	5-D	46,416	2,404	78
Indiana Univ. East, Richmond, IN 47374-1289	1971	$6,787(S)	NA	5-M	4,573	299	27
Indiana Univ. Kokomo, Kokomo, IN 46904-9003	1945	$6,810(S)	NA	5-M	4,180	220	27
Indiana Univ. Northwest, Gary, IN 46408-1197	1959	$6,853(S)	NA	5-M	6,052	386	29
Indiana Univ. of Pennsylvania, Indiana, PA 15705-1087	1875	$9,470(S)	$11,346	5-D	14,369	725	51
Indiana Univ.–Purdue Univ. Fort Wayne, Fort Wayne, IN 46805-1499	1917	$7,949(S)	$7,632	5-M	13,214	801	25
Indiana Univ.–Purdue Univ. Indianapolis, Indianapolis, IN 46202	1969	$8,909(S)	$7,981	5-D	30,690	3,302	44
Indiana Univ. South Bend, South Bend, IN 46634-7111	1922	$6,905(S)	$7,150	5-M	7,859	485	26
Indiana Univ. Southeast, New Albany, IN 47150-6405	1941	$6,827(S)	$6,280	5-M	6,442	499	32
Indiana Wesleyan Univ., Marion, IN 46953-4974	1920	$24,102	$3,797	2-D	3,018	290	71
Inter Amer. Univ. of Puerto Rico, Aguadilla campus, Aguadilla, PR 00605	1957	$4,814	NA	1-M	4,668	255	26
Inter Amer. Univ. of Puerto Rico, Arecibo campus, Arecibo, PR 00614-4050	1957	$4,852	NA	1-M	4,878	298	NA
Inter Amer. Univ. of Puerto Rico, Barranquitas campus, Barranquitas, PR 00794	1957	$4,660	NA	1-M	2,418	135	NA
Inter Amer. Univ. of Puerto Rico, Bayamón campus, Bayamón, PR 00957	1912	$5,860	NA	1-M	4,825	295	27
Inter Amer. Univ. of Puerto Rico, Fajardo campus, Fajardo, PR 00738-7003	1965	$178/cr.	NA	1-M	2,115	105	NA
Inter Amer. Univ. of Puerto Rico, Guayama campus, Guayama, PR 00785	1958	$5,534	NA	1-M	2,151	183	29
Inter Amer. Univ. of Puerto Rico, Metropolitan campus, San Juan, PR 00919-1293	1960	$7,011	NA	1-D	NA	590	28
Inter Amer. Univ. of Puerto Rico, Ponce campus, Mercedita, PR 00715-1602	1962	$4,866	NA	1-M	5,734	295	28
Inter Amer. Univ. of Puerto Rico, San Germán campus, San Germán, PR 00683-5008	1912	$5,920	$2,700	1-D	5,123	281	37
Iona Coll., New Rochelle, NY 10801-1890	1940	$34,030	$13,570	2-M	3,909	352	58
Iowa State Univ. of Sci. & Tech., Ames, IA 50011	1858	$7,736(S)	$8,070	5-D	34,435	1,802	69
Ithaca Coll., Ithaca, NY 14850	1892	$39,532	$14,332	1-D	6,587	778	78
Jackson State Univ., Jackson, MS 39217	1877	$6,602(S)	NA	5-D	9,508	564	43
Jacksonville State Univ., Jacksonville, AL 36265-1602	1883	$8,790(S)	$6,985	5-D	8,659	466	30
Jacksonville Univ., Jacksonville, FL 32211	1934	$31,370	$10,820	1-D	4,085	335	39
James Madison Univ., Harrisonburg, VA 22807	1908	$9,662(S)	$8,828	5-D	20,853	1,487	82
Jefferson Coll. of Health Sciences, Roanoke, VA 24013	1982	$23,380	$7,670	1-M	1,131	140	37
John Brown Univ., Siloam Springs, AR 72761-2121	1919	$24,468	$8,664	2-M	2,400	200	61

Name, address	Year founded	Tuition & fees	Room & board	Control, degree	Enroll-ment	Faculty	Grad. rate
John Carroll Univ., University Heights, OH 44118-4581	1886	$37,180	$10,920	2-M	3,700	423	71%
John F. Kennedy Univ., Pleasant Hill, CA 94523-4817 (4)	1964	$11,472	NA	1-D	1,580	237	NA
John Jay Coll. of Criminal Justice of the City Univ. of New York, New York, NY 10019-1093	1964	$6,059(S)	NA	11-M	15,008	NA	43
Johns Hopkins Univ., Baltimore, MD 21218-2699	1876	$49,210	$14,540	1-D	7,306	677	94
Johnson & Wales Univ., Charlotte, NC 28202	2004	$29,576	NA	1-B	2,255	120	49
Johnson & Wales Univ., Denver, CO 80220	1993	$29,576	NA	1-M	1,391	114	47
Johnson & Wales Univ., North Miami, FL 33181	1992	$29,576	NA	1-B	1,904	109	37
Johnson & Wales Univ., Providence, RI 02903-3703	1914	$29,576	NA	1-D	9,955	604	54
Johnson C. Smith Univ., Charlotte, NC 28216-5398	1867	$18,236	$7,100	1-M	1,402	173	43
Johnson State Coll., Johnson, VT 05656	1828	$9,600(S)	$9,414	5-M	1,662	179	35
Johnson Univ., Knoxville, TN 37998-1001	1893	$11,850	$5,550	2-D	1,031	85	54
Judson Univ., Elgin, IL 60123-1498	1963	$28,070	$9,450	2-D	1,288	159	50
Juniata Coll., Huntingdon, PA 16652-2119	1876	$40,600	$11,140	2-M	1,632	149	78
Kalamazoo Coll., Kalamazoo, MI 49006-3295	1833	$41,061	$8,679	2-B	1,461	124	77
Kansas State Univ., Manhattan, KS 66506	1863	$9,034(S)	$8,060	5-D	24,766	1,291	59
Kean Univ., Union, NJ 07083	1855	$11,244(S)	$12,200	5-D	14,359	1,371	48
Keene State Coll., Keene, NH 03435	1909	$12,938(S)	$9,712	5-M	4,957	434	63
Keiser Univ., Fort Lauderdale, FL 33309	1977	$17,596	NA	1-D	17,129	1,597	68
Kendall Coll., Chicago, IL 60201-2899	1934	NA	NA	3-B	2,545	209	37
Kennesaw State Univ., Kennesaw, GA 30144	1963	$6,932(S)	$7,914	5-D	25,714	1,438	43
Kent State Univ., Kent, OH 44242-0001	1910	$10,012(S)	$9,908	5-D	29,477	1,730	55
Kent State Univ. at Geauga, Burton, OH 44021-9500	1964	$5,664(S)	NA	5-M	2,725	148	20
Kent State Univ. at Stark, Canton, OH 44720-7599	1967	$5,664(S)	NA	5-M	4,678	262	27
Kentucky State Univ., Frankfort, KY 40601	1886	$7,404(S)	$6,690	12-D	1,895	150	20
Kenyon Coll., Gambier, OH 43022-9623	1824	$49,140	$11,890	1-B	1,662	203	89
Kettering Univ., Flint, MI 48504	1919	$36,980	$7,240	1-M	2,089	134	57
Keuka Coll., Keuka Park, NY 14478-0098	1890	$28,235	$10,800	2-M	1,999	477	47
Keystone Coll., La Plume, PA 18440	1868	$21,900	$9,900	1-M	1,484	249	36
King Univ., Bristol, TN 37620-2699	1867	$25,708	$8,180	2-D	2,898	505	54
King's Coll., Wilkes-Barre, PA 18711-0801	1946	$31,816	$11,686	2-M	2,308	230	62
Knox Coll., Galesburg, IL 61401	1837	$41,847	$9,012	1-B	1,399	145	80
Kutztown Univ. of Pennsylvania, Kutztown, PA 19530-0730	1866	$8,833(S)	$8,430	5-M	9,218	432	56
La Roche Coll., Pittsburgh, PA 15237-5898	1963	$25,500	$10,324	2-M	1,412	198	45
La Salle Univ., Philadelphia, PA 19141-1199	1863	$39,800	$13,940	2-D	6,255	469	67
La Sierra Univ., Riverside, CA 92515	1922	$30,470	$7,800	2-D	2,510	240	50
Lafayette Coll., Easton, PA 18042-1798	1826	$45,635	$13,520	2-B	2,503	279	88
Lake Erie Coll., Painesville, OH 44077-3389	1856	$29,162	$9,178	1-M	1,114	113	47
Lake Forest Coll., Lake Forest, IL 60045	1857	$42,644	$9,570	1-M	1,626	182	73
Lake Superior State Univ., Sault Sainte Marie, MI 49783	1946	$10,248(S)	$8,987	5-M	2,438	175	40
Lakeland Coll., Sheboygan, WI 53082-0359	1862	$22,950	$7,700	2-M	3,749	71	42
Lamar Univ., Beaumont, TX 77710	1923	$9,251(S)	$8,302	5-D	14,895	589	33
Lander Univ., Greenwood, SC 29649-2099	1872	$10,418(S)	$10,996	5-M	3,049	249	40
Lane Coll., Jackson, TN 38301-4598	1882	$9,780	$6,620	2-B	1,262	87	32
Langston Univ., Langston, OK 73050	1897	$4,801(S)	$8,720	5-D	2,576	200	44
Lasell Coll., Newton, MA 02466-2709	1851	$31,000	$12,750	1-M	2,127	237	57
Lawrence Tech. Univ., Southfield, MI 48075-1058	1932	$30,200	$8,986	1-D	4,015	413	45
Lawrence Univ., Appleton, WI 54911	1847	$42,657	$8,808	1-B	1,519	192	80
Le Moyne Coll., Syracuse, NY 13214	1946	$31,340	$12,130	2-M	3,381	337	72
Lebanon Valley Coll., Annville, PA 17003-1400	1866	$37,470	$10,100	2-D	1,901	240	75
Lee Univ., Cleveland, TN 37320-3450	1918	$15,000	$7,045	2-M	5,098	409	54
Lehigh Univ., Bethlehem, PA 18015-3094	1865	$44,890	$11,880	1-D	7,119	697	87
Lehman Coll. of the City Univ. of New York, Bronx, NY 10468-1589	1931	$6,429(S)	NA	11-M	12,220	912	36
LeMoyne-Owen Coll., Memphis, TN 38126-6595	1862	$10,900	$5,910	2-B	1,023	88	22
Lenoir-Rhyne Univ., Hickory, NC 28601	1891	$32,140	$11,060	2-M	2,143	231	54
Lesley Univ., Cambridge, MA 02138-2790 (4)	1909	$25,550	$14,830	1-D	4,422	249	58
LeTourneau Univ., Longview, TX 75607-7001	1946	$26,910	$9,300	2-M	2,667	202	52
Lewis & Clark Coll., Portland, OR 97219-7899	1867	$43,382	$11,000	1-D	3,504	417	79
Lewis-Clark State Coll., Lewiston, ID 83501-2698	1893	$5,900(S)	$6,194	5-B	4,304	251	31
Lewis Univ., Romeoville, IL 60446	1932	$29,040	$9,930	2-D	6,689	694	62
Liberty Univ., Lynchburg, VA 24515	1971	$22,000	$8,786	2-D	13,847	2,873	53
Life Univ., Marietta, GA 30060-2903	1974	$10,590	$12,480	1-D	2,754	199	27
LIM Coll., New York, NY 10022-5268 (4)	1939	$24,225	$19,850	3-M	1,737	194	48
Limestone Coll., Gaffney, SC 29340-3799	1845	$23,900	$8,200	1-M	1,263	106	28
Lincoln Memorial Univ., Harrogate, TN 37752-1901	1897	$20,546	$7,300	1-D	3,735	290	40
Lincoln Univ., Jefferson City, MO 65101	1866	$6,838(S)	$5,531	5-M	3,117	194	25
Lincoln Univ., Lincoln University, PA 19352	1854	$10,232(S)	$8,686	12-M	1,819	160	41
Lindenwood Univ., St. Charles, MO 63301-1695	1827	$15,580	$7,880	2-D	12,151	1,064	50
Lindsey Wilson Coll., Columbia, KY 42728	1903	$23,162	$8,900	2-D	2,641	245	34
Linfield Coll., McMinnville, OR 97128-6894	1849	$37,346	$10,330	2-B	1,683	194	69
Lipscomb Univ., Nashville, TN 37204-3951	1891	$27,390	$10,350	2-D	4,489	558	62
Livingstone Coll., Salisbury, NC 28144-5298	1879	$16,825	$6,596	2-B	1,175	73	NA
Lock Haven Univ. of Pennsylvania, Lock Haven, PA 17745-2390	1870	$9,276(S)	$8,752	5-M	4,917	230	50
Loma Linda Univ., Loma Linda, CA 92350	1905	NA	NA	2-D	4,270	840	NA
Long Island Univ.–LIU Brooklyn, Brooklyn, NY 11201-8423	1926	$34,852	$12,330	1-D	8,354	805	26
Long Island Univ.–LIU Post, Brookville, NY 11548-1300	1954	$34,852	$12,808	1-D	9,486	705	40
Longwood Univ., Farmville, VA 23909	1839	$11,910(S)	$10,272	5-M	5,096	303	66
Loras Coll., Dubuque, IA 52004-0178	1839	$29,729	$8,353	2-M	1,569	153	64
Louisiana Coll., Pineville, LA 71359-0001	1906	$14,570	$5,074	2-M	1,256	108	47
Louisiana State Univ. & Agr. & Mech. Coll., Baton Rouge, LA 70803	1860	$8,750(S)	$10,804	5-D	37,314	1,467	67
Louisiana State Univ. at Alexandria, Alexandria, LA 71302-9121	1960	$4,768(S)	$6,240	5-B	2,430	139	NA
Louisiana State Univ. Health Sciences Ctr., New Orleans, LA 70112-2223	1931	$5,540(S)	$3,708	5-D	2,828	893	NA
Louisiana State Univ. in Shreveport, Shreveport, LA 71115-2399	1965	$6,236(S)	NA	5-D	4,206	178	30
Louisiana Tech. Univ., Ruston, LA 71272	1894	$8,052(S)	$5,520	5-D	11,225	430	54
Lourdes Univ., Sylvania, OH 43560-2898	1958	$19,220	$9,100	2-M	1,780	228	26
Loyola Marymount Univ., Los Angeles, CA 90045-2659	1911	$41,372	$14,395	2-D	9,515	NA	78
Loyola Univ. Chicago, Chicago, IL 60660	1870	$39,179	$13,310	2-D	15,902	1,530	73
Loyola Univ. Maryland, Baltimore, MD 21210-2699	1852	$44,255	$12,790	2-D	5,977	577	84
Loyola Univ. New Orleans, New Orleans, LA 70118-6195	1912	$36,610	$12,660	2-D	4,686	441	55
Lubbock Christian Univ., Lubbock, TX 79407-2099	1957	$19,400	$6,908	2-M	1,902	180	43
Luther Coll., Decorah, IA 52101	1861	$39,190	$7,920	2-B	2,385	246	82
Luther Rice Coll. & Seminary, Lithonia, GA 30038-2454	1962	$5,352	NA	2-M	1,650	NA	NA
Lycoming Coll., Williamsport, PA 17701-5192	1812	$35,900	$10,884	2-B	1,357	119	62
Lynchburg Coll., Lynchburg, VA 24501-3199	1903	$34,545	$9,330	2-D	2,736	282	56
Lyndon State Coll., Lyndonville, VT 05851-0919	1911	$10,286(S)	$9,138	5-M	1,436	160	39
Lynn Univ., Boca Raton, FL 33431-5598	1962	$35,200	$11,300	1-D	2,613	199	40

Name, address	Year founded	Tuition & fees	Room & board	Control, degree	Enroll-ment	Faculty	Grad. rate
Macalester Coll., St. Paul, MN 55105-1899	1874	$1,521/cr. hr.	NA	2-B	2,039	238	87%
Madonna Univ., Livonia, MI 48150-1173	1947	$17,390	$8,610	2-D	3,947	327	59
Maharishi Univ. of Mgmt., Fairfield, IA 52557	1971	$26,530	$7,400	1-D	1,132	139	32
Maine Maritime Acad., Castine, ME 04420 (2)	1941	$12,400(S)	$9,830	5-M	1,066	93	73
Malone Univ., Canton, OH 44709	1892	$27,440	$9,266	2-M	1,980	197	51
Manchester Univ., North Manchester, IN 46962-1225	1889	$730/cr. hr.	NA	2-D	1,479	97	55
Manhattan Coll., Riverdale, NY 10471	1853	$37,498	$13,740	2-M	3,970	460	74
Manhattanville Coll., Purchase, NY 10577-2132	1841	$36,220	$14,520	1-D	2,865	310	61
Mansfield Univ. of Pennsylvania, Mansfield, PA 16933	1857	$9,526(S)	$10,936	5-M	2,752	165	54
Maranatha Baptist Univ., Watertown, WI 53094	1968	$13,510	$6,480	2-M	1,042	123	52
Marian Univ., Fond du Lac, WI 54935-4699	1936	$25,930	$6,490	2-D	2,130	271	56
Marian Univ., Indianapolis, IN 46222-1997	1851	$29,400	$9,140	2-D	2,776	273	53
Marietta Coll., Marietta, OH 45750-4000	1835	$33,140	$10,395	1-M	1,500	180	63
Marist Coll., Poughkeepsie, NY 12601-1387	1929	$32,500	$13,600	1-M	6,356	601	78
Marquette Univ., Milwaukee, WI 53201-1881	1881	$37,170	NA	2-D	11,745	1,168	79
Marshall Univ., Huntington, WV 25755	1837	$6,526(S)	$9,546	5-D	13,381	722	45
Mars Hill Univ., Mars Hill, NC 28754	1856	$30,174	$8,667	2-M	1,440	157	38
Martin Univ., Indianapolis, IN 46218-3867	1977	NA	NA	1-M	1,236	43	13
Mary Baldwin Coll., Staunton, VA 24401-3610 (4)	1842	$29,595	$8,650	1-D	1,754	219	43
Marygrove Coll., Detroit, MI 48221-2599 (4)	1905	NA	NA	2-M	2,953	64	34
Maryland Inst. Coll. of Art, Baltimore, MD 21217	1826	$40,890	$11,260	1-M	2,155	342	73
Marylhurst Univ., Marylhurst, OR 97036-0261	1893	$20,345	NA	2-M	1,273	NA	NA
Marymount California Univ., Rancho Palos Verdes, CA 90275-6299	1932	$31,657	$12,998	2-M	1,107	114	NA
Marymount Manhattan Coll., New York, NY 10021-4597	1936	$27,636	$15,000	1-B	1,858	302	44
Marymount Univ., Arlington, VA 22207-4299	1950	$27,470	$12,010	2-D	3,441	381	51
Maryville Coll., Maryville, TN 37804-5907	1819	$32,866	$10,442	2-B	1,213	108	55
Maryville Univ. of St. Louis, St. Louis, MO 63141-7299	1872	$25,884	$9,972	1-D	5,931	559	67
Marywood Univ., Scranton, PA 18509-1598	1915	$32,692	$13,900	2-D	3,056	419	69
Massachusetts Coll. of Art & Design, Boston, MA 02115-5882	1873	$11,225(S)	$13,000	5-M	2,100	269	70
Massachusetts Coll. of Liberal Arts, North Adams, MA 01247-4100	1894	$8,975(S)	$9,638	5-M	1,765	172	52
Massachusetts Inst. of Tech., Cambridge, MA 02139-4307	1861	$45,016	$13,224	1-D	11,319	1,504	91
Massachusetts Maritime Acad., Buzzards Bay, MA 02532-1803 (2)	1891	$7,280(S)	$11,120	5-M	1,497	114	70
The Master's Coll. & Seminary, Santa Clarita, CA 91321-1200	1927	$29,860	$9,720	2-D	1,515	186	62
Mayville State Univ., Mayville, ND 58257-1299	1889	$6,489(S)	$5,430	5-B	1,081	81	42
McDaniel Coll., Westminster, MD 21157-4390	1867	$38,350	$9,100	1-M	3,187	378	68
McKendree Univ., Lebanon, IL 62254-1299	1828	$27,930	$9,020	2-D	3,131	271	56
McMurry Univ., Abilene, TX 79697	1923	$24,844	$7,988	2-M	1,007	111	36
McNeese State Univ., Lake Charles, LA 70609	1939	$6,335(S)	$6,536	5-M	8,242	435	37
MCPHS Univ., Boston, MA 02115-5896	1823	$30,530	$15,240	1-D	6,935	NA	71
Medaille Coll., Buffalo, NY 14214-2695	1875	$25,002	$9,500	1-D	2,383	294	50
Medgar Evers Coll. of the City Univ. of New York, Brooklyn, NY 11225-2298	1969	$6,332(S)	NA	11-B	6,701	490	NA
Med. Univ. of South Carolina, Charleston, SC 29425	1824	NA	NA	5-D	2,775	223	NA
Mercer Univ., Macon, GA 31207	1833	$33,780	$10,678	2-D	6,729	720	64
Mercy Coll., Dobbs Ferry, NY 10522-1189	1951	$17,766	$12,690	1-D	11,272	1,037	30
Mercy Coll. of Ohio, Toledo, OH 43604 (4)	1993	$11,980	NA	2-B	1,193	167	94
Mercyhurst Univ., Erie, PA 16546	1926	$31,485	$10,800	2-M	3,011	260	61
Meredith Coll., Raleigh, NC 27607-5298	1891	$33,730	$10,040	1-M	1,885	216	62
Merrimack Coll., North Andover, MA 01845-5800	1947	$36,215	$13,255	2-M	3,354	357	68
Messiah Coll., Mechanicsburg, PA 17055	1909	$32,240	$9,630	2-M	3,234	331	80
Methodist Univ., Fayetteville, NC 28311-1498	1956	$27,930	$10,414	2-M	2,416	213	44
Metropolitan Coll. of New York, New York, NY 10013	1964	$17,760	NA	1-M	1,228	NA	36
Metropolitan State Univ., St. Paul, MN 55106-5000	1971	$6,642(S)	NA	5-D	8,354	NA	NA
Metropolitan State Univ. of Denver, Denver, CO 80217-3362	1963	$5,744(S)	NA	5-M	23,381	1,494	25
Miami Univ., Oxford, OH 45056	1809	$14,287(S)	$11,109	12-D	18,620	1,185	79
Miami Univ. Hamilton, Hamilton, OH 45011-3399	1968	$13,846(S)	$10,900	5-M	4,194	224	NA
Michigan State Univ., East Lansing, MI 48824	1855	$13,200(S)	$9,154	5-D	50,085	2,793	78
Michigan Tech. Univ., Houghton, MI 49931	1885	$14,040(S)	$9,516	5-D	7,104	453	64
MidAmerica Nazarene Univ., Olathe, KS 66062-1899	1966	$24,250	$7,550	2-M	1,862	82	55
Middle Georgia State Coll., Cochran, GA 31014-1599	1884	$3,028(S)	$7,736	5-B	3,614	170	NA
Middle Tennessee State Univ., Murfreesboro, TN 37132	1911	$7,876(S)	$8,302	5-D	22,729	1,256	46
Middlebury Coll., Middlebury, VT 05753-6002	1800	$46,044	$13,116	1-D	2,526	331	94
Midland Coll., Midland, TX 79705-6329	1969	$2,340(A)	NA	11-B	5,233	271	NA
Midway Coll., Midway, KY 40347-1120 (4)	1847	$22,000	$8,000	2-D	1,600	118	38
Midwestern State Univ., Wichita Falls, TX 76308	1922	$7,753(S)	$6,810	5-M	5,874	332	45
Miles Coll., Fairfield, AL 35064	1905	$12,276	$6,896	2-B	1,738	147	NA
Millersville Univ. of Pennsylvania, Millersville, PA 17551-0302	1855	$10,268(S)	$11,380	5-M	8,047	449	64
Milligan Coll., Milligan College, TN 37682	1866	$29,830	$6,500	2-M	1,191	134	58
Millikin Univ., Decatur, IL 62522-2084	1901	$29,620	$9,240	2-D	2,191	279	61
Mills Coll., Oakland, CA 94613-1000	1852	$42,918	$12,914	1-D	1,541	197	69
Milwaukee Sch. of Engineering, Milwaukee, WI 53202-3109 (2)	1903	$36,540	$8,613	1-M	2,810	258	56
Minnesota State Univ. Mankato, Mankato, MN 56001	1868	$8,481(S)	$8,042	5-D	15,407	754	49
Minnesota State Univ. Moorhead, Moorhead, MN 56563-0002	1885	$7,829(S)	$7,398	5-M	6,310	NA	42
Minot State Univ., Minot, ND 58707-0002	1913	$6,086(S)	$5,550	5-M	3,410	279	40
Misericordia Univ., Dallas, PA 18612-1098	1924	$29,010	$12,050	2-D	3,196	315	71
Mississippi Coll., Clinton, MS 39058	1826	$15,458	$8,408	2-D	5,070	461	62
Mississippi State Univ., Mississippi State, MS 39762	1878	$7,140(S)	$8,954	5-D	20,138	1,005	61
Mississippi Univ. for Women, Columbus, MS 39701-9998	1884	$5,640(S)	$6,381	5-D	2,696	216	41
Mississippi Valley State Univ., Itta Bena, MS 38941-1400	1946	$6,066(S)	$7,177	5-M	2,222	146	30
Missouri Baptist Univ., St. Louis, MO 63141-8660	1964	$22,760	$9,070	2-D	5,321	286	44
Missouri Southern State Univ., Joplin, MO 64801-1595	1937	$5,762(S)	$6,299	5-M	5,613	354	36
Missouri State Univ., Springfield, MO 65897	1905	$7,796(S)	$7,678	5-D	21,816	1,128	50
Missouri Univ. of Sci. & Tech., Rolla, MO 65409	1870	$9,537(S)	$9,540	5-D	8,642	491	63
Missouri Valley Coll., Marshall, MO 65340-3197	1889	$19,350	$8,100	2-M	1,659	90	26
Missouri Western State Univ., St. Joseph, MO 64507-2294	1915	$6,498(S)	$7,346	5-M	5,834	407	35
Molloy Coll., Rockville Centre, NY 11571-5002	1955	$26,850	$13,590	1-D	4,497	686	70
Monmouth Coll., Monmouth, IL 61462-1998	1853	$34,200	$8,060	2-B	1,300	133	56
Monmouth Univ., West Long Branch, NJ 07764-1898	1933	$32,310	$11,798	1-D	6,395	633	67
Monroe Coll., Bronx, NY 10468-5407	1933	$13,740	$9,200	3-M	7,215	251	71
Montana State Univ., Bozeman, MT 59717	1893	$5,330(S)	NA	5-D	15,421	960	50
Montana State Univ. Billings, Billings, MT 59101	1927	$5,780(S)	$6,980	5-M	4,781	342	27
Montana State Univ.–Northern, Havre, MT 59501-7751	1929	NA	NA	5-M	1,273	96	30
Montana Tech. of The Univ. of Montana, Butte, MT 59701-8997	1895	$6,752(S)	$8,238	5-D	2,945	228	42
Montclair State Univ., Montclair, NJ 07043-1624	1908	$11,540(S)	$14,010	5-D	20,022	1,738	64
Moody Bible Inst., Chicago, IL 60610-3284	1886	NA	NA	2-M	3,349	211	NA
Moravian Coll., Bethlehem, PA 18018-6650	1742	$37,572	$11,082	2-M	1,930	172	69

Name, address	Year founded	Tuition & fees	Room & board	Control, degree	Enroll-ment	Faculty	Grad. rate
Morehead State Univ., Morehead, KY 40351	1922	$7,866(S)	$7,888	5-D	11,053	492	45%
Morehouse Coll., Atlanta, GA 30314 (1)	1867	$26,339	$12,710	1-B	2,170	214	54
Morgan State Univ., Baltimore, MD 21251	1867	$7,378(S)	$9,232	5-D	7,005	558	100
Morningside Coll., Sioux City, IA 51106	1894	$27,180	$8,250	2-M	2,824	237	54
Morrisville State Coll., Morrisville, NY 13408-0901	1908	$7,642(S)	$12,858	5-B	2,911	261	NA
Mount Aloysius Coll., Cresson, PA 16630-1999	1939	$20,268	$8,830	2-M	1,867	204	NA
Mount Carmel Coll. of Nursing, Columbus, OH 43222 (4)	1903	$12,016	$5,000	1-M	1,084	98	64
Mount Holyoke Coll., South Hadley, MA 01075 (3)	1837	$43,886	$12,860	1-M	2,255	240	80
Mount Ida Coll., Newton, MA 02459-3310	1899	$30,447	$12,500	1-M	1,481	189	38
Mount Marty Coll., Yankton, SD 57078-3724	1936	$22,892	$6,978	2-M	1,236	61	54
Mount Mary Univ., Milwaukee, WI 53222-4597	1913	$25,852	$7,738	2-D	1,385	200	49
Mount Mercy Univ., Cedar Rapids, IA 52402-4797	1928	$28,226	$8,600	2-M	1,762	152	72
Mount St. Joseph Univ., Cincinnati, OH 45233-1670	1920	$26,850	$8,710	2-D	2,219	247	57
Mount St. Mary Coll., Newburgh, NY 12550-3494	1960	$27,312	$13,556	1-M	2,479	258	59
Mount St. Mary's Univ., Los Angeles, CA 90049-1599 (4)	1925	$35,944	$11,117	2-D	3,349	459	66
Mount St. Mary's Univ., Emmitsburg, MD 21727-7799	1808	$37,500	$12,400	2-M	2,305	203	64
Mount Vernon Nazarene Univ., Mount Vernon, OH 43050-9500	1964	$24,650	$7,260	2-M	2,141	247	58
Muhlenberg Coll., Allentown, PA 18104-5586	1848	$44,145	$10,450	2-B	2,440	278	85
Murray State Univ., Murray, KY 42071	1922	$7,608(S)	$8,206	5-D	11,207	681	52
Musians Inst., Hollywood, CA 90028	1976	NA	NA	3-B	1,337	204	NA
Muskingum Univ., New Concord, OH 43762	1837	$24,036	$7,818	2-M	2,099	NA	NA
National Louis Univ., Chicago, IL 60603	1886	NA	NA	1-D	5,737	521	20
National Paralegal Coll., Phoenix, AZ 85014	2002	$6,600	NA	3-M	1,150	33	NA
National Univ., La Jolla, CA 92037-1011	1971	$14,670	NA	1-M	17,608	1,092	46
Nazareth Coll. of Rochester, Rochester, NY 14618-3790	1924	$30,562	$12,598	1-D	2,818	475	76
Nebraska Methodist Coll., Omaha, NE 68114	1891	$18,109	$6,460	2-D	1,000	68	43
Nebraska Wesleyan Univ., Lincoln, NE 68504-2796	1887	$28,500	$7,950	2-M	2,083	233	69
Neumann Univ., Aston, PA 19014-1298	1965	$25,860	$11,800	2-D	3,047	327	54
Nevada State Coll. at Henderson, Henderson, NV 89015	2002	$4,463(S)	NA	5-B	2,988	94	17
New England Coll., Henniker, NH 03242-3293	1946	$34,566	$13,388	1-D	2,457	225	38
New England Inst. of Tech., East Greenwich, RI 02818	1940	$22,230	NA	1-M	2,922	341	NA
New Jersey City Univ., Jersey City, NJ 07305-1597	1927	$10,852(S)	$10,604	5-D	8,136	780	32
New Jersey Inst. of Tech., Newark, NJ 07102	1881	$15,648(S)	$13,280	5-D	10,646	678	58
New Mexico Highlands Univ., Las Vegas, NM 87701	1893	$4,500(S)	$7,404	5-M	3,546	291	18
New Mexico Inst. of Mining & Tech., Socorro, NM 87801	1889	$6,256(S)	$6,740	5-D	2,127	148	45
New Mexico State Univ., Las Cruces, NM 88003-8001	1888	$5,950(S)	$8,100	5-D	15,829	1,097	46
New Orleans Baptist Theol Seminary, New Orleans, LA 70126-4858 (2)	1917	NA	NA	2-D	2,036	NA	NA
The New Sch. for Public Engagement, New York, NY 10011-8603	1919	NA	NA	1-D	2,014	447	NA
New York City Coll. of Tech. of the City Univ. of New York, Brooklyn, NY 11201-2983	1946	$6,690(S)	NA	11-B	17,374	1,493	20
New York Inst. of Tech., Old Westbury, NY 11568-8000	1955	$32,180	$12,830	1-D	7,884	830	45
New York Univ., New York, NY 10012-1019	1831	$46,170	$16,782	1-D	49,274	6,843	82
Newberry Coll., Newberry, SC 29108-2197	1856	$24,300	$9,300	2-B	1,093	131	41
Newman Univ., Wichita, KS 67213-2097	1933	$24,730	$7,060	2-M	3,687	267	48
Niagara Univ., Niagara University, NY 14109	1856	$29,060	$11,950	2-D	4,015	384	64
Nicholls State Univ., Thibodaux, LA 70310	1948	$7,304(S)	$8,580	5-M	6,298	311	37
Nichols Coll., Dudley, MA 01571-5000	1815	$33,300	$12,600	1-M	1,495	81	48
Norfolk State Univ., Norfolk, VA 23504	1935	$9,060(S)	$8,624	5-D	6,027	NA	34
North Carolina Agr. & Tech. State Univ., Greensboro, NC 27411	1891	$5,535(S)	$6,755	5-D	10,725	710	47
North Carolina Central Univ., Durham, NC 27707-3129	1910	$5,525(S)	$8,165	5-D	7,687	557	47
North Carolina State Univ., Raleigh, NC 27695	1887	$8,296(S)	$10,030	5-D	33,989	1,819	76
North Carolina Wesleyan Coll., Rocky Mount, NC 27804-8677	1956	$28,150	$9,524	2-B	1,872	270	35
North Central Coll., Naperville, IL 60566-7063	1861	$34,230	$9,795	2-M	3,043	267	63
North Central Univ., Minneapolis, MN 55404-1322	1930	NA	NA	2-B	1,125	102	37
North Dakota State Univ., Fargo, ND 58108	1890	$7,820(S)	$7,282	5-D	14,747	891	56
North Greenville Univ., Tigerville, SC 29688-1892	1892	$16,290	$9,640	2-D	2,529	210	50
North Park Univ., Chicago, IL 60625-4895	1891	$24,600	$8,220	2-D	3,138	305	56
Northcentral Univ., Prescott Valley, AZ 86314	1996	$10,000	NA	3-D	13,091	494	NA
Northeastern Illinois Univ., Chicago, IL 60625-4699	1961	$8,612(S)	NA	5-M	10,813	631	20
Northeastern State Univ., Tahlequah, OK 74464-2399	1846	$5,285(S)	$6,300	5-D	8,332	525	31
Northeastern Univ., Boston, MA 02115-5096	1898	$43,440	$14,570	1-D	24,255	NA	82
Northern Arizona Univ., Flagstaff, AZ 86011	1899	$9,990(S)	$9,020	5-D	27,715	1,644	52
Northern Illinois Univ., DeKalb, IL 60115-2854	1895	$11,992(S)	$11,790	5-D	20,611	1,099	50
Northern Kentucky Univ., Highland Heights, KY 41099	1968	$8,856(S)	$8,964	5-D	15,090	978	38
Northern Michigan Univ., Marquette, MI 49855-5301	1899	$9,388(S)	$8,954	5-D	8,781	456	51
Northern New Mexico Coll., Española, NM 87532	1909	NA	NA	5-B	2,272	253	NA
Northern State Univ., Aberdeen, SD 57401-7198	1901	$8,043(S)	$6,942	5-M	3,531	169	54
Northwest Missouri State Univ., Maryville, MO 64468-6001	1905	$8,276(S)	$9,192	5-M	6,720	308	49
Northwest Nazarene Univ., Nampa, ID 83686-5897	1913	$27,950	$6,600	2-D	2,249	106	52
Northwest Univ., Kirkland, WA 98033	1934	$27,700	$7,790	2-D	1,634	252	43
Northwestern Coll., Orange City, IA 51041-1996	1882	$29,050	$8,750	2-M	1,205	138	63
Northwestern Oklahoma State Univ., Alva, OK 73717-2799	1897	$5,843(S)	$4,230	5-M	2,165	176	34
Northwestern State Univ. of Louisiana, Natchitoches, LA 71497	1884	$6,807(S)	$8,397	5-D	8,944	492	42
Northwestern Univ., Evanston, IL 60208	1851	$47,251	$14,389	1-D	21,108	1,629	94
Northwood Univ., Michigan campus, Midland, MI 48640-2398	1959	$23,132	$9,310	1-M	1,669	143	56
Norwich Univ., Northfield, VT 05663	1819	$32,812	$11,984	1-M	3,672	332	57
Notre Dame Coll., South Euclid, OH 44121-4293	1922	$25,694	$8,598	2-M	1,393	118	NA
Notre Dame de Namur Univ., Belmont, CA 94002-1908	1851	$31,822	$12,494	2-D	2,030	248	48
Notre Dame of Maryland Univ., Baltimore, MD 21210-2476 (4)	1873	$33,670	$10,930	2-D	2,764	136	56
Nova Southeastern Univ., Fort Lauderdale, FL 33314-7796	1964	$26,700	$10,580	1-D	24,148	1,725	46
Nyack Coll., Nyack, NY 10960	1882	$24,300	$8,950	2-D	2,896	282	42
Oakland City Univ., Oakland City, IN 47660-1099	1885	$22,800	$9,030	2-D	2,086	97	52
Oakland Univ., Rochester, MI 48309-4401	1957	$10,613(S)	$8,895	5-D	20,519	1,129	45
Oakwood Univ., Huntsville, AL 35896	1896	$16,720	$9,312	2-M	1,824	171	46
Oberlin Coll., Oberlin, OH 44074	1833	$50,564	$13,630	1-M	2,978	218	88
Occidental Coll., Los Angeles, CA 90041-3314	1887	$46,270	$12,940	1-M	2,117	266	85
Oglala Lakota Coll., Kyle, SD 57752-0490	1970	NA	NA	11-M	1,000	NA	NA
Oglethorpe Univ., Atlanta, GA 30319-2797	1835	$32,500	$11,700	1-B	1,095	96	51
Ohio Dominican Univ., Columbus, OH 43219-2099	1911	$29,430	$10,280	2-M	2,707	264	43
Ohio Northern Univ., Ada, OH 45810-1599	1871	$28,810	$10,890	2-D	3,695	307	65
The Ohio State Univ., Columbus, OH 43210	1870	$10,037(S)	$9,850	5-D	58,322	5,281	84
The Ohio State Univ. at Lima, Lima, OH 45804	1960	$7,140(S)	NA	5-M	1,056	83	33
The Ohio State Univ. at Marion, Marion, OH 43302-5695	1958	$7,140(S)	NA	5-M	1,204	104	43
The Ohio State Univ.–Mansfield campus, Mansfield, OH 44906-1599	1958	$7,140(S)	$5,205	5-M	1,188	100	42
The Ohio State Univ.–Newark campus, Newark, OH 43055-1797	1957	$7,140(S)	$7,185	5-M	2,396	150	39

Name, address	Year founded	Tuition & fees	Room & board	Control, degree	Enroll-ment	Faculty	Grad. rate
Ohio Univ., Athens, OH 45701-2979	1804	$10,602(S)	$10,478	5-D	29,217	1,301	67%
Ohio Univ.–Chillicothe, Chillicothe, OH 45601	1946	$4,908(S)	NA	5-M	2,200	NA	NA
Ohio Univ.–Lancaster, Lancaster, OH 43130-1097	1968	$4,908(S)	NA	5-M	1,728	NA	NA
Ohio Univ.–Southern campus, Ironton, OH 45638-2214	1956	NA	NA	5-M	1,836	NA	NA
Ohio Univ.–Zanesville, Zanesville, OH 43701-2695	1946	$4,908(S)	NA	5-B	2,042	130	NA
Ohio Wesleyan Univ., Delaware, OH 43015	1842	$41,920	$11,210	2-B	1,734	219	65
Oklahoma Baptist Univ., Shawnee, OK 74804	1910	$24,000	$6,780	2-M	1,979	181	51
Oklahoma Christian Univ., Oklahoma City, OK 73136-1100	1950	$19,890	$7,030	2-M	2,472	234	54
Oklahoma City Univ., Oklahoma City, OK 73106-1402	1904	$30,726	$9,750	2-D	3,014	283	59
Oklahoma Panhandle State Univ., Goodwell, OK 73939-0430	1909	$6,677(S)	$3,906	5-B	1,387	91	38
Oklahoma State Univ., Stillwater, OK 74078	1890	$7,442(S)	$7,390	5-D	25,854	1,327	61
Oklahoma Wesleyan Univ., Bartlesville, OK 74006-6299	1909	$23,180	$7,488	2-M	1,335	111	37
Old Dominion Univ., Norfolk, VA 23529	1930	$9,250(S)	$10,233	5-D	24,932	1,321	52
Olivet Coll., Olivet, MI 49076-9701	1844	$23,801	$3,950	2-M	1,059	90	39
Olivet Nazarene Univ., Bourbonnais, IL 60914	1907	$32,790	$7,900	2-D	4,861	463	56
Oral Roberts Univ., Tulsa, OK 74171	1963	$23,410	$9,765	2-D	3,612	269	53
Oregon Health & Sci. Univ., Portland, OR 97239-3098	1974	NA	NA	12-D	2,861	117	NA
Oregon Inst. of Tech., Klamath Falls, OR 97601-8801	1947	NA	NA	5-M	3,911	257	45
Oregon State Univ., Corvallis, OR 97331	1868	$9,122(S)	$11,151	5-D	28,886	1,596	63
Otis Coll. of Art & Design, Los Angeles, CA 90045-9785	1918	$38,330	NA	1-M	1,086	272	57
Otterbein Univ., Westerville, OH 43081	1847	$31,624	$9,460	2-D	2,984	333	60
Ouachita Baptist Univ., Arkadelphia, AR 71998-0001	1886	$23,320	$6,900	2-B	1,543	149	60
Our Lady of Holy Cross Coll., New Orleans, LA 70131-7399	1916	$9,950	NA	2-M	1,298	NA	NA
Our Lady of the Lake Coll., Baton Rouge, LA 70808	1990	$11,150	NA	2-M	1,704	164	29
Our Lady of the Lake Univ. of San Antonio, San Antonio, TX 78207-4689	1895	$24,596	$7,436	2-D	3,173	320	38
Pace Univ., New York, NY 10038	1906	$39,697	$15,774	1-D	12,857	1,339	55
Pacific Lutheran Univ., Tacoma, WA 98447	1890	$37,950	$10,330	2-D	3,275	353	68
Pacific Oaks Coll., Pasadena, CA 91103 (4)	1945	NA	NA	1-M	1,028	125	NA
Pacific Union Coll., Angwin, CA 94508-9707	1882	$28,131	$7,485	2-M	1,647	146	45
Pacific Univ., Forest Grove, OR 97116-1797	1849	$39,858	$11,448	1-D	3,640	414	59
Palm Beach Atlantic Univ., West Palm Beach, FL 33416-4708	1968	$26,274	$8,600	2-D	3,865	359	55
Palm Beach State Coll., Lake Worth, FL 33461-4796	1933	$2,378(S)	NA	5-B	29,174	1,185	NA
Palmer Coll. of Chiropractic, Davenport, IA 52803-5287	1897	NA	NA	1-D	2,310	15	NA
Palo Alto Univ., Palo Alto, CA 94304	1975	$20,428	NA	1-D	1,081	NA	NA
Park Univ., Parkville, MO 64152-3795	1875	$10,600	$7,980	1-M	9,800	174	42
Parsons The New Sch. for Design, New York, NY 10011-8878	1896	$40,140	$15,100	1-M	5,134	1,083	69
Patten Univ., Oakland, CA 94601-2699	1944	$3,432	NA	2-M	1,050	125	37
Peirce Coll., Philadelphia, PA 19102-4699 (4)	1865	$13,800	NA	1-M	1,833	NA	NA
Penn State Abington, Abington, PA 19001	1950	$13,942(S)	NA	12-B	3,952	271	47
Penn State Altoona, Altoona, PA 16601-3760	1939	$14,588(S)	$10,520	12-B	3,903	293	66
Penn State Berks, Reading, PA 19610-6009	1924	$14,588(S)	$11,500	12-B	2,839	220	59
Penn State Brandywine, Media, PA 19063-5596	1966	$13,942(S)	NA	12-B	1,488	142	43
Penn State Erie, The Behrend Coll., Erie, PA 16563-0001	1948	$14,588(S)	$10,520	12-M	4,138	309	68
Penn State Harrisburg, Middletown, PA 17057-4898	1966	$14,588(S)	$11,980	12-D	4,519	361	67
Penn State Univ. Park, University Park, PA 16802	1855	$17,502(S)	$10,520	12-D	47,040	3,069	86
Penn State Worthington Scranton, Dunmore, PA 18512-1699	1923	$13,882(S)	NA	12-B	1,126	95	47
Penn State York, York, PA 17403	1926	$13,930(S)	NA	12-M	1,172	99	49
Pennsylvania Coll. of Health Sciences, Lancaster, PA 17602 (4)	1903	$15,255	NA	1-M	1,447	197	NA
Pennsylvania Coll. of Tech., Williamsport, PA 17701-5778	1965	$15,450(S)	$10,836	12-B	5,623	474	NA
Pepperdine Univ., Malibu, CA 90263	1937	$46,692	$13,390	2-D	7,417	709	84
Peru State Coll., Peru, NE 68421	1867	$5,922(S)	$6,492	5-M	2,358	109	NA
Pfeiffer Univ., Misenheimer, NC 28109-0960	1885	$24,150	$9,230	2-M	2,019	150	59
Philadelphia Univ., Philadelphia, PA 19144	1884	$35,080	$11,610	1-D	3,757	531	66
Piedmont Coll., Demorest, GA 30535	1897	$21,350	$8,786	2-D	2,120	251	50
Pittsburg State Univ., Pittsburg, KS 66762	1903	$6,230(S)	$6,936	5-M	7,479	412	53
Pitzer Coll., Claremont, CA 91711-6101	1963	$46,992	$14,758	1-B	1,081	115	81
Plymouth State Univ., Plymouth, NH 03264-1595	1871	$12,677(S)	$10,728	5-D	4,887	413	58
Point Loma Nazarene Univ., San Diego, CA 92106-2899	1902	$31,406	$9,600	2-M	3,374	351	73
Point Park Univ., Pittsburgh, PA 15222-1984	1960	$27,190	$10,320	1-M	3,841	454	50
Point Univ., West Point, GA 31833	1937	$17,650	$6,350	2-B	1,522	120	36
Polk State Coll., Winter Haven, FL 33881-4299	1964	$3,367(S)	NA	5-B	11,887	388	NA
Polytechnic Univ. of Puerto Rico, Hato Rey, PR 00919	1966	$7,800	NA	1-D	4,507	253	18
Pomona Coll., Claremont, CA 91711	1887	$45,832	$14,700	1-B	1,650	232	93
Pontifical Catholic Univ. of Puerto Rico, Ponce, PR 00717-0777	1948	$5,560	$1,369	2-D	7,682	385	39
Portland State Univ., Portland, OR 97207-0751	1946	$7,752(S)	$11,349	5-D	27,696	1,540	39
Prairie View A&M Univ., Prairie View, TX 77446-0519	1878	$8,098(S)	$7,467	5-D	8,429	461	36
Pratt Inst., Brooklyn, NY 11205-3899	1887	$46,586	$11,496	1-M	4,556	1,068	64
Presbyterian Coll., Clinton, SC 29325	1880	$34,828	$9,344	2-D	1,460	135	65
Princeton Univ., Princeton, NJ 08544-1019	1746	$43,450	$14,160	1-D	8,088	1,103	96
Providence Coll., Providence, RI 02918	1917	$44,323	$13,060	2-M	4,687	482	86
Purchase Coll., State Univ. of New York, Purchase, NY 10577-1400	1967	$7,933(S)	$12,232	5-M	4,289	463	68
Purdue Univ., West Lafayette, IN 47907	1869	$10,002(S)	$10,030	5-D	38,770	2,243	74
Purdue Univ. Calumet, Hammond, IN 46323-2094	1951	$6,758(S)	$5,485	5-M	9,501	504	31
Purdue Univ. North Central, Westville, IN 46391-9542	1967	$7,186(S)	NA	5-M	6,177	289	21
Queens Coll. of the City Univ. of New York, Flushing, NY 11367-1597	1937	$6,638(S)	$11,000	11-M	19,310	1,464	57
Queens Univ. of Charlotte, Charlotte, NC 28274-0002	1857	$29,250	$10,642	2-M	2,386	254	59
Quincy Univ., Quincy, IL 62301-2699	1860	$26,998	$10,000	2-M	1,279	124	49
Quinnipiac Univ., Hamden, CT 06518-1940	1929	$42,270	$14,820	1-D	9,035	921	76
Radford Univ., Radford, VA 24142	1910	$9,360(S)	$8,406	5-D	9,798	717	59
Ramapo Coll. of New Jersey, Mahwah, NJ 07430-1680	1969	$8,650(S)	$11,550	5-M	6,003	465	72
Randolph-Macon Coll., Ashland, VA 23005-5505	1830	$36,340	$10,750	2-B	1,394	148	62
Rasmussen Coll. Lake Elmo/Woodbury, Lake Elmo, MN 55042	NA	$12,114	NA	3-B	1,360	23	NA
Rasmussen Coll. Ocala, Ocala, FL 34471	1984	$12,114	NA	3-B	1,194	36	NA
Reed Coll., Portland, OR 97202-8199	1908	$47,760	$12,200	1-M	1,394	151	79
Regent Univ., Virginia Beach, VA 23464-9800	1977	$17,150	$8,250	2-D	6,154	609	53
Regis Coll., Weston, MA 02493	1927	$35,750	$13,700	2-D	1,912	211	45
Regis Univ., Denver, CO 80221-1099	1877	$33,710	$9,830	2-D	9,208	855	60
Reinhardt Univ., Waleska, GA 30183-2981	1883	$20,266	$7,568	2-M	1,422	172	36
Rensselaer Polytechnic Inst., Troy, NY 12180-3590	1824	$47,908	$13,620	1-D	7,028	497	82
Rhode Island Coll., Providence, RI 02908-1991	1854	$7,602(S)	$10,094	5-D	8,641	746	43
Rhode Island Sch. of Design, Providence, RI 02903-2784	1877	$44,594	$12,640	1-M	2,449	463	87
Rhodes Coll., Memphis, TN 38112-1690	1848	$43,224	$10,746	1-M	2,054	210	80
Rice Univ., Houston, TX 77251-1892	1912	$40,566	$13,400	1-D	6,621	849	92
Rider Univ., Lawrenceville, NJ 08648-3001	1865	$36,830	$13,330	1-M	5,326	592	63
Ringling Coll. of Art & Design, Sarasota, FL 34234-5895	1931	$40,040	$13,580	1-B	1,219	148	66
Rivier Univ., Nashua, NH 03060	1933	$27,855	$10,570	2-D	2,441	193	49

Name, address	Year founded	Tuition & fees	Room & board	Control, degree	Enroll-ment	Faculty	Grad. rate
Roanoke Coll., Salem, VA 24153-3794	1842	$39,666	$12,370	2-B	2,054	224	64%
Robert Morris Univ., Moon Township, PA 15108-1189	1921	$26,054	$11,810	1-D	5,555	482	62
Robert Morris Univ. Illinois, Chicago, IL 60605	1913	$25,200	$12,600	1-M	3,205	234	79
Roberts Wesleyan Coll., Rochester, NY 14624-1997	1866	$28,068	$9,840	2-M	1,762	263	61
Rochester Inst. of Tech., Rochester, NY 14623-5603	1829	$36,038	$11,568	1-D	16,320	1,499	65
Rockford Univ., Rockford, IL 61108-2393	1847	$27,530	$7,710	1-M	1,284	166	45
Rockhurst Univ., Kansas City, MO 64110-2561	1910	$32,865	$9,080	2-D	3,002	244	69
Rocky Mountain Coll., Billings, MT 59102-1796	1878	$25,252	$7,944	2-M	1,031	124	41
Rocky Mountain Coll. of Art + Design, Lakewood, CO 80214	1963	$16,395	NA	3-M	1,045	159	48
Roger Williams Univ., Bristol, RI 02809	1956	$31,750	$14,546	1-D	4,884	410	62
Rogers State Univ., Claremore, OK 74017-3252	1909	$5,321(S)	$8,830	5-B	4,289	281	20
Rollins Coll., Winter Park, FL 32789-4499	1885	$43,080	$13,470	1-D	2,469	219	71
Roosevelt Univ., Chicago, IL 60605	1945	$27,300	$12,532	1-D	6,113	723	30
Rose-Hulman Inst. of Tech., Terre Haute, IN 47803-3999 (2)	1874	$41,283	$12,057	1-M	2,388	197	78
Rowan Univ., Glassboro, NJ 08028-1701	1923	$12,616(S)	$11,406	5-D	14,778	1,312	70
Rush Univ., Chicago, IL 60612-3832	1969	NA	NA	1-D	1,566	796	NA
Rust Coll., Holly Springs, MS 38635-2328	1866	$9,286	$4,000	2-B	1,031	50	NA
Rutgers, The State Univ. of New Jersey, Camden, Camden, NJ 08102-1401	1927	$13,683(S)	$11,438	5-D	6,321	614	52
Rutgers, The State Univ. of New Jersey, Newark, Newark, NJ 07102	1892	$13,297(S)	$12,509	5-D	11,314	875	66
Rutgers, The State Univ. of New Jersey, New Brunswick, Piscataway, NJ 08854-8097	1766	$13,813(S)	$11,749	5-D	48,378	4,875	80
Sacred Heart Univ., Fairfield, CT 06825-1000	1963	$35,750	$13,514	2-D	7,781	733	67
The Sage Colls., Troy, NY 12180	1916	$28,200	$11,830	1-D	2,877	271	59
Saginaw Valley State Univ., University Center, MI 48710	1963	$8,691(S)	$8,400	5-D	9,829	756	40
St. Ambrose Univ., Davenport, IA 52803-2898	1882	$26,740	$9,016	2-D	3,671	425	63
St. Anselm Coll., Manchester, NH 03102-1310	1889	$35,634	$12,690	2-B	1,968	209	75
St. Augustine Coll., Chicago, IL 60640-3501	1980	$9,576	NA	1-B	1,430	154	NA
St. Augustine's Univ., Raleigh, NC 27610-2298	1867	$745/cr. hr.	NA	2-B	1,016	100	NA
St. Bonaventure Univ., St. Bonaventure, NY 14778-2284	1858	$30,475	$11,100	2-M	2,147	222	68
St. Catherine Univ., St. Paul, MN 55105	1905	$36,420	$8,894	2-D	5,055	525	60
St. Cloud State Univ., St. Cloud, MN 56301-4498	1869	$7,554(S)	$7,560	5-D	16,245	880	47
St. Edward's Univ., Austin, TX 78704	1885	$38,720	$11,664	2-M	4,686	495	67
St. Francis Coll., Brooklyn Heights, NY 11201-4398	1884	$22,300	$12,000	2-M	2,749	301	55
St. Francis Univ., Loretto, PA 15940-0600	1847	$32,128	$11,082	2-D	2,387	232	72
St. John Fisher Coll., Rochester, NY 14618-3597	1948	$29,550	$11,158	2-D	3,856	458	72
St. John's Univ., Collegeville, MN 56321	1857	$38,704	$9,280	2-M	1,895	168	81
St. John's Univ., Queens, NY 11439	1870	$38,680	$16,390	2-D	20,445	1,452	59
St. Joseph's Coll., Rensselaer, IN 47978	1889	$27,485	$8,610	2-M	1,166	125	46
St. Joseph's Coll., Long Island campus, Patchogue, NY 11772-2399	1916	$24,130	NA	1-M	3,623	402	69
St. Joseph's Coll., New York, Brooklyn, NY 11205-3688	1916	$24,130	NA	1-M	1,356	190	65
St. Joseph's Coll. of Maine, Standish, ME 04084	1912	$30,990	$11,900	2-M	3,355	126	50
St. Joseph's Univ., Philadelphia, PA 19131-1395	1851	$40,580	$14,426	2-D	8,974	711	73
St. Lawrence Univ., Canton, NY 13617-1455	1856	$47,686	$12,286	1-M	2,508	211	85
St. Leo Univ., Saint Leo, FL 33574-6665	1889	$20,520	$9,870	2-D	6,058	203	40
St. Louis Coll. of Pharm., St. Louis, MO 63110-1088	1864	$28,264	$9,783	1-D	1,366	151	66
St. Louis Univ., St. Louis, MO 63103-2097	1818	$37,966	$10,380	2-D	13,287	1,301	72
St. Martin's Univ., Lacey, WA 98503	1895	$31,688	$9,990	2-M	1,760	223	48
St. Mary's Coll., Notre Dame, IN 46556 (3)	1844	$35,970	$10,930	2-B	1,519	195	81
St. Mary's Coll. of California, Moraga, CA 94575	1863	$41,380	$14,140	2-D	4,257	525	60
St. Mary's Coll. of Maryland, St. Mary's City, MD 20686-3001	1840	$13,824(S)	$11,930	5-M	1,804	214	81
St. Mary's Univ., San Antonio, TX 78228-8507	1852	$26,892	$8,894	2-D	3,712	384	63
St. Mary's Univ. of Minnesota, Winona, MN 55987-1399	1912	$31,335	$8,240	2-D	5,825	631	65
St. Michael's Coll., Colchester, VT 05439	1904	$40,750	$10,975	2-M	2,617	252	79
St. Norbert Coll., De Pere, WI 54115-2099	1898	$33,023	$8,455	2-M	2,169	202	70
St. Olaf Coll., Northfield, MN 55057-1098	1874	$42,940	$9,790	2-B	3,034	334	89
St. Petersburg Coll., St. Petersburg, FL 33733-3489	1927	$2,634(S)	NA	11-B	31,793	1,731	28
St. Peter's Univ., Jersey City, NJ 07306-5997	1872	$32,230	$13,458	2-D	3,302	323	53
St. Thomas Aquinas Coll., Sparkill, NY 10976	1952	$28,130	$11,680	1-M	1,942	176	57
St. Thomas Univ., Miami Gardens, FL 33054-6459	1961	$27,150	$5,150	2-D	2,225	230	35
St. Vincent Coll., Latrobe, PA 15650-2690	1846	$30,706	$9,538	2-D	1,829	198	73
St. Xavier Univ., Chicago, IL 60655-3105	1847	NA	NA	2-M	4,709	431	52
Salem Coll., Winston-Salem, NC 27101 (4)	1772	$25,356	$11,764	2-M	1,118	NA	65
Salem State Univ., Salem, MA 01970-5353	1854	$8,646(S)	$11,956	5-M	9,301	NA	46
Salisbury Univ., Salisbury, MD 21801-6837	1925	$8,560(S)	$10,620	5-D	8,770	660	66
Salve Regina Univ., Newport, RI 02840-4192	1934	$35,690	$12,860	2-D	2,739	277	67
Sam Houston State Univ., Huntsville, TX 77341	1879	$8,932(S)	$8,324	5-D	19,573	973	53
Samford Univ., Birmingham, AL 35229	1841	$28,370	$10,234	2-D	4,933	485	66
Samuel Merritt Univ., Oakland, CA 94609-3108 (4)	1909	$44,114	NA	1-D	1,580	278	NA
San Diego State Univ., San Diego, CA 92182	1897	$6,866(S)	$14,745	5-D	33,483	1,714	67
San Diego State Univ.–Imperial Valley campus, Calexico, CA 92231	1959	NA	NA	5-M	1,003	NA	NA
San Francisco State Univ., San Francisco, CA 94132-1722	1899	$6,468(S)	NA	5-D	29,465	NA	50
San Jose State Univ., San Jose, CA 95192-0001	1857	$7,323(S)	$11,810	5-M	32,697	1,694	51
Santa Clara Univ., Santa Clara, CA 95053	1851	$43,812	$12,921	2-D	9,015	917	85
Santa Fe Coll., Gainesville, FL 32606	1966	$3,164(S)	NA	11-B	15,745	829	NA
Sarah Lawrence Coll., Bronxville, NY 10708-5999	1926	$50,736	$14,504	1-M	1,761	304	77
Savannah Coll. of Art & Design, Savannah, GA 31402-3146	1978	$34,295	$13,710	1-M	11,973	655	65
Savannah State Univ., Savannah, GA 31404	1890	$6,498(S)	$7,330	5-M	4,915	252	28
Sch. of the Art Inst. of Chicago, Chicago, IL 60603-3103	1866	$42,230	$12,500	1-M	3,522	853	57
Sch. of Visual Arts, New York, NY 10010-3994	1947	$35,000	NA	3-M	4,397	971	66
Schreiner Univ., Kerrville, TX 78028-5697	1923	$24,360	$10,610	2-M	1,136	118	41
Seattle Pacific Univ., Seattle, WA 98119-1997	1891	$35,472	$10,086	2-D	4,217	384	75
Seattle Univ., Seattle, WA 98122-1090	1891	$38,205	$10,830	2-D	7,273	748	78
Seton Hall Univ., South Orange, NJ 07079-2697	1856	$36,926	$13,692	2-D	9,903	952	64
Seton Hill Univ., Greensburg, PA 15601	1883	$32,037	$10,739	2-M	1,959	192	60
Sewanee: The Univ. of the South, Sewanee, TN 37383-1000	1857	$38,700	$11,050	2-D	1,714	220	79
Shaw Univ., Raleigh, NC 27601-2399	1865	$16,480	$8,158	2-M	1,802	153	25
Shawnee State Univ., Portsmouth, OH 45662-4344	1986	$7,364(S)	$9,552	5-M	4,247	311	27
Shenandoah Univ., Winchester, VA 22601-5195	1875	$30,760	$9,920	2-D	3,693	427	55
Shepherd Univ., Shepherdstown, WV 25443	1871	$6,830(S)	$9,682	5-M	4,041	363	40
Shippensburg Univ. of Pennsylvania, Shippensburg, PA 17257-2299	1871	$9,774(S)	$11,160	5-D	7,355	374	55
Shorter Univ., Rome, GA 30165	1873	$20,250	$9,400	2-M	1,696	186	43
Siena Coll., Loudonville, NY 12211-1462	1937	$33,415	$13,595	2-M	3,184	350	80
Siena Heights Univ., Adrian, MI 49221-1796	1919	$22,740	$9,300	2-M	2,642	268	51
Simmons Coll., Boston, MA 02115	1899	$36,230	$13,736	1-D	4,800	710	71
Simpson Coll., Indianola, IA 50125-1297	1860	$32,550	$7,963	2-M	1,725	188	72
Simpson Univ., Redding, CA 96003-8606	1921	$25,200	$7,900	2-M	1,267	220	52

Name, address	Year founded	Tuition & fees	Room & board	Control, degree	Enroll-ment	Faculty	Grad. rate
Skidmore Coll., Saratoga Springs, NY 12866	1903	$47,314	$12,628	1-M	2,646	368	87%
Slippery Rock Univ. of Pennsylvania, Slippery Rock, PA 16057-1383	1889	$9,309(S)	$9,794	5-D	8,495	393	67
Smith Coll., Northampton, MA 01063	1871	$44,724	$14,950	1-D	2,989	298	87
Sonoma State Univ., Rohnert Park, CA 94928-3609	1960	$7,276(S)	$11,799	5-M	9,120	524	54
South Carolina State Univ., Orangeburg, SC 29117-0001	1896	$10,088(S)	$9,402	5-D	3,331	234	38
South Dakota Sch. of Mines & Tech., Rapid City, SD 57701-3995	1885	$10,040(S)	$6,370	5-D	2,798	178	52
South Dakota State Univ., Brookings, SD 57007	1881	$7,713(S)	$6,985	5-D	12,557	NA	57
Southeastern Baptist Theological Seminary, Wake Forest, NC 27588-1889	1950	NA	NA	2-D	2,266	85	NA
Southeastern Louisiana Univ., Hammond, LA 70402	1925	$6,547(S)	$7,100	5-D	14,498	610	36
Southeastern Oklahoma State Univ., Durant, OK 74701-0609	1909	$5,688(S)	$6,143	5-M	3,877	271	29
Southeastern Univ., Lakeland, FL 33801-6099	1935	$22,202	$9,297	2-D	3,834	276	42
Southeast Missouri State Univ., Cape Girardeau, MO 63701-4799	1873	$6,938(S)	$8,432	5-M	12,087	560	51
Southern Adventist Univ., Collegedale, TN 37315-0370	1892	$20,650	$5,900	2-D	3,175	174	45
Southern Arkansas Univ.–Magnolia, Magnolia, AR 71753	1909	$7,568(S)	$5,422	5-M	3,546	274	29
Southern Baptist Theological Seminary, Louisville, KY 40280-0004	1858	NA	NA	2-D	3,190	NA	NA
Southern Connecticut State Univ., New Haven, CT 06515-1355	1893	$9,157(S)	$11,289	5-D	10,825	1,005	53
Southern Illinois Univ. Carbondale, Carbondale, IL 62901-4701	1869	$12,248(S)	$9,694	5-D	17,989	928	44
Southern Illinois Univ. Edwardsville, Edwardsville, IL 62026-0001	1957	$9,738(S)	$8,781	5-D	13,972	907	50
Southern Methodist Univ., Dallas, TX 75275	1911	$48,190	$15,575	2-D	11,272	1,125	77
Southern Nazarene Univ., Bethany, OK 73008	1899	$22,680	$7,970	2-M	2,177	226	46
Southern New Hampshire Univ., Manchester, NH 03106-1045	1932	$3,752/course	NA	1-D	3,588	565	49
Southern Oregon Univ., Ashland, OR 97520	1926	$7,720(S)	$11,397	5-M	5,913	304	41
Southern Polytechnic State Univ., Marietta, GA 30060-2896	1948	NA	NA	5-M	6,202	309	37
Southern Tech. Coll., Fort Myers, FL 33907	1940	$13,860	NA	1-B	1,259	160	20
Southern Univ. & Agr. & Mech. Coll., Baton Rouge, LA 70813	1880	$6,534(S)	$7,501	5-D	7,699	546	30
Southern Univ. at New Orleans, New Orleans, LA 70126-1009 (4)	1959	NA	NA	5-M	3,141	102	5
Southern Utah Univ., Cedar City, UT 84720-2498	1897	$6,138(S)	$3,100	5-M	7,656	NA	38
Southern Wesleyan Univ., Central, SC 29630-1020	1906	$22,800	$7,950	2-M	1,883	193	39
Southwest Baptist Univ., Bolivar, MO 65613-2597	1878	$20,840	$6,800	2-D	3,696	287	48
Southwest Minnesota State Univ., Marshall, MN 56258	1963	$8,062(S)	$7,352	5-M	6,896	194	43
Southwestern Assemblies of God Univ., Waxahachie, TX 75165-5735	1927	$19,450	$6,340	2-M	1,984	161	39
Southwestern Coll., Winfield, KS 67156-2499	1885	$25,946	$7,080	2-D	1,627	167	54
Southwestern Oklahoma State Univ., Weatherford, OK 73096-3098	1901	$5,820(S)	$5,080	5-D	4,994	297	33
Southwestern Univ., Georgetown, TX 78626	1840	$37,560	$12,108	2-B	1,538	165	73
Spalding Univ., Louisville, KY 40203-2188	1814	$23,887	$8,400	2-D	2,311	NA	37
Spelman Coll., Atlanta, GA 30314-4399 (3)	1881	$25,496	$11,945	1-B	2,135	244	68
Spring Arbor Univ., Spring Arbor, MI 49283-9799	1873	$24,350	$8,460	2-M	3,961	135	57
Spring Hill Coll., Mobile, AL 36608-1791	1830	$32,468	$11,696	2-M	1,412	126	58
Springfield Coll., Springfield, MA 01109-3797	1885	$33,455	$11,210	1-D	3,286	353	69
Stanford Univ., Stanford, CA 94305-9991	1891	$45,729	$14,107	1-D	18,469	1,583	95
State Coll. of Florida Manatee-Sarasota, Bradenton, FL 34206-7046	1957	$3,074(S)	NA	5-B	10,314	442	NA
State Univ. of New York at Fredonia, Fredonia, NY 14063-1136	1826	$7,740(S)	$12,100	5-M	5,214	488	67
State Univ. of New York at New Paltz, New Paltz, NY 12561	1828	$7,418(S)	$10,896	5-M	7,692	658	74
State Univ. of New York at Oswego, Oswego, NY 13126	1861	$7,581(S)	$12,690	5-M	8,034	570	63
State Univ. of New York at Plattsburgh, Plattsburgh, NY 12901-2681	1889	$7,497(S)	$11,304	5-M	5,968	499	61
State Univ. of New York Coll. at Cortland, Cortland, NY 13045	1868	$7,719(S)	$12,040	5-M	6,958	649	67
State Univ. of New York Coll. at Geneseo, Geneseo, NY 14454-1401	1871	$7,774(S)	$11,518	5-M	5,658	349	78
State Univ. of New York Coll. at Old Westbury, Old Westbury, NY 11568-0210	1965	$7,323(S)	$10,390	5-M	4,504	337	37
State Univ. of New York Coll. at Oneonta, Oneonta, NY 13820-4015	1889	$7,548(S)	$11,530	5-M	6,023	483	67
State Univ. of New York Coll. at Potsdam, Potsdam, NY 13676	1816	$7,553(S)	$10,920	5-M	3,979	357	54
State Univ. of New York Coll. of Agr. & Tech. at Cobleskill, Cobleskill, NY 12043	1916	$7,609(S)	$12,140	5-B	2,532	173	50
State Univ. of New York Coll. of Environmental Sci. & Forestry, Syracuse, NY 13210-2779	1911	$7,398(S)	$15,120	5-D	2,457	184	68
State Univ. of New York Coll. of Tech. at Canton, Canton, NY 13617	1906	$7,509(S)	$11,300	5-B	3,278	265	31
State Univ. of New York Coll. of Tech. at Delhi, Delhi, NY 13753	1913	$7,530(S)	$10,970	5-M	3,616	245	63
State Univ. of New York Downstate Med. Ctr., Brooklyn, NY 11203-2098	1858	$6,755(S)	$8,944	5-D	1,694	981	NA
State Univ. of New York Empire State Coll., Saratoga Springs, NY 12866-4391	1971	$6,665(S)	NA	5-M	11,963	1,255	NA
State Univ. of New York Maritime Coll., Throggs Neck, NY 10465-4198	1874	$7,446(S)	$11,040	5-M	1,799	142	47
State Univ. of New York Polytechnic Inst., Utica, NY 13504-3050	1966	$7,440(S)	$11,236	5-M	2,737	250	43
State Univ. of New York Upstate Med. Univ., Syracuse, NY 13210-2334	1950	$6,600(S)	$10,500	5-D	1,787	54	NA
Stephen F. Austin State Univ., Nacogdoches, TX 75962	1923	$8,892(S)	$8,868	5-D	12,801	685	43
Stetson Univ., DeLand, FL 32723	1883	$41,590	$6,874	1-D	4,137	424	61
Stevens Inst. of Tech., Hoboken, NJ 07030	1870	$44,666	$14,214	1-D	5,541	406	79
Stevenson Univ., Stevenson, MD 21153	1952	$28,980	$12,490	1-M	4,323	461	63
Stillman Coll., Tuscaloosa, AL 35403-9990	1876	$15,865	$7,056	2-B	1,072	61	34
Stockton Univ., Galloway, NJ 08205-9441	1969	$12,568(S)	$11,164	5-D	8,570	660	67
Stonehill Coll., Easton, MA 02357	1948	$37,426	$14,290	2-B	2,401	274	82
Stony Brook Univ., State Univ. of New York, Stony Brook, NY 11794	1957	$8,430(S)	$11,648	5-D	24,607	1,627	69
Suffolk Univ., Boston, MA 02108-2770	1906	$32,660	$14,638	1-D	8,321	765	55
Sullivan Univ., Louisville, KY 40205	1864	NA	NA	3-D	4,394	319	NA
Sul Ross State Univ., Alpine, TX 79832	1920	$6,900(S)	$7,416	5-M	2,906	173	26
Summit Univ., Clarks Summit, PA 18411-1297	1932	$21,850	$5,800	2-D	1,001	47	36
Susquehanna Univ., Selinsgrove, PA 17870	1858	$40,350	$10,800	2-B	2,093	244	76
Swarthmore Coll., Swarthmore, PA 19081-1397	1864	$46,060	$13,550	1-B	1,534	206	92
Syracuse Univ., Syracuse, NY 13244	1870	$41,886	$14,460	1-D	21,492	1,597	80
Tarleton State Univ., Stephenville, TX 76402	1899	$8,246(S)	$9,042	5-D	11,697	672	43
Taylor Univ., Upland, IN 46989-1001	1846	$29,538	$8,283	2-M	2,209	210	74
Temple Univ., Philadelphia, PA 19122-6096	1884	$15,096(S)	$10,738	12-D	37,788	2,820	69
Tennessee State Univ., Nashville, TN 37209-1561	1912	$6,930(S)	$6,240	5-D	9,027	575	NA
Tennessee Tech. Univ., Cookeville, TN 38505	1915	$7,498(S)	$8,296	5-D	11,118	680	51
Tennessee Wesleyan Coll., Athens, TN 37303	1857	$22,900	$7,310	2-M	1,034	141	45
Texas A&M Intl. Univ., Laredo, TX 78041-1900	1969	$7,558(S)	$8,028	5-D	7,554	360	41
Texas A&M Univ., College Station, TX 77843	1876	$9,180(S)	$9,522	5-D	61,263	3,762	79
Texas A&M Univ.–Commerce, Commerce, TX 75429-3011	1889	$7,096(S)	$8,106	5-D	11,490	679	52
Texas A&M Univ.–Corpus Christi, Corpus Christi, TX 78412-5503	1947	$7,591(S)	$8,583	5-D	11,234	598	38
Texas A&M Univ.–Kingsville, Kingsville, TX 78363	1925	$7,554(S)	$7,554	5-D	8,728	460	36
Texas A&M Univ.–Texarkana, Texarkana, TX 75505-5518	1971	$5,794(S)	$5,910	5-M	1,653	NA	NA
Texas Christian Univ., Fort Worth, TX 76129-0002	1873	$38,600	$11,380	2-D	10,033	958	75
Texas Lutheran Univ., Seguin, TX 78155-5999	1891	$26,800	$9,240	2-M	1,320	125	46
Texas Southern Univ., Houston, TX 77004-4584	1947	$8,126(S)	$9,438	5-D	9,233	605	16
Texas State Univ., San Marcos, TX 78666	1899	$9,516(S)	$7,612	5-D	36,739	1,780	55
Texas Tech. Univ., Lubbock, TX 79409	1923	$9,308(S)	$8,405	5-D	35,158	1,636	59
Texas Wesleyan Univ., Fort Worth, TX 76105-1536	1890	$23,144	$8,238	2-D	2,606	229	39
Texas Woman's Univ., Denton, TX 76201 (4)	1901	$7,995(S)	$6,780	5-D	15,070	791	47
Thiel Coll., Greenville, PA 16125-2181	1866	$27,828	$10,900	2-B	1,074	101	36
Thomas Edison State Coll., Trenton, NJ 08608-1176	1972	$5,700(S)	NA	5-M	20,606	NA	NA
Thomas Jefferson Univ., Philadelphia, PA 19107	1824	NA	NA	1-D	3,326	NA	NA

Name, address	Year founded	Tuition & fees	Room & board	Control, degree	Enroll-ment	Faculty	Grad. rate
Thomas More Coll., Crestview Hills, KY 41017-3495	1921	$29,153	$7,770	2-M	1,655	128	46%
Thomas Univ., Thomasville, GA 31792-7499	1950	$14,740	$4,800	1-M	1,124	53	NA
Tiffin Univ., Tiffin, OH 44883-2161	1888	$21,560	$9,870	1-M	4,098	306	48
Touro Coll., New York, NY 10010	1971	$15,520	$10,600	1-D	17,544	NA	NA
Towson Univ., Towson, MD 21252-0001	1866	$8,650(S)	$11,260	5-D	22,285	1,671	68
Transylvania Univ., Lexington, KY 40508-1797	1780	$33,360	$9,300	2-B	1,014	110	70
Trevecca Nazarene Univ., Nashville, TN 37210-2877	1901	$23,126	$8,060	2-D	2,606	188	51
Trine Univ., Angola, IN 46703-1764	1884	$30,350	$10,200	1-M	2,832	358	53
Trinity Christian Coll., Palos Heights, IL 60463-0929	1959	$25,290	$9,390	2-M	1,406	154	58
Trinity Coll., Hartford, CT 06106-3100	1823	$50,776	$13,144	1-M	2,350	295	84
Trinity Intl. Univ., Deerfield, IL 60015-1284	1897	NA	NA	2-D	2,671	82	52
Trinity Univ., San Antonio, TX 78212-7200	1869	$36,214	$11,936	2-M	2,488	307	81
Trinity Washington Univ., Washington, DC 20017-1094 (3)	1897	$21,330	$9,658	2-M	1,630	NA	NA
Troy Univ., Troy, AL 36082	1887	$7,564(S)	$6,498	5-D	19,041	1,110	36
Truett-McConnell Coll., Cleveland, GA 30528	1946	$17,300	$7,120	2-M	1,681	128	22
Truman State Univ., Kirksville, MO 63501-4221	1867	$7,374(S)	NA	5-M	6,248	391	71
Tufts Univ., Medford, MA 02155	1852	$48,643	$12,634	1-D	10,917	1,061	92
Tulane Univ., New Orleans, LA 70118-5669	1834	$48,306	$12,556	1-D	13,531	1,211	83
Tusculum Coll., Greeneville, TN 37743-9997	1794	$22,670	$8,500	2-M	1,921	189	36
Tuskegee Univ., Tuskegee, AL 36088	1881	$19,120	$9,104	1-D	3,118	269	46
Union Coll., Barbourville, KY 40906-1499	1879	$24,075	$7,000	2-M	1,139	107	34
Union Coll., Schenectady, NY 12308-2311	1795	$48,384	$11,856	1-B	2,242	239	86
Union Inst. & Univ., Cincinnati, OH 45206-1925	1969	$11,904	NA	1-D	1,480	298	NA
Union Univ., Jackson, TN 38305-3697	1823	$28,190	$8,430	2-D	3,846	244	66
United States Air Force Acad., USAF Academy, CO 80840-5025	1954	$0(C)	NA	4-B	3,952	510	86
United States Military Acad., West Point, NY 10996 (2)	1802	$0(C)	NA	4-B	4,414	612	81
United States Naval Acad., Annapolis, MD 21402-5000	1845	$0(C)	NA	4-B	4,511	582	90
United Talmudical Seminary, Brooklyn, NY 11211 (1)	1949	NA	NA	2-M	1,500	NA	NA
Universidad Adventista de las Antillas, Mayagüez, PR 00681-0118	1957	$5,550	$2,900	2-M	1,322	95	30
Universidad del Este, Carolina, PR 00984	1949	$5,434	NA	1-M	13,317	NA	NA
Universidad del Turabo, Gurabo, PR 00778-3030	1972	$5,580	NA	1-D	17,325	993	19
Universidad Metropolitana, San Juan, PR 00928-1150	1980	$5,580	NA	1-D	13,773	1,149	25
Univ. at Albany, State Univ. of New York, Albany, NY 12222-0001	1844	$8,527(S)	$11,986	5-D	17,273	1,319	65
Univ. at Buffalo, the State Univ. of New York, Buffalo, NY 14260	1846	$8,871(S)	$12,400	5-D	29,944	1,797	72
Univ. of Advancing Tech., Tempe, AZ 85283-1042 (2)	1983	NA	NA	3-M	1,073	60	NA
The Univ. of Akron, Akron, OH 44325	1870	$10,260(S)	$10,968	5-D	23,976	1,601	40
The Univ. of Alabama, Tuscaloosa, AL 35487	1831	$9,826(S)	$8,866	5-D	36,047	1,776	66
The Univ. of Alabama at Birmingham, Birmingham, AL 35294	1969	$9,280(S)	$5,720	5-D	18,698	948	56
The Univ. of Alabama in Huntsville, Huntsville, AL 35899	1950	$9,158(S)	$8,433	5-D	7,348	484	46
Univ. of Alaska Anchorage, Anchorage, AK 99508	1954	$6,074(S)	$11,179	5-D	17,321	1,406	NA
Univ. of Alaska Fairbanks, Fairbanks, AK 99775-7520	1917	$7,370(S)	$8,242	5-D	8,700	993	43
Univ. of Alaska Southeast, Juneau, AK 99801	1972	$4,944(S)	$6,150	5-M	3,458	229	31
The Univ. of Arizona, Tucson, AZ 85721	1885	$10,581(S)	$9,700	5-D	42,236	1,834	60
Univ. of Arkansas, Fayetteville, AR 72701-1201	1871	$8,210(S)	$9,454	5-D	26,237	1,288	62
Univ. of Arkansas at Little Rock, Little Rock, AR 72204-1099	1927	$7,934(S)	$5,530	5-D	11,645	740	24
Univ. of Arkansas at Monticello, Monticello, AR 71656	1909	NA	NA	5-M	3,920	240	24
Univ. of Arkansas at Pine Bluff, Pine Bluff, AR 71601-2799	1873	$6,178(S)	$7,200	5-D	2,513	196	27
Univ. of Arkansas for Med. Sciences, Little Rock, AR 72205-7199	1879	$8,497(S)	$6,300	5-D	2,809	1,271	NA
Univ. of Arkansas–Fort Smith, Fort Smith, AR 72913-3649	1928	$5,891(S)	$8,077	11-B	6,823	412	27
Univ. of Baltimore, Baltimore, MD 21201-5779	1925	$8,018(S)	NA	5-D	3,526	405	NA
Univ. of Bridgeport, Bridgeport, CT 06604	1927	$29,920	$12,710	1-D	5,191	462	28
Univ. of California, Berkeley, Berkeley, CA 94720-1500	1868	$12,972(S)	$15,438	5-D	37,565	2,272	91
Univ. of California, Davis, Davis, CA 95616	1905	$13,896(S)	$14,218	5-D	34,508	1,792	83
Univ. of California, Irvine, Irvine, CA 92697	1965	$14,757(S)	$12,638	5-D	30,051	1,458	87
Univ. of California, Los Angeles, Los Angeles, CA 90095	1919	$13,029(S)	$13,135	5-D	43,239	2,657	91
Univ. of California, Merced, Merced, CA 95343	2005	$14,813(S)	$14,718	5-D	6,268	347	63
Univ. of California, Riverside, Riverside, CA 92521-0102	1954	$13,307(S)	$15,000	5-D	21,569	974	69
Univ. of California, San Diego, La Jolla, CA 92093	1959	NA	$12,254	5-D	28,294	1,213	86
Univ. of California, Santa Barbara, Santa Barbara, CA 93106-2014	1909	$13,860(S)	$14,128	5-D	23,051	1,079	81
Univ. of California, Santa Cruz, Santa Cruz, CA 95064	1965	$13,398(S)	$14,730	5-D	17,866	831	78
Univ. of Central Arkansas, Conway, AR 72035-0001	1907	$7,889(S)	$5,778	5-D	11,698	727	45
Univ. of Central Florida, Orlando, FL 32816	1963	$6,368(S)	$9,300	5-D	60,810	1,823	70
Univ. of Central Missouri, Warrensburg, MO 64093	1871	$7,265(S)	$7,828	5-M	13,379	635	54
Univ. of Central Oklahoma, Edmond, OK 73034-5209	1890	$6,686(S)	$9,862	5-M	16,840	900	37
Univ. of Charleston, Charleston, WV 25304-1099	1888	$24,200	$9,100	1-D	2,111	174	36
Univ. of Chicago, Chicago, IL 60637-1513	1891	$48,253	$14,205	1-D	12,558	1,748	93
Univ. of Cincinnati, Cincinnati, OH 45221	1819	$13,218(S)	$10,750	5-D	35,421	1,220	65
Univ. of Colorado Boulder, Boulder, CO 80309	1876	$10,789(S)	$12,810	5-D	32,080	1,927	70
Univ. of Colorado Colorado Springs, Colorado Springs, CO 80933-7150	1965	$9,143(S)	$9,150	5-D	11,463	745	47
Univ. of Colorado Denver, Denver, CO 80217-3364	1912	$9,985(S)	$11,140	5-D	22,791	3,816	40
Univ. of Connecticut, Storrs, CT 06269	1881	$13,364(S)	$12,174	5-D	26,541	1,589	81
Univ. of Dallas, Irving, TX 75062-4736	1955	$35,800	$11,300	2-D	2,548	234	70
Univ. of Dayton, Dayton, OH 45469	1850	$37,230	$11,840	2-D	11,343	929	76
Univ. of Delaware, Newark, DE 19716	1743	$12,342(S)	$11,558	12-D	21,895	1,654	81
Univ. of Denver, Denver, CO 80208	1864	$42,090	$11,109	1-D	11,808	1,282	76
Univ. of Detroit Mercy, Detroit, MI 48221	1877	$37,320	$8,528	2-D	5,725	NA	NA
Univ. of Dubuque, Dubuque, IA 52001-5099	1852	$26,950	$8,490	2-M	2,118	216	48
Univ. of Evansville, Evansville, IN 47722	1854	$31,776	$10,880	2-D	2,567	233	64
The Univ. of Findlay, Findlay, OH 45840-3653	1882	$30,640	$9,350	2-D	5,170	278	55
Univ. of Florida, Gainesville, FL 32611	1853	$4,477(S)	$9,630	5-D	50,350	3,782	88
Univ. of Georgia, Athens, GA 30602	1785	$10,836(S)	$9,246	5-D	35,197	NA	84
Univ. of Great Falls, Great Falls, MT 59405	1932	$21,556	$6,800	2-M	1,100	116	NA
Univ. of Guam, Mangilao, GU 96923	1952	$5,098(S)	$1,910	7-M	3,958	NA	29
Univ. of Hartford, West Hartford, CT 06117-1599	1877	$36,460	$11,638	1-D	6,817	788	55
Univ. of Hawaii at Hilo, Hilo, HI 96720-4091	1970	$7,548(S)	$9,970	5-D	3,924	338	38
Univ. of Hawaii at Manoa, Honolulu, HI 96822	1907	$10,584(S)	NA	5-D	19,507	1,512	56
Univ. of Hawaii–West Oahu, Kapolei, HI 96707	1976	$7,380(S)	NA	5-B	2,661	71	40
Univ. of Houston, Houston, TX 77204	1927	$10,518(S)	$9,278	5-D	40,914	2,018	48
Univ. of Houston–Clear Lake, Houston, TX 77058-1002	1971	$6,936(S)	$9,682	5-D	8,665	529	NA
Univ. of Houston–Downtown, Houston, TX 77002	1974	$6,614(S)	NA	5-M	14,439	668	19
Univ. of Houston–Victoria, Victoria, TX 77901-4450	1973	$6,749(S)	$7,108	5-M	4,407	239	NA
Univ. of Idaho, Moscow, ID 83844-2282	1889	$6,784(S)	$8,022	5-D	11,702	696	58
Univ. of Illinois at Chicago, Chicago, IL 60607-7128	1946	$13,634(S)	$10,871	5-D	27,563	1,856	60
Univ. of Illinois at Springfield, Springfield, IL 62703-5407	1969	$11,413(S)	$11,550	5-D	5,431	379	49
Univ. of Illinois at Urbana–Champaign, Champaign, IL 61820	1867	$15,602(S)	$10,848	5-D	44,942	1,893	84
Univ. of Indianapolis, Indianapolis, IN 46227-3697	1902	$26,170	$9,324	2-D	5,442	542	56

Name, address	Year founded	Tuition & fees	Room & board	Control, degree	Enroll-ment	Faculty	Grad. rate
The Univ. of Iowa, Iowa City, IA 52242-1316	1847	$8,104(S)	$9,728	5-D	31,387	1,616	70%
The Univ. of Kansas, Lawrence, KS 66045	1866	$9,707(S)	$7,896	5-D	27,180	1,773	60
Univ. of Kentucky, Lexington, KY 40506-0032	1865	$10,936(S)	$11,434	5-D	29,203	1,965	60
Univ. of La Verne, La Verne, CA 91750-4443	1891	$38,560	$12,510	1-D	4,876	459	59
Univ. of Louisiana at Lafayette, Lafayette, LA 70504	1898	$6,948(S)	$8,566	5-D	17,195	748	48
Univ. of Louisiana at Monroe, Monroe, LA 71209-0001	1931	$6,963(S)	$6,830	5-D	8,645	NA	NA
Univ. of Louisville, Louisville, KY 40292-0001	1798	$10,236(S)	$7,710	5-D	21,559	1,288	54
Univ. of Maine, Orono, ME 04469	1865	$10,606(S)	$9,296	5-D	11,286	845	60
Univ. of Maine at Augusta, Augusta, ME 04330-9410	1965	$7,448(S)	NA	5-B	4,664	282	12
Univ. of Maine at Farmington, Farmington, ME 04938-1990	1863	$9,217(S)	$8,970	5-M	1,960	173	54
Univ. of Maine at Fort Kent, Fort Kent, ME 04743-1292	1878	$7,575(S)	$7,720	5-B	1,327	93	52
Univ. of Maine at Presque Isle, Presque Isle, ME 04769-2888	1903	$7,435(S)	$7,656	5-B	1,138	98	46
Univ. of Mary, Bismarck, ND 58504-9652	1959	$15,665	$6,400	2-D	3,135	257	52
Univ. of Mary Hardin-Baylor, Belton, TX 76513	1845	$24,460	$7,020	2-D	3,740	294	48
Univ. of Mary Washington, Fredericksburg, VA 22401-5358	1908	$10,252(S)	$9,430	5-M	4,535	387	70
Univ. of Maryland, Baltimore County, Baltimore, MD 21250	1963	$10,384(S)	$10,562	5-D	13,979	785	65
Univ. of Maryland, College Park, College Park, MD 20742	1856	$9,427(S)	$10,633	5-D	37,610	2,442	85
Univ. of Maryland Eastern Shore, Princess Anne, MD 21853-1299	1886	$9,807(S)	$8,994	5-D	4,454	345	32
Univ. of Maryland Univ. Coll., Adelphi, MD 20783	1947	$6,744(S)	NA	5-D	47,906	2,599	NA
Univ. of Massachusetts Amherst, Amherst, MA 01003	1863	$13,443(S)	$11,457	5-D	28,635	1,470	76
Univ. of Massachusetts Boston, Boston, MA 02125-3393	1964	$11,966(S)	NA	5-D	16,756	1,219	42
Univ. of Massachusetts Dartmouth, North Dartmouth, MA 02747-2300	1895	$11,681(S)	$11,435	5-D	9,111	594	47
Univ. of Massachusetts Lowell, Lowell, MA 01854	1894	$12,447(S)	$11,278	5-D	17,184	1,043	54
Univ. of Memphis, Memphis, TN 38152	1912	$8,973(S)	$8,976	5-D	21,059	1,425	44
Univ. of Miami, Coral Gables, FL 33124	1925	$44,350	$12,684	1-D	16,774	1,542	82
Univ. of Michigan, Ann Arbor, MI 48109	1817	$13,486(S)	$10,246	5-D	43,625	3,259	91
Univ. of Michigan–Dearborn, Dearborn, MI 48128	1959	$11,222(S)	NA	5-D	8,923	563	50
Univ. of Michigan–Flint, Flint, MI 48502-1950	1956	$10,138(S)	$7,911	5-D	8,574	576	34
Univ. of Minnesota, Crookston, Crookston, MN 56716-5001	1966	$11,468(S)	$7,350	5-B	2,850	87	48
Univ. of Minnesota, Duluth, Duluth, MN 55812-2496	1947	$12,802(S)	$7,004	5-D	11,093	615	59
Univ. of Minnesota, Morris, Morris, MN 56267-2134	1959	$12,583(S)	$7,626	5-B	1,899	154	67
Univ. of Minnesota, Twin Cities campus, Minneapolis, MN 55455-0213	1851	$13,626(S)	$8,920	5-D	51,147	2,913	78
Univ. of Mississippi, University, MS 38677	1844	$7,096(S)	$9,908	5-D	22,503	2,063	61
Univ. of Mississippi Med. Ctr., Jackson, MS 39216-4505	1955	NA	NA	5-D	2,092	836	NA
Univ. of Missouri, Columbia, MO 65211	1839	$9,433(S)	$9,386	5-D	35,441	1,474	69
Univ. of Missouri–Kansas City, Kansas City, MO 64110-2499	1929	$9,476(S)	$9,815	5-D	16,160	1,172	51
Univ. of Missouri–St. Louis, St. Louis, MO 63121	1963	$10,065(S)	$9,052	5-D	17,085	961	46
Univ. of Mobile, Mobile, AL 36613	1961	$19,700	$9,550	2-M	1,600	172	42
The Univ. of Montana, Missoula, MT 59812-0002	1893	$6,330(S)	$8,006	5-D	13,952	853	50
The Univ. of Montana Western, Dillon, MT 59725-3598	1893	$4,797(S)	$6,536	5-B	1,470	94	54
Univ. of Montevallo, Montevallo, AL 35115	1896	$10,660(S)	$6,400	5-M	3,066	223	45
Univ. of Mount Olive, Mount Olive, NC 28365	1951	$17,800	$7,200	2-B	3,855	183	44
Univ. of Mount Union, Alliance, OH 44601-3993	1846	$27,990	$9,200	2-M	2,262	239	63
Univ. of Nebraska at Kearney, Kearney, NE 68849-0001	1903	$6,584(S)	$8,850	5-M	6,902	442	56
Univ. of Nebraska at Omaha, Omaha, NE 68182	1908	$6,750(S)	$8,408	5-D	15,227	1,044	42
Univ. of Nebraska–Lincoln, Lincoln, NE 68588	1869	$8,070(S)	$9,961	5-D	25,006	1,101	67
Univ. of Nebraska Med. Ctr., Omaha, NE 68198	1869	NA	NA	5-D	3,625	1,232	NA
Univ. of Nevada, Las Vegas, Las Vegas, NV 89154	1957	$6,590(S)	$10,730	5-D	28,525	1,444	39
Univ. of Nevada, Reno, Reno, NV 89557	1874	$6,872(S)	$10,868	5-D	19,934	1,041	50
Univ. of New England, Biddeford, ME 04005-9526	1831	$34,080	$12,670	1-D	6,429	499	61
Univ. of New Hampshire, Durham, NH 03824	1866	$16,552(S)	$10,360	5-D	15,169	1,032	77
Univ. of New Haven, West Haven, CT 06516-1916	1920	$34,630	$14,410	1-D	6,811	642	49
Univ. of New Mexico, Albuquerque, NM 87131-2039	1889	$6,447(S)	$8,580	5-D	27,889	1,624	48
Univ. of New Orleans, New Orleans, LA 70148	1958	$7,482(S)	$9,274	5-D	9,234	397	34
Univ. of North Alabama, Florence, AL 35632-0001	1830	$9,073(S)	$6,327	5-M	6,841	365	39
Univ. of North Carolina at Asheville, Asheville, NC 28804-3299	1927	$6,392(S)	$8,332	5-M	3,845	296	64
The Univ. of North Carolina at Chapel Hill, Chapel Hill, NC 27599	1789	$8,336(S)	$10,592	5-D	29,135	2,006	90
The Univ. of North Carolina at Charlotte, Charlotte, NC 28223-0001	1946	$6,277(S)	$9,270	5-D	27,238	1,494	55
The Univ. of North Carolina at Greensboro, Greensboro, NC 27412-5001	1891	$6,442(S)	$7,688	5-D	18,647	952	56
The Univ. of North Carolina at Pembroke, Pembroke, NC 28372-1510	1887	$5,287(S)	$8,101	5-M	6,269	421	79
The Univ. of North Carolina Wilmington, Wilmington, NC 28403-3297	1947	$6,392(S)	$9,124	5-D	14,570	997	71
Univ. of North Dakota, Grand Forks, ND 58202	1883	$7,741(S)	$6,810	5-D	14,906	753	53
Univ. of North Florida, Jacksonville, FL 32224	1965	$6,385(S)	$9,204	5-D	15,984	873	55
Univ. of North Georgia, Dahlonega, GA 30597	1873	$6,816(S)	$9,162	5-D	16,064	779	52
Univ. of North Texas, Denton, TX 76203	1890	$9,706(S)	$7,760	5-D	36,166	1,438	50
Univ. of Northern Colorado, Greeley, CO 80639	1890	$7,733(S)	$10,360	5-D	11,784	770	46
Univ. of Northern Iowa, Cedar Falls, IA 50614	1876	$7,749(S)	$8,046	5-D	11,928	790	64
Univ. of Northwestern Ohio, Lima, OH 45805-1498	1920	NA	NA	1-B	3,848	127	NA
Univ. of Northwestern–St. Paul, St. Paul, MN 55113-1598	1902	$28,870	$8,954	2-M	3,427	208	63
Univ. of Notre Dame, Notre Dame, IN 46556	1842	$46,237	$13,224	2-D	12,179	1,309	95
Univ. of Oklahoma, Norman, OK 73019-0390	1890	$7,695(S)	$9,126	5-D	27,261	1,409	67
Univ. of Oklahoma Health Sciences Ctr., Oklahoma City, OK 73190	1890	$6,318(S)	NA	5-D	3,315	454	NA
Univ. of Oregon, Eugene, OR 97403	1876	$9,918(S)	$11,442	5-D	24,096	1,633	69
Univ. of Pennsylvania, Philadelphia, PA 19104	1740	$47,668	$13,464	1-D	21,296	2,048	96
Univ. of Phoenix–Online campus, Phoenix, AZ 85034-7209	1989	NA	NA	3-D	292,797	11,477	NA
Univ. of Pikeville, Pikeville, KY 41501	1889	$18,840	$7,210	2-D	2,457	150	38
Univ. of Pittsburgh, Pittsburgh, PA 15260	1787	$17,772(S)	$10,800	12-D	28,617	2,178	82
Univ. of Pittsburgh at Bradford, Bradford, PA 16701-2812	1963	$13,322(S)	$8,480	12-B	1,499	165	53
Univ. of Pittsburgh at Greensburg, Greensburg, PA 15601-5860	1963	$13,372(S)	$9,490	12-B	1,578	100	53
Univ. of Pittsburgh at Johnstown, Johnstown, PA 15904-2990	1927	$13,374(S)	$9,080	12-B	2,957	NA	60
Univ. of Portland, Portland, OR 97203-5798	1901	$38,520	$11,444	2-D	4,169	339	80
Univ. of Puerto Rico in Aguadilla, Aguadilla, PR 00604	1972	$1,662(S)	NA	6-B	3,076	NA	NA
Univ. of Puerto Rico in Arecibo, Arecibo, PR 00613	1967	$1,662(S)	NA	6-B	4,352	NA	NA
Univ. of Puerto Rico in Bayamón, Bayamón, PR 00959	1971	$2,212(S)	NA	6-B	5,075	258	45
Univ. of Puerto Rico in Carolina, Carolina, PR 00984-4800	1974	$1,662(S)	NA	6-B	4,321	NA	NA
Univ. of Puerto Rico in Cayey, Cayey, PR 00736	1967	NA	NA	6-B	3,830	164	41
Univ. of Puerto Rico in Humacao, Humacao, PR 00791	1962	$2,019(S)	$8,280	6-B	3,774	257	45
Univ. of Puerto Rico in Ponce, Ponce, PR 00732-7186	1970	$2,019(S)	$8,280	6-B	3,229	188	38
Univ. of Puerto Rico in Utuado, Utuado, PR 00641-2500	1979	$1,662(S)	NA	6-B	1,623	107	NA
Univ. of Puerto Rico, Mayagüez campus, Mayagüez, PR 00681-9000	1911	$1,662(S)	NA	6-D	13,852	NA	NA
Univ. of Puerto Rico, Med. Sciences campus, San Juan, PR 00936-5067 (4)	1950	NA	NA	6-D	2,381	NA	NA
Univ. of Puerto Rico, Río Piedras campus, San Juan, PR 00931-3300	1903	$1,662(S)	NA	6-D	18,966	1,084	47
Univ. of Puget Sound, Tacoma, WA 98416	1888	$43,428	$11,180	1-D	2,826	284	76
Univ. of Redlands, Redlands, CA 92373-0999	1907	$43,186	$12,710	1-D	5,147	524	73
Univ. of Rhode Island, Kingston, RI 02881	1892	$12,506(S)	$7,256	5-D	16,571	1,123	59
Univ. of Richmond, University of Richmond, VA 23173	1830	$46,680	$10,790	1-D	3,514	416	84
Univ. of Rio Grande, Rio Grande, OH 45674	1876	$21,930	$9,450	1-M	2,161	175	39

Name, address	Year founded	Tuition & fees	Room & board	Control, degree	Enroll-ment	Faculty	Grad. rate
Univ. of Rochester, Rochester, NY 14627	1850	$46,960	$13,708	1-D	11,060	793	84%
Univ. of St. Francis, Joliet, IL 60435-6169	1920	$29,950	NA	2-D	2,414	294	56
Univ. of St. Francis, Fort Wayne, IN 46808-3994	1890	$27,220	$9,276	2-M	2,308	274	50
Univ. of St. Joseph, West Hartford, CT 06117-2700 (4)	1932	$36,140	$14,850	2-D	2,565	279	52
Univ. of St. Mary, Leavenworth, KS 66048-5082	1923	$24,450	$8,448	2-D	1,436	245	35
Univ. of St. Thomas, St. Paul, MN 55105-1096	1885	$36,682	$5,770	2-D	10,226	NA	72
Univ. of St. Thomas, Houston, TX 77006-4696	1947	$29,440	$8,250	2-D	3,522	356	52
Univ. of San Diego, San Diego, CA 92110-2492	1949	$42,908	$11,910	2-D	8,349	897	77
Univ. of San Francisco, San Francisco, CA 94117-1080	1855	$42,634	$13,650	2-D	10,701	NA	70
The Univ. of Scranton, Scranton, PA 18510	1888	$39,956	$13,566	2-D	5,589	525	80
Univ. of Sioux Falls, Sioux Falls, SD 57105-1699	1883	$25,480	$6,700	2-M	1,564	140	49
Univ. of South Alabama, Mobile, AL 36688-0002	1963	$8,610(S)	$7,100	5-D	15,805	991	37
Univ. of South Carolina, Columbia, SC 29208	1801	$11,158(S)	$9,248	5-D	32,971	2,373	NA
Univ. of South Carolina Aiken, Aiken, SC 29801	1961	$9,602(S)	$7,110	5-M	3,444	265	39
Univ. of South Carolina Beaufort, Bluffton, SC 29909	1959	$9,404(S)	$7,310	5-B	1,794	141	27
Univ. of South Carolina Upstate, Spartanburg, SC 29303-4999	1967	$10,518(S)	$7,682	5-M	5,509	429	38
The Univ. of South Dakota, Vermillion, SD 57069-2390	1862	$8,022(S)	$7,089	5-D	10,061	595	57
Univ. of South Florida, Tampa, FL 33620-9951	1956	$6,410(S)	$9,400	5-D	41,938	1,698	63
Univ. of South Florida, St. Petersburg, St. Petersburg, FL 33701	1965	$5,821(S)	$9,400	5-M	4,592	263	32
Univ. of South Florida Sarasota-Manatee, Sarasota, FL 34243	1956	$5,587(S)	NA	5-M	1,912	135	NA
Univ. of Southern California, Los Angeles, CA 90089	1880	$48,280	$13,334	1-D	42,469	3,268	91
Univ. of Southern Indiana, Evansville, IN 47712-3590	1965	$6,957(S)	$7,928	5-D	9,364	664	39
Univ. of Southern Maine, Portland, ME 04104-9300	1878	$8,920(S)	$9,150	5-D	8,428	622	31
Univ. of Southern Mississippi, Hattiesburg, MS 39406-0001	1910	$7,224(S)	$7,640	5-D	14,792	942	48
The Univ. of Tampa, Tampa, FL 33606-1490	1931	$26,330	$9,624	1-M	7,683	675	62
The Univ. of Tennessee, Knoxville, TN 37996	1794	$11,876(S)	$10,296	5-D	30,386	2,090	69
The Univ. of Tennessee at Chattanooga, Chattanooga, TN 37403-2598	1886	$8,138(S)	$8,110	5-D	11,670	766	40
The Univ. of Tennessee at Martin, Martin, TN 38238-1000	1900	$8,024(S)	$5,786	5-M	7,042	523	47
The Univ. of Texas at Arlington, Arlington, TX 76019	1895	$8,878(S)	$8,156	5-D	39,740	NA	42
The Univ. of Texas at Austin, Austin, TX 78712-1111	1883	$9,830(S)	$11,456	5-D	51,313	3,026	81
The Univ. of Texas at Brownsville, Brownsville, TX 78520-4991	1973	$5,011(S)	$6,706	5-D	8,612	NA	26
The Univ. of Texas at Dallas, Richardson, TX 75080	1969	$11,806(S)	$9,542	5-D	23,095	1,110	71
The Univ. of Texas at El Paso, El Paso, TX 79968-0001	1913	$7,255(S)	$9,180	5-D	8,036	NA	45
The Univ. of Texas at San Antonio, San Antonio, TX 78249-0617	1969	$8,737(S)	$7,624	5-D	28,628	NA	31
The Univ. of Texas at Tyler, Tyler, TX 75799-0001	1971	$7,312(S)	$8,979	5-D	8,036	512	45
The Univ. of Texas Health Sci. Ctr. at Houston, Houston, TX 77225-0036	1972	$6,507(S)	NA	5-D	4,556	128	NA
The Univ. of Texas Health Sci. Ctr. at San Antonio, San Antonio, TX 78229-3900	1976	NA	NA	5-D	3,093	NA	NA
The Univ. of Texas Med. Branch, Galveston, TX 77555	1891	NA	NA	5-D	2,430	NA	NA
The Univ. of Texas–Pan Amer., Edinburg, TX 78539	1927	$5,173(S)	$5,952	5-D	21,015	865	43
The Univ. of Texas of the Permian Basin, Odessa, TX 79762-0001	1969	$6,458(S)	$7,978	5-M	5,560	237	34
The Univ. of the Arts, Philadelphia, PA 19102-4944	1870	$38,410	$14,004	1-M	1,894	470	60
Univ. of the Cumberlands, Williamsburg, KY 40769-1372	1889	$22,000	$8,500	2-D	5,736	324	36
Univ. of the District of Columbia, Washington, DC 20008-1175	1976	$5,128(S)	$10,300	9-D	4,803	576	14
Univ. of the Incarnate Word, San Antonio, TX 78209-6397	1881	$27,798	$11,364	2-D	8,745	577	42
Univ. of the Pacific, Stockton, CA 95211-0197	1851	$41,342	$12,582	1-D	6,304	781	67
Univ. of the Sacred Heart, San Juan, PR 00914-0383	1935	$5,660	$2,900	2-M	5,666	367	35
Univ. of the Sciences, Philadelphia, PA 19104-4495	1821	$36,096	$14,108	1-D	2,748	365	74
Univ. of the Virgin Islands, Saint Thomas, VI 00802-9990	1962	$4,794(S)	NA	7-M	2,280	260	26
The Univ. of Toledo, Toledo, OH 43606-3390	1872	$9,463(S)	$10,304	5-D	20,626	1,088	45
The Univ. of Tulsa, Tulsa, OK 74104-3189	1894	$39,036	$10,680	1-D	4,682	444	70
Univ. of Utah, Salt Lake City, UT 84112-1107	1850	$7,835(S)	$8,528	5-D	31,515	1,865	62
Univ. of Vermont, Burlington, VT 05405	1791	$16,226(S)	$10,780	5-D	12,856	770	76
Univ. of Virginia, Charlottesville, VA 22903	1819	$12,998(S)	$10,052	5-D	23,732	1,415	94
The Univ. of Virginia's Coll. at Wise, Wise, VA 24293	1954	$8,868(S)	$10,340	5-B	2,182	209	42
Univ. of Washington, Seattle, WA 98195	1861	$12,394(S)	$10,833	5-D	44,784	4,277	84
Univ. of Washington, Bothell, Bothell, WA 98011-8246	1990	$12,517(S)	$10,833	5-M	4,962	297	67
Univ. of Washington, Tacoma, Tacoma, WA 98402-3100	1990	$12,262(S)	$10,833	5-D	4,477	295	55
The Univ. of West Alabama, Livingston, AL 35470	1835	$8,018(S)	$6,256	5-M	3,989	251	32
Univ. of West Florida, Pensacola, FL 32514-5750	1963	$8,400(S)	$9,912	5-D	12,602	598	48
Univ. of West Georgia, Carrollton, GA 30118	1933	$6,956(S)	$8,532	5-D	12,206	635	41
Univ. of Wisconsin–Eau Claire, Eau Claire, WI 54702-4004	1916	$8,744(S)	$6,986	5-D	10,689	542	69
Univ. of Wisconsin–Green Bay, Green Bay, WI 54311-7001	1968	$7,758(S)	$7,224	5-M	6,921	317	51
Univ. of Wisconsin–La Crosse, La Crosse, WI 54601-3742	1909	$8,794(S)	$5,910	5-D	10,536	602	70
Univ. of Wisconsin–Madison, Madison, WI 53706-1380	1848	$10,410(S)	$8,600	5-D	43,193	2,935	85
Univ. of Wisconsin–Milwaukee, Milwaukee, WI 53201-0413	1956	$9,391(S)	$9,126	5-D	28,013	1,644	44
Univ. of Wisconsin–Oshkosh, Oshkosh, WI 54901	1871	$7,437(S)	$7,386	5-D	14,411	628	54
Univ. of Wisconsin–Parkside, Kenosha, WI 53141-2000	1968	$8,334(S)	$6,572	5-M	4,584	231	31
Univ. of Wisconsin–Platteville, Platteville, WI 53818-3099	1866	$7,491(S)	$7,080	5-M	8,901	424	52
Univ. of Wisconsin–River Falls, River Falls, WI 54022	1874	$7,751(S)	$6,435	5-M	6,184	400	51
Univ. of Wisconsin–Stevens Point, Stevens Point, WI 54481-3897	1894	$7,669(S)	$6,786	5-D	9,292	532	61
Univ. of Wisconsin–Stout, Menomonie, WI 54751	1891	$9,025(S)	$6,434	5-D	9,371	489	NA
Univ. of Wisconsin–Superior, Superior, WI 54880-4500	1893	$7,994(S)	$6,320	5-M	2,589	218	43
Univ. of Wisconsin–Whitewater, Whitewater, WI 53190-1790	1868	$7,600(S)	$6,144	5-M	12,159	620	57
Univ. of Wyoming, Laramie, WY 82071	1886	$4,646(S)	$9,755	5-D	12,820	790	54
Upper Iowa Univ., Fayette, IA 52142-1857	1857	$28,073	$7,910	1-M	5,162	659	38
Urbana Univ., Urbana, OH 43078-2091	1850	$20,896	NA	1-M	1,551	120	NA
Ursinus Coll., Collegeville, PA 19426-1000	1869	$46,080	$11,500	1-B	1,681	172	81
Ursuline Coll., Pepper Pike, OH 44124-4398 (4)	1871	$28,520	$9,490	2-D	1,236	224	47
Utah State Univ., Logan, UT 84322	1888	$6,384(S)	$5,680	5-D	27,662	1,107	49
Utah Valley Univ., Orem, UT 84058-5999	1941	$5,270(S)	NA	5-M	31,332	1,708	25
Utica Coll., Utica, NY 13502-4892	1946	$33,736	$11,934	1-D	4,249	412	44
Valdosta State Univ., Valdosta, GA 31698	1906	$6,142(S)	$7,864	5-D	11,563	616	39
Valencia Coll., Orlando, FL 32802-3028	1967	$2,473(S)	NA	5-B	42,915	1,602	NA
Valley City State Univ., Valley City, ND 58072	1890	$6,674(S)	$5,938	5-M	1,378	NA	48
Valparaiso Univ., Valparaiso, IN 46383	1859	$34,760	$10,180	2-D	4,516	391	67
Vanderbilt Univ., Nashville, TN 37240-1001	1873	$43,838	$14,382	1-D	12,686	1,194	93
Vanguard Univ. of Southern California, Costa Mesa, CA 92626-9601	1920	$30,050	$9,420	2-M	2,255	243	55
Vassar Coll., Poughkeepsie, NY 12604	1861	$49,570	$11,570	1-M	2,418	333	92
Vaughn Coll. of Aeronautics & Tech., Flushing, NY 11369 (2)	1932	$21,830	$12,365	1-M	1,614	203	52
Vermont Tech. Coll., Randolph Center, VT 05061-0500	1866	$13,200(S)	$9,414	5-B	1,544	200	NA
Villanova Univ., Villanova, PA 19085-1699	1842	$45,966	$12,278	2-D	10,735	1,011	89
Virginia Coll. in Birmingham, Birmingham, AL 35209	1989	NA	NA	3-M	3,826	NA	NA
Virginia Commonwealth Univ., Richmond, VA 23284-9005	1838	$14,573(S)	$9,318	5-D	31,163	3,311	57
Virginia Military Inst., Lexington, VA 24450 (2)	1839	$15,518(S)	$8,372	5-B	1,700	188	76
Virginia Polytechnic Inst. & State Univ., Blacksburg, VA 24061	1872	$11,455(S)	$7,598	5-D	31,224	1,661	82
Virginia State Univ., Petersburg, VA 23806-0001	1882	$8,002(S)	$10,128	5-D	5,025	446	43
Virginia Union Univ., Richmond, VA 23220-1170	1865	$14,930	$8,074	2-D	1,715	120	26

Name, address	Year founded	Tuition & fees	Room & board	Control, degree	Enroll-ment	Faculty	Grad. rate
Virginia Wesleyan Coll., Norfolk, VA 23502-5599	1961	$34,428	$8,680	2-B	1,502	130	48%
Viterbo Univ., La Crosse, WI 54601-4797	1890	$25,050	$8,260	2-D	2,804	320	49
Wagner Coll., Staten Island, NY 10301-4495	1883	$40,750	$12,450	1-D	2,217	221	64
Wake Forest Univ., Winston-Salem, NC 27109	1834	$47,682	$12,996	1-D	7,788	732	88
Walden Univ., Minneapolis, MN 55401	1970	$14,310	NA	3-D	52,188	3,222	NA
Waldorf Coll., Forest City, IA 50436-1713	1903	$20,884	$6,994	2-M	1,457	46	31
Walla Walla Univ., College Place, WA 99324-1198	1892	$25,866	$6,855	2-M	1,887	NA	56
Walsh Coll. of Accountancy & Business Admin., Troy, MI 48007-7006	1922	$14,775	NA	1-M	2,753	185	NA
Walsh Univ., North Canton, OH 44720-3396	1958	$26,670	$9,580	2-D	2,918	334	55
Wartburg Coll., Waverly, IA 50677-0903	1852	$37,190	$9,010	2-B	1,661	166	63
Washburn Univ., Topeka, KS 66621	1865	$6,038(S)	$6,541	10-D	6,722	537	35
Washington Adventist Univ., Takoma Park, MD 20912	1904	$21,395	$8,300	2-M	1,493	134	26
Washington & Jefferson Coll., Washington, PA 15301	1781	$41,282	$10,884	1-B	1,362	154	76
Washington & Lee Univ., Lexington, VA 24450-0303	1749	$45,617	$10,645	1-D	2,264	361	88
Washington Coll., Chestertown, MD 21620-1197	1782	$43,840	$10,612	1-M	1,481	184	74
Washington State Univ., Pullman, WA 99164	1890	$12,428(S)	$11,276	5-D	28,686	1,825	65
Washington State Univ. Tri-Cities, Richland, WA 99352-1671	1989	$12,428(S)	$11,276	5-D	1,347	NA	NA
Washington State Univ. Vancouver, Vancouver, WA 98686	1989	NA	NA	5-M	3,096	NA	NA
Washington Univ. in St. Louis, St. Louis, MO 63130-4899	1853	$48,093	$15,280	1-D	14,348	1,270	95
Wayland Baptist Univ., Plainview, TX 79072-6998	1908	$16,980	$6,690	2-M	5,534	576	32
Waynesburg Univ., Waynesburg, PA 15370-1222	1849	$21,290	$8,860	2-D	2,039	263	60
Wayne State Coll., Wayne, NE 68787	1910	$5,604(S)	$6,420	5-M	3,470	220	46
Wayne State Univ., Detroit, MI 48202	1868	$12,350(S)	$9,713	5-D	27,578	1,804	34
Weber State Univ., Ogden, UT 84408-1001	1889	$5,184(S)	$8,400	5-M	25,954	1,280	43
Webster Univ., St. Louis, MO 63119-3194	1915	$24,500	$10,600	1-D	4,692	878	64
Wellesley Coll., Wellesley, MA 02481 (3)	1870	$45,078	$13,960	1-B	2,474	351	86
Wentworth Inst. of Tech., Boston, MA 02115-5998	1904	$30,765	$12,840	1-M	4,558	355	64
Wesleyan Univ., Middletown, CT 06459	1831	$48,974	$13,504	1-D	3,224	396	93
Wesley Coll., Dover, DE 19901-3875	1873	$24,100	$10,670	2-M	1,770	170	22
West Chester Univ. of Pennsylvania, West Chester, PA 19383	1871	$9,054(S)	$8,042	5-D	16,086	913	67
West Coast Univ., North Hollywood, CA 91606	1909	$11,325	NA	3-M	1,792	NA	NA
West Texas A&M Univ., Canyon, TX 79016-0001	1909	$6,105(S)	$7,196	5-D	8,972	445	40
West Virginia State Univ., Institute, WV 25112-1000	1891	$6,228(S)	$10,356	5-M	2,884	195	25
West Virginia Univ., Morgantown, WV 26506	1867	$6,960(S)	$9,582	5-D	29,175	1,475	57
West Virginia Univ. Inst. of Tech., Montgomery, WV 25136	1895	$6,048(S)	$8,902	5-B	1,261	102	20
West Virginia Wesleyan Coll., Buckhannon, WV 26201	1890	$28,792	$4,040	2-M	1,511	152	58
West Liberty Univ., West Liberty, WV 26074	1837	$6,412(S)	$8,550	5-M	2,694	NA	40
Western Carolina Univ., Cullowhee, NC 28723	1889	$6,531(S)	$8,016	5-D	10,382	676	58
Western Connecticut State Univ., Danbury, CT 06810-6885	1903	$9,077(S)	$11,311	5-D	6,025	586	44
Western Governors Univ., Salt Lake City, UT 84107	1998	$6,070	NA	1-M	57,821	1,654	NA
Western Illinois Univ., Macomb, IL 61455-1390	1899	$11,282(S)	$9,450	5-D	11,458	705	54
Western Intl. Univ., Phoenix, AZ 85021-2718	1978	NA	NA	3-M	2,993	369	NA
Western Kentucky Univ., Bowling Green, KY 42101	1906	$9,140(S)	$7,171	5-D	20,171	1,195	50
Western Michigan Univ., Kalamazoo, MI 49008	1903	$10,685(S)	$8,943	5-D	23,914	1,466	54
Western New England Univ., Springfield, MA 01119	1919	$33,466	$12,688	1-D	3,966	352	60
Western New Mexico Univ., Silver City, NM 88062-0680	1893	$4,723(S)	NA	5-M	2,697	259	NA
Western Oregon Univ., Monmouth, OR 97361-1394	1856	$8,723(S)	$9,416	5-M	5,996	393	46
Western State Colorado Univ., Gunnison, CO 81231	1901	$7,874(S)	$9,050	5-M	2,581	141	37
Western Washington Univ., Bellingham, WA 98225-5996	1893	$8,965(S)	$10,042	5-M	15,060	898	72
Westfield State Univ., Westfield, MA 01086	1838	$8,682(S)	$10,236	5-M	6,321	482	63
Westminster Coll., New Wilmington, PA 16172-0001	1852	$33,410	$10,160	2-M	1,608	163	74
Westminster Coll., Salt Lake City, UT 84105-3697	1875	$30,364	$8,456	1-M	2,992	387	61
Westmont Coll., Santa Barbara, CA 93108-1099	1937	$39,990	$12,580	2-B	1,378	151	77
Westwood Coll.–Anaheim, Anaheim, CA 92806	NA	NA	NA	3-B	1,206	82	NA
Westwood Coll.–Inland Empire, Upland, CA 91786	NA	NA	NA	3-B	1,140	94	NA
Westwood Coll.–Online campus, Westminster, CO 80021	NA	NA	NA	3-M	7,584	281	NA
Wheaton Coll., Wheaton, IL 60187-5593	1860	$31,900	$8,820	2-D	2,914	314	89
Wheaton Coll., Norton, MA 02766	1834	$46,423	$11,840	1-B	1,587	188	77
Wheeling Jesuit Univ., Wheeling, WV 26003-6295	1954	$28,030	$5,470	2-D	1,575	162	64
Wheelock Coll., Boston, MA 02215-4176 (4)	1888	$32,830	$13,600	1-M	1,331	180	55
Whitman Coll., Walla Walla, WA 99362-2083	1859	$44,800	$11,228	1-B	1,498	216	87
Whittier Coll., Whittier, CA 90608-0634	1887	$41,636	$12,245	1-D	2,290	170	65
Whitworth Univ., Spokane, WA 99251-0001	1890	$37,630	$10,278	2-M	2,654	305	75
Wichita State Univ., Wichita, KS 67260	1895	$7,265(S)	$8,373	5-D	15,003	857	46
Widener Univ., Chester, PA 19013-5792	1821	$39,830	$12,588	1-D	5,985	625	53
Wilkes Univ., Wilkes-Barre, PA 18766-0002	1933	$31,262	$12,808	1-D	4,562	314	56
Willamette Univ., Salem, OR 97301-3931	1842	$44,076	$10,820	2-D	3,060	271	78
William Carey Univ., Hattiesburg, MS 39401-5499	1906	$10,800	$4,050	2-M	3,248	NA	NA
William Jessup Univ., Rocklin, CA 95765	1939	$26,480	$10,278	2-M	1,212	187	67
William Jewell Coll., Liberty, MO 64068-1843	1849	$32,330	$8,880	1-M	1,060	141	60
William Paterson Univ. of New Jersey, Wayne, NJ 07470-8420	1855	$12,244(S)	$10,670	5-D	11,048	1,148	51
William Peace Univ., Raleigh, NC 27604-1194	1857	$25,850	$9,900	2-B	1,077	153	41
William Penn Univ., Oskaloosa, IA 52577-1799	1873	$23,210	$6,222	2-M	1,791	215	32
William Woods Univ., Fulton, MO 65251-1098	1870	$22,160	$8,960	2-D	2,031	266	52
Williams Coll., Williamstown, MA 01267	1793	$48,310	$12,760	1-M	2,099	346	95
Wilmington Coll., Wilmington, OH 45177	1870	$29,120	$9,392	2-M	1,458	119	52
Wilmington Univ., New Castle, DE 19720-6491	1967	$8,162	NA	1-D	14,989	1,636	34
Wingate Univ., Wingate, NC 28174	1896	$28,110	$10,600	2-D	3,034	281	53
Winona State Univ., Winona, MN 55987	1858	$8,750(S)	$7,890	5-D	8,655	620	57
Winston-Salem State Univ., Winston-Salem, NC 27110-0003	1892	$7,187(S)	$8,528	5-M	6,427	336	37
Winthrop Univ., Rock Hill, SC 29733	1886	$13,812(S)	$8,182	5-M	1,050	561	56
Wisconsin Lutheran Coll., Milwaukee, WI 53226-9942	1973	$25,960	$8,900	2-M	1,178	151	64
Wittenberg Univ., Springfield, OH 45501-0720	1845	$38,090	$10,028	2-M	1,964	185	69
Wofford Coll., Spartanburg, SC 29303-3663	1854	$37,120	$10,730	2-B	1,608	158	78
Woodbury Univ., Burbank, CA 91504-1099	1884	$33,150	$10,048	1-M	1,607	271	47
Worcester Polytechnic Inst., Worcester, MA 01609-2280	1865	$44,222	$13,082	1-D	6,381	485	85
Worcester State Univ., Worcester, MA 01602-2597	1874	$8,557(S)	$11,255	5-M	6,350	512	53
Wright State Univ., Dayton, OH 45435	1964	$8,730(S)	$9,108	5-D	16,842	654	39
Wright State Univ.–Lake campus, Celina, OH 45822-2921	1969	$5,842(S)	$7,754	5-M	1,147	NA	33
Xavier Univ., Cincinnati, OH 45207	1831	$33,960	$11,020	2-D	6,538	699	71
Xavier Univ. of Louisiana, New Orleans, LA 70125-1098	1925	$21,552	$8,500	2-D	2,976	245	43
Yale Univ., New Haven, CT 06520	1701	$47,600	$14,600	1-D	12,336	1,687	96
Yeshiva Univ., New York, NY 10033-3201	1886	$38,730	$11,250	1-D	6,438	1,298	85
York Coll. of Pennsylvania, York, PA 17405-7199	1787	$18,240	$10,160	1-D	5,067	519	61
York Coll. of the City Univ. of New York, Jamaica, NY 11451-0001	1967	$6,447(S)	NA	11-M	8,493	501	29
Young Harris Coll., Young Harris, GA 30582	1886	$26,571	$9,190	2-B	1,034	105	NA
Youngstown State Univ., Youngstown, OH 44555-0001	1908	$8,317(S)	$8,645	5-D	12,545	1,049	34

DIRECTORY

Associations and Organizations

Source: World Almanac research

Selected list, generally by category and first distinctive key word in each title. Listed by acronym when that is the official name. Year established is in parentheses. Entries for religious organizations include addresses and leadership information for 2015.

Academic and Educational

Academies, Natl. (1863): (202) 334-2000; www.nationalacademies.org
African American Life and History, Assn. for the Study of (1915): (202) 238-5910; www.asalh.org
Alpha Delta Kappa (1947): (816) 363-5525; www.alphadeltakappa.org
AMIDEAST (America-Mideast Educational and Training Services, Inc.) (1951): (202) 776-9600; www.amideast.org
Anthropological Assn., American (1902): (703) 528-1902; www.aaanet.org
Archaeological Institute of America (1879): (617) 353-9361; www.archaeological.org
Arts, Americans for the (1960): (202) 371-2830; www.artsusa.org
Arts and Sciences, American Academy of (1780): (617) 576-5000; www.amacad.org
Beta Gamma Sigma Inc. (1913): (314) 432-5650; www.betagammasigma.org
Beta Sigma Phi Intl. (1931): (816) 444-6800; www.betasigmaphi.org
Biological Sciences, American Institute of (1947): (703) 674-2500; www.aibs.org
Classical Studies, Society for (fmr. American Philological Assn.) (1869): (215) 898-4975; www.apaclassics.org
College Board (1900): (212) 713-8000; www.collegeboard.org
Colleges and Universities, Assn. of American (1915): (202) 387-3760; www.aacu.org
Community Colleges, American Assn. of (1920): (202) 728-0200; www.aacc.nche.edu
Consumer Interests, American Council on (1953): (727) 493-2131; www.consumerinterests.org
Delta Kappa Gamma Society Intl. (1929): (512) 478-5748; www.dkg.org
Education, American Council on (1918): (202) 939-9300; www.acenet.edu
Education, Council for Advancement and Support of (1974): (202) 328-2273; www.case.org
Education of Young Children, Natl. Assn. for the (1926): (202) 232-8777; www.naeyc.org
Educators for World Peace, Intl. Assn. of (1973): (256) 534-5501; www.iaewp.org
English-Speaking Union of the U.S. (1920): (212) 818-1200; www.esuus.org
Entomological Society of America (1889): (301) 731-4535; www.entsoc.org
Family Relations, Natl. Council on (1938): (888) 781-9331; www.ncfr.org
Foreign Study, American Institute for (1964): (866) 906-2437; www.aifs.com
Freedom of Information Coalition, Natl. (1958): (573) 882-4856; www.nfoic.org
French Institute/Alliance Française (1971): (212) 355-6100; www.fiaf.org
Genealogical Society, Natl. (1903): (703) 525-0050; www.ngsgenealogy.org
Genetic Assn., American (1914): (541) 867-0334; www.theaga.org
Geological Society of America (1888): (303) 357-1000; www.geosociety.org
Hemispheric Affairs, Council on (1975): (202) 223-4975; www.coha.org
Industrial and Applied Mathematics, Society for (1952): (215) 382-9800; www.siam.org
Intl. Education, Institute of (1919): (212) 883-8200; www.iie.org
Intl. Educational Exchange, Council on (1947): (207) 553-4000; www.ciee.org
Intl. Law, American Society of (1906): (202) 939-6000; www.asil.org
Irish American Cultural Inst. (1962): (973) 605-1991; www.iaci-usa.org
IRTS Foundation (fmr. Intl. Radio and TV Society Foundation) (1939): (212) 867-6650; www.irts.org
Law Libraries, American Assn. of (1906): (312) 939-4764; www.aallnet.org
Learned Societies, American Council of (1919): (212) 697-1505; www.acls.org
Libraries Assn., Special (1909): (703) 647-4900; www.sla.org
Linguistic Society of America (1924): (202) 835-1714; www.lsadc.org
Literacy Assn., Intl. (fmr. Intl. Reading Assn.) (1956): (302) 731-1600; www.reading.org
Mathematical Society, American (1888): (401) 455-4000; www.ams.org
Mensa, Ltd., American (1960): (817) 607-0060; www.us.mensa.org
Meteorological Society, American (1919): (617) 227-2425; www.ametsoc.org
Metric Assn., Inc., U.S. (1916): www.us-metric.org
Microbiology, American Society for (1899): (202) 737-3600; www.asm.org
Modern Language Assn. of America (1883): (646) 576-5000; www.mla.org
Museums, American Alliance of (1906): (202) 289-1818; www.aam-us.org
Music Education, Natl. Assn. for (fmr. Music Educators Natl. Conference) (1907): (703) 860-4000; www.nafme.org
Musicological Society, American (1934): (207) 798-4243; www.ams-net.org
Negro College Fund, United (1944): (800) 331-2244; www.uncf.org
Oriental Society, American (1842): (734) 647-4760; www.umich.edu/~aos/
ORT America (1922): (212) 505-7700; www.ortamerica.org
PEN American Center (1922): (212) 334-1660; www.pen.org
Phi Beta Kappa Society (1776): (202) 265-3808; www.pbk.org
Phi Theta Kappa Honor Society (1918): (800) 946-9995; www.ptk.org
Philosophical Assn., American (1900): (302) 831-1112; www.apaonline.org
Physics, American Inst. of (1931): (301) 209-3100; www.aip.org
Physiological Society, American (1887): (301) 634-7164; www.the-aps.org
Poetry Society of America (1910): (212) 254-9628; www.poetrysociety.org
Poets, Academy of American (1934): (212) 274-0343; www.poets.org
Political Science, Academy of (1880): (212) 870-2500; www.psqonline.org
Religion, American Academy of (1909): (404) 727-3049; www.aarweb.org
Science, American Assn. for the Advancement of (1848): (202) 326-6400; www.aaas.org
Science Fiction Society, World (1939): www.wsfs.org
Sciences, Natl. Academy of (1863): (202) 334-2000; www.nasonline.org
Sigma Beta Delta (1994): (314) 516-4723; www.sigmabetadelta.org
Sociological Assn., American (1905): (202) 383-9005; www.asanet.org
Tau Beta Pi Assn. (1885): (865) 546-4578; www.tbp.org
Teach For America (1990): (212) 279-2080; www.teachforamerica.org
Theological Schools in the U.S. and Canada, Assn. of (1918): (412) 788-6505; www.ats.edu
Theosophical Society in America (1875): (630) 668-1571; www.theosophical.org
Universities, Assn. of American (1900): (202) 408-7500; www.aau.edu
World Learning (1932): (802) 257-7751; www.worldlearning.org

Animal Welfare and Environment

Animal Welfare Institute (1951): (202) 337-2332; www.awionline.org
Animals, American Society for the Prevention of Cruelty to (ASPCA) (1866): (212) 876-7700; www.aspca.org
Animals, People for the Ethical Treatment of (PETA) (1980): (757) 622-7382; www.peta.org
Appalachian Trail Conservancy (1925): (304) 535-6331; www.appalachiantrail.org
Audubon Society, Natl. (1905): (212) 979-3000; www.audubon.org
Cat Fanciers' Assn., Inc., The (1906): (330) 680-4070; www.cfa.org
Conservation Intl. (1987): (703) 341-2400; www.conservation.org
Defenders of Wildlife (1947): (800) 385-9712; www.defenders.org
Ducks Unlimited (1937): (901) 758-3825; www.ducks.org
Forest History Society (1946): (919) 682-9319; www.foresthistory.org
Foresters, Society of American (1900): (301) 897-8720; www.safnet.org
Friends of the Earth (1969): (202) 783-7400; www.foe.org
Garden Club of America (1913): (212) 753-8287; www.gcamerica.org
Garden Clubs, Inc., Natl. (1929): (314) 776-7574; www.gardenclub.org
Geographic Society, Natl. (1888): (813) 979-6845; www.nationalgeographic.com
Green Mountain Club (1910): (802) 244-7037; www.greenmountainclub.org
Greenpeace (1971): (202) 462-1177; www.greenpeaceusa.org
Hiking Society, American (1976): (301) 565-6704; www.americanhiking.org
Horse Council, American (1969): (202) 296-4031; www.horsecouncil.org
Humane Society of the U.S., The (1954): (202) 452-1100; www.humanesociety.org
Natural Resources Defense Council (1970): (212) 727-2700; www.nrdc.org
Nature Conservancy, The (1951): (703) 841-5300; www.nature.org
Ocean Conservancy (1972): (202) 429-5609; www.oceanconservancy.org
Ornithologists' Union, American (1883): www.aou.org
Recreation and Park Assn., Natl. (1965): (800) 626-6772; www.nrpa.org
Recycling Coalition, Inc., Natl. (1978): (202) 618-2107; www.nrcrecycles.org
Rose Society, American (1892): (318) 938-5402; www.ars.org
Save the Redwoods League (1918): (415) 362-2352; www.savetheredwoods.org
Sierra Club (1892): (415) 977-5500; www.sierraclub.org
Water Environment Federation (1928): (800) 666-0206; www.wef.org
Wildflower Center, Lady Bird Johnson (1982): (512) 232-0100; www.wildflower.org
Wildlife Federation, Natl. (1936): (800) 822-9919; www.nwf.org
World Wildlife Fund (1961): (202) 293-4800; www.worldwildlife.org

Children and Social Services

Big Brothers Big Sisters of America (1904): (813) 720-8778; www.bbbs.org
Boy Scouts of America (1910): (972) 580-2000; www.scouting.org
Boys & Girls Clubs of America (1906): (404) 487-5700; www.bgca.org
Camp Fire (fmr. Camp Fire Boys & Girls) (1910): (816) 285-2010; www.campfire.org
Child Welfare League of America (1920): (202) 688-4200; www.cwla.org
Children's Aid Society (1913): (205) 251-7148; www.childrensaid.org
Children's Book Council, The (1945): (212) 966-1990; www.cbcbooks.org
Feeding America (fmr. America's Second Harvest) (1976): (800) 771-2303; feedingamerica.org
4-H Council, Natl. (1914): (301) 961-2800; www.4-h.org
Future Business Leaders of America-Phi Beta Lambda, Inc. (1942): (800) 325-2946; www.fbla-pbl.org
Future Farmers of America Org., Natl. (1928): (317) 802-6060; www.ffa.org

Gifted Children, Natl. Assn. for (1954): (202) 785-4268; www.nagc.org
Girl Scouts of the USA (1912): (212) 852-8000; www.girlscouts.org
Honor Society, Natl. (1921): (703) 860-0200; www.nhs.us
Junior Achievement USA®. (1919): (719) 540-8000; www.ja.org
Junior Auxiliaries, Inc., Natl. Assn. of (1941): (662) 332-3000; www.najanet.org
Junior Chamber Intl. USA (1914): (636) 778-3010; www.usjaycees.org
Junior Honor Society, Natl. (1929): (703) 860-0200; www.njhs.us
Missing and Exploited Children, Natl. Center for (1984): (703) 224-2150; www.missingkids.com
Pilot Intl. (1921): (478) 477-1208; www.pilotinternational.org
Student Councils, Natl. Assn. of (1931): (703) 860-0200; www.nasc.us

Fraternal

Eagles, Fraternal Order of (1898): (614) 883-2200; www.foe.com
Eastern Star, General Grand Chapter, Order of the (1876): (202) 667-4737; www.easternstar.org
Elks of the USA, Benevolent and Protective Order of (1868): (773) 755-4700; www.elks.org
Freemasonry, Scottish Rite of, Supreme Council, 33°, Northern Masonic Jurisdiction (1813): (781) 862-4410; www.scottishritenmj.org
Freemasonry, Scottish Rite of, Supreme Council, 33°, Southern Jurisdiction (1802): (202) 232-3579; www.srmason-sj.org
Kiwanis Intl. (1915): (317) 875-8755; www.kiwanis.org
Knights of Columbus (1882): (203) 752-4000; www.kofc.org
Knights of Pythias, Order of (1864): (781) 436-5966; www.pythias.org
Lions Clubs Intl. (1917): (630) 571-5466; www.lionsclubs.org
Men, Natl. Coalition for (1977): (888) 223-1280; www.ncfm.org
Moose Intl., Inc. (1888): (630) 859-2000; www.mooseintl.org
Odd Fellows, Independent Order of (1819): (336) 725-5955; www.ioof.org
Rotary Intl. (1905): (847) 866-3000; www.rotary.org
Shriners Intl. (1872): (813) 281-0300; www.shrinersinternational.org
Sons of Italy in America, Order (1905): (202) 547-2900; www.osia.org
Sons of Norway (1895): (612) 827-3611; www.sofn.com
Woodmen of America, Modern (1883): (800) 447-9811; www.modern-woodmen.org

Historical

Civil War Trust (1987): (202) 367-1861; www.civilwar.org
Colonial Dames XVII Century, Natl. Soc. (1915): (202) 293-1700; www.colonialdames17c.org
Daughters of the American Revolution (1890): (202) 628-1776; www.dar.org
Daughters of the Confederacy, United (1894): (804) 355-1636; www.hqudc.org
Historic Preservation, Natl. Trust for (1949): (202) 588-6000; www.preservationnation.org
Historical Assn., American (1884): (202) 544-2422; www.historians.org
Lewis and Clark Trail Heritage Foundation (1969): (406) 454-1234; lewisandclark.org
Mayflower Descendants, General Soc. of (1897): (508) 746-3188; www.themayflowersociety.org
Pilgrims, Natl. Soc. Sons and Daughters of the (1908): www.nssdp.com
Railway Historical Society, Natl. (1935): (215) 557-6606; www.nrhs.com
Sons of the American Revolution, Natl. Soc. (1889): (502) 589-1776; www.sar.org
Sons of Confederate Veterans (1896): (800) 380-1896; www.scv.org
State and Local History, American Assn. for (1940): (615) 320-3203; www.aaslh.org
Supreme Court Historical Society (1974): (202) 543-0400; www.supremecourthistory.org
Theodore Roosevelt Assn. (1920): (516) 921-6319; www.theodoreroosevelt.org
Thoreau Society (1941): (978) 369-5310; www.thoreausociety.org
Titanic Historical Society, Inc. (1963): (413) 543-4770; www.titanichistoricalsociety.org
Victorian Society in America (1966): (215) 636-9872; www.victoriansociety.org

Industrial and Trade

Aerospace Industries Assn. (1919): (703) 358-1000; www.aia-aerospace.org
Better Business Bureaus, Council of (1912): (703) 276-0100; www.bbb.org
Chamber of Commerce, U.S. (1912): (202) 659-6000; www.uschamber.com
Chemistry Council, American (1872): (202) 249-7000; www.americanchemistry.com
Construction Specifications Institute (1948): (800) 689-2900; www.csinet.org
CropLife America (1933): (202) 296-1585; www.croplifeamerica.org
Electrical Manufacturers Assn., Natl. (1926): (703) 841-3200; www.nema.org
Fire Protection Assn., Natl. (NFPA) (1896): (617) 770-3000; www.nfpa.org
Fisheries Soc., American (1870): (301) 897-8616; www.fisheries.org
Foreign Trade Council, Natl. (1914): (202) 887-0278; www.nftc.org
Funeral Consumers Alliance (1963): (802) 865-8300; www.funerals.org
Hotel & Lodging Assn., American (1910): (202) 289-3100; www.ahla.com
Insurance Assn., American (1866): (202) 828-7100; www.aiadc.org
Magazine Media, Assn. of (1919): (212) 872-3700; www.magazine.org
Manufacturers, Natl. Assn. of (1895): (202) 637-3000; www.nam.org
Newspaper Assn. of America (1992): (571) 366-1000; www.naa.org
Nuclear Society, American (1954): (708) 352-6611; www.ans.org
Orchestras, League of American (1942): (212) 262-5161; www.symphony.org
Petroleum Institute, American (1919): (202) 682-8000; www.api.org
Printing Industries of America, Inc. (1887): (412) 741-6860; www.printing.org
Publishers, Assn. of American (1970): (202) 347-3375; www.publishers.org
Retail Federation, Natl. (1908): (202) 783-7971; www.nrf.com
Safety Council, Natl. (1913): (630) 285-1121; www.nsc.org
Shipbuilders Council of America (1920): (202) 737-3234; www.shipbuilders.org
Small Business Assn., Natl. (1937): (800) 345-6728; www.nsba.biz
Software & Information Industry Assn. (1999): (202) 289-7442; www.siia.net
Tall Buildings and Urban Habitat, Council on (1969): (312) 567-3487; www.ctbuh.org
Toy Industry Assn., Inc. (1916): (212) 675-1141; www.toyassociation.org
Water Works Assn., American (1881): (303) 794-7711; www.awwa.org
Zoos & Aquariums, Assn. of (1924): (301) 562-0777; www.aza.org

Lifestyle and Travel

AAA (American Automobile Assn.) (1902): (407) 444-7000; www.aaa.com
AARP (fmr. American Assn. of Retired Persons) (1958): (888) 687-2277; www.aarp.org
AFS Intercultural Programs USA (1947): (800) 237-4636; www.afsusa.org
Aircraft Owners and Pilots Assn. (1939): (800) 872-2672; www.aopa.org
Appalachian Mountain Club (1876): (617) 523-0636; www.outdoors.org
Boat Owners Assn. of the U.S. (1966): (800) 395-2628; www.boatus.com
Camp Assn., American (1910): (765) 342-8456; www.acacamps.org
Consumer Federation of America (1968): (202) 387-6121; www.consumerfed.org
Consumers Union (1936): (914) 378-2000; www.consumersunion.org
Green America (fmr. Co-op America) (1982): (800) 584-7336; www.greenamerica.org
Helicopter Society Intl., American (1943): (703) 684-6777; www.vtol.org
Hostelling Intl. USA (1934): (240) 650-2100; www.hiusa.org
Jewish Community Centers Assn. of North America (1917): (212) 532-4949; www.jcca.org
Motorcyclist Assn., American (1924): (614) 856-1900; www.americanmotorcyclist.com
Parents Without Partners, Inc. (1957): (800) 637-7974; www.parentswithoutpartners.org
Planetary Society (1980): (626) 793-5100; www.planetary.org
SCRABBLE® Players Assn., N. American (2009): www.scrabbleplayers.org
Sports Car Club of America (1944): (785) 357-7222; www.scca.org
Toastmasters Intl. (1924): (949) 858-8255; www.toastmasters.org
YMCA (Young Men's Christian Assn.) of the USA (1851): (800) 872-9622; www.ymca.net
YWCA (Young Women's Christian Assn.) USA (1858): (202) 467-0801; www.ywca.org

Military and Veterans

Air Force Assn. (1946): (703) 247-5800; www.afa.org
American Legion (1919): (317) 630-1200; www.legion.org
American Legion Auxiliary (1919): (317) 569-4500; www.alaforveterans.org
AMVETS (American Veterans) (1944): (877) 726-8387; www.amvets.org
Army, Assn. of the United States (1950): (703) 841-4300; www.ausa.org
Blinded Veterans Assn. (1958): (202) 371-8880; www.bva.org
Civil Air Patrol (1941): (877) 227-9142; www.gocivilairpatrol.com
Coast Guard Combat Veterans Assn. (1985): (610) 539-1000; www.coastguardcombatvets.com
Disabled American Veterans (1920): (859) 441-7300; www.dav.org
82nd Airborne Division Assn., Inc. (1944): (910) 223-1182; www.82ndassociation.org
Ex-Prisoners of War, American (1942): (817) 649-2979; www.axpow.org
Fleet Reserve Assn. (1924): (703) 683-1400; www.fra.org
Iraq and Afghanistan Veterans of America (2004): (212) 982-9699; www.iava.org
Jewish War Veterans of the U.S.A. (1896): (202) 265-6280; www.jwv.org
Legion of Valor Museum (1991): (559) 498-0510; www.fresnovetsmuseum.com
Marine Corps League (1937): (703) 207-9588; www.mcleague.org
Military Officers Assn. of America (1929): (703) 549-2311; www.moaa.org
Military Order of the World Wars (1919): (703) 683-4911; www.moww.org
National Guard Assn. of the U.S. (1878): (202) 789-0031; www.ngaus.org
Naval Institute, U.S. (1873): (410) 268-6110; www.usni.org
Navy League of the United States (1902): (703) 528-1775; www.navyleague.org
Ninety-Nines, Inc. (Intl. Org. of Women Pilots) (1929): (405) 685-7969; www.ninety-nines.org
Non-Commissioned Officers Assn. (1960): (210) 653-6161; www.ncoausa.org
Paralyzed Veterans of America (1946): (800) 424-8200; www.pva.org
POW/MIA Families, Natl. League of (1970): (703) 465-7432; www.pow-miafamilies.org
Purple Heart, Military Order of the (1932): (703) 354-2140; www.purpleheart.org
Reserve Officers Assn. of the U.S. (1922): (202) 479-2200; www.roa.org
Sons of the American Legion (1932): (317) 630-1200; www.legion.org/sons
Tin Can Sailors (Natl. Assn. of Destroyer Veterans) (1976): (800) 223-5535; www.destroyers.org
Uniformed Services, Natl. Assn. for (1968): (800) 842-3451; www.naus.org

USO, Inc. (United Service Org.) (1941): (888) 484-3876; www.uso.org
USS Los Angeles CA-135 Assn. (1977): www.uss-la-ca135.org/2la-assoc.htm
USS Missouri Memorial Assn., Inc. (1998): (808) 455-1600; www.ussmissouri.org
Veterans of Foreign Wars (1899): (816) 756-3390; www.vfw.org
Veterans of Foreign Wars, Ladies Auxiliary to the (1914): (816) 561-8655; www.ladiesauxvfw.org
Vietnam Veterans of America (1978): (301) 585-4000; www.vva.org
Women's Army Corps Veterans' Assn. (1946): (256) 820-6824; www.armywomen.org
Wounded Warrior Project (2002): (877) 832-6997; www.woundedwarriorproject.org

Political

Abortion Federation, Natl. (1977): (202) 667-5881; www.prochoice.org
Action Network, American (2010): (202) 559-6420; americanactionnetwork.org
Advancement and Support of Education, Council for (1974): (202) 328-2273; www.case.org
American Indians, Natl. Congress of (1944): (202) 466-7767; www.ncai.org
American-Islamic Relations, Council on (1994): (202) 488-8787; www.cair.com
Brady Campaign to Prevent Gun Violence (1974): (202) 370-8100; www.bradycampaign.org
Center for Responsive Politics (1983): (202) 857-0044; www.opensecrets.org
Cities, Natl. League of (1924): (202) 626-3100; www.nlc.org
Civil Liberties Union, American (ACLU) (1920): (212) 549-2500; www.aclu.org
Coffee Party USA (2010): (301) 259-1869; www.coffeepartyusa.com
Common Cause (1970): (202) 833-1200; www.commoncause.org
Concerned Women for America (1979): (202) 488-7000; www.cwfa.org
Congress of Racial Equality (CORE) (1942): (212) 598-4000; www.core-online.org
Conservation Voters, League of (1969): (202) 785-8683; www.lcv.org
Constitution Party (1992): (717) 390-1993; www.constitutionparty.com
Crime and Delinquency, Natl. Council on (1907): (800) 306-6223; www.nccdglobal.org
Crossroads GPS (Grassroots Political Strategies) (2010): (202) 706-7051; www.crossroadsgps.org
Democratic Natl. Committee (1848): (202) 863-8000; www.democrats.org
Feminists for Life of America (1972): (703) 836-3354; www.feministsforlife.org
Future Fund, Amer. (2007): (515) 661-4233; www.americanfuturefund.com
Gay & Lesbian Alliance Against Defamation (GLAAD) (1985): (212) 629-3322; www.glaad.org
Governors Assn., Natl. (1908): (202) 624-5300; www.nga.org
Grange of the Order of Patrons of Husbandry, Natl. (1867): (202) 628-3507; www.nationalgrange.org
Gray Panthers (1970): (202) 737-6637
Greens/Green Party of the USA (1984): (202) 319-7191; www.gp.org
Homeless, Natl. Coalition for the (1984): (202) 462-4822; www.nationalhomeless.org
Human Rights Campaign (1980): (202) 628-4160; www.hrc.org
Immigration Equality (1994): (212) 714-2904; immigrationequality.org
Immigration Reform, Federation for American (FAIR) (1979): (202) 328-7004; www.fairus.org
Japanese American Citizens League (1929): (415) 921-5225; www.jacl.org
Jewish Committee, American (1906): (212) 751-4000; www.ajc.org
John Birch Society (1958): (920) 749-3780; www.jbs.org
LGBTQ Task Force, Natl. (fmr. Natl. Gay and Lesbian Task Force) (1973): (202) 393-5177; www.thetaskforce.org
Libertarian Party (1971): (202) 333-0008; www.lp.org
Marriage, Natl. Org. for (2007): (888) 894-3604; www.nationformarriage.org
Marry, Freedom to (2003): (212) 851-8418; www.freedomtomarry.org
Mayors, U.S. Conference of (1932): (202) 293-7330; www.usmayors.org
NAACP (Natl. Assn. for the Advancement of Colored People) (1909): (410) 580-5777; www.naacp.org
NRA (National Rifle Assn.) (1871): (800) 672-3888; www.nra.org
Parliamentarians, Natl. Assn. of (1930): (816) 833-3892; www.parliamentarians.org
Patriot Majority (2005): www.patriotmajority.org
Progress, Center for American (2003): (202) 682-1611; www.americanprogress.org
Reform Party Natl. Committee (1995): (972) 275-9297; www.reformparty.org
Republican Natl. Committee (1856): (202) 863-8500; www.rnc.org
Southern Christian Leadership Conference (1957): (404) 522-1420; sclcnational.org
Southern Poverty Law Center (1971): (334) 956-8200; www.splcenter.org
State Governments, Council of (1933): (859) 244-8000; www.csg.org
Tax Foundation (1937): (202) 464-6200; www.taxfoundation.org
Tax Reform, Americans for (1985): (202) 785-0266; www.atr.org
Taxpayers Union, Natl. (1969): (703) 683-5700; www.ntu.org
Tea Party Federation, Natl. (2010): www.thenationalteapartyfederation.com
Tea Party Patriots (2009): www.teapartypatriots.org
Term Limits, U.S. (1992): (202) 261-3532; www.termlimits.org
Urban League, Natl. (1910): (212) 558-5300; www.nul.org
Women, Natl. Organization for (NOW) (1966): (202) 628-8669; www.now.org
Women and Families, Natl. Partnership for (1971): (202) 986-2600; www.nationalpartnership.org
Women Voters, League of (1920): (202) 429-1965; www.lwv.org
Women's Christian Temperance Union (1874): (847) 864-1397; www.wctu.org
Zionist Organization of America (1897): (212) 481-1500; www.zoa.org

Religious

African Methodist Episcopal Church (1787): 500 8th Ave. S., Nashville, TN 37203; (615) 254-0911; www.ame-church.com; Gen. Sec., Dr. Jeffery Cooper
African Methodist Episcopal Zion Church (1796): 3225 West Sugar Creek Rd., Charlotte, NC 28269; (704) 599-4630; www.amez.org; Senior Bishop, George E. Battle Jr.
American Baptist Churches USA (1907): P.O. Box 851, Valley Forge, PA 19482; (610) 768-2000; www.abc-usa.org; Gen. Sec., A. Roy Medley
Antiochian Orthodox Christian Archdiocese of North America (1895): P.O. Box 5238, Englewood, NJ 07631; (201) 871-1355; www.antiochian.org; Primate, Archbishop Metropolitan Joseph
Armenian Apostolic Church of America: *Eastern Prelacy* (1958): 138 E. 39th St., New York, NY 10016; (212) 689-7810; www.armenianprelacy.org; Prelate, Archbishop Oshagan Choloyan; *Western Prelacy* (1973): 6252 Honolulu Ave., La Crescenta, CA 91214; (818) 248-7737; www.westernprelacy.org; Prelate, Archbishop Moushegh Mardirossian
Assemblies of God USA (1914): 1445 N. Boonville Ave., Springfield, MO 65802; (417) 862-2781; www.ag.org; Gen. Supt., Dr. George O. Wood
Atheists, American (1963): P.O. Box 158, Cranford, NJ 07016; (908) 276-7300; www.atheists.org; Pres., David P. Silverman
Bahá'ís of the U.S., Natl. Spiritual Assembly of the (1909): 1233 Central St., Evanston, IL 60201; (847) 733-3400; www.bahai.us; Sec., Kenneth E. Bowers
Baptist Bible Fellowship Intl. (1950): 720 E. Kearney St., Springfield, MO 65803; (417) 862-5001; www.bbfi.org; Pres., Eddie Lyons
Baptist Convention, Southern (1845): 901 Commerce St., Nashville, TN 37203; (615) 244-2355; www.sbc.net; Pres., Dr. Ronnie Floyd
Baptist Convention, USA, Inc., Natl. (1886): 1700 Baptist World Center Dr., Nashville, TN 37207; (615) 228-6292; www.nationalbaptist.com; Pres., Dr. Jerry Young
Baptist Convention of America Intl., Inc., Natl. (1880): 777 S.R.L. Thornton Fwy., Ste. 210, Dallas, TX 75203; (214) 942-3311; www.nbcainc.com; Pres., Rev. Samuel C. Tolbert Jr.
Baptist Conventional of America, Natl. Missionary (1880): 6925 Wofford Dr., Dallas, TX 75227; (877) 886-6222; www.nmbca.com; Pres., Dr. Nehemiah Davis
Bible Society, American (1816): 1865 Broadway, New York, NY 10023; (212) 408-1200; www.americanbible.org; Pres., Dr. Roy L. Peterson
Biblical Literature, Society of (1880): 825 Houston Mill Rd., Atlanta, GA 30329; (404) 727-3100; www.sbl-site.org; Exec. Dir., Dr. John F. Kutsko
B'nai B'rith Intl. (1843): 1120 20th St. NW, Ste. 300 N, Washington, DC 20036; (202) 857-6600; www.bnaibrith.org; Pres., Allan J. Jacobs
Brethren in Christ Church (c. 1778): 431 Grantham Rd., Mechanicsburg, PA 17055; (717) 697-2634; www.bic-church.org; Natl. Dir., Dr. Alan Robinson
Buddhist Churches of America (1899): 1710 Octavia St., San Francisco, CA 94109; (415) 776-5600; www.buddhistchurchesofamerica.org; Pres., Kent Matsuda
Catholic Bishops, U.S. Conference of (2001): 3211 4th St. NE, Washington, DC 20017; (202) 541-3000; www.usccb.org; Gen. Sec., Msgr. Ronny E. Jenkins
Christian Church (Disciples of Christ) (1832): Disciples Center, P.O. Box 1986, Indianapolis, IN 46206; (317) 635-3100; www.disciples.org; Gen. Min. and Pres., Rev. Dr. Sharon E. Watkins
Christian Methodist Episcopal Church (1870): 4466 Elvis Presley Blvd., Memphis, TN 38116; (901) 345-0580; www.thec-mechurch.org; Senior Bishop, Lawrence Reddick
Church of the Brethren (1708): General Offices, 1451 Dundee Ave., Elgin, IL 60120; (847) 742-5100; www.brethren.org; Gen. Sec., Stanley J. Noffsinger
Church of Christ (1830): P.O. Box 472, Independence, MO 64051; (816) 206-0147; www.churchofchrist-tl.org; Sec., Council of Apostles, Duane L. Ely
Church of God (Anderson, IN) (1881): Box 2420, Anderson, IN 46018; (765) 642-0256; www.jesusisthesubject.org; Gen. Dir., Jim Lyon
Church of God (Cleveland, TN) (1886): 2490 Keith St. NW, Cleveland, TN 37320; (423) 472-3361; www.churchofgod.org; Gen. Overseer, Dr. Mark Williams
Church of God in Christ (1897): Mason Temple, 930 Mason St., Memphis, TN 38126; (901) 947-9300; www.cogic.org; Presiding Bishop, Bishop Charles E. Blake Sr.
Church of Jesus Christ (1862): World Operations Ctr., 110 Walton Tea Room Rd., Greensburg, PA 15601; (412) 771-1686; www.thechurchofjesuschrist.org
Church of Jesus Christ of Latter-day Saints, The (Mormons) (1830): 50 W. North Temple St., Salt Lake City, UT 84150; (801) 240-2640; www.lds.org; Pres., Thomas S. Monson
Church of the Nazarene (1908): Global Ministry Center, 17001 Prairie Star Pkwy., Lenexa, KS 66220; (913) 577-0500; www.nazarene.org; Gen. Sec., David P. Wilson
Community of Christ (reorganized Church of Jesus Christ of Latter-Day Saints) (1830): Intl. Headquarters, 1001 W. Walnut, Independence, MO 64050; (816) 833-1000; www.cofchrist.org; Pres., Stephen M. Veazey

Community Churches, International Council of (1950): 21116 Washington Pkwy., Frankfort, IL 60423; (815) 464-5690; www.icccusa.com; Interim Exec. Dir., Don Ashmall
Conservative Judaism, United Synagogue of (1913): 820 Second Ave., New York, NY 10017; (212) 533-7800; www.uscj.org; Pres., Margo Gold
Converge Worldwide (fmr. Baptist General Conference) (1852): 2002 S. Arlington Heights Rd., Arlington Heights, IL 60005; (800) 323-4215; www.convergeworldwide.org; Pres., Scott Ridout
Cumberland Presbyterian Church (1810): 8207 Traditional Pl., Cordova, TN 38016; (901) 276-4572; www.cumberland.org
Episcopal Church (1789): 815 Second Ave., New York, NY 10017; (212) 716-6000; www.episcopalchurch.org; Presiding Bishop and Primate, Most Rev. Katharine Jefferts Schori
Evangelical Lutheran Church in America (1988): 8765 W. Higgins Rd., Chicago, IL 60631; (773) 380-2700; www.elca.org; Presiding Bishop, Rev. Elizabeth A. Eaton
First Church of Christ, Scientist, The (1879): 210 Massachusetts Ave., Boston, MA 02115; (617) 450-2000; www.christianscience.com; Pres., Beverley Beddoes-Mills
Free Methodist Church USA (1860): 770 N. High School Rd., Indianapolis, IN 46214; (317) 244-3660; www.fmcusa.org; Chief Operating Officer, Larry Roberts
Freedom From Religion Foundation (1978): P.O. Box 750, Madison, WI 53701; (608) 256-8900; www.ffrf.org
Friends General Conference (1900): 1216 Arch St., #2B, Philadelphia, PA 19107; (215) 561-1700; www.fgcquaker.org; Gen. Sec., Barry Crossno
Gideons Intl. (1899): P.O. Box 140800, Nashville, TN 37214; (615) 564-5000; www.gideons.org
Greek Orthodox Archdiocese of America (1922): 8 E. 79th St., New York, NY 10075; (212) 570-3500; www.goarch.org; Primate, Archbishop Demetrios
Hadassah, the Women's Zionist Organization of America, Inc. (1912): 40 Wall St., New York, NY 10005; (888) 303-3640; www.hadassah.org; Exec. Dir. and CEO, Janice Weinman
Interfaith Alliance (1994): 1250 24th St. NW, Ste. 300, Washington, DC 20037; (202) 466-0567; www.interfaithalliance.org; Exec. Dir., Rabbi Jack Moline
Islamic Society of North America: 6555 S. County Rd. 750 East, Plainfield, IN 46168; (317) 839-8157; www.isna.net; Pres., Azhar Azeez
Jehovah's Witnesses (1931): 25 Columbia Heights, Brooklyn, NY 11201; (718) 560-5000; www.jw.org
Jewish Congress, American (1918): 260 Madison Ave., 2nd Fl., New York, NY 10016; (212) 879-4500; www.ajcongress.org; Pres., Jack Rosen
Jewish Reconstructionist Communities (2012): 1299 Church Rd., Wyncote, PA 19095; (215) 576-0800; www.jewishrecon.org; Pres., Rabbi Deborah Waxman
Jewish Women, Natl. Council of (1893): 475 Riverside Dr., Ste. 1901, New York, NY 10115; (212) 645-4048; www.ncjw.org; Pres., Debbie Hoffmann
Lutheran Church—Missouri Synod (1847): 1333 S. Kirkwood Rd., St. Louis, MO 63122; (800) 248-1930; www.lcms.org; Pres., Rev. Dr. Matthew C. Harrison
Mennonite Church USA (2001): 718 N. Main St., Newton, KS 67114; (316) 283-5100; www.mennoniteusa.org; Exec. Dir., Ervin Stutzman
Moravian Church in North America (1735): www.moravian.org; *Northern Prov.*: 1021 Center St., P.O. Box 1245, Bethlehem, PA 18016; (610) 867-7566; Pres., Betsy Miller; *Southern Prov.*: 459 S. Church St., Winston-Salem, NC 27101; (336) 725-5811; Pres., Rt. Rev. David Guthrie
North American Shia Ithnasheri Muslim Communities, Org. of (1986): P.O. Box 29691, Minneapolis, MN 55429; (905) 763-7512; www.nasimco.org; Pres., Gulamabbas Najafi
Orthodox Union (1898): 11 Broadway, New York, NY 10004; (212) 563-4000; www.ou.org; Exec. Vice Pres., Allen Fagin
Pentecostal Assemblies of the World, Inc. (1906): 3939 N. Meadows Dr., Indianapolis, IN 46205; (317) 547-9541; www.pawinc.org; Presiding Bishop, Charles H. Ellis, III
Presbyterian Church (U.S.A.) (1983): 100 Witherspoon St., Louisville, KY 40202; (800) 728-7228; www.pcusa.org; Exec. Dir., Linda Valentine
Progressive Natl. Baptist Convention, Inc. (1961): 601 50th St. NE, Washington, DC 20019; (202) 396-0558; www.pnbc.org; Pres., Dr. James C. Perkins
Rabbis, Central Conference of American (1889): 355 Lexington Ave., New York, NY 10017; (212) 972-3636; www.ccarnet.org; Pres., Richard A. Block
Reform Judaism, Union for (1873): 633 3rd Ave., New York, NY 10017; (212) 650-4000; www.urj.org; Pres., Rabbi Rick Jacobs
Secular Humanism, Council for (1980): P.O. Box 664, Amherst, NY 14226; (716) 636-7571; www.secularhumanism.org; Pres. and CEO, Ronald A. Lindsay
Separation of Church and State, Americans United for (1947): 1301 K St. NW, Ste. 850E, Washington, DC 20005; (202) 466-3234; www.au.org; Exec. Dir., Rev. Barry W. Lynn
Seventh-day Adventist Church (1863): 12501 Old Columbia Pike, Silver Spring, MD 20904; (301) 680-6000; www.adventist.org; Pres., Ted N. C. Wilson
Unitarian Universalist Assn. of Congregations (1961): 24 Farnsworth St., Boston, MA 02210; (617) 742-2100; www.uua.org; Pres., Rev. Peter Morales
United Church of Christ (1957): 700 Prospect Ave., Cleveland, OH 44115; (216) 736-2100; www.ucc.org; Pres., Rev. Geoffrey A. Black
United Methodist Church (1968): 100 Maryland Ave. NE, Washington, DC 20002; (202) 488-5600; www.umc.org
United Pentecostal Church Intl. (1945): 8855 Dunn Rd., Hazelwood, MO 63042; (314) 837-7300; www.upci.org; Gen. Supt., David K. Bernard
Wesleyan Church (1843): 13300 Olio Rd., Fishers, IN 46037; (317) 774-7900; www.wesleyan.org; Gen. Supt., Dr. Jo Anne Lyon

Businesses and Corporations

Source: World Almanac research

Listed below are major corporations offering products and services to U.S. consumers, as of June 2015. Alphabetization is by first key word or founder last name. Listings generally include examples of products offered.

Company name (NYSE/Nasdaq symbol, if traded on those markets): Address; Telephone number; Website; Top executive; Business, products, or services.

A&P: see Great Atlantic & Pacific Tea Co., Inc.
Abbott Laboratories (ABT): 100 Abbott Park Rd., Abbott Park, IL 60064; (224) 667-6100; www.abbott.com; Miles D. White; develops, mfr. pharmaceutical, nutritional, diagnostic prods. Spun off indep. pharm. co. Abvie, 1/1/2013. Acquired CFR Pharmaceuticals, 9/26/2014.
ABC: see Walt Disney Co.
adidas Group: Adi-Dassler-Strasse 1, D-91074 Herzogenaurach, Germany; +49 (0) 9132-84-0; www.adidas-group.com; Herbert Hainer; apparel and accessories mfr. (Reebok, Rockport, Taylor Golf).
Advance Publications, Inc.: 950 W. Fingerboard Rd., Staten Island, NY, 10305; (718) 981-1234; www.advance.net; Steven Newhouse; communications, newspaper and magazine publisher (*Parade*; Condé Nast subsids.: *New Yorker*, *Vanity Fair*, *Vogue*).
Aetna, Inc. (AET): 151 Farmington Ave., Hartford, CT 06156; (860) 273-0123; www.aetna.com; Mark T. Bertolini; health care, employee benefits. Announced plans to acquire Humana, 7/3/2015.
Aflac, Inc. (AFL): 1932 Wynnton Rd., Columbus, GA 31999; (706) 596-3493; www.aflac.com; Daniel P. Amos; supplemental health and life insurance.
Alaska Air Group, Inc. (ALK): 19300 International Blvd., Seattle, WA 98188; (206) 433-3200; www.alaskaair.com; Bradley D. Tilden; airline carriers (Alaska Airlines, Horizon Air).
Alcatel-Lucent (ALU): 148/152 route de la Reine, Boulogne-Billancourt 92100, France; +33 (0) 15514-1010; www.alcatel-lucent.com; Michel Combes; telecom. equip., broadband networks. Announced plans to merge with Nokia, 4/15/2015.
Alcoa Inc. (AA): 201 Isabella St., Pittsburgh, PA 15212; (412) 553-4545; www.alcoa.com; Klaus Kleinfeld; prod., mfr. of aluminum, aluminum prods. (aerospace, automotive, industrial materials and components).
Alibaba Group (BABA): 969 West Wen Yi Road, Yu Hang District, Hangzhou 311121, China; +86 571-8502-2088; www.alibaba.com; Jack Yun; online shopping, logistics, marketing; data mgmt.; financial serv. Record-high U.S. IPO, 9/19/2014.
Allegheny Technologies Inc. (ATI): 1000 Six PPG Pl., Pittsburgh, PA 15222; (412) 394-2800; www.atimetals.com; Richard J. Harshman; specialty metals mfr. (titanium, alloys).
Allstate Corp. (ALL): 2775 Sanders Rd., Northbrook, IL 60062; (847) 402-5000; www.allstate.com; Thomas J. Wilson; personal property and casualty insurance; financial services.
Altria Group, Inc. (MO): 6601 W. Broad St., Richmond, VA 23230; (804) 484-8897; www.altria.com; Martin J. Barrington; tobacco co. (Marlboro, Merit, Parliament, Virginia Slims). (Altria spun off Philip Morris's intl. operations in 2008 but owns Philip Morris brands in U.S.)
Alphabet: see Google, Inc.
Amazon.com, Inc. (AMZN): 440 Terry Ave. N., Seattle, WA 98109; (206) 266-1000; www.amazon.com; Jeffrey P. Bezos; online retailer of books, music, other consumer and household prods. Agreed to acquire game platform Twitch Interactive, 8/25/2014.
American Airlines Group, Inc. (AAL): 4333 Amon Carter Blvd., Ft. Worth, TX 76155; (817) 963-1234; www.aa.com; Doug Parker; airlines (American Airlines, American Eagle, US Airways). Formed from merger of American Airlines and US Airways, 12/9/2013.
American Electric Power Co., Inc. (AEP): 1 Riverside Plz., Columbus, OH 43215; (614) 716-1000; www.aep.com; Nicholas K. Akins; public utilities.
American Express Co. (AXP): World Financial Ctr., 200 Vesey St., NY, NY 10285; (212) 640-2000; www.americanexpress.com; Kenneth I. Chenault; charge and credit cards, travel-related services.
American Greetings Corp.: 1 American Rd., Cleveland, OH 44144; (216) 252-7300; www.americangreetings.com; Morry Weiss; greeting cards, stationery, party goods, gift items. Acquired by Weiss Family, 8/7/2013.
American Intl. Group, Inc. (AIG): 180 Maiden Ln., NY, NY 10038; (212) 770-7000; www.aigcorporate.com; Peter D. Hancock; insurance, financial services. AIG received $182 bil in govt. bailouts, 2008.

AmerisourceBergen (ABC): 1300 Morris Dr., Chesterbrook, PA, 19087; (610) 727-7000; www.amerisourcebergen.com; Steven H. Collis; distrib. of generic and brand-name pharmaceuticals.

Anheuser-Busch InBev (BUD): Brouwerijplein 1, 3000 Leuven, Belgium; +32 (16) 276111; www.ab-inbev.com; Carlos Brito; brewers (Budweiser, Bud Light, Michelob, Busch), soft drinks. Acquired Oriental Brewery, 3/31/2014.

Anthem, Inc. (ANTM): 120 Monument Cir., Indianapolis, IN 46204; (317) 488-6000; www.anthem.com; Joseph R. Swedish; health insurance co. Fmr. WellPoint, Inc.; renamed 12/3/2014. Agreed to acquire Cigna, 7/24/2015.

Apple Inc. (AAPL): 1 Infinite Loop, Cupertino, CA 95014; (408) 996-1010; www.apple.com; Tim Cook; mfr. of computers (Mac), digital media devices (iPod, iPhone, iPad) and distrib. (iTunes store, Apple Music). Acquired Beats Music, Beats Electronics, 8/1/2014.

ARAMARK Corp. (ARMK): 1101 Market St., Philadelphia, PA 19107; (215) 238-3000; www.aramark.com; Eric J. Foss; food/support services to institutions and facilities, uniforms and career apparel. IPO, 12/12/2013.

ArcelorMittal USA, Inc.: 1 South Dearborn, Chicago, IL 60603; (312) 899-3440; www.arcelormittal.com; Lou Schorsch; steel; U.S. subsidiary of Arcelor Mittal, based in Luxembourg.

Archer Daniels Midland Co. (ADM): 4666 Faries Pkwy., Decatur, IL 62526; (217) 424-5200; www.adm.com; Juan R. Luciano; agricultural commodities and prods.

Armstrong World Industries, Inc. (AWI): 2500 Columbia Ave., P.O. Box 3001, Lancaster, PA 17604; (717) 397-0611; www.armstrong.com; Matthew J. Espe; mfr. of flooring, ceiling prods., cabinets.

ArvinMeritor, Inc.: see Meritor, Inc.

Ashland Inc. (ASH): 50 E. RiverCenter Blvd., P.O. Box 391, Covington, KY 41012; (859) 815-3333; www.ashland.com; William A. Wulfsohn; petroleum producer and refiner (Valvoline, plastics), chemicals, road construction.

AT&T Inc. (T): 208 S. Akard St., Dallas, TX 75202; (210) 821-4105; www.att.com; Randall L. Stephenson; telecommunications, global information management. Acquired Mexican wireless provider Iusacell, 1/16/2015; DirecTV, 7/24/2015.

AutoNation, Inc. (AN): 200 SW 1st Ave., Ste. 1600, Ft. Lauderdale, FL 33301; (954) 769-6000; www.autonation.com; Mike Jackson; auto retailer; new and used vehicles; auto parts, maintenance, and repair; auto finance and insurance.

Avon Products, Inc. (AVP): 777 Third Ave., NY, NY 10017; (212) 282-7000; www.avon.com; Sheri S. McCoy; cosmetics, fragrances, skin and personal care items; fashion.

Bank of America Corp. (BAC): 100 N. Tryon St., Charlotte, NC 28255; (704) 386-5681; www.bankofamerica.com; Brian T. Moynihan; banking and financial services.

Barnes & Noble, Inc. (BKS): 122 Fifth Ave., NY, NY 10011; (212) 633-3300; www.barnesandnobleinc.com; Leonard S. Riggio; leading U.S. bookseller (retail and college), publisher (Sterling Pub. Co.). Announced it would spin off college bookstores business into separate co., 2/26/2015.

Baxter International Inc. (BAX): 1 Baxter Pkwy., Deerfield, IL 60015; (224) 948-2000; www.baxter.com; Robert L. Parkinson Jr.; mfr. of health care prods. Spun off pharmaceutical business into Baxalta, 7/1/2015.

Beam Suntory: 510 Lake Cook Rd., Deerfield, IL 60015; (847) 948-8888; www.beamsuntory.com; Matt Shattock; spirits (Jim Beam, Maker's Mark, Courvoisier, Sauza). Beam Inc. acquired by Suntory Holdings, Ltd., renamed Beam Suntory, 4/30/2014.

Bear Stearns Cos. Inc.: see JPMorgan Chase & Co.

Becton, Dickinson & Co. (BDX): 1 Becton Dr., Franklin Lakes, NJ 07417; (201) 847-6800; www.bd.com; Vincent A. Forlenza; medical, laboratory, diagnostic prods. Acquired med. tech. firm Alverix, Inc., 1/7/2014.

Berkshire Hathaway Inc. (BRK.A): 3555 Farnam St., Ste. 1440, Omaha, NE 68131; (402) 346-1400; www.berkshirehathaway.com; Warren E. Buffett; diversified holdings incl. insurance (GEICO), building materials (Benjamin Moore & Co., Shaw), apparel (Fruit of the Loom), food (Dairy Queen). Agreed to buy Duracell from Procter & Gamble, 11/13/2014; agreed to acquire Precision Castparts, 8/10/2015.

Bertelsmann AG: Carl-Bertelsmann-Str. 270, 33311 Gütersloh, Germany; +49 (0) 5241-80-62321; www.bertelsmann.de; Thomas Rabe; intl. media corp., trade book publisher (Random House: Knopf, Doubleday). Formed Penguin Random House with Pearson, 7/1/2013.

Best Buy Co., Inc. (BBY): 7601 Penn Ave. S., Richfield, MN 55423; (612) 291-1000; www.bestbuy.com; Hubert Joly; retailer of software, appliances, cellular phones, consumer electronics.

Blackstone Group LP, The (BX): 345 Park Ave., NY, NY 10154; (212) 583-5000; www.blackstone.com; Stephen A. Schwarzman; asset mgmt., financial services.

Blockbuster LLC: see Dish Network.

Boeing Co. (BA): 100 N. Riverside, Chicago, IL 60606; (312) 544-2000; www.boeing.com; Dennis A. Muilenburg; world's leading aerospace co., mfr. of commercial jet and military aircraft; one of the largest U.S. defense contractors.

Brink's Co., The (BCO): 1801 Bayberry Ct., P.O. Box 18100, Richmond, VA 23226; (469) 549-6000; www.brinkscompany.com; Thomas C. Schievelbein; security (armored transport, money processing, trans. of valuables).

Bristol-Myers Squibb Co. (BMY): 345 Park Ave., NY, NY 10154; (212) 546-4000; www.bms.com; Giovanni Caforio; development, mfr., and sale of pharmaceuticals (Plavix, Abilify, Atripla).

Brown-Forman Corp. (BFB): 850 Dixie Hwy., Louisville, KY 40210; (502) 585-1100; www.brown-forman.com; Paul C. Varga; distilled spirits (Jack Daniel's, Southern Comfort, Finlandia), wine and champagne (Sonoma-Cutrer, Korbel).

Brown Shoe Co., Inc.: see Caleres.

Brunswick Corp. (BC): 1 N. Field Ct., Lake Forest, IL 60045; (847) 735-4700; www.brunswick.com; Dustan E. McCoy; leisure and recreation prods., incl. marine engines and boats; billiards, bowling, and fitness equip. bowling centers.

Burger King (BKW): see Restaurant Brands Intl.

Caleres (CAL): 8300 Maryland Ave., St. Louis, MO 63105; (314) 854-4000; www.caleres.com; Diane M. Sullivan; shoe mfr. (Buster Brown, Naturalizer, Dr. Scholl's, AVIA) and retailer (Famous Footwear). Sold shoes.com, 12/15/2014; fmr. Brown Shoe Co.; renamed 5/28/2015.

Cablevision Systems Corp. (CVC): 1111 Stewart Ave., Bethpage, NY 11714; (516) 803-2300; www.cablevision.com; James L. Dolan; cable and Internet services provider (Optimum); local media and programming; movie theaters (Clearview). Sold Optimum West to Charter, 7/1/2013.

Caesars Entertainment Corp. (CZR): One Caesars Palace Dr., Las Vegas, NV 89109; (702) 407-6000; www.caesars.com; Mark Frissora; casinos; gambling services (Caesars, Harrah's, Horseshoe, World Series of Poker). Operating unit filed for Ch. 11 reorganization, 1/15/2015.

Campbell Soup Co. (CPB): One Campbell Pl., Camden, NJ 08103; (856) 342-4800; www.campbellsoupcompany.com; Denise Morrison; soup mfr.; sauces (Pace, Prego), V8 juice, Pepperidge Farm prods. Acquired Garden Fresh Gourmet, 6/29/2015.

Cardinal Health, Inc. (CAH): 7000 Cardinal Pl., Dublin, OH 43017; (614) 757-5000; www.cardinalhealth.com; George S. Barrett; pharmaceutical and med. equip. dist. co. Acquired med. device mfr. AccessClosure, 5/12/2014.

Carlyle Group, The (CG): 1001 Pennsylvania Ave. NW, Washington, DC 20004; (202) 729-5399; www.carlyle.com; William E. Conway Jr.; private equity group.

Caterpillar Inc. (CAT): 100 NE Adams St., Peoria, IL 61629; (309) 675-1000; www.caterpillar.com; Douglas R. Oberhelman; mfr. of construction and mining equip. Acquired Berg Propulsion, 9/6/2013.

CBS Corp. (CBS): 51 W. 52nd St., NY, NY 10019; (212) 975-4321; www.cbscorporation.com; Leslie Moonves; TV networks (CBS, Showtime); TV distribution; radio stations; book publishing (Simon & Schuster).

CenturyLink, Inc. (CTL): 100 CenturyLink Dr., Monroe, LA 71203; (318) 388-9000; www.centurylink.com; Glen F. Post III; telecommunications provider.

Charter Communications, Inc. (CHTR): 400 Atlantic St., Stamford, CT 06901; (203) 905-7801; www.charter.com; Tom Rutledge; cable TV provider. Announced plan to buy Time Warner Cable and Bright House Networks, 5/26/2015.

Chevron Corp. (CVX): 6001 Bollinger Canyon Rd., San Ramon, CA 94583; (925) 842-1000; www.chevron.com; John S. Watson; integrated energy co.

Chiquita Brands Intl., Inc.: 550 S. Caldwell St., Charlotte, NC 28202; (980) 636-5000; www.chiquita.com; Brian W. Kocher; fruits and vegetables. Acquired by Cutrale-Safra, 1/6/2015.

CHS, Inc. (CHSCP): 5500 Cenex Dr., Inver Grove Heights, MN 55077; (651) 355-6000; www.chsinc.com; Carl Casale; grain marketing, oil refining, and pipeline operations.

Church & Dwight Co., Inc. (CHD): Princeton South Corporate Center, 500 Charles Ewing Blvd., Ewing, NJ 08628; (800) 524-1328; www.churchdwight.com; James R. Craigie; top world producer of sodium bicarbonate (ARM & HAMMER baking soda); household (OxiClean) and personal care prods. (Arrid, Trojan, First Response).

Cigna Corp. (CI): 900 Cottage Grove Rd., Bloomfield, CT 06002; (860) 226-6000; www.cigna.com; David M. Cordani; insurance provider. Acquisition by Anthem announced, 7/24/2015.

Cintas Corp. (CTAS): 6800 Cintas Blvd., Cincinnati, OH 45262; (513) 459-1200; www.cintas.com; Scott D. Farmer; uniform supplier.

Circuit City Stores, Inc.: see Systemax Inc.

Cisco Systems, Inc. (CSCO): 170 W. Tasman Dr., San Jose, CA 95134; (408) 526-4000; www.cisco.com; John T. Chambers; networking and communication prods.

Citigroup, Inc. (C): 399 Park Ave., NY, NY 10022; (212) 559-1000; www.citigroup.com; Michael L. Corbat; diversified financial services.

Clorox Co. (CLX): 1221 Broadway, Oakland, CA 94612; (510) 271-7000; www.clorox.com; Benno Dorer; consumer prods. (Clorox, Formula 409, Pine-Sol, S.O.S., Tilex; Scoop Away, Fresh Step cat litters; Kingsford charcoal; Hidden Valley dressing; Glad plastic bags; Brita water systems; Burt's Bees personal care prods.).

Coca-Cola Co. (KO): 1 Coca-Cola Plz., Atlanta, GA 30313; (404) 676-2121; www.coca-cola.com; Muhtar Kent; beverages (Coca-Cola, Sprite, DASANI water), juice prods. (Minute Maid).

Colgate-Palmolive Co. (CL): 300 Park Ave., NY, NY 10022; (212) 310-2000; www.colgate.com; Ian M. Cook; soap (Irish Spring), detergent (Palmolive), household cleansers (Ajax), toothpaste (Colgate, Tom's of Maine), pet food (Hill's Science Diet).

Comcast Corp. (CMCSA): 1701 JFK Blvd., Philadelphia, PA 19103; (215) 286-1700; www.comcast.com; Brian L. Roberts; cable provider; broadband media services; programming (E!, NBC, Bravo, USA, Telemundo).

Computer Sciences Corp. (CSC): 3170 Fairview Park Dr., Falls Church, VA 22042; (703) 876-1000; www.csc.com; Mike Lawrie; technology services.
ConAgra Foods, Inc. (CAG): 1 ConAgra Dr., Omaha, NE 68102; (402) 240-4000; www.conagrafoods.com; Sean Connolly; food processor (Chef Boyardee, Healthy Choice frozen dinners, Egg Beaters, Reddi-wip); food service supplier. Acquired Ralcorp Holdings, 1/29/2013.
ConocoPhillips Co. (COP): 600 N. Dairy Ashford, P.O. Box 2197, Houston, TX 77079; (281) 293-1000; www.conocophillips.com; Ryan M. Lance; oil and gas exploration and prod. co. Spun off refining and marketing segment, 5/1/2012, as Phillips 66.
Consolidated Edison, Inc. (ED): 4 Irving Pl., NY, NY 10003; (212) 460-4600; www.conedison.com; John McAvoy; electric, natural gas utilities.
Continental Airlines, Inc.: see United Continental Holdings, Inc.
Corning Inc. (GLW): 1 Riverfront Plz., Corning, NY 14831; (607) 974-9000; www.corning.com; Wendell P. Weeks; mfr. of telecommunications, specialty equip. fiber optics. Agreed to acquire Samsung's fiber-optics business, 12/2/2014.
Costco Wholesale Corp. (COST): 999 Lake Dr., Issaquah, WA 98027; (425) 313-8100; www.costco.com; W. Craig Jelinek; wholesale warehouse stores.
Countrywide Financial: see Bank of America Corp.
Crane Co. (CR): 100 First Stamford Pl., Stamford, CT 06902; (203) 363-7300; www.craneco.com; Max H. Mitchell; mfr. of fluid control devices, vending machines, aircraft components.
Crown Holdings, Inc. (CCK): 1 Crown Way, Philadelphia, PA 19154; (215) 698-5100; www.crowncork.com; John W. Conway; leading producer of packaging prods. Acquired Mivisa Envases, 4/23/2014; Empaque, 2/18/2015.
CSX Corp. (CSX): 500 Water St., 15th Fl., Jacksonville, FL 32202; (904) 359-3200; www.csx.com; Michael J. Ward; rail freight transport.
CVS Health (CVS): 1 CVS Dr., Woonsocket, RI 02895; (401) 765-1500; www.cvs.com; Larry J. Merlo; retail drugstores. Fmr. CVS Caremark Corp.; ended tobacco sales and renamed co., 9/3/2014. Agreed to acquire Target's pharmacy/clinic businesses, 6/15/2015.
Dana Holding Corp. (DAN): 3939 Technology Dr., Maumee, OH 43537; (419) 887-3000; www.dana.com; Roger J. Wood; truck and auto parts, supplies.
Darden Restaurants, Inc. (DRI): 1000 Darden Center Dr., Orlando, FL 32837; (407) 245-4000; www.darden.com; Eugene Lee Jr.; casual-dining restaurants (Olive Garden, LongHorn Steakhouse). Sold Red Lobster, 7/28/2014.
Dean Foods Co. (DF): 2711 N. Haskell Ave., Ste. 3400, Dallas, TX 75204; (214) 303-3400; www.deanfoods.com; Greg A. Tanner; milk and specialty dairy prods. (Land O' Lakes, Horizon Organic, Silk soy milk, International Delight coffee creamers). Spun off WhiteWave Foods Co., 5/23/2013.
Deere & Co. (DE): One John Deere Pl., Moline, IL 61265; (309) 765-8000; www.deere.com; Samuel R. Allen; mfr. of farm equip., industrial equip., lawn and garden tractors.
Dell Inc.: 1 Dell Way, Round Rock, TX 78682; (512) 338-4400; www.dell.com; Michael S. Dell; laptop and desktop computers, network accessories, peripherals, tablets, smartphones. Acquired by founder Michael Dell and Silver Lake Partners, 10/29/2013. Bought data mining co. StatSoft, 3/24/2014.
Delta Air Lines, Inc. (DAL): 1030 Delta Blvd., Atlanta, GA 30354; (404) 715-2600; www.delta.com; Richard H. Anderson; air transportation.
Diebold, Inc. (DBD): 5995 Mayfair Rd., North Canton, OH 44720; (330) 490-4000; www.diebold.com; Andy W. Mattes; mfr. ATMs, security systems and prods.
Dillard's, Inc. (DDS): 1600 Cantrell Rd., Little Rock, AR 72201; (501) 376-5200; www.dillards.com; William Dillard II; dept. store chain.
Dish Network Corp. (DISH): 9601 S. Meridian Blvd., Englewood, CO 80112; (303) 723-1000; www.dish.com; Charlie Ergen; satellite media services.
Walt Disney Co., The (DIS): 500 S. Buena Vista St., Burbank, CA 91521; (818) 560-1000; disney.go.com; Robert A. Iger; motion pictures (Lucasfilm, Touchstone, Pixar); TV (ABC, ESPN) and radio; publishing; theme parks (Walt Disney World, Disneyland) and resorts. Acquired Maker Studios, 3/24/2014.
Doctor's Associates Inc.: 325 Bic Dr., Milford, CT 06461; (203) 877-4281; www.subway.com; Frederick A. DeLuca; restaurants (Subway).
Dole Food Co., Inc.: One Dole Dr., Westlake Village, CA 91362; (818) 879-6600; www.dole.com; David Murdock; food prods., fresh fruits, vegetables.
Dollar Tree (DLTR): 500 Volvo Pkwy., Chesapeake, VA 23320; (757) 321-5000; www.dollartree.com; Bob Sasser; discount retailer. Acquired Family Dollar, 7/6/2015.
R. R. Donnelley & Sons Co. (RRD): 111 S. Wacker Dr., Chicago, IL 60606; (312) 326-8000; www.rrdonnelley.com; Thomas J. Quinlan III; commercial printing; photos/graphics, translation; printer of *The World Almanac*. Acquired Courier Corp., 6/8/2015.
Dow Chemical Co. (DOW): 2030 Dow Ctr., Midland, MI 48674; (989) 636-1000; www.dow.com; Andrew N. Liveris; chemicals, plastics. Agreed to sell most of chlorine assets to Olin Corp., 3/27/2015.
Dow Jones & Co., Inc.: see News Corp.
Dr Pepper Snapple Group, Inc. (DPS): 5301 Legacy Dr., Plano, TX 75024; (972) 673-7000; www.drpeppersnapplegroup.com; Larry D. Young; bottler and distrib. of nonalcoholic beverages (Dr Pepper, Hawaiian Punch, 7UP, Snapple, Mott's).
Duke Energy Corp. (DUK): 550 S. Tryon St., Charlotte, NC 28202; (704) 594-6200; www.duke-energy.com; Lynn J. Good; utilities, fiber optic networks.
Dun & Bradstreet Corp. (DNB): 103 JFK Pkwy., Short Hills, NJ 07078; (973) 921-5500; www.dnb.com; Bob Carrigan; business information, research.
Dupont (E. I. du Pont de Nemours & Co.) (DD): 1007 Market St., Wilmington, DE 19898; (302) 774-1000; www.dupont.com; Ellen J. Kullman; petroleum, consumer prods. Spun off Chemours, 7/1/2015.
Eastman Kodak Co. (KODK): 343 State St., Rochester, NY 14650; (585) 724-4000; www.kodak.com; Jeffrey J. Clarke; imaging technology and services. Emerged from Chap. 11 reorganization, 9/3/2013; relisted on NYSE, 11/1/2013.
Eaton Corp. (ETN): Eaton Ctr., 1111 Superior Ave., Cleveland, OH 44114; (216) 523-5000; www.eaton.com; Alexander M. Cutler; mfr. vehicle components, controls.
eBay Inc. (EBAY): 2065 Hamilton Ave., San Jose, CA 95125; (408) 376-7400; www.ebay.com; John Donahoe; e-commerce (StubHub). Spun off PayPal, 7/17/2015.
Edison Intl. (EIX): 2244 Walnut Grove Ave., Rosemead, CA 91770; (626) 302-2222; www.edison.com; Theodore F. Craver Jr.; electric utilities.
Electronic Arts Inc. (EA): 209 Redwood Shores Pkwy., Redwood City, CA 94065; (650) 628-1500; www.ea.com; Andrew Wilson; leading U.S. video game publisher (Madden NFL, Battlefield, The Sims, UFC).
Electronic Data Systems: see Hewlett-Packard Co.
Eli Lilly and Co. (LLY): Lilly Corporate Center, Indianapolis, IN 46285; (317) 276-2000; www.lilly.com; John C. Lechleiter; pharmaceutical research, development, and manufacturing (Prozac, Strattera, Cialis). Acquired Novartis Animal Health, 1/1/2015.
EMC Corp. (EMC): 176 South St., Hopkinton, MA 01748; (508) 435-1000; www.emc.com; Joseph M. Tucci; data storage/protection.
Emerson Electric Co. (EMR): 8000 W. Florissant Ave., St. Louis, MO 63136; (314) 553-2000; www.emerson.com; David N. Farr; electrical, electronics prods. and systems.
Energizer Holdings, Inc. (ENR): 533 Maryville Univ. Dr., St. Louis, MO 63141; (314) 985-2000; www.energizer.com; Alan R. Hoskins; batteries, flashlights, personal care prods.
Enterprise Products Partners L.P. (EPD): 1100 Louisiana St., Houston, TX 77002; (713) 381-6500; www.enterpriseproducts.com; Michael A. Creel; oil processing/transport and waterborne freight.
Estée Lauder Cos. Inc. (EL): 767 Fifth Ave., NY, NY 10153; (212) 572-4200; www.elcompanies.com; Fabrizio Freda; cosmetics (Clinique, Bobbi Brown), fragrance, skin care prods. Acquired GLAMGLOW, 1/16/2015.
Exelon Corp. (EXC): 10 S. Dearborn St., 48th Fl., Chicago, IL 60680; (800) 483-3220; www.exeloncorp.com; Christopher M. Crane; electricity generation/distrib.; natural gas. Agreed to acquire Pepco Holdings, 4/30/2014.
Express Scripts Holding Co. (ESRX): 1 Express Way, St. Louis, MO 63121; (314)-996-0900; www.express-scripts.com; George Paz; U.S. pharmacy benefits mgmt. co.
ExxonMobil Corp. (XOM): 5959 Las Colinas Blvd., Irving, TX 75039; (972) 444-1000; www.exxonmobil.com; Rex W. Tillerson; integrated energy, oil co.
Facebook, Inc. (FB): 1601 Willow Rd., Menlo Park, CA 94025; (650) 308-7300; www.facebook.com; Mark Zuckerberg; social networking platforms, services. Acquired Little Eye Labs, 1/7/2014; WhatsApp, 2/19/2014; Oculus VR, 7/21/2014.
Federal Home Loan Mortgage Corp. (Freddie Mac): 8200 Jones Branch Dr., McLean, VA 22102; (703) 903-2000; www.freddiemac.com; Donald H. Layton; residential mortgage provider. Under U.S. govt. mgmt. since 9/7/2008.
Federal Natl. Mortgage Assn. (Fannie Mae): 3900 Wisconsin Ave. NW, Washington, DC 20016; (202) 752-7000; www.fanniemae.com; Timothy J. Mayopoulos; provider of residential mortgage funds. Under U.S. govt. mgmt. since 9/7/2008.
FedEx Corp. (FDX): 942 S. Shady Grove Rd., Memphis, TN 38120; (901) 818-7500; www.fedex.com; Frederick W. Smith; delivery services. Announced plan to acquire Dutch co. TNT Express, 4/7/2015.
Fifth & Pacific Cos., Inc.: see Kate Spade & Co.
First Data Corp.: 5565 Glenridge Connector NE, Ste. 2000, Atlanta, GA 30342; (404) 890-2000; www.firstdata.com; Frank Bisignano; financial transaction processing.
FirstEnergy Corp. (FE): 76 S. Main St., Akron, OH 44308; (800) 736-3402; www.firstenergycorp.com; Charles E. Jones; public electricity supplier.
Fluor Corp. (FLR): 6700 Las Colinas Blvd., Irving, TX 75039; (469) 398-7000; www.fluor.com; David T. Seaton; international engineering and construction co.
Foot Locker, Inc. (FL): 112 W. 34th St., NY, NY 10120; (212) 720-3700; www.footlocker-inc.com; Richard A. Johnson; retail athletic stores (Footaction, Foot Locker, Champs Sports). Acquired Runners Point Group, 7/10/2013.
Ford Motor Co. (F): 1 American Rd., Dearborn, MI 48126; (313) 322-3000; www.ford.com; William C. Ford Jr.; auto mfr.; motor vehicle sales (Ford, Lincoln); auto financing (Ford Motor Credit).
Fortune Brands Home and Security, Inc. (FBHS): 520 Lake Cook Rd., Deerfield, IL 60015; (847) 484-4400; www.fbhs.com; Christopher Klein; cabinetry, plumbing (Moen), windows and doors, security and storage (Master Lock).
Fox: see News Corp.

Gannett Co., Inc. (GCI): 7950 Jones Branch Dr., McLean, VA 22107; (703) 854-6000; www.gannett.com; Robert Dickey; newspaper publisher (*USA Today*). Original Gannett Co., spun off network and cable TV and digital media divisions as TEGNA, Inc., 6/29/2015, newspapers as new entity retaining name.

Gap Inc. (GPS): 2 Folsom St., San Francisco, CA 94105; (650) 952-4400; www.gapinc.com; Art Peck; casual apparel retailer (Gap, Banana Republic, Old Navy).

General Dynamics Corp. (GD): 2941 Fairview Park Dr., Ste. 100, Falls Church, VA 22042; (703) 876-3000; www.generaldynamics.com; Phebe N. Novakovic; defense contractor: aerospace, combat systems, marine systems, computing devices.

General Electric Co. (GE): 3135 Easton Tpke., Fairfield, CT 06828; (203) 373-2211; www.ge.com; Jeffrey Immelt; electrical, electronic equip., financial services, radio and TV broadcasting, aircraft engines, power generation, appliances. Announced plans to acquire power businesses of French Alstom, 4/30/2014.

General Mills, Inc. (GIS): One General Mills Blvd., Minneapolis, MN 55426; (763) 764-7600; www.generalmills.com; Kendall J. Powell; food mfr. (Betty Crocker, Bisquick, Cheerios, Chex, Green Giant, Häagen-Dazs, Pillsbury, Progresso, Total, Wheaties, Yoplait). Acquired Annie's Homegrown, 10/21/2014.

General Motors Co. (GM): 300 Renaissance Ctr., Detroit, MI 48265; (313) 556-5000; www.gm.com; Mary T. Barra; auto mfr. (Chevrolet, Cadillac, Buick, GMC); auto financing (GM Financial); vehicle security (OnStar). General Motors Corp. filed for Chap. 11 reorganization, 6/1/2009; sold profitable components to a new, smaller co. called General Motors Co., 7/10/2009.

Genuine Parts Co. (GPC): 2999 Circle 75 Pkwy., Atlanta, GA 30339; (770) 953-1700; www.genpt.com; Thomas C. Gallagher; distrib. of auto (NAPA), industrial replacement parts.

Goldman Sachs Group, Inc. (GS): 200 West St., 29th Fl., NY, NY 10282; (212) 902-1000; www.goldmansachs.com; Lloyd C. Blankfein; investment banking, asset mgmt., securities services.

Goodyear Tire & Rubber Co. (GT): 200 Innovation Way, Akron, OH 44316; (330) 796-2121; www.goodyear.com; Richard J. Kramer; tires and other auto prods.

Google, Inc. (GOOG): 1600 Amphitheatre Pkwy., Mountain View, CA 94043; (650) 253-0000; www.google.com; Larry Page; Internet-related prods. and services (leading search engine, ad sales; YouTube). Acquired Nest Labs, Inc., 2/7/2014. Sold Motorola Mobility to Lenovo, 10/30/2014. Announced the company would reorganize under the name Alphabet, 8/10/2015.

W. R. Grace & Co. (GRA): 7500 Grace Dr., Columbia, MD 21044; (410) 531-4000; www.grace.com; Fred E. Festa; chemicals, construction prods. Emerged from Chap. 11 reorganization, 2/3/2014.

Graham Holdings Co. (GHC): 1150 15th St. NW, Washington, DC 20071; (202) 334-6000; www.ghco.com; Donald E. Graham; media (newspapers, Slate.com, TV), education (Kaplan), home health care. Fmr. Washington Post. Co.; renamed 11/29/2013 after sale of *Washington Post* newspaper to Amazon.com CEO Jeff Bezos, 10/1/2013.

Great Atlantic & Pacific Tea Co., Inc.: 2 Paragon Dr., Montvale, NJ 07645; (201) 573-9700; www.aptea.com; Paul Hertz; supermarkets (A&P, Food Basics, Food Emporium, Super Fresh, Waldbaum's, Pathmark).

Halliburton Co. (HAL): 3000 N. Sam Houston Pkwy. E., Houston, TX 77032; (281) 871-4000; www.halliburton.com; David J. Lesar; oil field mgmt., energy services. Agreed to acquire rival Baker Hughes Inc.,11/17/2014.

Hanesbrands Inc. (HBI): 1000 E. Hanes Mill Rd., Winston-Salem, NC 27105; (336) 519-8080; www.hanesbrands.com; Richard A. Noll; apparel mfr. (Hanes, barely there, Bali, Champion, Flexees, Glamorise, Gear for Sports, Just My Size, L'eggs, Lilyette, Playtex, Wonderbra). Acquired Maidenform Brands, Inc., 10/7/2013; DB Apparel, 9/3/2014; Knights Apparel, 4/8/2015.

Harley-Davidson, Inc. (HOG): 3700 W. Juneau Ave., Milwaukee, WI 53208; (414) 342-4680; www.harley-davidson.com; Keith E. Wandell; mfr. motorcycles, parts, and accessories.

Hartford Financial Services Group, Inc. (HIG): One Hartford Plz., Hartford, CT 06155; (860) 547-5000; www.thehartford.com; Christopher J. Swift; insurance, financial services.

Hasbro, Inc. (HAS): 1027 Newport Ave., Pawtucket, RI 02862; (401) 431-8697; www.hasbro.com; Brian Goldner; toy and game mfr. (Milton Bradley, Playskool, G.I. Joe, Parker Bros., Nerf, Play-Doh).

HCA Holdings, Inc. (HCA): 1 Park Plz., Nashville, TN 37203; (615) 344-9551; www.hcahealthcare.com; R. Milton Johnson; owns and operates hospitals; other diagnostic, surgical, health treatment centers. Agreed to acquire CareNow, 10/28/2014.

H. J. Heinz Co.: see Kraft Heinz Co.

Henkel Corp.: 19001 N. Scottsdale Rd., Scottsdale, AZ 85255; (480) 754-3425; www.henkelna.com; Jeffrey C. Piccolomini; consumer prods. (Dial soap, Purex detergent, Right Guard antiperspirant, Renuzit air fresheners); U.S. subsidiary of Germany's Henkel co.

Hershey Co., The (HSY): 100 Crystal A Dr., Hershey, PA 17033; (717) 534-4200; www.thehersheycompany.com; John P. Bilbrey; chocolate prods mfr. (Reese's, Kit Kat, Mounds, Almond Joy, Jolly Rancher, Twizzlers, Milk Duds, Good & Plenty, York, Krackel). Acquired Allan Candy Co., 12/4/2014.

Hertz Global Holdings, Inc. (HTZ): 225 Brae Blvd., Park Ridge, NJ 07656; (201) 307-2000; www.hertz.com; John P. Tague; car rentals.

Hess Corp. (HES): 1185 Ave. of the Americas, 40th Fl., NY, NY 10036; (212) 997-8500; www.hess.com; John B. Hess; integrated oil and gas co.

Hewlett-Packard Co. (HPQ): 3000 Hanover St., Palo Alto, CA 94304; (650) 857-1501; www.hp.com; Meg Whitman; computers, electronic prods. and systems. Announced plans to split into two cos., computer/printer businesses and corp. hardware/services, 10/6/2014. Agreed to Sell Snapfish to District Photo, 4/21/2015. Bought Wi-Fi equip. mfr. Arbua Networks, 5/19/2015.

Hillenbrand, Inc. (HI): One Batesville Blvd., Batesville, IN 47006; (812) 934-7000; www.hillenbrandinc.com; Joe Raver; holder of Batesville Caskets, coffin mfr.

Hill-Rom Holdings, Inc. (HRC): 1069 State Rte. 46 E., Batesville, IN 47006; (812) 934-7777; www.hill-rom.com; John J. Greisch; mfr. hospital beds, other hospital equip. Acquired Trumpf Medical Systems, 8/1/2014.

Hillshire Brands Co.: see Tyson Foods, Inc.

Hilton Worldwide (HLT): 7930 Jones Branch Dr., Ste. 1100, McLean, VA 22102; (703) 883-1000; www.hiltonworldwide.com; Christopher J. Nassetta; hotels and resorts (Doubletree, Embassy, Hampton). Sold landmark Waldorf Astoria, 2/11/2015.

Home Depot, Inc. (HD): 2455 Paces Ferry Rd. NW, Atlanta, GA 30339; (770) 433-8211; www.homedepot.com; Craig Menear; home improvement warehouse stores. Acquired Blinds.com, 1/23/2014.

Honeywell Intl. Inc. (HON): 101 Columbia Rd., Morristown, NJ 07962; (973) 455-2000; www.honeywell.com; David Cote; industrial and home control systems, aerospace guidance systems. Acquired Datamax-O'Neil, 3/2/2015.

Hormel Foods Corp. (HRL): 1 Hormel Pl., Austin, MN 55912; (507) 437-5611; www.hormelfoods.com; Jeffrey M. Ettinger; food processor, primarily meat (SPAM, Dinty Moore, Jennie-O, Skippy). Acquired Muscle Milk, 8/12/2014. Agreed to buy Applegate Farms, 5/26/2015.

Hostess Brands LLC: 1 E Armour Blvd., Kansas City, MO 64111; (816) 701-4600; www.hostessbrands.com; William Toler; baked goods wholesaler, distrib.

Houghton Mifflin Harcourt Co. (HMHC): 222 Berkeley St., Boston, MA 02116; (617) 351-5000; www.hmhco.com; Linda K. Zecher; publisher of textbooks and other educational prods. (Holt McDougal Clarion), trade and reference books. Emerged from Chap. 11 reorganization, 6/22/2012. Acquired online educational co. Tribal Nova, 4/11/2013; SchoolChapters, Inc., 7/1/2014. Agreed to buy Scholastic's educational tech. business, 4/24/2015.

H&R Block, Inc. (HRB): 1 H&R Block Way, Kansas City, MO 64105; (816) 854-3000; www.hrblock.com; William C. Cobb; tax return preparation; business and consulting services.

Humana Inc. (HUM): 500 W. Main St., Louisville, KY 40202; (502) 580-1000; www.humana.com; Bruce D. Broussard; managed health care service provider, related specialty prods.. Announced plans to merge with Aetna, 7/3/2015.

IAC/InterActiveCorp (IACI): 555 W. 18th St., NY, NY 10011; (212) 314-7300; www.iac.com; Barry Diller; Internet conglomerate (Ask.com, Match.com, Citysearch, Urbanspoon, Vimeo).

iHeartMedia, Inc.: 200 E. Basse Rd., San Antonio, TX 78209; (210) 822-2828; www.iheartmedia.com; Robert Pittman; radio stations; outdoor advertising. Fmr. Clear Channel Communications; renamed 9/16/2014.

Illinois Tool Works Inc. (ITW): 3600 W. Lake Ave., Glenview, IL 60026; (847) 724-7500; www.itw.com; E. Scott Santi; consumer, industrial tools; food equip. (Hobart), packaging (Zip-Pak).

Ingersoll-Rand plc (IR): 170/175 Lakeview Dr., Airside Business Park, Swords, Dublin, Ireland; 353-1-870-7400; company.ingersollrand.com; Michael W. Lamach; locks and security systems (Schlage, Kryptonite); refrigeration equip. (Thermo King, Hussmann); industrial equip.; air conditioning systems (Trane). Spun off Allegion security prods., 12/2/2013.

Ingram Micro Inc. (IM): 1600 E. St. Andrew Pl., Santa Ana, CA 92705; (714) 566-1000; www.ingrammicro.com; Alain Moné; IT equip. wholesaler and distrib. in over 160 countries.

Intel Corp. (INTC): 2200 Mission College Blvd., Santa Clara, CA 95054; (408) 765-8080; www.intel.com; Andy D. Bryant; mfr. semiconductors, microprocessors (Core, Centrino). Agreed to acquire Altera Corp., 6/1/2015.

International Business Machines Corp. (IBM): One New Orchard Rd., Armonk, NY 10504; (914) 499-1900; www.ibm.com; Virginia M. Rometty; advanced information processing technology equip., services. Sold chip-mfr. unit to GlobalFoundries, 7/1/2015.

International Paper Co. (IP): 6400 Poplar Ave., Memphis, TN 38197; (901) 419-7000; www.internationalpaper.com; Mark S. Sutton; paper/forest prods. Spun off distr. business xpedx, which merged with Unisource to form Veritiv Corp., 7/1/2014.

International Textile Group, Inc.: 804 Green Valley, Greensboro, NC 27408; (336) 379-6220; www.itg-global.com; Kenneth T. Kunberger; apparel and home textiles/fabrics.

INTL FCStone Inc. (INTL): 708 Third Ave., 15th Fl., NY, NY 10017; (212) 485-3500; www.intlfcstone.com; Sean O'Connor; securities and commodities advising.

J.C. Penney Co., Inc. (JCP): 6501 Legacy Dr., Plano, TX 75024; (972) 431-1000; www.jcpenney.net; Mike Ullman; dept. store retailer, general merchandise catalog sales.

J.Crew Group, Inc.: 770 Broadway, NY, NY 10003; (212) 209-2500; www.jcrew.com; Millard S. Drexler; retail and mail order apparel and accessories.

JetBlue Airways Corp. (JBLU): 27-01 Queens Plz. N., Long Island City, NY 11101; (718) 286-7900; www.jetblue.com; Robin Hayes; air transportation.

Jo-Ann Stores, Inc.: 5555 Darrow Rd., Hudson, OH 44236; (330) 656-2600; www.joann.com; Jill Soltau; specialty fabric and craft stores.

Johnson Controls, Inc. (JCI): 5757 N. Green Bay Ave., Milwaukee, WI 53209; (414) 524-1200; www.johnsoncontrols.com; Alex A. Molinaroli; equip. and controls for heating, ventilating, AC, refrigeration, and building security; auto interiors, batteries. Agreed to spin off auto interiors unit, 5/18/2014. Acquired Air Distribution Technologies, 6/16/2014.

Johnson & Johnson (JNJ): 1 Johnson & Johnson Plz., New Brunswick, NJ 08933; (732) 524-0400; www.jnj.com; Alex Gorsky; health care prods. (Band-Aid, Neosporin), pharmaceuticals (Tylenol, Motrin, Sudafed), toiletries (Neutrogena, Aveeno). Sold Ortho-Clinical Diagnostics, Inc. to The Carlyle Group, 6/30/2014.

S. C. Johnson & Son, Inc.: 1525 Howe St., Racine, WI 53403; (262) 260-2000; www.scjohnson.com; H. Fisk Johnson; cleaning and other household prods. (Johnson's Wax, Windex, Pledge, Fantastik, Raid, OFF!, Shout, Glade, Scrubbing Bubbles, Ziploc bags). Agreed to acquire UK-based Deb Group, 2/6/2015; HomeBrands A.S., 3/2/2015.

Jones Group, Inc.: 1411 Broadway, NY, NY 10018; (212) 642-3860; www.jny.com; Wesley R. Card; apparel (Jones New York, Gloria Vanderbilt), shoes (Nine West, Anne Klein); retail and outlet stores. Acquired by Sycamore Partners, 4/8/2014.

JPMorgan Chase & Co. (JPM): 270 Park Ave., Fl. 12, NY, NY 10017; (212) 270-6000; www.jpmorganchase.com; James Dimon; financial services.

Kate Spade & Co. (KATE): 2 Park Ave., NY, NY 10016; (212) 354-4900; www.katespadeand.company.com; Craig. A. Leavitt; women's apparel.

KBR, Inc. (KBR): 601 Jefferson St., Ste. 3400, Houston, TX 77002; (713) 753-2000; www.kbr.com; Stuart Bradie; engineering; construction mgmt. services.

Kellogg Co. (K): One Kellogg Sq., Battle Creek, MI 49016; (269) 961-2000; www.kelloggcompany.com; John A. Bryant; mfr. of ready-to-eat cereals, other food prods. (Frosted Flakes, Rice Krispies, Pop-Tarts, Nutri-Grain, Keebler, Eggo, Pringles).

Kelly Services, Inc. (KELYA): 999 W. Big Beaver Rd., Troy, MI 48084; (248) 362-4444; www.kellyservices.com; Carl T. Camden; temporary staffing services.

Kimberly-Clark Corp. (KMB): 351 Phelps Dr., Irving, TX 75038; (972) 281-1200; www.kimberly-clark.com; Thomas J. Falk; personal care prods. (Kleenex, Scott, Cottonelle, Huggies, Kotex).

Kinder Morgan, Inc. (KMI): 1001 Louisiana St., Ste. 1000, Houston, TX 77002; (713) 369-9000; www.kindermorgan.com; Richard D. Kinder; energy trans. and storage. Acquired Kinder Morgan Energy Partners, Kinder Morgan Management, and El Paso Pipeline Partners, 11/26/2014; Hiland Partners, 2/13/2015.

Kmart Corp.: see Sears Holdings Corp.

Koch Industries, Inc.: P.O. Box 2256, Wichita, KS 67201; (316) 828-5500; www.kochind.com; Charles G. Koch; forest prod. mfr.; oil refineries/pipeline; chemicals; pollution-control equip.; ranching.

Kraft Heinz Co. (KHC): 1 PPG Pl., Ste. 3100, Pittsburgh, PA 15222; (412) 456-5700; www.kraftheinzcompany.com; Bernardo Hees; food and beverage mfr. (Ore-Ida, 57 Varieties ketchup, Velveeta, Crystal Light, Maxwell House, Kool-Aid, Lunchables, Jell-O, Oscar Mayer). Formed from merger of Kraft Foods Group with H.J. Heinz Co., 7/2/2015.

Kroger Co. (KR): 1014 Vine St., Cincinnati, OH 45202; (513) 762-4000; www.thekrogerco.com; W. Rodney McMullen; grocery, convenience, and mall jewelry stores.

L Brands, Inc. (fmr. Limited Brands) (LB): 3 Limited Pkwy., Columbus, OH 43230; (614) 415-7000; www.lb.com; Leslie H. Wexner; apparel stores (La Senza, Victoria's Secret, PINK, Henri Bendel), home decor, personal care (Bath & Body Works).

La-Z-Boy Inc. (LZB): 1284 N. Telegraph Rd., Monroe, MI 48162; (734) 242-1444; www.la-z-boy.com; Kurt L. Darrow; reclining chairs, other furniture.

Leggett & Platt, Inc. (LEG): No. 1 Leggett Rd., Carthage, MO 64836; (417) 358-8131; www.leggett.com; David S. Haffner; furniture and its components, industrial materials, automotive seating suspension, control and power train cable systems.

Levi Strauss & Co.: 1155 Battery St., San Francisco, CA 94111; (415) 501-6000; www.levistrauss.com; Charles Bergh; blue jeans, casual sportswear (Dockers).

Lexmark Intl., Inc. (LXK): 740 W. New Circle Rd., Lexington, KY 40550; (859) 232-2000; www.lexmark.com; Paul Rooke; computer printers and peripherals.

Liberty Mutual Holding Co. Inc.: 175 Berkeley St., Boston, MA 02116; (617) 357-9500; www.libertymutual.com; David H. Long; insurance prods. and services.

LinkedIn Corp. (LNKD): 2029 Stierlin Ct., Ste. 200, Mountain View, CA, 94043; (650) 687-3600; www.linkedin.com; Jeff Weiner; social networking services. Agreed to acquire online learning co. lynda.com, 4/9/2015.

Liz Claiborne, Inc.: see J.C. Penney Co., Inc.

L.L.Bean, Inc.: 15 Casco St., Freeport, ME 04033; (207) 552-2000; www.llbean.com; Christopher J. McCormick; catalog and retail outdoor apparel, footwear, gear.

Lockheed Martin Corp. (LMT): 6801 Rockledge Dr., Bethesda, MD 20817; (301) 897-6000; www.lockheedmartin.com; Marillyn A. Hewson; leading U.S. defense contractor; aircraft, electronics, missiles, information tech., and communications. Acquired Zeta Associates, 8/18/2014; agreed to buy Sikorsky Aircraft from United Technologies, 7/20/2015.

Loews Corp. (L): 667 Madison Ave., NY, NY 10065; (212) 521-2000; www.loews.com; James S. Tisch; hotels, insurance (CNA Financial), offshore drilling (Diamond).

Lorillard, Inc.: see Reynolds American, Inc.

Lowe's Cos., Inc. (LOW): 1000 Lowe's Blvd., Mooresville, NC 28117; (704) 758-1000; www.lowes.com; Robert A. Niblock; building material and home improvement superstores.

Macy's, Inc. (M): 7 W. 7th St., Cincinnati, OH 45202; (513) 579-7000; www.macysinc.com; Terry J. Lundgren; dept. stores (Macy's, Bloomingdale's). Acquired cosmetics retailer Bluemercury, Inc., 3/9/2015.

ManpowerGroup (MAN): 100 Manpower Pl., Milwaukee, WI 53212; (414) 961-1000; www.manpowergroup.com; Jonas Prising; employment services.

Marathon Oil Corp. (MRO): 5555 San Felipe St., Houston, TX 77056; (713) 629-6600; www.marathonoil.com; Lee M. Tillman; integrated oil co.

Marriott International, Inc. (MAR): 10400 Fernwood Rd., Bethesda, MD 20817; (301) 380-3000; www.marriott.com; Arne M. Sorenson; hotels (Renaissance, Courtyard, Fairfield Inn, Ritz-Carlton). Acquired Protea Hospitality Group, 4/1/2014; Delta Hotels and Resorts, 4/1/2015.

Mars, Inc.: 6885 Elm St., McLean, VA 22101; (703) 821-4900; www.mars.com; Grant F. Reid; food mfr., including of chocolate (M&M's, Snickers, Dove), food (Uncle Ben's), pet food (Pedigree, Whiskas, Iams, Eukanuba, Natura, Innova, Sheba).

Masco Corp. (MAS): 21001 Van Born Rd., Taylor, MI 48180; (313) 274-7400; www.masco.com; Keith J. Allman; mfr. kitchen, bathroom prods. (Delta, Peerless faucets; Merillat cabinets); windows (Milgard); paints (Behr). Spun off TopBuild Corp., 7/1/2015.

Massachusetts Mutual Life Insurance Co. (MassMutual Financial Group): 1295 State St., Springfield, MA 01111; (413) 744-1000; www.massmutual.com; Roger W. Crandall; financial planning and investment, life insurance.

Mattel, Inc. (MAT): 333 Continental Blvd., El Segundo, CA 90245; (310) 252-2000; www.mattel.com; Bryan Stockton; toymaker (Barbie, Fisher-Price, Hot Wheels, Matchbox, American Girls). Acquired MEGA Brands, 4/30/2014.

McClatchy Co. (MNI): 2100 Q St., Sacramento, CA 95816; (916) 321-1855; www.mcclatchy.com; Patrick J. Talamantes; newspaper publisher.

McDonald's Corp. (MCD): 2111 McDonald's Dr., Oak Brook, IL 60523; (630) 623-3000; www.mcdonalds.com; Steve Easterbrook; fast food.

McGraw-Hill Financial (MHFI): 1221 Ave. of the Americas, NY, NY 10020; (212) 512-2000; www.mcgraw-hill.com; Douglas L. Peterson; information and financial services (Standard & Poor's).

McKesson Corp. (MCK): 1 Post St., San Francisco, CA 94104; (415) 983-8300; www.mckesson.com; John H. Hammergren; distrib. of drugs and toiletries; provides mgmt. software and services.

Medco Health Solutions, Inc.: see Express Scripts Holding Co.

Medtronic, Inc. (MDT): 710 Medtronic Pkwy., Minneapolis, MN 55432; (763) 514-4000; www.medtronic.com; Omar Ishrak; mfr. of implantable biomedical devices. Acquired medical tech. co. Covidien, 1/26/2015.

Merck & Co., Inc. (MRK): 1 Merck Dr., Whitehouse Station, NJ 08889; (908) 423-1000; www.merck.com; Kenneth C. Frazier; pharmaceuticals (Gardasil, Propecia, Singulair, Vytorin, Zocor); consumer health prods. (Claritin, Coppertone, Dr. Scholl's, MiraLAX). Acquired Idenix Pharmaceuticals, 8/5/2014; Cubist Pharmaceuticals, 1/21/2015.

Meredith Corp. (MDP): 1716 Locust St., Des Moines, IA 50309; (515) 284-3000; www.meredith.com; Stephen M. Lacy; magazine publishing (*Better Homes and Gardens*, *Ladies' Home Journal*, *Parents*, *Family Circle*, *Every Day With Rachael Ray*, *FamilyFun*), book publishing, broadcasting, online media (allrecipes.com).

Meritor, Inc. (MTOR): 2135 W. Maple Rd., Troy, MI 48084; (248) 435-1000; www.meritor.com; Ivor J. Evans; commercial vehicles systems and components.

Merrill Lynch & Co., Inc.: see Bank of America Corp.

MetLife, Inc. (MET): 200 Park Ave., NY, NY 10166; (212) 578-2211; www.metlife.com; Steven A. Kandarian; insurance, financial services.

MGM Resorts Intl. (MGM): 3600 Las Vegas Blvd. S., Las Vegas, NV 89109; (702) 693-7120; www.mgmresorts.com; James J. Murren; hotel-casino operator (Mirage, New York-New York, Luxor, Bellagio, Circus Circus, Monte Carlo). Announced formation of joint venture hotel co. MGM Hakkasan Hospitality, 4/15/2014.

Microsoft Corp. (MSFT): One Microsoft Way, Redmond, WA 98052; (425) 882-8080; www.microsoft.com; Satya Nadella; software (Windows, Word, Excel); video game consoles (Xbox). Acquired Nokia's devices and services businesses, 4/25/2014; Minecraft developer Mojang, 11/6/2014.

Miller Brewing Co.: see SABMiller plc.

Molson Coors Brewing Co. (TAP): 1225 17th St., Ste. 3200, Denver, CO 80202; (303) 927-2337; www.molsoncoors.com; Mark Hunter; brewer (Coors, Killian's, Molson, Heineken, Miller).

Mondelez International, Inc. (MDLZ): 3 Pkwy N., Northfield, IL 60093; (847) 646-2000; www.mondelezinternational.com; Irene B. Rosenfeld; global food mfr., including Nabisco (Oreo), Cadbury, Tang, Trident.

Morgan Stanley (MS): 1585 Broadway, NY, NY 10036; (212) 761-4000; www.morgan

stanley.com; James P. Gorman; diversified financial services.
Motorola Solutions, Inc. (MSI): 1303 E. Algonquin Rd., Schaumburg, IL 60196; (847) 576-5000; www.motorolasolutions.com; Gregory Q. Brown; electronic equip. and components; communication devices. Sold enterprise business to Zebra Tech. Corp., 10/27/2014.
Murphy Oil Corp. (MUR): 200 Peach St., El Dorado, AR 71730; (870) 862-6411; www.murphyoilcorp.com; Roger W. Jenkins; oil and gas exploration and production.
Nationwide Mutual Insurance Co.: One Nationwide Plz., Columbus, OH 43215; (614) 249-7111; www.nationwide.com; Stephen S. Rasmussen; property/casualty, life insurance; financial services.
Navistar Intl. Corp. (NAV): 2701 Navistar Dr., Lisle, IL 60532; (331) 332-5000; www.navistar.com; Troy Clarke; mfr. heavy-duty trucks, parts, school buses.
NBC Universal: 30 Rockefeller Plz., NY, NY 10112; (212) 664-4444; www.nbcuni.com; Stephen B. Burke; news/entertainment producer and developer; TV and CATV stations (NBC, Bravo, USA, Telemundo); film production. Owned by Comcast and General Electric.
NCR Corp. (NCR): 3097 Satellite Blvd., Duluth, GA 30096; (937) 445-1936; www.ncr.com; William R. Nuti; mfr. ATMs, retail technology, hardware and software; computer services and supplies.
Nestlé USA, Inc.: 800 N. Brand Blvd., Glendale, CA 91203; (818) 549-6000; www.nestleusa.com; Paul Grimwood; candy (Baby Ruth, Raisinets), beverages (Nestea, Juicy Juice), food (Buitoni, Coffee-Mate), frozen foods (Stouffer's, Häagen-Dazs, Lean Cuisine), pet foods (Purina, Alpo, Friskies). Subsidiary of Nestlé SA in Switzerland.
Netflix, Inc. (NFLX): 100 Winchester Cir., Los Gatos, CA 95032; (408) 540-3700; www.netflix.com; Reed Hastings; online DVD rentals; streaming video.
New York Life Insurance Co.: 51 Madison Ave., NY, NY 10010; (212) 576-7000; www.newyorklife.com; Theodore A. Mathas; life insurance, annuities, mutual funds.
New York Times Co. (NYT): 620 8th Ave., NY, NY 10018; (212) 556-1234; www.nytco.com; Arthur O. Sulzberger Jr.; newspapers. Sold New England Media Group (incl. *Boston Globe*), 10/24/2013.
Newell Rubbermaid Inc. (NWL): 3 Glenlake Pkwy., Atlanta, GA 30328; (770) 418-7000; www.newellrubbermaid.com; Michael B. Polk; housewares (Rubbermaid, Levolor, Calphalon); hair accessories (Goody); writing utensils (Parker, Sharpie, Paper Mate); hardware and tools (Irwin, Amerock); juvenile prods. (Graco).
News Corp. (NWS): 1211 Ave. of the Americas, NY, NY 10036; (212) 416-3400; www.newscorp.com; K. Rupert Murdoch; global newspaper, magazine, book publishing (HarperCollins; *Wall Street Journal*); TV and CATV stations (FOX, Fox News Channel, FX); film production; websites (Hulu). Split into 2 cos., publishing and entertainment, 6/28/2013. Acquired Harlequin Enterprises from Torstar Corp., 8/1/2014.
NIKE, Inc. (NKE): 1 Bowerman Dr., Beaverton, OR 97005; (503) 671-6453; nikeinc.com; Mark G. Parker; athletic footwear and apparel mfr.
Nordstrom, Inc. (JWN): 1617 6th Ave., Seattle, WA 98101; (206) 628-2111; www.nordstrom.com; Blake W. Nordstrom; upscale dept. store chain.
Norfolk Southern Corp. (NSC): Three Commercial Pl., Norfolk, VA 23510; (855) 667-3655; www.nscorp.com; James A. Squires; railway operator; freight carrier.
Northrop Grumman Corp. (NOC): 2980 Fairview Park Dr., Falls Church, VA 22042; (703) 280-2900; www.northropgrumman.com; Wes Bush; defense contractor: aircraft, electronics, data systems, information systems, missiles.
Northwest Airlines Corp.: see Delta Air Lines, Inc.
Northwestern Mutual Life Insurance Co.: 720 E. Wisconsin Ave., Milwaukee, WI 53202; (414) 271-1444; www.northwesternmutual.com; John E. Schlifske; life insurance, investment prods. and services, annuities. Sold Russell Investments to London Stock Exchange Group, 12/3/2014.
Occidental Petroleum Corp. (OXY): 5 Greenway Plz., Ste. 110, Houston, TX 77046; (713) 215-7000; www.oxy.com; Stephen I. Chazen; oil, natural gas, chemicals, plastics. Spun off California assets into separate co., 12/1/2014.
Office Depot, Inc. (ODP): 6600 N. Military Trl., Boca Raton, FL 33496; (561) 438-4800; www.officedepot.com; Roland C. Smith; office supply retail stores. Agreed to merge with Staples, Inc., 2/4/2015.
Omnicom Group Inc. (OMC): 437 Madison Ave., NY, NY 10022; (212) 415-3600; www.omnicomgroup.com; John D. Wren; advertising, marketing, interactive/digital media.
Oracle Corp. (ORCL): 500 Oracle Pkwy., Redwood City, CA 94065; (650) 506-7000; www.oracle.com; Lawrence J. Ellison; database and file mgmt. software. Acquired MICROS Systems, 9/8/2014. Agreed to buy Toa Technologies, 7/31/2014; Front Porch Digital; 9/14/2014; Datalogix, 12/22/2014.
Owens Corning (OC): 1 Owens Corning Pkwy., Toledo, OH 43659; (419) 248-8000; www.owenscorning.com; Michael H. Thaman; world leader in insulation, advanced glass, composite materials. Acquired Thermafiber, Inc., 6/3/2013.
Owens-Illinois, Inc. (OI): 1 Michael Owens Way, Perrysburg, OH 43551; (567) 336-5000; Albert P. L. Stroucken; www.o-i.com; mfr. of glass containers.
Payless ShoeSource, Inc.: 3231 SE 6th Ave., Topeka, KS 66607; (785) 233-5171; www.collectivebrands.com; W. Paul Jones; shoe mfr./retailer.
PepsiCo, Inc. (PEP): 700 Anderson Hill Rd., Purchase, NY 10577; (914) 253-2000; www.pepsico.com; Indra K. Nooyi; soft drinks and other beverages (Pepsi-Cola, Mountain Dew, Gatorade, Tropicana), snacks and cereals (Fritos, Lay's, Ruffles, Quaker).
Pfizer, Inc. (PFE): 235 E. 42nd St., NY, NY 10017; (212) 733-2323; www.pfizer.com; Ian Read; biopharmaceuticals (Celebrex, Lipitor, Viagra, Zoloft); human and animal health care prods. Announced plans to acquire Hospira, 2/5/2015.
PG&E Corp. (PCG): 77 Beale St., 24th Fl., San Francisco, CA 94105; (415) 973-8200; www.pgecorp.com; Anthony F. Earley Jr.; operates Pacific Gas and Electric public utility.
Philip Morris Intl. Inc. (PM): 120 Park Ave., NY, NY 10017; (917) 663-2000; www.pmi.com; André Calantzopoulos; intl. mfr. and distrib. of tobacco. (Altria spun off intl. Philip Morris operations in 2008 but owns Philip Morris brands in U.S.) Acquired Nicocigs, Ltd., 6/26/2014.
Phillips 66 Co. (PSX): P.O. Box 4428, Houston, TX 77210; (281) 293-6600; www.phillips66.com; Greg C. Garland; oil, gas refining and marketing. Spun off from ConocoPhillips, 5/1/2012.
Pitney Bowes Inc. (PBI): 1 Elmcroft Rd., Stamford, CT 06926; (203) 356-5000; www.pb.com; Marc B. Lautenbach; postage meters and mailing equip.
Plains All American Pipeline, L.P. (PAA): 333 Clay St., Ste. 1600, Houston, TX 77002; (713) 646-4100; www.plainsallamerican.com; Greg L. Armstrong; oil and natural gas transportation, storage.
Post Holdings, Inc. (POST): 2503 S. Hanley Rd., St. Louis, MO 63144; (314) 644-7600; www.postfoods.com; Robert V. Vitale; ready-to-eat cereals. Acquired MOM Brands Co., 5/4/2015.
PPG Industries, Inc. (PPG): 1 PPG Pl., Pittsburgh, PA 15272; (412) 434-3131; www.ppg.com; Charles E. Bunch; glass prods., silicas, fiberglass, chemicals, sealants. Acquired Masterwork Paint Co., 7/1/2014; Comex, 11/5/2014.
Procter & Gamble Co. (PG): 1 Procter & Gamble Plz., Cincinnati, OH 45202; (513) 983-1100; www.pg.com; Alan G. Lafley; soaps and detergents (Ivory, Cheer, Tide, Mr. Clean); toiletries (Crest, Scope, Head & Shoulders, Old Spice); pharmaceuticals (Pepto-Bismol, Vicks cough medicines); paper prods. (Charmin toilet tissues, Bounty towels), Tampax tampons; disposable diapers (Pampers, Luvs); CoverGirl and Max Factor cosmetics; Clairol hair care; Gillette razors. Agreed to sell Duracell to Berkshire Hathaway, 11/13/2014.
Prudential Financial, Inc. (PRU): 751 Broad St., Newark, NJ 07102; (973) 802-6000; www.prudential.com; John R. Strangfeld Jr.; insurance, financial services.
Publix Super Markets Inc.: 3300 Publix Corporate Pkwy., Lakeland, FL 33811; (863) 688-1188; www.publix.com; William Crenshaw; supermarket chain.
PVH Corp. (PVH): 200 Madison Ave., NY, NY 10016; (212) 381-3500; www.pvh.com; Emanuel Chirico; mfr. of apparel, including licensed brands (Calvin Klein, IZOD, Geoffrey Beene, Kenneth Cole, Tommy Hilfiger, Sean John).
Quest Diagnostics Inc. (DGX): 3 Giralda Farms, Madison, NJ 07940; (800) 222-0446; www.questdiagnostics.com; Stephen H. Rusckowski; leading clinical laboratory. Acquired Summit Health, 4/21/2014.
RadioShack Corp.: 300 RadioShack Cir., Fort Worth, TX 76102; (817) 415-3011; www.radioshack.com; Ron Garriques; consumer electronics retailer. Filed for Ch. 11 reorganization, 2/5/2015. General Wireless, Inc. acquired 1,743 remaining Radio Shack stores, 3/31/2015.
Ralcorp Holdings, Inc.: see ConAgra Foods, Inc.
Ralph Lauren Corp. (RL): 650 Madison Ave., NY, NY 10022; (212) 318-7000; www.ralphlauren.com; Ralph Lauren; men's and women's apparel, home furnishings, fragrances.
Raytheon Co. (RTN): 870 Winter St., Waltham, MA 02451; (781) 522-3000; www.raytheon.com; Thomas A. Kennedy; defense, communications systems. Acquired cybersecurity co. Websense, 5/29/2015.
Reader's Digest Assn., Inc.: 750 Third Ave., NY, NY 10017; (914) 238-1000; www.rda.com; Bonnie Kintzer; magazine publisher; marketer of books, music, video prods. Emerged from second Chap. 11 reorganization since 2010, 7/31/2013.
Republic Services, Inc. (RSG): 18500 N. Allied Way, Phoenix, AZ 85054; (480) 627-2700; www.republicservices.com; Donald W. Slager; waste mgmt. co.
Restaurant Brands Intl. (QSR): 226 Wyecroft Rd., Oakville, ON L6K 3X7, Canada; (905) 845-6511; www.rbi.com; Daniel Schwartz; fast food restaurants (Burger King, Tim Hortons). Co. formed through acquisition of Tim Hortons, Inc. by former co. Burger King Worldwide, 12/12/2014.
Revlon, Inc. (REV): 237 Park Ave., NY, NY 10017; (212) 527-4000; www.revlon.com; Lorenzo Delpani; cosmetics, skin care. Acquired The Colomer Group (TCG), 10/9/2013; CBBeauty, 4/30/2015.
Reynolds American Inc. (RAI): 401 N. Main St., Winston-Salem, NC 27101; (336) 741-2000; www.reynoldsamerican.com; Susan M. Cameron; cigarettes (Camel, Pall Mall, Doral, Newport), smokeless tobacco (Grizzly, Kodiak), e-cigarettes (VUSE). Acquired Lorillard, 6/12/2015.
Rite Aid Corp. (RAD): 30 Hunter Ln., Camp Hill, PA 17011; (717) 761-2633; www.riteaid.com; John T. Standley; retail drugstores. Agreed to buy pharmacy-benefit manager EnvisionRx, 2/11/2015.
Rockwell Automation, Inc. (ROK): 1201 S. 2nd St., Milwaukee, WI 53204; (414) 382-2000; www.rockwellautomation.com; Keith D. Nosbusch; industrial automation co.
Rohm and Haas Co.: see Dow Chemical Co.
Ryder System, Inc. (R): 11690 NW 105th St., Miami, FL 33178; (305) 500-3726; www.ryder.com; Robert E. Sanchez; truck-leasing service.
SABMiller plc: 1 Stanhope Gate, London, W1K 1AF, United Kingdom; + 44 1483 264000; www.sabmiller.com; Alan Clark; brewing company (Miller, Peroni, Grolsch).

Agreed to acquire Meantime Brewing Co., 5/15/2015.

Safeway Inc.: 5918 Stoneridge Mall Rd., Pleasanton, CA 94588; (925) 467-3000; www.safeway.com; Robert Edwards; supermarkets. Acquired by Albertson Holdings LLC, 1/30/2015.

Schering-Plough Corp.: see Merck & Co., Inc.

Sears Holdings Corp. (SHLD): 3333 Beverly Rd., Hoffman Estates, IL 60179; (847) 286-2500; www.searsholdings.com; Edward S. Lampert; U.S. retailer. Spun off Land's End, Inc., 4/4/2014.

Shell Oil Co.: 910 Louisiana St., Houston, TX 77002; (713) 241-6161; www.shell.us; Ben van Beurden; integrated oil co.; subsidiary of Royal Dutch Shell.

Sherwin-Williams Co. (SHW): 101 W. Prospect Ave., Cleveland, OH 44115; (216) 566-2000; www.sherwin-williams.com; Christopher M. Connor; paint and varnish producer (Dutch Boy, Krylon, Minwax).

Smithfield Foods, Inc.: 200 Commerce St., Smithfield, VA 23430; (757) 365-3000; www.smithfieldfoods.com; C. Larry Pope; pork producer and processor. Subsidiary of China-based WH Group since 9/26/2013.

J. M. Smucker Co. (SJM): One Strawberry Ln., Orrville, OH 44667; (330) 682-3000; www.smuckers.com; Timothy P. Smucker; leading producer of fruit spreads, peanut butter (Jif), oils (Crisco), coffee (Folgers), baking prods. (Pillsbury), pet foods (Milk-Bone, Kibbles 'n Bits). Acquired Big Heart Pet Brands, 3/23/2015.

Sony Corp. of America: 550 Madison Ave., NY, NY 10022; (212) 833-6800; www.sony.com; Michael Lynton; U.S. subsidiary of Japan-based Sony Corp.; electronics, movies, music.

Southwest Airlines Co. (LUV): 2702 Love Field Dr., Dallas, TX 75235; (214) 792-4000; www.southwest.com; Gary C. Kelly; air transportation.

Sprint Nextel Corp. (S): 6200 Sprint Pkwy., Overland Park, KS 66251; (703) 433-4000; www.sprint.com; Marcelo Claure; wireless and long-distance telecommunications. Sold 72% of co. shares to SoftBank Corp., 7/5/2013.

Stanley Black & Decker, Inc. (SWK): 1000 Stanley Dr., New Britain, CT 06053; (860) 225-5111; www.stanleyblackanddecker.com; John F. Lundgren; one of the top U.S. mfrs. of hand and power tools (DeWalt, Bostitch), household prods. (Kwikset, Baldwin).

Staples, Inc. (SPLS): 500 Staples Dr., Framingham, MA 01702; (508) 253-5000; www.staples.com; Ronald L. Sargent; office-supply retailer. Acquired online retail software co. Runa, 10/2/2013; PNI Digital Media, 7/11/2014. Agreed to acquire Office Depot, Inc., 2/4/2015.

Starbucks Corp. (SBUX): 2401 Utah Ave. S., Seattle, WA 98134; (206) 447-1575; www.starbucks.com; Howard D. Schultz; coffee producer; world's leading specialty coffee retailer.

Starwood Hotels & Resorts Worldwide, Inc. (HOT): 1 StarPoint, Stamford, CT 06902; (203) 964-6000; www.starwoodhotels.com; Adam Aron; hotel and resort co. (Westin, Sheraton, W Hotels).

State Farm Mutual Automobile Ins. Co.: 1 State Farm Plz., Bloomington, IL 61710; (309) 766-2311; www.statefarm.com; Edward B. Rust Jr.; auto/homeowners insurance. Sold Canadian operations to Desjardins Group, 1/1/2015.

Sun Microsystems, Inc.: see Oracle Corp.

SUPERVALU Inc. (SVU): East View Innovation Ctr., 7075 Flying Cloud Dr., Eden Prairie, MN 55344; (952) 828-4000; www.supervalu.com; Sam Duncan; food retailer, wholesale distrib. (Save-A-Lot, Cub Foods, Shoppers).

SYSCO Corp. (SYY): 1390 Enclave Pkwy., Houston, TX 77077; (281) 584-1390; www.sysco.com; William J. DeLaney; food-service distrib.

Systemax Inc. (SYX): 11 Harbor Park Dr., Port Washington, NY 11050; (516) 608-7000; www.systemax.com; Richard Leeds; computers, electronics, industrial prod. retailer.

Target Corp. (TGT): 1000 Nicollet Mall, Minneapolis, MN 55403; (612) 304-6073; www.target.com; Brian Cornell; discount retailer.

TEGNA, Inc. (TGNA): 7950 Jones Branch Dr., McLean, VA 22107; (703) 854-7000; www.tegna.com; Gracia Martore; network and cable TV, websites (careerbuilder.com, cars.com). Spun off from Gannett Co., 6/29/2015.

Tenneco Inc. (TEN): 500 N. Field Dr., Lake Forest, IL 60045; (847) 482-5000; www.tenneco.com; Gregg M. Sherrill; automotive parts (Monroe, Walker).

Texas Instruments Inc. (TXN): 12500 TI Blvd., Dallas, TX 75266; (972) 995-2011; www.ti.com; Richard K. Templeton; processors, semiconductors, software, handheld calculators.

Textron Inc. (TXT): 40 Westminster St., Providence, RI 02903; (401) 421-2800; www.textron.com; Scott C. Donnelly; aircraft (Cessna, Bell, Beechcraft); pilot training; industrial, auto prods.; financial services.

3M Co. (MMM): 3M Center, St. Paul, MN 55144; (651) 733-1110; www.3m.com; Inge G. Thulin; abrasives, adhesives, electrical, health care, cleaning (Scotch-Brite, O-Cel-O sponges, Scotchgard), printing, consumer prods. (Scotch Tape, Post-it).

TIAA-CREF: 730 Third Ave., NY, NY 10017; (212) 490-9000; www.tiaa-cref.org; Roger W. Ferguson Jr.; financial services provider. Bought Nuveen Investments, 10/1/2014.

Time Inc. (TIME): 1271 Ave. of the Americas, NY, NY, 10020; (212) 522-1212; www.timeinc.com; Joseph A. Ripp; magazine publishing (*Time*, *Sports Illustrated*, *People, Fortune*). Spun off from Time Warner, 6/9/2014.

Time Warner Inc. (TWX): One Time Warner Ctr., NY, NY 10019; (212) 484-8000; www.timewarner.com; Jeffrey L. Bewkes; TV and CATV (Cartoon Network, HBO, CNN, TBS, TNT), motion pictures (Warner Bros.), recordings. AOL and Time Warner completed the largest corporate merger in history in 2001; Time Warner spun off AOL, 12/9/2009. Spun off magazine holdings as Time Inc., 6/9/2014.

TJX Cos., Inc. (TJX): 770 Cochituate Rd., Framingham, MA 01701; (508) 390-1000; www.tjx.com; Carol Meyrowitz; off-price apparel retailer (T.J. Maxx, Marshalls); home furnishing retailer (HomeGoods).

Toro Co. (TTC): 8111 Lyndale Ave. S, Bloomington, MN 55420; (952) 888-8801; www.thetorocompany.com; Michael J. Hoffman; lawn and turf maintenance prods. (Lawn-Boy), snow removal equip.; irrigation systems.

Toys "R" Us, Inc.: 1 Geoffrey Way, Wayne, NJ 07470; (973) 617-3500; www.toysrus.com; David A. Brandon; children's specialty retailer.

Tribune Media Co. (TRCO): 435 N. Michigan Ave., Chicago, IL 60611; (312) 222-9100; www.tribunemedia.com; Peter Liguori; broadcasting (incl. WGN and 41 other owned/operated television stations, radio), Tribune Studios. Fmr. known as Tribune Co., renamed 8/4/2014. Spun off newspaper holdings (*L.A. Times*, *Chicago Tribune*) as Tribune Publishing Co., 8/4/2014.

Trinity Industries, Inc. (TRN): 2525 Stemmons Fwy., Dallas, TX 75207; (214) 631-4420; trinityindustries.com; Timothy R. Wallace; mfr. metal prods., rail and freight equip. Acquired Thomas & Betts' utility steel structures division, 8/18/2014.

Twitter, Inc. (TWTR): 1355 Market St., San Francisco, CA, 94103; (415) 222-9670; twitter.com; Jack Dorsey; microblogging/social networking services. Acquired video-streaming startup Periscope, 3/9/2015.

Tyco Intl. Ltd. (TYC): 9 Roszel Rd., Princeton, NJ 08540; (609) 720-4200; www.tyco.com; George R. Oliver; security and fire safety prods. Acquired Exacq Technologies, 7/29/2013. Bought fire protection services co. Westfire, 11/14/2013.

Tyson Foods, Inc. (TSN): 2200 W. Don Tyson Pkwy., Springdale, AR 72762; (479) 290-4000; www.tysonfoods.com; Donnie Smith; fresh and processed poultry; beef and pork prods. (Ball Park, Sara Lee, Hillshire Farm, Jimmy Dean). Acquired Hillshire Brands Co., 8/28/2014.

UBS Financial Services Inc.: 1285 Ave. of the Americas, NY, NY 10019; (212) 713-2000; www.ubs.com; financial services; subsidiary of Switzerland's UBS AG.

Unilever USA (UN/UL): 800 Sylvan Ave., Englewood Cliffs, NJ 07632; (201) 894-4000; www.unileverusa.com; Paul Polman; food (Hellmann's mayonnaise, Knorr soups, Wish-Bone salad dressing, Lipton, Slim-Fast), hygiene prods. (Dove, Q-tips, Vaseline). Subsidiary of Unilever NV (Neth.) and Unilever plc (UK). Agreed to acquire Dermalogica skincare, 6/24/2015; Murad Skincare, 7/2/2015.

Union Pacific Corp. (UNP): 1400 Douglas St., Omaha, NE, 68179; (402) 544-5000; www.up.com; John J. Koraleski; one of the largest railroad freight cos. in U.S.

Unisys Corp. (UIS): 801 Lakeview Dr., Ste. 100, Blue Bell, PA 19422; (215) 986-4011; www.unisys.com; Peter A. Altabef; designs, manuf. computer information systems; IT consulting.

United Continental Holdings, Inc. (UAL): 233 S. Wacker Dr., Chicago IL 60606; (312) 997-8000; www.unitedcontinentalholdings.com; Jeffery A. Smisek; air transportation (United Airlines, Continental Airlines).

United Parcel Service, Inc. (UPS): 55 Glenlake Pkwy. NE, Atlanta, GA 30328; (404) 828-6000; www.ups.com; David Abney; shipping, logistics. Acquired UK-based pharmaceutical logistics firm Polar Speed, 2/11/2014.

United States Steel Corp. (X): 600 Grant St., Pittsburgh, PA 15219; (412) 433-1121; www.ussteel.com; Mario Longhi; steel, tin prods., resource mgmt.

United Technologies Corp. (UTX): One Financial Plz., Hartford, CT 06103; (860) 728-7000; www.utc.com; Gregory J. Hayes; aerospace, industrial prods. and services (Carrier, Otis, Pratt & Whitney). Agreed to sell Sikorsky Aircraft to Lockheed Martin, 7/20/2015.

UnitedHealth Group Inc. (UNH): UHG Center, 9900 Bren Rd. E., Minnetonka, MN 55343; (952) 936-1300; www.unitedhealthgroup.com; Stephen J. Hemsley; health insurance. Agreed to acquire benefit mgmt. co. Catamaran Corp., 3/30/3015.

Valero Energy Corp. (VLO): One Valero Way, San Antonio, TX 78249; (210) 345-2000; www.valero.com; Joe Gorder; fuel mfg. and marketing. Spun off CST Brands, 5/1/2013.

Verizon Communications Inc. (VZ): 140 West St., NY, NY 10007; (212) 395-1000; www.verizon.com; Lowell C. McAdam; broadband, wireless, wireline services provider. Acquired Vodafone's 45% stake in Verizon Wireless, giving it full ownership, 2/21/2014. Agreed to sell CA, FL, TX wireline operations to Frontier Communications, 2/5/2015. Acquired AOL, 6/23/2015.

VF Corp. (VFC): 105 Corporate Center Blvd., Greensboro, NC 27408; (336) 424-6000; www.vfc.com; Eric C. Wiseman; apparel (Lee, Wrangler, North Face, Timberland).

Viacom Inc. (VIA): 1515 Broadway, NY, NY 10036; (212) 258-6000; www.viacom.com; Philippe P. Dauman; media networks (BET, Comedy Central, MTV, VH1, Nickelodeon); movies (Paramount).

Visteon Corp. (VC): One Village Center Dr., Van Buren Twp., MI 48111; (734) 710-5000; www.visteon.com; Sachin Lawande; automotive parts mfr. Acquired Johnson Controls' automotive electronics business, 7/1/2014.

Walgreens Boots Alliance, Inc.. (WBA): 108 Wilmot Rd., Deerfield, IL 60015; (847) 315-3700; www.walgreensbootsalliance.com; Stefano Pessina; retail drugstores, pharmaceutical wholesale/distrib. (Alliance Healthcare). Formed through merger of Swiss-based Boots Alliance with Walgreens Co., 12/31/2014.
Wal-Mart Stores, Inc. (WMT): 702 SW 8th St., Bentonville, AR 72716; (479) 273-4000; www.walmartstores.com; Doug McMillon; discount stores, discount warehouse clubs (Sam's Club).
Washington Post Co.: see Graham Holdings Co.
Waste Management, Inc. (WM): 1001 Fannin St., Ste. 4000, Houston, TX 77002; (713) 512-6200; www.wm.com; David P. Steiner; waste, recycling. Acquired Deffenbaugh Disposal, 3/26/2015.
WellPoint, Inc.: see Anthem, Inc.
Wells Fargo & Co. (WFC): 420 Montgomery St., San Francisco, CA 94163; (866) 249-3302; www.wellsfargo.com; John G. Stumpf; financial services.
Wendy's Co. (WEN): 1 Dave Thomas Blvd., Dublin, OH 43017; (614) 764-3100; www.aboutwendys.com; Emil J. Brolick; fast food restaurants.
Western Union Co. (WU): 12500 E. Belford Ave., Englewood, CO 80112; (720) 332-1000; www.westernunion.com; Hikmet Ersek; money transfers, payment services.
WestRock Co. (WRK): 501 S. 5th St., Richmond, VA 23219; (804) 444-1000; www.westrock.com; Steven C. Vorhees; packaging, shipping containers; chemicals. Formed through merger of Rock-Tenn Co. and MeadWestvaco Corp., 7/1/2015.
Weyerhaeuser Co. (WY): 33663 Weyerhaeuser Way S., Federal Way, WA 98001; (253) 924-2345; www.weyerhaeuser.com; Doyle R. Simons; produces, distributes wood prods.; real estate development.
Whirlpool Corp. (WHR): 2000 N. M-63, Benton Harbor, MI 49022; (269) 923-5000; www.whirlpoolcorp.com; Jeff M. Fettig; mfr. of major home appliances (KitchenAid, Amana, Maytag). Acquired American Dryer Corp., 7/3/2015.
Whole Foods Market, Inc. (WFM): 550 Bowie St., Austin, TX 78703; (512) 477-4455; www.wholefoodsmarket.com; John P. Mackey/Walter Robb; grocery stores specializing in natural/organic foods.
Winnebago Industries, Inc. (WGO): 605 W. Crystal Lake Rd., Forest City, IA 50436; (641) 585-3535; www.winnebagoind.com; Randy J. Potts; mfr. of motor homes, or recreational vehicles (RVs).
Wm. Wrigley Jr. Co.: see Mars, Inc.
World Fuel Services Corp. (INT): 9800 NW 41st St., Ste. 400, Miami, FL 33178; (305) 428-8000; www.wfscorp.com; Michael J. Kasbar; marketer and financer of fuel to large-scale aviation and marine-related firms. Acquired Watson Petroleum Ltd., 3/10/2014.
Xerox Corp. (XRX): 45 Glover Ave., P.O. Box 4505, Norwalk, CT 06856; (203) 968-3000; www.xerox.com; Ursula M. Burns; printers, multifunction devices, document publishing technology and support. Acquired Consilience Software, Inc., 10/3/2014.
Yahoo! Inc. (YHOO): 701 First Ave., Sunnyvale, CA 94089; (408) 349-3300; www.yahoo.com; Marissa Mayer; Internet media co. Acquired blogging platform and social networking site Tumblr, 6/20/2013; video advertising platform BrightRoll, 12/15/2014.
Yum! Brands, Inc. (YUM): 1441 Gardiner Ln., Louisville, KY 40213; (502) 874-8300; www.yum.com; David C. Novak; fast food restaurants (Pizza Hut, KFC, Taco Bell).

Labor Unions and Professional Organizations

Source: Bureau of Labor Statistics, U.S. Dept. of Labor; AFL-CIO; World Almanac research

= Member of Change to Win Federation, formed in 2005 by unions disaffiliated from AFL-CIO. * = Independent union or one not otherwise affiliated with Change to Win or AFL-CIO. All other unions listed are affiliated with AFL-CIO as of 2015. Year established is in parentheses.

Labor Unions

Air Line Pilots Assn. (ALPA) (1931): 49,763+ members, 31 U.S. and Canadian airlines; (703) 689-2270; www.alpa.org
American Federation of Labor and Congress of Industrial Organizations (AFL-CIO) (1955): federation of 56 unions, 12,741,859+ members; (202) 637-5000; www.aflcio.org
Automobile, Aerospace & Agricultural Implement Workers of America, International Union, United (UAW) (1935): 403,466 members, 750+ locals; (313) 926-5000; www.uaw.org
Bakery, Confectionery, Tobacco Workers, and Grain Millers International Union (BCTGM) (1886): 72,122 members, 143 locals; (301) 933-8600; www.bctgm.org
Bricklayers and Allied Craftworkers, International Union of (BAC) (1865): 72,855 members, 50 locals; (202) 783-3788; www.bacweb.org
***Carpenters and Joiners of America, United Brotherhood of** (UBC) (1881): nearly 500,000 members, 600+ locals; (202) 546-6206; www.carpenters.org
#Change to Win Federation (2005): 4 unions, ex-affiliates of AFL-CIO, 4,215,042 members; (202) 721-0660; www.changetowin.org
Communications Workers of America (CWA) (1938): 623,020 members, 1,200 locals; (202) 434-1100; www.cwa-union.org
***Education Assn., Natl.** (NEA) (1857): 2,963,121 members, 14,000+ affiliates; (202) 833-4000; www.nea.org
Electrical Workers, International Brotherhood of (IBEW) (1891): 658,812 members, 900 locals; (202) 833-7000; www.ibew.org
Engineers, International Union of Operating (IUOE) (1896): 374,521 members, 145 locals; (202) 429-9100; www.iuoe.org
#Farm Workers of America, United (UFW) (1962): 8,368 members; (661) 823-6151; www.ufw.org
***Federal Employees, Natl. Federation of** (NFFE; affiliated with IAMAW) (1917): 110,000 members, nearly 200 locals; (202) 216-4420; www.nffe.org
Fire Fighters, International Assn. of (IAFF) (1918): 296,931 members, 3,100+ locals; (202) 737-8484; www.iaff.org
Flight Attendants, Assn. of (AFA-CWA) (1945): 40,873 members, 19 airlines; merged with Communications Workers of America in 2004; (202) 434-1300; www.afanet.org
#Food and Commercial Workers International Union, United (UFCW) (1979): 1,271,804 members, 400+ locals; (202) 223-3111; www.ufcw.org
Glass, Molders, Pottery, Plastics and Allied Workers Intl. Union (GMP) (1842): 27,057 members, 250+ locals; (610) 565-5051; www.gmpiu.org
Government Employees, American Federation of (AFGE) (1932): 306,338 members, 1,100 locals; (202) 737-8700; www.afge.org
#Graphic Communications Conference (GCC/IBT) (1983): 67,806 members; merged with Teamsters in 2005; (202) 462-1400; www.gciu.org
Iron Workers, Intl. Assn. of Bridge, Structural, Ornamental, and Reinforcing (1896): 123,906 members, 200+ locals; (202) 383-4800; www.ironworkers.org
Laborers' International Union of North America (LiUNA) (1903): 557,870 members, 400 locals; (202) 737-8320; www.liuna.org
Letter Carriers, Natl. Assn. of (NALC) (1889): 270,203 members, 2,000+ locals; (202) 393-4695; www.nalc.org
#Locomotive Engineers and Trainmen, Brotherhood of (BLET) (1863): 54,272 members, 500+ locals; (216) 241-2630; www.ble-t.org
Longshoremen's Assn., Intl. (ILA) (1892): 40,437 members, approx. 200 locals; (212) 425-1200; www.ilaunion.org
Machinists and Aerospace Workers, International Assn. of (IAM) (1888): 569,373 members; affiliated with TCU in 2005; (301) 967-4500; www.goiam.org
#Maintenance of Way Employes, Division of the Intl. Brotherhood of Teamsters; Brotherhood of (BMWED) (1887): 36,025 members, 770 locals; merged with Teamsters in 2004; (248) 662-2660; www.bmwed.org (Note: In honor of tradition, the union maintains the variant spelling of "employes" in its logo.)
Mine Workers of America, United (UMWA) (1890): 73,937 members, 600 locals; (703) 291-2400; www.umwa.org
Musicians of the United States and Canada, American Federation of (AFM) (1896): 77,857 members, 240+ locals; (212) 869-1330; www.afm.org
Newspaper Guild—Communications Workers of America, The (TNG) (CWA) (1933): 34,000+ members, 90 locals; (202) 434-7177; www.newsguild.org
***Nurses Assn., American** (ANA) (1911): 146,000 members, 54 constituent state and territorial assns.; (301) 628-5000; www.nursingworld.org
Office and Professional Employees Intl. Union (OPEIU) (1945): 101,895 members, 200 locals; (800) 346-7348; www.opeiu.org
Painters and Allied Trades, International Union of (IUPAT) (1887): 103,416 members, 425 locals; (410) 564-5900; www.iupat.org
Plumbing and Pipe Fitting Industry of the U.S. and Canada, United Assn. of Journeymen and Apprentices of the (UA) (1889): 370,000+ members, 300+ locals; (410) 269-2000; www.ua.org
***Police, Fraternal Order of** (1915): 325,000+ members, 2,100+ affiliates; (615) 399-0900; www.grandlodgefop.org
Police Assns., International Union of (IUPA) (1979): 80,000 members; (941) 487-2560; www.iupa.org
Postal Workers Union, American (APWU) (1971): 238,926 members, 1,000+ locals; (202) 842-4200; www.apwu.org
Roofers, Waterproofers and Allied Workers, United Union of (1906): 20,617 members; (202) 463-7663; www.unionroofers.com
***Rural Letter Carriers' Assn., Natl.** (1903): 104,718 members, 50 state org.; (703) 684-5545; www.nrlca.org
***Security, Police, Fire Professionals of America, Intl. Union,** (SPFPA) (1948): 17,484 members, 200 locals; (586) 772-7250; www.spfpa.org
#Service Employees International Union (SEIU) (1921): 1,893,775 mil members, 150+ locals; (202) 730-7000; www.seiu.org
Sheet Metal, Air, Rail, and Transportation Workers, Int. Assn. of (SMART) (2008, from merger of Sheet Metal Workers' Intl. Assn. and United Transportation Union): 204,316 members, 700 locals; (202) 662-0800; www.smart-union.org
State, County, and Municipal Employees, American Federation of (AFSCME) (1932): 1,337,126 members, 3,400 locals; (202) 429-1000; www.afscme.org
Steel, Paper and Forestry, Rubber, Manufacturing, Energy, Allied Industrial and Service Workers International Union, United (USW) (2005): 589,907 members,

1,800+ locals; formed from merger of the unions United Steelworkers of America (USWA) (1936) and Paper, Allied-Industrial, Chemical and Energy Workers (PACE) (1999); (412) 562-2400; www.usw.org

Teachers, American Federation of (AFT) (1916): 1,597,140 members, 3,000+ locals; (202) 879-4400; www.aft.org

#Teamsters, International Brotherhood of (IBT) (1903): 1,305,773 members, 475 locals; (202) 624-6800; www.teamster.org

Theatrical Stage Employees, Moving Picture Technicians, Artists and Allied Crafts of the U.S., Its Territories, and Canada, Intl. Alliance of (IATSE) (1893): 118,829 members, 375+ locals; (212) 730-1770; www.iatse-intl.org

Transit Union, Amalgamated (ATU) (1892): 193,683 members, 270 locals; (202) 537-1645; www.atu.org

Transport Workers Union of America (TWU) (1934): 116,199 members, nearly 200 locals; (202) 719-3900; www.twu.org

Transportation Communications Intl. Union (TCU) (1899): affiliated with IAM in 2005; see Machinists and Aerospace Workers.

***Treasury Employees Union, Natl.** (NTEU) (1938): 79,588 members, 270+ chapters; (202) 572-5500; www.nteu.org

UNITE HERE (UNITE, 1900; HERE, 1891; merged 2004): 251,000+ members, 127 locals; (212) 265-7000; www.unitehere.org

#Workers United (affiliated with SEIU) (2009): 83,000 members

***Writers Guild of America, West** (1933): 21,162 members; (323) 951-4000; www.wga.org

Professional Organizations and Societies

Accountants, American Institute of Certified Public (1887): 412,000+ members; (888) 777-7077; www.aicpa.org

ACMP—The Chamber Music Network (1947): 5,400 members; (212) 645-7424; www.acmp.net

Actuaries, Soc. of (1949): 24,000 members; (847) 706-3500; www.soa.org

Administrative Professionals, Intl. Assn. of (1942): 24,000 members; (816) 891-6600; www.iaap-hq.org

Agricultural and Biological Engineers, American Soc. of (1907): 8,000+ members; (269) 429-0300; www.asabe.org

AIGA (fmr. American Institute of Graphic Arts) (1914): 25,000+ members; (212) 807-1990; www.aiga.org

Air & Waste Management Assn. (1907): 5,000+ members; (412) 232-3444; www.awma.org

AMSUS—The Society of the Federal Health Professionals (1891): nearly 8,000 members; (301) 897-8800; www.amsus.org

APICS—The Assn. for Operations Management (1957): 43,000+ members; (773) 867-1777; www.apics.org

Architects, American Institute of (1857): 85,000+ members; (202) 626-7300; www.aia.org

ASIS Intl. (fmr. Amer. Soc. for Industrial Security) (1955): 38,000+ members; (703) 519-6200; www.asisonline.org

Astrologers, Inc., American Federation of (1938): 4,000 members; (480) 838-1751; www.astrologers.com

Astronomical Society, American (1899): 7,000 members; (202) 328-2010; www.aas.org

Authors Guild, The (1912): 9,000+ members; (212) 563-5904; www.authorsguild.org

Bankers of America, Independent Community (1930): 6,000+ members; (202) 659-8111; www.icba.org

Bar Assn., American (1878): nearly 400,000 members; (312) 988-5000; www.abanet.org

Bar Assn., Federal (1920): 16,000+ members; (571) 481-9100; www.fedbar.org

Biochemistry and Molecular Biology, American Society for (1906): 12,000+ members; (240) 283-6600; www.asbmb.org

Broadcasters, Natl. Assn. of (1923): 8,300 members; (202) 429-5300; www.nab.org

Business Women's Assn., American (1949): 40,000 members; (800) 228-0007; www.abwa.org

Cartoonists Society, Natl. (1946): 500+ members; (407) 994-6703; www.reuben.org

Ceramic Society, American (1898): 9,500+ members; (240) 646-7054; www.ceramics.org

Chemical Society, American (1876): 158,000+ members; (202) 872-4600; www.chemistry.org

Chiefs of Police, Intl. Assn. of (1893): 23,000+ members; (703) 836-6767; www.theiacp.org

Chiropractic Assn., American (1963): 15,000 members; (703) 276-8800; www.acatoday.org

Civil Engineers, American Soc. of (1852): 146,000+ members; (703) 295-6300; www.asce.org

College Admission Counseling, Natl. Assn. for (1937): 14,000+ members; (703) 836-2222; www.nacacnet.org

Communication Assn., Natl. (1914): 8,000+ members; (202) 464-4622; www.natcom.org

Composers, Authors & Publishers, American Soc. of (ASCAP) (1914): 540,000+ members; (212) 621-6000; www.ascap.com

Computing Machinery, Assn. for (1947): 100,000+ members; (212) 626-0500; www.acm.org

Computing Professionals, Institute for the Certification of (1973): nearly 55,000 members; (847) 299-4227; www.iccp.org

Counseling Assn., American (1952): 50,000+ members; (800) 347-6647; www.counseling.org

Country Music Assn. (1958): 7,100+ members; (615) 244-2840; www.cmaworld.com

Dental Assn., American (1859): 157,000+ members; (312) 440-2500; www.ada.org

Directors Guild of America (1936): 15,000+ members; (310) 289-2000; www.dga.org

Electrical and Electronics Engineers, Institute of (1963): 426,000+ members; (732) 981-0060; www.ieee.org

Electronics Technicians, Intl. Soc. of Certified (1980): 50,000+ members; (817) 921-9101; www.iscet.org

Energy Engineers, Assn. of (1977): 16,000+ members; (770) 447-5083; www.aeecenter.org

Engineers, Natl. Society of Professional (1934): 35,000+ members; (703) 684-2800; www.nspe.org

Environmental Assessment Assn. (1972): 3,500 members; (877) 743-6806; www.eaa-assoc.org

Environmental Health Assn., Natl. (1937): 4,500+ members; (303) 756-9090; www.neha.org

Family Physicians, American Academy of (1947): 120,900 members; (913) 906-6000; www.aafp.org

Farm Bureau Federation, American (1919): 6.2 mil+ members; (202) 406-3600; www.fb.org

Farmers Union, Natl. (1902): 250,000 families; (202) 554-1600; www.nfu.org

Financial Professionals, Assn. for (1979): 16,000+ members; (301) 907-2862; www.afponline.org

Financial Service Professionals, Soc. of (1928): 11,000 members; (610) 526-2500; www.financialpro.org

Fire Chiefs, Intl. Assn. of (1873): nearly 12,000 members; (703) 273-0911; www.iafc.org

Fire Protection Engineers, Soc. of (1950): 4,000+ members; (301) 718-2910; www.sfpe.org

Food Technologists, Institute of (1939): 17,000+ members; (312) 782-8424; www.ift.org

Forensic Sciences, American Academy of (1948): 7,000 members; (719) 636-1100; www.aafs.org

Funeral Directors Assn., Natl. (1882): 19,000 members; (262) 789-1880; www.nfda.org

General Contractors of America, Associated (1918): 26,000+ cos.; (703) 548-3118; www.agc.org

Geographers, Assn. of American (1904): 10,000 members; (202) 234-1450; www.aag.org

Ground Water Assn., Natl. (1948): 12,000+ members; (614) 898-7791; www.ngwa.org

Heating, Refrigerating and Air-Conditioning Engineers, Inc., American Soc. of (1894): 53,000+ members; (404) 636-8400; www.ashrae.org

Home Builders, Natl. Assn. of (1942): 140,000+ members; (202) 266-8200; www.nahb.org

Human Resource Management, Soc. for (SHRM) (1948): 275,000+ members; (703) 548-3440; www.shrm.org

Illustrators, Society of (1901): 1,000 members; (212) 838-2560; www.societyillustrators.org

Industrial Designers Society of America (1965): 3,200+ members; (703) 707-6000; www.idsa.org

Intelligence Officers, Assn. of Former (1975): 24 chap., 5,000+ members; (703) 790-0320; www.afio.com

Interior Designers, American Soc. of (1975): 24,000+ members; (202) 546-3480; www.asid.org

Jail Assn., American (1981): 4,000+ members; (301) 790-3930; www.aja.org

Journalists, Society of Professional (1909): nearly 10,000 members; (317) 927-8000; www.spj.org

Judicature Society, American (1913): 6,000 members; (615) 873-4675; www.ajs.org

Landscape Architects, American Society of (1899): 15,000+ members; (202) 898-2444; www.asla.org

Legal Administrators, Assn. of (1971): nearly 10,000 members; (847) 267-1252; www.alanet.org

Library Assn., American (1876): 55,300+ members; (800) 545-2433; www.ala.org

Lifesaving Assn., U.S. (1964): 11,000 members; (866) 367-8752; www.usla.org

Logistics, Intl. Society of (SOLE) (1966): 3,000+ members; (301) 459-8446; www.sole.org

Magicians, Intl. Brotherhood of (1922): nearly 11,000 members; (636) 724-2400; www.magician.org

Management Accountants, Inst. of (1919): 70,000+ members; (201) 573-9000; www.imanet.org

Management Assn., American (1923): 4,100 cos., 38,000 ind.; (212) 903-7976; www.amanet.org

Marketing Assn., American (1937): 30,000+ members; (312) 542-9000; www.ama.org

Master Brewers Assn. of the Americas (1887): 3,000+ members; (651) 454-7250; www.mbaa.com

Material and Process Engineering, Soc. for the Advancement of (1944): 5,000+ members; (626) 331-0616; www.sampe.org

Mechanical Engineers, American Soc. of (1880): 140,000+ members; (973) 882-1170; www.asme.org

Medical Assn., American (1847): 250,000 members; (800) 621-8335; www.ama-assn.org

Medical Library Assn. (1898): 4,000+ members; (312) 419-9094; www.mlanet.org

Motion Picture Arts & Sciences, Academy of (1927): 7,000+ members; (310) 247-3000; www.oscars.org

Motion Picture and Television Engineers, Soc. of (1916): 6,000+ members; (914) 761-1100; www.smpte.org

Mystery Writers of America (1945): 3,000+ members; (212) 888-8171; www.mysterywriters.org

NALS...the association for legal professionals (fmr. the Natl. Assn. of Legal Secretaries) (1929): 6,000 members; (918) 582-5188; www.nals.org

Notaries, American Society of (1965): approx. 20,000 members; (850) 671-5164; www.notaries.org

Nursing, Natl. League for (1893): 40,000 members, 1,200 institutions; (800) 669-1656; www.nln.org

Operations Management, Assn. for (APICS) (1957): 43,000+ members, 300+ intl. partners; (773) 867-1777; www.apics.org

Optometric Assn., American (1898): 39,000 members; (800) 365-2219; www.aoa.org

Organists, American Guild of (1896): 17,000 members; (212) 870-2310; www.agohq.org

Pharmacists Assn., American (1852): 62,000+ members; (202) 628-4410; www.pharmacist.com

Physical Therapy Assn., American (1921): 90,000+ members; (703) 684-2782; www.apta.org

Plastics Engineers, Society of (1942): nearly 16,000 members; (203) 775-0471; www.4spe.org

Police Assn.—United States Section, Intl. (1962): 10,000 members; (855) 241-9998; www.ipa-usa.org

Population Assn. of America (1930): 3,000 members; (301) 565-6710; www.populationassociation.org

Postmasters of the U.S., Natl. Assn. of (1898): 42,000+ members, 95 clubs; (703) 683-9027; www.napus.org

Press Club, Natl. (1908): 3,500– members; (202) 662-7500; www.press.org

Professional Ball Players of America, Assn. of (1924): 11,000 members; (714) 528-2012; www.apbpa.org

Professional Beauty Assn. (1904): 12,000+ members; (480) 281-0424; www.probeauty.org

Psychiatric Assn., American (1844): 36,000+ members; (703) 907-7300; www.psychiatry.org

Psychological Assn., American (1892): nearly 122,500 members; (202) 336-5500; www.apa.org

Public Administration, American Soc. for (1939): 8,000 members; (202) 393-7878; www.aspanet.org

Public Health Assn., American (1872): 25,000+ members; (202) 777-2742; www.apha.org

Public Relations Soc. of America (1947): 22,000+ members; (212) 460-1400; www.prsa.org

Range Management, Society for (1948): 4,000+ members; (303) 986-3309; www.rangelands.org

Real Estate Appraisers, Natl. Assn. of (1966): 10,000+ members; (877) 743-6806; www.narea-assoc.org

Rehabilitation Assn., Natl. (1923): 5,600 members; (703) 836-0850; www.nationalrehab.org

Road & Transportation Builders Assn., American (1902): 6,000+ members; (202) 289-4434; www.artba.org

Safety Engineers, American Soc. of (1911): 37,000+ members; (847) 699-2929; www.asse.org

School Administrators, American Assn. of (1865): 13,000+ members; (703) 528-0700; www.aasa.org

Science Teachers Assn., Natl. (1944): 55,000 members; (703) 243-7100; www.nsta.org

Screen Actors Guild—American Federation of Television and Radio Artists (2012): 160,000 members; (855) 724-2387; www.sagaftra.org

Songwriters Guild of America (1931): 5,000+ members; (615) 742-9945; www.songwritersguild.com

Sportscasters Assn., American (1979): 500+ members; (212) 227-8080; www.americansportscastersonline.com

Surgeons, American College of (1913): 80,000+ members; (312) 202-5000; www.facs.org

Tax Administrators, Federation of (1937): (202) 624-5890; www.taxadmin.org

Teachers of English, Natl. Council of (1911): 35,000+ members; (217) 328-3870; www.ncte.org

Teachers of English to Speakers of Other Languages, Inc. (1966): 11,978 members; (703) 836-0774; www.tesol.org

Teachers of French, American Assn. of (1927): nearly 10,000 members; (815) 310-0490; www.frenchteachers.org

Teachers of German, American Assn. of (1926): 4,000+ members; (856) 795-5553; www.aatg.org

Teachers of Mathematics, Natl. Council of (1920): 80,000 members; (703) 620-9840; www.nctm.org

Teachers of Spanish and Portuguese, American Assn. of (1917): 11,000+ members; (248) 960-2180; www.aatsp.org

Television Arts and Sciences, Natl. Academy of (1955): (212) 586-8424; www.emmyonline.org

Theological Library Assn., American (1946): 800+ members; (312) 454-5100; www.atla.com

Transportation Engineers, Inst. of (1930): nearly 17,000 members; (202) 785-0060; www.ite.org

Travel Agents, American Soc. of (1931): 12,000 members; (703) 739-2782; www.asta.org

Underwriters, Soc. of Chartered Property and Casualty (1944): 20,000+ members; (800) 932-2728; www.cpcusociety.org

University Women, American Assn. of (1881): 100,000+ members; (202) 785-7700; www.aauw.org

Veterinary Medical Assn., American (1863): 86,500+ members; (800) 248-2862; www.avma.org

Women in Communications, The Assn. for (1909): 2,000+ members; (703) 370-7436; www.womcom.org

Women Engineers, Society of (1950): 27,000 members; (877) 793-4636; societyofwomenengineers.swe.org

Women in Media, Alliance for (1951): nearly 10,000 members; (202) 750-3664; www.allwomeninmedia.org

Professional Sports Organizations

Source: World Almanac research

Major League Baseball

Office of the Commissioner, 245 Park Ave., 31st Fl., New York, NY 10167; (212) 931-7800; www.mlb.com

American League

Baltimore Orioles (1953): 333 W. Camden St., Baltimore, MD 21201; (410) 685-9800; www.orioles.com

Boston Red Sox (1901): 4 Yawkey Way, Boston, MA 02215; (617) 267-9440; www.redsox.com

Chicago White Sox (1900, as Chicago White Stockings): 333 W. 35th St., Chicago, IL 60616; (312) 674-1000; www.whitesox.com

Cleveland Indians (1901, as Cleveland Blues): 2401 Ontario St., Cleveland, OH 44115; (216) 420-4200; www.indians.com

Detroit Tigers (1901): 2100 Woodward Ave., Detroit, MI 48201; (313) 471-2000; www.tigers.com

Houston Astros (1962, as Houston Colt 45s): 501 Crawford St., Houston, TX 77002; (713) 259-8000; www.astros.com. (The Astros were a National League team, 1962-2012; the franchise joined the AL West beginning with the 2013 season.)

Kansas City Royals (1969): One Royal Way, Kansas City, MO 64129; (816) 921-8000; www.royals.com

Los Angeles Angels of Anaheim (1961): 2000 Gene Autry Way, Anaheim, CA 92806; (714) 940-2000; www.angelsbaseball.com

Minnesota Twins (1960): 1 Twins Way, Minneapolis, MN 55403; (612) 659-3400; www.twinsbaseball.com

New York Yankees (1903): One E. 161st St., Bronx, NY 10451; (718) 293-4300; www.yankees.com

Oakland Athletics (1901, as Philadelphia Athletics): 7000 Coliseum Way, Oakland, CA 94621; (510) 638-4900; oakland.athletics.mlb.com

Seattle Mariners (1977): P.O. Box 4100, Seattle, WA 98194; (206) 346-4000; www.mariners.com

Tampa Bay Rays (1995, as Tampa Bay Devil Rays): One Tropicana Dr., St. Petersburg, FL 33705; (727) 825-3137; www.raysbaseball.com

Texas Rangers (1960, as Washington Senators): 1000 Ballpark Way, Arlington, TX 76011; (817) 273-5222; www.texasrangers.com

Toronto Blue Jays (1976): One Blue Jays Way, Ste. 3200, Toronto, ON M5V 1J1, Canada; (416) 341-1000; www.bluejays.com

National League

Arizona Diamondbacks (1998): 401 E. Jefferson St., Phoenix, AZ 85004; (602) 462-6500; www.dbacks.com

Atlanta Braves (1876, as Boston Red Stockings): 755 Hank Aaron Dr., Atlanta, GA 30315; (404) 522-7630; www.braves.com

Chicago Cubs (1876, as Chicago White Stockings): 1060 W. Addison, Chicago, IL 60613; (773) 404-2827; www.cubs.com

Cincinnati Reds (1869, as Cincinnati Red Stockings): 100 Main St., Cincinnati, OH 45202; (513) 765-7000; www.reds.com

Colorado Rockies (1991): 2001 Blake St., Denver, CO 80205; (303) 292-0200; www.coloradorockies.com

Houston Astros: see American League.

Los Angeles Dodgers (1890): 1000 Elysian Park Ave., Los Angeles, CA 90012; (323) 224-1500; www.dodgers.com

Miami Marlins (1991, as Florida Marlins): 501 Marlins Way, Miami, FL 33125; (305) 480-1300; www.marlins.com

Milwaukee Brewers (1970): One Brewers Way, Milwaukee, WI 53214; (414) 902-4400; www.brewers.com

New York Mets (1961): Citi Field, Flushing, NY 11368; (718) 507-6387; www.mets.com

Philadelphia Phillies (1883): One Citizens Bank Way, Philadelphia, PA 19148; (215) 463-6000; www.phillies.com

Pittsburgh Pirates (1887, as Pittsburgh Alleghenies): 115 Federal St., Pittsburgh, PA 15212; (412) 323-5000; www.pirates.com

St. Louis Cardinals (1892, as St. Louis Browns): 700 Clark St., St. Louis, MO 63102; (314) 345-9600; www.cardinals.com

San Diego Padres (1969): 100 Park Blvd., San Diego, CA 92101; (619) 795-5000; www.padres.com

San Francisco Giants (1883, as New York Gothams): 24 Willie Mays Plz., San Francisco, CA 94107; (415) 972-2000; www.sfgiants.com

Washington Nationals (1969, as Montréal Expos): 1500 South Capitol St., SE, Washington, DC 20003; (202) 675-6287; www.nationals.com

National Basketball Association

League Office, 645 Fifth Ave., New York, NY 10022; (212) 407-8000; www.nba.com

Atlanta Hawks (1949, as Tri-Cities Blackhawks): 101 Marietta St. NW, Ste. 1900, Atlanta, GA 30303; (866) 715-1500; www.nba.com/hawks/

Boston Celtics (1946): 226 Causeway St., 4th Fl., Boston, MA 02114; (866) 423-5849; www.nba.com/celtics/

Brooklyn Nets (1967, as New Jersey Americans): 15 MetroTech Ctr., 11th Fl., Brooklyn, NY 11201; (718) 933-3000; www.nba.com/nets/

Charlotte Hornets (2004, as Charlotte Bobcats): 333 E. Trade St., Charlotte, NC 28202; (704) 688-8600; www.nba.com/hornets/

Chicago Bulls (1966): 1901 W. Madison St., Chicago, IL 60612; (312) 455-4000; www.nba.com/bulls/

Cleveland Cavaliers (1970): One Center Ct., Cleveland, OH 44115; (216) 420-2000; www.nba.com/cavaliers/

Dallas Mavericks (1980): 2909 Taylor St., Dallas, TX 75226; (214) 747-6287; www.nba.com/mavericks/
Denver Nuggets (1967, as Denver Rockets): 1000 Chopper Cir., Denver, CO 80204; (303) 405-1100; www.nba.com/nuggets/
Detroit Pistons (1957): Six Championship Dr., Auburn Hills, MI 48326; (248) 377-0100; www.nba.com/pistons/
Golden State Warriors (1946, as Philadelphia Warriors): 1011 Broadway, Oakland, CA 94605; (510) 986-2200; www.nba.com/warriors/
Houston Rockets (1967, as San Diego Rockets): 1510 Polk St., Houston, TX 77002; (713) 627-3865; www.nba.com/rockets/
Indiana Pacers (1967): 125 S. Pennsylvania St., Indianapolis, IN 46204; (317) 917-2500; www.nba.com/pacers/
Los Angeles Clippers (1970, as Buffalo Braves): 1111 S. Figueroa St., Ste. 1100, Los Angeles, CA 90015; (213) 742-7500; www.nba.com/clippers/
Los Angeles Lakers (1947, as Minneapolis Lakers): 555 N. Nash St., El Segundo, CA 90245; (310) 426-6000; www.nba.com/lakers/
Memphis Grizzlies (1995, as Vancouver Grizzlies): 191 Beale St., Memphis, TN 38103; (901) 888-4667; www.nba.com/grizzlies/
Miami Heat (1988): 601 Biscayne Blvd., Miami, FL 33132; (786) 777-1000; www.nba.com/heat/
Milwaukee Bucks (1968): 1001 N. 4th St., Milwaukee, WI 53203; (414) 227-0500; www.nba.com/bucks/
Minnesota Timberwolves (1989): 600 1st Ave. North, Minneapolis, MN 55403; (612) 673-1600; www.nba.com/timberwolves/
New Orleans Pelicans (1988, as Charlotte Hornets): 5800 Airline Dr., Metairie, LA 70003; (504) 593-4700; www.nba.com/pelicans/
New York Knickerbockers (1946): Two Pennsylvania Plz., New York, NY 10121; (212) 465-6471; www.nba.com/knicks/
Oklahoma City Thunder (1967, as Seattle SuperSonics): 2 Leadership Square, 211 N. Robinson Ave., Ste. 300; Oklahoma City, OK 73102; (405) 208-4800; www.nba.com/thunder/
Orlando Magic (1989): 8701 Maitland Summit Blvd., Orlando, FL 32810; (407) 916-2400; www.nba.com/magic/
Philadelphia 76ers (1937, as Syracuse Nationals): 3601 S. Broad St., Philadelphia, PA 19148; (215) 339-7676; www.nba.com/sixers/
Phoenix Suns (1968): 201 E. Jefferson St., Phoenix, AZ 85004; (602) 379-7900; www.nba.com/suns/
Portland Trail Blazers (1970): One Center Ct., Ste. 200, Portland, OR 97227; (503) 234-9291; www.nba.com/blazers/
Sacramento Kings (1945, as Rochester Royals): One Sports Pkwy., Sacramento, CA 95834; (916) 928-0000; www.nba.com/kings/
San Antonio Spurs (1967, as Dallas Chaparrals): One AT&T Center, San Antonio, TX 78219; (210) 444-5000; www.nba.com/spurs/
Toronto Raptors (1995): 40 Bay St., Toronto, ON M5J 2X2, Canada; (416) 366-3865; www.nba.com/raptors/
Utah Jazz (1974, as New Orleans Jazz): 301 W. South Temple, Salt Lake City, UT 84101; (801) 325-2500; www.nba.com/jazz/
Washington Wizards (1961, as Chicago Packers): 601 F St. NW, Washington, DC 20004; (202) 661-5000; www.nba.com/wizards/

National Hockey League

NHL Headquarters, 1185 Ave. of the Americas, 15th Fl., New York, NY 10036; (212) 789-2000; www.nhl.com
Anaheim Ducks (1993): 2695 E. Katella Ave., Anaheim, CA 92806; (877) 945-3946; ducks.nhl.com
Arizona Coyotes (1979, as Winnipeg Jets): 9300 W. Maryland Ave., Glendale, AZ 85305; (623) 772-3200; coyotes.nhl.com
Boston Bruins (1924): 100 Legends Way, Boston, MA 02114; (617) 624-1900; bruins.nhl.com
Buffalo Sabres (1970): One Seymour H. Knox III Plz., Buffalo, NY 14203; (716) 855-4100; sabres.nhl.com
Calgary Flames (1980): P.O. Box 1540, Station M, Calgary, AB T2P 3B9, Canada; (403) 777-2177; flames.nhl.com
Carolina Hurricanes (1972, as New England Whalers): 1400 Edwards Mill Rd., Raleigh, NC 27607; (919) 467-7825; hurricanes.nhl.com
Chicago Blackhawks (1926): 1901 W. Madison St., Chicago, IL 60612; (312) 455-7000; blackhawks.nhl.com
Colorado Avalanche (1972, as Quebec Nordiques): 1000 Chopper Cir., Denver, CO 80204; (303) 405-1100; avalanche.nhl.com
Columbus Blue Jackets (2000): 200 W. Nationwide Blvd., Suite Level, Columbus, OH 43215; (614) 246-4625; bluejackets.nhl.com
Dallas Stars (1967, as Minnesota North Stars): 2601 Ave. of the Stars, Frisco, TX 75034; (214) 387-5500; stars.nhl.com
Detroit Red Wings (1926, as Detroit Cougars): 600 Civic Center Dr., Detroit, MI 48226; (313) 471-6606; redwings.nhl.com
Edmonton Oilers (1972, as Alberta Oilers): 11230 - 110 St., Edmonton, AB T5G 3H7, Canada; (780) 414-4000; oilers.nhl.com
Florida Panthers (1993): One Panther Pkwy., Sunrise, FL 33323; (954) 835-7000; panthers.nhl.com
Los Angeles Kings (1967): 1111 S. Figueroa St., Ste. 3100, Los Angeles, CA 90015; (213) 742-7100; kings.nhl.com
Minnesota Wild (2000): 317 Washington St., St. Paul, MN 55102; (651) 602-6000; wild.nhl.com
Montréal Canadiens (1917): 1909, avenue des Canadiens-de-Montréal, Montréal, QC H3C 5L2, Canada; (514) 932-2582; canadiens.nhl.com
Nashville Predators (1998): 501 Broadway, Nashville, TN 37203; (615) 770-2355; predators.nhl.com
New Jersey Devils (1974, as Kansas City Scouts): Prudential Center, 25 Lafayette St., Newark, NJ 07102; (973) 757-6100; devils.nhl.com
New York Islanders (1972): 1255 Hempstead Tpke., Uniondale, NY 11553; (516) 501-6700; islanders.nhl.com
New York Rangers (1926): Two Pennsylvania Plz., New York, NY 10121; (212) 465-6000; rangers.nhl.com
Ottawa Senators (1992): 1000 Palladium Dr., Ottawa, ON K2V 1A5, Canada; (613) 599-0250; senators.nhl.com
Philadelphia Flyers (1967): 3601 S. Broad St., Philadelphia, PA 19148; (215) 336-3600; flyers.nhl.com
Pittsburgh Penguins (1967): 1001 5th Ave., Pittsburgh, PA 15219; (412) 642-1800; penguins.nhl.com
St. Louis Blues (1967): 1401 Clark Ave. at Brett Hull Way, St. Louis, MO 63103; (314) 622-2500; blues.nhl.com
San Jose Sharks (1991): 525 W. Santa Clara St., San Jose, CA 95113; (408) 287-7070; sharks.nhl.com
Tampa Bay Lightning (1992): 401 Channelside Dr., Tampa, FL 33602; (813) 301-6500; lightning.nhl.com
Toronto Maple Leafs (1919, as Toronto St. Pats): 40 Bay St., Ste. 400, Toronto, ON M5J 2X2, Canada; (416) 815-5700; mapleleafs.nhl.com
Vancouver Canucks (1946, joined NHL in 1970): 800 Griffiths Way, Vancouver, BC V6B 6G1, Canada; (604) 899-7400; canucks.nhl.com
Washington Capitals (1974): 627 N. Glebe Rd., Ste. 850, Arlington, VA 22203; (202) 266-2200; capitals.nhl.com
Winnipeg Jets (1999, as Atlanta Thrashers): 345 Graham Ave., Winnipeg, MB R3C 5S6, Canada; (204) 987-7825; jets.nhl. com

National Football League

League Office, 345 Park Ave., New York, NY 10154; (212) 450-2000; www.nfl.com
Arizona Cardinals (1898, as Morgan Athletic Club): P.O. Box 888, Phoenix, AZ 85001; (602) 379-0101; www.azcardinals.com
Atlanta Falcons (1966): 4400 Falcon Pkwy., Flowery Branch, GA 30542; (770) 965-3115; www.atlantafalcons.com
Baltimore Ravens (1996): 1101 Russell St., Baltimore, MD 21230; (410) 261-7283; www.baltimoreravens.com
Buffalo Bills (1960): One Bills Dr., Orchard Park, NY 14127; (716) 648-1800; www.buffalobills.com
Carolina Panthers (1995): 800 S. Mint St., Charlotte, NC 28202; (704) 358-7000; www.panthers.com
Chicago Bears (1920, as Decatur Staleys): 1000 Football Dr., Lake Forest, IL 60045; (847) 615-2327; www.chicagobears.com
Cincinnati Bengals (1968): One Paul Brown Stadium, Cincinnati, OH 45202; (513) 621-3550; www.bengals.com
Cleveland Browns (1946): 76 Lou Groza Blvd., Berea, OH 44017; (440) 824-3434; www.clevelandbrowns.com
Dallas Cowboys (1960): One AT&T Way, Arlington, TX 76011; (817) 892-4000; www.dallascowboys.com
Denver Broncos (1960): 13655 Broncos Pkwy., Englewood, CO 80112; (303) 649-9000; www.denverbroncos.com
Detroit Lions (1930, as Portsmouth Spartans): 222 Republic Dr., Allen Park, MI 48101; (313) 262-2000; www.detroitlions.com
Green Bay Packers (1919): 1265 Lombardi Ave., Green Bay, WI 54304; (920) 569-7500; www.packers.com
Houston Texans (2002): Two NRG Park, Houston, TX 77054; (832) 667-2002; www.houstontexans.com
Indianapolis Colts (1953, as Baltimore Colts): 7001 W. 56th St., Indianapolis, IN 46254; (317) 297-2658; www.colts.com
Jacksonville Jaguars (1995): One EverBank Field Dr., Jacksonville, FL 32202; (904) 633-2000; www.jaguars.com
Kansas City Chiefs (1960, as Dallas Texans): One Arrowhead Dr., Kansas City, MO 64129; (816) 920-9300; www.kcchiefs.com
Miami Dolphins (1966): 347 Don Shula Dr., Miami Gardens, FL 33056; (305) 943-8000; www.miamidolphins.com
Minnesota Vikings (1961): 9520 Viking Dr., Eden Prairie, MN 55344; (952) 828-6500; www.vikings.com
New England Patriots (1960): One Patriot Pl., Foxboro, MA 02035; (508) 543-8200; www.patriots.com
New Orleans Saints (1967): 5800 Airline Dr., Metairie, LA 70003; (504) 733-0255; www.neworleanssaints.com
New York Giants (1925): MetLife Stadium, E. Rutherford, NJ 07073; (201) 935-8111; www.giants.com
New York Jets (1960, as New York Titans): One Jets Dr., Florham Park, NJ 07932; (800) 469-5387; www.newyorkjets.com
Oakland Raiders (1960): 1220 Harbor Bay Pkwy., Alameda, CA 94502; (510) 864-5000; www.raiders.com
Philadelphia Eagles (1933): One NovaCare Way, Philadelphia, PA 19145; (215) 463-2500; www.philadelphiaeagles.com
Pittsburgh Steelers (1933): 3400 S. Water. St., Pittsburgh, PA 15203; (412) 432-7800; www.steelers.com
St. Louis Rams (1937, as Cleveland Rams): One Rams Way, St. Louis, MO 63045; (314) 982-7267; www.stlouisrams.com
San Diego Chargers (1960, as Los Angeles Chargers): P.O. Box 609609, San Diego, CA 92160; (858) 874-4500; www.chargers.com
San Francisco 49ers (1946): 4900 Marie P. DeBartolo Way, Santa Clara, CA 95054; (408) 562-4949; www.49ers.com
Seattle Seahawks (1976): 12 Seahawks Way, Renton, WA 98056; (888) 635-4295; www.seahawks.com
Tampa Bay Buccaneers (1976): One Buccaneer Pl., Tampa, FL 33607; (813) 870-2700; www.buccaneers.com
Tennessee Titans (1960, as Houston Oilers): 460 Great Circle Rd., Nashville, TN 37228; (615) 565-4000; www.titansonline.com
Washington Redskins (1932, as Boston Braves): 21300 Redskin Park Dr., Ashburn, VA 20147; (703) 726-7000; www.redskins.com

Health Organizations

Source: World Almanac research

Entries are roughly alphabetized by the basic condition addressed or organization name. Year established is in parentheses. Always check with a physician before embarking on any new health-related undertaking.

Al-Anon Family Groups (1951): (757) 563-1600; www.al-anon.alateen.org
Alcoholics Anonymous (1935): (212) 870-3400; www.aa.org
Alcoholism and Drug Dependence, Inc., Natl. Council on (1944): (212) 269-7797; www.ncadd.org
Aging, Natl. Institute on (1974): (301) 496-1752; www.nia.nih.gov
Aging's Eldercare Locator, Admin. on (1991): (800) 677-1116; www.eldercare.gov
AIDSinfo: (800) 448-0440; www.aidsinfo.nih.gov
Allergy, Asthma and Immunology, American Academy of (1943): (414) 272-6071; www.aaaai.org
ALS Assn. [Lou Gehrig's disease] (1985): (202) 407-8580; www.alsa.org
Alzheimer's Assn. (1979): (312) 335-8700; www.alz.org
Anorexia Nervosa and Associated Disorders, Natl. Assn. of (1976): (630) 577-1333; www.anad.org
Arc of the United States, The (1950): (800) 433-5255; www.thearc.org
Arthritis Foundation (1948): (800) 283-7800; www.arthritis.org
Arthritis and Musculoskeletal and Skin Diseases, Natl. Institute of (1986): (877) 226-4267; www.niams.nih.gov
Asthma and Allergy Foundation of America (1953): (800) 727-8462; www.aafa.org
Autism Society (1965): (800) 328-8476; www.autism-society.org
Blind, American Council of the (1961): (202) 467-5081; (800) 424-8666; www.acb.org
Blind, Natl. Federation of the (1940): (410) 659-9314; www.nfb.org
Blindness, Foundation Fighting (1971): (800) 683-5555; www.blindness.org
Blindness, Prevent (1908): (800) 331-2020; www.preventblindness.org
Brain Tumor Society, Natl. (2008): (617) 924-9997; www.braintumor.org
Breast Cancer Diagnosis, After (ABCD) (1999): (414) 977-1780; (800) 977-4121; www.abcdbreastcancersupport.org
Cancer Institute's Cancer Information Service, Natl. (1975): (800) 422-6237; www.cancer.gov/aboutnci/cis/
Cancer Society, American (1913): (800) 227-2345; www.cancer.org
Centers for Disease Control and Prevention (CDC) (1946): (800) 232-4636; www.cdc.gov
Cerebral Palsy, United (1949): (202) 776-0406; (800) 872-5827; www.ucp.org
Child Abuse and Family Violence, Natl. Council on (1984): (202) 429-6695; www.nccafv.org
Childhelp Natl. Child Abuse Hotline (1959): (800) 422-4453; www.childhelp.org
Children, Natl. Center for Missing and Exploited (1984): (703) 224-2150; www.missingkids.com
Children's Tumor Foundation (1978): (212) 344-6633; www.ctf.org
Chronic Pain Assn., American (1980): (800) 533-3231; www.theacpa.org
Continence, Natl. Assn. for (1982): (843) 419-5307; (800) 252-3777; www.nafc.org
Cooley's Anemia Foundation (1954): (800) 522-7222; www.thalassemia.org
Crohn's and Colitis Foundation of America (1967): (800) 932-2423; www.ccfa.org
Cystic Fibrosis Foundation (1955): (800) 344-4823 or (301) 951-4422; www.cff.org
Deaf, Natl. Assn. of the (1880): (301) 587-1788, TTY (301) 587-1789; www.nad.org
Depression and Bipolar Support Alliance (1985): (800) 826-3632; www.dbsalliance.org
Diabetes Assn., American (1940): (800) 342-2383; www.diabetes.org
Diabetes and Digestive and Kidney Diseases, Natl. Institute of (1950): (800) 891-5390; www.kidney.niddk.nih.gov
Dial-A-Hearing Screening Test: (800) 222-EARS (222-3277)
Domestic Violence Hotline, Natl. (1996): (800) 799-7233; TTY (800) 787-3224; www.thehotline.org
Down Syndrome Congress, Natl. (1973): (800) 232-6372; www.ndsccenter.org
Down Syndrome Society, Natl. (1979): (800) 221-4602; www.ndss.org
Dyslexia Assn., Intl. (1949): (410) 296-0232; www.interdys.org
Easter Seals [special needs] (1919): (800) 221-6827; www.easterseals.com
Endometriosis Assn. (1980): (414) 355-2200; www.endometriosisassn.org
Epilepsy Foundation (1967): (800) 332-1000; www.epilepsyfoundation.org
Fat Acceptance, Natl. Assn. to Advance (1969): (916) 558-6880; www.naafa.org
First Candle [sudden infant death syndrome] (1987): (800) 221-7437; www.sidsalliance.org
FoodSafety.gov—Gateway to Federal Food Safety Information: Food: (888) 723-3366; Meat, poultry, eggs: (888) 674-6854; Illness or food poisoning: (800) 232-4636 (CDC)
Gamblers Anonymous (1957): (626) 960-3500; www.gamblersanonymous.org
Geriatrics Society, American (1942): (212) 308-1414; www.americangeriatrics.org
Headache Foundation, Natl. (1970): (888) 643-5552; www.headaches.org
HealthyWomen (1988): (877) 986-9472; www.healthywomen.org
Hearing Society, Intl. (1951): (734) 522-7200; www.ihsinfo.org
Heart Assn., American (1924): (800) 242-8721; www.heart.org
Hearts, Inc., Mended (1951): (888) 432-7899; www.mendedhearts.org
Hospice Education Institute (1985): (800) 331-1620; www.hospiceworld.org
Hospice Intl., Children's (1983): (703) 684-0330; www.chionline.org
Hospital Assn., American (1899): (312) 422-3000; (800) 424-4301; www.aha.org
Huntington's Disease Society of America (1967): (800) 345-4372; www.hdsa.org
JDRF (fmr. Juvenile Diabetes Research Foundation) (1970): (800) 533-2873; www.jdrf.org
Kidney Foundation, Natl. (1950): (800) 622-9010; www.kidney.org
Kidney Fund, American (1971): (800) 638-8299; www.kidneyfund.org
La Leche League Intl. [breastfeeding] (1957): (800) 525-3243; www.llli.org
Leukemia and Lymphoma Society (1949): (800) 955-4572; www.lls.org
Liver Foundation, American (1976): (800) 465-4837; www.liverfoundation.org
Living Bank [organ donation] (1968): (800) 528-2971; www.livingbank.org
Lung Assn., American (1904): (800) 586-4872; www.lung.org
Lung Line (1983): (800) 222-5864; www.nationaljewish.org/about/contact/lung-line/
Lupus Foundation of America, Inc. (1977): (800) 558-0121; www.lupus.org
March of Dimes [babies' health] (1938): (914) 997-4488; www.marchofdimes.org
Marfan Foundation, Natl. (1981): (800) 8-MARFAN (862-7326); www.marfan.org
Mayo Clinic (1889): (507) 284-2511; www.mayoclinic.com
ME/CFS Initiative, Solve [myalgic encephalomyelitis/chronic fatigue syndrome] (1987): (704) 364-0016; solvecfs.org
Mental Health, Natl. Institute of (1946): (866) 615-6464; www.nimh.nih.gov
Mental Health America (1909): (800) 969-6642; www.nmha.org
Mental Illness, Natl. Alliance on (1979): (888) 950-6264; www.nami.org
Multiple Sclerosis Society, Natl. (1946): (800) 344-4867; www.nationalmssociety.org
Muscular Dystrophy Assn. (1950): (800) 572-1717; www.mdausa.org
Myeloma Foundation, Intl. (1990): (800) 452-2873; www.myeloma.org
Narcotics Anonymous (1953): (818) 773-9999; www.na.org
Natl. Health Council (1920): (202) 785-3910; www.nationalhealthcouncil.org
Natl. Health Information Center (1979): (240) 453-8280; www.health.gov/NHIC/
Natl. Institutes of Health (NIH) (1887): (301) 496-4000; www.nih.gov
Neurological Disorders and Stroke, Natl. Institute of (1950): (800) 352- 9424; www.ninds.nih.gov
Organ Sharing, United Network for (1984): (804) 782-4800; www.unos.org
Osteoporosis Foundation, Natl. (1984): (800) 231-4222; www.nof.org
Overeaters Anonymous (1960): (505) 891-2664; www.oa.org
Parkinson Foundation, Natl. (1957): (800) 473-4636; www.parkinson.org
Parkinson's Disease Foundation (1957): (800) 457-6676; www.pdf.org
Pediatrics, American Academy of (1930): (800) 433-9016; www.aap.org
Phoenix House [substance abuse] (1967): (888) 671-9392; www.phoenixhouse.org
Planned Parenthood Federation of America, Inc. (1916): (800) 230-7526; www.plannedparenthood.org
Plastic Surgeons, American Society of (1931): (800) 514-5058; www.plasticsurgery.org
Post-Polio Health Intl. (1960): (314) 534-0475; www.post-polio.org
Psoriasis Foundation, Natl. (1966): (800) 723-9166; www.psoriasis.org
Rare Disorders, Natl. Org. for (1983): (203) 744-0100; www.rarediseases.org
Rehabilitation Information Center, Natl. (1977): (800) 346-2742; TTY (301) 459-5984; www.naric.com
Reye's Syndrome Foundation, Natl. (1974): (800) 233-7393; www.reyessyndrome.org
Runaway Safeline, Natl. (1971): (800) 786-2929; www.1800runaway.org
Scleroderma Foundation (1989): (800) 722-4673; www.scleroderma.org
Sexual Health Assn., American (1914): (919) 361-8400; www.ashastd.org
Sickle Cell Disease Assn. of America (1971): (800) 421-8453; www.sicklecelldisease.org
Sjögren's Syndrome Foundation (1983): (800) 475-6473; www.sjogrens.org
Speech-Language-Hearing Assn., American (1925): (800) 638-8255, TTY (301) 296-5650; www.asha.org
Spinal Assn., United (1946): (718) 803-3782; www.spinalcord.org
Stroke Assn., Natl. (1984): (800) 787-6537; www.stroke.org
Stuttering Assn., Natl. (1977): (212) 944-4050; (800) 937-8888; www.nsastutter.org
Stuttering Foundation of America (1947): (800) 992-9392; www.stutteringhelp.org
Substance Abuse and Mental Health Services Admin.: (877) 726-4727; www.samhsa.gov
Sudden Infant Death Syndrome Institute, Amer. (1983): (239) 431-5425; www.sids.org
Suicide Prevention Lifeline, Natl. (2004): (800) 273-TALK (8255); www.suicidepreventionlifeline.org
Therapy Dogs Intl. (1976): (973) 252-9800; www.tdi-dog.org
Tourette Assn. of America (fmr. Tourette Syndrome Assn.) (1972): (718) 224-2999; www.tsa-usa.org
Tuberous Sclerosis Alliance (1974): (800) 225-6872; www.tsalliance.org
Urological Assn., American (1902): (866) 746-4282; www.auanet.org
Visual Impairments, Natl. Assn. of Parents of Children with (1980): (800) 284-4422; www.napvi.org
Women's Health Network, Natl. (1975): (202) 682-2640; www.nwhn.org

UNITED STATES FACTS

Superlative U.S. Statistics

Source: U.S. Geological Survey, U.S. Dept. of the Interior; U.S. Census Bureau, U.S. Dept. of Commerce; World Almanac research

Superlative Statistics for the 50 States

Total area for 50 states and Washington, DC		3,796,742 sq mi
Land area for 50 states and Washington, DC		3,531,905 sq mi
Water area for 50 states and Washington, DC		264,837 sq mi
Largest state	Alaska	665,384 sq mi
Smallest state	Rhode Island	1,545 sq mi
Largest county (excluding Alaska)	San Bernardino County, CA	20,105 sq mi
Smallest county	Arlington County, VA[1]	26 sq mi
Largest incorporated city (by area, pop. 1,000+)	Sitka, AK	4,811 sq mi
Northernmost city	Barrow, AK	71°17′ N
Northernmost point	Point Barrow, AK	71°23′ N
Southernmost city	Hilo, HI	19°43′ N
Southernmost settlement	Naalehu, HI.	19°03′ N
Southernmost point	Ka Lae (South Cape), island of Hawaii	18°55′ N (155°41′ W)
Easternmost city	Eastport, ME	66°59′24″ W
Easternmost settlement[2]	Attu Station, AK	173°11′ E
Easternmost point[2]	Pochnoi Point, Semisopochnoi Island, AK	179°52′ E
Westernmost city	Adak Station, AK	173°11′ E
Westernmost settlement	Adak Station, AK	173°11′ E
Westernmost point	Amatignak Island, AK	179°09′ W
Highest incorporated city	Leadville, CO	10,158 ft
Lowest settlement	Bombay Beach, CA	–208 ft
Highest point on Atlantic coast	Cadillac Mountain, Mount Desert Island, ME	1,530 ft
Oldest national park	Yellowstone National Park (1872), WY-MT-ID	2,219,791 acres
Largest national park	Wrangell-St. Elias, AK	8,323,147 acres
Highest waterfall	Yosemite Falls—total in three sections (Upper Yosemite Fall, 1,430 ft; Cascades, 675 ft; Lower Yosemite Fall, 320 ft)	2,425 ft
Longest river system	Mississippi-Missouri-Red Rock	3,710 mi
Highest mountain	Denali (fmr. Mt. McKinley), AK	20,320 ft
Lowest point	Death Valley, CA	–282 ft
Deepest lake	Crater Lake, OR	1,949 ft
Rainiest spot	Mount Waialeale, Kauai, HI	annual avg. rainfall 422 in.
Largest gorge	Grand Canyon, Colorado River, AZ	277 mi long, 600 ft to 18 mi wide, 1 mi deep
Deepest gorge	Hells Canyon, Snake River, OR-ID	7,900 ft
Largest dam	New Cornelia Tailings, Ten Mile Wash, AZ[3]	274,026,000 cu yds material used
Tallest building	One World Trade Center, New York, NY	1,776 ft
Largest building	Boeing Manufacturing Plant, Everett, WA	472,000,000 cu ft; covers 98 acres
Largest office building	Pentagon, Arlington, VA	77,015,000 cu ft; covers 29 acres
Tallest supported structure	KVLY-TV Tower, Blanchard, ND	2,063 ft
Tallest freestanding tower	Stratosphere Tower, Las Vegas, NV	1,149 ft
Longest bridge span	Verrazano-Narrows Bridge, New York, NY	4,260 ft
Highest bridge	Royal Gorge Bridge, Cañon City, CO	1,053 ft above water
Deepest well (onshore)	Bertha Rogers No. 1 (inactive gas well), Washita County, OK	31,441 ft

Superlative Statistics for the 48 Contiguous States

Total area for 48 states and Washington, DC		3,129,611 sq mi
Land area for 48 states and Washington, DC		2,958,868 sq mi
Water area for 48 states and Washington, DC		170,743 sq mi
Largest state	Texas	268,596 sq mi
Northernmost city	Bellingham, WA	48°46′ N
Northernmost settlement	Angle Inlet, MN	49°20′ N
Northernmost point	Northwest Angle, MN	49°21′ N
Southernmost city	Key West, FL	24°33′ N
Southernmost mainland city	Florida City, FL	25°27′ N
Southernmost point	Ballast Key, FL	24°31′ N
Easternmost settlement	Lubec, ME	66°58′49″ W
Easternmost point	West Quoddy Head, ME	66°57′ W
Westernmost town	La Push, WA	124°38′ W
Westernmost point	Bodelteh Islands, WA	124°46′ W
Highest mountain	Mount Whitney, CA	14,505 ft

(1) Smallest county by land area is Kalawao County, Hawaii, at 12 sq mi; its total area (including water) is 53 sq mi. Superlative shown is for smallest total area. (2) Alaska's Aleutian Islands extend into the Eastern Hemisphere (across 180° longitude) and thus technically contain the easternmost point and settlement in the U.S. (3) Privately owned industrial dam composed of tailings, remnants of a mining process.

Highest and Lowest Elevations in U.S. States and Territories

Source: U.S. Geological Survey, U.S. Dept. of the Interior
(negative sign indicates below sea level)

	Highest point			Lowest point		
State/territory	Name	County	Elev. (ft)	Name	County	Elev. (ft)
Alabama	Cheaha Mountain	Cleburne	2,413	Gulf of Mexico		Sea level
Alaska	Denali (fmr. Mt. McKinley)	Denali	20,320	Pacific Ocean		Sea level
American Samoa	Lata Mountain	Tau Island	3,160	Pacific Ocean		Sea level
Arizona	Humphreys Peak	Coconino	12,637	Colorado R.	Yuma	70
Arkansas	Magazine Mountain	Logan	2,753	Ouachita R.	Ashley-Union	55
California	Mount Whitney	Inyo-Tulare	14,505	Death Valley	Inyo	–282
Colorado	Mount Elbert	Lake	14,440	Arikaree R.	Yuma	3,315
Connecticut	S. slope of Mt. Frissell	Litchfield	2,380	Long Island Sound		Sea level
Delaware	Ebright Azimuth	New Castle	448	Atlantic Ocean		Sea level
Dist. of Columbia	Tenleytown	NW quadrant	410	Potomac R.		1
Florida	Britton Hill	Walton	345	Atlantic Ocean		Sea level
Georgia	Brasstown Bald	Towns-Union	4,784	Atlantic Ocean		Sea level
Guam	Mount Lamlam	Agat District	1,332	Pacific Ocean		Sea level
Hawaii	Pu'u Wekiu, Mauna Kea	Hawaii	13,796	Pacific Ocean		Sea level
Idaho	Borah Peak	Custer	12,661	Snake R.	Nez Perce	710
Illinois	Charles Mound	Jo Daviess	1,235	Mississippi R.	Alexander	279
Indiana	Hoosier Hill	Wayne	1,257	Ohio R.	Posey	320
Iowa	Hawkeye Point	Osceola	1,670	Mississippi R.	Lee	480
Kansas	Mount Sunflower	Wallace	4,039	Verdigris R.	Montgomery	679
Kentucky	Black Mountain	Harlan	4,145	Mississippi R.	Fulton	257
Louisiana	Driskill Mountain	Bienville	535	New Orleans	Orleans	–8
Maine	Mount Katahdin	Piscataquis	5,268	Atlantic Ocean		Sea level
Maryland	Hoye Crest	Garrett	3,360	Atlantic Ocean		Sea level
Massachusetts	Mount Greylock	Berkshire	3,491	Atlantic Ocean		Sea level
Michigan	Mount Arvon	Baraga	1,979	Lake Erie		571
Minnesota	Eagle Mountain	Cook	2,301	Lake Superior		601
Mississippi	Woodall Mountain	Tishomingo	806	Gulf of Mexico		Sea level
Missouri	Taum Sauk Mountain	Iron	1,772	St. Francis R.	Dunklin	230
Montana	Granite Peak	Park	12,807	Kootenai R.	Lincoln	1,800
Nebraska	Panorama Point	Kimball	5,424	Missouri R.	Richardson	840
Nevada	Boundary Peak	Esmeralda	13,146	Colorado R.	Clark	479
New Hampshire	Mount Washington	Coos	6,288	Atlantic Ocean		Sea level
New Jersey	High Point	Sussex	1,803	Atlantic Ocean		Sea level
New Mexico	Wheeler Peak	Taos	13,166	Red Bluff Reservoir	Eddy	2,842
New York	Mount Marcy	Essex	5,344	Atlantic Ocean		Sea level
North Carolina	Mount Mitchell	Yancey	6,684	Atlantic Ocean		Sea level
North Dakota	White Butte	Slope	3,506	Red R. of the North	Pembina	750
Northern Mariana Isls.	Mount Agrihan	Agrihan Island	3,166	Pacific Ocean		Sea level
Ohio	Campbell Hill	Logan	1,550	Ohio R.	Hamilton	455
Oklahoma	Black Mesa	Cimarron	4,973	Little R.	McCurtain	289
Oregon	Mount Hood	Clackamas-Hood R.	11,240	Pacific Ocean		Sea level
Pennsylvania	Mount Davis	Somerset	3,213	Delaware R.	Delaware	Sea level
Puerto Rico	Cerro de Punta	Ponce District	4,390	Atlantic Ocean		Sea level
Rhode Island	Jerimoth Hill	Providence	812	Atlantic Ocean		Sea level
South Carolina	Sassafras Mountain	Pickens	3,560	Atlantic Ocean		Sea level
South Dakota	Harney Peak	Pennington	7,242	Big Stone Lake	Roberts	966
Tennessee	Clingmans Dome	Sevier	6,643	Mississippi R.	Shelby	178
Texas	Guadalupe Peak	Culberson	8,749	Gulf of Mexico		Sea level
Utah	Kings Peak	Duchesne	13,518	Beaver Dam Wash	Washington	2,000
Vermont	Mount Mansfield	Chittenden	4,393	Lake Champlain		95
Virginia	Mount Rogers	Grayson-Smyth	5,729	Atlantic Ocean		Sea level
Virgin Islands	Crown Mountain	St. Thomas Island	1,556	Atlantic Ocean		Sea level
Washington	Mount Rainier	Pierce	14,410	Pacific Ocean		Sea level
West Virginia	Spruce Knob	Pendleton	4,863	Potomac R.	Jefferson	240
Wisconsin	Timms Hill	Price	1,951	Lake Michigan		579
Wyoming	Gannett Peak	Fremont	13,810	Belle Fourche R.	Crook	3,099

U.S. Coastline by State

Source: National Oceanic and Atmospheric Administration, U.S. Dept. of Commerce
(in statute miles; only states with coastline or shoreline are shown)

	Coastline[1]	Shoreline[2]
Atlantic Coast	**2,069**	**28,673**
Connecticut	0	618
Delaware	28	381
Florida	580	3,331
Georgia	100	2,344
Maine	228	3,478
Maryland	31	3,190
Massachusetts	192	1,519
New Hampshire	13	131
New Jersey	130	1,792
New York	127	1,850
North Carolina	301	3,375
Pennsylvania	0	89
Rhode Island	40	384
South Carolina	187	2,876
Virginia	112	3,315

	Coastline[1]	Shoreline[2]
Gulf Coast	**1,631**	**17,141**
Alabama	53	607
Florida	770	5,095
Louisiana	397	7,721
Mississippi	44	359
Texas	367	3,359
Pacific Coast	**7,623**	**40,298**
Alaska	5,580	31,383
California	840	3,427
Hawaii	750	1,052
Oregon	296	1,410
Washington	157	3,026
Arctic Coast	**1,060**	**2,521**
United States	**12,383**	**88,633**

(1) Length of general outline of seacoast. Measurements were made in 1948 with a unit measure of 30 minutes of latitude on charts as near the scale of 1:1,200,000 as possible. Includes coastlines of large sounds and bays. (2) Shoreline of outer coast, offshore islands, sounds, bays, rivers, and creeks to the head of tidewater or to a point where tidal waters narrow to a width of 100 ft. Figures obtained in 1939-40 with a recording instrument on the largest-scale charts and maps then available.

States: Capitals, Key Dates, Geographic Data

Source: *Statistical Abstract of the United States*, U.S. Census Bureau, U.S. Dept. of Commerce

The 13 colonies that declared independence from Great Britain and fought the War of Independence (American Revolution) became the 13 original states. They were, in the order in which they ratified the Constitution: Delaware, Pennsylvania, New Jersey, Georgia, Connecticut, Massachusetts, Maryland, South Carolina, New Hampshire, Virginia, New York, North Carolina, and Rhode Island.

			Entered Union		Extent (mi)		Area (sq mi)			Rank
State	Settled[1]	Capital	Date	Order	Length (approx.	Width mean)	Land	Water	Total	by tot. area
AL	1702	Montgomery	Dec. 14, 1819	22	330	190	50,645	1,775	52,420	30
AK	1784	Juneau	Jan. 3, 1959	49	1,480[2]	810	570,641	94,743	665,384	1
AZ	1776	Phoenix	Feb. 14, 1912	48	400	310	113,594	396	113,990	6
AR	1686	Little Rock	June 15, 1836	25	260	240	52,035	1,143	53,179	29
CA	1769	Sacramento	Sept. 9, 1850	31	770	250	155,779	7,916	163,695	3
CO	1858	Denver	Aug. 1, 1876	38	380	280	103,642	452	104,094	8
CT	1634	Hartford	Jan. 9, 1788	5	110	70	4,842	701	5,543	48
DE	1638	Dover	Dec. 7, 1787	1	96	30	1,949	540	2,489	49
DC	NA	NA	NA	NA	NA	NA	61	7	68	51
FL	1565	Tallahassee	Mar. 3, 1845	27	447	361	53,625	12,133	65,758	22
GA	1733	Atlanta	Jan. 2, 1788	4	300	230	57,513	1,912	59,425	24
HI	1820	Honolulu	Aug. 21, 1959	50	NA	NA	6,423	4,509	10,932	43
ID	1842	Boise	July 3, 1890	43	479	305	82,643	926	83,569	14
IL	1720	Springfield	Dec. 3, 1818	21	390	210	55,519	2,395	57,914	25
IN	1733	Indianapolis	Dec. 11, 1816	19	270	140	35,826	593	36,420	38
IA	1788	Des Moines	Dec. 28, 1846	29	310	200	55,857	416	56,273	26
KS	1727	Topeka	Jan. 29, 1861	34	400	210	81,759	520	82,278	15
KY	1774	Frankfort	June 1, 1792	15	380	140	39,486	921	40,408	37
LA	1699	Baton Rouge	Apr. 30, 1812	18	380	130	43,204	9,174	52,378	31
ME	1624	Augusta	Mar. 15, 1820	23	320	190	30,843	4,537	35,380	39
MD	1634	Annapolis	Apr. 28, 1788	7	250	90	9,707	2,699	12,406	42
MA	1620	Boston	Feb. 6, 1788	6	190	50	7,800	2,754	10,554	44
MI	1668	Lansing	Jan. 26, 1837	26	490	240	56,539	40,175	96,714	11
MN	1805	St. Paul	May 11, 1858	32	400	250	79,627	7,309	86,936	12
MS	1699	Jackson	Dec. 10, 1817	20	340	170	46,923	1,509	48,432	32
MO	1735	Jefferson City	Aug. 10, 1821	24	300	240	68,742	965	69,707	21
MT	1809	Helena	Nov. 8, 1889	41	630	280	145,546	1,494	147,040	4
NE	1823	Lincoln	Mar. 1, 1867	37	430	210	76,824	524	77,348	16
NV	1849	Carson City	Oct. 31, 1864	36	490	320	109,781	791	110,572	7
NH	1623	Concord	June 21, 1788	9	190	70	8,953	397	9,349	46
NJ	1660	Trenton	Dec. 18, 1787	3	150	70	7,354	1,368	8,723	47
NM	1610	Santa Fe	Jan. 6, 1912	47	370	343	121,298	292	121,590	5
NY	1614	Albany	July 26, 1788	11	330	283	47,126	7,429	54,555	27
NC	1660	Raleigh	Nov. 21, 1789	12	500	150	48,618	5,201	53,819	28
ND	1812	Bismarck	Nov. 2, 1889	39	340	211	69,001	1,698	70,698	19
OH	1788	Columbus	Mar. 1, 1803	17	220	220	40,861	3,965	44,826	34
OK	1889	Oklahoma City	Nov. 16, 1907	46	400	220	68,595	1,304	69,899	20
OR	1811	Salem	Feb. 14, 1859	33	360	261	95,988	2,391	98,379	9
PA	1682	Harrisburg	Dec. 12, 1787	2	283	160	44,743	1,312	46,054	33
RI	1636	Providence	May 29, 1790	13	40	30	1,034	511	1,545	50
SC	1670	Columbia	May 23, 1788	8	260	200	30,061	1,960	32,020	40
SD	1859	Pierre	Nov. 2, 1889	40	370	210	75,811	1,305	77,116	17
TN	1769	Nashville	June 1, 1796	16	491	115	41,235	909	42,144	36
TX	1682	Austin	Dec. 29, 1845	28	790	660	261,232	7,365	268,596	2
UT	1847	Salt Lake City	Jan. 4, 1896	45	350	270	82,170	2,727	84,897	13
VT	1724	Montpelier	Mar. 4, 1791	14	160	80	9,217	400	9,616	45
VA	1607	Richmond	June 25, 1788	10	430	200	39,490	3,285	42,775	35
WA	1811	Olympia	Nov. 11, 1889	42	360	240	66,456	4,842	71,298	18
WV	1727	Charleston	June 20, 1863	35	240	130	24,038	192	24,230	41
WI	1766	Madison	May 29, 1848	30	310	260	54,158	11,339	65,496	23
WY	1834	Cheyenne	July 10, 1890	44	360	280	97,093	720	97,813	10

NA = Not applicable. **Note:** Land and water areas may not add up to totals because of rounding. (1) First permanent settlement by Europeans. (2) Does not include Aleutian Islands or Alexander Archipelago.

Continental Divide of the U.S.

The Continental Divide of the U.S., also known as the Great Divide, is located at the watershed created by the mountain ranges, or tablelands, of the Rocky Mountains. This watershed separates the waters that ultimately drain into the Atlantic Ocean and its marginal seas from those waters that drain into the Pacific Ocean. The majority of water flowing E in the U.S. drains into the Gulf of Mexico and then the Atlantic. The majority of water flowing W drains through the Columbia River or Colorado River, which flows into the Gulf of California before reaching the Pacific.

The location and route of the Continental Divide across the U.S. can be described as follows:

Beginning at the U.S.-Mexico border, near longitude 108°45′ W, the Divide, in a northerly direction, crosses New Mexico along the western edge of the Rio Grande drainage basin, entering Colorado near longitude 106°41′ W. From there by an irregular route N across Colorado along the western summits of the Rio Grande and Arkansas, South Platte, and North Platte river basins, and across Rocky Mountain National Park, entering Wyoming near longitude 106°52′ W.

From there in a northwesterly direction, forming the western rims of the North Platte, Big Horn, and Yellowstone river basins, crossing the SW portion of Yellowstone National Park. From there in a westerly and then northerly direction forming the boundary between Idaho and Montana, to a point on the boundary near longitude 114°00′ W. From there northeasterly and northwesterly through Montana and Glacier National Park, entering Canada near longitude 114°04′ W.

Depending on how a "divide" is defined, the U.S. can also be characterized as having a Northern (or Laurentian) Divide, Eastern Divide, and St. Lawrence Seaway Divide. Some of the waters at the Northern Divide drain into Hudson Bay and the Arctic Ocean. The Appalachian Mountains mark the Eastern Divide, with waters joining the Atlantic or Gulf of Mexico. The waters at the St. Lawrence Seaway Divide, near Chicago, flow into the Gulf of St. Lawrence or Gulf of Mexico.

Chronological List of Territories, With State Admissions to Union

Source: U.S. National Archives and Records Administration

Territory	Date of act creating territory	When act took effect	Date of admission as state	Years as terr.
Northwest Territory[1]	July 13, 1787	No fixed date	Mar. 1, 1803[2]	16
Territory southwest of Ohio River	May 26, 1790	No fixed date	June 1, 1796[3]	6
Mississippi	Apr. 7, 1798	When president acted	Dec. 10, 1817	19
Indiana	May 7, 1800	July 4, 1800	Dec. 11, 1816	16
Orleans	Mar. 26, 1804	Oct. 1, 1804	Apr. 30, 1812[4]	7
Michigan	Jan. 11, 1805	June 30, 1805	Jan. 26, 1837	31
Louisiana-Missouri[5]	Mar. 3, 1805	July 4, 1805	Aug. 10, 1821	16
Illinois	Feb. 3, 1809	Mar. 1, 1809	Dec. 3, 1818	9
Alabama	Mar. 3, 1817	When MS formed state govt.	Dec. 14, 1819	2
Arkansas	Mar. 2, 1819	July 4, 1819	June 15, 1836	17
Florida	Mar. 30, 1822	No fixed date	Mar. 3, 1845	23
Wisconsin	Apr. 20, 1836	July 3, 1836	May 29, 1848	12
Iowa	June 12, 1838	July 3, 1838	Dec. 28, 1846	8
Oregon	Aug. 14, 1848	Date of act	Feb. 14, 1859	10
Minnesota	Mar. 3, 1849	Date of act	May 11, 1858	9
New Mexico	Sept. 9, 1850	On president's proclamation	Jan. 6, 1912	61
Utah	Sept. 9, 1850	Date of act	Jan. 4, 1896	46
Washington	Mar. 2, 1853	Date of act	Nov. 11, 1889	36
Kansas	May 30, 1854	Date of act	Jan. 29, 1861	6
Nebraska	May 30, 1854	Date of act	Mar. 1, 1867	12
Colorado	Feb. 28, 1861	Date of act	Aug. 1, 1876	15
Dakota	Mar. 2, 1861	Date of act	Nov. 2, 1889	28
Nevada	Mar. 2, 1861	Date of act	Oct. 31, 1864	3
Arizona	Feb. 24, 1863	Date of act	Feb. 14, 1912	49
Idaho	Mar. 3, 1863	Date of act	July 3, 1890	27
Montana	May 26, 1864	Date of act	Nov. 8, 1889	25
Wyoming	July 25, 1868	When officers were qualified	July 10, 1890	22
Alaska	May 17, 1884[6]	No fixed date	Jan. 3, 1959	75
Oklahoma	May 2, 1890	Date of act	Nov. 16, 1907	17
Hawaii	Apr. 30, 1900	June 14, 1900	Aug. 21, 1959	59

(1) Included what is now Ohio, Indiana, Illinois, Michigan, Wisconsin, and E Minnesota. (2) Date of admission for Ohio, the first state created out of NW territory. (3) Admitted as the state of Tennessee. (4) Admitted as the state of Louisiana. (5) The act renaming Louisiana Territory as Missouri Territory (June 4, 1812) became effective Dec. 7, 1812. (6) Act constituted Alaska as a district, though it was often referred to and administered as a territory. The Territory of Alaska was formally organized by an act of Aug. 24, 1912.

U.S. Geographic Centers

Source: U.S. Geological Survey, U.S. Dept. of the Interior

There is no generally accepted definition of a geographic center and no uniform method for determining it. Geographic center is defined here as the center of gravity of the surface of an area, or that point on which an area would balance if it were a plane of uniform thickness.

No government agency has officially established any points marking the geographic center of the U.S., the conterminous U.S. (48 states), or the North American continent. In 1941, private citizens erected a monument in Lebanon, KS, marking it as the geographic center of the then U.S. (conterminous). A cairn in Rugby, ND, was completed in 1932 designating that location as the center of the North American continent. The geographic centers in the following list are approximate. They are indicated by county then city unless otherwise noted.

U.S. (50 states): W of Castle Rock, Butte County, South Dakota; 44°58´ N, 103°46´ W
Conterminous U.S. (48 states): nr. Lebanon, Smith County, Kansas; 39°50´ N, 98°35´ W
North American continent: 6 mi W of Balta, Pierce County, North Dakota; 48°10´ N, 100°10´ W
Alabama: Chilton, 12 mi SW of Clanton
Alaska: approx. 60 mi NW of Denali; 63°50´ N, 152° W
Arizona: Yavapai, 55 mi E-SE of Prescott
Arkansas: Pulaski, 12 mi NW of Little Rock
California: Madera, 38 mi E of Madera
Colorado: Park, 30 mi NW of Pikes Peak
Connecticut: Hartford, at East Berlin
Delaware: Kent, 11 mi S of Dover
District of Columbia: near 4th and L Sts. NW
Florida: Hernando, 12 mi N-NW of Brooksville
Georgia: Twiggs, 18 mi SE of Macon
Hawaii: off Maui; 20°15´ N, 156°20´ W
Idaho: Custer, SW of Challis
Illinois: Logan, 28 mi NE of Springfield
Indiana: Boone, 14 mi N-NW of Indianapolis
Iowa: Story, 5 mi NE of Ames
Kansas: Barton, 15 mi NE of Great Bend
Kentucky: Marion, 3 mi N-NW of Lebanon
Louisiana: Avoyelles, 3 mi SE of Marksville
Maine: Piscataquis, 18 mi N of Dover
Maryland: Prince George's, 4.5 mi NW of Davidsonville
Massachusetts: Worcester, N part of city of Worcester
Michigan: Wexford, 5 mi N-NW of Cadillac
Minnesota: Crow Wing, 10 mi SW of Brainerd
Mississippi: Leake, 9 mi W-NW of Carthage
Missouri: Miller, 20 mi SW of Jefferson City
Montana: Fergus, 11 mi W of Lewistown
Nebraska: Custer, 10 mi NW of Broken Bow
Nevada: Lander, 26 mi SE of Austin
New Hampshire: Belknap, 3 mi E of Ashland
New Jersey: Mercer, 5 mi SE of Trenton
New Mexico: Torrance, 12 mi S-SW of Willard
New York: Madison, 12 mi S of Oneida and 26 mi SW of Utica
North Carolina: Chatham, 10 mi NW of Sanford
North Dakota: Sheridan, 5 mi SW of McClusky
Ohio: Delaware, 25 mi N-NE of Columbus
Oklahoma: Oklahoma, 8 mi N of Oklahoma City
Oregon: Crook, 25 mi S-SE of Prineville
Pennsylvania: Centre, 2.5 mi SW of Bellefonte
Rhode Island: Kent, 1 mi S-SW of Crompton
South Carolina: Richland, 13 mi SE of Columbia
South Dakota: Hughes, 8 mi NE of Pierre
Tennessee: Rutherford, 5 mi NE of Murfreesboro
Texas: McCulloch, 15 mi NE of Brady
Utah: Sanpete, 3 mi N of Manti
Vermont: Washington, 3 mi E of Roxbury
Virginia: Buckingham, 5 mi SW of Buckingham
Washington: Chelan, 10 mi W-SW of Wenatchee
West Virginia: Braxton, 4 mi E of Sutton
Wisconsin: Wood, 9 mi SE of Marshfield
Wyoming: Fremont, 58 mi E-NE of Lander

Lengths of U.S. Boundaries

The length of the boundary between the U.S. and Canada is 5,525 mi—3,987 mi between the conterminous U.S. and Canada and 1,538 mi between Alaska and Canada. A 1925 treaty established the International Boundary Commission to maintain the boundary. The U.S.-Mexican border, first established by treaty in 1848, is 1,954-miles long. It largely follows the Rio Grande and Colorado River, from the Gulf of Mexico to the Pacific Ocean. It is overseen by the International Boundary and Water Commission.

Origins of the Names of U.S. States

Source: State officials; Smithsonian Institution; Topographic Division, U.S. Geological Survey, U.S. Dept. of the Interior

Alabama: Choctaw word for a Chickasaw tribe. First noted in accounts of Hernando de Soto expedition.

Alaska: Russian version of Aleutian (Eskimo) word *alakshak* for "peninsula," "great lands," or "land that is not an island."

Arizona: Spanish version of Pima Indian word for "little spring place" or Aztec *arizuma*, meaning "silver-bearing."

Arkansas: Algonquin name for Quapaw Indians, meaning "south wind."

California: Bestowed by Spanish conquistadors (possibly Hernán Cortés). It was the name of an imaginary island in the 1510 Spanish novel *Las Sergas de Esplandián*, by Garci Rodríguez de Montalvo. The Spanish first visited *Baja* (Lower) *California* in 1533. The present-day U.S. state was called *Alta* (Upper) *California*.

Colorado: From Spanish for "red," first applied to Colorado River.

Connecticut: From Mohican and other Algonquin words meaning "long river place."

Delaware: Named for Lord De La Warr, early governor of Virginia; first applied to river, then to Indian tribe (Lenni-Lenape).

District of Columbia: For Christopher Columbus, 1791.

Florida: Named by Juan Ponce de León *Pascua Florida*, "Flowery Easter," on Easter Sunday, 1513.

Georgia: Named by colonial administrator James Oglethorpe for King George II of England in 1732.

Hawaii: Possibly derived from *Hawaiki* or *Owhyhee*, Polynesian word for "homeland."

Idaho: Said to be a coined name with the invented meaning "gem of the mountains"; suggested for the Pikes Peak mining territory (Colorado), then applied to the new mining territory of the Pacific Northwest. Another theory suggests *Idaho* may be Kiowa Apache term for the Comanche.

Illinois: French for *Illini* or "land of *Illini*," Algonquin word meaning "men" or "warriors."

Indiana: Means "land of the Indians."

Iowa: Indian word variously translated as "here I rest" or "beautiful land." Named for the Iowa River, which was named for the Iowa Indians.

Kansas: Sioux word for "south wind people."

Kentucky: Indian word variously translated as "dark and bloody ground," "meadowland," and "land of tomorrow."

Louisiana: Part of territory called Louisiana by René-Robert Cavelier Sieur de La Salle for French King Louis XIV.

Maine: From Maine, ancient French province. Also descriptive, referring to the mainland as distinct from coastal islands.

Maryland: For Queen Henrietta Maria, wife of Charles I of England.

Massachusetts: From Indian tribe whose name meant "at or about the Great Hill" in Blue Hills region south of Boston.

Michigan: From Chippewa *mici gama*, meaning "great water," after lake of the same name.

Minnesota: From Dakota Sioux word meaning "cloudy water" or "sky-tinted water" of the Minnesota River.

Mississippi: Probably Chippewa *mici zibi*, meaning "great river" or "gathering-in of all the waters." Also Algonquin word *messipi*.

Missouri: Algonquin Indian term meaning "river of the big canoes."

Montana: Latin or Spanish for "mountainous."

Nebraska: From Omaha or Otos Indian word meaning "broad water" or "flat river," describing the Platte River.

Nevada: Spanish, meaning "snow-clad."

New Hampshire: Named by Capt. John Mason of Plymouth Council, in 1629, for his home county in England.

New Jersey: The Duke of York, in 1664, gave a patent to Lord John Berkeley and Sir George Carteret for *Nova Caesaria*, or New Jersey, after England's Isle of Jersey.

New Mexico: Spaniards in Mexico applied term to land north and west of Rio Grande in the 16th century.

New York: For James, Duke of York and Albany, who received patent for New Netherland from his brother Charles II and sent an expedition to capture it, 1664.

North Carolina: In 1619, Charles I gave patent to Sir Robert Heath for Province of Carolana, from *Carolus*, Latin name for Charles. Charles II granted a new patent to Earl of Clarendon and others. Divided into North and South Carolina, 1710.

North Dakota: Sioux word *Dakota*, meaning "friend" or "ally."

Ohio: Iroquois word for "fine or good river."

Oklahoma: Choctaw word meaning "red man," proposed by Rev. Allen Wright, Choctaw-speaking Indian.

Oregon: Origin unknown. One theory is that the name derives from *wauregan*, meaning "beautiful," term used by Indians in New England.

Pennsylvania: William Penn, Quaker who was made full proprietor of area by King Charles II in 1681, suggested "Sylvania," or "woodland," for his tract. The king's government owed 16,000 pounds to Penn's father, Adm. William Penn, and the land was granted as partial settlement. Charles II added "Penn" to "Sylvania," against the modest proprietor's desires, in honor of the admiral.

Puerto Rico: Spanish for "rich port."

Rhode Island: Origin unknown. One theory notes that Giovanni de Verrazano recorded observing an island about the size of the Greek island of Rhodes in 1524. Another theory is that Dutch explorer Adriaen Block named the state *Roode Eylandt* for its red clay.

South Carolina: See North Carolina.

South Dakota: See North Dakota.

Tennessee: *Tanasi* was the name of Cherokee villages on the Little Tennessee River. From 1784 to 1788, this was the State of Franklin, or Frankland.

Texas: Variant of word used by Caddo and other Indians meaning "friends" or "allies" and applied to them by the Spanish in eastern Texas. Also written *Texias*, *Tejas*, *Teysas*.

Utah: From a Navajo word meaning "upper," or "higher up," as applied to Shoshone tribe called Ute. Proposed name *Deseret*, "land of honeybees," from Book of Mormon, was rejected by Congress.

Vermont: From French words *vert* (green) and *mont* (mountain). The Green Mountains were said to have been named by Samuel de Champlain. When the state was formed in 1777, Dr. Thomas Young suggested combining *vert* and *mont*.

Virginia: Named by Sir Walter Raleigh, who outfitted an expedition in 1584, in honor of England's Queen Elizabeth, the Virgin Queen.

Washington: Named after George Washington. When the bill creating the Territory of Columbia was introduced in the 32nd Congress, its name was changed to Washington because of the existence of the District of Columbia.

West Virginia: So named when western counties of Virginia refused to secede from the U.S. in 1863.

Wisconsin: Indian name, spelled *Ouisconsin* or *Mesconsing* by early chroniclers, believed to mean "grassy place" in Chippewa. Congress made it *Wisconsin*.

Wyoming: From Algonquin words for "large prairie place," "at the big plains," or "on the great plain."

Territorial Sea of the U.S.

According to a Dec. 27, 1988, proclamation by Pres. Ronald Reagan, "The territorial sea of the United States henceforth extends to 12 nautical miles from the baselines of the United States determined in accordance with international law. In accordance with international law, as reflected in the applicable provisions of the 1982 United Nations Convention on the Law of the Sea, within the territorial sea of the United States, the ships of all countries enjoy the right of innocent passage and the ships and aircraft of all countries enjoy the right of transit passage through international straits."

Major Accessions of Territory by the U.S.

Source: U.S. Dept. of the Interior; U.S. Census Bureau, U.S. Dept. of Commerce

Not including territories such as the Panama Canal Zone and the Philippines, which are no longer under U.S. jurisdiction.

Accession	Date	Area (sq mi)	Accession	Date	Area (sq mi)	Accession	Date	Area (sq mi)
Territory in 1790[1]	NA	888,685	Mexican Cession	1848	529,017	Guam[3]	1899	212
Louisiana Purchase	1803	827,192	Gadsden Purchase	1853	29,640	American Samoa[4]	1900	76
Treaty of Florida	1819	72,003	Alaska	1867	586,412	U.S. Virgin Islands	1917	133
Texas	1845	390,143	Hawaii	1898	6,450	Northern Marianas[5]	1986	179
Oregon Territory	1846	285,680	Puerto Rico[2]	1899	3,435			

NA = Not applicable. (1) Includes that part of a drainage basin of Red River of the North, south of 49th parallel, sometimes considered part of Louisiana Purchase. (2) Ceded by Spain in 1898, ratified in 1899, and became the Commonwealth of Puerto Rico by Act of Congress on July 25, 1952. (3) Acquired in 1898; ratified 1899. (4) Acquired in 1899; ratified 1900. (5) Part of the UN Trust Territory of the Pacific Islands, which U.S. began administering in 1947; became U.S. commonwealth Nov. 3, 1986.

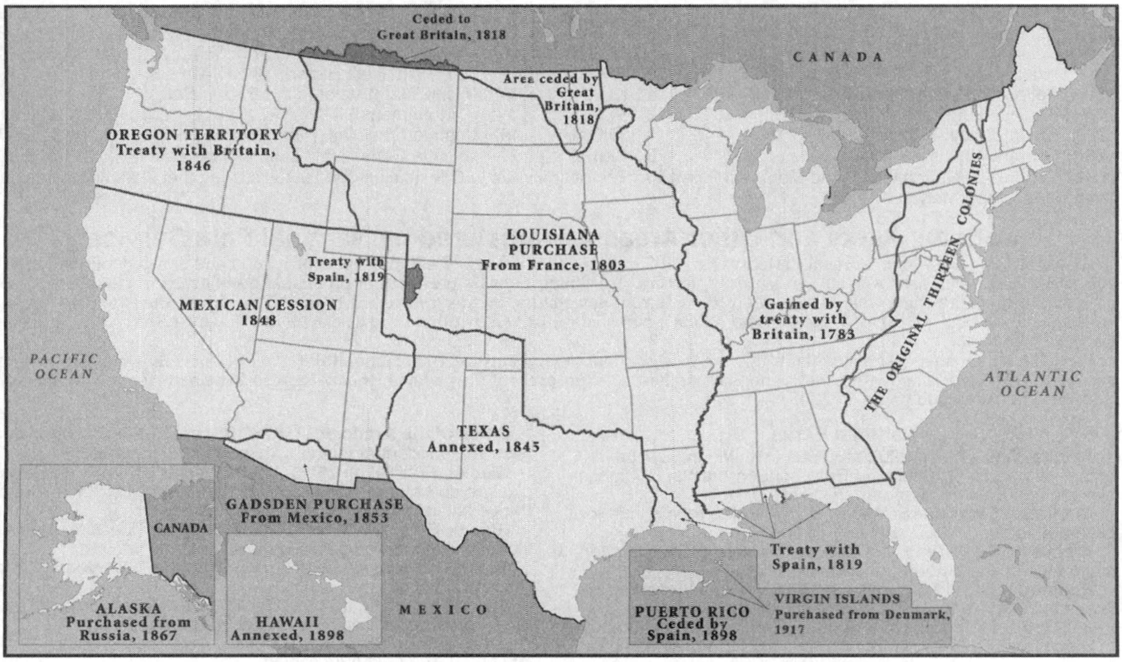

National Park System Recreation Visits, 1905-2014

Source: National Park Service (NPS), U.S. Dept. of the Interior

An NPS site, regardless of its designation (as a park, monument, or preserve, etc.), is generally referred to as a unit. Not all units report public use statistics.

Year	Units reporting visits	Recreation visits	Year	Units reporting visits	Recreation visits
1905	6	140,954	1990	316	255,581,467
1910	9	173,416	1995	328	269,564,307
1915	12	314,299	2000	344	285,891,275
1920	26	1,022,091	2001	345	279,873,926
1925	39	1,900,499	2002	349	277,299,880
1930	45	3,038,935	2003	353	266,230,290
1935	85	7,435,659	2004	356	276,908,337
1940	113	16,410,148	2005	356	273,488,751
1945	143	10,855,548	2006	359	272,623,980
1950	139	32,706,172	2007	360	275,581,547
1955	150	48,891,000	2008	360	274,852,949
1960	166	71,586,000	2009	360	285,579,941
1965	182	118,662,500	2010	363	281,303,769
1970	217	168,135,100	2011	367	278,939,216
1975	251	188,085,700	2012	367	282,765,682
1980	275	220,463,211	2013	370	273,630,895
1985	303	263,441,808	2014	376	292,800,082

Most-Visited Sites in the National Park System, 2014

Source: National Park Service (NPS), U.S. Dept. of the Interior

Attendance at 376 of 405 NPS sites totaled 292,800,082 recreation visits in 2014. (Not all units report public use statistics.)

Rank	Site (location)	Rec. visits
1.	Golden Gate Natl. Recreation Area (CA)	15,004,420
2.	Blue Ridge Parkway (NC-VA)	13,941,749
3.	Great Smoky Mountains Natl. Park (NC-TN)	10,099,276
4.	George Washington Memorial Parkway (DC-MD-VA)	7,472,150
5.	Lincoln Memorial (DC)	7,139,072
6.	Lake Mead Natl. Recreation Area (AZ-NV)	6,942,873
7.	Gateway Natl. Recreation Area (NJ-NY)	6,021,713
8.	Natchez Trace Parkway (MS-AL-TN)	5,846,474
9.	Chesapeake & Ohio Canal Natl. Historical Park (DC-MD-WV)	5,066,219
10.	Grand Canyon Natl. Park (AZ)	4,756,771
11.	Castle Clinton Natl. Monument (NY)	4,727,110
12.	Gulf Islands Natl. Seashore (FL-MS)	4,455,240
13.	Cape Cod Natl. Seashore (MA)	4,426,750
14.	Vietnam Veterans Memorial (DC)	4,403,467
15.	San Francisco Maritime Natl. Historical Park (CA)	4,256,888
16.	World War II Memorial (DC)	4,230,793
17.	Statue of Liberty Natl. Monument (NY)	4,198,815
18.	Delaware Water Gap Natl. Recreation Area (NJ-PA)	4,041,672
19.	Yosemite Natl. Park (CA)	3,882,642
20.	Korean War Veterans Memorial (DC)	3,767,287
21.	Independence Natl. Historical Park (PA)	3,648,050
22.	Yellowstone Natl. Park (ID-MT-WY)	3,513,484
23.	Rocky Mountain Natl. Park (CO)	3,434,751
24.	Colonial Natl. Historical Park (VA)	3,335,060
25.	Olympic Natl. Park (WA)	3,243,872
26.	Martin Luther King Jr. Memorial (DC)	3,199,136
27.	Zion Natl. Park (UT)	3,189,696
28.	Chattahoochee River Natl. Recreation Area (GA)	3,119,160
29.	Franklin Delano Roosevelt Memorial (DC)	2,938,239
30.	Grand Teton Natl. Park (WY)	2,791,392
31.	Thomas Jefferson Memorial (DC)	2,708,607
32.	Acadia Natl. Park (ME)	2,563,129
33.	Boston Natl. Historical Park (MA)	2,476,078
34.	Rock Creek Park (DC)	2,437,948
35.	Point Reyes Natl. Seashore (CA)	2,433,944
36.	Glen Canyon Natl. Recreation Area (AZ-UT)	2,368,452
37.	Glacier Natl. Park (MT)	2,338,528
38.	Cuyahoga Valley Natl. Park (OH)	2,189,849
39.	Assateague Island Natl. Seashore (MD-VA)	2,170,681
40.	Cape Hatteras Natl. Seashore (NC)	2,153,350
41.	Mount Rushmore Natl. Memorial (SD)	2,144,808
42.	Kennesaw Mountain Natl. Battlefield Park (GA)	2,119,013
43.	National Capital Parks Central[1] (DC)	1,999,232
44.	Valley Forge Natl. Historic Park (PA)	1,990,881
45.	Jefferson Natl. Expansion Memorial (MO)	1,817,091
46.	Hawaii Volcanoes Natl. Park (HI)	1,693,005
47.	Fort Point Natl. Historic Site (CA)	1,677,457
48.	World War II Valor in the Pacific Natl. Monument (HI-AK-CA)	1,620,814
49.	Joshua Tree Natl. Park (CA)	1,589,904
50.	Indiana Dunes Natl. Lakeshore (IN)	1,553,372

(1) Also known as National Mall and Memorial Parks. Incl. recreation visits to Constitution Gardens; visits to other sites within this unit are reported separately.

National Parks and Other Areas Administered by National Park Service

As of Dec. 31, 2014, the National Park Service (NPS) administered about 84,479,064 acres of federal and non-federal land across 405 sites. Date when area was authorized or established by Congress or by presidential proclamation is given in parentheses; any date that follows indicates when a site received its current designation or was transferred to the NPS. Figure after the date is gross area acres as of Dec. 31, 2014. Table does not include parks administered by other agencies, such as the Forest Service or Bureau of Land Management.

Pres. Barack Obama designated the following new national monuments in 2015: Honouliuli (HI), Pullman (IL), and Waco Mammoth (TX). The federal government has not yet purchased the property of the planned Ronald Reagan Boyhood Home Natl. Historic Site, designated by public law in 2002.

National Parks

Acadia, ME (1916/1929): 48,996. Incl. Mount Desert Isl., half of Isle au Haut, Schoodic Peninsula on mainland. Highest elevation on Eastern seaboard.

American Samoa, AS (1988): 8,257. Paleotropical rain forest, coral reef.

Arches, UT (1929/1971): 76,679. Contains giant red sandstone arches and other products of erosion.

Badlands, SD (1929/1978): 242,756. Reformations and native prairie; animal fossils 23-37 mil years old.

Big Bend, TX (1935): 801,163. Rio Grande, Chisos Mtns.

Biscayne, FL (1968/1980): 172,971. Aquatic park encompassing chain of islands south of Miami.

Black Canyon of the Gunnison, CO (1933/1999): 30,750. Has canyon 2,900 ft deep and 40 ft wide at narrowest part.

Bryce Canyon, UT (1923/1928): 35,835. Colorful display of erosion effects.

Canyonlands, UT (1964): 337,598. At junction of Colorado and Green Rivers; extensive evidence of prehistoric peoples.

Capitol Reef, UT (1937/1971): 241,904. 70-mi uplift of sandstone cliffs dissected by high-walled gorges.

Carlsbad Caverns, NM (1923/1930): 46,766. More than 110 limestone caves, incl. Carlsbad Cavern; Chihuahuan Desert.

Channel Islands, CA (1938/1980): 249,561. Sea lion breeding place, nesting seabirds, unique plants.

Congaree, SC (1976/2003): 26,276. Largest intact tract of old-growth bottomland hardwood forest in U.S.

Crater Lake, OR (1902): 183,224. Deepest U.S. lake, in crater of Mt. Mazama, volcano that erupted about 7,700 years ago.

Cuyahoga Valley, OH (1974/2000): 32,571. Along Ohio and Erie Canal system between Akron and Cleveland.

Death Valley, CA-NV (1933/1994): 3,373,063. Large desert. Incl. lowest point in Western Hemisphere and Scotty's Castle.

Denali, AK (1917/1980): 4,740,911. Formerly known as Mt. McKinley; highest mountain in U.S.

Dry Tortugas, FL (1935/1992): 64,701. Ft. Jefferson and seven coral reef and sand islands near Key West.

Everglades, FL (1934): 1,508,974. Largest remaining subtropical wilderness in continental U.S; incl. East Everglades Expansion Area acreage added in 1989.

Gates of the Arctic, AK (1978/1984): 7,523,897. Vast wilderness in north central region. Limited federal facilities.

Glacier, MT (1910): 1,013,322. Rocky Mt. scenery, numerous glaciers and glacial lakes. Part of Waterton-Glacier Intl. Peace Park established by U.S. and Canada in 1932.

Glacier Bay, AK (1925/1986): 3,223,383. Tidewater glaciers that move down mountainsides and break up into sea.

Grand Canyon, AZ (1893/1919): 1,201,647. Carved by Colorado River.

Grand Teton, WY (1929): 310,044. Incl. highest peaks of Teton Mtns.; summer feeding ground of largest American elk herd.

Great Basin, NV (1922/1986): 77,180. Incl. Wheeler Peak, Lexington Arch, Lehman Caves.

Great Sand Dunes, CO (1932/2000): 107,302. North America's tallest dunes.

Great Smoky Mountains, NC-TN (1926/1934): 522,427. Largest Eastern U.S. mountain range; magnificent forests.

Guadalupe Mountains, TX (1966): 86,367. Extensive Permian limestone fossil reef; tremendous earth fault.

Haleakalā, HI (1916/1960): 33,265. Dormant volcano on island of Maui with large craters.

Hawai'i Volcanoes, HI (1916/1961): 323,431. Contains Kilauea and Mauna Loa, active volcanoes.

Hot Springs, AR (1832/1921): 5,549. Waters from park's 47 hot springs used for bathing and drinking.

Isle Royale, MI (1931): 571,790. Largest island in Lake Superior.

Joshua Tree, CA (1936/1994): 790,636. Desert region incl. Joshua trees, other plant and animal life.

Katmai, AK (1918/1980): 3,674,368. "Valley of Ten Thousand Smokes," scene of 1912 volcanic eruption.

Kenai Fjords, AK (1978/1980): 669,984. Marine mammals, birdlife; Harding Icefield, one of four major icecaps in U.S.

Kings Canyon, CA (1890/1940): 461,901. Mountain wilderness, dominated by Kings River Canyons and High Sierra; giant sequoias.

Kobuk Valley, AK (1978/1980): 1,750,716. Contains geological and recreational sites. Limited federal facilities.

Lake Clark, AK (1978/1980): 2,619,836. Across Cook Inlet from Anchorage; scenic wilderness, fish and wildlife. Limited federal facilities.

Lassen Volcanic, CA (1907/1916): 106,452. Contains Lassen Peak, recently active volcano; other volcanic phenomena.

Mammoth Cave, KY (1926/1941): 52,830. Longest known cave system in world (more than 390 mi currently surveyed), river 300 ft below surface.

Mesa Verde, CO (1906): 52,485. Most notable and best preserved prehistoric cliff dwellings in U.S.

Mount Rainier, WA (1899): 236,381. Most glaciated peak in contiguous U.S.

North Cascades, WA (1968): 504,781. Mountainous region with many glaciers, lakes.

Olympic, WA (1909/1938): 922,650. Mountain wilderness containing remnant of Pacific Northwest rain forest, active glaciers, shoreline, rare elk.

Petrified Forest, AZ (1906/1962): 221,416. Extensive petrified wood and Indian artifacts. Contains part of Painted Desert.

Pinnacles, CA (1908/2013): 26,686. A release site for captive-bred California condors; talus caves.

Redwood, CA (1968): 138,999. 40 mi of Pacific coastline, groves of ancient redwoods and world's tallest trees.

Rocky Mountain, CO (1915): 265,795. On Continental Divide; incl. peaks over 14,000 ft.

Saguaro, AZ (1933/1994): 91,442. Part of Sonoran Desert; incl. giant saguaro cacti, unique to region.

Sequoia, CA (1890): 404,063. Giant sequoia groves; world's largest tree (by volume). Mt. Whitney, highest mountain in conterminous U.S.

Shenandoah, VA (1926): 199,117. Portion of Blue Ridge Mtns.; overlooks Shenandoah Valley; Skyline Drive.

Theodore Roosevelt, ND (1947/1978): 70,447. Contains part of Roosevelt's ranch and scenic badlands.

Virgin Islands, VI (1956): 14,948. Covers 75% of St. John Isl. and Hassel Isl.; beaches, Carib Indian petroglyphs, evidence of colonial Danes.

Voyageurs, MN (1971): 218,200. Abundant lakes, forests, wildlife.

Wind Cave, SD (1903): 33,847. Limestone caverns in Black Hills; extensive wildlife incl. bison herd.

Wrangell-St. Elias, AK (1978/1980): 8,323,147. Largest area in park system; most peaks over 16,000 ft. No federal facilities.

Yellowstone, ID-MT-WY (1872): 2,219,791. World's first national park. World's greatest geyser area with about 10,000 geysers, hot springs; falls and canyons of Yellowstone River; grizzly bear, moose, bison.

Yosemite, CA (1890): 761,348. Yosemite Valley, country's highest waterfall, grove of sequoias, mountains.

Zion, UT (1909/1919): 147,237. Unusual shapes, landscapes resulting from erosion and faulting; evidence of past volcanic activity; contains 2,394-ft monolith "Great White Throne."

National Historical Parks

Abraham Lincoln Birthplace, Hodgenville, KY (1916/1959): 345. Memorial building, sinking spring.

Adams, Quincy, MA (1946/1998): 24. Home of Pres. John Adams, John Quincy Adams, and descendants.

Appomattox Court House, VA (1930/1954): 1,774. Where Confederate Gen. Lee surrendered to Gen. Grant, signaling Civil War's end.

Blackstone River Valley, MA-RI (2014): 1,400. Preserves the valley's industrial heritage.

Boston, MA (1974): 44. Incl. Faneuil Hall, Old North Church, Bunker Hill, Paul Revere House.

Cane River Creole, LA (1994): 206. Preserves Creole culture as it developed along the Cane River.

Cedar Creek and Belle Grove, VA (2002): 3,712. Civil War battle site and an antebellum plantation in Shenandoah Valley.

Chaco Culture, NM (1907/1980): 33,960. Ruins of pueblos built by prehistoric peoples incl. Pueblo, Hopi, and Navajo.

Chesapeake & Ohio Canal, MD-DC-WV (1938/1971): 19,612. 184-mi historic canal; DC to Cumberland, MD.

Colonial, VA (1930/1936): 8,677. Incl. most of Jamestown Isl., site of first successful English colony; Yorktown, site of Cornwallis's surrender to George Washington; Colonial Parkway.

Cumberland Gap, KY-TN-VA (1940): 24,547. Mountain pass of Wilderness Road, which carried first great migration of pioneers into America's interior.

Dayton Aviation Heritage, OH (1992): 111. Commemorates area's involvement in aviation.

First State, DE-PA (2013/2014): NA. Locations date from colonial past of DE, first state to ratify Constitution.

George Rogers Clark, Vincennes, IN (1966): 26. Commemorates American defeat of British in West during Revolution.

Harpers Ferry, MD-VA-WV (1944/1963): 3,670. At confluence of Shenandoah and Potomac Rivers, the site of John Brown's 1859 raid on the Army arsenal.

Harriet Tubman Underground Railroad, MD (2013/2014): NA. Protects landscapes on the Eastern Shore, where Tubman was born and guided other slaves to freedom.

Hopewell Culture, OH (1923/1992): 1,765. Remains of ceremonial mounds built in the Ohio River Valley, 200 BCE-500 CE.

Independence, Philadelphia, PA (1948): 45. Several properties associated with American Revolution and founding of U.S., incl. Independence Hall, Liberty Bell Center.

Jean Lafitte (and Preserve), LA (1907/1978): 22,421. Incl. Chalmette, site of 1815 Battle of New Orleans; French Quarter.

Kalaupapa, HI (1980): 10,779. Former colony on Molokai Isl. for those with Hansen's disease (leprosy).

Kaloko-Honokohau, HI (1978): 1,163. Preserves native culture of Hawaii.

Keweenaw, MI (1992): 1,869. Site of first significant copper mine in U.S.

Klondike Gold Rush, AK-WA (1976): 12,996. Preserves Chilkoot Trail used in 1898 Gold Rush. Museum in Seattle.

Lewis and Clark, OR-WA (1958/2004): 3,410. Lewis and Clark encampment, 1805-06. Incorporates former Fort Clatsop Natl. Mem. Park and OR-WA state parks.

Lowell, MA (1978): 141. Textile mills, canal, 19th-cent. structures; park shows planned city of Industrial Revolution.

Lyndon B. Johnson, TX (1969/1980): 1,570. President's birthplace, boyhood home, ranch.

Marsh-Billings-Rockefeller, VT (1992): 643. Boyhood home of conservationist George Perkins Marsh.

Minute Man, MA (1959): 1,027. Where Minute Men battled British, Apr. 19, 1775. Also contains Nathaniel Hawthorne's home.

Morristown, NJ (1933): 1,711. Site of important military encampments during the American Revolution; Washington's headquarters, 1779-80.

Natchez, MS (1988): 108. Mansions, townhouses, and villas related to history of Natchez.

New Bedford Whaling, MA (1996): 34. Preserves structures and relics associated with the city's 19th-cent. whaling industry.

New Orleans Jazz, LA (1994): 5. Preserves, educates, and interprets jazz as it has evolved in New Orleans.

Nez Perce, ID-MT-OR-WA (1965): 4,565. Illustrates history and culture of Nez Perce, or Nimiipuu, homeland (38 separate sites).

Palo Alto Battlefield, TX (1978): 3,442. Scene of first battle of the Mexican War.

Paterson Great Falls, NJ (2011): 36. Falls helped make city one of U.S.'s earliest industrial centers.

Pecos, NM (1965/1990): 6,703. Ruins of ancient Pueblo of Pecos, archaeological sites, and two associated Spanish colonial missions from 17th and 18th centuries.

Pu'uhonua o Hōnaunau, HI (1955/1978): 420. Until 1819, a sanctuary for Hawaiians vanquished in battle and for those guilty of crimes or breaking taboos.

Rosie the Riveter/WWII Home Front, Richmond, CA (2000): 145. Site of shipyard that employed thousands of women during WWII; commemorates women who worked in wartime industries.

Salt River Bay (and Ecological Preserve), St. Croix, VI (1992): 989. Only known site where, in 1493, members of a Columbus party landed on what is now U.S. territory.

San Antonio Missions, TX (1978): 830. Four Spanish missions, 18th-cent. irrigation system.

San Francisco Maritime, CA (1988): 50. Artifacts, photographs, and historic vessels related to development of the Pacific Coast.

San Juan Island, WA (1966): 2,146. Commemorates peaceful relations between U.S., Canada, and Great Britain since the 1872 boundary disputes.

Saratoga, NY (1938): 3,410. Scene of a major 1777 battle that became a turning point in the American Revolution.

Sitka, AK (1910/1972): 116. Scene of last major resistance of Tlingit to the Russians, 1804.

Thomas Edison, West Orange, NJ (1955/1962): 21. Inventor's home and laboratory.

Tumacacori, AZ (1908/1990): 360. Historic Spanish mission building near site first visited by Father Kino in 1691.

Valley Forge, PA (1976): 3,468. Continental Army campsite in 1777-78 winter.

War in the Pacific, GU (1978): 2,037. Seven distinct units illustrating the Pacific theater of WWII. Limited federal facilities.

Women's Rights, NY (1980): 7. Seneca Falls site where Lucretia Mott, Elizabeth Cady Stanton organized movement in 1848.

National Battlefields/Parks/Sites

Antietam, MD (1890/1978): 3,230. Battle here ended first Confederate invasion of North, Sept. 17, 1862.

Big Hole, MT (1910/1963): 1,011. Site of major battle with Nez Perce Indians, Aug. 9-10, 1877.

Brices Cross Roads, Baldwyn, MS (1929): 1. Site of Confederate victory, June 10, 1864.

Cowpens, SC (1929/1972): 842. American Revolution battlefield, Jan. 17, 1781.

Fort Donelson, TN-KY (1928/1985): 1,308. Site of first major Union victory, Feb. 14-16, 1862.

Fort Necessity, PA (1931/1961): 903. Site of first battle of French and Indian War, July 3, 1754.

Kennesaw Mountain, GA (1917/1935): 2,853. Site of major battle of Atlanta campaign in Civil War.

Manassas, VA (1940): 5,073. Scene of two Civil War battles.

Monocacy, MD (1934/1976): 1,647. Civil War battle in defense of Washington, DC, fought here, July 9, 1864.

Moores Creek, Currie, NC (1926/1980): 88. Commemorates Feb. 27, 1776, battle between Patriots and Loyalists.

Petersburg, VA (1926/1962): 2,740. Scene of Union campaigns, 1864-65.

Richmond, VA (1936): 8,004. Site of battles defending Confederate capital.

River Raisin, Monroe, MI (2010): 42. Site of major battles of War of 1812.

Stones River, TN (1927/1960): 709. Scene of battle that began federal offensive to trisect Confederacy, Dec. 31, 1862-Jan. 2, 1863.

Tupelo, MS (1929/1961): 1. Site of crucial battle over Union Gen. Sherman's supply line, July 14-15, 1865.

Wilson's Creek, MO (1960/1970): 2,368. Scene of Civil War battle for control of Missouri, Aug. 10, 1861.

National Military Parks

Chickamauga and Chattanooga, GA-TN (1890): 9,078. Where Gen. Sherman and Union armies gained control of TN, 1863.

Fredericksburg and Spotsylvania, VA (1927/1933): 8,380. Sites of several major Civil War battles and campaigns.

Gettysburg, PA (1895/1933): 5,988. Site of decisive Confederate defeat in North, July 1863, and of Gettysburg Address.

Guilford Courthouse, NC (1917/1933): 250. American Revolution battle site.

Horseshoe Bend, AL (1956): 2,040. On Tallapoosa River, where Gen. Andrew Jackson broke power of Upper Creek Indian Confederacy on Mar. 27, 1814.

Kings Mountain, SC (1931/1933): 3,945. Site of American Revolution battle, fought on Oct. 7, 1780.

Pea Ridge, AR (1956): 4,300. Civil War battle, Mar. 7-8, 1862.

Shiloh, TN-MS (1894/1933): 6,048. Major Civil War battle site; incl. Indian burial mounds.

Vicksburg, MS-LA (1899/1933): 1,802. Union victory gave North control of Mississippi and split Confederate forces.

National Memorials

Arkansas Post, AR (1960): 758. First permanent French settlement in lower Mississippi River valley.

Arlington House, The Robert E. Lee Memorial, VA (1925/1972): 28. Lee's home overlooking the Potomac River.

Chamizal, El Paso, TX (1966/1974): 55. Commemorates 1963 settlement of 99-year border dispute with Mexico.

Coronado, AZ (1941/1952): 4,830. Commemorates first European exploration of the Southwest.

De Soto, Bradenton, FL (1948): 30. Commemorates 16th-cent. Spanish explorations.

Federal Hall, New York, NY (1939/1955): 0.45. First seat of U.S. government under the Constitution.

Flight 93, Shanksville, PA (2002): 2,320. Commemorates passengers and crew of Flight 93, who died thwarting an attack on Sept. 11, 2001. First features of memorial completed and dedicated in 2011.

Fort Caroline, Jacksonville, FL (1950): 138. On St. Johns River, site of first attempt by France, in 16th cent., at permanent North American settlement.

Franklin Delano Roosevelt Memorial, DC (1982): 8. Statues of Pres. Roosevelt and Eleanor Roosevelt; waterfalls and gardens.

General Grant, New York, NY (1958): 0.76. Tomb of Ulysses Grant and wife; largest mausoleum in U.S.

Hamilton Grange, New York, NY (1962): 1.04. Home of Alexander Hamilton.

Jefferson National Expansion, St. Louis, MO (1935): 193. Commemorates 19th cent. westward expansion; incl. Gateway Arch.

Johnstown Flood, PA (1964): 178. Commemorates 1889 flood.

Korean War Veterans Memorial, DC (1986): 1.56. Honors those who served in the Korean War.

Lincoln Boyhood, Lincoln City, IN (1962): 200. Site of Abraham Lincoln's boyhood home and grave site of his mother.

Lincoln Memorial, DC (1911/1933): 7. Marble statue of 16th president.

Lyndon Baines Johnson Memorial Grove on the Potomac, DC (1973): 17. Overlooks Potomac River; vista of the Capitol.

Martin Luther King Jr., DC (1996): 3. Granite statue of Dr. King close to where he delivered "I Have a Dream" speech.

Mount Rushmore, SD (1925): 1,278. World-famous sculpture of presidents Washington, Jefferson, Lincoln, T. Roosevelt.

Perry's Victory and International Peace Memorial, Put-in-Bay, OH (1936/1972): 25. World's most massive Doric column promotes pursuit of peace through arbitration and disarmament.

Port Chicago Naval Magazine, Danville, CA (2009): 5. Where 1944 munitions ship explosion killed 320 men.

Roger Williams, Providence, RI (1965): 5. Memorial to founder of Rhode Island.

Thaddeus Kosciuszko, Philadelphia, PA (1972): 0.02. Memorial to Polish hero of American Revolution.

Theodore Roosevelt Island, DC (1932/1933): 89. Statue of Roosevelt in wooded island sanctuary.

Thomas Jefferson Memorial, DC (1934): 18. Statue of Jefferson in an inscribed circular, colonnaded structure.

Vietnam Veterans Memorial, DC (1980): 2. Black granite wall with names of those missing or killed in action in Vietnam War.

Washington Monument, DC (1848/1933): 106. Obelisk honoring the first U.S. president.

World War I Memorial, DC (1981/2014): 1.76. Formerly Pershing Park, dedicated to Gen. John J. Pershing.

World War II Memorial, DC (1994/2004): 8. Oval plaza with central pool commemorating those who fought and died.

Wright Brothers, Kill Devil Hills, NC (1927/1953): 428. Site of first powered flight.

National Historic Sites

Allegheny Portage Railroad, PA (1964): 1,284. Linked Pennsylvania Canal system and the West.

Andersonville, GA (1970): 516. Civil War POW camp.

Andrew Johnson, Greeneville, TN (1935/1963): 17. Two homes and the tailor shop of 17th U.S. president.

Bent's Old Fort, CO (1960): 799. Replica of fort on Sante Fe Trail.

Boston African-American, MA (1980): 0.59. Pre-Civil War black-owned structures.

Brown v. Board of Education, Topeka, KS (1992): 1.85. Commemorates landmark 1954 U.S. Supreme Court decision, which ended legal segregation in schools.

Carl Sandburg Home, Flat Rock, NC (1968): 264. Home of Pulitzer Prize-winning poet and biographer.

Carter G. Woodson Home, DC (1976/2006): 0.15. Home of "Father of Black History."

Charles Pinckney, Mt. Pleasant, SC (1988): 28. Farm of a principal author and signer of the Constitution.

Christiansted, St. Croix, VI (1952/1961): 27. Commemorates Danish colony.

Clara Barton, Glen Echo, MD (1974): 9. Home of American Red Cross founder.

Edgar Allan Poe, Philadelphia, PA (1978/1980): 0.52. Writer's home.

Eisenhower, Gettysburg, PA (1967): 690. Home of 34th president.

Eleanor Roosevelt, Hyde Park, NY (1977): 181. Former first lady's personal retreat.

Eugene O'Neill, Danville, CA (1976): 13. Home where playwright wrote his final plays, incl. *The Iceman Cometh*.

First Ladies, Canton, OH (2000): 0.46. Home of first lady Ida Sexton McKinley. Library now devoted to America's first ladies.

Ford's Theatre, DC (1866/1970): 0.3. Incl. theater where Lincoln was assassinated, house where he died, and Lincoln Museum.

Fort Bowie, AZ (1964): 999. Focal point of operations against Geronimo and Apaches.

Fort Davis, TX (1961): 523. Frontier outpost in West Texas; established to guard the San Antonio-El Paso Road.

Fort Laramie, WY (1938/1960): 867. Military post on Oregon Trail.

Fort Larned, KS (1964/1966): 718. Military post on Santa Fe Trail.

Fort Point, CA (1970): 29. West Coast fortification; protected San Francisco during and after Civil War.

Fort Raleigh, NC (1941): 513. First attempted English settlement in North America.

Fort Scott, KS (1965/1978): 17. Commemorates U.S. frontier. Focal point of black troop activity, training during Civil War.

Fort Smith, AR-OK (1961): 75. One of the earliest U.S. posts in Missouri Territory, active 1817-90.

Fort Union Trading Post, MT-ND (1966): 440. Principal fur-trading post on upper Missouri, 1829-67.

Fort Vancouver, WA-OR (1948/1961): 207. Headquarters for Hudson's Bay Company.

Frederick Douglass, DC (1962/1988): 9. Home of black abolitionist, writer, orator.

Frederick Law Olmsted, Brookline, MA (1979): 7. Home of city planner, famous for designing Central Park in NYC.

Friendship Hill, PA (1978): 675. Home of Albert Gallatin, Jefferson's and Madison's secretary of treasury.

Golden Spike, UT (1957): 2,735. Commemorates completion of first transcontinental railroad in 1869.

Grant-Kohrs Ranch, MT (1972): 1,618. Ranch house owned by John Grant, 19th-cent. range-cattle industry pioneer.

Hampton, Towson, MD (1948): 62. 18th-cent. Georgian mansion, which in 1790 was largest house in U.S.

Harry S. Truman, MO (1983): 13. House of 33rd president from 1919 on and farm where he worked as young man.

Herbert Hoover, West Branch, IA (1965): 187. Birthplace and boyhood home of 31st president.

Home of Franklin D. Roosevelt, Hyde Park, NY (1944): 850. FDR's birthplace, home, and "summer White House."

Hopewell Furnace, PA (1938/1985): 848. 19th-cent. iron-making village.

Hubbell Trading Post, AZ (1965): 160. Oldest continuously operating trading post in SW; founded in 1878 on Navajo Nation.

James A. Garfield, Mentor, OH (1980): 8. Home of 20th president; site of his front-porch campaign.

Jimmy Carter, Plains, GA (1987): 72. Birthplace and home of 39th president.

John Fitzgerald Kennedy, Brookline, MA (1967): 0.09. Birthplace and childhood home of 35th president.

John Muir, Martinez, CA (1964): 344. Home of Sierra Club co-founder and "Father of the National Park Service."

Knife River Indian Villages, ND (1974): 1,749. Remnants of villages last occupied by Hidatsa and Mandan Indians.

Lincoln Home, Springfield, IL (1971): 12. Lincoln's residence when he was elected 16th president, 1860.

Little Rock Central High School, AR (1998): 27. Commemorates 1957 desegregation during which federal troops were called in to protect nine black students.

Longfellow House–Washington's Headquarters, Cambridge, MA (1972): 2. Poet's home, 1837-82; Washington's headquarters during Boston siege, 1775-76.

Maggie L. Walker, Richmond, VA (1978): 1.29. Home of black leader and first female bank president, daughter of former slave.

Manzanar, Lone Pine, CA (1992): 814. Manzanar War Relocation Ctr., a WWII Japanese-American internment camp.

Martin Luther King Jr., Atlanta, GA (1980): 39. Birthplace, grave, church of the civil rights leader.

Martin Van Buren, Kinderhook, NY (1974): 285. Lindenwald, home of 8th president.

Mary McLeod Bethune Council House, DC (1982/1991): 0.07. Commemorates Bethune's leadership in the black women's movement.

Minidoka, ID (2008): 396. WWII Japanese internment center.

Minuteman Missile, SD (1999): 44. Missile launch facilities dating back to Cold War era.

Nicodemus, KS (1996): 5. Only remaining Western town established by African Americans during Reconstruction.

Ninety Six, SC (1976): 1,022. Colonial trading village and site of Gen. Nathanael Greene's siege on Loyalist-held fort in 1781.

Pennsylvania Avenue, DC (1965): 19. Incl. area between Capitol and White House, encompassing U.S. Navy Memorial, Freedom Plaza, Old Post Office Pavilion, and other sites.

President William Jefferson Clinton Birthplace Home, Hope, AR (2010): 1. Birthplace and early home of 42nd president.

Pu'ukoholā Heiau, Kawaihae, HI (1972): 86. Ruins of temple built by King Kamehameha, first king of united Hawaiian islands.

Sagamore Hill, Oyster Bay, NY (1962): 83. Home of Pres. Theodore Roosevelt from 1885 until his death in 1919.

Saint-Gaudens, Cornish, NH (1964): 191. Home, studio, and gardens of American sculptor Augustus Saint-Gaudens.

Saint Paul's Church, New York, NY (1943): 6. Site associated with John Peter Zenger's "freedom of the press" trial.

Salem Maritime, MA (1938): 9. Major fishing and whaling port famous for 1692 witchcraft trials.

Sand Creek Massacre, CO (2000): 12,583. Site where more than 160 Cheyenne and Arapaho Indians were killed by U.S. soldiers in 1864.

San Juan, PR (1949): 75. 16th-cent. Spanish fortifications.

Saugus Iron Works, MA (1974): 9. Reconstructed 17th-cent. colonial ironworks.

Springfield Armory, MA (1974): 55. Small-arms manufacturing center for nearly 200 years.

Steamtown, Scranton, PA (1986): 62. Rail yard, roadhouse, repair shops of former Delaware, Lackawanna & Western Railroad.

Theodore Roosevelt Birthplace, New York, NY (1962): 0.11. Reconstructed brownstone where 26th president was born.

Theodore Roosevelt Inaugural, Buffalo, NY (1966): 1.18. Wilcox House, where 26th president took oath of office, 1901.

Thomas Stone, Port Tobacco, MD (1978): 328. Home of signer of Declaration of Independence.

Tuskegee Airmen, AL (1998): 90. Airfield where pilots of all-black WWII air corps unit received flight training.

Tuskegee Institute, AL (1974): 58. College founded by Booker T. Washington in 1881 for blacks.

Ulysses S. Grant, St. Louis, MO (1989): 10. Home of Grant during pre-Civil War years.

Vanderbilt Mansion, Hyde Park, NY (1940): 212. Mansion of 19th-cent. financier.

Washita Battlefield, OK (1996): 315. Scene of Nov. 27, 1868, battle between Plains tribes and U.S. army.

Weir Farm, Wilton, CT (1990): 74. Home and studio of American impressionist painter J. Alden Weir.

Whitman Mission, Walla Walla, WA (1936/1963): 139. Site of Protestant missionaries to Cayuse Indians beginning in 1830s.

William Howard Taft, Cincinnati, OH (1969): 4. Birthplace and early home of 27th president.

Name	Location	Year[1]	Acreage
National Lakeshores			
Apostle Islands	WI	1970	69,372
Indiana Dunes	IN	1966	15,314
Pictured Rocks	MI	1966	73,236
Sleeping Bear Dunes	MI	1970	71,210
National Monuments			
African Burial Ground	NY	2006	0.35
Agate Fossil Beds	NE	1965	3,058
Alibates Flint Quarries	TX	1965	1,371
Aniakchak[2]	AK	1978	137,176
Aztec Ruins	NM	1923	318
Bandelier	NM	1916	33,677
Booker T. Washington	VA	1956	239
Buck Island Reef	VI	1961	19,015
Cabrillo	CA	1913	160
Canyon de Chelly	AZ	1931	83,840
Cape Krusenstern	AK	1978	649,096
Capulin Volcano	NM	1916	793
Casa Grande Ruins	AZ	1889	473
Castillo de San Marcos	FL	1924	19
Castle Clinton	NY	1946	1
Cedar Breaks	UT	1933	6,155
César E. Chávez	CA	2012	117
Charles Young Buffalo Soldiers	OH	2013	60
Chiricahua	AZ	1924	12,025
Colorado	CO	1911	20,536
Craters of the Moon	ID	1924	53,571
Devils Postpile	CA	1911	800
Devils Tower	WY	1906	1,347
Dinosaur	CO-UT	1915	210,283
Effigy Mounds	IA	1949	2,526
El Malpais	NM	1987	114,314
El Morro	NM	1906	1,279
Florissant Fossil Beds	CO	1969	5,998
Fort Frederica	GA	1936	284
Fort Matanzas	FL	1924	300
Fort McHenry (and Historic Shrine)	MD	1925	43
Fort Monroe	VA	2011	325
Fort Pulaski	GA	1924	5,623
Fort Stanwix	NY	1935	16
Fort Sumter	SC	1948	235
Fort Union	NM	1954	721
Fossil Butte	WY	1972	8,198
George Washington Birthplace	VA	1930	662
George Washington Carver	MO	1943	210
Gila Cliff Dwellings	NM	1907	533
Governors Island	NY	2001	23
Grand Portage	MN	1951	710
Hagerman Fossil Beds	ID	1988	4,351
Hohokam Pima[3]	AZ	1972	1,690
Homestead NM of America	NE	1936	211
Hovenweep	CO-UT	1923	785
Jewel Cave	SD	1908	1,274
John Day Fossil Beds	OR	1974	14,062
Lava Beds	CA	1925	46,692
Little Bighorn Battlefield	MT	1879	765
Montezuma Castle	AZ	1906	1,016
Muir Woods	CA	1908	554
Natural Bridges	UT	1908	7,636
Navajo	AZ	1909	360
Ocmulgee	GA	1934	704
Oregon Caves	OR	1909	488
Organ Pipe Cactus	AZ	1937	330,689
Petroglyph	NM	1990	7,209
Pipe Spring	AZ	1923	40
Pipestone	MN	1937	282
Poverty Point[2]	LA	1988	911
Rainbow Bridge	UT	1910	160
Russell Cave	AL	1961	310
Salinas Pueblo Missions	NM	1909	1,071

Name	Location	Year[1]	Acreage
Scotts Bluff	NE	1919	3,005
Statue of Liberty	NJ-NY	1924	61
Sunset Crater Volcano	AZ	1930	3,040
Timpanogos Cave	UT	1922	250
Tonto	AZ	1907	1,120
Tule Springs Fossil Beds	NV	2014	22,650
Tuzigoot	AZ	1939	812
Virgin Islands Coral Reef	VI	2001	12,708
Walnut Canyon	AZ	1915	3,529
White Sands	NM	1933	143,733
World War II Valor in the Pacific	HI-CA	2008	59
Wupatki	AZ	1924	35,422
Yucca House[2]	CO	1919	34
National Parkways			
Blue Ridge	NC-VA	1933	96,107
George Washington Memorial	MD-DC-VA	1930	7,035
John D. Rockefeller Jr. Memorial	WY	1972	23,777
Natchez Trace	MS-TN-AL	1938	52,302
National Preserves			
Aniakchak[2]	AK	1980	464,118
Bering Land Bridge	AK	1980	2,697,391
Big Cypress[4]	FL	1974	720,564
Big Thicket	TX	1974	109,086
Craters of the Moon	ID	2002	410,733
Denali	AK	1917	1,334,118
Gates of the Arctic	AK	1978	948,608
Glacier Bay	AK	1925	58,406
Great Sand Dunes	CO	2000	41,686
Katmai	AK	1918	418,699
Lake Clark	AK	1978	1,410,294
Little River Canyon	AL	1992	15,288
Mojave	CA	1994	1,541,426
Noatak	AK	1978	6,587,071
Tallgrass Prairie	KS	1996	10,894
Timucuan Ecological and Historic	FL	1988	46,281
Valles Caldera	NM	2014	89,000
Wrangell-St. Elias	AK	1978	4,852,645
Yukon-Charley Rivers	AK	1978	2,526,512
National Recreation Areas			
Amistad	TX	1965	58,500
Bighorn Canyon	MT-WY	1966	120,296
Boston Harbor Islands	MA	1996	1,482
Chattahoochee River	GA	1978	9,800
Chickasaw	OK	1902	9,899
Curecanti	CO	1965	43,095
Delaware Water Gap	NJ-PA	1965	67,030
Gateway	NJ-NY	1972	26,607
Gauley River	WV	1988	11,589
Glen Canyon	AZ-UT	1958	1,254,117
Golden Gate	CA	1972	81,380
Lake Chelan	WA	1968	61,949
Lake Mead	AZ-NV	1936	1,495,806
Lake Meredith	TX	1965	44,978
Lake Roosevelt (fmr. Coulee Dam)	WA	1946	100,390
Ross Lake	WA	1968	117,575
Santa Monica Mountains	CA	1978	156,670
Whiskeytown-Shasta-Trinity[5]	CA	1965	42,503
National Reserves			
City of Rocks	ID	1988	14,407
Ebey's Landing Historical	WA	1978	19,333
National Rivers			
Big South Fork (and Rec. Area)	KY-TN	1976	123,679
Buffalo	AR	1972	94,293
Mississippi (and Rec. Area)	MN	1988	53,775
New River Gorge	WV	1978	72,186
Ozark Scenic Riverways	MO	1964	80,785
National Seashores			
Assateague Island[6]	MD-VA	1965	41,320
Canaveral	FL	1975	57,662
Cape Cod	MA	1961	43,607
Cape Hatteras	NC	1937	30,351
Cape Lookout	NC	1966	28,243
Cumberland Island	GA	1972	36,347
Fire Island	NY	1964	19,580
Gulf Islands	FL-MS	1971	138,306
Padre Island	TX	1962	130,434
Point Reyes	CA	1962	71,055
International Historic Site			
Saint Croix Island	ME	1949	7
Other Designations			
Catoctin Mountain Park	MD	1954	5,891
Constitution Gardens	DC	1974	39
Fort Washington Park	MD	1930	341
Greenbelt Park	MD	1950	1,175
National Capital Parks	DC-MD	1933	6,841
National Mall	DC	1933	156
Piscataway Park	MD	1961	4,626
Prince William Forest Park	VA	1948	16,081
Rock Creek Park	DC	1890	1,755
White House	DC	1933	18
Wolf Trap National Park for the Performing Arts	VA	1966	130

National Wild and Scenic Rivers

Rivers in this system are designated by Congress or the Secretary of the Interior. As of Dec. 2014, the system included 12,709 miles of 208 rivers in 39 states and Puerto Rico. Not all of the rivers that the NPS administers are official units of the park system. Only official NPS units are listed here.

Name	Location	Year[1]	Acreage
Alagnak Wild[2]	AK	1980	30,665
Bluestone Scenic	WV	1978	4,310
Delaware Scenic	NJ-PA	1978	1,973
Great Egg Harbor Scenic and Rec.	NJ	1992	43,311
Missouri Recreational	NE-SD	1991	34,159
Niobrara Scenic	NE	1991	29,101
Obed	TN	1976	5,073
Rio Grande	TX	1978	9,600
Saint Croix Scenic Riverway[7]	MN-WI	1968	92,746
Upper Delaware Scenic and Rec.	NY-PA	1978	75,000

Affiliated Areas

Affiliated areas are administered in connection with the NPS but are not owned by that agency.

Name	Location	Year[1]	Acreage
Aleutian World War II Natl. Historic Site (NHS)	AK	1996	81
American Memorial Park	MP	1978	133
Benjamin Franklin Natl. Memorial	PA	1972	NA
Chicago Portage NHS	IL	1952	91
Chimney Rock NHS	NE	1956	83
Fallen Timbers Battlefield and Fort Miamis NHS	OH	1999	185
Father Marquette Natl. Memorial	MI	1975	52
Gloria Dei (Old Swedes') Church NHS	PA	1942	4
Green Springs Natl. Historic Landmark District	VA	1974	14,000
Historic Camden Revolutionary War Site	SC	1982	107
Ice Age Natl. Scientific Reserve	WI	1964	32,500
International Peace Garden	ND-MB	1949	2,339
Iñupiat Heritage Center	AK	1999	NA
Jamestown NHS	VA	1940	23
Kate Mullany NHS	NY	2004	0.06
Lower East Side Tenement NHS	NY	1998	NA
New Jersey Coastal Heritage Trail Route	NJ	1988	NA
Oklahoma City Natl. Memorial	OK	2004	3
Pinelands Natl. Reserve	NJ	1978	1,100,000
Red Hill Patrick Henry Natl. Memorial	VA	1986	117
Roosevelt Campobello Intl. Park	NB	1964	2,861
Sewall-Belmont House NHS	DC	1974	0.35
Thomas Cole NHS	NY	1999	3
Touro Synagogue NHS	RI	1946	0.23
Wing Luke Museum of the Asian Pacific American Experience	WA	2013	NA

NA = Not available. (1) Year current designation received. (2) No federal facilities; state services may be available at certain sites. (3) Located on Gila River Indian Reservation; not open to the public. (4) Total incl. acreage added in 1988 expansion. (5) Shasta and Trinity units are administered by the Forest Service. Figure given is NPS acreage only. (6) Figure given includes acreage administered by Fish and Wildlife Service. (7) Total incl. Lower Saint Croix acreage added in 1972.

National Trails System

Source: National Park Service and Bureau of Land Management, U.S. Dept. of the Interior; U.S. Forest Service, USDA

As of mid-2015, the National Trails System included 11 national scenic trails, 19 national historic trails, more than 1,200 national recreation trails, and 6 connecting and side trails. National scenic trails and national historic trails are established by Congress and administered by the NPS, Forest Service, or BLM. Official NPS units are indicated by an asterisk.

Name	Location	Year[1]	Length (mi)[2]
National Scenic Trails			
*Appalachian	ME to GA	1968	2,185
Arizona	AZ	2009	800+
Continental Divide	MT, ID, WY, CO, NM	1978	3,100
Florida	FL	1983	1,300
Ice Age	WI	1980	1,200
*Natchez Trace	MS-AL-TN	1983	65
New England	MA-CT	2009	215
North Country	NY to ND	1980	4,500
Pacific Crest	CA-OR-WA	1968	2,650
Pacific Northwest	MT-ID-WA	2009	1,200
*Potomac Heritage	VA to PA	1983	830
National Historic Trails[3]			
Ala Kahakai	HI	2000	175
California	MO, NE to CA, OR	1992	5,839
Captain John Smith Chesapeake	VA, DC, MD, DE	2006	3,000
El Camino Real de los Tejas	TX-LA	2004	2,580
El Camino Real de Tierra Adentro	NM-TX	2000	404
Iditarod	AK	1978	2,300
Juan Bautista de Anza	AZ-CA	1990	1,200
Lewis and Clark	IL to Pacific	1978	3,700
Mormon Pioneer	IL to UT	1978	1,300
Nez Perce (Nee-Me-Poo)	OR to MT	1986	1,170
Old Spanish	NM to CA	2002	2,700
Oregon	MO to OR	1978	2,130
Overmountain Victory	NC, SC, TN, VA	1980	330
Pony Express	MO to CA	1992	1,900
Santa Fe	MO, KS, OK, CO, NM	1987	1,203
Selma to Montgomery	AL	1996	54
Star-Spangled Banner	VA-DC-MD	2008	560
Trail of Tears	GA, NC, KY to OK	1987	5,043
Washington-Rochambeau Revolutionary Route	MA to VA	2009	680

(1) Year designation was received. (2) Authorized or currently completed length. (3) Trails may include both overland and water routes.

U.S. Forest Service Special Designated Areas

Source: U.S. Forest Service, U.S. Dept. of Agriculture; as of Sept. 30, 2014

These areas within the National Forest System have been specially designated by presidential proclamation or act of Congress. Size does not include acreage within National Forest boundaries not federally owned or administered by the Forest Service. Not shown are national monuments designated in 2015 by Pres. Barack Obama: Berryessa Snow Mountain (CA) and Browns Canyon (CO).

NM = Natl. Monument; NRA = Natl. Recreation Area; NS(A) = Natl. Scenic (Area); NVM = Natl. Volcanic Monument; SMA = Special Management Area

Area	Location	Estab.	Acreage
Admiralty Island NM	AK	1980	985,567
Allegheny NRA	PA	1984	23,790
Ancient Bristlecone Pine Forest	CA	2009	31,825
Arapaho NRA	CO	1978	31,999
Barkshead (Ozark #2) Natl. Game Refuge	AR	1926	5,851
Bear Creek NSA	VA	2009	5,122
Beech Creek NSA & Botanical Area	OK	1988	8,580
Beech Creek NSA	OK	1988	8,042
Beech Creek Natl. Botanical Area	OK	1988	538
Big Levels Game Refuge	VA	1935	12,147
Black Mountain (Ozark #5) Natl. Game Refuge	AR	1926	18,929
Bowen Gulch Protection Area	CO	1993	13,234
Bridgeport Winter Recreation Area	CA	2009	7,250
Caney Creek (Ouachita #4) Natl. Game Refuge	AR	1935	8,038
Cascade Head NS Research Area	OR	1974	7,188
Catahoula Wildlife Mgmt. Preserve	LA	1941	37,586
Cherokee Natl. Game Refuge #1	TN	1924	9,862
Chimney Rock NM	CO	2012	4,724
Columbia River Gorge NSA	OR-WA	1986	82,788
Burdoin Mountain SMA	WA	1986	7,253
Gates of the Columbia River Gorge SMA	OR-WA	1986	53,431
Rowena SMA	OR-WA	1986	3,488
Wind Mountain SMA	WA	1986	14,801
Coosa Bald NSA	GA	1991	7,043
Cradle of Forestry in America Natl. Historic Area	NC	1968	7,793
Crystal Springs Watershed	OR	2009	2,094
Cultus Creek	OR	2009	278
Ed Jenkins NRA	GA	1991	23,540
Flaming Gorge NRA	UT-WY	1968	187,405
Fossil Ridge Rec. Mgmt. Area	CO	1993	43,363
Francis Marion Natl. Wildlife Pres.	SC	1948	54,430
Frank Church-River of No Return Special Mining Mgmt. Zone-Clear Creek	ID	1980	13,879
Giant Sequoia NM	CA	2000	328,374
Grand Canyon Natl. Game Preserve	AZ	1906	622,270
Grand Island NRA	MI	1990	13,334
Grey Towers Natl. Historic Site	PA	2004	95
Haw Creek (Ozark #4) Natl. Game Refuge	AR	1926	3,783
Hells Canyon NRA	OR-ID	1975	634,261
Indian Nations Scenic Wildlife Area	OK	1988	44,518
James Peak Protection Area	CO	2002	17,509
Jemez NRA	NM	1993	48,844
Jewel Cave NM	SD	1908	2,531
Kelly Butte SMA	WA	1998	5,669
Kings River SMA	CA	1987	50,886
Land Between the Lakes NRA	KY-TN	1998	171,251
Livingston (Ozark #1) Natl. Game Refuge	AR	1926	8,755
Misty Fiords NM	AK	1980	2,295,939
Moccasin (Ozark #3) Natl. Game Refuge	AR	1926	4,048
Mono Basin NSA	CA	1984	51,353
Moosalamoo NRA	VT	2006	15,913
Mount Baker NRA	WA	1984	8,789
Mount Hood NRA	OR	2009	34,465
Mount Pleasant NSA	VA	1994	6,864
Mount Rogers NRA	VA	1966	114,228
Mount St. Helens NVM	WA	1989	112,864
Newberry NVM	OR	1990	56,483
Noontootly Natl. Game Refuge	GA	1938	24,669
Norbeck Wildlife Preserve	SD	1920	27,630
North Cascades NSA	WA	1984	88,178
Oak Mountain (Ouachita #2) Natl. Game Refuge	AR	1935	8,551
Ocala Natl. Game Refuge	FL	1930	68,241
Opal Creek Scenic Recreation Area	OR	1996	13,011
Oregon Dunes NRA	OR	1972	30,440
Ouachita Natl. Wildlife Preserve	AR	1935	138,039
Quinault SMA	WA	1988	5,415
Piedra SMA	CO	1993	60,421
Pigeon Creek (Ouachita #1) Natl. Game Refuge	AR	1935	8,107
Pine Ridge NRA	NE	1986	6,636
Pisgah Natl. Game Preserve	NC	1916	71,895
Rattlesnake NRA	MT	1980	60,081
Red Dirt Natl. Wildlife Mgmt. Pres.	LA	1941	40,213
Robert S. Kerr Botanical Area	OK	1988	7,971
Robert T. Stafford White Rocks NRA	VT	1984	36,563
Roubideau SMA	CO	1993	18,696
Santa Rosa & San Jacinto Mtns. NM	CA	2000	69,434
Sawtooth NRA	ID	1972	730,864
Seng Mountain NSA	VA	2009	5,195
Sheep Mountain Game Refuge	WY	1924	21,526
Smith River NRA	CA	1990	321,348
Spring Mountains NRA	NV	1993	316,558
Spruce Knob-Seneca Rocks NRA	WV	1965	57,499
Tabeguache SMA	CO	1993	9,029
Upper Big Bottom	OR	2009	1,581
Whiskeytown-Shasta-Trinity NRA	CA	1965	173,064
Winding Stair Mountain NRA	OK	1988	26,617

National Heritage Areas

Source: National Park Service (NPS), U.S. Dept. of the Interior; Alliance of National Heritage Areas

National Heritage Areas (NHAs) are designated by Congress for their national importance. NHAs are not units of the National Park system, though the NPS advises and provides limited financial assistance. NHC = Natl. Heritage Corridor.

Name	Location	Year[1]	Size (sq mi)
Abraham Lincoln	IL	2008	25,975
Arabia Mountain	GA	2006	64
Atchafalaya	LA	2006	10,400
Augusta Canal	GA	1996	3+
Baltimore	MD	2009	18
Blue Ridge	NC	2003	10,515
Cache La Poudre River[2]	CO	2009	45
Cane River	LA	1994	181
Champlain Valley Natl. Heritage Partnership	NY-VT	2006	NA[3]
Crossroads of the American Revolution	NJ	2006	2,155
Delaware & Lehigh NHC[2]	PA	1988	165
Erie Canalway NHC	NY	2000	4,834
Essex	MA	1996	500
Freedom's Frontier	KS-MO	2006	31,021
Freedom's Way	MA-NH	2009	994
Great Basin Natl. Heritage Route	NV-UT	2006	15,704
Gullah Geechee Cultural Heritage Corridor	NC, SC, GA, FL	2006	12,818
Hudson River Valley[2]	NY	1996	154
Illinois & Michigan Canal NHC	IL	1984	862
John H. Chafee Blackstone River Valley NHC	MA-RI	1986	720+
Journey Through Hallowed Ground[2]	PA, MD, WV, VA	2008	180
Kenai Mountains-Turnagain Arm	AK	2009	NA
Lackawanna River Heritage Trail[2]	PA	2000	70
The Last Green Valley NHC	CT-MA	1994	1,086
Mississippi Delta	MS	2009	10,976
Mississippi Gulf Coast	MS	2004	4,289
Mississippi Hills	MS	2009	NA[4]
Mormon Pioneer	UT	2006	16,070
MotorCities	MI	1998	10,000+
Muscle Shoals	AL	2009	3,913
National Aviation Heritage Area	OH	2004	NA[5]
National Coal Heritage Area	WV	1996	5,300
Niagara Falls[2]	NY	2008	13
Northern Plains	ND	2009	800
Northern Rio Grande	NM	2006	10,000
Ohio & Erie Canalway[2]	OH	1996	110
Oil Region	PA	2004	708
Path of Progress Natl. Heritage Tour Route[2]	PA	1988	500
Rivers of Steel	PA	1996	5,000+
Sangre de Cristo	CO	2009	3,000+
Schuylkill River Valley	PA	2000	1,750
Shenandoah Valley Battlefields Natl. Historic District	VA	1996	3,939
Silos and Smokestacks	IA	1996	20,000+
South Carolina NHC[2]	SC	1996	240
South Park	CO	2009	1,800
Tennessee Civil War[6]	TN	1996	42,144
Upper Housatonic Valley	MA-CT	2006	964
Wheeling	WV	2000	12
Yuma Crossing	AZ	2000	21

NA = Not available. (1) Year designation was received. (2) Figure given is length of area. (3) Covers 11 counties in both states. (4) Parts of 30 counties. (5) 8 counties. (6) Spans entire state of Tennessee.

Attractions in and Around Washington, DC

Most attractions are free. Hours are subject to change, especially on holidays, when some attractions may be closed. For more details call the Washington, DC, Convention and Visitors Association at 1-800-422-8644 or visit www.washington.org.

Arlington National Cemetery

Arlington National Cemetery, on the former Custis-Lee estate in Arlington, VA, was first used as a burial site during the Civil War. It is the final resting place of Pres. William Howard Taft and Pres. John F. Kennedy and his wife, Jacqueline Bouvier Kennedy Onassis. More than 400,000 U.S. military personnel from every major war are buried at Arlington. The **Tomb of the Unknown Soldier**, dedicated in 1921, is guarded by soldiers 24 hrs. a day.

A number of monuments and memorials are located throughout the 624-acre cemetery. They include the **Women in Military Service for America Memorial** (dedicated 1997), which honors the 2.5 mil women who have served in the U.S. military.

Open daily 8 AM-5 PM (8 AM-7 PM, Apr.-Sept.). Arlington, VA; (877) 907-8585. **Website:** www.arlingtoncemetery.mil

The **U.S. Marine Corps War Memorial** stands north of Arlington National Cemetery. A bronze statue depicts the raising of the U.S. flag on Mt. Suribachi, Feb. 23, 1945, during the World War II battle of Iwo Jima. The memorial grounds are open daily 6 AM-midnight. (703) 289-2500. **Website:** www.nps.gov/gwmp/

Bureau of Engraving and Printing

The Bureau of Engraving and Printing of the U.S. Treasury Dept. is the headquarters for the making of U.S. paper money. Free, public tours are offered Mon.-Fri., 9 AM-3:45 PM (6 PM in spring and summer). 14th and C Sts. SW; (866) 874-2330. **Website:** www.moneyfactory.gov

The Capitol

The United States Capitol was originally designed by Dr. William Thornton, an amateur architect, whose submission in 1793 won him $500 and a city lot. Three other architects designed or supervised construction of the Capitol before its completion.

The present cast-iron dome at its greatest exterior height measures 135 ft, 5 in. and is topped by the bronze Statue of Freedom, which stands 19½ ft and weighs 14,985 lbs. On its base are the words *E Pluribus Unum* (out of many, one). Restoration work on the dome began in 2014.

The Capitol Visitor Center is open to the public Mon.-Sat., 8:30 AM-4:30 PM. Free guided tours are available by pass 8:45 AM to 3:30 PM.

To observe Congress while it is in session, those living in the U.S. may obtain tickets from their U.S. representative or senators. Visitors from other countries may obtain passes at the Visitor Center. Between Constitution and Independence Aves., bounded by First St.; (202) 226-8000. **Website:** www.visitthecapitol.gov

Federal Bureau of Investigation

The Federal Bureau of Investigation discontinued tours of its headquarters following the Sept. 11, 2001, terrorist attacks. The FBI launched a pilot program in 2014 opening an Education Center to the public. Visits must be arranged in advance through the office of one's congressional delegate. J. Edgar Hoover Bldg., Pennsylvania Ave., between 9th and 10th Sts. NW; (202) 324-3000. **Website:** www.fbi.gov

Folger Shakespeare Library

The Folger Shakespeare Library, on Capitol Hill, is a research institution with the world's largest collection of Shakespearean materials and other rare books and manuscripts of the Renaissance period. Open to the public Mon.-Sat., 10 AM-5 PM, and Sun., 12 PM-5 PM. Building and garden tours are available. 201 E. Capitol St. SE; (202) 544-4600. **Website:** www.folger.edu

Holocaust Memorial Museum

The U.S. Holocaust Memorial Museum (opened 1993) documents the Holocaust through displays, interactive videos, and lectures. The permanent exhibition is recommended for visitors age 11 and up.

The museum is open daily, 10 AM-5:20 PM, with extended hours in spring. Entry into the permanent exhibition is timed, Mar. through Aug. Timed passes are available at the door each day on a first-come, first-served basis; advance passes can be ordered online for a fee. 100 Raoul Wallenberg Pl. SW; (202) 488-0400. **Website:** www.ushmm.org

Jefferson Memorial

Dedicated Apr. 13, 1943, the Thomas Jefferson Memorial stands on the south shore of the Tidal Basin in West Potomac Park. The circular stone structure combines architectural elements of the dome of the Pantheon in Rome and the rotunda designed by Jefferson for the Univ. of Virginia.

The memorial is open 24 hrs. a day and staffed 9:30 AM-11:30 PM. Ohio and E. Basin Drs. SW; (202) 426-6841. **Website:** www.nps.gov/thje/

Kennedy Center

The John F. Kennedy Center for the Performing Arts opened in 1971. Designed by Edward Durell Stone, it includes an opera house, concert hall, theaters, restaurants, and a library. Free tours available Mon.-Fri., 10 AM-5 PM, and Sat.-Sun., 10 AM-1 PM. 2700 F St. NW; (800) 444-1324. **Website:** www.kennedy-center.org

Martin Luther King Jr. Memorial

The MLK Jr. Memorial (dedicated 2011) features a 30-ft figure of Dr. King emerging from a block of granite. The memorial, designed by sculptor Lei Yixin, is located on the Tidal Basin between the Lincoln and Jefferson Memorials.

The memorial is open 24 hrs. a day and staffed 9:30 AM-11:30 PM. Independence Ave. SW and West Basin Dr. SW; (202) 426-6841. **Website:** www.nps.gov/mlkm/

Korean War Veterans Memorial

The Korean War Veterans Memorial, dedicated 1995 at the Mall's west end, features a multiservice formation of 19 combat-ready soldiers in ponchos. A granite wall, with images of service members, juts into the Pool of Remembrance.

The memorial is open 24 hrs. a day. Independence Ave. SW and French Dr. SW; (202) 426-6841. **Website:** www.nps.gov/kowa/

Library of Congress

Established by and for Congress in 1800, the Library of Congress extends its services to other government agencies and libraries, scholars, and the public. It contains more than 160 mil items in some 470 languages, making it the world's largest library.

The Thomas Jefferson Building (Main Reading Room and exhibition galleries) is open Mon.-Sat., 8:30 AM-4:30 PM. The James Madison Memorial and John Adams Buildings have longer hours. 101 Independence Ave. SE; (202) 707-8000. **Website:** www.loc.gov

Lincoln Memorial

Designed by Henry Bacon and dedicated in 1922, the Lincoln Memorial in West Potomac Park is a large marble hall enclosing a statue, designed by Daniel Chester French, of Abraham Lincoln seated in an armchair. The text of the Gettysburg Address is engraved in the south chamber, that of Lincoln's second inaugural speech in the north chamber.

The memorial is open 24 hrs. a day and staffed 9:30 AM-11:30 PM. Independence Ave. and French Dr. SW; (202) 426-6841. **Website:** www.nps.gov/linc/

Mount Vernon

Mount Vernon, George Washington's estate, is about 15 mi from Washington, DC, in northern Virginia. The house is believed to be an enlargement of one built by Augustine Washington in 1735. His son Lawrence renamed the estate after British Adm. Edward Vernon. George Washington, Lawrence's half brother, inherited it in 1761. The estate has been restored to its 18th-cent. appearance. Washington and his wife, Martha, are buried on the grounds.

Open all year; hours vary seasonally; (703) 780-2000. Admission: adults $17, seniors (62+) $16, youth (6-11) $9, ages 5 and under free. **Website:** www.mountvernon.org

National Archives and Records

Original copies of the Declaration of Independence, the Constitution, and the Bill of Rights are on display at the National Archives Museum. The National Archives also holds other U.S. government records, historic maps, photographs, and manuscripts.

The museum is open daily 10 AM-5:30 PM. Constitution Ave. bet. 7th and 9th Sts. NW; (866) 272-6272. **Website:** www.archives.gov

National Gallery of Art

The National Gallery of Art, established by Congress, opened in 1941. The original West Building was designed by John Russell Pope. The East Building, opened in 1978, was designed by I. M. Pei. Galleries are open Mon.-Sat., 10 AM-5 PM, and Sun., 11 AM-6 PM. The Sculpture Garden has extended hours in summer. 4th St. and Constitution Ave NW; (202) 737-4215. **Website:** www.nga.gov

The Pentagon

The Pentagon, headquarters of the Dept. of Defense, is the largest office building in the U.S. It houses some 23,000 employees in offices occupying 3,705,793 sq ft. The building was severely damaged when struck by a plane on Sept. 11, 2001.

Tours are available by reservation only, which must be made online 14-90 days in advance. Non-U.S. citizens must present a foreign passport or permanent resident card to enter. Arlington, VA; (703) 697-1776. **Website:** pentagontours.osd.mil

Franklin Delano Roosevelt Memorial

Opened in 1997, the FDR Memorial features four spaces with bronze statues and panels depicting FDR through his four terms in office. The 8-acre memorial is on the Tidal Basin.

Open daily with staff on grounds 9:30 AM-11:30 PM. Ohio and W. Basin Drs. SW; (202) 426-6841. **Website:** www.nps.gov/fdrm/

Smithsonian Institution

The Smithsonian Institution, established in 1846, is the world's largest museum and research complex. It holds some 137 mil artifacts and specimens in its trust. Seventeen of its 19 museums and the National Zoo are in the DC area. The **Smithsonian Institution Building** (or The Castle) houses the Smithsonian Information Center. Also on the National Mall are the **National Museum of American History**, the **National Museum of Natural History**, the **National Air and Space Museum**, the **National Museum of the American Indian**, the **Hirshhorn Museum and Sculpture Garden**, the **Arthur M. Sackler Gallery**, the **Freer Gallery of Art**, the **National Museum of African Art**, and the **Arts and Industries Building** (reopening in 2016 as a special-events space). Located nearby are the **National Postal Museum**, the **National Museum of American Art**, the **National Portrait Gallery**, and the **Renwick Gallery**. The **Anacostia Community Museum** is in SE DC. The Air and Space Museum's **Udvar-Hazy Center** is near Dulles Airport in Virginia. The **National Museum of African American History and Culture** is expected to open on the Mall in 2016.

Most museums are open daily, 10 AM-5:30 PM (later in summer); (202) 633-1000. **Website:** www.si.edu

Vietnam Veterans Memorial

Originally dedicated in 1982, the Vietnam Veterans Memorial recognizes those who served in the Vietnam War. The names of more than 58,000 Americans who lost their lives or remain missing are inscribed on polished black-granite walls arranged to form a V, designed by Maya Ying Lin.

Two additions have been made to Lin's design, the Frederick Hart sculpture *Three Servicemen* (1984), and the Vietnam Women's Memorial (1993), designed by Glenna Goodacre, honoring the more than 11,500 women who served in Vietnam.

The memorial is open 24 hrs. a day. Constitution Ave. and Bacon Dr. NW; (202) 426-6841. **Website:** www.nps.gov/vive/

Washington Monument

The Washington Monument, dedicated in 1885, is a tapering shaft, or obelisk, of white marble, 554 ft, 7 11/32 in. in height and 55 ft, 1½ in. square at base. Eight small windows, two on each side, are located on the observation deck at the 500-ft level.

Open daily, 9 AM-5 PM (10 PM in summer). Same-day timed passes are available first-come, first-served; advance passes can be obtained for a fee. 15th St. and Constitution Ave. NW; (202) 426-6841. **Website:** www.nps.gov/wamo/

White House

The White House, the president's residence, stands on 18 acres on the south side of Pennsylvania Ave., between the Treasury and the old Executive Office Building. The sandstone walls, quarried at Aquia Creek, VA, were first made white with lime-based whitewash in 1798, though the name did not become official until 1901.

Free self-guided tours of the residence's public areas are available Tues.-Thurs., 7:30-11:30 AM, and Fri. and Sat., 7:30 AM-1:30 PM. Tour requests must be made at least 21 days in advance through one's member of Congress. Foreign visitors may make requests through their embassy. Tours are scheduled on a first-come, first-served basis. 1600 Pennsylvania Ave. NW; (202) 456-7041. **Website:** www.whitehouse.gov.

The White House Visitor Center at 1450 Pennsylvania Ave. NW is open daily 7:30 AM-4 PM; (202) 208-1631. **Website:** www.nps.gov/whho/

National World War II Memorial

The National WWII Memorial, opened in 2004, is dedicated to the approx. 16 mil veterans who served and the more than 400,000 who died in the war. The 8.25-acre site is at the east end of the Lincoln Memorial Reflecting Pool.

The 43-ft archways at the north and south entrances represent the Atlantic and Pacific theaters. A wall of 4,000 gold stars, each representing 100 American deaths, stands in an oval plaza surrounded by 56 pillars standing for the states, territories, and the Dist. of Columbia.

The memorial is open 24 hrs. a day and staffed 9:30 AM-11:30 PM. 17th St. and Independence Ave. SW; (202) 426-6841. **Website:** www.nps.gov/nwwm/

UNITED STATES HISTORY

This chapter includes the following sections:

Chronology of Events 436
Patrick Henry's Speech. 458
Declaration of Independence 458
Constitution of the U.S. 461
The Bill of Rights, Constitutional Amendments . . 466
How a Bill Becomes a Law 469
Presidential Oath of Office 469
Presidential Succession 469
Confederate States: Secession and Government 470
Gettysburg Address 470
U.S. National Motto. 470
Great Seal of the U.S. 471
Flag of the U.S. 471
U.S. National Anthem 489
Liberty Bell 489
Statue of Liberty National Monument 490

Chronology of Events

1492 **Christopher Columbus** and crew sighted land Oct. 12 in what is now the Bahamas.

1513 **Juan Ponce de León** explored Florida coast.

1524 **Giovanni da Verrazano** led French expedition along coast from Carolina north to Nova Scotia; entered New York Harbor.

1526 San Miguel de Guadalupe, **first European settlement** in what became U.S. territory, was established in the summer off South Carolina coast; abandoned in Oct.

1539 **Hernando de Soto** landed in Florida May 28; crossed Mississippi River, 1541.

1540 **Francisco Vásquez de Coronado** explored Southwest north of Rio Grande. **Hernando de Alarcón** reached Colorado River; **García López de Cárdenas** reached Grand Canyon. Others explored California coast.

1562 **First French colony** in what became U.S. territory founded on Parris Island off South Carolina coast; abandoned, 1564.

1565 **St. Augustine, FL**, oldest continuously occupied European settlement in U.S., founded Sept. 8 by Pedro Menéndez de Avilés. Spain ceded settlement to U.S. in 1821.

1579 **Sir Francis Drake** entered San Francisco Bay and claimed region for Britain.

1585 **First English colony** in America, sponsored by Sir Walter Raleigh, founded on **Roanoke Island**, off North Carolina coast; colony failed.

1587 Second colony attempted on Roanoke Island. Virginia Dare of colony became **first English infant born** in the New World. Settlers of second colony found to have vanished, 1590.

1607 Capt. **John Smith** and 105 cavaliers in three ships landed on Virginia coast and started Jamestown, **first permanent English settlement** in New World.

1609 **Henry Hudson**, English explorer of Northwest Passage, employed by Dutch, sailed into New York Harbor in Sept. and up Hudson to Albany. **Samuel de Champlain** explored Lake Champlain, to the north. Spaniards settled **Santa Fe, NM.**

1619 House of Burgesses, **first representative assembly** in New World, elected July 30 at Jamestown, VA. **First black laborers**—indentured servants—in English North American colonies, brought by Dutch to Jamestown in Aug. Chattel slavery legally recognized, 1650.

1620 **Pilgrims**, Puritan separatists, left Plymouth, England, Sept. 16 on *Mayflower*; reached Cape Cod Nov. 19; 103 passengers landed at Plymouth, Dec. 26. **Mayflower Compact**, signed Nov. 11, was agreement to form a self-government. Half of colony died during harsh winter.

1624 Dutch settled in Albany and along Hudson River, establishing the colony of **New Netherland** in May.

1626 Peter Minuit bought **Manhattan** for Dutch West India Co. from Manahatta Indians during summer for goods valued at $24; named island **New Amsterdam.**

1630 Settlement of **Boston** established by Massachusetts colonists led by John Winthrop; Winthrop began *The History of New England*. **William Bradford**, a governor of Plymouth Colony, began his chronicle *History of Plymouth Plantation (1620-1647)*, first published in entirety in 1856.

1634 **Maryland** founded as Catholic colony under charter to Lord Baltimore. Act of Toleration passed 1649 provided for religious tolerance.

1635 Boston Latin School, **oldest public school** in continuous existence in U.S., founded Apr. 23.

1636 Roger Williams founded **Providence, RI**, in June, as a democratically ruled colony with separation of church and state. Charter granted, 1644. **Harvard College** founded; oldest institution of higher learning in U.S.

1640 **First book printed** in America, the so-called *Bay Psalm Book.*

1647 **Liberal constitution** drafted in Rhode Island. First law in America providing for **free compulsory basic education** enacted in Massachusetts.

1660 British Parliament passed first **Navigation Act** Dec. 1, regulating colonial commerce to suit English needs.

1661 Missionary John Eliot's translation of the New Testament into Algonquian became the **first Bible printed** in North America.

1664 British troops Sept. 8 seized New Netherland from Dutch. Charles II granted New Netherland and city of New Amsterdam to brother, Duke of York; both renamed **New York**. Dutch recaptured colony 1673 but ceded it to Britain Nov. 10, 1674.

1670 **Charles Town, SC**, founded by English colonists in Apr.

1673 **Regular mail service** on horseback instituted Jan. 1 between New York and Boston. **Jacques Marquette** and **Louis Jolliet** reached the upper Mississippi and traveled down it.

1674 Future **Salem witch trial** judge Samuel Sewall began renowned diary covering events through 1729.

1676 Bloody **Indian war** in New England ended Aug. 12. King Philip, Wampanoag chief, and Narragansett Indians killed. **Nathaniel Bacon** led planters against autocratic British Gov. Sir William Berkeley, burned Jamestown, VA, Sept. 19. Rebellion collapsed when Bacon died; 23 followers executed.

1678 A book of poetry by **Anne Bradstreet** (first published in Britain) revised and expanded for posthumous publication in Massachusetts. Considered first female poet in American colonies.

1679 Fire destroyed 150 houses in Boston. City imported **first fire engines** from England.

1681 John Bunyan's ***The Pilgrim's Progress*** published in America; became best seller.

1682 **René-Robert Cavelier, Sieur de La Salle**, claimed lower Mississippi River country for France and called it Louisiana Apr. 9. Had French outposts built in Illinois and Texas, 1684. Killed during mutiny, 1687. Spanish colonists became the **first Europeans to settle Texas**, at site of present-day El Paso.

1683 William Penn signed treaty with Delaware Indians Apr. 23 and made payment for **Pennsylvania** lands. The **first German colonists** in America settled near Philadelphia.

1689 New York's English colonial governor, **Sir Edmund Andros**, resigned after armed uprising in Boston on Apr. 18.

1690 **First colonial newspaper**, *Publick Occurrences*, published by Benjamin Harris but shut down after one issue for lack of official permission. Harris also published *New England Primer* for use as elementary school textbook. Large-scale **whaling** operations began in Nantucket, MA.

1620: Pilgrims and other colonists sign the Mayflower Compact to form a "civil body politic."

1692: Witchcraft trials begin in Salem Village; 14 women and 6 men are executed.

1692 Hysteria over **witchcraft** began in Salem Village (now Danvers), MA; 14 women and 6 men were executed by special court.
1697 *The Essays* of **Sir Francis Bacon**, first published in England in 1597, was published in America; it became a best seller.
1699 Former privateer Capt. **William Kidd** arrested and sent to England; hanged for piracy, 1701. French settlements made in Mississippi, Louisiana.
1702 Legislation enacted making **Church of England** the established church in Maryland.
1704 Indians and French allies attacked **Deerfield**, MA, Feb. 29; killed 40, captured and marched off 100. *Boston News Letter*, **first regular newspaper**, started by postmaster John Campbell.
1710 British-colonial troops captured French fort, Port Royal, Nova Scotia, in **Queen Anne's War**, 1702-13. France yielded Nova Scotia by treaty, 1713.
1712 **Slaves revolted** in New York City Apr. 6; 21 were executed. Second uprising, 1741; 13 slaves hanged, 13 burned, 71 deported.
1716 **First theater** in colonies opened in Williamsburg, VA.
1726 **Great Awakening**, general revival of evangelical religion, began in colonies.
1731 America's **first subscription library** (paying members could freely borrow books) cofounded in Philadelphia by Benjamin Franklin.
1732 Benjamin Franklin published the **first *Poor Richard's Almanack***; published annually until 1757. Georgia, last of 13 colonies, chartered.
1733 **Influenza epidemic** swept through New York City and Philadelphia.
1735 Editor **John Peter Zenger** was acquitted of libel Aug. 5 in New York City after criticizing the British governor's conduct in office.
1739 A series of **slave uprisings** put down in South Carolina.
1741 Famous sermon "Sinners in the Hands of an Angry God," delivered July 8 at Enfield, MA, by Jonathan Edwards, one of the most important preachers in the **Great Awakening** religious revival. Danish navigator **Vitus Bering**, commanding Russian expedition, reached Alaska.
1744 **King George's War** pitted British and colonials versus French. Colonials captured Louisbourg, Cape Breton Isl., Nova Scotia, June 17, 1745. Returned to France 1748 by Treaty of Aix-la-Chapelle.
1752 According to legend, **Benjamin Franklin**, flying kite in thunderstorm, proved lightning is electricity, June 15; invented lightning rod. **Liberty Bell**, cast in England, was delivered to Pennsylvania.
1754 **French and Indian War** began with Ft. Necessity campaign in Pennsylvania. Skirmish May 28, battle at fort July 3-4. British moved Acadian French from Nova Scotia to Louisiana Oct. 8, 1755. British captured Québec Sept. 18, 1759, in battles in which French Gen. Joseph de Montcalm and British Gen. James Wolfe were killed. Peace pact signed Feb. 10, 1763. French lost Canada and Midwest. Delegates from seven colonies to New York for **Albany Congress**, July 19, approved plan of union by Benjamin Franklin; plan rejected by the colonies.
1757 **First streetlights** appeared in Philadelphia.
1764 **Sugar Act**, Apr. 5, placed duties on lumber, foodstuffs in colonies. First law passed by Parliament to specifically raise revenue from colonies, alleviate French and Indian War debts. British enforced this act, unlike with **Molasses Act** of 1733.
1765 **Stamp Act**, enacted by Parliament Mar. 22, required revenue stamps to help fund royal troops. Nine colonies, at Stamp Act Congress in New York Oct. 7-25, adopted Declaration of Rights. Stamp Act repealed Mar. 17, 1766. **Quartering Act**, requiring colonists to house British troops, went into effect Mar. 24.
1767 **Townshend Acts** levied taxes on glass, lead, paper, paint, and tea. In 1770 all duties except on tea were repealed.
1770 British troops fired Mar. 5 into Boston mob, killed five including **Crispus Attucks**, a black man, reportedly leader of group; later called **Boston Massacre**.
1773 East India Co. tea ships turned back at Boston, New York, and Philadelphia in May. Cargo ship burned at Annapolis, Oct. 14; cargo thrown overboard at **Boston Tea Party**, Dec. 16, to protest the tea tax. **First museum** in the colonies was officially established in Charleston, SC; later named the Charleston Museum.
1774 **"Intolerable Acts"** of Parliament curtailed Massachusetts self-rule; barred use of Boston Harbor until dumped tea was paid for. **First Continental Congress** held in Philadelphia Sept. 5-Oct. 26; called for civil disobedience against British. Rhode Island **abolished slavery**.
1775 **Patrick Henry** addressed Virginia convention, Mar. 23, said, "Give me liberty, or give me death!" **Paul Revere**, **William Dawes**, and Dr. **Samuel Prescott**, Apr. 18, rode to alert patriots that British were on their way to Concord, MA, to destroy arms. At **Lexington**, MA, Apr. 19, Minutemen lost eight. On return from **Concord**, British suffered 273 casualties. Col. Ethan Allen (joined by Col. Benedict Arnold) captured **Ft. Ticonderoga** in New York, May 10, also Crown Point. Colonials headed for **Bunker Hill** and fortified nearby Breed's Hill, Charlestown, MA. Repulsed British under Gen. William Howe twice before retreating, June 17. Continental Congress June 15 named **George Washington** commander in chief; established a postal system, July 26. Benjamin Franklin became the **first postmaster general**.
1776 **Thomas Paine**'s *Common Sense*, famous pro-independence pamphlet, published Jan. 10; quickly sold some 100,000 copies. France and Spain agreed May 2 to provide arms to U.S. In Continental Congress June 7, Richard Henry Lee (VA) moved "that these United Colonies are, and of right ought to be, free and independent states." Resolution adopted July 2. **Declaration of Independence** approved July 4, signed Aug. 2. Col. William Moultrie's batteries at **Charleston, SC**, repulsed British sea attack June 28. Washington lost **Battle of Long Island** Aug. 27; evacuated New York. **Nathan Hale** executed as spy by British Sept. 22. Brig. Gen. Arnold's Lake Champlain fleet was defeated in **Battle of Valcour Island** Oct. 11, but British returned to Canada. Howe failed to destroy Washington's army at White Plains, NY, Oct. 28. Hessians captured Ft. Washington, Manhattan, and 3,000 men, Nov. 16; captured Ft. Lee, NJ, Nov. 20. Washington, in Pennsylvania, recrossed **Delaware River** Dec. 25-26, defeated Hessians at **Battle of Trenton**, NJ, Dec. 26.
1777 Washington defeated Lord Charles Cornwallis at **Princeton**, NJ, Jan. 3. Continental Congress, June 14, authorized an **American flag**, the Stars and Stripes. Maj. Gen. John Burgoyne's force of 8,000 from Canada captured **Ft. Ticonderoga**, NY, July 6. Americans beat back Burgoyne at Bemis Heights, Oct. 7, cut off British escape route. Burgoyne surrendered 5,000 men at Saratoga, NY, Oct. 17. **Articles of Confederation** adopted by Continental Congress, Nov. 15; took effect Mar. 1, 1781.
1778 **France signed treaty** of aid with U.S. Feb. 6; sent fleet. British evacuated Philadelphia, June 18.
1779 **George Rogers Clark** took Ft. Vincennes in what is now Indiana in Feb. **John Paul Jones** on the *Bonhomme Richard* defeated *Serapis* in British North Sea waters, Sept. 23.
1780 Charleston, SC, fell to the British May 12, but Loyalists were defeated in battle of **Kings Mountain**, NC, Oct. 7 in what Thomas Jefferson called "the turn of the tide of success." **Benedict Arnold** found to be a traitor Sept. 23. Arnold escaped, made brigadier general in British army.
1781 Bank of North America, **first commercial bank**, incorporated May 26. Cornwallis retired to **Yorktown, VA.**

Adm. Francois Joseph de Grasse landed 3,000 French and stopped British fleet in **Hampton Roads**, VA. Washington and Jean Baptiste de Rochambeau joined forces, arrived near Williamsburg, Sept. 26. Siege of Cornwallis began, Oct. 6; **Cornwallis surrendered** Oct. 19.

1782 New British cabinet agreed in Mar. to **recognize U.S. independence**. Preliminary agreement signed in Paris, Nov. 30. Use of **scarlet letter A**, sewn on clothing or branded on skin of adulterers, discontinued in New England.

1783 Massachusetts Supreme Court decision in final Quock Walker trial **declared slavery illegal**. Newspapers typically published weekly; **first regular daily newspaper**, *Pennsylvania Evening Post*, went on sale in Philadelphia, May 30. Britain, U.S. signed **Paris peace treaty**, Sept. 3, recognizing American independence; Congress ratified it Jan. 14, 1784. Washington ordered army disbanded Nov. 3, bade farewell to his officers at Fraunces Tavern, New York City, Dec. 4.

1784 Thomas Jefferson's proposal to **ban slavery in new territories** after 1802 was narrowly defeated, Mar. 1.

1785 Regular **stagecoach routes** established between Albany, NY; New York City; and Philadelphia.

1786 Delegates from five states at Annapolis, MD, Sept. 11-14 asked Congress to call a **constitutional convention**.

1787 **Shays's Rebellion** of debt-ridden farmers in Massachusetts failed, Jan. 25. **Constitutional convention** opened in Philadelphia, May 25, with Washington presiding. Constitution accepted by delegates, Sept. 17. Delaware was first state to ratify it, Dec. 7; Pennsylvania and New Jersey followed. **Northwest Ordinance** adopted July 13 by Continental Congress for Northwest Territory, north of Ohio River, west of New York; made rules for statehood and guaranteed freedom of religion, support for schools, no slavery. ***Federalist Papers*** first appeared in *NY Independent Journal*.

1788 A large fire in **New Orleans**, then a Spanish territory, destroyed much of the city, Mar. 21. **Constitution adopted** June 21 after being ratified by the requisite ninth state (New Hampshire); also ratified by Georgia, Connecticut, Massachusetts, Maryland, South Carolina, Virginia, and New York throughout the year. **First U.S. senators elected** Sept. 30, from Pennsylvania.

1789 **George Washington** chosen president by all electors voting (73 eligible, 69 voting, 4 absent); **John Adams**, vice president, got 34 votes. **First Congress** met at Federal Hall, New York City, and declared Constitution in effect, Mar. 4; Washington inaugurated there Apr. 30; **first inaugural ball** held May 7. U.S. **State Dept.** established by Congress July 27. (Thomas Jefferson installed as first secretary of state Feb. 1790.) **War Dept.** created Aug. 7, with Henry Knox as secretary; **Treasury Dept.** created Sept. 2, with Alexander Hamilton to be secretary. **Supreme Court** created by Federal Judiciary Act, Sept. 24; **John Jay** confirmed by Congress as first Supreme Court chief justice, Sept. 26.

1790 **First Supreme Court session** held Feb. 2 in New York City. Congress, Mar. 1, authorized decennial **U.S. census**. Collection of data took 18 months. **Naturalization Act** (two-year residency) passed Mar. 26. John Carroll consecrated as **first American Catholic bishop**, Aug. 15. Congress met in **Philadelphia**, new temporary capital, Dec. 6.

1791 **Bill of Rights**, submitted to states, Sept. 25, 1789, went into effect Dec. 15. First Bank of the United States, **first bank chartered by federal government**, established in Philadelphia.

1792 Coinage Act established **U.S. Mint** in Philadelphia, Apr. 2. Gen. **"Mad" Anthony Wayne** made commander in Ohio-Indiana area, trained American Legion, established string of forts. Routed Indians at Fallen Timbers on Maumee River, Aug. 20, 1794; checked British at Fort Miami, OH, same year. **White House** cornerstone laid Oct. 13.

1793 **Washington** inaugurated for second term, Mar. 4, having received 132 electoral votes; **John Adams** again became vice president, having received second highest total, 77. Washington declared **U.S. neutrality**, Apr. 22, in war between Britain and France. Eli Whitney invented **cotton gin** (patented 1794), reviving Southern slavery.

1794 **Whiskey Rebellion**, western Pennsylvania farmers protesting liquor tax of 1791, suppressed by federal militia in Sept. **Jay's Treaty**, controversial treaty with Britain negotiated by John Jay, signed Nov. 19, ratified June 24, 1795. This treaty intended to settle long-standing differences between U.S. and Britain.

1793: Eli Whitney invents the cotton gin; U.S. cotton production grows exponentially and Southern slavery expands.

1795 U.S. bought peace from **Algerian pirates** by paying $1 mil ransom for 115 seamen Sept. 5, followed by annual tributes. Gen. Wayne signed **Treaty of Greenville** with Indians, opening Northwest Territory to settlers. Univ. of North Carolina became **first operating state university**.

1796 **Washington's farewell address** as president delivered Sept. 17. Warned against permanent alliances with foreign powers, big public debt, large military establishment, and devices of "small, artful, enterprising minority."

1797 **John Adams** inaugurated as second president Mar. 4, having received 71 electoral votes; **Thomas Jefferson** became vice president, having received 68. U.S. frigate *United States* launched at Philadelphia, July 10; ***Constellation*** at Baltimore, Sept. 7; ***Constitution*** (Old Ironsides) at Boston, Sept. 20.

1798 **Alien and Sedition Acts** passed by Federalists June-July; intended to silence political opposition. **War with France threatened** over French raids on U.S. shipping and rejection of U.S. diplomats. Navy (45 ships) and 365 privateers captured 84 French ships. USS *Constellation* took French warship *Insurgente*, 1799. Napoleon stopped French raids after becoming first consul.

1800 Federal government moved to **Washington, DC**.

1801 **John Marshall** named Supreme Court chief justice, Jan. 20. **Thomas Jefferson**, who had received same number of electoral votes as Aaron Burr in 1800 election, won out over Burr in House vote Feb. 17; Burr named vice president. **Tripoli declared war** June 10 against U.S., which refused added tribute to commerce-raiding Arab corsairs. Land and naval campaigns forced Tripoli to negotiate peace, June 4, 1805. **Oldest U.S. art institution**, Pennsylvania Academy of Fine Arts, founded in Philadelphia.

1802 Congress established U.S. Military Academy at **West Point**, NY.

1803 Supreme Court, in ***Marbury v. Madison***, overturned U.S. law for first time, Feb. 24. Napoleon sold all of Louisiana, stretching to Canadian border, to U.S. for $11.25 mil in bonds, plus $3.75 mil indemnities to American citizens with claims against France. U.S. took title Dec. 20. **Louisiana Purchase** doubled U.S. area.

1804 **Meriwether Lewis** and **William Clark** expedition ordered by Pres. Thomas Jefferson to explore what is now Northwest U.S. Started from St. Louis May 14; ended Sept. 23, 1806, back in St. Louis. Vice Pres. **Aaron Burr** shot Alexander Hamilton in duel July 11 in Weehawken, NJ; Hamilton died next day.

1805 U.S. Marines aided by Arab mercenaries, Apr. 27, captured Tripolitan port of Derna. Major victory in war against **Barbary pirates**; inspiration for "to the shores of Tripoli" in Marines Corps hymn.

1807 Robert Fulton made **first practical steamboat trip**; left New York City Aug. 17 and reached Albany, NY, 150 mi away, in 32 hr. **Embargo Act** banned all trade with foreign countries, forbidding ships to set sail for foreign ports Dec. 22.

1808 Slave importation outlawed. Some 250,000 slaves were illegally imported 1808-60.

1810 Third U.S. Census found population of 7,239,881. The slave population was put at 1,191,364 and the population of all other non-white free persons at 186,446.

1811 Indiana Territory governor William Henry Harrison defeated Indians led by Tenskwatawa, called the Prophet, in **Battle of Tippecanoe**, Nov. 7. Construction began on **Cumberland Road** in Cumberland, MD; road became important route to West. About 400 **slaves revolted** in Louisiana and marched on New Orleans. The insurrection was suppressed; two whites, some 75 slaves killed.

1812 War of 1812 had three main causes: Britain seized U.S. ships trading with France; Britain had seized 4,000 naturalized U.S. sailors by 1810; Britain armed Indians, who raided Western border. U.S. stopped trade with Europe 1807 and 1809. Trade with Britain only was stopped 1810. Unaware that Britain had raised blockade against France two days before, **Congress declared war** June 18. British took **Detroit** Aug. 16.

1813 Oliver H. Perry defeated British fleet at **Battle of Lake Erie**, Sept. 10. U.S. won **Battle of the Thames**, Ontario, Oct. 5, but failed in Canadian invasion attempts. York (Toronto) and Buffalo, NY, were burned.

1814 Troops under Andrew Jackson defeated Creek Indians led by Chief Weatherford at Battle of Horseshoe Bend in Alabama, Mar. 29, ending **Creek Indian War**, begun a year earlier. British landed in Maryland in Aug., defeated U.S. force Aug. 24, **burned Capitol and White House**. Maryland militia stopped British advance, Sept. 12. British bombardment of Ft. McHenry, Baltimore, for 25 hr., Sept. 13-14, failed, inspiring **Francis Scott Key** to write the words to **"The Star-Spangled Banner."** U.S. won naval **Battle of Lake Champlain** Sept. 11. Peace treaty with Great Britain signed at Ghent, Belgium, Dec. 24.

1815 Some 5,300 British, unaware of peace treaty, attacked U.S. entrenchments near **New Orleans**, Jan. 8. British had more than 2,000 casualties; Americans lost 71. U.S. flotilla finally ended attacks by **pirates** from Ottoman states of Algiers, Tunis, Tripoli.

1816 Second Bank of the U.S. chartered Apr. 10. The **American Colonization Society**, which sought to address slavery issue by transporting freed blacks to Africa, formed in Washington, DC, Dec. 1816-Jan. 1817.

1817 Thomas Hopkins Gallaudet established the **first free public school for the deaf** in Hartford, CT.

1818 Connecticut expanded **suffrage** among white male voters. Massachusetts followed suit in 1820, and New York in 1821, reducing or eliminating property qualifications.

1819 Spain ceded **Florida** to U.S. Feb. 22. American steamship *Savannah* made first part-steam-powered, part-sail-powered **crossing of Atlantic**, traveling from Savannah, GA, to Liverpool, England, in 29 days. **Washington Irving**'s *Sketch Book* became best seller.

1820 First organized immigration of blacks to Africa from U.S. began with 86 free blacks sailing to Sierra Leone in Feb. Henry Clay's **Missouri Compromise** bill passed by Congress, Mar. 3. Slavery was allowed in Missouri but not west of the Mississippi River, north of 36° 30′ (the southern line of Missouri). Compromise repealed 1854.

1821 Emma Willard founded Troy Female Seminary, **first U.S. women's college**. Stephen Austin established **first American community in Texas**, San Felipe de Austin. **James Fenimore Cooper**'s *The Spy*, novel set during American Revolution, published and became a best seller.

1822 Tension between sports and academics surfaced when Yale College Pres. Timothy Dwight banned a **primitive form of football**, setting fines for violators.

1823 Monroe Doctrine, opposing European intervention in the Americas, enunciated by Pres. James Monroe Dec. 2. The **Hudson River School**, painters who focused on the beauties of nature, began to receive public attention.

1824 Pawtucket, RI, **weavers strike**, first such action by women workers. **Slavery abolished** in state of Illinois Aug. 2.

1825 After a deadlocked election, **John Quincy Adams** was elected president by the House, Feb. 9. **Erie Canal** opened; first boat left Buffalo, NY, Oct. 26, reached New York City Nov. 4. John Stevens, of Hoboken, NJ, built and operated **first experimental steam locomotive** in U.S.

1826 Thomas Jefferson and **John Adams** both died July 4. **James Fenimore Cooper**'s *The Last of the Mohicans* published.

1827 Massachusetts became first state to pass a law providing for tax-supported **public high schools**.

1828 Baltimore & Ohio, the **first U.S. passenger railroad**, began operations July 4. South Carolina Dec. 19 declared right of **state nullification of federal laws**, opposing the "Tariff of Abominations." **Noah Webster** published his *American Dictionary of the English Language*.

1829 Andrew Jackson inaugurated as president, Mar. 4.

1830 Famous **debate** culminating Jan. 27 between Sen. **Daniel Webster** (MA) and Robert Hayne (SC), on state right to nullify federal law. **Mormon church** organized by Joseph Smith in Fayette, NY, Apr. 6. Pres. Jackson, May 28, signed **Indian Removal Act**, granting president authority to negotiate treaties whereby Indians living east of Mississippi R. give up lands in exchange for lands in West.

1831 William Lloyd Garrison began **abolitionist newspaper** *The Liberator* Jan. 1. **Nat Turner**, black slave in Virginia, led local slave rebellion, starting Aug. 21; 57 whites killed. Troops called in, 100 slaves killed. Turner captured, tried, and hanged Nov. 11.

1832 Black Hawk War in Illinois and Wisconsin Apr.-Sept. pushed Sauk and Fox Indians west across Mississippi.

1833 American Anti-Slavery Society founded in Philadelphia, Dec. 4. **Oberlin College** became first to adopt coeducation in U.S.

1835 According to tradition, the **Liberty Bell** cracked July 8 while tolling death of Chief Justice John Marshall. **Seminole Indians** in Florida under Osceola began attacks Nov. 1, protesting forced removal. The unpopular war ended Aug. 14, 1842; most of the Indians sent to Oklahoma. **Texas** proclaimed right to secede from Mexico; **Sam Houston** put in command of Texas army, Nov. 2-4. **Gold** discovered on Cherokee land in Georgia. Indians forced to cede lands, Dec. 20, and to cross Mississippi.

1836 Texans besieged at **Alamo** in San Antonio by Mexicans under Antonio López de Santa Anna, Feb. 23-Mar. 6; entire garrison killed. Texas independence had been declared, Mar. 2. At San Jacinto Apr. 21, Sam Houston and Texans defeated Mexicans. Ralph Waldo Emerson published his first work, *Nature*, espousing his philosophy of **transcendentalism**. Marcus Whitman, H. H. Spaulding, and wives reached Fort Walla Walla on Columbia River, OR, **first white women to cross the Continental Divide**, in the Rocky Mountains.

1838 Cherokee Indians forced to walk **"Trail of Tears"** from southeast U.S. to area in present-day Oklahoma. At least 4,000—nearly one-fifth of Cherokee population—are estimated to have died.

1841 First emigrant wagon train bound for California, 47 people, left Independence, MO, May 1; reached California Nov. 4. Edgar Allan Poe published one of the **first American detective stories**, *The Murders in the Rue Morgue*.

1842 Webster-Ashburton Treaty signed Aug. 9, fixing U.S.-Canada border in Maine and Minnesota. **First use of anesthetic** (sulfuric ether gas) in an operation performed by Georgia doctor Crawford Long.

1838: Cherokee Indians are marched from their homes in southeast U.S. to present-day Oklahoma on the "Trail of Tears."

1843 More than 1,000 settlers left Independence, MO, for Oregon May 22, arriving in Oct. via **Oregon Trail**.

1844 **First message over first telegraph line** sent May 24 by inventor Samuel F. B. Morse from Washington to Baltimore: "What hath God wrought?"

1845 Congress **overrode a presidential veto for the first time**, Mar. 3, after Pres. John Tyler vetoed a tariff bill. Congress of **Texas** voted for annexation by U.S., July 4; Texas admitted to Union, Dec. 29. **Edgar Allan Poe**'s poem "The Raven" published.

1846 **Mexican War** began after Pres. James K. Polk ordered Gen. Zachary Taylor to seize disputed Texan land settled by Mexicans. After border clash, U.S. declared war May 13; Mexico declared war May 23. About 12,000 U.S. troops took Vera Cruz Mar. 27, 1847, and Mexico City Sept. 14, 1847. Treaty signed Feb. 2, 1848, ended war, and Mexico ceded claims to Texas, California, and other territory. Bear flag of **Republic of California** raised by American settlers at Sonoma, June 14. Treaty with Britain June 15 set **Oregon territory** boundary at 49th parallel (extension of existing line). Expansionists had used slogan "54°40′ or fight." The term **"manifest destiny,"** coined by journalist in 1845, also came into play. **Mormons**, after violent clashes with settlers over polygamy, left Nauvoo, IL, for West under Brigham Young. They settled July 1847 at Salt Lake City, UT. Elias Howe invented **sewing machine**.

1847 **First adhesive U.S. postage stamps**—Benjamin Franklin 5¢, Washington 10¢—sold July 1. **Henry Wadsworth Longfellow**'s *Evangeline* published.

1848 **Gold** discovered Jan. 24 in California; 80,000 prospectors emigrated in 1849. Lucretia Mott and Elizabeth Cady Stanton led Seneca Falls, NY, **Women's Rights Convention** July 19-20.

1850 Sen. Henry Clay's **Compromise of 1850** admitted California as 31st state Sept. 9, with slavery forbidden; made Utah and New Mexico territories; made **Fugitive Slave Law** harsher; and ended District of Columbia slave trade. **Nathaniel Hawthorne**'s *The Scarlet Letter* published.

1851 **Herman Melville**'s *Moby-Dick* published.

1863: Pres. Abraham Lincoln's Gettysburg Address commemorates the deaths of thousands in fewer than 300 words.

1852 **Harriet Beecher Stowe**'s *Uncle Tom's Cabin* published.

1853 Japan receives Comm. Matthew C. Perry, July 14. He negotiated treaty to **open Japan** to U.S. ships. New York City hosted **first World's Fair** in the U.S., beginning July 14. **Stephen Foster** published "My Old Kentucky Home."

1854 **Republican Party** formed at Ripon, WI, Feb. 28. Opposed Kansas-Nebraska Act, which left issue of slavery to vote of settlers. Act became law May 30. Treaty ratified with Mexico Apr. 25, providing for **Gadsden Purchase** of a strip of land. **Henry David Thoreau**'s *Walden* published.

1855 **First railroad train crossed Mississippi River** on river's first bridge, between Rock Island, IL, and Davenport, IA, Apr. 21. **Walt Whitman**'s *Leaves of Grass* published.

1856 Proslavery group sacked **Lawrence, KS**, May 21; abolitionist John Brown led antislavery contingent against Missourians at Osawatomie, KS, Aug. 30. Antislavery Republican Party's **first presidential nominee**, John C. Frémont, defeated by James Buchanan. Abraham Lincoln made 50 speeches for Frémont. **First U.S. kindergarten** opened in Watertown, WI.

1857 In **Dred Scott** case, which involved determination of constitutionality of already-repealed Missouri Compromise, Supreme Court decided Mar. 6 that slaves did not become free in a free state, and blacks were not and could not be citizens. **Currier & Ives**, firm of American lithographers, issued their first print.

1858 **First Atlantic cable** completed by Cyrus W. Field Aug. 5. **Lincoln-Douglas debates** in Illinois, Aug. 21-Oct. 15.

1859 Edwin L. Drake drilled the **first commercially productive oil well** near Titusville, PA, Aug. 27. Abolitionist John Brown, with 21 men, seized U.S. armory at **Harpers Ferry**, WV, Oct. 16. U.S. Marines captured raiders, killing several. Brown was hanged for treason Dec. 2.

1860 Shoeworkers in Lynn, MA, went on strike Feb. 22. Within a week, strike spread to include 20,000 shoeworkers throughout New England in country's **largest strike to date**. **First Pony Express** between Sacramento, CA, and St. Joseph, MO, started Apr. 3. Republican **Abraham Lincoln** elected president Nov. 6 in four-way race.

1861 Seven southern states set up **Confederate States of America** Feb. 8, with **Jefferson Davis** as president. **Civil War** began as Confederates fired on **Ft. Sumter** in Charleston, SC, Apr. 12; they captured it Apr. 14. Pres. Lincoln called for 75,000 volunteers Apr. 15. Lincoln blockaded Southern ports Apr. 19, cutting off vital exports and aid. By May, 11 states had seceded. Confederates repelled Union forces at first **Battle of Bull Run**, July 21. **First transcontinental telegraph line** put in operation.

1862 Union forces were victorious in Western campaigns, took New Orleans May 1. Battles in East were largely inconclusive despite heavy casualties. The **Battle of Antietam**, in western Maryland Sept. 17, was bloodiest one-day battle of war; each side lost more than 2,000 men. **Homestead Act**, which granted free farms to settlers, approved May 20. **Land Grant Act**, which provided for public land sale to benefit agricultural education, approved July 7. It eventually led to establishment of state university systems.

1863 Pres. Lincoln issued **Emancipation Proclamation** Jan. 1, freeing "all slaves in areas still in rebellion." Union forces won major victory at Gettysburg, PA, July 1-3. Confederate forces under siege surrendered **Vicksburg, MS**, to Union forces under Gen. Ulysses S. Grant, July 4; control of Mississippi River in Union hands. About 1,000 were killed or wounded in **draft riots** in New York City; some blacks were hanged by mobs July 13-16. Pres. Lincoln gave his **Gettysburg Address** Nov. 19. Lincoln declared **Thanksgiving** a national holiday.

1864 Gen. **William Tecumseh Sherman** marched through Georgia, taking Atlanta Sept. 1 and Savannah Dec. 22. **Sand Creek massacre** of Cheyenne and Arapaho Indians Nov. 29. Soldiers drove Indians out of village; about 150 killed.

1865 Gen. **Robert E. Lee surrendered** 27,800 Confederate troops to Gen. Grant at Appomattox Court House in VA, Apr. 9. J. E. Johnston surrendered 31,200 to Sherman at Durham Station, NC, Apr. 18. Last rebel troops surrendered May 26. Pres. Lincoln shot Apr. 14 by **John Wilkes Booth** in Ford's Theater, Washington, DC; died the following morning. Vice Pres. **Andrew Johnson** was sworn in as president. Booth was hunted down and fatally wounded, perhaps by his own hand, Apr. 26. Four co-conspirators were hanged July 7. **13th Amendment**, abolishing slavery, ratified Dec. 6.

1890: Jacob Riis's *How the Other Half Lives* documents urban slums and tenements, instigating reform.

1866 Congress took control of Southern **Reconstruction**, backed freedmen's rights in legislation vetoed by Pres. Johnson; veto overridden by Congress, Apr. 9. **Ku Klux Klan** formed secretly in South to terrorize blacks who voted. Disbanded 1869-71.

1867 **Alaska** sold to U.S. by Russia for $7.2 mil Mar. 30, through efforts of Sec. of State William H. Seward. Fraternal society the **Grange** was organized Dec. 4 to protect farmer interests. **Horatio Alger**'s *Ragged Dick* published.

1868 Pres. Johnson dismissed Sec. of War Edwin M. Stanton without Senate approval. **Johnson impeached** by the House Feb. 24 for violation of Tenure of Office Act, though charges were actually made in response to his opposition to congressional Reconstruction. He was acquitted by the Senate Mar.-May. **14th Amendment**, providing for citizenship of all persons born or naturalized in U.S. and subject to the jurisdiction thereof, ratified July 9. **Louisa May Alcott**'s *Little Women* published. ***The World Almanac***, a publication of the *New York World* newspaper, appeared for first time.

1869 **Transcontinental railroad** completed; golden spike driven at Promontory Summit, UT, May 10, marking junction of Central Pacific and Union Pacific lines. Attempt to "corner" gold led to financial **"Black Friday"** in New York Sept. 24. **Woman suffrage law** passed in Wyoming Territory Dec. 10. **Knights of Labor** labor union formed in Philadelphia. By 1886, it had 700,000 members nationally.

1870 **15th Amendment**, making race no bar to voting rights, ratified Feb. 8. **First U.S. boardwalk** completed, in Atlantic City, NJ. **U.S. Weather Bureau** founded.

1871 **Great Chicago fire** destroyed city Oct. 8-11. **National Rifle Association (NRA)** founded.

1872 **Amnesty Act** May 22 restored civil rights to citizens of the South, except for 500 Confederate leaders. Congress established Yellowstone, **first national park**. James McNeill Whistler painted famous portrait known informally as **"Whistler's Mother."**

1873 **First U.S. postal card** issued May 1. **Jesse James** and his gang robbed their first passenger train July 21. Banks failed, panic began in Sept. **Depression** lasted five years. **"Boss" William Tweed** of New York City was convicted Nov. 19 of stealing public funds; he died in jail in 1878. New York's Bellevue Hospital started **first nursing school**.

1874 **Women's Christian Temperance Union** established in Cleveland. **First public zoo** in U.S. established in Philadelphia.

1875 Congress passed **Civil Rights Act** Mar. 1, giving equal rights to blacks in public accommodations and jury duty. Supreme Court invalidated act in 1883. First **Kentucky Derby** held May 17. First **Jim Crow segregation law** enacted, in Tennessee.

1876 **Alexander Graham Bell** patented the telephone Mar. 7. Col. **George A. Custer** and 264 soldiers of the 7th Cavalry were killed June 25 in "last stand," **Battle of the Little Bighorn**, MT, in Sioux Indian War. Democrat **Samuel J. Tilden** received majority of popular votes for president over Republican **Rutherford B. Hayes**, Nov. 7, but 22 electoral votes were in dispute. Congress agreed to certify Hayes as winner in Feb. 1877 after Republicans agreed to end federal Reconstruction of South.

1877 **Molly Maguires**—Irish terrorist society in mining areas of Scranton, PA—was broken up by hanging, June 21, of 11 leaders for murders of mine officials and police. Pres. Rutherford B. Hayes sent federal troops to control violent national **railroad strike**, which began in July.

1878 **First commercial telephone exchange** opened, New Haven, CT, Jan. 28. **Thomas A. Edison** founded Edison Electric Light Co. on Oct. 15.

1879 **F. W. Woolworth** opened his first five-and-ten store, in Utica, NY, Feb. 22. French actress **Sarah Bernhardt** made her U.S. debut Nov. 8 at New York City's Booth Theater. Economist and social philosopher **Henry George** published *Progress & Poverty*, advocating single tax on land.

1881 **Clara Barton** founded **American Red Cross** May 21. Pres. **James A. Garfield** shot in Washington, DC, July 2; died Sept. 19. Famous gun battle between the Earp brothers and outlaw rustlers Oct. 26 near the **OK Corral**, Tombstone, AZ. **Booker T. Washington** founded Tuskegee Institute for blacks. **Helen Hunt Jackson**'s *A Century of Dishonor*, about mistreatment of Indians, published.

1882 **Chinese Exclusion Act**, barring immigration of Chinese laborers for 10 years, later made permanent, passed by Congress May 6; prohibited naturalization of Chinese resident aliens.

1883 Civil Service Act, or **Pendleton Act**, passed Jan. 16, created foundations of American civil service system. The **Brooklyn Bridge** opened May 24 as world's longest suspension bridge. Transcontinental **Northern Pacific Railroad** was completed Sept. 8. **Buffalo Bill Cody**'s Wild West Show began its 30-year touring run.

1884 **First long-distance telephone call** completed, Mar. 27, between Boston and New York. Switchback Railway—**first U.S. roller coaster** built as amusement park ride—opened at Coney Island in New York City. **Mark Twain**'s *The Adventures of Huckleberry Finn* published.

1885 **Washington Monument** dedicated Feb. 21.

1886 **Haymarket riot** and bombing, May 4, followed labor battles for 8-hr. work day in Chicago; seven police and four workers died. Eight anarchists found guilty Aug. 20; four hanged Nov. 11. **Coca-Cola** first sold, May 8, at Jacob's Pharmacy in Atlanta. Apache Indian **Geronimo** surrendered Sept. 4, ending last major Indian war. **Statue of Liberty** dedicated Oct. 28. **American Federation of Labor** (AFL) formed Dec. 8 by 25 craft unions.

1887 **Interstate Commerce Act** enacted Feb. 4, created Interstate Commerce Commission.

1888 **Great blizzard** struck Eastern U.S. Mar. 11-14, causing about 400 deaths. Ernest Thayer's poem **"Casey at the Bat"** recited for first time in public at New York City theater in May.

1889 U.S. opened 2-mil acre **Oklahoma District** to settlement Apr. 22, initiating land run; "sooner" settlers illegally entered the territory before that date to stake favorable claims. More than 2,200 lives lost in **Johnstown flood** (PA) May 31. **Electric lights** installed at White House.

1890 **Sherman Antitrust Act** passed July 2, began federal effort to curb monopolies. Massacre at **Wounded Knee**, SD, Dec. 29, the last major conflict between Indians and U.S. troops; about 200 Indian men, women, and children and 29 soldiers were killed. **Jacob Riis**'s *How the Other Half Lives*, about city slums, published, instigating reform legislation in New York City. **Emily Dickinson**'s poems published, four years after her death.

1891 **Forest Reserve Act**, Mar. 3, let president close public forest land to settlement for establishment of national parks. **Carnegie Hall**, in New York City, opened May 5.

1892 **Ellis Island**, in New York Bay, opened Jan. 1 to receive immigrants; closed 1954. **Homestead strike** (PA) at Carnegie steel mills; 7 guards and 11 strikers and spectators shot to death July 6. James J. Corbett defeated John L. Sullivan Sept. 7 to become **first world heavyweight champion** under Marquess of Queensbury rules.

1893 **Columbian Exposition** world's fair held May-Oct. in Chicago. Financial panic led to four-year **depression**. **Mormon Temple** dedicated in Salt Lake City, UT.

1894 Thomas A. Edison's **kinetoscope**, for motion pictures (invented 1887), given first public showing Apr. 14. **Jacob S. Coxey** led army of unemployed from the Midwest, reaching Washington, DC, Apr. 30. Coxey arrested May 1 for trespassing on Capitol grounds; his army disbanded. **Pullman**

strike began May 11 at railroad car plant in Chicago. Milton Hershey started **Hershey Chocolate Company**.

1895 **"America, the Beautiful"** appeared for first time, in church publication, July 4. **Stephen Crane**'s *The Red Badge of Courage* published.

1896 Supreme Court, in *Plessy v. Ferguson*, May 18, approved racial segregation under the **"separate but equal"** doctrine. **William Jennings Bryan** delivered "Cross of Gold" speech July 9; won Democratic Party nomination. **John Philip Sousa** composed "Stars and Stripes Forever" on Dec. 25.

1897 **Olney-Pauncefote Treaty** with Britain, Jan. 11, gave wide scope to arbitration in settling disputes; never ratified by U.S. John J. McDermott won **first Boston Marathon** Apr. 19. First Klondike gold arrived in San Francisco July 14, helping set off **Klondike gold rush**. **First subway service** in country opens to public in Boston, Sept. 1.

1898 U.S. battleship ***Maine*** exploded Feb. 15 in Havana, Cuba; 260 killed. U.S. blockaded Cuba Apr. 22 in aid of independence forces. U.S. declared **war on Spain** Apr. 24; destroyed Spanish fleet in Philippines May 1; took Guam June 20. U.S. took **Puerto Rico** July 25-Aug. 12. Spain agreed Dec. 10 to cede Philippines, Puerto Rico, and Guam, and approved independence for Cuba. Annexation of **Hawaii** signed by Pres. William McKinley, July 7.

1899 Filipino insurgents, unable to get recognition of independence from U.S., started guerrilla war Feb. 4. Their leader, Emilio Aguinaldo, captured May 23, 1901. **Philippine insurrection** ended 1902. Killed were 20,000 Filipino troops and some 200,000 civilians, mostly from disease and starvation. Pres. McKinley signed treaty officially ending **Spanish-American War**, Feb. 10. U.S. declared **Open Door Policy** Sept. 6, to make China an open international market. Philosopher **John Dewey**'s *School and Society*, advocating progressive education ("learn by doing"), published. Pianist Scott Joplin's "Maple Leaf Rag" published, popularizing **ragtime music**.

1900 **International Ladies' Garment Workers Union** founded in New York City June 3. Fought sweatshop working conditions. **Carry Nation**, Kansas temperance leader, began raiding saloons with a hatchet. U.S. helped suppress **Boxer Rebellion** in Beijing, China. Eastman Kodak Co. introduced the **Brownie camera**, popularizing picture-taking.

1901 Texas had first significant oil strike at **Spindletop** well near Beaumont, Jan. 10. U.S. withdrew troops from **Cuba** May 20, and Cuba became independent. Pres. **McKinley** shot Sept. 6 in Buffalo, NY, by anarchist Leon Czolgosz; died Sept. 14. Vice Pres. **Theodore Roosevelt** sworn in as youngest-ever president, at age 42 years, 11 months. **Booker T. Washington**'s *Up From Slavery* published.

1902 Permanent **Bureau of the Census** established Mar. 6. **Helen Keller** autobiography appeared in serial form.

1903 Treaty between U.S. and Colombia to have U.S. dig **Panama Canal** signed Jan. 22, but rejected by Colombia's Congress; Panama declared independence from Colombia with U.S. support Nov. 3; recognized by Pres. Roosevelt Nov. 6. U.S., Panama signed canal treaty Nov. 18. Wisconsin set first **direct primary voting system**, May 23. **Henry Ford** founded Ford Motor Co., June 16. Boston defeated Pittsburgh, 5 games to 3, Oct. 13 in **first modern World Series**. **First successful flight** in heavier-than-air mechanically propelled airplane by **Orville Wright** Dec. 17 near Kitty Hawk, NC, 120 ft in 12 sec. Later flight same day by **Wilbur Wright**, 852 ft in 59 sec. Improved plane patented, 1906. **Iroquois Theater fire** in Chicago killed about 600 out of 1,900 in audience, Dec. 30. Pioneering film ***Great Train Robbery*** produced.

1904 St. Louis hosted **first Olympics in U.S.**, July 1-Nov. 23. First section of **New York City subway** system opened, Oct. 27. **Ida Tarbell** published muckraking *The History of the Standard Oil Company*. **Henry James**'s last major novel, *The Golden Bowl*, published.

1905 **Industrial Workers of the World**, which advocated Marxian theory of class struggle between workers and capitalists, founded in Chicago, June 27. **Rotary**, oldest service club organization in U.S., founded in Chicago.

1906 **San Francisco earthquake** and fire, Apr. 18-19, caused more than 3,000 deaths and $400 mil in damages. **Upton Sinclair**'s *The Jungle*, which exposed working conditions in meat-packing industry, published. Helped spur passage of the **Pure Food and Drug Act** and **Meat Inspection Act** June 30.

1907 Financial panic and **depression** started Mar. 13. Pres. Roosevelt sent **"Great White Fleet"** of 16 U.S. battleships around the world in show of power.

1908 Springfield, IL, torn by **anti-black rioting**, Aug. 14-15. Henry Ford introduced **Model T** car, priced at $850, Oct. 1.

1909 Adm. Robert E. Peary claimed to have reached **North Pole** Apr. 6 on sixth attempt, accompanied by black explorer Matthew Henson and four Inuit; may have fallen short. National Conference on the Negro convened May 30, leading to founding of **National Association for the Advancement of Colored People** (NAACP).

1910 **Boy Scouts** of America founded Feb. 8. Former Pres. Roosevelt called for **"new nationalism"** in famous speech in Kansas, Aug. 10.

1911 Building with New York City's **Triangle Shirtwaist Co.** factory caught fire Mar. 25; 146 died. Supreme Court ruled May 15 that **Standard Oil Co.** must be dissolved because it unreasonably restrained trade. **First transcontinental airplane flight** (with numerous stops) by C. P. Rodgers, from New York to Pasadena, CA, Sept. 17-Nov. 5; time in air 82 hr., 4 min.

1912 American Girl Guides founded Mar. 12; name changed in 1913 to **Girl Scouts**. U.S. Marines, Aug. 14, sent to **Nicaragua**, which was in default of loans to U.S. and Europe.

1913 **16th Amendment**, authorizing federal income tax, ratified Feb. 3. The **Armory Show** in New York City brought modern art to U.S. for first time, Feb. 17. **17th Amendment**, providing for direct popular election of U.S. senators, ratified Apr. 8. **Federal Reserve System** authorized Dec. 23, in major reform of U.S. banking and finance.

1914 **Ford Motor Co.** raised basic wage rates from $2.40 for 9-hr. day to $5 for 8-hr. day, Jan. 5, increasing stability in labor force. When U.S. sailors were arrested in Tampico, Mexico, Apr. 9, Atlantic fleet was sent to **Veracruz**, occupied city. Pres. Woodrow Wilson proclaimed **U.S. neutrality** in the European war, Aug. 4. The **Panama Canal** officially opened Aug. 15. The **Clayton Antitrust Act** passed Oct. 15, strengthening federal antimonopoly powers.

1915 **First transcontinental telephone call**, New York to San Francisco, completed Jan. 25 by Alexander Graham Bell and Thomas A. Watson. British ship ***Lusitania*** sunk May 7 by German submarine; 1,198 passengers died, including 128 Americans. (In notice in morning newspapers the day *Lusitania* set sail, Germany had warned Americans against taking passage on British vessels.) As result of U.S. campaign, Germany issued apology and promise of payments, Oct. 5. U.S. troops landed in **Haiti**, July 28. Haiti became virtual U.S. protectorate under Sept. 16 treaty. Pres. Wilson asked for a military fund increase, Dec. 7. D. W. Griffith's film ***The Birth***

1906: Damages caused by the San Francisco earthquake and subsequent fires leave 225,000 (more than half the area population) homeless.

1920: Prohibition of alcoholic beverages goes into effect, but "the noble experiment" fails broadly in subsequent years and is repealed in 1933.

of a Nation released. William J. Simmons partly inspired by film to revive **Ku Klux Klan**, which peaks in 1920s.

1916 Gen. **John J. Pershing** entered Mexico in Mar. to pursue **Francisco (Pancho) Villa**, who had raided U.S. border areas. Forces withdrew Feb. 5, 1917. **Rural Credits Acts** passed July 17, followed by **Warehouse Act** Aug. 11; both provided financial aid to farmers. Bomb exploded during **San Francisco Preparedness Day parade** July 22, killed 10. Thomas J. Mooney, labor organizer, and Warren K. Billings, shoeworker, convicted 1917; both later pardoned. U.S. bought **Virgin Islands** from Denmark Aug. 4. U.S. established military government in the **Dominican Republic** Nov. 29. Jeannette Rankin (R, MT) elected to House of Representatives, **first female member of Congress**.

1917 Germany, suffering from British blockade, declared almost unrestricted **submarine warfare** Jan. 31. U.S. cut diplomatic ties with Germany Feb. 3 and formally **declared war** Apr. 6. Jones Act, passed Mar. 2, made **Puerto Rico** a U.S. territory, its inhabitants U.S. citizens. **Conscription law** passed May 18. First U.S. troops arrived in Europe June 26.

1918 Pres. Wilson set out his **14 Points** as basis for peace, Jan. 8. More than 1 mil American troops were in Europe by July. Allied counteroffensive launched at Château-Thierry July 18. War ended with signing of **armistice** Nov. 11. **Influenza epidemic** killed an estimated 20 mil worldwide, 548,000 in U.S.

1919 **18th Amendment**, providing for prohibition of manufacture, sale, or transportation of alcoholic beverages, ratified Jan. 16, to take effect on Jan. 16, 1920. **First transatlantic flight**, by U.S. Navy seaplane, left Rockaway, NY, May 8; stopped at Newfoundland, Azores, Lisbon May 27. **Boston police strike** Sept. 9, earliest strike conducted by government employees. About 250 **foreign-born radicals** deported Dec. 21 to Soviet Union.

1920 In national **Red Scare**, some 2,700 Communists, anarchists, and other radicals were arrested Jan.-May. **League of Women Voters** founded Feb. 14. Senate refused Mar. 19 to ratify **League of Nations Covenant**. **Nicola Sacco** and **Bartolomeo Vanzetti** accused of killing two men in Massachusetts payroll holdup Apr. 15; found guilty 1921. A seven-year campaign for their release failed; both executed Aug. 23, 1927. Verdict repudiated 1977 by proclamation of Massachusetts Gov. Michael Dukakis. **19th Amendment** ratified Aug. 18, giving women the vote. **First regular licensed radio broadcasting** began Aug. 20. **Wall St. bombing** in New York City killed 30, injured 100, did $2 mil damage, Sept. 16. **Sinclair Lewis**'s *Main Street* published.

1921 Congress sharply curbed immigration, set **national quota system** May 19. Joint congressional resolution declaring **peace with Germany, Austria, and Hungary** signed July 2 by Pres. Warren G. Harding; treaties were signed in Aug. In so-called **Black Sox scandal**, eight Chicago White Sox players were banned from baseball Aug. 4 for conspiring with gamblers to throw the 1919 World Series. Limitation of Armaments Conference met in Washington, DC, Nov. 12-Feb. 6, 1922. Major powers agreed to curtail naval construction, outlaw poison gas, restrict submarine attacks on merchant vessels, and respect China's integrity.

1922 During nationwide coal strike, union miners killed some 21 strikebreakers at Herrin, IL, June 21-22, in incident referred to as the **Herrin Massacre**. **T. S. Eliot**'s *The Waste Land* published.

1923 **First sound-on-film motion picture**, *Phonofilm*, shown at Rivoli Theater, New York City, beginning in Apr. Pres. Calvin Coolidge addressed Congress, Dec. 6; **first radio broadcast of president's annual speech**.

1924 Law approved by Congress June 15 made all **Native Americans U.S. citizens**. **Nellie Tayloe Ross** elected governor of Wyoming, and **Miriam (Ma) Ferguson** elected governor of Texas Nov. 9. Ross inaugurated as nation's **first female governor** Jan. 5, 1925. Ferguson installed Jan. 20, 1925. **George Gershwin** wrote "Rhapsody in Blue."

1925 In so-called "Monkey Trial," John T. Scopes found guilty of having taught **evolution** in Dayton, TN, high school and fined, July 24. **F. Scott Fitzgerald**'s *The Great Gatsby* published.

1926 Dr. Robert H. Goddard, Mar. 16, demonstrated **first liquid-fuel rocket**. Congress established **Army Air Corps** July 2. **Air Commerce Act** passed Nov. 2, established government agencies for development of airports, radio navigation, and other services. **Ernest Hemingway**'s *The Sun Also Rises* published.

1927 Capt. **Charles A. Lindbergh** left Roosevelt Field, NY, May 20 alone in ***Spirit of St. Louis*** on first New York-Paris nonstop flight. Reached Le Bourget airfield May 21, 3,610 mi in 33½ hr. *The Jazz Singer*, **first feature-length film** in which **spoken dialogue was part of narrative action**, released Oct. 6. The musical *Show Boat* opened in New York City Dec. 27.

1928 **Amelia Earhart** became first woman to fly across the Atlantic, June 17. **Herbert Hoover** elected president Nov. 6, defeating New York Gov. Alfred E. Smith, a Catholic.

1929 Gangsters killed seven rivals in Chicago **St. Valentine's Day massacre** Feb. 14, which won Al Capone control of Chicago's underworld. Stock market crash Oct. 29 marked end of past prosperity as stock prices plummeted. Stock losses for 1929-31 estimated at $50 bil; beginning of **Great Depression**. Albert B. Fall, former interior sec., was convicted of accepting $10,000 bribe in leasing of the **Elk Hills (Teapot Dome)** naval oil reserve; sentenced Nov. 1 to a year in prison and fined. **William Faulkner**'s *The Sound and the Fury* published.

1930 London **Naval Reduction Treaty** signed by U.S., Britain, Italy, France, and Japan Apr. 22; in effect Jan. 1, 1931; expired Dec. 31, 1936. **Hawley-Smoot Tariff** signed; rate hikes slash world trade. **Sinclair Lewis** became first American to win a Nobel Prize in literature. **Dashiell Hammett**'s *The Maltese Falcon* published.

1931 **Empire State Building** opened in New York City May 1, displacing NYC's Chrysler Building as world's tallest. **Al Capone** convicted of tax evasion Oct. 17. **Pearl Buck**'s *The Good Earth* published. **Charlie Chaplin** film *City Lights* released.

1932 **Reconstruction Finance Corp.** established Jan. 22 to stimulate banking and business. Unemployment at 12 mil. Twenty-month-old **Charles Lindbergh Jr.** kidnapped Mar. 1; found dead May 12. Bruno Hauptmann found guilty Feb. 1935; executed Apr. 3, 1936. Unemployed World War I veterans demanding Congress pay promised bonus early launched **Bonus March** on Washington, DC, May 29. **Franklin D. Roosevelt** elected president for first time in Democratic landslide, Nov. 8. Chicago Bears won **first NFL title game** Dec. 18, defeating the Portsmouth (OH) Spartans, 9-0.

1933 Pres. Roosevelt named **Frances Perkins** U.S. sec. of labor; **first woman in U.S. cabinet**. Pres. Roosevelt ordered **all U.S. banks closed** Mar. 6. In a "100 days" special session, Mar. 9-June 16, Congress passed **New Deal**, including measures to regulate banks, distribute funds to the jobless, create jobs, raise agricultural prices, and set wage and production standards for industry. **Gold standard** dropped by U.S. in favor of "modified gold bullion standard"; announced by Pres. Roosevelt Apr. 19, ratified by Congress June 5. **Tennessee Valley Authority (TVA)** created by act of Congress, May 18. **Prohibition** ended in the U.S. as 36th state ratified **21st Amendment** Dec. 5. Pres. Roosevelt foreswore armed intervention in **Western Hemisphere** nations, Dec. 26.

1934 Pres. Roosevelt signed law creating **Securities and Exchange Commission**, June 6. U.S. troops pulled out of **Haiti**, Aug. 6.

1935 **Works Progress Administration (WPA)** instituted May 6. Rural Electrification Administration created May 11.

1936: Dorothea Lange's iconic "Migrant Mother" photo comes to represent the desperation felt nationwide during the long economic downturn of the Great Depression (1929-39).

National Industrial Recovery Act struck down by Supreme Court May 27. **Boulder Dam** (later renamed **Hoover Dam**) completed, May 29. **Social Security Act** passed by Congress Aug. 8-9. Comedian **Will Rogers** and aviator Wiley Post killed Aug. 15 in Alaska plane crash. **Huey Long**, Louisiana senator and national political leader, shot Sept. 8; died Sept. 10. George Gershwin's jazz opera ***Porgy and Bess*** opened Oct. 10 in New York. **Committee for Industrial Organization** (later Congress of Industrial Organizations) formed to expand industrial unionism Nov. 9.

1936 Jesse Owens won four gold medals at the **Berlin Olympics** in Aug. **Baseball Hall of Fame** founded in Cooperstown, NY. **Margaret Mitchell**'s *Gone With the Wind* published.

1937 Airship ***Hindenburg*** caught fire May 6 as it was landing in Lakehurst, NJ; 36 killed. **Golden Gate Bridge** in San Francisco opened May 27. **Joe Louis** knocked out James J. Braddock to become world heavyweight champ June 22. Aviator **Amelia Earhart** and copilot Fred Noonan disappeared July 2 near Howland Isl., in the Pacific. Pres. Roosevelt proposed judicial reforms that would allow him to appoint additional Supreme Court justices; his **"court-packing" plan** defeated. **Auto, steel labor unions** won first big contracts.

1938 National minimum wage enacted June 25. Orson Welles's radio dramatization of H. G. Wells's ***War of the Worlds***, Oct. 30, caused Martian invasion scare among some who had missed the introduction. **Seabiscuit** beat War Admiral in match race of the century, at Pimlico track, MD, Nov. 1. Artist Anna Mary Robertson, **"Grandma Moses,"** discovered. **Thornton Wilder**'s *Our Town* produced on Broadway.

1939 Opera singer **Marian Anderson** performed for integrated crowd of 75,000 at Lincoln Memorial Apr. 9 after Daughters of the American Revolution refused to let Anderson sing in DC's Constitution Hall. **New York World's Fair**—theme: "The World of Tomorrow"—opened Apr. 30, closed Oct. 31. Reopened for second season May 11-Oct. 27, 1940. **Lou Gehrig**, seriously ill with disease that would come to bear his name, said farewell to fans at Yankee Stadium, July 4. Albert Einstein alerted Pres. Roosevelt to **A-bomb possibilities** in Aug. 2 letter. **U.S. declared its neutrality** in European war Sept. 5. Pres. Roosevelt proclaimed limited **national emergency** Sept. 8, unlimited emergency May 27, 1941. Both ended by Pres. Harry Truman, Apr. 28, 1952.

Pocket Books, **first paperback publisher** in U.S., established. **John Steinbeck**'s *The Grapes of Wrath* published. ***The Wizard of Oz*** and ***Gone With the Wind*** released, the latter to become highest-grossing film of all time (inflation-adjusted).

1940 U.S. OK'd sale of **surplus war material** to Britain June 3; announced transfer of 50 overaged destroyers Sept. 3. **First peacetime military draft** in U.S. history approved, Sept. 14. **Forty-hour work week** went into effect, Oct. 24. Pres. **Roosevelt** elected Nov. 5 to third presidential term. **Richard Wright**'s *Native Son* published.

1941 Four Freedoms—freedom of speech and religion, freedom from want and fear—termed essential by Pres. Roosevelt in speech to Congress Jan. 6. **Lend-Lease Act** signed Mar. 11 provided $7 bil in military credits for Britain. Lend-lease for USSR approved in Nov. Pres. Roosevelt signed executive order June 25 barring federal government and war contractors from **racial discrimination**. Order also established Fair Employment Practice Committee. The **Atlantic Charter**, 8-point declaration of principles, issued by Pres. Roosevelt and British Prime Min. Winston Churchill, Aug. 14. Japan attacked **Pearl Harbor**, Hawaii, 7:55 AM Hawaiian time, Dec. 7; 19 ships sunk or damaged, 2,403 dead. Pres. Roosevelt called it "a date which will live in infamy." U.S. declared war on Japan Dec. 8. Germany and Italy declared war on U.S. Dec. 11. U.S. responded with declaration of war later on same day. Japanese invaded **Philippines**, Dec. 22; Wake Island fell, Dec. 23. ***Citizen Kane***, directed by Orson Welles, released.

1942 Pres. Roosevelt issued executive order Feb. 19 authorizing relocation of Japanese-Americans. Federal government began forcibly moving 110,000 Japanese-Americans from West Coast to **detention camps**; exclusion lasted three years. Japanese troops took **Bataan** peninsula Apr. 8 and **Corregidor** May 6. **Battle of Midway** June 4-7 was Japan's first major defeat. Marines landed on **Guadalcanal** Aug. 7; last Japanese not expelled until Feb. 9, 1943. U.S., Britain invaded **North Africa** Nov. 8. **First nuclear chain reaction** (fission of uranium isotope U-235) produced at Univ. of Chicago under physicists Arthur Compton, Enrico Fermi, others, Dec. 2. The movie ***Casablanca***, starring Humphrey Bogart and Ingrid Bergman, released.

1943 ***Oklahoma!*** opened Mar. 31 on Broadway. Pres. Roosevelt signed June 10 pay-as-you-go income tax bill. Starting July 1, wage and salary earners were subject to **paycheck withholding tax**. **Detroit race riot** June 21 left 34 dead, 700 injured. Six killed in riot in New York City's **Harlem** section Aug. 2. U.S., Britain invaded **Sicily** July 9, Italian **mainland** Sept. 3. Marines in Nov. recaptured the **Gilbert Islands**, captured by Japan in 1941 and 1942.

1944 U.S., Allied forces invaded Europe at Normandy, France, on **"D Day,"** June 6, in greatest amphibious landing in history. **GI Bill of Rights**, providing benefits to veterans, signed by Pres. Roosevelt June 22. Representatives of the U.S. and other major powers met at **Dumbarton Oaks**, Washington, DC, Aug. 21-Oct. 7, to work out formation of postwar world organization that would become the **United Nations**. U.S. forces landed on **Leyte**, Philippines, Oct. 20. Pres. **Roosevelt** elected to fourth term as president Nov. 7. **Battle of the Bulge**, failed Nazi counteroffensive, waged Dec. 16 to Jan. 28, 1945.

1945 Yalta Conference met in the Crimea, USSR, Feb. 4-11. Pres. Roosevelt, Prime Min. Churchill, and Soviet leader Joseph Stalin agreed that their countries, plus France, would occupy Germany and that the Soviet Union would enter war against Japan. Marines landed on **Iwo Jima** Feb. 19, won control Mar. 16 after heavy casualties. U.S. forces invaded **Okinawa** Apr. 1, captured it June 21. Pres. **Roosevelt** died in Warm Springs, GA, Apr. 12; Vice Pres. **Harry S. Truman** became president. Germany surrendered May 7; May 8 proclaimed **V-E Day**. **First atomic bomb**, produced at Los Alamos, NM, exploded at Alamogordo, NM, July 16. Bomb dropped on **Hiroshima**, Japan, Aug. 6, killing about 75,000; bomb dropped on **Nagasaki**, Japan, Aug. 9, killing about 40,000. Japan agreed to surrender Aug. 14; formally surrendered Sept. 2. At **Potsdam Conference**, July 17-Aug. 2, leaders of U.S., USSR, and Britain agreed on disarmament of Germany, occupation zones, war crimes trials. **Empire State Building** struck accidentally by Army B-25 bomber, July 28, killing 14. U.S. forces entered **Korea** south of 38th parallel to displace Japanese Sept. 8. Gen. **Douglas MacArthur** took over supervision of Japan Sept. 9.

1946 Steel strike by 750,000 started Jan. 21, settled in four weeks. Strike by 400,000 **mine workers** began Apr. 1 (settled May 29); other industries (including rail, maritime) followed. Former Prime Min. Winston Churchill employed the phrase **"Iron Curtain"** in Mar. 5 speech at Westminster

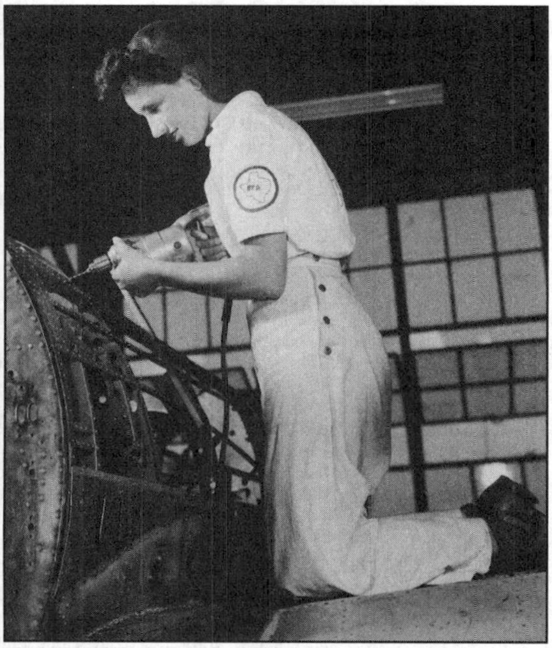

1941: The U.S. enters World War II with 12 million women in the workforce and adds another 6 million by 1945; 3 million women work in war-related factories.

College in Fulton, MO. Atomic bomb tested off **Bikini Atoll** in Pacific, July 1. In all, U.S. conducted 23 nuclear tests between 1946 and 1958. **Philippines** given independence by U.S. July 4. Mother Frances Xavier Cabrini **first American to be canonized**, July 7. Dr. Benjamin Spock's *Baby and Child Care* published as **baby boom** began.

1947 Pres. Truman asked Congress for financial and military aid for Greece and Turkey to help combat Communist subversion, Mar. 12; **Truman Doctrine** approved May 15. UN Security Council voted Apr. 2 to place under U.S. trusteeship the **Pacific islands** formerly mandated to Japan. **Jackie Robinson** joined Brooklyn Dodgers Apr. 11, breaking color barrier in major league baseball. The **Marshall Plan** for U.S. aid to European countries proposed by Sec. of State George C. Marshall June 5. Congress authorized some $12 bil in next four years. **Taft-Hartley Labor Act** restricting labor union power vetoed by Pres. Truman June 20; Congress overrode veto. Air Force Capt. **Chuck Yeager** broke sound barrier, Oct. 14, in X-1 rocket plane.

1948 Organization of American States (OAS) founded Apr. 30 by 21 countries. USSR halted all surface traffic into **West Berlin** June 24; in response, U.S. and British troops launched an **airlift**. Soviet blockade halted May 12, 1949; airlift ended Sept. 30. Pres. **Truman** elected Nov. 2, defeating NY Gov. Thomas E. Dewey in historic upset. **Alger Hiss** indicted Dec. 15 for perjury, after denying he had passed secret documents to Whittaker Chambers to go to a Communist spy ring; convicted Jan. 21, 1950. **Kinsey Report** on sexuality in the human male published.

1949 North Atlantic Treaty Organization (**NATO**) established Aug. 24 by U.S., Canada, and 10 Western European nations, agreeing that an armed attack against one would be considered an attack against all. Eleven leaders of U.S. **Communist Party** convicted Oct. 14 of advocating violent overthrow of U.S. government; sentenced to prison. Supreme Court upheld convictions, 1951. Pres. Truman, Oct. 26, signed legislation raising **federal minimum wage** from 40¢ an hour to 75¢. **Arthur Miller**'s *Death of a Salesman* opened on Broadway.

1950 Masked bandits robbed **Brink's, Inc.**, Boston express office, Jan. 17, of $2.8 mil. Case solved 1956; eight sentenced to life. Pres. Truman authorized production of **H-bomb** Jan. 31. Special Senate committee to investigate organized crime established May 3, chaired by Sen. **Estes Kefauver** (D, TN).

North Korean forces **invaded South Korea** June 25. UN asked for troops to restore peace. Pres. Truman ordered Air Force and Navy to Korea June 27. Truman approved ground forces, air strikes against North Korea June 30. U.S. sent 35 military advisers to **South Vietnam** June 27 and agreed to aid anti-Communist government. U.S. forces landed at **Inchon**, South Korea, Sept. 15. UN forces took Pyongyang Oct. 20, reached China border Nov. 20. China sent troops across border Nov. 26. U.S. banned shipments Dec. 8 to **Communist China** and to Asiatic ports trading with it.

Army **seized all railroads** Aug. 27 on Truman's order to prevent general strike; returned to owners in 1952. Two members of **Puerto Rican nationalist movement** tried to kill Pres. Truman Nov. 1.

Peanuts comic strip appeared in newspapers. Variety show ***Your Show of Shows*** debuted on TV. David Riesman's ***The Lonely Crowd*** published.

1951 22nd Amendment, limiting presidential term of office, ratified Feb. 27. **Julius Rosenberg**; his wife, **Ethel Rosenberg**; and **Morton Sobell** found guilty Mar. 29 of conspiracy to commit wartime espionage. Rosenbergs received death penalty. Sobell sentenced to 30 years; released 1969.

Pres. Truman removed Gen. **Douglas MacArthur** from Korea command Apr. 11 for unauthorized policy statements. **Korea cease-fire** talks began in July; lasted two years. Fighting ended July 27, 1953.

Transcontinental TV began Sept. 4 with Pres. Truman's address at Japanese Peace Treaty Conference in San Francisco. **Japanese peace treaty** signed in San Francisco Sept. 8 by U.S., Japan, and 47 other nations. **J. D. Salinger**'s *Catcher in the Rye* published. *I Love Lucy* sitcom premiered on TV.

1952 Pres. Truman ordered seizure of nation's **steel mills** Apr. 8 to avert strike; ruled illegal by Supreme Court June 2. **Peace contract** between West Germany, U.S., Great Britain, and France signed May 26. Last racial and ethnic barriers to naturalization removed, June 26-27, with passage of **Immigration and Naturalization Act** of 1952. **Puerto Rico** proclaimed commonwealth July 25, after referendum Mar. 3. Richard Nixon, as vice-pres. candidate, gave **"Checkers" speech**, so called because of sentimental reference to his dog Checkers, Sept. 23. **First hydrogen device explosion** Nov. 1 in Pacific. **Ralph Ellison**'s *Invisible Man* published.

1953 Federal jury in New York convicted 13 **Communist** leaders on conspiracy charges, Jan. 20. **Julius and Ethel Rosenberg** executed in electric chair, June 19, for relaying nuclear secrets to Soviet Union. **Korean War armistice** signed July 27. California Gov. **Earl Warren** sworn in Oct. 5 as 14th chief justice of U.S. Supreme Court.

1954 *Nautilus*, **first atomic-powered submarine**, launched at Groton, CT, Jan. 21. Five members of Congress were wounded in the House Mar. 1 by four **Puerto Rican independence supporters** who fired at random from a spectators' gallery.

At televised hearings, Apr. 22-June 17, before a Senate subcommittee, Army officials accused Sen. **Joseph McCarthy** (R, WI) of seeking preferential treatment for a draftee, and McCarthy accused Army of hindering probe of Communist infiltration. McCarthy was cleared in the hearings, but the Senate later voted to condemn him, 67-22, for abuse of the Senate during hearings and debates.

Supreme Court ruled unanimously May 17 that racial segregation in public schools was unconstitutional, in ***Brown v. Board of Education** of Topeka*. **Ernest Hemingway** won Nobel Prize in literature for *The Old Man and the Sea*.

1955 U.S. agreed Feb. 12 to help train **South Vietnamese army**. Supreme Court ordered "all deliberate speed" in **integration** of public schools, May 31. A summit meeting of leaders of **Big 4**—U.S., Britain, France, and USSR—took place July 18-23 in Geneva, Switzerland.

Rosa Parks refused Dec. 1 to give her seat to white man on bus in Montgomery, AL. Her arrest, detention, and conviction sparked boycott of bus system, organized by Rev. **Martin Luther King Jr.**, by Montgomery's black community, Dec. 5. Bus segregation ordinance declared unconstitutional by federal court in 1956. Boycott ended Dec. 23 of that year.

America's two largest labor organizations merged Dec. 5, creating **AFL-CIO**. Russian-born U.S. citizen **Vladimir Nabokov**'s *Lolita* published.

1956 Massive resistance to Supreme Court **desegregation rulings** was called for Mar. 12 by 101 Southern congressmen. U.S. Supreme Court, Apr. 23, unanimously ruled against **racial segregation** on intrastate buses.

Federal-Aid Highway Act signed June 29, creating **interstate highway system**. **First transatlantic telephone cable** activated Sept. 25. In Game 5, Oct. 8, Yankee right-hander

1955: Rosa Parks's arrest for refusing to give up her seat on a bus in Montgomery, Alabama, sparks a boycott that would desegregate public transportation.

Don Larsen pitched **only perfect World Series game**. **Eugene O'Neill**'s *Long Day's Journey Into Night* opened Nov. 7 on Broadway.

1957 Congress approved **Civil Rights Act of 1957**, Apr. 29, first such bill since Reconstruction to protect voting rights. Pres. Eisenhower signed act into law Sept. 9; provided for creation of Civil Rights Commission. The U.S. surgeon general July 12 said studies showed "direct link" between cigarette **smoking and lung cancer**.

Arkansas Gov. Orval Faubus (D) called National Guardsmen Sept. 4 to bar nine black students from entering all-white high school in **Little Rock**. Faubus complied Sept. 21 with federal court order to remove Guardsmen, but local authorities ordered black students to withdraw. Pres. Eisenhower sent troops Sept. 24 to enforce court order.

Jack Kerouac's *On the Road* published.

1958 Army launched **first U.S. Earth-orbiting satellite**, *Explorer I*, Jan. 31 from Cape Canaveral, FL; discovered Van Allen radiation belt. U.S. Marines sent to **Lebanon** to protect elected government from threatened overthrow July-Oct. Nuclear sub *Nautilus* made **first undersea crossing of North Pole** Aug. 5. Presidential aide **Sherman Adams** resigned Sept. 22 over scandal involving alleged improper gifts. **First domestic jet airline passenger service** in U.S. opened by National Airlines Dec. 10 between New York and Miami.

1959 **Alaska** admitted as 49th state, Jan. 3; **Hawaii** admitted as 50th, Aug. 21. **St. Lawrence Seaway** linking Atlantic Ocean and Great Lakes opened to traffic, Apr. 25.

Vice Pres. Richard Nixon, on tour of USSR, held **"kitchen debate,"** July 24, with Soviet Prem. Nikita Khrushchev at U.S. exhibit in Moscow. Prem. **Khrushchev** paid unprecedented visit to U.S. Sept. 15-27; made transcontinental tour.

Pres. Eisenhower issued injunction Oct. 12, upheld and made effective by Supreme Court Nov. 7, ending record **116-day steel strike**. In **quiz show scandal**, Columbia Univ. Prof. Charles Van Doren admitted to U.S. House subcommittee Nov. 2 that he had been coached before appearances on NBC-TV's *21* in 1956; he had won $129,000. William Wyler's ***Ben-Hur*** released; the movie won a record 11 Academy Awards the following year.

1960 **Sit-ins** began Feb. 1 when four black college students in Greensboro, NC, refused to move from a Woolworth lunch counter after being denied service. By Sept. 1961, more than 70,000 students, whites and blacks, had participated in sit-ins. Pres. Eisenhower signed **Civil Rights Act** May 6.

A U.S. **U-2 reconnaissance plane** was shot down in the Soviet Union May 1; pilot Gary Powers captured. The incident led to cancellation of Paris summit conference; Powers traded for Soviet spy, 1962. A **birth control pill** approved as safe for first time by Food and Drug Administration May 9. Vice Pres. **Richard Nixon** and Sen. **John F. Kennedy** faced each other Sept. 26 in first in series of televised debates. Kennedy defeated Nixon to win presidency, Nov. 8. U.S. announced Dec. 15 its backing of rightist group in **Laos**, which took power the next day.

Alfred Hitchcock film ***Psycho*** released.

1961 U.S. severed diplomatic and consular relations with Cuba Jan. 3, after disputes over nationalizations of U.S. firms, U.S. military presence at Guantánamo base. U.S.-directed invasion of Cuba's **Bay of Pigs** Apr. 17 by Cuban exiles unsuccessfully attempted to overthrow the regime of Prem. Fidel Castro.

Peace Corps created by executive order, Mar. 1. **23rd Amendment**, giving DC citizens the right to vote in presidential elections, ratified Mar. 29. Alan B. Shepard Jr. rocketed from Cape Canaveral, FL, in a Mercury capsule May 5, in **first U.S.-crewed suborbital space flight**.

"Freedom Rides" from Washington, DC, across Deep South were launched May 20 to protest segregation in interstate transportation.

Joseph Heller's *Catch-22* published.

1962 Pres. Kennedy said Feb. 14 that U.S. military advisers in **Vietnam** would fire if fired upon. Lt. Col. John H. Glenn Jr. became **first American in orbit** Feb. 20 when he circled the Earth three times in the Mercury capsule *Friendship 7*.

In ***Baker v. Carr***, Mar. 26, U.S. Supreme Court ruled that constitutional challenges to unequal distribution of voters among legislative districts could be resolved by federal courts. **James Meredith** became first black student at Univ. of Mississippi Oct. 1 after 3,000 federal troops put down riots.

A Soviet **offensive missile buildup** in Cuba was revealed Oct. 22 by Pres. Kennedy, who ordered naval and air quarantine on shipment of offensive military equipment to the island. He and Soviet Prem. Khrushchev agreed Oct. 28 on formula to end crisis. Kennedy announced Nov. 2 that missile bases in Cuba were being dismantled. **Rachel Carson**'s *Silent Spring* launched environmentalist movement.

1963 In ***Gideon v. Wainwright***, Mar. 18, Supreme Court ruled that all criminal defendants must have counsel.

March for civil rights began May 2 in Birmingham, AL; led to desegregation accord, which in turn sparked rioting and violence. Univ. of Alabama **desegregated** after Gov. George Wallace stepped aside when confronted by federally deployed National Guard troops June 11. Civil rights leader **Medgar Evers** assassinated June 12. On Aug. 28, 200,000 joined in **March on Washington** in support of black demands for equal rights led by **Rev. Martin Luther King Jr.**; highlight was King's **"I Have a Dream" speech**.

Supreme Court ruled June 17 that laws requiring **recitation of Lord's Prayer or Bible verses** in public schools were unconstitutional. Pres. Kennedy, on Europe trip, addressed huge crowd in **West Berlin**, June 23. **Limited nuclear test-ban treaty** agreed upon July 25 by the U.S., the Soviet Union, and Britain. Four black girls killed in bombing of **16th St. Baptist Church** in Birmingham, AL, Sept. 15.

South Vietnam Pres. **Ngo Dinh Diem** assassinated Nov. 2; U.S. had earlier withdrawn support. Pres. **Kennedy** shot and fatally wounded Nov. 22 as he rode in motorcade through downtown Dallas, TX. Vice Pres. **Lyndon B. Johnson** sworn in as president. **Lee Harvey Oswald** arrested and charged with murder but was himself shot and fatally wounded Nov. 24. Nightclub owner **Jack Ruby** convicted of Oswald's murder; Ruby died in 1967 while awaiting retrial following reversal of his conviction. **Betty Friedan**'s feminist work *The Feminine Mystique* published.

1964 **Panama** suspended relations with U.S. Jan. 9 after riots. U.S. offered Dec. 18 to negotiate new canal treaty. **The Beatles** appeared Feb. 9 on *The Ed Sullivan Show*. Supreme Court ruled Feb. 17 that **congressional districts** as near as practicable be equal in population. U.S. reported May 27 it was sending military planes to **Laos**.

Three **civil rights workers** reported missing in Mississippi June 22; bodies found Aug. 4. Eighteen white men tried. On Oct. 20, 1967, an all-white federal jury convicted seven of conspiracy in the slayings. Omnibus **civil rights bill** signed by Pres. Johnson July 2, banning discrimination in voting, jobs, public accommodations.

Congress Aug. 7 passed **Tonkin Gulf Resolution**, authorizing presidential action in Vietnam, after North Vietnamese boats reportedly attacked U.S. destroyers Aug. 2. Congress approved War on Poverty bill Aug. 11, providing for a domestic Peace Corps (**VISTA**), **Job Corps**, and antipoverty funding. The **Warren Commission** released a report Sept. 27 concluding that Lee Harvey Oswald was solely responsible for the Kennedy assassination. Pres. **Johnson** elected to full term, Nov. 3, defeating Sen. **Barry Goldwater** (R, AZ) in landslide. **Verrazano-Narrows Bridge** opened in New York City, Nov. 21, with world's then-longest suspension span.

1965 In State of the Union address Jan. 4, Pres. Johnson outlined plans for **"Great Society,"** program of civil rights, antipoverty, and health-care legislation. Johnson in Feb. ordered continuous bombing of **North Vietnam** below 20th parallel.

Malcolm X assassinated by Nation of Islam members Feb. 21 at New York City rally. March from **Selma to Montgomery**, AL, Mar. 21-25, by Rev. Martin Luther King Jr. to demand federal protection of blacks' voting rights. Some 14,000 U.S. troops sent to **Dominican Republic** during civil war Apr. 28. All troops withdrawn by next year. Bill establishing **Medicare**, government health insurance program for elderly, signed by Pres. Johnson July 30.

New **Voting Rights Act**, which banned literacy tests and other voter qualification tests, signed Aug. 6. Arrest of black motorist by white police officers precipitated **Watts riot** in predominantly-black Los Angeles neighborhood Aug. 11-16. Riots resulted in 34 deaths and $200 mil in property damage.

National **immigration quota system** abolished Oct. 3. **Electric power failure** blacked out most of northeastern U.S., parts of two Canadian provinces the night of Nov. 9-10.

1966 U.S. forces began firing into **Cambodia** May 1. Bombing of **Hanoi** area of North Vietnam by U.S. planes began June 29. By Dec. 31, 385,300 U.S. troops were stationed in South Vietnam, plus 60,000 offshore and 33,000 in Thailand.

Supreme Court ruled June 13, in ***Miranda v. Arizona***, that suspects must be read their rights before police questioning. **Medicare** began July 1. In **Univ. of Texas shooting** rampage, 25-year-old student Charles Whitman killed 15 and wounded 31 from tower observation deck on Austin campus, Aug. 1; shot dead by police.

Dept. of Transportation created, Oct. 15. Edward Brooke (R, MA) elected Nov. 8 as first black U.S. senator in 85 years. Robert C. Weaver named secretary of newly created Dept. of Housing and Urban Development, becoming **first black cabinet member**.

1967 Green Bay Packers beat Kansas City Chiefs, 35-10, in **first Super Bowl**, Jan. 15, in Los Angeles. Three astronauts died Jan. 27 in ***Apollo 1*** fire on ground at Cape Canaveral, FL. **25th Amendment**, providing for presidential succession, ratified Feb. 10. Pres. Johnson and Soviet Prem. **Aleksei Kosygin** met June 23 and 25 at Glassboro State College in New Jersey; agreed not to let any crisis push them into war.

1967: A major anti-Vietnam War demonstration, a march on the Pentagon, draws more than 70,000 protesters.

Riots erupted among residents of predominantly black **Newark**, NJ, July 12-17; 26 killed, 1,500 injured, more than 1,000 arrested. In **Detroit**, MI, July 23-30, 43 died, 2,000 injured; 5,000 left homeless by rioting, looting, and burning in city's black neighborhoods. **Thurgood Marshall** sworn in Oct. 2 as first black U.S. Supreme Court justice. **Antiwar march** on Washington, DC, Oct. 21-22, drew at least 70,000 participants. Carl B. Stokes (D, Cleveland) and Richard G. Hatcher (D, Gary, IN) elected **first black mayors** of major U.S. cities Nov. 7.

1968 In **"Tet offensive,"** Communist troops attacked several provincial capitals and other major cities, including Saigon, Jan. 30, but suffered heavy casualties. Pres. Johnson **curbed bombing** of North Vietnam Mar. 31. Peace talks began in Paris May 10. All bombing of North halted Oct. 31.

Rev. **Martin Luther King Jr.** assassinated Apr. 4 in Memphis, TN. **James Earl Ray**, an escaped convict, pleaded guilty to slaying, was sentenced to 99 years. Students at **Columbia Univ.**, Apr. 23-24, seized school buildings in protest against school's involvement in military research, among other issues. Sen. **Robert F. Kennedy** (D, NY) shot June 5 in Los Angeles after celebrating presidential primary victories, died June 6. **Sirhan Sirhan** convicted of murder, 1969; death sentence commuted to life in prison, 1972.

Vice Pres. Hubert Humphrey nominated for president at **Democratic National Convention** in Chicago, marked by clash between police and antiwar protesters, Aug. 26-29. Republican nominee **Richard Nixon** won presidency, defeating Humphrey in close race Nov. 5.

Apollo 8 **orbited moon** in five-day mission, Dec. 21-27. North Korea released 82-man crew of the **USS *Pueblo*** Dec. 22, 11 months after seizing the ship in Sea of Japan; one crew member had been killed in battle.

1969 Expanded four-party **Vietnam peace talks** began Jan. 18. U.S. force peaked at 543,400 in Apr.; withdrawal started July 8. Pres. Nixon set Vietnamization policy of expanding role of South Vietnamese forces Nov. 3. Earl Warren retired upon swearing in **Warren Burger**, June 23, as Supreme Court chief justice. In incident that marked birth of **gay rights** movement, police clashed with patrons of gay bar, the **Stonewall Inn**, in New York City June 27.

U.S. astronaut **Neil Armstrong**, commander of the *Apollo 11* mission, became the **first person to set foot on the moon**, July 20, followed by astronaut **Edwin "Buzz" Aldrin**. Astronaut **Michael Collins** remained aboard command module.

Woodstock rock music festival near Bethel, NY, drew 300,000-500,000 people, Aug. 15-18. **Anti-Vietnam War demonstrations** held in cities across the U.S., marking Vietnam Moratorium day, Oct. 15; on Nov. 15, some 250,000 marched in Washington, DC. Massacre of hundreds of civilians by U.S. troops at **My Lai**, South Vietnam, in 1968 reported Nov. 16. **Kurt Vonnegut**'s *Slaughterhouse Five* published. ***Sesame Street*** launched on public TV.

1970 A federal jury Feb. 18 found the **"Chicago 7"** antiwar activists not guilty of conspiring to incite riots during 1968 Democratic National Convention. However, five were convicted of crossing state lines with intent to incite riots.

Three astronauts safely returned to Earth Apr. 17 after oxygen tank on ***Apollo 13*** ruptured. Lunar landing had been canceled. Millions of Americans participated in antipollution demonstrations Apr. 22 to mark **first Earth Day**.

U.S. and South Vietnamese forces crossed **Cambodian** borders Apr. 30 to get at enemy bases. Four students killed May 4 at **Kent State Univ.** in Ohio by National Guardsmen during war protest. In protest at **Jackson State Univ.** in Mississippi, two killed when police fired on protesters.

First female U.S. generals appointed June 11. **Postal reform** measure signed Aug. 12 created an independent U.S. Postal Service. Pres. Nixon, Dec. 31, signed **clean air bill** calling for development of cleaner auto engine and national air quality standards for 10 major pollutants. Garry Trudeau's ***Doonesbury*** comic strip launched in 30 papers.

1969: *Apollo 11* lands on the lunar surface; Edwin "Buzz" Aldrin (pictured) and Neil Armstrong are first men to walk on the Moon.

1971 **Charles Manson** and three of his cult followers found guilty Jan. 25 of first-degree murder in 1969 slaying of actress Sharon Tate and six others. A court-martial jury Mar. 29 convicted Lt. **William Calley** in murder of 22 South Vietnamese at **My Lai** on Mar. 16, 1968. He was sentenced to life in prison Mar. 31, later reduced to 20 years.

Pres. Nixon, Apr. 14, relaxed 20-year **trade embargo with China**. *New York Times* began publishing June 13 classified **Pentagon Papers**, secret Pentagon study on U.S. involvement in Vietnam leaked by Daniel Ellsberg, military analyst consulting for government. Supreme Court June 30 upheld, 6-3, right to publish the documents. **26th Amendment**, lowering the minimum voting age to 18, ratified June 30. Pres. Nixon, Aug. 15, instituted 90-day **wage and price freeze**.

U.S. bombers initiated massive five-day strike Dec. 26 in North Vietnam in retaliation for alleged violations of agreements reached prior to 1968 bombing halt.

1972 Pres. Nixon arrived in **Beijing** Feb. 21 for eight-day visit to China, in "journey for peace." Joint communiqué released Feb. 27 called for increased Sino-U.S. contacts. Senate, Mar. 22, approved **Equal Rights Amendment** banning discrimination on basis of sex; sent measure to states for ratification.

North Vietnamese forces launched biggest attacks in four years across the demilitarized zone Mar. 30. The U.S. responded Apr. 15 with **resumption of bombing** of Hanoi and Haiphong. Pres. Nixon announced May 8 the mining of North Vietnam ports.

Gov. **George C. Wallace** (D, AL), campaigning for president at Laurel, MD, shopping center May 15, shot and seriously wounded. **Arthur Bremer** convicted Aug. 4, sentenced to 63 years for shooting Wallace and three others. In **first visit of U.S. president to Moscow**, Pres. Nixon arrived May 22 for summit talks with Kremlin leaders that culminated in landmark strategic arms pact (**SALT I**). Five men arrested June 17 for breaking into Democratic National Committee offices in **Watergate** office complex in Washington, DC. U.S. Supreme Court in *Furman v. Georgia* June 29 ruled **capital punishment** as practiced was unconstitutional.

Mark Spitz won seven gold medals in world record times at the Munich Olympics in Aug.-Sept.

Last U.S. combat troops left Vietnam Aug. 11. Pres. **Nixon** reelected Nov. 7 in landslide, carrying 49 states to defeat Sen. George McGovern (D, SD). Three astronauts, part of ***Apollo 17***, made 6th and last lunar landing on Dec. 11. Full-scale **bombing of North Vietnam** resumed after Paris peace negotiations reached impasse Dec. 18.

The Godfather, directed by Francis Ford Coppola, is released.

1973 In ***Roe v. Wade***, Supreme Court ruled, 7-2, Jan. 22, fetus not a person with constitutional rights and that right to privacy protected woman's decision to have abortion; states may not ban abortions during first three months of pregnancy but may regulate, not ban, abortions during second trimester.

Four-party **Vietnam peace pacts** signed in Paris Jan. 27. **End of military draft** announced on same day. Last U.S. troops left Vietnam Mar. 29. North Vietnam released some 590 U.S. prisoners by Apr. 1. Pres. Nixon announced, Apr. 30, resignation of top Nixon aides H. R. Haldeman and John Ehrlichman and firing of White House Counsel **John Dean** as a consequence of the widening **Watergate** scandal. Dean told Senate hearings June 25 that Nixon, his aides, and Justice Dept. had conspired to cover up Watergate facts. The U.S. officially ceased bombing in **Cambodia** at midnight Aug. 14 in accord with June congressional action.

Vice Pres. **Spiro Agnew**, Oct. 10, resigned and pleaded no contest to charge of tax evasion while Maryland governor. **Gerald R. Ford**, Oct. 12, became **first appointed vice president** under 25th Amendment; sworn in Dec. 6. The **"Saturday Night Massacre"** occurred Oct. 20, when Pres. Nixon ordered Atty. Gen. Elliot Richardson to fire Watergate special prosecutor **Archibald Cox**, who had sought handover of Nixon's subpoenaed **White House tapes**. Richardson refused to comply and resigned; Dep. Atty. Gen. William Ruckelshaus refused and was fired. Solicitor Gen. Robert Bork, as acting atty. gen., then fired Cox. Nixon administration named **Leon Jaworski**, Nov. 1, to succeed Cox.

Skylab, **first U.S. space station**, launched May 14. **Secretariat** became first Triple Crown winner since **Citation** in 1948 by winning Belmont Stakes June 9 in record time. **Billie Jean King** defeated Bobby Riggs in three straight sets in tennis's nationally televised "Battle of the Sexes," Sept. 20. Total **ban on oil exports** to U.S. imposed by Arab oil-producing nations Oct. 19-21 after outbreak of an Arab-Israeli war; lifted Mar. 1974. Congress overrode Nov. 7 Pres. Nixon's veto of **war powers bill** curbing president's power to commit forces to hostilities abroad without congressional approval.

1974 On Apr. 8, **Hank Aaron** of the Atlanta Braves hit his 715th career home run to break Babe Ruth's record.

House Judiciary Committee opened **impeachment** hearings May 9 against Pres. Nixon. John Ehrlichman and three **White House "plumbers"** found guilty July 12 of conspiring to violate the civil rights of the psychiatrist of **Pentagon Papers** leaker Daniel Ellsberg by breaking into psychiatrist's office. Supreme Court ruled, 8-0, July 24 that Pres. Nixon had to turn over 64 **audio tapes of White House conversations**. House Judiciary Committee, in televised hearings July 24-30, recommended **articles of impeachment** against Pres. Nixon, involving conspiracy to obstruct justice in Watergate cover-up, abuses of power, and defiance of committee subpoenas.

Pres. **Nixon** announced his **resignation**, Aug. 8, and stepped down the next day. His support in Congress had begun to collapse Aug. 5 after release of tapes appearing to implicate him in Watergate cover-up. Vice Pres. **Ford** sworn in Aug. 9 as 38th U.S. president. Pres. Ford, Aug. 20, nominated **Nelson Rockefeller** to be vice president; Rockefeller sworn in Dec. 10. Citing need to move on, Pres. Ford, Sept. 8, issued **pardon to Nixon** for any federal crimes he committed while president.

New York Times published article Dec. 22 on CIA engagement in illegal domestic surveillance. Reports of other apparently illegal CIA activities, recorded in **"family jewels"** file kept by the CIA, leaked out over the years.

1975 Former Atty. Gen. John Mitchell and ex-presidential advisers H. R. Haldeman and John Ehrlichman found guilty Jan. 1 of **Watergate cover-up** charges. Mitchell released 1979, last of 25 jailed over scandal to leave prison.

U.S. launched **evacuation from Saigon** of Americans and some South Vietnamese Apr. 29 as Communist forces completed takeover of South Vietnam; **South Vietnamese** government officially surrendered Apr. 30. U.S. merchant ship ***Mayaguez*** and its crew of 39 seized by Cambodian forces in Gulf of Siam May 12. In rescue operation, U.S. Marines attacked Koh Tang Island, recovered ship and crew but inadvertently left three Marines behind. Congress voted $405 mil for **South Vietnam refugees** May 16; 140,000 flown to U.S.

Publishing heiress **Patricia (Patty) Hearst**, kidnapped Feb. 5, 1974, by Symbionese Liberation Army (SLA), captured in San Francisco Sept. 18 with other militants. She was convicted Mar. 20, 1976, of bank robbery.

1976 In **right-to-die** case, New Jersey Supreme Court, Mar. 31, allowed comatose Karen Ann Quinlan to be removed from respirator; she survived until 1985. U.S. Supreme Court reinstated **death penalty**, July 2, subject to conditions.

U.S. celebrated **200th anniversary of independence** July 4 with festivals, parades, and New York City's Operation Sail, gathering of tall ships from around the world. **"Legionnaire's disease"** killed 29 people who attended American Legion convention July 21-24 in Philadelphia.

Viking I made successful landing on Mars, July 20. Two U.S. officers on routine mission near DMZ slain by **North Korean soldiers** Aug. 18; North Korea stated "regret."

1977 Convicted murderer Gary Gilmore executed by Utah firing squad Jan. 17; **first use of capital punishment** in U.S. since 1967. Pres. Jimmy Carter Jan. 21 pardoned most Vietnam War **draft evaders**.

Natural gas shortage caused by severe winter weather led Congress Feb. 2 to approve emergency gas bill temporarily authorizing reallocation from surplus areas. Pres. Carter signed act Aug. 4 creating new cabinet-level **Energy Dept.** FBI Dec. 7 released 40,000 pages of previously secret files relating to **Kennedy assassination**.

George Lucas's first ***Star Wars*** film released.

1978 Senate voted Apr. 18 to turn over **Panama Canal** to Panama on Dec. 31, 1999; Mar. 16 vote had given approval to treaty guaranteeing area's neutrality after the year 2000. Californians, June 6, approved **Proposition 13**, state constitutional amendment slashing property taxes.

Supreme Court, June 28, ruled that while race could be a factor in admission to institutions of higher education, **numerical quotas** could not be used.

Egyptian Pres. **Anwar al-Sadat** and Israeli Prem. **Menachem Begin** reached accord on "framework for peace," Sept. 17, after Pres. Carter-mediated talks at **Camp David**. New York's Chemical Bank Dec. 20 initiated industry-wide move to raise **lending rate** to near-record 11.75%.

1979 Partial meltdown released radioactive material Mar. 28 at nuclear reactor on **Three Mile Island** near Middletown, PA. American Airlines DC-10 **jetliner crashed** May 25 after losing an engine following takeoff from Chicago, killing 275 people.

In speech July 15, Pres. Carter spoke of national "crisis of confidence" and outlined proposed 10-year, $140-bil program to reduce **dependence on foreign oil**. Militant followers of **Ayatollah Khomeini** took hostage some 90 people, including 66 Americans, Nov. 4 at **American embassy in Tehran**, Iran. Khomeini demanded return of ailing former Shah Muhammad Reza Pahlavi to stand trial.

1980 Pres. Carter announced, Jan. 4, economic sanctions against USSR in retaliation for Soviet invasion of Afghanistan. At Carter's request, U.S. Olympic Committee voted, Apr. 12, against U.S. participation in **Moscow Summer Olympics**. At **Winter Olympics** in Lake Placid, NY, U.S. hockey team defeated Russian team Feb. 22 en route to gold medal in "miracle on ice."

Eight Americans were killed, Apr. 24, in ill-fated attempt to rescue hostages held by Iranian militants. **Mt. St. Helens**, in Washington state, erupted May 18. The blast, with others May 25 and June 12, left 57 dead. In sweeping victory, Nov. 4, **Ronald Reagan** (R) was elected 40th president, defeating incumbent Pres. Carter. Republicans gained control of Senate. Former Beatle **John Lennon** was shot and killed by Mark David Chapman, Dec. 8, in New York City.

1981 Minutes after Reagan's inauguration Jan. 20, 52 **American hostages in Iran** were freed after being held for 444 days. Pres. **Reagan** was shot and seriously wounded, Mar. 30, in Washington, DC; also seriously wounded were a Secret Service agent, a policeman, and Press Sec. **James Brady**. **John W. Hinckley Jr.** arrested, found not guilty by reason of insanity in 1982, and committed to mental institution.

1981: Pres. Ronald Reagan nominates Sandra Day O'Connor to be the first woman to serve on the U.S. Supreme Court.

World's **first reusable spacecraft**, space shuttle ***Columbia***, sent into space, Apr. 12. U.S. Centers for Disease Control, June 5, reported first cases of what became known as **AIDS**.

Air controllers went on **strike** Aug. 3; most were fired by Pres. Reagan after defying back-to-work order. Reagan signed into law Aug. 13 **tax-cut legislation**, expected to save taxpayers $750 bil over five years, largest tax cut to date. The Senate confirmed, Sept. 21, appointment of **Sandra Day O'Connor** as **first female Supreme Court justice**.

1982 The 13-year-old Justice Dept. lawsuit against **AT&T** was settled Jan. 8. AT&T agreed to give up 22 Bell System companies and was allowed to expand. **Equal Rights Amendment**, sent to states in 1972, defeated when deadline for ratification passed June 30 with support from only 35 of the 38 states needed. The economy showed signs of recovery from a **recession** that began in mid-1981, as Dow Jones Industrial Average hit 1,016.93 Oct. 13, its highest level in 18 months.

NFL strike ended Nov. 16 after 57 days when players and team owners settled with $1.6-bil pact. Singer **Michael Jackson**'s album *Thriller*, released Nov. 30, became monumental best-seller. Retired dentist Dr. Barney B. Clark became **first permanent artificial heart recipient**, Dec. 2; he died Mar. 23, 1983. The House, Dec. 16, cited EPA administrator Anne Gorsuch for contempt after she refused to release records relating to enforcement of **Superfund** law.

1983 Pres. Reagan, Jan. 3, declared Times Beach, MO, a federal disaster area because of toxic **dioxin** in soil, prompting evacuation of residents and town's closure. Harold Washington (D) elected Apr. 12 as **first black mayor of Chicago**. On Apr. 20, Pres. Reagan signed compromise bipartisan bill designed to save **Social Security** from bankruptcy.

Sally Ride became **first American woman to travel in space**, June 18, when space shuttle *Challenger* launched from Cape Canaveral, FL. On Sept. 1, **South Korean passenger jet** in Soviet air space and apparently misidentified was shot down; 269 people, including 61 Americans, killed.

On Oct. 23, 241 U.S. Marines and sailors were killed when TNT-laden **suicide truck bomb** blew up Marine barracks at Beirut International Airport in **Lebanon**. U.S. troops, with small force from six Caribbean nations, invaded **Grenada** Oct. 25; deposed Marxist regime.

1984 Seven regional companies took over **local telephone service** from AT&T, Jan. 1. On space shuttle *Challenger*'s fourth trip, launched Feb. 3, two astronauts became **first humans to fly free of a spacecraft**. On May 7, Vietnam War veterans reached out-of-court settlement with chemical companies in class-action suit over the herbicide **Agent Orange**.

Former Vice Pres. **Walter Mondale** won Democratic presidential nomination, June 6. He chose Rep. **Geraldine Ferraro** (D, NY) as vice presidential candidate, first woman to be nominated for position by major political party. Pres. Reagan signed bill July 17 cutting federal transportation aid to states that keep their **drinking age** under 21. Pres. **Reagan** reelected Nov. 6 in Republican landslide, carrying 49 states for record 525 electoral votes. **Bernhard Goetz** shot and wounded four allegedly menacing teenage boys on NYC subway train, Dec. 22; later acquitted of major charges but was successfully sued.

1985 Visiting Germany, Pres. Reagan, May 5, laid wreath at Bergen-Belsen Nazi concentration camp site and at military cemetery at **Bitburg**, where some Nazis were buried. Philadelphia police bombed a rowhouse occupied by **MOVE radical group**, May 13; 11 killed, and fire damaged two blocks of houses. On June 14, **terrorists seized TWA jet** after takeoff from Athens, Greece, with 153 passengers and crew. Thirty-nine Americans held hostage for 17 days; one U.S. service member killed.

Reversing an Apr. 23 decision to market "new" Coke, the **Coca-Cola Co.** said, July 10, it would resume marketing soda made under its original "Classic" formula. **Live Aid** rock concert broadcast around the world July 13, raised $70 mil for famine relief in Ethiopia.

On Oct. 7, four **Palestinian hijackers** seized Italian cruise ship ***Achille Lauro*** in the Mediterranean for two days. One American, Leon Klinghoffer, killed. For first time in six years U.S. and Soviet leaders met at **summit in Geneva**, Nov. 19-20. **General Electric** agreed Dec. 11 to buy RCA Corp.

1986 The U.S. officially observed **Martin Luther King Jr. Day** for first time Jan. 20. Space shuttle ***Challenger*** exploded 73 seconds after liftoff, Jan. 28, killing six astronauts and Teacher in Space Project participant Christa McAuliffe. In four-day extravaganza in July, the U.S. celebrated 100th birthday of the **Statue of Liberty**.

The Senate confirmed, Sept. 17, Reagan's nomination of **William Rehnquist** as chief justice and **Antonin Scalia** as associate justice of U.S. Supreme Court. Congress completed action Oct. 2 overriding a veto to place economic sanctions on **South Africa**. Lebanese newspaper first broke news of **Iran-Contra scandal** Nov. 3, involving secret U.S. sale of arms to Iran and diversion of some of the proceeds to support the Contras, a right-wing, anti-Communist insurgent movement in Nicaragua.

Financier **Ivan Boesky** agreed Nov. 14 to pay $100 mil in fines and illicit profits for **insider trading**. Robert Penn Warren named America's **first poet laureate**.

1987 Pres. Reagan produced nation's **first trillion-dollar budget**, Jan. 5. FDA approved, Mar. 20, AZT—first drug shown to be effective in fight against **AIDS**. Nearly 1.4 mil **illegal aliens** met May 4 deadline for applying for amnesty under immigration measure passed in 1986.

Joint public hearings by Senate and House committees investigating **Iran-Contra affair** opened May 5. Lt. Col. **Oliver North**, former National Security Council staff member, said he had believed all his activities were authorized by his superiors. Hearings ended Aug. 3. Pres. Reagan, Aug. 12, denied knowing of diversion of funds to Contras.

An **Iraqi missile** killed 37 sailors on the USS *Stark* in the Persian Gulf, May 17. Iraq called it an accident. The 200th anniversary of **U.S. Constitution** signing was observed, Sept. 17, in Philadelphia and around the U.S. **Stock market crashed**, Oct. 19, with the Dow Jones industrial average plummeting a then-record 508 points to 1,738, ending bull market that began mid-1982. Pres. Reagan and Soviet leader Mikhail Gorbachev Dec. 8, signed **pact to dismantle** all 1,752 U.S. and 859 Soviet intermediate- and shorter-range (300-3,400 mi) missiles.

1988 *Phantom of the Opera* opened Jan. 26; it would go on to be longest-running Broadway play ever. In report issued May 16, Surgeon Gen. C. Everett Koop declared **cigarettes addictive**. Congress approved, in June, expansion of **Medicare** benefits to protect against "catastrophic" medical costs; act was repealed in Nov. 1989.

A missile, fired from U.S. Navy warship *Vincennes* in the Persian Gulf, mistakenly struck a commercial **Iranian airliner**, July 3, killing all 290 aboard. **George H. W. Bush** (R) elected 41st U.S. president, Nov. 8, decisively defeating Massachusetts Gov. **Michael Dukakis** (D). **Pan Am Flight 103** exploded and crashed, due to terrorist bomb, into town of Lockerbie, Scotland, Dec. 21, killing all 259 people aboard and 11 on the ground. Investment firm **Drexel Burnham Lambert** agreed, Dec. 21, to plead guilty to insider trading and other violations, and pay penalties of $650 mil. U.S. suffered widespread **drought** conditions, the worst in over 50 years.

1989 Major oil spill occurred when ***Exxon Valdez*** struck Bligh Reef in Alaska's Prince William Sound, Mar. 24. Oliver North convicted, May 4, on charges related to **Iran-Contra scandal**. Conviction thrown out on appeal in 1991 because of his immunized testimony. TV comedy series ***Seinfeld*** premiered July 5 on NBC.

A measure to rescue **savings and loan industry** signed into law, Aug. 9, by Pres. Bush, launching largest federal rescue to date. Army Gen. **Colin Powell** became **first black chairman of Joint Chiefs of Staff** after being nominated Aug. 10 by Pres. Bush.

Baseball legend **Pete Rose** banned from game for life Aug. 24 for involvement with gamblers. **Hurricane Hugo** swept through the Carolinas Sept. 22, causing at least 86 deaths and $7 bil damage. An **earthquake** struck the San Francisco Bay area just before a World Series game, Oct. 17, causing 63 deaths.

L. Douglas Wilder (D) declared governor of Virginia Nov. 27, **first elected black governor** in U.S. history. U.S. troops invaded Panama, Dec. 20, overthrowing the government of **Manuel Noriega**. Noriega, wanted by U.S. authorities on drug charges, surrendered Jan. 3, 1990.

1990 Junk bond financier **Michael Milken** pleaded guilty to fraud-related charges, Apr. 14; agreed to pay $500 mil in restitution and sentenced Nov. 21 to 10 years in prison. Pres. Bush signed **Americans With Disabilities Act** barring discrimination against and requiring accommodations for the disabled, July 26.

Operation Desert Shield forces left for Saudi Arabia Aug. 7 to defend that country following invasion of **Kuwait** by Iraq, Aug. 2. David Souter confirmed Sept. 27 to serve on Supreme Court, replacing retiring Justice **William Brennan**. Pres. Bush Nov. 15 signed new **Clean Air Act**, focused on urban pollution, cancer-causing emissions from industrial sources.

1991 The U.S. and its allies defeated Iraq in **Persian Gulf War** and liberated Kuwait, which Iraq had invaded. On Jan. 17, the allies launched devastating air attacks, followed by rapid ground war starting Feb. 24. Pres. Bush ordered cease-fire Feb. 27.

An 8-month **recession** showed signs of having ended in Mar. The **Dow Jones** industrial average closed above 3,000 for first time, Apr. 17. Justice **Thurgood Marshall** announced, June 17, plans to retire. Senate, voting 52-48 on Oct. 15, confirmed nomination of **Clarence Thomas** to replace Marshall, after contentious hearings marked by allegations that Thomas had sexually harassed former aide Anita Hill. House Speaker Tom Foley announced Oct. 3 closure of **House Bank** by end of year after revelations that House members had written numerous bad checks.

1992 Retail giant **R.H. Macy & Co.** filed for bankruptcy, Jan. 27. Major U.S. carrier Trans World Airlines (**TWA**) filed for bankruptcy, Jan. 31. **Riots** swept South Central Los Angeles Apr. 29 after jury acquitted four white police officers on all but one count in 1991 videotaped beating of black motorist **Rodney King**. Death toll in L.A. violence was put at 53. **27th Amendment**, regarding congressional pay raises, ratified May 7.

Hurricane Andrew ravaged South Florida and Louisiana Aug. 24-26, causing 65 deaths. White supremacist and fugitive Randall Weaver surrendered Aug. 31 after 11-day **FBI siege** at his **Ruby Ridge**, ID, cabin, during which his wife, son, and a deputy sheriff were killed.

Bill Clinton (D) elected 42nd president, Nov. 3, defeating Pres. Bush (R) and independent Ross Perot. A UN-sanctioned military force, led by U.S. troops, arrived in **Somalia** Dec. 9. Presidents of U.S., Canada, and Mexico Dec. 17 signed North American Free Trade Agreement (**NAFTA**), which took effect Jan. 1, 1994.

1993 A bomb exploded in a parking garage beneath the **World Trade Center** in New York City, Feb. 26, killing six. Four men found guilty, Mar. 4, 1994. Four federal agents killed, Feb. 28, during unsuccessful raid on **Branch Davidian** compound near **Waco**, TX. A 51-day siege by agents ended Apr. 19

when the compound burned down, leaving more than 70 cult members dead. Eleven cult members acquitted Feb. 26, 1994, of deaths of federal agents.

Janet Reno became **first female attorney general** Mar. 12. Federal jury, Apr. 17, found two Los Angeles police officers guilty and two not guilty of violating civil rights of motorist **Rodney King** in 1991 videotaped beating.

In a May 14 plebiscite, voters in **Puerto Rico** supported continuing commonwealth status with U.S. **"Motor-voter" bill** signed by Pres. Clinton, May 20, easing voting procedures. **"Great Flood of 1993"** inundated parts of nine Midwestern states in summer, leaving about 50 dead and $15 bil in damages.

Pres. Clinton, July 2, approved recommendations that 33 major U.S. military bases be closed. On July 19 he announced **"don't ask, don't tell, don't pursue"** policy for homosexuals in the military. **Ruth Bader Ginsburg** sworn in, Aug. 10, as 107th Supreme Court justice, replacing retiring Justice **Byron White**. Pres. Clinton, Aug. 10, signed measure designed to **cut federal budget deficits** by $496 bil over five years, through spending cuts and new taxes. **Brady Bill**, a major gun-control measure, signed into law by Pres. Clinton Nov. 30.

1994 A predawn **earthquake** in the Los Angeles area, Jan. 17, claimed 61 lives. Pres. Clinton Feb. 3 lifted 19-year ban on U.S. trade with **Vietnam**. Byron De La Beckwith convicted Feb. 5 of 1963 murder of civil rights leader **Medgar Evers**. Longtime CIA officer **Aldrich Ames** and his wife charged, Feb. 21, with spying for Russians. Under plea bargain, he received life in prison, while she drew 63 months.

U.S. troops, Mar. 25, officially ended peacekeeping and humanitarian aid mission in **Somalia**, begun in 1992. Congressional committees, late July, began **Whitewater hearings**. Kenneth Starr named Aug. 5 as independent counsel to probe Whitewater affair. Major league **baseball players** went on strike following Aug. 11 games. World Series canceled; strike ended Apr. 25, 1995. Senate Majority Leader George Mitchell (D, ME), Sept. 26, dropped efforts to pass Pres. Clinton's **health-care reform** package.

Republicans gained control of both House and Senate in Nov. 8 elections after many years of Democratic control. House speaker **Tom Foley** (MA) was among the defeated Democrats.

1995 Newt Gingrich (R, GA) elected U.S. House speaker. A bill to end Congress's exemption from federal labor laws, first in series of measures in Republicans' **"Contract With America,"** cleared Congress Jan. 17; signed into law Jan. 23. Pres. Clinton, Jan. 31, authorized $20-bil loan to **Mexico**. Last UN peacekeeping troops withdrew from **Somalia** Feb. 28-Mar. 3, with aid of U.S. Marines. In **Haiti**, peacekeeping responsibilities were transferred from U.S. to UN forces Mar. 31, with U.S. providing 2,400 soldiers.

Truck **bomb exploded outside Oklahoma City federal office building** Apr. 19, killing 168 people; antigovernment extremist Timothy McVeigh arrested as key suspect, Apr. 21. U.S. space shuttle *Atlantis* made first in series of dockings with Russian space station *Mir*, June 29-July 4. The U.S. announced July 11 it was reestablishing **relations with Vietnam**.

Ten Muslim militants convicted, Oct. 1, in failed **plot to blow up UN Headquarters**, other buildings and assassinate political leaders. Former football star **O. J. Simpson** found not guilty Oct. 3 of June 1994 murders of former wife, Nicole Brown Simpson, and a friend of hers. Hundreds of thousands of black men participated in **Million Man March** and rally in Washington, DC, Oct. 16, organized by Rev. Louis Farrakhan.

Five Americans among seven killed, Nov. 13, in **bombing** of U.S. military post in **Riyadh, Saudi Arabia**. Budget impasse between Congress and Pres. Clinton led to partial **government shutdown** Nov. 14; operations resumed Nov. 20 under continuing resolutions. After talks outside Dayton, OH, warring parties in **Bosnia and Herzegovina** reached agreement Nov. 21 to end their conflict; treaty signed Dec. 14, and U.S. peacekeeping troops arrived. A 1973 federal law imposing **55-mph speed limit** repealed Nov. 28.

1996 Senate, Jan. 26, approved, 87-4, Second Strategic Arms Reduction Treaty (**START II**) with Russia. Congress, Mar. 27-28, approved **line item veto**; struck down by Supreme Court, June 1998.

1995: The Murrah Federal Building in Oklahoma City is targeted in the deadliest act of domestic terrorism in U.S. history.

James and Susan McDougal convicted May 28 of fraud and conspiracy in **Whitewater** case; Arkansas Gov. Jim Guy Tucker (D) convicted on similar charges. The antitax **Freemen** surrendered to federal authorities June 13 after 81-day standoff near Jordan, MT; four were convicted, July 1998, of conspiring to defraud banks.

Bomb exploded at **Khobar Towers** military complex near Dhahran, Saudi Arabia, June 25, killing 19 American service personnel. Homemade pipe bomb exploded July 27 in **Atlanta**, GA, park during **Summer Olympics**; one person killed. Extremist Eric Robert Rudolph, arrested in May 2003, pleaded guilty to this and other bombings.

Major **welfare reform bill** signed into law, Aug. 22. Federal Defense of Marriage Act (**DOMA**), passed by wide margins and signed Sept. 21, barred federal recognition of same-sex marriages and permitted states to disregard same-sex marriages from other states. U.S. signed **Comprehensive Test Ban Treaty**, Sept. 24, which banned all nuclear weapons tests and explosions; Senate failed to ratify treaty. Pres. **Clinton reelected**, Nov. 5.

1997 Madeleine Albright sworn in as sec. of state Jan. 23, becoming first female State Dept. head. Former CIA official Harold Nicholson pleaded guilty, Mar. 3, to **spying for Russia**. Thirty-nine members of **Heaven's Gate** religious cult found dead in Rancho Santa Fe, CA, house Mar. 26, in apparent mass suicide.

Timothy McVeigh convicted of conspiracy and murder, June 2, in 1995 **Oklahoma City** bombing; executed June 2001. Co-conspirator Terry Nichols convicted Dec. 23 on related charges; later sentenced to life in prison. Two Islamic militants convicted, Nov. 12, of key roles in 1993 bombing of **World Trade Center**. The film ***Titanic***, released Dec. 14, went on to win 11 Oscars and gross over $600 mil.

1998 Media outlets reported Jan. 21 on evidence of sexual relationship between Pres. Clinton and former White House intern **Monica Lewinsky**. Clinton initially denied affair, but in grand jury testimony and address to the nation, Aug. 17, acknowledged relationship that was "not appropriate." On Sept. 9, independent counsel **Kenneth Starr** sent findings to House; the Judiciary Committee, Oct. 5, voted 21-16 to recommend full inquiry. House, Dec. 19, approved two articles of **impeachment** charging Clinton with grand jury perjury and obstruction of justice in cover-up.

"Unabomber" Theodore Kaczynski, arrested in Montana in 1993, pleaded guilty Jan. 22 to California and New Jersey bombings that killed three people; sentenced in May to four life terms plus 30 years. Texas, Feb. 3, executed its first female convict in 135 years.

Bombs at U.S. embassies in Nairobi, Kenya, and Dar es Salaam, Tanzania, killed at least 257, Aug. 7; U.S. launched retaliatory strikes, Aug. 20, against targets in Afghanistan and Sudan. On Sept. 30, Pres. Clinton announced federal **budget surplus** of $70 bil for fiscal 1998, first since 1969.

Pres. Clinton, Nov. 13, settled suit by agreeing to pay $850,000 to **Paula Jones**, who alleged he had made an unwanted sexual advance in 1991. Biggest U.S. **tobacco companies**, in settlement Nov. 23, agreed to pay states and territories $206 bil over 25 years to cover public health costs.

1999 ***The Sopranos*** TV drama debuted, Jan. 10. Pres. **Clinton** was acquitted, Feb. 12, at end of Senate impeachment trial. Perjury article failed with 45 votes; obstruction of justice article drew 50-50 vote, short of the needed two-thirds.

Dr. **Jack Kevorkian** convicted of second-degree murder Mar. 26 in death of terminally ill man. One man pleaded guilty Apr. 5, another convicted Nov. 4, in 1998 kidnapping and beating death of **Matthew Shepard**, an openly gay student at the Univ. of Wyoming.

Eric Harris, 18, and Dylan Klebold, 17, killed 12 fellow students and a teacher Apr. 20 at **Columbine High School** in Littleton, CO, then fatally shot themselves. **John F. Kennedy Jr.** killed in crash of private plane July 16.

2000 Across U.S., midnight celebrations marked changeover to year 2000 on Jan. 1; feared **Y2K** computer glitch caused few problems. Vermont Gov. Howard Dean (D) on Apr. 26 signed first state law recognizing same-sex **civil unions**. Scientists from U.S. and Britain announced jointly, June 26, that they had determined structure of the **human genome**.

Six-year-old **Elián González** was returned to father in Cuba June 28, seven months after rescue from boat wreck in which his mother and other refugees drowned. **Tiger Woods** became youngest player, at age 24, to win all four of golf's majors, with record score in British Open, July 23.

Food and Drug Administration announced, Sept. 28, approval of **RU-486**, a pill that induces abortions. Seventeen U.S. sailors died Oct. 12 in terrorist bombing of **USS *Cole***, which was refueling in Aden, Yemen.

On election night, Nov. 7, the winner of **Florida's electoral votes** remained uncertain, leaving national result in doubt. Florida Supreme Court, Dec. 8, ordered manual recount of certain ballots; on Dec. 12, U.S. Supreme Court reversed that decision, and Vice Pres. **Al Gore** (D), next day, conceded to Texas Gov. **George W. Bush** (R).

2001 **AOL-Time Warner merger** completed Jan. 11. FBI agent **Robert Hanssen** arrested Feb. 20, charged with spying for Soviet Union and Russia over 20-year period; under plea bargain, sentenced in 2002 to life in prison. **U.S. Navy spy plane** collided with Chinese fighter plane over South China Sea Apr. 1, killing fighter pilot; 24 U.S. crew members detained in Hainan until U.S. apology, Apr. 12.

Sen. **James Jeffords** (R, VT) May 24 left his party, giving Democrats control of Senate. Pres. George W. Bush signed, June 7, $1.35-tril tax-cut package. Bush announced Aug. 9 he would allow federal funding of limited research on existing **stem-cell** lines from human embryos.

On morning of **Sept. 11**, two hijacked commercial airliners struck **World Trade Center twin towers** in New York City in **worst-ever terrorist attack** on American soil. A third hijacked plane destroyed a portion of the **Pentagon**; a fourth crashed in a field near Shanksville, PA. Some 3,000 people were killed, including about 2,750 at World Trade Center. Five people died and 14 became ill from exposure to **anthrax** through U.S. postal system, Oct. 4-Nov. 21.

U.S. and Britain, Oct. 7, launched airstrike campaign against Afghan-based terrorist organization **al-Qaeda** and Afghanistan's ruling **Taliban** militia. Pres. Bush created **Office of Homeland Security**, Oct. 8, and on Oct. 26 signed USA **Patriot Act**, with wide-ranging provisions aimed at preventing terrorism. **Taliban** surrendered Kabul, Nov. 13, and fled from Kandahar, their stronghold, Dec. 7. U.S. government, Dec. 11, indicted al-Qaeda member **Zacarias Moussaoui** as Sept. 11 co-conspirator; he pleaded guilty, sentenced in May 2006 to life in prison. Operation in Afghanistan's **Tora Bora** cave complex, Dec. 12-17, failed to capture al-Qaeda leader **Osama bin Laden**.

Leading energy-trading company **Enron** filed for bankruptcy, Dec. 2. Pres. Bush announced, Dec. 13, U.S. withdrawal from **1972 Antiballistic Missile Treaty** with Russians.

2002 Taliban and al-Qaeda fighters captured in Afghanistan flown to U.S. naval base at **Guantánamo Bay** in Cuba, starting Jan. 11.

In State of the Union address, Jan. 29, Pres. Bush called Iran, Iraq, and North Korea part of **"axis of evil."** By Mar. 6, 1,200 U.S. troops were involved in **Operation Anaconda** against al-Qaeda and Taliban forces in Afghanistan. Independent prosecutor's report, Mar. 20, found insufficient evidence that Pres. Clinton or Hillary Clinton committed any crime in connection with **Whitewater**. Pres. Bush, Mar. 27, signed into law McCain-Feingold **campaign-finance reform bill** banning unregulated, unrestricted "soft money" donations; part of bill struck down by Supreme Court, June 2007.

Ceremonial last girder removed May 30 from **World Trade Center** site, signaling end of massive clean-up and recovery operation. **WorldCom** filed for bankruptcy, July 21.

"Shoe-Bomber" Richard Reid pleaded guilty Oct. 4 to all charges stemming from incident aboard plane in Dec. 2001; sentenced Jan. 2003 to life in prison. On Oct. 10-11 the House, 296-133, and Senate, 77-23, gave Bush backing to use military force against **Iraq**. Bush administration revealed Oct. 16 that **North Korea** had acknowledged developing nuclear arms. Bush signed measure, Nov. 25, creating cabinet **Dept. of Homeland Security**.

U.S. Catholic bishops, Nov. 13, approved revised policies dealing with priests who sexually abuse minors. Cardinal **Bernard Law**, accused of covering up sexual abuse by priests, resigned as archbishop of Boston Dec. 13. **Trent Lott** (R, MS) bowed out as new Senate majority leader Dec. 20 after remarks apparently supporting segregation.

2003 On Jan. 10-11, Gov. George Ryan (R) pardoned or **commuted death sentences** of all 171 on Illinois death row.

Space shuttle ***Columbia*** broke apart Feb. 1 during descent toward planned landing; all seven crew members killed. Report issued Aug. 26 blamed damage sustained during liftoff; also cited "broken safety culture" at NASA. Senate, Mar. 6, approved the **Strategic Offensive Reductions Treaty** (Moscow Treaty) for reducing nuclear stockpiles signed in 2002 by U.S. and Russian leaders.

U.S.-led military offensive aimed at ousting **Saddam Hussein** got underway Mar. 19, when 40 Tomahawk cruise missiles hit targets in Baghdad. U.S. forces Mar. 21 seized oil fields near Basra. By Apr. 9, U.S. forces reported control over much of Baghdad. Pres. Bush, speaking from aircraft carrier May 1, declared **end of major combat operations in Iraq**; insurgents continued to mount attacks.

Pres. Bush signed bill May 28 providing $330 bil in **tax cuts** over several years. A power failure caused **blackouts** affecting some 50 mil people, mostly in northeastern U.S. and Canada, on Aug. 14.

The Roman Catholic archdiocese of Boston agreed to pay up to $85 mil in **sex abuse settlement** announced Sept. 9. Californians, Oct. 7, voted to recall Gov. Gray Davis (D) and replace him with actor-turned-politician **Arnold Schwarzenegger** (R). Rev. V. Gene Robinson consecrated Nov. 2 as Episcopal Church's **first openly gay bishop**.

Senate, Nov. 3, approved $87.5 bil for **U.S. military forces in Iraq** and help rebuilding the country. Virginia jury, Nov. 17, found **John Muhammad** guilty in 2002 Washington, DC, area **sniper attacks** that killed 10; sentenced to death. Another Virginia jury found accomplice **Lee Malvo** guilty, Dec. 18; sentenced to life without parole.

Pres. Bush signed bill Dec. 8 to overhaul **Medicare**, adding prescription drug benefit and expanding role of private insurance companies. **Saddam Hussein captured** by U.S. forces Dec. 13, in underground hideout southeast of Tikrit.

2004 ***The Lord of the Rings**: The Return of the King* won 11 Oscars, Feb. 29.

Photos showing abuse of **Abu Ghraib prison** inmates in Iraq by American soldiers emerged Apr. 3. On May 17, as a result of a Nov. 2003 court decision, Massachusetts became the first state in which **same-sex marriage** was legal.

U.S.-led coalition transferred power to interim Iraqi government, June 28. **9/11 Commission Report**, released July 22, called for restructuring U.S. intelligence operations.

Boston Red Sox won World Series Oct. 27, for first time since 1918.

Pres. **Bush reelected** Nov. 2, with 286 electoral votes, defeating Sen. John Kerry (D, MA), with 251. Republicans increased majorities in Senate and House. Pres. Bush signed intelligence reform bill Dec. 17, creating a director of national intelligence.

2005 Two U.S. soldiers found guilty, Jan. 14, in **Abu Ghraib** prisoner abuses in Iraq and sentenced to prison terms.

Condoleezza Rice became first black woman sec. of state, Jan. 26. **Alberto Gonzales** became first Hispanic U.S. atty. gen., Feb. 3. **Terri Schiavo**, in a persistent vegetative state since 1990, died Mar. 31, 13 days after feeding tube was removed following legal battle.

Vanity Fair article revealed May 31 that former FBI official W. Mark Felt was **"Deep Throat"**—key source for *Washington Post* reporters Bob Woodward and Carl Bernstein probing 1972 Watergate break-in.

Hurricane Katrina hit Gulf coast, Aug. 29, causing devastation in Louisiana, Mississippi, and Alabama. Breaches in levees on Lake Pontchartrain, Aug. 30, flooded New Orleans. Relief efforts widely criticized as insufficient.

Chief Justice **William H. Rehnquist** died Sept. 3. Bush Sept. 5 nominated as successor **John G. Roberts Jr.**; on Sept. 29 he was confirmed by Senate, 78-22, and sworn in as 17th chief justice. On Oct. 31 Bush nominated **Samuel A. Alito Jr.** to replace retiring Justice Sandra Day O'Connor; confirmed Jan. 31, 2006.

House Majority Leader **Tom DeLay** (R, TX) indicted in Texas Sept. 28 on money laundering charges; later convicted.

New York Times, Dec. 16, reported that Pres. Bush in 2002 had secretly authorized National Security Agency to **eavesdrop without court warrant** on people in U.S. suspected of terrorist activities. Congress passed and Bush, Dec. 30, signed **anti-torture legislation**.

2006 Former top Republican lobbyist **Jack Abramoff** pleaded guilty Jan. 3 to bribery and other charges; in plea agreement, promised to cooperate with investigation into his dealings with members of Congress.

U.S. Supreme Court ruled June 29 that Pres. Bush's system for trying terrorism detainees at **Guantánamo Bay** was unauthorized under federal law and Geneva Conventions. Bush, July 19, issued his **first veto**, on bill to end funding constraints on human embryonic **stem cell research**.

British authorities announced Aug. 10 they had foiled terrorist plot to use **liquid explosives** on flights between Britain and U.S. Pres. Bush Sept. 6 confirmed existence of **secret overseas prisons** for terrorism suspects run by CIA. Bush signed bill Oct. 26 authorizing 700-mi fence along **U.S.-Mexico border**.

Democrats won control of House and Senate in **midterm congressional elections** Nov. 7. Pres. Bush announced Nov. 8 that Defense Sec. **Donald Rumsfeld**, a focus of criticism over Iraq war, had resigned.

2007 Rep. Nancy Pelosi (D, CA) chosen Jan. 4 as **first woman Speaker of the House**. On Jan. 10, Pres. Bush announced **troop "surge"** in Iraq, backed by Lt. Gen. **David Petraeus**, new top U.S. commander there.

Reports of substandard conditions at **Walter Reed Army Medical Center** in Washington, DC, led to ousters of military officials, Mar. 1-2. I. Lewis **"Scooter" Libby**, former chief of staff for Vice Pres. Cheney, found guilty Mar. 6 of perjury and obstructing justice in investigation into a leak exposing undercover CIA agent; Bush commuted sentence.

A senior at **Virginia Tech** killed 27 students and five faculty members on Apr. 16 before killing himself. On Apr. 18, Supreme Court upheld, 5-4, a 2003 federal law that banned so-called **partial birth abortions**.

U.S. Senate and House May 24 approved Iraq and Afghanistan **war-funding bill** with benchmarks for withdrawal of U.S. troops from Iraq; Congress also raised federal **minimum wage** from $5.15 to $7.25 per hour over two years.

Dow Jones industrial average closed over 14,000 July 19, just 59 trading days after passing 13,000. Pres. Bush issued an executive order July 20 banning any "cruel, inhuman, or degrading" treatment of **imprisoned terror suspects**. *Harry Potter and the Deathly Hallows*, final novel in J. K. Rowling's series, released July 21, earning record U.S. sales.

A **Minneapolis highway bridge** collapsed Aug. 1, causing the deaths of 13 people. Congress, Aug. 4, cleared measure allowing **National Security Agency** to monitor communications without court warrants if believed related to terrorism. Barry Bonds tied Hank Aaron's all-time career **home-run record** at 755 on Aug. 4 in San Diego; hit No. 756 on Aug. 7.

José Padilla convicted of conspiracy in terrorism case, Aug. 16; sentenced to 17 years, 4 months. Atty. Gen. **Alberto Gonzales**, blamed for alleged politically motivated firings of U.S. attorneys, announced resignation Aug. 27.

Report by former U.S. Sen. George J. Mitchell, released Dec. 13, presented evidence of **performance-enhancing drug use** by 86 Major League Baseball players.

Under law signed Dec. 17, New Jersey became the first state to **repeal the death penalty** since U.S. Supreme Court reinstated it in 1976. An energy bill mandating an increase in automobile **fuel-economy standards** to 35 mi per gallon by 2030 signed by Pres. Bush Dec. 19.

2008 Sen. **John McCain** (AZ) won New Hampshire primary, Jan. 8; clinched 2008 Republican presidential nomination by early Mar. Among Democrats, Sen. **Barack Obama** (IL) moved ahead of closest rival Sen. **Hillary Clinton** (NY) to clinch nomination in early June.

The Federal Reserve cut key interest rates, Jan. 22 and 30, to aid U.S. economy; $168-bil **economic stimulus** package, signed Feb. 13 by Pres. Bush, provided tax rebates.

In Mar. 18 speech, Sen. Obama discussed America's racial divide and condemned inflammatory rhetoric used by Rev. **Jeremiah Wright**, his former pastor.

U.S. Supreme Court ruled June 12 that foreign prisoners at **Guantánamo Bay** could legally challenge detention. **Oil prices spiked** above $140 per barrel in June; national average price for gallon of regular gas topped $4.

Sec. of State Condoleezza Rice signed agreements in Czech Republic, July 8, and Poland, Aug. 20, to place components of a U.S. **missile defense system** there (agreements rescinded by

2005: Hurricane Katrina and subsequent failure of levees cause unprecedented destruction in New Orleans.

Obama administration, 2009). Measure signed July 10 by Pres. Bush expanded government power to spy on suspected terrorists. U.S., Sept. 1, gave Iraqi forces security responsibilities in Anbar province, formerly center of a Sunni insurgency. U.S. airstrike in **Afghanistan** village, Aug. 22, killed up to 90 civilians.

Meeting Aug. 25-28, Democrats nominated **Obama** for president and Sen. **Joe Biden** (DE) for vice president. Meeting Sept. 1-4, Republicans nominated **McCain** for president and Alaska Gov. **Sarah Palin** for vice president.

With financial system in crisis, federal government Sept. 7 took control of mortgage finance companies **Fannie Mae** and **Freddie Mac**. A week later, investment titan **Merrill Lynch** agreed to sell itself to Bank of America for $50 bil, and **Lehman Brothers** declared bankruptcy after finding no buyer. The Fed Sept. 16 took control of insurance giant **AIG**, giving it a credit line that expanded to $144 bil by Oct. 31.

On Sept. 20, a Treasury Dept. plan was introduced to purchase up to $700 bil of **"toxic" mortgage-backed securities** to restore confidence. Legislation to implement Troubled Assets Relief Program (**TARP**) failed in the House, Sept. 29, sending Dow Jones industrial average down 778 points. Revised **bailout plan** passed Senate Oct. 1, 74-25, and House Oct. 3, 263-171; gave Treasury immediate access to half of $700 bil in TARP funds. On Oct. 21 Fed pledged $540 bil as a backup to protect money market funds.

Barack Obama elected, Nov. 4, as **first African-American president** in U.S. history, earning 53% of popular vote and 365 of 538 electoral votes. Democrats also increased majorities in House and Senate. California voters approved **Proposition 8**, banning same-sex marriages in the state.

U.S. government Nov. 23 announced plan to provide $20 bil in cash and up to $306 bil more as backup to protect ailing **Citigroup** from potential mortgage losses. Pres.-elect Obama Nov. 24 named **Timothy Geithner** to be treasury sec.; he was confirmed Jan. 26, 2009. The Dow dropped 7.7% Dec. 1 after reports that manufacturing had hit 26-year low and that U.S. economy fell into **recession** in Dec. 2007.

Pres.-elect Obama named former rival **Hillary Clinton**, Dec. 1, to be sec. of state (confirmed Jan. 2009). Illinois Gov. **Rod Blagojevich** (D) arrested Dec. 9, accused of seeking to sell Senate seat being vacated by Obama. Convicted in a state senate trial, he was removed from office, Jan. 2009. **Bernard Madoff** arrested Dec. 11 for **Ponzi scheme**; sentenced to 150 years in jail in guilty plea, June 2009. Fed, Dec. 16, cut benchmark interest rate to near zero. On Dec. 19, Pres. Bush announced that $17 bil in **TARP funds** would be used to help keep **General Motors** and **Chrysler** afloat.

2009 Treasury Dept., Jan. 15, gained access to remaining $350 bil in TARP funds; acted to prop up **Bank of America**.

Barack Obama inaugurated Jan. 20 as 44th U.S. president. He issued executive orders Jan. 22 restricting CIA interrogation practices and calling for closing of U.S. military prison at **Guantánamo Bay**, Cuba, within a year (closing blocked by Congress). Treasury Sec. Geithner, Feb. 10, outlined $2-tril program to stabilize banking and ease credit markets with **"stress tests"** for banks. Obama signed **stimulus** bill Feb. 17, with $212 bil in tax cuts and $575 bil in new spending; introduced $275-bil program Feb. 18 to aid homeowners.

Pres. Obama announced, Feb. 17, that U.S. would send 17,000 more troops to **Afghanistan** and said, Feb. 27, that most U.S. troops would be out of Iraq by Aug. 2010. **California** legislators, ending 15-week deadlock, closed $42-bil budget gap, Feb. 19; revised plan passed July 24.

Treasury Sec. Geithner, Mar. 23, introduced Public-Private Investment Program (PPIP), offering incentives to encourage purchases of **"toxic assets."**

Vermont, Apr. 7, became first state to pass a law allowing **same-sex marriage** without prior judicial mandate. Obama administration Apr. 13 eased restrictions on family travel and remittances to **Cuba**.

Justice Dept. Apr. 16 released memos offering legal rationale for CIA interrogation methods, including **waterboarding**. On Aug. 24, Atty. Gen. Eric Holder appointed special prosecutor to investigate **possible detainee abuse**.

After outbreak of influenza A (H1N1), or **swine flu**, in Mexico and then in U.S., U.S. officials declared public health emergency Apr. 26.

Chrysler LLC filed for bankruptcy protection Apr. 30; union given stake in reorganized company. Pres. Obama, May 19, tightened **fuel efficiency** standards for vehicles. **General Motors** filed for bankruptcy June 1, under plan providing new federal funds. On June 9, 10 financial firms got permission from U.S. Treasury to return some $68 bil in **TARP funds**.

George Tiller, Kansas doctor who performed **late-term abortions**, murdered May 31; anti-abortion activist was convicted Jan. 2010 and sentenced Mar. 2010 to life in prison.

Speaking June 4 in Egypt, Pres. Obama called for "new beginning" in relations with **Muslim world**. U.S. military completed **withdrawal from Iraq's cities** and towns June 30. Obama, June 22, signed measure to regulate content and marketing of tobacco products. Obama and Russian Pres. Dmitri Medvedev, July 6, agreed to reduce **nuclear arsenals** and to allow U.S. flights to Afghanistan through Russian airspace.

Short-term federal **"cash for clunkers"** program, for trading in old gas-guzzling vehicles, began July 24.

Judge **Sonia Sotomayor** confirmed Aug. 6 for U.S. Supreme Court vacancy left by retirement of **David Souter**; sworn in Aug. 8, she became first Hispanic to join the court.

Airport shuttle driver Najibullah Zazi charged, Sept. 24, with plot to produce bombs for **terror attacks** in the New York City subway system; he later pleaded guilty.

Government reported Oct. 29 that real GDP grew at 3.5% annual rate in July-Sept., signaling technical end of **recession**. However, **unemployment** in Oct. passed 10%. Pres. Obama Nov. 6 signed measure extending unemployment benefits and $8,000 tax credit for first-time homebuyers.

Pres. Obama announced Oct. 30 end to U.S. travel and immigration restrictions on people with **AIDS**. On Nov. 5, 12 soldiers and a civilian were killed in shooting at **Ft. Hood**, TX; Army Maj. Nidal Malik Hasan, shot and captured by SWAT team, later sentenced to death. Obama Dec. 1 announced a **surge** of 30,000 additional troops to **Afghanistan**. He received **Nobel Peace Prize** Dec. 10 in Oslo, Norway. Obama brokered **greenhouse-gas accord**, Dec. 18 in Copenhagen, establishing nonbinding reduction goals.

Detroit-bound airline passengers, Dec. 25, thwarted attempt by Nigerian man to ignite **explosives hidden in his underwear**. On Dec. 30, a Jordanian CIA informant acting as a double agent set off bomb at CIA meeting site near Afghan-Pakistan border, killing himself and eight others.

2010 On Jan. 19, state sen. **Scott Brown** (R) elected to U.S. Senate seat long held by Sen. Edward Kennedy (D, MA) and ended Democrats' filibuster-proof majority. U.S. Supreme Court Jan. 21 held that corporations and unions could spend unlimited funds on advertising to influence election outcomes.

U.S. and other coalition troops launched offensive in **Helmand Province**, Afghanistan, Feb. 13, targeting Taliban.

Pres. Obama, Mar. 18, signed $18-bil **job-stimulus** measure providing tax cuts and other employer incentives.

On Mar. 21, the House voted, 219-212, with no Republican support, to approve **"Obamacare"** health-care reform bill as passed by Senate in Dec. 2009. The wide-ranging, controversial measure, signed by Pres. Obama on Mar. 23, aimed in part at extending health insurance to millions of uninsured.

Meeting Apr. 8 in Prague, Pres. Obama and Russian Pres. Dmitri Medvedev signed New Strategic Arms Reduction Treaty, or **New START** (ratified by Senate Dec. 2010; in force Feb. 2011). On Apr. 15, Obama outlined plans for **NASA** to send manned missions to an asteroid by 2025 and to Mars by the mid-2030s; defended termination of Bush administration program to return astronauts to the Moon by 2020.

On Apr. 20, a gas explosion and fire engulfed ***Deepwater Horizon*** drilling platform off Louisiana coast, killing 11 people on board and damaging the ecology and state economy.

Arizona Gov. Jan Brewer (R), Apr. 23, signed controversial **immigration measure**. (Key provisions struck down by U.S. Supreme Court, June 2012.) New York City police May 1 dismantled **car bomb in Times Square**; suspect pleaded guilty to terrorism charges.

Pres. Obama May 10 nominated **Elena Kagan** to the U.S. Supreme Court to replace retiring Justice **John Paul Stevens**; confirmed by Senate, Aug. 5.

Obama June 23 named Gen. **David Petraeus** as commander in Afghanistan, replacing Gen. Stanley McChrystal, who was forced to resign after remarks he made criticizing administration were published. Ten **Russian agents** were arrested June 27 on spy charges; later exchanged for four Russians convicted of having ties to U.S. and UK intelligence agencies.

Goldman Sachs agreed July 15 to pay $550 mil to settle case, brought by the SEC, alleging it had duped investors. Obama signed major **financial reform measure**, July 21.

More than 75,000 Afghanistan documents, many of them classified, were published July 25 on website run by **WikiLeaks** and in some news outlets. U.S. had filed charges, July 6, against Army Pfc. Bradley Manning, arrested May 26 in connection with earlier WikiLeaks releases.

Last U.S. combat unit left Iraq Aug. 19 and Pres. Obama, Aug. 31, declared **U.S. combat mission in Iraq ended**; however, 50,000 troops remained in noncombat units.

Congress passed measures to **aid small businesses** with loans and tax breaks; signed into law Sept. 27. **TARP program** reached two-year mark Oct. 3, the day its authority to make new commitments expired. Treasury Dept. estimated net cost at $51 bil or less, though this figure was disputed.

In Nov. 2 elections **Republicans gained control** of the U.S. House but fell short in the Senate. The Fed Nov. 3 announced plan to buy $600 bil worth of Treasury securities in effort to stimulate sluggish economy.

Bipartisan presidential commission chaired by former Clinton chief of staff **Erskine Bowles** and former Sen. **Alan Simpson** (R, WY), released report, Dec. 1, calling for deep cuts in government spending and entitlements and for lowering taxes while closing loopholes, to stabilize national debt. Obama, Dec. 17, signed $858-bil compromise measure that extended **Bush-era tax cuts** for two years and **unemployment** insurance benefits for 13 months, while reducing Social Security payroll tax for one year. **"Don't ask, don't tell"** policy for gays in the military was repealed, Dec. 22.

2011 The 112th Congress convened Jan. 5; **John Boehner** (R, OH) elected House Speaker. Gunman in Tucson, AZ, Jan. 8, killed six people and injured 13 others, including Rep. **Gabrielle Giffords** (D, AZ); shooter Jared Loughner sentenced, Nov. 2012, to seven life terms plus 140 years.

Atty. Gen. Eric Holder disclosed Feb. 23 that the Obama administration would no longer defend in court the 1996 **Defense of Marriage Act**.

A measure to limit **collective bargaining** by most public sector employees, championed by Wisconsin Gov. **Scott Walker** (R), passed state legislature Mar. 9-10.

With federal government shutdown looming, congressional leaders reached agreement Apr. 9 on omnibus appropriations bill. Pres. Obama outlined plan, Apr. 13, to cut $4 tril from projected deficits over 12 years by cutting spending and raising taxes on the wealthy. Two days later, House approved budget resolution based on plan by Rep. Paul Ryan (R, WI). **Ryan plan** would cut both spending and taxes, replace Medicaid with block grants to states, and change Medicare into subsidized private insurance for new recipients. House plan defeated in Senate, May 25.

Former baseball slugger **Barry Bonds** was convicted Apr. 13 of obstructing justice in 2003 for evasive answers to a grand jury investigating banned **performance-enhancing drugs**. Pres. Obama Apr. 27 denounced rumors by so-called birthers; released copies of his **birth certificate**.

On May 2, in Abbottabad, Pakistan, a CIA-led squadron of U.S. Navy SEALs breached hideout of al-Qaeda leader **Osama bin Laden**, and killed him.

The single **deadliest U.S. tornado** in more than a half-century hit Joplin, MO, May 22, claiming about 160 lives. Congress cleared and Obama, May 26, signed measure extending key provisions of USA **Patriot Act**.

2011: The U.S. Justice Dept. stops defending the federal law that bans recognition of same-sex marriages; beginning in 2004, a growing number of states legalize the practice via court decisions, legislative action, and popular vote.

House rejected measure to raise federal **debt ceiling** without compensating deficit reductions May 31. Budget control act shaped by Vice Pres. Biden and Senate minority leader Mitch McConnell (R, KY) passed by bipartisan votes in Congress, Aug. 1-2. It called for raising the debt ceiling and some $900 bil in spending cuts, with an additional $1.5 tril in cuts to be worked out by supercommittee. Standard & Poor's, Aug. 5, downgraded nation's **credit rating**.

U.S. stepped up **drone attacks** against jihadists in Yemen after Pres. Ali Abdullah Saleh and others were wounded June 3 in a rocket attack.

After jury failed to reach a verdict on most counts in Aug. 2010, former Illinois Gov. **Rod Blagojevich** (D) was convicted in a retrial on 17 felony corruption charges June 27; sentenced Dec. 7 to 14 years in prison. **Bank of America**, June 29, agreed to pay $8.5 bil to cover investor losses on mortgage-backed securities issued by its Countrywide unit.

Gen. **David Petraeus** confirmed June 30 to replace **Leon Panetta** as CIA director; Panetta confirmed July 1 to replace retiring Defense Sec. **Robert Gates**.

NASA's **space shuttle** program ended with landing of the *Atlantis*, July 21. Taliban insurgents in **Afghanistan** shot down U.S. transport helicopter Aug. 6, killing 38 people, including 17 Navy SEAL commandos.

Atty. Gen. Eric Holder announced Aug. 30 the departure of two senior Justice Dept. officials who had overseen **Operation Fast and Furious**, a failed gun-trafficking sting operation. Obama, Sept. 8, proposed $447-bil economic **stimulus plan**, to be paid for by limiting tax breaks and raising taxes on high incomes.

A left-wing movement that began Sept. 17 as **Occupy Wall Street** in New York City expanded to demonstrations across the U.S. and overseas. **Anwar al-Awlaki**, a U.S. citizen and Muslim cleric linked to terrorist attacks in U.S., was killed Sept. 30 in U.S. drone attack in Yemen.

Formalities Dec. 12-15 marked the end of the U.S. military mission in **Iraq**. Last U.S. troop convoy left Dec. 18. Since 2003 U.S.-led invasion, nearly 4,500 U.S. service members had been killed and 32,000 wounded.

Averting new government shutdown, Congress Dec. 16-17 passed $915-bil omnibus measure to fund agencies through 2012 fiscal year. Congress Dec. 23 also approved temporary extension of a **payroll tax** break and benefits for long-term unemployed.

2012 Pres. Barack Obama Feb. 10 announced compromise **health insurance** mandate that avoided requiring religiously affiliated employers to directly provide contraceptive coverage. Congress voted Feb. 17 to extend **payroll tax cut** through 2012.

In settlement Mar. 2 between oil-and-gas giant **BP** and victims of 2010 ***Deepwater Horizon*** explosion in Gulf of Mexico, BP agreed to cover medical expenses and accept court administration of a $20-bil escrow fund. BP later pleaded guilty to criminal charges and agreed to pay $4.5 bil.

Former Massachusetts Gov. **Mitt Romney** took 6 of 10 primary contests on "Super Tuesday," Mar. 6. By May 29, he had clinched the 2012 GOP presidential nomination.

Obama became first sitting president to endorse same-sex marriage, in May 9 TV interview. Social networking giant **Facebook**'s initial public offering raised $16 bil May 18.

Wisconsin Gov. **Scott Walker** (R) easily survived June 5 recall election. Obama June 15 announced executive action ending deportation of qualified young undocumented immigrants.

Jerry Sandusky, former assistant football coach at **Penn State** Univ., was convicted June 22 in sexual abuse of 10 boys. NCAA, July 23, announced penalties against the university for covering up his actions although many were later overturned.

U.S. Supreme Court, June 28, upheld **Obamacare** penalties for those who do not obtain health insurance. Twelve people were killed July 20, in movie-theater shooting in Aurora, CO; James Holmes arrested and charged. A gunman in an apparent hate crime opened fire Aug. 5 at a Sikh temple in Oak Creek, WI, leaving six dead, before killing himself.

NASA rover ***Curiosity*** landed on Mars Aug. 6.

Mitt Romney and running mate Rep. **Paul Ryan** (WI) were nominated at GOP convention Aug. 27-30. Meeting Sept. 4-6, Democrats nominated the Obama-Biden ticket. Leftist magazine *Mother Jones* Sept. 17 posted a video, covertly recorded at a May 2012 fundraiser, in which Romney appeared to write off 47% of Americans as dependent on government handouts.

U.S. facility in **Benghazi**, Libya, was attacked by terrorists Sept. 11-12 and ambassador J. Christopher Stevens and three other Americans died; report released Dec. 18 blamed State Dept. for "grossly inadequate" security. The **Fed** announced Sept. 13 it would begin buying mortgage-backed securities.

An inspector general's report, Sept. 19, cited serious flaws in Justice Dept. gun-buying Operation Fast and Furious. On Oct. 22, **Lance Armstrong**, accused in doping scandal, was banned from cycling.

Hurricane Sandy made landfall in the U.S. Oct. 29, devastating coastal areas, and leaving over 200 dead.

Pres. Obama was reelected Nov. 6, with 51% of popular vote. Voters in Maine, Maryland, and Washington approved ballot measures to legalize same-sex marriage, becoming the first states to do so by popular vote. Colorado and Washington became the first to vote to allow recreational use of **marijuana**.

Retired Army Gen. **David Petraeus** resigned as CIA director Nov. 9 after an FBI cybercrime investigation uncovered an extramarital affair. Adam Lanza fatally shot 20 small children and six adults before killing himself Dec. 14 at **Sandy Hook** Elementary School in Newtown, CT.

With "fiscal cliff" of automatic budget cuts (sequestration) and expiring tax breaks looming as of Jan. 1, 2013, Vice Pres. Biden and Senate Minority Leader Mitch McConnell (R, KY) negotiated compromise, Dec. 30-31, to make Bush-era tax cuts permanent up to certain ceilings, while deferring possible sequestration to Mar. 1, 2013.

2013 The House (257-167) and Senate (89-8) passed measure to temporarily avert **fiscal cliff** Jan. 1. Pres. Barack Obama was officially sworn in for a second term, Jan. 20. In hearings before Congress Jan. 23, outgoing Sec. of State Hillary Clinton defended response to Sept. 2012 **Benghazi** attack in Libya. Defense Sec. Leon Panetta, Jan. 24, reversed policy barring women from combat missions. Sen. **John Kerry** (D, MA) was easily confirmed as secretary of state, Jan. 29. Senate Feb. 26 voted, 58-41, to confirm former Sen. **Chuck Hagel** (R, NE) as defense secretary. Sequestration took effect Mar. 1, triggering $1.2 tril in spending cuts to defense and domestic programs over 10 years.

2013: Bombs explode near the Boston Marathon finish line, killing three and injuring more than 260.

Two bombs at the **Boston Marathon**, Apr. 15, killed three spectators and injured 264. Surveillance video identified bombers as young Chechen immigrant brothers Dzhokhar and Tamerlan Tsarnaev. In shootout Apr. 18 with police, Tamerlan was shot, run over by a vehicle driven by his brother, and died; Dzhokhar was captured Apr. 19.

Lois Lerner, director of **IRS** division handling tax-exempt organizations, apologized May 10 for singling out groups with "Tea Party" or "patriot" in their names but denied political motivation. She was suspended May 23 after invoking Fifth Amendment before a House committee and later resigned.

Boy Scouts of America voted May 23 to let openly gay youths join troops.

The *Guardian* newspaper, June 5, disclosed details of a classified Natl. Security Agency surveillance program that monitored phone records and tracked emails and Internet activity. **Edward Snowden**, a contractor for the CIA, claimed responsibility for leaks after having left U.S.

U.S. Supreme Court, 5-4, June 25, struck down a key provision of the 1965 Voting Rights Act. In 5-4 decisions, June 26, the court struck down provision in the 1996 Defense of Marriage Act (**DOMA**) that denied federal benefits to same-sex couples, and let stand a lower court ruling throwing out California's ban on same-sex marriage.

A jury found **George Zimmerman** not guilty July 13 in the 2012 killing of **Trayvon Martin**, an unarmed black teenager, in Sanford, FL. Zimmerman, a neighborhood watch volunteer, claimed self-defense; widespread protests broke out after verdict.

Detroit filed for bankruptcy protection, July 18. Once-fugitive mobster **James "Whitey" Bulger** was found guilty of murder and other charges Aug. 12 in Boston; sentenced to life in prison.

A military judge Aug. 21 sentenced Army Pfc. **Chelsea Manning** (formerly Bradley Manning), Aug. 21, to 30 years in prison for releasing over 700,000 U.S. military and diplomatic documents to the **WikiLeaks** website. Army Staff Sgt. **Robert Bales**, who pleaded guilty to having killed 16 Afghan civilians, was sentenced to life Aug. 23.

A gunman killed 12 people at the **Navy Yard** in Washington, DC, Sept. 16; he was killed by responding police.

After Congress failed to produce a budget agreement, the **U.S. government partially shut** down Oct. 1, leaving some 800,000 federal workers on furlough or working without pay. With the public widely opposed to the shutdown, the Senate, Oct. 16, 81-18, approved a compromise measure and the House went along (285-144). Federal and state **health insurance exchanges** opened Oct. 1 in rollout of a signature Obama care feature, but the federal website was plagued by design flaws and technical glitches.

In elections Nov. 5, **Terry McAuliffe** (D) won Virginia governorship, and Gov. **Chris Christie** (R) was reelected in New Jersey; **Bill de Blasio** (D) was elected mayor of New York City. **JPMorgan Chase** agreed, Nov. 19, to $13-bil settlement of charges of deceptive practices in sales of troubled mortgages. Senate Nov. 21 approved a procedural change allowing most presidential nominations to advance by majority vote.

White House panel, Dec. 18, issued sweeping recommendations aimed at limiting **NSA surveillance** and increasing oversight. **Dow Jones** industrial average closed 2013 up 26.5%, its biggest yearly gain since 1995.

2014 Some two years after U.S. troop withdrawal, Sunni militants commonly known as the Islamic State of Iraq and Syria (**ISIS**) wrested control of Fallujah from Iraqi forces Jan. 3 and gained further ground in Iraq.

U.S. Senate Jan. 6 voted, 56-26, to confirm **Janet Yellen** as the first woman to serve as **Federal Reserve** chair. Documents published Jan. 8 implicated a senior aide to New Jersey Gov. Chris Christie (R) and another Christie appointee in closing lanes to the **George Washington Bridge** as political retribution.

In State of the Union address Jan. 28, Pres. Barack Obama stressed the aim of reducing income inequality. The Dow Jones industrial average Feb. 3 dropped 326 points, or 2.1%.

Obama Feb. 7 signed five-year **farm bill** that cut $16.6 bil from agricultural subsidies and food assistance.

After years of stalling, **General Motors**, Feb. 7, began a recall of vehicles with defects linked to at least 13 deaths (revised to more than 100 deaths as of 2015); GM was later fined $35 mil for delay. Toyota agreed Mar. 19 to a $1.2-bil criminal fine on charges that the company concealed information about defective parts.

Pres. Obama reported Apr. 1 that 7.1 mil people had signed up for coverage via state and federal health insurance marketplaces, a key component of **Obamacare**, despite federal website glitches and other issues that led to changes in deadlines and requirements. Health and Human Services Sec. **Kathleen Sebelius** announced her resignation Apr. 10; she had faced criticism for the bungled rollout. Office of Management and Budget director **Sylvia Mathews Burwell** was confirmed as her replacement in June.

A heavily armed man killed 6 people and injured 13 others near the Univ. of California-Santa Barbara, May 23. U.S. Army Sgt. **Bowe Bergdahl**, captured by the Taliban in 2009, was freed in a prisoner exchange May 31; the U.S. released five Taliban members from Guantánamo Bay.

Veterans Affairs Sec. **Eric Shinseki** resigned May 30 after revelations that VA hospitals had manipulated schedules to disguise long waiting times for patients; former Procter & Gamble CEO **Robert McDonald** confirmed to replace him in July. Congress July 30-31 passed a bill allowing veterans to receive treatment at non-VA hospitals under certain conditions.

Environmental Protection Agency, June 2, proposed new regulations requiring states to reduce **carbon dioxide emissions** from power plants by 2030. **Seattle** city council voted June 2 to raise city's **minimum hourly wage** to $15 over the next few years.

House Majority Leader **Eric Cantor** (R, VA) lost Republican primary June 10 to **Dave Brat**, a Tea Party-backed political novice. Party members elected majority whip **Kevin McCarthy** (R, CA) majority leader June 19.

ISIS militants captured most of **Mosul**, Iraq, June 10, as they expanded control of territory in Iraq and Syria; the group declared a **"caliphate"** June 29. Obama June 19 announced the U.S. would send up to 300 military advisers to Iraq.

U.S. Supreme Court ruled June 30 that "closely held corporations" could not be required to offer **contraceptive** coverage under Obamacare provisions against owners' religious beliefs.

U.S. State Dept. announced, July 26, it had evacuated embassy staff from Libya's capital; by late Aug, Islamist forces held the city. Pres. Obama Aug. 7 authorized airstrikes to disrupt ISIS operations in Iraq.

A white police officer shot and killed unarmed black 18-year-old **Michael Brown**, Aug. 9, in **Ferguson**, MO, precipitating sometimes violent protests; National Guard deployed. Grand jury declined to indict the officer Nov. 24.

ISIS released video Aug. 19 showing beheading of kidnapped American journalist **James Foley**; beheading of a second American journalist, **Steven Sotloff**, was shown in a video released Sept 2.

Bank of America agreed Aug. 21 to settlement on charges it had misled investors into buying toxic mortgage-backed securities preceding the 2008 financial crisis.

Obama Sept. 10 said he would expand U.S. airstrikes against ISIS in Iraq and Syria and send more noncombat personnel.

U.S. announced Sept. 16 it would send 3,000 military personnel to West Africa in response to **Ebola** epidemic. A man armed with a knife broke into the White House, Sept. 19, sparking congressional inquiry into security lapses; **Secret Service** Dir. Julia Pierson resigned Oct. 1.

U.S. Congress passed bill authorizing $500 mil to arm and train Syrian rebels; signed Sept. 19 by Obama. Afghan and U.S. officials signed agreement Sept. 30 providing for 9,800 American and at least 2,000 NATO troops to remain beyond formal end of combat mission in Dec. 2014.

The **Dow Jones** industrial average, Oct. 15, fell 460 points before rebounding to close down 173 points.

U.S. federal jury Oct. 22 convicted four former guards employed by **Blackwater** security firm (now known as Academi) in 2007 shootings that killed 17 Iraqi civilians.

2014: The fatal police shooting of black 18-year-old Michael Brown sparks protests in Ferguson, MO, and draws attention to racial disparities in treatment by law enforcement.

New York City's One World Trade Center, now tallest building in the Western Hemisphere, welcomed first tenants Nov. 3.

GOP gained control of Senate and strengthened hold on House in **midterm elections** Nov. 4. Republicans also won 24 of 36 gubernatorial races. Obama Nov. 7 approved an approximate doubling of U.S. noncombat military personnel in Iraq, to about 3,000. Labor Dept. announced Nov. 7 that the Oct. unemployment rate had dipped to 5.8%, lowest since July 2008.

Obama and Chinese Pres. **Xi Jinping** announced agreement Nov. 12 to reduce carbon outputs in effort to fight climate change.

ISIS Nov. 16 released video showing the beheading of U.S. aid worker **Peter Kassig**.

Obama Nov. 20 announced **executive actions on immigration** that could affect an estimated 4-5 mil undocumented immigrants. (A lawsuit challenging the orders by Texas and 25 other states was pending in 2015.)

House Intelligence Committee report, released Nov. 21, found no intelligence failure prior to 2012 **Benghazi** attack but concluded there was inadequate protection at the facility in Libya. Defense Sec. Chuck Hagel announced resignation Nov. 24; Obama named former Pentagon official **Ashton Carter** to replace him.

A grand jury decided Dec. 3 not to indict a New York City police officer for using a non-regulation chokehold on detainee **Eric Garner**, who died in custody; protests broke out in New York City and other cities, turning violent in some. A black man shot and killed two New York City police officers in their patrol car, Dec. 20, then killed himself.

Senate Intelligence Committee report released Dec. 9 concluded that the CIA's use of **enhanced interrogation techniques** in secret overseas prisons was ineffective in uncovering unique lifesaving information and more brutal than acknowledged.

A $1.1-tril **appropriations bill** funding most of the federal government through fiscal year 2015 passed the House (219-206) and Senate (56-40); signed by Obama Dec. 16. Separate resolution funded Dept. of Homeland Security only through Feb. 27, 2015, in face of opposition over Obama's immigration actions.

Hackers gained access to Sony Pictures Entertainment data and, Dec. 16, threatened violence against U.S. theaters that showed ***The Interview***, a comedy about plot to assassinate North Korean dictator **Kim Jong Un**.

Pres. Obama and Cuban Pres. **Raúl Castro** Dec. 17 announced that their two countries would work to reestablish diplomatic relations, broken since 1959 Communist takeover.

A U.S.-led operation and multinational NATO alliance formally ended combat missions in **Afghanistan** Dec. 28 after over 13 years; 2,215 Americans had been killed and more than 20,000 wounded there since Oct. 2001. U.S. monthly **oil prices** fell to five-year-low by Dec. 31. The **Dow Jones** industrial average closed up 7.5%, in sixth straight year of growth.

Patrick Henry's Speech to the Virginia Convention

The following is an excerpt from Patrick Henry's speech to the Virginia Convention, which met at St. John's Church in Richmond, on Mar. 23, 1775, to react to British oppression.

Gentlemen may cry, peace, peace—but there is no peace. The war is actually begun! The next gale that sweeps from the north will bring to our ears the clash of resounding arms! Our brethren are already in the field! Why stand we here idle? What is it that gentlemen wish? What would they have? Is life so dear, or peace so sweet, as to be purchased at the price of chains and slavery? Forbid it, Almighty God! I know not what course others may take; but as for me, give me liberty, or give me death!

Adoption of the Declaration of Independence

On June 7, 1776, Richard Henry Lee, who had issued the first call for a congress of the colonies, introduced in the Continental Congress at Philadelphia a resolution declaring "that these United Colonies are, and of right ought to be, free and independent states, that they are absolved from all allegiance to the British Crown, and that all political connection between them and the state of Great Britain is, and ought to be, totally dissolved."

The resolution, seconded by John Adams on behalf of the Massachusetts delegation, came up again June 11 when a committee of five chaired by Thomas Jefferson (VA) was appointed to express the purpose of the resolution in a declaration of independence. The other four were John Adams, Benjamin Franklin (PA), Robert R. Livingston (NY), and Roger Sherman (CT).

Drafting the Declaration was assigned to Jefferson, who worked on a portable desk of his own construction in a room at Market and 7th St. The committee reported the result on June 28, 1776. The members of the Congress suggested a number of changes, which Jefferson called "deplorable." They did not approve Jefferson's arraignment of the British people and King George III for encouraging and fostering the slave trade, which Jefferson called "an execrable commerce." They eliminated 630 words and added 146, leaving 1,322 words in the final draft. In its final form, capitalization was erratic. Jefferson had written that men were endowed with "inalienable" rights; in the final copy it came out as "unalienable" and has been thus ever since.

The Lee-Adams resolution of independence was adopted by 12 yeas on July 2—the actual date of the act of independence. The Declaration, which explains the act, was adopted July 4.

After the Declaration was adopted, July 4, 1776, it was turned over to printer John Dunlap to be printed on broadsides. The original copy was lost and one of his broadsides was attached to a page in the journal of the Congress. It was read aloud July 8 in Philadelphia; Easton, PA; and Trenton, NJ. On July 9, it was read by order of Gen. George Washington to the troops assembled on the Common in New York City (now City Hall Park).

The Continental Congress of July 19, 1776, adopted the following resolution:

"Resolved, That the Declaration passed on the 4th, be fairly engrossed on parchment with the title and stile of 'The Unanimous Declaration of the thirteen United States of America' and that the same, when engrossed, be signed by every member of Congress." (Engrossing meant clearly writing out an official document.)

Not all delegates who signed the engrossed Declaration had been present on July 4. Among them were Robert Morris (PA), William Williams (CT), and Samuel Chase (MD), who signed on Aug. 2. Oliver Wolcott (CT), George Wythe (VA), Richard Henry Lee (VA), and Elbridge Gerry (MA) signed in Aug. and Sept.; Matthew Thornton (NH) joined the Congress Nov. 4 and signed later. Thomas McKean (DE) rejoined Washington's army before signing and said later that he signed in 1781.

Charles Carroll of Carrollton was appointed a delegate by Maryland on July 4, 1776, presented his credentials July 18, and signed the engrossed Declaration on Aug. 2. Born Sept. 19, 1737, he was 95 years old and the last surviving signer when he died Nov. 14, 1832.

Two Pennsylvania delegates who did not support the Declaration July 4, 1776, were replaced. The four New York delegates did not have authority from their state to vote on July 4. On July 9, the New York state convention authorized its delegates to approve the Declaration, and the Congress was so notified on July 15, 1776. The four signed the Declaration on Aug. 2.

Declaration of Independence

The Declaration of Independence was adopted by the Continental Congress in Philadelphia on July 4, 1776. John Hancock was president of the Congress, and Charles Thomson was secretary. A copy of the Declaration, engrossed (i.e., written in a clear hand) on parchment, was signed by members of Congress on and after Aug. 2, 1776. On Jan. 18, 1777, Congress ordered that "an authenticated copy, with the names of the members of Congress subscribing the same, be sent to each of the United States, and that they be desired to have the same put on record." Authenticated copies were printed in broadside form in Baltimore, where the Continental Congress was then in session. The following text is that of the original printed by John Dunlap in Philadelphia for the Continental Congress. The original is on display at the National Archives in Washington, DC.

In CONGRESS, July 4, 1776.
A DECLARATION
By the REPRESENTATIVES of the UNITED STATES OF AMERICA, In GENERAL CONGRESS assembled.

When in the Course of human Events, it becomes necessary for one People to dissolve the Political Bands which have connected them with another, and to assume among the Powers of the Earth, the separate and equal Station to which the Laws of Nature and of Nature's God entitle them, a decent Respect to the Opinions of Mankind requires that they should declare the causes which impel them to the Separation.

We hold these Truths to be self-evident, that all Men are created equal, that they are endowed by their Creator with certain unalienable Rights, that among these are Life, Liberty, and the Pursuit of Happiness—That to secure these Rights, Governments are instituted among Men, deriving their just Powers from the Consent of the Governed, that whenever any Form of Government becomes destructive of these Ends, it is the Right of the People to alter or to abolish it, and to institute new Government, laying its Foundation on such Principles, and organizing its Powers in such Form, as to them shall seem most likely to effect their Safety and Happiness. Prudence, indeed, will dictate that Governments long established should not be changed for light and transient Causes; and accordingly all Experience hath shewn, that Mankind are more disposed to suffer, while Evils are sufferable, than to right themselves by abolishing the Forms to which they are accustomed. But when a long Train of Abuses and Usurpations, pursuing invariably the same Object, evinces a Design to reduce them under absolute Despotism, it is their Right, it is their Duty, to throw off such Government, and to provide new Guards for their future Security. Such has been the patient Sufferance of these Colonies; and such is now the Necessity which constrains them to alter their former Systems of Government. The History of the present King of Great Britain is a History of repeated Injuries and Usurpations, all having in direct Object the Establishment of an absolute Tyranny over these States. To prove this, let Facts be submitted to a candid World.

He has refused his Assent to Laws, the most wholesome and necessary for the public Good.

He has forbidden his Governors to pass Laws of immediate and pressing Importance, unless suspended in their Operation till his Assent should be obtained; and when so suspended, he has utterly neglected to attend to them.

He has refused to pass other Laws for the Accommodation of large Districts of People, unless those People would relinquish the Right of Representation in the Legislature, a Right inestimable to them, and formidable to Tyrants only.

He has called together Legislative Bodies at Places unusual, uncomfortable, and distant from the Depository of their Public Records, for the sole Purpose of fatiguing them into Compliance with his Measures.

He has dissolved Representative Houses repeatedly, for opposing with manly Firmness his Invasions on the Rights of the People.

He has refused for a long Time, after such Dissolutions, to cause others to be elected; whereby the Legislative Powers, incapable of Annihilation, have returned to the People at large for their exercise; the State remaining in the mean time exposed to all the Dangers of Invasion from without, and Convulsions within.

He has endeavoured to prevent the Population of these States; for that Purpose obstructing the Laws for Naturalization of Foreigners; refusing to pass others to encourage their Migrations hither, and raising the Conditions of new Appropriations of Lands.

He has obstructed the Administration of Justice, by refusing his Assent to Laws for establishing Judiciary Powers.

He has made Judges dependent on his Will alone, for the Tenure of their Offices, and the Amount and payment of their Salaries.

He has erected a Multitude of new Offices, and sent hither Swarms of Officers to harrass our People, and eat out their Substance.

He has kept among us, in Times of Peace, Standing Armies, without the consent of our Legislatures.

He has affected to render the Military independent of, and superior to the Civil Power.

He has combined with others to subject us to a Jurisdiction foreign to our Constitution, and unacknowledged by our Laws; giving his Assent to their Acts of pretended Legislation:

For Quartering large bodies of armed troops among us:

For protecting them, by a mock Trial, from Punishment for any Murders which they should commit on the Inhabitants of these States:

For cutting off our Trade with all Parts of the World:

For imposing Taxes on us without our Consent:

For depriving us, in many Cases, of the Benefits of Trial by Jury:

For transporting us beyond Seas to be tried for pretended Offences:

For abolishing the free System of English Laws in a neighbouring Province, establishing therein an arbitrary Government, and enlarging its Boundaries, so as to render it at once an Example and fit Instrument for introducing the same absolute Rule into these Colonies:

For taking away our Charters, abolishing our most valuable Laws, and altering fundamentally the Forms of our Governments:

For suspending our own Legislatures, and declaring themselves invested with Power to legislate for us in all Cases whatsoever.

He has abdicated Government here, by declaring us out of his Protection and waging War against us.

He has plundered our Seas, ravaged our Coasts, burnt our towns, and destroyed the Lives of our People.

He is, at this Time, transporting large Armies of foreign Mercenaries to complete the works of Death, Desolation, and Tyranny, already begun with circumstances of Cruelty

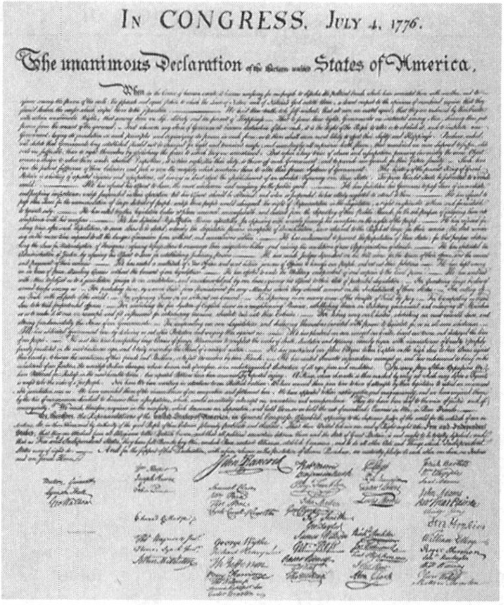
IN CONGRESS, JULY 4, 1776.

The unanimous Declaration of the thirteen united States of America,

John Hancock

and Perfidy, scarcely paralleled in the most barbarous Ages, and totally unworthy the Head of a civilized Nation.

He has constrained our fellow Citizens taken Captive on the high Seas to bear Arms against their Country, to become the Executioners of their Friends and Brethren, or to fall themselves by their Hands.

He has excited domestic Insurrections amongst us, and has endeavoured to bring on the Inhabitants of our Frontiers, the merciless Indian Savages, whose known Rule of Warfare, is an undistinguished Destruction, of all Ages, Sexes and Conditions.

In every stage of these Oppressions we have Petitioned for Redress in the most humble Terms: Our repeated Petitions have been answered only by repeated Injury. A Prince, whose Character is thus marked by every act which may define a Tyrant, is unfit to be the Ruler of a free People.

Nor have we been wanting in Attentions to our British Brethren. We have warned them from Time to Time of Attempts by their Legislature to extend an unwarrantable Jurisdiction over us. We have reminded them of the Circumstances of our Emigration and Settlement here. We have appealed to their native Justice and Magnanimity, and we have conjured them by the Ties of our common Kindred to disavow these Usurpations, which, would inevitably interrupt our Connections and Correspondence. They too have been deaf to the Voice of Justice and of Consanguinity. We must, therefore, acquiesce in the Necessity, which denounces our Separation, and hold them, as we hold the rest of Mankind, Enemies in War, in Peace, Friends.

We, therefore, the Representatives of the UNITED STATES OF AMERICA, in General Congress, Assembled, appealing to the Supreme Judge of the World for the Rectitude of our Intentions, do, in the Name, and by Authority of the good People of these Colonies, solemnly Publish and Declare, That these United Colonies are, and of Right ought to be, Free and Independent States; that they are absolved from all Allegiance to the British Crown, and that all political Connection between them and the State of Great Britain, is and ought to be totally dissolved; and that as Free and Independent States, they have full Power to levy War, conclude Peace, contract Alliances, establish Commerce, and to do all other Acts and Things which Independent States may of right do. And for the support of this declaration, with a firm Reliance on the Protection of Divine Providence, we mutually pledge to each other our lives, our Fortunes, and our sacred Honor.

JOHN HANCOCK, President.

Attest.

CHARLES THOMSON, Secretary.

Signers of the Declaration of Independence

Delegate (state)	Occupation	Birthplace	Born	Died
Adams, John (MA)	Lawyer	Braintree (Quincy), MA	Oct. 30, 1735	July 4, 1826
Adams, Samuel (MA)	Political leader	Boston, MA	Sept. 27, 1722	Oct. 2, 1803
Bartlett, Josiah (NH)	Physician, judge	Amesbury, MA	Nov. 21, 1729	May 19, 1795
Braxton, Carter (VA)	Farmer	Newington Plantation, VA	Sept. 10, 1736	Oct. 10, 1797
Carroll, Charles, of Carrollton (MD)	Merchant	Annapolis, MD	Sept. 19, 1737	Nov. 14, 1832
Chase, Samuel (MD)	Judge	Princess Anne, MD	Apr. 17, 1741	June 19, 1811
Clark, Abraham (NJ)	Surveyor	Elizabethtown, NJ	Feb. 15, 1726	Sept. 15, 1794
Clymer, George (PA)	Merchant	Philadelphia, PA	Mar. 16, 1739	Jan. 23, 1813
Ellery, William (RI)	Lawyer	Newport, RI	Dec. 22, 1727	Feb. 15, 1820
Floyd, William (NY)	Soldier	Brookhaven, NY	Dec. 17, 1734	Aug. 4, 1821
Franklin, Benjamin (PA)	Printer, publisher	Boston, MA	Jan. 17, 1706	Apr. 17, 1790
Gerry, Elbridge (MA)	Merchant	Marblehead, MA	July 17, 1744	Nov. 23, 1814
Gwinnett, Button (GA)	Merchant	Gloucester, England	c. 1735	May 19, 1777
Hall, Lyman (GA)	Physician	Wallingford, CT	Apr. 12, 1724	Oct. 19, 1790
Hancock, John (MA)	Merchant	Braintree (Quincy), MA	Jan. 12, 1737	Oct. 8, 1793
Harrison, Benjamin (VA)	Farmer	Charles City County, VA	Apr. 5, 1726	Apr. 24, 1791
Hart, John (NJ)	Farmer	Stonington, CT	c. 1711	May 11, 1779
Hewes, Joseph (NC)	Merchant	Kingston, NJ	Jan. 23, 1730	Nov. 10, 1779
Heyward, Thomas, Jr. (SC)	Lawyer, farmer	St. Luke's Parish, SC	July 28, 1746	Mar. 6, 1809
Hooper, William (NC)	Lawyer	Boston, MA	June 17, 1742	Oct. 14, 1790
Hopkins, Stephen (RI)	Judge, educator	Providence, RI	Mar. 7, 1707	July 13, 1785
Hopkinson, Francis (NJ)	Judge, author	Philadelphia, PA	Oct. 2, 1737	May 9, 1791
Huntington, Samuel (CT)	Judge	Windham, CT	July 3, 1731	Jan. 5, 1796
Jefferson, Thomas (VA)	Lawyer	Shadwell, VA	Apr. 13, 1743	July 4, 1826
Lee, Francis Lightfoot (VA)	Farmer	Westmoreland County, VA	Oct. 14, 1734	Jan. 11, 1797
Lee, Richard Henry (VA)	Farmer	Westmoreland County, VA	Jan. 20, 1732	June 19, 1794
Lewis, Francis (NY)	Merchant	Llandaff, Wales	Mar. 21, 1713	Dec. 31, 1802
Livingston, Philip (NY)	Merchant	Albany, NY	Jan. 15, 1716	June 12, 1778
Lynch, Thomas, Jr. (SC)	Farmer	Winyah, SC	Aug. 5, 1749	(at sea) 1779
McKean, Thomas (DE)	Lawyer	New London, PA	Mar. 19, 1734	June 24, 1817
Middleton, Arthur (SC)	Farmer	Charleston, SC	June 26, 1742	Jan. 1, 1787
Morris, Lewis (NY)	Farmer	Morrisania (Bronx County), NY	Apr. 8, 1726	Jan. 22, 1798
Morris, Robert (PA)	Merchant	Liverpool, England	Jan. 31, 1734	May 8, 1806
Morton, John (PA)	Judge	Ridley, PA	c. 1724	Apr. 1777
Nelson, Thomas, Jr. (VA)	Farmer	Yorktown, VA	Dec. 26, 1738	Jan. 4, 1789
Paca, William (MD)	Judge	Abingdon, MD	Oct. 31, 1740	Oct. 23, 1799
Paine, Robert Treat (MA)	Judge	Boston, MA	Mar. 11, 1731	May 12, 1814
Penn, John (NC)	Lawyer	Caroline County, VA	May 17, 1741	Sept. 14, 1788
Read, George (DE)	Judge	Cecil County, MD	Sept. 18, 1733	Sept. 21, 1798
Rodney, Caesar (DE)	Judge	Dover, DE	Oct. 7, 1728	June 29, 1784
Ross, George (PA)	Judge	New Castle, DE	May 10, 1730	July 14, 1779
Rush, Benjamin (PA)	Physician	Byberry Twp. (Philadelphia), PA	Jan. 4, 1746	Apr. 19, 1813
Rutledge, Edward (SC)	Lawyer	Charleston, SC	Nov. 23, 1749	Jan. 23, 1800
Sherman, Roger (CT)	Lawyer	Newton, MA	Apr. 19, 1721	July 23, 1793
Smith, James (PA)	Lawyer	Ireland	c. 1719	July 11, 1806
Stockton, Richard (NJ)	Lawyer	Princeton, NJ	Oct. 1, 1730	Feb. 28, 1781
Stone, Thomas (MD)	Lawyer	Charles County, MD	c. 1743	Oct. 5, 1787
Taylor, George (PA)	Ironmaster	Ireland	c. 1716	Feb. 23, 1781
Thornton, Matthew (NH)	Physician	Ireland	c. 1714	June 24, 1803
Walton, George (GA)	Judge	Cumberland County, VA	c. 1741	Feb. 2, 1804
Whipple, William (NH)	Merchant, judge	Kittery, ME	Jan. 14, 1730	Nov. 28, 1785
Williams, William (CT)	Merchant	Lebanon, CT	Apr. 8, 1731	Aug. 2, 1811
Wilson, James (PA)	Judge	Carskerdo, Scotland	Sept. 14, 1742	Aug. 21, 1798
Witherspoon, John (NJ)	Clergyman, educator	Gifford, Scotland	Feb. 5, 1723	Nov. 15, 1794
Wolcott, Oliver (CT)	Judge	Windsor, CT	Nov. 20, 1726	Dec. 1, 1797
Wythe, George (VA)	Lawyer	Elizabeth City County, VA	c. 1726	June 8, 1806

Origin of the Constitution

The War of Independence was conducted by delegates from the original 13 states, who composed the Congress of the United States of America, known as the Continental Congress. In 1777 the Congress submitted to the legislatures of the states the Articles of Confederation and Perpetual Union, which were ratified by New Hampshire, Massachusetts, Rhode Island, Connecticut, New York, New Jersey, Pennsylvania, Delaware, Virginia, North Carolina, South Carolina, Georgia, and finally, in 1781, Maryland.

The first article read: "The stile of this confederacy shall be the United States of America." This did not signify a sovereign nation, because the states delegated only those powers they could not handle individually, such as to wage war, make treaties, and contract debts for general expenses (e.g., paying the army). Taxes for payment of such debts were levied by the individual states. The president signed himself "President of the United States in Congress assembled," but here the United States were considered in the plural, a cooperating group.

When the war was over, it became evident that a stronger federal union was needed. The Congress left the initiative to the legislatures. Virginia in Jan. 1786 appointed commissioners to meet with representatives of other states; delegates from Virginia, Delaware, New York, New Jersey, and Pennsylvania met at Annapolis. Alexander Hamilton prepared their call asking delegates from all states to meet in Philadelphia in May 1787 "to render the Constitution of the federal government adequate to the exigencies of the union." Congress endorsed the plan on Feb. 21, 1787. Delegates were appointed by all states except Rhode Island.

The convention was called for May 14, 1787, but a quorum was not present until May 25. George Washington was chosen president (presiding officer). The states certified 65 delegates, but 10 did not attend. The work was done by 55, not all of whom were present at all sessions. Of the 55 attending delegates, 39 signed Sept. 17, 1787, some with reservations, and 16 failed to sign. Some historians have said 74 delegates (nine more than the 65 actually certified) were named, and 19 failed to attend. These additional persons refused the appointment, were never delegates, and were never counted as absentees. Washington sent the Constitution to Congress, and that body, Sept. 28, 1787, ordered it sent to the legislatures, "in order to be submitted to a convention of delegates chosen in each state by the people thereof."

The Constitution was ratified by votes of state conventions as follows: Delaware, Dec. 7, 1787, unanimous; Pennsylvania, Dec. 12, 1787, 46 to 23; New Jersey, Dec. 18, 1787, unanimous; Georgia, Jan. 2, 1788, unanimous; Connecticut, Jan. 9, 1788, 128 to 40; Massachusetts, Feb. 6, 1788, 187 to 168; Maryland, Apr. 28, 1788, 63 to 11; South Carolina, May 23, 1788, 149 to 73; New Hampshire, June 21, 1788, 57 to 46; Virginia, June 25, 1788, 89 to 79; New York, July 26, 1788, 30 to 27. Nine states were needed to establish the operation of the Constitution "between the states so ratifying the same," and New Hampshire was the ninth state. The government did not declare the Constitution in effect until the first Wednesday in Mar. 1789, which was Mar. 4. After that, North Carolina ratified it on Nov. 21, 1789, 194 to 77; and Rhode Island, May 29, 1790, 34 to 32. Vermont in convention ratified it on Jan. 10, 1791, and by act of Congress approved on Feb. 18, 1791, was admitted into the Union as the 14th state, Mar. 4, 1791.

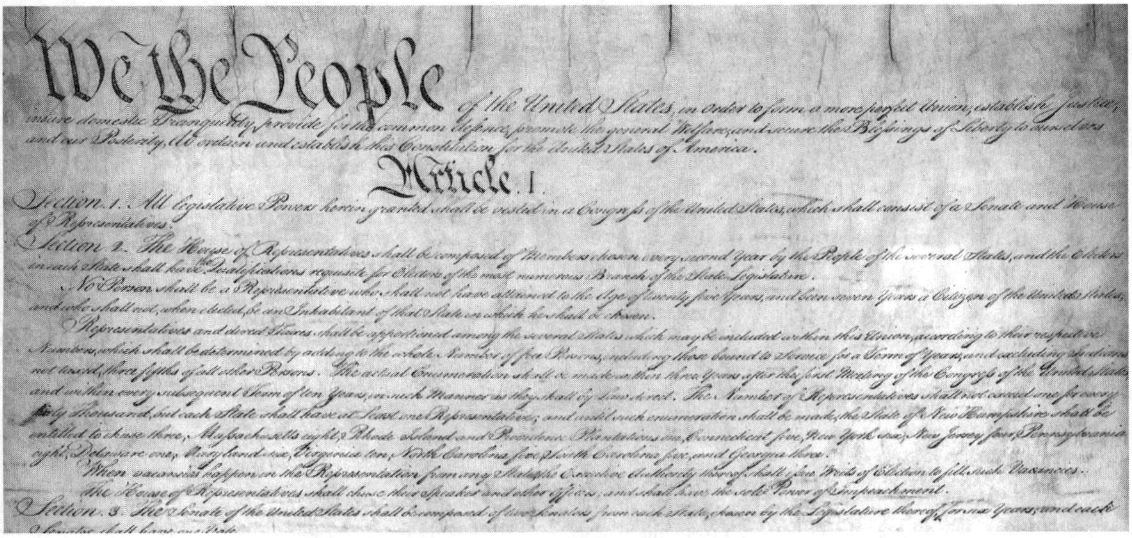

Constitution of the United States

The text of the Constitution given here is from the centennial edition of *The Constitution of the United States of America: Analysis and Interpretation*, prepared by the Library of Congress and issued by the U.S. Government Printing Office July 1, 2014. Text in brackets indicates that an item has been superseded or amended, or provides background information. **Boldface text** preceding an article, section, or amendment is a brief summary, added by *The World Almanac*.

The Original Seven Articles

PREAMBLE

We the People of the United States, in Order to form a more perfect Union, establish Justice, insure domestic Tranquility, provide for the common defence, promote the general Welfare, and secure the Blessings of Liberty to ourselves and our Posterity, do ordain and establish this Constitution for the United States of America.

ARTICLE I.

Section 1—Legislative powers, in whom vested.

All legislative Powers herein granted shall be vested in a Congress of the United States, which shall consist of a Senate and House of Representatives.

Section 2—House of Representatives, how and by whom chosen. Qualifications of a Representative. Representatives and direct taxes, how apportioned and enumerated. Vacancies to be filled. Choosing of officers and power of impeachment.

The House of Representatives shall be composed of Members chosen every second Year by the People of the several States, and the Electors in each State shall have the Qualifications requisite for Electors of the most numerous Branch of the State Legislature.

No Person shall be a Representative who shall not have attained to the Age of twenty five Years, and been seven Years a Citizen of the United States, and who shall not, when elected, be an Inhabitant of that State in which he shall be chosen.

[Representatives and direct Taxes shall be apportioned among the several States which may be included within this Union, according to their respective Numbers, which shall be determined by adding to the whole Number of free Persons, including those bound to Service for a Term of Years, and excluding Indians not taxed, three fifths of all other Persons.] *[The previous sentence was superseded by Amendment XIV, section 2.]* The actual Enumeration shall be made within three Years after the first Meeting of the Congress of the United States, and within every subsequent Term of ten Years, in such Manner as they shall by Law direct. The Number of Representatives shall not exceed one for every thirty Thousand, but each State shall have at Least one Representative; and until such enumeration shall be made, the State of New Hampshire shall be entitled to chuse three, Massachusetts eight, Rhode-Island and Providence Plantations one, Connecticut five, New York six, New Jersey four, Pennsylvania eight, Delaware one, Maryland six, Virginia ten, North Carolina five, South Carolina five, and Georgia three.

When vacancies happen in the Representation from any State, the Executive Authority thereof shall issue Writs of Election to fill such Vacancies.

The House of Representatives shall chuse their Speaker and other Officers; and shall have the sole Power of Impeachment.

Section 3—Senators, how and by whom chosen. How assembled. Qualifications of a Senator. President of the Senate. President pro tempore and other officers of the Senate, how chosen. Power to try impeachments. Judgment in cases of impeachment.

The Senate of the United States shall be composed of two Senators from each State, [chosen by the Legislature] *[The preceding words were superseded by Amendment XVII.]* thereof, for six Years; and each Senator shall have one Vote.

Immediately after they shall be assembled in Consequence of the first Election, they shall be divided as equally as may be into three Classes. The Seats of the Senators of the first Class shall be vacated at the Expiration of the second Year, of the second Class at the Expiration of the fourth Year, and of the third Class at the Expiration of the sixth Year, so that one third may be chosen every second Year; [and if Vacancies happen by Resignation, or otherwise, during the Recess of the Legislature of any State, the Executive thereof may make temporary Appointments until the next Meeting of the Legislature, which shall then fill such Vacancies.] *[The words in brackets were superseded by Amendment XVII.]*

No Person shall be a Senator who shall not have attained to the Age of thirty Years, and been nine Years a Citizen of the United States, and who shall not, when elected, be an Inhabitant of that State for which he shall be chosen.

The Vice President of the United States shall be President of the Senate, but shall have no Vote, unless they be equally divided.

The Senate shall chuse their other Officers, and also a President pro tempore, in the Absence of the Vice President, or when he shall exercise the Office of President of the United States.

The Senate shall have the sole Power to try all Impeachments. When sitting for that Purpose, they shall be on Oath or Affirmation. When the President of the United States is tried, the Chief Justice shall preside: And no Person shall be convicted without the Concurrence of two thirds of the Members present.

Judgment in Cases of Impeachment shall not extend further than to removal from Office, and disqualification to hold and enjoy any Office of honor, Trust or Profit under the United States: but the Party convicted shall nevertheless be liable and subject to Indictment, Trial, Judgment and Punishment, according to Law.

Section 4—Times, places, manner of elections. Time of assembly.

The Times, Places and Manner of holding Elections for Senators and Representatives, shall be prescribed in each State by the Legislature thereof; but the Congress may at any time by Law make or alter such Regulations, except as to the Places of chusing Senators.

The Congress shall assemble at least once in every Year, and such Meeting shall be [on the first Monday in December], *[The words in brackets were superseded by Amendment XX, section 2.]* unless they shall by Law appoint a different Day.

Section 5—Membership, quorums, adjournments. Rules of proceedings. Journal of proceedings. Time of adjournments.

Each House shall be the Judge of the Elections, Returns and Qualifications of its own Members, and a Majority of each shall constitute a Quorum to do Business; but a smaller Number may adjourn from day to day, and may be authorized to compel the Attendance of absent Members, in such Manner, and under such Penalties as each House may provide.

Each House may determine the Rules of its Proceedings, punish its Members for disorderly Behaviour, and, with the Concurrence of two thirds, expel a Member.

Each House shall keep a Journal of its Proceedings, and from time to time publish the same, excepting such Parts as may in their Judgment require Secrecy; and the Yeas and Nays of the Members of either House on any question shall, at the Desire of one fifth of those Present, be entered on the Journal.

Neither House, during the Session of Congress, shall, without the Consent of the other, adjourn for more than three days, nor to any other Place than that in which the two Houses shall be sitting.

Section 6—Compensation, privileges. Incompatible offices.

The Senators and Representatives shall receive a Compensation for their Services, to be ascertained by Law, and paid out of the Treasury of the United States. They shall in all Cases, except Treason, Felony and Breach of the Peace, be privileged from Arrest during their Attendance at the Session of their respective Houses, and in going to and returning from the same; and for any Speech or Debate in either House, they shall not be questioned in any other Place.

No Senator or Representative shall, during the Time for which he was elected, be appointed to any civil Office under the Authority of the United States, which shall have been created, or the Emoluments whereof shall have been encreased during such time; and no Person holding any Office under the United States, shall be a Member of either House during his Continuance in Office.

Section 7—House to originate revenue bills. Legislative process; bill presented to the President before becoming law. Passing of bill over objections of President, veto.

All Bills for raising Revenue shall originate in the House of Representatives; but the Senate may propose or concur with Amendments as on other Bills.

Every Bill which shall have passed the House of Representatives and the Senate, shall, before it become a Law, be presented to the President of the United States; If he approve he shall sign it, but if not he shall return it, with his Objections to that House in which it shall have originated, who shall enter the Objections at large on their Journal, and proceed to reconsider it. If after such Reconsideration two thirds of that House shall agree to pass the Bill, it shall be sent, together with the Objections, to the other House, by which it shall likewise be reconsidered, and if approved by two thirds of that House, it shall become a Law. But in all such Cases the Votes of both Houses shall be determined by Yeas and Nays, and the Names of the Persons voting for and against the Bill shall be entered on the Journal of each House respectively. If any Bill shall not be returned by the President within ten Days (Sundays excepted) after it shall have been presented to him, the Same shall be a Law, in like Manner as if he had signed it, unless the Congress by their Adjournment prevent its Return, in which Case it shall not be a Law.

Every Order, Resolution, or Vote to which the Concurrence of the Senate and House of Representatives may be necessary (except on a question of Adjournment) shall be presented to the President of the United States; and before the Same shall take Effect, shall be approved by him, or being disapproved by him, shall be repassed by two thirds of the Senate and House of Representatives, according to the Rules and Limitations prescribed in the Case of a Bill.

Section 8—Powers of Congress.

The Congress shall have Power To lay and collect Taxes, Duties, Imposts and Excises, to pay the Debts and provide for the common Defence and general Welfare of the United States; but all Duties, Imposts and Excises shall be uniform throughout the United States;

To borrow Money on the credit of the United States;

To regulate Commerce with foreign Nations, and among the several States, and with the Indian Tribes;

To establish an uniform Rule of Naturalization, and uniform Laws on the subject of Bankruptcies throughout the United States;

To coin Money, regulate the Value thereof, and of foreign Coin, and fix the Standard of Weights and Measures;

To provide for the Punishment of counterfeiting the Securities and current Coin of the United States;

To establish Post Offices and post Roads;

To promote the Progress of Science and useful Arts, by securing for limited Times to Authors and Inventors the exclusive Right to their respective Writings and Discoveries;

To constitute Tribunals inferior to the supreme Court;

To define and punish Piracies and Felonies committed on the high Seas, and Offences against the Law of Nations;

To declare War, grant Letters of Marque and Reprisal, and make Rules concerning Captures on Land and Water;

To raise and support Armies, but no Appropriation of Money to that Use shall be for a longer Term than two Years;

To provide and maintain a Navy;

To make Rules for the Government and Regulation of the land and naval Forces;

To provide for calling forth the Militia to execute the Laws of the Union, suppress Insurrections and repel Invasions;

To provide for organizing, arming, and disciplining, the Militia, and for governing such Part of them as may be employed in the Service of the United States, reserving to the States respectively, the Appointment of the Officers, and the Authority of training the Militia according to the discipline prescribed by Congress;

To exercise exclusive Legislation in all Cases whatsoever, over such District (not exceeding ten Miles square) as may, by Cession of particular States, and the Acceptance of Congress, become the Seat of the Government of the United States, and to exercise like Authority over all Places purchased by the Consent of the Legislature of the State in which the Same shall be, for the Erection of Forts, Magazines, Arsenals, dock-Yards, and other needful Buildings;—And

To make all Laws which shall be necessary and proper for carrying into Execution the foregoing Powers, and all other Powers vested by this Constitution in the Government of the United States, or in any Department or Officer thereof.

Section 9—Powers denied to Congress: Importation of slaves. Habeas corpus. Bills of attainder. Taxes, how apportioned. Export duty. Preference to ports. Money, how drawn from Treasury. Titles of nobility.

The Migration or Importation of such Persons as any of the States now existing shall think proper to admit, shall not be prohibited by the Congress prior to the Year one thousand eight hundred and eight, but a Tax or duty may be imposed on such Importation, not exceeding ten dollars for each Person.

The Privilege of the Writ of Habeas Corpus shall not be suspended, unless when in Cases of Rebellion or Invasion the public Safety may require it.

No Bill of Attainder or ex post facto Law shall be passed.

No Capitation, or other direct, Tax shall be laid, [unless in Proportion to the Census or Enumeration herein before directed to be taken]. *[Words in brackets modified by Amendment XVI.]*

No Tax or Duty shall be laid on Articles exported from any State.

No Preference shall be given by any Regulation of Commerce or Revenue to the Ports of one State over those of another: nor shall Vessels bound to, or from, one State, be obliged to enter, clear, or pay Duties in another.

No Money shall be drawn from the Treasury, but in Consequence of Appropriations made by Law; and a regular Statement and Account of the Receipts and Expenditures of all public Money shall be published from time to time.

No Title of Nobility shall be granted by the United States: And no Person holding any Office of Profit or Trust under them, shall, without the Consent of the Congress, accept of any present, Emolument, Office, or Title, of any kind whatever, from any King, Prince, or foreign State.

Section 10—States prohibited from the exercise of certain powers.

No State shall enter into any Treaty, Alliance, or Confederation; grant Letters of Marque and Reprisal; coin Money; emit Bills of Credit; make any Thing but gold and silver Coin a Tender in Payment of Debts; pass any Bill of Attainder, ex post facto Law, or Law impairing the Obligation of Contracts, or grant any Title of Nobility.

No State shall, without the Consent of the Congress, lay any Imposts or Duties on Imports or Exports, except what may be absolutely necessary for executing it's inspection Laws: and the net Produce of all Duties and Imposts, laid by any State on Imports or Exports, shall be for the Use of the Treasury of the United States; and all such Laws shall be subject to the Revision and Controul of the Congress.

No State shall, without the Consent of Congress, lay any Duty of Tonnage, keep Troops, or Ships of War in time of Peace, enter into any Agreement or Compact with another State, or with a foreign Power, or engage in War, unless actually invaded, or in such imminent Danger as will not admit of delay.

ARTICLE II.

Section 1—President, powers and term of office. Electors, number and how appointed. Electors to vote for President. Qualifications of President. On whom duties devolve in case of removal, death, etc., of President. President's compensation. Oath of office.

The executive Power shall be vested in a President of the United States of America. He shall hold his Office during the Term of four Years, and, together with the Vice President, chosen for the same Term, be elected, as follows:

Each State shall appoint, in such Manner as the Legislature thereof may direct, a Number of Electors, equal to the whole Number of Senators and Representatives to which the State may be entitled in the Congress: but no Senator or Representative, or Person holding an Office of Trust or Profit under the United States, shall be appointed an Elector.

[The Electors shall meet in their respective States, and vote by Ballot for two Persons, of whom one at least shall not be an Inhabitant of the same State with themselves. And they shall make a List of all the Persons voted for, and of the Number of Votes for each; which List they shall sign and certify, and transmit sealed to the Seat of the Government of the United States, directed to the President of the Senate. The President of the Senate shall, in the Presence of the Senate and House of Representatives, open all the Certificates, and the Votes shall then be counted. The Person having the greatest Number of Votes shall be the President, if such Number be a Majority of the whole Number of Electors appointed; and if there be more than one who have such Majority, and have an equal Number of Votes, then the House of Representatives shall immediately chuse by Ballot one of them for President; and if no Person have a Majority, then from the five highest on the List the said House shall in like Manner chuse the President. But in chusing the President, the Votes shall be taken by States, the Representation from each State having one Vote; A quorum for this Purpose shall consist of a Member or Members from two thirds of the States, and a Majority of all the States shall be necessary to a Choice. In every Case, after the Choice of the President, the Person having the greatest Number of Votes of the Electors shall be the Vice President. But if there should remain two or more who have equal Votes, the Senate shall chuse from them by Ballot the Vice President.] *[This clause was superseded by Amendment XII.]*

The Congress may determine the Time of chusing the Electors, and the Day on which they shall give their Votes; which Day shall be the same throughout the United States.

No Person except a natural born Citizen, or a Citizen of the United States, at the time of the Adoption of this Constitution, shall be eligible to the Office of President; neither shall any Person be eligible to that Office who shall not have attained to the Age of thirty five Years, and been fourteen Years a Resident within the United States. *[For qualification of the Vice President, see Amendment XII.]*

[In Case of the Removal of the President from Office, or of his Death, Resignation, or Inability to discharge the Powers and Duties of the said Office, the Same shall devolve on the Vice President, and the Congress may by Law provide for the Case of Removal, Death, Resignation or Inability, both of the President and Vice President, declaring what Officer shall then act as President, and such Officer shall act accordingly, until the Disability be removed, or a President shall be elected.] *[This clause was superseded by Amendment XXV.]*

The President shall, at stated Times, receive for his Services, a Compensation, which shall neither be encreased nor diminished during the Period for which he shall have been elected, and he shall not receive within that Period any other Emolument from the United States, or any of them.

Before he enter on the Execution of his Office, he shall take the following Oath or Affirmation:—

"I do solemnly swear (or affirm) that I will faithfully execute the Office of President of the United States, and will to the best of my Ability, preserve, protect and defend the Constitution of the United States."

Section 2—President to be Commander in Chief. Power to make treaties; nominations for, appointments to certain offices. Power to fill vacancies during Senate recess.

The President shall be Commander in Chief of the Army and Navy of the United States, and of the Militia of the several States, when called into the actual Service of the United States; he may require the Opinion, in writing, of the principal Officer in each of the executive Departments, upon any Subject relating to the Duties of their respective Offices, and he shall have Power to Grant Reprieves and Pardons for Offences against the United States, except in Cases of Impeachment.

He shall have Power, by and with the Advice and Consent of the Senate, to make Treaties, provided two thirds of the Senators present concur; and he shall nominate, and by and with the Advice and Consent of the Senate, shall appoint Ambassadors, other public Ministers and Consuls, Judges of the supreme Court, and all other Officers of the United States, whose Appointments are not herein otherwise provided for, and which shall be established by Law: but the Congress may by Law vest the Appointment of such inferior Officers, as they think proper, in the President alone, in the Courts of Law, or in the Heads of Departments.

The President shall have Power to fill up all Vacancies that may happen during the Recess of the Senate, by granting Commissions which shall expire at the End of their next Session.

Section 3—President shall communicate to, may convene and adjourn Congress; shall receive ambassadors, execute laws, and commission officers.

He shall from time to time give to the Congress Information on the State of the Union, and recommend to their Consideration such Measures as he shall judge necessary and expedient; he may, on extraordinary Occasions, convene both Houses, or either of them, and in Case of Disagreement between them, with Respect to the Time of Adjournment, he may adjourn them to such Time as he shall think proper; he shall receive Ambassadors and other public Ministers; he shall take Care that the Laws be faithfully executed, and shall Commission all the Officers of the United States.

Section 4—All civil offices forfeited for certain crimes.

The President, Vice President and all civil Officers of the United States, shall be removed from Office on Impeachment for, and Conviction of, Treason, Bribery, or other high Crimes and Misdemeanors.

ARTICLE III.

Section 1—Judicial powers, tenure, compensation.

The judicial Power of the United States, shall be vested in one supreme Court, and in such inferior Courts as the Congress may from time to time ordain and establish. The Judges, both of the supreme and inferior Courts, shall hold their Offices during good Behaviour, and shall, at stated Times, receive for their Services, a Compensation, which shall not be diminished during their Continuance in Office.

Section 2—Judicial power, cases to which it extends. Jurisdiction of Supreme Court. Trial by jury; where held.

The judicial Power shall extend to all Cases, in Law and Equity, arising under this Constitution, the Laws of the United States, and Treaties made, or which shall be made, under their Authority;—to all Cases affecting Ambassadors, other public Ministers and Consuls;—to all Cases of admiralty and maritime Jurisdiction;—to Controversies to which the United States shall be a Party;—to Controversies between two or more States;—[between a State and Citizens of another State;]—between Citizens of different States;—between Citizens of the same State claiming Lands under Grants of different States, [and between a State, or the Citizens thereof, and foreign States, Citizens or Subjects.] *[This section was modified by Amendment XI.]*

In all Cases affecting Ambassadors, other public Ministers and Consuls, and those in which a State shall be Party, the supreme Court shall have original Jurisdiction. In all the other Cases before mentioned, the supreme Court shall have appellate Jurisdiction, both as to Law and Fact, with such Exceptions, and under such Regulations as the Congress shall make.

The Trial of all Crimes, except in Cases of Impeachment, shall be by Jury; and such Trial shall be held in the State where the said Crimes shall have been committed; but when not committed within any State, the Trial shall be at such Place or Places as the Congress may by Law have directed.

Section 3—Treason defined. Punishment of.

Treason against the United States, shall consist only in levying War against them, or in adhering to their Enemies, giving them Aid and Comfort. No Person shall be convicted of Treason unless on the Testimony of two Witnesses to the same overt Act, or on Confession in open Court.

The Congress shall have Power to declare the Punishment of Treason, but no Attainder of Treason shall work Corruption of Blood, or Forfeiture except during the Life of the Person attainted.

ARTICLE IV.

Section 1—Each State to give credit to the public acts, etc., of every other State.

Full Faith and Credit shall be given in each State to the public Acts, Records, and judicial Proceedings of every other State. And the Congress may by general Laws prescribe the Manner in which such Acts, Records and Proceedings shall be proved, and the Effect thereof.

Section 2—Privileges of citizens of each State. Fugitives from justice to be delivered up. Fugitives from service or labor, to be delivered up.

The Citizens of each State shall be entitled to all Privileges and Immunities of Citizens in the several States.

A Person charged in any State with Treason, Felony, or other Crime, who shall flee from Justice, and be found in another State, shall on Demand of the executive Authority of the State from which he fled, be delivered up, to be removed to the State having Jurisdiction of the Crime.

[No Person held to Service or Labour in one State, under the Laws thereof, escaping into another, shall, in Consequence of any Law or Regulation therein, be discharged from such Service or Labour, but shall be delivered up on Claim of the Party to whom such Service or Labour may be due.] *[This clause was superseded by Amendment XIII.]*

Section 3—Admission of new States. Power of Congress over territory and other property.

New States may be admitted by the Congress into this Union; but no new State shall be formed or erected within the Jurisdiction of any other State; nor any State be formed by the Junction of two or more States, or Parts of States, without the Consent of the Legislatures of the States concerned as well as of the Congress.

The Congress shall have Power to dispose of and make all needful Rules and Regulations respecting the Territory or other Property belonging to the United States; and nothing in this Constitution shall be so construed as to Prejudice any Claims of the United States, or of any particular State.

Section 4—Republican form of government guaranteed; each State to be protected.

The United States shall guarantee to every State in this Union a Republican Form of Government, and shall protect each of them against Invasion; and on Application of the Legislature, or of the Executive (when the Legislature cannot be convened) against domestic Violence.

ARTICLE V.

Constitution, how amended; proviso.

The Congress, whenever two thirds of both Houses shall deem it necessary, shall propose Amendments to this Constitution, or, on the Application of the Legislatures of two thirds of the several States, shall call a Convention for proposing Amendments, which, in either Case, shall be valid to all Intents and Purposes, as Part of this Constitution, when ratified by the Legislatures of three fourths of the several States, or by Conventions in three fourths thereof, as the one or the other Mode of Ratification may be proposed by the Congress; Provided that no Amendment which may be made prior to the Year One thousand eight hundred and eight shall in any Manner affect the first and fourth Clauses in the Ninth Section of the first Article; and that no State, without its Consent, shall be deprived of its equal Suffrage in the Senate.

ARTICLE VI.

Certain debts and engagements shall be valid. Constitution, laws and treaties made, shall be supreme law of the United States. Oath to support Constitution, by whom taken; no religious test shall be required.

All Debts contracted and Engagements entered into, before the Adoption of this Constitution, shall be as valid against the United States under this Constitution, as under the Confederation.

This Constitution, and the Laws of the United States which shall be made in Pursuance thereof; and all Treaties made, or which shall be made, under the Authority of the United States, shall be the supreme Law of the Land; and the Judges in every State shall be bound thereby, any Thing in the Constitution or Laws of any State to the Contrary notwithstanding.

The Senators and Representatives before mentioned, and the Members of the several State Legislatures, and all executive and judicial Officers, both of the United States and of the several States, shall be bound by Oath or Affirmation, to support this Constitution; but no religious Test shall ever be required as a Qualification to any Office or public Trust under the United States.

ARTICLE VII.

Ratification to establish the Constitution.

The Ratification of the Conventions of nine States, shall be sufficient for the Establishment of this Constitution between the States so ratifying the Same.

The Word, "the," being interlined between the seventh and eighth Lines of the first Page, The Word "Thirty" being partly written on an Erazure in the fifteenth Line of the first Page, The Words "is tried" being interlined between the thirty second and thirty third Lines of the first Page and the Word "the" being interlined between the forty third and forty fourth Lines of the second Page.

Attest William Jackson Secretary

done in Convention by the Unanimous Consent of the States present the Seventeenth Day of September in the Year of our Lord one thousand seven hundred and Eighty seven and of the Independance of the United States of America the Twelfth. In witness whereof We have hereunto subscribed our Names,

G^{o}. Washington, Presid^{t}. and deputy from Virginia

New Hampshire—John Langdon, Nicholas Gilman

Massachusetts—Nathaniel Gorham, Rufus King

Connecticut—W^{m}. Saml. Johnson, Roger Sherman

New York—Alexander Hamilton

New Jersey—Wil: Livingston, David Brearley, W^{m}. Paterson, Jona: Dayton

Pennsylvania—B Franklin, Thomas Mifflin, Robt. Morris, Geo. Clymer, Thos. FitzSimons, Jared Ingersoll, James Wilson, Gouv Morris

Delaware—Geo: Read, Gunning Bedford jun, John Dickinson, Richard Bassett, Jaco: Broom

Maryland—James McHenry, Dan of St Thos. Jenifer, Danl Carroll

Virginia—John Blair, James Madison Jr.

North Carolina—W^{m}. Blount, Rich^{d}. Dobbs Spaight, Hu Williamson

South Carolina—J. Rutledge, Charles Cotesworth Pinckney, Charles Pinckney, Pierce Butler

Georgia—William Few, Abr Baldwin

Origin of the Bill of Rights

Congress, at its first session in New York, NY, submitted to the states 12 amendments Sept. 25, 1789, to clarify certain individual and state rights not named in the Constitution. They are generally called the Bill of Rights.

Influential in framing these amendments was the Declaration of Rights of Virginia, written by George Mason (1725-92) in 1776. Mason, a Virginia delegate to the Constitutional Convention, did not sign the Constitution and opposed its ratification on the ground that it did not sufficiently oppose slavery or safeguard individual rights.

In the preamble to the resolution offering the proposed amendments, Congress said: "The Conventions of a number of the States, having at the time of their adopting the Constitution, expressed a desire, in order to prevent misconstruction or abuse of its powers, that further declaratory and restrictive clauses should be added: And as extending the ground of public confidence in the Government, will best insure the beneficent ends of its institution."

Ten of these amendments, now commonly known as one to 10 inclusive, but originally three to 12 inclusive, were ratified by the states as follows: New Jersey, Nov. 20, 1789; Maryland, Dec. 19, 1789; North Carolina, Dec. 22, 1789; South Carolina, Jan. 19, 1790; New Hampshire, Jan. 25, 1790; Delaware, Jan. 28, 1790; New York, Feb. 27, 1790; Pennsylvania, Mar. 10, 1790; Rhode Island, June 7, 1790; Vermont, Nov. 3, 1791; Virginia, Dec. 15, 1791; Massachusetts, Mar. 2, 1939; Georgia, Mar. 18, 1939; Connecticut, Apr. 19, 1939. These original 10 ratified amendments follow as Amendments I to X inclusive.

Of the two original proposed amendments that were not ratified promptly by the necessary number of states, the first related to apportionment of Representatives; the second, relating to compensation of members of Congress, was ratified in 1992 and became Amendment XXVII.

The Bill of Rights

In force Dec. 15, 1791

AMENDMENT I.

Religious establishment prohibited. Freedom of speech and of press; right to assemble and to petition.

Congress shall make no law respecting an establishment of religion, or prohibiting the free exercise thereof; or abridging the freedom of speech, or of the press; or the right of the people peaceably to assemble, and to petition the Government for a redress of grievances.

AMENDMENT II.

Right to keep and bear arms.

A well regulated Militia, being necessary to the security of a free State, the right of the people to keep and bear Arms shall not be infringed.

AMENDMENT III.

Conditions for quartering of soldiers.

No Soldier shall, in time of peace be quartered in any house, without the consent of the Owner, nor in time of war, but in a manner to be prescribed by law.

AMENDMENT IV.

Protection from unreasonable search and seizure.

The right of the people to be secure in their persons, houses, papers, and effects, against unreasonable searches and seizures, shall not be violated, and no Warrants shall issue but upon probable cause, supported by Oath or affirmation, and particularly describing the place to be searched, and the persons or things to be seized.

AMENDMENT V.

Provisions concerning prosecution and due process of law. Compensation of private property taken for public use.

No person shall be held to answer for a capital, or otherwise infamous crime, unless on a presentment or indictment of a Grand Jury, except in cases arising in the land or naval forces, or in the Militia, when in actual service in time of War or public danger; nor shall any person be subject for the same offence to be twice put in jeopardy of life or limb; nor shall be compelled in any criminal case to be a witness against himself, nor be deprived of life, liberty, or property, without due process of law; nor shall private property be taken for public use, without just compensation.

AMENDMENT VI.

Rights of accused in criminal prosecutions.

In all criminal prosecutions, the accused shall enjoy the right to a speedy and public trial, by an impartial jury of the State and district wherein the crime shall have been committed, which district shall have been previously ascertained by law, and to be informed of the nature and cause of the accusation; to be confronted with the witnesses against him; to have compulsory process for obtaining witnesses in his favor, and to have the Assistance of Counsel for his defense.

AMENDMENT VII.

Right of trial by jury in civil cases.

In Suits at common law, where the value in controversy shall exceed twenty dollars, the right of trial by jury shall be preserved, and no fact tried by a jury, shall be otherwise reexamined in any Court of the United States, than according to the rules of the common law.

AMENDMENT VIII.

Excessive bail or fines; cruel and unusual punishment.

Excessive bail shall not be required, nor excessive fines imposed, nor cruel and unusual punishments inflicted.

AMENDMENT IX.

Unenumerated rights.

The enumeration in the Constitution, of certain rights, shall not be construed to deny or disparage others retained by the people.

AMENDMENT X.

Rights reserved to States.

The powers not delegated to the United States by the Constitution, nor prohibited by it to the States, are reserved to the States respectively, or to the people.

Amendments Since the Bill of Rights

AMENDMENT XI.

Judicial powers construed.

[Proposed by Congress Mar. 4, 1794. Ratification complete Feb. 7, 1795, though official announcement of ratification not made until Jan. 8, 1798.]

The Judicial power of the United States shall not be construed to extend to any suit in law or equity, commenced or prosecuted against one of the United States by Citizens of another State, or by Citizens or Subjects of any Foreign State.

AMENDMENT XII.

Election of President and Vice-President.

[Proposed by Congress Dec. 9, 1803; ratified June 15, 1804.]

The Electors shall meet in their respective states and vote by ballot for President and Vice-President, one of whom, at least, shall not be an inhabitant of the same state with themselves; they shall name in their ballots the person voted for as President, and in distinct ballots the person voted for as Vice-President, and they shall make distinct lists of all persons voted for as President, and of all persons voted for as Vice-President, and of the number of votes for each, which lists they shall sign and certify, and transmit sealed to the seat of the government of the United States, directed to the President of the Senate;—The President of the Senate shall, in the presence of the Senate and House of Representatives, open all the certificates and the votes shall then be counted;—The person having the greatest number of votes for President, shall be the President, if such number be a majority of the whole number of Electors appointed; and if no person have such majority, then from the persons having the highest numbers not exceeding three on the list of those voted for as President, the House of Representatives shall choose immediately, by ballot, the President. But in choosing the President, the votes shall be taken by states, the representation from each state having one vote; a quorum for this purpose shall consist of a member or members from two-thirds of the states, and a majority of all the states shall be necessary to a choice. [And if the House of Representatives shall not choose a President whenever the right of choice shall devolve upon them, before the fourth day of March next following, then the Vice-President shall act as President, as in the case of the death or other constitutional disability of the President.] *[The words in brackets were superseded by Amendment XX, section 3.]* The person having the greatest number of votes as Vice-President, shall be the Vice-President, if such number be a majority of the whole number of Electors appointed, and if no person have a majority, then from the two highest numbers on the list, the Senate shall choose the Vice-President; a quorum for the purpose shall consist of two-thirds of the whole number of Senators, and a majority of the whole number shall be necessary to a choice. But no person constitutionally ineligible to the office of President shall be eligible to that of Vice-President of the United States.

THE RECONSTRUCTION AMENDMENTS

[Amendments XIII, XIV, and XV are commonly known as the Reconstruction Amendments inasmuch as they followed the Civil War and were drafted by Republicans who wanted to impose their own policy of reconstruction on the South. Southern postbellum legislatures in states including Mississippi, South Carolina, and Georgia had set up laws that effectively perpetuated slavery under other names.]

AMENDMENT XIII.

Slavery abolished.

[Proposed by Congress Jan. 31, 1865; ratified Dec. 6, 1865.]

Section 1. Neither slavery nor involuntary servitude, except as a punishment for crime whereof the party shall have been duly convicted, shall exist within the United States, or any place subject to their jurisdiction.

Section 2. Congress shall have power to enforce this article by appropriate legislation.

AMENDMENT XIV.

Citizenship rights not to be abridged.

[Proposed by Congress June 13, 1866, ratified July 9, 1868, and declared to have been ratified in a proclamation by the Secretary of State, July 28, 1868.]

Section 1. All persons born or naturalized in the United States, and subject to the jurisdiction thereof, are citizens of the United States and of the State wherein they reside. No State shall make or enforce any law which shall abridge the privileges or immunities of citizens of the United States; nor shall any State deprive any person of life, liberty, or property, without due process of law; nor deny to any person within its jurisdiction the equal protection of the laws.

Section 2. Representatives shall be apportioned among the several States according to their respective numbers, counting the whole number of persons in each State, excluding Indians not taxed. But when the right to vote at any election for the choice of electors for President and Vice-President of the United States, Representatives in Congress, the Executive and Judicial officers of a State, or the members of the Legislature thereof, is denied to any of the male inhabitants of such State, being [twenty-one] *[The words in brackets were changed by Amendment XXVI.]* years of age, and citizens of the United States, or in any way abridged, except for participation in rebellion, or other crime, the basis of representation therein shall be reduced in the proportion which the number of such male citizens shall bear to the whole number of male citizens twenty-one years of age in such State.

Section 3. No person shall be a Senator or Representative in Congress, or elector of President and Vice-President, or hold any office, civil or military, under the United States, or under any State, who, having previously taken an oath, as a member of Congress, or as an officer of the United States, or as a member of any State legislature, or as an executive or judicial officer of any State, to support the Constitution of the United States, shall have engaged in insurrection or rebellion against the same, or given aid or comfort to the enemies thereof. But Congress may by a vote of two-thirds of each House, remove such disability.

Section 4. The validity of the public debt of the United States, authorized by law, including debts incurred for payment of pensions and bounties for services in suppressing insurrection or rebellion, shall not be questioned. But neither the United States nor any State shall assume or pay any debt or obligation incurred in aid of insurrection or rebellion against the United States, or any claim for the loss or emancipation of any slave; but all such debts, obligations and claims shall be held illegal and void.

Section 5. The Congress shall have power to enforce, by appropriate legislation, the provisions of this article.

AMENDMENT XV.

Race no bar to voting rights.

[Proposed by Congress Feb. 26, 1869; ratified Feb. 3, 1870.]

Section 1. The right of citizens of the United States to vote shall not be denied or abridged by the United States or by any State on account of race, color, or previous condition of servitude.

Section 2. The Congress shall have power to enforce this article by appropriate legislation.

AMENDMENT XVI.

Income taxes authorized.

[Proposed by Congress July 12, 1909; ratified Feb. 3, 1913.]

The Congress shall have power to lay and collect taxes on incomes, from whatever source derived, without apportionment among the several States, and without regard to any census or enumeration.

AMENDMENT XVII.

Popular election of Senators.

[Proposed by Congress May 13, 1912; ratified Apr. 8, 1913.]

The Senate of the United States shall be composed of two Senators from each State, elected by the people thereof, for six years; and each Senator shall have one vote. The electors in each State shall have the qualifications requisite for electors of the most numerous branch of the State legislatures.

When vacancies happen in the representation of any State in the Senate, the executive authority of such State shall issue writs of election to fill such vacancies: Provided, That the legislature of any State may empower the executive thereof to make temporary appointments until the people fill the vacancies by election as the legislature may direct.

This amendment shall not be so construed as to affect the election or term of any Senator chosen before it becomes valid as part of the Constitution.

AMENDMENT XVIII.

Liquor prohibition amendment.

[Proposed by Congress Dec. 18, 1917; ratified Jan. 16, 1919. Repealed by Amendment XXI, effective Dec. 5, 1933.]

Section 1. After one year from the ratification of this article the manufacture, sale, or transportation of intoxicating liquors within, the importation thereof into, or the exportation thereof from the United States and all territory subject to the jurisdiction thereof for beverage purposes is hereby prohibited.

Section 2. The Congress and the several States shall have concurrent power to enforce this article by appropriate legislation.

Section 3. This article shall be inoperative unless it shall have been ratified as an amendment to the Constitution by the legislatures of the several States, as provided in the Constitution, within seven years from the date of the submission hereof to the States by the Congress.

AMENDMENT XIX.

Nationwide suffrage to women.

[Proposed by Congress June 4, 1919; ratified Aug. 18, 1920.]

The right of citizens of the United States to vote shall not be denied or abridged by the United States or by any State on account of sex.

Congress shall have power to enforce this article by appropriate legislation.

AMENDMENT XX.

Commencement of terms of office

[Proposed by Congress Mar. 2, 1932; ratified Jan. 23, 1933.]

Section 1. The terms of the President and Vice President shall end at noon on the 20th day of January, and the terms of Senators and Representatives at noon on the 3d day of January, of the years in which such terms would have ended if this article had not been ratified; and the terms of their successors shall then begin.

Section 2. The Congress shall assemble at least once in every year, and such meeting shall begin at noon on the 3d day of January, unless they shall by law appoint a different day.

Section 3. If, at the time fixed for the beginning of the term of the President, the President elect shall have died, the Vice President elect shall become President. If a President shall not have been chosen before the time fixed for the beginning of his term, or if the President elect shall have failed to qualify, then the Vice President elect shall act as President until a President shall have qualified; and the Congress may by law provide for the case wherein neither a President elect nor a Vice President elect shall have qualified, declaring who shall then act as President, or the manner in which one who is to act shall be selected, and such person shall act accordingly until a President or Vice President shall have qualified.

Section 4. The Congress may by law provide for the case of the death of any of the persons from whom the House of Representatives may choose a President whenever the right of choice shall have devolved upon them, and for the case of the death of any of the persons from whom the Senate may choose a Vice President whenever the right of choice shall have devolved upon them.

Section 5. Sections 1 and 2 shall take effect on the 15th day of October following the ratification of this article.

Section 6. This article shall be inoperative unless it shall have been ratified as an amendment to the Constitution by the legislatures of three-fourths of the several States within seven years from the date of its submission.

AMENDMENT XXI.

Repeal of Amendment XVIII.

[Proposed by Congress Feb. 20, 1933; ratified Dec. 5, 1933.]

Section 1. The eighteenth article of amendment to the Constitution of the United States is hereby repealed.

Section 2. The transportation or importation into any State, Territory, or possession of the United States for delivery or use therein of intoxicating liquors, in violation of the laws thereof, is hereby prohibited.

Section 3. This article shall be inoperative unless it shall have been ratified as an amendment to the Constitution by conventions in the several States, as provided in the Constitution, within seven years from the date of the submission hereof to the States by the Congress.

AMENDMENT XXII.

Limit on presidential terms of office.

[Proposed by Congress Mar. 24, 1947; ratified Feb. 27, 1951.]

Section 1. No person shall be elected to the office of the President more than twice, and no person who has held the office of President, or acted as President, for more than two years of a term to which some other person was elected President shall be elected to the office of the President more than once. But this Article shall not apply to any person holding the office of President when this Article was proposed by Congress, and shall not prevent any person who may be holding the office of President, or acting as President, during the term within which this Article becomes operative from holding the office of President or acting as President during the remainder of such term.

Section 2. This Article shall be inoperative unless it shall have been ratified as an amendment to the Constitution by the legislatures of three-fourths of the several States within seven years from the date of its submission to the States by the Congress.

AMENDMENT XXIII.

Presidential vote for District of Columbia.

[Proposed by Congress June 16, 1960; ratified Mar. 29, 1961.]

Section 1. The District constituting the seat of Government of the United States shall appoint in such manner as the Congress may direct:

A number of electors of President and Vice President equal to the whole number of Senators and Representatives in Congress to which the District would be entitled if it were a State, but in no event more than the least populous State; they shall be in addition to those appointed by the States, but they shall be considered, for the purposes of the election of President and Vice President, to be electors appointed by a State; and they shall meet in the District and perform such duties as provided by the twelfth article of amendment.

Section 2. The Congress shall have power to enforce this article by appropriate legislation.

AMENDMENT XXIV.

Poll tax barred in federal elections.

[Proposed by Congress Sept. 14, 1962; ratified Jan. 23, 1964.]

Section 1. The right of citizens of the United States to vote in any primary or other election for President or Vice President, for electors for President or Vice President, or for

Senator or Representative in Congress, shall not be denied or abridged by the United States or any State by reason of failure to pay any poll tax or other tax.

Section 2. The Congress shall have power to enforce this article by appropriate legislation.

AMENDMENT XXV.

Presidential vacancy, inability, and succession.

[Proposed by Congress July 6, 1965; ratified Feb. 10, 1967.]

Section 1. In case of the removal of the President from office or of his death or resignation, the Vice President shall become President.

Section 2. Whenever there is a vacancy in the office of the Vice President, the President shall nominate a Vice President who shall take office upon confirmation by a majority vote of both Houses of Congress.

Section 3. Whenever the President transmits to the President pro tempore of the Senate and the Speaker of the House of Representatives his written declaration that he is unable to discharge the powers and duties of his office, and until he transmits to them a written declaration to the contrary, such powers and duties shall be discharged by the Vice President as Acting President.

Section 4. Whenever the Vice President and a majority of either the principal officers of the executive departments or of such other body as Congress may by law provide, transmit to the President pro tempore of the Senate and the Speaker of the House of Representatives their written declaration that the President is unable to discharge the powers and duties of his office, the Vice President shall immediately assume the powers and duties of the office as Acting President.

Thereafter, when the President transmits to the President pro tempore of the Senate and the Speaker of the House of Representatives his written declaration that no inability exists, he shall resume the powers and duties of his office unless the Vice President and a majority of either the principal officers of the executive department or of such other body as Congress may by law provide, transmit within four days to the President pro tempore of the Senate and the Speaker of the House of Representatives their written declaration that the President is unable to discharge the powers and duties of his office. Thereupon Congress shall decide the issue, assembling within forty-eight hours for that purpose if not in session. If the Congress, within twenty-one days after receipt of the latter written declaration, or, if Congress is not in session, within twenty-one days after Congress is required to assemble, determines by two-thirds vote of both Houses that the President is unable to discharge the powers and duties of his office, the Vice President shall continue to discharge the same as Acting President; otherwise, the President shall resume the powers and duties of his office.

AMENDMENT XXVI.

Voting age lowered to 18 years.

[Proposed by Congress Mar. 23, 1971; ratified July 1, 1971.]

Section 1. The right of citizens of the United States, who are eighteen years of age or older, to vote shall not be denied or abridged by the United States or by any State on account of age.

Section 2. The Congress shall have power to enforce this article by appropriate legislation.

AMENDMENT XXVII.

Congressional pay.

[Proposed by Congress Sept. 25, 1789; ratified May 7, 1992.]

No law, varying the compensation for the services of the Senators and Representatives, shall take effect, until an election of Representatives shall have intervened.

How a Bill Becomes a Law

A senator or representative introduces a bill in Congress by sending it to the clerk of the Senate or the House, who assigns it a number and title. This procedure is termed the first reading. The clerk then refers the bill to the appropriate committee of the Senate or House.

If the committee does not wish to consider the bill, it will table it. Otherwise, the committee holds hearings to listen to opinions and facts offered by members and other interested parties. The committee then debates the bill and may offer amendments. A vote is taken, and if favorable, the bill is sent back to the clerk of the Senate or House.

The clerk reads the bill to the house—the second reading. Members may then debate the bill and suggest amendments.

After debate and any amendments, the bill is given a third reading, simply of the title, and put to a voice or roll-call vote.

If the bill passes, it goes to the other house, where it may be defeated or passed, with or without amendments. If defeated, the bill dies. If passed with amendments, a conference committee made up of members of both houses works out the differences between the two bills and arrives at a compromise.

After passage of the final version by both houses, the bill is sent to the president. If the president signs it, the bill becomes a law. The president may instead veto the bill by refusing to sign it and sending it back to the house where it originated, with reasons for the veto.

The president's objections are then read and debated, and a roll-call vote is taken. If the bill receives less than a two-thirds majority, it is defeated. If it receives at least two-thirds, it is sent to the other house. If that house also passes it by at least a two-thirds majority, the president's veto is overridden, and the bill becomes a law.

If the president neither signs nor vetoes the bill within 10 days—not including Sundays—it automatically becomes a law even without the president's signature. However, if Congress adjourns within those 10 days, the bill is automatically killed; this indirect rejection is termed a pocket veto.

Under the Line Item Veto Act, effective Jan. 1, 1997, the president was authorized, under certain circumstances, to veto a bill in part. The legislation was found unconstitutional by the Supreme Court, June 25, 1998.

Presidential Oath of Office

The Constitution (Article II) directs that the president-elect shall take the following oath to be inaugurated: "I do solemnly swear [affirm] that I will faithfully execute the office of President of the United States, and will, to the best of my ability, preserve, protect, and defend the Constitution of the United States."

Custom decrees the addition of the words "So help me God" at the end of the oath when taken by the president-elect, with the left hand on the Bible for the duration of the oath, and the right hand slightly raised.

Presidential Succession

If, by reason of death, resignation, removal from office, inability, or failure to qualify, there is neither a president nor vice president to discharge the powers and duties of the office of president, then the speaker of the House of Representatives shall upon his resignation as speaker and as representative, act as president. The same rule shall apply in the case of the death, resignation, removal from office, or inability of an individual acting as president.

If, at the time when a speaker is to begin the discharge of the powers and duties of the office of president, there is no speaker, or the speaker fails to qualify as acting president, then the president pro tempore of the Senate, upon his resignation as president pro tempore and as senator, shall act as president.

An individual acting as president shall continue to act until the expiration of the then current presidential term, except that (1) if his discharge of the powers and duties of the office is founded in whole or in part in the failure of both the president-elect and the vice president-elect to qualify, then he shall act only until a president or vice president qualifies, and (2) if his discharge of the powers and duties of the office is founded in whole or in part on the inability of the president or vice president, then he shall act only until the removal of the disability of one of such individuals.

If, by reason of death, resignation, removal from office, or failure to qualify, there is no president pro tempore to act as president, then the officer of the United States who is highest on the following list, and who is not under any disability to discharge the powers and duties of president shall act as president: the secretaries of state, treasury, and defense; the attorney general; the secretaries of interior, agriculture, commerce, labor, health and human services, housing and urban development, transportation, energy, education, veterans affairs, and homeland security.

Legislation approved July 18, 1947; amended Sept. 9, 1965, Oct. 15, 1966, Aug. 4, 1977, Sept. 27, 1979, and Mar. 9, 2006. See also Constitutional Amendment XXV.

Confederate States: Secession and Government

The American Civil War (1861-65) grew out of sectional disputes over the continued existence of slavery in the South. Southern legislators contended that the states retained many rights, including the right to own slaves and the right to secede.

The war was not fought by state against state but by one federal regime against another. A Confederate government in Richmond, VA, assumed control over the economic, political, and military life of the seceding states, under protest from Georgia and South Carolina.

South Carolina voted unanimously in convention to secede from the Union, repealing its 1788 ratification of the U.S. Constitution on Dec. 20, 1860, to take effect on Dec. 24. Other states seceded in 1861. Their votes in conventions were: Mississippi, Jan. 9, 84-15; Florida, Jan. 10, 62-7; Alabama, Jan. 11, 61-39; Georgia, Jan. 19, 208-89; Louisiana, Jan. 26, 113-17; Texas, Feb. 1, 166-7, ratified by popular vote (34,794 to 11,325) Feb. 23; Virginia, Apr. 17, 88-55, ratified by popular vote (128,884 to 32,134) May 23; Arkansas, May 6, 69-1; Tennessee, May 7, ratified by popular vote (104,019 to 47,238) June 8; North Carolina, unanimous, May 20.

Missouri Unionists stopped secession in conventions Feb. 28 and Mar. 9, 1861. Under the protection of Confederate troops, secessionist members of the legislature adopted a resolution of secession at Neosho, Oct. 31. The Confederate Congress seated the secessionists' representatives.

Kentucky did not secede, and its government remained Unionist. In a part of the state occupied by Confederate troops, Kentuckians approved secession, and the Confederate Congress admitted their representatives.

The Maryland legislature voted against secession Apr. 27, 1861, 53-13. Delaware did not secede. Pro-Union residents of western Virginia held conventions at Wheeling and, on June 17, 1861, formed the Restored Government of Virginia. It was admitted to the Union as West Virginia on June 20, 1863. Its constitution provided for gradual abolition of slavery.

Forty-two delegates from South Carolina, Georgia, Alabama, Mississippi, Louisiana, and Florida met in convention in Montgomery, AL, on Feb. 4, 1861. They adopted a provisional constitution of the Confederate States of America and elected Jefferson Davis (MS) as provisional president and Alexander H. Stephens (GA) as provisional vice president.

A permanent constitution was adopted Mar. 11. It banned African slave trade, but it did not bar interstate commerce in slaves. On July 20 the Congress moved to Richmond. Davis was elected president in Nov. 1861 and was inaugurated Feb. 22, 1862.

The Congress adopted a flag consisting of a red field with a white stripe and a blue jack with a circle of white stars. Later, the more popular flag was the red field with blue diagonal crossbars that held 13 white stars, for the 11 states in the Confederacy plus Kentucky and Missouri.

The Gettysburg Address

Delivered by Pres. Abraham Lincoln at the dedication of the Soldiers' National Cemetery in Gettysburg, PA, on Nov. 19, 1863. Five handwritten copies of the Gettysburg Address as made by Lincoln are known to exist. The text differs slightly between copies. The Bliss copy, made for Alexander Bliss, is shown here. The copy is kept on display in the White House.

Four score and seven years ago our fathers brought forth on this continent, a new nation, conceived in Liberty, and dedicated to the proposition that all men are created equal.

Now we are engaged in a great civil war, testing whether that nation, or any nation so conceived and so dedicated, can long endure. We are met on a great battle-field of that war. We have come to dedicate a portion of that field, as a final resting place for those who here gave their lives that that nation might live. It is altogether fitting and proper that we should do this.

But, in a larger sense, we can not dedicate—we can not consecrate—we can not hallow—this ground. The brave men, living and dead, who struggled here, have consecrated it, far above our poor power to add or detract. The world will little note, nor long remember what we say here, but it can never forget what they did here.

It is for us the living, rather, to be dedicated here to the unfinished work which they who fought here have thus far so nobly advanced. It is rather for us to be here dedicated to the great task remaining before us—that from these honored dead we take increased devotion to that cause for which they gave the last full measure of devotion—that we here highly resolve that these dead shall not have died in vain—that this nation, under God, shall have a new birth of freedom—and that government of the people, by the people, for the people, shall not perish from the earth.

Origin of the United States National Motto

In God We Trust, designated as the U.S. National Motto by Congress in 1956, originated during the Civil War as an inscription for U.S. coins. On Nov. 13, 1861, the Rev. M. R. Watkinson, of Ridleyville, PA, wrote to Treasury Sec. Salmon P. Chase requesting "recognition of the Almighty God in some form on our coins." Chase ordered designs prepared with the inscription *In God We Trust* and backed coinage legislation that authorized use of this slogan. The motto first appeared on some U.S. coins in 1864 and sporadically thereafter until 1938, after which all U.S. coins bear the inscription. A joint resolution passed by the 84th Congress and signed by Pres. Dwight D. Eisenhower July 30, 1956, declared *In God We Trust* the national motto of the United States.

Great Seal of the U.S.

On July 4, 1776, the Continental Congress appointed a committee consisting of Benjamin Franklin, John Adams, and Thomas Jefferson "to bring in a device for a seal of the United States of America." The designs submitted by this and a subsequent committee were considered unacceptable. After many delays, a third committee, appointed early in 1782, presented a design prepared by lawyer William Barton. Charles Thomson, the secretary of Congress, suggested certain changes, and Congress finally approved the design on June 20, 1782. The obverse side of the seal shows an American bald eagle. In its mouth is a ribbon bearing the motto *E Pluribus Unum* (out of many, one). In the eagle's talons are 13 arrows of war and an olive branch of peace. The reverse side shows an unfinished pyramid with an eye (Eye of Providence) above it.

The Flag of the U.S.—The Stars and Stripes

The 50-star flag of the United States was raised for the first time officially at 12:01 AM on July 4, 1960, at Ft. McHenry National Monument in Baltimore, MD. The 50th star had been added for Hawaii; a year earlier the 49th, for Alaska.

There are so many myths and legends surrounding the history of the Stars and Stripes that the facts are difficult, and in some cases impossible, to establish. For example, it is not certain who designed the Stars and Stripes, who made the first such flag, or even whether it ever flew during any battle of the American Revolution.

Historians agree, however, that the Stars and Stripes originated as the result of a resolution offered by the Marine Committee of the Second Continental Congress at Philadelphia and adopted on June 14, 1777. It read:

"Resolved: that the flag of the United States be thirteen stripes, alternate red and white; that the union be thirteen stars, white in a blue field, representing a new constellation."

Congress gave no hint as to the designer of the flag, no instructions as to the arrangement of the stars, and no information on its appropriate uses.

The resolution establishing the flag was not published until Sept. 2, 1777. Despite repeated requests, Washington did not get the flags until 1783, after the war was over. And there is no certainty that they were the Stars and Stripes.

Early Flags

Many historians consider the first flag of the U.S. to have been the Grand Union (sometimes called Great Union) flag, although the Continental Congress never officially adopted it. This flag was a modification of the British Meteor flag, which had the red cross of St. George and the white cross of St. Andrew combined in the blue canton. For the Grand Union flag, six horizontal stripes were imposed on the red field, dividing it into 13 alternating red and white stripes. On Jan. 1, 1776, when the Continental Army came into formal existence, this flag was unfurled on Prospect Hill, Somerville, MA. Washington wrote that "we hoisted the Union Flag in compliment to the United Colonies."

One of several flags about which controversy has raged for years is in Easton, PA. Containing the devices of the national flag in reversed order, this flag has been in the public library at Easton for more than 150 years. Some contend that this flag was actually the first Stars and Stripes, first displayed on July 8, 1776. This flag has 13 red and white stripes in the canton, 13 white stars centered in a blue field.

A flag was hastily improvised from garments by the defenders of Ft. Schuyler at Rome, NY, Aug. 3-22, 1777. Historians believe it was the Grand Union Flag.

The Sons of Liberty had a flag of nine red and white stripes, to signify nine colonies, when they met in New York in 1765 to oppose the Stamp Tax. By 1775, the flag had grown to 13 red and white stripes, with a rattlesnake on it.

At Concord, Apr. 19, 1775, the minutemen from Bedford, MA, are said to have carried a flag having a silver arm with sword on a red field. At Cambridge, MA, the Sons of Liberty used a plain red flag with a green pine tree on it.

In June 1775, Washington went from Philadelphia to Boston to take command of the army. He was escorted to New York by the Philadelphia Light Horse Troop, which carried a yellow flag that had an elaborate coat of arms—the shield charged with 13 knots, the motto "For These We Strive"—and a canton of 13 blue and silver stripes.

In Feb. 1776, Col. Christopher Gadsden, a member of the Continental Congress, gave the South Carolina Provincial Congress a flag "such as is to be used by the commander-in-chief of the American Navy." It had a yellow field, with a rattlesnake about to strike and the words "Don't Tread on Me."

At the Battle of Bennington, Aug. 16, 1777, patriots used a flag of seven white and six red stripes with a blue canton extending down nine stripes and showing an arch of 11 white stars over the figure 76 and a star in each of the upper corners. The stars are seven-pointed. This flag is preserved in the historical museum in Bennington, VT.

At the Battle of Cowpens, Jan. 17, 1781, the 3rd Maryland Regiment is said to have carried a flag of 13 red and white stripes, with a blue canton containing 12 stars in a circle around one star.

Who Designed the Flag? No one knows for certain. Francis Hopkinson, designer of a naval flag, declared he had designed the flag and in 1781 asked Congress to reimburse him for his services. Congress did not do so.

Who Called the Flag "Old Glory"? The flag is said to have been named Old Glory by William Driver, a sea captain of Salem, MA. One legend has it that he did so when he raised the flag on his brig in 1824. But his daughter said he named it at his 21st birthday celebration on Mar. 17, 1824, when his mother presented the homemade flag to him.

The Betsy Ross Legend. The widely publicized legend that Betsy Ross made the first Stars and Stripes in June 1776, at the request of a committee composed of George Washington, Robert Morris, and George Ross, an uncle, was first made public in 1870, by a grandson of Ross. Historians have been unable to find a historical record of such a meeting or committee.

Adding New Stars

On the admission of Vermont and Kentucky to the Union, Congress designated that after May 1, 1795, the flag should have 15 stripes, alternating red and white, and 15 white stars on a blue field.

When more new states were admitted, it became evident that the flag would become burdened with stripes. Congress ordered that after July 4, 1818, the flag should have 13 stripes, symbolizing 13 original states; that the union have 20 stars, and that whenever a new state was admitted a new star should be added on the July 4 following admission.

No law designates the permanent arrangement of the stars. However, since 1912, when a new state has been admitted, the new design has been announced by executive order. No star is specifically identified with any state.

Code of Etiquette for Display and Use of the U.S. Flag

Source: Congressional Research Service

Although the Stars and Stripes originated in 1777, it was not until 146 years later that there was a serious attempt to establish a uniform code of etiquette for the U.S. flag. On Feb. 15, 1923, the War Department issued a circular on the rules of flag usage. A joint resolution of Congress June 22, 1942, amended by Public Law 94-344, July 7, 1976, codified "existing rules and customs pertaining to the display and use of the flag." Military branches have their own codes of etiquette regarding the flag; this guide is for civilian purposes.

An act of Congress approved on Feb. 8, 1917, provided certain penalties for the desecration, mutilation, or improper use of the flag within the District of Columbia. A 1968 federal law provided penalties of as much as a year's imprisonment or a $1,000 fine or both for publicly burning or otherwise desecrating any U.S. flag. In 1989, the Supreme Court ruled that no laws could prohibit political protesters from burning the flag. The decision had the effect of declaring unconstitutional the flag desecration laws of 48 states, as well as a similar federal statute, in cases of peaceful political expression.

The Supreme Court, in June 1990, declared that a new federal law making it a crime to burn or deface the American flag violated the free-speech guarantee of the First Amendment. The decision led to repeated attempts in Congress to pass a constitutional amendment to make it possible to prosecute flag burners. In 2005, the House passed a flag desecration amendment with the requisite two-thirds majority, but the measure failed by one vote to achieve two-thirds majority in the Senate in 2006.

The current code of etiquette clarifies U.S. customs and rules for flag display. No penalty or punishment is specified for display of the flag other than as suggested.

When to Display the Flag. The flag should be displayed on all days, especially on legal holidays and other special occasions, in or near every public institution, in or near polling places on election days, and in or near schools when in session. Citizens may fly the flag at any time. It is customary to display the flag only from sunrise to sunset on buildings and on stationary flagstaffs in the open. It may be displayed at night if properly illuminated.

Flying the Flag at Half-Staff. Flying the flag at half-staff is a signal of mourning. The flag should be hoisted to the top of the staff for an instant before being lowered to half-staff. It should be hoisted to the peak again before being lowered for the day.

The flag should fly at half-staff for 30 days from the day of death of a president or former president; for 10 days from the day of death of a vice president, chief justice or retired chief justice of the U.S., or speaker of the House of Representatives; from day of death until burial of an associate justice of the Supreme Court, cabinet member, former vice president, or governor; for a member of Congress, on day of death and the following day.

On Memorial Day, the flag should fly at half-staff until noon and then be raised to the peak.

How to Display the Flag. The flag should be hoisted briskly and lowered ceremoniously and should never be allowed to touch the ground or the floor. When the flag is hung over a sidewalk from a rope extending from a building to a pole, the union (the blue field with white stars) should be at the peak of the staff. When the flag is hung over the center of a street the union should be to the north in an east-west street and to the east in a north-south street. No other flag may be flown above or, if on the same level, to the right of the U.S. flag. At the United Nations Headquarters, however, the UN flag may be placed above flags of all member nations and other national flags may be flown with equal prominence or honor with the flag of the U.S.

When the flag is displayed horizontally or vertically against a wall, the stars should be uppermost and at the observer's left.

When used to cover a casket, the flag should be placed so that the union is at the head and over the left shoulder. It should not be lowered into the grave nor touch the ground.

How to Dispose of Worn Flags. When the flag is in such condition that it is no longer fit for display, it should be destroyed in a dignified way, preferably by burning.

Prohibited Uses of the Flag. The flag should not be dipped to any person or thing. (An exception—customarily, ships salute by dipping their colors.) It should never be displayed with the union down save as a distress signal. It should never be carried flat or horizontally, but always aloft and free.

The flag should not be draped over the hood, top, sides, or back of a vehicle, train, or boat; if displayed on a vehicle the staff should be fixed to the chassis or right fender. It should not be used as a receptacle for carrying anything. It should not be used to cover a statue or a monument.

The flag should never be used for advertising purposes, nor be embroidered on such articles as cushions or handkerchiefs, printed on boxes or anything that is designed for temporary use; or used as a costume or athletic uniform.

Pledge of Allegiance to the Flag

I pledge allegiance to the flag of the United States of America, and to the republic for which it stands, one nation under God, indivisible, with liberty and justice for all.

This, the current official version of the Pledge of Allegiance, developed from a pledge first published in the Sept. 8, 1892, issue of *Youth's Companion*, a weekly magazine. The original pledge contained the phrase "my flag," which was changed more than 30 years later to "flag of the United States of America." A 1954 act of Congress added the words "under God." (In 2002, the 9th Circuit U.S. Court of Appeals ruled that recitation of the pledge in public schools could not include that phrase. In 2004, however, the U.S. Supreme Court voted to decline to decide the case on a technicality. The lower court's decision was thus overturned.)

The authorship of the pledge was in dispute for many years. *Youth's Companion* stated in 1917 that the original draft was written by James B. Upham, an executive of the magazine who died in 1910. A leaflet circulated by the magazine later named Upham as the originator of the first draft.

Francis Bellamy, a former member of the *Youth's Companion* editorial staff, publicly claimed authorship of the pledge in 1923. In 1939, the United States Flag Association, acting on the advice of a committee named to study the controversy, upheld the claim of Bellamy, who had died eight years earlier. In 1957 the Library of Congress issued a report attributing the authorship to Bellamy.

According to the federal Flag Code, the pledge should be given while standing at attention facing the flag with the right hand over the heart. Those not in military uniform should remove any non-religious head coverings with their right hand and hold it at the left shoulder, the hand being over the heart. Those in uniform should remain silent, face the flag, and render a military salute.

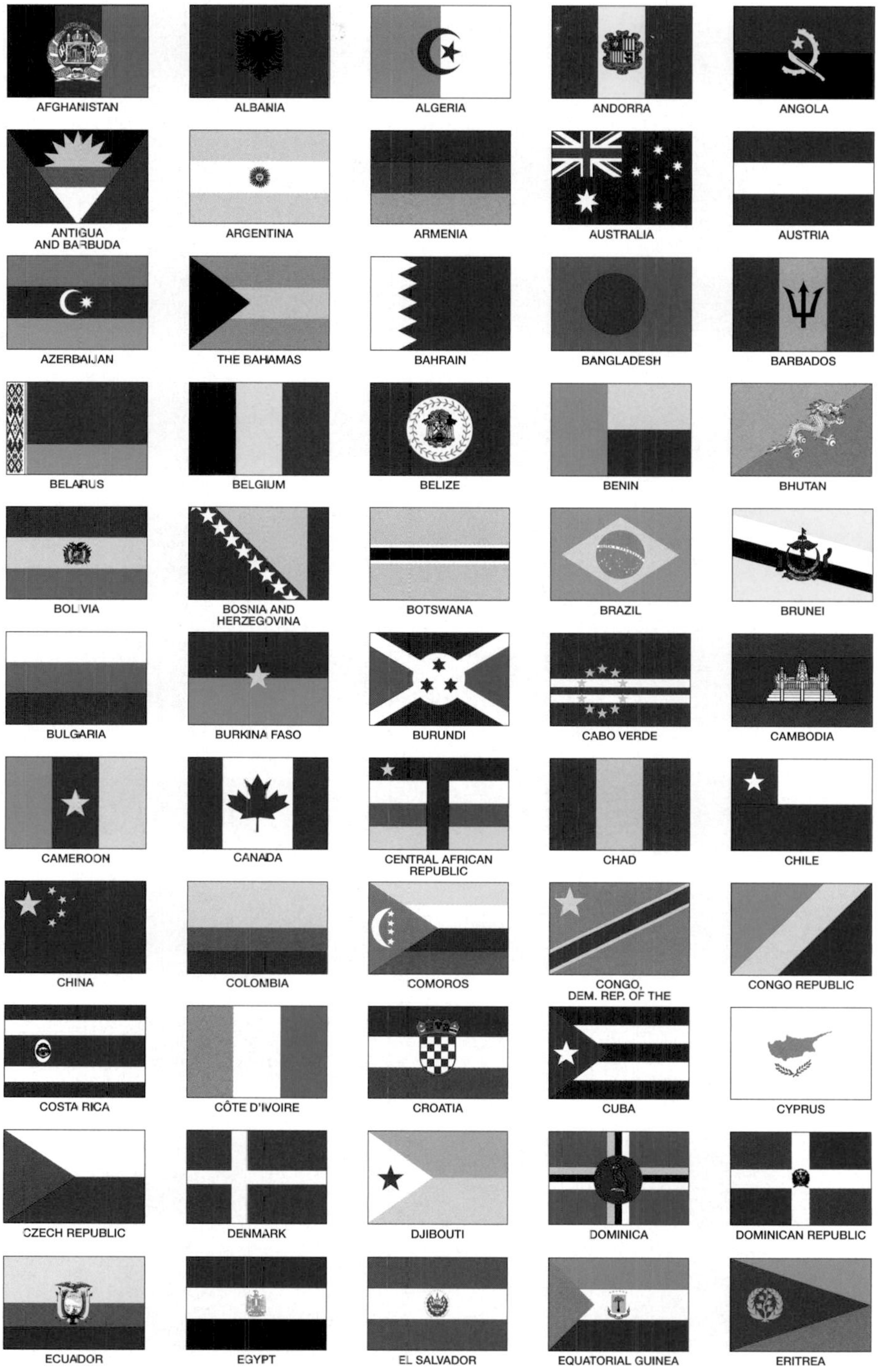
AFGHANISTAN
ALBANIA
ALGERIA
ANDORRA
ANGOLA
ANTIGUA AND BARBUDA
ARGENTINA
ARMENIA
AUSTRALIA
AUSTRIA
AZERBAIJAN
THE BAHAMAS
BAHRAIN
BANGLADESH
BARBADOS
BELARUS
BELGIUM
BELIZE
BENIN
BHUTAN
BOLIVIA
BOSNIA AND HERZEGOVINA
BOTSWANA
BRAZIL
BRUNEI
BULGARIA
BURKINA FASO
BURUNDI
CABO VERDE
CAMBODIA
CAMEROON
CANADA
CENTRAL AFRICAN REPUBLIC
CHAD
CHILE
CHINA
COLOMBIA
COMOROS
CONGO, DEM. REP. OF THE
CONGO REPUBLIC
COSTA RICA
CÔTE D'IVOIRE
CROATIA
CUBA
CYPRUS
CZECH REPUBLIC
DENMARK
DJIBOUTI
DOMINICA
DOMINICAN REPUBLIC
ECUADOR
EGYPT
EL SALVADOR
EQUATORIAL GUINEA
ERITREA

Note: Flag proportions have been standardized to fit page.

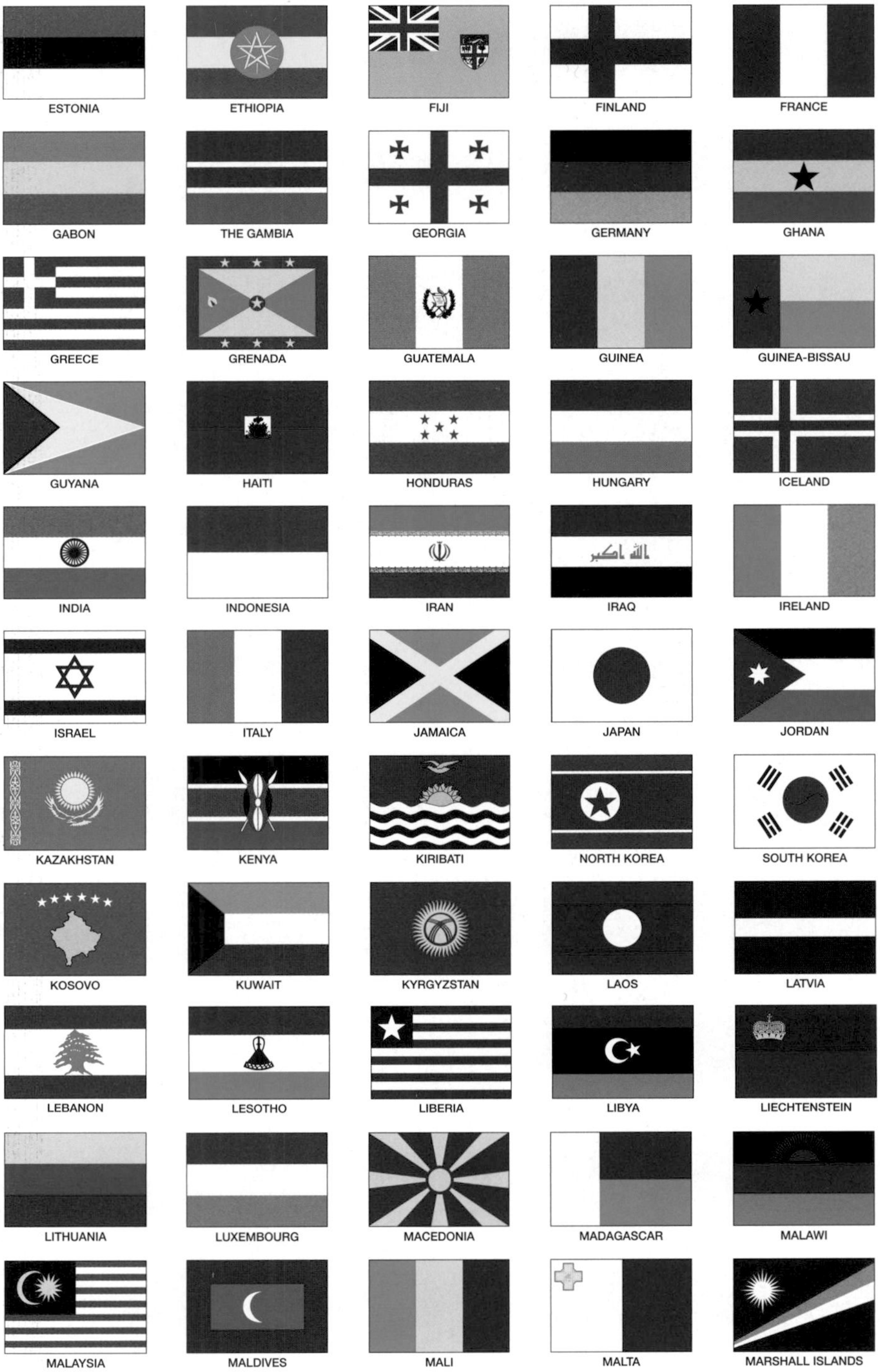

Note: Flag proportions have been standardized to fit page.

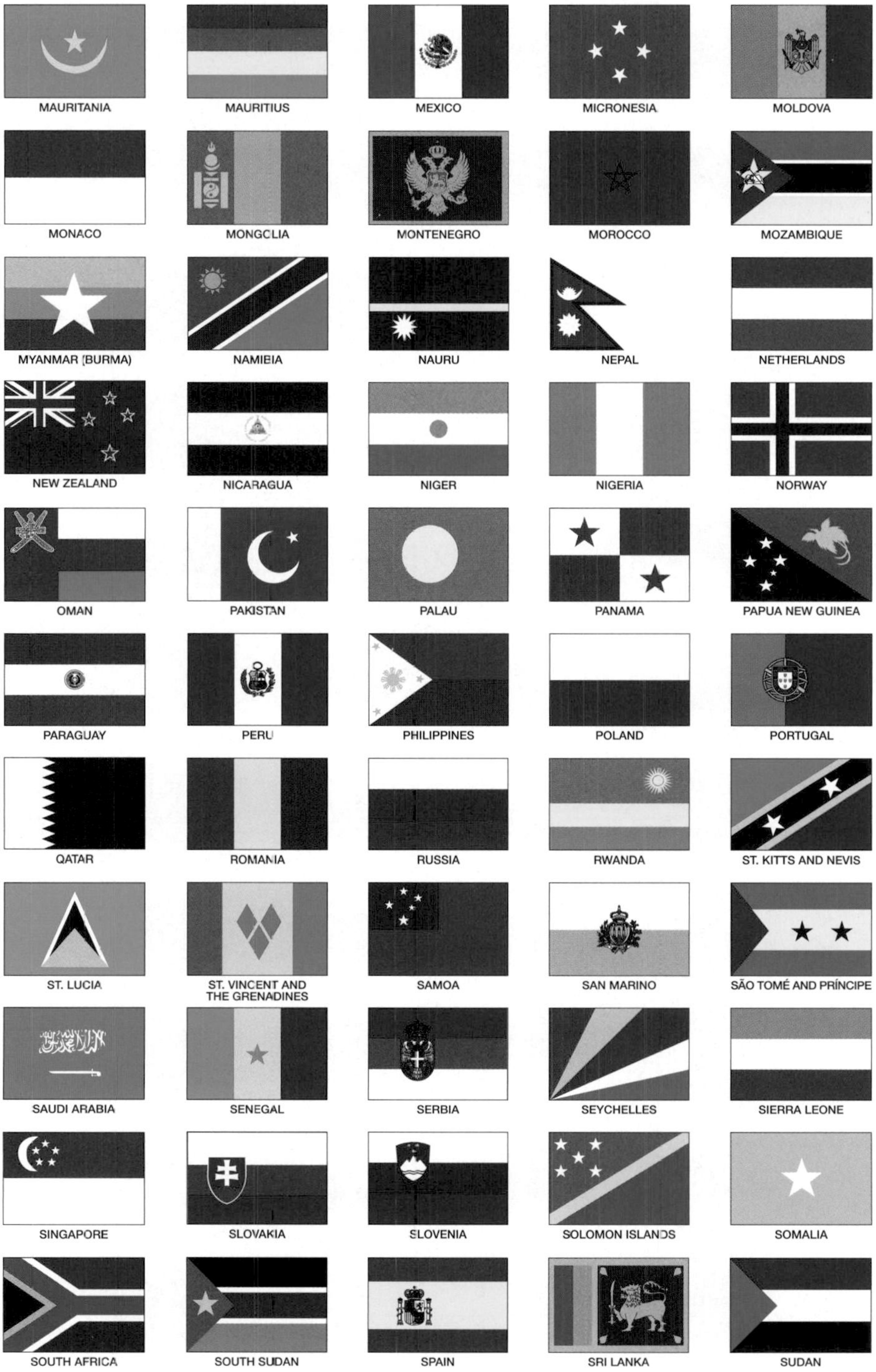
MAURITANIA
MAURITIUS
MEXICO
MICRONESIA
MOLDOVA
MONACO
MONGOLIA
MONTENEGRO
MOROCCO
MOZAMBIQUE
MYANMAR (BURMA)
NAMIBIA
NAURU
NEPAL
NETHERLANDS
NEW ZEALAND
NICARAGUA
NIGER
NIGERIA
NORWAY
OMAN
PAKISTAN
PALAU
PANAMA
PAPUA NEW GUINEA
PARAGUAY
PERU
PHILIPPINES
POLAND
PORTUGAL
QATAR
ROMANIA
RUSSIA
RWANDA
ST. KITTS AND NEVIS
ST. LUCIA
ST. VINCENT AND THE GRENADINES
SAMOA
SAN MARINO
SÃO TOMÉ AND PRÍNCIPE
SAUDI ARABIA
SENEGAL
SERBIA
SEYCHELLES
SIERRA LEONE
SINGAPORE
SLOVAKIA
SLOVENIA
SOLOMON ISLANDS
SOMALIA
SOUTH AFRICA
SOUTH SUDAN
SPAIN
SRI LANKA
SUDAN

Note: Flag proportions have been standardized to fit page.

SURINAME

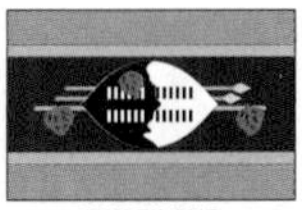
SWAZILAND

SWEDEN

SWITZERLAND

SYRIA

TAIWAN

TAJIKISTAN

TANZANIA

THAILAND

TIMOR-LESTE (EAST TIMOR)

TOGO

TONGA

TRINIDAD AND TOBAGO

TUNISIA

TURKEY

TURKMENISTAN

TUVALU

UGANDA

UKRAINE

UNITED ARAB EMIRATES

UNITED KINGDOM

UNITED STATES

URUGUAY

UZBEKISTAN

VANUATU

VATICAN CITY

VENEZUELA

VIETNAM

YEMEN

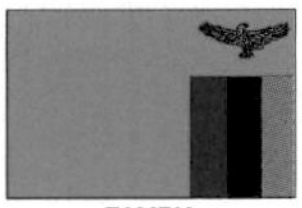
ZAMBIA

ZIMBABWE

INTERNATIONAL TIME ZONES

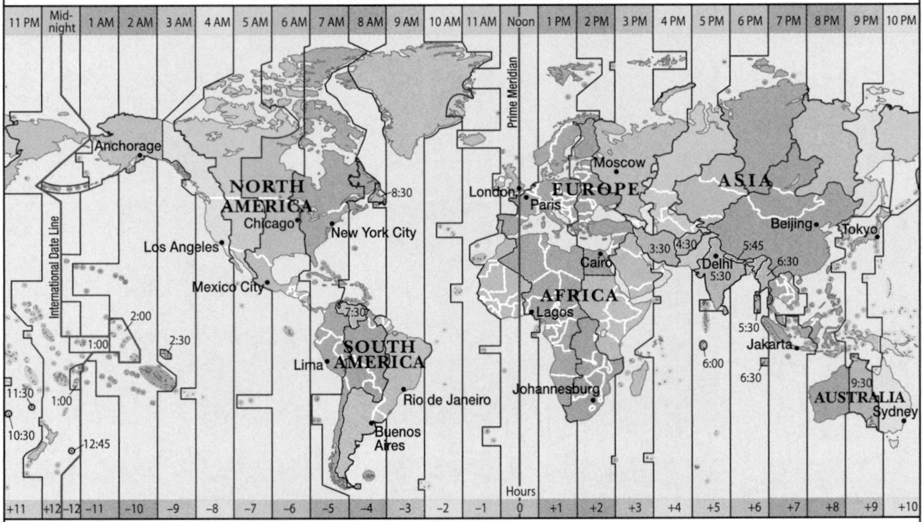

The world is divided into 24 time zones, each 15° longitude wide. The longitudinal meridian passing through Greenwich, England, is the starting point, and is called the *prime meridian*. The 12th zone is divided by the 180th meridian (International Date Line). When the line is crossed going west, the date is advanced one day; when crossed going east, the date becomes a day earlier.

Note: Flag proportions have been standardized to fit page.

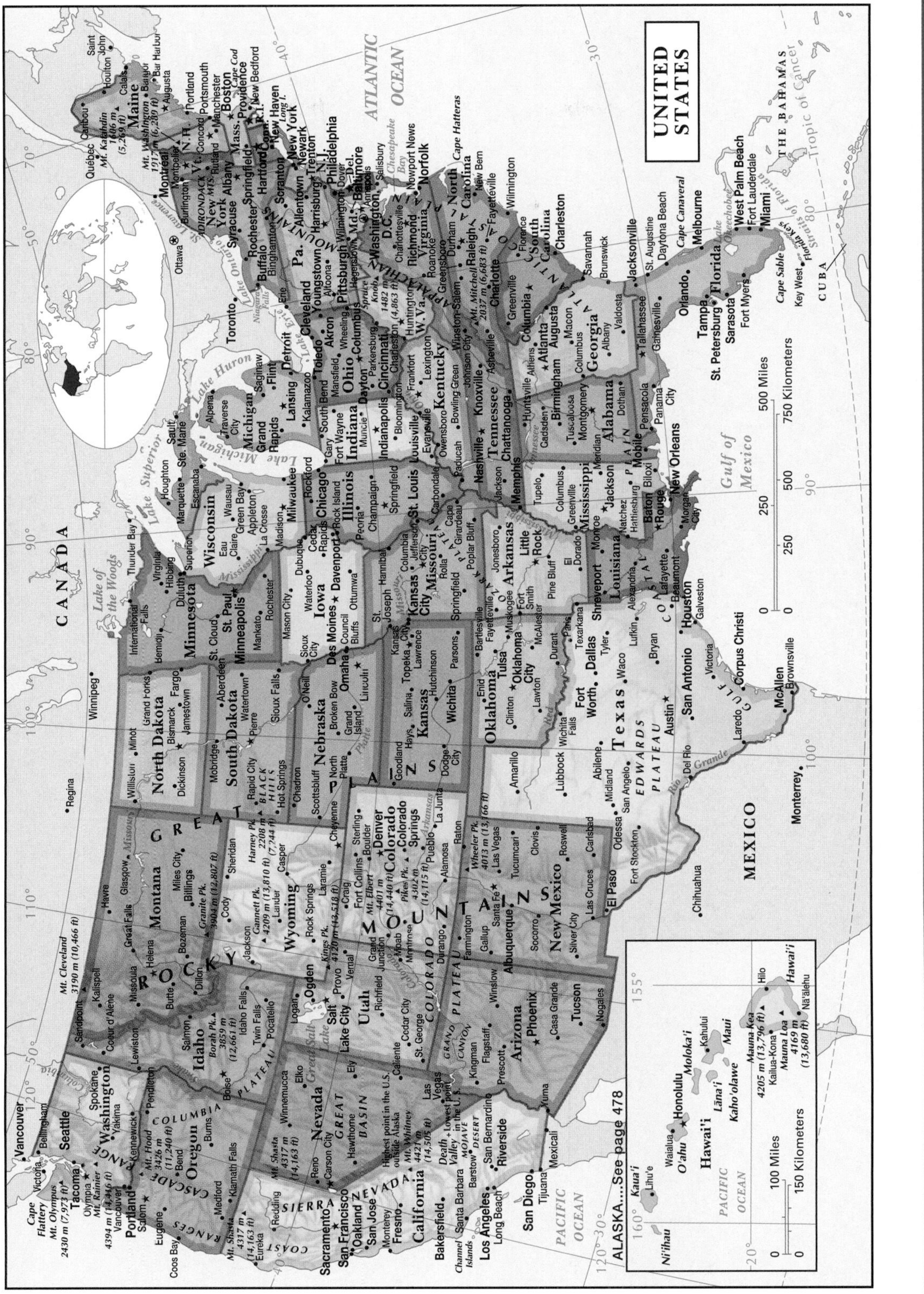
UNITED STATES
CANADA
MEXICO
ATLANTIC OCEAN
PACIFIC OCEAN
Gulf of Mexico
THE BAHAMAS
CUBA
Tropic of Cancer
Straits of Florida
Lake Superior
Lake Michigan
Lake Huron
Lake Erie
Lake Ontario
Lake of the Woods
Great Salt Lake
Chesapeake Bay
Lake Okeechobee
GREAT PLAINS
ROCKY MOUNTAINS
APPALACHIAN MOUNTAINS
COLUMBIA PLATEAU
COLORADO PLATEAU
GREAT BASIN
MOJAVE DESERT
EDWARDS PLATEAU
CASCADE RANGE
SIERRA NEVADA
COAST RANGES
COASTAL PLAIN
BLACK HILLS
ADIRONDACK MTS.
Washington
Oregon
California
Nevada
Idaho
Montana
Wyoming
Utah
Arizona
Colorado
New Mexico
North Dakota
South Dakota
Nebraska
Kansas
Oklahoma
Texas
Minnesota
Iowa
Missouri
Arkansas
Louisiana
Wisconsin
Illinois
Michigan
Indiana
Ohio
Kentucky
Tennessee
Mississippi
Alabama
Georgia
Florida
South Carolina
North Carolina
Virginia
W. Va.
Pa.
New York
Maine
Vt.
N.H.
Mass.
Conn.
R.I.
N.J.
Del.
Md.
Washington, D.C.
Seattle
Portland
San Francisco
Los Angeles
San Diego
Sacramento
Las Vegas
Phoenix
Salt Lake City
Denver
Dallas
Houston
San Antonio
New Orleans
Chicago
Detroit
St. Louis
Kansas City
Minneapolis
St. Paul
Atlanta
Miami
Boston
New York
Philadelphia
Baltimore
Mt. Whitney 4421 m (14,505 ft)
Death Valley Lowest point in the U.S.
Highest point in the U.S. outside Alaska
Mt. Rainier 4394 m (14,416 ft)
Mt. Elbert 4401 m (14,440 ft)
Mt. Mitchell 2037 m (6,683 ft)
Mt. Washington 1917 m (6,289 ft)
Cape Hatteras
Cape Cod
Cape Canaveral
Cape Sable
Florida Keys
0 250 500 Miles
0 250 500 750 Kilometers
Hawai'i
Ni'ihau
Kaua'i
O'ahu
Honolulu
Moloka'i
Lāna'i
Maui
Kaho'olawe
Mauna Kea 4205 m (13,796 ft)
Mauna Loa 4169 m (13,680 ft)
Hilo
0 100 Miles
0 150 Kilometers
ALASKA....See page 478

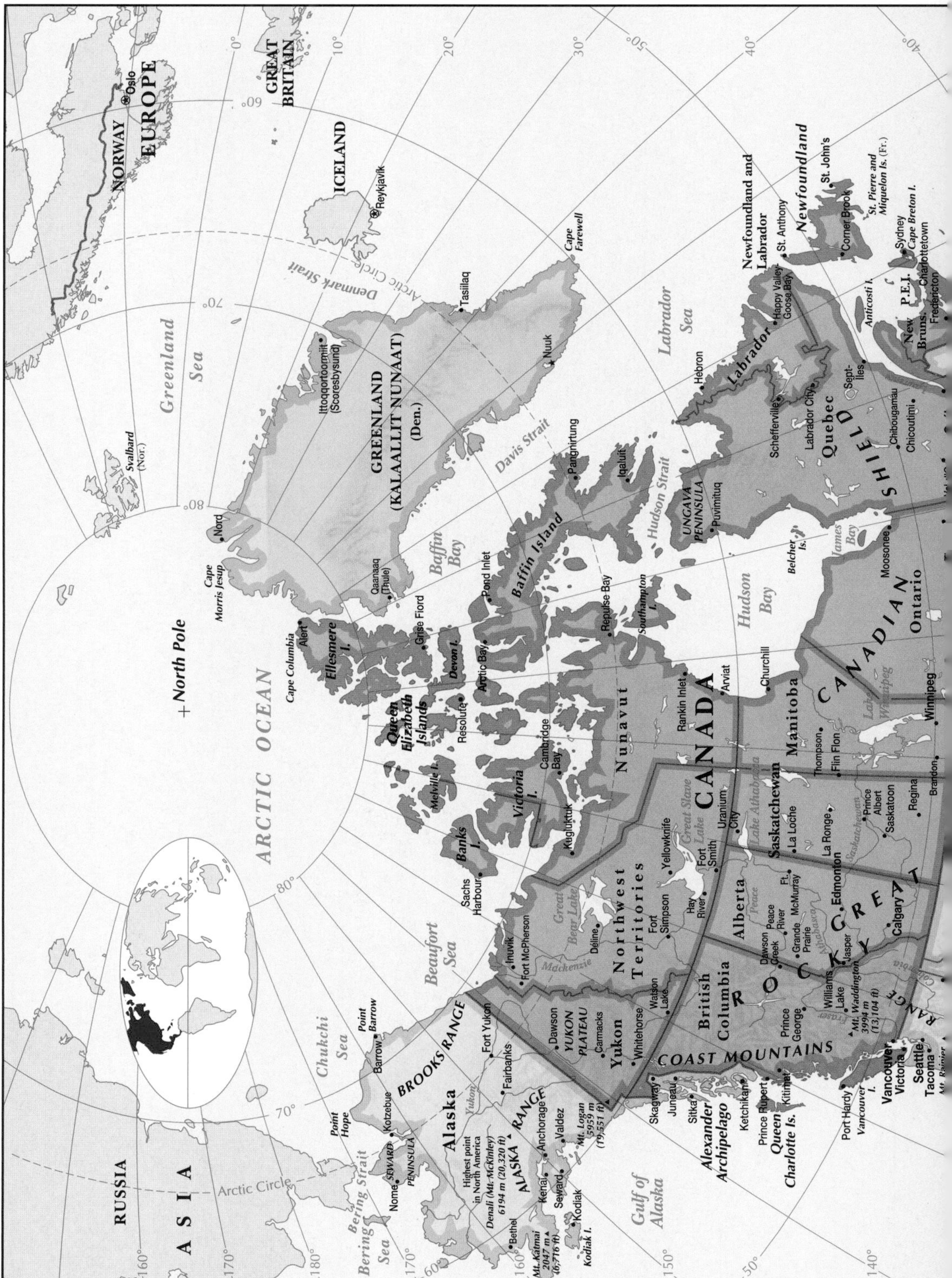

ARCTIC OCEAN
North Pole
NORWAY
Oslo
EUROPE
GREAT BRITAIN
ICELAND
Reykjavík
Denmark Strait
Arctic Circle
Greenland Sea
Svalbard (Nor.)
GREENLAND (KALAALLIT NUNAAT) (Den.)
Ittoqqortoormiit (Scoresbysund)
Tasiilaq
Cape Farewell
Nuuk
Cape Morris Jesup
Nord
Qaanaaq (Thule)
Baffin Bay
Davis Strait
Labrador Sea
Cape Columbia
Alert
Ellesmere I.
Grise Fiord
Devon I.
Queen Elizabeth Islands
Resolute
Arctic Bay
Pond Inlet
Baffin Island
Pangnirtung
Iqaluit
Hudson Strait
Southampton I.
Repulse Bay
Melville I.
Banks I.
Victoria I.
Cambridge Bay
Sachs Harbour
Kugluktuk
Nunavut
Rankin Inlet
Arviat
CANADA
Hudson Bay
Churchill
UNGAVA PENINSULA
Puvirnituq
Belcher Is.
James Bay
Moosonee
Hebron
Labrador
Schefferville
Labrador City
Sept-Îles
Happy Valley-Goose Bay
Newfoundland and Labrador
St. Anthony
Newfoundland
Corner Brook
St. John's
St. Pierre and Miquelon Is. (Fr.)
Sydney
Cape Breton I.
Charlottetown
Anticosti I.
P.E.I.
New Bruns.
Fredericton
Quebec
Chibougamau
Chicoutimi
CANADIAN SHIELD
Ontario
Manitoba
Lake Winnipeg
Winnipeg
Thompson
Flin Flon
Brandon
Saskatchewan
Prince Albert
Saskatoon
Regina
La Ronge
La Loche
Uranium City
Lake Athabasca
Great Slave Lake
Fort Smith
Yellowknife
Hay River
Northwest Territories
Fort Simpson
Great Bear Lake
Déline
Mackenzie
Inuvik
Fort McPherson
Beaufort Sea
Alberta
Peace
Peace River
Ft. McMurray
Edmonton
Grande Prairie
Dawson Creek
Jasper
Calgary
ROCKY
British Columbia
Williams Lake
Prince George
Mt. Waddington 3994 m (13,104 ft)
Fraser
COAST MOUNTAINS
Kitimat
Prince Rupert
Queen Charlotte Is.
Port Hardy
Vancouver I.
Vancouver
Victoria
Seattle
Tacoma
Ketchikan
Sitka
Juneau
Skagway
Alexander Archipelago
Whitehorse
Watson Lake
Yukon
Carmacks
YUKON PLATEAU
Dawson
Fort Yukon
Fairbanks
BROOKS RANGE
Point Barrow
Barrow
Chukchi Sea
Point Hope
Kotzebue
SEWARD PENINSULA
Nome
Alaska
Yukon
ALASKA RANGE
Highest point in North America
Denali (Mt. McKinley) 6194 m (20,320 ft)
Anchorage
Valdez
Mt. Logan 5959 m (19,551 ft)
Kenai
Seward
Kodiak
Kodiak I.
Bethel
Mt. Katmai 2047 m (6,716 ft)
Gulf of Alaska
Bering Strait
Bering Sea
RUSSIA
ASIA

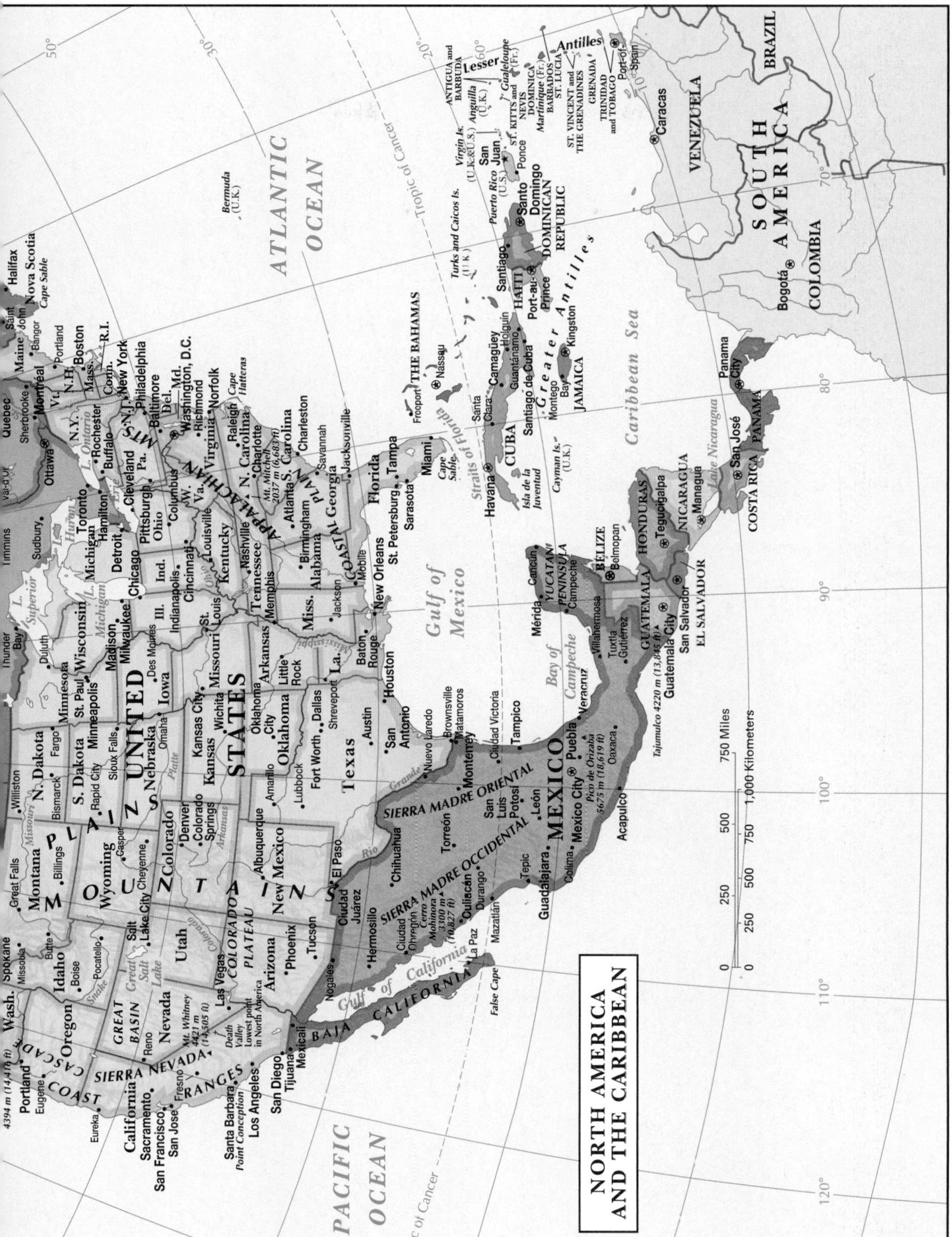
NORTH AMERICA AND THE CARIBBEAN
ATLANTIC OCEAN
PACIFIC OCEAN
Gulf of Mexico
Caribbean Sea
Bay of Campeche
Gulf of California
Tropic of Cancer
UNITED STATES
MEXICO
CUBA
HAITI
DOMINICAN REPUBLIC
JAMAICA
THE BAHAMAS
BELIZE
GUATEMALA
HONDURAS
EL SALVADOR
NICARAGUA
COSTA RICA
PANAMA
SOUTH AMERICA
VENEZUELA
COLOMBIA
BRAZIL
Greater Antilles
Lesser Antilles
ROCKY MOUNTAINS
GREAT PLAINS
APPALACHIAN MTS.
COASTAL PLAIN
GREAT BASIN
COLORADO PLATEAU
SIERRA NEVADA
COAST RANGES
CASCADE
SIERRA MADRE ORIENTAL
SIERRA MADRE OCCIDENTAL
BAJA CALIFORNIA
YUCATÁN PENINSULA
Washington, D.C.
Mexico City
Havana
Ottawa
Bermuda (U.K.)
0 250 500 750 Miles
0 250 500 750 1,000 Kilometers

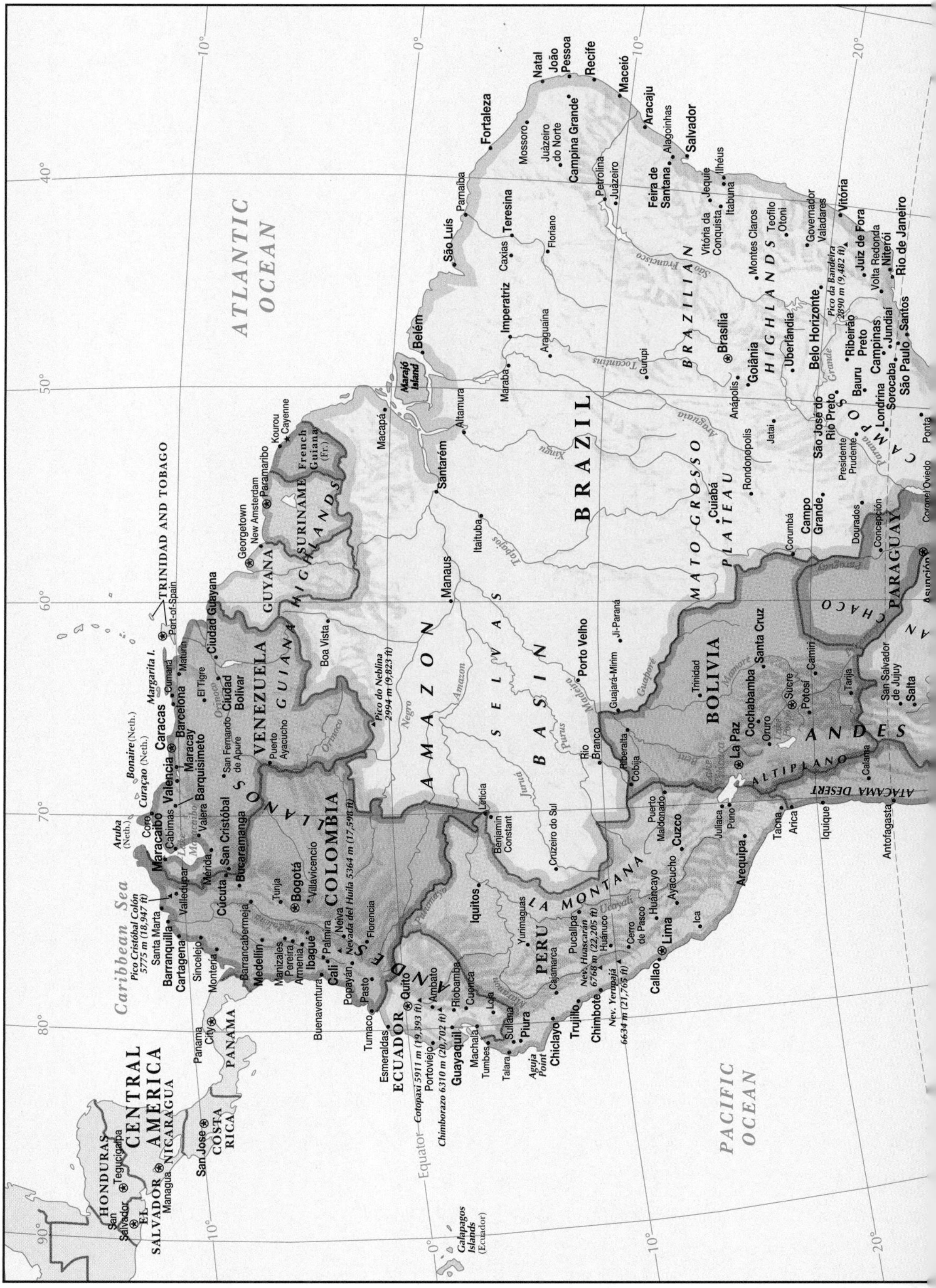
ATLANTIC OCEAN
PACIFIC OCEAN
Caribbean Sea
CENTRAL AMERICA
HONDURAS
Tegucigalpa
EL SALVADOR
San Salvador
NICARAGUA
Managua
COSTA RICA
San José
PANAMA
Panama City
Aruba (Neth.)
Bonaire (Neth.)
Curaçao (Neth.)
Margarita I.
TRINIDAD AND TOBAGO
Port-of-Spain
Pico Cristóbal Colón 5775 m (18,947 ft)
Barranquilla
Santa Marta
Cartagena
Sincelejo
Montería
Valledupar
Maracaibo
Coro
Cabimas
Lake Maracaibo
Valera
Mérida
San Cristóbal
Cúcuta
Bucaramanga
Barrancabermeja
Medellín
Manizales
Pereira
Armenia
Ibagué
Tunja
Bogotá
Villavicencio
Palmira
Cali
Buenaventura
Neiva
Florencia
Popayán
Pasto
Tumaco
Nevado del Huila 5364 m (17,598 ft)
COLOMBIA
LLANOS
VENEZUELA
Valencia
Caracas
Maracay
Barquisimeto
Barcelona
Cumaná
Maturín
El Tigre
Ciudad Bolívar
Ciudad Guayana
San Fernando de Apure
Puerto Ayacucho
Orinoco
GUIANA HIGHLANDS
GUYANA
Georgetown
SURINAME
New Amsterdam
Paramaribo
French Guiana (Fr.)
Kourou
Cayenne
Boa Vista
Pico do Neblina 2994 m (9,823 ft)
ECUADOR
Esmeraldas
Quito
Ambato
Riobamba
Cuenca
Guayaquil
Portoviejo
Machala
Loja
Cotopaxi 5911 m (19,393 ft)
Chimborazo 6310 m (20,702 ft)
Equator
Galapagos Islands (Ecuador)
PERU
Tumbes
Talara
Sullana
Piura
Aguja Point
Chiclayo
Cajamarca
Trujillo
Chimbote
Nev. Huascarán 6768 m (22,205 ft)
Nev. Yerupajá 6634 m (21,765 ft)
Huánuco
Cerro de Pasco
Callao
Lima
Ica
Huancayo
Ayacucho
Cuzco
Pucallpa
Yurimaguas
Iquitos
LA MONTANA
Ucayali
Marañon
Putumayo
Arequipa
Juliaca
Puno
Puerto Maldonado
Tacna
Arica
Iquique
Antofagasta
Calama
ATACAMA DESERT
ALTIPLANO
ANDES
Lake Titicaca
BOLIVIA
La Paz
Oruro
Cochabamba
Sucre
Potosí
Tarija
Trinidad
Santa Cruz
Camiri
Riberalta
Cobija
Guajará-Mirim
Lake Poopó
Beni
Mamoré
Guaporé
San Salvador de Jujuy
Salta
CHACO
PARAGUAY
Asunción
Concepción
Coronel Oviedo
AMAZON BASIN
SELVAS
Amazon
Negro
Juruá
Purus
Madeira
Tapajós
Xingu
Araguaia
Tocantins
São Francisco
Paraná
Grande
Paraguay
Leticia
Benjamin Constant
Cruzeiro do Sul
Rio Branco
Porto Velho
Ji-Paraná
Manaus
Itaituba
Santarém
Altamura
Macapá
Marajó Island
Belém
BRAZIL
São Luís
Parnaíba
Teresina
Fortaleza
Caxias
Floriano
Imperatriz
Marabá
Araguaína
Gurupi
Mossoró
Natal
João Pessoa
Juàzeiro do Norte
Campina Grande
Recife
Maceió
Aracaju
Petrolina
Juàzeiro
Feira de Santana
Alagoinhas
Salvador
Vitória da Conquista
Jequié
Ilhéus
Itabuna
Montes Claros
Teófilo Otoni
Governador Valadares
Vitória
BRAZILIAN HIGHLANDS
Brasília
Anápolis
Goiânia
Uberlândia
Belo Horizonte
Pico da Bandeira 2890 m (9,482 ft)
Juiz de Fora
Volta Redonda
Niterói
Rio de Janeiro
Ribeirão Preto
Campinas
Jundiaí
Santos
São Paulo
Sorocaba
Londrina
Bauru
São José do Rio Preto
Presidente Prudente
Jataí
Rondonópolis
Cuiabá
MATO GROSSO PLATEAU
Corumbá
Campo Grande
Dourados
CAMPOS
Ponta
10°
0°
20°
40°
50°
60°
70°
80°
90°

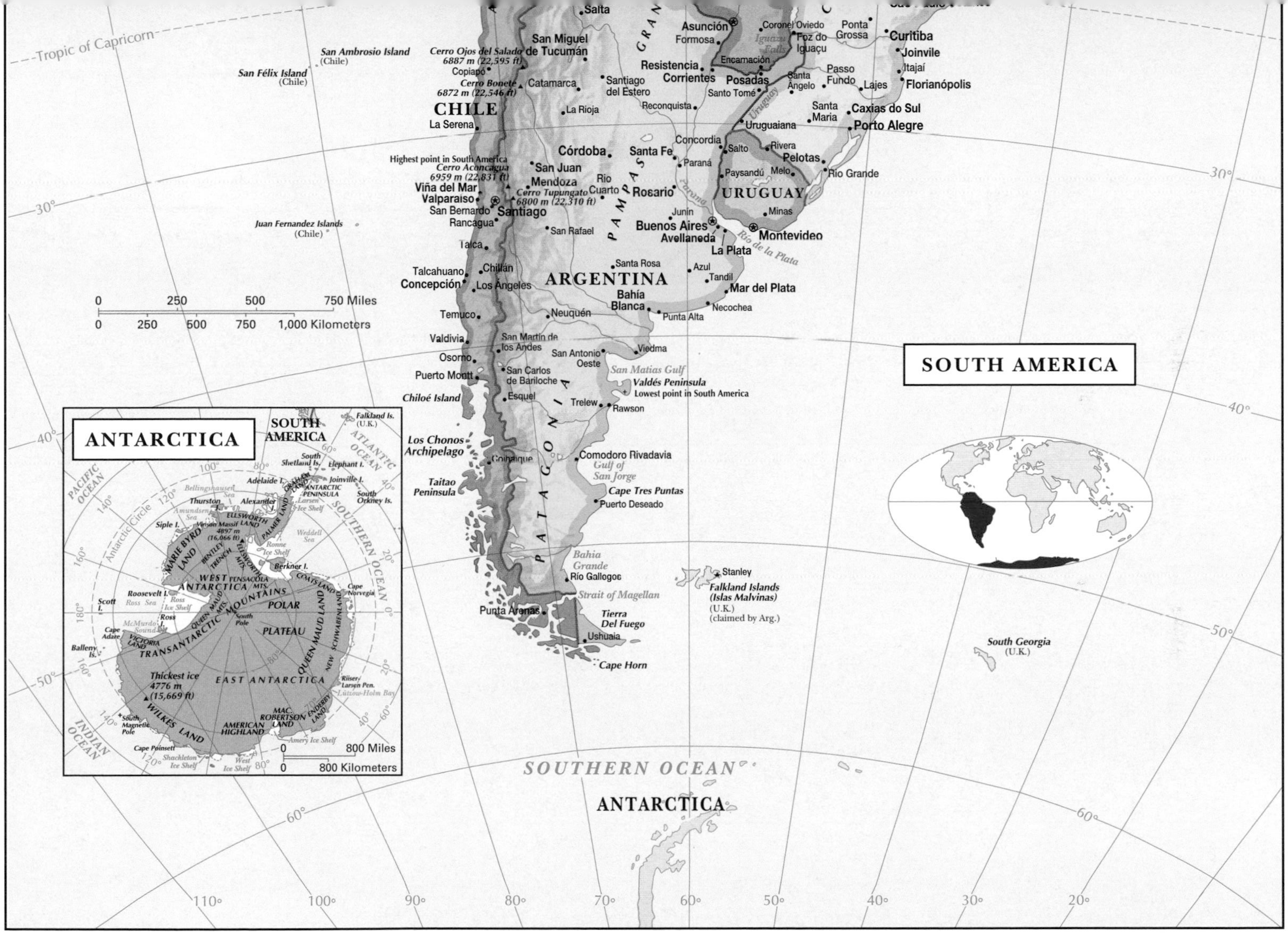
SOUTH AMERICA
Tropic of Capricorn
San Ambrosio Island (Chile)
San Félix Island (Chile)
Juan Fernandez Islands (Chile)
Cerro Ojos del Salado 6887 m (22,595 ft)
Cerro Bonete 6872 m (22,546 ft)
Highest point in South America Cerro Aconcagua 6959 m (22,831 ft)
Cerro Tupungato 6800 m (22,310 ft)
CHILE
ARGENTINA
URUGUAY
PAMPAS
PATAGONIA
Salta
San Miguel de Tucumán
Copiapó
Catamarca
La Rioja
Santiago del Estero
La Serena
Córdoba
San Juan
Mendoza
Viña del Mar
Valparaiso
Santiago
San Bernardo
Rancagua
Talca
Chillán
Talcahuano
Concepción
Los Ángeles
San Rafael
Rio Cuarto
Rosario
Santa Fe
Paraná
Concordia
Reconquista
Resistencia
Corrientes
Asunción
Formosa
Encarnación
Posadas
Santo Tomé
Coronel Oviedo
Foz do Iguaçu
Iguazu Falls
Ponta Grossa
Curitiba
Joinvile
Itajaí
Florianópolis
Passo Fundo
Santa Ângelo
Lajes
Santa Maria
Caxias do Sul
Porto Alegre
Uruguaiana
Salto
Rivera
Pelotas
Paysandú
Melo
Rio Grande
Minas
Montevideo
Junín
Buenos Aires
Avellaneda
La Plata
Río de la Plata
Santa Rosa
Azul
Tandil
Mar del Plata
Bahía Blanca
Punta Alta
Necochea
Neuquén
Temuco
Valdivia
San Martín de los Andes
Osorno
Puerto Montt
San Carlos de Bariloche
San Antonio Oeste
Viedma
San Matias Gulf
Valdés Peninsula
Lowest point in South America
Chiloé Island
Esquel
Trelew
Rawson
Los Chonos Archipelago
Coihaique
Comodoro Rivadavia
Gulf of San Jorge
Taitao Peninsula
Cape Tres Puntas
Puerto Deseado
Bahia Grande
Río Gallegos
Strait of Magellan
Punta Arenas
Tierra Del Fuego
Ushuaia
Cape Horn
Stanley
Falkland Islands (Islas Malvinas) (U.K.) (claimed by Arg.)
South Georgia (U.K.)
SOUTHERN OCEAN
ANTARCTICA
0 250 500 750 Miles
0 250 500 750 1,000 Kilometers
30° 40° 50° 60°
110° 100° 90° 80° 70° 60° 50° 40° 30° 20°
ANTARCTICA
SOUTH AMERICA
Falkland Is. (U.K.)
ATLANTIC OCEAN
PACIFIC OCEAN
INDIAN OCEAN
SOUTHERN OCEAN
South Shetland Is.
Elephant I.
Joinville I.
South Orkney Is.
Adelaide I.
ANTARCTIC PENINSULA
Larsen Ice Shelf
Bellingshausen Sea
Thurston I.
Alexander I.
Amundsen Sea
Siple I.
Vinson Massif 4897 m (16,066 ft)
ELLSWORTH LAND
PALMER LAND
Weddell Sea
Ronne Ice Shelf
MARIE BYRD LAND
BENTLEY TRENCH
ELLSWORTH MTS.
Berkner I.
WEST ANTARCTICA
PENSACOLA MTS.
COATS LAND
Cape Norvegia
Roosevelt I.
Ross Sea
Ross Ice Shelf
Scott I.
Ross I.
McMurdo Sound
TRANSANTARCTIC MOUNTAINS
QUEEN MAUD MTS.
South Pole
POLAR PLATEAU
QUEEN MAUD LAND
NEW SCHWABENLAND
Cape Adare
VICTORIA LAND
Balleny Is.
Antarctic Circle
Thickest ice 4776 m (15,669 ft)
EAST ANTARCTICA
Riiser-Larsen Pen.
Lützow-Holm Bay
South Magnetic Pole
WILKES LAND
AMERICAN HIGHLAND
MAC. ROBERTSON LAND
ENDERBY LAND
Amery Ice Shelf
Cape Poinsett
Shackleton Ice Shelf
West Ice Shelf
0 800 Miles
0 800 Kilometers

EUROPE
GREENLAND (KALAALLIT NUNAAT) (Denmark)
Arctic Circle
ICELAND
Ísafjördur
Akureyri
Keflavík
Reykjavík
Seydhisfjördhur
Norwegian Sea
Faroe Islands (Den.)
Torshavn
Shetland Islands (U.K.)
Orkney Islands
Hebrides
Thurso
Inverness
Scotland
Aberdeen
Dundee
Glasgow
Edinburgh
Ayr
Londonderry
Northern Ireland
Belfast
UNITED KINGDOM
Newcastle
IRELAND
Galway
Dublin
Limerick
Cork
Waterford
Liverpool
Manchester
Leeds
Kingston upon Hull
Sheffield
Birmingham
Coventry
Norwich
Wales
Swansea
Cardiff
England
Bristol
London
Thames
Plymouth
Land's End
Portsmouth
Dover
English Channel
ATLANTIC OCEAN
North Sea
NORWAY
SWEDEN
Narvik
Bodø
Namsos
Trondheim
Molde
Ålesund
Östersund
Sundsvall
Bergen
Haugesund
Stavanger
Oslo
Drammen
Skien
Kristiansand
Borlänge
Uppsala
Karlstad
Örebro
Stockholm
Vänern
Norrköping
Vättern
Linköping
Göteborg
Jönköping
Ålborg
Halmstad
Växjö
Öland
Jutland
Århus
Esbjerg
Copenhagen
Helsingborg
Malmö
DENMARK
Odense
Bornholm (Den.)
Baltic
Kiel
Lubeck
Rostock
Gdańsk
Groningen
Hamburg
Szczecin
NETHERLANDS
Amsterdam
Bremen
NORTHERN
Bydgoszcz
The Hague
Rotterdam
Hannover
Berlin
Antwerp
Bielefeld
Essen
Madgeburg
Oder
Poznań
Brussels
Cologne
GERMANY
POLAND
Lille
Kassel
Leipzig
BELGIUM
Liege
Bonn
Erfurt
Dresden
Wrocław
Channel Is. (U.K.)
Le Havre
Brest
Caen
Rouen
LUXEMBOURG
Luxembourg
Wiesbaden
Chemnitz
Liberec
Walbrzych
Frankfurt
Prague
Paris
Rennes
Mannheim
Plzen
Ostrava
Seine
Le Mans
Nancy
Saarbrucken
Nürnberg
CZECH REP.
Brno
Nantes
Orleans
Loire
Strasbourg
Rhine
Stuttgart
Regensburg
Tours
Dijon
Augsburg
Munich
Linz
Danube
Bratislava
Bay of Biscay
FRANCE
Basel
Zürich
Bern
Salzburg
Vienna
Limoges
Innsbruck
SWITZERLAND
LIECHTENSTEIN
AUSTRIA
Clermont-Ferrand
Lyon
Geneva
ALPS
Graz
Györ
HUNG
Bordeaux
Saint-Etienne
Mt. Blanc 4810 m (15,781 ft)
Matterhorn 4478 m (14,692 ft)
Klagenfurt
Garonne
Grenoble
Milan
Bergamo
Udine
SLOVENIA
Ljubljana
Zagreb
Pécs
Trieste
Rijeka
CROATIA
A Coruña
Gijón
Vigo
Santander
Leon
Bilbao
Donostia–San Sebastián
Toulouse
Rhone
Torino
Verona
Venice
Banja Luka
Porto
Braga
Vitoria-Gasteiz
Pamplona
Montpellier
Avignon
Genoa
Parma
Po
Bologna
BOS. & HERZ.
Duero
Valladolid
Pico de Aneto 3404 m (11,168 ft)
PYRENEES
Marseille
Nice
MONACO
SAN MARINO
DINARIC ALPS
Coimbra
IBERIAN
Salamanca
Ebro
Toulon
Pisa
Florence
Ancona
Split
Sarajevo
PORTUGAL
Zaragoza
ANDORRA
APENNINES
Perugia
Lisbon
Madrid
Barcelona
Corsica (Fr.)
Elba
Tiber
Adriatic Sea
Setubal
Tagus
Badajoz
Toledo
Tarragona
Ajaccio
Dubrovnik
SPAIN
Castellon de la Plana
VATICAN CITY
Rome
ITALY
Foggia
Valencia
PENINSULA
Majorca
Minorca
Sassari
Naples
Bari
Cape St. Vincent
Cordoba
Palma de Mallorca
Balearic Is. (Sp.)
Sardinia (It.)
Vesuvius 1277 m (4,190 ft)
Salerno
Taranto
Seville
Alicante
Murcia
Cádiz
Málaga
Granada
Cartagena
Cagliari
Tyrrhenian Sea
Ionian Sea
Strait of Gibraltar
GIBRALTAR (U.K.)
Almería
Mediterranean Sea
Messina
Palermo
Etna 3369 m (11,053 ft)
Reggio di Calabria
Sicily (It.)
Catania
Rabat
Algiers
Tunis
AFRICA
0 250 500 Miles
0 250 500 750 Kilometers
TUNISIA
MALTA
Valletta
MOROCCO
ALGERIA
70°
60°
50°
40°
30°
20°
10°
0°

Barents Sea
Novaya Zemlya
North Cape
Hammerfest
Vardø
Tromsø
Murmansk
Ivalo
LAPLAND
Apatity
KOLA PENINSULA
Kiruna
Rovaniemi
White Sea
Nar'yan-Mar
Pechora
Pechora
ASIA
URAL MOUNTAINS
Ukhta
Arkhangel'sk
RUSSIA
Luleå
Oulu
Belomorsk
Skellefteå
Syktyvkar
Dvina
Umeå
FINLAND
Gulf of Bothnia
Bereznik
Kotlas
Vaasa
Kuopio
Lake Onega
Perm'
Jyvaskyla
Lake Ladoga
Petrozavodsk
Kirov
Pori
Tampere
Lahti
Izhevsk
Kama
Ufa
Turku
Kotka
Cherepovets
Vologda
Naberezhnye Chelny
Helsinki
Gulf of Finland
St. Petersburg
Åland Is. (Fin.)
Tallinn
ESTONIA
Rybinsk
Kostroma
Yoshkar Ola
Kazan
Velikiy Novgorod
Yaroslavl'
Nizhniy Novgorod
Cheboksary
Sterlitamak
Tartu
Ivanovo
Pskov
Tver'
Ul'yanovsk
Orsk
Gotland (Swe.)
Riga
Vladimir
Tol'yatti
Orenburg
LATVIA
Moscow
Saransk
Samara
Liepaja
Ural
Daugavpils
Ryazan'
Penza
Klaipeda
LITHUANIA
Vitsyebsk
Kaluga
Volga
Kaunas
Vilnius
Smolensk
Tula
(RUSSIA)
Kaliningrad
Orsha
EUROPEAN PLAIN
Minsk
Mahilyow
Tambov
Lipetsk
Saratov
Bryansk
KAZAKHSTAN
Bialystok
Hrodna
Babruysk
BELARUS
Vistula
Homyel'
Voronezh
Warsaw
Brest
Pinsk
Kursk
Chernihiv
Belgorod
Łódź
Sumy
Radom
Lublin
Kyiv (Kiev)
Kharkiv
Volgograd
Kielce
Poltava
Katowice
Zhytomyr
Cherkasy
Luhansk
Astrakhan'
Kraków
L'viv
UKRAINE
Dnieper
Horlivka
Vinnytsia
Dnipropetrovs'k
Donetsk
Don
CARPATHIAN MOUNTAINS
SLOVAKIA
Chernivtsi
Rostov-na-Donu
Banska Bystrica
Kosice
Prut
Zaporizhzhia
Miskolc
MOLDOVA
Kryvyy Rih
Mariupol'
Budapest
Debrecen
Iasi
Chişinău
Mykolaiv
Caspian
Sea of Azov
Stavropol
HUNGARY
Oradea
Cluj-Napoca
Odesa
CRIMEA PENINSULA (disputed territory)
Krasnodar
Mt. Elbrus 5642 m (18,510 ft) Highest point in Europe
Grozny
Makhachkala
Kecskemét
Nal'chik
Vladikavkaz
Szeged
ROMANIA
Galati
Simferopol
CAUCASUS MTS.
Sea
Timişoara
Brasov
Sevastopol
Novi Sad
Ploieşti
GEORGIA
Bucharest
Constanța
Tbilisi
Baku
Belgrade
Craiova
Black Sea
AZERBAIJAN
SERBIA
Danube
Ruse
Varna
ARMENIA
Nis
Pleven
Yerevan
BULGARIA
MONTENEGRO
KOSOVO
Priština
Sofia
Burgas
Stara Zagora
AZER.
Podgorica
BALKAN
Skopje
Shkoder
Plovdiv
Istanbul
Durres
MACEDONIA
Tirana
PENINSULA
Kavala
ALBANIA
Thessaloniki
Vlore
Olympus 2917 m (9,570 ft)
Ankara
TURKEY
IRAN
Dardanelles
Larisa
Aegean Sea
Ioannina
Volos
Corfu
ASIA
GREECE
Patras
Athens
Corinth
Peloponnese
Kalamata
Sparta
Cyclades
SYRIA
Baghdad
IRAQ
Rhodes (Gr.)
Sea of Crete
Nicosia
Hania
Crete (Gr.)
Iraklion
CYPRUS
LEBANON
Beirut
Damascus
20°
30°
40°
50°
60°
70°

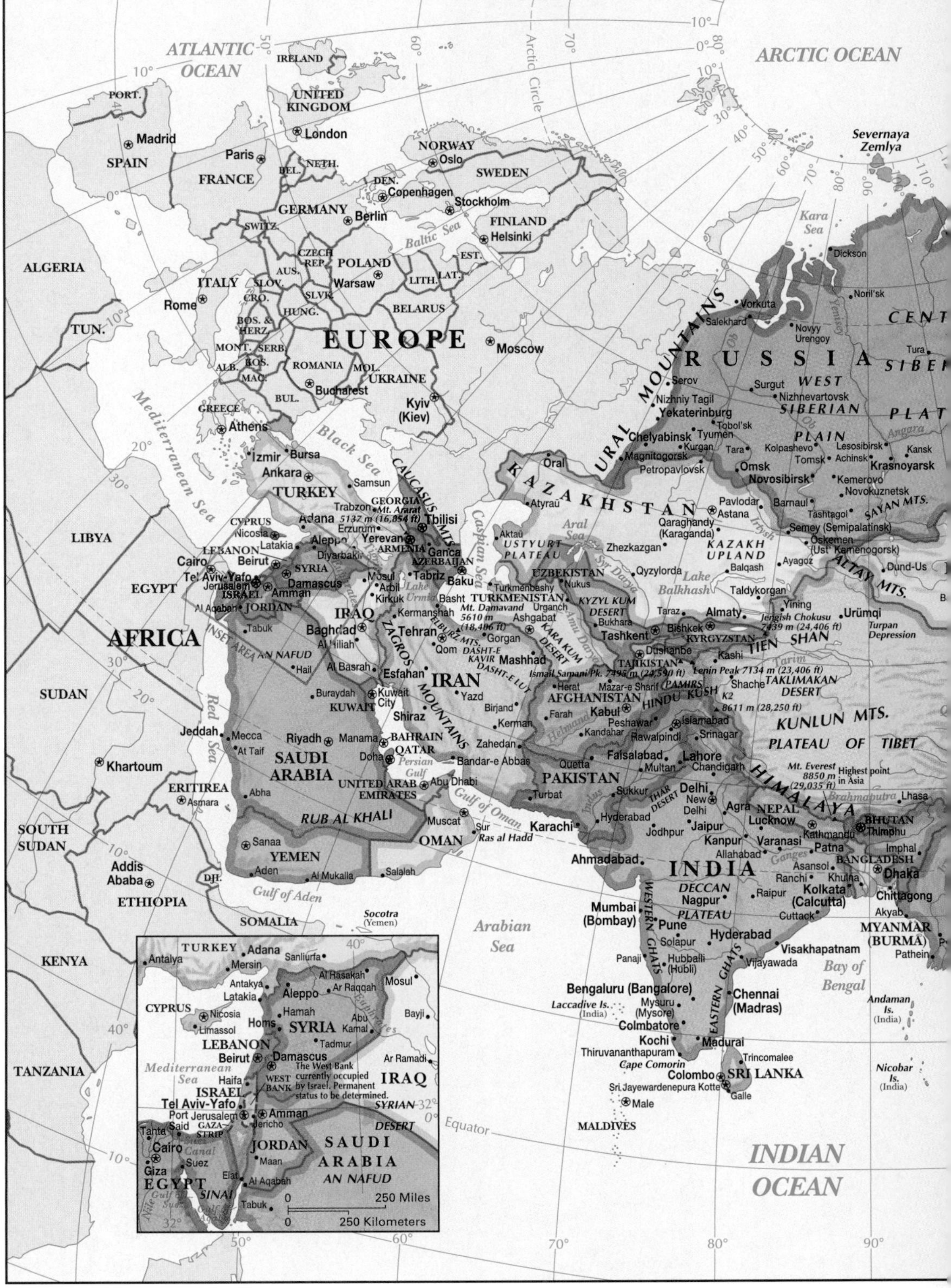

ATLANTIC OCEAN
ARCTIC OCEAN
Arctic Circle
IRELAND
UNITED KINGDOM
London
PORT.
Madrid
SPAIN
Paris
FRANCE
BEL.
NETH.
NORWAY
Oslo
SWEDEN
DEN.
Copenhagen
Stockholm
GERMANY
Berlin
FINLAND
Helsinki
Baltic Sea
SWITZ.
CZECH REP.
POLAND
EST.
ALGERIA
AUS.
Warsaw
LITH.
LAT.
ITALY
SLOV.
SLVK.
CRO.
HUNG.
BELARUS
Rome
TUN.
BOS. & HERZ.
EUROPE
Moscow
MONT.
SERB.
KOS.
ALB.
MAC.
ROMANIA
MOL.
UKRAINE
Bucharest
BUL.
Kyiv (Kiev)
Mediterranean Sea
GREECE
Athens
Black Sea
Izmir
Bursa
Ankara
TURKEY
Samsun
CAUCASUS MTS.
GEORGIA
Trabzon
Mt. Ararat 5137 m (16,854 ft)
Tbilisi
CYPRUS
Nicosia
Adana
Erzurum
Yerevan
ARMENIA
Ganca
AZERBAIJAN
LIBYA
LEBANON
Latakia
Aleppo
Diyarbakir
Beirut
SYRIA
Tigris
Mosul
Arbil
Kirkuk
Tabriz
Baku
Caspian Sea
Cairo
Tel Aviv-Yafo
Jerusalem
ISRAEL
Damascus
Amman
Lake Urmia
EGYPT
Al Aqabah
JORDAN
IRAQ
Kermanshah
Basht
Tabuk
Baghdad
Tehran
ELBURZ MTS.
AFRICA
INSET AREA
AN NAFUD
Al Hillah
Qom
Hail
Al Basrah
ZAGROS MOUNTAINS
Esfahan
IRAN
SUDAN
Red Sea
Buraydah
Kuwait City
KUWAIT
Yazd
Shiraz
Jeddah
Mecca
Riyadh
Manama
BAHRAIN
QATAR
Doha
At Taif
SAUDI ARABIA
Persian Gulf
Khartoum
UNITED ARAB EMIRATES
Abu Dhabi
ERITREA
Asmara
Abha
RUB AL KHALI
Muscat
Sur
Ras al Hadd
Gulf of Oman
SOUTH SUDAN
Sanaa
YEMEN
OMAN
Aden
Al Mukalla
Salalah
Addis Ababa
DJI.
ETHIOPIA
Gulf of Aden
SOMALIA
Socotra (Yemen)
KENYA
TANZANIA
Arabian Sea
Kerman
Birjand
Zahedan
Bandar-e Abbas
Mashhad
DASHT-E KAVIR
DASHT-E LUT
Gorgan
Mt. Damavand 5610 m (18,406 ft)
Ashgabat
TURKMENISTAN
Turkmenbashy
Nukus
UZBEKISTAN
KARA KUM DESERT
KYZYL KUM DESERT
Urganch
Bukhara
Amu Darya
Aktau
USTYURT PLATEAU
Aral Sea
Atyrau
KAZAKHSTAN
Oral
Zhezkazgan
Qyzylorda
Syr Darya
Lake Balkhash
Balqash
Qaraghandy (Karaganda)
KAZAKH UPLAND
Astana
Pavlodar
Irtysh
Semey (Semipalatinsk)
Oskemen (Ust' Kamenogorsk)
Ayagoz
Taldykorgan
Taraz
Almaty
Bishkek
KYRGYZSTAN
Tashkent
Dushanbe
TAJIKISTAN
Ismail Samani Pk. 7495 m (24,590 ft)
Lenin Peak 7134 m (23,406 ft)
Kashi
PAMIRS
Herat
Mazar-e Sharif
AFGHANISTAN
HINDU KUSH
Kabul
Farah
Helmand
Kandahar
Peshawar
Islamabad
Rawalpindi
Srinagar
Quetta
Faisalabad
Lahore
Multan
Chandigarh
PAKISTAN
Turbat
Sukkur
Indus
THAR DESERT
Delhi
New Delhi
Hyderabad
Karachi
Jodhpur
Jaipur
Agra
Kanpur
Lucknow
NEPAL
Kathmandu
Varanasi
Allahabad
Patna
Ganges
Ahmadabad
INDIA
DECCAN PLATEAU
Nagpur
Raipur
WESTERN GHATS
EASTERN GHATS
Mumbai (Bombay)
Pune
Solapur
Hyderabad
Panaji
Hubballi (Hubli)
Vijayawada
Visakhapatnam
Bengaluru (Bangalore)
Chennai (Madras)
Laccadive Is. (India)
Mysuru (Mysore)
Coimbatore
Kochi
Madurai
Thiruvananthapuram
Cape Comorin
Trincomalee
Colombo
SRI LANKA
Sri Jayewardenepura Kotte
Galle
Male
MALDIVES
Equator
INDIAN OCEAN
URAL MOUNTAINS
Vorkuta
Salekhard
Ob
RUSSIA
Serov
Nizhniy Tagil
Yekaterinburg
Chelyabinsk
Magnitogorsk
Kurgan
Tyumen
Tobol'sk
Petropavlovsk
Tara
Omsk
Novosibirsk
Surgut
Nizhnevartovsk
WEST SIBERIAN PLAIN
Kolpashevo
Tomsk
Lesosibirsk
Achinsk
Krasnoyarsk
Kansk
Angara
Kemerovo
Novokuznetsk
Barnaul
Tashtagol
SAYAN MTS.
ALTAY MTS.
Dund-Us
Yining
Jengish Chokusu 7439 m (24,406 ft)
Ürümqi
Turpan Depression
TIEN SHAN
Tarim
Shache
TAKLIMAKAN DESERT
K2 8611 m (28,250 ft)
KUNLUN MTS.
PLATEAU OF TIBET
Mt. Everest 8850 m (29,035 ft) Highest point in Asia
HIMALAYA
Brahmaputra
Lhasa
BHUTAN
Thimphu
Imphal
BANGLADESH
Dhaka
Asansol
Ranchi
Khulna
Kolkata (Calcutta)
Chittagong
Cuttack
Akyab
MYANMAR (BURMA)
Pathein
Bay of Bengal
Andaman Is. (India)
Nicobar Is. (India)
Kara Sea
Dickson
Noril'sk
Yenisey
Novyy Urengoy
Tura
CENT
SIBER
PLAT
Severnaya Zemlya
TURKEY
Antalya
Adana
Mersin
Sanliurfa
Al Hasakah
Ar Raqqah
Mosul
Antakya
Latakia
Aleppo
Euphrates
CYPRUS
Nicosia
Limassol
Hamah
Homs
SYRIA
Abu Kamal
Bayji
LEBANON
Tadmur
Beirut
Damascus
The West Bank currently occupied by Israel. Permanent status to be determined.
Ar Ramadi
Mediterranean Sea
Haifa
WEST BANK
ISRAEL
IRAQ
Tel Aviv-Yafo
SYRIAN DESERT
Port Said
Jerusalem
Amman
Tanta
GAZA STRIP
Jericho
Cairo
Suez Canal
Suez
JORDAN
SAUDI ARABIA
Maan
AN NAFUD
Giza
EGYPT
Elat
Al Aqabah
SINAI
Nile
Gulf of Suez
Gulf of Aqaba
Tabuk
0 250 Miles
0 250 Kilometers

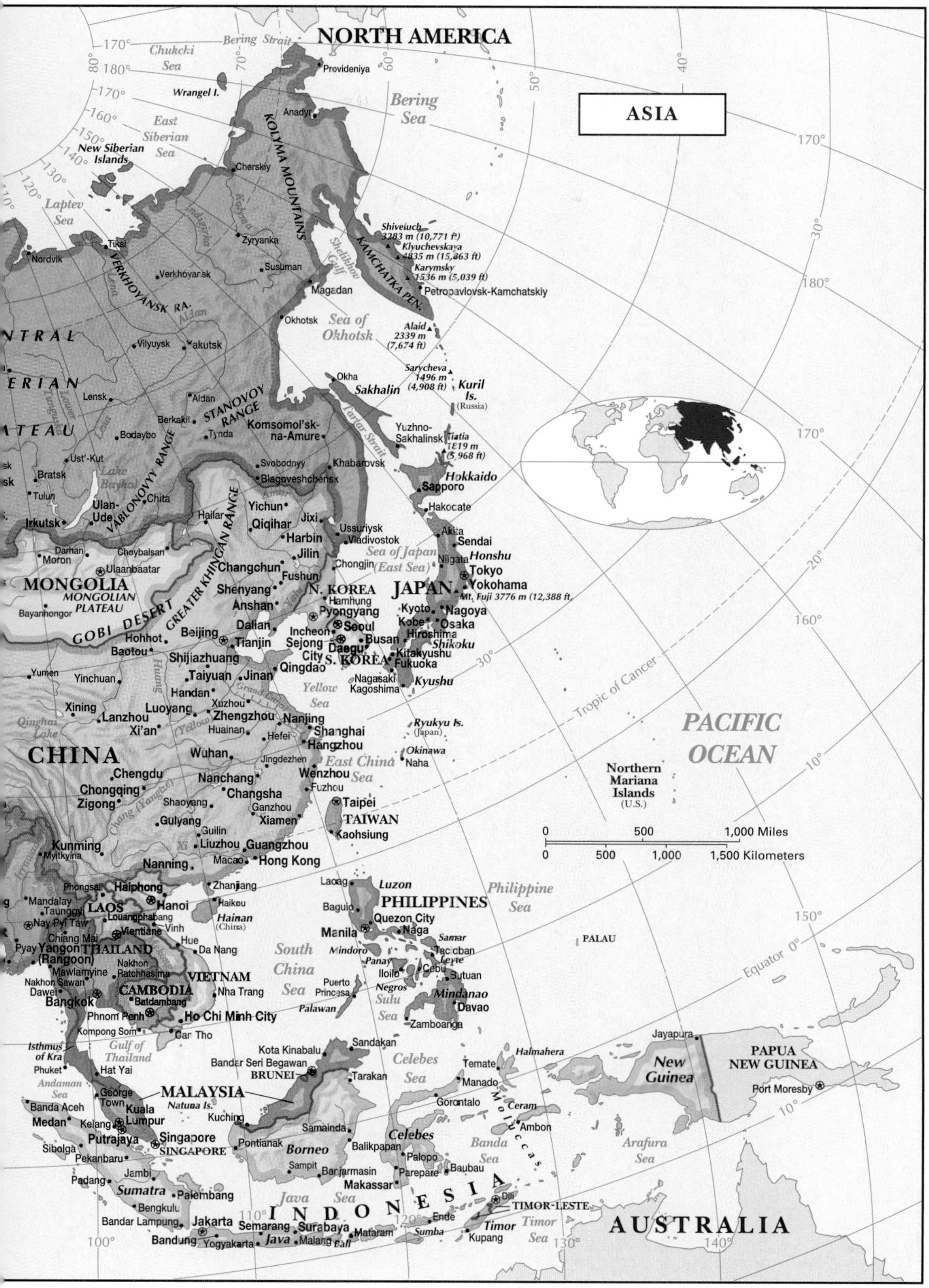

ASIA
NORTH AMERICA
Bering Strait
Chukchi Sea
Wrangel I.
Providenya
Bering Sea
Anadyr
East Siberian Sea
New Siberian Islands
Cherskiy
KOLYMA MOUNTAINS
Laptev Sea
Tiksi
Nordvik
VERKHOYANSK RA.
Verkhoyansk
Zyryanka
Susuman
Shelikhov Gulf
KAMCHATKA PEN.
Shiveluch 3283 m (10,771 ft)
Klyuchevskaya 4835 m (15,863 ft)
Karymsky 1536 m (5,039 ft)
Petropavlovsk-Kamchatskiy
Magadan
Okhotsk
Sea of Okhotsk
Alaid 2339 m (7,674 ft)
Vilyuysk
Yakutsk
Sarycheva 1496 m (4,908 ft)
Kuril Is. (Russia)
Okha
Sakhalin
Lensk
Aldan
STANOVOY RANGE
Berkakit
Tynda
Komsomol'sk-na-Amure
Tartar Strait
Yuzhno-Sakhalinsk
Tiatia 1819 m (5,968 ft)
Bodaybo
YABLONOVYY RANGE
Ust'-Kut
Bratsk
Lake Baykal
Tulun
Svobodnyy
Blagoveshchensk
Khabarovsk
Hokkaido
Sapporo
Hakodate
Ulan-Ude
Chita
Irkutsk
Hailar
Yichun
Qiqihar
Jixi
GREATER KHINGAN RANGE
Harbin
Ussuriysk
Vladivostok
Akita
Sendai
Honshu
Darhan
Moron
Choybalsan
Ulaanbaatar
Jilin
Sea of Japan (East Sea)
Niigata
Chongjin
Tokyo
Yokohama
MONGOLIA
MONGOLIAN PLATEAU
Changchun
Fushun
Shenyang
Anshan
N. KOREA
Hamhung
Pyongyang
JAPAN
Mt. Fuji 3776 m (12,388 ft)
Bayanhongor
GOBI DESERT
Dalian
Seoul
Incheon
Sejong City
Daegu
Busan
Kyoto
Nagoya
Kobe
Osaka
Hiroshima
Shikoku
Kitakyushu
Fukuoka
Hohhot
Beijing
Tianjin
Baotou
Shijiazhuang
Qingdao
S. KOREA
Yumen
Yinchuan
Taiyuan
Jinan
Handan
Yellow Sea
Nagasaki
Kagoshima
Kyushu
Xining
Lanzhou
Luoyang
Xuzhou
Grand Canal
Zhengzhou
Nanjing
Qinghai Lake
Xi'an
Huang (Yellow)
Huainan
Hefei
Shanghai
Hangzhou
Ryukyu Is. (Japan)
Okinawa
Naha
CHINA
Wuhan
Jingdezhen
East China Sea
Tropic of Cancer
PACIFIC OCEAN
Chengdu
Chongqing
Zigong
Nanchang
Changsha
Wenzhou
Fuzhou
Shaoyang
Ganzhou
Chang (Yangtze)
Taipei
TAIWAN
Kaohsiung
Xiamen
Guiyang
Guilin
Northern Mariana Islands (U.S.)
Kunming
Myitkyina
Liuzhou
Guangzhou
Macao
Hong Kong
Nanning
0 500 1,000 Miles
0 500 1,000 1,500 Kilometers
Irrawaddy
Phongsali
Haiphong
Zhanjiang
Laoag
Luzon
Mandalay
Taunggyi
LAOS
Hanoi
Haikou
Hainan (China)
Baguio
PHILIPPINES
Philippine Sea
Nay Pyi Taw
Louangphabang
Vinh
Vientiane
Quezon City
Manila
Naga
Chiang Mai
Hue
Samar
Pyay
Yangon (Rangoon)
THAILAND
Da Nang
South China Sea
Mindoro
Tacloban
Leyte
PALAU
Panay
Iloilo
Cebu
Butuan
Nakhon Ratchasima
Mawlamyine
Nakhon Sawan
VIETNAM
Negros
Equator 0°
Dawei
CAMBODIA
Nha Trang
Puerto Princesa
Sulu Sea
Mindanao
Davao
Bangkok
Batdambang
Palawan
Phnom Penh
Ho Chi Minh City
Zamboanga
Kompong Som
Can Tho
Jayapura
Isthmus of Kra
Gulf of Thailand
Kota Kinabalu
Sandakan
Celebes Sea
Halmahera
Phuket
Bandar Seri Begawan
BRUNEI
Ternate
New Guinea
PAPUA NEW GUINEA
Andaman Sea
Hat Yai
Tarakan
Manado
Port Moresby
George Town
MALAYSIA
Natuna Is.
Gorontalo
Moluccas
Ceram
Banda Aceh
Medan
Kelang
Kuala Lumpur
Kuching
Ambon
Putrajaya
Samarinda
Celebes
Sibolga
Singapore
SINGAPORE
Pontianak
Borneo
Balikpapan
Banda Sea
Arafura Sea
Pekanbaru
Palopo
Sampit
Parepare
Baubau
Jambi
Banjarmasin
Padang
Sumatra
Palembang
Makassar
Bengkulu
Java Sea
INDONESIA
Dili
TIMOR-LESTE
Ende
Bandar Lampung
Jakarta
Semarang
Surabaya
Mataram
Sumba
Timor
Timor Sea
AUSTRALIA
Bandung
Yogyakarta
Java
Malang
Bali
Kupang

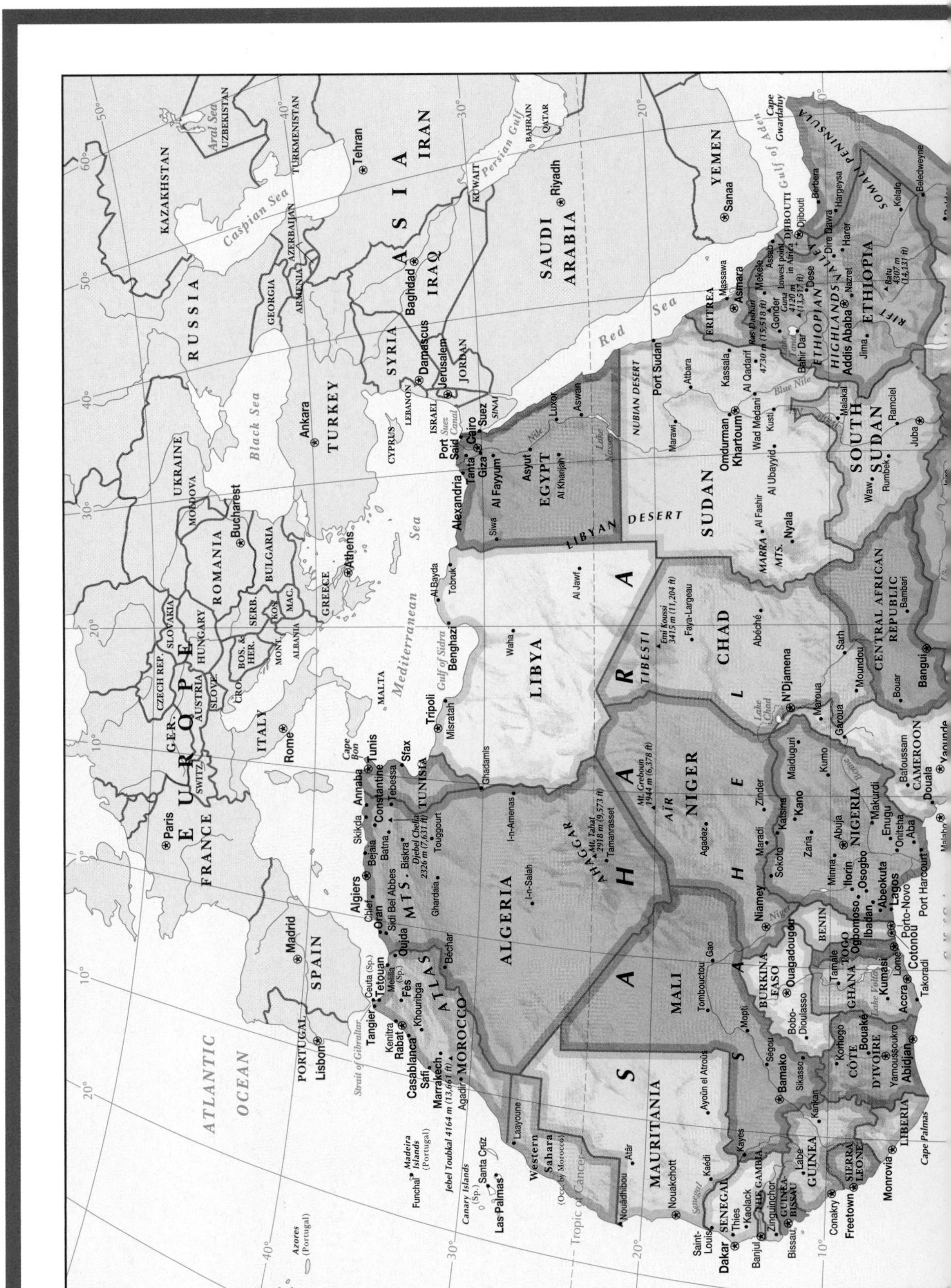
ATLANTIC
OCEAN
Azores (Portugal)
Madeira Islands (Portugal)
Funchal
Canary Islands (Sp.)
Santa Cruz
Las Palmas
Jebel Toubkal 4164 m (13,661 ft)
Tropic of Cancer
PORTUGAL
Lisbon
SPAIN
Madrid
Strait of Gibraltar
FRANCE
Paris
E U R O P E
SWITZ.
GER.
CZECH REP.
AUSTRIA
SLOVAKIA
HUNGARY
SLOV.
CRO.
BOS. & HER.
SERB.
MONT.
ALBANIA
KOS.
MAC.
ITALY
Rome
MALTA
GREECE
Athens
BULGARIA
ROMANIA
Bucharest
MOLDOVA
UKRAINE
RUSSIA
KAZAKHSTAN
UZBEKISTAN
Aral Sea
TURKMENISTAN
Caspian Sea
Black Sea
GEORGIA
ARMENIA
AZERBAIJAN
TURKEY
Ankara
CYPRUS
SYRIA
LEBANON
ISRAEL
JORDAN
Damascus
Jerusalem
IRAQ
Baghdad
IRAN
Tehran
A S I A
KUWAIT
Persian Gulf
BAHRAIN
QATAR
SAUDI ARABIA
Riyadh
YEMEN
Sanaa
Red Sea
Gulf of Aden
Cape Gwardafuy
Mediterranean Sea
Gulf of Sidra
Cape Bon
MOROCCO
Tangier
Ceuta (Sp.)
Tetouan
Melilla (Sp.)
Fès
Rabat
Kenitra
Casablanca
Khouribga
Safi
Marrakech
Agadir
ATLAS MTS.
Oujda
Béchar
ALGERIA
Algiers
Oran
Chlef
Sidi Bel Abbes
Bejaia
Skikda
Annaba
Constantine
Batna
Biskra
Tebessa
Djebel Chelia 2326 m (7,631 ft)
Ghardaia
Touggourt
I-n-Salah
I-n-Amenas
AHAGGAR
Mt. Tahat 2918 m (9,573 ft)
Tamanrasset
TUNISIA
Tunis
Sfax
LIBYA
Tripoli
Misratah
Benghazi
Al Bayda
Tobruk
Ghadamis
Waha
Al Jawf
EGYPT
Alexandria
Port Said
Suez Canal
Suez
Cairo
Giza
Tanta
SINAI
Al Fayyum
Asyut
Luxor
Aswan
Siwa
Al Kharijah
Nile
Lake Nasser
LIBYAN DESERT
NUBIAN DESERT
S A H A R A
TIBESTI
Emi Koussi 3415 m (11,204 ft)
Mt. Greboun 1944 m (6,378 ft)
AÏR
Western Sahara (Occ. by Morocco)
Laayoune
MAURITANIA
Nouakchott
Nouâdhibou
Atâr
Kaédi
Ayoûn el Atroûs
MALI
Tombouctou
Gao
Mopti
Ségou
Bamako
Kayes
Sikasso
SENEGAL
Senegal
Saint-Louis
Dakar
Thies
Kaolack
THE GAMBIA
Banjul
GUINEA-BISSAU
Bissau
Ziguinchor
GUINEA
Conakry
Labe
Kankan
SIERRA LEONE
Freetown
LIBERIA
Monrovia
Cape Palmas
CÔTE D'IVOIRE
Korhogo
Bouaké
Yamoussoukro
Abidjan
BURKINA FASO
Ouagadougou
Bobo-Dioulasso
GHANA
Tamale
Kumasi
Accra
Takoradi
TOGO
Lomé
BENIN
Cotonou
Porto-Novo
NIGER
Niamey
Agadez
Maradi
Zinder
NIGERIA
Sokoto
Katsina
Kano
Zaria
Maiduguri
Minna
Abuja
Ilorin
Ogbomoso
Osogbo
Ibadan
Abeokuta
Lagos
Makurdi
Enugu
Onitsha
Aba
Port Harcourt
Kumo
CHAD
Faya-Largeau
Abéché
N'Djamena
Lake Chad
Sarh
Moundou
CAMEROON
Maroua
Garoua
Bafoussam
Douala
Yaounde
Malabo
CENTRAL AFRICAN REPUBLIC
Bambari
Bouar
Bangui
SUDAN
Port Sudan
Atbara
Marawi
Kassala
Omdurman
Khartoum
Wad Medani
Kusti
Al Qadarif
Al Ubayyid
Al Fashir
Nyala
MARRA MTS.
Blue Nile
SOUTH SUDAN
Malakal
Waw
Rumbek
Ramciel
Juba
ERITREA
Asmara
Massawa
ETHIOPIA
ETHIOPIAN HIGHLANDS
Addis Ababa
Ras Dashen 4730 m (15,518 ft)
Mekele
Gonder
Bahir Dar
Lake Tana
Dese
Jima
Nazret
Dire Dawa
Harer
Batu 4307 m (14,131 ft)
RIFT VALLEY
DJIBOUTI
Djibouti
Assab
Guna 4120 m (13,517 ft)
lowest point in Africa
SOMALI PENINSULA
Berbera
Hargeysa
Kelafo
Beledweyne

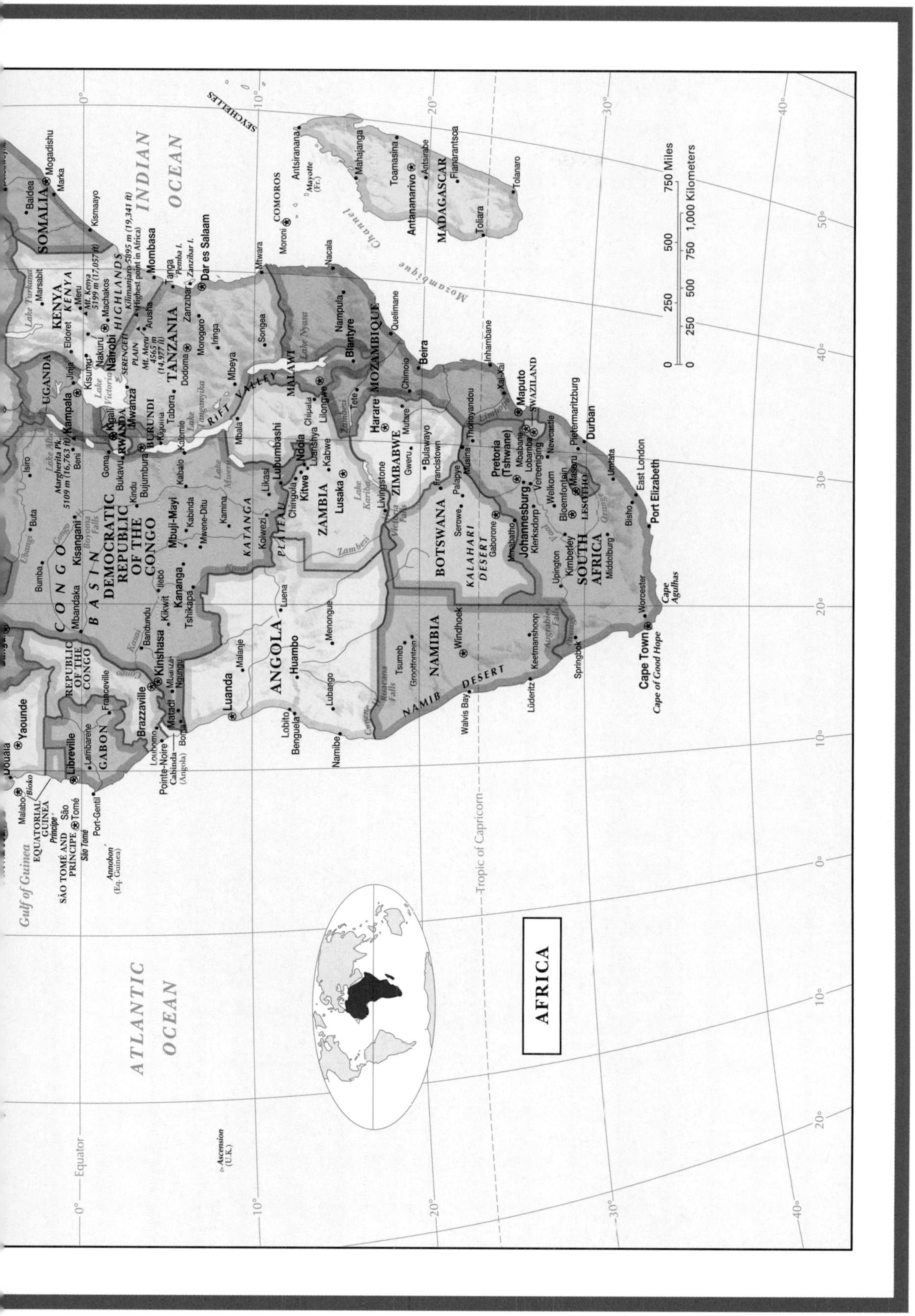

AFRICA
ATLANTIC OCEAN
INDIAN OCEAN
Gulf of Guinea
Equator
Tropic of Capricorn
SOMALIA
Mogadishu
Marka
Baldea
Kismayo
KENYA
Nairobi
Mombasa
Marsabit
Eldoret
Nakuru
Kisumu
Machakos
Meru
Mt. Kenya 5199 m (17,057 ft)
KENYA HIGHLANDS
Kilimanjaro 5895 m (19,341 ft) (Highest point in Africa)
Lake Turkana
UGANDA
Kampala
Jinja
Lake Victoria
TANZANIA
Dar es Salaam
Dodoma
Arusha
Tanga
Zanzibar
Zanzibar I.
Pemba I.
Morogoro
Iringa
Mbeya
Songea
Mwanza
Tabora
Kigoma
Mt. Meru 4565 m (14,977 ft)
SERENGETI PLAIN
Lake Tanganyika
RIFT VALLEY
RWANDA
Kigali
BURUNDI
Bujumbura
DEMOCRATIC REPUBLIC OF THE CONGO
Kinshasa
Kisangani
Lubumbashi
Mbuji-Mayi
Kananga
Kolwezi
Likasi
Kalemie
Kabalo
Kamina
Kindu
Bukavu
Goma
Beni
Isiro
Buta
Bumba
Mbandaka
Bandundu
Kikwit
Tshikapa
Ilebo
Kabinda
Mwene-Ditu
Matadi
Boma
Margherita Pk. 5109 m (16,763 ft)
Lake Albert
Lake Mweru
CONGO BASIN
KATANGA
KATANGA PLATEAU
REPUBLIC OF THE CONGO
Brazzaville
Pointe-Noire
Loubomo
Franceville
GABON
Libreville
Port-Gentil
Lambaréné
EQUATORIAL GUINEA
Malabo
Bioko
Yaounde
Douala
SÃO TOMÉ AND PRÍNCIPE
São Tomé
Príncipe
Annobon (Eq. Guinea)
Cabinda (Angola)
ANGOLA
Luanda
Huambo
Lobito
Benguela
Namibe
Lubango
Malanje
Luena
Menongue
ZAMBIA
Lusaka
Ndola
Kitwe
Chingola
Luanshya
Kabwe
Livingstone
Mbala
Lake Kariba
Victoria Falls
Zambezi
MALAWI
Lilongwe
Blantyre
Lake Nyasa
MOZAMBIQUE
Maputo
Beira
Nampula
Quelimane
Tete
Chimoio
Inhambane
Xai-Xai
Nacala
Mtwara
Mozambique Channel
ZIMBABWE
Harare
Bulawayo
Mutare
Gweru
BOTSWANA
Gaborone
Francistown
Serowe
Palapye
KALAHARI DESERT
Limpopo
NAMIBIA
Windhoek
Walvis Bay
Lüderitz
Keetmanshoop
Tsumeb
Grootfontein
NAMIB DESERT
Ruacana Falls
SOUTH AFRICA
Pretoria (Tshwane)
Johannesburg
Cape Town
Durban
Port Elizabeth
East London
Bloemfontein
Kimberley
Pietermaritzburg
Upington
Springbok
Worcester
Welkom
Klerksdorp
Vereeniging
Mmabatho
Musina
Thohoyandou
Newcastle
Umtata
Bisho
Middelburg
Augrabies Falls
Orange
Cape of Good Hope
Cape Agulhas
LESOTHO
Maseru
SWAZILAND
Mbabane
Lobamba
MADAGASCAR
Antananarivo
Toamasina
Mahajanga
Antsiranana
Fianarantsoa
Antsirabe
Toliara
Tolanaro
COMOROS
Moroni
Mayotte (Fr.)
SEYCHELLES
Ascension (U.K.)
0 250 500 750 Miles
0 250 500 750 1,000 Kilometers

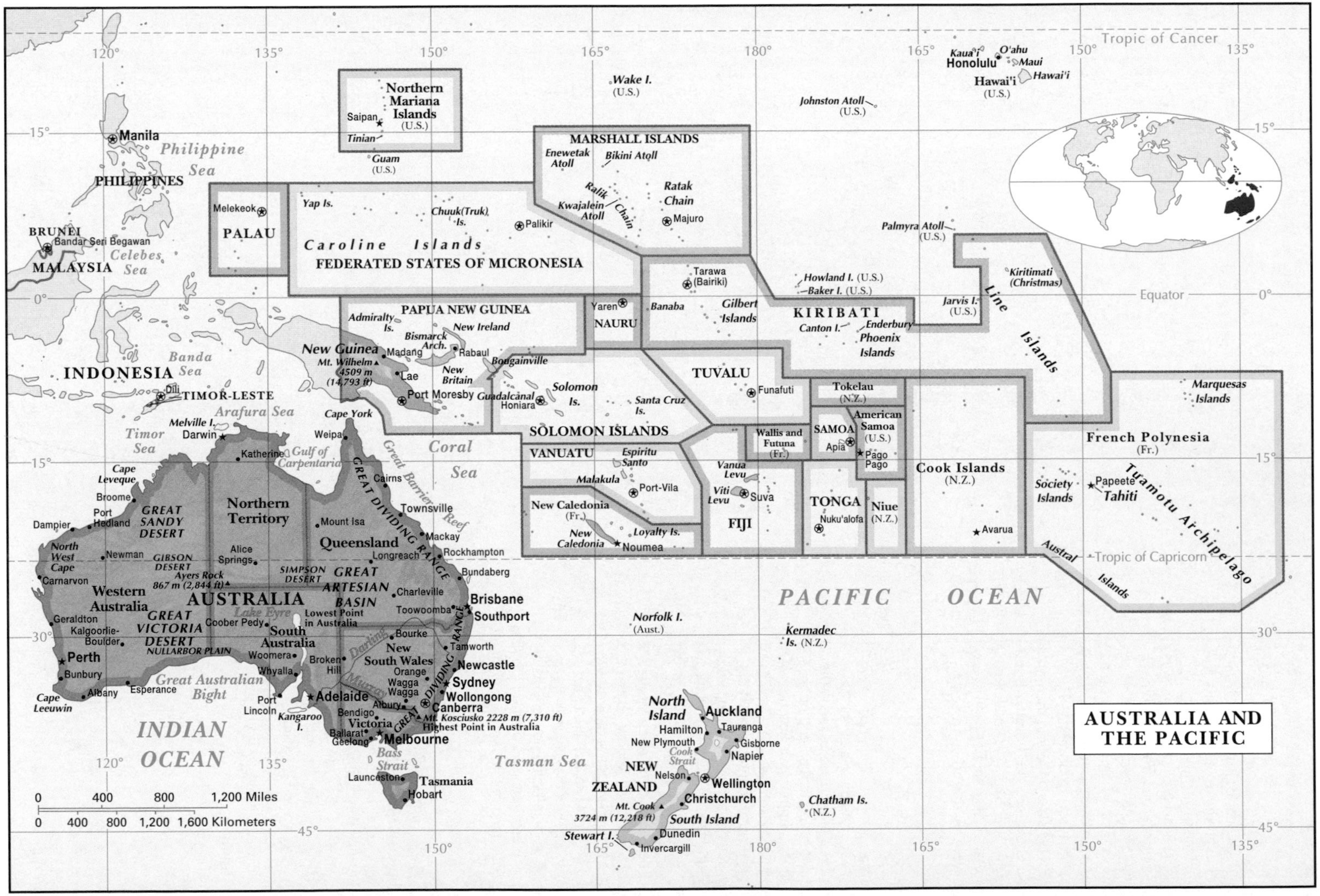
AUSTRALIA AND
THE PACIFIC
Tropic of Cancer
Equator
Tropic of Capricorn
Northern Mariana Islands (U.S.)
Saipan
Tinian
Guam (U.S.)
Wake I. (U.S.)
Johnston Atoll (U.S.)
Kaua'i
O'ahu
Honolulu
Maui
Hawai'i (U.S.)
Hawai'i
Manila
Philippine Sea
PHILIPPINES
BRUNEI
Bandar Seri Begawan
MALAYSIA
Celebes Sea
MARSHALL ISLANDS
Enewetak Atoll
Bikini Atoll
Ralik Chain
Kwajalein Atoll
Ratak Chain
Majuro
Melekeok
PALAU
Yap Is.
Chuuk(Truk) Is.
Palikir
Caroline Islands
FEDERATED STATES OF MICRONESIA
Palmyra Atoll (U.S.)
Tarawa (Bairiki)
Banaba
Gilbert Islands
Howland I. (U.S.)
Baker I. (U.S.)
KIRIBATI
Canton I.
Enderbury
Phoenix Islands
Jarvis I. (U.S.)
Kiritimati (Christmas)
Line Islands
Yaren
NAURU
PAPUA NEW GUINEA
Admiralty Is.
New Ireland
Bismarck Arch.
Rabaul
New Guinea
Mt. Wilhelm 4509 m (14,793 ft)
Madang
Lae
New Britain
Bougainville
Port Moresby
INDONESIA
Banda Sea
Dili
TIMOR-LESTE
Arafura Sea
Timor Sea
Melville I.
Darwin
Cape York
Weipa
Gulf of Carpentaria
Coral Sea
Great Barrier Reef
Guadalcanal
Honiara
Solomon Is.
Santa Cruz Is.
SOLOMON ISLANDS
TUVALU
Funafuti
Tokelau (N.Z.)
SAMOA
Apia
American Samoa (U.S.)
Pago Pago
Wallis and Futuna (Fr.)
VANUATU
Espiritu Santo
Malakula
Port-Vila
New Caledonia (Fr.)
New Caledonia
Loyalty Is.
Noumea
Vanua Levu
Viti Levu
Suva
FIJI
TONGA
Nuku'alofa
Niue (N.Z.)
Cook Islands (N.Z.)
Avarua
Marquesas Islands
French Polynesia (Fr.)
Society Islands
Papeete
Tahiti
Tuamotu Archipelago
Austral Islands
PACIFIC OCEAN
Norfolk I. (Aust.)
Kermadec Is. (N.Z.)
Chatham Is. (N.Z.)
Cape Leveque
Broome
Port Hedland
Dampier
North West Cape
Carnarvon
GREAT SANDY DESERT
GIBSON DESERT
Newman
Western Australia
AUSTRALIA
Ayers Rock 867 m (2,844 ft)
Alice Springs
Northern Territory
Katherine
Mount Isa
Queensland
Cairns
Townsville
Mackay
Rockhampton
Bundaberg
GREAT DIVIDING RANGE
SIMPSON DESERT
GREAT ARTESIAN BASIN
Longreach
Charleville
Lake Eyre
Lowest Point in Australia
Coober Pedy
South Australia
Toowoomba
Brisbane
Southport
Geraldton
Kalgoorlie-Boulder
GREAT VICTORIA DESERT
NULLARBOR PLAIN
Perth
Bunbury
Albany
Cape Leeuwin
Esperance
Great Australian Bight
Woomera
Whyalla
Port Lincoln
Kangaroo I.
Adelaide
Broken Hill
Darling
Murray
Bourke
New South Wales
Tamworth
Newcastle
Orange
Wagga Wagga
Sydney
Wollongong
Albury
Canberra
Mt. Kosciusko 2228 m (7,310 ft) Highest Point in Australia
Bendigo
Victoria
Ballarat
Geelong
Melbourne
Bass Strait
Launceston
Tasmania
Hobart
INDIAN OCEAN
Tasman Sea
North Island
Auckland
Hamilton
Tauranga
New Plymouth
Gisborne
Napier
Cook Strait
NEW ZEALAND
Nelson
Wellington
Christchurch
Mt. Cook 3724 m (12,218 ft)
South Island
Dunedin
Stewart I.
Invercargill
0 400 800 1,200 Miles
0 400 800 1,200 1,600 Kilometers
120°
135°
150°
165°
180°
15°
0°
30°
45°

History of the U.S. National Anthem

"The Star-Spangled Banner" was ordered played by the military and naval services by Pres. Woodrow Wilson in 1916. It was designated the national anthem by Act of Congress, Mar. 3, 1931. The words were written by Francis Scott Key, of Georgetown, MD, during the bombardment of Ft. McHenry in Baltimore, MD, Sept. 13-14, 1814. Key was a lawyer, a graduate of St. John's College, Annapolis, MD, and a volunteer in a light artillery company. When a friend, Dr. Beanes, a Maryland physician, was taken aboard Adm. Cockburn's British squadron for interfering with ground troops, Key and J. S. Skinner, carrying a note from Pres. Madison, went to the fleet under a flag of truce on a cartel ship to ask Beanes's release. Cockburn consented, but as the fleet was about to sail up the Patapsco to bombard Ft. McHenry, he detained them, first on HMS *Surprise* and then on a supply ship.

Key witnessed the bombardment from his own vessel. It began at 7 AM, Sept. 13, and lasted 25 hours. The British fired more than 1,500 shells, each weighing as much as 220 lbs. They were unable to approach closely because the U.S. had sunk 22 vessels to form a barrier. Only four Americans were killed and 24 wounded. A British bombship was disabled.

During the event, Key wrote a stanza on the back of an envelope. The next day at Indian Queen Inn in Baltimore, he wrote out the poem and gave it to his brother-in-law, Judge J. H. Nicholson. Nicholson suggested use of the tune, "Anacreon in Heaven" (attributed to a British composer named John Stafford Smith), and had the poem printed on broadsides, of which two copies survive. On Sept. 20 it appeared in the *Baltimore American*. Later Key made three copies; one is in the Library of Congress, and one in the Pennsylvania Historical Society.

The flag that Key saw during the bombardment is preserved in the Smithsonian Institution, Washington, DC. It measures 30 by 42 ft and has 15 alternating red and white stripes and 15 stars, for the original 13 states plus Kentucky and Vermont. It was sewn by flag maker Mary Pickersgill. Her house in Baltimore was restored in 1953 and is preserved as part of the Star-Spangled Banner Flag House museum.

The Star-Spangled Banner

I

Oh, say can you see by the dawn's early light
What so proudly we hailed at the twilight's last gleaming?
Whose broad stripes and bright stars thru the perilous fight,
O'er the ramparts we watched were so gallantly streaming?
And the rockets' red glare, the bombs bursting in air,
Gave proof through the night that our flag was still there.
Oh, say does that star-spangled banner yet wave
O'er the land of the free and the home of the brave?

II

On the shore, dimly seen through the mists of the deep,
Where the foe's haughty host in dread silence reposes,
What is that which the breeze, o'er the towering steep,
As it fitfully blows, half conceals, half discloses?
Now it catches the gleam of the morning's first beam,
In full glory reflected now shines in the stream:
'Tis the star-spangled banner! Oh long may it wave
O'er the land of the free and the home of the brave!

III

And where is that band who so vauntingly swore
That the havoc of war and the battle's confusion,
A home and a country should leave us no more!
Their blood has washed out their foul footsteps' pollution.
No refuge could save the hireling and slave
From the terror of flight, or the gloom of the grave:
And the star-spangled banner in triumph doth wave
O'er the land of the free and the home of the brave!

IV

Oh! thus be it ever, when freemen shall stand
Between their loved home and the war's desolation!
Blest with victory and peace, may the heav'n rescued land
Praise the Power that hath made and preserved us a nation.
Then conquer we must, when our cause it is just,
And this be our motto: "In God is our trust."
And the star-spangled banner in triumph shall wave
O'er the land of the free and the home of the brave!

History of the Liberty Bell

The Liberty Bell is housed in the Liberty Bell Center, located in Philadelphia's Independence National Historical Park.

The original bell was ordered by Isaac Norris, Assembly Speaker and Chairman of the State House Superintendents, from Thomas Lester of Whitechapel Foundry in London. It reached Philadelphia at the end of Aug. 1752. It bore an inscription from Leviticus 25:10: "Proclaim LIBERTY throughout all the land unto all the inhabitants thereof."

The bell was cracked by a stroke of its clapper in Sept. 1752 while it hung on a truss in the State House yard for testing. Pass & Stow, Philadelphia founders, recast the bell, adding 1½ ounces of copper to a pound of the original Whitechapel metal to reduce its high tone and brittleness. That proved to be too much copper, injuring its tone, so Pass & Stow recast it once more.

In June 1753, the bell was hung in the old wooden steeple of the State House. It rang out while the Continental Congress was in session in the State House. It proclaimed the Boston Tea Party as well as the first public reading of the Declaration of Independence, on July 8, 1776.

On Sept. 18, 1777, when the British Army was about to occupy Philadelphia, the Liberty Bell was moved in a baggage train to Allentown, PA, where it was hidden until June 27, 1778. The bell was moved back to Philadelphia after the British left the city.

In 1781, the wooden steeple became insecure and the bell was lowered into the brick section of the tower, where it remained until 1828. According to tradition, it cracked in 1835 as it tolled the death of U.S. Supreme Court Chief Justice John Marshall. It rang for the last time on Feb. 23, 1846, in honor of George Washington's birthday on the 22nd. In 1852 it was placed on exhibition in Independence Hall.

In 1876, when thousands of Americans visited Philadelphia for the Centennial Exposition, the bell was placed in its old wooden support in the tower hallway. In 1877, it was hung from the ceiling of the tower by a chain of 13 links. In 1896, it was placed within a glass case to prevent souvenir hunters and vandals from taking some of the metal. In 1915, the case was removed so that the public might touch the bell. To mark the opening of the Bicentennial Year, the bell was moved just after midnight on Jan. 1, 1976, to a new glass and steel pavilion behind Independence Hall for easier viewing.

On Oct. 9, 2003, the bell was transferred to its present location, where exhibits explain the bell's history.

Measurements of the bell: circumference around the lip, 12 ft ½ in.; circumference around the crown, 6 ft 11¼ in.; lip to the crown, 3 ft; height over the crown, 2 ft 3 in.; thickness at lip, 3 in.; thickness at crown, 1¼ in.; weight, 2,080 lbs; length of clapper, 3 ft 2 in.

Statue of Liberty National Monument

Since 1886, the Statue of Liberty, formally known as "Liberty Enlightening the World," has stood as a symbol of freedom in New York harbor. It also commemorates French-American friendship because it was given by the people of France to the people of the U.S. It was designed by French sculptor Frédéric Auguste Bartholdi (1834-1904).

On Washington's Birthday, Feb. 22, 1877, Congress approved the use of a site on Bedloe's Island suggested by Bartholdi. This island of 12 acres had been owned in the 17th cent. by a Walloon colonist named Isaac Bedloe. On Aug. 3, 1956, Pres. Dwight Eisenhower approved a measure changing the name to Liberty Island.

The statue was finished on May 21, 1884, and presented to the U.S. minister to France, Levi Parsons Morton, July 4, 1884, by Ferdinand de Lesseps, head of the Franco-American Union, promoter of the Panama Canal, and builder of the Suez Canal.

On Aug. 5, 1884, the cornerstone for the pedestal was laid on the foundations of Fort Wood, erected by the government in 1811. The American Committee for the Statue of Liberty had raised an inadequate $125,000, and *New York World* newspaper owner Joseph Pulitzer appealed Mar. 16, 1885, for general donations. By Aug. 11, 1885, he had raised $100,000. The statue itself arrived dismantled, in 214 packing cases, from Rouen, France, in June 1885. The last rivet of the statue was driven on Oct. 28, 1886, when Pres. Grover Cleveland dedicated the monument.

The Statue of Liberty National Monument was designated as such in 1924. It is administered by the National Park Service. A $2.5-mil building housing the American Museum of Immigration was opened by Pres. Richard Nixon on Sept. 26, 1972, at the base of the statue. It houses a permanent exhibition tracing the history of American immigration.

Four years of restoration work funded and led by the Statue of Liberty-Ellis Island Foundation were completed before the statue's 1986 centennial. The $87-mil project included the replacement of the 1,600 wrought iron bands that hold the statue's copper skin to its frame, replacement of the torch, and installation of an elevator. A four-day Liberty Weekend extravaganza of concerts, tall ships, ethnic festivals, and fireworks, July 3-6, 1986, celebrated the 100th anniversary. U.S. Supreme Court Chief Justice Warren E. Burger swore in 5,000 new citizens on Ellis Island, while 20,000 others across the country were sworn in through a satellite telecast. Other ceremonies followed on Oct. 28, 1986, the statue's exact 100th birthday.

After the Sept. 11, 2001, terrorist attacks, Liberty Island was closed to visitors. On Dec. 20, 2001, the secretary of the interior reopened the island after installing airport-type screening facilities at passenger embarkation areas at Battery Park in Manhattan and Liberty State Park in New Jersey.

The federal government needed to increase security throughout the park before reopening the statue. In addition to federally funded security upgrades, significant safety improvements were made to meet building codes. Access to the statue was restored on Aug. 3, 2004.

Following the 125th anniversary celebration Oct. 28, 2011, the statue was closed. A $30-mil renovation brought the statue up to contemporary safety standards and allowed for increased visitor access. The island remained open to visitors, and views of the statue were largely unobstructed, but visitors could not go inside. The statue interior reopened Oct. 28, 2012, but damages caused by Hurricane Sandy the next week forced all of Liberty Island to close again.

The island and the statue officially reopened for visitors July 4, 2013. Advance reservations are required to visit the museum, statue pedestal, or crown. Reservations are available by visiting www.statuecruises.com or by calling 1-877-LADY-TIX. Visitors to the statue's interior must follow a number of guidelines including ones on height restrictions and locker rentals, for which there is a $2 fee. (Inside the statue, visitors may carry only a camera, a ferry ticket with crown reservation, and necessary medication.) Park rangers conduct English-language tours throughout the day. Standard self-guided audio tours are available in nine languages; a children's version of the audio tour is available in five languages. For more information, visit www.nps.gov/stli/ and www.statueofliberty.org.

Statue Statistics

The statue weighs 450,000 lbs, or 225 tons. The copper sheeting weighs 200,000 lbs. There are 377 steps from the main lobby to the crown platform. There are 146 steps from the top of the pedestal (the statue's feet) to the crown platform.

Statue feature	Measurement Ft	In.
Height from base to torch tip	151	1
Foundation of pedestal to torch tip	305	1
Heel to top of head	111	1
Hand, length	16	5
Index finger, length	8	0
Fingernail size		13x10
Head from chin to cranium	17	3
Head thickness, ear to ear	10	0
Nose, length	4	6
Right arm, length	42	0
Right arm, max. thickness	12	0
Waist, thickness	35	0
Mouth, width	3	0
Tablet, length	23	7
Tablet, width	13	7

Ellis Island

Ellis Island was the gateway to America for over 12 mil immigrants between 1892 and 1924. In the late 18th cent., Samuel Ellis, a New York City merchant, purchased the island and gave it his name. From Ellis, it passed to New York state before the U.S. government bought it in 1808. On Jan. 1, 1892, the government opened the first federal immigration center in the U.S. there. The 27.5-acre site eventually supported more than 35 buildings, including the Main Building with its Great Hall, in which as many as 5,000 people a day were processed.

Closed as an immigration station in 1954, Ellis Island was proclaimed part of the Statue of Liberty National Monument in 1965 by Pres. Lyndon B. Johnson. After a six-year, $170-mil restoration project funded by the Statue of Liberty-Ellis Island Foundation, Ellis Island was reopened as a museum in 1990. Artifacts, historic photographs and documents, oral histories, and ethnic music depicting 400 years of American immigration are housed in the museum.

In 1998, the U.S. Supreme Court ruled that nearly 90% of the island (the 24.2 acres that are landfill) lies in New Jersey, while the original 3.3 acres, on which the museum is located, are in New York.

The American Family Immigration History Center opened in Apr. 2001. It contains an electronic database of ship passenger arrival information through the Port of New York and Ellis Island from 1892 to 1924. Data on over 22 mil individuals are available, as well as multimedia presentations on various immigrant groups and migration patterns, reproductions of original ships' passenger manifests, and pictures of over 800 immigrant ships. **Website:** www.libertyellisfoundation.org

Damage caused by storm surges from Hurricane Sandy in late Oct. 2012 forced Ellis Island to close for repairs. As of Sept. 2015, the island had reopened but parts of the Main Building and Museum remained closed and many artifacts and exhibits were inaccessible.

PRESIDENTS OF THE UNITED STATES

U.S. Presidents

	Name	Politics	Born	Birthplace	Inaug.	Age at inaug.	Died	Age at death
1.	George Washington	Fed.	1732, Feb. 22	VA	1789	57	1799, Dec. 14	67
2.	John Adams	Fed.	1735, Oct. 30	MA	1797	61	1826, July 4	90
3.	Thomas Jefferson	Dem.-Rep.	1743, Apr. 13	VA	1801	57	1826, July 4	83
4.	James Madison	Dem.-Rep.	1751, Mar. 16	VA	1809	57	1836, June 28	85
5.	James Monroe	Dem.-Rep.	1758, Apr. 28	VA	1817	58	1831, July 4	73
6.	John Quincy Adams	Dem.-Rep.	1767, July 11	MA	1825	57	1848, Feb. 23	80
7.	Andrew Jackson	Dem.	1767, Mar. 15	SC	1829	61	1845, June 8	78
8.	Martin Van Buren	Dem.	1782, Dec. 5	NY	1837	54	1862, July 24	79
9.	William Henry Harrison	Whig	1773, Feb. 9	VA	1841	68	1841, Apr. 4	68
10.	John Tyler	Whig	1790, Mar. 29	VA	1841	51	1862, Jan. 18	71
11.	James Knox Polk	Dem.	1795, Nov. 2	NC	1845	49	1849, June 15	53
12.	Zachary Taylor	Whig	1784, Nov. 24	VA	1849	64	1850, July 9	65
13.	Millard Fillmore	Whig	1800, Jan. 7	NY	1850	50	1874, Mar. 8	74
14.	Franklin Pierce	Dem.	1804, Nov. 23	NH	1853	48	1869, Oct. 8	64
15.	James Buchanan	Dem.	1791, Apr. 23	PA	1857	65	1868, June 1	77
16.	Abraham Lincoln	Rep.	1809, Feb. 12	KY	1861	52	1865, Apr. 15	56
17.	Andrew Johnson	(1)	1808, Dec. 29	NC	1865	56	1875, July 31	66
18.	Ulysses S. Grant	Rep.	1822, Apr. 27	OH	1869	46	1885, July 23	63
19.	Rutherford Birchard Hayes	Rep.	1822, Oct. 4	OH	1877	54	1893, Jan. 17	70
20.	James Abram Garfield	Rep.	1831, Nov. 19	OH	1881	49	1881, Sept. 19	49
21.	Chester Alan Arthur	Rep.	1829, Oct. 5	VT	1881	51	1886, Nov. 18	57
22.	Grover Cleveland	Dem.	1837, Mar. 18	NJ	1885	47	1908, June 24	71
23.	Benjamin Harrison	Rep.	1833, Aug. 20	OH	1889	55	1901, Mar. 13	67
24.	Grover Cleveland	Dem.	1837, Mar. 18	NJ	1893	55	1908, June 24	71
25.	William McKinley	Rep.	1843, Jan. 29	OH	1897	54	1901, Sept. 14	58
26.	Theodore Roosevelt	Rep.	1858, Oct. 27	NY	1901	42	1919, Jan. 6	60
27.	William Howard Taft	Rep.	1857, Sept. 15	OH	1909	51	1930, Mar. 8	72
28.	(Thomas) Woodrow Wilson	Dem.	1856, Dec. 28	VA	1913	56	1924, Feb. 3	67
29.	Warren Gamaliel Harding	Rep.	1865, Nov. 2	OH	1921	55	1923, Aug. 2	57
30.	(John) Calvin Coolidge	Rep.	1872, July 4	VT	1923	51	1933, Jan. 5	60
31.	Herbert Clark Hoover	Rep.	1874, Aug. 10	IA	1929	54	1964, Oct. 20	90
32.	Franklin Delano Roosevelt	Dem.	1882, Jan. 30	NY	1933	51	1945, Apr. 12	63
33.	Harry S. Truman	Dem.	1884, May 8	MO	1945	60	1972, Dec. 26	88
34.	Dwight David Eisenhower	Rep.	1890, Oct. 14	TX	1953	62	1969, Mar. 28	78
35.	John Fitzgerald Kennedy	Dem.	1917, May 29	MA	1961	43	1963, Nov. 22	46
36.	Lyndon Baines Johnson	Dem.	1908, Aug. 27	TX	1963	55	1973, Jan. 22	64
37.	Richard Milhous Nixon[2]	Rep.	1913, Jan. 9	CA	1969	56	1994, Apr. 22	81
38.	Gerald Rudolph Ford	Rep.	1913, July 14	NE	1974	61	2006, Dec. 26	93
39.	James Earl (Jimmy) Carter	Dem.	1924, Oct. 1	GA	1977	52		
40.	Ronald Wilson Reagan	Rep.	1911, Feb. 6	IL	1981	69	2004, June 5	93
41.	George Herbert Walker Bush	Rep.	1924, June 12	MA	1989	64		
42.	Wm. Jefferson (Bill) Clinton	Dem.	1946, Aug. 19	AR	1993	46		
43.	George Walker Bush	Rep.	1946, July 6	CT	2001	54		
44.	Barack Hussein Obama	Dem.	1961, Aug. 4	HI	2009	47		

(1) Andrew Johnson, a Democrat, had been nominated vice president by Republicans and elected with Lincoln on National Union ticket. (2) Resigned Aug. 9, 1974.

U.S. Presidents, Vice Presidents, Congresses

President	Service	Vice President	Congresses
1. George Washington	Apr. 30, 1789-Mar. 3, 1797	1. John Adams	1, 2, 3, 4
2. John Adams	Mar. 4, 1797-Mar. 3, 1801	2. Thomas Jefferson	5, 6
3. Thomas Jefferson	Mar. 4, 1801-Mar. 3, 1805	3. Aaron Burr	7, 8
	Mar. 4, 1805-Mar. 3, 1809	4. George Clinton	9, 10
4. James Madison	Mar. 4, 1809-Mar. 3, 1813	George Clinton[1]	11, 12
	Mar. 4, 1813-Mar. 3, 1817	5. Elbridge Gerry[2]	13, 14
5. James Monroe	Mar. 4, 1817-Mar. 3, 1825	6. Daniel D. Tompkins	15, 16, 17, 18
6. John Quincy Adams	Mar. 4, 1825-Mar. 3, 1829	7. John C. Calhoun	19, 20
7. Andrew Jackson	Mar. 4, 1829-Mar. 3, 1833	John C. Calhoun[3]	21, 22
	Mar. 4, 1833-Mar. 3, 1837	8. Martin Van Buren	23, 24
8. Martin Van Buren	Mar. 4, 1837-Mar. 3, 1841	9. Richard M. Johnson	25, 26
9. William Henry Harrison[4]	Mar. 4, 1841-Apr. 4, 1841	10. John Tyler	27
10. John Tyler	Apr. 6, 1841-Mar. 3, 1845	(None)	27, 28
11. James K. Polk	Mar. 4, 1845-Mar. 3, 1849	11. George M. Dallas	29, 30
12. Zachary Taylor[4]	Mar. 5, 1849-July 9, 1850	12. Millard Fillmore	31
13. Millard Fillmore	July 10, 1850-Mar. 3, 1853	(None)	31, 32
14. Franklin Pierce	Mar. 4, 1853-Mar. 3, 1857	13. William R. King[5]	33, 34
15. James Buchanan	Mar. 4, 1857-Mar. 3, 1861	14. John C. Breckinridge	35, 36
16. Abraham Lincoln	Mar. 4, 1861-Mar. 3, 1865	15. Hannibal Hamlin	37, 38
(4)	Mar. 4, 1865-Apr. 15, 1865	16. Andrew Johnson	39
17. Andrew Johnson	Apr. 15, 1865-Mar. 3, 1869	(None)	39, 40
18. Ulysses S. Grant	Mar. 4, 1869-Mar. 3, 1873	17. Schuyler Colfax	41, 42
	Mar. 4, 1873-Mar. 3, 1877	18. Henry Wilson[6]	43, 44
19. Rutherford B. Hayes	Mar. 4, 1877-Mar. 3, 1881	19. William A. Wheeler	45, 46
20. James A. Garfield[4]	Mar. 4, 1881-Sept. 19, 1881	20. Chester A. Arthur	47
21. Chester A. Arthur	Sept. 20, 1881-Mar. 3, 1885	(None)	47, 48
22. Grover Cleveland[7]	Mar. 4, 1885-Mar. 3, 1889	21. Thomas A. Hendricks[8]	49, 50
23. Benjamin Harrison	Mar. 4, 1889-Mar. 3, 1893	22. Levi P. Morton	51, 52
24. Grover Cleveland[7]	Mar. 4, 1893-Mar. 3, 1897	23. Adlai E. Stevenson	53, 54
25. William McKinley	Mar. 4, 1897-Mar. 3, 1901	24. Garret A. Hobart[9]	55, 56
(4)	Mar. 4, 1901-Sept. 14, 1901	25. Theodore Roosevelt	57
26. Theodore Roosevelt	Sept. 14, 1901-Mar. 3, 1905	(None)	57, 58
	Mar. 4, 1905-Mar. 3, 1909	26. Charles W. Fairbanks	59, 60
27. William H. Taft	Mar. 4, 1909-Mar. 3, 1913	27. James S. Sherman[10]	61, 62

President	Service	Vice President	Congresses
28. Woodrow Wilson	Mar. 4, 1913-Mar. 3, 1921	28. Thomas R. Marshall	63, 64, 65, 66
29. Warren G. Harding[4]	Mar. 4, 1921-Aug. 2, 1923	29. Calvin Coolidge	67
30. Calvin Coolidge	Aug. 3, 1923-Mar. 3, 1925	(None)	68
	Mar. 4, 1925-Mar. 3, 1929	30. Charles G. Dawes	69, 70
31. Herbert C. Hoover	Mar. 4, 1929-Mar. 3, 1933	31. Charles Curtis	71, 72
32. Franklin D. Roosevelt[11]	Mar. 4, 1933-Jan. 20, 1941	32. John N. Garner	73, 74, 75, 76, 77
	Jan. 20, 1941-Jan. 20, 1945	33. Henry A. Wallace	77, 78, 79
(4)	Jan. 20, 1945-Apr. 12, 1945	34. Harry S. Truman	79
33. Harry S. Truman	Apr. 12, 1945-Jan. 20, 1949	(None)	79, 80, 81
	Jan. 20, 1949-Jan. 20, 1953	35. Alben W. Barkley	81, 82, 83
34. Dwight D. Eisenhower	Jan. 20, 1953-Jan. 20, 1961	36. Richard M. Nixon	83, 84, 85, 86, 87
35. John F. Kennedy[4]	Jan. 20, 1961-Nov. 22, 1963	37. Lyndon B. Johnson	87, 88
36. Lyndon B. Johnson	Nov. 22, 1963-Jan. 20, 1965	(None)	88, 89
	Jan. 20, 1965-Jan. 20, 1969	38. Hubert H. Humphrey	89, 90, 91
37. Richard M. Nixon	Jan. 20, 1969-Jan. 20, 1973	39. Spiro T. Agnew[12]	91, 92, 93
(13)	Jan. 20, 1973-Aug. 9, 1974	40. Gerald R. Ford[14]	93
38. Gerald R. Ford[15]	Aug. 9, 1974-Jan. 20, 1977	41. Nelson A. Rockefeller[16]	93, 94, 95
39. Jimmy Carter	Jan. 20, 1977-Jan. 20, 1981	42. Walter F. Mondale	95, 96, 97
40. Ronald W. Reagan	Jan. 20, 1981-Jan. 20, 1989	43. George H. W. Bush	97, 98, 99, 100, 101
41. George H. W. Bush	Jan. 20, 1989-Jan. 20, 1993	44. Dan Quayle	101, 102, 103
42. Bill Clinton	Jan. 20, 1993-Jan. 20, 2001	45. Al Gore	103, 104, 105, 106, 107
43. George W. Bush	Jan. 20, 2001-Jan. 20, 2009	46. Dick Cheney	107, 108, 109, 110, 111
44. Barack H. Obama	Jan. 20, 2009-	47. Joe Biden	111, 112, 113

(1) Died Apr. 20, 1812. (2) Died Nov. 23, 1814. (3) Resigned Dec. 28, 1832, to become U.S. senator. (4) Died in office. (5) Died Apr. 18, 1853. (6) Died Nov. 22, 1875. (7) Terms not consecutive. (8) Died Nov. 25, 1885. (9) Died Nov. 21, 1899. (10) Died Oct. 30, 1912. (11) First president to be inaugurated under 20th Amendment, Jan. 20, 1937. (12) Resigned Oct. 10, 1973, after pleading no contest to a charge of tax evasion. (13) Resigned Aug. 9, 1974. (14) First nonelected vice president, chosen under 25th Amendment procedure. (15) First president never elected president or vice president. (16) Second nonelected vice president, chosen under 25th Amendment. Confirmed Dec. 19, 1974.

Vice Presidents of the U.S.

The numerals given vice presidents do not coincide with those given presidents because some presidents (Tyler, Fillmore, A. Johnson, Arthur) had none, and some had more than one.

Name	Birthplace	Born	Home	Inaug.	Politics/ party	Place of death	Died	Age at death
1. John Adams	Quincy, MA	1735	MA	1789	Fed.	Quincy, MA	1826	90
2. Thomas Jefferson	Shadwell, VA	1743	VA	1797	Dem.-Rep.	Monticello, VA	1826	83
3. Aaron Burr	Newark, NJ	1756	NY	1801	Dem.-Rep.	Staten Island, NY	1836	80
4. George Clinton	Little Britain, NY	1739	NY	1805	Dem.-Rep.	Washington, DC	1812	73
5. Elbridge Gerry	Marblehead, MA	1744	MA	1813	Dem.-Rep.	Washington, DC	1814	70
6. Daniel D. Tompkins	Scarsdale, NY	1774	NY	1817	Dem.-Rep.	Staten Island, NY	1825	51
7. John C. Calhoun[1]	Abbeville, SC	1782	SC	1825	Dem.-Rep.	Washington, DC	1850	68
8. Martin Van Buren	Kinderhook, NY	1782	NY	1833	Dem.	Kinderhook, NY	1862	79
9. Richard M. Johnson[2]	Louisville, KY	1780	KY	1837	Dem.	Frankfort, KY	1850	70
10. John Tyler	Greenway, VA	1790	VA	1841	Whig	Richmond, VA	1862	71
11. George M. Dallas	Philadelphia, PA	1792	PA	1845	Dem.	Philadelphia, PA	1864	72
12. Millard Fillmore	Cayuga Co., NY	1800	NY	1849	Whig	Buffalo, NY	1874	74
13. William R. King	Sampson Co., NC	1786	AL	1853	Dem.	Cahaba, AL	1853	67
14. John C. Breckinridge	Lexington, KY	1821	KY	1857	Dem.	Lexington, KY	1875	54
15. Hannibal Hamlin	Paris, ME	1809	ME	1861	Rep.	Bangor, ME	1891	81
16. Andrew Johnson	Raleigh, NC	1808	TN	1865	(3)	Carter Co., TN	1875	66
17. Schuyler Colfax	New York, NY	1823	IN	1869	Rep.	Mankato, MN	1885	62
18. Henry Wilson	Farmington, NH	1812	MA	1873	Rep.	Washington, DC	1875	63
19. William A. Wheeler	Malone, NY	1819	NY	1877	Rep.	Malone, NY	1887	68
20. Chester A. Arthur	Fairfield, VT	1829	NY	1881	Rep.	New York, NY	1886	57
21. Thomas A. Hendricks	Zanesville, OH	1819	IN	1885	Dem.	Indianapolis, IN	1885	66
22. Levi P. Morton	Shoreham, VT	1824	NY	1889	Rep.	Rhinebeck, NY	1920	96
23. Adlai E. Stevenson[4]	Christian Co., KY	1835	IL	1893	Dem.	Chicago, IL	1914	78
24. Garret A. Hobart	Long Branch, NJ	1844	NJ	1897	Rep.	Paterson, NJ	1899	55
25. Theodore Roosevelt	New York, NY	1858	NY	1901	Rep.	Oyster Bay, NY	1919	60
26. Charles W. Fairbanks	Unionville Centre, OH	1852	IN	1905	Rep.	Indianapolis, IN	1918	66
27. James S. Sherman	Utica, NY	1855	NY	1909	Rep.	Utica, NY	1912	57
28. Thomas R. Marshall	N. Manchester, IN	1854	IN	1913	Dem.	Washington, DC	1925	71
29. Calvin Coolidge	Plymouth Notch, VT	1872	MA	1921	Rep.	Northampton, MA	1933	60
30. Charles G. Dawes	Marietta, OH	1865	IL	1925	Rep.	Evanston, IL	1951	85
31. Charles Curtis	Topeka, KS	1860	KS	1929	Rep.	Washington, DC	1936	76
32. John Nance Garner	Red River Co., TX	1868	TX	1933	Dem.	Uvalde, TX	1967	98
33. Henry A. Wallace	Adair County, IA	1888	IA	1941	Dem.	Danbury, CT	1965	77
34. Harry S. Truman	Lamar, MO	1884	MO	1945	Dem.	Kansas City, MO	1972	88
35. Alben W. Barkley	Graves Co., KY	1877	KY	1949	Dem.	Lexington, VA	1956	78
36. Richard M. Nixon	Yorba Linda, CA	1913	CA	1953	Rep.	New York, NY	1994	81
37. Lyndon B. Johnson	Stonewall, TX	1908	TX	1961	Dem.	San Antonio, TX	1973	64
38. Hubert H. Humphrey	Wallace, SD	1911	MN	1965	Dem.	Waverly, MN	1978	66
39. Spiro T. Agnew[5]	Baltimore, MD	1918	MD	1969	Rep.	Berlin, MD	1996	77
40. Gerald R. Ford[6]	Omaha, NE	1913	MI	1973	Rep.	Rancho Mirage, CA	2006	93
41. Nelson A. Rockefeller[7]	Bar Harbor, ME	1908	NY	1974	Rep.	New York, NY	1979	70
42. Walter F. Mondale	Ceylon, MN	1928	MN	1977	Dem.			
43. George H. W. Bush	Milton, MA	1924	TX	1981	Rep.			
44. James Danforth (Dan) Quayle Jr.	Indianapolis, IN	1947	IN	1989	Rep.			
45. Albert A. Gore	Washington, DC	1948	TN	1993	Dem.			
46. Richard B. Cheney	Lincoln, NE	1941	WY	2001	Rep.			
47. Joseph R. Biden Jr.	Scranton, PA	1942	DE	2009	Dem.			

(1) Resigned Dec. 28, 1832, having been elected to the Senate to fill a vacancy. (2) Richard M. Johnson was the only vice president to be chosen by the Senate because of a tied vote in the Electoral College. (3) Democrat Andrew Johnson was nominated vice president by Republicans and elected with Lincoln on the National Union Ticket. (4) Grandfather of Democratic candidate for president in 1952 and 1956. (5) Resigned Oct. 10, 1973, after pleading no contest to a charge of tax evasion. (6) First nonelected vice president, chosen under 25th Amendment procedure. (7) Second nonelected vice president, chosen under 25th Amendment.

Biographies of the Presidents

George Washington (1789-97), first president, Federalist, was born on Feb. 22, 1732, in Wakefield on Pope's Creek, Westmoreland Co., VA, the son of Augustine and Mary Ball Washington. He spent his early childhood on a farm near Fredericksburg. His father died when Washington was 11. He studied mathematics and surveying, and at 16, he went to live with his elder half brother, Lawrence, who built and named Mount Vernon in Virginia. Washington surveyed the lands of Thomas Fairfax in the Shenandoah Valley. He accompanied Lawrence to Barbados, West Indies, where he contracted smallpox and was deeply scarred. Lawrence died in 1752, and Washington inherited his property. He valued land, and when he died, he owned 70,000 acres in Virginia and 40,000 acres in what is now West Virginia.

Washington's military service began in 1753, when Lt. Gov. Robert Dinwiddie of Virginia sent him on missions deep into Ohio country. He clashed with the French and had to surrender Fort Necessity on July 3, 1754. He was an aide to the British general Edward Braddock and was at his side when the army was ambushed and defeated (July 9, 1755) on a march to Fort Duquesne. He helped take Fort Duquesne from the French in 1758.

After Washington's marriage to Martha Dandridge Custis, a widow, in 1759, he managed his family estate at Mount Vernon. Although not in favor of independence initially, he opposed the repressive measures of the British crown and took charge of the Virginia troops before war broke out. He was made commander of the newly created Continental Army by the Continental Congress on June 15, 1775.

The American victory was due largely to Washington's leadership. He was resourceful, a disciplinarian, and a dependable force for unity. Washington favored a federal government. He became chairman of the Constitutional Convention of 1787 and helped get the Constitution ratified. Unanimously elected president by the Electoral College, he was inaugurated Apr. 30, 1789, on the balcony of New York's Federal Hall. He was reelected in 1792. Washington made an effort to avoid partisan politics as president.

Refusing to consider a third term, Washington retired to Mount Vernon in Mar. 1797. A ride in snow and rain around his estate led to what present-day doctors believe to have been an attack of acute epiglottitis. Doctors were unsuccessful in treating the inflammation in his throat, and Washington died Dec. 14, 1799.

John Adams (1797-1801), second president, Federalist, was born on Oct. 30, 1735, in Braintree (now Quincy), MA, the son of John and Susanna Boylston Adams. He was a great-grandson of Henry Adams, who came from England in 1636. He graduated from Harvard in 1755, then taught school and studied law. He married Abigail Smith in 1764. In 1770, he successfully defended in court the British soldiers who fired on civilians in the Boston Massacre. He was a delegate to the Continental Congress and a signer of the Declaration of Independence. In 1778, Congress sent Adams and John Jay to join Benjamin Franklin as diplomatic representatives in Europe. Because he ran second to Washington in Electoral College balloting in Feb. 1789, Adams became the nation's first vice president, a post he characterized as highly insignificant; he was reelected in 1792.

In 1796 Adams was chosen president by the electors. His administration was marked by growing conflict with fellow Federalist Alexander Hamilton and with others in his own cabinet who supported Hamilton's strongly anti-French position. Adams avoided full-scale war with France but became unpopular, especially after securing passage of the Alien and Sedition Acts in 1798. His foreign policy contributed significantly to the election of Thomas Jefferson in 1800.

Adams lived for a quarter century after he left office, during which time he wrote extensively. He died July 4, 1826, on the same day as his rival Thomas Jefferson (the 50th anniversary of the Declaration of Independence).

Thomas Jefferson (1801-09), third president, Democratic-Republican, was born on Apr. 13, 1743, in Shadwell in Goochland (now Albemarle) Co., VA, the son of Peter and Jane Randolph Jefferson. His father died when Jefferson was 14, leaving him 2,750 acres and his slaves. Jefferson attended (1760-62) the College of William and Mary, read Greek and Latin classics, and played the violin. In 1769 he was elected to the Virginia House of Burgesses. In 1770 he began building his home, Monticello, and in 1772 he married Martha Wayles Skelton, a wealthy widow. Jefferson helped establish the Virginia Committee of Correspondence. As a member of the Second Continental Congress he drafted the Declaration of Independence. He also was a member of the Virginia House of Delegates (1776-79) and was elected governor of Virginia in 1779. He was reelected in 1780 but resigned the next year after British troops invaded Virginia. During his term he wrote the statute on religious freedom. After his wife's death in 1782, Jefferson again became a delegate to the Congress, and in 1784 he drafted the report that was the basis for the Ordinances of 1784, 1785, and 1787. He was minister to France from 1785 to 1789, when George Washington appointed him secretary of state.

Jefferson's strong faith in the consent of the governed conflicted with the emphasis on executive control, favored by Sec. of the Treasury Alexander Hamilton, and Jefferson resigned as secretary of state on Dec. 31, 1793. In the 1796 election Jefferson was the Democratic-Republican candidate for president; John Adams won the election, and Jefferson became vice president. In 1800, Jefferson and Aaron Burr received equal numbers of Electoral College votes; the House of Representatives elected Jefferson president. Jefferson was a strong advocate of westward expansion; major events of his first term were the Louisiana Purchase (1803) and the Lewis and Clark expedition. An important development during his second term was passage of the Embargo Act, barring U.S. ships from setting sail to foreign ports. Jefferson established the Univ. of Virginia and designed its buildings. He died July 4, 1826, on the same day as John Adams (the 50th anniversary of the Declaration of Independence).

Analysis of contemporary accounts, plantation records, and DNA taken from descendants of Jefferson and of Sally Hemings, one of his slaves, has caused many historians to conclude Jefferson fathered one or more of her six children.

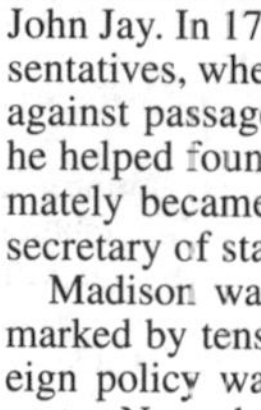

James Madison (1809-17), fourth president, Democratic-Republican, was born on Mar. 16, 1751, in Port Conway, King George Co., VA, the son of James and Eleanor Rose Conway Madison. Madison graduated from the College of New Jersey in 1771. He served in the Virginia Constitutional Convention (1776), and, in 1780, became a delegate to the Second Continental Congress. He was chief recorder at the Constitutional Convention in 1787 and supported ratification in the *Federalist Papers*, written with Alexander Hamilton and John Jay. In 1789, Madison was elected to the House of Representatives, where he helped frame the Bill of Rights and fought against passage of the Alien and Sedition Acts. In the 1790s, he helped found the Democratic-Republican Party, which ultimately became the Democratic Party. He became Jefferson's secretary of state in 1801.

Madison was elected president in 1808. His first term was marked by tensions with Great Britain, and his conduct of foreign policy was criticized by the Federalists and by his own party. Nevertheless, he was reelected in 1812, the year war was declared on Great Britain. The war that many considered a second American revolution ended with a treaty that did not settle any of the issues. Madison's most important action after the war was demilitarizing the U.S.-Canadian border.

In 1817, Madison retired to his estate, Montpelier, where he served as an elder statesman. He edited his famous papers on the Constitutional Convention and helped found the Univ. of Virginia, of which he became rector in 1826. He died June 28, 1836.

James Monroe (1817-25), fifth president, Democratic-Republican, was born on Apr. 28, 1758, in Westmoreland Co., VA, the son of Spence and Elizabeth Jones Monroe. He entered the College of William and Mary in 1774 but left to serve in the Third Virginia Regiment during the American Revolution. After the war, he studied law with Thomas Jefferson. In 1782 he was elected to the Virginia House of Delegates, and he served (1783-86) as a delegate to the Continental Congress. He opposed ratification of the Constitution because it lacked a bill of rights. Monroe was elected to the U.S. Senate in 1790. In 1794, Pres. Washington appointed Monroe minister to France. He was again minister to France (1803) under Pres. Jefferson as well as minister to Great Britain (1803-07). He served twice as governor of Virginia (1799-1802, 1811).

In 1816 Monroe was elected president; he was reelected in 1820 with all but one Electoral College vote. His administration became known as the Era of Good Feeling. He obtained Florida from Spain, settled boundary disputes with Britain over Canada, and eliminated border forts. He supported the antislavery position that led to the Missouri Compromise. His most significant contribution was the Monroe Doctrine, which opposed European intervention in the Western Hemisphere and became a cornerstone of U.S. foreign policy.

Although Monroe retired to Oak Hill, VA, financial problems forced him to sell his property and move to New York City. He died there on July 4, 1831.

John Quincy Adams (1825-29), sixth president, independent Federalist, later Democratic-Republican, was born on July 11, 1767, in Braintree (now Quincy), MA, the son of John and Abigail Adams. His father was the second president. He studied abroad and at Harvard College, from which he graduated in 1787. In 1803, he was elected to the U.S. Senate. President Monroe chose him as his secretary of state in 1817. In this capacity he negotiated the cession of Florida from Spain, supported exclusion of slavery in the Missouri Compromise, and helped formulate the Monroe Doctrine.

After no candidate won an Electoral College majority in 1824, the presidential election was decided by the House of Representatives. Adams won with support from rival Henry Clay, whom he named secretary of state, fueling accusations of a "corrupt bargain." His expansion of executive powers was strongly opposed, and in the 1828 election he lost to Andrew Jackson. In 1831 he entered the House of Representatives and served 17 years. He opposed slavery, the annexation of Texas, and the Mexican War. He helped establish the Smithsonian Institution.

Adams suffered a stroke in the House and died in the Speaker's Room on Feb. 23, 1848.

Andrew Jackson (1829-37), seventh president, Democratic-Republican, later a Democrat, was born on Mar. 15, 1767, in the Waxhaw district, on the border of North and South Carolina, the son of Andrew and Elizabeth Hutchinson Jackson. At the age of 13, he joined the militia to fight in the American Revolution and was captured. Orphaned at age 14, Jackson was raised by an uncle. By age 20, he was practicing law, and he later served as prosecuting attorney in Nashville, TN. In 1796 he helped draft the constitution of Tennessee, and for a year he occupied its one seat in the House of Representatives. The next year he served in the U.S. Senate.

In the War of 1812, Jackson crushed the Creek Indians at Horseshoe Bend, AL (1814), and, with a greatly outnumbered army consisting chiefly of backwoods militia members and volunteers, defeated Gen. Edward Pakenham's British troops at the Battle of New Orleans (1815). Nicknamed "Old Hickory" for his toughness, he emerged a national hero.

In 1818 Jackson briefly invaded Spanish Florida to quell Seminoles and outlaws who harassed frontier settlements. He ran for president against John Quincy Adams in 1824, but did not achieve a majority despite winning the most popular and electoral votes. The House of Representatives decided the election and chose Adams. In the 1828 election, however, Jackson defeated Adams, carrying the West and the South.

As president, Jackson introduced what became known as the spoils system—rewarding party members with government posts. A self-professed champion of the common man, he also viewed the Second Bank of the U.S. as a bastion of privilege and made it a major issue in the election of 1832, the first where candidates were chosen at national conventions rather than in congressional caucuses. Defeating Henry Clay, Jackson increasingly diverted funds from the national bank into so-called pet banks run by members of his own party. When South Carolina refused to collect imports under a federal tariff, which it declared null and void, Jackson won passage of legislation confirming his right to use military force to obtain compliance; eventually the tariff rate was reduced and the nullifiers backed down. After leaving office in 1837, he retired to the Hermitage, his estate outside Nashville, where he died on June 8, 1845.

Martin Van Buren (1837-41), eighth president, Democrat, was born on Dec. 5, 1782, in Kinderhook, NY, the son of Abraham and Maria Hoes Van Buren. After attending local schools, he studied law and became a lawyer at the age of 20. A consummate politician, Van Buren began his career in the New York state senate and then served as state attorney general (1816-19). He was elected to the U.S. Senate in 1821. He helped swing Eastern support to Andrew Jackson in the 1828 election and served as Jackson's secretary of state from 1829 to 1831. In 1832 he was elected vice president. Known as the "Little Magician," Van Buren was extremely influential in Jackson's administration.

In 1836, Van Buren defeated William Henry Harrison for president and took office as the financial panic of 1837 initiated a nationwide depression. Although he instituted the independent treasury system, his refusal to spend land revenues led to his defeat by William Henry Harrison in 1840. In 1844 he lost the Democratic nomination to James K. Polk. In 1848 he again ran for president on the Free Soil ticket but lost. He died in Kinderhook on July 24, 1862.

William Henry Harrison (1841), ninth president, Whig, who served only 31 days, was born on Feb. 9, 1773, in Berkeley, Charles City Co., VA, the son of Benjamin Harrison—a signer of the Declaration of Independence—and of Elizabeth Bassett Harrison. He attended Hampden-Sydney College. Harrison served as secretary of the Northwest Territory in 1798 and was its delegate to the House of Representatives in 1799. He was the first governor of Indiana Territory and served as superintendent of Indian affairs. With 900 men he put down a Shawnee uprising at Tippecanoe, IN, on Nov. 7, 1811. A generation later, in 1840, he waged a rousing presidential campaign using the slogan "Tippecanoe and Tyler Too." The Tyler of the slogan was his running mate, John Tyler.

Although born to one of the wealthiest, most prestigious, and most influential families in Virginia, Harrison also campaigned with the slogan "Log Cabin and Hard Cider." He caught pneumonia during his inauguration and died Apr. 4, 1841, after only one month in office.

John Tyler (1841-45), 10th president, independent Whig, was born on Mar. 29, 1790, in Greenway, Charles City Co., VA, the son of John and Mary Armistead Tyler. His father was governor of Virginia (1808-11). Tyler graduated from the College of William and Mary in 1807 and in 1811 was elected to the Virginia legislature. In 1816 he was chosen for the U.S. House of Representatives. He served in the Virginia legislature again from 1823 to 1825, when he was elected governor of Virginia. After a stint in the U.S. Senate (1827-36), he was elected vice president (1840).

When William Henry Harrison died only a month after taking office, Tyler succeeded him. Because he was the first person to occupy the presidency without having been elected to that office, he was referred to as "His Accidency." He gained passage of the Preemption Act of 1841, which gave squatters on government land the right to buy 160 acres at the minimum auction price. His last act as president was to sign a resolution annexing Texas. Tyler accepted renomination in 1844 from some Democrats but withdrew in favor of the official party candidate, James K. Polk. A strong advocate of states' rights, he served briefly in the Confederate House of Representatives before he died in Richmond, VA, on Jan. 18, 1862.

James Knox Polk (1845-49), 11th president, Democrat, was born on Nov. 2, 1795, in Mecklenburg Co., NC, the son of Samuel and Jane Knox Polk. He graduated from the Univ. of North Carolina in 1818 and served in the Tennessee state legislature from 1823 to 1825. He served in the U.S. House of Representatives from 1825 to 1839, the last four years as Speaker. He was governor of Tennessee from 1839 to 1841. In 1844, after the Democratic National Convention became deadlocked, it nominated Polk, who became the first "dark horse" candidate for president. He was nominated primarily because he favored annexation of Texas.

As president, Polk reestablished the independent treasury system originated by Van Buren. He was so intent on acquiring California from Mexico that he sent troops to the Mexican border and, when Mexicans attacked, declared that a state of war existed. The Mexican War ended with the annexation of California and much of the Southwest as part of America's "manifest destiny." Polk compromised on the Oregon boundary ("54-40 or fight!") by accepting the 49th parallel and yielding Vancouver Island to the British. Polk died in Nashville, TN, on June 15, 1849, a few months after leaving office.

Zachary Taylor (1849-50), 12th president, Whig, who served only 16 months, was born on Nov. 24, 1784, in Orange Co., VA, the son of Richard and Sarah Strother Taylor. He grew up on his father's plantation near Louisville, KY, where he was educated by private tutors. In 1808 Taylor joined the regular army and was commissioned first lieutenant. He fought in the War of 1812, the Black Hawk War (1832), and the second Seminole War (beginning in 1837). He was called "Old Rough and Ready." In 1846 Pres. Polk sent him with an army to the Rio Grande. When the Mexicans attacked him, Polk declared war. Outnumbered four to one, Taylor defeated Antonio López de Santa Anna at Buena Vista (1847).

A national hero, Taylor received the Whig nomination in 1848 and was elected president, even though he had never bothered to vote. He resumed the spoils system and, though a slaveholder, worked to admit California as a free state. He fell ill, likely from a case of acute gastroenteritis, and died in office on July 9, 1850.

Millard Fillmore (1850-53), 13th president, Whig, was born on Jan. 7, 1800, in Cayuga Co., NY, the son of Nathaniel and Phoebe Millard Fillmore. Although he had little schooling, he became a law clerk at the age of 22 and was admitted to the bar a year later. He was elected to the New York state assembly in 1828 and served until 1831. From 1833 until 1835 and again from 1837 to 1843, he represented his district in the U.S. House of Representatives. He opposed the entrance of Texas as a slave state and voted for a protective tariff. In 1844 he was defeated for governor of New York.

In 1848, he was elected vice president; he became president after Taylor's death. Fillmore favored the Compromise of 1850 and signed the Fugitive Slave Law. His policies pleased neither expansionists nor slaveholders, and he was not renominated in 1852. In 1856 he was nominated by the American (Know-Nothing) Party, but despite the support of the Whigs, he was defeated by James Buchanan. He died in Buffalo, NY, on Mar. 8, 1874.

Franklin Pierce (1853-57), 14th president, Democrat, was born on Nov. 23, 1804, in Hillsboro, NH, the son of Benjamin Pierce, Revolutionary War general and governor of New Hampshire, and Anna Kendrick. He graduated from Bowdoin College in 1824 and was admitted to the bar in 1827. He was elected to the New Hampshire state legislature in 1829 and was chosen Speaker in 1831. He went to the U.S. House in 1833 and was elected a U.S. senator in 1837. He enlisted in the Mexican War and became brigadier general under Gen. Winfield Scott.

In 1852 Pierce was nominated as the Democratic presidential candidate on the 49th ballot. He decisively defeated Gen. Scott, his Whig opponent, in the election. Although he was against slavery, Pierce was influenced by proslavery Southerners. He supported the controversial Kansas-Nebraska Act, which left the question of slavery in the new territories of Kansas and Nebraska to popular vote. Pierce signed a reciprocity treaty with Canada and approved the Gadsden Purchase, from Mexico, of a border area on a proposed railroad route. Denied renomination, he spent most of his remaining years in Concord, NH, where he died on Oct. 8, 1869.

James Buchanan (1857-61), 15th president, Federalist, later Democrat, was born on Apr. 23, 1791, near Mercersburg, PA, the son of James and Elizabeth Speer Buchanan. He graduated from Dickinson College in 1809 and was admitted to the bar in 1812. He fought in the War of 1812 as a volunteer. He was twice elected to the Pennsylvania general assembly, and in 1821 he entered the U.S. House of Representatives. After briefly serving (1832-33) as minister to Russia, he was elected U.S. senator from Pennsylvania. As Polk's secretary of state (1845-49), he ended the Oregon dispute with Britain and supported the Mexican War and annexation of Texas. As minister to Great Britain, he signed the Ostend Manifesto (1854), declaring a U.S. right to take Cuba by force should efforts to purchase it fail.

Nominated by Democrats, Buchanan was elected president in 1856. On slavery he favored popular sovereignty and choice by state constitutions but did not consistently uphold this position. He denied the right of states to secede but opposed coercion and attempted to keep peace by not provoking secessionists. Buchanan left office having failed to deal decisively with the situation. He died at Wheatland, his estate, near Lancaster, PA, on June 1, 1868.

Abraham Lincoln (1861-65), 16th president, Whig, then Republican, was born on Feb. 12, 1809, in a log cabin on a farm in Hardin (now Larue) Co., KY, the son of Thomas and Nancy Hanks Lincoln. The Lincolns moved to Spencer Co., IN, near Gentryville, when Lincoln was 7. After Lincoln's mother died, his father married Mrs. Sarah Bush Johnston in 1819. In 1830 the family moved to Macon Co., IL.

Defeated in 1832 in a race for the state legislature, Lincoln was elected on the Whig ticket two years later and served in the lower house from 1834 to 1842. In 1837 Lincoln was admitted to the bar and became partner in a Springfield, IL, law office. In 1846, he was elected to Congress, where he attracted attention during a single term for his opposition to the Mexican War and his position on slavery. In 1856 he campaigned for the newly founded Republican Party, and in 1858 he became its senatorial candidate against Stephen A. Douglas. Although he lost the election, Lincoln gained national recognition from his debates with Douglas.

In 1860, Lincoln was nominated for president by the Republican Party on a platform of restricting slavery. He ran against Douglas, a northern Democrat; John C. Breckinridge, a Southern proslavery Democrat; and John Bell, of the Constitutional Union Party. In response to Lincoln's victory, South Carolina seceded from the Union on Dec. 20, 1860, soon followed by six other Southern states.

The Civil War erupted when South Carolina's Fort Sumter, which Lincoln decided to resupply, was attacked by Confederate forces on Apr. 12, 1861. Lincoln called for recruits from the North, and four more Southern states seceded. Hundreds of thousands of Union and Confederate soldiers were killed or wounded in four years of battle that followed. On Sept. 22, 1862, five days after the Battle of Antietam, Lincoln announced that slaves in territory then in rebellion would be free Jan. 1, 1863, under his Emancipation Proclamation. His speeches, including his Gettysburg and inaugural addresses, are remembered for their eloquence.

Lincoln was reelected, in 1864, over Gen. George B. McClellan, a Democrat. Confederate Gen. Robert E. Lee surrendered on Apr. 9, 1865. On Apr. 14, Lincoln was shot by actor

John Wilkes Booth in Ford's Theater, in Washington, DC. He died the next day.

Andrew Johnson (1865-69), 17th president, Democrat, was born on Dec. 29, 1808, in Raleigh, NC, the son of Jacob and Mary McDonough Johnson. He was apprenticed to a tailor as a youth but ran away after two years and eventually settled in Greeneville, TN, where he was elected councilman and later mayor. In 1835 he was sent to the state general assembly. In 1843 he was elected to the U.S. House of Representatives, where he served for 10 years. Johnson was also governor of Tennessee from 1853 to 1857, when he was elected to the U.S. Senate. Although Johnson had held slaves, he opposed secession and tried to prevent Tennessee from seceding. In Mar. 1862, Lincoln appointed him military governor of occupied Tennessee.

In 1864, in order to balance Lincoln's ticket with a Southern Democrat, the Republicans nominated Johnson for vice president. He was elected vice president with Lincoln and succeeded to the presidency upon Lincoln's death. Soon afterward, in conflict with Congress over the president's power over the South, he proclaimed an amnesty to all Confederates, except certain leaders, if they would ratify the 13th Amendment abolishing slavery. States doing so added anti-Negro provisions that enraged Congress, which restored military control over the South. When Johnson removed Sec. of War Edwin M. Stanton without notifying the Senate, the House impeached him in Feb. 1868 on the charge of violating the Tenure of Office Act. In reality, the House was responding to his opposition to harsh congressional Reconstruction, expressed in repeated vetoes. He was acquitted in the Senate by one-vote margins on each of two counts.

Johnson was denied renomination but remained politically active. He was reelected to the Senate in 1874. Johnson died July 31, 1875, at Carter Station, TN.

Ulysses S. Grant (1869-77), 18th president, Republican, was born on Apr. 27, 1822, in Point Pleasant, OH, the son of Jesse R. and Hannah Simpson Grant. The next year the family moved to Georgetown, OH. Grant was named Hiram Ulysses. Upon entering West Point in 1839, he found his name had been put down as Ulysses S. Grant, with his middle name first and his mother's maiden name as his middle name. He eventually adopted it as his true name but maintained the "S" did not stand for anything. Grant graduated in 1843. During the Mexican War, Grant served under both Gen. Zachary Taylor and Gen. Winfield Scott. In 1854, he resigned his commission because of loneliness and drinking problems, and in the following years he engaged in generally unsuccessful farming and business ventures. With the start of the Civil War, he was named colonel and then brigadier general of the Illinois Volunteers. He took Forts Henry and Donelson and fought at Shiloh. His brilliant campaign against Vicksburg and his victory at Chattanooga made him so prominent that Lincoln placed him in command of all Union armies. Grant accepted Confederate Gen. Robert E. Lee's surrender at Appomattox Court House on Apr. 9, 1865.

Grant was nominated for president by the Republicans in 1868 and elected over Democrat Horatio Seymour. The 15th Amendment, the amnesty bill, and peaceful settlement of disputes with Great Britain were events of his administration. The Liberal Republicans and Democrats opposed him with Horace Greeley in the 1872 election, but Grant was reelected. His second administration was marked by scandals, including the Crédit Mobilier affair, the Whiskey Ring, in which high-ranked officials conspired to defraud the government of taxes, and the impeachment of his secretary of war. An attempt by the Stalwarts (Old Guard Republicans) to nominate him in 1880 failed. Left penniless by the 1884 collapse of an investment firm in which he was a partner, he wrote his well-regarded memoirs while suffering from cancer to provide income for his family. He died at Mt. McGregor, NY, on July 23, 1885.

Rutherford Birchard Hayes (1877-81), 19th president, Republican, was born on Oct. 4, 1822, in Delaware, OH, the son of Rutherford and Sophia Birchard Hayes. He was reared by his uncle, Sardis Birchard. Hayes graduated from Kenyon College in 1842 and from Harvard Law School in 1845. He practiced law in Lower Sandusky (now Fremont), OH, and was city solicitor of Cincinnati from 1858 to 1861. During the Civil War, he was major of the 23rd Ohio Volunteers. He was wounded several times, and by the end of the war he had risen to the rank of brevet major general. While serving (1865-67) in the U.S. House of Representatives, Hayes supported Reconstruction and Johnson's impeachment. He was twice elected governor of Ohio (1867, 1869). After losing a race for the U.S. House in 1872, he was reelected governor of Ohio in 1875.

In 1876, Hayes was nominated for president. He believed he had lost the election to Democrat Samuel J. Tilden. But a few Southern states submitted two sets of electoral votes, and the result was in dispute. An electoral commission, consisting of 8 Republicans and 7 Democrats, awarded all disputed votes to Hayes, allowing him to become president by one electoral vote. Hayes, keeping a promise to Southerners, withdrew troops from areas still occupied in the South, ending the era of Reconstruction. He proposed civil service reforms, alienating those favoring the spoils system, and advocated repeal of the Tenure of Office Act restricting presidential power to dismiss officials. He supported sound money and specie payments.

Hayes died in Fremont, OH, on Jan. 17, 1893.

James Abram Garfield (1881), 20th president, Republican, was born on Nov. 19, 1831, in Orange, Cuyahoga Co., OH, the son of Abram and Eliza Ballou Garfield. His father died in 1833, and he was reared in poverty by his mother. He worked as a canal bargeman, a farmer, and a carpenter. He attended Western Reserve Eclectic Institute and graduated from Williams College in 1856. He returned to Western Reserve to teach and in 1857, at age 25, he became the school's president. In 1859 he was elected to the Ohio legislature. Antislavery and antisecession, he volunteered for military service in the Civil War, becoming colonel of the 42nd Ohio Infantry and brigadier in 1862. He fought at Shiloh, TN, was chief of staff for Gen. William Starke Rosecrans, and was made major general for gallantry at Chickamauga, GA. He entered Congress as a radical Republican in 1863, calling for execution or exile of Confederate leaders, but he moderated his views after the Civil War. On the electoral commission in 1877 he voted for Hayes against Tilden on strict party lines.

Garfield was a senator-elect in 1880 when he became the Republican nominee for president. He was chosen as a compromise over Gen. Grant, James G. Blaine, and John Sherman, and won election despite some bitterness among Grant's supporters. For much of his brief tenure as president, Garfield was concerned with a fight with New York Sen. Roscoe Conkling, who opposed two major appointments made by Garfield. On July 2, 1881, Garfield was shot and seriously wounded by a mentally disturbed office seeker, Charles J. Guiteau, while entering a railroad station in Washington, DC. He died on Sept. 19, 1881, in Elberon, NJ.

Chester Alan Arthur (1881-85), 21st president, Republican, was born on Oct. 5, 1829, in Fairfield, VT, to William and Malvina Stone Arthur. He graduated from Union College in 1848, taught school in Vermont, then studied law and practiced in New York City. In 1853, he argued in a fugitive slave case that slaves transported through New York State were thereby freed. In 1871, he was appointed collector of the Port of New York. Pres. Hayes, an opponent of the spoils system, forced him to resign in 1878. This made the New York machine enemies of Hayes. Arthur and the Stalwarts (Old Guard Republicans) tried to nominate Grant for a third term as president in 1880. When Garfield was nominated, Arthur was nominated for vice president in the interests of harmony.

Upon Garfield's assassination, Arthur became president. Despite his past connections, he signed major civil service reform legislation. Arthur tried to dissuade Congress from enacting the high protective tariff of 1883. He was defeated for renomination in 1884 by James G. Blaine. He died in New York City on Nov. 18, 1886.

Grover Cleveland (1885-89; 1893-97) *(According to a State Dept. ruling, Grover Cleveland should be counted as both the 22nd and the 24th president because his two terms were not consecutive)*, Democrat, was born Stephen Grover Cleveland on Mar. 18, 1837, in Caldwell, NJ, the son of Richard F. and Ann Neal Cleveland. When he was a small boy, his family moved to New York. Prevented by his father's death from attending college, he studied on his own and was admitted to the bar in Buffalo, NY, in 1859. In succession he became assistant district attorney (1863), sheriff (1871), mayor (1881), and governor of New York (1882). He was an independent, honest administrator who hated corruption. Cleveland was nominated for president over opposition from New York City's Tammany Hall in 1884 and defeated Republican James G. Blaine.

As president, he enlarged the civil service and vetoed many pension raids on the Treasury. In the 1888 election he was defeated by Benjamin Harrison, although his popular vote was larger. Reelected over Harrison in 1892, he faced a money crisis brought about by a lowered gold reserve, circulation of paper, and exorbitant silver purchases under the Sherman Silver Purchase Act. He obtained a repeal of the Sherman Act but was unable to secure effective tariff reform. A severe economic depression and labor troubles racked his administration, but he refused to interfere in business matters and rejected Jacob Coxey's demand for unemployment relief. In 1894, he broke the Pullman strike. Cleveland was not renominated in 1896. He died in Princeton, NJ, on June 24, 1908.

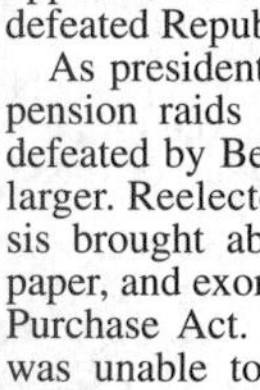

Benjamin Harrison (1889-93), 23rd president, Republican, was born on Aug. 20, 1833, in North Bend, OH, the son of John Scott and Elizabeth Irwin Harrison. His great-grandfather, Benjamin Harrison, was a signer of the Declaration of Independence; his grandfather, William Henry Harrison, was the ninth president; his father was a member of Congress. He attended school on his father's farm and graduated from Miami Univ. in Oxford, OH, in 1852. He was admitted to the bar in 1854 and practiced in Indianapolis, IN. During the Civil War, he rose to the rank of brevet brigadier general and fought at Kennesaw Mountain, Peachtree Creek, Nashville, and in the Atlanta campaign. He lost the 1876 gubernatorial election in Indiana but succeeded in becoming a U.S. senator in 1881.

In 1888 he defeated Cleveland for president despite receiving fewer popular votes. As president, he expanded the pension list and signed the McKinley high tariff bill, the Sherman Antitrust Act, and the Sherman Silver Purchase Act. During his administration, six states were admitted to the Union. He was defeated for reelection in 1892. He died in Indianapolis, IN, on Mar. 13, 1901.

William McKinley (1897-1901), 25th president, Republican, was born on Jan. 29, 1843, in Niles, OH, the son of William and Nancy Allison McKinley. McKinley briefly attended Allegheny College. When the Civil War broke out in 1861, he enlisted and served for the duration. He rose to captain and in 1865 was made brevet major. After studying law in Albany, NY, he opened a law office in Canton, OH (1867). He served twice in the U.S. House (1877-83; 1885-91) and led the fight there for the McKinley Tariff, passed in 1890; he was not reelected to the House as a result. He served two terms (1892-96) as governor of Ohio.

In 1896 he was elected president as a proponent of a protective tariff and sound money (gold standard) over William Jennings Bryan, the Democrat and a proponent of free silver. McKinley was reluctant to intervene in Cuba, but the loss of the battleship *Maine* at Havana crystallized opinion. He demanded Spain's withdrawal from Cuba; Spain made some concessions, but Congress announced a state of war as of Apr. 21, 1898. He was reelected in the 1900 campaign, defeating Bryan's anti-imperialist arguments with the promise of a "full dinner pail." He was known for a conservative stance on business issues. On Sept. 6, 1901, at the Pan-American Exposition, in Buffalo, NY, he was shot by Leon Czolgosz, an anarchist. He died Sept. 14.

Theodore Roosevelt (1901-09), 26th president, Republican, was born on Oct. 27, 1858, in New York City, the son of Theodore and Martha Bulloch Roosevelt. He was a fifth cousin of Franklin D. Roosevelt and an uncle of Eleanor Roosevelt. Roosevelt graduated from Harvard Univ. in 1880. He attended Columbia Law School briefly but abandoned law to enter politics. He was elected to the New York State Assembly in 1881 and served until 1884. He spent the next two years ranching and hunting in the Dakota Territory. In 1886, he ran unsuccessfully for mayor of New York City. He was civil service commissioner in Washington, DC, from 1889 to 1895. From 1895 to 1897, he served as New York City's police commissioner. He was assistant secretary of the Navy under McKinley. The Spanish-American War made him nationally known. He organized the First U.S. Volunteer Cavalry (Rough Riders) and, as lieutenant colonel, led the charge up Kettle Hill in San Juan, Cuba. Elected New York governor in 1898, he fought the spoils system and achieved taxation of corporation franchises.

Nominated for vice president in 1900, Roosevelt became the nation's youngest president when McKinley was assassinated. He was reelected in 1904. As president he fought corruption of politics by big business, dissolved the Northern Securities Co. and others for violating antitrust laws, intervened in the 1902 coal strike on behalf of the public, obtained the Elkins Law (1903) forbidding rebates to favored corporations, and helped pass the Hepburn Railway Rate Act of 1906 (extending jurisdiction of the Interstate Commerce Commission). He helped obtain passage of the Pure Food and Drug Act (1906) and of employers' liability laws. Roosevelt vigorously organized conservation efforts. He mediated the peace between Japan and Russia in 1905, for which he won the Nobel Peace Prize. He abetted the 1903 revolution in Panama that led to U.S. acquisition of territory for the Panama Canal.

In 1908 Roosevelt obtained the nomination of William H. Taft, who was elected. Feeling that Taft had abandoned his policies, he unsuccessfully sought the nomination in 1912. He then ran on the Progressive "Bull Moose" ticket against Taft and Woodrow Wilson, splitting the Republicans and ensuring Wilson's election. During the campaign he was shot by a mentally deranged man but was not seriously wounded. In 1916, after unsuccessfully seeking the presidential nomination, he supported the Republican candidate, Charles E. Hughes. He strongly promoted U.S. intervention in World War I.

Roosevelt was a voracious reader and wrote some 40 books, including *The Winning of the West*. He died Jan. 6, 1919, at Sagamore Hill, his home in Oyster Bay, NY.

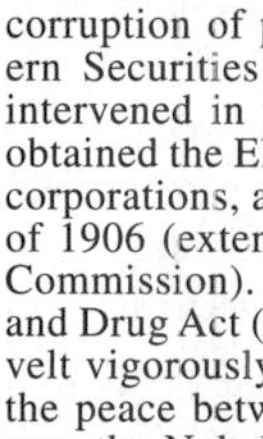

William Howard Taft (1909-13), 27th president, Republican, and 10th chief justice of the U.S., was born on Sept. 15, 1857, in Cincinnati, OH, the son of Alphonso and Louisa Maria Torrey Taft. His father was secretary of war and attorney general in Grant's cabinet and minister to Austria and Russia under Arthur. Taft graduated from Yale in 1878 and from Cincinnati Law School in 1880. After working as a law reporter for Cincinnati newspapers, he served as assistant prosecuting attorney (1881-82), assistant county solicitor (1885), superior court judge (1887), U.S. solicitor-general (1890), and federal circuit judge (1892). In 1900 he became head of the U.S. Philippines Commission and was the first civil governor of the Philippines (1901-04). In 1904 he served as secretary of war, and in 1906 he was sent to Cuba to help avert a threatened revolution.

Taft was groomed for the presidency by Theodore Roosevelt and elected over William Jennings Bryan in 1908. Taft vigorously continued Roosevelt's trust-busting, instituted the Dept. of Labor, and drafted amendments calling for direct election of senators and an income tax. However, his tariff and conservation policies angered progressives. Although renominated in 1912, he was opposed by Roosevelt, who ran on the Progressive Party ticket; the result was Wilson's election.

Taft, with reservations, supported the League of Nations. After leaving office, he was professor of constitutional law at Yale (1913-21) and chief justice of the U.S. (1921-30). Taft was the only person to have been both president and chief justice. He died in Washington, DC, on Mar. 8, 1930.

(Thomas) Woodrow Wilson (1913-21), 28th president, Democrat, was born on Dec. 28, 1856, in Staunton, VA, the son of Joseph Ruggles and Janet (Jessie) Woodrow Wilson. He grew up in Georgia and South Carolina. He attended Davidson College in North Carolina before graduating from Princeton Univ. in 1879. He studied law at the Univ. of Virginia and political science at Johns Hopkins Univ., where he received his PhD in 1886. He taught at Bryn Mawr (1885-88) and at Wesleyan (1888-90) before joining the faculty at Princeton. He was president of Princeton from 1902 until 1910, when he was elected governor of New Jersey. In 1912 he was nominated for president with the aid of William Jennings Bryan, who sought to block James "Champ" Clark and New York City's Tammany Hall. Wilson won because Theodore Roosevelt, running as a "Bull Moose" Progressive, siphoned votes away from Republican candidate Taft.

As president, Wilson protected American interests in revolutionary Mexico and fought for American rights on the high seas. He oversaw the creation of the Federal Reserve system, cut the tariff, and developed a reputation as a reformer. His sharp warnings to Germany led to the resignation of his secretary of state, Bryan, a pacifist. In 1916 he was reelected by a slim margin with the slogan "He kept us out of war," although his attempts to mediate in the war failed. After several American ships were sunk by the Germans, he secured a declaration of war against Germany on Apr. 6, 1917.

Wilson outlined his peace program on Jan. 8, 1918, in the Fourteen Points, a state paper that enunciated a doctrine of self-determination for the settlement of territorial disputes. The Germans accepted his terms and an armistice on Nov. 11, 1918. Wilson went to Paris to help negotiate the peace treaty, the crux of which he considered the League of Nations. The Senate demanded reservations that would not make the U.S. subordinate to the votes of other nations in case of war. Wilson refused and toured the country to get support. After he suffered a severe stroke in Oct. 1919, his wife, Edith Wilson, concealed the extent of his infirmity, controlled access to him, and in effect largely acted in his place.

Wilson was awarded the 1919 Nobel Peace Prize, but the treaty embodying the League of Nations was ultimately rejected by the Senate in 1920. He left the White House in Mar. 1921. He died in Washington, DC, on Feb. 3, 1924.

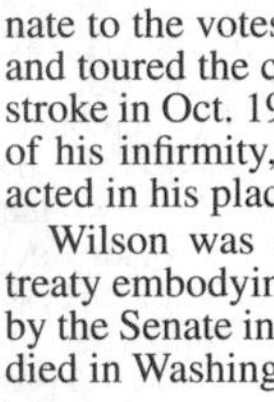

Warren Gamaliel Harding (1921-23), 29th president, Republican, was born on Nov. 2, 1865, near Corsica (now Blooming Grove), OH, the son of George Tyron and Phoebe Elizabeth Dickerson Harding. He attended Ohio Central College, studied law, and became editor and publisher of a county newspaper. He entered the political arena as state senator (1901-04) and then served as lieutenant governor (1904-06). In 1910 he ran unsuccessfully for governor of Ohio; in 1914 he was elected to the U.S. Senate. In the Senate he voted for antistrike legislation, women's suffrage, and the Volstead Prohibition Enforcement Act over Pres. Wilson's veto. He opposed the League of Nations.

In 1920 he was nominated for president and defeated James M. Cox in the election. The Republicans capitalized on war weariness and fear that Wilson's League of Nations would curtail U.S. sovereignty. Harding stressed a return to "normalcy" and worked for tariff revision and the repeal of excess profits law and high income taxes. In what became known as the Teapot Dome scandal, his secretary of the interior, Albert B. Fall, resigned and was later convicted of accepting bribes in the leasing of government-owned oil reserves to private companies.

As rumors began to circulate about the corruption in his administration, Harding fell ill after a trip to Alaska, and he died suddenly in San Francisco on Aug. 2, 1923. Harding's letters to a longtime mistress were made public by the Library of Congress in 2014, and DNA evidence in 2015 confirmed another mistress's claim that he had fathered her daughter.

(John) Calvin Coolidge (1923-29), 30th president, Republican, was born on July 4, 1872, in Plymouth Notch, VT, the son of John Calvin and Victoria J. Moor Coolidge. Coolidge graduated from Amherst College in 1895. He entered Republican state politics and served as mayor of Northampton, MA, as state senator, as lieutenant governor, and, in 1919, as governor. In Sept. 1919, Coolidge attained national prominence by calling out the state guard in the Boston police strike. He declared, "There is no right to strike against the public safety by anybody, anywhere, anytime." This brought his name before the Republican convention of 1920, where he was nominated for vice president.

Coolidge succeeded to the presidency on Harding's death. As president, he opposed the League of Nations and the soldiers' bonus bill, which was passed over his veto. In 1924 he was elected to the presidency by a huge majority. He substantially reduced the national debt. He twice vetoed legislation to aid financially hard-pressed farmers.

With Republicans eager to renominate him, Coolidge simply announced on Aug. 2, 1927, "I do not choose to run for president in 1928." He died in Northampton, MA, on Jan. 5, 1933.

Herbert Clark Hoover (1929-33), 31st president, Republican, was born on Aug. 10, 1874, in West Branch, IA, the son of Jesse Clark and Hulda Randall Minthorn Hoover. Hoover grew up in Indian Territory (now Oklahoma) and Oregon and graduated from Stanford Univ. with a degree in geology in 1895. He worked briefly with the U.S. Geological Survey and then managed mines in Australia, Asia, Europe, and Africa. While chief engineer of imperial mines in China, he directed food relief for victims of the Boxer Rebellion. He gained a reputation not only as an engineer but as a humanitarian as he directed the American Relief Committee, London (1914-15) and the U.S. Commission for Relief in Belgium (1915-19). He was U.S. Food Administrator (1917-19), American Relief Administrator (1918-23), and in charge of Russian Relief (1918-23). He served as secretary of commerce under both Harding and Coolidge. Some historians believe that he was the most effective secretary of commerce ever to hold that office.

In 1928 Hoover was elected president over Alfred E. Smith. In 1929 the stock market crashed, and the economy collapsed. During the Great Depression, Hoover inaugurated some government assistance programs, but he was opposed to administration of aid through a federal bureaucracy. As the effects of the Depression continued, he was defeated in the 1932 election by Franklin D. Roosevelt. Hoover remained active after leaving office. Pres. Truman named him coordinator of the European Food Program (1946) and chairman of the Commission on Organization of the Executive Branch (1947-49); he was later appointed by Pres. Eisenhower to serve in the same role (1953-55).

Hoover died in New York City on Oct. 20, 1964.

Franklin Delano Roosevelt (1933-45), 32nd president, Democrat, was born on Jan. 30, 1882, in Hyde Park, NY, the son of James and Sara Delano Roosevelt. He graduated from Harvard Univ. in 1903. He attended Columbia University Law School without taking a degree and was admitted to the New York State bar in 1907. His political career began when he was elected to the New York State senate in 1910. In 1913 Pres. Wilson appointed him assistant secretary of the navy, a post he held during World War I.

In 1920 Roosevelt ran for vice president with James Cox and was defeated. From 1921 to 1928 he worked in his New York law office and was also vice president of a bank. In Aug. 1921, he was stricken with poliomyelitis, which left his legs paralyzed. As a result of therapy he was able to stand and walk a few steps with the aid of leg braces.

Roosevelt served two terms as governor of New York (1929-33). In 1932, Democratic convention delegate W. G. McAdoo, pledged to nominee John N. Garner, threw his votes to Roosevelt, who was nominated for president. The Depression and the promise to repeal Prohibition ensured his election. He asked for emergency powers, proclaimed the New Deal, and put into effect a vast number of administrative changes. Foremost was the use of public funds for relief and public works, resulting in deficit financing. He greatly expanded the federal government's regulation of business and by an excess profits tax and progressive income taxes produced a redistribution of earnings on an unprecedented scale. He also promoted legislation establishing the Social Security system. He was the last president inaugurated on Mar. 4 (1933) and the first inaugurated on Jan. 20 (1937).

Roosevelt was the first president to use radio for "fireside chats." When the Supreme Court nullified some New Deal laws, he sought power to "pack" the Court with additional justices, but Congress refused to give him the authority. He was the first president to break the no-third-term tradition (1940) and was elected to a fourth term in 1944 despite failing health.

Roosevelt was openly hostile to fascist governments before World War II and launched a lend-lease program on behalf of the Allies. With British Prime Min. Winston Churchill he wrote a declaration of principles to be followed after Nazi defeat (the Atlantic Charter of Aug. 14, 1941) and urged the Four Freedoms (freedom of speech, of worship, from want, from fear) Jan. 6, 1941. After Japan attacked Pearl Harbor on Dec. 7, 1941, the U.S. entered the war. Roosevelt guided the nation through the war and conferred with allied heads of state but did not live to see the end of the war. He died of a cerebral hemorrhage in Warm Springs, GA, on Apr. 12, 1945.

Harry S. Truman (1945-53), 33rd president, Democrat, was born on May 8, 1884, in Lamar, MO, the son of John Anderson and Martha Ellen Young Truman. A family disagreement over whether his middle name should be Shipp or Solomon, after his two grandfathers, resulted in his using only the middle initial S. After graduating from high school (1901) in Independence, MO, he worked in the mailroom of the *Kansas City Star*, as a railroad timekeeper, and as a clerk in Kansas City banks until about 1905. He ran his family's farm from 1906 to 1917, then served in France during World War I. After the war he opened a haberdashery, was a judge on the Jackson Co. Court (1922-24), and attended Kansas City School of Law (1923-25).

Truman was elected to the U.S. Senate in 1934 and reelected in 1940. In 1944, with Roosevelt's backing, he was nominated for vice president and elected. On Roosevelt's death in 1945, Truman became president. In 1948, in a famous upset victory, he defeated Republican Thomas E. Dewey to win a new term.

Truman authorized the first uses of the atomic bomb (Hiroshima and Nagasaki, Aug. 6 and 9, 1945), bringing World War II to a rapid end. He was responsible for what came to be called the Truman Doctrine to aid nations such as Greece and Turkey threatened by Communist takeover, and his strong commitment to NATO and to the Marshall Plan helped bring the two about. In 1948-49, he broke a Soviet blockade of West Berlin with a massive airlift. When Communist North Korea invaded South Korea (June 1950), he won UN approval for a "police action" and, without prior congressional consent, sent in forces under Gen. Douglas MacArthur. When MacArthur opposed his policy of limited objectives, Truman removed him.

He died in Kansas City, MO, on Dec. 26, 1972.

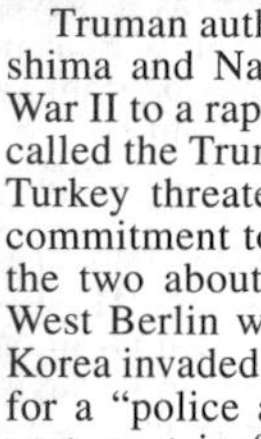

Dwight David Eisenhower (1953-61), 34th president, Republican, was born on Oct. 14, 1890, in Denison, TX, the son of David Jacob and Ida Elizabeth Stover Eisenhower, as David Dwight Eisenhower. He grew up on a small farm in Abilene, KS, and graduated from West Point in 1915. He was on the staff of Gen. Douglas MacArthur in the Philippines from 1935 to 1939. In 1942, he was made commander of Allied forces landing in North Africa; the next year he was made full general. He became supreme Allied commander in Europe that same year and led the Normandy invasion (June 6, 1944). He was subsequently given the rank of general of the Army.

On May 7, 1945, Eisenhower received the surrender of Germany at Rheims, France. He returned to the U.S. to serve as chief of staff (1945-48). His memoir, *Crusade in Europe* (1948), was a best-seller. In 1948 he became president of Columbia Univ.; in 1950 he became commander of NATO forces.

Eisenhower was nominated for president by the Republicans in 1952. He defeated Illinois Gov. Adlai E. Stevenson in the 1952 election and defeated Stevenson in 1956 to win reelection. Eisenhower called himself a moderate, favored the "free market system" versus government price and wage controls, kept government out of labor disputes, reorganized the defense establishment, and promoted missile programs. He continued foreign aid, helped negotiate a cease-fire truce in the Korean War, endorsed Taiwan and SE Asia defense treaties, backed the UN in condemning the Anglo-French raid on Egypt, and advocated the "open skies" policy of mutual inspection with the USSR. He sent U.S. troops into Little Rock, AR, in Sept. 1957, to enforce school integration.

Eisenhower died on Mar. 28, 1969, in Washington, DC.

John Fitzgerald Kennedy (1961-63), 35th president, Democrat, was born on May 29, 1917, in Brookline, MA, the son of Joseph P. and Rose Fitzgerald Kennedy. He graduated from Harvard Univ. in 1940. While serving in the Navy (1941-45), he commanded a PT (patrol torpedo) boat in the Solomons and won the Navy and Marine Corps Medal. In 1956, while recovering from spinal surgery, he wrote *Profiles in Courage*, which won a Pulitzer Prize in 1957. He served in the U.S. House of Representatives from 1947 to 1953 and was elected to the Senate in 1952 and 1958. In 1960, he won the Democratic nomination for president and narrowly defeated Republican Vice Pres. Richard M. Nixon. Kennedy was the youngest president ever elected to the office and the first Catholic.

Despite the image of youth and vigor he conveyed to the public, Kennedy suffered from serious medical problems, including Addison's disease and severe chronic back pain that required him to wear a back brace. The public was not aware of the extent of these problems or of his frequent sexual liaisons.

In Apr. 1961, the new Kennedy administration suffered a severe setback when an invasion force of anti-Castro Cubans, trained and directed by the CIA, failed to establish a beachhead at the Bay of Pigs in Cuba. But he weathered a major foreign crisis with his successful demand on Oct. 22, 1962, that the Soviet Union dismantle its missile bases in Cuba. Kennedy also defied Soviet attempts to force the Allies out of Berlin. He established the Peace Corps, spurred space exploration, and won passage of other "New Frontier" legislation. But Congress balked at initiatives such as medical coverage for the aged and aid to education. After some delay he introduced major civil rights legislation, but death intervened before it could be passed.

On Nov. 22, 1963, Kennedy was assassinated while riding in a motorcade in Dallas, TX. A commission chaired by Chief Justice Earl Warren concluded in Sept. 1964 that the sole assassin had been Lee Harvey Oswald, a former U.S. Marine and an ardent Marxist. Oswald was captured a short time after the assassination and charged, but two days later, he was shot dead by nightclub owner Jack Ruby while being moved to a county jail.

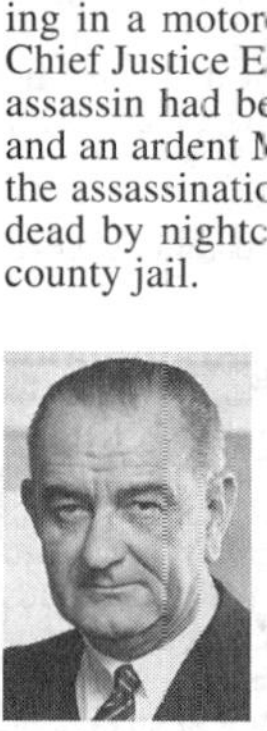

Lyndon Baines Johnson (1963-69), 36th president, Democrat, was born on Aug. 27, 1908, near Stonewall, TX, the son of Sam Ealy and Rebekah Baines Johnson. He graduated from Southwest Texas State Teachers College in 1930 and attended Georgetown University Law School. He taught public speaking in Houston (1930-31) and then served as secretary to Rep. R. M. Kleberg (1931-35). In 1937 Johnson won an election to fill the vacancy left by the death of a U.S. representative. In 1938 he was elected to the first of five full terms. During 1941 and 1942 he also served in the Navy in the Pacific, earning a Silver Star for bravery. He was elected U.S. senator in 1948 and reelected in 1954. He became Democratic leader of the Senate in 1953. Johnson had strong support for the Democratic presidential nomination at the 1960 convention and was elected vice president on the ticket led by the successful Democratic nominee, John F. Kennedy.

Johnson became president when Kennedy was assassinated. He was elected to a full term in 1964. Johnson's domestic program was of considerable importance. He won passage of major civil rights, anti-poverty, aid to education, and health-care (Medicare, Medicaid) legislation—the "Great Society" program. However, his escalation of the war in Vietnam came to overshadow the achievements of his administration. In the face of increasing division in the nation and in his own party over his handling of the war, Johnson declined to seek another term.

Johnson died on Jan. 22, 1973, in San Antonio, TX.

Richard Milhous Nixon (1969-74), 37th president, Republican, was born on Jan. 9, 1913, in Yorba Linda, CA, the son of Francis Anthony and Hannah Milhous Nixon. He graduated from Whittier College in 1934 and from Duke University Law School in 1937. After practicing law in Whittier, CA, and serving briefly in the Office of Price Administration in 1942, he entered the Navy and served in the South Pacific. Nixon was elected to the U.S. House of Representatives in 1946 and 1948. He achieved prominence as the House Un-American Activities Committee member who forced the showdown leading to the Alger Hiss perjury conviction. In 1950 he was elected to the Senate.

Nixon was elected vice president in the Eisenhower landslides of 1952 and 1956. He won the Republican nomination for president in 1960 but was narrowly defeated by John F. Kennedy. He ran unsuccessfully for governor of California in 1962. In 1968 he again won the GOP presidential nomination, then defeated Hubert Humphrey for the presidency.

As president, Nixon appointed four Supreme Court justices, including the chief justice, moving the court to the right. As a New Federalist, he sought to shift greater responsibility to state and local governments. At the same time, he championed important federal initiatives, including creation of the Office of Management and Budget and the Environmental Protection Agency. The economy suffered periods of high unemployment and inflation, and he imposed wage and price controls in 1971.

In foreign affairs, Nixon dramatically altered relations with China, which he visited in 1972—the first U.S. president to do so. With adviser Henry Kissinger, he pursued détente with the Soviet Union, signing major arms limitation and other treaties and increasing trade. He began a gradual withdrawal from Vietnam, but U.S. troops remained there through his first term. He ordered an incursion into Cambodia (1970) and the bombing of Hanoi and mining of Haiphong Harbor (1972). Reelected by a large majority in Nov. 1972, he secured a Vietnam cease-fire in Jan. 1973.

Nixon's second term was cut short by scandal, after disclosures relating to a June 1972 burglary of Democratic Party headquarters in the Watergate office complex in DC. The courts and Congress sought tapes of Nixon's office conversations; Nixon claimed executive privilege, but the Supreme Court ruled against him. In July 1974, the House Judiciary Committee recommended adoption of three impeachment articles charging him with obstruction of justice, abuse of power, and contempt of Congress. On Aug. 5, he released transcripts of conversations that linked him to cover-up activities. He resigned on Aug. 9, becoming the first president ever to do so.

In later years, Nixon emerged as an elder statesman. He died Apr. 22, 1994, in New York City.

Gerald Rudolph Ford (1974-77), 38th president, Republican, was born on July 14, 1913, in Omaha, NE, the son of Leslie and Dorothy Gardner King, and was named Leslie Lynch King Jr. When he was two, his parents divorced, and he and his mother moved to Grand Rapids, MI. There she married Gerald R. Ford, who formally adopted him and gave him his name. Ford graduated from the Univ. of Michigan in 1935 and from Yale Law School in 1941. He began practicing law in Grand Rapids, but in 1942, he joined the Navy and served in the Pacific, leaving the service in 1946 as a lieutenant commander. He entered the U.S. House of Representatives in 1949 and spent 25 years in the House, eight of them as Republican leader.

On Oct. 12, 1973, after Vice Pres. Spiro T. Agnew resigned, Pres. Nixon nominated Ford to replace him. It was the first use of the procedures set out in the 25th Amendment. When Nixon resigned, Aug. 9, 1974, because of the Watergate scandal, Ford became president; he was the only president who was never elected either to the presidency or to the vice presidency.

Ford was widely credited with having contributed to rebuilding morale after the Nixon presidency. But he was also criticized by many when he pardoned Nixon for any federal crimes he might have committed as president. Ford vetoed 48 bills in his first 21 months in office, mostly in the interest of fighting high inflation; he was less successful in curbing high unemployment. In foreign policy, Ford continued to pursue détente.

Ford was narrowly defeated in the 1976 election. He died Dec. 26, 2006, at home in Rancho Mirage, CA.

James Earl (Jimmy) Carter (1977-81), 39th president, Democrat, was the first president from the Deep South since before the Civil War. He was born on Oct. 1, 1924, in Plains, GA, the son of James and Lillian Gordy Carter. Carter graduated from the U.S. Naval Academy in 1946 and in 1952 entered the Navy's nuclear submarine program as an aide to Capt. (later Adm.) Hyman Rickover. He studied nuclear physics at Union College. Carter's father died in 1953, and he left the Navy to take over the family peanut farming businesses. He served in the Georgia state senate (1963-67) and as governor of Georgia (1971-75). In 1976, Carter won the Democratic nomination and defeated Pres. Gerald R. Ford.

On his first full day in office, Carter pardoned all Vietnam draft evaders. He played a major role in the negotiations leading to the 1979 peace treaty between Israel and Egypt, and he won passage of new treaties with Panama providing for U.S. control of the Panama Canal to end in 2000. Carter was widely criticized, however, for the poor state of the economy and was viewed by some as weak in his handling of foreign policy. In Nov. 1979, Iranian student militants attacked the U.S. embassy in Tehran and held members of the embassy staff hostage. Efforts to obtain release of the hostages were a major preoccupation during the rest of his term. He reacted to the Soviet invasion of Afghanistan by imposing a grain embargo and boycotting the Moscow Olympic Games.

Carter was defeated by Ronald Reagan in the 1980 election. The 52 American hostages in Iran were finally released on inauguration day, 1981, just after Reagan officially became president. After leaving office, Carter played an active role in diplomatic and humanitarian efforts around the world, especially through the Carter Center, which he founded with his wife, Rosalynn, in 1982. He was awarded the Nobel Peace Prize in 2002. In Aug. 2015, Carter disclosed that he was being treated for cancer.

Ronald Wilson Reagan (1981-89), 40th president, Republican, was born on Feb. 6, 1911, in Tampico, IL, the son of John Edward and Nellie Wilson Reagan. Reagan graduated from Eureka College in 1932, after which he worked as a sports announcer in Des Moines, IA. He began a successful career as a movie actor in 1937. During World War II Reagan served in the Army Air Force, making training films. He was president of the Screen Actors Guild in 1947-52 and in 1959-60. Reagan was elected governor of California in 1966 and reelected in 1970.

In 1980, Reagan gained the Republican presidential nomination and won a landslide victory over Jimmy Carter. He was easily reelected in 1984. Reagan forged a bipartisan coalition in Congress, which led to enactment of his program of large-scale tax cuts, cutbacks in many government programs, and a major defense buildup. He signed a Social Security reform bill designed to provide for the long-term solvency of the system. In 1986, he signed into law a major tax-reform bill. He was shot and seriously wounded in 1981 by John Hinckley, who was tried and found not guilty by reason of insanity.

In 1982, the U.S. joined France and Italy in maintaining a peacekeeping force in Beirut, Lebanon; the next year Reagan sent a task force to invade Grenada after two Marxist coups on the island. Reagan's opposition to international terrorism led to the U.S. bombing of Libyan military installations in 1986. He strongly supported El Salvador, the Nicaraguan contras, and other anticommunist governments and forces throughout the world. He also held four summit meetings with Soviet leader Mikhail Gorbachev and signed a treaty in 1987 eliminating short- and medium-range missiles from Europe.

In 1986, it was revealed that the U.S. had sold weapons through Israeli brokers to Iran in exchange for the release of U.S. hostages being held in Lebanon and that subsequently some of the money had been illegally diverted to the Nicaraguan contras. The scandal led to the resignation of leading White House aides, but no proof of Reagan's involvement was discovered. As Reagan left office in Jan. 1989, the nation was experiencing its sixth consecutive year of economic prosperity, while also piling up large budget deficits.

In 1994, Reagan revealed that he was suffering from Alzheimer's disease. He died on June 5, 2004, in Los Angeles, CA, from complications of the disease.

George Herbert Walker Bush (1989-93), 41st president, Republican, was born on June 12, 1924, in Milton, MA, the son of Prescott and Dorothy Walker Bush. He served as a U.S. Navy pilot in World War II. After graduating from Yale Univ. in 1948, he settled in Texas, where, in 1953, he helped found an oil company. After losing a bid for a U.S. Senate seat in 1964, he was elected to the House of Representatives in 1966 and 1968. He lost a second U.S. Senate race in 1970. Subsequently he served as U.S. ambassador to the United Nations (1971-73), headed the U.S. Liaison Office in Beijing (1974-75), and was director of the CIA (1976-77). Following an unsuccessful bid for the 1980 Republican presidential nomination, Bush became Ronald Reagan's running mate, and served as vice president from 1981 to 1989.

In 1988, Bush gained the GOP presidential nomination and defeated Gov. Michael Dukakis (D, MA) to win the presidency. Bush took office faced with U.S. budget and trade deficits, and insolvent U.S. savings and loan institutions. He faced a severe budget deficit annually, struggled with military cutbacks, and vetoed abortion-rights legislation. In 1990 he agreed to a budget deficit-reduction plan that included tax hikes, despite a campaign promise to the contrary, angering many conservatives.

Bush supported Soviet reforms, Eastern Europe democratization, and good relations with Beijing. In Dec. 1989, he sent troops to Panama; they overthrew the government and captured military dictator Gen. Manuel Noriega. Bush reacted to Iraq's Aug. 1990 invasion of Kuwait by sending U.S. forces to the Persian Gulf area and assembling a UN-backed coalition, including NATO and Arab League members. After a month-long air war, in Feb. 1991, Allied forces retook Kuwait in a four-day ground assault. The quick victory, with extremely light casualties on the U.S. side, gave Bush at that time one of the highest presidential approval ratings in history. His popularity plummeted by the end of 1991, however, as the economy slipped into recession. He was defeated by Bill Clinton in the 1992 election.

Bush saw his son George W. inaugurated as the 43rd president in 2001. In 2005 the elder Bush teamed with former Pres. Clinton to raise money for natural disaster victims.

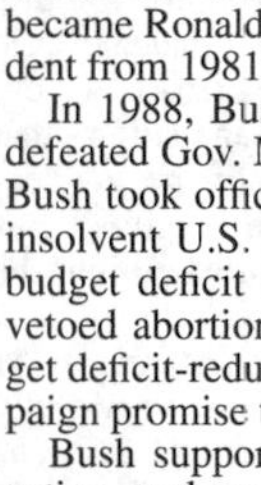

William Jefferson (Bill) Clinton (1993-2001), 42nd president, Democrat, was born Aug. 19, 1946, in Hope, AR, son of William Blythe and Virginia Cassidy Blythe, and was named William Jefferson Blythe IV. Blythe died in an auto accident before his son was born. His widow married Roger Clinton, whose last name Bill Clinton then took. Clinton earned his undergraduate degree from Georgetown Univ. in 1968. While attending Oxford Univ. as a Rhodes scholar, he legally avoided the draft and possible service in Vietnam, according to some critics by misleading his draft board. Clinton worked on George McGovern's 1972 presidential campaign and earned a degree from Yale Law School in 1973. He taught at the Univ. of Arkansas law school until 1976, when he was elected state attorney general. In 1978 he was elected governor, becoming the nation's youngest at the time. Though defeated for reelection in 1980, he was returned to office several times thereafter. He married law school classmate Hillary Rodham in 1975.

Clinton won most of the 1992 presidential primaries, moving his party toward the center as he tried to broaden his appeal; as the Democratic nominee he defeated Pres. George H. W. Bush and independent candidate H. Ross Perot in the Nov. election. In 1993, Clinton won passage of a deficit reduction measure and congressional approval of the North American Free Trade Agreement. However, his administration's plan for major health care reform legislation died in Congress. After 1994 midterm elections, Clinton faced Republican majorities in both houses of Congress. He followed a centrist course at home, sent troops to Bosnia to help implement a peace settlement, and cultivated relations with Russia and China.

Though accused of improprieties in his involvement in the Whitewater Development Corp., an Arkansas land-development venture, Clinton won reelection with 49% of the vote in 1996. Independent prosecutor Kenneth Starr did not find wrongdoing related to Whitewater, but did report evidence of an affair between Clinton and White House intern Monica Lewinsky. In 1998, Clinton became only the second U.S. president to be impeached by the House of Representatives. He was charged with perjury and obstruction of justice in an attempted cover-up of the affair but was acquitted by the Senate.

In 1999 the United States joined other NATO nations in an aerial bombing campaign that induced Serbia to withdraw troops from Kosovo, where they had been terrorizing ethnic Albanians. On Clinton's last full day in office, the Whitewater investigation ended in a deal; Clinton admitted having given false testimony and agreed to penalties. After leaving office he actively supported the political career of his wife, Hillary Clinton, who became a U.S. senator (D, NY), ran unsuccessfully for the 2008 Democratic presidential nomination, and ran for the party's 2016 presidential nomination, after having served as Pres. Obama's secretary of state. He took a leadership role in various humanitarian programs and founded what became the Bill, Hillary and Chelsea Clinton Foundation, to promote practical solutions to global problems.

George Walker Bush (2001-09), 43rd president, Republican, was born on July 6, 1946, in New Haven, CT. He was the oldest of six children born to the 41st president, George Herbert Walker Bush, and the former Barbara Pierce. He became the first son of a former president to occupy the White House since John Quincy Adams took office in 1825.

Bush grew up in Midland and Houston, TX. He attended Phillips Academy in Andover, MA, and then Yale Univ., graduating in 1968. Eligible for the draft, he fulfilled his military service requirement with the Texas Air National Guard. After earning a master's degree from Harvard Business School, he returned to Midland in 1975 and went into the oil business. Two years later he married Laura Welch, a librarian; they had twin daughters, Barbara and Jenna, in 1981. After aiding his father's winning 1988 presidential campaign, he became managing partner of the Texas Rangers baseball team. He was elected governor of Texas in 1994 and reelected in 1998.

In 2000, Bush won the Republican presidential nomination and, with running mate Dick Cheney, defeated the Democratic ticket led by Vice Pres. Al Gore, in one of the closest-ever U.S. presidential elections. The result was not settled until a mid-Dec. ruling by the U.S. Supreme Court left Florida's crucial electoral votes in Bush's column.

In May 2001, Bush won passage of a tax cut package projected at $1.35 tril over 10 years. After the Sept. 11, 2001, terrorist attacks on the U.S., he rallied support for a "war against terrorism." By Dec. 2001, the U.S. military, aided by forces from other nations, had deposed Afghanistan's Taliban regime, which was sheltering al-Qaeda terrorists. In Mar. 2003, the U.S., aided mainly by UK forces, launched an air and ground war against Iraq and deposed its autocratic leader, Saddam Hussein. No evidence was found that his regime had developed weapons of mass destruction, the key rationale for the war. A sovereign government was formed in June 2004, but insurgent violence and U.S. troop casualties continued.

Bush was reelected in Nov. 2004 with 51% of the popular vote, but his push for Social Security and immigration reforms in his second term failed in Congress, and his administration drew criticism for its response to Hurricane Katrina in Aug.-Sept. 2005. In 2006, Bush exercised his first veto to maintain restrictions on federal funding for stem cell research.

After Democrats won majorities in House and Senate 2006 midterm elections, Bush accepted the resignation of Defense Sec. Donald Rumsfeld, a target of widespread criticism over the Iraq war. Two months later, he announced a "surge" in U.S. troop strength in Iraq. A sharp drop in casualties ensued, aided also by a shift in alliances, and in late 2008 the administration reached an agreement with Iraq allowing U.S. troops to remain there through but not beyond 2011. But the Taliban was gaining strength in Afghanistan and Pakistan, and the Bush administration was damaged by revelations of prisoner abuse and extreme interrogation methods.

The U.S. economy fell into recession in Dec. 2007; Bush and congressional leaders responded with a $168-bil stimulus plan. Problems in home finance and credit markets triggered a deep economic crisis in Sept. and the Treasury Dept. announced a bailout of mortgage finance firms Fannie Mae and Freddie Mac. Lehman Bros. filed for bankruptcy, and the Federal Reserve rescued insurance giant AIG with a line of credit reaching $144 bil. A Bush administration-backed plan to buy up to $700 bil in devalued mortgage-related assets cleared Congress Oct. 3, after a severe stock market plunge bolstered support. The crisis added to Bush's unpopularity and contributed to the 2008 defeat of GOP presidential candidate Sen. John McCain (AZ).

In early 2010 Bush and former Pres. Clinton established a nonprofit organization to raise funds for earthquake relief in Haiti. Bush published a memoir entitled *Decision Points* (Nov. 2010) and a biography of his father, *41* (Nov. 2014).

Barack Hussein Obama (2009-), 44th president, Democrat, was born Aug. 4, 1961, in Honolulu, HI. His father, Barack Obama Sr., was a black Kenyan, and his mother, Stanley Ann Dunham, a white American. They divorced and, after his mother remarried, the family moved to Indonesia. Obama lived with his maternal grandparents in Hawaii while attending high school. He graduated from Columbia Univ. (1983) and, after working as a community organizer in Chicago, earned a law degree from Harvard Univ. (1991), where he was president of the law review. Obama practiced civil rights law in Chicago and taught at the Univ. of Chicago Law School. In 1992, he married attorney Michelle Robinson. They have two daughters, Malia and Natasha (Sasha).

Obama served eight years (1997-2004) in the Illinois state senate. He lost the Democratic nomination for a U.S. House seat in 2000, but was nominated to a U.S. Senate seat in a Mar. 2004 primary. Already somewhat known for his 1995 memoir, *Dreams From My Father*, he gained national attention with his keynote address at the Democratic National Convention in July 2004 and was easily elected in Nov. His second book, *The Audacity of Hope* (2006), was an immediate best-seller.

Stressing his opposition to the Iraq war and aim to bring change to Washington, Obama won the 2008 Democratic presidential nomination in a tight race against expected front-runner Sen. Hillary Clinton (NY). As a major recession deepened, Obama, with running mate Sen. Joe Biden (DE), defeated the Republican ticket, headed by Sen. John McCain (R, AZ), and became the nation's first African-American president. Sen. Clinton served as secretary of state in Obama's first term.

Pres. Obama called early on for a reset in relations with Russia and a new beginning in relations with the Muslim world, and was awarded the 2009 Nobel Peace Prize. He gradually pulled U.S. troops from Iraq, with no residual force left after 2011. In Afghanistan, after implementing a temporary troop surge, he began force reductions. But he stepped up drone strikes against Islamist militants in Afghanistan and Pakistan and authorized a 2011 raid that killed al-Qaeda leader Osama bin Laden. He supported calls for the resignation of repressive Egyptian Pres. Hosni Mubarak, a longtime U.S. ally, and authorized U.S. participation in NATO air strikes leading to the overthrow and death of Libyan dictator Muammar al-Qaddafi. The U.S. ambassador and three other Americans were killed in an attack by Islamist radicals on the U.S. consulate in Benghazi, Libya, in Sept. 2012. Inadequate security was blamed, and several congressional investigations found no evidence of deliberate wrongdoing on the part of the administration.

On the domestic front, the administration, early in 2009, won passage of a $787-bil economic stimulus package, and the U.S. pulled out of recession, though economic growth was slow. Obama's approval rating, close to 70% when he took office, fell by 2010 to the mid-40s. In 2010, Obama won passage of a top priority, a controversial health care reform bill aimed in part at extending coverage to uninsured Americans; fiercely opposed by Republicans, it survived several Supreme Court challenges. After Democrats lost their U.S. House majority in Nov. 2010 elections, Obama reached a compromise with Republicans on an $858-bil spending plan that included temporary extension of all G.W. Bush-era tax cuts along with unemployment benefits. A fight with Republicans over raising the federal debt limit led to agreement for compensating cuts to be worked out by a bipartisan congressional committee. When a deal could not be reached, large automatic cuts ("sequester") in both domestic and defense spending were slated to take effect in 2013. Obama, in 2012, became the first sitting president to publicly support same-sex marriage, and signed an executive order ending deportations for most young undocumented immigrants who came to the U.S. as children.

Obama and Biden were reelected in Nov. 2012, defeating a GOP ticket headed by former Massachusetts Gov. Mitt Romney. A compromise in Congress averted a year-end "fiscal cliff" by making expiring Bush tax cuts permanent for most people, while postponing the sequester. Further negotiations failed, and the sequester took effect, Mar. 1, 2013. In another showdown, the government (Oct. 2013) partially shut down for lack of funding authorization, with Republicans balking over Obamacare; they yielded after 16 days. The administration was embattled over reports in 2013 that the Internal Revenue Service had singled out Tea Party organizations for special scrutiny and was embarrassed by the botched rollout of Obamacare. In June 2013, Edward Snowden, a Natl. Security Agency (NSA) contractor, leaked extensive classified information about the wide scope of U.S. surveillance programs; Obama defended the NSA program while pledging limited reform. The Boston Marathon bombing, which killed three in Apr. 2013, was a reminder that the U.S. homeland remained vulnerable to terrorist attacks. In 2014, revelations of mismanagement at the Dept. of Veterans Affairs that jeopardized care of veterans led to resignation of the VA secretary, and controversy over illegal immigration heightened as increasing numbers of unaccompanied children flooded into the U.S. from Central America.

Abroad, Russian forces annexed the Crimean region of Ukraine (Mar. 2014) and pro-Russian separatists, reportedly bolstered by Russian forces, expanded their control in areas of eastern Ukraine. Obama joined Europe in limited economic sanctions against Russia in response. In the Middle East, the administration revived Arab-Israeli peace talks, but they broke down, and Israel (July 2014) launched a major operation in Gaza, with heavy civilian casualties, following rocket attacks by the militant Islamic group Hamas. Obama called for an end to the repressive regime of Syria's Bashar al-Assad, pitted against rebel factions in a bloody civil war since 2011. But when Assad forces appeared to have launched a chemical weapons attack on civilians in 2013, crossing what Obama had called a "red line," the president held back from punitive action, agreeing to a Russian-brokered pact with the regime. Meanwhile, the Sunni extremist group Islamic State in Iraq and Syria (ISIS), aided by foreign recruits, took over large areas of both countries, proclaiming a Sunni Islamic caliphate (June 2014) and driving out or massacring religious minorities. Obama authorized sending U.S. military advisers to Iraq and, after ISIS released videos showing executions of abducted Americans and others, he announced (Sept. 2014) a plan involving extended U.S. airstrikes against ISIS in both Iraq and Syria, along with some arms to aid moderate Syrian rebels.

After Nov. 2014 midterm elections the Obama administration faced Republican majorities in both houses of Congress. Relations between the administration and congressional Republicans remained highly polarized. Obama moved decisively in restoring relations with Cuba, after a half-century, and concluding, with five other nations and Iran, an accord intended to curb Iranian nuclear weapons development in return for ending economic sanctions. (The agreement was vulnerable to a congressional vote of disapproval, but Obama lobbied Congress to ensure it could not survive his veto.) Obama also won fast-track trade authority aimed at facilitating eventual congressional approval of a trade pact being negotiated with Asian-Pacific nations—a cause opposed by many within his own party. But Russian assertiveness, the disastrous civil war in Syria, the resultant refugee crisis, the growing power of ISIS, and the continuing threat of terrorism remained as challenges for the administration. On the domestic front, he issued controversial executive orders that delayed deportations of many immigrants in the country illegally and unveiled a major plan to fight climate change by cutting emissions from coal-burning power plants.

In his eulogy at the funeral of a black pastor and state senator, fatally shot (June 2015) with eight other African Americans at a church in Charleston, SC, Obama continued to address the issue of race relations. Race had been in the forefront of public debates over the past year as peaceful demonstrations, sometimes-violent protests, and even riots took place in response to the deaths of black men in encounters with police in Ferguson, MO (Aug. 2014), Baltimore, MD, and other cities.

Presidential Facts

Oldest president: Ronald Reagan, who was 77 when he left office
Youngest president: Theodore Roosevelt, who was 42 when sworn in after McKinley's death
Youngest person elected president: John F. Kennedy, who was 43 when elected in 1960
Tallest president: Abraham Lincoln, who was 6 feet, 4 inches
Shortest president: James Madison, who was 5 feet, 4 inches
Heaviest president: William Howard Taft, who was 332 pounds in 1911
First president to live in the White House: John Adams, who moved there in 1800
First president inaugurated in Washington, DC: Thomas Jefferson, in 1801
First president whose parents were immigrants: Andrew Jackson; his parents emigrated from Ireland in 1765
First president born a U.S. citizen: Martin Van Buren, in Kinderhook, NY, 1782
First president born outside the original colonies: Abraham Lincoln, in Kentucky, 1809
First president born west of the Mississippi: Herbert Hoover, in West Branch, IA, 1874
Most common presidential home state: Virginia, with 8 presidents
First president born in a hospital: Jimmy Carter, in Plains, GA, 1924
First president to have a telephone in the White House: Rutherford B. Hayes, in 1879
First president to travel outside U.S. while in office: Theodore Roosevelt visited Panama Canal site, 1906
First president to address the nation on radio: Warren G. Harding, in 1922
First president to appear on TV: Franklin D. Roosevelt, at opening ceremonies for the 1939 World's Fair
First president to give a live, televised news conference: John F. Kennedy, in 1961
First president to hold an Internet chat: Bill Clinton, in 1999
Presidents who lost the popular vote while winning election: John Quincy Adams, in 1824 (elected by the House after general election failed to produce a majority); Rutherford B. Hayes, in 1876; Benjamin Harrison, in 1888; George W. Bush, in 2000 (Popular vote totals before 1824 are unknown.)
Only presidents chosen by the House of Representatives: Thomas Jefferson (1st term) and John Quincy Adams
Only president never elected either president or vice president: Gerald Ford; named vice president when Spiro Agnew resigned (1973), became president when Nixon resigned (1974)
Left-handed presidents: James Garfield, Herbert Hoover, Harry Truman, Gerald Ford, Ronald Reagan, George H. W. Bush, Bill Clinton, and Barack Obama
Only Catholic president: John F. Kennedy; the most common religious affiliations have been Episcopalian (11) and Presbyterian (7)
Only bachelor presidents: James Buchanan, who never married, and Grover Cleveland, who married Frances Folsom in the White House in 1886
Only divorced president: Ronald Reagan; divorced from Jane Wyman in 1948, married Nancy Davis in 1952
Presidents who died on July 4: John Adams and Thomas Jefferson (both 1826) and James Monroe (1831)
Only president buried in Washington, DC: Woodrow Wilson, interred at Washington National Cathedral

Presidential Libraries

Presidential libraries are coordinated by the National Archives and Records Administration (www.archives.gov/presidential-libraries/). Materials for presidents before Herbert Hoover are held by private institutions. The Barack Obama Foundation announced in May 2015 that his presidential library would be located on Chicago's South Side. Under the Presidential Records Act, material is available to the public through Freedom of Information Act requests starting five years after a president has left office. Pres. George W. Bush's records became available Jan. 20, 2014.

Herbert Hoover Library and Museum
210 Parkside Dr.
West Branch, IA 52358
Phone: (319) 643-5301
Email: hoover.library@nara.gov
Website: hoover.archives.gov

Franklin D. Roosevelt Library and Museum
4079 Albany Post Rd.
Hyde Park, NY 12538-1990
Phone: (800) FDR-VISIT
Email: roosevelt.library@nara.gov
Website: www.fdrlibrary.marist.edu

Harry S. Truman Library and Museum
500 West U.S. Hwy. 24
Independence, MO 64050-2481
Phone: (800) 833-1225
Email: truman.library@nara.gov
Website: www.trumanlibrary.org

Dwight D. Eisenhower Library
200 SE 4th St.
Abilene, KS 67410-2900
Phone: (877) RING-IKE
Email: eisenhower.library@nara.gov
Website: eisenhower.archives.gov

John F. Kennedy Library and Museum
Columbia Pt.
Boston, MA 02125-3312
Phone: (866) JFK-1960
Email: kennedy.library@nara.gov
Website: www.jfklibrary.org

Lyndon Baines Johnson Library and Museum
2313 Red River St.
Austin, TX 78705-5737
Phone: (512) 721-0200
Email: johnson.library@nara.gov
Website: www.lbjlibrary.org

Richard Nixon Library and Museum
18001 Yorba Linda Blvd.
Yorba Linda, CA 92886-3903
Phone: (714) 983-9120
Email: nixon@nara.gov
Website: www.nixonlibrary.gov
MD office: Natl. Archives at College Park
8601 Adelphi Rd.
College Park, MD 20740-6001
Phone: (301) 837-3290

Gerald R. Ford Library and Museum
Library: 1000 Beal Ave.
Ann Arbor, MI 48109-2109
Phone: (734) 205-0555
Museum: 303 Pearl St. NW
Grand Rapids, MI 49504-5353
Phone: (616) 254-0400
Email: ford.library@nara.gov
Website: www.fordlibrarymuseum.gov

Jimmy Carter Library and Museum
441 Freedom Pkwy.
Atlanta, GA 30307-1498
Phone: (404) 865-7100
Email: carter.library@nara.gov
Website: www.jimmycarterlibrary.gov

Ronald Reagan Library and Museum
40 Presidential Dr.
Simi Valley, CA 93065-0600
Phone: (800) 410-8354
Email: reagan.library@nara.gov
Website: www.reagan.utexas.edu

George Bush Library and Museum
1000 George Bush Dr. West
College Station, TX 77845
Phone: (979) 691-4000
Email: library.bush@nara.gov
Website: bushlibrary.tamu.edu

William J. Clinton Library and Museum
1200 President Clinton Ave.
Little Rock, AR 72201
Phone: (501) 374-4242
Email: clinton.library@nara.gov
Website: www.clintonlibrary.gov

George W. Bush Library and Museum
2943 SMU Blvd.
Dallas, TX 75205
Phone: (214) 346-1650
Email: gwbush.library@nara.gov
Website: www.georgewbushlibrary.smu.edu

Presidential Impeachment in U.S. History

The U.S. Constitution provides for impeachment and removal from office of federal officials on grounds of "Treason, Bribery, or other high Crimes and Misdemeanors" (Article II, Sect. 4). Impeachment is the bringing of charges by the House of Representatives. It is followed by a Senate trial; a two-thirds majority vote of Senators present is needed for conviction and removal from office.

In 1868, **Andrew Johnson** became the first president impeached by the House, for his removal of Sec. of War Edwin M. Stanton without first notifying the Senate. He was tried but not convicted. In 1974, impeachment articles against Pres. **Richard Nixon**, in connection with the Watergate scandal, were adopted by the House Judiciary Committee. He resigned Aug. 9, and the House accepted the committee report without taking further action. In 1998, Pres. **Bill Clinton** was impeached by the House in connection with his cover-up of a sexual relationship with former White House intern Monica Lewinsky. He was tried in the Senate in 1999 and acquitted.

Wives and Children of the Presidents

Name (born-died; married)	State	Sons/ daughters
Martha Dandridge Custis Washington (1731-1802; 1759)	VA	None
Abigail Smith Adams (1744-1818; 1764)	MA	3/2
Martha Wayles Skelton Jefferson (1748-82; 1772)	VA	1/5
Dolley Payne Todd Madison (1768-1849; 1794)	NC	None
Elizabeth Kortright Monroe (1768-1830; 1786)	NY	1/2
Louisa Catherine Johnson Adams (1775-1852; 1797)	MD[1]	3/1
Rachel Donelson Robards Jackson (1767-1828; 1791)	VA	1/0[2]
Hannah Hoes Van Buren (1783-1819; 1807)	NY	4/0
Anna Tuthill Symmes Harrison (1775-1864; 1795)	NJ	6/4
Letitia Christian Tyler (1790-1842; 1813)	VA	3/5
Julia Gardiner Tyler (1820-89; 1844)	NY	5/2
Sarah Childress Polk (1803-91; 1824)	TN	None
Margaret (Peggy) Mackall Smith Taylor (1788-1852; 1810)	MD	1/5
Abigail Powers Fillmore (1798-1853; 1826)	NY	1/1
Caroline Carmichael McIntosh Fillmore (1813-81; 1858)	NJ	None
Jane Means Appleton Pierce (1806-63; 1834)	NH	3/0
Mary Todd Lincoln (1818-82; 1842)	KY	4/0
Eliza McCardle Johnson (1810-76; 1827)	TN	3/2
Julia Boggs Dent Grant (1826-1902; 1848)	MO	3/1
Lucy Ware Webb Hayes (1831-89; 1852)	OH	7/1
Lucretia Rudolph Garfield (1832-1918; 1858)	OH	5/2
Ellen Lewis Herndon Arthur (1837-80; 1859)	VA	2/1
Frances Folsom Cleveland (1864-1947; 1886)	NY	2/3
Caroline Lavinia Scott Harrison (1832-92; 1853)	OH	1/1
Mary Scott Lord Dimmick Harrison (1858-1948; 1896)	PA	0/1
Ida Saxton McKinley (1847-1907; 1871)	OH	0/2
Alice Hathaway Lee Roosevelt (1861-84; 1880)	MA	0/1
Edith Kermit Carow Roosevelt (1861-1948; 1886)	CT	4/1
Helen Herron Taft (1861-1943; 1886)	OH	2/1
Ellen Louise Axson Wilson (1860-1914; 1885)	GA	0/3
Edith Bolling Galt Wilson (1872-1961; 1915)	VA	None
Florence Kling De Wolfe Harding (1860-1924; 1891)	OH	None
Grace Anna Goodhue Coolidge (1879-1957; 1905)	VT	2/0
Lou Henry Hoover (1875-1944; 1899)	IA	2/0
Anna Eleanor Roosevelt (1884-1962; 1905)	NY	5/1
Elizabeth Virginia (Bess) Wallace Truman (1885-1982; 1919)	MO	0/1
Mamie Geneva Doud Eisenhower (1896-1979; 1916)	IA	2/0
Jacqueline Lee Bouvier Kennedy (1929-94; 1953)	NY	2/1
Claudia (Lady Bird) Alta Taylor Johnson (1912-2007; 1934)	TX	0/2
Thelma Catherine Patricia Ryan Nixon (1912-93; 1940)	NV	0/2
Elizabeth (Betty) Bloomer Warren Ford (1918-2011; 1948)	IL	3/1
Eleanor Rosalynn Smith Carter (1927- ; 1946)	GA	3/1
Anne Frances (Nancy) Robbins Davis Reagan (1921- ; 1952)	NY	1/1[3]
Barbara Pierce Bush (1925- ; 1945)	NY	4/2
Hillary Diane Rodham Clinton (1947- ; 1975)	IL	0/1
Laura Lane Welch Bush (1946- ; 1977)	TX	0/2
Michelle LaVaughn Robinson Obama (1964- ; 1992)	IL	0/2

Note: Pres. Buchanan was unmarried. Children not born to the marriages shown are not listed unless otherwise noted. (1) Born in London, father a MD citizen. (2) Adopted son. (3) Pres. Reagan's first wife, whom he later divorced, was Jane Wyman. They had a daughter who died in infancy, a daughter who lived past infancy, and an adopted son.

First Lady Michelle Obama

Michelle Robinson Obama was born in Chicago, IL, Jan. 17, 1964. She graduated from Princeton Univ., 1985, earned a law degree from Harvard Univ., 1988, and joined Chicago law firm Sidley & Austin. She served as assistant commissioner of planning and development for the city of Chicago, then as founding executive director of the Chicago chapter of Public Allies, an AmeriCorps program. She began working for the Univ. of Chicago in 1996, first as associate dean of student services, then as the Univ. of Chicago Medical Center's vice president of community and external affairs. Michelle and Barack Obama were married in 1992; in 1998, their daughter Malia was born, followed by Natasha (Sasha) in 2001.

As First Lady, Michelle Obama has focused on supporting military families, helping women balance career and family, encouraging national service, and promoting the arts and arts education. She also launched a major campaign to deal with the problem of childhood obesity in the U.S.

Burial Places of the Presidents

President	Burial place
Washington	Mt. Vernon, VA
J. Adams	Quincy, MA
Jefferson	Charlottesville, VA
Madison	Montpelier Station, VA
Monroe	Richmond, VA
J. Q. Adams	Quincy, MA
Jackson	Nashville, TN
Van Buren	Kinderhook, NY
W. H. Harrison	North Bend, OH
Tyler	Richmond, VA
Polk	Nashville, TN
Taylor	Louisville, KY
Fillmore	Buffalo, NY
Pierce	Concord, NH
Buchanan	Lancaster, PA
Lincoln	Springfield, IL
A. Johnson	Greeneville, TN
Grant	New York, NY
Hayes	Fremont, OH
Garfield	Cleveland, OH
Arthur	Albany, NY
Cleveland	Princeton, NJ
B. Harrison	Indianapolis, IN
McKinley	Canton, OH
T. Roosevelt	Oyster Bay, NY
Taft	Arlington Natl. Cem., VA
Wilson	Wash. Natl. Cathedral, DC
Harding	Marion, OH
Coolidge	Plymouth Notch, VT
Hoover	West Branch, IA
F. Roosevelt	Hyde Park, NY
Truman	Independence, MO
Eisenhower	Abilene, KS
Kennedy	Arlington Natl. Cem., VA
L. B. Johnson	Stonewall, TX
Nixon	Yorba Linda, CA
Ford	Grand Rapids, MI
Reagan	Simi Valley, CA

PRESIDENTIAL ELECTIONS

Electoral and Popular Vote, 2008 and 2012

Source: Federal Election Commission

	2012					2008					
	Electoral vote		Popular vote			Electoral vote		Popular vote			
State	Obama	Romney	Obama	Romney	Johnson	Obama	McCain	Obama	McCain	Nader	State
AL	0	9	795,696	1,255,925	12,328	0	9	813,479	1,266,546	6,788	AL
AK	0	3	122,640	164,676	7,392	0	3	123,594	193,841	3,783	AK
AZ	0	11	1,025,232	1,233,654	32,100	0	10	1,034,707	1,230,111	11,301	AZ
AR	0	6	394,409	647,744	16,276	0	6	422,310	638,017	12,882	AR
CA	55	0	7,854,285	4,839,958	143,221	55	0	8,274,473	5,011,781	108,381	CA
CO	9	0	1,323,102	1,185,243	35,545	9	0	1,288,633	1,073,629	13,352	CO
CT	7	0	905,083	634,892	12,580	7	0	997,772	629,428	19,162	CT
DE	3	0	242,584	165,484	3,882	3	0	255,459	152,374	2,401	DE
DC	3	0	267,070	21,381	2,083	3	0	245,800	17,367	958	DC
FL	29	0	4,237,756	4,163,447	44,726	27	0	4,282,074	4,045,624	28,124	FL
GA	0	16	1,773,827	2,078,688	45,324	0	15	1,844,123	2,048,759	1,158	GA
HI	4	0	306,658	121,015	3,840	4	0	325,871	120,566	3,825	HI
ID	0	4	212,787	420,911	9,453	0	4	236,440	403,012	7,175	ID
IL	20	0	3,019,512	2,135,216	56,229	21	0	3,419,348	2,031,179	30,948	IL
IN	0	11	1,152,887	1,420,543	50,111	11	0	1,374,039	1,345,648	909	IN
IA	6	0	822,544	730,617	12,926	7	0	828,940	682,379	8,014	IA
KS	0	6	440,726	692,634	20,456	0	6	514,765	699,655	10,527	KS
KY	0	8	679,370	1,087,190	17,063	0	8	751,985	1,048,462	15,378	KY
LA	0	8	809,141	1,152,262	18,157	0	9	782,989	1,148,275	6,997	LA
ME	4	0	401,306	292,276	9,352	4	0	421,923	295,273	10,636	ME
MD	10	0	1,677,844	971,869	30,195	10	0	1,629,467	959,862	14,713	MD
MA	11	0	1,921,290	1,188,314	30,920	12	0	1,904,097	1,108,854	28,841	MA
MI	16	0	2,564,569	2,115,256	7,774	17	0	2,872,579	2,048,639	33,085	MI
MN	10	0	1,546,167	1,320,225	35,098	10	0	1,573,354	1,275,409	30,152	MN
MS	0	6	562,949	710,746	6,676	0	6	554,662	724,597	4,011	MS
MO	0	10	1,223,796	1,482,440	43,151	0	11	1,441,911	1,445,814	17,813	MO
MT	0	3	201,839	267,928	14,165	0	3	231,667	242,763	3,686	MT
NE[1]	0	5	302,081	475,064	11,109	1	4	333,319	452,979	5,406	NE[1]
NV	6	0	531,373	463,567	10,968	5	0	533,736	412,827	6,150	NV
NH	4	0	369,561	329,918	8,212	4	0	384,826	316,534	3,503	NH
NJ	14	0	2,125,101	1,477,568	21,045	15	0	2,215,422	1,613,207	21,298	NJ
NM	5	0	415,335	335,788	27,788	5	0	472,422	346,832	5,327	NM
NY	29	0	4,485,741	2,490,431	47,256	31	0	4,804,945	2,752,771	41,249	NY
NC	0	15	2,178,391	2,270,395	44,515	15	0	2,142,651	2,128,474	1,448	NC
ND	0	3	124,827	188,163	5,231	0	3	141,278	168,601	4,189	ND
OH	18	0	2,827,709	2,661,437	49,493	20	0	2,940,044	2,677,820	42,337	OH
OK	0	7	443,547	891,325	—	0	7	502,496	960,165	—	OK
OR	7	0	970,488	754,175	24,089	7	0	1,037,291	738,475	18,614	OR
PA	20	0	2,990,274	2,680,434	49,991	21	0	3,276,363	2,655,885	42,977	PA
RI	4	0	279,677	157,204	4,388	4	0	296,571	165,391	4,829	RI
SC	0	9	865,941	1,071,645	16,321	0	8	862,449	1,034,896	5,053	SC
SD	0	3	145,039	210,610	5,795	0	3	170,924	203,054	4,267	SD
TN	0	11	960,709	1,462,330	18,623	0	11	1,087,437	1,479,178	11,560	TN
TX	0	38	3,308,124	4,569,843	88,580	0	34	3,528,633	4,479,328	5,751	TX
UT	0	6	251,813	740,600	12,572	0	5	327,670	596,030	8,416	UT
VT	3	0	199,239	92,698	3,487	3	0	219,262	98,974	3,339	VT
VA	13	0	1,971,820	1,822,522	31,216	13	0	1,959,532	1,725,005	11,483	VA
WA	12	0	1,755,396	1,290,670	42,202	11	0	1,750,848	1,229,216	29,489	WA
WV	0	5	238,269	417,655	6,302	0	5	303,857	397,466	7,219	WV
WI	10	0	1,620,985	1,410,966	20,439	10	0	1,677,211	1,262,393	17,605	WI
WY	0	3	69,286	170,962	5,326	0	3	82,868	164,958	2,525	WY
Total	**332**	**206**	**65,915,795**	**60,933,504**	**1,275,971**	**365**	**173**	**69,498,516**	**59,948,323**	**739,034**	**Total**

— = Not listed on state's ballot. (1) Nebraska is one of two states (the other is Maine) that allows electoral votes to be split between candidates.

Presidential Popular Vote, 2012

Candidate (party)	Vote total	Percent of vote
Barack Obama (Democrat)	65,915,795	51.06%
Mitt Romney (Republican)	60,933,504	47.20
Gary Johnson (Libertarian)	1,275,971	0.99
Jill Stein (Green)	469,627	0.36
Virgil Goode (Constitution/U.S. Taxpayers)	122,389	0.09
Roseanne Barr (Peace and Freedom)	67,326	0.05
Ross C. "Rocky" Anderson (Justice/ Natural Law)	43,018	0.03
Tom Hoefling (American Independent, America's Party)	40,628	0.03
Randall Terry (Independent/no party affiliation)	13,107	0.01
Richard Duncan (Independent)	12,557	0.01
Peta Lindsay (Socialism and Liberation)	7,791	0.01
Chuck Baldwin (Reform)	5,017	<0.01
Will Christensen (Constitution)	4,453	<0.01
Stewart Alexander (Socialist)	4,405	<0.01
James Harris (Socialist Workers)	4,117	<0.01
Thomas Robert Stevens (Objectivist)	4,091	<0.01%
Jim Carlson (Grassroots)	3,149	<0.01
Jill Reed (Unaffiliated)	2,877	<0.01
Merlin Miller (American Third Position)	2,701	<0.01
Sheila "Samm" Tittle (We the People)	2,572	<0.01
Gloria La Riva (Socialism and Liberation)	1,608	<0.01
Jerry White (Socialist Equality)	1,279	<0.01
Dean Morstad (Constitutional Govt.)	1,094	<0.01
Jerry Litzel (nominated by petition)	1,027	<0.01
Barbara Dale Washer (Reform)	1,016	<0.01
Jeff Boss (NSA Did 911)	1,007	<0.01
Andre Barnett (Reform)	956	<0.01
Jack Fellure (Prohibition)	518	<0.01
Write-in votes (other/miscellaneous)	136,040	0.11
None of these candidates (Nevada)	5,770	<0.01
Total	**129,085,410**	
Voting age population, Nov. 2012	235,248,000	
Percentage casting vote for president		54.87%

Note: Party designations vary from one state to another; party label listed may not necessarily represent a political party organization. Vote totals for the candidates listed above include any write-in votes they received.

The Electoral College

The president and the vice president are the only elective federal officials not chosen by direct vote of the people. They are elected by the members of the Electoral College, an institution provided for in the U.S. Constitution.

On presidential election day, the first Tuesday after the first Monday in Nov. of every fourth year, each state chooses as many electors as it has senators and representatives in Congress. In 1964, for the first time, as provided by the 23rd Amendment to the Constitution, the District of Columbia voted for three electors. Thus, with 100 senators and 435 representatives, there are 538 members of the Electoral College, with a majority of 270 electoral votes needed to elect the president and vice president.

Political parties were not part of the Founding Fathers' original plan. But today, each political party chooses its electors, by nomination at a state convention or by vote of the party central committee in each state. In some states, electors' names may be printed below the names of the presidential and vice presidential candidates on the Nov. ballot. In any case, the electors of the party receiving the highest vote are elected. Two states, Maine and Nebraska, allow for proportional allocation.

The electors meet on the first Monday after the second Wednesday in Dec. in their respective state capitals or in some other place prescribed by state legislatures. By long-established custom, they vote for their party nominees, although this is not required by federal law. They may be bound to do so by state law or party pledge.

The Constitution requires electors to cast a ballot for at least one person who is not an inhabitant of that elector's home state. This ensures that presidential and vice presidential candidates from the same party will not be from the same state. (In 2000, Republican vice presidential nominee Dick Cheney changed his voter registration to Wyoming, where he grew up and which he'd once represented in Congress, from George W. Bush's home state of Texas.) Also, an elector cannot be a member of Congress or hold federal office.

Certified and sealed lists of the votes of the electors in each state are sent to the president of the U.S. Senate. He or she then opens them in the presence of members of the Senate and House of Representatives in a joint session held in early Jan. The electoral votes of all the states are then officially counted.

If no candidate for president has a majority, the House of Representatives chooses a president from the top three candidates, with all representatives from each state combining to cast one vote for that state. The House decided the outcome of the 1800 and 1824 presidential elections. If no candidate for vice president has a majority, the Senate chooses from the top two, with the senators voting as individuals. The Senate chose the vice president following the 1836 election.

Under the electoral college system, a candidate who fails to be the top vote getter in the popular vote still may win a majority of electoral votes. This happened in the elections of 1876, 1888, and 2000.

Electoral Votes for President, 2012

Electoral votes based on the 2010 Census were in force beginning with the 2012 elections.

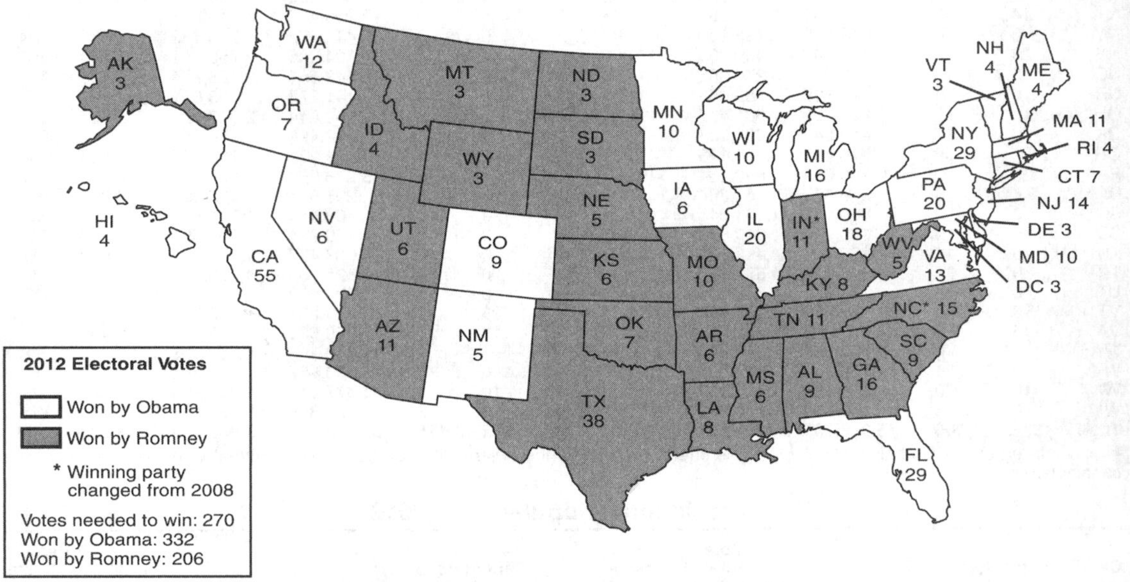

Voter Turnout in Presidential Elections, 1932-2012

Source: U.S. Census Bureau, U.S. Dept. of Commerce; Office of the Clerk, U.S. House of Representatives

Year	Candidates	Voter participation (% of voting-age population)
1932	F. D. Roosevelt-Hoover	52.6%
1936	F. D. Roosevelt-Landon	56.9
1940	F. D. Roosevelt-Willkie	58.8
1944	F. D. Roosevelt-Dewey	56.1
1948	Truman-Dewey	51.1
1952	Eisenhower-Stevenson	61.6
1956	Eisenhower-Stevenson	59.3
1960	Kennedy-Nixon	62.8
1964	L. B. Johnson-Goldwater	61.4
1968	Nixon-Humphrey	60.7
1972	Nixon-McGovern	55.1(1)
1976	Carter-Ford	53.6%
1980	Reagan-Carter	52.8
1984	Reagan-Mondale	53.3
1988	G. H. W. Bush-Dukakis	50.3
1992	Clinton-G. H. W. Bush-Perot	55.2
1996	Clinton-Dole-Perot	49.0
2000	G. W. Bush-Gore	50.3
2004	G. W. Bush-Kerry	55.7
2008	Obama-McCain	57.1
2012	Obama-Romney	54.9

(1) The drop in voter participation followed the expansion of eligibility with the enfranchisement of 18- to 20-year-olds.

Major-Party Nominees for President and Vice President, 1856-2012

Asterisk (*) denotes winning ticket.

Democratic			Republican		
Year	President	Vice President	Year	President	Vice President
1856	James Buchanan*	John Breckinridge	1856	John Frémont	William Dayton
1860	Stephen A. Douglas[1]	Herschel V. Johnson	1860	Abraham Lincoln*	Hannibal Hamlin
1864	George McClellan	G. H. Pendleton	1864	Abraham Lincoln*	Andrew Johnson
1868	Horatio Seymour	Francis Blair	1868	Ulysses S. Grant*	Schuyler Colfax
1872	Horace Greeley	B. Gratz Brown	1872	Ulysses S. Grant*	Henry Wilson
1876	Samuel J. Tilden	Thomas Hendricks	1876	Rutherford B. Hayes*	William Wheeler
1880	Winfield Hancock	William English	1880	James A. Garfield*	Chester A. Arthur
1884	Grover Cleveland*	Thomas Hendricks	1884	James G. Blaine	John Logan
1888	Grover Cleveland	A. G. Thurman	1888	Benjamin Harrison*	Levi Morton
1892	Grover Cleveland*	Adlai Stevenson	1892	Benjamin Harrison	Whitelaw Reid
1896	William J. Bryan	Arthur Sewall	1896	William McKinley*	Garret Hobart
1900	William J. Bryan	Adlai Stevenson	1900	William McKinley*	Theodore Roosevelt
1904	Alton Parker	Henry Davis	1904	Theodore Roosevelt*	Charles Fairbanks
1908	William J. Bryan	John Kern	1908	William H. Taft*	James Sherman
1912	Woodrow Wilson*	Thomas Marshall	1912	William H. Taft	James Sherman[2]
1916	Woodrow Wilson*	Thomas Marshall	1916	Charles E. Hughes	Charles Fairbanks
1920	James M. Cox	Franklin D. Roosevelt	1920	Warren G. Harding*	Calvin Coolidge
1924	John W. Davis	Charles W. Bryan	1924	Calvin Coolidge*	Charles G. Dawes
1928	Alfred E. Smith	Joseph T. Robinson	1928	Herbert Hoover*	Charles Curtis
1932	Franklin D. Roosevelt*	John N. Garner	1932	Herbert Hoover	Charles Curtis
1936	Franklin D. Roosevelt*	John N. Garner	1936	Alfred M. Landon	Frank Knox
1940	Franklin D. Roosevelt*	Henry A. Wallace	1940	Wendell L. Willkie	Charles McNary
1944	Franklin D. Roosevelt*	Harry S. Truman	1944	Thomas E. Dewey	John W. Bricker
1948	Harry S. Truman*	Alben W. Barkley	1948	Thomas E. Dewey	Earl Warren
1952	Adlai E. Stevenson	John J. Sparkman	1952	Dwight D. Eisenhower*	Richard M. Nixon
1956	Adlai E. Stevenson	Estes Kefauver	1956	Dwight D. Eisenhower*	Richard M. Nixon
1960	John F. Kennedy*	Lyndon B. Johnson	1960	Richard M. Nixon	Henry Cabot Lodge
1964	Lyndon B. Johnson*	Hubert H. Humphrey	1964	Barry M. Goldwater	William E. Miller
1968	Hubert H. Humphrey	Edmund S. Muskie	1968	Richard M. Nixon*	Spiro T. Agnew
1972	George S. McGovern	R. Sargent Shriver Jr.[3]	1972	Richard M. Nixon*	Spiro T. Agnew
1976	Jimmy Carter*	Walter F. Mondale	1976	Gerald R. Ford	Bob Dole
1980	Jimmy Carter	Walter F. Mondale	1980	Ronald Reagan*	George H. W. Bush
1984	Walter F. Mondale	Geraldine Ferraro	1984	Ronald Reagan*	George H. W. Bush
1988	Michael S. Dukakis	Lloyd Bentsen	1988	George H. W. Bush*	Dan Quayle
1992	Bill Clinton*	Al Gore	1992	George H. W. Bush	Dan Quayle
1996	Bill Clinton*	Al Gore	1996	Bob Dole	Jack Kemp
2000	Al Gore	Joseph Lieberman	2000	George W. Bush*	Richard Cheney
2004	John Kerry	John Edwards	2004	George W. Bush*	Richard Cheney
2008	Barack Obama*	Joe Biden	2008	John McCain	Sarah Palin
2012	Barack Obama*	Joe Biden	2012	Mitt Romney	Paul Ryan

(1) Douglas and Johnson were nominated at the Baltimore convention. An earlier convention in Charleston, SC, failed to reach a consensus and resulted in a split in the party. The Southern faction of the Democrats nominated John Breckinridge for president and Joseph Lane for vice president. (2) Died Oct. 30; replaced on ballot by Nicholas Butler. (3) Chosen by Democratic National Committee after Thomas Eagleton withdrew because of controversy over past treatments for depression.

Third-Party and Independent Presidential Candidates

In most elections since 1860, fewer than one vote in 20 has been cast for a third-party candidate. Still, independent and third-party candidates often bring attention to prominent issues and can affect the outcome between major-party candidates.

Major vote getters among third-party and independent candidates include James B. Weaver (People's Party), 1892; former Pres. Theodore Roosevelt (Progressive Party), 1912; Robert M. La Follette (Progressive Party), 1924; George C. Wallace (American Independent Party), 1968; and H. Ross Perot, as an independent in 1992 and with the Reform Party in 1996. In these six elections, non-major-party candidates combined polled at least 10% of the vote.

Roosevelt outpolled the Republican candidate, William Howard Taft, in 1912, capturing 28% of the popular vote and 88 electoral votes. In 1948, Strom Thurmond (States' Rights [Dixiecrat]) won 39 electoral votes from five Southern states; however, third-party candidates received only 5.75% of the popular vote. George Wallace's popularity in the same region in 1968 allowed him to get 46 electoral votes and 13.5% of the popular vote.

In 1992, Ross Perot captured 19% of the popular vote but failed to win a single electoral vote. In 1996, Perot won 8% of the popular vote; all third-party candidates combined won just over 10%. In 2000, Ralph Nader (Green, independent) won about 3% of the vote.

Notable Third-Party and Independent Campaigns by Year

Party	Presidential nominee	Year	Issues	Strength in
Anti-Masonic	William Wirt	1832	Against secret societies and oaths	PA, VT
Liberty	James G. Birney	1844	Anti-slavery	North
Free Soil	Martin Van Buren	1848	Anti-slavery	NY, OH
American (Know-Nothing)	Millard Fillmore	1856	Anti-immigrant	Northeast, South
Greenback	Peter Cooper	1876	For "cheap money," labor rights	National
Greenback	James B. Weaver	1880	For "cheap money," labor rights	National
Prohibition	John P. St. John	1884	Anti-liquor	National
People's (Populist)	James B. Weaver	1892	For "cheap money," end of national banks	South, West
Socialist	Eugene V. Debs	1900-12; 1920	For public ownership	National
Progressive (Bull Moose)	Theodore Roosevelt	1912	Against high tariffs	Midwest, West
Progressive	Robert M. La Follette	1924	For farmer and labor rights	Midwest, West
Socialist	Norman Thomas	1928-48	For liberal reforms	National
Union	William Lemke	1936	Anti-New Deal	National
States' Rights (Dixiecrat)	Strom Thurmond	1948	For states' rights	South
Progressive	Henry A. Wallace	1948	Anti-Cold War	NY, CA
American Independent	George C. Wallace	1968	For states' rights	South
American	John G. Schmitz	1972	For "law and order"	West, OH, LA
None (independent)	John B. Anderson	1980	A third choice	National
None (independent)	H. Ross Perot	1992	Federal budget deficit	National
Reform	H. Ross Perot	1996	Deficit, campaign finance	National
Green, independent	Ralph Nader	2000-08	Corporate power, domestic priorities	National
Libertarian	Gary Johnson	2012	Public debt, civil liberties	National

Popular and Electoral Vote for President, 1789-2012

(D) Democrat; (DR) Democratic Republican; (F) Federalist; (LB) Libertarian; (LR) Liberal Republican; (NR) National Republican; (P) People's; (PR) Progressive; (R) Republican; (W) Whig; * = See notes below table.

Year	President elected	Popular	Elec.	Major losing candidate(s)	Popular	Elec.
1789	George Washington	Unknown	69	No major opposition	—	—
1792	George Washington	Unknown	132	No major opposition	—	—
1796	John Adams (F)	Unknown	71	Thomas Jefferson (DR)	Unknown	68
1800*	Thomas Jefferson (DR)	Unknown	73	Aaron Burr (DR)	Unknown	73
1804	Thomas Jefferson (DR)	Unknown	162	Charles Pinckney (F)	Unknown	14
1808	James Madison (DR)	Unknown	122	Charles Pinckney (F)	Unknown	47
1812	James Madison (DR)	Unknown	128	DeWitt Clinton (F)	Unknown	89
1816	James Monroe (DR)	Unknown	183	Rufus King (F)	Unknown	34
1820	James Monroe (DR)	Unknown	231	John Quincy Adams (DR)	Unknown	1
1824*	John Quincy Adams (DR)	113,122	84	Andrew Jackson (DR)	151,271	99
				Henry Clay (DR)	46,587	37
				William H. Crawford (DR)	44,282	41
1828	Andrew Jackson (D)	642,553	178	John Quincy Adams (NR)	500,897	83
1832	Andrew Jackson (D)	701,780	219	Henry Clay (NR)	484,205	49
1836	Martin Van Buren (D)	764,176	170	William H. Harrison (W)	550,816	73
1840	William H. Harrison (W)	1,275,390	234	Martin Van Buren (D)	1,128,854	60
1844	James K. Polk (D)	1,339,494	170	Henry Clay (W)	1,300,004	105
1848	Zachary Taylor (W)	1,361,393	163	Lewis Cass (D)	1,223,460	127
				Martin Van Buren (Free Soil)	291,501	—
1852	Franklin Pierce (D)	1,607,510	254	Winfield Scott (W)	1,386,942	42
1856	James Buchanan (D)	1,836,072	174	John C. Fremont (R)	1,342,345	114
				Millard Fillmore (W-American)	873,053	8
1860	Abraham Lincoln (R)	1,865,908	180	Stephen A. Douglas (D)	848,019	12
				John C. Breckinridge (D)	845,763	72
				John Bell (Constitutional Union)	589,581	39
1864	Abraham Lincoln (R)	2,218,388	212	George McClellan (D)	1,812,807	21
1868	Ulysses S. Grant (R)	3,013,650	214	Horatio Seymour (D)	2,708,744	80
1872*	Ulysses S. Grant (R)	3,598,235	286	Horace Greeley (D-LR)	2,834,671	—
1876*	Rutherford B. Hayes (R)	4,034,311	185	Samuel J. Tilden (D)	4,288,546	184
1880	James A. Garfield (R)	4,446,158	214	Winfield S. Hancock (D)	4,444,260	155
1884	Grover Cleveland (D)	4,874,621	219	James G. Blaine (R)	4,848,936	182
1888	Benjamin Harrison (R)	5,443,892	233	Grover Cleveland (D)	5,534,488	168
1892	Grover Cleveland (D)	5,551,883	277	Benjamin Harrison (R)	5,179,244	145
				James Weaver (P)	1,027,329	22
1896	William McKinley (R)	7,108,480	271	William J. Bryan (D-P)	6,511,495	176
1900	William McKinley (R)	7,218,039	292	William J. Bryan (D)	6,358,345	155
1904	Theodore Roosevelt (R)	7,626,593	336	Alton B. Parker (D)	5,082,898	140
1908	William H. Taft (R)	7,676,258	321	William J. Bryan (D)	6,406,801	162
1912	Woodrow Wilson (D)	6,293,152	435	Theodore Roosevelt (PR)	4,119,207	88
				William H. Taft (R)	3,483,922	8
1916	Woodrow Wilson (D)	9,126,300	277	Charles E. Hughes (R)	8,546,789	254
1920	Warren G. Harding (R)	16,153,115	404	James M. Cox (D)	9,133,092	127
1924	Calvin Coolidge (R)	15,719,921	382	John W. Davis (D)	8,386,704	136
				Robert M. La Follette (PR)	4,822,856	13
1928	Herbert Hoover (R)	21,437,277	444	Alfred E. Smith (D)	15,007,698	87
1932	Franklin D. Roosevelt (D)	22,829,501	472	Herbert Hoover (R)	15,760,684	59
1936	Franklin D. Roosevelt (D)	27,757,333	523	Alfred Landon (R)	16,684,231	8
1940	Franklin D. Roosevelt (D)	27,313,041	449	Wendell Willkie (R)	22,348,480	82
1944	Franklin D. Roosevelt (D)	25,612,610	432	Thomas E. Dewey (R)	22,117,617	99
1948	Harry S. Truman (D)	24,179,345	303	Thomas E. Dewey (R)	21,991,291	189
				Strom Thurmond (States' Rights)	1,169,021	39
				Henry A. Wallace (PR)	1,157,172	—
1952	Dwight D. Eisenhower (R)	33,936,234	442	Adlai E. Stevenson (D)	27,314,992	89
1956*	Dwight D. Eisenhower (R)	35,590,472	457	Adlai E. Stevenson (D)	26,022,752	73
1960*	John F. Kennedy (D)	34,226,731	303	Richard M. Nixon (R)	34,108,157	219
1964	Lyndon B. Johnson (D)	43,129,566	486	Barry M. Goldwater (R)	27,178,188	52
1968	Richard M. Nixon (R)	31,785,480	301	Hubert H. Humphrey (D)	31,275,166	191
				George C. Wallace (Amer. Indep.)	9,906,473	46
1972*	Richard M. Nixon (R)	47,169,911	520	George S. McGovern (D)	29,170,383	17
1976*	Jimmy Carter (D)	40,830,763	297	Gerald R. Ford (R)	39,147,793	240
1980	Ronald Reagan (R)	43,904,153	489	Jimmy Carter (D)	35,483,883	49
				John B. Anderson (independent)	5,719,437	—
1984	Ronald Reagan (R)	54,455,075	525	Walter F. Mondale (D)	37,577,185	13
1988*	George H. W. Bush (R)	48,886,097	426	Michael S. Dukakis (D)	41,809,074	111
1992	Bill Clinton (D)	44,908,254	370	George H. W. Bush (R)	39,102,343	168
				H. Ross Perot (independent)	19,741,065	—
1996	Bill Clinton (D)	45,590,703	379	Bob Dole (R)	37,816,307	159
				H. Ross Perot (Reform)	7,866,284	—
2000*	George W. Bush (R)	50,459,211	271	Al Gore (D)	51,003,894	266
				Ralph Nader (Green)	2,834,410	—
2004*	George W. Bush (R)	62,040,610	286	John Kerry (D)	59,028,444	251
2008	Barack H. Obama (D)	69,498,516	365	John McCain (R)	59,948,283	173
2012	Barack H. Obama (D)	65,915,796	332	Mitt Romney (R)	60,933,500	206

***1800**—Elected by House of Representatives because of tied electoral vote. **1824**—Elected by House of Representatives because no candidate polled a majority. By 1824, the Democratic Republicans had become a loose coalition of competing political groups. By 1828, the supporters of Jackson were known as Democrats and John Q. Adams and Henry Clay supporters as National Republicans. **1872**—Greeley died Nov. 29, 1872. His electoral votes were split among four individuals. **1876**—FL, LA, OR, and SC election returns were disputed. Congress in joint session (Mar. 2, 1877) declared Hayes and Wheeler elected president and vice president. **1956**—Democrats elected 74 electors, but one from AL refused to vote for Stevenson. **1960**—Sen. Harry F. Byrd (D, VA) received 15 electoral votes. **1972**—John Hospers of CA received a vote from an elector of VA. **1976**—Ronald Reagan of CA received a vote from an elector of WA. **1988**—Sen. Lloyd Bentsen (D, TX) received a vote from an elector of WV. **2000**—One Gore elector from Washington, DC, abstained. Nader was listed as "independent" on the ballot in some states; he was not on the ballot in all states. **2004**—One MN elector voted for VP candidate John Edwards for both president and vice president.

Presidential Election Results by State, 1960-2012

Source: Federal Election Commission; local secretaries of state; state elections offices. State election results may vary slightly from those provided by the FEC.

Alabama

	2012		2008	
County	**Obama (D)**	**Romney (R)**	**Obama (D)**	**McCain (R)**
Autauga	6,363	17,379	6,093	17,403
Baldwin	18,424	66,016	19,386	61,271
Barbour	5,912	5,550	5,697	5,866
Bibb	2,202	6,132	2,299	6,262
Blount	2,970	20,757	3,522	20,389
Bullock	4,061	1,251	4,011	1,391
Butler	4,374	5,087	4,188	5,485
Calhoun	15,511	30,278	16,334	32,348
Chambers	6,871	7,626	6,799	8,067
Cherokee	2,132	7,506	2,306	7,298
Chilton	3,397	13,932	3,674	13,960
Choctaw	3,786	4,152	3,636	4,223
Clarke	6,334	7,470	5,914	7,466
Clay	1,777	4,817	1,760	4,984
Cleburne	971	5,272	1,168	5,216
Coffee	4,925	14,666	5,079	14,919
Colbert	9,166	13,936	9,703	14,739
Conecuh	3,555	3,439	3,429	3,470
Coosa	2,191	3,049	2,273	3,248
Covington	3,158	12,153	3,240	12,444
Crenshaw	2,050	4,331	1,938	4,319
Cullman	5,052	28,999	5,864	28,896
Dale	5,286	13,108	5,270	13,886
Dallas	14,612	6,288	13,986	6,798
De Kalb	5,239	18,331	5,658	17,957
Elmore	8,954	26,253	8,301	25,777
Escambia	5,489	9,287	5,188	9,375
Etowah	12,803	29,130	13,497	30,595
Fayette	1,817	6,054	1,994	5,883
Franklin	3,171	7,567	3,469	8,048
Geneva	2,039	9,175	2,134	9,417
Greene	4,521	804	4,408	876
Hale	5,411	3,210	4,982	3,200
Henry	3,083	5,628	3,018	5,585
Houston	12,367	29,270	12,225	29,254
Jackson	5,822	14,439	6,374	14,083
Jefferson	159,876	141,683	166,121	149,921
Lamar	1,646	5,457	1,614	5,419
Lauderdale	12,511	23,911	13,329	24,068
Lawrence	5,069	8,874	5,164	9,277
Lee	21,381	32,194	21,498	32,230
Limestone	9,829	25,295	9,536	23,598
Lowndes	5,747	1,756	5,449	1,809
Macon	9,045	1,331	9,450	1,396
Madison	62,015	90,884	64,117	86,965
Marengo	6,167	5,336	5,926	5,516
Marion	2,249	9,697	2,600	9,536
Marshall	6,299	25,867	7,038	25,727
Mobile	78,760	94,893	82,181	98,049
Monroe	4,914	5,741	5,025	6,175
Montgomery	63,085	38,332	62,166	42,031
Morgan	13,439	35,391	13,895	36,014
Perry	4,568	1,506	4,457	1,679
Pickens	4,455	5,124	4,594	5,434
Pike	6,035	7,963	5,879	8,004
Randolph	3,078	7,224	3,064	7,175
Russell	10,500	8,278	10,085	8,705
St. Clair	5,801	29,031	6,091	27,649
Shelby	20,051	71,436	20,625	69,060
Sumter	5,421	1,586	5,264	1,731
Talladega	13,905	19,246	13,779	20,112
Tallapoosa	6,319	12,396	6,063	13,116
Tuscaloosa	32,048	45,748	32,796	45,405
Walker	6,557	21,651	7,420	20,722
Washington	2,976	5,761	3,067	5,654
Wilcox	4,868	1,679	4,612	1,868
Winston	1,286	8,312	1,757	8,103
Totals	**795,696**	**1,255,925**	**813,479**	**1,266,546**

Alabama Vote Since 1960

2012: Romney, R, 1,255,925; Obama, D, 795,696; Johnson, Ind., 12,328; Stein, Ind., 3,397; Goode, Ind., 2,981.

2008: McCain, R, 1,266,546; Obama, D, 813,479; Nader, Ind., 6,788; Barr, Ind., 4,991; Baldwin, Ind., 4,310.

2004: Bush, R, 1,176,394; Kerry, D, 693,933; Nader, Ind., 6,701; Badnarik, Ind., 3,529; Peroutka, Ind., 1,994.

2000: Bush, R, 941,173; Gore, D, 692,611; Nader, Ind., 18,323; Buchanan, Ind., 6,351; Browne, LB, 5,893; Phillips, Ind., 775; Hagelin, Ind., 447.

1996: Dole, R, 769,044; Clinton, D, 662,165; Perot, RF, 92,149; Browne, LB, 5,290; Phillips, Ind., 2,365; Hagelin, Natural Law, 1,697; Harris, Ind., 516.

1992: Bush, R, 804,283; Clinton, D, 690,080; Perot, Ind., 183,109; Marrou, LB, 5,737; Fulani, New Alliance, 2,161.

1988: Bush, R, 815,576; Dukakis, D, 549,506; Paul, LB, 8,460; Fulani, Ind., 3,311.

1984: Reagan, R, 872,849; Mondale, D, 551,899; Bergland, LB, 9,504.

1980: Reagan, R, 654,192; Carter, D, 636,730; Anderson, Ind., 16,481; Rarick, Amer. Ind., 15,010; Clark, LB, 13,318; Bubar, Statesman, 1,743; Hall, Comm., 1,629; DeBerry, Soc. Workers, 1,303; McReynolds, Soc., 1,006; Commoner, Citizens, 517.

1976: Carter, D, 659,170; Ford, R, 504,070; Maddox, Amer. Ind., 9,198; Bubar, Prohib., 6,669; Hall, Comm., 1,954; MacBride, LB, 1,481.

1972: Nixon, R, 728,701; McGovern, D, 219,108 plus 37,815 Natl. Dem. Party of AL; Schmitz, Conservative, 11,918; Munn, Prohib., 8,551.

1968: Wallace, 3rd party, 691,425; Humphrey, D, 196,579; Nixon, R, 146,923; Munn, Prohib., 4,022.

1964: Goldwater, R, 479,085; D (electors unpledged), 209,848; scattered, 105.

1960: Kennedy, D, 324,050; Nixon, R, 237,981; Faubus, States' Rights, 4,367; Decker, Prohib., 2,106; King, Afro-Americans, 1,485; scattered, 236.

Alaska

	2012		2008	
	Obama (D)	**Romney (R)**	**Obama (D)**	**McCain (R)**
Totals	**122,640**	**164,676**	**123,594**	**193,841**

Alaska Vote Since 1960

2012: Romney, R, 164,676; Obama, D, 122,640; Johnson, LB, 7,392; Stein, Green, 2,917.

2008: McCain, R, 193,841; Obama, D, 123,594; Nader, Ind., 3,783; Baldwin, AK Ind., 1,660; Barr, LB, 1,589.

2004: Bush, R, 190,889; Kerry, D, 111,025; Nader, Populist, 5,069; Peroutka, AK Ind., 2,092; Badnarik, LB, 1,675; Cobb, Green, 1,058.

2000: Bush, R, 167,398; Gore, D, 79,004; Nader, Green, 28,747; Buchanan, RF, 5,192; Browne, LB, 2,636; Hagelin, Natural Law, 919; Phillips, Const., 596.

1996: Dole, R, 122,746; Clinton, D, 80,380; Perot, RF, 26,333; Nader, Green, 7,597; Browne, LB, 2,276; Phillips, U.S. Taxpayers, 925; Hagelin, Natural Law, 729.

1992: Bush, R, 102,000; Clinton, D, 78,294; Perot, Ind., 73,481; Gritz, Populist/America First, 1,379; Marrou, LB, 1,378.

1988: Bush, R, 119,251; Dukakis, D, 72,584; Paul, LB, 5,484; Fulani, New Alliance, 1,024.

1984: Reagan, R, 138,377; Mondale, D, 62,007; Bergland, LB, 6,378.

1980: Reagan, R, 86,112; Carter, D, 41,842; Clark, LB, 18,479; Anderson, Ind., 11,155; write-in, 857.

1976: Ford, R, 71,555; Carter, D, 44,058; MacBride, LB, 6,785.

1972: Nixon, R, 55,349; McGovern, D, 32,967; Schmitz, Amer., 6,903.

1968: Nixon, R, 37,600; Humphrey, D, 35,411; Wallace, 3rd party, 10,024.

1964: Johnson, D, 44,329; Goldwater, R, 22,930.

1960: Nixon, R, 30,953; Kennedy, D, 29,809.

Arizona

	2012		2008	
County	**Obama (D)**	**Romney (R)**	**Obama (D)**	**McCain (R)**
Apache	17,147	8,250	15,390	8,551
Cochise	18,546	29,497	18,943	29,026
Coconino	29,257	21,220	31,433	22,186
Gila	7,697	13,455	7,884	14,095
Graham	3,609	8,076	3,487	8,376
Greenlee	1,310	1,592	1,165	1,712
La Paz	1,880	3,714	1,929	3,509
Maricopa	602,288	749,885	602,166	746,448
Mohave	19,533	49,168	22,092	44,333
Navajo	16,945	19,884	15,579	19,761
Pima	201,251	174,779	206,254	182,406
Pinal	44,306	62,079	44,254	59,421
Santa Cruz	9,486	4,235	8,683	4,518
Yavapai	33,918	64,468	36,889	61,192
Yuma	18,059	23,352	18,559	24,577
Totals	**1,025,232**	**1,233,654**	**1,034,707**	**1,230,111**

Arizona Vote Since 1960

2012: Romney, R, 1,233,654; Obama, D, 1,025,232; Johnson, LB, 32,100; Stein, Green, 7,816.

2008: McCain, R, 1,230,111; Obama, D, 1,034,707; Barr, LB, 12,555; Nader, New Prog., 11,301; McKinney, Green, 3,406.

2004: Bush, R, 1,104,294; Kerry, D, 893,524; Badnarik, LB, 11,856.

2000: Bush, R, 781,652; Gore, D, 685,341; Nader, Green, 45,645; Buchanan, RF, 12,373; Smith, LB, 5,775; Hagelin, Natural Law, 1,120.

1996: Clinton, D, 653,288; Dole, R, 622,073; Perot, RF, 112,072; Browne, LB, 14,358.

1992: Bush, R, 572,086; Clinton, D, 543,050; Perot, Ind., 353,741; Gritz, Populist/America First, 8,141; Marrou, LB, 6,759; Hagelin, Natural Law, 2,267.

1988: Bush, R, 702,541; Dukakis, D, 454,029; Paul, LB, 13,351; Fulani, New Alliance, 1,662.

1984: Reagan, R, 681,416; Mondale, D, 333,854; Bergland, LB, 10,585.

1980: Reagan, R, 529,688; Carter, D, 246,843; Anderson, Ind., 76,952; Clark, LB, 18,784; DeBerry, Soc. Workers, 1,100; Commoner, Citizens, 551; Hall, Comm., 25; Griswold, Workers World, 2.

1976: Ford, R, 418,642; Carter, D, 295,602; McCarthy, Ind., 19,229; MacBride, LB, 7,647; Camejo, Soc. Workers, 928; Anderson, Amer., 564; Maddox, Amer. Ind., 85.

1972: Nixon, R, 402,812; McGovern, D, 198,540; Jenness, Soc. Workers, 30,945; Schmitz, Amer. Ind., 21,208.

1968: Nixon, R, 266,721; Humphrey, D, 170,514; Wallace, 3rd party, 46,573; McCarthy, New Party, 2,751; Cleaver, Peace/Freedom, 217; Halstead, Soc. Workers, 85; Blomen, Soc. Labor, 75.

1964: Goldwater, R, 242,535; Johnson, D, 237,753; Hass, Soc. Labor, 482.

1960: Nixon, R, 221,241; Kennedy, D, 176,781; Hass, Soc. Labor, 469.

Arkansas

	2012		2008	
County	**Obama (D)**	**Romney (R)**	**Obama (D)**	**McCain (R)**
Arkansas	2,455	3,897	2,619	4,185
Ashley	2,859	4,867	2,976	5,406
Baxter	5,172	13,688	6,539	12,852
Benton	22,636	54,646	23,331	51,124
Boone	3,772	11,159	4,435	10,575
Bradley	1,449	2,134	1,680	2,262
Calhoun	660	1,458	691	1,462
Carroll	3,696	6,125	4,172	6,083
Chicot	2,649	1,670	3,043	2,119
Clark	3,811	4,343	4,267	4,608
Clay	1,738	3,225	2,244	3,032
Cleburne	2,620	8,693	2,951	7,962
Cleveland	845	2,313	911	2,451
Columbia	3,557	5,790	3,554	5,861
Conway	3,005	4,514	3,149	4,691
Craighead	10,527	20,350	11,294	18,881
Crawford	4,881	15,145	5,238	14,688
Crittenden	9,487	6,998	10,330	7,650
Cross	2,279	4,269	2,580	4,393
Dallas	1,337	1,665	1,471	1,757
Desha	2,443	1,896	2,569	1,999
Drew	2,630	3,887	2,598	3,860
Faulkner	13,621	26,722	14,955	25,362
Franklin	1,726	4,631	1,869	4,411
Fulton	1,452	2,949	1,819	2,702
Garland	13,804	26,014	15,899	26,825
Grant	1,468	4,829	1,562	5,023
Greene	4,000	9,071	4,541	8,578
Hempstead	2,468	4,284	2,869	4,273
Hot Spring	3,830	7,097	4,288	7,209
Howard	1,471	2,892	1,746	2,957
Independence	3,281	8,728	3,688	8,255
Izard	1,524	3,575	1,792	3,193
Jackson	2,095	3,072	2,207	3,118
Jefferson	17,470	9,520	18,465	10,655
Johnson	2,799	5,064	3,034	4,922
Lafayette	1,173	1,713	1,133	1,685
Lawrence	1,788	3,536	2,138	3,357
Lee	2,107	1,280	2,263	1,454
Lincoln	1,425	2,199	1,710	2,513
Little River	1,552	3,385	1,753	3,247
Logan	2,009	5,079	2,286	5,350
Lonoke	5,625	17,880	5,968	17,242
Madison	2,099	4,263	2,144	3,972
Marion	2,037	4,774	2,384	4,524
Miller	4,518	10,622	4,869	9,913
Mississippi	6,467	6,603	6,667	6,976
Monroe	1,583	1,585	1,615	1,754
Montgomery	920	2,369	1,092	2,365
Nevada	1,314	1,996	1,474	2,062
Newton	993	2,508	1,182	2,588
Ouachita	4,633	5,521	4,346	5,427
Perry	1,187	2,581	1,352	2,743
Phillips	5,202	2,598	5,695	3,097
Pike	851	2,847	1,089	2,727
Poinsett	2,390	4,974	2,742	4,903
Polk	1,556	5,955	1,957	5,473
Pope	5,126	14,763	6,002	15,568
Prairie	880	2,153	1,048	2,223
Pulaski	87,248	68,984	88,854	70,212
Randolph	2,046	3,701	2,469	3,615
St. Francis	4,910	3,368	5,486	3,917
Saline	12,869	32,963	12,695	30,981
Scott	897	2,631	1,053	2,791
Searcy	814	2,699	961	2,726
Sebastian	13,092	29,169	13,673	28,637
Sevier	1,042	3,136	1,291	3,125
Sharp	2,092	4,921	2,436	4,535
Stone	1,356	3,776	1,598	3,534
Union	6,196	10,699	6,190	10,677
Van Buren	1,832	4,365	2,151	4,276
Washington	28,236	39,688	29,021	37,963
White	5,765	20,011	6,732	19,467
Woodruff	1,340	1,227	1,412	1,206
Yell	1,722	4,042	2,003	3,808
Totals	**394,409**	**647,744**	**422,310**	**638,017**

Arkansas Vote Since 1960

2012: Romney, R, 647,744; Obama, D, 394,409; Johnson, LB, 16,276; Stein, Green, 9,305; Lindsay, Socialism/Liberation, 1,734.

2008: McCain, R, 638,017; Obama, D, 422,310; Nader, Ind., 12,882; Barr, LB, 4,776; Baldwin, Const., 4,023; McKinney, Green, 3,470; La Riva, Socialism/Liberation, 1,139.

2004: Bush, R, 572,898; Kerry, D, 469,953; Nader, Populist, 6,171; Badnarik, LB, 2,352; Peroutka, Const., 2,083; Cobb, Green, 1,488.

2000: Bush, R, 472,940; Gore, D, 422,768; Nader, Green, 13,421; Buchanan, RF, 7,358; Browne, LB, 2,781; Phillips, Const., 1,415; Hagelin, Natural Law, 1,098.

1996: Clinton, D, 475,171; Dole, R, 325,416; Perot, RF, 69,884; Nader, Ind., 3,649; Browne, Ind., 3,076; Phillips, Ind., 2,065; Forbes, Ind., 932; Collins, Ind., 823; Masters, Ind., 749; Moorehead, Ind., 747; Hagelin, Ind., 729; Hollis, Ind., 538; Dodge, Ind., 483.

1992: Clinton, D, 505,823; Bush, R, 337,324; Perot, Ind., 99,132; Phillips, U.S. Taxpayers, 1,437; Marrou, LB, 1,261; Fulani, New Alliance, 1,022.

1988: Bush, R, 466,578; Dukakis, D, 349,237; Duke, Populist, 5,146; Paul, LB, 3,297.

1984: Reagan, R, 534,774; Mondale, D, 338,646; Bergland, LB, 2,220.

1980: Reagan, R, 403,164; Carter, D, 398,041; Anderson, Ind., 22,468; Clark, LB, 8,970; Commoner, Citizens, 2,345; Bubar, Statesman, 1,350; Hall, Comm., 1,244.

1976: Carter, D, 498,604; Ford, R, 267,903; McCarthy, Ind., 639; Anderson, Amer. Ind., 389.

1972: Nixon, R, 445,751; McGovern, D, 198,899; Schmitz, Amer. Ind., 3,016.

1968: Wallace, 3rd party, 235,627; Nixon, R, 189,062; Humphrey, D, 184,901.

1964: Johnson, D, 314,197; Goldwater, R, 243,264; Kasper, Natl. States' Rights, 2,965.

1960: Kennedy, D, 215,049; Nixon, R, 184,508; Faubus, Natl. States' Rights, 28,952.

California

	2012		2008	
County	**Obama (D)**	**Romney (R)**	**Obama (D)**	**McCain (R)**
Alameda	469,684	108,182	489,106	119,555
Alpine	389	236	422	252
Amador	6,830	10,281	7,813	10,561
Butte	42,669	44,479	49,013	46,706
Calaveras	8,670	12,365	9,813	12,835
Colusa	2,314	3,601	2,569	3,733
Contra Costa	290,824	136,517	306,983	136,436
Del Norte	3,791	4,614	4,323	4,967
El Dorado	35,166	50,973	40,529	50,314
Fresno	129,129	124,490	136,706	131,015
Glenn	3,301	5,632	3,734	5,910
Humboldt	34,457	18,825	39,692	21,713
Imperial	25,136	12,777	24,162	14,008
Inyo	3,422	4,340	3,743	4,523
Kern	89,495	126,618	93,457	134,793
Kings	12,979	17,671	14,747	19,710
Lake	13,163	9,200	14,854	9,935
Lassen	3,053	7,296	3,586	7,483
Los Angeles	2,216,903	885,333	2,295,853	956,425

	2012		2008	
County	Obama (D)	Romney (R)	Obama (D)	McCain (R)
Madera	16,018	22,852	17,952	23,583
Marin	99,896	30,880	109,320	28,384
Mariposa	3,498	5,140	4,100	5,298
Mendocino	23,193	9,658	27,843	10,721
Merced	33,005	27,581	34,031	28,704
Modoc	1,111	2,777	1,313	2,981
Mono	2,733	2,285	3,093	2,354
Monterey	82,920	37,390	88,453	38,797
Napa	35,870	19,526	38,849	19,484
Nevada	24,663	24,986	28,617	25,663
Orange	512,440	582,332	549,558	579,064
Placer	66,818	99,921	75,112	94,647
Plumas	4,026	5,721	4,715	6,035
Riverside	329,063	318,127	325,017	310,041
Sacramento	300,503	202,514	316,506	213,583
San Benito	11,276	7,343	11,917	7,425
San Bernardino	305,109	262,358	315,720	277,408
San Diego	626,957	536,726	666,581	541,032
San Francisco	301,723	47,076	322,220	52,292
San Joaquin	114,121	86,071	113,974	91,607
San Luis Obispo	61,258	59,967	68,176	61,055
San Mateo	206,085	72,756	222,826	75,057
Santa Barbara	94,129	64,606	105,614	65,585
Santa Clara	450,818	174,843	462,241	190,039
Santa Cruz	90,805	24,047	98,745	25,244
Shasta	25,819	48,067	28,867	49,588
Sierra	653	1,056	743	1,158
Siskiyou	8,046	11,077	9,292	11,520
Solano	96,783	52,092	102,095	56,035
Sonoma	153,942	54,784	168,888	55,127
Stanislaus	77,724	73,459	80,279	77,497
Sutter	12,192	18,122	13,412	18,911
Tehama	7,934	14,235	8,945	14,843
Trinity	2,674	2,716	3,233	2,940
Tulare	41,752	56,956	43,634	59,765
Tuolumne	9,998	13,880	11,532	14,988
Ventura	170,929	147,958	187,601	145,853
Yolo	48,715	23,368	53,488	24,592
Yuba	7,711	11,275	8,866	12,007
Totals	**7,854,285**	**4,839,958**	**8,274,473**	**5,011,781**

California Vote Since 1960

2012: Obama, D, 7,854,285; Romney, R, 4,839,958; Johnson, LB, 143,221; Stein, Green, 85,638; Barr, Peace/Freedom, 53,824; Hoefling, Amer. Ind., 38,372.

2008: Obama, D, 8,274,473; McCain, R, 5,011,781; Nader, Peace/Freedom, 108,381; Barr, LB, 67,582; Alan Keyes, Amer. Ind., 40,673; McKinney, Green, 38,774.

2004: Kerry, D, 6,745,485; Bush, R, 5,509,826; Badnarik, LB, 50,165; Cobb, Green, 40,771; Peltier, Peace/Freedom, 27,607; Peroutka, Amer. Ind., 26,645.

2000: Gore, D, 5,861,203; Bush, R, 4,567,429; Nader, Green, 418,707; Browne, LB, 45,520; Buchanan, RF, 44,987; Phillips, Amer. Ind., 17,042; Hagelin, Natural Law, 10,934.

1996: Clinton, D, 5,119,835; Dole, R, 3,828,380; Perot, RF, 697,847; Nader, Green, 237,016; Browne, LB, 73,600; Feinland, Peace/Freedom, 25,332; Phillips, Amer. Ind., 21,202; Hagelin, Natural Law, 15,403.

1992: Clinton, D, 5,121,325; Bush, R, 3,630,575; Perot, Ind., 2,296,006; Marrou, LB, 48,139; Daniels, Ind., 18,597; Phillips, U.S. Taxpayers, 12,711.

1988: Bush, R, 5,054,917; Dukakis, D, 4,702,233; Paul, LB, 70,105; Fulani, Ind., 31,181.

1984: Reagan, R, 5,305,410; Mondale, D, 3,815,947; Bergland, LB, 48,400.

1980: Reagan, R, 4,524,858; Carter, D, 3,083,661; Anderson, Ind., 739,833; Clark, LB, 148,434; Commoner, Ind., 61,063; Smith, Peace/Freedom, 18,116; Rarick, Amer. Ind., 9,856.

1976: Ford, R, 3,882,244; Carter, D, 3,742,284; McCarthy, write-in, 58,412; MacBride, LB, 56,388; Maddox, Amer. Ind., 51,098; Wright, People's, 41,731; Camejo, Soc. Workers, 17,259; Hall, Comm., 12,766; write-in, 4,935.

1972: Nixon, R, 4,602,096; McGovern, D, 3,475,847; Schmitz, Amer. Ind., 232,554; Spock, Peace/Freedom, 55,167; Hospers, LB, 980; Jenness, Soc. Workers, 574; Hall, Comm., 373; Fisher, Soc. Labor, 197; Munn, Prohib., 53; Green, Universal, 21.

1968: Nixon, R, 3,467,664; Humphrey, D, 3,244,318; Wallace, 3rd party, 487,270; Peace/Freedom, 27,707; McCarthy, Alternative, 20,721; Gregory, write-in, 3,230; Blomen, Soc. Labor, 341; Mitchell, Comm., 260; Munn, Prohib., 59; Soeters, Defense, 17.

1964: Johnson, D, 4,171,877; Goldwater, R, 2,879,108; Hass, Soc. Labor, 489; DeBerry, Soc. Workers, 378; Munn, Prohib., 305; Hensley, Universal, 19.

1960: Nixon, R, 3,259,722; Kennedy, D, 3,224,099; Decker, Prohib., 21,706; Hass, Soc. Labor, 1,051.

Colorado

	2012		2008	
County	Obama (D)	Romney (R)	Obama (D)	McCain (R)
Adams	100,649	70,972	93,443	63,976
Alamosa	3,811	2,705	3,521	2,635
Arapahoe	153,905	125,588	148,218	113,866
Archuleta	2,679	3,872	2,836	3,638
Baca	467	1,559	536	1,572
Bent	815	1,075	799	1,077
Boulder	125,091	49,981	124,159	44,904
Broomfield	16,966	15,008	16,168	12,757
Chaffee	5,086	5,070	4,861	4,873
Cheyenne	172	889	198	890
Clear Creek	3,119	2,430	3,332	2,300
Conejos	2,213	1,835	2,154	1,653
Costilla	1,340	446	1,245	415
Crowley	535	924	552	976
Custer	868	1,788	912	1,672
Delta	4,622	10,915	5,084	10,067
Denver	222,018	73,111	204,882	62,567
Dolores	334	859	369	818
Douglas	61,094	104,397	61,960	88,108
Eagle	12,792	9,411	13,187	8,179
El Paso	111,819	170,952	108,899	160,318
Elbert	3,603	10,266	3,819	9,108
Fremont	6,704	13,174	6,844	12,668
Garfield	11,305	12,535	11,357	11,359
Gilpin	1,892	1,346	1,954	1,253
Grand	3,684	4,253	4,037	4,128
Gunnison	5,044	3,341	5,556	3,131
Hinsdale	229	353	240	344
Huerfano	1,953	1,646	1,989	1,580
Jackson	216	600	277	624
Jefferson	159,296	144,197	158,153	131,627
Kiowa	118	677	178	650
Kit Carson	838	2,785	912	2,455
La Plata	15,489	12,794	16,057	11,503
Lake	1,839	1,098	1,859	1,078
Larimer	92,747	82,376	89,822	73,641
Las Animas	3,445	3,263	3,562	3,086
Lincoln	552	1,687	546	1,717
Logan	2,712	6,179	2,846	6,002
Mesa	23,846	47,472	24,008	44,578
Mineral	291	344	270	334
Moffat	1,330	4,695	1,582	4,135
Montezuma	4,542	7,401	4,661	6,961
Montrose	6,138	13,552	6,495	12,199
Morgan	3,912	6,602	3,813	6,272
Otero	3,647	4,382	3,546	4,393
Ouray	1,646	1,481	1,636	1,367
Park	3,862	5,236	4,250	4,896
Phillips	588	1,637	622	1,612
Pitkin	6,849	3,024	7,349	2,484
Prowers	1,519	3,230	1,487	3,043
Pueblo	42,551	31,894	41,097	30,257
Rio Blanco	568	2,724	655	2,437
Rio Grande	2,478	2,918	2,448	2,930
Routt	7,547	5,469	8,270	4,725
Saguache	1,865	964	1,730	953
San Juan	266	212	264	218
San Miguel	2,992	1,154	3,349	933
Sedgwick	419	881	468	857
Summit	9,347	5,571	9,802	4,883
Teller	4,333	8,702	4,513	8,146
Washington	468	2,076	529	1,949
Weld	49,050	63,775	47,292	56,526
Yuma	987	3,490	1,117	3,286
Totals	**1,323,102**	**1,185,243**	**1,288,633**	**1,073,629**

Colorado Vote Since 1960

2012: Obama, D, 1,323,102; Romney, R, 1,185,243; Johnson, LB, 35,545; Stein, Green, 7,508; Goode, Const., 6,234; Barr, Peace/Freedom, 5,059; Reed, unaff., 2,589; Anderson, Justice, 1,260; Tittle, We the People, 792; Hoefling, Amer. Ind., 679; La Riva, Socialism/Liberation, 317; Alexander, Soc. USA, 308; Miller, A3P, 266; Stevens, Objectivist, 235; Harris, Soc. Workers, 192; White, Soc. Equality, 189.

2008: Obama, D, 1,288,633; McCain, R, 1,073,629; Nader, Unaff., 13,352; Barr, LB, 10,898; Baldwin, Const., 6,233; Alan Keyes, Amer. Ind., 3,051; McKinney, Green, 2,822; McEnulty, unaff., 829; Jay, Boston Tea, 598; Allen, HeartQuake '08, 348; Stevens, Objectivist, 336; Moore, Soc. USA, 226; La Riva, Socialism/Liberation, 158; Harris, Soc. Workers, 154; Lyttle, U.S. Pacifist, 110; Amondson, Prohib., 85.

2004: Bush, R, 1,101,255; Kerry, D, 1,001,732; Nader, RF, 12,718; Badnarik, LB, 7,664; Peroutka, Amer. Const., 2,562; Cobb, Green, 1,591; Andress, Ind., 804; Amondson, Concerns of People, 378; Van Auken, Soc. Equal., 329; Harris, Soc. Workers, 241; Brown, Soc., 216; Dodge, Prohib., 140.

2000: Bush, R, 883,748; Gore, D, 738,227; Nader, Green, 91,434; Browne, LB, 12,799; Buchanan, RF, 10,465; Hagelin,

RF, 2,240; Phillips, Amer. Const., 1,319; McReynolds, Soc., 712; Harris, Soc. Workers, 216; Dodge, Prohib., 208.
1996: Dole, R, 691,848; Clinton, D, 671,152; Perot, RF, 99,629; Nader, Green, 25,070; Browne, LB, 12,392; Phillips, Amer. Const., 2,813; Collins, Ind., 2,809; Hagelin, Natural Law, 2,547; Hollis, Soc., 669; Moorehead, Workers World, 599; Templin, Amer., 557; Dodge, Prohib., 375; Harris, Soc. Workers, 244.
1992: Clinton, D, 629,681; Bush, R, 562,850; Perot, Ind., 366,010; Marrou, LB, 8,669; Fulani, New Alliance, 1,608.
1988: Bush, R, 728,177; Dukakis, D, 621,453; Paul, LB, 15,482; Dodge, Prohib., 4,604.
1984: Reagan, R, 821,817; Mondale, D, 454,975; Bergland, LB, 11,257.
1980: Reagan, R, 652,264; Carter, D, 367,973; Anderson, Ind., 130,633; Clark, LB, 25,744; Commoner, Citizens, 5,614; Bubar, Statesman, 1,180; Pulley, Soc., 520; Hall, Comm., 487.
1976: Ford, R, 584,367; Carter, D, 460,353; McCarthy, Ind., 26,107; MacBride, LB, 5,330; Bubar, Prohib., 2,882.
1972: Nixon, R, 597,189; McGovern, D, 329,980; Schmitz, Amer., 17,269; Fisher, Soc. Labor, 4,361; Spock, People's, 2,403; Hospers, LB, 1,111; Jenness, Soc. Workers, 555; Munn, Prohib., 467; Hall, Comm., 432.
1968: Nixon, R, 409,345; Humphrey, D, 335,174; Wallace, 3rd party, 60,813; Blomen, Soc. Labor, 3,016; Gregory, New Party, 1,393; Munn, Prohib., 275; Halstead, Soc. Workers, 235.
1964: Johnson, D, 476,024; Goldwater, R, 296,767; DeBerry, Soc. Workers, 2,537; Munn, Prohib., 1,356; Hass, Soc. Labor, 302.
1960: Nixon, R, 402,242; Kennedy, D, 330,629; Hass, Soc. Labor, 2,803; Dobbs, Soc. Workers, 572.

Connecticut

	2012		2008	
City	**Obama (D)**	**Romney (R)**	**Obama (D)**	**McCain (R)**
Bridgeport	32,135	5,168	33,976	6,507
Bristol	14,146	10,004	15,966	10,203
Danbury	15,290	10,590	16,028	10,732
East Hartford	14,149	4,556	14,811	5,195
Fairfield	15,283	14,357	17,236	13,071
Greenwich	13,079	16,456	16,233	13,937
Hamden	19,181	7,482	19,960	8,531
Hartford	31,735	2,138	31,741	2,686
Manchester	15,565	7,961	17,782	8,457
Meriden	14,886	6,880	15,913	7,363
Middletown	13,834	6,105	15,143	5,907
Milford	13,668	11,462	14,873	11,772
New Britain	16,052	4,783	16,742	5,442
New Haven	39,865	4,430	39,112	5,098
Norwalk	22,369	12,773	24,489	12,651
Shelton	8,362	10,327	9,655	10,428
Southington	10,727	10,452	12,066	9,845
Stamford	29,623	17,473	31,733	17,510
Stratford	13,483	9,324	14,626	10,199
Wallingford	11,560	9,259	12,833	9,372
Waterbury	20,931	11,043	22,599	12,821
West Hartford	21,069	10,511	23,576	10,021
West Haven	14,286	5,789	14,186	7,005
Other	483,805	425,569	546,493	414,675
Totals	**905,083**	**634,892**	**997,772**	**629,428**

Connecticut Vote Since 1960

2012: Obama, D, 905,083; Romney, R, 634,892; Johnson, LB, 12,580; Anderson, Ind., 5,487.
2008: Obama, D, 997,772; McCain, R, 629,428; Nader, Ind., 19,162.
2004: Kerry, D, 857,488; Bush, R, 693,826; Nader, petitioning cand., 12,969; Cobb, Green, 9,564; Badnarik, LB, 3,367; Peroutka, Concerned Citizens, 1,543.
2000: Gore, D, 816,015; Bush, R, 561,094; Nader, Green, 64,452; Phillips, Concerned Citizens, 9,695; Buchanan, RF, 4,731; Browne, LB, 3,484.
1996: Clinton, D, 735,740; Dole, R, 483,109; Perot, RF, 139,523; Nader, Green, 24,321; Browne, LB, 5,788; Phillips, Concerned Citizens, 2,425; Hagelin, Natural Law, 1,703.
1992: Clinton, D, 682,318; Bush, R, 578,313; Perot, Ind., 348,771; Marrou, LB, 5,391; Fulani, New Alliance, 1,363.
1988: Bush, R, 750,241; Dukakis, D, 676,584; Paul, LB, 14,071; Fulani, New Alliance, 2,491.
1984: Reagan, R, 890,877; Mondale, D, 569,597.
1980: Reagan, R, 677,210; Carter, D, 541,732; Anderson, Ind., 171,807; Clark, LB, 8,570; Commoner, Citizens, 6,130; scattered, 836.
1976: Ford, R, 719,261; Carter, D, 647,895; Maddox, George Wallace Party, 7,101; LaRouche, U.S. Labor, 1,789.
1972: Nixon, R, 810,763; McGovern, D, 555,498; Schmitz, Amer., 17,239; scattered, 777.
1968: Humphrey, D, 621,561; Nixon, R, 556,721; Wallace, 3rd party, 76,650; scattered, 1,300.
1964: Johnson, D, 826,269; Goldwater, R, 390,996; scattered, 1,313.
1960: Kennedy, D, 657,055; Nixon, R, 565,813.

Delaware

	2012		2008	
County	**Obama (D)**	**Romney (R)**	**Obama (D)**	**McCain (R)**
Kent	35,527	32,135	36,392	29,827
New Castle	167,082	81,230	178,768	74,608
Sussex	39,975	52,119	40,299	47,939
Totals	**242,584**	**165,484**	**255,459**	**152,374**

Delaware Vote Since 1960

2012: Obama, D, 242,584; Romney, R, 165,484; Johnson, LB, 3,882; Stein, Green, 1,940.
2008: Obama, D, 255,459; McCain, R, 152,374; Nader, Ind. (DE), 2,401; Barr, LB, 1,109; Baldwin, Const., 626; McKinney, Green, 385; Calero, Soc. Workers, 58.
2004: Kerry, D, 200,152; Bush, R, 171,660; Nader, Ind., 2,153; Badnarik, LB, 586; Peroutka, Const., 289; Cobb, Green, 250; Brown, Natural Law, 100.
2000: Gore, D, 180,068; Bush, R, 137,288; Nader, Green, 8,307; Buchanan, RF, 777; Browne, LB, 774; Phillips, Const., 208; Hagelin, Natural Law, 107.
1996: Clinton, D, 140,355; Dole, R, 99,062; Perot, RF, 28,719; Browne, LB, 2,052; Phillips, U.S. Taxpayers, 348; Hagelin, Natural Law, 274.
1992: Clinton, D, 126,054; Bush, R, 102,313; Perot, Ind., 59,213; Fulani, New Alliance, 1,105.
1988: Bush, R, 139,639; Dukakis, D, 108,647; Paul, LB, 1,162; Fulani, New Alliance, 443.
1984: Reagan, R, 152,190; Mondale, D, 101,656; Bergland, LB, 268.
1980: Reagan, R, 111,252; Carter, D, 105,754; Anderson, Ind., 16,288; Clark, LB, 1,974; Greaves, Amer., 400.
1976: Carter, D, 122,596; Ford, R, 109,831; McCarthy, nonpartisan, 2,437; Anderson, Amer., 645; LaRouche, U.S. Labor, 136; Bubar, Prohib., 103; Levin, Soc. Labor, 86.
1972: Nixon, R, 140,357; McGovern, D, 92,283; Schmitz, Amer., 2,638; Munn, Prohib., 238.
1968: Nixon, R, 96,714; Humphrey, D, 89,194; Wallace, 3rd party, 28,459.
1964: Johnson, D, 122,704; Goldwater, R, 78,078; Munn, Prohib., 425; Hass, Soc. Labor, 113.
1960: Kennedy, D, 99,590; Nixon, R, 96,373; Faubus, States' Rights, 354; Decker, Prohib., 284; Hass, Soc. Labor, 82.

District of Columbia

	2012		2008	
	Obama (D)	**Romney (R)**	**Obama (D)**	**McCain (R)**
Totals	**267,070**	**21,381**	**245,800**	**17,367**

District of Columbia Vote Since 1964

2012: Obama, D, 267,070; Romney, R, 21,381; Stein, DC Statehood Green, 2,458; Johnson, LB, 2,083.
2008: Obama, D, 245,800; McCain, R, 17,367; Nader, Ind., 958; McKinney, Green, 590.
2004: Kerry, D, 202,970; Bush, R, 21,256; Nader, Ind., 1,485; Cobb, DC Statehood Green, 737; Badnarik, LB, 502; Harris, Soc. Workers, 130.
2000: Gore, D, 171,923; Bush, R, 18,073; Nader, Green, 10,576; Browne, LB, 669; Harris, Soc. Workers, 114.
1996: Clinton, D, 158,220; Dole, R, 17,339; Nader, Green, 4,780; Perot, RF, 3,611; Browne, LB, 588; Hagelin, Natural Law, 283; Harris, Soc. Workers, 257.
1992: Clinton, D, 192,619; Bush, R, 20,698; Perot, Ind., 9,681; Fulani, New Alliance, 1,459; Daniels, Ind., 1,186.
1988: Dukakis, D, 159,407; Bush, R, 27,590; Fulani, New Alliance, 2,901; Paul, LB, 554.
1984: Mondale, D, 180,408; Reagan, R, 29,009; Bergland, LB, 279.
1980: Carter, D, 130,231; Reagan, R, 23,313; Anderson, Ind., 16,131; Commoner, Citizens, 1,826; Clark, LB, 1,104; Hall, Comm., 369; DeBerry, Soc. Workers, 173; Griswold, Workers World, 52; write-in, 690.
1976: Carter, D, 137,818; Ford, R, 27,873; Camejo, Soc. Workers, 545; MacBride, LB, 274; Hall, Comm., 219; LaRouche, U.S. Labor, 157.
1972: McGovern, D, 127,627; Nixon, R, 35,226; Reed, Soc. Workers, 316; Hall, Comm., 252.
1968: Humphrey, D, 139, 566; Nixon, R, 31,012.
1964: Johnson, D, 169,796; Goldwater, R, 28,801.

Florida

	2012		2008	
County	**Obama (D)**	**Romney (R)**	**Obama (D)**	**McCain (R)**
Alachua	69,699	48,797	75,565	48,513
Baker	2,311	8,975	2,327	8,672
Bay	22,051	56,876	23,653	56,683
Bradford	3,325	8,219	3,430	8,136
Brevard	122,993	159,300	127,620	157,589
Broward	508,312	244,101	492,640	237,729
Calhoun	1,664	4,366	1,821	4,345

County	2012 Obama (D)	2012 Romney (R)	2008 Obama (D)	2008 McCain (R)
Charlotte	35,906	47,996	39,031	45,205
Citrus	28,460	44,662	31,460	43,706
Clay	25,759	70,022	26,697	67,203
Collier	51,698	96,520	54,450	86,379
Columbia	8,462	18,429	9,171	18,670
De Soto	4,174	5,587	4,383	5,632
Dixie	1,798	5,052	1,925	5,194
Duval	196,737	211,615	202,618	210,537
Escambia	58,185	88,711	61,572	91,411
Flagler	23,207	26,969	24,726	23,951
Franklin	1,845	3,570	2,134	3,818
Gadsden	15,770	6,630	15,582	6,811
Gilchrist	1,885	5,917	1,996	5,656
Glades	1,603	2,344	1,381	1,938
Gulf	2,014	4,995	2,149	4,980
Hamilton	2,228	3,138	2,364	3,179
Hardee	2,463	4,696	2,568	4,763
Hendry	4,751	5,355	4,998	5,780
Hernando	37,830	44,938	41,886	45,021
Highlands	16,148	25,915	18,135	26,221
Hillsborough	286,467	250,186	272,963	236,355
Holmes	1,264	6,919	1,446	7,033
Indian River	27,492	43,450	29,710	40,176
Jackson	7,342	13,418	7,671	13,717
Jefferson	3,945	3,808	4,088	3,797
Lafayette	687	2,668	642	2,679
Lake	61,799	87,643	62,948	82,802
Lee	110,157	154,163	119,701	147,608
Leon	90,881	55,805	91,747	55,705
Levy	6,119	12,054	6,711	11,754
Liberty	942	2,301	895	2,339
Madison	4,176	4,474	4,270	4,544
Manatee	66,503	85,627	70,034	80,721
Marion	66,831	93,043	70,839	89,628
Martin	30,107	48,183	33,508	44,143
Miami-Dade	541,440	332,981	499,831	360,551
Monroe	19,404	19,234	20,907	18,933
Nassau	10,251	29,929	10,618	27,403
Okaloosa	23,421	70,168	25,872	68,789
Okeechobee	4,856	7,328	5,108	7,561
Orange	273,665	188,589	273,009	186,832
Osceola	67,239	40,592	59,962	40,086
Palm Beach	349,651	247,398	361,271	226,037
Pasco	98,263	112,427	102,417	110,104
Pinellas	239,104	213,258	248,299	210,066
Polk	114,622	131,577	113,865	128,878
Putnam	11,667	19,326	13,236	19,637
St. Johns	35,190	78,513	35,791	69,222
St. Lucie	65,869	56,202	67,125	52,512
Santa Rosa	17,768	58,186	19,470	55,972
Sarasota	95,119	110,504	102,686	102,897
Seminole	96,445	109,943	99,335	105,070
Sumter	19,524	40,646	17,655	30,866
Suwannee	4,751	12,672	4,916	12,534
Taylor	2,764	6,249	2,803	6,457
Union	1,339	3,980	1,300	3,940
Volusia	114,748	117,490	127,795	113,938
Wakulla	5,175	9,290	5,311	8,877
Walton	6,671	21,490	7,174	19,561
Washington	2,820	8,038	2,863	8,178
Totals	**4,237,756**	**4,163,447**	**4,282,074**	**4,045,624**

Florida Vote Since 1960

2012: Obama, D, 4,237,756; Romney, R, 4,163,447; Johnson, LB, 44,726; Stein, Green, 8,947; Barr, Peace/Freedom, 8,154; Stevens, Objectivist, 3,856; Goode, Const., 2,607; Anderson, Justice, 1,754; Hoefling, Amer. Ind., 946; Barnett, RF, 820; Alexander, Soc., 799; Lindsay, Socialism/Liberation, 322.

2008: Obama, D, 4,282,074; McCain, R, 4,045,624; Nader, Ecology (FL), 28,124; Barr, LB, 17,218; Baldwin, Const., 7,915; McKinney, Green, 2,887; Keyes, Amer. Ind., 2,550; La Riva, Socialism/Liberation, 1,516; Jay, Boston Tea, 795; Harris, Soc. Workers, 533; Stevens, Objectivist, 419; Moore, Soc. USA, 405; Amondson, Prohib., 293.

2004: Bush, R, 3,964,522; Kerry, D, 3,583,544; Nader, RF, 32,971; Badnarik, LB, 11,996; Peroutka, Const., 6,626; Cobb, Green, 3,917; Brown, Soc., 3,502; Harris, Soc. Workers, 2,732.

2000: Bush, R, 2,912,790; Gore, D, 2,912,253; Nader, Green, 97,488; Buchanan, RF, 17,484; Browne, LB, 16,415; Hagelin, Natural Law, 2,281; Moorehead, Workers World, 1,804; Phillips, Const., 1,371; McReynolds, Soc., 622; Harris, Soc. Workers, 562.

1996: Clinton, D, 2,545,968; Dole, R, 2,243,324; Perot, RF, 483,776; Browne, LB, 23,312.

1992: Bush, R, 2,171,781; Clinton, D, 2,071,651; Perot, Ind., 1,052,481; Marrou, LB, 15,068.

1988: Bush, R, 2,616,597; Dukakis, D, 1,655,851; Paul, LB, 19,796, Fulani, New Alliance, 6,655.

1984: Reagan, R, 2,728,775; Mondale, D, 1,448,344.

1980: Reagan, R, 2,046,951; Carter, D, 1,419,475; Anderson, Ind., 189,692; Clark, LB, 30,524; write-in, 285.

1976: Carter, D, 1,636,000; Ford, R, 1,469,531; McCarthy, Ind., 23,643; Anderson, Amer., 21,325.

1972: Nixon, R, 1,857,759; McGovern, D, 718,117; scattered, 7,407.

1968: Nixon, R, 886,804; Humphrey, D, 676,794; Wallace, 3rd party, 624,207.

1964: Johnson, D, 948,540; Goldwater, R, 905,941.

1960: Nixon, R, 795,476; Kennedy, D, 748,700.

Georgia

County	2012 Obama (D)	2012 Romney (R)	2008 Obama (D)	2008 McCain (R)
Appling	1,758	5,233	1,846	5,085
Atkinson	930	1,938	938	1,941
Bacon	791	3,093	817	3,089
Baker	794	785	846	828
Baldwin	8,483	7,589	8,587	7,823
Banks	780	5,354	1,027	5,120
Barrow	6,028	18,725	6,657	17,625
Bartow	8,396	26,876	9,662	25,976
Ben Hill	2,512	3,396	2,590	3,417
Berrien	1,273	4,843	1,471	4,901
Bibb	38,585	25,623	38,987	27,037
Bleckley	1,269	3,587	1,380	3,657
Brantley	939	4,964	1,119	5,080
Brooks	3,138	3,554	2,669	3,507
Bryan	3,707	9,560	3,636	9,112
Bulloch	9,593	14,174	9,586	14,174
Burke	5,405	4,301	5,233	4,344
Butts	2,968	6,306	3,065	5,947
Calhoun	1,298	883	1,342	862
Camden	6,377	11,343	6,482	10,502
Candler	1,157	2,344	1,209	2,286
Carroll	12,688	28,280	14,334	28,661
Catoosa	5,365	17,858	6,025	18,218
Charlton	1,197	2,527	1,197	2,466
Chatham	60,246	47,204	62,755	46,829
Chattahoochee	729	735	830	811
Chattooga	2,232	5,452	2,596	5,572
Cherokee	19,841	76,514	22,350	70,279
Clarke	25,431	13,815	29,591	15,333
Clay	862	537	879	558
Clayton	81,479	14,164	82,527	16,506
Clinch	852	1,598	989	1,678
Cobb	133,124	171,722	141,216	170,957
Coffee	5,057	9,248	4,811	8,872
Colquitt	3,973	9,243	4,139	9,185
Columbia	16,451	41,765	15,703	39,322
Cook	2,042	3,935	2,075	3,782
Coweta	15,168	39,653	15,521	37,571
Crawford	1,706	3,368	1,832	3,358
Crisp	3,167	4,182	3,085	4,424
Dade	1,411	4,471	1,612	4,703
Dawson	1,241	8,847	1,632	8,242
Decatur	4,591	5,824	4,424	5,890
DeKalb	238,224	64,392	254,594	65,581
Dodge	2,442	5,214	2,595	5,543
Dooly	2,285	1,985	2,138	1,991
Dougherty	26,295	11,449	26,135	12,547
Douglas	28,441	26,241	27,825	26,812
Early	2,765	2,557	2,603	2,711
Echols	173	917	201	981
Effingham	4,947	15,596	4,936	15,230
Elbert	3,181	4,859	3,366	4,868
Emanuel	2,927	5,100	3,068	5,110
Evans	1,268	2,268	1,374	2,462
Fannin	2,028	7,857	2,611	7,807
Fayette	19,736	38,075	20,313	38,501
Floyd	9,640	22,733	10,691	23,132
Forsyth	14,571	65,908	15,406	59,166
Franklin	1,499	6,114	1,914	6,069
Fulton	255,470	137,124	272,000	130,136
Gilmer	1,958	8,926	2,614	8,408
Glascock	176	1,135	210	1,202
Glynn	11,950	20,893	12,676	20,479
Gordon	3,440	13,197	4,268	13,113
Grady	3,419	5,924	3,539	5,775
Greene	3,201	5,071	3,339	4,532
Gwinnett	132,509	159,855	129,025	158,746
Habersham	2,301	12,166	2,900	11,766
Hall	12,999	47,481	14,457	44,962
Hancock	3,308	769	3,535	795
Haralson	1,789	8,446	2,248	8,658
Harris	4,145	11,197	4,184	10,648
Hart	2,870	6,517	3,365	6,537
Heard	948	3,160	1,042	3,133
Henry	43,761	46,774	40,567	47,157
Houston	22,702	34,662	22,094	33,392
Irwin	1,141	2,538	1,197	2,605
Jackson	4,238	19,135	4,950	17,776
Jasper	1,845	4,136	1,935	3,916

	2012		2008	
County	**Obama (D)**	**Romney (R)**	**Obama (D)**	**McCain (R)**
Jeff Davis	1,275	3,996	1,356	3,867
Jefferson	4,261	2,999	4,149	3,061
Jenkins	1,488	1,887	1,482	1,936
Johnson	1,305	2,440	1,198	2,426
Jones	4,274	7,744	4,572	7,782
Lamar	2,602	4,899	2,752	4,873
Lanier	1,114	1,820	1,062	1,787
Laurens	7,513	11,950	7,769	12,052
Lee	3,196	10,314	3,100	9,925
Liberty	10,457	5,565	10,474	5,828
Lincoln	1,586	2,807	1,650	2,731
Long	1,442	2,306	1,288	2,119
Lowndes	17,470	21,327	17,597	21,269
Lumpkin	2,055	8,647	2,586	8,326
Macon	3,211	1,545	3,251	1,712
Madison	2,494	8,443	2,965	8,226
Marion	1,412	1,733	1,381	1,772
McDuffie	4,044	5,475	3,989	5,400
McIntosh	2,864	3,409	2,905	3,282
Meriwether	4,331	4,856	4,465	4,982
Miller	852	1,905	818	1,899
Mitchell	4,081	4,155	3,872	4,201
Monroe	3,785	8,361	4,106	7,933
Montgomery	1,135	2,662	1,045	2,521
Morgan	2,753	6,186	3,091	5,987
Murray	2,542	8,443	3,026	8,180
Muscogee	42,573	27,510	44,158	29,568
Newton	21,851	20,982	20,827	20,337
Oconee	4,421	13,098	4,825	12,120
Oglethorpe	1,914	4,251	2,232	4,144
Paulding	15,825	40,846	17,229	39,192
Peach	6,148	5,287	5,927	5,173
Pickens	1,975	10,547	2,595	10,004
Pierce	1,124	5,667	1,253	5,500
Pike	1,356	6,668	1,575	6,547
Polk	3,615	9,811	4,052	9,850
Pulaski	1,219	2,444	1,377	2,553
Putnam	2,926	6,215	3,102	5,966
Quitman	612	510	597	509
Rabun	1,559	5,754	2,001	5,487
Randolph	1,770	1,271	1,833	1,370
Richmond	52,560	25,845	52,100	26,842
Rockdale	22,023	15,716	20,526	16,921
Schley	448	1,286	479	1,252
Screven	2,774	3,287	3,024	3,423
Seminole	1,478	2,245	1,660	2,315
Spalding	9,898	14,911	10,141	14,885
Stephens	2,131	7,221	2,705	7,689
Stewart	1,323	745	1,305	783
Sumter	6,375	5,378	6,454	5,717
Talbot	2,265	1,202	2,369	1,301
Taliaferro	636	323	643	339
Tattnall	1,897	4,706	1,932	4,730
Taylor	1,572	1,948	1,536	2,021
Telfair	1,805	2,480	1,862	2,486
Terrell	2,544	1,834	2,501	1,890
Thomas	7,653	11,156	7,720	10,642
Tift	4,660	9,185	4,749	9,431
Toombs	2,746	6,524	2,964	6,658
Towns	1,273	4,876	1,391	4,292
Treutlen	1,074	1,652	1,112	1,826
Troup	10,547	15,179	10,455	15,391
Turner	1,510	2,028	1,427	2,096
Twiggs	2,270	1,907	2,402	2,087
Union	2,139	8,773	2,486	8,013
Upson	3,959	7,230	4,061	7,291
Walker	5,274	16,247	6,095	17,110
Walton	8,148	29,036	8,469	27,253
Ware	3,900	7,941	4,034	8,311
Warren	1,529	990	1,554	1,087
Washington	4,714	4,035	4,607	4,216
Wayne	2,596	7,557	2,858	7,601
Webster	582	601	515	588
Wheeler	772	1,366	794	1,408
White	1,671	8,651	2,174	8,467
Whitfield	7,210	19,305	8,167	19,230
Wilcox	1,060	2,053	978	2,159
Wilkes	2,087	2,635	2,315	2,705
Wilkinson	2,181	2,246	2,298	2,349
Worth	2,487	5,869	2,542	5,780
Totals	**1,773,827**	**2,078,688**	**1,844,123**	**2,048,759**

Georgia Vote Since 1960

2012: Romney, R, 2,078,688; Obama, D, 1,773,827; Johnson, LB, 45,324.
2008: McCain, R, 2,048,759; Obama, D, 1,844,123; Barr, LB, 28,731.
2004: Bush, R, 1,914,254; Kerry, D, 1,366,149; Badnarik, LB, 18,387.
2000: Bush, R, 1,419,720; Gore, D, 1,116,230; Browne, LB, 36,332; Buchanan, Ind., 10,926.
1996: Dole, R, 1,080,843; Clinton, D, 1,053,849; Perot, RF, 146,337; Browne, LB, 17,870.
1992: Clinton, D, 1,008,966; Bush, R, 995,252; Perot, Ind., 309,657; Marrou, LB, 7,110.
1988: Bush, R, 1,081,331; Dukakis, D, 714,792; Paul, LB, 8,435; Fulani, New Alliance, 5,099.
1984: Reagan, R, 1,068,722; Mondale, D, 706,628.
1980: Carter, D, 890,955; Reagan, R, 654,168; Anderson, Ind., 36,055; Clark, LB, 15,627.
1976: Carter, D, 979,409; Ford, R, 483,743; write-in, 4,306.
1972: Nixon, R, 881,496; McGovern, D, 289,529; Schmitz, Amer., 812; scattered, 2,935.
1968: Wallace, 3rd party, 535,550; Nixon, R, 380,111; Humphrey, D, 334,440; write-in, 162.
1964: Goldwater, R, 616,600; Johnson, D, 522,557.
1960: Kennedy, D, 458,638; Nixon, R, 274,472; write-in, 239.

Hawaii

	2012		2008	
County	**Obama (D)**	**Romney (R)**	**Obama (D)**	**McCain (R)**
Hawaii	47,224	14,753	50,819	14,866
Honolulu	204,349	88,461	214,909	88,301
Kauai	18,641	6,121	20,416	6,245
Maui	36,052	11,602	39,727	11,154
Overseas	392	78	NA	NA
Totals	**306,658**	**121,015**	**325,871**	**120,566**

Hawaii Vote Since 1960

2012: Obama, D, 306,658; Romney, R, 121,015; Johnson, LB, 3,840; Stein, Green, 3,184.
2008: Obama, D, 325,871; McCain, R, 120,566; Nader, Ind. (HI), 3,825; Barr, LB, 1,314; Baldwin, Const., 1,013; McKinney, Green, 979.
2004: Kerry, D, 231,708; Bush, R, 194,191; Cobb, Green, 1,737; Badnarik, LB, 1,377.
2000: Gore, D, 205,286; Bush, R, 137,845; Nader, Green, 21,623; Browne, LB, 1,477; Buchanan, RF, 1,071; Phillips, Const., 343; Hagelin, Natural Law, 306.
1996: Clinton, D, 205,012; Dole, R, 113,943; Perot, RF, 27,358; Nader, Green, 10,386; Browne, LB, 2,493; Hagelin, Natural Law, 570; Phillips, Taxpayers, 358.
1992: Clinton, D, 179,310; Bush, R, 136,822; Perot, Ind., 53,003; Gritz, Populist/America First, 1,452; Marrou, LB, 1,119.
1988: Dukakis, D, 192,364; Bush, R, 158,625; Paul, LB, 1,999; Fulani, New Alliance, 1,003.
1984: Reagan, R, 184,934; Mondale, D, 147,098; Bergland, LB, 2,167.
1980: Carter, D, 135,879; Reagan, R, 130,112; Anderson, Ind., 32,021; Clark, LB, 3,269; Commoner, Citizens, 1,548; Hall, Comm., 458.
1976: Carter, D, 147,375; Ford, R, 140,003; MacBride, LB, 3,923.
1972: Nixon, R, 168,865; McGovern, D, 101,409.
1968: Humphrey, D, 141,324; Nixon, R, 91,425; Wallace, 3rd party, 3,469.
1964: Johnson, D, 163,249; Goldwater, R, 44,022.
1960: Kennedy, D, 92,410; Nixon, R, 92,295.

Idaho

	2012		2008	
County	**Obama (D)**	**Romney (R)**	**Obama (D)**	**McCain (R)**
Ada	77,137	97,554	82,236	93,328
Adams	577	1,413	728	1,517
Bannock	13,214	21,010	14,792	19,356
Bear Lake	302	2,489	502	2,377
Benewah	1,164	2,596	1,407	2,646
Bingham	3,822	13,440	4,424	12,230
Blaine	5,992	3,939	6,947	3,439
Boise	1,053	2,284	1,240	2,433
Bonner	6,500	11,367	7,840	11,145
Bonneville	9,903	32,276	11,417	29,334
Boundary	1,225	3,138	1,484	3,078
Butte	258	1,001	318	1,056
Camas	159	402	187	422
Canyon	19,866	44,369	20,147	42,752
Caribou	386	2,608	553	2,656
Cassia	1,098	7,154	1,332	6,309
Clark	66	235	64	305
Clearwater	1,032	2,541	1,211	2,569
Custer	530	1,744	611	1,694
Elmore	2,513	5,227	2,591	5,665
Franklin	325	5,195	600	4,246
Fremont	810	4,907	1,065	4,700
Gem	1,957	5,311	2,166	5,585
Gooding	1,287	3,696	1,489	3,765
Idaho	1,708	5,921	2,017	5,895

	2012		2008	
County	Obama (D)	Romney (R)	Obama (D)	McCain (R)
Jefferson	1,303	9,895	1,641	8,540
Jerome	1,699	4,804	1,794	4,897
Kootenai	18,851	39,381	22,120	38,387
Latah	8,306	7,589	9,195	7,988
Lemhi	960	3,029	1,061	2,938
Lewis	396	1,173	479	1,275
Lincoln	469	1,141	545	1,232
Madison	832	13,445	1,627	11,131
Minidoka	1,390	5,442	1,630	5,087
Nez Perce	6,451	9,967	7,123	10,357
Oneida	217	1,838	381	1,724
Owyhee	833	2,794	944	3,024
Payette	2,271	6,004	2,415	5,988
Power	982	1,870	1,027	1,754
Shoshone	2,277	2,699	2,521	2,953
Teton	1,926	2,458	2,302	2,263
Twin Falls	7,541	19,773	8,621	19,032
Valley	2,095	2,664	2,405	2,772
Washington	1,104	3,128	1,241	3,168
Totals	**212,787**	**420,911**	**236,440**	**403,012**

Idaho Vote Since 1960

2012: Romney, R, 420,911; Obama, D, 212,787; Johnson, LB, 9,453; Stein, Ind., 4,402; Anderson, Ind., 2,499; Goode, Const., 2,222.
2008: McCain, R, 403,012; Obama, D, 236,440; Nader, Ind., 7,175; Baldwin, Const., 4,747; Barr, LB, 3,658.
2004: Bush, R, 409,235; Kerry, D, 181,098; Badnarik, LB, 3,844; Peroutka, Const., 3,084.
2000: Bush, R, 336,937; Gore, D, 138,637; Buchanan, RF, 7,615; Browne, LB, 3,488; Phillips, Const., 1,469; Hagelin, Natural Law, 1,177.
1996: Dole, R, 256,595; Clinton, D, 165,443; Perot, RF, 62,518; Browne, LB, 3,325; Phillips, U.S. Taxpayers, 2,230; Hagelin, Natural Law, 1,600.
1992: Bush, R, 202,645; Clinton, D, 137,013; Perot, Ind., 130,395; Gritz, Populist/America First, 10,281; Marrou, LB, 1,167.
1988: Bush, R, 253,881; Dukakis, D, 147,272; Paul, LB, 5,313; Fulani, Ind., 2,502.
1984: Reagan, R, 297,523; Mondale, D, 108,510; Bergland, LB, 2,823.
1980: Reagan, R, 290,699; Carter, D, 110,192; Anderson, Ind., 27,058; Clark, LB, 8,425; Rarick, Amer., 1,057.
1976: Ford, R, 204,151; Carter, D, 126,549; Maddox, Amer., 5,935; MacBride, LB, 3,558; LaRouche, U.S. Labor, 739.
1972: Nixon, R, 199,384; McGovern, D, 80,826; Schmitz, Amer., 28,869; Spock, People's, 903.
1968: Nixon, R, 165,369; Humphrey, D, 89,273; Wallace, 3rd party, 36,541.
1964: Johnson, D, 148,920; Goldwater, R, 143,557.
1960: Nixon, R, 161,597; Kennedy, D, 138,853.

Illinois

	2012		2008	
County	Obama (D)	Romney (R)	Obama (D)	McCain (R)
Adams	9,648	20,416	11,794	18,711
Alexander	1,965	1,487	2,189	1,692
Bond	3,020	4,095	3,843	3,947
Boone	9,883	11,096	11,333	10,403
Brown	787	1,513	986	1,544
Bureau	8,134	8,164	8,889	7,911
Calhoun	1,080	1,440	1,423	1,221
Carroll	3,665	3,555	3,965	3,596
Cass	2,053	2,707	2,690	2,617
Champaign	40,831	35,312	48,597	33,871
Christian	5,494	8,885	6,918	7,872
Clark	2,591	5,144	3,742	4,409
Clay	1,584	4,190	2,425	3,926
Clinton	5,596	10,524	7,657	9,357
Coles	9,262	11,631	11,716	10,978
Cook	1,488,537	495,542	1,629,024	487,736
Crawford	2,358	5,585	3,883	5,070
Cumberland	1,641	3,509	2,055	3,156
DeKalb	21,207	18,934	25,784	18,266
DeWitt	2,601	4,579	3,308	4,348
Douglas	2,430	5,334	3,228	5,005
DuPage	199,460	195,046	228,698	183,626
Edgar	2,565	5,132	3,743	4,398
Edwards	754	2,405	1,140	2,137
Effingham	3,861	12,501	5,262	11,323
Fayette	2,853	5,951	3,967	5,499
Ford	1,656	4,229	2,227	4,079
Franklin	7,254	10,267	8,880	9,404
Fulton	8,328	6,632	9,732	6,251
Gallatin	1,029	1,492	1,587	1,212
Greene	2,023	3,451	2,619	3,053
Grundy	9,451	11,343	11,063	10,687
Hamilton	1,269	2,566	1,796	2,353
Hancock	3,650	5,271	4,141	5,161
Hardin	742	1,535	892	1,330
Henderson	1,978	1,541	2,215	1,541
Henry	12,332	11,583	13,181	11,263
Iroquois	3,413	9,120	4,643	8,695
Jackson	13,319	9,864	15,248	9,687
Jasper	1,436	3,514	2,063	2,964
Jefferson	6,089	9,811	7,462	9,302
Jersey	3,667	6,039	5,042	5,329
Jo Daviess	5,667	5,534	6,403	5,170
Johnson	1,572	3,963	1,871	3,912
Kane	90,332	88,335	106,756	83,963
Kankakee	21,595	23,136	24,750	22,527
Kendall	22,471	24,047	24,742	21,380
Knox	13,451	9,408	14,191	9,419
Lake	153,757	129,764	177,242	118,545
LaSalle	23,073	23,256	27,443	21,872
Lawrence	2,011	3,857	3,016	3,403
Lee	6,937	8,059	7,765	8,258
Livingston	5,020	9,753	6,189	9,191
Logan	3,978	7,844	5,250	7,429
Macon	22,780	25,309	25,487	24,948
Macoupin	9,464	10,946	12,090	9,891
Madison	58,922	60,608	68,979	57,177
Marion	6,225	9,248	8,345	8,691
Marshall	2,455	3,290	3,081	3,145
Mason	2,867	3,265	3,542	3,141
Massac	2,092	4,278	2,693	4,371
McDonough	5,967	6,147	6,783	6,055
McHenry	59,797	71,598	72,288	64,845
McLean	31,883	39,947	37,689	36,767
Menard	2,100	3,948	2,706	3,672
Mercer	4,507	3,876	4,887	3,833
Monroe	6,215	10,888	7,953	9,881
Montgomery	5,058	6,776	6,491	6,150
Morgan	5,806	7,972	7,467	7,591
Moultrie	2,144	3,784	2,668	3,471
Ogle	9,514	13,422	11,253	13,144
Peoria	40,209	36,774	45,906	34,579
Perry	3,819	5,507	4,701	5,086
Piatt	3,090	5,413	3,859	4,991
Pike	2,278	4,860	3,024	4,457
Pope	650	1,512	845	1,343
Pulaski	1,389	1,564	1,638	1,593
Putnam	1,559	1,502	1,900	1,378
Randolph	5,759	8,290	7,395	7,538
Richland	2,362	4,756	3,181	4,329
Rock Island	39,157	24,934	42,210	25,364
St. Clair	67,285	50,125	76,160	47,958
Saline	3,701	6,806	5,083	6,099
Sangamon	42,107	50,225	51,300	46,945
Schuyler	1,727	2,069	1,900	1,833
Scott	910	1,587	1,090	1,455
Shelby	3,342	6,843	4,245	6,396
Stark	1,095	1,528	1,357	1,513
Stephenson	10,165	10,512	11,349	9,909
Tazewell	24,438	35,335	29,384	33,247
Union	3,137	4,957	3,918	5,003
Vermilion	12,878	16,892	16,246	16,054
Wabash	1,590	3,478	2,462	3,254
Warren	4,044	3,618	4,286	3,637
Washington	2,450	4,792	3,342	4,473
Wayne	1,514	5,988	2,547	5,390
White	2,188	4,731	3,315	3,987
Whiteside	14,833	10,448	15,607	10,883
Will	144,229	128,969	160,406	122,597
Williamson	10,647	17,909	12,914	17,387
Winnebago	61,732	55,138	70,034	53,886
Woodford	5,572	12,961	6,999	12,191
Totals	**3,019,512**	**2,135,216**	**3,419,348**	**2,031,179**

Illinois Vote Since 1960

2012: Obama, D, 3,019,512; Romney, R, 2,135,216; Johnson, LB, 56,229; Stein, Green, 30,222.
2008: Obama, D, 3,419,348; McCain, R, 2,031,179; Nader, Ind., 30,948; Barr, LB, 19,642; McKinney, Green, 11,838; Baldwin, Const., 8,256; Polachek, New Party, 1,149.
2004: Kerry, D, 2,891,550; Bush, R, 2,345,946; Badnarik, LB, 32,442.
2000: Gore, D, 2,589,026; Bush, R, 2,019,421; Nader, Green, 103,759; Buchanan, Ind., 16,106; Browne, LB, 11,623; Hagelin, RF, 2,127.
1996: Clinton, D, 2,341,744; Dole, R, 1,587,021; Perot, RF, 346,408; Browne, LB, 22,548; Phillips, U.S. Taxpayers, 7,606; Hagelin, Natural Law, 4,606.

1992: Clinton, D, 2,453,350; Bush, R, 1,734,096; Perot, Ind., 840,515; Marrou, LB, 9,218; Fulani, New Alliance, 5,267; Gritz, Populist/America First, 3,577; Hagelin, Natural Law, 2,751; Warren, Soc. Workers, 1,361.
1988: Bush, R, 2,310,939; Dukakis, D, 2,215,940; Paul, LB, 14,944; Fulani, Solidarity, 10,276.
1984: Reagan, R, 2,707,103; Mondale, D, 2,086,499; Bergland, LB, 10,086.
1980: Reagan, R, 2,358,049; Carter, D, 1,981,413; Anderson, Ind., 346,754; Clark, LB, 38,939; Commoner, Citizens, 10,692; Hall, Comm., 9,711; Griswold, Workers World, 2,257; DeBerry, Soc. Workers, 1,302; write-in, 604.
1976: Ford, R, 2,364,269; Carter, D, 2,271,295; McCarthy, Ind., 55,939; Hall, Comm., 9,250; MacBride, LB, 8,057; Camejo, Soc. Workers, 3,615; Levin, Soc. Labor, 2,422; LaRouche, U.S. Labor, 2,018; write-in, 1,968.
1972: Nixon, R. 2,788,179; McGovern, D, 1,913,472; Fisher, Soc. Labor, 12,344; Hall, Comm., 4,541; Schmitz, Amer., 2,471; others, 2,229.
1968: Nixon, R, 2,174,774; Humphrey, D, 2,039,814; Wallace, 3rd party, 390,958; Blomen, Soc. Labor, 13,878; write-in, 325.
1964: Johnson, D, 2,796,833; Goldwater, R, 1,905,946; write-in, 62.
1960: Kennedy, D, 2,377,846; Nixon, R, 2,368,988; Hass, Soc. Labor, 10,560; write-in, 15.

Indiana

	2012		2008	
County	**Obama (D)**	**Romney (R)**	**Obama (D)**	**McCain (R)**
Adams	3,806	8,937	4,928	8,404
Allen	60,036	84,613	71,263	77,793
Bartholomew	10,625	18,083	13,567	17,067
Benton	1,159	2,329	1,563	2,183
Blackford	1,927	2,711	2,677	2,690
Boone	8,328	18,808	9,752	16,622
Brown	3,060	4,332	3,854	4,060
Carroll	2,635	4,999	3,736	4,858
Cass	5,371	8,443	7,011	8,346
Clark	20,807	25,450	21,953	25,326
Clay	3,460	7,096	4,954	6,267
Clinton	3,308	6,338	5,307	6,919
Crawford	2,041	2,421	2,286	2,393
Daviess	2,437	7,638	3,370	7,098
Dearborn	6,528	15,394	7,123	14,886
Decatur	2,941	7,119	3,892	6,449
DeKalb	5,419	10,587	7,175	9,780
Delaware	22,654	21,251	28,384	20,916
Dubois	6,522	11,654	8,748	9,526
Elkhart	24,399	42,378	31,398	39,396
Fayette	3,555	5,045	4,389	4,917
Floyd	14,812	19,878	16,263	19,957
Fountain	2,237	4,664	3,094	4,158
Franklin	2,909	7,424	3,404	7,018
Fulton	2,621	5,317	3,702	5,147
Gibson	4,928	9,487	6,455	8,449
Grant	9,589	15,151	11,293	14,734
Greene	4,350	8,457	5,709	7,691
Hamilton	43,796	90,747	49,704	78,401
Hancock	9,319	22,796	11,874	22,008
Harrison	6,607	10,640	7,288	10,551
Hendricks	21,112	44,312	24,548	39,728
Henry	7,613	10,838	10,059	10,896
Howard	15,135	20,327	17,871	20,248
Huntington	4,596	10,862	5,843	10,291
Jackson	5,838	10,419	7,354	9,726
Jasper	4,672	7,955	5,044	7,669
Jay	3,063	4,645	3,748	4,401
Jefferson	5,728	7,096	6,255	7,053
Jennings	3,821	6,120	5,312	6,261
Johnson	17,260	39,513	21,553	36,487
Knox	5,228	9,612	7,569	8,639
Kosciusko	6,862	22,558	9,236	20,488
LaGrange	2,898	6,231	3,663	5,702
Lake	130,897	68,431	139,301	67,742
LaPorte	24,107	18,615	28,258	17,918
Lawrence	5,779	11,622	7,208	11,018
Madison	24,407	26,769	30,152	26,403
Marion	216,336	136,509	241,987	134,313
Marshall	6,137	11,260	7,889	10,406
Martin	1,351	3,262	1,706	3,122
Miami	4,222	8,174	5,564	8,312
Monroe	33,436	22,481	41,450	21,118
Montgomery	4,271	9,824	6,013	9,060
Morgan	7,969	19,591	10,330	18,129
Newton	2,212	3,291	2,625	3,301
Noble	5,229	10,680	7,064	9,673
Ohio	994	1,759	1,158	1,713
Orange	2,939	4,617	3,390	4,536
Owen	2,823	5,062	3,570	4,415
Parke	2,110	4,234	2,924	3,909
Perry	4,316	3,403	5,141	3,202
Pike	2,125	3,627	2,700	3,221
Porter	37,252	34,406	39,178	33,857
Posey	4,533	7,430	5,828	6,804
Pulaski	1,899	3,366	2,466	3,388
Putnam	4,507	9,005	6,334	8,086
Randolph	3,769	6,218	4,839	5,788
Ripley	3,241	7,484	4,187	7,794
Rush	2,221	4,633	3,229	4,271
St. Joseph	56,460	52,578	68,710	48,510
Scott	3,998	4,539	4,271	4,445
Shelby	5,359	10,978	6,987	10,333
Spencer	4,026	5,515	5,039	5,001
Starke	3,809	4,738	4,778	4,473
Steuben	4,853	8,547	6,284	7,674
Sullivan	3,191	4,902	4,284	4,343
Switzerland	1,437	1,872	1,638	1,940
Tippecanoe	26,711	28,757	37,781	29,822
Tipton	2,432	4,773	3,250	4,452
Union	1,018	2,022	1,224	2,061
Vanderburgh	31,725	39,389	39,423	37,512
Vermillion	2,979	3,426	4,003	3,010
Vigo	19,712	19,369	25,040	18,121
Wabash	3,973	8,644	5,456	8,238
Warren	1,324	2,377	1,755	2,166
Warrick	8,793	15,351	12,329	16,013
Washington	3,909	6,533	4,562	6,519
Wayne	10,591	14,321	13,459	14,558
Wells	3,436	9,256	4,403	8,504
White	3,637	5,970	4,839	5,731
Whitley	4,420	10,258	5,862	9,124
Totals	**1,152,887**	**1,420,543**	**1,374,039**	**1,345,648**

Indiana Vote Since 1960

2012: Romney, R, 1,420,543; Obama, D, 1,152,887; Johnson, LB, 50,111.
2008: Obama, D, 1,374,039; McCain, R, 1,345,648; Barr, LB, 29,257.
2004: Bush, R, 1,479,438; Kerry, D, 969,011; Badnarik, LB, 18,058.
2000: Bush, R, 1,245,836; Gore, D, 901,980; Buchanan, Ind., 16,959; Browne, LB, 15,530.
1996: Dole, R, 1,006,693; Clinton, D, 887,424; Perot, RF, 224,299; Browne, LB, 15,632.
1992: Bush, R, 989,375; Clinton, D, 848,420; Perot, Ind., 455,934; Marrou, LB, 7,936; Fulani, New Alliance, 2,583.
1988: Bush, R, 1,297,763; Dukakis, D, 860,643; Fulani, New Alliance, 10,215.
1984: Reagan, R, 1,377,230; Mondale, D, 841,481; Bergland, LB, 6,741.
1980: Reagan, R, 1,255,656; Carter, D, 844,197; Anderson, Ind., 111,639; Clark, LB, 19,627; Commoner, Citizens, 4,852; Greaves, Amer., 4,750; Hall, Comm., 702; DeBerry, Soc., 610.
1976: Ford, R, 1,185,958; Carter, D, 1,014,714; Anderson, Amer., 14,048; Camejo, Soc. Workers, 5,695; LaRouche, U.S. Labor, 1,947.
1972: Nixon, R, 1,405,154; McGovern, D, 708,568; Reed, Soc. Workers, 5,575; Spock, Peace/Freedom, 4,544; Fisher, Soc. Labor, 1,688.
1968: Nixon, R, 1,067,885; Humphrey, D, 806,659; Wallace, 3rd party, 243,108; Munn, Prohib., 4,616; Halstead, Soc. Workers, 1,293; Gregory, write-in, 36.
1964: Johnson, D, 1,170,848; Goldwater, R, 911,118; Munn, Prohib., 8,266; Hass, Soc. Labor, 1,374.
1960: Nixon, R, 1,175,120; Kennedy, D, 952,358; Decker, Prohib., 6,746; Hass, Soc. Labor, 1,136.

Iowa

	2012		2008	
County	**Obama (D)**	**Romney (R)**	**Obama (D)**	**McCain (R)**
Adair	1,790	2,114	1,924	2,060
Adams	1,028	1,108	1,118	1,046
Allamakee	3,553	3,264	3,971	2,965
Appanoose	2,951	3,161	2,970	3,086
Audubon	1,611	1,802	1,739	1,634
Benton	6,862	6,940	7,058	6,447
Black Hawk	39,821	26,235	39,184	24,662
Boone	7,512	6,556	7,356	6,293
Bremer	6,763	6,405	6,940	5,741
Buchanan	5,911	4,450	6,050	4,139
Buena Vista	3,700	4,554	4,075	4,223
Butler	3,329	4,106	3,364	3,700
Calhoun	2,238	2,891	2,341	2,741
Carroll	4,947	5,601	5,302	4,922

	2012		2008	
County	**Obama (D)**	**Romney (R)**	**Obama (D)**	**McCain (R)**
Cass	2,858	4,217	3,211	4,006
Cedar	4,972	4,529	5,221	4,289
Cerro Gordo	13,316	10,128	14,405	9,375
Cherokee	2,634	3,662	2,890	3,372
Chickasaw	3,554	2,836	3,923	2,557
Clarke	2,189	2,124	2,218	2,118
Clay	3,385	4,951	3,925	4,355
Clayton	4,806	4,164	5,195	3,651
Clinton	15,141	9,432	15,018	9,324
Crawford	3,066	3,595	3,715	3,345
Dallas	16,576	20,988	15,149	16,954
Davis	1,520	2,138	1,680	2,029
Decatur	1,791	1,947	1,986	2,020
Delaware	4,616	4,636	4,649	4,113
Des Moines	11,888	8,136	12,462	7,721
Dickinson	4,095	5,912	4,625	5,162
Dubuque	28,768	21,280	28,611	18,651
Emmet	2,099	2,507	2,570	2,373
Fayette	5,732	4,492	5,908	4,205
Floyd	4,680	3,472	4,822	3,051
Franklin	2,266	2,823	2,575	2,501
Fremont	1,637	1,972	1,848	1,989
Greene	2,375	2,380	2,371	2,349
Grundy	2,635	4,215	2,790	3,945
Guthrie	2,569	3,171	2,625	3,074
Hamilton	3,782	3,991	4,018	3,913
Hancock	2,521	3,317	2,805	3,016
Hardin	4,075	4,670	4,393	4,315
Harrison	3,136	4,065	3,555	3,909
Henry	4,460	5,035	4,349	4,822
Howard	2,768	1,795	2,941	1,722
Humboldt	1,972	3,099	2,160	2,895
Ida	1,321	2,286	1,454	2,036
Iowa	4,144	4,569	4,202	4,188
Jackson	5,907	4,177	6,102	3,673
Jasper	10,257	8,877	10,250	8,794
Jefferson	4,798	3,436	5,070	3,324
Johnson	50,666	23,698	51,027	20,732
Jones	5,534	4,721	5,446	4,405
Keokuk	2,303	2,843	2,518	2,712
Kossuth	3,850	4,937	4,625	4,329
Lee	10,714	7,785	9,821	7,062
Linn	68,581	47,622	68,037	43,626
Louisa	2,452	2,420	2,523	2,314
Lucas	1,987	2,254	2,029	2,330
Lyon	1,423	4,978	1,675	4,471
Madison	3,630	4,638	3,733	4,579
Mahaska	4,213	6,448	4,464	6,271
Marion	7,507	9,828	7,421	9,256
Marshall	10,257	8,472	10,023	8,278
Mills	2,848	4,216	2,976	4,183
Mitchell	2,831	2,643	3,179	2,469
Monona	2,101	2,557	2,295	2,411
Monroe	1,731	2,026	1,798	2,000
Montgomery	1,922	3,001	2,326	2,887
Muscatine	11,323	8,168	10,920	7,929
O'Brien	1,969	5,266	2,338	4,894
Osceola	912	2,230	1,037	2,027
Page	2,613	4,348	2,900	4,351
Palo Alto	2,139	2,660	2,428	2,294
Plymouth	4,164	8,597	4,629	7,765
Pocahontas	1,523	2,396	1,800	2,138
Polk	128,465	96,096	120,984	89,668
Pottawattamie	19,644	21,860	20,436	21,237
Poweshiek	5,357	4,424	5,519	4,340
Ringgold	1,186	1,368	1,236	1,401
Sac	2,122	3,094	2,256	2,705
Scott	50,652	38,251	48,927	36,365
Shelby	2,469	3,911	2,863	3,488
Sioux	2,700	14,407	3,030	13,490
Story	26,192	19,668	26,548	18,995
Tama	4,768	4,098	4,899	3,820
Taylor	1,262	1,683	1,347	1,607
Union	3,043	2,813	3,000	2,781
Van Buren	1,402	2,064	1,546	1,986
Wapello	8,663	6,789	8,820	6,663
Warren	12,551	13,052	12,299	12,144
Washington	5,115	5,562	5,170	5,247
Wayne	1,251	1,583	1,357	1,565
Webster	9,537	8,469	9,917	8,337
Winnebago	2,903	2,906	3,254	2,730
Winneshiek	6,256	4,622	6,829	4,273
Woodbury	22,302	21,841	21,983	22,219
Worth	2,350	1,744	2,567	1,612
Wright	2,836	3,349	3,102	3,198
Totals	**822,544**	**730,617**	**828,940**	**682,379**

Iowa Vote Since 1960

2012: Obama, D, 822,544; Romney, R, 730,617; Johnson, LB, 12,926; Stein, Green, 3,769; Goode, Const., 3,038; Litzel, Ind., 1,027; Harris, Soc. Workers, 445; La Riva, Socialism/Liberation, 372.

2008: Obama, D, 828,940; McCain, R, 682,379; Nader, Peace/Freedom, 8,014; Barr, LB, 4,590; Baldwin, Const., 4,445; McKinney, Green, 1,423; Harris, Soc. Workers, 292; Moore, Soc. USA, 182; La Riva, Socialism/Liberation, 121.

2004: Bush, R, 751,957; Kerry, D, 741,898; Nader, petitioning cand., 5,973; Badnarik, LB, 2,992; Peroutka, Const., 1,304; Cobb, Green, 1,141; Harris, Soc. Workers, 373; Van Auken, petitioning cand., 176.

2000: Gore, D, 638,517; Bush, R, 634,373; Nader, Green, 29,374; Buchanan, RF, 5,731; Browne, LB, 3,209; Hagelin, Ind., 2,281; Phillips, Const., 613; Harris, Soc. Workers, 190; McReynolds, Soc., 107.

1996: Clinton, D, 620,258; Dole, R, 492,644; Perot, RF, 105,159; Nader, Green, 6,550; Hagelin, Natural Law, 3,349; Browne, LB, 2,315; Phillips, Taxpayers, 2,229; Harris, Soc. Workers, 331.

1992: Clinton, D, 586,353; Bush, R, 504,891; Perot, Ind., 253,468; Hagelin, Natural Law, 3,079; Gritz, Populist/America First, 1,177; Marrou, LB, 1,076.

1988: Dukakis, D, 670,557; Bush, R, 545,355; LaRouche, Ind., 3,526; Paul, LB, 2,494.

1984: Reagan, R, 703,088; Mondale, D, 605,620; Bergland, LB, 1,844.

1980: Reagan, R, 676,026; Carter, D, 508,672; Anderson, Ind., 115,633; Clark, LB, 13,123; Commoner, Citizens, 2,273; McReynolds, Soc., 534; Hall, Comm., 298; DeBerry, Soc. Workers, 244; Greaves, Amer., 189; Bubar, Statesman, 150; scattered, 519.

1976: Ford, R, 632,863; Carter, D, 619,931; McCarthy, Ind., 20,051; Anderson, Amer., 3,040; MacBride, LB, 1,452.

1972: Nixon, R, 706,207; McGovern, D, 496,206; Schmitz, Amer., 22,056; Jenness, Soc. Workers, 488; Hall, Comm., 272; Green, Universal, 199; Fisher, Soc. Labor, 195; scattered, 321.

1968: Nixon, R, 619,106; Humphrey, D, 476,699; Wallace, 3rd party, 66,422; Halstead, Soc. Workers, 3,377; Cleaver, Peace/Freedom, 1,332; Munn, Prohib., 362; Blomen, Soc. Labor, 241.

1964: Johnson, D, 733,030; Goldwater, R, 449,148; Munn, Prohib., 1,902; Hass, Soc. Labor, 182; DeBerry, Soc. Workers, 159.

1960: Nixon, R, 722,381; Kennedy, D, 550,565; Hass, Soc. Labor, 230; write-in, 634.

Kansas

	2012		2008	
County	**Obama (D)**	**Romney (R)**	**Obama (D)**	**McCain (R)**
Allen	1,869	3,316	2,189	3,552
Anderson	944	2,276	1,175	2,362
Atchison	2,567	3,917	3,241	3,791
Barber	482	1,772	598	1,833
Barton	2,297	7,874	3,027	7,802
Bourbon	1,996	4,102	2,394	4,240
Brown	1,076	2,829	1,317	2,985
Butler	7,282	18,157	9,159	18,155
Chase	358	875	383	976
Chautauqua	280	1,304	401	1,418
Cherokee	2,930	5,456	3,594	5,886
Cheyenne	233	1,159	323	1,148
Clark	174	805	245	897
Clay	834	2,788	1,009	2,998
Cloud	974	2,954	1,233	3,121
Coffey	898	2,903	1,121	3,054
Comanche	143	767	194	765
Cowley	4,319	8,081	5,012	8,492
Crawford	6,826	7,708	7,957	7,735
Decatur	266	1,218	343	1,189
Dickinson	2,020	5,832	2,422	6,081
Doniphan	902	2,414	1,115	2,372
Douglas	29,267	17,401	34,398	17,929
Edwards	298	1,059	333	995
Elk	281	1,049	363	1,042
Ellis	3,057	8,399	4,010	8,207
Ellsworth	702	1,930	851	2,021
Finney	2,682	6,219	3,275	6,926
Ford	2,600	5,602	2,991	5,730
Franklin	3,694	6,984	4,433	7,079
Geary	3,332	4,372	3,491	4,492
Gove	176	1,168	261	1,136
Graham	256	1,056	325	1,060
Grant	456	1,811	635	1,995
Gray	324	1,603	436	1,643
Greeley	113	543	151	591
Greenwood	478	1,590	622	1,619
Hamilton	163	693	233	844
Harper	550	1,759	736	1,999
Harvey	5,373	8,588	6,318	9,006

County	2012 Obama (D)	2012 Romney (R)	2008 Obama (D)	2008 McCain (R)
Haskell	215	1,159	278	1,277
Hodgeman	179	868	211	865
Jackson	1,901	3,527	2,308	3,811
Jefferson	2,977	4,827	3,542	5,220
Jewell	229	1,235	313	1,231
Johnson	110,526	158,401	127,091	152,627
Kearny	268	1,097	309	1,159
Kingman	733	2,397	963	2,603
Kiowa	163	976	200	912
Labette	3,117	4,742	3,839	5,001
Lane	172	739	193	814
Leavenworth	11,357	17,059	13,255	16,791
Lincoln	289	1,165	347	1,204
Linn	1,170	3,177	1,425	3,086
Logan	197	1,126	225	1,187
Lyon	5,111	6,470	5,924	6,698
Marion	1,385	3,889	1,801	4,159
Marshall	1,469	3,195	1,784	3,157
McPherson	3,449	8,545	4,218	8,937
Meade	258	1,428	357	1,540
Miami	4,712	9,858	5,742	9,382
Mitchell	584	2,327	701	2,440
Montgomery	3,501	8,630	4,338	9,309
Morris	718	1,773	907	1,875
Morton	189	1,072	229	1,153
Nemaha	1,000	3,930	1,432	3,817
Neosho	2,050	4,272	2,563	4,473
Ness	218	1,209	289	1,207
Norton	398	1,878	497	1,878
Osage	2,268	4,427	2,534	4,820
Osborne	324	1,479	403	1,490
Ottawa	558	2,295	704	2,323
Pawnee	718	1,836	882	1,946
Phillips	382	2,135	525	2,105
Pottawatomie	2,335	6,804	2,599	6,929
Pratt	980	2,771	1,294	2,822
Rawlins	190	1,223	273	1,247
Reno	8,085	15,718	9,916	16,112
Republic	477	2,134	640	1,978
Rice	911	2,676	1,163	2,780
Riley	8,977	11,507	10,495	12,111
Rooks	361	2,038	468	2,068
Rush	367	1,166	504	1,225
Russell	593	2,553	736	2,509
Saline	7,040	13,840	8,186	14,165
Scott	277	1,728	321	1,823
Sedgwick	71,977	106,506	82,337	106,849
Seward	1,490	3,617	1,493	3,791
Shawnee	36,975	37,782	41,235	41,476
Sheridan	168	1,154	254	1,108
Sherman	577	1,976	688	1,959
Smith	358	1,624	446	1,719
Stafford	404	1,385	542	1,495
Stanton	143	605	188	628
Stevens	252	1,749	283	1,815
Sumner	2,658	6,260	3,353	6,737
Thomas	598	2,788	787	2,837
Trego	291	1,261	420	1,225
Wabaunsee	918	2,256	1,036	2,395
Wallace	68	719	96	690
Washington	524	2,316	659	2,248
Wichita	157	821	163	840
Wilson	1,636	5,650	1,170	2,850
Woodson	380	1,035	512	1,055
Wyandotte	34,302	15,496	39,865	16,506
Totals	**440,726**	**692,634**	**514,765**	**699,655**

Kansas Vote Since 1960

2012: Romney, R, 692,634; Obama, D, 440,726; Johnson, LB, 20,456; Baldwin, RF, 5,017.

2008: McCain, R, 699,655; Obama, D, 514,765; Nader, Ind., 10,527; Barr, LB, 6,706; Baldwin, RF, 4,148.

2004: Bush, R, 736,456; Kerry, D, 434,993; Nader, RF, 9,348; Badnarik, LB, 4,013; Peroutka, Ind., 2,899.

2000: Bush, R, 622,332; Gore, D, 399,276; Nader, Ind., 36,086; Buchanan, RF, 7,370; Browne, LB, 4,525; Hagelin, Ind., 1,373; Phillips, Const., 1,254.

1996: Dole, R, 583,245; Clinton, D, 387,659; Perot, RF, 92,639; Browne, LB, 4,557; Phillips, Ind., 3,519; Hagelin, Ind., 1,655.

1992: Bush, R, 449,951; Clinton, D, 390,434; Perot, Ind., 312,358; Marrou, LB, 4,314.

1988: Bush, R, 554,049; Dukakis, D, 422,636; Paul, Ind., 12,553; Fulani, Ind., 3,806.

1984: Reagan, R, 674,646; Mondale, D, 332,471; Bergland, LB, 3,585.

1980: Reagan, R, 566,812; Carter, D, 326,150; Anderson, Ind., 68,231; Clark, LB, 14,470; Shelton, Amer., 1,555; Hall, Comm., 967; Bubar, Statesman, 821; Rarick, Conservative, 789.

1976: Ford, R, 502,752; Carter, D, 430,421; McCarthy, Ind., 13,185; Anderson, Amer., 4,724; MacBride, LB, 3,242; Maddox, Conservative, 2,118; Bubar, Prohib., 1,403.

1972: Nixon, R, 619,812; McGovern, D, 270,287; Schmitz, Conservative, 21,808; Munn, Prohib., 4,188.

1968: Nixon, R, 478,674; Humphrey, D, 302,996; Wallace, 3rd party, 88,921; Munn, Prohib., 2,192.

1964: Johnson, D, 464,028; Goldwater, R, 386,579; Munn, Prohib., 5,393; Hass, Soc. Labor, 1,901.

1960: Nixon, R, 561,474; Kennedy, D, 363,213; Decker, Prohib., 4,138.

Kentucky

County	2012 Obama (D)	2012 Romney (R)	2008 Obama (D)	2008 McCain (R)
Adair	1,660	5,841	1,668	5,512
Allen	1,808	5,184	2,024	5,258
Anderson	3,315	6,822	3,462	6,885
Ballard	1,189	2,647	1,427	2,537
Barren	5,400	10,922	5,434	11,133
Bath	1,770	2,275	2,210	2,234
Bell	2,224	7,127	2,782	6,681
Boone	15,629	35,922	16,292	33,812
Bourbon	3,075	4,692	3,385	4,820
Boyd	7,776	10,884	8,886	11,430
Boyle	4,471	7,703	4,769	7,701
Bracken	1,147	2,029	1,241	2,066
Breathitt	1,562	3,318	2,205	2,671
Breckinridge	2,825	5,025	3,110	5,281
Bullitt	9,971	21,306	10,177	20,102
Butler	1,293	3,716	1,555	3,696
Caldwell	1,852	3,904	2,212	3,866
Calloway	5,317	9,440	6,165	8,991
Campbell	15,080	24,240	15,622	24,046
Carlisle	750	1,835	879	1,699
Carroll	1,629	1,999	1,716	2,032
Carter	3,383	5,279	4,316	5,252
Casey	1,086	4,904	1,219	4,679
Christian	8,252	13,475	8,880	13,699
Clark	5,228	9,931	5,749	9,664
Clay	1,111	6,176	1,552	5,710
Clinton	752	3,569	761	3,366
Crittenden	960	2,839	1,254	2,604
Cumberland	599	2,216	697	2,056
Daviess	16,208	25,092	19,282	23,692
Edmonson	1,374	3,232	1,652	3,562
Elliott	1,186	1,126	1,535	902
Estill	1,356	3,749	1,555	3,685
Fayette	62,080	60,795	66,042	59,884
Fleming	1,911	3,780	2,279	3,432
Floyd	4,733	9,784	7,530	7,741
Franklin	11,535	11,345	11,767	11,911
Fulton	1,022	1,425	1,238	1,530
Gallatin	1,238	1,758	1,278	1,840
Garrard	1,661	5,310	2,012	5,118
Grant	2,810	5,664	3,112	5,510
Graves	4,547	10,699	5,843	10,056
Grayson	2,744	6,404	3,154	6,605
Green	1,165	3,634	1,204	3,785
Greenup	6,027	8,855	6,621	8,849
Hancock	1,833	2,212	2,135	1,928
Hardin	15,214	23,357	15,650	23,896
Harlan	1,830	8,652	2,586	7,165
Harrison	2,471	4,556	2,916	4,520
Hart	2,283	4,257	2,290	4,397
Henderson	8,091	10,296	10,049	9,523
Henry	2,530	3,940	2,725	4,081
Hickman	686	1,431	812	1,406
Hopkins	5,789	13,681	7,104	11,916
Jackson	612	4,365	743	4,407
Jefferson	186,181	148,423	196,435	153,957
Jessamine	6,001	14,233	6,236	13,711
Johnson	1,723	7,095	2,407	5,948
Kenton	24,920	41,389	26,480	40,714
Knott	1,420	4,130	2,612	3,070
Knox	2,484	8,467	3,074	8,150
LaRue	1,733	3,911	1,913	4,153
Laurel	3,905	18,151	4,618	17,660
Lawrence	1,520	3,995	2,036	3,503
Lee	595	1,977	752	1,978
Leslie	433	4,439	766	3,574
Letcher	1,702	6,811	2,623	5,367
Lewis	1,342	3,326	1,510	3,213
Lincoln	2,582	6,416	2,752	6,273
Livingston	1,346	3,089	1,622	2,890
Logan	3,469	6,899	3,811	6,925
Lyon	1,373	2,412	1,577	2,220
Madison	11,512	21,128	12,392	19,694
Magoffin	1,433	3,391	2,105	2,434
Marion	3,418	3,800	3,596	3,842
Marshall	5,022	10,402	5,683	9,512
Martin	574	3,180	808	2,824

	2012		2008	
County	Obama (D)	Romney (R)	Obama (D)	McCain (R)
Mason	2,592	4,197	2,891	4,102
McCracken	10,062	19,979	11,285	19,043
McCreary	1,069	4,564	1,258	4,078
McLean	1,432	2,705	1,963	2,386
Meade	4,122	6,606	4,343	6,691
Menifee	1,048	1,484	1,276	1,155
Mercer	2,966	6,820	3,159	6,781
Metcalfe	1,425	2,676	1,350	2,734
Monroe	936	3,762	1,067	3,537
Montgomery	3,701	6,398	4,234	5,947
Morgan	1,369	3,021	1,879	2,396
Muhlenberg	4,771	7,762	6,221	6,447
Nelson	7,611	10,673	7,654	10,139
Nicholas	948	1,583	1,272	1,634
Ohio	2,987	6,470	4,059	5,687
Oldham	9,240	20,179	10,000	18,997
Owen	1,501	2,971	1,694	2,969
Owsley	283	1,279	381	1,279
Pendleton	1,859	3,556	2,027	3,676
Perry	2,047	8,040	3,444	6,762
Pike	5,646	17,590	9,525	12,655
Powell	1,620	2,766	2,065	2,837
Pulaski	4,976	20,714	5,590	19,862
Robertson	340	579	451	533
Rockcastle	1,097	5,028	1,410	4,757
Rowan	3,438	4,035	4,074	3,907
Russell	1,445	6,346	1,569	5,779
Scott	7,532	12,679	7,712	11,782
Shelby	6,634	11,790	6,871	11,451
Simpson	2,650	4,355	2,775	4,437
Spencer	2,549	5,726	2,519	5,378
Taylor	3,285	7,551	3,165	7,568
Todd	1,403	3,247	1,543	3,336
Trigg	2,115	4,520	2,246	4,189
Trimble	1,355	2,133	1,484	2,239
Union	1,942	3,955	2,804	3,120
Warren	16,805	26,384	17,669	25,993
Washington	1,669	3,495	1,890	3,305
Wayne	1,855	5,289	2,201	4,868
Webster	1,765	3,607	2,390	3,037
Whitley	2,683	10,232	3,484	10,015
Wolfe	976	1,542	1,493	1,408
Woodford	4,883	7,219	5,027	7,130
Totals	**679,370**	**1,087,190**	**751,985**	**1,048,462**

Kentucky Vote Since 1960

2012: Romney, R, 1,087,190; Obama, D, 679,370; Johnson, LB, 17,063; Terry, Ind., 6,872; Stein, Green, 6,337.
2008: McCain, R, 1,048,462; Obama, D, 751,985; Nader, Ind., 15,378; Barr, LB, 5,989; Baldwin, Const., 4,694.
2004: Bush, R, 1,069,439; Kerry, D, 712,733; Nader, Ind., 8,856; Badnarik, LB, 2,619; Peroutka, Const., 2,213.
2000: Bush, R, 872,520; Gore, D, 638,923; Nader, Green, 23,118; Buchanan, RF, 4,152; Browne, LB, 2,885; Hagelin, Natural Law, 1,513; Phillips, Const., 915.
1996: Clinton, D, 636,614; Dole, R, 623,283; Perot, RF, 120,396; Browne, LB, 4,009; Phillips, U.S. Taxpayers, 2,204; Hagelin, Natural Law, 1,493.
1992: Clinton, D, 665,104; Bush, R, 617,178; Perot, Ind., 203,944; Marrou, LB, 4,513.
1988: Bush, R, 734,281; Dukakis, D, 580,368; Duke, Populist, 4,494; Paul, LB, 2,118.
1984: Reagan, R, 815,345; Mondale, D, 536,756.
1980: Reagan, R, 635,274; Carter, D, 616,417; Anderson, Ind., 31,127; Clark, LB, 5,531; McCormack, Respect for Life, 4,233; Commoner, Citizens, 1,304; Pulley, Soc., 393; Hall, Comm., 348.
1976: Carter, D, 615,717; Ford, R, 531,852; Anderson, Amer., 8,308; McCarthy, Ind., 6,837; Maddox, Amer. Ind., 2,328; MacBride, LB, 814.
1972: Nixon, R, 676,446; McGovern, D, 371,159; Schmitz, Amer., 17,627; Spock, People's, 1,118; Jenness, Soc. Workers, 685; Hall, Comm., 464.
1968: Nixon, R, 462,411; Humphrey, D, 397,547; Wallace, 3rd party, 193,098; Halstead, Soc. Workers, 2,843.
1964: Johnson, D, 669,659; Goldwater, R, 372,977; Kasper, Natl. States' Rights, 3,469.
1960: Nixon, R, 602,607; Kennedy, D, 521,855.

Louisiana

	2012		2008	
Parish	Obama (D)	Romney (R)	Obama (D)	McCain (R)
Acadia	6,560	19,931	7,028	19,229
Allen	2,617	6,495	2,891	6,333
Ascension	16,349	33,856	14,625	31,239
Assumption	4,754	6,083	4,756	5,981
Avoyelles	6,077	10,670	6,327	10,236
Beauregard	2,828	11,112	3,071	10,718
Bienville	3,490	3,641	3,589	3,776
Bossier	12,956	34,988	12,703	32,713
Caddo	58,042	52,459	55,536	52,228
Calcasieu	28,359	51,850	30,244	50,449
Caldwell	1,016	3,640	1,118	3,696
Cameron	408	3,260	613	3,089
Catahoula	1,408	2,744	1,659	3,486
Claiborne	3,014	3,649	3,025	3,750
Concordia	3,833	5,450	3,766	5,668
DeSoto	5,553	7,353	5,242	6,883
East Baton Rouge	102,656	92,292	99,652	95,390
East Carroll	2,478	1,508	2,267	1,254
East Feliciana	4,648	5,397	4,383	5,432
Evangeline	5,330	10,181	5,853	9,793
Franklin	2,921	6,294	2,961	6,278
Grant	1,422	7,082	1,474	6,907
Iberia	12,132	20,892	12,492	20,127
Iberville	9,548	7,271	9,023	7,185
Jackson	2,305	5,132	2,456	5,190
Jefferson	70,384	102,536	65,096	113,191
Jefferson Davis	3,484	10,014	3,923	9,278
Lafayette	31,768	64,992	32,145	62,055
Lafourche	9,623	28,592	9,662	27,089
LaSalle	764	5,726	860	5,602
Lincoln	7,956	10,739	8,292	10,680
Livingston	7,451	45,513	6,681	43,269
Madison	3,154	2,000	3,100	2,152
Morehouse	5,888	6,591	5,792	7,258
Natchitoches	7,942	9,077	7,801	9,054
Orleans	126,722	28,003	117,102	28,130
Ouachita	26,645	40,948	24,813	41,741
Plaquemines	3,599	6,471	3,380	6,894
Pointe Coupee	5,436	6,548	5,516	6,702
Rapides	20,045	37,193	20,127	36,611
Red River	2,253	2,483	2,080	2,484
Richland	3,387	5,846	3,311	5,751
Sabine	2,194	7,738	2,245	7,226
St. Bernard	5,059	8,501	3,491	9,643
St. Charles	8,896	15,937	8,522	16,457
St. Helena	3,780	2,529	3,567	2,522
St. James	7,059	5,209	6,994	5,432
St. John the Baptist	13,179	7,620	12,424	8,912
St. Landry	19,668	21,475	20,268	21,650
St. Martin	9,422	15,653	9,419	14,443
St. Mary	9,450	13,885	9,345	13,183
St. Tammany	25,728	84,723	24,596	83,078
Tangipahoa	17,722	31,590	16,438	31,434
Tensas	1,564	1,230	1,646	1,367
Terrebonne	12,074	29,503	11,581	28,210
Union	3,075	7,561	3,103	7,619
Vermilion	5,720	18,910	6,266	18,069
Vernon	3,173	12,150	3,534	11,946
Washington	6,466	11,798	6,122	12,215
Webster	6,802	11,400	6,610	11,417
West Baton Rouge	5,692	6,922	5,043	6,654
West Carroll	853	3,628	878	4,045
West Feliciana	2,441	3,257	2,415	3,150
Winn	1,919	4,541	2,047	4,632
Totals	**809,141**	**1,152,262**	**782,989**	**1,148,275**

Louisiana Vote Since 1960

2012: Romney, R, 1,152,262; Obama, D, 809,141; Johnson, LB, 18,157; Stein, Green, 6,978; Goode, Const., 2,508; Tittle, We the People, 1,767; Anderson, Justice, 1,368; Lindsay, Socialism/Liberation, 622; Fellure, Prohib., 518; Harris, Soc. Workers, 389; White, Soc. Equality, 355.
2008: McCain, R, 1,148,275; Obama, D, 782,989; Paul, LA Taxpayers, 9,368; McKinney, Green, 9,187; Nader, Ind., 6,997; Baldwin, Const., 2,581; Harris, Soc. Workers, 735; La Riva, Socialism/Liberation, 354; Amondson, Prohib., 275.
2004: Bush, R, 1,102,169; Kerry, D, 820,299; Nader, Better Life, 7,032; Peroutka, Const., 5,203; Badnarik, LB, 2,781; Brown, Protect Working Families, 1,795; Amondson, Prohib., 1,566; Cobb, Green, 1,276; Harris, Soc. Workers, 985.
2000: Bush, R, 927,871; Gore, D, 792,344; Nader, Green, 20,473; Buchanan, RF, 14,356; Phillips, Const., 5,483; Browne, LB, 2,951; Harris, Soc. Workers, 1,103; Hagelin, Natural Law, 1,075.
1996: Clinton, D, 927,837; Dole, R, 712,586; Perot, RF, 123,293; Browne, LB, 7,499; Nader, Liberty, Ecology, Community, 4,719; Phillips, U.S. Taxpayers, 3,366; Hagelin, Natural Law, 2,981; Moorehead, Workers World, 1,678.
1992: Clinton, D, 815,971; Bush, R, 733,386; Perot, Ind., 211,478; Gritz, Populist/America First, 18,545; Marrou, LB, 3,155; Daniels, Ind., 1,663; Phillips, U.S. Taxpayers, 1,552; Fulani, New Alliance, 1,434; LaRouche, Ind., 1,136.

1988: Bush, R, 883,702; Dukakis, D, 717,460; Duke, Populist, 18,612; Paul, LB, 4,115.
1984: Reagan, R, 1,037,299; Mondale, D, 651,586; Bergland, LB, 1,876.
1980: Reagan, R, 792,853; Carter, D, 708,453; Anderson, Ind., 26,345; Rarick, Amer. Ind., 10,333; Clark, LB, 8,240; Commoner, Citizens, 1,584; DeBerry, Soc. Workers, 783.
1976: Carter, D, 661,365; Ford, R, 587,446; Maddox, Amer., 10,058; Hall, Comm., 7,417; McCarthy, Ind., 6,588; MacBride, LB, 3,325.
1972: Nixon, R, 686,852; McGovern, D, 298,142; Schmitz, Amer., 52,099; Jenness, Soc. Workers, 14,398.
1968: Wallace, 3rd party, 530,300; Humphrey, D, 309,615; Nixon, R, 257,535.
1964: Goldwater, R, 509,225; Johnson, D, 387,068.
1960: Kennedy, D, 407,339; Nixon, R, 230,890; States' Rights (unpledged), 169,572.

Maine

	2012		2008	
County	**Obama (D)**	**Romney (R)**	**Obama (D)**	**McCain (R)**
Androscoggin	28,989	22,232	31,017	22,671
Aroostook	17,777	15,196	19,345	15,898
Cumberland	101,950	57,821	105,218	56,186
Franklin	9,367	6,369	10,113	6,627
Hancock	17,569	12,324	18,895	12,686
Kennebec	35,068	26,519	37,238	27,482
Knox	13,223	8,248	13,728	8,816
Lincoln	11,315	8,899	11,886	9,287
Oxford	16,330	11,996	17,940	12,863
Penobscot	38,811	36,547	41,614	37,495
Piscataquis	4,149	4,530	4,430	4,785
Sagadahoc	11,821	8,429	12,152	8,721
Somerset	12,216	11,800	13,335	11,867
Waldo	11,296	9,058	11,967	9,423
Washington	7,803	7,550	8,246	8,077
York	61,551	43,900	64,799	42,389
Outside U.S.	2,071	858	NA	NA
Totals	**401,306**	**292,276**	**421,923**	**295,273**

Maine Vote Since 1960

2012: Obama, D, 401,306; Romney, R, 292,276; Johnson, LB, 9,352; Stein, Green, 8,119.
2008: Obama, D, 421,923; McCain, R, 295,273; Nader, Ind., 10,636; McKinney, Green, 2,900.
2004: Kerry, D, 396,842; Bush, R, 330,201; Nader, Better Life, 8,069; Cobb, Green, 2,936; Badnarik, LB, 1,965; Peroutka, Const., 735.
2000: Gore, D, 319,951; Bush, R, 286,616; Nader, Green, 37,127; Buchanan, RF, 4,443; Browne, LB, 3,074; Phillips, Const., 579.
1996: Clinton, D, 312,788; Dole, R, 186,378; Perot, RF, 85,970; Nader, Green, 15,279; Browne, LB, 2,996; Phillips, Taxpayers, 1,517; Hagelin, Natural Law, 825.
1992: Clinton, D, 263,420; Perot, Ind., 206,820; Bush, R, 206,504; Marrou, LB, 1,681.
1988: Bush, R, 307,131; Dukakis, D, 243,569; Paul, LB, 2,700; Fulani, New Alliance, 1,405.
1984: Reagan, R, 336,500; Mondale, D, 214,515.
1980: Reagan, R, 238,522; Carter, D, 220,974; Anderson, Ind., 53,327; Clark, LB, 5,119; Commoner, Citizens, 4,394; Hall, Comm., 591; write-in, 84.
1976: Ford, R, 236,320; Carter, D, 232,279; McCarthy, Ind., 10,874; Bubar, Prohib., 3,495.
1972: Nixon, R, 256,458; McGovern, D, 160,584; scattered, 229.
1968: Humphrey, D, 217,312; Nixon, R, 169,254; Wallace, 3rd party, 6,370.
1964: Johnson, D, 262,264; Goldwater, R, 118,701.
1960: Nixon, R, 240,608; Kennedy, D, 181,159.

Maryland

	2012		2008	
County	**Obama (D)**	**Romney (R)**	**Obama (D)**	**McCain (R)**
Allegany	9,805	19,230	10,693	18,405
Anne Arundel	126,635	126,832	125,015	129,682
Baltimore	220,322	154,908	214,151	158,714
Calvert	20,529	23,952	20,299	23,095
Caroline	4,970	8,098	4,971	8,015
Carroll	27,939	56,761	28,060	54,503
Cecil	16,557	24,806	17,665	23,855
Charles	48,774	25,178	43,635	25,732
Dorchester	7,257	7,976	6,912	8,168
Frederick	55,146	58,798	54,013	55,170
Garrett	3,124	9,743	3,736	8,903
Harford	49,729	72,911	48,552	71,751
Howard	91,393	57,758	87,120	55,393
Kent	4,842	4,870	4,953	4,905
Montgomery	323,400	123,353	314,444	118,608
Prince George's	347,938	35,734	332,396	38,833
Queen Anne's	8,556	15,823	8,575	15,087
St. Mary's	19,711	26,797	19,023	24,705
Somerset	5,240	5,042	4,779	5,037
Talbot	8,808	11,339	9,035	10,995
Washington	25,042	36,074	26,245	34,169
Wicomico	19,635	21,764	19,436	21,849
Worcester	11,014	15,951	11,374	15,607
City				
Baltimore	221,478	28,171	214,385	28,681
Totals	**1,677,844**	**971,869**	**1,629,467**	**959,862**

Maryland Vote Since 1960

2012: Obama, D, 1,677,844; Romney, R, 971,869; Johnson, LB, 30,195; Stein, Green, 17,110.
2008: Obama, D, 1,629,467; McCain, R, 959,862; Nader, MD Ind., 14,713; Barr, LB, 9,842; McKinney, Green, 4,747; Baldwin, RF, 3,760.
2004: Kerry, D, 1,334,493; Bush, R, 1,024,703; Nader, Populist, 11,854; Badnarik, LB, 6,094; Cobb, Green, 3,632; Peroutka, Const., 3,421.
2000: Gore, D, 1,144,008; Bush, R, 813,827; Nader, Green, 53,768; Browne, LB, 5,310; Buchanan, RF, 4,248; Phillips, Const., 918.
1996: Clinton, D, 966,207; Dole, R, 681,530; Perot, RF, 115,812; Browne, LB, 8,765; Phillips, Taxpayers, 3,402; Hagelin, Natural Law, 2,517.
1992: Clinton, D, 988,571; Bush, R, 707,094; Perot, Ind., 281,414; Marrou, LB, 4,715; Fulani, New Alliance, 2,786.
1988: Bush, R, 876,167; Dukakis, D, 826,304; Paul, LB, 6,748; Fulani, New Alliance, 5,115.
1984: Reagan, R, 879,918; Mondale, D, 787,935; Bergland, LB, 5,721.
1980: Carter, D, 726,161; Reagan, R, 680,606; Anderson, Ind., 119,537; Clark, LB, 14,192.
1976: Carter, D, 759,612; Ford, R, 672,661.
1972: Nixon, R, 829,305; McGovern, D, 505,781; Schmitz, Amer., 18,726.
1968: Humphrey, D, 538,310; Nixon, R, 517,995; Wallace, 3rd party, 178,734.
1964: Johnson, D, 730,912; Goldwater, R, 385,495; write-in, 50.
1960: Kennedy, D, 565,800; Nixon, R, 489,538.

Massachusetts

	2012		2008	
County	**Obama (D)**	**Romney (R)**	**Obama (D)**	**McCain (R)**
Barnstable	70,822	60,446	74,264	55,694
Berkshire	48,843	14,252	49,558	14,876
Bristol	142,962	93,752	146,861	90,531
Dukes	7,978	2,792	7,913	2,442
Essex	210,302	150,480	208,976	137,129
Franklin	27,072	9,344	27,919	9,545
Hampden	123,619	73,392	121,454	71,350
Hampshire	57,359	21,480	56,869	20,618
Middlesex	471,804	267,321	464,484	245,766
Nantucket	3,830	2,187	4,073	1,863
Norfolk	202,714	148,393	200,675	136,841
Plymouth	131,845	121,086	131,817	112,904
Suffolk	223,896	59,999	207,127	57,194
Worcester	198,244	163,390	202,107	152,101
Totals	**1,921,290**	**1,188,314**	**1,904,097**	**1,108,854**

Massachusetts Vote Since 1960

2012: Obama, D, 1,921,290; Romney, R, 1,188,314; Johnson, LB, 30,920; Stein, Green, 20,691.
2008: Obama, D, 1,904,097; McCain, R, 1,108,854; Nader, Ind., 28,841; Barr, LB, 13,189; McKinney, Green, 6,550; Baldwin, RF, 4,971.
2004: Kerry, D, 1,803,800; Bush, R, 1,071,109; Badnarik, LB, 15,022; Cobb, Green, 10,623.
2000: Gore, D, 1,616,487; Bush, R, 878,502; Nader, Green, 173,564; Browne, LB, 16,366; Buchanan, RF, 11,149; Hagelin, Natural Law, 2,884.
1996: Clinton, D, 1,571,509; Dole, R, 718,058; Perot, RF, 227,206; Browne, LB, 20,424; Hagelin, Natural Law, 5,183; Moorehead, Workers World, 3,276.
1992: Clinton, D, 1,318,639; Bush, R, 805,039; Perot, Ind., 630,731; Marrou, LB, 9,021; Fulani, New Alliance, 3,172; Phillips, U.S. Taxpayers, 2,218; Hagelin, Natural Law, 1,812; LaRouche, Ind., 1,027.
1988: Dukakis, D, 1,401,415; Bush, R, 1,194,635; Paul, LB, 24,251; Fulani, New Alliance, 9,561.
1984: Reagan, R, 1,310,936; Mondale, D, 1,239,606.
1980: Reagan, R, 1,057,631; Carter, D, 1,053,802; Anderson, Ind., 382,539; Clark, LB, 22,038; DeBerry, Soc. Workers, 3,735; Commoner, Citizens, 2,056; McReynolds, Soc., 62; Bubar, Statesman, 34; Griswold, Workers World, 19; scattered, 2,382.

1976: Carter, D, 1,429,475; Ford, R, 1,030,276; McCarthy, Ind., 65,637; Camejo, Soc. Workers, 8,138; Anderson, Amer., 7,555; LaRouche, U.S. Labor, 4,922; MacBride, LB, 135.
1972: McGovern, D, 1,332,540; Nixon, R, 1,112,078; Jenness, Soc. Workers, 10,600; Schmitz, Amer., 2,877; Fisher, Soc. Labor, 129; Spock, People's, 101; Hall, Comm., 46; Hospers, LB, 43; scattered, 342.
1968: Humphrey, D, 1,469,218; Nixon, R, 766,844; Wallace, 3rd party, 87,088; Blomen, Soc. Labor, 6,180; Munn, Prohib., 2,369; scattered, 53; blank, 25,394.
1964: Johnson, D, 1,786,422; Goldwater, R, 549,727; Hass, Soc. Labor, 4,755; Munn, Prohib., 3,735; scattered, 159; blank, 48,104.
1960: Kennedy, D, 1,487,174; Nixon, R, 976,750; Hass, Soc. Labor, 3,892; Decker, Prohib., 1,633; others, 31; blank and void, 26,024.

Michigan

	2012		2008	
County	**Obama (D)**	**Romney (R)**	**Obama (D)**	**McCain (R)**
Alcona	2,472	3,571	2,896	3,404
Alger	2,212	2,330	2,472	2,188
Allegan	20,806	31,123	24,165	30,061
Alpena	6,549	7,298	7,705	7,125
Antrim	5,107	7,917	6,079	7,506
Arenac	3,669	4,057	4,155	3,807
Baraga	1,574	1,866	1,725	1,846
Barry	11,491	16,655	13,449	16,431
Bay	27,877	24,911	32,589	23,795
Benzie	4,685	5,075	5,451	4,687
Berrien	33,465	38,209	40,381	36,130
Branch	6,913	10,035	8,413	9,534
Calhoun	29,267	28,333	34,561	28,553
Cass	9,591	12,659	12,083	11,114
Charlevoix	5,939	8,000	6,817	7,306
Cheboygan	5,831	7,286	6,720	6,920
Chippewa	7,100	8,278	8,184	8,267
Clare	6,338	6,988	7,496	6,793
Clinton	18,191	20,650	20,005	19,726
Crawford	2,994	3,744	3,441	3,561
Delta	8,330	9,534	9,974	8,763
Dickinson	4,952	7,688	5,995	7,049
Eaton	27,913	26,197	30,742	25,900
Emmet	7,225	10,253	8,515	9,314
Genesee	128,978	71,808	143,927	72,451
Gladwin	5,760	6,661	6,590	6,391
Gogebic	4,058	3,444	4,757	3,330
Grand Traverse	20,875	26,534	23,258	24,716
Gratiot	7,610	8,241	9,105	8,322
Hillsdale	7,106	11,727	8,765	11,221
Houghton	6,801	8,196	7,476	8,101
Huron	6,518	8,806	8,367	8,434
Ingham	80,847	45,306	93,994	46,483
Ionia	11,018	14,315	12,565	14,156
Iosco	6,242	6,909	7,309	6,583
Iron	2,687	3,224	3,080	2,947
Isabella	13,038	10,800	16,679	11,220
Jackson	32,301	36,298	37,480	35,692
Kalamazoo	69,051	52,662	77,051	51,554
Kalkaska	3,272	4,901	3,780	4,527
Kent	133,408	155,925	149,909	148,336
Keweenaw	582	774	610	756
Lake	2,752	2,487	2,919	2,269
Lapeer	18,796	23,734	21,457	22,831
Leelanau	6,576	7,483	7,355	6,938
Lenawee	21,776	22,351	24,640	22,225
Livingston	37,216	60,083	42,349	55,592
Luce	991	1,580	1,191	1,490
Mackinac	2,652	3,397	3,027	3,268
Macomb	208,016	191,913	223,784	187,663
Manistee	6,473	5,737	7,235	5,510
Marquette	18,115	13,606	19,635	12,906
Mason	6,856	7,580	7,817	7,147
Mecosta	7,515	9,176	9,101	9,238
Menominee	5,242	5,564	5,981	4,855
Midland	17,450	23,919	20,701	22,263
Missaukee	2,274	4,665	2,898	4,469
Monroe	36,310	35,593	39,180	35,858
Montcalm	11,430	13,621	13,208	13,291
Montmorency	2,049	2,928	2,403	2,841
Muskegon	44,436	30,884	53,821	29,145
Newaygo	8,728	12,457	10,790	11,862
Oakland	349,002	296,514	372,566	276,956
Oceana	5,063	6,239	6,405	5,860
Ogemaw	4,791	5,437	5,391	5,133
Ontonagon	1,586	1,906	1,966	1,823
Osceola	3,981	6,141	4,855	5,973
Oscoda	1,657	2,308	1,887	2,320
Otsego	4,681	7,011	5,634	6,752
Ottawa	42,737	88,166	50,828	83,330
Presque Isle	3,192	3,794	3,722	3,606
Roscommon	6,198	6,701	7,082	6,727
Saginaw	54,381	42,720	60,276	42,225
St. Clair	33,983	39,271	40,677	38,536
St. Joseph	10,112	12,978	12,322	12,886
Sanilac	7,212	10,963	9,047	10,679
Schoolcraft	1,865	2,142	2,184	2,058
Shiawassee	17,197	15,962	19,397	16,268
Tuscola	11,425	14,240	13,503	13,740
Van Buren	16,290	16,141	18,588	15,534
Washtenaw	120,890	56,412	130,578	53,946
Wayne	595,846	213,814	660,085	219,582
Wexford	6,184	8,450	7,379	8,044
Totals	**2,564,569**	**2,115,256**	**2,872,579**	**2,048,639**

Michigan Vote Since 1960

2012: Obama, D, 2,564,569; Romney, R, 2,115,256; Stein, Green, 21,897; Goode, U.S. Taxpayers, 16,119; Johnson, Ind., 7,774, Anderson, Natural Law, 5,147;
2008: Obama, D, 2,872,579; McCain, R, 2,048,639; Nader, Natural Law, 33,085; Barr, LB, 23,716; Baldwin, U.S. Taxpayers, 14,685; McKinney, Green, 8,892.
2004: Kerry, D, 2,479,183; Bush, R, 2,313,746; Nader, Ind., 24,035; Badnarik, LB, 10,552; Cobb, Green, 5,325; Peroutka, U.S. Taxpayers, 4,980; Brown, Natural Law, 1,431.
2000: Gore, D, 2,170,418; Bush, R, 1,953,139; Nader, Green, 84,165; Browne, LB, 16,711; Phillips, U.S. Taxpayers, 3,791; Hagelin, Natural Law, 2,426.
1996: Clinton, D, 1,989,653; Dole, R, 1,481,212; Perot, RF, 336,670; Browne, LB, 27,670; Hagelin, Natural Law, 4,254; Moorehead, Workers World, 3,153; White, Soc. Equality, 1,554.
1992: Clinton, D, 1,871,182; Bush, R, 1,554,940; Perot, Ind., 824,813; Marrou, LB, 10,175; Phillips, U.S. Taxpayers, 8,263; Hagelin, Natural Law, 2,954.
1988: Bush, R, 1,965,486; Dukakis, D, 1,675,783; Paul, LB, 18,336; Fulani, Ind., 2,513.
1984: Reagan, R, 2,251,571; Mondale, D, 1,529,638; Bergland, LB, 10,055.
1980: Reagan, R, 1,915,225; Carter, D, 1,661,532; Anderson, Ind., 275,223; Clark, LB, 41,597; Commoner, Citizens, 11,930; Hall, Comm., 3,262; Griswold, Workers World, 30; Greaves, Amer., 21; Bubar, Statesman, 9.
1976: Ford, R, 1,893,742; Carter, D, 1,696,714; McCarthy, Ind., 47,905; MacBride, LB, 5,406; Wright, People's, 3,504; Camejo, Soc. Workers, 1,804; LaRouche, U.S. Labor, 1,366; Levin, Soc. Labor, 1,148; scattered, 2,160.
1972: Nixon, R, 1,961,721; McGovern, D, 1,459,435; Schmitz, Amer., 63,321; Fisher, Soc. Labor, 2,437; Jenness, Soc. Workers, 1,603; Hall, Comm., 1,210.
1968: Humphrey, D, 1,593,082; Nixon, R, 1,370,665; Wallace, 3rd party, 331,968; Halstead, Soc. Workers, 4,099; Blomen, Soc. Labor, 1,762; Cleaver, New Politics, 4,585; Munn, Prohib., 60; scattered, 29.
1964: Johnson, D, 2,136,615; Goldwater, R, 1,060,152; DeBerry, Soc. Workers, 3,817; Hass, Soc. Labor, 1,704; Prohib. (no candidate listed), 699; scattered, 145.
1960: Kennedy, D, 1,687,269; Nixon, R, 1,620,428; Dobbs, Soc. Workers, 4,347; Decker, Prohib., 2,029; Daly, Tax Cut, 1,767; Hass, Soc. Labor, 1,718; Ind. Amer. (unpledged), 539.

Minnesota

	2012		2008	
County	**Obama (D)**	**Romney (R)**	**Obama (D)**	**McCain (R)**
Aitkin	4,412	4,533	4,595	4,589
Anoka	88,614	93,430	86,976	91,357
Becker	6,829	9,204	7,687	8,851
Beltrami	11,818	9,637	12,019	9,762
Benton	8,173	10,849	8,454	10,338
Big Stone	1,345	1,385	1,552	1,362
Blue Earth	18,164	14,916	19,325	14,782
Brown	5,630	7,938	5,809	7,456
Carlton	11,389	6,586	11,501	6,549
Carver	20,745	31,155	20,654	28,156
Cass	6,858	8,957	7,276	8,660
Chippewa	3,083	2,967	3,280	2,907
Chisago	12,524	16,227	12,783	15,789
Clay	15,208	12,920	16,666	11,978
Clearwater	1,753	2,359	1,877	2,291
Cook	1,993	1,221	2,019	1,240
Cottonwood	2,433	3,316	2,759	3,157
Crow Wing	14,760	19,415	15,859	18,567
Dakota	116,255	109,516	116,778	104,364
Dodge	4,487	5,522	4,463	5,468
Douglas	8,653	11,884	9,256	11,241
Faribault	3,407	4,104	3,736	4,196
Fillmore	5,713	4,913	5,921	4,993
Freeborn	9,326	6,969	9,915	6,955
Goodhue	12,212	12,986	12,420	12,775
Grant	1,647	1,748	1,850	1,646

County	2012 Obama (D)	2012 Romney (R)	2008 Obama (D)	2008 McCain (R)
Hennepin	423,982	240,073	420,958	231,054
Houston	5,281	4,951	5,906	4,743
Hubbard	4,676	6,622	4,872	6,558
Isanti	8,024	11,675	8,248	11,324
Itasca	12,852	10,501	13,460	10,309
Jackson	2,268	3,044	2,618	2,858
Kanabec	3,593	4,328	3,743	4,479
Kandiyohi	9,805	11,240	10,125	11,319
Kittson	1,241	1,095	1,492	1,016
Koochiching	3,451	2,841	3,649	2,962
Lac Qui Parle	1,974	1,938	2,160	1,912
Lake	4,043	2,610	4,174	2,636
Lake of the Woods	859	1,306	971	1,278
Le Sueur	6,753	7,715	6,994	7,636
Lincoln	1,429	1,595	1,517	1,491
Lyon	5,465	6,594	6,110	6,315
Mahnomen	1,276	871	1,436	843
Marshall	1,998	2,569	2,311	2,285
Martin	4,054	6,657	4,413	6,053
McLeod	6,968	11,069	7,505	10,993
Meeker	4,969	6,913	5,380	6,737
Mille Lacs	5,829	6,951	6,072	7,049
Morrison	6,153	10,159	6,547	9,735
Mower	11,129	6,938	11,605	7,075
Murray	2,160	2,504	2,345	2,320
Nicollet	9,652	8,214	9,887	7,968
Nobles	3,793	4,581	4,244	4,368
Norman	1,730	1,384	2,129	1,204
Olmsted	39,338	36,832	38,711	36,202
Otter Tail	12,165	18,860	13,856	18,077
Pennington	3,024	3,305	3,394	3,248
Pine	6,750	6,845	7,084	6,862
Pipestone	1,725	2,826	2,023	2,652
Polk	6,773	7,615	7,850	7,148
Pope	2,981	3,142	3,317	3,069
Ramsey	184,938	86,800	182,974	88,942
Red Lake	928	978	1,120	983
Redwood	3,008	4,570	3,250	4,308
Renville	3,394	4,149	3,904	3,956
Rice	17,054	14,384	17,381	13,723
Rock	1,946	2,810	2,079	2,775
Roseau	2,772	4,409	3,097	4,438
St. Louis	73,378	39,131	77,351	38,742
Scott	29,712	40,323	29,208	36,724
Sherburne	17,597	27,848	17,957	26,140
Sibley	2,916	4,693	2,998	4,492
Stearns	33,551	43,015	35,690	41,194
Steele	8,706	9,903	9,016	10,068
Stevens	2,742	2,766	2,781	2,710
Swift	2,751	2,248	2,907	2,184
Todd	4,819	6,719	5,277	6,637
Traverse	943	861	1,043	933
Wabasha	5,415	6,049	5,646	5,935
Wadena	2,492	4,143	2,882	4,128
Waseca	4,370	5,116	4,401	5,211
Washington	70,203	69,137	70,277	64,334
Watonwan	2,494	2,517	2,562	2,526
Wilkin	1,258	1,884	1,550	1,786
Winona	14,980	11,480	16,308	10,975
Wright	25,741	40,466	26,343	37,779
Yellow Medicine	2,465	2,806	2,816	2,579
Totals	**1,546,167**	**1,320,225**	**1,573,354**	**1,275,409**

Minnesota Vote Since 1960

2012: Obama, D, 1,546,167; Romney, R, 1,320,225; Johnson, LB, 35,098; Stein, Green, 13,023; Goode, Const., 3,722; Carlson, Grassroots, 3,149; Anderson, Justice, 1,996; Morstad, Constitutional, 1,092; Harris, Soc. Workers, 1,051; Lindsay, Socialism/Liberation, 397.

2008: Obama, D, 1,573,354; McCain, R, 1,275,409; Nader, Ind., 30,152; Barr, LB, 9,174; Baldwin, Const., 6,787; McKinney, Green, 5,174; Calero, Soc. Workers, 790.

2004: Kerry, D, 1,445,014; Bush, R, 1,346,695; Nader, Better Life, 18,683; Badnarik, LB, 4,639; Cobb, Green, 4,408; Peroutka, Const., 3,074; Harens, other, 2,387; Van Auken, Soc. Equal., 539; Calero, Soc. Workers, 416.

2000: Gore, D, 1,168,266; Bush, R, 1,109,659; Nader, Green, 126,696; Buchanan, RF MN, 22,166; Browne, LB, 5,282; Phillips, Const., 3,272; Hagelin, RF, 2,294; Harris, Soc. Workers, 1,022.

1996: Clinton, D, 1,120,438; Dole, R, 766,476; Perot, RF, 257,704; Nader, Green, 24,908; Browne, LB, 8,271; Peron, Grass Roots, 4,898; Phillips, U.S. Taxpayers, 3,416; Hagelin, Natural Law, 1,808; Birrenbach, Ind. Grass Roots, 787; Harris, Soc. Workers, 684; White, Soc. Equality, 347.

1992: Clinton, D, 1,020,997; Bush, R, 747,841; Perot, Ind., 562,506; Marrou, LB, 3,373; Gritz, Populist/America First, 3,363; Hagelin, Natural Law, 1,406.

1988: Dukakis, D, 1,109,471; Bush, R, 962,337; McCarthy, MN Prog., 5,403; Paul, LB, 5,109.

1984: Mondale, D, 1,036,364; Reagan, R, 1,032,603; Bergland, LB, 2,996.

1980: Carter, D, 954,173; Reagan, R, 873,268; Anderson, Ind., 174,997; Clark, LB, 31,593; Commoner, Citizens, 8,406; Hall, Comm., 1,117; DeBerry, Soc. Workers, 711; Griswold, Workers World, 698; McReynolds, Soc., 536; write-in, 281.

1976: Carter, D, 1,070,440; Ford, R, 819,395; McCarthy, Ind., 35,490; Anderson, Amer., 13,592; Camejo, Soc. Workers, 4,149; MacBride, LB, 3,529; Hall, Comm., 1,092.

1972: Nixon, R, 898,269; McGovern, D, 802,346; Schmitz, Amer., 31,407; Fisher, Soc. Labor, 4,261; Spock, People's, 2,805; Jenness, Soc. Workers, 940; Hall, Comm., 662; scattered, 962.

1968: Humphrey, D, 857,738; Nixon, R, 658,643; Wallace, 3rd party, 68,931; Cleaver, Peace/Freedom, 935; Halstead, Soc. Workers, 808; McCarthy, write-in, 585; Mitchell, Comm., 415; Blomen, Industrial Govt., 285; scattered, 2,613.

1964: Johnson, D, 991,117; Goldwater, R, 559,624; Hass, Industrial Govt., 2,544; DeBerry, Soc. Workers, 1,177.

1960: Kennedy, D, 779,933; Nixon, R, 757,915; Dobbs, Soc. Workers, 3,077; Hass, Industrial Govt., 962.

Mississippi

County	2012 Obama (D)	2012 Romney (R)	2008 Obama (D)	2008 McCain (R)
Adams	9,061	6,293	9,021	6,566
Alcorn	3,511	11,111	4,130	10,805
Amite	3,242	4,414	3,348	4,245
Attala	3,927	5,126	3,849	5,273
Benton	2,051	2,041	2,227	2,329
Bolivar	10,582	4,701	10,334	4,891
Calhoun	2,586	4,412	2,522	4,467
Carroll	2,007	3,960	2,037	3,902
Chickasaw	4,378	3,994	4,588	4,395
Choctaw	1,428	2,812	1,459	2,624
Claiborne	4,838	625	4,682	748
Clarke	3,111	5,049	3,121	5,229
Clay	6,712	4,291	6,558	4,466
Coahoma	7,792	2,712	7,597	2,917
Copiah	7,749	6,282	7,710	6,701
Covington	3,878	5,405	3,852	5,523
DeSoto	21,575	43,559	19,627	44,222
Forrest	13,272	16,574	11,622	15,296
Franklin	1,726	2,735	1,733	2,909
George	1,359	8,376	1,532	7,700
Greene	1,325	4,531	1,366	4,361
Grenada	5,288	5,986	5,029	6,234
Hancock	3,917	12,964	3,768	13,020
Harrison	23,119	39,470	22,673	38,757
Hinds	76,112	29,664	75,401	32,949
Holmes	7,812	1,435	7,765	1,714
Humphreys	3,903	1,293	3,634	1,462
Issaquena	479	302	579	364
Itawamba	1,706	7,393	2,084	7,663
Jackson	17,299	35,747	17,781	35,993
Jasper	5,097	4,193	5,025	4,135
Jefferson	3,951	468	3,883	551
Jefferson Davis	4,267	2,507	4,454	2,871
Jones	9,211	20,687	8,846	20,157
Kemper	3,239	1,789	3,256	1,935
Lafayette	8,091	11,075	7,997	10,278
Lamar	5,494	19,101	5,159	18,497
Lauderdale	13,814	18,700	13,332	19,582
Lawrence	2,468	4,192	2,587	4,369
Leake	4,079	4,863	4,151	5,148
Lee	12,563	22,415	12,021	22,694
Leflore	9,119	3,587	8,914	4,105
Lincoln	5,471	10,839	5,505	10,781
Lowndes	13,388	13,518	13,209	13,994
Madison	20,722	28,507	19,831	27,203
Marion	4,393	8,237	4,422	8,513
Marshall	9,650	6,473	9,685	6,683
Monroe	7,056	9,723	7,169	10,184
Montgomery	2,675	2,947	2,609	3,071
Neshoba	3,089	7,837	3,114	8,209
Newton	3,319	6,394	3,218	6,579
Noxubee	4,920	1,325	5,030	1,525
Oktibbeha	9,095	8,761	9,326	9,320
Panola	9,079	7,629	8,690	7,620
Pearl River	4,366	17,549	4,320	17,881
Perry	1,527	4,137	1,533	4,067
Pike	9,650	8,181	9,276	8,651
Pontotoc	2,804	9,448	2,982	9,727
Prentiss	2,817	7,075	3,020	7,703
Quitman	2,837	1,116	2,803	1,334

County	2012 Obama (D)	2012 Romney (R)	2008 Obama (D)	2008 McCain (R)
Rankin	14,988	48,444	14,372	48,140
Scott	5,031	6,089	5,025	6,584
Sharkey	1,782	737	1,907	873
Simpson	4,723	7,424	4,817	7,641
Smith	1,979	6,049	1,968	6,265
Stone	2,003	5,420	1,996	5,149
Sunflower	8,199	2,929	7,838	3,245
Tallahatchie	3,959	2,499	4,105	2,786
Tate	4,933	7,332	5,003	7,678
Tippah	2,317	6,717	2,623	6,937
Tishomingo	1,643	6,133	1,962	6,249
Tunica	3,475	883	3,279	1,017
Union	2,742	8,498	2,985	9,072
Walthall	3,422	4,051	3,456	4,253
Warren	10,786	10,457	10,489	11,152
Washington	13,981	5,651	13,148	6,347
Wayne	4,148	6,111	3,890	6,070
Webster	1,190	3,992	1,349	4,072
Wilkinson	3,412	1,415	3,534	1,560
Winston	4,607	5,168	4,653	5,497
Yalobusha	3,030	3,276	3,151	3,628
Yazoo	6,603	4,941	6,116	5,290
Totals	**562,949**	**710,746**	**554,662**	**724,597**

Mississippi Vote Since 1960

2012: Romney, R, 710,746; Obama, D, 562,949; Johnson, LB, 6,676; Goode, Const., 2,609; Stein, Green, 1,588; Washer, RF, 1,016.

2008: McCain, R, 724,597; Obama, D, 554,662; Nader, Ind., 4,011; Baldwin, Const., 2,551; Barr, LB, 2,529; McKinney, Green, 1,034; Weill, RF, 481.

2004: Bush, R, 684,981; Kerry, D, 458,094; Nader, RF, 3,177; Badnarik, LB, 1,793; Percutka, Const., 1,759; Harris, Ind., 1,268; Cobb, Green, 1,073.

2000: Bush, R, 572,844; Gore, D, 404,614; Nader, Ind., 8,122; Phillips, Const., 3,267; Buchanan, RF, 2,265; Browne, LB, 2,009; Harris, Ind., 613; Hagelin, Natural Law, 450.

1996: Dole, R, 439,838; Clinton, D, 394,022; Perot, RF, 52,222; Browne, LB, 2,809; Phillips, U.S. Taxpayers, 2,314; Hagelin, Natural Law, 1,447; Collins, Ind., 1,205.

1992: Bush, R, 487,793; Clinton, D, 400,258; Perot, Ind., 85,626; Fulani, New Alliance, 2,625; Marrou, LB, 2,154; Phillips, U.S. Taxpayers, 1,652; Hagelin, Natural Law, 1,140.

1988: Bush, R, 557,890; Dukakis, D, 363,921; Duke, Ind., 4,232; Paul, LB, 3,329.

1984: Reagan, R, 582,377; Mondale, D, 352,192; Bergland, LB, 2,336.

1980: Reagan, R, 441,089; Carter, D, 429,281; Anderson, Ind., 12,036; Clark, LB, 5,465; Griswold, Workers World, 2,402; Pulley, Soc. Workers, 2,347.

1976: Carter, D, 381,309; Ford, R, 366,846; Anderson, Amer., 6,678; McCarthy, Ind., 4,074; Maddox, Ind., 4,049; Camejo, Soc. Workers, 2,805; MacBride, LB, 2,609.

1972: Nixon, R, 505,125; McGovern, D, 126,782; Schmitz, Amer., 11,598; Jenness, Soc. Workers, 2,458.

1968: Wallace, 3rd party, 415,349; Humphrey, D, 150,644; Nixon, R, 88,516.

1964: Goldwater, R, 356,528; Johnson, D, 52,618.

1960: D. (electors unpledged), 116,248; Kennedy, D, 108,362; Nixon, R, 73,561. *Mississippi's victorious slate of 8 unpledged Democratic electors cast their votes for Sen. Harry F. Byrd (D, VA).

Missouri

County	2012 Obama (D)	2012 Romney (R)	2008 Obama (D)	2008 McCain (R)
Adair	4,219	5,651	5,735	5,891
Andrew	2,649	5,457	3,345	5,279
Atchison	756	1,902	1,000	1,936
Audrain	3,539	6,186	4,434	6,167
Barry	3,667	9,832	4,630	9,758
Barton	1,230	4,418	1,455	4,414
Bates	2,557	5,020	3,271	4,833
Benton	2,925	6,069	3,629	5,759
Bollinger	1,213	4,095	1,690	3,972
Boone	39,847	37,404	47,062	36,849
Buchanan	15,594	18,660	19,164	19,110
Butler	4,363	12,248	5,316	11,805
Caldwell	1,312	2,721	1,814	2,654
Callaway	6,071	11,745	7,580	11,389
Camden	6,458	15,092	7,773	14,074
Cape Girardeau	9,728	25,370	12,208	24,768
Carroll	1,154	3,072	1,535	2,955
Carter	754	1,978	984	1,840
Cass	17,044	30,912	19,844	29,695
Cedar	1,537	4,376	2,060	4,194
Chariton	1,339	2,402	1,799	2,339
Christian	9,813	27,473	11,883	25,382
Clark	1,398	1,730	1,572	1,782
Clay	47,310	56,191	53,761	54,516
Clinton	3,688	5,931	4,545	5,709
Cole	12,005	24,490	13,959	24,385
Cooper	2,474	4,887	2,996	4,902
Crawford	2,951	6,434	3,911	6,007
Dade	939	2,895	1,184	2,864
Dallas	2,122	4,992	2,656	4,895
Daviess	1,125	2,290	1,400	2,263
DeKalb	1,194	3,056	1,692	2,889
Dent	1,585	4,883	2,056	4,655
Douglas	1,710	4,649	2,140	4,405
Dunklin	3,636	6,850	4,540	7,044
Franklin	16,347	29,396	21,256	27,355
Gasconade	2,099	4,895	2,899	4,763
Gentry	937	1,988	1,235	1,964
Greene	46,219	76,900	56,181	77,683
Grundy	1,212	3,030	1,580	3,006
Harrison	984	2,624	1,287	2,512
Henry	3,606	6,229	4,869	6,095
Hickory	1,733	2,835	2,171	2,850
Holt	551	1,725	802	1,794
Howard	1,723	3,017	2,036	2,708
Howell	4,395	11,544	5,736	10,982
Iron	1,669	2,252	2,213	2,090
Jackson	78,283	93,199	90,722	92,833
Jasper	12,809	31,349	15,730	31,667
Jefferson	41,564	53,978	53,467	50,804
Johnson	7,667	12,763	9,480	12,183
Knox	698	1,205	759	1,212
Laclede	4,093	10,934	5,218	10,875
Lafayette	5,655	9,803	6,902	9,442
Lawrence	4,017	11,421	5,097	11,263
Lewis	1,508	2,677	1,837	2,594
Lincoln	7,734	14,332	10,234	12,924
Linn	2,041	3,344	2,638	3,140
Livingston	1,906	4,006	2,435	3,993
Macon	2,309	4,701	2,784	4,586
Madison	1,588	3,227	2,042	2,897
Maries	1,299	3,165	1,599	2,853
Marion	4,031	7,923	4,703	7,705
McDonald	1,920	5,694	2,454	5,499
Mercer	353	1,255	519	1,169
Miller	2,651	8,099	3,553	7,797
Mississippi	1,858	2,997	2,247	3,034
Moniteau	1,608	4,704	2,084	4,467
Monroe	1,398	2,564	1,703	2,533
Montgomery	1,740	3,490	2,347	3,428
Morgan	2,773	5,733	3,565	5,451
New Madrid	2,814	4,284	3,370	4,593
Newton	6,425	18,181	7,450	17,637
Nodaway	3,172	5,593	4,493	5,568
Oregon	1,419	2,886	1,811	2,652
Osage	1,473	5,329	1,907	5,062
Ozark	1,261	3,080	1,661	2,918
Pemiscot	2,671	3,598	3,029	3,954
Perry	2,184	5,669	3,005	5,527
Pettis	5,904	10,842	6,932	11,018
Phelps	5,798	11,895	7,394	11,706
Pike	2,582	4,577	3,487	4,268
Platte	19,175	25,618	21,459	24,460
Polk	3,580	9,252	4,553	8,956
Pulaski	4,199	9,092	5,249	9,552
Putnam	587	1,673	695	1,591
Ralls	1,736	3,231	2,041	2,987
Randolph	3,031	6,667	3,984	6,457
Ray	4,275	5,815	5,241	5,593
Reynolds	1,157	1,931	1,418	1,782
Ripley	1,396	3,743	1,795	3,407
St. Charles	71,838	110,784	84,183	102,550
St. Clair	1,460	3,019	1,886	2,981
St. Francois	8,829	13,248	11,540	12,660
St. Louis Co.	297,097	224,742	333,123	221,705
Ste. Genevieve	3,813	4,055	4,979	3,732
Saline	3,790	5,104	4,712	4,962
Schuyler	697	1,174	775	1,139
Scotland	643	1,246	793	1,249
Scott	5,122	11,623	6,258	11,563
Shannon	1,302	2,262	1,637	2,075
Shelby	966	2,188	1,114	2,166
Stoddard	3,153	9,496	3,899	9,172
Stone	3,923	11,787	5,029	11,147
Sullivan	908	1,610	1,173	1,607
Taney	5,479	15,746	6,683	14,736

	2012		2008	
County	Obama (D)	Romney (R)	Obama (D)	McCain (R)
Texas	2,871	7,618	3,410	7,215
Vernon	2,580	5,758	3,381	5,334
Warren	5,219	9,150	6,705	8,675
Washington	3,417	5,071	4,711	4,706
Wayne	1,813	3,790	2,243	3,784
Webster	4,409	10,708	5,685	10,431
Worth	341	664	427	707
Wright	1,953	5,830	2,557	5,784
City				
Kansas City	105,670	29,509	120,102	31,854
St. Louis	118,780	22,943	132,925	24,662
Totals	**1,223,796**	**1,482,440**	**1,441,911**	**1,445,814**

Missouri Vote Since 1960

2012: Romney, R, 1,482,440; Obama, D, 1,223,796; Johnson, LB, 43,151; Goode, Const., 7,936.
2008: McCain, R, 1,445,814; Obama, D, 1,441,911; Nader, Ind., 17,813; Barr, LB, 11,386; Baldwin, Const., 8,201.
2004: Bush, R, 1,455,713; Kerry, D, 1,259,171; Badnarik, LB, 9,831; Peroutka, Const., 5,355.
2000: Bush, R, 1,189,924; Gore, D, 1,111,138; Nader, Green, 38,515; Buchanan, RF, 9,818; Browne, LB, 7,436; Phillips, Const., 1,957; Hagelin, Natural Law, 1,104.
1996: Clinton, D, 1,025,935; Dole, R, 890,016; Perot, RF, 217,188; Phillips, U.S. Taxpayers, 11,521; Browne, LB, 10,522; Hagelin, Natural Law, 2,287.
1992: Clinton, D, 1,053,873; Bush, R, 811,159; Perot, Ind., 518,741; Marrou, LB, 7,497.
1988: Bush, R, 1,084,953; Dukakis, D, 1,001,619; Fulani, New Alliance, 6,656; Paul, write-in, 434.
1984: Reagan, R, 1,274,188; Mondale, D, 848,583.
1980: Reagan, R, 1,074,181; Carter, D, 931,182; Anderson, Ind., 77,920; Clark, LB, 14,422; DeBerry, Soc. Workers, 1,515; Commoner, Citizens, 573; write-in, 31.
1976: Carter, D, 999,163; Ford, R, 928,808; McCarthy, Ind., 24,329.
1972: Nixon, R, 1,154,058; McGovern, D, 698,531.
1968: Nixon, R, 811,932; Humphrey, D, 791,444; Wallace, 3rd party, 206,126.
1964: Johnson, D, 1,164,344; Goldwater, R, 653,535.
1960: Kennedy, D, 972,201; Nixon, R, 962,221.

Montana

	2012		2008	
County	Obama (D)	Romney (R)	Obama (D)	McCain (R)
Beaverhead	1,371	3,289	1,617	3,008
Big Horn	2,882	1,667	3,516	1,628
Blaine	1,616	1,178	1,702	1,139
Broadwater	764	2,152	857	1,875
Carbon	2,146	3,533	2,443	3,108
Carter	96	678	111	573
Cascade	15,232	18,345	17,664	16,857
Chouteau	978	1,758	1,122	1,634
Custer	1,833	3,373	2,267	3,047
Daniels	237	740	343	694
Dawson	1,219	3,029	1,593	2,639
Deer Lodge	2,860	1,448	3,402	1,502
Fallon	237	1,128	318	1,064
Fergus	1,640	4,257	1,933	4,108
Flathead	13,892	28,309	16,138	25,559
Gallatin	21,961	24,358	24,205	22,578
Garfield	66	622	110	598
Glacier	2,924	1,415	3,423	1,451
Golden Valley	110	351	124	343
Granite	533	1,107	601	1,013
Hill	3,403	3,164	3,596	2,787
Jefferson	2,272	4,055	2,582	3,538
Judith Basin	337	854	397	801
Lake	5,805	7,135	6,766	6,498
Lewis and Clark	15,620	16,803	17,114	14,966
Liberty	257	702	367	594
Lincoln	2,552	6,057	3,025	5,704
Madison	1,289	3,130	1,607	2,822
McCone	223	745	321	726
Meagher	269	670	298	624
Mineral	700	1,216	845	1,053
Missoula	32,824	22,652	36,531	20,743
Musselshell	492	1,833	636	1,581
Park	3,783	4,709	4,173	4,376
Petroleum	49	240	68	227
Phillips	471	1,688	638	1,423
Pondera	975	1,673	1,223	1,588
Powder River	170	833	208	802
Powell	888	1,806	1,021	1,683
Prairie	167	520	211	503
Ravalli	7,285	14,307	8,400	13,002
Richland	1,002	3,510	1,203	3,184
Roosevelt	2,086	1,514	2,564	1,473
Rosebud	1,422	2,004	1,919	1,768
Sanders	1,720	3,980	1,970	3,563
Sheridan	665	1,207	953	987
Silver Bow	10,857	5,430	11,676	4,818
Stillwater	1,248	3,337	1,512	2,991
Sweet Grass	475	1,594	541	1,494
Teton	1,082	2,113	1,294	1,874
Toole	582	1,440	737	1,317
Treasure	114	319	156	314
Valley	1,385	2,337	1,645	2,121
Wheatland	272	693	289	657
Wibaux	98	421	146	379
Yellowstone	26,403	40,500	32,038	36,483
Totals	**201,839**	**267,928**	**231,667**	**242,763**

Montana Vote Since 1960

2012: Romney, R, 267,928; Obama, D, 201,839; Johnson, LB, 14,165.
2008: McCain, R, 242,763; Obama, D, 231,667; Paul, Const., 10,638; Nader, Ind., 3,686; Barr, LB, 1,355.
2004: Bush, R, 266,063; Kerry, D, 173,710; Nader, Ind., 6,168; Peroutka, Const., 1,764; Badnarik, LB, 1,733; Cobb, Green, 996.
2000: Bush, R, 240,178; Gore, D, 137,126; Nader, Green, 24,437; Buchanan, RF, 5,697; Browne, LB, 1,718; Phillips, Const., 1,155; Hagelin, Natural Law, 675.
1996: Dole, R, 179,652; Clinton, D, 167,922; Perot, RF, 55,229; Browne, LB, 2,526; Hagelin, Natural Law, 1,754.
1992: Clinton, D, 154,507; Bush, R, 144,207; Perot, Ind., 107,225; Gritz, Populist/America First, 3,658.
1988: Bush, R, 190,412; Dukakis, D, 168,936; Paul, LB, 5,047; Fulani, New Alliance, 1,279.
1984: Reagan, R, 232,450; Mondale, D, 146,742; Bergland, LB, 5,185.
1980: Reagan, R, 206,814; Carter, D, 118,032; Anderson, Ind., 29,281; Clark, LB, 9,825.
1976: Ford, R, 173,703; Carter, D, 149,259; Anderson, Amer., 5,772.
1972: Nixon, R, 183,976; McGovern, D, 120,197; Schmitz, Amer., 13,430.
1968: Nixon, R, 138,835; Humphrey, D, 114,117; Wallace, 3rd party, 20,015; Munn, Prohib., 510; Caton, New RF, 470; Halstead, Soc. Workers, 457.
1964: Johnson, D, 164,246; Goldwater, R, 113,032; Kasper, Natl. States' Rights, 519; Munn, Prohib., 499; DeBerry, Soc. Workers, 332.
1960: Nixon, R, 141,841; Kennedy, D, 134,891; Decker, Prohib., 456; Dobbs, Soc. Workers, 391.

Nebraska

	2012		2008	
County	Obama (D)	Romney (R)	Obama (D)	McCain (R)
Adams	4,062	8,316	4,685	8,252
Antelope	571	2,596	757	2,383
Arthur	30	227	39	217
Banner	55	346	62	348
Blaine	29	268	43	266
Boone	615	2,138	742	2,042
Box Butte	1,692	2,869	1,886	2,932
Boyd	188	873	250	839
Brown	224	1,302	311	1,208
Buffalo	5,365	13,570	5,867	13,097
Burt	1,291	2,029	1,413	1,907
Butler	1,045	2,738	1,190	2,557
Cass	4,367	7,556	4,753	7,120
Cedar	958	3,278	1,190	2,912
Chase	254	1,584	341	1,477
Cherry	436	2,557	599	2,360
Cheyenne	1,084	3,449	1,173	3,572
Clay	667	2,232	780	2,177
Colfax	969	2,051	1,125	2,018
Cuming	1,031	2,876	1,274	2,732
Custer	1,083	4,296	1,192	4,301
Dakota	2,922	3,094	2,994	3,292
Dawes	1,132	2,478	1,285	2,376
Dawson	2,199	5,460	2,399	5,460
Deuel	215	763	243	732
Dixon	870	1,745	946	1,785
Dodge	5,673	8,995	6,689	8,557
Douglas	106,456	113,220	116,810	106,291
Dundy	176	792	218	783
Fillmore	807	2,007	962	1,913
Franklin	384	1,112	442	1,079
Frontier	271	1,007	349	1,034
Furnas	423	1,782	556	1,725
Gage	3,903	5,513	4,473	5,435
Garden	242	829	283	844

	2012		2008	
County	Obama (D)	Romney (R)	Obama (D)	McCain (R)
Garfield	149	769	212	800
Gosper	230	734	260	776
Grant	30	322	41	318
Greeley	340	820	458	715
Hall	7,161	12,646	7,855	12,977
Hamilton	1,146	3,600	1,332	3,389
Harlan	354	1,395	402	1,329
Hayes	51	476	85	461
Hitchcock	274	1,178	346	1,001
Holt	882	3,922	1,089	3,746
Hooker	59	330	75	355
Howard	914	1,890	1,083	1,847
Jefferson	1,195	2,166	1,520	2,103
Johnson	790	1,225	914	1,142
Kearney	773	2,349	876	2,224
Keith	928	3,044	974	2,942
Keya Paha	80	393	115	409
Kimball	395	1,235	439	1,346
Knox	1,059	2,885	1,255	2,728
Lancaster	62,015	62,434	65,734	59,398
Lincoln	4,450	10,728	5,046	10,817
Logan	68	356	81	327
Loup	62	290	86	302
Madison	3,485	10,062	4,142	9,655
McPherson	41	237	45	240
Merrick	925	2,490	986	2,375
Morrill	455	1,681	557	1,725
Nance	481	1,106	549	1,116
Nemaha	1,128	2,012	1,240	2,134
Nuckolls	568	1,574	657	1,498
Otoe	2,561	4,258	2,915	4,033
Pawnee	400	899	483	859
Perkins	238	1,135	310	1,092
Phelps	880	3,400	1,050	3,360
Pierce	637	2,707	783	2,385
Platte	3,148	10,061	3,796	9,373
Polk	528	1,890	668	1,822
Red Willow	952	3,891	1,216	3,735
Richardson	1,191	2,443	1,513	2,342
Rock	103	672	139	640
Saline	2,289	2,557	2,674	2,434
Sarpy	26,671	43,213	28,010	38,816
Saunders	3,307	6,770	3,767	6,188
Scotts Bluff	4,327	9,648	4,745	9,708
Seward	2,386	5,003	2,703	4,647
Sheridan	390	2,021	454	1,941
Sherman	552	927	585	950
Sioux	101	624	117	603
Stanton	614	1,949	664	1,781
Thayer	728	1,874	860	1,749
Thomas	42	360	51	331
Thurston	1,247	939	1,120	972
Valley	498	1,657	706	1,657
Washington	3,132	6,899	3,711	6,425
Wayne	1,074	2,493	1,249	2,503
Webster	442	1,258	552	1,233
Wheeler	93	345	96	334
York	1,373	4,874	1,607	4,848
Totals	**302,081**	**475,064**	**333,319**	**452,979**

Nebraska Vote Since 1960

2012: Romney, R, 475,064; Obama, D, 302,081; Johnson, LB, 11,109; Terry, petitioning cand., 2,408.
2008: McCain, R, 452,979; Obama, D, 333,319; Nader, petitioning cand., 5,406; Baldwin, Nebraska, 2,972; Barr, LB, 2,740; McKinney, Green, 1,028.
2004: Bush, R, 512,814; Kerry, D, 254,328; Nader, petitioning cand., 5,698; Badnarik, LB, 2,041; Peroutka, Nebraska, 1,314; Cobb, Green, 978; Calero, petitioning cand., 82.
2000: Bush, R, 433,862; Gore, D, 231,780; Nader, Green, 24,540; Buchanan, Ind., 3,646; Browne, LB, 2,245; Hagelin, Natural Law, 478; Phillips, Ind., 468.
1996: Dole, R, 363,467; Clinton, D, 236,761; Perot, RF, 71,278; Browne, LB, 2,792; Phillips, Ind., 1,928; Hagelin, Natural Law, 1,189.
1992: Bush, R, 343,678; Clinton, D, 216,864; Perot, Ind., 174,104; Marrou, LB, 1,340.
1988: Bush, R, 397,956; Dukakis, D, 259,235; Paul, LB, 2,534; Fulani, New Alliance, 1,740.
1984: Reagan, R, 459,135; Mondale, D, 187,475; Bergland, LB, 2,075.
1980: Reagan, R, 419,214; Carter, D, 166,424; Anderson, Ind., 44,854; Clark, LB, 9,041.
1976: Ford, R, 359,219; Carter, D, 233,287; McCarthy, Ind., 9,383; Maddox, Amer. Ind., 3,378; MacBride, LB, 1,476.
1972: Nixon, R, 406,298; McGovern, D, 169,991; scattered, 817.
1968: Nixon, R, 321,163; Humphrey, D, 170,784; Wallace, 3rd party, 44,904.
1964: Johnson, D, 307,307; Goldwater, R, 276,847.
1960: Nixon, R, 380,553; Kennedy, D, 232,542.

Nevada

	2012		2008	
County	Obama (D)	Romney (R)	Obama (D)	McCain (R)
Churchill	2,961	7,061	3,494	6,832
Clark	389,936	289,053	380,765	257,078
Douglas	9,297	16,276	10,672	14,648
Elko	3,511	12,014	4,541	10,969
Esmeralda	92	317	104	303
Eureka	107	663	144	564
Humboldt	1,737	3,810	1,909	3,586
Lander	534	1,580	577	1,466
Lincoln	400	1,691	518	1,498
Lyon	7,380	13,520	8,405	12,154
Mineral	863	1,080	1,082	1,131
Nye	6,320	10,566	7,226	9,537
Pershing	632	1,167	673	1,075
Storey	920	1,321	1,102	1,247
Washoe	95,409	88,453	99,671	76,880
White Pine	983	2,601	1,230	2,440
City				
Carson City	10,291	12,394	11,623	11,419
Totals	**531,373**	**463,567**	**533,736**	**412,827**

Nevada Vote Since 1960

2012: Obama, D, 531,373; Romney, R, 463,567; Johnson, LB, 10,968; None of These Candidates, 5,770; Goode, Ind. Amer., 3,240.
2008: Obama, D, 533,736; McCain, R, 412,827; None of These Candidates, 6,267; Nader, Ind., 6,150; Barr, LB, 4,263; Baldwin, Const., 3,194; McKinney, Green, 1,411.
2004: Bush, R, 418,690; Kerry, D, 397,190; Nader, Ind., 4,838; None of These Candidates, 3,688; Badnarik, LB, 3,176; Peroutka, Ind. Amer., 1,152; Cobb, Green, 853.
2000: Bush, R, 301,575; Gore, D, 279,978; Nader, Green, 15,008; Buchanan, Citizens First, 4,747; None of These Candidates, 3,315; Browne, LB, 3,311; Phillips, Ind. Amer., 621; Hagelin, Natural Law, 415.
1996: Clinton, D, 203,974; Dole, R, 199,244; Perot, RF, 43,986; None of These Candidates, 5,608; Nader, Green, 4,730; Browne, LB, 4,460; Phillips, Ind. Amer., 1,732; Hagelin, Natural Law, 545.
1992: Clinton, D, 189,148; Bush, R, 175,828; Perot, Ind., 132,580; Gritz, Populist/America First, 2,892; Marrou, LB, 1,835.
1988: Bush, R, 206,040; Dukakis, D, 132,738; Paul, LB, 3,520; Fulani, New Alliance, 835.
1984: Reagan, R, 188,770; Mondale, D, 91,655; Bergland, LB, 2,292.
1980: Reagan, R, 155,017; Carter, D, 66,666; Anderson, Ind., 17,651; Clark, LB, 4,358.
1976: Ford, R, 101,273; Carter, D, 92,479; MacBride, LB, 1,519; Maddox, Amer. Ind., 1,497; scattered, 5,108.
1972: Nixon, R, 115,750; McGovern, D, 66,016.
1968: Nixon, R, 73,188; Humphrey, D, 60,598; Wallace, 3rd party, 20,432.
1964: Johnson, D, 79,339; Goldwater, R, 56,094.
1960: Kennedy, D, 54,880; Nixon, R, 52,387.

New Hampshire

	2012		2008	
County	Obama (D)	Romney (R)	Obama (D)	McCain (R)
Belknap	15,890	17,571	16,796	16,402
Carroll	13,977	14,207	15,221	13,387
Cheshire	25,380	15,156	26,971	15,205
Coos	9,095	6,342	9,532	6,558
Grafton	29,826	18,208	31,446	17,687
Hillsborough	102,303	99,991	104,820	97,178
Merrimack	44,756	34,524	45,078	34,010
Rockingham	80,142	87,921	83,723	81,917
Strafford	36,026	26,729	37,990	25,021
Sullivan	12,166	9,269	13,249	9,169
Totals	**369,561**	**329,918**	**384,826**	**316,534**

New Hampshire Vote Since 1960

2012: Obama, D, 369,561; Romney, R, 329,918; Johnson, LB, 8,212; Goode, Const., 708.
2008: Obama, D, 384,826; McCain, R, 316,534; Nader, Ind., 3,503; Barr, LB, 2,217; Phillies, LB, 531.
2004: Kerry, D, 340,511; Bush, R, 331,237; Nader, Ind., 4,479.
2000: Bush, R, 273,559; Gore, D, 266,348; Nader, Green, 22,198; Browne, LB, 2,757; Buchanan, Independence, 2,615; Phillips, Const., 328.
1996: Clinton, D, 246,166; Dole, R, 196,486; Perot, RF, 48,387; Browne, LB, 4,214; Phillips, Taxpayers, 1,344.

1992: Clinton, D, 209,040; Bush, R, 202,484; Perot, Ind., 121,337; Marrou, LB, 3,548.
1988: Bush, R, 281,537; Dukakis, D, 163,696; Paul, LB, 4,502; Fulani, New Alliance, 790.
1984: Reagan, R, 267,051; Mondale, D, 120,377; Bergland, LB, 735.
1980: Reagan, R, 221,705; Carter, D, 108,864; Anderson, Ind., 49,693; Clark, LB, 2,067; Commoner, Citizens, 1,325; Hall, Comm., 129; Griswold, Workers World, 76; DeBerry, Soc. Workers, 72; scattered, 68.
1976: Ford, R, 185,935; Carter, D, 147,645; McCarthy, Ind., 4,095; MacBride, LB, 936; Reagan, write-in, 388; LaRouche, U.S. Labor, 186; Camejo, Soc. Workers, 161; Levin, Soc. Labor, 66; scattered, 215.
1972: Nixon, R, 213,724; McGovern, D, 116,435; Schmitz, Amer., 3,386; Jenness, Soc. Workers, 368; scattered, 142.
1968: Nixon, R, 154,903; Humphrey, D, 130,589; Wallace, 3rd party, 11,173; New Party, 421; Halstead, Soc. Workers, 104.
1964: Johnson, D, 182,065; Goldwater, R, 104,029.
1960: Nixon, R, 157,989; Kennedy, D, 137,772.

New Jersey

	2012		2008	
County	**Obama (D)**	**Romney (R)**	**Obama (D)**	**McCain (R)**
Atlantic	65,600	46,522	67,830	49,902
Bergen	212,754	169,070	225,367	186,118
Burlington	126,377	87,401	131,219	89,626
Camden	153,682	69,476	159,259	73,819
Cape May	21,657	25,781	22,893	27,288
Cumberland	34,055	20,658	34,919	22,360
Essex	236,618	64,406	240,306	74,063
Gloucester	74,013	59,456	77,267	60,315
Hudson	153,108	42,369	154,140	55,360
Hunterdon	26,876	38,687	29,776	39,092
Mercer	104,377	47,355	107,926	50,223
Middlesex	190,555	107,310	193,812	123,695
Monmouth	133,145	147,513	148,737	160,433
Morris	100,146	124,947	112,275	132,331
Ocean	102,300	146,474	110,189	160,677
Passaic	115,926	64,523	113,257	72,552
Salem	14,719	14,334	16,044	14,816
Somerset	74,592	66,603	79,321	70,085
Sussex	26,104	40,625	28,840	44,184
Union	139,752	68,314	141,417	78,768
Warren	18,745	25,744	20,628	27,500
Totals	**2,125,101**	**1,477,568**	**2,215,422**	**1,613,207**

New Jersey Vote Since 1960

2012: Obama, D, 2,125,101; Romney, R, 1,477,568; Johnson, LB, 21,045; Stein, Green, 9,888; Goode, Const., 2,064; Anderson, Justice, 1,724; Boss, Ind., 1,007; Harris, Soc. Workers, 710; Miller, A3P, 664; Lindsay, Socialism/Liberation, 521.
2008: Obama, D, 2,215,422; McCain, R, 1,613,207; Nader, Ind., 21,298; Barr, Ind., 8,441; Baldwin, Ind., 3,956; McKinney, Ind., 3,636; Moore, Ind., 699; Boss, Ind., 639; Calero, Ind., 523; La Riva, Ind., 416.
2004: Kerry, D, 1,911,430; Bush, R, 1,670,003; Nader, Ind., 19,418; Badnarik, Ind., 4,514; Peroutka, Ind., 2,750; Cobb, Ind., 1,807; Brown, Ind., 664; Van Auken, Ind., 575; Calero, Ind., 530.
2000: Gore, D, 1,788,850; Bush, R, 1,284,173; Nader, Ind., 94,554; Buchanan, Ind., 6,989; Browne, Ind., 6,312; Hagelin, Ind., 2,215; McReynolds, Ind., 1,880; Phillips, Ind., 1,409; Harris, Ind., 844.
1996: Clinton, D, 1,652,361; Dole, R, 1,103,099; Perot, RF, 262,134; Nader, Green, 32,465; Browne, LB, 14,763; Hagelin, Natural Law, 3,887; Phillips, U.S. Taxpayers, 3,440; Harris, Soc. Workers, 1,837; Moorehead, Workers World, 1,337; White, Soc. Equality, 537.
1992: Clinton, D, 1,436,206; Bush, R, 1,356,865; Perot, Ind., 521,829; Marrou, LB, 6,822; Fulani, New Alliance, 3,513; Phillips, U.S. Taxpayers, 2,670; LaRouche, Ind., 2,095; Warren, Soc. Workers, 2,011; Daniels, Ind., 1,996; Gritz, Populist/America First, 1,867; Hagelin, Natural Law, 1,353.
1988: Bush, R, 1,740,604; Dukakis, D, 1,317,541; Lewin, Peace/Freedom, 9,953; Paul, LB, 8,421.
1984: Reagan, R, 1,933,630; Mondale, D, 1,261,323; Bergland, LB, 6,416.
1980: Reagan, R, 1,546,557; Carter, D, 1,147,364; Anderson, Ind., 234,632; Clark, LB, 20,652; Commoner, Citizens, 8,203; McCormack, Right to Life, 3,927; Lynen, Middle Class, 3,694; Hall, Comm., 2,555; Pulley, Soc. Workers, 2,198; McReynolds, Soc., 1,973; Gahres, Down With Lawyers, 1,718; Griswold, Workers World, 1,288; Wendelken, Ind., 923.
1976: Ford, R, 1,509,688; Carter, D, 1,444,653; McCarthy, Ind., 32,717; MacBride, LB, 9,449; Maddox, Amer., 7,716; Levin, Soc. Labor, 3,686; Hall, Comm., 1,662; LaRouche, U.S. Labor, 1,650; Camejo, Soc. Workers, 1,184; Wright, People's, 1,044; Bubar, Prohib., 554; Zeidler, Soc., 469.
1972: Nixon, R, 1,845,502; McGovern, D, 1,102,211; Schmitz, Amer., 34,378; Spock, People's, 5,355; Fisher, Soc. Labor, 4,544; Jenness, Soc. Workers, 2,233; Mahalchik, America First, 1,743; Hall, Comm., 1,263.
1968: Nixon, R, 1,325,467; Humphrey, D, 1,264,206; Wallace, 3rd party, 262,187; Halstead, Soc. Workers, 8,667; Gregory, Peace/Freedom, 8,084; Blomen, Soc. Labor, 6,784.
1964: Johnson, D, 1,867,671; Goldwater, R, 963,843; DeBerry, Soc. Workers, 8,181; Hass, Soc. Labor, 7,075.
1960: Kennedy, D, 1,385,415; Nixon, R, 1,363,324; Dobbs, Soc. Workers, 11,402; Lee, Conservative, 8,708; Hass, Soc. Labor, 4,262.

New Mexico

	2012		2008	
County	**Obama (D)**	**Romney (R)**	**Obama (D)**	**McCain (R)**
Bernalillo	150,739	106,408	171,556	110,521
Catron	560	1,494	664	1,398
Chaves	6,604	13,088	8,197	13,651
Cibola	4,961	2,998	5,827	3,131
Colfax	2,828	2,699	3,490	2,805
Curry	4,022	9,251	4,670	9,599
De Baca	287	586	359	676
Doña Ana	37,139	27,322	40,282	28,068
Eddy	6,142	12,583	7,351	12,500
Grant	7,090	5,358	8,142	5,406
Guadalupe	1,488	557	1,557	620
Harding	260	327	260	358
Hidalgo	995	899	993	936
Lea	4,080	12,548	5,108	13,347
Lincoln	2,942	5,961	3,535	6,001
Los Alamos	5,191	4,796	5,824	5,064
Luna	3,583	3,670	4,311	3,870
McKinley	15,841	5,546	16,572	6,382
Mora	1,955	595	2,168	569
Otero	6,829	12,451	8,610	12,806
Quay	1,383	2,202	1,547	2,367
Rio Arriba	11,465	3,397	12,703	4,086
Roosevelt	1,727	4,043	2,303	4,311
San Juan	15,855	28,849	18,028	27,869
San Miguel	8,850	2,303	10,320	2,478
Sandoval	27,236	24,387	32,669	25,193
Santa Fe	50,872	15,500	55,567	15,807
Sierra	1,964	2,928	2,352	3,017
Socorro	4,058	2,722	4,696	3,032
Taos	11,978	2,730	13,816	2,866
Torrance	2,428	3,529	3,087	3,735
Union	472	1,236	492	1,227
Valencia	13,511	12,825	15,366	13,136
Totals	**415,335**	**335,788**	**472,422**	**346,832**

New Mexico Vote Since 1960

2012: Obama, D, 415,335; Romney, R, 335,788; Johnson, LB, 27,788; Stein, Green, 2,691; Anderson, Ind., 1,174; Goode, Const., 982.
2008: Obama, D, 472,422; McCain, R, 346,832; Nader, Ind., 5,327; Barr, LB, 2,428; Baldwin, Const., 1,597; McKinney, Green, 1,552.
2004: Bush, R, 376,930; Kerry, D, 370,942; Nader, Ind., 4,053; Badnarik, LB, 2,382; Cobb, Green, 1,226; Peroutka, Const., 771.
2000: Gore, D, 286,783; Bush, R, 286,417; Nader, Green, 21,251; Browne, LB, 2,058; Buchanan, RF, 1,392; Hagelin, Natural Law, 361; Phillips, Const., 343.
1996: Clinton, D, 273,495; Dole, R, 232,751; Perot, RF, 32,257; Nader, Green, 13,218; Browne, LB, 2,996; Phillips, Taxpayers, 713; Hagelin, Natural Law, 644.
1992: Clinton, D, 261,617; Bush, R, 212,824; Perot, Ind., 91,895; Marrou, LB, 1,615.
1988: Bush, R, 270,341; Dukakis, D, 244,497; Paul, LB, 3,268; Fulani, New Alliance, 2,237.
1984: Reagan, R, 307,101; Mondale, D, 201,769; Bergland, LB, 4,459.
1980: Reagan, R, 250,779; Carter, D, 167,826; Anderson, Ind., 29,459; Clark, LB, 4,365; Commoner, Citizens, 2,202; Bubar, Statesman, 1,281; Pulley, Soc. Workers, 325.
1976: Ford, R, 211,419; Carter, D, 201,148; Camejo, Soc. Workers, 2,462; MacBride, LB, 1,110; Zeidler, Soc., 240; Bubar, Prohib., 211.
1972: Nixon, R, 235,606; McGovern, D, 141,084; Schmitz, Amer., 8,767; Jenness, Soc. Workers, 474.
1968: Nixon, R, 169,692; Humphrey, D, 130,081; Wallace, 3rd party, 25,737; Chavez, 1,519; Halstead, Soc. Workers, 252.
1964: Johnson, D, 194,017; Goldwater, R, 131,838; Hass, Soc. Labor, 1,217; Munn, Prohib., 543.
1960: Kennedy, D, 156,027; Nixon, R, 153,733; Decker, Prohib., 777; Hass, Soc. Labor, 570.

New York

County	2012 Obama (D)	2012 Romney (R)	2008 Obama (D)	2008 McCain (R)
Albany	87,556	45,064	93,937	50,586
Allegany	6,139	10,390	7,016	11,013
Bronx[1]	339,211	29,967	338,261	41,683
Broome	41,970	37,641	47,204	40,077
Cattaraugus	12,649	16,569	14,307	17,770
Cayuga	17,007	13,454	18,128	15,243
Chautauqua	23,812	27,971	29,129	28,579
Chemung	16,797	17,612	18,888	19,364
Chenango	9,116	9,713	10,100	10,337
Clinton	18,961	11,115	20,216	12,579
Columbia	16,221	12,225	17,556	13,337
Cortland	10,482	8,695	11,861	9,678
Delaware	8,304	9,938	9,462	10,524
Dutchess	65,312	56,025	71,060	59,628
Erie	237,356	169,675	256,299	178,815
Essex	9,784	6,647	10,390	7,913
Franklin	9,894	5,740	10,571	6,676
Fulton	8,607	10,814	9,695	11,709
Genesee	9,601	14,607	10,762	15,705
Greene	9,030	11,174	9,850	12,059
Hamilton	1,128	1,932	1,225	2,141
Herkimer	11,273	13,282	12,094	14,619
Jefferson	17,099	18,122	18,166	20,220
Kings (Brooklyn)[1]	604,443	124,551	603,525	151,872
Lewis	4,724	5,651	4,986	5,969
Livingston	11,705	14,448	13,655	16,030
Madison	13,871	13,622	14,692	14,434
Monroe	193,501	133,362	207,371	144,262
Montgomery	8,493	9,334	9,080	10,711
Nassau	302,695	259,308	342,185	288,776
New York (Manhattan)[1]	502,674	89,559	572,126	89,906
Niagara	43,986	43,240	47,303	46,348
Oneida	40,468	44,530	43,506	49,256
Onondaga	122,254	78,831	129,317	84,972
Ontario	23,087	23,820	25,103	25,171
Orange	73,315	65,367	78,326	72,042
Orleans	5,787	8,594	6,614	9,708
Oswego	23,515	19,980	24,777	23,571
Otsego	12,117	11,461	13,570	12,026
Putnam	19,512	24,083	21,613	25,145
Queens[1]	470,732	118,589	480,692	155,221
Rensselaer	37,408	29,113	39,753	32,840
Richmond (Staten Island)[1]	78,181	74,223	79,311	86,062
Rockland	65,657	57,363	69,543	61,752
St. Lawrence	21,353	15,138	23,706	16,956
Saratoga	52,957	50,382	56,645	52,855
Schenectady	36,844	26,568	38,611	29,758
Schoharie	5,427	7,467	6,009	8,071
Schuyler	3,674	4,281	3,933	4,542
Seneca	7,094	5,889	7,422	7,038
Steuben	15,787	21,954	17,148	24,203
Suffolk	304,079	282,131	346,549	307,021
Sullivan	15,268	12,705	16,850	13,900
Tioga	8,930	12,117	10,172	12,536
Tompkins	27,244	11,107	29,826	11,927
Ulster	47,752	29,759	54,320	33,300
Warren	14,806	14,119	16,281	15,429
Washington	11,523	11,085	12,741	12,533
Wayne	16,635	20,060	18,184	22,239
Westchester	240,785	143,122	261,810	147,824
Wyoming	5,661	10,348	6,379	10,998
Yates	4,488	4,798	4,890	5,269
Totals	**4,485,741**	**2,490,431**	**4,804,945**	**2,752,771**

(1) Borough of New York City.

New York Vote Since 1960

2012: Obama, D, 4,485,741; Romney, R, 2,490,431; Johnson, LB, 47,256; Stein, Green, 39,982; Goode, Const., 6,274; Lindsay, Socialism/Liberation, 2,050.

2008: Obama, D, 4,804,945; McCain, R, 2,752,771; Nader, Populist, 41,249; Barr, LB, 19,596; McKinney, Green, 12,801; Calero, Soc. Workers, 3,615; La Riva, Socialism/Liberation, 1,639.

2004: Kerry, D, 4,314,280; Bush, R, 2,962,567; Nader, Ind., 99,873; Badnarik, LB, 11,607; Calero, Soc. Workers, 2,405.

2000: Gore, D, 4,112,965; Bush, R, 2,405,570; Nader, Green, 244,360; Buchanan, RF, 31,554; Hagelin, Independence, 24,369; Browne, LB, 7,664; Harris, Soc. Workers, 1,790; Phillips, Const., 1,503.

1996: Clinton, D, 3,756,177; Dole, R, 1,933,492; Perot, RF, 503,458; Nader, Green, 75,956; Phillips, Right to Life, 23,580; Browne, LB, 12,220; Hagelin, Natural Law, 5,011; Moorehead, Workers World, 3,473; Harris, Soc. Workers, 2,762.

1992: Clinton, D, 3,444,450; Bush, R, 2,346,649; Perot, Ind., 1,090,721; Warren, Soc. Workers, 15,472; Marrou, LB, 13,451; Fulani, New Alliance, 11,318; Hagelin, Natural Law, 4,420.

1988: Dukakis, D, 3,347,882; Bush, R, 3,081,871; Marra, Right to Life, 20,497; Fulani, New Alliance, 15,845.

1984: Reagan, R, 3,664,763; Mondale, D, 3,119,609; Bergland, LB, 11,949.

1980: Reagan, R, 2,893,831; Carter, D, 2,728,372; Anderson, Liberal, 467,801; Clark, LB, 52,648; McCormack, Right to Life, 24,159; Commoner, Citizens, 23,186; Hall, Comm., 7,414; DeBerry, Soc. Workers, 2,068; Griswold, Workers World, 1,416; scattered, 1,064.

1976: Carter, D, 3,389,558; Ford, R, 3,100,791; MacBride, LB, 12,197; Hall, Comm., 10,270; Camejo, Soc. Workers, 6,996; LaRouche, U.S. Labor, 5,413; blank, void, and scattered, 143,037.

1972: Nixon, R, 3,824,642; McGovern, D, 2,767,956 and Liberal, 183,128 (total, 2,951,084); Reed, Soc. Workers, 7,797; Fisher, Soc. Labor, 4,530; Hall, Comm., 5,641; blank, void, and scattered, 161,641.

1968: Humphrey, D, 3,378,470; Nixon, R, 3,007,932; Wallace, 3rd party, 358,864; Gregory, Peace/Freedom, 24,517; Halstead, Soc. Workers, 11,851; Blomen, Soc. Labor, 8,432; blank, void, and scattered, 171,624.

1964: Johnson, D, 4,913,156; Goldwater, R, 2,243,559; Hass, Soc. Labor, 6,085; DeBerry, Soc. Workers, 3,215; scattered, 188; blank and void, 151,383.

1960: Kennedy, D, 3,423,909 and Liberal, 406,176 (total, 3,830,085); Nixon, R, 3,446,419; Dobbs, Soc. Workers, 14,319; scattered, 256; blank and void, 88,896.

North Carolina

County	2012 Obama (D)	2012 Romney (R)	2008 Obama (D)	2008 McCain (R)
Alamance	28,875	38,170	28,918	34,859
Alexander	4,611	12,253	5,167	11,790
Alleghany	1,583	3,390	2,021	3,124
Anson	7,019	4,166	6,456	4,207
Ashe	4,116	8,242	4,872	7,916
Avery	1,882	5,766	2,178	5,681
Beaufort	9,435	13,977	9,454	13,460
Bertie	6,695	3,387	6,365	3,376
Bladen	8,062	7,748	7,853	7,532
Brunswick	22,038	34,743	21,331	30,753
Buncombe	70,625	54,701	69,716	52,494
Burke	13,701	22,267	14,901	22,102
Cabarrus	32,849	49,557	31,546	45,924
Caldwell	10,898	23,229	12,081	22,526
Camden	1,508	3,109	1,597	3,140
Carteret	10,301	24,775	11,130	23,131
Caswell	5,348	5,594	5,545	5,208
Catawba	24,069	44,538	25,656	42,993
Chatham	18,361	16,665	17,862	14,668
Cherokee	3,378	9,278	3,785	8,643
Chowan	3,556	3,891	3,688	3,773
Clay	1,579	3,973	1,734	3,707
Cleveland	17,062	25,793	17,363	26,078
Columbus	11,050	12,941	11,076	12,994
Craven	18,763	26,928	19,352	24,901
Cumberland	75,792	50,666	74,693	52,151
Currituck	3,562	7,496	3,737	7,234
Dare	7,393	10,248	8,074	9,745
Davidson	20,624	49,383	22,433	45,419
Davie	5,735	14,687	6,178	13,981
Duplin	9,033	11,416	8,958	10,834
Durham	111,224	33,769	103,456	32,353
Edgecombe	18,310	8,546	17,403	8,445
Forsyth	92,323	79,768	91,085	73,674
Franklin	13,436	14,603	13,085	13,273
Gaston	33,171	56,138	31,384	52,507
Gates	2,786	2,564	2,830	2,547
Graham	1,119	2,750	1,265	2,824
Granville	13,598	12,405	13,074	11,447
Greene	3,778	4,411	3,796	4,272
Guilford	146,365	104,789	142,101	97,718
Halifax	17,176	8,763	16,047	8,961
Harnett	17,331	25,565	16,785	23,579
Haywood	11,833	15,633	12,730	14,910
Henderson	18,642	32,994	20,082	30,930
Hertford	7,843	3,007	7,513	3,089
Hoke	10,076	6,819	9,227	6,293
Hyde	1,163	1,193	1,241	1,212
Iredell	26,076	49,299	27,318	45,148
Jackson	8,095	8,254	8,766	7,854
Johnston	27,290	48,427	26,795	43,622
Jones	2,352	2,837	2,378	2,817
Lee	10,801	13,158	10,784	12,775
Lenoir	13,948	13,980	13,378	13,401
Lincoln	11,024	25,267	11,713	23,631

County	2012 Obama (D)	2012 Romney (R)	2008 Obama (D)	2008 McCain (R)
Macon	5,712	10,835	6,620	10,317
Madison	4,484	5,404	5,026	5,192
Martin	6,583	5,995	6,539	5,957
McDowell	6,031	11,775	6,571	11,534
Mecklenburg	272,262	171,668	253,958	153,848
Mitchell	1,838	5,806	2,238	5,499
Montgomery	4,706	6,404	4,926	6,155
Moore	16,505	29,495	17,624	27,314
Nash	24,313	23,842	23,099	23,728
New Hanover	48,668	53,385	49,145	50,544
Northampton	7,232	3,483	6,903	3,671
Onslow	18,490	32,243	19,499	30,278
Orange	53,901	21,539	53,806	20,266
Pamlico	2,647	4,051	2,838	3,823
Pasquotank	10,282	7,633	10,272	7,778
Pender	9,632	14,617	9,907	13,618
Perquimans	2,759	3,822	2,772	3,678
Person	8,418	10,496	8,446	10,030
Pitt	41,843	36,214	40,501	33,927
Polk	4,013	6,236	4,396	5,990
Randolph	14,773	45,160	16,414	40,998
Richmond	9,904	9,332	9,713	9,424
Robeson	24,988	17,510	23,058	17,433
Rockingham	16,351	25,227	17,255	23,899
Rowan	22,650	38,775	23,391	37,451
Rutherford	9,374	18,954	9,641	18,769
Sampson	11,566	14,422	11,836	14,038
Scotland	8,215	5,831	8,151	6,005
Stanly	8,431	19,904	8,878	19,329
Stokes	6,018	15,237	6,875	14,488
Surry	9,112	19,923	10,475	18,730
Swain	2,618	2,976	2,806	2,900
Transylvania	6,826	9,634	7,275	9,401
Tyrrell	837	930	933	960
Union	32,473	61,107	31,189	54,123
Vance	13,323	7,429	13,166	7,606
Wake	267,262	211,596	250,891	187,001
Warren	6,978	3,140	7,086	3,063
Washington	3,833	2,622	3,748	2,670
Watauga	13,002	13,861	14,558	13,344
Wayne	23,314	27,641	22,671	26,952
Wilkes	8,148	20,515	8,934	20,288
Wilson	20,875	17,954	19,652	17,375
Yadkin	3,957	12,578	4,527	12,409
Yancey	3,981	5,278	4,486	5,045
Totals	**2,178,391**	**2,270,395**	**2,142,651**	**2,128,474**

North Carolina Vote Since 1960

2012: Romney, R, 2,270,395; Obama, D, 2,178,391; Johnson, LB, 44,515.
2008: Obama, D, 2,142,651; McCain, R, 2,128,474; Barr, LB, 25,722.
2004: Bush, R, 1,961,166; Kerry, D, 1,525,849; Badnarik, LB, 11,731.
2000: Bush, R, 1,631,163; Gore, D, 1,257,692; Browne, LB, 13,891; Buchanan, RF, 8,874.
1996: Dole, R, 1,225,938; Clinton, D, 1,107,849; Perot, RF, 168,059; Browne, LB, 8,740; Hagelin, Natural Law, 2,771.
1992: Bush, R, 1,134,661; Clinton, D, 1,114,042; Perot, Ind., 357,864; Marrou, LB, 5,171.
1988: Bush, R, 1,237,258; Dukakis, D, 890,167; Fulani, New Alliance, 5,682; Paul, write-in, 1,263.
1984: Reagan, R, 1,346,481; Mondale, D, 824,287; Bergland, LB, 3,794.
1980: Reagan, R, 915,018; Carter, D, 875,635; Anderson, Ind., 52,800; Clark, LB, 9,677; Commoner, Citizens, 2,287; DeBerry, Soc. Workers, 416.
1976: Carter, D, 927,365; Ford, R, 741,960; Anderson, Amer., 5,607; MacBride, LB, 2,219; LaRouche, U.S. Labor, 755.
1972: Nixon, R, 1,054,889; McGovern, D, 438,705; Schmitz, Amer., 25,018.
1968: Nixon, R, 627,192; Wallace, 3rd party, 496,188; Humphrey, D, 464,113.
1964: Johnson, D, 800,139; Goldwater, R, 624,844.
1960: Kennedy, D, 713,136; Nixon, R, 655,420.

North Dakota

County	2012 Obama (D)	2012 Romney (R)	2008 Obama (D)	2008 McCain (R)
Adams	328	918	435	788
Barnes	2,394	2,964	2,741	2,826
Benson	1,235	868	1,569	773
Billings	89	472	114	375
Bottineau	1,183	2,280	1,387	2,059
Bowman	414	1,280	478	1,107
Burke	230	769	286	640
Burleigh	14,122	27,951	15,600	25,443
Cass	34,712	36,855	37,622	32,566
Cavalier	818	1,195	930	1,128
Dickey	853	1,610	1,044	1,525
Divide	385	733	464	630
Dunn	508	1,506	527	1,080
Eddy	486	634	583	548
Emmons	383	1,435	546	1,230
Foster	607	1,030	687	914
Golden Valley	162	742	210	642
Grand Forks	14,032	15,060	16,104	14,520
Grant	334	1,025	280	587
Griggs	536	771	598	682
Hettinger	313	1,000	406	893
Kidder	393	870	422	752
LaMoure	740	1,377	868	1,310
Logan	232	810	299	726
McHenry	943	1,678	981	1,374
McIntosh	459	1,035	579	916
McKenzie	927	2,458	933	1,740
McLean	1,670	3,141	1,867	2,767
Mercer	1,166	3,152	1,476	2,789
Morton	4,469	8,680	5,079	7,869
Mountrail	1,403	1,962	1,477	1,406
Nelson	767	865	907	800
Oliver	281	693	332	682
Pembina	1,253	1,899	1,494	1,722
Pierce	660	1,465	792	1,301
Ramsey	2,164	2,665	2,314	2,361
Ransom	1,343	1,009	1,371	998
Renville	398	851	505	799
Richland	3,198	4,229	3,513	3,900
Rolette	3,353	1,092	3,403	1,045
Sargent	1,075	879	1,115	778
Sheridan	163	642	229	555
Sioux	900	225	1,145	215
Slope	83	341	106	297
Stark	2,812	8,521	3,802	7,024
Steele	518	498	614	404
Stutsman	3,585	5,685	4,056	5,499
Towner	516	623	621	536
Traill	1,811	1,996	2,136	1,845
Walsh	1,985	2,656	2,325	2,415
Ward	8,441	16,230	10,144	15,061
Wells	673	1,654	841	1,468
Williams	2,322	7,184	2,921	6,291
Totals	**124,827**	**188,163**	**141,278**	**168,601**

North Dakota Vote Since 1960

2012: Romney, R, 188,163; Obama, D, 124,827; Johnson, LB, 5,231; Stein, Green, 1,361; Goode, Const., 1,185.
2008: McCain, R, 168,601; Obama, D, 141,278; Nader, Ind., 4,189; Barr, LB, 1,354; Baldwin, Const., 1,199.
2004: Bush, R, 196,651; Kerry, D, 111,052; Nader, Ind., 3,756; Badnarik, LB, 851; Peroutka, Const., 514.
2000: Bush, R, 174,852; Gore, D, 95,284; Nader, Ind., 9,486; Buchanan, RF, 7,288; Browne, Ind., 660; Phillips, Const., 373; Hagelin, Ind., 313.
1996: Dole, R, 125,050; Clinton, D, 106,905; Perot, RF, 32,515; Browne, LB, 847; Phillips, Ind., 745; Hagelin, Natural Law, 349.
1992: Bush, R, 136,244; Clinton, D, 99,168; Perot, Ind., 71,084.
1988: Bush, R, 166,559; Dukakis, D, 127,739; Paul, LB, 1,315; LaRouche, Natl. Econ. Recovery, 905.
1984: Reagan, R, 200,336; Mondale, D, 104,429; Bergland, LB, 703.
1980: Reagan, R, 193,695; Carter, D, 79,189; Anderson, Ind., 23,640; Clark, LB, 3,743; Commoner, LB, 429; McLain, Natl. People's League, 296; Greaves, Amer., 235; Hall, Comm., 93; DeBerry, Soc. Workers, 89; McReynolds, Soc., 82; Bubar, Statesman, 54.
1976: Ford, R, 153,470; Carter, D, 136,078; Anderson, Amer., 3,698; McCarthy, Ind., 2,952; Maddox, Amer. Ind., 269; MacBride, LB, 256; scattered, 371.
1972: Nixon, R, 174,109; McGovern, D, 100,384; Schmitz, Amer., 5,646; Jenness, Soc. Workers, 288; Hall, Comm., 87.
1968: Nixon, R, 138,669; Humphrey, D, 94,769; Wallace, 3rd party, 14,244; Halstead, Soc. Workers, 128; Munn, Prohib., 38; Troxell, Ind., 34.
1964: Johnson, D, 149,784; Goldwater, R, 108,207; DeBerry, Soc. Workers, 224; Munn, Prohib., 174.
1960: Nixon, R, 154,310; Kennedy, D, 123,963; Dobbs, Soc. Workers, 158.

Ohio

County	2012 Obama (D)	2012 Romney (R)	2008 Obama (D)	2008 McCain (R)
Adams	3,976	6,865	4,170	6,914
Allen	17,914	29,502	19,521	29,941
Ashland	8,281	15,519	9,300	15,158

	2012		2008	
County	Obama (D)	Romney (R)	Obama (D)	McCain (R)
Ashtabula	23,803	18,298	25,027	18,949
Athens	18,307	8,543	20,722	9,742
Auglaize	5,831	17,169	6,727	16,395
Belmont	14,156	16,758	16,302	15,422
Brown	7,107	11,916	7,503	12,192
Butler	62,388	105,176	66,030	105,340
Carroll	5,543	7,315	6,423	7,097
Champaign	7,044	11,045	7,385	11,141
Clark	31,297	31,820	31,958	33,634
Clermont	30,458	64,208	31,611	62,559
Clinton	5,791	12,009	6,558	12,410
Columbiana	19,821	25,251	21,882	25,585
Coshocton	6,940	8,390	7,689	8,675
Crawford	7,507	11,852	8,288	12,316
Cuyahoga	447,273	190,660	458,204	199,864
Darke	6,826	18,108	7,964	17,290
Defiance	7,732	10,176	8,399	10,407
Delaware	37,292	60,194	36,653	54,778
Erie	21,793	16,952	23,148	17,432
Fairfield	29,890	41,034	29,250	41,580
Fayette	4,249	6,620	4,401	7,102
Franklin	346,373	215,997	334,684	218,478
Fulton	9,073	11,738	9,900	11,689
Gallia	4,557	7,750	4,777	8,247
Geauga	19,659	30,589	21,250	29,096
Greene	32,256	49,819	33,540	48,936
Guernsey	7,450	8,993	7,625	9,197
Hamilton	219,927	193,326	224,644	195,107
Hancock	12,564	22,443	13,870	22,420
Hardin	4,619	7,489	5,013	7,749
Harrison	2,950	4,019	3,683	3,872
Henry	5,658	8,257	6,320	8,239
Highland	6,054	11,413	6,857	11,908
Hocking	6,157	6,285	6,231	6,326
Holmes	2,608	8,702	3,141	7,720
Huron	11,006	13,060	12,076	12,884
Jackson	5,166	7,904	5,397	8,219
Jefferson	15,385	17,034	17,635	17,559
Knox	10,470	17,266	11,014	16,640
Lake	57,680	58,744	60,155	59,142
Lawrence	10,744	14,651	11,262	15,415
Licking	34,201	45,503	33,896	46,886
Logan	7,062	13,633	7,936	13,848
Lorain	81,464	59,405	85,276	59,068
Lucas	136,616	69,940	142,852	73,706
Madison	6,845	10,342	6,532	10,603
Mahoning	77,059	42,641	79,173	45,319
Marion	12,504	14,265	12,870	15,454
Medina	38,785	50,418	40,924	48,189
Meigs	4,027	5,895	4,094	6,015
Mercer	4,745	16,561	5,853	15,100
Miami	16,383	34,606	18,372	33,417
Monroe	3,035	3,548	3,705	3,066
Montgomery	137,139	124,841	145,997	128,679
Morgan	2,814	3,179	2,966	3,440
Morrow	5,933	9,865	6,177	10,067
Muskingum	17,002	19,264	17,730	20,549
Noble	2,131	3,563	2,474	3,450
Ottawa	11,503	10,538	12,049	10,618
Paulding	3,538	5,354	4,165	5,317
Perry	7,033	7,627	7,261	7,721
Pickaway	9,684	14,037	9,077	14,228
Pike	5,684	5,685	6,033	6,162
Portage	39,453	35,242	41,856	34,822
Preble	6,211	13,535	6,999	13,562
Putnam	4,318	13,721	5,281	13,072
Richland	22,687	33,867	25,727	34,034
Ross	14,569	15,008	14,455	16,759
Sandusky	14,541	13,755	15,601	14,190
Scioto	15,077	15,492	14,926	16,994
Seneca	11,353	13,243	13,087	13,823
Shelby	6,343	17,142	7,317	15,924
Stark	89,432	88,581	96,990	86,743
Summit	153,041	111,001	155,105	110,499
Trumbull	61,672	38,279	64,145	40,164
Tuscarawas	18,407	22,242	21,498	20,454
Union	8,805	16,289	8,761	15,744
Van Wert	4,029	9,585	5,178	9,168
Vinton	2,436	2,856	2,463	3,021
Warren	32,909	76,564	33,398	71,691
Washington	11,651	17,284	12,368	17,019
Wayne	19,808	30,251	21,712	29,342
Williams	7,266	10,047	8,174	9,880
Wood	32,802	29,704	34,285	29,648
Wyandot	4,137	6,180	4,461	6,270
Totals	**2,827,709**	**2,661,437**	**2,940,044**	**2,677,820**

Ohio Vote Since 1960

2012: Obama, D, 2,827,709; Romney, R, 2,661,437; Johnson, LB, 49,493; Stein, Green, 18,573; Duncan, Ind., 12,502; Goode, Const., 8,152; Alexander, Soc., 2,944.

2008: Obama, D, 2,940,044; McCain, R, 2,677,820; Nader, Ind., 42,337; Barr, LB, 19,917; Baldwin, Const., 12,565; McKinney, Green, 8,518; Duncan, Ind., 3,905; Moore, Soc., 2,735.

2004: Bush, R, 2,859,768; Kerry, D, 2,741,167; Badnarik, nonpartisan, 14,676; Peroutka, nonpartisan, 939.

2000: Bush, R, 2,351,209; Gore, D, 2,186,190; Nader, Ind., 117,857; Buchanan, Ind., 26,724; Browne, LB, 13,475; Hagelin, Natural Law, 6,169; Phillips, Ind., 3,823.

1996: Clinton, D, 2,148,222; Dole, R, 1,859,883; Perot, RF, 483,207; Browne, Ind., 12,851; Moorehead, Ind., 10,813; Hagelin, Natural Law, 9,120; Phillips, Ind., 7,361.

1992: Clinton, D, 1,984,942; Bush, R, 1,894,310; Perot, Ind., 1,036,426; Marrou, LB, 7,252; Fulani, New Alliance, 6,413; Gritz, Populist/America First, 4,699; Hagelin, Natural Law, 3,437; LaRouche, Ind., 2,446.

1988: Bush, R, 2,416,549; Dukakis, D, 1,939,629; Fulani, Ind., 12,017; Paul, Ind., 11,926.

1984: Reagan, R, 2,678,559; Mondale, D, 1,825,440; Bergland, LB, 5,886.

1980: Reagan, R, 2,206,545; Carter, D, 1,752,414; Anderson, Ind., 254,472; Clark, LB, 49,033; Commoner, Citizens, 8,564; Hall, Comm., 4,729; Congress, Ind., 4,029; Griswold, Workers World, 3,790; Bubar, Statesman, 27.

1976: Carter, D, 2,011,621; Ford, R, 2,000,505; McCarthy, Ind., 58,258; Maddox, Amer. Ind., 15,529; MacBride, LB, 8,961; Hall, Comm., 7,817; Camejo, Soc. Workers, 4,717; LaRouche, U.S. Labor, 4,335; scattered, 130.

1972: Nixon, R, 2,441,827; McGovern, D, 1,558,889; Schmitz, Amer., 80,067; Fisher, Soc. Labor, 7,107; Hall, Comm., 6,437; Wallace, Ind., 460.

1968: Nixon, R, 1,791,014; Humphrey, D, 1,700,586; Wallace, 3rd party, 467,495; Gregory, 372; Blomen, Soc. Labor, 120; Halstead, Soc. Workers, 69; Mitchell, Comm., 23; Munn, Prohib., 19.

1964: Johnson, D, 2,498,331; Goldwater, R, 1,470,865.

1960: Nixon, R, 2,217,611; Kennedy, D, 1,944,248.

Oklahoma

	2012		2008	
County	Obama (D)	Romney (R)	Obama (D)	McCain (R)
Adair	2,127	4,381	2,052	4,638
Alfalfa	322	1,761	411	2,023
Atoka	1,243	3,538	1,370	3,511
Beaver	244	2,062	265	2,199
Beckham	1,417	5,508	1,625	5,772
Blaine	992	2,824	1,011	3,101
Bryan	3,681	9,520	4,426	9,307
Caddo	3,164	5,687	3,404	6,413
Canadian	10,537	35,625	11,426	36,428
Carter	4,908	12,214	5,603	13,241
Cherokee	6,144	8,162	7,194	9,186
Choctaw	1,494	3,572	1,860	3,730
Cimarron	115	1,082	152	1,119
Cleveland	34,771	59,116	39,681	64,749
Coal	649	1,710	600	1,672
Comanche	12,521	17,664	14,120	20,127
Cotton	657	1,796	690	1,793
Craig	1,747	3,559	2,073	3,858
Creek	7,128	18,986	8,318	20,187
Custer	2,359	7,446	2,660	7,842
Delaware	4,196	10,080	5,085	10,277
Dewey	301	1,792	346	1,857
Ellis	226	1,575	282	1,627
Garfield	4,733	15,177	5,545	17,067
Garvin	2,559	6,925	3,028	7,710
Grady	4,786	14,833	5,520	15,195
Grant	393	1,675	514	1,836
Greer	488	1,344	566	1,548
Harmon	264	659	333	757
Harper	173	1,261	221	1,342
Haskell	1,175	3,069	1,474	3,207
Hughes	1,370	2,838	1,709	3,134
Jackson	1,954	5,965	2,264	6,719
Jefferson	605	1,634	805	1,652
Johnston	1,137	2,649	1,249	2,708
Kay	4,627	11,499	5,463	13,230
Kingfisher	898	4,870	1,009	5,372
Kiowa	1,106	2,316	1,226	2,537
Latimer	1,170	2,628	1,313	2,860
Le Flore	4,662	11,177	5,136	11,605
Lincoln	3,273	9,553	3,504	10,470
Logan	4,724	12,314	5,717	12,556
Love	1,034	2,436	1,257	2,589
Major	446	2,700	515	2,956
Marshall	1,396	3,744	1,643	3,730
Mayes	4,823	9,637	5,749	10,234
McClain	3,194	11,112	3,551	11,193

County	2012 Obama (D)	2012 Romney (R)	2008 Obama (D)	2008 McCain (R)
McCurtain	2,440	7,635	2,794	7,745
McIntosh	2,779	4,509	3,320	4,903
Murray	1,540	3,606	1,592	3,746
Muskogee	9,952	13,404	11,294	15,289
Noble	1,143	3,488	1,174	3,881
Nowata	1,244	2,832	1,411	3,031
Okfuskee	1,256	2,335	1,480	2,643
Oklahoma	106,982	149,728	116,182	163,172
Okmulgee	5,432	7,731	6,191	8,727
Osage	6,704	11,242	7,498	12,160
Ottawa	3,509	6,466	4,268	6,905
Pawnee	1,813	4,232	2,063	4,533
Payne	9,198	16,481	10,601	18,435
Pittsburg	4,831	10,841	5,457	11,752
Pontotoc	3,947	8,945	4,512	9,750
Pottawatomie	7,188	16,250	7,910	17,753
Pushmataha	1,043	3,087	1,265	3,208
Roger Mills	272	1,402	287	1,502
Rogers	9,148	27,553	10,772	27,743
Seminole	2,600	4,856	2,977	5,600
Sequoyah	4,193	9,578	4,454	9,466
Stephens	3,939	12,908	4,538	14,394
Texas	862	4,930	923	5,336
Tillman	906	1,815	1,042	2,195
Tulsa	82,744	145,062	96,133	158,363
Wagoner	7,791	20,900	8,810	21,441
Washington	5,532	15,668	6,308	16,457
Washita	822	3,494	1,052	3,724
Woods	671	2,727	873	3,043
Woodward	1,133	5,945	1,350	6,404
Totals	**443,547**	**891,325**	**502,496**	**960,165**

Oklahoma Vote Since 1960

2012: Romney, R, 891,325; Obama, D, 443,547.
2008: McCain, R, 960,165; Obama, D, 502,496.
2004: Bush, R, 959,792; Kerry, D, 503,966.
2000: Bush, R, 744,337; Gore, D, 474,276; Buchanan, RF, 9,014; Browne, LB, 6,602.
1996: Dole, R, 582,315; Clinton, D, 488,105; Perot, RF, 130,788; Browne, LB, 5,505.
1992: Bush, R, 592,929; Clinton, D, 473,066; Perot, Ind., 319,878; Marrou, LB, 4,486.
1988: Bush, R, 678,367; Dukakis, D, 483,423; Paul, LB, 6,261; Fulani, New Alliance, 2,985.
1984: Reagan, R, 861,530; Mondale, D, 385,080; Bergland, LB, 9,066.
1980: Reagan, R, 695,570; Carter, D, 402,026; Anderson, Ind., 38,284; Clark, LB, 13,828.
1976: Ford, R, 545,708; Carter, D, 532,442; McCarthy, Ind., 14,101.
1972: Nixon, R, 759,025; McGovern, D, 247,147; Schmitz, Amer., 23,728.
1968: Nixon, R, 449,697; Humphrey, D, 301,658; Wallace, 3rd party, 191,731.
1964: Johnson, D, 519,834; Goldwater, R, 412,665.
1960: Nixon, R, 533,039; Kennedy, D, 370,111.

Oregon

County	2012 Obama (D)	2012 Romney (R)	2008 Obama (D)	2008 McCain (R)
Baker	2,369	5,702	2,805	5,650
Benton	27,776	14,991	29,901	15,264
Clackamas	95,493	88,592	103,476	83,595
Clatsop	9,861	7,249	10,701	7,192
Columbia	12,004	10,772	13,390	10,413
Coos	12,845	14,673	14,401	15,354
Crook	3,104	6,790	3,632	6,371
Curry	4,625	6,598	5,230	6,646
Deschutes	36,961	42,463	38,819	39,064
Douglas	17,145	30,776	20,298	30,919
Gilliam	371	639	430	648
Grant	853	2,926	1,006	2,785
Harney	832	2,607	950	2,595
Hood River	6,058	3,429	6,302	3,265
Jackson	44,468	49,020	49,090	49,043
Jefferson	3,301	4,642	3,682	4,402
Josephine	14,953	23,673	17,412	22,973
Klamath	8,302	18,898	9,370	19,113
Lake	770	2,808	957	2,638
Lane	102,652	62,509	114,037	63,835
Lincoln	13,401	8,686	14,258	8,791
Linn	20,378	28,944	22,163	28,071
Malheur	2,759	6,851	2,949	7,157
Marion	56,376	60,190	61,816	59,059
Morrow	1,202	2,532	1,410	2,509
Multnomah	274,887	75,302	279,696	75,171
Polk	16,292	17,819	17,536	17,714
Sherman	319	678	385	634
Tillamook	6,293	5,684	7,072	5,757
Umatilla	8,584	15,499	9,484	15,254
Union	3,973	7,636	4,613	7,581
Wallowa	1,253	2,804	1,492	2,836
Wasco	5,211	5,229	5,906	5,103
Washington	135,291	93,974	141,544	89,185
Wheeler	266	545	281	498
Yamhill	19,260	22,045	20,797	21,390
Totals	**970,488**	**754,175**	**1,037,291**	**738,475**

Oregon Vote Since 1960

2012: Obama, D, 970,488; Romney, R, 754,175; Johnson, LB, 24,089; Stein, Pacific Green, 19,427; Christensen, Const., 4,432; Anderson, OR Prog., 3,384.
2008: Obama, D, 1,037,291; McCain, R, 738,475; Nader, Peace Party of OR, 18,614; Baldwin, Const., 7,693; Barr, LB, 7,635; McKinney, Pacific Green, 4,543.
2004: Kerry, D, 943,163; Bush, R, 866,831; Badnarik, LB, 7,260; Cobb, Pacific Green, 5,315; Peroutka, Const., 5,257.
2000: Gore, D, 720,342; Bush, R, 713,577; Nader, Green, 77,357; Browne, LB, 7,447; Buchanan, Ind., 7,063; Hagelin, RF, 2,574; Phillips, Const., 2,189.
1996: Clinton, D, 649,641; Dole, R, 538,152; Perot, RF, 121,221; Nader, Pacific, 49,415; Browne, LB, 8,903; Phillips, Taxpayers, 3,379; Hagelin, Natural Law, 2,798; Hollis, Soc., 1,922.
1992: Clinton, D, 621,314; Bush, R, 475,757; Perot, Ind., 354,091; Marrou, LB, 4,277; Fulani, New Alliance, 3,030.
1988: Dukakis, D, 616,206; Bush, R, 560,126; Paul, LB, 14,811; Fulani, Ind., 6,487.
1984: Reagan, R, 658,700; Mondale, D, 536,479.
1980: Reagan, R, 571,044; Carter, D, 456,890; Anderson, Ind., 112,389; Clark, LB, 25,838; Commoner, Citizens, 13,642; scattered, 1,713.
1976: Ford, R, 492,120; Carter, D, 490,407; McCarthy, Ind., 40,207; write-in, 7,142.
1972: Nixon, R, 486,686; McGovern, D, 392,760; Schmitz, Amer., 46,211; write-in, 2,289.
1968: Nixon, R, 408,433; Humphrey, D, 358,866; Wallace, 3rd party, 49,683; write-ins: McCarthy, 1,496; N. Rockefeller, 69; others, 1,075.
1964: Johnson, D, 501,017; Goldwater, R, 282,779; write-in, 2,509.
1960: Nixon, R, 408,060; Kennedy, D, 367,402.

Pennsylvania

County	2012 Obama (D)	2012 Romney (R)	2008 Obama (D)	2008 McCain (R)
Adams	15,091	26,767	17,633	26,349
Allegheny	352,687	262,039	373,153	272,347
Armstrong	9,045	20,142	11,138	18,542
Beaver	37,055	42,344	40,499	42,895
Bedford	4,788	16,702	6,059	16,124
Berks	83,011	54,702	97,047	80,513
Blair	16,276	33,319	19,813	32,708
Bradford	8,624	14,410	10,306	15,057
Bucks	160,521	156,579	179,031	150,248
Butler	28,550	59,761	32,260	57,074
Cambria	24,249	35,163	32,451	31,995
Cameron	724	1,359	879	1,323
Carbon	11,580	13,504	13,464	12,957
Centre	34,176	34,001	41,950	32,992
Chester	124,311	124,840	137,833	114,421
Clarion	5,056	10,828	6,756	10,737
Clearfield	11,121	20,347	14,555	18,662
Clinton	5,734	7,303	7,097	7,504
Columbia	10,937	14,236	13,230	14,477
Crawford	13,883	20,901	16,780	20,750
Cumberland	44,367	64,809	48,306	63,739
Dauphin	64,965	57,450	69,975	58,238
Delaware	171,792	110,853	178,870	115,273
Elk	5,463	7,579	7,290	6,676
Erie	68,036	49,025	75,775	50,351
Fayette	21,971	26,018	25,866	26,081
Forest	896	1,383	1,038	1,366
Franklin	18,995	43,260	21,169	41,906
Fulton	1,310	4,814	1,576	4,642
Greene	5,852	8,428	7,829	7,889
Huntingdon	5,409	11,979	6,621	11,745
Indiana	14,473	21,257	17,065	19,727
Jefferson	4,787	13,048	6,447	12,057
Juniata	2,547	6,862	3,068	6,484
Lackawanna	61,838	35,085	67,520	39,488
Lancaster	88,481	130,669	99,586	126,568
Lawrence	17,513	21,047	19,711	21,851
Lebanon	19,900	35,872	23,310	34,314
Lehigh	78,283	66,874	87,089	63,382
Luzerne	64,307	58,325	72,492	61,127

County	2012 Obama (D)	2012 Romney (R)	2008 Obama (D)	2008 McCain (R)
Lycoming	15,203	30,658	18,381	30,280
McKean	5,297	9,545	6,465	9,224
Mercer	24,232	25,925	26,411	26,565
Mifflin	4,273	11,939	5,375	10,929
Monroe	35,221	26,867	39,453	28,293
Montgomery	233,356	174,381	253,393	165,552
Montour	3,053	4,652	3,364	4,574
Northampton	67,606	61,446	75,255	58,551
Northumberland	13,072	19,518	14,329	19,018
Perry	5,685	13,120	6,396	13,058
Philadelphia	588,806	96,467	595,980	117,221
Pike	10,210	12,786	11,493	12,518
Potter	1,897	5,231	2,300	5,109
Schuylkill	24,546	32,278	28,300	33,767
Snyder	4,687	10,073	5,382	9,900
Somerset	9,436	23,984	12,878	21,686
Sullivan	1,034	1,868	1,233	1,841
Susquehanna	6,935	10,800	8,381	10,633
Tioga	5,357	11,342	6,390	11,326
Union	6,109	9,896	7,333	9,859
Venango	7,945	13,815	9,238	13,718
Warren	6,995	10,010	8,537	9,685
Washington	40,345	53,230	46,122	50,752
Wayne	8,396	12,896	9,892	12,702
Westmoreland	63,722	103,932	72,721	102,294
Wyoming	5,061	6,587	5,985	6,983
York	73,191	113,304	82,839	109,268
Totals	**2,990,274**	**2,680,434**	**3,276,363**	**2,655,885**

Pennsylvania Vote Since 1960

2012: Obama, D, 2,990,274; Romney, R, 2,680,434; Johnson, LB, 49,991; Stein, Green, 21,341.
2008: Obama, D, 3,276,363; McCain, R, 2,655,885; Nader, Ind., 42,977; Barr, LB, 19,912.
2004: Kerry, D, 2,938,095; Bush, R, 2,793,847; Badnarik, LB, 21,185; Cobb, Green, 6,319; Peroutka, Const., 6,318.
2000: Gore, D, 2,485,967; Bush, R, 2,281,127; Nader, Green, 103,392; Buchanan, RF, 16,023; Phillips, Const., 14,428; Browne, LB, 11,248.
1996: Clinton, D, 2,215,819; Dole, R, 1,801,169; Perot, RF, 430,984; Browne, LB, 28,000; Phillips, Const., 19,552; Hagelin, Natural Law, 5,783.
1992: Clinton, D, 2,239,164; Bush, R, 1,791,841; Perot, Ind., 902,667; Marrou, LB, 21,477; Fulani, New Alliance, 4,661.
1988: Bush, R, 2,300,087; Dukakis, D, 2,194,944; McCarthy, Consumer, 19,158; Paul, LB, 12,051.
1984: Reagan, R, 2,584,323; Mondale, D, 2,228,131; Bergland, LB, 6,982.
1980: Reagan, R, 2,261,872; Carter, D, 1,937,540; Anderson, Ind., 292,921; Clark, LB, 33,263; DeBerry, Soc. Workers, 20,291; Commoner, Consumer, 10,430; Hall, Comm., 5,184.
1976: Carter, D, 2,328,677; Ford, R, 2,205,604; McCarthy, Ind., 50,584; Maddox, Const., 25,344; Camejo, Soc. Workers, 3,009; LaRouche, U.S. Labor, 2,744; Hall, Comm., 1,891; others, 2,934.
1972: Nixon, R, 2,714,521; McGovern, D, 1,796,951; Schmitz, Amer., 70,593; Jenness, Soc. Workers, 4,639; Hall, Comm., 2,686; others, 2,715.
1968: Humphrey, D, 2,259,405; Nixon, R, 2,090,017; Wallace, 3rd party, 378,582; Gregory, Peace/Freedom, 7,821; Blomen, Soc. Labor, 4,977; Halstead, Soc. Workers, 4,862; others, 2,264.
1964: Johnson, D, 3,130,954; Goldwater, R, 1,673,657; DeBerry, Soc. Workers, 10,456; Hass, Soc. Labor, 5,092; scattered, 2,531.
1960: Kennedy, D, 2,556,282; Nixon, R, 2,439,956; Hass, Soc. Labor, 7,185; Dobbs, Soc. Workers, 2,678; scattered, 440.

Rhode Island

City	2012 Obama (D)	2012 Romney (R)	2008 Obama (D)	2008 McCain (R)
Bristol	6,359	3,707	6,833	3,834
Coventry	9,122	6,969	9,622	7,367
Cranston	21,388	13,008	22,520	13,981
Cumberland	9,291	7,106	9,707	6,941
East Providence	14,095	5,752	15,380	6,216
Johnston	7,503	5,417	7,763	6,066
Lincoln	6,028	4,866	6,264	4,831
Newport	6,174	2,959	6,989	3,215
North Kingstown	7,847	6,451	8,562	6,285
North Providence	9,613	5,404	9,954	5,933
Pawtucket	18,155	5,228	18,486	6,098
Providence	43,617	7,282	46,276	8,548
Smithfield	5,293	4,681	5,464	4,660
South Kingstown	8,611	4,720	9,336	4,689
Warwick	24,448	15,027	25,802	16,541
West Warwick	6,956	4,332	7,475	4,735
Westerly	6,071	4,382	6,490	4,710
Woonsocket	7,985	4,114	8,678	4,398
Other	60,853	45,746	64,970	46,343
Totals	**279,677**	**157,204**	**296,571**	**165,391**

Rhode Island Vote Since 1960

2012: Obama, D, 279,677; Romney, R, 157,204; Johnson, LB, 4,388; Stein, Green, 2,421; Goode, Const., 430; Anderson, Justice, 416; Lindsay, Socialism/Liberation, 132.
2008: Obama, D, 296,571; McCain, R, 165,391; Nader, Ind., 4,829; Barr, LB, 1,382; McKinney, Green, 797; Baldwin, Const., 675; La Riva, Socialism/Liberation, 122.
2004: Kerry, D, 259,765; Bush, R, 169,046; Nader, RF, 4,651; Cobb, Green, 1,333; Badnarik, LB, 907; Peroutka, Const., 339; Parker, Workers World, 253.
2000: Gore, D, 249,508; Bush, R, 130,555; Nader, Ind., 25,052; Buchanan, RF, 2,273; Browne, Ind., 742; Hagelin, Ind., 271; Moorehead, Ind., 199; Phillips, Ind., 97; McReynolds, Ind., 52; Harris, Ind., 34.
1996: Clinton, D, 233,050; Dole, R, 104,683; Perot, RF, 43,723; Nader, Green, 6,040; Browne, LB, 1,109; Phillips, U.S. Taxpayers, 1,021; Hagelin, Natural Law, 435; Moorehead, Workers World, 186.
1992: Clinton, D, 213,299; Bush, R, 131,601; Perot, Ind., 105,045; Fulani, New Alliance, 1,878.
1988: Dukakis, D, 225,123; Bush, R, 177,761; Paul, LB, 825; Fulani, New Alliance, 280.
1984: Reagan, R, 212,080; Mondale, D, 197,106; Bergland, LB, 277.
1980: Carter, D, 198,342; Reagan, R, 154,793; Anderson, Ind., 59,819; Clark, LB, 2,458; Hall, Comm., 218; McReynolds, Soc., 170; DeBerry, Soc. Workers, 90; Griswold, Workers World, 77.
1976: Carter, D, 227,636; Ford, R, 181,249; MacBride, LB, 715; Camejo, Soc. Workers, 462; Hall, Comm., 334; Levin, Soc. Labor, 188.
1972: Nixon, R, 220,383; McGovern, D, 194,645; Jenness, Soc. Workers, 729.
1968: Humphrey, D, 246,518; Nixon, R, 122,359; Wallace, 3rd party, 15,678; Halstead, Soc. Workers, 383.
1964: Johnson, D, 315,463; Goldwater, R, 74,615.
1960: Kennedy, D, 258,032; Nixon, R, 147,502.

South Carolina

County	2012 Obama (D)	2012 Romney (R)	2008 Obama (D)	2008 McCain (R)
Abbeville	4,543	5,981	4,593	6,264
Aiken	25,322	44,042	26,101	42,849
Allendale	3,297	838	3,029	947
Anderson	22,405	48,709	24,132	48,690
Bamberg	4,624	2,194	4,426	2,309
Barnwell	5,188	4,659	4,931	4,769
Beaufort	29,848	42,687	30,396	37,821
Berkeley	28,542	38,475	27,755	36,205
Calhoun	4,045	3,707	3,970	3,695
Charleston	81,487	77,629	82,698	69,822
Cherokee	7,231	13,314	7,215	13,305
Chester	7,891	6,367	7,478	6,318
Chesterfield	7,958	8,490	7,842	8,325
Clarendon	9,091	7,071	8,673	6,758
Colleton	8,475	8,443	8,616	8,525
Darlington	15,457	14,434	14,505	14,544
Dillon	7,523	5,427	7,408	5,874
Dorchester	23,445	32,531	21,806	29,929
Edgefield	4,967	6,512	5,075	6,334
Fairfield	7,777	3,999	7,591	3,912
Florence	28,614	28,961	28,012	29,861
Georgetown	14,163	16,526	14,199	15,790
Greenville	68,070	121,685	70,886	116,363
Greenwood	11,972	16,348	12,348	16,995
Hampton	5,834	3,312	5,816	3,439
Horry	38,885	72,127	38,879	64,609
Jasper	5,757	4,169	5,389	3,365
Kershaw	11,259	16,324	11,226	16,466
Lancaster	13,419	19,333	12,139	16,441
Laurens	10,318	14,746	10,578	15,334
Lee	5,977	2,832	5,960	3,074
Lexington	34,148	76,662	33,303	74,960
Marion	9,688	5,164	9,608	5,416
Marlboro	6,100	3,676	6,794	3,996
McCormick	2,653	2,467	2,755	2,437

County	2012 Obama (D)	2012 Romney (R)	2008 Obama (D)	2008 McCain (R)
Newberry	6,913	9,260	6,708	9,616
Oconee	8,550	21,611	9,481	21,164
Orangeburg	30,720	12,022	27,263	12,115
Pickens	11,156	33,474	11,691	32,552
Richland	103,989	53,105	105,656	57,941
Saluda	3,328	5,135	3,323	5,191
Spartanburg	41,461	66,969	41,632	65,042
Sumter	27,589	19,274	25,431	18,581
Union	5,796	6,584	5,935	7,449
Williamsburg	11,335	4,824	11,279	5,004
York	39,131	59,546	37,918	54,500
Totals	**865,941**	**1,071,645**	**862,449**	**1,034,896**

South Carolina Vote Since 1960

2012: Romney, R, 1,071,645; Obama, D, 865,941; Johnson, LB, 16,321; Stein, Green, 5,446; Goode, Const., 4,765.
2008: McCain, R, 1,034,896; Obama, D, 862,449; Barr, LB, 7,283; Baldwin, Const., 6,827; Nader, petitioning cand., 5,053; McKinney, Green, 4,461.
2004: Bush, R, 937,974; Kerry, D, 661,699; Nader, Ind., 5,520; Peroutka, Const., 5,317; Badnarik, LB, 3,608; Brown, United Citizens, 2,124; Cobb, Green, 1,488.
2000: Bush, R, 786,892; Gore, D, 566,039; Nader, United Citizens, 20,279; Browne, LB, 4,898; Buchanan, RF, 3,309; Phillips, Const., 1,682; Hagelin, Natural Law, 943.
1996: Dole, R, 573,458; Clinton, D, 506,283; Perot, RF./Patriot, 64,386; Browne, LB, 4,271; Phillips, U.S. Taxpayers, 2,043; Hagelin, Natural Law, 1,248.
1992: Bush, R, 577,507; Clinton, D, 479,514; Perot, Ind., 138,872; Marrou, LB, 2,719; Phillips, U.S. Taxpayers, 2,680; Fulani, New Alliance, 1,235.
1988: Bush, R, 606,443; Dukakis, D, 370,554; Paul, LB, 4,935; Fulani, United Citizens, 4,077.
1984: Reagan, R, 615,539; Mondale, D, 344,459; Bergland, LB, 4,359.
1980: Reagan, R, 439,277; Carter, D, 428,220; Anderson, Ind., 13,868; Clark, LB, 4,807; Rarick, Amer. Ind., 2,086.
1976: Carter, D, 450,807; Ford, R, 346,149; Anderson, Amer., 2,996; Maddox, Amer. Ind., 1,950; write-in, 681.
1972: Nixon, R, 477,044; McGovern, D, 184,559, and United Citizens, 2,265 (total, 186,824); Schmitz, Amer., 10,075; write-in, 17.
1968: Nixon, R, 254,062; Wallace, 3rd party, 215,430; Humphrey, D, 197,486.
1964: Goldwater, R, 309,048; Johnson, D, 215,700; write-ins: Wallace, 5; Nixon, 1; Powell, 1; Thurmond, 1.
1960: Kennedy, D, 198,129; Nixon, R, 188,558; write-in, 1.

South Dakota

County	2012 Obama (D)	2012 Romney (R)	2008 Obama (D)	2008 McCain (R)
Aurora	556	804	655	794
Beadle	2,881	4,230	3,493	4,054
Bennett	548	626	557	614
Bon Homme	1,167	1,830	1,367	1,712
Brookings	5,827	6,220	7,207	6,431
Brown	7,250	8,321	9,041	8,067
Brule	824	1,499	965	1,407
Buffalo	472	166	454	156
Butte	1,002	3,073	1,306	2,821
Campbell	153	616	243	591
Charles Mix	1,483	2,230	1,807	2,109
Clark	713	1,067	830	1,065
Clay	2,955	2,147	3,808	2,296
Codington	4,588	6,696	5,595	6,374
Corson	648	515	837	535
Custer	1,335	3,062	1,475	2,909
Davison	3,042	4,757	3,554	4,731
Day	1,497	1,320	1,785	1,372
Deuel	941	1,175	1,054	1,088
Dewey	1,207	663	1,328	659
Douglas	332	1,334	424	1,293
Edmunds	622	1,264	819	1,213
Fall River	1,140	2,258	1,338	2,348
Faulk	331	765	426	739
Grant	1,493	2,034	1,786	1,951
Gregory	599	1,507	771	1,423
Haakon	138	940	187	939
Hamlin	921	1,803	1,043	1,661
Hand	575	1,242	718	1,247
Hanson	760	1,627	961	1,426
Harding	82	638	135	575
Hughes	2,786	5,219	3,037	5,298
Hutchinson	923	2,451	1,242	2,285
Hyde	189	531	226	547
Jackson	426	661	435	668
Jerauld	452	538	542	546
Jones	108	490	147	463
Kingsbury	1,092	1,451	1,277	1,435
Lake	2,724	3,419	3,033	2,993
Lawrence	3,973	7,025	4,932	6,787
Lincoln	7,982	13,611	8,642	11,803
Lyman	605	933	710	894
Marshall	1,061	889	1,261	900
McCook	905	1,655	1,219	1,646
McPherson	272	921	441	915
Meade	2,928	7,566	3,751	7,515
Mellette	375	381	373	445
Miner	479	636	605	577
Minnehaha	34,674	40,342	39,838	39,251
Moody	1,429	1,535	1,663	1,508
Pennington	15,125	28,232	17,802	27,603
Perkins	319	1,205	499	1,102
Potter	339	1,029	482	937
Roberts	2,302	1,883	2,672	1,781
Sanborn	389	688	500	669
Shannon	2,937	188	2,971	331
Spink	1,300	1,670	1,550	1,660
Stanley	435	1,063	510	1,017
Sully	186	613	233	581
Todd	1,976	498	2,208	571
Tripp	737	1,905	914	1,859
Turner	1,411	2,715	1,681	2,538
Union	2,782	4,698	3,244	4,310
Walworth	671	1,731	923	1,668
Yankton	4,226	5,495	4,838	5,039
Ziebach	439	314	554	312
Totals	**145,039**	**210,610**	**170,924**	**203,054**

South Dakota Vote Since 1960

2012: Romney, R, 210,610; Obama, D, 145,039; Johnson, LB, 5,795; Goode, Const., 2,371.
2008: McCain, R, 203,054; Obama, D, 170,924; Nader, Ind., 4,267; Baldwin, Const., 1,895; Barr, Ind., 1,835.
2004: Bush, R, 232,584; Kerry, D, 149,244; Nader, Ind., 4,320; Peroutka, Const., 1,103; Badnarik, LB, 964.
2000: Bush, R, 190,700; Gore, D, 118,804; Buchanan, RF, 3,322; Phillips, Ind., 1,781; Browne, LB, 1,662.
1996: Dole, R, 150,543; Clinton, D, 139,333; Perot, RF, 31,250; Browne, LB, 1,472; Phillips, Taxpayers, 912; Hagelin, Natural Law, 316.
1992: Bush, R, 136,718; Clinton, D, 124,888; Perot, Ind., 73,295.
1988: Bush, R, 165,415; Dukakis, D, 145,560; Paul, LB, 1,060; Fulani, New Alliance, 730.
1984: Reagan, R, 200,267; Mondale, D, 116,113.
1980: Reagan, R, 198,343; Carter, D, 103,855; Anderson, Ind., 21,431; Clark, LB, 3,824; Pulley, Soc. Workers, 250.
1976: Ford, R, 151,505; Carter, D, 147,068; MacBride, LB, 1,619; Hall, Comm., 318; Camejo, Soc. Workers, 168.
1972: Nixon, R, 166,476; McGovern, D, 139,945; Jenness, Soc. Workers, 994.
1968: Nixon, R, 149,841; Humphrey, D, 118,023; Wallace, 3rd party, 13,400.
1964: Johnson, D, 163,010; Goldwater, R, 130,108.
1960: Nixon, R, 178,417; Kennedy, D, 128,070.

Tennessee

County	2012 Obama (D)	2012 Romney (R)	2008 Obama (D)	2008 McCain (R)
Anderson	10,122	18,968	11,396	19,675
Bedford	4,211	10,034	5,027	10,217
Benton	2,258	3,850	2,645	3,696
Bledsoe	1,267	3,022	1,517	3,166
Blount	12,934	35,441	15,253	35,571
Bradley	8,037	27,422	9,357	28,333
Campbell	3,328	8,604	3,867	8,535
Cannon	1,564	3,309	2,011	3,322
Carroll	3,475	7,225	3,980	7,455
Carter	4,789	15,503	5,587	15,852
Cheatham	4,659	10,268	5,498	10,702
Chester	1,624	4,684	1,797	4,587
Claiborne	2,433	7,617	3,078	7,175
Clay	1,037	1,747	1,248	1,676
Cocke	2,804	8,459	3,340	8,945
Coffee	5,870	13,023	7,132	13,250
Crockett	1,669	3,783	1,967	3,994
Cumberland	6,261	18,653	7,889	17,436
Davidson	143,120	97,622	158,423	102,915
Decatur	1,303	2,874	1,566	3,101
DeKalb	2,174	4,143	2,832	4,085
Dickson	6,233	11,296	7,506	11,677
Dyer	3,757	9,921	4,411	9,859
Fayette	6,688	12,689	6,892	12,173
Fentress	1,561	5,243	1,831	4,789

	2012		2008	
County	Obama (D)	Romney (R)	Obama (D)	McCain (R)
Franklin	5,603	10,262	6,613	10,539
Gibson	6,564	12,883	7,406	13,516
Giles	3,760	6,915	4,614	6,902
Grainger	1,668	5,470	2,066	5,297
Greene	6,225	17,245	7,110	17,151
Grundy	1,643	2,516	1,971	2,563
Hamblen	5,234	14,522	6,807	15,508
Hamilton	58,836	79,933	64,246	81,702
Hancock	475	1,527	604	1,588
Hardeman	5,482	4,865	5,919	5,225
Hardin	2,467	7,886	2,794	7,077
Hawkins	5,088	14,382	5,930	14,756
Haywood	4,569	2,960	4,893	3,165
Henderson	2,517	7,421	3,021	7,669
Henry	4,339	8,193	5,153	8,182
Hickman	2,698	4,758	3,563	4,784
Houston	1,400	1,579	1,678	1,608
Humphreys	2,905	3,833	3,600	3,818
Jackson	1,739	2,383	2,224	2,185
Jefferson	4,232	13,038	5,178	13,092
Johnson	1,483	4,611	1,837	4,621
Knox	59,399	109,707	70,215	113,015
Lake	884	1,163	1,024	1,175
Lauderdale	4,011	4,616	4,322	4,933
Lawrence	4,237	10,770	5,161	10,566
Lewis	1,447	3,117	1,804	2,951
Lincoln	3,290	9,803	3,695	9,231
Loudon	5,058	16,707	6,058	15,815
Macon	1,552	5,260	2,060	5,145
Madison	18,367	21,993	20,209	23,290
Marion	3,953	6,272	4,506	6,746
Marshall	3,725	6,832	4,320	6,755
Maury	11,825	20,708	13,058	20,288
McMinn	4,609	12,967	5,541	12,989
McNairy	2,645	7,015	3,131	7,135
Meigs	1,163	2,734	1,372	2,797
Monroe	4,372	11,731	5,053	11,484
Montgomery	24,499	30,245	25,716	30,175
Moore	705	2,053	881	2,010
Morgan	1,725	4,669	1,969	4,717
Obion	3,321	8,814	4,308	8,873
Overton	2,805	4,775	3,419	4,497
Perry	992	1,578	1,329	1,596
Pickett	712	1,712	854	1,786
Polk	1,856	4,108	2,124	4,267
Putnam	7,802	17,254	9,739	17,101
Rhea	2,628	7,802	2,907	8,042
Roane	6,018	14,724	7,224	15,658
Robertson	8,290	17,643	9,318	17,903
Rutherford	36,414	60,846	40,460	59,892
Scott	1,452	5,117	1,720	4,931
Sequatchie	1,489	3,541	1,717	3,610
Sevier	7,418	25,984	8,604	24,922
Shelby	232,443	135,649	256,297	145,458
Smith	2,470	4,495	2,992	4,563
Stewart	2,069	2,963	2,470	2,956
Sullivan	15,321	43,562	18,354	44,808
Sumner	18,579	46,003	21,487	44,949
Tipton	7,133	16,672	7,931	17,165
Trousdale	1,240	1,612	1,475	1,688
Unicoi	1,913	5,032	2,107	5,011
Union	1,478	4,282	1,829	4,467
Van Buren	875	1,386	849	1,294
Warren	4,752	8,010	5,515	8,562
Washington	14,325	32,808	15,941	32,341
Wayne	1,163	4,253	1,355	4,076
Weakley	3,548	8,605	4,596	8,855
White	2,795	6,197	3,372	6,103
Williamson	25,142	69,850	27,886	64,858
Wilson	14,695	36,109	15,886	34,595
Totals	**960,709**	**1,462,330**	**1,087,437**	**1,479,178**

Tennessee Vote Since 1960

2012: Romney, R, 1,462,330; Obama, D, 960,709; Johnson, Ind., 18,623; Stein, Green, 6,515; Goode, Const., 6,022; Anderson, Ind., 2,639, Miller, Ind., 1,739.

2008: McCain, R, 1,479,178; Obama, D, 1,087,437; Nader, Ind., 11,560; Barr, Ind., 8,547; Baldwin, Ind., 8,191; McKinney, Ind., 2,499; Moore, Ind., 1,326; Jay, Ind., 1,011.

2004: Bush, R, 1,384,375; Kerry, D, 1,036,477; Nader, Ind., 8,992; Badnarik, Ind., 4,866; Peroutka, Ind., 2,570.

2000: Bush, R, 1,061,949; Gore, D, 981,720; Nader, Green, 19,781; Browne, LB, 4,284; Buchanan, RF, 4,250; Brown, Ind., 1,606; Phillips, Ind., 1,015; Hagelin, RF, 613; Venson, Ind., 535.

1996: Clinton, D, 909,146; Dole, R, 863,530; Perot, RF, 105,918; Nader, Ind., 6,427; Browne, Ind., 5,020; Phillips, Ind., 1,818; Collins, Ind., 688; Hagelin, Ind., 636; Michael, Ind., 408; Dodge, Ind., 324.

1992: Clinton, D, 933,521; Bush, R, 841,300; Perot, Ind., 199,968; Marrou, LB, 1,847.

1988: Bush, R, 947,233; Dukakis, D, 679,794; Paul, Ind., 2,041; Duke, Ind., 1,807.

1984: Reagan, R, 990,212; Mondale, D, 711,714; Bergland, LB, 3,072.

1980: Reagan, R, 787,761; Carter, D, 783,051; Anderson, Ind., 35,991; Clark, LB, 7,116; Commoner, Citizens, 1,112; Bubar, Statesman, 521; McReynolds, Soc., 519; Hall, Comm., 503; DeBerry, Soc. Workers, 490; Griswold, Workers World, 400; write-in, 152.

1976: Carter, D, 825,879; Ford, R, 633,969; Anderson, Amer., 5,769; McCarthy, Ind., 5,004; Maddox, Amer. Ind., 2,303; MacBride, LB, 1,375; Hall, Comm., 547; LaRouche, U.S. Labor, 512; Bubar, Prohib., 442; Miller, Ind., 316; write-in, 230.

1972: Nixon, R, 813,147; McGovern, D, 357,293; Schmitz, Amer., 30,373; write-in, 369.

1968: Nixon, R, 472,592; Wallace, 3rd party, 424,792; Humphrey, D, 351,233.

1964: Johnson, D, 635,047; Goldwater, R, 508,965; write-in, 34.

1960: Nixon, R, 556,577; Kennedy, D, 481,453; Faubus, States' Rights, 11,304; Decker, Prohib., 2,458.

Texas

	2012		2008	
County	Obama (D)	Romney (R)	Obama (D)	McCain (R)
Anderson	3,813	12,262	4,630	11,884
Andrews	795	3,639	790	3,816
Angelina	7,834	20,303	9,379	19,569
Aransas	2,704	6,830	3,006	6,693
Archer	525	3,600	740	3,595
Armstrong	98	828	128	856
Atascosa	5,133	7,461	4,415	5,462
Austin	2,252	9,265	2,821	8,786
Bailey	466	1,339	682	1,618
Bandera	1,864	7,426	2,250	6,935
Bastrop	9,864	14,033	11,687	13,817
Baylor	267	1,297	366	1,262
Bee	3,452	4,356	3,645	4,471
Bell	35,512	49,574	40,413	49,242
Bexar	264,856	241,617	275,527	246,275
Blanco	1,220	3,638	1,467	3,418
Borden	32	324	40	316
Bosque	1,367	5,885	1,797	5,762
Bowie	10,196	24,869	10,815	24,162
Brazoria	34,421	70,862	36,480	67,515
Brazos	17,477	37,209	20,502	37,465
Brewster	1,765	1,976	1,970	1,855
Briscoe	117	578	205	617
Brooks	1,886	507	1,747	556
Brown	1,904	11,895	2,822	12,052
Burleson	1,705	4,671	2,053	4,547
Burnet	3,674	12,843	4,608	12,059
Caldwell	4,791	6,021	5,403	6,107
Calhoun	2,410	4,144	2,729	4,106
Callahan	751	4,378	1,063	4,589
Cameron	49,975	26,099	48,480	26,671
Camp	1,428	2,881	1,734	2,798
Carson	292	2,451	406	2,548
Cass	2,924	8,763	3,490	8,279
Castro	630	1,470	719	1,562
Chambers	2,790	11,787	3,188	9,988
Cherokee	3,875	12,094	4,610	11,695
Childress	320	1,665	497	1,782
Clay	740	4,266	1,085	4,213
Cochran	256	649	284	758
Coke	179	1,218	299	1,252
Coleman	442	3,012	643	3,011
Collin	101,415	196,888	109,047	184,897
Collingsworth	177	962	234	943
Colorado	2,029	6,026	2,508	5,795
Comal	11,450	39,318	12,384	35,233
Comanche	890	3,944	1,334	3,813
Concho	194	793	257	807
Cooke	2,246	11,951	3,051	11,871
Coryell	5,158	11,220	6,619	11,550
Cottle	180	555	187	509
Crane	275	985	319	1,119
Crockett	480	957	512	1,026
Crosby	639	1,132	684	1,221
Culberson	568	295	492	257
Dallam	253	1,248	302	1,269
Dallas	405,571	295,813	422,989	310,000
Dawson	1,019	2,591	1,152	2,906
Deaf Smith	1,239	3,042	1,247	3,466
Delta	454	1,524	589	1,580
Denton	80,978	157,579	91,160	149,935
DeWitt	1,467	5,122	1,716	4,888
Dickens	216	793	234	730
Dimmit	2,141	762	2,692	874

	2012		2008	
County	Obama (D)	Romney (R)	Obama (D)	McCain (R)
Donley	226	1,287	291	1,374
Duval	3,331	980	3,298	1,076
Eastland	970	5,444	1,271	5,165
Ector	8,118	24,010	9,123	26,199
Edwards	232	642	346	673
El Paso	112,952	57,150	122,021	61,783
Ellis	13,881	39,574	15,333	38,078
Erath	1,965	10,329	3,128	10,768
Falls	2,033	3,356	2,225	3,328
Fannin	2,486	8,161	3,464	8,092
Fayette	2,315	8,106	3,014	7,582
Fisher	512	1,094	687	1,083
Floyd	551	1,523	730	1,784
Foard	140	348	198	327
Fort Bend	101,144	116,126	98,368	103,206
Franklin	751	3,446	1,036	3,392
Freestone	1,850	5,646	2,034	5,205
Frio	2,376	1,559	2,405	1,644
Gaines	535	3,484	650	3,385
Galveston	39,511	69,059	41,805	62,258
Garza	279	1,263	375	1,356
Gillespie	2,055	10,306	2,576	9,563
Glasscock	44	526	52	502
Goliad	1,127	2,294	1,329	2,298
Gonzales	1,777	4,216	2,167	4,076
Gray	886	6,443	1,153	6,924
Grayson	10,670	30,936	13,900	31,136
Gregg	12,398	28,742	13,166	29,203
Grimes	2,339	6,141	2,704	5,562
Guadalupe	15,744	33,117	16,156	30,869
Hale	2,243	6,490	2,708	7,171
Hall	265	832	324	930
Hamilton	591	2,918	863	2,876
Hansford	159	1,788	240	1,847
Hardeman	302	1,176	373	1,199
Hardin	3,359	17,746	3,939	16,603
Harris	587,044	586,073	590,982	571,883
Harrison	8,456	17,512	8,887	17,103
Hartley	184	1,708	250	1,711
Haskell	553	1,424	699	1,388
Hays	25,537	31,661	28,431	29,638
Hemphill	192	1,298	216	1,345
Henderson	6,106	21,231	7,913	20,857
Hidalgo	97,969	39,865	90,261	39,668
Hill	2,752	9,132	3,811	9,264
Hockley	1,486	5,546	1,797	5,795
Hood	3,843	18,409	5,087	17,299
Hopkins	2,777	9,836	3,530	9,299
Houston	2,265	5,880	2,656	5,872
Howard	2,110	6,453	2,545	7,029
Hudspeth	379	471	430	458
Hunt	6,671	21,011	8,594	20,573
Hutchinson	1,045	6,804	1,322	7,361
Irion	112	668	164	644
Jack	303	2,580	470	2,528
Jackson	1,070	3,906	1,301	3,723
Jasper	3,423	9,957	3,658	9,022
Jeff Davis	440	719	468	749
Jefferson	44,668	43,242	44,888	42,905
Jim Hogg	1,301	356	1,336	472
Jim Wells	6,492	4,598	6,706	4,841
Johnson	10,496	37,661	12,912	36,685
Jones	1,226	4,262	1,528	4,203
Karnes	1,325	2,825	1,760	2,736
Kaufman	9,472	24,846	11,161	23,735
Kendall	3,043	14,508	3,599	12,971
Kenedy	82	84	108	94
Kent	66	335	99	342
Kerr	4,338	17,274	5,570	16,752
Kimble	217	1,667	342	1,487
King	5	139	8	151
Kinney	522	880	633	907
Kleberg	4,754	4,058	5,256	4,540
Knox	332	1,160	367	986
La Salle	965	669	1,052	714
Lamar	4,181	12,826	5,243	12,952
Lamb	998	3,058	1,156	3,344
Lampasas	1,479	5,621	1,903	5,651
Lavaca	1,428	6,796	1,869	6,293
Lee	1,632	4,507	2,000	4,312
Leon	1,062	5,814	1,418	5,566
Liberty	5,202	17,323	5,991	15,448
Limestone	2,208	5,288	2,516	5,079
Lipscomb	119	1,044	155	1,093
Live Oak	919	3,154	1,048	3,095
Llano	1,822	7,610	2,250	7,281
Loving	9	54	12	67
Lubbock	26,271	63,469	30,486	66,304
Lynn	506	1,439	627	1,473
Madison	967	3,028	1,146	2,891

	2012		2008	
County	Obama (D)	Romney (R)	Obama (D)	McCain (R)
Marion	1,495	2,733	1,644	2,567
Martin	248	1,368	314	1,389
Mason	380	1,565	546	1,544
Matagorda	3,980	8,040	4,440	7,835
Maverick	8,303	2,171	8,554	2,316
McCulloch	537	2,419	728	2,263
McLennan	25,694	47,903	29,998	49,044
McMullen	67	431	132	400
Medina	4,784	11,079	5,147	10,480
Menard	171	665	295	712
Midland	8,286	35,689	9,691	36,155
Milam	2,636	5,481	3,044	5,217
Mills	279	1,882	398	1,753
Mitchell	538	1,756	586	1,815
Montague	1,116	6,549	1,597	6,245
Montgomery	32,920	137,969	36,703	119,884
Moore	964	3,968	1,123	4,282
Morris	1,858	3,232	2,055	3,158
Motley	55	538	67	522
Nacogdoches	6,465	13,925	8,393	14,828
Navarro	4,350	10,847	5,400	10,810
Newton	1,677	4,112	1,751	3,446
Nolan	1,216	3,282	1,521	3,485
Nueces	45,772	48,966	47,912	52,391
Ochiltree	253	2,719	243	2,851
Oldham	71	790	102	813
Orange	6,800	23,366	7,646	21,509
Palo Pinto	1,811	7,393	2,499	7,264
Panola	2,211	7,950	2,586	7,582
Parker	7,853	39,243	10,502	36,974
Parmer	529	2,011	719	2,969
Pecos	1,591	2,512	1,476	2,480
Polk	4,859	14,071	6,230	13,731
Potter	7,126	18,918	8,939	20,761
Presidio	1,282	504	1,252	489
Rains	761	3,279	1,048	3,146
Randall	7,574	41,447	9,468	41,948
Reagan	158	676	197	795
Real	277	1,236	375	1,238
Red River	1,482	3,549	1,539	3,461
Reeves	1,655	1,188	1,606	1,445
Refugio	998	1,663	1,382	1,855
Roberts	33	468	41	477
Robertson	2,798	4,419	2,675	3,980
Rockwall	8,120	27,113	8,492	23,300
Runnels	519	3,104	720	3,118
Rusk	4,451	13,924	4,983	13,646
Sabine	807	3,727	1,077	3,749
San Augustine	1,193	2,469	1,328	2,342
San Jacinto	2,410	7,107	2,721	6,151
San Patricio	7,856	12,005	8,854	12,404
San Saba	323	1,905	487	1,941
Schleicher	221	787	324	970
Scurry	838	4,124	1,088	4,414
Shackelford	131	1,218	208	1,284
Shelby	2,322	6,879	2,548	6,630
Sherman	121	908	127	884
Smith	21,456	57,331	23,726	55,187
Somervell	613	2,871	799	2,677
Starr	10,260	1,547	8,274	1,492
Stephens	475	2,892	626	2,869
Sterling	31	459	97	520
Stonewall	160	507	206	524
Sutton	369	1,110	381	1,189
Swisher	579	1,655	813	1,683
Tarrant	253,071	348,920	274,880	348,420
Taylor	9,750	32,904	12,690	34,317
Terrell	184	358	186	323
Terry	1,059	2,602	1,379	2,879
Throckmorton	109	700	166	671
Titus	2,648	6,084	3,145	6,028
Tom Green	9,294	26,878	11,158	27,362
Travis	232,788	140,152	254,017	136,981
Trinity	1,614	4,537	1,925	4,095
Tyler	1,668	5,910	2,166	5,644
Upshur	2,971	12,015	3,790	11,222
Upton	333	953	288	898
Uvalde	3,825	4,529	4,126	4,590
Val Verde	6,285	5,635	6,982	5,752
Van Zandt	3,084	15,794	4,505	15,734
Victoria	8,802	19,692	9,832	19,878
Walker	6,252	12,140	7,334	11,623
Waller	6,514	9,244	7,153	8,265
Ward	841	2,366	899	2,667
Washington	3,381	10,857	4,034	10,176
Webb	37,597	11,078	33,452	13,119
Wharton	4,235	9,750	4,937	9,431
Wheeler	232	1,878	314	1,918
Wichita	10,525	29,812	13,868	31,731
Wilbarger	971	2,956	1,196	3,283

County	2012 Obama (D)	2012 Romney (R)	2008 Obama (D)	2008 McCain (R)
Willacy	3,600	1,416	3,409	1,456
Williamson	61,875	97,006	67,691	88,323
Wilson	4,821	12,218	5,362	10,904
Winkler	398	1,311	477	1,529
Wise	3,221	17,207	4,471	15,973
Wood	3,056	14,351	4,010	13,658
Yoakum	409	1,698	450	1,989
Young	992	6,225	1,303	5,942
Zapata	2,527	997	1,939	919
Zavala	3,042	574	3,263	596
Totals	**3,308,124**	**4,569,843**	**3,528,633**	**4,479,328**

Texas Vote Since 1960

2012: Romney, R, 4,569,843; Obama, D, 3,308,124; Johnson, LB, 88,580; Stein, Green, 24,657.
2008: McCain, R, 4,479,328; Obama, D, 3,528,633 Barr, LB, 56,116.
2004: Bush, R, 4,526,917; Kerry, D, 2,832,704; Badnarik, LB, 38,787.
2000: Bush, R, 3,799,639; Gore, D, 2,433,746; Nader, Green, 137,994; Browne, LB, 23,160; Buchanan, Ind., 12,394.
1996: Dole, R, 2,736,167; Clinton, D, 2,459,683; Perot, RF, 378,537; Browne, LB, 20,256; Phillips, U.S. Taxpayers, 7,472; Hagelin, Natural Law, 4,422.
1992: Bush, R, 2,496,071; Clinton, D, 2,281,815; Perot, Ind., 1,354,781; Marrou, LB, 19,699.
1988: Bush, R, 3,036,829; Dukakis, D, 2,352,748; Paul, LB, 30,355; Fulani, New Alliance, 7,208.
1984: Reagan, R, 3,433,428; Mondale, D, 1,949,276.
1980: Reagan, R, 2,510,705; Carter, D, 1,881,147; Anderson, Ind., 111,613; Clark, LB, 37,643; write-in, 528.
1976: Carter, D, 2,082,319; Ford, R, 1,953,300; McCarthy, Ind., 20,118; Anderson, Amer., 11,442; Camejo, Soc. Workers, 1,723; write-in, 2,982.
1972: Nixon, R, 2,298,896; McGovern, D, 1,154,289; Jenness, Soc. Workers, 8,664; Schmitz, Amer., 6,039; others, 3,393.
1968: Humphrey, D, 1,266,804; Nixon, R, 1,227,844; Wallace, 3rd party, 584,269; write-in, 489.
1964: Johnson, D, 1,663,185; Goldwater, R, 958,566; Lightburn, Const., 5,060.
1960: Kennedy, D, 1,167,932; Nixon, R, 1,121,699; Sullivan, Const., 18,169; Decker, Prohib., 3,870; write-in, 15.

Utah

County	2012 Obama (D)	2012 Romney (R)	2008 Obama (D)	2008 McCain (R)
Beaver	346	2,174	542	1,902
Box Elder	1,984	17,101	3,311	15,228
Cache	6,244	35,039	10,294	29,127
Carbon	2,275	5,090	3,468	4,091
Daggett	94	406	131	297
Davis	21,889	96,861	30,477	77,341
Duchesne	581	5,698	911	4,689
Emery	569	3,777	973	3,358
Garfield	308	1,832	405	1,710
Grand	1,727	1,996	2,067	1,871
Iron	2,148	14,200	3,258	12,518
Juab	451	3,448	741	2,683
Kane	744	2,522	856	2,212
Millard	431	4,478	758	3,653
Morgan	403	4,114	689	3,311
Piute	74	697	141	635
Rich	83	915	154	831
Salt Lake	146,147	223,811	176,988	176,692
San Juan	2,139	3,074	2,406	2,638
Sanpete	980	8,406	1,631	6,664
Sevier	738	7,207	1,359	6,394
Summit	8,072	8,884	9,532	6,956
Tooele	4,524	14,268	5,830	10,998
Uintah	997	10,421	1,462	8,441
Utah	17,281	156,950	29,567	122,224
Wasatch	2,191	7,220	2,892	5,430
Washington	8,337	44,698	10,826	37,311
Wayne	215	1,089	335	940
Weber	19,841	54,224	25,666	45,885
Totals	**251,813**	**740,600**	**327,670**	**596,030**

Utah Vote Since 1960

2012: Romney, R, 740,600; Obama, D, 251,813; Johnson, LB, 12,572; Anderson, Justice, 5,335; Stein, Green, 3,817; Goode, Const., 2,871; La Riva, unaff., 393.
2008: McCain, R, 596,030; Obama, D, 327,670; Baldwin, Const., 12,012; Nader, unaff., 8,416; Barr, LB, 6,966; McKinney, unaff., 982; La Riva, unaff., 262.
2004: Bush, R, 663,742; Kerry, D, 241,199; Nader, Ind., 11,305; Peroutka, Const., 6,841; Badnarik, LB, 3,375; Jay, Personal Choice, 946; Harris, Soc. Workers, 393.
2000: Bush, R, 515,096; Gore, D, 203,053; Nader, Green, 35,850; Buchanan, RF, 9,319; Browne, LB, 3,616; Phillips, Ind. American, 2,709; Hagelin, Natural Law, 763; Harris, Soc. Workers, 186; Youngkeit, Ind., 161.
1996: Dole, R, 361,911; Clinton, D, 221,633; Perot, RF, 66,461; Nader, Green, 4,615; Browne, LB, 4,129; Phillips, Taxpayers, 2,601; Templin, Ind. American, 1,290; Crane, Ind., 1,101; Hagelin, Natural Law, 1,085; Moorehead, Workers World, 298; Harris, Soc. Workers, 235; Dodge, Prohib., 111.
1992: Bush, R, 322,632; Perot, Ind., 203,400; Clinton, D, 183,429; Gritz, Populist/America First, 28,602; Marrou, LB, 1,900; Hagelin, Natural Law, 1,319; LaRouche, Ind., 1,089.
1988: Bush, R, 428,442; Dukakis, D, 207,352; Paul, LB, 7,473; Dennis, Amer., 2,158.
1984: Reagan, R, 469,105; Mondale, D, 155,369; Bergland, LB, 2,447.
1980: Reagan, R, 439,687; Carter, D, 124,266; Anderson, Ind., 30,284; Clark, LB, 7,226; Commoner, Citizens, 1,009; Greaves, Amer., 965; Rarick, Amer. Ind., 522; Hall, Comm., 139; DeBerry, Soc. Workers, 124.
1976: Ford, R, 337,908; Carter, D, 182,110; Anderson, Amer., 13,304; McCarthy, Ind., 3,907; MacBride, LB, 2,438; Maddox, Amer. Ind., 1,162; Camejo, Soc. Workers, 268; Hall, Comm., 121.
1972: Nixon, R, 323,643; McGovern, D, 126,284; Schmitz, Amer., 28,549.
1968: Nixon, R, 238,728; Humphrey, D, 156,665; Wallace, 3rd party, 26,906; Peace/Freedom, 180; Halstead, Soc. Workers, 89.
1964: Johnson, D, 219,628; Goldwater, R, 181,785.
1960: Nixon, R, 205,361; Kennedy, D, 169,248; Dobbs, Soc. Workers, 100.

Vermont

County	2012 Obama (D)	2012 Romney (R)	2008 Obama (D)	2008 McCain (R)
Addison	12,257	5,203	13,202	5,667
Bennington	11,514	5,687	12,524	6,133
Caledonia	8,192	5,088	8,900	5,472
Chittenden	53,626	21,571	59,611	22,237
Essex	1,539	1,164	1,733	1,284
Franklin	12,057	7,405	13,179	7,853
Grand Isle	2,531	1,471	2,694	1,490
Lamoille	8,371	3,342	8,914	3,515
Orange	9,076	4,588	9,799	5,047
Orleans	7,117	4,306	7,998	4,482
Rutland	17,088	10,835	19,355	11,584
Washington	20,351	8,093	22,324	9,129
Windham	16,026	5,347	17,585	5,997
Windsor	19,494	8,598	21,444	9,084
Totals	**199,239**	**92,698**	**219,262**	**98,974**

Vermont Vote Since 1960

2012: Obama, D, 199,239; Romney, R, 92,698; Johnson, LB, 3,487; Anderson, Justice, 1,128; Lindsay, Socialism/Liberation, 695.
2008: Obama, D, 219,262; McCain, R, 98,974; Nader, Ind., 3,339; Barr, LB, 1,067; Baldwin, Const., 500; Calero, Soc. Workers, 150; La Riva, Socialism/Liberation, 149; Moore, Liberty Union, 141.
2004: Kerry, D, 184,067; Bush, R, 121,180; Nader, Ind., 4,494; Badnarik, LB, 1,102; Parker, Liberty Union, 265; Calero, Soc. Workers, 244.
2000: Gore, D, 149,022; Bush, R, 119,775; Nader, Green, 20,374; Buchanan, RF, 2,192; Lane, Grass Roots, 1,044; Browne, LB, 784; Hagelin, Natural Law, 219; McReynolds, Liberty Union, 161; Phillips, Const., 153; Harris, Soc. Workers, 70.
1996: Clinton, D, 137,894; Dole, R, 80,352; Perot, RF, 31,024; Nader, Green, 5,585; Browne, LB, 1,183; Hagelin, Natural Law, 498; Peron, Grass Roots, 480; Phillips, Taxpayers, 382; Hollis, Liberty Union, 292; Harris, Soc. Workers, 199.
1992: Clinton, D, 133,590; Bush, R, 88,122; Perot, Ind., 65,985.
1988: Bush, R, 124,331; Dukakis, D, 115,775; Paul, LB, 1,000; LaRouche, Ind., 275.
1984: Reagan, R, 135,865; Mondale, D, 95,730; Bergland, LB, 1,002.
1980: Reagan, R, 94,598; Carter, D, 81,891; Anderson, Ind., 31,760; Commoner, Citizens, 2,316; Clark, LB, 1,900; McReynolds, Liberty Union, 136; Hall, Comm., 118; DeBerry, Soc. Workers, 75; scattered, 413.
1976: Ford, R, 100,387; Carter, D, 77,798 and Ind. Vermonters, 991 (total, 79,789); McCarthy, Ind., 4,001; Camejo, Soc. Workers, 430; LaRouche, U.S. Labor, 196; scattered, 99.
1972: Nixon, R, 117,149; McGovern, D, 68,174; Spock, Liberty Union, 1,010; Jenness, Soc. Workers, 296; scattered, 318.
1968: Nixon, R, 85,142; Humphrey, D, 70,255; Wallace, 3rd party, 5,104; Gregory, New Party, 579; Halstead, Soc. Workers, 295.
1964: Johnson, D, 107,674; Goldwater, R, 54,868.
1960: Nixon, R, 98,131; Kennedy, D, 69,186.

Virginia

County	2012 Obama (D)	2012 Romney (R)	2008 Obama (D)	2008 McCain (R)
Accomack	7,655	8,213	7,607	7,833
Albemarle	29,757	23,297	29,792	20,576
Alleghany	3,403	3,595	3,553	3,715
Amelia	2,490	4,331	2,488	3,970
Amherst	5,900	8,876	6,094	8,470
Appomattox	2,453	5,340	2,641	4,903
Arlington	81,269	34,474	78,994	29,876
Augusta	9,451	23,624	9,825	23,120
Bath	894	1,274	1,043	1,349
Bedford	10,209	26,679	11,017	24,420
Bland	735	2,144	864	2,031
Botetourt	5,452	12,479	5,693	11,471
Brunswick	4,994	2,968	4,973	2,877
Buchanan	3,094	6,436	4,063	4,541
Buckingham	3,750	3,569	3,489	3,428
Campbell	7,595	17,695	8,091	17,444
Caroline	7,276	6,151	7,163	5,617
Carroll	3,685	8,736	4,109	8,187
Charles City	2,772	1,396	2,838	1,288
Charlotte	2,503	3,311	2,705	3,372
Chesterfield	77,694	90,934	74,310	86,413
Clarke	3,239	4,296	3,457	3,840
Craig	830	1,757	877	1,695
Culpeper	8,285	11,580	8,802	10,711
Cumberland	2,422	2,538	2,255	2,418
Dickenson	2,473	4,274	3,278	3,324
Dinwiddie	6,550	6,875	6,246	6,526
Essex	3,016	2,602	2,934	2,379
Fairfax	315,273	206,773	310,359	200,994
Fauquier	13,965	21,034	14,616	19,227
Floyd	2,732	4,673	2,937	4,441
Fluvanna	5,893	6,678	6,185	6,420
Franklin	9,090	16,718	9,618	15,414
Frederick	12,690	22,858	12,961	20,149
Giles	2,730	4,660	3,192	4,462
Gloucester	6,764	12,137	6,916	12,089
Goochland	4,676	8,448	4,813	7,643
Grayson	2,068	4,801	2,480	4,540
Greene	3,290	5,569	3,174	4,980
Greensville	3,135	1,766	3,122	1,729
Halifax	7,766	8,694	8,126	8,600
Hanover	18,294	39,940	18,447	37,344
Henrico	89,594	70,449	86,323	67,381
Henry	10,317	13,984	11,118	13,758
Highland	459	924	590	930
Isle of Wight	8,761	11,802	8,573	11,258
James City	17,879	22,843	17,352	20,912
King and Queen	1,745	1,865	1,918	1,763
King George	4,477	6,604	4,473	5,888
King William	3,344	5,466	3,344	4,966
Lancaster	3,149	3,753	3,235	3,647
Lee	2,583	6,847	3,219	5,825
Loudoun	82,479	75,292	74,845	63,336
Louisa	6,953	9,215	6,978	8,182
Lunenburg	2,684	2,969	2,703	2,900
Madison	2,639	3,869	2,862	3,758
Mathews	1,807	3,488	1,934	3,456
Mecklenburg	6,921	7,973	7,127	7,817
Middlesex	2,370	3,619	2,391	3,545
Montgomery	19,903	20,006	21,031	19,028
Nelson	4,171	3,947	4,391	3,647
New Kent	3,555	7,246	3,493	6,385
Northampton	3,741	2,676	3,800	2,713
Northumberland	3,191	4,310	3,312	4,041
Nottoway	3,344	3,409	3,413	3,499
Orange	6,870	9,244	7,107	8,506
Page	3,724	6,344	4,235	6,041
Patrick	2,417	5,622	2,879	5,491
Pittsylvania	10,858	19,263	11,415	18,730
Powhatan	4,088	11,200	4,237	10,088
Prince Edward	5,132	3,952	5,101	4,174
Prince George	6,991	8,879	7,130	8,752
Prince William	103,331	74,458	93,435	67,621
Pulaski	5,292	8,920	5,918	8,857
Rappahannock	1,980	2,311	2,105	2,227
Richmond	1,574	2,160	1,618	2,092
Roanoke	18,711	31,624	19,812	30,571
Rockbridge	4,088	5,898	4,347	5,732
Rockingham	10,065	24,186	10,453	22,468
Russell	3,718	8,180	4,932	6,389
Scott	2,395	7,439	2,725	6,980
Shenandoah	6,469	12,538	6,912	12,005
Smyth	4,171	8,379	4,239	7,817
Southampton	4,437	4,733	4,402	4,583
Spotsylvania	25,165	31,844	24,897	28,610
Stafford	27,182	32,480	25,716	29,221
Surry	2,576	1,671	2,626	1,663
Sussex	3,358	2,021	3,301	2,026
Tazewell	3,661	13,843	5,596	11,201
Warren	6,452	9,869	6,997	8,879
Washington	7,076	18,141	8,063	16,077
Westmoreland	4,295	3,731	4,577	3,719
Wise	3,760	11,076	4,995	8,914
Wythe	3,783	8,324	4,107	8,207
York	13,183	20,204	13,700	19,833
City				
Alexandria	52,199	20,249	50,473	19,181
Bedford	1,225	1,527	1,208	1,497
Bristol	2,492	4,780	2,665	4,579
Buena Vista	919	1,564	1,108	1,282
Charlottesville	16,510	4,844	15,705	4,078
Chesapeake	55,052	53,900	53,994	52,625
Colonial Heights	2,544	5,941	2,562	6,161
Covington	1,319	975	1,304	1,020
Danville	12,218	7,763	12,352	8,361
Emporia	1,793	886	1,702	897
Fairfax	6,651	4,775	6,575	4,691
Falls Church	5,015	2,147	4,695	1,970
Franklin	2,833	1,496	2,819	1,576
Fredericksburg	7,131	4,060	6,155	3,413
Galax	900	1,332	1,052	1,317
Hampton	46,966	18,640	46,917	20,476
Harrisonburg	8,654	6,565	8,444	6,048
Hopewell	5,179	3,739	5,285	4,149
Lexington	1,486	1,146	1,543	914
Lynchburg	15,948	19,806	16,269	17,638
Manassas	8,478	6,463	7,518	5,975
Manassas Park	2,879	1,699	2,463	1,634
Martinsville	3,855	2,312	4,139	2,311
Newport News	51,100	27,230	51,972	28,667
Norfolk	62,687	23,147	62,819	24,814
Norton	566	895	743	744
Petersburg	14,283	1,527	13,774	1,583
Poquoson	1,679	5,312	1,748	5,229
Portsmouth	32,501	12,858	32,327	13,984
Radford	2,732	2,520	2,930	2,418
Richmond	75,921	20,050	73,623	18,649
Roanoke	24,134	14,991	24,934	15,394
Salem	4,760	7,299	5,164	7,088
Staunton	5,728	5,272	5,569	5,330
Suffolk	24,267	17,820	22,446	17,165
Virginia Beach	94,299	99,291	98,885	100,319
Waynesboro	3,840	4,790	3,906	4,815
Williamsburg	4,903	2,682	4,328	2,353
Winchester	5,094	4,946	5,268	4,725
Totals	**1,971,820**	**1,822,522**	**1,959,532**	**1,725,005**

Virginia Vote Since 1960

2012: Obama, D, 1,971,820; Romney, R, 1,822,522; Johnson, LB, 31,216; Goode, Const., 13,058; Stein, Green, 8,627.

2008: Obama, D, 1,959,532; McCain, R, 1,725,005; Nader, Ind., 11,483; Barr, LB, 11,067; Baldwin, Ind. Green, 7,474; McKinney, Green, 2,344.

2004: Bush, R, 1,716,959; Kerry, D, 1,454,742; Badnarik, LB, 11,032; Peroutka, Const., 10,161.

2000: Bush, R, 1,437,490; Gore, D, 1,217,290; Nader, Green, 59,398; Browne, LB, 15,198; Buchanan, RF, 5,455; Phillips, Const., 1,809.

1996: Dole, R, 1,138,350; Clinton, D, 1,091,060; Perot, RF, 159,861; Phillips, Taxpayers, 13,687; Browne, LB, 9,174; Hagelin, Natural Law, 4,510.

1992: Bush, R, 1,150,517; Clinton, D, 1,038,650; Perot, Ind., 348,639; LaRouche, Ind., 11,937; Marrou, LB, 5,730; Fulani, New Alliance, 3,192.

1988: Bush, R, 1,309,162; Dukakis, D, 859,799; Fulani, Ind., 14,312; Paul, LB, 8,336.

1984: Reagan, R, 1,337,078; Mondale, D, 796,250.

1980: Reagan, R, 989,609; Carter, D, 752,174; Anderson, Ind., 95,418; Commoner, Citizens, 14,024; Clark, LB, 12,821; DeBerry, Soc. Workers, 1,986.

1976: Ford, R, 836,554; Carter, D, 813,896; Camejo, Soc. Workers, 17,802; Anderson, Amer., 16,686; LaRouche, U.S. Labor, 7,508; MacBride, LB, 4,648.

1972: Nixon, R, 988,493; McGovern, D, 438,887; Schmitz, Amer., 19,721; Fisher, Soc. Labor, 9,918.

1968: Nixon, R, 590,319; Humphrey, D, 442,387; Wallace, 3rd party, 320,272; Blomen, Soc. Labor, 4,671; Gregory, Peace/Freedom, 1,680; Munn, Prohib., 601. *10,561 votes for Wallace were omitted in the count.

1964: Johnson, D, 558,038; Goldwater, R, 481,334; Hass, Soc. Labor, 2,895.

1960: Nixon, R, 404,521; Kennedy, D, 362,327; Coiner, Conservative, 4,204; Hass, Soc. Labor, 397.

Washington

County	2012 Obama (D)	2012 Romney (R)	2008 Obama (D)	2008 McCain (R)
Adams	1,540	3,171	1,552	3,222
Asotin	4,003	5,654	4,139	5,451
Benton	28,145	49,461	26,288	45,345
Chelan	13,112	18,402	13,781	17,605
Clallam	18,580	18,437	19,470	18,199
Clark	93,382	92,951	95,356	84,212
Columbia	645	1,568	686	1,499
Cowlitz	22,726	20,746	24,597	19,554
Douglas	5,166	9,425	5,848	9,098
Ferry	1,294	1,995	1,467	1,916
Franklin	8,398	13,748	7,361	12,037
Garfield	336	913	385	968
Grant	8,950	17,852	9,601	17,153
Gray's Harbor	15,960	11,914	16,354	12,104
Island	21,478	19,605	22,058	19,426
Jefferson	12,739	6,405	13,252	6,330
King	668,004	275,700	648,230	259,716
Kitsap	67,277	52,846	68,624	53,297
Kittitas	7,949	9,782	8,030	9,471
Klickitat	4,598	5,316	4,965	4,944
Lewis	12,664	20,452	13,624	20,278
Lincoln	1,673	4,063	2,032	3,803
Mason	14,764	12,761	15,050	12,600
Okanogan	7,108	9,221	7,613	8,798
Pacific	5,711	4,499	6,094	4,555
Pend Oreille	2,508	3,952	2,562	3,717
Pierce	186,430	148,467	181,824	141,673
San Juan	7,125	3,111	7,374	2,958
Skagit	28,688	25,071	30,053	24,687
Skamania	2,628	2,687	2,817	2,524
Snohomish	188,516	133,016	187,294	126,722
Spokane	102,295	115,285	105,786	108,314
Stevens	7,762	13,691	8,499	13,132
Thurston	74,037	49,287	75,882	48,366
Wahkiakum	1,094	1,119	1,121	1,105
Walla Walla	9,768	14,648	10,081	14,182
Whatcom	57,089	42,703	58,236	40,205
Whitman	8,037	8,507	9,070	8,104
Yakima	33,217	42,239	33,792	41,946
Totals	**1,755,396**	**1,290,670**	**1,750,848**	**1,229,216**

Washington Vote Since 1960

2012: Obama, D, 1,755,396; Romney, R, 1,290,670; Johnson, LB, 42,202; Stein, Green, 20,928; Goode, Const., 8,851; Anderson, Justice, 4,946; Lindsay, Socialism/Liberation, 1,318; Harris, Soc. Workers, 1,205.

2008: Obama, D, 1,750,848; McCain, R, 1,229,216; Nader, Ind., 29,489; Barr, LB, 12,728; Baldwin, Const., 9,432; McKinney, Green, 3,819; La Riva, Socialism/Liberation, 705; Harris, Soc. Workers, 641.

2004: Kerry, D, 1,510,201; Bush, R, 1,304,894; Nader, Ind., 23,283; Badnarik, LB, 11,955; Peroutka, Const., 3,922; Cobb, Green, 2,974; Parker, Workers World, 1,077; Harris, Soc. Workers, 547; Van Auken, Soc. Equality, 231.

2000: Gore, D, 1,247,652; Bush, R, 1,108,864; Nader, Green, 103,002; Browne, LB, 13,135; Buchanan, Freedom, 7,171; Hagelin, Natural Law, 2,927; Phillips, Const., 1,989; Moorehead, Workers World, 1,729; McReynolds, Soc., 660; Harris, Soc. Workers, 304.

1996: Clinton, D, 1,123,323; Dole, R, 840,712; Perot, RF, 201,003; Nader, Ind., 60,322; Browne, LB, 12,522; Hagelin, Natural Law, 6,076; Phillips, U.S. Taxpayers, 4,578; Collins, Ind., 2,374; Moorehead, Workers World, 2,189; Harris, Soc. Workers, 738.

1992: Clinton, D, 993,037; Bush, R, 731,234; Perot, Ind., 541,780; Marrou, LB, 7,533; Gritz, Populist/America First, 4,854; Hagelin, Natural Law, 2,456; Phillips, U.S. Taxpayers, 2,354; Fulani, New Alliance, 1,776; Daniels, Ind., 1,171.

1988: Dukakis, D, 933,516; Bush, R, 903,835; Paul, LB, 17,240; LaRouche, Ind., 4,412.

1984: Reagan, R, 1,051,670; Mondale, D, 798,352; Bergland, LB, 8,844.

1980: Reagan, R, 865,244; Carter, D, 650,193; Anderson, Ind., 185,073; Clark, LB, 29,213; Commoner, Citizens, 9,403; DeBerry, Soc. Workers, 1,137; McReynolds, Soc., 956; Hall, Comm., 834; Griswold, Workers World, 341.

1976: Ford, R, 777,732; Carter, D, 717,323; McCarthy, Ind., 36,986; Maddox, Amer. Ind., 8,585; Anderson, Amer., 5,046; MacBride, LB, 5,042; Wright, People's, 1,124; Camejo, Soc. Workers, 905; LaRouche, U.S. Labor, 903; Hall, Comm., 817; Levin, Soc. Labor, 713; Zeidler, Soc., 358.

1972: Nixon, R, 837,135; McGovern, D, 568,334; Schmitz, Amer., 58,906; Spock, Ind., 2,644; Hospers, LB, 1,537; Fisher, Soc. Labor, 1,102; Jenness, Soc. Workers, 623; Hall, Comm., 566.

1968: Humphrey, D, 616,037; Nixon, R, 588,510; Wallace, 3rd party, 96,990; Cleaver, Peace/Freedom, 1,609; Blomen, Soc. Labor, 488; Mitchell, Free Ballot, 377; Halstead, Soc. Workers, 270.

1964: Johnson, D, 779,699; Goldwater, R, 470,366; Hass, Soc. Labor, 7,772; DeBerry, Freedom Soc., 537.

1960: Nixon, R, 629,273; Kennedy, D, 599,298; Hass, Soc. Labor, 10,895; Curtis, Const., 1,401; Dobbs, Soc. Workers, 705.

West Virginia

County	2012 Obama (D)	2012 Romney (R)	2008 Obama (D)	2008 McCain (R)
Barbour	1,768	3,824	2,419	3,685
Berkeley	14,275	22,156	15,994	20,841
Boone	2,790	5,467	4,529	3,632
Braxton	1,998	2,725	2,704	2,629
Brooke	4,005	5,060	4,717	4,961
Cabell	13,568	17,985	15,292	18,793
Calhoun	818	1,319	993	1,366
Clay	931	1,971	1,421	1,755
Doddridge	575	2,130	735	2,218
Fayette	5,419	8,350	7,242	7,658
Gilmer	840	1,595	1,004	1,445
Grant	718	3,783	997	3,166
Greenbrier	4,710	7,930	5,881	7,567
Hampshire	2,299	5,523	2,983	5,222
Hancock	4,627	7,226	5,504	7,518
Hardy	1,482	3,536	1,901	3,376
Harrison	9,732	15,876	13,582	17,824
Jackson	3,854	7,408	4,861	7,148
Jefferson	10,398	11,258	11,687	10,600
Kanawha	32,480	41,364	40,594	40,952
Lewis	1,736	4,375	2,109	4,335
Lincoln	2,227	4,383	3,029	3,637
Logan	3,469	8,222	5,873	7,326
Marion	8,959	12,054	11,618	11,501
Marshall	4,484	8,135	5,996	7,759
Mason	3,778	5,741	4,484	5,853
McDowell	2,109	3,959	3,430	2,882
Mercer	5,432	15,450	7,450	13,246
Mineral	2,885	7,833	3,750	7,616
Mingo	2,428	6,191	3,582	4,587
Monongalia	13,826	16,831	17,060	15,775
Monroe	1,455	3,616	2,014	3,397
Morgan	2,363	4,513	2,721	4,428
Nicholas	2,664	5,898	4,357	4,804
Ohio	6,786	10,768	8,593	10,694
Pendleton	1,074	2,095	1,310	2,035
Pleasants	955	1,825	1,142	1,772
Pocahontas	1,303	2,182	1,548	2,011
Preston	2,931	7,889	4,205	7,325
Putnam	7,256	16,032	9,334	15,162
Raleigh	7,739	20,614	10,237	17,548
Randolph	3,342	6,160	4,539	6,060
Ritchie	768	2,921	998	2,781
Roane	1,939	2,982	2,511	2,943
Summers	1,621	2,981	2,290	2,891
Taylor	1,941	3,840	2,462	3,605
Tucker	880	2,176	1,288	2,123
Tyler	890	2,314	1,241	2,415
Upshur	2,158	5,939	2,925	5,911
Wayne	4,931	8,688	6,137	8,947
Webster	947	1,710	1,552	1,386
Wetzel	2,217	3,473	2,942	3,342
Wirt	676	1,427	782	1,496
Wood	11,230	22,183	12,573	22,896
Wyoming	1,583	5,769	2,735	4,621
Totals	**238,269**	**417,655**	**303,857**	**397,466**

West Virginia Vote Since 1960

2012: Romney, R, 417,655; Obama, D, 238,269; Johnson, LB, 6,302; Stein, Mountain, 4,406; Terry, NPA, 3,806.

2008: McCain, R, 397,466; Obama, D, 303,857; Nader, unaff., 7,219; Baldwin, Const., 2,465; McKinney, Mountain, 2,355.

2004: Bush, R, 423,778; Kerry, D, 326,541; Nader, Ind., 4,063; Badnarik, LB, 1,405.

2000: Bush, R, 336,475; Gore, D, 295,497; Nader, Green, 10,680; Buchanan, RF, 3,169; Browne, LB, 1,912; Hagelin, Natural Law, 367.

1996: Clinton, D, 327,812; Dole, R, 233,946; Perot, RF, 71,639; Browne, LB, 3,062.

1992: Clinton, D, 331,001; Bush, R, 241,974; Perot, Ind., 108,829; Marrou, LB, 1,873.

1988: Dukakis, D, 341,016; Bush, R, 310,065; Fulani, New Alliance, 2,230.

1984: Reagan, R, 405,483; Mondale, D, 328,125.

1980: Carter, D, 367,462; Reagan, R, 334,206; Anderson, Ind., 31,691; Clark, LB, 4,356.

1976: Carter, D, 435,864; Ford, R, 314,726.

1972: Nixon, R, 484,964; McGovern, D, 277,435.

1968: Humphrey, D, 374,091; Nixon, R, 307,555; Wallace, 3rd party, 72,560.

1964: Johnson, D, 538,087; Goldwater, R, 253,953.

1960: Kennedy, D, 441,786; Nixon, R, 395,995.

Wisconsin

County	2012 Obama (D)	2012 Romney (R)	2008 Obama (D)	2008 McCain (R)
Adams	5,542	4,644	5,806	3,974
Ashland	5,399	2,820	5,818	2,634
Barron	10,890	11,443	12,078	10,457
Bayfield	6,033	3,603	5,972	3,365
Brown	62,526	64,836	67,269	55,854
Buffalo	3,570	3,364	3,949	2,923
Burnett	3,986	4,550	4,337	4,200
Calumet	11,489	14,539	13,295	12,722
Chippewa	15,237	15,322	16,239	13,492
Clark	6,172	7,412	7,454	6,383
Columbia	17,175	13,026	16,661	12,193
Crawford	4,629	3,067	4,987	2,830
Dane	216,071	83,644	205,984	73,065
Dodge	18,762	25,211	19,183	23,015
Door	9,357	8,121	10,142	7,112
Douglas	14,863	7,705	15,830	7,835
Dunn	11,316	10,224	13,002	9,566
Eau Claire	30,666	23,256	33,146	20,959
Florence	953	1,645	1,134	1,512
Fond du Lac	22,379	30,355	23,463	28,164
Forest	2,425	2,172	2,673	1,963
Grant	13,594	10,255	14,875	9,068
Green	11,206	7,857	11,502	6,730
Green Lake	3,793	5,782	4,000	5,393
Iowa	8,105	4,287	7,987	3,829
Iron	1,784	1,790	1,914	1,464
Jackson	5,298	3,900	5,572	3,552
Jefferson	20,158	23,517	21,448	21,096
Juneau	6,242	5,411	6,186	5,148
Kenosha	44,867	34,977	45,836	31,609
Kewaunee	5,153	5,747	5,902	4,711
La Crosse	36,693	25,751	38,524	23,701
Lafayette	4,536	3,314	4,732	2,984
Langlade	4,573	5,816	5,182	5,081
Lincoln	7,563	7,455	8,424	6,519
Manitowoc	20,403	21,604	22,428	19,234
Marathon	32,363	36,617	36,367	30,345
Marinette	9,882	10,619	11,195	9,726
Marquette	4,014	3,992	4,068	3,654
Menominee	1,191	179	1,257	185
Milwaukee	332,438	154,924	319,819	149,445
Monroe	9,515	9,675	10,198	8,666
Oconto	8,865	10,741	9,927	8,755
Oneida	10,452	10,917	11,907	9,630
Outagamie	45,659	47,372	50,294	39,677
Ozaukee	19,159	36,077	20,579	32,172
Pepin	1,876	1,794	2,102	1,616
Pierce	10,235	10,397	11,803	9,812
Polk	10,073	12,094	10,876	11,282
Portage	22,075	16,615	24,817	13,810
Price	3,887	3,884	4,559	3,461
Racine	53,008	49,347	53,408	45,954
Richland	4,969	3,573	5,041	3,298
Rock	49,219	30,517	50,529	27,364
Rusk	3,397	3,676	3,855	3,253
St. Croix	19,910	25,503	21,177	22,837
Sauk	18,736	12,838	18,617	11,562
Sawyer	4,486	4,442	4,765	4,199
Shawano	9,000	11,022	10,259	9,538
Sheboygan	27,918	34,072	30,395	30,801
Taylor	3,763	5,601	4,563	4,586
Trempealeau	7,605	5,707	8,321	4,808
Vernon	8,044	5,942	8,463	5,367
Vilas	5,951	7,749	6,491	7,055
Walworth	22,552	29,006	24,177	25,485
Washburn	4,447	4,699	4,693	4,303
Washington	23,166	54,765	25,719	47,729
Waukesha	78,779	162,798	85,339	145,152
Waupaca	11,578	14,002	12,952	12,232
Waushara	5,335	6,562	5,868	5,770
Winnebago	45,449	42,122	48,167	37,946
Wood	18,581	19,704	21,710	16,581
Totals	**1,620,985**	**1,407,966**	**1,677,211**	**1,262,393**

Wisconsin Vote Since 1960

2012: Obama, D, 1,620,985; Romney, R, 1,407,966; Johnson, LB, 20,439; Stein, Green, 7,665; White, Soc. Equality, 553; La Riva, Socialism/Liberation, 526.
2008: Obama, D, 1,677,211; McCain, R, 1,262,393; Nader, Ind., 17,605; Barr, LB, 8,858; Baldwin, Ind., 5,072; McKinney, Green, 4,216; Wamboldt, Ind., 764; Moore, Ind., 540; La Riva, Ind., 237.
2004: Kerry, D, 1,489,504; Bush, R, 1,478,120; Nader, Ind., 16,390; Badnarik, LB, 6,464; Cobb, Green, 2,661; Brown, Ind., 471; Harris, Ind., 411.
2000: Gore, D, 1,242,987; Bush, R, 1,237,279; Nader, Green, 94,070; Buchanan, RF, 11,446; Browne, LB, 6,640; Phillips, Const., 2,042; Moorehead, Workers World, 1,063; Hagelin, RF, 878; Harris, Soc. Workers, 306.
1996: Clinton, D, 1,071,971; Dole, R, 845,029; Perot, RF, 227,339; Nader, Green, 28,723; Phillips, U.S. Taxpayers, 8,811; Browne, LB, 7,929; Hagelin, Natural Law, 1,379; Moorehead, Workers World, 1,333; Hollis, Soc., 848; Harris, Soc. Workers, 483.
1992: Clinton, D, 1,041,066; Bush, R, 930,855; Perot, Ind., 544,479; Marrou, LB, 2,877; Gritz, Populist/America First, 2,311; Daniels, Ind., 1,883; Phillips, U.S. Taxpayers, 1,772; Hagelin, Natural Law, 1,070.
1988: Dukakis, D, 1,126,794; Bush, R, 1,047,499; Paul, LB, 5,157; Duke, Populist, 3,056.
1984: Reagan, R, 1,198,584; Mondale, D, 995,740; Bergland, LB, 4,883.
1980: Reagan, R, 1,088,845; Carter, D, 981,584; Anderson, Ind., 160,657; Clark, LB, 29,135; Commoner, Citizens, 7,767; Rarick, Const., 1,519; McReynolds, Soc., 808; Hall, Comm., 772; Griswold, Workers World, 414; DeBerry, Soc. Workers, 383; scattered, 1,337.
1976: Carter, D, 1,040,232; Ford, R, 1,004,987; McCarthy, Ind., 34,943; Maddox, Amer. Ind., 8,552; Zeidler, Soc., 4,298; MacBride, LB, 3,814; Camejo, Soc. Workers, 1,691; Wright, People's, 943; Hall, Comm., 749; LaRouche, U.S. Labor, 738; Levin, Soc. Labor, 389; scattered, 2,839.
1972: Nixon, R, 989,430; McGovern, D, 810,174; Schmitz, Amer., 47,525; Spock, Ind., 2,701; Fisher, Soc. Labor, 998; Hall, Comm., 663; Reed, Ind., 506; scattered, 893.
1968: Nixon, R, 809,997; Humphrey, D, 748,804; Wallace, 3rd party, 127,835; Blomen, Soc. Labor, 1,338; Halstead, Soc. Workers, 1,222; scattered, 2,342.
1964: Johnson, D, 1,050,424; Goldwater, R, 638,495; DeBerry, Soc. Workers, 1,692; Hass, Soc. Labor, 1,204.
1960: Nixon, R, 895,175; Kennedy, D, 830,805; Dobbs, Soc. Workers, 1,792; Hass, Soc. Labor, 1,310.

Wyoming

County	2012 Obama (D)	2012 Romney (R)	2008 Obama (D)	2008 McCain (R)
Albany	7,458	7,866	8,644	7,936
Big Horn	868	4,285	1,108	4,045
Campbell	2,163	14,953	2,990	13,011
Carbon	2,110	4,148	2,336	4,331
Converse	1,089	5,043	1,380	4,922
Crook	426	3,109	612	2,967
Fremont	5,333	11,075	6,016	11,083
Goshen	1,458	4,178	1,832	3,942
Hot Springs	523	1,895	619	1,834
Johnson	749	3,363	908	3,334
Laramie	14,295	23,904	16,072	24,549
Lincoln	1,287	7,144	1,823	6,485
Natrona	8,961	22,132	10,475	21,906
Niobrara	200	1,022	244	1,017
Park	2,927	11,234	3,757	10,839
Platte	1,223	3,136	1,407	3,002
Sheridan	3,618	10,267	4,458	10,177
Sublette	767	3,472	936	3,316
Sweetwater	4,774	11,428	5,762	10,360
Teton	6,213	4,858	7,472	4,565
Uinta	1,628	6,615	2,317	5,763
Washakie	794	3,014	1,042	2,956
Weston	422	2,821	658	2,618
Totals	**69,286**	**170,962**	**82,868**	**164,958**

Wyoming Vote Since 1960

2012: Romney, R, 170,962; Obama, D, 69,286; Johnson, LB, 5,326; Goode, Const., 1,452.
2008: McCain, R, 164,958; Obama, D, 82,868; Nader, Ind., 2,525; Barr, LB, 1,594; Baldwin, Ind., 1,192.
2004: Bush, R, 167,629; Kerry, D, 70,776; Nader, Ind., 2,741; Badnarik, LB, 1,171; Peroutka, Ind., 631.
2000: Bush, R, 147,947; Gore, D, 60,481; Buchanan, RF, 2,724; Browne, LB, 1,443; Phillips, Ind., 720; Hagelin, Natural Law, 411.
1996: Dole, R, 105,388; Clinton, D, 77,934; Perot, RF, 25,928; Browne, LB, 1,739; Hagelin, Natural Law, 582.
1992: Bush, R, 79,347; Clinton, D, 68,160; Perot, Ind., 51,263.
1988: Bush, R, 106,867; Dukakis, D, 67,113; Paul, LB, 2,026; Fulani, New Alliance, 545.
1984: Reagan, R, 133,241; Mondale, D, 53,370; Bergland, LB, 2,357.
1980: Reagan, R, 110,700; Carter, D, 49,427; Anderson, Ind., 12,072; Clark, LB, 4,514.
1976: Ford, R, 92,717; Carter, D, 62,239; McCarthy, Ind., 624; Reagan, Ind., 307; Anderson, Amer., 290; MacBride, LB, 89; Brown, Ind., 47; Maddox, Amer. Ind., 30.
1972: Nixon, R, 100,464; McGovern, D, 44,358; Schmitz, Amer., 748.
1968: Nixon, R, 70,927; Humphrey, D, 45,173; Wallace, 3rd party, 11,105.
1964: Johnson, D, 80,718; Goldwater, R, 61,998.
1960: Nixon, R, 77,451; Kennedy, D, 63,331.

UNITED STATES GOVERNMENT

EXECUTIVE BRANCH	LEGISLATIVE BRANCH	JUDICIAL BRANCH
President **Vice President** **Executive Office of the President** Council of Economic Advisers Council on Environmental Quality Executive Residence National Security Council Office of Administration Office of Management and Budget Office of National Drug Control Policy Office of Science and Technology Policy Office of the U.S. Trade Representative Office of the Vice President White House Office*	**CONGRESS** **Senate/House of Representatives** Architect of the Capitol Congressional Budget Office Government Accountability Office Government Printing Office Library of Congress Medicare Payment Advisory Commission Stennis Center for Public Service U.S. Botanic Garden	**Supreme Court of the United States** Courts of Appeals District Courts Territorial Courts Court of International Trade Court of Federal Claims Bankruptcy Courts Tax Court Court of Appeals for the Armed Forces Court of Appeals for Veterans Claims Administrative Office of the Courts Federal Judicial Center Sentencing Commission Judicial Panel on Multidistrict Litigation

*Includes Domestic Policy Council, National Security Advisor, National Economic Council, Office of Cabinet Affairs, Office of the Chief of Staff, Office of Communications, Office of Digital Strategy, Office of the First Lady, Office of Legislative Affairs, Office of Management and Administration, Oval Office Operations, Office of Presidential Personnel, Office of Public Engagement and Intergovernmental Affairs, Office of Scheduling and Advance, Office of the Staff Secretary, and Office of the White House Counsel.

The Obama Administration

As of Aug. 2015; mailing addresses are for Washington, DC, except where otherwise noted.
Terms of office of the president and vice president: Jan. 20, 2013, to Jan. 20, 2017.

President: By law, Pres. Barack H. Obama received an annual salary of $400,000 (taxable) and an annual expense allowance of $50,000 (nontaxable) for costs resulting from official duties. This does not include amounts available for expenditures within the Executive Office of the President, including $3,850,000 for necessary expenses for the White House, up to $100,000 a year for travel expenses, and up to $19,000 for official entertainment.

Website: www.whitehouse.gov/administration/president-obama

Vice President: By law, Vice Pres. Joseph R. Biden received an annual salary of $235,300 (taxable) and an annual expense allowance of $20,000 for costs resulting from official duties, plus $90,000 for official entertainment expenses (nontaxable).

Website: www.whitehouse.gov/administration/vice-president-biden

Cabinet Department Heads

(Salary: $203,700 per year)

Secretary of State: John Kerry
Secretary of the Treasury: Jack Lew
Secretary of Defense: Ashton Carter
Attorney General (Dept. of Justice): Loretta E. Lynch
Secretary of the Interior: Sally Jewell
Secretary of Agriculture: Thomas J. Vilsack
Secretary of Commerce: Penny Pritzker
Secretary of Labor: Thomas E. Perez
Secretary of Health and Human Services: Sylvia Mathews Burwell
Secretary of Housing and Urban Development: Julián Castro
Secretary of Transportation: Anthony Foxx
Secretary of Energy: Ernest Moniz
Secretary of Education: Arne Duncan
Secretary of Veterans Affairs: Robert A. McDonald
Secretary of Homeland Security: Jeh Johnson

Executive Agencies

Council of Economic Advisers: Jason Furman, chair; www.whitehouse.gov/administration/eop/cea/
Council on Environmental Quality: Christy Goldfuss, managing dir.; www.whitehouse.gov/administration/eop/ceq/
Office of Administration: vacant; www.whitehouse.gov/administration/eop/oa/
Office of Management and Budget: Shaun L. S. Donovan, dir.; www.whitehouse.gov/omb/
Office of Natl. Drug Control Policy: Michael Botticelli, dir.; www.whitehouse.gov/ondcp/
Office of Science and Technology Policy: John Holdren, dir.; www.whitehouse.gov/administration/eop/ostp/
Office of the U.S. Trade Representative: Amb. Michael Froman; www.ustr.gov

White House Staff

1600 Pennsylvania Ave. NW, 20500;
www.whitehouse.gov

Counselor to the President: vacant
Director, National Intelligence: James R. Clapper
Assistants to the President:
Chief of Staff: Denis McDonough
Deputy Chief of Staff for Implementation: Kristie Canegallo
Deputy Chief of Staff for Operations: Anita Breckenridge
Cabinet Secretary: Broderick D. Johnson
Counsel to the President: Warren N. Eggleston
White House Press Secretary: Joshua R. Earnest
National Security Advisor: Susan Rice
Deputy National Security Advisors: Avril D. Haines, Benjamin J. Rhodes
Director of Communications: Jennifer R. Psaki
Director of the Domestic Policy Council: Cecilia Muñoz
Economic Policy and Director of the National Economic Council: Jeffrey D. Zients
Homeland Security and Counterterrorism: Lisa O. Monaco
Director of Legislative Affairs: Katherine B. Fallon
Director of Political Strategy and Outreach: David M. Simas
Director of Speechwriting: Cody S. Keenan
Director of Scheduling and Advance: Chase M. Cushman
Management and Administration: Katy A. Kale
Senior Advisors: Brian C. Deese, Valerie B. Jarrett, Shailagh J. Murray
Physician to the President: Ronny L. Jackson
Chief of Staff to the Vice President: Steve Ricchetti
White House Social Secretary: Deesha Dyer
Chief of Staff to the First Lady: Christina M. Tchen
Senior Adviser to the First Lady: Melissa E. Winter

The U.S. Cabinet

The heads of major executive departments of the federal government constitute the Cabinet. This institution, not provided for in the U.S. Constitution, developed as an advisory body out of the desire of presidents to consult on policy matters. Aside from its advisory role, the Cabinet as a body has no formal function and wields no executive authority. Individual members exercise authority as heads of their departments, reporting to the president. The Cabinet meets at times set by the president. In addition, the Cabinet commonly includes other officials designated by the president as being of Cabinet rank.

The officials so designated by Pres. Barack Obama include Vice Pres. Joseph R. Biden, White House Chief of Staff Denis McDonough, Environmental Protection Agency Administrator Gina McCarthy, Office of Management and Budget Director Shaun L. S. Donovan, U.S. Trade Representative Ambassador Michael Froman, U.S. Ambassador to the United Nations Samantha Power, Council of Economic Advisers Chair Jason Furman, and Small Business Administration Administrator Maria Contreras-Sweet.

Department of State

2201 C St. NW, 20520; www.state.gov

The Dept. of Foreign Affairs was created by act of Congress on July 27, 1789, and the name changed to Dept. of State on Sept. 15, 1789. Conducts U.S. foreign policy. The Foreign Service protects American citizens and interests through embassies in some 180 countries under eight geographic bureaus. Maintains contact with foreign governments, negotiates agreements and treaties, and supports U.S. foreign trade. Promotes democracy, international security, human rights—including issues related to AIDS, human trafficking, war crimes, and migration—and arms and narcotics control. Represents the nation in international organizations. Issues passports to U.S. citizens and visas to foreigners. **Budget:** $26.0 bil (2013); $27.5 bil (2014); $30.5 bil (est. 2015). Budget for other intl. programs: $19.7 bil (2013); $18.7 bil (2014); $24.0 bil (est. 2015).

- Intl. Boundary and Water Commission (4171 North Mesa, Ste. C-100, El Paso, TX 79902); www.ibwc.gov
- Intl. Information Programs (2201 C St. NW, SA-5, Rm. 5B17, 20520); www.state.gov/r/iip/
- Intl. Narcotics and Law Enforcement Affairs (2201 C St. NW, Rm. 7826 HST, 20520); www.state.gov/j/inl/
- Intl. Organization Affairs (2201 C St. NW, Rm. 6323, 20520); www.state.gov/p/io/
- Population, Refugees, and Migration (2201 C St. NW, Rm. 6825 HST, 20520); www.state.gov/j/prm/
- U.S. Global AIDS Coordinator (2201 C St. NW, Ste. 10300, SA-22, 20520); www.state.gov/s/gac/

Secretaries of State

President	Secretary	Home	Sworn in
Washington	Thomas Jefferson	VA	1789
	Edmund J. Randolph	VA	1794
	Timothy Pickering	PA	1795
Adams, J.	Timothy Pickering	PA	1797
	John Marshall	VA	1800
Jefferson	James Madison	VA	1801
Madison	Robert Smith	MD	1809
	James Monroe	VA	1811
Monroe	John Quincy Adams	MA	1817
Adams, J. Q.	Henry Clay	KY	1825
Jackson	Martin Van Buren	NY	1829
	Edward Livingston	LA	1831
	Louis McLane	DE	1833
	John Forsyth	GA	1834
Van Buren	John Forsyth	GA	1837
Harrison, W. H.	Daniel Webster	MA	1841
Tyler	Daniel Webster	MA	1841
	Abel P. Upshur	VA	1843
	John C. Calhoun	SC	1844
Polk	John C. Calhoun	SC	1845
	James Buchanan	PA	1845
Taylor	James Buchanan	PA	1849
	John M. Clayton	DE	1849
Fillmore	John M. Clayton	DE	1850
	Daniel Webster	MA	1850
	Edward Everett	MA	1852
Pierce	William L. Marcy	NY	1853
Buchanan	William L. Marcy	NY	1857
	Lewis Cass	MI	1857
	Jeremiah S. Black	PA	1860
Lincoln	Jeremiah S. Black	PA	1861
	William H. Seward	NY	1861
Johnson, A.	William H. Seward	NY	1865
Grant	Elihu B. Washburne	IL	1869
	Hamilton Fish	NY	1869
Hayes	Hamilton Fish	NY	1877
	William M. Evarts	NY	1877
Garfield	William M. Evarts	NY	1881
	James G. Blaine	ME	1881
Arthur	James G. Blaine	ME	1881
	F. T. Frelinghuysen	NJ	1881
Cleveland	F. T. Frelinghuysen	NJ	1885
	Thomas F. Bayard	DE	1885
Harrison, B.	Thomas F. Bayard	DE	1889
	James G. Blaine	ME	1889
	John W. Foster	IN	1892
Cleveland	Walter Q. Gresham	IN	1893
	Richard Olney	MA	1895
McKinley	Richard Olney	MA	1897
	John Sherman	OH	1897
	William R. Day	OH	1898
	John M. Hay	DC	1898
Roosevelt, T.	John M. Hay	DC	1901
	Elihu Root	NY	1905
	Robert Bacon	NY	1909
Taft	Robert Bacon	NY	1909
	Philander C. Knox	PA	1909
Wilson	Philander C. Knox	PA	1913
	William J. Bryan	NE	1913
	Robert Lansing	NY	1915
	Bainbridge Colby	NY	1920
Harding	Charles E. Hughes	NY	1921
Coolidge	Charles E. Hughes	NY	1923
	Frank B. Kellogg	MN	1925
Hoover	Frank B. Kellogg	MN	1929
	Henry L. Stimson	NY	1929
Roosevelt, F. D.	Cordell Hull	TN	1933
	Edward R. Stettinius Jr.	VA	1944
Truman	Edward R. Stettinius Jr.	VA	1945
	James F. Byrnes	SC	1945
	George C. Marshall	PA	1947
	Dean G. Acheson	CT	1949
Eisenhower	John Foster Dulles	NY	1953
	Christian A. Herter	MA	1959
Kennedy	D. Dean Rusk	NY	1961
Johnson, L. B.	D. Dean Rusk	NY	1963
Nixon	William P. Rogers	NY	1969
	Henry A. Kissinger	DC	1973
Ford	Henry A. Kissinger	DC	1974
Carter	Cyrus R. Vance	NY	1977
	Edmund S. Muskie	ME	1980
Reagan	Alexander M. Haig Jr.	CT	1981
	George P. Shultz	CA	1982
Bush, G. H. W.	James A. Baker III	TX	1989
	Lawrence S. Eagleburger	MI	1992
Clinton	Warren M. Christopher	CA	1993
	Madeleine K. Albright	DC	1997
Bush, G. W.	Colin L. Powell	NY	2001
	Condoleezza Rice	AL	2005
Obama	Hillary Rodham Clinton	NY	2009
	John Kerry	MA	2013

Department of the Treasury

1500 Pennsylvania Ave. NW, 20220; www.treasury.gov

Organized by act of Congress on Sept. 2, 1789. Responsible for the fiscal affairs of the U.S. Serves as the government's financial agent; collects, borrows, and disburses funds for the federal government. Monitors the nation's financial infrastructure and economic development; recommends domestic and international financial, monetary, economic, trade, and tax policies. Manufactures currency and coins. Carries out monetary and tax law enforcement activities, sanctions, embargoes, and fights illicit finance—counterfeiting, money laundering, narcotics trafficking, terrorist financing. **Budget** (including interest on the public debt): $399.1 bil (2013); $446.9 bil (2014); $506.4 bil (est. 2015).

- Alcohol and Tobacco Tax and Trade Bureau (1310 G St. NW, Box 12, 20005); www.ttb.gov
- Bureau of Engraving and Printing (14th and C Sts. SW, 20228); www.moneyfactory.gov
- Bureau of the Fiscal Service (401 14th St. SW, 20227); www.fiscal.treasury.gov
- Financial Crimes Enforcement Network (P.O. Box 39, Vienna, VA 22183); www.fincen.gov
- Internal Revenue Service (1111 Constitution Ave. NW, 20224); www.irs.gov
- U.S. Mint (801 9th St. NW, 20220); www.usmint.gov

Secretaries of the Treasury

President	Secretary	Home	Sworn in
Washington	Alexander Hamilton	NY	1789
	Oliver Wolcott Jr.	CT	1795
Adams, J.	Oliver Wolcott Jr.	CT	1797
	Samuel Dexter	MA	1801
Jefferson	Samuel Dexter	MA	1801
	Albert Gallatin	PA	1801
Madison	Albert Gallatin	PA	1809
	George W. Campbell	TN	1814
	Alexander J. Dallas	PA	1814
	William H. Crawford	GA	1816
Monroe	William H. Crawford	GA	1817
Adams, J. Q.	Richard Rush	PA	1825

President	Secretary	Home	Sworn in
Jackson	Samuel D. Ingham	PA	1829
	Louis McLane	DE	1831
	William J. Duane	PA	1833
	Roger B. Taney	MD	1833
	Levi Woodbury	NH	1834
Van Buren	Levi Woodbury	NH	1837
Harrison, W. H.	Thomas Ewing	OH	1841
Tyler	Thomas Ewing	OH	1841
	Walter Forward	PA	1841
	John C. Spencer	NY	1843
	George M. Bibb	KY	1844
Polk	Robert J. Walker	MS	1845
Taylor	William M. Meredith	PA	1849
Fillmore	Thomas Corwin	OH	1850
Pierce	James Guthrie	KY	1853
Buchanan	Howell Cobb	GA	1857
	Phillip F. Thomas	MD	1860
	John A. Dix	NY	1861
Lincoln	Salmon P. Chase	OH	1861
	William P. Fessenden	ME	1864
	Hugh McCulloch	IN	1865
Johnson, A.	Hugh McCulloch	IN	1865
Grant	George S. Boutwell	MA	1869
	William A. Richardson	MA	1873
	Benjamin H. Bristow	KY	1874
	Lot M. Morrill	ME	1876
Hayes	John Sherman	OH	1877
Garfield	William Windom	MN	1881
Arthur	Charles J. Folger	NY	1881
	Walter Q. Gresham	IN	1884
	Hugh McCulloch	IN	1884
Cleveland	Daniel Manning	NY	1885
	Charles S. Fairchild	NY	1887
Harrison, B.	William Windom	MN	1889
	Charles Foster	OH	1891
Cleveland	John G. Carlisle	KY	1893
McKinley	Lyman J. Gage	IL	1897
Roosevelt, T.	Lyman J. Gage	IL	1901
	Leslie M. Shaw	IA	1902
	George B. Cortelyou	NY	1907
Taft	Franklin MacVeagh	IL	1909
Wilson	William G. McAdoo	NY	1913
	Carter Glass	VA	1918
	David F. Houston	MO	1920
Harding	Andrew W. Mellon	PA	1921
Coolidge	Andrew W. Mellon	PA	1923
Hoover	Andrew W. Mellon	PA	1929
	Ogden L. Mills	NY	1932
Roosevelt, F. D.	William H. Woodin	NY	1933
	Henry Morgenthau Jr.	NY	1934
Truman	Fred M. Vinson	KY	1945
	John W. Snyder	MO	1946
Eisenhower	George M. Humphrey	OH	1953
	Robert B. Anderson	CT	1957
Kennedy	C. Douglas Dillon	NJ	1961
Johnson, L. B.	C. Douglas Dillon	NJ	1963
	Henry H. Fowler	VA	1965
	Joseph W. Barr	IN	1968
Nixon	David M. Kennedy	IL	1969
	John B. Connally	TX	1971
	George P. Shultz	IL	1972
	William E. Simon	NJ	1974
Ford	William E. Simon	NJ	1974
Carter	W. Michael Blumenthal	MI	1977
	G. William Miller	RI	1979
Reagan	Donald T. Regan	NY	1981
	James A. Baker III	TX	1985
	Nicholas F. Brady	NJ	1988
Bush, G. H. W.	Nicholas F. Brady	NJ	1989
Clinton	Lloyd M. Bentsen	TX	1993
	Robert E. Rubin	NY	1995
	Lawrence H. Summers	CT	1999
Bush, G. W.	Paul H. O'Neill	MO	2001
	John W. Snow	OH	2003
	Henry M. Paulson Jr.	FL	2006
Obama	Timothy F. Geithner	NY	2009
	Jack Lew	NY	2013

Department of Defense

1400 Defense Pentagon, 20301; www.defense.gov

The Dept. of Defense, originally designated the National Military Establishment, was created on Sept. 18, 1947. Directs and controls the armed forces and assists the president in protecting the nation's security. Military departments of the Army, Navy, and Air Force are each separately organized under its own secretary but all function under the command of the secretary of defense. They conduct military operations as unified commands. The chairman of the Joint Chiefs of Staff is the principal military adviser to the president. Undersecretaries supervise acquisition, technology, and logistics; intelligence; personnel and readiness; and policy. **Budget** for military programs: $607.8 bil (2013); $577.9 bil (2014); $567.7 bil (est. 2015). **Budget** for civil programs: $63.1 bil (2013); $63.9 bil (2014); $67.2 bil (est. 2015).

- Def. Advanced Research Projects Agency (675 N. Randolph St., Arlington, VA 22203); www.darpa.mil
- Def. Intelligence Agency (200 MacDill Blvd., 20340); www.dia.mil
- Def. Security Cooperation Agency (2800 Defense Pentagon, 20301); www.dsca.mil
- Missile Def. Agency (5700 18th St., Bldg. 245, Fort Belvoir, VA 22060-5573); www.mda.mil
- Natl. Geospatial-Intelligence Agency (7500 GEOINT Dr., Springfield, VA 22150); www.nga.mil
- Natl. Security Agency/Central Security Service (9800 Savage Rd., Ft. Meade, MD 20755); www.nsa.gov

Secretaries of Defense

President	Secretary	Home	Sworn in
Truman	James V. Forrestal	NY	1947
	Louis A. Johnson	WV	1949
	George C. Marshall	PA	1950
	Robert A. Lovett	NY	1951
Eisenhower	Charles E. Wilson	MI	1953
	Neil H. McElroy	OH	1957
	Thomas S. Gates Jr.	PA	1959
Kennedy	Robert S. McNamara	MI	1961
Johnson, L. B.	Robert S. McNamara	MI	1963
	Clark M. Clifford	MD	1968
Nixon	Melvin R. Laird	WI	1969
	Elliot L. Richardson	MA	1973
	James R. Schlesinger	VA	1973
Ford	James R. Schlesinger	VA	1974
	Donald H. Rumsfeld	IL	1975
Carter	Harold Brown	CA	1977
Reagan	Caspar W. Weinberger	CA	1981
	Frank C. Carlucci	PA	1987
Bush, G. H. W.	Richard B. Cheney	WY	1989
Clinton	Les Aspin	WI	1993
	William J. Perry	CA	1994
	William S. Cohen	ME	1997
Bush, G. W.	Donald H. Rumsfeld	IL	2001
	Robert M. Gates	TX	2006
Obama	Robert M. Gates	TX	2009
	Leon E. Panetta	CA	2011
	Chuck Hagel	NE	2013
	Ashton Carter	PA	2015

Secretaries of War

The War Dept. (which included jurisdiction over the Navy until 1798) was created by act of Congress on Aug. 7, 1789.

President	Secretary	Home	Sworn in
Washington	Henry Knox	MA	1789
	Timothy Pickering	PA	1795
	James McHenry	MD	1796
Adams, J.	James McHenry	MD	1797
	Samuel Dexter	MA	1800
Jefferson	Henry Dearborn	MA	1801
Madison	William Eustis	MA	1809
	John Armstrong	NY	1813
	James Monroe	VA	1814
	William H. Crawford	GA	1815
Monroe	John C. Calhoun	SC	1817
Adams, J. Q.	James Barbour	VA	1825
	Peter B. Porter	NY	1828
Jackson	John H. Eaton	TN	1829
	Lewis Cass	MI	1831
	Benjamin F. Butler	NY	1837
Van Buren	Joel R. Poinsett	SC	1837
Harrison, W. H.	John Bell	TN	1841
Tyler	John Bell	TN	1841
	John C. Spencer	NY	1841
	James M. Porter	PA	1843
	William Wilkins	PA	1844
Polk	William L. Marcy	NY	1845
Taylor	George W. Crawford	GA	1849
Fillmore	Charles M. Conrad	LA	1850
Pierce	Jefferson Davis	MS	1853

President	Secretary	Home	Sworn in
Buchanan	John B. Floyd	VA	1857
	Joseph Holt	KY	1861
Lincoln	Simon Cameron	PA	1861
	Edwin M. Stanton	PA	1862
Johnson, A.	Edwin M. Stanton	PA	1865
	John M. Schofield	IL	1868
Grant	John A. Rawlins	IL	1869
	William T. Sherman	OH	1869
	William W. Belknap	IA	1869
	Alphonso Taft	OH	1876
	James D. Cameron	PA	1876
Hayes	George W. McCrary	IA	1877
	Alexander Ramsey	MN	1879
Garfield	Robert T. Lincoln	IL	1881
Arthur	Robert T. Lincoln	IL	1881
Cleveland	William C. Endicott	MA	1885
Harrison, B.	Redfield Proctor	VT	1889
	Stephen B. Elkins	WV	1891
Cleveland	Daniel S. Lamont	NY	1893
McKinley	Russell A. Alger	MI	1897
	Elihu Root	NY	1899
Roosevelt, T.	Elihu Root	NY	1901
	William H. Taft	OH	1904
	Luke E. Wright	TN	1908
Taft	Jacob M. Dickinson	TN	1909
	Henry L. Stimson	NY	1911
Wilson	Lindley M. Garrison	NJ	1913
	Newton D. Baker	OH	1916
Harding	John W. Weeks	MA	1921
Coolidge	John W. Weeks	MA	1923
	Dwight F. Davis	MO	1925
Hoover	James W. Good	IL	1929
	Patrick J. Hurley	OK	1929
Roosevelt, F. D.	George H. Dern	UT	1933
	Harry H. Woodring	KS	1937
	Henry L. Stimson	NY	1940
Truman	Robert P. Patterson	NY	1945
	Kenneth C. Royall[1]	NC	1947

(1) Last member of Cabinet with this title. The War Dept. became the Dept. of the Army with the creation of the Defense Dept. in 1947, though the Army secretary maintained Cabinet-level status until 1949.

Secretaries of the Navy

The Navy Dept. was created by act of Congress on Apr. 30, 1798. The Marine Corps is part of this department.

President	Secretary	Home	Sworn in
Adams, J.	Benjamin Stoddert	MD	1798
Jefferson	Benjamin Stoddert	MD	1801
	Robert Smith	MD	1801
Madison	Paul Hamilton	SC	1809
	William Jones	PA	1813
	Benjamin W. Crowninshield	MA	1814
Monroe	Benjamin W. Crowninshield	MA	1817
	Smith Thompson	NY	1818
	Samuel L. Southard	NJ	1823
Adams, J. Q.	Samuel L. Southard	NJ	1825
Jackson	John Branch	NC	1829
	Levi Woodbury	NH	1831
	Mahlon Dickerson	NJ	1834
Van Buren	Mahlon Dickerson	NJ	1837
	James K. Paulding	NY	1838
Harrison, W. H.	George E. Badger	NC	1841
Tyler	George E. Badger	NC	1841
	Abel P. Upshur	VA	1841
	David Henshaw	MA	1843
	Thomas W. Gilmer	VA	1844
	John Y. Mason	VA	1844
Polk	George Bancroft	MA	1845
	John Y. Mason	VA	1846
Taylor	William B. Preston	VA	1849
Fillmore	William A. Graham	NC	1850
	John P. Kennedy	MD	1852
Pierce	James C. Dobbin	NC	1853
Buchanan	Isaac Toucey	CT	1857
Lincoln	Gideon Welles	CT	1861
Johnson, A.	Gideon Welles	CT	1865
Grant	Adolph E. Borie	PA	1869
	George M. Robeson	NJ	1869
Hayes	Richard W. Thompson	IN	1877
	Nathan Goff Jr.	WV	1881
Garfield	William H. Hunt	LA	1881
Arthur	William E. Chandler	NH	1882
Cleveland	William C. Whitney	NY	1885
Harrison, B.	Benjamin F. Tracy	NY	1889
Cleveland	Hilary A. Herbert	AL	1893
McKinley	John D. Long	MA	1897
Roosevelt, T.	John D. Long	MA	1901
	William H. Moody	MA	1902
	Paul Morton	IL	1904
	Charles J. Bonaparte	MD	1905
	Victor H. Metcalf	CA	1906
	Truman H. Newberry	MI	1908
Taft	George von L. Meyer	MA	1909
Wilson	Josephus Daniels	NC	1913
Harding	Edwin Denby	MI	1921
Coolidge	Edwin Denby	MI	1923
	Curtis D. Wilbur	CA	1924
Hoover	Charles Francis Adams	MA	1929
Roosevelt, F. D.	Claude A. Swanson	VA	1933
	Charles Edison	NJ	1940
	Frank Knox	IL	1940
	James V. Forrestal	NY	1944
Truman	James V. Forrestal[1]	NY	1945

(1) Last member of Cabinet with this title. The Navy Dept. became a branch of the Dept. of Defense when the latter was created in 1947, though the Navy secretary maintained Cabinet-level status until 1949.

Department of Justice

950 Pennsylvania Ave. NW, 20530; www.justice.gov

The Office of Attorney General was established by act of Congress on Sept. 24, 1789. It officially reached Cabinet rank in Mar. 1792, when the first attorney general, Edmund Randolph, attended his initial Cabinet meeting. The Dept. of Justice, headed by the attorney general, was created June 22, 1870. Provides for the enforcement of federal laws and investigation of violations; furnishes legal counsel in cases involving the federal government and interprets laws relating to the activities of other federal departments; supervises federal penal institutions. The attorney general and Office of Legal Counsel render legal advice, upon request, to the president and department heads. The solicitor general conducts all suits brought before the U.S. Supreme Court in which the federal government is concerned. The Civil Division represents the U.S. government in many civil or criminal matters. The 94 U.S. attorneys are the principal litigators in the U.S. and its territories. **Budget:** \$29.7 bil (2013); \$28.6 bil (2014); \$36.1 bil (est. 2015).

- Bureau of Alcohol, Tobacco, Firearms, and Explosives (99 New York Ave. NE, 20226); www.atf.gov
- Bureau of Prisons (320 First St. NW, 20534); www.bop.gov
- Drug Enforcement Admin. (8701 Morrissette Dr., Springfield, VA 22152); www.dea.gov
- Executive Office for Immigration Review (5107 Leesburg Pike, Falls Church, VA 20530); www.justice.gov/eoir/
- Federal Bureau of Investigation (935 Pennsylvania Ave. NW, 20535); www.fbi.gov
- INTERPOL Washington (U.S. Natl. Central Bureau) (20530); www.justice.gov/interpol-washington/
- U.S. Marshals Service (2604 Jefferson Davis Hwy., Alexandria, VA 22301-1025); www.usmarshals.gov
- U.S. Parole Commission (90 K St. NE, 3rd Fl., 20530); www.justice.gov/uspc/

Attorneys General

President	Attorney General	Home	Sworn in
Washington	Edmund J. Randolph	VA	1789
	William Bradford	PA	1794
	Charles Lee	VA	1795
Adams, J.	Charles Lee	VA	1797
Jefferson	Levi Lincoln	MA	1801
	John Breckenridge	KY	1805
	Caesar A. Rodney	DE	1807
Madison	Caesar A. Rodney	DE	1807
	William Pinkney	MD	1811
	Richard Rush	PA	1814
Monroe	Richard Rush	PA	1817
	William Wirt	VA	1817
Adams, J. Q.	William Wirt	VA	1825

President	Attorney General	Home	Sworn in
Jackson	John M. Berrien	GA	1829
	Roger B. Taney	MD	1831
	Benjamin F. Butler	NY	1833
Van Buren	Benjamin F. Butler	NY	1837
	Felix Grundy	TN	1838
	Henry D. Gilpin	PA	1840
Harrison, W. H.	John J. Crittenden	KY	1841
Tyler	John J. Crittenden	KY	1841
	Hugh S. Legaré	SC	1841
	John Nelson	MD	1843
Polk	John Y. Mason	VA	1845
	Nathan Clifford	ME	1846
	Isaac Toucey	CT	1848
Taylor	Reverdy Johnson	MD	1849
Fillmore	John J. Crittenden	KY	1850
Pierce	Caleb Cushing	MA	1853
Buchanan	Jeremiah S. Black	PA	1857
	Edwin M. Stanton	PA	1860
Lincoln	Edward Bates	MO	1861
	James Speed	KY	1864
Johnson, A.	James Speed	KY	1865
	Henry Stanbery	OH	1866
	William M. Evarts	NY	1868
Grant	Ebenezer R. Hoar	MA	1869
	Amos T. Akerman	GA	1870
	George H. Williams	OR	1871
	Edwards Pierrepont	NY	1875
	Alphonso Taft	OH	1876
Hayes	Charles Devens	MA	1877
Garfield	I. Wayne MacVeagh	PA	1881
Arthur	Benjamin H. Brewster	PA	1882
Cleveland	Augustus H. Garland	AR	1885
Harrison, B.	William H. H. Miller	IN	1889
Cleveland	Richard Olney	MA	1893
	Judson Harmon	OH	1895
McKinley	Joseph McKenna	CA	1897
	John W. Griggs	NJ	1898
	Philander C. Knox	PA	1901
Roosevelt, T.	Philander C. Knox	PA	1901
	William H. Moody	MA	1904
	Charles J. Bonaparte	MD	1906
Taft	George W. Wickersham	NY	1909
Wilson	James C. McReynolds	TN	1913
	Thomas W. Gregory	TX	1914
	A. Mitchell Palmer	PA	1919
Harding	Harry M. Daugherty	OH	1921
Coolidge	Harry M. Daugherty	OH	1923
	Harlan F. Stone	NY	1924
	John G. Sargent	VT	1925
Hoover	William D. Mitchell	MN	1929
Roosevelt, F. D.	Homer S. Cummings	CT	1933
	Frank Murphy	MI	1939
	Robert H. Jackson	NY	1940
	Francis Biddle	PA	1941
Truman	Thomas C. Clark	TX	1945
	J. Howard McGrath	RI	1949
	James P. McGranery	PA	1952
Eisenhower	Herbert Brownell Jr.	NY	1953
	William P. Rogers	MD	1957
Kennedy	Robert F. Kennedy	MA	1961
Johnson, L. B.	Robert F. Kennedy	MA	1963
	Nicholas Katzenbach	IL	1964
	W. Ramsey Clark	TX	1967
Nixon	John N. Mitchell	NY	1969
	Richard G. Kleindienst	AZ	1972
	Elliot L. Richardson	MA	1973
	William B. Saxbe	OH	1974
Ford	William B. Saxbe	OH	1974
	Edward H. Levi	IL	1975
Carter	Griffin B. Bell	GA	1977
	Benjamin R. Civiletti	MD	1979
Reagan	William French Smith	CA	1981
	Edwin Meese III	CA	1985
	Richard L. Thornburgh	PA	1988
Bush, G. H. W.	Richard L. Thornburgh	PA	1989
	William P. Barr	NY	1991
Clinton	Janet Reno	FL	1993
Bush, G. W.	John Ashcroft	MO	2001
	Alberto R. Gonzales	TX	2005
	Michael B. Mukasey	NY	2007
Obama	Eric H. Holder Jr.	DC	2009
	Loretta E. Lynch	NY	2015

Department of the Interior

1849 C St. NW, 20240; www.doi.gov

Created by act of Congress on Mar. 3, 1849. Custodian of natural resources. Has the responsibility of protecting and conserving the country's land, water, minerals, fish, and wildlife; of promoting the wise use of all these natural resources; of maintaining national parks and recreation areas; and of preserving historic places. It also provides for the welfare of American Indian reservation communities and of inhabitants of island territories under U.S. administration. **Budget:** $9.6 bil (2013); $11.3 bil (2014); $13.0 bil (est. 2015).

- Bureau of Indian Affairs (MS-3658-MIB, 1849 C St. NW, 20240); www.indianaffairs.gov
- Bureau of Land Management (1849 C St. NW, 20240); www.blm.gov
- Bureau of Ocean Energy Management (1849 C St. NW, 20240); www.boem.gov
- Bureau of Reclamation (1849 C St. NW, 20240); www.usbr.gov
- Bureau of Safety and Environmental Enforcement (1849 C St. NW, 20240); www.bsee.gov
- National Park Service (1849 C St. NW, 20240); www.nps.gov
- Office of Surface Mining Reclamation and Enforcement (1951 Constitution Ave. NW, 20240); www.osmre.gov
- U.S. Fish and Wildlife Service (1849 C St. NW, 20240); www.fws.gov
- U.S. Geological Survey (12201 Sunrise Valley Dr., Reston, VA 20192); www.usgs.gov

Secretaries of the Interior

President	Secretary	Home	Sworn in
Taylor	Thomas Ewing	OH	1849
Fillmore	Thomas M. T. McKennan	PA	1850
	Alex H. H. Stuart	VA	1850
Pierce	Robert McClelland	MI	1853
Buchanan	Jacob Thompson	MS	1857
Lincoln	Caleb B. Smith	IN	1861
	John P. Usher	IN	1863
Johnson, A.	John P. Usher	IN	1865
	James Harlan	IA	1865
	Orville H. Browning	IL	1866
Grant	Jacob D. Cox	OH	1869
	Columbus Delano	OH	1870
	Zachariah Chandler	MI	1875
Hayes	Carl Schurz	MO	1877
Garfield	Samuel J. Kirkwood	IA	1881
Arthur	Henry M. Teller	CO	1882
Cleveland	Lucius Q. C. Lamar	MS	1885
	William F. Vilas	WI	1888
Harrison, B.	John W. Noble	MO	1889
Cleveland	M. Hoke Smith	GA	1893
	David R. Francis	MO	1896
McKinley	Cornelius N. Bliss	NY	1897
	Ethan A. Hitchcock	MO	1898
Roosevelt, T.	Ethan A. Hitchcock	MO	1901
	James R. Garfield	OH	1907
Taft	Richard A. Ballinger	WA	1909
	Walter L. Fisher	IL	1911
Wilson	Franklin K. Lane	CA	1913
	John B. Payne	IL	1920
Harding	Albert B. Fall	NM	1921
	Hubert Work	CO	1923
Coolidge	Hubert Work	CO	1923
	Roy O. West	IL	1929
Hoover	Ray Lyman Wilbur	CA	1929
Roosevelt, F. D.	Harold L. Ickes	IL	1933
Truman	Harold L. Ickes	IL	1945
	Julius A. Krug	WI	1946
	Oscar L. Chapman	CO	1949
Eisenhower	Douglas McKay	OR	1953
	Fred A. Seaton	NE	1956
Kennedy	Stewart L. Udall	AZ	1961
Johnson, L. B.	Stewart L. Udall	AZ	1963
Nixon	Walter J. Hickel	AK	1969
	Rogers C. B. Morton	MD	1971
Ford	Rogers C. B. Morton	MD	1971
	Stanley K. Hathaway	WY	1975
	Thomas S. Kleppe	ND	1975
Carter	Cecil D. Andrus	ID	1977
Reagan	James G. Watt	CO	1981
	William P. Clark	CA	1983
	Donald P. Hodel	OR	1985
Bush, G. H. W.	Manuel Lujan	NM	1989
Clinton	Bruce Babbitt	AZ	1993
Bush, G. W.	Gale Norton	CO	2001
	Dirk Kempthorne	ID	2006
Obama	Kenneth L. Salazar	CO	2009
	Sally Jewell	WA	2013

Department of Agriculture

1400 Independence Ave. SW, 20250; www.usda.gov

Created by act of Congress on May 15, 1862. On Feb. 8, 1889, its commissioner was renamed secretary of agriculture and became a member of the Cabinet. Provides leadership on food, agriculture, and natural resources; supports scientific research and education for agriculture, nutrition, and food safety. Develops nutrition assistance programs, promotes healthy eating, supplies food stamps, grades and inspects the commercial supply of food. Responsible for the health of the land through sustainable management and conservation, manages public lands in national forests and grasslands; safeguards against invasive pests and diseases; ensures the health and care of animals and plants. Oversees assistance and conservation programs for farmers and ranchers and programs to improve the rural economy and quality of life. Facilitates domestic and international marketing of U.S. agricultural products. **Budget:** $155.9 bil (2013); $141.8 bil (2014); $147.5 bil (est. 2015).

- Agricultural Research Service (1400 Independence Ave. SW, 20250); www.ars.usda.gov
- Economic Research Service (1400 Independence Ave. SW, Mail Stop 1800, 20250); www.ers.usda.gov
- Food and Nutrition Service (3101 Park Center Dr., Alexandria, VA 22302); www.fns.usda.gov
- Food Safety and Inspection Service (1400 Independence Ave. SW, 20250); www.fsis.usda.gov
- Foreign Agricultural Service (1400 Independence Ave. SW, Mail Stop 1001, 20250); www.fas.usda.gov
- Forest Service (1400 Independence Ave. SW, 20250); www.fs.fed.us
- Natl. Agricultural Statistics Service (1400 Independence Ave. SW, 20250); www.nass.usda.gov
- Natural Resources Conservation Service (1400 Independence Ave. SW, 20250); www.nrcs.usda.gov

Secretaries of Agriculture

President	Secretary	Home	Sworn in
Cleveland	Norman J. Colman	MO	1889
Harrison, B.	Jeremiah M. Rusk	WI	1889
Cleveland	J. Sterling Morton	NE	1893
McKinley	James Wilson	IA	1897
Roosevelt, T.	James Wilson	IA	1901
Taft	James Wilson	IA	1909
Wilson	David F. Houston	MO	1913
	Edwin T. Meredith	IA	1920
Harding	Henry C. Wallace	IA	1921
Coolidge	Henry C. Wallace	IA	1923
	Howard M. Gore	WV	1924
	William M. Jardine	KS	1925
Hoover	Arthur M. Hyde	MO	1929
Roosevelt, F. D.	Henry A. Wallace	IA	1933
	Claude R. Wickard	IN	1940
Truman	Clinton P. Anderson	NM	1945
	Charles F. Brannan	CO	1948
Eisenhower	Ezra Taft Benson	UT	1953
Kennedy	Orville L. Freeman	MN	1961
Johnson, L. B.	Orville L. Freeman	MN	1963
Nixon	Clifford M. Hardin	IN	1969
	Earl L. Butz	IN	1971
Ford	Earl L. Butz	IN	1974
	John A. Knebel	VA	1976
Carter	Bob Bergland	MN	1977
Reagan	John R. Block	IL	1981
	Richard E. Lyng	CA	1986
Bush, G. H. W.	Clayton K. Yeutter	NE	1989
	Edward Madigan	IL	1991
Clinton	Mike Espy	MS	1993
	Dan Glickman	KS	1995
Bush, G. W.	Ann M. Veneman	CA	2001
	Mike Johanns	NE	2005
	Ed Schafer	ND	2008
Obama	Thomas J. Vilsack	IA	2009

Department of Commerce

1401 Constitution Ave. NW, 20230; www.commerce.gov

The Dept. of Commerce was formed by Congress Mar. 4, 1913, when it divided the Dept. of Commerce and Labor into two departments. Fosters, serves, and promotes the nation's economic development and technological advancement; supports the comprehension and use of the environment and its oceanic life; assists states, communities, and individuals with economic progress; promotes trade abroad and ensures an effective export control and treaty compliance system. Issues trademarks and patents, maintains measurement standards, and manages the federal telecommunications spectrum. Collects, analyzes, and distributes statistics regarding the nation and the economy through the Bureaus of the Census and of Economic Analysis. NOAA explores, monitors, and conserves oceans and coasts, tracks weather and other environmental data. **Budget:** $9.1 bil (2013); $7.9 bil (2014); $10.0 bil (est. 2015).

- Bureau of the Census (4600 Silver Hill Rd., 20233); www.census.gov
- Bureau of Economic Analysis (1441 L St. NW, 20005); www.bea.gov
- Minority Business Development Agency (1401 Constitution Ave. NW, 20230); www.mbda.gov
- Natl. Institute of Standards and Technology (100 Bureau Dr., Stop 1070, Gaithersburg, MD 20899); www.nist.gov
- Natl. Oceanic and Atmospheric Admin. (1401 Constitution Ave. NW, Rm. 5128, 20230); www.noaa.gov
- Natl. Technical Information Service (5301 Shawnee Rd., Alexandria, VA 22312); www.ntis.gov
- Natl. Telecommunications and Information Admin. (1401 Constitution Ave. NW, 20230); www.ntia.doc.gov

Secretaries of Commerce

President	Secretary	Home	Sworn in
Wilson	William C. Redfield	NY	1913
	Joshua W. Alexander	MO	1919
Harding	Herbert C. Hoover	CA	1921
Coolidge	Herbert C. Hoover	CA	1923
	William F. Whiting	MA	1928
Hoover	Robert P. Lamont	IL	1929
	Roy D. Chapin	MI	1932
Roosevelt, F. D.	Daniel C. Roper	SC	1933
	Harry L. Hopkins	NY	1939
	Jesse H. Jones	TX	1940
	Henry A. Wallace	IA	1945
Truman	Henry A. Wallace	IA	1945
	W. Averell Harriman	NY	1947
	Charles W. Sawyer	OH	1948
Eisenhower	Sinclair Weeks	MA	1953
	Lewis L. Strauss	NY	1958
	Frederick H. Mueller	MI	1959
Kennedy	Luther H. Hodges	NC	1961
Johnson, L. B.	Luther H. Hodges	NC	1963
	John T. Connor	NJ	1965
	Alex B. Trowbridge	NJ	1967
	Cyrus R. Smith	NY	1968
Nixon	Maurice H. Stans	MN	1969
	Peter G. Peterson	IL	1972
	Frederick B. Dent	SC	1973
Ford	Frederick B. Dent	SC	1974
	Rogers C. B. Morton	MD	1975
	Elliot L. Richardson	MA	1975
Carter	Juanita M. Kreps	NC	1977
	Philip M. Klutznick	IL	1979
Reagan	Malcolm Baldrige	CT	1981
	C. William Verity Jr.	OH	1987
Bush, G. H. W.	Robert A. Mosbacher	TX	1989
	Barbara H. Franklin	PA	1992
Clinton	Ronald H. Brown	DC	1993
	Mickey Kantor	CA	1996
	William M. Daley	IL	1997
	Norman Y. Mineta	CA	2000
Bush, G. W.	Donald L. Evans	TX	2001
	Carlos M. Gutierrez	MI	2005
Obama	Gary F. Locke	WA	2009
	John Bryson	CA	2011
	Penny Pritzker	IL	2013

Secretaries of Commerce and Labor

The Dept. of Commerce and Labor was created by Congress on Feb. 14, 1903.

President	Secretary	Home	Sworn in
Roosevelt, T.	George B. Cortelyou	NY	1903
	Victor H. Metcalf	CA	1904
	Oscar S. Straus	NY	1906
Taft	Charles Nagel	MO	1909

Department of Labor

200 Constitution Ave. NW, 20210; www.dol.gov

The Dept. of Labor was formed by Congress Mar. 4, 1913, when it divided the Dept. of Commerce and Labor into two departments. Administers federal labor laws to foster, promote, and develop the welfare of job seekers, wage earners, and retirees of the U.S.; to improve working conditions; and to advance opportunities for profitable employment. Administers standards for wages and overtime pay, safety and health conditions, workers' compensation. Tracks changes in employment, prices, and other national economic measurements. Regulates pension and welfare benefit plans, the hiring and employment of migrant and seasonal workers, and requirements pertaining to the mining, construction, and transportation industries. Monitors labor unions and their funds. **Budget:** $80.3 bil (2013); $56.8 bil (2014); $52.8 bil (est. 2015).

- Bureau of Labor Statistics (2 Massachusetts Ave. NE, 20212); www.bls.gov
- Employment and Training Admin. (200 Constitution Ave. NW, 20210); www.doleta.gov
- Mine Safety and Health Admin. (1100 Wilson Blvd., 21st Fl., Arlington, VA 22209); www.msha.gov
- Occupational Safety and Health Admin. (200 Constitution Ave. NW, 20210); www.osha.gov
- Office of Federal Contract Compliance Programs (200 Constitution Ave. NW, 20210); www.dol.gov/ofccp/
- Office of Labor-Management Standards (200 Constitution Ave. NW, 20210); www.dol.gov/olms/
- Office of Workers' Compensation Programs (200 Constitution Ave. NW, 20210); www.dol.gov/owcp/
- Wage and Hour Div. (200 Constitution Ave. NW, 20210); www.dol.gov/whd/

Secretaries of Labor

President	Secretary	Home	Sworn in
Wilson	William B. Wilson	PA	1913
Harding	James J. Davis	PA	1921
Coolidge	James J. Davis	PA	1923
Hoover	James J. Davis	PA	1929
	William N. Doak	VA	1930
Roosevelt, F. D.	Frances Perkins	NY	1933
Truman	L. B. Schwellenbach	WA	1945
	Maurice J. Tobin	MA	1949
Eisenhower	Martin P. Durkin	IL	1953
	James P. Mitchell	NJ	1953
Kennedy	Arthur J. Goldberg	IL	1961
	W. Willard Wirtz	IL	1962
Johnson, L. B.	W. Willard Wirtz	IL	1963
Nixon	George P. Shultz	IL	1969
	James D. Hodgson	CA	1970
	Peter J. Brennan	NY	1973
Ford	Peter J. Brennan	NY	1974
	John T. Dunlop	CA	1975
	W. J. Usery Jr.	GA	1976
Carter	F. Ray Marshall	TX	1977
Reagan	Raymond J. Donovan	NJ	1981
	William E. Brock	TN	1985
	Ann D. McLaughlin	DC	1987
Bush, G. H. W.	Elizabeth H. Dole	NC	1989
	Lynn Martin	IL	1991
Clinton	Robert B. Reich	MA	1993
	Alexis M. Herman	AL	1997
Bush, G. W.	Elaine L. Chao	KY	2001
Obama	Hilda L. Solis	CA	2009
	Thomas E. Perez	MD	2013

Department of Housing and Urban Development

451 7th St. SW, 20410; www.hud.gov

Created by act of Congress on Sept. 9, 1965. Responsible for housing needs and the improvement and development of urban areas. Supports affordable housing, provides grants for community development and redevelopment. Enforces fair and safe housing standards. Provides funds to assist homeless individuals and families with emergency and transitional shelters. The FHA provides mortgage insurance on loans made by approved lenders. **Budget:** $56.6 bil (2013); $38.5 bil (2014); $42.4 bil (est. 2015).

- Fannie Mae (Federal Natl. Mortgage Association) (3900 Wisconsin Ave. NW, 20016); www.fanniemae.com
- Federal Housing Admin. (451 7th St. SW, 20410); www.fha.gov
- Freddie Mac (Federal Home Loan Mortgage Corporation) (8200 Jones Branch Dr., McLean, VA 22102); www.freddiemac.com
- Ginnie Mae (Government Natl. Mortgage Association) (451 7th St. SW, Rm. B-133, 20410); www.ginniemae.gov

Note: Fannie Mae and Freddie Mac are government-sponsored enterprises (GSEs).

Secretaries of Housing and Urban Development

President	Secretary	Home	Sworn in
Johnson, L. B.	Robert C. Weaver	WA	1966
	Robert C. Wood	MA	1969
Nixon	George W. Romney	MI	1969
	James T. Lynn	OH	1973
Ford	James T. Lynn	OH	1974
	Carla Anderson Hills	CA	1975
Carter	Patricia Roberts Harris	DC	1977
	Moon Landrieu	LA	1979
Reagan	Samuel R. Pierce Jr.	NY	1981
Bush, G. H. W.	Jack F. Kemp	NY	1989
Clinton	Henry G. Cisneros	TX	1993
	Andrew M. Cuomo	NY	1997
Bush, G. W.	Mel Martinez	FL	2001
	Alphonso Jackson	TX	2004
	Steve Preston	VA	2008
Obama	Shaun L. S. Donovan	NY	2009
	Julián Castro	TX	2014

Department of Transportation

1200 New Jersey Ave. SE, 20590; www.transportation.gov

Created by act of Congress on Oct. 15, 1966. Promotes and develops rapid, safe, efficient, and convenient transportation in the U.S.; monitors and administers assistance to transportation industries; negotiates and implements international transportation agreements. Manages airspace, commercial space transportation, and the movement of hazardous materials. Resolves railroad rate and service disputes and reviews proposed railroad mergers. Analyzes and shares research and statistics to develop and improve transportation through RITA. Develops and enforces regulations on the nation's pipeline transportation system. The Maritime Administration maintains a fleet of cargo ships in reserve for war or national emergencies and commissions officers of the merchant marines. Operates the U.S. portion of the St. Lawrence Seaway between Montréal and Lake Erie. **Budget:** $76.3 bil (2013); $76.2 bil (2014); $80.2 bil (est. 2015).

- Federal Aviation Admin. (800 Independence Ave. SW, 20591); www.faa.gov
- Federal Highway Admin. (1200 New Jersey Ave. SE, 20590); www.fhwa.dot.gov
- Federal Railroad Admin. (1200 New Jersey Ave. SE, 20590); www.fra.dot.gov
- Federal Transit Admin. (East Bldg., 1200 New Jersey Ave. SE, 20590); www.fta.dot.gov
- Maritime Admin. (1200 New Jersey Ave. SE, 20590); www.marad.dot.gov
- Natl. Highway Traffic Safety Admin. (West Bldg., 1200 New Jersey Ave. SE, 20590); www.nhtsa.gov
- Office of the Asst. Sec. for Research and Technology (1200 New Jersey Ave. SE, 20590); www.rita.dot.gov

Secretaries of Transportation

President	Secretary	Home	Sworn in
Johnson, L. B.	Alan S. Boyd	FL	1966
Nixon	John A. Volpe	MA	1969
	Claude S. Brinegar	CA	1973
Ford	Claude S. Brinegar	CA	1974
	William T. Coleman Jr.	PA	1975
Carter	Brock Adams	WA	1977
	Neil E. Goldschmidt	OR	1979
Reagan	Andrew L. Lewis Jr.	PA	1981
	Elizabeth H. Dole	NC	1983
	James H. Burnley	NC	1987
Bush, G. H. W.	Samuel K. Skinner	IL	1989
	Andrew H. Card Jr.	MA	1992
Clinton	Federico F. Peña	CO	1993
	Rodney E. Slater	AR	1997
Bush, G. W.	Norman Y. Mineta	CA	2001
	Mary E. Peters	AZ	2006
Obama	Raymond L. LaHood	IL	2009
	Anthony Foxx	NC	2013

Department of Energy

1000 Independence Ave. SW, 20585; energy.gov

Created by federal law on Aug. 4, 1977. Secures the nation's energy and promotes scientific and technological innovation. Oversees the national energy supply and electric grid. Investigates and promotes clean and reliable energy. Manages and cleans up nuclear and other radioactive material, including nuclear weapons. The OSTI supports much of America's scientific research through program offices, education initiatives, national laboratories, and technology centers. Four power administrations sell power from federal hydroelectric projects across the West and Southeast. **Budget:** $24.7 bil (2013); $23.6 bil (2014); $30.1 bil (est. 2015).

- Energy Information Admin. (1000 Independence Ave. SW, 20585); www.eia.gov
- Federal Energy Regulatory Commission (independent regulatory agency) (888 1st St. NE, 20426); www.ferc.gov
- Natl. Nuclear Security Admin. (1000 Independence Ave. SW, 20585); www.nnsa.energy.gov
- Office of Scientific and Technical Information (P.O. Box 62, Oak Ridge, TN 37831); www.osti.gov

Secretaries of Energy

President	Secretary	Home	Sworn in
Carter	James R. Schlesinger	VA	1977
	Charles W. Duncan Jr.	WY	1979
Reagan	James B. Edwards	SC	1981
	Donald P. Hodel	OR	1982
	John S. Herrington	CA	1985
Bush, G. H. W.	James D. Watkins	CA	1989
Clinton	Hazel R. O'Leary	MN	1993
	Federico F. Peña	CO	1997
	Bill Richardson	NM	1998
Bush, G. W.	Spencer Abraham	MI	2001
	Samuel W. Bodman	MA	2005
Obama	Steven Chu	CA	2009
	Ernest Moniz	MA	2013

Department of Health and Human Services

200 Independence Ave. SW, 20201; www.hhs.gov

The Dept. of Health, Education, and Welfare was created by Congress on Apr. 11, 1953. On Sept. 27, 1979, Congress approved creation of a separate Dept. of Education. The existing department was renamed the Dept. of Health and Human Services. Administers a wide range of programs in the fields of health care and social services that affect nearly all Americans. Medicare and Medicaid provide health care insurance for one in four Americans. The HRSA improves health care services for people who are uninsured, isolated, or medically vulnerable; also oversees organ, tissue, and blood cell donations. The FDA assures the safety of food, drugs, cosmetics, biological products, and medical devices. The CDC monitors and safeguards against disease outbreaks. The NIH supports research projects nationwide and 27 health institutes and centers. The surgeon general is the nation's chief health educator and leads the U.S. Public Health Service Commissioned Corps. **Budget:** $886.3 bil (2013); $936.0 bil (2014); $1.0 tril (est. 2015).

- Agency for Healthcare Research and Quality (540 Gaither Rd., Rockville, MD 20850); www.ahrq.gov
- Centers for Disease Control and Prevention (1600 Clifton Rd., Atlanta, GA 30329); www.cdc.gov
- Centers for Medicare and Medicaid Services (7500 Security Blvd., Baltimore, MD 21244); www.cms.gov
- Food and Drug Admin. (10903 New Hampshire Ave., Silver Spring, MD 20993); www.fda.gov
- Health Resources and Services Admin. (5600 Fishers Ln., Rockville, MD 20857); www.hrsa.gov
- Natl. Institutes of Health (9000 Rockville Pike, Bethesda, MD 20892); www.nih.gov
- Office of the Surgeon General (Tower Bldg., Plaza Level 1, Rm. 100, 1101 Wootton Pkwy., Rockville, MD 20852); www.surgeongeneral.gov

Secretaries of Health and Human Services

President	Secretary	Home	Sworn in
Carter	Patricia Roberts Harris	DC	1979
Reagan	Richard S. Schweiker	PA	1981
	Margaret M. Heckler	MA	1983
Reagan	Otis R. Bowen	IN	1985
Bush, G. H. W.	Louis W. Sullivan	GA	1989
Clinton	Donna E. Shalala	WI	1993
Bush, G. W.	Tommy Thompson	WI	2001
	Michael O. Leavitt	UT	2005
Obama	Kathleen Sebelius	KS	2009
	Sylvia Mathews Burwell	WV	2014

Secretaries of Health, Education, and Welfare

President	Secretary	Home	Sworn in
Eisenhower	Oveta Culp Hobby	TX	1953
	Marion B. Folsom	NY	1955
	Arthur S. Flemming	OH	1958
Kennedy	Abraham A. Ribicoff	CT	1961
	Anthony J. Celebrezze	OH	1962
Johnson, L. B.	Anthony J. Celebrezze	OH	1963
	John W. Gardner	NY	1965
	Wilbur J. Cohen	MI	1968
Nixon	Robert H. Finch	CA	1969
	Elliot L. Richardson	MA	1970
	Caspar W. Weinberger	CA	1973
Ford	Caspar W. Weinberger	CA	1974
	Forrest D. Mathews	AL	1975
Carter	Joseph A. Califano Jr.	DC	1977
	Patricia Roberts Harris	DC	1979

Department of Education

400 Maryland Ave. SW, 20202; www.ed.gov

The Dept. of Health, Education, and Welfare was created by Congress on Apr. 11, 1953. On Sept. 27, 1979, Congress approved creation of a separate Dept. of Education. Works with state agencies and local systems to ensure equal access to all levels of education and seeks to improve the quality of that education through federal support, research programs, and information sharing. Oversees a variety of financial aid distributed through competition, need-based requests, or a set formula. Sets policy goals and initiatives like No Child Left Behind. Conducts research and gathers educational information to disseminate to educators and the general public. **Budget:** $40.9 bil (2013); $59.6 bil (2014); $103.3 bil (est. 2015).

Secretaries of Education

President	Secretary	Home	Sworn in
Carter	Shirley Hufstedler	CA	1979
Reagan	Terrel H. Bell	UT	1981
	William J. Bennett	NY	1985
	Lauro F. Cavazos	TX	1988
Bush, G. H. W.	Lauro F. Cavazos	TX	1989
	Lamar Alexander	TN	1991
Clinton	Richard W. Riley	SC	1993
Bush, G. W.	Roderick R. Paige	TX	2001
	Margaret Spellings	TX	2005
Obama	Arne Duncan	IL	2009

Department of Veterans Affairs

810 Vermont Ave. NW, 20420; www.va.gov

Pres. Ronald Reagan signed a bill in 1988 granting Cabinet-level status to the Veterans Administration. The agency became the Dept. of Veterans Affairs on Mar. 15, 1989. Supports veterans and their families with nationwide programs for health care, financial assistance, and burial benefits. Compensates for disabilities incurred during wartime. Provides pensions for veterans with low incomes, education assistance, loan guaranty, and life insurance. Manages America's largest medical education and health professions training program which includes hospitals, clinics, nursing homes, veterans centers, rehabilitation treatment, readjustment counseling, and home-care programs. Also funds medical research pertaining to veterans issues. Manages 131 national cemeteries; provides headstones and markers. **Budget:** $138.5 bil (2013); $149.1 bil (2014); $160.8 bil (est. 2015).

Secretaries of Veterans Affairs

President	Secretary	Home	Sworn in
Bush, G. H. W.	Edward J. Derwinski	IL	1989
Clinton	Jesse Brown	IL	1993
	Togo D. West Jr.	NC	1998
Bush, G. W.	Anthony J. Principi	CA	2001
	R. James Nicholson	CO	2005
	James B. Peake	MO	2007
Obama	Eric K. Shinseki	VA	2009
	Robert A. McDonald	OH	2014

Department of Homeland Security

20528 (requires no street address); www.dhs.gov

Created by act of Congress on Nov. 25, 2002. Provides a unified core for the national network of organizations and institutions involved in efforts to secure the U.S., its borders, infrastructure, and major events. Provides funding, intelligence, and training for law enforcement and disaster relief. Leads and coordinates response teams to natural and manmade emergencies. Identifies threats, administers the Natl. Terrorism Advisory System. **Budget:** $57.2 bil (2013); $43.3 bil (2014); $45.7 bil (est. 2015).

- Fed. Emergency Management Agency (500 C St. SW, 20472); www.fema.gov
- Immigration and Customs Enforcement (500 12th St. SW, 20536); www.ice.gov
- Transportation Security Admin. (601 S. 12th St., Arlington, VA 20598); www.tsa.gov
- U.S. Citizenship and Immigration Services (20 Massachusetts Ave. NW, 20529); www.uscis.gov
- U.S. Coast Guard (2703 Martin Luther King Jr. Ave. SE, 20593); www.uscg.mil
- U.S. Customs and Border Protection (1300 Pennsylvania Ave. NW, 20229); www.cbp.gov
- U.S. Fire Admin. (16825 S. Seton Ave., Emmitsburg, MD 21727); www.usfa.fema.gov
- U.S. Secret Service (245 Murray Dr., Bldg. 410, 20223); www.secretservice.gov

Secretaries of Homeland Security

President	Secretary	Home	Sworn in
Bush, G. W.	Thomas Ridge	PA	2003
	Michael Chertoff	NJ	2005
Obama	Janet A. Napolitano	AZ	2009
	Jeh Johnson	NY	2014

Other Notable U.S. Government Agencies

Source: *The U.S. Government Manual*; National Archives and Records Administration; World Almanac research

All addresses are for Washington, DC, unless otherwise noted; as of Aug. 2015.

Administrative Conference of the U.S.: Paul R. Verkuil, chair (1120 20th St. NW, Ste. 706S, 20036); www.acus.gov
African Development Foundation: Shari Berenbach, pres. and CEO (1400 I St. NW, Ste. 1000, 20005); www.adf.gov
AMTRAK: Joseph H. Boardman, pres. and CEO (60 Massachusetts Ave. NE, 20002); www.amtrak.com
Broadcasting Board of Governors: Jeff Shell, chair (330 Independence Ave. SW, 20237); www.bbg.gov
Central Intelligence Agency: John O. Brennan, dir. (20505); www.cia.gov
Commodity Futures Trading Commission: Timothy G. Massad, chair (1155 21st St. NW, 20581); www.cftc.gov
Consumer Financial Protection Bureau: Rich Cordray, dir. (P.O. Box 4503, Iowa City, IA 52244); www.consumerfinance.gov
Consumer Product Safety Commission: Elliot F. Kaye, chair (4330 East West Hwy., Bethesda, MD 20814); www.cpsc.gov
Corp. for Natl. and Community Service: Wendy Spencer, CEO (1201 New York Ave. NW, 20525); www.nationalservice.gov
Court Services and Offender Supervision Agency for DC: Nancy M. Ware, dir. (633 Indiana Ave. NW, 20004); www.csosa.gov
Defense Nuclear Facilities Safety Board: Jessie Hill Roberson, act. chair (625 Indiana Ave. NW, Ste. 700, 20004); www.dnfsb.gov
Election Assistance Commission: Christy McCormick, chair (1335 East West Hwy., Ste. 4300, Silver Spring, MD 20910); www.eac.gov
Environmental Protection Agency: Gina McCarthy, admin. (Cabinet rank) (1200 Pennsylvania Ave. NW, 20460); www.epa.gov
Equal Employment Opportunity Commission: Jenny R. Yang, chair (131 M St. NE, 20507); www.eeoc.gov
Export-Import Bank of the U.S.: Fred P. Hochberg, pres. and chair (811 Vermont Ave. NW, 20571); www.exim.gov
Farm Credit Admin.: Kenneth A. Spearman, chair and CEO (1501 Farm Credit Dr., McLean, VA 22102); www.fca.gov
Federal Communications Commission: Tom Wheeler, chair (445 12th St. SW, 20554); www.fcc.gov
Federal Deposit Insurance Corp.: Martin J. Gruenberg, chair (550 17th St. NW, 20429); www.fdic.gov
Federal Election Commission: Ann M. Ravel, chair (999 E St. NW, 20463); www.fec.gov
Federal Housing Finance Agency: Melvin L. Watt, dir. (400 7th St. SW, 20024); www.fhfa.gov
Federal Labor Relations Authority: Carol Waller Pope, chair (1400 K St. NW, 20424); www.flra.gov
Federal Maritime Commission: Mario Cordero, chair (800 N. Capitol St. NW, 20573); www.fmc.gov
Federal Mediation and Conciliation Service: Allison Beck, dir. (2100 K St. NW, 20427); www.fmcs.gov
Federal Mine Safety and Health Review Commission: Mary Lu Jordan, chair (1331 Pennsylvania Ave. NW, Ste. 520N, 20004); www.fmshrc.gov
Federal Reserve System: Janet L. Yellen, chair (20th St. and Constitution Ave. NW, 20551); www.federalreserve.gov
Federal Retirement Thrift Investment Board: Michael D. Kennedy, chair (77 K St. NE, 20002); www.frtib.gov
Federal Trade Commission: Edith Ramirez, chair (600 Pennsylvania Ave. NW, 20580); www.ftc.gov
General Services Admin.: Denise Turner Roth, admin. (1800 F St. NW, 20405); www.gsa.gov
Institute of Museum and Library Services: Maura Marx, act. dir. (1800 M St. NW, 9th Fl., 20036); www.imls.gov
Inter-American Foundation: Robert N. Kaplan, pres. (1331 Pennsylvania Ave. NW, Ste. 1200N, 20004); www.iaf.gov
Merit Systems Protection Board: Susan Tsui Grundmann, chair (1615 M St. NW, 20419); www.mspb.gov
Natl. Aeronautics and Space Admin.: Charles F. Bolden Jr., admin. (300 E. Street SW, Suite 5R30, 20546); www.nasa.gov
Natl. Archives and Records Admin.: David S. Ferriero, archivist (8601 Adelphi Rd., College Park, MD 20740); www.archives.gov
Natl. Capital Planning Commission: L. Preston Bryant Jr., chair (401 9th St. NW, N. Lobby, Ste. 500, 20004); www.ncpc.gov
Natl. Council on Disability: Jeff Rosen, chair (1331 F St. NW, Ste. 850, 20004); www.ncd.gov
Natl. Credit Union Admin.: Debbie Matz, chair (1775 Duke St., Alexandria, VA 22314); www.ncua.gov
Natl. Endowment for the Arts: Jane Chu, chair (400 7th St. SW, 20506); www.arts.gov
Natl. Endowment for the Humanities: William Adams, chair (400 7th St. SW, 20506); www.neh.gov
Natl. Indian Gaming Commission: Jonodev Osceola Chaudhuri, chair (1849 C St. NW, Mail Stop #1621, 20240); www.nigc.gov
Natl. Labor Relations Board: Mark G. Pearce, chair (1015 Half St. SE, 20570); www.nlrb.gov
Natl. Mediation Board: Nicholas Geale, chair (1301 K St. NW, Ste. 250 East, 20005); www.nmb.gov
Natl. Science Foundation: France A. Córdova, dir. (4201 Wilson Blvd., Arlington, VA 22230); www.nsf.gov
Natl. Transportation Safety Board: Christopher A. Hart, chair (490 L'Enfant Plaza SW, 20594); www.ntsb.gov
Nuclear Regulatory Commission: Stephen G. Burns, chair (20555); www.nrc.gov
Nuclear Waste Technical Review Board: Rodney C. Ewing, chair (2300 Clarendon Blvd., Ste. 1300, Arlington, VA 22201); www.nwtrb.gov
Occupational Safety and Health Review Commission: Cynthia L. Attwood, act chair (1120 20th St. NW, 9th Fl., 20036); www.oshrc.gov
Office of the Dir. of Natl. Intelligence: James R. Clapper, dir. (20511); www.dni.gov
Office of Government Ethics: Walter M. Shaub Jr., dir. (1201 New York Ave. NW, Ste. 500, 20005); www.oge.gov
Office of Personnel Management: Beth F. Cobert, act. dir. (1900 E St. NW, 20415); www.opm.gov
Office of Special Counsel: Carolyn Lerner, spec. counsel (1730 M St. NW, Ste. 218, 20036); osc.gov
Overseas Private Investment Corp.: Elizabeth L. Littlefield, pres. and CEO (1100 New York Ave. NW, 20527); www.opic.gov
Peace Corps: Carrie Hessler-Radelet, dir. (1111 20th St. NW, 20526); www.peacecorps.gov
Pension Benefit Guaranty Corp.: Alice Maroni, act. dir. (1200 K St. NW, 20005); www.pbgc.gov
Postal Regulatory Commission: Robert G. Taub, act. chair (901 New York Ave. NW, Ste. 200, 20268); www.prc.gov
Railroad Retirement Board: Michael S. Schwartz, chair (844 N. Rush St., Chicago, IL 60611); www.rrb.gov
Securities and Exchange Commission: Mary Jo White, chair (100 F St. NE, 20549); www.sec.gov
Selective Service System: Lawrence G. Romo, dir. (Natl. Headquarters, Arlington, VA 22209); www.sss.gov
Small Business Admin.: Maria Contreras-Sweet, admin. (Cabinet rank) (409 3rd St. SW, 20416); www.sba.gov
Social Security Admin.: Carolyn W. Colvin, act. comm. (1100 West High Rise, 6401 Security Blvd., Baltimore, MD 21235); www.ssa.gov
Tennessee Valley Authority: Bill Johnson, CEO and pres. (400 W. Summit Hill Dr., Knoxville, TN 37902); www.tva.gov
U.S. Agency for Intl. Development: Alfonso E. Lenhardt, act. admin. (1300 Pennsylvania Ave. NW, 20523); www.usaid.gov
U.S. Commission on Civil Rights: Martin R. Castro, chair (1331 Pennsylvania Ave. NW, Ste. 1150, 20425); www.usccr.gov
U.S. Intl. Trade Commission: Meredith M. Broadbent, chair (500 E St. SW, 20436); www.usitc.gov
U.S. Postal Service: Megan J. Brennan, postmaster general and CEO (475 L'Enfant Plaza SW, 20260); www.usps.com
U.S. Trade and Development Agency: Leocadia I. Zak, dir. (1000 Wilson Blvd., Ste. 1600, Arlington, VA 22209); www.ustda.gov

Floor Leaders in the U.S. Senate, 1920-2015

Majority leaders

Name	Party	State	Tenure
Charles Curtis[1]	Rep.	KS	1925-1929
James E. Watson	Rep.	IN	1929-1933
Joseph T. Robinson	Dem.	AR	1933-1937
Alben W. Barkley	Dem.	KY	1937-1947
Wallace H. White	Rep.	ME	1947-1949
Scott W. Lucas	Dem.	IL	1949-1951
Ernest W. McFarland	Dem.	AZ	1951-1953
Robert A. Taft	Rep.	OH	1953
William F. Knowland	Rep.	CA	1953-1955
Lyndon B. Johnson	Dem.	TX	1955-1961
Mike Mansfield	Dem.	MT	1961-1977
Robert C. Byrd	Dem.	WV	1977-1981
Howard H. Baker Jr.	Rep.	TN	1981-1985
Robert J. Dole	Rep.	KS	1985-1987
Robert C. Byrd	Dem.	WV	1987-1989
George J. Mitchell	Dem.	ME	1989-1995
Robert J. Dole	Rep.	KS	1995-1996
Trent Lott	Rep.	MS	1996-2001[3]
Thomas A. Daschle	Dem.	SD	2001-2003[3]
William Frist	Rep.	TN	2003-2007[4]
Harry M. Reid	Dem.	NV	2007-2015
Mitch McConnell	Rep.	KY	2015-

Minority leaders

Name	Party	State	Tenure
Oscar W. Underwood[2]	Dem.	AL	1920-1923
Joseph T. Robinson	Dem.	AR	1923-1933
Charles L. McNary	Rep.	OR	1933-1944
Wallace H. White	Rep.	ME	1944-1947
Alben W. Barkley	Dem.	KY	1947-1949
Kenneth S. Wherry	Rep.	NE	1949-1951
Henry Styles Bridges	Rep.	NH	1952-1953
Lyndon B. Johnson	Dem.	TX	1953-1955
William F. Knowland	Rep.	CA	1955-1959
Everett M. Dirksen	Rep.	IL	1959-1969
Hugh D. Scott	Rep.	PA	1969-1977
Howard H. Baker Jr.	Rep.	TN	1977-1981
Robert C. Byrd	Dem.	WV	1981-1987
Robert J. Dole	Rep.	KS	1987-1995
Thomas A. Daschle	Dem.	SD	1995-2001[3]
Trent Lott	Rep.	MS	2001-2002[3,4]
Thomas A. Daschle	Dem.	SD	2003-2005
Harry M. Reid	Dem.	NV	2005-2007
Mitch McConnell	Rep.	KY	2007-2015
Harry M. Reid	Dem.	NV	2015-

Note: The offices of party (majority and minority) leaders in the Senate did not evolve until the 20th century. (1) First Republican to be formally designated floor leader. Henry Cabot Lodge (MA) served as unofficial party leader prior to Curtis's election. (2) First Democrat to be designated floor leader. (3) Democrats held the majority Jan. 3, 2001, until Dick Cheney (R) was installed as vice pres., Jan. 20. Republicans subsequently lost the majority when Jim Jeffords (VT) switched from Republican to Independent, June 6, 2001. (4) Trent Lott resigned from Republican leadership Dec. 20, 2002. William Frist was elected Republican leader Dec. 23, 2002, and began service Jan. 7, 2003, as majority leader.

Speakers of the U.S. House of Representatives, 1789-2015

Name	Party	State	Tenure
Frederick A. C. Muhlenberg	Federalist	PA	1789-1791
Jonathan Trumbull	Federalist	CT	1791-1793
Frederick A. C. Muhlenberg	Federalist	PA	1793-1795
Jonathan Dayton	Federalist	NJ	1795-1799
Theodore Sedgwick	Federalist	MA	1799-1801
Nathaniel Macon	Dem.-Rep.	NC	1801-1807
Joseph B. Varnum	Dem.-Rep.	MA	1807-1811
Henry Clay	Dem.-Rep.	KY	1811-1814
Langdon Cheves	Dem.-Rep.	SC	1814-1815
Henry Clay	Dem.-Rep.	KY	1815-1820
John W. Taylor	Dem.-Rep.	NY	1820-1821
Philip P. Barbour	Dem.-Rep.	VA	1821-1823
Henry Clay	Dem.-Rep.	KY	1823-1825
John W. Taylor	Dem.	NY	1825-1827
Andrew Stevenson	Dem.	VA	1827-1834
John Bell	Dem.	TN	1834-1835
James K. Polk	Dem.	TN	1835-1839
Robert M. T. Hunter	Dem.	VA	1839-1841
John White	Whig	KY	1841-1843
John W. Jones	Dem.	VA	1843-1845
John W. Davis	Dem.	IN	1845-1847
Robert C. Winthrop	Whig	MA	1847-1849
Howell Cobb	Dem.	GA	1849-1851
Linn Boyd	Dem.	KY	1851-1855
Nathaniel P. Banks	American	MA	1856-1857
James L. Orr	Dem.	SC	1857-1859
William Pennington	Rep.	NJ	1860-1861
Galusha A. Grow	Rep.	PA	1861-1863
Schuyler Colfax	Rep.	IN	1863-1869
Theodore M. Pomeroy	Rep.	NY	1869
James G. Blaine	Rep.	ME	1869-1875
Michael C. Kerr	Dem.	IN	1875-1876
Samuel J. Randall	Dem.	PA	1876-1881
J. Warren Keifer	Rep.	OH	1881-1883
John G. Carlisle	Dem.	KY	1883-1889
Thomas B. Reed	Rep.	ME	1889-1891
Charles F. Crisp	Dem.	GA	1891-1895
Thomas B. Reed	Rep.	ME	1895-1899
David B. Henderson	Rep.	IA	1899-1903
Joseph G. Cannon	Rep.	IL	1903-1911
Champ Clark	Dem.	MO	1911-1919
Frederick H. Gillett	Rep.	MA	1919-1925
Nicholas Longworth	Rep.	OH	1925-1931
John N. Garner	Dem.	TX	1931-1933
Henry T. Rainey	Dem.	IL	1933-1934
Joseph W. Byrns	Dem.	TN	1935-1936
William B. Bankhead	Dem.	AL	1936-1940
Sam Rayburn	Dem.	TX	1940-1947
Joseph W. Martin Jr.	Rep.	MA	1947-1949
Sam Rayburn	Dem.	TX	1949-1953
Joseph W. Martin Jr.	Rep.	MA	1953-1955
Sam Rayburn	Dem.	TX	1955-1961
John W. McCormack	Dem.	MA	1962-1971
Carl B. Albert	Dem.	OK	1971-1977
Thomas P. O'Neill Jr.	Dem.	MA	1977-1987
James C. Wright Jr.	Dem.	TX	1987-1989
Thomas S. Foley	Dem.	WA	1989-1995
Newt Gingrich	Rep.	GA	1995-1999
J. Dennis Hastert	Rep.	IL	1999-2007
Nancy Pelosi	Dem.	CA	2007-2011
John Boehner	Rep.	OH	2011-2015

Political Divisions of Congress, 1901-2015

Source: Office of the Clerk, U.S. House of Representatives; Congressional Research Service, Library of Congress

All figures reflect post-election party breakdown except where noted; **boldface** denotes party in majority immediately after election.

		SENATE					HOUSE OF REPRESENTATIVES				
Congress	Years	Total members	Dem.	Rep.	Other parties	Vacant	Total members	Dem.	Rep.	Other parties	Vacant
57th	1901-1903	90	32	**56**	2		357	151	**200**	6	
58th	1903-1905	90	33	**57**			386	176	**207**	3	
59th	1905-1907	90	32	**58**			386	135	**251**		
60th	1907-1909	92	31	**61**			391	167	**223**	1	
61st	1909-1911	92	32	**60**			391	172	**219**		
62nd	1911-1913	96	44	**52**			394	**230**	162	2	
63rd	1913-1915	96	**51**	44	1		435	**291**	134	10	
64th	1915-1917	96	**56**	40			435	**230**	196	9	
65th	1917-1919	96	**54**	42			435	214[1]	**215**	6	
66th	1919-1921	96	47	**49**			435	192	**240**	2	1
67th	1921-1923	96	37	**59**			435	131	**302**	2	
68th	1923-1925	96	42	**53**	1		435	207	**225**	3	

		SENATE					HOUSE OF REPRESENTATIVES				
Congress	Years	Total members	Dem.	Rep.	Other parties	Vacant	Total members	Dem.	Rep.	Other parties	Vacant
69th	1925-1927	96	41	**54**	1		435	183	**247**	5	
70th	1927-1929	96	46	**48**	1	1	435	194	**238**	3	
71st	1929-1931	96	39	**56**	1		435	164	**270**	1	
72nd	1931-1933	96	47	**48**	1		435	216[2]	**218**	1	
73rd	1933-1935	96	**59**	36	1		435	**313**	117	5	
74th	1935-1937	96	**69**	25	2		435	**322**	103	10	
75th	1937-1939	96	**76**	16	4		435	**334**	88	13	
76th	1939-1941	96	**69**	23	4		435	**262**	169	4	
77th	1941-1943	96	**66**	28	2		435	**267**	162	6	
78th	1943-1945	96	**57**	38	1		435	**222**	209	4	
79th	1945-1947	96	**57**	38	1		435	**242**	191	2	
80th	1947-1949	96	45	**51**			435	188	**246**	1	
81st	1949-1951	96	**54**	42			435	**263**	171	1	
82nd	1951-1953	96	**49**	47			435	**235**	199	1	
83rd	1953-1955	96	47	**48**	1		435	213	**221**	1	
84th	1955-1957	96	**48**	47	1		435	**232**	203		
85th	1957-1959	96	**49**	47			435	**234**	201		
86th	1959-1961	100	**65**	35			437[3]	**283**	153	1	
87th	1961-1963	100	**64**	36			437[3]	**263**	174		
88th	1963-1965	100	**66**	34			435	**259**	176		
89th	1965-1967	100	**68**	32			435	**295**	140		
90th	1967-1969	100	**64**	36			435	**247**	187		1
91st	1969-1971	100	**57**	43			435	**243**	192		
92nd	1971-1973	100	**54**	44	2		435	**255**	180		
93rd	1973-1975	100	**56**	42	2		435	**242**	192	1	
94th	1975-1977	100	**60**	38	2		435	**291**	144		
95th	1977-1979	100	**61**	38	1		435	**292**	143		
96th	1979-1981	100	**58**	41	1		435	**277**	158		
97th	1981-1983	100	46	**53**	1		435	**242**	192	1	
98th	1983-1985	100	46	**54**			435	**269**	166		
99th	1985-1987	100	47	**53**			435	**253**	182		
100th	1987-1989	100	**55**	45			435	**258**	177		
101st	1989-1991	100	**55**	45			435	**260**	175		
102nd	1991-1993	100	**56**	44			435	**267**	167	1	
103rd	1993-1995	100	**57**	43			435	**258**	176	1	
104th	1995-1997	100	48	**52**			435	204	**230**	1	
105th	1997-1999	100	45	**55**			435	206	**228**	1	
106th	1999-2001	100	45	**55**			435	211	**223**	1	
107th	2001-2003	100	50	50[4]			435	212	**221**	2	
108th	2003-2005	100	48	**51**	1		435	204	**229**	1	1
109th	2005-2007	100	44	**55**	1		435	202	**232**	1	
110th	2007-2009	100	49	49	2[5]		435	**233**	202		
111th	2009-2011	100	**57**	41	2[5]		435	**257**	178		
112th	2011-2013	100	**51**	47	2[5]		435	193	**242**		
113th	2013-2015	100	**53**	45	2[5]		435	201	**234**		
114th	2015-	100	44	**54**	2[5]		435	188	**246**		1

(1) Democrats organized the House with help of other parties. (2) Democrats organized the House because of Republican deaths. (3) Number of House seats was increased temporarily when proclamations were issued declaring Alaska (Jan. 3, 1959) and Hawaii (Aug. 21, 1959) new states. (4) While the Senate was split 50-50, control was held by whichever party had an incumbent vice president. Republican Sen. Jim Jeffords (VT) changed his party designation to Independent on June 6, 2001, switching control of the Senate to Democrats. (5) Both Independent senators chose to caucus with the Democrats.

Congressional Bills Vetoed, 1789-2015

Source: Virtual Reference Desk, U.S. Senate; as of June 30, 2015

The president has 10 days (excluding Sundays) to sign a bill passed by Congress. Veto power can be exercised on bills or joint resolutions. Only a two-thirds vote in both the Senate and the House can override the president's veto.

President	Regular vetoes	Pocket vetoes	Total vetoes	Vetoes overridden
Washington	2	—	2	—
J. Adams	—	—	—	—
Jefferson	—	—	—	—
Madison	5	2	7	—
Monroe	1	—	1	—
J. Q. Adams	—	—	—	—
Jackson	5	7	12	—
Van Buren	—	1	1	—
W. H. Harrison	—	—	—	—
Tyler	6	4	10	1
Polk	2	1	3	—
Taylor	—	—	—	—
Fillmore	—	—	—	—
Pierce	9	—	9	5
Buchanan	4	3	7	—
Lincoln	2	5	7	—
A. Johnson	21	8	29	15
Grant	45	48	93	4
Hayes	12	1	13	1
Garfield	—	—	—	—
Arthur	4	8	12	1
Cleveland[1]	304	110	414	2
B. Harrison	19	25	44	1
Cleveland[2]	42	128	170	5
McKinley	6	36	42	—
T. Roosevelt	42	40	82	1
Taft	30	9	39	1
Wilson	33	11	44	6
Harding	5	1	6	—
Coolidge	20	30	50	4
Hoover	21	16	37	3
F. D. Roosevelt	372	263	635	9
Truman	180	70	250	12
Eisenhower	73	108	181	2
Kennedy	12	9	21	—
L. Johnson	16	14	30	—
Nixon	26	17	43	7
Ford	48	18	66	12
Carter	13	18	31	2
Reagan	39	39	78	9
G. H. W. Bush[3]	29	15	44	1
Clinton[4]	36	1	37	2
G. W. Bush	12	—	12	4
Obama	4	—	4	—
Total[3,4]	**1,500**	**1,066**	**2,566**	**110**

— = 0. (1) First term only. (2) Second term only. (3) Excluded from the figures are two bills that Pres. George H. W. Bush claimed to be pocket vetoed but which Congress considered to be enacted because the president had failed to return them during a Congressional recess. (4) Does not include line-item vetoes, which were ruled unconstitutional by the U.S. Supreme Court on June 25, 1998.

Congressional Firsts and Milestones

Cities where Congress has convened: New York City (1789-90); Philadelphia (1790-1800); Washington, DC (1800-).

First meeting of Congress in the Capitol Building: Nov. 17, 1800.

First Congressional override of a presidential veto: Pres. John Tyler's veto of an appropriation bill, Mar. 3, 1845.

House of Representatives

First House meeting: Mar. 4, 1789, at Federal Hall in New York, NY. A quorum of 30 representatives was not reached until Apr. 1, 1789.

First House meeting in its current Capitol Building chamber: Dec. 16, 1857.

First former president to serve as representative: John Quincy Adams (MA, 1831-48); president, 1825-29.

First woman representative: Jeannette Rankin (R, MT, 1917-19, 1941-43).

First woman House speaker: Nancy Pelosi (D, CA), on Jan. 4, 2007.

First black representative: Joseph Rainey (R, SC, 1870-79).

First black woman representative: Shirley Chisholm (D, NY, 1969-83).

First elected Hispanic-American representative: Romualdo Pacheco (R, CA, 1877-83); Pacheco was born in California when it was Mexican territory.

First Asian-Pacific American representative: India-born Dalip Saund (D, CA, 1957-63).

Longest-serving representative: John Dingell Jr. (D, MI, 1955-2015), with more than 59 years of service.

Longest-serving House speaker: Sam Rayburn (D, TX, 1913-61) served as House speaker for 17 years, 2 months, and 2 days (non-consecutive).

Longest consecutive service by a single family: A member of the Dingell family has represented one of Michigan's districts since 1933: John Dingell (D, 1933-55), John Dingell Jr. (D, 1955-2015), and Debbie Dingell (D, 2015-).

Oldest representative: Ralph Hall (D-R, TX, 1981-2015); retired at age 91.

Oldest-known freshman representative: James B. Bowler (D, IL), who won a special election July 7, 1953, aged 78.

Youngest representative: William Charles Cole Claiborne (TN), who was elected at 22 years of age and began service Nov. 23, 1797. The House chose to seat him both times despite the Constitutional requirement that U.S. representatives be at least 25 years of age.

First live-TV broadcast of House proceedings: Mar. 19, 1979, by public television and C-SPAN. Al Gore Jr. (D, TN) was the first representative to give a speech before cameras that day.

First declaration of war made by the House: June 4, 1812, against Great Britain and Ireland.

The Senate

First Senate meeting: Mar. 4, 1789, at Federal Hall in New York, NY. A quorum of senators was not reached until Apr. 6, 1789.

First Senate meeting in its current chamber in the Capitol Building: Jan. 4, 1859.

First woman senator: Rebecca Felton (D, GA, 1922). Appointed to a seat left vacant by a death, 87-year-old Felton served only 24 hours after being sworn in Nov. 21. (Felton was also the oldest freshman senator and the last senator to have been a slave owner.)

First elected woman senator: Hattie Caraway (D, AR, 1931-45). Appointed in 1931 to fill the vacancy left by the death of her husband, Thaddeus H. Caraway, she was elected in 1932.

First black senator: Hiram R. Revels (R, MS, 1870-71).

First black woman senator: Carol Moseley-Braun (D, IL, 1993-99).

First American Indian senators: Charles Curtis (R, KS, 1907-13, 1915-29) and Robert Owen (D, OK, 1907-25).

First Hispanic-American senator: Mexico-born Octaviano Larrazolo (R, NM, 1928-29).

First Asian-American senator: Hiram L. Fong (R, HI, 1959-77).

First Jewish senator: David Levy Yulee (D, FL, 1845-51, 1855-61).

Longest-serving senator: Robert C. Byrd (D, WV, 1959-2010) died while in office, having served 51 years, 5 months, and 26 days.

Oldest senator: Strom Thurmond (R, SC), who turned 100 years of age on Dec. 5, 2002, one month before he retired from office.

Youngest senator: John H. Eaton (TN), who was 28 years, 5 months old when he was sworn in Nov. 16, 1818, despite the Constitutional requirement that U.S. senators be at least 30 years old.

Longest speech by a senator (since 1900): 24 hours, 18 minutes, by Strom Thurmond (D, SC) in his filibuster against the 1957 Civil Rights Act, Aug. 28-29, 1957.

First Senate impeachment trial of a president: Pres. Andrew Johnson, on Mar. 5, 1868; he was acquitted by a one-vote margin.

Number of Senate impeachment trials: 19, resulting in 7 acquittals, 8 convictions, 3 dismissals, and 1 resignation with no further action.

First regular live-TV broadcast from the Senate chamber: June 2, 1986, by the C-SPAN network.

Number of senators who have received the Nobel Peace Prize: 5 (Elihu Root, Frank Kellogg, Cordell Hull, Al Gore, Barack Obama). Root is the only one of the five to receive the award while serving as senator.

Number of senators who have changed party affiliation during their Senate service (since 1890): 21.

Congressional Activity, 1947-2014

Source: *Congressional Record*, U.S. Govt. Printing Office; THOMAS database, Library of Congress

Congress in recent years has been widely perceived as being less productive than in previous sessions. The data below shows the number of public laws and measures passed in every session of Congress since 1947.

Congress (years)	Public laws passed	Measures passed
80th (1947-48)	906	4,132
81st (1949-50)	921	5,764
82nd (1951-52)	594	4,593
83rd (1953-54)	781	5,201
84th (1955-56)	1,028	5,713
85th (1957-58)	936	5,126
86th (1959-60)	800	4,165
87th (1961-62)	885	4,769
88th (1963-64)	666	3,425
89th (1965-66)	810	4,116
90th (1967-68)	640	3,390
91st (1969-70)	695	3,318
92nd (1971-72)	607	2,840
93rd (1973-74)	649	3,088
94th (1975-76)	588	3,176
95th (1977-78)	633	3,211
96th (1979-80)	613	2,960
97th (1981-82)	473	2,267
98th (1983-84)	623	2,670
99th (1985-86)	664	2,698
100th (1987-88)	713	2,932
101st (1989-90)	650	2,691
102nd (1991-92)	590	2,615
103rd (1993-94)	465	2,054
104th (1995-96)	333	1,834
105th (1997-98)	394	2,077
106th (1999-00)	580	2,779
107th (2001-02)	377	2,163
108th (2003-04)	498	2,674
109th (2005-06)	482	2,684
110th (2007-08)	460	3,336
111th (2009-10)	383	2,939
112th (2011-12)	283	1,744
113th (2013-14)	296	1,788

Note: Measures passed refers to bills, joint resolutions, concurrent resolutions, or simple resolutions passed by the House or Senate. Public laws must be signed into law by the president.

Members of the 114th Congress: U.S. Senate

Source: *Statistics of the Congressional Election*, Clerk of the U.S. House of Representatives

54 Republicans, 44 Democrats, 2 independents (who caucus with Democrats). Boldface denotes the 2014 election winner. * = Incumbent. Third-party or independent candidates receiving fewer than 50,000 votes are not necessarily listed.

Terms are for six years and end Jan. 3 of the year preceding the senator's name in the following table. Annual salary, $174,000; President Pro Tempore, Majority Leader, and Minority Leader, $193,400. To be eligible to serve in the Senate, a person must be at least 30 years old, a U.S. citizen for at least nine years, and a resident of the state from which elected.

D = Democrat; **R** = Republican; **DFL** = Dem.-Farmer-Labor; **I** = Independent; **LB** = Libertarian; **NPL** = Nonpartisan League.

Term ends	Senator/candidate (party); service from[1]	2014 election results
Alabama		
2017	Richard Shelby (R); 1/6/1987	
2021	**Jeff Sessions* (R); 1/7/1997**	**Unopposed**
Alaska		
2017	Lisa Murkowski (R); 12/20/2002	
2021	**Dan Sullivan (R); 1/6/2015**	**135,445**
	Mark Begich* (D); 1/6/2009	129,431
Arizona		
2017	John McCain (R); 1/6/1987	
2019	Jeff Flake (R); 2013	
Arkansas		
2017	John Boozman (R); 1/5/2011	
2021	**Tom Cotton (R); 1/6/2015**	**478,819**
	Mark Pryor* (D); 1/7/2003	334,174
California		
2017	Barbara Boxer (D); 1993	
2019	Dianne Feinstein (D); 11/10/1992	
Colorado		
2017	Michael F. Bennet (D); 1/22/2009	
2021	**Cory Gardner (R); 1/6/2015**	**983,891**
	Mark Udall* (D); 1/6/2009	944,203
Connecticut		
2017	Richard Blumenthal (D); 1/5/2011	
2019	Christopher S. Murphy (D); 2013	
Delaware		
2019	Thomas R. Carper (D); 2001	
2021	**Christopher Coons* (D); 11/15/2010**	**130,655**
	Kevin Wade (R)	98,823
Florida		
2017	Marco Rubio (R); 1/5/2011	
2019	Bill Nelson (D); 2001	
Georgia		
2017	Johnny Isakson (R); 2005	
2021	**David Perdue (R); 1/6/2015**	**1,358,088**
	Michelle Nunn (D)	1,160,811
Hawaii		
2017	**Brian Schatz* (D); 12/26/2012[2]**	**246,827**
	Cam Cavasso (R)	98,006
2019	Mazie K. Hirono (D); 2013	
Idaho		
2017	Mike Crapo (R); 1/6/1999	
2021	**Jim Risch* (R); 1/6/2009**	**285,596**
	Nels Mitchell (D)	151,574
Illinois		
2017	Mark Kirk (R); 11/29/2010	
2021	**Richard J. Durbin* (D); 1/7/1997**	**1,929,637**
	Jim Oberweis (R)	1,538,522
	Sharon Hansen (LB)	135,316
Indiana		
2017	Dan Coats (R); 1/5/2011	
2019	Joe Donnelly (D); 2013	
Iowa		
2017	Chuck Grassley (R); 1981	
2021	**Joni Ernst (R); 1/6/2015**	**588,575**
	Bruce Braley (D)	494,370
Kansas		
2017	Jerry Moran (R); 1/5/2011	
2021	**Pat Roberts* (R); 1/7/1997**	**460,350**
	Greg Orman (I)	368,372
Kentucky		
2017	Rand Paul (R); 1/5/2011	
2021	**Mitch McConnell* (R); 1985**	**806,787**
	Alison Lundergan Grimes (D)	584,698
Louisiana		
2017	David Vitter (R); 2005	
2021[3]	**Bill Cassidy (R)**	**712,379**
	Mary L. Landrieu* (D); 1/7/1997	561,210
Maine		
2019	Angus King (I); 2013	
2021	**Susan M. Collins* (R); 1/7/1997**	**413,505**
	Shenna Bellows (D)	190,254
Maryland		
2017	Barbara Ann Mikulski (D); 1/6/1987	
2019	Benjamin L. Cardin (D); 2007	
Massachusetts		
2019	Elizabeth A. Warren (D); 2013	
2021	**Ed Markey* (D); 7/16/2013**	**1,289,944**
	Brian Herr (R)	791,950
Michigan		
2019	Debbie Stabenow (D); 2001	
2021	**Gary Peters (D); 1/6/2015**	**1,704,936**
	Terri Lynn Land (R)	1,290,199
	Jim Fulner (LB)	62,897
Minnesota		
2019	Amy Klobuchar (DFL); 2007	
2021	**Al Franken* (DFL); 7/7/2009**	**1,053,205**
	Mike McFadden (R)	850,227
Mississippi		
2019	Roger F. Wicker (R); 12/31/2007	
2021	**Thad Cochran* (R); 12/27/1978**	**378,481**
	Travis Childers (D)	239,439
Missouri		
2017	Roy Blunt (R); 1/5/2011	
2019	Claire McCaskill (D); 2007	
Montana		
2019	Jon Tester (D); 2007	
2021	**Steve Daines (R); 1/6/2015**	**213,709**
	Amanda Curtis (D)	148,184
Nebraska		
2019	Deb Fischer (R); 2013	
2021	**Ben Sasse (R); 1/6/2015**	**347,636**
	Dave Domina (D)	170,127
Nevada		
2017	Harry Reid (D); 1/6/1987	
2019	Dean Heller (R); 5/9/2011	
New Hampshire		
2017	Kelly Ayotte (R); 1/5/2011	
2021	**Jeanne Shaheen* (D); 1/6/2009**	**251,184**
	Scott Brown (R)	235,347

Term ends	Senator/candidate (party); service from[1]	2014 election results
New Jersey		
2019	Robert Menendez (D); 1/18/2006	
2021	**Cory Booker* (D); 10/31/2013**	**1,043,866**
	Jeff Bell (R)	791,297
New Mexico		
2019	Martin Heinrich (D); 2013	
2021	**Tom Udall* (D); 1/6/2009**	**286,409**
	Allen E. Weh (R)	229,097
New York		
2017	Charles E. Schumer (D); 1/6/1999	
2019	Kirsten E. Gillibrand (D); 1/27/2009	
North Carolina		
2017	Richard Burr (R); 2005	
2021	**Thom Tillis (R); 1/6/2015**	**1,423,259**
	Kay Hagan* (D); 1/6/2009	1,377,651
	Sean Haugh (LB)	109,100
North Dakota		
2017	John Hoeven (R); 1/5/2011	
2019	Heidi Heitkamp (D-NPL); 2013	
Ohio		
2017	Rob Portman (R); 1/5/2011	
2019	Sherrod Brown (D); 2007	
Oklahoma		
2017[4]	**James Lankford (R); 1/6/2015**	**557,002**
	Connie Johnson (D)	237,923
2021	**James M. Inhofe* (R); 11/21/1994**	**558,166**
	Matt Silverstein (D)	234,307
Oregon		
2017	Ron Wyden (D); 2/6/1996	
2021	**Jeff Merkley* (D); 1/6/2009**	**814,537**
	Monica Wehby (R)	538,847
Pennsylvania		
2017	Pat Toomey (R); 1/5/2011	
2019	Bob Casey Jr. (D); 2007	
Rhode Island		
2019	Sheldon Whitehouse (D); 2007	
2021	**Jack Reed* (D); 1/7/1997**	**223,675**
	Mark Zaccaria (R)	92,684
South Carolina		
2017[5]	**Tim Scott* (R); 1/3/2013**	**757,215**
	Joyce Dickerson (D)	459,583
2021	**Lindsey Graham* (R); 1/7/2003**	**672,941**
	Brad Hutto (D)	456,726
South Dakota		
2017	John Thune (R); 2005	
2021	**Mike Rounds (R); 1/6/2015**	**140,741**
	Rick Weiland (D)	82,456
Tennessee		
2019	Bob Corker (R); 2007	
2021	**Lamar Alexander* (R); 1/7/2003**	**850,087**
	Gordon Ball (D)	437,848
Texas		
2019	Ted Cruz (R); 2013	
2021	**John Cornyn* (R); 12/2/2002**	**2,861,531**
	David Alameel (D)	1,597,387
	Rebecca Paddock (LB)	133,751
	Emily Sanchez (Green)	54,701
Utah		
2017	Mike Lee (R); 1/5/2011	
2019	Orrin G. Hatch (R); 1977	
Vermont		
2017	Patrick Leahy (D); 1975	
2019	Bernard Sanders (I); 2007	
Virginia		
2019	Timothy M. Kaine (D); 2013	
2021	**Mark Warner* (D); 1/6/2009**	**1,073,667**
	Ed Gillespie (R)	1,055,940
	Robert Sarvis (LB)	53,102
Washington		
2017	Patty Murray (D); 1993	
2019	Maria Cantwell (D); 2001	
West Virginia		
2019	Joe Manchin III (D); 11/15/2010	
2021	**Shelley Moore Capito (R); 1/6/2015**	**281,820**
	Natalie Tennant (D)	156,360
Wisconsin		
2017	Ron Johnson (R); 1/5/2011	
2019	Tammy Baldwin (D); 2013	
Wyoming		
2019	John Barrasso (R); 6/22/2007	
2021	**Michael B. Enzi* (R); 1/7/1997**	**121,554**
	Charlie Hardy (D)	29,377

(1) Jan. 3, unless otherwise noted. (2) Sen. Daniel Inouye (D) died in office Dec. 17, 2012; Schatz was appointed to fill the seat until the 2014 general election, when a special election was held. (3) Result of a runoff the top two vote recipients held Dec. 6, 2014. (4) Sen. Tom Coburn (R) announced Jan. 16, 2014, that he would retire when the 113th Congress expired. The special election held on the date of the 2014 general election filled the seat for the two years remaining in his term. (5) Sen. Jim DeMint (R) resigned effective Jan. 1, 2013; Scott was appointed to fill the seat until the 2014 general election, when a special election was held.

Members of the 114th Congress: U.S. House of Representatives

Source: *Statistics of the Congressional Election*, Clerk of the U.S. House of Representatives

247 Republicans, 188 Democrats as of Sept. 30, 2015. Boldface denotes the 2014 election winner. * = Incumbent. Third-party or independent candidates receiving fewer than 10,000 votes are not necessarily listed.

Terms are for two years ending on Jan. 3, 2017. Annual salary, $174,000; Majority Leader and Minority Leader, $196,400; Speaker of the House, $223,500. To be eligible for membership, a person must be at least 25 years of age, a U.S. citizen for at least seven years, and a resident of the state from which elected.

D = Democrat; **R** = Republican; **Amer. Elect** = Americans Elect; **CP** = Constitution Party; **DFL** = Dem.-Farmer-Labor; **I** = Independent; **Indep. Amer.** = Independent American Party; **IP** = Independence Party; **LB** = Libertarian; **NPA** = No party affiliation; **NPD** = No party designation; **NPL** = Nonpartisan League; **PFP** = Peace and Freedom Party; **Prog.** = Progressive.

Dist.	Representative/candidate (party)	2014 election results
Alabama		
1	**Bradley Byrne* (R)**	**103,758**
	Burton LeFlore (D)	48,278
2	**Martha Roby* (R)**	**113,103**
	Erick Wright (D)	54,692
3	**Mike Rogers* (R)**	**103,558**
	Jesse Smith (D)	52,816
4	**Robert B. Aderholt* (R)**	**Unopposed**
5	**Mo Brooks* (R)**	**115,338**
	Mark Bray (I)	39,005
6	**Gary Palmer (R)**	**135,945**
	Mark Lester (D)	42,291
7	**Terri A. Sewell* (D)**	**Unopposed**
Alaska		
	Don Young* (R)	**142,572**
	Forrest Dunbar (D)	114,602
	Jim McDermott (LB)	21,290
Arizona		
1	**Ann Kirkpatrick* (D)**	**97,391**
	Andy Tobin (R)	87,723

Dist.	Representative/candidate (party)	2014 election results
2	**Martha McSally (R)**	**109,704**
	Ron Barber* (D)	109,543
3	**Raúl M. Grijalva* (D)**	**58,192**
	Gabriela Saucedo Mercer (R)	46,185
4	**Paul A. Gosar* (R)**	**122,560**
	Mike Weisser (D)	45,179
5	**Matt Salmon* (R)**	**124,867**
	James Woods (D)	54,596
6	**David Schweikert* (R)**	**129,578**
	W. John Williamson (D)	70,198
7	**Ruben Gallego (D)**	**54,235**
	Joe Cobb (LB)	10,715
8	**Trent Franks* (R)**	**128,710**
	Stephen Dolgos (Amer. Elect)	41,066
9	**Kyrsten Sinema* (D)**	**88,609**
	Wendy Rogers (R)	67,841
Arkansas		
1	**Rick Crawford* (R)**	**124,139**
	Jackie McPherson (D)	63,555
2	**French Hill (R)**	**123,073**
	Patrick Henry Hays (D)	103,477
	Debbie Standiford (LB)	10,590
3	**Steve Womack* (R)**	**151,630**
	Grant Brand (LB)	39,305
4	**Bruce Westerman (R)**	**110,789**
	James Lee Witt (D)	87,742
California		
1	**Doug LaMalfa* (R)**	**132,052**
	Heidi Hall (D)	84,320
2	**Jared Huffman* (D)**	**163,124**
	Dale K. Mensing (R)	54,400
3	**John Garamendi* (D)**	**79,224**
	Dan Logue (R)	71,036
4	**Tom McClintock* (R)**	**126,784**
	Art Moore (R)	84,350
5	**Mike Thompson* (D)**	**129,613**
	James Hinton (I)	41,535
6	**Doris O. Matsui* (D)**	**97,008**
	Joseph McCray Sr. (R)	36,448
7	**Ami Bera* (D)**	**92,521**
	Doug Ose (R)	91,066
8	**Paul Cook* (R)**	**77,480**
	Bob Conaway (D)	37,056
9	**Jerry McNerney* (D)**	**63,475**
	Antonio C. "Tony" Amador (R)	57,729
10	**Jeff Denham* (R)**	**70,582**
	Michael Eggman (D)	55,123
11	**Mark DeSaulnier (D)**	**117,502**
	Tue Phan (R)	57,160
12	**Nancy Pelosi* (D)**	**160,067**
	John Dennis (R)	32,197
13	**Barbara Lee* (D)**	**168,491**
	Dakin Sundeen (R)	21,940
14	**Jackie Speier* (D)**	**114,389**
	Robin Chew (R)	34,757
15	**Eric Swalwell* (D)**	**99,756**
	Hugh Bussell (R)	43,150
16	**Jim Costa* (D)**	**46,277**
	Johnny Tacherra (R)	44,943
17	**Mike Honda* (D)**	**69,561**
	Ro Khanna (D)	64,847
18	**Anna G. Eshoo* (D)**	**133,060**
	Richard Fox (R)	63,326
19	**Zoe Lofgren* (D)**	**85,888**
	Robert Murray (D)	41,900
20	**Sam Farr* (D)**	**106,034**
	Ronald Paul Kabat (NPD)	35,010
21	**David G. Valadao* (R)**	**45,907**
	Amanda Renteria (D)	33,470
22	**Devin Nunes* (R)**	**96,053**
	Suzanna "Sam" Aguilera-Marrero (D)	37,289
23	**Kevin McCarthy* (R)**	**100,317**
	Raul Garcia (D)	33,726
24	**Lois Capps* (D)**	**103,228**
	Chris Mitchum (R)	95,566
25	**Steve Knight (R)**	**60,847**
	Tony Strickland (R)	53,225
26	**Julia Brownley* (D)**	**87,176**
	Jeff Gorell (R)	82,653

Dist.	Representative/candidate (party)	2014 election results
27	**Judy Chu* (D)**	**75,728**
	Jack Orswell (R)	51,852
28	**Adam B. Schiff* (D)**	**91,996**
	Steve Stokes (NPD)	28,268
29	**Tony Cárdenas* (D)**	**50,096**
	Will Leader (R)	17,045
30	**Brad Sherman* (D)**	**86,568**
	Mark S. Reed (R)	45,315
31	**Pete Aguilar (D)**	**51,622**
	Paul Chabot (R)	48,162
32	**Grace F. Napolitano* (D)**	**50,353**
	Arturo Alas (R)	34,053
33	**Ted Lieu (D)**	**108,331**
	Elan Carr (R)	74,700
34	**Xavier Becerra* (D)**	**44,697**
	Adrienne Edwards (D)	16,924
35	**Norma J. Torres (D)**	**39,502**
	Christina Gagnier (D)	22,753
36	**Raul Ruiz* (D)**	**72,682**
	Brian Nestande (R)	61,457
37	**Karen Bass* (D)**	**96,787**
	Adam King (R)	18,051
38	**Linda T. Sánchez* (D)**	**58,192**
	Benjamin Campos (R)	40,288
39	**Ed Royce* (R)**	**91,319**
	Peter Anderson (D)	41,906
40	**Lucille Roybal-Allard* (D)**	**30,208**
	David Sanchez (D)	19,171
41	**Mark Takano* (D)**	**46,948**
	Steve Adams (R)	35,936
42	**Ken Calvert* (R)**	**74,540**
	Tim Sheridan (D)	38,850
43	**Maxine Waters* (D)**	**69,681**
	John Wood Jr. (R)	28,521
44	**Janice Hahn* (D)**	**59,670**
	Adam Shbeita (PFP)	9,192
45	**Mimi Walters (R)**	**106,083**
	Drew E. Leavens (D)	56,819
46	**Loretta Sanchez* (D)**	**49,738**
	Adam Nick (R)	33,577
47	**Alan Lowenthal* (D)**	**69,091**
	Andy Whallon (R)	54,309
48	**Dana Rohrabacher* (R)**	**112,082**
	Suzanne Joyce Savary (D)	62,713
49	**Darrell E. Issa* (R)**	**98,161**
	Dave Peiser (D)	64,981
50	**Duncan D. Hunter* (R)**	**111,997**
	James Kimber (D)	45,302
51	**Juan Vargas* (D)**	**56,373**
	Stephen Meade (R)	25,577
52	**Scott Peters* (D)**	**98,826**
	Carl DeMaio (R)	92,746
53	**Susan A. Davis* (D)**	**87,104**
	Larry A. Wilske (R)	60,940
Colorado		
1	**Diana DeGette* (D)**	**183,281**
	Martin Walsh (R)	80,682
2	**Jared Polis* (D)**	**196,300**
	George Leing (R)	149,645
3	**Scott R. Tipton* (R)**	**163,011**
	Abel J. Tapia (D)	100,364
	Tisha Casida (I)	11,294
4	**Ken Buck (R)**	**185,292**
	Vic Meyers (D)	83,727
5	**Doug Lamborn* (R)**	**157,182**
	Irv Halter (D)	105,673
6	**Mike Coffman* (R)**	**143,467**
	Andrew Romanoff (D)	118,847
7	**Ed Perlmutter* (D)**	**148,225**
	Don Ytterberg (R)	120,918
Connecticut		
1	**John B. Larson* (D)**	**135,825**
	Matthew Corey (R)	78,609
2	**Joe Courtney* (D)**	**141,948**
	Lori Hopkins-Cavanagh (R)	80,837
3	**Rosa L. DeLauro* (D)**	**140,485**
	James Brown (R)	69,454
4	**Jim Himes* (D)**	**106,873**
	Dan Debicella (R)	91,922

Dist.	Representative/candidate (party)	2014 election results
5	**Elizabeth Esty* (D)**	**113,564**
	Mark Greenberg (R)	97,767
Delaware		
	John C. Carney Jr.* (D)	**137,251**
	Rose Izzo (R)	85,146
Florida		
1	**Jeff Miller* (R)**	**165,086**
	Jim Bryan (D)	54,976
	Mark Wichern (NPA)	15,281
2	**Gwen Graham (D)**	**126,096**
	Steve Southerland II* (R)	123,262
3	**Ted Yoho* (R)**	**148,691**
	Marihelen Wheeler (D)	73,910
4	**Ander Crenshaw* (R)**	**177,887**
	Paula Moser-Bartlett (NPA)	35,663
	Gary L. Koniz (NPA)	13,690
5	**Corrine Brown* (D)**	**112,340**
	Glo Smith (R)	59,237
6	**Ron DeSantis* (R)**	**166,254**
	David Cox (D)	99,563
7	**John L. Mica* (R)**	**144,474**
	Wes Neuman (D)	73,011
8	**Bill Posey* (R)**	**180,728**
	Gabriel Rothblatt (D)	93,724
9	**Alan Grayson* (D)**	**93,850**
	Carol Platt (R)	74,963
10	**Daniel Webster* (R)**	**143,128**
	Michael McKenna (D)	89,426
11	**Richard B. Nugent* (R)**	**181,508**
	Dave Koller (D)	90,786
12	**Gus M. Bilirakis* (R)**	**Unopposed**
13	**David W. Jolly* (R)**	**168,172**
	Lucas Overby (LB)	55,318
14	**Kathy Castor* (D)**	**Unopposed**
15	**Dennis A. Ross* (R)**	**128,750**
	Alan Cohn (D)	84,832
16	**Vern Buchanan* (R)**	**169,126**
	Henry Lawrence (D)	105,483
17	**Tom Rooney* (R)**	**141,493**
	Will Bronson (D)	82,263
18	**Patrick Murphy* (D)**	**151,478**
	Carl Domino (R)	101,896
19	**Curt Clawson* (R)**	**159,354**
	April Freeman (D)	80,824
20	**Alcee L. Hastings* (D)**	**128,498**
	Jay Bonner (R)	28,968
21	**Ted Deutch* (D)**	**Unopposed**
22	**Lois Frankel* (D)**	**125,404**
	Paul Spain (R)	90,685
23	**Debbie Wasserman Schultz* (D)**	**103,269**
	Joe Kaufman (R)	61,519
24	**Frederica S. Wilson* (D)**	**129,192**
	Dufirstson Neree (R)	15,239
25	**Mario Diaz-Balart* (R)**	**Unopposed**
26	**Carlos Curbelo (R)**	**83,031**
	Joe Garcia* (D)	78,306
27	**Ileana Ros-Lehtinen* (R)**	**Unopposed**
Georgia		
1	**Buddy Carter (R)**	**95,337**
	Brian Reese (D)	61,175
2	**Sanford D. Bishop Jr.* (D)**	**96,363**
	Greg Duke (R)	66,537
3	**Lynn A. Westmoreland* (R)**	**Unopposed**
4	**Henry "Hank" Johnson* (D)**	**Unopposed**
5	**John Lewis* (D)**	**Unopposed**
6	**Tom Price* (R)**	**139,018**
	Robert Montigel (D)	71,486
7	**Rob Woodall* (R)**	**113,557**
	Thomas Wight (D)	60,112
8	**Austin Scott* (R)**	**Unopposed**
9	**Doug Collins* (R)**	**146,059**
	David Vogel (D)	34,988
10	**Jody Hice (R)**	**130,703**
	Ken Dious (D)	65,777
11	**Barry Loudermilk (R)**	**Unopposed**
12	**Rick W. Allen (R)**	**91,336**
	John Barrow* (D)	75,478
13	**David Scott* (D)**	**Unopposed**
14	**Tom Graves* (R)**	**Unopposed**

Dist.	Representative/candidate (party)	2014 election results
Hawaii		
1	**Mark Takai (D)**	**93,390**
	Charles K. Djou (R)	86,454
2	**Tulsi Gabbard* (D)**	**142,010**
	Kawika Crowley (R)	33,630
Idaho		
1	**Raul R. Labrador* (R)**	**143,580**
	Shirley Ringo (D)	77,277
2	**Mike Simpson* (R)**	**131,492**
	Richard Stallings (D)	82,801
Illinois		
1	**Bobby L. Rush* (D)**	**162,268**
	Jimmy Lee Tillman (R)	59,749
2	**Robin L. Kelly* (D)**	**160,337**
	Eric M. Wallace (R)	43,799
3	**Daniel Lipinski* (D)**	**116,764**
	Sharon Brannigan (R)	64,091
4	**Luis V. Gutierrez* (D)**	**79,666**
	Hector Concepcion (R)	22,278
5	**Mike Quigley* (D)**	**116,364**
	Vince Kolber (R)	56,350
	Nancy Wade (Green)	11,305
6	**Peter J. Roskam* (R)**	**160,287**
	Michael Mason (D)	78,465
7	**Danny K. Davis* (D)**	**155,110**
	Robert Bumpers (R)	27,168
8	**Tammy Duckworth* (D)**	**84,178**
	Larry Kaifesh (R)	66,878
9	**Janice D. Schakowsky* (D)**	**141,000**
	Susanne Atanus (R)	72,384
10	**Robert Dold (R)**	**95,992**
	Brad Schneider* (D)	91,136
11	**Bill Foster* (D)**	**93,436**
	Darlene Senger (R)	81,335
12	**Mike Bost (R)**	**110,038**
	William L. Enyart* (D)	87,860
	Paula Bradshaw (Green)	11,840
13	**Rodney Davis* (R)**	**123,337**
	Ann Callis (D)	86,935
14	**Randy Hultgren* (R)**	**145,369**
	Dennis Anderson (D)	76,861
15	**John Shimkus* (R)**	**166,274**
	Eric Thorsland (D)	55,652
16	**Adam Kinzinger* (R)**	**153,388**
	Randall Olsen (D)	63,810
17	**Cheri Bustos* (D)**	**110,560**
	Bobby Schilling (R)	88,785
18	**Darin LaHood (R)**[1]	**34,907**
	Rob Mellon (D)	15,840
Indiana		
1	**Peter J. Visclosky* (D)**	**86,579**
	Mark Leyva (R)	51,000
2	**Jackie Walorski* (R)**	**85,583**
	Joe Bock (D)	55,590
3	**Marlin A. Stutzman* (R)**	**97,892**
	Justin Kuhnle (D)	39,771
	Scott Wise (LB)	11,130
4	**Todd Rokita* (R)**	**94,998**
	John Dale (D)	47,056
5	**Susan Brooks* (R)**	**105,277**
	Shawn Denney (D)	49,756
6	**Luke Messer* (R)**	**102,187**
	Susan Hall Heitzman (D)	45,509
7	**André Carson* (D)**	**61,443**
	Catherine "Cat" Ping (R)	46,887
8	**Larry Bucshon* (R)**	**103,344**
	Tom Spangler (D)	61,384
9	**Todd C. Young* (R)**	**101,594**
	Bill Bailey (D)	55,016
Iowa		
1	**Rod Blum (R)**	**147,762**
	Pat Murphy (D)	141,145
2	**David Loebsack* (D)**	**143,431**
	Mariannette Miller-Meeks (R)	129,455
3	**David Young (R)**	**148,814**
	Staci Appel (D)	119,109
4	**Steve King* (R)**	**169,834**
	Jim Mowrer (D)	105,504

Dist.	Representative/candidate (party)	2014 election results
Kansas		
1	**Tim Huelskamp* (R)**	**138,764**
	James "Jim" Sherow (D)	65,397
2	**Lynn Jenkins* (R)**	**128,742**
	Margie Wakefield (D)	87,153
3	**Kevin Yoder* (R)**	**134,493**
	Kelly Kultala (D)	89,584
4	**Mike Pompeo* (R)**	**138,757**
	Perry Schuckman (D)	69,396
Kentucky		
1	**Ed Whitfield* (R)**	**173,022**
	Charles Hatchett (D)	63,596
2	**S. Brett Guthrie* (R)**	**156,936**
	Ron Leach (D)	69,898
3	**John A. Yarmuth* (D)**	**157,056**
	Michael Macfarlane (R)	87,981
4	**Thomas Massie* (R)**	**150,464**
	Peter Newberry (D)	71,694
5	**Harold "Hal" Rogers* (R)**	**171,350**
	Kenneth Stepp (D)	47,617
6	**Garland "Andy" Barr* (R)**	**147,404**
	Elisabeth Jensen (D)	98,290
Louisiana		
1	**Steve Scalise* (R)**	**189,250**
	M. V. "Vinny" Mendoza (D)	24,761
	Lee A. Dugas (D)	21,286
2	**Cedric L. Richmond* (D)**	**152,201**
	Gary Landrieu (D)	37,805
	David Brooks (NPA)	16,327
	Samuel Davenport (LB)	15,237
3	**Charles W. Boustany Jr.* (R)**	**185,867**
	Russell Richard (NPA)	28,342
	Bryan Barrilleaux (R)	22,059
4	**John Fleming* (R)**	**152,683**
	Randall Lord (LB)	55,236
5[2]	**Ralph Abraham (R)**	**134,616**
	Jamie Mayo (D)	75,006
6[2]	**Garrett Graves (R)**	**139,209**
	Edwin Edwards (D)	83,781
Maine		
1	**Chellie Pingree* (D)**	**186,674**
	Isaac Misiuk (R)	94,751
	Richard Murphy (I)	27,410
2	**Bruce Poliquin (R)**	**133,320**
	Emily Cain (D)	118,568
	Blaine Richardson (I)	31,337
Maryland		
1	**Andy Harris* (R)**	**176,342**
	Bill Tilghman (D)	73,843
2	**C. A. Dutch Ruppersberger* (D)**	**120,412**
	David Banach (R)	70,411
3	**John P. Sarbanes* (D)**	**128,594**
	Charles Long (R)	87,029
4	**Donna F. Edwards* (D)**	**134,628**
	Nancy Hoyt (R)	54,217
5	**Steny H. Hoyer* (D)**	**144,725**
	Chris Chaffee (R)	80,752
6	**John Delaney* (D)**	**94,704**
	Dan Bongino (R)	91,930
7	**Elijah E. Cummings* (D)**	**144,639**
	Corrogan R. Vaughn (R)	55,860
8	**Chris Van Hollen* (D)**	**136,722**
	Dave Wallace (R)	87,859
Massachusetts		
1	**Richard E. Neal* (D)**	**Unopposed**
2	**James P. McGovern* (D)**	**Unopposed**
3	**Niki Tsongas* (D)**	**139,104**
	Ann Wofford (R)	81,638
4	**Joseph P. Kennedy III* (D)**	**Unopposed**
5	**Katherine M. Clark* (D)**	**Unopposed**
6	**Seth W. Moulton (D)**	**149,638**
	Richard R. Tisei (R)	111,989
	Chris Stockwell (I)	10,373
7	**Michael E. Capuano* (D)**	**Unopposed**
8	**Stephen F. Lynch* (D)**	**Unopposed**
9	**Bill Keating* (D)**	**140,413**
	John Chapman (R)	114,971
Michigan		
1	**Dan Benishek* (R)**	**130,414**
	Jerry Cannon (D)	113,263
2	**Bill Huizenga* (R)**	**135,568**
	Dean Vanderstelt (D)	70,851
3	**Justin Amash* (R)**	**125,754**
	Bob Goodrich (D)	84,720
4	**John Moolenaar (R)**	**123,962**
	Jeff Holmes (D)	85,777
5	**Daniel T. Kildee* (D)**	**148,182**
	Allen Hardwick (R)	69,222
6	**Fred Upton* (R)**	**116,801**
	Paul Clements (D)	84,391
7	**Tim Walberg* (R)**	**119,564**
	Pam Byrnes (D)	92,083
8	**Mike Bishop (R)**	**132,739**
	Eric Schertzing (D)	102,269
9	**Sander M. Levin* (D)**	**136,342**
	George Brikho (R)	81,470
10	**Candice S. Miller* (R)**	**157,069**
	Chuck Stadler (D)	67,143
11	**Dave Trott (R)**	**140,435**
	Bobby McKenzie (D)	101,681
12	**Debbie Dingell (D)**	**134,346**
	Terry Bowman (R)	64,716
13	**John Conyers Jr.* (D)**	**132,710**
	Jeff Gorman (R)	27,234
14	**Brenda Lawrence (D)**	**165,272**
	Christina Barr (R)	41,801
Minnesota		
1	**Tim Walz* (DFL)**	**122,851**
	Jim Hagedorn (R)	103,536
2	**John Kline* (R)**	**137,778**
	Mike Obermueller (DFL)	95,565
	Paula Overby (IP)	12,319
3	**Erik Paulsen* (R)**	**167,515**
	Sharon Sund (DFL)	101,846
4	**Betty McCollum* (DFL)**	**147,857**
	Sharna Wahlgren (R)	79,492
	Dave Thomas (IP)	14,059
5	**Keith Ellison* (DFL)**	**167,079**
	Doug Daggett (R)	56,577
	Lee Bauer (IP)	12,001
6	**Tom Emmer (R)**	**133,328**
	Joe Perske (DFL)	90,926
	John Denney (IP)	12,457
7	**Collin C. Peterson* (DFL)**	**130,546**
	Torrey Westrom (R)	109,955
8	**Richard Nolan* (DFL)**	**129,090**
	Stewart Mills (R)	125,358
	Ray Sandman (Green)	11,450
Mississippi		
1[3]	**Trent Kelly (R)**	**69,516**
	Walter Howard Zinn Jr. (D)	29,831
2	**Bennie G. Thompson* (D)**	**100,688**
	Troy Ray (I)	36,465
	Shelley Shoemake (Reform)	11,493
3	**Gregg Harper* (R)**	**117,771**
	Douglas Magee (D)	47,744
4	**Steven M. Palazzo* (R)**	**108,776**
	Matt Moore (D)	37,869
Missouri		
1	**Wm. Lacy Clay* (D)**	**119,315**
	Dan Elder (R)	35,273
2	**Ann Wagner* (R)**	**148,191**
	Arthur Lieber (D)	75,384
3	**Blaine Luetkemeyer* (R)**	**130,940**
	Courtney Denton (D)	52,021
4	**Vicky Hartzler* (R)**	**120,014**
	Nate Irvin (D)	46,464
5	**Emanuel Cleaver* (D)**	**79,256**
	Jacob Turk (R)	69,071
6	**Sam Graves* (R)**	**124,616**
	W. A. "Bill" Hedge (D)	55,157
7	**Billy Long* (R)**	**104,054**
	Jim Evans (D)	47,282
	Kevin Craig (LB)	12,584
8	**Jason T. Smith* (R)**	**106,124**
	Barbara Stocker (D)	38,721

Dist.	Representative/candidate (party)	2014 election results
Montana		
	Ryan Zinke (R)	**203,871**
	John Lewis (D)	148,690
	Mike Fellows (LB)	15,402
Nebraska		
1	**Jeff Fortenberry* (R)**	**123,219**
	Dennis Crawford (D)	55,838
2	**Brad Ashford (D)**	**83,872**
	Lee Terry* (R)	78,157
3	**Adrian Smith* (R)**	**139,440**
	Mark Sullivan (D)	45,524
Nevada		
1	**Dina Titus* (D)**	**45,643**
	Annette Teijeiro (R)	30,413
2	**Mark E. Amodei* (R)**	**122,402**
	Kristen Spees (D)	52,016
	Janine Hansen (Indep. Amer.)	11,792
3	**Joe Heck* (R)**	**88,528**
	Erin Bilbray (D)	52,644
4	**Cresent Hardy (R)**	**63,466**
	Steven A. Horsford* (D)	59,844
New Hampshire		
1	**Frank Guinta (R)**	**125,508**
	Carol Shea-Porter* (D)	116,769
2	**Ann McLane Kuster* (D)**	**130,700**
	Marilinda Garcia (R)	106,871
New Jersey		
1	**Donald Norcross (D)**	**93,315**
	Garry Cobb (R)	64,073
2	**Frank A. LoBiondo* (R)**	**108,875**
	Bill Hughes (D)	66,026
3	**Tom MacArthur (R)**	**100,471**
	Aimee Belgard (D)	82,537
4	**Chris Smith* (R)**	**118,826**
	Ruben M. Scolavino (D)	54,415
5	**Scott Garrett* (R)**	**104,678**
	Roy Cho (D)	81,808
6	**Frank Pallone Jr.* (D)**	**72,190**
	Anthony E. Wilkinson (R)	46,891
7	**Leonard Lance* (R)**	**104,287**
	Janice Kovach (D)	68,232
8	**Albio Sires* (D)**	**61,510**
	Jude Anthony Tiscornia (R)	15,141
9	**Bill Pascrell Jr.* (D)**	**82,498**
	Dierdre Paul (R)	36,246
10	**Donald M. Payne Jr.* (D)**	**95,734**
	Yolanda Dentley (R)	14,154
11	**Rodney P. Frelinghuysen* (R)**	**109,455**
	Mark Dunec (D)	65,477
12	**Bonnie Watson Coleman (D)**	**90,430**
	Alieta Eck (R)	54,168
New Mexico		
1	**Michelle Lujan Grisham* (D)**	**105,474**
	Mike Frese (R)	74,558
2	**Steve Pearce* (R)**	**95,209**
	Roxanne "Rocky" Lara (D)	52,499
3	**Ben Ray Luján* (D)**	**113,249**
	Jefferson L. Byrd (R)	70,775
New York		
1	**Lee M. Zeldin (R)**	**94,035**
	Timothy H. Bishop* (D)	78,722
2	**Peter T. King* (R)**	**95,177**
	Patricia Maher (D)	41,814
3	**Steve Israel* (D)**	**90,032**
	Grant M. Lally (R)	74,269
4	**Kathleen M. Rice (D)**	**89,793**
	Bruce Blakeman (R)	80,127
5	**Gregory W. Meeks* (D)**	**75,712**
	Allen Steinhardt (I)	3,870
6	**Grace Meng* (D)**	**Unopposed**
7	**Nydia M. Velázquez* (D)**	**56,593**
	Jose Luis Fernandez (R)	5,713
8	**Hakeem S. Jeffries* (D)**	**77,255**
	Alan Bellone (Conservative)	6,673
9	**Yvette D. Clarke* (D)**	**82,659**
	Daniel Cavanagh (Conservative)	9,727
10	**Jerrold Nadler* (D)**	**89,080**
	Ross Brady (Conservative)	12,042

Dist.	Representative/candidate (party)	2014 election results
11[4]	**Dan Donovan (R)**	**23,409**
	Vincent J. Gentile (D)	15,808
12	**Carolyn B. Maloney* (D)**	**90,603**
	Nick Di Iorio (R)	22,731
13	**Charles B. Rangel* (D)**	**68,396**
	Daniel Vila Rivera (Green)	9,806
14	**Joseph Crowley* (D)**	**50,352**
	Elizabeth Perri (Conservative)	6,735
15	**José E. Serrano* (D)**	**54,906**
	Eduardo Ramirez (Conservative)	1,047
16	**Eliot L. Engel* (D)**	**Unopposed**
17	**Nita M. Lowey* (D)**	**98,150**
	Chris E. Day (R)	75,781
18	**Sean Patrick Maloney* (D)**	**88,993**
	Nan Hayworth (R)	85,660
19	**Christopher P. Gibson* (R)**	**131,594**
	Sean Eldridge (D)	72,470
20	**Paul Tonko* (D)**	**125,111**
	Jim Fischer (R)	79,104
21	**Elise Stefanik (R)**	**96,226**
	Aaron Woolf (D)	59,063
	Matthew Funiciello (Green)	19,238
22	**Richard L. Hanna* (R)**	**Unopposed**
23	**Thomas Reed* (R)**	**113,130**
	Martha Robertson (D)	70,242
24	**John Katko (R)**	**118,474**
	Daniel B. Maffei* (D)	80,304
25	**Louise McIntosh Slaughter* (D)**	**96,803**
	Mark W. Assini (R)	95,932
26	**Brian Higgins* (D)**	**113,210**
	Kathleen A. Weppner (R)	52,909
27	**Chris Collins* (R)**	**144,675**
	Jim O'Donnell (D)	58,911
North Carolina		
1	**G. K. Butterfield* (D)**	**154,333**
	Arthur Rich (R)	55,990
2	**Renee L. Ellmers* (R)**	**122,128**
	Clay Aiken (D)	85,479
3	**Walter B. Jones* (R)**	**139,415**
	Marshall Adame (D)	66,182
4	**David E. Price* (D)**	**169,946**
	Paul Wright (R)	57,416
5	**Virginia Foxx* (R)**	**139,279**
	Josh Brannon (D)	88,973
6	**Mark Walker (R)**	**147,312**
	Laura Fjeld (D)	103,758
7	**David Rouzer (R)**	**134,431**
	Jonathan Barfield Jr. (D)	84,054
8	**Richard Hudson* (R)**	**121,568**
	Antonio Blue (D)	65,854
9	**Robert Pittenger* (R)**	**Unopposed**
10	**Patrick T. McHenry* (R)**	**133,504**
	Tate MacQueen (D)	85,292
11	**Mark Meadows* (R)**	**144,682**
	Tom Hill (D)	85,342
12	**Alma Adams (D)**	**130,096**
	Vince Coakley (R)	42,568
13	**George Holding* (R)**	**153,991**
	Brenda Cleary (D)	114,718
North Dakota		
	Kevin Cramer* (R)	**138,100**
	George Sinner (Dem.-NPL)	95,678
	Robert J. "Jack" Seaman (LB)	14,531
Ohio		
1	**Steve Chabot* (R)**	**124,779**
	Fred Kundrata (D)	72,604
2	**Brad Wenstrup* (R)**	**132,658**
	Marek Tyszkiewicz (D)	68,453
3	**Joyce Beatty* (D)**	**91,769**
	John Adams (R)	51,475
4	**Jim Jordan* (R)**	**125,907**
	Janet Garrett (D)	60,165
5	**Robert "Bob" Latta* (R)**	**134,449**
	Robert Fry (D)	58,507
6	**Bill Johnson* (R)**	**111,026**
	Jennifer Garrison (D)	73,561
7	**Bob Gibbs* (R)**	**Unopposed**

Dist.	Representative/candidate (party)	2014 election results
8	**John Boehner* (R)**	**126,539**
	Tom Poetter (D)	51,534
	Jim Condit (CP)	10,257
9	**Marcy Kaptur* (D)**	**108,870**
	Richard May (R)	51,704
10	**Mike Turner* (R)**	**130,752**
	Robert Klepinger (D)	63,249
11	**Marcia Fudge* (D)**	**137,105**
	Mark Zetzer (R)	35,461
12	**Pat Tiberi* (R)**	**150,573**
	David Tibbs (D)	61,360
13	**Tim Ryan* (D)**	**120,230**
	Thomas Pekarek (R)	55,233
14	**David P. Joyce* (R)**	**135,736**
	Michael Wager (D)	70,856
15	**Steve Stivers* (R)**	**128,496**
	Scott Wharton (D)	66,125
16	**Jim Renacci* (R)**	**132,176**
	Pete Crossland (D)	75,199
Oklahoma		
1	**Jim Bridenstine* (R)**	**Unopposed**
2	**Markwayne Mullin* (R)**	**110,925**
	Earl E. Everett (D)	38,964
3	**Frank D. Lucas* (R)**	**133,335**
	Frankie Robbins (D)	36,270
4	**Tom Cole* (R)**	**117,721**
	Bert Smith (D)	40,998
5	**Steve Russell (R)**	**95,632**
	Al McAffrey (D)	57,790
Oregon		
1	**Suzanne Bonamici* (D)**	**160,038**
	Jason Yates (R)	96,245
	James Foster (LB)	11,213
	Steven C. Reynolds (Pacific Green)	11,163
2	**Greg Walden* (R)**	**202,374**
	Aelea Christofferson (D)	73,785
	Sharon Durbin (LB)	10,491
3	**Earl Blumenauer* (D)**	**211,748**
	James Buchal (R)	57,424
	Michael Meo (Pacific Green)	12,106
4	**Peter A. DeFazio* (D)**	**181,624**
	Art Robinson (R)	116,534
5	**Kurt Schrader* (D)**	**150,944**
	Tootie Smith (R)	110,332
Pennsylvania		
1	**Robert A. Brady* (D)**	**131,248**
	Megan Ann Rath (R)	27,193
2	**Chaka Fattah* (D)**	**181,141**
	Armond James (R)	25,397
3	**Mike Kelly* (R)**	**113,859**
	Dan LaVallee (D)	73,931
4	**Scott Perry* (R)**	**147,090**
	Linda D. Thompson (D)	50,250
5	**Glenn W. Thompson* (R)**	**115,018**
	Kerith Strano Taylor (D)	65,839
6	**Ryan A. Costello (R)**	**119,643**
	Manan Trivedi (D)	92,901
7	**Patrick Meehan* (R)**	**145,869**
	Mary Ellen Balchunis (D)	89,256
8	**Michael G. Fitzpatrick* (R)**	**137,731**
	Kevin Strouse (D)	84,767
9	**Bill Shuster* (R)**	**110,094**
	Alanna K. Hartzok (D)	63,223
10	**Tom Marino* (R)**	**112,851**
	Scott Brion (D)	44,737
	Nick Troiano (I)	22,734
11	**Lou Barletta* (R)**	**122,464**
	Andy Ostrowski (D)	62,228
12	**Keith J. Rothfus* (R)**	**127,993**
	Erin McClelland (D)	87,928
13	**Brendan Boyle (D)**	**123,601**
	Dee Adcock (R)	60,549
14	**Mike Doyle* (D)**	**Unopposed**
15	**Charles W. Dent* (R)**	**Unopposed**
16	**Joseph R. Pitts* (R)**	**101,722**
	Tom Houghton (D)	74,513
17	**Matthew Cartwright (D)**	**93,680**
	David Moylan (R)	71,371
18	**Tim Murphy* (R)**	**Unopposed**

Dist.	Representative/candidate (party)	2014 election results
Rhode Island		
1	**David N. Cicilline* (D)**	**87,060**
	Cormick Lynch (R)	58,877
2	**Jim Langevin* (D)**	**105,716**
	Rhue Reis (R)	63,844
South Carolina		
1	**Mark Sanford* (R)**	**Unopposed**
2	**Joe Wilson* (R)**	**121,649**
	Phil Black (D)	68,719
3	**Jeff Duncan* (R)**	**116,741**
	Barbara Jo Mullis (D)	47,181
4	**Trey Gowdy* (R)**	**126,452**
	Curtis McLaughlin (LB)	21,969
5	**Mick Mulvaney* (R)**	**103,078**
	Tom Adams (D)	71,985
6	**James E. Clyburn* (D)**	**125,747**
	Anthony Culler (R)	44,311
7	**Tom Rice* (R)**	**102,833**
	Gloria Bromell-Tinubu (D)	68,576
South Dakota		
	Kristi L. Noem* (R)	**183,834**
	Corinna Robinson (D)	92,485
Tennessee		
1	**Phil Roe* (R)**	**115,533**
	Robert Franklin (I)	9,906
	Robert Smith (Green)	9,869
2	**John J. Duncan Jr.* (R)**	**120,883**
	Bob Scott (D)	37,612
3	**Chuck Fleischmann* (R)**	**97,344**
	Mary M. Headrick (D)	53,983
4	**Scott DesJarlais* (R)**	**84,815**
	Lenda Sherrell (D)	51,357
5	**Jim Cooper* (D)**	**96,148**
	Bob Ries (R)	55,078
6	**Diane Black* (R)**	**115,231**
	Amos Powers (D)	37,232
7	**Marsha Blackburn* (R)**	**110,534**
	Daniel Cramer (D)	42,280
8	**Stephen Fincher* (R)**	**122,255**
	Wes Bradley (D)	42,433
9	**Steve Cohen* (D)**	**87,376**
	Charlotte Bergmann (R)	27,173
Texas		
1	**Louie Gohmert* (R)**	**115,084**
	Shirley J. McKellar (D)	33,476
2	**Ted Poe* (R)**	**101,936**
	Niko Letsos (D)	44,462
3	**Sam Johnson* (R)**	**113,404**
	Paul Blair (Green)	24,876
4	**John Ratcliffe (R)**	**Unopposed**
5	**Jeb Hensarling* (R)**	**88,998**
	Ken Ashby (LB)	15,264
6	**Joe Barton* (R)**	**92,334**
	David Cozad (D)	55,027
7	**John Culberson* (R)**	**90,606**
	James Cargas (D)	49,478
8	**Kevin Brady* (R)**	**125,066**
	Ken Petty (LB)	14,947
9	**Al Green* (D)**	**78,109**
	Johnny Johnson (LB)	7,894
10	**Michael T. McCaul* (R)**	**109,726**
	Tawana Walter-Cadien (D)	60,243
11	**Mike Conaway* (R)**	**107,939**
	Ryan Lange (LB)	11,635
12	**Kay Granger* (R)**	**113,186**
	Mark Greene (D)	41,757
13	**Mac Thornberry* (R)**	**110,842**
	Mike Minter (D)	16,822
14	**Randy Weber* (R)**	**90,116**
	Don Brown (D)	52,545
15	**Rubén Hinojosa* (D)**	**48,708**
	Eddie Zamora (R)	39,016
16	**Beto O'Rourke* (D)**	**49,338**
	Corey Roen (R)	21,324
17	**Bill Flores* (R)**	**85,807**
	Nick Haynes (D)	43,049
18	**Sheila Jackson Lee* (D)**	**76,097**
	Sean Seibert (R)	26,249
19	**Randy Neugebauer* (R)**	**90,160**
	Neal Marchbanks (D)	21,458
20	**Joaquin Castro* (D)**	**66,554**
	Jeffrey Blunt (LB)	21,410

Dist.	Representative/candidate (party)	2014 election results
21	**Lamar Smith* (R)**	**135,660**
	Antonio Diaz (Green)	27,831
	Ryan Shields (LB)	25,505
22	**Pete Olson* (R)**	**100,861**
	Frank Briscoe (D)	47,844
23	**Will Hurd (R)**	**57,459**
	Pete P. Gallego* (D)	55,037
24	**Kenny Marchant* (R)**	**93,712**
	Patrick McGehearty (D)	46,548
25	**Roger Williams* (R)**	**107,120**
	Marco Montoya (D)	64,463
26	**Michael C. Burgess* (R)**	**116,944**
	Mark Boler (LB)	24,526
27	**Blake Farenthold* (R)**	**83,342**
	Wesley Reed (D)	44,152
28	**Henry Cuellar* (D)**	**62,508**
	William Aikens (LB)	10,153
29	**Gene Green* (D)**	**41,321**
	James Stanczak (LB)	4,822
30	**Eddie Bernice Johnson* (D)**	**93,041**
	Max Koch (LB)	7,154
31	**John R. Carter* (R)**	**91,607**
	Louie Minor (D)	45,715
32	**Pete Sessions* (R)**	**96,495**
	Frank Perez (D)	55,325
33	**Marc Veasey* (D)**	**43,769**
	Jason Reeves (LB)	6,823
34	**Filemon Vela* (D)**	**47,503**
	Larry Smith (R)	30,811
35	**Lloyd Doggett* (D)**	**60,124**
	Susan Narvaiz (R)	32,040
36	**Brian Babin (R)**	**101,663**
	Michael K. Cole (D)	29,543
Utah		
1	**Rob Bishop* (R)**	**84,231**
	Donna McAleer (D)	36,422
2	**Chris Stewart* (R)**	**88,915**
	Luz Robles (D)	47,585
3	**Jason Chaffetz* (R)**	**102,952**
	Brian Wonnacott (D)	32,059
4	**Mia Love (R)**	**74,936**
	Doug Owens (D)	67,425
Vermont		
	Peter Welch* (D)	**123,349**
	Mark Donka (R)	59,432
Virginia		
1	**Robert J. Wittman* (R)**	**131,861**
	Norm Mosher (D)	72,059
2	**Scott Rigell* (R)**	**101,558**
	Suzanne Patrick (D)	71,178
3	**Bobby Scott* (D)**	**Unopposed**
4	**J. Randy Forbes* (R)**	**120,684**
	Elliott Fausz (D)	75,270
5	**Robert Hurt* (R)**	**124,735**
	Lawrence Gaughan (D)	73,482
6	**Bob Goodlatte* (R)**	**133,898**
	Will Hammer (LB)	22,161
	Elaine Hildebrandt (Indep. Green)	21,447
7	**David Brat (R)**	**148,026**
	Jack Trammell (D)	89,914
8	**Donald S. Beyer Jr.* (D)**	**128,102**
	Micah Edmond (R)	63,810
9	**H. Morgan Griffith* (R)**	**117,465**
	William Carr (I)	39,412
10	**Barbara Comstock (R)**	**125,914**
	John Foust (D)	89,957
11	**Gerry Connolly* (D)**	**106,780**
	Suzanne Scholte (R)	75,796
Washington		
1	**Suzan DelBene* (D)**	**101,428**
	Pedro Celis (R)	124,151
2	**Rick Larsen* (D)**	**122,173**
	B.J. Guillot (R)	79,518
3	**Jaime Herrera Beutler* (R)**	**124,796**
	Bob Dingethal (D)	78,018
4	**Dan Newhouse (R)**	**77,772**
	Clint Didier (R)	75,307
5	**Cathy McMorris Rodgers* (R)**	**135,470**
	Joseph Pakootas (D)	87,772
6	**Derek Kilmer* (D)**	**141,265**
	Marty McClendon (R)	83,025
7	**Jim McDermott* (D)**	**203,954**
	Craig Keller (R)	47,921
8	**Dave Reichert* (R)**	**125,741**
	Jason Ritchie (D)	73,003
9	**Adam Smith* (D)**	**118,132**
	Doug Basler (R)	48,662
10	**Denny Heck* (D)**	**99,279**
	Joyce McDonald (R)	82,213
West Virginia		
1	**David B. McKinley* (R)**	**92,491**
	Glen Gainer (D)	52,109
2	**Alex Mooney (R)**	**72,619**
	Nick Casey (D)	67,687
3	**Evan Jenkins (R)**	**77,713**
	Nick J. Rahall II* (D)	62,688
Wisconsin		
1	**Paul Ryan* (R)**	**182,316**
	Rob Zerban (D)	105,552
2	**Mark Pocan* (D)**	**224,920**
	Peter Theron (R)	103,619
3	**Ron Kind* (D)**	**155,368**
	Tony Kurtz (R)	119,540
4	**Gwen Moore* (D)**	**179,045**
	Dan Sebring (R)	68,490
5	**F. James Sensenbrenner Jr.* (R)**	**231,160**
	Chris Rockwood (D)	101,190
6	**Glenn Grothman (R)**	**169,767**
	Mark Harris (D)	122,212
7	**Sean P. Duffy* (R)**	**169,8[illegible]**
	Kelly Westlund (D)	112,94[illegible]
8	**Reid J. Ribble* (R)**	**188,553**
	Ron Gruett (D)	101,34[illegible]
Wyoming		
	Cynthia M. Lummis* (R)	**113,03[illegible]**
	Richard Grayson (D)	37,80[illegible]

(1) Aaron Schock resigned seat effective Mar. 31, 2015. Result of a special election held Sept. 10, 2015. LaHood was sworn into Congress Sept. 17, 2015. (2) Result of a runoff between the top two vote recipients held Dec. 6, 2014. (3) Alan Nunnelee died in office Feb. 6, 2015. Result of a runoff between top two special election vote recipients held June 2, 2015. Kelly was sworn in June 9, 2015. (4) Michael Grimm resigned seat effective Jan. 5, 2015. Result of a special election held May 5, 2015. Donovan was sworn in May 12, 2015.

Members of the 114th Congress: Nonvoting Members

Representative/candidate (party)	2014 election results
American Samoa	
Aumua Amata (R)	**4,306**
Eni F.H. Faleomavaega* (D)	3,157
District of Columbia	
Eleanor Holmes Norton* (D)	**143,923**
Nelson Rimensnyder (R)	11,673
Guam	
Madeleine Z. Bordallo* (D)	**20,693**
Margaret Metcalfe (R)	14,956
Northern Mariana Islands	
Gregorio Kilili Camacho Sablan* (I)	**8,54[illegible]**
Andrew Sablan Salas (D)	4,54[illegible]
Puerto Rico—Resident Commissioner[1]	
Pedro R. Pierluisi (New Prog./D)	
Virgin Islands	
Stacey Plaskett (D)	**21,22[illegible]**
Vince Danet (R)	1,96[illegible]

(1) The resident commissioner of Puerto Rico is the only member of the House of Representatives who serves a four-year term. Pierluisi was elected in Nov. 2012.

Justices of the U.S. Supreme Court

The Supreme Court comprises the chief justice of the U.S. and eight associate justices, all appointed for life by the president with advice and consent of the U.S. Senate. Names of chief justices are in **boldface**. Terms of service begin with the year each justice took the judicial oath. Service years are the number of complete years served by a justice. Current salaries: chief justice, $255,500; associate justice, $244,400. The U.S. Supreme Court Building is at 1 First St. NE, Washington, DC 20543.

Website: www.supremecourt.gov

Current membership. Chief justice: John G. Roberts Jr.; associate justices in seniority order: Antonin Scalia, Anthony M. Kennedy, Clarence Thomas, Ruth Bader Ginsburg, Stephen G. Breyer, Samuel A. Alito Jr., Sonia Sotomayor, Elena Kagan.

Name, appointed from	Service Term	Service Yrs.	Born	Died
John Jay, NY	1789-1795	5	1745	1829
John Rutledge, SC[1]	1790-1791	1	1739	1800
William Cushing, MA	1790-1810*	20	1732	1810
James Wilson, PA	1789-1798	8	1742	1798
John Blair, VA	1790-1795*	5	1732	1800
James Iredell, NC	1790-1799	9	1751	1799
Thomas Johnson, MD	1792-1793	<1	1732	1819
William Paterson, NJ	1793-1806	13	1745	1806
John Rutledge, SC[2,3]	1795	<1	1739	1800
Samuel Chase, MD	1796-1811	15	1741	1811
Oliver Ellsworth, CT	1796-1800	4	1745	1807
Bushrod Washington, VA	1799-1829*	30	1762	1829
Alfred Moore, NC	1800-1804	3	1755	1810
John Marshall, VA	1801-1835	34	1755	1835
William Johnson, SC	1804-1834	30	1771	1834
Henry B. Livingston, NY	1807-1823	16	1757	1823
Thomas Todd, KY	1807-1826	18	1765	1826
Gabriel Duvall, MD	1811-1835	23	1752	1844
Joseph Story, MA	1812-1845*	33	1779	1845
Smith Thompson, NY	1823-1843	20	1768	1843
Robert Trimble, KY	1826-1828	2	1777	1828
John McLean, OH	1830-1861*	31	1785	1861
Henry Baldwin, PA	1830-1844	14	1780	1844
James M. Wayne, GA	1835-1867	32	1790	1867
Roger B. Taney, MD	1836-1864	28	1777	1864
Philip P. Barbour, VA	1836-1841	4	1783	1841
John Catron, TN	1837-1865	28	1786	1865
John McKinley, AL	1838-1852*	14	1780	1852
Peter V. Daniel, VA	1842-1860*	18	1784	1860
Samuel Nelson, NY	1845-1872	27	1792	1873
Levi Woodbury, NH	1845-1851	5	1789	1851
Robert C. Grier, PA	1846-1870	23	1794	1870
Benjamin R. Curtis, MA	1851-1857	5	1809	1874
John A. Campbell, AL	1853-1861*	8	1811	1889
Nathan Clifford, ME	1858-1881	23	1803	1881
Noah H. Swayne, OH	1862-1881	18	1804	1884
Samuel F. Miller, IA	1862-1890	28	1816	1890
David Davis, IL	1862-1877	14	1815	1886
Stephen J. Field, CA	1863-1897	33	1816	1899
Salmon P. Chase, OH	1864-1873	8	1808	1873
William Strong, PA	1870-1880	10	1808	1895
Joseph P. Bradley, NJ	1870-1892	21	1813	1892
Ward Hunt, NY	1873-1882	9	1810	1886
Morrison R. Waite, OH	1874-1888	14	1816	1888
John M. Harlan, KY	1877-1911	33	1833	1911
William B. Woods, GA	1881-1887	6	1824	1887
Stanley Matthews, OH	1881-1889	7	1824	1889
Horace Gray, MA	1882-1902	20	1828	1902
Samuel Blatchford, NY	1882-1893	11	1820	1893
Lucius Q. C. Lamar, MS	1888-1893	5	1825	1893
Melville W. Fuller, IL	1888-1910	21	1833	1910
David J. Brewer, KS	1890-1910	20	1837	1910
Henry B. Brown, MI	1891-1906	15	1836	1913
George Shiras Jr., PA	1892-1903	10	1832	1924
Howell E. Jackson, TN	1893-1895	2	1832	1895
Edward D. White, LA[1]	1894-1910	16	1845	1921
Rufus W. Peckham, NY	1896-1909	13	1838	1909
Joseph McKenna, CA	1898-1925	26	1843	1926
Oliver W. Holmes, MA	1902-1932	29	1841	1935
William R. Day, OH	1903-1922	19	1849	1923
William H. Moody, MA	1906-1910	3	1853	1917
Horace H. Lurton, TN	1910-1914	4	1844	1914
Charles E. Hughes, NY[1]	1910-1916	5	1862	1948
Willis Van Devanter, WY	1911-1937	26	1859	1941
Joseph R. Lamar, GA	1911-1916	5	1857	1916
Edward D. White, LA[2]	1910-1921	10	1845	1921
Mahlon Pitney, NJ	1912-1922	10	1858	1924
James C. McReynolds, TN	1914-1941	26	1862	1946
Louis D. Brandeis, MA	1916-1939	22	1856	1941
John H. Clarke, OH	1916-1922	5	1857	1945
William H. Taft, CT	1921-1930	8	1857	1930
George Sutherland, UT	1922-1938	15	1862	1942
Pierce Butler, MN	1923-1939	16	1866	1939
Edward T. Sanford, TN	1923-1930	7	1865	1930
Harlan F. Stone, NY[1]	1925-1941	16	1872	1946
Charles E. Hughes, NY[2]	1930-1941	11	1862	1948
Owen J. Roberts, PA	1930-1945	15	1875	1955
Benjamin N. Cardozo, NY	1932-1938	6	1870	1938
Hugo L. Black, AL	1937-1971	34	1886	1971
Stanley F. Reed, KY	1938-1957	19	1884	1980
Felix Frankfurter, MA	1939-1962	23	1882	1965
William O. Douglas, CT	1939-1975	36[4]	1898	1980
Frank Murphy, MI	1940-1949	9	1890	1949
Harlan F. Stone, NY[2]	1941-1946	4	1872	1946
James F. Byrnes, SC	1941-1942	1	1879	1972
Robert H. Jackson, NY	1941-1954	13	1892	1954
Wiley B. Rutledge, IA	1943-1949	6	1894	1949
Harold H. Burton, OH	1945-1958	13	1888	1964
Fred M. Vinson, KY	1946-1953	7	1890	1953
Tom C. Clark, TX	1949-1967	17	1899	1977
Sherman Minton, IN	1949-1956	7	1890	1965
Earl Warren, CA	1953-1969	15	1891	1974
John Marshall Harlan, NY	1955-1971	16	1899	1971
William J. Brennan Jr., NJ	1956-1990	33	1906	1997
Charles E. Whittaker, MO	1957-1962	5	1901	1973
Potter Stewart, OH	1958-1981	22	1915	1985
Byron R. White, CO	1962-1993	31	1917	2002
Arthur J. Goldberg, IL	1962-1965	2	1908	1990
Abe Fortas, TN	1965-1969	3	1910	1982
Thurgood Marshall, NY	1967-1991	24	1908	1993
Warren E. Burger, VA	1969-1986	17	1907	1995
Harry A. Blackmun, MN	1970-1994	24	1908	1999
Lewis F. Powell Jr., VA	1972-1987	15	1907	1998
William H. Rehnquist, AZ[1]	1972-1986	14	1924	2005
John Paul Stevens, IL	1975-2010	34	1920	
Sandra Day O'Connor, AZ	1981-2006	24	1930	
William H. Rehnquist, VA[2]	1986-2005	18	1924	2005
Antonin Scalia, VA	1986-		1936	
Anthony M. Kennedy, CA	1988-		1936	
David H. Souter, NH	1990-2009	18	1939	
Clarence Thomas, GA	1991-		1948	
Ruth Bader Ginsburg, NY	1993-		1933	
Stephen G. Breyer, MA	1994-		1938	
John G. Roberts Jr., MD	2005-		1955	
Samuel A. Alito Jr., NJ	2006-		1950	
Sonia Sotomayor, NY	2009-		1954	
Elena Kagan, MA	2010-		1960	

* = Because of inadequate government record keeping, date of oath is estimated. (1) Later, chief justice, as listed. (2) Formerly associate justice. (3) Named acting chief justice; confirmation rejected by the Senate. (4) Longest term of service.

Supreme Court History and Notable Firsts

The U.S. Supreme Court first convened Feb. 1, 1790, in New York, NY. Acting on the authority of Congress as outlined in the Judiciary Act of 1789, the Court consisted of Chief Justice John Jay and five associate justices who held sessions for a few weeks in Feb. and Aug. The justices also served twice a year in each of the nation's then-13 judicial districts, a requirement known as riding circuit.

The Court's first major legal decision, *Chisholm v. Georgia* (1793), ruled that federal courts held jurisdiction over disputes between individual states and citizens of other states. (The 11th Amendment, which the states ratified in 1795, removed that jurisdiction.)

Since it was established, 112 justices have served on the Court for an average of 16 years. Of 160 nominations to the Court (including chief justice nominations), just 12 have been rejected by the Senate, most recently Robert Bork in 1987. (George W. Bush nominee Harriet Miers withdrew her nomination before the Senate considered it, in 2005.) Justices may be removed from the Court by impeachment. In 1805, the House of Representatives impeached Samuel Chase; he was later acquitted by the Senate.

The Court over time has expanded its impact on the nation's affairs. Since 1803 it has declared unconstitutional 170 acts of Congress and more than 1,070 state and territorial laws and municipal statutes. Operating on an est. $85-mil budget, the Court receives approximately 10,000 petitions annually and hears oral arguments in about 75-80 cases per term.

The Court begins its term the first Monday in October and recesses in late June or early July.

First fully vested justice: James Wilson took the Constitutional Oath of the Court Oct. 5, 1789

First Jewish justice: Louis D. Brandeis (1916-39)

First and only person to serve as both U.S. president and chief justice: William Howard Taft (president, 1909-13; chief justice, 1921-30)

First justice to take an oath at the White House: Frank Murphy, Jan. 18, 1940

First African-American justice: Thurgood Marshall (1967-91)

First woman justice: Sandra Day O'Connor (1981-2006)

First Hispanic justice: Sonia Sotomayor (2009-)

U.S. Supreme Court Decisions by Issue and Leadership Era, 1946-2015

Source: The Supreme Court Database, supremecourtdatabase.org

Decisions through the end of the 2014-15 term. Figures are the number of cases decided in each issue category (number of 5-4 decisions in parentheses).

	Number of decisions under Chief Justice—				
Issue	**Vinson (1946-53)**	**Warren (1953-69)**	**Burger (1969-86)**	**Rehnquist (1986-2005)**	**Roberts (2005-)**
Attorneys[1]	2 (0)	12 (1)	37 (5)	31 (7)	16 (2)
Civil rights	74 (7)	316 (27)	555 (78)	324 (69)	133 (30)
Criminal procedure	123 (29)	462 (70)	627 (109)	509 (136)	228 (58)
Due process	47 (6)	40 (5)	144 (18)	86 (23)	20 (5)
Economic activity	224 (37)	493 (48)	450 (52)	346 (40)	163 (18)
Federal taxation	49 (2)	118 (5)	75 (7)	56 (3)	12 (2)
Federalism	30 (1)	94 (3)	108 (6)	124 (26)	39 (8)
First amendment	44 (8)	206 (44)	236 (56)	140 (36)	41 (14)
Interstate relations	12 (2)	14 (0)	40 (0)	23 (1)	6 (1)
Judicial power	135 (18)	300 (20)	366 (33)	286 (28)	99 (22)
Miscellaneous[2]	1 (0)	12 (0)	12 (0)	19 (0)	5 (1)
Privacy	4 (0)	2 (0)	48 (9)	42 (6)	16 (1)
Private action[3]	0 (0)	0 (0)	0 (0)	0 (0)	2 (1)
Unions	41 (4)	131 (8)	109 (24)	55 (11)	17 (4)
Total	**786 (114)**	**2,200 (231)**	**2,807 (397)**	**2,041 (386)**	**797 (167)**

Note: Decision types include orally argued judgments, per curiams, and opinions; per curiams without oral arguments; equally divided votes; and decrees. (1) Includes cases on commercial fees, attorneys' fees, admission to state or federal bar, attorney discipline, and disbarment. (2) Includes cases that could not be classified. (3) Includes cases on civil procedures, commercial transactions, contracts, evidence, personal and real property, torts, and wills and trusts.

Selected Landmark Decisions of the U.S. Supreme Court, 1803-2014

1803: *Marbury v. Madison*. The Court ruled that Congress exceeded its power in the Judiciary Act of 1789. The Court thus established its power to review acts of Congress and to declare invalid those it found to be in conflict with the Constitution.

1819: *Trustees of Dartmouth College v. Woodward*. The Court ruled that a state could not arbitrarily alter the terms of a college's contract. The Court later used a similar principle to limit the states' ability to interfere with business contracts.

1819: *McCulloch v. Maryland*. The Court ruled that Congress had the authority to charter a national bank, under the Constitution's granting of power to enact all laws "necessary and proper" to responsibilities of government.

1824: *Gibbons v. Ogden*. The Court ruled that New York state had overstepped its authority in granting a monopoly to two steamboat operators. According to the ruling, Congress's power to regulate interstate commerce included transportation.

1857: *Dred Scott v. Sandford*. The Court declared unconstitutional the already-repealed Missouri Compromise of 1820 because it deprived a person of property—a slave—without due process of law. The Court also ruled that slaves were not citizens of any state nor of the U.S. The latter part of the decision was overturned by ratification of the 14th Amendment in 1868.

1880: *Strauder v. West Virginia*. The Court struck down a state law mandating that jurors must be white, ruling it a violation of the right to equal protection under the 14th Amendment.

1896: *Plessy v. Ferguson*. The Court ruled that a state law requiring federal railroad trains to provide separate but equal facilities for black and white passengers neither infringed upon federal authority to regulate interstate commerce nor violated the 13th and 14th Amendments. The "separate but equal" doctrine remained effective until the 1954 ***Brown v. Board of Education*** decision.

1904: *Northern Securities Co. v. U.S.* The Court ruled that a holding company formed solely to eliminate competition between two railroad lines was a combination in restraint of trade, violating the 1890 federal Sherman Antitrust Act.

1908: *Muller v. Oregon*. The Court upheld a state law limiting the working hours of women. (Louis D. Brandeis, counsel for the state, cited evidence from social workers, physicians, and factory inspectors that the number of hours women worked affected their health and morals.)

1911: *Standard Oil Co. of New Jersey v. U.S.* The Court ruled that the Standard Oil Trust must be dissolved because of its unreasonable restraint of trade.

1919: *Schenck v. U.S.* The Court sustained the Espionage Act of 1917, maintaining that freedom of speech and press could be constrained if "the words used ... create a clear and present danger."

1925: *Gitlow v. New York*. The Court ruled that the 1st Amendment prohibition against government abridgment of the freedom of speech applied to the states as well as to the federal government. The decision was the first of a number of rulings holding that the 14th Amendment extended the guarantees of the Bill of Rights to state action.

1935: *Schechter Poultry Corp. v. U.S.* The Court ruled that Congress exceeded its authority to delegate legislative powers and to regulate interstate commerce when it enacted the National Industrial Recovery Act (1933), which afforded the U.S. president too much discretionary power.

1944: *Korematsu v. U.S.* The Court upheld the constitutionality of an order barring all persons of Japanese ancestry, including U.S. citizens, from much of the West Coast, forcing them into internment camps, ruling that the need to prevent espionage outweighed the petitioner's civil rights. The ruling, never officially overturned, followed ***Hirabayashi v. U.S.*** (1943), in which the Court upheld the imposition of curfews on minority populations perceived to be a potential wartime threat.

1951: *Dennis v. U.S.* The Court upheld convictions under the Smith Act of 1940 for invoking Communist theory advocating the forcible overthrow of the government. In ***Yates v. U.S.*** (1957), the Court moderated this ruling by allowing such advocacy in the abstract, if not connected to action to achieve the goal.

1952: *Youngstown Sheet & Tube Co. v. Sawyer.* The Court ruled that the president had exceeded his wartime power in ordering the seizure of private steel mills during a nationwide steelworkers' strike. The Court held that neither the Constitution nor his role as commander-in-chief gave the president the authority to interfere in labor issues.

1954: *Brown v. Board of Education of Topeka.* The Court ruled that separate public schools for black and white students were inherently unequal, so state-sanctioned segregation in public schools violated the equal protection guarantee of the 14th Amendment. And in ***Bolling v. Sharpe*** the same year, the Court ruled that the congressionally mandated segregated public school system in the District of Columbia violated the 5th Amendment's due process guarantee of personal liberty. The Brown ruling also led to abolition of state-sponsored segregation in other public facilities.

1957: *Roth v. U.S.*; *Alberts v. California.* The Court ruled obscene material—defined as appealing primarily to "prurient interest" in the view of "the average person, applying contemporary community standards"—was not protected by 1st Amendment guarantees of freedom of speech and press, being "utterly without redeeming social importance." This definition was modified in later decisions, including ***Miller v. California*** (1973).

1958: *Cooper v. Aaron.* The Court held that Arkansas could not nullify ***Brown v. Board of Education*** by arguing mandatory school desegregation was unconstitutional. The opinion of the Court affirmed its reading of the Constitution as the "supreme law of the land."

1961: *Mapp v. Ohio.* The Court ruled that evidence obtained in violation of the 4th Amendment guarantee against unreasonable search and seizure must be excluded from use in state as well as federal trials.

1962: *Baker v. Carr.* The Court held that constitutional challenges to the unequal distribution of voters among legislative districts could be resolved by federal courts.

1962: *Engel v. Vitale.* The Court held that government bodies could not encourage the recitation of a state-composed prayer in public schools, even if nondenominational, because that would be an unconstitutional attempt to establish religion.

1963: *Gideon v. Wainwright.* The Court ruled that defendants in state cases must have access to an attorney even if they could not afford one.

1964: *New York Times Co. v. Sullivan.* The Court ruled that the 1st Amendment protected the press from libel suits for defamatory reports about public officials unless an injured party could prove that a defamatory report was made out of "actual malice," with "reckless disregard" for the truth.

1964: *Heart of Atlanta Motel v. U.S.* The Court upheld the constitutionality of Title II of the 1964 Civil Rights Act banning racial discrimination in motels/hotels engaged in interstate commerce (by accommodating travelers from other states). The Court in ***Katzenbach v. McClung*** (1964) held that Title II also applied to restaurants and businesses that purchased a substantial percentage of food or goods from other states.

1965: *Griswold v. Connecticut.* The Court ruled that a state unconstitutionally interfered with privacy in a marriage when it prohibited all persons, including married couples, from using contraceptives.

1966: *Miranda v. Arizona.* The Court ruled that, under the guarantee of due process, suspects in custody, before being questioned, must be informed that they have the right to remain silent, that anything they say may be used against them, and that they have the right to counsel.

1968: *Terry v. Ohio.* The Court ruled that a "stop and frisk" performed without a warrant or probable cause was not a violation of 4th Amendment rights, provided that the law enforcement officer had a reasonable suspicion that the subject was armed and dangerous, or had committed or was about to commit a crime.

1973: *Roe v. Wade*; *Doe v. Bolton.* The Court ruled that the fetus was not a "person" with constitutional rights and that a right to privacy inherent in the 14th Amendment's due process guarantee of personal liberty protected a woman's decision to have an abortion. During the first trimester of pregnancy, the Court maintained, the decision should be left entirely to a woman and her physician. Some regulation of abortion procedures was allowed in the second trimester and some restriction of abortion in the third.

1974: *U.S. v. Nixon.* The Court ruled that neither the separation of powers nor the need to preserve the confidentiality of presidential communications could alone justify an absolute executive privilege of immunity from judicial demands for evidence to be used in a criminal trial.

1976: *Gregg v. Georgia*; *Proffitt v. Florida*; *Jurek v. Texas.* The Court held that death, as a punishment for persons convicted of first-degree murder, was not in and of itself cruel and unusual punishment in violation of the 8th Amendment. But the Court ruled that the sentencing judge and jury must consider the character of the offender and the circumstances of the particular crime.

1978: *Regents of the Univ. of Calif. v. Bakke.* The Court ruled that an admissions program for a state medical school, under which a set number of places were reserved for minorities, violated the 1964 Civil Rights Act, which forbids the exclusion of anyone from a federally funded program based on race. However, the Court ruled that race could be considered as one of a complex of factors.

1985: *New Jersey v. T.L.O.* The Court ruled that officials who carry out searches on school grounds do not violate students' 4th Amendment rights because students' privacy rights can be outweighed by schools' need to maintain learning environments. The ruling put in place less stringent standards of required "reasonableness" for such searches.

1986: *Bowers v. Hardwick.* The Court refused to extend any right of privacy to homosexual activity, upholding a Georgia antisodomy law that in effect made such activity a crime. Georgia's supreme court struck down the law in 1998, and in ***Lawrence v. Texas*** (2003), the U.S. Supreme Court struck down all state antisodomy laws as violations of liberty prohibited in the 14th Amendment's due process clause. In ***Romer v. Evans*** (1996), the Court struck down a Colorado constitutional provision that barred homosexuals from recognition as a protected class, ruling that it violated the 14th Amendment's Equal Protection clause.

1989: *Texas v. Johnson.* The Court held the actions of a political activist who burned an American flag outside of the 1984 Republican National Convention were expressive and therefore protected by the 1st Amendment. The ruling invalidated laws in 48 states prohibiting flag desecration.

1990: *Cruzan v. Missouri.* The Court ruled that while a person had the right to refuse life-sustaining medical treatment, a state could require evidence that a comatose patient would not have wanted to live before withholding treatment. In two 1997 rulings, ***Washington v. Glucksberg*** and ***Vacco v. Quill***, the Court ruled that states could ban doctor-assisted suicide.

1995: *U.S. Term Limits, Inc. v. Thornton.* The Court ruled that neither states nor Congress could limit terms of members of Congress because the Constitution reserves to the people the right to choose federal lawmakers.

1995: *Adarand Constructors, Inc. v. Peña.* The Court held that federal programs that classify people by race, unless "narrowly tailored" to further a "compelling governmental interest," may violate the right to equal protection and are thus subject to strict scrutiny.

1997: *Clinton v. Jones.* Rejecting an appeal by Pres. Clinton in a sexual harassment suit, the Court ruled that a sitting president did not have temporary immunity from a lawsuit for actions outside the realm of official duties.

1997: *City of Boerne v. Flores.* The Court overturned the portion of a 1993 law banning enforcement of state laws that "substantially burden" religious practice unless there is a "compelling governmental interest" to do so. The Court held that the act was an unwarranted intrusion by Congress on states' prerogatives and an infringement of the judiciary's role.

1997: *Reno v. ACLU.* Citing the right to free expression, the Court overturned a provision making it a crime to display or distribute "obscene or indecent" or "patently offensive" material on the Internet. The Court ruled, however, in ***NEA v. Finley*** (1998) that "general standards of decency" may be used as a criterion in federal arts funding.

1998: *Clinton v. City of New York.* The Court struck down the Line-Item Veto Act (1996), holding that it unconstitutionally gave the president "the unilateral power to change the text of duly enacted statutes."

1998: *Faragher v. City of Boca Raton*; *Burlington Industries, Inc. v. Ellerth.* The Court issued new guidelines for workplace sexual harassment suits, holding employers responsible for misconduct by supervisory employees. And in ***Oncale v. Sundowner Offshore Services, Inc.***, the Court ruled that the law against discrimination based on sex applies regardless of whether the harasser and harassed are the same sex.

1999: *Dept. of Commerce v. U.S. House of Representatives.* Upholding a challenge to plans for the 2000 census, the Court prohibited statistical sampling, favored by Democrats, in apportioning seats in the U.S. House. The Court maintained that an actual head count was required.

1999: *Alden v. Maine*; *Florida Prepaid v. College Savings Bank*; *College Savings Bank v. Florida Prepaid.* In a series of rulings, the Court applied the principle of sovereign immunity to shield states in large part from being sued under federal law.

2000: *Boy Scouts of America v. Dale.* The Court ruled that the Boy Scouts could dismiss a troop leader after learning he was gay, holding that the right to freedom of association outweighed a New Jersey antidiscrimination statute.

2000: *Bush v. Gore.* The Court ruled that manual recounts in Florida of ballots cast in the 2000 presidential election could not proceed because inconsistent evaluation standards violated the equal protection clause. In effect, the ruling meant the existing official results would stand, making George W. Bush the narrow winner of the election.

2001: *Good News Club v. Milford Central School.* The justices found that a private religious organization could not be denied equal access to a public school facility for after-school meetings because that would be a violation of the group's free speech rights.

2002: *Federal Maritime Commission v. South Carolina State Ports Authority.* The Court ruled that the 11th Amendment gave states immunity from private lawsuits involving federal agencies.

2002: *Atkins v. Virginia.* The Court ruled that the execution of mentally retarded criminals violated the 8th Amendment ban on cruel and unusual punishment. The Court ruled in ***Roper v. Simmons*** (2005) that executions of convicts who committed their crimes before age 18 were also prohibited on the same grounds.

2002: *Zelman v. Simmons-Harris.* The Court ruled that publicly funded tuition vouchers could be used at religious schools without violating the separation of church and state.

2003: *Grutter v. Bollinger*; *Gratz v. Bollinger.* The Court upheld the use of race as a factor in the Univ. of Michigan Law School's admissions policies because of the school's interest in a diverse student body. In a second decision, however, the Court ruled against a strict point system based on racial and ethnic backgrounds as used in the university's undergraduate admissions process.

2004: *Tennessee v. Lane.* The Court ruled that disabled individuals could sue states under the Americans With Disabilities Act (1990) for failing to provide adequate access to state courthouses, despite states' usual immunity from private lawsuits in federal court under the 11th Amendment, which the Court ruled on in ***Federal Maritime Commission v. South Carolina State Ports Authority*** (2002).

2004: *Locke v. Davey.* The justices decided that a scholarship program provided by the state of Washington did not violate the right to free exercise of religion in denying aid to students preparing for the clergy.

2004: *Ashcroft v. ACLU.* The Court struck down federal legislation passed in 1998 to restrict online access to pornography by minors, on the basis that the law violated the 1st Amendment right of free speech.

2005: *Kelo v. City of New London.* The Court ruled that local governments could force property owners to sell their land in order to facilitate private development projects deemed to be economically beneficial to the community.

2006: *Garcetti v. Ceballos.* The Court ruled that the 1st Amendment guarantee of free speech did not protect statements made by public employees in the course of their official duties.

2006: *Hamdan v. Rumsfeld.* The Court ruled that Pres. George W. Bush's system for trying terrorism detainees at the U.S. military base in Guantánamo Bay, Cuba, was unauthorized under federal law and the international Geneva Conventions. The Court furthermore ruled in ***Boumediene v. Bush*** (2008) that detainees had a right to challenge their detention in federal court by applying for a writ of habeas corpus.

2007: *Gonzales v. Carhart*; *Gonzales v. Planned Parenthood Federation of America.* The Court upheld a 2003 federal law prohibiting the abortion procedure known as intact dilation and extraction, or "partial-birth" abortion.

2007: *Parents Involved in Community Schools v. Seattle School District No. 1*; *Meredith v. Jefferson County Board of Education.* The Court ruled that two school districts could not, to encourage diversity, use "racial classifications in making school assignments."

2008: *Crawford v. Marion County Election Board.* The Court upheld the constitutionality of an Indiana law requiring voters to present valid government photo identification.

2008: *District of Columbia v. Heller.* The Court overturned DC's handgun ban, ruling that the 2nd Amendment protected an individual's right to own guns for personal use.

2010: *Citizens United v. Federal Election Commission.* The Court ruled that a federal law barring corporations from using general funds to finance campaign advertisements was unconstitutional. The decision cast doubt on many laws restricting political spending by corporations and unions.

2011: *Snyder v. Phelps.* The justices found that an antigay church whose members protested at the funeral of a Marine could not be held liable for intrusion or the emotional distress of the father of the deceased because the protests were protected by the 1st Amendment.

2012: *U.S. v. Jones.* The Court ruled that attaching a GPS tracking device to a suspect's car and monitoring its movements requires a search warrant, as the 4th Amendment prohibition against unreasonable search and seizure applies.

2012: *Miller v. Alabama.* The Court ruled that mandatory life sentences without the possibility of parole violate juvenile offenders' 8th Amendment right to freedom from cruel and unusual punishment. The decision extended ***Graham v. Florida***, a 2010 case in which the Court held that juveniles may not receive life sentences for crimes that do not result in homicides.

2012: *Natl. Federation of Independent Business v. Sebelius.* The Court ruled Congress acted within its powers of taxation in enacting the individual-mandate provision of the Patient Protection and Affordable Care Act (ACA), which required Americans without government- or employer-provided health insurance to purchase it or pay a fine. The Court ruled unconstitutional the provision of the act's Medicaid expansion that threatened non-compliant states with loss of funding.

2013: *Shelby County v. Holder.* The justices ruled that a key provision of the 1965 Voting Rights Act, meant to prevent discriminatory voting regulations from being enacted, was unconstitutional because it relied on outdated information to identify areas for additional scrutiny.

2013: *U.S. v. Windsor.* The Court struck down the central provision of the 1996 federal Defense of Marriage Act (DOMA), which prohibited federal recognition of same-sex marriages. A separate decision, in ***Hollingsworth v. Perry***, had the effect of legalizing same-sex marriage in California.

2014: *Riley v. California*; *U.S. v. Wurie*. The Court unanimously decided that police generally could not search the mobile telephones of arrested individuals without first obtaining a search warrant.

2014: *Burwell v. Hobby Lobby Stores* and *Conestoga Wood Specialties Corp. v. Burwell*. The justices ruled that some closely held corporations could claim an exemption—based on their owners' religious beliefs and the 1993 Religious Freedom Restoration Act—from a 2010 ACA mandate requiring many businesses to provide health insurance that covers contraception.

See also Year in Review: Notable Supreme Court Decisions.

STATES AND OTHER AREAS OF THE U.S.

Sources: Population: Decennial Censuses and Population Estimates Program, U.S. Census Bureau, U.S. Dept. of Commerce; population as of July 1, 2014, unless otherwise noted. Pop. density is for land area only. **Racial distribution** categories are abbreviated; their full forms are white, black or African American, Asian, American Indian and Alaska Native, Native Hawaiian and Other Pacific Islander, two or more races. Categories may not add up to 100% due to rounding. **Hispanic** or Latino persons may be of any race. **Area:** Geography Division, U.S. Census Bureau, U.S. Dept. of Commerce. **Acres forested:** U.S. Forest Service, U.S. Dept. of Agriculture; source year may vary. **Chief airports:** Federal Aviation Admin., U.S. Dept. of Transportation. Chief airports had 500,000+ boardings in 2014. All **Economy** data as of 2014 unless otherwise noted. **Chief manuf. goods:** Manufacturing and Construction Division, U.S. Census Bureau, U.S. Dept. of Commerce. **Chief crops:** Natl. Agricultural Statistics Service, U.S. Dept. of Agriculture. **Farm income:** Economic Research Service, U.S. Dept. of Agriculture; cash receipts. **Nonfuel minerals:** Office of Mineral Information, U.S. Dept. of Interior; preliminary data. Some states exclude small amounts to avoid disclosing proprietary data. **Commercial fishing:** Natl. Marine Fisheries Service, U.S. Dept. of Commerce. **Gross state product** and **Per cap. pers. income:** Bureau of Economic Analysis, U.S. Dept. of Commerce; as of Dec. 2014. **Sales tax:** Federation of Tax Administrators; as of Jan. 1, 2015. **Gasoline tax:** American Petroleum Institute; as of July 1, 2015; incl. state excise tax, federal excise tax (18.4 cents per gallon), and other state fees. **Employment distrib.** and **Unemployment:** Bureau of Labor Statistics, U.S. Dept. of Labor; distribution is for non-farm jobs as of May 2014. **New private housing:** Manufacturing and Construction Division, U.S. Census Bureau, U.S. Dept. of Commerce. Figures are building permits issued and est. value of the construction. **Broadband Internet:** Industry Analysis and Tech. Division, Fed. Communications Commission. Broadband connections have minimum speeds of at least 768 kilobytes per second (Kbps) downstream and 200 Kbps upstream as of Dec., 2013; figure given is broadband as a percentage of total Internet connections. **Commercial banks** and **Savings institutions:** Federal Deposit Insurance Corp., as of June 30, 2014; FDIC-insured institutions only. **Lottery:** North American Assn. of State and Provincial Lotteries. Data may be unaudited and in some cases were gathered by third party. Some states report round sums; others report exact figures. **Federal employees:** Office of Personnel Mgmt., U.S. Dept. of Labor; as of Dec. 2014. **Education:** Natl. Ctr. for Education Statistics; high school graduation rates as of 2012-13 school year; number of colleges/univ. as of 2013-14. Data for private 4-yr. institutions does not include for-profit colleges/universities. **Energy:** Energy Information Admin., U.S. Dept. of Energy; average per capita monthly electricity consumption and cost for residential customers in 2013. **Tourism:** U.S. Travel Assn.; tourist spending in 2013. Other information from sources in individual states. NA = Not available.

Famous persons lists may include non-natives associated with the state as well as persons born there. **Websites** are subject to change and are not endorsed by *The World Almanac*.

Alabama (AL)

Heart of Dixie, Camellia State

People. Population: 4,849,377; rank: 23. **Pop. change** (2010-14): 1.5%. **Pop. density:** 95.8 per sq mi. **Racial distribution:** 69.7% white; 26.7% black; 1.3% Asian; 0.7% Amer. Ind.; 0.1% Hawaiian/Pacific Islander; 2 or more races, 1.5%. **Hispanic pop.:** 3.8%.

Geography. Total area: 52,420 sq mi; rank: 30. **Land area:** 50,645 sq mi; rank: 28. **Acres forested:** 23.1 mil. **Location:** East South Central state extending N-S from Tennessee to the Gulf of Mexico; E of the Mississippi R. **Climate:** long, hot summers; mild winters; generally abundant rain. **Topography:** coastal plains, including Prairie Black Belt, give way to hills, broken terrain; highest elevation 2,407 ft. **Capital:** Montgomery. **Chief airports:** Birmingham, Huntsville.

Economy. Chief industries: chemicals, electronics, apparel, primary metals, lumber and wood products, food processing, fabricated metals, automotive tires, oil and gas exploration. **Chief manuf. goods:** poultry processing, paper and paperboard, iron and steel, petroleum, automotive tires, aerospace, aluminum, auto body and parts. **Chief crops:** cotton, greenhouse and nursery, hay, peanuts, corn, soybeans. **Farm income:** crops, $1.28 bil; livestock/animal prods., $5.16 bil. **Nonfuel minerals:** $1.1 bil; cement (portland), stone (crushed), lime, sand and gravel (construction), cement (masonry). **Commercial fishing:** $55.6 mil. **Chief port:** Mobile. **Gross state product:** $199.4 bil. **Sales tax:** 4.0%. **Gasoline tax:** 39.27 cents/gal. **Employment distrib.:** 19.6% govt.; 19.2% trade/trans./util.; 12.9% mfg.; 11.7% ed./health; 11.7% prof./bus. serv.; 9.9% leisure/hosp.; 4.9% finance; 4.7% constr./mining/log.; 1.2% info.; 4.1% other serv. **Unemployment:** 6.8%. **Per cap. pers. income:** $37,493. **New private housing:** 13,369 units/$2.2 bil. **Broadband Internet:** 85.5%. **Commercial banks:** 159; deposits: $87.9 bil. **Savings institutions:** 11; deposits: $991.0 mil.

Federal govt. Fed. civ. employees: 38,257; **avg. salary:** $80,155. **Notable fed. facilities:** Redstone Arsenal; Ft. Rucker; Marshall Space Flight Ctr.; Anniston Army Depot; Maxwell AFB and Gunter Annex; Army Corps of Engineers, Mobile District.

Education. High school grad. rate: 80.0%. **4-year public coll./univ.:** 14; **2-yr. public:** 25; **4-yr. private:** 19.

Energy. Electricity use/cost: 1,211 kWh, $136.36.

State data. Motto: Audemus Jura Nostra Defendere (We dare defend our rights). **Flower:** Camellia. **Bird:** Northern flicker (yellowhammer is local nickname). **Tree:** Southern longleaf pine. **Song:** "Alabama." **Entered union:** Dec. 14, 1819; rank: 22nd.

Tourism. Tourist spending: $8.5 bil. **Attractions:** First White House of the Confederacy, Civil Rights Memorial, Alabama Shakespeare Festival, in Montgomery; Ivy Green (Helen Keller birthplace), Tuscumbia; Barber Vintage Motorsports Museum, Civil Rights Institute, Vulcan Park and Museum (world's largest cast iron statue), in Birmingham; G. W. Carver Interpretive Museum, Tuskegee; W. C. Handy Home, Museum, and Library, Frank Lloyd Wright's Rosenbaum House, in Florence; U.S. Space & Rocket Ctr., Huntsville; Moundville Archaeological Park; USS *Alabama* Memorial Park, Mobile; Gulf State Park, Gulf Shores. **Information:** Alabama Tourism Dept., 401 Adams Ave., Ste. 126, P.O. Box 4927, Montgomery, AL 36103; 1-800-ALABAMA, (334) 242-4169; www.alabama.travel

History. Alabama was inhabited by the Creek, Cherokee, Chickasaw, Alabama, and Choctaw peoples when Spanish explorers arrived in the early 1500s. The French made the first permanent settlement at Ft. Louis, 1702, and founded Mobile, 1711. France later gave up the entire region to England under the Treaty of Paris, 1763. Spanish forces took control of the Mobile Bay area, 1780, and it remained under Spanish control until seized by U.S. troops, 1813. Most of present-day Alabama was held by the Creeks until Gen. Andrew Jackson broke their power, 1814. When Alabama became a state, 1819, black slaves made up about one-third of the population. The Indian Removal Act of 1830 forced most remaining Creeks west. The state seceded, 1861, and the Confederate states were organized Feb. 4, at Montgomery, the first capital. The state was readmitted, 1868. Birmingham, founded 1871, became a center for iron- and steelmaking. The Montgomery bus boycott, 1955, sparked by Rosa Parks, helped launch the civil rights movement. Other confrontations occurred at Birmingham, 1963, and Selma, 1965. The leading political figure from the 1960s through the '80s, four-term gov. George Wallace, started as a segregationist but later won with black support. Growth in the auto industry boosted the state economy as the 21st cent. began. A string of tornadoes in western Alabama in Apr. 2011 killed at least 248. Jefferson County, which includes the city of Birmingham, filed for the then-most expensive municipal bankruptcy in history in Nov. 2011.

Famous Alabamians. Hank Aaron, Tallulah Bankhead, Charles Barkley, Hugo L. Black, Paul "Bear" Bryant, George Washington Carver, Nat King Cole, Courteney Cox, William Christopher "W. C." Handy, Polly Holliday, Bo Jackson, Helen Keller, Coretta Scott King, Harper Lee, Joe Louis, Willie Mays, Jim Nabors, Jesse Owens, Terrell Owens, Rosa Parks, Condoleezza Rice, Lionel Richie, Octavia Spencer, Channing Tatum, George C. Wallace, Booker T. Washington, Hank Williams.

Website. www.alabama.gov

Alaska (AK)

The Last Frontier (unofficial)

People. Population: 736,732; rank: 48. **Pop. change** (2010-14): 3.7%. **Pop. density:** 1.3 per sq mi. **Racial distribution:** 66.9% white; 3.9% black; 6.1% Asian; 14.8% Amer. Ind.; 1.3% Hawaiian/Pacific Islander; 2 or more races, 7.1%. **Hispanic pop.:** 5.3%.

Geography. Total area: 665,384 sq mi; rank: 1. **Land area:** 570,641 sq mi; rank: 1. **Acres forested:** 15.3 mil. **Location:** NW corner of North America, bordered on E by Canada.

Climate: SE, SW, and central regions, moist and mild; far N extremely dry. Extended summer days, winter nights throughout. **Topography:** includes Pacific and Arctic mountain systems, central plateau, and Arctic slope. Denali, formerly Mt. McKinley, 20,320 ft, is the highest point in N. America. **Capital:** Juneau. **Chief airport:** Anchorage.

Economy. Chief industries: petroleum, tourism, fishing, mining, forestry, transportation, aerospace. **Chief manuf. goods:** petroleum, seafood. **Chief crops:** greenhouse products, barley, oats, hay, potatoes, carrots. **Farm income:** crops, $26.22 mil; livestock/animal prods., $5.78 mil. **Nonfuel minerals:** $3.5 bil; zinc, gold, lead, silver, sand and gravel (construction). **Commercial fishing:** $1.9 bil. **Chief ports:** Anchorage, Dutch Harbor, Kodiak, Juneau, Sitka, Valdez. **Gross state product:** $57.1 bil. **Sales tax:** none. **Gasoline tax:** 30.65 cents/gal. **Employment distrib.:** 24.3% govt.; 20.3% trade/trans./util.; 3.2% mfg.; 14.1% ed./health; 8.6% prof./bus. serv.; 10.2% leisure/hosp.; 3.4% finance; 10.5% constr./mining/log.; 1.8% info.; 3.5% other serv. **Unemployment:** 6.8%. **Per cap. pers. income:** $52,901. **New private housing:** 1,518 units/$353.7 mil. **Broadband Internet:** 86.2%. **Commercial banks:** 6; deposits: $10.4 bil. **Savings institutions:** 1; deposits: $268.0 mil.

Federal govt. Fed. civ. employees: 10,609; **avg. salary:** $78,447. **Notable fed. facilities:** Joint Base Elmendorf-Richardson; Ft. Wainwright; Eielson AFB; Ft. Greely.

Education. High school grad. rate: 71.8%. **4-year public coll./univ.:** 3; **2-yr. public:** 3; **4-yr. private:** 2.

Energy. Electricity use/cost: 632 kWh, $114.56.

State data. Motto: North to the future. **Flower:** Forget-me-not. **Bird:** Willow ptarmigan. **Tree:** Sitka spruce. **Song:** "Alaska's Flag." **Entered union:** Jan. 3, 1959; rank: 49th.

Tourism. Tourist spending: $2.4 bil. **Attractions:** Portage Glacier, in Chugach Natl. Forest; Mendenhall Glacier, in Tongass Natl. Forest; Totem Heritage Ctr., Ketchikan; Glacier Bay Natl. Park and Preserve; Denali (formerly Mt. McKinley, N. America's highest peak), in Denali Natl. Park and Preserve; Mt. Roberts Tramway, Juneau; Alaska Maritime Natl. Wildlife Refuge; St. Michael's Cathedral, Alaska Raptor Ctr., in Sitka; White Pass & Yukon Route railroad, Skagway; Katmai Natl. Park and Preserve; Univ. of Alaska Museum of the North, Fairbanks. **Information:** Alaska Travel Industry Association, 2600 Cordova St., Ste. 201, Anchorage, AK 99503; 1-800-327-9372; www.travelalaska.com

History. Early inhabitants included the Tlingit-Haida and Athabascan peoples. Ancestors of the Aleut and Inuit (Eskimo) probably arrived from Siberia between 10,000 and 6,000 years ago. Vitus Bering, a Dane sailing for Russia, was the first European to land in Alaska, 1741. Russians, pursuing the fur trade, established a permanent settlement on Kodiak Island, 1784. Sec. of State William H. Seward bought Alaska from Russia for $7.2 mil in 1867, a deal some called "Seward's Folly." Discovery of gold in the Klondike region of Canada's Yukon Territory, 1896, triggered an Alaskan gold rush. Alaska became a territory, 1912, and a state, 1959. A huge oil find at Prudhoe Bay, 1968, led to construction of the Trans-Alaska Pipeline, 1974-77. The *Exxon Valdez* supertanker ran aground, 1989, spilling about 11 mil gallons of crude oil; the cleanup cost more than $2.2 bil. Repeated attempts by Congress members to pass a bill permitting oil and gas drilling in the Arctic National Wildlife Refuge have failed.

Famous Alaskans. Tom Bodett, Susan Butcher, Ernest Gruening, Jewel (Kilcher), Tony Knowles, Sydney Laurence, Sarah Palin, Libby Riddles, Curt Schilling, Jefferson "Soapy" Smith.

Website. www.alaska.gov

Arizona (AZ)

Grand Canyon State

People. Population: 6,731,484; rank: 15. **Pop. change** (2010-14): 5.3%. **Pop. density:** 59.3 per sq mi. **Racial distribution:** 83.7% white; 4.7% black; 3.3% Asian; 5.3% Amer. Ind.; 0.3% Hawaiian/Pacific Islander; 2 or more races, 2.7%. **Hispanic pop.:** 28.2%.

Geography. Total area: 113,990 sq mi; rank: 6. **Land area:** 113,594 sq mi; rank: 6. **Acres forested:** 18.6 mil. **Location:** southwestern U.S. **Climate:** clear and dry in southern regions and northern plateau; high central areas have heavy winter snows. **Topography:** Colorado Plateau in the N, containing the Grand Canyon; Mexican Highlands run NW to SE; Sonoran Desert in the SW. **Capital:** Phoenix. **Chief airports:** Phoenix, Tucson, Mesa.

Economy. Chief industries: manufacturing, construction, tourism, mining, agriculture. **Chief manuf. goods:** aerospace, semiconductors, navigational instruments, cement, plastics, structural metals, dairy, printing, furniture. **Chief crops:** cotton, grapes, apples, lettuce, hay, potatoes, sorghum, barley, corn, wheat. **Farm income:** crops, $2.02 bil; livestock/animal prods., $2.38 bil. **Nonfuel minerals:** $8.1 bil; copper, molybdenum concentrates, sand and gravel (construction), cement (portland), stone (crushed). **Gross state product:** $284.2 bil. **Sales tax:** 5.6%. **Gasoline tax:** 37.40 cents/gal. **Employment distrib.:** 15.8% govt.; 18.8% trade/trans./util.; 6.0% mfg.; 15.0% ed./health; 15.0% prof./bus. serv.; 11.5% leisure/hosp.; 7.4% finance; 5.4% constr./mining/log.; 1.7% info.; 3.6% other serv. **Unemployment:** 6.9%. **Per cap. pers. income:** $37,895. **New private housing:** 26,997 units/$5.7 bil. **Broadband Internet:** 84.7%. **Commercial banks:** 61; deposits: $94.4 bil. **Savings institutions:** 6; deposits: $2.9 bil. **Lottery:** total sales: $724.0 mil; profit: $175.4 mil.

Federal govt. Fed. civ. employees: 30,643; **avg. salary:** $67,972. **Notable fed. facilities:** Luke AFB; Davis-Monthan AFB; Ft. Huachuca; Yuma Proving Ground.

Education. High school grad. rate: 75.1%. **4-year public coll./univ.:** 8; **2-yr. public:** 20; **4-yr. private:** 13.

Energy. Electricity use/cost: 1,049 kWh, $122.85.

State data. Motto: Ditat Deus (God enriches). **Flower:** Blossom of the saguaro cactus. **Bird:** Cactus wren. **Tree:** Paloverde. **Song:** "Arizona." **Entered union:** Feb. 14, 1912; rank: 48th.

Tourism. Tourist spending: $16.6 bil. **Attractions:** Grand Canyon; Painted Desert, in Grand Canyon and Petrified Forest Natl. Parks; Glen Canyon Natl. Recreation Area; Canyon de Chelly Natl. Monument; Meteor Crater, near Winslow; London Bridge, Lake Havasu City; Biosphere 2, Oracle; Navajo Natl. Monument; Tombstone historic mining town; Tempe Town Lake. **Information:** Arizona Office of Tourism, 1110 W. Washington St., Ste. 155, Phoenix, AZ 85007; 1-866-275-5816; www.visitarizona.com

History. Paleo-Indians hunted large game in the area at least 12,000 years ago. Anasazi, Mogollon, and Hohokam civilizations lived there c. 300 BCE-1300 CE; Navajo and Apache came c. 15th cent. Marcos de Niza, a Franciscan, and Estevanico, a black former slave, explored, 1539; Spanish explorer Francisco Vásquez de Coronado visited, 1540. Eusebio Francisco Kino, a Jesuit missionary, taught Indians, 1692-1711, and left missions. Tubac, a Spanish fort, became the first European settlement, 1752. Spain ceded Arizona to Mexico, 1821. The U.S. took over, 1848, after the Mexican War. The area below the Gila R. came from Mexico in the Gadsden Purchase, 1853. Arizona became a territory, 1863. Apache wars ended with Geronimo's surrender, 1886. Arizona became a state, 1912, and grew rapidly after 1960 with a fourfold rise in population over the next four decades. Barry Goldwater was a leading conservative voice in the U.S. Senate (1953-65, 1969-87). The border with Mexico is a major gateway for illegal immigration to the U.S. In 2012, the U.S. Supreme Court struck down most provisions of a 2010 state immigration law that allowed police to make warrantless arrests of those reasonably suspected of having immigrated illegally, but left a provision requiring police to check the immigration status of those stopped or arrested for any other reason.

Famous Arizonans. Bruce Babbitt, Cochise, Alice Cooper, Geronimo, Gabrielle Giffords, Barry Goldwater, Zane Grey, Carl Hayden, George W. P. Hunt, Helen Hull Jacobs, Bil Keane, Percival Lowell, John McCain, John J. Rhodes, Linda Ronstadt, Emma Stone, Morris K. Udall, Stewart L. Udall, Frank Lloyd Wright.

Website. www.az.gov

Arkansas (AR)

Natural State, Razorback State

People. Population: 2,966,369; rank: 32. **Pop. change** (2010-14): 1.7%. **Pop. density:** 57.0 per sq mi. **Racial distribution:** 79.7% white; 15.6% black; 1.5% Asian; 1.0% Amer. Ind.; 0.3% Hawaiian/Pacific Islander; 2 or more races, 1.9%. **Hispanic pop.:** 6.3%.

Geography. Total area: 53,179 sq mi; rank: 29. **Land area:** 52,035 sq mi; rank: 27. **Acres forested:** 19 mil. **Location:** West South Central state. **Climate:** long, hot summers, mild winters; generally abundant rainfall. **Topography:** eastern delta and prairie, southern lowland forests, and the northwestern highlands, which include the Ozark Plateaus. **Capital:** Little Rock. **Chief airports:** Little Rock, Bentonville.

Economy. Chief industries: manufacturing, agriculture, tourism, forestry. **Chief manuf. goods:** poultry processing, motor vehicles and parts, iron and steel, paper and paperboard, plastics, preserved fruits and vegetables, aerospace, rubber. **Chief crops:** rice, soybeans, cotton, hay, wheat, corn, sorghum, tomatoes, peaches, watermelons, pecans, blueberries, grapes. **Farm income:** crops, $4.65 bil; livestock/animal prods., $5.75 bil. **Nonfuel minerals:** $1.0 bil; cement (portland), stone (crushed), bromine, sand and gravel (industrial), sand and gravel (construction). **Chief port:** Helena. **Gross state product:** $121.4 bil. **Sales tax:** 6.5%. **Gasoline tax:** 40.20 cents/gal. **Employment distrib.:** 17.8% govt.; 20.4% trade/trans./util.; 12.7% mfg.; 14.5% ed./health; 11.4% prof./bus. serv.; 9.6% leisure/hosp.; 4.2% finance; 4.7% constr./mining/log.; 1.1% info.; 3.6% other serv. **Unemployment:** 6.1%. **Per cap. pers. income:** $37,751. **New private housing:** 7,666 units/$1.3 bil. **Broadband Internet:** 88.8%. **Commercial banks:** 133; deposits: $53.2 bil. **Savings institutions:** 4; deposits: $624.0 mil. **Lottery:** total sales: $410.1 mil; profit: $81.5 mil.

Federal govt. Fed. civ. employees: 13,182; **avg. salary:** $66,437. **Notable fed. facilities:** Little Rock AFB; Pine Bluff Arsenal; Natl. Ctr. for Toxicological Research, Jefferson.

Education. High school grad. rate: 84.9%. **4-year public coll./univ.:** 11; **2-yr. public:** 22; **4-yr. private:** 12.

Energy. Electricity use/cost: 1,133 kWh, $108.64.

State data. Motto: Regnat Populus (The people rule). **Flower:** Apple blossom. **Bird:** Mockingbird. **Tree:** Pine. **Song:** "Arkansas." **Entered union:** June 15, 1836; rank: 25th.

Tourism. Tourist spending: $6.3 bil. **Attractions:** Eureka Springs; Ozark Folk Ctr. State Park, Mountain View; Blanchard Springs Caverns, in Ozark Natl. Forest; Crater of Diamonds State Park, Murfreesboro; Toltec Mounds Archeological State Park, Scott; Buffalo Natl. River; Hot Springs Natl. Park; Pea Ridge Natl. Military Park; William J. Clinton Presidential Library and Museum, Little Rock Central High School Natl. Historic Site, in Little Rock; Crystal Bridges Museum of American Art, Bentonville. **Information:** Arkansas Dept. of Parks & Tourism, 1 Capitol Mall, Little Rock, AR 72201; 1-800-NATURAL; www.arkansas.com

History. Quapaw, Caddo, Osage, Cherokee, and Choctaw peoples lived in the area at the time of European contact. The first European explorers were Hernando de Soto, 1541; Jacques Marquette and Louis Jolliet, 1673; and René-Robert Cavelier, sieur de La Salle, 1682. French fur trader Henri de Tonty founded the first settlement, 1686, at Arkansas Post. In 1762, the area was ceded by France to Spain, then given back, 1800, and was part of the Louisiana Purchase, 1803. It was made a territory, 1819, and entered the Union as a slave state, 1836. Arkansas seceded in 1861, after the Civil War began; it was readmitted, 1868. Pres. Eisenhower sent federal troops, 1957, to keep Gov. Orval Faubus from blocking racial integration at Central High School in Little Rock. Wal-Mart, now the world's leading retailer, opened its first store in Rogers, 1962. Elected five times as governor, Bill Clinton later served two terms as president (1993-2001). His presidential library opened, 2004, in Little Rock.

Famous Arkansans. Daisy Bates, Dee Brown, Paul "Bear" Bryant, Glen Campbell, Hattie Wyatt Caraway, Johnny Cash, Wesley Clark, Bill Clinton, Jay Hanna "Dizzy" Dean, Orval Faubus, James William Fulbright, Al Green, John Grisham, Levon Helm, John H. Johnson, Douglas MacArthur, John Little McClellan, James S. McDonnell, Scottie Pippen, Dick Powell, Brooks Robinson, Winthrop Rockefeller, Mary Steenburgen, Edward Durell Stone, Billy Bob Thornton, Sam Walton, Archibald Yell.

Website. www.arkansas.gov

California (CA)

Golden State

People. Population: 38,802,500; rank: 1. **Pop. change** (2010-14): 4.2%. **Pop. density:** 249.1 per sq mi. **Racial distribution:** 73.2% white; 6.5% black; 14.4% Asian; 1.7% Amer. Ind.; 0.5% Hawaiian/Pacific Islander; 2 or more races, 3.7%. **Hispanic pop.:** 36.1%.

Geography. Total area: 163,695 sq mi; rank: 3. **Land area:** 155,779 sq mi; rank: 3. **Acres forested:** 32.1 mil. **Location:** western coast of U.S. **Climate:** moderate temperatures and rainfall along the coast; extremes in the interior. **Topography:** long mountainous coastline; central valley; Sierra Nevada on the E; desert basins in southern interior; rugged mountains in N. **Capital:** Sacramento. **Chief airports:** Los Angeles, San Francisco, San Diego, Oakland, San Jose, Santa Ana, Sacramento, Ontario, Burbank, Long Beach, Palm Springs, Fresno.

Economy. Chief industries: agriculture, tourism, apparel, electronics, telecommunications, entertainment. **Chief manuf. goods:** petroleum, aerospace, precision instruments, semiconductors, telecom. and broadcasting equip., pharmaceutical, wineries, plastics, medical equip., preserved fruits and vegetables, printing, dairy, cut and sew apparel, motor vehicles. **Chief crops:** grapes, nursery products, almonds, lettuce, hay, strawberries, floriculture, tomatoes, cotton, oranges, pistachios, walnuts, broccoli, carrots, rice, peaches, lemons. **Farm income:** crops, $38.66 bil; livestock/animal prods., $15.32 bil. **Nonfuel minerals:** $3.5 bil; sand and gravel (construction), cement (portland), boron minerals, stone (crushed), gold. **Commercial fishing:** $255.4 mil. **Chief ports:** Long Beach, Los Angeles, San Diego, Port Hueneme, Richmond, Oakland, San Francisco, Stockton. **Gross state product:** $2.3 tril. **Sales tax:** 7.5%. **Gasoline tax:** 60.75 cents/gal. **Employment distrib.:** 15.5% govt.; 18.1% trade/trans./util.; 7.9% mfg.; 15.5% ed./health; 15.8% prof./bus. serv.; 11.4% leisure/hosp.; 4.9% finance; 4.6% constr./mining/log.; 2.9% info.; 3.4% other serv. **Unemployment:** 7.5%. **Per cap. pers. income:** $50,109. **New private housing:** 83,645 units/$18.7 bil. **Broadband Internet:** 89.8%. **Commercial banks:** 235; deposits: $1.1 tril. **Savings institutions:** 20; deposits: $15.4 bil. **Lottery:** total sales: $5.0 bil; profit: $1.4 bil.

Federal govt. Fed. civ. employees: 136,401; **avg. salary:** $81,337. **Notable fed. facilities:** USMC Camp Pendleton; Naval Base Coronado; Marine Corps Air Ground Combat Ctr., 29 Palms; Marine Corps Air Station Miramar; Travis AFB; Naval Research Lab, Monterey; Lawrence Livermore Natl. Lab; Lawrence Berkeley Natl. Lab; NASA Jet Propulsion Lab; Edwards AFB (NASA Dryden Flight Research Ctr., AF Test Ctr.); San Francisco Mint.

Education. High school grad. rate: 80.4%. **4-year public coll./univ.:** 35; **2-yr. public:** 114; **4-yr. private:** 140.

Energy. Electricity use/cost: 557 kWh, $90.19.

State data. Motto: Eureka (I have found it). **Flower:** Golden poppy. **Bird:** California valley quail. **Tree:** California redwood. **Song:** "I Love You, California." **Entered union:** Sept. 9, 1850; rank: 31st.

Tourism. Tourist spending: $116.0 bil. **Attractions:** *Queen Mary*, Aquarium of the Pacific, in Long Beach; Palomar Observatory, Palomar Mountain; Disneyland Resort, Anaheim; Getty Center, Universal Studios Hollywood, Griffith Observatory, in Los Angeles; Tournament of Roses and Rose Bowl, Pasadena; The California Museum, California State Railroad Museum, in Sacramento; San Diego Zoo, USS *Midway* Museum, in San Diego; Yosemite Valley; Lassen Volcanic, Sequoia, and Kings Canyon Natl. Parks; Mojave and Sonoran Deserts; Death Valley; Golden Gate Park, Alcatraz Island, in San Francisco; Napa Valley wine region; Monterey Bay Aquarium, Monterey Peninsula; Ancient Bristlecone Pine Forest (oldest known living trees on Earth), in Inyo Natl. Forest; Redwood Natl. and State Parks; Muir Woods Natl. Monument, Mill Valley. **Information:** California Tourism, P.O. Box 1499, Sacramento, CA 95812-1499; 1-877-225-4367; www.visitcalifornia.com

History. Early inhabitants included more than 100 different Native American tribes with multiple dialects. The first European explorers were Juan Rodríguez Cabrillo, 1542, and Sir Francis Drake, 1579. The first settlement was the Spanish Alta California mission at San Diego, 1769, first in a string founded by Franciscan Father Junípero Serra. California became a province of independent Mexico, 1821. U.S. traders and settlers arrived in the 19th cent. and staged the Bear Flag revolt, 1846, in protest against Mexican rule; later that year U.S. forces occupied California. At the end of the Mexican War, Mexico ceded the territory to the U.S., 1848; that same year gold was discovered, and the famed gold rush began. California became a state, 1850. An economic downturn in the 1870s spurred riots against Chinese immigrants, who had come as laborers in the boom years. An earthquake and related fires devastated San Francisco, 1906. During World War II, Japanese Americans, many of them U.S. citizens, were held in detention camps, 1942-45. Ronald Reagan, a former movie actor, became state governor (1967-75) and U.S. president (1981-89). A budget crisis, 2003, resulted in the recall of Gov. Gray Davis and the election of another actor, Arnold Schwarzenegger. Led by Hollywood in entertainment and Silicon Valley in technology, the state's economy dwarfs that of most nations. Still, billion-dollar budget deficits have been a perennial problem. As much of the state entered the fourth year of a devastating drought, Gov. Jerry Brown Apr. 1, 2015, ordered a mandatory statewide reduction in water use for residents and businesses.

Famous Californians. Tom Brady, Edmund G. (Pat) Brown, Jerry Brown, Luther Burbank, Julia Child, Ted Danson, Cameron Diaz, Leonardo DiCaprio, Joe DiMaggio, Landon Donovan, Clint Eastwood, Dianne Feinstein, John C. Fremont, Tom Hanks, Bret Harte, William Randolph Hearst, Helen Hunt, Steve Jobs, Jimmie Johnson, Angelina Jolie, Jack Kemp, Jason Kidd, Lisa Leslie, Monica Lewinsky, Jack London, George Lucas, Phil Mickelson, Marilyn Monroe, John Muir, Richard M. Nixon, Gwyneth Paltrow, George S. Patton Jr., Gregory Peck, Nancy Pelosi, Ronald Reagan, Sally K. Ride, William Saroyan, Arnold Schwarzenegger, Father Junípero Serra, O. J. Simpson, Kevin Spacey, Leland Stanford, Gwen Stefani, John Steinbeck, Shirley Temple, Earl Warren, Serena Williams, Ted Williams, Venus Williams, Tiger Woods.

Website. www.ca.gov

Colorado (CO)

Centennial State

People. Population: 5,355,866; rank: 22. **Pop. change** (2010-14): 6.5%. **Pop. density:** 51.7 per sq mi. **Racial distribution:** 87.7% white; 4.5% black; 3.1% Asian; 1.6% Amer. Ind.; 0.2% Hawaiian/Pacific Islander; 2 or more races, 2.9%. **Hispanic pop.:** 19.4%.

Geography. Total area: 104,094 sq mi; rank: 8. **Land area:** 103,642 sq mi; rank: 8. **Acres forested:** 22.9 mil. **Location:** W central U.S. **Climate:** low relative humidity, abundant sunshine, wide daily/seasonal temperature ranges; alpine conditions in the high mountains. **Topography:** eastern dry high plains; hilly to mountainous central plateau; western Rocky Mts. of high ranges with broad valleys, deep, narrow canyons. **Capital:** Denver. **Chief airports:** Denver, Colorado Springs.

Economy. Chief industries: manufacturing, construction, government, tourism, agriculture, aerospace, electronics equip. **Chief manuf. goods:** animal slaughtering, beer, petroleum, pharmaceuticals, aerospace, medical equip., precision instruments, printing, semiconductors. **Chief crops:** hay, corn, potatoes, wheat, onions, dry edible beans, sunflowers, sugar beets, barley, proso millet, cabbage, peaches, lettuce, apples, cantaloupes. **Farm income:** crops, $2.22 bil; livestock/animal prods., $5.24 bil. **Nonfuel minerals:** $2.3 bil; molybdenum concentrates, sand and gravel (construction), cement (portland), gold, stone (crushed). **Gross state product:** $306.7 bil. **Sales tax:** 2.9%. **Gasoline tax:** 40.40 cents/gal. **Employment distrib.:** 16.9% govt.; 17.1% trade/trans./util.; 5.5% mfg.; 12.5% ed./health; 15.5% prof./bus. serv.; 12.1% leisure/hosp.; 6.2% finance; 7.5% constr./mining/log.; 2.7% info.; 4.0% other serv. **Unemployment:** 5.0%. **Per cap. pers. income:** $48,730. **New private housing:** 28,686 units/$6.5 bil. **Broadband Internet:** 87.2%. **Commercial banks:** 135; deposits: $106.9 bil. **Savings institutions:** 13; deposits: $2.5 bil. **Lottery:** total sales: $545.0 mil; profit: $130.1 mil.

Federal govt. Fed. civ. employees: 35,727; **avg. salary:** $79,822. **Notable fed. facilities:** U.S. Air Force Academy; Peterson AFB; Denver Mint; Ft. Carson; Natl. Renewable Energy Lab; Transportation Tech. Ctr.; NORAD and USNORTHCOM Alt. Command Ctr., Cheyenne Mtn. Complex; Denver Federal Ctr.; Natl. Ctr. for Atmospheric Research; Natl. Inst. of Standards & Tech., Boulder; Natl. Wildlife Research Ctr.; NOAA Earth System Environmental Lab.

Education. High school grad. rate: 76.9%. **4-year public coll./univ.:** 14; **2-yr. public:** 14; **4-yr. private:** 15.

Energy. Electricity use/cost: 712 kWh, $84.91.

State data. Motto: Nil Sine Numine (Nothing without Providence). **Flower:** Rocky Mountain columbine. **Bird:** Lark bunting. **Tree:** Colorado blue spruce. **Songs:** "Where the Columbines Grow"; "Rocky Mountain High." **Entered union:** Aug. 1, 1876; rank: 38th.

Tourism. Tourist spending: $16.7 bil. **Attractions:** Denver Museum of Nature & Science, Denver Botanic Gardens, Denver Zoo; Red Rocks Park and Amphitheatre, Morrison; Natl. Ctr. for Atmospheric Research, Boulder; Rocky Mountain, Black Canyon of the Gunnison, and Mesa Verde (Anasazi cliff dwellings) Natl. Parks; Aspen, Breckenridge, Steamboat, and Vail ski resorts; Garden of the Gods, Colorado Springs; Great Sand Dunes Natl. Park and Preserve; Dinosaur and Colorado Natl. Monuments; Pikes Peak and Mount Evans; Grand Mesa Natl. Forest; historic mining towns of Central City, Silverton, Cripple Creek; Bent's Old Fort Natl. Historic Site, near La Junta; Georgetown Loop Historic Mining and Railroad Park; Durango & Silverton Narrow Gauge Railroad Museum, Durango; Cumbres & Toltec Scenic Railroad, Antonito; gambling in Black Hawk, Central City, Cripple Creek and on tribal land in Ignacio and Towaoc. **Information:** Colorado Tourism Office, 1625 Broadway, Ste. 1700, Denver, CO 80202; 1-800-COLORADO; www.colorado.com

History. Paleo-Indians hunted big game in the area at least 11,000 years ago. Anasazi cliff dwellers flourished around Mesa Verde until about 1300 CE; other Native Americans were the Ute, Pueblo, Cheyenne, and Arapaho. The region was claimed by Spain but passed to France, 1800. The U.S. acquired eastern Colorado in the Louisiana Purchase, 1803. Lt. Zebulon M. Pike explored the area, 1806, sighting the peak that bears his name. After the Mexican War, 1846-48, U.S. immigrants settled in the east, former Mexicans in the south. Gold was discovered in 1858, causing a population boom. Congress created Colorado Territory, 1861. Conflict between newcomers and displaced Native Americans led to the Sand Creek Massacre, 1864, in which U.S. soldiers and settlers killed some 150 Cheyenne and Arapaho. U.S. Army troops forced the removal to reservations (mostly in present-day Oklahoma) of most Native Americans in the state, 1867. The 1870s brought statehood, 1876, and rich silver finds that turned Leadville into a boomtown. Federal military and civilian employment in Colorado surged in the 1940s and '50s; since then, tourism and technology have fueled the economy. The state's Hispanic population grew from 5.8% in 1980 to 20.7% in 2010. Colorado became the first state in the U.S. to legalize the sale of recreational marijuana in Jan. 2014. The state raised $63 mil in tax revenue from combined medical and recreational marijuana sales in 2014.

Famous Coloradans. Tim Allen, Chauncey Billups, Frederick Bonfils, Molly Brown, William N. Byers, M. Scott Carpenter, Lon Chaney, Jack Dempsey, Mamie Eisenhower, Douglas Fairbanks, Barney Ford, Roy Halladay, Chief Ourey, Trey Parker, "Baby Doe" Tabor, Lowell Thomas, Byron R. White, Paul Whiteman.

Website. www.colorado.gov

Connecticut (CT)

Constitution State, Nutmeg State

People. Population: 3,596,677; rank: 29. **Pop. change** (2010-14): 0.6%. **Pop. density:** 742.8 per sq mi. **Racial distribution:** 81.2% white; 11.5% black; 4.5% Asian; 0.5% Amer. Ind.; 0.1% Hawaiian/Pacific Islander; 2 or more races, 2.2%. **Hispanic pop.:** 13.3%.

Geography. Total area: 5,543 sq mi; rank: 48. **Land area:** 4,842 sq mi; rank: 48. **Acres forested:** 1.8 mil. **Location:** New England state in NE corner of U.S. **Climate:** moderate; winters avg. slightly below freezing; warm, humid summers. **Topography:** western upland, the Berkshires, in the NW, highest elevations; narrow central lowland N-S; hilly eastern upland drained by rivers. **Capital:** Hartford. **Chief airport:** Windsor Locks.

Economy. Chief industries: manufacturing, retail trade, government, services, finances, insurance, real estate. **Chief manuf. goods:** aerospace, chemicals, fabricated metals, precision instruments, toiletries, medical equip., printing, plastics. **Chief crops:** nursery stock, Christmas trees, mushrooms, sweet corn, apples, tobacco, hay. **Farm income:** crops, $381.71 mil; livestock/animal prods., $247.67 mil. **Nonfuel minerals:** $202 mil; stone (crushed), sand and gravel (construction), clays (common), gemstones (natural). **Commercial fishing:** $14.6 mil. **Chief ports:** New Haven, Bridgeport, New London. **Gross state product:** $253.0 bil. **Sales tax:** 6.35%. **Gasoline tax:** 59.26 cents/gal. **Employment distrib.:** 14.3% govt.; 18.0% trade/trans./util.; 9.4% mfg.; 19.4% ed./health; 12.7% prof./bus. serv.; 9.4% leisure/hosp.; 7.6% finance; 3.5% constr./mining/log.; 1.9% info.; 3.7% other serv. **Unemployment:** 6.6%. **Per cap. pers. income:** $62,467. **New private housing:** 5,329 units/$1.1 bil. **Broadband Internet:** 87.2%. **Commercial banks:** 32; deposits: $78.6 bil. **Savings institutions:** 32; deposits: $34.6 bil. **Lottery:** total sales: $1.1 bil; profit: $319.5 mil.

Federal govt. Fed. civ. employees: 7,998; **avg. salary:** $81,414. **Notable fed. facilities:** U.S. Coast Guard Academy; Naval Sub Base New London.

Education. High school grad. rate: 85.5%. **4-year public coll./univ.:** 9; **2-yr. public:** 12; **4-yr. private:** 19.

Energy. Electricity use/cost: 752 kWh, $132.07.

State data. Motto: Qui Transtulit Sustinet (He who transplanted still sustains). **Flower:** Mountain laurel. **Bird:** American robin. **Tree:** White oak. **Song:** "Yankee Doodle." **Fifth** of the 13 original states to ratify the Constitution, Jan. 9, 1788.

Tourism. Tourist spending: $10.0 bil. **Attractions:** Mark Twain House and Museum, Hartford; Yale Univ. Art Gallery, Peabody Museum of Natural History, in New Haven; Mystic Seaport, Mystic Aquarium; Barnum Museum, Bridgeport; Gillette Castle State Park, East Haddam; USS *Nautilus* (1st nuclear-powered submarine) at Submarine Force Library and Museum, Groton; Mashantucket Pequot Museum and Research Ctr.; Foxwoods Resort Casino, Ledyard; Mohegan Sun, Uncasville; Lake Compounce (est. 1846; oldest continuously operating amusement park in U.S.), Bristol; Philip Johnson Glass House, New Canaan. **Information:** Connecticut Commission on Culture and Tourism, One Constitution Plz., 2nd Fl., Hartford, CT 06103; 1-888-CTVISIT, (860) 256-2800; www.ctvisit.com

History. At the time of European contact, inhabitants of the area were Algonquian peoples, including the Mohegan and Pequot. Dutch explorer Adriaen Block was the first European visitor, 1614. By 1634, settlers from Plymouth Bay had started colonies along the Connecticut R.; in 1637 they defeated the Pequots. The Colony of Connecticut was chartered by England, 1662; New Haven colony was added, 1665. A Patriot stronghold in the American Revolution, the state actively supported the antislavery movement and the Union cause in the Civil War. The state economy prospered in the 20th cent. from insurance- and defense-related industries. *Nautilus*, the first nuclear-powered submarine, was launched at Groton, 1954. Connecticut Sen. Joseph Lieberman was the Democratic nominee for vice president in 2000. American Indian casinos, starting with Foxwoods in 1992, were an economic boon to the state, but tourism revenues declined sharply with the recession that began in late 2007. Twenty children and six staff members were killed in a mass shooting at Sandy Hook Elementary School in Newtown, Dec. 14, 2012.

Famous "Nutmeggers." Ethan Allen, P. T. Barnum, Michael Bolton, Glenn Close, Samuel Colt, Ann Coulter, Jonathan Edwards, Nathan Hale, Katharine Hepburn, Isaac Hull, Norman Lear, Seth MacFarlane, John Mayer, Robert Mitchum, J. P. Morgan, Ralph Nader, Israel Putnam, Wallace Stevens, Harriet Beecher Stowe, Mark Twain, Noah Webster, Eli Whitney.

Website. www.ct.gov

Delaware (DE)

First State, Diamond State

People. Population: 935,614; rank: 45. **Pop. change** (2010-14): 4.2%. **Pop. density:** 480.0 per sq mi. **Racial distribution:** 70.8% white; 22.2% black; 3.8% Asian; 0.7% Amer. Ind.; 0.1% Hawaiian/Pacific Islander; 2 or more races, 2.5%. **Hispanic pop.:** 7.8%.

Geography. Total area: 2,489 sq mi; rank: 49. **Land area:** 1,949 sq mi; rank: 49. **Acres forested:** 0.4 mil. **Location:** Delmarva Peninsula on the Atlantic coastal plain. **Climate:** moderate. **Topography:** Piedmont Plateau to the N, sloping to a near sea-level plain. **Capital:** Dover.

Economy. Chief industries: chemicals, agriculture, finance, poultry, shellfish, tourism, auto assembly, food processing, transportation equip. **Chief manuf. goods:** pharmaceuticals, poultry processing, soap and cleaning compounds, precision instruments, basic chemicals, plastics. **Chief crops:** soybeans, corn, greenhouse and nursery, wheat, potatoes, barley, hay, watermelons, lima beans, green peas, pumpkins, mushrooms, cabbage. **Farm income:** crops, $315.21 mil; livestock/animal prods., $1.16 bil. **Nonfuel minerals:** $14.4 mil; sand and gravel (construction), magnesium compounds, stone (crushed), gemstones (natural). **Commercial fishing:** $7.4 mil. **Chief port:** Wilmington. **Gross state product:** $62.8 bil. **Sales tax:** none. **Gasoline tax:** 41.40 cents/gal. **Employment distrib.:** 14.9% govt.; 17.7% trade/trans./util.; 5.7% mfg.; 16.6% ed./health; 13.7% prof./bus. serv.; 11.1% leisure/hosp.; 10.3% finance; 4.7% constr./mining/log.; 1.0% info.; 4.2% other serv. **Unemployment:** 5.7%. **Per cap. pers. income:** $45,942. **New private housing:** 5,194 units/$615.5 mil. **Broadband Internet:** 85.9%. **Commercial banks:** 36; deposits: $412.0 bil. **Savings institutions:** 5; deposits: $3.5 bil. **Lottery:** total sales: $597.2 mil; profit: $214.5 mil.

Federal govt. Fed. civ. employees: 3,125; **avg. salary:** $69,731. **Notable fed. facilities:** Dover AFB; Bombay Hook National Wildlife Refuge.

Education. High school grad. rate: 80.4%. **4-year public coll./univ.:** 2; **2-yr. public:** 3; **4-yr. private:** 4.

Energy. Electricity use/cost: 944 kWh, $122.25.

State data. Motto: Liberty and independence. **Flower:** Peach blossom. **Bird:** Blue hen chicken. **Tree:** American holly. **Song:** "Our Delaware." **First** of original 13 states to ratify the Constitution, Dec. 7, 1787.

Tourism. Tourist spending: $1.8 bil. **Attractions:** Fort Christina (site of founding of colony of New Sweden), Holy Trinity (Old Swedes) Church (erected 1698, oldest church in U.S. still standing as built and in use), Hagley Museum and Library, Nemours Mansion and Gardens, in Wilmington; Winterthur Museum, Garden, and Library, near Wilmington; New Castle Historic District; John Dickinson "Penman of the Revolution" Plantation, First State Heritage Park, Dover Intl. Speedway, in Dover; Rehoboth Beach. **Information:** Delaware Tourism Office, 99 Kings Hwy., Dover, DE 19901; 1-866-2VISITDE; www.visitdelaware.com

History. The Lenni Lenape (Delaware) people lived in the region at the time of European contact. Henry Hudson located the Delaware R., 1609. In 1610, English explorer Samuel Argall entered Delaware Bay and named the area after Virginia's governor, Lord De La Warr. Dutch, Swedish, and Finnish settlers were followed by the British, who took control in 1664. After 1682, Delaware became part of Pennsylvania, and in 1704 it was granted its own assembly. It adopted a constitution as the state of Delaware, 1776, and was the first state to ratify the federal Constitution, 1787. Although it remained in the Union during the Civil War, Delaware retained slavery until the 13th Amendment abolished it in 1865. The DuPont company, founded as a gunpowder mill in 1802, became an industrial giant in the 20th cent. making nylon, Teflon, and other synthetics. Pro-business laws drew many out-of-state firms to incorporate in Delaware. In 2000, Ruth Ann Minner was elected Delaware's first woman governor.

Famous Delawareans. Thomas F. Bayard, Joseph Biden, Henry Seidel Canby, E. I. du Pont, John P. Marquand, Howard Pyle, Caesar Rodney, Susan Stroman.

Website. www.delaware.gov

Florida (FL)

Sunshine State

People. Population: 19,893,297; rank: 3. **Pop. change** (2010-14): 5.8%. **Pop. density:** 371.0 per sq mi. **Racial distribution:** 77.8% white; 16.8% black; 2.8% Asian; 0.5% Amer. Ind.; 0.1% Hawaiian/Pacific Islander; 2 or more races, 2.0%. **Hispanic pop.:** 21.2%.

Geography. Total area: 65,758 sq mi; rank: 22. **Land area:** 53,625 sq mi; rank: 26. **Acres forested:** 17.3 mil. **Location:** peninsula jutting southward 500 mi between the Atlantic and Gulf of Mexico. **Climate:** subtropical N of Bradenton-Lake Okeechobee-Vero Beach line; tropical S of line. **Topography:** land is flat or rolling; highest point is 345 ft in the NW. **Capital:** Tallahassee. **Chief airports:** Miami, Orlando, Fort Lauderdale, Tampa, Fort Myers, West Palm Beach, Jacksonville, Sanford, Pensacola, Clearwater, Sarasota.

Economy. Chief industries: tourism, agriculture, manufacturing, construction, services, international trade. **Chief manuf. goods:** navigational instruments, medical equip., cement, broadcasting equip., beverages, phosphatic fertilizer, preserved fruits and vegetables, structural metal, printing. **Chief crops:** greenhouse and nursery, oranges, sugarcane, tomatoes, green peppers, grapefruit, strawberries, snap beans, sweet corn, potatoes, cucumbers, tangerines. **Farm income:** crops, $5.83 bil; livestock/animal prods., $2.38 bil. **Nonfuel minerals:** $3.0 bil; phosphate rock, stone (crushed), cement (portland), sand and gravel (construction), cement (masonry). **Commercial fishing:** $230.2 mil. **Chief ports:** Pensacola, Tampa, Port Manatee, Miami, Port Everglades, Jacksonville, Canaveral. **Gross state product:** $839.9 bil. **Sales tax:** 6.0%. **Gasoline tax:** 54.82 cents/gal. **Employment distrib.:** 13.5% govt.; 20.6% trade/trans./util.; 4.1% mfg.; 14.9% ed./health; 14.9% prof./bus. serv.; 14.2% leisure/hosp.; 6.6% finance; 5.3% constr./mining/log.; 1.7% info.; 4.2% other serv. **Unemployment:** 6.3%. **Per cap. pers. income:** $42,645. **New private housing:** 84,075 units/$19.5 bil. **Broadband Internet:** 93.0%. **Commercial banks:** 242; deposits: $437.1 bil. **Savings institutions:** 25; deposits: $25.3 bil. **Lottery:** total sales: $5.4 bil; profit: $1.5 bil.

Federal govt. Fed. civ. employees: 74,916; **avg. salary:** $75,266. **Notable fed. facilities:** John F. Kennedy Space Ctr.; Eglin AFB; MacDill AFB; Hurlburt Field; Pensacola NAS; Jacksonville NAS; Mayport Naval Sta.

Education. High school grad. rate: 75.6%. **4-year public coll./univ.:** 36; **2-yr. public:** 5; **4-yr. private:** 61.

Energy. Electricity use/cost: 1,078 kWh, $121.53.

State data. Motto: In God we trust. **Flower:** Orange blossom. **Bird:** Mockingbird. **Tree:** Sabal palmetto palm. **Song:** "Old Folks at Home." **Entered union:** Mar. 3, 1845; rank: 27th.

Tourism. Tourist spending: $78.7 bil. **Attractions:** Miami Beach; Castillo de San Marcos Natl. Monument, St. Augustine Lighthouse & Museum, Lightner Museum, in St. Augustine (oldest permanent European settlement in U.S.); Walt Disney World Resort, SeaWorld Orlando, Universal Studios, Discovery Cove, in Orlando; Kennedy Space Ctr., U.S. Astronaut Hall of Fame; Everglades Natl. Park; Ringling Museum of Art, Ringling Circus Museum, in Sarasota; Cypress Gardens at Legoland Florida, Winter Haven; Busch Gardens, Big Cat Rescue, in Tampa; Florida Caverns State Park, Marianna; Key West. **Information:** Visit Florida, 2540 W. Executive Center Cir., Ste. 200, Tallahassee, FL 32301; 1-888-7FLA-USA; www.visitflorida.com

History. Florida has been inhabited for at least 12,000 years. Timucua, Apalachee, and Calusa peoples were living in the region when the earliest Europeans came; later the Seminole migrated from Georgia to Florida, becoming dominant there in the early 18th cent. The first European to see Florida was Ponce de León, 1513. France established a colony, Ft. Caroline, on the St. Johns R., 1564. Spain settled St. Augustine, 1565, and Spanish troops massacred most of the French. Britain's Sir Francis Drake burned St. Augustine, 1586. In 1763, Spain ceded Florida to Great Britain, which held the area 20 years before returning it to Spain. Florida was ceded to the U.S. in the Adams-Onís Treaty, 1819. The Seminole War, 1835-42, resulted in the removal of most Native Americans to Indian Territory. Florida joined the Union in 1845, seceded in 1861, and was readmitted in 1868. In the late 19th cent., hotel and railroad builder Henry M. Flagler laid the foundations of the tourism industry. The state experienced phenomenal population growth in the 20th cent., especially after 1950. The first U.S. astronaut was launched into space from Cape Canaveral, 1961. Walt Disney World opened near Orlando, 1971. Hurricane Andrew slammed Florida, 1992, causing at least $25 bil in property damage. A dispute over Florida's presidential vote in 2000 was decided by the U.S. Supreme Court and resulted in George W. Bush's Electoral College victory. Four hurricanes hit the state in 2004, causing more than $40 bil in damages.

Famous Floridians. Edna Buchanan, Jeb Bush, Marjory Stoneman Douglas, Henry Morrison Flagler, Carl Hiaasen, Perez Hilton, Zora Neale Hurston, James Weldon Johnson, Deacon Jones, MacKinlay Kantor, Osceola, Claude Pepper, Tom Petty, Henry B. Plant, A. Philip Randolph, Marjorie Kinnan Rawlings, Janet Reno, Marco Rubio, Deion Sanders, Emmitt Smith, Joseph W. Stilwell, Amar'e Stoudemire, Charles P. Summerall.

Website. www.myflorida.com

Georgia (GA)

Empire State of the South, Peach State

People. Population: 10,097,343; rank: 8. **Pop. change** (2010-14): 4.2%. **Pop. density:** 175.6 per sq mi. **Racial distribution:** 62.1% white; 31.5% black; 3.8% Asian; 0.5% Amer. Ind.; 0.1% Hawaiian/Pacific Islander; 2 or more races, 2.0%. **Hispanic pop.:** 8.5%.

Geography. Total area: 59,425 sq mi; rank: 24. **Land area:** 57,513 sq mi; rank: 21. **Acres forested:** 24.7 mil. **Location:** South Atlantic state. **Climate:** maritime tropical air masses dominate in summer; polar air masses in winter; E central area drier. **Topography:** most southerly of the Blue Ridge Mts. cover NE and N central; central Piedmont extends to the fall line of rivers; coastal plain levels to the coast flatlands. **Capital:** Atlanta. **Chief airports:** Atlanta, Savannah.

Economy. Chief industries: services, manufacturing, retail trade. **Chief manuf. goods:** carpet and rugs, animal slaughtering and processing, motor vehicles and parts, plastics, aircrafts, paper, chemicals, food. **Chief crops:** cotton, greenhouse and nursery, peanuts, pecans, corn, tomatoes, cucumbers, onions, watermelons, tobacco, squash, blueberries, hay, cabbage, soybeans, peaches, snap beans, wheat. **Farm income:** crops, $3.44 bil; livestock/animal prods., $6.67 bil. **Nonfuel minerals:** $1.6 bil; clays (kaolin), stone (crushed), cement (portland), clays (fuller's earth), sand and gravel (construction). **Commercial fishing:** $11.8 mil. **Chief ports:** Savannah, Brunswick. **Gross state product:** $476.5 bil. **Sales tax:** 4.0%. **Gasoline tax:** 51.02 cents/gal. **Employment distrib.:** 16.0% govt.; 21.0% trade/trans./util.; 8.7% mfg.; 12.7% ed./health; 15.2% prof./bus. serv.; 10.8% leisure/hosp.; 5.5% finance; 3.9% constr./mining/log.; 2.5% info.; 3.6% other serv. **Unemployment:** 7.2%. **Per cap. pers. income:** $39,097. **New private housing:** 39,423 units/$6.5 bil. **Broadband Internet:** 86.9%. **Commercial banks:** 242; deposits: $193.4 bil. **Savings institutions:** 17; deposits: $3.6 bil. **Lottery:** total sales: $4.0 bil; profit: $945.1 mil.

Federal govt. Fed. civ. employees: 70,229; **avg. salary:** $74,828. **Notable fed. facilities:** Ft. Benning; Ft. Stewart; Fed. Law Enforcement Training Ctr.; Robins AFB; Ft. Gordon; Naval Sub Base Kings Bay; Moody AFB; Centers for Disease Control; Marine Corps Logistics Base Albany.

Education. High school grad. rate: 71.7%. **4-year public coll./univ.:** 27; **2-yr. public:** 30; **4-yr. private:** 33.

Energy. Electricity use/cost: 1,088 kWh, $124.67.

State data. Motto: Wisdom, justice, and moderation. **Flower:** Cherokee rose. **Bird:** Brown thrasher. **Tree:** Live oak. **Song:** "Georgia on My Mind." **Fourth** of the 13 original states to ratify the Constitution, Jan. 2, 1788.

Tourism. Tourist spending: $25.0 bil. **Attractions:** Georgia State Capitol, Stone Mountain, Centennial Olympic Park, Six Flags Over Georgia, Martin Luther King Jr. Natl. Historic Site, Jimmy Carter Library and Museum, Atlanta Botanical Garden, Georgia Aquarium (largest in Western Hemisphere), in Atlanta; Kennesaw Mountain Natl. Battlefield Park; Chickamauga and Chattanooga Natl. Military Park; Chattahoochee-Oconee Natl. Forest; Dahlonega, site of earliest U.S. gold rush; Brasstown Bald (highest mtn. in state); Franklin D. Roosevelt's Little White House Historic Site, Warm Springs; Callaway Gardens, Pine Mountain; Andersonville Natl. Historic Site (Confederate military prison); Okefenokee Natl. Wildlife Refuge; Jekyll, St. Simons, and Cumberland barrier islands; Savannah Historic District. **Information:** Dept. of Economic Development, 75 Fifth St., NW, Ste. 1200, Atlanta, GA 30308; 1-800-VISITGA; www.exploregeorgia.org

History. Creek and Cherokee peoples were living in the region when Spaniards founded Santa Catalina mission, 1566, on Saint Catherines Island. Gen. James Oglethorpe established a colony at Savannah, 1733, for the poor and religiously persecuted. Oglethorpe defeated a Spanish army from Florida at Bloody Marsh, 1742. Georgia was a battleground in the American Revolution, with the British finally evacuating Savannah in 1782. When Georgia entered the Union, 1788, its plantation economy relied on slaves for rice and cotton growing. The Cherokee were removed to Indian Territory, 1838-39, and thousands died on the long march, known as the Trail of Tears. By 1860 the number of slaves exceeded 462,000 (nearly 44% of the total population). Georgia seceded from the Union, 1861, and was invaded by Union forces, 1864, under Gen. William T. Sherman, who took Atlanta, Sept. 2, and proceeded on his famous "march to the sea," ending in Savannah in Dec. Georgia was readmitted, 1870. Born 1929 in Atlanta, Martin Luther King Jr. made the city his base during the civil rights struggles of the 1960s. Atlanta became the leading city of the "New South," world headquarters of Coca-Cola and CNN, and host of the 1996 Summer Olympic Games. Hispanics are a rapidly growing economic and political force in the state. Eight Atlanta educators received prison sentences in Apr. 2015 for conspiring to elevate students' scores on standardized tests.

Famous Georgians. Kim Basinger, Griffin Bell, James Brown, Erskine Caldwell, Jimmy Carter, Ray Charles, Ty Cobb, James Dickey, Walt Frazier, John C. Fremont, Newt Gingrich, Nancy Grace, Joel Chandler Harris, "Doc" Holliday, Larry Holmes, Holly Hunter, Alan Jackson, Martin Luther King Jr., Gladys Knight, Sidney Lanier, Little Richard, Juliette Gordon Low, Margaret Mitchell, Jessye Norman, Sam Nunn, Flannery O'Connor, Otis Redding, Burt Reynolds, Julia Roberts, Jackie Robinson, Ryan Seacrest, Clarence Thomas, Travis Tritt, Ted Turner, Carl Vinson, Alice Walker, Herschel Walker, Joanne Woodward, Trisha Yearwood, Andrew Young.

Website. www.georgia.gov

Hawai'i (HI)

Aloha State

People. Population: 1,419,561; rank: 40. **Pop. change** (2010-14): 4.4%. **Pop. density:** 221.0 per sq mi. **Racial distribution:** 26.7% white; 2.5% black; 37.5% Asian; 0.4% Amer. Ind.; 10.0% Hawaiian/Pacific Islander; 2 or more races, 23.0%. **Hispanic pop.:** 8.5%.

Geography. Total area: 10,932 sq mi; rank: 43. **Land area:** 6,423 sq mi; rank: 47. **Acres forested:** 1.7 mil. **Location:**

Pacific archipelago of hundreds of islands 2,000 mi SW of U.S. mainland. **Climate:** subtropical, with wide variations in rainfall; Mt. Waialeale, on Kaua'i, wettest spot in U.S. (annual rainfall 422 in.). **Topography:** islands are tops of a chain of submerged volcanic mountains; Mauna Loa, Kilauea are active volcanoes. **Capital:** Honolulu. **Chief airports:** Honolulu, Kahului, Kailua Kona, Lihue, Hilo.

Economy. Chief industries: tourism, defense, sugar, pineapples. **Chief manuf. goods:** concrete, printing, baked goods, sugar, preserved fruits and vegetables, apparel. **Chief crops:** flowers and nursery, pineapples, seed crops, sugarcane, macadamia nuts, coffee, algae, papayas, tomatoes, bananas, basil, ginger. **Farm income:** crops, $566.44 mil; livestock/animal prods., $150.21 mil. **Nonfuel minerals:** $107 mil; stone (crushed), sand and gravel (construction), gemstones (natural). **Commercial fishing:** $108.0 mil. **Chief ports:** Honolulu, Hilo, Barbers Point, Kahului. **Gross state product:** $77.4 bil. **Sales tax:** 4.0%. **Gasoline tax:** 63.50 cents/gal. **Employment distrib.:** 20.1% govt.; 18.9% trade/trans./util.; 2.1% mfg.; 12.7% ed./health; 13.2% prof./bus. serv.; 18.0% leisure/hosp.; 4.4% finance; 5.1% constr./mining/log.; 1.3% info.; 4.4% other serv. **Unemployment:** 4.4%. **Per cap. pers. income:** $46,396. **New private housing:** 3,066 units/$1.0 bil. **Broadband Internet:** 91.2%. **Commercial banks:** 8; deposits: $30.3 bil. **Savings institutions:** 5; deposits: $6.3 bil.

Federal govt. Fed. civ. employees: 21,512; **avg. salary:** $74,518. **Notable fed. facilities:** Joint Base Pearl Harbor-Hickam; Schofield Barracks; Marine Corps Base Hawaii, Kaneohe Bay; Tripler Army Med. Ctr.; Ft. Shafter; Wheeler Army Airfield; Prince Kuhio Federal Bldg.

Education. High school grad. rate: 82.4%. **4-year public coll./univ.:** 4; **2-yr. public:** 6; **4-yr. private:** 7.

Energy. Electricity use/cost: 515 kWh, $190.36.

State data. Motto: Ua mau ke ea o ka aina i ka pono (The life of the land is perpetuated in righteousness). **Flower:** Yellow hibiscus. **Bird:** Hawaiian goose. **Tree:** Kukui (candlenut). **Song:** "Hawai'i Pono'i" (Hawai'i's Own). **Entered union:** Aug. 21, 1959; rank: 50th.

Tourism. Tourist spending: $19.9 bil. **Attractions:** Oahu Isl.: Natl. Memorial Cemetery of the Pacific, Waikiki Beach, Diamond Head, in Honolulu; USS *Arizona* Memorial, Pearl Harbor; Polynesian Cultural Ctr., Laie; Hanauma Bay; Nu'uanu Pali. Kaua'i Isl.: Waimea Canyon. Maui Isl.: Haleakala Natl. Park. Hawai'i Isl.: Hawaii Volcanoes Natl. Park, Wailoa and Wailuku River State Parks. **Information:** Hawaii Visitors and Conventions Bureau, 2270 Kalakaua Ave., Ste. 801, Honolulu, HI 96815; 1-800-GOHAWAII; www.gohawaii.com

History. Polynesians from islands 2,000 mi to the S settled the Hawaiian Islands, probably 300-600 CE. The first European visitor was British captain James Cook, 1778. King Kamehameha I united the islands by 1810. Christian missionaries arrived, 1819, bringing Western culture. Under the reign, 1825-54, of King Kamehameha III, a constitution, legislature, and public school system were instituted. Sugar production began, 1835, and it became the dominant industry. Queen Liliuokalani was deposed, 1893, and a republic was established, 1894, headed by Sanford B. Dole. Annexation by the U.S. came in 1898. The Japanese attack on Pearl Harbor, Dec. 7, 1941, brought the U.S. into World War II. Hawai'i attained statehood, 1959. Hurricane Iniki pounded Kaua'i, 1992, causing about $1 bil in damage. In 2006, Pres. George W. Bush designated the Northwestern Hawaiian Islands Natl. Monument, a marine area of 140,000 sq mi.

Famous Islanders. Bernice Pauahi Bishop, Tia Carrere, Alexander Cartwright, St. Damien de Veuster, Don Ho, Daniel K. Inouye, Duke Kahanamoku, King Kamehameha, Nicole Kidman, Brook Mahealani Lee, Jason Scott Lee, Queen Liliuokalani, Bruno Mars, Bette Midler, Barack Obama, Ellison S. Onizuka, Michelle Wie.

Website. www.ehawaii.gov

Idaho (ID)

Gem State

People. Population: 1,634,464; rank: 39. **Pop. change** (2010-14): 4.3%. **Pop. density:** 19.8 per sq mi. **Racial distribution:** 93.5% white; 0.8% black; 1.4% Asian; 1.7% Amer. Ind.; 0.2% Hawaiian/Pacific Islander; 2 or more races, 2.3%. **Hispanic pop.:** 10.8%.

Geography. Total area: 83,569 sq mi; rank: 14. **Land area:** 82,643 sq mi; rank: 11. **Acres forested:** 21.5 mil. **Location:** northwestern Mountain state bordering British Columbia. **Climate:** tempered by Pacific westerly winds; drier, colder, continental climate in SE; altitude an important factor. **Topography:** Snake R. plains in the S; central region of mountains, canyons, gorges (Hells Canyon, 7,900 ft, deepest in N. America); subalpine northern region. **Capital:** Boise. **Chief airport:** Boise.

Economy. Chief industries: manufacturing, agriculture, tourism, lumber, mining, electronics. **Chief manuf. goods:** computers and electronics, preserved fruits and vegetables, cheese, lumber. **Chief crops:** potatoes, wheat, hay, sugar beets, barley, greenhouse and nursery, onions, dry beans, corn, mint, apples, hops, peaches, lentils, peas, cherries, plums and prunes, oats. **Farm income:** crops, $3.19 bil; livestock/animal prods., $5.47 bil. **Nonfuel minerals:** $1.2 bil; molybdenum concentrates, phosphate rock, sand and gravel (construction), silver, lead. **Chief port:** Lewiston. **Gross state product:** $64.0 bil. **Sales tax:** 6.0%. **Gasoline tax:** 50.40 cents/gal. **Employment distrib.:** 18.2% govt.; 20.1% trade/trans./util.; 9.0% mfg.; 14.2% ed./health; 12.0% prof./bus. serv.; 10.0% leisure/hosp.; 5.2% finance; 6.4% constr./mining/log.; 1.3% info.; 3.6% other serv. **Unemployment:** 4.8%. **Per cap. pers. income:** $37,533. **New private housing:** 8,797 units/$1.7 bil. **Broadband Internet:** 81.1%. **Commercial banks:** 33; deposits: $20.1 bil. **Savings institutions:** 1; deposits: $457.0 mil. **Lottery:** total sales: $208.9 mil; profit: $49.0 mil.

Federal govt. Fed. civ. employees: 8,036; **avg. salary:** $67,237. **Notable fed. facilities:** Idaho Natl. Lab; Mountain Home AFB.

Education. High school grad. rate: NA. **4-year public coll./univ.:** 4; **2-yr. public:** 4; **4-yr. private:** 6.

Energy. Electricity use/cost: 1,055 kWh, $98.35.

State data. Motto: Esto Perpetua (It is perpetual). **Flower:** Syringa. **Bird:** Mountain bluebird. **Tree:** White pine. **Song:** "Here We Have Idaho." **Entered union:** July 3, 1890; rank: 43rd.

Tourism. Tourist spending: $4.2 bil. **Attractions:** Hells Canyon (deepest river gorge in N. America); World Ctr. for Birds of Prey, Boise Art Museum, in Boise; Craters of the Moon Natl. Monument and Preserve; Sun Valley; Shoshone Falls, near Twin Falls; Lava Hot Springs; Lake Coeur d'Alene; Sawtooth Natl. Recreation Area; Frank Church-River of No Return Wilderness Area; Nez Perce Natl. Historical Park. **Information:** Idaho Division of Tourism Development, 700 W. State St., P.O. Box 83720, Boise, ID 83720; 1-800-VISITID; www.visitid.org

History. Paleo-Indian hunters roamed the land over 13,000 years ago; later inhabitants included Shoshone, Northern Paiute, Bannock, and Nez Percé peoples. The Meriwether Lewis and William Clark Expedition took place 1804-06. Next came fur traders, 1809-34, and missionaries, 1830s-50s. Mormons made their first permanent settlement at Franklin, 1860. Idaho's gold rush began the same year and brought thousands of permanent settlers. A series of Indian wars followed, including a remarkable campaign by Chief Joseph and the Nez Percé that ended with his surrender in Montana, 1877. Idaho became a territory, 1863, and a state, 1890. In the 20th cent., it emerged as a leader in potato, lumber, and silver output. The Sun Valley ski resort opened in 1936, boosting tourism. Startup of Lewiston's river port, 1975, opened Idaho to oceangoing trade. Fueled by technology job growth, the state's population jumped 21.2% in 2000-10.

Famous Idahoans. William Borah, Frank Church, Lou Dobbs, Fred Dubois, W. Mark Felt, Chief Joseph, Harmon Killebrew, Ezra Pound, Marilynne Robinson, Sacagawea, Picabo Street, Lana Turner.

Website. www.idaho.gov

Illinois (IL)

Prairie State

People. Population: 12,880,580; rank: 5. **Pop. change** (2010-14): 0.4%. **Pop. density:** 232.0 per sq mi. **Racial distribution:** 77.5% white; 14.7% black; 5.3% Asian; 0.6% Amer. Ind.; 0.1% Hawaiian/Pacific Islander; 2 or more races, 1.8%. **Hispanic pop.:** 15.7%.

Geography. Total area: 57,914 sq mi; rank: 25. **Land area:** 55,519 sq mi; rank: 24. **Acres forested:** 5 mil. **Location:** East North Central state; western, southern, and eastern boundaries formed by Mississippi, Ohio, and Wabash Rivers, respectively. **Climate:** temperate; typically cold, snowy winters, hot summers. **Topography:** prairie and fertile plains throughout; open hills in the southern region. **Capital:** Springfield. **Chief airports:** Chicago (2).

Economy. Chief industries: services, manufacturing, travel, wholesale and retail trade, finance, insurance, real estate, construction, health care, agriculture. **Chief manuf. goods:** food, petroleum, plastics, chemicals, agricultural machinery, pharmaceuticals, motor vehicles, printing. **Chief crops:** corn, soybeans, hay, wheat, greenhouse and nursery, apples, peaches, sorghum. **Farm income:** crops, $15.40 bil; livestock/animal prods., $3.20 bil. **Nonfuel minerals:** $1.5 bil; sand and gravel (industrial), stone (crushed), sand and gravel (construction), cement (portland), tripoli. **Chief port:** Chicago. **Gross state product:** $745.9 bil. **Sales tax:** 6.25%. **Gasoline tax:** 54.39 cents/gal. **Employment distrib.:** 14.1% govt.; 19.9% trade/trans./util.; 9.6% mfg.; 15.2% ed./health; 15.8% prof./bus. serv.; 9.6% leisure/hosp.; 6.1% finance; 3.8% constr./mining/log.; 1.7% info.; 4.3% other serv. **Unemployment:** 7.1%. **Per cap. pers. income:** $48,120. **New private housing:** 20,578 units/$4.2 bil. **Broadband Internet:** 89.8%. **Commercial banks:** 512; deposits: $412.1 bil. **Savings institutions:** 77; deposits: $22.4 bil. **Lottery:** total sales: $2.8 bil; profit: $815.4 mil.

Federal govt. Fed. civ. employees: 41,307; **avg. salary:** $80,952. **Notable fed. facilities:** Great Lakes Naval Station; Fermi Natl. Accelerator Lab; Argonne Natl. Lab; Scott AFB; Rock Island Arsenal.

Education. High school grad. rate: 83.2%. **4-year public coll./univ.:** 12; **2-yr. public:** 48; **4-yr. private:** 80.

Energy. Electricity use/cost: 755 kWh, $80.57.

State data. Motto: State sovereignty, national union. **Flower:** Native violet. **Bird:** Cardinal. **Tree:** White oak. **Song:** "Illinois." **Entered union:** Dec. 3, 1818; rank: 21st.

Tourism. Tourist spending: $34.6 bil. **Attractions:** Art Institute of Chicago, Field Museum of Natural History, Shedd Aquarium, Millennium Park, Navy Pier, in Chicago; Illinois State Museum, Abraham Lincoln Presidential Library and Museum, in Springfield; Cahokia Mounds State Historic Site, Collinsville; Starved Rock State Park; Crab Orchard Natl. Wildlife Refuge; Forts Kaskaskia, de Chartres, Massac; Shawnee Natl. Forest; Dickson Mounds Museum, Lewistown. **Information:** Illinois Bureau of Tourism, 100 W. Randolph St., Ste. 3-400, Chicago, IL 60601; 1-800-2CONNECT; www.enjoyillinois.com

History. The region has been inhabited for at least 10,000 years; seminomadic Algonquian peoples, including the Peoria, Illinois, Kaskaskia, and Tamaroa, lived there at the time of European contact. Fur traders were the first Europeans in Illinois, followed shortly by Louis Jolliet and Jacques Marquette, 1673, and René-Robert Cavelier, sieur de La Salle, 1680, who built a fort near present-day Peoria. French priests established the first permanent settlements at Cahokia, near present-day St. Louis, 1699, and Kaskaskia, 1703. France ceded the area to Britain, 1763, and in 1778, American Gen. George Rogers Clark took Kaskaskia from the British without a shot. Illinois became a separate territory, 1809, and a state, 1818. Defeat of Native American tribes in the Black Hawk War, 1832, and canal, rail, and road construction brought rapid change. Mormon settlers at Nauvoo, 1839, met with hostility, and a Carthage mob killed Mormon leader Joseph Smith and his brother, 1844. The Great Chicago Fire, 1871, destroyed the city's downtown. Illinois became a center for the labor movement, leading to bitter conflicts such as the Haymarket riot, 1886, and Pullman strike, 1894. Social reformer Jane Addams founded Hull House, 1889, to aid immigrants and the poor. As manufacturing expanded, 1900-70, many African Americans arrived from the southern U.S. Chicago police violently suppressed antiwar protests at the 1968 Democratic National Convention. Dennis Hastert was the longest serving Republican Speaker of the House, 1999-2007. Barack Obama, elected in 2004, was only the fifth African American to serve in the U.S. Senate; he became the 44th U.S. president in 2009. Political corruption and criminality have plagued the state for decades; since 1960, five former governors have been charged with criminal offenses.

Famous Illinoisans. Jane Addams, Saul Bellow, John Belushi, Jack Benny, Ray Bradbury, Gwendolyn Brooks, St. Frances Xavier Cabrini, Al Capone, Hillary Rodham Clinton, Clarence Darrow, John Deere, Stephen A. Douglas, Katherine Dunham, Wyatt Earp, Roger Ebert, James T. Farrell, Marshall Field, Harrison Ford, Betty Friedan, Benny Goodman, Ulysses S. Grant, Dennis Hastert, Hugh Hefner, Ernest Hemingway, Charlton Heston, Jennifer Hudson, Henry J. Hyde, Abraham Lincoln, Vachel Lindsay, David Mamet, Edgar Lee Masters, Oscar Mayer, Cyrus McCormick, Eliot Ness, Bob Newhart, Michelle Obama, Ronald Reagan, Shonda Rhimes, Donald Rumsfeld, Carl Sandburg, Shel Silverstein, Adlai E. Stevenson, James Watson, Frank Lloyd Wright, Philip K. Wrigley.

Website. www.illinois.gov

Indiana (IN)

Hoosier State

People. Population: 6,596,855; rank: 16. **Pop. change** (2010-14): 1.7%. **Pop. density:** 184.1 per sq mi. **Racial distribution:** 86.1% white; 9.6% black; 2.0% Asian; 0.4% Amer. Ind.; 0.1% Hawaiian/Pacific Islander; 2 or more races, 1.9%. **Hispanic pop.:** 5.9%.

Geography. Total area: 36,420 sq mi; rank: 38. **Land area:** 35,826 sq mi; rank: 38. **Acres forested:** 4.9 mil. **Location:** East North Central state; Lake Michigan on N border. **Climate:** four distinct seasons with temperate climate. **Topography:** hilly southern region; fertile rolling plains of central region; flat, heavily glaciated N; dunes along Lake Michigan shore. **Capital:** Indianapolis. **Chief airport:** Indianapolis.

Economy. Chief industries: manufacturing, services, agriculture, government, wholesale and retail trade, transportation and public utilities. **Chief manuf. goods:** motor vehicles and parts, iron and steel mills, pharmaceuticals, petroleum, plastics, medical equip., printing. **Chief crops:** corn, soybeans, greenhouse and nursery, wheat, hay, tomatoes, watermelons, apples. **Farm income:** crops, $8.45 bil; livestock/animal prods., $4.29 bil. **Nonfuel minerals:** $818 mil; stone (crushed), cement (portland), lime, sand and gravel (construction), cement (masonry). **Chief ports:** Burns Harbor-Portage, Mt. Vernon, Jeffersonville. **Gross state product:** $317.8 bil. **Sales tax:** 7.0%. **Gasoline tax:** 54.04 cents/gal. **Employment distrib.:** 14.3% govt.; 19.5% trade/trans./util.; 16.9% mfg.; 14.6% ed./health; 10.7% prof./bus. serv.; 10.1% leisure/hosp.; 4.2% finance; 4.3% constr./mining/log.; 1.2% info.; 4.2% other serv. **Unemployment:** 6.0%. **Per cap. pers. income:** $39,433. **New private housing:** 17,816 units/$3.2 bil. **Broadband Internet:** 87.5%. **Commercial banks:** 130; deposits: $101.7 bil. **Savings institutions:** 35; deposits: $6.3 bil. **Lottery:** total sales: $1.0 bil; profit: $250.7 mil.

Federal govt. Fed. civ. employees: 22,017; **avg. salary:** $71,119. **Notable fed. facilities:** Nav. Surface Warfare Ctr., Crane Div.; Grissom Air Reserve Base.

Education. High school grad. rate: 87.0%. **4-year public coll./univ.:** 15; **2-yr. public:** 1; **4-yr. private:** 39.

Energy. Electricity use/cost: 1,005 kWh, $110.44.

State data. Motto: Crossroads of America. **Flower:** Peony. **Bird:** Cardinal. **Tree:** Tulip poplar. **Song:** "On the Banks of the Wabash, Far Away." **Entered union:** Dec. 11, 1816; rank: 19th.

Tourism. Tourist spending: $10.1 bil. **Attractions:** Lincoln Boyhood Natl. Memorial, Lincoln City; George Rogers Clark Natl. Historical Park, Vincennes; Tippecanoe Battlefield Museum and Park, Battle Ground; Benjamin Harrison Presidential Site, Indianapolis Motor Speedway and Hall of Fame Museum, Indianapolis Museum of Art, in Indianapolis; Indiana Dunes Natl. Lakeshore, Chesterton; College Football Hall of Fame, Studebaker Natl. Museum, in South Bend; Hoosier Natl. Forest. **Information:** Indiana Office of Tourism Development, 1 North Capital, Ste. 600, Indianapolis, IN 46204; 1-800-677-9800; www.visitindiana.com

History. When the Europeans arrived, Miami, Potawatomi, Kickapoo, Piankashaw, Wea, and Shawnee peoples inhabited the region. René-Robert Cavelier, sieur de La Salle, visited the present South Bend area, 1679 and 1681. The first French fort was built near present-day Lafayette, 1717. A French trading post was established, 1731-32, at Vincennes. France ceded the area to Britain, 1763. During the American Revolution, American Gen. George Rogers Clark captured Vincennes, 1778, and defeated British forces, 1779. Indiana became a territory, 1800, and a state, 1816. The Miami were beaten, 1794, at Fallen Timbers, and Gen. William H. Harrison defeated Tecumseh's Indian confederation, 1811, at Tippecanoe. Manufacturing grew rapidly after the Civil War. U.S. Steel founded Gary, 1906. An automotive test track was the site of the first Indianapolis 500 race, 1911. The auto industry remains key to the state economy; in 2008, Honda opened a $550-mil plant near Greensburg. Heavy rain in June 2008 flooded southwest and central Indiana. Some rights groups and businesses criticized the state's Religious Freedom Restoration Act as discriminatory to LGBT individuals; the legislature passed an amended version of the bill in response.

Famous "Hoosiers." Larry Bird, Ambrose Burnside, Meg Cabot, Hoagy Carmichael, Jim Davis, James Dean, Eugene V. Debs, John Dillinger, Theodore Dreiser, Paul Dresser, Jeff Gordon, Benjamin Harrison, Gil Hodges, Michael Jackson, David Letterman, Carole Lombard, Marjorie Main, John Mellencamp,

Jane Pauley, Cole Porter, Gene Stratton Porter, Ernie Pyle, Dan Quayle, James Whitcomb Riley, Oscar Robertson, Red Skelton, Tony Stewart, Booth Tarkington, Kurt Vonnegut, Lew Wallace, Ryan White, Wendell L. Willkie, Wilbur Wright.

Website. www.in.gov

Iowa (IA)

Hawkeye State

People. Population: 3,107,126; rank: 30. **Pop. change** (2010-14): 2.0%. **Pop. density:** 55.6 per sq mi. **Racial distribution:** 92.1% white; 3.4% black; 2.2% Asian; 0.5% Amer. Ind.; 0.1% Hawaiian/Pacific Islander; 2 or more races, 1.7%. **Hispanic pop.:** 4.9%.

Geography. Total area: 56,273 sq mi; rank: 26. **Land area:** 55,857 sq mi; rank: 23. **Acres forested:** 3 mil. **Location:** West North Central state bordered by Mississippi R. on the E, Missouri R. on the W. **Climate:** humid, continental. **Topography:** watershed from NW to SE; soil especially rich and land level in the N central counties. **Capital:** Des Moines. **Chief airports:** Des Moines, Cedar Rapids.

Economy. Chief industries: agriculture, communications, construction, finance, insurance, trade, services, manufacturing. **Chief manuf. goods:** machinery, vegetable oils, animal slaughtering and processing, laundry equip., plastics, motor vehicles and parts. **Chief crops:** corn, soybeans, hay, greenhouse and nursery, oats. **Farm income:** crops, $14.04 bil; livestock/animal prods., $16.88 bil. **Nonfuel minerals:** $757 mil; stone (crushed), cement (portland), sand and gravel (industrial), sand and gravel (construction), lime. **Gross state product:** $170.6 bil. **Sales tax:** 6.0%. **Gasoline tax:** 50.40 cents/gal. **Employment distrib.:** 16.7% govt.; 20.0% trade/trans./util.; 13.7% mfg.; 14.4% ed./health; 8.7% prof./bus. serv.; 9.2% leisure/hosp.; 6.6% finance; 5.3% constr./mining/log.; 1.6% info.; 3.9% other serv. **Unemployment:** 4.4%. **Per cap. pers. income:** $45,115. **New private housing:** 10,256 units/$1.9 bil. **Broadband Internet:** 85.5%. **Commercial banks:** 341; deposits: $73.1 bil. **Savings institutions:** 8; deposits: $2.6 bil. **Lottery:** total sales: $314.0 mil; profit: $73.9 mil.

Federal govt. Fed. civ. employees: 8,514; **avg. salary:** $67,435. **Notable fed. facilities:** Ames Lab; Natl. Animal Disease Ctr.

Education. High school grad. rate: 89.7%. **4-year public coll./univ.:** 3; **2-yr. public:** 16; **4-yr. private:** 34.

Energy. Electricity use/cost: 908 kWh, $100.30.

State data. Motto: Our liberties we prize, and our rights we will maintain. **Flower:** Wild rose. **Bird:** Eastern goldfinch. **Tree:** Oak. **Song:** "The Song of Iowa." **Entered union:** Dec. 28, 1846; rank: 29th.

Tourism. Tourist spending: $8.0 bil. **Attractions:** Des Moines Art Ctr., Iowa State Fairgrounds, Iowa State Capitol, in Des Moines; Natl. Czech & Slovak Museum & Library, Cedar Rapids; Herbert Hoover Natl. Historic Site, Presidential Library and Museum, in West Branch; Effigy Mounds Natl. Monument, Marquette; Amana Colonies; Figge Art Museum, Davenport; Living History Farms, Urbandale; Adventureland, Altoona; Boone & Scenic Valley Railroad and Museum; riverboat cruises and casino gambling, Mississippi and Missouri Rivers; Iowa Great Lakes, Okoboji; American Gothic House, Eldon; *Field of Dreams* movie site, Dyersville; Natl. Mississippi River Museum & Aquarium, Dubuque. **Information:** Iowa Tourism Office, Iowa Dept. of Economic Development, 200 E. Grand Ave., Des Moines, IA 50309; 1-888-472-6035; www.traveliowa.com

History. Early inhabitants were Mound Builders who dwelt on Iowa's fertile plains. Later, Iowa and Yankton Sioux lived in the area. The first Europeans, Jacques Marquette and Louis Jolliet, gave France its claim to the area, 1673. In 1762, France ceded the region to Spain, but Napoleon took it back, 1800. It became part of the U.S. through the Louisiana Purchase, 1803. Native American Sauk and Fox tribes moved into the area but relinquished their land in defeat after the 1832 uprising led by Sauk chieftain Black Hawk. Iowa became a territory in 1838 and entered as a free state, 1846, strongly supporting the Union. Fertile land lured farmers from eastern states, 1850-1900, and the population rose rapidly. Growth slowed in the 20th cent., as farming became mechanized. Surging demand for ethanol fuel from Iowa corn contributed more than $2.6 bil to the state economy in 2005. Severe flooding in eastern Iowa in June 2008 caused billions of dollars in damages and forced the evacuation of thousands of residents.

Famous Iowans. Tom Arnold, Johnny Carson, William F. "Buffalo Bill" Cody, Mamie Dowd Eisenhower, Michael Emerson, Bob Feller, George Gallup, Susan Glaspell, James Norman Hall, Herbert Hoover, Shawn Johnson, Ashton Kutcher, Ann Landers, Cloris Leachman, Glenn Miller, Lillian Russell, Billy Sunday, James A. Van Allen, Abigail Van Buren, Carl Van Vechten, Henry Wallace, Kurt Warner, John Wayne, Meredith Willson, Elijah Wood, Grant Wood.

Website. www.iowa.gov

Kansas (KS)

Sunflower State

People. Population: 2,904,021; rank: 34. **Pop. change** (2010-14): 1.8%. **Pop. density:** 35.5 per sq mi. **Racial distribution:** 86.8% white; 6.3% black; 2.8% Asian; 1.2% Amer. Ind.; 0.1% Hawaiian/Pacific Islander; 2 or more races, 2.8%. **Hispanic pop.:** 10.3%.

Geography. Total area: 82,278 sq mi; rank: 15. **Land area:** 81,759 sq mi; rank: 13. **Acres forested:** 2.5 mil. **Location:** West North Central state with Missouri R. on E. **Climate:** temperate but continental, with great extremes between summer and winter. **Topography:** hilly Osage Plains in the E; central region level prairie and hills; high plains in the W. **Capital:** Topeka. **Chief airport:** Wichita.

Economy. Chief industries: manufacturing, finance, insurance, real estate, services. **Chief manuf. goods:** animal slaughtering, aerospace, petroleum, plastics, machinery, navigational instruments, printing. **Chief crops:** wheat, corn, soybeans, hay, sorghum, sunflowers, cotton, potatoes. **Farm income:** crops, $5.85 bil; livestock/animal prods., $10.47 bil. **Nonfuel minerals:** $1.0 bil; helium (Grade A), cement (portland), salt, stone (crushed), helium (crude). **Chief port:** Kansas City. **Gross state product:** $147.1 bil. **Sales tax:** 6.15%. **Gasoline tax:** 42.43 cents/gal. **Employment distrib.:** 18.6% govt.; 18.8% trade/trans./util.; 11.5% mfg.; 13.7% ed./health; 12.1% prof./bus. serv.; 9.1% leisure/hosp.; 5.7% finance; 5.2% constr./mining/log.; 2.0% info.; 3.5% other serv. **Unemployment:** 4.5%. **Per cap. pers. income:** $45,546. **New private housing:** 7,459 units/$1.4 bil. **Broadband Internet:** 87.0%. **Commercial banks:** 314; deposits: $59.6 bil. **Savings institutions:** 15; deposits: $7.0 bil. **Lottery:** total sales: $258.1 mil; profit: $74.3 mil.

Federal govt. Fed. civ. employees: 15,971; **avg. salary:** $68,107. **Notable fed. facilities:** Ft. Riley; Leavenworth Fed. Pen.; McConnell AFB; Colmery-O'Neil VA Medical Ctr.; Dwight D. Eisenhower VA Medical Ctr.

Education. High school grad. rate: 85.7%. **4-year public coll./univ.:** 8; **2-yr. public:** 25; **4-yr. private:** 24.

Energy. Electricity use/cost: 926 kWh, $107.85.

State data. Motto: Ad Astra per Aspera (To the stars through difficulties). **Flower:** Native sunflower. **Bird:** Western meadowlark. **Tree:** Cottonwood. **Song:** "Home on the Range." **Entered union:** Jan. 29, 1861; rank: 34th.

Tourism. Tourist spending: $7.0 bil. **Attractions:** Eisenhower Presidential Library and Museum, Abilene; Natl. Agricultural Ctr. and Hall of Fame, Bonner Springs; Boot Hill Museum, Dodge City; Old Cowtown Museum, Wichita; Ft. Scott and Ft. Larned Natl. Historic Sites; Kansas Cosmosphere and Space Ctr., Hutchinson; U.S. Cavalry Museum, Ft. Riley; Tallgrass Prairie Natl. Preserve, Strong City; Kansas Speedway, Kansas City. **Information:** Kansas Dept. of Commerce, Travel and Tourism Div., 1000 SW Jackson St., Ste. 100, Topeka, KS 66612; (785) 296-2009; www.travelks.com

History. Wichita, Pawnee, Kansa, and Osage peoples lived in the area when Francisco de Coronado explored it in 1541. These Native Americans—hunters who also farmed—were joined on the Plains by the nomadic Cheyenne, Arapaho, Comanche, and Kiowa about 1800. France claimed the region, 1682, ceded its claim to Spain, 1762, then regained control, 1800, before selling it to the U.S. in the Louisiana Purchase, 1803. After 1830, thousands of Native Americans were removed from more eastern states to Kansas. Organized as a territory, 1854, the area witnessed violent clashes between pro- and antislavery settlers and became known as "Bleeding Kansas." It entered the Union as a free state, 1861. After the Civil War, rail construction and huge cattle drives from Texas turned Abilene and Dodge City into cowboy capitals. Russian Mennonite immigrants brought a new strain of winter wheat, 1874, transforming Kansas agriculture. Carry Nation launched her anti-saloon crusade in the 1890s. Part of the Dust Bowl, the state experienced drought and depression in the 1930s. Topeka was the focus of the famous *Brown v. Board of Education* decision, 1954, that led to desegregation of U.S. public schools. Bob Dole represented Kansas in the U.S. Senate (1969-96) but failed in several efforts to win higher office.

Famous Kansans. Kirstie Alley, Roscoe "Fatty" Arbuckle, Ed Asner, John Brown, Walter P. Chrysler, Glenn Cunningham, John Steuart Curry, Robert Joseph "Bob" Dole, Amelia Earhart, Dwight D. Eisenhower, Melissa Etheridge, Ron Evans, Georgia Neese Clark Gray, Maurice Greene, James Butler "Wild Bill" Hickok, Cyrus K. Holliday, Dennis Hopper, William Inge, Don Johnson, Walter Johnson, Nancy Landon Kassebaum, Buster Keaton, Emmett Kelly, Alfred M. "Alf" Landon, Hattie McDaniel, Oscar Micheaux, Carry Nation, Charlie Parker, Gordon Parks, Jim Ryun, Barry Sanders, Vivian Vance, William Allen White, Jess Willard.

Website. www.kansas.gov

Kentucky (KY)

Bluegrass State

People. Population: 4,413,457; rank: 26. **Pop. change** (2010-14): 1.7%. **Pop. density:** 111.8 per sq mi. **Racial distribution:** 88.3% white; 8.2% black; 1.4% Asian; 0.3% Amer. Ind.; 0.1% Hawaiian/Pacific Islander; 2 or more races, 1.8%. **Hispanic pop.:** 3.0%.

Geography. Total area: 40,408 sq mi; rank: 37. **Land area:** 39,486 sq mi; rank: 37. **Acres forested:** 12.5 mil. **Location:** East South Central state bordered on N by Illinois, Indiana, Ohio; on E by West Virginia and Virginia; on S by Tennessee; on W by Missouri. **Climate:** moderate, with plentiful rainfall. **Topography:** mountainous in E; rounded hills of the Knobs region in the N; Bluegrass region in heart of state; wooded rocky hillsides of the Pennyroyal Plateau; Western Coal Field; the fertile Jackson Purchase region in the SW. **Capital:** Frankfort. **Chief airports:** Greater Cincinnati, Louisville, Lexington.

Economy. Chief industries: manufacturing, services, finance, insurance and real estate, retail trade, public utilities. **Chief manuf. goods:** motor vehicles and parts, aluminum, basic chemicals, plastics, iron and steel, rubber, printing. **Chief crops:** hay, corn, soybeans, tobacco, wheat. **Farm income:** crops, $2.88 bil; livestock/animal prods., $3.66 bil. **Nonfuel minerals:** $857 mil; stone (crushed), lime, cement (portland), sand and gravel (construction), sand and gravel (industrial). **Chief ports:** Louisville, Hickman-Fulton County. **Gross state product:** $188.6 bil. **Sales tax:** 6.0%. **Gasoline tax:** 44.40 cents/gal. **Employment distrib.:** 17.3% govt.; 20.1% trade/trans./util.; 12.5% mfg.; 14.1% ed./health; 11.4% prof./bus. serv.; 10.2% leisure/hosp.; 4.8% finance; 4.8% constr./mining/log.; 1.4% info.; 3.4% other serv. **Unemployment:** 6.5%. **Per cap. pers. income:** $37,654. **New private housing:** 9,536 units/$1.3 bil. **Broadband Internet:** 90.5%. **Commercial banks:** 193; deposits: $69.8 bil. **Savings institutions:** 15; deposits: $1.5 bil. **Lottery:** total sales: $858.9 mil; profit: $225.5 mil.

Federal govt. Fed. civ. employees: 22,521; **avg. salary:** $64,049. **Notable fed. facilities:** U.S. Bullion Depository, Ft. Knox; Ft. Campbell; Fed. Medical Ctr., Lexington; Army Corps of Engineers, Louisville District.

Education. High school grad. rate: 86.1%. **4-year public coll./univ.:** 8; **2-yr. public:** 16; **4-yr. private:** 27.

Energy. Electricity use/cost: 1,154 kWh, $112.95.

State data. Motto: United we stand, divided we fall. **Flower:** Goldenrod. **Bird:** Cardinal. **Tree:** Tulip poplar. **Song:** "My Old Kentucky Home." **Entered union:** June 1, 1792; rank: 15th.

Tourism. Tourist spending: $8.3 bil. **Attractions:** Churchill Downs (Kentucky Derby), Louisville Slugger Museum and Factory, in Louisville; Land Between the Lakes Natl. Recreation Area (Kentucky and Barkley Lakes); Mammoth Cave Natl. Park (world's longest known cave system); Abraham Lincoln Birthplace Natl. Historical Park, Hodgenville; My Old Kentucky Home State Park, Bardstown; Cumberland Gap Natl. Historical Park, Middlesboro; Kentucky Horse Park, Lexington; Shaker Village of Pleasant Hill, Harrodsburg; Natl. Corvette Museum, Bowling Green. **Information:** Kentucky Dept. of Travel, Capital Plaza Tower, 22nd Fl., 500 Mero St., Frankfort, KY 40601; 1-800-225-8747; www.kentuckytourism.com

History. Paleo-Indians first arrived about 14,000 years ago. Much later, Shawnee, Wyandot, Delaware, and Cherokee peoples also used the area mostly for hunting. Explored by Thomas Walker and Christopher Gist, 1750-51, Kentucky was the first area W of the Alleghenies settled by American pioneers. The first permanent settlement was Harrodsburg, 1774. Daniel Boone blazed the Wilderness Trail through the Cumberland Gap and founded Ft. Boonesborough, 1775. Clashes with Native Americans were frequent, 1774-94. Virginia dropped its claims to the region, and Kentucky became a state, 1792. Tobacco growing, horse breeding, coal mining, and bourbon whiskey making were major industries in the 19th cent. A slave state, Kentucky tried to stay neutral in the Civil War, but then opted for the Union; many Kentuckians sided with the Confederacy. The U.S. gold depository at Ft. Knox opened, 1937. Prior to the 2008 economic downturn, auto manufacturing had grown in recent decades. An ice storm in southwestern Kentucky in Jan. 2009 killed 14 and caused severe power outages.

Famous Kentuckians. Muhammad Ali, Alben W. Barkley, Ned Beatty, Louis D. Brandeis, John C. Breckinridge, Kit Carson, Albert B. "Happy" Chandler, Henry Clay, George Clooney, Rosemary Clooney, Jefferson Davis, D. W. Griffith, "Casey" Jones, Jennifer Lawrence, Abraham Lincoln, Mary Todd Lincoln, Thomas Hunt Morgan, Carry Nation, Colonel Harland Sanders, Diane Sawyer, Jesse Stuart, Zachary Taylor, Hunter S. Thompson, Robert Penn Warren, Whitney M. Young Jr.

Website. www.kentucky.gov

Louisiana (LA)

Pelican State

People. Population: 4,649,676; rank: 25. **Pop. change** (2010-14): 2.6%. **Pop. density:** 107.6 per sq mi. **Racial distribution:** 63.4% white; 32.5% black; 1.8% Asian; 0.8% Amer. Ind.; 0.1% Hawaiian/Pacific Islander; 2 or more races, 1.5%. **Hispanic pop.:** 4.1%.

Geography. Total area: 52,378 sq mi; rank: 31. **Land area:** 43,204 sq mi; rank: 33. **Acres forested:** 15 mil. **Location:** West South Central state on the Gulf Coast. **Climate:** subtropical, affected by continental weather patterns. **Topography:** lowlands of marshes and Mississippi R. floodplain; Red R. Valley lowlands; upland hills in the Florida Parishes; avg. elevation, 100 ft. **Capital:** Baton Rouge. **Chief airport:** Metairie.

Economy. Chief industries: wholesale and retail trade, tourism, manufacturing, construction, transportation, communication, public utilities, finance, insurance, real estate, mining. **Chief manuf. goods:** petroleum, chemicals, plastics material and resin, pesticides and fertilizers, cleaning prods., paper and paperboard, ships, structural metals. **Chief crops:** sugarcane, cotton, rice, soybeans, corn, sweet potatoes. **Farm income:** crops, $2.65 bil; livestock/animal prods., $1.34 bil. **Nonfuel minerals:** $554 mil; salt, sand and gravel (construction), stone (crushed), sand and gravel (industrial), lime. **Commercial fishing:** $399.9 mil. **Chief ports:** New Orleans, Baton Rouge, Lake Charles, Port of S. Louisiana (La Place), Shreveport, Plaquemine, St. Bernard, Alexandria. **Gross state product:** $251.4 bil. **Sales tax:** 4.0%. **Gasoline tax:** 38.41 cents/gal. **Employment distrib.:** 16.4% govt.; 19.6% trade/trans./util.; 7.5% mfg.; 15.3% ed./health; 10.7% prof./bus. serv.; 11.5% leisure/hosp.; 4.7% finance; 9.3% constr./mining/log.; 1.4% info.; 3.6% other serv. **Unemployment:** 6.4%. **Per cap. pers. income:** $42,287. **New private housing:** 15,255 units/$2.9 bil. **Broadband Internet:** 91.1%. **Commercial banks:** 130; deposits: $91.7 bil. **Savings institutions:** 22; deposits: $4.4 bil. **Lottery:** total sales: $449.0 mil; profit: $170.7 mil.

Federal govt. Fed. civ. employees: 17,887; **avg. salary:** $69,944. **Notable federal facilities:** Ft. Polk (Joint Readiness Training Ctr.); Barksdale AFB; Strategic Petroleum Reserve, Michoud Assembly Facility, USDA Southern Regional Research Ctr., New Orleans NAS JRB.

Education. High school grad. rate: 73.5%. **4-year public coll./univ.:** 17; **2-yr. public:** 17; **4-yr. private:** 10.

Energy. Electricity use/cost: 1,273 kWh, $119.98.

State data. Motto: Union, justice, and confidence. **Flower:** Magnolia. **Bird:** Eastern brown pelican. **Tree:** Cypress. **Song:** "Give Me Louisiana." **Entered union:** Apr. 30, 1812; rank: 18th.

Tourism. Tourist spending: $10.6 bil. **Attractions:** Mardi Gras, French Quarter, Bourbon Street, in New Orleans; Jean Lafitte Natl. Historical Park and Preserve; Longfellow-Evangeline State Historic Site, St. Martinville; Kent Plantation House, Alexandria; Oak Alley Plantation, Vacherie; Hodges Gardens State Park, Florien; USS *Kidd* Veterans Memorial, Baton Rouge. **Information:** Louisiana Office of Tourism, P.O. Box 94291, Baton Rouge, LA 70804-9291; 1-800-677-4082; www.louisianatravel.com

History. Caddo, Tunica, Choctaw, Chitimacha, and Chawash peoples lived in the region at the time of European contact. Spanish explorers in the early 16th cent. reached the mouth of the Mississippi. René-Robert Cavelier, sieur de La Salle, 1682, claimed the region for France. Early French and Spanish settlers were the ancestors of Louisiana Creoles. Cajuns descended from the Acadians, French settlers expelled by the British from Nova Scotia, Canada, in 1755. France ceded the Louisiana region to Spain, 1762, took it back, 1800, and sold it to the U.S., 1803, in the Louisiana Purchase. Admitted as a state in 1812, Louisiana witnessed the Battle of New Orleans, 1815. Cotton and sugar plantations relied on black slaves, who made up close to 47% of the population in 1860, on the eve of the Civil War. Louisiana seceded, 1861, and was readmitted, 1868. Jazz was born in New Orleans in the early 20th cent. As governor (1928-32), Huey Long pushed populist programs. Many tropical storms and floods have battered Louisiana, including Hurricane Katrina and subsequent flooding, 2005, which devastated New Orleans. The offshore oil and gas industry developed after World War II. An oil rig explosion off the state's Gulf coast spilled millions of barrels of oil, damaging coastal wetlands and many of the state's marine-dependent industries in 2010.

Famous Louisianans. Louis Armstrong, Pierre Beauregard, Judah P. Benjamin, Braxton Bragg, Kate Chopin, Harry Connick Jr., Ellen DeGeneres, Fats Domino, George "Buddy" Guy, Lillian Hellman, Grace King, Jerry Lee Lewis, Bob Livingston, Huey Long, Eli Manning, Peyton Manning, Wynton Marsalis, Tim McGraw, Leonidas K. Polk, Anne Rice, Bill Russell, Henry Miller Shreve, Britney Spears, Madam C. J. Walker (Sarah Breedlove), Edward Douglass White Jr.

Website. www.louisiana.gov

Maine (ME)

Pine Tree State

People. Population: 1,330,089; rank: 41. **Pop. change** (2010-14): 0.1%. **Pop. density:** 43.1 per sq mi. **Racial distribution:** 95% white; 1.4% black; 1.2% Asian; 0.7% Amer. Ind.; <0.05% Hawaiian/Pacific Islander; 2 or more races, 1.6%. **Hispanic pop.:** 1.3%.

Geography. Total area: 35,380 sq mi; rank: 39. **Land area:** 30,843 sq mi; rank: 39. **Acres forested:** 17.5 mil. **Location:** New England state at northeastern tip of U.S. **Climate:** southern interior and coast influenced by air masses from the S and W; northern clime harsher, avg. over 100 in. snow in winter. **Topography:** Appalachian Mts. extend through state; western borders have rugged terrain; long sand beaches on southern coast; northern coast mainly rocky promontories, peninsulas, fjords. **Capital:** Augusta. **Chief airport:** Portland.

Economy. Chief industries: manufacturing, agriculture, fishing, services, trade, government, finance, insurance, real estate, construction. **Chief manuf. goods:** paper, ships and boats, cardboard, frozen/canned fruits and vegetables, plastics, baked goods. **Chief crops:** potatoes, greenhouse and nursery, wild blueberries, apples, hay, maple syrup. **Farm income:** crops, $433.16 mil; livestock/animal prods., $404.79 mil. **Nonfuel minerals:** $95 mil; sand and gravel (construction), cement (portland), stone (crushed), stone (dimension), cement (masonry). **Commercial fishing:** $475.4 mil. **Chief ports:** Searsport, Portland, Eastport. **Gross state product:** $55.8 bil. **Sales tax:** 5.5%. **Gasoline tax:** 48.41 cents/gal. **Employment distrib.:** 16.7% govt.; 19.3% trade/trans./util.; 8.1% mfg.; 20.2% ed./health; 10.8% prof./bus. serv.; 10.4% leisure/hosp.; 5.1% finance; 4.5% constr./mining/log.; 1.2% info.; 3.5% other serv. **Unemployment:** 5.7%. **Per cap. pers. income:** $42,071. **New private housing:** 3,242 units/$612.9 mil. **Broadband Internet:** 87.7%. **Commercial banks:** 11; deposits: $27.1 bil. **Savings institutions:** 21; deposits: $10.7 bil. **Lottery:** total sales: $230.1 mil; profit: $51.9 mil.

Federal govt. Fed. civ. employees: 9,484; **avg. salary:** $67,135. **Notable fed. facilities:** Portsmouth Naval Shipyard.

Education. High school grad. rate: 86.4%. **4-year public coll./univ.:** 8; **2-yr. public:** 7; **4-yr. private:** 12.

Energy. Electricity use/cost: 551 kWh, $79.13.

State data. Motto: Dirigo (I direct). **Flower:** White pine cone and tassel. **Bird:** Black-capped chickadee. **Tree:** Eastern white pine. **Song:** "State of Maine Song." **Entered union:** Mar. 15, 1820; rank: 23rd.

Tourism. Tourist spending: $3.4 bil. **Attractions:** Acadia Natl. Park, Bar Harbor, on Mt. Desert Island; Old Orchard Beach; Old Port historic waterfront, Victoria Mansion, Portland; Portland Head Light, Cape Elizabeth; Maine Maritime Museum, Bath; Baxter State Park; L.L. Bean flagship store and outlet shopping, Freeport. **Information:** Maine Office of Tourism, 59 State House Station, Augusta, ME 04333; 1-888-624-6345; www.visitmaine.com

History. Paleo-Indians arrived about 11,500 years ago. Maine was inhabited by Algonquian peoples including the Abnaki, Penobscot, and Passamaquoddy at the time of European contact. French settled, 1604, at the St. Croix R., English, c. 1607, on the Kennebec; both settlements failed. A royal charter, 1691, made Maine part of Massachusetts. Maine broke off, 1819, and became a separate state, 1820. Drawing on vast forest resources, the pulp and paper industry developed after the Civil War. Bath Iron Works began building U.S. Navy vessels and other ships in the 1890s. Mail-order and retail giant L.L. Bean was founded, 1912. Women have fared well in state politics: Margaret Chase Smith became the first woman to serve in both houses of Congress (House, 1940-49; Senate, 1949-73), and Olympia Snowe and Susan Collins represented Maine in the Senate since the mid-1990s (Snowe retired in Jan. 2013).

Famous "Down Easters." Leon Leonwood (L. L.) Bean, James G. Blaine, Patrick Dempsey, Hannibal Hamlin, Sarah Orne Jewett, Stephen King, Henry Wadsworth Longfellow, Sir Hiram and Hudson Maxim, Edna St. Vincent Millay, George J. Mitchell, Edmund Muskie, Judd Nelson, Edwin Arlington Robinson, Joan Benoit Samuelson, Liv Tyler, Kate Douglas Wiggin, Ben Ames Williams.

Website. www.maine.gov

Maryland (MD)

Old Line State, Free State

People. Population: 5,976,407; rank: 19. **Pop. change** (2010-14): 3.5%. **Pop. density:** 615.7 per sq mi. **Racial distribution:** 60.1% white; 30.3% black; 6.4% Asian; 0.6% Amer. Ind.; 0.1% Hawaiian/Pacific Islander; 2 or more races, 2.6%. **Hispanic pop.:** 7.9%.

Geography. Total area: 12,406 sq mi; rank: 42. **Land area:** 9,707 sq mi; rank: 42. **Acres forested:** 2.5 mil. **Location:** South Atlantic state stretching from the ocean to the Allegheny Mts. **Climate:** continental in the W; humid subtropical in the E. **Topography:** coastal plain on Eastern Shore separated by Chesapeake Bay from coastal plain, Piedmont Plateau, and the Blue Ridge. **Capital:** Annapolis. **Chief airport:** Glen Burnie.

Economy. Chief industries: manufacturing, biotechnology and information technology, services, tourism. **Chief manuf. goods:** navigational instruments, pharmaceutical and medicine, broadcasting equip., plastics, printing, milk and ice cream. **Chief crops:** greenhouse and nursery, corn, soybeans, wheat, hay, tomatoes, watermelons, barley, potatoes, apples. **Farm income:** crops, $947.78 mil; livestock/animal prods., $1.47 bil. **Nonfuel minerals:** $277 mil; cement (portland), stone (crushed), sand and gravel (construction), cement (masonry), stone (dimension). **Commercial fishing:** $75.9 mil. **Chief port:** Baltimore. **Gross state product:** $348.6 bil. **Sales tax:** 6.0%. **Gasoline tax:** 50.50 cents/gal. **Employment distrib.:** 19.3% govt.; 17.1% trade/trans./util.; 3.8% mfg.; 16.5% ed./health; 16.1% prof./bus. serv.; 10.4% leisure/hosp.; 5.4% finance; 5.9% constr./mining/log.; 1.4% info.; 4.2% other serv. **Unemployment:** 5.8%. **Per cap. pers. income:** $55,143. **New private housing:** 16,331 units/$2.9 bil. **Broadband Internet:** 86.9%. **Commercial banks:** 87; deposits: $117.9 bil. **Savings institutions:** 29; deposits: $5.7 bil. **Lottery:** total sales: $2.3 bil; profit: $941.7 mil.

Federal govt. Fed. civ. employees: 128,462; **avg. salary:** $99,553. **Notable fed. facilities:** U.S. Naval Academy; Beltsville Agriculture Res. Ctr.; Ft. Meade; Aberdeen Proving Ground; Joint Base Andrews; Naval Air Sys. Command; Goddard Space Flight Ctr.; Natl. Inst. of Health; Natl. Inst. of Standards & Technology; Food & Drug Admin.; Bureau of the Census; Walter Reed Natl. Military Med. Ctr., Bethesda; Natl. Marine Fisheries Serv.; Natl. Oceanic and Atmospheric Admin.

Education. High school grad. rate: 85.0%. **4-year public coll./univ.:** 13; **2-yr. public:** 16; **4-yr. private:** 22.

Energy. Electricity use/cost: 1,031 kWh, $136.63.

State data. Motto: Fatti Maschii, Parole Femine (Manly deeds, womanly words). **Flower:** Black-eyed Susan. **Bird:** Baltimore oriole. **Tree:** White oak. **Song:** "Maryland, My Maryland." **Seventh** of original 13 states to ratify the Constitution, Apr. 28, 1788.

Tourism. Tourist spending: $15.1 bil. **Attractions:** Ocean City; Ft. McHenry—the defense of which inspired Francis

Scott Key to write "The Star-Spangled Banner," Pimlico Race Course (Preakness Stakes), Edgar Allan Poe House and Museum, Oriole Park at Camden Yards, Natl. Aquarium, Inner Harbor, in Baltimore; Antietam Natl. Battlefield, Sharpsburg; South Mountain State Battlefield, Middletown; U.S. Naval Academy, Maryland State House (oldest in continuous legislative use in U.S.), in Annapolis; Natl. Cryptologic Museum, Ft. Meade. **Information:** Maryland Office of Tourism Development, 401 E. Pratt St., 14th Fl., Baltimore, MD 21202; 1-866-639-3526; www.visitmaryland.org

History. Europeans encountered Algonquian-speaking Nanticoke and Piscataway and Iroquois-speaking Susquehannock when they first visited the area. Italian navigator Giovanni da Verrazano reached the Chesapeake region in the early 16th cent. English Capt. John Smith explored and mapped the area, 1608. William Claiborne set up a trading post on Kent Island in Chesapeake Bay, 1631. King Charles I granted land to Cecilius Calvert, Lord Baltimore, 1632; Calvert's brother Leonard, with about 200 settlers, founded St. Mary's, 1634. During the Revolutionary War, Baltimore (1776-77) and Annapolis (1783-84) served as temporary capitals of the U.S. When a British fleet tried to take Ft. McHenry in the War of 1812, Marylander Francis Scott Key wrote "The Star-Spangled Banner," 1814. Born into slavery at Tuckahoe in 1818, Frederick Douglass became a leading abolitionist. Although a slaveholding state, Maryland stayed in the Union during the Civil War and was the site of the battle of Antietam, 1862. Gov. Spiro Agnew, elected U.S. vice pres., 1968 and 1972, pleaded no contest to tax evasion and resigned, 1973. Israeli and Egyptian leaders reached a historic peace accord at the Camp David presidential retreat, 1978. A major effort is under way to clean up pollution in the Chesapeake Bay watershed. The death of Freddie Gray, a young black man in police custody, touched off a week of sometimes violent protests in Baltimore in Apr. 2015. Six law enforcement officers were charged in his death.

Famous Marylanders. John Astin, Benjamin Banneker, Tom Clancy, Frederick Douglass, Matthew Henson, Francis Scott Key, H. L. Mencken, Kweisi Mfume, Ogden Nash, Charles Willson Peale, Michael Phelps, William Pinkney, Edgar Allan Poe, Cal Ripken Jr., Babe Ruth, Upton Sinclair, Roger B. Taney, Harriet Tubman, John Waters, Montel Williams.

Website. www.maryland.gov

Massachusetts (MA)

Bay State, Old Colony

People. Population: 6,745,408; rank: 14. **Pop. change** (2010-14): 3.0%. **Pop. density:** 864.8 per sq mi. **Racial distribution:** 82.6% white; 8.3% black; 6.3% Asian; 0.5% Amer. Ind.; 0.1% Hawaiian/Pacific Islander; 2 or more races, 2.2%. **Hispanic pop.:** 9.3%.

Geography. Total area: 10,554 sq mi; rank: 44. **Land area:** 7,800 sq mi; rank: 45. **Acres forested:** 3 mil. **Location:** New England state on Atlantic seaboard. **Climate:** temperate, with colder, drier clime in western region. **Topography:** jagged indented coast from Rhode Island around Cape Cod; flat land yields to stony upland pastures near central region and gentle hilly country in W; except in W, land is rocky, sandy, and not fertile. **Capital:** Boston. **Chief airport:** Boston.

Economy. Chief industries: services, trade, manufacturing. **Chief manuf. goods:** electronics and instruments, pharmaceuticals, telecom. and broadcasting equip., plastics, medical equip., printing. **Chief crops:** greenhouse and nursery, cranberries, tomatoes, sweet corn, apples, hay, tobacco. **Farm income:** crops, $315.09 mil; livestock/animal prods., $144.03 mil. **Nonfuel minerals:** $293 mil; stone (crushed), sand and gravel (construction), stone (dimension), lime, clays (common). **Commercial fishing:** $566.9 mil. **Chief ports:** Boston, Fall River. **Gross state product:** $459.9 bil. **Sales tax:** 6.25%. **Gasoline tax:** 44.94 cents/gal. **Employment distrib.:** 13.5% govt.; 16.1% trade/trans./util.; 7.1% mfg.; 21.6% ed./health; 15.3% prof./bus. serv.; 10.1% leisure/hosp.; 6.0% finance; 3.9% constr./mining/log.; 2.5% info.; 3.9% other serv. **Unemployment:** 5.8%. **Per cap. pers. income:** $59,182. **New private housing:** 14,486 units/$3.3 bil. **Broadband Internet:** 85.8%. **Commercial banks:** 72; deposits: $279.6 bil. **Savings institutions:** 106; deposits: $66.6 bil. **Lottery:** total sales: $4.8 bil; profit: $971.0 mil.

Federal govt. Fed. civ. employees: 24,420; **avg. salary:** $82,724. **Notable fed. facilities:** Thomas P. O'Neill Jr. Fed. Bldg.; J.W. McCormack Bldg.; JFK Fed. Bldg.; Hanscom AFB; Army Natick Soldier Systems Ctr.

Education. High school grad. rate: 85.0%. **4-year public coll./univ.:** 14; **2-yr. public:** 16; **4-yr. private:** 82.

Energy. Electricity use/cost: 638 kWh, $100.97.

State data. Motto: Ense Petit Placidam Sub Libertate Quietem (By the sword we seek peace, but peace only under liberty). **Flower:** Mayflower. **Bird:** Black-capped chickadee. **Tree:** American elm. **Song:** "All Hail to Massachusetts." **Sixth** of original 13 states to ratify the Constitution, Feb. 6, 1788.

Tourism. Tourist spending: $18.5 bil. **Attractions:** Provincetown art colony; Cape Cod; Plymouth Rock, Plimoth Plantation, Mayflower II, in Plymouth; Freedom Trail, Museum of Fine Arts, New England Aquarium, Faneuil Hall, Boston Harbor Isls. Natl. Recreation Area, Boston Public Garden, in Boston; Tanglewood, Hancock Shaker Village, Berkshire Scenic Railway Museum, Norman Rockwell Museum, in the Berkshires region; Peabody Essex Museum, House of the Seven Gables, in Salem; Old Sturbridge Village; Historic Deerfield; Walden Pond, Louisa May Alcott's Orchard House, in Concord; Naismith Memorial Basketball Hall of Fame, Springfield. **Information:** Massachusetts Office of Travel & Tourism, 10 Park Plz., Ste. 4510, Boston, MA 02116; 1-800-227-MASS; www.massvacation.com

History. Early inhabitants were Algonquian peoples: Nauset, Wampanoag, Massachuset, Pennacook, Nipmuc, and Pocumtuc. Pilgrims settled in Plymouth, 1620, giving thanks for their survival with the first Thanksgiving Day, 1621. About 20,000 new settlers arrived, 1630-40. Colonist-Native American relations deteriorated, leading to King Philip's War, 1675-76, which the colonists won. Witch trials at Salem, 1692, led to the execution of 20 people. Demonstrations against British restrictions set off the Boston Massacre, 1770, and the Boston Tea Party, 1773. The first bloodshed of American Revolution was at Lexington, 1775. After statehood, Massachusetts prospered from shipbuilding, seafaring, and the making of textiles, shoes, and metal goods, while artists, writers, and social reformers flourished. The controversial Sacco-Vanzetti case, 1920-27, ended with the execution of two Italian immigrants on murder and robbery charges. After World War II, old industries declined, knowledge-intensive enterprises thrived, and the Kennedys became a dominant political family. The state's highest court ruled, 2003, that same-sex couples could legally marry. Two bombs exploded Apr. 15, 2013, near the finish line of the Boston Marathon, killing three and injuring more than 250. Dzhokhar Tsarnaev was convicted on bombing charges in Apr. 2015 and sentenced to death.

Famous "Bay Staters." John Adams, John Quincy Adams, Samuel Adams, Louisa May Alcott, Horatio Alger, Susan B. Anthony, Crispus Attucks, Clara Barton, Michael Bloomberg, George H. W. Bush, Steve Carell, John Cheever, E. E. Cummings, Bette Davis, Emily Dickinson, Charles Eliot, Ralph Waldo Emerson, William Lloyd Garrison, Edward Everett Hale, John Hancock, Nathaniel Hawthorne, Oliver Wendell Holmes Jr., Winslow Homer, Elias Howe, John F. Kennedy, Jack Kerouac, John Kerry, Emeril Lagasse, Jack Lemmon, James Russell Lowell, Cotton Mather, Maria Mitchell, Samuel F. B. Morse, Conan O'Brien, Paul Revere, Norman Rockwell, Dr. Seuss (Theodor Seuss Geisel), Henry David Thoreau, Barbara Walters, James Abbott McNeil Whistler, John Greenleaf Whittier.

Website. www.mass.gov

Michigan (MI)

Great Lakes State, Wolverine State

People. Population: 9,909,877; rank: 10. **Pop. change** (2010-14): 0.3%. **Pop. density:** 175.3 per sq mi. **Racial distribution:** 79.9% white; 14.2% black; 2.9% Asian; 0.7% Amer. Ind.; <0.05% Hawaiian/Pacific Islander; 2 or more races, 2.3%. **Hispanic pop.:** 4.4%.

Geography. Total area: 96,714 sq mi; rank: 11. **Land area:** 56,539 sq mi; rank: 22. **Acres forested:** 20.3 mil. **Location:** East North Central state bordering four of the Great Lakes, divided into an Upper and Lower Peninsula by the Straits of Mackinac, which link Lakes Michigan and Huron. **Climate:** well-defined seasons tempered by the Great Lakes. **Topography:** low rolling hills give way to northern tableland of hilly belts in Lower Peninsula; Upper Peninsula is level in the E with swampy areas; western region is higher and more rugged. **Capital:** Lansing. **Chief airports:** Detroit, Grand Rapids.

Economy. Chief industries: manufacturing, services, tourism, agriculture, forestry/lumber. **Chief manuf. goods:** motor vehicles and parts, plastics, metalworking machinery, non-wood office furniture, fabricated metals. **Chief crops:** greenhouse and nursery, soybeans, corn, wheat, sugar beets, apples, blueberries, potatoes, dry beans, cherries, hay, cucumbers, tomatoes, grapes. **Farm income:** crops, $4.64 bil; livestock/animal prods., $3.95 bil. **Nonfuel minerals:** $2.4 bil; iron ore (usable shipped), cement (portland), sand and gravel (construction), stone (crushed), salt. **Commercial fishing:** $10.5 mil. **Chief ports:** Detroit, Escanaba, Calcite, Port Inland, Muskegon, Port Huron. **Gross state product:** $451.5 bil. **Sales tax:** 6.0%. **Gasoline tax:** 54.39 cents/gal. **Employment distrib.:** 13.9% govt.; 17.8% trade/trans./util.; 13.8% mfg.; 15.3% ed./health; 15.1% prof./bus. serv.; 10.0% leisure/hosp.; 4.9% finance; 3.9% constr./mining/log.; 1.3% info.; 4.0% other serv. **Unemployment:** 7.3%. **Per cap. pers. income:** $40,556. **New private housing:** 15,933 units/$3.3 bil. **Broadband Internet:** 87.7%. **Commercial banks:** 136; deposits: $167.6 bil. **Savings institutions:** 15; deposits: $9.3 bil. **Lottery:** total sales: $2.6 bil; profit: $743.1 mil.

Federal govt. Fed. civ. employees: 25,173; **avg. salary:** $79,114. **Notable fed. facilities:** Army TACOM Life Cycle Mgmt., Detroit Arsenal; DLA Logistics Info. Service; Selfridge Air Natl. Guard Base; Hart-Dole-Inouye Fed. Ctr.

Education. High school grad. rate: 77.0%. **4-year public coll./univ.:** 16; **2-yr. public:** 30; **4-yr. private:** 51.

Energy. Electricity use/cost: 665 kWh, $96.95.

State data. Motto: Si Quaeris Peninsulam Amoenam, Circumspice (If you seek a pleasant peninsula, look about you). **Flower:** Apple blossom. **Bird:** Robin. **Tree:** White pine. **Song:** "Michigan, My Michigan." **Entered union:** Jan. 26, 1837; rank: 26th.

Tourism. Tourist spending: $17.3 bil. **Attractions:** Henry Ford Museum and Greenfield Village, Dearborn; Frederik Meijer Gardens and Sculpture Park, Grand Rapids; Tahquamenon Falls (of Longfellow's poem *Song of Hiawatha*); De Zwaan windmill, Tulip Time Festival, in Holland; Soo Locks (bet. Lakes Superior and Huron), Sault Ste. Marie; Air Zoo, Portage; Mackinac Island; Belle Isle Park, Detroit Institute of Arts, Charles H. Wright Museum of African-American History, Motown Historical Museum, in Detroit. **Information:** Michigan Economic Development Corp., 300 N. Washington Sq., Lansing, MI 48913; 1-888-784-7328; www.michigan.org

History. Hunting and fishing peoples lived in the region as early as 11,000 years ago. Ojibwa, Ottawa, Miami, Potawatomi, and Huron inhabited the area at the time of European contact. French fur traders and missionaries arrived in the 17th cent. and established a settlement at Sault Ste. Marie, 1668. British took over, 1763, and crushed a Native American uprising led by Ottawa chieftain Pontiac. Treaty of Paris ceded the area to U.S., 1783, but the British remained until 1796. Michigan was organized as a territory, 1805. The British seized Ft. Mackinac and Detroit, 1812, but the U.S. regained control, 1814. The opening of the Erie Canal, 1825, and new land laws and Native American cessions led the way for a flood of settlers. Strongly antislavery, Michigan became a state, 1837, and supplied 90,000 soldiers to the Union army in the Civil War. In the 20th cent., automobile manufacturing was the backbone of the economy. Henry Ford launched the Model T car, 1908; the United Auto Workers union was founded, 1935. Motown music flourished in Detroit in the 1960s, but riots in 1967 dealt the city a heavy blow. As the auto industry faltered, Michigan lost more than 20% of its automotive-related jobs in 2002-07. In 2009, the federal government loaned billions of dollars to GM and Chrysler to keep them solvent. Detroit formally emerged from a 17-month bankruptcy process—the largest in municipal history—in Dec. 2014, having shed nearly $7 bil in debts.

Famous Michiganders. Ralph Bunche, Paul de Kruif, Thomas Edison, Eminem (Marshall Mathers), Edna Ferber, Gerald R. Ford, Henry Ford, Aretha Franklin, Edgar Guest, Lee Iacocca, Magic Johnson, Casey Kasem, Will Kellogg, Ring Lardner, Elmore Leonard, Charles Lindbergh, Joe Louis, Madonna, Malcolm X, Terry McMillan, Michael Moore, Larry Page, Pontiac, Gilda Radner, Mitt Romney, Diana Ross, Tom Selleck, Sinbad (David Adkins), John Smoltz, Lily Tomlin, Serena Williams.

Website. www.michigan.gov

Minnesota (MN)

North Star State, Gopher State

People. Population: 5,457,173; rank: 21. **Pop. change** (2010-14): 2.9%. **Pop. density:** 68.5 per sq mi. **Racial distribution:** 85.7% white; 5.9% black; 4.7% Asian; 1.3% Amer. Ind.; 0.1% Hawaiian/Pacific Islander; 2 or more races, 2.3%. **Hispanic pop.:** 4.6%.

Geography. Total area: 86,936 sq mi; rank: 12. **Land area:** 79,627 sq mi; rank: 14. **Acres forested:** 17.5 mil. **Location:** West North Central state bounded on the E by Wisconsin and Lake Superior, on the N by Canada, on the W by the Dakotas, and on the S by Iowa. **Climate:** northern part of state lies in the moist Great Lakes storm belt; the western border lies at the edge of the semiarid Great Plains. **Topography:** central hill and lake region covers approx. half the state; to the NE, rocky ridges and deep lakes; to the NW, flat plain; to the S, rolling plains and deep river valleys. **Capital:** St. Paul. **Chief airport:** Minneapolis.

Economy. Chief industries: agribusiness, forest products, mining, manufacturing, tourism. **Chief manuf. goods:** petroleum and asphalt, computers and electronics, milk and cheese, printing, animal slaughtering, paper and prod., medical equip. **Chief crops:** corn, soybeans, hay, sugar beets, wheat, potatoes, greenhouse and nursery, dry edible beans, green peas, sunflowers. **Farm income:** crops, $10.00 bil; livestock/animal prods., $8.85 bil. **Nonfuel minerals:** $4.7 bil; iron ore (usable shipped), sand and gravel (industrial), sand and gravel (construction), stone (crushed), stone (dimension). **Commercial fishing:** $0.3 mil. **Chief ports:** Two Harbors, Silver Bay, Duluth, St. Paul. **Gross state product:** $316.2 bil. **Sales tax:** 6.875%. **Gasoline tax:** 47.00 cents/gal. **Employment distrib.:** 14.8% govt.; 18.4% trade/trans./util.; 11.0% mfg.; 17.7% ed./health; 12.5% prof./bus. serv.; 9.3% leisure/hosp.; 6.3% finance; 4.1% constr./mining/log.; 1.9% info.; 4.0% other serv. **Unemployment:** 4.1%. **Per cap. pers. income:** $48,711. **New private housing:** 16,990 units/$3.7 bil. **Broadband Internet:** 87.1%. **Commercial banks:** 378; deposits: $251.1 bil. **Savings institutions:** 21; deposits: $3.7 bil. **Lottery:** total sales: $531.5 mil; profit: $127.9 mil.

Federal govt. Fed. civ. employees: 15,733; **avg. salary:** $75,864. **Notable fed. facilities:** Bishop Henry Whipple Fed. Bldg.; Minneapolis-St. Paul Air Reserve Station.

Education. High school grad. rate: 79.8%. **4-year public coll./univ.:** 12; **2-yr. public:** 31; **4-yr. private:** 34.

Energy. Electricity use/cost: 817 kWh, $96.51.

State data. Motto: L'Etoile du Nord (The star of the north). **Flower:** Pink and white lady's-slipper. **Bird:** Common loon. **Tree:** Red pine. **Song:** "Hail! Minnesota." **Entered union:** May 11, 1858; rank: 32nd.

Tourism. Tourist spending: $12.5 bil. **Attractions:** Minneapolis Institute of Arts, Walker Art Center, Minneapolis Sculpture Garden, Minnehaha Falls (in Longfellow's poem *Song of Hiawatha*), Guthrie Theater, in Minneapolis; Mall of America, Bloomington; Ordway Ctr. for the Performing Arts, Science Museum of Minnesota, in St. Paul; Voyageurs Natl. Park; Mayo Clinic, Rochester; North Shore (Lake Superior); Lake Minnetonka; Boundary Waters Canoe Area Wilderness; Superior Natl. Forest; Aerial Lift Bridge, Duluth. **Information:** Explore Minnesota Tourism, Metro Square, 121 7th Pl. E., Ste. 100, St. Paul, MN 55101; 1-888-TOURISM; www.exploreminnesota.com

History. Inhabited for at least 10,000 years, the region was home to Dakota Sioux when Europeans arrived. French fur traders Pierre Esprit Radisson and Médard Chouart, sieur des Groseilliers, explored in the mid-17th cent. In 1679, Daniel Greysolon, sieur Duluth, claimed the entire region for France. Ojibwa arrived in the 18th cent. and warred with the Sioux for over 100 years. Britain took the area east of the Mississippi, 1763. The U.S. took over that portion after the American Revolution and gained the western area, 1803, in the Louisiana Purchase. The U.S. built Ft. St. Anthony (now Ft. Snelling), 1819, and bought Native American lands, 1837, spurring an influx of settlers from the east. Minnesota became a territory, 1849, and a state, 1858. Sioux staged a bloody uprising, the Battle of Wood Lake, 1862, and were driven from the state. Railroad construction after the Civil War spurred the growth of the grain, timber, and iron mining industries. The opening of the St. Lawrence Seaway, 1959, aided the port of Duluth. Elected as a reformer, former wrestler Jesse Ventura served as governor, 1999-2003. Two-term Sen. Paul Wellstone, one of a long line of liberal Minnesota Democrats, died when his campaign plane crashed, 2002. The I-35W Mississippi River Bridge in Minneapolis collapsed in 2007, killing 13.

Famous Minnesotans. Andrews Sisters, Warren E. Burger, Ethan and Joel Coen, Bob Dylan, F. Scott Fitzgerald, Al Franken, Judy Garland, Cass Gilbert, Hubert H. Humphrey, Garrison Keillor, Sister Elizabeth Kenny, Jessica Lange, Sinclair Lewis, Paul Manship, E. G. Marshall, William J. and Charles H. Mayo, Eugene McCarthy, Walter F. Mondale, Prince (Prince Rogers Nelson), Charles M. Schulz, Ann Sothern, Harold Stassen, Thorstein Veblen, Jesse Ventura, Lindsey Vonn, Paul Wellstone.

Website. www.minnesota.gov

Mississippi (MS)

Magnolia State

People. Population: 2,994,079; rank: 31. **Pop. change** (2010-14): 0.9%. **Pop. density:** 63.8 per sq mi. **Racial distribution:** 59.7% white; 37.5% black; 1.0% Asian; 0.6% Amer. Ind.; 0.1% Hawaiian/Pacific Islander; 2 or more races, 1.2%. **Hispanic pop.:** 2.7%.

Geography. Total area: 48,432 sq mi; rank: 32. **Land area:** 46,923 sq mi; rank: 31. **Acres forested:** 19.4 mil. **Location:** East South Central state bordered on the W by the Mississippi R., on the S by the Gulf of Mexico. **Climate:** semitropical, with abundant rainfall and long growing season. **Topography:** low, fertile delta between the Yazoo and Mississippi Rivers; loess bluffs stretch around delta border; sandy gulf coastal terraces followed by piney woods and prairie; rugged, high sandy hills in extreme NE followed by Prairie Black Belt, Pontotoc Ridge, and flatwoods into the N central highlands. **Capital:** Jackson. **Chief airport:** Jackson.

Economy. Chief industries: warehousing and distribution, services, manufacturing, government, wholesale and retail trade. **Chief manuf. goods:** petroleum, upholstered furniture, poultry processing, motor vehicle parts, plastics, ships and boats, chemicals. **Chief crops:** cotton, soybeans, rice, hay, corn, sweet potatoes. **Farm income:** crops, $2.87 bil; livestock/animal prods., $3.79 bil. **Nonfuel minerals:** $192 mil; sand and gravel (construction), stone (crushed), clays (fuller's earth), clays (ball), clays (bentonite). **Commercial fishing:** $35.0 mil. **Chief ports:** Pascagoula, Vicksburg, Gulfport, Biloxi, Greenville. **Gross state product:** $104.9 bil. **Sales tax:** 7.0%. **Gasoline tax:** 37.18 cents/gal. **Employment distrib.:** 21.9% govt.; 19.5% trade/trans./util.; 12.4% mfg.; 12.1% ed./health; 8.9% prof./bus. serv.; 11.7% leisure/hosp.; 3.9% finance; 4.8% constr./mining/log.; 1.2% info.; 3.4% other serv. **Unemployment:** 7.8%. **Per cap. pers. income:** $34,333. **New private housing:** 6,871 units/$1.0 bil. **Broadband Internet:** 74.4%. **Commercial banks:** 98; deposits: $47.3 bil. **Savings institutions:** 6; deposits: $586.0 mil.

Federal govt. Fed. civ. employees: 17,938; **avg. salary:** $67,553. **Notable fed. facilities:** Keesler AFB; Meridian NAS; Columbus AFB; NASA Stennis Space Ctr.; Army Corps of Eng. Waterways Experiment Sta.; Naval Constr. Battalion Ctr., Gulfport.

Education. High school grad. rate: 75.5%. **4-year public coll./univ.:** 9; **2-yr. public:** 15; **4-yr. private:** 9.

Energy. Electricity use/cost: 1,220 kWh, $131.49.

State data. Motto: Virtute et Armis (By valor and arms). **Flower:** Magnolia. **Bird:** Mockingbird. **Tree:** Magnolia. **Song:** "Go, Mississippi!" **Entered union:** Dec. 10, 1817; rank: 20th.

Tourism. Tourist spending: $6.1 bil. **Attractions:** Vicksburg Natl. Military Park and Cemetery; Natchez Trace Parkway; antebellum home tours in Natchez and other cities; Tupelo Natl. Battlefield, Elvis Presley Birthplace, in Tupelo; Smith Robertson Museum and Cultural Ctr., Mynelle Gardens, Eudora Welty House, in Jackson; Mardi Gras parades on Gulf Coast; Beauvoir (Jefferson Davis Home and Presidential Library), Biloxi; Gulf Islands Natl. Seashore; Delta Blues Museum, Clarksdale. **Information:** Mississippi Division of Tourism, P.O. Box 849, Jackson, MS 39205; 1-866-SEE-MISS; www.visitmississippi.org

History. Choctaw, Chickasaw, and Natchez peoples were living in the region at the time of European contact. The Spaniard Hernando de Soto explored the area, 1540-41. René-Robert Cavelier, sieur de La Salle, traced the Mississippi R. from Illinois to its mouth and claimed the entire Mississippi Valley for France, 1682. The first settlement was the French Ft. Maurepas, 1699, on Biloxi Bay. The region was ceded to Britain, 1763, and claimed by Spain, 1779-98, then became a U.S. territory, 1798, and a state, 1817. Slavery spread along with cotton plantations, and slaves made up 55% of the population, 1860. Mississippi seceded, 1861. In the Civil War, Union forces captured Vicksburg, 1863, and caused extensive damage elsewhere. Mississippi reentered the Union, 1870. For the next 100 years, resistance to desegregation and violence against blacks made the state a battleground for the civil rights movement. Hurricanes Camille, 1969, and Katrina, 2005, caused substantial damage to the Gulf Coast. Since the early 1990s, casino gambling has boosted the economy, but the state's poverty rate remained the highest in the nation in 2010.

Famous Mississippians. Margaret Walker Alexander, Dana Andrews, Jimmy Buffett, Bo Diddley, Medgar Evers, William Faulkner, Brett Favre, Shelby Foote, Morgan Freeman, John Grisham, Fannie Lou Hamer, Jim Henson, Faith Hill, John Lee Hooker, Robert Johnson, James Earl Jones, B. B. King, L. Q. C. Lamar, Trent Lott, Gerald McRaney, Willie Morris, Walter Payton, Elvis Presley, Leontyne Price, Charley Pride, LeAnn Rimes, Robin Roberts, Muddy Waters, Eudora Welty, Tennessee Williams, Oprah Winfrey, Johnny Winter, Richard Wright, Tammy Wynette.

Website. www.ms.gov

Missouri (MO)

Show Me State

People. Population: 6,063,589; rank: 18. **Pop. change** (2010-14): 1.2%. **Pop. density:** 88.2 per sq mi. **Racial distribution:** 83.5% white; 11.8% black; 1.9% Asian; 0.5% Amer. Ind.; 0.1% Hawaiian/Pacific Islander; 2 or more races, 2.1%. **Hispanic pop.:** 3.5%.

Geography. Total area: 69,707 sq mi; rank: 21. **Land area:** 68,742 sq mi; rank: 18. **Acres forested:** 15.5 mil. **Location:** West North Central state near the geographic center of the conterminous U.S.; bordered on the E by Mississippi R., on the NW by Missouri R. **Climate:** continental, susceptible to cold Canadian air; moist, warm Gulf air; and drier SW air. **Topography:** rolling hills, open, fertile plains, and well-watered prairie N of the Missouri R.; S of the river, land is rough and hilly with deep, narrow valleys; alluvial plain in the SE; low elevation in the W. **Capital:** Jefferson City. **Chief airports:** St. Louis, Kansas City.

Economy. Chief industries: agriculture, manufacturing, aerospace, tourism. **Chief manuf. goods:** motor vehicles and parts, aerospace, pharmaceuticals, plastics, soap, animal slaughtering and processing, printing. **Chief crops:** soybeans, corn, hay, cotton and cottonseed, wheat, rice, sorghum. **Farm income:** crops, $5.66 bil; livestock/animal prods., $5.26 bil. **Nonfuel minerals:** $2.5 bil; cement (portland), stone (crushed), lead, lime, sand and gravel (industrial). **Gross state product:** $284.5 bil. **Sales tax:** 4.225%. **Gasoline tax:** 35.70 cents/gal. **Employment distrib.:** 16.1% govt.; 18.9% trade/trans./util.; 9.4% mfg.; 15.7% ed./health; 12.8% prof./bus. serv.; 10.8% leisure/hosp.; 6.0% finance; 4.2% constr./mining/log.; 2.1% info.; 4.1% other serv. **Unemployment:** 6.1%. **Per cap. pers. income:** $41,613. **New private housing:** 16,003 units/$2.7 bil. **Broadband Internet:** 92.8%. **Commercial banks:** 324; deposits: $133.2 bil. **Savings institutions:** 27; deposits: $24.5 bil. **Lottery:** total sales: $1.2 bil; profit: $267.3 mil.

Federal govt. Fed. civ. employees: 33,827; **avg. salary:** $67,249. **Notable fed. facilities:** Federal Reserve banks; Ft. Leonard Wood; Jefferson Barracks Natl. Cem.; Natl. Personnel Records Ctr.; Whiteman AFB.

Education. High school grad. rate: 85.7%. **4-year public coll./univ.:** 13; **2-yr. public:** 14; **4-yr. private:** 51.

Energy. Electricity use/cost: 1,086 kWh, $121.98.

State data. Motto: Salus Populi Suprema Lex Esto (Let the welfare of the people be the supreme law). **Flower:** Hawthorn. **Bird:** Bluebird. **Tree:** Dogwood. **Song:** "Missouri Waltz." **Entered union:** Aug. 10, 1821; rank: 24th.

Tourism. Tourist spending: $12.9 bil. **Attractions:** Silver Dollar City, Branson; Mark Twain Boyhood Home and Museum, Hannibal; Pony Express Natl. Museum, St. Joseph; Harry S. Truman Library and Museum, Independence; Gateway Arch (part of Jefferson Natl. Expansion Memorial), Ulysses S. Grant Natl. Historic Site, St. Louis Zoo, in St. Louis; Worlds of Fun amusement park, Kansas City; Lake of the Ozarks; Ozark Natl. Scenic Riverways; Natl. Churchill Museum, Fulton; State Capitol, Jefferson City; Wilson's Creek Natl. Battlefield; George Washington Carver Natl. Monument, Diamond; Bass Pro Shops Outdoor World, Springfield. **Information:** Missouri Division of Tourism, P.O. Box 1055, Jefferson City, MO 65102; 1-800-519-2100; www.visitmo.com

History. In the 17th cent., when French explorers arrived, Algonquian Sauk, Fox, and Illinois and Siouan Osage, Missouri, Iowa, and Kansa peoples were living in the region; few remained by the 1830s. French hunters and lead miners made the first settlement c. 1735, at Ste. Genevieve. The territory was ceded to Spain by the French, 1762, then returned to France, 1800, and acquired by the U.S. in the Louisiana Purchase, 1803. Powerful earthquakes rocked New Madrid, 1811-12. Missouri became a territory, 1812, and entered the Union as a slave state, 1821. St. Louis became the gateway for pioneers heading West. Though Missouri stayed with the Union, pro- and antislavery forces battled there during the Civil War. In the late 19th cent. railroad building and the cattle trade made Kansas City a boomtown. The most notable Missourian of the 20th cent., Harry S. Truman, was U.S. president, 1945-53. The state, a political bellwether, voted for the winner in every presidential election from 1960 to 2004. In May 2011, a tornado in Joplin killed about 162. The police-shooting death of Michael Brown in Ferguson in Aug. 2014 touched off major protests that spread nationwide and revived debate over the relationship between law enforcement officers and the communities they serve.

Famous Missourians. Maya Angelou, Robert Altman, John Ashcroft, Burt Bacharach, Josephine Baker, Scott Bakula, Thomas Hart Benton, Yogi Berra, Chuck Berry, George Caleb Bingham, Daniel Boone, Omar Bradley, William S. Burroughs, Kate Capshaw, Dale Carnegie, George Washington Carver, Bob Costas, Walter Cronkite, Sheryl Crow, Walt Disney, T. S. Eliot, Richard "Dick" Gephardt, John Goodman, Betty Grable, Jon Hamm, Edwin Hubble, Jesse James, Rush Limbaugh, Marianne Moore, Reinhold Niebuhr, J. C. Penney, John J. Pershing, Brad Pitt, Joseph Pulitzer, Ginger Rogers, Bess Truman, Harry S. Truman, Kathleen Turner, Tina Turner, Mark Twain, Dick Van Dyke, Tennessee Williams, Lanford Wilson, Shelley Winters, Jane Wyman.

Website. www.mo.gov

Montana (MT)

Treasure State

People. Population: 1,023,579; rank: 44. **Pop. change** (2010-14): 3.5%. **Pop. density:** 7.0 per sq mi. **Racial distribution:** 89.4% white; 0.6% black; 0.8% Asian; 6.6% Amer. Ind.; 0.1% Hawaiian/Pacific Islander; 2 or more races, 2.6%. **Hispanic pop.:** 2.8%.

Geography. Total area: 147,040 sq mi; rank: 4. **Land area:** 145,546 sq mi; rank: 4. **Acres forested:** 25.8 mil. **Location:** Mountain state bounded on the E by the Dakotas, on the S by Wyoming, on the SSW by Idaho, on the N by Canada. **Climate:** colder, continental climate with low humidity. **Topography:** Rocky Mts. in western third of state; eastern two-thirds gently rolling northern Great Plains. **Capital:** Helena.

Economy. Chief industries: agriculture, timber, mining, tourism, oil and gas. **Chief manuf. goods:** sawmills, softwood veneer and plywood, petroleum. **Chief crops:** wheat, barley, hay, sugar beets, potatoes, dry beans, flaxseed, cherries, corn, oats. **Farm income:** crops, $2.27 bil; livestock/animal prods., $2.27 bil. **Nonfuel minerals:** $1.3 bil; palladium metal, copper, molybdenum concentrates, platinum metal, gold. **Gross state product:** $44.3 bil. **Sales tax:** none. **Gasoline tax:** 46.15 cents/gal. **Employment distrib.:** 19.6% govt.; 21.0% trade/trans./util.; 4.0% mfg.; 15.2% ed./health; 8.7% prof./bus. serv.; 12.8% leisure/hosp.; 5.8% finance; 7.7% constr./mining/log.; 1.4% info.; 4.0% other serv. **Unemployment:** 4.7%. **Per cap. pers. income:** $40,601. **New private housing:** 3,884 units/$647.0 mil. **Broadband Internet:** 76.1%. **Commercial banks:** 68; deposits: $20.1 bil. **Savings institutions:** 3; deposits: $508.0 mil. **Lottery:** total sales: $53.3 mil; profit: $12.1 mil.

Federal govt. Fed. civ. employees: 8,959; **avg. salary:** $65,505. **Notable fed. facilities:** Malmstrom AFB and missile silos; Ft. Peck, Hungry Horse, Libby, Yellowtail, and other dams.

Education. High school grad. rate: 84.4%. **4-year public coll./univ.:** 6; **2-yr. public:** 11; **4-yr. private:** 4.

Energy. Electricity use/cost: 860 kWh, $88.85.

State data. Motto: Oro y Plata (Gold and silver). **Flower:** Bitterroot. **Bird:** Western meadowlark. **Tree:** Ponderosa pine. **Song:** "Montana." **Entered union:** Nov. 8, 1889; rank: 41st.

Tourism. Tourist spending: $4.0 bil. **Attractions:** Glacier and Yellowstone Natl. Parks; Museum of the Rockies, Bozeman; Museum of the Plains Indian, Blackfeet Reservation, in Browning; Custer Natl. Cemetery at Little Bighorn Battlefield Natl. Monument; Lewis and Clark Caverns State Park, Whitehall; Lewis and Clark Natl. Historic Trail Interpretive Ctr., Great Falls. **Information:** Travel Montana, Dept. of Commerce, 301 S. Park Ave., P.O. Box 200533, Helena, MT 59601; 1-800-VISITMT; www.visitmt.com

History. Paleo-Indian hunters reached the area over 12,000 years ago. Cheyenne, Blackfoot, Crow, Assiniboin, Salish (Flatheads), Kootenai, and Kalispel peoples lived in the region before Europeans arrived. French explorers visited the region, 1742. The U.S. acquired the area partly through the Louisiana Purchase, 1803, partly through the Lewis and Clark Expedition, 1804-06. Fur traders and missionaries established posts in the early 19th cent. Gold was discovered on Grasshopper Creek, 1862, and Montana Territory was established, 1864. Indian uprisings reached their peak with the defeat of Gen. George Custer at the Battle of Little Bighorn, 1876. Chief Joseph and the Nez Percé tribe surrendered here, 1877, after a long trek across the state. Mining activity and the coming of the Northern Pacific Railway, 1883, brought population growth. Montana became a state, 1889. Copper wealth from the Butte pits resulted in the turn of the century "War of Copper Kings" as feuding factions contended for "the richest hill on earth." During the first half of the 20th cent., the Anaconda Copper firm wielded enormous political influence. Jeannette Rankin, a suffragist and pacifist, was the first woman elected to Congress, 1916. Mike Mansfield served 34 years in Congress and was Senate Democratic leader, 1961-77. An 18-year hunt for notorious "Unabomber" Theodore Kaczynski ended with his arrest, 1996, at his cabin near Lincoln.

Famous Montanans. Dana Carvey, Gary Cooper, Marcus Daly, Chet Huntley, Phil Jackson, Will James, Myrna Loy, David Lynch, Mike Mansfield, Brent Musburger, Jeannette Rankin, Charles M. Russell, Lester Thurow.

Website. www.mt.gov

Nebraska (NE)

Cornhusker State

People. Population: 1,881,503; rank: 37. **Pop. change** (2010-14): 3.0%. **Pop. density:** 24.5 per sq mi. **Racial distribution:** 89.4% white; 4.9% black; 2.2% Asian; 1.4% Amer. Ind.; 0.1% Hawaiian/Pacific Islander; 2 or more races, 2.0%. **Hispanic pop.:** 8.9%.

Geography. Total area: 77,348 sq mi; rank: 16. **Land area:** 76,824 sq mi; rank: 15. **Acres forested:** 1.6 mil. **Location:** West North Central state with the Missouri R. for a border on NE and E. **Climate:** continental semiarid. **Topography:** till plains of the central lowland in the eastern third rises to the Great Plains and hill country of the N central and NW. **Capital:** Lincoln. **Chief airport:** Omaha.

Economy. Chief industries: agriculture, manufacturing. **Chief manuf. goods:** animal slaughtering, grain and oilseed, farm machinery, medical equip., motor vehicle parts, printing, structural metals. **Chief crops:** corn, sorghum, soybeans, hay, wheat, dry beans, oats, potatoes, sugar beets. **Farm income:** crops, $10.19 bil; livestock/animal prods., $14.53 bil. **Nonfuel minerals:** $326 mil; cement (portland), stone (crushed), sand and gravel (construction), sand and gravel (industrial), lime. **Gross state product:** $112.2 bil. **Sales tax:** 5.5%. **Gasoline tax:** 45.40 cents/gal. **Employment distrib.:** 17.5% govt.; 20.3% trade/trans./util.; 9.4% mfg.; 15.1% ed./health; 11.3% prof./bus. serv.; 8.8% leisure/hosp.; 7.3% finance; 4.7% constr./mining/log.; 1.7% info.; 3.8% other serv. **Unemployment:** 3.3%. **Per cap. pers. income:** $47,073. **New private housing:** 7,605 units/$1.2 bil. **Broadband Internet:** 80.0%. **Commercial banks:** 205; deposits: $53.4 bil. **Savings institutions:** 10; deposits: $4.7 bil. **Lottery:** total sales: $157.9 mil; profit: $38.0 mil.

Federal govt. Fed. civ. employees: 9,679; **avg. salary:** $70,319. **Notable fed. facilities:** Offutt AFB.

Education. High school grad. rate: 88.5%. **4-year public coll./univ.:** 7; **2-yr. public:** 8; **4-yr. private:** 16.

Energy. Electricity use/cost: 1,034 kWh, $125.71.

State data. Motto: Equality before the law. **Flower:** Goldenrod. **Bird:** Western meadowlark. **Tree:** Cottonwood. **Song:** "Beautiful Nebraska." **Entered union:** Mar. 1, 1867; rank: 37th.

Tourism. Tourist spending: $4.5 bil. **Attractions:** Univ. of Nebraska State Museum at Morrill Hall, Nebraska State Capitol, in Lincoln; Stuhr Museum of the Prairie Pioneer, Grand Island; Boys Town; Omaha's Henry Doorly Zoo and Aquarium, Joslyn Art Museum, The Durham Museum, in Omaha; Ashfall Fossil Beds State Hist. Park, near Royal; Strategic Air and Space Museum, Ashland; Arbor Lodge State Historical Park, Nebraska City; Buffalo Bill Ranch State Historical Park, North Platte; Pioneer Village, Minden; Oregon Trail landmarks, incl. at Scotts Bluff Natl. Monument and Chimney Rock Natl. Historic Site; Great Platte River Road Archway, Museum of Nebraska Art, in Kearney. **Information:** Nebraska Division of Travel and Tourism, 301 Centennial Mall S., Lincoln, NE 68508; 1-888-444-1867; www.visitnebraska.com

History. When Europeans arrived, Pawnee, Ponca, Omaha, and Oto peoples lived in the region. Spanish and French explorers and fur traders visited the area prior to its acquisition in the Louisiana Purchase, 1803. Meriwether Lewis and William Clark passed through, 1804-06. The first permanent settlement was Bellevue, near Omaha, 1823.

The 1834 Indian Intercourse Act declared Nebraska Indian country and excluded white settlement, but conflicts with settlers eventually forced Native Americans to move to reservations. Nebraska became a territory, 1854, and a state, 1867. Many Civil War veterans settled under free land terms of the 1862 Homestead Act; as agriculture grew, struggles followed between homesteaders and ranchers. Since the mid-1930s, Nebraska has been the only state with a unicameral legislature. A leader in agribusiness, Nebraska has also become a major telemarketing center. The "Oracle of Omaha," investor Warren Buffett, one of the world's wealthiest men, announced in 2006 he would give most of his $44-bil fortune to charity.

Famous Nebraskans. Grover Cleveland Alexander, Fred Astaire, Marlon Brando, Charles W. Bryan, William Jennings Bryan, Warren Buffett, Johnny Carson, Willa Cather, Dick Cavett, Dick Cheney, Loren Eiseley, Father Edward J. Flanagan, Henry Fonda, Bob Gibson, Rollin Kirby, Harold Lloyd, Malcolm X, J. Sterling Morton, John G. Neihardt, Nick Nolte, George W. Norris, Tom Osborne, Roscoe Pound, Red Cloud, Mari Sandoz, Robert Taylor, Darryl F. Zanuck.

Website. www.nebraska.gov

Nevada (NV)

Sagebrush State, Battle Born State, Silver State

People. Population: 2,839,099; rank: 35. **Pop. change** (2010-14): 5.1%. **Pop. density:** 25.9 per sq mi. **Racial distribution:** 76.2% white; 9.1% black; 8.3% Asian; 1.6% Amer. Ind.; 0.7% Hawaiian/Pacific Islander; 2 or more races, 4.0%. **Hispanic pop.:** 25.2%.

Geography. Total area: 110,572 sq mi; rank: 7. **Land area:** 109,781 sq mi; rank: 7. **Acres forested:** 10.6 mil. **Location:** Mountain state bordered on N by Oregon and Idaho, on E by Utah, on SE by Arizona, and on SW and W by California. **Climate:** semiarid and arid. **Topography:** rugged N-S mountain ranges; highest elevation, Boundary Peak, 13,146 ft; southern area is within the Mojave Desert; lowest elevation, Colorado R., at southern tip of state, 479 ft. **Capital:** Carson City. **Chief airports:** Las Vegas, Reno.

Economy. Chief industries: gaming, tourism, mining, manufacturing, government, retailing, warehousing, trucking. **Chief manuf. goods:** gaming machines, cement and concrete, plastics, printing, architectural and structural metals, electricity instruments. **Chief crops:** hay, onions, potatoes, alfalfa, wheat, garlic, mint, barley. **Farm income:** crops, $264.12 mil; livestock/animal prods., $602.81 mil. **Nonfuel minerals:** $7.5 bil; gold, copper, silver, lime, diatomite. **Gross state product:** $132.1 bil. **Sales tax:** 6.85%. **Gasoline tax:** 52.25 cents/gal. **Employment distrib.:** 12.5% govt.; 18.6% trade/trans./util.; 3.3% mfg.; 9.7% ed./health; 12.6% prof./bus. serv.; 28.2% leisure/hosp.; 4.6% finance; 6.4% constr./mining/log.; 1.1% info.; 2.9% other serv. **Unemployment:** 7.8%. **Per cap. pers. income:** $40,077. **New private housing:** 13,016 units/$1.8 bil. **Broadband Internet:** 91.7%. **Commercial banks:** 37; deposits: $54.1 bil. **Savings institutions:** 8; deposits: $94.5 bil.

Federal govt. Fed. civ. employees: 10,436; **avg. salary:** $71,259. **Notable fed. facilities:** Nevada Natl. Security Site; Hawthorne Army Depot; Creech AFB; Nellis AFB; Fallon NAS; Natl. Wild Horse & Burro Ctr. at Palomino Valley.

Education. High school grad. rate: 70.7%. **4-year public coll./univ.:** 6; **2-yr. public:** 1; **4-yr. private:** 3.

Energy. Electricity use/cost: 924 kWh, $109.94.

State data. Motto: All for our country. **Flower:** Sagebrush. **Bird:** Mountain bluebird. **Trees:** Single-leaf piñon and bristlecone pine. **Song:** "Home Means Nevada." **Entered union:** Oct. 31, 1864; rank: 36th.

Tourism. Tourist spending: $32.0 bil. **Attractions:** Legalized gambling, incl. at Lake Tahoe, Reno, Las Vegas, Laughlin, and Elko; Hoover Dam, Lake Mead Natl. Recreation Area, near Boulder City; Great Basin Natl. Park; Valley of Fire State Park; Red Rock Canyon Natl. Conservation Area; Las Vegas Strip, Fremont St., Natl. Atomic Testing Museum, Pinball Hall of Fame, Las Vegas Motor Speedway, in Las Vegas; Natl. Automobile Museum, Reno. **Information:** Commission on Tourism, 401 N. Carson St., Carson City, NV 89701; 1-800-NEVADA-8; www.travelnevada.com

History. Shoshone, Paiute, Bannock, and Washoe peoples lived in the area at the time of European contact. Nevada was first explored by Spaniards, 1776. In the 1820s, fur traders Peter Skene Ogden and Jedediah Smith separately explored the area. It was acquired by the U.S., 1848, at the end of the Mexican War. A trading post at Mormon Station, now Genoa, was established, 1850. Discovery of the Comstock Lode, rich in gold and silver, 1859, spurred a population boom. Nevada became a territory, 1861, and a state, 1864. Hoover Dam was built, 1931-36. With gambling legal since 1931, a surge in resort casino construction after World War II turned Las Vegas into one of the nation's most popular tourist destinations. An influx of Hispanics and Asians, attracted by service-industry and construction jobs, helped make Nevada the fastest-growing state in the U.S. in 1990-2005 and again in 2007. The recession in recent years has had an equally powerful effect. Nevada had the highest state unemployment and home foreclosure rates in 2011.

Famous Nevadans. Andre Agassi, Kyle Busch, Walter Van Tilburg Clark, George W. G. Ferris, Sarah Winnemucca Hopkins, Paul Laxalt, Dat So La Lee, John William Mackay, Anne Henrietta Martin, Pat McCarran, Key Pittman, William Morris Stewart.

Website. www.nv.gov

New Hampshire (NH)

Granite State

People. Population: 1,326,813; rank: 42. **Pop. change** (2010-14): 0.8%. **Pop. density:** 148.2 per sq mi. **Racial distribution:** 94% white; 1.5% black; 2.5% Asian; 0.3% Amer. Ind.; <0.05% Hawaiian/Pacific Islander; 2 or more races, 1.6%. **Hispanic pop.:** 2.8%.

Geography. Total area: 9,349 sq mi; rank: 46. **Land area:** 8,953 sq mi; rank: 44. **Acres forested:** 4.8 mil. **Location:** New England state bounded on S by Massachusetts, on W by Vermont, on N by Canada, on E by Maine and the Atlantic Ocean. **Climate:** highly varied, due to its nearness to high mountains and ocean. **Topography:** low, rolling coast followed by countless hills and mountains rising out of a central plateau. **Capital:** Concord. **Chief airport:** Manchester.

Economy. Chief industries: tourism, manufacturing, agriculture, trade, mining. **Chief manuf. goods:** navigational instruments, circuit boards, electrical equip., fabricated metal, machinery, medical equip., plastics. **Chief crops:** greenhouse and nursery, apples, sweet corn, hay, Christmas trees, berries, maple syrup. **Farm income:** crops, $106.47 mil; livestock/animal prods., $143.83 mil. **Nonfuel minerals:** $111 mil; sand and gravel (construction), stone (crushed), stone (dimension), gemstones (natural). **Commercial fishing:** $20.2 mil. **Chief port:** Portsmouth. **Gross state product:** $71.6 bil. **Sales tax:** none. **Gasoline tax:** 42.23 cents/gal. **Employment distrib.:** 14.0% govt.; 21.2% trade/trans./util.; 10.2% mfg.; 17.8% ed./health; 11.2% prof./bus. serv.; 10.3% leisure/hosp.; 5.5% finance; 3.9% constr./mining/log.; 1.9% info.; 4.0% other serv. **Unemployment:** 4.3%. **Per cap. pers. income:** $53,149. **New private housing:** 3,403 units/$653.4 mil. **Broadband Internet:** 81.5%. **Commercial banks:** 17; deposits: $21.6 bil. **Savings institutions:** 25; deposits: $7.3 bil. **Lottery:** total sales: $276.0 mil; profit: $72.5 mil.

Federal govt. Fed. civ. employees: 4,129; **avg. salary:** $84,153. **Notable fed. facilities:** Army Cold Regions Res. and Engineering Lab.

Education. High school grad. rate: 87.3%. **4-year public coll./univ.:** 5; **2-yr. public:** 7; **4-yr. private:** 11.

Energy. Electricity use/cost: 629 kWh, $102.66.

State data. Motto: Live free or die. **Flower:** Purple lilac. **Bird:** Purple finch. **Tree:** White birch. **Song:** "Old New Hampshire." **Ninth** of original 13 states to ratify the Constitution, June 21, 1788.

Tourism. Tourist spending: $3.8 bil. **Attractions:** Mt. Washington Cog Railway, Mt. Washington (highest peak in Northeast); Lake Winnipesaukee; Crawford, Franconia, Pinkham Notches (mountain passes), Flume Gorge, Cannon Mountain Aerial Tramway, in White Mountains region; Strawbery Banke Museum, Portsmouth; Canterbury Shaker Village; Saint-Gaudens Natl. Historic Site, Cornish; Mt. Monadnock; Santa's Village, Jefferson. **Information:** Division of Travel & Tourism Development, 172 Pembroke Rd., P.O. Box 1856; Concord, NH 03302; 1-800-FUN-IN-NH; www.visitnh.gov

History. The area has been inhabited for about 10,000 years. Algonquian-speaking peoples, including the Pennacook, lived in the region when the Europeans arrived. The first explorers to visit the area were England's Martin Pring, 1603, and France's Samuel de Champlain, 1605. The first settlement was Odiorne's Point (now port of Rye), 1623. Before the American Revolution, New Hampshire residents raided a British fort at Portsmouth, 1774, and drove the royal governor out, 1775. New Hampshire became the first colony to adopt its own constitution, 1776. After statehood, 1788, New Hampshire became a textile manufacturing center. The mill towns declined in the first half of the 20th cent., but tourism and technology industries, lured by low taxes, have revived the economy since the 1960s. A state law requires it to hold the first primary of the presidential campaign season.

Famous New Hampshirites. Dan Brown, Salmon P. Chase, Ralph Adams Cram, Mary Baker Eddy, Daniel Chester French, Robert Frost, Horace Greeley, Sarah Josepha Buell Hale, John Irving, Seth Meyers, Bode Miller, Franklin Pierce, Augustus Saint-Gaudens, Adam Sandler, Alan B. Shepard Jr., Sarah Silverman, David H. Souter, Daniel Webster.

Website. www.nh.gov

New Jersey (NJ)

Garden State

People. Population: 8,938,175; rank: 11. **Pop. change** (2010-14): 1.7%. **Pop. density:** 1,215.4 per sq mi. **Racial distribution:** 73% white; 14.8% black; 9.4% Asian; 0.6% Amer. Ind.; 0.1% Hawaiian/Pacific Islander; 2 or more races, 2.1%. **Hispanic pop.:** 17.4%.

Geography. Total area: 8,723 sq mi; rank: 47. **Land area:** 7,354 sq mi; rank: 46. **Acres forested:** 2 mil. **Location:** Middle Atlantic state bounded on N and E by New York and Atlantic Ocean, on S and W by Delaware and Pennsylvania. **Climate:** moderate, with marked difference between NW and SE extremities. **Topography:** Appalachian Valley in NW also has highest elevation, High Pt., 1,803 ft; Appalachian Highlands, flat-topped NE-SW mountain ranges; Piedmont Plateau, low plains broken by high ridges (Palisades) rising 400-500 ft; Coastal Plain, covering three-fifths of state in SE, rises from sea level to gentle slopes. **Capital:** Trenton. **Chief airports:** Newark, Atlantic City.

Economy. Chief industries: pharmaceuticals, telecommunications, biotechnology, printing and publishing. **Chief manuf. goods:** petroleum, pharmaceuticals, toiletries, chemicals, plastics, printing, navigational instruments, medical equip., paper prod. **Chief crops:** greenhouse and nursery, blueberries, peaches, corn, hay, tomatoes, bell peppers, cranberries, soybeans, apples. **Farm income:** crops, $888.35 mil; livestock/animal prods., $132.77 mil. **Nonfuel minerals:** $288 mil; stone (crushed), sand and gravel (construction), sand and gravel (industrial), greensand marl, peat. **Commercial fishing:** $133.1 mil. **Chief ports:** Newark-Elizabeth, Camden. **Gross state product:** $549.1 bil. **Sales tax:** 7.0%. **Gasoline tax:** 32.90 cents/gal. **Employment distrib.:** 15.6% govt.; 21.0% trade/trans./util.; 6.1% mfg.; 16.2% ed./health; 15.7% prof./bus. serv.; 9.1% leisure/hosp.; 6.1% finance; 3.8% constr./mining/log.; 1.9% info.; 4.3% other serv. **Unemployment:** 6.6%. **Per cap. pers. income:** $56,807. **New private housing:** 28,155 units/$4.1 bil. **Broadband Internet:** 85.3%. **Commercial banks:** 90; deposits: $216.8 bil. **Savings institutions:** 58; deposits: $69.6 bil. **Lottery:** total sales: $2.9 bil; profit: $965.0 mil.

Federal govt. Fed. civ. employees: 20,627; **avg. salary:** $87,870. **Notable fed. facilities:** Joint Base McGuire- Dix-Lakehurst; Picatinny Arsenal; FAA William J. Hughes Technical Ctr.

Education. High school grad. rate: 87.5%. **4-year public coll./univ.:** 13; **2-yr. public:** 19; **4-yr. private:** 28.

Energy. Electricity use/cost: 687 kWh, $108.10.

State data. Motto: Liberty and prosperity. **Flower:** Purple violet. **Bird:** Eastern goldfinch. **Tree:** Red oak. **Third** of the original 13 states to ratify the Constitution, Dec. 18, 1787.

Tourism. Tourist spending: $20.1 bil. **Attractions:** 130 mi of beaches, boardwalks on the Jersey Shore at Atlantic City (with gambling), Seaside Heights, Ocean City, Wildwood; Grover Cleveland Birthplace, Caldwell; Cape May Historic District; Thomas Edison Natl. Historical Park, West Orange; Six Flags Great Adventure, Jackson; Liberty State Park, Liberty Science Ctr., in Jersey City; Pine Barrens wilderness; Princeton Univ., Princeton Battlefield State Park, in Princeton; Morristown Natl. Historical Park; Adventure Aquarium, Battleship *New Jersey*, Walt Whitman House, in Camden. **Information:** Dept. of State, Division of Travel and Tourism, P.O. Box 460, Trenton, NJ 08625; 1-800-VISITNJ; www.visitnj.org

History. The Lenni Lenape (Delaware) peoples lived in the region and had mostly peaceful relations with European colonists, who arrived after the explorers Giovanni da Verrazano, 1524, and Henry Hudson, 1609. The first permanent European settlement was Dutch, at Bergen (now Jersey City), 1660. When the British took New Netherland, 1664, the area between the Delaware and Hudson Rivers was given to Lord John Berkeley and Sir George Carteret. During the American Revolution, New Jersey was the scene of many major battles, including Trenton, 1776; Princeton, 1777; and Monmouth, 1778. New Jersey was the third state to ratify the Constitution, 1787, and the first to approve the Bill of Rights, 1789. In a duel at Weehawken, 1804, Vice Pres. Aaron Burr fatally shot Alexander Hamilton. Canal and railroad building stimulated the growth of cities and industries in the 19th cent. The 20th-cent. arrival of large numbers of African Americans, Italians, Irish, European Jews, Puerto Ricans, South Asians, and other groups made New Jersey one of the most diverse states in the U.S. Construction of resort casinos in Atlantic City from the late 1970s revitalized tourism. Gov. James McGreevey resigned, 2004, after acknowledging an extramarital affair with a man identified as his former homeland security adviser. An estimated 37 people in New Jersey were killed when Hurricane Sandy (by then downgraded to a tropical storm) made landfall in 2012. Former members of Gov. Chris Christie's administration faced federal charges in 2014-15 over allegations that officials had created traffic jams on a toll bridge to punish a political opponent.

Famous New Jerseyans. Buzz Aldrin, Jason Alexander, Samuel Alito, Count Basie, Judy Blume, Jon Bon Jovi, Bill Bradley, Aaron Burr, Grover Cleveland, Stephen Crane, Danny DeVito, Thomas Edison, Albert Einstein, James Gandolfini, Allen Ginsberg, Alexander Hamilton, Ed Harris, Whitney Houston, Joyce Kilmer, Jack Nicholson, Shaquille O'Neal, Thomas Paine, Bill Parcells, Dorothy Parker, Joe Pesci, Molly Pitcher, Paul Robeson, Philip Roth, Antonin Scalia, Wally Schirra, H. Norman Schwarzkopf, Frank Sinatra, Bruce Springsteen, Martha Stewart, Meryl Streep, Dave Thomas, John Travolta, Walt Whitman, William Carlos Williams, Woodrow Wilson.

Website. www.nj.gov

New Mexico (NM)

Land of Enchantment

People. Population: 2,085,572; rank: 36. **Pop. change** (2010-14): 1.3%. **Pop. density:** 17.2 per sq mi. **Racial distribution:** 82.8% white; 2.5% black; 1.7% Asian; 10.4% Amer. Ind.; 0.2% Hawaiian/Pacific Islander; 2 or more races, 2.5%. **Hispanic pop.:** 45.7%.

Geography. Total area: 121,590 sq mi; rank: 5. **Land area:** 121,298 sq mi; rank: 5. **Acres forested:** 24.7 mil. **Location:** southwestern state bounded by Colorado on the N; Oklahoma, Texas, and Mexico on the E and S; Arizona on the W. **Climate:** dry, with temperatures rising or falling 5°F with every 1,000 ft elevation. **Topography:** eastern third, Great Plains; central third, Rocky Mts. (85% of the state is over 4,000-ft elevation); western third, high plateau. **Capital:** Santa Fe. **Chief airport:** Albuquerque.

Economy. Chief industries: government, services, trade. **Chief manuf. goods:** semiconductors, medical equip., navigational/measuring/medical/control instruments, aircraft, chemicals, jewelry. **Chief crops:** hay, pecans, corn, greenhouse and nursery, chiles, onions, cotton, wheat, peanuts. **Farm income:** crops, $706.13 mil; livestock/animal prods., $2.96 bil. **Nonfuel minerals:** $1.9 bil; copper, potash, sand and gravel (construction), molybdenum concentrates, stone (crushed). **Gross state product:** $93.0 bil. **Sales tax:** 5.125%. **Gasoline tax:** 37.28 cents/gal. **Employment distrib.:** 23.5% govt.; 16.6% trade/trans./util.; 3.3% mfg.; 16.0% ed./health; 12.1% prof./bus. serv.; 11.3% leisure/hosp.; 4.0% finance; 8.3% constr./mining/log.; 1.6% info.; 3.3% other serv. **Unemployment:** 6.5%. **Per cap. pers. income:** $37,605. **New private housing:** 4,799 units/$881.9 mil. **Broadband Internet:** 83.2%. **Commercial banks:** 56; deposits: $27.4 bil. **Savings institutions:** 7; deposits: $830.0 mil. **Lottery:** total sales: $136.0 mil; profit: $40.9 mil.

Federal govt. Fed. civ. employees: 21,560; **avg. salary:** $70,525. **Notable fed. facilities:** Kirtland, Cannon, Holloman AF Bases; Los Alamos Natl. Lab; White Sands Missile Range; Natl. Solar Observatory; Natl. Radio Astronomy Observatory (Very Large Array); Sandia Natl. Labs.

Education. High school grad. rate: 70.3%. **4-year public coll./univ.:** 9; **2-yr. public:** 19; **4-yr. private:** 3.

Energy. Electricity use/cost: 655 kWh, $76.56.

State data. Motto: Crescit Eundo (It grows as it goes). **Flower:** Yucca. **Bird:** Roadrunner. **Tree:** Piñon. **Songs:** "O, Fair New Mexico"; "Asi Es Nuevo Mexico." **Entered union:** Jan. 6, 1912; rank: 47th.

Tourism. Tourist spending: $6.6 bil. **Attractions:** Carlsbad Caverns Natl. Park (with Lechuguilla Cave, among world's longest caves); Petroglyph Natl. Monument, Sandia Peak Tramway, in Albuquerque; New Mexico History Museum, Museum of Intl. Folk Art, in Santa Fe (oldest U.S. capital); White Sands Natl. Monument (world's largest gypsum dune field); Chaco Culture Natl. Historical Park; Acoma Pueblo, or Sky City, built atop a 367-ft mesa; Taos Art Colony, Taos Ski Valley; Elephant Butte Lake State Park; Shiprock volcanic remnant; Intl. UFO Museum and Research Ctr., Roswell. **Information:** New Mexico Dept. of Tourism, 491 Old Santa Fe Trl., Santa Fe, NM 87501; 1-800-733-6396; www.newmexico.org

History. Inhabited for more than 10,000 years, the region was home to Sandia, Clovis, Folsom, Mogollon, and Anasazi cultures, followed by the Pueblo people, Anasazi descendants; later, nomadic Navajo and Apache came. Franciscan Marcos de Niza and a former black slave, Estevanico, explored the area, 1539, seeking gold; Coronado followed, 1540. First settlements were near San Juan Pueblo, 1598, and at Santa Fe, 1610. Settlers alternately traded and fought with the Apache, Comanche, and Navajo. Trade on the Santa Fe Trail to Missouri started, 1821. After the Mexican War began, 1846, Gen. Stephen Kearny took Santa Fe without firing a shot, and declared New Mexico part of the U.S. All Hispanic New Mexicans and Pueblo became U.S. citizens by terms of the 1848 treaty ending the war. New Mexico became a territory, 1850, but did not attain statehood until 1912. Pancho Villa raided Columbus, 1916, and U.S. troops were sent to the area. The world's first atomic bomb was exploded at a test site near Alamogordo, 1945. An underground nuclear waste depository opened near Carlsbad, 1999. Spaceport America, a state-owned commercial spaceport, hosted its first test launch in 2006.

Famous New Mexicans. Ben Abruzzo, Maxie Anderson, Jeff Bezos, William Bonney (Billy the Kid), Kit Carson, Bob Foster, Neil Patrick Harris, Tony Hillerman, Peter Hurd, Jean Baptiste Lamy, Nancy Lopez, Bill Mauldin, Georgia O'Keeffe, Bill Richardson, Kim Stanley, Al Unser, Bobby Unser.

Website. www.newmexico.gov

New York (NY)

Empire State

People. Population: 19,746,227; rank: 4. **Pop. change** (2010-14): 1.9%. **Pop. density:** 419.0 per sq mi. **Racial distribution:** 70.4% white; 17.6% black; 8.5% Asian; 1.0% Amer. Ind.; 0.1% Hawaiian/Pacific Islander; 2 or more races, 2.4%. **Hispanic pop.:** 17.3%.

Geography. Total area: 54,555 sq mi; rank: 27. **Land area:** 47,126 sq mi; rank: 30. **Acres forested:** 18.9 mil. **Location:** Middle Atlantic state bordered by the New England states, Atlantic Ocean on E; New Jersey and Pennsylvania on S; Lakes Ontario and Erie on W; Canada on N. **Climate:** variable; the SE region moderated by the ocean. **Topography:** highest and most rugged mountains in the NE Adirondack upland; St. Lawrence-Champlain lowlands extend from Lake Ontario NE along the Canadian border; Hudson-Mohawk lowland follows rivers N and W, 10-30 mi wide; Atlantic coastal plain in the SE; Appalachian Highlands, covering half the state westward from the Hudson Valley, include the Catskill Mts., Finger Lakes; plateau of Erie-Ontario lowlands. **Capital:** Albany. **Chief airports:** New York (2), Buffalo, Albany, Rochester, Syracuse, White Plains, Islip.

Economy. Chief industries: manufacturing, finance, communications, tourism, transportation, services. **Chief manuf. goods:** pharmaceuticals, photographic chemicals, electronics, automotive parts, toiletries, printing, plastics, apparel. **Chief crops:** greenhouse and nursery, apples, corn, hay, cabbage, onions, soybeans, potatoes, snap beans, grapes, squash, pumpkins, tomatoes, wheat, cucumbers, green peas. **Farm income:** crops, $2.10 bil; livestock/animal prods., $4.26 bil. **Nonfuel minerals:** $1.4 bil; salt, stone (crushed), sand and gravel (construction), cement (portland), wollastonite. **Commercial fishing:** $57.0 mil. **Chief ports:** New York, Buffalo, Albany. **Gross state product:** $1.4 tril. **Sales tax:** 4.0%. **Gasoline tax:** 64.39 cents/gal. **Employment distrib.:** 15.7% govt.; 16.9% trade/trans./util.; 4.9% mfg.; 20.6% ed./health; 13.6% prof./bus. serv.; 9.7% leisure/hosp.; 7.5% finance; 3.9% constr./mining/log.; 2.8% info.; 4.4% other serv. **Unemployment:** 6.3%. **Per cap. pers. income:** $56,231. **New private housing:** 36,286 units/$5.6 bil. **Broadband Internet:** 87.2%. **Commercial banks:** 155; deposits: $1.2 tril. **Savings institutions:** 58; deposits: $69.9 bil. **Lottery:** total sales: $9.2 bil; profit: $3.2 bil.

Federal govt. Fed. civ. employees: 52,261; **avg. salary:** $78,440. **Notable fed. facilities:** Ft. Drum; West Point Military Academy; Merchant Marine Academy; NY Fed. Reserve; U.S. Army Watervliet Arsenal; Brookhaven Natl. Lab; U.S. Mission to the United Nations.

Education. High school grad. rate: 76.8%. **4-year public coll./univ.:** 43; **2-yr. public:** 36; **4-yr. private:** 165.

Energy. Electricity use/cost: 602 kWh, $113.17.

State data. Motto: Excelsior (Ever upward). **Flower:** Rose. **Bird:** Bluebird. **Tree:** Sugar maple. **Song:** "I Love New York." **Eleventh** of original 13 states to ratify the Constitution, July 26, 1788.

Tourism. Tourist spending: $62.2 bil. **Attractions:** New York City; Adirondack and Catskill Mountains; Watkins Glen State Park; Thousand Islands region; Niagara Falls; Saratoga Race Course, Saratoga Springs; Philipsburg Manor, Old Dutch Church of Sleepy Hollow, in Sleepy Hollow; Washington Irving's Sunnyside, Tarrytown; Corning Museum of Glass; Fenimore Art Museum, Natl. Baseball Hall of Fame and Museum, in Cooperstown; Ft. Ticonderoga; New York State Capitol, Albany; Home of Franklin D. Roosevelt Natl. Historic Site, Hyde Park; Long Island beaches; Sagamore Hill (Theodore Roosevelt's "Summer White House"), Oyster Bay. **Information:** Empire State Development, Travel Information Center, 30 South Pearl St., Albany, NY 12245; 1-800-CALL-NYS; www.iloveny.com

History. When Europeans arrived, Algonquians including the Mahican, Wappinger, and Lenni Lenape inhabited the region, as did the Iroquoian Mohawk, Oneida, Onondaga, Cayuga, and Seneca tribes, who established the League of the Five Nations. Giovanni da Verrazano entered New York harbor, 1524. In 1609, Henry Hudson visited the river later named for him, and Samuel de Champlain explored the lake that now bears his name. The first permanent settlement was Dutch, near present-day Albany, 1624. New Amsterdam was settled, 1626, at the southern tip of Manhattan island. A British fleet seized New Netherland, 1664. Key battles of the American Revolution included Saratoga, 1777. In the 19th cent., New York City emerged as one of the world's great metropolitan areas, a center for trade, finance, and arts, and a haven for millions of immigrants. Completion of Erie Canal, 1825, established the state as a gateway to the West. The first women's rights convention was held in Seneca Falls, 1848. Although the state backed the Union in the Civil War, an 1863 military draft triggered three days of riots in New York City. Industry declined in the 20th cent., and California and Texas passed New York in population. Attica was the scene of a bloody prison revolt, 1971. Two jet aircraft hijacked by terrorists on Sept. 11, 2001, destroyed the World Trade Center in lower Manhattan. Gov. Eliot Spitzer resigned in Mar. 2008 after 14 months in office; he was alleged to have patronized a prostitution ring. An estimated 65 people in New York state were killed when Hurricane Sandy (by then downgraded to a tropical storm) made landfall in Oct. 2012. Citing concerns over health risks, Gov. Andrew Cuomo in Dec. 2014 announced a statewide ban on hydraulic fracturing (or "fracking") as a method to access the state's natural gas resources.

Famous New Yorkers. Woody Allen, Susan B. Anthony, James Baldwin, Lucille Ball, Ann Bancroft, L. Frank Baum, Milton Berle, Humphrey Bogart, Barbara Boxer, Mel Brooks, Benjamin Cardozo, De Witt Clinton, James Fenimore Cooper, Peter Cooper, Aaron Copland, Francis Ford Coppola, Tom Cruise, Robert De Niro, George Eastman, Jimmy Fallon, Millard Fillmore, Lou Gehrig, George and Ira Gershwin, Ruth Bader Ginsburg, Rudolph Giuliani, Jackie Gleason, Stephen Jay Gould, Julia Ward Howe, Charles Evans Hughes, Washington Irving, Henry and William James, John Jay, Edward Koch, Fiorello LaGuardia, Herman Melville, Arthur Miller, J. Pierpont Morgan Jr., Eddie Murphy, Joyce Carol Oates, Carroll O'Connor, Rosie O'Donnell, Eugene O'Neill, Jerry Orbach, George Pataki, Colin Powell, Nancy Reagan, John Roberts, John D. Rockefeller, Nelson Rockefeller, Richard Rodgers, Ray Romano, Eleanor Roosevelt, Franklin D. Roosevelt, Theodore Roosevelt, Tim Russert, J. D. Salinger, Caroline Kennedy Schlossberg, Jerry Seinfeld, Al Sharpton, Paul Simon, Alfred E. Smith, Elizabeth Cady Stanton, Barbra Streisand, Donald Trump, William (Boss) Tweed, Martin Van Buren, Luther Vandross, Gore Vidal, Denzel Washington, Edith Wharton, Walt Whitman, Mark Zuckerberg.

Website. www.ny.gov

North Carolina (NC)

Tar Heel State, Old North State

People. Population: 9,943,964; rank: 9. **Pop. change** (2010-14): 4.3%. **Pop. density:** 204.5 per sq mi. **Racial**

distribution: 71.5% white; 22.1% black; 2.7% Asian; 1.6% Amer. Ind.; 0.1% Hawaiian/Pacific Islander; 2 or more races, 2.1%. **Hispanic pop.:** 8.0%.

Geography. Total area: 53,819 sq mi; rank: 28. **Land area:** 48,618 sq mi; rank: 29. **Acres forested:** 18.8 mil. **Location:** South Atlantic state bounded on N by Virginia, on S by South Carolina, on SW by Georgia, on W by Tennessee, and on E by Atlantic. **Climate:** subtropical in SE, medium-continental in mountain region; tempered by the Gulf Stream and mountains in W. **Topography:** coastal plain and tidewater in two-fifths of state, extending to the fall line of the rivers; Piedmont Plateau in another two-fifths has gentle to rugged hills; southern Appalachian Mts. contain the Blue Ridge and Great Smoky Mts. **Capital:** Raleigh. **Chief airports:** Charlotte, Raleigh, Greensboro.

Economy. Chief industries: manufacturing, agriculture, tourism. **Chief manuf. goods:** transportation, tobacco, pharmaceuticals, toiletries, plastics, animal slaughtering and processing, household furniture, fabric and apparel. **Chief crops:** greenhouse and nursery, tobacco, cotton, soybeans, corn, Christmas trees, sweet potatoes, wheat, peanuts, blueberries, cucumbers, tomatoes, hay, potatoes. **Farm income:** crops, $4.27 bil; livestock/animal prods., $8.85 bil. **Nonfuel minerals:** $1.3 bil; stone (crushed), phosphate rock, sand and gravel (construction), sand and gravel (industrial), clays (common). **Commercial fishing:** $79.1 mil. **Chief ports:** Morehead City, Wilmington. **Gross state product:** $483.1 bil. **Sales tax:** 4.75%. **Gasoline tax:** 54.65 cents/gal. **Employment distrib.:** 17.2% govt.; 18.5% trade/trans./util.; 10.7% mfg.; 13.6% ed./health; 13.9% prof./bus. serv.; 11.0% leisure/hosp.; 5.1% finance; 4.6% constr./mining/log.; 1.7% info.; 3.6% other serv. **Unemployment:** 6.1%. **Per cap. pers. income:** $39,646. **New private housing:** 49,911 units/$8.6 bil. **Broadband Internet:** 84.4%. **Commercial banks:** 76; deposits: $334.8 bil. **Savings institutions:** 24; deposits: $5.0 bil. **Lottery:** total sales: $1.8 bil; profit: $503.1 mil.

Federal govt. Fed. civ. employees: 41,728; **avg. salary:** $70,788. **Notable fed. facilities:** Ft. Bragg; Camp Lejeune Marine Base, Marine Corps Air Station Cherry Point; NOAA Natl. Centers for Environmental Information.; Natl. Inst. of Environmental Health Sciences, EPA Research and Dev. Labs, all in Research Triangle Park.

Education. High school grad. rate: 82.5%. **4-year public coll./univ.:** 16; **2-yr. public:** 59; **4-yr. private:** 49.

Energy. Electricity use/cost: 1,098 kWh, $120.52.

State data. Motto: Esse Quam Videri (To be rather than to seem). **Flower:** Dogwood. **Bird:** Cardinal. **Tree:** Pine. **Song:** "The Old North State." **Twelfth** of the original 13 states to ratify the Constitution, Nov. 21, 1789.

Tourism. Tourist spending: $21.0 bil. **Attractions:** Cape Hatteras and Cape Lookout Natl. Seashores; Great Smoky Mountains Natl. Park; Guilford Courthouse Natl. Military Park; Moore's Creek Natl. Battlefield (1776 victory ended British rule in colony); Bennett Place (site of largest troop surrender of Civil War), Durham; Ft. Raleigh Natl. Historic Site, North Carolina Aquarium, on Roanoke Island; Wright Brothers Natl. Mem., Kill Devil Hills; USS *North Carolina*, Wilmington; North Carolina Zoo, Asheboro; North Carolina Symphony, Marbles Kids Museum, North Carolina Museum of Art, North Carolina Museum of Natural Sciences, in Raleigh; Carl Sandburg Home, Flat Rock; Biltmore House and Gardens, North Carolina Arboretum, in Asheville; U.S. Natl. Whitewater Ctr., Discovery Place, in Charlotte; Fort Macon State Park, Atlantic Beach. **Information:** North Carolina Division of Tourism, Film and Sports Development, 4324 Mail Service Ctr., Raleigh, NC 27699; 1-800-VISIT-NC, (919) 733-8372; www.visitnc.com

History. Algonquian, Siouan, and Iroquoian peoples lived in the region at the time of European contact. Sir Walter Raleigh tried to found a colony, 1584-87; the "Lost Colony" on Roanoke Island, 1587, seemingly disappeared without a trace. Permanent settlers came from Virginia in the mid-17th cent. The province's congress was the first to vote for independence, 1776. In the Revolutionary War, Gen. Charles Cornwallis's forces were defeated at Kings Mountain, 1780, and forced out after Guilford Courthouse, 1781. The state ratified the Constitution, 1789, only after Congress passed the Bill of Rights. North Carolina, where one-third of the population was slaves, seceded from the Union, 1861, and provided more troops to the Confederacy than any other state; it was readmitted, 1868. The Wright brothers made the first powered airplane flight at Kitty Hawk, 1903. Sit-ins at segregated Greensboro lunch counters, 1960, drew national attention to the civil rights movement. Long reliant on tobacco, textiles, and wood products, North Carolina has prospered since the 1960s from advanced technologies in the Raleigh-Durham-Chapel Hill area and banking in Charlotte. The hurricane-prone state was hit hard by Hazel, 1954, Fran, 1996, and Floyd, 1999.

Famous North Carolinians. David Brinkley, Shirley Caesar, John Coltrane, Rick Dees, Elizabeth Hanford Dole, Dale Earnhardt Sr., John Edwards, Ava Gardner, Richard Jordan Gatling, Billy Graham, Andy Griffith, O. Henry, Andrew Jackson, Andrew Johnson, Michael Jordan, William Rufus King, Charles Kuralt, Meadowlark Lemon, Dolley Madison, Thelonious Monk, Edward R. Murrow, Richard Petty, James K. Polk, Charlie Rose, Carl Sandburg, Enos Slaughter, Dean Smith, James Taylor, Thomas Wolfe.

Website. www.nc.gov

North Dakota (ND)

Peace Garden State

People. Population: 739,482; rank: 47. **Pop. change** (2010-14): 9.9%. **Pop. density:** 10.7 per sq mi. **Racial distribution:** 89.1% white; 2.1% black; 1.3% Asian; 5.4% Amer. Ind.; 0.1% Hawaiian/Pacific Islander; 2 or more races, 2%. **Hispanic pop.:** 1.8%.

Geography. Total area: 70,698 sq mi; rank: 19. **Land area:** 69,001 sq mi; rank: 17. **Acres forested:** 0.8 mil. **Location:** West North Central state situated exactly in the middle of North America, bounded on the N by Canada, on the E by Minnesota, on the S by South Dakota, on the W by Montana. **Climate:** continental, with a wide range of temperatures and moderate rainfall. **Topography:** Central Lowland in the E comprises the flat Red R. Valley and the Rolling Drift Prairie; Missouri Plateau of the Great Plains on the W. **Capital:** Bismarck.

Economy. Chief industries: agriculture, mining, tourism, manufacturing, telecommunications, energy, food processing. **Chief manuf. goods:** machinery, wood prods., motor vehicles and parts, furniture, processed foods. **Chief crops:** wheat, soybeans, corn, sugar beets, barley, dry beans, sunflowers, canola, potatoes, flaxseed, hay, dry peas, lentils, oats. **Farm income:** crops, $6.56 bil; livestock/animal prods., $1.61 bil. **Nonfuel minerals:** $232 mil; sand and gravel (construction), lime, stone (crushed), clays (common), sand and gravel (industrial). **Gross state product:** $55.1 bil. **Sales tax:** 5.0%. **Gasoline tax:** 41.40 cents/gal. **Employment distrib.:** 18.0% govt.; 22.8% trade/trans./util.; 5.6% mfg.; 12.7% ed./health; 7.7% prof./bus. serv.; 8.9% leisure/hosp.; 5.2% finance; 13.9% constr./mining/log.; 1.4% info.; 3.8% other serv. **Unemployment:** 2.8%. **Per cap. pers. income:** $54,951. **New private housing:** 12,178 units/$1.6 bil. **Broadband Internet:** 82.1%. **Commercial banks:** 93; deposits: $23.3 bil. **Savings institutions:** 2; deposits: $1.6 bil. **Lottery:** total sales: $27.0 mil; profit: $7.8 mil.

Federal govt. Fed. civ. employees: 5,401; **avg. salary:** $64,676. **Notable fed. facilities:** Minot AFB; Grand Forks AFB; Northern Prairie Wildlife Res. Ctr.; Garrison Dam Natl. Fish Hatchery; Grand Forks Human Nutrition Res. Ctr.

Education. High school grad. rate: 87.5%. **4-year public coll./univ.:** 9; **2-yr. public:** 5; **4-yr. private:** 6.

Energy. Electricity use/cost: 1,205 kWh, $109.85.

State data. Motto: Liberty and union, now and forever, one and inseparable. **Flower:** Wild prairie rose. **Bird:** Western meadowlark. **Tree:** American elm. **Song:** "North Dakota Hymn." **Entered union:** Nov. 2, 1889; rank: 39th.

Tourism. Tourist spending: $3.1 bil. **Attractions:** North Dakota Heritage Ctr., North Dakota State Capitol, in Bismarck; Bonanzaville, West Fargo; Ft. Union Trading Post Natl. Historic Site; Intl. Peace Garden, Dunseith; Elkhorn Ranch site, in Theodore Roosevelt Natl. Park; Ft. Abraham Lincoln State Park and Museum, Mandan; Dakota Dinosaur Museum, Dickinson; Knife River Indian Villages Natl. Historic Site; Scandinavian Heritage Park, Minden. **Information:** North Dakota Tourism Division, Century Center, 1600 E. Century Ave., Ste. 2, P.O. Box 2057, Bismarck, ND 58502; 1-800-435-5663; www.ndtourism.com

History. Paleo-Indian peoples hunted in the area at least 11,000 years ago. At the time of European contact, the Ojibwa, Yanktonai and Teton Sioux, Mandan, Arikara, and Hidatsa peoples lived in the region. Pierre de Varennes, sieur de La Vérendrye, was the first French fur trader in the area, 1738, followed by the English at the end of the 18th cent. Lewis and Clark built Ft. Mandan, near present-day Washburn, 1804-05, and wintered there. The first permanent settlement was at Pembina, 1812. Missouri River steamboats reached the area, 1832. Dakota Territory was organized, 1861. The first railroad arrived,

1872. The "bonanza farm" craze of the 1870s-80s led to statehood, 1889. The Nonpartisan League, a farmers' group favoring state ownership of industries, helped elect Lynn Frazier as governor, 1916, but he and others were ousted in a recall vote, 1921. The predominantly agricultural state has one of the nation's lowest unemployment rates, mostly due to surging oil production since late 2008 in the state's Bakken formation.

Famous North Dakotans. Maxwell Anderson, Angie Dickinson, Josh Duhamel, John Bernard Flannagan, Phil Jackson, Louis L'Amour, Peggy Lee, Roger Maris, Eric Sevareid, Vilhjalmur Stefansson, Lawrence Welk.

Website. www.nd.gov

Ohio (OH)

Buckeye State

People. Population: 11,594,163; rank: 7. **Pop. change** (2010-14): 0.5%. **Pop. density:** 283.7 per sq mi. **Racial distribution:** 83% white; 12.6% black; 2.0% Asian; 0.3% Amer. Ind.; 0.1% Hawaiian/Pacific Islander; 2 or more races, 2.1%. **Hispanic pop.:** 3.1%.

Geography. Total area: 44,826 sq mi; rank: 34. **Land area:** 40,861 sq mi; rank: 35. **Acres forested:** 8.2 mil. **Location:** East North Central state bounded on the N by Michigan and Lake Erie; on the E and S by Pennsylvania, West Virginia, and Kentucky; on the W by Indiana. **Climate:** temperate but variable; weather subject to much precipitation. **Topography:** generally rolling plain; Allegheny Plateau in E; Lake Erie Plains extend southward; central plains in the W. **Capital:** Columbus. **Chief airports:** Cleveland, Columbus, Dayton, Akron.

Economy. Chief industries: manufacturing, trade, services. **Chief manuf. goods:** motor vehicles and parts, petroleum, plastics and rubber, iron and steel, aircraft, machinery, fabricated metal, printing. **Chief crops:** corn, soybeans, hay, wheat, grapes, potatoes, tomatoes, apples, strawberries, tobacco. **Farm income:** crops, $6.17 bil; livestock/animal prods., $4.11 bil. **Nonfuel minerals:** $1.2 bil; stone (crushed), salt, sand and gravel (construction), lime, cement (portland). **Commercial fishing:** $5.8 mil. **Chief ports:** Cincinnati, Toledo, Conneaut, Cleveland, Ashtabula. **Gross state product:** $583.3 bil. **Sales tax:** 5.75%. **Gasoline tax:** 46.40 cents/gal. **Employment distrib.:** 14.2% govt.; 18.5% trade/trans./util.; 12.7% mfg.; 16.5% ed./health; 13.1% prof./bus. serv.; 10.4% leisure/hosp.; 5.4% finance; 3.8% constr./mining/log.; 1.3% info.; 3.9% other serv. **Unemployment:** 5.7%. **Per cap. pers. income:** $42,571. **New private housing:** 19,872 units/$3.8 bil. **Broadband Internet:** 84.0%. **Commercial banks:** 161; deposits: $240.3 bil. **Savings institutions:** 88; deposits: $31.2 bil. **Lottery:** total sales: $2.7 bil; profit: $904.3 mil.

Federal govt. Fed. civ. employees: 47,781; **avg. salary:** $78,732. **Notable fed. facilities:** Wright-Patterson AFB; Defense Supply Ctr., Columbus; NASA Glenn Research Ctr.; Joint Systems Manufacturing Center.

Education. High school grad. rate: 82.2%. **4-year public coll./univ.:** 35; **2-yr. public:** 25; **4-yr. private:** 68.

Energy. Electricity use/cost: 892 kWh, $107.07.

State data. Motto: With God, all things are possible. **Flower:** Scarlet carnation. **Bird:** Cardinal. **Tree:** Buckeye. **Song:** "Beautiful Ohio." **Entered union:** Mar. 1, 1803; rank: 17th.

Tourism. Tourist spending: $17.7 bil. **Attractions:** Hopewell Culture Natl. Historical Park, Chillicothe; Cuyahoga Valley Natl. Park; Armstrong Air and Space Museum, Wapakoneta; Natl. Museum of the U.S. Air Force, near Dayton; Pro Football Hall of Fame, First Ladies Natl. Historic Site, in Canton; Kings Island amusement park, Mason; Lake Erie Islands, Cedar Point amusement park, in Sandusky; birthplaces, homes of, and memorials to presidents W. H. Harrison, Grant, Hayes, Garfield, B. Harrison, McKinley, Taft, and Harding; Amish Country, particularly in Holmes County; German Village historic neighborhood, Franklin Park Conservatory and Botanical Gardens, in Columbus; Rock and Roll Hall of Fame and Museum, West Side Market, Cleveland Metroparks Zoo, in Cleveland; Cincinnati Museum Center at Union Terminal; Toledo Zoo. **Information:** Division of Travel and Tourism, P.O. Box 1001, Columbus, OH 43216; 1-800-BUCKEYE; www.discoverohio.com

History. Paleo-Indians hunted in the area about 11,000 years ago; the Adena and Hopewell cultures followed. Wyandot, Delaware, Miami, and Shawnee peoples sparsely occupied the area when the first Europeans arrived. René-Robert Cavelier, sieur de La Salle, visited the region, 1669. France claimed it, 1682, but ceded it to Britain, 1763. After the American Revolution, Ohio became part of the Northwest Territory, 1787. The first permanent settlement was at Marietta, 1788. Cincinnati was also founded, 1788; Cleveland, 1796. Indian warfare abated with the Treaty of Greenville, 1795. Ohio became a state, 1803. In the War of 1812, Oliver Hazard Perry's victory on Lake Erie and William Henry Harrison's invasion of Canada, 1813, ended British incursions. Columbus, founded 1812, became the state capital, 1816. Before the Civil War, Ohioans aided the Underground Railroad, helping runaway slaves. Agricultural for much of the 19th cent., the state became an industrial powerhouse in the 20th cent. but struggled to replace well-paying manufacturing jobs that began disappearing even before the 2007-09 recession. No Republican has ever won the presidency without winning Ohio's electoral votes.

Famous Ohioans. Berenice Abbott, Sherwood Anderson, Neil Armstrong, George Bellows, Halle Berry, Ambrose Bierce, Erma Bombeck, Drew Carey, Hart Crane, George Custer, Clarence Darrow, Paul Laurence Dunbar, Thomas Edison, Clark Gable, John Glenn, Zane Grey, Bob Hope, William Dean Howells, LeBron James, Maya Lin, Toni Morrison, Paul Newman, Jack Nicklaus, Annie Oakley, Jesse Owens, Jack Paar, Pontiac, Eddie Rickenbacker, John D. Rockefeller Sr. and Jr., Roy Rogers, Pete Rose, Arthur Schlesinger Jr., Gen. William Sherman, Steven Spielberg, Gloria Steinem, Harriet Beecher Stowe, Robert A. Taft, William H. Taft, Tecumseh, James Thurber, Ted Turner, Orville and Wilbur Wright.

Website. www.ohio.gov

Oklahoma (OK)

Sooner State

People. Population: 3,878,051; rank: 28. **Pop. change** (2010-14): 3.4%. **Pop. density:** 56.5 per sq mi. **Racial distribution:** 75.1% white; 7.7% black; 2.1% Asian; 9.0% Amer. Ind.; 0.2% Hawaiian/Pacific Islander; 2 or more races, 5.9%. **Hispanic pop.:** 8.6%.

Geography. Total area: 69,899 sq mi; rank: 20. **Land area:** 68,595 sq mi; rank: 19. **Acres forested:** 12.3 mil. **Location:** West South Central state bounded on the N by Colorado and Kansas, on the E by Missouri and Arkansas, on the S and W by Texas and New Mexico. **Climate:** temperate; southern humid belt merging with colder northern continental; humid eastern and dry western zones. **Topography:** high plains predominate in the W, hills and small mountains in the E; the E central region is dominated by the Arkansas R. Basin, and the S by the Red R. Plains. **Capital:** Oklahoma City. **Chief airports:** Oklahoma City, Tulsa.

Economy. Chief industries: manufacturing, mineral and energy exploration and production, agriculture, services. **Chief manuf. goods:** animal slaughtering and processing, petroleum, plastics and rubber, fabricated metals, machinery, motor vehicles and parts. **Chief crops:** wheat, greenhouse and nursery, hay, cotton, corn, soybeans, pecans, sorghum, peanuts. **Farm income:** crops, $1.34 bil; livestock/animal prods., $6.23 bil. **Nonfuel minerals:** $734 mil; stone (crushed), cement (portland), sand and gravel (industrial), sand and gravel (construction), helium (Grade A). **Chief port:** Catoosa. **Gross state product:** $183.5 bil. **Sales tax:** 4.5%. **Gasoline tax:** 35.40 cents/gal. **Employment distrib.:** 21.3% govt.; 18.2% trade/trans./util.; 8.0% mfg.; 13.7% ed./health; 11.3% prof./bus. serv.; 9.8% leisure/hosp.; 4.8% finance; 7.9% constr./mining/log.; 1.3% info.; 3.7% other serv. **Unemployment:** 4.5%. **Per cap. pers. income:** $43,138. **New private housing:** 14,179 units/$2.5 bil. **Broadband Internet:** 95.2%. **Commercial banks:** 237; deposits: $74.4 bil. **Savings institutions:** 4; deposits: $5.0 bil. **Lottery:** total sales: $191.2 mil; profit: $66.9 mil.

Federal govt. Fed. civ. employees: 36,398; **avg. salary:** $66,839. **Notable fed. facilities:** Tinker AFB; FAA Mike Monroney Aeronautical Ctr.; Ft. Sill; Altus AFB; McAlester Army Ammunition Plant; Vance AFB; Natl. Severe Storms Lab.

Education. High school grad. rate: 84.8%. **4-year public coll./univ.:** 17; **2-yr. public:** 13; **4-yr. private:** 14.

Energy. Electricity use/cost: 1,142 kWh, $110.55.

State data. Motto: Labor Omnia Vincit (Labor conquers all things). **Flower:** Mistletoe. **Bird:** Scissor-tailed flycatcher. **Tree:** Redbud. **Song:** "Oklahoma!" **Entered union:** Nov. 16, 1907; rank: 46th.

Tourism. Tourist spending: $7.5 bil. **Attractions:** Cherokee Heritage Ctr., Tahlequah; Oklahoma City Natl. Memorial and Museum, Natl. Cowboy and Western Heritage Museum, White Water Bay and Frontier City amusement parks, Museum of Osteology, Bricktown neighborhood, in Oklahoma City; Will Rogers Memorial Museums, Claremore and Oologah; Philbrook Museum of Art, Gilcrease Museum, in

Tulsa; Wichita Mountains Wildlife Refuge; Woolaroc Museum and Wildlife Preserve, Price Tower Arts Center, in Bartlesville; Sequoyah's Cabin, Sallisaw; Sam Noble Museum of Natural History, Norman. **Information:** Travel and Tourism Division, 120 N. Robinson, 6th Fl., P.O. Box 52002, Oklahoma City, OK 73152-2002; 1-800-652-6552; www.travelok.com

History. Few Native Americans inhabited the region when the Spanish explorer Coronado arrived, 1541; in the 16th and 17th cent., French traders visited. Part of the Louisiana Purchase, 1803, Oklahoma was known as Indian Country and, from 1834, Indian Territory. It became home to the "Five Civilized Tribes"—Cherokee, Choctaw, Chickasaw, Creek, and Seminole—after the forced removal of Indians from the eastern U.S., 1828-46. The land was also used by Comanche, Osage, and other Plains Indians. As white settlers pressed west, land was opened for homesteading by "runs" and lottery. The first run was in 1889; the most famous run, 1893, was to the Cherokee Outlet. Oklahoma became a state, 1907. In the early 20th cent., oil finds brought wealth to the Tulsa area; the Greenwood section of the city, then known as the "Negro Wall Street," was devastated by a white mob, 1921. Depression and drought drove many "Okies" from the Dust Bowl to California in the 1930s. A truck bomb in Oklahoma City, 1995, destroyed a federal office building, killing 168 people; Timothy McVeigh was executed for the crime, 2001. A tornado in Moore killed 23 people May 20, 2013; the widest tornado on record touched down in El Reno May 31, 2013, killing 10 people. Since 2010, Oklahoma has experienced thousands of earthquakes believed to be connected with the use of disposal wells for waste from oil and gas operations.

Famous Oklahomans. Troy Aikman, Carl Albert, Gene Autry, Johnny Bench, William Boyd (Hopalong Cassidy), Garth Brooks, Lon Chaney, Gordon Cooper, Ralph Ellison, John Hope Franklin, James Garner, Vince Gill, Woody Guthrie, Paul Harvey, Ron Howard, Patrick J. Hurley, Ben Johnson, Jeane Kirkpatrick, Louis L'Amour, Shannon Lucid, Wilma Mankiller, Mickey Mantle, Reba McEntire, Wiley Post, Tony Randall, Oral Roberts, Will Rogers, Barry Switzer, Maria Tallchief, Jim Thorpe, Carrie Underwood, J. C. Watts Jr.

Website. www.ok.gov

Oregon (OR)

Beaver State

People. Population: 3,970,239; rank: 27. **Pop. change** (2010-14): 3.6%. **Pop. density:** 41.4 per sq mi. **Racial distribution:** 87.9% white; 2.0% black; 4.3% Asian; 1.8% Amer. Ind.; 0.4% Hawaiian/Pacific Islander; 2 or more races, 3.6%. **Hispanic pop.:** 11.3%.

Geography. Total area: 98,379 sq mi; rank: 9. **Land area:** 95,988 sq mi; rank: 10. **Acres forested:** 29.7 mil. **Location:** Pacific state bounded on N by Washington, on E by Idaho, on S by Nevada and California, on W by the Pacific. **Climate:** mild and humid on coast; continental dryness and extreme temperatures in the interior. **Topography:** Coast Range of rugged mountains; fertile Willamette R. Valley to E and S; Cascade Mt. Range of volcanic peaks E of the valley; plateau E of Cascades, remaining two-thirds of state. **Capital:** Salem. **Chief airport:** Portland.

Economy. Chief industries: manufacturing, services, trade, finance, insurance, real estate, government, construction. **Chief manuf. goods:** wood prods., frozen produce, printing, computers and electronics, transportation equip., industrial machinery. **Chief crops:** greenhouse and nursery, grass seed, hay, wheat, potatoes, Christmas trees, onions, pears, hazelnuts, corn, grapes, cherries, blackberries, blueberries, peppermint, snap beans, apples, hops. **Farm income:** crops, $3.30 bil; livestock/animal prods., $1.90 bil. **Nonfuel minerals:** $357 mil; stone (crushed), sand and gravel (construction), cement (portland), diatomite, perlite (crude). **Commercial fishing:** $179.2 mil. **Chief ports:** Portland, Coos Bay. **Gross state product:** $215.7 bil. **Sales tax:** none. **Gasoline tax:** 49.47 cents/gal. **Employment distrib.:** 17.4% govt.; 18.5% trade/trans./util.; 10.5% mfg.; 14.6% ed./health; 12.9% prof./bus. serv.; 10.7% leisure/hosp.; 5.2% finance; 4.9% constr./mining/log.; 1.9% info.; 3.4% other serv. **Unemployment:** 6.9%. **Per cap. pers. income:** $41,681. **New private housing:** 16,645 units/$3.2 bil. **Broadband Internet:** 88.5%. **Commercial banks:** 48; deposits: $61.1 bil. **Savings institutions:** 7; deposits: $906.0 mil. **Lottery:** total sales: $1.1 bil; profit: $516.7 mil.

Federal govt. Fed. civ. employees: 18,328; **avg. salary:** $72,954. **Notable fed. facilities:** Bonneville Power Admin.

Education. High school grad. rate: 68.7%. **4-year public coll./univ.:** 9; **2-yr. public:** 17; **4-yr. private:** 24.

Energy. Electricity use/cost: 976 kWh, $96.58.

State data. Motto: She flies with her own wings. **Flower:** Oregon grape. **Bird:** Western meadowlark. **Tree:** Douglas fir. **Song:** "Oregon, My Oregon." **Entered union:** Feb. 14, 1859; rank: 33rd.

Tourism. Tourist spending: $9.7 bil. **Attractions:** John Day Fossil Beds Natl. Monument; Multnomah Falls, Columbia River Gorge; Timberline Lodge, Mount Hood Natl. Forest; Crater Lake Natl. Park; Oregon Dunes Natl. Recreation Area; Ft. Clatsop (Lewis and Clark Natl. Historical Park), Astoria Column, in Astoria; Oregon Caves Natl. Monument; Intl. Rose Test Garden, Lan Su Chinese Garden, Pittock Mansion, Oregon Museum of Science and Industry, in Portland; Oregon Shakespeare Festival, Ashland; High Desert Museum, Bend; "Spruce Goose" (largest aircraft ever built), Evergreen Aviation and Space Museum, McMinnville; Yaquina Head Outstanding Natural Area, Oregon Coast Aquarium, in Newport. **Information:** Travel Oregon, 670 Hawthorne SE, Ste. 240, Salem, OR 97301; 1-800-547-7842; www.traveloregon.com

History. More than 100 Native American tribes inhabited the area at the time of European contact, including the Chinook, Yakima, Cayuse, Modoc, and Nez Percé. Capt. Robert Gray sighted and sailed into the Columbia R., 1792. Lewis and Clark, traveling overland, wintered at its mouth, 1805-06. Fur traders sent by John Jacob Astor established the Astoria trading post in the Columbia River region, 1811. Settlers arrived in the Willamette Valley, 1834. In 1843, the first large wave of settlers arrived via the Oregon Trail. Oregon became a territory, 1848, and a state, 1859. Early in the 20th cent., the "Oregon System"—political reforms that included initiative, referendum, recall, direct primary, and woman suffrage—was adopted. Originally dominated by forest products, the economy diversified after World War II, with technology firms clustering in the "Silicon Forest" area around Portland. Oregonians were the first in the U.S. to pass measures allowing physician-assisted suicide for terminally ill patients, 1994, and establishing an all-mail voting system, 1998. Gov. John Kitzhaber resigned a month into his unprecedented fourth term in 2015, amidst an ethics scandal.

Famous Oregonians. Ernest Bloch, Bill Bowerman, Ty Burrell, Beverly Cleary, Matt Groening, Ernest Haycox, Chief Joseph, Ken Kesey, Phil Knight, Ursula K. Le Guin, Edwin Markham, Tom McCall, John McLoughlin, Joaquin Miller, Bob Packwood, Linus Pauling, Steve Prefontaine, John "Jack" Reed, Alberto Salazar, Mary Decker Slaney, William Simon U'Ren.

Website. www.oregon.gov

Pennsylvania (PA)

Keystone State

People. Population: 12,787,209; rank: 6. **Pop. change** (2010-14): 0.7%. **Pop. density:** 285.8 per sq mi. **Racial distribution:** 82.9% white; 11.6% black; 3.3% Asian; 0.3% Amer. Ind.; 0.1% Hawaiian/Pacific Islander; 2 or more races, 1.8%. **Hispanic pop.:** 5.6%.

Geography. Total area: 46,054 sq mi; rank: 33. **Land area:** 44,743 sq mi; rank: 32. **Acres forested:** 17 mil. **Location:** Middle Atlantic state bordered on the E by the Delaware R., on the S by the Mason-Dixon Line, on the W by West Virginia and Ohio, on the N/NE by Lake Erie and New York. **Climate:** continental with wide fluctuations in seasonal temperatures. **Topography:** Allegheny Mts. run SW-NE, with Piedmont and Coast Plain in the SE triangle; Allegheny Front a diagonal spine across the state's center; N and W rugged plateau falls to Lake Erie Lowland. **Capital:** Harrisburg. **Chief airports:** Philadelphia, Pittsburgh, Harrisburg.

Economy. Chief industries: agribusiness, advanced manufacturing, health care, travel and tourism, depository institutions, biotechnology, printing and publishing, research and consulting, trucking and warehousing, transportation by air, engineering and management, legal services. **Chief manuf. goods:** petroleum, pharmaceuticals, plastics, iron and steel, printing, paper and paperboard, confectionery and snacks, animal slaughtering and processing. **Chief crops:** greenhouse and nursery, mushrooms, corn, hay, soybeans, apples, tomatoes, wheat, grapes, peaches, potatoes, strawberries, tobacco. **Farm income:** crops, $2.60 bil; livestock/animal prods., $5.69 bil. **Nonfuel minerals:** $1.6 bil; stone (crushed), cement (portland), lime, sand and gravel (construction), sand and gravel (industrial). **Commercial fishing:** $0.1 mil. **Chief ports:** Philadelphia, Pittsburgh. **Gross state**

product: $662.9 bil. **Sales tax:** 6.0%. **Gasoline tax:** 70.00 cents/gal. **Employment distrib.:** 12.2% govt.; 19.1% trade/trans./util.; 9.7% mfg.; 20.2% ed./health; 13.0% prof./bus. serv.; 9.7% leisure/hosp.; 5.4% finance; 4.8% constr./mining/log.; 1.4% info.; 4.4% other serv. **Unemployment:** 5.8%. **Per cap. pers. income:** $47,727. **New private housing:** 25,059 units/$4.7 bil. **Broadband Internet:** 86.6%. **Commercial banks:** 156; deposits: $264.0 bil. **Savings institutions:** 75; deposits: $54.4 bil. **Lottery:** total sales: $3.8 bil; profit: $1.1 bil.

Federal govt. Fed. civ. employees: 58,740; **avg. salary:** $72,705. **Notable fed. facilities:** Army War College, Carlisle Barracks; NAVSUP Weapon Systems Support, Mechanicsburg; Philadelphia Mint, Defense Supply Ctr., Naval Surface Warfare Ctr., in Phila.; DLA Distribution Ctr. Susquehanna, New Cumberland, Mechanicsburg; Tobyhanna Army Depot; Letterkenny Army Depot.

Education. High school grad. rate: 85.5%. **4-year public coll./univ.:** 45; **2-yr. public:** 17; **4-yr. private:** 105.

Energy. Electricity use/cost: 857 kWh, $124.29.

State data. Motto: Virtue, liberty, and independence. **Flower:** Mountain laurel. **Bird:** Ruffed grouse. **Tree:** Hemlock. **Song:** "Pennsylvania." **Second** of the original 13 states to ratify the Constitution, Dec. 12, 1787.

Tourism. Tourist spending: $23.6 bil. **Attractions:** Liberty Bell Ctr. at Independence Natl. Historical Park, Franklin Institute, Philadelphia Museum of Art, in Philadelphia; Valley Forge Natl. Historical Park, King of Prussia; Gettysburg Natl. Military Park; Pennsylvania Dutch Country, Lancaster County; Hersheypark, Hershey; Duquesne Incline, Carnegie Museums of Pittsburgh, Heinz Hall for the Performing Arts, in Pittsburgh; Pocono Mountains; Pine Creek Gorge (Pennsylvania Grand Canyon), Allegheny Natl. Forest; Fallingwater (house designed by Frank Lloyd Wright), Mill Run; Johnstown Flood Natl. Memorial; Steamtown Natl. Historic Site, Scranton; U.S. Brig *Niagara*, Erie Maritime Museum, Presque Isle State Park, in Erie; Oil Region Natl. Heritage Area; Longwood Gardens, Kennett Square. **Information:** Pennsylvania Tourism Office, Dept. of Community and Economic Development, Commonwealth Keystone Building, 4th Fl., 400 North St., Harrisburg, PA 17120-0225; 1-800-VISITPA; www.visitpa.com

History. When Europeans came, Algonquian-speaking Lenni Lenape (Delaware) and Shawnee and the Iroquoian Susquehannocks, Erie, and Seneca occupied the region. Swedish explorers made the first permanent settlement, 1643, on Tinicum Island. The Dutch seized the settlement, 1655, but lost it to the British, 1664. The region was given by Charles II to William Penn, 1681. Philadelphia ("brotherly love") was the capital of the colonies during most of the American Revolution and of the U.S., 1790-1800; the Declaration of Independence, 1776, and Constitution, 1787, were signed here. Philadelphia was taken by the British, 1777. George Washington's troops encamped at Valley Forge in the bitter winter of 1777-78. Slavery was abolished, 1780. Union victory at the Battle of Gettysburg, July 1-3, 1863, marked a turning point in the Civil War. A dam collapse at Johnstown, 1889, killed at least 2,200 people. From the late 19th to the mid-20th cent., Pittsburgh prospered from coal and steel; later, heavy industry declined, but the city revived as a hub of finance, health care, and research. The Three Mile Island nuclear plant near Harrisburg had a near-meltdown, 1979. One of four hijacked planes on Sept. 11, 2001, crashed near Shanksville; the Flight 93 national memorial was officially dedicated on the site in 2011.

Famous Pennsylvanians. Marian Anderson, Maxwell Anderson, George Blanda, Kobe Bryant, James Buchanan, Andrew Carnegie, Rachel Carson, Wilt Chamberlain, Noam Chomsky, Perry Como, Bill Cosby, Cyrus H. K. Curtis, Thomas Eakins, Tina Fey, Stephen Foster, Benjamin Franklin, Robert Fulton, Martha Graham, Milton Hershey, Gene Kelly, Grace Kelly (Princess Grace of Monaco), Dan Marino, George C. Marshall, Chris Matthews, John J. McCloy, Margaret Mead, Andrew W. Mellon, Joe Montana, Stan Musial, Joe Namath, John O'Hara, Arnold Palmer, Robert E. Peary, Mike Piazza, Pink (Alecia Beth Moore), Tom Ridge, Mary Roberts Rinehart, Fred Rogers, Betsy Ross, Will Smith, Jimmy Stewart, Taylor Swift, Jim Thorpe, Johnny Unitas, John Updike, Honus Wagner, Andy Warhol, Benjamin West.

Website. www.pa.gov

Rhode Island (RI)

Little Rhody, Ocean State

People. Population: 1,055,173; rank: 43. **Pop. change** (2010-14): 0.2%. **Pop. density:** 1,020.5 per sq mi. **Racial distribution:** 85.1% white; 7.7% black; 3.5% Asian; 0.9% Amer. Ind.; 0.2% Hawaiian/Pacific Islander; 2 or more races, 2.6%. **Hispanic pop.:** 12.4%.

Geography. Total area: 1,545 sq mi; rank: 50. **Land area:** 1,034 sq mi; rank: 50. **Acres forested:** 0.4 mil. **Location:** New England state. **Climate:** invigorating and changeable. **Topography:** eastern lowlands of Narragansett Basin; western uplands of flat and rolling hills. **Capital:** Providence. **Chief airport:** Warwick.

Economy. Chief industries: services, manufacturing. **Chief manuf. goods:** plastics, fabricated metals, electrical equip., jewelry. **Chief crops:** greenhouse and nursery, sweet corn, berries, potatoes, apples, hay. **Farm income:** crops, $49.37 mil; livestock/animal prods., $26.01 mil. **Nonfuel minerals:** $69.2 mil; sand and gravel (construction), stone (crushed), sand and gravel (industrial), gemstones (natural). **Commercial fishing:** $86.4 mil. **Chief ports:** Providence, Davisville, Newport. **Gross state product:** $55.0 bil. **Sales tax:** 7.0%. **Gasoline tax:** 52.40 cents/gal. **Employment distrib.:** 12.6% govt.; 15.4% trade/trans./util.; 8.6% mfg.; 21.9% ed./health; 12.9% prof./bus. serv.; 12.1% leisure/hosp.; 6.7% finance; 3.3% constr./mining/log.; 1.8% info.; 4.9% other serv. **Unemployment:** 7.7%. **Per cap. pers. income:** $48,838. **New private housing:** 952 units/$195.0 mil. **Broadband Internet:** 87.3%. **Commercial banks:** 11; deposits: $24.0 bil. **Savings institutions:** 11; deposits: $3.0 bil. **Lottery:** total sales: $837.9 mil; profit: $376.3 mil.

Federal govt. Fed. civ. employees: 6,933; **avg. salary:** $87,440. **Notable fed. facilities:** Naval War College; Naval Undersea Warfare Ctr.; EPA Atlantic Ecology Div. Lab.

Education. High school grad. rate: 79.7%. **4-year public coll./univ.:** 2; **2-yr. public:** 1; **4-yr. private:** 10.

Energy. Electricity use/cost: 602 kWh, $91.48.

State data. Motto: Hope. **Flower:** Violet. **Bird:** Rhode Island red chicken. **Tree:** Red maple. **Song:** "Rhode Island." **Thirteenth** of original 13 states to ratify the Constitution, May 29, 1790.

Tourism. Tourist spending: $1.9 bil. **Attractions:** Block Island; mansions (The Breakers, The Elms, others), Cliff Walk, Intl. Tennis Hall of Fame and Museum, Touro Synagogue (completed 1763, oldest in U.S.), in Newport; First Baptist Church in America, Rhode Island School of Design Museum of Art, WaterFire art installation, in Providence; Slater Mill Historic Site, Pawtucket; Gilbert Stuart Birthplace and Museum, Saunderstown. **Information:** Rhode Island Tourism Division, 315 Iron Horse Way, Ste. 101, Providence, RI 02908; 1-800-556-2484; www.visitrhodeisland.com

History. When Europeans arrived, Narragansett, Niantic, Nipmuc, and Wampanoag peoples lived in the region. Giovanni da Verrazano visited the area, 1524. The first permanent settlement was founded at Providence, 1636, by Roger Williams, who was exiled from the Massachusetts Bay Colony. Anne Hutchinson, also exiled, settled Portsmouth, 1638. Quaker and Jewish immigrants seeking freedom of worship began arriving, 1650s-60s. The colonists broke the power of the Narragansett in the Great Swamp Fight, 1675, the decisive battle in King Philip's War. The colony was the first to formally renounce all allegiance to King George III, May 4, 1776. Initially opposed to joining the Union, Rhode Island was the last of the 13 colonies to ratify the Constitution, 1790. Trade, textiles, and metal goods dominated the economy in the 19th cent., and Newport became a fashionable resort after the Civil War. The U.S. Navy was the state's largest civilian employer, 1945-73, until the destroyer force was relocated from Newport. A nightclub fire in West Warwick killed 100 people in 2003.

Famous Rhode Islanders. Ambrose Burnside, George M. Cohan, Nelson Eddy, Jabez Gorham, Nathanael Greene, Elisabeth Hasselbeck, Christopher and Oliver La Farge, Cormac McCarthy, John McLaughlin, Matthew C. and Oliver Hazard Perry, Gilbert Stuart, Meredith Vieira.

Website. www.ri.gov

South Carolina (SC)

Palmetto State

People. Population: 4,832,482; rank: 24. **Pop. change** (2010-14): 4.5%. **Pop. density:** 160.8 per sq mi. **Racial distribution:** 68.3% white; 27.8% black; 1.5% Asian; 0.5% Amer. Ind.; 0.1% Hawaiian/Pacific Islander; 2 or more races, 1.7%. **Hispanic pop.:** 4.9%.

Geography. Total area: 32,020 sq mi; rank: 40. **Land area:** 30,061 sq mi; rank: 40. **Acres forested:** 13 mil.

Location: South Atlantic state bordered by North Carolina on the N; Georgia on the SW and W; the Atlantic Ocean on the E, SE, and S. **Climate:** humid subtropical. **Topography:** Blue Ridge province in NW has highest peaks; piedmont lies between the mountains and the fall line; coastal plain covers two-thirds of state. **Capital:** Columbia. **Chief airports:** Charleston, Greer, Myrtle Beach.

Economy. Chief industries: tourism, agriculture, manufacturing. **Chief manuf. goods:** chemicals and synthetics, motor vehicles and parts, plastics, paper and paper prods., turbines, rubber, textiles. **Chief crops:** greenhouse and nursery, tobacco, soybeans, cotton, corn, peaches, wheat, tomatoes, peanuts. **Farm income:** crops, $1.12 bil; livestock/animal prods., $1.59 bil. **Nonfuel minerals:** $581 mil; cement (portland), stone (crushed), sand and gravel (construction), sand and gravel (industrial), cement (masonry). **Commercial fishing:** $21.6 mil. **Chief ports:** Charleston, Georgetown. **Gross state product:** $190.3 bil. **Sales tax:** 6.0%. **Gasoline tax:** 35.15 cents/gal. **Employment distrib.:** 18.2% govt.; 18.9% trade/trans./util.; 11.6% mfg.; 11.6% ed./health; 13.4% prof./bus. serv.; 12.1% leisure/hosp.; 4.7% finance; 4.5% constr./mining/log.; 1.3% info.; 3.6% other serv. **Unemployment:** 6.4%. **Per cap. pers. income:** $36,934. **New private housing:** 27,537 units/$5.4 bil. **Broadband Internet:** 83.2%. **Commercial banks:** 77; deposits: $68.8 bil. **Savings institutions:** 14; deposits: $1.2 bil. **Lottery:** total sales: $1.3 bil; profit: $323.4 mil.

Federal govt. Fed. civ. employees: 20,223; **avg. salary:** $70,295. **Notable fed. facilities:** Ft. Jackson; Joint Base Charleston; Marine Corps Recruit Depot Parris Island; Shaw AFB; USMC Air Station Beaufort; Savannah River Site.

Education. High school grad. rate: 77.6%. **4-year public coll./univ.:** 13; **2-yr. public:** 20; **4-yr. private:** 22.

Energy. Electricity use/cost: 1,124 kWh, $134.86.

State data. Motto: Dum Spiro Spero (While I breathe, I hope). **Flower:** Yellow jessamine. **Bird:** Carolina wren. **Tree:** Palmetto. **Song:** "Carolina." **Eighth** of the original 13 states to ratify the Constitution, May 23, 1788.

Tourism. Tourist spending: $12.3 bil. **Attractions:** Historic Charleston, Waterfront Park, Charleston Museum (est. 1773, oldest in U.S.), Middleton Place, Magnolia Plantation and Gardens, Drayton Hall, in Charleston; Ft. Sumter Natl. Monument (where first shots of Civil War were fired), in Charleston Harbor; Cypress Gardens, Moncks Corner; Boone Hall Plantation and Gardens, Mt. Pleasant; Brookgreen Gardens, Murrells Inlet; Myrtle Beach; Hilton Head Island; Andrew Jackson State Park, Lancaster; South Carolina State Museum, Riverbanks Zoo, in Columbia. **Information:** SC Dept. of Parks, Recreation, and Tourism, 1205 Pendleton St., Columbia, SC 29201; 1-866-224-9339, (803) 734-1700; www.discoversouthcarolina.com

History. When Europeans arrived, Cherokee, Catawba, and Muskogean peoples lived in the area. Spanish and French came in the 16th cent. The first English colonists settled near the Ashley R., 1670, and moved to the site of present-day Charleston, 1680. The colonists seized the government, 1775, and the royal governor fled. The British took Charleston, 1780, but were defeated at Kings Mountain that same year and at Cowpens, 1781. In the 1830s, South Carolinians, angered by federal protective tariffs, adopted the Nullification Doctrine, holding that a state can void an act of Congress. Plantation agriculture relied on slave labor to cultivate rice and cotton; slaves made up 57% of the population in 1860, when South Carolina was the first state to secede from the Union. Confederate troops fired on and forced the surrender of U.S. troops at Ft. Sumter, in Charleston Harbor, 1861, launching the Civil War. The state was readmitted to the Union, 1868. Strom Thurmond, who ran for president as a segregationist in 1948, later served 48 years in the U.S. Senate (1955-2003). Formerly dependent on textiles, the state has attracted new industries by courting foreign investment. The state removed the Confederate flag from its capitol grounds in July 2015 after a white supremacist shooter killed nine black parishioners at a Charleston church the previous month.

Famous South Carolinians. Charles F. Bolden Jr., James F. Byrnes, John C. Calhoun, Stephen Colbert, Marian Wright Edelman, Joe Frazier, DuBose Heyward, Ernest F. Hollings, Andrew Jackson, Jesse Jackson, "Shoeless" Joe Jackson, Jasper Johns, Andie MacDowell, Francis Marion, Ronald E. McNair, Charles Pinckney, John Rutledge, Thomas Sumter, Strom Thurmond, John B. Watson.

Website. www.sc.gov

South Dakota (SD)

Coyote State, Mount Rushmore State

People. Population: 853,175; rank: 46. **Pop. change** (2010-14): 4.8%. **Pop. density:** 11.3 per sq mi. **Racial distribution:** 85.7% white; 1.9% black; 1.3% Asian; 8.9% Amer. Ind.; 0.1% Hawaiian/Pacific Islander; 2 or more races, 2.2%. **Hispanic pop.:** 2.6%.

Geography. Total area: 77,116 sq mi; rank: 17. **Land area:** 75,811 sq mi; rank: 16. **Acres forested:** 1.9 mil. **Location:** West North Central state bounded on the N by North Dakota, on the E by Minnesota and Iowa, on the S by Nebraska, on the W by Wyoming and Montana. **Climate:** characterized by extremes of temperature, persistent winds, low precipitation and humidity. **Topography:** Prairie Plains in the E; rolling hills of the Great Plains in the W; the Black Hills, rising 3,500 ft, in the SW corner. **Capital:** Pierre.

Economy. Chief industries: agriculture, services, manufacturing. **Chief manuf. goods:** animal slaughtering, machinery, semiconductors, surgical appliances. **Chief crops:** corn, soybeans, wheat, hay, sunflowers, sorghum, oats, barley. **Farm income:** crops, $6.13 bil; livestock/animal prods., $4.65 bil. **Nonfuel minerals:** $311 mil; gold, cement (portland), stone (crushed), sand and gravel (construction), lime. **Gross state product:** $45.9 bil. **Sales tax:** 4.0%. **Gasoline tax:** 48.40 cents/gal. **Employment distrib.:** 18.4% govt.; 20.0% trade/trans./util.; 10.2% mfg.; 16.1% ed./health; 7.0% prof./bus. serv.; 10.9% leisure/hosp.; 6.9% finance; 5.5% constr./mining/log.; 1.4% info.; 3.7% other serv. **Unemployment:** 3.4%. **Per cap. pers. income:** $46,345. **New private housing:** 4,722 units/$689.2 mil. **Broadband Internet:** 81.6%. **Commercial banks:** 80; deposits: $415.5 bil. **Savings institutions:** 5; deposits: $2.4 bil. **Lottery:** total sales: $645.0 mil; profit: $104.7 mil.

Federal govt. Fed. civ. employees: 8,063; **avg. salary:** $62,599. **Notable fed. facilities:** Ellsworth AFB.

Education. High school grad. rate: 82.7%. **4-year public coll./univ.:** 7; **2-yr. public:** 5; **4-yr. private:** 7.

Energy. Electricity use/cost: 1,055 kWh, $108.21.

State data. Motto: Under God, the people rule. **Flower:** Pasqueflower. **Bird:** Chinese ring-necked pheasant. **Tree:** Black Hills spruce. **Song:** "Hail, South Dakota." **Entered union:** Nov. 2, 1889; rank: 40th.

Tourism. Tourist spending: $2.7 bil. **Attractions:** Mt. Rushmore Natl. Memorial, Keystone; Harney Peak (tallest E of Rockies); Custer State Park; Crazy Horse Memorial (mtn. carving in progress); Wind Cave Natl. Park, near Hot Springs; Black Hills Natl. Forest; Needles Hwy., part of Peter Norbeck Natl. Scenic Byway; Minuteman Missile Natl. Historic Site; Deadwood (1876 gold rush town); Jewel Cave Natl. Monument, near Custer; Badlands Natl. Park; Great Lakes of South Dakota; Great Plains Zoo and Delbridge Museum of Natural History, Sioux Falls; Corn Palace, Mitchell; Reptile Gardens, Chapel in the Hills, Bear Country USA, in Rapid City. **Information:** Dept. of Tourism and State Development, Capitol Lake Plaza, 711 E. Wells Ave., c/o 500 E. Capitol Ave., Pierre, SD 57501; 1-800-SDAKOTA; www.travelsd.com

History. Paleo-Indians hunted in the region at least 11,500 years ago. At the time of first European contact, Mandan, Hidatsa, Arikara, and Sioux lived in the area. The French Vérendrye brothers explored the region, 1742-43. The U.S. acquired the territory in the Louisiana Purchase, 1803, and Meriwether Lewis and William Clark passed through, 1804-06. In 1817 a trading post opened at what would become Ft. Pierre. Dakota Territory was established, 1861. Gold was discovered, 1874, in the Black Hills on Lakota Sioux land; the "Great Dakota Boom" began in 1879. South Dakota became a state, 1889. Massacre of more than 200 Native American men, women, and children at Wounded Knee, 1890, ended Sioux resistance. Armed supporters of the American Indian Movement, a Native American rights group, occupied the area, leading to a 70-day standoff, 1973. Major economic activities include agribusiness and, since the 1980s, credit card services. Republicans scored a key election victory, 2004, with the defeat of three-term U.S. Sen. Tom Daschle, a national Democratic leader.

Famous South Dakotans. Sparky Anderson, Bob Barker, Black Elk, Tom Brokaw, Crazy Horse, Tom Daschle, Myron Floren, Mary Hart, Cheryl Ladd, Ernest O. Lawrence, George McGovern, Russell Means, Billy Mills, Allen H. Neuharth, Pat O'Brien, Sitting Bull.

Website. www.sd.gov

Tennessee (TN)

Volunteer State

People. Population: 6,549,352; rank: 17. **Pop. change** (2010-14): 3.2%. **Pop. density:** 158.8 per sq mi. **Racial distribution:** 78.9% white; 17.1% black; 1.7% Asian; 0.4% Amer. Ind.; 0.1% Hawaiian/Pacific Islander; 2 or more races, 1.7%. **Hispanic pop.:** 4.4%.

Geography. Total area: 42,144 sq mi; rank: 36. **Land area:** 41,235 sq mi; rank: 34. **Acres forested:** 14 mil. **Location:** East South Central state bounded on the N by Kentucky and Virginia; on the E by North Carolina; on the S by Georgia, Alabama, and Mississippi; on the W by Arkansas and Missouri. **Climate:** humid continental to the N; humid subtropical to the S. **Topography:** rugged country in the E; the Great Smoky Mts. of the Unakas; low ridges of the Appalachian Valley; flat Cumberland Plateau; slightly rolling terrain and knobs of the Interior Low Plateau, the largest region; Eastern Gulf Coastal Plain to the W, laced with streams; Mississippi Alluvial Plain, a narrow strip of swamp and floodplain in the extreme W. **Capital:** Nashville. **Chief airports:** Nashville, Memphis, Alcoa.

Economy. Chief industries: manufacturing, trade, services, tourism, finance, insurance, real estate. **Chief manuf. goods:** motor vehicles and parts, computers and electronics, food, chemicals, plastics, printing, appliances, aluminum. **Chief crops:** greenhouse and nursery, soybeans, cotton, corn, tobacco, hay, tomatoes, wheat. **Farm income:** crops, $2.41 bil; livestock/animal prods., $1.82 bil. **Nonfuel minerals:** $1.1 bil; stone (crushed), zinc, cement (portland), sand and gravel (construction), sand and gravel (industrial). **Chief ports:** Memphis, Nashville, Chattanooga. **Gross state product:** $300.6 bil. **Sales tax:** 7.0%. **Gasoline tax:** 39.80 cents/gal. **Employment distrib.:** 15.0% govt.; 21.0% trade/trans./util.; 11.5% mfg.; 14.2% ed./health; 13.2% prof./bus. serv.; 10.9% leisure/hosp.; 5.0% finance; 4.0% constr./mining/log.; 1.5% info.; 3.7% other serv. **Unemployment:** 6.7%. **Per cap. pers. income:** $40,654. **New private housing:** 27,632 units/$4.6 bil. **Broadband Internet:** 83.3%. **Commercial banks:** 205; deposits: $118.6 bil. **Savings institutions:** 14; deposits: $3.5 bil. **Lottery:** total sales: $1.4 bil; profit: $337.3 mil.

Federal govt. Fed. civ. employees: 26,116; **avg. salary:** $69,366. **Notable fed. facilities:** Tennessee Valley Authority; Oak Ridge Natl. Lab; Arnold Engineering Development Ctr.; Ft. Campbell; NSA Mid-South, Millington.

Education. High school grad. rate: 86.3%. **4-year public coll./univ.:** 9; **2-yr. public:** 13; **4-yr. private:** 47.

Energy. Electricity use/cost: 1,245 kWh, $124.25.

State data. Motto: Agriculture and commerce. **Flower:** Iris. **Bird:** Mockingbird. **Tree:** Tulip poplar. **Songs:** "My Homeland, Tennessee"; "When It's Iris Time in Tennessee"; "My Tennessee"; "Tennessee Waltz"; "Rocky Top"; "Smoky Mountain Rain." **Entered union:** June 1, 1796; rank: 16th.

Tourism. Tourist spending: $16.7 bil. **Attractions:** Lookout Mountain, Tennessee Aquarium, Ruby Falls, in Chattanooga; Great Smoky Mountains Natl. Park; Lost Sea (largest underground lake in U.S.), Sweetwater; Cherokee Natl. Forest; Cumberland Gap Natl. Historical Park; James K. Polk Ancestral Home, Columbia; American Museum of Science and Energy, Oak Ridge; The Hermitage (home of Pres. Andrew Jackson), Country Music Hall of Fame and Museum, Ryman Auditorium, Belle Meade Plantation, Parthenon replica, Grand Ole Opry, in Nashville; Dollywood theme park, Pigeon Forge; Graceland (home of Elvis Presley), Sun Studio, in Memphis; Alex Haley Museum and Interpretive Ctr., Henning; Casey Jones Village, Jackson; Bristol Motor Speedway. **Information:** Dept. of Tourist Development, Wm. Snodgrass/ Tennessee Tower, 312 Rosa L. Parks Ave., 25th Fl., Nashville, TN 37243; 1-800-462-8366; www.tnvacation.com

History. Inhabited for at least 20,000 years, the region was home to Creek and Yuchi peoples when the first Europeans arrived; the Cherokee moved into the region in the early 18th cent. Spanish explorers visited the area, 1540. English traders crossed the Great Smoky Mtns. from the east, while France's Jacques Marquette and Louis Jolliet sailed down the Mississippi on the west, 1673. The first permanent settlement was of Virginians on the Watauga R., 1769. After the American Revolution, in which Tennesseans fought in eastern campaigns, the region became a territory, 1790, and a state, 1796. Slavery was widespread in western Tennessee, where cotton was the main crop, but much less common in the east. The state seceded, 1861, and saw many Civil War engagements; some 187,000 Tennesseans fought for the Confederacy and 51,000 for the Union. Tennessee was readmitted in 1866, the only former Confederate state not to have a postwar military government. The famous Scopes trial, 1925, questioned the teaching of evolution in public schools. In the 1930s, the Tennessee Valley Authority, a federal program, brought electric power to rural areas. Nashville became the capital of country music while Memphis fostered the blues and, with Elvis Presley in the 1950s, rock 'n' roll. Martin Luther King Jr. was assassinated in Memphis, 1968. Since the 1970s, auto plants have become major employers, as has Federal Express. Al Gore Jr., U.S. vice pres. (1993-2001), lost his 2000 presidential bid partly because he failed to carry his home state of Tennessee. Record amounts of rainfall flooded parts of Tennessee, including Nashville, in May 2010.

Famous Tennesseans. Roy Acuff, Kenny Chesney, Davy Crockett, David Farragut, Ernie Ford, Aretha Franklin, Bill Frist, Al Gore Jr., Alex Haley, William C. Handy, Sam Houston, Cordell Hull, Andrew Jackson, Andrew Johnson, Casey Jones, Estes Kefauver, Grace Moore, Dolly Parton, Minnie Pearl, James Polk, Elvis Presley, Wilma Rudolph, Dinah Shore, Bessie Smith, Fred Thompson, Justin Timberlake, Tina Turner, Hank Williams Jr., Alvin York.

Website. www.tn.gov

Texas (TX)

Lone Star State

People. Population: 26,956,958; rank: 2. **Pop. change** (2010-14): 7.2%. **Pop. density:** 103.2 per sq mi. **Racial distribution:** 80% white; 12.5% black; 4.5% Asian; 1.0% Amer. Ind.; 0.1% Hawaiian/Pacific Islander; 2 or more races, 1.8%. **Hispanic pop.:** 35.1%.

Geography. Total area: 268,596 sq mi; rank: 2. **Land area:** 261,232 sq mi; rank: 2. **Acres forested:** 61.8 mil. **Location:** southwestern state bounded on the SE by the Gulf of Mexico; on the SW by Mexico, separated by the Rio Grande; surrounding states are Louisiana, Arkansas, Oklahoma, New Mexico. **Climate:** extremely varied; driest region is the Trans-Pecos; wettest is the NE. **Topography:** Gulf Coast Plain in the S and SE; North Central Plains slope upward with some hills; the Great Plains extend over the Panhandle, are broken by low mountains; the Trans-Pecos is the southern extension of the Rockies. **Capital:** Austin. **Chief airports:** Fort Worth, Houston (2), Austin, Dallas, San Antonio, El Paso, Midland.

Economy. Chief industries: manufacturing, trade, oil and gas extraction, services. **Chief manuf. goods:** petroleum, chemicals and resins, computers and electronics, animal slaughtering and processing, plastics, aerospace. **Chief crops:** cotton, greenhouse and nursery, corn, wheat, sorghum, hay, peanuts, onions, rice, pecans, grapefruit. **Farm income:** crops, $7.84 bil; livestock/animal prods., $17.03 bil. **Nonfuel minerals:** $4.2 bil; stone (crushed), cement (portland), sand and gravel (construction), sand and gravel (industrial), salt. **Commercial fishing:** $268.0 mil. **Chief ports:** Houston, Galveston, Brownsville, Beaumont, Port Arthur, Corpus Christi, Texas City, Freeport. **Gross state product:** $1.6 tril. **Sales tax:** 6.25%. **Gasoline tax:** 38.40 cents/gal. **Employment distrib.:** 15.8% govt.; 20.0% trade/trans./util.; 7.3% mfg.; 13.3% ed./health; 13.4% prof./bus. serv.; 10.8% leisure/hosp.; 6.0% finance; 8.1% constr./mining/log.; 1.7% info.; 3.5% other serv. **Unemployment:** 5.1%. **Per cap. pers. income:** $45,426. **New private housing:** 166,982 units/$26.3 bil. **Broadband Internet:** 93.3%. **Commercial banks:** 534; deposits: $648.7 bil. **Savings institutions:** 45; deposits: $71.1 bil. **Lottery:** total sales: $3.7 bil; profit: $995.5 mil.

Federal govt. Fed. civ. employees: 110,471; **avg. salary:** $73,383. **Notable fed. facilities:** Ft. Hood; Ft. Bliss; Sheppard, Dyess, Goodfellow AF Bases; Joint Base San Antonio; NASA Johnson Space Ctr.; Naval Air Training School, Corpus Christi NAS; Red River Army Depot; Western Currency Facility, Ft. Worth.

Education. High school grad. rate: 88.0%. **4-year public coll./univ.:** 44; **2-yr. public:** 63; **4-yr. private:** 58.

Energy. Electricity use/cost: 1,174 kWh, $133.33.

State data. Motto: Friendship. **Flower:** Bluebonnet. **Bird:** Mockingbird. **Tree:** Pecan. **Song:** "Texas, Our Texas." **Entered union:** Dec. 29, 1845; rank: 28th.

Tourism. Tourist spending: $61.2 bil. **Attractions:** Big Bend and Guadalupe Mountains Natl. Parks; Fort Davis Natl. Historic Site; Six Flags Over Texas, Arlington; SeaWorld San Antonio, Six Flags Fiesta Texas, The Alamo, San Antonio Missions Natl. Historical Park, San Antonio River Walk, in San Antonio; Natl. Cowgirl Museum and Hall of Fame, Kimbell Art Museum, Ft. Worth Zoo, Bureau of Engraving and Printing, in Ft. Worth; Lyndon B. Johnson Natl. Historical Park, Johnson City; LBJ Presidential Library and Museum, Bullock Texas State History Museum, Austin; George Bush Presidential Library and Museum, College Station; Dallas Arboretum and Botanical Garden, Sixth Floor Museum at Dealey Plaza, George W. Bush Presidential Library and Museum, in Dallas; USS *Lexington*, Texas State Aquarium, Padre Island Natl. Seashore, in Corpus Christi. **Information:** Texas Tourism, P.O. Box 141009, Austin, TX 78714; 1-800-452-9292, (512) 486-5876; www.traveltex.com

History. Humans have lived in the region for at least 12,000 years. Coahuiltecan, Karankawa, Caddo, Jumano, and Tonkawa peoples were in the area when the first Europeans came; later, Apache, Comanche, Cherokee, and Wichita arrived. Early Spanish explorers included Alonso Alvarez de Pineda, who sailed along the Texas coast, 1519; Cabeza de Vaca, shipwrecked near Galveston along with the former slave Estevanico, 1528; and Coronado, who crossed the Panhandle, 1541. Spaniards made the first settlement at Ysleta, near El Paso, 1682. Americans moved into the land early in the 19th cent. Mexico, of which Texas was a part, won independence from Spain, 1821. Texans rebelled, 1836, losing to Santa Anna at the Alamo but winning decisively under Sam Houston at San Jacinto. With Houston as president, 1836-38 and 1841-44, the Republic of Texas functioned as a nation until admitted to the Union. With a slave population of 30%, Texas seceded, 1861; mostly unscathed by the Civil War, it was readmitted, 1870. In 1900 a powerful hurricane lashed Galveston, killing at least 8,000. Cotton and cattle were dominant until 1901, when the Spindletop gusher, near Beaumont, launched the petroleum and petrochemical industries. By 2000, the state population ranked second in the U.S. With wealth and population came political power, notably in the presidencies of Lyndon B. Johnson (1963-69), George H. W. Bush (1989-93), and George W. Bush (2001-09). A fertilizer plant in the town of West exploded Apr. 17, 2013, killing 15 people. Texas led a coalition of 26 states in a federal lawsuit asserting that Pres. Barack Obama's executive actions on immigration in 2012 and late 2014 were unconstitutional.

Famous Texans. Lance Armstrong, Stephen F. Austin, Lloyd Bentsen, James Bowie, Drew Brees, Carol Burnett, George H. W. Bush, George W. Bush, Joan Crawford, J. Frank Dobie, Dwight D. Eisenhower, Morgan Fairchild, Farrah Fawcett, Sam Houston, Howard Hughes, Kay Bailey Hutchison, Molly Ivins, Lyndon B. Johnson, Tommy Lee Jones, Janis Joplin, Barbara Jordan, Beyoncé Knowles, Mary Martin, Matthew McConaughey, Chester Nimitz, Sandra Day O'Connor, H. Ross Perot, Katherine Anne Porter, Dan Rather, Sam Rayburn, Ann Richards, Sissy Spacek, George Strait, Babe Didrikson Zaharias.

Website. www.texas.gov

Utah (UT)

Beehive State

People. Population: 2,942,902; rank: 33. **Pop. change** (2010-14): 6.5%. **Pop. density:** 35.8 per sq mi. **Racial distribution:** 91.4% white; 1.3% black; 2.4% Asian; 1.5% Amer. Ind.; 1.0% Hawaiian/Pacific Islander; 2 or more races, 2.4%. **Hispanic pop.:** 12.2%.

Geography. Total area: 84,897 sq mi; rank: 13. **Land area:** 82,170 sq mi; rank: 12. **Acres forested:** 18.3 mil. **Location:** middle Rocky Mountain state; its SE corner touches Colorado, New Mexico, and Arizona and is the only spot in the U.S. where four states join. **Climate:** arid; ranges from warm desert in SW to alpine in NE. **Topography:** high Colorado Plateau is cut by brilliantly colored canyons of the SE; broad, flat, desertlike Great Basin of the W; the Great Salt Lake and Bonneville Salt Flats to the NW; Middle Rockies in the NE run E-W; valleys and plateaus of the Wasatch Front. **Capital:** Salt Lake City. **Chief airport:** Salt Lake City.

Economy. Chief industries: services, trade, manufacturing, government, transportation, utilities. **Chief manuf. goods:** food, petroleum, nonferrous metal, motor vehicles and parts, aerospace, sporting goods, fabricated metal, computers and electronics. **Chief crops:** hay, greenhouse and nursery, wheat, cherries, onions, apples, barley, peaches, corn. **Farm income:** crops, $532.11 mil; livestock/animal prods., $1.84 bil. **Nonfuel minerals:** $4.2 bil; copper, gold, molybdenum concentrates, magnesium metal, potash. **Gross state product:** $141.4 bil. **Sales tax:** 5.95%. **Gasoline tax:** 42.91 cents/gal. **Employment distrib.:** 17.3% govt.; 18.9% trade/trans./util.; 9.1% mfg.; 13.1% ed./health; 14.1% prof./bus. serv.; 9.9% leisure/hosp.; 5.6% finance; 6.8% constr./mining/log.; 2.5% info.; 2.8% other serv. **Unemployment:** 3.8%. **Per cap. pers. income:** $37,766. **New private housing:** 17,510 units/$3.4 bil. **Broadband Internet:** 88.3%. **Commercial banks:** 58; deposits: $389.7 bil. **Savings institutions:** 5; deposits: $58.8 bil.

Federal govt. Fed. civ. employees: 26,656; **avg. salary:** $67,437. **Notable fed. facilities:** Hill AFB; Tooele Army Depot; Army Dugway Proving Ground; NSA Utah Data Ctr.

Education. High school grad. rate: 83.0%. **4-year public coll./univ.:** 7; **2-yr. public:** 1; **4-yr. private:** 10.

Energy. Electricity use/cost: 798 kWh, $82.79.

State data. Motto: Industry. **Flower:** Sego lily. **Bird:** (California) sea gull. **Tree:** Blue spruce. **Song:** "Utah, This Is the Place." **Entered union:** Jan. 4, 1896; rank: 45th.

Tourism. Tourist spending: $7.5 bil. **Attractions:** Temple Square (site of Mormon Church headquarters), Salt Lake City; Great Salt Lake; Zion, Canyonlands, Bryce Canyon, Arches, and Capitol Reef Natl. Parks; Dinosaur, Rainbow Bridge, Timpanogos Cave, and Natural Bridges Natl. Monuments; Lake Powell; Flaming Gorge Natl. Recreation Area; Utah Olympic Park, Sundance Film Festival, in Park City. **Information:** Utah Office of Tourism, Council Hall/Capitol Hill, 300 N. State St., Salt Lake City, UT 84114; 1-800-200-1160; www.utah.com

History. Ute, Gosiute, Southern Paiute, and Navajo peoples lived in the region at the time of European contact. Spanish Franciscans visited the area, 1776; American fur traders followed. Permanent settlement began with the arrival of the Latter-day Saints, or Mormons, 1847; they made the arid land bloom and created a prosperous economy. Organized in 1849, the State of Deseret asked admission to the Union; instead, Congress established Utah Territory, 1850, and Brigham Young was appointed governor. The Union Pacific and Central Pacific railroads met near Promontory Point, May 10, 1869, creating the first transcontinental railroad. Statehood was not achieved until 1896, after a long controversy over the Mormon practices of economic isolationism and polygamy (the church renounced the latter in 1890). The 20th cent. brought expansion in mining, defense-related industries, and, more recently, information technologies. More than two-thirds of Utahans are Mormons; the church has its world headquarters in Salt Lake City. Utah experienced 60% population growth, 1990-2010, and has the highest birthrate and lowest median age of any state in the U.S.

Famous Utahans. Maude Adams, Roseanne Barr, Ezra Taft Benson, John Moses Browning, Butch Cassidy, Marriner S. Eccles, Philo T. Farnsworth, David M. Kennedy, J. Willard Marriott, Merlin Olsen, the Osmonds, Ivy Baker Priest, George W. Romney, Wallace Stegner, Brigham Young, Loretta Young.

Website. www.utah.gov

Vermont (VT)

Green Mountain State

People. Population: 626,562; rank: 50. **Pop. change** (2010-14): 0.1%. **Pop. density:** 68.0 per sq mi. **Racial distribution:** 95% white; 1.2% black; 1.6% Asian; 0.4% Amer. Ind.; <0.05% Hawaiian/Pacific Islander; 2 or more races, 1.8%. **Hispanic pop.:** 1.5%.

Geography. Total area: 9,616 sq mi; rank: 45. **Land area:** 9,217 sq mi; rank: 43. **Acres forested:** 4.5 mil. **Location:** northern New England state. **Climate:** temperate, with considerable temperature extremes; heavy snowfall in mountains. **Topography:** Green Mts. N-S backbone 20-36 mi wide; avg. altitude 1,000 ft. **Capital:** Montpelier. **Chief airport:** Burlington.

Economy. Chief industries: manufacturing, tourism, agriculture, trade, finance, insurance, real estate, government. **Chief manuf. goods:** dairy, plastics, printing, wood furniture, sporting goods, metalworking machinery. **Chief crops:** greenhouse and nursery, hay, maple syrup, apples, berries, sweet corn. **Farm income:** crops, $178.43 mil; livestock/animal prods., $813.60 mil. **Nonfuel minerals:** $128 mil; stone (crushed), sand and gravel (construction), stone (dimension), talc (crude), gemstones (natural). **Gross state product:** $29.6 bil. **Sales tax:** 6.0%. **Gasoline tax:** 49.21 cents/gal. **Employment distrib.:** 18.3% govt.; 17.9% trade/trans./util.; 10.0% mfg.; 20.5% ed./health; 8.7% prof./bus. serv.; 10.6% leisure/hosp.; 3.9% finance; 5.1% constr./mining/log.; 1.6% info.; 3.4% other serv. **Unemployment:** 4.1%. **Per cap. pers. income:** $47,330. **New private housing:** 1,546 units/$281.5 mil. **Broadband Internet:** 85.4%.

Commercial banks: 13; deposits: $6.9 bil. **Savings institutions:** 10; deposits: $4.9 bil. **Lottery:** total sales: $102.3 mil; profit: $22.6 mil.

Federal govt. Fed. civ. employees: 3,198; **avg. salary:** $72,586. **Notable fed. facilities:** Law Enforcement Support Ctr.

Education. High school grad. rate: 86.6%. **4-year public coll./univ.:** 5; **2-yr. public:** 1; **4-yr. private:** 17.

Energy. Electricity use/cost: 569 kWh, $97.50.

State data. Motto: Freedom and unity. **Flower:** Red clover. **Bird:** Hermit thrush. **Tree:** Sugar maple. **Song:** "These Green Mountains." **Entered union:** Mar. 4, 1791; rank: 14th.

Tourism. Tourist spending: $2.2 bil. **Attractions:** Shelburne Museum; Shelburne Farms; Vermont Marble Museum, Proctor; Bennington Battle Monument; Pres. Calvin Coolidge Homestead, Plymouth; Ben & Jerry's Factory, Waterbury; Stowe, Killington, and Burke ski resorts: Hildene (Robert Todd Lincoln home), Manchester; Marsh-Billings-Rockefeller Natl. Historical Park, Woodstock. **Information:** Vermont Dept. of Tourism and Marketing, Natl. Life Building, 6th Fl., Montpelier, VT 05620; 1-800-VERMONT, (802) 828-3237; www.vermontvacation.com

History. Inhabited for 10,000 years or more, the region attracted Abenaki and Mahican peoples before Europeans arrived. Champlain explored the lake that now bears his name, 1609. The first European settlement was on Isle la Motte in Lake Champlain, 1666. During the American Revolution, Ethan Allen and the Green Mountain Boys captured Ft. Ticonderoga (NY), 1775. Under a constitution that provided for public schools and abolished slavery, settlers declared a republic, 1777. Vermont joined the Union, 1791. Agriculture dominated in the 19th cent. Still mainly rural, the state expanded tourism and manufacturing after World War II, and IBM became the largest private employer. Vermont was the first state to recognize same-sex civil unions (2000) and to enact equal same-sex marriage rights via legislation (2009).

Famous Vermonters. Ethan Allen, Chester A. Arthur, Calvin Coolidge, Howard Dean, John Deere, George Dewey, John Dewey, Stephen A. Douglas, Dorothy Canfield Fisher, James Fisk, James "Jim" Jeffords, Jody Williams.

Website. www.vermont.gov

Virginia (VA)

Old Dominion

People. Population: 8,326,289; rank: 12. **Pop. change** (2010-14): 4.1%. **Pop. density:** 210.8 per sq mi. **Racial distribution:** 70.5% white; 19.7% black; 6.3% Asian; 0.5% Amer. Ind.; 0.1% Hawaiian/Pacific Islander; 2 or more races, 2.8%. **Hispanic pop.:** 7.6%.

Geography. Total area: 42,775 sq mi; rank: 35. **Land area:** 39,490 sq mi; rank: 36. **Acres forested:** 15.9 mil. **Location:** South Atlantic state bounded by the Atlantic Ocean on the E and surrounded by North Carolina, Tennessee, Kentucky, West Virginia, and Maryland. **Climate:** mild and equable. **Topography:** mountain and valley region in the W, including the Blue Ridge Mts.; rolling Piedmont Plateau; tidewater, or coastal plain, including the Eastern Shore. **Capital:** Richmond. **Chief airports:** Dulles, Arlington, Highland Springs, Norfolk.

Economy. Chief industries: services, trade, government, manufacturing, tourism, agriculture. **Chief manuf. goods:** beverages and tobacco, transportation equip., animal slaughtering and processing, plastics, textiles, paper and paper prods., printing, pharmaceuticals, furniture, chemicals. **Chief crops:** greenhouse and nursery, soybeans, tomatoes, corn, tobacco, hay, cotton, apples, wheat, peanuts, potatoes. **Farm income:** crops, $1.34 bil; livestock/animal prods., $2.83 bil. **Nonfuel minerals:** $1.1 bil; stone (crushed), cement (portland), lime, sand and gravel (construction), sand and gravel (industrial). **Commercial fishing:** $163.3 mil. **Chief ports:** Norfolk Harbor, Newport News, Richmond, Hopewell. **Gross state product:** $463.6 bil. **Sales tax:** 5.3%. **Gasoline tax:** 40.73 cents/gal. **Employment distrib.:** 18.6% govt.; 16.8% trade/trans./util.; 6.1% mfg.; 13.2% ed./health; 18.0% prof./bus. serv.; 10.0% leisure/hosp.; 5.1% finance; 5.1% constr./mining/log.; 1.9% info.; 5.2% other serv. **Unemployment:** 5.2%. **Per cap. pers. income:** $49,710. **New private housing:** 28,682 units/$4.7 bil. **Broadband Internet:** 85.6%. **Commercial banks:** 132; deposits: $205.0 bil. **Savings institutions:** 7; deposits: $34.9 bil. **Lottery:** total sales: $1.8 bil; profit: $538.6 mil.

Federal govt. Fed. civ. employees: 132,613; **avg. salary:** $89,382. **Notable fed. facilities:** Pentagon; Norfolk Naval Sta., Shipyard, and other Hampton Roads military bases; Ft. Belvoir; Joint Base Langley-Eustis; NASA Langley Res. Ctr.; CIA George Bush Ctr. for Intelligence, Langley; FBI Academy, Quantico USMC Base; Dahlgren Nav. Surface Warfare Ctr. and Lab; USDA Food and Nutrition Serv.; U.S. Geological Survey Natl. Ctr.

Education. High school grad. rate: 84.5%. **4-year public coll./univ.:** 16; **2-yr. public:** 24; **4-yr. private:** 38.

Energy. Electricity use/cost: 1,156 kWh, $125.36.

State data. Motto: Sic Semper Tyrannis (Thus always to tyrants). **Flower:** Dogwood. **Bird:** Cardinal. **Tree:** Dogwood. **Song emeritus:** "Carry Me Back to Old Virginia." **Tenth** of original 13 states to ratify the Constitution, June 25, 1788.

Tourism. Tourist spending: $22.0 bil. **Attractions:** Colonial Williamsburg, Busch Gardens Williamsburg, Jamestown Settlement, in Williamsburg; Yorktown Victory Ctr.; Wolf Trap Natl. Park for the Performing Arts, near Vienna; Arlington Natl. Cemetery; George Washington's Mount Vernon; Thomas Jefferson's Monticello, Charlottesville; Stratford Hall (Robert E. Lee birthplace); Appomattox Court House Natl. Historical Park; Shenandoah Natl. Park; Blue Ridge Natl. Parkway; Virginia Beach; Kings Dominion amusement park, Doswell. **Information:** Virginia Tourism Corp., 901 E. Byrd St., Richmond, VA 23219; 1-800-VISITVA; www.virginia.org

History. Cherokee and Susquehanna peoples and the Algonquians of the Powhatan Confederacy were in the region when Europeans arrived. English settlers founded Jamestown, 1607. Virginians were indispensable to the founding of the American republic, and four of the first five U.S. presidents—Washington, Jefferson, Madison, and Monroe—came from there. The conclusive battle of the American Revolution took place at Yorktown, 1781. The state profited from tobacco, cotton, and the slave trade; in 1860, slaves made up nearly one-third of the population. Virginia seceded from the Union, 1861, and Richmond became the capital of the Confederacy. Western counties, loyal to the Union, split off to become West Virginia, 1863. The war ended with Robert E. Lee's surrender to Ulysses S. Grant at Appomattox, 1865, and Virginia was readmitted to the Union, 1870. In the 20th cent., expansion of federal civilian jobs and military facilities transformed the economy. State officials pledged "massive resistance" to racial integration in the mid-1950s, but eventually accommodated. In 1989, L. Douglas Wilder became the first elected black governor in U.S. history. On Sept. 11, 2001, terrorist hijackers crashed a jet into U.S. defense headquarters at the Pentagon, in Arlington. Seven-term Rep. Eric Cantor became the first House majority leader ever to lose a primary in 2014. Former Gov. Robert McDonnell and his estranged wife were both found guilty in a corruption trial in 2014.

Famous Virginians. Arthur Ashe, Sandra Bullock, Richard E. Byrd, James B. Cabell, Henry Clay, Katie Couric, Gabby Douglas, Jubal Early, Jerry Falwell, William Henry Harrison, Patrick Henry, A. P. Hill, Thomas Jefferson, Joseph E. Johnston, Robert E. Lee, Meriwether Lewis and William Clark, James Madison, John Marshall, George Mason, James Monroe, Sean Parker, George Pickett, Pocahontas, Edgar Allan Poe, John Randolph, Walter Reed, Rev. Pat Robertson, John Smith, J. E. B. Stuart, William Styron, Zachary Taylor, John Tyler, Maggie Walker, Booker T. Washington, George Washington, L. Douglas Wilder, Woodrow Wilson.

Website. www.virginia.gov

Washington (WA)

Evergreen State

People. Population: 7,061,530; rank: 13. **Pop. change** (2010-14): 5.0%. **Pop. density:** 106.3 per sq mi. **Racial distribution:** 80.7% white; 4.1% black; 8.2% Asian; 1.9% Amer. Ind.; 0.7% Hawaiian/Pacific Islander; 2 or more races, 4.5%. **Hispanic pop.:** 10.7%.

Geography. Total area: 71,298 sq mi; rank: 18. **Land area:** 66,456 sq mi; rank: 20. **Acres forested:** 22.2 mil. **Location:** Pacific state bordered by Canada on the N, Idaho on the E, Oregon on the S, and the Pacific Ocean on the W. **Climate:** mild, dominated by the Pacific Ocean and protected by the Cascades. **Topography:** Olympic Mts. on NW peninsula; open land along coast to Columbia R.; flat terrain of Puget Sound Lowland; high peaks of Cascade Mts. to the E; Columbia Basin in central portion; highlands to the NE; mountains to the SE. **Capital:** Olympia. **Chief airports:** Seattle, Spokane, Bellingham.

Economy. Chief industries: advanced technology, aerospace, biotechnology, intl. trade, forestry, tourism, recycling, agriculture and food processing. **Chief manuf. goods:** aerospace, petroleum, food, paper, milled lumber, plastics, structural metals, computers and electronics. **Chief crops:** apples, potatoes, wheat, hay, cherries, greenhouse and nursery, forest products, pears, grapes, onions, hops, sweet corn, Christmas trees, mint, raspberries. **Farm income:** crops, $6.86 bil; livestock/animal prods., $3.16 bil. **Nonfuel minerals:** $890 mil; sand and gravel (construction), stone (crushed), gold, cement (portland), diatomite. **Commercial fishing:** $365.5 mil. **Chief ports:** Seattle, Tacoma, Vancouver, Kelso-Longview, Anacortes. **Gross state product:** $427.1 bil. **Sales tax:** 6.5%. **Gasoline tax:** 55.90 cents/gal. **Employment distrib.:** 18.0% govt.; 18.4% trade/trans./util.; 9.2% mfg.; 14.8% ed./health; 12.2% prof./bus. serv.; 9.6% leisure/hosp.; 5.0% finance; 5.7% constr./mining/log.; 3.5% info.; 3.7% other serv. **Unemployment:** 6.2%. **Per cap. pers. income:** $49,583. **New private housing:** 33,898 units/$7.0 bil. **Broadband Internet:** 89.0%. **Commercial banks:** 77; deposits: $115.7 bil. **Savings institutions:** 15; deposits: $7.2 bil. **Lottery:** total sales: $595.1 mil; profit: $148.3 mil.

Federal govt. Fed. civ. employees: 51,680; **avg. salary:** $74,046. **Notable fed. facilities:** Bonneville Power Admin.; Lewis-McChord Joint Base; Fairchild AFB; DOE Hanford Nuclear Site; Naval Base Kitsap (Bremerton and Bangor); Whidbey Island NAS; Pacific Northwest Natl. Lab.

Education. High school grad. rate: 76.4%. **4-year public coll./univ.:** 18; **2-yr. public:** 25; **4-yr. private:** 23.

Energy. Electricity use/cost: 1,041 kWh, $90.55.

State data. Motto: Alki (By and by). **Flower:** Western rhododendron. **Bird:** Willow goldfinch. **Tree:** Western hemlock. **Song:** "Washington, My Home." **Entered union:** Nov. 11, 1889; rank: 42nd.

Tourism. Tourist spending: $14.5 bil. **Attractions:** Seattle Center, Space Needle, EMP Museum, Museum of Flight, Pike Place Market, Underground Tour, in Seattle; Mount Rainier, Olympic, and North Cascades Natl. Parks; Mount St. Helens Natl. Volcanic Monument; Puget Sound; San Juan Islands; Grand Coulee Dam; Columbia R. Gorge Natl. Scenic Area; Riverfront Park, Spokane; Snoqualmie Falls. **Information:** WA State Tourism Office, 128 10th Ave. SW, P.O. Box 42525, Olympia, WA 98504; 1-866-964-8913; www.experiencewa.com

History. People of the Clovis culture lived in the region 11,000 years ago. At the time of European contact, Native Americans in the area included Nez Percé, Spokane, Yakima, Cayuse, Okanogan, Walla Walla, and Colville peoples in the interior, and Nooksak, Chinook, Nisqually, Clallam, Makah, Quinault, and Puyallup peoples along the coast. Spain's Bruno de Heceta sailed the coast, 1775. In 1792, British naval officer George Vancouver mapped the Puget Sound area, and American Capt. Robert Gray sailed up the Columbia R. Fur traders and missionaries arrived in the first half of the 19th cent. Final agreement on the border of Washington and Canada was made with Britain, 1846. Completion in 1883 of a transcontinental rail link between Puget Sound and the eastern U.S. aided immigration, and Washington became a state in 1889. In the 20th cent., cheap hydroelectric power spurred growth in the aluminum and aircraft industries. Founded in 1975, Microsoft became a computer software giant. Mount St. Helens erupted, 1980. With grunge music, Starbucks coffee, and Amazon.com, Seattle became a national trendsetter in the 1990s. Violent street protests disrupted a World Trade Organization meeting there in 1999. Gary Locke, in office 1997-2005, was the first U.S. governor of Chinese ancestry. A mudslide in Mar. 2014 killed 43 people in a rural area north of Seattle.

Famous Washingtonians. Paul Allen, Glenn Beck, Raymond Carver, Kurt Cobain, Bing Crosby, William O. Douglas, Bill Gates, Jimi Hendrix, Henry M. Jackson, Gary Larson, Mary McCarthy, Robert Motherwell, Edward R. Murrow, Apolo Ohno, Theodore Roethke, Ann Rule, Hope Solo, Hilary Swank, Julia Sweeney, Adam West, Marcus Whitman, Minoru Yamasaki.

Website. access.wa.gov

West Virginia (WV)

Mountain State

People. Population: 1,850,326; rank: 38. **Pop. change** (2010-14): –0.1%. **Pop. density:** 77.0 per sq mi. **Racial distribution:** 93.7% white; 3.6% black; 0.8% Asian; 0.2% Amer. Ind.; <0.05% Hawaiian/Pacific Islander; 2 or more races, 1.6%. **Hispanic pop.:** 1.2%.

Geography. Total area: 24,230 sq mi; rank: 41. **Land area:** 24,038 sq mi; rank: 41. **Acres forested:** 12.2 mil. **Location:** South Atlantic state bounded on the N by Pennsylvania, Maryland; on the S, W, and NW by Virginia, Kentucky, Ohio; on the E by Maryland and Virginia. **Climate:** humid continental climate except for marine modification in the lower panhandle. **Topography:** hilly to mountainous; Allegheny Plateau in the W covers two-thirds of state; mountains here are the highest in the state, over 4,000 ft. **Capital:** Charleston.

Economy. Chief industries: manufacturing, services, mining, tourism. **Chief manuf. goods:** chemicals, aluminum, motor vehicle parts, lumber and plywood, primary and fabricated metals. **Chief crops:** hay, apples, corn, peaches, soybeans, tobacco, wheat. **Farm income:** crops, $148.49 mil; livestock/animal prods., $682.67 mil. **Nonfuel minerals:** $371 mil; stone (crushed), cement (portland), lime, sand and gravel (industrial), cement (masonry). **Chief port:** Huntington. **Gross state product:** $75.3 bil. **Sales tax:** 6.0%. **Gasoline tax:** 53.00 cents/gal. **Employment distrib.:** 20.4% govt.; 17.7% trade/trans./util.; 6.4% mfg.; 16.8% ed./health; 8.9% prof./bus. serv.; 9.6% leisure/hosp.; 3.9% finance; 7.7% constr./mining/log.; 1.3% info.; 7.3% other serv. **Unemployment:** 6.5%. **Per cap. pers. income:** $36,644. **New private housing:** 2,677 units/$395.4 mil. **Broadband Internet:** 93.1%. **Commercial banks:** 74; deposits: $30.2 bil. **Savings institutions:** 4; deposits: $802.0 mil. **Lottery:** total sales: $1.2 bil; profit: $553.1 mil.

Federal govt. Fed. civ. employees: 14,888; **avg. salary:** $72,755. **Notable fed. facilities:** Natl. Radio Astronomy Observatory, Green Bank; Bureau of the Fiscal Service Bldg.; Alderson Fed. Prison Camp; FBI Criminal Justice Information Services.

Education. High school grad. rate: 81.4%. **4-year public coll./univ.:** 13; **2-yr. public:** 10; **4-yr. private:** 9.

Energy. Electricity use/cost: 1,118 kWh, $106.44.

State data. Motto: Montani Semper Liberi (Mountaineers are always free). **Flower:** Big rhododendron. **Bird:** Cardinal. **Tree:** Sugar maple. **Songs:** "The West Virginia Hills"; "This Is My West Virginia"; "West Virginia, My Home, Sweet Home." **Entered union:** June 20, 1863; rank: 35th.

Tourism. Tourist spending: $2.9 bil. **Attractions:** Harpers Ferry Natl. Historical Park, Appalachian Trail Conservancy and Visitor Ctr., in Harpers Ferry; Clay Center for the Arts and Sciences and Avampato Discovery Museum, Charleston; The Greenbrier resort, White Sulphur Springs; Berkeley Springs State Park; Seneca Rocks State Park; New River Gorge Natl. River; Beckley Exhibition Coal Mine; Monongahela Natl. Forest; Fenton Art Glass Company, Williamstown; Mountain State Forest Festival, Elkins; Mountain State Art & Craft Fair, Ripley; Natl. Radio Astronomy Observatory in Green Bank (with world's largest fully steerable radio telescope); Cass Scenic Railroad State Park. **Information:** West Virginia Division of Tourism, Capitol Complex, Bldg. 6, Rm. 525, Charleston, WV 25305; 1-800-CALLWVA; gotowv.com

History. Sparsely inhabited at the time of European contact, the area was primarily Native American hunting grounds. British explorers Thomas Batts and Robert Fallam reached the New R., 1671. Coal, discovered in 1742, was mined extensively by the mid-19th cent. White settlement led to conflicts with Native Americans, including a major battle in which settlers defeated an Indian confederacy at Point Pleasant, 1774. The region joined the Union as part of Virginia, 1788. Longstanding tensions between the E and W parts of the state came to a head in 1861, when Virginia seceded. Delegates of western counties, meeting at Wheeling, repudiated the act and created a new state, Kanawha, later renamed West Virginia, which was admitted to the Union in 1863. Poverty has been a problem for much of the state's subsequent history. It continued to rank low in per capita personal income, despite billions of dollars in federal contracts brought to the state by nine-term U.S. Sen. Robert Byrd, who passed away in 2010. Coal mining, though dangerous, continues to be a major industry; nearly 30 miners were killed in a mine explosion in 2010. In Jan. 2014, Gov. Earl Ray Tomblin banned water use for some 300,000 people for up to 10 days after coal processing chemicals leaked into a waterway.

Famous West Virginians. George Brett, Pearl S. Buck, Robert C. Byrd, Henry Louis Gates Jr., Stonewall Jackson, Don Knotts, Michael Joseph Owens, Brad Paisley, Mary Lou Retton, Walter Reuther, Cyrus Vance, Jerry West, Charles "Chuck" Yeager.

Website. www.wv.gov

Wisconsin (WI)

Badger State

People. Population: 5,757,564; rank: 20. **Pop. change** (2010-14): 1.2%. **Pop. density:** 106.3 per sq mi. **Racial distribution:** 87.8% white; 6.6% black; 2.6% Asian; 1.1% Amer. Ind.; <0.05% Hawaiian/Pacific Islander; 2 or more races, 1.8%. **Hispanic pop.:** 5.8%.

Geography. Total area: 65,496 sq mi; rank: 23. **Land area:** 54,158 sq mi; rank: 25. **Acres forested:** 17.1 mil. **Location:** East North Central state bounded on the N by Lake Superior and Upper Michigan, on the E by Lake Michigan, on the S by Illinois, on the W by the St. Croix and Mississippi Rivers. **Climate:** long, cold winters and short, warm summers tempered by the Great Lakes. **Topography:** narrow Lake Superior Lowland plain met by Northern Highland, which slopes gently to the sandy crescent Central Plain; Western Upland in the SW; three broad parallel limestone ridges running N-S are separated by wide and shallow lowlands in the SE. **Capital:** Madison. **Chief airports:** Milwaukee, Madison.

Economy. Chief industries: services, manufacturing, trade, government, agriculture, tourism. **Chief manuf. goods:** transportation, dairy, animal slaughtering and processing, paper, printing, plastics, computers and electronics. **Chief crops:** corn, greenhouse and nursery, soybeans, potatoes, cranberries, hay, wheat, snap beans, apples, peas. **Farm income:** crops, $3.48 bil; livestock/animal prods., $9.41 bil. **Nonfuel minerals:** $1.8 bil; sand and gravel (industrial), sand and gravel (construction), stone (crushed), lime, stone (dimension). **Commercial fishing:** $6.1 mil. **Chief ports:** Superior, Milwaukee, Green Bay. **Gross state product:** $292.9 bil. **Sales tax:** 5.0%. **Gasoline tax:** 51.30 cents/gal. **Employment distrib.:** 14.5% govt.; 18.1% trade/trans./util.; 16.3% mfg.; 15.1% ed./health; 10.7% prof./bus. serv.; 9.6% leisure/hosp.; 5.3% finance; 3.9% constr./mining/log.; 1.7% info.; 4.8% other serv. **Unemployment:** 5.5%. **Per cap. pers. income:** $44,585. **New private housing:** 14,622 units/$2.6 bil. **Broadband Internet:** 90.3%. **Commercial banks:** 247; deposits: $124.9 bil. **Savings institutions:** 31; deposits: $11.6 bil. **Lottery:** total sales: $568.8 mil; profit: $168.3 mil.

Federal govt. Fed. civ. employees: 14,959; **avg. salary:** $69,438. **Notable fed. facilities:** Ft. McCoy; USDA Forest Products Lab.

Education. High school grad. rate: 88.0%. **4-year public coll./univ.:** 14; **2-yr. public:** 17; **4-yr. private:** 30.

Energy. Electricity use/cost: 703 kWh, $95.21.

State data. Motto: Forward. **Flower:** Wood violet. **Bird:** Robin. **Tree:** Sugar maple. **Song:** "On, Wisconsin!" **Entered union:** May 29, 1848; rank: 30th.

Tourism. Tourist spending: $10.2 bil. **Attractions:** Wade House, Greenbush; Villa Louis, Prairie du Chien; Circus World Museum, Baraboo; Wisconsin Dells; Old World Wisconsin, Eagle; shoreline and state parks of Door County; Chequamegon-Nicolet Natl. Forest; House on the Rock, Taliesin, in Spring Green; Monona Terrace Community and Convention Ctr., Madison; Milwaukee Art Museum, Pabst Mansion, in Milwaukee. **Information:** Wisconsin Dept. of Tourism, 201 W. Washington Ave., P.O. Box 8690, Madison, WI 53708; 1-800-432-TRIP; www.travelwisconsin.com

History. At the time of European contact, Ojibwa, Menominee, Winnebago, Kickapoo, Sauk, Fox, and Potawatomi peoples inhabited the area. French explorer Jean Nicolet reached Green Bay, 1634; French missionaries and fur traders followed. The British took over, 1763. The U.S. won the land after the American Revolution but did not wield control until forts were established at Green Bay and Prairie du Chien, 1816. Native Americans rebelled against the seizure of tribal lands in the Black Hawk War, 1832, but were defeated and relocated to reservations. Wisconsin became a territory, 1836, and a state, 1848. Some 96,000 soldiers served the Union cause during the Civil War. Many immigrants arrived from Germany, Poland, and Scandinavia. Wisconsin agriculture focused on dairy; Milwaukee became a manufacturing center. As governor, 1901-06, Robert La Follette pushed Progressive reforms such as direct primary voting and consumer protection laws. An era of McCarthyism ended when anti-Communist crusader U.S. Sen. Joseph McCarthy was censured by the Senate, 1954. The state legislature passed controversial measures in 2011 to restrict collective bargaining by some 170,000 public-sector employees and in 2014 became the 25th state to pass a "right-to-work" law allowing private-sector workers to choose not to join unions and avoid paying dues even if they are benefiting from union contracts.

Famous Wisconsinites. Don Ameche, Carrie Chapman Catt, Willem Dafoe, Edna Ferber, Hamlin Garland, King Camp Gillette, Harry Houdini, Robert La Follette, (Vladzio Valentino) Liberace, Alfred Lunt, Pat O'Brien, Georgia O'Keeffe, Danica Patrick, Les Paul, William H. Rehnquist, John Ringling, Donald K. "Deke" Slayton, Spencer Tracy, Orson Welles, Laura Ingalls Wilder, Thornton Wilder, Frank Lloyd Wright.

Website. www.wisconsin.gov

Wyoming (WY)

Equality State, Cowboy State

People. Population: 584,153; rank: 51. **Pop. change** (2010-14): 3.6%. **Pop. density:** 6.0 per sq mi. **Racial distribution:** 92.7% white; 1.6% black; 1.0% Asian; 2.7% Amer. Ind.; 0.1% Hawaiian/Pacific Islander; 2 or more races, 2.0%. **Hispanic pop.:** 8.6%.

Geography. Total area: 97,813 sq mi; rank: 10. **Land area:** 97,093 sq mi; rank: 9. **Acres forested:** 10.5 mil. **Location:** Mountain state in the high western plateaus of the Great Plains. **Climate:** semidesert conditions throughout; true desert in the Bighorn and Great Divide Basins. **Topography:** eastern Great Plains rise to the foothills of the Rocky Mts.; the Continental Divide crosses the state from the NW to the SE. **Capital:** Cheyenne.

Economy. Chief industries: mineral extraction, oil, natural gas, tourism and recreation, agriculture. **Chief manuf. goods:** petroleum, chemicals, fabricated metal, beet sugar, lumber. **Chief crops:** hay, sugar beets, barley, dry beans, wheat, corn, greenhouse and nursery, oats. **Farm income:** crops, $392.62 mil; livestock/animal prods., $1.43 bil. **Livestock:** $1.18 bil. **Nonfuel minerals:** $2.4 bil; soda ash, helium (Grade A), clays (bentonite), sand and gravel (construction), cement (portland). **Gross state product:** $44.2 bil. **Sales tax:** 4.0%. **Gasoline tax:** 42.40 cents/gal. **Employment distrib.:** 24.9% govt.; 18.9% trade/trans./util.; 3.3% mfg.; 9.5% ed./health; 6.5% prof./bus. serv.; 12.2% leisure/hosp.; 4.0% finance; 16.1% constr./mining/log.; 1.3% info.; 3.3% other serv. **Unemployment:** 4.3%. **Per cap. pers. income:** $54,810. **New private housing:** 1,901 units/$502.6 mil. **Broadband Internet:** 79.4%. **Commercial banks:** 44; deposits: $13.6 bil. **Savings institutions:** 2; deposits: $371.0 mil.

Federal govt. Fed. civ. employees: 5,412; **avg. salary:** $62,976. **Notable fed. facilities:** Warren AFB.

Education. High school grad. rate: 77.0%. **4-year public coll./univ.:** 1; **2-yr. public:** 7; **4-yr. private:** 1.

Energy. Electricity use/cost: 894 kWh, $90.85.

State data. Motto: Equal rights. **Flower:** Indian paintbrush. **Bird:** Western meadowlark. **Tree:** Plains cottonwood. **Song:** "Wyoming." **Entered union:** July 10, 1890; rank: 44th.

Tourism. Tourist spending: $3.0 bil. **Attractions:** Yellowstone Natl. Park (est. 1872, first U.S. national park); Grand Teton Natl. Park; Natl. Elk Refuge, Jackson; Devils Tower Natl. Monument; Ft. Laramie Natl. Historic Site; Oregon Trail ruts, Guernsey; Buffalo Bill Historical Ctr., Cody; Cheyenne Frontier Days. **Information:** Wyoming Travel and Tourism, 1520 Etchepare Cir., Cheyenne, WY 82007; 1-800-225-5996; www.wyomingtourism.org

History. Inhabited for at least 12,000 years, the region supported Shoshone, Crow, Cheyenne, Oglala Sioux, and Arapaho peoples when Europeans arrived. France's Vérendrye brothers were the first Europeans to see the region, 1742-43. John Colter, an American, traversed the Yellowstone area, 1807-08. Trappers and fur traders followed in the 1820s. Forts Laramie and Bridger became important stops on trails to the West Coast. Population grew after the Union Pacific crossed the state, 1867-68. Wyoming became a territory, 1868, and the first to extend full voting rights to women, 1869. Statehood was attained, 1890. Disputes between large landowners and small ranchers culminated in the Johnson County Cattle War, 1892; federal troops were called in to restore order. Nellie Tayloe Ross was the first woman governor to take office in the U.S., 1925. Wyoming, the least populous state, has relied on the energy, tourism, and ranching industries in recent decades. Dick Cheney, Wyoming's representative in the U.S. House, 1979-89, served as U.S. vice pres. (2001-09).

Famous Wyomingites. James Bridger, Dick Cheney, William F. "Buffalo Bill" Cody, Curt Gowdy, Esther Hobart Morris, Nellie Tayloe Ross.

Website. www.wyoming.gov

District of Columbia (DC)

People. Population: 658,893; rank: 49. **Pop. change** (2010-14): 9.5%. **Pop. density:** 10,801.5 per sq mi. **Racial distribution:** 43.6% white; 49.0% black; 4.0% Asian; 0.6% Amer. Ind.; 0.2% Hawaiian/Pacific Islander; 2 or more races, 2.6%. **Hispanic pop.:** 8.3%.

Geography. Total area: 68 sq mi; rank: 51. **Land area:** 61 sq mi; rank: 51. **Acres forested:** NA. **Location:** at the confluence of the Potomac and Anacostia Rivers, flanked by Maryland on the N, E, and SE and by Virginia on the SW. **Climate:** hot humid summers, mild winters. **Topography:** low hills rise toward the N away from the Potomac R. and slope to the S; highest elevation, 410 ft; lowest on Potomac R., 1 ft.

Economy. Chief industries: government, legal, publishing, medical, service, tourism. **Gross state product:** $115.5 bil. **Sales tax:** 5.75%. **Gasoline tax:** 41.90 cents/gal. **Employment distrib.:** 30.8% govt.; 4.1% trade/trans./util.; 0.1% mfg.; 16.7% ed./health; 21.3% prof./bus. serv.; 9.4% leisure/hosp.; 4.0% finance; 1.9% constr./mining/log.; 2.5% info.; 9.4% other serv. **Unemployment:** 7.8%. **Per cap. pers. income:** $76,532. **New private housing:** 4,189 units/$374.4 mil. **Broadband Internet:** 81.8%. **Commercial banks:** 31; deposits: $41.1 bil. **Savings institutions:** 3; deposits: $166.0 mil. **Lottery:** total sales: $216.2 mil; profit: $55.0 mil.

Federal govt. Fed. civ. employees: 169,318; **avg. salary:** $108,263.

Education. High school grad. rate: 62.3%. **4-year public coll./univ.:** 2; **2-yr. public:** 0; **4-yr. private:** 13.

Energy. Electricity use/cost: 720 kWh, $90.51.

District data. Motto: Justitia omnibus (Justice for all). **Flower:** American beauty rose. **Bird:** Wood thrush. **Tree:** Scarlet oak.

Tourism. Tourist spending: $9.7 bil. **Attractions:** See Attractions in and Around Washington, DC, pp. 444-45. **Information:** Destination DC, 901 7th St. NW, 4th Fl., Washington, DC, 20001-3719; 1-800-422-8644; www.washington.org

History. The District of Columbia, coextensive with the city of Washington, is the seat of the U.S. federal government. It lies on the west central edge of Maryland on the Potomac R., opposite Virginia. The Piscataway, an Algonquian-speaking people, were living in the region when Europeans arrived in the 17th cent. Proposals for a "federal town" for the deliberations of the Continental Congress were made in 1783. Authorized by Congress, 1790, Pres. George Washington chose the Potomac site and persuaded landowners to sell their holdings to the government. Its area was originally 100 sq mi taken from the sovereignty of Maryland and Virginia. Virginia's portion south of the Potomac was given back to that state in 1846.

Pres. Washington chose Pierre Charles L'Enfant, a Frenchman, to plan the capital. Surveyor Andrew Ellicott finished the official map and design of the city, assisted by Benjamin Banneker, a black architect and astronomer. Washington laid the cornerstone of the north wing of the Capitol building, 1793, and Pres. John Adams moved to the new national capital, 1800. The City of Washington was incorporated, 1802. British troops invaded, 1814, setting fire to the Capitol, the President's House (as the White House was then called), and other buildings. Pres. Abraham Lincoln ended slavery in the district, 1862. Many African Americans arrived after the Civil War, but racial segregation remained legal until the mid-20th cent. After federal government expansion spurred population growth, 1930-50, an exodus to the suburbs shrank the city's population, 1950-2005.

The 23rd Amendment (1961) granted residents the right to vote for president and vice president. Congress, which has legislative authority over the District under the Constitution, approved legislation in 1970 giving the District one delegate to the House of Representatives, who could vote in committee but not on the floor. Voters approved, 1974, a congressionally drafted charter giving them the right to elect their own mayor and city council. The district won the right to levy taxes, but Congress retained power to veto council actions and approve the city budget. Security measures were dramatically increased after terrorists attacked the U.S. on Sept. 11, 2001. After a 34-year absence, major league baseball returned to the city in 2005.

Famous Washingtonians. Edward Albee, Michael Chabon, Frederick Douglass, John Foster Dulles, Kevin Durant, Edward Kennedy "Duke" Ellington, Marvin Gaye, Katharine Graham, Goldie Hawn, J. Edgar Hoover, Bill Nye, Pete Sampras, John Philip Sousa.

Website. www.dc.gov

OUTLYING U.S. AREAS

American Samoa (AS)

People. Population (2015 est.): 54,343. **Pop. change** (2010-15): –2.1%. **Pop. density:** 715.0 per sq mi. **Racial distribution** (2010): 92.6% Hawaiian/Pacific Islander; 3.6% Asian; 0.9% white; 0.1% other; 2 or more races 2.7%. **Languages:** Samoan, English, Tongan.

Geography. Total area: 581 sq mi. **Land area:** 76 sq mi. **Acres forested:** 43,631. **Location:** most southerly of all lands under U.S. sovereign, about 2,300 mi SW of Honolulu. It is an unincorporated territory consisting of seven islands: Samoan group: **Tutuila** (52.59 sq mi), **Aunu'u** (0.59 sq mi); Manu'a group: **Ta'u** (17.57 sq mi), **Olosega** (2.03 sq mi), **Ofu** (2.83 sq mi); and the atolls **Rose** (0.03 sq mi) and **Swains** (1.38 sq mi). **Climate:** marine tropical, avg. temp 82°F with little seasonal variation; avg. annual rainfall about 36 in. **Topography:** volcanic islands, rugged peaks, and limited coastal plains. About 70% of the land is bush and mountains. **Capital:** Pago Pago on Tutuila. **Airport:** Pago Pago.

Economy. Chief industries: tuna fishing and processing, trade, services, tourism. **Chief crops:** giant taro, taro, yams, coconuts, breadfruits, bananas, papayas. **Livestock** (2008): 35,709 chickens, 16,904 hogs/pigs. **Nonfuel minerals:** crushed stone, traprock. **Commercial fishing** (2008): $9.7 mil. **Unemployment** (2007): 29.8%. **Gross domestic product** (2013 est.): $711.0 mil. **Broadband Internet:** NA. **Commercial banks:** 2; deposits: $161.0 mil.

Education. 4-year public coll./univ.: 1; **2-yr. public:** 0; **4-yr. private:** 0.

Energy. Electricity production (2013 est.): 156.4 mil kWh.

Fed. civ. employees (Dec. 2014): 81; **avg. salary:** $64,956.

Misc. data. Motto: Samoa Muamua le Atua (In Samoa, God is first). **Flower:** Paogo (Ula-fala). **Plant:** Ava. **Song:** "Amerika Samoa."

Tourism. Attractions: Natl. Park of American Samoa; Natl. Marine Sanctuary of American Samoa; Jean P. Haydon Museum. **Information:** Office of Tourism, Dept. of Commerce, American Samoa Govt., P.O. Box 1147, Pago Pago, AS 96799; (684) 699-9411; www.amsamoatourism.com

History. A tripartite agreement between Great Britain, Germany, and the U.S. in 1899 gave the U.S. sovereignty over the eastern islands of the Samoan group; these islands became American Samoa. Local chiefs ceded Tutuila and Aunu'u to the U.S. in 1900 and the Manu'a group and Rose Island in 1904; Swains Island was annexed in 1925. Samoa (Western), comprising the larger islands of the Samoan group, was a New Zealand mandate and UN Trusteeship until it became independent Jan. 1, 1962 (now called Samoa).

From 1900 to 1951, American Samoa was under the jurisdiction of the U.S. Navy. Since 1951, it has been under the Interior Dept. On Jan. 3, 1978, the first popularly elected Samoan governor and lieutenant governor were inaugurated. Previously, the governor was appointed by the Sec. of the Interior. American Samoa has a bicameral legislature and elects a delegate to the U.S. House of Representatives who has a voice but no vote, except in committees.

Five of the seven islands are volcanoes. Scientists discovered a rapidly growing volcano, Vailulu'u, between Ta'u and Rose in 1975.

The tuna canning industry has been the backbone of the economy since the 1950s, but one of the two canneries closed in 2009. An 8.1-magnitude earthquake in Sept. 2009 triggered a tsunami that severely damaged Tutuila.

American Samoans are of Polynesian origin. They are nationals of the U.S. As of 2010, 109,637 lived in the U.S., including 18,287 in Hawaii and 40,100 in California.

Website. www.americansamoa.gov

Guam (GU)

People. Population (2015 est.): 161,785. **Pop change** (2010-15): 1.5%. **Pop. density:** 770.4 per sq mi. **Racial/ethnic distribution** (2010 est.): 37.3% Chamorro; 26.3% Filipino; 12.0% other Pac. Isl.; 7.1% white. **Languages:** English, Chamorro, Philippine/other Pacific Island languages.

Geography. Total area: 571 sq mi. **Land area:** 210 sq mi. **Acres forested:** 63,830. **Location:** largest and southernmost of the Mariana Islands in the West Pacific, 3,700 mi W of Hawaii. **Climate:** tropical, with temperatures from 70° to 90°F; rainy July to Nov., avg. annual rainfall about 80-100 in. **Topography:** coralline limestone plateau in the N; southern chain of low volcanic mountains slope gently to the W, more steeply to coastal cliffs on the E; general elevation, 500 ft; highest point, Mt. Lamlam, 1,332 ft. **Capital:** Hagåtña. **Chief airport:** Tamuning.

Economy. Chief industries: U.S. military, tourism, construction, shipping, concrete products, printing and publishing. **Chief manuf. goods:** textiles, foods. **Chief crops:** watermelons, cucumbers, eggplant, long beans, bananas, corn. **Livestock** (2007): 533 chickens, 112 cattle, 635 hogs/pigs, 124 goats. **Nonfuel minerals** (2008): $3.8 mil; crushed stone. **Commercial fishing** (2008): $499,095. **Chief port:** Apra Harbor. **Gross domestic product** (2013 est.): $4.9 bil. **Employment distrib.** (Dec. 2012): 30.2% trade/trans; 26.7% serv.; 25.5% govt.; 10.6% constr.; 2.7% mfg.; 0.2% agric. **Unemployment** (2013 est.): 8.4%. **Per capita income** (2010): $12,864. **Broadband Internet:** 100.0%. **Commercial banks:** 5; deposits: $2.3 bil. **Savings institutions:** 1; deposits: $95.0 mil.

Education. 4-year public coll./univ.: 1; **2-yr. public:** 1; **4-yr. private:** 1.

Energy. Electricity production (2013 est.): 1.6 bil kWh.

Federal govt. Fed. employees (Dec. 2014): 2,357; **avg. salary:** $65,499. **Notable fed. facilities:** Andersen AFB.

Misc. data. Motto: Where America's day begins. **Flower:** Puti Tai Nobio (Bougainvillea). **Bird:** Ko'ko (Guam rail). **Tree:** Ifit (Intsia bijuga). **Song:** "Stand Ye Guamanians."

Tourism. Attractions: Ritidian Point, Guam Natl. Wildlife Refuge; War in the Pacific Natl. Historical Park; Chamorro Village; Two Lovers Point. **Information:** Guam Visitors Bureau, 401 Pale San Vitores Rd., Tumon, Guam 96913; (671) 646-5278; www.visitguam.org

History. Guam was probably settled by voyagers from the Indonesian-Philippine archipelago by 3rd cent. BCE. Pottery, rice cultivation, and megalithic technology show strong East Asian cultural influence. Centralized, village clan-based communities engaged in agriculture and offshore fishing. The estimated population by the early 16th cent. was 50,000-75,000. Ferdinand Magellan arrived in the Marianas Mar. 6, 1521. They were colonized in 1668 by Spanish missionaries, who named them the Mariana Islands in honor of Maria Anna, queen of Spain. When Spain ceded Guam to the U.S., it sold the other Marianas to Germany. Japan obtained a League of Nations mandate over the German islands in 1919; in Dec. 1941 it seized Guam, which was retaken by the U.S. in July-Aug. 1944.

Guam is a self-governing organized unincorporated U.S. territory. The Organic Act of 1950 provided for a governor, elected to a four-year term, and a 21-member unicameral legislature, elected biennially by the residents, who are American citizens. In 1970, the first governor was elected. In 1972, a U.S. law gave Guam one delegate to the U.S. House of Representatives who has a voice but no vote, except in committees.

Guam's quest to change its status to a U.S. commonwealth began in the late 1970s. The Guam Commission on Self-Determination, created in 1984, developed a draft Commonwealth Act. In 1993, legislation proposing a change of status was submitted to the U.S. Congress. In 1994, the U.S. Congress passed legislation transferring 3,200 acres of land on Guam from federal to local control. The Navy approved in 2015 a plan to move 5,000 Marines stationed in Okinawa, Japan, to Guam.

Website. www.guam.gov

Commonwealth of the Northern Mariana Islands (MP)

People. Population (2015 est.): 52,344. **Pop. change** (2010-15): –2.9%. **Pop. density:** 287.6 per sq mi. **Racial/ethnic distribution** (2010 est.): 50.0% Asian; 34.9% Hawaiian/Pacific Islander; 2.5% other; 2 or more races/ethnicities, 12.7%. **Languages:** Philippine languages, Chinese, Chamorro (official), English (official), other Pacific Island languages.

Geography. Total area: 1,976 sq mi. **Land area:** 182 sq mi. **Acres forested:** 50,218. **Location:** between Guam and the Tropic of Cancer, the 14 islands of the Northern Marianas form a 300-mi long archipelago. The indigenous population is concentrated on the three largest of the six inhabited islands: **Saipan**, the seat of government and commerce, **Rota**, and **Tinian**. **Climate:** tropical, with avg. temperature around 82°F, moderated by NE trade winds; avg. annual rainfall 80-100 in. **Topography:** limestone southern islands with even terraces, coral reefs; volcanic northern isles. **Capital:** Saipan. **Airport:** Saipan.

Economy. Chief industries: banking, construction, fishing, mining, tourism, apparel manufacturing, retail. **Chief manuf. goods:** apparel, stone, clay and glass prods. **Chief crops:** bananas, cucumbers, sweet potatoes, taro, watermelons. **Livestock** (2007): 9,700 chickens, 1,395 cattle, 1,483 hogs/pigs. **Commercial fishing** (2010 est.): $608,971. **Chief port:** Saipan. **Gross domestic product** (2013 est.): $682.0 mil. **Employment distrib.:** 1.9% agriculture; 10.0% industry; 88.1% services. **Unemployment** (2010): 11.2%. **Broadband Internet:** NA. **Commercial banks:** 3; deposits: $550.0 mil.

Education. 4-year public coll./univ.: 1; **2-yr. public:** 0; **4-yr. private:** 0.

Energy. Electricity production (2009): 60,600 kWh.

Federal govt. Fed. civ. employees (Dec. 2014): 64; **avg. salary:** $59,183.

Misc. data. Flower: Plumeria. **Bird:** Mariana fruit-dove. **Tree:** Flame tree. **Song:** "Gi Talo Gi Halom Tasi" (In the Middle of the Sea).

Tourism. Attractions: House of Taga; American Memorial Park; Banzai Cliff. **Information:** Marianas Visitors Authority, P.O. Box 500861, Saipan, MP 96950; (670) 664-3200; www.mymarianas.com

History. The people of the Northern Marianas are predominantly of Chamorro cultural extraction, although Carolinians and immigrants from other areas of E. Asia and Micronesia have also settled in the islands. English is among the several languages commonly spoken.

The German-controlled Northern Marianas were placed under Japanese control by a League of Nations mandate after World War I. The U.S. captured the islands during World War II. From July 18, 1947, the U.S. had administered the Northern Marianas under a trusteeship agreement with the UN Security Council. In 1975, the residents voted to become a U.S. commonwealth.

The Northern Mariana Islands has been self-governing since 1978, when a constitution drafted and adopted by the people became effective and a popularly elected bicameral legislature (two-year term), with offices of governor (four-year term) and lieut. governor, was inaugurated. Pres. Ronald Reagan proclaimed the Northern Marianas a commonwealth, 1986, and the UN formally ended its trusteeship, 1990. In 2008, U.S. law gave the islands one delegate to the U.S. House of Representatives who has a voice but no vote, except in committees.

Under the 1976 Commonwealth Covenant with the U.S., the islands are exempt from federal immigration and import laws, and minimum wage is lower than on the mainland. The garment-making industry, which has since boomed, has drawn accusations of sweatshop conditions from some critics. Legislation passed in 2007 was intended to raise the minimum wage to the federal rate by 2015, but it stood at $6.05 in 2015 with another 50-cent increase scheduled for Sept. 2016.

Website. gov.mp

Commonwealth of Puerto Rico (PR)

Estado Libre Asociado de Puerto Rico

People. Population (2015 est.): 3,598,357 (about 4.6 mil additional Puerto Ricans reside in the mainland U.S.). **Pop. change** (2010-15): –3.4%. **Pop. density:** 1,050.9 per sq mi. **Racial distribution:** 75.8% white; 12.4% black; 0.2% Asian; 0.5% Amer. Ind.; <0.05% Hawaiian/Pacific Islander; 2 or more races, 3.3%. **Hispanic pop.:** 99.0%. **Languages:** Spanish and English are joint official languages.

Geography. Total area: 5,325 sq mi. **Land area:** 3,424 sq mi. **Acres forested:** 1.2 mil. **Location:** island lying between the Atlantic to the N and the Caribbean to the S; it is easternmost of the West Indies group called the Greater Antilles, of which Cuba, Hispaniola, and Jamaica are the larger islands. **Climate:** mild, with a mean temperature of 77°F. **Topography:** mountainous throughout three-fourths of its rectangular area, surrounded by a broken coastal plain; highest peak, Cerro de Punto, 4,390 ft. **Capital:** San Juan. **Chief airport:** San Juan.

Economy. Chief industries: manufacturing, service, tourism. **Chief manuf. goods:** pharmaceuticals, medical equip., electronics, apparel, food products. **Chief crops:** pumpkins, coffee, watermelons, plantains, yams, oranges, pineapples, sugarcane, bananas. **Livestock** (2007): 1.4 mil chickens, 5.1 mil broilers, 490,817 cattle, 11,137 sheep, 69,892 hogs/pigs. **Nonfuel minerals** (2008): $164 mil; crushed stone, lime, salt, cement (portland), clays (common). **Commercial fishing** (2008): $3.8 mil. **Chief ports:** San Juan, Ponce, Mayaguez. **Gross domestic product** (2013): $101.5 bil. **Employment distrib.:** 25.5% govt.; 19.2% trade/trans./util.; 8.1% mfg.; 14.3% ed./health; 12.5% prof./bus. serv.; 8.9% leisure/hosp.; 4.6% finance; 2.7% constr./mining/log.; 2.3% info.; 1.9% other serv. **Unemployment** (2014 est.): 14.2%. **Per capita income** (est. 2010): $15,203. **Broadband Internet:** 94.2%. **Commercial banks:** 8; deposits: $55.0 bil. **Lottery** (2009): total sales: $421.2 mil; profit: $146.9 mil.

Federal govt. Fed. civ. employees (Dec. 2014): 9,190; **avg. salary:** $65,499. **Notable fed. facilities:** PR Natl. Guard Training Area at Camp Santiago; Ft. Buchanan; Intl. Inst. of Tropical Forestry; Vieques Natl. Wildlife Refuge; USGS Caribbean Water Science Ctr.

Education. 4-year public coll./univ.: 14; **2-yr. public:** 4; **4-yr. private:** 45.

Energy. Electricity production (2011 est.): 20.0 bil kWh.

Misc. data. Motto: Joannes Est Nomen Eius (John is his name). **Flower:** Maga. **Bird:** Reinita. **Tree:** Ceiba. **Anthem:** "La Borinqueña."

Tourism. Attractions: Museo de Arte de Ponce; San Felipe del Morro and San Cristóbal forts, San Juan Natl. Historic Site, Walled City of Old San Juan, Casa Blanca in San Juan; Arecibo Observatory; Cordillera Central mtn. range; El Yunque Natl. Forest (only tropical rain forest in Natl. Forest system); Cathedral of San Juan Bautista; Porta Coeli (Doorway to Heaven) Church and Religious Art Museum, San Germán; Rio Camuy Cave Park, Camuy; Mosquito Bay. **Information:** The Puerto Rico Tourism Company, La Princesa Bldg. #2, Paseo La Princesa, Old San Juan, PR 00902; (800) 866-7827; www.seepuertorico.com

History. Puerto Rico (or Borinquen, after the original Arawak Indian name, Boriquen) was visited by Christopher Columbus on his second voyage, Nov. 19, 1493. In 1508, the Spanish arrived.

Sugarcane was introduced, 1515, and slaves were imported three years later. Gold mining petered out, 1570. Spaniards fought off a series of British and Dutch attacks; slavery was abolished, 1873. Under the Treaty of Paris, Puerto Rico was ceded to the U.S. after the Spanish-American War, 1898. In 1952 the people voted in favor of commonwealth status.

The Commonwealth of Puerto Rico is a self-governing part of the U.S. with a primarily Hispanic culture. The island's citizens have virtually the same control over their internal affairs as do the 50 states of the U.S. However, they do not vote in national general elections, only in national primaries.

Puerto Rico is represented in the U.S. House of Representatives by a Resident Commissioner who has a voice but no vote, except in committees.

No federal income tax is collected from residents on income earned from local sources in Puerto Rico. Nevertheless, as part of the U.S. legal system, Puerto Rico is subject to the provisions of the U.S. Constitution; most federal laws apply as they do in the 50 states.

Puerto Rico's famous "Operation Bootstrap," begun in the late 1940s, succeeded in changing the island from the "Poorhouse of the Caribbean" to an area with the highest per capita income in Latin America. This program encouraged manufacturing and development of the tourist trade by selective tax exemption, low-interest loans, and other incentives. Despite the marked success of Puerto Rico's development efforts over an extended period of time, per capita income in Puerto Rico is low in comparison to that of the 50 states.

In plebiscites held in 1967, 1993, and 1998, voters chose to retain commonwealth status. Protests mounted in the late-1990s over the U.S. Navy's use of Vieques Island for live ammunition training; official military exercises there were terminated, 2003. Puerto Rico went into default for the first time in its history Aug. 2015 after it missed a bond payment. The island had a total debt load of about $70 bil.

Cultural facilities and events. Festival Casals classical music concerts, mid-June; Puerto Rico Symphony Orchestra at Music Conservatory; Botanical Garden and Museum of Anthropology, Art, and History at the Univ. of Puerto Rico; Institute of Puerto Rican Culture, at the Dominican Convent.

Famous Puerto Ricans. Julia de Burgos, Marta Casals Istomin, Pablo Casals, José Celso Barbosa, Orlando Cepeda, Roberto Clemente, José de Diego, José Feliciano, Doña Felisa Rincón de Gautier, Luis A. Ferré, José Ferrer, Commodore Diégo E. Hernández, Miguel Hernández Agosto, Rafael Hernández (El Jibarito), Rafael Hernández Colón, Raúl Juliá, René Marqués, Ricky Martin, Concha Meléndez, Rita Moreno, Luis Muñoz Marín, Luis Palés Matos, Joaquin Phoenix, Adm. Horacio Rivero.

Website. www.pr.gov (in Spanish)

Virgin Islands (VI)

St. John, St. Croix, St. Thomas

People. Population (2015 est.): 103,574. **Pop. change** (2010-15): –2.7%. **Pop. density:** 772.9 per sq mi. **Racial distribution** (2010): 76.0% black; 15.6% white; 6.2% other race; 2 or more races, 2.1%. **Languages:** English (official), Spanish, Creole.

Geography. Total area: 733 sq mi. **Land area:** 134 sq mi. **Acres forested:** 45,163. **Location:** 3 larger and 50 smaller islands and cays in the S and W of the V.I. group (British V.I. colony to the N and E), which is situated 70 mi E of Puerto Rico; W of Anegada Passage, a major channel connecting the Atlantic Ocean and Caribbean Sea. **Climate:** subtropical; sun tempered by gentle trade winds; humidity is low; avg. temperature 78°F. **Topography:** St. Thomas is mainly a ridge of hills running E-W and has little tillable land; St. Croix rises abruptly in the N but slopes to flatlands and lagoons in the S; St. John has steep, lofty hills and valleys with little level tillable land. **Capital:** Charlotte Amalie on St. Thomas. **Chief airport:** Charlotte Amalie.

Economy. Chief industries: retail, petroleum, tourism, prof. consulting. **Chief manuf. goods:** rum, stone, glass and clay products, electronics, textiles. **Chief crops:** cucumbers, coconuts, mangoes, tomatoes, bananas. **Livestock** (2007): 699 chickens, 776 cattle, 2,981 sheep, 1,125 hogs/pigs, 2,331 goats. **Nonfuel minerals:** crushed stone, limestone, traprock. **Commercial fishing** (2011): $7.1 mil. **Chief port:** Charlotte Amalie. **Gross domestic product** (2013 est.): $3.8 bil. **Employment distrib.:** 28.3% govt.; 21.4% trade/trans./util.; 1.6% mfg.; 6.3% ed./health; 9.0% prof./bus. serv.; 19.6% leisure/hosp.; 5.6% finance; 4.2% constr./mining/log.; 1.9% info.; 2.1% other serv. **Unemployment** (June 2011): 9.4%. **Per capita income** (2012): $19,982. **Broadband Internet:** 94.5%. **Commercial banks:** 4; deposits: $1.7 bil.

Education. 4-year public coll./univ.: 1; **2-yr. public:** 0; **4-yr. private:** 0.

Energy. Electricity production (2012 est.): 707 mil kWh.

Federal govt. Fed. civ. employees (Dec. 2014): 354; **avg. salary:** $66,426.

Misc. data. Motto: United in pride and hope. **Flower:** Yellow cedar. **Bird:** Yellow breast. **Song:** "Virgin Islands March."

Tourism. Attractions: St. Croix Isl.: Salt River Bay Natl. Historic Park and Ecological Preserve, Christiansted Natl. Historic Site. St. John and Hassel Isls.: Virgin Islands Natl. Park. St. Thomas Isl.: Blackbeard's Castle, Coral World Ocean Park, Magens Bay, 99 Steps. **Information:** USVI Division of Tourism, P.O. Box 6400, St. Thomas 00804; 1-800-372-USVI; www.visitusvi.com

History. The islands were visited by Columbus in 1493. Spanish forces, 1555, defeated the Caribes and claimed the territory; by 1596 the native population was annihilated. The first permanent settlement in the U.S. territory, 1672, was by the Danes; U.S. purchased the islands, 1917, for defense purposes.

The Virgin Islands has a republican form of government, headed by a governor and lieut. governor elected, since 1970, by popular vote for four-year terms. There is a 15-member unicameral legislature, elected by popular vote for a two-year term. Residents of the V.I. have been U.S. citizens since 1927. Since 1973 they have elected a delegate to the U.S. House of Representatives, who has a voice but no vote, except in committees.

Website. www.gov.vi

Other Islands

Navassa lies between Haiti and Jamaica, 100 mi S of Guantánamo Bay, Cuba, in the Caribbean. It covers 1,147 acres and is uninhabited. Claimed 1857, a USCG lighthouse was built 1917, now inoperative. Natl. Wildlife Refuge since 1999. Administered by the Dept. of Interior.

The three coral islands of **Wake Atoll—Wake, Wilkes**, and **Peale**—lie in the Pacific Ocean on a direct route from Hawaii to Hong Kong, about 2,300 mi W of Honolulu and 1,500 mi NE of Guam. The group is 4.5 mi long, 1.5 mi wide. Land area totals 2.5 sq mi. The U.S. annexed Wake Atoll Jan. 17, 1899. Japan occupied Wake 1941-45. Designated a National Historic Landmark in 1985. Wake is owned by the U.S. Air Force, administered by the Dept. of Interior, and used by the Army as a missile launch facility. The population consists of military personnel and contractors. Most infrastructure was damaged by super typhoon Ioke in 2006.

The following mostly uninhabited islands are part of the **Pacific/Remote Islands National Wildlife Refuge Complex**, which along with Wake Atoll are administered by the Dept. of Interior: **Midway Atoll**, acquired in 1867, has three main islands—Sand, Spit, and Eastern—1,250 mi WNW of Honolulu, with an area of about 1,500 acres. Naval activity ended in 1997. Has the world's largest colony of Laysan albatross. **Johnston Atoll**, 800 mi WSW of Honolulu, is two natural and two artificial islands across 107 sq mi administered by the Navy. Johnston was a nuclear test site in 1958, 1962; the Army disposed of chemical weapons 1990-2000. Cleanup ended in 2005. **Kingman Reef** is a barren, coral atoll 932 mi S of Hawaii, annexed 1922. **Palmyra Atoll** is 54 islets over 753 sq mi, 1,052 mi S of Hawaii; annexed with Hawaii in 1898. Part privately owned by the Nature Conservancy. **Jarvis Island** covers 1,086 acres, 1,300 mi S of Honolulu near the equator. West of Jarvis are **Howland and Baker Islands**, 36 mi apart and about 1,600 mi SW of Honolulu.

100 MOST POPULOUS U.S. CITIES

Sources: Population: Decennial Census and Population Estimates Program, U.S. Census Bureau, U.S. Dept. of Commerce. Population is as of July 1, 2014; population rank is indicated within parentheses. **Pop. density** specifies the number of persons per square mile (sq mi) of land **area**. Unless otherwise noted, **all other figures** are estimates for 2009-13 from the American Community Survey, U.S. Census Bureau. **Racial distribution** categories are abbreviated; their full forms are white, black or African American, Asian, American Indian and Alaska Native, Native Hawaiian and Other Pacific Islander, some other race, two or more races. **Hispanic** or Latino persons may be of any race. **Language** is what is spoken at home; languages other than Spanish spoken by less than 5% of the population age 5 and over are omitted. **Employment:** Bureau of Labor Statistics, U.S. Dept. of Labor, for 2014. **Per capita income:** Bureau of Economic Analysis, U.S. Dept. of Commerce; figures apply to MSAs for 2013. **Educational attainment** is the percentage of persons ages 25 and up who have graduated high school (HS) and who have a bachelor's degree or higher. **Avg. commute** is the time it takes for workers 16 years and over to travel from home to work. "Drive" includes only those who drive to work alone. Forms of transport used by less than 10% are omitted. **Avg. home:** National Association of Realtors®. Figures represent median 2014 sales price of existing single-family homes in the metropolitan area; data not available for all cities. **Avg. rent** is the median gross rent (rent asked plus est. avg. cost of utilities) per month. **Mayor** (or other city leader) and **website:** World Almanac research as of mid-2015; subject to change. A nonpartisan mayor is one whose party affiliation was not indicated on the ballot.

Included here are the 100 most populous U.S. cities, according to U.S. Census Bureau estimates released in May 2015. Most data are for the city proper; some, where noted, apply to the Metropolitan Statistical Area (MSA). Inc. = incorporated; est. = established.

Albuquerque, New Mexico

Population: 557,169 (32). **Pop. density:** 2,961. **Pop. change (2010-14):** 1.8%. **Area:** 188.1 sq mi. **Racial distribution:** 71.2% white; 3.3% black; 2.7% Asian; 4.3% Amer. Ind.; 0.1% Pac. Isl.; 14.4% other; 2+ races 4.0%. **Hispanic pop.:** 46.7%. **Foreign born:** 10.8%. **U.S. citizens:** 93.1%. **Language:** 70.4% English only; 24.3% Spanish.

Employment: 251,415 employed; 5.9% unemployed. **Per capita income:** $36,287; change (2012-13): –0.3%. **Below poverty level:** 17.9%; 14.1% of families. **Educational attainment:** 88.5% HS; 33.0% bachelor's. **Avg. commute:** 21.2 min. 79.7% drive. **Housing units:** 240,277; 92.6% occupied. **Home ownership:** 60.0%. **Avg. home:** $177,600; change (2012-14): 4.3%. **Avg. rent:** $789.

Mayor: Richard J. Berry, nonpartisan

History: Founded 1706 by the Spanish; inc. 1890.

Website: www.cabq.gov

Anaheim, California

Population: 346,997 (56). **Pop. density:** 6,943. **Pop. change (2010-14):** 2.9%. **Area:** 50.0 sq mi. **Racial distribution:** 62.6% white; 2.6% black; 15.3% Asian; 0.4% Amer. Ind.; 0.5% Pac. Isl.; 15.5% other; 2+ races 3.1%. **Hispanic pop.:** 52.6%. **Foreign born:** 37.1%. **U.S. citizens:** 79.0%. **Language:** 39.0% English only; 44.2% Spanish.

Employment: 157,832 employed; 6.9% unemployed. **Per capita income:** $48,425; change (2012-13): 1.4%. **Below poverty level:** 16.1%; 13.3% of families. **Educational attainment:** 74.7% HS; 24.2% bachelor's. **Avg. commute:** 27 min. 75.9% drive; 12.9% carpool. **Housing units:** 104,724; 94.6% occupied. **Home ownership:** 47.8%. **Avg. home:** $687,900; change (2012-14): 26.8%. **Avg. rent:** $1,344.

Mayor: Tom Tait, nonpartisan

History: Founded 1857; inc. 1870. Home of Disneyland, the Anaheim Ducks, and the Los Angeles Angels.

Website: www.anaheim.net

Anchorage, Alaska

Population: 301,010 (64). **Pop. density:** 177. **Pop. change (2010-14):** 2.6%. **Area:** 1,704.9 sq mi. **Racial distribution:** 66.2% white; 5.9% black; 8.2% Asian; 6.9% Amer. Ind.; 2.1% Pac. Isl.; 1.6% other; 2+ races 9.1%. **Hispanic pop.:** 8.0%. **Foreign born:** 9.4%. **U.S. citizens:** 95.8%. **Language:** 82.7% English only; 4.6% Spanish.

Employment: 151,731 employed; 5.1% unemployed. **Per capita income:** $52,696; change (2012-13): 0.5%. **Below poverty level:** 7.9%; 5.4% of families. **Educational attainment:** 92.5% HS; 32.8% bachelor's. **Avg. commute:** 19.4 min. 75.1% drive; 12.6% carpool. **Housing units:** 113,278; 92.9% occupied. **Home ownership:** 60.6%. **Avg. rent:** $1,142.

Mayor: Ethan Berkowitz, nonpartisan

History: Founded 1914 as a construction camp for railroad; HQ of Alaska Defense Command, WWII. Severely damaged in earthquake, 1964. Current population center of Alaska.

Website: www.muni.org

Arlington, Texas

Population: 383,204 (51). **Pop. density:** 3,996. **Pop. change (2010-14):** 4.6%. **Area:** 95.9 sq mi. **Racial distribution:** 65.3% white; 19.4% black; 7.2% Asian; 0.6% Amer. Ind.; <0.05% Pac. Isl.; 5.1% other; 2+ races 2.4%. **Hispanic pop.:** 28.2%. **Foreign born:** 19.7%. **U.S. citizens:** 87.3%. **Language:** 67.6% English only; 22.3% Spanish.

Employment: 194,960 employed; 5.0% unemployed. **Per capita income:** $46,989; change (2012-13): 1.3%. **Below poverty level:** 16.6%; 13.2% of families. **Educational attainment:** 84.3% HS; 29.1% bachelor's. **Avg. commute:** 25.9 min. 81.2% drive; 12.0% carpool. **Housing units:** 146,424; 91.2% occupied. **Home ownership:** 57.4%. **Avg. home:** $188,300; change (2012-14): 18.2%. **Avg. rent:** $841.

Mayor: Jeff Williams, nonpartisan

History: Settled in 1840s; inc. 1884.

Website: www.arlington-tx.gov

Atlanta, Georgia

Population: 456,002 (39). **Pop. density:** 3,426. **Pop. change (2010-14):** 7.9%. **Area:** 133.1 sq mi. **Racial distribution:** 39.3% white; 53.5% black; 3.6% Asian; 0.2% Amer. Ind.; <0.05% Pac. Isl.; 1.4% other; 2+ races 1.9%. **Hispanic pop.:** 5.3%. **Foreign born:** 7.7%. **U.S. citizens:** 94.6%. **Language:** 89.3% English only; 4.9% Spanish.

Employment: 213,278 employed; 7.8% unemployed. **Per capita income:** $41,307; change (2012-13): 1.4%. **Below poverty level:** 25.0%; 20.2% of families. **Educational attainment:** 88.0% HS; 46.8% bachelor's. **Avg. commute:** 25.1 min. 68.0% drive; 10.3% public trans. **Housing units:** 225,051; 79.7% occupied. **Home ownership:** 45.4%. **Avg. home:** $159,500; change (2012-14): 57.3%. **Avg. rent:** $948.

Mayor: Kasim Reed, nonpartisan

History: Founded as Terminus 1837; renamed Atlanta 1845; inc. 1847. Played major role in Civil War; became permanent state capital 1877. Birthplace of civil rights movement; host to 1996 Centennial Olympic Games.

Website: www.atlantaga.gov

Aurora, Colorado

Population: 353,108 (54). **Pop. density:** 2,295. **Pop. change (2010-14):** 8.3%. **Area:** 153.8 sq mi. **Racial distribution:** 65.4% white; 15.8% black; 4.8% Asian; 1.0% Amer. Ind.; 0.2% Pac. Isl.; 7.3% other; 2+ races 5.3%. **Hispanic pop.:** 29.0%. **Foreign born:** 20.4%. **U.S. citizens:** 86.0%. **Language:** 68.6% English only; 21.0% Spanish.

Employment: 170,754 employed; 5.6% unemployed. **Per capita income:** $51,946; change (2012-13): 1.0%. **Below poverty level:** 16.7%; 13.0% of families. **Educational attainment:** 85.9% HS; 26.4% bachelor's. **Avg. commute:** 28.4 min. 76.0% drive; 11.6% carpool. **Housing units:** 130,682; 93.4% occupied. **Home ownership:** 57.9%. **Avg. home:** $310,200; change (2012-14): 22.9%. **Avg. rent:** $947.

Mayor: Steve Hogan, nonpartisan

History: Founded 1891; originally called Fletcher; renamed Aurora 1907; inc. 1929. Early growth stimulated by presence of military bases; fast-growing trade, technology, and med. science center.

Website: www.auroragov.org

Austin, Texas

Population: 912,791 (11). **Pop. density:** 2,922. **Pop. change (2010-14):** 11.9%. **Area:** 312.4 sq mi. **Racial distribution:** 73.2% white; 8.0% black; 6.2% Asian; 0.5% Amer. Ind.; 0.1% Pac. Isl.; 9.0% other; 2+ races 2.9%. **Hispanic pop.:** 34.6%. **Foreign born:** 18.6%. **U.S. citizens:** 86.0%. **Language:** 67.7% English only; 24.9% Spanish.

Employment: 510,565 employed; 3.7% unemployed. **Per capita income:** $44,760; change (2012-13): 0.5%. **Below poverty level:** 19.1%; 13.5% of families. **Educational attainment:** 86.7% HS; 45.6% bachelor's. **Avg. commute:** 22.9 min. 72.9% drive; 10.4% carpool. **Housing units:** 366,459; 92.2% occupied. **Home ownership:** 45.0%. **Avg. home:** $240,700; change (2012-14): 16.8%. **Avg. rent:** $978.

Mayor: Steve Adler, nonpartisan

History: First permanent settlement 1835; capital of Rep. of Texas 1839; named after Stephen Austin; inc. 1840.

Website: www.austintexas.gov

Bakersfield, California

Population: 368,759 (52). **Pop. density:** 2,482. **Pop. change (2010-14):** 5.7%. **Area:** 148.5 sq mi. **Racial distribution:** 65.5% white; 8.2% black; 6.4% Asian; 1.1% Amer. Ind.; 0.1% Pac. Isl.; 14.3% other; 2+ races 4.3%. **Hispanic pop.:** 46.0%. **Foreign born:** 18.7%. **U.S. citizens:** 88.5%. **Language:** 62.1% English only; 31.2% Spanish.

Employment: 163,465 employed; 9.3% unemployed. **Per capita income:** $35,847; change (2012-13): 2.0%. **Below**

poverty level: 20.4%; 16.7% of families. **Educational attainment:** 78.5% HS; 20.0% bachelor's. **Avg. commute:** 22.9 min. 79.4% drive; 13.5% carpool. **Housing units:** 118,474; 92.8% occupied. **Home ownership:** 57.8%. **Avg. rent:** $979.

Mayor: Harvey L. Hall, nonpartisan

History: Named after Col. Thomas Baker, an early settler; inc. 1898.

Website: www.bakersfieldcity.us

Baltimore, Maryland

Population: 622,793 (26). **Pop. density:** 7,694. **Pop. change (2010-14):** 0.2%. **Area:** 80.9 sq mi. **Racial distribution:** 30.3% white; 63.2% black; 2.4% Asian; 0.4% Amer. Ind.; <0.05% Pac. Isl.; 1.4% other; 2+ races 2.3%. **Hispanic pop.:** 4.3%. **Foreign born:** 7.4%. **U.S. citizens:** 95.4%. **Language:** 91.2% English only; 3.7% Spanish.

Employment: 268,824 employed; 8.7% unemployed. **Per capita income:** $54,457; change (2012-13): 0.6%. **Below poverty level:** 23.8%; 19.1% of families. **Educational attainment:** 80.2% HS; 26.8% bachelor's. **Avg. commute:** 30.1 min. 60.5% drive; 17.8% public trans.; 10.1% carpool. **Housing units:** 296,256; 81.5% occupied. **Home ownership:** 48.3%. **Avg. home:** $244,100; change (2012-14): 18.5%. **Avg. rent:** $924.

Mayor: Stephanie C. Rawlings-Blake, Democrat

History: Founded by Maryland legislature 1729; inc. 1797; War of 1812 British artillery barrage of Ft. McHenry (1814) inspired Francis Scott Key to write "Star-Spangled Banner." Birthplace of America's railroads 1828; rebuilt after fire 1904. Site of National Aquarium.

Website: www.baltimorecity.gov

Baton Rouge, Louisiana

Population: 228,895 (96). **Pop. density:** 2,956. **Pop. change (2010-14):** –0.3%. **Area:** 77.4 sq mi. **Racial distribution:** 39.3% white; 54.3% black; 3.5% Asian; 0.2% Amer. Ind.; <0.05% Pac. Isl.; 0.9% other; 2+ races 1.8%. **Hispanic pop.:** 3.4%. **Foreign born:** 5.4%. **U.S. citizens:** 96.5%. **Language:** 91.5% English only; 2.9% Spanish.

Employment: 109,466 employed; 6.4% unemployed. **Per capita income:** $41,776; change (2012-13): 2.4%. **Below poverty level:** 25.4%; 17.2% of families. **Educational attainment:** 85.4% HS; 32.8% bachelor's. **Avg. commute:** 20.8 min. 78.0% drive; 11.5% carpool. **Housing units:** 100,615; 87.1% occupied. **Home ownership:** 50.9%. **Avg. home:** $171,300; change (2012-14): 4.3%. **Avg. rent:** $776.

Mayor-President: Melvin "Kip" Holden, Democrat

History: Claimed by Spain at time of Louisiana Purchase 1803; est. independence by rebellion 1810; inc. as town 1817. Became state capital 1849; Union-held most of Civil War.

Website: www.brgov.com

Boise, Idaho

Population: 216,282 (99). **Pop. density:** 2,687. **Pop. change (2010-14):** 4.8%. **Area:** 80.5 sq mi. **Racial distribution:** 89.9% white; 1.4% black; 3.6% Asian; 0.7% Amer. Ind.; 0.3% Pac. Isl.; 1.2% other; 2+ races 2.9%. **Hispanic pop.:** 7.4%. **Foreign born:** 7.3%. **U.S. citizens:** 95.6%. **Language:** 90.3% English only; 4.1% Spanish.

Employment: 111,011 employed; 3.9% unemployed. **Per capita income:** $36,780; change (2012-13): 2.7%. **Below poverty level:** 15.6%; 10.2% of families. **Educational attainment:** 93.8% HS; 38.3% bachelor's. **Avg. commute:** 17.8 min. 78.7% drive. **Housing units:** 92,005; 93.9% occupied. **Home ownership:** 61.0%. **Avg. home:** $172,900; change (2012-14): 24.7%. **Avg. rent:** $784.

Mayor: David H. Bieter, nonpartisan

History: Gold discovered in area, 1862; inc., proclaimed capital of Idaho Terr., 1964; on Oregon Trail.

Website: www.cityofboise.org

Boston, Massachusetts

Population: 655,884 (24). **Pop. density:** 13,561. **Pop. change (2010-14):** 5.7%. **Area:** 48.4 sq mi. **Racial distribution:** 53.7% white; 25.1% black; 9.0% Asian; 0.4% Amer. Ind.; <0.05% Pac. Isl.; 7.3% other; 2+ races 4.5%. **Hispanic pop.:** 18.0%. **Foreign born:** 26.5%. **U.S. citizens:** 85.5%. **Language:** 64.2% English only; 15.8% Spanish.

Employment: 335,583 employed; 5.3% unemployed. **Per capita income:** $61,754; change (2012-13): 0.8%. **Below poverty level:** 21.4%; 16.4% of families. **Educational attainment:** 85.0% HS; 43.9% bachelor's. **Avg. commute:** 28.8 min. 38.3% drive; 33.3% public trans.; 15.2% walk. **Housing units:** 273,118; 91.3% occupied. **Home ownership:** 34.1%. **Avg. home:** $389,800; change (2012-14): 11.0%. **Avg. rent:** $1,281.

Mayor: Martin J. Walsh, nonpartisan

History: Settled 1630 by John Winthrop; capital of Mass. Bay Colony; figured strongly in American Revolution, earning distinction as the "Cradle of Liberty"; inc. 1822.

Website: www.cityofboston.gov

Buffalo, New York

Population: 258,703 (76). **Pop. density:** 6,406. **Pop. change (2010-14):** –0.9%. **Area:** 40.4 sq mi. **Racial distribution:** 50.2% white; 37.6% black; 3.8% Asian; 0.5% Amer. Ind.; <0.05% Pac. Isl.; 4.4% other; 2+ races 3.4%. **Hispanic pop.:** 9.7%. **Foreign born:** 8.4%. **U.S. citizens:** 95.0%. **Language:** 84.4% English only; 7.1% Spanish.

Employment: 103,005 employed; 7.9% unemployed. **Per capita income:** $44,301; change (2012-13): 1.1%. **Below poverty level:** 30.7%; 26.7% of families. **Educational attainment:** 82.3% HS; 24.4% bachelor's. **Avg. commute:** 20 min. 67.3% drive; 12.0% public trans. **Housing units:** 134,839; 83.1% occupied. **Home ownership:** 42.2%. **Avg. home:** $129,000; change (2012-14): 1.7%. **Avg. rent:** $682.

Mayor: Byron W. Brown, Democrat

History: Settled 1780 by Seneca Indians; raided twice by British in War of 1812. Served as western terminus for Erie Canal; became a center for trade and manufacturing; inc. 1832. A last stop on the Underground Railroad. Key point for Canada-U.S. political, trade, and social relations.

Website: www.city-buffalo.com

Chandler, Arizona

Population: 254,276 (78). **Pop. density:** 3,937. **Pop. change (2010-14):** 7.4%. **Area:** 64.6 sq mi. **Racial distribution:** 77.8% white; 5.3% black; 8.6% Asian; 1.2% Amer. Ind.; 0.2% Pac. Isl.; 2.9% other; 2+ races 3.9%. **Hispanic pop.:** 23.1%. **Foreign born:** 14.4%. **U.S. citizens:** 92.6%. **Language:** 77.0% English only; 13.2% Spanish.

Employment: 131,054 employed; 5.1% unemployed. **Per capita income:** $38,745; change (2012-13): 0.7%. **Below poverty level:** 9.1%; 6.5% of families. **Educational attainment:** 91.9% HS; 39.4% bachelor's. **Avg. commute:** 23.8 min. 78.5% drive; 11.5% carpool. **Housing units:** 94,065; 91.4% occupied. **Home ownership:** 63.5%. **Avg. home:** $198,500; change (2012-14): 34.5%. **Avg. rent:** $1,079.

Mayor: Jay Tibshraeny, nonpartisan

History: Formed 1912; population doubled in 1990s as the self-proclaimed high-tech oasis in the Silicon Desert.

Website: www.chandleraz.gov

Charlotte, North Carolina

Population: 809,958 (17). **Pop. density:** 2,669. **Pop. change (2010-14):** 9.6%. **Area:** 303.4 sq mi. **Racial distribution:** 52.4% white; 35.0% black; 5.2% Asian; 0.4% Amer. Ind.; 0.1% Pac. Isl.; 4.4% other; 2+ races 2.6%. **Hispanic pop.:** 13.3%. **Foreign born:** 15.0%. **U.S. citizens:** 89.6%. **Language:** 80.3% English only; 11.6% Spanish.

Employment: 406,259 employed; 5.1% unemployed. **Per capita income:** $41,645; change (2012-13): 0.5%. **Below poverty level:** 17.1%; 13.4% of families. **Educational attainment:** 88.0% HS; 39.8% bachelor's. **Avg. commute:** 24.3 min. 76.5% drive; 10.6% carpool. **Housing units:** 325,609; 90.7% occupied. **Home ownership:** 56.3%. **Avg. home:** $193,800; change (2012-14): 23.8%. **Avg. rent:** $882.

Mayor: Daniel Clodfelter, Democrat

History: Settled by Scotch-Irish immigrants 1740s; inc. 1768 and named after Queen Charlotte, British King George III's wife. Scene of first major U.S. gold discovery 1799.

Website: charmeck.org

Chesapeake, Virginia

Population: 233,371 (92). **Pop. density:** 685. **Pop. change (2010-14):** 4.4%. **Area:** 340.8 sq mi. **Racial distribution:** 62.7% white; 30.0% black; 3.2% Asian; 0.3% Amer. Ind.; 0.1% Pac. Isl.; 0.9% other; 2+ races 2.8%. **Hispanic pop.:** 4.6%. **Foreign born:** 4.8%. **U.S. citizens:** 97.9%. **Language:** 92.6% English only; 3.3% Spanish.

Employment: 110,362 employed; 5.3% unemployed. **Per capita income:** $44,756; change (2012-13): 0.5%. **Below poverty level:** 8.5%; 6.9% of families. **Educational attainment:** 90.2% HS; 29.3% bachelor's. **Avg. commute:** 24.4 min. 86.6% drive. **Housing units:** 84,403; 94.1% occupied. **Home ownership:** 72.5%. **Avg. home:** $196,000; change (2012-14): 4.5%. **Avg. rent:** $1,160.

Mayor: Alan P. Krasnoff, Independent

History: Region settled in 1620s with first English colonies on banks of Elizabeth River; home to Great Dismal Swamp Canal, first envisioned by George Washington in 1763. Battle of Great Bridge fought here Dec. 1775; inc. 1963.

Website: www.cityofchesapeake.net

Chicago, Illinois

Population: 2,722,389 (3). **Pop. density:** 11,953. **Pop. change (2010-14):** 0.9%. **Area:** 227.8 sq mi. **Racial distribution:** 47.8% white; 32.3% black; 5.7% Asian; 0.3% Amer. Ind.; <0.05% Pac. Isl.; 11.8% other; 2+ races 2.1%. **Hispanic pop.:** 28.7%. **Foreign born:** 21.0%. **U.S. citizens:** 87.6%. **Language:** 64.2% English only; 24.4% Spanish.

Employment: 1,264,234 employed; 7.7% unemployed. **Per capita income:** $49,071; change (2012-13): 1.3%. **Below poverty level:** 22.6%; 18.6% of families. **Educational attainment:** 81.1% HS; 34.2% bachelor's. **Avg. commute:** 33.3 min. 50.3% drive; 26.7% public trans. **Housing units:** 1,192,790; 86.2% occupied. **Home ownership:** 45.3%. **Avg. home:** $205,900; change (2012-14): 17.5%. **Avg. rent:** $949.

Mayor: Rahm Emanuel, nonpartisan

History: Site acquired from Indians 1795; significant white settlement began with completion of Erie Canal 1825; chartered as city 1837. Boomed with arrival of railroads and canal to Mississippi R.; one-third of city destroyed by fire 1871. Major grain and livestock market.

Website: www.cityofchicago.org

Chula Vista, California

Population: 260,988 (75). **Pop. density:** 5,259. **Pop. change (2010-14):** 6.6%. **Area:** 49.6 sq mi. **Racial distribution:** 68.2% white; 4.4% black; 14.2% Asian; 0.6% Amer. Ind.; 0.3% Pac. Isl.; 7.3% other; 2+ races 5.0%. **Hispanic pop.:** 58.5%. **Foreign born:** 31.1%. **U.S. citizens:** 85.3%. **Language:** 42.9% English only; 46.0% Spanish; 6.4% Tagalog.

Employment: 110,351 employed; 8.0% unemployed. **Per capita income:** $51,384; change (2012-13): 1.4%. **Below poverty level:** 11.8%; 10.2% of families. **Educational attainment:** 81.3% HS; 26.9% bachelor's. **Avg. commute:** 26.8 min. 79.2% drive; 10.9% carpool. **Housing units:** 83,732; 90.5% occupied. **Home ownership:** 58.7%. **Avg. home:** $497,900; change (2012-14): 29.2%. **Avg. rent:** $1,255.

Mayor: Mary Casillas Salas, nonpartisan

History: Visited by Spanish in 1542; became part of Spanish land grant in 1795; came into the U.S. during the Mexican War in 1847; inc. 1911. WWII brought aircraft industry and growth.

Website: www.chulavistaca.gov

Cincinnati, Ohio

Population: 298,165 (65). **Pop. density:** 3,826. **Pop. change (2010-14):** 0.4%. **Area:** 77.9 sq mi. **Racial distribution:** 50.8% white; 43.4% black; 2.0% Asian; 0.3% Amer. Ind.; <0.05% Pac. Isl.; 0.9% other; 2+ races 2.6%. **Hispanic pop.:** 3.1%. **Foreign born:** 5.2%. **U.S. citizens:** 96.6%. **Language:** 92.4% English only; 3.1% Spanish.

Employment: 134,575 employed; 5.9% unemployed. **Per capita income:** $43,923; change (2012-13): 1.2%. **Below poverty level:** 30.4%; 24.7% of families. **Educational attainment:** 84.3% HS; 31.5% bachelor's. **Avg. commute:** 22.4 min. 71.9% drive. **Housing units:** 162,315; 80.1% occupied. **Home ownership:** 39.8%. **Avg. home:** $140,500; change (2012-14): 9.5%. **Avg. rent:** $640.

Mayor: John Cranley, nonpartisan

History: Founded 1788; named after the Society of Cincinnati, an organization of Revolutionary War officers; chartered as village 1802; inc. 1819.

Website: www.cincinnati-oh.gov

Cleveland, Ohio

Population: 389,521 (48). **Pop. density:** 5,013. **Pop. change (2010-14):** –1.6%. **Area:** 77.7 sq mi. **Racial distribution:** 40.4% white; 52.3% black; 1.7% Asian; 0.4% Amer. Ind.; <0.05% Pac. Isl.; 2.3% other; 2+ races 3.0%. **Hispanic pop.:** 9.8%. **Foreign born:** 4.6%. **U.S. citizens:** 97.7%. **Language:** 88.2% English only; 7.2% Spanish.

Employment: 149,983 employed; 8.0% unemployed. **Per capita income:** $45,747; change (2012-13): 1.8%. **Below poverty level:** 35.4%; 30.6% of families. **Educational attainment:** 77.4% HS; 14.9% bachelor's. **Avg. commute:** 24.3 min. 70.3% drive; 10.9% public trans. **Housing units:** 212,640; 78.5% occupied. **Home ownership:** 44.9%. **Avg. home:** $122,600; change (2012-14): 11.5%. **Avg. rent:** $659.

Mayor: Frank G. Jackson, nonpartisan

History: Surveyed in 1796; given recognition as village 1815; inc. 1836; annexed Ohio City 1854.

Website: www.city.cleveland.oh.us

Colorado Springs, Colorado

Population: 445,830 (42). **Pop. density:** 2,288. **Pop. change (2010-14):** 6.0%. **Area:** 194.9 sq mi. **Racial distribution:** 80.1% white; 6.2% black; 2.8% Asian; 0.7% Amer. Ind.; 0.3% Pac. Isl.; 4.8% other; 2+ races 5.1%. **Hispanic pop.:** 16.6%. **Foreign born:** 8.2%. **U.S. citizens:** 95.7%. **Language:** 86.9% English only; 8.0% Spanish.

Employment: 203,843 employed; 5.9% unemployed. **Per capita income:** $41,250; change (2012-13): 0.2%. **Below poverty level:** 13.7%; 9.8% of families. **Educational attainment:** 93.0% HS; 36.3% bachelor's. **Avg. commute:** 20.8 min. 79.1% drive; 10.2% carpool. **Housing units:** 180,259; 93.3% occupied. **Home ownership:** 59.0%. **Avg. home:** $222,300; change (2012-14): 10.3%. **Avg. rent:** $860.

Mayor: John Suthers, nonpartisan

History: Founded 1871 at the foot of Pike's Peak; inc. 1872.

Website: coloradosprings.gov

Columbus, Ohio

Population: 835,957 (15). **Pop. density:** 3,835. **Pop. change (2010-14):** 5.8%. **Area:** 218.0 sq mi. **Racial distribution:** 62.2% white; 27.7% black; 4.2% Asian; 0.2% Amer. Ind.; <0.05% Pac. Isl.; 2.0% other; 2+ races 3.5%. **Hispanic pop.:** 5.6%. **Foreign born:** 10.9%. **U.S. citizens:** 93.1%. **Language:** 86.0% English only; 4.5% Spanish.

Employment: 417,562 employed; 4.8% unemployed. **Per capita income:** $43,867; change (2012-13): 1.9%. **Below poverty level:** 22.4%; 17.0% of families. **Educational attainment:** 88.3% HS; 33.1% bachelor's. **Avg. commute:** 21.3 min. 80.7% drive. **Housing units:** 376,002; 86.7% occupied. **Home ownership:** 46.9%. **Avg. home:** $156,300; change (2012-14): 14.5%. **Avg. rent:** $809.

Mayor: Michael B. Coleman, nonpartisan

History: First settlement 1797; laid out as new state capital 1812 with current name; inc. 1834.

Website: www.columbus.gov

Corpus Christi, Texas

Population: 320,434 (58). **Pop. density:** 1,996. **Pop. change (2010-14):** 4.9%. **Area:** 160.5 sq mi. **Racial distribution:** 84.7% white; 4.5% black; 1.8% Asian; 0.4% Amer. Ind.; <0.05% Pac. Isl.; 6.4% other; 2+ races 2.1%. **Hispanic pop.:** 60.2%. **Foreign born:** 8.0%. **U.S. citizens:** 95.3%. **Language:** 61.1% English only; 36.2% Spanish.

Employment: 146,998 employed; 4.9% unemployed. **Per capita income:** $42,331; change (2012-13): 1.7%. **Below poverty level:** 18.2%; 14.2% of families. **Educational attainment:** 80.7% HS; 20.8% bachelor's. **Avg. commute:** 19.4 min. 79.5% drive; 11.6% carpool. **Housing units:** 125,520; 89.0% occupied. **Home ownership:** 57.3%. **Avg. home:** $171,100; change (2012-14): 19.9%. **Avg. rent:** $844.

Mayor: Nelda Martinez, nonpartisan

History: Settled 1839; inc. 1852. One of the largest U.S. ports.

Website: www.cctexas.com

Dallas, Texas

Population: 1,281,047 (9). **Pop. density:** 3,753. **Pop. change (2010-14):** 6.7%. **Area:** 341.4 sq mi. **Racial distribution:** 56.2% white; 24.5% black; 3.0% Asian; 0.3% Amer. Ind.; <0.05% Pac. Isl.; 13.8% other; 2+ races 2.2%. **Hispanic pop.:** 41.9%. **Foreign born:** 24.4%. **U.S. citizens:** 80.9%. **Language:** 57.5% English only; 37.6% Spanish.

Employment: 605,501 employed; 5.2% unemployed. **Per capita income:** $46,989; change (2012-13): 1.3%. **Below poverty level:** 23.8%; 20.3% of families. **Educational attainment:** 74.2% HS; 29.4% bachelor's. **Avg. commute:** 25.2 min. 77.4% drive; 10.9% carpool. **Housing units:** 523,645; 88.2% occupied. **Home ownership:** 43.6%. **Avg. home:** $188,300; change (2012-14): 18.2%. **Avg. rent:** $838.

Mayor: Mike Rawlings, nonpartisan

History: First settled 1841; platted 1846; inc. 1871. Developed as financial and commercial center of Southwest; headquarters of regional Federal Reserve Bank; major center for distribution and high-tech manufacturing.

Website: www.dallascityhall.com

Denver, Colorado

Population: 663,862 (21). **Pop. density:** 4,338. **Pop. change (2010-14):** 10.0%. **Area:** 153.0 sq mi. **Racial distribution:** 74.1% white; 10.0% black; 3.4% Asian; 1.1% Amer. Ind.; 0.1% Pac. Isl.; 8.0% other; 2+ races 3.3%. **Hispanic pop.:** 31.4%. **Foreign born:** 15.8%. **U.S. citizens:** 89.2%. **Language:** 73.1% English only; 20.3% Spanish.

Employment: 352,427 employed; 4.9% unemployed. **Per capita income:** $51,946; change (2012-13): 1.0%. **Below poverty level:** 19.1%; 14.5% of families. **Educational attainment:** 85.4% HS; 42.9% bachelor's. **Avg. commute:** 24.6 min. 69.6% drive. **Housing units:** 287,735; 92.5% occupied. **Home ownership:** 50.2%. **Avg. home:** $310,200; change (2012-14): 22.9%. **Avg. rent:** $883.

Mayor: Michael B. Hancock, nonpartisan

History: Settled 1858 by gold prospectors and miners; inc. 1861; became territorial capital 1867; growth spurred by gold and silver boom. Became financial, industrial, cultural center of Rocky Mt. region.

Website: www.denvergov.org

Detroit, Michigan

Population: 680,250 (18). **Pop. density:** 4,903. **Pop. change (2010-14):** –4.4%. **Area:** 138.8 sq mi. **Racial distribution:** 11.8% white; 81.7% black; 1.2% Asian; 0.3% Amer. Ind.; <0.05% Pac. Isl.; 2.9% other; 2+ races 2.0%. **Hispanic pop.:** 7.1%. **Foreign born:** 5.1%. **U.S. citizens:** 96.5%. **Language:** 90.4% English only; 6.0% Spanish.

Employment: 209,692 employed; 16.7% unemployed. **Per capita income:** $42,887; change (2012-13): 0.8%. **Below poverty level:** 39.3%; 33.9% of families. **Educational attainment:** 77.6% HS; 12.7% bachelor's. **Avg. commute:** 26.6 min. 70.1%

drive; 12.4% carpool. **Housing units:** 363,194; 70.7% occupied. **Home ownership:** 51.9%. **Avg. home:** $63,400 (2012). **Avg. rent:** $761.

Mayor: Mike Duggan, nonpartisan

History: Founded by French 1701; controlled by British 1760; acquired by U.S. 1796; destroyed by fire 1805; fought over during War of 1812; inc. 1815; capital of state 1837-47. Auto manufacturing began 1890.

Website: www.detroitmi.gov

Durham, North Carolina

Population: 251,893 (81). **Pop. density:** 2,322. **Pop. change (2010-14):** 9.9%. **Area:** 108.5 sq mi. **Racial distribution:** 46.2% white; 39.9% black; 4.8% Asian; 0.4% Amer. Ind.; <0.05% Pac. Isl.; 5.4% other; 2+ races 3.2%. **Hispanic pop.:** 13.9%. **Foreign born:** 14.6%. **U.S. citizens:** 89.2%. **Language:** 79.8% English only; 13.0% Spanish.

Employment: 123,559 employed; 4.5% unemployed. **Per capita income:** $45,018; change (2012-13): –0.3%. **Below poverty level:** 20.0%; 13.8% of families. **Educational attainment:** 86.6% HS; 46.8% bachelor's. **Avg. commute:** 21.1 min. 74.0% drive; 12.5% carpool. **Housing units:** 105,326; 91.2% occupied. **Home ownership:** 50.5%. **Avg. home:** $199,100; change (2012-14): 7.2%. **Avg. rent:** $852.

Mayor: William V. Bell, nonpartisan

History: Inc. 1869. Trinity College moved to Durham in 1892, renamed Duke Univ. in 1924.

Website: durhamnc.gov

El Paso, Texas

Population: 679,036 (19). **Pop. density:** 2,645. **Pop. change (2010-14):** 4.2%. **Area:** 256.7 sq mi. **Racial distribution:** 81.8% white; 3.4% black; 1.2% Asian; 0.5% Amer. Ind.; 0.2% Pac. Isl.; 10.6% other; 2+ races 2.3%. **Hispanic pop.:** 80.0%. **Foreign born:** 25.0%. **U.S. citizens:** 86.2%. **Language:** 28.8% English only; 69.0% Spanish.

Employment: 272,959 employed; 6.0% unemployed. **Per capita income:** $31,156; change (2012-13): 1.3%. **Below poverty level:** 21.5%; 18.3% of families. **Educational attainment:** 76.4% HS; 22.7% bachelor's. **Avg. commute:** 22.6 min. 79.5% drive; 11.3% carpool. **Housing units:** 233,307; 93.0% occupied. **Home ownership:** 59.3%. **Avg. home:** $140,800; change (2012-14): 1.6%. **Avg. rent:** $724.

Mayor: Oscar Leeser, nonpartisan

History: First settled 1598; inc. 1873; arrival of railroad, 1881, boosted city's population and industries.

Website: www.elpasotexas.gov

Fort Wayne, Indiana

Population: 258,522 (77). **Pop. density:** 2,337. **Pop. change (2010-14):** 1.9%. **Area:** 110.6 sq mi. **Racial distribution:** 74.3% white; 15.9% black; 3.2% Asian; 0.3% Amer. Ind.; 0.1% Pac. Isl.; 2.9% other; 2+ races 3.2%. **Hispanic pop.:** 8.0%. **Foreign born:** 7.6%. **U.S. citizens:** 95.4%. **Language:** 89.0% English only; 5.9% Spanish.

Employment: 113,667 employed; 6.1% unemployed. **Per capita income:** $37,537; change (2012-13): 0.1%. **Below poverty level:** 18.7%; 14.6% of families. **Educational attainment:** 87.9% HS; 25.6% bachelor's. **Avg. commute:** 19.7 min. 85.3% drive. **Housing units:** 113,145; 89.2% occupied. **Home ownership:** 63.7%. **Avg. home:** $108,200; change (2012-14): 1.9%. **Avg. rent:** $656.

Mayor: Tom Henry, Democrat

History: French fort 1680; U.S. fort 1794; settled by 1832; inc. 1840 prior to Wabash-Erie Canal completion in 1843.

Website: www.cityoffortwayne.org

Fort Worth, Texas

Population: 812,238 (16). **Pop. density:** 2,384. **Pop. change (2010-14):** 8.9%. **Area:** 340.7 sq mi. **Racial distribution:** 64.6% white; 19.0% black; 3.5% Asian; 0.6% Amer. Ind.; 0.1% Pac. Isl.; 9.6% other; 2+ races 2.6%. **Hispanic pop.:** 34.2%. **Foreign born:** 17.5%. **U.S. citizens:** 87.6%. **Language:** 67.3% English only; 27.4% Spanish.

Employment: 371,661 employed; 4.9% unemployed. **Per capita income:** $46,989; change (2012-13): 1.3%. **Below poverty level:** 19.3%; 15.1% of families. **Educational attainment:** 79.9% HS; 26.5% bachelor's. **Avg. commute:** 25.9 min. 81.6% drive; 11.1% carpool. **Housing units:** 294,218; 90.1% occupied. **Home ownership:** 58.5%. **Avg. home:** $188,300; change (2012-14): 18.2%. **Avg. rent:** $857.

Mayor: Betsy Price, nonpartisan

History: Established as military post 1849; inc. 1873; oil discovered 1917.

Website: fortworthtexas.gov

Fremont, California

Population: 228,758 (97). **Pop. density:** 2,953. **Pop. change (2010-14):** 6.6%. **Area:** 77.5 sq mi. **Racial distribution:** 30.5% white; 3.6% black; 51.1% Asian; 0.5% Amer. Ind.; 0.5% Pac. Isl.; 7.5% other; 2+ races 6.3%. **Hispanic pop.:** 14.8%. **Foreign born:** 43.7%. **U.S. citizens:** 80.8%. **Language:** 41.6% English only; 9.9% Spanish; 15.6% Chinese; 7.1% Hindi; 5.8% other Asian languages.

Employment: 109,454 employed; 4.6% unemployed. **Per capita income:** $69,127; change (2012-13): 1.6%. **Below poverty level:** 6.0%; 3.9% of families. **Educational attainment:** 91.0% HS; 50.9% bachelor's. **Avg. commute:** 29.7 min. 75.0% drive; 10.9% carpool. **Housing units:** 75,033; 94.7% occupied. **Home ownership:** 63.2%. **Avg. home:** $737,600; change (2012-14): 35.6%. **Avg. rent:** $1,566.

Mayor: Bill Harrison, nonpartisan

History: Area first settled by Spanish 1769; inc. 1956 with consolidation of five communities.

Website: www.fremont.gov

Fresno, California

Population: 515,986 (34). **Pop. density:** 4,557. **Pop. change (2010-14):** 3.8%. **Area:** 113.2 sq mi. **Racial distribution:** 53.1% white; 7.9% black; 12.8% Asian; 1.0% Amer. Ind.; 0.2% Pac. Isl.; 20.3% other; 2+ races 4.7%. **Hispanic pop.:** 47.2%. **Foreign born:** 20.9%. **U.S. citizens:** 87.0%. **Language:** 58.3% English only; 28.3% Spanish.

Employment: 206,531 employed; 12.6% unemployed. **Per capita income:** $35,635; change (2012-13): 3.2%. **Below poverty level:** 28.9%; 23.4% of families. **Educational attainment:** 75.0% HS; 20.3% bachelor's. **Avg. commute:** 21.7 min. 77.4% drive; 11.9% carpool. **Housing units:** 173,000; 92.0% occupied. **Home ownership:** 48.0%. **Avg. rent:** $884.

Mayor: Ashley Swearengin, nonpartisan

History: Founded by railroad company 1872; inc. 1885.

Website: www.fresno.gov

Garland, Texas

Population: 235,501 (91). **Pop. density:** 4,129. **Pop. change (2010-14):** 3.6%. **Area:** 57.0 sq mi. **Racial distribution:** 45.0% white; 13.5% black; 10.4% Asian; 0.4% Amer. Ind.; 0.1% Pac. Isl.; 24.3% other; 2+ races 6.3%. **Hispanic pop.:** 39.2%. **Foreign born:** 27.0%. **U.S. citizens:** 82.5%. **Language:** 54.0% English only; 34.0% Spanish.

Employment: 115,260 employed; 5.3% unemployed. **Per capita income:** $46,989; change (2012-13): 1.3%. **Below poverty level:** 16.2%; 12.8% of families. **Educational attainment:** 76.7% HS; 21.4% bachelor's. **Avg. commute:** 27.6 min. 78.6% drive; 13.8% carpool. **Housing units:** 79,482; 93.3% occupied. **Home ownership:** 63.7%. **Avg. home:** $188,300; change (2012-14): 18.2%. **Avg. rent:** $932.

Mayor: Douglas Athas, nonpartisan

History: Settled 1850s; inc. 1891.

Website: www.garlandtx.gov

Gilbert, Arizona

Population: 239,277 (86). **Pop. density:** 3,525. **Pop. change (2010-14):** 14.1%. **Area:** 67.9 sq mi. **Racial distribution:** 83.8% white; 3.5% black; 6.6% Asian; 0.7% Amer. Ind.; 0.1% Pac. Isl.; 2.0% other; 2+ races 3.3%. **Hispanic pop.:** 14.9%. **Foreign born:** 9.5%. **U.S. citizens:** 96.1%. **Language:** 84.6% English only; 7.7% Spanish.

Employment: 117,207 employed; 4.7% unemployed. **Per capita income:** $38,745; change (2012-13): 0.7%. **Below poverty level:** 6.7%; 5.4% of families. **Educational attainment:** 95.5% HS; 39.6% bachelor's. **Avg. commute:** 26.7 min. 78.5% drive; 11.6% carpool. **Housing units:** 75,658; 92.9% occupied. **Home ownership:** 71.4%. **Avg. home:** $198,500; change (2012-14): 34.5%. **Avg. rent:** $1,269.

Mayor: John Lewis, nonpartisan

History: Est. 1891; inc. 1920.

Website: www.gilbertaz.gov

Glendale, Arizona

Population: 237,517 (88). **Pop. density:** 4,043. **Pop. change (2010-14):** 4.9%. **Area:** 58.8 sq mi. **Racial distribution:** 76.2% white; 6.0% black; 3.6% Asian; 1.7% Amer. Ind.; 0.1% Pac. Isl.; 8.8% other; 2+ races 3.5%. **Hispanic pop.:** 37.0%. **Foreign born:** 16.0%. **U.S. citizens:** 89.8%. **Language:** 69.6% English only; 24.4% Spanish.

Employment: 105,227 employed; 6.3% unemployed. **Per capita income:** $38,745; change (2012-13): 0.7%. **Below poverty level:** 20.5%; 16.1% of families. **Educational attainment:** 82.9% HS; 21.5% bachelor's. **Avg. commute:** 26.5 min. 73.5% drive; 15.2% carpool. **Housing units:** 89,570; 87.5% occupied. **Home ownership:** 57.8%. **Avg. home:** $198,500; change (2012-14): 34.5%. **Avg. rent:** $854.

Mayor: Jerry Weiers, nonpartisan

History: Est. 1892; inc. 1910.

Website: www.glendaleaz.com

Greensboro, North Carolina

Population: 282,586 (67). **Pop. density:** 2,231. **Pop. change (2010-14):** 4.8%. **Area:** 126.7 sq mi. **Racial distribution:** 49.4%

white; 40.9% black; 4.2% Asian; 0.4% Amer. Ind.; 0.1% Pac. Isl.; 2.8% other; 2+ races 2.4%. **Hispanic pop.:** 7.5%. **Foreign born:** 10.7%. **U.S. citizens:** 92.9%. **Language:** 86.3% English only; 6.5% Spanish.

Employment: 130,192 employed; 5.9% unemployed. **Per capita income:** $37,092; change (2012-13): 0.2%. **Below poverty level:** 20.3%; 15.0% of families. **Educational attainment:** 87.7% HS; 35.7% bachelor's. **Avg. commute:** 20.1 min. 81.3% drive. **Housing units:** 125,852; 88.7% occupied. **Home ownership:** 53.1%. **Avg. home:** $136,600; change (2012-14): 9.5%. **Avg. rent:** $742.

Mayor: Nancy Vaughan, nonpartisan

History: Settled 1749; site of Revolutionary War conflict 1781 between Generals Nathanael Greene and Cornwallis; inc. 1807. Origin of civil rights sit-in movement.

Website: www.greensboro-nc.gov

Henderson, Nevada

Population: 277,440 (71). **Pop. density:** 2,651. **Pop. change (2010-14):** 7.6%. **Area:** 104.7 sq mi. **Racial distribution:** 78.8% white; 5.7% black; 7.9% Asian; 0.5% Amer. Ind.; 0.4% Pac. Isl.; 3.0% other; 2+ races 3.7%. **Hispanic pop.:** 13.8%. **Foreign born:** 12.0%. **U.S. citizens:** 96.0%. **Language:** 82.9% English only; 8.0% Spanish.

Employment: 130,662 employed; 7.8% unemployed. **Per capita income:** $37,457; change (2012-13): –0.1%. **Below poverty level:** 9.8%; 6.9% of families. **Educational attainment:** 92.5% HS; 30.7% bachelor's. **Avg. commute:** 23.2 min. 81.8% drive. **Housing units:** 114,681; 88.4% occupied. **Home ownership:** 64.0%. **Avg. home:** $198,000; change (2012-14): 47.7%. **Avg. rent:** $1,156.

Mayor: Andy A. Hafen, nonpartisan

History: Early growth spurred by WWII magnesium mining; inc. 1953.

Website: www.cityofhenderson.com

Hialeah, Florida

Population: 235,563 (90). **Pop. density:** 10,991. **Pop. change (2010-14):** 4.4%. **Area:** 21.4 sq mi. **Racial distribution:** 93.7% white; 2.1% black; 0.5% Asian; 0.1% Amer. Ind.; <0.05% Pac. Isl.; 2.8% other; 2+ races 0.8%. **Hispanic pop.:** 95.1%. **Foreign born:** 73.1%. **U.S. citizens:** 62.8%. **Language:** 7.2% English only; 92.1% Spanish.

Employment: 104,489 employed; 7.0% unemployed. **Per capita income:** $45,377; change (2012-13): 1.3%. **Below poverty level:** 24.5%; 21.7% of families. **Educational attainment:** 69.6% HS; 13.2% bachelor's. **Avg. commute:** 24 min. 78.9% drive. **Housing units:** 73,828; 95.5% occupied. **Home ownership:** 50.3%. **Avg. home:** $266,000; change (2012-14): 31.0%. **Avg. rent:** $989.

Mayor: Carlos Hernandez, nonpartisan

History: Founded 1917; inc. 1925. Industrial and residential city NW of Miami; site of Hialeah Park Horse Racing Track.

Website: www.hialeahfl.gov

Honolulu, Hawaii

Population: 350,399 (55). **Pop. density:** 5,790. **Pop. change (2010-14):** 3.5%. **Area:** 60.5 sq mi. **Racial distribution:** 18.2% white; 1.7% black; 54.5% Asian; 0.2% Amer. Ind.; 8.1% Pac. Isl.; 0.7% other; 2+ races 16.7%. **Hispanic pop.:** 6.0%. **Foreign born:** 28.2%. **U.S. citizens:** 86.9%. **Language:** 63.0% English only; 1.4% Spanish; 7.1% Chinese; 6.8% Japanese; 5.0% Tagalog; 8.6% other Pac. Isl. languages.

Employment: 444,678 employed; 4.1% unemployed. **Per capita income:** $48,798; change (2012-13): 1.1%. **Below poverty level:** 12.1%; 8.1% of families. **Educational attainment:** 87.9% HS; 35.0% bachelor's. **Avg. commute:** 22.4 min. 57.5% drive; 12.8% carpool; 12.4% public trans. **Housing units:** 142,767; 89.1% occupied. **Home ownership:** 43.3%. **Avg. home:** $682,800; change (2012-14): 8.6%. **Avg. rent:** $1,251.

Mayor: Kirk Caldwell, nonpartisan

History: Europeans entered harbor 1778; declared capital of kingdom of Hawaii by King Kamehameha III 1850. Pearl Harbor naval base attacked by Japanese Dec. 7, 1941.

Website: www.honolulu.gov

Houston, Texas

Population: 2,239,558 (4). **Pop. density:** 3,734. **Pop. change (2010-14):** 6.5%. **Area:** 599.7 sq mi. **Racial distribution:** 57.9% white; 23.5% black; 6.2% Asian; 0.4% Amer. Ind.; <0.05% Pac. Isl.; 10.1% other; 2+ races 1.8%. **Hispanic pop.:** 43.6%. **Foreign born:** 28.3%. **U.S. citizens:** 79.5%. **Language:** 53.7% English only; 37.6% Spanish.

Employment: 1,095,948 employed; 4.7% unemployed. **Per capita income:** $51,930; change (2012-13): 1.1%. **Below poverty level:** 22.9%; 19.5% of families. **Educational attainment:** 75.4% HS; 29.2% bachelor's. **Avg. commute:** 25.9 min. 75.7% drive; 12.3% carpool. **Housing units:** 907,494; 86.1% occupied. **Home ownership:** 45.4%. **Avg. home:** $198,400; change (2012-14): 20.4%. **Avg. rent:** $848.

Mayor: Annise D. Parker, Democrat

History: Founded 1836; inc. 1837; capital of Rep. of Texas 1837-39; developed rapidly after completion of channel to Gulf of Mexico 1914. World center of oil, natural gas technology.

Website: www.houstontx.gov

Indianapolis, Indiana

Population: 848,788 (14). **Pop. density:** 2,348. **Pop. change (2010-14):** 3.3%. **Area:** 361.5 sq mi. **Racial distribution:** 62.1% white; 27.8% black; 2.3% Asian; 0.2% Amer. Ind.; <0.05% Pac. Isl.; 4.9% other; 2+ races 2.7%. **Hispanic pop.:** 9.4%. **Foreign born:** 8.7%. **U.S. citizens:** 93.4%. **Language:** 87.4% English only; 8.4% Spanish.

Employment: 397,298 employed; 6.5% unemployed. **Per capita income:** $42,542; change (2012-13): 0.8%. **Below poverty level:** 20.9%; 16.6% of families. **Educational attainment:** 84.3% HS; 27.3% bachelor's. **Avg. commute:** 22.6 min. 81.9% drive; 2.1% public trans. **Housing units:** 380,531; 85.9% occupied. **Home ownership:** 55.2%. **Avg. home:** $144,600; change (2012-14): 11.6%. **Avg. rent:** $770.

Mayor: Gregory A. Ballard, Republican

History: Settled 1820; became capital 1825.

Website: www.indy.gov

Irvine, California

Population: 248,531 (82). **Pop. density:** 3,790. **Pop. change (2010-14):** 16.5%. **Area:** 65.6 sq mi. **Racial distribution:** 52.2% white; 2.0% black; 38.5% Asian; 0.4% Amer. Ind.; 0.2% Pac. Isl.; 2.3% other; 2+ races 4.5%. **Hispanic pop.:** 9.8%. **Foreign born:** 36.0%. **U.S. citizens:** 84.8%. **Language:** 55.2% English only; 5.8% Spanish; 9.7% Chinese; 7.0% Korean.

Employment: 116,794 employed; 4.1% unemployed. **Per capita income:** $48,425; change (2012-13): 1.4%. **Below poverty level:** 12.2%; 6.2% of families. **Educational attainment:** 96.3% HS; 64.9% bachelor's. **Avg. commute:** 23.6 min. 78.7% drive. **Housing units:** 85,866; 94.4% occupied. **Home ownership:** 49.8%. **Avg. home:** $687,900; change (2012-14): 26.8%. **Avg. rent:** $1,846.

Mayor: Steven S. Choi, nonpartisan

History: Univ. of CA–Irvine campus announced 1959; planned city developed around campus 1960s; inc. 1971.

Website: www.cityofirvine.org

Irving, Texas

Population: 232,406 (93). **Pop. density:** 3,467. **Pop. change (2010-14):** 7.2%. **Area:** 67.0 sq mi. **Racial distribution:** 58.2% white; 13.0% black; 14.5% Asian; 0.5% Amer. Ind.; <0.05% Pac. Isl.; 11.1% other; 2+ races 2.6%. **Hispanic pop.:** 40.6%. **Foreign born:** 33.5%. **U.S. citizens:** 75.5%. **Language:** 47.7% English only; 36.1% Spanish.

Employment: 118,354 employed; 4.8% unemployed. **Per capita income:** $46,989; change (2012-13): 1.3%. **Below poverty level:** 16.1%; 13.7% of families. **Educational attainment:** 79.7% HS; 34.1% bachelor's. **Avg. commute:** 22.7 min. 79.3% drive; 11.8% carpool. **Housing units:** 90,543; 90.8% occupied. **Home ownership:** 38.8%. **Avg. home:** $188,300; change (2012-14): 18.2%. **Avg. rent:** $893.

Mayor: Beth Van Duyne, nonpartisan

History: Founded 1903; inc. 1914; remained small until 1950s.

Website: cityofirving.org

Jacksonville, Florida

Population: 853,382 (12). **Pop. density:** 1,142. **Pop. change (2010-14):** 3.6%. **Area:** 747.4 sq mi. **Racial distribution:** 60.4% white; 30.6% black; 4.3% Asian; 0.3% Amer. Ind.; 0.1% Pac. Isl.; 1.2% other; 2+ races 3.1%. **Hispanic pop.:** 8.0%. **Foreign born:** 9.7%. **U.S. citizens:** 95.3%. **Language:** 86.5% English only; 6.0% Spanish.

Employment: 408,495 employed; 6.5% unemployed. **Per capita income:** $43,149; change (2012-13): 0.6%. **Below poverty level:** 17.3%; 13.3% of families. **Educational attainment:** 87.5% HS; 25.5% bachelor's. **Avg. commute:** 23.7 min. 80.5% drive; 10.4% carpool. **Housing units:** 367,330; 84.9% occupied. **Home ownership:** 61.6%. **Avg. home:** $181,100; change (2012-14): 41.3%. **Avg. rent:** $927.

Mayor: Lenny Curry, Republican

History: Settled 1816 as Cowford; renamed after Andrew Jackson 1822; inc. 1832; rechartered 1851; scene of conflicts in Seminole and Civil Wars.

Website: www.coj.net

Jersey City, New Jersey

Population: 262,146 (74). **Pop. density:** 17,722. **Pop. change (2010-14):** 5.4%. **Area:** 14.8 sq mi. **Racial distribution:** 35.2% white; 26.1% black; 24.2% Asian; 0.5% Amer. Ind.; <0.05% Pac. Isl.; 11.0% other; 2+ races 3.1%. **Hispanic pop.:** 27.4%. **Foreign born:** 39.0%. **U.S. citizens:** 78.6%. **Language:** 47.9% English only; 22.6% Spanish; 5.6% Tagalog.

Employment: 129,195 employed; 6.6% unemployed. **Per capita income:** $59,246; change (2012-13): 0.5%. **Below poverty level:** 18.4%; 15.5% of families. **Educational attainment:**

84.8% HS; 42.0% bachelor's. **Avg. commute:** 35.2 min. 46.2% public trans.; 33.9% drive. **Housing units:** 110,031; 87.5% occupied. **Home ownership:** 30.0%. **Avg. home:** $394,900; change (2012-14): 4.1%. **Avg. rent:** $1,174.

Mayor: Steven M. Fulop, nonpartisan

History: Site bought from Indians 1630; chartered as town by British 1668; scene of Revolutionary War conflict 1779; chartered under present name 1838. Important station on Underground Railroad.

Website: www.cityofjerseycity.com

Kansas City, Missouri

Population: 470,800 (37). **Pop. density:** 1,495. **Pop. change (2010-14):** 2.2%. **Area:** 315.0 sq mi. **Racial distribution:** 60.0% white; 29.2% black; 2.4% Asian; 0.5% Amer. Ind.; 0.2% Pac. Isl.; 4.2% other; 2+ races 3.5%. **Hispanic pop.:** 10.1%. **Foreign born:** 7.6%. **U.S. citizens:** 95.4%. **Language:** 88.0% English only; 7.2% Spanish.

Employment: 234,212 employed; 6.7% unemployed. **Per capita income:** $45,558; change (2012-13): 1.2%. **Below poverty level:** 19.1%; 14.5% of families. **Educational attainment:** 87.5% HS; 31.3% bachelor's. **Avg. commute:** 21.3 min. 80.4% drive. **Housing units:** 225,145; 85.6% occupied. **Home ownership:** 56.3%. **Avg. home:** $158,800; change (2012-14): 11.4%. **Avg. rent:** $789.

Mayor: Sly James, nonpartisan

History: Settled by 1838 at confluence of Missouri and Kansas Rivers; inc. 1850.

Website: kcmo.gov

Laredo, Texas

Population: 252,309 (80). **Pop. density:** 2,734. **Pop. change (2010-14):** 6.4%. **Area:** 92.3 sq mi. **Racial distribution:** 93.4% white; 0.4% black; 0.6% Asian; 0.4% Amer. Ind.; <0.05% Pac. Isl.; 4.5% other; 2+ races 0.7%. **Hispanic pop.:** 95.4%. **Foreign born:** 27.3%. **U.S. citizens:** 80.4%. **Language:** 8.9% English only; 90.5% Spanish.

Employment: 101,383 employed; 4.8% unemployed. **Per capita income:** $27,102; change (2012-13): 0.8%. **Below poverty level:** 30.8%; 26.3% of families. **Educational attainment:** 65.3% HS; 17.7% bachelor's. **Avg. commute:** 21.3 min. 79.3% drive; 13.7% carpool. **Housing units:** 69,394; 92.2% occupied. **Home ownership:** 63.2%. **Avg. rent:** $747.

Mayor: Pete Saenz, nonpartisan

History: Founded by Spanish colonists in 1755; part of U.S. from 1848. Fast growth fueled by immigration; principal port of entry into Mexico.

Website: www.cityoflaredo.com

Las Vegas, Nevada

Population: 613,599 (29). **Pop. density:** 4,609. **Pop. change (2010-14):** 4.9%. **Area:** 133.1 sq mi. **Racial distribution:** 67.7% white; 11.2% black; 6.4% Asian; 0.7% Amer. Ind.; 0.6% Pac. Isl.; 9.1% other; 2+ races 4.3%. **Hispanic pop.:** 31.7%. **Foreign born:** 21.3%. **U.S. citizens:** 86.8%. **Language:** 66.6% English only; 24.8% Spanish.

Employment: 269,350 employed; 8.0% unemployed. **Per capita income:** $37,457; change (2012-13): –0.1%. **Below poverty level:** 17.1%; 12.8% of families. **Educational attainment:** 82.5% HS; 21.4% bachelor's. **Avg. commute:** 25 min. 77.9% drive; 11.3% carpool. **Housing units:** 248,308; 85.7% occupied. **Home ownership:** 53.6%. **Avg. home:** $198,000; change (2012-14): 47.7%. **Avg. rent:** $993.

Mayor: Caroline G. Goodman, nonpartisan

History: Occupied by Mormons 1855-57; bought by railroad 1903; inc. 1911; gambling legalized 1931.

Website: www.lasvegasnevada.gov

Lexington, Kentucky

Population: 310,797 (61). **Pop. density:** 1,096. **Pop. change (2010-14):** 4.8%. **Area:** 283.6 sq mi. **Racial distribution:** 76.2% white; 14.3% black; 3.5% Asian; 0.3% Amer. Ind.; <0.05% Pac. Isl.; 3.0% other; 2+ races 2.6%. **Hispanic pop.:** 6.8%. **Foreign born:** 8.9%. **U.S. citizens:** 93.4%. **Language:** 88.1% English only; 6.2% Spanish.

Employment: 158,803 employed; 4.8% unemployed. **Per capita income:** $40,391; change (2012-13): 0.7%. **Below poverty level:** 18.9%; 12.2% of families. **Educational attainment:** 88.6% HS; 40.1% bachelor's. **Avg. commute:** 19.7 min. 79.7% drive. **Housing units:** 135,987; 90.6% occupied. **Home ownership:** 55.2%. **Avg. home:** $144,000; change (2012-14): 0.6%. **Avg. rent:** $756.

Mayor: Jim Gray, nonpartisan

History: Site founded and named in 1775 after site of the Revolutionary War's opening battle at Lexington, MA; settled 1779; chartered 1782; inc. 1832.

Website: www.lexingtonky.gov

Lincoln, Nebraska

Population: 272,996 (72). **Pop. density:** 3,019. **Pop. change (2010-14):** 5.4%. **Area:** 90.4 sq mi. **Racial distribution:** 87.2% white; 4.2% black; 4.1% Asian; 0.8% Amer. Ind.; 0.1% Pac. Isl.; 1.1% other; 2+ races 2.6%. **Hispanic pop.:** 6.4%. **Foreign born:** 7.6%. **U.S. citizens:** 95.5%. **Language:** 88.2% English only; 4.5% Spanish.

Employment: 148,891 employed; 2.9% unemployed. **Per capita income:** $42,743; change (2012-13): 1.1%. **Below poverty level:** 16.5%; 10.4% of families. **Educational attainment:** 93.4% HS; 36.1% bachelor's. **Avg. commute:** 17.7 min. 81.1% drive. **Housing units:** 111,168; 94.7% occupied. **Home ownership:** 57.5%. **Avg. home:** $145,600; change (2012-14): 4.3%. **Avg. rent:** $714.

Mayor: Chris Beutler, nonpartisan

History: Originally called Lancaster; chosen state capital 1867, renamed after Abraham Lincoln; inc. 1869.

Website: lincoln.ne.gov

Long Beach, California

Population: 473,577 (36). **Pop. density:** 9,415. **Pop. change (2010-14):** 2.3%. **Area:** 50.3 sq mi. **Racial distribution:** 52.8% white; 13.5% black; 12.8% Asian; 0.9% Amer. Ind.; 0.8% Pac. Isl.; 13.1% other; 2+ races 6.2%. **Hispanic pop.:** 40.9%. **Foreign born:** 26.0%. **U.S. citizens:** 85.5%. **Language:** 55.2% English only; 32.3% Spanish.

Employment: 218,484 employed; 9.0% unemployed. **Per capita income:** $48,425; change (2012-13): 1.4%. **Below poverty level:** 20.2%; 16.4% of families. **Educational attainment:** 79.3% HS; 28.5% bachelor's. **Avg. commute:** 28.7 min. 72.4% drive; 10.3% carpool. **Housing units:** 175,755; 93.2% occupied. **Home ownership:** 40.9%. **Avg. home:** $449,500; change (2012-14): 37.3%. **Avg. rent:** $1,106.

Mayor: Robert Garcia, nonpartisan

History: Settled as early as 1784 by Spanish; by 1884, present site developed on harbor; inc. 1888; oil discovered 1921.

Website: www.longbeach.gov

Los Angeles, California

Population: 3,928,864 (2). **Pop. density:** 8,383. **Pop. change (2010-14):** 3.5%. **Area:** 468.7 sq mi. **Racial distribution:** 52.4% white; 9.4% black; 11.4% Asian; 0.5% Amer. Ind.; 0.2% Pac. Isl.; 22.8% other; 2+ races 3.4%. **Hispanic pop.:** 48.6%. **Foreign born:** 38.8%. **U.S. citizens:** 77.3%. **Language:** 39.8% English only; 43.1% Spanish.

Employment: 1,839,546 employed; 8.7% unemployed. **Per capita income:** $48,425; change (2012-13): 1.4%. **Below poverty level:** 22.0%; 17.8% of families. **Educational attainment:** 74.5% HS; 31.1% bachelor's. **Avg. commute:** 29.2 min. 67.1% drive; 11.0% public trans.; 10.1% carpool. **Housing units:** 1,422,368; 92.9% occupied. **Home ownership:** 37.6%. **Avg. home:** $449,500; change (2012-14): 37.3%. **Avg. rent:** $1,175.

Mayor: Eric Garcetti, nonpartisan

History: Founded by Spanish 1781; captured by U.S. 1846; inc. 1850; grew rapidly after coming of railroads, 1876 and 1885. Hollywood is a district of L.A.

Website: www.lacity.org

Louisville, Kentucky

Population: 612,780 (30). **Pop. density:** 2,323. **Pop. change (2010-14):** 2.4%. **Area:** 263.8 sq mi. **Racial distribution:** 71.5% white; 22.7% black; 2.2% Asian; 0.1% Amer. Ind.; <0.05% Pac. Isl.; 0.8% other; 2+ races 2.7%. **Hispanic pop.:** 4.6%. **Foreign born:** 6.5%. **U.S. citizens:** 95.8%. **Language:** 91.6% English only; 3.9% Spanish.

Employment: 355,616 employed; 6.1% unemployed. **Per capita income:** $41,477; change (2012-13): 0.2%. **Below poverty level:** 18.4%; 14.0% of families. **Educational attainment:** 86.7% HS; 26.9% bachelor's. **Avg. commute:** 22.2 min. 81.5% drive. **Housing units:** 272,876; 89.7% occupied. **Home ownership:** 61.1%. **Avg. home:** $142,800; change (2012-14): 4.2%. **Avg. rent:** $700.

Mayor: Greg Fischer, Democrat

History: Settled 1778; named for Louis XVI of France; inc. 1828; base for Union forces in Civil War.

Website: www.louisvilleky.gov

Lubbock, Texas

Population: 243,839 (85). **Pop. density:** 1,992. **Pop. change (2010-14):** 5.7%. **Area:** 122.4 sq mi. **Racial distribution:** 77.3% white; 8.1% black; 2.3% Asian; 0.5% Amer. Ind.; 0.1% Pac. Isl.; 8.4% other; 2+ races 3.3%. **Hispanic pop.:** 33.1%. **Foreign born:** 5.8%. **U.S. citizens:** 96.6%. **Language:** 77.8% English only; 19.0% Spanish.

Employment: 119,642 employed; 3.9% unemployed. **Per capita income:** $38,695; change (2012-13): 3.0%. **Below poverty level:** 21.8%; 14.1% of families. **Educational attainment:** 85.2% HS; 29.2% bachelor's. **Avg. commute:** 15.1 min. 82.1% drive; 10.5% carpool. **Housing units:** 97,658; 90.5% occupied. **Home ownership:** 54.8%. **Avg. rent:** $794.

Mayor: Glen Robertson, nonpartisan

History: Settled 1879; laid out 1891; inc. 1909 through merger of two towns.

Website: www.mylubbock.us

Madison, Wisconsin

Population: 245,691 (83). **Pop. density:** 3,204. **Pop. change (2010-14):** 5.2%. **Area:** 76.7 sq mi. **Racial distribution:** 80.3% white; 7.4% black; 7.6% Asian; 0.3% Amer. Ind.; <0.05% Pac. Isl.; 1.3% other; 2+ races 3.1%. **Hispanic pop.:** 6.5%. **Foreign born:** 10.4%. **U.S. citizens:** 93.0%. **Language:** 85.4% English only; 5.1% Spanish.

Employment: 144,129 employed; 3.7% unemployed. **Per capita income:** $49,917; change (2012-13): 2.8%. **Below poverty level:** 19.4%; 9.3% of families. **Educational attainment:** 94.6% HS; 53.8% bachelor's. **Avg. commute:** 19.1 min. 63.2% drive. **Housing units:** 108,143; 95.5% occupied. **Home ownership:** 49.3%. **Avg. home:** $228,200; change (2012-14): 8.4%. **Avg. rent:** $906.

Mayor: Paul R. Soglin, nonpartisan

History: Settled 1832; selected as site for state capital, named after James Madison, 1836; chartered 1856.

Website: www.cityofmadison.com

Memphis, Tennessee

Population: 656,861 (23). **Pop. density:** 2,070. **Pop. change (2010-14):** 0.7%. **Area:** 317.4 sq mi. **Racial distribution:** 30.4% white; 63.0% black; 1.7% Asian; 0.2% Amer. Ind.; <0.05% Pac. Isl.; 3.0% other; 2+ races 1.7%. **Hispanic pop.:** 6.4%. **Foreign born:** 6.2%. **U.S. citizens:** 95.5%. **Language:** 90.9% English only; 5.9% Spanish.

Employment: 260,358 employed; 8.7% unemployed. **Per capita income:** $40,987; change (2012-13): 0.9%. **Below poverty level:** 26.9%; 22.2% of families. **Educational attainment:** 82.5% HS; 23.7% bachelor's. **Avg. commute:** 21.4 min. 79.1% drive; 13.0% carpool. **Housing units:** 294,641; 83.2% occupied. **Home ownership:** 51.1%. **Avg. home:** $138,600; change (2012-14): 18.3%. **Avg. rent:** $812.

Mayor: A. C. Wharton, nonpartisan

History: French, Spanish, and U.S. forts by 1797; settled by 1819; inc. as town 1826, as city 1840; surrendered charter to state 1879 after yellow fever epidemics; rechartered as city 1893.

Website: www.cityofmemphis.org

Mesa, Arizona

Population: 464,704 (38). **Pop. density:** 3,377. **Pop. change (2010-14):** 5.6%. **Area:** 137.6 sq mi. **Racial distribution:** 83.6% white; 3.4% black; 1.9% Asian; 2.1% Amer. Ind.; 0.4% Pac. Isl.; 5.8% other; 2+ races 2.7%. **Hispanic pop.:** 26.0%. **Foreign born:** 12.3%. **U.S. citizens:** 91.3%. **Language:** 78.6% English only; 17.6% Spanish.

Employment: 206,617 employed; 5.9% unemployed. **Per capita income:** $38,745; change (2012-13): 0.7%. **Below poverty level:** 15.7%; 11.7% of families. **Educational attainment:** 87.5% HS; 24.3% bachelor's. **Avg. commute:** 24.8 min. 77.0% drive; 12.2% carpool. **Housing units:** 199,496; 83.6% occupied. **Home ownership:** 61.9%. **Avg. home:** $198,500; change (2012-14): 34.5%. **Avg. rent:** $867.

Mayor: John Giles, nonpartisan

History: Founded by Mormons 1878; inc. 1883. Population boomed fivefold 1960-80.

Website: www.mesaaz.gov

Miami, Florida

Population: 430,332 (44). **Pop. density:** 11,990. **Pop. change (2010-14):** 7.3%. **Area:** 35.9 sq mi. **Racial distribution:** 74.9% white; 19.8% black; 0.9% Asian; 0.1% Amer. Ind.; <0.05% Pac. Isl.; 3.1% other; 2+ races 1.1%. **Hispanic pop.:** 70.3%. **Foreign born:** 57.7%. **U.S. citizens:** 67.6%. **Language:** 22.7% English only; 69.9% Spanish.

Employment: 194,468 employed; 7.0% unemployed. **Per capita income:** $45,377; change (2012-13): 1.3%. **Below poverty level:** 29.9%; 24.9% of families. **Educational attainment:** 70.9% HS; 23.1% bachelor's. **Avg. commute:** 26.2 min. 68.8% drive; 11.3% public trans.; 10.2% carpool. **Housing units:** 187,938; 80.3% occupied. **Home ownership:** 32.8%. **Avg. home:** $266,000; change (2012-14): 31.0%. **Avg. rent:** $946.

Mayor: Tomás Regalado, nonpartisan

History: Site of fort 1836; settlement began 1870; inc. 1896. Modern city developed into financial and recreation center; land speculation in 1920s added to city's growth, as did Cuban, Central and South American, and Haitian immigration since 1960.

Website: www.miamigov.com

Milwaukee, Wisconsin

Population: 599,642 (31). **Pop. density:** 6,239. **Pop. change (2010-14):** 0.8%. **Area:** 96.1 sq mi. **Racial distribution:** 47.4% white; 39.4% black; 3.7% Asian; 0.5% Amer. Ind.; <0.05% Pac. Isl.; 5.3% other; 2+ races 3.6%. **Hispanic pop.:** 17.3%. **Foreign born:** 10.0%. **U.S. citizens:** 93.2%. **Language:** 80.7% English only; 13.5% Spanish.

Employment: 262,154 employed; 8.1% unemployed. **Per capita income:** $47,688; change (2012-13): 1.1%. **Below poverty level:** 29.1%; 24.9% of families. **Educational attainment:** 81.2% HS; 22.1% bachelor's. **Avg. commute:** 22 min. 70.5% drive; 11.6% carpool. **Housing units:** 257,857; 88.8% occupied. **Home ownership:** 43.7%. **Avg. home:** $207,800; change (2012-14): 10.9%. **Avg. rent:** $775.

Mayor: Tom Barrett, Democrat

History: Indian trading post by 1674; settlement began 1835; inc. 1848. Famous beer industry.

Website: city.milwaukee.gov

Minneapolis, Minnesota

Population: 407,207 (46). **Pop. density:** 7,539. **Pop. change (2010-14):** 6.3%. **Area:** 54.0 sq mi. **Racial distribution:** 67.0% white; 17.5% black; 5.9% Asian; 1.6% Amer. Ind.; <0.05% Pac. Isl.; 3.5% other; 2+ races 4.5%. **Hispanic pop.:** 10.0%. **Foreign born:** 15.2%. **U.S. citizens:** 90.7%. **Language:** 79.7% English only; 8.3% Spanish.

Employment: 219,658 employed; 3.8% unemployed. **Per capita income:** $51,183; change (2012-13): 0.7%. **Below poverty level:** 22.5%; 15.7% of families. **Educational attainment:** 88.3% HS; 45.7% bachelor's. **Avg. commute:** 22.3 min. 61.9% drive; 13.4% public trans. **Housing units:** 179,731; 92.0% occupied. **Home ownership:** 49.2%. **Avg. home:** $210,100; change (2012-14): 22.3%. **Avg. rent:** $836.

Mayor: Betsy Hodges, Democrat (DFL)

History: Site visited by French missionary Louis Hennepin 1680; located on military-reservation land 1819; inc. 1867.

Website: minneapolismn.gov

Nashville, Tennessee

Population: 644,014 (25). **Pop. density:** 1,353. **Pop. change (2010-14):** 6.5%. **Area:** 475.9 sq mi. **Racial distribution:** 61.6% white; 28.4% black; 3.2% Asian; 0.2% Amer. Ind.; <0.05% Pac. Isl.; 4.3% other; 2+ races 2.2%. **Hispanic pop.:** 10.0%. **Foreign born:** 11.9%. **U.S. citizens:** 92.1%. **Language:** 84.2% English only; 8.6% Spanish.

Employment: 335,888 employed; 5.1% unemployed. **Per capita income:** $45,759; change (2012-13): 1.2%. **Below poverty level:** 18.9%; 14.3% of families. **Educational attainment:** 86.2% HS; 35.3% bachelor's. **Avg. commute:** 23.3 min. 79.8% drive; 10.2% carpool. **Housing units:** 275,536; 89.9% occupied. **Home ownership:** 54.2%. **Avg. home:** $183,000; change (2012-14): 13.9%. **Avg. rent:** $835.

Mayor: Karl Dean, nonpartisan

History: Settled 1779; first chartered 1806; became permanent state capital 1843. Home of Grand Ole Opry.

Website: www.nashville.gov

New Orleans, Louisiana

Population: 384,320 (50). **Pop. density:** 2,268. **Pop. change (2010-14):** 10.4%. **Area:** 169.4 sq mi. **Racial distribution:** 33.6% white; 59.8% black; 3.0% Asian; 0.4% Amer. Ind.; 0.1% Pac. Isl.; 1.6% other; 2+ races 1.5%. **Hispanic pop.:** 5.3%. **Foreign born:** 5.9%. **U.S. citizens:** 96.7%. **Language:** 90.2% English only; 4.7% Spanish.

Employment: 166,019 employed; 7.0% unemployed. **Per capita income:** $44,746; change (2012-13): 0.5%. **Below poverty level:** 27.3%; 22.4% of families. **Educational attainment:** 84.5% HS; 33.7% bachelor's. **Avg. commute:** 23 min. 69.8% drive; 10.4% carpool. **Housing units:** 190,127; 78.1% occupied. **Home ownership:** 47.3%. **Avg. home:** $165,000; change (2012-14): 5.6%. **Avg. rent:** $926.

Mayor: Mitchell J. Landrieu, Democrat

History: Founded by French 1718; became major seaport on Mississippi R.; acquired by U.S. as part of Louisiana Purchase 1803; inc. 1805. Americans defeated British forces at Battle of New Orleans in 1815.

Website: www.nola.gov

New York, New York

Population: 8,491,079 (1). **Pop. density:** 28,163. **Pop. change (2010-14):** 3.7%. **Area:** 301.5 sq mi. **Racial distribution:** 44.3% white; 24.9% black; 13.0% Asian; 0.4% Amer. Ind.; 0.1% Pac. Isl.; 14.4% other; 2+ races 3.0%. **Hispanic pop.:** 28.7%. **Foreign born:** 37.0%. **U.S. citizens:** 82.3%. **Language:** 51.2% English only; 24.6% Spanish; 5.7% Chinese.

Employment: 3,826,673 employed; 7.2% unemployed. **Per capita income:** $59,246; change (2012-13): 0.5%. **Below poverty level:** 20.3%; 17.3% of families. **Educational attainment:** 79.8% HS; 34.5% bachelor's. **Avg. commute:** 39.2 min. 55.9% public trans.; 22.4% drive; 10.2% walk. **Housing units:** 3,380,513; 90.8% occupied. **Home ownership:** 32.2%. **Avg. home:** $394,900; change (2012-14): 4.1%. **Avg. rent:** $1,200.

Mayor: Bill de Blasio, Democrat

History: Trading post est. 1624; British took control from Dutch 1664, named city New York; briefly U.S. capital; under new charter, 1898, city expanded to include five boroughs: Bronx, Brooklyn, Queens, and Staten Island, as well as Manhattan. Sept. 11, 2001, terrorist attacks destroyed World Trade Center, killed more than 2,750.

Website: www.nyc.gov

Newark, New Jersey

Population: 280,579 (69). **Pop. density:** 11,598. **Pop. change (2010-14):** 1.1%. **Area:** 24.2 sq mi. **Racial distribution:** 25.9% white; 51.7% black; 1.5% Asian; 0.3% Amer. Ind.; 0.1% Pac. Isl.; 14.4% other; 2+ races 6.1%. **Hispanic pop.:** 34.1%. **Foreign born:** 27.2%. **U.S. citizens:** 81.9%. **Language:** 54.6% English only; 31.1% Spanish; 8.3% Portuguese.

Employment: 106,757 employed; 10.2% unemployed. **Per capita income:** $59,246; change (2012-13): 0.5%. **Below poverty level:** 29.1%; 26.0% of families. **Educational attainment:** 70.8% HS; 12.7% bachelor's. **Avg. commute:** 32.3 min. 48.5% drive; 26.3% public trans.; 13.7% carpool. **Housing units:** 109,722; 84.2% occupied. **Home ownership:** 22.7%. **Avg. home:** $381,500; change (2012-14): 3.2%. **Avg. rent:** $968.

Mayor: Ras J. Baraka, nonpartisan

History: Settled by Puritans 1666; used as supply base by George Washington 1776; inc. as town 1833, as city 1836.

Website: www.ci.newark.nj.us

Norfolk, Virginia

Population: 245,428 (84). **Pop. density:** 4,538. **Pop. change (2010-14):** 1.0%. **Area:** 54.1 sq mi. **Racial distribution:** 48.2% white; 42.6% black; 3.4% Asian; 0.4% Amer. Ind.; 0.2% Pac. Isl.; 1.6% other; 2+ races 3.5%. **Hispanic pop.:** 6.9%. **Foreign born:** 6.4%. **U.S. citizens:** 96.5%. **Language:** 90.4% English only; 4.8% Spanish.

Employment: 105,789 employed; 6.4% unemployed. **Per capita income:** $44,756; change (2012-13): 0.5%. **Below poverty level:** 19.2%; 15.1% of families. **Educational attainment:** 86.0% HS; 25.3% bachelor's. **Avg. commute:** 21.5 min. 70.8% drive; 10.2% carpool. **Housing units:** 95,271; 89.8% occupied. **Home ownership:** 44.5%. **Avg. home:** $196,000; change (2012-14): 4.5%. **Avg. rent:** $948.

Mayor: Paul D. Fraim, nonpartisan

History: Founded 1682; burned by colonists to prevent capture by British during Revolutionary War; rebuilt and inc. as town 1805, as city 1845. Site of world's largest naval base; major East Coast commercial port and cruise terminal.

Website: www.norfolk.gov

North Las Vegas, Nevada

Population: 230,788 (94). **Pop. density:** 2,355. **Pop. change (2010-14):** 6.4%. **Area:** 98.0 sq mi. **Racial distribution:** 52.4% white; 19.5% black; 5.8% Asian; 0.6% Amer. Ind.; 1.0% Pac. Isl.; 15.8% other; 2+ races 4.9%. **Hispanic pop.:** 40.3%. **Foreign born:** 22.4%. **U.S. citizens:** 85.8%. **Language:** 59.9% English only; 33.7% Spanish.

Employment: 96,690 employed; 8.5% unemployed. **Per capita income:** $37,457; change (2012-13): –0.1%. **Below poverty level:** 16.0%; 12.9% of families. **Educational attainment:** 77.1% HS; 15.0% bachelor's. **Avg. commute:** 27 min. 82.5% drive; 10.2% carpool. **Housing units:** 76,273; 87.2% occupied. **Home ownership:** 57.3%. **Avg. home:** $198,000; change (2012-14): 47.7%. **Avg. rent:** $1,118.

Mayor: John J. Lee, nonpartisan

History: Inc. 1946.

Website: www.cityofnorthlasvegas.com

Oakland, California

Population: 413,775 (45). **Pop. density:** 7,403. **Pop. change (2010-14):** 5.6%. **Area:** 55.9 sq mi. **Racial distribution:** 39.4% white; 27.0% black; 16.5% Asian; 0.7% Amer. Ind.; 0.6% Pac. Isl.; 10.3% other; 2+ races 5.7%. **Hispanic pop.:** 25.7%. **Foreign born:** 27.0%. **U.S. citizens:** 84.6%. **Language:** 60.1% English only; 21.8% Spanish; 7.5% Chinese.

Employment: 193,461 employed; 7.3% unemployed. **Per capita income:** $69,127; change (2012-13): 1.6%. **Below poverty level:** 20.5%; 16.6% of families. **Educational attainment:** 80.2% HS; 38.1% bachelor's. **Avg. commute:** 28.3 min. 55.2% drive; 18.3% public trans.; 11.2% carpool. **Housing units:** 170,977; 90.5% occupied. **Home ownership:** 40.4%. **Avg. home:** $737,600; change (2012-14): 35.6%. **Avg. rent:** $1,087.

Mayor: Libby Schaaf, nonpartisan

History: Area settled by Spanish 1820; inc. 1854.

Website: www.oaklandnet.com

Oklahoma City, Oklahoma

Population: 620,602 (27). **Pop. density:** 1,023. **Pop. change (2010-14):** 6.6%. **Area:** 606.7 sq mi. **Racial distribution:** 67.0% white; 14.5% black; 4.0% Asian; 3.2% Amer. Ind.; <0.05% Pac. Isl.; 4.5% other; 2+ races 6.9%. **Hispanic pop.:** 17.7%. **Foreign born:** 12.0%. **U.S. citizens:** 91.6%. **Language:** 80.8% English only; 14.2% Spanish.

Employment: 288,842 employed; 3.9% unemployed. **Per capita income:** $44,280; change (2012-13): 1.0%. **Below poverty level:** 18.2%; 14.1% of families. **Educational attainment:** 84.8% HS; 28.1% bachelor's. **Avg. commute:** 20.3 min. 82.1% drive; 11.3% carpool. **Housing units:** 257,544; 88.4% occupied. **Home ownership:** 59.4%. **Avg. home:** $150,300; change (2012-14): 3.7%. **Avg. rent:** $747.

Mayor: Mick Cornett, nonpartisan

History: Settled during land rush in Midwest 1889; inc. 1890; became capital 1910; oil discovered 1928. Bomb in 1995 destroyed federal office bldg., killed 168 people.

Website: www.okc.gov

Omaha, Nebraska

Population: 446,599 (41). **Pop. density:** 3,439. **Pop. change (2010-14):** 5.2%. **Area:** 129.9 sq mi. **Racial distribution:** 75.9% white; 13.1% black; 2.6% Asian; 0.7% Amer. Ind.; 0.1% Pac. Isl.; 4.6% other; 2+ races 3.0%. **Hispanic pop.:** 13.1%. **Foreign born:** 9.9%. **U.S. citizens:** 93.0%. **Language:** 84.7% English only; 10.3% Spanish.

Employment: 221,848 employed; 3.6% unemployed. **Per capita income:** $47,736; change (2012-13): 1.6%. **Below poverty level:** 16.6%; 11.8% of families. **Educational attainment:** 87.9% HS; 33.1% bachelor's. **Avg. commute:** 18.2 min. 80.8% drive; 10.8% carpool. **Housing units:** 182,199; 91.7% occupied. **Home ownership:** 58.5%. **Avg. home:** $149,000; change (2012-14): 7.0%. **Avg. rent:** $776.

Mayor: Jean Stothert, nonpartisan

History: Founded 1854; inc. 1857. Large food-processing, telecommunications, information-processing center.

Website: www.cityofomaha.org

Orlando, Florida

Population: 262,372 (73). **Pop. density:** 2,555. **Pop. change (2010-14):** 9.6%. **Area:** 102.7 sq mi. **Racial distribution:** 58.9% white; 28.6% black; 3.5% Asian; 0.4% Amer. Ind.; <0.05% Pac. Isl.; 6.0% other; 2+ races 2.6%. **Hispanic pop.:** 26.1%. **Foreign born:** 18.2%. **U.S. citizens:** 89.9%. **Language:** 67.5% English only; 22.5% Spanish.

Employment: 143,686 employed; 5.5% unemployed. **Per capita income:** $36,992; change (2012-13): 0.9%. **Below poverty level:** 19.2%; 15.0% of families. **Educational attainment:** 88.4% HS; 32.9% bachelor's. **Avg. commute:** 24.6 min. 78.3% drive. **Housing units:** 122,261; 82.5% occupied. **Home ownership:** 39.0%. **Avg. home:** $180,000; change (2012-14): 34.3%. **Avg. rent:** $983.

Mayor: Buddy Dyer, nonpartisan

History: Ft. Gatlin built just south of present-day Orlando in 1838; name changed from Jernigan to Orlando 1856; inc. 1875. Walt Disney World opened in 1971.

Website: www.cityoforlando.net

Philadelphia, Pennsylvania

Population: 1,560,297 (5). **Pop. density:** 11,635. **Pop. change (2010-14):** 2.1%. **Area:** 134.1 sq mi. **Racial distribution:** 41.5% white; 43.3% black; 6.5% Asian; 0.3% Amer. Ind.; 0.1% Pac. Isl.; 5.8% other; 2+ races 2.5%. **Hispanic pop.:** 12.7%. **Foreign born:** 12.2%. **U.S. citizens:** 93.8%. **Language:** 78.5% English only; 9.9% Spanish.

Employment: 634,036 employed; 8.0% unemployed. **Per capita income:** $52,503; change (2012-13): 1.2%. **Below poverty level:** 26.5%; 21.1% of families. **Educational attainment:** 81.2% HS; 23.9% bachelor's. **Avg. commute:** 31.8 min. 50.5% drive; 26.1% public trans. **Housing units:** 668,806; 86.7% occupied. **Home ownership:** 53.3%. **Avg. home:** $220,700; change (2012-14): 3.4%. **Avg. rent:** $893.

Mayor: Michael A. Nutter, Democrat

History: First settled by Swedes 1638; Swedes surrendered to Dutch 1654; settled by English and Scottish Quakers 1678; named Philadelphia 1682; chartered 1701. Continental Congresses convened 1774, 1775; Declaration of Independence signed here 1776; natl. capital 1790-1800; state capital 1683-1799.

Website: www.phila.gov

Phoenix, Arizona

Population: 1,537,058 (6). **Pop. density:** 2,970. **Pop. change (2010-14):** 6.0%. **Area:** 517.5 sq mi. **Racial distribution:** 77.3% white; 6.8% black; 3.2% Asian; 1.9% Amer. Ind.; 0.2% Pac. Isl.; 7.8% other; 2+ races 2.9%. **Hispanic pop.:** 40.3%. **Foreign born:** 20.2%. **U.S. citizens:** 85.5%. **Language:** 63.7% English only; 30.2% Spanish.

Employment: 693,153 employed; 6.2% unemployed. **Per capita income:** $38,745; change (2012-13): 0.7%. **Below poverty level:** 22.8%; 18.0% of families. **Educational attainment:** 80.6% HS; 26.3% bachelor's. **Avg. commute:** 24.4 min. 74.9% drive; 12.3% carpool. **Housing units:** 599,124; 86.4% occupied. **Home ownership:** 55.5%. **Avg. home:** $198,500; change (2012-14): 34.5%. **Avg. rent:** $870.

Mayor: Greg Stanton, nonpartisan

History: Founded 1867; inc. 1881; became territorial capital 1889.

Website: www.phoenix.gov

Pittsburgh, Pennsylvania

Population: 305,412 (62). **Pop. density:** 5,515. **Pop. change (2010-14):** –0.1%. **Area:** 55.4 sq mi. **Racial distribution:** 66.4% white; 25.3% black; 4.7% Asian; 0.2% Amer. Ind.; <0.05% Pac.

Isl.; 0.6% other; 2+ races 2.9%. **Hispanic pop.:** 2.6%. **Foreign born:** 7.4%. **U.S. citizens:** 95.3%. **Language:** 90.2% English only; 2.0% Spanish.

Employment: 148,518 employed; 5.6% unemployed. **Per capita income:** $49,049; change (2012-13): 1.6%. **Below poverty level:** 22.6%; 15.7% of families. **Educational attainment:** 90.4% HS; 35.5% bachelor's. **Avg. commute:** 22.8 min. 54.8% drive; 17.5% public trans.; 11.2% walk; 10.1% carpool. **Housing units:** 156,224; 85.1% occupied. **Home ownership:** 48.8%. **Avg. rent:** $767.

Mayor: William "Bill" Peduto, Democrat

History: Settled around Ft. Pitt 1758; inc. 1816; became an inland port; by Civil War, already a center for iron production.

Website: pittsburghpa.gov

Plano, Texas

Population: 278,480 (70). **Pop. density:** 3,886. **Pop. change (2010-14):** 6.6%. **Area:** 71.7 sq mi. **Racial distribution:** 69.8% white; 7.1% black; 18.2% Asian; 0.5% Amer. Ind.; 0.1% Pac. Isl.; 1.7% other; 2+ races 2.7%. **Hispanic pop.:** 14.6%. **Foreign born:** 23.9%. **U.S. citizens:** 87.1%. **Language:** 67.9% English only; 11.6% Spanish.

Employment: 146,804 employed; 4.5% unemployed. **Per capita income:** $46,989; change (2012-13): 1.3%. **Below poverty level:** 7.7%; 5.7% of families. **Educational attainment:** 93.4% HS; 54.2% bachelor's. **Avg. commute:** 25.4 min. 81.7% drive. **Housing units:** 105,759; 94.7% occupied. **Home ownership:** 64.0%. **Avg. home:** $188,300; change (2012-14): 18.2%. **Avg. rent:** $1,087.

Mayor: Harry LaRosiliere, nonpartisan

History: Settled 1846; inc. 1873.

Website: www.plano.gov

Portland, Oregon

Population: 619,360 (28). **Pop. density:** 4,641. **Pop. change (2010-14):** 5.8%. **Area:** 133.5 sq mi. **Racial distribution:** 77.4% white; 6.3% black; 7.5% Asian; 0.8% Amer. Ind.; 0.6% Pac. Isl.; 3.1% other; 2+ races 4.4%. **Hispanic pop.:** 9.4%. **Foreign born:** 13.8%. **U.S. citizens:** 92.0%. **Language:** 81.1% English only; 7.1% Spanish.

Employment: 322,712 employed; 5.9% unemployed. **Per capita income:** $43,728; change (2012-13): 1.2%. **Below poverty level:** 17.8%; 12.0% of families. **Educational attainment:** 90.5% HS; 43.8% bachelor's. **Avg. commute:** 24.4 min. 59.0% drive; 11.6% public trans. **Housing units:** 266,581; 93.8% occupied. **Home ownership:** 53.4%. **Avg. home:** $227,700; change (2012-14): 3.7%. **Avg. rent:** $915.

Mayor: Charlie Hales, nonpartisan

History: Settled by pioneers 1845; developed as trading center, aided by California Gold Rush 1849; chartered 1851.

Website: www.portlandoregon.gov

Raleigh, North Carolina

Population: 439,896 (43). **Pop. density:** 3,052. **Pop. change (2010-14):** 8.3%. **Area:** 144.1 sq mi. **Racial distribution:** 60.4% white; 29.5% black; 4.3% Asian; 0.3% Amer. Ind.; 0.1% Pac. Isl.; 3.4% other; 2+ races 2.1%. **Hispanic pop.:** 11.2%. **Foreign born:** 13.7%. **U.S. citizens:** 90.4%. **Language:** 82.2% English only; 9.9% Spanish.

Employment: 220,050 employed; 4.5% unemployed. **Per capita income:** $43,947; change (2012-13): 0.6%. **Below poverty level:** 16.2%; 11.8% of families. **Educational attainment:** 90.0% HS; 47.5% bachelor's. **Avg. commute:** 21.6 min. 79.3% drive. **Housing units:** 178,910; 90.9% occupied. **Home ownership:** 53.6%. **Avg. home:** $208,600; change (2012-14): 10.7%. **Avg. rent:** $897.

Mayor: Nancy McFarlane, nonpartisan

History: Named after Sir Walter Raleigh; site chosen for state capital 1788; laid out 1792; inc. 1795; occupied by Union Gen. William Sherman 1865.

Website: www.raleighnc.gov

Reno, Nevada

Population: 236,995 (89). **Pop. density:** 2,210. **Pop. change (2010-14):** 4.7%. **Area:** 107.2 sq mi. **Racial distribution:** 79.6% white; 3.1% black; 6.4% Asian; 1.0% Amer. Ind.; 0.7% Pac. Isl.; 5.5% other; 2+ races 3.7%. **Hispanic pop.:** 25.0%. **Foreign born:** 16.9%. **U.S. citizens:** 90.0%. **Language:** 74.6% English only; 17.8% Spanish.

Employment: 110,920 employed; 7.5% unemployed. **Per capita income:** $45,168; change (2012-13): 0.2%. **Below poverty level:** 18.6%; 13.6% of families. **Educational attainment:** 85.7% HS; 28.9% bachelor's. **Avg. commute:** 19.4 min. 77.0% drive; 10.1% carpool. **Housing units:** 101,400; 88.8% occupied. **Home ownership:** 47.4%. **Avg. home:** $247,500; change (2012-14): 45.8%. **Avg. rent:** $867.

Mayor: Hillary Schieve, nonpartisan

History: Founded 1857; originally named Lakes Crossing; name changed to Reno, after a Union Civil War general, 1868, with arrival of transcontinental railroad.

Website: www.reno.gov

Richmond, Virginia

Population: 217,853 (98). **Pop. density:** 3,642. **Pop. change (2010-14):** 6.7%. **Area:** 59.8 sq mi. **Racial distribution:** 43.4% white; 49.2% black; 2.3% Asian; 0.3% Amer. Ind.; <0.05% Pac. Isl.; 1.4% other; 2+ races 3.4%. **Hispanic pop.:** 6.2%. **Foreign born:** 7.0%. **U.S. citizens:** 94.9%. **Language:** 90.2% English only; 5.6% Spanish.

Employment: 105,134 employed; 6.1% unemployed. **Per capita income:** $46,118; change (2012-13): 0.8%. **Below poverty level:** 25.6%; 20.1% of families. **Educational attainment:** 81.5% HS; 34.8% bachelor's. **Avg. commute:** 21.7 min. 70.3% drive; 11.1% carpool. **Housing units:** 98,579; 86.1% occupied. **Home ownership:** 43.1%. **Avg. home:** $220,200; change (2012-14): 13.7%. **Avg. rent:** $883.

Mayor: Dwight C. Jones, nonpartisan

History: First settled 1607; became capital of Commonwealth of Virginia 1779; attacked by British under Benedict Arnold 1781; inc. 1782; capital of Confederate States of America 1861-65.

Website: www.richmondgov.com

Riverside, California

Population: 319,504 (59). **Pop. density:** 3,936. **Pop. change (2010-14):** 4.5%. **Area:** 81.2 sq mi. **Racial distribution:** 67.0% white; 6.5% black; 6.6% Asian; 1.0% Amer. Ind.; 0.2% Pac. Isl.; 13.9% other; 2+ races 4.8%. **Hispanic pop.:** 51.3%. **Foreign born:** 23.0%. **U.S. citizens:** 86.0%. **Language:** 57.4% English only; 35.3% Spanish.

Employment: 134,264 employed; 7.9% unemployed. **Per capita income:** $33,025; change (2012-13): 2.2%. **Below poverty level:** 19.1%; 13.8% of families. **Educational attainment:** 77.7% HS; 22.2% bachelor's. **Avg. commute:** 28.5 min. 76.4% drive; 12.6% carpool. **Housing units:** 98,636; 91.7% occupied. **Home ownership:** 56.3%. **Avg. home:** $273,900; change (2012-14): 44.7%. **Avg. rent:** $1,135.

Mayor: Rusty Bailey, nonpartisan

History: Founded 1870; inc. 1886. Known for its citrus industry, home of the parent navel orange tree; historic Mission Inn resort.

Website: www.riversideca.gov

Sacramento, California

Population: 485,199 (35). **Pop. density:** 4,955. **Pop. change (2010-14):** 3.8%. **Area:** 97.9 sq mi. **Racial distribution:** 50.3% white; 13.9% black; 18.3% Asian; 0.9% Amer. Ind.; 1.4% Pac. Isl.; 8.4% other; 2+ races 6.8%. **Hispanic pop.:** 27.2%. **Foreign born:** 21.9%. **U.S. citizens:** 89.2%. **Language:** 63.5% English only; 17.1% Spanish.

Employment: 209,080 employed; 7.7% unemployed. **Per capita income:** $46,499; change (2012-13): 2.2%. **Below poverty level:** 21.9%; 17.3% of families. **Educational attainment:** 82.4% HS; 29.3% bachelor's. **Avg. commute:** 24 min. 72.2% drive; 12.6% carpool. **Housing units:** 193,273; 91.8% occupied. **Home ownership:** 48.4%. **Avg. home:** $268,700; change (2012-14): 52.0%. **Avg. rent:** $999.

Mayor: Kevin Johnson, nonpartisan

History: Settled 1839; important trading center during California Gold Rush 1840s; became state capital 1854.

Website: www.cityofsacramento.org

St. Louis, Missouri

Population: 317,419 (60). **Pop. density:** 5,124. **Pop. change (2010-14):** –0.6%. **Area:** 62.0 sq mi. **Racial distribution:** 44.9% white; 48.6% black; 2.8% Asian; 0.2% Amer. Ind.; <0.05% Pac. Isl.; 0.9% other; 2+ races 2.5%. **Hispanic pop.:** 3.6%. **Foreign born:** 6.7%. **U.S. citizens:** 95.6%. **Language:** 90.4% English only; 3.1% Spanish.

Employment: 148,984 employed; 7.7% unemployed. **Per capita income:** $45,992; change (2012-13): 1.4%. **Below poverty level:** 27.4%; 22.1% of families. **Educational attainment:** 82.9% HS; 29.6% bachelor's. **Avg. commute:** 23.9 min. 71.1% drive. **Housing units:** 175,593; 80.1% occupied. **Home ownership:** 44.6%. **Avg. home:** $141,700; change (2012-14): 14.4%. **Avg. rent:** $724.

Mayor: Francis Slay, Democrat

History: Founded 1764 as fur trading post by French; acquired by U.S. 1803; chartered 1822; became independent city 1876. Lies on Mississippi R. near confluence with Missouri R.

Website: www.stlouis-mo.gov

St. Paul, Minnesota

Population: 297,640 (66). **Pop. density:** 5,726. **Pop. change (2010-14):** 4.3%. **Area:** 52.0 sq mi. **Racial distribution:** 61.1% white; 15.7% black; 15.5% Asian; 0.9% Amer. Ind.; 0.1% Pac. Isl.; 2.5% other; 2+ races 4.2%. **Hispanic pop.:** 9.7%. **Foreign born:** 17.9%. **U.S. citizens:** 90.2%. **Language:** 73.1% English only; 7.2% Spanish; 9.0% Hmong.

Employment: 146,059 employed; 4.1% unemployed. **Per capita income:** $51,183; change (2012-13): 0.7%. **Below poverty level:** 23.0%; 17.3% of families. **Educational attainment:** 86.2% HS; 38.3% bachelor's. **Avg. commute:** 22.3 min. 70.0%

drive; 10.6% carpool. **Housing units:** 120,077; 93.2% occupied. **Home ownership:** 50.4%. **Avg. home:** $210,100; change (2012-14): 22.3%. **Avg. rent:** $810.

Mayor: Chris Coleman, nonpartisan

History: Founded in early 1840s as Pig's Eye Landing; became capital of Minnesota territory 1849; chartered as St. Paul 1854.

Website: www.stpaul.gov

St. Petersburg, Florida

Population: 253,693 (79). **Pop. density:** 4,108. **Pop. change (2010-14):** 3.4%. **Area:** 61.8 sq mi. **Racial distribution:** 68.7% white; 24.4% black; 3.3% Asian; 0.2% Amer. Ind.; 0.1% Pac. Isl.; 0.9% other; 2+ races 2.4%. **Hispanic pop.:** 7.0%. **Foreign born:** 10.6%. **U.S. citizens:** 95.4%. **Language:** 88.3% English only; 5.0% Spanish.

Employment: 127,793 employed; 5.6% unemployed. **Per capita income:** $40,425; change (2012-13): 1.3%. **Below poverty level:** 16.9%; 11.9% of families. **Educational attainment:** 87.9% HS; 28.7% bachelor's. **Avg. commute:** 21.9 min. 80.4% drive. **Housing units:** 127,713; 82.2% occupied. **Home ownership:** 60.5%. **Avg. home:** $151,500; change (2012-14): 13.1%. **Avg. rent:** $924.

Mayor: Rick Kriseman, nonpartisan

History: Founded 1888; inc. 1903. Site of Salvador Dali Museum.

Website: www.stpete.org

San Antonio, Texas

Population: 1,436,697 (7). **Pop. density:** 3,117. **Pop. change (2010-14):** 7.7%. **Area:** 461.0 sq mi. **Racial distribution:** 75.7% white; 6.8% black; 2.4% Asian; 0.7% Amer. Ind.; 0.1% Pac. Isl.; 11.6% other; 2+ races 2.7%. **Hispanic pop.:** 63.2%. **Foreign born:** 14.0%. **U.S. citizens:** 91.2%. **Language:** 54.6% English only; 41.7% Spanish.

Employment: 645,195 employed; 4.5% unemployed. **Per capita income:** $39,951; change (2012-13): 1.0%. **Below poverty level:** 19.9%; 16.0% of families. **Educational attainment:** 80.7% HS; 24.6% bachelor's. **Avg. commute:** 23.3 min. 78.9% drive; 11.3% carpool. **Housing units:** 528,607; 90.3% occupied. **Home ownership:** 55.7%. **Avg. home:** $182,100; change (2012-14): 14.2%. **Avg. rent:** $818.

Mayor: Ivy R. Taylor, nonpartisan

History: First Spanish garrison 1718; Battle of the Alamo 1836; city subsequently captured by Texans; inc. 1837; first town meeting in Texas took place here in 1845.

Website: www.sanantonio.gov

San Bernardino, California

Population: 215,213 (100). **Pop. density:** 3,499. **Pop. change (2010-14):** 2.4%. **Area:** 61.5 sq mi. **Racial distribution:** 51.0% white; 13.8% black; 4.4% Asian; 0.9% Amer. Ind.; 0.3% Pac. Isl.; 24.4% other; 2+ races 5.1%. **Hispanic pop.:** 60.6%. **Foreign born:** 22.7%. **U.S. citizens:** 85.3%. **Language:** 53.3% English only; 41.5% Spanish.

Employment: 74,488 employed; 10.2% unemployed. **Per capita income:** $33,025; change (2012-13): 2.2%. **Below poverty level:** 32.4%; 27.8% of families. **Educational attainment:** 67.7% HS; 11.2% bachelor's. **Avg. commute:** 27 min. 74.0% drive; 15.6% carpool. **Housing units:** 64,329; 90.7% occupied. **Home ownership:** 49.4%. **Avg. home:** $273,900; change (2012-14): 44.7%. **Avg. rent:** $930.

Mayor: R. Carey Davis, nonpartisan

History: Named by Spanish Franciscan missionaries 1810; major Mormon settlement in the 1850s, later recalled to Utah; inc. 1854. Population grew in 1860s when gold was discovered nearby; later became a transportation hub.

Website: www.sbcity.org

San Diego, California

Population: 1,381,069 (8). **Pop. density:** 4,247. **Pop. change (2010-14):** 5.7%. **Area:** 325.2 sq mi. **Racial distribution:** 64.8% white; 6.7% black; 16.4% Asian; 0.6% Amer. Ind.; 0.5% Pac. Isl.; 6.4% other; 2+ races 4.7%. **Hispanic pop.:** 29.3%. **Foreign born:** 26.2%. **U.S. citizens:** 87.2%. **Language:** 60.2% English only; 22.5% Spanish.

Employment: 650,376 employed; 6.1% unemployed. **Per capita income:** $51,384; change (2012-13): 1.4%. **Below poverty level:** 15.6%; 10.8% of families. **Educational attainment:** 87.0% HS; 41.7% bachelor's. **Avg. commute:** 22.5 min. 74.9% drive. **Housing units:** 516,951; 92.2% occupied. **Home ownership:** 47.9%. **Avg. home:** $497,900; change (2012-14): 29.2%. **Avg. rent:** $1,329.

Mayor: Kevin L. Faulconer, nonpartisan

History: Claimed by Spanish 1542; first mission est. 1769; scene of conflict during Mexican-American War 1846; inc. 1850.

Website: www.sandiego.gov

San Francisco, California

Population: 852,469 (13). **Pop. density:** 18,179. **Pop. change (2010-14):** 5.8%. **Area:** 46.9 sq mi. **Racial distribution:** 50.3% white; 5.9% black; 33.3% Asian; 0.4% Amer. Ind.; 0.4% Pac. Isl.; 5.4% other; 2+ races 4.2%. **Hispanic pop.:** 15.2%. **Foreign born:** 35.6%. **U.S. citizens:** 86.3%. **Language:** 55.0% English only; 11.6% Spanish; 18.4% Chinese.

Employment: 509,338 employed; 4.4% unemployed. **Per capita income:** $69,127; change (2012-13): 1.6%. **Below poverty level:** 13.5%; 8.2% of families. **Educational attainment:** 86.3% HS; 52.4% bachelor's. **Avg. commute:** 30.5 min. 37.0% drive; 32.6% public trans.; 10.1% walk. **Housing units:** 378,186; 91.3% occupied. **Home ownership:** 36.6%. **Avg. home:** $737,600; change (2012-14): 35.6%. **Avg. rent:** $1,488.

Mayor: Edwin M. Lee, nonpartisan

History: Nearby Farallon Islands sighted by Spanish 1542; city settled by 1776; claimed by U.S. 1846; became major city during California Gold Rush 1849; inc. 1850. Devastated by earthquake 1906.

Website: www.sfgov.org

San Jose, California

Population: 1,015,785 (10). **Pop. density:** 5,753. **Pop. change (2010-14):** 6.3%. **Area:** 176.6 sq mi. **Racial distribution:** 45.9% white; 3.1% black; 32.8% Asian; 0.6% Amer. Ind.; 0.3% Pac. Isl.; 12.4% other; 2+ races 4.8%. **Hispanic pop.:** 33.2%. **Foreign born:** 38.6%. **U.S. citizens:** 82.3%. **Language:** 43.9% English only; 23.8% Spanish; 10.2% Vietnamese; 6.2% Chinese.

Employment: 501,029 employed; 5.8% unemployed. **Per capita income:** $69,205; change (2012-13): 3.2%. **Below poverty level:** 12.2%; 8.8% of families. **Educational attainment:** 82.3% HS; 37.4% bachelor's. **Avg. commute:** 25.9 min. 77.5% drive; 11.3% carpool. **Housing units:** 319,700; 96.0% occupied. **Home ownership:** 58.0%. **Avg. home:** $860,000; change (2012-14): 33.3%. **Avg. rent:** $1,474.

Mayor: Sam Liccardo, nonpartisan

History: Founded by Spanish, 1777, between San Francisco and Monterey; state capital 1849-51; inc. 1850.

Website: www.sanjoseca.gov

Santa Ana, California

Population: 334,909 (57). **Pop. density:** 12,337. **Pop. change (2010-14):** 2.9%. **Area:** 27.1 sq mi. **Racial distribution:** 45.4% white; 1.3% black; 10.0% Asian; 0.5% Amer. Ind.; 0.1% Pac. Isl.; 40.9% other; 2+ races 1.7%. **Hispanic pop.:** 78.5%. **Foreign born:** 47.8%. **U.S. citizens:** 67.1%. **Language:** 17.1% English only; 72.7% Spanish; 6.9% Vietnamese

Employment: 149,150 employed; 6.3% unemployed. **Per capita income:** $48,425; change (2012-13): 1.4%. **Below poverty level:** 21.5%; 18.5% of families. **Educational attainment:** 53.6% HS; 11.8% bachelor's. **Avg. commute:** 24.9 min. 70.5% drive; 15.8% carpool. **Housing units:** 76,089; 95.7% occupied. **Home ownership:** 46.0%. **Avg. home:** $687,900; change (2012-14): 26.8%. **Avg. rent:** $1,294.

Mayor: Miguel Pulido, nonpartisan

History: Founded 1769; inc. 1869.

Website: www.santa-ana.org

Scottsdale, Arizona

Population: 230,512 (95). **Pop. density:** 1,253. **Pop. change (2010-14):** 6.0%. **Area:** 183.9 sq mi. **Racial distribution:** 89.8% white; 2.1% black; 3.8% Asian; 1.1% Amer. Ind.; 0.1% Pac. Isl.; 1.6% other; 2+ races 1.5%. **Hispanic pop.:** 9.8%. **Foreign born:** 10.9%. **U.S. citizens:** 94.9%. **Language:** 85.9% English only; 6.4% Spanish.

Employment: 118,270 employed; 4.7% unemployed. **Per capita income:** $38,745; change (2012-13): 0.7%. **Below poverty level:** 8.7%; 5.5% of families. **Educational attainment:** 96.1% HS; 52.7% bachelor's. **Avg. commute:** 21.8 min. 77.0% drive; 10.6% work at home. **Housing units:** 125,466; 79.9% occupied. **Home ownership:** 67.8%. **Avg. home:** $198,500; change (2012-14): 34.5%. **Avg. rent:** $1,122.

Mayor: W. J. "Jim" Lane, nonpartisan

History: Founded 1888 by Army Chaplain Winfield Scott; inc. 1951; slogan "West's Most Western Town" adopted same year.

Website: www.scottsdaleaz.gov

Seattle, Washington

Population: 668,342 (20). **Pop. density:** 7,972. **Pop. change (2010-14):** 9.5%. **Area:** 83.8 sq mi. **Racial distribution:** 70.6% white; 7.4% black; 14.1% Asian; 0.7% Amer. Ind.; 0.4% Pac. Isl.; 1.6% other; 2+ races 5.2%. **Hispanic pop.:** 6.4%. **Foreign born:** 17.7%. **U.S. citizens:** 91.6%. **Language:** 77.6% English only; 4.6% Spanish.

Employment: 391,190 employed; 4.1% unemployed. **Per capita income:** $55,190; change (2012-13): 1.1%. **Below poverty level:** 13.6%; 7.2% of families. **Educational attainment:** 93.2% HS; 57.4% bachelor's. **Avg. commute:** 25.4 min. 51.5% drive; 19.2% public trans. **Housing units:** 309,205; 93.3% occupied. **Home ownership:** 46.8%. **Avg. home:** $355,800; change (2012-14): 18.4%. **Avg. rent:** $1,091.

Mayor: Ed Murray, nonpartisan

History: Settled 1851; inc. 1869. Suffered severe fire 1889; played prominent role during Alaska Gold Rush 1897; growth followed opening of Panama Canal 1914. Center of aircraft industry during WWII.

Website: www.seattle.gov

Stockton, California

Population: 302,389 (63). **Pop. density:** 4,904. **Pop. change (2010-14):** 3.3%. **Area:** 61.7 sq mi. **Racial distribution:** 44.6% white; 11.6% black; 21.6% Asian; 1.0% Amer. Ind.; 0.6% Pac. Isl.; 13.4% other; 2+ races 7.2%. **Hispanic pop.:** 41.1%. **Foreign born:** 26.2%. **U.S. citizens:** 85.5%. **Language:** 54.0% English only; 27.2% Spanish.

Employment: 112,502 employed; 11.5% unemployed. **Per capita income:** $34,755; change (2012-13): 2.9%. **Below poverty level:** 24.3%; 20.1% of families. **Educational attainment:** 74.4% HS; 17.7% bachelor's. **Avg. commute:** 27 min. 75.4% drive; 16.4% carpool. **Housing units:** 100,011; 90.4% occupied. **Home ownership:** 51.2%. **Avg. rent:** $959.

Mayor: Anthony Silva, nonpartisan

History: Site purchased 1842; settled 1849; inc. 1850. Chief distribution point for agric. products of San Joaquin Valley.

Website: www.stocktongov.com

Tampa, Florida

Population: 358,699 (53). **Pop. density:** 3,163. **Pop. change (2010-14):** 6.5%. **Area:** 113.4 sq mi. **Racial distribution:** 64.1% white; 26.0% black; 3.5% Asian; 0.7% Amer. Ind.; 0.1% Pac. Isl.; 2.8% other; 2+ races 2.9%. **Hispanic pop.:** 23.7%. **Foreign born:** 15.6%. **U.S. citizens:** 91.6%. **Language:** 74.7% English only; 18.3% Spanish.

Employment: 174,724 employed; 5.9% unemployed. **Per capita income:** $40,425; change (2012-13): 1.3%. **Below poverty level:** 21.4%; 16.6% of families. **Educational attainment:** 85.9% HS; 33.1% bachelor's. **Avg. commute:** 22.6 min. 77.6% drive. **Housing units:** 160,290; 86.5% occupied. **Home ownership:** 50.9%. **Avg. home:** $151,500; change (2012-14): 13.1%. **Avg. rent:** $940.

Mayor: Bob Buckhorn, nonpartisan

History: U.S. army fort on site 1824; inc. 1851. Ybor City, Tampa's Latin Quarter, a Natl. Historical Landmark District.

Website: www.tampagov.net

Toledo, Ohio

Population: 281,031 (68). **Pop. density:** 3,482. **Pop. change (2010-14):** –2.1%. **Area:** 80.7 sq mi. **Racial distribution:** 65.1% white; 27.0% black; 1.1% Asian; 0.4% Amer. Ind.; 0.1% Pac. Isl.; 2.2% other; 2+ races 4.0%. **Hispanic pop.:** 7.5%. **Foreign born:** 3.2%. **U.S. citizens:** 98.3%. **Language:** 93.9% English only; 3.3% Spanish.

Employment: 120,046 employed; 6.9% unemployed. **Per capita income:** $38,604; change (2012-13): 1.8%. **Below poverty level:** 27.2%; 22.3% of families. **Educational attainment:** 84.8% HS; 17.2% bachelor's. **Avg. commute:** 19 min. 81.9% drive. **Housing units:** 138,382; 85.4% occupied. **Home ownership:** 55.2%. **Avg. home:** $87,200; change (2012-14): 8.5%. **Avg. rent:** $629.

Mayor: Paula Hicks-Hudson, nonpartisan

History: Site of Ft. Industry 1794; Battle of Ft. Meigs 1812; figured in Toledo War 1835-36 between OH and MI over borders; inc. 1837.

Website: toledo.oh.gov

Tucson, Arizona

Population: 527,972 (33). **Pop. density:** 2,288. **Pop. change (2010-14):** 1.3%. **Area:** 230.8 sq mi. **Racial distribution:** 75.7% white; 5.1% black; 2.7% Asian; 2.6% Amer. Ind.; 0.1% Pac. Isl.; 10.1% other; 2+ races 3.6%. **Hispanic pop.:** 42.1%. **Foreign born:** 15.0%. **U.S. citizens:** 90.8%. **Language:** 66.5% English only; 28.4% Spanish.

Employment: 233,573 employed; 6.5% unemployed. **Per capita income:** $37,063; change (2012-13): 1.0%. **Below poverty level:** 25.2%; 18.5% of families. **Educational attainment:** 84.1% HS; 24.7% bachelor's. **Avg. commute:** 21.7 min. 73.5% drive; 10.5% carpool. **Housing units:** 231,237; 87.9% occupied. **Home ownership:** 50.4%. **Avg. home:** $175,800; change (2012-14): 17.3%. **Avg. rent:** $742.

Mayor: Jonathan Rothschild, Democrat

History: Settled 1775 by Spanish as a presidio; acquired by U.S. in Gadsden Purchase 1853; inc. 1877.

Website: www.tucsonaz.gov

Tulsa, Oklahoma

Population: 399,682 (47). **Pop. density:** 2,030. **Pop. change (2010-14):** 1.9%. **Area:** 196.9 sq mi. **Racial distribution:** 66.6% white; 15.2% black; 2.4% Asian; 4.3% Amer. Ind.; 0.1% Pac. Isl.; 4.2% other; 2+ races 7.2%. **Hispanic pop.:** 14.4%. **Foreign born:** 9.9%. **U.S. citizens:** 92.8%. **Language:** 84.8% English only; 11.3% Spanish.

Employment: 185,374 employed; 4.2% unemployed. **Per capita income:** $47,297; change (2012-13): 1.2%. **Below poverty level:** 20.1%; 16.1% of families. **Educational attainment:** 86.8% HS; 30.0% bachelor's. **Avg. commute:** 18.2 min. 81.1% drive; 11.0% carpool. **Housing units:** 186,311; 87.8% occupied. **Home ownership:** 53.3%. **Avg. home:** $145,500; change (2012-14): 6.7%. **Avg. rent:** $727.

Mayor: Dewey F. Bartlett Jr., Republican

History: Settled in 1836 by Creek Indians; modern town founded 1882; inc. 1898; oil discovered early 20th century. Emerging telecommunications hub.

Website: www.cityoftulsa.org

Virginia Beach, Virginia

Population: 450,980 (40). **Pop. density:** 1,806. **Pop. change (2010-14):** 2.7%. **Area:** 249.7 sq mi. **Racial distribution:** 68.6% white; 19.2% black; 6.4% Asian; 0.3% Amer. Ind.; 0.1% Pac. Isl.; 1.1% other; 2+ races 4.3%. **Hispanic pop.:** 6.9%. **Foreign born:** 8.7%. **U.S. citizens:** 96.5%. **Language:** 88.3% English only; 4.1% Spanish.

Employment: 220,342 employed; 4.9% unemployed. **Per capita income:** $44,756; change (2012-13): 0.5%. **Below poverty level:** 7.9%; 6.1% of families. **Educational attainment:** 93.6% HS; 32.9% bachelor's. **Avg. commute:** 22.9 min. 81.9% drive. **Housing units:** 178,753; 92.3% occupied. **Home ownership:** 64.2%. **Avg. home:** $196,000; change (2012-14): 4.5%. **Avg. rent:** $1,235.

Mayor: William D. Sessoms Jr., nonpartisan

History: Area founded by Capt. John Smith 1607; formed by merger with Princess Anne Co. 1963.

Website: www.vbgov.com

Washington, District of Columbia

Population: 658,893 (22). **Pop. density:** 10,777. **Pop. change (2010-14):** 8.9%. **Area:** 61.1 sq mi. **Racial distribution:** 40.1% white; 50.1% black; 3.5% Asian; 0.3% Amer. Ind.; <0.05% Pac. Isl.; 3.6% other; 2+ races 2.3%. **Hispanic pop.:** 9.6%. **Foreign born:** 13.8%. **U.S. citizens:** 91.7%. **Language:** 84.2% English only; 7.6% Spanish.

Employment: 348,049 employed; 7.8% unemployed. **Per capita income:** $61,507; change (2012-13): –0.6%. **Below poverty level:** 18.6%; 14.8% of families. **Educational attainment:** 88.4% HS; 52.4% bachelor's. **Avg. commute:** 29.7 min. 38.4% public trans.; 34.0% drive; 12.2% walk. **Housing units:** 298,327; 88.4% occupied. **Home ownership:** 42.1%. **Avg. home:** $383,800; change (2012-14): 9.0%. **Avg. rent:** $1,242.

Mayor: Muriel Bowser, Democrat

History: U.S. capital; site on Potomac R. chosen by George Washington 1790 on land ceded from VA and MD (portion S of Potomac returned to VA 1846); Congress first met 1800; inc. 1802; sacked by British, War of 1812. Sept. 11, 2001, terrorist attack on the Pentagon killed 125.

Website: dc.gov

Wichita, Kansas

Population: 388,413 (49). **Pop. density:** 2,421. **Pop. change (2010-14):** 1.5%. **Area:** 160.4 sq mi. **Racial distribution:** 74.7% white; 11.2% black; 5.0% Asian; 1.0% Amer. Ind.; 0.1% Pac. Isl.; 3.6% other; 2+ races 4.5%. **Hispanic pop.:** 15.5%. **Foreign born:** 10.2%. **U.S. citizens:** 93.8%. **Language:** 83.5% English only; 10.7% Spanish.

Employment: 178,167 employed; 5.6% unemployed. **Per capita income:** $42,060; change (2012-13): 1.6%. **Below poverty level:** 17.6%; 13.2% of families. **Educational attainment:** 87.2% HS; 28.2% bachelor's. **Avg. commute:** 17.6 min. 85.0% drive. **Housing units:** 167,131; 90.0% occupied. **Home ownership:** 60.9%. **Avg. home:** $125,700; change (2012-14): 7.5%. **Avg. rent:** $690.

Mayor: Jeff Longwell, nonpartisan

History: Founded 1864; inc. 1871. Established itself as aircraft manufacturing hub between WWI and WWII.

Website: www.wichita.gov

Winston-Salem, North Carolina

Population: 239,269 (87). **Pop. density:** 1,806. **Pop. change (2010-14):** 4.0%. **Area:** 132.5 sq mi. **Racial distribution:** 56.4% white; 34.8% black; 2.1% Asian; 0.2% Amer. Ind.; 0.1% Pac. Isl.; 4.5% other; 2+ races 2.0%. **Hispanic pop.:** 15.1%. **Foreign born:** 11.2%. **U.S. citizens:** 91.3%. **Language:** 82.9% English only; 13.7% Spanish.

Employment: 104,694 employed; 5.6% unemployed. **Per capita income:** $37,943; change (2012-13): 0.3%. **Below poverty level:** 23.2%; 17.5% of families. **Educational attainment:** 85.0% HS; 32.6% bachelor's. **Avg. commute:** 19.2 min. 82.5% drive. **Housing units:** 105,026; 87.6% occupied. **Home ownership:** 56.7%. **Avg. home:** $135,200; change (2012-14): 9.4%. **Avg. rent:** $706.

Mayor: Allen Joines, Democrat

History: Salem founded 1766; Winston founded 1849; became Winston-Salem 1913. The Reynolds Building, completed 1929, used as model for Empire State Building (designed by same architects).

Website: www.cityofws.org

UNITED STATES POPULATION

Census Origins and Methods

A census is conducted in the U.S. every 10 years. The primary purpose is to apportion seats in the House of Representatives. Census data is also used to determine the boundaries of state legislative districts and the distribution of federal funds to local, state, and tribal governments.

The first U.S. census, mandated by Article 1, Section 2 of the Constitution, was conducted in 1790, a little more than a year after George Washington became president. It counted the numbers of free white males ages 16 and over (as a measure of available workers and military personnel), free white males under 16, free white females, all other free persons, and slaves. The data was collected over 18 months, at a cost of about $44,000, or $1.1 million in current dollars. The 1790 census counted a total of 3.9 million people, resulting in an increase from 65 to 105 seats in the U.S. House of Representatives.

As the nation grew, so did the scope of the census. The first inquiries on manufacturing were made in 1810. Questions on "the pursuits, industry, education, and resources of the country" were added to the 1840 census. It took a full 10 years to publish the results of the 1880 and 1890 censuses because of the number of questions asked. Because of those delays, Congress limited the 1900 census to questions on population, mortality, agriculture, and manufacturing.

Today, the secretary of commerce and the Census Bureau are directed by law to collect data on population, housing, employment, agriculture, manufacturing, trade, construction, transportation, and governments, among other things, at stated intervals. They also conduct smaller-scale surveys on behalf of other federal agencies.

U.S. marshals administered the earliest decennial censuses by visiting each household and reporting to the president (1790), to the secretary of state (1800-40), or to the secretary of the interior (1850-70). Trained census-takers were hired for the 1880 census and thereafter. In 1902, Congress authorized a permanent Census Office within the Interior Department. In 1903, the agency was transferred to the new Department of Commerce and Labor and remained with the Commerce Department when a separate labor department was created in 1913.

The 1790 through 1820 decennial censuses were officially enumerated the first Monday in Aug. The 1830-1900 censuses were as of June 1, though the 1890 census was not started until June 2 (June 1 was a Sunday). The 1910 census was as of Apr. 15, the 1920 census as of Jan. 1, and every census since 1930 has been for Apr. 1.

The Census Bureau began using statistical sampling techniques in the 1940s, the first modern computer in the 1950s, and enumeration by mail in the 1960s. These innovations allowed the Bureau to publish data more quickly, at a lower cost and with less burden on the public. Any personally identifiable information gathered is withheld from the public for 72 years, after which records are made available through the National Archives. The 1940 Census records, the most recent set to be released, can be accessed at 1940census.archives.gov.

Prior to 2010, about five in six households responded to the short-form census while one in six households answered a long-form questionnaire, which asked about details such as ancestry, marital status, and occupation. The 2005 implementation of the American Community Survey (ACS) made the long-form questionnaire no longer necessary. Conducted yearly on a random sample of the population, the ACS gathers demographic, economic, and housing information on communities across the country.

U.S. Population by State and Region, 2000, 2014

Source: Population Estimates Program and Decennial Census, U.S. Census Bureau, U.S. Dept. of Commerce

(ranked by 2014 resident population)

Rank	State	2014[1]	2000[2]	% change, 2000-14
1.	California	38,802,500	33,871,653	14.6%
2.	Texas	26,956,958	20,851,790	29.3
3.	Florida	19,893,297	15,982,824	24.5
4.	New York	19,746,227	18,976,821	4.1
5.	Illinois	12,880,580	12,419,647	3.7
6.	Pennsylvania	12,787,209	12,281,054	4.1
7.	Ohio	11,594,163	11,353,145	2.1
8.	Georgia	10,097,343	8,186,816	23.3
9.	North Carolina	9,943,964	8,046,485	23.6
10.	Michigan	9,909,877	9,938,480	–0.3
11.	New Jersey	8,938,175	8,414,347	6.2
12.	Virginia	8,326,289	7,079,030	17.6
13.	Washington	7,061,530	5,894,141	19.8
14.	Massachusetts	6,745,408	6,349,105	6.2
15.	Arizona	6,731,484	5,130,632	31.2
16.	Indiana	6,596,855	6,080,517	8.5
17.	Tennessee	6,549,352	5,689,267	15.1
18.	Missouri	6,063,589	5,596,683	8.3
19.	Maryland	5,976,407	5,296,507	12.8
20.	Wisconsin	5,757,564	5,363,715	7.3
21.	Minnesota	5,457,173	4,919,492	10.9
22.	Colorado	5,355,866	4,302,015	24.5
23.	Alabama	4,849,377	4,447,351	9.0
24.	South Carolina	4,832,482	4,011,816	20.5
25.	Louisiana	4,649,676	4,468,958	4.0
26.	Kentucky	4,413,457	4,042,285	9.2
27.	Oregon	3,970,239	3,421,436	16.0
28.	Oklahoma	3,878,051	3,450,652	12.4
29.	Connecticut	3,596,677	3,405,602	5.6%
30.	Iowa	3,107,126	2,926,382	6.2
31.	Mississippi	2,994,079	2,844,656	5.3
32.	Arkansas	2,966,369	2,673,400	11.0
33.	Utah	2,942,902	2,233,198	31.8
34.	Kansas	2,904,021	2,688,824	8.0
35.	Nevada	2,839,099	1,998,257	42.1
36.	New Mexico	2,085,572	1,819,046	14.7
37.	Nebraska	1,881,503	1,711,265	9.9
38.	West Virginia	1,850,326	1,808,350	2.3
39.	Idaho	1,634,464	1,293,956	26.3
40.	Hawaii	1,419,561	1,211,537	17.2
41.	Maine	1,330,089	1,274,923	4.3
42.	New Hampshire	1,326,813	1,235,786	7.4
43.	Rhode Island	1,055,173	1,048,319	0.7
44.	Montana	1,023,579	902,195	13.5
45.	Delaware	935,614	783,600	19.4
46.	South Dakota	853,175	754,844	13.0
47.	North Dakota	739,482	642,200	15.1
48.	Alaska	736,732	626,931	17.5
49.	Dist. of Columbia	658,893	572,059	15.2
50.	Vermont	626,562	608,827	2.9
51.	Wyoming	584,153	493,782	18.3
	United States	**318,857,056**	**281,424,603**	**13.3**
	Northeast[3]	56,152,333	53,594,784	4.8
	Midwest[4]	67,745,108	64,395,194	5.2
	South[5]	119,771,934	100,235,846	19.5
	West[6]	75,187,681	63,198,779	19.0

Note: The U.S. resident population consists of individuals whose usual residence, or where they live and sleep most of the time, is in one of the 50 states or DC. It excludes overseas U.S. military personnel and civilian U.S. citizens living abroad. (1) Estimates are as of July 1. (2) Figures are for Apr. 1 of decennial census year. Population figures may reflect revisions/corrections to initial tabulated census counts. (3) Incl. the states of the New England (Connecticut, Maine, Massachusetts, New Hampshire, Rhode Island, Vermont) and Middle Atlantic (New Jersey, New York, Pennsylvania) divisions. (4) Incl. the states of the East North Central (Illinois, Indiana, Michigan, Ohio, Wisconsin) and West North Central (Iowa, Kansas, Minnesota, Missouri, Nebraska, North Dakota, South Dakota) divisions. (5) Incl. the states of the South Atlantic (Delaware, DC, Florida, Georgia, Maryland, North Carolina, South Carolina, Virginia, West Virginia), East South Central (Alabama, Kentucky, Mississippi, Tennessee), and West South Central (Arkansas, Louisiana, Oklahoma, Texas) divisions. (6) Incl. the states of the Mountain (Arizona, Colorado, Idaho, Montana, Nevada, New Mexico, Utah, Wyoming) and Pacific (Alaska, California, Hawaii, Oregon, Washington) divisions.

U.S. Population by Official

Source: Decennial Censuses, U.S. Census Bureau,
(population figures for 1790-1860

State	1790	1800	1810	1820	1830	1840	1850	1860	1870	1880	1890	1900	1910	1920
AL	—	1	9	128	310	591	772	964	996,992	1,262,505	1,513,401	1,828,697	2,138,093	2,348,174
AK	—	—	—	—	—	—	—	—	—	33,426	32,052	63,592	64,356	55,036
AZ	—	—	—	—	—	—	—	—	9,658	40,440	88,243	122,931	204,354	334,162
AR	—	—	1	14	30	98	210	435	484,471	802,525	1,128,211	1,311,564	1,574,449	1,752,204
CA	—	—	—	—	—	—	93	380	560,247	864,694	1,213,398	1,485,053	2,377,549	3,426,861
CO	—	—	—	—	—	—	—	34	39,864	194,327	413,249	539,700	799,024	939,629
CT	238	251	262	275	298	310	371	460	537,454	622,700	746,258	908,420	1,114,756	1,380,631
DE	59	64	73	73	77	78	92	112	125,015	146,608	168,493	184,735	202,322	223,003
DC[1]	—	8	15	23	30	34	52	75	131,700	177,624	230,392	278,718	331,069	437,571
FL	—	—	—	—	35	54	87	140	187,748	269,493	391,422	528,542	752,619	968,470
GA	83	163	251	341	517	691	906	1,057	1,184,109	1,542,180	1,837,353	2,216,331	2,609,121	2,895,832
HI	—	—	—	—	—	—	—	—	—	—	—	154,001	191,874	255,881
ID	—	—	—	—	—	—	—	—	14,999	32,610	88,548	161,772	325,594	431,866
IL	—	—	12	55	157	476	851	1,712	2,539,891	3,077,871	3,826,352	4,821,550	5,638,591	6,485,280
IN	—	6	25	147	343	686	988	1,350	1,680,637	1,978,301	2,192,404	2,516,462	2,700,876	2,930,390
IA	—	—	—	—	—	43	192	675	1,194,020	1,624,615	1,912,297	2,231,853	2,224,771	2,404,021
KS	—	—	—	—	—	—	—	107	364,399	996,096	1,428,108	1,470,495	1,690,949	1,769,257
KY[1]	74	221	407	564	688	780	982	1,156	1,321,011	1,648,690	1,858,635	2,147,174	2,289,905	2,416,630
LA	—	—	77	153	216	352	518	708	726,915	939,946	1,118,588	1,381,625	1,656,388	1,798,509
ME[2]	97	152	229	298	399	502	583	628	626,915	648,936	661,086	694,466	742,371	768,014
MD	320	342	381	407	447	470	583	687	780,894	934,943	1,042,390	1,188,044	1,295,346	1,449,661
MA[2]	379	423	472	523	610	738	995	1,231	1,457,351	1,783,085	2,238,947	2,805,346	3,366,416	3,852,356
MI	—	—	5	7	28	212	398	749	1,184,059	1,636,937	2,093,890	2,420,982	2,810,173	3,668,412
MN	—	—	—	—	—	—	6	172	439,706	780,773	1,310,283	1,751,394	2,075,708	2,387,125
MS	—	8	31	75	137	376	607	791	827,922	1,131,597	1,289,600	1,551,270	1,797,114	1,790,618
MO	—	—	20	67	140	384	682	1,182	1,721,295	2,168,380	2,679,185	3,106,665	3,293,335	3,404,055
MT	—	—	—	—	—	—	—	—	20,595	39,159	142,924	243,329	376,053	548,889
NE	—	—	—	—	—	—	—	29	122,993	452,402	1,062,656	1,066,300	1,192,214	1,296,372
NV	—	—	—	—	—	—	—	7	42,491	62,266	47,355	42,335	81,875	77,407
NH	142	184	214	244	269	285	318	326	318,300	346,991	376,530	411,588	430,572	443,083
NJ	184	211	246	278	321	373	490	672	906,096	1,131,116	1,444,933	1,883,669	2,537,167	3,155,900
NM	—	—	—	—	—	—	62	94	91,874	119,565	160,282	195,310	327,301	360,350
NY	340	589	959	1,373	1,919	2,429	3,097	3,881	4,382,759	5,082,871	6,003,174	7,268,894	9,113,614	10,385,227
NC	394	478	557	639	738	753	869	993	1,071,361	1,399,750	1,617,949	1,893,810	2,206,287	2,559,123
ND[3]	—	—	—	—	—	—	—	—	2,405	36,909	190,983	319,146	577,056	646,872
OH	—	42	231	581	938	1,519	1,980	2,340	2,665,260	3,198,062	3,672,329	4,157,545	4,767,121	5,759,394
OK[4]	—	—	—	—	—	—	—	—	—	—	258,657	790,391	1,657,155	2,028,283
OR	—	—	—	—	—	—	12	52	90,923	174,768	317,704	413,536	672,765	783,389
PA	434	602	810	1,049	1,348	1,724	2,312	2,906	3,521,951	4,282,891	5,258,113	6,302,115	7,665,111	8,720,017
RI	69	69	77	83	97	109	148	175	217,353	276,531	345,506	428,556	542,610	604,397
SC	249	346	415	503	581	594	669	704	705,606	995,577	1,151,149	1,340,316	1,515,400	1,683,724
SD[3]	—	—	—	—	—	—	—	5	11,776	98,268	348,600	401,570	583,888	636,547
TN	36	106	262	423	682	829	1,003	1,110	1,258,520	1,542,359	1,767,518	2,020,616	2,184,789	2,337,885
TX	—	—	—	—	—	—	213	604	818,579	1,591,749	2,235,527	3,048,710	3,896,542	4,663,228
UT	—	—	—	—	—	—	11	40	86,336	143,963	210,779	276,749	373,351	449,396
VT	85	154	218	236	281	292	314	315	330,551	332,286	332,422	343,641	355,956	352,428
VA[1]	692	808	878	938	1,044	1,025	1,119	1,220	1,225,163	1,512,565	1,655,980	1,854,184	2,061,612	2,309,187
WA	—	—	—	—	—	—	1	12	23,955	75,116	357,232	518,103	1,141,990	1,356,621
WV[1]	56	79	105	137	177	225	302	377	442,014	618,457	762,794	958,800	1,221,119	1,463,701
WI	—	—	—	—	—	31	305	776	1,054,670	1,315,497	1,693,330	2,069,042	2,333,860	2,632,067
WY	—	—	—	—	—	—	—	—	9,118	20,789	62,555	92,531	145,965	194,402
U.S.[5]	**3,929**	**5,308**	**7,240**	**9,638**	**12,861**	**17,063**	**23,192**	**31,443**	**38,558,371**	**50,189,209**	**62,979,766**	**76,212,168**	**92,228,496**	**106,021,537**

Note: With some exceptions, pop. shown is number of residents in a state (or territory of the same name) at the time of each decennial census. Figures may differ from originally published census data because of revisions. Excl. overseas U.S. military personnel and civilian U.S. citizens living abroad. (1) 1790-1860 VA figures are for present-day boundaries. That is, they incl. pop. in areas then part of DC (1800-40) and excl. pop. of areas that went to KY (1790) and WV (1790-1860). (2) 1790-1810 figures for MA do not incl. district taken to form state of ME in 1820. (3) 1860 SD figure is for area reported as "unorganized Dakota"; 1870-80 figures are for present-day ND and SD. (4) 1890-1900 figures incl. pop. for Indian Terr. (5) 1830-40 totals excl. persons (5,318 in 1830; 6,100 in 1840) on public ships in service of the U.S. not credited to any state. 1890 total incl. Indian Terr. and Indian Reservations pop. (325,464) specially enumerated.

Estimated Population of American Colonies, 1630-1780

Source: U.S. Census Bureau, U.S. Dept. of Commerce
(numbers in thousands)

Colony	1630	1650	1670	1690	1700	1720	1740	1750	1760	1770	1780
Total	**4.6**	**50.4**	**111.9**	**210.4**	**250.9**	**466.2**	**905.6**	**1,170.8**	**1,593.6**	**2,148.1**	**2,780.4**
Connecticut	—	4.1	12.6	21.6	26.0	58.8	89.6	111.3	142.5	183.9	206.7
Delaware	—	0.2	0.7	1.5	2.5	5.4	19.9	28.7	33.3	35.5	45.4
Georgia	—	—	—	—	—	—	2.0	5.2	9.6	23.4	56.1
Kentucky[1]	—	—	—	—	—	—	—	—	—	15.7	45.0
Maine (counties)[2]	0.4	1.0	—	—	—	—	—	—	20.0	31.3	49.1
Maryland	—	4.5	13.2	24.0	29.6	66.1	116.1	141.1	162.3	202.6	245.5
Massachusetts and Plymouth[2,3]	0.9	15.6	35.3	56.9	55.9	91.0	151.6	188.0	202.6	235.3	268.6
New Hampshire	0.5	1.3	1.8	4.2	5.0	9.4	23.3	27.5	39.1	62.4	87.8
New Jersey	—	—	1.0	8.0	14.0	29.8	51.4	71.4	93.8	117.4	139.6
New York	0.4	4.1	5.8	13.9	19.1	36.9	63.7	76.7	117.1	162.9	210.5
North Carolina	—	—	3.9	7.6	10.7	21.3	51.8	73.0	110.4	197.2	270.1
Pennsylvania	—	—	—	11.4	18.0	31.0	85.6	119.7	183.7	240.1	327.3
Rhode Island	—	0.8	2.2	4.2	5.9	11.7	25.3	33.2	45.5	58.2	52.9
South Carolina	—	—	0.2	3.9	5.7	17.0	45.0	64.0	94.1	124.2	180.0
Tennessee[4]	—	—	—	—	—	—	—	—	—	1.0	10.0
Vermont[5]	—	—	—	—	—	—	—	—	—	10.0	47.6
Virginia	2.5	18.7	35.3	53.0	58.6	87.8	180.4	231.0	339.7	447.0	538.0

Note: With the exception of KY, ME, Plymouth, TN, and VT, colonies shown are the original 13 states. (1) Admitted as state 1792. (2) For 1660-1750, the pop. of ME counties are included with MA. ME was annexed by MA in the 1650s but became a separate state in 1820. (3) Plymouth became part of Prov. of Massachusetts in 1691. (4) Admitted as state 1796. (5) Admitted as state 1791.

Census, 1790-2010

U.S. Dept. of Commerce
only are in thousands)

1930	1940	1950	1960	1970	1980	1990	2000	2010	State
2,646,248	2,832,961	3,061,743	3,266,740	3,444,354	3,894,025	4,040,389	4,447,351	4,779,753	AL
59,278	72,524	128,643	226,167	302,583	401,851	550,043	626,931	710,235	AK
435,573	499,261	749,587	1,302,161	1,775,399	2,716,546	3,665,339	5,130,632	6,392,017	AZ
1,854,482	1,949,387	1,909,511	1,786,272	1,923,322	2,286,357	2,350,624	2,673,400	2,915,919	AR
5,677,251	6,907,387	10,586,223	15,717,204	19,971,069	23,667,764	29,758,213	33,871,653	37,253,956	CA
1,035,791	1,123,296	1,325,089	1,753,947	2,209,596	2,889,735	3,294,473	4,302,015	5,029,196	CO
1,606,903	1,709,242	2,007,280	2,535,234	3,032,217	3,107,564	3,287,116	3,405,602	3,574,097	CT
238,380	266,505	318,085	446,292	548,104	594,338	666,168	783,600	897,934	DE
486,869	663,091	802,178	763,956	756,668	638,432	606,900	572,059	601,767	DC
1,468,211	1,897,414	2,771,305	4,951,560	6,791,418	9,746,961	12,938,071	15,982,824	18,801,332	FL
2,908,506	3,123,723	3,444,578	3,943,116	4,587,930	5,462,982	6,478,149	8,186,816	9,687,850	GA
368,300	422,770	499,794	632,772	769,913	964,691	1,108,229	1,211,537	1,360,301	HI
445,032	524,873	588,637	667,191	713,015	944,127	1,006,734	1,293,956	1,567,652	ID
7,630,654	7,897,241	8,712,176	10,081,158	11,110,285	11,427,409	11,430,602	12,419,647	12,830,632	IL
3,238,503	3,427,796	3,934,224	4,662,498	5,195,392	5,490,210	5,544,156	6,080,517	6,483,802	IN
2,470,939	2,538,268	2,621,073	2,757,537	2,825,368	2,913,808	2,776,831	2,926,382	3,046,355	IA
1,880,999	1,801,028	1,905,299	2,178,611	2,249,071	2,364,236	2,477,588	2,688,824	2,853,118	KS
2,614,589	2,845,627	2,944,806	3,038,156	3,220,711	3,660,324	3,686,892	4,042,285	4,339,367	KY
2,101,593	2,363,880	2,683,516	3,257,022	3,644,637	4,206,116	4,220,164	4,468,958	4,533,372	LA
797,423	847,226	913,774	969,265	993,722	1,125,043	1,227,928	1,274,923	1,328,361	ME
1,631,526	1,821,244	2,343,001	3,100,689	3,923,897	4,216,933	4,780,753	5,296,507	5,773,626	MD
4,249,614	4,316,721	4,690,514	5,148,578	5,689,170	5,737,093	6,016,425	6,349,105	6,547,629	MA
4,842,325	5,256,106	6,371,766	7,823,194	8,881,826	9,262,044	9,295,287	9,938,480	9,883,706	MI
2,563,953	2,792,300	2,982,483	3,413,864	3,806,103	4,075,970	4,375,665	4,919,492	5,303,925	MN
2,009,821	2,183,796	2,178,914	2,178,141	2,216,994	2,520,770	2,575,475	2,844,656	2,967,297	MS
3,629,367	3,784,664	3,954,653	4,319,813	4,677,623	4,916,766	5,116,901	5,596,683	5,988,927	MO
537,606	559,456	591,024	674,767	694,409	786,690	799,065	902,195	989,415	MT
1,377,963	1,315,834	1,325,510	1,411,330	1,485,333	1,569,825	1,578,417	1,711,265	1,826,341	NE
91,058	110,247	160,083	285,278	488,738	800,508	1,201,675	1,998,257	2,700,551	NV
465,293	491,524	533,242	606,921	737,681	920,610	1,109,252	1,235,786	1,316,470	NH
4,041,334	4,160,165	4,835,329	6,066,782	7,171,112	7,365,011	7,730,188	8,414,347	8,791,909	NJ
423,317	531,818	681,187	951,023	1,017,055	1,303,302	1,515,069	1,819,046	2,059,181	NM
12,588,066	13,479,142	14,830,192	16,782,304	18,241,391	17,558,165	17,990,778	18,976,821	19,378,102	NY
3,170,276	3,571,623	4,061,929	4,556,155	5,084,411	5,880,095	6,632,448	8,046,485	9,535,483	NC
680,845	641,935	619,636	632,446	617,792	652,717	638,800	642,200	672,591	ND
6,646,697	6,907,612	7,946,627	9,706,397	10,657,423	10,797,603	10,847,115	11,353,145	11,536,504	OH
2,396,040	2,336,434	2,233,351	2,328,284	2,559,463	3,025,487	3,145,576	3,450,652	3,751,351	OK
953,786	1,089,684	1,521,341	1,768,687	2,091,533	2,633,156	2,842,337	3,421,436	3,831,074	OR
9,631,350	9,900,180	10,498,012	11,319,366	11,800,766	11,864,720	11,882,842	12,281,054	12,702,379	PA
687,497	713,346	791,896	859,488	949,723	947,154	1,003,464	1,048,319	1,052,567	RI
1,738,765	1,899,804	2,117,027	2,382,594	2,590,713	3,120,729	3,486,310	4,011,816	4,625,364	SC
692,849	642,961	652,740	680,514	666,257	690,768	696,004	754,844	814,191	SD
2,616,556	2,915,841	3,291,718	3,567,089	3,926,018	4,591,023	4,877,203	5,689,267	6,346,105	TN
5,824,715	6,414,824	7,711,194	9,579,677	11,198,655	14,225,513	16,986,335	20,851,790	25,145,565	TX
507,847	550,310	688,862	890,627	1,059,273	1,461,037	1,722,850	2,233,198	2,763,885	UT
359,611	359,231	377,747	389,881	444,732	511,456	562,758	608,827	625,741	VT
2,421,851	2,677,773	3,318,680	3,966,949	4,651,448	5,346,797	6,189,197	7,079,030	8,001,024	VA
1,563,396	1,736,191	2,378,963	2,853,214	3,413,244	4,132,353	4,866,669	5,894,141	6,724,540	WA
1,729,205	1,901,974	2,005,552	1,860,421	1,744,237	1,950,186	1,793,477	1,808,350	1,852,994	WV
2,939,006	3,137,587	3,434,575	3,951,777	4,417,821	4,705,642	4,891,769	5,363,715	5,686,986	WI
225,565	250,742	290,529	330,066	332,416	469,557	453,589	493,782	563,626	WY
123,202,624	**132,164,569**	**151,325,798**	**179,323,175**	**203,302,031**	**226,542,199**	**248,718,302**	**281,424,603**	**308,746,065**	**U.S.**

U.S. Center of Population, 1790-2010

Source: Decennial Censuses, Geography Division, U.S. Census Bureau, U.S. Dept. of Commerce

The country's **(mean) center of population** is the center of population gravity. In other words, it is the point upon which the U.S. would balance if the country were a rigid, weightless plane and its population was distributed thereon, with each individual assuming an equal weight.

Census year	N Lat °	′	″	W Long °	′	″	Approximate location
1790	39	16	30	76	11	12	Kent Co., MD, 23 miles east of Baltimore
1800	39	16	6	76	56	30	Howard Co., MD, 18 miles west of Baltimore
1810	39	11	30	77	37	12	Loudoun Co., VA, 40 miles northwest by west of Washington, DC
1820	39	5	42	78	33	0	Hardy Co., WV(1), 16 miles east of Moorefield
1830	38	57	54	79	16	54	Grant Co., WV(1), 19 miles west-southwest of Moorefield
1840	39	2	0	80	18	0	Upshur Co., WV(1), 16 miles south of Clarksburg
1850	38	59	0	81	19	0	Wirt Co., WV(1), 23 miles southeast of Parkersburg
1860	39	0	24	82	48	48	Pike Co., OH, 20 miles south by east of Chillicothe
1870	39	12	0	83	35	42	Highland Co., OH, 48 miles east by north of Cincinnati
1880	39	4	8	84	39	40	Boone Co., KY, 8 miles west by south of Cincinnati, OH
1890	39	11	56	85	32	53	Decatur Co., IN, 20 miles east of Columbus
1900	39	9	36	85	48	54	Bartholomew Co., IN, 6 miles southeast of Columbus
1910	39	10	12	86	32	20	Monroe Co., IN, in the city of Bloomington
1920	39	10	21	86	43	15	Owen Co., IN, 8 miles south-southeast of Spencer
1930	39	3	45	87	8	6	Greene Co., IN, 3 miles northeast of Linton
1940	38	56	54	87	22	35	Sullivan Co., IN, 2 miles southeast by east of Carlisle
1950	38	50	21	88	9	33	Richland Co., IL, 8 miles north-northwest of Olney
1950(2)	38	48	15	88	22	8	Clay Co., IL, 3 miles northeast of Louisville
1960(2)	38	35	58	89	12	35	Clinton Co., IL, 6.5 miles northwest of Centralia
1970(2)	38	27	47	89	42	22	St. Clair Co., IL, 5 miles east-southeast of Mascoutah
1980(2)	38	8	13	90	34	26	Jefferson Co., MO, 0.25 mile west of DeSoto
1990(2)	37	52	20	91	12	55	Crawford Co., MO, 9.7 miles southeast of Steelville
2000(2)	37	41	49	91	48	34	Phelps Co., MO, 2.8 miles east of Edgar Springs
2010(2)	37	31	3	92	10	23	Texas Co., MO, 2.7 miles northeast of Plato

(1) Pres. Lincoln signed a bill Dec. 31, 1862, approving statehood for West Virginia (made up of former Virginia counties). It was admitted to the Union June 20, 1863. (2) Incl. Alaska and Hawaii.

Density of U.S. Population by State, 1930-2010

Source: Decennial Censuses, U.S. Census Bureau, U.S. Dept. of Commerce

(per square mile of land area, as measured for the 2010 census)

State	1930	1950	1970	1990	2010	State	1930	1950	1970	1990	2010
AL	52.3	60.5	68.0	79.8	94.4	MT	3.7	4.1	4.8	5.5	6.8
AK	0.1	0.2	0.5	1.0	1.2	NE	17.9	17.3	19.3	20.5	23.8
AZ	3.8	6.6	15.6	32.3	56.3	NV	0.8	1.5	4.5	10.9	24.6
AR	35.6	36.7	37.0	45.2	56.0	NH	52.0	59.6	82.4	123.9	147.0
CA	36.4	68.0	128.1	191.0	239.1	NJ	549.5	657.5	974.7	1,051.1	1,195.5
CO	10.0	12.8	21.3	31.8	48.5	NM	3.5	5.6	8.4	12.5	17.0
CT	331.8	414.5	626.1	678.8	738.1	NY	267.1	314.7	387.0	381.7	411.2
DE	122.3	163.2	281.3	341.9	460.8	NC	65.2	83.5	104.5	136.3	196.1
DC	7,975.1	13,140.0	12,392.0	9,941.3	9,856.5	ND	9.9	9.0	9.0	9.3	9.7
FL	27.4	51.7	126.6	241.3	350.6	OH	162.7	194.5	260.7	265.5	282.3
GA	50.6	59.9	79.8	112.6	168.4	OK	34.9	32.6	37.3	45.9	54.7
HI	57.3	77.8	119.7	172.6	211.8	OR	9.9	15.8	21.8	29.6	39.9
ID	5.4	7.1	8.6	12.2	19.0	PA	215.3	234.6	263.6	265.6	283.9
IL	137.4	156.9	200.2	205.9	231.1	RI	665.0	766.0	915.8	970.6	1,018.1
IN	90.4	109.8	145.0	154.8	181.0	SC	57.8	70.4	86.2	116.0	153.9
IA	44.2	46.9	50.6	49.7	54.5	SD	9.1	8.6	8.8	9.2	10.7
KS	23.0	23.3	27.5	30.3	34.9	TN	63.5	79.8	95.2	118.3	153.9
KY	66.2	74.6	81.5	93.3	109.9	TX	22.3	29.5	42.9	65.0	96.3
LA	48.6	62.1	84.3	97.7	104.9	UT	6.2	8.4	12.9	21.0	33.6
ME	25.9	29.6	32.2	39.8	43.1	VT	39.0	41.0	48.2	61.1	67.9
MD	168.1	241.4	404.1	492.6	594.8	VA	61.3	84.0	117.7	156.7	202.6
MA	544.8	601.3	729.4	771.3	839.4	WA	23.5	35.8	51.3	73.2	101.2
MI	85.6	112.7	157.0	164.4	174.8	WV	71.9	83.4	72.6	74.6	77.1
MN	32.2	37.5	47.8	54.9	66.6	WI	54.3	63.4	81.6	90.3	105.0
MS	42.8	46.4	47.2	54.8	63.2	WY	2.3	3.0	3.4	4.7	5.8
MO	52.8	57.5	68.0	74.4	87.1	**U.S.**	**34.7**	**42.6**	**57.5**	**70.4**	**87.4**

Note: For the sake of comparison, the densities of Alaska and Hawaii in 1930 and 1950 are included though they were not yet states.

U.S. Area and Population, 1790-2010

Source: Decennial Censuses, U.S. Census Bureau, U.S. Dept. of Commerce

	AREA (square miles)			RESIDENT POPULATION			
						Increase over preceding census	
Census date	Total area[1]	Land area	Water area[1]	Number	Per sq mi of land	Number	%
1790 (Aug. 2)	891,364	864,746	24,065	3,929,214	4.5	—	—
1800 (Aug. 4)	891,364	864,746	24,065	5,308,483	6.1	1,379,269	35.1%
1810 (Aug. 6)	1,722,685	1,681,828	34,175	7,239,881	4.3	1,931,398	36.4
1820 (Aug. 7)	1,792,552	1,749,462	38,544	9,638,453	5.5	2,398,572	33.1
1830 (June 1)	1,792,552	1,749,462	38,544	12,860,702	7.4	3,222,249	33.4
1840 (June 1)	1,792,552	1,749,462	38,544	17,063,453	9.8	4,203,751	32.7
1850 (June 1)	2,991,655	2,940,042	52,705	23,191,876	7.9	6,128,423	35.9
1860 (June 1)	3,021,295	2,969,640	52,747	31,443,321	10.6	8,251,445	35.6
1870 (June 1)	3,612,299	3,540,705	68,082	38,558,371	10.9	7,115,050	22.6
1880 (June 1)	3,612,299	3,540,705	68,082	50,189,209	14.2	11,630,838	30.2
1890 (June 1)	3,612,299	3,540,705	68,082	62,979,766	17.8	12,790,557	25.5
1900 (June 1)	3,618,770	3,547,314	67,901	76,212,168	21.5	13,232,402	21.0
1910 (Apr. 15)	3,618,770	3,547,045	68,170	92,228,496	26.0	16,016,328	21.0
1920 (Jan. 1)	3,618,770	3,546,931	68,284	106,021,537	29.9	13,793,041	15.0
1930 (Apr. 1)	3,618,770	3,554,608	60,607	123,202,624	34.7	17,181,087	16.2
1940 (Apr. 1)	3,618,770	3,554,608	60,607	132,164,569	37.2	8,961,945	7.3
1950 (Apr. 1)	3,618,770	3,552,206	63,005	151,325,798	42.6	19,161,229	14.5
1960 (Apr. 1)	3,618,770	3,540,911	74,212	179,323,175	50.6	27,997,377	18.5
1970 (Apr. 1)	3,618,770	3,536,855	78,444	203,302,031	57.5	23,978,856	13.4
1980 (Apr. 1)	3,618,770	3,539,289	79,481	226,542,199	64.0	23,240,168	11.4
1990 (Apr. 1)	3,717,796	3,536,278	181,518	248,718,302	70.3	22,176,103	9.8
2000 (Apr. 1)	3,794,083	3,537,438	256,645	281,424,603	79.6	32,706,301	13.1
2010 (Apr. 1)	3,796,742	3,531,905	264,837	308,746,065	87.4	27,321,462	9.7

Note: Area and population density figures represent the area within the boundaries of the U.S. under its jurisdiction on the date in question including, in some cases, considerable areas not organized or settled and not covered by the census. Beginning in 1870, area data include Alaska; from 1900 on, data include Hawaii. Population figures may reflect revisions/corrections to initial tabulated census counts. (1) Figures for 1790-1980 cover inland water only. Figures for 1990 include inland, coastal, and Great Lakes water. Figures for 2000-10 include additional territorial water.

U.S. Congressional Apportionment by Census Year, 1850-2010

Source: Decennial Censuses, U.S. Census Bureau, U.S. Dept. of Commerce

The U.S. Constitution, in Article 1, Section 2, mandates that the population be counted every 10 years so that the number of U.S. representatives can be apportioned among the states. Every state is entitled to at least one House seat. The size of a state's resident population, both citizens and noncitizens, determines if it may send additional representatives to Congress. A congressional apportionment has been made after every decennial census except for that of 1920. Prior to 1870, slaves were counted as being only three-fifths of a person in the apportionment population. Since the 1970 census (excluding 1980), overseas military personnel and federal civilian employees as well as their dependents have been allocated to a home state for apportionment purposes. Residents of the District of Columbia, Puerto Rico, and U.S. island areas are not included in the apportionment population as they lack voting seats in the U.S. House.

Under a law approved in 1941, House seats are allocated using the Huntington-Hill, or equal proportions, method. It allows for the least possible variation in the average number of people each House member represents.

The first House of Representatives, in 1789, had 65 members as provided by the Constitution. The states with the most representatives were Virginia (10), Massachusetts (8), and Pennsylvania (8). As the nation's population grew, the number of representatives was increased. A 1911 act fixed the total membership of the House at 435. (Alaska and Hawaii each gained one House seat when they became states, temporarily raising the total to 437 representatives until after the 1960 census was conducted.)

State	2010	2000	1990	1970	1950	1900	1850
AL	7	7	7	7	9	9	7
AK	1	1	1	1	1	NA	NA
AZ	9	8	6	4	2	NA	NA
AR	4	4	4	4	6	7	2
CA	53	53	52	43	30	8	2
CO	7	7	6	5	4	3	NA
CT	5	5	6	6	6	5	4
DE	1	1	1	1	1	1	1
FL	27	25	23	15	8	3	1
GA	14	13	11	10	10	11	8
HI	2	2	2	2	1	NA	NA
ID	2	2	2	2	2	1	NA
IL	18	19	20	24	25	25	9
IN	9	9	10	11	11	13	11
IA	4	5	5	6	8	11	2
KS	4	4	4	5	6	8	NA
KY	6	6	6	7	8	11	10
LA	6	7	7	8	8	7	4
ME	2	2	2	2	3	4	6
MD	8	8	8	8	7	6	6
MA	9	10	10	12	14	14	11
MI	14	15	16	19	18	12	4
MN	8	8	8	8	9	9	2
MS	4	4	5	5	6	8	5
MO	8	9	9	10	11	16	7
MT	1	1	1	2	2	1	NA
NE	3	3	3	3	4	6	NA
NV	4	3	2	1	1	1	NA
NH	2	2	2	2	2	2	3
NJ	12	13	13	15	14	10	5
NM	3	3	3	2	2	NA	NA
NY	27	29	31	39	43	37	33
NC	13	13	12	11	12	10	8
ND	1	1	1	1	2	2	NA
OH	16	18	19	23	23	21	21
OK	5	5	6	6	6	5	NA
OR	5	5	5	4	4	2	1
PA	18	19	21	25	30	32	25
RI	2	2	2	2	2	2	2
SC	7	6	6	6	6	7	6
SD	1	1	1	2	2	2	NA
TN	9	9	9	8	9	10	10
TX	36	32	30	24	22	16	2
UT	4	3	3	2	2	1	NA
VT	1	1	1	1	1	2	3
VA	11	11	11	10	10	10	13
WA	10	9	9	7	7	3	NA
WV	3	3	3	4	6	5	NA
WI	8	8	9	9	10	11	3
WY	1	1	1	1	1	1	NA
Total	**435**	**435**	**435**	**435**	**437**	**391**	**237**

NA = Not applicable.

U.S. Slave and "Free Colored" Population, 1790, 1820, 1860

Source: Decennial Censuses, U.S. Census Bureau, U.S. Dept. of Commerce

	1790 census			1820 census			1860 census		
	Slaves	% slaves[1]	Free colored	Slaves	% slaves[1]	Free colored	Slaves	% slaves[1]	Free colored
Northern states[2]	**40,354**	**2.1%**	**27,070**	**19,108**	**0.4%**	**99,307**	**18**	**0.0%**	**225,224**
Connecticut	2,764	1.2	2,808	97	0.0	7,870	0	0.0	8,627
New Jersey	11,423	6.2	2,762	7,557	2.7	12,460	18	0.0	25,318
New York	21,324	6.3	4,654	10,088	0.7	29,279	0	0.0	49,005
Pennsylvania	3,737	0.9	6,537	211	0.0	30,202	0	0.0	56,949
Border/disputed states	**124,353**	**27.5**	**12,056**	**248,860**	**22.4**	**55,794**	**429,403**	**13.2**	**118,652**
Delaware	8,887	15.0	3,899	4,509	6.2	12,958	1,798	1.6	19,829
Kansas	—	—	—	—	—	—	2	0.0	625
Kentucky	12,430	16.9	114	126,732	22.5	2,759	225,483	19.5	10,684
Maryland	103,036	32.2	8,043	107,397	26.4	39,730	87,189	12.7	83,942
Missouri	—	—	—	10,222	15.4	347	114,931	9.7	3,572
Southern states	**532,974**	**35.3**	**20,401**	**1,265,534**	**37.8**	**75,775**	**3,521,110**	**38.7**	**132,760**
Alabama	—	—	—	41,879	32.7	571	435,080	45.1	2,690
Arkansas	—	—	—	1,617	11.3	59	111,115	25.5	144
Florida	—	—	—	—	—	—	61,745	44.0	932
Georgia	29,264	35.5	398	149,656	43.9	1,763	462,198	43.7	3,500
Louisiana	—	—	—	69,064	45.0	10,476	331,726	46.9	18,647
Mississippi	—	—	—	32,814	43.5	458	436,631	55.2	773
North Carolina	100,572	25.5	4,975	204,917	32.1	14,712	331,059	33.4	30,463
South Carolina	107,094	43.0	1,801	258,475	51.4	6,826	402,406	57.2	9,914
Tennessee	3,417	9.6	361	80,107	18.9	2,737	275,719	24.8	7,300
Texas	—	—	—	—	—	—	182,566	30.2	355
Virginia	292,627	39.1	12,866	427,005	39.7	38,173	490,865	30.7	58,042
Total territories[3]	—	—	—	**4,520**	**19.4**	**2,758**	**3,229**	**1.1**	**11,434**
Total states and territories	**697,681**	**17.8**	**59,527**	**1,538,022**	**16.0**	**233,634**	**3,953,760**	**12.6**	**488,070**

Note: "Free colored" was an official Census Bureau designation in these decades. States are grouped roughly by allegiance in the Civil War. (1) Percentage of total pop., all races. (2) The following states are not listed separately but are included in totals for Northern states (relevant census years in parentheses): CA (1860), IL (1820, 1860), IN (1820, 1860), IA (1860), ME (1790, 1820, 1860), MA (1790, 1820, 1860), MI (1820, 1860), MN (1860), NH (1790, 1820, 1860), OH (1820, 1860), OR (1860), RI (1790, 1820, 1860), VT (1790, 1820, 1860), WI (1820, 1860). (3) Incl. AZ (1860), CO (1860), Dakota (1860), DC (1820, 1860), NE (1860), NV (1860), NM (1860), UT (1860), WA (1860).

U.S. Population by Sex, Race, Residence, and Median Age, 1790-2010

Source: Decennial Censuses, U.S. Census Bureau, U.S. Dept. of Commerce

(numbers in thousands, unless otherwise noted)

	SEX		RACE[2]				RESIDENCE		MEDIAN AGE (years)		
				Black							
Census date	Male	Female	White	Number	% tot. pop	Other	Urban[3]	Rural	All races	White[2]	Black[2]
Conterminous U.S.[1]											
1790 (Aug. 2)	NA	NA	3,172	757	19.3%	NA	202	3,728	NA	NA	NA
1800 (Aug. 4)	NA	NA	4,306	1,002	18.9	NA	322	4,986	NA	NA	NA
1810 (Aug. 6)	NA	NA	5,862	1,378	19.0	NA	525	6,714	NA	16.0	NA
1820 (Aug. 7)	4,897	4,742	7,867	1,772	18.4	NA	693	8,945	16.7	16.6	17.2
1830 (June 1)	6,532	6,334	10,537	2,329	18.1	NA	1,127	11,733	17.2	17.3	17.2
1840 (June 1)	8,689	8,381	14,196	2,874	16.8	NA	1,845	15,218	17.8	17.9	17.6
1850 (June 1)	11,838	11,354	19,553	3,639	15.7	NA	3,574	19,617	18.9	19.2	17.4
1860 (June 1)	16,085	15,358	26,923	4,442	14.1	79	6,217	25,227	19.4	19.7	17.5
1870 (June 1)	19,494	19,065	33,589	4,880	12.7	89	9,902	28,656	20.2	20.4	18.5
1880 (June 1)	25,519	24,637	43,403	6,581	13.1	172	14,130	36,059	20.9	21.4	18.0
1890 (June 1)	32,237	30,711	55,101	7,489	11.9	358	22,106	40,874	22.0	22.5	17.8
1900 (June 1)	38,816	37,178	66,809	8,834	11.6	351	30,215	45,997	22.9	23.4	19.4
1910 (Apr. 15)	47,332	44,640	81,732	9,828	10.7	413	42,064	50,164	24.1	24.5	20.8
1920 (Jan. 1)	53,900	51,810	94,821	10,463	9.9	427	54,253	51,768	25.3	25.5	22.3
1930 (Apr. 1)	62,137	60,638	110,287	11,891	9.7	597	69,161	54,042	26.5	26.9	23.5
1940 (Apr. 1)	66,062	65,608	118,215	12,866	9.8	589	74,705	57,459	29.0	29.5	25.3
United States											
1950 (Apr. 1)	74,833	75,864	135,150	15,045	10.0	713	96,847	54,479	30.2	30.8	26.1
1960 (Apr. 1)	88,331	90,992	158,832	18,872	10.5	1,620	125,269	54,054	29.5	30.3	23.5
1970 (Apr. 1)	98,926	104,309	178,098	22,581	11.1	2,557	149,647	53,565	28.1	28.9	22.4
1980 (Apr. 1)	110,053	116,493	194,713	26,683	11.8	5,150	167,051	59,495	30.0	30.9	24.9
1990 (Apr. 1)	121,284	127,507	208,741	30,517	12.3	9,533	187,053	61,656	32.8	33.7	27.9
2000 (Apr. 1)	138,054	143,368	194,553	34,658	12.3	13,118	222,361	59,061	35.3	38.6	30.2
2010 (Apr. 1)	151,781	156,964	196,818	38,929	12.6	18,147	249,253	59,492	37.2	42.0	32.4

NA = Not available. **Note:** Population figures may reflect revisions/corrections to initial tabulated census counts. (1) Excludes Alaska and Hawaii. (2) New race categories were introduced in the 2000 census. Race data for 2000 and on are for people who reported being of one race alone. "White" does not include people who reported being of Hispanic or Latino origin. "Other" comprises Asians, Native Hawaiians and other Pacific Islanders, American Indians and Alaska Natives. Because of these changes, race data from 2000 on are not comparable to figures from previous years. (3) The Census Bureau's definition of "urban" has changed over time. Figures for 2000 and 2010 include residents of urbanized areas (50,000 or more inhabitants) and urban clusters (at least 2,500 but fewer than 50,000 inhabitants).

U.S. Population by Race and Hispanic Origin, 2000-10

Source: Decennial Censuses, U.S. Census Bureau, U.S. Dept. of Commerce

	2010		2000		% change, 2000-10[2]	
	One race alone	One or more races[1]	One race alone	One or more races[1]	One race alone	One or more races
Total population	**299,736,465**	**308,746,065**	**274,595,678**	**281,421,906**	**9.2%**	**9.7%**
Race						
White	223,553,265	231,040,398	211,460,626	216,930,975	5.7	6.5
Black or African American	38,929,319	42,020,743	34,658,190	36,419,434	12.3	15.4
Asian	14,674,252	17,320,856	10,242,998	11,898,828	43.3	45.6
American Indian and Alaska Native	2,932,248	5,220,579	2,475,956	4,119,301	18.4	26.7
Native Hawaiian and other Pac. Isl.	540,013	1,225,195	398,835	874,414	35.4	40.1
Some Other Race	19,107,368	21,748,084	15,359,073	18,521,486	24.4	17.4
Hispanic origin and race						
Hispanic or Latino, any race	47,435,002	50,477,594	33,081,736	35,305,818	43.4	43.0
Not Hispanic or Latino	252,301,463	258,267,944	241,513,942	246,116,088	4.5	4.9
White	196,817,552	201,856,108	194,552,774	198,177,900	1.2	1.9
Black or African American	37,685,848	40,123,525	33,947,837	35,383,751	11.0	13.4
Asian	14,465,124	16,722,710	10,123,169	11,579,494	42.9	44.4
American Indian and Alaska Native	2,247,098	4,029,675	2,068,883	3,444,700	8.6	17.0
Native Hawaiian and other Pac. Isl.	481,576	1,014,888	353,509	748,149	36.2	35.7
Some Other Race	604,265	1,033,866	467,770	1,770,645	29.2	–41.6

Note: Population figures may reflect revisions/corrections to initial tabulated census counts. (1) Alone or in combination with one or more of the other races listed. Numbers do not add up to totals because of individuals reporting more than one race. (2) An error in data processing resulted in the overstatement in the 2000 census of the number of people reporting more than one race, in particular race combinations involving Some Other Race. Percent change in multiple-race populations between 2000 and 2010 should ideally be calculated with specific race combinations (e.g., White and Black or White and Asian).

U.S. Population Growth by Race and Hispanic Origin, 1970-2030

Source: Decennial Censuses and Population Projections Program, U.S. Census Bureau, U.S. Dept. of Commerce
(numbers in millions)

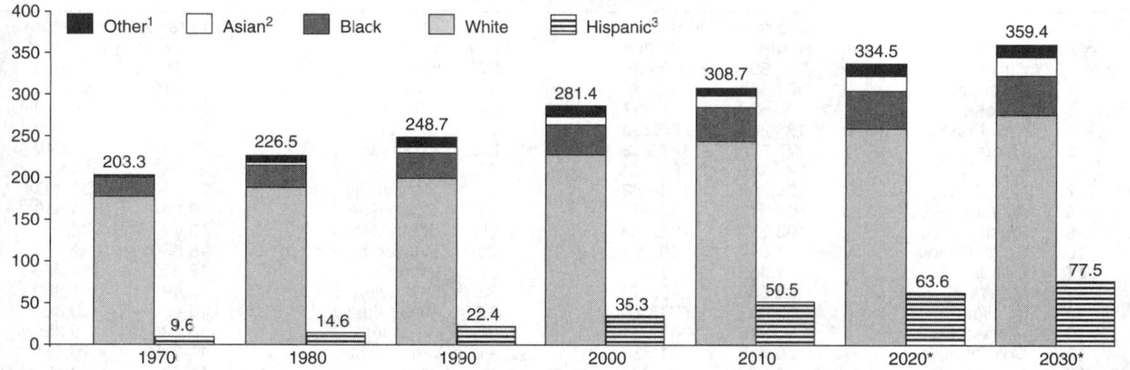

*Projected. **Note:** Because of changes in census questions and methods, data on race and Hispanic origin are not wholly comparable over time. Population figures may reflect revisions/corrections to initial tabulated census counts. (1) Includes American Indians and Alaska Natives as well as other races not shown. For 2000 and on, this category also includes Native Hawaiians and other Pacific Islanders along with persons reporting two or more races. (2) Figures for 1970-90 include Pacific Islanders. (3) May be of any race.

U.S. Race and Minority Group Percentages by State, 2010

Source: Decennial Census, U.S. Census Bureau, U.S. Dept. of Commerce
(percentage of state or country's total population)

	One race alone[1] (%)							
State	**White**	**Black or African American**	**Asian**	**American Indian and Alaska Native**	**Native Hawaiian and other Pacific Islander**	**Some other race**	**Two or more races[1] (%)**	**Hispanic or Latino, any race (%)**
Alabama	67.0%	26.0%	1.1%	0.5%	0.04%	0.08%	1.3%	3.9%
Alaska	64.1	3.1	5.3	14.4	1.02	0.16	6.4	5.5
Arizona	57.8	3.7	2.7	4.0	0.17	0.13	1.8	29.6
Arkansas	74.5	15.3	1.2	0.7	0.19	0.07	1.6	6.4
California	40.1	5.8	12.8	0.4	0.35	0.23	2.6	37.6
Colorado	70.0	3.8	2.7	0.6	0.11	0.15	2.0	20.7
Connecticut	71.2	9.4	3.8	0.2	0.03	0.34	1.7	13.4
Delaware	65.3	20.8	3.2	0.3	0.03	0.17	2.0	8.2
District of Columbia	34.8	50.0	3.5	0.2	0.04	0.24	2.1	9.1
Florida	57.9	15.2	2.4	0.3	0.05	0.26	1.5	22.5
Georgia	55.9	30.0	3.2	0.2	0.05	0.20	1.6	8.8
Hawaii	22.7	1.5	37.7	0.2	9.43	0.14	19.4	8.9
Idaho	84.0	0.6	1.2	1.1	0.14	0.10	1.7	11.2
Illinois	63.7	14.3	4.5	0.1	0.02	0.12	1.4	15.8
Indiana	81.5	9.0	1.6	0.2	0.03	0.13	1.5	6.0
Iowa	88.7	2.9	1.7	0.3	0.06	0.07	1.4	5.0
Kansas	78.2	5.7	2.3	0.8	0.07	0.10	2.3	10.5
Kentucky	86.3	7.7	1.1	0.2	0.05	0.11	1.5	3.1
Louisiana	60.3	31.8	1.5	0.6	0.03	0.15	1.3	4.2
Maine	94.4	1.1	1.0	0.6	0.02	0.08	1.4	1.3
Maryland	54.7	29.0	5.5	0.2	0.04	0.21	2.2	8.2
Massachusetts	76.1	6.0	5.3	0.2	0.02	0.94	1.9	9.6
Michigan	76.6	14.0	2.4	0.6	0.02	0.10	1.9	4.4
Minnesota	83.1	5.1	4.0	1.0	0.04	0.11	1.9	4.7
Mississippi	58.0	36.9	0.9	0.5	0.03	0.06	0.9	2.7
Missouri	81.0	11.5	1.6	0.4	0.10	0.09	1.8	3.5
Montana	87.8	0.4	0.6	6.1	0.06	0.05	2.2	2.9
Nebraska	82.1	4.4	1.7	0.8	0.05	0.12	1.6	9.2
Nevada	54.1	7.7	7.1	0.9	0.57	0.18	2.9	26.5
New Hampshire	92.3	1.0	2.1	0.2	0.02	0.14	1.4	2.8
New Jersey	59.3	12.8	8.2	0.1	0.02	0.31	1.5	17.7
New Mexico	40.5	1.7	1.3	8.5	0.06	0.18	1.4	46.3
New York	58.3	14.4	7.3	0.3	0.03	0.42	1.7	17.6
North Carolina	65.3	21.2	2.2	1.1	0.06	0.16	1.6	8.4
North Dakota	88.9	1.1	1.0	5.3	0.04	0.05	1.5	2.0
Ohio	81.1	12.0	1.7	0.2	0.03	0.13	1.8	3.1
Oklahoma	68.7	7.3	1.7	8.2	0.11	0.08	5.1	8.9
Oregon	78.5	1.7	3.6	1.1	0.33	0.14	2.9	11.7
Pennsylvania	79.5	10.4	2.7	0.1	0.02	0.13	1.4	5.7
Rhode Island	76.4	4.9	2.8	0.4	0.03	0.84	2.2	12.4
South Carolina	64.1	27.7	1.3	0.4	0.05	0.12	1.4	5.1
South Dakota	84.7	1.2	0.9	8.5	0.04	0.06	1.8	2.7
Tennessee	75.6	16.5	1.4	0.3	0.04	0.10	1.4	4.6
Texas	45.3	11.5	3.8	0.3	0.07	0.14	1.3	37.6
Utah	80.4	0.9	2.0	1.0	0.87	0.13	1.8	13.0
Vermont	94.3	0.9	1.3	0.3	0.02	0.09	1.6	1.5
Virginia	64.8	19.0	5.5	0.3	0.06	0.19	2.3	7.9
Washington	72.5	3.4	7.1	1.3	0.58	0.18	3.7	11.2
West Virginia	93.2	3.4	0.7	0.2	0.02	0.06	1.3	1.2
Wisconsin	83.3	6.2	2.3	0.9	0.03	0.07	1.4	5.9
Wyoming	85.9	0.8	0.8	2.1	0.06	0.08	1.5	8.9
United States	**63.7**	**12.2**	**4.7**	**0.7**	**0.16**	**0.20**	**1.9**	**16.3**

Note: Population figures may reflect revisions/corrections to initial tabulated census counts. (1) Not Hispanic or Latino.

American Indian and Alaska Native Population by State, 2010

Source: Decennial Census, U.S. Census Bureau, U.S. Dept. of Commerce
(ranked by one race alone)

Rank	State	One race alone[1]	More than one race[2]
1.	California	362,801	360,424
2.	Oklahoma	321,687	161,073
3.	Arizona	296,529	56,857
4.	New Mexico	193,222	26,290
5.	Texas	170,972	144,292
6.	North Carolina	122,110	61,972
7.	New York	106,906	114,152
8.	Alaska	104,871	33,441
9.	Washington	103,869	95,129
10.	South Dakota	71,817	10,256
11.	Florida	71,458	91,104
12.	Montana	62,555	16,046
13.	Michigan	62,007	77,088
14.	Minnesota	60,916	40,984
15.	Colorado	56,010	51,822
16.	Wisconsin	54,526	31,702
17.	Oregon	53,203	56,020
18.	Illinois	43,963	57,488
19.	North Dakota	36,591	6,405
20.	Utah	32,927	17,137
21.	Georgia	32,151	51,873
22.	Nevada	32,062	23,883
23.	Louisiana	30,579	24,500
24.	Virginia	29,225	51,699
25.	New Jersey	29,026	41,690
26.	Alabama	28,218	28,900
27.	Kansas	28,150	30,980
28.	Missouri	27,376	45,000
29.	Pennsylvania	26,843	54,249
30.	Ohio	25,292	64,832
31.	Arkansas	22,248	25,340
32.	Idaho	21,441	14,944
33.	Maryland	20,420	38,237
34.	Tennessee	19,994	34,880
35.	South Carolina	19,524	22,647
36.	Massachusetts	18,850	31,855
37.	Indiana	18,462	31,276
38.	Nebraska	18,427	11,389
39.	Mississippi	15,030	10,880
40.	Wyoming	13,336	5,260
41.	Connecticut	11,256	19,884
42.	Iowa	11,084	13,427
43.	Kentucky	10,120	21,235
44.	Maine	8,568	9,914
45.	Rhode Island	6,058	8,336
46.	Delaware	4,181	5,718
47.	Hawaii	4,164	29,306
48.	West Virginia	3,787	9,527
49.	New Hampshire	3,150	7,374
50.	Vermont	2,207	5,172
51.	District of Columbia	2,079	4,442
	United States	**2,932,248**	**2,288,331**

(1) Respondents who self-identified as American Indian and Alaska Native (AIAN) alone. (2) Respondents who self-identified as AIAN in combination with one or more other races.

American Indian and Alaska Native Population by Selected Tribal Groupings, 2010

Source: Decennial Census, U.S. Census Bureau, U.S. Dept. of Commerce
(ranked by American Indian and Alaska Native [AIAN] alone, one tribal grouping alone)

	AIAN alone		AIAN alone or in combination
Tribal grouping	One tribal grouping alone[1]	One or more tribal groupings[2]	One or more tribal groupings[3]
Total	**2,879,638**	**2,932,248**	**5,220,579**
AIAN tribes, not specified	693,709	693,709	1,545,963
Amer. Ind. tribes, specified	1,935,363	2,032,133	3,397,251
Navajo	286,731	295,016	332,129
Cherokee	284,247	300,463	819,105
Mexican Amer. Ind.	121,221	123,550	175,494
Chippewa	112,757	115,402	170,742
Sioux	112,176	116,477	170,110
Choctaw	103,910	110,308	195,764
Apache	63,193	69,694	111,810
Lumbee	62,306	62,957	73,691
Pueblo	49,695	52,026	62,540
Creek	48,352	52,948	88,332
Iroquois	40,570	42,461	81,002
Chickasaw	27,973	30,206	52,278
Blackfeet	27,279	31,798	105,304
Pima	22,040	23,205	26,655
Yaqui	21,679	23,195	32,595
S. Amer. Ind.	20,901	21,380	47,233
Potawatomi	20,412	20,874	33,771
Tohono O'Odham	19,522	20,247	23,478
Central Amer. Ind.	15,882	16,454	27,844
Puget Sound Salish	14,320	14,535	20,260
Seminole	14,080	16,448	31,971
Spanish Amer. Ind.	13,460	13,758	19,951
Hopi	12,580	14,634	18,327
Comanche	12,284	13,471	23,330
Cheyenne	11,375	12,493	19,051
Crow	10,332	10,860	15,203
Kiowa	9,437	10,355	13,787
Paiute	9,340	10,205	13,767
Osage	8,938	10,063	18,576
Yakama	8,786	9,096	11,527
Menominee	8,374	8,627	11,133
Houma	8,169	8,240	10,768
Colville	8,114	8,314	10,549
Arapaho	8,014	8,402	10,861
Shoshone	7,852	8,462	13,002
Delaware	7,843	8,215	18,264
Yuman	7,727	8,278	10,089
Ute	7,435	8,220	11,491
Ottawa	7,272	8,048	13,033
Canadian and French Amer. Ind.	6,433	7,051	14,822
Cree	2,211	2,950	7,983
All other tribes	270,141	282,747	429,629
Amer. Ind. tribes, not specified	131,943	132,060	234,320
AK Native tribes, specified	98,892	103,086	138,850
Yup'ik	28,927	29,618	33,889
Inupiat[4]	24,859	25,736	33,360
Alaskan Athabascan	15,623	16,427	22,484
Tlingit-Haida	15,256	16,115	26,080
Aleut	11,920	12,643	19,282
Tsimshian	2,307	2,547	3,755
AK Native tribes, not specified	19,731	19,904	29,933

Note: This table measures the number of responses, not respondents. Respondents who self-identified with multiple tribal groupings are counted more than once. A tribal grouping refers to combined individual tribes (e.g., Fort Sill Apache and San Carlos Apache as Apache or King Salmon Tribe and Native Village of Kanatak as Aleut). (1) For example, Navajo or Alaskan Athabascan. (2) As in footnote 1 or in combination with other tribal groupings (e.g., Yakama and Aleut). (3) As in footnotes 1 or 2 or in combination with another race (e.g., Apache, Navajo, and white; or Inupiat, white, and black). (4) Eskimo in previous censuses.

Largest U.S. Metropolitan Areas by Population, 2000-14

Source: Population Estimates Program and Decennial Censuses, U.S. Census Bureau, U.S. Dept. of Commerce

(ranked by 2014 population; 2014 estimates are as of July 1; 2000 and 2010 decennial census figures are for Apr. 1)

Metropolitan Statistical Areas (MSAs) are defined, or delineated geographically, for federal statistical use by the Office of Management and Budget (OMB) with technical assistance from the Census Bureau. The standards used to define metropolitan areas are revised before each decennial census. Areas are delineated using the most recently issued standards and are updated between census years.

An MSA consists of at least one urbanized area of 50,000 or more inhabitants, plus adjacent territory closely integrated socially and economically with the core as measured by commuting ties. The OMB's most recent definitions, issued in Feb. 2013, designates 381 MSAs in the U.S. About 85.5% of the resident population resided in an MSA in 2014.

Rank	Metropolitan Statistical Area	Population			Percent change	
		2014	2010	2000	2010-14	2000-14
1.	New York-Newark-Jersey City, NY-NJ-PA	20,092,883	19,567,410	18,944,519	2.7%	6.1%
2.	Los Angeles-Long Beach-Anaheim, CA	13,262,220	12,828,837	12,365,627	3.4	7.3
3.	Chicago-Naperville-Elgin, IL-IN-WI	9,554,598	9,461,105	9,098,316	1.0	5.0
4.	Dallas-Fort Worth-Arlington, TX	6,954,330	6,426,214	5,204,126	8.2	33.6
5.	Houston-The Woodlands-Sugar Land, TX	6,490,180	5,920,416	4,693,161	9.6	38.3
6.	Philadelphia-Camden-Wilmington, PA-NJ-DE-MD	6,051,170	5,965,343	5,687,147	1.4	6.4
7.	Washington-Arlington-Alexandria, DC-VA-MD-WV	6,033,737	5,636,232	4,837,428	7.1	24.7
8.	Miami-Fort Lauderdale-West Palm Beach, FL	5,929,819	5,564,635	5,007,564	6.6	18.4
9.	Atlanta-Sandy Springs-Roswell, GA	5,614,323	5,286,728	4,263,438	6.2	31.7
10.	Boston-Cambridge-Newton, MA-NH	4,732,161	4,552,402	4,391,344	3.9	7.8
11.	San Francisco-Oakland-Hayward, CA	4,594,060	4,335,391	4,123,740	6.0	11.4
12.	Phoenix-Mesa-Scottsdale, AZ	4,489,109	4,192,887	3,251,876	7.1	38.0
13.	Riverside-San Bernardino-Ontario, CA	4,441,890	4,224,851	3,254,821	5.1	36.5
14.	Detroit-Warren-Dearborn, MI	4,296,611	4,296,250	4,452,557	0.0	–3.5
15.	Seattle-Tacoma-Bellevue, WA	3,671,478	3,439,809	3,043,878	6.7	20.6
16.	Minneapolis-St. Paul-Bloomington, MN-WI	3,495,176	3,348,859	3,031,918	4.4	15.3
17.	San Diego-Carlsbad, CA	3,263,431	3,095,313	2,813,833	5.4	16.0
18.	Tampa-St. Petersburg-Clearwater, FL	2,915,582	2,783,243	2,395,997	4.8	21.7
19.	St. Louis, MO-IL	2,806,207	2,787,701	2,675,343	0.7	4.9
20.	Baltimore-Columbia-Towson, MD	2,785,874	2,710,489	2,552,994	2.8	9.1
21.	Denver-Aurora-Lakewood, CO	2,754,258	2,543,482	2,179,240	8.3	26.4
22.	Charlotte-Concord-Gastonia, NC-SC	2,380,314	2,217,012	1,717,372	7.4	38.6
23.	Pittsburgh, PA	2,355,968	2,356,285	2,431,087	0.0	–3.1
24.	Portland-Vancouver-Hillsboro, OR-WA	2,348,247	2,226,009	1,927,881	5.5	21.8
25.	San Antonio-New Braunfels, TX	2,328,652	2,142,508	1,711,703	8.7	36.0
26.	Orlando-Kissimmee-Sanford, FL	2,321,418	2,134,411	1,644,561	8.8	41.2
27.	Sacramento–Roseville–Arden-Arcade, CA	2,244,397	2,149,127	1,796,857	4.4	24.9
28.	Cincinnati, OH-KY-IN	2,149,449	2,114,580	1,994,830	1.6	7.8
29.	Kansas City, MO-KS	2,071,133	2,009,342	1,811,254	3.1	14.3
30.	Las Vegas-Henderson-Paradise, NV	2,069,681	1,951,269	1,375,765	6.1	50.4
31.	Cleveland-Elyria, OH	2,063,598	2,077,240	2,148,143	–0.7	–3.9
32.	Columbus, OH	1,994,536	1,901,974	1,675,013	4.9	19.1
33.	Indianapolis-Carmel-Anderson, IN	1,971,274	1,887,877	1,658,462	4.4	18.9
34.	San Jose-Sunnyvale-Santa Clara, CA	1,952,872	1,836,911	1,735,819	6.3	12.5
35.	Austin-Round Rock, TX	1,943,299	1,716,289	1,249,763	13.2	55.5
36.	Nashville-Davidson–Murfreesboro–Franklin, TN	1,792,649	1,670,890	1,381,287	7.3	29.8
37.	Virginia Beach-Norfolk-Newport News, VA-NC	1,716,624	1,676,822	1,580,057	2.4	8.6
38.	Providence-Warwick, RI-MA	1,609,367	1,600,852	1,582,997	0.5	1.7
39.	Milwaukee-Waukesha-West Allis, WI	1,572,245	1,555,908	1,500,741	1.0	4.8
40.	Jacksonville, FL	1,419,127	1,345,596	1,122,750	5.5	26.4
41.	Memphis, TN-MS-AR	1,343,230	1,324,829	1,213,230	1.4	10.7
42.	Oklahoma City, OK	1,336,767	1,252,987	1,095,421	6.7	22.0
43.	Louisville-Jefferson County, KY-IN	1,269,702	1,235,708	1,121,109	2.8	13.3
44.	Richmond, VA	1,260,029	1,208,101	1,055,683	4.3	19.4
45.	New Orleans-Metairie, LA	1,251,849	1,189,866	1,337,726	5.2	–6.4
46.	Raleigh, NC	1,242,974	1,130,490	797,071	10.0	55.9
47.	Hartford-West Hartford-East Hartford, CT	1,214,295	1,212,381	1,148,618	0.2	5.7
48.	Salt Lake City, UT	1,153,340	1,087,873	939,122	6.0	22.8
49.	Birmingham-Hoover, AL	1,143,772	1,128,047	1,052,238	1.4	8.7
50.	Buffalo-Cheektowaga-Niagara Falls, NY	1,136,360	1,135,509	1,170,111	0.1	–2.9
51.	Rochester, NY	1,083,393	1,079,671	1,062,452	0.3	2.0
52.	Grand Rapids-Wyoming, MI	1,027,703	988,938	930,670	3.9	10.4
53.	Tucson, AZ	1,004,516	980,263	843,746	2.5	19.1
54.	Urban Honolulu, HI	991,788	953,207	876,156	4.0	13.2
55.	Tulsa, OK	969,224	937,478	859,532	3.4	12.8
56.	Fresno, CA	965,974	930,450	799,407	3.8	20.8
57.	Bridgeport-Stamford-Norwalk, CT	945,438	916,829	882,567	3.1	7.1
58.	Worcester, MA-CT	930,473	916,980	860,054	1.5	8.2
59.	Albuquerque, NM	904,587	887,077	729,649	2.0	24.0
60.	Omaha-Council Bluffs, NE-IA	904,421	865,350	767,041	4.5	17.9
61.	Albany-Schenectady-Troy, NY	880,167	870,716	825,875	1.1	6.6
62.	Bakersfield, CA	874,589	839,631	661,645	4.2	32.2
63.	Greenville-Anderson-Mauldin, SC	862,463	824,112	725,680	4.7	18.8
64.	New Haven-Milford, CT	861,277	862,477	824,008	–0.1	4.5
65.	Knoxville, TN	857,585	837,571	748,259	2.4	14.6
66.	Oxnard-Thousand Oaks-Ventura, CA	846,178	823,318	753,197	2.8	12.3
67.	El Paso, TX	836,698	804,123	682,966	4.1	22.5
68.	McAllen-Edinburg-Mission, TX	831,073	774,769	569,463	7.3	45.9
69.	Allentown-Bethlehem-Easton, PA-NJ	829,835	821,173	740,395	1.1	12.1
70.	Baton Rouge, LA	825,478	802,484	705,973	2.9	16.9
71.	Dayton, OH	800,836	799,232	805,816	0.2	–0.6
72.	Columbia, SC	800,495	767,598	647,158	4.3	23.7

Largest U.S. Cities by Population, 1850-2014

Source: Population Estimates Program and Decennial Censuses, U.S. Census Bureau, U.S. Dept. of Commerce
(ranked by 2014 population)

Rank	City	2014	2000	1990	1980	1970	1950	1900	1850
1.	New York, NY	8,491,079	8,008,654	7,322,564	7,071,639	7,895,563	7,891,957	3,437,202	515,547
2.	Los Angeles, CA	3,928,864	3,694,742	3,485,557	2,968,528	2,811,801	1,970,358	102,479	1,610
3.	Chicago, IL	2,722,389	2,896,016	2,783,726	3,005,072	3,369,357	3,620,962	1,698,575	29,963
4.	Houston, TX	2,239,558	1,953,631	1,630,864	1,595,138	1,233,535	596,163	44,633	2,396
5.	Philadelphia, PA	1,560,297	1,517,550	1,585,577	1,688,210	1,949,996	2,071,605	1,293,697	121,376
6.	Phoenix, AZ	1,537,058	1,321,045	983,392	789,704	584,303	106,818	5,544	—
7.	San Antonio, TX	1,436,697	1,144,646	935,393	785,940	654,153	408,442	53,321	3,488
8.	San Diego, CA	1,381,069	1,223,400	1,110,623	875,538	697,471	334,387	17,700	—
9.	Dallas, TX	1,281,047	1,188,580	1,007,618	904,599	844,401	434,462	42,638	—
10.	San Jose, CA	1,015,785	894,943	782,224	629,400	459,913	95,280	21,500	—
11.	Austin, TX	912,791	656,562	465,648	345,890	253,539	132,459	22,258	629
12.	Jacksonville, FL[1]	853,382	735,617	635,230	540,920	504,265	204,517	28,429	1,045
13.	San Francisco, CA[2]	852,469	776,733	723,959	678,974	715,674	775,357	342,782	34,776
14.	Indianapolis, IN[1]	848,788	791,926	741,915	710,868	746,992	427,173	169,164	8,091
15.	Columbus, OH	835,957	711,470	632,945	565,021	540,025	375,901	125,560	17,882
16.	Fort Worth, TX	812,238	534,694	447,619	385,164	393,455	278,778	26,688	—
17.	Charlotte, NC	809,958	540,167	395,934	315,474	241,420	134,042	18,091	1,065
18.	Detroit, MI	680,250	951,270	1,027,974	1,203,368	1,514,063	1,849,568	285,704	21,019
19.	El Paso, TX	679,036	563,662	515,342	425,259	322,261	130,485	15,906	—
20.	Seattle, WA	668,342	563,376	516,259	493,846	530,831	467,591	80,671	—
21.	Denver, CO	663,862	553,693	467,610	492,686	514,678	415,786	133,859	—
22.	Washington, DC	658,893	572,059	606,900	638,432	756,668	802,178	278,718	40,001
23.	Memphis, TN	656,861	650,100	610,337	646,174	623,988	396,000	102,320	8,841
24.	Boston, MA	655,884	589,141	574,283	562,994	641,071	801,444	560,892	136,881
25.	Nashville-Davidson, TN[1]	644,014	569,892	510,786	477,811	447,877	174,307	80,865	10,165
26.	Baltimore, MD	622,793	651,154	736,014	786,741	905,787	949,708	508,957	169,054
27.	Oklahoma City, OK	620,602	506,132	444,724	404,014	368,164	243,504	10,037	—
28.	Portland, OR	619,360	529,121	438,802	368,148	379,967	373,628	90,426	—
29.	Las Vegas, NV	613,599	479,137	258,204	164,674	125,787	24,624	—	—
30.	Louisville/Jefferson Co., KY[1]	612,780	256,231	269,555	298,694	361,706	369,129	204,731	43,194
31.	Milwaukee, WI	599,642	596,974	628,088	636,297	717,372	637,392	285,315	20,061
32.	Albuquerque, NM	557,169	448,607	384,619	332,619	244,920	96,815	6,238	—
33.	Tucson, AZ	527,972	486,699	405,371	330,537	262,933	45,454	7,531	—
34.	Fresno, CA	515,986	427,652	354,091	217,491	165,655	91,669	12,470	—
35.	Sacramento, CA	485,199	407,018	369,365	275,741	257,105	137,572	29,282	6,820
36.	Long Beach, CA	473,577	461,522	429,321	361,498	358,879	250,767	2,252	—
37.	Kansas City, MO	470,800	441,545	434,829	448,028	507,330	456,622	163,752	—
38.	Mesa, AZ	464,704	396,375	288,104	152,404	63,049	16,790	722	—
39.	Atlanta, GA	456,002	416,267	393,929	425,022	495,039	331,314	89,872	2,572
40.	Virginia Beach, VA	450,980	425,257	393,089	262,199	172,106	5,390	—	—
41.	Omaha, NE	446,599	390,007	335,719	313,939	346,929	251,117	102,555	—
42.	Colorado Springs, CO	445,830	360,890	280,430	215,105	135,517	45,472	21,085	—
43.	Raleigh, NC	439,896	276,094	212,092	150,255	122,830	65,679	13,643	4,518
44.	Miami, FL	430,332	362,470	358,648	346,681	334,859	249,276	1,681	—
45.	Oakland, CA	413,775	399,484	372,242	339,337	361,561	384,575	66,960	—
46.	Minneapolis, MN	407,207	382,747	368,383	370,951	434,400	521,718	202,718	—
47.	Tulsa, OK	399,682	393,049	367,302	360,919	330,350	182,740	1,390	—
48.	Cleveland, OH	389,521	477,459	505,616	573,822	750,879	914,808	381,768	17,034
49.	Wichita, KS	388,413	346,753	304,017	279,838	276,554	168,279	24,671	—
50.	New Orleans, LA	384,320	484,674	496,938	557,927	593,471	570,445	287,104	116,375
51.	Arlington, TX	383,204	332,969	261,717	160,113	90,229	7,692	1,079	—
52.	Bakersfield, CA	368,759	246,889	174,978	105,611	69,515	34,784	4,836	—
53.	Tampa, FL	358,699	303,447	280,015	271,577	277,714	124,681	15,839	—
54.	Aurora, CO	353,108	275,921	222,103	158,588	74,974	11,421	202	—
55.	Urban Honolulu, HI[3]	350,399	371,657	365,272	365,048	324,871	248,034	39,306	—
56.	Anaheim, CA	346,997	328,014	266,406	219,494	166,408	14,556	1,456	—
57.	Santa Ana, CA	334,909	337,977	293,827	204,023	155,710	45,533	4,933	—
58.	Corpus Christi, TX	320,434	277,454	257,453	232,134	204,525	108,287	4,703	—
59.	Riverside, CA	319,504	255,166	226,546	170,591	140,089	46,764	7,973	—
60.	St. Louis, MO	317,419	348,189	396,685	452,801	622,236	856,796	575,238	77,860
61.	Lexington-Fayette Urban Co., KY[1]	310,797	260,512	225,366	204,165	108,137	55,534	26,369	8,159
62.	Pittsburgh, PA	305,412	334,563	369,879	423,959	520,089	676,806	321,616	46,601
63.	Stockton, CA	302,389	243,771	210,943	148,283	109,963	70,853	17,506	—
64.	Anchorage, AK	301,010	260,283	226,338	174,431	48,081	11,254	—	—
65.	Cincinnati, OH	298,165	331,285	364,040	385,409	453,514	503,998	325,902	115,435
66.	St. Paul, MN	297,640	286,840	272,235	270,230	309,866	311,349	163,065	1,112
67.	Greensboro, NC	282,586	223,891	183,894	155,642	144,076	74,389	10,035	—
68.	Toledo, OH	282,313	313,782	332,943	354,635	383,062	303,616	131,822	3,829
69.	Newark, NJ	280,579	272,537	275,221	329,248	381,930	438,776	246,070	38,894
70.	Plano, TX	278,480	222,030	127,885	72,331	17,872	2,126	1,304	—
71.	Henderson, NV	277,440	175,381	64,948	24,363	16,395	—	—	—
72.	Lincoln, NE	272,996	225,581	191,972	171,932	149,518	98,884	40,169	—
73.	Orlando, FL	262,372	185,951	164,674	128,291	99,006	52,367	2,481	—
74.	Jersey City, NJ	262,146	240,055	228,517	223,532	260,350	299,017	206,433	6,856
75.	Chula Vista, CA	260,988	173,556	135,160	83,927	67,901	15,927	—	—
76.	Buffalo, NY	258,703	292,648	328,175	357,870	462,768	580,132	352,387	42,261
77.	Fort Wayne, IN	258,522	205,727	172,971	172,391	178,269	133,607	45,115	4,282
78.	Chandler, AZ	254,276	176,581	89,862	29,673	13,763	3,799	—	—
79.	St. Petersburg, FL	253,693	248,232	240,318	238,647	216,159	96,738	1,575	—
80.	Laredo, TX	252,309	176,576	122,899	91,449	69,024	51,910	13,429	—

Rank	City	2014	2000	1990	1980	1970	1950	1900	1850
81.	Durham, NC	251,893	187,035	136,612	101,149	95,438	71,311	6,679	—
82.	Irvine, CA	248,531	143,072	110,330	62,134	—	—	—	—
83.	Madison, WI	245,691	208,054	190,766	170,616	171,809	96,056	19,164	1,525
84.	Norfolk, VA	245,428	234,403	261,250	266,979	307,951	213,513	46,624	14,326
85.	Lubbock, TX	243,839	199,564	186,206	174,361	149,101	71,747	—	—
86.	Gilbert, AZ	239,277	109,697	29,122	5,717	1,971	1,114	—	—
87.	Winston-Salem, NC	239,269	185,776	143,485	131,885	133,683	87,811	13,650	—
88.	Glendale, AZ	237,517	218,812	147,864	97,172	36,228	8,179	—	—
89.	Reno, NV	236,995	180,480	133,850	100,756	72,863	32,497	4,500	—
90.	Hialeah, FL	235,563	226,419	188,008	145,254	102,452	19,676	—	—
91.	Garland, TX	235,501	215,768	180,635	138,857	81,437	10,571	819	—
92.	Chesapeake, VA	233,371	199,184	151,982	114,486	89,580	—	—	—
93.	Irving, TX	232,406	191,615	155,037	109,943	97,260	2,621	—	—
94.	North Las Vegas, NV	230,788	115,488	47,849	42,739	46,067	3,875	—	—
95.	Scottsdale, AZ	230,512	202,705	130,075	88,622	67,823	—	—	—
96.	Baton Rouge, LA	228,895	227,818	219,531	220,394	165,291	125,629	11,269	3,905
97.	Fremont, CA	228,758	203,413	173,339	131,945	100,869	—	—	—
98.	Richmond, VA	217,853	197,790	202,798	219,214	249,332	230,310	85,050	27,570
99.	Boise City, ID	216,282	185,787	125,551	102,249	74,990	34,393	5,957	—
100.	San Bernardino, CA	215,213	185,401	164,676	117,389	108,794	63,058	6,150	—

Note: 2014 population estimates are as of July 1. Decennial census figures for 1950-2010 are for Apr. 1; 1850 and 1900 are for June 1. Figures may reflect revisions/corrections to initial tabulated census counts. Cities are incorporated places unless otherwise noted. (1) Consolidated city-county government. For years predating consolidation, city population figures are shown. (2) 1850 figure is for 1852, from state census. 1850 census results were destroyed by fire. (3) Census designated place (CDP). Figures for years prior to 2014 are for Honolulu CDP and are not directly comparable.

Population Change in Largest U.S. Cities, 2010-14

Source: Population Estimates Program and Decennial Census, U.S. Census Bureau, U.S. Dept. of Commerce
(ranked by % change, 2010-14; 2014 estimates are as of July 1; 2010 decennial census figures are for Apr. 1)

Cities With Most Growth

Rank	City	Population 2014	Population 2010	% change, 2010-14
1.	Irvine, CA	248,531	212,375	17.0%
2.	Austin, TX	912,791	790,390	15.5
3.	Gilbert, AZ	239,277	208,453	14.8
4.	New Orleans, LA	384,320	343,829	11.8
5.	Charlotte, NC	809,958	731,424	10.7
6.	Denver, CO	663,862	600,158	10.6
7.	Durham, NC	251,893	228,330	10.3
8.	Orlando, FL	262,372	238,300	10.1
9.	Seattle, WA	668,342	608,660	9.8
10.	Fort Worth, TX	812,238	741,206	9.6
11.	Washington, DC	658,893	601,723	9.5
12.	Omaha, NE	446,599	408,958	9.2
13.	Raleigh, NC	439,896	403,892	8.9
14.	Aurora, CO	353,108	325,078	8.6
15.	Atlanta, GA	456,002	420,003	8.6
16.	San Antonio, TX	1,436,697	1,327,407	8.2
17.	Miami, FL	430,332	399,457	7.7
18.	Chandler, AZ	254,276	236,123	7.7
19.	Henderson, NV	277,440	257,729	7.6
20.	Irving, TX	232,406	216,290	7.5

Cities With Least Growth

Rank	City	Population 2014	Population 2010	% change, 2010-14
1.	Detroit, MI	680,250	713,777	–4.7%
2.	Toledo, OH	281,031	287,208	–2.2
3.	Cleveland, OH	389,521	396,815	–1.8
4.	Buffalo, NY	258,703	261,310	–1.0
5.	St. Louis, MO	317,419	319,294	–0.6
6.	Baton Rouge, LA	228,895	229,493	–0.3
7.	Pittsburgh, PA	305,412	305,704	–0.1
8.	Baltimore, MD	622,793	620,961	0.3
9.	Cincinnati, OH	298,165	296,943	0.4
10.	Milwaukee, WI	599,642	594,833	0.8
11.	Chicago, IL	2,722,389	2,695,598	1.0
12.	Norfolk, VA	245,428	242,803	1.1
13.	Newark, NJ	280,579	277,140	1.2
14.	Tucson, AZ	527,972	520,116	1.5
15.	Memphis, TN	656,861	646,889	1.5
16.	Wichita, KS	388,413	382,368	1.6
17.	Fort Wayne, IN	258,522	253,691	1.9
18.	Tulsa, OK	399,682	391,906	2.0
19.	Albuquerque, NM	557,169	545,852	2.1
20.	Philadelphia, PA	1,560,297	1,526,006	2.2

Note: This table shows which of the 100 largest U.S. cities by 2014 population size experienced the most and least population growth since 2010. Figures may reflect revisions/corrections to initial tabulated census counts. Cities are typically incorporated places.

Largest U.S. Counties by Population, 2000, 2014

Source: Population Estimates Program and Decennial Census, U.S. Census Bureau, U.S. Dept. of Commerce
(ranked by 2014 population; 2014 estimates are as of July 1; 2000 decennial census figures are for Apr. 1)

Rank	County	2014	2000	% change, 2000-14
1.	Los Angeles Co., CA	10,116,705	9,519,338	6.3%
2.	Cook Co., IL	5,246,456	5,376,815	–2.4
3.	Harris Co., TX	4,441,370	3,400,578	30.6
4.	Maricopa Co., AZ	4,087,191	3,072,149	33.0
5.	San Diego Co., CA	3,263,431	2,813,833	16.0
6.	Orange Co., CA	3,145,515	2,846,289	10.5
7.	Miami-Dade Co., FL	2,662,874	2,253,779	18.2
8.	Kings Co., NY	2,621,793	2,465,525	6.3
9.	Dallas Co., TX	2,518,638	2,218,774	13.5
10.	Riverside Co., CA	2,329,271	1,545,387	50.7
11.	Queens Co., NY	2,321,580	2,229,379	4.1
12.	San Bernardino Co., CA	2,112,619	1,709,434	23.6
13.	King Co., WA	2,079,967	1,737,044	19.7
14.	Clark Co., NV	2,069,681	1,375,765	50.4
15.	Tarrant Co., TX	1,945,360	1,446,219	34.5
16.	Santa Clara Co., CA	1,894,605	1,682,585	12.6%
17.	Broward Co., FL	1,869,235	1,623,018	15.2
18.	Bexar Co., TX	1,855,866	1,392,931	33.2
19.	Wayne Co., MI	1,764,804	2,061,162	–14.4
20.	New York Co., NY	1,636,268	1,537,372	6.4
21.	Alameda Co., CA	1,610,921	1,443,741	11.6
22.	Middlesex Co., MA	1,570,315	1,466,394	7.1
23.	Philadelphia Co., PA	1,560,297	1,517,550	2.8
24.	Suffolk Co., NY	1,502,968	1,419,369	5.9
25.	Sacramento Co., CA	1,482,026	1,223,499	21.1
26.	Bronx Co., NY	1,438,159	1,332,650	7.9
27.	Palm Beach Co., FL	1,397,710	1,131,191	23.6
28.	Nassau Co., NY	1,358,627	1,334,544	1.8
29.	Hillsborough Co., FL	1,316,298	998,948	31.8
30.	Cuyahoga Co., OH	1,259,828	1,393,845	–9.6

Note: Decennial pop. figures may reflect revisions/corrections to initial tabulated census counts. The 10 smallest counties by estimated 2014 population: (1) Loving Co., TX (pop. 86); (2) Kalawao Co., HI (89); (3) King Co., TX (262); (4) Kenedy Co., TX (400); (5) Arthur Co., NE (453); (6) Petroleum Co., MT (485); (7) McPherson Co., NE (498); (8) Blaine Co., NE (504); (9) Loup Co., NE (588); and (10) Grant Co., NE (619).

Mobility of U.S. Population by Selected Characteristics, 2013-14

Source: Annual Social and Economic Supplement, Current Population Survey (CPS), U.S. Census Bureau, U.S. Dept. of Commerce

(numbers in thousands)

	Total movers	Location of new residence: Same county	Diff. county, same state	Diff. state	Abroad
Sex					
Male	17,737	11,705	3,204	2,227	599
Female	17,944	11,731	3,242	2,438	534
Age					
1 to 14 years	7,881	5,477	1,300	916	188
15 years and older	27,799	17,962	5,145	3,748	945
25 years and older	20,274	13,014	3,781	2,785	694
65 years and older	1,474	885	315	235	39
85 years and older	183	100	50	29	5
Educational attainment[1]					
Not a h.s. graduate	2,469	1,728	381	239	121
High school graduate	5,390	3,635	1,037	599	118
Some college or associate degree	5,648	3,683	1,083	759	123
Bachelor's degree	4,368	2,678	810	692	187
Prof. or grad. degree	2,401	1,287	471	497	145
Marital status[2]					
Married, spouse present	9,629	5,862	1,805	1,573	390
Married, spouse absent	519	348	71	58	42
Widowed	753	493	154	86	20
Divorced	3,097	2,050	648	352	48
Separated	1,013	727	155	103	28
Never married	12,788	8,480	2,313	1,577	417
Nativity					
Native	30,631	20,302	5,787	4,145	397
Foreign born	5,050	3,134	660	519	736
Tenure					
In owner-occupied unit	10,345	6,644	2,130	1,265	306
In renter-occupied unit[3]	25,337	16,792	4,317	3,400	827
Total movers	**35,681**	**23,436**	**6,446**	**4,666**	**1,133**

Note: Total movers consists of persons ages 1 and older who moved to a new residence in the 12 months preceding the administering of the survey. Figures may not add up to totals due to rounding. (1) Ages 25 and older. (2) Ages 15 and older. (3) Includes units occupied without payment of cash rent.

Population by Urban and Rural, 1790-2010

Source: Decennial Censuses, U.S. Census Bureau, U.S. Dept. of Commerce

The Census Bureau currently defines an area as urban if it has at least 2,500 people (at least 1,500 of which are not in institutional group quarters, such as a correctional facility). All other areas are considered rural. Prior to 1950, the definition of urban was limited to incorporated places and other areas meeting certain criteria.

Year	Total pop.	No. of places of 2,500 or more	% of total pop.: Urban	Rural
Pre-1950 urban definition				
1790	3,929,214	24	5.1%	94.9%
1800	5,308,483	33	6.1	93.9
1810	7,239,881	46	7.3	92.7
1820	9,638,453	61	7.2	92.8
1830	12,860,702	90	8.8	91.2
1840	17,063,353	131	10.8	89.2
1850	23,191,876	237	15.4	84.6
1860	31,443,321	392	19.8	80.2
1870	38,558,371	663	25.7	74.3
1880	50,189,209	939	28.2	71.8
1890	62,979,766	1,348	35.1	64.9
1900	76,212,168	1,740	39.6	60.4
1910	92,228,496	2,266	45.6	54.4
1920	106,021,537	2,725	51.2	48.8
1930	123,202,624	3,183	56.1%	43.9%
1940	132,164,569	3,485	56.5	43.5
1950	151,325,798	4,077	59.6	40.4
1960	179,323,175	5,023	63.1	36.9
1950-90 urban definition				
1950	151,325,798	4,307	64.0	36.0
1960	179,323,175	5,445	69.9	30.1
1970	203,302,031	6,433	73.6	26.3
1980	226,542,199	7,749	73.7	26.3
1990	248,718,302	8,510	75.2	24.8
Current urban definition				
1990	248,718,302	8,510	78.0	22.0
2000	281,424,603	9,063	79.0	21.0
2010	308,746,065	9,644	80.7	19.3

Note: Figures may not add up to 100 due to rounding.

U.S. Households by Size, 1900-2010

Source: Decennial Censuses, U.S. Census Bureau, U.S. Dept. of Commerce

The household population does not include those living in group quarters (either institutionalized like a correctional facility or noninstitutionalized like a college dormitory). Data not available for 1930; 1950 figures are based on a sample of the population. Average household size is shown above each bar.

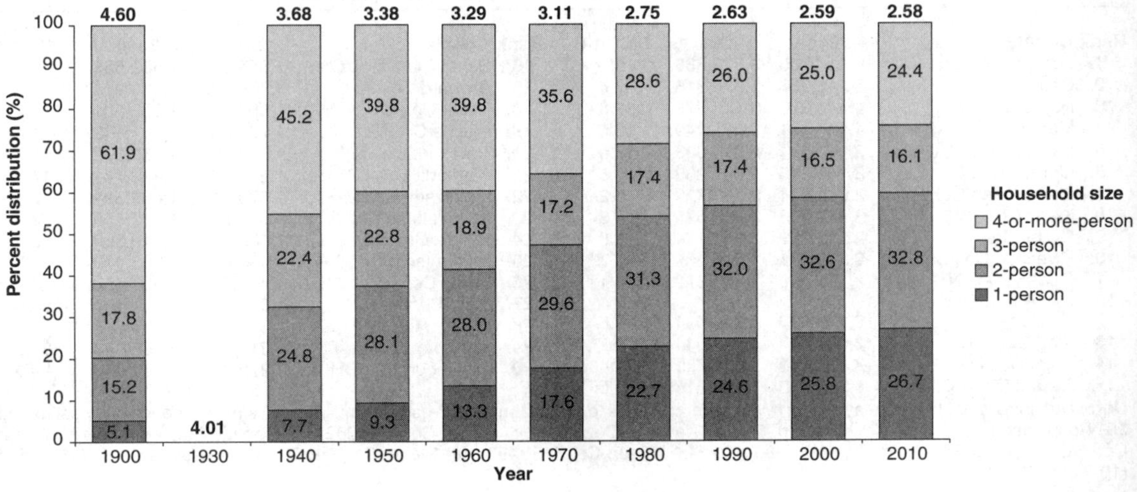

U.S. Population by Age, Sex, and Household, 2014

Source: American Community Survey (ACS), U.S. Census Bureau, U.S. Dept. of Commerce

	Number	% of tot.
Total population[1]	**318,857,056**	**100.0%**
Age		
Under 5 years	19,773,010	6.2
5 to 14 years	41,313,376	13.0
15 to 17 years	12,491,037	3.9
15 to 44 years	128,119,504	40.2
18 years and over	245,279,633	76.9
Male	119,274,182	37.4
Female	126,005,451	39.5
18 to 24 years	31,554,009	9.9
25 to 34 years	43,323,099	13.6
35 to 44 years	40,751,359	12.8
45 to 54 years	43,353,277	13.6
55 to 64 years	40,082,996	12.6
65 years and over	46,214,893	14.5
75 years and over	19,796,689	6.2
85 years and over	6,045,970	1.9
Median age (years)	37.7	NA

	Number	% of tot.
Sex		
Male	156,890,101	49.2%
Female	161,966,955	50.8
Total households[2]	**117,259,427**	**100.0%**
Family households	77,152,072	65.8
2-person household	33,522,309	28.6
3-person household	17,437,286	14.9
4-person household	14,754,728	12.6
5-or-more-person household	11,437,749	9.8
Married-couple family household	56,114,671	47.9
Male HH, no wife present	5,765,116	4.9
Female HH, no husband present	15,272,285	13.0
Nonfamily households	40,107,355	34.2
1-person household, or HH living alone	32,593,690	27.8
HH 65 years and over	12,122,226	10.3
2-person household	6,087,175	5.2
3-or-more-person household	1,426,490	1.2
Average household size	2.65	NA

NA = Not applicable. HH = Householder, or person in whose name a home is owned or rented. **Note:** Data based on sample and subject to sampling variability. (1) Includes population living in group quarters (institutional and noninstitutional, e.g., correctional facilities, university housing). (2) Number of occupied housing units, not household members. Group quarters are not considered households.

Elderly U.S. Population, 1900-2060

Source: Decennial Censuses and Population Projections Program, U.S. Census Bureau, U.S. Dept. of Commerce
(numbers of resident population in thousands)

	65 and over		85 and over	
Year	**Number**	**% tot. pop.**	**Number**	**% tot. pop.**
1900[1]	3,080	4.1%	122	0.2%
1920[1]	4,933	4.7	210	0.2
1940[1]	9,019	6.8	365	0.3
1960	16,560	9.2	929	0.5
1980	25,549	11.3	2,240	1.0
2000	34,992	12.4	4,240	1.5
2010	40,268	13.0%	5,493	1.8%
2020	56,441	16.9	6,727	2.0
2030	74,107	20.6	9,132	2.5
2040	82,344	21.7	14,634	3.9
2050	87,996	22.1	18,972	4.8
2060	98,164	23.6	19,724	4.7

Note: 1900 figures are for June 1; 1920 figures are for Jan. 1; and 1940-2010 figures are for Apr. 1. 2020-60 projections are as of July 1. (1) Excludes Alaska and Hawaii.

U.S. Population Projections by Age, 2020-60

Source: Population Projections Program, U.S. Census Bureau, U.S. Dept. of Commerce
(numbers of resident population in thousands)

	2020		2030		2040		2050		2060	
Age	**No.**	**% distrib.**	**No.**	**% distrib.**	**No.**	**% distrib.**	**No.**	**% distrib.**	**No.**	**% distrib.**
Total	**334,503**	**100.0%**	**359,402**	**100.0%**	**380,219**	**100.0%**	**398,328**	**100.0%**	**416,795**	**100.0%**
Under 5 years	20,568	6.2	21,178	5.9	21,471	5.7	22,147	5.6	22,778	5.5
5 to 13 years	36,824	11.0	38,322	10.7	39,087	10.3	39,887	10.0	41,193	9.9
14 to 17 years	16,737	5.0	16,773	4.7	17,627	4.6	17,854	4.5	18,338	4.4
18 to 24 years	30,555	9.1	30,794	8.6	31,815	8.4	32,717	8.2	33,300	8.0
25 to 44 years	89,518	26.8	95,795	26.7	96,854	25.5	99,653	25.0	103,010	24.7
45 to 64 years	83,861	25.1	82,434	22.9	91,021	23.9	98,074	24.6	100,013	24.0
65 years and over	56,441	16.9	74,107	20.6	82,344	21.7	87,996	22.1	98,164	23.6
85 years and over	6,727	2.0	9,132	2.5	14,634	3.9	18,972	4.8	19,724	4.7
100 years and over	89	0.0	138	0.0	193	0.1	387	0.1	604	0.1

Note: Projections are as of July 1 of given year. They are based on assumptions about future births, deaths, and net international migration.

Disability Status of U.S. Population by Age, 2014

Source: American Community Survey (ACS), U.S. Census Bureau, U.S. Dept. of Commerce
(numbers in thousands, by disability type)

Characteristic	Number	% of pop.
Total population (all ages)	**313,890**	**100.00%**
With a disability[1]	39,675	12.64
Under 5 years	154	0.05
Under 18 years	3,054	0.97
18 to 64 years	20,460	6.52
65 years and over	16,161	5.15
With a hearing difficulty	11,238	3.58
Under 5 years	105	0.03
Under 18 years	438	0.14
18 to 64 years	4,058	1.29
65 years and over	6,742	2.15
With a vision difficulty	7,346	2.34
Under 5 years	89	0.03
Under 18 years	544	0.17
18 to 64 years	3,803	1.21
65 years and over	2,999	0.96

Characteristic	Number	% of pop.
Total population (5 and over)	**294,119**	**100.00%**
With a cognitive difficulty[2]	14,985	5.09
5 to 17 years	2,215	0.75
18 to 64 years	8,669	2.95
65 years and over	4,100	1.39
With an ambulatory difficulty[3]	20,917	7.11
5 to 17 years	341	0.12
18 to 64 years	10,225	3.48
65 years and over	10,351	3.52
With a self-care difficulty[4]	7,943	2.70
5 to 17 years	512	0.17
18 to 64 years	3,645	1.24
65 years and over	3,785	1.29
Total population (18 and over)	**240,450**	**100.00%**
With an independent living difficulty[5]	14,073	5.85
18 to 64 years	7,224	3.00
65 years and over	6,849	2.85

Note: Data based on sample and subject to sampling variability. Does not include military personnel and civilian institutionalized population (i.e., those under formal supervision or custody in a facility). (1) Identified by the ACS as persons "who exhibit difficulty with specific functions and may, in the absence of accommodation, have a disability." (2) Concentrating, remembering, or making decisions. (3) Walking or climbing stairs. (4) Dressing or bathing. (5) Doing errands alone, such as visiting a doctor's office or shopping.

Marital Status of the U.S. Population, 1960-2014

Source: Annual Social and Economic Supplements, Current Population Surveys (CPS), U.S. Census Bureau, U.S. Dept. of Commerce
(numbers in millions)

Marital status	Both sexes 2014	2000	1980	1960	Male 2014	2000	1980	1960	Female 2014	2000	1980	1960
Total	**252.2**	**213.8**	**171.9**	**124.9**	**122.4**	**103.1**	**81.9**	**60.3**	**129.9**	**110.7**	**89.9**	**64.6**
Married[1]	132.6	120.2	104.8	84.4	65.9	59.7	51.8	41.8	66.7	60.5	53.0	42.6
Never married	80.0	60.0	44.5	27.5	42.7	32.3	24.2	15.3	37.3	27.8	20.2	12.3
Divorced	25.3	19.9	9.9	2.8	10.7	8.6	3.9	1.1	14.6	11.3	6.0	1.7
Widowed	14.3	13.7	12.7	10.2	3.1	2.6	2.0	2.1	11.2	11.1	10.8	8.1
% of total or subset pops.												
Married[1]	52.6%	56.2%	61.0%	67.6%	53.8%	57.9%	63.2%	69.3%	51.4%	54.7%	58.9%	65.9%
Never married	31.7	28.1	25.9	22.0	34.9	31.3	29.6	25.3	28.7	25.1	22.5	19.0
Divorced	10.0	9.3	5.8	2.3	8.8	8.3	4.8	1.8	11.3	10.2	6.6	2.6
Widowed	5.7	6.4	7.4	8.1	2.5	2.5	2.4	3.5	8.6	10.0	12.0	12.5

Note: Total population for 1980, 2000, and 2014 is persons ages 15 and older and for 1960, persons ages 14 and older. Data is based on sample of occupied households in the civilian noninstitutional population. Figures may not add up to totals due to rounding. (1) Comprises subcategories Married, spouse present; Married, spouse absent; and Separated.

Living Arrangements of Children in the U.S. by Parental Presence, 1970-2014

Source: Annual Social and Economic Supplements, Current Population Surveys (CPS), U.S. Census Bureau, U.S. Dept. of Commerce

		% of children (within selected population at left) living with—								
			Mother only—							
Race and Hispanic origin/year	**No. of children (thous.)**	**Both parents[4]**	**Total[5]**	**Married spouse absent**	**Divorced**	**Widowed**	**Never married**	**Father only**	**Neither parent**
All children									
2014	73,692	69%	24%	1%	7%	1%	11%	4%	4%
White alone[1]									
1970	58,791	90	8	3	3	2	Z	1	2
1980	52,242	83	14	4	7	2	1	2	2
1990	51,390	79	16	4	8	1	3	3	2
2000	56,455	75	17	NA	NA	NA	NA	4	3
2014	53,881	74	19	1	7	1	7	4	3
Black alone[1]									
1970	9,422	58	30	16	5	4	4	2	10
1980	9,375	42	44	16	11	4	13	2	12
1990	10,018	38	51	12	10	2	27	4	8
2000	11,412	38	49	NA	NA	NA	NA	4	9
2014	11,080	39	51	2	8	1	35	4	6
Hispanic[2]									
1970[3]	4,006	78	NA	NA	NA	NA	NA	NA	NA
1980	5,459	75	20	8	6	2	4	2	3
1990	7,174	67	27	10	7	2	8	3	3
2000	11,613	65	25	NA	NA	NA	NA	4	5
2014	17,871	65	28	2	6	1	13	3	4

NA = Not available. Z = Less than 1%. **Note:** Children are defined as all persons under 18 years of age excluding those who are a family reference person or spouse. Data based on sample of occupied households in the civilian noninstitutional population. (1) One race only, not in combination with another race. (2) May be of any race. (3) Data based on 1970 decennial census. (4) Includes married and unmarried couples. (5) Includes children whose mothers are separated, a subcategory not shown in detail here.

Children in the U.S. by Parental Presence, 2014

Source: Annual Social and Economic Supplement, Current Population Survey (CPS), U.S. Census Bureau, U.S. Dept. of Commerce
(numbers in thousands)

	Number	% of total
Total children	**73,692**	**100.0%**
Living with 2 parents	50,602	68.7
Married parents	47,491	64.4
Unmarried parents	3,111	4.2
Biological mother and father	45,717	62.0
Married parents	43,011	58.4
Biological mother and stepfather	2,896	3.9
Biological father and stepmother	911	1.2
Biological mother and adoptive father	165	0.2
Biological father and adoptive mother	35	0.0
Adoptive mother and father	651	0.9
Other[1]	228	0.3

	Number	% of total
Living with 1 parent	20,257	27.5%
Mother only	17,410	23.6
Biological	17,017	23.1
Father only	2,848	3.9
Biological	2,728	3.7
Living with no parent	2,833	3.8
Grandparents only	1,591	2.2
Other relatives only	673	0.9
Nonrelatives only	457	0.6
Other arrangement	111	0.2
Living with at least 1 biological parent	69,468	94.3
Living with at least 1 stepparent	4,201	5.7
Living with at least 1 adoptive parent	1,220	1.7

Note: Children are defined as all persons under 18 years of age excluding those who are a family reference person or spouse. Data based on sample of occupied households in the civilian noninstitutional population. (1) Includes children living with one adoptive parent and one stepparent, or two stepparents.

Unmarried-Partner Households in the U.S. by Sex of Partners, 2014

Source: American Community Survey (ACS), U.S. Census Bureau, U.S. Dept. of Commerce

Type of household	Number	% of total	% of cat.
Total households	**117,259,427**	**100.0%**	—
Unmarried-partner households	7,175,477	6.1	100.0%
Male HH, female partner	3,432,899	2.9	47.8
Female HH, male partner	3,294,307	2.8	45.9

Type of household	Number	% of total	% of cat.
Female HH, female partner	233,607	0.2%	3.3%
Male HH, male partner	214,664	0.2	3.0
All other households	110,083,950	93.9	100.0

HH = Householder, or person in whose name a home is owned or rented. **Note:** Data based on sample and subject to sampling variability. A household includes all people occupying a housing unit; the household population does not include people living in group quarters (e.g., correctional facilities, university housing).

Persons Granted Lawful Permanent Resident Status by State, 2013

Source: Office of Immigration Statistics, U.S. Dept. of Homeland Security
(ranked by fiscal year 2013 number)

State/territory	Number	State/territory	Number	State/territory	Number	State/territory	Number
Total	**990,553**	North Carolina	16,798	Kentucky	5,159	New Hampshire	2,227
California	191,806	Arizona	16,097	Kansas	5,000	Idaho	2,120
New York	133,601	Ohio	13,819	Oklahoma	4,648	Mississippi	1,716
Florida	102,939	Minnesota	12,781	Louisiana	4,355	Alaska	1,460
Texas	92,674	Colorado	11,108	South Carolina	4,266	North Dakota	1,234
New Jersey	53,082	Connecticut	10,985	Nebraska	4,141	South Dakota	1,231
Illinois	35,988	Nevada	9,886	Iowa	4,105	Guam	1,210
Massachusetts	29,482	Tennessee	8,380	Alabama	3,848	Maine	1,208
Virginia	27,861	Indiana	7,668	New Mexico	3,664	Vermont	838
Maryland	25,361	Oregon	7,171	Rhode Island	3,337	West Virginia	760
Pennsylvania	24,720	Missouri	6,345	District of Columbia	2,981	Wyoming	522
Georgia	24,387	Hawaii	6,226	Puerto Rico	2,942	Montana	445
Washington	22,994	Wisconsin	5,918	Arkansas	2,900	Other[1]	1,379
Michigan	16,952	Utah	5,503	Delaware	2,325		

Note: Applicants for lawful permanent resident (LPR) status, or "green cards," may already live in the U.S. They include refugees and asylees, temporary workers, foreign students, family members of U.S. citizens, and unauthorized immigrants. Applicants from outside the U.S. enter on a visa and are granted LPR status upon admittance. (1) Includes other U.S. territories and armed forces posts.

Persons Granted Lawful Permanent Resident Status by Top Areas of Residence, 2013

Source: Office of Immigration Statistics, U.S. Dept. of Homeland Security
(ranked by fiscal year 2013 number)

Core Based Statistical Area (CBSA)[1]	Number	% of total
Total	**990,553**	**100.0%**
New York-Northern New Jersey-Long Island, NY-NJ-PA	167,393	16.9
Los Angeles-Long Beach-Santa Ana, CA	79,893	8.1
Miami-Fort Lauderdale-Pompano Beach, FL	66,636	6.7
Washington-Arlington-Alexandria, DC-VA-MD-WV	39,170	4.0
Chicago-Joliet-Naperville, IL-IN-WI	32,819	3.3
Houston-Sugar Land-Baytown, TX	31,953	3.2
San Francisco-Oakland-Fremont, CA	30,600	3.1
Dallas-Fort Worth-Arlington, TX	26,760	2.7
Boston-Cambridge-Quincy, MA-NH	23,867	2.4
Atlanta-Sandy Springs-Marietta, GA	20,054	2.0
Philadelphia-Camden-Wilmington, PA-NJ-DE-MD	18,121	1.8
Seattle-Tacoma-Bellevue, WA	17,865	1.8
San Jose-Sunnyvale-Santa Clara, CA	17,292	1.7
San Diego-Carlsbad-San Marcos, CA	16,567	1.7
Riverside-San Bernardino-Ontario, CA	14,026	1.4
Detroit-Warren-Livonia, MI	11,131	1.1
Phoenix-Mesa-Glendale, AZ	11,025	1.1
Minneapolis-St. Paul-Bloomington, MN-WI	10,478	1.1
Orlando-Kissimmee-Sanford, FL	10,200	1.0
Baltimore-Towson, MD	8,599	0.9
Las Vegas-Paradise, NV	8,381	0.8
Tampa-St. Petersburg-Clearwater, FL	8,360	0.8
Sacramento–Arden-Arcade–Roseville, CA	7,504	0.8
Denver-Aurora-Broomfield, CO	7,498	0.8
Austin-Round Rock-San Marcos, TX	6,015	0.6
Portland-Vancouver-Hillsboro, OR-WA	5,934	0.6%
El Paso, TX	5,261	0.5
San Antonio-New Braunfels, TX	5,082	0.5
Charlotte-Gastonia-Rock Hill, NC-SC	5,053	0.5
Columbus, OH	4,868	0.5
Honolulu, HI	4,656	0.5
Bridgeport-Stamford-Norwalk, CT	4,468	0.5
Nashville-Davidson–Murfreesboro–Franklin, TN	4,275	0.4
Providence-New Bedford-Fall River, RI-MA	4,263	0.4
Indianapolis-Carmel, IN	3,944	0.4
Raleigh-Cary, NC	3,798	0.4
Kansas City, MO-KS	3,696	0.4
Salt Lake City, UT	3,403	0.3
Hartford-West Hartford-East Hartford, CT	3,373	0.3
McAllen-Edinburg-Mission, TX	3,267	0.3
St. Louis, MO-IL	3,187	0.3
Jacksonville, FL	3,170	0.3
Cleveland-Elyria-Mentor, OH	3,076	0.3
Fresno, CA	2,853	0.3
Worcester, MA	2,853	0.3
Oxnard-Thousand Oaks-Ventura, CA	2,801	0.3
Cincinnati-Middletown, OH-KY-IN	2,762	0.3
San Juan-Caguas-Guaynabo, PR	2,706	0.3
Milwaukee-Waukesha-West Allis, WI	2,686	0.3
Pittsburgh, PA	2,645	0.3
Other CBSAs	191,377	19.3
Non-CBSA or unknown	12,889	1.3

Note: Applicants for lawful permanent resident (LPR) status, or "green cards," may already live in the U.S. They include refugees and asylees, temporary workers, foreign students, family members of U.S. citizens, and unauthorized immigrants. Applicants from outside the U.S. enter on a visa and are granted LPR status upon admittance. (1) CBSAs refer collectively to metropolitan and micropolitan statistical areas. These areas are defined for federal statistical use by the Office of Management and Budget with technical assistance from the Census Bureau.

Unauthorized Immigrant Population in the U.S., 2000, 2012

Source: Office of Immigration Statistics, U.S. Dept. of Homeland Security
(ranked by 2012 est. population; as of Jan. of given year)

Country of Birth

Country	Est. population 2012	Est. population 2000	% change, 2000-12
All countries	**11,430,000**	**8,460,000**	**35.1%**
Mexico	6,720,000	4,680,000	43.6
El Salvador	690,000	430,000	60.5
Guatemala	560,000	290,000	93.1
Honduras	360,000	160,000	125.0
Philippines	310,000	200,000	55.0
India	260,000	120,000	116.7
Korea[1]	230,000	180,000	27.8
China	210,000	190,000	10.5
Ecuador	170,000	110,000	54.5
Vietnam	160,000	160,000	0.0
Other countries	1,760,000	1,940,000	–9.3

State of Residence

State	Est. population 2012	Est. population 2000	% change, 2000-12
All states	**11,430,000**	**8,460,000**	**35.1%**
California	2,820,000	2,510,000	12.4
Texas	1,830,000	1,090,000	67.9
Florida	730,000	800,000	–8.8
New York	580,000	540,000	7.4
Illinois	540,000	440,000	22.7
New Jersey	430,000	350,000	22.9
Georgia	400,000	220,000	81.8
North Carolina	360,000	260,000	38.5
Arizona	350,000	330,000	6.1
Washington	270,000	170,000	58.8
Other states	3,110,000	1,750,000	77.7

Note: Unauthorized immigrant population estimates are made using the residual method. The estimated size of the legally resident foreign-born pop. (i.e., lawful permanent residents, asylees, refugees, and nonimmigrants such as temporary workers) is subtracted from the total foreign-born pop. Numbers may not add up to totals because of rounding. (1) Incl. North and South Korea.

U.S. Foreign-Born Population

Source: Annual Social and Economic Supplements, Current Population Surveys (CPS), U.S. Census Bureau, U.S. Dept. of Commerce

Percentage of Population That Is Foreign-Born, 1900-2014

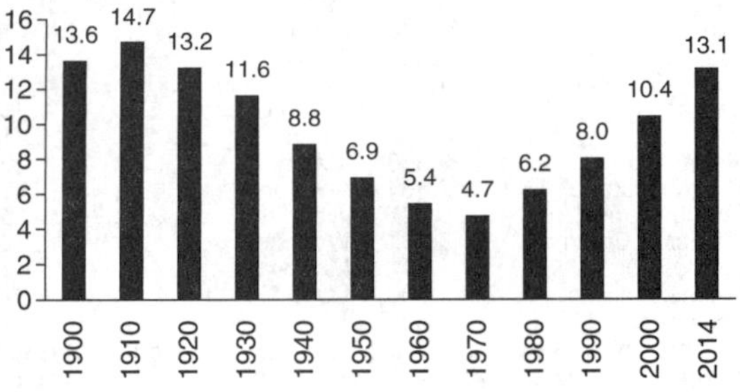

Foreign-Born Population by Region of Birth, 1995-2012

(numbers in thousands)

Region	2012[1] No.	2012[1] %	2000	1995
Asia	11,587	29.0%	7,246	6,121
Under 18	843	32.3	657	767
Europe	4,546	11.4	4,355	3,937
Under 18	214	8.2	250	232
Latin America	21,034	52.6	14,477	11,777
Under 18	1,278	48.9	1,684	1,481
Other[2]	2,809	7.0	2,301	2,658
Under 18	277	10.6	245	275
All regions	**39,976**	**100.0**	**28,379**	**24,493**
Under 18	**2,612**	**100.0**	**2,837**	**2,726**

(1) Figures are percentage of total foreign-born population or of all foreign-born under 18 years of age. (2) Including those born at sea.

U.S. Foreign-Born Population: Top Countries of Origin, 1880-2014

Source: American Community Survey (ACS), Decennial Censuses, U.S. Census Bureau, U.S. Dept. of Commerce

(numbers in thousands; percentage is of all foreign-born)

1880			1920			1960			2000			2014[4]		
Country	**No.**	**%**	**Country**	**No.**	**%**	**Country**	**No.**	**%**	**Country**	**No.**	**%**	**Country**	**No.**	**%**
Germany	1,967	29.4	Germany	1,686	12.1	Italy	1,257	12.9	Mexico	9,177	29.5	Mexico	11,714	27.6
Ireland	1,855	27.8	Italy	1,610	11.6	Germany	990	10.2	China[2]	1,519	4.9	China[2]	2,520	5.9
UK	918	13.7	U.S.S.R.	1,400	10.1	Canada	953	9.8	Philippines	1,369	4.4	India	2,206	5.2
Canada	717	10.7	Poland	1,140	8.2	UK	765	7.9	India	1,023	3.3	Philippines	1,926	4.5
Sweden	194	2.9	Canada	1,138	8.2	Poland	748	7.7	Vietnam	988	3.2	El Salvador	1,315	3.1
Norway	182	2.7	UK	1,135	8.2	U.S.S.R.	691	7.1	Cuba	873	2.8	Vietnam	1,292	3.0
France	107	1.6	Ireland	1,037	7.5	Mexico	576	5.9	Korea[3]	864	2.8	Cuba	1,173	2.8
China[1]	104	1.6	Sweden	626	4.5	Ireland	339	3.5	Canada	821	2.6	Korea[3]	1,080	2.5
Switzerland	89	1.3	Austria	576	4.1	Austria	305	3.1	El Salvador	817	2.6	Dominican Republic	998	2.4
Czech.	85	1.3	Mexico	486	3.5	Hungary	245	2.5	Germany	707	2.3	Guatemala	916	2.2
Total	**6,680**	**100.0**	**Total**	**13,921**	**100.0**	**Total**	**9,738**	**100.0**	**Total**	**31,108**	**100.0**	**Total**	**42,391**	**100.0**

(1) Incl. Taiwan. (2) Incl. Hong Kong and Taiwan. (3) North and South Korea. (4) Data based on sample and subject to sampling variability. The Census Bureau collects data from foreign-born persons regardless of their immigration status, so data implicitly incl. unauthorized migrants.

Language Spoken at Home by the U.S. Population, 2014

Source: American Community Survey (ACS), U.S. Census Bureau, U.S. Dept. of Commerce

(number of speakers ages 5 and older, by language or language group)

Language	Number (thous.)	% of tot. pop.	% English inability[1]
Total population	**299,084.0**	**100.0%**	**8.6%**
Speak only English	**235,905.6**	**78.9**	**NA**
Speak another language	**63,178.5**	**21.1**	**40.5**
Spanish			
Spanish or Spanish Creole	39,254.3	13.12	41.7
Other Indo-European languages			
Armenian	240.6	0.08	43.1
French (incl. Patois, Cajun)	1,219.8	0.41	19.9
French Creole	795.5	0.27	41.1
German	934.4	0.31	15.6
Greek	289.4	0.10	24.8
Gujarati	388.9	0.13	34.9
Hindi	723.8	0.24	21.6
Italian	641.4	0.21	25.5
Persian	416.1	0.14	38.5
Polish	533.9	0.18	38.9
Portuguese or Portuguese Creole	680.6	0.23	35.7
Russian	890.1	0.30	45.8
Scandinavian languages	120.6	0.04	11.7
Serbo-Croatian	246.2	0.08	38.2
Urdu	477.7	0.16	30.6
Yiddish	154.7	0.05	42.7
Other Indic languages	955.1	0.32	40.6
Other Slavic languages	318.7	0.11%	37.7%
Other West Germanic langs.	318.0	0.11	25.3
Other Indo-European langs.	462.9	0.15	34.2
Asian and Pacific Island languages			
Chinese	3,139.4	1.05	55.8
Hmong	236.4	0.08	43.9
Japanese	437.5	0.15	43.3
Korean	1,131.3	0.38	54.8
Laotian	146.2	0.05	47.7
Mon-Khmer, Cambodian	216.5	0.07	49.9
Tagalog	1,688.5	0.56	31.3
Thai	157.4	0.05	52.5
Vietnamese	1,458.2	0.49	59.2
Other Asian languages	1,092.7	0.37	31.4
Other Pacific Island langs.	430.7	0.14	39.4
All other languages			
African languages	1,060.6	0.35	31.6
Arabic	1,117.3	0.37	38.0
Hebrew	213.2	0.07	17.1
Hungarian	78.2	0.03	29.3
Navajo	164.4	0.05	18.3
Other Native North American languages	201.3	0.07	15.7
Other and unspecified langs.	145.9	0.05	42.3

NA = Not applicable. **Note:** Data based on sample and subject to sampling variability. (1) Percent of respondents described by the characteristic/language at left who indicated that they spoke English less than "very well." For example, 43.1% of respondents who use Armenian at home do not speak English very well.

U.S. Population by Ancestry Reported, 2014

Source: American Community Survey (ACS), U.S. Census Bureau, U.S. Dept. of Commerce
(numbers in thousands; ranked by number)

Ancestry	Number	% of total
Total population	**318,857**	**100.0%**
German	46,047	14.4
Irish	33,148	10.4
English	24,382	7.6
American	22,097	6.9
Italian	17,221	5.4
Polish	9,249	2.9
French (excl. Basque)	8,154	2.6
Scottish	5,365	1.7
Norwegian	4,445	1.4%
Dutch	4,243	1.3
Swedish	3,887	1.2
European	3,679	1.2
Sub-Saharan African[1]	3,224	1.0
Scotch-Irish[2]	2,979	0.9
West Indian (excl. Hispanic groups)[3]	2,865	0.9
Russian	2,763	0.9
French Canadian	2,099	0.7%
Arab[4]	1,927	0.6
Welsh	1,758	0.6
Czech	1,420	0.4
Hungarian	1,406	0.4
Portuguese	1,340	0.4
Other ancestry not shown here	138,246	43.4
Unclassified or not reported	48,426	15.2

Note: Data based on sample and subject to sampling variability. Because respondents could self-identify with more than one ancestry, numbers do not add up to total. (1) Incl. Cabo Verdean, Ethiopian, Ghanian, Kenyan, Liberian, Nigerian, Senegalese, Sierra Leonean, Somalian, South African, Sudanese, Ugandan, Zimbabwean, African, and other sub-Saharan African. (2) Excl. persons reporting Irish-Scotch ancestry. (3) Incl. Bahamian, Barbadian, Belizean, Bermudan, British or Dutch West Indian, Haitian, Jamaican, Trinidadian and Tobagonian, U.S. Virgin Islander, West Indian, and other West Indian. (4) Incl. Egyptian, Iraqi, Jordanian, Lebanese, Moroccan, Palestinian, Syrian, Arab, and other Arab.

U.S. Race and Minority Group Populations by Age, 2014

Source: American Community Survey (ACS), U.S. Census Bureau, U.S. Dept. of Commerce

Race and origin/age	Number	% of race
White (not Hispanic or Latino)	**197,409,353**	**100.0%**
Under 5 years	9,839,867	5.0
Under 18 years	38,053,239	19.3
18 to 64 years	123,185,572	62.4
65 years and over	36,170,542	18.3
85 years and over	4,989,845	2.5
Black or African American	**40,379,066**	**100.0**
Under 5 years	2,790,249	6.9
Under 18 years	10,449,293	25.9
18 to 64 years	25,844,176	64.0
65 years and over	4,085,597	10.1
85 years and over	443,742	1.1
Asian	**16,686,960**	**100.0**
Under 5 years	923,004	5.5
Under 18 years	3,425,262	20.5
18 to 64 years	11,399,203	68.3
65 years and over	1,862,495	11.2
85 years and over	198,488	1.2
American Indian and Alaska Native	**2,601,714**	**100.0**
Under 5 years	186,872	7.2
Under 18 years	724,299	27.8
18 to 64 years	1,643,369	63.2
65 years and over	234,046	9.0
85 years and over	18,577	0.7
Native Hawaiian and other Pacific Islander	**557,154**	**100.0%**
Under 5 years	35,870	6.4
Under 18 years	143,898	25.8
18 to 64 years	374,697	67.3
65 years and over	38,559	6.9
85 years and over	2,189	0.4
Some other race	**15,063,263**	**100.0**
Under 5 years	1,281,234	8.5
Under 18 years	4,598,716	30.5
18 to 64 years	9,724,135	64.6
65 years and over	740,412	4.9
85 years and over	65,694	0.4
Two or more races	**9,605,771**	**100.0**
Under 5 years	1,437,060	15.0
Under 18 years	4,484,212	46.7
18 to 64 years	4,648,842	48.4
65 years and over	472,717	4.9
85 years and over	43,593	0.5
Hispanic or Latino (any race)	**55,279,452**	**100.0**
Under 5 years	5,096,665	9.2
Under 18 years	17,911,107	32.4
18 to 64 years	33,845,563	61.2
65 years and over	3,522,782	6.4
85 years and over	366,938	0.7

Note: Data based on sample and subject to sampling variability. Categories are for one race alone, not in combination with any other race, unless otherwise noted.

Educational Attainment of the U.S. Population, 2014

Source: American Community Survey (ACS), U.S. Census Bureau, U.S. Dept. of Commerce
(numbers in thousands; population 25 years of age and over)

Race and origin/highest ed. completed	Number	% of race
White (not Hispanic or Latino)	**142,032**	**100.0%**
Less than H.S. diploma	11,353	8.0
H.S. diploma or equiv. credential	40,031	28.2
Some college or associate's degree	42,878	30.2
Bachelor's degree or higher	47,770	33.6
Black or African American	**25,133**	**100.0**
Less than H.S. diploma	3,931	15.6
H.S. diploma or equiv. credential	7,934	31.6
Some college or associate's degree	8,318	33.1
Bachelor's degree or higher	4,950	19.7
Asian	**11,604**	**100.0**
Less than H.S. diploma	1,594	13.7
H.S. diploma or equiv. credential	1,798	15.5
Some college or associate's degree	2,232	19.2
Bachelor's degree or higher	5,980	51.5
American Indian and Alaska Native	**1,580**	**100.0**
Less than H.S. diploma	327	20.7
H.S. diploma or equiv. credential	504	31.9
Some college or associate's degree	530	33.5
Bachelor's degree or higher	219	13.9
Native Hawaiian and other Pacific Islander	**340**	**100.0%**
Less than H.S. diploma	46	13.6
H.S. diploma or equiv. credential	127	37.3
Some college or associate's degree	115	33.8
Bachelor's degree or higher	52	15.3
Some other race	**8,563**	**100.0**
Less than H.S. diploma	3,402	39.7
H.S. diploma or equiv. credential	2,393	27.9
Some college or associate's degree	1,847	21.6
Bachelor's degree or higher	921	10.8
Two or more races	**3,918**	**100.0**
Less than H.S. diploma	526	13.4
H.S. diploma or equiv. credential	908	23.2
Some college or associate's degree	1,357	34.6
Bachelor's degree or higher	1,127	28.8
Hispanic or Latino (any race)	**30,696**	**100.0**
Less than H.S. diploma	10,639	34.7
H.S. diploma or equiv. credential	8,347	27.2
Some college or associate's degree	7,299	23.8
Bachelor's degree or higher	4,411	14.4

H.S. = High school. **Note:** Data based on sample and subject to sampling variability. Categories are for one race alone, not in combination with any other race, unless otherwise noted.

Populations, ZIP, and Area Codes for U.S. Places of 10,000 or More

Source: Decennial Census and Population Estimates Program, U.S. Census Bureau, U.S. Dept. of Commerce; NeuStar Inc.; www.usps.com

The following is a list of places of 10,000 or more residents according to the U.S. Census Bureau's population estimates for 2014 and the results of the 2010 census.

This list includes **places incorporated** under state law as cities, towns, villages, or boroughs, and **Census designated places (CDPs)**, marked with a (c). This list also includes, in *italics*, **minor civil divisions (MCDs)** in Connecticut, Maine, Massachusetts, New Hampshire, Rhode Island, and Vermont. **Townships are not included.** Neither CDPs nor MCDs are incorporated areas. The Census Bureau delineates CDPs as statistical counterparts to incorporated places. Unless an exception is noted, the Census Bureau does not include CDPs in its estimates program. MCDs, while not automatically recognized as CDPs, are often the primary political or administrative divisions of a county. (Balance) indicates that the population given is for a consolidated area minus the residents of any incorporated places within.

An asterisk (*) denotes that the **ZIP code** given is for general delivery; mail routes and/or P.O. boxes within the place may use a different one. Telephone **area codes** are given in parentheses. New phone numbers may be assigned a different area code from that of existing phone numbers in an area. These areas of overlay are noted. When two or more area codes are listed for one place, consult local operators for assistance. Area codes based on latest information as of Sept. 2015. — = Not available.

Alabama

Area code 938 overlays area code 256.

ZIP	Place	Area code	2010 population	2014 estimate
*35007	Alabaster	(205)	30,352	31,545
*35950	Albertville	(256)	21,160	21,458
*35010	Alexander City	(256)	14,875	14,849
*36201	Anniston	(256)	23,106	22,457
*35611	Athens	(256)	21,897	24,522
*36502	Atmore	(251)	10,194	10,006
*36830	Auburn	(334)	53,380	60,258
*35020	Bessemer	(205)	27,456	26,949
*35203	Birmingham	(205)	212,237	212,247
35040	Calera	(205)	11,620	12,972
*35215	Center Point	(205)	16,921	16,777
35043	Chelsea	(205)	10,183	11,758
*35055	Cullman	(256)	14,775	15,145
36526	Daphne	(251)	21,570	24,395
*35601	Decatur	(256)	55,683	55,532
*36301	Dothan	(334)	65,496	68,409
*36330	Enterprise	(334)	26,562	27,772
*36027	Eufaula	(334)	13,137	12,781
35064	Fairfield	(205)	11,117	10,988
*36532	Fairhope	(251)	15,326	18,089
*35630	Florence	(256)	39,319	40,215
*36535	Foley	(251)	14,618	16,243
35214	Forestdale (c)	(205)	10,162	—
*35967	Fort Payne	(256)	14,012	14,125
*35901	Gadsden	(256)	36,856	36,295
35071	Gardendale	(205)	13,893	13,729
36542	Gulf Shores	(251)	9,741	10,963
35640	Hartselle	(256)	14,255	14,459
*35080	Helena	(205)	16,793	17,883
*35209	Homewood	(205)	25,167	25,802
*35216	Hoover	(205)	81,619	84,353
*35023	Hueytown	(205)	16,105	15,815
*35801	Huntsville	(256)	180,105	188,226
35210	Irondale	(205)	12,349	12,444
36265	Jacksonville	(256)	12,548	12,250
*35501	Jasper	(205)	14,352	14,109
35094	Leeds	(205)	11,773	11,939
*35758	Madison	(256)	42,938	46,450
36054	Millbrook	(334)	14,640	15,169
*36602	Mobile	(251)	195,111	194,675
*36104	Montgomery	(334)	205,764	200,481
35004	Moody	(205)	11,726	12,457
*35223	Mountain Brook	(205)	20,413	20,734
*35661	Muscle Shoals	(256)	13,146	13,614
*35476	Northport	(205)	23,330	24,709
*36801	Opelika	(334)	26,477	29,171
36203	Oxford	(256)	21,348	21,155
*36360	Ozark	(334)	14,907	14,700
35124	Pelham	(205)	21,352	22,699
*35125	Pell City	(205)	12,695	13,573
*36867	Phenix City	(334)	32,822	37,540
35127	Pleasant Grove	(205)	10,110	10,325
*36066	Prattville	(334)	33,960	35,317
36610	Prichard	(251)	22,659	22,312
36206	Saks (c)	(256)	10,744	—
36571	Saraland	(251)	13,405	13,744
*35768	Scottsboro	(256)	14,770	14,748
*36701	Selma	(334)	20,756	19,814
*35150	Sylacauga	(256)	12,749	12,703
*35160	Talladega	(256)	15,676	16,012
36619	Tillman's Corner (c)	(251)	17,398	—
*36081	Troy	(334)	18,033	19,138
35173	Trussville	(205)	19,933	20,702
*35401	Tuscaloosa	(205)	90,468	96,122
*35216	Vestavia Hills	(205)	34,033	34,124

Alaska

Area code 907 applies to the entire state.

ZIP	Place	2010 population	2014 estimate
*99501	Anchorage	291,826	301,010
99711	Badger (c)	19,482	—
*99708	College (c)	12,964	—
*99701	Fairbanks	31,535	32,469
*99801	Juneau	31,275	32,406
99654	Knik-Fairview (c)	14,923	—

Arizona

ZIP	Place	Area code	2010 population	2014 estimate
85086	Anthem (c)	(623)	21,700	—
*85119	Apache Junction	(480)	35,840	38,131
85123	Arizona City (c)	(520)	10,475	—
*85323	Avondale	(623)	76,238	79,646
*85326	Buckeye	(623)	50,876	59,470
*86442	Bullhead City	(928)	39,540	39,364
86322	Camp Verde	(928)	10,873	11,097
*85122	Casa Grande	(520)	48,571	51,478
85740	Casas Adobes (c)	(520)	66,795	—
85718	Catalina Foothills (c)	(520)	50,796	—
*85225	Chandler	(480)	236,123	254,276
86323	Chino Valley	(928)	10,817	11,019
85128	Coolidge	(520)	11,825	12,209
86326	Cottonwood	(928)	11,265	11,595
*85607	Douglas	(520)	17,378	16,744
85746	Drexel Heights (c)	(520)	27,749	—
85335	El Mirage	(623)	31,797	33,532
85131	Eloy	(520)	16,631	16,738
*86004	Flagstaff	(928)	65,870	68,785
85132	Florence	(520)	25,536	26,912
85705	Flowing Wells (c)	(520)	16,419	—
*86427	Fort Mohave (c)	(928)	14,364	—
85367	Fortuna Foothills (c)	(928)	26,265	—
*85268	Fountain Hills	(480)	22,489	23,573
*85234	Gilbert	(480)	208,453	239,277
*85302	Glendale	(623)	226,721	237,517
85118	Gold Canyon (c)	(480)	10,159	—
*85338	Goodyear	(623)	65,275	75,664
*85622	Green Valley (c)	(520)	21,391	—
*86401	Kingman	(928)	28,068	28,549
*86403	Lake Havasu City	(928)	52,527	53,103
*85653	Marana	(520)	34,961	39,888
*85138	Maricopa	(520)	43,482	47,442
*85201	Mesa	(480)	439,041	464,704
86401	New Kingman-Butler (c)	(928)	12,134	—
*85087	New River (c)	(623)	14,952	—
*85621	Nogales	(520)	20,837	20,407
*85737	Oro Valley	(520)	41,011	42,018
85253	Paradise Valley	(480)	12,820	13,663
*85541	Payson	(928)	15,301	15,245
*85345	Peoria	(623)	154,065	166,934
*85003	Phoenix	(480)/(602)/(623)	1,445,632	1,537,058
*86301	Prescott	(928)	39,843	40,958
*86314	Prescott Valley	(928)	38,822	41,075
*85142	Queen Creek	(480)	26,361	32,236
85648	Rio Rico (c)	(520)	18,962	—
85629	Sahuarita	(520)	25,259	27,547
85349	San Luis	(928)	25,505	31,091
*85142	San Tan Valley (c)	(480)	81,321	—
*85251	Scottsdale	(480)	217,385	230,512
*86336	Sedona	(928)	10,031	10,281
*85901	Show Low	(928)	10,660	10,841
*85635	Sierra Vista	(520)	43,888	43,806
85650	Sierra Vista Southeast (c)	(520)	14,797	—
85350	Somerton	(928)	14,287	14,912
*85351	Sun City (c)	(623)	37,499	—
*85375	Sun City West (c)	(623)	24,535	—
85248	Sun Lakes (c)	(480)	13,975	—
*85374	Surprise	(623)	117,517	126,275
85749	Tanque Verde (c)	(520)	16,901	—
*85282	Tempe	(480)	161,719	172,816
*85701	Tucson	(520)	520,116	527,972
85735	Tucson Estates (c)	(520)	12,192	—
85641	Vail (c)	(520)	10,208	—
86326	Verde Village (c)	(928)	11,605	—
*85364	Yuma	(928)	93,064	93,400

Arkansas

ZIP	Place	Area code	2010 population	2014 estimate
*71923	Arkadelphia	(870)	10,714	10,649
*72501	Batesville	(870)	10,248	10,497
*72714	Bella Vista	(479)	26,461	27,688
*72015	Benton	(501)	30,681	33,625
*72712	Bentonville	(479)	35,301	41,613

ZIP	Place	Area code	2010 population	2014 estimate
*72315	Blytheville	(870)	15,620	14,884
*72022	Bryant	(501)	16,688	19,625
72023	Cabot	(501)	23,776	25,627
*71701	Camden	(870)	12,183	11,569
*72719	Centerton	(479)	9,515	11,193
*72032	Conway	(501)	58,908	64,490
*71730	El Dorado	(870)	18,884	18,352
*72701	Fayetteville	(479)	73,580	80,621
*72335	Forrest City	(870)	15,371	14,823
*72901	Fort Smith	(479)	86,209	87,351
*72601	Harrison	(870)	12,943	13,130
72342	Helena-West Helena	(870)	12,282	11,320
*71801	Hope	(870)	10,095	10,004
*71901	Hot Springs	(501)	35,193	35,673
*71909	Hot Springs Village (c)	(501)	12,807	—
*72076	Jacksonville	(501)	28,364	28,808
*72401	Jonesboro	(870)	67,263	72,210
*72201	Little Rock	(501)	193,524	197,706
*71753	Magnolia	(870)	11,577	11,489
*72104	Malvern	(501)	10,318	10,826
72364	Marion	(870)	12,345	12,321
*72113	Maumelle	(501)	17,163	17,804
*72653	Mountain Home	(870)	12,448	12,278
*72114	North Little Rock	(501)	62,304	66,810
*72450	Paragould	(870)	26,113	27,465
*71601	Pine Bluff	(870)	49,083	45,332
*72756	Rogers	(479)	55,964	61,464
*72801	Russellville	(479)	27,920	28,993
*72143	Searcy	(501)	22,858	23,983
*72120	Sherwood	(501)	29,523	30,407
72761	Siloam Springs	(479)	15,039	15,944
*72764	Springdale	(479)	69,797	76,565
71854	Texarkana	(870)	29,919	30,014
*72956	Van Buren	(479)	22,791	23,070
*72301	West Memphis	(870)	26,245	25,423

California

Area code 424 overlays area code 310. Area code 442 overlays 760. Area code 628 overlays 415. Area code 657 overlays 714. Area code 669 overlays 408. Area code 747 overlays 818.

ZIP	Place	Area code	2010 population	2014 estimate
92301	Adelanto	(760)	31,765	32,728
*91301	Agoura Hills	(818)	20,330	20,843
*94501	Alameda	(510)	73,812	77,660
94507	Alamo (c)	(925)	14,570	—
94706	Albany	(510)	18,539	19,488
*91801	Alhambra	(626)	83,089	85,569
92656	Aliso Viejo	(949)	47,823	50,231
*91901	Alpine (c)	(619)	14,236	—
*91001	Altadena (c)	(626)	42,777	—
95127	Alum Rock (c)	(408)	15,536	—
*94503	American Canyon	(707)	19,454	20,470
*92805	Anaheim	(714)	336,265	346,997
96007	Anderson	(530)	9,932	10,209
95843	Antelope (c)	(916)	45,770	—
*94509	Antioch	(925)	102,372	108,930
*92307	Apple Valley	(760)	69,135	71,595
*91006	Arcadia	(626)	56,364	58,232
*95521	Arcata	(707)	17,231	17,730
*95825	Arden-Arcade (c)	(916)	92,186	—
*93420	Arroyo Grande	(805)	17,252	17,908
*90701	Artesia	(562)	16,522	16,895
93203	Arvin	(661)	19,304	20,583
94577	Ashland (c)	(510)	21,925	—
*93422	Atascadero	(805)	28,310	29,134
95301	Atwater	(209)	28,168	29,022
*95603	Auburn	(530)	13,330	13,960
93204	Avenal	(559)	15,505	13,308
91746	Avocado Heights (c)	(626)	15,411	—
91702	Azusa	(626)	46,361	48,799
*93301	Bakersfield	(661)	347,483	368,759
91706	Baldwin Park	(626)	75,390	77,119
92220	Banning	(951)	29,603	30,769
*92310	Barstow	(760)	22,639	23,498
94565	Bay Point (c)	(925)	21,349	—
92223	Beaumont	(951)	36,877	42,277
*90201	Bell	(323)	35,477	36,217
*90201	Bell Gardens	(213)/(323)/(562)	42,072	43,146
*90706	Bellflower	(562)	76,616	78,236
94002	Belmont	(650)	25,835	27,073
94510	Benicia	(707)	26,997	27,930
*94704	Berkeley	(510)	112,580	118,853
*90210	Beverly Hills	(213)/(310)/(323)	34,109	34,871
*92314	Big Bear City (c)	(909)	12,304	—
92316	Bloomington (c)	(951)	23,851	—
*92225	Blythe	(760)	20,817	19,258
*91902	Bonita (c)	(619)	12,538	—
92021	Bostonia (c)	(619)	15,379	—
92227	Brawley	(760)	24,953	25,820
*92821	Brea	(562)/(714)	39,282	41,508
94513	Brentwood	(925)	51,481	57,019
*90620	Buena Park	(714)	80,530	83,105
*91502	Burbank	(818)	103,340	105,368
*94010	Burlingame	(650)	28,806	30,298
91301	Calabasas	(818)	23,058	24,296
*92231	Calexico	(760)	38,572	39,799
*93505	California City	(760)	14,120	13,263
*93010	Camarillo	(805)	65,201	66,923
95682	Cameron Park (c)	(530)	18,228	—
92058	Camp Pendleton South (c)	(760)	10,616	—
*95008	Campbell	(408)	39,349	41,119
92587	Canyon Lake	(951)	10,561	11,010
95010	Capitola	(831)	9,918	10,146
*92008	Carlsbad	(760)	105,328	112,299
*95608	Carmichael (c)	(916)	61,762	—
*93013	Carpinteria	(805)	13,040	13,671
*90745	Carson	(310)	91,714	93,271
92077	Casa de Oro-Mt. Helix (c)	(619)	18,762	—
*91384	Castaic (c)	(661)	19,015	—
*94546	Castro Valley (c)	(510)	61,388	—
*92234	Cathedral City	(760)	51,200	53,437
95307	Ceres	(209)	45,417	47,343
90703	Cerritos	(562)	49,041	50,004
*94541	Cherryland (c)	(510)	14,728	—
*95926	Chico	(530)	86,187	89,180
*91708	Chino	(909)	77,983	84,723
91709	Chino Hills	(909)	74,799	77,005
93610	Chowchilla	(559)	18,720	18,909
*91910	Chula Vista	(619)	243,916	260,988
91702	Citrus (c)	(626)	10,866	—
*95610	Citrus Heights	(916)	83,301	86,145
91711	Claremont	(909)	34,926	36,054
94517	Clayton	(925)	10,897	11,690
95422	Clearlake	(707)	15,250	15,089
*93612	Clovis	(559)	95,631	102,189
92236	Coachella	(760)	40,704	44,132
93210	Coalinga	(559)	13,380	16,452
92324	Colton	(909)	52,154	54,053
*90040	Commerce	(323)	12,823	13,076
*90221	Compton	(310)	96,455	98,597
*94520	Concord	(925)	122,067	127,522
*93212	Corcoran	(559)	24,813	22,815
*92882	Corona	(951)	152,374	161,486
*92118	Coronado	(619)	18,912	24,910
*92626	Costa Mesa	(714)/(949)	109,960	112,784
92679	Coto de Caza (c)	(949)	14,866	—
*91722	Covina	(626)	47,796	49,002
92325	Crestline (c)	(909)	10,770	—
90201	Cudahy	(323)	23,805	24,291
*90230	Culver City	(310)	38,883	39,691
*95014	Cupertino	(408)	58,302	60,668
90630	Cypress	(714)	47,802	49,240
*94015	Daly City	(415)/(650)	101,123	106,094
*92629	Dana Point	(949)	33,351	34,116
*94526	Danville	(925)	42,039	43,909
*95616	Davis	(530)	65,622	66,742
90250	Del Aire (c)	(310)/(323)	10,001	—
*93215	Delano	(661)	53,041	52,651
95315	Delhi (c)	(209)	10,755	—
*92240	Desert Hot Springs	(760)	25,938	28,164
91765	Diamond Bar	(909)	55,544	56,784
95619	Diamond Springs (c)	(530)	11,037	—
93618	Dinuba	(559)	21,453	23,667
*94514	Discovery Bay (c)	(925)	13,352	—
95620	Dixon	(707)	18,351	19,164
*90240	Downey	(562)	111,772	114,172
*91008	Duarte	(626)	21,321	22,006
94568	Dublin	(925)	46,036	54,695
92544	East Hemet (c)	(951)	17,418	—
90022	East Los Angeles (c)	(323)	126,496	—
94303	East Palo Alto	(650)	28,155	29,530
90221	East Rancho Dominguez (c)	(310)/(323)	15,135	—
91775	East San Gabriel (c)	(626)	14,874	—
*91752	Eastvale[1]	(909)/(951)	53,668	57,016
*92020	El Cajon	(619)	99,478	103,091
*92243	El Centro	(760)	42,598	43,763
94530	El Cerrito	(510)	23,549	24,599
95762	El Dorado Hills (c)	(916)	42,108	—
*91731	El Monte	(626)	113,475	116,631
*93446	El Paso de Robles (Paso Robles)	(805)	29,793	31,287
90245	El Segundo	(310)	16,654	17,063
*94803	El Sobrante (c) (Contra Costa Co.)	(510)	12,669	—
92503	El Sobrante (c) (Riverside Co.)	(714)/(909)	12,723	—
*95624	Elk Grove	(916)	153,015	163,553
*94608	Emeryville	(510)	10,080	11,227
*92024	Encinitas	(760)	59,518	62,254
*92025	Escondido	(760)	143,911	150,243
*95501	Eureka	(707)	27,191	26,925
93221	Exeter	(559)	10,334	10,558
95628	Fair Oaks (c)	(916)	30,912	—
*94533	Fairfield	(707)	105,321	111,125
94541	Fairview (c)	(510)	10,003	—

ZIP	Place	Area code	2010 population	2014 estimate
*92028	Fallbrook (c)	(760)	30,534	—
93223	Farmersville	(559)	10,588	10,786
*93015	Fillmore	(805)	15,002	15,420
90001	Florence-Graham (c)	(323)	63,387	—
95828	Florin (c)	(916)	47,513	—
*95630	Folsom	(916)	72,203	75,361
*92335	Fontana	(909)	196,069	204,950
95841	Foothill Farms (c)	(916)	33,121	—
95540	Fortuna	(707)	11,926	11,888
94404	Foster City	(650)	30,567	32,754
*92704	Fountain Valley	(714)	55,313	57,010
*94538	Fremont	(510)	214,089	228,758
92596	French Valley (c)	(951)	23,067	—
*93706	Fresno	(559)	494,665	515,986
*92831	Fullerton	(714)	135,161	139,677
95632	Galt	(209)	23,647	24,817
95215	Garden Acres (c)	(209)	10,648	—
*92843	Garden Grove	(714)	170,883	175,078
*90247	Gardena	(310)	58,829	60,395
*95020	Gilroy	(408)	48,821	52,533
92509	Glen Avon (c)	(951)	20,199	—
*91201	Glendale	(818)	191,719	200,167
*91741	Glendora	(626)	50,073	51,442
*93117	Goleta	(805)	29,888	30,797
*92313	Grand Terrace	(951)	12,040	12,414
95746	Granite Bay (c)	(916)	20,402	—
*95945	Grass Valley	(530)	12,860	12,878
93927	Greenfield	(831)	16,330	16,929
*93433	Grover Beach	(805)	13,156	13,505
91745	Hacienda Heights (c)	(626)	54,038	—
94019	Half Moon Bay	(650)	11,324	12,371
*93230	Hanford	(559)	53,967	55,065
90716	Hawaiian Gardens	(562)	14,254	14,557
*90250	Hawthorne	(310)/(323)	84,293	87,583
*94544	Hayward	(510)	144,186	154,612
95448	Healdsburg	(707)	11,254	11,656
*92543	Hemet	(951)	78,657	83,032
94547	Hercules	(510)	24,060	25,086
90254	Hermosa Beach	(310)	19,506	19,891
*92344	Hesperia	(760)	90,173	92,749
92346	Highland	(909)	53,104	54,651
94010	Hillsborough	(650)	10,825	11,413
*95023	Hollister	(831)	34,928	37,086
92879	Home Gardens (c)	(909)	11,570	—
*92647	Huntington Beach	(714)	189,992	200,809
90255	Huntington Park	(323)	58,114	59,362
92251	Imperial	(760)	14,758	16,811
*91932	Imperial Beach	(619)	26,324	27,149
*92201	Indio	(760)	76,036	85,633
*90301	Inglewood	(310)/(323)	109,673	111,905
*92602	Irvine	(714)/(949)	212,375	248,531
93117	Isla Vista (c)	(805)	23,096	—
*91752	Jurupa Valley[2]	(951)	95,004	98,842
93630	Kerman	(559)	13,544	14,394
93930	King City	(831)	12,874	13,580
93631	Kingsburg	(559)	11,382	11,732
*91011	La Cañada Flintridge	(818)	20,246	20,662
*91214	La Crescenta-Montrose (c)	(818)	19,653	—
*90631	La Habra	(562)/(949)	60,239	62,066
*91941	La Mesa	(619)	57,065	59,177
*90638	La Mirada	(562)/(714)	48,527	49,459
90623	La Palma	(562)/(714)	15,568	15,911
91977	La Presa (c)	(619)	34,169	—
*91744	La Puente	(626)	39,816	40,735
*92253	La Quinta	(760)	37,467	39,964
95401	La Riviera (c)	(916)	10,802	—
91750	La Verne	(909)	31,063	32,288
92694	Ladera Ranch (c)	(949)	22,980	—
94549	Lafayette	(925)	23,893	25,473
*92652	Laguna Beach	(949)	22,723	23,341
*92653	Laguna Hills	(949)	30,344	30,972
*92677	Laguna Niguel	(949)	62,979	65,448
*92637	Laguna Woods	(949)	16,192	16,415
92352	Lake Arrowhead (c)	(909)	12,424	—
*92530	Lake Elsinore	(951)	51,821	60,029
92630	Lake Forest	(949)	77,264	80,148
*93535	Lake Los Angeles (c)	(661)	12,328	—
92530	Lakeland Village (c)	(909)/(951)	11,541	—
92040	Lakeside (c)	(619)	20,648	—
*90714	Lakewood	(562)	80,048	81,653
93241	Lamont (c)	(661)	15,120	—
*93534	Lancaster	(661)	156,633	161,043
*94939	Larkspur	(415)	11,926	12,325
95330	Lathrop	(209)	18,023	20,075
*90260	Lawndale	(310)	32,769	33,442
*91945	Lemon Grove	(619)	25,320	26,511
95824	Lemon Hill (c)	(916)	13,729	—
93245	Lemoore	(559)	24,531	25,186
90304	Lennox (c)	(310)	22,753	—
95648	Lincoln	(916)	42,819	45,902
95901	Linda (c)	(530)	17,773	—
93247	Lindsay	(559)	11,768	13,192
95062	Live Oak (c)	(831)	17,158	—
*94550	Livermore	(925)	80,968	86,870

ZIP	Place	Area code	2010 population	2014 estimate
95334	Livingston	(209)	13,058	13,815
*95240	Lodi	(209)	62,134	63,950
92354	Loma Linda	(951)	23,261	23,853
90717	Lomita	(310)	20,256	20,768
*93436	Lompoc	(805)	42,434	44,013
*90802	Long Beach	(310)/(562)	462,257	473,577
*90720	Los Alamitos	(562)/(949)	11,449	11,716
*94022	Los Altos	(650)	28,976	30,288
*90012	Los Angeles	(213)/(310)/(323)	3,792,621	3,928,864
93635	Los Banos	(209)	35,972	37,126
*95030	Los Gatos	(408)	29,413	30,735
*93402	Los Osos (c)	(805)	14,276	—
90262	Lynwood	(213)/(310)/(323)	69,772	71,839
*93638	Madera	(559)	61,416	63,605
95954	Magalia (c)	(530)	11,310	—
*90265	Malibu	(310)	12,645	12,958
*90266	Manhattan Beach	(310)	35,135	35,881
*95336	Manteca	(209)	67,096	73,494
93933	Marina	(831)	19,718	20,817
94553	Martinez	(925)	35,824	37,567
95901	Marysville	(530)	12,072	12,231
90270	Maywood	(323)	27,395	27,937
93250	McFarland	(661)	12,707	13,605
*95521	McKinleyville (c)	(707)	15,177	—
92570	Mead Valley (c)	(951)	18,510	—
93640	Mendota	(559)	11,014	11,412
*92586	Menifee	(951)	77,519	85,182
*94025	Menlo Park	(650)	32,026	33,309
*95340	Merced	(209)	78,958	81,743
*94941	Mill Valley	(415)	13,903	14,403
94030	Millbrae	(650)	21,532	22,703
*95035	Milpitas	(408)	66,790	73,672
91752	Mira Loma (c)	(951)	21,930	—
*92691	Mission Viejo	(949)	93,305	97,209
*95350	Modesto	(209)	201,165	209,286
*91016	Monrovia	(626)	36,590	37,415
91763	Montclair	(909)	36,664	38,465
90640	Montebello	(323)	62,500	63,929
*93940	Monterey	(831)	27,810	28,276
*91754	Monterey Park	(323)/(626)/(818)	60,269	61,458
*93021	Moorpark	(805)	34,421	35,550
*94556	Moraga	(925)	16,016	17,032
*92551	Moreno Valley	(951)	193,365	202,976
*95037	Morgan Hill	(408)	37,882	42,068
*93442	Morro Bay	(805)	10,234	10,544
*94041	Mountain View	(650)	74,066	79,378
*92562	Murrieta	(951)	103,466	108,368
92407	Muscoy (c)	(909)	10,644	—
*94558	Napa	(707)	76,915	80,011
*91950	National City	(619)	58,582	60,343
94560	Newark	(510)	42,573	44,723
95360	Newman	(209)	10,224	10,748
*92657	Newport Beach	(949)	85,186	87,266
93444	Nipomo (c)	(805)	16,714	—
92860	Norco	(951)	27,063	26,959
95603	North Auburn (c)	(530)	13,022	—
94025	North Fair Oaks (c)	(650)	14,687	—
95660	North Highlands (c)	(916)	42,694	—
92705	North Tustin (c)	(714)/(949)	24,917	—
*90650	Norwalk	(562)	105,549	107,096
*94947	Novato	(415)	51,904	55,005
*91377	Oak Park (c)	(805)/(818)	13,811	—
95361	Oakdale	(209)	20,675	21,854
*94601	Oakland	(510)	390,724	413,775
94561	Oakley	(925)	35,432	39,224
*92056	Oceanside	(760)	167,086	174,558
93308	Oildale (c)	(661)	32,684	—
95961	Olivehurst (c)	(530)	13,656	—
*91761	Ontario	(909)	163,924	169,089
*92868	Orange	(714)	136,416	139,812
95662	Orangevale (c)	(916)	33,960	—
*93455	Orcutt (c)	(805)	28,905	—
94563	Orinda	(925)	17,643	19,003
*95965	Oroville	(530)	15,546	16,220
*93030	Oxnard	(805)	197,899	205,437
93950	Pacific Grove	(831)	15,041	15,601
94044	Pacifica	(650)	37,234	39,088
*92260	Palm Desert	(760)	48,445	51,202
*92262	Palm Springs	(760)	44,552	46,854
*93550	Palmdale	(661)	152,750	158,279
*94303	Palo Alto	(650)	64,403	66,955
*90274	Palos Verdes Estates	(310)	13,438	13,680
*95969	Paradise	(530)	26,218	26,449
90723	Paramount	(562)	54,098	55,406
95823	Parkway (c)	(916)	14,670	—
93648	Parlier	(559)	14,494	14,990
*91101	Pasadena	(323)/(626)/(818)	137,122	140,881
	Paso Robles. *See* El Paso de Robles			
95363	Patterson	(209)	20,413	21,212
92509	Pedley (c)	(951)	12,672	—
*92570	Perris	(951)	68,386	73,756
*94952	Petaluma	(707)	57,941	59,953
*92371	Phelan (c)	(760)	14,304	—
*90660	Pico Rivera	(562)	62,942	64,235

ZIP	Place	Area code	2010 population	2014 estimate
*94611	Piedmont	(510)	10,667	11,236
94564	Pinole	(510)	18,390	19,100
94565	Pittsburg	(925)	63,264	68,140
*92870	Placentia	(714)	50,533	52,397
95667	Placerville	(530)	10,389	10,556
94523	Pleasant Hill	(925)	33,152	34,497
*94566	Pleasanton	(925)	70,285	77,682
*91765	Pomona	(909)	149,058	153,350
*93041	Port Hueneme	(805)	21,723	22,139
*93257	Porterville	(559)	54,165	55,466
*92064	Poway	(858)	47,811	49,848
93907	Prunedale (c)	(831)	17,560	—
*93536	Quartz Hill (c)	(661)	10,912	—
92065	Ramona (c)	(760)	20,292	—
*95670	Rancho Cordova	(916)	64,776	69,740
*91730	Rancho Cucamonga	(909)	165,269	174,305
92270	Rancho Mirage	(760)	17,218	17,982
90275	Rancho Palos Verdes	(310)	41,643	42,726
*92019	Rancho San Diego (c)	(619)	21,208	—
92688	Rancho Santa Margarita	(949)	47,853	49,359
96080	Red Bluff	(530)	14,076	14,057
*96001	Redding	(530)	89,861	91,593
*92373	Redlands	(909)	68,747	70,622
*90277	Redondo Beach	(310)	66,748	68,149
*94063	Redwood City	(650)	76,815	82,881
93654	Reedley	(559)	24,194	25,426
*92377	Rialto	(909)	99,171	102,741
*94801	Richmond	(510)	103,701	108,565
*93555	Ridgecrest	(760)	27,616	28,726
95673	Rio Linda (c)	(916)	15,106	—
95366	Ripon	(209)	14,297	14,966
95367	Riverbank	(209)	22,678	23,798
*92501	Riverside	(951)	303,871	319,504
*95677	Rocklin	(916)	56,974	60,344
*94928	Rohnert Park	(707)	40,971	42,262
93560	Rosamond (c)	(661)	18,150	—
93314	Rosedale (c)	(661)	14,058	—
*91770	Rosemead	(626)	53,764	54,947
95826	Rosemont (c)	(916)	22,681	—
*95678	Roseville	(916)	118,788	128,615
90720	Rossmoor (c)	(714)	10,244	—
91748	Rowland Heights (c)	(626)	48,993	—
*92519	Rubidoux (c)	(951)	34,280	—
*95814	Sacramento	(916)	466,488	485,199
95368	Salida (c)	(209)	13,722	—
*93907	Salinas	(831)	150,441	156,677
*94960	San Anselmo	(415)	12,336	12,676
*92401	San Bernardino	(909)	209,924	215,213
94066	San Bruno	(650)	41,114	43,009
*93001	San Buenaventura (Ventura)	(805)	106,433	109,484
94070	San Carlos	(650)	28,406	29,803
*92672	San Clemente	(949)	63,522	65,326
*92101	San Diego	(619)/(858)	1,307,402	1,381,069
92065	San Diego Country Estates (c)	(760)	10,109	—
91773	San Dimas	(909)	33,371	34,637
*91340	San Fernando	(818)	23,645	24,587
*94102	San Francisco	(415)	805,235	852,469
*91775	San Gabriel	(626)	39,718	40,519
*92582	San Jacinto	(951)	44,199	46,490
*95113	San Jose	(408)	945,942	1,015,785
*92675	San Juan Capistrano	(949)	34,593	36,282
*94577	San Leandro	(510)	84,950	89,351
94580	San Lorenzo (c)	(510)	23,452	—
*93401	San Luis Obispo	(805)	45,119	46,730
*92069	San Marcos	(760)	83,781	92,929
*91108	San Marino	(626)	13,147	13,423
*94402	San Mateo	(650)	97,207	102,893
94806	San Pablo	(510)	29,139	30,050
*94901	San Rafael	(415)	57,713	59,237
*94583	San Ramon	(925)	72,148	75,332
93657	Sanger	(559)	24,270	24,810
*92701	Santa Ana	(714)/(949)	324,528	334,909
*93101	Santa Barbara	(805)	88,410	91,196
*95050	Santa Clara	(408)	116,468	122,192
*91350	Santa Clarita	(661)	176,320	181,557
*95060	Santa Cruz	(831)	59,946	63,364
90670	Santa Fe Springs	(562)	16,223	17,537
*93454	Santa Maria	(805)	99,553	103,410
*90401	Santa Monica	(310)	89,736	92,987
*93060	Santa Paula	(805)	29,321	30,441
*95401	Santa Rosa	(707)	167,815	174,170
*92071	Santee	(619)	53,413	57,052
*95070	Saratoga	(408)	29,926	31,001
*95066	Scotts Valley	(831)	11,580	11,858
90740	Seal Beach	(562)	24,168	24,662
93955	Seaside	(831)	33,025	34,182
93662	Selma	(559)	23,219	24,283
93263	Shafter	(661)	16,988	17,559
*96019	Shasta Lake	(916)	10,164	10,166
*91024	Sierra Madre	(626)	10,917	11,165
*90755	Signal Hill	(562)	11,016	11,526
*93065	Simi Valley	(805)	124,237	126,871
92075	Solana Beach	(858)	12,867	13,337
93960	Soledad	(831)	25,738	25,336
95476	Sonoma	(707)	10,648	11,017
91733	South El Monte	(626)	20,116	20,569
90280	South Gate	(323)/(562)	94,396	96,312
*96150	South Lake Tahoe	(530)	21,403	21,529
*91030	South Pasadena	(213)/(323)/(626)/(818)	25,619	26,156
*94080	South San Francisco	(650)	63,632	67,009
91744	South San Jose Hills (c)	(626)	20,551	—
90605	South Whittier (c)	(562)	57,156	—
*91977	Spring Valley (c) (San Diego Co.)	(619)	28,205	—
*94305	Stanford (c)	(650)	13,809	—
90680	Stanton	(714)	38,186	38,719
91381	Stevenson Ranch (c)	(661)	17,557	—
*95202	Stockton	(209)	291,707	302,389
*94585	Suisun City	(707)	28,111	29,256
93543	Sun Village (c)	(661)	11,565	—
*94086	Sunnyvale	(408)	140,081	149,980
*96130	Susanville	(530)	17,947	15,543
94941	Tamalpais-Homestead Valley (c)	(415)	10,735	—
*93561	Tehachapi	(661)	14,414	13,236
*92590	Temecula	(951)	100,097	109,428
92883	Temescal Valley (c)	(951)	22,535	—
91780	Temple City	(626)	35,558	36,334
*91360	Thousand Oaks	(805)	126,683	129,342
*90503	Torrance	(310)	145,438	148,495
*95376	Tracy	(209)	82,922	85,841
*96161	Truckee	(916)	16,180	16,297
*93274	Tulare	(559)	59,278	61,867
*95380	Turlock	(209)	68,549	71,245
*92780	Tustin	(714)/(949)	75,540	80,621
*92277	Twentynine Palms	(760)	25,048	25,902
*95482	Ukiah	(707)	16,075	15,977
94587	Union City	(510)	69,516	73,621
*91784	Upland	(909)	73,732	76,043
*95687	Vacaville	(707)	92,428	95,856
91744	Valinda (c)	(626)	22,822	—
92343	Valle Vista (c)	(951)	14,578	—
*94590	Vallejo	(707)	115,942	120,228
	Ventura. *See* San Buenaventura			
*92393	Victorville	(760)	115,903	121,901
90043	View Park-Windsor Hills (c)	(310)	11,075	—
91722	Vincent (c)	(925)	15,922	—
95829	Vineyard (c)	(916)	24,836	—
*93291	Visalia	(559)	124,442	129,281
*92083	Vista	(760)	93,834	98,079
*91789	Walnut	(626)	29,172	30,214
*94596	Walnut Creek	(925)	64,173	67,673
90255	Walnut Park (c)	(213)	15,966	—
93280	Wasco	(661)	25,545	26,303
*95076	Watsonville	(831)	51,199	53,111
90502	West Carson (c)	(310)	21,699	—
*91790	West Covina	(626)	106,098	108,455
*90069	West Hollywood	(310)/(323)	34,399	35,883
91746	West Puente Valley (c)	(626)	22,636	—
*95691	West Sacramento	(916)	48,744	51,847
*90606	West Whittier-Los Nietos (c)	(562)	25,540	—
*92683	Westminster	(714)	89,701	92,068
*90047	Westmont (c)	(323)	31,853	—
*90602	Whittier	(562)	85,331	87,318
92595	Wildomar	(951)	32,176	35,377
*90222	Willowbrook (c)	(323)	35,983	—
95492	Windsor	(707)	26,801	27,414
92040	Winter Gardens (c)	(619)	20,631	—
95388	Winton (c)	(209)	10,613	—
92504	Woodcrest (c)	(909)/(951)	14,347	—
*95695	Woodland	(530)	55,468	57,432
*92886	Yorba Linda	(714)	64,234	67,826
*95991	Yuba City	(530)	64,925	65,773
92399	Yucaipa	(909)	51,367	53,096
*92284	Yucca Valley	(760)	20,700	21,485

(1) Place was incorporated after the 2010 Census was conducted. Data in 2010 column is for Eastvale CDP. (2) Place was incorporated after the 2010 Census was conducted. Data in 2010 column is Census Bureau estimate.

Colorado

Area code 720 overlays area code 303.

ZIP	Place	Area code	2010 population	2014 estimate
*80004	Arvada	(303)	106,433	113,574
*80010	Aurora	(303)	325,078	353,108
80221	Berkley (c)	(970)	11,207	—
*80908	Black Forest (c)	(719)	13,116	—
*80302	Boulder	(303)	97,385	105,112
*80601	Brighton	(303)	33,352	36,765
*80020	Broomfield	(303)	55,889	62,138
*81212	Cañon City	(719)	16,400	16,337
80108	Castle Pines[1]	(303)	10,360	10,796
*80104	Castle Rock	(303)	48,231	55,747

ZIP	Place	Area code	2010 population	2014 estimate
*80015	Centennial	(303)	100,377	107,201
80111	Cherry Creek (c)	(303)	11,120	—
81222	Cimarron Hills (c)	(719)	16,161	—
81520	Clifton (c)	(970)	19,889	—
*80903	Colorado Springs	(719)	416,427	445,830
*80128	Columbine (c)	(303)	24,280	—
*80022	Commerce City	(303)	45,913	51,762
80304	Dakota Ridge (c)	(303)	32,005	—
*80202	Denver	(303)	600,158	663,862
*81301	Durango	(970)	16,887	17,834
81632	Edwards (c)	(970)	10,266	—
*80110	Englewood	(303)	30,255	32,480
80516	Erie	(303)	18,135	20,493
80620	Evans	(970)	18,537	20,473
80221	Federal Heights	(303)	11,467	12,178
*80520	Firestone	(303)	10,147	11,537
80913	Fort Carson (c)	(719)	13,813	—
*80525	Fort Collins	(970)	143,986	156,480
*80701	Fort Morgan	(970)	11,315	11,329
80817	Fountain	(719)	25,846	27,631
*80530	Frederick	(303)	8,679	10,927
*81521	Fruita	(970)	12,646	12,761
*80401	Golden	(303)	18,867	20,201
*81501	Grand Junction	(970)	58,566	60,210
*80631	Greeley	(970)	92,889	98,596
*80111	Greenwood Village	(303)	13,925	15,385
*80126	Highlands Ranch (c)	(303)	96,713	—
80534	Johnstown	(970)	9,887	13,306
80127	Ken Caryl (c)	(303)	32,438	—
80026	Lafayette	(303)	24,453	27,081
*80226	Lakewood	(303)	142,980	149,643
*80120	Littleton	(303)	41,737	44,669
*80124	Lone Tree	(303)	10,218	13,545
*80501	Longmont	(303)	86,270	90,237
80027	Louisville	(303)	18,376	20,112
*80538	Loveland	(970)	66,859	72,651
*81401	Montrose	(970)	19,132	19,045
*80233	Northglenn	(303)	35,789	38,596
*80134	Parker	(303)	45,297	49,857
*81003	Pueblo	(719)	106,595	108,423
81007	Pueblo West (c)	(719)	29,637	—
80911	Security-Widefield (c)	(719)	32,882	—
80221	Sherrelwood (c)	(303)	18,287	—
*80487	Steamboat Springs	(970)	12,088	12,260
80751	Sterling	(970)	14,777	14,629
80027	Superior	(303)	12,483	12,855
80134	The Pinery (c)	(303)	10,517	—
*80229	Thornton	(303)	118,772	130,307
80229	Welby (c)	(303)	14,846	—
*80030	Westminster	(303)	106,114	112,090
*80033	Wheat Ridge	(303)	30,166	31,034
*80550	Windsor	(970)	18,644	21,106

(1) Place was incorporated after the 2010 Census was conducted. Data in 2010 column is Census Bureau estimate.

Connecticut

Area code 475 overlays area code 203. Area code 959 overlays 860. See introductory note.

ZIP	Place	Area code	2010 population	2014 estimate
06401	Ansonia	(203)	19,249	18,959
06001	*Avon*	(860)	18,098	18,421
06037	*Berlin*	(860)	19,866	20,610
06801	*Bethel*	(203)	18,584	19,372
06002	*Bloomfield*	(860)	20,486	20,819
06405	*Branford*	(203)	28,026	28,225
*06604	Bridgeport	(203)	144,229	147,612
*06010	Bristol	(860)	60,477	60,570
06804	*Brookfield*	(203)	16,452	17,055
06019	*Canton*	(860)	10,292	10,345
*06410	*Cheshire*	(203)	29,261	29,250
06413	*Clinton*	(860)	13,260	13,129
*06415	*Colchester*	(860)	16,068	16,192
06238	*Coventry*	(860)	12,435	12,419
06416	*Cromwell*	(860)	14,005	14,113
*06810	Danbury	(203)	80,893	83,784
06820	*Darien*	(203)	20,732	21,689
06418	Derby	(203)	12,902	12,768
*06424	*East Hampton*	(860)	12,959	12,874
*06108	*East Hartford*	(860)	51,252	51,033
*06512	*East Haven*	(203)	29,257	29,044
06333	*East Lyme*	(860)	19,159	19,140
*06088	*East Windsor*	(860)	11,162	11,423
06029	*Ellington*	(860)	15,602	15,795
*06082	*Enfield*	(860)	44,654	44,626
*06825	*Fairfield*	(203)	59,404	61,347
*06032	*Farmington*	(860)	25,340	25,627
06033	*Glastonbury*	(860)	34,427	34,754
*06035	*Granby*	(860)	11,282	11,310
*06830	*Greenwich*	(203)	61,171	62,610
*06830	Greenwich (c)	(203)	12,942	—
06351	*Griswold*	(860)	11,951	11,916
06340	*Groton*	(860)	40,115	40,167
06437	*Guilford*	(203)	22,375	22,413
*06514	*Hamden*	(203)	60,960	61,422
*06101	Hartford	(860)	124,775	124,705
*06239	*Killingly*	(860)	17,370	17,172
06339	*Ledyard*	(860)	15,051	15,121
06443	*Madison*	(203)	18,269	18,259
*06040	*Manchester*	(860)	58,241	58,106
*06040	Manchester (c)	(860)	30,577	—
*06250	*Mansfield*	(860)	26,543	25,977
*06450	Meriden	(203)	60,868	60,293
06457	Middletown	(860)	47,648	47,043
*06460	Milford (balance)	(203)	51,271	51,857
*06460	*Milford*	(203)	52,759	53,358
06468	*Monroe*	(203)	19,479	19,867
06353	*Montville*	(860)	19,571	19,635
06770	Naugatuck	(203)	31,862	31,659
*06051	New Britain	(860)	73,206	72,878
*06840	*New Canaan*	(203)	19,738	20,314
06812	*New Fairfield*	(203)	13,881	14,149
*06511	New Haven	(203)	129,779	130,282
06320	New London	(860)	27,620	27,374
06776	*New Milford*	(860)	28,142	27,474
*06111	*Newington*	(860)	30,562	30,685
06470	*Newtown*	(203)	27,560	28,152
06471	*North Branford*	(203)	14,407	14,322
06473	*North Haven*	(203)	24,093	23,909
*06850	Norwalk	(203)	85,603	88,145
06360	Norwich	(860)	40,493	40,178
06475	*Old Saybrook*	(860)	10,242	10,217
06477	*Orange*	(203)	13,956	13,955
06478	*Oxford*	(203)	12,683	12,914
06374	*Plainfield*	(860)	15,405	15,135
06062	*Plainville*	(860)	17,716	17,801
06782	*Plymouth*	(860)	12,243	11,914
*06877	*Ridgefield*	(203)	24,638	25,205
06067	*Rocky Hill*	(860)	19,709	20,094
*06483	*Seymour*	(203)	16,540	16,537
06484	Shelton	(203)	39,559	41,295
06070	*Simsbury*	(860)	23,511	23,975
06071	*Somers*	(860)	11,444	11,303
06074	*South Windsor*	(860)	25,709	25,823
06488	*Southbury*	(203)	19,904	19,881
06489	*Southington*	(860)	43,069	43,815
*06075	*Stafford*	(860)	12,087	11,881
*06901	Stamford	(203)	122,643	128,278
06378	*Stonington*	(860)	18,545	18,512
*06268	Storrs (c)	(860)	15,344	—
*06614	*Stratford*	(203)	51,384	52,734
*06078	*Suffield*	(860)	15,735	15,814
06084	*Tolland*	(860)	15,052	14,872
*06790	Torrington	(860)	36,383	35,190
06611	*Trumbull*	(203)	36,018	36,578
06066	*Vernon*	(860)	29,179	29,098
*06492	*Wallingford*	(203)	45,135	45,074
06492	Wallingford Center (c)	(203)	18,209	—
*06702	Waterbury	(203)	110,366	109,307
*06385	*Waterford*	(860)	19,517	19,427
*06795	*Watertown*	(860)	22,514	22,046
*06105	*West Hartford*	(860)	63,268	63,324
06516	West Haven	(203)	55,564	54,905
06883	*Weston*	(203)	10,179	10,388
*06880	*Westport*	(203)	26,391	27,561
*06109	*Wethersfield*	(860)	26,668	26,446
06226	Willimantic (c)	(860)	17,737	—
06897	*Wilton*	(203)	18,062	18,692
*06094	*Winchester*	(860)	11,242	10,929
*06280	*Windham*	(860)	25,268	25,005
*06095	*Windsor*	(860)	29,044	29,069
06096	*Windsor Locks*	(860)	12,498	12,565
*06716	*Wolcott*	(203)	16,680	16,716

Delaware

Area code 302 applies to the entire state.

ZIP	Place	2010 population	2014 estimate
19701	Bear (c)	19,371	—
19713	Brookside (c)	14,353	—
*19901	Dover	36,047	37,355
19702	Glasgow (c)	14,303	—
19707	Hockessin (c)	13,527	—
19709	Middletown	18,871	19,910
19963	Milford	9,559	10,179
*19711	Newark	31,454	33,008
19808	Pike Creek Valley (c)	11,217	—
19977	Smyrna	10,023	11,170
*19801	Wilmington	70,851	71,817

District of Columbia

Area code 202 applies to the entire district.

ZIP	Place	2010 population	2014 estimate
*20001	Washington	601,723	658,893

Florida

Part of area code 321 overlays area code 407. Area code 754 overlays 954. Area code 786 overlays 305.

ZIP	Place	Area code	2010 population	2014 estimate
*32828	Alafaya (c)	(407)	78,113	—
*32701	Altamonte Springs	(407)	41,496	42,225
33572	Apollo Beach (c)	(813)	14,055	—
*32712	Apopka	(407)	41,542	47,084
*32233	Atlantic Beach	(904)	12,655	13,031
33823	Auburndale	(863)	13,507	14,518
*33160	Aventura	(305)	35,762	37,451
32807	Azalea Park (c)	(407)	12,556	—
*33830	Bartow	(863)	17,298	18,420
34667	Bayonet Point (c)	(727)	23,467	—
33507	Bayshore Gardens (c)	(941)	16,323	—
*33756	Bellair-Meadowbrook Terrace (c)	(904)	13,343	—
33430	Belle Glade	(561)	17,467	18,061
*34420	Bellview (c)	(352)	23,355	—
*33509	Bloomingdale (c)	(813)	22,711	—
*33431	Boca Raton	(561)	84,392	91,332
*34135	Bonita Springs	(239)	43,914	49,299
*33436	Boynton Beach	(561)	68,217	73,124
*34201	Bradenton	(941)	49,546	52,769
*33510	Brandon (c)	(813)	103,483	—
32503	Brent (c)	(850)	21,804	—
33142	Brownsville (c)	(305)	15,313	—
34743	Buenaventura Lakes (c)	(407)	26,079	—
32404	Callaway	(850)	14,405	15,006
32920	Cape Canaveral	(321)	9,912	10,049
*33914	Cape Coral	(239)	154,305	169,854
*33618	Carrollwood (c)	(813)	33,365	—
*32707	Casselberry	(407)	26,241	26,707
33558	Cheval (c)	(813)	10,702	—
33624	Citrus Park (c)	(813)	24,252	—
*33755	Clearwater	(727)	107,685	110,703
*34711	Clermont	(352)	28,742	30,600
*32922	Cocoa	(321)	17,140	17,419
*32931	Cocoa Beach	(321)	11,231	11,400
*33063	Coconut Creek	(954)	52,909	58,536
32809	Conway (c)	(407)	13,467	—
*33328	Cooper City	(954)	28,547	34,923
*33134	Coral Gables	(305)	46,780	51,227
*33065	Coral Springs	(954)	121,096	127,952
33157	Coral Terrace (c)	(305)	24,376	—
33015	Country Club (c)	(305)	47,105	—
33196	Country Walk (c)	(305)	15,997	—
*32536	Crestview	(850)	20,978	22,955
*33189	Cutler Bay	(305)	40,286	44,321
33919	Cypress Lake (c)	(239)	11,846	—
*33004	Dania Beach	(954)	29,639	31,117
*33314	Davie	(954)	91,992	98,895
*32114	Daytona Beach	(386)	61,005	63,011
*32713	DeBary	(386)	19,320	19,648
*33441	Deerfield Beach	(954)	75,018	78,881
*32720	DeLand	(386)	27,031	29,194
*33444	Delray Beach	(561)	60,522	65,055
*32738	Deltona	(407)	85,182	86,890
*32541	Destin	(850)	12,305	13,355
32836	Doctor Phillips (c)	(407)	10,981	—
*33166	Doral	(305)	45,704	54,116
*34698	Dunedin	(727)	35,321	35,819
33610	East Lake (c)	(813)	30,962	—
33619	East Lake-Orient Park (c)	(813)	22,753	—
32583	East Milton (c)	(850)	11,074	—
*32132	Edgewater	(386)	20,750	21,121
33614	Egypt Lake-Leto (c)	(813)	35,282	—
34680	Elfers (c)	(727)	13,986	—
*34223	Englewood (c)	(941)	14,863	—
32534	Ensley (c)	(850)	20,602	—
*33928	Estero (c)	(239)	22,612	—
*32726	Eustis	(352)	18,558	19,455
32804	Fairview Shores (c)	(305)	10,239	—
*32034	Fernandina Beach	(904)	11,487	12,103
32514	Ferry Pass (c)	(850)	28,921	—
33547	Fish Hawk (c)	(813)	14,087	—
32003	Fleming Island (c)	(904)	27,126	—
*33034	Florida City	(305)	11,245	12,062
32960	Florida Ridge (c)	(772)	18,164	—
32714	Forest City (c)	(407)	13,854	—
*33301	Fort Lauderdale	(954)	165,521	176,013
*33901	Fort Myers	(239)	62,298	70,918
*34981	Fort Pierce	(772)	41,590	43,601
*32548	Fort Walton Beach	(850)	19,507	21,558
33172	Fountainebleau (c)	(305)	59,764	—
34747	Four Corners (c)	(863)	26,116	—
32259	Fruit Cove (c)	(904)	29,362	—
34232	Fruitville (c)	(941)	13,224	—
*32601	Gainesville	(352)	124,354	128,460
33534	Gibsonton (c)	(813)	14,234	—
33138	Gladeview (c)	(954)	11,535	—
33143	Glenvar Heights (c)	(305)	16,898	—
34116	Golden Gate (c)	(239)	23,961	—
33055	Golden Glades (c)	(305)	33,145	—
32733	Goldenrod (c)	(407)	12,039	—
32560	Gonzalez (c)	(850)	13,273	—
33170	Goulds (c)	(305)	10,103	—
*33463	Greenacres	(561)	37,573	39,157
*34736	Groveland	(352)	8,729	10,460
33581	Gulf Gate Estates (c)	(941)	10,911	—
*33737	Gulfport	(727)	12,029	12,198
*33844	Haines City	(863)	20,535	22,072
*33009	Hallandale Beach	(954)	37,113	39,051
*33010	Hialeah	(305)	224,669	235,563
*33016	Hialeah Gardens	(305)	21,744	23,555
33846	Highland City (c)	(863)	10,834	—
*33455	Hobe Sound (c)	(772)	11,521	—
*34690	Holiday (c)	(727)	22,403	—
*32125	Holly Hill	(386)	11,659	11,765
*33019	Hollywood	(954)	140,768	148,047
*33030	Homestead	(305)	60,512	65,524
34447	Homosassa Springs (c)	(352)	13,791	—
34787	Horizon West (c)	(352)	14,000	—
*34667	Hudson (c)	(727)	12,158	—
32837	Hunters Creek (c)	(407)	14,321	—
*34142	Immokalee (c)	(239)	24,154	—
33908	Iona (c)	(239)	15,369	—
33162	Ives Estates (c)	(305)	19,525	—
*32210	Jacksonville	(904)	821,784	853,382
*32250	Jacksonville Beach	(904)	21,362	22,665
33568	Jasmine Estates (c)	(727)	18,989	—
*34957	Jensen Beach (c)	(772)	11,707	—
*33458	Jupiter	(561)	55,156	60,681
33478	Jupiter Farms (c)	(561)	11,994	—
33183	Kendale Lakes (c)	(305)	56,148	—
*33156	Kendall (c)	(305)	75,371	—
33193	Kendall West (c)	(305)	36,154	—
33149	Key Biscayne	(305)	12,344	12,924
33037	Key Largo (c)	(305)	10,433	—
*33040	Key West	(305)	24,649	25,704
33556	Keystone (c)	(813)	24,039	—
*34744	Kissimmee	(407)	59,682	66,722
*32159	Lady Lake	(352)	13,926	14,455
32054	Lake Butler (c)	(386)	15,400	—
*32055	Lake City	(386)	12,046	12,100
33612	Lake Magdalene (c)	(813)	28,509	—
*32746	Lake Mary	(407)	13,822	15,801
*33853	Lake Wales	(863)	14,225	15,140
*33460	Lake Worth	(561)	34,910	37,097
*33801	Lakeland	(863)	97,422	102,346
33801	Lakeland Highlands (c)	(863)	11,056	—
32073	Lakeside (c)	(904)	30,943	—
34951	Lakewood Park (c)	(772)	11,323	—
*34639	Land O' Lakes (c)	(813)	31,996	—
*33465	Lantana	(561)	10,423	10,996
*33770	Largo	(727)	77,648	79,019
*33319	Lauderdale Lakes	(954)	32,593	34,410
*33313	Lauderhill	(954)	66,887	70,626
33714	Lealman (c)	(727)	19,879	—
*34748	Leesburg	(352)	20,117	21,524
*33936	Lehigh Acres (c)	(239)	86,784	—
*33033	Leisure City (c)	(305)	22,655	—
*33074	Lighthouse Point	(954)	10,344	10,953
32810	Lockhart (c)	(407)	13,060	—
*32750	Longwood	(407)	13,657	13,877
*33549	Lutz (c)	(813)	19,344	—
32444	Lynn Haven	(850)	18,493	19,792
*32751	Maitland	(407)	15,751	16,823
33550	Mango (c)	(813)	11,313	—
*34145	Marco Island	(239)	16,413	17,460
*33063	Margate	(954)	53,284	56,061
32824	Meadow Woods (c)	(407)	25,558	—
*32901	Melbourne	(321)	76,068	78,490
*32953	Merritt Island (c)	(321)	34,743	—
*33125	Miami	(305)	399,457	430,332
*33140	Miami Beach	(305)	87,779	91,732
*33014	Miami Gardens	(305)	107,167	112,265
*33014	Miami Lakes	(305)	29,361	30,791
33138	Miami Shores	(305)	10,493	10,861
*33266	Miami Springs	(305)	13,809	14,415
*32068	Middleburg (c)	(904)	13,008	—
32563	Midway (c) (Santa Rosa Co.)	(850)	16,115	—
34715	Minneola	(352)	9,403	10,351
*33023	Miramar	(954)	122,041	134,989
*32757	Mount Dora	(352)	12,370	13,182
32526	Myrtle Grove (c)	(850)	15,870	—
*34102	Naples	(239)	19,537	20,968
32566	Navarre (c)	(850)	31,378	—
*34653	New Port Richey	(727)	14,911	15,527
34653	New Port Richey East (c)	(727)	10,036	—
*32168	New Smyrna Beach	(386)	22,464	23,658
*32578	Niceville	(850)	12,749	14,387
*33917	North Fort Myers (c)	(239)	39,407	—
*33068	North Lauderdale	(954)	41,023	43,214
*33161	North Miami	(305)	58,786	61,420
*33160	North Miami Beach	(305)	41,523	43,664
*33408	North Palm Beach	(561)	12,015	12,483

ZIP	Place	Area code	2010 population	2014 estimate
*34286	North Port	(941)	57,357	60,380
33624	Northdale (c)	(813)	22,079	—
33860	Oak Ridge (c)	(407)	22,685	—
*33334	Oakland Park	(954)	41,363	43,800
32065	Oakleaf Plantation (c)	(904)	20,315	—
*34470	Ocala	(352)	56,315	57,586
34761	Ocoee	(407)	35,579	41,073
*33163	Ojus (c)	(305)	18,036	—
34677	Oldsmar	(813)	13,591	13,913
*33265	Olympia Heights (c)	(305)	13,488	—
*33054	Opa-locka	(305)	15,219	16,460
*32763	Orange City	(386)	10,599	11,056
*32801	Orlando	(407)	238,300	262,372
*32174	Ormond Beach	(386)	38,137	39,075
*32765	Oviedo	(407)	33,342	38,020
32571	Pace (c)	(850)	20,039	—
*32177	Palatka	(386)	10,558	10,387
*32905	Palm Bay	(321)	103,190	105,838
*33410	Palm Beach Gardens	(561)	48,452	51,919
*34990	Palm City (c)	(772)	23,120	—
*32137	Palm Coast	(386)	75,180	80,600
*34683	Palm Harbor (c)	(727)	57,439	—
*33601	Palm River-Clair Mel (c)	(813)	21,024	—
*33406	Palm Springs	(561)	18,928	21,728
32082	Palm Valley (c)	(904)	20,019	—
*34221	Palmetto	(941)	12,606	13,082
*33157	Palmetto Bay	(305)	23,410	24,513
33157	Palmetto Estates (c)	(305)	13,535	—
*32401	Panama City	(850)	36,484	37,681
*32417	Panama City Beach	(850)	12,018	12,408
*33067	Parkland	(954)	23,962	28,131
*33026	Pembroke Pines	(954)	154,750	164,626
*32502	Pensacola	(850)	51,923	53,068
*32809	Pine Castle (c)	(407)	10,805	—
*32808	Pine Hills (c)	(407)	60,076	—
33156	Pinecrest	(305)	18,223	19,251
*33781	Pinellas Park	(727)	49,079	50,946
33168	Pinewood (c)	(305)	16,520	—
*33566	Plant City	(813)	34,721	36,627
*33311	Plantation	(954)	84,955	91,457
*34758	Poinciana (c)	(407)	53,193	—
*33060	Pompano Beach	(954)	99,845	106,105
*33952	Port Charlotte (c)	(941)	54,392	—
*32129	Port Orange	(386)	56,048	58,742
32927	Port St. John (c)	(321)	12,267	—
*34953	Port St. Lucie	(772)	164,603	174,110
34992	Port Salerno (c)	(772)	10,091	—
*33032	Princeton (c)	(305)	22,038	—
*33950	Punta Gorda	(941)	16,641	17,596
33177	Richmond West (c)	(305)	31,973	—
*33569	Riverview (c)	(813)	71,050	—
*33404	Riviera Beach	(561)	32,488	33,649
*32955	Rockledge	(321)	24,926	26,071
*33411	Royal Palm Beach	(561)	34,140	37,015
*33570	Ruskin (c)	(813)	17,208	—
*34695	Safety Harbor	(727)	16,884	17,234
*32084	Saint Augustine	(904)	12,975	13,841
*34769	Saint Cloud	(407)	35,183	43,005
*33701	Saint Petersburg	(727)	244,769	253,693
33912	San Carlos Park (c)	(239)	16,824	—
*32771	Sanford	(407)	53,570	57,525
*34231	Sarasota	(941)	51,917	54,214
33577	Sarasota Springs (c)	(941)	14,395	—
32937	Satellite Beach	(321)	10,109	10,418
*32958	Sebastian	(772)	21,929	23,344
*33870	Sebring	(863)	10,491	10,372
*33770	Seminole	(813)	17,233	17,923
34610	Shady Hills (c)	(727)	11,523	—
33505	South Bradenton (c)	(941)	22,178	—
32121	South Daytona	(386)	12,252	12,397
*33243	South Miami	(305)	11,657	12,183
33157	South Miami Heights (c)	(305)	35,696	—
33595	South Venice (c)	(941)	13,949	—
32824	Southchase (c)	(407)	15,921	—
*34604	Spring Hill (c)	(352)	98,621	—
*34994	Stuart	(772)	15,593	16,197
*33573	Sun City Center (c)	(813)	19,258	—
33160	Sunny Isles Beach	(305)	20,832	21,946
*33325	Sunrise	(954)	84,439	91,256
*33283	Sunset (c)	(305)	16,389	—
33144	Sweetwater	(305)	13,499	20,751
*32301	Tallahassee	(850)	181,376	188,107
*33321	Tamarac	(954)	60,427	63,793
*33184	Tamiami (c)	(305)	55,271	—
*33602	Tampa	(813)	335,709	358,699
*34689	Tarpon Springs	(727)	23,484	24,239
32778	Tavares	(352)	13,951	14,930
*33687	Temple Terrace	(813)	24,541	25,419
33412	The Acreage (c)	(561)	38,704	—
33186	The Crossings (c)	(305)	22,758	—
33196	The Hammocks (c)	(305)	51,003	—
*32162	The Villages (c)	(352)	51,442	—
33592	Thonotosassa (c)	(813)	13,014	—
33186	Three Lakes (c)	(305)	15,047	—
*32780	Titusville	(321)	43,761	44,557
33615	Town 'n' Country (c)	(813)	78,442	—
34655	Trinity (c)	(813)	10,907	—
33613	University (c) (Hillsborough Co.)	(813)	41,163	—
32826	University (c) (Orange Co.)	(407)	31,084	—
33165	University Park (c)	(305)	26,995	—
32401	Upper Grand Lagoon (c)	(850)	13,963	—
*33594	Valrico (c)	(813)	35,545	—
*34285	Venice	(941)	20,748	21,730
*32960	Vero Beach	(772)	15,220	16,017
32960	Vero Beach South (c)	(772)	23,092	—
32955	Viera East (c)	(321)	10,757	—
33901	Villas (c)	(239)	11,569	—
32507	Warrington (c)	(850)	14,531	—
32779	Wekiwa Springs (c)	(407)	21,998	—
*33414	Wellington	(561)	56,508	61,485
*33544	Wesley Chapel (c)	(813)	44,092	—
33714	West Lealman (c)	(727)	15,651	—
33138	West Little River (c)	(305)	34,699	—
*32912	West Melbourne	(321)	18,355	20,078
*33401	West Palm Beach	(561)	99,919	104,031
33023	West Park	(954)	14,156	14,914
32505	West Pensacola (c)	(850)	21,339	—
33626	Westchase (c)	(813)	21,747	—
33165	Westchester (c)	(305)	29,862	—
*33326	Weston	(954)	65,333	69,100
33165	Westwood Lakes (c)	(305)	11,838	—
*33305	Wilton Manors	(954)	11,632	12,243
*34787	Winter Garden	(407)	34,568	38,746
*33880	Winter Haven	(863)	33,874	36,371
*32789	Winter Park	(407)	27,852	29,442
*32708	Winter Springs	(407)	33,282	34,169
32092	World Golf Village (c)	(904)	12,310	—
32547	Wright (c)	(850)	23,127	—
*32097	Yulee (c)	(904)	11,491	—
*33540	Zephyrhills	(813)	13,288	14,381

Georgia

Area codes 404/470/678 overlay area code 770. Area code 762 overlays 706.

ZIP	Place	Area code	2010 population	2014 estimate
*30101	Acworth	(770)	20,425	21,867
*31701	Albany	(229)	77,434	75,769
*30004	Alpharetta	(770)	57,551	63,038
*31709	Americus	(229)	17,041	16,283
*30601	Athens-Clarke Co. (balance)	(706)	115,452	119,648
*30301	Atlanta	(404)	420,003	456,002
*30901	Augusta-Richmond Co. (balance)	(706)	195,844	196,741
*39817	Bainbridge	(229)	12,697	12,496
30032	Belvedere Park (c)	(404)	15,152	—
30326	Brookhaven[1]	(404)	49,217	51,079
*31520	Brunswick	(912)	15,383	15,903
*30518	Buford	(404)	12,225	13,392
*30701	Calhoun	(706)	15,650	16,052
30032	Candler-McAfee (c)	(404)	23,025	—
*30114	Canton	(770)	22,958	24,801
*30117	Carrollton	(770)	24,388	26,690
*30120	Cartersville	(770)	19,731	20,015
*30341	Chamblee	(770)	9,892	16,112
30337	College Park	(404)	13,942	14,598
*31907	Columbus	(706)	189,885	200,887
*30013	Conyers	(404)	15,195	15,718
*31015	Cordele	(229)	11,147	10,939
*30014	Covington	(770)	13,118	13,667
31805	Cusseta-Chattahoochee Co.	(706)	11,267	11,837
*30132	Dallas	(770)	11,544	12,629
*30720	Dalton	(706)	33,128	33,529
*30030	Decatur	(404)	19,335	20,380
*30340	Doraville	(770)	8,330	10,714
*31533	Douglas	(912)	11,589	11,665
*30134	Douglasville	(404)	30,961	32,523
30333	Druid Hills (c)	(404)	14,568	—
*31021	Dublin	(478)	16,201	16,182
*30096	Duluth	(404)	26,600	28,838
*30338	Dunwoody	(770)	46,267	48,000
*30344	East Point	(404)	33,712	35,488
30809	Evans (c)	(706)	29,011	—
30213	Fairburn	(770)	12,950	13,696
*30214	Fayetteville	(404)	15,945	16,725
*30297	Forest Park	(404)	18,468	18,949
*30501	Gainesville	(770)	33,804	36,306
39854	Georgetown (c)	(912)	11,823	—
*30223	Griffin	(770)	23,643	23,329
30813	Grovetown	(706)	11,216	12,746
*31313	Hinesville	(912)	33,437	34,815
*30114	Holly Springs	(770)	9,189	10,237
*31546	Jesup	(912)	10,214	10,285
30022	Johns Creek	(770)	76,728	83,102

ZIP	Place	Area code	2010 population	2014 estimate
*30144	Kennesaw	(404)	29,783	32,400
31548	Kingsland	(912)	15,946	16,416
*30240	LaGrange	(706)	29,588	30,557
*30045	Lawrenceville	(404)	28,546	30,212
*30047	Lilburn	(404)	11,596	12,543
30122	Lithia Springs (c)	(770)	15,491	—
30052	Loganville	(770)	10,458	11,022
30126	Mableton (c)	(404)	37,115	—
*31201	Macon-Bibb Co.[1]	(478)	155,292	153,691
*30060	Marietta	(404)	56,579	60,014
30907	Martinez (c)	(706)	35,795	—
*30253	McDonough	(770)	22,084	23,004
*31061	Milledgeville	(478)	17,715	19,211
*30004	Milton	(770)	32,661	36,662
*30655	Monroe	(770)	13,234	13,664
*31768	Moultrie	(229)	14,268	14,507
30087	Mountain Park (c)	(404)	11,554	—
*30263	Newnan	(770)	33,039	36,203
*30071	Norcross	(770)	9,116	16,349
30319	North Atlanta (c)	(404)	40,456	—
30033	North Decatur (c)	(404)	16,698	—
30033	North Druid Hills (c)	(404)	18,947	—
*30269	Peachtree City	(404)	34,364	35,063
*30092	Peachtree Corners[1]	(770)	38,011	40,531
31069	Perry	(478)	13,839	15,144
31322	Pooler	(912)	19,140	22,251
30127	Powder Springs	(404)	13,940	14,590
30074	Redan (c)	(404)	33,015	—
31324	Richmond Hill	(912)	9,281	11,229
*30274	Riverdale	(404)	15,134	15,669
*30161	Rome	(706)	36,303	35,997
*30077	Roswell	(404)	88,346	94,089
31558	Saint Marys	(912)	17,121	17,949
31522	Saint Simons (c)	(912)	12,743	—
*30328	Sandy Springs	(404)	93,853	101,908
*31401	Savannah	(912)	136,286	144,352
30079	Scottdale (c)	(404)	10,631	—
*30080	Smyrna	(404)	51,271	54,958
*30078	Snellville	(404)	18,242	19,439
*30458	Statesboro	(912)	28,422	30,367
30281	Stockbridge	(404)	25,636	27,619
30518	Sugar Hill	(404)	18,522	20,821
30024	Suwanee	(770)	15,355	18,164
*31792	Thomasville	(229)	18,413	18,700
*31794	Tifton	(229)	16,350	16,701
*30084	Tucker (c)	(404)	27,581	—
30291	Union City	(404)	19,456	20,427
*31601	Valdosta	(229)	54,518	56,595
*30474	Vidalia	(912)	10,473	10,670
30180	Villa Rica	(770)	13,956	14,700
*31088	Warner Robins	(478)	66,588	73,271
*31501	Waycross	(912)	14,649	14,166
31410	Wilmington Island (c)	(912)	15,138	—
30680	Winder	(770)	14,099	14,930
*30188	Woodstock	(770)	23,896	27,823

(1) Place was incorporated after the 2010 Census was conducted. Data in 2010 column is Census Bureau estimate.

Hawaii

Area code 808 applies to the entire state.

ZIP	Place	2000 population	2010 population
96821	East Honolulu (c)	—	49,914
96706	Ewa Beach (c)	14,650	14,955
96706	Ewa Gentry (c)	4,939	22,690
96701	Halawa (c)	13,891	14,014
96749	Hawaiian Paradise Park (c)	7,051	11,404
*96720	Hilo (c)	40,759	43,263
*96813	Honolulu, urban (c)	371,657	350,399[1]
*96732	Kahului (c)	20,146	26,337
96740	Kailua (c) (Hawaii Co.)	9,870	11,975
96734	Kailua (c) (Honolulu Co.)	36,513	38,635
96744	Kaneohe (c)	34,970	34,597
96746	Kapaa (c)	9,472	10,699
*96707	Kapolei (c)	—	15,186
96753	Kihei (c)	16,749	20,881
*96761	Lahaina (c)	9,118	11,704
96707	Makakilo (c)	13,156	18,248
96789	Mililani Mauka (c)	—	21,039
96789	Mililani Town (c)	28,608	27,629
96792	Nanakuli (c)	10,814	12,666
96782	Pearl City (c)	30,976	47,698
96797	Royal Kunia (c)	—	14,525
96857	Schofield Barracks (c)	14,428	16,370
96786	Wahiawa (c)	16,151	17,821
96792	Waianae (c)	10,506	13,177
96793	Wailuku (c)	12,296	15,313
96701	Waimalu (c)	29,371	13,730
96797	Waipahu (c)	33,108	38,216
96797	Waipio (c)	11,672	11,674

(1) 2014 estimate.

Idaho

Area code 208 applies to the entire state.

ZIP	Place	2010 population	2014 estimate
*83401	Ammon	13,816	14,685
83221	Blackfoot	11,899	11,814
*83702	Boise	205,671	216,282
83318	Burley	10,345	10,480
*83605	Caldwell	46,237	50,224
83202	Chubbuck	13,922	14,229
*83814	Coeur d'Alene	44,137	47,912
83616	Eagle	19,908	22,502
*83714	Garden City	10,972	11,420
83835	Hayden	13,294	13,870
*83402	Idaho Falls	56,813	58,691
83338	Jerome	10,890	11,189
83634	Kuna	15,210	16,999
83501	Lewiston	31,894	32,482
*83642	Meridian	75,092	87,743
*83843	Moscow	23,800	24,767
83647	Mountain Home	14,206	13,780
*83651	Nampa	81,557	88,211
*83201	Pocatello	54,255	54,292
*83854	Post Falls	27,574	29,896
*83440	Rexburg	25,484	27,094
*83301	Twin Falls	44,125	46,528

Illinois

Area code 224 overlays area code 847. Area code 331 overlays 630. Area code 779 overlays 815. Area code 872 overlays 312/773.

ZIP	Place	Area code	2010 population	2014 estimate
60101	Addison	(630)	36,942	37,297
*60102	Algonquin	(847)	30,046	30,410
60803	Alsip	(708)	19,277	19,427
62002	Alton	(618)	27,865	27,177
60002	Antioch	(847)	14,430	14,411
*60005	Arlington Heights	(847)	75,101	76,024
*60505	Aurora	(630)	197,899	200,456
*60010	Barrington	(847)	10,327	10,373
*60103	Bartlett	(630)	41,208	41,632
*60510	Batavia	(630)	26,045	26,424
*60083	Beach Park	(847)	13,638	13,988
*62220	Belleville	(618)	44,478	42,529
60104	Bellwood	(708)	19,071	19,152
61008	Belvidere	(815)	25,585	25,282
*60106	Bensenville	(630)	18,352	18,487
60402	Berwyn	(708)	56,657	56,693
*60108	Bloomingdale	(630)	22,018	22,299
*61701	Bloomington	(309)	76,610	78,730
*60406	Blue Island	(708)	23,706	23,785
*60440	Bolingbrook	(630)	73,366	74,180
60914	Bourbonnais	(815)	18,631	18,534
60915	Bradley	(815)	15,895	15,677
60455	Bridgeview	(708)	16,446	16,491
60513	Brookfield	(708)	18,978	19,023
60089	Buffalo Grove	(847)	41,496	41,701
60459	Burbank	(708)	28,925	29,218
60527	Burr Ridge	(630)	10,559	10,761
62206	Cahokia	(618)	15,241	14,588
60409	Calumet City	(708)	37,042	37,213
*60119	Campton Hills	(630)/(847)	11,131	11,317
61520	Canton	(309)	14,704	14,307
*62901	Carbondale	(618)	25,902	26,324
*60188	Carol Stream	(630)	39,711	40,349
60110	Carpentersville	(847)	37,691	38,407
60013	Cary	(847)	18,271	17,991
62801	Centralia	(618)	13,032	12,742
*61821	Champaign	(217)	81,055	84,513
60410	Channahon	(815)	12,560	12,616
61920	Charleston	(217)	21,838	21,838
62629	Chatham	(217)	11,500	12,212
*60607	Chicago	(312)/(773)	2,695,598	2,722,389
*60411	Chicago Heights	(708)	30,276	30,436
60415	Chicago Ridge	(708)	14,305	14,434
60804	Cicero	(708)	83,891	84,354
62234	Collinsville	(618)	25,579	24,883
62236	Columbia	(618)	9,707	10,121
60478	Country Club Hills	(708)	16,541	16,865
60435	Crest Hill	(815)	20,837	20,771
60445	Crestwood	(708)	10,950	11,029
*60014	Crystal Lake	(815)	40,743	40,493
*61832	Danville	(217)	33,027	32,243
60561	Darien	(630)	22,086	22,315
*62521	Decatur	(217)	76,122	74,010
60015	Deerfield	(847)	18,225	18,385
60115	DeKalb	(815)	43,862	44,054
*60018	Des Plaines	(847)	58,364	58,947
61021	Dixon	(815)	15,733	15,285
60419	Dolton	(708)	23,153	23,307
*60515	Downers Grove	(630)	47,833	49,715
61244	East Moline	(309)	21,302	21,175
*61611	East Peoria	(309)	23,402	23,375
*62201	East St. Louis	(618)	27,006	26,672
*62025	Edwardsville	(618)	24,293	24,758

ZIP	Place	Area code	2010 population	2014 estimate
62401	Effingham	(217)	12,328	12,577
*60120	Elgin	(847)	108,188	111,117
*60007	Elk Grove Village	(847)	33,127	33,379
60126	Elmhurst	(630)	44,121	45,751
60707	Elmwood Park	(708)	24,883	24,954
*60201	Evanston	(847)	74,486	75,658
60805	Evergreen Park	(708)	19,852	19,935
*62208	Fairview Heights	(618)	17,078	16,901
*60130	Forest Park	(708)	14,167	14,196
60020	Fox Lake	(847)	10,579	10,578
60423	Frankfort	(815)	17,782	18,446
*60131	Franklin Park	(847)	18,333	18,404
61032	Freeport	(815)	25,638	24,851
60030	Gages Lake (c)	(847)	10,198	—
*61401	Galesburg	(309)	32,195	31,659
60134	Geneva	(630)	21,495	21,742
62034	Glen Carbon	(618)	12,934	12,947
*60137	Glen Ellyn	(630)	27,450	27,763
*60139	Glendale Heights	(630)	34,208	34,530
*60025	Glenview	(847)	44,692	46,767
62035	Godfrey	(618)	17,982	17,782
62040	Granite City	(618)	29,849	29,183
60030	Grayslake	(847)	20,957	21,018
60031	Gurnee	(847)	31,295	31,207
60133	Hanover Park	(630)	37,973	38,476
*60426	Harvey	(708)	25,282	25,347
60429	Hazel Crest	(708)	14,100	14,182
62948	Herrin	(618)	12,501	12,852
*60457	Hickory Hills	(708)	14,049	14,177
*60035	Highland Park	(847)	29,763	29,871
*60521	Hinsdale	(630)	16,816	17,446
*60195	Hoffman Estates	(847)	51,895	52,347
*60491	Homer Glen	(708)	24,220	24,364
*60430	Homewood	(708)	19,323	19,464
60142	Huntley	(847)	24,291	25,603
*62650	Jacksonville	(217)	19,446	19,159
*60436	Joliet	(815)	147,433	147,928
60458	Justice	(708)	12,926	13,022
60901	Kankakee	(815)	27,537	26,860
61443	Kewanee	(309)	12,916	12,596
60525	La Grange	(708)	15,550	15,759
60526	La Grange Park	(708)	13,579	13,665
60045	Lake Forest	(847)	19,375	19,379
*60102	Lake in the Hills	(847)	28,965	28,893
*60047	Lake Zurich	(847)	19,631	20,054
60438	Lansing	(708)	28,331	28,522
*60439	Lemont	(630)	16,000	16,661
*60048	Libertyville	(847)	20,315	20,512
62656	Lincoln	(217)	14,504	14,162
*60645	Lincolnwood	(847)	12,590	12,687
60046	Lindenhurst	(847)	14,462	14,468
60532	Lisle	(630)	22,390	22,827
*60441	Lockport	(815)	24,839	25,119
60148	Lombard	(630)	43,165	43,893
*61130	Loves Park	(815)	23,996	23,551
60534	Lyons	(708)	10,729	10,773
*61115	Machesney Park	(815)	23,499	23,036
61455	Macomb	(309)	19,288	18,943
62959	Marion	(618)	17,193	17,438
*60426	Markham	(708)	12,508	12,688
*60443	Matteson	(708)	19,009	19,156
61938	Mattoon	(217)	18,555	18,211
*60153	Maywood	(708)	24,090	24,133
*60050	McHenry	(815)	26,992	26,630
*60160	Melrose Park	(708)	25,411	25,511
60445	Midlothian	(708)	14,819	14,911
60447	Minooka	(815)	10,924	11,194
60448	Mokena	(708)	18,740	19,447
*61265	Moline	(309)	43,483	42,685
60538	Montgomery	(630)	18,438	19,301
60450	Morris	(815)	13,636	14,135
61550	Morton	(309)	16,267	16,499
60053	Morton Grove	(847)	23,270	23,497
60056	Mount Prospect	(847)	54,167	54,951
62864	Mount Vernon	(618)	15,277	15,177
60060	Mundelein	(847)	31,064	31,562
*60540	Naperville	(630)	141,853	146,128
60451	New Lenox	(815)	24,394	25,426
60714	Niles	(847)	29,803	30,000
*61761	Normal	(309)	52,497	54,594
*60634	Norridge	(708)	14,572	14,674
60542	North Aurora	(630)	16,760	17,342
*60064	North Chicago	(847)	32,574	30,395
*60062	Northbrook	(847)	33,170	33,655
60164	Northlake	(708)	12,323	12,372
60452	Oak Forest	(708)	27,962	28,174
*60453	Oak Lawn	(708)	56,690	57,034
*60301	Oak Park	(708)	51,878	52,008
62269	O'Fallon	(618)	28,281	29,069
*60462	Orland Park	(708)	56,767	58,666
60543	Oswego	(630)	30,355	33,099
61350	Ottawa	(815)	18,768	18,428
*60067	Palatine	(847)	68,557	69,387
60463	Palos Heights	(708)	12,515	12,597
60465	Palos Hills	(708)	17,484	17,627
60466	Park Forest	(708)	21,975	22,034
60068	Park Ridge	(847)	37,480	37,856
*61554	Pekin	(309)	34,094	33,824
*61602	Peoria	(309)	115,007	115,828
61354	Peru	(815)	10,295	10,016
*60544	Plainfield	(815)	39,581	42,138
60545	Plano	(630)	10,856	11,175
61764	Pontiac	(815)	11,931	11,599
60070	Prospect Heights	(847)	16,256	16,418
*62301	Quincy	(217)	40,633	40,805
61866	Rantoul	(217)	12,941	13,100
60471	Richton Park	(708)	13,646	13,751
60305	River Forest	(708)	11,172	11,208
60171	River Grove	(708)	10,227	10,271
60827	Riverdale	(708)	13,549	13,604
*61201	Rock Island	(309)	39,018	38,642
*61101	Rockford	(815)	152,871	149,123
60008	Rolling Meadows	(847)	24,099	24,279
60446	Romeoville	(815)	39,680	39,679
61073	Roscoe	(815)	10,785	10,603
60172	Roselle	(630)	22,763	23,030
60073	Round Lake	(847)	18,289	18,536
60073	Round Lake Beach	(847)	28,175	28,012
*60174	Saint Charles	(630)	32,974	33,387
60411	Sauk Village	(708)	10,506	10,545
*60193	Schaumburg	(847)	74,227	74,896
*60176	Schiller Park	(847)	11,793	11,857
*62269	Shiloh	(618)	12,651	12,907
*60436	Shorewood	(815)	15,615	16,569
*60077	Skokie	(847)	64,784	65,112
60177	South Elgin	(847)	21,985	22,226
60473	South Holland	(708)	22,030	22,144
*62703	Springfield	(217)	116,250	116,809
61081	Sterling	(815)	15,370	15,011
60107	Streamwood	(630)	39,858	40,345
61364	Streator	(815)	13,710	13,289
60501	Summit	(708)	11,054	11,447
*62221	Swansea	(618)	13,430	13,651
60178	Sycamore	(815)	17,519	17,753
62568	Taylorville	(217)	11,246	10,971
*60477	Tinley Park	(708)	56,703	57,280
*61801	Urbana	(217)	41,250	42,044
60061	Vernon Hills	(847)	25,113	25,911
60181	Villa Park	(630)	21,904	22,038
60555	Warrenville	(630)	13,140	13,336
61571	Washington	(309)	15,134	15,816
62298	Waterloo	(618)	9,811	10,178
60084	Wauconda	(847)	13,603	13,896
*60085	Waukegan	(847)	89,078	88,915
*60185	West Chicago	(630)	27,086	27,507
60154	Westchester	(708)	16,718	16,807
60558	Western Springs	(708)	12,975	13,284
60559	Westmont	(630)	24,685	24,963
*60187	Wheaton	(630)	52,894	53,644
60090	Wheeling	(847)	37,648	38,010
60091	Wilmette	(847)	27,087	27,446
60093	Winnetka	(847)	12,187	12,490
*60191	Wood Dale	(630)	13,770	13,945
62095	Wood River	(618)	10,657	10,355
60517	Woodridge	(630)	32,971	33,378
60098	Woodstock	(815)	24,770	25,178
60482	Worth	(708)	10,789	10,838
60560	Yorkville	(630)	16,921	18,096
60099	Zion	(847)	24,413	24,264

Indiana

Area code 463 overlays area code 317 effective Oct. 17, 2016. Area code 930 overlays 812.

ZIP	Place	Area code	2010 population	2014 estimate
*46011	Anderson	(765)	56,129	55,455
46706	Auburn	(260)	12,731	12,834
46123	Avon	(317)	12,446	15,971
47421	Bedford	(812)	13,413	13,355
46107	Beech Grove	(317)	14,192	14,514
*47408	Bloomington	(812)	80,405	83,322
46112	Brownsburg	(317)	21,285	23,322
*46032	Carmel	(317)	79,191	86,682
46303	Cedar Lake	(219)	11,560	11,854
46304	Chesterton	(219)	13,068	13,403
*47129	Clarksville	(812)	21,724	21,879
*47201	Columbus	(812)	44,061	46,124
47331	Connersville	(765)	13,481	13,032
47933	Crawfordsville	(765)	15,915	15,988
*46307	Crown Point	(219)	27,317	28,623
*46311	Dyer	(219)	16,390	16,169
46312	East Chicago	(219)	29,698	28,990
*46514	Elkhart	(574)	50,949	51,421
*47708	Evansville	(812)	117,429	120,346
*46038	Fishers	(317)	76,794	86,325
*46802	Fort Wayne	(260)	253,691	258,522
*46041	Frankfort	(765)	16,422	16,153

ZIP	Place	Area code	2010 population	2014 estimate
46131	Franklin	(317)	23,712	24,356
*46402	Gary	(219)	80,294	77,909
*46526	Goshen	(574)	31,719	32,267
46530	Granger (c)	(574)	30,465	—
46135	Greencastle	(765)	10,326	10,362
46140	Greenfield	(317)	20,602	21,398
47240	Greensburg	(812)	11,492	11,817
*46142	Greenwood	(317)	49,791	54,491
46319	Griffith	(219)	16,893	16,516
*46320	Hammond	(219)	80,830	78,384
*46322	Highland	(219)	23,727	23,127
46342	Hobart	(219)	29,059	28,635
46750	Huntington	(260)	17,391	17,166
*46201	Indianapolis (balance)	(317)	820,445	848,788
*47546	Jasper	(812)	15,038	15,325
*47130	Jeffersonville	(812)	44,953	46,440
*46902	Kokomo	(765)	45,468	57,085
*46350	La Porte	(219)	22,053	22,007
*47901	Lafayette	(765)	67,140	70,654
46405	Lake Station	(219)	12,572	12,175
46226	Lawrence	(317)	46,001	47,550
46052	Lebanon	(765)	15,792	15,836
46947	Logansport	(574)	18,396	18,019
47250	Madison	(812)	11,967	12,035
*46952	Marion	(765)	29,948	29,308
46151	Martinsville	(765)	11,828	11,744
*46410	Merrillville	(219)	35,246	35,450
*46360	Michigan City	(219)	31,479	31,487
*46544	Mishawaka	(574)	48,252	48,174
*47302	Muncie	(765)	70,085	70,211
46321	Munster	(219)	23,603	23,103
*47150	New Albany	(812)	36,372	36,589
47362	New Castle	(765)	18,114	17,653
46774	New Haven	(260)	14,794	15,608
*46060	Noblesville	(317)	51,969	57,584
*46970	Peru	(765)	11,417	11,079
*46168	Plainfield	(317)	27,631	30,409
46563	Plymouth	(574)	10,033	10,095
46368	Portage	(219)	36,828	36,760
47907	Purdue University (c)	(765)	12,183	—
*47374	Richmond	(765)	36,812	36,159
46373	Saint John	(219)	14,850	16,117
46375	Schererville	(219)	29,243	28,926
47274	Seymour	(812)	17,503	19,094
46176	Shelbyville	(765)	19,191	19,163
*46601	South Bend	(574)	101,168	101,190
46224	Speedway	(317)	11,812	12,101
*47802	Terre Haute	(812)	60,785	60,956
*46383	Valparaiso	(219)	31,730	32,369
47591	Vincennes	(812)	18,423	18,032
46992	Wabash	(260)	10,666	10,433
*46580	Warsaw	(574)	13,559	14,280
47501	Washington	(812)	11,509	12,020
*47906	West Lafayette	(765)	29,596	32,109
*46074	Westfield	(317)	30,068	35,297
47396	Yorktown	(765)	9,405	11,220
46077	Zionsville	(317)	14,160	25,734

Iowa

ZIP	Place	Area code	2010 population	2014 estimate
50009	Altoona	(515)	14,541	16,105
*50010	Ames	(515)	58,965	63,266
*50021	Ankeny	(515)	45,582	53,801
52722	Bettendorf	(563)	33,217	35,122
*50036	Boone	(515)	12,661	12,633
52601	Burlington	(319)	25,663	25,539
51401	Carroll	(712)	10,103	10,007
*50613	Cedar Falls	(319)	39,260	40,859
*52401	Cedar Rapids	(319)	126,326	129,195
*52732	Clinton	(563)	26,885	26,246
50325	Clive	(515)	15,447	17,052
52241	Coralville	(319)	18,907	20,349
*51501	Council Bluffs	(712)	62,230	62,245
*52802	Davenport	(563)	99,685	102,448
*50315	Des Moines	(515)	203,433	209,220
*52001	Dubuque	(563)	57,637	58,436
50501	Fort Dodge	(515)	25,206	24,594
52627	Fort Madison	(319)	11,051	10,764
50125	Indianola	(515)	14,782	15,305
*52240	Iowa City	(319)	67,862	73,415
50131	Johnston	(515)	17,278	20,359
52632	Keokuk	(319)	10,780	10,692
52302	Marion	(319)	34,768	36,774
50158	Marshalltown	(641)	27,552	27,727
*50401	Mason City	(641)	28,079	27,458
52761	Muscatine	(563)	22,886	23,888
50208	Newton	(641)	15,254	15,150
52317	North Liberty	(319)	13,374	15,386
52577	Oskaloosa	(641)	11,463	11,541
52501	Ottumwa	(641)	25,023	24,682
50219	Pella	(641)	10,352	10,337
*51101	Sioux City	(712)	82,684	82,517
51301	Spencer	(712)	11,233	11,206
50588	Storm Lake	(712)	10,600	10,895
*50322	Urbandale	(515)	39,463	43,150
*50701	Waterloo	(319)	68,406	68,364
50263	Waukee	(515)	13,790	17,705
50677	Waverly	(319)	9,874	10,106
*50265	West Des Moines	(515)	56,609	63,325

Kansas

ZIP	Place	Area code	2010 population	2014 estimate
67002	Andover	(316)	11,791	12,509
67005	Arkansas City	(620)	12,415	12,205
66002	Atchison	(913)	11,021	10,771
67037	Derby	(316)	22,158	23,234
*67801	Dodge City	(620)	27,340	28,117
67042	El Dorado	(316)	13,021	12,879
66801	Emporia	(620)	24,916	24,560
*67846	Garden City	(620)	26,658	27,004
*66030	Gardner	(913)	19,123	20,667
67530	Great Bend	(620)	15,995	15,840
*67601	Hays	(785)	20,510	21,044
67060	Haysville	(316)	10,826	11,112
*67501	Hutchinson	(620)	42,080	41,642
*66441	Junction City	(785)	23,353	24,665
*66102	Kansas City	(913)	145,786	149,636
66043	Lansing	(913)	11,265	11,713
*66044	Lawrence	(785)	87,643	92,763
*66048	Leavenworth	(913)	35,251	36,000
*66211	Leawood	(913)	31,867	34,395
*66215	Lenexa	(913)	48,190	51,042
*67901	Liberal	(620)	20,525	21,012
*66502	Manhattan	(785)	52,281	56,078
67460	McPherson	(620)	13,155	13,189
*66202	Merriam	(913)	11,003	11,290
*67114	Newton	(316)	19,132	19,120
*66061	Olathe	(913)	125,872	133,062
66067	Ottawa	(785)	12,649	12,403
*66204	Overland Park	(913)	173,372	184,525
67357	Parsons	(620)	10,500	10,174
*66762	Pittsburg	(620)	20,233	20,394
*66208	Prairie Village	(913)	21,447	21,877
*67401	Salina	(785)	47,707	47,867
*66203	Shawnee	(913)	62,209	64,599
*66603	Topeka	(785)	127,473	127,215
*67202	Wichita	(316)	382,368	388,413
67156	Winfield	(620)	12,301	12,258

Kentucky

Area code 364 overlays area code 270.

ZIP	Place	Area code	2010 population	2014 estimate
*41101	Ashland	(606)	21,684	21,335
40004	Bardstown	(502)	11,700	12,998
*40403	Berea	(859)	13,561	14,658
*42101	Bowling Green	(270)	58,067	62,479
41005	Burlington (c)	(859)	15,926	—
*42718	Campbellsville	(270)	9,108	11,282
*41011	Covington	(859)	40,640	40,944
*40422	Danville	(859)	16,218	16,620
*42701	Elizabethtown	(270)	28,531	29,974
*41018	Erlanger	(859)	18,082	18,647
*41042	Florence	(859)	29,951	31,888
42223	Fort Campbell North (c)	(270)	13,685	—
40121	Fort Knox (c)	(270)	10,124	—
41075	Fort Thomas	(859)	16,325	16,329
*40601	Frankfort	(502)	25,527	27,557
40324	Georgetown	(502)	29,098	31,653
*42141	Glasgow	(270)	14,028	14,339
*42420	Henderson	(270)	28,757	28,900
*42240	Hopkinsville	(270)	31,577	32,634
41051	Independence	(859)	24,757	26,378
*40269	Jeffersontown	(502)	26,595	26,949
40342	Lawrenceburg	(502)	10,505	11,093
*40507	Lexington-Fayette	(859)	295,803	310,797
*40202	Louisville-Jefferson Co. (balance)	(502)	597,337	612,780
*40252	Lyndon	(502)	11,002	11,311
42431	Madisonville	(270)	19,591	19,622
42066	Mayfield	(270)	10,024	10,122
40047	Mount Washington	(502)	9,117	12,246
42071	Murray	(270)	17,741	18,630
*41071	Newport	(859)	15,273	15,426
*40356	Nicholasville	(859)	28,015	29,097
*42301	Owensboro	(270)	57,265	58,374
*42003	Paducah	(270)	25,024	24,978
*40160	Radcliff	(502)	21,688	22,952
*40475	Richmond	(859)	31,364	33,556
*40207	Saint Matthews	(502)	17,472	17,911
*40066	Shelbyville	(502)	14,045	14,985
40165	Shepherdsville	(502)	11,222	11,856
*40216	Shively	(502)	15,264	15,643
*42501	Somerset	(606)	11,196	11,422
*40391	Winchester	(859)	18,368	18,443

Louisiana

ZIP	Place	Area code	2010 population	2014 estimate
*70510	Abbeville	(337)	12,257	12,446
*71301	Alexandria	(318)	47,723	48,175
70714	Baker	(225)	13,895	13,776
71220	Bastrop	(318)	11,365	10,881
*70801	Baton Rouge	(225)	229,493	228,895
70360	Bayou Blue (c)	(985)	12,352	—
*70364	Bayou Cane (c)	(985)	19,355	—
*70037	Belle Chasse (c)	(504)	12,679	—
*70427	Bogalusa	(985)	12,232	11,926
*71111	Bossier City	(318)	61,315	67,472
70518	Broussard	(337)	8,197	10,356
70837	Central	(225)	26,864	28,119
*70043	Chalmette (c)	(504)	16,751	—
70433	Claiborne (c)	(985)	11,507	—
*70526	Crowley	(337)	13,265	13,189
*70726	Denham Springs	(225)	10,215	10,097
70634	DeRidder	(337)	10,578	10,799
70047	Destrehan (c)	(985)	11,535	—
70072	Estelle (c)	(504)	16,377	—
70535	Eunice	(337)	10,398	10,330
70810	Gardere (c)	(225)	10,580	—
*70737	Gonzales	(225)	9,781	10,457
*70053	Gretna	(504)	17,736	17,845
*70401	Hammond	(985)	20,019	20,363
*70058	Harvey (c)	(504)	20,348	—
*70360	Houma	(985)	33,727	34,124
70121	Jefferson (c)	(504)	11,193	—
70546	Jennings	(337)	10,383	10,183
*70062	Kenner	(504)	66,702	67,064
*70501	Lafayette	(337)	120,623	126,066
*70601	Lake Charles	(337)	71,993	74,889
*70068	LaPlace (c)	(985)	29,872	—
70070	Luling (c)	(985)	12,119	—
*70471	Mandeville	(985)	11,560	12,236
*70072	Marrero (c)	(504)	33,141	—
*70001	Metairie (c)	(504)	138,481	—
*71055	Minden	(318)	13,082	12,808
*71201	Monroe	(318)	48,815	49,601
*70380	Morgan City	(985)	12,404	11,943
70611	Moss Bluff (c)	(337)	11,557	—
*71457	Natchitoches	(318)	18,323	18,384
*70560	New Iberia	(337)	30,617	30,745
*70112	New Orleans	(504)	343,829	384,320
*70570	Opelousas	(337)	16,634	16,617
*71360	Pineville	(318)	14,555	14,425
70769	Prairieville (c)	(225)	26,895	—
70394	Raceland (c)	(985)	10,193	—
70123	River Ridge (c)	(504)	13,494	—
*71270	Ruston	(318)	21,859	22,301
70817	Shenandoah (c)	(318)	18,399	—
*71102	Shreveport	(318)	199,311	198,242
*70458	Slidell	(985)	27,068	27,622
*70663	Sulphur	(337)	20,410	20,206
70056	Terrytown (c)	(504)	23,319	—
*70301	Thibodaux	(985)	14,566	14,603
70056	Timberlane (c)	(504)	10,243	—
70094	Waggaman (c)	(504)	10,015	—
*71291	West Monroe	(318)	13,065	12,985
70058	Woodmere (c)	(504)	12,080	—
70592	Youngsville	(337)	8,105	11,006
70791	Zachary	(225)	14,960	16,219

Maine

Area code 207 applies to the entire state. See introductory note.

ZIP	Place	2010 population	2014 estimate
*04210	Auburn	23,055	22,912
*04330	Augusta	19,136	18,705
*04401	Bangor	33,039	32,568
*04005	Biddeford	21,277	21,337
04011	*Brunswick*	20,278	20,441
04011	Brunswick (c)	15,175	—
04105	*Falmouth*	11,185	11,734
04038	*Gorham*	16,381	17,024
04043	*Kennebunk*	10,798	11,111
*04240	Lewiston	36,592	36,299
*04473	*Orono*	10,362	10,670
*04101	Portland	66,194	66,666
04072	Saco	18,482	19,014
04073	Sanford[1]	20,798	20,906
*04074	*Scarborough*	18,919	19,524
*04106	South Portland	25,002	25,424
04084	*Standish*	9,874	10,020
*04901	Waterville	15,722	16,182
04090	*Wells*	9,589	10,009
*04092	Westbrook	17,494	17,886
*04062	*Windham*	17,001	17,589
03909	*York*	12,529	12,803

(1) Place was incorporated after the 2010 Census was conducted. Data in 2010 column is Census Bureau estimate for Sanford MCD.

Maryland

Area code 240 overlays area code 301. Area codes 443/667 overlay 410.

ZIP	Place	Area code	2010 population	2014 estimate
21001	Aberdeen	(410)	14,959	15,434
20607	Accokeek (c)	(301)	10,573	—
*20783	Adelphi (c)	(301)	15,086	—
*21401	Annapolis	(410)	38,394	38,856
21403	Annapolis Neck (c)	(410)	10,950	—
21227	Arbutus (c)	(410)	20,483	—
21012	Arnold (c)	(410)	23,106	—
*20906	Aspen Hill (c)	(301)	48,759	—
21220	Ballenger Creek (c)	(410)	18,274	—
21201	Baltimore	(410)	620,961	622,793
*21014	Bel Air	(410)	10,120	10,264
21050	Bel Air North (c)	(410)	30,568	—
21014	Bel Air South (c)	(410)	47,709	—
*20705	Beltsville (c)	(301)	16,772	—
20603	Bensville (c)	(301)	11,923	—
*20814	Bethesda (c)	(301)	60,858	—
*20715	Bowie	(301)	54,727	57,646
21225	Brooklyn Park (c)	(410)	14,373	—
20619	California (c)	(301)	11,857	—
20705	Calverton (c)	(301)	17,724	—
21613	Cambridge	(410)	12,326	12,569
*20748	Camp Springs (c)	(301)	19,096	—
21234	Carney (c)	(410)	29,941	—
*21228	Catonsville (c)	(410)	41,567	—
20657	Chesapeake Ranch Estates (c)	(301)	10,519	—
20782	Chillum (c)	(301)	33,513	—
20871	Clarksburg (c)	(301)	13,766	—
20735	Clinton (c)	(301)	35,970	—
20904	Cloverly (c)	(301)	15,126	—
21030	Cockeysville (c)	(410)	20,776	—
*20904	Colesville (c)	(301)	14,647	—
*20740	College Park	(301)	30,413	32,256
*21045	Columbia (c)	(410)	99,615	—
21114	Crofton (c)	(410)	27,348	—
*21502	Cumberland	(301)	20,859	20,235
20872	Damascus (c)	(301)	15,257	—
21222	Dundalk (c)	(410)	63,597	—
20737	East Riverdale (c)	(301)	15,509	—
*21601	Easton	(410)	15,945	16,675
21040	Edgewood (c)	(410)	25,562	—
21784	Eldersburg (c)	(410)	30,531	—
21075	Elkridge (c)	(410)	15,593	—
*21921	Elkton	(410)	15,443	15,852
*21043	Ellicott City (c)	(410)	65,834	—
21221	Essex (c)	(410)	39,262	—
20904	Fairland (c)	(301)	23,681	—
21061	Ferndale (c)	(410)	16,746	—
*20747	Forestville (c)	(301)	12,353	—
*20744	Fort Washington (c)	(301)	23,717	—
*21701	Frederick	(301)	65,239	68,400
*20877	Gaithersburg	(301)	59,933	66,816
*20874	Germantown (c)	(301)	86,395	—
20745	Glassmanor (c)	(301)	17,295	—
*21061	Glen Burnie (c)	(410)	67,639	—
20906	Glenmont (c)	(301)	13,529	—
20769	Glenn Dale (c)	(301)	13,466	—
*20770	Greenbelt	(301)	23,068	24,125
*21740	Hagerstown	(301)	39,662	40,364
21740	Halfway (c)	(301)	10,701	—
21078	Havre de Grace	(410)	12,952	13,512
20748	Hillcrest Heights (c)	(301)	16,469	—
*20781	Hyattsville	(301)	17,557	18,420
21043	Ilchester (c)	(410)	23,476	—
21085	Joppatowne (c)	(410)	12,616	—
20902	Kemp Mill (c)	(301)	12,564	—
*20774	Kettering (c)	(301)	12,790	—
*21122	Lake Shore (c)	(410)	19,477	—
20785	Landover (c)	(301)	23,078	—
*20787	Langley Park (c)	(301)	18,755	—
*20706	Lanham (c)	(301)	10,157	—
*20774	Largo (c)	(301)	10,709	—
*20707	Laurel	(301)	25,115	26,160
20653	Lexington Park (c)	(410)	11,626	—
21090	Linthicum (c)	(410)	10,324	—
21207	Lochearn (c)	(410)	25,333	—
20724	Maryland City (c)	(301)	16,093	—
21093	Mays Chapel (c)	(410)	11,420	—
21220	Middle River (c)	(410)	25,191	—
21207	Milford Mill (c)	(410)	29,042	—
*20716	Mitchellville (c)	(301)	10,967	—
*20886	Montgomery Village (c)	(301)	32,032	—
20784	New Carrollton	(301)	12,135	12,708
*20852	North Bethesda (c)	(301)	43,828	—
20878	North Potomac (c)	(301)	24,410	—
21811	Ocean Pines (c)	(410)	11,710	—
21113	Odenton (c)	(410)	37,132	—
*20832	Olney (c)	(301)	33,844	—
21236	Overlea (c)	(410)	12,275	—
21117	Owings Mills (c)	(410)	30,622	—

ZIP	Place	Area code	2010 population	2014 estimate
*20745	Oxon Hill (c)	(301)	17,722	—
21234	Parkville (c)	(410)	30,734	—
21401	Parole (c)	(410)	15,922	—
*21122	Pasadena (c)	(410)	24,287	—
21128	Perry Hall (c)	(410)	28,474	—
*21207	Pikesville (c)	(410)	30,764	—
*20850	Potomac (c)	(301)	44,965	—
21133	Randallstown (c)	(301)	32,430	—
20855	Redland (c)	(301)	17,242	—
*21136	Reisterstown (c)	(410)	25,968	—
*21122	Riviera Beach (c)	(410)	12,677	—
*20850	Rockville	(301)	61,209	65,937
20772	Rosaryville (c)	(301)	10,697	—
21237	Rosedale (c)	(410)	19,257	—
21221	Rossville (c)	(410)	15,147	—
*21801	Salisbury	(410)	30,343	32,563
20723	Scaggsville (c)	(301)	24,333	—
*20706	Seabrook (c)	(301)	17,287	—
21144	Severn (c)	(410)	44,231	—
21146	Severna Park (c)	(410)	37,634	—
*20901	Silver Spring (c)	(301)	71,452	—
20707	South Laurel (c)	(301)	26,112	—
*20746	Suitland (c)	(301)	25,825	—
21842	Summerfield (c)	(410)	10,898	—
*20912	Takoma Park	(301)	16,715	17,670
*21204	Towson (c)	(410)	55,197	—
20854	Travilah (c)	(301)	12,159	—
*20602	Waldorf (c)	(301)	67,752	—
20743	Walker Mill (c)	(301)	11,302	—
*21157	Westminster	(410)	18,590	18,724
*20902	Wheaton (c)	(301)	48,284	—
20904	White Oak (c)	(301)	17,403	—
21207	Woodlawn (c) (Baltimore Co.)	(410)	37,879	—

Massachusetts

Area code 339 overlays area code 781. Area code 351 overlays 978. Area code 774 overlays 508. Area code 857 overlays 617. See introductory note.

ZIP	Place	Area code	2010 population	2014 estimate
02351	*Abington*	(781)	15,985	16,197
*01720	*Acton*	(978)	21,924	23,237
*02743	*Acushnet*	(508)	10,303	10,410
01001	Agawam	(413)	28,438	28,772
01913	Amesbury	(978)	16,283	16,794
*01002	*Amherst*	(413)	37,819	39,774
*01002	Amherst Center (c)	(413)	19,065	—
*01810	*Andover*	(978)	33,201	35,085
*02476	*Arlington*	(781)	42,844	44,461
01721	*Ashland*	(508)	16,593	17,312
*01331	*Athol*	(978)	11,584	11,621
02703	Attleboro	(508)	43,593	43,970
01501	*Auburn*	(508)	16,188	16,387
02630	Barnstable	(508)	45,193	44,529
*01730	*Bedford*	(781)	13,320	14,205
01007	*Belchertown*	(413)	14,649	14,846
02019	*Bellingham*	(508)	16,332	16,770
*02478	*Belmont*	(781)	24,729	25,496
01915	Beverly	(978)	39,502	40,952
*01821	*Billerica*	(978)	40,243	42,264
*02108	Boston	(617)	617,594	655,884
*02532	*Bourne*	(508)	19,754	19,711
*02184	Braintree	(781)	35,744	37,362
*02324	*Bridgewater*	(508)	26,563	27,472
*02301	Brockton	(508)	93,810	94,779
*02446	*Brookline*	(617)	58,732	59,334
*01803	*Burlington*	(781)	24,498	25,683
*02139	Cambridge	(617)	105,162	109,694
02021	*Canton*	(781)	21,561	22,510
*02330	*Carver*	(508)	11,509	11,583
01507	*Charlton*	(508)	12,981	13,312
01824	*Chelmsford*	(978)	33,802	34,960
02150	Chelsea	(617)	35,177	38,861
*01020	Chicopee	(413)	55,298	55,795
01510	*Clinton*	(978)	13,606	13,749
01742	*Concord*	(978)	17,668	19,535
01923	*Danvers*	(978)	26,493	27,460
*02747	*Dartmouth*	(508)	34,032	34,415
*02026	*Dedham*	(781)	24,729	25,473
02638	*Dennis*	(508)	14,207	14,037
01826	*Dracut*	(978)	29,457	31,079
01571	*Dudley*	(508)	11,390	11,818
*02332	*Duxbury*	(781)	15,059	15,384
02333	*East Bridgewater*	(508)	13,794	14,243
*01028	*East Longmeadow*	(413)	15,720	16,123
01027	Easthampton	(413)	16,053	16,036
*02334	*Easton*	(508)	23,112	23,907
02149	Everett	(617)	41,667	44,231
02719	*Fairhaven*	(508)	15,873	16,034
*02720	Fall River	(508)	88,857	88,712
*02540	*Falmouth*	(508)	31,531	31,631
01420	Fitchburg	(978)	40,318	40,445
02035	*Foxborough*	(508)	16,865	17,376
*01701	*Framingham*	(508)	68,318	70,746
02038	Franklin	(508)	31,635	32,836
*01440	Gardner	(978)	20,228	20,381
*01930	Gloucester	(978)	28,789	29,626
01519	*Grafton*	(508)	17,765	18,371
*01301	Greenfield	(413)	17,456	17,368
*01450	*Groton*	(978)	10,646	11,222
*02339	*Hanover*	(781)	13,879	14,360
*02341	*Hanson*	(781)	10,209	10,441
02645	*Harwich*	(508)	12,243	12,188
*01830	Haverhill	(978)	60,879	62,488
*02043	*Hingham*	(781)	22,157	22,964
02343	*Holbrook*	(781)	10,791	11,026
01520	*Holden*	(508)	17,346	18,476
01746	*Holliston*	(508)	13,547	14,388
*01040	Holyoke	(413)	39,880	40,124
01748	*Hopkinton*	(508)	14,925	16,311
01749	*Hudson*	(978)	19,063	19,754
01749	Hudson (c)	(978)	14,907	—
02045	*Hull*	(781)	10,293	10,365
01938	*Ipswich*	(978)	13,175	13,661
02364	*Kingston*	(781)	12,629	13,154
02347	*Lakeville*	(508)	10,602	11,208
*01840	Lawrence	(978)	76,377	78,197
01524	*Leicester*	(508)	10,970	11,270
01453	Leominster	(978)	40,759	41,150
*02420	*Lexington*	(781)	31,394	33,075
*01028	*Longmeadow*	(413)	15,784	15,882
*01850	Lowell	(978)	106,519	109,945
01056	*Ludlow*	(413)	21,103	21,436
*01462	*Lunenburg*	(978)	10,086	11,107
*01901	Lynn	(781)	90,329	92,137
01940	*Lynnfield*	(781)	11,596	12,668
02148	Malden	(781)	59,450	60,859
*02048	*Mansfield*	(508)	23,184	23,595
01945	*Marblehead*	(781)	19,808	20,454
01752	Marlborough	(508)	38,499	39,612
*02050	*Marshfield*	(781)	25,132	25,635
02649	*Mashpee*	(508)	14,006	14,049
01754	*Maynard*	(978)	10,106	10,474
02052	*Medfield*	(508)	12,024	12,394
*02155	Medford	(781)	56,173	57,437
02053	*Medway*	(508)	12,752	13,184
02176	Melrose	(781)	26,983	27,969
01844	Methuen	(978)	47,255	49,112
*02346	*Middleborough*	(508)	23,116	24,103
01757	*Milford*	(508)	27,999	28,439
01757	Milford (c)	(508)	25,055	—
*01527	*Millbury*	(508)	13,261	13,460
02186	*Milton*	(617)	27,003	27,360
*02584	*Nantucket*	(508)	10,172	10,856
01760	*Natick*	(508)	33,006	35,523
*02494	*Needham*	(781)	28,886	30,205
*02740	New Bedford	(508)	95,072	94,845
01950	Newburyport	(978)	17,416	17,926
*02456	Newton	(617)	85,146	88,287
02056	*Norfolk*	(508)	11,227	11,800
01247	North Adams	(413)	13,708	13,354
01845	*North Andover*	(978)	28,352	29,478
*02760	*North Attleborough*	(508)	28,712	28,908
*01864	*North Reading*	(978)	14,892	15,509
*01060	Northampton	(413)	28,549	28,554
01532	*Northborough*	(508)	14,155	14,834
01534	*Northbridge*	(508)	15,707	16,407
*02766	*Norton*	(508)	19,031	19,396
02061	*Norwell*	(781)	10,506	10,817
02062	*Norwood*	(781)	28,602	29,056
01540	*Oxford*	(508)	13,709	13,853
01069	Palmer	(413)	12,140	12,174
*01960	Peabody	(978)	51,251	52,376
*02359	*Pembroke*	(781)	17,837	18,197
01463	*Pepperell*	(978)	11,497	11,975
*01201	Pittsfield	(413)	44,737	43,697
*02360	*Plymouth*	(508)	56,468	58,271
*02169	Quincy	(617)	92,271	93,397
02368	*Randolph*	(781)	32,112	33,629
*02767	*Raynham*	(508)	13,383	13,691
01867	*Reading*	(781)	24,747	25,508
02769	*Rehoboth*	(508)	11,608	11,926
02151	Revere	(781)	51,755	54,157
02370	*Rockland*	(781)	17,489	17,761
*01970	Salem	(978)	41,340	42,824
*02563	*Sandwich*	(508)	20,675	20,536
01906	*Saugus*	(781)	26,628	27,921
*02066	*Scituate*	(781)	18,133	18,413
02771	*Seekonk*	(508)	13,722	14,683
02067	*Sharon*	(781)	17,612	18,121
*01545	*Shrewsbury*	(508)	35,608	36,580
*02725	*Somerset*	(508)	18,165	18,278
*02143	Somerville	(617)	75,754	78,901
01075	*South Hadley*	(413)	17,514	17,691
02664	South Yarmouth (c)	(508)	11,092	—

ZIP	Place	Area code	2010 population	2014 estimate
01550	Southbridge	(508)	16,719	16,825
01562	*Spencer*	(508)	11,688	11,805
*01103	Springfield	(413)	153,060	153,991
02180	*Stoneham*	(781)	21,437	21,886
02072	*Stoughton*	(781)	26,962	28,396
01776	*Sudbury*	(978)	17,659	18,766
01907	*Swampscott*	(781)	13,787	14,014
02777	*Swansea*	(508)	15,865	16,150
*02780	Taunton	(508)	55,874	56,544
01876	*Tewksbury*	(978)	28,961	30,260
01879	*Tyngsborough*	(978)	11,292	12,149
01569	*Uxbridge*	(508)	13,457	13,783
01880	*Wakefield*	(781)	24,932	26,774
02081	*Walpole*	(508)	24,070	24,933
*02451	Waltham	(781)	60,632	63,014
02571	*Wareham*	(508)	21,822	22,473
*02742	Watertown	(617)	31,915	34,127
01778	*Wayland*	(508)	12,994	13,541
01570	*Webster*	(508)	16,767	16,844
01570	Webster (c)	(508)	11,412	—
*02457	*Wellesley*	(781)	27,982	29,362
*01089	West Springfield	(413)	28,391	28,627
*01581	*Westborough*	(508)	18,272	18,756
*01085	Westfield	(413)	41,094	41,608
01886	*Westford*	(978)	21,951	23,678
02493	*Weston*	(781)	11,261	11,992
02790	*Westport*	(508)	15,532	15,742
02090	*Westwood*	(781)	14,618	14,979
*02188	Weymouth	(781)	53,743	55,643
02382	*Whitman*	(781)	14,489	14,790
01095	*Wilbraham*	(413)	14,219	14,509
01887	*Wilmington*	(978)	22,325	23,370
01475	*Winchendon*	(978)	10,300	10,615
01890	*Winchester*	(781)	21,374	22,270
02152	Winthrop	(617)	17,497	18,352
*01801	Woburn	(781)	38,120	39,272
*01602	Worcester	(508)	181,045	183,016
*02093	*Wrentham*	(508)	10,955	11,422
*02675	*Yarmouth*	(508)	23,793	23,592

Michigan

Area code 947 overlays area code 248.

ZIP	Place	Area code	2010 population	2014 estimate
49221	Adrian	(517)	21,133	20,840
48101	Allen Park	(313)	28,210	27,566
49401	Allendale (c)	(616)	17,579	—
49707	Alpena	(989)	10,483	10,247
*48103	Ann Arbor	(734)	113,934	117,770
*48321	Auburn Hills	(248)	21,412	21,845
*49014	Battle Creek	(269)	52,347	51,833
*48708	Bay City	(989)	34,932	34,149
48505	Beecher (c)	(810)	10,232	—
*49022	Benton Harbor	(269)	10,038	10,018
48072	Berkley	(248)	14,970	15,273
48025	Beverly Hills	(248)	10,267	10,448
49307	Big Rapids	(231)	10,601	10,443
*48012	Birmingham	(248)	20,103	20,757
*48509	Burton	(810)	29,999	28,974
49601	Cadillac	(231)	10,355	10,335
*48017	Clawson	(248)	11,825	12,049
49036	Coldwater	(517)	10,945	10,811
49321	Comstock Park (c)	(616)	10,088	—
49508	Cutlerville (c)	(616)	14,370	—
*48120	Dearborn	(313)	98,153	95,535
*48127	Dearborn Heights	(313)	57,774	56,415
*48201	Detroit	(313)	713,777	680,250
*49506	East Grand Rapids	(616)	10,694	11,258
*48823	East Lansing	(517)	48,579	48,648
48021	Eastpointe	(586)	32,442	32,654
49829	Escanaba	(906)	12,616	12,413
*48333	Farmington	(248)	10,372	10,554
*48331	Farmington Hills	(248)	79,740	81,435
48430	Fenton	(810)	11,756	11,463
48220	Ferndale	(248)	19,900	20,256
*48502	Flint	(810)	102,434	99,002
49506	Forest Hills (c)	(616)	25,867	—
48026	Fraser	(586)	14,480	14,622
*48135	Garden City	(734)	27,692	27,052
49417	Grand Haven	(616)	10,412	10,965
*49503	Grand Rapids	(616)	188,040	193,792
*49418	Grandville	(616)	15,378	15,857
48230	Grosse Pointe Park	(313)	11,555	11,288
48230	Grosse Pointe Woods	(313)	16,135	15,835
*48212	Hamtramck	(313)	22,423	22,099
48225	Harper Woods	(313)	14,236	13,907
48840	Haslett (c)	(517)	19,220	—
48030	Hazel Park	(248)	16,422	16,604
48203	Highland Park	(313)	11,776	10,375
*49423	Holland	(616)	33,051	33,644
48842	Holt (c)	(517)	23,973	—
48141	Inkster	(313)/(734)	25,369	24,786
48846	Ionia	(616)	11,394	11,439
*49201	Jackson	(517)	33,534	33,200
*49428	Jenison (c)	(616)	16,538	—
*49001	Kalamazoo	(269)	74,262	75,922
*49508	Kentwood	(616)	48,707	50,764
*48915	Lansing	(517)	114,297	114,620
48146	Lincoln Park	(313)	38,144	37,231
*48150	Livonia	(734)	96,942	94,958
48071	Madison Heights	(248)	29,694	30,267
49855	Marquette	(906)	21,355	21,441
48122	Melvindale	(313)	10,715	10,441
*48640	Midland	(989)	41,863	41,957
*48161	Monroe	(734)	20,733	20,198
*48046	Mount Clemens	(586)	16,314	16,408
*48858	Mount Pleasant	(989)	26,016	25,971
*49440	Muskegon	(231)	38,401	38,393
49444	Muskegon Heights	(231)	10,856	10,799
*48047	New Baltimore	(586)	12,084	12,269
*49120	Niles	(269)	11,600	11,400
49505	Northview (c)	(616)	14,541	—
*49441	Norton Shores	(231)	23,994	24,081
*48374	Novi	(248)	55,224	58,416
48237	Oak Park	(248)	29,319	29,834
*48805	Okemos (c)	(517)	21,369	—
*48867	Owosso	(906)	15,194	14,779
*48340	Pontiac	(248)	59,515	59,808
*48060	Port Huron	(810)	30,184	29,168
*49024	Portage	(269)	46,292	47,837
*48192	Riverview	(734)	12,486	12,222
*48308	Rochester	(248)	12,711	12,995
*48306	Rochester Hills	(248)	70,995	73,125
48174	Romulus	(313)/(734)	23,989	23,496
48066	Roseville	(586)	47,299	47,598
*48067	Royal Oak	(248)	57,236	59,069
*48601	Saginaw	(989)	51,508	49,844
*48080	Saint Clair Shores	(313)	59,715	60,036
*49783	Sault Ste. Marie	(906)	14,144	13,959
48178	South Lyon	(248)	11,327	11,713
*48033	Southfield	(248)	71,739	73,002
48195	Southgate	(734)	30,047	29,416
*48310	Sterling Heights	(586)	129,699	131,741
49091	Sturgis	(269)	10,994	10,901
48180	Taylor	(313)/(734)	63,131	61,594
*49684	Traverse City	(231)	14,674	15,042
48183	Trenton	(734)	18,853	18,427
*48083	Troy	(248)	80,980	83,107
49534	Walker	(616)	23,537	24,468
*48088	Warren	(586)	134,056	135,099
48917	Waverly (c)	(517)	23,925	—
48184	Wayne	(734)	17,593	17,091
*48185	Westland	(313)/(734)	84,094	82,314
48393	Wixom	(248)	13,498	13,744
48183	Woodhaven	(734)	12,875	12,594
*48192	Wyandotte	(734)	25,883	25,151
*49509	Wyoming	(616)	72,125	74,826
*48197	Ypsilanti	(734)	19,435	20,081

Minnesota

ZIP	Place	Area code	2010 population	2014 estimate
56007	Albert Lea	(507)	18,016	17,815
56308	Alexandria	(320)	11,070	11,680
*55304	Andover	(763)	30,598	31,996
*55303	Anoka	(612)	17,142	17,276
55124	Apple Valley	(952)	49,084	50,487
55912	Austin	(507)	24,718	24,716
*56601	Bemidji	(218)	13,431	14,453
55309	Big Lake	(763)	10,060	10,360
*55014	Blaine	(763)	57,186	61,190
*55420	Bloomington	(952)	82,893	86,314
*56401	Brainerd	(218)	13,590	13,425
*55430	Brooklyn Center	(763)	30,104	30,729
*55443	Brooklyn Park	(763)	75,781	78,728
55313	Buffalo	(763)	15,453	15,912
*55337	Burnsville	(651)	60,306	61,630
55316	Champlin	(763)	23,089	23,828
55317	Chanhassen	(952)	22,952	24,967
55318	Chaska	(952)	23,770	24,838
55720	Cloquet	(218)	12,124	12,081
55421	Columbia Heights	(612)	19,496	19,675
*55433	Coon Rapids	(763)	61,476	62,112
55016	Cottage Grove	(651)	34,589	35,630
*55422	Crystal	(763)	22,151	22,605
*55802	Duluth	(218)	86,265	86,238
*55121	Eagan	(651)	64,206	66,084
*55005	East Bethel	(763)	11,626	11,642
*55344	Eden Prairie	(952)	60,797	63,228
*55424	Edina	(952)	47,941	49,596
55330	Elk River	(763)	22,974	23,746
*56031	Fairmont	(507)	10,666	10,328
55021	Faribault	(507)	23,352	23,594
55024	Farmington	(651)	21,086	22,571
*56537	Fergus Falls	(218)	13,138	13,304

ZIP	Place	Area code	2010 population	2014 estimate
55025	Forest Lake	(651)	18,375	19,399
*55432	Fridley	(763)	27,208	27,670
*55427	Golden Valley	(763)	20,371	20,866
*55744	Grand Rapids	(218)	10,869	11,097
*55304	Ham Lake	(763)	15,296	15,888
55033	Hastings	(651)	22,172	22,566
*55746	Hibbing	(218)	16,361	16,302
*55343	Hopkins	(952)	17,591	18,056
55038	Hugo	(651)	13,332	14,239
55350	Hutchinson	(320)	14,178	13,872
*55076	Inver Grove Heights	(651)	33,880	34,709
55044	Lakeville	(952)	55,954	59,866
*55014	Lino Lakes	(651)	20,216	20,948
*55109	Little Canada	(651)	9,773	10,228
*56001	Mankato	(507)	39,309	40,411
*55311	Maple Grove	(763)	61,567	66,945
*55109	Maplewood	(651)	38,018	40,199
56258	Marshall	(507)	13,680	13,641
*55118	Mendota Heights	(651)	11,071	11,222
*55401	Minneapolis	(612)	382,578	407,207
*55345	Minnetonka	(952)	49,734	51,486
*55362	Monticello	(763)	12,759	13,136
*56560	Moorhead	(218)	38,065	39,857
55112	Mounds View	(763)	12,155	12,657
55112	New Brighton	(651)	21,456	22,266
*54427	New Hope	(763)	20,339	20,792
56073	New Ulm	(507)	13,522	13,258
55056	North Branch	(651)	10,125	10,160
*56002	North Mankato	(507)	13,394	13,432
55109	North St. Paul	(651)	11,460	12,224
55057	Northfield	(507)	20,007	20,356
*55128	Oakdale	(651)	27,378	28,033
*55330	Otsego	(763)	13,571	15,047
55060	Owatonna	(507)	25,599	25,625
*55446	Plymouth	(763)	70,576	75,057
55372	Prior Lake	(952)	22,796	25,039
*55303	Ramsey	(763)	23,668	25,598
55066	Red Wing	(651)	16,459	16,470
55423	Richfield	(612)	35,228	36,179
55422	Robbinsdale	(763)	13,953	14,320
*55901	Rochester	(507)	106,769	111,402
55374	Rogers	(763)	8,597	12,393
55068	Rosemount	(651)	21,874	22,998
*55113	Roseville	(651)	33,660	35,319
*56301	Saint Cloud	(320)	65,842	66,389
*55416	Saint Louis Park	(952)	45,250	47,502
55376	Saint Michael	(763)	16,399	17,087
*55101	Saint Paul	(651)	285,068	297,640
56082	Saint Peter	(507)	11,196	11,570
56377	Sartell	(320)	15,876	16,523
56379	Sauk Rapids	(320)	12,773	13,348
55378	Savage	(952)	26,911	29,208
*55379	Shakopee	(952)	37,076	39,677
55126	Shoreview	(651)	25,043	26,194
*55075	South St. Paul	(651)	20,160	20,487
*55082	Stillwater	(651)	18,225	18,800
*55127	Vadnais Heights	(651)	12,302	13,143
*55387	Waconia	(952)	10,697	11,774
*55118	West St. Paul	(651)	19,540	19,806
*55110	White Bear Lake	(651)	23,797	24,986
56201	Willmar	(320)	19,610	19,570
55987	Winona	(507)	27,592	27,384
*55125	Woodbury	(651)	61,961	66,807
56187	Worthington	(507)	12,764	12,932

Mississippi

Area code 769 overlays area code 601.

ZIP	Place	Area code	2010 population	2014 estimate
39520	Bay St. Louis	(228)	9,260	11,388
*39530	Biloxi	(228)	44,054	44,984
*39042	Brandon	(601)	21,705	23,156
*39601	Brookhaven	(601)	12,513	12,470
39272	Byram	(601)	11,489	11,556
39046	Canton	(601)	13,189	13,713
*38614	Clarksdale	(662)	17,962	17,011
*38732	Cleveland	(662)	12,334	12,412
*39056	Clinton	(601)	25,216	25,411
*39701	Columbus	(662)	23,640	23,248
*38834	Corinth	(662)	14,573	14,865
39540	D'Iberville	(228)	9,486	10,962
39553	Gautier	(228)	18,572	18,596
*38701	Greenville	(662)	34,400	32,704
*38930	Greenwood	(662)	15,205	15,730
*38901	Grenada	(662)	13,092	12,956
*39501	Gulfport	(228)	67,793	71,750
*39401	Hattiesburg	(601)	45,989	47,016
38632	Hernando	(662)	14,090	15,290
38637	Horn Lake	(662)	26,066	26,766
*38751	Indianola	(662)	10,683	10,078
*39201	Jackson	(601)	173,514	171,155
*39440	Laurel	(601)	18,540	18,868
39560	Long Beach	(228)	14,792	15,448
*39110	Madison	(601)	24,149	25,455
*39648	McComb	(601)	12,790	12,703
*39301	Meridian	(601)	41,148	40,196
*39563	Moss Point	(228)	13,704	13,671
*39120	Natchez	(601)	15,792	15,269
*39564	Ocean Springs	(228)	17,442	17,530
38654	Olive Branch	(662)	33,484	35,457
*38655	Oxford	(662)	18,916	21,757
*39567	Pascagoula	(228)	22,392	22,224
*39208	Pearl	(601)	25,092	26,388
39465	Petal	(601)	10,454	10,727
39466	Picayune	(601)	10,878	10,749
*39157	Ridgeland	(601)	24,047	24,221
*38671	Southaven	(662)	48,982	51,824
*39759	Starkville	(662)	23,888	24,886
*38801	Tupelo	(662)	34,546	35,688
*39180	Vicksburg	(601)	23,856	23,392
39773	West Point	(662)	11,307	11,093
39194	Yazoo City	(662)	11,403	11,366

Missouri

ZIP	Place	Area code	2010 population	2014 estimate
63123	Affton (c)	(314)	20,307	—
63010	Arnold	(636)	20,808	21,243
*63011	Ballwin	(636)	30,404	30,505
63137	Bellefontaine Neighbors	(314)	10,860	10,807
64012	Belton	(816)	23,116	23,165
*64015	Blue Springs	(816)	52,575	53,573
*65613	Bolivar	(417)	10,325	10,572
*65616	Branson	(417)	10,520	11,340
63044	Bridgeton	(314)	11,550	11,782
*63701	Cape Girardeau	(573)	37,941	39,167
64836	Carthage	(417)	14,378	14,271
*63017	Chesterfield	(636)	47,484	47,777
*63105	Clayton	(314)	15,939	15,882
*65201	Columbia	(573)	108,500	116,906
*63128	Concord (c)	(314)	16,421	—
63126	Crestwood	(314)	11,912	11,951
63141	Creve Coeur	(314)	17,833	17,868
*63366	Dardenne Prairie	(636)	11,494	12,783
63025	Eureka	(636)	10,189	10,543
64024	Excelsior Springs	(816)	11,084	11,488
63640	Farmington	(573)	16,240	17,915
63135	Ferguson	(314)	21,203	21,086
63028	Festus	(636)	11,602	11,885
*63031	Florissant	(314)	52,158	52,303
65473	Fort Leonard Wood (c)	(573)	15,061	—
65251	Fulton	(573)	12,790	12,864
*64118	Gladstone	(816)	25,410	26,800
64029	Grain Valley	(816)	12,854	13,236
64030	Grandview	(816)	24,475	25,290
63401	Hannibal	(573)	17,916	17,893
*63042	Hazelwood	(314)	25,703	25,666
*64050	Independence	(816)	116,830	117,494
63755	Jackson	(573)	13,758	14,677
*65101	Jefferson City	(573)	43,079	43,132
63136	Jennings	(314)	14,712	14,737
*64801	Joplin	(417)	50,150	51,316
*64106	Kansas City	(816)	459,787	470,800
63857	Kennett	(573)	10,932	10,796
63501	Kirksville	(660)	17,505	17,633
63122	Kirkwood	(314)	27,540	27,660
63367	Lake St. Louis	(636)	14,545	15,014
65536	Lebanon	(417)	14,474	14,650
*64063	Lee's Summit	(816)	91,364	93,864
63125	Lemay (c)	(314)	16,645	—
*64068	Liberty	(816)	29,149	30,376
*63011	Manchester	(636)	18,094	18,197
65340	Marshall	(660)	13,065	13,042
63043	Maryland Heights	(314)	27,472	27,405
64468	Maryville	(660)	11,972	12,007
63129	Mehlville (c)	(314)	28,380	—
65265	Mexico	(573)	11,543	11,664
65270	Moberly	(660)	13,974	13,890
*64850	Neosho	(417)	11,835	12,134
65714	Nixa	(417)	19,022	20,570
63129	Oakville (c)	(314)	36,143	—
63366	O'Fallon	(636)	79,329	84,009
63034	Old Jamestown (c)	(314)	19,184	—
63114	Overland	(314)	16,062	15,985
65721	Ozark	(417)	17,820	18,871
*63901	Poplar Bluff	(573)	17,023	17,242
64083	Raymore	(816)	19,206	19,963
*64133	Raytown	(816)	29,526	29,481
65738	Republic	(417)	14,751	15,680
*65401	Rolla	(573)	19,559	19,926
63074	Saint Ann	(314)	13,020	12,955
*63301	Saint Charles	(636)	65,794	68,090
*64501	Saint Joseph	(816)	76,780	76,967
*63101	Saint Louis	(314)	319,294	317,419
*63376	Saint Peters	(636)	52,575	56,076
*65301	Sedalia	(660)	21,387	21,492
63801	Sikeston	(573)	16,318	16,370

ZIP	Place	Area code	2010 population	2014 estimate
63138	Spanish Lake (c).	(314)	19,650	—
*65804	Springfield.	(417)	159,498	165,378
63017	Town and Country.	(314)	10,815	10,975
63379	Troy.	(314)	10,540	11,355
63084	Union	(636)	10,204	10,859
63130	University City.	(314)	35,371	35,115
64093	Warrensburg	(660)	18,838	19,963
63090	Washington.	(636)	13,982	14,020
64870	Webb City.	(417)	10,996	11,075
63119	Webster Groves	(314)	22,995	23,186
63385	Wentzville	(636)	29,070	33,912
*65775	West Plains.	(417)	11,986	12,275
*63011	Wildwood	(314)	35,517	35,820

Montana

Area code 406 applies to the entire state.

ZIP	Place	2010 population	2014 estimate
*59101	Billings	104,170	108,869
*59715	Bozeman	37,280	41,660
*59701	Butte-Silver Bow (balance)	33,525	33,980
*59401	Great Falls	58,505	59,152
*59601	Helena	28,190	29,943
*59901	Kalispell	19,927	21,518
*59801	Missoula	66,788	69,821

Nebraska

Area code 531 overlays area code 402.

ZIP	Place	Area code	2010 population	2014 estimate
68310	Beatrice	(402)	12,459	12,055
*68005	Bellevue	(402)	50,137	53,936
68138	Chalco (c)	(402)	10,994	—
*68601	Columbus	(402)	22,111	22,630
*68025	Fremont	(402)	26,397	26,500
*68801	Grand Island.	(308)	48,520	51,236
*68901	Hastings	(402)	24,907	24,915
*68847	Kearney	(308)	30,787	32,469
*68128	La Vista.	(402)	15,758	17,636
68850	Lexington	(308)	10,230	10,146
*68502	Lincoln	(402)	258,379	272,996
*68701	Norfolk	(402)	24,210	24,444
*69101	North Platte.	(308)	24,733	24,327
*68104	Omaha	(402)	408,958	446,599
*68046	Papillion	(402)	18,894	23,270
*69361	Scottsbluff.	(308)	15,039	14,875
68776	South Sioux City.	(402)	13,353	13,360

Nevada

Area code 725 overlays area code 702.

ZIP	Place	Area code	2010 population	2014 estimate
*89005	Boulder City	(702)	15,023	15,386
*89701	Carson City.	(775)	55,274	54,522
*89801	Elko.	(775)	18,297	20,300
89124	Enterprise (c)	(702)	108,481	—
89408	Fernley	(775)	19,368	19,204
89410	Gardnerville Ranchos (c)	(775)	11,312	—
*89015	Henderson	(702)	257,729	277,440
*89101	Las Vegas.	(702)	583,756	613,599
*89027	Mesquite.	(702)	15,276	16,970
*89030	North Las Vegas	(702)	216,961	230,788
*89048	Pahrump (c)	(775)	36,441	—
*89121	Paradise (c)	(702)	223,167	—
*89501	Reno.	(775)	225,221	236,995
*89441	Spanish Springs (c)	(775)	15,064	—
*89431	Sparks	(775)	90,264	94,708
89815	Spring Creek (c)	(702)	12,361	—
89147	Spring Valley (c)	(702)	178,395	—
89135	Summerlin South (c).	(702)	24,085	—
*89433	Sun Valley (c)	(775)	189,372	—
89110	Sunrise Manor (c).	(702)	19,299	—
89122	Whitney (c)	(702)	38,585	—
89101	Winchester (c).	(702)	27,978	—

New Hampshire

Area code 603 applies to the entire state. See introductory note.

ZIP	Place	2010 population	2014 estimate
03031	*Amherst*	11,201	11,266
03110	*Bedford*	21,203	21,689
03743	Claremont.	13,355	13,074
*03301	Concord	42,695	42,444
03038	*Derry*.	33,109	33,307
03038	Derry (c)	22,015	—
*03820	Dover	29,987	30,665
03824	*Durham*.	14,638	15,759
03824	Durham (c)	10,345	—
03833	*Exeter*	14,306	14,543
03045	*Goffstown*	17,651	17,972
*03842	*Hampton*.	15,430	15,208
03755	*Hanover*	11,260	11,379
03106	*Hooksett*	13,451	13,771
03051	*Hudson*.	24,467	24,775
*03431	Keene	23,409	23,034
*03246	Laconia.	15,951	16,067
*03766	Lebanon	13,151	13,589
03053	*Londonderry*.	24,129	24,403
03053	Londonderry (c)	11,037	—
*03103	Manchester.	109,565	110,448
03054	*Merrimack*	25,494	25,659
03055	*Milford*	15,115	15,153
*03060	Nashua	86,494	87,259
03076	*Pelham*	12,897	13,219
*03801	Portsmouth.	20,779	21,598
03077	*Raymond*	10,138	10,280
*03867	Rochester	29,752	29,991
03079	*Salem*	28,776	29,005
03878	Somersworth	11,766	11,777
03087	*Windham*	13,592	14,250

New Jersey

Area code 551 overlays area code 201. Area code 848 overlays 732. Area code 862 overlays 973.

ZIP	Place	Area code	2010 population	2014 estimate
07712	Asbury Park	(732)	16,116	15,778
*08401	Atlantic City	(609)	39,558	39,415
07001	Avenel (c)	(732)	17,011	—
07002	Bayonne	(201)	63,024	65,975
08722	Beachwood.	(732)	11,045	11,253
*08031	Bellmawr.	(856)	11,583	11,454
07621	Bergenfield	(201)	26,764	27,406
08805	Bound Brook.	(732)	10,402	11,116
08807	Bradley Gardens (c)	(908)	14,206	—
08302	Bridgeton	(856)	25,349	25,347
08015	Browns Mills (c)	(609)	11,223	—
*08101	Camden	(856)	77,344	77,332
07008	Carteret.	(732)	22,844	24,114
08002	Cherry Hill Mall (c)	(856)	14,171	—
07010	Cliffside Park.	(201)	23,594	25,503
*07015	Clifton	(973)	84,136	85,927
*08108	Collingswood	(856)	13,926	13,962
07067	Colonia (c)	(732)	17,795	—
*07801	Dover	(973)	18,157	18,313
07628	Dumont.	(201)	17,479	17,863
*07019	East Orange	(973)	64,270	65,078
*07724	Eatontown.	(732)	12,709	12,257
08043	Echelon (c)	(856)	10,743	—
07020	Edgewater.	(201)	11,513	12,343
*07201	Elizabeth.	(908)	124,969	128,705
07407	Elmwood Park	(201)	19,403	20,374
*07631	Englewood	(201)	27,147	27,670
07410	Fair Lawn	(201)/(973)	32,457	33,549
07022	Fairview	(201)	13,835	14,317
07932	Florham Park	(973)	11,696	11,829
08863	Fords (c)	(732)	15,187	—
07024	Fort Lee	(201)	35,345	37,026
07417	Franklin Lakes	(201)	10,590	10,837
08823	Franklin Park (c)	(732)	13,295	—
07728	Freehold	(732)	12,052	11,973
07026	Garfield.	(973)	30,487	31,486
08028	Glassboro	(856)	18,579	19,007
07452	Glen Rock.	(201)	11,601	11,901
08030	Gloucester City.	(856)	11,456	11,317
*08053	Greentree (c)	(856)	11,367	—
07093	Guttenberg	(201)	11,176	11,481
*07601	Hackensack	(201)	43,010	44,519
08033	Haddonfield	(856)	11,593	11,411
08690	Hamilton Square (c)	(609)	12,784	—
08037	Hammonton	(609)	14,791	14,765
07029	Harrison	(973)	13,620	15,376
07604	Hasbrouck Heights	(201)	11,842	12,147
*07506	Hawthorne	(973)	18,791	19,048
08904	Highland Park.	(732)	13,982	14,436
07642	Hillsdale	(201)	10,219	10,482
07030	Hoboken	(201)	50,005	53,312
*08753	Holiday City-Berkeley (c)	(732)	12,831	—
07843	Hopatcong	(973)	15,147	14,684
08830	Iselin (c)	(732)	18,695	—
*07303	Jersey City	(201)	247,597	262,146
*07032	Kearny . . . . (201)/(973)		40,684	41,837
07405	Kinnelon	(973)	10,248	10,381
08701	Lakewood (c)	(732)	53,805	—
07035	Lincoln Park	(973)	10,521	10,482
07036	Linden.	(732)/(908)	40,499	41,651
08021	Lindenwold	(856)	17,613	17,417
07643	Little Ferry.	(201)	10,626	10,866
07644	Lodi.	(201)/(973)	24,136	24,654
07740	Long Branch.	(732)	30,719	30,522
07940	Madison	(973)	15,845	16,122
08835	Manville	(908)	10,344	10,388

ZIP	Place	Area code	2010 population	2014 estimate
08053	Marlton (c)	(856)	10,133	—
08836	Martinsville (c)	(908)	11,980	—
08619	Mercerville (c)	(609)	13,230	—
08840	Metuchen	(732)	13,574	13,826
08846	Middlesex	(732)	13,635	13,888
08332	Millville	(856)	28,400	28,497
08057	Moorestown-Lenola (c)	(856)	14,217	—
*07960	Morristown	(973)	18,411	19,085
*08901	New Brunswick	(732)	55,181	57,080
07646	New Milford	(201)	16,341	16,678
07974	New Providence	(908)	12,171	12,422
*07102	Newark	(973)	277,140	280,579
07031	North Arlington	(201)	15,392	15,723
*07060	North Plainfield	(908)	21,936	22,029
07436	Oakland	(201)	12,754	13,046
*08050	Ocean Acres (c)	(609)	16,142	—
08226	Ocean City	(609)	11,701	11,374
08857	Old Bridge (c)	(732)	23,753	—
07650	Palisades Park	(201)	19,622	20,471
*07652	Paramus	(201)	26,342	26,832
07055	Passaic	(973)	69,781	71,509
*07510	Paterson	(973)	146,199	146,753
08070	Pennsville (c)	(856)	11,888	—
*08861	Perth Amboy	(732)	50,814	52,328
08865	Phillipsburg	(908)	14,950	14,570
08021	Pine Hill	(856)	10,233	10,464
*07061	Plainfield	(908)	49,808	50,955
*08232	Pleasantville	(609)	20,249	20,467
08742	Point Pleasant	(732)	18,392	18,665
07442	Pompton Lakes	(973)	11,097	11,166
*08540	Princeton	(609)	12,307	30,108
08536	Princeton Meadows (c)	(609)	13,834	—
07065	Rahway	(732)	27,346	28,528
07446	Ramsey	(201)	14,473	14,800
*07701	Red Bank	(732)	12,206	12,445
07657	Ridgefield	(201)	11,032	11,289
07660	Ridgefield Park	(201)	12,729	12,996
*07451	Ridgewood	(201)/(973)	24,958	25,496
07456	Ringwood	(973)	12,228	12,377
07661	River Edge	(201)	11,340	11,579
07751	Robertsville (c)	(732)	11,297	—
07203	Roselle	(908)	21,085	21,551
07204	Roselle Park	(908)	13,297	13,595
07070	Rutherford	(201)	18,061	18,464
*08872	Sayreville	(732)	42,704	45,262
*07094	Secaucus	(201)	16,264	18,416
07078	Short Hills (c)	(973)	13,165	—
08244	Somers Point	(609)	10,795	10,756
*08873	Somerset (c)	(732)	22,083	—
08876	Somerville	(908)	12,098	12,153
07080	South Plainfield	(732)/(908)	23,385	23,960
*08882	South River	(732)	16,008	16,334
08003	Springdale (c)	(856)	14,518	—
*07901	Summit	(908)	21,457	22,071
07670	Tenafly	(201)	14,488	14,816
*07724	Tinton Falls	(732)	17,892	17,898
*08753	Toms River (c)	(732)	88,791	—
*07512	Totowa	(973)	10,804	10,937
*08650	Trenton	(609)	84,913	84,034
07087	Union City	(201)	66,455	68,668
07043	Upper Montclair (c)	(973)	11,565	—
08406	Ventnor City	(609)	10,650	10,597
*08360	Vineland	(856)	60,724	61,171
07057	Wallington	(201)/(973)	11,335	11,626
07465	Wanaque	(201)/(973)	11,116	11,447
07728	West Freehold (c)	(732)/(908)	13,613	—
07093	West New York	(201)	49,708	52,597
*07091	Westfield	(732)/(908)	30,316	30,890
*07675	Westwood	(201)	10,908	11,149
08094	Williamstown (c)	(609)/(856)	15,567	—
07095	Woodbridge (c)	(732)/(908)	19,265	—
*08096	Woodbury	(856)	10,174	10,016
07424	Woodland Park	(973)	11,819	12,403

New Mexico

ZIP	Place	Area code	2010 population	2014 estimate
*88310	Alamogordo	(575)	30,403	31,060
*87101	Albuquerque	(505)	545,852	557,169
*88210	Artesia	(575)	11,301	11,842
*88220	Carlsbad	(575)	26,138	28,103
*88021	Chaparral (c)	(505)	14,631	—
*88101	Clovis	(575)	37,775	39,860
*88030	Deming	(575)	14,855	14,605
*87532	Española	(505)	10,224	10,130
*87401	Farmington	(505)	45,877	44,445
*87301	Gallup	(505)	21,678	22,469
*88240	Hobbs	(575)	34,122	37,118
*88001	Las Cruces	(575)	97,618	101,408
*87701	Las Vegas	(505)	13,753	13,518
*87544	Los Alamos (c)	(505)	12,019	—
87031	Los Lunas	(505)	14,835	15,206
*88260	Lovington	(575)	11,009	11,840
87107	North Valley (c)	(505)	11,333	—
*88130	Portales	(575)	12,280	12,233
*87124	Rio Rancho	(505)	87,521	93,820
*88201	Roswell	(575)	48,366	48,608
*87501	Santa Fe	(505)	67,947	70,297
*88061	Silver City	(575)	10,315	10,172
87105	South Valley (c)	(505)	40,976	—
*88063	Sunland Park	(575)	14,106	15,400

New York

Area codes 347/929 overlay area code 718. Area codes 646/917 overlay 212. Area code 934 overlays 631 effective July 16, 2016.

ZIP	Place	Area code	2010 population	2014 estimate
*12202	Albany	(518)	97,856	98,566
12010	Amsterdam	(518)	18,620	18,135
*13021	Auburn	(315)	27,687	27,019
11702	Babylon	(631)	12,166	12,172
11510	Baldwin (c)	(516)	24,033	—
*14020	Batavia	(585)	15,465	15,077
11706	Bay Shore (c)	(631)	26,337	—
12508	Beacon	(845)	15,541	14,238
11710	Bellmore (c)	(516)	16,218	—
11714	Bethpage (c)	(516)	16,429	—
*13901	Binghamton	(607)	47,376	46,299
11716	Bohemia (c)	(631)	10,180	—
11717	Brentwood (c)	(631)	60,664	—
*14610	Brighton (c)	(585)	36,609	—
*14201	Buffalo	(716)	261,310	258,703
*14424	Canandaigua	(585)	10,545	10,488
11720	Centereach (c)	(631)	31,578	—
*11722	Central Islip (c)	(516)	34,450	—
*14227	Cheektowaga (c)	(716)	75,178	—
12047	Cohoes	(518)	16,168	16,212
11725	Commack (c)	(631)	36,124	—
11726	Copiague (c)	(631)	22,993	—
11727	Coram (c)	(631)	39,113	—
*14830	Corning	(607)	11,183	10,993
13045	Cortland	(607)	19,204	19,164
11729	Deer Park (c)	(631)	27,745	—
14043	Depew	(716)	15,303	15,205
*11746	Dix Hills (c)	(631)	26,892	—
10522	Dobbs Ferry	(914)	10,875	11,098
*14048	Dunkirk	(716)	12,563	12,216
11730	East Islip (c)	(631)	14,475	—
11758	East Massapequa (c)	(516)	19,069	—
11554	East Meadow (c)	(516)	38,132	—
11731	East Northport (c)	(631)	20,217	—
11772	East Patchogue (c)	(631)	22,469	—
10709	Eastchester (c)	(914)	19,554	—
14226	Eggertsville (c)	(716)	15,019	—
*14901	Elmira	(607)	29,200	28,647
11003	Elmont (c)	(516)	33,198	—
11731	Elwood (c)	(631)	11,177	—
*13760	Endicott	(607)	13,392	13,083
13762	Endwell (c)	(607)	11,446	—
13219	Fairmount (c)	(315)	10,224	—
11738	Farmingville (c)	(631)	15,481	—
*11001	Floral Park	(516)	15,863	15,967
13603	Fort Drum (c)	(315)	12,955	—
11768	Fort Salonga (c)	(631)	10,008	—
11010	Franklin Square (c)	(516)	29,320	—
14063	Fredonia	(716)	11,230	10,792
11520	Freeport	(516)	42,860	43,304
13069	Fulton	(315)	11,896	11,648
*11530	Garden City	(516)	22,371	22,616
14456	Geneva	(315)	13,261	13,160
11542	Glen Cove	(516)	26,964	27,314
12801	Glens Falls	(518)	14,700	14,428
12078	Gloversville	(518)	15,665	15,122
*11023	Great Neck	(516)	9,989	10,118
14616	Greece (c)	(585)	14,519	—
11740	Greenlawn (c)	(631)	13,742	—
11946	Hampton Bays (c)	(631)	13,603	—
10528	Harrison	(914)	27,472	28,151
*11788	Hauppauge (c)	(631)	20,882	—
10927	Haverstraw	(845)	11,910	12,172
*11550	Hempstead	(516)	53,891	55,527
*11801	Hicksville (c)	(516)	41,547	—
11741	Holbrook (c)	(631)	27,195	—
11742	Holtsville (c)	(631)	19,714	—
11743	Huntington (c)	(631)	18,046	—
*11746	Huntington Station (c)	(631)	33,029	—
*14617	Irondequoit (c)	(585)	51,692	—
11751	Islip (c)	(631)	18,689	—
*14850	Ithaca	(607)	30,014	30,720
*14701	Jamestown	(716)	31,146	30,429
10535	Jefferson Valley-Yorktown (c)	(914)	14,142	—
11753	Jericho (c)	(516)	13,567	—
13790	Johnson City	(607)	15,174	14,832
*14217	Kenmore	(716)	15,423	15,236
11754	Kings Park (c)	(631)	17,282	—

ZIP	Place	Area code	2010 population	2014 estimate
*12401	Kingston	(845)	23,893	23,557
10950	Kiryas Joel	(845)	20,175	22,246
14218	Lackawanna	(716)	18,141	17,955
11755	Lake Grove	(631)	11,163	11,241
11779	Lake Ronkonkoma (c)	(631)	20,155	—
*14086	Lancaster	(716)	10,352	10,294
11756	Levittown (c)	(516)	51,881	—
11757	Lindenhurst	(631)	27,253	27,321
*14094	Lockport	(716)	21,165	20,743
11561	Long Beach	(516)	33,275	33,664
11563	Lynbrook	(516)	19,427	19,558
10543	Mamaroneck	(914)	18,929	19,302
11949	Manorville (c)	(631)	14,314	—
11758	Massapequa (c)	(516)	21,685	—
11762	Massapequa Park	(516)	17,008	17,206
13662	Massena	(315)	10,936	10,723
11950	Mastic (c)	(631)	15,481	—
11951	Mastic Beach[1]	(631)	12,930	14,874
11763	Medford (c)	(631)	24,142	—
11747	Melville (c)	(631)	18,985	—
11566	Merrick (c)	(516)	22,097	—
11953	Middle Island (c)	(631)	10,483	—
*10940	Middletown	(845)	28,086	27,728
11764	Miller Place (c)	(631)	12,339	—
11501	Mineola	(516)	18,799	19,028
10952	Monsey (c)	(845)	18,412	—
10549	Mount Kisco	(914)	10,877	11,103
11766	Mount Sinai (c)	(631)	12,118	—
*10550	Mount Vernon	(914)	67,292	68,458
10954	Nanuet (c)	(845)	17,882	—
11767	Nesconset (c)	(631)	13,387	—
11590	New Cassel (c)	(516)	14,059	—
10956	New City (c)	(845)	33,559	—
*10801	New Rochelle	(914)	77,062	79,637
*10001	New York	(212)/(718)	8,175,133	8,491,079
*12550	Newburgh	(845)	28,866	28,358
*14301	Niagara Falls	(716)	50,193	49,219
11701	North Amityville (c)	(631)	17,862	—
11703	North Babylon (c)	(631)	17,509	—
11706	North Bay Shore (c)	(631)	18,944	—
11710	North Bellmore (c)	(516)	19,941	—
11713	North Bellport (c)	(631)	11,545	—
11757	North Lindenhurst (c)	(631)	11,652	—
11758	North Massapequa (c)	(516)	17,886	—
11566	North Merrick (c)	(516)	12,272	—
11040	North New Hyde Park (c)	(516)	14,899	—
14120	North Tonawanda	(716)	31,568	30,929
11580	North Valley Stream (c)	(516)	16,628	—
11793	North Wantagh (c)	(516)	11,960	—
11572	Oceanside (c)	(516)	32,109	—
13669	Ogdensburg	(315)	11,128	10,895
14760	Olean	(585)/(716)	14,452	14,043
13421	Oneida	(315)	11,393	11,192
13820	Oneonta	(607)	13,901	13,838
10562	Ossining	(914)	25,060	25,359
13126	Oswego	(315)	18,142	17,988
11772	Patchogue	(631)	11,798	12,364
10965	Pearl River (c)	(845)	15,876	—
10566	Peekskill	(914)	23,583	24,058
11803	Plainview (c)	(516)	26,217	—
*12901	Plattsburgh	(518)	19,989	19,740
10573	Port Chester	(914)	28,967	29,522
11050	Port Washington (c)	(516)	15,846	—
*12601	Poughkeepsie	(845)	32,736	30,513
11961	Ridge (c)	(631)	13,336	—
11901	Riverhead (c)	(631)	13,299	—
*14604	Rochester	(585)	210,565	209,983
*11570	Rockville Centre	(516)	24,023	24,191
11778	Rocky Point (c)	(631)	14,014	—
*13440	Rome	(315)	33,725	32,645
11779	Ronkonkoma (c)	(631)	19,082	—
11575	Roosevelt (c)	(516)	16,258	—
12303	Rotterdam (c)	(518)	20,652	—
10580	Rye	(914)	15,720	16,000
11780	Saint James (c)	(631)	13,338	—
13454	Salisbury (c)	(315)	12,093	—
12866	Saratoga Springs	(518)	26,586	27,436
11782	Sayville (c)	(631)	16,853	—
*10583	Scarsdale	(914)	17,166	17,729
*12305	Schenectady	(518)	66,135	65,936
11783	Seaford (c)	(516)	15,294	—
11784	Selden (c)	(631)	19,851	—
11733	Setauket-East Setauket (c)	(631)	15,477	—
11967	Shirley (c)	(631)	27,854	—
10591	Sleepy Hollow	(914)	9,870	10,208
*11787	Smithtown (c)	(631)	26,470	—
11735	South Farmingdale (c)	(516)	14,486	—
10977	Spring Valley	(845)	31,347	32,510
*11790	Stony Brook (c)	(631)	13,740	—
10980	Stony Point (c)	(845)	12,147	—
*10901	Suffern	(845)	10,723	10,991
11791	Syosset (c)	(516)	18,829	—
*13202	Syracuse	(315)	145,170	144,263
10591	Tarrytown	(914)	11,277	11,537
11776	Terryville (c)	(631)	11,849	—
*14150	Tonawanda	(716)	15,130	14,976
*14150	Tonawanda (c)	(716)	58,144	—
*12180	Troy	(518)	50,129	49,910
*11553	Uniondale (c)	(516)	24,759	—
*13501	Utica	(315)	62,235	61,332
*11580	Valley Stream	(516)	37,511	37,832
11793	Wantagh (c)	(516)	18,871	—
*13601	Watertown	(315)	27,023	27,590
12189	Watervliet	(518)	10,254	10,233
*11704	West Babylon (c)	(631)	43,213	—
10993	West Haverstraw	(845)	10,165	10,417
11552	West Hempstead (c)	(516)	18,862	—
11795	West Islip (c)	(631)	28,335	—
*14224	West Seneca (c)	(716)	44,711	—
*11590	Westbury	(516)	15,146	15,329
*10601	White Plains	(914)	56,853	58,035
11797	Woodbury	(516)	10,686	10,814
11598	Woodmere (c)	(516)	17,121	—
11798	Wyandanch (c)	(631)	11,647	—
*10701	Yonkers	(914)	195,976	200,667

(1) Place was incorporated after the 2010 Census was conducted. Data in 2010 column is for Mastic Beach CDP.

North Carolina

Area code 743 overlays area code 336 effective May 23, 2016. Area code 980 overlays 704. Area code 984 overlays 919.

ZIP	Place	Area code	2010 population	2014 estimate
28315	Albemarle	(910)	15,903	15,976
*27502	Apex	(919)	37,476	43,907
27263	Archdale	(336)	11,415	11,539
*27203	Asheboro	(336)	25,012	25,886
*28801	Asheville	(828)	83,393	87,882
28012	Belmont	(704)	10,076	10,456
*28607	Boone	(828)	17,122	18,130
*27215	Burlington	(336)	49,963	51,812
27510	Carrboro	(919)	19,582	20,984
*27511	Cary	(919)	135,234	155,227
*27514	Chapel Hill	(919)	57,233	59,376
*28204	Charlotte	(704)	731,424	809,958
*27520	Clayton	(919)	16,116	18,445
27012	Clemmons	(336)	18,627	19,522
*28025	Concord	(704)	79,066	85,560
28031	Cornelius	(704)	24,866	27,481
*28036	Davidson	(704)	10,944	11,981
*27701	Durham	(919)	228,330	251,893
*27288	Eden	(336)	15,527	15,407
*27909	Elizabeth City	(252)	18,683	18,047
*28301	Fayetteville	(910)	200,564	203,948
27526	Fuquay-Varina	(919)	17,937	22,644
27529	Garner	(919)	25,745	27,814
*28052	Gastonia	(704)	71,741	73,698
*27530	Goldsboro	(919)	36,437	35,947
27253	Graham	(336)	14,153	14,479
*27401	Greensboro	(336)	269,666	282,586
*27834	Greenville	(252)	84,554	89,852
28075	Harrisburg	(704)	11,526	14,132
*28532	Havelock	(252)	20,735	20,706
*27536	Henderson	(252)	15,368	15,265
*28739	Hendersonville	(828)	13,137	13,650
*28601	Hickory	(828)	40,010	40,143
*27260	High Point	(336)	104,371	108,629
27540	Holly Springs	(919)	24,661	30,157
28348	Hope Mills	(910)	15,176	16,301
*28078	Huntersville	(704)	46,773	51,567
28079	Indian Trail	(704)	33,518	36,360
*28540	Jacksonville	(910)	70,145	69,047
*28081	Kannapolis	(704)	42,625	45,245
*27284	Kernersville	(336)	23,123	23,739
28086	Kings Mountain	(704)	10,296	10,644
*28501	Kinston	(252)	21,677	21,392
*27545	Knightdale	(919)	11,401	13,871
*28352	Laurinburg	(910)	15,962	15,593
28451	Leland	(910)	13,527	17,015
*28645	Lenoir	(828)	18,228	17,920
27023	Lewisville	(336)	12,639	13,342
*27292	Lexington	(336)	18,931	19,257
*28092	Lincolnton	(704)	10,486	10,732
*28358	Lumberton	(910)	21,542	21,716
*28105	Matthews	(704)	27,198	30,008
27302	Mebane	(919)	11,393	13,277
28227	Mint Hill	(704)	22,722	25,076
*28110	Monroe	(704)	32,797	34,331
*28115	Mooresville	(704)	32,711	35,300
*28655	Morganton	(828)	16,918	16,690
27560	Morrisville	(919)	18,576	22,772
*27030	Mount Airy	(336)	10,388	10,383
28120	Mount Holly	(704)	13,656	14,016
28411	Murraysville (c)	(910)	14,215	—
*28560	New Bern	(252)	29,524	30,291
28658	Newton	(828)	12,968	13,005
*28374	Pinehurst	(910)	13,124	15,434
28399	Piney Green (c)	(910)	13,293	—

ZIP	Place	Area code	2010 population	2014 estimate
*27601	Raleigh	(919)	403,892	439,896
*27320	Reidsville	(336)	14,520	14,073
27870	Roanoke Rapids	(252)	15,754	15,495
*27801	Rocky Mount	(252)	57,477	56,325
*28144	Salisbury	(704)	33,662	33,710
*27330	Sanford	(919)	28,094	29,116
*28150	Shelby	(704)	20,323	20,276
27577	Smithfield	(919)	10,966	11,735
*28387	Southern Pines	(910)	12,334	13,235
*28390	Spring Lake	(910)	11,964	13,370
28104	Stallings	(704)	13,831	14,968
*28677	Statesville	(704)	24,532	25,722
27358	Summerfield	(336)	10,232	10,753
27886	Tarboro	(252)	11,415	11,310
*27360	Thomasville	(336)	26,757	27,002
*27587	Wake Forest	(919)	30,117	36,693
28173	Waxhaw	(704)	9,859	12,750
28104	Weddington	(704)	9,459	10,322
*28401	Wilmington	(910)	106,476	113,657
*27893	Wilson	(252)	49,167	49,395
*27101	Winston-Salem	(336)	229,617	239,269

North Dakota

Area code 701 applies to the entire state.

ZIP	Place	2010 population	2014 estimate
*58501	Bismarck	61,272	68,896
*58601	Dickinson	17,787	22,322
*58102	Fargo	105,549	115,863
*58201	Grand Forks	52,838	56,057
*58401	Jamestown	15,427	15,446
58554	Mandan	18,331	20,820
*58701	Minot	40,888	47,997
58078	West Fargo	25,830	31,771
*58801	Williston	14,716	24,562

Ohio

Area code 220 overlays area code 740. Area code 234 overlays 330. Area code 380 overlays 614 effective Feb. 27, 2016. Area code 567 overlays 419.

ZIP	Place	Area code	2010 population	2014 estimate
*44301	Akron	(330)	199,110	197,859
44601	Alliance	(330)	22,322	22,078
44001	Amherst	(440)	12,021	12,143
44805	Ashland	(419)	20,362	20,218
*44004	Ashtabula	(440)	19,124	18,508
45701	Athens	(740)	23,832	24,024
44202	Aurora	(330)	15,548	15,734
44515	Austintown (c)	(330)	29,677	—
44011	Avon	(440)	21,193	22,302
44012	Avon Lake	(440)	22,581	23,204
44203	Barberton	(330)	26,550	26,302
44140	Bay Village	(440)	15,651	15,435
44122	Beachwood	(216)	11,953	11,797
45434	Beavercreek	(937)	45,193	45,934
44146	Bedford	(216)/(440)	13,074	12,805
*44146	Bedford Heights	(216)/(440)	10,751	10,675
43311	Bellefontaine	(937)	13,370	13,167
44017	Berea	(440)	19,093	18,986
43209	Bexley	(614)	13,057	13,517
*45242	Blue Ash	(513)	12,114	12,149
*44512	Boardman (c)	(330)	35,376	—
*43402	Bowling Green	(419)	30,028	31,591
44141	Brecksville	(440)	13,656	13,469
45211	Bridgetown (c)	(513)	14,407	—
44147	Broadview Heights	(440)	19,400	19,254
44142	Brook Park	(216)/(440)	19,212	18,886
44144	Brooklyn	(216)	11,169	10,947
44212	Brunswick	(330)	34,255	34,604
44820	Bucyrus	(419)	12,362	11,973
*43725	Cambridge	(740)	10,635	10,485
*44703	Canton	(330)	73,007	72,297
*45822	Celina	(419)	10,400	10,373
*45458	Centerville	(937)	23,999	23,915
45601	Chillicothe	(740)	21,901	21,738
*45202	Cincinnati	(513)	296,943	298,165
43113	Circleville	(740)	13,314	13,455
45315	Clayton	(937)	13,209	13,170
*44102	Cleveland	(216)	396,815	389,521
*44118	Cleveland Heights	(216)	46,121	45,181
*43201	Columbus	(614)	787,033	835,957
44030	Conneaut	(440)	12,841	12,813
43812	Coshocton	(740)	11,216	11,107
*44221	Cuyahoga Falls	(330)	49,652	49,210
*45401	Dayton	(937)	141,527	141,003
43512	Defiance	(419)	16,494	16,776
43015	Delaware	(740)	34,753	37,372
*45247	Dent (c)	(513)	10,497	—
44622	Dover	(330)	12,826	12,857
*43016	Dublin	(614)/(740)	41,751	44,214
*44112	East Cleveland	(216)	17,843	17,432
43920	East Liverpool	(330)	11,195	10,951
*44095	Eastlake	(440)	18,577	18,321
*44035	Elyria	(440)	54,533	53,972
45322	Englewood	(937)	13,465	13,457
*44117	Euclid	(216)	48,920	47,893
45324	Fairborn	(937)	32,352	33,329
*45011	Fairfield	(513)	42,510	42,770
44126	Fairview Park	(440)	16,826	16,481
*45839	Findlay	(419)	41,202	41,098
*45224	Finneytown (c)	(513)	12,741	—
45240	Forest Park	(513)	18,720	18,723
45230	Forestville (c)	(513)	10,532	—
44830	Fostoria	(419)	13,441	13,182
45005	Franklin	(513)	11,771	11,811
43420	Fremont	(419)	16,734	16,448
43230	Gahanna	(614)	33,248	34,257
44833	Galion	(419)	10,512	10,175
*44125	Garfield Heights	(216)	28,849	28,229
44232	Green	(330)	25,699	25,917
45331	Greenville	(937)	13,227	13,037
43123	Grove City	(614)	35,575	38,519
*45011	Hamilton	(513)	62,477	62,486
45030	Harrison	(513)	9,897	10,479
43056	Heath	(740)	10,310	10,456
43026	Hilliard	(614)/(740)	28,435	32,465
45424	Huber Heights	(937)	38,101	38,162
*44236	Hudson	(330)	22,262	22,448
45638	Ironton	(740)	11,129	10,995
*44240	Kent	(330)	28,904	29,639
*45429	Kettering	(937)	56,163	55,705
44107	Lakewood	(216)	52,131	50,926
43130	Lancaster	(740)	38,780	39,595
45036	Lebanon	(513)	20,033	20,434
*45801	Lima	(419)	38,771	38,265
43140	London	(740)	9,904	10,056
*44052	Lorain	(440)	64,097	63,776
*45140	Loveland	(513)	12,081	12,405
44124	Lyndhurst	(216)/(440)	14,001	13,733
*44056	Macedonia	(330)	11,188	11,579
*45248	Mack (c)	(513)	11,585	—
*44901	Mansfield	(419)	47,821	46,824
44137	Maple Heights	(216)	23,138	22,735
45750	Marietta	(740)	14,085	13,954
*43302	Marion	(740)	36,837	36,620
*43040	Marysville	(937)	22,094	22,708
45040	Mason	(513)	30,712	31,613
*44646	Massillon	(330)	32,149	32,274
43537	Maumee	(419)	14,286	14,036
44124	Mayfield Heights	(440)	19,155	18,849
*44256	Medina	(330)	26,678	26,523
*44060	Mentor	(440)	47,159	46,870
*45343	Miamisburg	(937)	20,181	20,092
44130	Middleburg Heights	(216)/(440)	15,946	15,751
*45042	Middletown	(513)	48,694	48,791
45211	Monfort Heights (c)	(513)	11,948	—
*45050	Monroe	(513)	12,442	13,279
45242	Montgomery	(513)	10,251	10,440
43050	Mount Vernon	(740)	16,990	16,788
*44216	New Franklin	(330)	14,227	14,292
44663	New Philadelphia	(330)	17,288	17,438
*43055	Newark	(740)	47,573	47,839
44446	Niles	(330)	19,266	18,778
*44720	North Canton	(330)	17,488	17,490
44070	North Olmsted	(440)	32,718	32,130
*44039	North Ridgeville	(440)	29,465	31,871
44133	North Royalton	(440)	30,444	30,327
45239	Northbrook (c)	(513)	10,668	—
44203	Norton	(330)	12,085	12,042
44857	Norwalk	(419)	17,012	16,898
*45212	Norwood	(513)	19,207	19,405
*43616	Oregon	(419)	20,291	20,196
45056	Oxford	(513)	21,371	21,782
44077	Painesville	(440)	19,563	19,840
*44129	Parma	(216)/(440)	81,601	80,015
44130	Parma Heights	(216)/(440)	20,718	20,330
43062	Pataskala	(740)	14,962	15,192
*43551	Perrysburg	(419)	20,623	21,368
43147	Pickerington	(614)/(740)	18,291	19,408
45356	Piqua	(937)	20,522	20,759
*45662	Portsmouth	(740)	20,226	20,326
43065	Powell	(614)	11,500	12,511
44266	Ravenna	(330)	11,724	11,643
*45215	Reading	(513)	10,385	10,354
43068	Reynoldsburg	(614)/(740)	35,893	36,711
44143	Richmond Heights	(216)/(440)	10,546	10,495
45431	Riverside	(937)	25,201	25,040
44116	Rocky River	(440)	20,213	20,433
44460	Salem	(330)	12,303	12,087
*44870	Sandusky	(419)	25,793	25,346
44131	Seven Hills	(216)/(440)	11,804	11,702
*44122	Shaker Heights	(216)	28,448	27,790
45241	Sharonville	(513)	13,560	13,581

ZIP	Place	Area code	2010 population	2014 estimate
*45365	Sidney	(937)	21,229	20,905
44139	Solon	(440)	23,348	23,075
*44121	South Euclid	(216)	22,295	21,869
45066	Springboro	(513)	17,409	18,017
45246	Springdale	(513)	11,223	11,212
*45501	Springfield	(937)	60,608	59,956
*43952	Steubenville	(740)	18,659	18,303
44224	Stow	(330)	34,837	34,773
44241	Streetsboro	(330)	16,028	16,238
*44136	Strongsville	(440)	44,750	44,654
44471	Struthers	(330)	10,713	10,441
43560	Sylvania	(419)	18,965	18,965
44278	Tallmadge	(330)	17,537	17,527
44883	Tiffin	(419)	17,963	17,739
*43601	Toledo	(419)	287,208	281,031
45067	Trenton	(513)	11,869	12,260
*45426	Trotwood	(937)	24,431	24,171
*45373	Troy	(937)	25,058	25,564
44087	Twinsburg	(330)	18,795	18,837
*44122	University Heights	(216)	13,539	13,203
*43221	Upper Arlington	(614)	33,771	34,609
43078	Urbana	(937)	11,793	11,524
45891	Van Wert	(419)	10,846	10,768
45377	Vandalia	(937)	15,246	15,139
*44089	Vermilion	(440)	10,594	10,478
*44281	Wadsworth	(330)	21,567	21,893
*44481	Warren	(330)	41,557	40,633
*44122	Warrensville Heights	(216)	13,542	13,286
43160	Washington Court House	(740)	14,192	14,085
*45449	West Carrollton	(937)	13,143	13,018
*43081	Westerville	(614)	36,120	37,667
44145	Westlake	(440)	32,729	32,424
*45239	White Oak (c)	(513)	19,167	—
43213	Whitehall	(614)	18,062	18,558
44092	Wickliffe	(440)	12,750	12,584
*44094	Willoughby	(440)	22,268	22,453
44095	Willowick	(440)	14,171	14,009
45177	Wilmington	(937)	12,520	12,375
44691	Wooster	(330)	26,119	26,540
43085	Worthington	(614)	13,575	14,384
45385	Xenia	(937)	25,719	25,911
*44503	Youngstown	(330)	66,982	65,062
*43701	Zanesville	(740)	25,487	25,372

Oklahoma

Area code 539 overlays area code 918.

ZIP	Place	Area code	2010 population	2014 estimate
*74820	Ada	(580)	16,810	17,130
*73521	Altus	(580)	19,813	19,531
*73401	Ardmore	(580)	24,283	25,226
*74003	Bartlesville	(918)	35,750	36,498
73008	Bethany	(405)	19,051	19,580
74008	Bixby	(918)	20,884	24,008
*74012	Broken Arrow	(918)	98,850	104,726
*73018	Chickasha	(405)	16,036	16,334
73020	Choctaw	(405)	11,146	11,992
*74017	Claremore	(918)	18,581	18,971
*73115	Del City	(405)	21,332	22,008
*73533	Duncan	(580)	23,431	23,173
*74701	Durant	(580)	15,856	17,041
*73034	Edmond	(405)	81,405	88,605
73036	El Reno	(405)	16,749	18,153
*73644	Elk City	(580)	11,693	12,680
*73701	Enid	(580)	49,379	51,386
*74033	Glenpool	(918)	10,808	11,855
73044	Guthrie	(405)	10,191	11,096
73942	Guymon	(580)	11,442	12,128
74037	Jenks	(918)	16,924	19,951
*73501	Lawton	(580)	96,867	97,017
*74501	McAlester	(918)	18,383	18,247
*74354	Miami	(918)	13,570	13,671
*73110	Midwest City	(405)	54,371	57,039
*73160	Moore	(405)	55,081	59,196
*74401	Muskogee	(918)	39,223	38,616
73064	Mustang	(405)	17,395	19,638
*73069	Norman	(405)	110,925	118,040
*73102	Oklahoma City	(405)	579,999	620,602
74447	Okmulgee	(918)	12,321	12,227
74055	Owasso	(918)	28,915	33,773
*74601	Ponca City	(580)	25,387	24,766
74063	Sand Springs	(918)	18,906	19,553
*74066	Sapulpa	(918)	20,544	20,432
*74801	Shawnee	(405)	29,857	31,254
*74074	Stillwater	(405)	45,688	48,406
*74464	Tahlequah	(918)	15,753	16,496
*74103	Tulsa	(918)	391,906	399,682
*73112	Warr Acres	(405)	10,043	10,408
73096	Weatherford	(580)	10,833	11,989
*73801	Woodward	(580)	12,051	12,963
*73099	Yukon	(405)	22,709	25,349

Oregon

Area code 458 overlays area code 541. Area code 971 overlays 503.

ZIP	Place	Area code	2010 population	2014 estimate
*97321	Albany	(541)	50,158	51,980
*97006	Aloha (c)	(503)	49,425	—
97601	Altamont (c)	(541)	19,257	—
97520	Ashland	(541)	20,078	20,684
*97005	Beaverton	(503)	89,803	95,109
*97701	Bend	(541)	76,639	84,080
97229	Bethany (c)	(503)	20,646	—
97013	Canby	(503)	15,829	17,010
97291	Cedar Mill (c)	(503)	14,546	—
97502	Central Point	(541)	17,169	17,724
97420	Coos Bay	(541)	15,967	16,039
97113	Cornelius	(503)	11,869	12,185
*97333	Corvallis	(541)	54,462	54,953
97338	Dallas	(503)	14,583	15,102
*97009	Damascus	(503)	10,539	10,893
*97401	Eugene	(541)	156,185	160,561
97116	Forest Grove	(503)	21,083	23,096
97301	Four Corners (c)	(503)	15,947	—
97027	Gladstone	(503)	11,497	11,888
*97526	Grants Pass	(541)	34,533	35,272
*97030	Gresham	(503)	105,594	109,892
*97015	Happy Valley	(503)	13,903	17,319
97303	Hayesville (c)	(503)	19,936	—
97838	Hermiston	(541)	16,745	17,137
*97123	Hillsboro	(503)	91,611	99,393
*97303	Keizer	(503)	36,478	37,303
*97601	Klamath Falls	(541)	20,840	21,119
97850	La Grande	(541)	13,082	13,026
*97034	Lake Oswego	(503)	36,619	37,999
97355	Lebanon	(541)	15,518	15,982
97128	McMinnville	(503)	32,187	33,393
*97501	Medford	(541)	74,907	78,557
*97269	Milwaukie	(503)	20,291	20,640
97132	Newberg	(503)	22,068	22,692
97365	Newport	(541)	9,989	10,116
97268	Oak Grove (c)	(503)	16,629	—
97006	Oak Hills (c)	(503)	11,333	—
97267	Oatfield (c)	(503)	13,415	—
97914	Ontario	(541)	11,366	10,982
97045	Oregon City	(503)	31,859	35,266
97801	Pendleton	(541)	16,612	16,904
*97201	Portland	(503)	583,776	619,360
97756	Redmond	(541)	26,215	27,941
97470	Roseburg	(541)	21,181	21,903
97051	Saint Helens	(503)	12,883	13,061
*97301	Salem	(503)	154,637	161,637
97055	Sandy	(503)	9,570	10,309
97140	Sherwood	(503)	18,194	18,978
*97477	Springfield	(541)	59,403	60,263
97058	The Dalles	(541)	13,620	15,162
*97223	Tigard	(503)	48,035	50,787
97060	Troutdale	(503)	15,962	16,552
97062	Tualatin	(503)	26,054	26,907
97068	West Linn	(503)	25,109	26,289
97070	Wilsonville	(503)	19,509	22,026
97071	Woodburn	(503)	24,080	24,734

Pennsylvania

Area code 267 overlays area code 215. Area code 272 overlays 570. Area code 484 overlays 610. Area code 878 overlays 412/724.

ZIP	Place	Area code	2010 population	2014 estimate
*18101	Allentown	(610)	118,032	119,104
15101	Allison Park (c)	(412)/(724)	21,552	—
*16601	Altoona	(814)	46,320	45,558
19003	Ardmore (c)	(610)	12,455	—
15234	Baldwin	(412)	19,767	19,740
18603	Berwick	(570)	10,477	10,316
15102	Bethel Park	(412)	32,313	32,257
*18016	Bethlehem	(610)	74,982	75,135
*17815	Bloomsburg	(570)	14,855	14,727
19008	Broomall (c)	(610)	10,789	—
*16001	Butler	(724)	13,757	13,369
*17013	Carlisle	(717)	18,682	18,916
15108	Carnot-Moon (c)	(412)	11,372	—
*17201	Chambersburg	(717)	20,268	20,602
*19013	Chester	(610)	33,972	34,133
19320	Coatesville	(610)	13,100	13,164
17109	Colonial Park (c)	(717)	13,229	—
17512	Columbia	(717)	10,400	10,383
19023	Darby	(610)	10,687	10,695
19026	Drexel Hill (c)	(610)	28,043	—
*18512	Dunmore	(570)	14,057	13,791
*18042	Easton	(610)	26,800	27,052
17022	Elizabethtown	(717)	11,545	11,611
*18049	Emmaus	(610)	11,211	11,335
17522	Ephrata	(717)	13,394	13,837
*16501	Erie	(814)	101,786	99,452
16063	Fernway (c)	(724)	12,414	—
15237	Franklin Park	(412)	13,470	14,269

ZIP	Place	Area code	2010 population	2014 estimate
18052	Fullerton (c)	(610)	14,925	—
*15601	Greensburg	(724)	14,892	14,571
*17331	Hanover	(717)	15,289	15,454
*17101	Harrisburg	(717)	49,528	49,082
*18201	Hazleton	(570)	25,340	24,932
16148	Hermitage	(724)	16,220	16,118
17033	Hershey (c)	(717)	14,257	—
19044	Horsham (c)	(215)	14,842	—
*15701	Indiana	(724)	13,975	14,194
15025	Jefferson Hills	(412)	10,619	11,232
*15901	Johnstown	(814)	20,978	20,184
*19406	King of Prussia (c)	(610)	19,936	—
18704	Kingston	(570)	13,182	12,994
*17601	Lancaster	(717)	59,322	59,302
19446	Lansdale	(215)	16,269	16,487
19050	Lansdowne	(610)	10,620	10,641
*17042	Lebanon	(717)	25,477	25,573
*19055	Levittown (c)	(215)	52,983	—
15068	Lower Burrell	(724)	11,761	11,531
*15132	McKeesport	(412)	19,731	19,561
*16335	Meadville	(814)	13,388	13,238
*15146	Monroeville	(412)/(724)	28,386	28,285
18936	Montgomeryville (c)	(215)	12,624	—
18707	Mountain Top (c)	(570)	10,982	—
15120	Munhall	(412)	11,406	11,305
*15668	Murraysville	(412)/(724)	20,079	20,162
18634	Nanticoke	(570)	10,465	10,301
*16108	New Castle	(724)	23,273	22,575
*15068	New Kensington	(724)	13,116	12,796
*19401	Norristown	(610)	34,324	34,484
16301	Oil City	(814)	10,557	10,227
*19107	Philadelphia	(215)	1,526,006	1,560,297
*19460	Phoenixville	(610)	16,440	16,599
*15201	Pittsburgh	(412)	305,704	305,412
15239	Plum	(412)	27,126	27,532
*19464	Pottstown	(610)	22,377	22,684
17901	Pottsville	(570)	14,324	13,940
*19601	Reading	(610)	88,082	87,812
15857	Saint Marys	(814)	13,070	12,793
*18505	Scranton	(570)	76,089	75,281
*16146	Sharon	(724)	14,038	13,669
17404	Shiloh (c)	(717)	11,218	—
15129	South Park Twp. (c)	(814)	13,416	—
*16801	State College	(814)	42,034	42,100
15401	Uniontown	(724)	10,372	10,064
15241	Upper St. Clair (c)	(412)	19,229	—
15301	Washington	(724)	13,663	13,551
*17268	Waynesboro	(717)	10,568	10,760
17315	Weigelstown (c)	(717)	12,875	—
*19380	West Chester	(610)	18,461	19,189
*15122	West Mifflin	(412)	20,313	20,175
18052	Whitehall	(412)	13,944	13,896
*18701	Wilkes-Barre	(570)	41,498	40,814
15221	Wilkinsburg	(412)	15,930	15,813
*17701	Williamsport	(570)	29,381	29,197
19090	Willow Grove (c)	(215)	15,726	—
19610	Wyomissing	(610)	10,461	10,472
19050	Yeadon	(610)	11,443	11,525
*17401	York	(717)	43,718	43,865

Rhode Island

Area code 401 applies to the entire state. See introductory note.

ZIP	Place	2010 population	2014 estimate
02806	*Barrington*	16,310	16,236
02809	*Bristol*	22,954	22,332
*02830	*Burrillville*	15,955	16,246
02863	Central Falls	19,376	19,328
*02816	*Coventry*	35,014	35,021
*02905	Cranston	80,387	81,037
02864	*Cumberland*	33,506	34,301
02818	*East Greenwich*	13,146	13,147
02914	East Providence	47,037	47,331
02919	*Johnston*	28,769	29,144
*02865	*Lincoln*	21,105	21,507
02842	*Middletown*	16,150	16,105
*02882	*Narragansett*	15,868	15,705
*02840	Newport	24,672	24,089
02843	Newport East (c)	11,769	—
02852	*North Kingstown*	26,486	26,291
*02908	*North Providence*	32,078	32,366
02896	*North Smithfield*	11,967	12,218
*02860	Pawtucket	71,148	71,499
02871	*Portsmouth*	17,389	17,373
*02904	Providence	178,042	179,154
*02857	*Scituate*	10,329	10,496
*02917	*Smithfield*	21,430	21,507
*02879	*South Kingstown*	30,639	30,750
02878	*Tiverton*	15,780	15,813
02864	Valley Falls (c)	11,547	—
02885	*Warren*	10,611	10,492
*02886	Warwick	82,672	81,963
02893	*West Warwick*	29,191	28,880
02891	*Westerly*	22,787	22,731
02891	Westerly (c)	17,936	—
02895	Woonsocket	41,186	41,228

South Carolina

Area code 854 overlays area code 843.

ZIP	Place	Area code	2010 population	2014 estimate
*29801	Aiken	(803)	29,524	30,258
*29621	Anderson	(864)	26,686	27,181
*29906	Beaufort	(843)	12,361	13,130
29611	Berea (c)	(864)	14,295	—
*29910	Bluffton	(843)	12,530	15,199
29033	Cayce	(803)	12,528	12,951
*29401	Charleston	(843)	120,083	130,113
*29631	Clemson	(864)	13,905	15,072
*29201	Columbia	(803)	129,272	132,067
*29526	Conway	(843)	17,103	20,175
29204	Dentsville (c)	(803)	14,062	—
*29640	Easley	(864)	19,993	20,549
29681	Five Forks (c)	(864)	14,140	—
*29501	Florence	(843)	37,056	37,961
29206	Forest Acres	(803)	10,361	10,603
*29715	Fort Mill	(803)	10,811	13,087
*29341	Gaffney	(864)	12,414	12,597
29605	Gantt (c)	(864)	14,229	—
29445	Goose Creek	(843)	35,938	40,370
*29601	Greenville	(864)	58,409	62,252
*29646	Greenwood	(864)	23,222	23,236
*29650	Greer	(864)	25,515	27,676
*29406	Hanahan	(843)	17,997	19,865
*29928	Hilton Head Island	(843)	37,099	40,039
29063	Irmo	(803)	11,097	11,893
29412	James Island[1]	(843)	11,187	11,630
29456	Ladson (c)	(843)	13,790	—
*29072	Lexington	(803)	17,870	19,893
29662	Mauldin	(864)	22,889	24,823
*29464	Mount Pleasant	(843)	67,843	77,796
*29575	Myrtle Beach	(843)	27,109	29,992
29108	Newberry	(803)	10,277	10,268
*29841	North Augusta	(803)	21,348	22,300
*29410	North Charleston	(843)	97,471	106,749
*29582	North Myrtle Beach	(843)	13,752	15,174
29073	Oak Grove (c)	(803)	10,291	—
*29115	Orangeburg	(803)	13,964	13,553
29611	Parker (c)	(864)	11,431	—
29935	Port Royal	(843)	10,678	11,870
29020	Red Hill (c)	(843)	13,223	—
*29730	Rock Hill	(803)	66,154	69,967
29407	Saint Andrews (c)	(803)	20,493	—
29210	Seven Oaks (c)	(803)	15,144	—
*29681	Simpsonville	(864)	18,238	20,125
29577	Socastee (c)	(843)	19,952	—
*29306	Spartanburg	(864)	37,013	37,525
*29483	Summerville	(843)	43,392	46,974
*29150	Sumter	(803)	40,524	40,929
29687	Taylors (c)	(864)	21,617	—
29607	Wade Hampton (c)	(864)	20,622	—
*29169	West Columbia	(803)	14,988	15,920

(1) Place was incorporated after the 2010 Census was conducted. Data in 2010 column is Census Bureau estimate.

South Dakota

Area code 605 applies to the entire state.

ZIP	Place	2010 population	2014 estimate
*57401	Aberdeen	26,091	27,800
*57006	Brookings	22,056	23,225
*57350	Huron	12,592	13,163
57301	Mitchell	15,254	15,693
57501	Pierre	13,646	14,054
*57701	Rapid City	67,956	72,638
*57103	Sioux Falls	153,888	168,586
*57783	Spearfish	10,494	11,091
57069	Vermillion	10,571	10,699
57201	Watertown	21,482	22,057
57078	Yankton	14,454	14,552

Tennessee

Area code 629 overlays area code 615.

ZIP	Place	Area code	2010 population	2014 estimate
38002	Arlington	(901)	11,517	11,634
*37303	Athens	(423)	13,458	13,664
*38133	Bartlett	(901)	54,613	58,264
*37027	Brentwood	(615)	37,060	40,982
*37620	Bristol	(423)	26,702	26,729
*37402	Chattanooga	(423)	167,674	173,778
*37040	Clarksville	(931)	132,929	146,806
*37311	Cleveland	(423)	41,285	43,182
37315	Collegedale	(423)	8,282	10,729

ZIP	Place	Area code	2010 population	2014 estimate
*38017	Collierville	(901)	43,965	48,655
*38401	Columbia	(931)	34,681	36,071
*38501	Cookeville	(931)	30,435	31,335
*38555	Crossville	(931)	10,795	11,330
*37055	Dickson	(615)	14,538	14,993
*38024	Dyersburg	(731)	17,145	16,839
37412	East Ridge	(423)	20,979	21,317
*37643	Elizabethton	(423)	14,176	14,271
*37922	Farragut	(865)	20,676	21,687
*37064	Franklin	(615)	62,487	70,612
37066	Gallatin	(615)	30,278	33,347
*38138	Germantown	(901)	38,844	39,267
*37072	Goodlettsville	(615)	15,921	16,991
*37743	Greeneville	(423)	15,062	15,035
*37075	Hendersonville	(615)	51,372	55,153
*38301	Jackson	(731)	65,211	67,319
*37601	Johnson City	(423)	63,152	65,813
*37660	Kingsport	(423)	48,205	53,028
*37902	Knoxville	(865)	178,874	184,281
*37086	La Vergne	(615)	32,588	34,274
38002	Lakeland	(901)	12,430	12,564
38464	Lawrenceburg	(931)	10,428	10,498
*37087	Lebanon	(615)	26,190	29,427
37091	Lewisburg	(931)	11,100	11,371
37355	Manchester	(931)	10,102	10,349
38237	Martin	(731)	11,473	11,322
*37801	Maryville	(865)	27,465	28,329
*37110	McMinnville	(931)	13,605	13,620
*38103	Memphis	(901)	646,889	656,861
37343	Middle Valley (c)	(423)	12,684	—
*38053	Millington	(901)	10,176	11,080
*37813	Morristown	(423)	29,137	29,304
*37122	Mount Juliet	(615)	23,671	29,387
*37130	Murfreesboro	(615)	108,755	120,954
*37201	Nashville-Davidson (balance)	(615)	601,222	644,014
*37830	Oak Ridge	(865)	29,330	29,303
38242	Paris	(731)	10,156	10,156
37148	Portland	(615)	11,480	12,218
37415	Red Bank	(423)	11,651	11,784
*37862	Sevierville	(865)	14,807	16,355
37865	Seymour (c)	(865)	10,919	—
*37160	Shelbyville	(931)	20,335	21,037
37167	Smyrna	(615)	39,974	45,274
*37379	Soddy-Daisy	(423)	12,714	13,190
37174	Spring Hill	(931)	29,036	34,269
37172	Springfield	(615)	16,440	16,752
*37388	Tullahoma	(931)	18,655	18,899
*38261	Union City	(731)	10,895	10,666
37188	White House	(615)	10,255	11,042

Texas

Area code 346 overlays area codes 281/713/832. Area code 430 overlays 903. Area codes 469/972 overlay 214. Area code 682 overlays 817. Area code 737 overlays 512.

ZIP	Place	Area code	2010 population	2014 estimate
*79603	Abilene	(325)	117,063	120,958
75001	Addison	(214)	13,056	15,457
78516	Alamo	(956)	18,353	19,224
77039	Aldine (c)	(713)	15,869	—
*78332	Alice	(361)	19,104	19,395
*75002	Allen	(214)	84,246	94,179
78573	Alton	(956)	12,341	15,497
*77511	Alvin	(713)	24,236	25,525
*79109	Amarillo	(806)	190,695	197,254
79714	Andrews	(432)	11,088	13,245
*77515	Angleton	(979)	18,862	19,472
75409	Anna	(972)	8,249	10,571
*76001	Arlington	(817)	365,438	383,204
77346	Atascocita (c)	(281)	65,844	—
*75751	Athens	(903)	12,710	12,819
*78712	Austin	(512)	790,390	912,791
*76020	Azle	(817)	10,947	11,530
*75180	Balch Springs	(214)	23,728	25,120
*77414	Bay City	(979)	17,614	17,368
*77520	Baytown	(713)	71,802	76,127
*77707	Beaumont	(409)	118,296	117,585
*76021	Bedford	(817)	46,979	48,908
*78102	Beeville	(361)	12,863	13,303
*77401	Bellaire	(713)	16,855	18,252
*76704	Bellmead	(254)	9,901	10,184
76513	Belton	(254)	18,216	20,128
*76126	Benbrook	(817)	21,234	22,419
*79720	Big Spring	(432)	27,282	28,472
*78006	Boerne	(830)	10,471	12,835
75418	Bonham	(903)	10,127	10,058
*79007	Borger	(806)	13,251	12,978
*77833	Brenham	(979)	15,716	16,297
*78520	Brownsville	(956)	175,023	183,046
*76801	Brownwood	(325)	19,288	18,972
78717	Brushy Creek (c)	(512)	21,764	—
*77801	Bryan	(979)	76,201	80,913
78610	Buda	(512)	7,295	11,461
76354	Burkburnett	(940)	10,811	11,142
*76028	Burleson	(817)	36,690	41,818
*79015	Canyon	(806)	13,303	14,432
*78130	Canyon Lake (c)	(830)	21,262	—
*75006	Carrollton	(214)	119,097	128,353
*75104	Cedar Hill	(214)	45,028	48,084
*78613	Cedar Park	(512)	48,937	63,574
77530	Channelview (c)	(713)	38,289	—
78108	Cibolo	(210)	15,349	25,280
77450	Cinco Ranch (c)	(281)	18,274	—
*76031	Cleburne	(817)	29,337	29,848
77015	Cloverleaf (c)	(713)	22,942	—
77531	Clute	(979)	11,211	11,392
*77840	College Station	(979)	93,857	103,483
76034	Colleyville	(817)	22,807	24,952
*77301	Conroe	(936)	56,207	65,871
78109	Converse	(210)	18,198	21,054
*75019	Coppell	(214)	38,659	40,678
76522	Copperas Cove	(254)	32,032	32,943
*76205	Corinth	(940)	19,935	20,836
*78401	Corpus Christi	(361)	305,215	320,434
*75110	Corsicana	(903)	23,770	23,989
76036	Crowley	(817)	12,838	14,572
*75201	Dallas	(214)	1,197,816	1,281,047
77536	Deer Park	(281)	32,010	33,719
*78840	Del Rio	(830)	35,591	36,079
*75020	Denison	(903)	22,682	22,907
*76201	Denton	(940)	113,383	128,205
*75115	DeSoto	(214)	49,047	51,934
77539	Dickinson	(281)	18,680	19,595
78537	Donna	(956)	15,798	16,448
79029	Dumas	(806)	14,691	14,937
*75116	Duncanville	(214)	38,524	39,707
*78852	Eagle Pass	(830)	26,248	28,329
*78539	Edinburg	(956)	77,100	83,014
77437	El Campo	(979)	11,602	11,577
*79910	El Paso	(915)	649,121	679,036
*75119	Ennis	(214)	18,513	18,823
*76039	Euless	(817)	51,277	53,630
*75234	Farmers Branch	(214)	28,616	32,560
*75022	Flower Mound	(214)	64,669	69,650
76119	Forest Hill	(817)	12,355	12,795
75126	Forney	(214)	14,661	17,536
76544	Fort Hood (c)	(254)	29,589	—
*76133	Fort Worth	(817)	741,206	812,238
77498	Four Corners (c)	(281)	12,382	—
78624	Fredericksburg	(830)	10,530	10,886
*77541	Freeport	(979)	12,049	12,191
77545	Fresno (c)	(281)	19,069	—
*77546	Friendswood	(281)	35,805	38,248
*75034	Frisco	(214)	116,989	145,035
*76240	Gainesville	(940)	16,002	16,095
77547	Galena Park	(713)	10,887	11,178
*77550	Galveston	(409)	47,743	49,608
*75040	Garland	(214)	226,876	235,501
*76528	Gatesville	(254)	15,751	15,872
*78626	Georgetown	(512)	47,400	59,102
75154	Glenn Heights	(214)	11,278	11,915
*75051	Grand Prairie	(214)	175,396	185,453
*76051	Grapevine	(817)	46,334	50,844
77479	Greatwood (c)	(281)	11,538	—
*75401	Greenville	(903)	25,557	26,180
77619	Groves	(409)	16,144	15,753
*76117	Haltom City	(817)	42,409	43,913
76548	Harker Heights	(254)	26,700	28,526
*78550	Harlingen	(956)	64,849	65,914
*75652	Henderson	(903)	13,712	13,604
79045	Hereford	(806)	15,370	15,216
76643	Hewitt	(254)	13,549	14,166
78557	Hidalgo	(956)	11,198	13,497
75067	Highland Village	(214)	15,056	15,995
*79927	Horizon City	(915)	16,735	19,332
*77002	Houston	(713)	2,099,451	2,239,558
*77338	Humble	(713)	15,133	15,616
*77340	Huntsville	(936)	38,548	40,435
*76053	Hurst	(817)	37,337	38,733
78634	Hutto	(512)	14,698	21,170
*75062	Irving	(214)	216,290	232,406
77029	Jacinto City	(281)	10,553	10,809
75766	Jacksonville	(903)	14,544	14,675
78729	Jollyville (c)	(512)	16,151	—
*77449	Katy	(713)	14,102	15,591
*76248	Keller	(817)	39,627	43,924
*78028	Kerrville	(830)	22,347	22,905
*75662	Kilgore	(903)	12,975	14,948
*76541	Killeen	(254)	127,921	138,154
*78363	Kingsville	(361)	26,213	26,529
78640	Kyle	(512)	28,016	32,881
78572	La Homa (c)	(956)	11,985	—
77568	La Marque	(409)	14,509	15,521
*77571	La Porte	(281)	33,800	35,039
77566	Lake Jackson	(979)	26,849	27,604
*78734	Lakeway	(512)	11,391	13,685
*75146	Lancaster	(214)	36,361	38,453

ZIP	Place	Area code	2010 population	2014 estimate
*78041	Laredo	(956)	236,091	252,309
*77573	League City	(281)	83,560	94,403
*78641	Leander	(512)	26,521	34,172
*78268	Leon Valley	(210)	10,151	11,015
*79336	Levelland	(806)	13,542	13,954
*75067	Lewisville	(214)	95,290	102,889
75068	Little Elm	(214)	25,898	35,414
*78233	Live Oak	(210)	13,131	15,116
78644	Lockhart	(512)	12,698	13,232
*75601	Longview	(903)	80,455	81,593
*79401	Lubbock	(806)	229,573	243,839
*75901	Lufkin	(936)	35,067	36,141
77657	Lumberton	(409)	11,943	12,312
76063	Mansfield	(817)	56,368	62,246
*75670	Marshall	(903)	23,523	24,701
*78501	McAllen	(956)	129,877	138,596
*75070	McKinney	(214)	131,117	156,767
78570	Mercedes	(956)	15,570	16,591
*75149	Mesquite	(214)	139,824	144,416
*79701	Midland	(432)	111,147	128,037
76065	Midlothian	(214)	18,037	20,934
*76067	Mineral Wells	(940)	16,788	15,362
*78572	Mission	(956)	77,058	82,431
*77083	Mission Bend (c)	(281)	36,501	—
*77489	Missouri City	(713)	67,358	71,710
*75455	Mount Pleasant	(903)	15,564	16,021
*75094	Murphy	(214)	17,708	20,230
*75961	Nacogdoches	(936)	32,996	33,687
77627	Nederland	(409)	17,547	17,108
*78130	New Braunfels	(830)	57,740	66,394
77479	New Territory (c)	(281)	15,186	—
*76117	North Richland Hills	(817)	63,343	68,529
*79761	Odessa	(432)	99,940	114,597
*77630	Orange	(409)	18,595	18,913
*75801	Palestine	(903)	18,712	18,393
*79065	Pampa	(806)	17,994	18,399
*75460	Paris	(903)	25,171	24,895
*77506	Pasadena	(713)	149,043	153,887
*77581	Pearland	(713)	91,252	103,441
78721	Pecan Grove (c)	(254)	15,963	—
*78660	Pflugerville	(512)	46,936	54,644
78577	Pharr	(956)	70,400	75,382
*79072	Plainview	(806)	22,194	21,166
*75074	Plano	(214)	259,841	278,480
*77640	Port Arthur	(409)	53,818	54,548
77979	Port Lavaca	(361)	12,248	12,399
77651	Port Neches	(409)	13,040	12,755
78374	Portland	(361)	15,099	15,915
75078	Prosper	(214)	9,423	14,416
*78580	Raymondville	(965)	11,284	11,117
*75154	Red Oak	(214)	10,769	11,560
76140	Rendon (c)	(817)	12,552	—
*75080	Richardson	(214)	99,223	108,617
*77469	Richmond	(713)	11,679	12,018
78582	Rio Grande City	(956)	13,834	14,227
76701	Robinson	(254)	10,509	11,416
78380	Robstown	(361)	11,487	11,657
*78382	Rockport	(361)	8,766	10,323
*75087	Rockwall	(214)	37,490	41,785
78584	Roma	(956)	9,765	10,088
*77471	Rosenberg	(832)	30,618	34,468
*78681	Round Rock	(512)	99,887	112,744
*75088	Rowlett	(214)	56,199	58,407
75189	Royse City	(214)	9,349	10,757
75048	Sachse	(214)	20,329	23,681
*76179	Saginaw	(817)	19,806	21,703
*76901	San Angelo	(325)	93,200	98,975
*78201	San Antonio	(210)	1,327,407	1,436,697
78586	San Benito	(956)	24,250	24,506
79849	San Elizario (c)	(915)	13,603	—
78589	San Juan	(956)	33,856	36,174
*78666	San Marcos	(512)	44,894	58,892
*77510	Santa Fe	(409)	12,222	12,860
*78154	Schertz	(210)	31,465	36,896
77586	Seabrook	(281)	11,952	12,792
75159	Seagoville	(214)	14,835	15,723
*78155	Seguin	(830)	25,175	27,041
*75090	Sherman	(903)	38,521	39,943
77459	Sienna Plantation (c)	(281)	13,721	—
*79549	Snyder	(325)	11,202	11,571
*79927	Socorro	(915)	32,013	32,909
77587	South Houston	(713)	16,983	17,536
76092	Southlake	(817)	26,575	29,086
*77373	Spring (c)	(713)	54,298	—
*77477	Stafford	(713)	17,693	18,344
*76401	Stephenville	(254)	17,123	19,374
*77478	Sugar Land	(713)	78,817	86,777
*75482	Sulphur Springs	(903)	15,449	15,975
79556	Sweetwater	(325)	10,906	10,805
76574	Taylor	(512)	15,191	16,483
*76501	Temple	(254)	66,102	70,765
*75160	Terrell	(214)	15,816	16,561
*75501	Texarkana	(903)	36,411	37,225
*77590	Texas City	(409)	45,099	46,639
75056	The Colony	(214)	36,328	41,352
*77381	The Woodlands (c)	(281)	93,847	—
78260	Timberwood Park (c)	(830)	13,447	—
*77375	Tomball	(713)	10,753	11,299
76262	Trophy Club	(817)	8,024	11,227
*75702	Tyler	(903)	96,900	101,421
*78148	Universal City	(210)	18,530	19,721
75205	University Park	(214)	23,068	24,396
*78801	Uvalde	(830)	15,751	16,412
*76384	Vernon	(940)	11,002	10,531
*77901	Victoria	(361)	62,592	66,094
*77662	Vidor	(409)	10,579	10,920
*76704	Waco	(254)	124,805	130,194
*76148	Watauga	(817)	23,497	24,345
*75165	Waxahachie	(214)	29,621	32,344
*76086	Weatherford	(817)	25,250	27,769
77598	Webster	(281)	10,400	11,115
78728	Wells Branch (c)	(512)	12,120	—
*78596	Weslaco	(956)	35,670	37,601
79764	West Odessa (c)	(432)	22,707	—
77005	West University Place	(713)	14,787	15,604
76108	White Settlement	(817)	16,116	16,896
*76301	Wichita Falls	(940)	104,553	105,114
75098	Wylie	(214)	41,427	45,913

Utah

Area code 385 overlays area code 801.

ZIP	Place	Area code	2010 population	2014 estimate
84004	Alpine	(801)	9,555	10,131
84003	American Fork	(801)	26,263	28,152
*84010	Bountiful	(801)	42,552	43,385
84302	Brigham City	(435)	17,899	18,631
*84720	Cedar City	(435)	28,857	29,483
84062	Cedar Hills	(801)	9,796	10,261
84014	Centerville	(801)	15,335	16,819
*84015	Clearfield	(801)	30,112	30,484
84015	Clinton	(801)	20,426	21,104
*84047	Cottonwood Heights	(801)	33,433	34,166
84020	Draper	(801)	42,274	46,202
*84005	Eagle Mountain	(801)	21,415	25,593
84025	Farmington	(801)	18,275	22,159
*84032	Heber City	(435)	11,362	13,599
*84096	Herriman	(801)	21,785	28,556
84003	Highland	(801)	15,523	17,456
*84117	Holladay	(801)	26,472	27,129
84737	Hurricane	(435)	13,748	15,032
84037	Kaysville	(801)	27,300	29,494
84118	Kearns (c)	(801)	35,731	—
*84041	Layton	(801)	67,311	72,231
*84043	Lehi	(801)	47,407	56,275
84042	Lindon	(801)	10,070	10,723
*84321	Logan	(435)	48,174	48,997
84044	Magna (c)	(801)	26,505	—
84047	Midvale	(801)	27,964	31,725
84109	Millcreek (c)	(801)	62,139	—
*84107	Murray	(801)	46,746	48,822
*84404	North Ogden	(801)	17,357	18,172
84054	North Salt Lake	(801)	16,322	19,193
*84401	Ogden	(801)	82,825	84,316
*84057	Orem	(801)	88,328	91,781
*84651	Payson	(801)	18,294	19,331
84062	Pleasant Grove	(801)	33,509	37,064
*84601	Provo	(801)	112,488	114,801
*84065	Riverton	(801)	38,753	41,457
*84067	Roy	(801)	36,884	37,877
*84770	Saint George	(435)	72,897	78,505
*84101	Salt Lake City	(801)	186,440	190,884
*84070	Sandy	(801)	87,461	91,148
84655	Santaquin	(801)	9,128	10,106
84043	Saratoga Springs	(801)	17,781	24,356
84335	Smithfield	(435)	9,495	11,014
84095	South Jordan	(801)	50,418	62,781
84403	South Ogden	(801)	16,532	16,852
*84115	South Salt Lake	(801)	23,617	24,748
84660	Spanish Fork	(801)	34,691	37,527
*84663	Springville	(801)	29,466	31,464
84075	Syracuse	(801)	24,331	26,639
*84118	Taylorsville	(801)	58,652	60,433
84074	Tooele	(435)	31,605	32,573
*84078	Vernal	(435)	9,089	10,844
84780	Washington	(435)	18,761	23,360
84401	West Haven	(801)	10,272	11,582
*84084	West Jordan	(801)	103,712	110,920
84015	West Point	(801)	9,511	10,204
*84119	West Valley City	(801)	129,480	134,495
84010	Woods Cross	(801)	9,761	11,097

Vermont

Area code 802 applies to the entire state. See introductory note.

ZIP	Place	2010 population	2014 estimate
05201	*Bennington*	15,764	15,431
*05301	*Brattleboro*	12,046	11,765

ZIP	Place	2010 population	2014 estimate
*05401	Burlington	42,417	42,211
*05446	*Colchester*	17,067	17,384
*05452	*Essex*	19,587	20,724
05468	*Milton*	10,352	10,667
*05701	Rutland	16,495	15,942
*05403	South Burlington	17,904	18,743

Virginia

Area code 571 overlays area code 703.

ZIP	Place	Area code	2010 population	2014 estimate
*22314	Alexandria	(703)	139,966	150,575
22003	Annandale (c)	(703)	41,008	—
*22201	Arlington (c)	(703)	207,627	—
*20146	Ashburn (c)	(703)	43,511	—
22041	Bailey's Crossroads (c)	(703)	23,643	—
*24060	Blacksburg	(540)	42,620	43,985
23235	Bon Air (c)	(804)	16,366	—
23112	Brandermill (c)	(804)	13,173	—
*24201	Bristol	(276)	17,835	17,184
20148	Broadlands (c)	(703)	12,313	—
20111	Buckhall (c)	(703)	16,293	—
20109	Bull Run (c)	(703)	14,983	—
*22015	Burke (c)	(703)	41,055	—
22015	Burke Centre (c)	(703)	17,326	—
*20165	Cascades (c)	(434)	11,912	—
24018	Cave Spring (c)	(540)	24,922	—
*20120	Centreville (c)	(703)	71,135	—
*20151	Chantilly (c)	(703)	23,039	—
*22901	Charlottesville	(434)	43,475	45,593
22026	Cherry Hill (c)	(703)	16,000	—
*23320	Chesapeake	(757)	222,209	233,371
*23831	Chester (c)	(804)	20,987	—
*24073	Christiansburg	(540)	21,041	21,805
23834	Colonial Heights	(804)	17,411	17,731
20165	Countryside (c)	(703)	10,072	—
22701	Culpeper	(540)	16,379	17,411
22193	Dale City (c)	(703)	65,969	—
*24541	Danville	(434)	43,055	42,444
20170	Dranesville (c)	(703)	11,921	—
23222	East Highland Park (c)	(804)	14,796	—
22033	Fair Oaks (c)	(703)	30,223	—
*22030	Fairfax	(703)	22,565	24,483
22039	Fairfax Station (c)	(703)	12,030	—
*22046	Falls Church	(703)	12,332	13,601
22308	Fort Hunt (c)	(703)	16,045	—
*22310	Franconia (c)	(703)	18,245	—
20171	Franklin Farm (c)	(703)	19,288	—
*22401	Fredericksburg	(540)	24,286	28,350
22630	Front Royal	(540)	14,440	15,038
*20155	Gainesville (c)	(703)	11,481	—
*23060	Glen Allen (c)	(804)	14,774	—
22066	Great Falls (c)	(703)	15,427	—
22306	Groveton (c)	(703)	14,598	—
*23669	Hampton	(757)	137,436	136,879
*22801	Harrisonburg	(540)	48,914	52,478
*20170	Herndon	(703)	23,292	24,554
23075	Highland Springs (c)	(804)	15,711	—
24019	Hollins (c)	(540)	14,673	—
23860	Hopewell	(804)	22,591	22,196
22303	Huntington (c)	(703)	11,267	—
22306	Hybla Valley (c)	(703)	15,801	—
22043	Idylwood (c)	(703)	17,288	—
22038	Kings Park West (c)	(703)	13,390	—
22315	Kingstowne (c)	(703)	15,556	—
22192	Lake Ridge (c)	(540)	41,058	—
23228	Lakeside (c)	(804)	11,849	—
20176	Lansdowne (c)	(703)	11,253	—
23060	Laurel (c)	(804)	16,713	—
*20175	Leesburg	(703)	42,616	49,496
22312	Lincolnia (c)	(703)	22,855	—
20136	Linton Hall (c)	(703)	35,725	—
*22079	Lorton (c)	(703)	18,610	—
20165	Lowes Island (c)	(703)	10,756	—
*24501	Lynchburg	(434)	75,568	79,047
24572	Madison Heights (c)	(434)	11,285	—
*20110	Manassas	(703)	37,821	42,081
*20111	Manassas Park	(703)	14,273	15,174
23235	Manchester (c)	(804)	10,804	—
*24112	Martinsville	(276)	13,821	13,711
22191	Marumsco (c)	(703)	35,036	—
*22101	McLean (c)	(703)	48,115	—
20171	McNair (c)	(703)	17,513	—
23234	Meadowbrook (c)	(804)	18,312	—
*23111	Mechanicsville (c)	(804)	36,348	—
*22081	Merrifield (c)	(703)	15,212	—
22025	Montclair (c)	(703)	19,570	—
22121	Mount Vernon (c)	(703)	12,416	—
22191	Neabsco (c)	(703)	12,068	—
22122	Newington (c)	(703)	12,943	—
22153	Newington Forest (c)	(703)	12,442	—
*23607	Newport News	(757)	180,719	182,965
*23502	Norfolk	(757)	242,803	245,428
*22124	Oakton (c)	(703)	34,166	—
*23801	Petersburg	(804)	32,420	32,701
23662	Poquoson	(757)	12,150	12,048
*23707	Portsmouth	(757)	95,535	96,004
*24141	Radford	(540)	16,408	17,646
*20190	Reston (c)	(703)	58,404	—
*23232	Richmond	(804)	204,214	217,853
*24017	Roanoke	(540)	97,032	99,428
24281	Rose Hill (c) (Fairfax Co.)	(276)	20,226	—
*24153	Salem	(540)	24,802	25,483
23233	Short Pump (c)	(804)	24,729	—
20152	South Riding (c)	(703)	24,256	—
*22150	Springfield (c)	(703)	30,484	—
*24401	Staunton	(540)	23,746	24,538
*20164	Sterling (c)	(703)	27,822	—
20109	Sudley (c)	(703)	16,203	—
*23434	Suffolk	(757)	84,585	86,806
20164	Sugarland Run (c)	(703)	11,799	—
24502	Timberlake (c)	(434)	12,183	—
23229	Tuckahoe (c)	(804)	44,990	—
*22102	Tysons Corner (c)	(703)	19,627	—
*22180	Vienna	(703)	15,687	16,459
*23450	Virginia Beach	(757)	437,994	450,980
23888	Wakefield (c)	(757)	11,275	—
22980	Waynesboro	(540)	21,006	21,366
*22042	West Falls Church (c)	(703)	29,207	—
22152	West Springfield (c)	(703)	22,460	—
*23185	Williamsburg	(757)	14,068	14,691
*22601	Winchester	(540)	26,203	27,543
24592	Wolf Trap (c)	(703)	16,131	—
24381	Woodlawn (c) (Fairfax Co.)	(276)	20,804	—

Washington

ZIP	Place	Area code	2010 population	2014 estimate
98520	Aberdeen	(360)	16,896	16,255
*98221	Anacortes	(360)	15,778	16,232
98223	Arlington	(360)	17,926	18,808
98335	Artondale (c)	(253)	12,653	—
*98002	Auburn	(253)	70,180	76,347
98110	Bainbridge Island	(206)	23,025	23,293
98604	Battle Ground	(360)	17,571	18,930
*98004	Bellevue	(425)	122,363	136,426
*98225	Bellingham	(360)	80,885	83,365
*98390	Bonney Lake	(360)	17,374	18,809
*98011	Bothell	(425)	33,505	36,567
98036	Bothell West (c)	(425)	16,607	—
*98337	Bremerton	(360)	37,729	38,572
98178	Bryn Mawr-Skyway (c)	(206)	15,645	—
*98166	Burien	(206)	33,313	50,188
98607	Camas	(360)	19,355	21,220
98531	Centralia	(360)	16,336	16,623
99004	Cheney	(509)	10,590	11,420
98072	Cottage Lake (c)	(425)	22,494	—
98042	Covington	(253)	17,575	19,134
*98198	Des Moines	(206)	29,673	31,011
*98031	East Hill-Meridian (c)	(253)	29,878	—
98056	East Renton Highlands (c)	(425)	11,140	—
98802	East Wenatchee	(509)	13,190	13,505
98204	Eastmont (c)	(425)	20,101	—
*98020	Edmonds	(425)	39,709	40,896
98387	Elk Plain (c)	(253)	14,205	—
*98926	Ellensburg	(509)	18,174	18,774
98022	Enumclaw	(360)	10,669	11,548
*98201	Everett	(425)	103,019	106,736
98058	Fairwood (c) (King Co.)	(425)	19,102	—
*98001	Federal Way	(253)	89,306	93,425
98248	Ferndale	(360)	11,415	12,704
98597	Five Corners (c)	(360)	18,159	—
98433	Fort Lewis (c)	(253)	11,046	—
98375	Frederickson (c)	(253)	18,719	—
98338	Graham (c)	(253)	23,491	—
98930	Grandview	(509)	10,862	11,140
98665	Hazel Dell (c)	(360)	19,435	—
98011	Inglewood-Finn Hill (c)	(425)	22,707	—
*98027	Issaquah	(425)	30,434	34,056
98626	Kelso	(360)	11,925	11,788
98028	Kenmore	(425)	20,460	21,839
*99336	Kennewick	(509)	73,917	77,421
*98031	Kent	(253)/(425)	92,411	125,560
98033	Kingsgate (c)	(425)	13,065	—
*98033	Kirkland	(425)	48,787	85,763
98029	Klahanie (c)	(425)	10,674	—
*98503	Lacey	(360)	42,393	45,446
98155	Lake Forest Park	(206)	12,598	13,184
98042	Lake Morton-Berrydale (c)	(253)/(425)	10,160	—
98258	Lake Stevens	(425)	28,069	30,284
98391	Lake Tapps (c)	(253)	11,859	—
98002	Lakeland North (c)	(253)	12,942	—
98002	Lakeland South (c)	(253)	11,574	—
*98498	Lakewood	(253)	58,163	59,610

ZIP	Place	Area code	2010 population	2014 estimate
98632	Longview	(360)	36,648	36,483
98264	Lynden	(360)	11,951	13,165
*98036	Lynnwood	(425)	35,836	36,687
98290	Maltby (c)	(360)/(425)	10,830	—
98038	Maple Valley	(425)	22,684	25,125
98012	Martha Lake (c)	(425)	15,473	—
*98270	Marysville	(360)	60,020	65,087
98040	Mercer Island	(206)	22,699	24,326
*98082	Mill Creek	(425)	18,244	19,200
98012	Mill Creek East (c)	(425)	15,709	—
98272	Monroe	(360)	17,304	17,899
98837	Moses Lake	(509)	20,366	21,713
*98273	Mount Vernon	(360)	31,743	33,132
98043	Mountlake Terrace	(425)	19,909	20,817
98275	Mukilteo	(425)	20,254	20,993
*98059	Newcastle	(425)	10,380	11,201
98037	North Lynnwood (c)	(425)	16,574	—
*98277	Oak Harbor	(360)	22,075	22,306
*98501	Olympia	(360)	46,478	49,218
98662	Orchards (c)	(360)	19,556	—
*98444	Parkland (c)	(253)	35,803	—
*99301	Pasco	(509)	59,781	68,648
*98362	Port Angeles	(360)	19,038	19,256
*98366	Port Orchard	(360)	11,144	13,266
98390	Prairie Ridge (c)	(360)	11,464	—
*99163	Pullman	(509)	29,799	31,682
*98371	Puyallup	(253)	37,022	39,105
*98052	Redmond	(425)	54,144	59,285
*98058	Renton	(425)	90,927	98,404
*99352	Richland	(509)	48,058	53,019
98686	Salmon Creek (c)	(360)	19,686	—
*98074	Sammamish	(425)	45,780	51,229
*98148	SeaTac	(206)	26,909	28,126
*98101	Seattle	(206)/(425)	608,660	668,342
98284	Sedro-Woolley	(360)	10,540	10,764
*98133	Shoreline	(206)	53,007	55,174
98208	Silver Firs (c)	(206)/(425)	20,891	—
*98315	Silverdale (c)	(360)	19,204	—
*98065	Snoqualmie	(425)	10,670	12,630
*98373	South Hill (c)	(253)	52,431	—
98387	Spanaway (c)	(253)	27,227	—
*99201	Spokane	(509)	208,916	212,052
*99216	Spokane Valley	(509)	89,755	91,729
98944	Sunnyside	(509)	15,858	16,140
*98402	Tacoma	(253)	198,397	205,159
*98138	Tukwila	(206)	19,107	19,920
*98501	Tumwater	(360)	17,371	18,820
98053	Union Hill-Novelty Hill (c)	(425)	18,805	—
*98466	University Place	(253)	31,144	32,282
*98661	Vancouver	(360)	161,791	169,294
*98013	Vashon (c)	(206)	10,624	—
99362	Walla Walla	(509)	31,731	31,910
98671	Washougal	(360)	14,095	14,999
*98801	Wenatchee	(509)	31,925	33,261
*99353	West Richland	(509)	11,811	13,351
98166	White Center (c)	(206)	13,495	—
*98072	Woodinville	(425)	10,938	11,372
*98903	Yakima	(509)	91,067	93,357

West Virginia

Area code 681 overlays area code 304; both apply to the entire state.

ZIP	Place	2010 population	2014 estimate
*25801	Beckley	17,614	17,238
24701	Bluefield	10,447	10,448
*25301	Charleston	51,400	50,404
*26301	Clarksburg	16,578	16,242
*26554	Fairmont	18,704	18,740
*25701	Huntington	49,138	48,807
*25401	Martinsburg	17,227	17,743
*26505	Morgantown	29,660	31,073
*26101	Parkersburg	31,492	30,981
25177	Saint Albans	11,044	10,835
*25303	South Charleston	13,450	13,214
*25526	Teays Valley (c)	13,175	—
*26105	Vienna	10,749	10,562
26062	Weirton	19,746	19,362
26003	Wheeling	28,486	27,790

Wisconsin

Area code 534 overlays area code 715.

ZIP	Place	Area code	2010 population	2014 estimate
54301	Allouez	(920)	13,975	13,943
*54911	Appleton	(920)	72,623	73,971
*54304	Ashwaubenon	(920)	16,963	17,111
53913	Baraboo	(608)	12,048	12,085
53916	Beaver Dam	(920)	16,214	16,536
54311	Bellevue	(920)	14,570	15,215
*53511	Beloit	(608)	36,966	36,881
*53045	Brookfield	(262)	37,920	37,982
*53209	Brown Deer	(414)	11,999	12,102
53105	Burlington	(262)	10,464	10,541
53108	Caledonia	(262)	24,705	24,708
53012	Cedarburg	(262)	11,412	11,506
*54729	Chippewa Falls	(715)	13,661	13,965
53110	Cudahy	(414)	18,267	18,341
54115	De Pere	(920)	23,800	24,555
*54703	Eau Claire	(715)	65,883	67,684
*53711	Fitchburg	(608)	25,260	27,154
*54935	Fond du Lac	(920)	43,021	42,917
53538	Fort Atkinson	(920)	12,368	12,430
53132	Franklin	(414)	35,451	36,278
53022	Germantown	(262)	19,749	19,901
*53209	Glendale	(414)	12,872	12,887
53024	Grafton	(262)	11,459	11,531
*54303	Green Bay	(920)	104,057	104,891
53129	Greendale	(414)	14,046	14,332
*53220	Greenfield	(414)	36,720	37,157
53027	Hartford	(262)	14,223	14,280
*54303	Howard	(920)	17,399	18,987
*54016	Hudson	(715)	12,719	13,415
*53545	Janesville	(608)	63,575	64,009
54130	Kaukauna	(920)	15,462	15,799
*53140	Kenosha	(262)	99,218	99,894
*54601	La Crosse	(608)	51,320	52,440
54140	Little Chute	(920)	10,449	10,813
*53714	Madison	(608)	233,209	245,691
*54220	Manitowoc	(920)	33,736	33,102
54143	Marinette	(715)	10,968	10,897
*54449	Marshfield	(715)	19,118	18,691
54952	Menasha	(920)	17,353	17,604
*53051	Menomonee Falls	(262)	35,626	35,974
54751	Menomonie	(715)	16,264	16,237
*53092	Mequon	(262)	23,132	23,509
53562	Middleton	(608)	17,442	18,671
*53202	Milwaukee	(414)	594,833	599,642
53566	Monroe	(608)	10,827	10,781
*53406	Mount Pleasant	(262)	26,197	26,293
53150	Muskego	(262)	24,135	24,621
*54956	Neenah	(920)	25,501	25,855
*53151	New Berlin	(262)	39,584	39,842
53154	Oak Creek	(414)	34,451	35,053
53066	Oconomowoc	(262)	15,759	16,319
54650	Onalaska	(608)	17,736	18,385
*54901	Oshkosh	(920)	66,083	66,621
53072	Pewaukee	(262)	13,195	13,942
53818	Platteville	(608)	11,224	12,281
*53158	Pleasant Prairie	(262)	19,719	20,400
54467	Plover	(715)	12,123	12,326
53074	Port Washington	(262)	11,250	11,586
53901	Portage	(608)	10,324	10,178
*53402	Racine	(262)	78,860	78,065
*53076	Richfield	(262)	11,300	11,460
54022	River Falls	(715)	15,000	15,175
*53081	Sheboygan	(920)	49,288	48,775
53211	Shorewood	(414)	13,162	13,331
53172	South Milwaukee	(414)	21,156	21,236
*54481	Stevens Point	(715)	26,717	26,658
53589	Stoughton	(608)	12,611	13,039
*54173	Suamico	(920)	11,346	11,878
*53590	Sun Prairie	(608)	29,364	31,752
54880	Superior	(715)	27,244	26,705
53089	Sussex	(262)	10,518	10,740
*54241	Two Rivers	(920)	11,712	11,437
53593	Verona	(608)	10,619	12,003
*53094	Watertown	(920)	23,861	23,891
*53186	Waukesha	(262)	70,718	71,489
53597	Waunakee	(608)	12,097	13,067
53963	Waupun	(920)	11,340	11,377
*54403	Wausau	(715)	39,106	39,302
*53213	Wauwatosa	(414)	46,396	47,102
*53214	West Allis	(414)	60,411	60,624
*53095	West Bend	(262)	31,078	31,692
*54476	Weston	(715)	14,868	14,988
*53217	Whitefish Bay	(414)	14,110	14,122
53190	Whitewater	(262)	14,390	15,040
*54494	Wisconsin Rapids	(715)	18,367	17,966

Wyoming

Area code 307 applies to the entire state.

ZIP	Place	2010 population	2014 estimate
*82609	Casper	55,316	60,086
*82001	Cheyenne	59,466	62,845
*82930	Evanston	12,359	12,190
*82716	Gillette	29,087	31,971
*82935	Green River	12,515	12,630
*83001	Jackson	9,577	10,449
*82072	Laramie	30,816	32,081
82501	Riverton	10,615	10,953
*82901	Rock Springs	23,036	24,045
82801	Sheridan	17,444	17,916

WORLD HISTORY

Chronology of World History

Note: In this section, the notation BCE (before the common era) is applied to years dating to the traditional BC (before Christ) era, and CE (common era) is applied to AD (anno domini) dates. This notation is now preferred in scientific and academic publications. The traditional Gregorian Calendar system and its dates and years are unaltered except by these labels.

Other abbreviations used in this chapter include the following: KYA = thousand years ago, MYA = million years ago, c. = circa, fl. = flourished, r. = ruled, b. = born, d. = died.

Prehistory: Our Ancestors Emerge

Reviewed by Albert Rolls, Ph.D., June 2013

Evidence of the origins of *Homo sapiens sapiens*, the genus, species, and subspecies to which all living humans belong, comes from a small but increasing number of fossils, from genetic and anatomical studies, and from interpretation of the geological and archaeological records. The latest evidence suggests that humans evolved from apelike primate ancestors that lived in eastern and central Africa 7 to 5 million years ago (MYA). Although all humans living today are members of a single species, the fossil record confirms that our ancestors coexisted with a number of similar species throughout our evolutionary history. Current theories trace the first hominin[1] (upright, bipedal, humanlike primate) to Africa, where several distinct genera appeared 6-4 MYA. They lived in a variety of environments throughout most of the continent, including swampy forest margins, woodlands, and open savannas (usually near lakes or springs). In addition to *Australopithecus afarensis*—better known as "Lucy," a 3.2 MYA Ethiopian specimen found in 1974—these earliest hominins include such recent discoveries as *Sahelanthropus* (c. 6.5 MYA, from Chad), *Ardipithecus* (c. 5 MYA, Kenya), *Kenyanthropus* (c. 3.5 MYA, Kenya), and *Orrorin* (c. 5 MYA, Kenya). Later, between 4 and 3 MYA, these earliest hominins gave rise to at least two groups of savanna/lake-edge adapted "man-apes." Called australopithecines, they are divided into "gracile" and "robust" lineages, both containing a number of species. The robust australopithecines were characterized by enormous molar and premolar teeth; they probably went extinct around 1 MYA or slightly thereafter. Although it is uncertain from which australopithecine species humans descended, the most likely species are usually assigned to the gracile lineage.

Our genus, *Homo*, arose 3-2 MYA, when hominins began to produce primitive stone tools. The oldest tools are dated to c. 2.5 MYA from the Kada Gona site, in Ethiopia, and were used for scrapping and cutting meat, sinew, and wood. It is not known whether these early hominins had the ability to speak, but they were social animals, lived in groups of 12-20 individuals, aggregated and dispersed seasonally, had campsites, and subsisted by gathering plants and small animals and by scavenging other kills. A closer ancestor, *Homo ergaster*, appeared in E Africa around 1.9 MYA and was the first to leave the continent, spreading throughout Eurasia by c. 1.8 MYA. *H. ergaster* is sometimes grouped with *H. erectus*, a species first identified in the 1890s on the island of Java. It was capable of hunting large and medium-sized hoofed animals, such as antelopes and horses, learned to make and control fire—by c. 500 thousand years ago (KYA) in Europe, possibly earlier in Africa—and almost certainly had primitive language skills.

After about 350 KYA, Europe provides a particularly rich set of fossil evidence usually assigned to *H. erectus*. By a near-universal consensus, this species gave rise to the Neanderthals, who appeared c. 200 KYA. Neanderthals were humanlike in most respects: they could speak, were proficient hunters of large game, had sophisticated tools and weapons and a developed social organization, and were well adapted to the harsh climates of Ice Age Europe. Recent advances in molecular biology support the theory that Neanderthals were a distinct population or species that in some places coexisted and may have interbred with early modern humans (also called Crô-Magnons). *H. antecessor*, a new species (c. 870 KYA) identified at the Trinchera Dolina site in north-central Spain, might help clarify the relationship between the earliest representatives of *Homo* in western Europe, and the Neanderthals. A similar situation may have occurred in E Asia, where more primitive *Homo* species coexisted with early modern humans after c. 40 KYA, and possibly as recently as 18 KYA, on the island of Flores, in Indonesia.

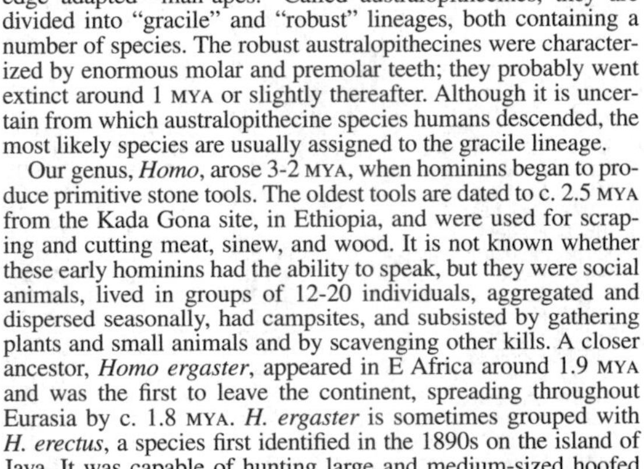

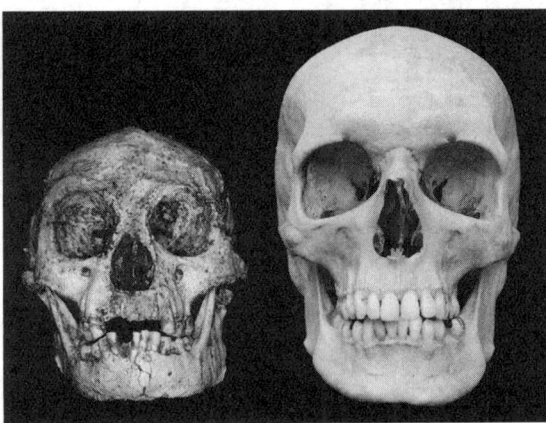

The 18,000-year-old "hobbit" skull (left) found on Flores in Indonesia in 2004 appears to show that the primitive species coexisted with modern humans (skull on right).

Genetic evidence indicates that the first *Homo sapiens* originated in E Africa between 200 and 100 KYA. The oldest modern human fossils date to c. 160 KYA and were found at the Herto site in Ethiopia's Middle Awash Valley. The species quickly spread, displacing, extinguishing, outcompeting, and/or genetically swamping the archaic humans it encountered. Modern humans were living in Israel by c. 100 KYA, and in Romania by c. 35 KYA. Migration from Asia to Australia took place as early as 60 KYA. First confirmation for the crossing from Asia to the Americas by the Bering land bridge dates to the end of the last Ice Age, at 14 KYA. However, genetic data suggests that small, isolated groups of hunter-gatherers arrived in the Americas up to 10,000 years earlier, settling in both continents. Their arrival was rapidly followed by the extinction of the indigenous Pleistocene megafauna (e.g., mammoths, mastodonts), due either to overexploitation by humans, an extraterrestrial impact c. 12,900 years ago, or a combination of both.

As human cognitive capacities slowly expanded over the Pleistocene (1.7-0.01 MYA), a variety of behavioral modes—in toolmaking, diet, shelter, social arrangements, and spiritual expression—arose as humans adapted to different geographic and climatic zones. By about 13,000 years ago, sites from all over the world show seasonal migration patterns and efficient exploitation of a wide range of plant and animal foods, some of which were eventually domesticated.

The ability to make fire at will enormously expanded the human food niche. Fire-making possibly began as early as 1 MYA in Africa and is clearly documented throughout Eurasia after c. 500 KYA. Hearths were found in northern Israel by c. 750 KYA and by 465 KYA in southwestern France. Fire-hardened wooden throwing spears about 3 m long were fashioned by big-game hunters 400 KYA at the Schoeningen lignite mine in Germany. Scraping tools, dated after 750 KYA in Europe, N Africa, the Middle East, and Central Asia, suggest the preparation of hides for clothing. The oldest relatively unambiguous evidence of personal adornment—perforated shell beads—dates to c. 120 KYA at Skhul Cave on Mount Carmel in Israel. Although they were probably invented much earlier, impressions in burnt clay from the Czech Republic document the ability to weave cloth baskets and nets by 28 KYA. By the time Australia was settled, human ancestors had learned to navigate in boats over considerable distances in open water. The earliest-known bone tools were fashioned some 90 KYA at Semliki, in the Congo basin, by fishermen who crafted sophisticated bone harpoons to catch giant catfish.

About 60 KYA, the earliest immigrants to Australia carved and painted designs on rocks. Although the painted caves of Cosquer and Chauvet in southern France have (contested) radiocarbon dates of c. 32 KYA, painting, engraving, and bodily decoration flourished in Europe 15 KYA, along with stone and ivory sculpture. More than 200 western European caves show remarkable examples of naturalistic wall painting. A few musical instruments—bone flutes with precisely bored holes—have been found in sites dated after 40 KYA. Over the course of the Upper Pleistocene (c. 130-12 KYA), the number of people who survived to become grandparents slowly increased. With more adults available to provide child care, humans began to develop more complex, multigenerational social systems.

The reach of social memory increased accordingly. Shortly after 12 KYA, among widely separated foraging communities in both hemispheres, a series of dramatic technological and social changes occurred, marking the Neolithic, or New Stone, Age. As the world climate became drier and warmer, population/resource imbalances ensued, creating the conditions that allowed for increased human interference in the life cycles of certain plants and animals. This interference ultimately resulted in the appearance of domestication economies, initially in the northern Middle East. Domesticated plants and animals encouraged population growth and the appearance of permanent settlements, which in turn reduced birth spacing and spurred more population growth. Agricultural economies increasingly replaced hunting and gathering. Reliance upon domesticated plants and animals, coupled with technological advances like pottery-making, precipitated a dramatic increase in world population and social complexity. Genetic research suggests that mutations related to traits currently found in some human populations, such as Europeans' unusually light skin pigmentation and ability to process lactose, arose after c. 12 KYA.

Sites in the Americas, SE Europe, and the Middle East show roughly contemporaneous (12-6 KYA) evidence of Neolithic domestication economies; similar evidence of E and S Asian, W European, and sub-Saharan African Neolithic adaptations dates to 10-7 KYA. From W Asian sources, farming and the herding of sheep and goats spread rapidly throughout the Mediterranean Basin, perhaps in as short a time interval as 100-200 years. The variety of crops—wheat, barley, rice, maize, squash, beans, and tubers—and a mix of other characteristics suggest that this adaptation occurred independently in as many as 12 or 13 places in both hemispheres. Evidence for fermented beverages likewise coincides with the early Neolithic settled farming lifestyle. Northern Chinese farmers concocted a wine-like drink from rice, honey, and fruit between 9 and 8 KYA. In highland W Asia, in what is today Iran, vintners were fermenting grapes and making wine by c. 7.4 KYA. The plants and animals associated with the Neolithic Revolution provided the basis for all subsequent social and cultural evolution worldwide.

(1) Although "hominid" was standard usage several decades ago, "hominin" is now more commonly used in reference to human ancestors because of new developments in the interpretation of primate evolution.

Earliest Civilizations: 4000-1000 BCE

Mesopotamia. If history began with writing, the first chapter opened in Mesopotamia, the Tigris-Euphrates river valley. The Sumerians used clay tablets with pictographs to keep records after 4000 BCE. A **cuneiform** (wedge-shaped) script evolved by 3000 BCE as a full syllabic alphabet. Neighboring peoples adapted the script for their own use.

Sumerian life centered, from 4000 BCE, on large cities (Eridu, Ur, Uruk, Nippur, Kish, and Lagash) organized around temples and priestly bureaucracies, with surrounding plains watered by vast irrigation works and worked with traction plows. Sailboats, wheeled vehicles, potter's wheels, and kilns were used. Copper was smelted and tempered from c. 4000 BCE; bronze was produced not long after. Ores, as well as precious stones and metals, were obtained through long-distance ship and caravan trade. Iron was used from c. 2000 BCE. Improved ironworking, developed partly by the Hittites, became widespread by 1200 BCE.

Sumerian political primacy passed among cities and their kingly dynasties. Semitic-speaking peoples, with cultures derived from the Sumerian, founded a succession of dynasties that ruled in Mesopotamia and neighboring areas for most of 1,800 years. Among them were the **Akkadians** (first under Sargon I, c. 2350 BCE), the Amorites (whose laws, codified by **Hammurabi**, c. 1792-1750 BCE, have biblical parallels), and the Assyrians, with interludes of rule by the Hittites, Kassites, and Mitanni.

Mesopotamian learning, preserved in vast libraries, was practically oriented. Scribes maintained lists of astronomical phenomena, plants, animals, and stones. Medical texts listed ailments and herbal cures. The Sumerians worshipped anthropomorphic gods representing natural forces. Sacrifices were made at **ziggurats**, or huge stepped temples.

The Syria-Palestine area, site of some of the earliest urban remains (Jericho, 7000 BCE) and of the recently uncovered **Ebla** civilization (fl. 2500 BCE), experienced Egyptian cultural and political influence along with Mesopotamian. The **Phoenician** coast was an active commercial center. A phonetic alphabet was invented here before 1600 BCE. It became the ancestor of many other alphabets.

Egypt. Agricultural villages along the Nile R. were united by around 3300 BCE into two kingdoms, Upper and Lower Egypt. They were unified (c. 3100 BCE) under the pharaoh Menes. A bureaucracy supervised construction of canals and monuments (**pyramids** starting 2700 BCE). Control over Nubia to the S was asserted from 2600 BCE. Brilliant **Old Kingdom** period achievements in architecture, sculpture, and painting reached their height during the 3rd and 4th dynasties. **Hieroglyphic writing** appeared by 3200 BCE, recording a sophisticated literature that included religious writings, philosophy, history, and science. An ordered hierarchy of gods, including totemistic animal elements, was served by a powerful priesthood in Memphis. The pharaoh was identified with the falcon god Horus. Other trends included belief in an afterlife and short-lived quasi-monotheistic reforms introduced by the pharaoh **Akhenaton** (c. 1379-1362 BCE), who was married to Nefertiti.

After a period of dominance by Semitic Hyksos from Asia (c. 1700-1550 BCE), the **New Kingdom** established an empire in Syria. Egypt became increasingly embroiled in Asiatic wars and diplomacy. Conquered by Persia in 525 BCE, it eventually faded away as an independent culture.

India. An urban civilization with an as-yet undeciphered writing system stretched across the Indus Valley and along the Arabian Sea c. 3000-1500 BCE. Major sites are Harappa and **Mohenjo-Daro** in Pakistan, well-planned geometric cities with underground sewers and vast granaries. The entire region may have been ruled as a single state. Bronze was used, and arts and crafts were well developed. Religious life apparently took the form of fertility cults. Indus civilization was in decline before the arrival of **Aryan** migrants who arrived from the NW, speaking an Indo-European language. Led by a warrior aristocracy whose legendary deeds are in the **Rig Veda**, the Aryans spread E and S, bringing their sky gods, priestly (Brahman) ritual, and the beginnings of the caste system. Local customs and beliefs were assimilated by the conquerors.

Europe. On Crete, the Bronze Age **Minoan civilization** emerged c. 2500 BCE. A prosperous economy and richly decorative art was supported by seaborne commerce. Mycenae and other cities in mainland Greece and Asia Minor (e.g., **Troy**) preserved elements of the culture until c. 1200 BCE. Cretan Linear A script (c. 2000-1700 BCE) remains undeciphered; Linear B script (c. 1300-1200 BCE) records an early Greek dialect. The possible connection between Mycenaean monumental stonework and the megalithic monuments of Western Europe, Iberia, and Malta (c. 4000-1500 BCE) is unclear.

China. Proto-Chinese Neolithic cultures had long covered N and SE China when the first large political state was organized in the N by the **Shang dynasty** (c. 1523 BCE). Shang kings

The Great Sphinx of Giza is believed to have been built during Egypt's 4th dynasty (c. 2575-2465 BCE).

called themselves Sons of Heaven, and they presided over a cult of human and animal sacrifice to ancestors and nature gods. The Chou dynasty, starting c. 1027 BCE, expanded the area of the Sons of Heaven's dominion, but feudal states exercised most temporal power. A writing system with 2,000 characters was already in use under the Shang, with **pictographs** later supplemented by phonetic characters. Many of its principles and symbols, despite changes in spoken Chinese, were preserved in later writing systems. Technical advances allowed urban specialists to create fine ceramic and jade products, and bronze casting after 1500 BCE was the most advanced in the world. Bronze artifacts discovered in northern Thailand date from 3600 BCE, hundreds of years before similar Middle Eastern finds.

Americas. **Olmecs** settled (1500 BCE) on the Gulf coast of Mexico and developed the first known civilization in the Western Hemisphere. Temple cities and huge stone sculptures date from 1200 BCE. A rudimentary calendar and writing system existed. Olmec religion—centered on a jaguar god—and art forms influenced later Mesoamerican cultures.

Formation of Classical Societies: 1000-400 BCE

Greece. After a period of decline during the Dorian Greek invasions (1200-1000 BCE), the Aegean area developed a unique civilization. Drawing on Mycenaean traditions, Mesopotamian learning (weights and measures, lunisolar calendar, astronomy, musical scales), the Phoenician alphabet (modified for Greek), and Egyptian art, **Greek city-states** saw a rich elaboration of intellectual life. The two great epic poems attributed to **Homer**, the *Iliad* and the *Odyssey*, were probably composed around the 8th cent. BCE. Long-range commerce was aided by metal coinage (introduced by the Lydians in Asia Minor before 700 BCE). Colonies were founded around the Mediterranean (Cumae in Italy in 760 BCE; Massalia in France c. 600 BCE) and Black Sea shores.

Philosophy, starting with Ionian speculation on the nature of matter (Thales, c. 634-546 BCE), continued by other "Pre-Socratics" (e.g., Heraclitus, c. 535-415 BCE; Parmenides, b. c. 515 BCE), reached a high point in Athens in the rationalist idealism of **Plato** (c. 428-347 BCE), a disciple of **Socrates** (c. 469-399 BCE; executed for alleged impiety), and in **Aristotle** (384-322 BCE), a pioneer in many fields, from natural sciences to logic, ethics, and metaphysics. The **arts** were highly valued. Architecture culminated in the **Parthenon** (438 BCE) by Phidias (fl. 490-430 BCE). Poetry (Sappho, c. 610-580 BCE; Pindar, c. 518-438 BCE) and **drama** (Aeschylus, 525-456 BCE; Sophocles, c. 496-406 BCE; Euripides, c. 484-406 BCE) thrived. Male beauty and strength, a chief artistic theme, were celebrated at the national games at Olympia.

Ruled by local tyrants or **oligarchies**, the Greeks were not politically united but managed to resist inclusion in the Persian Empire. Persian king Darius was defeated at Marathon (490 BCE), his son Xerxes at Salamis (480 BCE), and the Persian army at Plataea (479 BCE). Democracy sprouted in Athens as statesman Pericles (495-429 BCE) sought participation in government from all citizens. Local warfare was common; the **Peloponnesian Wars** (431-404 BCE) ended in Sparta's victory over Athens. Greek political power subsequently waned, but Greek cultural forms spread far and wide.

Hebrews. Nomadic Hebrew tribes entered Canaan before 1200 BCE, settling among other Semitic peoples speaking the same language. They brought from the desert a **monotheistic** faith said to have been revealed to Abraham in Canaan c. 1800 BCE and Moses at Mt. Sinai c. 1250 BCE, after the Hebrews' escape from bondage in Egypt. David (r. 1000-961 BCE) and Solomon (r. 961-922 BCE) united them in a kingdom that briefly dominated the area. **Phoenicians** to the N founded Mediterranean colonies (Carthage, c. 814 BCE) and sailed into the Atlantic.

A temple in Jerusalem became the national religious center, with sacrifices performed by a hereditary priesthood. Polytheistic influences, especially of the fertility cult of Baal, were opposed by **prophets** (Elijah, Amos, Isaiah).

Divided into **two kingdoms** after Solomon, the Hebrews were unable to resist the revived Assyrian empire, which conquered Israel, the northern kingdom, in 722 BCE. Judah, the southern kingdom, was conquered in 586 BCE by the Babylonians under Nebuchadnezzar II. With the fixing of most of the biblical canon by the mid-4th cent. BCE and the emergence of rabbis, Judaism successfully survived the loss of Hebrew autonomy. A Jewish kingdom was revived under the Hasmoneans (168-42 BCE).

China. During the **Eastern Zhou** dynasty (770-256 BCE), Chinese culture spread E to the sea and S to the Yangtze R. Large feudal states on the periphery of the empire contended for preeminence but continued to recognize the Son of Heaven (king), who retained a purely ritual role enriched with courtly music and dance. In the Age of Warring States (403-221 BCE), when the first sections of the **Great Wall** were built, the Qin state in the W gained supremacy and finally united all of China.

Iron tools entered China c. 500 BCE. Casting techniques were advanced, aiding agriculture. Peasants owned their land and owed civil and military service to nobles. China's cities grew in number and size; barter remained the chief trade medium.

Intellectual ferment among noble scribes and officials produced a classical age of Chinese literature and philosophy. **Confucius** (551-479 BCE) urged a restoration of a supposedly harmonious social order of the past through proper conduct in accordance with one's station and through filial and ceremonial piety. The *Analects* attributed to him are revered throughout E Asia.

Among other thinkers, **Mencius** (d. 289 BCE) added the view that the Mandate of Heaven can be removed from an unjust dynasty. The Legalists sought to curb the supposed natural wickedness of people through new institutions and harsh laws. The Naturalists emphasized the balance of opposites—yin, yang—in the world. **Daoists** sought mystical knowledge through meditation and disengagement.

India. The political and cultural center of India shifted from the Indus to the Ganges River Valley. Buddhism, Jainism, and mystical revisions of orthodox Vedism all developed c. 500-300 BCE. The *Upanishads*, last part of the *Veda*, urged escape from the cycle of rebirth into the physical world. Vedism remained the preserve of the Brahman caste.

In contrast, **Buddhism**, founded by Siddhartha Gautama (c. 563-c. 483 BCE)—Buddha ("Enlightened One")—appealed to merchants in the urban centers and took hold at first (and most lastingly) on the geographic fringes of Indian civilization. The classic Indian epics were composed in this era: the ***Ramayana*** perhaps c. 300 BCE, the ***Mahabharata*** over a period starting around 400 BCE.

Northern India was divided into a large number of monarchies and aristocratic republics, probably derived from tribal groupings, when the Magadha kingdom was formed in Bihar c. 542 BCE. It soon became the dominant power. The **Maurya** dynasty, founded by Chandragupta c. 321 BCE, expanded the kingdom, uniting most of Northern India in a centralized bureaucratic empire. The third Mauryan king, **Asoka** (r. c. 274-236 BCE), conquered most of the subcontinent. He converted to Buddhism, inscribed its tenets on pillars throughout India, and downplayed the caste system.

Before its final decline in India, Buddhism developed into a popular worship of heavenly Bodhisattvas ("enlightened beings"), and it produced a refined architecture (the Great Stupa [shrine] at Sanchi, 100 CE) and sculpture (Gandhara reliefs, 1-400 CE).

China's Great Wall, first built during the Age of Warring States (403-221 BCE), was rebuilt, extended, and modified over thousands of years to protect China from invaders.

Persia. Aryan peoples (Persians, Medes) dominated the area of present Iran by the beginning of the 1st millennium BCE. The prophet **Zoroaster** (b. c. 628 BCE) introduced a dualistic religion in which the forces of good (Ahura Mazda, "Lord of Wisdom") and evil (Ahriman) battle for dominance; individuals are judged by their actions and earn damnation or salvation. Zoroaster's hymns (*Gathas*) are included in the *Avesta*, the Zoroastrian scriptures. A version of this faith became the established religion of the Persian Empire.

Africa. Nubia, periodically occupied by Egypt since about 2600 BCE, ruled Egypt c. 750-661 BCE and survived as an independent Egyptianized kingdom (**Kush**; capital Meroe) for 1,000 years. The Iron Age Nok culture flourished c. 500 BCE-200 CE on the Benue Plateau of **Nigeria**.

Americas. The Chavin culture controlled Northern Peru c. 900 BCE to 200 BCE. Its ceremonial centers, featuring the jaguar god, survived long after. Its architecture, ceramics, and textiles had influenced other Peruvian cultures. **Mayan civilization** began to develop in Central America as early as 1500 BCE.

Great Empires Unite the Classical World: 400 BCE-400 CE

Persia and the Mediterranean. **Cyrus**, ruler of a small kingdom in Persia from 559 BCE, united the Persians and Medes within 10 years and conquered Asia Minor and Babylonia in another 10. His son Cambyses, followed by **Darius** (r. 522-486 BCE), added vast lands to the E and N as far as the Indus Valley and Central Asia, as well as Egypt and Thrace. The whole empire was ruled by an international bureaucracy and army, with Persians holding the chief positions. The resources and styles of all the subject civilizations were exploited to create a rich syncretic art.

The kingdom of Macedon, which under Philip II dominated the Greek world and Egypt, was passed on to Philip's son **Alexander** in 336 BCE. Within 13 years, Alexander had conquered all the Persian dominions. Imbued by his tutor Aristotle with Greek ideals, Alexander encouraged colonization, and Greek-style cities were founded. After his death in 323 BCE, wars of succession divided the empire into three significant dynasties—the **Antigonids** in Asia Minor and Macedon, the **Ptolemies** in Egypt, and the **Seleucids** in Mesopotamia. In the ensuing 300 years (the **Hellenistic Era**), a cosmopolitan Greek-oriented culture permeated the ancient world from Western Europe to the borders of India, absorbing native elites everywhere.

Hellenistic philosophy stressed the private individual's search for happiness. The Cynics followed Diogenes (c. 372-287 BCE), who stressed self-sufficiency and restriction of desires and expressed contempt for luxury and social convention. Zeno (c. 335-c. 263 BCE) and the **Stoics** exalted reason, identified it with virtue, and counseled an ascetic disregard for misfortune. The **Epicureans** tried to build lives of moderate pleasure without political or emotional involvement. Hellenistic arts imitated life realistically, especially in sculpture and literature (comedies of Menander, 342-292 BCE).

The sciences thrived, especially at Alexandria, where the Ptolemies financed a great library and museum. Fields of study included mathematics (**Euclid**'s geometry, c. 300 BCE); astronomy (heliocentric theory of Aristarchus, 310-230 BCE; Julian calendar, 45 BCE; **Ptolemy**'s *Almagest*, c. 150 CE); geography (world map of Eratosthenes, 276-194 BCE); hydraulics (**Archimedes**, 287-212 BCE); medicine (Galen, 130-200 CE); and chemistry. Inventors refined uses for siphons, valves, gears, springs, screws, levers, cams, and pulleys.

A restored Persian empire under the **Parthians** (northern Iranian tribespeople) controlled the eastern Hellenistic world from 250 BCE to 229 CE. The Parthians and the succeeding **Sassanian dynasty** (c. 224-651 CE) fought with Rome periodically. The Sassanians revived Zoroastrianism as a state religion and patronized a nationalistic artistic and scholarly renaissance.

Rome. The city of Rome was founded, according to legend, by Romulus in 753 BCE. Through military expansion and colonization, and by granting citizenship to leading members of conquered tribes, the city annexed all of Italy S of the Po R. in the 100-year period before 268 BCE. The Latin and other Italic tribes were annexed first, followed by the **Etruscans** (founders of a great civilization N of Rome) and Greek colonies in the S. With a large standing army and reserve forces of several hundred thousand, Rome was able to defeat **Carthage** in the three **Punic Wars** (264-241 BCE, 218-201 BCE, 149-146 BCE), despite the invasion of Italy by **Hannibal** (218 BCE), thus gaining Sicily and territory in Spain and N Africa.

Rome exploited local disputes to conquer Greece and Asia Minor in the 2nd cent. BCE and Egypt in the 1st (after the defeat and suicide of **Antony and Cleopatra**, 30 BCE). The Mediterranean civilized world, up to the disputed Parthian border, was now Roman and remained so for 500 years. Less civilized regions were added to the Empire: Gaul (conquered by **Julius Caesar**, 58-51 BCE), Britain (43 CE), and Dacia NE of the Danube (107 CE).

The original aristocratic republican government, with democratic features added in the 5th and 4th cent. BCE, deteriorated under the pressures of empire and class conflict (**Gracchus** brothers, social reformers, murdered in 133 BCE and 121 BCE; slave revolts in 135 BCE and 73 BCE). After a series of civil wars (Marius vs. Sulla, 88-82 BCE; Caesar vs. **Pompey**, 49-45 BCE; triumvirate vs. Caesar's assassins, 44-43 BCE; Antony vs. Octavian, 32-30 BCE), the empire came under the rule of a deified monarch (first emperor, **Augustus**, 27 BCE-14 CE).

Provincials (nearly all granted citizenship by Caracalla, 212 CE) came to dominate the army and civil service. Traditional **Roman law**, systematized and interpreted by independent jurists, and local self-rule in provincial cities were supplanted by a vast tax-collecting bureaucracy in the 3rd and 4th cent. The legal rights of women, children, and slaves were strengthened.

Roman innovations in **civil engineering** included water mills, windmills, and rotary mills and the use of cement that hardened under water. Monumental architecture (baths, theaters, temples) relied on the arch and the dome. A network of roads (some still standing) stretched 53,000 mi, passing through mountain tunnels as long as 3.5 mi. Aqueducts brought water to cities; underground sewers removed waste.

Roman art and literature were derivative of Greek models. Innovations were made in sculpture (naturalistic busts, equestrian statues), decorative wall painting (as at Pompeii), satire (**Juvenal**, 60-127 CE), history (**Tacitus**, 56-120 CE), and prose romance (**Petronius**, d. 66 CE). Gladiatorial contests dominated public amusements, which were supported by the state.

India. The **Gupta** monarchs reunited Northern India c. 320 CE. Their peaceful and prosperous reign saw a revival of Hindu religious thought and Brahman power. The old Vedic traditions were combined with devotion to many indigenous deities (who were seen as manifestations of Vedic gods). Caste lines were reinforced, and Buddhist practices gradually disappeared or were integrated with **Hindu** traditions. The art (often erotic), architecture, and literature of the period, patronized by the Gupta court, are considered among India's finest achievements (Kalidasa, poet and dramatist, fl. c. 400 CE). Mathematical innovations included the use of zero and decimal numbers. Invasions by White Huns from the NW led to the empire's destruction c. 550 CE. Rich cultures also developed in Southern India during this period. Emotional Tamil religious poetry contributed to the Hindu revival. The Pallava kingdom controlled much of Southern India c. 350-880 CE and helped to spread Indian civilization to SE Asia.

China. The Qin ruler Shih Huang Ti (r. 221-210 BCE), known as the First Emperor, centralized political authority; standardized the written language, laws, weights, measures, and coinage; and conducted a census. But he tried to destroy most philosophical texts. The **Han** dynasty (202 BCE-220 CE) instituted the Mandarin bureaucracy, which lasted 2,000 years. Local officials were selected by examination in Confucian classics and trained at the imperial university and provincial schools.

The invention of **paper** facilitated this bureaucratic system. Agriculture was promoted, but peasants bore most of the tax burden. Irrigation was improved, water clocks and sundials were used, astronomy and mathematics thrived, and landscape painting was perfected.

With the expansion S and W (to nearly the present borders of today's China), trade was opened with India, SE Asia, and the Middle East over sea and caravan routes. Indian missionaries brought Mahayana Buddhism to China by the 1st cent. CE and spawned a variety of sects. Daoism was revived and merged with popular superstitions. **Daoist and Buddhist monasteries** and convents multiplied in the turbulent centuries after the collapse of the Han dynasty in 220 CE.

Monotheism Spreads: 1-750 CE

Roman Empire. Polytheism was practiced in the Roman Empire, and religions indigenous to particular Middle Eastern nations became international. Roman citizens worshiped **Isis** of Egypt, **Mithras** of Persia, **Demeter** of Greece, and the great mother **Cybele** of Phrygia. Their cults centered on mysteries (secret ceremonies) and the promise of an afterlife, symbolized by the death and rebirth of the god. The Jews of the empire preserved their monotheistic religion, Judaism, the world's oldest (c. 1300 BCE) continuous religion. Its teachings are contained in the Bible (the Old Testament). 1st-cent. CE Judaism embraced several sects, including the **Sadducees**, mostly drawn from the Temple priesthood, who were culturally Hellenized; the **Pharisees**, who upheld the full range of traditional customs and practices as of equal weight to literal scriptural law and elaborated synagogue worship; and the **Essenes**, an ascetic, millenarian sect. Messianic fervor led to repeated, unsuccessful rebellions against Rome (66-70, 135 CE). As a result, the Temple in Jerusalem was destroyed and the population decimated; this event marked the beginning of the Diaspora (living in exile). To preserve the faith, codification of law was begun at the academy of Yavneh. The work continued for some 500 years in Palestine and in Babylonia, ending in the final redaction (c. 600) of the **Talmud**, a huge collection of legal and moral debates, rulings, liturgy, biblical exegesis, and legendary materials.

Christianity. Emerging as a distinct sect by the second half of the 1st cent. CE, Christianity is based on the teachings of **Jesus**, whom believers considered the Savior (Messiah or Christ) and son of God. Missionary activities of the Apostles and such early leaders as **Paul of Tarsus** spread the faith. Intermittent persecution, as in Rome under Nero in 64 CE, on grounds of suspected disloyalty, failed to disrupt Christian communities. Each congregation, generally urban and of plebeian character, was tightly organized under a leader (bishop), elders (presbyters or priests), and assistants (deacons). The four **Gospels** (accounts of the life and teachings of Jesus) and the Acts of the Apostles were written down in the late 1st and early 2nd cent. and circulated along with letters of Paul and other Christian leaders. An authoritative canon of these writings was not fixed until the 4th cent.

A school for priests was established at Alexandria in the 2nd cent. Its teachers (**Origen**, c. 182-251) helped define doctrine and promote the faith in Greek-style philosophical works. Neoplatonism underwent Christian coloration in the writings of Church Fathers such as **Augustine** (354-430). Christian hermits began to associate in monasteries, first in Egypt (St. Pachomius, c. 290-345), then in other eastern lands, then in the W (**St. Benedict's rule**, 529). Devotion to saints, especially Mary, mother of Jesus, spread. Under **Constantine** (r. 306-37), Christianity became in effect the established religion of the Empire. Pagan temples were expropriated, state funds were used to build churches and support the hierarchy, and laws were adjusted in accordance with Christian ideas. Pagan worship was banned by the end of the 4th cent., and severe restrictions were placed on Judaism.

The newly established church was rocked by doctrinal disputes, often exacerbated by regional rivalries. Chief heresies (as defined by church councils, backed by imperial authority) were **Arianism**, which denied the divinity of Jesus; **Monophysitism**, denying the human nature of Christ; **Donatism**, which regarded as invalid any sacraments administered by sinful clergy; and **Pelagianism**, which denied the necessity of unmerited divine aid (grace) for salvation.

Islam. The earliest Arab civilization emerged by the end of the 2nd millennium BCE in the watered highlands of Yemen. Seaborne and caravan trade in frankincense and myrrh connected the area with the Nile and Fertile Crescent. The Minaean, Sabean (Sheba), and Himyarite states successively held sway. By Muhammad's time (7th cent. CE), the region was a province of Sassanian Persia. In the N, the Nabataean kingdom at Petra and the kingdom of Palmyra were Aramaicized, Romanized, and finally absorbed, as neighboring Judea had been, into the Roman Empire. Nomads shared the central region with a few trading towns and oases. Wars between tribes and raids on communities were common and were celebrated in a poetic tradition that by the 6th cent. helped establish a classic literary Arabic.

About 610, **Muhammad**, a 40-year-old Arab man of Mecca, emerged as a prophet. He proclaimed a revelation from the one true God, calling on contemporaries to abandon idolatry and restore the faith of Abraham. He introduced his religion as **Islam**, meaning "submission" to the one God, Allah, as a continuation of the biblical faith of Abraham, Moses, and Jesus, all respected as prophets in this system. His teachings, recorded in the Quran, in many ways were inclusive of Abrahamic monotheistic ideas known to the Jews and Christians in Arabia. A key aspect of the Abrahamic connection was insistence on justice in society, which led to severe opposition among the aristocrats in Mecca. As conditions worsened for Muhammad and his followers, he decided in 622 to make a ***hegira*** (flight) to Medina, 200 mi to the N. This event marks the beginning of the Muslim lunar calendar. Hostilities between Mecca and Medina increased, and in 629 Muhammad conquered Mecca. By the time he died in 632, nearly all the Arabian peninsula accepted his political and religious leadership.

After his death the majority of Muslims (later known as **Sunni** Muslims) recognized the leadership of the **caliph** (successor) Abu Bakr (632-34), followed by Umar (634-44), Uthman (644-56), and Ali (656-60). A minority, the **Shiites**, insisted instead on the leadership of Ali, Muhammad's cousin and son-in-law. By 644, **Muslim rule** over Arabia was confirmed. Muslim armies had threatened the Byzantine and Persian empires, which were weakened by wars and disaffection among subject peoples (including Coptic and Syriac Christians opposed to the Byzantine Orthodox establishment). Syria, Palestine, Egypt, Iraq, and Persia fell to Muslim armies. The new administration assimilated existing systems in the region; hence the conquered peoples participated in running the empire. The Quran recognized the so-called Peoples of the Book, i.e., Christians, Jews, and Zoroastrians, as tolerated monotheists, and Muslim policy was relatively tolerant to minorities living as "protected" peoples. An expanded tax system, based on conquests of the Persian and Byzantine empires, provided revenue to organize campaigns against neighboring non-Muslim regions.

Under the **Umayyads** (661-750) and **Abbasids** (750-1256), territorial expansion led Muslim armies across N Africa and into Spain (711). Muslim armies in the W were stopped at Tours, France, in 732 by the Frankish ruler **Charles Martel**. Asia Minor, the Indus Valley, and Transoxiana were conquered in the E. The conversion of conquered peoples to Islam was gradual. In many places the official Arabic language supplanted the local tongues. But in the eastern regions the Arab rulers and their armies adopted Persian cultures and language as part of their Muslim identity.

Disputes over succession and pious opposition to injustices in society led to a number of oppositional movements, which led to the factionalization of Muslim community. The **Shiites** supported leadership candidates descended from Muhammad, believing them to be carriers of some kind of divine authority. The **Kharijites** supported an egalitarian system derived from the Quran, opposing and even engaging in battle against those who did not agree with them.

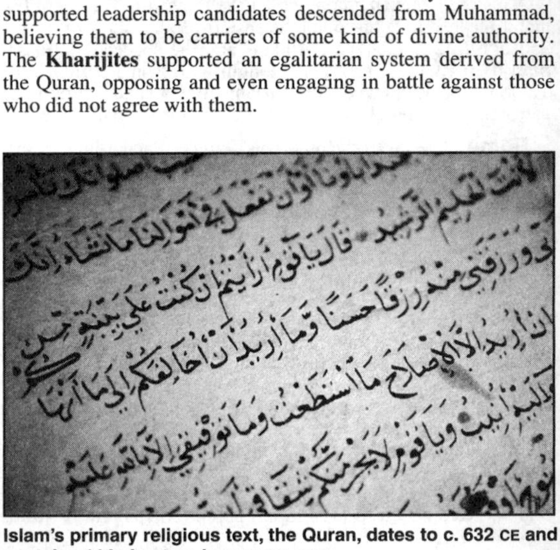

Islam's primary religious text, the Quran, dates to c. 632 CE and contains 114 chapters known as *sura*.

New Peoples Enter World History: 400-900 CE

Barbarian invasions and fall of Rome. Germanic tribes infiltrated S and E from their Baltic homeland during the 1st millennium BCE, reaching southern Germany by 100 BCE and the Black Sea by 214 CE. Organized into large federated tribes under elected kings, most resisted Roman domination and raided the empire in times of civil war (Goths took Dacia in 214, raided Thrace in 251-69). Germanic troops and commanders dominated the Roman armies by the end of the 4th cent. **Huns**, invaders from Asia, entered Europe in 372, driving more Germans into the empire. Emperor Valens allowed Visigoths to cross the Danube in 376. Huns under Attila (d. 453) raided Gaul, Italy, and the Balkans.

The western empire, weakened by overtaxation and social stagnation, was overrun in the 5th cent. Gaul was effectively lost in 406-07, Spain in 409, Britain in 410, and Africa in 429-39. Rome was sacked in 410 by Visigoths under Alaric and in 455 by Vandals. The **last western emperor**, Romulus Augustulus, was deposed in 476 by the Germanic chief Odoacer.

Celts. Celtic cultures, which in pre-Roman times covered most of W Europe, were confined almost entirely to the British Isles after the Germanic invasions. **St. Patrick** completed (c. 457-92) the conversion of Ireland and a strong monastic tradition took hold. Irish monastic missionaries in Scotland, England, and on the continent (Columba, c. 521-97; Columbanus, c. 543-615) helped restore Christianity after the Germanic invasions. **Monasteries** became centers of classic and Christian learning and presided over the recording of a Christianized Celtic mythology, elaborated by secular writers and bards. An intricate decorative art style developed, especially in book illumination (Lindisfarne Gospels, c. 700; Book of Kells, 8th cent.).

Successor states. The Visigothic kingdom in Spain (from 419) and much of France (to 507) saw continuation of Roman administration, language, and law (Breviary of Alaric, 506) until its destruction by the Muslims (711). The Vandal kingdom in Africa (from 429) was conquered by the Byzantines in 533. Italy was ruled successively by an Ostrogothic kingdom under Byzantine suzerainty (489-554), direct Byzantine government, and German Lombards (568-774). The Lombards divided the peninsula with the Byzantines and papacy under the dynamic reformer **Pope Gregory the Great** (590-604) and successors.

King Clovis (r. 481-511) united the Franks on both sides of the Rhine and, after his conversion to Christianity, defeated the Arian heretics, Burgundians (after 500), and Visigoths (507) with the support of native clergy and the papacy. Under the **Merovingian** kings, a feudal system emerged: power was fragmented among hierarchies of military landowners. Social stratification, which in late Roman times had acquired legal, hereditary sanction, was reinforced.

The Carolingians (747-987) expanded the kingdom and restored central power. **Charlemagne** (r. 768-814) conquered nearly all the Germanic lands, including Lombard Italy. He was crowned emperor by Pope Leo III in Rome in 800. A centuries-long decline in commerce and arts was reversed under Charlemagne's patronage. He welcomed Jews to his kingdom, which became a center of Jewish learning (Rashi, 1040-1105). He sponsored the Carolingian Renaissance of learning under the Anglo-Latin scholar Alcuin (c. 732-804), who reformed church liturgy.

Byzantine Empire. Under **Diocletian** (r. 284-305) the Roman empire had been divided into two parts to facilitate administration and defense. **Constantine** founded (330) **Constantinople** (at old Byzantium) as a fully Christian city. Commerce and taxation financed a sumptuous, orientalized court, a class of hereditary bureaucratic families, and magnificent urban construction (Hagia Sophia, 532-37). The city's fortifications and naval innovations repelled assaults by Goths, Huns, Slavs, Bulgars, Avars, Arabs, and Scandinavians. Greek replaced Latin as the official language by c. 700. **Byzantine art**, a solemn, sacral, and stylized variation of late classical styles (mosaics at the Church of San Vitale, Ravenna, Italy, 526-48), was a starting point for medieval art in Eastern and Western Europe.

Justinian (r. 527-65) briefly reconquered parts of Spain, N Africa, and Italy, codified **Roman law** (Codex Justinianus [529] was medieval Europe's chief legal text), closed the Platonic Academy at Athens, and ordered all pagans to convert. Lombards in Italy and Arabs in Africa retook most of his conquests. The Isaurian dynasty from Anatolia (from 717) and the Macedonian dynasty (867-1054) restored military and commercial power. The Iconoclast controversy (726-843) over the permissibility of images helped alienate the Eastern Church from the papacy.

Abbasid Empire. Baghdad (established 762) became seat of the **Abbasid dynasty** (established 750), while Umayyads continued to rule in Spain. A brilliant cosmopolitan civilization emerged, inaugurating a Muslim-Arab golden age. Arabic was the lingua franca of the empire; intellectual sources from Persian, Sanskrit, Greek, and Syriac were rendered into Arabic. Christians and Jews equally participated in this translation movement, which also involved interaction between Jewish legal thought and Islamic law, as much as between Christian theology and Muslim scholasticism. Persian-style court life, with art and music, flourished at the court of **Harun al-Rashid** (786-809), celebrated in the masterpiece known to English readers as *The Arabian Nights*. The sciences, medicine, and mathematics were pursued at Baghdad, Cordova, and Cairo (c. 969). The culmination of this intellectual synthesis in Islamic civilization came with the scientific and philosophical works of **Avicenna** (Ibn Sina, 980-1037), **Averroes** (Ibn Rushd, 1126-98), and **Maimonides** (1135-1204), a Jew who wrote in Arabic. This intellectual tradition was translated into Latin and opened a new period in Christian thought.

The decentralization of the Abbasid empire, from 874, led to the establishment of various Muslim dynasties under different ethnic groups. Persians, Berbers, and Turks ruled different regions, retaining connection with the Abbasid caliph at the religious level. The Abbasid period also saw various religious movements against the orthodox position held by governing authorities. This situation in Muslim religion led to the establishment of different legal, theological, and mystical schools of thought. The most influential mass movement was **Sufism**, which aimed at the reaching out of the average individual in quest of a spiritual path. Al-Ghazali (1058-1111) is credited with reconciling personal Sufism with orthodox Sunni tradition.

Africa. Immigrants from Saba in S Arabia helped set up the **Axum** kingdom in Ethiopia in the 1st cent. (their language, Ge'ez, is preserved by the Ethiopian Church). In the 3rd cent., when the kingdom became Christianized, it defeated Kushite Meroe and expanded its influence into Yemen. Axum was the center of a vast ivory trade and controlled the Red Sea coast until c. 1100. Arab conquest in Egypt cut Axum's political and economic ties with Byzantium.

The Iron Age entered W Africa by the end of the 1st millennium BCE. **Ghana**, the first known sub-Saharan state, ruled in the upper Senegal-Niger region c. 400-1240, controlling the trade of gold from mines in the S to trans-Sahara caravan routes to the N. The **Bantu** peoples, probably of W African origin, began to spread E and S perhaps 2,000 years ago, displacing the Pygmies and Bushmen of central and southern Africa during a 1,500-year period.

Japan. The advanced Neolithic Yayoi period, when irrigation, rice farming, and iron and bronze casting techniques were introduced from China or Korea, persisted to c. 400 CE. The myriad Japanese states were then united by the **Yamato** clan, under an emperor who acted as chief priest of the animistic Shinto cult. Japanese political and military intervention by the 6th cent. in Korea, then under strong Chinese influence, quickened a Chinese cultural invasion of Japan, bringing Buddhism, the Chinese language (which long remained a literary and governmental medium), Chinese ideographs, and Buddhist styles in painting, sculpture, literature, and architecture (7th cent., Horyuji temple at Nara). The Taika Reforms (646) tried unsuccessfully to centralize Japan according to Chinese bureaucratic and Buddhist philosophical values.

A nativist reaction against the Buddhist **Nara** period (710-94) ushered in the **Heian** period (794-1185) centered at the new capital, Kyoto. Japanese elegance and simplicity modified Chinese styles in architecture, scroll painting, and literature; the writing system was also simplified. The courtly novel *Tale of Genji* (1010-20) testifies to the enhanced role of women in medieval Japanese literature and culture.

Southeast Asia. The historic peoples of SE Asia began arriving some 2,500 years ago from China and Tibet, displacing scattered aborigines. Their agriculture relied on rice and yams. Indian cultural influences were strongest; literacy and Hindu and Buddhist ideas followed the S India-China trade route. From the

The Khmer empire (fl. 800-1300) erected the Angkor complex—including dozens of temples, reservoirs, and canals—over a period of hundreds of years.

southern tip of Indochina, the kingdom of **Funan** (1st-7th cent.) traded as far W as Persia. It was absorbed by Chenla, itself conquered by the **Khmer** empire (800-1300). The Khmers, under Hindu god-kings (Suryavarman II, 1113-c. 1150), built the monumental Angkor Wat temple center for the royal phallic cult. The **Nam-Viet** kingdom in Annam, dominated by China and Chinese culture for 1,000 years, emerged in the 10th cent., growing at the expense of the Khmers, who also lost ground in the NW to the new, highly organized **Thai** kingdom. On Sumatra, the **Srivijaya** empire controlled vital sea lanes (7th-10th cent.). A Buddhist dynasty, the Sailendras, ruled central **Java** (8th-9th cent.), building at Borobudur one of the largest stupas (dome-shaped Buddhist shrines) in the world.

China. The Sui dynasty (581-618) ushered in a period of commercial, artistic, and scientific achievement in China, which continued under the **Tang** dynasty (618-906). Inventions like the magnetic compass, gunpowder, the abacus, and printing were introduced or perfected. Medical innovations included cataract surgery. The state, from its cosmopolitan capital, Chang-an, supervised foreign trade, which exchanged Chinese silks, porcelains, and art for spices and ivory over Central Asian caravan routes and sea routes reaching Africa. A golden age of poetry bequeathed valuable works to later generations (Tu Fu, 712-70; Li Po, 701-62). Landscape painting flourished.

Commercial and industrial expansion continued under the **Northern Sung** dynasty (960-1126), facilitated by paper money and credit notes. But commerce never achieved full respectability; government monopolies expropriated successful merchants. The population, long stable at 50 million, doubled in 200 years with the introduction of early-ripening rice and the double harvest. In art, native Chinese styles were revived.

Americas. From 300 to 600, a Native American empire stretched from the Valley of Mexico to Guatemala, centering on the huge city **Teotihuacán** (founded 100 BCE). To the S, in Guatemala, a high **Mayan** civilization developed (150-900) around hundreds of rural ceremonial centers. The Mayans improved on Olmec writing and the calendar and pursued astronomy and mathematics. In South America, a widespread pre-Inca culture grew from **Tiahuanacu**, Bolivia, near Lake Titicaca (Gateway of the Sun doorway, c. 700).

Christian Europe Regroups and Expands: 900-1300

Scandinavia. Pagan Danish and Norse (Viking) adventurers, traders, and pirates raided the coasts of the British Isles (Dublin, c. 831), France, and even the Mediterranean for over 200 years beginning in the late 8th cent. Inland settlement in the W was limited to Great Britain (King Canute, 994-1035) and Normandy, settled (911) under Rollo, as a fief of France. Vikings also reached Iceland (874), Greenland (c. 986), and North America (**Leif Ericson** and others, c. 1000). Norse traders (**Varangians**) developed Russian river commerce from the 8th to the 11th cent. and helped set up a state at Kiev in the late 9th cent. Conversion to Christianity occurred in the 10th cent., reaching Sweden 100 years later. In the 11th cent. Norman bands conquered Southern Italy and Sicily, and Duke **William of Normandy** conquered (1066) England, bringing feudal government and the French language, essential elements in later English civilization.

Central and East Europe. Slavs began to expand from about 150 CE in all directions in Europe. By the 7th cent. they reached as far S as the Adriatic and Aegean seas. In the Balkan Peninsula they dislocated Romanized local populations or assimilated newcomers (Bulgarians, a Turkic people). The first **Slavic states** were Moravia (628) in Central Europe and the Bulgarian state (680) in the Balkans. Byzantine missions of St. Methodius and Cyril (whose Greek-based cyrillic alphabet is still used by some Southern and Eastern Slavs) converted (863) Moravia.

The Eastern Slavs, part-civilized under the overlordship of the Turkish-Jewish **Khazar** trading empire (7th-10th cent.), gravitated toward Constantinople by the 9th cent. The **Kievan** state adopted (989) Eastern Christianity under Prince Vladimir. King Boleslav I (992-1025) began **Poland**'s long history of conquest. The Magyars (**Hungarians**), in present-day Hungary since 896, accepted (1001) Latin Christianity.

Germany. The German kingdom that emerged after the breakup of Charlemagne's Western Empire remained a confederation of largely autonomous states. Otto I, a Saxon who was king from 936, established the **Holy Roman Empire**—a union of Germany and Northern Italy—in alliance with Pope John XII, who crowned (962) him emperor; he defeated (955) the Magyars. Imperial power was greatest under the **Hohenstaufens** (1138-1254), despite the growing opposition of the papacy, which ruled central Italy, and the Lombard League cities. Frederick II (1194-1250) improved administration and patronized the arts. After his death, German influence was removed from Italy.

Christian Spain. From its northern mountain redoubts, Christian rule slowly migrated S through the 11th cent., when Muslim unity collapsed. After the capture (1085) of **Toledo**, the kingdoms of Portugal, Castile, and Aragon undertook repeated crusades of reconquest, finally completed in 1492. Elements of Islamic civilization persisted in recaptured areas, influencing all Western Europe.

Crusades. **Pope Urban II** called for a crusade (1095) to restore Asia Minor to Byzantium and the Holy Land to Christendom. This first crusade captured Jerusalem and led to the foundation of four Frankish states in the Levant. The defeat inflicted upon crusaders at the Battle of Hattin (1187) by **Saladin** (c. 1137-93), the Kurdish ruler of Egypt and Syria, effectively negated territorial gains. Many crusades followed until 1291. The 4th crusade sacked Constantinople (1204). Other crusades were launched against Christian heretics (Albigensian Crusade, 1229), pagans, and enemies of the papacy.

Economy. The agricultural base of European life benefited from improvements in **plow design** (c. 1000) and by the draining of lowlands and clearing of forests, leading to a rural population increase. Towns grew in Northern Italy, Flanders, and Northern Germany (Hanseatic League). Improvements in **loom design** permitted factory textile production. **Guilds** dominated urban trades from the 12th cent. Banking (centered in Italy, 12th-15th cent.) facilitated long-distance trade.

Christianity. The split between the Eastern and Western churches was formalized in 1054. Western and Central Europe was divided into 500 bishoprics under one united hierarchy, but conflicts between secular and church authorities were frequent (German **Investiture Controversy**, 1075-1122). Clerical power was first strengthened through the international monastic reform begun at Cluny in 910. Popular religious enthusiasm often expressed itself in heretical movements (Waldensians from 1173), but was channeled by the **Dominican** (1215) and **Franciscan** (1223) friars into the religious mainstream.

Arts. **Romanesque** architecture (9th to mid-12th cent.) expanded on late Roman models, using the rounded arch and massed stone to support enlarged basilicas. Painting and sculpture followed Byzantine models. The literature of **chivalry** was exemplified by the epic (*Chanson de Roland*, c. 1100) and by courtly love poems of the troubadours of Provence and minnesingers of Germany. **Gothic** architecture emerged in France (choir of St. Denis, c. 1140) and spread along with French cultural influence. Rib vaulting and pointed arches were used to combine soaring heights with delicacy, and they freed walls for display of stained glass. Exteriors were covered with painted relief sculpture and embellished with elaborate architectural detail.

Learning. Law, medicine, and philosophy were advanced at independent **universities** (Bologna, Paris, 12th cent.), originally corporations of students and masters. Twelfth-cent. translations of Greek classics, especially by Aristotle, encouraged an analytic approach. Scholastic philosophy, from Anselm (1033-1109) to **Aquinas** (1225-74), attempted to understand revelation through reason.

Apogee of Central Asian Power and the Spread of Islam: 1250-1500

Turks. Turkic peoples, of Central Asian ancestry, were a military threat to the Byzantine and Persian Empires from the 6th cent. After several waves of invasions, during which most of the Turks adopted Islam, the **Seljuk Turks** took (1055) Baghdad. They ruled Persia, Iraq, and, after 1071, Asia Minor, where massive numbers of Turks settled. The empire was divided in the 12th cent. into smaller states ruled by Seljuks, Kurds, and Mamluks (a military caste of former Turk, Kurd, and Circassian slaves), which governed Egypt and the Middle East until the Ottoman era (c. 1290-1922).

Osman I (r. c. 1290-1326) and succeeding sultans united Anatolian Turkish warriors in a militaristic state that waged holy war against Byzantium and Balkan Christians. Most of the Balkans had been subdued and Anatolia united when Constantinople fell (1453). By the mid-16th cent., Hungary, the Middle East, and N Africa had been conquered. The Turkish advance was stopped at Vienna (1529) and at the naval battle of Lepanto (1571) by Spain, Venice, and the papacy.

The **Ottoman state** was governed in accordance with orthodox Muslim law. Greek, Armenian, and Jewish communities were segregated and were ruled by religious leaders responsible for taxation; they dominated trade. Many state offices and most army ranks were filled by slaves, in part through a system of child conscription among Christians.

India. Mahmud of Ghazni (971-1030) led repeated Turkish raids into N India. Turkish power was consolidated in 1206 with the start of the **Sultanate at Delhi**. Centralization of state power under the early Delhi sultans went far beyond traditional Indian practice. Muslim rule of much of the subcontinent lasted until the British conquest 600 years later, though Hinduism remained the majority religion.

Mongols. Genghis Khan (c. 1167-1227) first united the feuding Mongol tribes and built their armies into an effective offensive force around a core of highly mobile cavalry. He and his immediate successors created the largest land empire in history; by 1279 it stretched from the E coast of Asia to the Danube and from the Siberian steppes to the Arabian Sea. East-West trade and contacts were facilitated (Marco Polo, c. 1254-1324). The western Mongols were Islamized by 1295; successor states soon lost their Mongol character by assimilation. They were briefly reunited under the Turk Tamerlane (1336-1405).

Kublai Khan ruled China from his new capital Beijing (established c. 1264). Naval campaigns against Japan (1274, 1281) and Java (1293) were defeated, the latter by the Hindu-Buddhist maritime kingdom of Majapahit. The **Yuan** dynasty used Mongols and other foreigners (including Europeans) in official posts and tolerated the return of Nestorian Christianity (suppressed 841-45) and the spread of Islam in the S and W. A native reaction expelled the Mongols in 1367-68.

Russia. The Kievan state in Russia, weakened by the decline of Byzantium and the rise of the Catholic Polish-Lithuanian state, was overrun (1238-40) by the Mongols. Only the northern trading republic of Novgorod remained independent. The grand dukes of Moscow emerged as leaders of a coalition of princes that eventually (by 1481) defeated the Mongols. After the fall of Constantinople in 1453, the **Tsars** (Caesars) at Moscow (from Ivan III, r. 1462-1505) set up an independent Russian Orthodox Church. Commerce failed to revive. The isolated Russian state remained agrarian with the peasant class falling into serfdom.

Persia. A revival of Persian literature, making use of the Arab alphabet and literary forms, began in the 10th cent. (epic of Firdausi, 935-1020). An art revival, influenced by Chinese styles introduced after the Mongols came to power in Iran, began in the 13th cent. Persian cultural and political forms, and often the Persian language, were used for centuries by Turkish and Mongol elites from the Balkans to India. Persian mystics from Rumi (1207-73) to Jami (1414-92) promoted **Sufism** in their poetry.

Africa. Two militant Islamic Berber dynasties emerged from the Sahara to carve out empires from the Sahel to central Spain—the **Almoravids** (c. 1050-1140) and the fanatical **Almohads** (c. 1125-1269). The Ghanaian empire was replaced in the upper Niger by Mali (c. 1230-1340), whose Muslim rulers imported Egyptians to help make **Timbuktu** a center of commerce (in gold, leather, and slaves) and learning. The Songhay empire (to 1590) replaced Mali. To the S, forest kingdoms produced refined artworks (Ife terra cotta, **Benin** bronzes).

Other **Muslim states** in Nigeria (Hausas) and Chad originated in the 11th cent. and continued in some form until the 19th-cent. European conquest. Less-developed Bantu kingdoms existed across central Africa.

Some 40 Muslim Arab-Persian trading colonies and city-states were established all along the E African coast from the 10th cent. (Kilwa, Mogadishu). The interchange with Bantu peoples produced the **Swahili** language and culture. Gold, palm oil, and slaves were brought from the interior, stimulating the growth of the Monamatapa kingdom of the Zambezi (15th cent.). The Christian Ethiopian empire (from 13th cent.) continued the traditions of Axum.

Southeast Asia. Islam was introduced into Malaya and the Indonesian islands by Arab, Persian, and Indian traders. Coastal Muslim cities and states (starting before 1300) soon dominated the interior. Chief among these was the **Malacca** state (c. 1400-1511), on the Malay peninsula.

Arts and Statecraft Thrive in Europe; New Asian Empires Rise: 1350-1600

Italy. Distinctive Italian achievements in literature and fine arts during the late Middle Ages (**Dante**, 1265-1321; Giotto, 1276-1337) led to the vigorous new styles of the Renaissance (14th-16th cent.). Patronized by the rulers of the quarreling petty states of Italy (**Medicis** in Florence and the papacy, c. 1400-1737), the plastic arts perfected realistic techniques, including **perspective** (Masaccio, 1401-28; Leonardo **da Vinci**, 1452-1519). Classical motifs were used in architecture, and increased talent and expense were put into secular buildings. The Florentine dialect was refined as a national literary language (**Petrarch**, 1304-74). Greek refugees from the E strengthened the respect of humanist scholars for the classic sources. Soon an international movement aided by the spread of **printing** (Gutenberg, c. 1397-1468), **humanism** was optimistic about the power of human reason (Erasmus of Rotterdam, 1466-1536, **More**'s *Utopia*, 1516) and valued individual effort in the arts and in politics (**Machiavelli**, 1469-1527).

France. The French monarchy, strengthened in its repeated struggles with powerful nobles (Burgundy, Flanders, Aquitaine) by alliances with the growing commercial towns, consolidated bureaucratic control under Philip IV (r. 1285-1314) and extended French influence into Germany and Italy (popes at Avignon, France, 1309-1417). The **Hundred Years War** (1337-1453) ended English dynastic claims in France (battles of Crécy, 1346, and Poitiers, 1356; Joan of Arc executed, 1431). A French Renaissance, dating from royal invasions (1494, 1499) of Italy, was encouraged at the court of Francis I (r. 1515-47), who centralized taxation and law. French vernacular literature consciously asserted its independence (La Pléiade, 1549).

England. The evolution of England's political institutions began with the **Magna Carta** (1215), by which King John guaranteed the privileges of nobles and church against the monarchy and assured jury trial. After the **Wars of the Roses** (1455-85), the **Tudor** dynasty reasserted royal prerogatives (Henry VIII, r. 1509-47), but the trend toward independent departments and ministerial government also continued. English trade (wool exports from c. 1340) was protected by the nation's growing maritime power (**Spanish Armada** destroyed, 1588).

Queen Elizabeth I, who ruled England for more than 40 years (1558-1603), presided over the age in which Shakespeare, Spenser, and Marlowe flourished.

English replaced French and Latin in the late 14th cent. in law and literature (**Chaucer**, c. 1340-1400), and English translation of the Bible began (Wycliffe, 1380s). **Elizabeth I** (r. 1558-1603) presided over the development of poetry (Spenser, 1552-99), drama (**Shakespeare**, 1564-1616), and music.

German Empire. From among a welter of minor feudal states, church lands, and independent cities, the **Habsburgs** assembled a far-flung territorial domain, based in Austria from 1276. Family members held the title of Holy Roman Emperor from 1438 to the Empire's dissolution in 1806 but failed to centralize its domains, leaving Germany disunited for centuries. Resistance to Turkish expansion brought Hungary under Austrian control from the 16th cent. The Netherlands, Luxembourg, and Burgundy were added in 1477, curbing French expansion.

The Flemish painting tradition of naturalism, technical proficiency, and bourgeois subject matter began in the 15th cent. (Jan **van Eyck**, c. 1390-1441), the earliest northern manifestation of the Renaissance. Albrecht **Dürer** (1471-1528) typified the merging of late Gothic and Italian trends in 16th-cent. German art. Imposing civic architecture flourished in the prosperous commercial cities.

Black Death. The bubonic plague reached Europe from the E in 1348, killing up to half the population by 1350 (and recurring periodically in most areas until the early 18th cent.). Labor scarcity forced wages to rise and brought greater freedom to the peasantry, making possible **peasant uprisings** (Jacquerie in France, 1358; Wat Tyler's rebellion in England, 1381).

Spain. Despite the unification of Castile and Aragon in 1479, the two countries retained separate governments, and the nobility, especially in Aragon and Catalonia, retained many privileges. Spanish lands in Italy (Naples, Sicily) and the Netherlands entangled the country in European wars through the mid-17th cent., while explorers, traders, and conquerors built up a Spanish empire in the Americas and the Philippines.

From the late 15th cent., a **golden age** of literature and art produced works of social satire (plays of Lope de Vega, 1562-1635; **Cervantes**, 1547-1616), as well as spiritual intensity (**El Greco**, 1541-1614; **Velázquez**, 1599-1660).

Explorations. Organized European maritime exploration began, seeking to evade the Venice-Ottoman monopoly of eastern trade and to promote Christianity. A key goal was to satisfy a growing taste for Asian goods. Beginning in 1418, expeditions from Portugal explored the W coast of Africa, until Vasco da Gama rounded the Cape of Good Hope in 1497 and reached India. A Portuguese trading empire was consolidated by the seizure of Goa (1510) and Malacca (1551). Japan was reached in 1542. The voyages of Christopher **Columbus** (1492-1504) uncovered a world new to Europeans, which Spain hastened to subdue. Navigation schools in Spain and Portugal, the development of large sailing ships (carracks) mounted with cannons, and the invention (c. 1475) of the rifle aided European penetration.

Mughals and Safavids. E of the Ottoman Empire, two Muslim dynasties ruled unchallenged in the 16th and 17th cent. The Mughal dynasty of India, founded by Persianized Turkish invaders from the NW under Babur, dates from their 1526 conquest of the Delhi Sultanate. The dynasty ruled most of India for more than 200 years, surviving nominally until 1857. **Akbar** (r. 1556-1605) consolidated administration at his glorious court, where the Urdu language (Persian-influenced Hindi) developed. Trade relations with Europe increased. Under Shah Jahan (1629-58), a secularized art fusing Hindu and Muslim elements flourished in miniature painting and in architecture (**Taj Mahal**). **Sikhism** (founded late 15th cent.) combined elements of both faiths. Suppression of Hindus and Shiite Muslims in S India in the late 17th cent. weakened the empire.

Intense devotion to the Shiite sect characterized the Safavids (1502-1736) of Persia and led to hostilities with the Sunni Ottomans for more than a century. The prosperity and the strength of the empire are evidenced by the mosques at its capital city, **Isfahan**. The Safavids enhanced Iranian national consciousness.

China. The **Ming** emperors (1368-1644), the last native dynasty in China, wielded strong personal power. European trade (Portuguese monopoly through **Macao** from 1557) was strictly controlled. Jesuit scholars and scientists (Matteo Ricci, 1552-1610) introduced some Western science; their writings familiarized the West with China. The arts thrived, especially in the areas of painting and ceramics. Chinese manufacturing boomed, bringing in new profits from world trade.

Japan. After the decline of the first hereditary *shogunate* (chief generalship) at **Kamakura** (1185-1333), fragmentation of power accelerated, as did the consequent social mobility. Under Kamakura and the Ashikaga shogunate (1338-1573), the *daimyos* (lords) and *samurai* (warriors) grew more powerful and promoted a martial ideology. Japanese pirates and traders plied the China coast. Popular Buddhist movements included the nationalist Nichiren sect (from c. 1250) and **Zen** (brought from China, 1191), which stressed meditation and a disciplined aesthetic (tea ceremony, gardening, martial arts, *No* drama).

Change and Expansion in Europe: 1500-1700

Reformation. Theological debate and protests against real and perceived clerical corruption existed in the medieval Christian world, expressed by such dissenters as John **Wycliffe** (c. 1320-84) and his followers (the Lollards) in England, and **Huss** (burned as a heretic, 1415) in Bohemia.

Martin **Luther** (1483-1546) preached that faith alone, without the mediation of clergy or good works, leads to salvation. He attacked the authority of the pope, rejected priestly celibacy, and recommended individual study of the Bible (which he translated into German c. 1525). His 95 Theses (1517) led to his excommunication (1521). John **Calvin** (1509-64) said that God's elect were predestined for salvation and all others for damnation; good conduct and success were signs of election. Calvin in Geneva and John **Knox** (1505-72) in Scotland established theocratic states.

Henry VIII asserted English national authority and secular power by breaking away (1534) from the Catholic Church, creating what would become the Anglican Church. Monastic property was confiscated, and some Protestant doctrines given official sanction.

Religious wars. A century and a half of religious wars began with a southern German peasant uprising (1524), repressed with Luther's support. Radical sects—democratic, pacifist, millenarian—arose (Anabaptists ruled Münster, 1534-35) and were suppressed violently. Civil war in France from 1562 between **Huguenots** (Protestant nobles and merchants) and Catholics ended with the 1598 **Edict of Nantes**, tolerating Protestants (revoked 1685). Habsburg attempts to restore Catholicism in Germany were resisted in 25 years of fighting.

The 1555 Peace of Augsburg guarantee of religious independence to local princes and cities was confirmed only after the **Thirty Years' War** (1618-48), when much of Germany was devastated by local and foreign armies (Sweden, France).

A Catholic Reformation, or **Counter-Reformation**, met the Protestant challenge, defining an official theology at the Council of Trent (1545-63). The **Jesuit** order (Society of Jesus), founded in 1534 by Ignatius Loyola (1491-1556), helped reconvert large areas of Poland, Hungary, and S Germany and sent missionaries to the New World, India, and China. The **Inquisition** suppressed heresy in Catholic countries. A revival of religious fervor appeared in devotional literature (Teresa of Avila, 1515-82) and in grandiose **Baroque** art (Bernini, 1598-1680).

Scientific Revolution. The late nominalist thinkers (Ockham, c. 1300-49) of Paris and Oxford challenged Aristotelian orthodoxy, allowing for a freer scientific approach. At the same time, metaphysical values, such as the Neoplatonic faith in an orderly, mathematical cosmos, still motivated and directed inquiry. Nicolaus **Copernicus** (1473-1543) promoted the heliocentric theory, which was confirmed when Johannes **Kepler** (1571-1630) discovered the mathematical laws describing the elliptical orbits of the planets. The traditional Christian-Aristotelian belief that the heavens and the Earth were fundamentally different collapsed when **Galileo Galilei** (1564-1642) discovered moving sunspots, irregular moon topography, and moons around Jupiter, but he faced religious opposition (Galileo's retraction, 1633). He and Sir Isaac **Newton** (1642-1727) developed a mechanics that unified cosmic and earthly phenomena. Newton and Gottfried von **Leibniz** (1646-1716) invented calculus. René **Descartes** (1596-1650), best known for his influential philosophy, also invented analytic geometry.

An explosion of **observational science** included the discovery of blood circulation (Harvey, 1578-1657) and microscopic life (Leeuwenhoek, 1632-1723) and advances in anatomy (Vesalius, 1514-64, dissected corpses) and chemistry (Boyle, 1627-91). Scientific research institutes were founded in Florence (1657), London (**Royal Society**, 1660), and Paris (1666). Inventions proliferated (Savery's steam engine, 1696).

Arts. Mannerist trends of the High Renaissance (**Michelangelo**, 1475-1564) exploited virtuosity, grace, novelty, and exotic subjects and poses. The notion of artistic genius was promoted. Private connoisseurs entered the art market. These trends were elaborated in the 17th cent. **Baroque** era on a grander scale. Dynamic movement in painting and sculpture was emphasized by sharp lighting effects, rich materials (colored marble, gilt), and realistic details. Curved facades, broken lines, rich detail, and ceiling decoration characterized Baroque architecture. Monarchs, princes, and prelates, usually Catholic, used Baroque art to enhance and embellish their authority, as in royal portraits (Velázquez, 1599-1660; Van Dyck, 1599-1641).

National styles emerged. In France, a taste for rectilinear order and serenity (Poussin, 1594-1665), linked to the new rational philosophy, was expressed in classical forms. The influence of **classical values** in French literature (tragedies of **Racine**, 1639-99) gave rise to the "battle of the Ancients and Moderns." New forms included the essay (**Montaigne**, 1533-92) and novel (*Princesse de Clèves*, La Fayette, 1678).

Dutch painting of the 17th cent. was unique in its wide social distribution. The Flemish tradition of undemonstrative realism reached its peak in **Rembrandt** (1606-69) and Jan Vermeer (1632-75).

Economy. European economic expansion, known as the **commercial revolution**, was stimulated by new trade with the East, by New World gold and silver, and by a doubling of population (50 million in 1450, 100 million in 1600). **New business and financial techniques** were developed and refined, such as joint-stock companies, insurance, and letters of credit and exchange. The Bank of Amsterdam (1609) and the Bank of England (1694) broke the old monopoly of private banking families. The rise of a business mentality was typified by the spread of clock towers in cities in the 14th cent. By the mid-15th cent., portable clocks were available; the first watch was invented in 1502.

By 1650, most governments had adopted the **mercantile system**, in which they sought to amass metallic wealth by protecting merchants' foreign and colonial trade monopolies. The rise in prices and the new coin-based economy undermined craft guild and feudal manorial systems. Expanding industries (clothweaving, mining) benefited from technical advances. Coal began to replace wood as the chief fuel; it was used to fuel new 16th-cent. blast furnaces making cast iron.

The exact purpose of the Incan city of Machu Picchu, built in the 15th century and abandoned less than 150 years later, is unknown; one theory is that it served as a royal retreat.

New World. The **Aztecs** united much of the Mesoamerican area in a militarist empire by 1519 from their capital, Tenochtitlán (pop. 300,000), which was the center of a cult requiring ritual human sacrifice. Most of the civilized areas of South America were ruled by the centralized Inca Empire (1476-1534), stretching 2,000 mi from Ecuador to NW Argentina. Lavish and sophisticated traditions in pottery, weaving, sculpture, and architecture were maintained in both regions.

These empires, beset by revolts, fell in two short campaigns to gold-seeking Spanish forces based in the Antilles and Panama. Hernán **Cortés** took Mexico (1519-21); Francisco **Pizarro**, Peru (1532-35). From these centers, land and sea expeditions claimed most of North and South America for Spain. The indigenous high cultures did not survive the impact of **Christian missionaries** and the new upper class of whites. Although the Spanish administration intermittently concerned itself with their welfare, the population was devastated by European diseases and remained impoverished at most levels. New World silver and such native products as potatoes, tobacco, corn, peanuts, chocolate, and rubber exercised a major economic influence on Europe.

Brazil, which the Portuguese reached in 1500 and settled after 1530, and the Caribbean colonies of several European nations developed a plantation economy where sugarcane, tobacco, cotton, coffee, rice, indigo, and lumber were grown by slaves. From the early 16th to late 19th cent., 10 million Africans were transported to **slavery** in the Americas and Caribbean islands.

Netherlands. The urban, Calvinist northern provinces of the Netherlands rebelled (1568) against Habsburg Spain and founded an oligarchic mercantile republic. Their control of the Baltic grain market enabled them to exploit Mediterranean food shortages. Religious refugees—French and Belgian Protestants, Iberian Jews—added to the commercial talent pool. After Spain absorbed Portugal (1580), the Dutch seized Portuguese possessions and created a vast commercial empire ultimately centered in parts of the Caribbean and in Indonesia. The Dutch also challenged or supplanted Portuguese traders in China and Japan. Revolution in 1640 restored Portuguese independence.

England. Anglicanism became firmly established under **Elizabeth I** after a brief Catholic interlude under "Bloody" Mary I (1553-58). But religious and political conflicts led to a rebellion (1642) by Parliament. Forces of the Roundheads (Puritans) defeated the Cavaliers (Royalists); Charles I was beheaded (1649). The new Commonwealth was ruled as a military dictatorship by Oliver **Cromwell**, who also brutally crushed (1649-51) an Irish rebellion. Conflicts within the Puritan camp (democratic Levelers defeated, 1649) aided the Stuart restoration (1660), but Parliament was strengthened and the peaceful **"Glorious Revolution"** (1688) advanced political and religious liberties (writings of **Locke**, 1632-1704). British privateers (Drake, 1540-96) challenged Spanish control of the New World and penetrated Asian trade routes (Madras taken, 1639). North American colonies (Jamestown, 1607; Plymouth, 1620) provided an outlet for private enterprise and religious dissenters from Europe. The British East India company gained growing sway in 18th-cent. India, as Mughal power declined.

France. Emerging from the religious civil wars in 1628, France regained military and commercial great power status (under the ministries of **Richelieu**, Mazarin, and Colbert). Under **Louis XIV** (r. 1643-1715), royal absolutism triumphed over nobles and local *parlements* (defeat of Fronde, 1648-53). Durable colonies were founded in Canada (1608), the Caribbean (1626), and India (1674).

Sweden. Sweden seceded from the Scandinavian Union in 1523. The thinly populated agrarian state (with copper, iron, and timber exports) was united by the Vasa kings, whose conquests by the mid-17th cent. made Sweden the dominant Baltic power. The empire collapsed in the Great Northern War (1700-21).

Poland. After the union with Lithuania in 1447, Poland ruled vast territories from the Baltic to the Black Sea, resisting German and Turkish incursions. Catholic nobles failed to gain the loyalty of their Orthodox Christian subjects in the E; commerce and trades were practiced by German and Jewish immigrants. The bloody 1648-49 Cossack uprising began the kingdom's dismemberment.

Russia. Growing authority of the tsars continued with advancing serfdom. Around 1700, **Peter the Great** imported new Western styles and technologies. Steady territorial expansion created a vast territory touching China, the Ottoman Empire, and east-central Europe.

China. A new dynasty, the **Manchus**, invaded from the NE, seized power in 1644, and expanded Chinese control to its greatest extent in Central and SE Asia. Trade and diplomatic contact with Europe grew, carefully controlled by China. New crops (sweet potato, maize, peanut) allowed economic and population growth (pop. 300 million, in 1800). Traditional arts and literature were pursued with increased sophistication (*Dream of the Red Chamber*, novel, mid-18th cent.).

Japan. Tokugawa Ieyasu, shogun from 1603, finally unified and pacified feudal Japan. Hereditary nobles (daimyos and samurai) monopolized government office and the professions. An urban merchant class grew, literacy spread, and a cultural renaissance occurred (**haiku**, a verse innovation of the poet Basho, 1644-94). Fear of European domination led to persecution of Christian converts from 1597 and to substantial isolation from outside contact from 1640.

Philosophy, Industry, and Revolution: 1700-1800

Science and reason. Greater faith in reason and empirical observation, instead of tradition and religious beliefs, espoused since the Renaissance (Francis Bacon, 1561-1626), was bolstered by scientific discoveries. René **Descartes** (1596-1650) used a rationalistic approach modeled on geometry and introspection to discover "self-evident" truths as a foundation of knowledge. Sir Isaac **Newton** emphasized induction from experimental observation. Baruch de **Spinoza** (1632-77), who called for political and intellectual freedom, developed a systematic rationalistic philosophy in his classic work *Ethics*.

French philosophers assumed leadership of the **Enlightenment** in the 18th cent. Montesquieu (1689-1755) used British history to support his notions of limited government. **Voltaire**'s (1694-1778) diaries and novels of exotic travel illustrated the intellectual trends toward secular ethics and relativism. Jean-Jacques **Rousseau**'s (1712-78) radical concepts of the **social contract** and of the inherent goodness of the common man gave impetus to antimonarchical republicanism. The *Encyclopedia* (1751-72, edited by Diderot and d'Alembert), designed as a monument to reason, was largely devoted to practical technology.

In England, ideals of liberty were connected with empiricist philosophy and science in the followers of John **Locke**. But British empiricism, especially as developed by the skeptical David **Hume** (1711-76), radically reduced the role of reason in philosophy, as did the evolutionary approach to law and politics of Edmund Burke (1729-97) and the utilitarian ethics of Jeremy Bentham (1748-1832). Adam Smith (1723-90) and other economists called for a rationalization of economic activity by removing artificial barriers to a supposedly natural free exchange of goods known as **laissez-faire**.

German writers participated in the new philosophical trends popularized by Christian von Wolff (1679-1754). Immanuel **Kant**'s (1724-1804) transcendental idealism, unifying an empirical epistemology with a priori moral and logical concepts, directed German thought away from skepticism. Italian contributions included work on electricity (Galvani, 1737-98; Volta, 1745-1827), the pioneer historiography of Vico (1668-1744), and writings on penal reform (Beccaria, 1738-94). Benjamin Franklin (1706-90) was celebrated in Europe for his varied achievements.

The growth of the **press** (*Spectator*, 1711-12) and the wide distribution of sentimental **novels** attested to the increase of a large bourgeois public.

New technological developments, including mechanized manufacturing processes and innovations in power sources, enabled the industrial revolution from about 1760 on.

Arts. **Rococo** art, characterized by extravagant decorative effects, asymmetries copied from organic models, and artificial pastoral subjects, was favored by the continental aristocracy for most of the century (Watteau, 1684-1721) and had musical analogies in the ornamentalized polyphony of late Baroque. The **Neoclassical** art after 1750, associated with the new scientific archaeology, was more streamlined and was infused with the supposed moral and geometric rectitude of the Roman Republic (David, 1748-1825). In England, **town planning** on a grand scale began.

Industrial Revolution in England. Agricultural improvements, such as the sowing drill (1701) and livestock breeding, were implemented on the large fields provided by enclosure of common lands by private owners. Profits from agriculture and from colonial and foreign trade (1800 volume, £54 mil) were channeled through hundreds of banks and the **Stock Exchange** (est. 1773) into new industrial processes.

The Newcomen steam pump (1712) aided coal mining. Coal fueled the new efficient steam engines patented by James Watt in 1769, and coke-smelting produced cheap, sturdy iron for machinery by the 1730s. The **flying shuttle** (1733) and **spinning jenny** (c. 1764) were used in the large new cotton textile factories, where women and children were much of the workforce. Goods were transported cheaply over **canals** (2,000 mi; built 1760-1800). By the early 19th cent., industrialization spread in Western Europe and North America.

American Revolution. The British colonies in North America attracted a mass immigration of religious dissenters and poor people throughout the 17th and 18th cent., coming from the British Isles, Germany, the Netherlands, and other countries including imported African slaves. The population reached 3 million non-natives by the 1770s. The indigenous population was greatly reduced by European diseases and by wars with the various colonies. British attempts to control colonial trade and to tax the colonists to pay for the costs of colonial administration and defense clashedwith local self-government and eventually provoked the colonies to a successful rebellion.

Central and East Europe. The monarchs of the three states that dominated E Europe—Austria, Prussia, and Russia—expanded royal power and centralized institutions in their kingdoms, which were enlarged by the division (1772-95) of Poland.

Under **Frederick II** (the Great) (r. 1740-86) Prussia, with its efficient modern army, doubled in size. State monopolies and tariff protection fostered industry, and some legal reforms were introduced. Austria's heterogeneous realms were unified under **Maria Theresa** (r. 1740-80) and **Joseph II** (r. 1765-90). Reforms in education, law, and religion were enacted, and the Austrian serfs were freed (1781). With its defeat in the Seven

Years' War in 1763, Austria failed to regain Silesia, which had been seized by Prussia, but it was compensated by expansion to the E and S (Hungary, Slavonia, 1699; Galicia, 1772).

Russia, whose borders continued to expand, adopted some Western bureaucratic and economic policies under **Peter I** (r. 1682-1725) and **Catherine II** (r. 1762-96). Trade and cultural contacts with the West multiplied from the new Baltic Sea capital, **St. Petersburg** (est. 1703).

French Revolution. The growing French middle class lacked political power and resented aristocratic tax privileges, especially in light of the successful American Revolution. Peasants lacked adequate land and were burdened with feudal obligations to nobles. War with Britain led to the loss of French Canada and drained the treasury, finally forcing the king to call the **Estates-General** in 1789 for the first time since 1614, in an atmosphere of food riots (poor crop in 1788).

Aristocratic resistance to absolutism was soon overshadowed by the reformist Third Estate (middle class), which proclaimed itself the **National Constituent Assembly** June 17 and took the "Tennis Court oath" on June 20 to secure a constitution. The storming of the **Bastille** on July 14, 1789, by Parisian artisans was followed by looting and the seizure of aristocratic property throughout France. Assembly reforms included abolition of class and regional privileges, a Declaration of Rights, suffrage by taxpayers (75% of male population), and the **Civil Constitution of the Clergy** providing for election and loyalty oaths for priests. A republic was declared Sept. 22, 1792, in spite of royalist pressure from Austria and Prussia, which had declared war in Apr. (joined by Britain the next year). Louis XVI was beheaded Jan. 21, 1793, and Queen Marie Antoinette was beheaded Oct. 16, 1793.

Royalist uprisings in La Vendée and military reverses led to institution of a **reign of terror** in which tens of thousands of opponents of the Revolution and criminals were executed. Radical reforms in the **Convention** period (Sept. 1793-Oct. 1795) included the abolition of colonial slavery, economic measures to aid the poor, support of public education, and a short-lived de-Christianization.

Division among radicals (execution of Hebert, Danton, and Robespierre, 1794) aided the ascendancy of a moderate **Directory**, which consolidated military victories. **Napoleon Bonaparte** (1769-1821), a popular young general, exploited political divisions and participated in a coup Nov. 9, 1799, making himself first consul (dictator).

India. Sikh and Hindu rebels (Rajputs, Marathas) and Afghans destroyed the power of the Mughals during the 18th cent. After France's defeat (1763) in the Seven Years' War, Britain was the primary European trade power in India. Its control of inland **Bengal** and **Bihar** was recognized (1765) by the Mughal shah, who granted the **British East India Co.** (under Clive, 1725-74) the right to collect land revenue there. Despite objections from Parliament (1784 India Act), the company's involvement in local wars and politics led to repeated acquisitions of new territory. The company exported Indian textiles, sugar, and indigo, but industry was discouraged to promote British imports.

Nationalism Gathers Momentum: 1800-40

French ideals and empire spread. Inspired by the ideals of the French Revolution, and supported by the expanding French armies, new republican regimes arose near France: the **Batavian** Republic in the Netherlands (1795-1806), the **Helvetic** Republic in Switzerland (1798-1803), the **Cisalpine** Republic in Northern Italy (1797-1805), the **Ligurian** Republic in Genoa (1797-1805), and the **Parthenopean** Republic in Southern Italy (1799). A Roman Republic existed briefly in 1798 after Pope Pius VI was arrested by French troops. In Italy and Germany, new nationalist sentiments were stimulated both in imitation of and in reaction to developments in France (anti-French and anti-Jacobin peasant uprisings in Italy, 1796-99).

From 1804, when Napoleon declared himself emperor, to 1812, a succession of military victories (Austerlitz, 1805; Jena, 1806) extended his control over most of Europe through puppet states (**Confederation of the Rhine** united W German states for the first time and **Grand Duchy of Warsaw** revived Polish national hopes), expansion of the empire, and alliances.

Among the lasting reforms initiated under Napoleon's absolutist reign were establishment of the Bank of France, centralization of tax collection, codification of law along Roman models (Code Napoléon), and reform and extension of secondary and university education. In an 1801 concordat, the papacy recognized the effective autonomy of the French Catholic Church.

Napoleon's continental successes were offset by a British victory under Adm. Horatio Nelson in the **Battle of Trafalgar** (1805). Some 400,000 French soldiers were killed in the Napoleonic Wars, along with about 600,000 foreign troops.

Last gasp of old regimes. The disastrous 1812 invasion of Russia exposed Napoleon's overextension. After Napoleon's 1814 exile at Elba, his armies were defeated (1815) at **Waterloo** by British and Prussian troops.

At the **Congress of Vienna**, the monarchs and princes of Europe redrew their boundaries, to the advantage of Prussia (in Saxony and the Ruhr), Austria (in Illyria and Venetia), and Russia (in Poland and Finland). British conquest of Dutch and French colonies (S Africa, Ceylon, Mauritius) was recognized. France, under the restored Bourbons, retained its expanded 1792 borders. The settlement brought 50 years of international peace to Europe.

But the Congress was unable to check the advance of liberal ideals and of nationalism among the smaller European nations. The 1825 **Decembrist uprising** by liberal officers in Russia was easily suppressed. But an independence movement in **Greece**, stirred by commercial prosperity and a cultural revival, succeeded in expelling Ottoman rule by 1831, with the aid of Britain, France, and Russia.

A constitutional monarchy was secured in France by the **1830 Revolution**; Louis Philippe became king. The revolutionary contagion spread to **Belgium**, which gained its independence (1830) from the Dutch monarchy, to **Poland**, whose rebellion was defeated (1830-31) by Russia, and to Germany.

Romanticism. A new style in intellectual and artistic life replaced Neoclassicism and Rococo after the mid-18th cent. By the early 19th cent., Romanticism prevailed in Europe.

Rousseau had begun the reaction against rationalism; in education (*Émile*, 1762) he stressed subjective spontaneity over regularized instruction. German writers (Lessing, 1729-81; Herder, 1744-1803) favorably compared the German folk song to classical forms and began a cult of Shakespeare, whose passion and "natural" wisdom was a model for the romantic *Sturm und Drang*

Haiti's Toussaint L'Ouverture was a leader of the revolution that led to Haiti's establishment as a free, self-governing state in 1804.

(Storm and Stress) movement. **Goethe**'s *Sorrows of Young Werther* (1774) set the model for the tragic, passionate genius.

A new interest in **Gothic architecture** in England after 1760 (Walpole, 1717-97) spread through Europe, associated with an aesthetic Christian and mystic revival (**Blake**, 1757-1827). Celtic, Norse, and German mythology and folk tales were revived or imitated (Grimm's Fairy Tales, 1812-22). The medieval revival (Scott's *Ivanhoe*, 1819) led to a new interest in history, stressing national differences and organic growth (**Carlyle**, 1795-1881; Michelet, 1798-1874), corresponding to theories of natural evolution (Lamarck's *Philosophie Zoologique*, 1809; Lyell's *Geology*, 1830-33). A reaction against classicism characterized the English **romantic poets** (beginning with **Wordsworth**, 1770-1850). Revolution and war fed an emphasis on freedom and conflict, expressed by both poets (**Byron**, 1788-1824; **Hugo**, 1802-85) and philosophers (**Hegel**, 1770-1831).

Wild gardens replaced the formal French variety, and painters favored rural, stormy, and mountainous landscapes (**Turner**, 1775-1851; **Constable**, 1776-1837). Clothing became freer, with wigs, hoops, and ruffles discarded. Originality and genius were expected in the life and work of inspired artists (Murger's *Scenes From Bohemian Life*, 1847-49). Exotic locales and themes (as in Gothic horror stories) were used in art and literature (Delacroix, 1798-1863; **Poe**, 1809-49). Music exhibited the new dramatic style and a breakdown of classical forms (**Beethoven**, 1770-1827). The use of folk melodies and modes aided the growth of distinct national traditions (Glinka in Russia, 1804-57).

Latin America. François **Toussaint L'Ouverture** led a successful slave revolt in Haiti, which subsequently became the first Caribbean state to achieve independence (1804). The mainland Spanish colonies won their independence (1810-24) under such leaders as Simón **Bolívar** (1783-1830). Brazil became an independent empire (1822) under the Portuguese prince regent. A new class of military officers divided power with large landholders and the church.

United States. Territory under U.S. control nearly doubled in size with the **Louisiana Purchase** (1803). Heavy immigration and exploitation of ample natural resources fueled rapid economic growth. The spread of the franchise, public education, and antislavery sentiment were signs of a widespread democratic ethic.

China. Failure to keep pace with Western arms technology exposed China to greater European influence and hampered efforts to bar imports of opium, which had damaged Chinese society and drained wealth overseas. In the **Opium War** (1839-42), Britain forced China to expand trade opportunities and to cede Hong Kong.

New Complexities: Reforms and Imperialism: 1840-80

Idea of progress. As a result of the cumulative scientific, economic, and political changes of the preceding eras, the idea took hold among literate people in the West that continuing growth and improvement constituted the usual state of human and natural life.

Charles **Darwin**'s statement of the **theory of evolution** and survival of the fittest (*On the Origin of Species*, 1859), defended by intellectuals and scientists against theological objections, was taken as confirmation that progress was the natural direction of life. The controversy helped define popular ideas of the dedicated scientist and of science's increasing control over the world (Foucault's demonstration of Earth's rotation, 1851; **Pasteur**'s germ theory, 1861).

Liberals following Ricardo (1772-1823) in their faith that unrestrained competition would bring continuous economic expansion sought to adjust political life to new social realities and believed that unregulated competition of ideas would yield truth (**Mill**, 1806-73). In England, successive reform bills (1832, 1867, 1884) gave representation to the new industrial towns and extended the franchise to the middle and lower classes and to Catholics, Dissenters, and Jews. On both sides of the Atlantic, reformists tried to improve conditions for the mentally ill (**Dix**, 1802-87), women (Anthony, 1820-1906), and prisoners. Slavery was barred in the British Empire (1833), the U.S. (1865), and Brazil (1888).

Socialist theories based on ideas of human perfectibility or progress were widely disseminated. Utopian socialists such as Saint-Simon (1760-1825) envisaged an orderly, just society directed by a technocratic elite. A model factory town, New Lanark, Scotland, was set up by utopian Robert Owen (1771-1858), and communal experiments were tried in the U.S. (Brook Farm, MA, 1841-47).

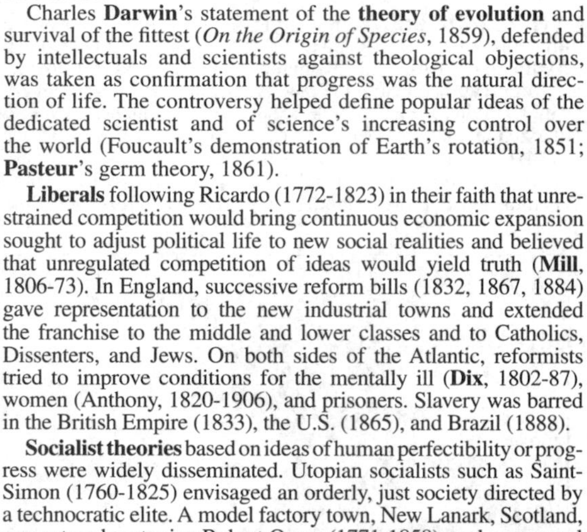

Louis Daguerre's 10-minute exposure of Boulevard du Temple in Paris (1838) omits moving traffic but includes the earliest candid image of a person: a man having his shoes polished.

Bakunin's (1814-76) anarchism represented the opposite extreme of total freedom. Karl **Marx** (1818-83) posited the inevitable triumph of socialism in industrial countries through a dialectical process of class conflict. Effective development of oceanic steamship lines (Cunard Lines, 1840s) and the opening of the **Suez Canal** accelerated shipping and commerce. Telegraph lines (Australia-Europe, 1871) sped communication. International organizations included the General (later Universal) Postal Union (1874) and conferences to limit epidemics like cholera. The initial **Geneva Convention** (1864) regulated treatment of prisoners of war.

Spread of industry. The technical processes and managerial innovations of the English industrial revolution spread to Europe (especially Germany) and the U.S., causing an explosion of industrial production, demand for raw materials, and competition for markets. Inventors, both trained and self-taught, provided means for larger-scale production (Bessemer steel, 1856; sewing machine, 1846). Many inventions were shown at the universal prosperity-themed 1851 London Great Exhibition at the **Crystal Palace**.

Local specialization and long-distance trade were aided by a revolution in transportation and communication. Railroads were first introduced in the 1820s in England and the U.S. Over 150,000 mi of track had been laid worldwide by 1880, with another 100,000 mi laid in the next decade. Steamships were improved (*Savannah* crossed Atlantic, 1819). The **telegraph**, perfected by 1844 (Morse), connected the Old and New Worlds by cable in 1866 and quickened the pace of international commerce and politics. The first commercial **telephone** exchange went into operation in the U.S. in 1878.

The new class of industrial workers, uprooted from their rural homes, lacked job security and suffered from dangerous overcrowding at work and at home. Many responded by organizing **trade unions** (legalized in England, 1824; France, 1884). The U.S. Knights of Labor had 700,000 members by 1886. The First International (1864-76) tried to unite workers worldwide around a Marxist program. The quasi-Socialist Paris Commune uprising (1871) was violently suppressed. Acts to reduce child labor and regulate conditions were passed (1833-50 in England). Social security measures were introduced by the Bismarck regime (1883-89) in Germany.

Revolutions of 1848. Among the causes of the continent-wide revolutions were an international collapse of credit and resulting unemployment, bad harvests in 1845-47, and a cholera epidemic. The new urban proletariat and expanding bourgeoisie demanded greater political roles. Republics were proclaimed in France, Rome, and Venice. Nationalist feelings reached fever pitch in the Habsburg empire, as Hungary declared independence under Kossuth, a Slav Congress demanded equality, and Piedmont tried to drive Austria from Lombardy. A national liberal assembly at Frankfurt called for German unification.

But riots fueled bourgeois fear of socialism (**Marx** and **Engels**, *Communist Manifesto*, 1848), and peasants remained conservative. The old establishment—the Papacy, the Habsburgs with the help of the Tsarist Russian army—was able to rout the revolutionaries by 1849. The French Republic succumbed to a renewed monarchy by 1852 (Emperor Napoleon III).

Great nations unified. Using the "blood and iron" tactics of Bismarck from 1862, Prussia controlled N Germany by 1867 (war with Denmark, 1864; Austria, 1866). After defeating France in 1870 (annexation of Alsace-Lorraine), it won the allegiance of S German states. A new **German Empire** was proclaimed (1871). **Italy**, inspired by Giuseppe Mazzini (1805-72) and Giuseppe Garibaldi (1807-82), was unified by the reformed Piedmont kingdom through uprisings, plebiscites, and war.

The **United States** expanded its area after the 1846-48 Mexican War and defeated (1861-65) a secession attempt by Southern states in the **Civil War**. Canadian provinces were united in an autonomous **Dominion of Canada** (1867). Control in **India** was removed from the East India Co. and centralized under British administration after the 1857-58 Sepoy rebellion, laying the groundwork for the modern Indian state. Queen Victoria was named Empress of India (1876).

Europe dominates Asia. The Ottoman Empire began to weaken in the face of Balkan nationalisms and European imperial incursions in N Africa (**Suez Canal**, 1869). The Ottomans had lost control of most of both regions by 1882. Russia completed its expansion S by 1884 (despite the temporary setback of the **Crimean War** with Turkey, Britain, and France, 1853-56), taking Turkestan, all the Caucasus, and Chinese areas in the E and sponsoring Balkan Slavs against the Turks. A succession of reformist and reactionary regimes presided over a slow modernization (serfs freed, 1861). Persian independence suffered as Russia and British India competed for influence.

China was forced to sign a series of unequal treaties with European powers and Japan. Overpopulation and an inefficient dynasty brought misery and caused rebellions (Taiping, Muslims) leaving tens of millions dead. **Japan** was forced by the U.S. (Commodore Perry's visits, 1853-54) and Europe to end its isolation. The Meiji restoration (1868) gave power to a Westernizing oligarchy, abolishing feudalism and expanding education. Intensified empire-building gave Burma to Britain (1824-85) and Indochina to France (1862-95). Christian missionary activity followed imperial and trade expansion in Asia.

Arts. The official **Beaux Arts** school in Paris set an international style of imposing public buildings (Paris Opera, 1861-74; Vienna Opera, 1861-69) and uplifting statues (Bartholdi's Statue of Liberty, 1884). Realist painting, influenced by photography (Daguerre, 1837), appealed to a new mass audience with social or historical narrative (Wilkie, 1785-1841; Poynter, 1836-1919) or with serious religious, moral, or social messages (pre-Raphaelites, Millet's *Angelus*, 1858), often drawn from ordinary life. The **Impressionists** (Monet, 1840-1926; Pissarro, 1830-1903; Renoir, 1841-1919) rejected the formalism, sentimentality, and precise techniques of academic art in favor of a spontaneous, undetailed rendering of the world through careful representation of the effect of natural light on objects. They were strongly influenced by Asian and African styles.

Realistic **novelists** presented the full panorama of social classes and personalities but retained sentimentality and moral judgment (**Dickens**, 1812-70; **Eliot**, 1819-80; **Tolstoy**, 1828-1910; **Balzac**, 1799-1850).

Veneer of Stability: 1880-1900

Imperialism triumphant. The vast **African** interior, visited by European explorers (Barth, 1821-65; Livingstone, 1813-73), was conquered by the European powers in rapid, competitive thrusts from their coastal bases after 1880, mostly for domestic political and international strategic reasons. W African Muslim kingdoms (Fulani), Arab slave traders (Zanzibar), and Bantu military confederations (Zulu) were alike subdued. Only Christian Ethiopia (defeat of Italy, 1896) and Liberia resisted successfully. France (W Africa) and Britain ("Cape to Cairo," **Boer War**, 1899-1902) were the major beneficiaries. The ideology of "the white man's burden" (Kipling, *Barrack Room Ballads*, 1892) justified the conquests, which in fact reflected Europe's weapons superiority.

W European foreign capital investment soared to nearly $40 bil by 1914, but most was in E Europe (France, Germany), the Americas (Britain), and Europe's colonies. The foundation of the modern interdependent world economy was laid, with cartels dominating raw material trade. Global developments included a new agreement on international patents (1883), the modern Olympics (1896), and the global spread of department stores.

An industrious world. Industrial and technological proficiency characterized the two new great powers—Germany and the U.S. Coal and iron deposits enabled Germany to reach second- or third-place status in iron, steel, and shipbuilding by the 1900s. German electrical and chemical industries were world leaders. The U.S. post-Civil War boom (interrupted by financial panics—1884, 1893, 1896) was shaped by massive immigration from S and E Europe from 1880, government subsidy of railroads, and huge private monopolies (Standard Oil, 1870; U.S. Steel, 1901). The **Spanish-American War**, 1898 (Philippine Insurrection, 1899-1902), and the **Open Door policy** in China (1899) made the U.S. a world power.

England led in **urbanization**, with London the world capital of finance, insurance, and shipping. Sewer systems (Paris, 1850s), electric subways (London, 1890), parks, and bargain department stores helped improve living standards for most of the urban population of the industrial world. Birthrates declined in the West while infant mortality rates plunged (demographic transition, 1880-1920).

Upheavals in Asia. Asian reaction to European economic, military, and religious incursions took the form of imitation of Western techniques and adoption of Western ideas of progress and freedom. The Chinese "self-strengthening" movement of the 1860s and 1870s included rail, port, and arsenal improvements and metal and textile mills. Reformers such as **K'ang** Yu-wei (1858-1927) won liberalizing reforms in 1898, right after the European and Japanese "scramble for concessions."

A universal education system in Japan and importation of foreign industrial, scientific, and military experts aided Japan's rapid modernization after 1868 under the authoritarian Meiji regime. Japan's victory in the **Sino-Japanese War** (1894-95) put Formosa and Korea in its power. Industrialization began in earnest by 1890.

In India, the British alliance with the remaining princely states masked reform sentiment among the Westernized urban elite; higher education had been conducted largely in English for 50 years. The **Indian National Congress**, founded in 1885, demanded a larger government role for Indians.

***Fin-de-siècle* sophistication.** **Naturalist** writers pushed realism to its extreme limits, adopting a quasi-scientific attitude and writing about formerly taboo subjects such as sex, crime, extreme poverty, and corruption (Flaubert, 1821-80; Zola, 1840-1902; Hardy, 1840-1928). Unseen or repressed psychological motivations were explored in the clinical and theoretical works of Sigmund **Freud** (1856-1939) and in works of fiction (**Dostoyevsky**, 1821-81; Henry James, 1843-1916; Schnitzler, 1862-1931).

A contempt for bourgeois life or a desire to shock a complacent audience was shared by the French **symbolist** poets (Verlaine, 1844-96; Rimbaud, 1854-91), by neopagan English writers (Swinburne, 1837-1909), by continental dramatists (**Ibsen**, 1828-1906), and by satirists (**Wilde**, 1854-1900). The German philosopher Friedrich **Nietzsche** (1844-1900) was influential in his elitism and pessimism.

Postimpressionist art neglected long-cherished conventions of representation (**Cézanne**, 1839-1906) and showed a willingness to learn from primitive and non-European art (**Gauguin**, 1848-1903; Japanese prints).

Racism. Gobineau (1816-82) gave a pseudobiological foundation to modern racist theories, which spread in Europe in the latter 19th cent., along with **Social Darwinism**, the belief that societies are and should be organized as a struggle for survival of the fittest. The medieval period was interpreted as an era of natural Germanic rule (Chamberlain, 1855-1927), and notions of racial superiority were associated with German national aspirations (Treitschke, 1834-96). **Anti-Semitism**, with a new racist rationale, became a significant political force in Germany (Anti-Semitic Petition, 1880), Austria (Lueger, 1844-1910), and France (**Dreyfus affair**, 1894-1906).

Imperialism's High Point: 1900-09

Alliances. While the peace of Europe (and its dependencies) continued to hold (1907 **Hague Conference** extended the rules of war and international arbitration procedures), imperial rivalries, protectionist trade practices (in Germany and France), and the escalating arms race (British *Dreadnought* battleship launched; Germany widens Kiel canal, 1906) exacerbated minor disputes (German-French Moroccan "crises," 1905, 1911).

Security was sought through balance-of-power alliances: **Triple Alliance** (Germany, Austria-Hungary, Italy; renewed in 1902 and 1907); Anglo-Japanese Alliance (1902), Franco-Russian Alliance (1899), **Entente Cordiale** (Britain, France, 1904), Anglo-Russian Treaty (1907), German-Ottoman friendship. Global developments included the establishment of an international court in The Hague, the first transatlantic radio transmission (1901), and the creation of the first international association for European football (1904).

Ottomans decline. The Ottoman government was unable to resist further loss of territory, and earlier reform efforts gave way to greater authoritarianism. Nearly all European lands were lost in 1912 to Serbia, Greece, Montenegro, and Bulgaria. Italy took Libya and the Dodecanese islands the same year. Britain took Kuwait (1899) and the Sinai (1906). The **Young Turk** revolution in 1908 forced the sultan to restore a constitution, and it introduced some social reform and secularization.

British Empire. British trade and cultural influence remained dominant in the empire, but constitutional reforms presaged its eventual dissolution. The colonies of **Australia** were united in 1901 under a self-governing commonwealth. **New Zealand** acquired dominion status in 1907. The old Boer republics joined Cape Colony and Natal in the self-governing Union of **South Africa** in 1910.

The 1909 Indian Councils Act enhanced the role of elected province legislatures in **India**. The Muslim League (founded 1906) sought separate communal representation.

East Asia. Japan exploited its growing industrial power to expand its empire. Victory in the 1904-05 war against Russia (naval battle of Tsushima, 1905) assured Japan's domination of **Korea** (annexed 1910) and Manchuria (Port Arthur taken, 1905).

In China, central authority began to crumble (empress died, 1908). Reforms (Confucian exam system ended 1905, modernization of the army, building of railroads) were inadequate, and secret societies of reformers and nationalists, inspired by the Westernized **Sun** Yat-sen (1866-1925), fomented periodic uprisings in the S.

Siam, whose independence had been guaranteed by Britain and France in 1896, was split into spheres of influence by those countries in 1907.

Russia. The population of the Russian Empire approached 150 million in 1900. Reforms in education, in law, and in local institutions (*zemstvos*) and an industrial boom starting in the 1880s (oil, railroads) created the beginnings of a modern society, despite the autocratic tsarist regime. Liberals (1903 Union of Liberation), Socialists (Social Democrats founded 1898, Bolsheviks split off 1903), and populists (Social Revolutionaries founded 1901) were periodically repressed, and national minorities were persecuted (anti-Jewish pogroms, 1903, 1905-06).

An industrial crisis after 1900 and harvest failures aggravated poverty among urban workers, and the 1904-05 defeat by Japan (which checked Russia's Asian expansion) sparked the **Revolution of 1905-06**. A **Duma** (parliament) was created under Tsar Nicholas II. Agricultural reform (under Stolypin, prime minister, 1906-11) created a large class of land-owning peasants (*kulaks*).

Emigration from densely populated European countries soared in the early 20th century; many landed on Ellis Island, en route to American cities.

The world shrinks. Developments in transportation and communication and mass population movements helped create an awareness of an interdependent world. Early **automobiles** (Daimler, Benz, 1885) were experimental or were designed as luxuries. Assembly-line mass production (Ford Motor Co., 1903) made the invention practical, and by 1910 nearly 500,000 motor vehicles were registered in the U.S. alone. **Heavier-than-air flights** began in 1903 in the U.S. (Wright brothers' *Flyer*), preceded by glider, balloon, and model plane advances in several countries. Trade was advanced by improvements in **ship design** (gyrocompass, 1910), speed (*Lusitania* crossed Atlantic in five days, 1907), and reach (Panama Canal begun, 1904).

The first transatlantic **radio** telegraphic transmission occurred in 1901, six years after Marconi discovered radio. Radio transmission of human speech had been made in 1900. Telegraphic transmission of photos was achieved in 1904, lending immediacy to news reports. **Phonographs**, popularized by Caruso's recordings (starting 1902), made for quick international spread of musical styles (ragtime). **Motion pictures**, perfected in the 1890s (Dickson, Lumière brothers), became a popular and artistic medium after 1900; newsreels appeared in 1909.

Emigration from crowded European centers soared in the decade: 9 million migrated to the U.S., and millions more went to Siberia, Canada, Argentina, Australia, South Africa, and Algeria. Some 70 million Europeans emigrated in the century before 1914. Several million Chinese, Indians, and Japanese migrated to SE Asia, where their urban skills often enabled them to take a predominant economic role.

Social reform. The social and economic problems of the poor were kept in the public eye by realist fiction writers (Dreiser's *Sister Carrie*, 1900; Gorky's *Lower Depths*, 1902; Sinclair's *The Jungle*, 1906), journalists (U.S. **muckrakers**—Steffens, Tarbell), and artists (Ashcan school). Frequent labor strikes and occasional assassinations by anarchists or radicals (Empress Elizabeth of Austria, 1898; King Umberto I of Italy, 1900; U.S. Pres. McKinley, 1901; Russian Interior Min. Plehve, 1904; Portugal's King Carlos, 1908) added to social tension and fear of revolution. Feminist agitators for the vote surfaced in several countries.

But democratic reformism responded in part. In Germany, Bernstein's (1850-1932) **revisionist Marxism**, downgrading revolution, was accepted by the powerful Social Democrats and trade unions. The British Fabian Society (the Webbs, Shaw) and the Labour Party (founded 1906) worked for reforms such as social security and union rights (1906), while woman suffragists grew more militant. U.S. **progressives** fought big business (Pure Food and Drug Act, 1906). In France, the 10-hour workday (1904) and separation of church and state (1905) were reform victories, as was universal suffrage in Austria (1907).

Arts. An unprecedented period of experimentation, centered in France, produced several new **painting styles**: Fauvism exploited bold color areas (Matisse, *Woman With Hat*, 1905); expressionism reflected powerful inner emotions (Brücke group, 1905); Cubism combined several views of an object on one flat surface (Picasso, *Demoiselles*, 1906-07); futurism tried to depict speed and motion (Italian Futurist Manifesto, 1910). **Architects** explored new uses of steel structures, with facades either neoclassical (Adler and Sullivan in U.S.), curvilinear Art Nouveau (Gaudi's Casa Mila, 1905-10), or functionally streamlined (Wright's Robie House, 1909).

Music and dance shared the experimental spirit. Ruth St. Denis (1877-1968) and Isadora Duncan (1878-1927) pioneered modern dance, while Sergei Diaghilev in Paris revitalized classic ballet from 1909. Composers explored atonal music (Debussy, 1862-1918) and dissonance (Schoenberg, 1874-1951) or revolutionized classical forms (Stravinsky, 1882-1971), often showing jazz or folk music influences.

War and Revolution: 1910-19

War threatens. Germany under Wilhelm II sought a political and imperial role consonant with its industrial strength, challenging Britain's world supremacy and threatening France, which was still resenting the loss (1871) of Alsace-Lorraine. Austria wanted to curb an expanded Serbia (after 1912) and the threat it posed to its own Slav lands. Russia feared Austrian and German political and economic aims in the Balkans and Turkey.

An accelerated arms race resulted from these circumstances. The German standing army rose to more than 2 million men by 1914. Russia and France had more than a million each, and Austria and the British Empire nearly a million each. Dozens of enormous battleships were built by the powers after 1906.

The **assassination of Austrian Archduke Franz Ferdinand** by a Serbian nationalist, June 28, 1914, was the trigger for war. The system of alliances made the conflict Europe-wide; Germany's invasion of Belgium to outflank France forced Britain to enter the war. Patriotic fervor was nearly unanimous among all classes in most countries.

World War I. German forces were stopped in France in one month. The rival armies dug **trench networks**. Artillery and improved machine guns prevented either side from any lasting advance despite repeated assaults (600,000 dead at **Verdun**, Feb.-July 1916). Poison gas, used by Germany in 1915, proved ineffective. The entrance of more than 1 million U.S. troops tipped the balance after mid-1917, forcing Germany to sue for peace the next year. The formal armistice was signed on Nov. 11, 1918, and the German emperor abdicated.

In the E, the Russian armies were thrown back (battle of **Tannenberg**, Aug. 20, 1914), and the war grew unpopular in Russia. An allied attempt to relieve Russia through Turkey failed (**Gallipoli**, 1915). The **Russian Revolution** (1917) abolished the monarchy. The new Bolshevik regime signed the capitulatory Brest-Litovsk peace in Mar. 1918. Italy entered the war on the allied side in May 1915 but was pushed back by Oct. 1917. A renewed offensive with Allied aid in Oct.-Nov. 1918 forced Austria to surrender.

The British Navy successfully blockaded Germany, which responded with submarine U-boat attacks; **unrestricted submarine warfare** against neutrals after Jan. 1917 helped bring the U.S. into the war. Other battlefields included Palestine and Mesopotamia, both of which Britain wrested from the Turks in 1917, and the African and Pacific colonies of Germany, most of which fell to Britain, France, Australia, Japan, and South Africa.

Settlement. At the **Paris Peace Conference** (Jan.-June 1919), concluded by the **Treaty of Versailles**, and in subsequent negotiations and local wars (Russian-Polish War, 1920), the **map of Europe** was redrawn with a nod to U.S. Pres. Woodrow Wilson's principle of self-determination. Austria and Hungary were separated, and much of their land was given to Yugoslavia (formerly Serbia), Romania, Italy, and the newly independent Poland and Czechoslovakia. Germany lost territory in the W, N, and E, while Finland and the Baltic states were detached from Russia. The Ottoman Empire ended (1922) and most of its Arab lands went to British-sponsored Arab states or to direct French and British rule. Belgium's sovereignty was recognized.

From 1916, the civilian populations and economies of both sides were mobilized to an unprecedented degree. Hardships intensified among fighting nations in 1917 (French mutiny crushed in May). More than 10 million soldiers died in the war.

A huge **reparations** burden and partial demilitarization were imposed on Germany. Pres. Wilson obtained approval for a League of Nations, but the U.S. Senate refused to allow the U.S. to join.

Russian revolution. Military defeats and high casualties caused a contagious lack of confidence in Tsar Nicholas, who was forced to abdicate Mar. 1917. A liberal provisional government failed to end the war, and massive desertions, riots, and fighting between factions followed. A moderate socialist government under Aleksandr Kerensky was overthrown (Nov. 1917) in a violent coup by the **Bolsheviks** in Petrograd under **Lenin**, who later disbanded the elected Constituent Assembly.

The Bolsheviks brutally suppressed all opposition and ended the war with Germany in Mar. 1918. **Civil war** broke out in the summer between the Red Army (the Bolsheviks and their supporters), and monarchists, anarchists, minority nationalities (Ukrainians, Georgians, Poles), and others. Small U.S., British, French, and Japanese units also opposed the Bolsheviks (1918-19; Japan in Vladivostok to 1922). The civil war, anarchy, and pogroms devastated the country until the 1920 Red Army victory. The **Communist Party** leadership retained absolute power.

Other European revolutions. An unpopular monarchy in **Portugal** was overthrown in 1910. The new republic took severe anticlerical measures in 1911.

After a century of Home Rule agitation, during which **Ireland** was devastated by famine (1 million dead, 1846-47) and emigration, republican militants staged an unsuccessful uprising in Dublin during **Easter 1916**. The execution of the leaders and mass arrests by the British won popular support for the rebels. The **Irish Free State**, comprising all but the six northern counties, achieved dominion status in 1922.

In the aftermath of the world war, radical revolutions were attempted in Germany (**Spartacist** uprising, Jan. 1919), **Hungary** (Kun regime, 1919), and elsewhere. All were suppressed or failed for lack of support.

Chinese revolution. The Manchu Dynasty was overthrown and a republic proclaimed in Oct. 1911. First Pres. Sun Yat-sen resigned in favor of strongman Yuan Shih-k'ai. Sun organized the parliamentarian **Kuomintang** party.

Students launched protests on May 4, 1919, against League of Nations concessions in China to Japan. Nationalist, liberal, and socialist ideas and political groups spread. The **Communist Party** was founded in 1921. A Communist regime took power in Mongolia with Soviet support in 1921.

India restive. Indian objections to British rule erupted in nationalist riots as well as in the nonviolent tactics of Mahatma **Gandhi** (1869-1948). Nearly 400 unarmed demonstrators were shot at **Amritsar** in Apr. 1919. Britain approved limited self-rule that year.

Mexican revolution. Under the long Diaz dictatorship (1877-1911) the economy advanced, but Indian and mestizo lands were confiscated, and concessions to foreigners (mostly U.S.) damaged the middle class. A revolution in 1910 led to civil wars and U.S. intervention (1914, 1916-17). Land reform and a more democratic constitution (1917) were achieved.

Sciences. Scientific specialization prevailed by the 20th cent. Advances in knowledge and technological aptitude increased with the geometric rise in the number of practitioners. Physicists challenged common-sense views of causality, observation, and a mechanistic universe, putting science further beyond popular grasp (**Einstein**'s general theory of relativity, 1915-16; Bohr's quantum mechanics, 1913; Heisenberg's uncertainty principle, 1927).

Both sides in World War I (1914-19) developed elaborate networks of dug-in trenches from which to fight.

Aftermath of War: 1920-29

U.S. Easy credit, technological ingenuity, and war-related industrial decline in Europe caused a long economic boom, in which ownership of new products—**autos, phones, radios**—became more democratized. **Prosperity**, an increase in women workers, women's suffrage (19th Amendment ratified, 1920), and drastic change in fashion (**flappers**, mannish bob for women, clean-shaven men) created a wide perception of social change despite prohibition of alcoholic beverages (1919-33). Union membership and strikes increased. Fear of radicals led to Palmer raids (1919-20) and the Sacco-Vanzetti case (1921-27).

Europe sorts itself out. Germany's liberal **Weimar constitution** (1919) could not guarantee a stable government in the face of rightist violence (Rathenau assassinated, 1922) and Communist refusal to cooperate with Socialists. Reparations and Allied occupation of the Rhineland caused staggering inflation that destroyed middle-class savings, but economic expansion resumed after mid-decade, aided by U.S. loans. A sophisticated, **innovative culture** developed in architecture and design (Bauhaus, 1919-28), film (Lang, *M*, 1931), painting (Grosz), music (Weill, *Threepenny Opera*, 1928), theater (Brecht, *A Man's a Man*, 1926), criticism (Benjamin), philosophy (Jung), and fashion. This culture was considered decadent and socially disruptive by rightists.

England elected its first Labour governments (Jan. 1924, June 1929). A 10-day general strike in support of coal miners failed in May 1926. In **Italy**, strikes, political chaos, and violence by small Fascist bands culminated in the Oct. 1922 Fascist March on Rome, which established **Mussolini**'s dictatorship. Strikes were outlawed (1926), and Italian influence was pressed in the Balkans (Albania made a protectorate, 1926). A conservative dictatorship was also established in **Portugal** in a 1926 military coup.

Czechoslovakia, the only stable democracy to emerge from the war in Central or E Europe, faced opposition from Germans (in the Sudetenland), Ruthenians, and some Slovaks. As the industrial heartland of the old Habsburg empire, it remained fairly prosperous. With French backing, it formed the Little Entente with Yugoslavia (1920) and **Romania** (1921) to block Austrian or Hungarian irredentism. Croats and Slovenes in **Yugoslavia** demanded a federal state until King Alexander I proclaimed (1929) a royal dictatorship. Poland faced internal nationality problems as well (Germans, Ukrainians, Jews); Pilsudski ruled as dictator from 1926. The Baltic states were threatened by traditionally dominant ethnic Germans and by Soviet-supported Communists.

Howard Carter's 1922 discovery of the tomb of Tutankhamun, who ruled as pharaoh in the 14th century BCE, is considered the archaeological find of the century.

An economic collapse and famine in **Russia** (1921-22) claimed 5 million lives. The New Economic Policy (1921) allowed land ownership by peasants and some private commerce and industry. **Stalin** was absolute ruler within four years of Lenin's death (1924). He inaugurated a brutal collectivization program (1929-32) and used foreign Communist parties for Soviet state advantage. Industrialization advanced rapidly.

Internationalism. Revulsion against World War I led to pacifist agitation, to the Kellogg-Briand Pact renouncing aggressive war (1928), and to **naval disarmament** pacts (Washington, 1922; London, 1930). But the League of Nations was able to arbitrate only minor disputes (Greece-Bulgaria, 1925). A number of countries pulled back from global contacts, as with American isolationism and Russia's separation from international capitalism.

Middle East. Mustafa Kemal (**Ataturk**) led **Turkish** nationalists in resisting Italian, French, and Greek military advances (1919-23). The sultanate was abolished (1922), and elaborate reforms were passed, including secularization of law and adoption of the Latin alphabet. Ethnic conflict led to persecution of **Armenians** (more than 1 million dead in 1915, 1 million expelled), Greeks (forced Greek-Turk population exchange, 1923), and Kurds (1925 uprising).

With evacuation of the Turks from **Arab** lands, the puritanical Wahabi dynasty of E Arabia conquered (1919-25) what is now Saudi Arabia. British, French, and Arab dynastic and nationalist maneuvering resulted in the creation of two more Arab monarchies in 1921—Iraq and Transjordan (both under British control)—and two French mandates—Syria and Lebanon. Jewish immigration into British-mandated **Palestine**, inspired by the Zionist movement, was resisted by Arabs, at times violently (1921, 1929 massacres).

Reza Khan ruled **Persia** after his 1921 coup (shah from 1925), centralized control, and created the trappings of a modern secular state.

In 1922, English archaeologist Howard Carter discovered the tomb of the boy pharaoh **Tutankhamun** in the Valley of the Kings in Egypt.

China. The Kuomintang under **Chiang Kai-shek** (1887-1975) subdued the warlords by 1928. The Communists were brutally suppressed after their alliance with the Kuomintang was broken in 1927. Relative peace thereafter allowed for industrial and financial improvements, with some Russian, British, and U.S. cooperation.

Arts. Nearly all bounds of subject matter, style, and attitude were broken in the arts of the period. **Abstract** art first took inspiration from natural forms or narrative themes (Kandinsky from 1911) and then worked free of any representational aims (Malevich's suprematism, 1915-19; Mondrian's geometric style from 1917). The **Dada** movement (from 1916) mocked artistic pretension with absurd collages and constructions. Paradox, illusion, and psychological taboos were exploited by **surrealists** by the late 1920s (Dali, Magritte). Architectural schools celebrated industrial values, whether vigorous abstract constructivism (Tatlin, *Monument to the Third International*, 1919) or the machined, streamlined **Bauhaus** style, which was extended to many design fields (Helvetica typeface).

Prose writers explored revolutionary narrative modes related to dreams (Kafka's *Trial*, 1925), internal monologue (Joyce's *Ulysses*, 1922), and word play (Stein's *Making of Americans*, 1925). Poets and novelists wrote of modern alienation (Eliot's ***Waste Land***, 1922) and aimlessness ("The Lost Generation").

Rise of Totalitarians: 1930-39

Depression. A worldwide financial panic and economic depression began with the Oct. 1929 U.S. stock market crash and the May 1931 failure of the Austrian Credit-Anstalt. A credit crunch caused international bankruptcies and **unemployment**: 12 million jobless by 1932 in the U.S., 5.6 million in Germany, 2.7 million in England. Governments responded with **tariff restrictions** (Smoot-Hawley Act, 1930; Ottawa Imperial Conference, 1932), which dried up world trade. Government public works programs were vitiated by deflationary budget balancing.

Germany. Years of agitation by violent extremists were brought to a head by the Depression. Nazi leader Adolf Hitler was named chancellor in Jan. 1933 and given dictatorial power by the Reichstag in Mar. Opposition parties were disbanded, strikes banned, and all aspects of economic, cultural, and religious life were brought under central government and Nazi party control and manipulated by sophisticated propaganda. Severe persecution of Jews began (**Nuremberg Laws**, Sept. 1935). Many Jews, political opponents, and others were sent to concentration camps (Dachau, 1933), where thousands died or were killed. Public works, renewed conscription (1935), arms production, and a four-year plan (1936) all but ended unemployment.

Hitler's expansionism started with reincorporation of the Saar (1935), occupation of the **Rhineland** (Mar. 1936), and annexation of Austria (Mar. 1938). At **Munich** (Sept. 1938)

Britain and France attempted to appease Hitler and avoid war by successfully encouraging Czechoslovakia's surrender of the Sudetenland territory.

Russia. Rapid industrialization was achieved through successive **five-year plans** starting in 1928, using severe labor discipline and mass forced labor. Industry was financed by exploitation of agriculture, which was almost totally collectivized by the early 1930s (*kolkhoz* [collective farm]; *sovkhoz* [state farm], often in newly worked lands). Millions perished in a series of manufactured disasters: extermination (1929-34) of kulaks (peasant landowners), severe famine (1932-33), party purges and show trials (Great Purge, 1936-38), suppression of nationalities, and poor conditions in labor camps. Purges also increased Stalin's power in the Communist party.

Spain. An industrial revolution during World War I created an urban proletariat, which was attracted to socialism and anarchism; Catalan nationalists challenged central authority. The five years after King Alfonso left Spain in Apr. 1931 were dominated by tension between intermittent leftist and anticlerical governments and clericals, monarchists, and other rightists. Anarchist and Communist rebellions were crushed, but a July 1936 extreme right rebellion led by Gen. Francisco **Franco** and aided by Nazi Germany and Fascist Italy succeeded after a three-year **civil war** (more than 1 million dead in battles and atrocities). The war polarized international public opinion.

Italy. Despite propaganda for the ideal of the Corporate State, few domestic reforms were attempted. An entente with Hungary and Austria (Mar. 1934), a pact with Germany and Japan (Nov. 1937), and intervention by 50,000-75,000 troops in Spain (1936-39) sealed Italy's identification with the fascist bloc (anti-Semitic laws after Mar. 1938). Ethiopia was conquered (1935-36) and Albania annexed (Jan. 1939) in conscious imitation of ancient Rome.

Eastern Europe. Repressive regimes fought for power against an active opposition (liberals, socialists, Communists, peasants, Nazis). Minority groups and Jews were restricted within national boundaries that did not coincide with ethnic population patterns. In the destruction of **Czechoslovakia**, Hungary occupied S Slovakia (Nov. 1938) and Ruthenia (Mar. 1939), and a pro-Nazi regime took power in the rest of Slovakia. Other boundary disputes (e.g., Poland-Lithuania, Yugoslavia-Bulgaria, and Romania-Hungary) doomed attempts to build joint fronts against Germany or Russia. Economic depression was severe.

East Asia. After a period of liberalism in **Japan**, nativist militarists dominated the government with peasant support. Manchuria was seized (Sept. 1931-Feb. 1932), and a puppet state was set up (Manchukuo). Adjacent Jehol (Inner Mongolia) was occupied in 1933. **China** proper was invaded in July 1937; large areas were conquered by Oct. 1938. Hundreds of thousands of rapes, murders, and other atrocities were attributed to the Japanese.

Communist forces left Kuomintang-besieged strongholds in the S of China in a Long March (1934-35) to the N. The Kuomintang-Communist civil war was suspended in Jan. 1937 in the face of threatening Japan.

Democracies. The Roosevelt Administration, in office Mar. 1933, embarked on an extensive program of **New Deal** social reform and economic stimulation, including protection for labor unions (heavy industries organized), Social Security, public works, wage-and-hour laws, and assistance to farmers. Isolationist sentiment (1937 Neutrality Act) prevented U.S. intervention in Europe, but military expenditures were increased in 1939.

French political instability and polarization prevented resolution of economic and international security questions. The **Popular Front** government under Leon Blum (June 1936-Apr. 1938) passed social reforms (40-hour work week) and raised arms spending. National coalition governments, which ruled Britain from Aug. 1931, brought economic recovery but failed to define a consistent international policy until Chamberlain's government (from May 1937), which practiced **appeasement** of Germany and Italy.

Italy's Benito Mussolini and Germany's Adolf Hitler affirmed their total political and military alliance with 1939's Pact of Steel.

India. Twenty years of agitation for autonomy and then for independence (Gandhi's **salt march**, 1930) achieved some constitutional reform (extended provincial powers, 1935) despite Muslim-Hindu strife. Social issues assumed prominence with peasant uprisings (1921), strikes (1928), Gandhi's efforts for untouchables (1932 "fast unto death"), and social and agrarian reform by the provinces after 1937.

Arts. The streamlined, geometric design motifs of Art Deco (from 1925) prevailed through the 1930s. **Abstract art** flourished (Moore sculptures from 1931) alongside a new **realism** related to social and political concerns (Socialist Realism, the official Soviet style from 1934; Mexican muralist Rivera, 1886-1957; and Orozco, 1883-1949), which were also expressed in fiction and poetry (Steinbeck's *Grapes of Wrath*, 1939; Sandburg's *The People, Yes*, 1936). Modern architecture (International Style, 1932) was unchallenged in its use of artificial materials (concrete, glass), lack of decoration, and monumentality (Rockefeller Center, 1929-40). Larger-than-life U.S.-made films captured a worldwide audience (*Gone With the Wind*, *The Wizard of Oz*, both 1939).

War, Hot and Cold: 1940-49

War in Asia-Pacific. Japan occupied Indochina in Sept. 1940, dominated Thailand in Dec. 1941, and attacked Hawaii (**Pearl Harbor**), the Philippines, Hong Kong, and Malaya on Dec. 7, 1941 (precipitating U.S. entrance into the war). Indonesia was attacked in Jan. 1942, and Burma was conquered in Mar. 1942. The Battle of **Midway** (June 1942) turned back the Japanese advance. "Island-hopping" battles (**Guadalcanal**, Aug. 1942-Jan. 1943; **Leyte Gulf**, Oct. 1944; **Iwo Jima**, Feb.-Mar. 1945; **Okinawa**, Apr. 1945) and massive bombing raids on Japan from June 1944 wore out Japanese defenses. U.S. atom bombs, dropped Aug. 6 and 9 on **Hiroshima** and **Nagasaki**, forced Japan to agree, on Aug. 14, to surrender; formal surrender was on Sept. 2, 1945.

War in Europe. The Nazi-Soviet nonaggression pact (Aug. 1939) freed Germany to attack Poland (Sept. 1939). Britain and France, which had guaranteed Polish independence, declared war on Germany. Russia seized E Poland (Sept. 1939), attacked Finland (Nov. 1939), and took the Baltic states (July 1940). Mobile German forces staged *blitzkrieg* attacks during Apr.-June 1940, conquering neutral Denmark, Norway, and the Low Countries and defeating France; 350,000 British and French troops were evacuated at **Dunkirk**, France (May). The **Battle of Britain** (June-Dec. 1940) denied Germany air superiority. German-Italian campaigns won the Balkans by Apr. 1941. Three million Axis troops **invaded Russia** in June 1941, marching through Ukraine to the Caucasus, and through White Russia and the Baltic republics to Moscow and Leningrad.

The U.S. bombing of Hiroshima and Nagasaki, Japan, in 1945 demonstrated the deadly, destructive power of atomic weapons and forced an end to World War II.

Russian winter counterthrusts (1941-42 and 1942-43) stopped the German advance (**Stalingrad**, Sept. 1942-Feb. 1943). Sustaining great casualties, the Russians drove the Axis from all E Europe and the Balkans in the next two years. Invasions of N Africa (Nov. 1942), Italy (Sept. 1943), and **Normandy** (launched on D-Day, June 6, 1944) brought U.S., British, Free French, and allied troops to Germany by spring 1945. In Feb. 1945, the three Allied leaders, Winston **Churchill** (Britain), Joseph **Stalin** (USSR), and Franklin D. **Roosevelt** (U.S.), met in Yalta to discuss strategy and resolve political issues, including the postwar Allied occupation of Germany. Germany surrendered May 7, 1945.

Atrocities. The war brought 20th-cent. cruelty to its peak. The Nazi regime systematically killed an estimated 5-6 million Jews, including some 3 million who died in death camps (e.g., **Auschwitz**). Gypsies, political opponents, people with mental or physical disabilities, and others deemed undesirable were also murdered by the Nazis, as were vast numbers of Slavs.

German bombs killed 70,000 British civilians. More than 100,000 Chinese civilians were killed by Japanese forces in the capture and occupation of Nanking. Severe retaliation by the Soviet army, E European partisans, Free French, and others took a heavy toll. U.S. and British bombing of Germany killed hundreds of thousands, as did U.S. bombing of Japan (80,000-200,000 at Hiroshima alone). Some 45 million people died in the war.

Settlement. The **United Nations** charter was signed in San Francisco on June 26, 1945, by 50 nations. The International Tribunal at **Nuremberg** convicted 22 German leaders for war crimes in Sept. 1946; 23 Japanese leaders were convicted in Nov. 1948. Postwar border changes included large gains in territory for the USSR, losses for Germany, a shift to the W in Polish borders, and minor losses for Italy. Communist regimes, supported by Soviet troops, took power in most of Eastern Europe, including Soviet-occupied Germany (GDR, a.k.a. East Germany, proclaimed Oct. 1949). Japan lost all overseas lands. Global developments involved establishing new economic coordinating bodies like the International Monetary Fund (1944) and the Universal Declaration of Human Rights (1948).

Recovery. Basic political and social changes were imposed on Japan and W Germany by the Western allies (Japan constitution adopted, Nov. 1946; W German basic law, May 1949). U.S. **Marshall Plan** aid ($12 bil, 1947-51) spurred W European economic recovery after a period of severe inflation and strikes in Europe and the U.S. The British Labour Party introduced a national health service and nationalized basic industries in 1946.

Cold War. Western fears of further Soviet advances (Cominform formed in Oct. 1947; Czechoslovakia coup, Feb. 1948; Berlin blockade, Apr. 1948-Sept. 1949) led to the formation of **NATO**. Civil war in Greece and Soviet pressure on Turkey led to U.S. aid under the **Truman Doctrine** (Mar. 1947). Other anti-Communist security pacts were the Organization of American States (Apr. 1948) and the SE Asia Treaty Organization (Sept. 1954). A new wave of **Soviet purges** and repression intensified in the last years of Stalin's rule, extending to E Europe (Slansky trial in Czechoslovakia, 1951). Only Yugoslavia resisted Soviet control (expelled by Cominform, June 1948; U.S. aid, June 1949).

China, Korea. Communist forces emerged from World War II strengthened by the Soviet takeover of industrial Manchuria. In four years of fighting, the Kuomintang was driven from the mainland; the People's Republic of China was proclaimed Oct. 1, 1949. Korea was divided by USSR and U.S. occupation forces. Separate republics were proclaimed in the two zones in Aug.-Sept. 1948.

India. India and Pakistan became independent dominions on Aug. 15, 1947. Millions of Hindu and Muslim refugees were created by the partition. Riots (1946-47) took hundreds of thousands of lives. Mahatma **Gandhi** was assassinated in Jan. 1948. Burma became completely independent in Jan. 1948; Ceylon took dominion status in Feb.

Middle East. The UN approved partition of Palestine into Jewish and Arab states. **Israel** was proclaimed a state, May 14, 1948. Arabs rejected partition, but failed to defeat Israel in war (May 1948-July 1949). Immigration from Europe and the Middle East swelled Israel's Jewish population. British and French forces left Lebanon and Syria in 1946. Transjordan occupied most of Arab Palestine.

Southeast Asia. Communists and others fought against restoration of French rule in **Indochina** from 1946; a non-Communist government was recognized by France in Mar. 1949, but fighting continued. Both Indonesia and the Philippines became independent; the former in 1949 after four years of war with the Netherlands, the latter in 1946. Philippine economic and military ties with the U.S. remained strong; a Communist-led peasant rising was checked in 1948.

Arts. New York became the center of the world art market; **abstract expressionism** was the chief mode (Pollock from 1943, de Kooning from 1947). Literature and philosophy explored **existentialism** (Camus's *The Stranger*, 1942; Sartre's *Being and Nothingness*, 1943). Non-Western attempts to revive or create regional styles (Senghor's Négritude, Mishima's novels) were responses to global cultural influences. Radio and phonograph records spread American popular music (swing, bebop) around the world.

The Cold War Decade: 1950-59

Decolonization. The relatively peaceful decline of European political and military power in Asia and Africa accelerated in the 1950s. Nearly all of **N Africa** was freed by 1956, but France fought a bitter war to retain Algeria, with its large European minority, until 1962. **Ghana**, independent in 1957, led a parade of new black African nations (more than two dozen by 1962), which altered the political character of the UN. Ethnic disputes often exploded in the new nations after decolonization (UN troops in Cyprus, 1964; **Nigerian civil war**, 1967-70). Leaders of the new states, mostly sharing socialist ideologies, tried to create an Afro-Asian bloc (Bandung Conference, 1955), but Western economic influence and U.S. political ties remained strong (Baghdad Pact, 1955).

Trade. World trade volume soared, in an atmosphere of monetary stability assured by international accords (**Bretton Woods**, 1944). In Europe, economic integration advanced (**European Economic Community**, 1957; European Free Trade Association, 1960). Comecon (1949) coordinated the economies of Soviet-bloc countries. Global developments included transcontinental jet travel (first South Africa to Britain flight, 1952; introduction of term "jet lag," 1965) and the increasing spread of English in global business, sports, and transportation.

U.S. Economic growth produced an abundance of consumer goods (9.3 million motor vehicles sold, 1955). Suburban housing changed life patterns for middle and working classes (Levittown, NY, 1947-51). Pres. Dwight **Eisenhower**'s landslide election victories (1952, 1956) reflected consensus politics. A system of alliances and military bases bolstered U.S. influence on all continents. Trade and payments surpluses were balanced by overseas investments and foreign aid ($50 bil, 1950-59).

USSR. In the "thaw" after Stalin's death in 1953, relations with the West improved (evacuation of Vienna, Geneva summit conference, both 1955). Repression of scientific and cultural life eased, and many prisoners were freed culminating in **de-Stalinization** (1956). Nikita **Khrushchev**'s leadership aimed at consumer sector growth, but farm production lagged, despite the virgin lands program (from 1954). Soviet crushing of the 1956 Hungarian revolution, the 1960 U-2 spy plane episode, and other incidents renewed E-W tension and domestic curbs.

Eastern Europe. Resentment of Russian domination and Stalinist repression combined with nationalist, economic, and religious factors to produce periodic violence. E Berlin workers rioted (1953), Polish workers rioted in Poznan (June 1956), and a broad-based **revolution** broke out in **Hungary** (Oct. 1956). All were suppressed by Soviet force or threats (at least 7,000 dead in Hungary), but Poland was allowed to restore private ownership of farms, and a degree of personal and economic freedom returned to Hungary. Yugoslavia experimented with worker self-management and a market economy.

Korea. The 1945 division of Korea along the 38th parallel left industry in the N, which was organized into a militant regime and armed by the USSR. The S was politically disunited. More than 60,000 N Korean troops invaded the S on June 25, 1950. The U.S., backed by the UN Security Council, sent troops. **UN troops** reached the Chinese border in Nov. Some 200,000 Chinese troops crossed the Yalu R. and drove back UN forces. By spring 1951, battle lines had become stabilized near the original 38th parallel border, but heavy fighting continued. Finally, an armistice was signed on July 27, 1953. U.S. troops remained in the S, and U.S. economic and military aid continued. The war stimulated rapid economic recovery in Japan.

China. Starting in 1952, industry, agriculture, and social institutions were forcibly collectivized. In a massive purge, as many as several million people were executed as Kuomintang supporters or as class and political enemies. The **Great Leap Forward** (1958-60) unsuccessfully tried to force the pace of development by substituting labor for investment.

Southeast Asia. Ho Chi Minh's forces, aided by the USSR and the new Chinese Communist government, fought French and pro-French Vietnamese forces to a standstill and captured the strategic **Dien Bien Phu** camp in May 1954. The Geneva Agreements divided Vietnam in half pending elections (never held) and recognized Laos and Cambodia as independent. The U.S. aided the anti-Communist Republic of Vietnam in the S.

Middle East. Arab revolutions placed leftist, militantly nationalist regimes in power in Egypt (1952) and Iraq (1958). But Arab unity attempts failed (United Arab Republic joined Egypt, Syria, Yemen, 1958-61). Arab refusal to recognize Israel (Arab League economic blockade began Sept. 1951) led to a permanent **state of war**, with repeated incidents (Gaza, 1955). Israel occupied Sinai, and Britain and France took (Oct. 1956) the Suez Canal, but were replaced by the UN Emergency Force. The Mossadegh government in Iran nationalized (May 1951) the British-owned oil industry in May, but was overthrown (Aug. 1953) in a U.S.-aided coup.

Latin America. Argentinian dictator Juan **Perón**, in office 1946, crushed opposition and enforced land reform, some nationalization, welfare state measures, and curbs on the Roman Catholic Church. A Sept. 1955 coup deposed Perón. The 1952 revolution in Bolivia brought land reform, nationalization of tin mines, and improvement in the status of Native Americans, who nevertheless remained poor. The Batista regime in Cuba was overthrown (Jan. 1959) by Fidel **Castro**, who imposed a Communist dictatorship, aligned Cuba with the USSR and improved education and health care. A U.S.-backed anti-Castro invasion (**Bay of Pigs**, Apr. 1961) was crushed. Self-government advanced in the British Caribbean.

Technology. Large outlays on research and development in the U.S. and the USSR focused on military applications (H-bomb in U.S., 1952; USSR, 1953; Britain, 1957; intercontinental missiles, late 1950s). Soviet launching of the **Sputnik** satellite (Oct. 4, 1957) spurred increases in U.S. science education funds (National Defense Education Act).

Literature and film. Alienation from social and literary conventions reached an extreme in the theater of the absurd (Beckett's *Waiting for Godot*, 1952), the "new novel" (Robbe-Grillet's *Voyeur*, 1955), and avant-garde film (Antonioni's *L'Avventura*, 1960). U.S. beatniks (Kerouac's *On the Road*, 1957) and others rejected the supposed conformism of Americans (Riesman's *The Lonely Crowd*, 1950).

Rising Expectations and New Protests: 1960-69

Global economy. The longest sustained economic boom on record spanned almost the entire decade in the capitalist world; the closely watched GNP figure doubled (1960-70) in the U.S., fueled by **Vietnam War**-related budget deficits. The **General Agreement on Tariffs and Trade** (1967) stimulated Western European prosperity, which spread to peripheral areas (Spain, Italy, E Germany). Japan became a top economic power. Foreign investment aided the industrialization of Brazil. There were limited Soviet economic reform attempts. Outside the Soviet zone the global economy was marked by the growing role of multinational corporations (3,000 in 1914; 6,000 by 1970). International nongovernmental organizations (NGOs) also multiplied rapidly (Amnesty International, 1961).

Reform and radicalization. Pres. John F. **Kennedy**, inaugurated 1961, emphasized youthful idealism and vigor; his assassination Nov. 22, 1963, was a national trauma. Political and social reform movements took root in U.S. and other countries. Blacks demonstrated nonviolently and with partial success against segregation and poverty (1963 March on Washington; 1964 **Civil Rights Act**), but some urban areas erupted in riots (Watts, 1965; Detroit, 1967; **Martin Luther King Jr.** assassination, Apr. 4, 1968). New concern for the poor (Harrington's *Other America*, 1963) helped lead to Pres. Lyndon Johnson's **"Great Society"** programs (Medicare, Water Quality Act, Higher Education Act, all 1965). Concern for the **environment** surged (Carson's *Silent Spring*, 1962).

Feminism revived as a cultural and political movement (Friedan's *Feminine Mystique*, 1963; National Organization for Women founded, 1966), and a movement for homosexual rights emerged (Stonewall riot in NYC, 1969). Pope John XXIII called the **Second Vatican Council** (1962-65), which liberalized Roman Catholic liturgy and some other aspects of Catholicism.

Opposition to U.S. involvement in Vietnam, especially among university students (**Moratorium** protest, Nov. 1969), turned violent (Weatherman Chicago riots, Oct. 1969). **New Left** and Marxist theories became popular, and membership in radical groups (Students for a Democratic Society, Black Panthers) increased. Maoist groups, especially in Europe, called for total transformation of society. In France, students sparked a nationwide strike affecting 10 million workers in May-June 1968.

China. China's revolutionary militancy under **Mao** Zedong led to border disputes and other conflict with the USSR under "revisionist" Khrushchev, starting in 1960. The **"Great**

Independence did not ensure post-colonial democracy: Congo's first elected prime minister, Patrice Lumumba (left), was assassinated (1961) shortly after his 12-week-old government was deposed by Pres. Joseph Kasa-Vubu (right).

Proletarian Cultural Revolution" tried to impose a utopian egalitarian program in China and spread revolution abroad; political struggle, often violent, convulsed China in 1965-68.

Southeast Asia. Communist-led guerrillas aided by N Vietnam fought from 1960 against the S Vietnam government of Ngo Dinh Diem (killed 1963). The U.S. military role increased after the 1964 **Tonkin Gulf** incident. Laotian and Cambodian neutrality were threatened by Communist insurgencies, with N Vietnamese aid, and U.S. intrigues.

Developing world. A bloc of authoritarian leftist regimes among the newly independent nations came to dominate the conference of nonaligned nations (Belgrade, 1961; Cairo, 1964; Lusaka, 1970). Soviet political ties and military bases were established in Cuba, Egypt, Algeria, Guinea, and other countries. Some leaders were ousted in coups by pro-Western groups—Dem. Rep. of the Congo's Patrice Lumumba (killed 1961), Ghana's Kwame Nkrumah (exiled 1966), and Indonesia's Sukarno (effectively ousted in 1965 after a Communist coup failed).

Middle East. Arab-Israeli tension erupted into a brief war June 1967. Israel emerged from the war as a major regional power. Military shipments before and after the war increased Soviet influence in much of the Arab world. Most Arab states broke U.S. diplomatic ties, while Communist countries cut their ties to Israel. Intra-Arab disputes continued: Egypt and Saudi Arabia supported rival factions in a bloody Yemen civil war 1962-70; Lebanese troops fought Palestinian commandos 1969.

Eastern Europe. To stop the large-scale exodus of citizens, E German authorities built (Aug. 1961) a fortified **wall across Berlin**. Soviet sway in the Balkans was weakened by Albania's support of China (USSR broke ties in Dec. 1961) and Romania's assertion (1964) of limited autonomy. Liberalization (spring 1968) in Czechoslovakia was crushed with massive force by troops of five Warsaw Pact countries. W German treaties (1970) with the USSR and Poland facilitated transfer of German technology and confirmed postwar boundaries.

Arts and styles. The boundary between fine and popular arts was blurred to some extent by Pop Art (Warhol) and rock musicals (*Hair*, 1968). Informality and exaggeration prevailed in fashion (beards, miniskirts). A nonpolitical "counterculture" developed, rejecting traditional bourgeois life goals and personal habits, and use of marijuana and hallucinogens spread (**Woodstock** festival, Aug. 1969). **The Beatles** brought unprecedented sophistication to rock music.

Science. Achievements in space (**humans on the moon**, July 1969) and electronics (lasers, integrated circuits) encouraged a faith in scientific solutions to problems in agriculture ("green revolution"), medicine (heart transplants, 1967), and other areas. Harmful technology, it was believed, could be controlled (1963 Limited Test Ban Treaty, 1968 Nuclear Nonproliferation Treaty).

New Global Balances and Religious Revivals: 1970-79

U.S.: Caution and neoconservatism. A sluggish economy, energy shortages, and environmental problems contributed to a **"limits of growth"** philosophy. Suspicion of science and technology killed or delayed some projects (supersonic transport dropped, 1971). The Three Mile Island nuclear reactor accident (Mar. 1979) reinforced fears of nuclear energy.

There was some backlash against social change. School busing and racial quotas were opposed (Bakke decision, June 1978); Equal Rights Amendment for women languished; legislation aimed at protecting homosexuals was opposed.

Completion of Communist forces' takeover of **South Vietnam** (evacuation of U.S. civilians, Apr. 1975), revelations of Central Intelligence Agency misdeeds (Rockefeller Commission report, June 1975), and **Watergate** scandals (Nixon resigned in Aug. 1974) reduced faith in U.S. moral and material capacity to influence world affairs. Revelations of Soviet crimes (Solzhenitsyn's *Gulag Archipelago*, 1974) and Soviet intervention in Africa helped foster a revival of anti-Communist sentiment.

Economy sluggish. The 1960s boom faltered in the 1970s; a severe recession in the U.S. and Europe (1974-75) followed a huge oil price hike (Dec. 1973). Monetary instability (U.S. cut ties to gold in Aug. 1971), the decline of the dollar, and protectionist moves by industrial countries (1977-78) threatened trade. Business investment declined. Severe inflation plagued many countries (25% in Britain, 1975; 18% in U.S., 1979).

The fall of Saigon (1975) marked the end of the war in Vietnam as Americans and some South Vietnamese evacuated the city.

China readjusts. After the 1976 deaths of Mao Zedong and Zhou Enlai, pragmatists won the struggle for leadership. A nationwide purge of orthodox Maoists ensued, and the **Gang of Four**, led by Mao's widow, Chiang Ching, was arrested. The new leaders freed more than 100,000 political prisoners and reduced public adulation of Mao. Political and trade ties expanded Japan, Europe, and the U.S. in the late 1970s, as relations worsened with the USSR, Cuba, and Vietnam (four-week invasion by China, 1979). Ideological guidelines, were reversed (bonuses to workers, Dec. 1977; exams for college entrance, Oct. 1977). Some restrictions on cultural expression were eased.

Europe. European unity moves (EEC-EFTA trade accord, 1972) faltered as economic problems appeared (Britain floated pound, 1972; France floated franc, 1974). Germany and Switzerland curbed guest workers from S Europe. Greece and Turkey quarreled over Cyprus and Aegean oil rights.

All non-Communist Europe was under democratic rule after free elections (June 1976) in **Spain** seven months after the death of Franco. The conservative, colonialist regime in **Portugal** was overthrown in Apr. 1974. In **Greece** the seven-year military dictatorship yielded power in 1974. The **British** Labour government imposed (1975) wage curbs and suspended nationalization schemes. Terrorism in **Germany** (1972 Munich Olympics killings) led to laws curbing some civil liberties. **French** "new philosophers" rejected leftist ideologies, and the Socialist-Communist coalition lost a 1978 election bid.

Religion and politics. The improvement in **Muslim** countries' political fortunes by the 1950s (with the exception of Central Asia under Soviet and Chinese rule) and the growth of Arab oil wealth were followed by a resurgence of traditional religious fervor. Libyan dictator Muammar al-**Qaddafi** mixed Islamic laws with socialism. The illegal Muslim Brotherhood in **Egypt** was accused of violence, while extreme groups bombed (1977) theaters to protest Western and secular values.

In **Turkey**, the National Salvation Party was the first Islamic group to share (1974) power since secularization in the 1920s. In **Iran**, Ayatollah Ruhollah **Khomeini** led a revolution that deposed the secular shah (Jan. 1979) and created an Islamic republic. Religiously motivated Muslims took part in an insurrection in **Saudi Arabia** that briefly seized (1979) the Grand Mosque in Mecca. Muslim puritan opposition to **Pakistan** Pres. Zulfikar Ali-Bhutto helped lead to his overthrow in July 1977. Muslim solidarity, however, could not prevent Pakistan's eastern province (**Bangladesh**) from declaring (Dec. 1971) independence after a bloody civil war.

Muslim and Hindu resentment of coerced sterilization in **India** helped defeat the Indira Gandhi government, and a coalition including religious Hindu parties replaced it (Mar. 1977). Muslims in the S **Philippines**, aided by Libya, rebelled against central rule from 1973. The Buddhist Soka Gakkai movement launched (1964) the Komeito party in **Japan**, which became a major opposition party in 1972 and 1976 elections.

Evangelical Protestant groups grew in the U.S. A revival of interest in Orthodox Christianity occurred among **Russian** intellectuals (Solzhenitsyn). The secularist **Israeli** Labor party, after decades of rule, was ousted in 1977 by conservatives led by Menachem Begin; religious militants founded settlements on the disputed West Bank, part of biblically promised Israel. Reform Judaism in U.S. revived many traditional practices.

Religious wars raged in **Northern Ireland** (Catholic vs. Protestant, 1969-97) and **Lebanon** (Christian vs. Muslim, 1975-90), while religious militancy complicated the Israel-Arab dispute (1973 Israel-Arab war). The Camp David Accords in 1978, negotiated by Egyptian Pres. Anwar al-Sadat, Israeli Prime Min. Menachem Begin, and U.S. Pres. Jimmy Carter, facilitated the landmark 1979 **Egypt-Israel peace treaty**, but increased militancy on the West Bank impeded further progress.

Latin America. Repressive conservative regimes strengthened their hold, with a violent coup against the elected (Sept. 1973) **Allende** government in **Chile**, military coup in **Argentina** (1976), and coups against reformist regimes in **Bolivia** (1971, 1979) and **Peru** (1976). In Central America, increasing liberal and leftist militancy led to the ouster (1979) of the **Somoza** regime of **Nicaragua** and to civil conflict in **El Salvador**.

Southeast Asia. Communist victories in Vietnam, Cambodia, and Laos by May 1975 led to new turmoil. The **Pol Pot** regime in **Cambodia** ordered millions to resettle in rural areas, in a program of forced labor and terrorism that cost more than 1 million lives (1975-79) and caused hundreds of thousands to flee. The Vietnamese invasion of Cambodia (1979) swelled the refugee population and contributed to widespread starvation.

Russian expansion. Soviet influence, checked in some countries (troops ousted by Egypt, 1972), was projected farther afield, often with the use of Cuban troops (Angola, 1975-89; Ethiopia, 1977-88). **Détente** with the West—1972 Berlin pact, 1972 strategic arms pact (**SALT**)—gave way to a more antagonistic relationship in the late 1970s, exacerbated by the Soviet invasion (1979) of **Afghanistan**.

Africa. The last remaining European colonies were granted independence (**Spanish Sahara**, 1976; **Djibouti**, 1977), and, after 10 years of civil war, a black government took over (1979) in **Zimbabwe** (Rhodesia); white domination remained in **South Africa**. European involvement in local wars (Russia in **Angola**, **Ethiopia**; France in **Chad**, **Zaire**, **Mauritania**) and the use of tens of thousands of Cuban troops were denounced by some African leaders. Ethnic or tribal clashes made Africa a locus of sustained warfare during the late 1970s.

End of the Cold War and Demand for Democracy: 1980-89

Global developments. International contacts accelerated thanks to new openness in China (1978) and USSR (1985); global consumerism was symbolized by the rapid spread of McDonald's restaurants (Japan, 1971; Russia, 1990).

USSR, Eastern Europe. The late 1980s saw the remaking of the Soviet state and the beginning of the disintegration of the Soviet empire. After the deaths of Gen. Sec. Leonid **Brezhnev** (1982) and two successors, the harsh treatment of dissent and restriction of emigration, and the Soviet invasion (Dec. 1979) of Afghanistan, Gen. Sec. Mikhail **Gorbachev** (in office 1985-91) promoted ***glasnost*** and ***perestroika***—economic, political, and social reform. Supported by the Communist Party (July 1988), he signed (Dec. 1987) the INF nuclear disarmament treaty. Military withdrawal from Afghanistan was completed in Feb. 1989, and the Soviet people chose (Mar. 1989) part of the new Congress of People's Deputies from competing candidates. By decade's end the **Cold War** appeared to be fading away.

In **Poland**, Solidarity, the labor union founded (1980) by Lech Walesa, was outlawed in 1982 but legalized in 1988, after years of unrest. Poland's first free election since the Communist takeover brought **Solidarity** victory (June 1989); Tadeusz Mazowiecki, a Walesa adviser, became prime minister in a government with the Communists. In fall 1989 the failure of Marxist economies in **Hungary**, **East Germany**, **Czechoslovakia**, **Bulgaria**, and **Romania** brought the collapse of the Communist monopoly and a demand for democracy. In a historic step, the **Berlin Wall** was opened in Nov. 1989.

The Berlin Wall, which had divided East and West Berlin since 1961, was opened in Nov. 1989.

U.S. The **"Reagan Years"** (1981-88) featured new economic policies via budget and tax cuts, deregulation, "junk bond" financing, leveraged buyouts, and mergers. However, there was a stock market crash (Oct. 1987), and federal budget deficits and the trade deficit increased. Foreign policy showed a **strong anti-Communist stance**, via increased defense spending, aid to anti-Communists in Central America, invasion of Cuba-threatened Grenada, and championing of the "Star Wars" missile defense program. Four Reagan-Gorbachev summits (1985-88) climaxed in the INF treaty (1987). The **Iran-Contra affair** (Oliver North testimony, July 1987) was a major political scandal.

Middle East. The Middle East remained militarily unstable, with sharp divisions along economic, political, racial, and religious lines. In **Iran**, the Islamic revolution of 1979 created a strong anti-U.S. stance (hostage crisis, Nov. 1979-Jan. 1981). In Sept. 1980, **Iraq** repudiated its border agreement with Iran and began major hostilities that led to an eight-year war in which hundreds of thousands were killed.

Libya's support for international terrorism induced the U.S. to close (May 1981) its diplomatic mission there and embargo (Mar. 1982) Libyan oil. Following an attack on a West Berlin disco frequented by U.S. military, U.S. bombed targets in Libya (Apr. 1986).

Israel affirmed (July 1980) all Jerusalem as its capital, destroyed (June 1981) an Iraqi atomic reactor, and invaded **Lebanon**, citing terrorism from the Palestine Liberation Organization; PLO withdrew from Lebanon after cease-fire. A **Palestinian uprising** began (Dec. 1987) in Israeli-occupied Gaza and spread to the West Bank; troops responded with force, killing 300 by the end of 1988, with 6,000 more in detention camps. Israeli withdrawal from Lebanon began in Feb. 1985 and ended in June 1985, as Lebanon continued to be torn by military and political conflict. Artillery duels (Mar.-Apr. 1989) between Christian East Beirut and Muslim West Beirut left 200 dead.

Latin America. In **Nicaragua**, the leftist Sandinista National Liberation Front, in power after the 1979 civil war, faced problems as a result of Nicaragua's military aid to leftist guerrillas in El Salvador and U.S. backing of antigovernment contras. The CIA admitted (1984) having directed the mining of Nicaraguan ports, and the U.S. sent humanitarian (1985) and military (1986) aid. Profits from U.S. **secret arms sales** to Iran were found (1987) diverted to contras. Cease-fire talks between the Sandinista government and contras came in 1988, and elections were held in Nicaragua in Feb. 1990.

In **El Salvador**, a military coup (Oct. 1979) failed to halt extremist terrorism. Archbishop Oscar Romero was assassinated in Mar. 1980; from Jan. to June some 4,000 civilians were killed

The Chinese government responded to pro-democracy demonstrations in Tiananmen Square with force (1989).

in the civil unrest. In 1984, newly elected Pres. José Napoleon Duarte worked to stem human rights abuses, but violence continued. In **Chile**, Gen. Augusto Pinochet yielded the presidency after a democratic election (Dec. 1989) but remained as head of the army. He had ruled the country since 1973, imposing harsh measures against leftists and dissidents.

Africa. The 1980s saw continuing economic decline in virtually all African countries, a result of accelerating desertification, the world economic recession, heavy indebtedness to overseas creditors, rapid population growth, and political instability. Some 60 million Africans faced prolonged hunger in 1981. Much of Africa had one of the worst **droughts** ever in 1983, and by year's end, one-third of the population, or about 150 million, were near **famine**. Live Aid, a marathon rock concert, was presented in July 1985, and the U.S. and Western nations sent aid in Sept. 1985. Wars in Ethiopia and Sudan and military strife in several other nations continued. **HIV/AIDS** took a heavy toll.

Anti-apartheid sentiment gathered force in **South Africa**, with demonstrations meeting violent police response. White voters approved (Nov. 1983) the first constitution to give "Coloureds" (people of mixed-race background) and Asians a voice, while still excluding the black majority. The U.S. imposed economic sanctions in Aug. 1985, and 11 Western nations followed in Sept. Pres. P. W. **Botha** was succeeded (Sept. 1989) by F. W. **de Klerk**, who promised negotiation with the black population.

Asia and the Pacific. Benazir **Bhutto** became the first woman to lead a majority-Muslim nation as prime minister of **Pakistan** (Dec. 1988). The "people power" revolt in the **Philippines** ousted Ferdinand **Marcos** (Feb. 1986) after two decades as president; he was replaced by Corazon **Aquino**.

During the 1980s **China**'s Communist government and paramount leader **Deng** Xiaoping expanded commercial and technical ties to the West and the role of market forces. In Apr. 1989 student demonstrators camped out in **Tiananmen Square**, Beijing, in a peaceful call for political reform. Some 100,000 students and workers marched; at least 20 other cities saw protests. In response, martial law was imposed. Army troops crushed the demonstration in and around Tiananmen Square on June 3-4, with death toll estimates of 500-7,000, up to 10,000 dissidents arrested, and 31 people tried and executed. The conciliatory Communist Party chief was ousted; the Politburo adopted (July 1989) reforms against official corruption.

Japan's relations with other nations, especially the U.S., were dominated by **trade imbalances** favoring Japan. Western Europe and the U.S. accused Japan of restrictive trade policies.

Europe. With the addition of Greece, Portugal, and Spain, the European Community became a common market of more than 300 million people. Margaret **Thatcher** became the first British prime minister in the 20th cent. to win a third consecutive term (1987). **France** elected (1981) its first socialist president, François **Mitterrand**, who was reelected in 1988. Elections in 1983 brought **Italy** its first socialist premier, Bettino **Craxi**.

International terrorism. With the 1979 **overthrow of the shah** of Iran and with instablity in the Middle East, terrorism became a prominent tactic. In 1979-81, Iranian militants held 52 **U.S. hostages in Iran** for 444 days. In 1983 a TNT-laden suicide terrorist blew up U.S. Marine headquarters in Beirut, Lebanon, killing 241 Americans; almost simultaneously, a truck bomb blew up a French paratrooper barracks, killing 58. The ***Achille Lauro*** cruise ship was hijacked in Oct. 1985, and an American passenger killed. Incidents rose to 700 in 1985 and to 1,000 in 1988. **Assassinated leaders** included Egypt's Pres. Anwar al-**Sadat** (1981), India's Prime Min. Indira **Gandhi** (1984), and Lebanese Prem. Rashid **Karami** (1987).

New Regional Tensions in the Post-Cold War World: 1990-99

Global developments. Nations in the 1990s made post-Cold War adjustments; a growing awareness of globalization developed with growth of the **Internet** and spread of democracy and economic cooperation (Group of 20 formed, Sept. 1999). Some elements of globalization met with massive protests (World Trade Org. meeting in Seattle, Nov.-Dec. 1999). Efforts to deal with environmental change intensified with tentative agreements in Kyoto, Japan (1997).

Soviet Empire breakup. The breakup of the Soviet Union into 15 independent states began with declarations of independence by the Baltic republics of **Lithuania**, **Latvia**, and **Estonia** during an abortive coup against Mikhail **Gorbachev** (Aug. 1991). Other republics followed. In Dec. 1991, **Russia**, **Ukraine**, and **Belarus** declared the Soviet Union dead; Gorbachev resigned. The Warsaw Pact and the Council for Mutual Economic Assistance (Comecon) were disbanded. Most of the former Soviet republics joined in a loose confederation called the **Commonwealth of Independent States**. Russia's people suffered severe economic hardship as the nation, under Pres. Boris **Yeltsin**, moved to reboot the economy under a free market system.

The Muslim republic of **Chechnya** declared independence from Russia, leading to an invasion by Russian troops (Dec. 1994). A cease-fire took hold in 1996, and Russians withdrew. In 1999 Russia forcibly suppressed Muslim insurgents in Dagestan and entered Chechnya, again fighting separatist rebels. Yeltsin resigned Dec. 31, 1999, to be replaced by Vladimir **Putin** (elected in his own right, Mar. 2000).

Europe. **Yugoslavia** broke apart, and hostilities ensued along ethnic and religious lines. **Croatia**, **Slovenia**, and **Macedonia** declared independence (1991), followed by **Bosnia-Herzegovina** (1992). **Serbia** and **Montenegro** remained as the republic of Yugoslavia. Bitter fighting followed, especially in Bosnia, where Serbs reportedly engaged in **"ethnic cleansing"** of the Muslim population; a peace plan (Dayton accord, 1995), was brokered by the U.S., with **NATO** responsible for policing its implementation. In spring 1999, NATO conducted a bombing campaign aimed at stopping Yugoslavia from driving out ethnic Albanians from the **Kosovo** region; a peace accord

South African anti-apartheid activist Nelson Mandela served over 27 years in jail before release; he was elected president of South Africa four years later (1994).

was reached in June under which NATO peacekeeping troops entered Kosovo.

The **two Germanys were reunited** after 45 years (Oct. 1990). The union was greeted with jubilation, but economic stresses followed. Czechoslovakia broke apart peacefully (Jan. 1993), becoming the **Czech Republic** and **Slovakia**. In **Poland**, labor leader Lech **Walesa** was elected president (Dec. 1991).

NATO approved the **Partnership for Peace** Program (Jan. 1994) coordinating the defense of E and Central European countries, which Russia later joined. NATO signed a pact with **Russia** (1997) providing for NATO expansion into the former Soviet-bloc countries. The Czech Republic, **Hungary**, and Poland became NATO members in Jan. 1999. Efforts toward European unity continued with adoption of a single market (Jan. 1993) and conversion of the European Community to the **European Union** as the Maastricht Treaty took effect (Nov. 1993). Agreement was reached for 11 EU members to adopt a common currency **(euro)** in Jan. 1999.

An intraparty revolt forced Margaret **Thatcher** out as prime minister of the **UK**, to be succeeded by John **Major** (Nov. 1990); seven years later, Labour was returned to power under Tony **Blair** (May 1997). The divorce of Prince **Charles and Diana**, followed by the death of Diana (Aug. 1997), made headlines around the world. Talks on peace in **Northern Ireland** that included Sinn Fein, political arm of the Irish Republican Army, led to a peace plan, approved in an all-Ireland vote (May 1998). In Dec. 1999, Northern Ireland was granted home rule. In **Scotland** voters overwhelmingly approved establishment of a regional legislature (1997), and in **Wales** voters narrowly approved establishment of a local assembly (1997). The Church of England began to ordain women as priests (1994).

Middle East. In Aug. 1990, **Iraq**'s Saddam Hussein ordered troops to invade **Kuwait**. The UN approved military action (Nov. 1990). An international military force led by the U.S. bombed Iraq (Jan. 1991) and launched a land attack, crushing the invasion (Feb. 1991). Iraq accepted the terms of a cease-fire (Apr. 1991), and U.S. troops withdrew. The UN imposed **sanctions** on Iraq for failure to abide by the cease-fire. Iraq's reported failure to cooperate with UN inspectors seeking to eliminate **weapons of mass destruction** led to airstrikes by the U.S. and Britain (1998, 2001).

Israel and the **PLO** signed a peace accord (Sept. 1993) providing for Palestinian self-government in the West Bank and Gaza Strip. Prime Min. Yitzhak **Rabin** and Foreign Min. Shimon **Peres** of Israel and Yasir **Arafat** of the PLO received the Nobel Peace Prize for their efforts (1994). Six Arab nations relaxed boycott against Israel (1994), and Israel and **Jordan** signed a peace treaty (Oct. 1994). Rabin was assassinated (Nov. 1995) by an Israeli opponent of the peace process. Benjamin **Netanyahu** became prime minister (May 1996). Arafat was elected to the presidency of the Palestinian Authority (Jan. 1996).

Asia and the Pacific. **Hong Kong** was returned to **China** (July 1997) after 156 years as a British colony, and **Macao** reverted to China (Dec. 1999) after over 400 years of Portuguese rule. Both were to retain their legal and economic systems for 50 years. **Jiang** Zemin, general secretary of the Chinese Communist Party, assumed the additional post of president of China (Mar. 1993). China released from prison—and exiled—some well-known dissidents but continued to earn criticism for **human rights abuses**. In Nov. 1999 the U.S. and China signed a landmark pact normalizing trade relations. China's annual economic growth reached 10% and more.

After years of prosperity, **Thailand**, **Indonesia**, and **South Korea** in 1997 began to suffer economic reverses that had a worldwide ripple effect. All three received IMF bailout packages. In **Indonesia**, protests over mismanagement led to the resignation of Pres. Suharto (May 1998) after 32 years of nearly autocratic rule. In a referendum (Aug. 1999), **East Timor** voted overwhelmingly for independence; pro-Indonesian militias rampaged through the territory, but a multinational **peacekeeping force** helped restore order (Sept. 1999). In South Korea, former dissident **Kim** Dae-jung was elected president (Dec. 1997).

In Japan members of a religious cult released the nerve gas sarin on **Tokyo subway**, killing 12 people and injuring more than 5,500 (Mar. 1995). Tamil rebels continued their armed conflict in **Sri Lanka**. In **Afghanistan** the **Taliban**, an extreme Islamic fundamentalist group, gained control of Kabul (Sept. 1996) and, eventually, most of the country. In **North Korea**, longtime dictator **Kim Il Sung** died (July 1994), to be succeeded by son **Kim Jong Il**. In the same year the country signed an agreement with the U.S. setting a timetable for North Korea to eliminate its **nuclear program**. The country also suffered from severe drought and famine conditions.

Margaret Thatcher, Britain's longest-serving prime minister of the 20th century, was replaced in 1990 by John Major, a member of her own Conservative Party.

Indian army troops repeatedly clashed with pro-independence demonstrators in the disputed Muslim region of **Kashmir**, exacerbating relations with **Pakistan**. India and Pakistan both conducted nuclear tests in 1998. Conflict in Pakistan between government and the military led to a bloodless coup (Oct. 1999).

Africa. **South Africa**'s Pres. F. W. **de Klerk** released dissident Nelson **Mandela** from prison (Feb. 1990) after 27 years, and lifted a ban on the black nationalist African National Congress. The white minority government repealed apartheid laws (1990, 1991). Mandela was elected president (Apr. 1994), and a new constitution became law (Dec. 1996). In **Nigeria**, Gen. Olusegun Obasanjo was elected (Feb. 1999), the country's first civilian leader in 15 years. The decades-long rule of **Mobutu** Sese Seko in **Zaire** came to an end (May 1997) at the hands of rebel forces led by Laurent **Kabila**. Kabila changed the country's name back to **Democratic Republic of the Congo**; conditions remained unstable.

Factional fighting erupted in **Somalia** (Jan. 1991). The UN sent a U.S.-led **peacekeeping force**, but it was unsuccessful in restoring order. The UN ended its mission (Mar. 1995) with no durable government in place. **Liberia** endured factional fighting that lasted almost five years and claimed over 150,000 lives; a cease-fire was reached in Aug. 1995.

After the presidents of **Burundi** and **Rwanda** were killed in an airplane crash (Apr. 1994), violence erupted in Rwanda; Hutu extremists killed hundreds of thousands of minority Tutsis and moderate Hutus in a genocide. The World Health Organization reported (1995) that Africa accounted for 70% of **AIDS** cases worldwide.

A 16-year civil war appeared to end in **Angola** (May 1991) when the government signed a peace accord with the rebel UNITA faction. **Namibia** officially became independent in Mar. 1990 after almost 20 years under UN trusteeship. In **Algeria**, the army cancelled a second round of parliamentary elections (Jan. 1992) after the Islamic party won a first round. Ensuing violence by **Islamic fundamentalists** claimed thousands of lives; a peace plan was worked out in 1999.

North America. The **North American Free Trade Agreement** (NAFTA), liberalizing trade between the U.S., Canada, and Mexico, went into effect Jan. 1, 1994. In **Canada**, liberal Jean **Chrétien** became prime minister (Nov. 1993). The new Canadian territory of Nunavut, a large area formerly part of Northwest Territories, was created (Apr. 1999).

In the **U.S.**, Pres. Bill **Clinton** (D) proposed (Feb. 1998) the first balanced federal budget in nearly 30 years. In Dec. 1998 Clinton was **impeached** by the U.S. House; he was acquitted by the Senate in Feb. 1999.

In **Mexico**, Ernesto Zedillo of the ruling PRI party was elected president (July 1994) after the party's first candidate was assassinated. The country soon faced a crisis affecting the value of the peso, but recovered with the help of a U.S. bailout package.

Central America and the Caribbean. In **Haiti**, Jean-Bertrand **Aristide** was elected president (Dec. 1990) but was ousted in a military coup after nine months. A delegation headed by former U.S. Pres. Jimmy Carter arranged (Sept. 1994) for the junta to step aside for Aristide, who served until 1996. In **Nicaragua**, Violeta Chamorro defeated Daniel **Ortega** in the presidential election (Feb. 1990), thus ousting the Sandinistas. In **Panama**, U.S. troops invaded and overthrew the government of Manuel **Noriega** (Dec. 1989). Noriega was captured Jan. 1990; he was convicted and jailed on drug-related charges in U.S. in 1992 and in France in 2010. On Dec. 31, 1999, Panama assumed full control of the **Panama Canal**, in accord with a treaty with the U.S.

South America. Alberto **Fujimori** was elected president of **Peru** in June 1990 and, despite his suppression of the constitution (1992), reelected in 1995. Leftist guerrillas took hostages at an ambassador's residence in Lima (Dec. 1996); one hostage was killed during a government rescue attempt (Apr. 1997). Peronist Pres. Carlos Saúl **Menem** served as **Argentina**'s president for much of the decade, imposing economic austerity.

Former Chilean Pres. Augusto **Pinochet** continued to head the army until Mar. 1998; he was arrested in London (Oct. 1998) on human rights charges but judged unfit for trial. In **Brazil**, Fernando Henrique **Cardoso** was elected president (Oct. 1994) and reelected in 1998 despite an economic slump; the IMF announced a $42-bil aid package for the country (Nov. 1998). In **Venezuela** two coup attempts were thwarted (1992); coup leader Hugo **Chávez**, a leftist populist, was elected president in Dec. 1998.

Terrorism. The U.S. was a target of terrorism linked to radical Islam. A bomb exploded in a garage beneath New York City's **World Trade Center**, killing six people (Feb. 1993). Bombs set off outside **U.S. embassies** in Kenya and Tanzania killed over 220 people (Aug. 1998); the U.S. retaliated with airstrikes at alleged terrorist-linked sites in Afghanistan and Sudan. In the U.S.'s deadliest instance of domestic terrorism, 168 people were killed in the bombing of a federal building in **Oklahoma City**, OK (Apr. 1995), by anti-government extremists.

Science and technology. The powerful **Hubble Space Telescope** was launched in Apr. 1990. U.S. space shuttle ***Atlantis*** docked with the orbiting Russian space station ***Mir*** (June 1995) in first of several joint missions. In Nov. 1998 the first component for a new **International Space Station** was launched into space from Kazakhstan.

Scottish scientists announced (Feb. 1997) the **cloning** of a sheep—the first mammal successfully cloned from a cell from an adult animal.

Tim Berners-Lee launched the first **World Wide Web** server (1990). User-friendly graphical browsers (Mosaic, 1993; Netscape, 1994) and consumer-friendly Internet service providers followed, expanding the reach of the **Internet**.

Globalization and Global Realignments: 2000-09

Terrorism and crime. The decade saw a surge in terrorism associated with radical **Islam**. In Oct. 2000, 17 were killed aboard the **USS *Cole*** in Aden, **Yemen**, in a suicide bombing tied to **al-Qaeda**, a terrorist network based in Afghanistan. Terrorism reached a new level **Sept. 11, 2001**, when hijackers crashed two jetliners into the twin towers of the **World Trade Center** in New York City and another into the **Pentagon** outside Washington, DC, with a fourth crashing in a Pennsylvania field. The attacks, linked to al-Qaeda and its leader **Osama bin Laden**, destroyed both towers and killed about 3,000 people.

Among other incidents tied to Islamic radicals, a car bomb on the Indonesian island of **Bali** (Oct. 2002) killed about 200. **Commuter trains** were bombed in **Madrid**, Spain, killing 191 (Mar. 2004). Subway trains and a bus were bombed in **London** (July 2005); 56 died. Eight explosions killed 207 on commuter trains in **Mumbai**, India (July 2006); also in Mumbai (Nov. 2008), terrorists launched coordinated attacks on sites frequented by foreigners, killing some 170. **Chechen** separatist guerrillas were implicated in an attack on a **Moscow** movie theater (Oct. 2002; over 100 hostages died), bombings in Moscow's subways (Feb. 2004), explosions on two Russian planes (Aug. 2004; 89 died), and takeover of a school in Beslan (Sept. 2004; over 330 died).

Global economic crisis. Rapid economic growth in China and other developing countries contrasted with sluggish rates in traditional economic powers. A global **recession**, beginning in late 2007, led to a **financial meltdown** (Sept. 2008). **Iceland**'s banking system collapsed (Oct. 2008), rescued by loans and austerity. **Dubai**'s state-controlled investment company Dubai World was bailed out (Dec. 2009) by Abu Dhabi. Soaring food and **fuel prices** led to unrest, including an attempted general strike in **Egypt** and riots in **Haiti** (Apr. 2008). **Austerity** measures spurred protests in several European countries.

The attacks of Sept. 11, 2001, killed more than 2,500 people in New York.

War in Iraq and Afghanistan. The U.S., with Great Britain, invaded **Iraq** (Mar. 2003) to oust the regime of Saddam **Hussein**. Troops took control of Baghdad and other cities, and U.S. Pres. George W. **Bush** declared major combat ended by May, but insurgents caused continuing casualties. No **weapons of mass destruction**, cited as major grounds for the invasion, were found. Hussein was captured by U.S. troops (Dec. 2003) and convicted and executed by Iraqi authorities for crimes against humanity (Dec. 2006). Iraqis voted in elections for a transitional assembly (Jan. 2005), democratic constitution (Oct. 2005), and parliament (Dec. 2005); negotiations produced a Shiite coalition government under Prime Min. Nouri al-**Maliki** (May 2006). With **insurgent violence** intensifying, Bush announced (Jan. 2007) a **"surge"** of additional U.S. troops; casualties fell sharply, aided by a cease-fire with Shiite militias and a shift by minority Sunni away from support for al-Qaeda.

In **Afghanistan**, a U.S.-led military coalition ousted the **Taliban** regime. A transitional government was installed (Dec. 2001), but the Taliban remained strong as NATO assumed control of multinational forces in Aug. 2003. Afghans elected Hamid **Karzai** as president (Nov. 2004). From 2007, Taliban and other Islamist militants stepped up activities, often operating from safe havens inside Pakistan. The U.S. increased its troop strength in Afghanistan (2009) and expanded use of **drones**.

Middle East. Suicide bombings by Palestinians and retaliation by Israelis escalated violence. Israel launched major **West Bank offensive** (Mar. 2002) and reoccupied much of the West Bank after briefly withdrawing. The U.S., Russia, UN, and EU initiated (Apr. 2003) a **"road map"** for peace negotiations; little progress was made. After Palestinian leader Yasir **Arafat** died (Nov. 2004), Mahmoud **Abbas** was elected in his place. The militant Palestinian party **Hamas** won a parliamentary majority over the long-ruling **Fatah** party (Jan. 2006).

Israel launched attacks on **Lebanon** (July 2006) after a raid into N Israel by Lebanon-based **Hezbollah** guerrillas; a cease-fire was declared a month later. In reaction to Hamas rocket and mortar attacks, Israel launched an offensive in the **Gaza Strip** (Dec. 2008), which killed an estimated 1,300 Palestinians. Prime Min. Ehud **Olmert**, in office from 2006 on, resigned amid corruption inquiries; Feb. 2009 elections led to a coalition government headed by conservative former Prime Min. Benjamin **Netanyahu**.

In **Yemen**, U.S. used **drones** to target al-Qaeda beginning in 2002. The government of longtime Pres. Ali Abdullah **Saleh** also battled a growing insurgency from Shiite Houthi rebels, believed to be supported by Iran.

Asia. Gen. Pervez **Musharraf**, brought to power in a 1999 coup, assumed **Pakistan**'s presidency (June 2001). After the Sept. 11, 2001, terrorist attacks, Pakistan agreed to help in fighting Taliban and al-Qaeda militants. Pakistan and **India** restored ties (May 2003) and declared a cease-fire in disputed territory (Nov. 2003); relations remained tense. After former Pakistani Prime Min. Benazir **Bhutto** was assassinated in a bombing (Dec. 2007), her party won parliamentary elections (Feb. 2008) and her widower, Asif Ali **Zardari**, was elected president (Sept. 2008). In May 2009, the government launched an offensive against Taliban insurgents in the Swat Valley. The UN Intl. Atomic Energy Agency (IAEA) censured **Iran** (Dec. 2003) for covering up aspects of its **nuclear** program. Iran continued enriching uranium in defiance of IAEA deadlines. Pres. Mahmoud **Ahmadinejad** was declared landslide winner in June 2009 elections widely perceived as rigged; massive **protests** were crushed by police and paramilitaries. In **Kyrgyzstan**, protests (Mar. 2005) against election fraud brought down Pres. Askar Akayev in a **"tulip revolution." South Korean** Pres. Kim Dae-jung and **North Korean** ruler Kim Jong Il agreed to seek peace at a summit (June 2000), but tensions rose after North Korea admitted to a **nuclear weapons** development program (Oct. 2002). At multination talks, North Korea agreed (Feb. 2007) to end its nuclear program in exchange for aid but reneged, conducting tests Apr.-May 2009.

A **tsunami** (Dec. 2004) swept ashore in Indian Ocean nations, leaving some 228,000 dead. **Earthquakes** struck Kashmir and other parts of Pakistan and India (Oct. 2005), killing nearly 80,000, and hit China's Sichuan province (May 2008), killing nearly 70,000. With the retirement of **China**'s Pres. Jiang Zemin, **Hu** Jintao was named Communist party chief (Nov. 2002) and president (Mar. 2003). In **Japan**, Liberal Democrats, in virtually uninterrupted power since the 1950s, were dispatched in parliamentary elections (Aug. 2009).

Myanmar's military junta cracked down on hundreds of thousands of protesters (Sept. 2007). Over 80,000 people were killed in a **cyclone** there (May 2008); the regime thwarted aid agencies. After stepping up an offensive against **Tamil guerrillas, Sri Lanka** government declared an end (May 2009) to a rebellion that since 1983 had claimed at least 80,000 lives.

Europe. The **EU** admitted 10 East European nations in May 2004; two more joined in Jan. 2007, for a total of 27 members. By 2008 the **euro** was the common currency in 15 EU nations. Voters in France and the Netherlands rejected a treaty to establish a new **EU constitution** (May-June 2005). A modified plan (called the **Treaty of Lisbon)** came into force after Irish voters approved it (Oct. 2009).

In Oct. 2000, Yugoslav strongman Slobodan **Milosevic** yielded power after a disputed election. Milosevic surrendered to Serbian authorities; he went on trial in The Hague (Feb. 2002) for **war crimes** during 1990s ethnic conflicts in the Balkans but died of an apparent heart attack (Mar. 2006) before a verdict. Former Bosnian Serb leader Radovan **Karadzic** was arraigned on war crimes charges (July 2008). **Kosovo** unilaterally declared independence (Feb. 2008).

Germany elected its first East German and first woman chancellor (Nov. 2005) in Angela **Merkel**, a Christian Democrat. Rioting shook France's immigrant communities in 300 cities and towns (Nov. 2005). A Danish newspaper's publication of cartoon **caricatures of Muhammad** sparked protests by Muslims (Jan.-Feb. 2006).

British Prime Min. Tony **Blair** won reelection twice (2001, 2005), becoming the first Labour prime minister to earn three straight terms. He stepped down in June 2007, to be succeeded by fellow Labourite Gordon **Brown**. **France** saw the election (May 2007) of conservative Nicolas **Sarkozy** as president and rejoined NATO's military command (Apr. 2009) after more than 40 years. Vladimir **Putin**, in power in Russia since 1999, was constitutionally barred from a new presidential term in 2008; his protégé, Dmitri **Medvedev**, was elected (May 2008). In **Ukraine**, a tainted presidential runoff election (Nov. 2004) led to the country's **"orange revolution"**; a recount gave power to nationalist Viktor **Yushchenko**.

Africa. Ethiopia and Eritrea signed a **peace treaty** (Dec. 2000). Laurent **Kabila**, president of **Dem. Rep. of the Congo**, was assassinated (Jan. 2001). Liberian Pres. Charles **Taylor** went into exile (Aug. 2003) as part of a deal to end a 14-year civil war; other accords were reached aimed at ending civil wars in **Angola** (Apr. 2002) and **Côte d'Ivoire** (Jan. 2003).

A peace agreement in Dem. Rep. of the Congo (Apr. 2003) did not end violence there; the nation agreed to work with Rwanda to disarm Hutu rebels (Nov. 2007). In **Sudan** a power-sharing accord between the Muslim-led government and rebels from the Christian south was signed, Jan. 2005, giving the south limited autonomy. Rebellion in the **Darfur** area of western Sudan led to large-scale violence. Arab militias (**janjaweed**), reportedly backed by the government, were accused of displacing over 2 mil people in acts bordering on **genocide**; by the end of 2009 over 300,000 people had been killed. The Intl. Criminal Court issued an arrest warrant for Sudanese Pres. Omar al-**Bashir** for war crimes (Mar. 2009); he remained in power.

Disputed elections sparked violence in **Kenya** (Jan. 2008) and **Zimbabwe** (Apr. 2008). Under Pres. Robert Mugabe's rule, unemployment in Zimbabwe topped 90% and hyperinflation left the currency virtually worthless. **Guinea-Bissau**'s defense chief and then its president were assassinated in turn by rival groups (Mar. 2009).

Americas and the Caribbean. In Jan. 2001, Republican George W. **Bush** was inaugurated as **U.S.** president, after one of the closest elections in U.S. history. Democrats claimed the White House with the Nov. 2008 election of Barack **Obama**, first-ever black U.S. president. The long-supreme **Institutional Revolutionary Party** lost power in **Mexico** with the election of two successive presidents from a center-right party, Vicente **Fox** and Felipe **Calderón** (July 2000, July 2006). Calderón launched a crackdown on drug trafficking (Dec. 2006); from then through the end of 2010, more than 30,000 people were killed in violence fueled by **drug cartels**.

In **Brazil**, reformist candidate Luiz Inácio **Lula da Silva** won a runoff (Oct. 2002) to become president. **Chile** was ruled by Socialist governments under Ricardo **Lagos** Escobar (from 2000) and Michelle **Bachelet** (from 2006). In **Venezuela**, leftist populist Pres. Hugo **Chávez** regained power after a 48-hour coup (Dec. 2002) and consolidated it, in part through a referendum (Feb. 2009) that eliminated presidential term limits. In **Bolivia**, Evo **Morales**, another leftist populist, won election as president (Dec. 2005) and passage of a new constitution (Jan. 2009). In **Honduras**, leftist leader Manuel **Zelaya** was elected president (Nov. 2005) but was ousted by the military (June 2009) after seeking constitutional changes; conservative Porfirio (Pepe) **Lobo** was elected (Nov. 2009) to succeed him.

Peronist Nestor **Kirchner** won election as president of **Argentina** (Apr. 2003); his wife, Cristina Kirchner, was elected (Oct. 2007) to succeed him. **Haiti** was wracked by antigovernment protests, leading to the resignation of Jean-Bertrand **Aristide** in Feb. 2004; a UN peacekeeping mission was brought in. **Canada**'s Liberal Party was defeated in Jan. 2006 elections; Conservative Stephen **Harper** became prime minister, heading a minority government. Pres. **Fidel Castro**, **Cuba**'s leader since 1959, ceded powers to his brother, **Raúl**, to undergo surgery (July 2006); he formally resigned in Feb. 2008.

Religion. Pope **John Paul II** died, Apr. 2005, after 26 years in the papacy; German Cardinal Joseph Ratzinger was elected as his successor, taking the name **Benedict XVI**. During the decade, reports of **sexual abuse** by Catholic priests and evidence of inaction by church officials emerged.

Science and technology. The U.S. **space shuttle *Columbia*** broke up on reentering Earth's atmosphere (Feb. 2003), killing all seven crew members; space shuttle program resumed July 2005. **NASA** landed two rovers, *Spirit* and *Opportunity*, on **Mars** (Jan. 2004), and verified the presence of water ice on the planet (June 2008). **China** launched its first manned space flight, Oct. 2003. China, Oct. 2010, unveiled the Tianhe-1A **supercomputer**, the world's fastest. **Internet** penetration and access to technology expanded exponentially; online commerce, social networking (Facebook, 2004; Twitter, 2006), mobile computing (iPhone, 2007), and file-sharing services became commonplace.

Environment and health. Under the **Kyoto Protocol**, which took effect Feb. 2005, most industrialized nations agreed to specific reductions in emissions of **greenhouse gases** linked to global warming by 2012. A NASA report (Jan. 2010) found that 2000-09 had the warmest average global temperatures since modern records began in the 1880s.

Worldwide **AIDS** estimates were revised (Nov. 2007) to show new infections had peaked in the late 1990s. An epidemic of **swine flu**, or influenza A (H1N1), broke out in **Mexico** (Apr. 2009) and spread, killing more than 18,000.

Searching for Resolutions: 2010-June 2015

Terrorism. Osama **bin Laden**, leader of radical Islamist organization al-Qaeda, was **killed in Pakistan** in a raid by U.S. special forces (May 2011). Core al-Qaeda leadership showed signs of weakening, but **al-Qaeda** affiliates and other groups motivated by radical Islam, including the increasingly powerful **Islamic State in Iraq and Syria (ISIS)**, launched attacks on civilians in many countries. Global deaths from terrorist acts were up 81% in 2014 from the year before.

Among other incidents, **al-Shabab** militants based in Somalia and linked to al-Qaeda were responsible for July 2010 bombings in Kampala, **Uganda** (more than 70 World Cup soccer watchers killed), Sept. 2013 shootings at a Nairobi, **Kenya**, shopping mall (over 70 killed), and an Apr. 2015 massacre at a college in Garissa, Kenya (close to 150 killed). Al-Qaeda in the Arabian Peninsula (**AQAP**) launched attacks in **Yemen**, including one on a military parade rehearsal (May 2012; over 90 killed) and on a hospital (Dec. 2013; over 50 died). The radical Islamist group **Boko Haram**, active in **Nigeria**, executed kidnappings (including abduction of over 200 schoolgirls, Apr. 2014); bombings (Kano mosque, Nov. 2014; over 100 killed); and massacres of villagers (thousands killed in 2014 alone).

Two immigrants from Chechnya set off bombs, killing three and injuring 264, near finish line of **Boston Marathon** (Apr. 2013). In Ottawa, **Canada**, a Muslim gunman killed a sentry and attacked Parliament (Oct. 2014) before being killed. In **Pakistan**, seven **Taliban** gunmen attacked a Peshawar school (Dec. 2014), killing some 150 people, mostly children. In **France** terrorists possibly linked to AQAP killed 17 people in and around Paris (Jan. 2015), including 12 at offices of *Charlie Hebdo*, a magazine notorious for cartoons offensive to Islam. In Mar. 2015, gunmen attacked museum in **Tunisia**'s capital (more than 20 killed, mostly foreign tourists). Close to 140 people died in Mar. 2015 bombings of two mosques in Sanaa, **Yemen**; **ISIS**, known mostly for attacks in Iraq and Syria, claimed responsibility.

In other outbreaks of terrorism, an anti-Muslim extremist in **Norway** killed 77 people in a rampage, July 2011.

War in Iraq and Afghanistan. The last U.S. combat unit withdrew from **Iraq**, Aug. 2010, and the U.S. military left in Dec. 2011. Death toll: about 4,500 U.S. service members, 300 from allied countries, with Iraqi civilian deaths estimated at over 100,000. Sectarian violence accelerated after U.S. left, reaching some 17,000 civilian deaths in 2014.

As Sunni disaffection grew, **ISIS**, a Sunni Muslim al-Qaeda offshoot and sometime rival, incubated in Syria, gained ground in Iraq (**Fallujah**, Jan. 2014; **Mosul**, June 2014; **Ramadi**, May 2015), and declared (June 2014) an Islamic state in a large swath of Iraq and Syria. ISIS imposed strict Islamic law; terrorized and murdered Christians, Yazidi, and other minorities, Shiite Muslims, and resisters; and videotaped beheadings of captives (such as American James Foley, Aug. 2014) for propaganda purposes. Separatist Kurds controlled parts of Iraq and fought ISIS on the ground; U.S., aided by other countries, conducted airstrikes and sent in advisers to train Iraqi troops. Prime Min. Nouri al-**Maliki**'s Shiite party won a plurality in Apr. 2014 elections, but he lost party support. Haider **al-Abadi** formed a new, possibly less sectarian Shiite government (Sept. 2014). U.S. troop withdrawal from **Afghanistan** began in 2011; U.S. and UK formally ended combat operations (Oct. 2014). The only U.S. prisoner in **Taliban** custody was freed (May 2014) in exchange for five Taliban prisoners in Guantánamo. U.S. and NATO-led International Security Assistance Force (ISAF) combat operations officially ended in Dec. 2014. Death toll in 13 years: over 2,215 U.S. troops, 1,130 ISAF forces; at least 17,774 civilians (UN estimate, since 2009 only). Some 13,000 troops remained after Dec. to support and train Afghan forces, under agreement reached in Sept. 2014 after Ashraf **Ghani** and chief executive Abdullah **Abdullah** took office in the country's first democratic power transfer since 2001. Taliban showed strength in attack on Afghan Parliament that killed two (June 2015).

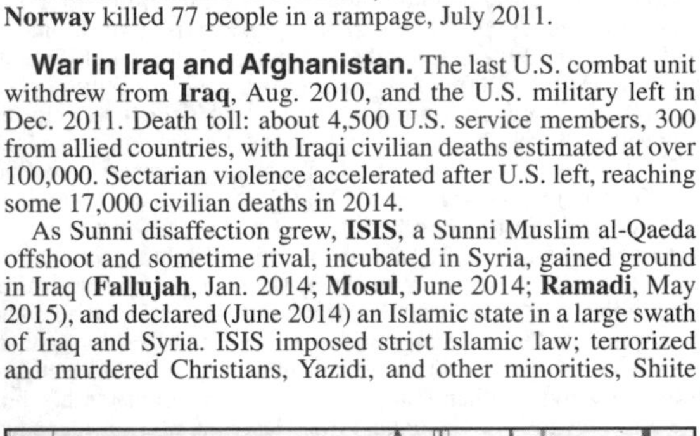

The Sunni extremist group known commonly as ISIS expanded its territorial control and declared an Islamic state in a large part of Iraq and Syria in 2014.

Middle East. UN General Assembly granted nonmember observer state status to **Palestine** (Nov. 2012). Arab-Israeli **peace talks** resumed, July 2013, but foundered as Fatah and militant Hamas factions agreed (Apr. 2014) to aim at unification. Israel began airstrikes on **Gaza** (July 2014) after rocket attacks by Hamas-affiliated groups; at least 2,000 Palestinians and 60 Israeli soldiers were dead by the end of Aug. 2014, when a cease-fire was established. Israeli Prime Min. Benjamin **Netanyahu** retained power after Mar. 2015 elections, forming a right-wing government. Relations between Israel's Netanyahu-led government and the U.S. were strained, in part by differences over Iran's nuclear program. Nuclear negotiations (with five permanent UN Security Council nations plus Germany) led to a framework agreement (Apr. 2015) to cut back Iranian nuclear development in return for removal of sanctions.

Poverty, religious and ethnic conflict, and government corruption and repression fueled revolts that challenged several entrenched Arab regimes. But this so-called **Arab Spring** led in most cases to increased violence and chaos rather than to democracies. Protests forced the ouster of **Tunisian** Pres. Zine al-Abidine Ben Ali (Jan. 2011); elections followed and a new constitution (Jan. 2014) recognized civil liberties. In **Egypt**, after mass protests led to the overthrow of longtime Pres. Hosni **Mubarak** (Feb. 2011), the **Muslim Brotherhood**-dominated government (elected June 2012) provoked protests and fell in a military coup (July 2013). Raids (over 600 killed, Aug. 2013) and mass arrests followed. Coup leader Abdel Fattah **al-Sisi** was elected president, May 2014. In **Yemen**, protests, starting in Jan. 2011, led to fall of the government (Nov. 2011); the new president also resigned (Jan. 2015) and fled after Shia Houthi rebels took over the capital city. A **Saudi**-led coalition of Arab states began a bombing campaign (Mar. 2015) against the Houthi.

In **Libya**, insurgents with NATO military backing overthrew dictator Muammar al-**Qaddafi**, who was killed (Oct. 2011). The country became a battleground for rival Islamist factions, with ISIS gaining a foothold; refugees seeking asylum in Europe fled by boat, and Westerners faced dangers (U.S. consulate attack in **Benghazi**, Sept. 2012; multiple embassy closures). In **Syria**, Pres. Bashar al-**Assad** launched a ferocious offensive against antigovernment protesters (beginning Mar. 2011), giving rise to civil war. After about 1,400 people were killed in chemical attacks (Aug. 2013) attributed to the Assad regime, the government accepted Russian-backed plan for surrender of chemical weapons. Some 200,000 had been killed in the conflict by government forces and by rebel groups, including the dominant **ISIS**, which won a major victory in capturing **Palmyra** (May 2015). By mid-2015, an estimated 6.5 mil people were internally displaced; more than 3 mil others had fled the country.

Europe. The EU, with IMF help, provided loan packages to bail out **Greece** (beginning May 2010) and **Ireland** (Nov. 2010), but popular opposition to austerity measures and installation of a leftist government after Jan. 2015 elections left Greece's financial future in doubt. The European Central Bank bailed out **Portugal** (May 2011). The EU provided a bank bailout for **Spain** (June 2012) and reached a bailout agreement with **Cyprus** (Mar. 2013). Far-right parties scored big gains in **European Parliament** elections (May 2014).

Britain returned conservatives to power in a coalition government under David **Cameron** (May 2010); Cameron's conservatives won an outright majority in June 2015 elections. Nationalists swept Scotland's seats, though their cause had been set back by a Sept. 2014 referendum in which Scots voted to remain in the UK. In **France**, socialist François **Hollande** defeated conservative Nicolas **Sarkozy** to become president (May 2012). Elections in **Poland** (May 2015) and **Denmark** (June 2015) put center-right parties in power.

Amid accusations of corruption and voter fraud, Vladimir **Putin** won third term as **Russia**'s president (Mar. 2012). He gave asylum to fugitive U.S. secrets leaker Edward Snowden (Aug. 2013) and strengthened ties to China with a 30-year natural gas deal (May 2014). In **Ukraine**, the pro-Russian Viktor **Yanukovich** was elected president (Feb. 2010), but his rebuff to EU integration (Nov. 2013) led to mass protests, with protesters fired on; he fled and was removed by Parliament. Claiming a danger to ethnic Russians, Putin sent troops to **Crimea** and, in Mar. 2014, annexed the region. With pro-Russian separatists fighting for control of East Ukraine, apparently with Russian backing, a pro-European moderate, Petro **Poroshenko**, was elected Ukraine's president (May 2014); he signed EU trade agreement, June 2014. Talks between Ukraine and France, Germany, and Russia led to a fragile cease-fire, Feb. 2015; UN estimated close to 6,000 people had been killed up to then, while some 1.5 mil had fled the country or were internally displaced.

A **Germanwings Airbus crashed** in the French Alps (Mar. 2015), killing 150, in apparent suicide by copilot. In May 2015, traditionally Catholic **Ireland** became the first country to legalize same-sex marriage by popular vote.

Asia and the Pacific. Monsoon **floods** (July-Aug. 2010) in **Pakistan** left millions homeless. An **earthquake** and tsunami (Mar. 2011) struck Japan, killing more than 16,000 and leading to meltdowns at nuclear reactors. Over 8,500 were killed in two earthquakes in **Nepal** (Apr.-May 2015). A **Malaysian airliner** en route to Beijing with 239 aboard veered off course and **vanished** (Mar. 2014). In **Kyrgyzstan**, Kurmanbek **Bakiyev** was ousted (Apr. 2010) after clashes with protesters left at least 85 dead. Despite ethnic violence (up to 2,000 killed), a referendum was held (June 2010) and new constitution approved. Almazbek **Atambayev** was elected president (Oct. 2011). **North Korean** dictator **Kim Jong Il** died (Dec. 2011) and was succeeded by youngest son **Kim Jong Un**, who launched numerous missile tests, threatened the U.S., and sought to consolidate power (executed uncle, Dec. 2013). Moderately reformist cleric Hassan **Rouhani** won the June 2013 presidential election in **Iran**, strengthening hopes for international agreement on nuclear program.

Myanmar's military junta was dissolved (Mar. 2011) following the country's first election in 20 years (Nov. 2010), which brought the military-backed USDP party to power; the party led by dissident Aung San **Suu Kyi** gained seats in interim elections (Apr. 2012). Violence against the segregated Muslim Rohingya minority continued. Mass protests in **Thailand** led to country's 12th military coup (May 2014).

Upon Chinese Pres. **Hu** Jintao's retirement, **Xi** Jinping was named Communist party chief (Nov. 2012) and president (Mar. 2013). The party retained firm control (**Hong Kong** prodemocracy protests, Sept.-Dec. 2014). Liberal Democrats in **Japan** regained power in Dec. 2012 elections. In **Australia**, Prime Min. Kevin **Rudd** was displaced (June 2010) by his deputy, Julia **Gillard**, who became Australia's first female prime minister; Rudd ousted her and again became prime minister, June 2013. The Hindu nationalist Bharatiya Janata party won a majority in May 2014 elections in **India**, ousting the dominant Indian Congress Party; Narendra **Modi** became prime minister.

Pope Benedict XVI, the leader of the world's 1.2 billion Roman Catholics, resigned in 2013 and was replaced by Pope Francis, the first pontiff from the Americas.

Africa. Coups ousted **Niger**'s president (Feb. 2010) and ended elections in **Guinea-Bissau** (Apr. 2012); in both cases, civilian rule returned following new elections. In a referendum, southern Sudanese (mostly Christian or indigenous beliefs) voted overwhelmingly for separation from the north (mostly Arab Muslim), and **South Sudan** was granted independence as of July 2011. However, a power struggle between rival leaders plunged the new country into ethnic warfare, leaving thousands dead by 2015. Low-level soldiers staged a coup in **Mali** (Mar. 2012). The junta ceded power to civilians, but Islamic rebels seized control in the north. French and West African forces intervened; a peace deal was reached (June 2013) but proved fragile. In **Burkina Faso**, Pres. Blaise **Campaoré**, in power for 27 years, resigned and fled amid protests (Oct. 2014). In **Nigeria**, former dictator and opposition candidate Muhammadu **Buhari**, pledging action against Boko Haram, was elected president (Mar. 2015). An **Ebola outbreak** in **W Africa** began in early 2014, causing more than 11,000 deaths by mid-2015, mostly in Guinea, Liberia, and Sierra Leone.

Americas and the Caribbean. **Haiti** was devastated by an earthquake (Jan. 2010) that killed more than 200,000; an epidemic of **cholera**, likely introduced by UN peacekeepers, left over 8,000 dead by the end of 2013. **Canada**'s Conservatives, under Prime Min. Stephen **Harper**, won an outright majority in May 2011 elections; Liberals lost heavily, leaving New Democratic Party as official opposition. **Mexico**'s Institutional Revolutionary Party regained power with election of Enrique **Peña Nieto** (July 2012). In **Brazil**, reformist Pres. **Lula da Silva**'s chosen successor, Dilma **Rousseff**, was elected (Oct. 2010); she narrowly won reelection (Oct. 2014) but faced protests in 2015 over corruption scandal and economic slump. In **Venezuela**, leftist Pres. Hugo **Chávez** was reelected (Oct. 2012) but died (Mar. 2013) before he could be inaugurated; ally Nicolás **Maduro** Moros was elected to replace him (Apr. 2013); more than 40 killed and hundreds arrested in antigovernment protests starting Feb. 2014. Barack **Obama** was reelected **U.S.** president in Nov. 2012. In major foreign policy change, U.S. and **Cuba** (Dec. 2014) restored relations, broken since two years after the 1959 Cuban Revolution.

Religion. **Benedict XVI** resigned after eight years as pope (Feb. 2013); Argentinean Cardinal Jorge Mario Bergoglio succeeded him, taking the name **Francis** and becoming the first pope from the Americas. U.S. Commission on International Religious Freedom cited (Apr. 2015) 17 countries for severe violations of **religious freedom**.

Science, technology, environment. **WikiLeaks**, a nonprofit group formed in 2007 to expose government secrets, began disseminating documents related to Iraq and Afghanistan wars (Apr., July 2010). After 30 years, **NASA**'s space shuttle program ended with return of ***Atlantis*** to Earth (July 2011). NASA's rover ***Curiosity*** landed on Mars, Aug. 2012. **China** landed unmanned ***Yulu*** rover on the Moon, Dec. 2013.

UN-sponsored Intergovernmental Panel on Climate Change, in reports issued in 2013-14, stressed "human influence" as "dominant cause" of **global warming**. Presidents of **U.S.** and **China** agreed (Nov. 2014) on plan to limit future carbon dioxide emissions. **Pope Francis** released encyclical (June 2015), focusing on climate change and the environment.

HISTORICAL FIGURES

Note: Information accurate as of Sept. 2015.

Ancient Greeks and Romans

Greeks

Aeschines, orator, 389-314 BCE
Aeschylus, dramatist, 525-456 BCE
Aesop, fableist, c. 620-c. 560 BCE
Alcibiades, politician, 450-404 BCE
Anacreon, poet, c. 582-c. 485 BCE
Anaxagoras, philosopher, c. 500-428 BCE
Anaximander, philosopher, 611-546 BCE
Anaximenes, philosopher, c. 570-500 BCE
Antiphon, speechwriter, c. 480-411 BCE
Apollonius, mathematician, c. 265-170 BCE
Archimedes, mathematician, 287-212 BCE
Aristophanes, dramatist, c. 448-380 BCE
Aristotle, philosopher, 384-322 BCE
Athenaeus, scholar, fl. c. 200
Callicrates, architect, fl. 5th cent. BCE
Callimachus, poet, c. 305-240 BCE
Cratinus, comic dramatist, 520-421 BCE
Democritus, philosopher, c. 460-370 BCE
Demosthenes, orator, 384-322 BCE
Diodorus, historian, fl. 20 BCE
Diogenes, philosopher, 372-c. 287 BCE
Dionysius, historian, d. c. 7 BCE
Empedocles, philosopher, c. 490-430 BCE
Epicharmus, dramatist, c. 530-440 BCE
Epictetus, philosopher, c. 55-c. 135
Epicurus, philosopher, 341-270 BCE
Eratosthenes, scientist, 276-194 BCE
Euclid, mathematician, fl. c. 300 BCE
Euripides, dramatist, c. 484-406 BCE
Galen, physician, 129-216
Heraclitus, philosopher, c. 540-c. 475 BCE
Herodotus, historian, c. 484-420 BCE
Hesiod, poet, 8th cent. BCE
Hippocrates, physician, c. 460-377 BCE
Homer, poet, fl. c. 8th cent. BCE
Isocrates, orator, 436-338 BCE
Menander, dramatist, 342-292 BCE
Parmenides, philosopher, b. c. 515 BCE
Pericles, statesman, c. 495-429 BCE
Phidias, sculptor, c. 500-435 BCE
Pindar, poet, c. 518-c. 438 BCE
Plato, philosopher, c. 428-347 BCE
Plutarch, biographer, c. 46-120
Polybius, historian, c. 200-c. 118 BCE
Praxiteles, sculptor, 400-330 BCE
Pythagoras, phil., math., c. 580-c. 500 BCE
Sappho, poet, c. 610-c. 580 BCE
Simonides, poet, 556-c. 468 BCE
Socrates, philosopher, 469-399 BCE
Solon, statesman, 640-560 BCE
Sophocles, dramatist, c. 496-406 BCE
Strabo, geographer, c. 63 BCE-24 CE
Thales, philosopher, c. 634-546 BCE
Themistocles, politician, c. 524-c. 460 BCE
Theocritus, poet, c. 310-250 BCE
Theophrastus, phil., c. 372-c. 287 BCE
Thucydides, historian, fl. 5th cent. BCE
Timon, philosopher, c. 320-c. 230 BCE
Xenophon, historian, c. 434-c. 355 BCE
Zeno, philosopher, c. 335-c. 263 BCE

Romans

Ammianus, historian, c. 330-395
Apuleius, satirist, c. 124-c. 170
Boethius, scholar, c. 480-524
Caesar, Julius, leader, 100-44 BCE
Catiline, politician, c. 108-62 BCE
Cato (Elder), statesman, 234-149 BCE
Catullus, poet, c. 84-54 BCE
Cicero, orator, 106-43 BCE
Claudian, poet, c. 370-c. 404
Ennius, poet, 239-170 BCE
Gellius, author, c. 130-c. 165
Horace, poet, 65-8 BCE
Juvenal, satirist, 60-127
Livy, historian, 59 BCE-17 CE
Lucan, poet, 39-65
Lucilius, poet, c. 180-c.102 BCE
Lucretius, poet, c. 99-c. 55 BCE
Martial, epigrammatist, c. 38-c. 103
Nepos, historian, c. 100-c. 25 BCE
Ovid, poet, 43 BCE-17 CE
Persius, satirist, 34-62
Plautus, dramatist, c. 254-c. 184 BCE
Pliny the Elder, scholar, 23-79
Pliny the Younger, author, 62-113
Quintilian, rhetorician, c. 35-c. 97
Sallust, historian, 86-34 BCE
Seneca, philosopher, 4 BCE-65 CE
Silius, poet, c. 25-101
Statius, poet, c. 45-c. 96
Suetonius, biographer, c. 69-c. 122
Tacitus, historian, 56-120
Terence, dramatist, 195/185-c. 159 BCE
Tibullus, poet, c. 55-c. 19 BCE
Vergil, poet, 70-19 BCE
Vitruvius, architect, fl. 1st cent. BCE

Roman Rulers

From Romulus to the end of the Empire in the West (Rome). Rulers in the East sat in Constantinople and, for a brief period, in Nicaea, until the capture of Constantinople by the Turks in 1453, when Byzantium was succeeded by the Ottoman Empire.

The Kingdom

BCE
753 Romulus (Quirinus)
715 Numa Pompilius
673 Tullus Hostilius
641 Ancus Marcius
616 L. Tarquinius Priscus
579 Servius Tullius
534 L. Tarquinius Superbus

The Republic

509 Consulate established; Quaestorship instituted
498 Dictatorship introduced
494 Plebeian Tribunate created; Plebeian Aedileship created
444 Consular Tribunate organized
435 Censorship instituted
366 Praetorship established; Curule Aedileship created
362 Military Tribunate elected
326 Proconsulate introduced
311 Naval Duumvirate elected
217 Dictatorship of Fabius Maximus
133 Tribunate of Tiberius Gracchus
123 Tribunate of Gaius Gracchus
82 Dictatorship of Sulla
60 First Triumvirate formed (Caesar, Pompeius, Crassus)
47 Dictatorship of Caesar
43 Second Triumvirate formed (Octavianus, Antonius, Lepidus)

The Empire

27 Augustus (or Octavian)
CE
14 Tiberius
37 Caligula
41 Claudius
54 Nero
68 Galba
69 Otho; Vitellius; Vespasian, established Flavian Dynasty
79 Titus
81 Domitian, end of Flavian Dynasty
96 Nerva
98 Trajan
117 Hadrian
138 Antoninus Pius
161 Marcus Aurelius and Lucius Verus
169 Marcus Aurelius (alone)
177 Marcus Aurelius and Commodus
180 Commodus
193 Pertinax
193 Didius Julianus
193 Septimius Severus, founded Severan Dynasty
211 Caracalla and Geta
212 Caracalla (alone)
217 Macrinus
218 Elagabalus (or Heliogabalus)
222 Alexander Severus, end of dynasty
235 Maximinus (the Thracian)
238 Gordian I and Gordian II
238 Pupienus and Balbinus
238 Gordian III
244 Philip (the Arabian)
249 Decius
251 Gallus and Volusianus
253 Aemilian
253 Valerian and Gallienus
258 Gallienus (alone)
268 Claudius II (or Claudius Gothicus)
270 Quintillus
270 Aurelian
275 Tacitus
276 Florian
276 Probus
282 Carus
283 Carinus and Numerian
284 Diocletian
286 Diocletian and Maximian
305 Galerius and Constantius I
306 Galerius, Maximinus (or Maximinus Daia), Severus
307 Galerius, Maximinus (Daia), Constantine I, Licinius, Maxentius
311 Maximinus (Daia), Constantine I, Licinius, Maxentius
314 Constantine I, Licinius
324 Constantine I (the Great), first Christian emperor
337 Constantine II, Constans I, Constantius II
340 Constantius II and Constans I
353 Constantius II (alone)
361 Julian (the Apostate)
363 Jovian

West (Rome) and East (Constantinople)

364 Valentinian I (West), Valens (East)
367 Valentinian I with Gratian (W), Valens (E)
375 Gratian with Valentinian II (W), Valens (E)
379 Gratian with Valentinian II (W), Theodosius I (E)
383 Magnus Maximus and Valentinian II (W), Theodosius I (E)
388 Valentinian II (W), Theodosius I (E)
392 Eugenius (W), Theodosius I (E)
394 Theodosius I (the Great)
395 Honorius (W), Arcadius (E)
408 Honorius (W), Theodosius II (E)
423 Valentinian III (W), Theodosius II (E)
450 Valentinian III (W), Marcian (E)
455 Petronius Maximus (W), Marcian (E)
455 Avitus (W), Marcian (E)
457 Majorian (W), Leo I (E)
461 Libius Severus (W), Leo I (E)
467 Anthemius (W), Leo I (E)
472 Olybrius (W), Leo I (E)
473 Glycerius (W), Leo I (E)
474 Julius Nepos (W), Leo II (E)
475 Romulus Augustulus (W), Zeno (E)
476 End of Empire in W when Romulus Augustulus deposed by Germanic chief Odoacer, who was later murdered by King Theodoric of Ostrogoths, 493

Rulers of England and the United Kingdom

Reign began	Name	Age at death[1]
	England: Saxons and Danes	
829	Egbert, king of Wessex, won allegiance of all English	NA
839	Ethelwulf, son of Egbert, king of Wessex, Sussex, Kent, Essex	NA
858	Ethelbald, eldest son of Ethelwulf, displaced father in Wessex	NA
860	Ethelbert, 2nd son of Ethelwulf, united Kent and Wessex	NA
866	Ethelred I, 3rd son of Ethelwulf, king of Wessex, fought Danes	NA
871	Alfred (the Great), 4th son of Ethelwulf, defeated Danes, fortified London	52
899	Edward (the Elder), son of Alfred, united English, claimed Scotland	55
924	Athelstan (the Glorious), eldest son of Edward, king of Mercia, Wessex	45
940	Edmund, 3rd son of Edward, king of Wessex, Mercia	25
946	Edred, 4th son of Edward	32
955	Edwy (the Fair), eldest son of Edmund, king of Wessex	18
959	Edgar (the Peaceful), 2nd son of Edmund, ruled all English	32
975	Edward (the Martyr), eldest son of Edgar, murdered by stepmother	17
978; 1014[2]	Ethelred II (the Unready), 2nd son of Edgar, married Emma of Normandy	48
1016	Edmund II (Ironside), son of Ethelred II, king of London	27
1016	Canute (the Dane), son of Sweyn, who conquered English territory; gave Wessex to Edmund II; married Emma, Ethelred II's widow	40
1035	Harold I (Harefoot), illegitimate son of Canute	NA
1040	Hardecanute, son of Canute by Emma, also king of Denmark	24
1042	Edward (the Confessor), son of Ethelred II, canonized 1161	62
1066	Harold II, Edward's brother-in-law, last Saxon king	44
	England: House of Normandy	
1066	William I (the Conqueror), son of Duke Robert I of Normandy, defeated Harold II at Hastings	60
1087	William II (Rufus), 3rd son of William I, killed by arrow while hunting in possible assassination	43
1100	Henry I (Beauclerc), youngest son of William I	67
	England: House of Blois	
1135	Stephen, son of Adela, daughter of William I, and Count of Blois	50
	England: House of Plantagenet	
1154	Henry II, son of Geoffrey Plantagenet (Angevin) by Matilda, daughter of Henry I	56
1189	Richard I (Coeur de Lion), son of Henry II, crusader	42
1199	John (Lackland), son of Henry II, approved Magna Carta, 1215	50
1216	Henry III, son of John, acceded at 9, under regency until 1227	65
1272	Edward I (Longshanks), son of Henry III	68
1307	Edward II, son of Edward I, deposed by Parliament	43
1327	Edward III (of Windsor), son of Edward II	65
1377	Richard II, grandson of Edward III, deposed	33
	England: House of Lancaster	
1399	Henry IV (of Bolingbroke), son of John of Gaunt, duke of Lancaster, son of Edward III	47
1413	Henry V, son of Henry IV, victor over French at Agincourt	34
1422; 1470	Henry VI, son of Henry V, overthrown by Edward IV in 1461 but was returned to throne in 1470. Deposed, died in Tower of London, 1471	49
	England: House of York	
1461; 1471	Edward IV, great-great-grandson of Edward III, son of duke of York. Acclaimed king by Parliament, 1461. Driven into exile in 1470 but regained throne, 1471	40
1483	Edward V, son of Edward IV, murdered in Tower of London	13
1483	Richard III, brother of Edward IV, fell in battle at Bosworth Field against Henry Tudor	32
	England: House of Tudor	
1485	Henry VII, son of Edmund Tudor, earl of Richmond, whose father had married Henry V's widow. Descended from Edward III through mother, Margaret Beaufort, via John of Gaunt. Married Elizabeth of York, eldest daughter of Edward IV, to unite Lancaster and York	53
1509	Henry VIII, 2nd son of Henry VII, by Elizabeth	56
1547	Edward VI, son of Henry VIII, by Jane Seymour, his 3rd queen. Ruled under regents, was forced to name Lady Jane Grey his successor. Council of State proclaimed her queen, July 10, 1553. Mary Tudor won Council, was proclaimed queen, July 19. Mary had Jane beheaded for treason, 1554	16
1553	Mary I, daughter of Henry VIII, by his 1st wife, Catherine of Aragon	43
1558	Elizabeth I, daughter of Henry VIII, by his 2nd wife, Anne Boleyn	69
	Great Britain: House of Stuart	
1603	James I (James VI of Scotland), son of Mary, Queen of Scots. First to call self king of Great Britain; this became official with Acts of Union, 1707	59
1625	Charles I, only surviving son of James I	48
	Great Britain: Commonwealth	
1649	Declared upon execution of Charles I	—
	Great Britain: Protectorate	
1653	Oliver Cromwell, served on Council of State, executive body of Commonwealth, following overthrow of monarchy. Named Lord Protector upon creation of Protectorate by 1653 Instrument of Government	59
1658	Richard Cromwell, 3rd son of Oliver Cromwell. Resigned as Lord Protector amid civil war, 1659	86
	Great Britain: House of Stuart (restored)	
1660	Charles II, eldest son of Charles I, Restoration put him back on throne, died without issue	55
1685	James II, 2nd son of Charles I, deposed 1688	68
1689	William III, son of William, Prince of Orange, by Mary, daughter of Charles I. Offered joint rule of throne with wife by Parliament	51
1689	Mary II, eldest daughter of James II and wife of William III, died 1694	33
1702	Anne, 2nd daughter of James II, sister-in-law of William III, assumed throne on William's death	49
	United Kingdom of Great Britain[3]: House of Hanover	
1714	George I, son of Elector of Hanover by Sophia, granddaughter of James I	67
1727	George II, only son of George I, married Caroline of Brandenburg	77
1760	George III, grandson of George II, married Charlotte of Mecklenburg	81
1820	George IV, eldest son of George III, prince regent from Feb. 1811	67
1830	William IV, 3rd son of George III, married Adelaide of Saxe-Meiningen	71
1837	Victoria, daughter of Edward, 4th son of George III; married Prince Albert of Saxe-Coburg and Gotha, 1840	81
	United Kingdom of Great Britain[3]: House of Saxe-Coburg-Gotha	
1901	Edward VII, eldest son of Victoria, married Alexandra, Princess of Denmark	68

Reign began	United Kingdom of Great Britain[3]: House of Windsor[4]	Age at death[1]
1910	George V, 2nd son of Edward VII, married Princess Mary of Teck	70
1936	Edward VIII, eldest son of George V, acceded Jan. 20, abdicated Dec. 11	77
1936	George VI, 2nd son of George V, married Lady Elizabeth Bowes-Lyon	56
1952	Elizabeth II, elder daughter of George VI, acceded Feb. 6	

NA = Age/birthdate not certain. (1) Except where noted, year of death is year of accession of succeeding ruler. (2) King Sweyn I of Denmark invaded England in 1013 and declared himself king. Ethelred II reclaimed the throne upon Sweyn's death in 1014. (3) Officially the United Kingdom of Great Britain and Ireland after Act of Union 1801 and the United Kingdom of Great Britain and Northern Ireland after Anglo-Irish Treaty of 1921 (name formalized 1927). (4) Name adopted by proclamation of George V, July 17, 1917, because of anti-German feeling during World War I.

Rulers of Scotland

Reign began	Name
846	Kenneth I, first Scot to rule both Scots and Picts
1005	Malcolm II, son of Kenneth II
1034	Duncan I, grandson, first general ruler
1040	Macbeth, seized kingdom, slain by Malcolm Canmore
1057	Malcolm III (Canmore), eldest son of Duncan I
1093	Donald III (the Fair), younger brother
1094	Duncan II, eldest son of Malcolm III by first wife
1095	Donald III (restored)
1097	Edgar, 4th son of Malcolm III and Queen Margaret
1107	Alexander I, brother
1124	David I, brother
1153	Malcolm IV (the Maiden), grandson
1165	William (the Lion), brother
1214	Alexander II, son
1249	Alexander III, son
1286	Margaret (Maid of Norway), granddaughter; died 1290 at age 8. (Interregnum, 1290-92)
1292	John Balliol, proclaimed king of Scotland by Edward I of England. (Interregnum, 1296-1306[1])
1306	Robert I (the Bruce), victor at Bannockburn, 1314. Treaty with England and secured throne, 1328
1329	David II, only surviving son
1371	Robert II (the Steward), son of Robert I's daughter Marjorie and Walter, steward of Scotland. First of Stewart line
1390	Robert III, son
1406	James I, son, assassinated
1437	James II, son
1460	James III, eldest son, possibly assassinated
1488	James IV, eldest son
1513	James V, eldest son, died at Battle of Flodden
1542	Mary (Queen of Scots), daughter, became queen before she was 1 week old. Married Francis II (d. 1560), son of King Henry II of France, 1558. Married her cousin, Henry Stewart, Lord Darnley (d. 1567), 1565. Married James Hepburn, Earl of Bothwell, 1567. Imprisoned by Elizabeth I, 1568; beheaded, 1587
1567	James VI, son of Mary and Lord Darnley, became James I, king of England, on Elizabeth's death, 1603. (Legislative union of Scotland and England as United Kingdom of Great Britain not official until Acts of Union, 1707)

Note: Not all rulers before 1005 are shown. (1) Edward I decreed annexation of Scotland to England, 1296, after defeating Balliol in battle. William Wallace led resistance, 1297-1305.

Prime Ministers of the United Kingdom

Cl. = Coalition; C = Conservative; La. = Labour; Li. = Liberal; P = Peelite; T = Tory; W = Whig

Entered office	Name (party)
1721	Sir Robert Walpole (W)[1]
1742	Earl of Wilmington (W)
1743	Henry Pelham (W)
1754	Duke of Newcastle (W)
1756	Duke of Devonshire (W)
1757	Duke of Newcastle (W)
1762	Earl of Bute (T)
1763	George Grenville (W)
1765	Marquess of Rockingham (W)
1766	William Pitt the Elder (Earl of Chatham) (W)
1768	Duke of Grafton (W)
1770	Frederick North (Lord North) (T)
1782	Marquess of Rockingham (W)
1782	Earl of Shelburne (W)
1783	Duke of Portland (Cl.)
1783	William Pitt the Younger (T)
1801	Henry Addington (T)
1804	William Pitt the Younger (T)
1806	William Wyndham Grenville, Baron Grenville (W)
1807	Duke of Portland (T)
1809	Spencer Perceval (T)
1812	Earl of Liverpool (T)
1827	George Canning (T)
1827	Viscount Goderich (T)
1828	Duke of Wellington (T)
1830	Earl Grey (W)
1834	Viscount Melbourne (W)
1834	Sir Robert Peel (C)
1835	Viscount Melbourne (W)
1841	Sir Robert Peel (C)
1846	Lord (later Earl) John Russell (W)
1852	Earl of Derby (C)
1852	Earl of Aberdeen (P)
1855	Viscount Palmerston (Li.)
1858	Earl of Derby (C)
1859	Viscount Palmerston (Li.)
1865	Earl Russell (Li.)
1866	Earl of Derby (C)
1868	Benjamin Disraeli (C)
1868	William E. Gladstone (Li.)
1874	Benjamin Disraeli (C)
1880	William E. Gladstone (Li.)
1885	Marquess of Salisbury (C)
1886	William E. Gladstone (Li.)
1886	Marquess of Salisbury (C)
1892	William E. Gladstone (Li.)
1894	Earl of Rosebery (Li.)
1895	Marquess of Salisbury (C)
1902	Arthur J. Balfour (C)
1905	Sir Henry Campbell-Bannerman (Li.)
1908	Herbert H. Asquith (Li.)
1915	Herbert H. Asquith (Cl.)
1916	David Lloyd George (Cl.)
1922	Andrew Bonar Law (C)
1923	Stanley Baldwin (C)
1924	James Ramsay MacDonald (La.)
1924	Stanley Baldwin (C)
1929	James Ramsay MacDonald (La.)
1931	James Ramsay MacDonald (Cl.)
1935	Stanley Baldwin (Cl.)
1937	Neville Chamberlain (Cl.)
1940	Winston Churchill (Cl.)
1945	Winston Churchill (C)
1945	Clement Attlee (La.)
1951	Sir Winston Churchill (C)
1955	Sir Anthony Eden (C)
1957	Harold Macmillan (C)
1963	Sir Alec Douglas-Home (C)
1964	Harold Wilson (La.)
1970	Edward Heath (C)
1974	Harold Wilson (La.)
1976	James Callaghan (La.)
1979	Margaret Thatcher (C)
1990	John Major (C)
1997	Tony Blair (La.)
2007	Gordon Brown (La.)
2010	David Cameron (Cl.)

Note: Prime ministers prior to 1801 are for Great Britain. The Conservative Party was formed in 1834, an outgrowth of the Tory party. (1) Walpole is commonly regarded as the first prime minister of Britain, though the title was not commonly used then and did not become official until 1905.

Prime Ministers of Canada

C = Conservative; Li. = Liberal; PC = Progressive Conservative; U = Unionist

Entered office	Name (party)
1867	Sir John A. Macdonald (C)
1873	Alexander Mackenzie (Li.)
1878	Sir John A. Macdonald (C)
1891	Sir John J. C. Abbott (C)
1892	Sir John S. D. Thompson (C)
1894	Sir Mackenzie Bowell (C)
1896[1]	Sir Charles Tupper (C)
1896	Sir Wilfrid Laurier (Li.)
1911	Sir Robert Laird Borden (C/U)[2]
1920	Arthur Meighen (U)
1921	W. L. Mackenzie King (Li.)
1926[3]	Arthur Meighen (C)
1926	W. L. Mackenzie King (Li.)
1930	Richard Bedford Bennett (C)
1935	W. L. Mackenzie King (Li.)
1948	Louis St. Laurent (Li.)
1957	John G. Diefenbaker (PC)
1963	Lester Bowles Pearson (Li.)
1968	Pierre Elliott Trudeau (Li.)
1979	Joe Clark (PC)
1980	Pierre Elliott Trudeau (Li.)
1984[3]	John Napier Turner (Li.)
1984	Brian Mulroney (PC)
1993[4]	Kim Campbell (PC)
1993	Jean Chrétien (Li.)
2003	Paul Martin (Li.)
2006	Stephen Harper (C)

(1) May-July. (2) Conservative 1911-17, Unionist 1917-20. (3) June-Sept. (4) June-Oct.

Rulers of France

Caesar to Charlemagne

Julius Caesar subdued the Gauls, native tribes of Gaul (France), 58 to 51 BCE. The Romans ruled 500 years. The Franks, a Teutonic tribe, reached the Somme from the east c. 250 CE. By the 5th cent., the Merovingian Franks ousted the Romans. In 451, with the help of Visigoths, Burgundians, and others, they defeated Attila and the Huns at Châlons-sur-Marne.

Childeric I became leader of the Merovingians, 458. His son Clovis I, crowned 481, founded the dynasty. After defeating the Alemanni (Germans), 496, he was baptized a Christian and made Paris his capital. His line ruled until Childeric III was deposed, 751.

The West Merovingians were called Neustrians, the eastern Austrasians. Pepin of Herstal (687-714), major domus (head of the palace) of Austrasia, took over Neustria as dux (leader) of the Franks. Pepin's son, Charles, called Martel (the Hammer), defeated the Saracens at Tours-Poitiers, 732; was succeeded by his son, Pepin the Short, 741, who deposed Childeric III and ruled as king until 768.

His son, Charlemagne, or Charles the Great (742-814), became king of the Franks, 768, with his brother Carloman (751-71). Charlemagne ruled France, Germany, parts of Italy, Spain, and Austria, and enforced Christianity. Crowned Emperor of the Romans by Pope Leo III in Rome, Dec. 25, 800. Succeeded by son, Louis I (the Pious), 814. At death, 840, Louis left empire to sons Lothair (Roman emperor), Pepin I (king of Aquitaine), Louis II (the German), and Charles II (the Bald, of France). They quarreled and, by the Treaty of Verdun, 843, divided the empire.

The date preceding each entry is year of accession.

Carolingian Dynasty

843 Charles II (the Bald), Roman emperor, 875
877 Louis II (the Stammerer), son
879 Louis III (d. 882), son, and brother Carloman
885 Charles II (the Fat), Roman emperor, 881
888 Eudes (Odo), elected by nobles
898 Charles III (the Simple), son of Louis II, defeated by Robert
922 Robert, brother of Eudes, killed in war
923 Rudolph (Raoul), duke of Burgundy
936 Louis IV, son of Charles III
954 Lothair, son, aged 13, defeated by Capet
986 Louis V (the Sluggard), left no heirs

House of Capet

987 Hugh Capet, son of Hugh the Great
996 Robert II (the Pious), son
1031 Henry I, son
1060 Philip I (the Fair), son
1108 Louis VI (the Fat), son
1137 Louis VII (the Younger), son
1180 Philip II (Augustus), son, crowned at Reims
1223 Louis VIII (the Lion), son
1226 Louis IX, son, arbitrated disputes with English King Henry III; led crusades, 1248 (captured in Egypt, 1250) and 1270, when he died of plague in Tunis. Canonized as St. Louis, 1297
1270 Philip III (the Hardy), son
1285 Philip IV (the Fair), son, king at 17
1314 Louis X (the Headstrong), son. His posthumous son, John I, lived and reigned only five days
1316 Philip V (the Tall), brother of Louis X
1322 Charles IV (the Fair), brother of Louis X

House of Valois

1328 Philip VI (of Valois), grandson of Philip III
1350 John II (the Good), son, retired to England
1364 Charles V (the Wise), son
1380 Charles VI (the Beloved), son
1422 Charles VII (the Victorious), son. In 1429, Joan of Arc (Jeanne d'Arc) defeated English at Orleans and Patay and had Charles crowned at Reims, July 17. Joan was captured May 24, 1430, and executed May 30, 1431, at Rouen for heresy. Charles ordered her rehabilitation, effected 1455.
1461 Louis XI (the Cruel), son, civil reformer
1483 Charles VIII (the Affable), son
1498 Louis XII, great-grandson of Charles V
1515 Francis I, of Angouleme, nephew, son-in-law. Fought four major wars, was patron of the arts
1547 Henry II, son, killed at joust. Husband of Catherine de Médicis and lover of Diane de Poitiers. Catherine was daughter of Lorenzo de Medici. By marriage to Henry II, she became the mother of Francis II, Charles IX, Henry III, and Queen Margaret (Reine Margot), wife of Henry IV (of Navarre).
1559 Francis II, son. Betrothed in 1548 at age 4 to Mary, Queen of Scots, aged 6; they were married 1558. Francis died 1560, aged 16. Mary returned to rule Scotland, 1561.
1560 Charles IX, brother
1574 Henry III, brother, assassinated

House of Bourbon

1589 Henry IV (of Navarre), grandson of Queen Margaret of Navarre. Made enemies when he gave tolerance to Protestants by Edict of Nantes, 1598. Married Margaret of Valois, daughter of Henry II and Catherine de Médicis; was divorced. Married Marie de Médicis, 1600. She became regent upon Henry's assassination, 1610-17, for her son, Louis XIII; she was exiled by Richelieu, 1631.
1610 Louis XIII (the Just), son, married Anne of Austria. His chief minister (1622-42), Cardinal Richelieu, determined his policies.
1643 Louis XIV (the Sun King), son; was king 72 years. Until 1661, Anne of Austria was regent with Cardinal Mazarin as chief minister; Louis then ruled absolutely. Known for his lavish court and arts patronage, he exhausted a prosperous country in wars for thrones and territory.
1715 Louis XV (the Beloved), great-grandson. Married a Polish princess, lost Canada to the English. His favorite mistresses, Mme. de Pompadour and Mme. Du Barry, influenced policies. Mme. Pompadour's saying "Après moi, le déluge" (After me, the deluge) often incorrectly attributed to Louis XV
1774 Louis XVI, grandson, married Marie Antoinette, daughter of Empress Maria Therese of Austria. King and queen beheaded by Revolution, 1793. Their son, called Louis XVII, died in prison, never ruled

First Republic

1792 National Convention of the French Revolution
1795 Directory, under Barras and others
1799 Consulate, Napoleon Bonaparte, first consul. Elected consul for life, 1802

First Empire

1804 Napoleon I (Napoleon Bonaparte), emperor. Josephine (de Beauharnais), empress, 1804-09; Marie Louise, empress, 1810-14. Son, Napoleon II (1811-32), titular king of Rome, later duke of Reichstadt, never ruled. Napoleon I abdicated 1814; died in exile, 1821.

House of Bourbon (restored)

1814 Louis XVIII, brother of Louis XVI, king
1824 Charles X, brother, reactionary, deposed by the July Revolution, 1830

House of Orleans

1830 Louis-Philippe (the Citizen King)

Second Republic

1848 Louis Napoleon Bonaparte, nephew of Napoleon I, president

Second Empire

1852 Napoleon III (Louis Napoleon Bonaparte), emperor; Eugenie (de Montijo), empress. Lost Franco-Prussian war, deposed 1870. Son, Prince Imperial (1856-79), died in Zulu War. Eugenie died 1920.

Third Republic

1871 Louis Adolphe Thiers (1797-1877), president
1873 Marshal Patrice M. de MacMahon (1808-93)
1879 Paul J. Grevy (1807-91)
1887 M. Sadi-Carnot (1837-94), assassinated
1894 Jean P. P. Casimir-Perier (1847-1907)
1895 François Felix Faure (1841-99)
1899 Emile Loubet (1838-1929)
1906 C. Armand Fallieres (1841-1931)
1913 Raymond Poincaré (1860-1934)
1920 Paul Deschanel (1856-1922)
1920 Alexandre Millerand (1859-1943)
1924 Gaston Doumergue (1863-1937)
1931 Paul Doumer (1857-1932), assassinated
1932 Albert Lebrun (1871-1950), resigned 1940

Vichy Regime

1940 Henri Philippe Petain (1856-1951), chief of state, 1940-44, under German armistice

Provisional Government

1944 Charles Andre J. M. de Gaulle (1890-1970)
1946 Felix Gouin (1884-1977)
1946 Georges Bidault (1899-1983)

Fourth Republic

1947 Vincent Auriol (1884-1966), president
1954 Rene Coty (1882-1962)

Fifth Republic

1959 Charles Andre J. M. De Gaulle (1890-1970), president
1969 Georges Pompidou (1911-74)
1974 Valéry Giscard d'Estaing (1926-)
1981 François Mitterrand (1916-96)
1995 Jacques Chirac (1932-)
2007 Nicolas Sarkozy (1955-)
2012 François Hollande (1954-)

Rulers of Middle Europe and Germany

Carolingian Dynasty

Charles I (the Great), or Charlemagne, made Roman emperor by pope in Rome, 800. Ruled France, Italy, and Middle Europe; established Ostmark (later Austria). Died 814.

Louis I (Ludwig) (the Pious), son, crowned co-emperor by Charlemagne, 813. Divided empire among sons. Died 840; sons fought for control.

Louis II (the German), son, succeeded to East Francia (Germany), 843-76, with Treaty of Verdun.

Charles III (the Fat), son, inherited Swabia, 876. With brothers' deaths, acquired East Francia and West Francia (France), reuniting empire. Crowned emperor by pope, 881; deposed 887.

Arnulf, nephew, 887-99, took over East Francia; partition of empire.

Louis IV (the Child), son, 900-11, last direct descendant of Charlemagne.

Conrad I, duke of Franconia, first elected German king, 911-18.

Saxon Dynasty; First Reich

Henry I (the Fowler), duke of Saxony, elected king 919-36.

Otto I (the Great), son, 936-73, crowned Holy Roman Emperor by pope, 962.

Otto II, son, 961-83, ruled with Otto I as king, then emperor, 967.

Otto III, son, 983-1002, crowned Holy Roman Emperor, 996.

Henry II (the Saint), great-grandson of Otto the Great, duke of Bavaria, 1002-24. Crowned emperor, 1014.

Salian Dynasty

Conrad II, 1024-39, elected king of Germany.

Henry III (the Black), son, 1039-56, deposed three popes; annexed Burgundy.

Henry IV, son, 1056-1106, with mother, Agnes of Poitou, as regent in early years. He and Pope Gregory VII tried to depose each other. Civil war lasted about 20 years.

Henry V, son, 1106-25, last of Salian Dynasty.

Lothair, duke of Saxony, elected king 1125-37. Crowned emperor in Rome, 1133.

Hohenstaufen Dynasty

Conrad III, duke of Franconia, 1138-52, in Second Crusade.

Frederick I (Barbarossa, Italian for "Redbeard"), nephew, 1152-90.

Henry VI, son, 1190-97, gained kingdom of Sicily through marriage.

Philip of Swabia, brother, 1197-1208. Otto IV, nephew of King Richard I of England, 1198-1215, was elected rival king. Philip's murder, in 1208, led to Otto's win in new election same year. Civil war followed before Otto was deposed, 1215.

Frederick II, son of Henry VI, elected 1212-50. Had earlier succeeded father as king of Sicily; crowned himself king of Jerusalem, 1229, in Sixth Crusade.

Conrad IV, son, 1250-54. Conquered Naples.

(Interregnum, 1254-73. Conradin, son of Conrad IV and last legitimate Hohenstaufen, defeated by Charles of Anjou—brother of King Louis IX of France—and executed, 1268. Rise of electors of German monarch.)

Transition

Rudolf I, of Hapsburg, 1273-91, defeated King Ottocar II of Bohemia, 1278. Bequeathed duchies of Austria and Styria to sons.

Adolf of Nassau, 1292-98, killed in war with Albert I.

Albert I, elder son of Rudolf I, 1298-1308, assassinated.

Henry VII, of Luxemburg, 1308-13. Gained Bohemia, 1310; crowned Holy Roman Emperor, 1312.

Louis IV, of Wittelsbach, 1314-46. Also elected was a son of Albert I, Frederick of Austria, whom Louis defeated in 1322. Rejected need for papal confirmation of elected German king.

Charles IV, of Luxemburg, grandson of Henry VII, 1346-78. Took Brandenburg.

Wenceslaus, son, 1378-1400; deposed.

Rupert, of Wittelsbach, elector palatine, 1400-10.

Sigismund, brother of Wenceslaus, 1410-37.

Hapsburg Dynasty

Albert II, duke of Austria, son-in-law of Sigismund, elected German king, 1438-39; king of Hungary and Holy Roman Emperor.

Frederick III, cousin, 1440-93, fought Turks.

Maximilian I, son, 1493-1519, archduke of Austria.

Charles V, grandson, 1519-58. King of Spain; assumed title of Holy Roman Emperor. Martin Luther, who had been excommunicated by pope, appeared at Diet of Worms, 1521. Charles attempted church reform and conciliation between Catholicism and Protestantism; abdicated.

Ferdinand I, brother, 1558-64; king of Hungary and Bohemia, 1526 (successive leaders through Maria Theresa will rule these lands as well).

Maximilian II, son, 1564-76.

Rudolf II, son, 1576-1612.

Matthias, brother, 1612-19.

Ferdinand II, grandson of Ferdinand I, 1619-37. Bohemian Protestants, unhappy with Ferdinand's support of Catholic Counter-Reformation, crowned Frederick V, elector palatine. Frederick became known as "Winter King" with defeat in battle, 1620; start of Thirty Years' War.

Ferdinand III, son, 1637-57. Treaties signed, 1648, in Peace of Westphalia ended war.

Leopold I, son, 1658-1705.

Joseph I, son, 1705-11.

Charles VI, brother, 1711-40; died without male heir.

Maria Theresa, daughter, 1740-80. Appointed husband, Francis Stephen of Lorraine, co-regent. Dispute over her inheritance led to War of the Austrian Succession. Charles VII, also known as Charles Albert, elected in opposition to Francis, 1742-45. After Charles's death, she obtained election of her husband as Holy Roman Emperor Francis I, 1745-65. Fought Seven Years' War with Frederick II of Prussia.

Hapsburg-Lorraine Dynasty

Joseph II, son, 1765-90, reformer. Ruled jointly with Maria Theresa until her death. Participated in first partition of Poland, with Prussia and Russia.

Leopold II, brother, 1790-92; king of Hungary and Bohemia.

Francis II, son, 1792-1806; king of Hungary and Bohemia. Proclaimed first emperor of Austria, 1804-35. Unsuccessfully fought against Napoleon; forced to abdicate, 1806, as Holy Roman Emperor, last use of title.

Ferdinand, son, 1835-48, emperor of Austria; king of Hungary and Bohemia. Abdicated in favor of nephew after revolution broke out in Vienna.

Austro-Hungarian Monarchy

Francis Joseph I, nephew, 1848-1916, emperor of Austria and king of Hungary. Defeated in Austro-Prussian War, 1866 Formed dual monarchy of Austria-Hungary, 1867. After Serbian nationalist assassinated Francis Joseph's nephew and heir, Archduke Francis Ferdinand, June 28, 1914, Austrian diplomacy precipitated World War I.

Charles I, grandnephew, 1916-18, last emperor of Austria and king of Hungary. Abdicated Nov. 1918; died in exile, 1922.

Second and Third Reichs

William I, brother of Frederick William IV, 1861-88, king of Prussia. Appointed Otto von Bismarck chancellor, 1862. Franco-Prussian War, also known as Franco-German War, 1870-71, unified German states. William proclaimed German emperor, 1871: beginning of Second Reich.

Frederick III, son, 1888.

William II, son, 1888-1918, led Germany into World War I Abdicated Nov. 1918; died in exile in the Netherlands, 1941.

Germany adopted constitution at Weimar, July 1, 1919, setting up Weimar Republic. Presidents included Friedrich Ebert 1919-25, and Paul von Hindenburg, 1925-34, field marshal in World War I. Hindenburg appointed Adolf Hitler chancellor 1933, at beginning of Third Reich. Following Hindenburg's death, Hitler succeeded as Führer and chancellor, 1934-45, with dictatorial powers. Annexed Austria, 1938. Precipitated World War II, 1939-45. Hitler committed suicide, 1945.

Germany After 1945

After World War II, Germany was split between democratic West and Soviet-dominated East. West German chancellors Konrad Adenauer, 1949-63; Ludwig Erhard, 1963-66; Kurt Georg Kiesinger, 1966-69; Willy Brandt, 1969-74; Helmut Schmidt, 1974-82; Helmut Kohl, 1982-90. East German Communist party leaders: Walter Ulbricht, 1950-71; Erich Honecker 1971-89; Egon Krenz, 1989. (Berlin Wall fell, Nov. 1989.)

Germany reunited Oct. 3, 1990. Post-reunification chancellors: Helmut Kohl, 1990-98; Gerhard Schröder, 1998-2005; Angela Merkel, 2005- .

Rulers of Hungary

The first king of Hungary was Stephen I, of the Arpad Dynasty, 1000-38. Feuds followed his death.

Charles I, also known as Charles Robert, became king, 1308-42.

Louis I (the Great), son, 1342-82. Succeeded uncle Casimir III as ruler of Poland, 1370.

Mary, elder daughter, 1382-95, ruled with husband, Sigismund of Luxemburg, 1387-1437, who also became king of Bohemia, Germany and Holy Roman Emperor. Hedwig (Jadwiga), younger daughter of Louis I, became queen of Poland. (See **Rulers of Poland**.)

Albert II, duke of Austria, son-in-law of Sigismund, 1438-39. Also king of Germany and Holy Roman Emperor.

Vladislaus I, 1440-44, king of Poland.

Ladislaus V, posthumous son of Albert II, 1444-57, not crowned until 1453. Janos Hunyadi acted as governor under young king, 1446-52; fought Turks.

Matthias I (Corvinus), son of Janos Hunyadi, 1458-90. Shared title of king of Bohemia. Captured Vienna, 1485; annexed Styria, Carinthia.

Vladislaus II, 1490-1516, king of Bohemia.

Louis II, son, 1516-26. Died in Battle of Mohács against Suleiman (the Magnificent), head of Ottoman Empire.

Ferdinand I, of Austria, brother-in-law, and John I, also known as John Zapolya of Transylvania, elected rival kings. Suleiman claimed part of Hungary for Ottoman Empire. Hungary partitioned. (Refer to **Hapsburg Dynasty** for continuation.)

Rulers of Prussia

Nucleus of Prussia was the margravate of Brandenburg, an electorate of the Holy Roman Empire. Frederick VI, burgrave of Nuremberg, was made elector of Brandenburg, 1415. Rise of Hohenzollern Dynasty in territory that included Brandenburg and duchy of Prussia.

Frederick William (the Great Elector), 1640-88, elector of Brandenburg.

Frederick III, son, 1688-1713, elector of Brandenburg. Crowned Frederick I, king in Prussia, 1701.

Frederick William I, son, 1713-40.

Frederick II (the Great), son, 1740-86; military strategist who expanded Prussia's holdings.

Frederick William II, nephew, 1786-97.

Frederick William III, son, 1797-1840; Napoleonic Wars.

Frederick William IV, son, 1840-61. Revolution of 1848; constitution adopted, 1850. (Refer to **Second and Third Reichs** for continuation.)

Rulers of Poland

House of Piast

Mieszko I, c. 963-92, duke of Poland; Poland Christianized, 966. Expansion under three with name Boleslaus (reigns not consecutive): Boleslaus I (the Brave), son, 992-1025, crowned first king of Poland, 1025; Boleslaus II (the Bold), great-grandson, 1058-79, exiled after killing bishop of Krakow, Stanislaus (who became a patron saint of Poland); Boleslaus III (the Wry-Mouthed), nephew, 1102-38, divided Poland among four sons with oldest also in control of crown. Period of feudal division followed.

A Polish duke, Conrad of Masovia, asked the Teutonic Knights—a German military religious order—to crusade against Prussia, 1226. Teutonic Knights conquered lands; thereafter warred with Poland. Mongols/Tatars invaded Poland, 1241.

Vladislaus I, 1306-33, reunited most Polish territories; crowned king, 1320. Casimir III (the Great), son, 1333-70, developed economy, cultural life, foreign policy. No male heir. Succeeded by Louis I, nephew, 1370-82, who was also Louis I (the Great) of Hungary.

Jadwiga, daughter, 1384-99.

House of Jagiello

Vladislaus Jagiello, grand duke of Lithuania, married Jadwiga, 1386, and ruled jointly as Vladislaus II, 1386-1434. Poland and Lithuania united; Lithuania converted to Christianity. Defeated Teutonic Knights at Grunwald (Tannenberg), 1410.

Vladislaus III, son, 1434-44, also king of Hungary. Fought Turks; killed in Battle of Varna, 1444.

Casimir IV, brother, 1447-92, put son Vladislaus on throne of Bohemia and Hungary. Victorious over Teutonic Knights; signed treaty, 1466, after 13-year war.

John I, son, 1492-1501.

Alexander I, brother, 1501-05.

Sigismund I, brother, 1506-48, patronized sciences and arts; his and son's reign were golden age. Grand Master of Teutonic Order, Albert Hohenzollern, converted to Protestantism; secularized his state and made first duke of Prussia by Sigismund, 1525.

Sigismund II, son, 1548-72; Union of Lublin, 1569, established dual state of Poland and Lithuania. No male heir.

Elective Kings

Henry of Valois, 1573-74, first king elected by nobility. Left Poland to assume crown of France after brother's death. Interregnum.

Stephen Bathory, 1576-86, prince of Transylvania, married Anna, sister of Sigismund II. Fought Russians.

Sigismund III Vasa, nephew of Sigismund II and son of king of Sweden, 1587-1632. Fought to reclaim Swedish crown, which he'd lost because of his Catholicism; battled Russians and Turks.

Vladislaus IV Vasa, son, 1632-48.

John II Casimir Vasa, brother, 1648-68. Fought Cossacks, Swedish, Russians, Turks, Tatars; period of invasions known as "the Deluge."

Michael Korybut Wisniowiecki, 1669-73.

John III Sobieski, 1674-96, freed Vienna from besieging Turks, 1683.

Augustus II (the Strong), 1697-1733, elector of Saxony.

Augustus III, son, 1733-63, elector of Saxony.

Stanislaus II, 1764-95, last king. Encouraged reforms; first modern constitution in Europe, 1791. Poland lost territory to Russia, Austria, and Prussia in three partitions (1772, 1793, 1795). Thaddeus Kosciusko, American-Polish general, attempted unsuccessful insurrection, 1794.

Poland Under Foreign Rule

Grand duchy of Warsaw created by Napoleon I out of Prussian (formerly Polish) territory. Frederick Augustus I, king of Saxony, ruled grand duchy, 1807-15. Defeat of Napoleon led to Congress of Vienna, 1814-15; part of Poland claimed as kingdom by Russia. Polish uprisings against Russia (1830, 1863) and Austria (1846) repressed. Poland regained independence following World War I.

Second Republic

Jozef Pilsudski, 1918-22, head of state. Presidents: Gabriel Narutowicz, 1922, assassinated by extremist; Stanislaus Wojciechowski, 1922-26, resigned after coup d'état by Pilsudski; Ignacy Moscicki, 1926-39, ruled with Pilsudski (d. 1935) and Pilsudski's military colleagues as virtual dictator during what came to be known as Sanacja (meaning "cleansing" or "healing") regime.

Poland Under Foreign Occupation, Influence

After Hitler and Stalin signed nonaggression pact, Germany invaded Poland Sept. 1, 1939; Russia invaded Sept. 17. Polish government-in-exile was in France, then England. Vladislaus Raczkiewicz, 1939-47, president; Gen. Vladislaus Sikorski, 1939-43, and Stanislaus Mikolajczyk, 1943-44, prime ministers. Polish residents were sent to German concentration camps and Soviet labor camps; about 3 million Jewish Poles were killed in the Holocaust. Thousands of Polish prisoners of war, mostly military officers, massacred in Katyn Forest by Soviet secret police, 1940. Soviet-sponsored Polish Committee of National Liberation took formative role in new government, 1945, renamed Polish People's Republic in 1952. Communist Polish United Workers' Party ruled the country. Brief period of liberalization followed Stalin's death in 1953. Vladislaus Gomulka, 1956-70, and Edward Gierek, 1970-80, led country as first secretary of Polish United Workers' Party.

Election of Cardinal Karol Wojtyla, archbishop of Krakow, as pope (John Paul II) inspired Poles, 1978. Strikes in 1980 prompted creation of Solidarity, an independent trade union headed by Lech Walesa. Solidarity gained control of government in partly free elections, 1985.

Third Republic

Presidents: Lech Walesa, 1990-95; Aleksander Kwasniewski, 1995-2005; Lech Kaczynski, 2005-10, died in plane crash; Bronislaus Komorowski and Grzegorz Schetyna, acting, 2010; Komorowski, 2010-15; Andrzej Duda, 2015- .

Rulers of Denmark, Sweden, Norway

Denmark

Canute (the Great) ruled area that included England, Denmark, and Norway, 1016-35. Valdemar IV Atterdag reunited Denmark, 1361. Margaret I, daughter, married to Haakon VI, king of Norway, 1363. After Valdemar's death, Olaf, Margaret's infant son, made king of Denmark, 1375. He was also crowned king of Norway after death of Haakon, 1380. Following Olaf's death, 1387, Margaret served as regent of Denmark, Norway, and Sweden. She effected the Union of Kalmar of the three kingdoms, 1397. She had her grandnephew, Eric of Pomerania, crowned (she held actual power until her death, 1412).

Succeeding rulers were unable to enforce their claims on Sweden until Christian II, 1512-23, conquered the country, 1520. He was soon deposed; accession of Gustavus I as king of Sweden, 1523, ended Kalmar Union. Denmark continued to dominate Norway until the Napoleonic Wars when Frederick VI, 1808-39, allied with Napoleon I after Danish fleet was attacked by Britain, 1807. By 1814 treaty, Denmark was forced to cede Norway to Sweden.

Succession: House of Oldenborg (began with Christian I, 1448): Christian VIII, 1839-48; Frederick VII, son, 1848-63. House of Glücksborg: Christian IX, 1863-1906; Frederick VIII, son, 1906-12; Christian X, son, 1912-47; Frederick IX, son, 1947-72; Margrethe II, daughter, 1972- .

Sweden

Under King Magnus Ladulas, hereditary nobility established around 1280. Swedish nobles opposed to Albert of Mecklenburg accepted Margaret I, regent of Denmark, as ruler, 1389. Sweden joined Kalmar Union, 1397. After internal unrest, Sweden was conquered anew by Denmark's Christian II, 1520. Execution of Christian's opponents in "Stockholm Bloodbath" led to uprising under Gustavus Vasa, who was elected Swedish king, 1523-60. Gustavus established an independent kingdom with centralized power, state church, and hereditary throne. Gustavus II Adolphus, 1611-32, fought Russia, Poland, Germany and was called the Lion of the North; died in battle.

Later rulers: Christina, daughter, 1632-54, abdicated; Charles X Gustavus, cousin, 1654-60; Charles XI, son, 1660-97; Charles XII, son, 1697-1718; Ulrika Eleonora, sister, 1718-20, abdicated; Frederick I, of Hesse, husband, 1720-51; Adolphus Frederick, 1751-71; Gustavus III, son, 1771-92; Gustavus IV Adolphus, son, 1792-1809, deposed; Charles XIII, uncle, 1809-18. Charles XIV John (born Jean Baptiste Bernadotte, a general under Napoleon I), 1818-44, founded House of Bernadotte.

Succession: Oscar I, son, 1844-59; Charles XV, son, 1859-72; Oscar II, brother, 1872-1907; Gustavus V, son, 1907-50; Gustavus VI Adolf, son, 1950-73; Carl XVI Gustavus, grandson, 1973- .

Norway

Harald I (Fairhair) overcame rivals to become first king of Norway, c. 885-c. 933. Olaf II Haraldsson, 1015-28, Christianized country; became patron saint of Norway. Haakon V Magnusson, 1299-1319, died without male heir. His daughter Ingeborg was married to Erik, a son of the Norwegian king; their son Magnus VII Eriksson became ruler of Norway, 1319-55, and Sweden, 1319-63. Haakon VI Magnusson, son, 1355-80, married Margaret of Denmark. Olaf IV, son, became king of Norway, 1380-87, and Denmark, 1375-87, with mother as regent. Margaret took over rule upon his death, 1387. Union of Kalmar, 1397, united Norway, Denmark, and Sweden.

After Napoleonic Wars, Denmark ceded Norway to Sweden, 1814. A strong nationalist movement forced Sweden to recognize Norway as an independent kingdom under the Swedish kings. Norwegian constitution, adopted 1814, allowed for creation of the Storting (Norwegian parliament), which governed country domestically. In 1905, the union was dissolved. Prince Charles of Denmark elected king of Norway as Haakon VII, 1905-57; founded House of Glücksburg. Succession: Olav V, son, 1957-91; Harald V, son, 1991- .

Rulers of the Netherlands and Belgium

The Netherlands

William I, son of Prince William V of Orange, came to power after French rule ended in the Netherlands, 1813; crowned king with approval of Congress of Vienna, 1815. Started House of Orange-Nassau. Northern Netherlands was known as Holland. Belgians, in southern Netherlands, rebelled against the Dutch and seceded, Oct. 4, 1830. Dutch formally recognized Belgian independence, Apr. 19, 1839. William I abdicated, 1840.

Succession: William II, son, 1840-49; William III, son, 1849-90; Wilhelmina, daughter, 1890-1948; Juliana, daughter, 1948-80; Beatrix, daughter, 1980-2013; Willem-Alexander, son, 2013- .

Belgium

A national congress elected Prince Leopold of Saxe-Coburg as king. He took the throne July 21, 1831, as Leopold I.

Succession: Leopold II, son, 1865-1909; Albert I, nephew, 1909-34; Leopold III, son, 1934-51, in exile after Germany invaded Belgium, later abdicated; Prince Charles, brother, acted as regent 1944-50; Baudouin I, son of Leopold III, 1951-93; Albert II, brother, 1993-2013; Philippe, son, 2013- .

Rulers of Modern Italy

After the fall of Napoleon, the Congress of Vienna, 1814-15, restored Italy as a political patchwork, comprising the Kingdom of the Two Sicilies (Naples and Sicily), the Papal States, and smaller units. King Victor Emmanuel I of Savoy ruled Sardinia, Piedmont, and Genoa.

Victor Emmanuel I abdicated 1821. Charles Felix, brother, 1821-31, died without issue. Succeeded by Charles Albert, 1831-49; he abdicated upon defeat by the Austrians. Succeeded by Victor Emmanuel II, son, 1849-61. United Italy emerged under Camillo Benso di Cavour, prime minister of the Kingdom of Sardinia, 1852-61. Giuseppe Mazzini and Giuseppe Garibaldi were also figures in Risorgimento ("resurgence") period before Italy's unification.

In 1859, France forced Austria to cede Lombardy to Sardinia. In 1860, Garibaldi led more than 1,000 volunteers in a campaign against King Francis II of the Two Sicilies, taking Sicily and Naples. The House of Savoy subsequently annexed the Two Sicilies, Tuscany, Parma, Modena, Romagna, the Marches, and Umbria. Victor Emmanuel II assumed leadership of a united Kingdom of Italy, Mar. 17, 1861.

In 1866, Victor Emmanuel II allied with Prussia in the Austro-Prussian War and, with Prussia's victory, received Venetia. On Sept. 20, 1870, Italian troops entered Rome, ending the temporal power of the Roman Catholic Church. (The 1929 Lateran Treaty established papal sovereignty in Vatican City.)

Succession: Umberto I, son, 1878-1900, assassinated; Victor Emmanuel III, son, 1900-46; Umberto II, son, 1946, ruled a month. In 1919, Benito Mussolini helped found the nationalist Fasci di Combattimento (Fighting Leagues), or Fascists. After Mussolini organized March on Rome, 1922, Victor Emmanuel III agreed to a coalition government. Mussolini eventually became dictator (Il Duce). He entered World War II as an ally of Hitler, 1940. He was dismissed by the king, 1943; executed, 1945.

At a plebiscite, 1946, voters approved a republic. Prime minister Alcide de Gasperi was chief of state, 1945-53; Enrico de Nicola was provisional president. Successive presidents: Luigi Einaudi, 1948-55; Giovanni Gronchi, 1955-62; Antonio Segni, 1962-64; Giuseppe Saragat, 1964-71; Giovanni Leone, 1971-78; Alessandro Pertini, 1978-85; Francesco Cossiga, 1985-92; Oscar Luigi Scalfaro, 1992-99; Carlo Azeglio Ciampi, 1999-2006; Giorgio Napolitano, 2006-15; Sergio Mattarella, 2015- .

Rulers of Spain

From 8th to 11th centuries, Spain was dominated by the Moors (Muslims from North Africa of Arab and Berber origin). A number of small kingdoms—Aragon, Asturias, Castile, Catalonia, Leon, Navarre, and Valencia—undertook a Christian reconquest. In 1474, Isabella became Queen of Castile and Leon. By the Catholic Monarchs' request, Pope Sixtus IV authorized the Inquisition, 1478. Isabella's husband, Ferdinand V, acceded to the throne of Aragon, 1479. Last Moorish kingdom, Granada, seized 1492. Spain sponsored Christopher Columbus, who led European exploration of New World, 1492. Isabella was succeeded by daughter, Joanna (the Mad), but Ferdinand acted as regent until his death, 1516.

Charles I, son of Joanna and grandson of Hapsburg Emperor Maximilian I, became Holy Roman Emperor as Charles V, 1520;

abdicated 1556. Philip II, son, 1556-98, inherited only part of empire. He conquered Portugal, fought against Ottoman Empire, sent Armada in unsuccessful invasion of England. Succession: Philip III, son, 1598-1621; Philip IV, son, 1621-65; Charles II, son, 1665-1700, no issue, left Spain to Philip of Anjou, grandson of Louis XIV of France. As Philip V, he was first of Bourbon dynasty in Spain, 1700-46 (his son Louis ruled briefly in 1724); Ferdinand VI, son, 1746-59; Charles III, brother, 1759-88; Charles IV, son, 1788-1808, abdicated.

Joseph Bonaparte made king of Spain, 1808-13, by his brother Napoleon. Ferdinand VII, son of Charles IV, 1808, 1814-33, lost American colonies except Cuba, Puerto Rico. Maria Christina of the Two Sicilies, wife, was regent until 1843 for Isabella II, daughter, who was driven into exile by revolution, 1868. Amadeo of Savoy elected king by the Cortes (parliament), 1870-73. First Republic, 1873-74. Alfonso XII, son of Isabella II, 1875-85; Alfonso XIII, posthumous son, 1901-31, with mother Maria Christina as regent before he assumed throne. Spain ceded territory after loss in Spanish-American War, 1898. Primo de Rivera ruled as dictator after military coup but was forced to resign after losing support, 1923-30. Alfonso agreed to exile without formal abdication. Monarchy abolished; Second Republic established with socialist backing. Presidents: Niceto Alcala Zamora, 1931-36; Manuel Azaña, 1936-39.

Revolt by military started Spanish Civil War, 1936-39. Gen. Francisco Franco ruled as head of Nationalist regime, 1939-73. Monarchy restored after 1947 referendum. Juan Carlos, grandson of Alfonso XIII, acceded to throne after Franco's death in 1975; abdicated, 2014. Felipe VI, son, 2014- .

Leaders in the South American Wars of Liberation

Francisco de Miranda, José de San Martín, and Simón Bolívar led early 19th-cent. struggles of South American nations to free themselves from Spain.

Miranda (1750-1816), a Venezuelan, served as an officer in the Spanish army. After a dispute with the army, he fled to the U.S., 1783, where he met leaders of the American Revolution. He traveled seeking support for South American independence from other world leaders. Miranda unsuccessfully attempted a revolt in Venezuela, 1806. Napoleon's invasion of Spain, 1808, prompted the start of a revolution in Venezuela. Miranda returned, 1810, and headed the revolution with dictatorial powers. Venezuela declared independence, 1811. Overcome by royalist forces, 1812, Miranda surrendered and was arrested; he died in a Spanish prison.

San Martín (1778-1850) was born in present-day Argentina. He served in Spanish campaigns in Europe until 1811. He returned to Argentina and joined the independence movement, 1812. In 1817, he invaded Chile through the Andean mountain passes. He and Bernardo O'Higgins defeated the Spanish at Chacabuco, 1817. Chile gained independence, 1819; O'Higgins became first director of Chile, 1817-23. In 1821, San Martín entered Lima and took the port of Callao; he became protector of an independent Peru.

Bolívar (1783-1830) was born into an aristocratic family in Venezuela. He served under Miranda until Miranda's surrender in 1812. Bolívar continued to fight; he captured Caracas and was named Liberator, 1813. But he was forced to flee by royalist forces, 1814. In 1817, Bolívar again fought for control of Venezuela. With Francisco de Paula Santander and José Antonio Páez, he defeated the Spanish at the Battle of Boyacá, 1819, freeing New Granada (present-day Colombia). New Granada, Venezuela, and the area that is now Panama and Ecuador were joined as the Republic of Colombia, or Gran Colombia, with Bolívar as president later that same year, though parts of the republic remained under Spanish control. He decisively defeated the Spanish in the Battle of Carabobo in Venezuela, 1821.

Antonio José de Sucre, Bolívar's chief lieutenant, overcame Spanish forces at the Battle of Pichincha in Ecuador, 1822. Bolívar convinced San Martín to resign as protector of Peru. Peru was declared independent after Bolívar and Sucre won the Battle of Junin, Aug. 1824, and Sucre triumphed at the Battle of Ayacucho, Dec. 1824.

Sucre organized Upper Peru as Republica Bolívar (now Bolivia), 1825, and acted as president in place of Bolívar, who wrote its constitution.

Civil strife caused the Colombian federation to break apart. Bolívar gave up the presidency, 1830.

Rulers of Russia; Leaders of the USSR and Russian Federation

The Varangian (Viking) prince Rurik is considered to be the first leader of the Russians; he established himself at Novgorod, c. 862 CE. His successor, Oleg, and those who followed Oleg ruled as princes of Kiev. Vladimir I, or Saint Vladimir, married sister of Byzantine emperor and converted to Christianity, 988. Yaroslav I (the Wise), brother, 1019-54, was important organizer and lawgiver; his daughters married kings of Norway, Hungary, and France. In 1169, Andrew Bogolyubsky conquered Kiev and began the line of Vladimir.

Daniel, a son of grand prince of Vladimir, Alexander Nevsky, was first to be called prince of Muscovy (Moscow), 1263-1303. Dmitri Ivanovich (Donskoi), prince of Moscow, defeated the Tatars at the Battle of Kulikovo, 1380. His successors were grand princes of Moscow. Ivan III (the Great), 1462-1505, achieved considerable territorial expansion.

Ivan III married Sofia Palaeologus, niece of the last Byzantine emperor. Succession: Vasily III, son. Ivan IV (the Terrible), son, crowned 1547 as Tsar of Russia, ruled until 1584. Fyodor I, son, 1584-98, was weak; Boris Godunov had control before becoming tsar, 1598-1605. After years of internal strife ("Time of Troubles"), the Russians united under 16-year-old Michael Romanov, distantly related to Ivan IV's first wife. He ruled 1613-45, establishing the Romanov line.

Tsars, or emperors, of Russia (Romanovs): Peter I (the Great), 1682-1725, with Ivan V, brother, as co-ruler, 1682-96. Catherine I, his widow, 1725-27. Peter II, grandson of Peter I, 1727-30. Anna, daughter of Ivan V and niece of Peter I, 1730-40. Ivan VI, nephew, 1740-41; deposed by Elizabeth, daughter of Peter I, 1741-62. Peter III, nephew, 1762; deposed by his wife, Catherine II (the Great), former princess of Anhalt Zerbst (Germany), 1762-96. Paul I, son, 1796-1801, assassinated. Alexander I, son, 1801-25, defeated Napoleon. Nicholas I, brother, 1825-55. Alexander II, son, 1855-81, assassinated. Alexander III, son, 1881-94. Nicholas II, son, 1894-1917, last tsar of Russia, was forced to abdicate by revolutionaries following losses to Germany in WWI. The tsar, empress, tsarevich (crown prince), and tsar's four daughters were murdered by the Bolsheviks, July 1918.

Premiers of provisional government: Prince Georgi Lvov, followed by Alexander Kerensky, 1917.

Union of Soviet Socialist Republics

Bolshevik Revolution, Nov. 7, 1917, (also known as the October Revolution, based on Russia's then use of the Julian calendar) removed Kerensky from power. Council of People's Commissars formed with Lenin (Vladimir Ilyich Ulyanov) as chair (or premier), 1917-24. Aleksei Rykov (executed 1938) and Vyacheslav M. Molotov held the office, but effective ruler was Joseph Stalin (Joseph Vissarionovich Dzhugashvili), general secretary of the Communist Party. Stalin was chair of the Council of People's Commissars from 1941 until his death in 1953. Succeeded by Georgi M. Malenkov, who also briefly served as general secretary of the Communist Party before being ousted from the position by Nikita S. Khrushchev. Malenkov was forced to resign as premier, 1955, and was expelled from the Communist Party, 1961. Nikolai A. Bulganin was premier, 1955-58, until his replacement by Khrushchev, 1958-64.

Leonid I. Brezhnev ousted Khrushchev as general secretary of the party, a post he held until his death in 1982. Aleksei N. Kosygin was premier, 1964-80. The Central Committee elected former KGB (state security) head Yuri V. Andropov general secretary, 1982-84. After Andropov's death, Konstantin U. Chernenko was chosen for the position, 1984-85. Upon Chernenko's death, he was succeeded by Mikhail Gorbachev. Gorbachev assumed the newly created position of president of the Soviet Union, 1990. Boris Yeltsin was sworn in July 1991 as the Russian Republic's first elected president. Under Yeltsin, Russia became a founding member of the Commonwealth of Independent States. Gorbachev resigned the presidency, Dec. 25, 1991, and the Soviet Union officially disbanded Dec. 31. Each of the 15 former Soviet constituent republics became independent.

Post-Soviet Russia

Presidents of the Russian Federation: Boris Yeltsin, 1991-99; Vladimir Putin, 2000-08; Dmitry Medvedev, 2008-12; Putin, 2012- .

Governments of China

Where dynastic dates overlap, the rulers or events referred to appeared in different areas of China.

Years in power	Government
c. 1994-c. 1766 BCE	Xia dynasty, first hereditary Chinese dynasty
c. 1766-c. 1027 BCE	Shang dynasty
c. 1027-770 BCE	Western Zhou dynasty, capital near present-day Xi'an
770-256 BCE	Eastern Zhou dynasty, new capital established at Luoyang
403-221 BCE	Period of the Warring States
221-206 BCE	Qin dynasty, quasi-feudal states unified for first time; name of China derived from this dynasty
206 BCE-9 CE	Earlier, or Western Han dynasty, founded by rebel leader Liu Bang; Chinese state expanded under Emperor Wudi (born Liu Che), 140-87 BCE, who represented zenith of power
9-23	Xin dynasty, established by courtier Wang Mang, who deposed infant emperor for whom he had been acting as regent
25-220	Later, or Eastern Han dynasty
220-265[1]	Wei dynasty, established by son of Han general Cao Cao
221-263[1]	Shu Han dynasty in SW China
222-280[1]	Wu dynasty in SE China
265-317	Western Jin dynasty, established by Sima Yan, Wei dynasty general
317-420	Eastern Jin dynasty, established by prince of Sima family
420-589	Southern dynasties, four short-lived dynasties with capital at Jiankang (present-day Nanjing)
589-618	Sui dynasty, reunified China; first ruler was Emperor Wendi (born Yang Jian), military appointee who usurped throne of non-Chinese Northern Zhou, 581
618-906	Tang dynasty, founded by Li Yuan (known as Emperor Gaozu), who led rebellion against the Sui. Early rulers included former imperial concubine Empress Wu, 683-705; Xuanzong, 712-56
907-960	Five Dynasties, period of disunion with short-lived dynasties in N; Ten Kingdoms (or states) mostly in S
907-1125	Liao dynasty, of Khitan Mongols, capital at Yanjing (present-day Beijing)
960-1126	Northern Song dynasty, established by military leader Zhao Kuangyin, capital at Kaifeng
1122-1234	Jin dynasty, of Juchen people of Manchuria; drove Song out of N China
1127-1279	Southern Song dynasty, capital at Lin'an (present-day Hangzhou)
1279-1368	Yuan dynasty, of Mongols; Kublai Khan, grandson of Genghis Khan, high point of Mongol power
1368-1644	Ming dynasty, founded by rebel leader Zhu Yuanzhang, former Buddhist monk. Country again under Chinese rule, capital in present-day Nanjing, then Beijing after defeat of Mongolian tribes
1644-1912	Qing, or Manchu dynasty, under rule of Manchu people. Power of Chinese empire reached highest point in its 2,000-year history. Last imperial dynasty; Emperor Xuantong, or Puyi, last emperor. Sun Yat-sen led revolution, 1911. Republic of China formed, 1912
1912-1949	Rep. of China, Gen. Yuan Shikai elected first president. Power passed to provincial warlords upon his death, 1916. Gen. Chiang Kai-shek sought to reunify China under Kuomintang (Nationalist party), with new national government at Nanjing, 1928. War with Japan, then civil war, led to Nationalist authority collapse, Communist declaration of People's Rep. of China, 1949

(1) Also known as the period of the Three Kingdoms because of warfare between the Wei, Shu Han, and Wu dynasties.

Leaders of People's Republic of China

Name	Title/position, years in power
Mao Zedong	Chairman, 1949-59; Communist Party of China (CPC) Chairman, 1949-76
Zhou Enlai	Premier, 1949-76; foreign minister, 1949-76
Deng Xiaoping	Deputy Premier, 1952-66, 1973-76; "paramount leader," 1977-97
Liu Shaoqi	Chairman, 1959-68
Hua Guofeng	Premier, 1976-80; CPC Chairman, 1976-81
Hu Yaobang	CPC General Secretary, 1980-87; CPC Chairman, 1981-82[1]
Zhao Ziyang	Premier, 1980-87; CPC General Secretary, 1987-89
Li Xiannian	President, 1983-88
Yang Shangkun	President, 1988-93
Li Peng	Premier, 1988-98
Jiang Zemin	CPC General Secretary, 1989-2002; President, 1993-2003
Zhu Rongji	Premier, 1998-2003
Hu Jintao	CPC General Secretary, 2002-12; President, 2003-13
Wen Jiabao	Premier, 2003-13
Xi Jinping	CPC General Secretary, 2012- ; President, 2013-
Li Keqiang	Premier, 2013-

(1) Position of CPC chairman was abolished in 1982, making the CPC general secretary the party's highest-ranking official.

Historical Periods of Japan

Years in power	Period	Founding event
c. 300-592	Yamato	Conquest of Yamato plain
592-710	Asuka	Accession of Empress Suiko
710-794	Nara	Heijo (Nara) completed; capital moved to Nagaoka, 784
794-1185	Heian	Heian (Kyoto) completed
858-1160	Fujiwara	Fujiwara-no-Yoshifusa became regent
1160-1185	Taira	Taira-no-Kiyomoro assumed control; Minamoto-no-Yoritomo victor over Taira, 1185
1192-1333	Kamakura	Yoritomo became shogun
1334-1392	Namboku	Emperor Godaigo restored; established Southern Court at Yoshino, 1336
1392-1573	Muromachi	Unification of Southern and Northern Courts
1467-1600	Sengoku	Onin war began
1573-1603	Momoyama	Oda Nobunaga entered Kyoto, 1568, deposed last Ashikaga shogun, 1573. Tokugawa Ieyasu victor at Sekigahara, 1600
1603-1867	Edo	Ieyasu became shogun
1868-1912	Meiji	Meiji (Mutsuhito) ascended throne in Meiji Restoration; Charter Oath, 1868, led to Westernization
1912-1926	Taisho	Accession of Emperor Taisho (Yoshihito)
1926-1989	Showa	Accession of Emperor Hirohito
1989-	Heisei	Accession of Emperor Akihito

WORLD EXPLORATION AND GEOGRAPHY

Early Explorers of the Western Hemisphere

Genetic evidence suggests that beginning around 14,000 years before the present (BP), the earliest immigrants crossed the Bering Land Bridge, which was up to 1,000-km (621-mi) wide in places, between Siberia and Alaska and spread rapidly south through the Americas, arriving at S America's southern tip by c. 10,700 BP. The Anzick child (c. 12,600 BP), uncovered in Montana in 1968; Kennewick Man (9,600-9,200 BP), found in Washington's Columbia River in 1996; and Luzia (11,500 BP) from Brazil are examples of these early arrivals. Modern Native Americans appear to be descended from peoples indigenous to N and Central Asia who arrived in subsequent waves. Genetic, skeletal, and linguistic evidence documents their migration throughout the Americas.

Archaeologists have confirmed evidence of habitation by 12,900 BP at sites along the shores of ancient lakes in Chile's Atacama Desert. One theory holds that a glacier covered much of N America from c. 20,000 to 13,000 BP; those who settled in S America might have traveled there in small boats skirting the pack ice along the W coast or spread from the N through an ice-free corridor in what today is western Canada. Other theories posit that they arrived before continental glaciation blocked migration or came from Iberia in skin boats. Remains from a burial at Santana do Riacho in Brazil (8,000-10,000 BP) seem to suggest that some of the early immigrants may have originated in Africa, coming via the land bridge from Siberia.

Long before Europeans arrived, the Americas were, for the most part, populated by hunter-gatherers and small-scale horticulturalists. In a few areas (SE U.S., Mesoamerica, coastal Peru and Chile), complex chiefdoms and state-level societies had appeared. Irrigation canals dating to 4,700 BP provide evidence for the origins of large-scale agriculture along the western slopes of Peru's Andes Mountains. The earliest known state in the Americas occupied a 700-sq-mi area spanning four river valleys in coastal Peru between 3,500 and 500 BP.

The Norse (Vikings sailing out of Iceland and Greenland), led by Leif Ericson, are usually credited with having been the first Europeans to reach America, with at least five voyages occurring about 1000 CE to areas they called Helluland, Markland, and Vinland—possibly what are known today as Baffin Island, Labrador, and either Newfoundland or somewhere farther south in New England. L'Anse aux Meadows, on the northern tip of Newfoundland, is the only documented settlement, with evidence of a small village with workshops and a forge dating to c. 1000 CE. The Norse abandoned Greenland and Newfoundland after failing to import farming and herding economies.

Sustained contact between the hemispheres began with the first voyage of Christopher Columbus (born Cristoforo Colombo, c. 1451, near Genoa, Italy). Columbus made four voyages to the New World under the authority of the Spanish monarchs Ferdinand II and Isabella. He left Palos, Spain, Aug. 3, 1492, with a fleet of three vessels—the *Niña*, *Pinta*, and *Santa María*—and 88 men, landing at San Salvador (Watlings Island, The Bahamas) on Oct. 12, 1492. He also visited Cuba, Hispaniola, and many smaller Caribbean islands, then populated by the Taíno Indians. A second expedition left Cadíz, Spain, Sept. 25, 1493, with 17 ships and 1,400 men, reaching the island of Dominica in the Lesser Antilles on Nov. 3, 1493. His third voyage took him from Sanlucar, Spain, on May 30, 1498, with six ships, to the island of Trinidad and to the adjacent coast of S America, where he made landfall at the mouth of the Orinoco River. A fourth voyage departed Cadíz on May 9, 1502, and reached the E coast of Mexico, Honduras, Panama, and what he christened Santiago (the present-day island of Jamaica). Columbus died in Spain, on May 20, 1506, still convinced he had reached Asia by sailing west.

In N America, John and Sebastian Cabot, Italian explorers sailing for the English crown, reached Newfoundland and possibly Nova Scotia in 1497. John's second voyage (1498), in search of the fabled Northwest Passage trade route to Asia, resulted in the loss of his entire fleet.

In 1497 and 1499, Amerigo Vespucci (for whom the Americas are named), an Italian explorer sailing for Spain, passed along the N and E coasts of S America. He was the first to argue that these lands were previously unknown and not part of Asia. For most of the 16th cent., exploration was dominated by the Spanish and Portuguese empires. Some early explorations are listed below.

Year	Explorer	Nationality (sponsor, if different)	Area reached or explored
1497-98	Vasco da Gama	Portuguese	Cape of Good Hope (Africa), India
1499	Alonso de Ojeda	Spanish	Northern S Amer. coast, Venezuela
1500	Vicente Yañez Pinzón	Spanish	S American coast, Amazon R.
1500	Pedro Álvarez Cabral	Portuguese	Brazil
1501	Rodrigo de Bastidas	Spanish	Central America
1513	Vasco Núñez de Balboa	Spanish	Panama, Pacific Ocean
1513	Juan Ponce de León	Spanish	Florida, Yucatán Peninsula
1515	Juan de Solis	Spanish	Río de la Plata
1519	Alonso de Pineda	Spanish	Mouth of Mississippi R.
1519	Hernán Cortés	Spanish	Mexico
1519-20	Ferdinand Magellan	Portuguese (Spanish)	Straits of Magellan, Tierra del Fuego
1524	Giovanni da Verrazano	Italian (French)	Atlantic coast, incl. New York Harbor
1528	Álvar Núñez Cabeza de Vaca	Spanish	Texas coast and interior
1532	Francisco Pizarro	Spanish	Peru
1534	Jacques Cartier	French	Canada, Gulf of St. Lawrence
1536	Pedro de Mendoza	Spanish	Buenos Aires
1539	Francisco de Ulloa	Spanish	California coast
1539	Marcos de Niza	Italian (Spanish)	SW United States
1539-41	Hernando de Soto	Spanish	Mississippi R., near Memphis, TN
1540	Francisco de Coronado	Spanish	SW United States
1540	Hernando de Alarcón	Spanish	Colorado R.
1540	Garcia Lopez de Cárdenas	Spanish	Colorado, Grand Canyon
1541	Francisco de Orellana	Spanish	Amazon R.
1542	Juan Rodriguez Cabrillo	Portuguese (Spanish)	Western Mexico, San Diego Harbor
1565	Pedro Menéndez de Avilés	Spanish	St. Augustine, FL
1576	Sir Martin Frobisher	English	Frobisher Bay, Canada
1577-80	Sir Francis Drake	English	California coast, on voyage around world
1582	Antonio de Espejo	Spanish	SW U.S. (New Mexico)
1584	Philip Amadas and Arthur Barlowe (for Raleigh)	English	Virginia
1585-87	Sir Walter Raleigh's men	English	Roanoke Isl., NC
1595	Sir Walter Raleigh	English	Orinoco R.
1603-09	Samuel de Champlain	French	Canadian interior, Lake Champlain
1607	John Smith	English	Atlantic coast
1609-10	Henry Hudson	English (Dutch)	Hudson R., Hudson Bay
1634	Jean Nicolet	French	Lake Michigan, Wisconsin
1673	Jacques Marquette and Louis Jolliet	French	Mississippi R., south to Arkansas
1682	René-Robert Cavelier, sieur de La Salle	French	Mississippi R., south to Gulf of Mexico
1727-29	Vitus Bering	Danish (Russian)	Bering Strait, Alaska
1789	Sir Alexander Mackenzie	Canadian	NW Canada
1804-06	Meriwether Lewis and William Clark	American	Missouri R., Rocky Mts., Columbia R.

Arctic Exploration

Early Explorers

1587: John Davis (Eng.) traveled Davis Strait to Sanderson's Hope, 72°12´N.

1596-97: Willem Barents and Jacob van Heemskerck (Dutch) discovered Bear Isl., touched NW tip of Spitsbergen, 79°49´N, rounded Novaya Zemlya, where they were forced to winter ashore, first W Europeans to successfully do so in the Arctic.

1607: Henry Hudson (Eng.) went north along Greenland's E coast to Cape Hold-with-Hope, 73°30´, then north of Spitsbergen to 80°23´. Explored Hudson's Touches (Jan Mayen).

1616: William Baffin and Robert Bylot (Eng.) traveled Baffin Bay to Smith Sound.

1728: Vitus Bering (Dan./Russ.) sailed through strait (Bering), proving Asia and America are separate.

1733-40: Great Northern Expedition (Russ.) surveyed Siberian Arctic coast.

1741: Vitus Bering (Dan./Russ.) sighted Alaska, named Mount St. Elias. His lieutenant, Aleksei Chirikof, explored coast.

1771: Samuel Hearne (Brit., Hudson's Bay Co.) went overland from Prince of Wales Fort (Churchill) on Hudson Bay to mouth of Coppermine R.

1778: James Cook (Brit.) sailed through Bering Strait to Icy Cape, AK, and North Cape, Siberia.

1789: Sir Alexander Mackenzie (Scot., North West Co.). Montreal to mouth of Mackenzie R.

1806: William Scoresby (Brit.). North of Spitsbergen to 81°30´.

1820-23: Ferdinand von Wrangel (Russ.) surveyed Siberian Arctic coast. His exploration joined James Cook's at North Cape, confirming separation of the continents.

1827: William Edward Parry (Brit.), attempting to reach North Pole via Spitsbergen, reached 82°45´N via sledge.

1831: James Clark Ross (Brit.) was first to reach north magnetic pole.

1878-79: Baron Adolf Erik Nordenskiöld (Swed.) was first to navigate the Northeast Passage—an ocean route connecting Europe's North Sea, along the Arctic coast of Asia and through the Bering Sea, to the Pacific Ocean.

1881: The U.S. steamer *Jeannette*, led by Lt. Cmdr. George W. DeLong, was trapped in ice and crushed, June. DeLong and 11 others died; 12 survived.

1881-84: Adolphus Greely led 24-person U.S. expedition to Ellesmere Isl. Only he and five others survived after failed attempts to reach them left the expedition with few supplies.

1888: Fridtjof Nansen (Nor.) crossed Greenland ice cap.

1893-96: Nansen in *Fram* drifted from New Siberian Isls. to Spitsbergen; tried polar dash in 1895, reached Franz Josef Land, 86°14´N.

1897: Salomon A. Andrée (Swed.) and two others started in balloon from Spitsbergen, July 11; they drifted across pole to U.S. before disappearing. Their bodies were found, Aug. 6, 1930, on White Isl., 82°57´N, 29°52´E.

1903-06: Roald Amundsen (Nor.) was first to sail whole length of Northwest Passage—ocean route linking the Atlantic Ocean to the Pacific via Canada's marine waterways.

North Pole Exploration

Robert E. Peary (U.S.) explored Greenland's coast, 1891-92; tried for North Pole, 1893. In 1900, he reached northern limit of Greenland and 83°50´N; in 1902, he reached 84°17´N; in 1906, he went from Ellesmere Isl. to 87°06´N. He sailed in the *Roosevelt*, July 1908, to winter off Cape Sheridan, Grant Land. The dash for the North Pole began Mar. 1 from Cape Columbia, Ellesmere Isl. Peary reportedly reached the pole, 90°N, Apr. 6, 1909; recent research suggests he may have fallen short of his goal by c. 30-60 mi. (Dr. Frederick Cook claimed to have reached the North Pole in 1908.) The first surface expedition independently confirmed to have reached the North Pole was that of Ralph Plaisted in 1968.

Peary had several support groups carrying supplies until the last group turned back at 87°47´N. Peary, Matthew Henson, and four Inuit (or Eskimos) proceeded with dog teams and sleds. They were said to have crossed the pole several times, then built an igloo there and rested before returning south.

1914: Donald MacMillan (U.S.) traveled 200 mi from Axel Heiberg Isl. in search of Peary-named Crocker Land; MacMillan realized Peary had seen a Fata Morgana, mirage whereby pack ice in distance appears to be land.

1915-17: Vilhjalmur Stefansson (Can.) discovered Borden, Brock, Meighen, and Lougheed Isls.

1918-20: Roald Amundsen (Nor.) sailed Northeast Passage.

1925: Amundsen and Lincoln Ellsworth (U.S.) reached 87°44´N in attempt to fly to North Pole from Spitsbergen.

1926: Richard E. Byrd and Floyd Bennett (U.S.) reputedly flew over North Pole, May 9.

Amundsen, Ellsworth, and Umberto Nobile (Ital.) flew over North Pole May 12 in dirigible *Norge*.

1928: Nobile crossed North Pole in airship, May 24; crashed, May 25. Amundsen died attempting rescue.

North Pole Exploration Records

1958: Nuclear-powered submarine USS *Nautilus*, under Cmdr. William R. Anderson, crossed the North Pole beneath the ice, Aug. 3.

1960: In Aug., the nuclear submarine USS *Seadragon* (Cmdr. George P. Steele II) made the first E-W underwater transit through Northwest Passage. Traveling mostly submerged, it made the 850-mi trek from Baffin Bay to the Beaufort Sea in six days.

1968: Ralph Plaisted (U.S.) and three amateur explorers on snowmobiles became first independently confirmed surface expedition to reach North Pole, Apr. 19.

1977: Soviet nuclear icebreaker *Arktika* became first surface ship to reach North Pole, Aug. 16.

1978: On Apr. 30, Naomi Uemura (Jpn.) became first person to reach the North Pole alone, traveling by dog sled in a 54-day, 600-mi trek over the frozen Arctic.

1982: In Apr., Sir Ranulph Fiennes and Charles Burton, Brit. explorers, reached the North Pole and became first to circle the Earth from pole to pole. They had reached the South Pole 16 months earlier. The 52,000-mi trek took three years, involved 23 people, and cost an estimated $18 mil.

1986: Six explorers reached the North Pole assisted only by dogs, May 2. They became first to reach the pole without aerial logistics support since at least 1909. The explorers—Americans Will Steger, Paul Schurke, Ann Bancroft, and Geoff Carroll and Canadians Brent Boddy and Richard Weber—completed the 500-mi journey in 56 days.

1995: Weber and Mikhail Malakhov (Russ.) became first pair to make it to North Pole and back without any mechanical assistance, June 15. The 940-mi trip, made entirely on skis, took 121 days.

2003: Pen Hadow (Brit.) became first to reach North Pole from Canada, solo and without resupply, May 20. The 377-mi journey across the ice took 64 days.

2006: Prince Albert II of Monaco became first royal to reach North Pole, Apr. 16.

Antarctic Exploration

Antarctica has been approached since 1773-75, when Capt. James Cook (Brit.) reached 71°10´S. Many seas and landmarks bear the names of early explorers. Fabian von Bellingshausen (Russ.) discovered Peter I and Alexander I Isls., 1819-21. Nathaniel Palmer (U.S.) traveled throughout Palmer Peninsula, 60°W, 1820. Capt. John Davis (U.S.) made the first known Antarctic landing on Feb. 7, 1821. In 1823, James Weddell (Brit.) found Weddell Sea, 74°15´S, the southernmost point that had been reached.

First to announce existence of the continent of Antarctica was Charles Wilkes (U.S.), who followed the coast for 1,500 mi, 1840. Adelie Coast, 140°E, was found by Dumont d'Urville (Fr.), 1840. Ross Ice Shelf was found by James Clark Ross (Brit.), 1841-42.

1895: Leonard Kristensen (Nor.) landed a party on Victoria Land. They were first ashore on main continental mass. C. E. Borchgrevink, a member of that party, returned in 1899 with a Brit. expedition, first to winter on Antarctica.

1902-04: Robert Falcon Scott (Brit.) explored Edward VII Peninsula to 82°17´S, 146°33´E from McMurdo Sound.

1908-09: Ernest Shackleton (Brit.) was first to use Manchurian ponies in Antarctic sledging. He reached 88°23´S, discovering route onto plateau by way of Beardmore Glacier and pioneering the way to the pole.

1911: Roald Amundsen (Nor.) with four men and dog teams reached South Pole, Dec. 14.

1912: Scott reached the pole from Ross Isl., Jan. 18, with four companions. They died from starvation and exposure on return. Their bodies and expedition notes were found, Nov. 12.

1928: Sir George Hubert Wilkins (Austral.) was first to use airplane over Antarctica.

1929: Richard E. Byrd (U.S.) established Little America on Bay of Whales. On 1,600-mi airplane flight begun Nov. 28, he crossed South Pole, Nov. 29, with three others.

1934-35: Byrd led second expedition to Little America, explored 450,000 sq mi, wintered alone at 80°08´S.

1934-37: John Rymill (Austral.) led British Graham Land Expedition; discovered Palmer Peninsula was part of mainland.

1935: Lincoln Ellsworth (U.S.) flew south along E Coast of Palmer Peninsula, then crossed continent to Little America, making four landings.

1939-41: U.S. Navy planes discovered about 150,000 sq mi of new land.

1940: Byrd charted most of coast between Ross Sea and Palmer Peninsula.

1946-47: U.S. Navy undertook Operation Highjump, commanded by Byrd, which included 13 ships and 4,000 men. Airplanes photomapped coastline and penetrated beyond pole.

1946-48: Ronne Antarctic Research Expedition Cmdr. Finn Ronne, USNR, determined Antarctic to be only one continent with no strait between Weddell Sea and Ross Sea; explored 250,000 sq mi of land by flights to 79°S.

1955-57: U.S. Navy's Operation Deep Freeze led by Byrd. Supporting U.S. scientific efforts for International Geophysical Year (IGY), the operation established five coastal stations fronting Indian, Pacific, and Atlantic Oceans and three interior stations; explored more than 1 mil sq mi in Wilkes Land.

1957-58: During IGY, July 1957 through Dec. 1958, scientists from 12 countries conducted research within network of some 60 stations on Antarctica.

Dr. Vivian E. Fuchs (Brit.) led 12-person Trans-Antarctic Expedition on first land crossing of Antarctica. Starting from the Weddell Sea, they reached Scott Station, Mar. 2, 1958, after traveling 2,158 mi in 99 days.

1958: A group of five U.S. scientists led by seismologist Edward C. Thiel, moving by tractor from Ellsworth Station on Weddell Sea, identified a mountain range 5,000 ft above the ice sheet and 9,000 ft above sea level. The range, originally seen by a Navy plane, was named Dufek Massif, for Rear Adm. George Dufek.

1959: Argentina, Australia, Belgium, Chile, France, Japan, New Zealand, Norway, South Africa, USSR, UK, and U.S. signed a treaty suspending territorial claims for 30 years and reserving the continent south of 60°S for research.

1961-62: Scientists discovered Bentley Trench, running from Ross Ice Shelf into Marie Byrd Land, near the end of the Ellsworth Mts., toward Weddell Sea.

1962: U.S. nuclear power plant went online at McMurdo Sound; in operation until 1972.

1963: On Feb. 22, a U.S. plane made the region's longest nonstop flight from McMurdo Station south past the pole to Shackleton Mts., southeast to "area of inaccessibility," and back to McMurdo Station, covering 3,600 mi in 10 hours.

1964: New Zealanders mapped the mountain area from Cape Adare west some 400 mi to Pennell Glacier.

1985: Researcher Igor A. Zotikov (Russ.) discovered sediments in Ross Ice Shelf that seem to support continental drift theory. Ocean Drilling Project finds that the ice sheets of E Antarctica are 37 mil years old.

1989: Victoria Murden and Shirley Metz became first women as well as first Americans to reach South Pole overland when they arrived with nine others, Jan. 17.

1991: 24 nations approved environmental protection protocol to 1959 Antarctica Treaty, Oct. 4; in force in 1998. New provisions include banning oil and other mineral exploration for 50 years.

1994: On Dec. 25, after 50-day trek, Liv Arnesen (Nor.) became first woman to ski alone and unaided to South Pole.

1995: Borge Ousland (Nor.) reached South Pole on skis, Dec. 22, becoming first to reach both N and S Poles solo.

1996-97: Ousland became first to traverse Antarctica alone; reached South Pole Dec. 19, 1996. Traveled 1,675 mi in 64 days, ending Jan. 18, 1997.

2000-01: Ann Bancroft (U.S.) and Arnesen became first women to ski unaided across Antarctica, Feb. 11, 2001. The 1,717-mi journey took 94 days.

2008: Norwegians Christian Eide, Rune Midtgaard, Morten Andvig, and Mads Agerup reached the South Pole unaided, Dec. 26, in record 24 days, 8 hr., 50 min.

Volcanoes

Source: *Volcanoes of the World*, Geoscience Press; Global Volcanism Program, Smithsonian Institution, www.volcano.si.edu

Eruptions have been documented in about 550 volcanoes. More than half to three-quarters of these historically active volcanoes can be found on the so-called **Ring of Fire**, which runs along the W coast of the Americas from the southern tip of Chile to Alaska, down the E coast of Asia from Kamchatka to Indonesia, and continues from New Guinea to New Zealand. The Ring of Fire marks the boundaries between tectonic plates underlying the Pacific Ocean and those of the surrounding continents. Volcanic activity also occurs along rift zones like Iceland, where plates pull apart, or over hot spots such as Hawaii, where plumes of molten material rise from the mantle to the Earth's crust. The majority of Earth's volcanism takes place at submarine rift zones, on the seafloor.

Notable Volcanic Eruptions

In approximately 5,700 BC, Mount Mazama, in southern Oregon, erupted violently, ejecting large amounts of ash and pumice and sending out pyroclastic flows (mixture of volcanic debris and gases). The ash spread over the northwestern U.S. and southern Canada. The eruption collapsed the top of the mountain, leaving a caldera about 6 mi across and 1 mi deep. This depression filled with water from rain and snow to form what is now called Crater Lake.

In 79 CE, Mount Vesuvius, a volcano overlooking Naples Bay, became active after several centuries of apparent inactivity. On Aug. 24 of that year, heated mud and ash swept down the mountain, engulfing the cities of Pompeii, Herculaneum, and Stabiae with debris more than 60 ft deep. About 10% of the population of the three towns were killed.

In 1883, an eruption similar to the Mazama eruption occurred on the island of Krakatau. At least 2,000 people died in pyroclastic flows on Aug. 26. The next day, the 2,640-ft peak of the volcano collapsed to 1,000 ft below sea level, sinking most of the island and killing over 3,000. The eruptions and collapse generated a series of tsunamis that killed more than 31,000 people in Java and Sumatra. Ash from the eruption colored sunsets around the world for two years.

Date	Volcano	Est. deaths
Aug. 24, 79 CE	Vesuvius, Italy	16,000
1586	Kelut, Java, Indon.	10,000
Dec. 15, 1631	Vesuvius, Italy	4,000
Aug. 12, 1772	Papandayan, Java, Indon.	3,000
June 8, 1783	Laki, Iceland	9,350
May 21, 1792	Unzen, Japan	14,500
Apr. 10-12, 1815	Tambora, Sumbawa, Indon.	92,000[1]
Aug. 26-27, 1883	Krakatau, Indon.	36,000[2]
Apr. 24, 1902	Santa María, Guatemala	1,000[3]
May 8, 1902	Pelée, Martinique	28,000
Jan. 30, 1911	Taal, Philippines	1,400
June 6-8, 1912	Novarupta, AK, U.S.[4]	1
May 19, 1919	Kelut, Java, Indon.	5,000
Jan. 17-21, 1951	Lamington, New Guinea	3,000
May 18, 1980	St. Helens, WA, U.S.	57
Mar. 28, 1982	El Chichón, Mexico	1,880
Nov. 13, 1985	Nevado del Ruiz, Colombia	23,000
Aug. 21, 1986	Lake Nyos, Cameroon	1,700[5]
June 15, 1991	Pinatubo, Luzon, Philippines	800[6]

(1) Of these, about 10,000 were directly related to the eruption. Released gases and particles altered the global climate, leading to additional deaths from starvation and disease when crops failed. (2) Collapse of volcano generated tsunamis, which were responsible for the majority of deaths. (3) An additional 3,000 deaths due to a malaria outbreak are sometimes attributed to the eruption. (4) Biggest eruption of 20th cent. by volume. (5) Caused by release of massive amount of carbon dioxide from crater lake. (6) Of these, about 500 were associated with post-eruption lahars (volcanic mudflows).

Notable Active Volcanoes

Source: Global Volcanism Program, Smithsonian Inst.; Volcano Hazards Program, U.S. Geological Survey, U.S. Dept. of the Interior

Active volcanoes display a wide range of activity, including the production of ash plumes and seismic swarms. An eruption may involve the explosive ejection of fragmental material and escape of liquid lava. Year of a volcano's last known or confirmed eruption, as of June 2015, is given. Volcanoes are listed by height, which does not reflect eruptive magnitude. Submarine volcanoes are not included.

Volcano (latest eruption)	Location	Height (ft)
Africa		
Cameroon (2000)	Cameroon	13,435
Nyiragongo (2013)	Dem. Rep. of the Congo	11,385
Nyamuragira (2014)	Dem. Rep. of the Congo	10,033
Ol Doinyo Lengai (2013)	Tanzania	9,718
Fogo (2015)	Cape Verde Isls.	9,281
Piton de la Fournaise (2015)	Réunion Isl. (Fr.), Indian O.	8,635
Karthala (2007)	Comoros	7,746
Nabro (2012)	Eritrea	7,277
Antarctica		
Erebus (2014)	Ross Isl.	12,448
Michael (2012)	Saunders Isl. (UK)	3,248
Asia and Oceania		
Klyuchevskoy (2015)	Kamchatka, Russia	15,597
Kerinci (2009)	Sumatra, Indon.	12,467
Fuji (1708)	Honshu, Japan	12,388
Rinjani (2010)	Lombok, Indon.	12,224
Semeru (2014)	Java, Indon.	12,060
Tolbachik (2013)	Kamchatka, Russia	11,847
Koryaksky (2009)	Kamchatka, Russia	11,339
Slamet (2014)	Java, Indon.	11,247
Raung (2008)	Java, Indon.	10,932
Shiveluch (2014)	Kamchatka, Russia	10,771
Ontake (2014)	Honshu, Japan	10,062
Merapi (2014)	Java, Indon.	9,738
Zhupanovsky (2015)	Kamchatka, Russia	9,511
Marapi (2014)	Sumatra, Indon.	9,485
Bezymianny (2013)	Kamchatka, Russia	9,455
Peuet Sague (2000)	Sumatra, Indon.	9,190
Ruapehu (2007)	New Zealand	9,177
Heard (2014)	Australia	9,006
Changbaishan (1903)	China-North Korea	9,003
Papandayan (2002)	Java, Indon.	8,743
Asama (2009)	Honshu, Japan	8,425
Dieng Volcanic Complex (2009)	Java, Indon.	8,415
Mayon (2014)	Luzon, Philippines	8,077
Sinabung (2015)	Sumatra, Indon.	8,071
Kanlaon (2006)	Negros Isl., Philippines	7,989
Niigata-Yakeyama (1998)	Honshu, Japan	7,874
Kizimen (2013)	Kamchatka, Russia	7,657
Ulawun (2013)	Papua New Guinea	7,657
Tengger Caldera (2012)	Java, Indon.	7,641
Alaid (2012)	Kuril Isls., Russia	7,497
Chokai (1974)	Honshu, Japan	7,336
Galunggung (1984)	Java, Indon.	7,113
Tangkubanparahu (2015)	Java, Indon.	6,837
Tongariro (2012)	New Zealand	6,490
Azuma (1977)	Honshu, Japan	6,394
Sangeang Api (2014)	Lesser Sunda Isls., Indon.	6,394
Nasu (1963)	Honshu, Japan	6,283
Bagana (2015)	Papua New Guinea	6,086
Karkar (2014)	Papua New Guinea	6,033
Chachadake (Tiatia) (1981)	Kunashir Isl., Japan-admin. by Russia	5,978
Bandai (1888)	Honshu, Japan	5,958
Manam (2015)	Papua New Guinea	5,928
Gorely (2010)	Kamchatka, Russia	5,902
Kuju (1996)	Kyushu, Japan	5,876
Karangetang (Api Siau) (2014)	Sangihe Isls., Indon.	5,853
Soputan (2015)	Sulawesi, Indon.	5,853
Chikurachki (2015)	Kuril Isls., Russia	5,843
Kelut (2014)	Java, Indon.	5,679
Adatara (1996)	Honshu, Japan	5,669
Gamalama (2014)	Halmahera, Indon.	5,627
Lewotobi (2014)	Flores Isl., Indonesia	5,587
Kirishima (2011)	Kyushu, Japan	5,577
Gamkonora (2007)	Halmahera, Indon.	5,364
Aso (2015)	Kyushu, Japan	5,223
Lokon-Empung (2013)	Sulawesi, Indon.	5,184
Bulusan (2011)	Luzon, Philippines	5,135
Karymsky (2015)	Kamchatka, Russia	4,964
Akan (2008)	Hokkaido, Japan	4,918
Aoba (2011)	Vanuatu	4,908
Sarychev Peak (2009)	Kuril Isls., Russia	4,908
Pinatubo (1993)	Luzon, Philippines	4,875
Unzen (1996)	Kyushu, Japan	4,865
Lopevi (2007)	Vanuatu	4,636
Akita-Yakeyama (1997)	Honshu, Japan	4,482
Dukono (2015)	Halmahera, Indon.	4,380
Ambrym (2015)	Vanuatu	4,377
Langila (2012)	Papua New Guinea	4,364
Ibu (2013)	Halmahera, Indon	4,347
Awu (2004)	Sangihe Isls., Indon.	4,331

Volcano (latest eruption)	Location	Height (ft)
Central America and West Indies		
Tacaná (1986)	Mexico-Guatemala	13,333
Acatenango (1972)	Guatemala	13,045
Santa María (2015)	Guatemala	12,375
Fuego (2015)	Guatemala	12,346
Irazú (1994)	Costa Rica	11,260
Turrialba (2015)	Costa Rica	10,958
Poás (2014)	Costa Rica	8,885
Pacaya (2015)	Guatemala	8,373
Santa Ana (2005)	El Salvador	7,812
San Miguel (2015)	El Salvador	6,988
Rincón de la Vieja (2014)	Costa Rica	6,286
San Cristóbal (2015)	Nicaragua	5,725
Concepción (2011)	Nicaragua	5,577
Arenal (2010)	Costa Rica	5,479
Soufrière Guadeloupe (1977)	Guadeloupe Isl. (France)	4,813
Pelée (1932)	Martinique (France)	4,573
Momotombo (1905)	Nicaragua	4,255
North America		
Pico de Orizaba (1846)	Mexico	18,619
Popocatépetl (2013)	Mexico	17,802
Rainier (1894)	Washington	14,409
Shasta (1786)	California	14,163
Wrangell (2002)	Alaska	14,163
Colima (2015)	Mexico	12,631
Spurr (1992)	Alaska	11,070
Lassen Peak (1917)	California	10,456
Redoubt (2009)	Alaska	10,197
Iliamna (1876)	Alaska	10,016
Shishaldin (2015)	Aleutian Isls., AK	9,373
St. Helens (2008)	Washington	8,363
Veniaminof (2013)	Alaska	8,225
Pavlof (2014)	Alaska	8,179
Katmai (1912)	Alaska	6,716
Makushin (1995)	Aleutian Isls., AK	5,906
Great Sitkin (1974)	Aleutian Isls., AK	5,709
Cleveland (2014)	Aleutian Isls., AK	5,676
Gareloi (1989)	Aleutian Isls., AK	5,161
Korovin (2007)	Aleutian Isls., AK	5,030
South America		
Llullaillaco (1877)	Chile-Argentina	22,110
San Pedro (1960)	Chile	20,161
Guallatiri (1960)	Chile	19,918
Sabancaya (2014)	Peru	19,577
Cotopaxi (1940)	Ecuador	19,393
El Misti (1985)	Peru	19,101
Ubinas (2015)	Peru	18,609
Tupungatito (1987)	Chile-Argentina	18,570
Láscar (2013)	Chile	18,346
Nevado del Huila (2012)	Colombia	17,598
Nevado del Ruiz (2015)	Colombia	17,320
Sangay (2015)	Ecuador	17,159
Irruputuncu (1995)	Chile-Bolivia	16,939
Tungurahua (2015)	Ecuador	16,480
Guagua Pichincha (2002)	Ecuador	15,696
Puracé (1977)	Colombia	15,256
Galeras (2013)	Colombia	14,029
Planchón-Peteroa (2011)	Chile	13,048
Lautaro (1979)	Chile	11,834
Reventador (2015)	Ecuador	11,686
Llaima (2009)	Chile	10,253
Copahue (2014)	Chile-Argentina	9,688
Villarrica (2015)	Chile	9,341
Europe		
Etna (2015)	Italy	10,925
Vesuvius (1944)	Italy	4,203
Stromboli (2013)	Italy	3,031
Santorini (1950)	Greece	1,204
Mid-Atlantic		
Jan Mayen (1985)	N Atlantic O. (Norway)	7,470
Bardarbunga (2015)	Iceland	6,591
Grímsvötn (2011)	Iceland	5,659
Eyjafjallajökull (2010)	Iceland	5,466
Hekla (2000)	Iceland	4,892
Mid-Pacific		
Mauna Loa (1984)	Hawaii, HI	13,681
Haleakala (1750)	Maui, HI	10,023
Kilauea (2015)	Hawaii, HI	4,009

Mountains

North America

Source: U.S. Geological Survey, U.S. Dept. of the Interior; Natural Resources Canada. Survey dates and elevation sources may differ.

Peak, state/prov., country	Height (ft)
Denali (fmr. McKinley), AK	20,320
Logan, Yukon, Canada	19,551
Pico de Orizaba, Mexico	18,619
St. Elias, AK-YT, U.S.-Can.	18,009
Popocatépetl, Mexico	17,802
Foraker, AK	17,400
Iztaccíhuatl, Mexico	17,154
Lucania, YT, Canada	17,146
King Peak, YT, Canada	16,972
Steele, YT, Canada	16,624
Bona, AK	16,500
Blackburn, AK	16,390
Sanford, AK	16,237
South Buttress, AK	15,885
Wood, YT, Canada	15,873
Vancouver, AK-YT, U.S.-Can.	15,699
Churchill, AK	15,638
Nevado de Toluca (Xinantécatl), Mexico	15,350
Fairweather, AK-BC, U.S.-Can.	15,299
Macaulay, YT, Canada	15,299
Slaggard, YT, Canada	15,299
Hubbard, AK-YT, U.S.-Can.	15,016
Bear, AK	14,831
Walsh, YT, Canada	14,780
East Buttress, AK	14,730
Matlalcueyetl, Mexico	14,636
Hunter, AK	14,573
Browne Tower, AK	14,530
Whitney, CA	14,505
Alverstone, AK-YT, U.S.-Can.	14,500
University Peak, AK	14,470
Elbert, CO	14,440
Massive, CO	14,421
Harvard, CO	14,421
Rainier, WA	14,410
Williamson, CA	14,376
Blanca Peak, CO	14,345
La Plata Peak, CO	14,336
Uncompahgre Peak, CO	14,321
Crestone Peak, CO	14,294
Lincoln, CO	14,293
Castle Peak, CO	14,279
Grays Peak, CO	14,278
Antero, CO	14,276
Torreys Peak, CO	14,275
Quandary Peak, CO	14,271
Evans, CO	14,265
Longs Peak, CO	14,259
McArthur, YT, Canada	14,253
White Mountain Peak, CA	14,252
North Palisade, CA	14,248
Wilson, CO	14,246
Cameron, CO	14,238
Shavano, CO	14,231
Princeton, CO	14,204
Belford, CO	14,203
Yale, CO	14,200
Crestone Needle, CO	14,197
Bross, CO	14,172
Kit Carson, CO	14,165
Point Success, WA	14,164
Shasta, CA	14,163
Wrangell, AK	14,163
Maroon Peak, CO	14,163
Tabeguache, CO	14,162
Oxford, CO	14,160
El Diente Peak, CO	14,159
Sill, CA	14,159
Democrat, CO	14,155
Sneffels, CO	14,150
Capitol Peak, CO	14,130
Liberty Cap, WA	14,118
Pikes Peak, CO	14,115
Snowmass, CO	14,099
Russell, CA	14,094
Eolus, CO	14,083
Windom, CO	14,082
Challenger Point, CO	14,081

Note: The highest point in the West Indies is Pico Duarte (10,417 ft), in the Dominican Republic.

Other Notable U.S. Mountains

Peak, state	Height (ft)
Gannett Peak, WY	13,810
Grand Teton, WY	13,775
Kings, UT	13,518
Cloud, WY	13,171
Wheeler, NM	13,166
Boundary, NV	13,146
Granite, MT	12,807
Borah, ID	12,661
Humphreys, AZ	12,637
Adams, WA	12,281
San Gorgonio, CA	11,503
Hood, OR	11,240
Lassen, CA	10,461
Granite, CA	10,325
Guadalupe, TX	8,751
Olympus, WA	7,973
Harney, SD	7,244
Mitchell, NC	6,683
Clingmans Dome, NC-TN	6,643
Washington, NH	6,289
Rogers, VA	5,729
Marcy, NY	5,344
Katahdin, ME	5,269
Spruce Knob, WV	4,863
Mansfield, VT	4,393
Black Mountain, KY	4,145

South America

Peak, country	Height (ft)
Aconcagua, Argentina	22,835
Ojos del Salado, Arg.-Chile	22,595
Bonete, Argentina	22,546
Tupungato, Argentina-Chile	22,310
Pissis, Argentina	22,241
Mercedario, Argentina	22,211
Huascarán, Peru	22,205
Llullaillaco, Argentina-Chile	22,109
El Libertador, Argentina	22,047
Cachi, Argentina	22,047
Yerupajá, Peru	21,765
Incahuasi, Argentina-Chile	21,720
Galan, Argentina	21,654
El Muerto, Argentina-Chile	21,457
Sajama, Bolivia	21,391
Nacimiento, Argentina	21,302
Illimani, Bolivia	21,201
Coropuna, Peru	21,083
Laudo, Argentina	20,997
Ancohuma, Bolivia	20,958
Ausangate, Peru	20,945
Toro, Argentina-Chile	20,932
Illampu, Bolivia	20,873
Tres Cruces, Argentina-Chile	20,853
Huandoy, Peru	20,852
Parinacota, Bolivia-Chile	20,768
Tortolas, Argentina-Chile	20,745
Ampato, Peru	20,702
Chimborazo, Ecuador	20,702
El Condor, Argentina	20,669
Salcantay, Peru	20,574
Huancarhuas, Peru	20,531
Famatina, Argentina	20,505
Pumasillo, Peru	20,492
Solo, Argentina	20,492
Polleras, Argentina	20,456
Pular, Chile	20,423
Chani, Argentina	20,341
Aucanquilcha, Chile	20,295
Juncal, Argentina-Chile	20,276
Negro, Argentina	20,184
Quela, Argentina	20,128
Condoriri, Bolivia	20,095
Palermo, Argentina	20,079
Solimana, Peru	20,068
San Juan, Argentina-Chile	20,049
Sierra Nevada, Argentina-Chile	20,023
Antofalla, Argentina	20,013
Marmolejo, Argentina-Chile	20,013
Chachani, Peru	19,931

Africa

Peak, country	Height (ft)
Kilimanjaro, Tanzania	19,341
Kenya, Kenya	17,057
Margherita Pk., Uganda-Congo	16,763
Ras Dashan, Ethiopia	15,158
Meru, Tanzania	14,977
Karisimbi, Congo-Rwanda	14,787
Elgon, Kenya-Uganda	14,178
Batu, Ethiopia	14,131
Guna, Ethiopia	13,881
Gughe, Ethiopia	13,780
Toubkal, Morocco	13,661
Cameroon, Cameroon	13,435

Australia, New Zealand, SE Asian Islands

Peak, country	Height (ft)
Jaya, New Guinea, Indon.	16,024
Trikora, New Guinea, Indon.	15,585
Mandala, New Guinea, Indon.	15,420
Wilhelm, Papua New Guinea	14,793
Kinabalu, Malaysia	13,436
Kerinci, Sumatra, Indon.	12,467
Aoraki/Cook, New Zealand	12,218
Semeru, Java, Indonesia	12,060
Kosciusko, Australia	7,310

Height of Mount Everest

Mt. Everest, the world's highest mountain, was considered 29,002 ft when Edmund Hillary and Tenzing Norgay became the first to scale it, in 1953. In 1954, the Surveyor General of the Republic of India set the height at 29,028 ft, plus or minus 10 ft because of snow. In 1999, a team of climbers sponsored by Boston's Museum of Science and the National Geographic Society measured the height at the summit using satellite-based technology. The new measurement, of 29,035 ft, was accepted by other authorities, including the U.S. National Imagery and Mapping Agency.

Climbers typically ascend Everest on its north (Tibet) or south face (Nepal). By the end of the 2014 climbing season, which runs from April through May, about 4,142 climbers had made successful ascents while around 267 climbers had died in the attempt. Among the dead were 16 Sherpas killed in an avalanche triggered by falling ice Apr. 18, 2014. Concerns about additional avalanches, the increasing number of tourists on Everest, and fair worker compensation contributed to the decision by most tour operators to cancel the rest of the 2014 season on the south face. Expeditions were called off on both sides of the mountain after a 7.8-magnitude earthquake hit Nepal Apr. 25, 2015. The earthquake triggered avalanches that swept through Everest Base Camp on the south side, killing 19 and injuring more than 60.

Europe

Peak, country	Height (ft)
Alps	
Mont Blanc, France-Italy	15,781
Monte Rosa (highest peak of group), Switzerland	15,203
Dom, Switzerland	14,911
Liskamm, It.-Switzerland	14,852
Weisshorn, Switzerland	14,780
Taschhorn, Switzerland	14,733
Matterhorn, It.-Switzerland	14,692
Dent Blanche, Switzerland	14,293
Nadelhorn, Switzerland	14,196
Grand Combin, Switzerland	14,154
Lenzpitze, Switzerland	14,088
Finsteraarhorn, Switzerland	14,022
Castor, Switzerland	13,865
Zinalrothorn, Switzerland	13,849
Hohberghom, Switzerland	13,842
Alphubel, Switzerland	13,799
Rimpfischhom, Switzerland	13,776
Aletschorn, Switzerland	13,763
Strahlhorn, Switzerland	13,747
Dent D'Herens, Switzerland	13,686
Breithorn, It.-Switzerland	13,665
Bishorn, Switzerland	13,645
Jungfrau, Switzerland	13,642
Ecrins, France	13,461
Monch, Switzerland	13,448
Pollux, Switzerland	13,422
Schreckhorn, Switzerland	13,379
Ober Gabelhorn, Switzerland	13,330
Gran Paradiso, Italy	13,323
Bernina, It.-Switzerland	13,284
Fiescherhorn, Switzerland	13,283
Grunhorn, Switzerland	13,266
Lauteraarhorn, Switzerland	13,261
Durrenhorn, Switzerland	13,238
Allalinhorn, Switzerland	13,213
Weissmies, Switzerland	13,199
Lagginhorn, Switzerland	13,156
Zupo, Switzerland	13,120
Fletschhorn, Switzerland	13,110
Adlerhorn, Switzerland	13,081
Gletscherhorn, Switzerland	13,068
Schalihorn, Switzerland	13,040
Scerscen, Switzerland	13,028
Eiger, Switzerland	13,025
Jagerhorn, Switzerland	13,024
Rottalhorn, Switzerland	13,022
Pyrenees	
Aneto, Spain	11,168
Posets, Spain	11,073
Perdido, Spain	11,007
Vignemale, France-Spain	10,820
Long, Spain	10,479
Estats, Spain	10,304
Montcalm, Spain	10,105
Caucasus (Europe-Asia)	
Elbrus, Russia	18,510
Shkhara, Georgia	17,064
Dykh Tau, Russia	17,054
Kashtan Tau, Russia	16,877
Janqi, Georgia	16,565
Kazbek, Georgia	16,558

Asia (Mainland)

Peak, country/region	Height (ft)
Everest, Nepal-Tibet	29,035
K2 (Godwin Austen), Kashmir	28,251
Kanchenjunga, India-Nepal	28,169
Lhotse I (Everest), Nepal-Tibet	27,923
Makalu I, Nepal-Tibet	27,824
Lhotse II (Everest), Nepal-Tibet	27,560
Dhaulagiri, Nepal	26,795
Manaslu I, Nepal	26,781
Cho Oyu, Nepal-Tibet	26,750
Nanga Parbat, Kashmir	26,660
Annapurna I, Nepal	26,545
Annapurna II, Nepal	26,545
Gasherbrum, Kashmir	26,470
Broad, Kashmir	26,400
Gosainthan, Nepal-Tibet	26,287
Gyachung Kang, Nepal-Tibet	25,910
Disteghil Sar, Kashmir	25,868
Himalchuli, Nepal	25,801
Nuptse (Everest), Nepal-Tibet	25,726
Masherbrum, Kashmir	25,660
Nanda Devi, India	25,645
Rakaposhi, Kashmir	25,550
Kamet, India-Tibet	25,447
Namcha Barwa, Tibet	25,445
Gurla Mandhata, Tibet	25,355
Ulugh Muztagh, Xinjiang, China-Tibet	25,340
Kungur, Xinjiang, China	25,325
Tirich Mir, Pakistan	25,230
Makalu II, Nepal-Tibet	25,120
Minya Konka, China	24,900
Annapurna III, Nepal	24,786
Kula Gangri, Bhutan-Tibet	24,784
Changtse (Everest), Nepal-Tibet	24,780
Muztagh Ata, Xinjiang, China	24,757
Skyang Kangri, Kashmir	24,750
Annapurna IV, Nepal	24,688
Ismail Samani Peak, Tajikistan	24,590
Jongsong Peak, India-Nepal-China	24,472
Jengish Chokusu, Xinjiang, China-Kyrgyzstan	24,406
Sia Kangri, Kashmir	24,350
Haramosh Peak, Pakistan	24,270
Istoro Nal, Pakistan	24,240
Kirat Chuli, India-Nepal	24,165
Chomo Lhari, Bhutan-Tibet	24,040
Chamlang, Nepal	24,012
Kabru, India-Nepal	24,002
Alung Gangri, Tibet	24,000
Baltoro Kangri, Kashmir	23,990
Mana, India	23,860
Baruntse, Nepal	23,688
Nepal Peak, India-Nepal	23,500
Amne Machin, China	23,490
Gauri Sankar, Nepal-Tibet	23,440
Badrinath, India	23,420
Nunkun, Kashmir	23,410
Lenin Peak, Tajikistan	23,406
Pyramid, India-Nepal	23,400
Api, Nepal	23,399
Pauhunri, India-Tibet	23,385
Trisul, India	23,360
Kangto, India-Tibet	23,260
Nyenchen Thanglha, Tibet	23,255
Trisuli, India	23,210
Pumori, Nepal-Tibet	23,190
Dunagiri, India	23,184
Lombo Kangra, Tibet	23,165
Saipal, Nepal	23,106
Macha Pucchare, Nepal	22,958
Khan Tengri, Kazakhstan-Kyrgyzstan-Xinjiang, China	22,949
Numbar, Nepal	22,817
Kanjiroba, Nepal	22,580
Ama Dablam, Nepal	22,350
Cho Polu, Nepal	22,093
Lingtren, Nepal-Tibet	21,972
Khumbutse, Nepal-Tibet	21,785
Hlako Gangri, Tibet	21,266
Grosvenor, China	21,190
Thagchhab Gangri, Tibet	20,976
Damavand, Iran	18,406
Ararat, Turkey	16,854

Antarctica

Peak	Height (ft)
Vinson Massif	16,066
Tyree	15,919
Shinn	15,750
Gardner	15,375
Epperly	15,100
Kirkpatrick	14,855
Elizabeth	14,698
Markham	14,290
Bell	14,117
Mackellar	14,098
Anderson	13,957
Bentley	13,934
Kaplan	13,878
Andrew Jackson	13,750
Sidley	13,720
Ostenso	13,710
Minto	13,668
Miller	13,650
Long Gables	13,620
Dickerson	13,517
Giovinetto	13,412
Wade	13,400
Fisher	13,386
Fridtjof Nansen	13,350
Wexler	13,202
Lister	13,200
Shear	13,100
Odishaw	13,008
Donaldson	12,894
Ray	12,808
Sellery	12,779
Waterman	12,730
Anne	12,703
Press	12,566
Falla	12,549
Rucker	12,520
Goldthwait	12,510
Morris	12,500
Erebus	12,450
Campbell	12,434
Don Pedro Christophersen	12,355
Lysaght	12,326

Notable Islands and Their Areas

Figures are for total area in square miles. Boldface figures in parentheses show rank among the world's 10 largest individual islands. Only the largest islands in an island group are shown. Table does not include islands smaller than 10 sq mi in area. Canada's Manitoulin Island (1,068 sq mi), in Lake Huron, is the world's largest island in a freshwater lake.

Antarctica

Adelaide	1,400
Alexander	16,700
Berkner	18,500
Roosevelt	2,900

Arctic Ocean

Amund Ringnes, NU, Can.	2,029
Axel Heiberg, NU, Can.	16,671
Baffin, NU, Can. **(5)**	195,928
Banks, NT, Can.	27,038
Bathurst, NU, Can.	6,194
Bolshoy Lyakhovsky, Russia	1,776
Borden, NT-NU, Can.	1,079
Bylot, NU, Can.	4,273
Coats, NU, Can.	2,123
Cornwallis, NU, Can.	2,701
Devon, NU, Can.	21,331
Disko, Greenland, Denmark	3,312
Ellef Ringnes, NU, Can.	4,361
Ellesmere, NU, Can. **(10)**	75,767
Faddayevskiy, Russia	1,930
Franz Josef Land, Russia	8,000
Iturup (Etorofu), Russia	2,596
King William, NU, Can.	5,062
Kotelny, Russia	4,504
Mackenzie King, NT, Can.	1,949
Melville, NT-NU, Can.	16,274
Milne Land, Greenland, Den.	1,400
New Siberian Isls., Russia	14,500
Novaya Zemlya, Russia (2 isls.)	31,730
Prince Charles, NT, Can.	3,676
Prince Patrick, NT, Can.	6,119
Prince of Wales, NU, Can.	12,872
Severnaya Zemlya, Russia (tot. group)	14,175
Bol'shevik	4,368
Komsomolets	3,477
Oktyabr'skoy Revolyutsii	5,471
Somerset, NU, Can.	9,570
Southampton, NU, Can.	15,913
Svalbard, Norway (tot. group)	23,561
Nordaustlandet	5,410
Spitsbergen	14,546
Traill, Greenland, Denmark	1,300
Victoria, NT-NU, Can. **(8)**	83,897
Wrangel, Russia	2,937

Atlantic Ocean

Anticosti, QC, Can.	3,066
Ascension, UK	35
Azores, Portugal (tot. group)	868
Faial	67
San Miguel	291
Bahama Isls. (tot. group)	5,382
Andros	2,300
Bermuda Isls., UK (tot. group)	21
Bioko Isl., Equatorial Guinea	785
Block Island, RI, U.S.	21
Cabo Verde	1,557
Canary Isls., Spain (tot. group)	2,807
Fuerteventura	688
Gran Canaria	592
Tenerife	795
Cape Breton, NS, Can.	3,981
Caviana, Pará, Brazil	1,918
Channel Isls., UK (tot. group)	75
Guernsey	24
Jersey	45
Falkland Isls., UK (tot. group)	4,700
East Falkland	2,550
West Falkland	1,750
Faroe Isls., Denmark	539
Great Britain, UK **(9)**	80,823
Greenland, Denmark **(1)**	836,330
Gurupá, Pará, Brazil	1,878
Hebrides, Scotland, UK	2,744
Iceland	39,958
Ireland, Ireland-UK	32,589
Isle of Man, UK	221
Isle of Wight, England, UK	147
Long Island, NY, U.S.	1,320
Madeira Isls., Portugal	306
Marajo, Brazil	15,444
Martha's Vineyard, MA, U.S.	89
Mount Desert, ME, U.S.	104
Nantucket, MA, U.S.	45
Newfoundland, Canada	42,031
Orkney Isls., Scotland, UK	383
Prince Edward Isl. (main), Can.	2,170
St. Helena, UK	47
Shetland Isls., Scotland, UK	555
Skye, Scotland, UK	647
South Georgia, UK	1,450
Tierra del Fuego, Chile-Arg.	18,800
Tristan da Cunha, UK	38

Baltic Sea

Aland Isls., Finland	610
Bornholm, Denmark	228
Funen, Denmark	1,154
Gotland, Sweden	1,159
Zealand, Denmark	2,722

Caribbean Sea

Antigua	108
Aruba, Netherlands	69
Barbados	166
Cuba	42,804
Isle of Youth	926
Cayman Isls., UK (tot. group)	102
Curaçao, Netherlands	171
Dominica	290
Guadeloupe, France	687
Hispaniola (Haiti and Dominican Rep.)	29,389
Jamaica	4,244
Martinique, France	436
Puerto Rico, U.S.	3,425
Tobago	116
Trinidad	1,864
Virgin Isls., UK	59
Virgin Isls., U.S.	134

East Indies

Bali, Indonesia	2,171
Bangka, Indonesia	4,375
Borneo, Indonesia-Malaysia-Brunei **(3)**	290,321
Bougainville, Papua New Guinea	3,880
Buru, Indonesia	3,670
Celebes, Indonesia	69,000
Flores, Indonesia	5,500
Halmahera, Indonesia	6,865
Java (Jawa), Indonesia	48,900
Madura, Indonesia	2,113
Moluccas, Indonesia	32,307
New Britain, PNG	14,093
New Guinea, Indon.-PNG **(2)**	303,381
New Ireland, PNG	3,707
Seram, Indonesia	6,621
Sumatra, Indonesia **(6)**	182,543
Sumba, Indonesia	4,306
Sumbawa, Indonesia	5,965
Timor, Indon.–Timor-Leste	13,094
Yos Sudarsa, Indonesia	4,500

Indian Ocean

Andaman Isls., India	2,500
Kerguelen, France	2,247
Madagascar **(4)**	226,917
Mauritius	720
Pemba, Tanzania	380
Réunion, France	970
Seychelles	176
Sri Lanka	25,332
Zanzibar, Tanzania	640

Mediterranean Sea

Balearic Isls., Spain	1,927
Corfu, Greece	229
Corsica, France	3,369
Crete, Greece	3,189
Cyprus	3,572
Elba, Italy	86
Euboea, Greece	1,411
Malta	95
Rhodes, Greece	540
Sardinia, Italy	9,301
Sicily, Italy	9,926

Pacific Ocean

Admiralty, AK, U.S.	1,709
Aleutian Isls., AK, U.S. (tot. group)	6,912
Adak	275
Amchitka	116
Attu	350
Kanaga	142
Kiska	106
Tanaga	195
Umnak	686
Unalaska	1,051
Unimak	1,571
Baranof, AK, U.S.	1,636
Chichagof, AK, U.S.	2,062
Chiloe, Chile	3,241
Diomede (Big), Russia	11
Easter Isl. (Rapa Nui), Chile	63
Fiji (tot. group)	7,056
Vanua Levu	2,242
Viti Levu	4,109
Galapagos Isls., Ecuador	3,043
Graham Isl., BC, Can.	2,456
Guadalcanal, Solomon Isls.	2,180
Guam, U.S.	210
Hainan, China	13,000
Hawaiian Isls., HI, U.S. (tot. group)	6,428
Hawaii	4,028
Oahu	597
Hong Kong, China	31
Hoste, Chile	1,590
Japan (tot. group)	145,931
Hokkaido	30,110
Honshu **(7)**	88,022
Kyushu	14,190
Okinawa	467
Shikoku	7,066
Kangaroo, South Australia	1,705
Kiritimati (Christmas), Kiribati	150
Kodiak, AK, U.S.	3,485
Kupreanof, AK, U.S.	1,084
Marquesas Isls., France	492
Marshall Islands	70
Melville, Northern Terr., Australia	2,234
Micronesia	271
New Caledonia, France	6,530
New Zealand (tot. group)	103,362
Chatham Isls.	372
North	44,075
South	58,076
Stewart	649
Northern Mariana Isls., U.S.	179
Nunivak, AK, U.S.	1,600
Palau	188
Philippines (tot. group)	115,831
Leyte	2,787
Luzon	40,680
Mindanao	36,775
Mindoro	3,690
Negros	4,907
Palawan	4,554
Panay	4,446
Samar	5,050
Prince of Wales, AK, U.S.	2,770
Revillagigedo, AK, U.S.	1,134
Riesco, Chile	1,973
St. Lawrence, AK, U.S.	1,780
Sakhalin, Russia	29,500
Samoa Isls. (tot. group)	1,177
American Samoa, U.S.	77
Savaii, Samoa	659
Tutuila, U.S.	55
Upolu, Samoa	432
Santa Catalina, CA, U.S.	75
Santa Ines, Chile	1,407
Tahiti, France	402
Taiwan (tot. group)	13,892
Jinmen Dao (Quemoy)	56
Tasmania, Australia	26,178
Tonga	288
Vancouver Isl., BC, Can.	12,079
Vanuatu	4,707
Wellington, Chile	2,549

Persian Gulf

Bahrain	295

Notable Deserts of the World

Deserts are defined as regions of the Earth receiving less than 10 in. of precipitation annually, usually in combination with an evaporation rate exceeding precipitation.

In addition to areas listed below, the continent of Antarctica, with an area of about 5.4 mil sq mi (roughly doubled by ice in winter), is generally considered a desert. Annual precipitation averages 8 in. along the coast and far less in the deep interior; however, there is little evaporation.

Arabian (Eastern), 86,000 sq mi in Egypt between the Nile R. and Red Sea, extending south into Sudan
Atacama, 600-mi-long area rich in nitrate and copper deposits in northern Chile
Chihuahuan, 140,000 sq mi in TX, NM, AZ, and Mexico
Dasht-e Kavir, approx. 500 mi long by 200 mi wide in north-central Iran
Dasht-e Lut, approx. 300 mi long by 200 mi wide in south-central Iran
Death Valley, 3,300 sq mi in CA and NV
Gibson, 120,000 sq mi in the interior of western Australia
Gobi, 500,000 sq mi in Mongolia and China
Great Sandy, 103,186 sq mi in western Australia
Great Victoria, 134,653 sq mi in southwestern Australia
Kalahari, 275,000 sq mi in southern Africa
Kara Kum, 115,000 sq mi in Turkmenistan
Kyzyl Kum, 115,000 sq mi in Kazakhstan and Uzbekistan
Libyan, 425,000 sq mi in the Sahara, extending from Libya through southwestern Egypt into Sudan
Mojave, 15,000 sq mi in southern CA
Namib, long narrow area (varies 30-100 mi wide) extending 800 mi along SW coast of Africa
Nubian, 157,000 sq mi in the Sahara in northeastern Sudan
Painted Desert, section of high plateau in northern AZ extending 200 mi southeast from Grand Canyon
Patagonia, 300,000 sq mi in southern Argentina
Rub al-Khali (Empty Quarter), 225,000 sq mi in the S Arabian Peninsula
Sahara, 3,500,000 sq mi in N Africa, extending west to the Atlantic. Largest desert in the world
Sonoran, 70,000 sq mi in southwestern AZ and southeastern CA extending into NW Mexico
Syrian, 100,000 sq mi over much of northern Saudi Arabia, eastern Jordan, southern Syria, and western Iraq
Taklamakan, 140,000 sq mi in Xinjiang Prov., China
Thar (Great Indian), 100,000-sq-mi area extending 400 mi along India-Pakistan border

Areas and Average Depths of Oceans, Seas, and Gulfs

Geographers and mapmakers recognize at least four major bodies of water: the Pacific, Atlantic, Indian, and Arctic Oceans. The Atlantic and Pacific Oceans are considered divided at the equator into N and S. The Arctic Ocean is the name for waters north of the continental landmasses in the region of the Arctic Circle. The International Hydrographic Organization delimited a fifth world ocean in 2000. The Southern Ocean extends from the coast of Antarctica north to 60°S latitude, encompassing portions of the Atlantic, Indian, and Pacific Oceans. A Woods Hole Oceanographic Institution study published in 2010 calculated a mean depth of 12,081 ft for the world's oceans.

Body of water	Area (sq mi)	Avg. depth (ft)
Pacific Ocean	60,060,869	14,040
Atlantic Ocean	29,637,962	11,810
Indian Ocean	26,469,609	12,800
Southern Ocean	7,848,295	14,450
Arctic Ocean	5,427,050	4,300
South China Sea	1,148,500	4,802
Caribbean Sea	971,400	8,448
Mediterranean Sea	969,100	4,926
Bering Sea	873,000	4,893
Gulf of Mexico	582,100	5,297
Sea of Okhotsk	537,500	3,192
Sea of Japan	391,100	5,468
Hudson Bay	281,900	305
East China Sea	256,600	620
Andaman Sea	218,100	3,667
Black Sea	196,100	3,906
Red Sea	174,900	1,764
North Sea	164,900	308
Baltic Sea	147,500	180
Yellow Sea	113,500	121
Persian Gulf	88,800	328
Gulf of California	59,100	2,375

Principal Ocean Depths

Source: National Geospatial-Intelligence Agency, U.S. Dept. of Defense

Body of water	Location (lat.)	Location (long.)	Depth (meters)	Depth (fathoms)	Depth (feet)
Pacific Ocean					
Mariana Trench	11°22′ N	142°36′ E	10,994	6,012	36,069
Tonga Trench	23°16′ S	174°44′ W	10,800	5,906	35,433
Philippine Trench	10°38′ N	126°36′ E	10,057	5,499	32,995
Kermadec Trench	31°53′ S	177°21′ W	10,047	5,494	32,963
Bonin Trench	24°30′ N	143°24′ E	9,994	5,464	32,788
Kuril Trench	44°15′ N	150°34′ E	9,750	5,331	31,988
Izu Trench	31°05′ N	142°10′ E	9,695	5,301	31,808
New Britain Trench	06°19′ S	153°45′ E	8,940	4,888	29,331
Yap Trench	08°33′ N	138°02′ E	8,527	4,663	27,976
Japan Trench	36°08′ N	142°43′ E	8,412	4,600	27,599
Peru-Chile Trench	23°18′ S	71°14′ W	8,064	4,409	26,457
Palau Trench	07°52′ N	134°56′ E	8,054	4,404	26,424
Aleutian Trench	50°51′ N	177°11′ E	7,679	4,199	25,194
New Hebrides Trench	20°36′ S	168°37′ E	7,570	4,139	24,836
North Ryukyu Trench	24°00′ N	126°48′ E	7,181	3,927	23,560
Middle America Trench	14°02′ N	93°39′ W	6,662	3,643	21,857
Atlantic Ocean					
Puerto Rico Trench	19°55′ N	65°27′ W	8,605	4,705	28,232
South Sandwich Trench	55°42′ S	25°56′ W	8,325	4,552	27,313
Romanche Gap	0°13′ S	18°26′ W	7,728	4,226	25,354
Cayman Trench	19°12′ N	80°00′ W	7,535	4,120	24,721
Brazil Basin	09°10′ S	23°02′ W	6,119	3,346	20,076
Indian Ocean					
Java Trench	10°19′ S	109°58′ E	7,125	3,896	23,376
Ob' Trench	09°45′ S	67°18′ E	6,874	3,759	22,553
Diamantina Trench	35°50′ S	105°14′ E	6,602	3,610	21,660
Vema Trench	09°08′ S	67°15′ E	6,402	3,501	21,004
Agulhas Basin	45°20′ S	26°50′ E	6,195	3,387	20,325
Arctic Ocean					
Eurasia Basin	82°23′ N	19°31′ E	5,450	2,980	17,881
Mediterranean Sea					
Ionian Basin	36°32′ N	21°06′ E	5,150	2,816	16,896

Note: Greater depths have been reported in some areas but have not been officially confirmed by research vessels.

Major World Rivers

North American rivers are listed in a separate table.

River	Source or upper limit of length	Outflow	Length (mi)
Africa			
Chari	Bamingui-Bangoran region, Central African Republic	Lake Chad	650
Congo	Junction of Lualaba and Luvua Rivers, Dem. Rep. of Congo	Atlantic Ocean	2,720
Cubango (fmr. Okavango)	Central Angola	Okavango Delta	1,000
Gambia	Fouta Djallon, Guinea	Atlantic Ocean	700
Kasai	Central Angola	Congo River	1,100
Limpopo	Junction of Marico and Ngotwane Rivers, South Africa	Indian Ocean	1,100
Lualaba	Southeastern Dem. Rep. of Congo	Congo River	1,100
Niger	Fouta Djallon, Guinea	Gulf of Guinea	2,600
Nile	Luvironza River, Burundi	Mediterranean Sea	4,160
Orange	Maluti Mountains, northern Lesotho	Atlantic Ocean	1,300
Sénégal	Junction of Bafing and Bakoy Rivers, Mali	Atlantic Ocean	1,000
Ubangi	Junction of Uele and Bomu Rivers, Dem. Rep. of Congo	Congo River	700
Zambezi	Northwestern Zambia	Indian Ocean	1,700
Asia			
Amu Darya	Junction of Wakhsh and Panj Rivers, Tajikistan	Aral Sea	1,660
Amur	Junction of Shilka and Argun Rivers, China-Russia	Tartar Strait	1,780
Angara	Lake Baykal, Russia	Yenisei River	1,150
Ayeyarwady (fmr. Irrawaddy)	Junction of Mali and Nmai Rivers, Myanmar	Andaman Sea	1,000
Brahmaputra	Kailas Range, Himalayas, southwestern Tibet	Bay of Bengal	1,800
Chang-Jiang	Tibetan Plateau, southwestern Qinghai, China	East China Sea	3,450
Euphrates	Junction of Kara (Sarasu) and Murat Rivers, Turkey	Shatt al-Arab	1,700
Ganges	Gangotri glacier, Himalayas, India	Bay of Bengal	1,560
Godavari	Western Ghats, Maharashtra, India	Bay of Bengal	900
Hsi (see Xi He)			
Huang-He	Kunlun Mountains, Qinghai, China	Yellow Sea	3,000
Indus	Kailas Range, Himalayas, Tibet	Arabian Sea	1,900
Irtysh	Kazakhstan-Russia	Ob River	2,650
Jordan	Junction of Dan, Banias, and Hazbani streams, Israel	Dead Sea	200
Kolyma	Kolyma and Cherskogo Ranges, Russia	Arctic Ocean	1,500
Krishna	Western Ghats, Maharashtra, India	Bay of Bengal	800
Kura	Northeastern Turkey	Caspian Sea	950
Lena	Western Baikal Range, Russia	Laptev Sea	2,648
Mekong	Eastern Tibetan Plateau, China	South China Sea	2,700
Narmada	Madhya Pradesh, India	Arabian Sea	775
Ob	Junction of Biya and Katun Rivers, Russia	Gulf of Ob	2,300
Salween	Eastern Tibet, China	Gulf of Martaban	1,750
Songhua Jiang	Changbai Mountains, Jilin, China	Amur River	1,150
Sungari (see Songhua Jiang)			
Sutlej	Kailas Range, Himalayas, Tibet	Indus River	900
Syr	Junction of Naryn and Kara Darya Rivers, Uzbekistan	Aral Sea	1,380
Tarim	Junction of Kashi and Yarkant Rivers, China	Lop Nor	1,300
Tigris	Taurus Mountains, Turkey	Shatt al-Arab	1,150
Xi He	Eastern Yunnan, China	South China Sea	1,250
Yamuna	Yamnotri glacier, Uttarakhand, India	Ganges River	850
Yangtze (see Chang-Jiang)			
Yellow (see Huang-He)			
Yenisei	Kyzyl, Tuva Republic, Russia	Kara Sea	2,500
Australia			
Darling	Eastern Highlands, NE New South Wales/SE Queensland	Murray River	1,702
Murray	Australian Alps, SE New South Wales	Southern Ocean	1,558
Murrumbidgee	Australian Alps, SE New South Wales	Murray River	923
Europe			
Buh, Southern	NW of Khmel'nyts'kyy, Ukraine	Black Sea	532
Buh, Western	ENE of Zolochiv, Ukraine	Wisla River	500
Danube	Brege and Brigach Rivers, Black Forest, southwestern Germany	Black Sea	1,770
Dnieper	W of Sychevka, Smolensk, Russia	Black Sea	1,420
Dniester	Carpathian Mountains, Ukraine	Black Sea	850
Don	SE of Tula, Russia	Sea of Azov	1,200
Drava	Carnic Alps, northern Italy	Danube River	450
Dvina, North	Near Veliki Ustyug, Vologda, Russia	White Sea	465
Dvina, West	Valdai Hills, Russia	Gulf of Riga	635
Ebro	Cantabrian Mountains, northern Spain	Mediterranean Sea	575
Elbe	Giant Mountains, northwestern Czech Republic	North Sea	725
Garonne	Central Pyrenees, Spain	Bay of Biscay	402
Kama	Ural Mountains, N of Kuliga, Russia	Volga River	1,260
Loire	Mt. Gerbier-de-Jonc, Vivrais Mountains, France	Atlantic Ocean	630
Marne	Langres Plateau, northeastern France	Seine River	325
Meuse	Langres Plateau, northeastern France	North Sea	560
Oder	Sudetes Mountains, northeastern Czech Republic	Baltic Sea	562
Oka	S of Orël, Russia	Volga River	925
Pechora	Northern Ural Mountains, Russia	Barents Sea	1,120
Po	Cottian Alps, Piedmont, northwestern Italy	Adriatic Sea	405
Rhine	Swiss Alps	North Sea	820

River	Source or upper limit of length	Outflow	Length (mi)
Rhône	Rhône glacier, northeastern Valais, Switzerland	Mediterranean Sea	505
Seine	Langres Plateau, northern Burgundy, France	English Channel	480
Shannon	Near Cuilcagh Mountain, northwestern Cavan County, Ireland	Atlantic Ocean	240
Tagus	E of Madrid, Spain	Atlantic Ocean	585
Thames	4 headstreams in the Cotswold Hills, Gloucestershire, England, UK	North Sea	215
Tiber	Etruscan Apennines, Italy	Tyrrhenian Sea	251
Tisza	N of Rakhiv, western Ukraine	Danube River	700
Ural	Southern Ural Mountains, northeastern Bashkortostan, Russia	Caspian Sea	1,580
Volga	Valdai Hills, Smolensk, Russia	Caspian Sea	2,290
Weser	Junction of Fulda and Werra Rivers, Germany	North Sea	273
Wisla	W Beskid range, Carpathian Mountains, southwestern Poland	Gulf of Gdansk	665
South America			
Amazon	Junction of Ucayali and Marañón Rivers, Andes Mountains, Peru	Atlantic Ocean	3,900
Araguaía	Serra das Araras, Goiás-Mato Grosso, Brazil	Tocantins River	1,100
Beni	Cordillera Real, La Paz, Bolivia	Madeira River	1,000
Caquetá-Japura	Andes Mountains, southwestern Colombia	Amazon River	1,750
Juruá	Cerros de Canchyuaya, eastern Peru	Amazon River	1,500
Madeira	Junction of Beni and Mamoré Rivers, Bolivia	Amazon River	2,100
Magdalena	Cordillera Central, southwestern Colombia	Caribbean Sea	1,000
Negro	Southeastern Colombia	Amazon River	1,400
Orinoco	Near Mt. Delgado Chalbaud, Guiana Highlands, S Venezuela	Atlantic Ocean	1,600
Paraguay	Central Mato Grosso highlands, Brazil	Paraná River	1,584
Paraná	Junction of Paranaíba and Rio Grande Rivers, SE Brazil	Rio de la Plata	2,485
Pilcomayo	E of Lake Poopó, Bolivia	Paraguay River	1,000
Purus	Andes Mountains, eastern Peru	Amazon River	2,100
Putumayo	Andes Mountains, southern Colombia	Amazon River	1,000
Rio de la Plata	Estuary of Paraná and Uruguay Rivers, Argentina-Uruguay	Atlantic Ocean	170
São Francisco	Serra de Canastra, southwestern Minas Gerais, Brazil	Atlantic Ocean	1,800
Tocantins	South-central Goiás, Brazil	Para River	1,640
Ucayali	Junction of Apurímac and Urubamba Rivers, eastern Peru	Marañón River	1,000
Uruguay	Southern Brazil	Rio de la Plata	1,000
Xingu	Central Mato Grosso, Brazil	Amazon River	1,230

Major Rivers in North America

River	Source or upper limit of length	Outflow	Length (mi)
Alabama	Gilmer County, GA	Mobile River	729
Albany	Lake St. Joseph, ON, Can.	James Bay	610
Allegheny	Potter County, PA	Ohio River	325
Altamaha-Ocmulgee	Junction of Yellow and South Rivers, Newton Co., GA	Atlantic Ocean	392
Apalachicola-Chattahoochee	Towns County, GA	Gulf of Mexico	524
Arkansas	Lake County, CO	Mississippi River	1,459
Assiniboine	Eastern Saskatchewan, Can.	Red River	450
Attawapiskat	Attawapiskat, ON, Can.	James Bay	465
Back (NT)	Contwoyto Lake, NT, Can.	Chantrey Inlet, Arctic Ocean	605
Big Black	Webster County, MS	Mississippi River	330
Brazos	Junction of Salt and Double Mountain Forks, Stonewall Co., TX	Gulf of Mexico	1,280
Canadian	Las Animas County, CO	Arkansas River	906
Cedar (IA)	Dodge County, MN	Iowa River	329
Cheyenne	Junction of Antelope Creek and Dry Fork, Converse Co., WY	Missouri River	290
Churchill, Labrador	Lake Ashuanipi, NL, Can.	Atlantic Ocean	532
Churchill, Manitoba	Methy Lake, SK, Can.	Hudson Bay	1,000
Cimarron	Colfax County, NM	Arkansas River	600
Colorado (AZ)	Rocky Mountain Natl. Park, CO	Gulf of California	1,450
Colorado (TX)	Dawson County, TX	Matagorda Bay	862
Columbia	Columbia Lake, BC, Can.	Pacific Ocean, bet. OR and WA	1,243
Columbia, Upper	Columbia Lake, BC, Can.	Mouth of Snake River	890
Connecticut	Third Connecticut Lake, NH	Long Island Sound, CT	407
Coppermine	Lac de Gras, NT, Can.	Coronation Gulf, Arctic Ocean	525
Cumberland	Letcher County, KY	Ohio River	720
Delaware	Schoharie County, NY	Liston Point, Delaware Bay	390
Fraser	Near Mount Robson (on Continental Divide)	Strait of Georgia	850
Gila	Catron County, NM	Colorado River	649
Green (UT-WY)	Junction of Wells and Trail Creeks, Sublette County, WY	Colorado River	730
Hudson	Henderson Lake, Essex County, NY	Upper New York Bay	306
Illinois	St. Joseph County, IN	Mississippi River	420
James (ND-SD)	Wells County, ND	Missouri River	710
James (VA)	Junction of Jackson and Cowpasture Rivers, Botetourt Co., VA	Hampton Roads	340
Kanawha-New	Junction of North and South Forks of New River, NC	Ohio River	352
Kentucky	Junction of North and Middle Forks, Lee County, KY	Ohio River	259
Klamath	Lake Ewauna, Klamath Falls, OR	Pacific Ocean	250

River	Source or upper limit of length	Outflow	Length (mi)
Kootenay	Kootenay Lake, BC, Can.	Columbia River	485
Koyukuk	Endicott Mountains, AK	Yukon River	470
Kuskokwim	Alaska Range	Kuskokwim Bay	724
Liard	Southern Yukon, AK	Mackenzie River	693
Little Missouri	Crook County, WY	Missouri River	560
Mackenzie	Great Slave Lake, NT, Can.	Arctic Ocean	2,635
Milk	Junction of North and South Forks, AB, Can.	Missouri River	625
Minnesota	Big Stone Lake, MN	Mississippi River	332
Mississippi	Lake Itasca, Clearwater County, MN	Gulf of Mexico	2,340
Mississippi-Missouri-Red Rock	Source of Red Rock, Beaverhead County, MT	Gulf of Mexico	3,710
Missouri	Junction of Jefferson, Madison, and Gallatin Rivers, Gallatin County, MT	Mississippi River	2,315
Missouri-Red Rock	Source of Red Rock, Beaverhead County, MT	Mississippi River	2,540
Mobile-Alabama-Coosa	Gilmer County, GA	Mobile Bay	774
Nelson	Lake Winnipeg, MB, Can.	Hudson Bay	410
Neosho	Morris County, KS	Arkansas River, OK	460
Niobrara	Niobrara County, WY	Missouri River, NE	431
North Canadian	Union County, NM	Canadian River, OK	800
North Platte	Junction of Grizzly and Little Grizzly Creeks, Jackson Co., CO	Platte River, NE	618
Ohio	Junction of Allegheny and Monongahela Rivers, Pittsburgh, PA	Mississippi River	981
Ohio-Allegheny	Potter County, PA	Mississippi River	1,310
Osage	East-central Kansas	Missouri River	500
Ottawa	Lake Capimitchigama, QC, Can.	St. Lawrence River	790
Ouachita	Polk County, AR	Black River	605
Peace	Junction of Finlay and Parsnip Rivers, BC, Can.	Slave River	1,210
Pearl	Neshoba County, MS	Gulf of Mexico	411
Pecos	Mora County, NM	Rio Grande	926
Pee Dee-Yadkin	Watauga County, NC	Winyah Bay	435
Pend Oreille-Clark Fork	Near Butte, MT	Columbia River	531
Platte	Junction of North Platte and South Platte Rivers, NE	Missouri River	310
Porcupine	Ogilvie Mountains, AK	Yukon River, AK	569
Potomac	Garrett County, MD	Chesapeake Bay	383
Powder	Junction of South and Middle Forks, WY	Yellowstone River	375
Red (River of the South)	Curry County, NM	Atchafalaya River, LA	1,290
Red River of the North	Junction of Otter Tail and Bois de Sioux Rivers, Wilkin Co., MN	Lake Winnipeg	545
Republican	Junction of North Fork and Arikaree Rivers, NE	Kansas River	445
Rio Grande (Rio Bravo)	San Juan County, CO	Gulf of Mexico	1,900
Roanoke	Junction of North and South Forks, Montgomery Co., VA	Albemarle Sound	380
Rock (IL-WI)	Dodge County, WI	Mississippi River	300
Sabine	Junction of South and Caddo Forks, Hunt Co., TX	Sabine Lake	380
Sacramento	Siskiyou County, CA	Suisun Bay	377
St. Francis	Iron County, MO	Mississippi River	425
St. John	Northwestern Maine	Bay of Fundy	418
St. Lawrence	Lake Ontario, NY-ON, Can.	Gulf of St. Lawrence, Atlantic Ocean	800
Saguenay	Lake St. John, QC, Can.	St. Lawrence River	434
Salmon (ID)	Custer County, ID	Snake River	420
San Joaquin	Junction of South and Middle Forks, Madera Co., CA	Suisun Bay	350
San Juan	Silver Lake, Archuleta County, CO	Colorado River	360
Santee-Wateree-Catawba	McDowell County, NC	Atlantic Ocean	538
Saskatchewan, North	Rocky Mountains, AB, Can.	Saskatchewan R.	800
Saskatchewan, South	Rocky Mountains, AB, Can.	Saskatchewan R.	865
Savannah	Junction of Seneca and Tugaloo Rivers, Anderson Co., SC	Atlantic Ocean, GA-SC	314
Severn (ON)	Sandy Lake, ON, Can.	Hudson Bay	610
Smoky Hill	Cheyenne County, CO	Kansas River, KS	540
Snake	Teton County, WY	Columbia River, WA	1,038
South Platte	Junction of South and Middle Forks, Park County, CO	Platte River	424
Susitna	Alaska Range	Cook Inlet	313
Susquehanna	Otsego Lake, Otsego County, NY	Chesapeake Bay	447
Tallahatchie	Tippah County, MS	Yazoo River	301
Tanana	Wrangell Mountains, AK	Yukon River	659
Tennessee	Junction of French Broad and Holston Rivers, TN	Ohio River	652
Tennessee-French Broad	Courthouse Creek, Transylvania County, NC	Ohio River	886
Tombigbee	Prentiss County, MS	Mobile River	525
Trinity	N of Dallas, TX	Galveston Bay	360
Usumacinta	Junction of Pasión and Chixoy Rivers, Guatemala	Bay of Campeche, Mex.	600
Wabash	Darke County, OH	Ohio River	512
Washita	Hemphill County, TX	Red River, OK	500
White (AR-MO)	Madison County, AR	Mississippi River	722
Willamette	Douglas County, OR	Columbia River	309
Wind-Bighorn	Junction of Wind and Little Wind Rivers, Fremont Co., WY (source of Wind R. is Togwotee Pass, Teton Co., WY)	Yellowstone River	338
Wisconsin	Lac Vieux Desert, Vilas County, WI	Mississippi River	430
Yellowstone	Park County, WY	Missouri River	682
Yukon	McNeil River, YT, Can.	Bering Sea	1,979

Major Natural Lakes of the World

Source: U.S. Geological Survey, U.S. Dept. of the Interior; Natural Resources Canada

A lake is generally defined as a body of water surrounded by land. By this definition some bodies of water that are called seas, such as the Caspian Sea and the Aral Sea, are really lakes. In the following table, the word "lake" is omitted when it is part of the name.

Name	Continent	Area (sq mi)	Length (mi)	Maximum depth (ft)	Elevation (ft)
Caspian Sea[1]	Asia-Europe	143,244	760	3,363	–92
Superior	North America	31,700	350	1,330	600
Victoria	Africa	26,828	250	270	3,720
Huron	North America	23,000	206	750	579
Michigan	North America	22,300	307	923	579
Tanganyika	Africa	12,700	420	4,823	2,534
Baykal	Asia	12,162	395	5,315	1,493
Great Bear	North America	12,096	192	1,463	512
Nyasa (Malawi)	Africa	11,150	360	2,280	1,550
Great Slave	North America	11,030	298	2,014	512
Erie	North America	9,910	241	210	570
Winnipeg	North America	9,416	266	200	712
Ontario	North America	7,340	193	802	245
Balkhash[1]	Asia	7,115	376	85	1,115
Ladoga	Europe	6,835	124	738	13
Maracaibo	South America	5,217	133	115	sea level
Aral Sea[1,2]	Asia	4,040	260	180	175
Onega	Europe	3,710	145	328	108
Eyre[1]	Australia	3,600[3]	90	4	–52
Titicaca	South America	3,200	122	922	12,500
Nicaragua	North America	3,100	102	230	102
Athabasca	North America	3,064	208	407	699
Reindeer	North America	2,568	143	720	1,106
Tonle Sap	Asia	2,500[3]	70	45	NA
Turkana (Rudolf)	Africa	2,473	154	240	1,230
Issyk Kul[1]	Asia	2,355	115	2,303	5,279
Torrens[1]	Australia	2,230[3]	130	(3)	92
Vänern	Europe	2,181	91	328	144
Nettilling	North America	2,140	67	(3)	98
Winnipegosis	North America	2,075	141	38	833
Albert	Africa	2,075	100	168	2,030
Nipigon	North America	1,872	72	540	853
Gairdner[1]	Australia	1,840[3]	90	(3)	112
Urmia[1]	Asia	1,815	90	49	4,177
Manitoba	North America	1,799	140	21	813
Chad	Africa	521[4]	175	24	787

NA = Not available. (1) Salt lake. (2) The diversion of its two feeder rivers since the 1960s has devastated the Aral—once the world's fourth-largest lake (26,000 sq mi) with length, max. depth, and elevation shown. By 2000, the Aral had effectively become three lakes, with the total area shown. (3) Subject to great seasonal variation. (4) Once fourth-largest lake in Africa (about 10,000 sq mi in the 1960s), Chad had shrunk to around 5% of its original size by 2006 as a result of irrigation and long-term drought.

The Great Lakes

Source: National Ocean Service, National Oceanic and Atmospheric Administration, U.S. Dept. of Commerce

The Great Lakes form the world's **largest freshwater body** (in surface area) and with their connecting waterways are the largest inland water transportation unit. Draining the north-central basin of the U.S., they enable shipping to get to the Atlantic via their outlet, the St. Lawrence R.; the Gulf of Mexico can be reached via the Illinois Waterway, between Lake Michigan and the Mississippi R. A third outlet connects with the Hudson R. and then the Atlantic via the New York State Barge Canal System. Illinois Waterway and NYS Barge Canal System traffic is limited to recreational boating and small shipping vessels.

Only Lake Michigan is wholly in the U.S.; the other lakes are shared with Canada. Ships move from the shores of Lake Superior to Whitefish Bay in the east, then through the Soo Locks in Sault Ste. Marie, MI, onto St. Mary's R. and into Lake Huron. To reach the Port of Indiana-Burns Harbor and South Chicago, IL, ships travel west from Lake Huron to Lake Michigan through the Straits of Mackinac. Low water datum is based on the International Great Lakes Datum (1985), with Rimouski, Quebec, as the reference zero point. The distance between Duluth, MN, and Lake Ontario's east end is 1,156 mi.

	Superior	Michigan	Huron	Erie	Ontario
Length (mi)	350	307	206	241	193
Breadth (mi)	160	118	183	57	53
Deepest soundings (ft)	1,333	923	750	210	802
Volume of water (cu mi)	2,935	1,180	850	116	393
Area (sq mi) water surface—U.S.	20,600	22,300	9,100	4,980	3,460
Canada	11,100	NA	13,900	4,930	3,880
Area (sq mi) entire drainage basin—U.S.	16,900	45,600	16,200	18,000	15,200
Canada	32,400	NA	35,500	4,720	12,100
Total area (sq mi), U.S. and Canada	**81,000**	**67,900**	**74,700**	**32,630**	**34,850**
Low water datum above mean water level at Rimouski, QC, avg. level (ft)	601.10	577.50	577.50	569.20	243.30
Latitude, N	46°25′	41°37′	43°00′	41°23′	43°11′
	49°00′	46°06′	46°17′	42°52′	44°15′
Longitude, W	84°22′	84°45′	79°43′	78°51′	76°03′
	92°06′	88°02′	84°45′	83°29′	79°53′
National boundary line (mi)	282.8	NA	260.8	251.5	174.6
U.S. shoreline (mainland only) (mi)	863	1,400	580	431	300

NA = Not applicable.

Notable Waterfalls

Source: National Geographic Society

The magnitude of a waterfall is determined not only by height but also by volume and steadiness of flow, crest width, the angle of a drop, and the number of leaps it may make. A series of low falls over a considerable distance is known as a cascade. Waterfalls are highly variable and few authoritative figures exist. For more information and some alternative measurements, see the World Waterfall Database at www.worldwaterfalldatabase.com.

Estimated mean annual flow (ft^3/sec): Niagara, 212,200; Paulo Afonso, 100,000; Iguazú, 61,000; Victoria, 35,400.

Height is total drop in feet in one or more leaps. If river name is not shown, it is the same as the waterfall. # = more than one leap; * = diminishes greatly seasonally; ** = reduces to a trickle or is dry for part of each year; R. = river; (C) = cascade.

Name, location	Height (ft)
Africa	
Angola	
Ruacana, Cunene R.	406
Lesotho	
Maletsunyane*	630
South Africa	
Augrabies, Orange R.*	480
Tugela#	2,800
Tanzania-Zambia	
Kalambo*	704
Zimbabwe-Zambia	
Victoria, Zambezi R.*	343
Asia and Oceania	
Australia	
New South Wales	
Wentworth	614
Wollomombi	722
Queensland	
Tully**	984
Wallaman, Stony Creek	879
India	
Sivasamudram	320
Jog, Sharavati R.*	829
Japan	
Kegon, Lake Chuzenji*	350
New Zealand	
Helena	722
Sutherland, Arthur R.#	1,904
Europe	
Austria	
Gastein#	487
Krimml#	1,246
France	
Gavarnie*	1,385
Italy	
Toce (C)	470
Norway	
Mardalsfossen#**	2,154
Skykje**	984
Vetti, Morka-Koldedola R.	900
Sweden	
Handol#	345
Switzerland	
Giessbach (C)	984
Reichenbach#	820
Staubbach	984
Trümmelbach#	1,312
United Kingdom	
Glomach, Scotland	370
Pistyll Rhaeadr, Wales	240
North America	
Canada	
Alberta	
Panther, Nigel Creek	600
British Columbia	
Della#	1,444
Takakkaw, Daly Glacier#	992
Ontario	
Niagara (Horseshoe)	167
Québec	
Montmorency	276
United States	
Alabama	
Noccalula Falls	90
California	
Feather*	640
Yosemite National Park	
Bridalveil*	620
Illilouette*	370
Nevada, Merced R.*	594
Ribbon**	1,612
Silver Strand, Meadow Brook**	574
Vernal, Merced R.*	317
Yosemite#**	2,425
Colorado	
Seven Falls, S. Cheyenne Creek#	300
Hawaii	
Akaka, Kolekole Stream	420
Idaho	
Shoshone, Snake R.**	212
Kentucky	
Cumberland	68
Maryland	
Great, Potomac R. (C)*	76
Minnesota	
Minnehaha**	53
New Jersey	
Great, Passaic R.	70
New York	
Niagara (American)	120
Taughannock*	215
Oregon	
Multnomah#	850
Tennessee	
Fall Creek	256
Washington	
Sluiskin, Paradise R.	300
Snoqualmie**	268
Wisconsin	
Big Manitou, Black R. (C)*	165
Wyoming	
Tower	132
Yellowstone (lower)*	308
Yellowstone (upper)*	109
South America	
Argentina-Brazil	
Iguazú	269
Brazil	
Cachoeira da Fumaça*	1,312
Paulo Afonso, São Francisco R.	275
Colombia	
Tequendama, Bogota R.*	482
Ecuador	
Agoyan, Pastaza R.*	200
Guyana	
Kaieteur, Potaro R.	741
King George VI, Kamarang R.	1,600
Marina, Ipobe R.#	500
Venezuela	
Angel (Kerepakupai Merú), Churún#*	3,212
Cuquenan	2,000

Latitude and Longitude of World Cities

Source: National Geospatial-Intelligence Agency, U.S. Dept. of Defense

City, country	Lat. °	Lat. ′	Long. °	Long. ′
Athens, Greece	37	59 N	23	44 E
Bangkok, Thailand	13	45 N	100	31 E
Beijing, China	39	55 N	116	23 E
Berlin, Germany	52	31 N	13	24 E
Bogotá, Colombia	4	38 N	74	3 W
Buenos Aires, Argentina	34	35 S	58	40 W
Cairo, Egypt	30	4 N	31	17 E
Jakarta, Indonesia	6	10 S	106	49 E
Jerusalem, Israel	31	45 N	35	0 E
Johannesburg, South Africa	26	12 S	28	2 E
Kiev, Ukraine	50	26 N	30	31 E
Lagos, Nigeria	6	35 N	3	45 E
London, UK (Greenwich)	51	28 N	0	0
Manila, Philippines	14	35 N	121	0 E
Mexico City, Mexico	19	26 N	99	8 W
Moscow, Russia	55	45 N	37	36 E
Mumbai (Bombay), India	18	59 N	72	50 E
New Delhi, India	28	36 N	77	12 E
Paris, France	48	52 N	2	20 E
Rio de Janeiro, Brazil	22	52 S	43	16 W
Rome, Italy	41	54 N	12	29 E
Santiago, Chile	33	27 S	70	40 W
Seoul, South Korea	37	35 N	127	0 E
Sydney, Australia	33	51 S	151	12 E
Tehran, Iran	35	40 N	51	25 E
Tokyo, Japan	35	41 N	139	45 E

Highest and Lowest Continental Elevations

Source: National Geographic Society

Continent	Highest point	Elev. (ft)
Asia	Everest, Nepal-Tibet	29,035
South America	Aconcagua, Argentina	22,835
North America	Denali (fmr. McKinley), Alaska	20,320
Africa	Kilimanjaro, Tanzania	19,341
Europe	Elbrus, Russia	18,510
Antarctica	Vinson Massif	16,066
Australia	Kosciusko, New South Wales	7,310

Continent	Lowest point	Ft below sea level
Antarctica	Bentley Subglacial Trench	8,333[1]
Asia	Dead Sea, Israel-Jordan	1,348
Africa	Lake Assal, Djibouti	512
North America	Death Valley, California	282
South America	Valdes Peninsula, Argentina	131
Europe	Caspian Sea, Russia, Azerbaijan	92
Australia	Lake Eyre, South Australia	49

(1) Estimated level of the continental floor. Lower points that have yet to be discovered may exist beneath the ice.

Latitude, Longitude, and Elevation of U.S. and Canadian Cities

Source: U.S. geographic positions and altitudes provided by U.S. Geological Survey, U.S. Dept. of the Interior. Canadian geographic positions and altitudes provided by Natural Resources Canada.

City, state/province	Lat. N °	′	″	Long. W °	′	″	Elev. (ft)
Albany, NY	42	39	9	73	45	22	148
Albuquerque, NM	35	5	4	106	39	4	4,954
Anchorage, AK	61	13	5	149	54	1	102
Annapolis, MD	38	58	42	76	29	32	43
Atlanta, GA	33	44	56	84	23	17	1,050
Augusta, GA	33	28	15	81	58	29	141
Augusta, ME	44	18	38	69	46	46	121
Austin, TX	30	16	2	97	44	35	489
Baltimore, MD	39	17	25	76	36	44	33
Baton Rouge, LA	30	27	3	91	9	16	46
Billings, MT	45	47	0	108	30	2	3,123
Birmingham, AL	33	31	14	86	48	9	614
Bismarck, ND	46	48	30	100	47	1	1,696
Boise, ID	43	36	49	116	12	12	2,700
Boston, MA	42	21	30	71	3	35	46
Buffalo, NY	42	53	11	78	52	42	600
Burlington, VT	44	28	33	73	12	43	197
Calgary, AB	51	2	45	114	3	27	3,557
Carson City, NV	39	9	50	119	46	3	4,682
Casper, WY	42	52	0	106	18	47	5,105
Cedar Rapids, IA	42	0	30	91	38	39	807
Charleston, SC	32	46	36	79	55	51	10
Charleston, WV	38	20	59	81	37	57	597
Charlotte, NC	35	13	38	80	50	35	761
Charlottetown, PE	46	14	25	63	8	5	160
Cheyenne, WY	41	8	24	104	49	13	6,086
Chicago, IL	41	51	0	87	39	0	587
Churchill, MB	58	46	51	94	11	13	94
Cleveland, OH	41	29	58	81	41	43	653
Colorado Springs, CO	38	50	2	104	49	17	6,010
Columbia, SC	34	0	3	81	2	5	302
Columbus, OH	39	57	40	82	59	56	781
Concord, NH	43	12	29	71	32	15	272
Corpus Christi, TX	27	48	2	97	23	47	7
Dallas, TX	32	46	59	96	48	24	420
Denver, CO	39	44	21	104	59	5	5,279
Des Moines, IA	41	36	2	93	36	33	873
Detroit, MI	42	19	53	83	2	45	597
Dover, DE	39	9	29	75	31	27	30
Durham, NC	35	59	39	78	53	55	400
Edmonton, AB	53	32	4	113	29	25	2,200
El Paso, TX	31	45	31	106	29	13	3,717
Eugene, OR	44	3	7	123	5	12	430
Evansville, IN	37	58	29	87	33	21	387
Fairbanks, AK	64	50	16	147	42	59	446
Fargo, ND	46	52	38	96	47	23	902
Ft. Smith, AR	35	23	9	94	23	55	440
Ft. Wayne, IN	41	7	50	85	7	44	810
Ft. Worth, TX	32	43	31	97	19	15	653
Frankfort, KY	38	12	3	84	52	24	505
Fredericton, NB	45	56	43	66	40	0	67
Greensboro, NC	36	4	21	79	47	31	827
Greenville, SC	34	51	9	82	23	38	984
Gulfport, MS	30	22	3	89	5	34	20
Halifax, NS	44	52	0	63	42	58	477
Hamilton, ON	43	14	34	79	59	22	780
Harrisburg, PA	40	16	25	76	53	4	331
Hartford, CT	41	45	49	72	41	6	30
Helena, MT	46	35	34	112	2	10	4,045
Hilo, HI	19	43	21	155	5	13	20
Honolulu, HI	21	18	25	157	51	30	16
Houston, TX	29	45	48	95	21	48	36
Idaho Falls, ID	43	28	0	112	2	3	4,705
Indianapolis, IN	39	46	6	86	9	29	718
Iqaluit, NU	63	45	0	68	31	0	112
Jackson, MS	32	17	56	90	11	5	279
Jacksonville, FL	30	19	56	81	39	20	16
Jefferson City, MO	38	34	36	92	10	25	630
Jersey City, NJ	40	43	41	74	4	40	33
Juneau, AK	58	18	7	134	25	11	56
Kansas City, MO	39	5	59	94	34	43	899
Knoxville, TN	35	57	38	83	55	15	906
Lansing, MI	42	43	57	84	33	20	853
Laredo, TX	27	30	23	99	30	27	413
Las Vegas, NV	36	10	30	115	8	14	2,001
Lexington, KY	37	59	19	84	28	40	968
Lincoln, NE	40	48	0	96	40	0	1,201
Little Rock, AR	34	44	47	92	17	23	335
Los Angeles, CA	34	3	8	118	14	37	292
Louisville, KY	38	15	15	85	45	34	466
Madison, WI	43	4	23	89	24	4	873
Manchester, NH	42	59	44	71	27	17	259
Memphis, TN	35	8	58	90	2	56	259
Miami, FL	25	46	27	80	11	37	7
Milwaukee, WI	43	2	20	87	54	23	614
Minneapolis, MN	44	58	48	93	15	50	830
Mobile, AL	30	41	40	88	2	35	10
Montgomery, AL	32	22	0	86	18	0	239
Montpelier, VT	44	15	36	72	34	31	525
Montréal, QC	45	31	0	73	39	0	221
Nashville, TN	36	9	57	86	47	4	568
New Orleans, LA	29	57	17	90	4	30	0
New York, NY	40	42	51	74	0	22	33
Newark, NJ	40	44	8	74	10	21	33
Nome, AK	64	30	4	165	24	23	36
Oklahoma City, OK	35	28	3	97	30	59	1,197
Olympia, WA	47	2	16	122	54	3	92
Omaha, NE	41	15	31	95	56	16	1,060
Ottawa, ON	45	20	0	75	35	3	382
Overland Park, KS	38	58	56	94	40	15	1,083
Philadelphia, PA	39	57	8	75	9	50	46
Phoenix, AZ	33	26	54	112	4	27	1,086
Pierre, SD	44	22	6	100	21	3	1,480
Pittsburgh, PA	40	26	26	79	59	45	764
Portland, OR	45	31	24	122	40	34	33
Providence, RI	41	49	26	71	24	46	10
Provo, UT	40	14	2	111	39	31	4,550
Québec, QC	46	49	0	71	13	0	244
Raleigh, NC	35	46	20	78	38	19	315
Rapid City, SD	44	4	50	103	13	52	3,241
Regina, SK	50	27	17	104	36	24	1,894
Reno, NV	39	31	47	119	48	50	4,505
Richmond, VA	37	33	14	77	27	37	210
Rochester, NY	43	9	17	77	36	56	505
Sacramento, CA	38	34	54	121	29	40	20
St. John's, NL	47	28	56	52	47	49	461
St. Louis, MO	38	37	38	90	11	52	466
St. Paul, MN	44	56	34	93	5	36	794
Salem, OR	44	56	35	123	2	6	157
Salt Lake City, UT	40	45	39	111	53	28	4,265
San Antonio, TX	29	25	27	98	29	37	650
San Diego, CA	32	42	55	117	9	26	62
San Francisco, CA	37	46	30	122	25	10	52
San Jose, CA	37	20	22	121	53	42	82
San Juan, PR	18	27	59	66	6	21	26
Santa Fe, NM	35	41	13	105	56	16	6,995
Saskatoon, SK	52	8	23	106	41	10	1,653
Savannah, GA	32	5	1	81	5	59	20
Seattle, WA	47	36	22	122	19	55	177
Shreveport, LA	32	31	31	93	45	1	151
Sioux City, IA	42	30	0	96	24	1	1,201
Sioux Falls, SD	43	33	0	96	42	1	1,473
Spokane, WA	47	39	32	117	25	34	1,877
Springfield, IL	39	48	6	89	38	37	600
Tacoma, WA	47	15	10	122	26	39	249
Tampa, FL	27	56	51	82	27	30	16
Topeka, KS	39	2	54	95	40	41	948
Toronto, ON	43	44	30	79	22	24	251
Trenton, NJ	40	13	1	74	44	35	59
Tucson, AZ	32	13	18	110	55	35	2,490
Tulsa, OK	36	9	14	95	59	34	722
Vancouver, BC	49	15	40	123	6	50	14
Victoria, BC	48	25	42	123	21	53	63
Virginia Beach, VA	36	51	11	75	58	41	10
Washington, DC	38	53	42	77	2	11	23
Whitehorse, YT	60	41	46	135	4	51	2,305
Wichita, KS	37	41	32	97	20	15	1,302
Wilmington, DE	39	44	45	75	32	48	92
Wilmington, NC	34	13	32	77	56	42	50
Winnipeg, MB	49	53	4	97	8	47	783
Yakima, WA	46	36	7	120	30	21	1,070
Yellowknife, NT	62	27	13	114	22	12	675

RELIGION

Religious Group Membership in the U.S.

Source: Todd M. Johnson, ed. *World Christian Database* (Leiden/Boston: Brill, Aug. 2015), except where indicated.

Figures are latest available from the source and generally are based on collected reports made by each denomination and include only persons affiliated with a congregation of the denomination. Reporting practices vary from one denomination to another, but generally include all members, not only full communicants. Religious groups with fewer than 40,000 members not generally shown. Broad religious groups indicated in **boldface** are estimates for adherents, based on self-identification in surveys and other data, and are updated on a continuing basis.

Group (congregations)	Members
African Methodist Episcopal Church (8,915)	2,697,000
African Methodist Episcopal Zion Church (3,305)	1,596,000
Agnosticism (NA)	**49,049,536**
American Baptist Assn. (1,720)	349,000
American Baptist Churches in the USA (5,724)	1,692,000
American Evangelistic Assn. (560)	270,000
Antiochian Orthodox Christian, North America (247)	450,000
Apostolic Assemblies of Christ Intl. (300)	45,600
Apostolic Assembly of the Faith in Christ Jesus (759)	90,000
Armenian Apostolic Church of America (37)	350,000
Armenian Church of North America (94)	370,000
Armenian Evangelical Union of Churches (58)	44,100
Assemblies of God Fellowship Intl. (853)	820,000
Assemblies of God USA (12,516)	3,102,000
Assemblies of the Lord Jesus Christ (300)	50,000
Associate Reformed Presbyterian Church (275)	48,700
Assn. of Faith Churches and Ministries (1,111)	202,000
Assn. of Free Lutheran Congregations (271)	44,500
Assn. of Intl. Gospel Assemblies (260)	270,000
Assyrian Church of the East (22)	114,000
Atheism (NA)	**2,842,405**
Baha'i Faith (NA)	**547,727**
Baptist Bible Fellowship Intl. (4,500)	1,669,000
Baptist General Conference (1,200)	180,000
Baptist Missionary Assn. of America (1,250)	230,000
Bible Way Churches of Our Lord Jesus Christ World-Wide (1,400)	340,000
Brethren in Christ Church (222)	46,300
Buddhism (NA)	**4,145,566**
Calvary Chapels Intl. (1,111)	500,000
Charismatic Episcopal Church of N. America (85)	40,000
Chinese Folk Religions[1] (NA)	**113,795**
Christian and Missionary Alliance (2,021)	432,471
Christian Brethren (Open) (1,200)	110,000
Christian Church (Disciples of Christ) (3,691)	658,869
Christian Churches and Churches of Christ (5,007)	1,174,000
Christian Congregation (1,550)	125,000
Christian Methodist Episcopal Church (3,592)	919,000
Christian Reformed Church in N. America (1,062)	269,000
Christianity (all)[2] (NA)	**253,213,274**
Church of Christ, Scientist (2,206)	848,000
Church of God (Anderson, IN) (2,305)	259,000
Church of God (Cleveland, OH) (6,542)	1,334,000
Church of God (Huntsville, AL) (1,645)	84,800
Church of God in Christ (22,401)	8,016,000
Church of God of Prophecy (1,841)	98,800
Church of Jesus Christ (655)	150,000
Church of Jesus Christ of Latter-day Saints (13,601)	6,144,582
Church of Our Lord Jesus Christ of Apostolic Faith (535)	650,000
Church of the Brethren (1,047)	152,000
Church of the Living God (170)	42,000
Church of the Nazarene (5,130)	793,000
Churches of Christ (Non-Instrumental) (13,067)	1,402,000
Churches of God General Conference (320)	40,000
Churches on the Rock Intl. (188)	206,000
Congregational Christian Churches (400)	67,000
Conservative Baptist Assn. of America (1,250)	245,000
Conservative Congregational Christian Conference (296)	42,296
Coptic Orthodox Church (170)	130,000
Covenant Ministries Intl. (31)	101,000
Cumberland Presbyterian Church (740)	76,500
Czechoslovak Hussite Church (38)	59,900
Elim Assemblies Fellowship (240)	41,000
Episcopal Church in the USA (5,007)	1,923,046
Ethiopian Orthodox Church in the USA (77)	80,200
Ethnoreligious[1] (NA)	**1,136,159**
Evangelical Covenant Church of America (850)	150,000
Evangelical Fellowship Intl. (270)	80,000
Evangelical Free Church of America (1,355)	396,000
Evangelical Lutheran Church in America (10,498)	4,603,000
Evangelical Presbyterian Church (271)	113,762
Evangelistic Messengers Assn. (556)	131,000
Faith Christian Fellowship Intl. (331)	230,000

Group (congregations)	Members
Free Methodist Church of North America (1,053)	75,586
Full Gospel Baptist Church Fellowship (500)	165,000
Full Gospel Fellowship of Churches and Ministers (1,273)	432,632
General Assn. of General Baptists (840)	98,000
General Assn. of Regular Baptist Churches (1,321)	132,700
General Conference of Mennonite Brethren Churches (464)	111,000
Global Network of Christian Ministries (270)	40,000
Grace Gospel Fellowship (Network of Ministers) (41)	44,300
Grace Intl. (102)	120,000
Greater Emmanuel Intl. Fellowship of Churches and Ministries (47)	47,800
Greek Orthodox Archdiocese of America (525)	1,500,000
Hinduism (NA)	**1,469,446**
Independent Assemblies Fellowship (457)	91,200
Independent Assemblies of God Intl. (300)	120,000
Independent Churches of the Latter Rain Revival (706)	70,400
Independent Fundamental Churches of America (630)	59,000
Indian Pentecostal Church of America (361)	220,000
Interdenominational Ministries Intl. (163)	45,600
Intl. Church of the Foursquare Gospel (1,971)	480,000
Intl. Churches of Christ (142)	45,000
Intl. Convention of Faith Ministries (410)	100,000
Intl. Council of Community Churches (137)	69,276
Intl. Evangelical Church (100)	50,000
Intl. Evangelism Crusades (65)	65,000
Intl. Fellowship of Faith Ministries (2,618)	261,000
Intl. Gospel Assemblies (655)	460,000
Intl. Ministers Forum (492)	170,000
Intl. Pentecostal Holiness Church (2,024)	330,054
Islam[3] (NA)	**4,418,642**
Jainism (NA)	**89,410**
Jehovah's Witnesses (12,995)	2,710,000
Jesus Is Lord Church (245)	40,700
Judaism[4] (NA)	**5,707,235**
Korean American Presbyterian Church (817)	81,500
Korean Full Gospel Churches of America (914)	293,000
Korean Presbyterian Church of America (1,793)	569,000
Latin American Council of Christian Churches (226)	117,000
Lighthouse Gospel Fellowship (425)	50,500
Living Faith Christian Centers (533)	53,200
Lutheran Church-Missouri Synod (6,138)	2,327,000
Malankara Orthodox Syrian Church of the East (92)	45,000
Mennonite Church USA (920)	140,000
Ministers Fellowship Intl. (723)	65,300
Missionary Church (361)	52,200
Missionary Gospel Church Intl. (750)	45,000
Moravian Church in America (170)	42,200
Natl. Assn. of Free Will Baptists (2,400)	233,000
Natl. Baptist Convention of America (12,300)	4,200,000
Natl. Baptist Convention, USA (40,000)	9,364,000
Natl. Baptist Evangelical Life and Soul Saving Assembly (287)	85,800
Natl. David Spiritual Temple of Christ (73)	67,900
Natl. Missionary Baptist Conv. of America (280)	449,000
Natl. Primitive Baptist Convention (1,565)	600,000
Native American Church of North America (400)	200,000
Network of Kingdom Churches (1,210)	291,000
Network of Restoration Churches (163)	40,700
New Apostolic Church USA (320)	50,000
New Religion[1] (NA)	**1,697,239**
North American Baptist Conference (422)	90,900
North American Old Roman Catholic Church (137)	65,200
Old Order Amish Mennonite Church (950)	115,000
Open Bible Standard Churches (330)	40,000
Orthodox Church in America (551)	2,700,000
Pentecostal Assemblies of the Apostolic Faith (77)	59,400
Pentecostal Assemblies of the World (1,650)	1,300,000
Pentecostal Church of God (1,134)	98,579
Pentecostal Churches of the Apostolic Faith (246)	72,000
Presbyterian Church (USA) (10,746)	2,749,000

Group (congregations)	Members
Presbyterian Church in America (1,365)	377,000
Primitive Baptists (2,897)	132,000
Progressive Natl. Baptist Convention (1,200)	2,087,000
Reformed Church in America (896)	250,938
Reorganized Church of Jesus Christ of Latter-Day Saints (920)	175,000
Rhema Bible Churches (560)	170,000
Roman Catholic Church[5] (18,538)	70,655,599
Romanian Orthodox Episcopate of America (37)	105,000
Russian Orthodox Church Outside Russia (221)	90,100
Salvation Army (1,228)	377,000
Serbian Orthodox Church in N. and S. America (123)	68,760
Seventh-day Adventist Church (4,917)	1,241,000
Shintoism (NA)	**65,666**
Sikhism (NA)	**364,143**
Southern Baptist Convention (45,854)	20,678,000
Spanish Christian Churches (346)	85,100
Spiritism (NA)	**235,911**
Taoism (or Daoism) (NA)	**13,005**
Trinity Church Network (20)	131,000
Unitarian Universalist Assn. (1,048)	221,367
United Baptist Churches (410)	56,800
United Church of Christ (5,232)	1,086,000
United Church of Jesus Christ (Apostolic) (114)	131,000
United Evangelical Churches (294)	78,800
United Free Will Baptist Church (706)	104,000
United House of Prayer for All People (161)	1,632,000
United Methodist Church (33,869)	7,526,642
United Pentecostal Church Intl. (4,748)	830,000
Unity School of Christianity (661)	115,000
Universal Fellowship of Metropolitan Community Churches (220)	40,000
Victory Fellowship of Ministries (160)	57,000
Vineyard Churches (USA) (556)	189,000
Volunteers of America (300)	45,400
Way of the Cross Church of Christ (72)	75,000
Wesleyan Church (1,716)	139,008
Willow Creek Assn. of Churches (2,000)	400,000
Wisconsin Evangelical Lutheran Synod (1,259)	378,196
Word of Faith Fellowship/Ministries (25)	45,600
World Council of Independent Christian Churches (327)	54,700
World Harvest Ministerial Alliance (163)	59,000
World Ministry Fellowship (290)	50,000
World Missionary Church (163)	40,700
World Salt (82)	50,500
Worldwide Missionary Evangelism (231)	45,600
Worldwide/Last Churches (220)	156,000
Zoroastrianism (NA)	**18,474**

(1) See definition in World Adherents table on p. 698. (2) 2015 estimate. Self-identified; affiliated Christians in the U.S. were estimated at 206,672,494 in 2015. (3) Other sources vary. The Council on American-Islamic Relations estimates a total of 2,000 mosques and 6-7 mil Muslims in the U.S. (4) Includes congregations of Jewish Reconstructionist Federation (about 100), Union of Orthodox Jewish Congregations of America (1,930), Union for Reform Judaism (850), and United Synagogue of Conservative Judaism (600). Among Jewish adherents in the U.S., about 35% classify themselves as Reform, 18% as Conservative, 10% as Orthodox, 2% as Reconstructionist, the rest as "just Jewish." Source: Ira M. Sheskin and Arnold Dashefsky, "Jewish Population of the United States," in *The American Jewish Year Book* (Dordrecht: Springer, 2015). (This source estimates the total American Jewish population at 6.8 mil.) (5) According to another estimate, by the U.S. Center for Research in the Apostolate, there were 79.7 mil self-identified Roman Catholics in the U.S. in 2014.

World Adherents of Religions by Continental Area, 2014

Source: *2015 Encyclopædia Britannica Book of the Year*. All figures are midyear estimates.

Religion (no. of countries)	Africa	Asia	Europe	Latin America	Northern America	Oceania	World
Baha'is (224)	2,381,000	3,603,000	137,000	962,000	593,000	118,000	7,794,000
Buddhists (152)	274,000	507,766,000	1,865,000	794,000	4,632,000	620,000	515,951,000
Chinese folk religionists (120)	144,000	449,460,000	565,000	200,000	815,000	108,000	451,292,000
Christians (234)	553,046,000	372,552,000	580,784,000	575,606,000	279,417,000	28,534,000	2,389,939,000
Roman Catholics (234)	199,125,000	146,234,000	277,068,000	504,971,000	89,298,000	9,326,000	1,226,022,000
Protestants (231)	209,681,000	93,681,000	94,079,000	62,884,000	62,003,000	12,921,000	535,249,000
Independents (231)	119,783,000	147,535,000	15,082,000	53,960,000	71,855,000	2,035,000	410,250,000
Orthodox (137)	50,533,000	18,748,000	202,831,000	1,104,000	7,770,000	1,048,000	282,034,000
Confucianists (17)	21,300	8,334,000	16,000	500	0	52,200	8,424,000
Ethnoreligionists (146)	97,718,000	152,630,000	1,169,000	3,792,000	1,269,000	394,000	256,972,000
Hindus (144)	3,163,000	967,028,000	1,159,000	796,000	1,909,000	542,000	974,597,000
Jains (19)	106,000	5,332,800	19,800	1,500	104,000	3,100	5,567,200
Jews (147)	132,000	6,302,000	1,519,000	457,000	5,608,000	124,000	14,142,000
Muslims (214)	473,121,000	1,147,503,000	45,404,000	1,669,000	5,284,000	609,000	1,673,590,000
Sunnis (212)	465,892,000	945,963,000	43,247,000	1,224,000	3,651,000	502,000	1,460,479,000
Shiites (148)	2,817,000	192,170,000	2,125,000	432,000	1,039,000	104,000	198,687,000
New religionists (121)	216,900	60,786,000	646,000	1,929,200	2,465,300	122,400	66,165,800
Shintoists (8)	0	2,746,000	0	8,100	64,900	0	2,819,000
Sikhs (64)	81,600	23,561,300	582,000	7,700	633,000	52,400	24,918,000
Spiritists (59)	3,100	2,200	146,400	13,751,000	252,000	8,300	14,163,000
Taoists (6)	0	8,642,200	0	0	12,900	4,900	8,660,000
Zoroastrians (27)	1,100	164,500	5,800	0	21,900	2,700	196,000
All religious adherents (234)	**1,130,409,000**	**3,716,413,000**	**634,018,000**	**599,974,000**	**303,081,000**	**31,295,000**	**6,415,190,000**
Nonreligious (233)	7,820,000	625,842,000	108,795,000	23,448,000	55,155,000	7,534,000	828,594,000
Agnostics (233)	7,181,000	510,568,000	94,076,000	20,423,000	52,886,000	6,977,000	692,111,000
Atheists (223)	639,000	115,274,000	14,719,000	3,025,000	2,269,000	557,000	136,483,000

Note: Figures may not add up to totals due to rounding. "Religious adherents," or those who indicate attachment to religion, may or may not consider themselves as belonging to a particular religious denomination. They are estimated to make up 88.6% of the world population. Figures shown for adherents to specific religious groups are estimates generally based on self-definition as reported in censuses, surveys, and other data; these people may not all be actually affiliated with a particular congregation as members. Some individuals report attachment to more than one religious group, and subdivisions shown in this table are not necessarily exhaustive. Continental areas are as per UN demographic terminology; "Asia" is defined to include the former Soviet Central Asian states, while "Europe" includes all of Russia, extending to the Pacific coast. Figures in parentheses indicate the number of countries where the religion or type of belief has a significant following. **Buddhists** include Mahayana (72%), Theravada or Hinayana (25%), and Tantrayana (incl. Lamaists, Tibetans) (3%). **Chinese folk religionists** are followers of traditional Chinese religion; it may involve worship of local deities, ancestor veneration, Confucian ethics, divination, and Buddhist or Taoist elements, among other beliefs and practices. **Christians** are usually baptized members of a church belonging to one of the major Christian traditions shown here. Those characterized as Independents belong to sects or groups that consider themselves independent of historical mainstream institutionalized Christianity; these include groups such as Unitarians, Mormons, and Jehovah's Witnesses. **Confucianists** are followers of Confucius, mostly living in China or elsewhere in East/Southeast Asia. **Ethnoreligionists** are followers of local, tribal, animistic, or shamanistic religions, generally belonging to a single ethnic group. **Hindus** include Vaishnavites (68%); Shaivites (27%); and Saktists, neo-Hindi, and reformed Hindi (5%). **New religionists** include followers of Asian new religions, radical new crisis religions, and non-Christian syncretistic mass religions.

Episcopal Church Liturgical Colors and Calendar, 2015-19

The most common liturgical colors in the Episcopal Church are as follows: **White**—Christmas Day through first Sunday after Epiphany; Maundy Thursday (as an alternative to crimson at the Eucharist); from the Vigil of Easter to the Day of Pentecost (Whitsunday); Trinity Sunday; Feasts of the Lord (except Holy Cross Day); the Confession of St. Peter; the Conversion of St. Paul; St. Joseph; St. Mary Magdalene; St. Mary the Virgin; St. Michael and All Angels; All Saints' Day; St. John the Evangelist; memorials of other saints who were not martyred; Independence Day and Thanksgiving Day; weddings and funerals. **Red**—the Day of Pentecost; Holy Cross Day; feasts of apostles and evangelists (except those previously mentioned); feasts and memorials of martyrs (including Holy Innocents' Day). **Violet**—Advent and Lent. **Crimson** or oxblood (dark red)—Holy Week. **Green**—the seasons after Epiphany and after Pentecost. **Black**—optional alternative for funerals and Good Friday.

The days of fasting are Ash Wednesday and Good Friday. Other days of special devotion (penitence) include the 40 days of Lent. Ember days are days of prayer for the church's ministry. They fall on the Wednesday, Friday, and Saturday after the first Sunday in Lent, the Day of Pentecost, Holy Cross Day, and Dec. 13. Rogation Days, the three days before Ascension Day, are days of prayer for God's blessing on the crops, on commerce and industry, and for conservation of the Earth's resources.

Holy days and other variables	2015	2016	2017	2018	2019
Golden Number	2	3	4	5	6
Sunday Letter	D	C/B	A	G	F
Sundays after Epiphany	6	5	8	6	8
Ash Wednesday	Feb. 18	Feb. 10	Mar. 1	Feb. 14	Mar. 6
First Sunday in Lent	Feb. 22	Feb. 14	Mar. 5	Feb. 18	Mar. 10
Passion/Palm Sunday	Mar. 29	Mar. 20	Apr. 9	Mar. 25	Apr. 14
Good Friday	Apr. 3	Mar. 25	Apr. 14	Mar. 30	Apr. 19
Easter Day	Apr. 5	Mar. 27	Apr. 16	Apr. 1	Apr. 21
Ascension Day	May 14	May 5	May 25	May 10	May 30
Day of Pentecost	May 24	May 15	June 4	May 20	June 9
Trinity Sunday	May 31	May 22	June 11	May 27	June 16
Numbered Proper of 2 Pentecost	#5	#4	#6	#4	#7
First Sunday of Advent	Nov. 29	Nov. 27	Dec. 3	Dec. 2	Dec. 1

Greek Orthodox Movable Ecclesiastical Dates, 2015-19

Feast days and fasting days are determined annually on the basis of the date of Holy Pascha (Easter). This ecclesiastical cycle begins with the first day of the Triodion and ends with the Sunday of All Saints, a total of 18 weeks.

Holy days and observances	2015	2016	2017	2018	2019
Triodion begins	Feb. 1	Feb. 21	Feb. 5	Jan. 28	Feb. 18
1st Saturday of Souls	Feb. 14	Mar. 5	Feb. 18	Feb. 10	Mar. 2
Meat-Fare Sunday	Feb. 15	Mar. 6	Feb. 19	Feb. 11	Mar. 3
2nd Saturday of Souls	Feb. 21	Mar. 12	Feb. 25	Feb. 17	Mar. 9
Lent begins	Feb. 23	Mar. 14	Feb. 27	Feb. 19	Mar. 11
St. Theodore—3rd Saturday of Souls	Feb. 28	Mar. 19	Mar. 4	Feb. 24	Mar. 16
Sunday of Orthodoxy	Mar. 1	Mar. 20	Mar. 5	Feb. 25	Mar. 17
Saturday of Lazarus	Apr. 4	Apr. 23	Apr. 8	Mar. 31	Apr. 20
Palm Sunday	Apr. 5	Apr. 24	Apr. 9	Apr. 1	Apr. 21
Holy (Good) Friday	Apr. 10	Apr. 29	Apr. 14	Apr. 6	Apr. 26
Western Easter	Apr. 5	Mar. 27	Apr. 16	Apr. 1	Apr. 21
Orthodox Easter	Apr. 12	May 1	Apr. 16	Apr. 8	Apr. 28
Ascension	May 21	June 9	May 25	May 17	June 6
Saturday of Souls	May 30	June 18	June 3	May 26	June 15
Pentecost	May 31	June 19	June 4	May 27	June 16
All Saints	June 7	June 26	June 11	June 3	June 23
Fast of Holy Apostles (first day)	June 8	June 27	June 12	June 4	June 24

Jewish Holy Days, 5775-5779 (2014-19)

The Jewish calendar consists of 12 lunar months, alternating between 29 and 30 days. It is lunisolar and adjusts for the solar cycle by adding an extra month (Adar II) in the 3rd, 6th, 8th, 11th, 14th, 17th, and 19th years of a 19-year cycle. The calendar starts on the day of Creation, reckoned in the 2nd-3rd cent. BCE as Tishrei 1, 3,761 years before the common era.

The religious calendar begins with the month Nisan, from which all other months are counted, and the civil calendar with Tishrei. The months are 1) Nisan, 2) Iyar, 3) Sivan, 4) Tammuz, 5) Av (also Abh), 6) Elul, 7) Tishrei, 8) Cheshvan (also Marcheshvan), 9) Kislev, 10) Tevet (also Tebeth), 11) Shevat (also Shebhat), 12) Adar, and 12a) Adar Sheni (II), added in leap years.

All holidays listed below begin at sunset of the previous day and end at nightfall on the last day shown.

Holiday	Date on Jewish cal.	(5775) 2014-15		(5776) 2015-16		(5777) 2016-17		(5778) 2017-18		(5779) 2018-19	
Rosh Hashanah (New Year)	Tishrei 1	Sept. 25	Thu.	Sept. 14	Mon.	Oct. 3	Mon.	Sept. 21	Thu.	Sept. 10	Mon.
	Tishrei 2	Sept. 26	Fri.	Sept. 15	Tue.	Oct. 4	Tue.	Sept. 22	Fri.	Sept. 11	Tue.
Yom Kippur (Day of Atonement)	Tishrei 10	Oct. 4	Sat.	Sept. 23	Wed.	Oct. 12	Wed.	Sept. 30	Sat.	Sept. 19	Wed.
Sukkot	Tishrei 15	Oct. 9	Thu.	Sept. 28	Mon.	Oct. 17	Mon.	Oct. 5	Thu.	Sept. 24	Mon.
	Tishrei 21	Oct. 15	Wed.	Oct. 4	Sun.	Oct. 23	Sun.	Oct. 11	Wed.	Sept. 30	Sun.
Shemini Atzeret	Tishrei 22	Oct. 16	Thu.	Oct. 5	Mon.	Oct. 24	Mon.	Oct. 12	Thu.	Oct. 1	Mon.
Simchat Torah	Tishrei 23	Oct. 17	Fri.	Oct. 6	Tue.	Oct. 25	Tue.	Oct. 13	Fri.	Oct. 2	Tue.
Hanukkah	Kislev 25	Dec. 17	Wed.	Dec. 7	Mon.	Dec. 25	Sun.	Dec. 13	Wed.	Dec. 3	Mon.
	Tevet 2 or 3	Dec. 24	Wed.	Dec. 14	Mon.	Jan. 1	Sun.	Dec. 20	Wed.	Dec. 10	Mon.
Purim	Adar 14	Mar. 5	Thu.	Mar. 24	Thu.	Mar. 12	Sun.	Mar. 1	Thu.	Mar. 21	Thu.
Pesach (Passover)	Nisan 15	Apr. 4	Sat.	Apr. 23	Sat.	Apr. 11	Tue.	Mar. 31	Sat.	Apr. 20	Sat.
	Nisan 22	Apr. 11	Sat.	Apr. 30	Sat.	Apr. 18	Tue.	Apr. 7	Sat.	Apr. 27	Sat.
Shavuot (Pentecost)	Sivan 6	May 24	Sun.	June 12	Sun.	May 31	Wed.	May 20	Sun.	June 9	Sun.
	Sivan 7	May 25	Mon.	June 13	Mon.	June 1	Thu.	May 21	Mon.	June 10	Mon.
Fast of the 9th of Av	Av 9	July 26	Sun.*	Aug. 14	Sun.*	Aug. 1	Tue.	July 22	Sun.*	Aug. 11	Sun.*

*Date changed to avoid Sabbath.

Hindu Festivals, 2015-19

There are various traditional lunisolar Hindu calendars. Most have similar names for the 12 lunar months, with days beginning at dawn or sunrise, but they differ in various ways, including the numbering of years and the starting point of months. The Indian civil (Saka) calendar, adopted in 1957, is solar-based, and begins Mar. 22 (Mar. 21 in leap years). The year 1938 on the Saka calendar begins Mar. 21, 2016. There are many Hindu holidays and festivals; some are observed only in certain regions. Below are three of the most widely observed.

Festival	2015	2016	2017	2018	2019
Maha Shivaratri (Night of Shiva)[1]	Feb. 17	Mar. 8	Feb. 25	Feb. 14	Mar. 5
Holi (Festival of Color)	Mar. 6	Mar. 23	Mar. 13	Mar. 2	Mar. 21
Diwali (Festival of Lights)	Nov. 11	Oct. 30	Oct. 19	Nov. 7	Oct. 27

(1) Begins the night of the previous day.

Islamic Holy Days, 1436-40 AH (late 2014-19)

The Islamic calendar is a strict lunar calendar reckoned from the year of the Hijra (anno Hegirae, or AH)—Muhammad's flight from Mecca to Medina, in 622 CE. Each year consists of 12 lunar months of 29 or 30 days beginning and ending with each new moon's visible crescent. Common years have 354 days; leap years have 355 days. Some Muslim countries employ a conventionalized calendar with the leap day added to the last month, Dhu'l-Hijja, but for religious purposes the leap date is taken into account by tracking each new moon sighting.

Holy days begin at sunset of the day previous to the day cited. The actual dates may vary slightly from what is shown below, depending on the locality and the times of actual moon sightings as determined by different authorities.

Holy day (date)	(1436) 2014-15	(1437) 2015-16	(1438) 2016-17	(1439) 2017-18	(1440) 2018-19
New Year's Day (Muharram 1)	Oct. 25 2014	Oct. 14, 2015	Oct. 2, 2016	Sept. 21, 2017	Sept. 12, 2018
Ashura (Muharram 10)	Nov. 3, 2014	Oct. 23, 2015	Oct. 11, 2016	Sept. 30, 2017	Sept. 21, 2018
Mawlid (Rabi' I 12)	Jan. 3, 2015	Dec. 23, 2015	Dec. 12, 2016	Dec. 1, 2017	Nov. 21, 2018
Ramadan begins (Ramadan 1)	June 18, 2015	June 6, 2016	May 27, 2017	May 16, 2018	May 6, 2019
Eid al-Fitr (Shawwal 1)	July 17, 2015	July 7, 2016	June 26, 2017	June 15, 2018	June 5, 2019
Eid al-Adha (Dhu'l-Hijja 10)	Sept. 23, 2015	Sept. 11, 2016	Sept. 1, 2017	Aug. 22, 2018	Aug. 12, 2019

Ash Wednesday and Easter Sunday (Western Churches), 2001-2100

Year	Ash Wed.	Easter Sunday	Year	Ash Wed.	Easter Sunday	Year	Ash Wed.	Easter Sunday	Year	Ash Wed.	Easter Sunday	Year	Ash Wed.	Easter Sunday
2001	Feb. 28	Apr. 15	2021	Feb. 17	Apr. 4	2041	Mar. 6	Apr. 21	2061	Feb. 23	Apr. 10	2081	Feb. 12	Mar. 30
2002	Feb. 13	Mar. 31	2022	Mar. 2	Apr. 17	2042	Feb. 19	Apr. 6	2062	Feb. 8	Mar. 26	2082	Mar. 4	Apr. 19
2003	Mar. 5	Apr. 20	2023	Feb. 22	Apr. 9	2043	Feb. 11	Mar. 29	2063	Feb. 28	Apr. 15	2083	Feb. 17	Apr. 4
2004	Feb. 25	Apr. 11	2024	Feb. 14	Mar. 31	2044	Mar. 2	Apr. 17	2064	Feb. 20	Apr. 6	2084	Feb. 9	Mar. 26
2005	Feb. 9	Mar. 27	2025	Mar. 5	Apr. 20	2045	Feb. 22	Apr. 9	2065	Feb. 11	Mar. 29	2085	Feb. 28	Apr. 15
2006	Mar. 1	Apr. 16	2026	Feb. 18	Apr. 5	2046	Feb. 7	Mar. 25	2066	Feb. 24	Apr. 11	2086	Feb. 13	Mar. 31
2007	Feb. 21	Apr. 8	2027	Feb. 10	Mar. 28	2047	Feb. 27	Apr. 14	2067	Feb. 16	Apr. 3	2087	Mar. 5	Apr. 20
2008	Feb. 6	Mar. 23	2028	Mar. 1	Apr. 16	2048	Feb. 19	Apr. 5	2068	Mar. 7	Apr. 22	2088	Feb. 25	Apr. 11
2009	Feb. 25	Apr. 12	2029	Feb. 14	Apr. 1	2049	Mar. 3	Apr. 18	2069	Feb. 27	Apr. 14	2089	Feb. 16	Apr. 3
2010	Feb. 17	Apr. 4	2030	Mar. 6	Apr. 21	2050	Feb. 23	Apr. 10	2070	Feb. 12	Mar. 30	2090	Mar. 1	Apr. 16
2011	Mar. 9	Apr. 24	2031	Feb. 26	Apr. 13	2051	Feb. 15	Apr. 2	2071	Mar. 4	Apr. 19	2091	Feb. 21	Apr. 8
2012	Feb. 22	Apr. 8	2032	Feb. 11	Mar. 28	2052	Mar. 6	Apr. 21	2072	Feb. 24	Apr. 10	2092	Feb. 13	Mar. 30
2013	Feb. 13	Mar. 31	2033	Mar. 2	Apr. 17	2053	Feb. 19	Apr. 6	2073	Feb. 8	Mar. 26	2093	Feb. 25	Apr. 12
2014	Mar. 5	Apr. 20	2034	Feb. 22	Apr. 9	2054	Feb. 11	Mar. 29	2074	Feb. 28	Apr. 15	2094	Feb. 17	Apr. 4
2015	Feb. 18	Apr. 5	2035	Feb. 7	Mar. 25	2055	Mar. 3	Apr. 18	2075	Feb. 20	Apr. 7	2095	Mar. 9	Apr. 24
2016	Feb. 10	Mar. 27	2036	Feb. 27	Apr. 13	2056	Feb. 16	Apr. 2	2076	Mar. 4	Apr. 19	2096	Feb. 29	Apr. 15
2017	Mar. 1	Apr. 16	2037	Feb. 18	Apr. 5	2057	Mar. 7	Apr. 22	2077	Feb. 24	Apr. 11	2097	Feb. 13	Mar. 31
2018	Feb. 14	Apr. 1	2038	Mar. 10	Apr. 25	2058	Feb. 27	Apr. 14	2078	Feb. 16	Apr. 3	2098	Mar. 5	Apr. 20
2019	Mar. 6	Apr. 21	2039	Feb. 23	Apr. 10	2059	Feb. 12	Mar. 30	2079	Mar. 8	Apr. 23	2099	Feb. 25	Apr. 12
2020	Feb. 26	Apr. 12	2040	Feb. 15	Apr. 1	2060	Mar. 3	Apr. 18	2080	Feb. 21	Apr. 7	2100	Feb. 10	Mar. 28

Roman Catholic Church Hierarchy

The Roman Catholic Church is headed by the pope, or bishop of Rome. He is assisted and advised by members of the College of Cardinals. The church is governed through a central administrative body, the Roman Curia. Dioceses around the world are headed by bishops appointed by the pope; collectively they also play a part in leadership of the church as a whole.

The Papacy

Roman Catholics consider Peter the Apostle to have been the first bishop of Rome and first in a line of popes extending to the present. He is said to have arrived in Rome c. 42 CE and to have been martyred there c. 67; he was later canonized as a saint. Popes through history have had both religious and secular roles. The pope today is the head of state of Vatican City as well as leader of the church.

German-born Pope **Benedict XVI**, formerly Cardinal Joseph Ratzinger, who was elected in Apr. 2005, resigned effective Feb. 28, 2013, citing his age (85) and declining health. Assuming the title of supreme pontiff emeritus, he took up residence in a restored convent near the Vatican.

At a papal conclave in Mar. 2013, 115 cardinals from 48 countries chose Argentinean Cardinal Jorge Mario Bergoglio as pope. He took the name **Francis**, after St. Francis of Assisi (1182-1226), known for his life of poverty and devotion to the poor. Pope Francis was the first member of the Society of Jesus (Jesuits) to become pope, and the first born outside Europe since Syrian-born Gregory III, who died in 741.

Chronological List of Popes

Source: *Annuario Pontificio*

Table lists year of accession of each pope. * = antipope, an illegitimate claimant to the papal throne.

Year	Pope	Year	Pope	Year	Pope	Year	Pope	Year	Pope
	St. Peter	530	Boniface II	882	Marinus I	1102	Albert*	1431	Eugene IV
67	St. Linus	530	Dioscorus*	884	St. Adrian III	1105	Sylvester IV*	1439	Felix V*
76	St. Anacletus,	533	John II	885	Stephen V (VI)	1118	Gelasius II	1447	Nicholas V
	or Cletus	535	St. Agapitus I	891	Formosus	1118	Gregory VIII*	1455	Callistus III
88	St. Clement I	536	St. Silverius, Martyr	896	Boniface VI	1119	Callistus II	1458	Pius II
97	St. Evaristus	537	Vigilius	896	Stephen VI (VII)	1124	Honorius II	1464	Paul II
105	St. Alexander I	556	Pelagius I	897	Romanus	1124	Celestine II*	1471	Sixtus IV
115	St. Sixtus I	561	John III	897	Theodore II	1130	Innocent II	1484	Innocent VIII
125	St. Telesphorus	575	Benedict I	898	John IX	1130	Anacletus II*	1492	Alexander VI
136	St. Hyginus	579	Pelagius II	900	Benedict IV	1138	Victor IV*	1503	Pius III
140	St. Pius I	590	St. Gregory I	903	Leo V	1143	Celestine II	1503	Julius II
155	St. Anicetus	604	Sabinian	903	Christopher*	1144	Lucius II	1513	Leo X
166	St. Soter	607	Boniface III	904	Sergius III	1145	Bl. Eugene III	1522	Adrian VI
175	St. Eleutherius	608	St. Boniface IV	911	Anastasius III	1153	Anastasius IV	1523	Clement VII
189	St. Victor I	615	St. Deusdedit,	913	Landus	1154	Adrian IV	1534	Paul III
199	St. Zephyrinus		or Adeodatus	914	John X	1159	Alexander III	1550	Julius III
217	St. Callistus I	619	Boniface V	928	Leo VI	1159	Victor IV*	1555	Marcellus II
217	St. Hippolytus*	625	Honorius I	928	Stephen VII (VIII)	1164	Paschal III*	1555	Paul IV
222	St. Urban I	640	Severinus	931	John XI	1168	Callistus III*	1559	Pius IV
230	St. Pontian	640	John IV	936	Leo VII	1179	Innocent III*	1566	St. Pius V
235	St. Anterus	642	Theodore I	939	Stephen VIII (IX)	1181	Lucius III	1572	Gregory XIII
236	St. Fabian	649	St. Martin I, Martyr	942	Marinus II	1185	Urban III	1585	Sixtus V
251	St. Cornelius	654	St. Eugene I	946	Agapitus II	1187	Clement III	1590	Urban VII
251	Novatian*	657	St. Vitalian	955	John XII	1187	Gregory VIII	1590	Gregory XIV
253	St. Lucius I	672	Adeodatus II	963	Leo VIII	1191	Celestine III	1591	Innocent IX
254	St. Stephen I	676	Donus	964	Benedict V	1198	Innocent III	1592	Clement VIII
257	St. Sixtus II	678	St. Agatho	965	John XIII	1216	Honorius III	1605	Leo XI
259	St. Dionysius	682	St. Leo II	973	Benedict VI	1227	Gregory IX	1605	Paul V
269	St. Felix I	684	St. Benedict II	974	Boniface VII*	1241	Celestine IV	1621	Gregory XV
275	St. Eutychian	685	John V	974	Benedict VII	1243	Innocent IV	1623	Urban VIII
283	St. Caius	686	Conon	983	John XIV	1254	Alexander IV	1644	Innocent X
296	St. Marcellinus	687	Theodore*	985	John XV	1261	Urban IV	1655	Alexander VII
308	St. Marcellus I	687	Paschal*	996	Gregory V	1265	Clement IV	1667	Clement IX
309	St. Eusebius	687	St. Sergius I	997	John XVI*	1271	Bl. Gregory X	1670	Clement X
311	St. Melchiades	701	John VI	999	Sylvester II	1276	Bl. Innocent V	1676	Bl. Innocent XI
314	St. Sylvester I	705	John VII	1003	John XVII	1276	Adrian V	1689	Alexander VIII
336	St. Marcus	708	Sisinnius	1004	John XVIII	1276	John XXI	1691	Innocent XII
337	St. Julius I	708	Constantine	1009	Sergius IV	1277	Nicholas III	1700	Clement XI
352	Liberius	715	St. Gregory II	1012	Benedict VIII	1281	Martin IV	1721	Innocent XIII
355	Felix II*	731	St. Gregory III	1012	Gregory*	1285	Honorius IV	1724	Benedict XIII
366	St. Damasus I	741	St. Zachary	1024	John XIX	1288	Nicholas IV	1730	Clement XII
366	Ursinus*	752	Stephen II (III)[1]	1032	Benedict IX	1294	St. Celestine V	1740	Benedict XIV
384	St. Siricius	757	St. Paul I	1045	Sylvester III	1294	Boniface VIII	1758	Clement XIII
399	St. Anastasius I	767	Constantine*	1045	Benedict IX	1303	Bl. Benedict XI	1769	Clement XIV
401	St. Innocent I	768	Philip*	1045	Gregory VI	1305	Clement V	1775	Pius VI
417	St. Zosimus	768	Stephen III (IV)	1046	Clement II	1316	John XXII	1800	Pius VII
418	St. Boniface I	772	Adrian I	1047	Benedict IX	1328	Nicholas V*	1823	Leo XII
418	Eulalius*	795	St. Leo III	1048	Damasus II	1334	Benedict XII	1829	Pius VIII
422	St. Celestine I	816	Stephen IV (V)	1049	St. Leo IX	1342	Clement VI	1831	Gregory XVI
432	St. Sixtus III	817	St. Paschal I	1055	Victor II	1352	Innocent VI	1846	Pius IX
440	St. Leo I	824	Eugene II	1057	Stephen IX (X)	1362	Bl. Urban V	1878	Leo XIII
461	St. Hilary	827	Valentine	1058	Benedict X*	1370	Gregory XI	1903	St. Pius X
468	St. Simplicius	827	Gregory IV	1059	Nicholas II	1378	Urban VI	1914	Benedict XV
483	St. Felix III (II)	844	John*	1061	Alexander II	1378	Clement VII*	1922	Pius XI
492	St. Gelasius I	844	Sergius II	1061	Honorius II*	1389	Boniface IX	1939	Pius XII
496	Anastasius II	847	St. Leo IV	1073	St. Gregory VII	1394	Benedict XIII*	1958	St. John XXIII
498	St. Symmachus	855	Benedict III	1080	Clement III*	1404	Innocent VII	1963	Paul VI
498	Lawrence* (also in	855	Anastasius*	1086	Bl. Victor III	1406	Gregory XII	1978	John Paul I
	501-505)	858	St. Nicholas I	1088	Bl. Urban II	1409	Alexander V*	1978	St. John Paul II
514	St. Hormisdas	867	Adrian II	1099	Paschal II	1410	John XXIII*	2005	Benedict XVI
523	St. John I, Martyr	872	John VIII	1100	Theodoric*	1417	Martin V	2013	Francis
526	St. Felix IV (III)								

Bl. = Blessed. (1) After St. Zachary, a Roman priest named Stephen was elected who died before assuming the papacy. Another Stephen was then elected to succeed Zachary as Stephen II. He is sometimes listed as Stephen III.

Pope Francis

Pope Francis was born Jorge Mario Bergoglio in Buenos Aires, Argentina, Dec. 17, 1936; his parents were Italian immigrants. He joined the Jesuits in 1958 and was ordained a priest in 1969. Bergoglio served as a parish priest, theology professor, college administrator, and head of the Jesuit province covering Argentina and Uruguay. Ordained a bishop in 1992, he was named archbishop of Buenos Aires in 1998 and made a cardinal in 2001. He was said to have placed second in the balloting for pope in 2005.

Soon after his election in 2013, Francis took steps to illustrate his commitment to the ideals of St. Francis; for example, he chose to live in a modest apartment, rather than in the elaborate papal suite overlooking St. Peter's Square. He approved measures for reform of the scandal-ridden Vatican Bank and established a commission to advise the church on clerical sex abuse. In June 2015, Francis released an encyclical focusing on consumerism, climate change, and the environment.

College of Cardinals

Members of the Sacred College of Cardinals are chosen by the pope to be his chief assistants and advisers in the administration of the church. Among their duties is the election of the pope.

In its present form, the College of Cardinals dates from the 12th century. The first cardinals, from about the 6th century, were deacons and priests of the leading churches of Rome and were bishops of neighboring dioceses. The title of cardinal was limited to members of the college in 1567. The number of cardinals was set at 70 in 1586. Pope John XXIII began to increase the number in 1959; however, the number eligible to participate in papal elections was limited to 120. Previous limitations were set aside by Pope John Paul II when he created new cardinals. In 1918, the Code of Canon Law specified that all cardinals must be priests. Pope John XXIII in 1962 ruled that cardinals must ordinarily be bishops. In 1971, Pope Paul VI decreed that at age 80, cardinals must retire from curial departments and offices and cannot be summoned to participate in papal elections.

As of Sept. 2015, there were 219 cardinals from 74 countries, of whom 118, from 58 countries, remained eligible to vote.

North American Cardinals

Name	Office	Born	Named cardinal
Raymond L. Burke	Prefect, Supreme Tribunal of the Apostolic Signature	1948	2010
Thomas C. Collins[1]	Archbishop of Toronto, ON, Canada	1947	2012
Daniel N. DiNardo[2]	Archbishop of Galveston-Houston	1949	2007
Timothy M. Dolan	Archbishop of New York	1950	2012
James M. Harvey	Archpriest of St. Paul Outside-the-Walls	1949	2012
William Henry Keeler[3]	Archbishop emeritus of Baltimore	1931	1994
Gérald Cyprien Lacroix	Archbishop of Québec, Canada	1957	2014
Bernard F. Law[3]	Archbishop emeritus of Boston	1931	1985
William Levada	Archbishop emeritus of San Francisco	1936	2006
Javier Lozano Barragán[3]	Archbishop emeritus of Zacatecas, Mexico	1933	2003
Roger Mahony	Archbishop emeritus of Los Angeles	1936	1991
Adam Joseph Maida[3]	Archbishop emeritus of Detroit	1930	1994
Theodore McCarrick[3]	Archbishop emeritus of Washington, DC	1930	2001
Edwin F. O'Brien	Grand Master of the Knights of the Holy Sepulcher	1939	2012
Sean O'Malley[4]	Archbishop of Boston	1944	2006
Marc Ouellet	Prefect, Congregation for Bishops; archbishop emeritus of Québec, Canada	1944	2003
Justin F. Rigali[3]	Archbishop emeritus of Philadelphia	1935	2003
Norberto Rivera Carrera[2]	Archbishop of Mexico City, Mexico	1942	1998
José Francisco Robles Ortega	Archbishop of Guadalajara, Mexico	1949	2007
Juan Sandoval Íñiguez[3]	Archbishop emeritus of Guadalajara, Mexico	1933	1994
James F. Stafford[3]	Archbishop emeritus of Denver	1932	1998
Alberto Suárez Inda	Archbishop of Morelia, Mexico	1939	2015
Donald W. Wuerl	Archbishop of Washington, DC	1940	2010

(1) Member, Commission of Cardinals Overseeing the Institute for Works of Religion (Vatican Bank). (2) Member, Council for the Economy. (3) Ineligible to vote in a papal conclave because of age. (4) Member, Council of Cardinals and Pontifical Commission for the Protection of Minors.

The Ten Commandments

In the Hebrew Bible (Old Testament) the Ten Commandments (also called the Decalogue, from the Greek meaning "ten words") were revealed by God to Moses on Mt. Sinai. They form the covenant between God and the Israelites and the moral code that is the basis for the Jewish and Christian religions. The Ten Commandments appear in two places in the Old Testament—Exodus 20:1-17 and Deuteronomy 5:6-21.

Most Protestant, Anglican, and Orthodox Christians follow Jewish tradition, as shown here, which considers the introduction ("I am the Lord ...") the first commandment and makes the prohibition against idolatry the second. Roman Catholic and Lutheran traditions combine I and II and split the last commandment into two that separately prohibit coveting of a neighbor's wife and of a neighbor's goods. This arrangement alters the numbering of the other commandments by one.

Following is the text as it appears in Exodus 20:1-17, in the King James version of the Bible [Roman numerals added]:

And God spake all these words, saying,

I. I *am* the LORD thy God, which have brought thee out of the land of Egypt, out of the house of bondage. Thou shalt have no other gods before me.

II. Thou shalt not make unto thee any graven image, or any likeness of *any thing* that *is* in heaven above, or that *is* in the earth beneath, or that *is* in the water under the earth. Thou shalt not bow down thyself to them, nor serve them: for I the LORD thy God *am* a jealous God, visiting the iniquity of the fathers upon the children unto the third and fourth *generation* of them that hate me; and shewing mercy unto thousands of them that love me, and keep my commandments.

III. Thou shalt not take the name of the LORD thy God in vain: for the LORD will not hold him guiltless that taketh his name in vain.

IV. Remember the sabbath day, to keep it holy. Six days shalt thou labour, and do all thy work: but the seventh day *is* the sabbath of the LORD thy God: *in it* thou shalt not do any work, thou, nor thy son, nor thy daughter, thy manservant, nor thy maidservant, nor thy cattle, nor thy stranger that *is* within thy gates: for *in* six days the LORD made heaven and earth, the sea, and all that in them *is*, and rested the seventh day: wherefore the LORD blessed the sabbath day, and hallowed it.

V. Honour thy father and thy mother: that thy days may be long upon the land which the LORD thy God giveth thee.

VI. Thou shalt not kill.

VII. Thou shalt not commit adultery.

VIII. Thou shalt not steal.

IX. Thou shalt not bear false witness against thy neighbour.

X. Thou shalt not covet thy neighbour's house, thou shalt not covet thy neighbour's wife, nor his manservant, nor his maidservant, nor his ox, nor his ass, nor any thing that *is* thy neighbour's.

Books of the Bible

Old Testament—Standard Protestant List				New Testament List		
Genesis	I Kings	Ecclesiastes	Obadiah	Matthew	Ephesians	Hebrews
Exodus	II Kings	Song of Solomon	Jonah	Mark	Philippians	James
Leviticus	I Chronicles	Isaiah	Micah	Luke	Colossians	I Peter
Numbers	II Chronicles	Jeremiah	Nahum	John	I Thessalonians	II Peter
Deuteronomy	Ezra	Lamentations	Habakkuk	Acts	II Thessalonians	I John
Joshua	Nehemiah	Ezekiel	Zephaniah	Romans	I Timothy	II John
Judges	Esther	Daniel	Haggai	I Corinthians	II Timothy	III John
Ruth	Job	Hosea	Zechariah	II Corinthians	Titus	Jude
I Samuel	Psalms	Joel	Malachi	Galatians	Philemon	Revelation
II Samuel	Proverbs	Amos				

The standard Protestant Old Testament consists of the same 39 books as in the Bible of Judaism, but the latter is organized differently. The Old Testament used by Roman Catholics has 7 additional deuterocanonical books, plus some additional parts of books. The 7 are **Tobit**, **Judith**, **Wisdom**, **Sirach (Ecclesiasticus)**, **Baruch**, **I Maccabees**, and **II Maccabees**. Both Catholic and Protestant versions of the New Testament have 27 books with the same names.

Figures in the Hebrew Bible (Old Testament)

Aaron: First of Hebrew high priests; brother of Moses and Miriam.
Abel: Second son of Adam and Eve; slain by Cain.
Abraham: Founder of monotheism; patriarch; also called Abram.
Adam: First human according to Genesis.
Amos: Herdsman; prophesized against social injustice and oppression of the poor.
Bathsheba: Seduced by King David; mother of King Solomon.
Cain: First son of Adam and Eve; killed his brother Abel.
Cyrus: Persian ruler; sent Jews home from exile.
Daniel: Cast into lion's den for violating decree of King Darius; saved.
David: Israel's greatest king; shepherd, warrior, musician, psalmist.
Deborah: Prophet and judge; ruled over Israel.
Elijah: Great prophet; was victorious over the priests of the Phoenician god Baal.
Elisha: Prophet; successor to Elijah.
Esther: Jewish wife of the king of Persia; saved Jews from annihilation.
Eve: First woman according to Genesis.
Ezekiel: Visionary; prophesized hope to exiled Jews in Babylon.
Ezra: Great Jewish leader; rededicated worship and Torah law after exile.
Goliath: Giant Philistine warrior; slain by David.
Hannah: Childless; promised child to God; mother to the prophet Samuel.
Hosea: Enacted prophecy; asked God's forgiveness for Israel's unfaithfulness.
Isaac: Son of Abraham and Sarah; saved from sacrificial altar.
Isaiah: Highly educated prophet; avoided war with Assyria; Israel destroyed; Jerusalem survived.
Jacob: Son of Isaac; father of the Twelve Tribes; renamed "Israel" by angel.
Jeremiah: Confronted leaders; urged surrender to Babylon.
Jezebel: Phoenician queen of King Ahab; had Israelite prophets killed.
Job: "Blameless" man; allowed by God to lose family, health, and possessions in a test of his faith.
Jonah: Swallowed by a great fish; prophesied destruction of Nineveh, averted when the people repented.
Jonathan: Son of King Saul; friend of David.
Joseph: Favorite of Jacob; interpreted Pharaoh's dreams; brought Hebrews to Egypt.
Joshua: Successor of Moses; led Hebrews into Canaan.
Josiah: Reformist king; repaired Solomon's Temple; restored worship; reintroduced Passover.
Leah: Matriarch; older sister of Rachel; Jacob's wife.
Micah: Prophet; predicted the end of war and beginning of peace.
Miriam: Prophet and great leader of the Hebrews; sister to Moses and Aaron.
Moses: Most important Hebrew prophet; leader of the Israelites; received the Torah.
Nathan: Prophet; confronted King David over his seduction of Bathsheba.
Nebuchadnezzar: Babylonian king; destroyed Jerusalem.
Nehemiah: Led Jews back to Jerusalem from Babylonian exile.
Noah: Man of great faith who, according to Genesis, saved his family and two of every living thing on Earth from a great flood.
Rachel: Matriarch; younger sister of Leah; Jacob's wife; Joseph's mother.
Rebecca: Matriarch; wife of Isaac; mother of Jacob.
Ruth: Moabite convert; ancestor of David.
Samson: Judge and military leader of Israel; possessed superhuman strength.
Samuel: Prophet; anointed Saul king of Israel and later anointed David to succeed him.
Sarah: First matriarch of Israel; wife of Abraham; mother of Isaac.
Saul: First king of Israel; father of Jonathan.
Solomon: King of Israel at its zenith; known for great wisdom.
Zechariah: Prophet; encouraged rebuilding of Solomon's Temple destroyed by Babylonians.

Figures in the New Testament

Andrew: One of the Twelve Apostles; brother of Peter and former fisherman; one of the earlier disciples.
Barabbas: Imprisoned with Jesus; set free by Pilate on Passover.
Barnabas: Disciple of Jesus; closely connected with Paul.
Bartholomew: A lesser-known member of the Twelve Apostles; cheerful and prayed often.
Cornelius: Roman convert; defended by Peter, allowing Gentiles to become Christians.
Elizabeth: Mother of John the Baptist; relation of the Virgin Mary.
Gabriel: Archangel; appeared to the Virgin Mary to announce that she was to give birth to the Messiah.
Herod: May refer to Herod the Great, who ordered the death of children after Jesus's birth, or to his son, Herod, who had John the Baptist beheaded.
James: May refer to either of two apostles: James, son of Zebedee, brother of John the Apostle, or the lesser-known James, son of Alphaeus.
Jesus: Central figure of the Gospels; believed to be the Messiah and son of God; crucified by the Romans.
John (Apostle): Beloved disciple of Jesus; one of the Twelve; possible author of fourth Gospel; brother of James.
John (Baptist): Known as John the Baptist; important prophet and forerunner to Jesus; relation of the Virgin Mary.
Joseph: Husband of the Virgin Mary; descendant of King David.
Judas Iscariot: Betrayer of Jesus; prominent member of the Apostles; committed suicide.
Judas Thaddeus: One of the Twelve; also called Jude to distinguish him from Judas Iscariot.
Lazarus: Brother of the disciples Martha and Mary of Bethany; raised from the dead by Jesus at their request; possibly the same Lazarus who appears in Jesus's parable of the rich man.
Luke: Traditional author of the Gospel of Luke; possibly a follower of Paul.
Mark: Traditional author of the Gospel of Mark; possibly a disciple of Peter.
Mary, the mother of Jesus: Traditionally believed to be a virgin who conceived without sin; wife of Joseph.
Mary Magdalene: Important female disciple of Jesus; witness to his death and resurrection.
Matthew: One of the Twelve; possible author of the Gospel of Matthew; former tax collector.
Matthias: Often included on lists of the Twelve Apostles as the apostle who replaced Judas Iscariot after his betrayal.
Paul (Saul): Writer of nearly a quarter of the New Testament; a former persecutor of Christians, converted after a vision; played a significant role in spreading Christianity.
Peter: Considered the foremost of the Twelve Apostles; traditionally the first pope and "rock" of the Christian church; author of epistles; also called Simon and Simon Peter.
Philip: One of the Twelve; considered pragmatic and sensible.
Pilate, Pontius: A Roman prefect; played large role in the trial and crucifixion of Jesus.
Simon: One of the Twelve; known as "the Zealot" to distinguish from Simon Peter.
Stephen: Fervently preached that Jesus was the Messiah; stoned to death by angry mob, including Saul; important figure in Saul's conversion.
Thomas: One of the Twelve; known as "Doubting Thomas" because he did not believe Jesus was risen until he could touch him.
Timothy: A disciple closely connected with Paul; recipient of epistles.
Zacharias: Father of John the Baptist; husband of Elizabeth; struck dumb when he doubted his barren wife could become pregnant.

Major Christian Denominations:

Brackets indicate some features that tend to

Denomination	Origins	Organization	Authority	Special rites
Baptists	In radical Reformation, objections to infant baptism, demands for church and state separation; John Smyth, English Separatist, in 1609; Roger Williams, 1638, Providence, RI.	Congregational; each local church is autonomous.	Scripture; some Baptists, particularly in the South, interpret the Bible literally.	[Baptism, usually early teen years and after, by total immersion]; Lord's Supper.
Church of Christ (Disciples)	Among evangelical Presbyterians in KY (1804) and PA (1809), in distress over Protestant factionalism and decline of fervor; organized in 1832.	Congregational.	["Where the Scriptures speak, we speak; where the Scriptures are silent, we are silent."]	Adult baptism; Lord's Supper (weekly).
Episcopalians	Henry VIII separated English Catholic Church from Rome, 1534, for political reasons; Protestant Episcopal Church in U.S. founded in 1789.	[Diocesan bishops, in apostolic succession, are elected by parish representatives; the national Church is headed by General Convention and Presiding Bishop; part of the Anglican Communion.]	Scripture as interpreted by tradition, especially 39 Articles (1563); tri-annual convention of bishops, priests, and lay people.	Infant baptism, Eucharist, and other sacraments; sacrament taken to be symbolic, but as having real spiritual effect.
Jehovah's Witnesses	Founded in 1870 in PA by Charles Taze Russell; incorporated as Watch Tower Bible and Tract Society of PA, 1884; name Jehovah's Witnesses adopted in 1931.	A governing body located in NY coordinates worldwide activities; each congregation cared for by a body of elders; each Witness considered a minister.	The Bible.	Baptism by immersion; annual Lord's Meal ceremony.
Latter-day Saints (Mormons)	In a vision of the Father and the Son reported by Joseph Smith (1820s) in NY; Smith also reported receiving new scripture on golden tablets: the Book of Mormon.	Theocratic; 1st Presidency (church president, two counselors), 12 Apostles preside over international church; local congregations headed by lay priesthood leaders.	Revelation to living prophet (church president). The Bible, Book of Mormon, and other revelations to Smith and his successors.	Baptism at age 8; laying on of hands (which confers the gift of the Holy Ghost); Lord's Supper; temple rites: baptism for the dead, marriage for eternity, others.
Lutherans	Begun by Martin Luther in Wittenberg, Germany, in 1517; objection to Catholic doctrine of salvation and sale of indulgences; break complete, 1519.	Varies from congregational to episcopal; in U.S., a combination of regional synods and congregational polities is most common.	Scripture alone; the *Book of Concord* (1580), which includes the three Ecumenical Creeds, is subscribed to as a correct exposition of Scripture.	Infant baptism; Lord's Supper; Christ's true body and blood present "in, with, and under the bread and wine."
Methodists	Rev. John Wesley began movement in 1738, within Church of England; first U.S. denomination in Baltimore (1784).	Conference and superintendent system; [in United Methodist Church, general superintendents are bishops—not a priestly order, only an office—who are elected for life].	Scripture as interpreted by tradition, reason, and experience.	Baptism of infants or adults; Lord's Supper commanded; other rites: marriage, ordination, solemnization of personal commitments.
Orthodox	Developed in original Christian proselytizing; broke with Rome in 1054 after centuries of doctrinal disputes and diverging traditions.	Synods of bishops in autonomous, usually national, churches elect a patriarch, archbishop, or metropolitan; these men, as a group, are the heads of the church.	Scripture, tradition, and the first seven church councils up to Nicaea II in 787; bishops in council have authority in doctrine and policy.	Seven sacraments: infant baptism and anointing, Eucharist, ordination, penance, marriage, and anointing of the sick.
Pentecostal	In Topeka, KS (1901) and Los Angeles (1906), in reaction to perceived loss of evangelical fervor among Methodists and others.	Originally a movement, not a formal organization, Pentecostalism now has a variety of organized forms and continues also as a movement.	Scripture; individual charismatic leaders, the teachings of the Holy Spirit.	[Spirit baptism, especially as shown in "speaking in tongues"; healing and sometimes exorcism]; adult baptism; Lord's Supper.
Presbyterians	In 16th-cent. Calvinist reformation; differed with Lutherans over sacraments, church government; John Knox founded Scotch Presbyterian church about 1560.	[Highly structured representational system of ministers and lay persons (presbyters) in local, regional, and national bodies (synods).]	Scripture.	Infant baptism; Lord's Supper; bread and wine symbolize Christ's spiritual presence.
Roman Catholics	Traditionally, founded by Jesus who named St. Peter the first vicar; developed in early Christian proselytizing, especially after the conversion of imperial Rome in the 4th cent.	[Hierarchy with supreme power vested in pope elected by cardinals]; councils of bishops advise on matters of doctrine and policy.	[The pope, when speaking for the whole church in matters of faith and morals, and tradition (which is expressed in church councils and in part contained in Scripture).]	Mass; seven sacraments: baptism, reconciliation, Eucharist, confirmation, marriage, ordination, and anointing of the sick (unction).
United Church of Christ	[By ecumenical union, in 1957, of Congregationalists and Evangelical and Reformed, representing both Calvinist and Lutheran traditions.]	Congregational; a General Synod, representative of all congregations, sets general policy.	Scripture.	Infant baptism; Lord's Supper.

How Do They Differ?

distinguish a denomination sharply from others.

Practice	Ethics	Doctrine	Other	Denomination
Worship style varies from staid to evangelistic; extensive missionary activity.	Usually opposed to alcohol and tobacco; some tendency toward a perfectionist ethical standard.	[No creed; true church is of believers only, who are all equal.]	Believing no authority can stand between the believer and God, the Baptists are strong supporters of church and state separation.	**Baptists**
Tries to avoid any rite not considered part of the 1st-cent. church; some congregations may reject instrumental music.	Some tendency toward perfectionism; increasing interest in social action programs.	Simple New Testament faith; avoids any elaboration not firmly based on Scripture.	Highly tolerant in doctrinal and religious matters; strongly supportive of scholarly education.	**Church of Christ (Disciples)**
Formal, based on *Book of Common Prayer*, updated 1979; services range from austerely simple to highly liturgical.	Tolerant, sometimes permissive; some social action programs.	Scripture; the "historic creeds," which include the Apostles, Nicene, and Athanasian, and the *Book of Common Prayer*; ranges from Anglo-Catholic to low church, with Calvinist influences.	Strongly ecumenical, holding talks with many branches of Christendom.	**Episcopalians**
Meetings are held in Kingdom Halls and members' homes for study and worship; [extensive door-to-door visitations].	High moral code; stress on marital fidelity and family values; avoidance of tobacco and blood transfusions.	[God, by his first creation, Christ, will soon destroy all wickedness; 144,000 faithful ones will rule in heaven with Christ over others on a paradise earth.]	Total allegiance proclaimed only to God's kingdom or heavenly government by Christ; main periodical, *The Watchtower*, is printed in over 200 languages.	**Jehovah's Witnesses**
Simple service with prayers, hymns, sermon; private temple ceremonies may be more elaborate.	Temperance; strict moral code; [tithing]; a strong work ethic with communal self-reliance; [strong missionary activity]; family emphasis.	Jesus Christ is the Son of God, the Eternal Father. Jesus's atonement saves all humans; those who are obedient to God's laws may become joint-heirs with Christ in God's kingdom.	Mormons believe theirs is the true church of Jesus Christ, restored by God through Joseph Smith. Official name: The Church of Jesus Christ of Latter-day Saints.	**Latter-day Saints (Mormons)**
Relatively simple, formal liturgy with emphasis on the sermon.	Generally conservative in personal and social ethics; doctrine of "two kingdoms" (worldly and holy) supports conservatism in secular affairs.	Salvation by grace alone through faith; Lutheranism has made major contributions to Protestant theology.	Though still somewhat divided along ethnic lines (German, Swedish, etc.), main divisions are between fundamentalists and liberals.	**Lutherans**
Worship style varies widely by denomination, local church, geography.	Originally pietist and perfectionist; always strong social activist elements.	No distinctive theological development; 25 articles abridged from Church of England's 39, not binding.	In 1968, The United Methodist Church was formed by the union of The Methodist Church and The Evangelical United Brethren Church.	**Methodists**
Elaborate liturgy, usually in the vernacular, though extremely traditional; the liturgy is the essence of Orthodoxy; veneration of icons.	Tolerant; little stress on social action; divorce, remarriage permitted in some cases; bishops are celibate; priests need not be.	Emphasis on Christ's resurrection, rather than crucifixion; the Holy Spirit proceeds from God the Father only.	Orthodox Church in America originally under Patriarch of Moscow, was granted autonomy in 1970; Greek Orthodox do not recognize this autonomy.	**Orthodox**
Loosely structured service with rousing hymns and sermons, culminating in spirit baptism.	Usually, emphasis on perfectionism, with varying degrees of tolerance.	Simple traditional beliefs, usually Protestant, with emphasis on the immediate presence of God in the Holy Spirit.	Once confined to lower-class "holy rollers," Pentecostalism now appears in mainline churches and has established middle-class congregations.	**Pentecostal**
A simple, sober service in which the sermon is central.	Traditionally, a tendency toward strictness, with firm church- and self-discipline; otherwise tolerant.	Emphasizes the sovereignty and justice of God; no longer dogmatic.	Although traces of belief in predestination (that God has foreordained salvation for the "elect") remain, this idea is no longer a central element in Presbyterianism.	**Presbyterians**
Relatively elaborate ritual centered on the Mass; also rosary recitation, novenas, etc.	Traditionally strict but increasingly tolerant in practice; divorce and remarriage not accepted, but annulments sometimes granted; celibate clergy, except in Eastern rite.	Highly elaborated; salvation by merit gained through grace; dogmatic; special veneration of Mary, the mother of Jesus.	Relatively rapid change followed Vatican Council II; Mass now in vernacular instead of Latin; more stress on social action, tolerance, ecumenism.	**Roman Catholics**
Usually simple service with emphasis on the sermon.	Tolerant; some social action emphasis.	Standard Protestant; Statement of Faith (1959) is not binding.	Two main churches in the 1957 union represented earlier unions with small groups of almost every Protestant denomination.	**United Church of Christ**

Major Non-Christian Religions

Source: Baha'i reviewed by the Baha'i Community Relations Center; Islam reviewed by Natana Delong-Bas, Lecturer in Islamic Studies, Boston Coll.; Hinduism and Judaism reviewed by Anthony Padovano, PhD, STD, Prof. of Literature & Relig. Studies, Ramapo College, NJ, Adj. Prof. of Theol., Fordham Univ.; Sikhism reviewed by The Sikh Coalition of New York, NY.

Islam

Founded: Muhammad received his first revelation in 610 CE.

Founder: Muhammad (c. 570-632 CE), the Prophet.

Sacred texts: Two texts constitute the Muslim sacred canon, the *Quran* (Koran) and the *Hadith*. The Quran provides the foundation for Islamic religion and culture. It is regarded as the final, perfect, and complete word of God as revealed to Muhammad over the course of his life. Received by Muhammad in the Arabic language, it is memorized in Arabic by adherents regardless of their native language. It is divided into 114 chapters of unequal length, the shortest containing only 3 verses, and the longest containing 286 verses. The Quran is the ultimate source of everything Islamic, from metaphysics to theology to sacred history, to ethics and law, to art. The Hadith, which describes Muhammad's actions, attitudes, and teachings, complements the Quran. Due to its long history of oral transmission, the Hadith's lessons are seen as somewhat vulnerable to human error. It is not said to contain God's unadulterated voice as is the Quran but functions as a powerful spiritual and behavioral code nonetheless.

Organization: Muhammad was both the last prophet and a statesman. Muslim leaders have often assumed both civil and moral functions within Islamic states. Within the larger community, there are cultural and national groups, held together by a common religious law, the *Sharia*. Muslims believe that God is the ultimate lawgiver and that human beings cannot devise laws that oppose divine laws. Still, the Sharia is approached differently in different parts of the Islamic world. Over the centuries, Sunnis have developed four major schools of law: the Hanafi, the Shafi'i, the Hanbali, and the Maliki. The Ja'fari is the most important and well-known Shiite school. Before the 20th century, religious scholars known as the *ulama* held much legal power. Judges (*qadis*) and law-interpreters (*muftis*) are people learned in religious law who lead congregational prayers in mosques and perform other religious duties.

Practice: Five duties (of both men and women), known as the Pillars of Islam, are regarded as cardinal in Islam and as central to the life of the Islamic community. In accordance with Islam's absolute commitment to monotheism, the first duty is the profession of faith (the *Shahadah*): "There is no God but Allah and Muhammad is His Prophet." A Muslim must profess this belief publicly at least once in his or her lifetime; it defines the membership of an individual in the Islamic community. The second duty is that of five daily prayers organized in intervals throughout the day: sunrise, early afternoon, late afternoon, immediately after sunset, and before midnight. During prayer, Muslims face the Kaaba, a small, cube-shaped structure in the courtyard of al-Haram (the "inviolate place"), at the Grand Mosque of Mecca. All five prayers in Islam are congregational and are to be offered in a mosque, but they may be offered individually if one cannot be present with a congregation. Congregational prayer is required only at the early afternoon prayer on Friday for men. The third cardinal duty of a Muslim is to pay alms, or *zakat*, which should be 2.5% of one's total wealth. This was originally the tax levied by Muhammad on the wealthy members of the community, primarily to help the poor. Only when zakat has been paid is the rest of a Muslim's property considered purified and legitimate. The fourth duty is the fast of the lunar month of Ramadan. During the fasting month, one must abstain from eating, drinking, smoking, impure thoughts, and sexual intercourse from dawn until sunset, and feed at least one poor person, if able. The fifth duty is the pilgrimage to the Kaaba, known as the hajj, which a Muslim must undertake, with exceptions for poverty and ill health, at least once during his or her lifetime.

Divisions: There are two major groups: the majority Sunni (84% of the worldwide Muslim population) and the minority Shiites (14%). Sects first appeared in Islam at the time of Muhammad's death. The group that came to be known as Sunni accepted Abu Bakr, an early convert, as his successor (caliph), while a smaller number, which became the Shia, believed that Ali ibn Abi Talib, the son-in-law and first cousin of the prophet, should have become his successor (Imam). Imams are believed to interpret the Quran infallibly. **Shiites** fall into three major branches: Fivers, Seveners, and Twelvers, reflecting the number of Imams they recognize. Twelvers believe that the 12th Imam has lived an invisible existence since 874, and will return as the Mahdi (a messiah figure) who will usher in a 1,000-year reign of peace and justice. **Sufism** (mystical dimension of Islam) emphasizes personal relation to God and obedience informed by love of God; it is prevalent among both Sunni and Shiites.

Location: W Africa to Philippines, across a band including E Africa, Central Asia and western China, India, Malaysia, Indonesia. Islam has several million adherents in North America and about 30 mil in Europe.

Beliefs: Strictly monotheistic. God is creator of the universe, omnipotent, omniscient, just, forgiving, and merciful. God revealed the Koran to Muhammad to guide humanity to truth and justice. Those who sincerely "submit" (literal meaning of "Islam") to God attain salvation.

World's Largest Muslim Populations

Source: "Global Religious Landscape," Pew Research Center's Forum on Religion & Public Life, Dec. 2012; based on 2010 ests.

Rank	Country	Muslim population	% of country's pop.
1.	Indonesia	209,120,000	87.2%
2.	India	176,190,000	14.4
3.	Pakistan	167,410,000	96.4
4.	Bangladesh	133,540,000	89.8
5.	Nigeria	77,300,000	48.8
6.	Egypt	76,990,000	94.9
7.	Iran	73,570,000	99.0+
8.	Turkey	71,330,000	98.0
9.	Algeria	34,730,000	97.9
10.	Morocco	31,940,000	99.0+
11.	Iraq	31,340,000	99.0
12.	Afghanistan	31,330,000	99.0+
13.	Sudan[1]	30,490,000	90.7
14.	Ethiopia	28,680,000	34.6
15.	Uzbekistan	26,550,000	96.7
16.	Saudi Arabia	25,520,000	93.0
17.	China	24,690,000	1.8
18.	Yemen	23,830,000	99.0+
19.	Syria	18,930,000	92.8
20.	Malaysia	18,100,000	63.7

(1) Excluding what is now South Sudan.

Baha'i

Founded: Mid-19th century.

Founder: Mirza Husayn-Ali Nuri (1817-92), later known as Baha'u'llah (Arabic for "Glory of God").

Sacred texts: The writings of Baha'u'llah and of his herald the Bab (Siyyid Ali-Muhammad, 1819-50). The primary text is *Kitab-i-Aqdas* (Most Holy Book).

Organization: The Baha'i administrative system consists of elected nine-member councils at the local, national, and international levels. There are also more than 180 National Spiritual Assemblies and an elected, international governing body known as the Universal House of Justice.

Practice: Prayer, meditation, and fasting are key components of the Baha'i Faith. Work performed in a spirit of service to humanity is considered an important form of worship. The Baha'i Faith has no clergy and minimal ritual and congregational worship.

Divisions: In a religion in which unity is perhaps the central spiritual value, the Baha'i Faith has avoided separating into sects with differentiated theologies and practices.

Location: Worldwide.

Beliefs: God has progressively revealed His will and purpose through a series of Divine manifestations including Jesus, Buddha, Muhammad, Zoroaster, and Baha'u'llah. Baha'u'llah's teachings include the oneness of humanity, the equality of men and women, the harmony of science and religion, and the need to abandon all forms of prejudice and eliminate extremes of poverty and wealth.

Buddhism

Founded: About 525 BCE, reportedly near Benares, India.

Founder: Gautama Siddhartha (c. 563-483 BCE), the Buddha, who achieved enlightenment through intense meditation.

Sacred texts: The *Tripitaka*, a collection of the Buddha's teachings, rules of monastic life, and philosophical commentaries on the teachings; also a vast body of Buddhist teachings and commentaries, many of which are called *sutras*.

Organization: The basic institution is the *sangha*, or monastic order, through which traditions are passed down. Monastic life tends to be democratic and antiauthoritarian.

Practice: Varies widely according to the sect and ranges from austere meditation to magical chanting and elaborate temple rites. Many practices, such as exorcism of devils, reflect pre-Buddhist beliefs.

Divisions: A variety of sects grouped into three primary branches: Theravada, which emphasizes the importance of pure thought and deed; Mahayana (includes Zen and Sokagakkai), which ranges from philosophical schools to belief in the saving grace of higher beings or ritual practices and to practical meditative disciplines; and Vajrayana, or Tantrism, a combination of belief in ritual magic and sophisticated philosophy.

Location: Mainly in Asia, from Sri Lanka to Japan.

Beliefs: Life is suffering, and there is no ultimate reality behind it. The cycle of birth and rebirth continues because of desire and attachment to the unreal "self." Meditation and deeds will end the cycle and achieve Nirvana (nothingness, enlightenment).

Hinduism

Founded: About 1500 BCE by Aryans who migrated to India, where their Vedic religion intermixed with the practices and beliefs of the native peoples.

Sacred texts: The *Veda*, including the *Upanishads*, a collection of rituals and commentaries; a vast number of epic stories about gods, heroes, and saints, including the *Bhagavadgita*, a part of the *Mahabharata*, and the *Ramayana*.

Organization: None, strictly speaking. Generally, rituals should be performed or assisted by Brahmins, the priestly caste, but in practice, simpler rituals can be performed by anyone. Brahmins are the final judges of ritual purity, the vital element in Hindu life. Temples and religious organizations are usually presided over by Brahmins.

Practice: Primarily passage rites (e.g., initiation, marriage, death) and daily devotions. Of the public rites, the *puja*, a ceremonial dinner for a god, is the most common.

Divisions: There is no concept of orthodoxy in Hinduism, which presents a variety of sects. The three major living traditions are those devoted to the gods Vishnu and Shiva and to the goddess Shakti. Numerous folk beliefs and practices, often in amalgamation with the above groups, exist side by side with philosophical schools.

Location: Mainly India, Nepal, Malaysia, Guyana, Suriname, and Sri Lanka.

Beliefs: There is only one divine principle; the many gods are only aspects of that unity. Life in all its forms is an aspect of the divine, but it appears as a separation from the divine, a meaningless cycle of birth and rebirth (*samsara*) determined by the purity or impurity of past deeds (*karma*). To improve one's karma or escape samsara by pure acts, thought, and/or devotion is the aim of every Hindu.

Judaism

Founded: About 2000 BCE.

Founder: Abraham is regarded as the founding patriarch.

Sacred texts: The five books of Moses (the Torah), the basic source of teachings.

Organization: Originally theocratic, Judaism has evolved into a congregational polity. The basic institution is the local synagogue or temple, operated by the congregation and led by a rabbi of their choice. Chief rabbis in France and Great Britain have authority only over those who accept it; in Israel, the two chief rabbis have civil authority in family law.

Practice: Among traditional practitioners, almost all areas of life are governed by strict discipline. Sabbath and holidays are marked by observances, and attendance at public worship is considered especially important. Chief annual observances are Passover, celebrating liberation of the Israelites from Egypt and marked by the Seder meal in homes, and the 10 days from Rosh Hashanah (New Year) to Yom Kippur (Day of Atonement), a period of penitence.

Divisions: Judaism is an unbroken spectrum from ultraconservative to ultraliberal, largely reflecting different points of view regarding the binding character of the prohibitions and duties—particularly the dietary and Sabbath observations—traditionally prescribed for the daily life of the Jew.

Location: Mainly in Israel and the U.S.

Beliefs: Strictly monotheistic. God is the creator and ruler of the universe. God established a particular relationship with the Hebrew people: by obeying a divine law God gave them, they would be a special witness to God's mercy and justice. Judaism stresses ethical behavior (and, among the traditional, careful ritual obedience) as true worship of God.

Sikhism

Founded: Late 15th century in South Asia.

Founder: Guru Nanak Dev ji, Sikhism's first Guru.

Sacred texts: The *Guru Granth Sahib* was compiled by the Sikh Gurus and contains their experiences of the Divine. It also contains writings by other saintly figures of different faiths.

Organization: Each Sikh must make her or his own spiritual journey and not depend on clergy. Congregational prayer led by both men and women takes place in local *Gurdwaras*. Harmandir Sahib in Amritsar, Punjab (northern India), is the central place of worship.

Practice: Prayers are required in the morning, evening, and before sleeping. The most important mode of congregational prayer is the singing of hymns from the Guru Granth Sahib. The "Five Ks" are five articles of faith required of all Sikhs: *Kes* (uncut hair), *Kangha* (comb), *Kara* (steel bracelet), *Kirpan* (sword), and *Kaccha* (short pants).

Divisions: The last living Guru, Guru Gobind Singh (1666-1708) crystallized the practices and beliefs of the faith and determined that no future living Guru was needed. Today the religion is guided by joint sovereignty of Guru Granth and Guru Panth. Guru Granth is the Sikh scripture, as the spiritual manifestation of the Guru, while the Guru Panth is the collectivity of all initiated Sikhs worldwide, as the physical manifestation of the Guru.

Location: Many Sikhs have Punjabi backgrounds. The Punjab region was divided between India and Pakistan with the end of British rule.

Beliefs: Sikhism preaches a message of devotion, remembrance of God at all times, truthful living, equality between all human beings, and social justice, while denouncing what is considered superstition and blind ritualism. Sikhism is a monotheistic religion based on revelation.

LANGUAGE

New Words in English

The following words and definitions were provided by Merriam-Webster Inc., publishers of *Merriam-Webster's Collegiate Dictionary, Eleventh Edition*, released in 2003. The words are among those that the Merriam-Webster editors decided had achieved enough currency in English to be added to the latest printing of this edition.

aji: a chili pepper that ranges in pungency from mild to very hot
alpha test: a test of a nearly complete prototype of a product especially by employees of the company developing the product
aquaponics: a system of growing plants in the water that has been used to cultivate aquatic organisms
auto-tune: to adjust or alter a recording of a voice with audio-editing software to correct sung notes that are out of tune
big data: an accumulation of data that is too large or complex for processing by traditional database management tools
caprese: a salad consisting of slices of mozzarella and tomatoes, basil, and olive oil or Italian dressing
catfish: a person who sets up a false personal profile on a social networking site for fraudulent or deceptive purposes
colonography: noninvasive visualization of the interior of the colon by means of a computed tomography or magnetic resonance imaging
commentariat: a group of powerful and influential commentators
crop top: a short upper body garment for women that does not cover the midriff
digital divide: the economic, educational, and social inequalities between those who have computers and online access and those who do not
double down: to become more tenacious, zealous, or resolute in a position or undertaking
e-waste: waste consisting of discarded electronic products (as computers, televisions, and cell phones)
freegan: an activist who scavenges for free food in waste receptacles as a means of reducing consumption of resources
gamification: the process of adding games or gamelike elements to something (as a task) so as to encourage participation
heteronormative: of, relating to, or based on the attitude that heterosexuality is the only normal and natural expression of sexuality
macchiato: espresso topped with a thin layer of foamed milk
muffin top: the fatty flesh that hangs over tightly worn pants
pho: a soup made of beef or chicken broth and rice noodles
planogram: a schematic drawing or plan for displaying merchandise in a store so as to maximize sales
poutine: a dish of French fries covered with brown gravy and cheese curds
pushback: resistance or opposition to a policy or regulation especially by those affected
schmutz: dirt, grime
skate park: an outdoor area having structures and surfaces for roller-skating and skateboarding
ski cross: a skiing race in which competitors race directly against each other down a sloped course that features jumps and banked curves
social networking: the creation and maintenance of personal and business relationships especially online
stalkerazzo: a freelance photographer or videographer who aggressively stalks celebrities for candid photographs or videos
Yooper: a native or inhabitant of the Upper Peninsula of Michigan—used as a nickname
yuzu: a green or yellow citrus fruit whose acidic rind and juice are often used in Japanese cuisine
zip tie: a plastic strip that can be threaded through its end and tightened so as to fasten something

Words About Words

alliteration: repetition of same, initial consonant sounds of two or more words in sequence or in short intervals. Ex.: "I have **s**tood **s**till and **s**topped the **s**ound of feet." —Robert Frost, "Acquainted With the Night"
anagram: word or word sequence that is a rearrangement, typically clever, of letters in another word or word sequence. Ex.: The Leaning Tower of Pisa = I spot one giant flaw here.
assonance: repetition of same or similar vowel sounds in words located near each other. Ex.: "Gr**ee**n as a dr**ea**m, and d**ee**p as death." —Rupert Brooke, "The Old Vicarage, Grantchester"
back-formation: creation of a word from an existing word, whose forms seem to suggest that the previously existing word derived from the newer word. Ex.: The verb "edit" is a back-formation of the word "editor."
cliché: a saying or expression that has been used so often it has lost its effect. Ex.: work like a dog
euphemism: a mild, indirect expression used instead of a plainer one that might be harsh, unpleasant, or offensive. Ex.: restroom instead of toilet; pass away, or pass, instead of die
hyperbole: exaggeration for emphasis or effect. Ex.: "And fired the shot heard round the world." —Ralph Waldo Emerson, "Concord Hymn"
irony: deliberate use of an expression in which the literal or surface meaning is contrary to a hidden intended, often opposite meaning that can be inferred. Ex.: "Yet Brutus says he was ambitious; / And Brutus is an honorable man." —William Shakespeare, *Julius Caesar*
litotes: intentional understatement made by negating the opposite of what is meant. Ex.: This was no small matter.
metaphor: a stated equivalence between two dissimilar things or a reference to one thing rather than another, so as to imply a comparison. Ex.: "Life is a tale told by an idiot, full of sound and fury, signifying nothing." —William Shakespeare, *Macbeth*
metonymy: substitution of one word for another that it suggests. Ex.: The pen is mightier than the sword.
onomatopoeia: words that imitate the sounds they describe. Ex.: buzz, murmur
oxymoron: expression containing seemingly contradictory words. Ex.: deafening silence
palindrome: word or phrase that reads the same backward and forward. Ex: radar, Hannah, "Madam, I'm Adam"
paradox: a statement that is phrased to seem contradictory, odd, or opposed to common sense or expectation, while being presented as true. Ex.: "What a pity that youth must be wasted on the young." —George Bernard Shaw
personification: treatment of objects or abstractions as if they were persons. Ex.: "Because I could not stop for Death— / He kindly stopped for me." —Emily Dickinson, "Because I Could Not Stop for Death"
simile: a comparison between two dissimilar things using the words "like" or "as." Ex.: "My love is like a red, red rose" —Robert Burns, "A Red, Red Rose"
spoonerism: play on words in which the initial sounds of two or more words are transposed, creating different phrases whose meanings when compared can be humorous. Ex.: blushing crow instead of crushing blow
synecdoche: a form of metonymy; the use of a part for the whole, or the whole for the part. Ex.: All hands on deck!
tautology: useless, often unwitting repetition of the same idea in different wording. Ex.: close proximity. In logic, a proposition that would be self-contradictory to deny. Ex.: All bachelors are male.

National Spelling Bee

The annual Scripps National Spelling Bee, conducted by The E.W. Scripps Company and other newspapers since 1941, was instituted by *The Courier-Journal* of Louisville, KY, in 1925. Students under 16 who are not beyond 8th grade are eligible to compete locally for a chance to advance to the national competition in Washington, DC. In 2015, for the second year in a row, there was a tie for first place. Co-winners were Vanya Shivashankar of Olathe, KS, and Gokul Venkatachalam of Chesterfield, MO. They both correctly spelled the last words available in the final round. Cole Shafer-Ray of Norman, OK, placed third.

Here are the last words given and spelled correctly at the National Spelling Bee in recent years.

1983	Purim	1990	fibranne	1997	euonym	2004	autochthonous	2011	cymotrichous
1984	luge	1991	antipyretic	1998	chiaroscurist	2005	appoggiatura	2012	guetapens
1985	milieu	1992	lyceum	1999	logorrhea	2006	Ursprache	2013	knaidel
1986	odontalgia	1993	kamikaze	2000	demarche	2007	serrefine	2014	feuilleton
1987	staphylococci	1994	antediluvian	2001	succedaneum	2008	guerdon		stichomythia
1988	elegiacal	1995	xanthosis	2002	prospicience	2009	Laodicean	2015	scherenschnitte
1989	spoliator	1996	vivisepulture	2003	pococurante	2010	stromuhr		nunatak

Commonly Misspelled English Words

a lot
accidentally
accommodate
accumulate
achieve
acknowledgment
acquainted
acquire
all right
already
amateur
appearance
appropriate
assassinate
assimilate
believe
broccoli
bureau
business
calendar
Caribbean
cemetery
changeable
Cincinnati
collectible
commission
commitment
committee
connoisseur
conscience
conscious
convenience
deceive
defendant
definitely
desirable
desperate
deterrent
doesn't
eighth
eligible
embarrass
environment
existence
fascinating
February
fluorescent
forty
gauge
government
grammar
harass
humorous
incidentally
independent
indispensable
innocuous
inoculate
irresistible
jewelry
judgment
laboratory
leisure
liaison
license
lieutenant
lightning
liquefy
maintenance
management
marriage
Massachusetts
medieval
millennium
miniature
miscellaneous
Mississippi
misspelled
mnemonic
mysterious
necessary
noticeable
occasionally
occurrence
omitted
opportunity
parallel
patience
performance
permanent
permissible
perseverance
personnel
pharaoh
possession
potatoes
precede
preferred
prescient
privilege
propaganda
questionnaire
raspberry
receipt
receive
recommend
rhythm
ridiculous
sacrilegious
seize
separate
sergeant
sheriff
siege
sincerely
success
supersede
temperament
temperature
thorough
tomorrow
transferred
transsexual
truly
twelfth
vaccinate
vacillate
vacuum
vicious
Wednesday
weird
wherever
wholly

Foreign Words and Phrases

(A = Arabic; F = French; Ger = German; Gr = Greek; I = Italian; J = Japanese; L = Latin; R = Russian; S = Spanish; Y = Yiddish)

ad hoc (L; ad-HOK): for the end or purpose at hand; impromptu
ad hominem (L; ad-HOH-mee-nem): argument that criticizes an opponent, often unfairly, rather than addressing an issue directly
al fresco (I; ahl-FRAYS-koh): outdoors
anime (J: A-nuh-may): Japanese-style animation
antebellum (L; AHN-teh-BEL-lum): pre-war
au courant (F; oh-koo-RAHN): up-to-date, fashionable
belles lettres (F; bel-LET-truh): writing aspiring to artistic merit
bête noire (F; bet-NWAHR): a thing or person viewed with particular dislike or fear
bildungsroman (Ger; BIL-doongs-roh-mahn): novel embodying coming-of-age story
bodega (S; boh-DAY-gah): grocery store
bon vivant (F; bon-vee-VAHN): a person with refined tastes, especially for food and drink
bonhomie (F; boh-noh-MEE): friendliness
bourgeois (F; boo-ZHWAH): middle-class; materialistic
carte blanche (F; kahrt-BLANSH): full discretionary power
cause célèbre (F; kawz-suh-LEB): a notorious incident
chutzpah (Y, HUHTS-pah): audacity, nerve
comme il faut (F; cum-eel-FOH): proper; as it should be
contretemps (F; kon-truh-TAHN): awkward situation
coup de grâce (F; kooh-duh-GRAHS): the decisive final blow
cum laude/magna cum laude/summa cum laude (L; kuhm-LOU-day; MAG-na ... ; SOO-ma ...): with praise or honor/with great praise or honor/with the highest praise or honor
de facto (L; day-FAK-toh): in fact, if not by law
de jure (L; dee-JOOR-ee, day-YOOR-ay): by right or by law
de rigueur (F; duh-ree-GUR): required by convention or etiquette
détente (F; day-TAHNT): an easing of strained relations
deus ex machina (L; DAY-uhs-eks-MAH-keh-nah): person/event that provides a solution unexpectedly or suddenly, espec. (in literature) a contrived solution to a plot
doppelgänger (Ger; DAH-pul-gang-ur): a double or ghostly counterpart of a person
double entendre (F; DOO-blahn-TAHN-druh): expression with a double meaning, one meaning of which is often risqué
e pluribus unum (L; eh-PLOO-ree-boos-OO-noom): out of many, one (U.S. motto)
éminence grise (F; ay-meh-nahns-GREEZ): one who wields power behind the scenes
ennui (F; ah-NOOEE): boredom; world-weariness; annoyance
ersatz (Ger; EHR-zats): artificial; being a (usually inferior) substitute
ex post facto (L; eks-pohst-FAK-toh): retroactive(ly)
fait accompli (F; fayt-uh-kom-PLEE): an accomplished fact
fatwa (A; FAHT-wah): in Islam, a legal or religious decree
faux pas (F; foh-PAH): false step; breach of etiquette
habeas corpus (L; HAY-bee-ahs-KOR-pus): an order for a prisoner to be brought to court to challenge his or her detention
hoi polloi (Gr; hoy-puh-LOY): the masses
impresario (I; im-prah-SAH-ri-oh): manager, promoter, or sponsor of a musical or theatrical program or company
imprimatur (L; im-prah-MAH-toor): approval or official permission to print, espec. by the Roman Catholic church
in loco parentis (L; in-LOH-koh-puh-REN-tis): in place of parent
in medias res (L; in-MAY-dee-oos-rays): into the middle of things
intelligentsia (R; in-te-luh-JEN-see-uh): elite social class made up of intellectuals and educated people
ipso facto (L; ip-soh-FAK-toh): by that fact itself
je ne sais quoi (F; zhuh-nuh-say-KWAH): literally, "I don't know what"; the little something that eludes description
jihad (A; jih-HAHD): Islamic holy war; struggle in devotion to Islam
joie de vivre (F; zhwah-duh-VEEV-ruh): zest for life
kvetch (Y; Kuh-VETCH): complain, gripe
leitmotif (Ger; lyt-moh-TEEF): the central theme or idea, particularly in art and literature
mano a mano (S; MAH-noh-ah-MAH-noh): hand to hand; in direct combat
mea culpa (L; MAY-uh-CUL-puh): through my fault
mensch (Y; MENTSCH): an upright, noble, admirable person
modus operandi (L; MOH-duhs-op-uh-RAN-dee): method of operation
mujahedeen (A; moo-jah-ha-DEEN): Islamic holy warrior
noblesse oblige (F; noh-BLES-oh-BLEEZH): the obligation of nobility to help the less fortunate
nolo contendere (L; NOH-loh-kohn-TEN-duh-ree): a plea of no contest to charges, without admitting guilt
non compos mentis (L; non-KOM-puhs-MEN-tis): not of sound mind
non sequitur (L; non-SEH-kwi-tour): a conclusion that does not logically follow from what preceded it
nouveau riche (F; noo-voh-REESH): a newly rich person, espec. one who spends money conspicuously
ombudsman (Swedish; AHM-budz-muhn): person who receives, investigates, and settles complaints
par excellence (F; par-ek-seh-LANS): best of all; incomparable
persona non grata (L; per-SOH-nah-non-GRAH-tah): unwelcome person
pièce de résistance (F; pee-es-duh-ray-ZEES-tonz): the outstanding item in a series or group
prima facie (L; pry-muh-FAY-shee-ee; pry-muh-FAY-shuh): true at first glance; presumptively valid
pro bono (L; proh-BOH-noh): (work) donated for the public good
quid pro quo (L; kwid-proh-KWOH): something given or received for something else
raison d'être (F; RAY-zohnn-DET-ruh): reason for being
savoir faire (F; sav-wahr-FAIR): dexterity in social affairs
schadenfreude (Ger; SHAH-duhn-froy-deh): joy at another's misfortune
semper fidelis (L; SEM-puhr-fee-DAY-lis): always faithful
sobriquet (F; SOH-bri-kay): nickname or informal descriptive name for someone
sotto voce (I; sah-toh-VOH-chee); in a low voice
sui generis (L; soo-ee-JEN-er-is); unique; one of a kind
terra firma (L; TER-uh-FUR-muh): solid ground
verboten (Ger; ver-BOH-ten): forbidden
vis-à-vis (F; vee-zuh-VEE): compared with; with regard to
voir dire (F; vwar-DEER): examination by lawyers or judge to determine the suitability of a witness or a prospective juror
zeitgeist (Ger; ZITE-gyste): the general intellectual, moral, and cultural climate of an era

Names for Animal Young

calf: cattle, elephant, hippo, camel, others
cheeper: grouse, partridge, quail
chick: chicken, penguin, other birds
cockerel: rooster
codling, sprag: codfish
colt: horse, zebra (male)
cria: llama, alpaca
cub: lion, bear, shark, fox, others
cygnet: swan
duckling: duck
elver: eel
ephyra: jellyfish
eyas: hawk, others
fawn: deer, antelope
filly: horse, zebra (female)
fingerling, fry: fish generally
fledgling, nestling: birds generally
foal: horse, zebra, others
gosling: goose
heifer: cow
hoglet: hedgehog
joey: kangaroo, opossum, wombat
kid: goat
kit: beaver, rabbit, ferret, others
kitten: cat, other small mammals
lamb: sheep
larva: frog, sea urchin, insects generally
parr, smolt, grilse: salmon
piglet, shoat, farrow, suckling: pig
polliwog, tadpole: frog
poult: turkey
pullet: hen
pup: dog, fox, seal, rat, others
spat: oyster, other bivalves
spiderling: spider
spike, blinker, tinker: mackerel
squab: pigeon
whelp: dog, tiger, other carnivores
yearling: cattle, sheep, horse, others

Names for Animal Collectives

alligators: congregation
ants: army, colony, swarm
apes: shrewdness, troop
bears: sleuth, sloth
bees: colony, swarm, hive, grist
birds: flight, volery
buffalo: gang, obstinacy
butterflies: flutter
buzzards: wake
camels: caravan, flock, train
cats: clowder, cluster, pounce
cattle: drove
cheetahs: coalition
cockroaches: intrusion
cranes: sedge, siege
crocodiles: bask, nest, float
crows: murder, horde
dolphins: pod
doves: dule, pitying
ducks: brace, team
eagles: convocation, aerie
ferrets: business
finches: charm
fish: school, shoal
flamingos: stand, flamboyance
foxes: skulk
geese: flock, gaggle, skein
giraffes: corps, herd, tower
goats: tribe, trip
gorillas: band, troop, whoop
grasshoppers: cloud
hawks: cast, kettle
hedgehogs: array, prickle
hippopotamuses: bloat
horses: pair, team
hounds: cry, mute, pack
hyenas: cackle
iguanas: mess
jellyfish: smack
kangaroos: mob, troop
larks: exaltation
leopards: leap
lions: pride
locusts: plague, swarm
moles: labor
monkeys: troop
mules: barren, span
nightingales: watch
otters: romp
owls: parliament
oxen: yoke
peacocks: muster
pheasants: nest, nide, bouquet
ponies: string
raccoons: gaze
ravens: unkindness
rhinoceroses: crash
seals: pod
sheep: flock, drove, hurtle
snakes: nest
squirrels: dray, scurry
starlings: flock, murmuration
swans: bevy
tigers: streak
toads: knot
trout: hover
turkeys: rafter
turtles: bale
vultures: committee
whales: gam, herd, pod
woodchucks: fall
woodpeckers: descent
zebras: herd, zeal

Some Common Abbreviations and Acronyms

Acronyms are pronounceable words formed from first letters (or syllables) of other words. Some abbreviations below (e.g., AIDS, NATO) are thus acronyms. Some acronyms are words coined as abbreviations and written in lowercase (e.g., sonar, yuppie). Capitalization usage may vary from what is shown here. Some acronyms may have other meanings not given here. Italicized words preceding parenthetical definitions below are Latin unless otherwise noted.

A: ampere
AA: Alcoholics Anonymous; Associate in Arts; administrative assistant
ABA: American Bar Association
AC: alternating current; air-conditioning
ACA: Affordable Care Act
ACLU: American Civil Liberties Union
AD: *anno Domini* (in the year of the Lord)
ADD: attention deficit disorder
AFL-CIO: American Federation of Labor and Congress of Industrial Organizations
AFSCME: American Federation of State, County, and Municipal Employees
AFT: American Federation of Teachers
AI: artificial intelligence
AIDS: acquired immune deficiency syndrome
ALA: American Library Association
a.m. or **AM:** *ante meridiem* (before noon)
AP: Associated Press
APO: army post office
APR: annual percentage rate
AQAP: al-Qaeda in the Arabian Peninsula
ARM: adjustable rate mortgage
ASCAP: American Society of Composers, Authors, and Publishers
ASCII: American Standard Code for Information Interchange
ATM: automated teller machine
Ave.: Avenue
AWOL: absent without leave
BA: Bachelor of Arts
bbl: barrel(s)
BC: before Christ
BCE: before Common, or Christian, Era
bpd: barrels per day
BS: Bachelor of Science
Btu: British thermal unit(s)
bu: bushel(s)
BYOB: bring your own bottle
C: Celsius, centigrade
c: *circa* (about); copyright
CAT: computerized axial tomography
CD: compact disc
CDC: Centers for Disease Control and Prevention; Community Development Corporation
CE: Common Era; Christian Era
CEO: chief executive officer
cf.: *confer* (compare)
CFO: chief financial officer
CIA: Central Intelligence Agency
CIF: cost, insurance, and freight
COBRA: Consolidated Omnibus Budget Reconciliation Act (health insurance continuation)
COD: cash (or collect) on delivery
COL or **Col.:** Colonel
COLA: cost of living adjustment
COO: chief operating officer
CPA: certified public accountant
CPI: consumer price index
CPL or **Cpl.:** Corporal
CPR: cardiopulmonary resuscitation
CPU: central processing unit
CST: central standard time
CV: curriculum vitae
DA: district attorney
DC: direct current
DD: Doctor of Divinity
DDS: Doctor of Dental Surgery
DEA: Drug Enforcement Agency
DHS: Department of Homeland Security
DMD: Doctor of Dental Medicine
DMZ: demilitarized zone
DNA: deoxyribonucleic acid
DNC: Democratic National Committee
DNR: do not resuscitate
DOA: dead on arrival
DOB: date of birth
DoD: Department of Defense
dpi: dots per inch
DPT: diphtheria, pertussis, tetanus
DUI: driving under the influence
DVD: digital video disc
DVM: Doctor of Veterinary Medicine
DWI: driving while intoxicated
ECB: European Central Bank
ed.: edited; edition; editor
EEG: electroencephalogram
e.g.: *exempli gratia* (for example)
EKG or **ECG:** electrocardiogram
EOE: equal opportunity employer
EP: extended play
EPA: Environmental Protection Agency
ERA: Equal Rights Amendment; earned run average
ESL: English as a second language
ESP: extrasensory perception
Esq.: Esquire
EST: eastern standard time
et al.: *et alii* (and others)
etc.: *et cetera* (and so forth)
EU: European Union
F: Fahrenheit
Fannie Mae: Federal National Mortgage Association
FAQ: frequently asked questions
FBI: Federal Bureau of Investigation
FDA: Food and Drug Administration
FDIC: Federal Deposit Insurance Corporation
FEC: Federal Election Commission
FEMA: Federal Emergency Management Agency
ff.: and those following
FICA: Federal Insurance Contributions Act (Social Security)
FIFA: Fédération Internationale de Football Association
fl.: *floruit* (flourished), used for historical figures when life dates uncertain
Freddie Mac: Federal Home Loan Mortgage Corporation
FTP: file transfer protocol
FWIW: for what it's worth
FY: fiscal year
FYI: for your information
GATT: General Agreement on Tariffs and Trade
GB: gigabyte(s)
GDP: gross domestic product
GED: general equivalency diploma
GMT: Greenwich mean time
GOP: Grand Old Party (Republican Party)
GPS: Global Positioning System
GUI: graphical user interface
ha: hectare
hazmat: HAZardous MATerial
HDTV: high-definition television
HIV: human immunodeficiency virus
HMO: health maintenance organization
HMS: His/Her Majesty's Ship (UK)
Hon.: the Honorable
HOV: high-occupancy vehicle
HRH: Her (His) Royal Highness (UK)
HTML: hypertext markup language
HTTP: hypertext transfer protocol
HUD: Department of Housing and Urban Development
HVAC: heating, ventilating, and air-conditioning
Hz: hertz
ibid: *ibidem* (in the same place)
ICU: intensive care unit
i.e.: *id est* (that is)
IM: instant messaging
IMF: International Monetary Fund
IM(H)O: in my (humble) opinion
INS: Immigration and Naturalization Service
IPO: initial public offering
IQ: intelligence quotient
IRA: individual retirement account; Irish Republican Army
IRS: Internal Revenue Service
ISBN: International Standard Book Number
ISIL or **ISIS:** Islamic State of Iraq in the Levant, or of Iraq and Syria (two names for the extremist group that calls itself the Islamic State)
ISP: Internet service provider
IVF: in vitro fertilization
JD: *Juris Doctor* (Doctor of Law)
k: karat; **K:** Kelvin
kWh: kilowatt-hour(s)
laser: Light Amplification by Stimulated Emission of Radiation
lb: pound
LGBT: lesbian, gay, bisexual, and transgender
LLP: limited liability partnership
loc. cit.: *loco citato* (in the place cited)

LOL: laughing out loud
LSAT: Law School Admission Test
LT or **Lt.:** Lieutenant
MA: Master of Arts
MB: megabyte(s)
MBA: Master of Business Administration
MCAT: Medical College Admission Test
MD: *Medicinae Doctor* (Doctor of Medicine)
MIA: missing in action
modem: MOdulator-DEModulator
MP: member of Parliament (UK)
mph: miles per hour
MRI: magnetic resonance imaging
ms, mss: manuscript(s)
MS: Master of Science; multiple sclerosis
MSG: monosodium glutamate
MST: mountain standard time
MVP: most valuable player
NA: not applicable; not available
NAACP: National Association for the Advancement of Colored People
NAFTA: North American Free Trade Agreement
NASA: National Aeronautics and Space Administration
NATO: North Atlantic Treaty Organization
NB or **n.b.:** *nota bene* (note carefully)
NCAA: National Collegiate Athletic Association
NEA: National Education Association
NIH: National Institutes of Health
NOW: National Organization for Women
NPR: National Public Radio
NRA: National Rifle Association
NSA: National Security Agency
obs.: obsolete
OECD: Organization for Economic Cooperation and Development
OED: Oxford English Dictionary
OMB: Office of Management and Budget
op: *opus* (work)
OPEC: Organization of Petroleum Exporting Countries
OTC: over-the-counter
oz: ounce
p, pp: page(s)
PA: public address
PAC: political action committee
PC: personal computer; politically correct
PDA: personal digital assistant
PETA: People for the Ethical Treatment of Animals
PhD: *Philosophiae Doctor* (Doctor of Philosophy)
PIN: personal identification number
p.m. or **PM:** *post meridiem* (after noon)
POTUS: President of the United States
PPO: preferred provider organization, a type of health-care provider network
PS: *post scriptum* (postscript)
PST: Pacific standard time
pt: part(s); pint(s); point(s)
PVT or **Pvt.:** Private
QC: Queen's Council (UK)
QED: *quod erat demonstrandum* (which was to be demonstrated)
q.v.: *quod vide* (which see)
radar: RAdio Detecting And Ranging
RAM: random access memory
RCMP: Royal Canadian Mounted Police
REM: rapid eye movement
Rev.: Reverend
rev.: revised; reviewed
RIP: *requiescat in pace* (may he/she rest in peace)
RN: registered nurse
RNA: ribonucleic acid
RNC: Republican National Committee
ROM: read only memory
ROTC: Reserve Officers' Training Corps
rpm: revolutions per minute
RSVP: *répondez s'il vous plaît* (Fr.) (please reply)
SARS: severe acute respiratory syndrome
SASE: self-addressed stamped envelope
SEC: Securities and Exchange Commission
SETI: Search for Extraterrestrial Intelligence
SGT or **Sgt.:** Sergeant
SIDS: sudden infant death syndrome
SJ: Society of Jesus (Jesuits)
sonar: SOund NAvigation and Ranging
SOTU: State of the Union
SPCA: Society for the Prevention of Cruelty to Animals
SSI: Supplementary Security Income
St.: Saint; Street
STEM: science, technology, engineering, math
TB: tuberculosis; terabyte(s)
TBA: to be announced
TBD: to be determined
tbsp: tablespoon
TEFL: teaching English as a foreign language
TPP: Trans-Pacific Partnership (trade agreement)
TSA: Transportation Security Administration
tsp: teaspoon
UFO: unidentified flying object
UPC: Universal Product Code
URL: Universal Resource Locator
USDA: United States Department of Agriculture
USS: United States ship
UTC: coordinated universal time
VA: Department of Veterans Affairs
var.: variant
VAT: value-added tax
VCR: videocassette recorder
viz: *videlicet* (namely)
VP: vice president
W: watt(s)
WHO: World Health Organization
WMD: weapon of mass destruction
WPM: words per minute
WTF: what the f--- [expletive]
WTO: World Trade Organization
WWW: World Wide Web
YMCA/YWCA: Young Men's/Women's Christian Association
YTD: year to date
yuppie: young urban professional
ZIP: zone improvement plan (U.S. Postal Service)

Top 10 First Names of Americans by Decade or Year of Birth

Source: U.S. Social Security Administration

All names are from Social Security card applications for births that occurred in the United States after 1879. Rankings are based on one spelling of the name; variant spellings and similar names are considered separate names.

BOYS

1880-1889 . . . . John, William, James, George, Charles, Frank, Joseph, Henry, Robert, Thomas
1890-1899 . . . . John, William, James, George, Charles, Joseph, Frank, Robert, Edward, Henry
1900-1909 . . . . John, William, James, George, Charles, Robert, Joseph, Frank, Edward, Thomas
1910-1919 . . . . John, William, James, Robert, Joseph, George, Charles, Edward, Frank, Thomas
1920-1929 . . . . Robert, John, James, William, Charles, George, Joseph, Richard, Edward, Donald
1930-1939 . . . . Robert, James, John, William, Richard, Charles, Donald, George, Thomas, Joseph
1940-1949 . . . . James, Robert, John, William, Richard, David, Charles, Thomas, Michael, Ronald
1950-1959 . . . . Michael, David, James, John, Robert, Mark, William, Richard, Thomas, Jeffrey
1960-1969 . . . . Michael, David, John, James, Robert, Mark, William, Richard, Thomas, Jeffrey
1970-1979 . . . . Michael, Christopher, Jason, David, James, John, Robert, Brian, William, Matthew
1980-1989 . . . . Michael, Christopher, Matthew, Joshua, David, James, Daniel, Robert, John, Joseph
1990-1999 . . . . Michael, Christopher, Matthew, Joshua, Jacob, Nicholas, Andrew, Daniel, Tyler, Joseph
2000-2009 . . . . Jacob, Michael, Joshua, Matthew, Daniel, Christopher, Andrew, Ethan, Joseph, William
2014 . . . . Noah, Liam, Mason, Jacob, William, Ethan, Michael, Alexander, James, Daniel

GIRLS

1880-1889 . . . . Mary, Anna, Emma, Elizabeth, Margaret, Minnie, Ida, Bertha, Clara, Alice
1890-1899 . . . . Mary, Anna, Margaret, Helen, Elizabeth, Ruth, Florence, Ethel, Emma, Marie
1900-1909 . . . . Mary, Helen, Margaret, Anna, Ruth, Elizabeth, Dorothy, Marie, Florence, Mildred
1910-1919 . . . . Mary, Helen, Dorothy, Margaret, Ruth, Mildred, Anna, Elizabeth, Frances, Virginia
1920-1929 . . . . Mary, Dorothy, Helen, Betty, Margaret, Ruth, Virginia, Doris, Mildred, Frances
1930-1939 . . . . Mary, Betty, Barbara, Shirley, Patricia, Dorothy, Joan, Margaret, Nancy, Helen
1940-1949 . . . . Mary, Linda, Barbara, Patricia, Carol, Sandra, Nancy, Sharon, Judith, Susan
1950-1959 . . . . Mary, Linda, Patricia, Susan, Deborah, Barbara, Debra, Karen, Nancy, Donna
1960-1969 . . . . Lisa, Mary, Susan, Karen, Kimberly, Patricia, Linda, Donna, Michelle, Cynthia
1970-1979 . . . . Jennifer, Amy, Melissa, Michelle, Kimberly, Lisa, Angela, Heather, Stephanie, Nicole
1980-1989 . . . . Jessica, Jennifer, Amanda, Ashley, Sarah, Stephanie, Melissa, Nicole, Elizabeth, Heather
1990-1999 . . . . Jessica, Ashley, Emily, Sarah, Samantha, Amanda, Brittany, Elizabeth, Taylor, Megan
2000-2009 . . . . Emily, Madison, Emma, Olivia, Hannah, Abigail, Isabella, Samantha, Elizabeth, Ashley
2014 . . . . Emma, Olivia, Sophia, Isabella, Ava, Mia, Emily, Abigail, Madison, Charlotte

Origins of Popular American Given Names

Source: World Almanac research

Some names are commonly used for either sex but are listed here under the more traditionally associated sex. Some names listed here have variant spellings that are not shown.

Boys

Aiden: Gaelic *Aodhan*, "little fire," from name of Celtic sun god
Alexander: Gr. *Alexandros*, "defender of man"
Andrew: Gr. *andreios*, "manly"
Anthony: Roman *Antonius*, possibly from Gr. *anthos*, "flower"
Benjamin: Heb. *Binyamin*, "son of the right hand"
Brandon: Eng. place name, "gorse-covered hill"
Brian: Irish, perhaps Celtic *Brigonos*, "high" or "noble"
Charles: Ger. *ceorl*, "free man"
Christopher: Gr. *Christophoros*, "bearing Christ"
Daniel: Heb. "God is my judge"
David: Heb. *Dodavehu*, perhaps "darling"
Edward: Old Eng. *Eadweard*, "wealth-guard"
Elijah: Heb. "the Lord is my God"
Ethan: Heb. "solid, firm"
Francis, Frank: Late Lat. *Franciscus*, "Frenchman"
George: Gr. *georgos*, "soil tiller," "farmer"
Henry: Ger. *Haimric*, "home-power"
Jack: nickname for or variant of John
Jacob: Heb. *Yaakov*, "God protects" or "supplanter"
James: Late Lat. *Iacomus*, form of Jacob
Jason: Gr. *Iason*, "healer"
Jayden: prob. from Jay (short form for many *J* names) and Hayden (Old Eng. "little hollow")
Jeffrey: Norman Fr., from Ger. *Gaufrid*, "land-peace," or *Gisfrid*, "pledge-peace"
John: Heb. *Yohanan*, "God is gracious"
Jonathan: Heb. "God has given"
José: Heb. and Aramaic *Yose*, variant of Joseph
Joseph: Heb. *Yosef*, "[God] shall add"
Joshua: Heb. *Yoshua*, "God saves"
Liam: Gaelic form of William
Logan: Scot. "little hollow"
Mark: Lat. *Marcus*, perhaps from Mars, Roman god of war
Mason: Fr. "stone worker," related to Old Eng. "work"
Matthew: Heb. *Mattathia*, "gift of God"
Michael: Heb. "who could ever be like God?"
Nathan: Heb. "God has given"; modern short form of Nathaniel or Jonathan
Nicholas: Gr. *Nikolaos*, "victory-people"
Noah: Heb. "rest"
Patrick: Lat. *Patricius*, "of noble origin"
Richard: Ger. "power-hardy"
Robert: Ger. *Hrodberht*, "fame-bright"
Ryan: prob. from Irish surname, Gaelic "king"
Samuel: Heb. *Shemuel*, "God heard"
Sean: Gaelic form of John
Steven: Gr. *stephanos*, "crown" or "garland"
Thomas: Aramaic "twin"
Tyler: Old Eng. *tigeler*, "tile layer"
William: Ger. *Wilhelm*, "will-helmet"

Girls

Abigail: Heb. "my father is joy"
Addison: Eng. "son of Adam"
Alexandra, Sandra: fem. forms of Alexander
Alexis: Gr. "helper" or "defender"
Alyssa: variant of Alicia (Eng., Sp.) or Alice (Eng., Fr.); may mean "noble"
Amanda: 17th-cent. invention from Lat. "lovable"
Amelia: Ger. "hard-working," or from Lat. *aemulus*, "striving"
Amy: Old Fr. *Amee*, "beloved"
Andrea: fem. form of Andrew
Angela: Gr. *angelos*, "messenger [of God]"
Anna: Lat., Gr. form of Hannah; variants include Ann (Eng.), Ana (Sp.), Anne (Eng., Fr., Ger.)
Ashley: Eng. place name, "ash grove"
Aubrey: Fr., orig. from Ger. *Alberic*, "king of elves"
Ava: prob. modern form of Eva, Lat. form of Heb. *Eve*
Avery: Eng., common place name; may also mean "elf counsel" or "elf ruler"
Barbara: Gr. *barbarus*, "foreign"
Brianna: modern fem. form of Brian
Carol, Charlotte: fem. forms of Charles
Chloe: Gr. "young shoot," "blooming"
Claire, Clara: Lat. *clarus*, "famous"
Deborah: Heb. "bee"
Donna: Ital. "lady"
Dorothy: Gr. *Dorothea*, "gift of God"
Elizabeth: Heb. *Elisheba*, perhaps "God is my oath" or "God is good fortune"
Ella: prob. variant or nickname for Ellen, variant of Helen, or Eleanor
Emily: see Amelia
Emma: Ger. *ermen*, "whole" or "entire"
Eve, Evelyn: Heb. "life-giving"
Grace: Lat. *gratia*, "grace," "blessing"
Hailey: Eng. place name, "hay clearing"
Hannah: Heb. "He [God] has favored me"
Harper: Old Eng. "harp player"
Heather: Middle Eng. *hathir*, "heather"
Helen: Gr. *Helene*, possibly "sunbeam"
Isabella, Isabel: Lat., Sp. variant of Elizabeth
Jennifer: Cornish form of Welsh *Gwenhwyfar*, "fair-smooth"
Jessica: Shakesp. invention, prob. fem. form of *Jesse*, Heb. "God exists"
Judith: Heb. "Jewish woman"
Julia: fem. form of Julius, Roman family name, or Lat. "youthful"
Kaitlyn: American spelling of Caitlin, the Irish form of Katherine
Karen: Danish form of Katherine
Katherine: Egyptian *Aikaterine*, later modified to resemble Gr. *katharos*, "pure"
Kelly: Irish Gaelic *Ceallagh*, perhaps "churchgoer" or "bright-headed"
Kimberly: Eng. place name, "Cyneburgh's clearing"
Laura: Lat. *laurus*, "laurel"
Lily: for the flower, symbol of purity
Linda: Sp. "pretty" or Ger. "tender"
Lisa: nickname for Elizabeth
Madison: Middle Eng. surname, "son of Madeline or Maud"
Margaret: Gr. *margaron*, "pearl"
Maria, Marie, Mary: Lat., Fr., Eng. forms for Heb. *Maryam*, perhaps "seeress" or "wished-for child"
Megan: Welsh form of Margaret
Melissa: Gr. "bee"
Mia: Nordic or Ital., short for Maria, etc.
Michelle: Fr. fem. form of Michael
Nancy: medieval Eng. nickname for Agnes (Gr. *hagnos*, "holy"), later also for Ann
Natalie: Fr., from Lat. *natalia*, "birthday [of Christ]"
Nicole: Fr. fem. form of Nicholas
Olivia: Lat. *oliva*, "olive tree"
Patricia: Lat. fem. form of Patrick
Rachel: Heb. "ewe"
Rose, Rosa: for the flower, suggesting beauty
Ruth: Heb., perhaps "companion"
Samantha: colonial American invention, prob. combining Sam from Samuel with *-antha* from Gr. *anthos*, "flower"
Sarah: Heb. "princess"
Sharon: Biblical place name, Heb. "plain"
Sofia, Sophia: Gr. "wisdom"
Stephanie: Fr. fem. form of Steven
Susan: Eng. form of Heb. *Shoshana*, "lily"
Teresa: Sp., perhaps "woman from Therasia"
Victoria: Lat. *victoria*, "victory"

Eponyms

(words named for people)

boycott: to avoid trade or dealings with, as a protest; after Charles C. Boycott, an English land agent in County Mayo, Ireland, ostracized in 1880 for refusing to reduce rents
derrick: a type of crane consisting of a boom connected to the base of an upright mast; after Derrick, early 17th-cent. English hangman who used a gallows that operated via cables and pulleys
draconian: harsh; after Draco, statesman who codified laws with severe punishments in Athens c. 621 BCE
gerrymander: to draw an election district in such a way as to favor a political party; after Elbridge Gerry, who created (1812) just such an election district (shaped like a salamander) during his governorship of Massachusetts
guillotine: a machine for beheading; after Joseph Guillotin, French physician who proposed its use in 1789 as more humane than hanging
Luddite: one who opposes new technology; from Ned Ludd, leader of a group of textile workers in England who destroyed machinery in the early 1800s
maudlin: excessively sentimental; from scriptural figure Mary Magdalene, who is often shown weeping in depictions
milquetoast: a timid, unassertive person; after Caspar Milquetoast, comic strip character created by American cartoonist Harold Tucker Webster in 1924
salmonella: bacteria that can cause infections when contaminated food or water is consumed; named after Daniel Elmer Salmon, American veterinarian and public health official
sandwich: two or more slices of bread with a filling in-between; after John Montagu, 4th Earl of Sandwich (1718-92), who supposedly ate these at the gaming table
shrapnel: originally, a projectile with lead balls designed to inflict maximum damage in explosions, later pieces of shell casings; from Henry Shrapnel (1761-1842), British artillery officer who designed the projectile
silhouette: an outline image; from Étienne de Silhouette (1709-67), a stingy French finance minister
Zamboni: an ice resurfacing machine; after American inventor Frank Zamboni, who owned an ice skating rink

American Manual Alphabet

In the American Manual Alphabet, each letter of the alphabet is represented by a position of the fingers. This system was originally developed in France by Charles-Michel de l'Épée in the 1700s. Laurent Clerc and Thomas Gallaudet further refined it into the American Manual Alphabet, which a person may use to spell out a word with no American Sign Language equivalent.

A B C D E F G H I

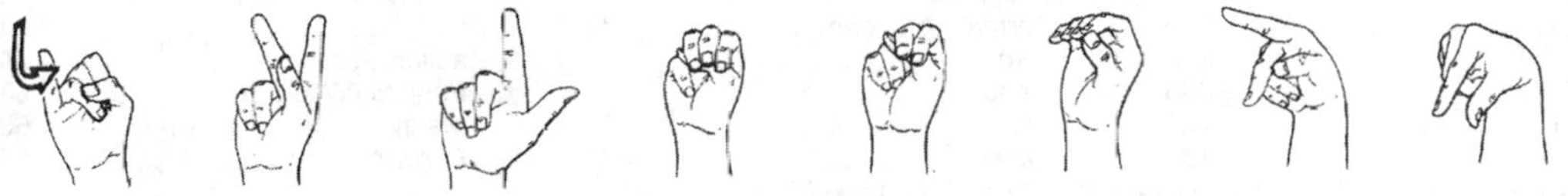

J K L M N O P Q

R S T U V W X Y Z

Words and Expressions in Common Languages

English	Arabic	Chinese[1]	French	German	Hebrew	Russian	Spanish
Hello/hi	Salam	Ni hao	Bonjour	Hallo	Shalom	Privet (informal)	Hola
Good morning	Sabah el kheer	Zao shang hao	Bonjour	Guten Morgen	Boker tov	Dobraye utra	Buenos días
Good night	Tosbeho 'ala khair	Wan an	Bonne nuit	Gute Nacht	Layla tov	Spakoynay noci	Buenas noches
Good-bye	Ma'a salama	Zai jian	Au revoir	Auf wiedersehen	Lehitraot	Da svidan'ya	Adiós
Please	Men fadlek	Qing	S'il vous plaît	Bitte	Bevakasha	Pazhalusta	Por favor
Thank you very much	Shokran jazeelan	Xie xie	Merci beaucoup	Danke schön	Toda raba	Spasiba	Muchas gracias
You're welcome	Al' afw	Huan ying	De rien/pas de quoi	Keine Ursache	Bevakasha	Pazhalusta	De nada
How are you?	Kaifa haloka?	Ni hao?	Comment allez-vous?	Wie geht's dir/Ihnen?	Ma shelomkha?	Kak dela?	Cómo estás?
I'm fine	Ana bekhair	Hen hao	Je vais bien	Mir geht's gut	Tov	Harasho	Estoy bien
I'm sorry	Aasef	Bao qian	Je suis désolé	Entschuldigung	Ani mamash mitstaer	Prastite	Lo siento
Excuse me	Alma'derah	Bao qian	Pardon	Darf ich mal vorbei?	Selikha	Izvinite	Perdone
yes	na'am	shi [it is so]	oui	ja	ken	da	si
no	laa	bu [not]	non	nein	lo	nyet	no
one	wahed	yi	un	eins	ekhad	adin	uno
two	ithnaan	er	deux	zwei	shenayim	dva	dos
three	thalatha	san	trois	drei	shelosha	tri	tres
four	arba'a	si	quatre	vier	arbaa	chityri	cuatro
five	khamsa	wu	cinq	fünf	khamisha	p'at	cinco

Note: Actual form or usage of some words and expressions may vary depending on dialect, grammar, or circumstances. Transliterations for languages not in Latin alphabet vary. (1) Mandarin.

Language Diversity

Source: *Ethnologue: Languages of the World, 17th Edition*; United Nations Educational, Scientific, and Cultural Organization (UNESCO); World Almanac research

There are more than 7,100 individual languages spoken somewhere in the world. But more than 40% of the world's people speak one of the eight most common languages as their native tongue, and more than 75% speak one of the top 85 languages. Some 3,700 languages have fewer than 10,000 native speakers, and about 700 languages have fewer than 100.

Using classifications developed by linguists, about 2,400 languages spoken today are said to be at least threatened or unsustainably losing speakers. In some cases, people of the childbearing generation still use the language but do not transmit it to their children. In others, only those in the grandparent generation or older use a language, though they may have little occasion to do so. *Ethnologue* classifies 432 languages as nearly extinct and another 188 as dormant—that is, having no speakers with more than a "symbolic proficiency." Some languages disappear when the last native speaker dies.

Some say communities should determine whether a language remains worth using; a language should be allowed to die naturally. Others give more value to language preservation in the name of cultural diversity. Some experts have concluded that as languages die out, knowledge of the local environment and physical world is lost. A recent study of the Amesha tribe in the Peruvian Amazon found that as their severely endangered language faded, crop diversity decreased.

UNESCO supports efforts to preserve various endangered languages. In one, experts created a system for writing down words in the Khang language (spoken in parts of northwest Vietnam), which had no written version. In addition, they produced recordings, word lists, grammars, and other materials for use in language classes aimed at reviving and perpetuating the use of Khang.

Principal Languages of the World

Source: Lewis, M. Paul, Gary F. Simons, Charles D. Fennig (eds.). *Ethnologue: Languages of the World, 17th Edition.* www.ethnologue.com. As updated in 2015. Used by permission, © SIL International.

Languages shown in italics are macrolanguages, or language groups that are equivalent in some ways to individual languages. Each language group consists of a number of variants, which may be mutually unintelligible; these variants, when they have 2.5 million speakers or more, will also appear in the larger table below, and occasionally have the same name as the macrolanguage. Numbers are estimates and count only speakers for whom the language is a first language, or mother tongue.

Languages Spoken by the Most People

Language	Speakers (mil)	Language	Speakers (mil)	Language	Speakers (mil)
Chinese[1]	1,197	Japanese	128	Turkish	71
Spanish	399	*Lahnda*	89	Tamil	69
English	335	Javanese	84	Vietnamese	68
Hindi	260	German (standard)	78	Urdu	64
Arabic	242	Korean	77	Italian	64
Portuguese	203	French	76	Punjabi (Western)	63
Bengali	189	Telugu	74	*Malay*	60
Russian	166	Marathi	72	*Persian*	57

(1) Includes Mandarin (848 mil speakers), Wu (77 mil), and Yue (62 mil).

Languages With at Least 2.5 Million Speakers

Primary country is country of origin, not necessarily the country where the most speakers reside (e.g., Portugal is the primary country for Portuguese, but more Portuguese speakers live in Brazil). Number of speakers is worldwide total for each language.

Primary country	Language	Countries	Speakers (mil)
Afghanistan	Pashto, Southern	4	10.8
	Dari	2	9.6
	Uzbek, Southern	2	3.0
Albania	*Albanian*	16	5.4
Algeria	Arabic, Algerian Spoken	1	26.7
	Kabyle	1	5.6
Angola	Umbundu	1	6.0
	Kimbundu	1	4.0
Armenia	Armenian	14	5.9
Austria	Bavarian	4	14.1
Azerbaijan	Azerbaijani, North	4	7.3
Bangladesh	Bengali	4	189.3
	Rangpuri	2	15.0
	Chittagonian	1	13.0
	Sylheti	2	10.3
Belarus	Belarusan	4	3.2
Bolivia	*Aymara*	4	2.8
	Quechua, South Bolivian	2	2.8
	Aymara, Central	4	2.6
Botswana	Tswana	4	5.2
Brazil	Hunsrik	1	3.0
Bulgaria	Bulgarian	8	7.8
Burkina Faso	Mòoré	2	5.1
Burundi	Rundi	1	10.2
Cambodia	Khmer, Central	2	14.2
China	*Chinese*	33	1,197.3
	Chinese, Mandarin	12	847.8
	Chinese, Wu	1	77.2
	Chinese, Yue	10	62.2
	Chinese, Min Nan	10	46.6
	Chinese, Jinyu	1	45.0
	Chinese, Xiang	1	36.0
	Chinese, Hakka	13	30.1
	Chinese, Gan	1	20.6
	Zhuang	2	14.9
	Uyghur	4	10.4
	Chinese, Min Bei	2	10.3
	Chinese, Min Dong	6	9.1
	Hmong	10	7.7
	Chinese, Huizhou	1	4.6
	Mongolian, Peripheral	2	3.4
	Chinese, Min Zhong	1	3.1
	Bouyei	2	2.6
	Chinese, Pu-Xian	3	2.6
Congo, Dem. Rep. of	Luba-Kasai	1	6.3
	Kongo	3	5.6
	Koongo	3	5.0
	Kituba	1	4.2
Côte d'Ivoire	Jula	3	2.6
Croatia	Croatian	8	5.6
Czech Republic	Czech	5	10.6
Denmark	Danish	3	5.5
Egypt	Arabic, Egyptian Spoken	1	55.0
	Arabic, Sa'idi Spoken	1	19.0
Ethiopia	Amharic	2	21.8
	Oromo	3	17.5
	Oromo, West Central	1	8.9
	Tigrigna	3	6.9
	Oromo, Eastern	1	4.5
	Oromo, Borana-Arsi-Guji	3	3.9
	Sidamo	1	3.0
Finland	Finnish	3	5.4
France	French	53	75.9
Georgia	Georgian	3	4.2
Germany	German, Standard	18	78.1
	Mainfränkisch	1	4.9
Ghana	Akan	1	8.3
	Ghanaian Pidgin English	1	5.0
	Éwé	2	3.1
Greece	Greek	9	13.4
Guinea	*Mandingo*	7	6.5
	Maninkakan, Eastern	3	3.5
	Pular	4	2.9
Haiti	Haitian	2	7.7
Hungary	Hungarian	9	12.6
India	Hindi	4	260.3
	Telugu	2	74.0
	Marathi	1	71.8
	Tamil	6	68.8
	Gujarati	6	46.6
	Bhojpuri	3	39.7
	Kannada	1	37.7
	Maithili	2	33.9
	Malayalam	2	33.6
	Oriya	4	32.7
	Oriya	1	32.1
	Punjabi, Eastern	3	29.5
	Marwari	3	19.7
	Magahi	1	14.0
	Chhattisgarhi	1	13.3
	Assamese	1	12.8
	Deccan	1	12.8
	Rajasthani	3	12.4
	Kanauji	1	9.5
	Haryanvi	1	8.0
	Varhadi-Nagpuri	1	7.0
	Santhali	3	6.2
	Konkani	4	6.1
	Indian Sign Language	2	5.9
	Marwari	2	5.6
	Kashmiri	2	5.6
	Malvi	1	5.6
	Mewari	1	5.1
	Lambadi	1	4.2
	Dogri	1	4.0
	Merwari	1	3.9
	Mina	1	3.8
	Konkani, Goan	2	3.6
	Bhili	1	3.3

Primary country	Language	Countries	Speakers (mil)
India (cont.)	Sadri	2	3.3
	Bundeli	1	3.1
	Awadhi	2	3.0
	Shekhawati	1	3.0
	Godwari	1	3.0
	Garhwali	1	2.9
	Bagheli	2	2.9
	Wagdi	1	2.5
Indonesia	Javanese	3	84.3
	Sunda	1	34.0
	Indonesian	1	23.2
	Madura	2	6.8
	Minangkabau	1	5.5
	Bugis	2	5.0
	Betawi	1	5.0
	Banjar	2	3.5
	Aceh	1	3.5
	Bali	1	3.3
	Musi	1	3.1
Iran	*Persian*	29	57.0
	Persian, Iranian	6	47.4
	Azerbaijani	15	24.2
	Azerbaijani, South	4	16.9
	Domari	13	4.0
	Gilaki	1	3.3
	Mazanderani	1	3.3
	Kurdish, Southern	2	3.0
Iraq	*Kurdish*	31	30.0
	Arabic, Mesopotamian Spoken	4	15.1
	Kurdish, Central	2	6.8
	Arabic, North Mesopotamian Spoken	3	6.3
Israel	Hebrew	1	5.3
Italy	Italian	11	63.8
	Napoletano-Calabrese	1	5.7
	Sicilian	1	4.7
	Lombard	2	3.9
	Venetian	4	3.9
Jamaica	Jamaican Creole English	3	3.2
Japan	Japanese	2	128.1
Jordan	Arabic, South Levantine Spoken	3	6.5
Kazakhstan	Kazakh	6	12.9
Kenya	Gikuyu	1	6.6
	Oluluyia	3	5.1
	Kalenjin	3	4.8
	Dholuo	2	4.2
	Kamba	1	3.9
Korea, South	Korean	5	77.2
Kuwait	Arabic, Gulf Spoken	9	5.3
Kyrgyzstan	Kyrgyz	5	4.3
Laos	Lao	3	3.3
Lesotho	Sotho, Southern	2	5.6
Libya	Arabic, Libyan Spoken	3	4.3
Lithuania	Lithuanian	2	3.0
Madagascar	*Malagasy*	5	17.6
	Malagasy, Plateau	2	7.5
Malawi	Chichewa	4	10.0
	Yao	4	3.1
	Tumbuka	2	2.6
Malaysia	*Malay*	13	60.5
	Malay	3	15.8
	Malay, Kedah	2	2.6
Mali	Bamanankan	2	4.1
Mauritania	Hassaniyya	7	3.2
Mongolia	*Mongolian*	6	5.8
Morocco	Arabic, Moroccan Spoken	2	21.0
	Tachelhit	2	3.9
	Tamazight, Central Atlas	1	2.5
Mozambique	Makhuwa	1	3.1
Myanmar (Burma)	Burmese	1	32.0
	Shan	3	3.3
Nepal	*Nepali*	5	16.1
	Nepali	3	15.4
Netherlands	Dutch	7	21.9
Nigeria	Hausa	9	25.1
	Yoruba	2	19.4
	Igbo	1	18.0
Nigeria (cont.)	Fulfulde, Nigerian	3	11.6
	Kanuri	6	3.8
	Kanuri, Central	5	3.2
Norway	Norwegian	1	4.7
Pakistan	*Lahnda*	6	88.7
	Urdu	6	64.0
	Punjabi, Western	2	62.6
	Pushto	9	38.3
	Pashto, Northern	3	21.0
	Sindhi	3	20.3
	Saraiki	2	20.1
	Baluchi	8	7.4
	Pashto, Central	1	6.5
	Brahui	3	4.2
	Balochi, Southern	4	3.8
	Pahari-Potwari	2	2.5
Paraguay	*Guarani*	5	4.9
	Guarani, Paraguayan	1	4.9
Peru	*Quechua*	6	8.9
Philippines	Tagalog	3	24.3
	Cebuano	1	15.8
	Ilocano	1	7.0
	Hiligaynon	1	5.8
	Bikol	1	3.6
	Waray-Waray	1	2.6
	Bikol, Central	1	2.5
Poland	Polish	9	38.6
Portugal	Portuguese	12	203.4
Romania	Romanian	6	23.7
	Romany	41	2.6
Russia	Russian	16	166.2
	Tatar	4	5.2
Rwanda	Rwanda	3	7.2
Saudi Arabia	*Arabic*	60	242.4
	Arabic, Najdi Spoken	4	9.9
	Arabic, Hijazi Spoken	2	6.0
Senegal	*Fulah*	20	22.3
	Wolof	2	4.0
	Pulaar	6	3.7
Serbia	*Serbo-Croatian*	27	15.7
	Serbian	10	8.6
	Albanian, Gheg	6	3.4
Slovakia	Slovak	8	5.2
Somalia	Somali	4	14.8
South Africa	Zulu	5	12.0
	Xhosa	2	8.2
	Afrikaans	6	7.1
	Sotho, Northern	1	4.6
	Tsonga	4	4.0
Spain	Spanish	31	398.9
	Catalan	4	4.1
Sri Lanka	Sinhala	2	15.6
Sudan	Arabic, Sudanese Spoken	3	16.9
Sweden	Swedish	3	9.2
Switzerland	German, Swiss	5	6.3
Syria	Arabic, North Levantine Spoken	2	14.8
Tajikistan	Tajiki	4	7.9
Tanzania	*Swahili*	15	15.4
	Swahili	8	15.4
	Sukuma	1	5.4
Thailand	Thai	2	20.4
	Thai, Northeastern	1	15.0
	Thai, Northern	2	6.0
	Thai, Southern	1	4.5
Tunisia	Arabic, Tunisian Spoken	1	11.2
Turkey	Turkish	8	70.9
	Kurdish, Northern	9	20.2
Turkmenistan	Turkmen	4	7.6
Uganda	Ganda	1	4.1
Ukraine	Ukrainian	9	34.9
United Kingdom	English	101	335.5
Uzbekistan	*Uzbek*	14	27.0
	Uzbek, Northern	6	24.0
Vietnam	Vietnamese	3	67.8
Yemen	Arabic, Sanaani Spoken	1	7.6
	Arabic, Ta'izzi-Adeni Spoken	2	7.1
Zambia	Bemba	2	4.1
Zimbabwe	Shona	3	10.7

BUILDINGS, BRIDGES, AND TUNNELS

100 Tallest Buildings in the World

Source: Phorio, phorio.com; Council on Tall Buildings and Urban Habitat (CTBUH), Illinois Inst. of Technology, www.ctbuh.org

Structures under construction and topped out architecturally are denoted by an asterisk (*). Year in parentheses is date of completion or projected completion. Only buildings that are completed or under construction and topped out as of Oct. 1, 2015, are included here. Height is generally measured from the lowest significant open-air pedestrian entrance to the architectural top, including penthouses, spires, and other decorative features that are an integral part of the design. Stories generally counted from street level. NA = Not available.

Building	Ht. (ft)	Stories
Burj Khalifa, Dubai, United Arab Emirates (2010)	2,717	163
Shanghai Tower, Shanghai, China (2015)	2,073	128
Makkah Royal Clock Tower Hotel, Mecca, Saudi Arabia (2012)	1,972	120
*Ping An Finance Center, Shenzhen, China (2016)	1,965	115
*Goldin Finance 117, Tianjin, China (2016)	1,957	128
One World Trade Center, New York, NY, U.S. (2014)	1,776	94
*Guangzhou CTF Finance Centre, Guangzhou, China (2016)	1,739	111
Taipei 101, Taipei, Taiwan (2004)	1,667	101
Shanghai World Financial Center, Shanghai, China (2008)	1,614	101
International Commerce Centre, Hong Kong, China (2010)	1,588	108
Petronas Twin Tower I, Kuala Lumpur, Malaysia (1998)	1,483	88
Petronas Twin Tower II, Kuala Lumpur, Malaysia (1998)	1,483	88
Zifeng Tower, Nanjing, China (2010)	1,476	66
Willis (formerly Sears) Tower, Chicago, IL, U.S. (1974)	1,451	108
KK100, Shenzhen, China (2011)	1,449	100
Guangzhou International Finance Center, Guangzhou, China (2010)	1,439	103
*Wuhan Center Tower, Wuhan, China (2016)	1,437	88
*Marina 101, Dubai, UAE (2015)	1,399	101
432 Park Avenue, New York, NY, U.S. (2015)	1,397	85
Trump International Hotel & Tower, Chicago, IL, U.S. (2009)	1,389	98
Jin Mao Tower, Shanghai, China (1999)	1,380	88
Princess Tower, Dubai, UAE (2012)	1,356	101
Al Hamra Tower, Kuwait City, Kuwait (2011)	1,354	80
Two International Finance Centre, Hong Kong, China (2003)	1,352	88
23 Marina, Dubai, UAE (2012)	1,287	88
CITIC Plaza, Guangzhou, China (1996)	1,280	80
*Capital Market Authority Tower, Riyadh, Saudi Arabia (2015)	1,263	76
Shun Hing Square, Shenzhen, China (1996)	1,260	69
*Eton Place Dalian Tower 1, Dalian, China (2015)	1,257	80
Burj Mohammed Bin Rashid, Abu Dhabi, UAE (2014)	1,251	88
Empire State Building, New York, NY, U.S. (1931)	1,250	102
Elite Residence, Dubai, UAE (2012)	1,248	87
Central Plaza, Hong Kong, China (1992)	1,227	78
*Federation Towers-Vostok Tower, Moscow, Russia (2015)	1,226	95
*Dalian International Trade Center, Dalian, China (2016)	1,214	86
Bank of China Tower, Hong Kong, China (1990)	1,205	72
Bank of America Tower, New York, NY, U.S. (2009)	1,200	55
Almas Tower, Dubai, UAE (2008)	1,181	68
JW Marriott Marquis Hotel Dubai Tower 2, Dubai, UAE (2013)	1,166	82
JW Marriott Marquis Hotel Dubai Tower 1, Dubai, UAE (2012)	1,166	82
Emirates Office Tower, Dubai, UAE (2000)	1,163	54
OKO-Residential Tower, Moscow, Russia (2015)	1,160	90
The Torch, Dubai, UAE (2011)	1,155	86
*Forum 66 Tower 1, Shenyang, China (2015)	1,150	68
The Pinnacle, Guangzhou, China (2012)	1,149	60
T&C Tower, Kaohsiung, Taiwan (1997)	1,140	85
Aon Center, Chicago, IL, U.S. (1973)	1,136	83
The Center, Hong Kong, China (1998)	1,135	73
John Hancock Center, Chicago, IL, U.S. (1969)	1,128	100
*Ahmed Abdul Rahim Al Attar Tower, Dubai, UAE (2016)	1,122	76
*ADNOC Headquarters, Abu Dhabi, UAE (2015)	1,122	76
Mercury City Tower, Moscow, Russia (2013)	1,112	75
Chongqing World Financial Center, Chongqing, China (2015)	1,112	72
Wuxi International Finance Square, Wuxi, China (2014)	1,112	68
*DAMAC Heights, Dubai, UAE (2016)	1,100	88
*Tianjin Modern City Office Tower, Tianjin, China (2016)	1,109	65
Tianjin World Financial Center, Tianjin, China (2011)	1,105	75
Shimao International Plaza, Shanghai, China (2006)	1,094	60
Rose Rayhaan by Rotana, Dubai, UAE (2007)	1,093	71
Minsheng Bank Building, Wuhan, China (2008)	1,086	68
*Ryugyong Hotel, Pyongyang, North Korea (NA)	1,083	105
China World Tower, Beijing, China (2010)	1,083	74
*Yuexiu Fortune Center Tower 1, Wuhan, China (2016)	1,083	66
*Hon Kwok City Center, Shenzhen, China (2016)	1,081	80
Keangnam Hanoi Landmark Tower, Hanoi, Vietnam (2012)	1,078	72
Longxi International Hotel, Jiangyin, China (2011)	1,076	72
Al Yaqoub Tower, Dubai, UAE (2013)	1,076	69
Wuxi Suning Plaza 1, Wuxi, China (2014)	1,076	67
The Index, Dubai, UAE (2010)	1,070	80
The Landmark, Abu Dhabi, UAE (2013)	1,063	72
Deji Plaza, Nanjing, China (2013)	1,063	62
*Yantai Shimao No. 1 The Harbour, Yantai, China (2015)	1,060	59
Q1 Tower, Gold Coast, Australia (2005)	1,058	78
Wenzhou Trade Center, Wenzhou, China (2011)	1,056	68
Burj Al Arab, Dubai, UAE (1999)	1,053	56
Nina Tower, Hong Kong, China (2006)	1,051	80
*Sinar Mas Center 1, Shanghai, China (2016)	1,048	66
Chrysler Building, New York, NY, U.S. (1930)	1,046	77
*Global City Square, Guangzhou, China (2016)	1,046	67
New York Times Tower, New York, NY, U.S. (2007)	1,046	52
HHHR Tower, Dubai, UAE (2010)	1,042	72
*Chongqing IFS T1, Chongqing, China (2016)	1,037	62
Nanjing International Youth Cultural Centre Tower, Nanjing, China (2015)	1,032	68
*MahaNakhon, Bangkok, Thailand (2016)	1,031	75
Bank of America Plaza, Atlanta, GA, U.S. (1992)	1,023	55
Moi Center Tower A, Shenyang, China (2014)	1,020	75
US Bank Tower, Los Angeles, CA, U.S. (1990)	1,018	73
Ocean Heights, Dubai, UAE (2010)	1,017	83
Menara Telekom, Kuala Lumpur, Malaysia (2001)	1,017	55
Fortune Center, Guangzhou, China (2015)	1,015	73
Pearl River Tower, Guangzhou, China (2013)	1,015	71
Emirates Tower Two, Dubai, UAE (2000)	1,014	56
Stalnaya Vershina, Moscow, Russia (2015)	1,013	72
Burj Rafal, Riyadh, Saudi Arabia (2014)	1,010	68
*Wanda Plaza 1, Kunming, China (2016)	1,008	67
*Wanda Plaza 2, Kunming, China (2016)	1,008	67
Franklin Center-North Tower, Chicago, IL, U.S. (1989)	1,007	60
One57, New York, NY, U.S. (2014)	1,005	75
Cayan Tower, Dubai, UAE (2013)	1,005	73
East Pacific Center Tower A, Shenzhen, China (2013)	1,004	85

Tallest Free-Standing Towers in the World

Source: Phorio, phorio.com; Council on Tall Buildings and Urban Habitat (CTBUH), Illinois Inst. of Technology, www.ctbuh.org
Year is date of completion or projected completion. As of Oct. 1, 2015.

Tower	Ht. (ft)	Year
Tokyo Sky Tree, Tokyo, Japan	2,080	2012
Canton Tower, Guangzhou, China	1,969	2010
CN Tower, Toronto, ON, Canada	1,815	1976
Ostankino Tower, Moscow, Russia	1,772	1967
Oriental Pearl Television Tower, Shanghai, China	1,535	1995
Milad Tower, Tehran, Iran	1,427	2008
Manara Kuala Lumpur, Kuala Lumpur, Malaysia	1,379	1996
Tianjin Radio & TV Tower, Tianjin, China	1,362	1991
Central Radio & TV Tower, Beijing, China	1,347	1992
Henan Province Radio & Television Emission Tower, Zhengzhou, China	1,273	2010
Kiev TV Tower, Kiev, Ukraine	1,263	1974
Tashkent Tower, Tashkent, Uzbekistan	1,230	1985
Liberation Tower, Kuwait City, Kuwait	1,220	1996
Alma-Ata Tower, Almaty, Kazakhstan	1,217	1982
TV Tower, Riga, Latvia	1,208	1987
Berliner Fernsehturm, Berlin, Germany	1,207	1969
Stratosphere Tower, Las Vegas, NV, U.S.	1,149	1996
Lotus Tower, Colombo, Sri Lanka	1,148	2016
West Pearl Tower, Chengdu, China	1,112	2004
Macau Tower, Macau, China	1,109	2001
Europaturm, Frankfurt, Germany	1,106	1979

Tall Buildings in Selected North American Cities

Source: Phorio, phorio.com; Council on Tall Buildings and Urban Habitat (CTBUH), Illinois Inst. of Technology, www.ctbuh.org

List includes freestanding towers and other structures that do not have stories and are not technically considered buildings. Structures still under construction as of Oct. 1, 2015, are denoted by an asterisk (*). Year in parentheses is date of completion or projected completion. Height is generally measured from the lowest significant open-air pedestrian entrance to the architectural top, including penthouses, spires, and other decorative features that are an integral part of the design. Stories generally counted from street level. NA = Not applicable/available.

Building/structure	Ht. (ft)	Stories
Atlanta, GA		
Bank of America Plaza (incl. spire), 600 Peachtree St. NE (1992)	1,023	55
SunTrust Plaza, 303 Peachtree St. NE (1993)[1]	867	60
One Atlantic Center, 1201 W. Peachtree St. (1987)	820	50
191 Peachtree Tower (1991)	770	50
Westin Peachtree Plaza, 210 Peachtree St. NW (1976)[2]	723	73
Georgia Pacific Tower, 133 Peachtree St. NE (1981)	697	51
Promenade II (incl. spire), 1230 Peachtree St. NE (1989)	691	40
AT&T Building, 675 W. Peachtree St. (1980)	677	47
Sovereign, 3344 Peachtree (2008)	665	48
1180 Peachtree (2006)	657	41
GLG Grand/Four Seasons Hotel, 75 14th St. NE (1992)	609	53
The Mansion on Peachtree, 3376 Peachtree Rd. NE (2008)	580	42
Atlantic, 270 17th St. NW (2009)	577	46
State of Georgia Building, 2 Peachtree St. NW (1967)[3]	556	44
Marriott Marquis, 265 Peachtree Center Ave. NE (1985)	554	52
Viewpoint, 855 Peachtree St. NE (2008)	501	36

(1) 902 ft incl. antenna. (2) 883 ft incl. antenna. (3) 599 ft incl. antenna.

Building/structure	Ht. (ft)	Stories
Austin, TX		
Austonian, 200 Congress Ave. (2010)	683	56
*Fairmont Austin (incl. spire), 101 Red River St. (2017)	595	36
360 Condominiums (incl. spire), 360 Nueces St. (2008)	581	45
Frost Bank Tower, 401 N. Congress Ave. (2004)	516	33
Boston, MA		
200 Clarendon St. (1976)	790	62
Prudential Tower, 800 Boylston St. (1964)[1]	750	52
*Millennium Tower, Washington St. (2016)	685	55
Federal Reserve Bldg., 600 Atlantic Ave. (1978)	604	32
BNY Mellon Center at One Boston Place, 201 Washington St. (1970)	602	41
One International Place, 100 Oliver St. (1987)	600	46
100 Federal St. (1971)	591	37
One Financial Center, 10 Dewey Square (1984)	590	46
111 Huntington Ave. (2002)	564	36
Two International Place (1993)	538	35
One Post Office Square (1981)	525	40
1 Federal St. (1975)	520	38
Exchange Place, 53 State St. (1984)	510	39
Sixty State St. (1977)	509	38
1 Beacon St. (1972)	507	36
State Street Financial Center (incl. spire), 1 Lincoln St. (2003)	503	36
28 State St. (1970)	500	40

(1) 920 ft incl. antenna.

Building/structure	Ht. (ft)	Stories
Burnaby, BC, Canada		
*Solo District-Altus (2016)	602	48
*4670 Assembly Way (2018)	535	57
Sovereign, 4509 Kingsway (2014)	511	45
Calgary, AB, Canada		
*Brookfield Place Tower One, 225 6th Ave. (2018)	810	56
The Bow, 510 Centre St. (2012)	779	57
*Telus Sky (2018)	729	59
Petro Canada Centre West Tower, 150 6th Ave. SW (1984)	705	53
Eighth Avenue Place East Tower, 8th Ave. and 5th St. SW (2011)	696	49
Bankers Hall West Tower, 888 3rd St. SW (2000)	645	50
Bankers Hall East Tower, 855 2nd St. SW (1989)	645	50
Calgary Tower, 101 9th Ave. SW (1967)	626	NA
Centennial Place 1 (incl. spire), 520 3rd Ave. SW (2010)	599	40
TransCanada Tower, 450 1st St. SW (2001)	581	38
Canterra Tower, 400 3rd Ave. SW (1988)	580	46
Eighth Avenue Place West Tower, 8th Ave. and 5th St. SW (2014)	580	40
Jamieson Place (incl. spires), 302 4th Ave. SW (2009)	568	38
First Canadian Centre, 350 7th Ave. SW (1982)	547	41
Western Canadian Place-North Tower, 707 6th St. SW (1983)	538	41
Canada Trust, Calgary Eatons Centre, 421 7th Ave. SW (1991)	530	40
*City Centre I, 339 2nd Ave. SW (2015)	530	36
Scotia Centre, 700 2nd St. SW (1976)	509	42
Nexen Building, 801 7th Ave. SW (1982)	500	37
Charlotte, NC		
Bank of America Corporate Center, 100 N. Tryon St. (1992)	871	60
Duke Energy Center, 534 S. Tryon St. (2010)	786	48
Hearst Tower, 214 N. Tryon St. (2002)	659	47
One Wells Fargo Center, 301 S. College St. (1988)	588	42
The Vue, 400 W. 5th St. (2010)	574	50
Bank of America Plaza, 101 S. Tryon St. (1974)	503	40
Chicago, IL		
Willis (fmr. Sears) Tower, 233 S. Wacker Dr. (1974)[1]	1,451	108
Trump International Hotel & Tower (incl. spire), 401 N. Wabash Ave. (2009)	1,389	98
Aon Center, 200 E. Randolph St. (1973)	1,136	83
John Hancock Center, 875 N. Michigan Ave. (1969)[2]	1,128	100
Franklin Center-North Tower (incl. spires), 227 W. Monroe St. (1989)	1,007	60
Two Prudential Plaza (incl. spire), 180 N. Stetson Ave. (1990)	995	64
311 S. Wacker Dr. (1990)	961	65
900 N. Michigan Ave. (1989)	871	66
Aqua, 225 N. Columbus Dr. (2009)	859	86
Water Tower Place, 845 N. Michigan Ave. (1976)	859	74
Chase Tower, 21 S. Clark St. (1969)	850	60
Park Tower, 800 N. Michigan Ave. (2000)	844	68
The Legacy at Millennium Park, 21-39 S. Wabash (2010)	818	73
300 N. LaSalle (2009)	785	60
3 First National Plaza, 70 W. Madison St. (1981)	767	57
Chicago Title & Trust Center, 161 N. Clark St. (1992)	756	50
Blue Cross HQ, 300 E. Randolph St. (2010)	744	54
*River Point, 444 W. Lake St. (2017)	732	50
Olympia Centre, 737 N. Michigan Ave. (1986)	731	63
One Museum Park, 1215 S. Prairie Ave. (2009)	726	62
AMA Plaza, 330 N. Wabash Ave. (1973)	695	52
Waldorf Astoria Chicago, 940 N. Rush St. (2009)	686	60
111 S. Wacker Dr. (2005)	681	51
181 W. Madison St. (1990)	680	50
Hyatt Center, 71 S. Wacker Dr. (2005)	679	48
One Magnificent Mile, 980 N. Michigan Ave. (1983)	673	57
340 on the Park, 340 W. Randolph St. (2007)	672	64
United Bldg., 77 W. Wacker Dr. (1992)	668	49
*150 North Riverside (2017)	665	49
UBS Tower, 1 N. Wacker Dr. (2001)	652	50
Daley Center, 55 W. Washington St. (1965)	648	31
55 E. Erie St. (2004)	647	56
Lake Point Tower, 505 N. Lake Shore Dr. (1968)	645	70
River East Center, 350 E. Illinois St. (2001)	644	58
Grand Plaza I (incl. spire), 540 N. State St. (2003)	641	57
155 N. Wacker Dr. (2009)	638	45
Leo Burnett Bldg., 35 W. Wacker Dr. (1989)	635	46
The Heritage at Millennium Park, 125 N. Wabash Ave. (2005)	631	57
NBC Tower (incl. spire), 455 N. Cityfront Plaza Dr. (1989)	627	37
353 N. Clark (2009)	623	44
OneEleven, 111 W. Wacker Dr. (2014)	616	58
Millennium Centre, 33 W. Ontario St. (2003)	610	58
Board of Trade (incl. statue), 141 W. Jackson Blvd. (1930)	609	44
Chicago Place, 700 N. Michigan Ave. (1991)	608	49
CNA Plaza, 325 S. Wabash St. (1972)	601	44
One Prudential Plaza, 130 E. Randolph St. (1955)[3]	601	41
Heller International Tower, 500 W. Monroe St. (1992)	600	45
One Madison Plaza, 200 W. Madison St. (1982)	599	44
One Museum Park West, 201 E. Roosevelt Rd. (2010)	595	54
1000 Lake Shore Plaza (1964)	590	55
The Clare at Water Tower, 55 E. Pearson St. (2008)	589	52
Citigroup Center, 500 W. Madison St. (1987)	588	42
*Optima Chicago Center II, 220 E. Illinois St. (2018)	587	57
The Park Monroe, 65 E. Monroe St. (1972)	583	49
Crain Communications Bldg., 150 N. Michigan Ave. (1983)	582	41
North Pier Apts., 474 N. Lake Shore Dr. (1990)	581	61
Citadel Center, 131 S. Dearborn St. (2003)	580	39
The Fordham, 25 E. Superior St. (2003)	574	52
190 S. LaSalle St. (1987)	573	40

Building/structure	Ht. (ft)	Stories
One South Dearborn (2005)	571	39
Onterie Center, 446 E. Ontario St. (1986)	570	58
Loews North Park Drive, 455 North Park Dr. (2015)	569	51
Chicago Temple, 77 W. Washington St. (1924)	568	23
Palmolive Building (incl. beacon), 919 N. Michigan Ave. (1929)	565	37
Marina City I, 300 N. State St. (1964)	562	61
Marina City II, 301 N. Dearborn St. (1964)	562	61
Kluczynski Federal Building, 230 S. Dearborn St. (1975)	562	42
Huron Plaza Apts., 30 E. Huron St. (1983)	560	56
Boeing International Headquarters, 100 N. Riverside Plz. (1990)	560	36
The Parkshore, 195 N. Harbor Dr. (1991)	556	56
North Harbor Tower, 175 N. Harbor Dr. (1988)	556	55
Civic Opera Bldg., 20 N. Wacker Dr. (1929)	555	45
Streeter Place, 351 E. Ohio St. (2009)	554	55
Harbor Point, 155 N. Harbor Dr. (1975)	554	54
Newberry Plaza, 1000 N. State St. (1974)	553	53
Michigan Plaza South, 205 N. Michigan Ave. (1985)	553	46
30 N. LaSalle St. (1975)	553	44
Pittsfield Building, 55 E. Washington St. (1927)	551	38
One S. Wacker Dr. (1982)	550	40
Park Millennium, 222 N. Columbus Dr. (2002)	544	57
AMLI River North, 401 N. Clark St. (2013)	543	49
Franklin Center-South Tower, 125 S. Franklin St. (1992)	538	35
The Pinnacle, 21 E. Huron St. (2004)	535	48
LaSalle National Bank, 135 S. LaSalle St. (1934)	535	45
Park Place Tower, 655 W. Irving Park Rd. (1971)	531	56
One N. LaSalle St. (1930)	530	48
The Elysees, 111 E. Chestnut St. (1973)	529	56
River Plaza, 405 N. Wabash St. (1977)	524	56
35 E. Wacker Drive (1927)	523	40
Kemper Building, 1 E. Wacker Dr. (1962)	522	41
Mather Tower, 75 E. Wacker Dr. (1928)	521	41
Chicago Mercantile Exchange, 10 S. Wacker Dr. (1987)	520	40
Chicago Mercantile Exchange, 30 S. Wacker Dr. (1983)	520	40
The Columbian, 1180 S. Michigan Ave. (2008)	517	47
*200 N. Michigan (2016)	517	44
191 N. Wacker Drive (2002)	516	37
401 E. Ontario St. (1990)	515	51
One Financial Place, 440 S. LaSalle St. (1985)	515	39
The Streeter, 345 E. Ohio St. (2006)	514	50
Park Tower Condominiums, 5415 N. Sheridan Rd. (1973)	513	54
600 North Lake Shore Drive-South Tower (2009)	513	47
LaSalle-Wacker Building, 221 N. LaSalle St. (1930)	512	41
Harris Bank III, 115 S. LaSalle St. (1974)	510	38
321 N. Clark St. (1987)	510	35
215 West, 215 W. Washington St. (2010)	509	50
400 E. Ohio St. (1982)	505	50
Carbide & Carbon Bldg., 230 N. Michigan Ave. (1929)	503	37
One Superior Place, 1 W. Superior St. (1999)	502	52
120 N. LaSalle St. (1992)	501	39
10 S. LaSalle St. (1986)	501	37
The Tides, 360 E. South Water St. (2008)	500	51
200 S. Wacker Drive (1981)	500	41

(1) 1,729 ft incl. antenna. (2) 1,499 ft incl. antenna. (3) 912 ft incl. antenna.

Cleveland, OH

Building/structure	Ht. (ft)	Stories
Key Tower (incl. spire), 127 Public Sq. (1991)	947	57
Terminal Tower, 50 Public Sq. (1928)[1]	708	52
200 Public Sq. (1985)	658	46
Tower at Erieview, 1301 E. 9th St. (1964)	529	40

(1) 771 ft incl. flagpole.

Columbus, OH

Building/structure	Ht. (ft)	Stories
James A. Rhodes State Office Tower, 30 E. Broad St. (1973)	624	41
Leveque-Lincoln Tower, 50 W. Broad St. (1927)	555	47
William Green Building, 30 W. Spring St. (1990)	530	33
Huntington Center, 41 S. High St. (1983)	512	37
Vern Riffe State Office Tower, 77 S. High St. (1988)	503	33

Dallas, TX

Building/structure	Ht. (ft)	Stories
Bank of America Plaza, 901 Main St. (1985)	921	72
Renaissance Tower (incl. spire), 1201 Elm St. (1974)	886	56
Comerica Bank Tower, 1717 Main St. (1987)	787	60
JPMorgan Chase Tower, 2200 Ross Ave. (1987)	738	55
Fountain Place, 1445 Ross Ave. (1986)	720	58
Trammel Crow Center, 2001 Ross Ave. (1984)	686	50
1700 Pacific Ave. (1983)	655	50
Thanksgiving Tower, 1600 Pacific Ave. (1982)	645	50
Energy Plaza, 1601 Bryan St. (1983)	629	49
Elm Place, 1401 Elm St. (1965)	628	52
Gables Republic Tower (incl. spire), 300 N. Ervay (1954)	602	36
Republic Center Tower II, 325 N. St. Paul (1964)	598	50
One AT&T Plaza, 208 S. Akard St. (1984)	580	37
Ross Tower, 500 N. Akard St. (1984)	579	45
Museum Tower, 2112 Flora St. (2013)	560	42
Cityplace Center East, 2711 N. Haskell Ave. (1989)	560	42
Reunion Tower, 300 Reunion Blvd. (1976)	560	NA
Sheraton Dallas Hotel Center Tower, 400 Olive St. (1959)	550	42
Mercantile Bldg. (incl. spire), 1700 Main St. (1943)	523	31
Bryan Tower, 2001 Bryan St. (1973)	512	40

Denver, CO

Building/structure	Ht. (ft)	Stories
Republic Plaza, 330 17th St. (1984)	714	56
1801 California St. (1982)	709	52
Wells Fargo Center, 1700 Lincoln Ave. (1983)	698	50
Four Seasons Hotel and Private Residences, 1111 14th St. (2010)	639	45
*1144 Fifteenth (2018)	617	40
1999 Broadway (1985)	544	43
707 17th St. (1981)	522	42
555 17th St. (1978)	507	40

Detroit, MI

Building/structure	Ht. (ft)	Stories
Marriott Hotel, Renaissance Center I (1977)[1]	727	70
One Detroit Center, 500 Woodward Ave. (1991)	619	43
Penobscot Building, 633 Griswold Ave. (1928)[2]	565	47
Renaissance Center 100 Tower (1976)	508	39
Renaissance Center 200 Tower (1976)	508	39
Renaissance Center 300 Tower (1976)	508	39
Renaissance Center 400 Tower (1976)	508	39

(1) 755 ft incl. antenna. (2) 665 ft incl. antenna.

Fort Worth, TX

Building/structure	Ht. (ft)	Stories
Burnett Plaza, 801 Cherry St. (1983)	567	40
D.R. Horton Tower, 301 Commerce St. (1984)	547	38
Carter Burgess Plaza, 777 Main St. (1982)	525	40

Hartford, CT

Building/structure	Ht. (ft)	Stories
City Place I, 185 Asylum St. (1980)	535	38
Travelers Tower, 26 Grove St. (1919)	527	24
Goodwin Square, 225 Asylum St. (1990)	522	30

Houston, TX

Building/structure	Ht. (ft)	Stories
JPMorganChase Tower, 600 Travis St. (1982)	1,002	75
Wells Fargo Plaza, 1000 Louisiana St. (1983)	992	71
Williams Tower, 2800 Post Oak Blvd. (1982)	901	64
Bank of America Center, 700 Louisiana St. (1983)	780	56
Texaco Heritage Plaza, 1111 Bagby St. (1987)	762	53
*609 Main at Texas (2017)	757	49
Enterprise Plaza, 1100 Louisiana St. (1980)[1]	756	55
Centerpoint Energy Plaza, 1111 Louisiana St. (1996)	741	53
1600 Smith St. (1984)	732	55
Fulbright Tower, 1301 McKinney St. (1982)	725	52
One Shell Plaza, 900 Louisiana St. (1970)[2]	714	50
1400 Smith St. (1983)	691	50
3 Allen Center, 333 Clay St. (1980)	685	50
LyondellBassell Tower, 1221 McKinney St. (1978)	678	47
First City Tower, 1001 Fannin St. (1984)	662	47
BG Group Place, 811 Main St. (2011)	632	46
San Felipe Plaza, 5847 San Felipe Blvd. (1984)	625	45
ExxonMobil Building, 800 Bell Ave. (1962)	606	44
1500 Louisiana St. (2002)	600	40
America General Center, 2929 Allen Pkwy. (1983)	590	42
Two Houston Center, 909 Fannin St. (1974)	579	40
San Jacinto Monument, La Porte (1939)	570	NA
Marathon Oil Tower, 5555 San Felipe Blvd. (1983)	562	41
Wedge International Tower, 1415 Louisiana St. (1983)	550	44
KBR Tower, 601 Jefferson St. (1973)	550	40
*2929 Weslayan (2015)	533	40
Pennzoil Place I, 700 Milam St. (1976)	523	36
Pennzoil Place II, 700 Louisiana St. (1976)	523	36
Devon Energy Center, 1200 Smith St. (1978)	521	36
RRI Energy Plaza, 1000 Main St. (2003)	518	36
Total Plaza, 1201 Louisiana St. (1971)	518	35
The Huntington, 2121 Kirby Dr. (1982)	503	34
*Market Square Tower, 777 Preston St. (2017)	502	40
El Paso Energy Building, 1010 Milam St. (1962)	502	33
One Park Place, 1500 McKinney St. (2009)	501	37
Memorial Hermann Tower, 929 Gessner Rd. (2009)	500	35

(1) 782 ft incl. antenna. (2) 999 ft incl. antenna.

Indianapolis, IN

Building/structure	Ht. (ft)	Stories
Chase Tower, 111 Monument Cir. (1990)[1]	701	49
One America Tower, 200 N. Illinois St. (1982)	533	38
One Indiana Square, 200 N. Delaware St. (1970)	504	36

(1) 811 ft incl. antenna.

Jersey City, NJ

Building/structure	Ht. (ft)	Stories
30 Hudson St. (2004)	781	42
*URL Harborside Tower 1 (2016)	700	71
*J3 (2016)	574	53

Building/structure	Ht. (ft)	Stories
101 Hudson St. (1992)	548	42
Trump Plaza I, 88 Morgan St. (2008)	532	55
Newport Tower, 525 Washington Blvd. (1990)	531	37
70 Columbus (2015)	529	50
Exchange Place Center, 10 Exchange Pl. (incl. spire) (1990)	516	32
Hudson Green East Tower, 77 Hudson St. (2009)	509	48
Hudson Green West Tower, 77 Hudson St. (2010)	501	48

Las Vegas, NV

Building/structure	Ht. (ft)	Stories
Stratosphere Tower, 2000 Las Vegas Blvd. S. (1996)	1,149	NA
*Fontainebleau Resort Hotel, 2755 Las Vegas Blvd. S. (NA)	735	63
*Resorts World Las Vegas Tower I (2018)	674	57
The Palazzo, 3339 Las Vegas Blvd. S. (2007)	642	53
Encore at Wynn Las Vegas, 3145 Las Vegas Blvd. S. (2008)	631	52
Trump International Hotel and Tower 1, 3128 Las Vegas Blvd. S. (2008)	622	64
Wynn Las Vegas, 3145 Las Vegas Blvd. S. (2005)	613	45
Cosmopolitan Casino Spa Tower, Las Vegas Blvd. and Harmon Ave. (2010)	603	52
Cosmopolitan Beach Resort Tower, Las Vegas Blvd. and Harmon Ave. (2010)	603	50
Aria Resort and Casino (2009)	600	60
Planet Hollywood Towers, 3667 Las Vegas Blvd. S. (2009)	597	50
VDARA, 2551 W. Harmon Ave. (2009)	556	55
Eiffel Tower, Paris Hotel and Casino, 3645 Las Vegas Blvd. S. (1998)	540	NA
Mandarin Oriental Hotel Las Vegas, 3750 Las Vegas Blvd. S. (2009)	539	47
New York, New York Hotel and Casino, 3790 Las Vegas Blvd. S. (1997)	529	48
Palms Place, 4321 W. Flamingo Rd. (2008)	518	50
Bellagio Hotel and Casino, 3600 Las Vegas Blvd. S. (1998)	508	36
Sky Las Vegas, 2780 Las Vegas Blvd. S. (2007)	500	45

Los Angeles, CA

Building/structure	Ht. (ft)	Stories
*Wilshire Grand Center (2017)	1,100	73
US Bank Tower, 633 W. 5th St. (1990)	1,018	73
Aon Center, 707 Wilshire Blvd. (1974)	858	62
Two California Plaza, 350 S. Grand Ave. (1992)	750	52
Gas Company Tower, 555 W. 5th St. (1991)	749	52
Bank of America Plaza, 333 South Hope St. (1975)	735	55
777 Tower, 777 S. Figueroa St. (1991)	725	53
Wells Fargo Tower, 333 S. Grand Ave. (1983)	723	54
Figueroa at Wilshire, 601 S. Figueroa St. (1989)	717	52
City National Tower, 555 S. Flower St. (1971)	699	52
Paul Hastings Tower, 515 S. Flower St. (1971)	699	52
*Oceanside Plaza Tower I (2018)	677	49
Ritz Carlton/Marriott Marquis Los Angeles, 900 W. Olympic Blvd. (2010)	667	54
*Metropolis Tower D (2019)	647	58
Citigroup Center, 444 S. Flower St. (1979)	625	48
611 Place, 611 W. 6th St. (1967)	620	42
KPMG Tower, 355 S. Grand Ave. (1984)	606	45
One California Plaza, 300 S. Grand Ave. (1985)	578	42
Century Plaza Tower 1, 2029 Century Park East (1973)	571	44
Century Plaza Tower 2, 2049 Century Park East (1973)	571	44
Ernst & Young, LLP Plaza, 725 S. Figueroa St. (1986)	534	41
AIG-SunAmerica Ctr., 1999 Ave. of the Stars (1989)	533	39
*Oceanwide Plaza Tower II (2018)	530	40
*Oceanwide Plaza Tower III (2018)	530	40
TCW Tower, 865 S. Figueroa St. (1990)	517	37
Union Bank Plaza, 445 S. Figueroa St. (1968)	516	40
10 Universal City Plaza (1984)	506	36

Mexico City, Mexico

Building/structure	Ht. (ft)	Stories
*Torre Reforma, Paseo de la Reforma 483 (2016)	800	57
*Punto Chapultepec, Reforma 509 (2018)	780	59
*Torre BBVA Bancomer, Paseo de la Reforma 506 (2015)	771	50
*Torre Paradox, Av. Santa Fe 562 (2017)	768	62
Torre Mayor, Paseo de la Reforma 505 (2003)	738	55
Torre Ejecutiva Pemex, Marina Nacional 329 Col. Huasteca (1984)	693	51
Torre Altus, Paseo de los Laureles 416 (1999)	640	44
Torre Latino Americana (incl. spire), Eje Central Lazaro Cardenas 2 (1956)	597	45
*Torre Cuarzo, Paseo de la Reforma 26 (2016)	591	40
*Miyana Tower 1 (2017)	577	43
World Trade Center, Montecito 38 Col. Napoles (1972)	565	50
*Siroco Elite Residences, Av. Santa Fe 482 (2015)	561	43
*Torre Punta Reforma, Paseo de la Reforma 180 (2015)	558	37
Peninsula Tower, Av. Santa Fe 1240 (2014)	539	50
Arcos Torre II, Paseo de los Tamarindos 400 (2008)	529	35
Arcos Torre I, Paseo de los Tamarindos 400 (1997)	529	35
*Torre Diana, Rio Lerma 232 (2016)	519	33

Miami, FL

Building/structure	Ht. (ft)	Stories
*Panorama Tower, 1101 Brickell Ave. (2017)	822	80
Four Seasons Hotel & Tower, 1441 Brickell Ave. (2003)	789	64
Wachovia Financial Ctr., 200 S. Biscayne Blvd. (1983)	764	55
*One Thousand Museum, 1000 Biscayne Blvd. (2017)	706	60
Marquis, 1100 Biscayne Blvd. (2009)	679	63
Met 2 Office Tower, 200 SE 3rd St. (2010)	655	47
900 Biscayne Bay, 900 Biscayne Blvd. (2008)	650	63
*Echo Brickell, 1451 Brickell Ave. (2017)	637	60
*Brickell CityCentre Office Tower 3 (2018)	634	45
Mint at Riverfront, 90 SW 3rd St. (2009)	631	55
Infinity at Brickell, 60 W. 13th St. (2008)	630	52
Miami Tower, 100 SE 2nd St. (1987)	625	47
Marinablue, 888 Biscayne Blvd. (2007)	615	57
Plaza on Brickell Tower I, 901 Brickell Ave. (2007)	610	56
Epic Residences & Hotel, 300 Biscayne Blvd. Way (2009)	601	54
*One Paraiso, 620 NE 31st St. (2017)	601	53
*SLS Brickell, 1300 S. Miami Ave. (2016)	599	52
*SLS Lux Brickell, 801 S. Miami Ave. (2016)	595	57
Icon Brickell North Tower, 495 Brickell Ave. (2008)	586	58
Icon Brickell South Tower, 495 Brickell Ave. (2008)	586	58
Ten Museum Park, 1040 Biscayne Blvd. (2007)	585	50
*Solitair Brickell, 80 SW 8th St. (2016)	555	48
Paramount at Edgewater Square, 2066 N. Bayshore Dr. (2009)	555	47
50 Biscayne Blvd. (2007)	554	55
Quantum on the Bay South Tower, 1900 N. Bayshore Dr. (2008)	554	51
*Biscayne Beach, 701 NE 29th St. (2016)	550	51
*Brickell Heights North Tower, 850 S. Miami Ave. (2016)	549	52
*Paraiso Bay Tower 1, 600 NE 31st St. (2017)	548	55
*Paraiso Bay Tower 2, 600 NE 31st St. (2017)	548	55
*1010 Brickell (2017)	548	50
*Met Square, 340 SE 3rd St. (2017)	545	46
Opera Tower, 1750 N. Bayshore Dr. (2007)	543	56
Vizcayne North Tower, 244 Biscayne Blvd. (2008)	538	49
Vizcayne South Tower, 244 Biscayne Blvd. (2008)	538	49
Quantum on the Bay North Tower, 1900 N. Bayshore Dr. (2008)	536	44
*Aria on the Bay, 1770 N. Bayshore Dr. (2017)	535	50
*Brickell Heights South Tower, 850 S. Miami Ave. (2016)	529	52
Jade at Brickell Bay, 1331 Brickell Bay Dr. (2004)	528	49
Plaza on Brickell Tower II, 901 Brickell Ave. (2007)	525	48
*North Squared, BrickellCityCentre (2018)	522	48
Santa Maria, 1643 Brickell Ave. (1997)	520	51
*Rise, Brickell CityCentre (2015)	520	45
*EAST, Miami, Brickell CityCentre, 89 SE 8th St. (2015)	516	41
The Ivy, 90-95 SW 3rd St. (2008)	512	45
Stephen P. Clark Center, 111 NW 1st St. (1985)	510	28
BrickellHouse, 1300 Brickell Bay Dr. (2014)	509	48
*Reach, Brickell CityCentre (2015)	503	44
Met 2 Marriott Marquis, 200 SE 3rd St. (2010)	502	41
Wind, 330 S. Miami Ave. (2008)	501	41
*Paraiso Bayviews (2018)	500	44
1450 Brickell (2010)	500	34

Milwaukee, WI

Building/structure	Ht. (ft)	Stories
U.S. Bank Center, 777 E. Wisconsin Ave. (1973)	601	42
*Northwestern Mutual Tower (2017)	550	33
100 E. Wisconsin Ave. (1989)	549	37

Minneapolis, MN

Building/structure	Ht. (ft)	Stories
IDS Tower, 80 S. 8th St. (1973)[1]	792	55
Capella Tower, 225 S. 6th St. (1992)	776	56
Wells Fargo Center, 90 S. 7th St. (1988)	775	56
33 South 6th St. (1983)	668	52
Campbell Mithun Tower, 222 S. 9th St. (1985)	582	42
US Bank Plaza I, 200 S. 6th St. (1981)	561	40
RBC Plaza, 60 S. 6th St. (1992)	539	40
Fifth Street Towers II, 150 S. 5th St. (1988)	504	36

(1) 910 ft incl. antenna.

Monterrey, Mexico

Building/structure	Ht. (ft)	Stories
*Torre Koi, San Pedro Garza Garcia (2016)	906	67
*Metropolitan Center Torre III, San Pedro Garza Garcia (2016)	689	50
*Pabellon M (2015)	682	47
Torre Avalanz, San Pedro Garza Garcia (2000)	597	43
*Metropolitan Center Torre II, San Pedro Garza Garcia (2016)	594	52
Centro de Gobierno Plaza Civica (2010)	591	36

Building/structure	Ht. (ft)	Stories
Torre Helicon, San Pedro Garza Garcia (2012)	512	33

Montréal, QC, Canada

Building/structure	Ht. (ft)	Stories
1250 Boulevard Rene Levesque (incl. spire) (1992)	743	47
1000 Rue de la Gauchetiere (1992)	673	51
Tour de la Bourse, 800 Place Victoria (1964)	624	47
1 Place Villa Marie (1962)	616	43
La Tour CIBC, 1155 Rene Levesque Blvd. (1962)[1]	604	45
*L'Avenue (2017)	574	50
Montreal Tower (1987)	574	NA
*Tour Avenue des Canadiens (2016)	548	50
Tour McGill College, 1501 McGill College (1992)	519	38

(1) 740 ft incl. antenna.

New Orleans, LA

Building/structure	Ht. (ft)	Stories
One Shell Square, 701 Poydras St. (1972)	697	51
CapitalOne Center, 201 St. Charles Ave. (1985)	645	53
Plaza Tower, 1001 Howard Ave. (1969)	531	45
Energy Centre, 1100 Poydras St. (1984)	530	39

New York, NY

Building/structure	Ht. (ft)	Stories
One World Trade Center (incl. spire) (2014)	1,776	94
*Central Park Tower, 217 West 57th St. (2019)	1,550	99
*111 W. 57th St. (2017)	1,438	80
432 Park Avenue (2015)	1,397	85
*30 Hudson Yards (2019)	1,268	73
Empire State Building, 350 5th Ave. (1931)[1]	1,250	102
Bank of America (incl. spire), One Bryant Park (2009)	1,200	55
*Three World Trade Center, 175 Greenwich St. (2018)	1,079	80
*53 West 53rd (2018)	1,050	77
Chrysler Building. (incl. spire), 405 Lexington Ave. (1930)	1,046	77
New York Times Tower (incl. spire), 620 8th Ave. (2007)	1,046	52
*35 Hudson Yards (2018)	1,009	72
One57, 157 W. 57th St. (2014)	1,005	75
*One Manhattan West, 401 9th Ave. (2019)	995	69
4 World Trade Center, 150 Greenwich St. (2014)	977	65
70 Pine (incl. spire) (1932)	952	67
*220 Central Park South (2017)	950	66
*30 Park Place, 99 Church St. (2016)	937	67
The Trump Bldg., 40 Wall St. (1930)	927	71
Citigroup Center, 153 E. 53rd St. (1977)	915	59
*15 Hudson Yards (2018)	914	70
*425 Park Avenue (2018)	893	42
*10 Hudson Yards (2016)	878	50
New York by Gehry at Eight Spruce Street (2011)	870	76
Trump World Tower, 845 UN Plaza (2001)	861	72
Comcast Building, 30 Rockefeller Center (1933)	850	70
*56 Leonard Street (2016)	821	57
Cityspire Center, 150 W. 56th St. (1987)	814	75
28 Liberty (1961)	813	60
4 Times Square (1999)[2]	809	48
MetLife Building, 200 Park Ave. (1963)	808	59
Bloomberg Tower, 731 Lexington Ave. (2005)[3]	806	54
*101 Murray Street (2018)	792	58
Woolworth Building, 233 Broadway (1913)	792	57
*520 Park Avenue (2017)	781	52
*55 Hudson Yards (2017)	780	51
*50 West, 50 West St. (2017)	778	64
*45 East 22nd Street (2017)	778	63
1 Worldwide Plaza, 935 8th Ave. (1989)	778	47
Carnegie Hall Tower, 152 W. 57th St. (1991)	757	60
383 Madison Avenue (2001)	755	47
1717 Broadway (2013)	753	67
AXA Center, 787 7th Ave. (1985)	752	51
One Penn Plaza, 250 W. 34th St. (1972)	750	57
1251 Avenue of the Americas (1971)	750	54
Time Warner Center North Tower, 10 Columbus Cir. (2004)	749	55
Time Warner Center South Tower, 10 Columbus Cir. (2004)	749	55
Goldman Sachs HQ, 200 Murray St. (2010)	749	44
60 Wall Street (1989)	745	55
One Astor Plaza, 1515 Broadway (1972)	745	54
One Liberty Plaza, 165 Broadway (1972)	743	54
7 World Trade Center (2006)	743	49
Twenty Exchange, 20 Exchange Place (1931)	741	57
Three World Financial Center, 200 Vesey St. (1986)	739	51
1540 Broadway (incl. spire) (1990)	732	42
Times Square Tower, 1459 Broadway (2004)	726	47
Metropolitan Tower, 142 W. 57th St. (1985)	716	68
*252 E. 57th Street (2017)	715	59
*100 E. 53rd Street (2017)	712	66
JPMorganChase World Headquarters, 270 Park Ave. (1960)	707	52
General Motors Building, 767 5th Ave. (1968)	705	50
*3 Manhattan West, 401 W. 31st St. (2017)	702	64
*118 Fulton Street (2018)	700	63
*One Manhattan Square, 250 South St. (2018)	700	56
Metropolitan Life Tower, 1 Madison Ave. (1909)	700	50
500 5th Avenue (1931)	697	59
Americas Tower, 1177 Ave. of the Americas (1992)	692	48
Solow Building, 9 W. 57th St. (1974)	689	49
HSBC Bank Building, 140 Broadway (1967)	688	52
55 Water Street (1972)	687	53
277 Park Avenue (1963)	687	50
*The Beekman Hotel & Residences, 5 Beekman St. (2016)	687	47
1585 Broadway (1989)	685	42
Random House/Park Imperial, 1739 Broadway (2003)	684	52
Four Seasons Hotel, 57 E. 57th St. (1993)	682	52
*Sky, 605 W. 42nd St. (2015)	676	61
McGraw-Hill Building, 1221 Ave. of the Americas (1972)	674	51
Barclay Tower, 10 Barclay St. (2007)	673	56
One Grand Central Place, 60 E. 42nd St. (1930)	673	53
Citigroup Building, 1 Court Sq., Queens (1990)	673	50
*One Seaport, 161 Maiden Ln. (2018)	670	60
Paramount Plaza, 1633 Broadway (1970)	670	48
Trump Tower, 725 5th Ave. (1982)	664	58
Bank of New York Building, 1 Wall St. (1932)	654	50
Silver Towers East, 600 W. 42nd St. (2009)	653	58
Silver Towers West, 600 W. 42nd St. (2009)	653	58
599 Lexington Avenue (1986)	653	51
712 5th Avenue (1990)	650	53
Chanin Building, 122 E. 42nd St. (1929)	649	56
245 Park Avenue (1967)	648	47
550 Madison Avenue (1983)	647	37
*28 on 28th, 42-12 28th St., Queens (2017)	646	58
Two World Financial Center, 225 Liberty St. (1986)	645	44
1095 Avenue of the Americas (1974)	645	43
570 Lexington Avenue (1931)	642	50
1 New York Plaza, 1 Water St. (1969)	640	50
1 MiMA Tower, 440 W. 42nd St. (2011)	638	63
1 Dag Hammarskjold Plaza, 885 2nd Ave. (1972)	637	48
345 Park Avenue (1968)	634	44
Langham Place, 400 5th Ave. (2010)	632	58
Mercantile Bldg., 10 E. 40th St. (1929)	632	48
W New York Downtown Hotel & Residences, 123 Washington St. (2010)	631	57
Grace Plaza, 1114 Ave. of the Americas (1972)	630	50
Home Insurance Plaza, 59 Maiden Ln. (1966)	630	44
101 Park Avenue (1982)	629	49
Central Park Place, 301 W. 57th St. (1988)	628	56
888 7th Avenue (1971)	628	45
Burlington House, 1345 Ave. of the Americas (1969)	625	50
Waldorf Astoria New York, 301 Park Ave. (1931)	625	47
Trump Palace, 200 E. 69th St. (1991)	623	54
One Madison Park, 20 E. 23rd St. (2010)	621	51
Olympic Tower, 645 5th Ave. (1976)	620	51
425 Fifth Avenue (2003)	618	55
The Epic, 125 W. 31st St. (2007)	615	58
919 3rd Avenue (1970)	615	47
Tower 49, 12 E. 49th St. (1985)	615	44
750 7th Avenue (incl. spire) (1989)	615	35
New York Life, 51 Madison Ave. (1928)	615	33
Eventi, 851 6th Ave. (2010)	614	46
*551 10th Avenue (2016)	612	52
Credit Lyonnais Building, 1301 Ave. of the Americas (1964)	609	46
Baccarat Hotel & Residences, 20 West 53rd St. (2014)	605	47
The Orion, 350 W. 42nd St. (2006)	604	58
590 Madison Avenue (1983)	603	41
250 W. 55th Street (2013)	602	40
Eleven Times Square, 644 8th Ave. (2011)	601	40
1166 Avenue of the Americas (1974)	600	44
Hawthorn Park, 160 W. 62nd St. (2014)	598	54
*43-22 Queens St., Queens (NA)	598	54
Hearst Magazine Tower, 959 8th Ave. (2006)	597	46
*Avalon Willoughby West, 100 Willoughby St., Brooklyn (2015)	596	57
3 Lincoln Center, 160 W. 66th St. (1993)	595	60
Celanese Building, 1211 Ave. of the Americas (1973)	592	45
The London NYC, 151 W. 54th St. (1990)	590	54
388 Bridge Street, Brooklyn (2014)	590	51
Thurgood Marshall U.S. Courthouse, 505 Pearl St. (1936)	590	37
Museum Tower Apts., 21 W. 53rd St. (1985)	589	52
The Millenium Hilton Hotel, 55 Church St. (1992)	588	58
Sky House, 11 E. 29th St. (2008)	588	55
Time-Life Building, 1271 Ave. of the Americas (1959)	587	48
Jacob K. Javits Federal Bldg., 26 Federal Plz. (1967)	587	41
W Times Square, 1567 Broadway (2000)	584	53
Trump International Hotel & Tower, 15 Columbus Cir. (1970)	583	44
Stevens Tower, 1185 Ave. of the Americas (1971)	580	42
Municipal Building, 1 Centre St. (1914)	580	34

Building/structure	Ht. (ft)	Stories
520 Madison Avenue (1981)	577	43
One World Financial Center, 200 Liberty St. (1985)	577	37
Merchandise Mart, 41 Madison Ave. (1973)	576	42
Park Avenue Plaza, 55 E. 52nd St. (1981)	575	44
300 Madison Avenue (2003)	575	38
Lehman Building, 745 7th Ave. (2001)	575	38
One Financial Square, 33 Old Slip (1987)	575	37
Marriott Marquis Times Square, 1531 Broadway (1985)	574	50
299 Park Avenue (1967)	574	42
5 Times Square, 590 7th Ave. (2002)	574	40
Socony Mobil Building, 150 E. 42nd St. (1956)	572	42
1290 Avenue of the Americas (1963)	571	43
780 3rd Avenue (1983)	570	49
600 3rd Avenue (1971)	570	42
*590 Fulton St., Brooklyn (2016)	568	51
450 Lexington Avenue (1991)	568	38
Paramount Tower, 240 E. 39th St. (1998)	567	51
230 Park Avenue (1928)	565	35
*The Hub, 333 Schermerhorn St., Brooklyn (2016)	563	52
New York Palace Hotel, 455 Madison Ave. (1980)	563	51
Continental Bank Building, 30 Broad St. (1932)	562	48
Park Avenue Tower, 65 E. 55th St. (1986)	561	36
Nelson Tower, 450 7th Ave. (1931)	560	46
Sherry-Netherland, 781 5th Ave. (1927)	560	40
623 5th Avenue (1990)	560	36
South Park Tower, 124 W. 60th St. (1986)	558	51
100 UN Plaza, 327 E. 48th St. (1986)	557	52
Continental Can, 633 3rd Ave. (1962)	557	39
3 Park Avenue (1975)	556	42
Continental Center, 180 Maiden Ln. (1983)	555	41
Sperry & Hutchinson Bldg., 330 Madison Ave. (1964)	555	41
Equitable Building, 120 Broadway (1915)	555	38
Reuters Building, 3 Times Sq. (2001)[4]	555	30
Tower 111, 885 6th Ave. (2011)	554	48
The Belvedere, 10 E. 29th St. (1999)	554	48
Inmont Bldg., 1133 Ave. of the Americas (1970)	552	45
Downtown by Philippe Starck, 15 Broad St. (1927)	551	42
Hyatt Times Square, 135 W. 45th St. (2013)	550	53
Biltmore Tower, 267 W. 47th St. (2003)	550	51
Unisys Building, 605 3rd Ave. (1963)	550	44
2 Grand Central Tower, 140 E. 45th St. (1982)	550	43
The Tower at 15 Central Park West (2008)	550	35
AT&T Long Lines Building, 33 Thomas St. (1974)	550	29
50 UN Plaza, 345 E. 46th St. (2015)	548	44
Bankers Trust, 33 E. 48th St. (1971)	547	41
The Corinthian, 330 E. 38th St. (1988)	546	55
Transportation Building, 225 Broadway (1928)	546	44
MillenniumTower, 101 W. 67th St. (1995)	545	54
The Galleria, 117 E. 57th St. (1975)	544	56
2 Gold Street (2005)	543	51
220 Riverside Blvd. at Trump Place (2003)	542	49
17 State Street (1988)	542	41
Grand Central Plaza, 622 3rd Ave. (1973)	542	38
*626 1st Avenue West Tower (2016)	540	46
New York Telephone, 375 Pearl St. (1976)	540	42
1285 Avenue of the Americas (1960)	540	42
Ritz Tower, 109 E. 57th St. (1925)	540	41
14 Wall (1912)	540	29
Tribeca Tower, 105 Duane St. (1990)	537	53
Lefcourt Colonial Building, 295 Madison Ave. (1929)	537	45
*175 W. 60th Street (2016)	533	48
1700 Broadway (1969)	533	41
Westin Hotel New York, 43rd St. and 8th Ave. (2002)	532	45
515 Park Avenue (1999)	532	43
DuMont Building, 515 Madison Ave. (1931)	532	42
The Brooklyner, 111 Lawrence St., Brooklyn (2010)	531	52
One East River Place, 525 E. 72nd St. (1989)	530	49
*21 West End Avenue (2016)	529	45
The Metropolis, 150 E. 44th St. (2001)	528	50
William Beaver House, 15 William St. (2010)	528	47
North American Plywood, 800 3rd Ave. (1972)	526	41
Hotel Pierre, 2 E. 61st St. (1928)	525	44
767 3rd Avenue (1980)	525	39

(1) 1,455 ft incl. antenna. (2) 1,118 ft incl. antenna. (3) 941 ft incl. antenna. (4) 659 ft incl. antenna.

Philadelphia, PA

Building/structure	Ht. (ft)	Stories
*Comcast Innovation and Technology Center, 1800 Arch St. (2018)	1,121	59
Comcast Center, 1701 JFK Blvd. (2008)	974	57
One Liberty Place (incl. spire), 1650 Market St. (1987)	945	61
Two Liberty Place (incl. spire), 1601 Chestnut St. (1989)	848	58
Mellon Bank Center, 1735 Market St. (1990)	792	54
Three Logan, 1717 Arch St. (1991)	739	55
*FMC Tower at Cira Centre South (2017)	730	49
G. Fred DiBona Jr. Building, 1901 Market St. (1990)	625	45
Commerce Square #2, 2001 Market St. (1992)	572	40
Commerce Square #1, 2005 Market St. (1990)	572	40
City Hall (incl. statue) (1901)	548	7
Residences at Ritz-Carlton, 1416 S. Penn Sq. (2009)	518	46
1818 Market St. (1974)	500	40

Pittsburgh, PA

Building/structure	Ht. (ft)	Stories
US Steel Tower, 600 Grant St. (1970)	841	64
One Mellon Bank Center, 500 Grant St. (1983)	725	54
One PPG Place (1984)	635	40
Fifth Avenue Place, 120 5th Ave. (1987)	616	32
One Oxford Centre, 301 Grant St. (1982)	615	46
Gulf Tower, 707 Grant St. (1932)	582	44
*The Tower at PNC Plaza (2015)	564	33
University of Pittsburgh Cathedral of Learning, 4200 5th Ave. (1936)	535	42
3 Mellon Bank Center, 525 Wm. Penn Way (1951)	520	41
K&L Gates Center, 210 6th Ave. (1968)	511	39

Portland, OR

Building/structure	Ht. (ft)	Stories
Wells Fargo Center, 1300 SW 5th Ave. (1973)	546	40
U.S. Bancorp Tower, 111 SW 5th Ave. (1983)	536	42
*Park Avenue West, 728 SW 9th Ave. (2015)	515	33
Koin Center, 222 SW Columbia St. (1984)	509	31

St. Louis, MO

Building/structure	Ht. (ft)	Stories
Gateway Arch (1965)	630	NA
Metropolitan Square Tower, 211 N. Broadway (1988)	593	42
AT&T Center, 900 Pine St. (1984)	588	44
Thomas F. Eagleton Federal Courthouse, 111 S. 10th St. (2000)	557	29

San Francisco, CA

Building/structure	Ht. (ft)	Stories
*Salesforce Tower, 415 Mission St. (2017)	1,070	61
Sutro Tower (1972)	977	NA
Transamerica Pyramid, 600 Montgomery St. (1972)	853	48
*181 Fremont (2017)	802	54
555 California St. (1969)	779	52
345 California Center (1986)	695	48
Millennium Tower, 301 Mission St. (2009)	645	58
One Rincon Hill South Tower, 425 First St. (2008)	605	54
101 California Street (1982)	600	48
50 Fremont Center (1985)	600	43
Chevron Tower, 575 Market St. (1975)	573	40
Four Embarcadero Center, 55 Clay St. (1984)	570	45
One Embarcadero Center, 355 Clay St. (1970)	569	45
44 Montgomery Street (1967)	565	43
Spear Tower, 1 Market St. (1976)	565	42
One Sansome Street (1984)	550	43
One Rincon Hill North Tower, 425 First St. (2014)	541	45
Shaklee Terrace Building, 444 Market St. (1982)	537	38
First Market Tower, 525 Market St. (1972)	529	38
McKesson Plaza, 1 Post St. (1969)	529	38
425 Market Street (1973)	524	38
Telsis Tower, 1 Montgomery St. (1982)	500	38

Seattle, WA

Building/structure	Ht. (ft)	Stories
Columbia Center, 701 5th Ave. (1985)	933	76
1201 Third Avenue Tower, 1201 3rd Ave. (1988)	772	55
Two Union Square, 601 Union St. (1989)	740	56
Seattle Municipal Tower, 700 5th Ave. (1990)	722	57
*The Mark, 811 5th Ave. (2017)	660	43
Safeco Plaza, 1001 4th Ave. (1969)	630	50
City Centre, 1420 5th Ave. (1989)	606	44
Space Needle, 203 6th Ave. (1962)	605	NA
Russell Investments Center, 1301 2nd Ave. (2006)	598	42
Wells Fargo Center, 999 3rd Ave. (1983)	574	47
Bank of America Fifth Ave. Plz., 800 5th Ave. (1981)	543	42
901 5th Avenue (1973)	536	41
*Amazon Tower I, 2021 7th Ave. (2016)	524	37
*Amazon Tower II, 2021 7th Ave. (2017)	521	37
*Amazon Tower III, 2021 7th Ave. (2017)	520	37
Rainier Tower, 1301 5th Ave. (1977)	514	31
Fourth & Madison Building, 915 4th Ave. (2003)	512	40
1918 8th Avenue (2009)	500	36

Sunny Isles Beach, FL

Building/structure	Ht. (ft)	Stories
*Muse, 17141 Collins Ave. (2017)	649	47
*Mansions at Acqualina, 17749 Collins Ave. (2015)	643	46
*Porsche Design Tower, 18555 Collins Ave. (2016)	641	57
*Jade Signature, 16901 Collins Ave. (2017)	636	55
Jade on the Beach Condominiums, 17001 Collins Ave. (2008)	574	51
Trump Royale, 18201 Collins Ave. (2008)	551	43
Trump Palace, 18101 Collins Ave. (2005)	551	43
Acqualina Ocean Residences, 17875 Collins Ave. (2004)	550	51
Jade Ocean, 17121 Collins Ave. (2009)	543	51

Tampa, FL

Building/structure	Ht. (ft)	Stories
Regions Building, 100 N. Tampa St. (1992)	579	42
Bank of America Plaza, 101 E. Kennedy Blvd. (1986)	577	42
One Tampa City Center, 201 N. Franklin St. (1981)	537	39
SunTrust Financial Center, 401 E. Jackson St. (1992)	525	36

Toronto, ON, Canada

Building/structure	Ht. (ft)	Stories
CN Tower, 310 Front St. West (1976)	1,815	NA
First Canadian Place, 100 King St. West (1975)[1]	978	72
Trump International Hotel & Tower (incl. spire), 325 Bay St. (2012)	908	63
Scotia Tower, 40 King St. West (1989)	902	68
Aura at College Park, 388 Yonge St. (2014)	892	78
Brookfield Place (incl. spire), 161 Bay St. (1990)	856	53
*Number One Bloor, 1 Bloor St. East (2016)	844	75
Commerce Court West, 199 Bay St. (1973)[2]	784	57
Ice Condos at York Centre 2, 16 York St. (2015)	768	67
*Harbour Plaza Residences East, 90 Harbour St. (2017)	764	66
*Eau de Soleil 1, 2183 Lake Shore Blvd. West, Etobicoke (2017)	749	66
*Ten York (2017)	735	65
*Harbour Plaza Residences West, 90 Harbour St. (2017)	735	62
TD Centre-Toronto Dominion Bank Tower, 66 Wellington St. West (1967)	730	56
Bay-Adelaide Center West Tower, 335 Bay St. (2010)	704	52
Living Shangri-La Toronto, 180 University Ave. (2012)	702	65
Ritz-Carlton Hotel and Residences, 185 Wellington St. West (2011)	687	54
*Massey Tower, 199 Yonge St. (2018)	683	60
BCE Place, Bay-Wellington Tower, 181 Bay St. (1991)	679	49
L Tower, 1 Front St. (2014)	673	58
*88 Scott Street (2017)	669	58
Four Seasons Private Residences West, 48 Yorkville Ave. (2012)	669	55
Ice Condos at York Centre 1, 16 York St. (2014)	663	57
*YC Condos, 460 Yonge St. (2019)	651	60
*Bay-Adelaide Center East Tower, 40 Adelaide St. (2016)	643	44
*E Condos South, 8 Eglington Ave. (2017)	642	58
*Wellesley on the Park, 11 Wellesley St. West (2017)	637	60
*EY Tower, 100 Adelaide St. West (2017)	617	40
RBC Centre, 155 Wellington St. West (2009)	607	42
*CASA II, 42 Charles St. East (2016)	605	57
*U Condominiums East Tower, 50 St. Joseph St. (2015)	604	55
TD North Tower, 77 King St. West (1969)	600	46
Maple Leaf Square North Tower, 65 Bremmer Blvd. (2010)	595	54
*Eau de Soleil 2, 2183 Lake Shore Blvd. West, Etobicoke (2017)	593	49
*CASA III, 50 Charles St. East (NA)	589	55
*INDX Condominiums, 70 Temperance St. (2016)	587	54
1 King West (2005)	578	51
Success Tower 2, 33 Bay St. (2010)	569	55
*One York Street (2016)	569	35
Royal Bank Plaza-South Tower, 200 Bay St. (1976)	567	41
Maple Leaf Square South Tower, 55 Bremmer Blvd. (2010)	562	50
Hullmark Centre I, 4789 Yonge St. (2015)	557	45
*Lago at the Waterfront, 2151 Lake Shore Blvd. West, Etobicoke (2016)	550	49
44 Charles Street West (1974)	545	51
*Karma, 9 Grenville St. (2016)	544	50
Quantum 2, 2195 Yonge St. (2008)	541	51
Residences @ College Park I, 763 Bay St. (2006)	535	51
Burano, 832 Bay St. (2012)	535	50
Success Tower 1, 18 Harbour St. (2011)	531	52
X2, 580 Jarvis St. (2015)	529	44
*FIVE, 606 Yonge St. (2015)	528	48
Three Hundred, 300 Front St. West (2014)	518	52
The Uptown, 35 Balmuto St. (2011)	518	48
Theatre Park, 224 King St. West (2015)	515	47
Southcore Financial Centre Delta Hotel, 75 Lower Simcoe St. (2014)	515	47
Festival Tower, 330 King St. West (2011)	514	42
*87 Peter (NA)	505	49
*U Condominiums West Tower, 50 St. Joseph St. (2015)	505	45
TD South Tower, 79 Wellington St. West (1985)	504	39
35 Mariner (2005)	503	49
Westlake Village 1 (2015)	503	48
Montage, 20 Fort York Blvd. (2009)	502	48

(1) 1,116 ft incl. antenna. (2) 942 ft incl. antenna.

Tulsa, OK

Building/structure	Ht. (ft)	Stories
BOK Tower, 1 E. 2nd St. (1975)	667	52
Cityplex Central Tower, 2448 E. 81st St. (1979)	648	60
First Place Tower, 15 E. 5th St. (1973)	516	40
Mid-Continent Tower, 401 S. Boston St. (1984)	513	36

Vancouver, BC, Canada

Building/structure	Ht. (ft)	Stories
Shangri-La Vancouver, 1120 W. Georgia St. (2009)	659	59
*Trump International Hotel & Tower, 1153 W. Georgia (2016)	616	58
*Telus Garden Residential Tower (2016)	550	53
Hotel Georgia, 667 Howe St. (2012)	520	50

Other Tall Buildings in North America

Building/structure	Location	Ht. (ft)	Stories
Devon Energy Center (2012)	Oklahoma City, OK	844	52
*Stantec Tower (2018)	Edmonton, AB, Can.	823	70
RSA Battle House Tower (incl. spire) (2007)	Mobile, AL	745	35
Revel Hotel (2012)	Atlantic City, NJ	718	53
Hotel Riu Plaza Guadalajara (2011)	Guadalajara, Mex.	705	44
Great American Tower at Queen City Square (2011)	Cincinnati, OH	665	40
The Tower at First National Center (2002)	Omaha, NE	634	45
801 Grand (1991)	Des Moines, IA	630	44
*Delta Hotel and Residences (2018)	Edmonton, AB, Can.	627	56
One Kansas City Place (incl. spire) (1988)	Kansas City, MO	623	42
Tower of the Americas (1968)	San Antonio, TX	622	NA
Bank of America Tower (1990)	Jacksonville, FL	617	42
AT&T Building (1994)	Nashville TN	617	33
Town Pavilion (1986)	Kansas City, MO	591	38
Erastus Corning II Tower (1973)	Albany, NY	589	44
Niagara Falls Hilton Phase 2 (2009)	Niagara Falls, ON, Can.	581	58
Absolute World 56 (2012)	Mississauga, ON, Can.	576	56
Carew Tower (1931)[1]	Cincinnati, OH	574	49
*Torre NVBOLA (2016)	Puebla, Mex.	574	43
Concourse Corporate Ctr. V (incl. spire) (1988)	Sandy Springs, GA	570	34
Torre Aura Altitude (2008)	Zapopan, Mex.	563	44
Blue Diamond Tower (2000)	Miami Beach, FL	559	44
Green Diamond Tower (2000)	Miami Beach, FL	559	44
Washington Monument (1884)	Washington, DC	555	NA
Concourse Corporate Ctr. VI (incl. spire) (1991)	Sandy Springs, GA	553	34
AEGON Center (1992)	Louisville, KY	549	35
Metropolitan Tower (1986)	Little Rock, AR	546	40
Marriott Rivercenter (incl. spires) (1988)	San Antonio, TX	546	38
RBC Plaza (incl. spire) (2008)	Raleigh, NC	538	32
Modis Tower (1975)	Jacksonville, FL	535	37
Legg Mason Building (1973)	Baltimore, MD	529	40
One Seneca Tower (1970)	Buffalo NY	529	38
Vehicle Assembly Bldg. (1965)	Cape Canaveral, FL	526	40
Harrah's Waterfront Tower (2008)	Atlantic City, NJ	525	44
Skylon (1965)	Niagara Falls, ON, Can.	520	NA
Absolute World 50 (2012)	Mississauga, ON, Can.	518	50
*3 Civic Plaza (2016)	Surrey, BC, Can.	516	50
Bank of America (1924)	Baltimore, MD	509	37
The Westin Virginia Beach Town Center and Residences (2007)	Virginia Beach, VA	508	38
The Beach Club Tower 2 (2006)	Hallandale Beach, FL	505	50
Chase Tower (1971)	Oklahoma City, OK	500	36
One American Plaza (1991)	San Diego, CA	500	34

(1) 623 ft incl. antenna.

Selected Bridge Styles

Bridges support weight through tension (pulling), compression (pushing), or a combination of both. **Suspension** and **cable-stayed** bridges are characterized by cables under tension. While the deck of a suspension bridge hangs from suspenders, that of a cable-stayed bridge ties directly to a bridge tower. The elements of a **truss** form triangles, which distribute the forces of tension and compression. Truss bridges can thus carry more weight than beam bridges. Steel plates can be welded or bolted together to make a **plate girder**, a kind of beam. A common form is the **box girder**.

A bridge can have a **simple** configuration, whereby its load is supported at both ends. If a bridge is **continuous**, its load extends across multiple supports. In a **cantilever** configuration, structural elements (e.g., trusses or girders) supported at one end project out, or cantilever, to carry a span.

Notable North American Bridges

Source: World Almanac research; Office of Bridge Technology, Federal Highway Administration, U.S. Dept. of Transportation

Asterisk (*) designates a bridge that carries railroads only. All other bridges carry roads or roads and rail unless otherwise noted. Year is date of completion or projected completion. Span of bridge is the distance between its main supports. As of mid-2015.

Suspension

Year	Bridge	Location	Main span (ft)
1964	Verrazano-Narrows	New York, NY	4,260
1937	Golden Gate	San Francisco Bay, CA	4,200
1957	Mackinac	Straits of Mackinac, MI	3,800
1931	George Washington	New York, NY-Fort Lee, NJ	3,500
1950/2007	Tacoma Narrows (twin)	Tacoma, WA	2,800
2003	Al Zampa Memorial (New Carquinez) (westbound)	Carquinez Strait, CA	2,388
1936	San Francisco-Oakland Bay (West Span)[1]	San Francisco-Yerba Buena Isl., CA	2,310
1939	Bronx-Whitestone	East R., New York, NY	2,300
1970	Pierre Laporte	Quebec City, QC, Can.	2,190
1951/68	Delaware Mem. (twin)	Pennsville, NJ-New Castle, DE	2,150
1957	Walt Whitman	Philadelphia, PA	2,000
1929	Ambassador	Detroit, MI-Windsor, ON, Can.	1,850
1961	Throgs Neck	New York, NY	1,801
1926	Benjamin Franklin	Phila., PA-Camden, NJ	1,750
1924	Bear Mountain	Hudson R., Peekskill, NY	1,632
1969	Claiborne Pell/Newport	Narragansett Bay, RI	1,600
1952/73	William Preston Lane Jr. Memorial (twin)	Sandy Point, MD	1,600
1903	Williamsburg	East R., New York, NY	1,600
1883	Brooklyn	East R., New York, NY	1,596
1938	Lions Gate	Vancouver, BC, Can.	1,550
1963	Vincent Thomas	L.A. Harbor, CA	1,500
1930	Mid-Hudson	Poughkeepsie, NY	1,495
1909	Manhattan	East R., New York, NY	1,470
1955	Angus L. Macdonald	Halifax, NS, Can.	1,447
1970	A. Murray MacKay	Halifax, NS, Can.	1,400
1936	Triborough (Harlem R. Lift/Bronx Crossing/East R. Suspension)	East R., New York, NY	1,380
2013	San Francisco-Oakland Bay (SAS)[2]	San Francisco Bay, CA	1,263

Cantilever

Year	Bridge	Location	Main span (ft)
1917	Quebec	Quebec City, QC, Can.	1,800
1974	Commodore Barry	Chester, PA-Bridgeport, NJ	1,644
1958/88	Crescent City Connection (twin)	Mississippi R., New Orleans, LA	1,575
1995	Veterans Memorial	Gramercy, LA	1,460
1968	Baton Rouge	Mississippi R., LA	1,235
1955	Tappan Zee (I-287)	Hudson R., Tarrytown, NY	1,212
1930	Lewis and Clark	Longview, WA-Rainier, OR	1,200
1909	Queensboro	East R., New York, NY	1,182
1958	Carquinez (eastbound)	San Francisco Bay, CA	1,100
1930	Jacques Cartier	Montreal, QC, Can.	1,097
1968	Isaiah D. Hart	Jacksonville, FL	1,088
1956	Richmond-San Rafael (twin)	San Francisco Bay, CA	1,070
1963/80	Newburgh-Beacon (twin)	Hudson R., NY	1,000

Truss

Year	Bridge	Location	Main span (ft)
1966	Astoria-Megler (U.S. 101)	Columbia R., OR-WA	1,232
1976	Francis Scott Key	Baltimore, MD	1,200
1981	Ravenswood	Ohio R., Ravenswood, WV	902
1995	Taylor-Southgate, Ohio R.	Cincinnati, OH-Newport, KY	850
1943	Julien Dubuque (U.S. 20)	Mississippi R., IA-IL	845
1966	Charles Braga	Fall River, MA	840
1956	Shawneetown (KY 56) (twin)	Ohio R., IL-KY	825
1953	John E. Mathews	Jacksonville, FL	810
1992	Cooper R.	Charleston, SC	800
1957	Kingston-Rhinecliff	Hudson R., NY	800
1950	Maurice J. Tobin	Boston, MA	800
1940	Gov. Nice Mem.	Newburg, MD-Dahlgren, VA	800
1986	Rochester-Monaca	Rochester-Monaca, PA	780
1973/88	Atchafalaya R. (U.S. 190) (twin)	Krotz Springs, LA	780
1988	Phil G. McDonald (Glade Creek)	Beckley, WV	784
1917	*Sciotoville RR (twin)	Sciotoville, OH-KY	775
1981	Sewickley	Sewickley, PA	750
1977	Jennings Randolph	Chester, WV-E. Liverpool, OH	750
1974	Carroll C. Cropper (I-275)	Ohio R., IN-KY	750
1940	Glover Cary	Ohio R., Owensboro, KY-IN	750
1984	13th Street	Ohio R., Ashland, KY-OH	740
1959	Monaca-E. Rochester	Monaca-E. Rochester, PA	730
1976	Betsy Ross	Philadelphia, PA	729
2013	Milton-Madison (U.S. 421)	Ohio R., KY-IN	727
1967	Matthew E. Welsh	Ohio R., Mauckport, IN-KY	725
1994	Robert C. Byrd	Huntington, WV	720
1971	Atchafalaya R. (LA 1)	Simmesport, LA	720
1962	U.S. 41 Twin	Ohio R., Evansville, IN-Henderson, KY	720
1929	Irvin S. Cobb (U.S. 45)	Ohio R., Brookport, IL-Paducah, KY	716
1970	Vanport	Vanport, PA	715
1962	Champlain	Montreal, QC, Can.	707
1973	Girard Point	Philadelphia, PA	700
1963	John F. Kennedy (I-65)	Ohio R., Louisville, KY-Jeffersonville, IN	700
1923	*Mears Mem., Tanana R.	Nenana, AK	700

Plate and Box Girder

Year	Bridge	Location	Main span (ft)
1997	Confederation[3]	Prince Edward Isl.-NB, Can.	820
1978	Shubenacadie R.	S. Maitland, NS, Can.	790
2010	Kanawha R. (I-64)	S. Charleston-Dunbar, WV	760
1982	Jesse H. Jones Mem.	Houston, TX	750
1977	LA 27, Intracoastal Canal	Gibbstown, LA	750
1976	LA 82, Intracoastal Canal	Forked Isl., LA	750
1967	San Mateo-Hayward	San Francisco Bay, CA	750
1992	Jamestown-Verrazano	Narragansett Bay, RI	674
2002	Vietnam Veterans Memorial	James R., Richmond, VA	672
1986	Umatilla	Columbia R., OR-WA	660
1969	San Diego-Coronado (twin)	San Diego Bay, CA	660
2007	Benicia-Martinez (new)	Carquinez Strait, CA	659
1967	Poplar St./William L. Clay Sr.	Miss. R., St. Louis, MO-IL	647
1978	Stanislaus R.	Parrots Ferry, CA	640
1992/94	Acosta (twin)	Jacksonville, FL	630
1973	Loop 610/Sidney Sherman	Houston, TX	630
1981	Juneau-Douglas	Gastineau Channel, AK	620
1981	Glenn Jackson (I-205)	Columbia R., OR-WA	600

Cable-Stayed

Year	Bridge	Location	Main span (ft)
2012	Baluarte Bicentennial	Sinaloa-Durango states, Mex.	1,706
2011	John James Audubon	Pointe Coupee-West Feliciana, LA	1,583
2005	Arthur Ravenel Jr.	Charleston, SC	1,546
2012	Port Mann	Vancouver, BC, Can.	1,542
1986	Alex Fraser	Vancouver, BC, Can.	1,526
2014	Stan Musial Veterans Mem. (I-70)	Miss. R., St. Louis, MO-IL	1,500
2010	U.S. 82, Mississippi R.	Greenville, MS-Lake Village, AR	1,378
1994	Clark	Alton, IL-MO	1,360
1989	Dames Point	Jacksonville, FL	1,300
2003	Sidney Lanier	Brunswick, GA	1,250
1995	Fred Hartman	Houston Ship Channel, Baytown, TX	1,250
2007	Veterans' Glass City Skyway	Maumee R., Toledo, OH	1,225
1983	Hale Boggs Memorial	Luling, LA	1,222
2016/18	New NY (I-287) (twin)	Hudson R., Tarrytown, NY	1,200
2002	William Natcher, Ohio R.	Owensboro, KY-IN	1,200
1987	Sunshine Skyway (I-275)	Tampa Bay, FL	1,200
2012	Margaret Hunt Hill	Trinity R., Dallas, TX	1,197
1988	Tampico	Panuco R., Mex.	1,181
2006	Penobscot Narrows	Bucksport, ME	1,161
2003	Bill Emerson Memorial	Cape Girardeau, MO-IL	1,150
1988	Skybridge[4]	Vancouver, BC, Can.	1,115
1991	Talmadge Memorial	Savannah, GA	1,100
2000	Maysville (Wm. H. Harsha)	Savannah, GA	1,050

Steel Arch

Year	Bridge	Location	Main span (ft)
1977	New River Gorge	Fayetteville, WV	1,700
1931	Bayonne (Kill Van Kull)	Bayonne, NJ-New York, NY	1,675
1973	Fremont	Portland, OR	1,255
1964	Port Mann	Vancouver, BC, Can.	1,200
1967	Laviolette	Trois-Rivières, QC, Can.	1,100
1990	Roosevelt Lake	Roosevelt Lake, AZ	1,080

Year	Bridge	Location	Main span (ft)
1959	Glen Canyon	Page, AZ	1,028
1962	Lewiston-Queenston	NY-ON, Can.	1,001
1976	Perrine	Twin Falls, ID	993
1916	*Hell Gate	East R., New York, NY	978
1941	Rainbow	Niagara Falls, NY-ON, Can.	950
1997	Second Blue Water	Port Huron, MI-ON, Can.	922
1977	Moundsville	Ohio R., WV	912
1983/92	Jefferson Barracks (I-255) (twin)	Mississippi R., IL-MO	910
1973	Hernando DeSoto (I-40) (two spans)	Mississippi R., AR-TN	900
2008	Blennerhassett (U.S. 50)	Parkersburg, WV-OH	878
1936	Henry Hudson	Harlem R., New York, NY	840
1966	Bob Cummings Lincoln Trail	Ohio R., IN-KY	825
1978	I-57, Mississippi R.	Cairo, IL	821
1980	I-65, Mobile R.	Mobile, AL	800
1961	Sherman Minton (I-64)	IN-Louisville, KY	800
1978	I-470, Ohio R.	Wheeling, WV	780
1932	West End	Pittsburgh, PA	780
1971	Piscataqua R. (I-95 High Level)	Portsmouth, NH-Kittery, ME	756
1995	Navajo	Marble Canyon, AZ	726

Movable Bridges

Vertical Lift

Year	Bridge	Location	Main span (ft)
1959	*Arthur Kill	New York, NY-Elizabeth, NJ	558
1935	*Cape Cod Canal	Buzzards Bay, MA	544
1896	*Delair	Pennsauken, NJ-Phila., PA	542
1937	Marine Pkwy. Hodges Mem.	Jamaica Bay, New York, NY	540
1931	Burlington-Bristol	Delaware R., NJ-PA	540
1908	*Burlington Northern RR[5]	Portland, OR	516
1968	*Second Narrows Railway	Vancouver, BC, Can.	499
1911	*Armour-Swift-Burlington	Missouri R., Kansas City, MO	428
1945	*Harry S Truman	Kansas City, MO	427

Bascule

Year	Bridge	Location	Main span (ft)
1940	Charles Berry Memorial	Lorain, OH	333
1917	Market St./Ch. John Ross	Chattanooga, TN	310
2003	SW 2nd Avenue	Miami, FL	302

Swing

Year	Bridge	Location	Main span (ft)
1927	Fort Madison (Santa Fe)	Mississippi R., IA	525
1952	George P. Coleman Mem.	Yorktown, VA	500
1991	SW Spokane St.	Seattle, WA	480
1899	*Illinois Central RR	Chicago, IL	479
1914	*Coos Bay RR	Coos Bay, OR	458
1913	East Haddam (Rt. 82)	Connecticut R., CT	456

Floating Pontoon[6]

Year	Bridge	Location	Main span (ft)
1963	Evergreen Pt. (SR 520)[7]	Seattle, WA	7,578
1961	Hood Canal (SR 104)	Kitsap Co.-Jefferson Co., WA	7,450
1993	Lacey V. Murrow (I-90)	Seattle, WA	6,561
1989	Homer M. Hadley (I-90)	Seattle, WA	5,736

Other Notable North American Bridges

Year	Bridge	Type	Location	Tot. length (ft)
1956/69	Lake Pontchartrain Causeway[8]	Twin concrete trestle	Metairie-Mandeville, LA	126,055
1979	Manchac Swamp	Twin concrete trestle	Manchac, LA	120,384
1973	Atchafalaya Basin (I-10)	Twin concrete trestle	Baton Rouge, LA	95,040
1982	Seven Mile (Overseas Hwy, U.S. 1)	Segmental concrete	Florida Keys	35,867
2009/11	I-10 Twin Spans	Twin concrete trestle	Slidell-New Orleans, LA	29,040
2002	Croatan Sound	Continuous post-tensioned girder	Manteo, NC	27,000
1993	Choctawhatchee Mid-Bay	Segmental concrete	Destin-Niceville, FL	19,265
1962	International	Arch truss	Sault Ste. Marie, MI-ON, Can.	9,278
2009	Walkway Over the Hudson[9]	Pedestrian	Poughkeepsie-Highland, NY	6,768
1874	Eads, Mississippi R.[10]	Steel arch	St. Louis, MO-IL	6,442
1987	Powder Point	Tropical hardwood	Duxbury, MA	2,200
1969	Silver Memorial, Ohio R.[11]	Cantilever	Pt. Pleasant, WV-OH	1,964
2010	Mike O'Callaghan-Pat Tillman Mem. (U.S. 93)[12]	Concrete arch	Colorado R., AZ-NV	1,900
1994	Natchez Trace Parkway	Concrete arch	Franklin, TN	1,572
1901	Hartland[13]	Covered	St. John R., Hartland, NB, Can.	1,282

(1) Two complete bridges each 2,310-ft long, which share an anchor point. (2) Self-Anchored Suspension Span (SAS); the world's longest single-tower, self-anchored suspension bridge. (3) World's longest bridge crossing ice-covered water, with total length of 8 mi. (4) World's longest cable-stayed bridge carrying mass transit only. (5) Vertical lift replaced swing span in 1989. (6) Length listed is of bridge's floating section. (7) To be replaced by new, wider SR 520 floating pontoon, with expected opening in 2016. (8) World's second-longest bridge over water, behind China's Qingdao Bay Bridge (25.8 mi). (9) Originally opened in 1889 as a railroad bridge. (10) World's first major structure made of alloy steel. (11) Replaced Silver Bridge, the collapse of which in 1967 led to the creation of National Bridge Inspection Standards in the U.S. (12) Longest single-span concrete arch in Western Hemisphere. (13) World's longest covered bridge.

Oldest U.S. Bridges in Continuous Use

Built in 1697, the stone-arch Frankford Ave. Bridge (U.S. 13) crosses Pennypack Creek in Philadelphia, PA. It consists of three spans and has a total length of 154 ft. The bridge was constructed as part of the King's Road, which connected Philadelphia to New York.

The oldest covered bridge, completed in 1829, is the double-span, 256-ft-long Bath-Haverhill Bridge, which spans the Ammonoosuc River between the towns of Bath and Haverhill, NH. The bridge was bypassed in 1999. It has since reopened to pedestrian traffic only.

Notable World Bridges

Source: World Almanac research; Laboratory of Bridge Engineering, Aalto Univ. School of Science and Technology
Year is date of completion or projected completion. Span of bridge is the distance between its main supports. As of mid-2015.

Suspension

Year	Bridge	Location	Main span (ft)
1998	Akashi Kaikyo	Japan	6,532
2009	Xihoumen	China	5,413
1998	Storebælt (Great Belt, East Bridge)	Denmark	5,328
2012	Yi Sun-sin (Gwangyang)	South Korea	5,069
2005	Runyang Yangtze R. (south)	China	4,888
2012	Nanjing Fourth Yangtze R.	China	4,652
1981	Humber	England	4,626
2015	Yavuz Sultan Selim (Third Bosphorus)	Turkey	4,619
1999	Jiangyin Yangtze R.	China	4,544
1997	Tsing Ma	China	4,518
2013	Hardanger	Norway	4,298
2007	Yangluo Yangtze R.	China	4,199
1997	Höga Kusten	Sweden	3,970
2012	Aizhai	China	3,858
2015	Ulsan Grand	South Korea	3,773
2008	Huangpu	China	3,635
1988	Minami Bisan-Seto	Japan	3,609
1988	Fatih Sultan Mehmet (Bosphorus II)	Turkey	3,576
2010	Baling R.	China	3,570
2012	Taizhou Yangtze R.[1]	China	3,543
1973	Bosphorus	Turkey	3,524
1999	Kurushima III	Japan	3,379
1999	Kurushima II	Japan	3,346
1966	Ponte 25 de Abril, Tagus R.	Portugal	3,323
1964	Forth Road	Scotland	3,300

(1) Two consecutive spans of equal length.

Steel Arch

Year	Bridge	Location	Main span (ft)
2009	Chaotianmen Yangtze R.	China	1,811
2003	Lupu	China	1,804
1932	Sydney Harbour	Australia	1,650
2005	Wushan Yangtze R.	China	1,614
2016	Chenab (rail)[1]	India	1,532
2013	Xijiang (rail)	China	1,476
2007	Xinguang	China	1,404
2007	Caiyuanba	China	1,378
2010	Daning R.	China	1,312
2008	Hiroshima Airport	Japan	1,247

Year	Bridge	Location	Main span (ft)
1959	Sloboda	Croatia	1,224
2000	Yajisha	China	1,181
1962	Bridge of the Americas	Panama	1,128
1967	Zdakov	Czech Republic	1,083
1961	Runcorn-Widnes	England	1,082
1935	Birchenough	Zimbabwe	1,080

(1) Will be world's highest rail bridge (1,178 ft) upon completion.

Concrete Arch

Year	Bridge	Location	Main span (ft)
1997	Wanxian Yangtze R.	China	1,378
2015	Nanpanjiang (rail)	China	1,365
1980	Krk I	Croatia	1,280
2015	Almonte Viaduct	Spain	1,260
2012	Zhaohua Jialing R.	China	1,194
1995	Jiangjiehe	China	1,083
2015	Tajo Railway	Spain	1,063
1996	Yongjiang	China	1,024
1964	Gladesville	Australia	1,000

Cantilever

Year	Bridge	Location	Main span (ft)
1890	Forth Rail[1]	Scotland	1,710
1974	Minato	Japan	1,673
1943	Rabindra Setu (Howrah)	India	1,500

(1) Two spans of equal length.

Plate and Box Girder

Year	Bridge	Location	Main span (ft)
2006	Shibanpo	China	1,083
1998	Stolmasundet	Norway	988
1998	Raftsundet	Norway	978
1974	Pres. Costa e Silva (Rio-Niterói)	Brazil	984
1978	Neckar Valley Viaduct, Weitingen	Germany	863
1956	Branko's	Serbia	856
1989	Third	Brazil	853
1966	Zoobrücke	Germany	850

Cable-Stayed

Year	Bridge	Location	Main span (ft)
2012	Russky Island	Russia	3,622
2008	Sutong Yangtze R.	China	3,570
2009	Stonecutters	China	3,340
2009	Edong	China	3,038
1999	Tatara	Japan	2,920
1995	Normandy	France	2,808
2010	Jingyue Yangtze R.	China	2,677
2009	Incheon	South Korea	2,625
2012	Zolotoy Rog	Russia	2,418
2009	Shanghai Yangtze R.	China	2,395
2009	Minpu	China	2,323
2005	Third Nanjing Yangtze R.	China	2,126
2001	Second Nanjing Yangtze R.	China	2,060
2000	Third Wuhan Yangtze R. (Baishazhou)	China	2,028
2002	Qingzhou Minjiang R.	China	1,985
1993	Yangpu	China	1,975
1998	Meiko Chuo	Japan	1,936
1997	Xupu	China	1,936
2004	Rion-Antirion	Greece	1,837
2014	Bukhang	South Korea	1,772
1991	Skarnsundet	Norway	1,739
1999	Shantou Queshi	China	1,699
1995	Tsurumi Tsubasa	Japan	1,673
2008	Tianxingzhou Yangtze R.	China	1,654
2012	Mokpo	South Korea	1,640
2007	Kanchanaphisek	Thailand	1,640
2002	Jingsha	China	1,640
2000	Øresund	Denmark-Sweden	1,608
1991	Ikuchi	Japan	1,608
1994	Higashi Kobe	Japan	1,591
2011	Geo Geum	South Korea	1,575
1998	Zhanjiang	China	1,575
1997	Ting Kau	China	1,558
1999	Seohae Grand	South Korea	1,542
1989	Yokohama Bay	Japan	1,509

Other Notable World Bridges[1]

Year	Bridge	Location	Length (ft)
2011	Danyang-Kunshan Grand (rail)[2]	China	538,000
2000	Bang Na Espressway[3]	Thailand	180,446
2011	Qingdao Bay[4]	China	136,417
2007	Hangzhou Bay	China	118,000
2005	Donghai	China	106,627
2013	Jiashao	China	33,136
1978	Demerara Harbour (floating)	Guyana	6,074
1994	Nordhordland (floating)	Norway	4,088

(1) Length listed is total length of bridge. (2) World's longest bridge. (3) World's longest road bridge. (4) World's longest oversea bridge.

World's Longest Railway Tunnels

Source: World Almanac research

Year is date of opening or projected opening unless otherwise noted. As of mid-2015.

Year	Tunnel	Location	Operating railway	Length (mi)
2016	Gotthard Base (twin)	Switzerland-Italy	Swiss Federal Railways (SBB)	35.4/35.5
1988	Seikan	Japan	Japan Railways Group	33.5
1994	English Channel (Chunnel) (twin)	UK-France	Eurotunnel	31.1
2007	Lötschberg Base (twin)	Switzerland	BLS Lötschbergbahn AG	21.0
2007	Guadarrama (twin)	Spain	Renfe	17.6
2009	Taihang (twin)	China	China's Ministry of Railways	17.3
2005	Hakkoda	Japan	Japan Railways Group	16.4
2018	Guangzhou-Shenzhen-Hong Kong Express Rail Link (XRL), Hong Kong section	China	MTR Corporation	16.2
2002	Iwate-Ichinohe	Japan	Japan Railways Group	16.0
NA[1]	Pajares (twin)	Spain	Renfe	15.3
2015	Iiyama	Japan	Japan Railways Group	13.8
1982	Daishimizu	Japan	Japan Railways Group	13.8
2008-09	Geumjeong	South Korea	Korea Railroad Corporation	12.6
2006	Wushaoling (twin)	China	China's Ministry of Railways	12.5
1906/22	Simplon No. 1 and 2	Switzerland-Italy	BLS Lötschbergbahn AG	12.3
1999	Vereina	Switzerland	Rhätische Bahn (RhB)	11.8
2007	High Speed 1 (Channel Tunnel Rail Link, or CTRL) (twin)	UK-France	London & Continental Railways (LCR)	11.8
1975	Shin-Kanmon (twin)	Japan	Japan Railways Group	11.6
1934	Apennine	Italy	Ferrovie dello Stato (FS)	11.5
2002	Qinling (twin)	China	China's Ministry of Railways	11.5
2006	Vaglia	Italy	Ferrovie dello Stato (FS)	10.4
2014	West Qinling (twin)	China	China's Ministry of Railways	10.3
1972	Rokko	Japan	Japan Railways Group	10.1

NA = Not available. (1) Tunnels have been dug but are not yet in operation.

Underwater Vehicular Tunnels in North America

Source: World Almanac research

(more than 5,000 ft in length; year is date of opening)

Year	Name	Location	Waterway	Length (ft)
1950	Brooklyn Battery (twin)	New York, NY	East River	9,117
1927	Holland (twin)	New York, NY-Jersey City, NJ	Hudson River	8,558/8,371
1937/45/57	Lincoln (center/north/south tubes)	New York, NY-Weehawken, NJ	Hudson River	8,216/7,482/8,006
1985	Fort McHenry (twin)	Baltimore, MD	Patapsco River	7,920
1957/76	Hampton Roads (twin)	Hampton, VA	Hampton Roads	7,479
1957	Baltimore Harbor (twin)	Baltimore, MD	Baltimore Harbor	7,392
1940	Queens Midtown (twin)	New York, NY	East River	6,414
1934	Sumner	Boston, MA	Boston Harbor	5,653
1964	Thimble Shoal	Northampton Co., VA	Chesapeake Bay	5,552
1964	Chesapeake Channel	Northampton Co., VA	Chesapeake Bay	5,237
1930	Detroit-Windsor	Detroit, MI-Windsor, ON, Canada	Detroit River	5,160
1961	Callahan	Boston, MA	Boston Harbor	5,070

Land Vehicular Tunnels in the U.S.

Source: World Almanac research; Federal Highway Administration, U.S. Dept. of Transportation
(3,400 ft or more in length)

Name	Location	Length (ft)
Anton Anderson Memorial[1]	Whittier, AK	13,300
Edwin C. Johnson Memorial (eastbound)	I-70, Clear Creek Co.-Summit Co., CO	8,960
Eisenhower Mem. (westbound)	I-70, Clear Creek Co.-Summit Co., CO	8,939
Ted Williams[2]	MA Turnpike, Boston, MA	8,448
Thomas P. O'Neill Jr.	I-93, Boston, MA	7,920
Allegheny (twin)	PA Turnpike	6,070
Liberty (twin)	Pittsburgh, PA	5,920
Zion-Mount Carmel	Zion Natl. Park, UT	5,808
East River Mountain (twin)	I-77, Rocky Gap, VA-Bluefield, WV	5,412
Tuscarora Mountain (twin)	PA Turnpike	5,326
Tetsuo Harano (twin)	H-3 Freeway, HI	5,165
Kittatinny Mountain (twin)	PA Turnpike	4,727
Cumberland Gap (twin)	U.S. 25E, KY-TN	4,600
Lehigh (twin)	PA Tpke., NE Extension	4,461/4,380
Blue Mountain (twin)	PA Turnpike	4,339
Wawona	Yosemite Natl. Pk., CA	4,233
Big Walker Mountain (twin)	Bland Co., VA	4,229
Squirrel Hill	Pittsburgh, PA	4,225
Tom Lantos/Devil's Slide (twin)	San Mateo Co., CA	4,200
Hanging Lake (twin)	Glenwood Canyon, CO	4,000
Caldecott (4 tubes)	Oakland, CA	3,771/3,610/3,610/3,389
Fort Pitt (twin)	Pittsburgh, PA	3,614
Mount Baker	Seattle, WA	3,456
Dingess	Mingo Co., WV	3,400
Mall	Washington, DC	3,400

(1) Vehicles and trains take turns using the tunnel's one lane. (2) Total length of tunnel is 8,448 ft, 3,960 ft of which is underwater.

Major U.S. Dams and Reservoirs

Source: 2013 National Inventory of Dams, U.S. Army Corps of Engineers

Highest U.S. Dams

Rank	Dam	River	State	Type	Height		Year completed
					Feet	Meters	
1.	Oroville	Feather	California	E	770	235	1968
2.	Hoover	Colorado	Nevada	A-G	730	221	1935
3.	Dworshak	N. Fork Clearwater	Idaho	G	717	219	1973
4.	Glen Canyon	Colorado	Arizona	A	710	216	1963
5.	New Bullards Bar	North Yuba	California	A	645	197	1970
6.	Mossyrock	Cowlitz	Washington	A	606	185	1968
7.	Shasta	Sacramento	California	G	602	183	1945
8.	Don Pedro	Tuolumne	California	E	585	178	1971
9.	New Melones	Stanislaus	California	E-R	578	176	1979
10.	Hungry Horse	S. Fork Flathead	Montana	A	564	172	1952

A = Arch; E = Embankment, earthfill; R = Embankment, rockfill; G = Gravity. **Note:** The height of a dam is the vertical distance between the original streambed or excavated foundation and the dam's crest, parapet wall, or maximum design water level. Tailings and other mining dams (i.e., dams built from the waste generated by mining operations) are not included in this list.

Largest U.S. Embankment Dams

Rank	Dam	River	State	Volume		Year completed
				Cubic yards (thousands)	Cubic meters (thousands)	
1.	Fort Peck	Missouri	Montana	125,628	96,049	1957
2.	Oahe	Missouri	South Dakota	92,000	70,339	1966
3.	Oroville	Feather	California	80,000	61,164	1968
4.	B. F. Sisk	San Luis Creek	California	77,670	59,383	1967
5.	Garrison	Missouri	North Dakota	66,500	50,843	1953
6.	Scotts Flat	Deer Creek	California	66,300	50,690	1948
7.	Cochiti	Rio Grande	New Mexico	65,000	49,696	1975
8.	Herbert Hoover	North New River Canal	Florida	54,700	41,821	1965
9.	Fort Randall	Missouri	South Dakota	50,200	38,381	1954
10.	Castaic	Castaic Creek	California	44,000	33,640	1973

Note: An embankment dam is any dam constructed with excavated material, including earth, rocks, and mining or other industrial waste. (In contrast, gravity, arch, and buttress dams are generally made out of concrete or masonry.) The majority of the world's dams are embankment dams. All dams in this list are earthfill, or formed primarily out of layers of compacted earth.

Largest-Capacity U.S. Reservoirs

Rank	Dam	Reservoir	State	Max. reservoir capacity		Year completed
				Acre feet (thousands)	Cubic meters (thousands)	
1.	Hoover	Lake Mead	Nevada	30,237	37,296,790	1935
2.	Glen Canyon	Lake Powell	Arizona	29,875	36,850,270	1963
3.	Garrison	Lake Sakakawea	North Dakota	24,500	30,220,305	1953
4.	Oahe	Lake Oahe	South Dakota	23,600	29,110,172	1966
5.	Fort Peck	Fort Peck Lake	Montana	19,100	23,559,503	1957
6.	Grand Coulee	Lake Roosevelt	Washington	9,562	11,794,553	1941
7.	Herbert Hoover	Lake Okeechobee	Florida	8,519	10,508,032	1965
8.	Kentucky	Kentucky Lake	Kentucky	7,535	9,294,779	1944
9.	Sam Rayburn	Sam Rayburn Lake	Texas	6,520	8,042,302	1965
10.	Wright Patman	Wright Patman Lake	Texas	6,505	8,023,799	1954

Note: A reservoir is a body of water created by a dam for storage. This water may serve a single or multiple purposes, such as irrigation, flood reduction, and electricity generation.

Major Dams and Reservoirs of the World

Source: World Register of Dams, Intl. Commission on Large Dams (ICOLD)
Asterisk (*) designates structure is planned or under construction as of mid-2015.

World's Highest Dams

Rank	Dam	Country	Height above lowest formation Meters	Feet
1.	*Rogun	Tajikistan	335	1,099
2.	*Bakhtiari	Iran	315	1,033
3.	Jinping I	China	305	1,001
4.	Nurek	Tajikistan	300	984
5.	Lianghekou	China	295	968
6.	Xiaowan (Yunnan Gorge)	China	294	965
7.	Xiluodu	China	286	938
8.	Grande Dixence	Switzerland	285	935
9.	*Baihetan	China	277	909
10.	Inguri	Georgia	272	892
11.	*Yusufeli	Turkey	270	886
12.	Chicoasén	Mexico	262	860
13.	Vajont	Italy	262	860
14.	Nuozhadu	China	262	860
15.	Khersan 2	Iran	260	853

World's Largest Embankment Dams

Rank	Dam	Country	Volume cubic meters (thousands)
1.	Tarbela	Pakistan	129,200
2.	Fort Peck	U.S.	96,049
3.	Ataturk	Turkey	84,500
4.	Yacyreta	Argentina/Paraguay	81,000
5.	Tucurui	Brazil	80,865
6.	*Rogun	Tajikistan	75,500
7.	Oahe	U.S.	70,339
8.	Guri	Venezuela	70,000
9.	Parambikulam	India	69,165
10.	High Island West	China	67,000
11.	Gardiner	Canada	65,440
12.	Mangla	Pakistan	64,991
13.	Afsluitdijk	Netherlands	63,400
14.	Oroville	U.S.	61,164
15.	B. F. Sisk	U.S.	59,378

World's Largest-Capacity Reservoirs

Rank	Dam	Country	Max. capacity cubic meters (millions)
1.	Kariba	Zimbabwe/Zambia	180,600
2.	Bratsk	Russia	169,000
3.	High Aswan	Egypt	162,000
4.	Akosombo (Lake Volta)	Ghana	150,000
5.	Daniel-Johnson	Canada	141,851
6.	Guri	Venezuela	135,000
7.	W. A. C. Bennett	Canada	74,300
8.	Krasnoyarsk	Russia	73,300
9.	Zeya	Russia	68,400
10.	*Hidase	Ethiopia	63,000
11.	Robert-Bourassa (La Grande 2)	Canada	61,715
12.	La Grande 3	Canada	60,020
13.	Ust-Ilim	Russia	59,300
14.	Boguchany	Russia	58,200
15.	Kuibyshev	Russia	58,000

World's Largest-Capacity Hydro Plants

Rank	Dam	Country	Installed capacity (MW)
1.	Sanxia (Three Gorges Dam)	China	22,500
2.	Itaipu	Brazil/Paraguay	14,000
3.	*Baihetan	China	14,000
4.	Xiluodu	China	13,860
5.	*Belo Monte	Brazil	11,234
6.	Guri	Venezuela	10,000
7.	Tucuruí	Brazil	8,370
8.	Grand Coulee	U.S.	6,809
9.	Sayano-Shushenskaya	Russia	6,400
10.	Xiangjiaba	China	6,400
11.	Longtan	China	6,300
12.	Krasnoyarsk	Russia	6,000
13.	Nuozhadu	China	5,850
14.	Robert-Bourassa	Canada	5,616
15.	*Hidase	Ethiopia	5,250

Timeline of Selected Architectural Styles and Structures

Asterisk (*) denotes part of a UNESCO World Heritage site.

Style and period	Location; characteristics; significant examples
Mesopotamian c. 3500-539 BCE	City-states of Sumer, Akkad, Babylon, Assyria (modern-day Iraq). Mud-brick rectangular temples on oval platforms with simple corbel vaults, later ziggurats. Painted terra-cotta mosaics and murals; carved reliefs on columns and walls. **Ziggurat of Nanna**, Ur (Muqayyar, Iraq), ordered by Ur-Nammu, c. 2100 BCE **Anu Ziggurat and White Temple**, Uruk (Warka, Iraq), c. 3000 BCE
Egyptian c. 3000-30 BCE	Along Nile R. Mud-brick and limestone tombs and massive, geometric pyramids, post-and-lintel construction. Highly decorative with colorful hieroglyphics, carvings, columns, obelisks, paintings, and sculpture. ***Stepped Pyramid of Pharaoh Djoser** (Saqqara, Egypt), by Imhotep, c. 2737-2717 BCE ***Great Pyramid of Khufu** (Giza, Egypt), c. 2250 BCE ***Great Temple of Amon-Ra** (Karnak, Egypt), c. 1530-300 BCE ***Mortuary Temple of Queen Hatshepsut**, Deir el-Bahari (Thebes, Egypt), by Senenmut, c. 1479-1458 BCE
Three Dynasties c. 2100-221 BCE	China. Single-level mud-brick or mud-smeared timber structures on earthen platforms with thatched roofs. Later, bracketed wooden-framed structures with brick-tiled floors, roofs with overhanging eaves. **City of Erlitou** (Yanshi, China), c. 1900-1500 BCE
Minoan c. 1800-1450 BCE	Crete. Palaces, tombs in monumental style adapted from Mesopotamia and Egypt. Multilevel stone palaces with large central court, no fortifications. Walls made of doors (*polythyron*); stone porticoes and lintels; wooden ceilings and columns; beehive-shaped tombs (*tholi*). **Palace at Knossos** (Heraklion, Crete, Greece), c. 1700 BCE
Mycenaean c. 1600-1100 BCE	Greece. Adapted Minoan style, with large stone masonry, huge walls, and fortified citadels with complex palaces (*megaron*). ***Treasury of Atreus** (Mycenae, Greece), c. 1250 BCE
Olmec c. 1200-400 BCE	Mexico Gulf Coast. Many religious structures, including stone temple-pyramids centered in cities; also large stone sculptures and mosaic pavement with natural and animistic themes. **Great Pyramid** (La Venta, Mexico), c. 800-400 BCE
Mayan c. 900 BCE-900 CE	Central America. Religious structures with plaster-surfaced stone temple-pyramids with stairs containing tombs. Decorative animistic and geometric relief sculptures, lintels, and stone monuments with hieroglyphics. ***Pyramid of the Magician** (Uxmal, Mexico), c. 700-910 CE ***North Acropolis** (Tikal, Guatemala), c. 200 BCE

Style and period	Location; characteristics; significant examples
Greek c. 750-323 BCE	Greek peninsula, Asia Minor, North Africa, western Mediterranean. Religious, civic buildings in monumental style, inspired by Egypt, based on strict rules of form and human proportion; many ornamental details. Marble and limestone structures (including rectangular temples) with pediment, colonnaded porticoes in diverse regional styles, defined by orders of architecture like Ionic, Doric, Corinthian. Most early buildings with timber supports; solid stone in later temples. ***Parthenon, Acropolis** (Athens, Greece), by Ictinus and Callicrates, 447-436 BCE ***Temple of Zeus** (Olympia, Greece), by Libon of Elis, mid-5th cent. BCE **Mausoleum of Halicarnassus** (Bodrum, Turkey), by Pythis, c. 353 BCE (destroyed) ***Temple of Apollo Epicurius** (Bassae, Greece), by Ictinus, c. 420 BCE
Achaemenid c. 550-334 BCE	Persian Empire (Eastern Mediterranean to Indus R.). Palatial complexes influenced by cultures absorbed by the empire; limestone and mud-brick complexes on raised stone terraces with ornamental stairways, rectangular pillared audience halls with porticoes and corner towers; pleasure gardens (*bâgh*) as focal point of architecture. ***Pasargadae** (Iran), founded by Cyrus II, after 547 BCE ***Persepolis** (Iran), founded by Darius I, around 518 BCE
Roman c. 500 BCE-400 CE	Roman Empire. Civic and religious structures with grandiose limestone brick and concrete construction in systematic, practical layout. Adapted Greek orders in many structures, including circular temples and large covered halls (basilica), but emphasized movement with rounded arches and domes, geometric vaults. ***Pantheon** (Rome, Italy), ordered by Emperor Hadrian, 118-128 CE ***Colosseum** (Rome, Italy), ordered by Emperor Vespasian, 70-82 CE ***Roman Forum** (Rome, Italy), 500s BCE-608 CE
Qin and Han c. 221 BCE-220 CE	China. Massive public works, palaces, tombs, and planned cities; systematic layout and design determined by divination techniques (geomancy). Multistoried timber palace complexes with gardens, courtyards laid along a long hall with a south-north axis for weather; decorative roof with overhanging eaves. ***The Great Wall** (China), ordered by Qin Shi Huang, 220 BCE-c. 1600 CE ***Mausoleum of the First Qin Emperor** (Xianyang [Xi'an], China), c. 210 BCE
Sassanian 226-651	Iran. Mud-brick, mortared rubble, and stone palaces on platforms. Tall, vaulted entry chambers with one open side (*iwans*). Three-aisled hall chambers covered with rudimentary barrel vaults. Parabolic domes abandoned for square courtyards in later Sassanian period. **Palace of Ardashir I** (Firuzabad, Iran), c. 224 **Taq-i Kisra** [Arch of Khosrau] (Ctesiphon, Iraq), c. 260 or c. 550
Byzantine 330-1453	Byzantine Empire, Italy, Russia. Religious structures with masonry construction based on Roman architecture, many salvaged pieces. Centralized cross-in-square layout, with large central dome supported by vaults. Highly decorative, with iconographic frescoes, glass mosaics. ***Hagia Sophia** (Istanbul, Turkey), by Anthemius and Isidorus, 532-37 ***St. Mark's Basilica** (Venice, Italy), ordered by Domenico Contarini, 1063-94
Sui and Tang 581-906	China. Includes influences from other cultures; geomancy used to enhance harmony and social status. Rectangular, multistory modular timber structures with interlinking corridors; single-eaved roofs with exposed beams. **Daming Palace** (Xi'an, China), 634 (destroyed) ***Hall of the Great Buddha**, Foguang Temple (Mount Wutai, China), ordered rebuilt by Xuan Zhong, 857
Early Islamic (Umayyad) 692-c. 1000	Syria, Middle East, North Africa, southern Spain. Mosques in adapted Sassanian style. Austere exteriors; simple columned halls with minarets and mihrabs (prayer niches), walled courtyards and gardens, onion domes. Highly decorative interiors with patterned marble, mosaics. ***Dome of the Rock** [Qubbat al-Sakhra] (Jerusalem), ordered by Abd al-Malik, 692 ***Great Mosque of Córdoba** (Spain), ordered by Abd al-Rahman I, 784-86
Khmer c. 880-1200s	Indochina. Hindu or Buddhist temple complexes, including brick, later sandstone beehive-shaped shrines with arches atop terraced temple "mountains" symbolizing Mount Meru, Hindu and Buddhist center of the universe, where the gods dwell. Concentric layout of structures mimics the cosmos, relating religious narrative in carved reliefs. ***Angkor Wat** (Cambodia), ordered by Suryavarman II, 12th cent.
Romanesque (Norman) c. 900s-1100s	Western Europe. Churches and monasteries in localized Roman style; many reused material from Roman structures. Austere, heavy, simple masonry construction with thick walls, concealed buttresses, small windows, barrel arches, and vaults. Churches like Roman basilica with arched central nave, lower side aisles, apse, transept formed Latin cross. Monumental art and ornaments with Christian narrative throughout, especially on façade and portals. ***Durham Cathedral** (England, UK), ordered by Bishop William de Saint-Calais, 1093-1133 ***Cathedral, Baptistery, and "Leaning" Tower** (Pisa, Italy), by various architects, begun in 1063, tower not completed until 1372
Gothic c. 1100s-1500s	France, Europe. Cathedrals meant to inspire spirituality with design like Roman basilica: pointed arches and spires that reach toward heavens, skeletal masonry, revealed structure like flying buttresses, ribbed vaults to allow better lighting, large stained-glass windows. **Abbey Church of Saint-Denis** (France), ordered by Abbot Suger, 1136-47 ***Cathedral of Notre-Dame** (Paris, France), ordered by Bishop Maurice de Sully, 1163-1351 ***Chartres Cathedral** (France), 1194-1260 ***Cologne Cathedral** (Cologne, Germany), ordered by Archbishop Konrad von Hochstaden, 1248-1880 ***St. Vitus Cathedral** (Prague, Czech Republic), by Matthias of Arras, later Peter Parler, 1344-1929
Yuan and Ming 1279-1644	China. Mongol-influenced timber and some brick structures influenced by geomancy. Emphasized monumental mass in low-lying, sprawling structures with simple rectangular pavilions, great halls, elaborate wooden latticework, carved and painted details. ***Forbidden City** (Beijing, China), ordered by Emperor Yongle, 1406-20
Renaissance 1420s-1520s	Italy. The rebirth or rediscovery of ancient Roman design, grounded in a scholarly approach to architecture. Followed rules of proportion in perspective and symmetry, classical orders, and simple but perfected geometric forms; emphasis on human scale. ***Pazzi Chapel** (Florence, Italy), by Filippo Brunelleschi, 1429-61 ***Palazzo Medici-Riccardi** (Florence, Italy), by Michelozzo di Bartolomeo, 1444-60 ***Tempietto San Pietro** (Rome, Italy), by Donato Bramante, 1502-10 ***Villa Almerico Capra, or La Rotonda** (near Vicenza, Italy), by Andrea Palladio, later Vincenzo Scamozzi, 1566-1610

Style and period	Location; characteristics; significant examples
Mughal 1526-1858	India. Monumental palaces and mosques blending Hindu and Islamic architecture. Sandstone with marble inlay; highly decorative, with semiprecious stones, vegetal and Koranic motifs. Formulaic four-part pleasure gardens (*charbâgh*), exemplified by grounds of Taj Mahal. ***Humayun's Tomb** (Delhi, India), by Sayyid Muhammad, 1562-72 ***Taj Mahal** (Agra, India), ordered by Emperor Shah Jahan, 1631-48
Baroque 1630s-1700s	Italy, later Western Europe. Elaborate and theatrical religious and civic structures, focused on dramatic overall effect. Complex geometric shapes and elaborate sculptures meant to be viewed from many angles. **St. Carlo alle Quattro Fontane** (Rome, Italy), by Francesco Borromini, 1638-41 ***Palace of Versailles** (Versailles, France), royal hunting lodge (built 1631-34) expanded under Louis XIV, 1661-1710 **Church of San Lorenzo** (Turin, Italy), by Guarino Guarini, 1666-79 **Church of St. John of Nepomuk, or Asamkirche** (Munich, Germany), by Cosmas Damian and Egid Quirin Asam, 1733-46
Rococo 1690s-1700s	Europe. Mostly interior, simplified but still fanciful Baroque designs; ornate with natural motifs, gold trim, light and creamy colors, asymmetrical designs, and unusual materials. ***Sanssouci Palace** (Potsdam, Germany), by Georg Wenzeslaus von Knobelsdorff, 1745-47
Neoclassicism 1750-1830	Europe, Americas. Civic, commercial, and religious structures; chaste, non-decorative designs in reaction to Baroque excess. Grounded in Enlightenment-era principles and simple, strict adherence to classic (Greek, Roman, Renaissance) forms and details. Palladian style in England, Federal style in U.S. **Chiswick House** (Chiswick, England, UK), by Richard Boyle, 1725-29 ***Monticello** (Charlottesville, VA), by Thomas Jefferson, 1768-1809
Neo-Gothic 1837-1900s	Britain, U.S. Civic, commercial, and religious structures utilizing Gothic forms in new commercial enterprises like railway stations and hotels. Traditional masonry façade disguised modern structural material like iron and glass. ***Westminster Palace** (London, England, UK), by Charles Barry and A.W.N. Pugin, 1840-47 **Hotel fronting St. Pancras Railway Station** (London, England, UK), by George Gilbert Scott, 1865-71
Arts and Crafts 1850s-1930s	England, U.S. Residential structures made of brick and other indigenous materials with pastoral and traditional elements like gabled roofs. Conceived as a reaction against homogenization of style following the Industrial Revolution. **Red House** (Bexley Heath, England, UK), by Philip Webb, 1859 **Tigbourne Court** (Surrey, England, UK), by Edwin Lutyens, 1898
Beaux-Arts 1870s-1930s	France, U.S. Grandiose, highly decorative style, using a mix of classical forms taught at the École des Beaux-Arts (School of Fine Arts) in Paris: columns, wall projections, elaborate rooftops, high-relief decoration. **Boston Public Library** (Boston, MA), by McKim, Mead, and White, 1888-95 **Grand Central Terminal** (New York, NY), Reed & Stem and Warren & Wetmore, 1903-13
Art Nouveau 1884-1905	Europe (esp. Brussels, Belgium; France). Civic and residential structures using industrial products like metal and glass to mimic natural forms; airy, fluid, and ornate. ***Hôtel Tassel** (Brussels, Belgium), by Victor Horta, 1892-93 **Entrances to Métro (subway)** (Paris, France), by Hector Guimard, 1900
Prairie 1893-1917	U.S. Mostly residences, some civic buildings in adapted Arts and Crafts style. Inspired by American Midwest and small-town values. Frank Lloyd Wright most notable architect of the style. Buildings centered on chimney, with overhanging eaves and horizontal emphasis, long bands of windows. **Robie House** (Chicago, IL), by Frank Lloyd Wright, 1908-10 **National Farmer's Bank** (Owatonna, MN), by Louis Sullivan, 1906-08
Futurism 1913-14	Italy. Purely theoretical style that produced no actual structures. Emphasized concrete, glass, and steel construction; pure geometric forms and straight lines; and exposed structure and utilities. **La Città Nuova (The New City)** (sketches), by Antonio Sant'Elia, 1913
Constructivism 1914-20s	Russia, Europe. Public buildings based on socialist philosophies. Purely utilitarian industrial design, modern materials. **Rusakov Club** (Moscow, Russia), by Konstantin Melnikov, 1927-28
De Stijl 1917-31	Netherlands. Building and fixtures designed as a complete, sculpture-like piece of art; emphasis on primary colors, simple but asymmetrical geometry. Name is Dutch for "The Style." ***Schröder House** (Utrecht, Netherlands), by Gerrit Thomas Rietveld, 1924
Bauhaus 1919-33	Weimar Republic Germany. Art and design school founded by Walter Gropius with philosophy that the machine is the modern medium. Concrete, glass, and steel construction that united industrial crafts and fine arts with simple geometric forms and colors. ***Bauhaus** (Dessau, Germany), by Walter Gropius, 1925-26
International Style 1920s-70s	Asia, Europe, North America. Reinforced concrete and steel structures, mostly commercial buildings with some residences and civic structures. Post-and-slab construction meant walls no longer supported weight so façades could be continuous strip (ribbon) glass "curtain-walls" with modular interiors. Emphasis on simple forms; glass, marble, and stainless steel; minimal decoration. **Philadelphia Savings Fund Society Building** (Philadelphia, PA), by George Howe and William Lescaze, 1926-32 **Villa Savoye** (Poissy, France), by Le Corbusier, 1928-31 **Seagram Building** (New York, NY), by Ludwig Mies Van Der Rohe with Philip Johnson, 1954-58
Art Deco 1925-30s	Europe, U.S. Traditional, symmetric, elegant construction like Beaux-Arts whimsically mixed with modern styles like geometric forms and steel or chrome features. **Chrysler Building** (New York, NY), by William van Alen, 1928-30 **Empire State Building** (New York, NY), by Shreve, Lamb & Harmon, 1930-31
Postmodernism 1970s-present	Asia, Europe, North America. Playful reaction against generic, mainstream "orthodox modern architecture," according to Robert Venturi. Token references to traditional architectural elements like pediments or gables on houses; aim to present, Venturi wrote, "old clichés in new settings." **Vanna Venturi House** (Philadelphia, PA), by Robert Venturi, 1962 **Public Service Building** (Portland, OR), by Michael Graves, 1980-82

World Population Growth

The global population in ancient times can only be very roughly estimated, but there were perhaps 50 mil people in the world in 1000 BCE. The United Nations (UN) Population Division estimates a figure of 300 mil for 1 CE. This diagram shows estimated population growth since then.

Although different sources may provide varying estimates, they agree that the world's population began growing more rapidly in the 18th and 19th centuries and increased at an even greater rate in the 20th century. According to the UN, the total population reached 1 bil in 1804; rose to 2 bil 123 years later, in 1927; to 3 bil 33 years after that, in 1960; to 4 bil in 1974; to 5 bil in 1987; and to 6 bil in 1999.

The U.S. Census Bureau, which also issues estimates and projections, put the world population in mid-2015 at about 7.3 bil. It projects that the population will reach 8 bil by 2025.

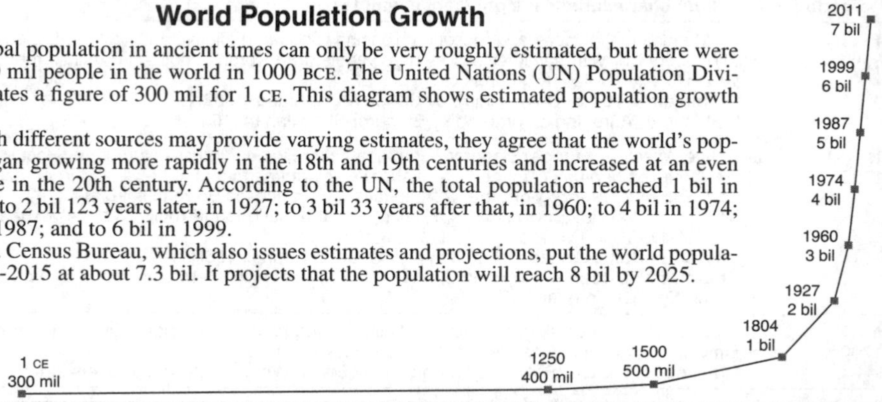

Area and Population of the World by Continent/Region

Source: International Data Base, International Programs Center, U.S. Census Bureau, U.S. Dept. of Commerce; *The World Factbook*, Central Intelligence Agency (CIA)

Composition of geographical (continental) regions are as defined by the United Nations. Figures may not add up to totals due to rounding.

Continent/ region	Land area (sq mi)	Land area (sq km)	% of Earth's land	Population (midyear) 1950	1975	2000	2015	% of world total, 2015	2025[1]
Asia	11,921,254	30,875,906	21.2	1,437,565,483	2,413,723,561	3,693,777,378	4,343,450,503	59.9	4,714,839,381
Africa	11,494,762	29,771,296	20.4	229,058,740	416,195,934	802,705,164	1,156,434,405	15.9	1,442,127,980
Europe[2]	8,559,255	22,168,368	15.2	547,140,324	678,635,710	730,523,121	745,615,793	10.3	750,004,442
N. America	7,879,373	20,407,482	14.0	165,945,185	238,783,486	313,388,332	356,602,286	4.9	385,028,748
Latin America[3]	7,762,306	20,104,280	13.8	165,442,794	320,629,690	517,756,498	617,243,759	8.5	673,313,198
Oceania	3,278,295	8,490,744	5.8	12,476,128	21,114,852	30,420,890	37,143,265	0.5	41,266,804
Antarctica[4]	5,405,430	14,000,000	9.6	NA	NA	NA	NA	NA	NA
World	**56,300,674**	**145,818,075**	**100.0**	**2,557,628,654**	**4,089,083,233**	**6,088,571,383**	**7,256,490,011**	**100.0**	**8,006,580,553**

NA = Not applicable. (1) Projected. (2) Includes all of Russia. (3) Includes the Caribbean. (4) Antarctica has no indigenous inhabitants, though people are present at permanent and seasonal research stations.

Population of the World's Largest Urban Areas

Source: *World Urbanization Prospects*, Dept. of Economic and Social Affairs, UN Population Division

Population figures are midyear estimates for urban agglomerations, i.e., whole metropolitan areas comprising an urban center and surrounding settlements of lower density. The UN releases an update every two years. Population counts for 2015 and 2030 are projections. Data may differ from figures elsewhere in *The World Almanac*. MMA = Major Metropolitan Area.

(ranked by mid-2015 population)

Rank	Urban area, country	Population (thous.) 1975	2000	2015	2030	Rate of change (%) 1975-2000	2000-15	2015-30	Pop. of urban area as % of country's 2015 pop.
1.	Tokyo, Japan	26,615	34,450	38,001	37,190	29.4%	10.3%	–2.1%	29.9%
2.	Delhi, India	4,426	15,732	25,703	36,060	255.4	63.4	40.3	2.1
3.	Shanghai, China	5,627	13,959	23,741	30,751	148.1	70.1	29.5	1.7
4.	São Paulo, Brazil	9,614	17,014	21,066	23,444	77.0	23.8	11.3	10.3
5.	Mumbai (Bombay), India	7,082	16,367	21,043	27,797	131.1	28.6	32.1	1.7
6.	Mexico City, Mexico	10,734	18,457	20,999	23,865	71.9	13.8	13.6	17.2
7.	Beijing, China	4,828	10,162	20,384	27,706	110.5	100.6	35.9	1.5
8.	Kinki MMA (Osaka), Japan	16,298	18,660	20,238	19,976	14.5	8.5	–1.3	15.9
9.	Cairo, Egypt	6,450	13,626	18,772	24,502	111.3	37.8	30.5	21.2
10.	New York-Newark, NY-NJ, U.S.	15,880	17,813	18,593	19,885	12.2	4.4	6.9	5.8
11.	Dhaka, Bangladesh	2,221	10,285	17,598	27,374	363.1	71.1	55.6	10.4
12.	Karachi, Pakistan	3,989	10,032	16,618	24,838	151.5	65.6	49.5	8.3
13.	Buenos Aires, Argentina	8,745	12,407	15,180	16,956	41.9	22.4	11.7	35.0
14.	Kolkata (Calcutta), India	7,888	13,058	14,865	19,092	65.5	13.8	28.4	1.2
15.	Istanbul, Turkey	3,600	8,744	14,164	16,694	142.9	62.0	17.9	17.8
16.	Chongqing, China	2,545	7,863	13,332	17,380	209.0	69.6	30.4	1.0
17.	Lagos, Nigeria	1,890	7,281	13,123	24,239	285.2	80.2	84.7	7.2
18.	Manila, Philippines	4,999	9,962	12,946	16,756	99.3	30.0	29.4	12.8
19.	Rio de Janeiro, Brazil	7,733	11,307	12,902	14,174	46.2	14.1	9.9	6.3
20.	Guangzhou, Guangdong, China	1,698	7,330	12,458	17,574	331.7	70.0	41.1	0.9
21.	Los Angeles-Long Beach-Santa Ana, CA, U.S.	8,926	11,798	12,310	13,257	32.2	4.3	7.7	3.8
22.	Moscow, Russia	7,623	10,005	12,166	12,200	31.2	21.6	0.3	8.5
23.	Kinshasa, Dem. Rep. of the Congo	1,482	6,140	11,587	19,996	314.3	88.7	72.6	14.6
24.	Tianjin, China	3,527	6,670	11,210	14,655	89.1	68.1	30.7	0.8
25.	Paris, France	8,558	9,737	10,843	11,803	13.8	11.4	8.9	16.3
26.	Shenzhen, China	36	6,550	10,749	12,673	18,094.4	64.1	17.9	0.8
27.	Jakarta, Indonesia	4,813	8,390	10,323	13,812	74.3	23.0	33.8	4.0
28.	London, UK	7,546	8,613	10,313	11,467	14.1	19.7	11.2	16.1
29.	Bangalore, India	2,111	5,567	10,087	14,762	163.7	81.2	46.3	0.8
30.	Lima, Peru	3,696	7,294	9,897	12,221	97.3	35.7	23.5	32.5

National Rankings by Population, Area, Population Density, 2015

Source: International Data Base, International Programs Center, U.S. Census Bureau, U.S. Dept. of Commerce; *The World Factbook*, Central Intelligence Agency (CIA)

Population figures are for midyear. The world had an estimated population of 7.3 bil in mid-2015. China was the most populous nation, with nearly one-fifth of the world total. A country's land area does not include inland water. Refer to Nations of the World for a country's total area. Population density is calculated using land area.

Largest Populations

Rank	Country	Population
1.	China[1]	1,367,485,388
2.	India	1,251,695,584
3.	United States	321,368,864
4.	Indonesia	255,993,674
5.	Brazil	204,259,812
6.	Pakistan	199,085,847
7.	Nigeria	181,562,056
8.	Bangladesh	168,957,745
9.	Russia	142,423,773
10.	Japan	126,919,659

Smallest Populations

Rank	Country	Population
1.	Vatican City[2]	842
2.	Nauru	9,540
3.	Tuvalu	10,869
4.	Palau	21,265
5.	Monaco	30,535
6.	San Marino	33,020
7.	Liechtenstein	37,624
8.	Saint Kitts and Nevis	51,936
9.	Marshall Islands	72,191
10.	Dominica	73,607

Largest Land Areas

Rank	Country	Area (sq mi)	Area (sq km)
1.	Russia	6,323,482	16,377,742
2.	China	3,600,947	9,326,410
3.	United States	3,537,455	9,161,966
4.	Canada	3,511,023	9,093,507
5.	Brazil	3,227,096	8,358,140
6.	Australia	2,966,153	7,682,300
7.	India	1,147,956	2,973,193
8.	Argentina	1,056,642	2,736,690
9.	Kazakhstan	1,042,360	2,699,700
10.	Algeria	919,595	2,381,741

Smallest Land Areas

Rank	Country	Area (sq mi)	Area (sq km)
1.	Vatican City	0.17	0.44
2.	Monaco	0.77	2
3.	Nauru	8	21
4.	Tuvalu	10	26
5.	San Marino	24	61
6.	Liechtenstein	62	160
7.	Marshall Islands	70	181
8.	Saint Kitts and Nevis	101	261
9.	Maldives	115	298
10.	Malta	122	316

Most Densely Populated

Rank	Country	Persons per sq mi	Persons per sq km
1.	Monaco	39,542.6	15,267.5
2.	Singapore	21,392.7	8,259.8
3.	Vatican City[2]	4,956.3	1,913.6
4.	Bahrain	4,589.1	1,771.9
5.	Maldives	3,417.9	1,319.6
6.	Malta	3,392.9	1,310.0
7.	Bangladesh	3,361.7	1,298.0
8.	Taiwan	1,879.9	725.8
9.	Barbados	1,750.4	675.8
10.	Mauritius	1,709.4	660.0

Least Densely Populated

Rank	Country	Persons per sq mi	Persons per sq km
1.	Mongolia	5.0	1.9
2.	Namibia	7.0	2.7
3.	Australia	7.7	3.0
4.	Iceland	8.6	3.3
5.	Mauritania	9.0	3.5
6.	Libya	9.4	3.6
7.	Suriname	9.6	3.7
8.	Guyana	9.7	3.7
9.	Botswana	10.0	3.9
10.	Canada	10.0	3.9

(1) Does not include mid-2015 population of Hong Kong (7,141,106) and Macao (592,731). (2) Population is for mid-2014.

Current Population and Projections for Countries and Other Areas

Source: International Data Base, International Programs Center, U.S. Census Bureau, U.S. Dept. of Commerce; *The World Factbook*, Central Intelligence Agency (CIA)

(midyear figures)

Country/area	2015	2025	2050
Afghanistan	32,564,342	41,117,073	63,795,418
Albania	3,029,278	3,104,932	2,824,012
Algeria	39,542,166	45,841,317	55,444,735
American Samoa	54,343	53,316	49,308
Andorra	85,580	85,112	74,765
Angola	19,625,353	25,673,282	45,888,061
Anguilla	16,418	19,749	26,980
Antigua and Barbuda	92,436	103,830	122,930
Argentina	43,431,886	47,164,630	53,511,279
Armenia	3,056,382	2,961,175	2,468,311
Aruba	112,162	126,130	150,730
Australia	22,751,014	25,053,669	29,012,740
Austria	8,665,550	8,987,330	9,107,912
Azerbaijan	9,780,780	10,533,598	11,209,644
Bahamas, The	324,597	349,116	371,219
Bahrain	1,346,613	1,579,899	1,847,072
Bangladesh	168,957,745	197,673,655	250,155,274
Barbados	290,604	297,015	282,041
Belarus	9,589,689	9,325,020	8,339,664
Belgium	11,323,973	12,037,746	12,772,233
Belize	347,369	411,007	543,690
Benin	10,448,647	13,564,964	22,118,545
Bermuda	70,196	72,851	69,874
Bhutan	741,919	820,143	951,873
Bolivia	10,800,882	12,463,434	16,003,638
Bosnia and Herzegovina	3,867,055	3,787,402	3,216,039
Botswana	2,182,719	2,425,114	2,871,345
Brazil	204,259,812	218,259,140	232,304,177
Brunei	429,646	498,756	638,157
Bulgaria	7,186,893	6,728,056	5,531,820
Burkina Faso	18,931,686	25,384,628	47,429,509

Country/area	2015	2025	2050
Burundi	10,742,276	14,791,662	30,391,856
Cabo Verde	545,993	619,168	741,842
Cambodia	15,708,756	18,037,946	22,338,891
Cameroon	23,739,218	30,508,842	51,912,309
Canada	35,099,836	37,558,781	41,135,648
Cayman Islands	56,092	67,661	91,118
Central African Republic	5,391,539	6,637,613	10,338,863
Chad	11,631,456	13,914,726	20,473,601
Chile	17,508,260	18,764,737	19,688,474
China	1,367,485,388	1,407,006,788	1,301,627,048
Colombia	46,736,728	51,194,904	56,227,630
Comoros	780,971	905,545	1,169,893
Congo, Dem. Rep. of	79,375,136	99,162,003	144,805,434
Congo Republic	4,755,097	5,947,999	10,201,971
Cook Islands	9,838	7,621	5,460
Costa Rica	4,814,144	5,353,218	6,065,989
Côte d'Ivoire	23,295,302	27,651,498	37,111,782
Croatia	4,464,844	4,374,007	3,864,201
Cuba	11,031,433	10,784,894	9,161,479
Curaçao	148,406	153,501	150,128
Cyprus	1,189,197	1,329,908	1,392,078
Czech Republic	10,644,842	10,696,842	10,209,638
Denmark	5,581,503	5,697,913	5,575,147
Djibouti	828,324	1,016,919	1,395,810
Dominica	73,607	74,374	64,772
Dominican Republic	10,478,756	11,702,846	13,690,264
Ecuador	15,868,396	17,867,616	21,102,550
Egypt	88,487,396	103,742,157	137,872,522
El Salvador	6,141,350	6,288,430	6,181,181
Equatorial Guinea	740,743	935,553	1,428,139
Eritrea	6,527,689	7,987,458	11,381,250
Estonia	1,265,420	1,182,920	923,335

Country/area	2015	2025	2050
Ethiopia	99,465,819	131,260,566	228,066,276
Faroe Islands	50,196	53,200	57,112
Fiji	909,389	956,003	1,013,636
Finland	5,476,922	5,630,882	5,475,753
France	66,553,766	68,860,292	69,484,481
French Polynesia	282,703	305,484	324,712
Gabon	1,705,336	2,063,339	3,229,741
Gambia, The	1,967,709	2,369,298	3,210,223
Gaza Strip	1,869,055	2,350,255	3,392,849
Georgia	4,931,226	4,929,789	4,714,548
Germany	80,854,408	79,226,209	71,541,906
Ghana	26,327,649	32,610,058	52,415,526
Gibraltar	29,258	29,753	28,423
Greece	10,775,643	10,670,697	10,035,935
Greenland	57,733	57,174	49,356
Grenada	110,694	114,741	114,205
Guam	161,785	176,770	201,610
Guatemala	14,918,999	17,564,073	22,995,434
Guernsey	66,080	67,710	66,521
Guinea	11,780,162	15,240,839	26,407,254
Guinea-Bissau	1,726,170	2,061,262	2,894,545
Guyana	735,222	781,231	878,028
Haiti	10,110,019	11,252,370	13,352,710
Honduras	8,746,673	10,143,828	12,948,839
Hong Kong	7,141,106	7,296,877	6,623,263
Hungary	9,897,541	9,615,020	8,489,811
Iceland	331,918	366,578	406,766
India	1,251,695,584	1,396,046,308	1,656,553,632
Indonesia	255,993,674	276,746,433	300,183,166
Iran	81,824,270	90,481,226	100,044,564
Iraq	37,056,169	47,656,612	76,519,418
Ireland	4,892,305	5,417,947	6,333,836
Isle of Man	87,545	92,606	92,840
Israel	8,049,314	9,305,235	12,364,874
Italy	61,855,120	62,591,055	61,415,852
Jamaica	2,950,210	3,151,611	3,554,571
Japan	126,919,659	123,385,521	107,209,536
Jersey	97,294	104,140	107,581
Jordan	8,117,564	8,320,007	11,411,275
Kazakhstan	18,157,122	19,809,426	22,237,156
Kenya	45,925,301	53,196,255	70,755,460
Kiribati	105,711	117,779	139,738
Korea, North	24,983,205	26,242,210	26,969,396
Korea, South	49,115,196	49,372,307	43,368,983
Kosovo	1,870,981	1,999,461	2,222,619
Kuwait	2,788,534	3,169,497	3,863,453
Kyrgyzstan	5,664,939	6,218,713	7,063,351
Laos	6,911,544	7,971,675	10,068,995
Latvia	1,986,705	1,772,796	1,249,812
Lebanon	6,184,701	5,396,843	5,621,049
Lesotho	1,947,701	1,970,540	1,920,225
Liberia	4,195,666	5,283,774	8,192,118
Libya	6,411,776	7,374,566	8,970,664
Liechtenstein	37,624	40,505	43,610
Lithuania	2,884,433	2,573,431	1,801,002
Luxembourg	570,252	680,527	864,238
Macao	592,731	630,434	620,184
Macedonia	2,096,015	2,119,511	1,990,728
Madagascar	23,812,681	30,182,920	45,807,534
Malawi	17,964,697	24,957,849	51,780,996
Malaysia	30,513,848	34,683,300	42,928,546
Maldives	393,253	388,681	444,429
Mali	16,955,536	22,533,811	38,395,414
Malta	413,965	421,239	395,639
Marshall Islands	72,191	83,203	103,092
Mauritania	3,596,702	4,425,089	6,536,272
Mauritius	1,339,827	1,412,384	1,441,100
Mexico	121,736,809	134,828,700	150,567,503
Micronesia	105,216	98,948	74,483
Moldova	3,546,847	3,176,863	2,261,208
Monaco	30,535	31,706	29,810
Mongolia	2,992,908	3,301,176	3,669,264
Montenegro	647,073	635,537	577,654
Montserrat	5,241	5,529	5,707
Morocco	33,322,699	36,484,418	42,026,448
Mozambique	25,303,113	32,306,018	58,998,457
Myanmar (Burma)	56,320,206	61,747,758	70,673,160
Namibia	2,212,307	2,283,845	2,149,815
Nauru	9,540	10,008	11,995
Nepal	31,551,305	36,622,606	45,984,605
Netherlands	16,947,904	17,572,113	17,906,594
New Caledonia	271,615	307,452	370,511
New Zealand	4,438,393	4,775,930	5,198,992
Nicaragua	5,907,881	6,493,913	7,233,620
Niger	18,045,729	24,618,828	44,221,854
Nigeria	181,562,056	230,570,741	391,296,754
Northern Mariana Islands	52,344	61,985	77,842
Norway	5,207,689	5,682,068	6,364,008
Oman	3,286,936	3,981,057	5,401,957
Pakistan	199,085,847	228,385,138	290,847,790
Palau	21,265	22,102	22,894
Panama	3,657,024	4,117,882	4,859,334
Papua New Guinea	6,672,429	7,823,210	10,110,027
Paraguay	6,783,272	7,602,853	8,840,105
Peru	30,444,999	33,283,408	36,943,693
Philippines	100,998,376	117,445,897	155,380,252
Poland	38,562,189	37,753,766	32,738,308
Portugal	10,825,309	10,806,202	9,933,334
Puerto Rico	3,598,357	3,476,473	2,984,291
Qatar	2,194,817	2,562,764	2,558,854
Romania	21,666,350	20,872,127	18,060,354
Russia	142,423,773	140,139,049	129,908,086
Rwanda	12,661,733	16,080,729	27,506,207
Saint Barthelemy	7,237	7,056	6,527
Saint Helena	7,795	7,888	7,296
Saint Kitts and Nevis	51,936	55,405	56,362
Saint Lucia	163,922	168,519	162,356
Saint Martin	31,754	33,048	34,601
Saint Pierre and Miquelon	5,657	5,030	3,516
Saint Vincent and the Grenadines	102,627	100,409	93,507
Samoa	197,773	210,369	245,010
San Marino	33,020	35,203	35,178
São Tomé and Príncipe	194,006	227,395	309,457
Saudi Arabia	27,752,316	31,877,311	40,250,628
Senegal	13,975,834	17,580,816	27,244,158
Serbia	7,176,794	6,845,638	5,869,146
Seychelles	92,430	98,843	100,391
Sierra Leone	5,879,098	7,500,140	13,593,862
Singapore	5,674,472	6,732,999	8,609,518
Sint Maarten	40,888	46,560	53,001
Slovakia	5,445,027	5,405,646	4,850,540
Slovenia	1,983,412	1,907,560	1,596,947
Solomon Islands	622,469	747,001	1,015,731
Somalia	10,616,380	13,274,251	22,626,120
South Africa	53,675,563	59,108,375	68,528,850
South Sudan	12,042,910	16,615,122	26,843,710
Spain	48,146,134	51,415,437	52,490,640
Sri Lanka	22,053,488	23,563,343	25,166,733
Sudan	36,108,853	42,733,103	59,129,521
Suriname	579,633	636,782	717,936
Swaziland	1,435,613	1,585,439	1,834,151
Sweden	9,801,616	10,587,441	12,011,256
Switzerland	8,121,830	8,665,531	9,539,097
Syria	17,064,854	24,537,876	31,225,740
Taiwan	23,415,126	23,642,264	20,834,040
Tajikistan	8,191,958	9,510,130	12,132,365
Tanzania	51,045,882	66,904,889	118,586,412
Thailand	67,976,405	69,588,429	66,063,997
Timor-Leste	1,231,116	1,539,173	2,191,749
Togo	7,552,318	9,741,450	16,583,950
Tonga	106,501	104,648	78,995
Trinidad and Tobago	1,222,363	1,183,838	1,023,741
Tunisia	11,037,225	11,849,537	12,180,271
Turkey	79,414,269	84,544,177	89,290,126
Turkmenistan	5,231,422	5,800,391	6,607,083
Turks and Caicos Islands	50,280	61,293	84,240
Tuvalu	10,869	11,819	13,423
Uganda	37,101,745	50,692,201	93,476,229
Ukraine	44,429,471	42,887,993	37,148,031
United Arab Emirates	5,779,760	7,063,346	8,018,904
United Kingdom	64,088,222	67,243,723	71,153,797
United States	321,368,864	347,334,912	398,328,349
Uruguay	3,341,893	3,431,610	3,495,238
Uzbekistan	29,199,942	31,823,964	35,116,374
Vanuatu	272,264	323,464	432,658
Vatican City[2]	842	NA	NA
Venezuela	29,275,460	33,188,608	40,255,592
Vietnam	94,348,835	102,458,828	111,173,583
Virgin Islands, British	33,454	41,324	59,618
Virgin Islands, U.S.	103,574	95,902	68,933
Wallis and Futuna	15,613	16,023	15,598
West Bank	2,785,366	3,328,248	4,376,251
Western Sahara	570,866	735,697	1,173,350
Yemen	26,737,317	32,822,216	46,080,625
Zambia	15,066,266	20,104,997	38,992,619
Zimbabwe	14,229,541	17,370,260	25,198,196
World[1]	**7,256,490,011**	**8,006,580,553**	**9,408,141,302**

NA = Not available. **Note:** Figures for countries do not include the population of any dependencies listed separately in this table. For example, China's population estimate and projections do not include Hong Kong nor Macao. (1) Total projected populations do not include countries for which projections were not available. (2) Current pop. is as of 2014.

Countries Ranked by Gross Domestic Product and Per Capita GDP, 2014

Source: *The World Factbook*, Central Intelligence Agency (CIA)

Estimates of gross domestic product (GDP)—the value of all final goods and services that a country produced in a year—were made based on purchasing power parity exchange rates. Per capita GDP is calculated using the estimated population size as of July 1 in a given year. Data may differ from estimates made by the U.S. Bureau of Economic Analysis. GDP figures are for 2014 unless otherwise noted.

GDP (in mil) Highest		GDP (in mil) Lowest		Per capita GDP Highest		Per capita GDP Lowest	
1. China[1]	$17,630,000	1. Tuvalu	$35	1. Qatar	$143,400	1. Central African Republic	$600
2. U.S.	17,460,000	2. Nauru[2]	60	2. Luxembourg	92,400	Somalia[6]	600
3. India	7,277,000	3. Marshall Islands	178	3. Liechtenstein[4]	89,400	3. Congo, Dem. Rep. of	700
4. Japan	4,807,000	4. Kiribati	180	4. Singapore	81,300	4. Malawi	800
5. Germany	3,621,000	5. Palau	272	5. Monaco[5]	78,700	5. Burundi	900
6. Russia	3,568,000	6. Micronesia[3]	331	6. Brunei	77,700	Liberia	900
7. Brazil	3,073,000	7. Tonga	523	7. Kuwait	71,000	7. Niger	1,000
8. France	2,587,000	8. São Tomé and Príncipe	612	8. Norway	65,900	8. Mozambique	1,100
9. Indonesia	2,554,000	9. Vanuatu	687	9. United Arab Emirates	65,000	9. Eritrea	1,200
10. UK	2,435,000	10. Dominica	757	10. Switzerland	55,200	10. Guinea	1,300
11. Mexico	2,143,000	11. Samoa	995	11. San Marino[5]	55,000	11. Guinea-Bissau	1,400
12. Italy	2,066,000	12. Solomon Islands	1,046	12. U.S.	54,800	Madagascar	1,400
13. Korea, South	1,786,000	13. St. Vincent and the Grenadines	1,198	13. Saudi Arabia	52,800	13. Ethiopia	1,500
14. Saudi Arabia	1,616,000	14. Comoros	1,211	14. Bahrain	51,400	Togo	1,500
15. Canada	1,579,000	15. St. Kitts and Nevis	1,220	15. Netherlands	47,400	15. Mali	1,600
16. Spain	1,534,000	16. Grenada	1,248	16. Ireland	46,800	Kiribati	1,600
17. Turkey	1,512,000	17. St. Lucia	1,893	17. Australia	46,600	17. Comoros	1,700
18. Iran	1,284,000	18. Antigua and Barbuda	1,989	18. Austria	45,400	Burkina Faso	1,700
19. Australia	1,100,000	19. San Marino	2,007	19. Sweden	44,700	Rwanda	1,700
20. Nigeria	1,058,000	20. Seychelles	2,304	Germany	44,700	Gambia, The	1,700

(1) Does not include Hong Kong ($400.6 bil GDP) or Macao ($51.7 bil GDP in 2013). (2) 2005 est. (3) Supplemented by grant aid, averaging perhaps $100 mil annually. (4) 2009 est. (5) 2013 est. (6) 2010 est.

Gold Reserves of Selected Central Banks and Governments, 1975-2014

Source: *International Financial Statistics*, International Monetary Fund (IMF)
(in mil fine troy ounces)

Year end	All countries	Canada	China[1]	France	Germany[2]	India	Italy	Japan	Netherlands	Russia	Switzerland	UK	U.S.
1975	1,188.0	22.0	NA	100.9	117.6	7.0	82.5	21.1	54.3	NA	83.2	21.0	274.7
1980	1,152.2	21.0	12.8	81.9	95.2	8.6	66.7	24.2	43.9	NA	83.3	18.8	264.3
1985	1,147.4	20.1	12.7	81.9	95.2	9.4	66.7	24.2	43.9	NA	83.3	19.0	262.7
1990	1,144.2	14.8	12.7	81.9	95.2	10.7	66.7	24.2	43.9	NA	83.3	18.9	261.9
1995	1,114.4	3.4	12.7	81.9	95.2	12.8	66.7	24.2	34.8	9.4	83.3	18.4	261.7
2000	1,066.0	1.2	12.7	97.2	111.5	11.5	78.8	24.5	29.3	12.4	77.8	15.7	261.6
2002	1,045.2	0.6	19.3	97.2	110.8	11.5	78.8	24.6	27.4	12.5	61.6	10.1	262.0
2003	1,027.4	0.1	19.3	97.2	110.6	11.5	78.8	24.6	25.0	12.5	52.5	10.1	261.5
2004	1,010.7	0.1	19.3	96.0	110.4	11.5	78.8	24.6	25.0	12.4	43.5	10.0	261.6
2005	991.3	0.1	19.3	90.9	110.2	11.5	78.8	24.6	22.3	12.4	41.5	10.0	261.6
2006	979.6	0.1	19.3	87.4	110.0	11.5	78.8	24.6	20.6	12.9	41.5	10.0	261.5
2007	963.3	0.1	19.3	83.7	109.9	11.5	78.8	24.6	20.0	14.5	36.8	10.0	261.5
2008	963.9	0.1	19.3	80.1	109.7	11.5	78.8	24.6	19.7	16.7	33.4	10.0	261.5
2009	980.8	0.1	33.9	78.3	109.5	17.9	78.8	24.6	19.7	20.9	33.4	10.0	261.5
2010	991.5	0.1	33.9	78.3	109.3	17.9	78.8	24.6	19.7	25.4	33.4	10.0	261.5
2011	1,003.3	0.1	33.9	78.3	109.2	17.9	78.8	24.6	19.7	28.4	33.4	10.0	261.5
2012	1,018.6	0.1	33.9	78.3	109.0	17.9	78.8	24.6	19.7	30.8	33.4	10.0	261.5
2013	1,024.1	0.1	33.9	78.3	108.9	17.9	78.8	24.6	19.7	33.3	33.4	10.0	261.5
2014	1,030.0	0.1	33.9	78.3	108.8	17.9	78.8	24.6	19.7	38.8	33.4	10.0	261.5

NA = Not available. (1) Figures are for mainland China only and do not include Hong Kong (0.07 mil oz t in 2014) or Macao. (2) West Germany prior to 1991.

Consumer Price Changes in Selected Countries, 1975-2014

Source: International Monetary Fund (IMF); World Development Indicators, The World Bank
(annual average % change)

Country	1975-80	1980-85	1985-90	1990-95	1995-2000	2000-05	2006-07	2008-09	2009-10	2010-11	2011-12	2012-13	2013-14
Canada	8.7%	7.5%	4.5%	2.3%	1.7%	2.3%	2.1%	0.3%	1.8%	2.9%	1.5%	0.9%	1.9%
China[1]	NA	NA	9.5	13.1	1.8	1.4	4.8	–0.7	3.3	5.4	2.7	2.6	2.0
France	10.5	9.7	3.1	2.2	1.2	1.9	1.5	0.1	1.5	2.1	2.0	0.9	0.5
Germany	NA	NA	NA	2.8	1.3	1.5	2.3	0.3	1.1	2.1	2.0	1.5	0.9
Italy	16.4	13.8	5.7	5.0	2.4	2.4	1.8	0.8	1.5	2.7	3.0	1.2	0.2
Japan	6.6	2.8	1.3	1.4	0.3	–0.4	0.1	–1.3	–0.7	–0.3	–0.03	0.4	2.7
Spain	18.6	12.2	6.5	5.2	2.6	3.2	2.8	–0.3	1.8	3.2	2.4	1.4	–0.1
Sweden	10.5	9.0	6.2	4.2	0.5	1.5	2.2	–0.5	1.2	3.0	0.9	–0.04	–0.2
Switzerland	2.3	4.3	2.5	3.2	0.7	0.8	0.7	–0.5	0.7	0.2	–0.7	–0.2	–0.01
United Kingdom	NA	NA	2.4	3.8	1.6	1.4	2.3	2.2	3.3	4.5	2.8	2.6	1.5
United States	8.9	5.5	4.0	3.1	2.5	2.6	2.9	–0.4	1.6	3.2	2.1	1.5	1.6
All countries	**11.3**	**15.0**	**16.1**	**19.2**	**6.0**	**3.7**	**3.7**	**2.4**	**3.6**	**4.8**	**3.8**	**3.6**	**3.2**

NA = Not available. (1) Figures for mainland China only and do not include Hong Kong (4.4% in 2013-14) or Macao (6.0% in 2013-14).

Hourly Compensation Costs in Manufacturing in Selected Countries, 1996-2013

Source: International Labor Comparisons Program, U.S. Bureau of Labor Statistics, U.S. Dept. of Labor; The Conference Board

For all workers in manufacturing, including part-time and temporary employees. Compensation costs, or employer labor costs, include direct pay (pay for time worked and directly-paid benefits), social insurance expenditures, and labor-related taxes.

(in U.S. dollars)

Country	1996	2000	2004	2007	2010	2013	Country	1996	2000	2004	2007	2010	2013
Argentina	7.43	8.16	4.51	8.04	12.77	19.97	Korea, South	9.55	9.62	12.63	19.43	17.88	21.96
Australia	19.17	16.40	26.72	33.28	39.56	47.09	Mexico	3.05	4.70	5.26	6.17	6.13	6.82
Austria	28.13	21.92	31.12	38.06	40.12	44.37	Netherlands	NA	21.00	32.95	38.23	39.45	42.26
Belgium	32.72	26.08	39.88	47.38	50.66	54.88	New Zealand	12.11	8.95	14.74	18.80	20.39	25.85
Brazil	7.07	4.34	3.82	7.10	10.00	10.69	Norway	NA	24.53	39.33	52.09	57.51	65.86
Canada	18.63	18.34	23.68	31.25	34.35	36.33	Philippines	1.31	0.99	1.08	1.58	1.85	2.12
Czech Republic	3.38	3.40	6.57	9.81	11.43	12.17	Poland	NA	3.52	4.91	7.81	8.46	9.25
Denmark	NA	22.24	35.66	44.41	48.50	51.07	Portugal	7.10	5.90	9.20	11.16	12.00	12.90
Estonia	NA	2.55	4.86	8.73	9.45	11.66	Singapore	11.93	11.72	13.20	15.70	19.41	23.95
Finland	25.01	19.83	32.41	39.05	40.35	44.57	Slovakia	2.73	2.60	5.20	8.53	10.71	12.31
France	27.82	21.33	32.11	37.96	39.04	42.85	Spain	15.48	12.38	19.79	24.75	26.61	28.09
Germany	33.24	25.37	37.67	43.72	44.25	48.98	Sweden	27.16	23.43	34.73	42.59	42.69	51.10
Greece	12.61	9.94	15.87	19.72	22.33	18.96	Switzerland	35.53	26.95	39.39	43.51	51.12	63.23
Hungary	3.11	2.96	6.17	8.66	8.40	9.44	Taiwan	7.10	7.31	7.27	8.18	8.31	9.37
Ireland	17.64	16.40	28.28	36.70	40.66	41.98	United Kingdom	17.77	20.63	28.47	35.21	28.99	31.00
Israel	10.90	12.25	12.81	15.72	19.22	22.25	United States	22.46	24.95	29.30	32.07	34.75	36.34
Italy	21.00	16.61	27.06	31.76	33.81	36.92	**OECD countries[1]**	**NA**	**16.57**	**22.12**	**26.72**	**28.71**	**30.83**
Japan	23.67	25.03	25.26	23.72	31.75	29.13							

NA = Not available. **Note:** China and India are not shown here because data for those countries are not strictly comparable. (1) All countries in this table except for Argentina, Brazil, the Philippines, Singapore, and Taiwan are members of the Organisation for Economic Co-operation and Development (OECD), but not all OECD members are shown.

Unemployment Rates in Selected Countries, 1970-2014

Source: International Labor Comparisons Program, U.S. Bureau of Labor Statistics, U.S. Dept. of Labor; The Conference Board

Year	U.S.	Australia	Canada	France	Germany[1]	Italy	Japan	Netherlands	Sweden	UK
1970	4.9%	1.7%	5.7%	2.5%	0.5%	3.2%	1.2%	NA	1.5%	NA
1975	8.5	4.9	6.9	3.6	3.4	3.4	1.9	5.1%	1.6	4.5%
1980	7.1	6.1	7.3	5.6	2.8	4.4	2.0	6.0	2.0	6.8
1985	7.2	8.3	10.1	9.0	7.2	6.0	2.5	9.6	2.8	11.4
1990	5.6	6.9	7.7	8.0	5.0	7.0	2.0	7.6	1.8	7.1
1995	5.6	8.5	8.6	10.2	8.2	11.3	2.9	7.1	9.1	8.7
1997	4.9	8.5	8.4	10.8	9.9	11.3	3.1	5.6	10.1	7.0
1999	4.2	6.9	7.0	10.1	8.5	11.0	4.2	3.5	7.1	6.0
2000	4.0	6.3	6.1	8.6	7.8	10.1	4.4	3.1	5.8	5.5
2001	4.7	6.8	6.5	7.8	7.9	9.1	4.5	2.5	5.0	5.1
2002	5.8	6.4	7.0	8.0	8.6	8.6	4.9	3.0	5.1	5.2
2003	6.0	5.9	6.9	8.6	9.3	8.5	4.6	4.1	5.8	5.0
2004	5.5	5.4	6.4	9.0	10.3	8.1	4.2	5.0	6.6	4.8
2005	5.1	5.0	6.0	9.0	11.2	7.8	3.8	5.2	7.7	4.9
2006	4.6	4.8	5.5	8.9	10.3	6.9	3.6	4.3	7.0	5.5
2007	4.6	4.4	5.2	8.1	8.7	6.2	3.6	3.6	6.1	5.4
2008	5.8	4.2	5.3	7.5	7.6	6.8	3.7	3.1	6.1	5.7
2009	9.3	5.6	7.3	9.2	7.8	7.9	4.8	3.7	8.3	7.6
2010	9.6	5.2	7.1	9.4	7.1	8.5	4.7	4.5	8.5	7.9
2011	8.9	5.1	6.5	9.3	5.9	8.5	4.2	4.5	7.7	8.1
2012	8.1	5.2	6.3	9.9	5.5	10.8	3.9	5.3	7.9	8.0
2013	7.4	5.6	6.1	10.4	5.3	12.3	3.4	6.7	8.0	7.6
2014[2]	6.2	6.0	5.9	10.4	5.1	12.8	3.0	6.9	7.9	NA

NA = Not available. **Note:** Unemployment rates are for the civilian working-age population. Data from other countries have been adjusted to U.S. concepts so that comparisons can be made. Because of changes in survey methodology, some data may not be fully comparable over time. (1) For former West Germany only through 1990; data after 1991 are for unified Germany. (2) Preliminary est.

Personal Tax Payments in Selected Countries, 2014

Source: *Taxing Wages*, Organisation for Economic Co-operation and Development (OECD)

Rates are averages for a single person without children at the income level of the average worker.

(as % of gross wage earnings before taxes, in U.S. dollars with equal purchasing power; ranked by total payment rate)

Country	Total payment rate[1]	Income tax	Employee soc. sec. contribs.	Gross earnings	Country	Total payment rate[1]	Income tax	Employee soc. sec. contribs.	Gross earnings
Belgium	42.3%	28.3%	14.0%	$55,225	Sweden	24.4%	17.4%	7.0%	$46,379
Germany	39.5	19.1	20.4	57,628	United Kingdom	23.7	14.4	9.3	50,865
Denmark	38.4	35.6	2.8	52,161	Australia	23.4	23.4	0.0	53,170
Austria	34.6	16.5	18.1	50,373	Canada	23.3	15.6	7.7	39,438
Hungary	34.5	16.0	18.5	23,133	Czech Republic	23.1	12.1	11.0	23,058
Slovenia	33.2	11.1	22.1	29,758	Spain	23.0	16.6	6.4	39,029
Italy	31.6	22.1	9.5	40,426	Slovakia	22.9	9.5	13.4	20,559
Netherlands	31.4	16.1	15.3	59,280	Japan	21.7	7.6	14.1	46,884
Finland	30.7	22.6	8.0	46,165	Ireland	20.5	16.5	4.0	41,958
Luxembourg	29.9	17.6	12.3	60,158	Estonia	19.7	17.7	2.0	22,537
Norway	28.8	20.6	8.2	59,355	Switzerland	17.4	11.1	6.3	66,506
France	28.7	14.7	14.1	44,136	New Zealand	17.3	17.3	0.0	37,226
Iceland	28.5	28.1	0.4	50,001	Israel	16.5	8.8	7.7	32,865
Turkey	27.4	12.4	15.0	24,054	South Korea	13.4	5.0	8.3	46,664
Portugal	27.3	16.3	11.0	29,805	Mexico	10.0	8.7	1.4	12,373
Greece	24.9	8.9	16.0	32,467	Chile	7.0	0.0	7.0	19,071
United States	24.8	17.2	7.7	50,075					
Poland	24.8	7.0	17.8	23,403	**OECD countries[2]**	**25.5**	**15.6**	**9.9**	**40,770**

(1) Figures may not add up to totals due to rounding. (2) The 34 countries shown here.

Refugees and Other Populations of Concern, 2005-14

Source: *UNHCR Global Trends*, United Nations High Commissioner for Refugees (UNHCR)

Refugees are persons recognized under the 1951 UN Refugee Convention/1967 Protocol or the 1969 OAU (Org. of African Unity) Refugee Convention, those recognized in accordance with the UNHCR Statute, and persons granted or receiving protection. The UNHCR also extends assistance to internally displaced persons (IDPs), although they legally remain under their home country's protection. Stateless persons are not considered nationals under any state under the operation of its laws. Others of concern comprises persons who do not necessarily belong in any one category. Because of changes in classification and methodology, figures from 2005 are not fully comparable with figures for later years. Population as of year-end.

Category	2005	2008	2010	2011	2012	2013	2014	% change, 2013-14
Refugees	8,662,000	10,489,800	10,549,700	10,404,800	10,498,000	11,699,300	14,380,100	22.9%
Asylum-seekers (pending cases)	802,100	825,800	837,500	895,300	942,800	1,164,400	1,796,200	54.3
Returned refugees[1]	1,105,600	603,800	197,700	531,900	525,900	414,600	126,900	–69.4
IDPs	6,616,800	14,442,200	14,697,900	15,473,400	17,670,400	23,925,500	32,274,600	34.9
Returned IDPs[1]	519,400	1,361,400	2,923,300	3,245,800	1,545,400	1,356,200	1,822,700	34.4
Stateless persons	2,383,700	6,572,200	3,463,000	3,477,100	3,335,800	3,469,200	3,492,100	0.7
Others of concern	960,400	166,900	1,255,600	1,411,800	1,329,700	836,100	1,052,800	25.9
Total	**21,050,000**	**34,462,100**	**33,924,700**	**35,440,100**	**35,848,000**	**42,865,300**	**54,945,400**	**28.2**

(1) Persons who have returned to their place of origin in that year.

Refugees and People in a Refugee-Like Situation, 2014

Source: *UNHCR Global Trends*, United Nations High Commissioner for Refugees (UNHCR)

Refugees are persons recognized under the 1951 UN Refugee Convention/1967 Protocol or the 1969 OAU (Org. of African Unity) Refugee Convention, those recognized in accordance with the UNHCR Statute, and persons granted or receiving protection. Persons outside of their country or territory of origin who face protection risks—but whose refugee status has not been ascertained—are described as being in a refugee-like situation. Only countries hosting 50,000 or more refugees and people in a refugee-like situation are shown; of those countries, only places originating 5,000 or more refugees and people in a refugee-like situation are given, in decreasing order. As of year-end.

Place of asylum	Origin of most refugees (excl. asylum seekers with pending cases)	Number
Africa		**4,126,779**
Algeria	Western Sahara	94,128
Burundi	Dem. Rep. of the Congo	52,936
Cameroon	Central African Republic, Nigeria	264,126
Chad	Sudan, Central African Republic	452,897
Congo, Dem. Rep. of	Central African Republic, Rwanda, Burundi	119,754
Congo Republic	Dem. Rep. of the Congo, Central African Republic, Rwanda	54,842
Egypt	Syria, Palestinian[1], Sudan, Somalia, Iraq	236,090
Ethiopia	South Sudan, Somalia, Eritrea, Sudan	659,524
Kenya	Somalia, South Sudan, Ethiopia, Dem. Rep. of the Congo	551,352
Mauritania	Mali, Western Sahara	75,635
Niger	Mali, Nigeria	77,830
Rwanda	Dem. Rep. of the Congo	73,820
South Africa	Somalia, Dem. Rep. of the Congo, Ethiopia, Zimbabwe, Congo Republic	112,192
South Sudan	Sudan, Dem. Rep. of the Congo	248,152
Sudan	South Sudan, Eritrea, Chad, Ethiopia	277,833
Tanzania	Dem. Rep. of the Congo, Burundi	88,492
Uganda	Dem. Rep. of the Congo, South Sudan, Somalia, Rwanda, Burundi	385,513
Asia		**7,942,132**
Afghanistan	Pakistan	300,423
Bangladesh	Myanmar (Burma)	232,472
China	Vietnam	301,052
India	China, Sri Lanka, Myanmar (Burma), Afghanistan	199,937
Iran	Afghanistan, Iraq	982,027
Iraq	Syria, Turkey, Iran, Palestinian[1]	271,143
Jordan	Syria, Iraq	654,141
Lebanon	Syria, Iraq	1,154,040
Malaysia	Myanmar (Burma)	99,381
Pakistan	Afghanistan	1,505,525
Syria	Iraq	149,140
Thailand	Myanmar (Burma)	130,238
Turkey	Syria, Iraq	1,587,374
Yemen	Somalia, Ethiopia	257,645
Europe		**1,495,283**
Austria[2]	Russia, Afghanistan	55,598
France	Sri Lanka, Dem. Rep. of the Congo, Russia, Serbia-Kosovo, Cambodia, Turkey, Vietnam, Laos, Guinea, Mauritania	252,264
Germany	Iraq, Syria, Afghanistan, Turkey, Iran, Serbia-Kosovo	216,973
Italy	Eritrea, Somalia, Afghanistan, Nigeria, Pakistan, Mali	93,715
Netherlands	Somalia, Iraq, Syria, Eritrea, Afghanistan	82,494
Russia	Ukraine	235,750
Sweden	Syria, Iraq, Somalia, Eritrea, stateless[3], Afghanistan	142,207
Switzerland	Eritrea, Syria	62,620
United Kingdom	Eritrea, Iran, Zimbabwe, Afghanistan, Somalia, Pakistan	117,161
Latin America and the Caribbean		**352,668**
Ecuador[2]	Colombia	122,161
Venezuela	Colombia	173,600
North America		**416,385**
Canada	Colombia, China, Sri Lanka, Pakistan, Haiti, Mexico	149,163
United States	China, Haiti, Colombia, Ethiopia, Egypt, El Salvador, Venezuela, Nepal, Russia, Guatemala, Iraq, Cameroon	267,222
Oceania		**46,847**
TOTAL		**14,380,094**

(1) Number includes Palestinians under the UNHCR mandate only. (2) Number as of year-end 2013/year-start 2014. (3) Persons not considered nationals under any state under the operation of its laws.

Internally Displaced Persons, 2014

Source: Internal Displacement Monitoring Centre, Norwegian Refugee Council

Internally displaced persons (IDPs) are people who have been forced to flee due to armed conflict or human rights violations but who have not crossed into another country. As such, they are not protected by international refugee law and legally remain under the protection of their home country. Estimates are as of year-end 2014 and may comprise only registered IDPs or those displaced from a certain area of a country.

Country	Number	Country	Number	Country	Number
Afghanistan	805,400+	India	853,900+	Philippines	77,700+
Armenia	<8,400	Indonesia	84,000+	Russia	25,400+
Azerbaijan	<568,900	Iraq	3.3 mil+	Senegal	24,000
Bangladesh	431,000+	Kenya	309,200	Serbia	97,300
Bosnia and Herzegovina	100,400+	Kosovo	17,100+	Somalia	1.1 mil
Burundi	<77,600	Laos	<4,500	South Sudan[3]	1.5 mil
Cameroon	40,000+	Lebanon	19,700	Sri Lanka	<90,000
Central African Republic	<438,500	Liberia	23,000	Sudan[3]	3.1 mil+
Chad	<71,000	Libya	400,000+	Syria	7.6 mil+
Colombia[1]	6.0 mil	Macedonia	200+	Thailand	<35,000
Congo, Dem. Rep. of	2.8 mil	Mali	61,600+	Timor-Leste	900+
Congo Republic	<7,800	Mexico	281,400+	Togo	10,000
Côte d'Ivoire	300,900+	Myanmar (Burma)	645,300	Turkey	953,700+
Cyprus	<212,400	Nepal	<50,000	Turkmenistan	4,000+
El Salvador	<288,900	Niger	11,000	Uganda	<29,800
Eritrea	<10,000	Nigeria	1.1 mil+	Ukraine	646,500+
Ethiopia	397,200	Pakistan	1.9 mil+	Uzbekistan	3,400+
Georgia	<232,700	Palestine[2]	275,000+	Yemen	334,100
Guatemala	248,500+	Papua New Guinea	7,500+	Zimbabwe	<36,000
Honduras	29,400+	Peru	150,000+	**Total**	**38.0 mil**

Note: The number of IDPs in Algeria, Israel, and Rwanda was undetermined. (1) Cumulative since 1985. (2) Occupied Palestinian Territory. (3) Number does not incl. an est. 20,000 IDPs from Abyei Area, disputed territory between Sudan and South Sudan.

Mortality Rate by Cause of Death in Selected Nations, 2012

Source: World Health Organization (WHO)

(per 100,000 population; ranked by deaths from communicable, maternal, neonatal, and nutritional conditions)

Rank	Country	Communicable, maternal, neonatal, and nutritional conditions	Non-communicable diseases	Injuries	All causes
1.	Sierra Leone	1,327.4	963.5	149.5	2,440.4
2.	Central African Republic	1,212.1	550.8	107.9	1,870.9
3.	Lesotho	1,110.5	671.8	142.5	1,924.7
4.	Chad	1,070.9	712.6	114.5	1,897.9
5.	Mozambique	998.1	593.7	175.3	1,767.0
6.	Somalia	927.2	550.7	188.5	1,666.3
7.	Congo, Dem. Rep. of	920.7	724.4	137.1	1,782.2
8.	Swaziland	884.3	702.4	119.5	1,706.2
9.	Angola	873.3	768.4	137.8	1,779.4
10.	Guinea-Bissau	869.8	764.7	111.6	1,746.2
96.	Russia	73.8	790.3	102.8	966.9
121.	China	41.4	576.3	50.4	668.2
129.	Japan	33.9	244.2	40.5	318.6
133.	United States	31.3	412.8	44.2	488.4
138.	United Kingdom	28.5	358.8	21.5	408.8
149.	Canada	22.6	318.0	31.3	372.0
151.	Germany	21.6	365.1	23.0	409.7
153.	France	21.4	313.2	34.6	369.1
165.	Italy	15.5	303.6	20.1	339.2
170.	Austria	12.6	359.5	30.6	402.7

Estimated HIV Infection and Reported AIDS Cases, 2014

Source: Joint United Nations Programme on HIV/AIDS (UNAIDS)

UNAIDS announced in July 2015 that the UN Millennium Development Goal of halting and reversing the spread of HIV had been met. Between 2000, when the goal was set, and 2014, the number of new HIV infections each year dropped 35%, from 3.1 million to 2 million. This reduction was particularly notable among children, as pregnant women were increasingly able to access antiretroviral therapy. The cost of antiretroviral therapy has become more affordable as well. In 2014, the price of a year's worth of first-line formulations for one person was about $100. The annual number of AIDS-related deaths fell by 42% from 2004 to 2014, though tuberculosis remained a leading cause of death among those living with HIV.

Worldwide, an estimated $187 billion had been spent on the HIV/AIDS epidemic since 2000. Current investment in fighting HIV/AIDS is about $22 billion a year. Despite a decline in the number of countries that restricted the entry, stay, and residence of those living with HIV/AIDS, 37 countries still had such discriminatory laws as of Apr. 2015.

Current and New HIV/AIDS Cases and Deaths by Region, 2014

Source: Joint United Nations Programme on HIV/AIDS (UNAIDS)

Region	Number living with HIV/AIDS	Percent of world total[1]	New HIV infections	AIDS-related deaths
East and Southern Africa	19,200,000	52.0%	940,000	460,000
West and Central Africa	6,600,000	17.9	420,000	330,000
Asia and the Pacific	5,000,000	13.5	340,000	240,000
Western and Central Europe and North America	2,400,000	6.5	85,000	26,000
Latin America	1,700,000	4.6	87,000	41,000
Eastern Europe and Central Asia	1,500,000	4.1	140,000	62,000
Caribbean	280,000	0.8	13,000	8,800
Middle East and North Africa	240,000	0.7	22,000	12,000
World[2]	**36,900,000**	**100.0**	**2,000,000**	**1,200,000**

(1) Population within a region living with HIV/AIDS as a percentage of population worldwide living with HIV/AIDS. (2) Figures may not add up to totals because of rounding.

Drinking Water and Sanitation, 2015

Source: World Health Organization (WHO); United Nations Children's Fund (UNICEF)

In 2015, an estimated 91% of the world's population had access to improved drinking-water sources, although service and water quality were inconsistent. Meanwhile, the UN's Millennium Development Goal for access to improved sanitation (target 77%) has yet to be reached. As of 2015, only 68% of people worldwide used improved sanitation facilities. One in eight people still practiced open defecation. Those without access to improved sanitation are at increased risk of contracting a variety of infectious and parasitic diseases such as diarrhea, malaria, and hepatitis A.

The G7 countries have near-universal (99% or greater) access to improved water and sanitation. In comparison, while 97% of Russia's population had access to improved drinking-water sources, only 72% had access to improved sanitation in 2015. In China, the figures were 95% and 76%, respectively.

Lowest Access to Improved Sanitation Facilities, 2015

Source: World Health Organization (WHO); United Nations Children's Fund (UNICEF)

Sanitation facilities are considered improved if they are private and not shared with other households, incl. sewer or septic system connections, ventilated improved pit latrines, and composting toilets.

(ranked by % of total pop. with access)

Rank	Country	% of pop. with access: Total	Urban	Rural
1.	South Sudan	6.7%	16.4%	4.5%
2.	Niger	10.9	37.9	4.6
3.	Togo	11.6	24.7	2.9
4.	Madagascar	12.0	18.0	8.7
5.	Chad	12.1	31.4	6.5
6.	Sierra Leone	13.3	22.8	6.9
7.	Ghana	14.9	20.2	8.6
8.	Congo Republic	15.0	20.0	5.6
9.	Tanzania	15.6	31.3	8.3
10.	Eritrea	15.7	44.5	7.3
11.	Liberia	16.9	28.0	5.9
12.	Papua New Guinea	18.9	56.4	13.3
13.	Uganda	19.1	28.5	17.3
14.	Benin	19.7	35.6	7.3
15.	Burkina Faso	19.7	50.4	6.7
16.	Guinea	20.1	34.1	11.8
17.	Mozambique	20.5%	42.4%	10.1%
18.	Guinea-Bissau	20.8	33.5	8.5
19.	Central African Republic	21.8	43.6	7.2
20.	Côte d'Ivoire	22.5	32.8	10.3
	Caucasus and Central Asia	95.9	96.3	95.7
	Eastern Asia	77.4	87.3	64.3
	Latin America and the Caribbean	83.1	87.9	64.1
	Northern Africa	89.5	92.2	86.1
	Oceania	35.5	75.9	23.2
	South-eastern Asia	72.2	80.8	64.3
	Southern Asia	46.9	67.2	36.0
	Sub-Saharan Africa	29.7	40.3	23.3
	Western Asia	93.8	95.8	89.2
	Developed countries	95.6	96.8	91.4
	World	**67.6**	**82.2**	**50.5**

Lowest Access to Improved Drinking-Water Sources, 2015

Source: World Health Organization (WHO); United Nations Children's Fund (UNICEF)

Improved drinking-water sources protect from outside contamination and incl. household connections, public taps or standpipes, dug wells, and rainwater collection.

(ranked by % of total pop. with access)

Rank	Country/area	% of pop. with access: Total	Urban	Rural
1.	Papua New Guinea	40.0%	88.0%	32.8%
2.	Equatorial Guinea	47.9	72.5	31.5
3.	Angola	49.0	75.4	28.2
4.	Chad	50.8	71.8	44.8
5.	Mozambique	51.1	80.6	37.0
6.	Madagascar	51.5	81.6	35.3
7.	Congo, Dem. Rep. of	52.4	81.1	31.2
8.	Afghanistan	55.3	78.2	47.0
9.	Tanzania	55.6	77.2	45.5
10.	Ethiopia	57.3	93.1	48.6
11.	Haiti	57.7	64.9	47.6
12.	Eritrea	57.8	73.2	53.3
13.	Mauritania	57.9	58.4	57.1
14.	Niger	58.2	100.0	48.6
15.	Palestine	58.4	50.7	81.5
16.	South Sudan	58.7	66.7	56.9
17.	Sierra Leone	62.6%	84.9%	47.8%
18.	Togo	63.1	91.4	44.2
19.	Kenya	63.2	81.6	56.8
20.	Mongolia	64.4	66.4	59.2
	Caucasus and Central Asia	88.6	97.8	81.4
	Eastern Asia	95.6	97.6	93.0
	Latin America and the Caribbean	94.6	97.4	83.9
	Northern Africa	92.8	94.9	90.2
	Oceania	55.7	94.2	44.1
	South-eastern Asia	90.3	95.5	85.6
	Southern Asia	92.5	95.5	91.0
	Sub-Saharan Africa	67.7	86.8	56.1
	Western Asia	94.6	96.5	90.1
	Developed countries	99.2	99.5	97.9
	World	**90.9**	**96.4**	**84.5**

Foreign Development Aid Donors, 2013-14

Source: Development Assistance Committee (DAC), Organisation for Economic Co-operation and Development (OECD)

Listed below is the amount of official development assistance (ODA)—in the form of grants or loans—each DAC member country disbursed in a given year to developing countries. The numbers are net flows, or amounts disbursed less repayments on earlier loans. Both bilateral ODA (made directly to an aid recipient) and multilateral ODA (made to an agency like the World Bank) are included.

(ranked by size of ODA as % of 2014 gross national income [GNI]; 2014 figures are prelim.)

Rank	Donor	ODA as % of GNI 2013	ODA as % of GNI 2014	ODA in mil of current U.S. dollars 2013	ODA in mil of current U.S. dollars 2014
1.	Sweden	1.01%	1.10%	$5,827.29	$6,222.55
2.	Luxembourg	1.00	1.07	429.32	426.76
3.	Norway	1.07	0.99	5,581.36	5,024.28
4.	Denmark	0.85	0.85	2,927.46	2,995.97
5.	United Kingdom	0.70	0.71	17,870.71	19,386.50
6.	Netherlands	0.67	0.64	5,435.45	5,572.03
7.	Finland	0.54	0.60	1,435.36	1,634.58
8.	Switzerland	0.45	0.49	3,200.12	3,547.59
9.	Belgium	0.45	0.45	2,299.54	2,384.51
10.	Germany	0.38	0.41	14,228.26	16,248.67
11.	Ireland	0.46	0.38	845.85	808.80
12.	France	0.41	0.36	11,338.93	10,370.87
13.	New Zealand	0.26	0.27	457.31	502.28
14.	Australia	0.33	0.27	4,845.55	4,203.42
15.	Austria	0.27	0.26	1,171.49	1,144.39
16.	Canada	0.27	0.24	4,947.24	4,196.45
17.	Iceland	0.25%	0.21%	$34.91	$35.41
18.	Japan	0.23	0.19	11,581.59	9,188.29
19.	United States	0.18	0.19	31,496.57	32,728.62
20.	Portugal	0.23	0.19	488.32	418.96
21.	Italy	0.17	0.16	3,430.07	3,342.05
22.	Spain	0.18	0.14	2,374.57	1,893.28
23.	Korea, South	0.13	0.13	1,755.38	1,850.67
24.	Slovenia	0.13	0.13	61.63	61.53
25.	Czech Rep.	0.11	0.11	210.88	208.99
26.	Greece	0.10	0.11	239.07	248.44
27.	Slovakia	0.09	0.08	86.04	81.24
28.	Poland	0.10	0.08	471.90	437.08
Total DAC		**0.30**	**0.29**	**135,072.17**	**135,164.21**
Avg. country effort		0.39	0.39		
G7 countries[1]		**0.27**	**0.27**	**94,893.37**	**95,461.45**
EU institutions		**NA**	**NA**	**15,959.20**	**16,105.70**

NA = Not applicable/available. (1) Canada, France, Germany, Italy, Japan, the UK, and the U.S.

Recipients of U.S. Official Development Assistance, 2012-13

Source: Development Assistance Committee (DAC), Organisation for Economic Co-operation and Development (OECD)

(net flows of total official development assistance in mil of current U.S. dollars; ranked by 2013 numbers)

Rank	Country	2012	2013
1.	Afghanistan	$2,773.13	$1,700.19
2.	West Bank and Gaza Strip	288.27	966.26
3.	Kenya	817.83	819.88
4.	Syria	150.77	748.26
5.	Tanzania	568.74	734.11
6.	Ethiopia	732.61	619.40
7.	Pakistan	624.76	569.47
8.	Nigeria	419.11	551.06
9.	Mozambique	435.49	543.68
10.	Jordan	556.64	529.11
11.	Iraq	582.80	483.87
12.	South Africa	$505.27	$479.35
13.	South Sudan	773.34	457.94
14.	Uganda	394.25	451.97
15.	Haiti	427.64	405.38
16.	Sudan	63.51	373.50
17.	Zambia	305.09	313.21
18.	Colombia	326.93	291.18
19.	Congo, Dem. Rep. of	291.76	262.62
20.	Morocco	167.23	260.25
All developing countries		**25,471.15**	**26,383.17**

Nuclear Powers of the World

As of Aug. 2015, eight countries were acknowledged nuclear weapons states: the **UK**, **France**, **China**, **India**, **Pakistan**, **Russia**, **North Korea**, and the **U.S.** **Israel** was presumed to have an arsenal. **South Africa** announced in 1993 that it had built six nuclear weapons and partially completed a seventh, but that they had all been dismantled. **Argentina** and **Brazil** established a joint inspection agency in the early 1990s after committing to the peaceful use of nuclear energy.

All of the more than 40 nations with the knowledge or technology to produce nuclear weapons have signed the Nuclear Non-Proliferation Treaty (NPT) with the exception of Israel, India, and Pakistan. After expelling Intl. Atomic Energy Agency (IAEA) inspectors in Dec. 2002, North Korea announced on Jan. 10, 2003, its withdrawal from the NPT effective the following day.

North Korea has conducted three nuclear tests to date, in 2006, 2009, and 2013. Analysts believe the country has sufficient weapons-grade plutonium for at least six bombs but lacks the means to deliver them via missile. North Korea is also suspected of attempting to enrich uranium. (Enriched uranium can be used as reactor fuel or in a nuclear weapon.)

Iran had argued that as an NPT signatory, it had a right to pursue the peaceful application of nuclear technology. The IAEA maintained the country had withheld information on the extent of its nuclear activities in violation of the NPT. Iran continued its activities despite multiple UN Security Council resolutions against the transfer of nuclear technology to Iran and numerous international economic sanctions. Iranian president Hassan Rouhani, elected in June 2013, agreed to new talks. Iran and the so-called P5+1 (the five permanent members of the UN Security Council plus Germany) signed a Joint Comprehensive Plan of Action July 14, 2015. Under the agreement, Iran would curb its ability to enrich uranium as well as reduce its current stockpile of the material. Iran's "breakout" time—the amount of time it would need to accumulate enough material for one nuclear bomb—would be increased to at least one year. The IAEA would monitor Iran's compliance in return for the lifting of sanctions.

Estimated Numbers of Nuclear Weapons by Country, 1945-2015

Source: *Bulletin of the Atomic Scientists*; Carnegie Endowment for International Peace; Federation of American Scientists (FAS); Natural Resources Defense Council (NRDC); Nuclear Threat Initiative (NTI); Stockholm International Peace Research Institute (SIPRI)

Year	United States	USSR/Russia	United Kingdom	France	China	Israel[1]	India	Pakistan	Total[2]
1945	6	—	—	—	—	—	—	—	6
1950	369	5	—	—	—	—	—	—	374
1960	20,434	1,605	30	—	—	—	—	—	22,069
1970	26,662	11,643	280	36	75	8	—	—	38,696
1980	24,304	30,062	350	250	280	31	—	—	55,246
1990	21,004	37,000	300	505	430	53	—	—	59,239
2000	10,577	21,000	185	470	400	72	—	—	32,632
2010	9,400	12,300	225	300	240	60-80	60-80	70-90	22,400
2015	7,200	7,500	215	300	250	80	90-110	100-120	15,700

(1) Israel is widely presumed to have a nuclear stockpile although it has never confirmed nor denied its nuclear status. (2) Numbers may not add up to total due to rounding and uncertainty over size of stockpiles and operational status of warheads.

Nuclear Arms Treaties and Negotiations: A Historical Overview

Aug. 5, 1963: Partial (Limited) Test Ban Treaty signed by the UK, U.S., and USSR, went into effect Oct. 10, 1963. Prohibits parties from testing or participating in the testing of nuclear weapons in the atmosphere, in outer space, and under water.

July 1, 1968: Nuclear Non-Proliferation Treaty (NPT) opened to signatures, went into effect Mar. 5, 1970. With the UK, U.S., and USSR as major signers, the parties agree not to help non-nuclear nations get or make nuclear weapons, though such nations can pursue the peaceful application of nuclear energy.

On May 11, 1995, parties to the treaty voted to extend it indefinitely. As of Aug. 2015, 191 states were party to the treaty, not including North Korea, which withdrew in 2003. Israel, India, and Pakistan were not signatories.

May 26, 1972: The **Strategic Arms Limitation Talks (SALT I)** led to the signing of two agreements by the U.S. and USSR: the **Treaty on the Limitation of Anti-Ballistic Missile Systems** (or **ABM Treaty**) and an interim agreement. These agreements cap the numbers of intercontinental ballistic missile (ICBM) launchers and submarine-launched ballistic missile (SLBM) launchers.

July 3, 1974: Treaty on the Limitation of Underground Nuclear Weapon Tests (or **Threshold Test Ban Treaty**) signed by the U.S. and USSR. Limits underground testing of nuclear weapons to yields of 150 kilotons or less. On May 28, 1976, U.S. and Russia signed the **Peaceful Nuclear Explosions Treaty**, governing explosions outside weapons test sites. Both treaties entered into force Dec. 11, 1990.

June 18, 1979: Strategic Offensive Arms Limitation Treaty (or **SALT II**) signed by the U.S. and USSR. Limited each side to 2,400 missile launchers and heavy bombers; ceiling to apply until Jan. 1, 1985. Never ratified; superseded by START I.

Dec. 8, 1987: Intermediate-Range Nuclear Forces (INF) Treaty signed by the U.S. and USSR. Eliminates all U.S. and Soviet intermediate- and shorter-range nuclear missiles. For the first time, a treaty eliminated an entire category of nuclear weapons and established a comprehensive verification system. Entered into force June 1, 1988.

July 31, 1991: Strategic Arms Reduction Treaty (START I) signed by the USSR and U.S. to reduce long-range nuclear forces no later than seven years after the treaty entered into force. This was the first treaty to mandate reductions in so-called strategic nuclear weapons by the superpowers.

With the Soviet Union breakup in Dec. 1991, four former republics became independent nations with strategic nuclear arms: Russia, Ukraine, Kazakhstan, and Belarus. Under the **Lisbon Protocol** of May 1992, Ukraine, Kazakhstan, and Belarus agreed to accede to the NPT as non-nuclear-weapon states, to destroy or transfer their nuclear weapons to Russia, and to ratify START I. START I expired on Dec. 5, 2009.

Jan. 3, 1993: START II signed by the U.S. and Russia, ratified by the two on Jan. 26, 1996, and Apr. 14, 2000, respectively. Called for further reductions in their long-range nuclear arsenals. Both sides withdrew from the treaty before it went into force.

Sept. 24, 1996: Comprehensive Nuclear-Test-Ban Treaty (CTBT) signed by 71 countries, including the five nuclear-weapons states (China, France, Russia, UK, U.S.). The CTBT bans all nuclear explosions. It is intended to prevent the nuclear powers from developing more advanced weapons while limiting the ability of other states to acquire such devices. As of Aug. 2015, the CTBT had been signed by 183 nations. It had been ratified by 164 but not the U.S. or China. It will enter into force only after ratification by all Annex 2 states—the 44 states with nuclear technology capabilities at the time of the treaty's final negotiations. Only 36 have done so to date.

Dec. 13, 2001: The U.S. announced its intention to withdraw from the **ABM Treaty** in 180 days, arguing that it hindered the government in protecting itself from "future terrorist or rogue state missile attacks." Russia responded by withdrawing from **START II**, stating that U.S. withdrawal from the ABM Treaty effectively invalidated START II.

May 24, 2002: Strategic Offensive Reductions Treaty (SORT or **Moscow Treaty)** signed by the U.S. and Russia, entered into force June 1, 2003. Committed both countries to cutting nuclear arsenals to 1,700-2,200 warheads each by Dec. 31, 2012. SORT lapsed upon entry into force of the New START Treaty.

Apr. 8, 2010: New START Treaty signed by the U.S. and Russia, entered into force Feb. 5, 2011. It limits each country's arsenal of deployed strategic nuclear warheads to 1,550.

Major International Organizations

African Union (AU), inaugurated July 9, 2002, in Durban, South Africa, following disbanding of the Organization of African Unity (OAU). All of Africa's countries, with the exception of Morocco, make up its 54 members. (Morocco withdrew after the OAU admitted Western Sahara [Sahrawi Arab Dem. Rep.], a territory claimed by Morocco.) The AU is focused on achieving greater socioeconomic integration and unity among its member states. The AU's founding document authorized the organization to intervene to stop genocide, war crimes, or human rights abuses within individual member nations. **Headquarters:** Addis Ababa, Ethiopia. **Website:** www.au.int

Asia-Pacific Economic Cooperation (APEC), founded Nov. 1989 as a forum to further cooperation on trade and investment between nations of the region and the rest of the world. Its 21 members are Australia, Brunei, Canada, Chile, China, Hong Kong, Indonesia, Japan, Malaysia, Mexico, New Zealand, Papua New Guinea, Peru, Philippines, Russia, Singapore, South Korea, Taiwan, Thailand, the U.S., and Vietnam. **Secretariat:** Singapore. **Website:** www.apec.org

Association of Southeast Asian Nations (ASEAN), formed Aug. 8, 1967, to promote economic, social, and cultural cooperation and development among the states of Southeast Asia. Its members are Brunei, Cambodia, Indonesia, Laos, Malaysia, Myanmar, Philippines, Singapore, Thailand, and Vietnam. **Headquarters:** Jakarta, Indonesia. **Website:** www.asean.org

Caribbean Community and Common Market (CARICOM), established Aug. 1, 1973, to increase cooperation in economics, health, education, culture, science and technology, and tax administration, as well as the coordination of foreign policy. Its 15 members are Antigua and Barbuda, The Bahamas, Barbados, Belize, Dominica, Grenada, Guyana, Haiti, Jamaica, Montserrat, St. Kitts and Nevis, St. Lucia, St. Vincent and the Grenadines, Suriname, and Trinidad and Tobago. Anguilla, Bermuda, British Virgin Islands, Cayman Islands, and Turks and Caicos Islands are associate members. **Secretariat:** Georgetown, Guyana. **Website:** www.caricom.org

The Commonwealth, originally called the British Commonwealth of Nations, then the Commonwealth of Nations, is an association of nations and dependencies, most part of the former British Empire. Queen Elizabeth II, the current British monarch, is the symbolic head of the Commonwealth. (The secretary-general is chosen by Commonwealth leaders.)

There are 53 independent, sovereign nations in the Commonwealth. Regular members include the UK and 15 other nations recognizing the British monarch, represented by a governor-general, as their head of state. **Secretariat:** London, UK. **Website:** www.thecommonwealth.org

Commonwealth of Independent States (CIS), established in Dec. 1991 as an alliance of former Soviet constituent republics. Its members are Armenia, Azerbaijan, Belarus, Kazakhstan, Kyrgyzstan, Moldova, Russia, Tajikistan, Turkmenistan, Ukraine, and Uzbekistan. Georgia withdrew from the organization in 2009 following fighting with Russia over disputed territory. Policy is set through coordinating bodies such as the Council of the Heads of States and Council of the Heads of Governments. **Headquarters:** Minsk, Belarus. **Website:** www.cis.minsk.by or www.cisstat.com/eng/

European Free Trade Association (EFTA), created May 3, 1960, to promote free trade and economic integration. The European Economic Area (EEA) agreement, in force since 1994, set up a single market, with free flow of goods, services, capital, and labor, among EU nations and Iceland, Liechtenstein, and Norway, the EFTA members party to the EEA. Switzerland, the fourth EFTA member, has bilateral agreements with the EU. **Headquarters:** Geneva, Switzerland. **Website:** www.efta.int

European Union (EU), known as the European Community (EC) until 1993, aims to integrate economies, coordinate social developments, and foster political partnerships between member states. As of Jan. 1, 1993, there has been a single market, with no restrictions on the movement of people, goods, services, and money, within the EU.

The EU has its origins in such organizations as the European Coal and Steel Community (ECSC), established by the 1951 Treaty of Paris, and the European Economic Community (EEC, or Common Market) and European Atomic Energy Community (Euratom), created by the 1957 Treaties of Rome. A merger of the three communities' executives went into effect in 1967. As of Aug. 2015, there were 28 EU members: the 12 original members (Belgium, Denmark, France, Germany, Greece, Ireland, Italy, Luxembourg, Netherlands, Portugal, Spain, and UK); 3 that entered in 1995 (Austria, Finland, Sweden); 10 that joined in 2004 (Cyprus, Czech Republic, Estonia, Hungary, Latvia, Lithuania, Malta, Poland, Slovakia, Slovenia); 2 that joined in 2007 (Bulgaria, Romania); and 1 that joined in 2013 (Croatia). Albania, Macedonia, Montenegro, Serbia, and Turkey were candidate countries. All 79 member-states of the Africa, Caribbean, and Pacific Group of States (APC) with the exception of Cuba are affiliated with the EU under the Cotonou Agreement (for the 20-year period ending in 2020). **De facto capital:** Brussels, Belgium. **Website:** europa.eu

Leaders of the then-12 member nations signed the Treaty on European Union, also known as the Maastricht Treaty, on Feb. 7, 1992. It went into effect in 1993, committing the organization to launching a common currency; to establishing common foreign policies; and to taking a lead on social policy among other issues. The European Central Bank was established in 1998. In 1999, 11 of the then-15 EU countries began using the euro. By 2002, national currencies in those 11 countries and Greece were removed from circulation, leaving the euro as the only currency of legal tender. EU peacekeeping forces replaced NATO troops in Macedonia, 2003, the first such mission for the organization. A Treaty Establishing a Constitution for Europe was signed in 2004 by EU members but was never ratified.

Group of Eight (G8), forum of major industrialized countries. France, Germany, Italy, Japan, the UK, and the U.S. first met in 1975 as the Group of Six. Canada joined in 1976 and Russia in 1998. The EU is also represented at summits. In Mar. 2014, group members condemned Russia for its annexation of Crimea, a region of Ukraine. They boycotted a planned G8 summit in Russia and have met as the Group of Seven since June 2014.

International Criminal Police Organization (INTERPOL), created 1923 as the International Criminal Police Commission before changing its name in 1956, is the world's largest international police organization. There were 190 member nations as of Aug. 2015. **General Secretariat:** Lyon, France. **Website:** www.interpol.int

League of Arab States (Arab League), created Mar. 22, 1945. The League promotes economic, social, political, and military cooperation, mediates disputes, and represents Arab states in certain international negotiations. Its members are Algeria, Bahrain, Comoros, Djibouti, Egypt, Iraq, Jordan, Kuwait, Lebanon, Libya, Mauritania, Morocco, Oman, Palestine (considered an independent state by the League), Qatar, Saudi Arabia, Somalia, Sudan, Syria, Tunisia, United Arab Emirates, and Yemen. **Headquarters:** Cairo, Egypt. **Website:** www.lasportal.org

North Atlantic Treaty Organization (NATO), created with the signing of what is popularly known as the Washington Treaty Apr. 4, 1949 (in effect Aug. 24, 1949). Its 28 members as of Aug. 2015 are Albania, Belgium, Bulgaria, Canada, Croatia, Czech Republic, Denmark, Estonia, France, Germany, Greece, Hungary, Iceland, Italy, Latvia, Lithuania, Luxembourg, Netherlands, Norway, Poland, Portugal, Romania, Slovakia, Slovenia, Spain, Turkey, UK, and U.S.

Members agree to settle disputes by peaceful means, to develop their capacity to resist armed attack, to regard an attack on one as an attack on all, and to take necessary action to repel an attack under Article 51 of the UN Charter. **Headquarters:** Brussels, Belgium. **Website:** www.nato.int

NATO's military representatives include the Military Committee; the International Military Staff, the committee's executive body; and the military command structure (Allied Command Operations and Allied Command Transformation). The North Atlantic Council is NATO's main political decision-making body.

With the end of the Cold War in the early 1990s, members put greater stress on political action and on creating a rapid deployment force to react to local crises. By the mid-1990s, Russia and other former Soviet republics, among other countries, had joined with NATO in the so-called Partnership for Peace program, established in 1994, which provides for limited joint military exercises and peacekeeping missions. NATO also engages with countries through its Mediterranean Dialogue and Istanbul Cooperation Initiative and cooperates with countries it considers "partners across the globe."

A NATO-led multinational force was deployed to help keep the peace in Bosnia and Herzegovina in 1995. In 1999, a force was deployed in Kosovo. Following the Sept. 2001 terrorist attacks on the U.S., the NATO Council agreed to invoke for the first time Article 5 of the treaty, which stipulates mutual defense of alliance members. NATO assumed control of the International Security Assistance Force in Afghanistan (ISAF), Aug. 2003, marking the first time NATO led a mission outside Europe.

Organization of American States (OAS), which describes itself as the world's oldest regional organization, was officially formed by the signing of a charter on Apr. 30, 1948. The General Assembly of member states meets annually. The assembly assigns functions to the Permanent Council and the Inter-American Council for Integral Development.

The OAS's 35 members are Antigua and Barbuda, Argentina, The Bahamas, Barbados, Belize, Bolivia, Brazil, Canada, Chile, Colombia, Costa Rica, Cuba, Dominica, Dominican Republic, Ecuador, El Salvador, Grenada, Guatemala, Guyana, Haiti, Honduras, Jamaica, Mexico, Nicaragua, Panama, Paraguay, Peru, St. Kitts and Nevis, St. Lucia, St. Vincent and the Grenadines, Suriname, Trinidad and Tobago, U.S., Uruguay, and Venezuela. **Headquarters:** Washington, DC. **Website:** www.oas.org

Organization for Economic Cooperation and Development (OECD), established Dec. 14, 1960, to promote the economic and social welfare of all its member countries and to stimulate efforts on behalf of developing nations. Its 34 members are Australia, Austria, Belgium, Canada, Chile, Czech Republic, Denmark, Estonia, Finland, France, Germany, Greece, Hungary, Iceland, Ireland, Israel, Italy, Japan, Luxembourg, Mexico, Netherlands, New Zealand, Norway, Poland, Portugal, Slovakia, Slovenia, South Korea, Spain, Sweden, Switzerland, Turkey, UK, and the U.S. **Headquarters:** Paris, France. **Website:** www.oecd.org

Organization of Petroleum Exporting Countries (OPEC), created Sept. 14, 1960, by Iran, Iraq, Kuwait, Saudi Arabia, and Venezuela. This group made up of most but not all the major petroleum exporting nations seeks to stabilize the oil market and set world oil prices by controlling production. In addition to the founding countries, members include Algeria, Angola, Ecuador, Indonesia (suspended membership starting in Jan. 2009), Libya, Nigeria, Qatar, and United Arab Emirates. Gabon withdrew from OPEC in 1995. **Secretariat/headquarters:** Vienna, Austria. **Website:** www.opec.org

Organization for Security and Cooperation in Europe (OSCE), established in 1972 as the Conference on Security and Cooperation in Europe; current name adopted 1995. The group, formed by NATO and Warsaw Pact members, seeks improved East-West relations through a commitment to nonaggression and human rights, and cooperation in economics, science and technology, cultural exchange, and environmental protection. There were 57 member states as of Aug. 2015, making it the world's largest regional security organization. **Secretariat:** Vienna, Austria. **Website:** www.osce.org

United Nations

The 70th regular session of the United Nations General Assembly convened Sept. 15, 2015, attended by world leaders and other delegates from 193 nations. The UN headquarters is located on 18 acres, considered international territory, in New York, NY.

Proposals to establish an organization for maintenance of world peace led to the convening of the United Nations Conference on International Organization in San Francisco, Apr. 25-June 26, 1945, where the UN charter was drawn. It was signed June 26 by 50 nations and on Oct. 15 by Poland. It went into effect Oct. 24, 1945, upon ratification by the permanent members of the Security Council and a majority of the other signatories.

Purposes. To maintain international peace and security; to develop friendly relations among nations; to achieve international cooperation in solving economic, social, cultural, and humanitarian problems and in promoting respect for human rights and basic freedoms; to be a center for harmonizing the actions of nations in attaining these common ends.

Visitors to the UN. The UN headquarters is open every day except New Year's Day, President's Day, Good Friday, Memorial Day, Independence Day, Eid al-Fitr, Labor Day, Eid al-Adha, Thanksgiving, and Christmas. It is closed to the public during the UN general debate and may also close on short notice at other times for meetings of heads of state and government. Guided one-hour tours are conducted on weekdays only. Tickets can be purchased online. A limited number of tickets for same-day tours may be sold on-site. Groups of 40 or more can reserve directly with the UN via the website. For safety reasons, children under 5 years of age are not admitted on tours. **Website:** visit.un.org

The UN Visitor Center, in the basement of the General Assembly Building, is the only area open to the public on weekends. It includes a bookstore, gift shops, and cafe. All visitors over age 16 must present a government-issued photo ID to enter UN headquarters.

United Nations Secretaries General

Took office	Secretary, nation
1946	Trygve Lie, Norway
1953	Dag Hammarskjöld, Sweden
1961	U Thant, Burma (Myanmar)
1972	Kurt Waldheim, Austria
1982	Javier Pérez de Cuéllar, Peru
1992	Boutros Boutros-Ghali, Egypt
1997	Kofi Annan, Ghana
2007	Ban Ki-moon, South Korea

Six Main Organs of the United Nations

The United Nations consists of six principal organs, 15 agencies, and many programs and other bodies. The six principal organs are the General Assembly, the Security Council, the Secretariat, the Economic and Social Council, the International Court of Justice, and the Trusteeship Council.

General Assembly. The General Assembly is composed of representatives of all the member nations. Each nation is entitled to one vote. The General Assembly meets in regular annual sessions and in special session when convoked at the request of the Security Council or a majority of UN members. On important questions a two-thirds majority of members present and voting is required; on other questions a simple majority is sufficient.

The General Assembly must approve the UN budget and apportion expenses among members. A member in arrears can lose its vote if the amount of arrears equals or exceeds the amount of the contributions due for the preceding two full years. **Website:** www.un.org/en/ga/

Security Council. The Security Council consists of 15 members, five with permanent seats. The remaining 10 are elected for two-year terms by the General Assembly.

The permanent members of the Council are China, France, Russia, United Kingdom, and the United States. Nonpermanent members with terms expiring Dec. 31, 2015, are Chad, Chile, Jordan, Lithuania, and Nigeria; those with terms expiring Dec. 31, 2016, are Angola, Malaysia, New Zealand, Spain, and Venezuela.

The Security Council has the primary responsibility within the UN for maintaining international peace and security. The Council may investigate any dispute that threatens international peace and security.

Any UN member may participate in Council discussions at its invitation. Decisions on procedural questions are made by an affirmative vote of nine members. On all other matters the affirmative vote of nine members must include the concurring votes of all permanent members (giving them veto power).

The Security Council directs the various peacekeeping forces deployed throughout the world. **Website:** www.un.org/en/sc/

Secretariat. The Secretariat is responsible for the UN's day-to-day operations. It is headed by the secretary-general, who is the chief administrative officer of the UN. This person is appointed by the General Assembly, on the recommendation of the Security Council, for a five-year, renewable term. The secretary-general reports to the General Assembly and may bring to the attention of the Security Council any matter that threatens international peace. The Secretariat maintains an international staff of about 44,000. **Website:** www.un.org/en/sections/about-un/secretariat/

Economic and Social Council. The Economic and Social Council consists of 54 members elected by the General Assembly to overlapping three-year terms. The council is responsible for economic, social, and environmental matters. It meets with academics, non-governmental organizations, and private-sector representatives throughout the year. A month-long substantive session takes place each July. These sessions are alternately held in New York and Geneva, Switzerland. **Website:** www.un.org/en/ecosoc/

International Court of Justice (World Court). The International Court of Justice is the principal judicial organ of the UN. The Court has jurisdiction over cases that UN members or parties to the court's statute submit to it. In addition to rendering judgments, the Court gives advisory opinions.

The court's 15 judges are elected to nine-year terms by the General Assembly and the Security Council. No two judges come from the same nation, and they represent the world's principal legal systems. Once elected, the judges no longer act as representatives of a government. The Court remains permanently in session, except during vacations. All questions are decided by a majority. The International Court of Justice sits in The Hague, Netherlands. **Website:** www.icj-cij.org

Trusteeship Council. The Trusteeship Council, made up of the five permanent Security Council members, supervised the administration of UN trust territories. All 11 trust territories have since attained their right to self-determination. The Council formally suspended its work on Nov. 1, 1994, with Palau's independence.

The text of the **UN Charter** is online at www.un.org/en/documents/charter/.

Selected UN Programs and Funds, Specialized Agencies, and Related Organizations

UN programs and funds operate with voluntary funding. UN specialized agencies and related organizations are autonomous groups that have a functional relationship or working agreement with the UN. Their financing comes from voluntary and assessed contributions. The location in parentheses is the primary office or headquarters.

Food and Agriculture Org. (FAO) helps countries modernize farms, forests, and fisheries; improves food distribution; and raises levels of nutrition. (Rome, Italy) **Website:** www.fao.org

International Atomic Energy Agency (IAEA) promotes safe, peaceful uses of atomic energy. (Vienna, Austria) **Website:** www.iaea.org

International Civil Aviation Org. (ICAO) sets international civil aviation standards and regulations. (Montréal, Quebec, Canada) **Website:** www.icao.int

International Fund for Agricultural Development (IFAD) seeks to alleviate poverty in rural areas of developing countries. (Rome, Italy) **Website:** www.ifad.org

International Labor Org. (ILO) promotes decent and productive employment practices, the improvement of labor conditions, social security, and vocational training. (Geneva, Switzerland) **Website:** www.ilo.org

International Maritime Org. (IMO) seeks cooperation on technical matters affecting international shipping. (London, England, UK) **Website:** www.imo.org

International Monetary Fund (IMF) promotes international monetary cooperation, currency stabilization, and the expansion of international trade. (Washington, DC) **Website:** www.imf.org

International Telecommunication Union (ITU) regulates all aspects of global communication, including setting standards for radio, telegraph, telephone, and space radio-communications, and allocating radio frequencies. (Geneva, Switzerland) **Website:** www.itu.int

Office of the United Nations High Commissioner for Refugees (UNHCR) safeguards the rights of and provides essential assistance for refugees. (Geneva, Switzerland) **Website:** www.unhcr.org

United Nations Children's Fund (UNICEF) provides financial aid and development assistance to programs for children and mothers in developing countries. (New York, NY) **Website:** www.unicef.org

United Nations Educational, Scientific, and Cultural Org. (UNESCO) works to improve education around the world and to preserve historical and cultural sites. (Paris, France) **Website:** www.unesco.org

United Nations Industrial Development Org. (UNIDO) helps developing and transitional nations pursue sustainable industrial development while promoting international industrial cooperation. (Vienna, Austria) **Website:** www.unido.org

Universal Postal Union (UPU) facilitates international collaboration among postal service providers. (Berne, Switzerland) **Website:** www.upu.int

World Bank Group is focused on ending extreme poverty and promoting the sharing of prosperity worldwide. It encompasses five institutions. The **International Bank for Reconstruction and Development (IBRD)** provides loans and technical assistance for projects in developing member countries. The **International Development Assn. (IDA)** provides funds for development projects on concessionary terms to the poorest countries. The IBRD and IDA make up the World Bank. The **International Finance Corp. (IFC)** promotes private-sector growth in developing countries; encourages the development of local capital markets; and stimulates the international flow of private capital. The **Multilateral Investment Guarantee Agency (MIGA)** promotes foreign direct investment in developing countries by guaranteeing investments from noncommercial political risks. The **International Center for Settlement of Investment Disputes (ICSID)** provides conciliation and arbitration services for disputes between foreign investors and host governments that arise out of an investment. (Washington, DC) **Website:** www.worldbank.org, www.ifc.org, www.miga.org

World Health Org. (WHO) responds to public-health emergencies and works to eradicate life-threatening diseases. (Geneva, Switzerland) **Website:** www.who.int

World Intellectual Property Org. (WIPO) protects literary, industrial, scientific, and artistic works through international cooperation. (Geneva, Switzerland) **Website:** www.wipo.int

World Meteorological Org. (WMO) coordinates the free exchange of world meteorological data. (Geneva, Switzerland) **Website:** www.wmo.int

World Tourism Org. (UNWTO) advocates for responsible, sustainable, and universally accessible tourism. (Madrid, Spain) **Website:** www.unwto.org

World Trade Org. (WTO) administers trade agreements and treaties between nations, attempts to settle disputes, and keeps track of trade measures and statistics. (Geneva, Switzerland) **Website:** www.wto.org

Ongoing UN Peacekeeping Missions, 2015

Source: Dept. of Peacekeeping Operations (DPKO), Dept. of Field Support, Dept. of Management; United Nations Secretariat

Unless otherwise noted, numbers are for peacekeeping operations only (not including political and peacebuilding missions), as of June 30, 2015. Year given in graphic is the year each mission started.

Uniformed personnel (troops, police, military observers)	105,394
Countries contributing uniformed personnel	122
Civilian personnel:	
International	5,315
Local	11,476
Total personnel serving in 16 peacekeeping operations	123,945
Approved budget for July 1, 2015-June 30, 2016	$8.27 bil
Peacekeeping operations since 1948	71
Total fatalities in peace operations since 1948	3,372
Est. total cost of operations, 1948 to June 30, 2010	$69 bil

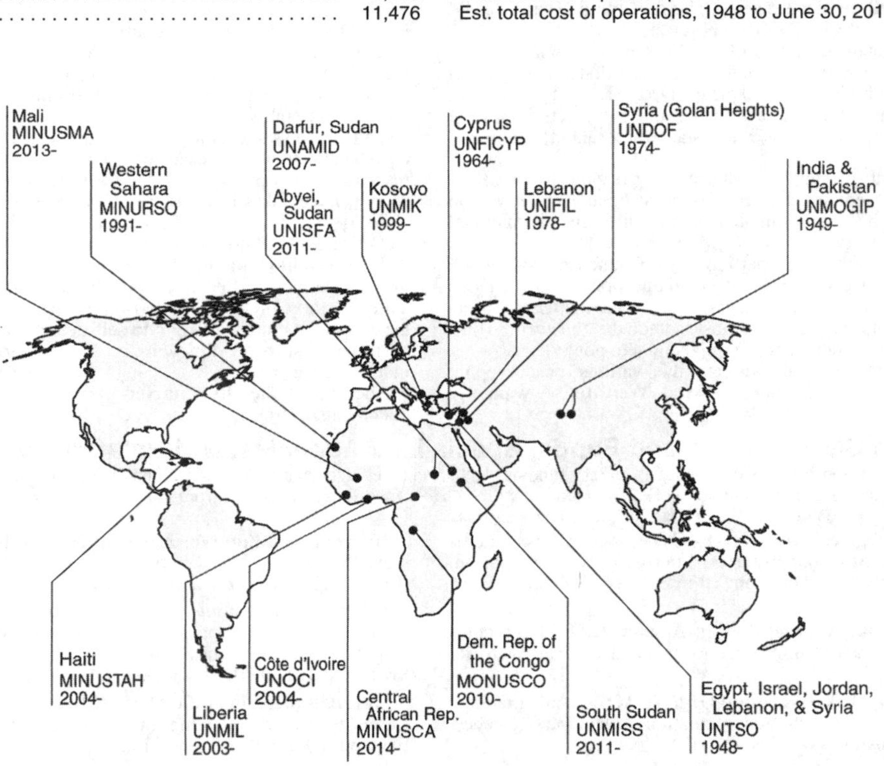

Roster of the United Nations

Listed below are the 193 members of the United Nations, with the years in which they were admitted (as of Aug. 2015). Vatican City, Kosovo, and China (Taiwan)[1] are not members. Taiwan's repeated bids for UN membership have so far been unsuccessful. Palestine and Vatican City are non-member states of the UN with permanent observer status.

Member	Year
Afghanistan	1946
Albania	1955
Algeria	1962
Andorra	1993
Angola	1976
Antigua and Barbuda	1981
Argentina	1945
Armenia	1992
Australia	1945
Austria	1955
Azerbaijan	1992
Bahamas, The	1973
Bahrain	1971
Bangladesh	1974
Barbados	1966
Belarus	1945
Belgium	1945
Belize	1981
Benin	1960
Bhutan	1971
Bolivia	1945
Bosnia and Herzegovina[2]	1992
Botswana	1966
Brazil	1945
Brunei	1984
Bulgaria	1955
Burkina Faso	1960
Burundi	1962
Cabo Verde	1975
Cambodia	1955
Cameroon	1960
Canada	1945
Central African Rep.	1960
Chad	1960
Chile	1945
China[1]	1945
Colombia	1945
Comoros	1975
Congo, Dem. Rep. of	1960
Congo Republic	1960
Costa Rica	1945
Côte d'Ivoire	1960
Croatia[2]	1992
Cuba	1945
Cyprus	1960
Czech Republic[3]	1993
Denmark	1945
Djibouti	1977
Dominica	1978
Dominican Republic	1945
Ecuador	1945
Egypt[4]	1945
El Salvador	1945
Equatorial Guinea	1968
Eritrea	1993
Estonia	1991
Ethiopia	1945
Fiji	1970
Finland	1955
France	1945
Gabon	1960
Gambia, The	1965
Georgia	1992
Germany[5]	1973
Ghana	1957
Greece	1945
Grenada	1974
Guatemala	1945
Guinea	1958
Guinea-Bissau	1974
Guyana	1966
Haiti	1945
Honduras	1945
Hungary	1955
Iceland	1946
India	1945
Indonesia[6]	1950
Iran	1945
Iraq	1945
Ireland	1955
Israel	1949
Italy	1955
Jamaica	1962
Japan	1956
Jordan	1955
Kazakhstan	1992
Kenya	1963
Kiribati	1999
Korea, North	1991
Korea, South	1991
Kuwait	1963
Kyrgyzstan	1992
Laos	1955
Latvia	1991
Lebanon	1945
Lesotho	1966
Liberia	1945
Libya	1955
Liechtenstein	1990
Lithuania	1991
Luxembourg	1945
Macedonia[2,7]	1993
Madagascar	1960
Malawi	1964
Malaysia[8]	1957
Maldives	1965
Mali	1960
Malta	1964
Marshall Islands	1991
Mauritania	1961
Mauritius	1968
Mexico	1945
Micronesia	1991
Moldova	1992
Monaco	1993
Mongolia	1961
Montenegro[2,9]	2006
Morocco	1956
Mozambique	1975
Myanmar (Burma)	1948
Namibia	1990
Nauru	1999
Nepal	1955
Netherlands	1945
New Zealand	1945
Nicaragua	1945
Niger	1960
Nigeria	1960
Norway	1945
Oman	1971
Pakistan	1947
Palau	1994
Panama	1945
Papua New Guinea	1975
Paraguay	1945
Peru	1945
Philippines	1945
Poland	1945
Portugal	1955
Qatar	1971
Romania	1955
Russia[10]	1945
Rwanda	1962
Saint Kitts and Nevis	1983
Saint Lucia	1979
Saint Vincent and the Grenadines	1980
Samoa	1976
San Marino	1992
São Tomé and Príncipe	1975
Saudi Arabia	1945
Senegal	1960
Serbia[2,9]	2000
Seychelles	1976
Sierra Leone	1961
Singapore[8]	1965
Slovakia[3]	1993
Slovenia[2]	1992
Solomon Islands	1978
Somalia	1960
South Africa[11]	1945
South Sudan[12]	2011
Spain	1955
Sri Lanka	1955
Sudan[12]	1956
Suriname	1975
Swaziland	1968
Sweden	1946
Switzerland	2002
Syria[3]	1945
Tajikistan	1992
Tanzania[13]	1961
Thailand	1946
Timor-Leste	2002
Togo	1960
Tonga	1999
Trinidad and Tobago	1962
Tunisia	1956
Turkey	1945
Turkmenistan	1992
Tuvalu	2000
Uganda	1962
Ukraine	1945
United Arab Emirates	1971
United Kingdom	1945
United States	1945
Uruguay	1945
Uzbekistan	1992
Vanuatu	1981
Venezuela	1945
Vietnam	1977
Yemen[14]	1947
Zambia	1964
Zimbabwe	1980

(1) The General Assembly (GA) voted in 1971 to expel the Chinese government in Taiwan and admit the government in Beijing. (2) The Socialist Federal Republic of Yugoslavia was an original UN member. After four of its six republics (Bosnia and Herzegovina, Croatia, Macedonia, and Slovenia) declared independence in 1991-92, the two remaining republics, Montenegro and Serbia, reconstituted as the Federal Republic of Yugoslavia. They sought to take over the former Yugoslavia's UN seat in 1992 but were expelled a few months later by GA vote. The Federal Republic of Yugoslavia was granted membership in 2000. In 2003, the country changed its name to Serbia and Montenegro. (3) Czechoslovakia, an original UN member from 1945 to 1992, was succeeded by both the Czech Republic and Slovakia in 1993. (4) Egypt and Syria were original UN members. In 1958, Egypt and Syria established the United Arab Republic and continued under a single UN membership. In 1961, Syria resumed separate membership following independence. (5) The Federal Republic of Germany and the German Democratic Republic became UN members in 1973. In 1990, the two formed one sovereign state. (6) Withdrew from the UN in 1965; rejoined in 1966. (7) Provisionally referred to as the former Yugoslav Republic of Macedonia within the UN pending settlement of Greece's objection to its constitutional name. (8) The Federation of Malaya joined the UN in 1957. In 1963, it changed its name to Malaysia following the accession of Singapore, Sabah, and Sarawak. Singapore became an independent UN member in 1965. (9) After Montenegro declared independence in 2006, the Republic of Serbia continued Serbia and Montenegro's UN membership. Montenegro was admitted to the UN as the Republic of Montenegro the same month. (10) The USSR was an original UN member. After the USSR's dissolution in 1991, Russia informed the UN it would continue the Soviet Union's membership in the Security Council and all other UN organs with the support of the Commonwealth of Independent States (comprising most of the former Soviet republics). (11) Readmitted in 1994. Its delegation had been suspended from participation in 1974 because of apartheid. (12) The Republic of South Sudan seceded from the Republic of the Sudan in 2011 and was admitted to the UN the same year. (13) Tanganyika was a UN member from 1961 and Zanzibar from 1963. The two countries united in 1964 to form the United Republic of Tanganyika and Zanzibar, which continued a single UN membership. It later changed its name to the United Republic of Tanzania. (14) The Yemen Arab Republic was admitted in 1947; the People's Democratic Republic of Yemen in 1967. In 1990, the two nations formed the Republic of Yemen.

U.S. Representatives to the United Nations, 1946-2015

The U.S. Permanent Representative to the United Nations is head of the U.S. Mission to the UN in New York. He or she is appointed by the president and confirmed by the Senate. This individual holds the rank and status of Ambassador Extraordinary and Plenipotentiary. Year given is the year each took office.

Year	Representative
1946	Edward R. Stettinius Jr.
1946	Herschel V. Johnson (act.)
1947	Warren R. Austin
1953	Henry Cabot Lodge Jr.
1960	James J. Wadsworth
1961	Adlai E. Stevenson
1965	Arthur J. Goldberg
1968	George W. Ball
1968	James Russell Wiggins
1969	Charles W. Yost
1971	George H. W. Bush
1973	John A. Scali
1975	Daniel P. Moynihan
1976	William W. Scranton
1977	Andrew Young
1979	Donald McHenry
1981	Jeane J. Kirkpatrick
1985	Vernon A. Walters
1989	Thomas R. Pickering
1992	Edward J. Perkins
1993	Madeleine K. Albright
1997	Bill Richardson
1998	A. Peter Burleigh (act.)
1999	Richard C. Holbrooke
2001	James B. Cunningham (act.)
2001	John D. Negroponte
2004	John C. Danforth
2005	Anne W. Patterson (act.)
2005	John R. Bolton
2006	Alejandro D. Wolff (act.)
2007	Zalmay M. Khalilzad
2009	Susan E. Rice
2013	Samantha Power

International Criminal Court

The International Criminal Court (ICC) was created when 120 nations signed the Rome Statute on July 17, 1998. Its mission is to try individuals accused of genocide, war crimes, or other crimes against humanity, which was undertaken in the past by temporary tribunals. The statute came into force on July 1, 2002. As of Aug. 2015, 123 nations were state parties to the Rome Statute of the ICC. China, Russia, and the U.S. have not yet joined.

The ICC, unlike the International Court of Justice (or World Court), is not part of the UN. It is an independent international agency with its own administration and budget, which is made up of funds from member states and voluntary contributions by other institutions, international groups, individuals, and corporations. It consists of 18 judges elected by member nations. An absolute majority of these 18 judges elect three from among themselves to serve as president, first vice president, and second vice president in three-year, renewable terms. A Registry handles the nonjudicial aspects of administration. The Office of the Prosecutor reviews, investigates, and, prosecutes cases referred to it by a state or by the UN Security Council.

As of Aug. 2015, 22 cases in 9 situations had been brought before the ICC. Two situations were in the Central African Republic and one each in Côte d'Ivoire; Dem. Rep. of the Congo; Kenya; Libya; Mali; Darfur, Sudan; and Uganda. It was conducting preliminary examinations in Afghanistan, Colombia, Georgia, Guinea, Honduras, Iraq, Nigeria, Palestine, and Ukraine. The court issued its first-ever conviction Mar. 14, 2012, when it found the warlord Thomas Lubanga Dyilo guilty of war crimes for his use of child soldiers in the Dem. Rep. of the Congo.

Though jurisdiction is limited to member nations, the ICC is a court of last resort. It may also initiate cases involving non-member nations if it deems the country's authorities have not taken steps to investigate or prosecute a case. The ICC is based in The Hague, Netherlands, though it may sit elsewhere.

Website: www.icc-cpi.int

Geneva Conventions

The Geneva Conventions are four international treaties governing the protection of civilians in times of war, the treatment of prisoners of war, and the care of the wounded and sick in the armed forces. The first convention, covering the sick and wounded in war, was concluded in Geneva, Switzerland, in 1864, at a conference convened by the Swiss government at the urging of the International Committee of the Red Cross. The convention was amended and expanded in 1906. In 1929, two more conventions covering the wounded and prisoners of war were signed. Outrage at the treatment of prisoners and civilians during WWII by some belligerents, notably Germany and Japan, prompted the conclusion, on Aug. 12, 1949, of four new conventions. Three of these restated and strengthened the previous conventions. The fourth codified general principles of international law governing the treatment of civilians in wartime.

The 1949 convention for civilians provided for special safeguards for wounded persons, children under 15 years of age, pregnant women, and the elderly. Discrimination on racial, religious, national, or political grounds was forbidden. Torture, collective punishment, reprisals, unwarranted destruction of property, and forced use of civilians for an occupier's armed forces were also prohibited. Also included was a pledge for the humane treatment, adequate feeding, and delivery of supplies to prisoners. They were not to be forced to disclose more than minimal information. Two additional protocols were adopted in June 1977 dealing with the protection of victims, especially civilians, in international and non-international armed conflicts. (A third protocol, adopted in 2005, created the Red Crystal emblem for use along with the Red Cross and Red Crescent.)

Most countries have formally accepted all or most of the humanitarian conventions as binding. However, there is no permanent international machinery in place to enforce these treaties.

Genocide

Source: Convention on the Prevention and Punishment of the Crime of Genocide, United Nations Treaty Series 277; Rome Statute of the International Criminal Court

The term "genocide" (which combines Greek and Latin roots to mean "murder of a race") was coined by Polish-Jewish lawyer Raphael Lemkin in 1944 to describe the intentional destruction or attempted destruction of a national, ethnic, racial, or religious group, whether in wartime or peacetime. Genocide is defined as killing members of a group, causing serious bodily harm to members of a group, or otherwise attempting to bring about a group's destruction, including efforts to prevent births or transfer children away from a group. Although the legal definition of genocide does not extend to political groups, the term is often used colloquially to refer to large-scale political violence.

The prohibition against genocide is part of customary international law and is codified in the Convention on the Prevention and Punishment of the Crime of Genocide, which entered into force on Jan. 12, 1951. As of Aug. 2015, 146 nations, including the U.S., were parties to it. Genocide is also prohibited by the domestic laws of many nations.

The first modern trials for genocide were conducted by the Allies after WWII. Although the charter of the Nuremberg Tribunal—the international court set up to try Nazi war criminals—did not use the term genocide, its definition of "crimes against humanity" included persecution on racial or religious grounds. More recently, the UN Security Council created ad hoc tribunals to try those responsible for genocide and other serious crimes in the former Yugoslavia and in Rwanda. The International Criminal Court (ICC) also has jurisdiction to try perpetrators of genocide. The ICC issued two arrest warrants for Sudanese Pres. Omar Hassan al-Bashir on multiple counts of genocide, crimes against humanity, and war crimes after the UN Security Council referred the situation in Darfur to the ICC prosecutor.

Examples of Genocides Since 1900

Year	Event	Location	Est. deaths
1915	Extermination of Armenians by the Young Turks	Turkey/Ottoman Empire	1,000,000+
1930s	Intentional infliction of famine on Ukraine	Soviet Union (Ukraine)	6,000,000-7,000,000
1933-45	Attempted destruction of European Jewry (Holocaust)	Europe	6,000,000
1975-79	Khmer Rouge campaign of extermination under Pol Pot[1]	Cambodia	1,500,000-2,000,000
1981-83	Army and paramilitary killings of indigenous Mayan during civil war	Guatemala	200,000+
1988	Anfal Campaign (named by the Iraqi government) against Iraqi Kurds	Iraq	100,000-200,000
1992-95	Ethnic killings during the breakup of Yugoslavia, chiefly Serbs against Bosnian Muslims (known as Bosniaks)	Bosnia-Herzegovina, Serbia, Croatia	200,000
1994	Hutu massacre of Tutsis	Rwanda	800,000
2003-present	Rebel group and government-backed Arab militia attacks on non-Arab southern tribes, black population[2]	Darfur region, Sudan	200,000-400,000

Note: Estimates based on historical evidence. The legal definition of "genocide" does not include politically motivated mass killings. Therefore, instances of mass violence against political or class enemies, such as Josef Stalin's purges of some 20 mil Soviets in the 1930s, and Mao Zedong's Cultural Revolution, which killed several million Chinese, are not included. (1) The mass killings during Cambodia's Khmer Rouge regime are often spoken of as genocide, though many of the murders were politically or class motivated. (2) In 2005, a UN commission concluded that although the "international offenses ... that have been committed in Darfur may be no less serious and heinous than genocide," it did not term the situation there a genocide.

NATIONS OF THE WORLD

As of mid-2015, there were **196 nations** in the world. This number includes three nations that are not United Nations (UN) members—Kosovo, Taiwan, and Vatican City (Holy See). Certain regions and territories can be found under the entry for their governing nation. **Sources:** FAOSTAT and AQUASTAT, Food and Agric. Org. of the UN (FAO); Joint UN Programme on HIV/AIDS (UNAIDS); Intl. Data Base, U.S. Census Bureau; International Energy Statistics, Energy Information Admin., U.S. Dept. of Energy; *International Financial Statistics*, Intl. Monetary Fund (IMF); *Key Indicators of the Labour Market*, International Labour Organization; ITU World Telecommunication/ICT Indicators Database, Intl. Telecommunication Union; *The Military Balance*, Intl. Inst. for Strategic Studies; *Oil & Gas Journal*, PennWell Corp.; UN Educational, Scientific, and Cultural Org. (UNESCO); *UNWTO World Tourism Barometer* © World Tourism Org.; U.S. Dept. of State; WardsAuto Group, a div. of Penton; The World Bank; *The World Factbook*, Central Intelligence Agency (CIA); *Trends in International Migrant Stock* and *World Urbanization Prospects*, Population Div., UN Dept. of Economic and Social Affairs.

Note: Because of rounding or incomplete enumeration, percentages may not add up to 100%. FY = Fiscal year. NA = Not available/applicable. **Population, age distrib.**, and **pop. density** are mid-2015 ests. **Growth** gives the avg. annual percent change in the pop. resulting from **births** and **deaths** in 2015 as well as the flow of migrants into and out of a country. International **migrants**, including foreign-born citizens and refugees, as a percent of the total pop. is for 2013. Percent of total pop. living in **urban** areas, as defined by each country, are mid-2015 ests. **Languages** are ranked with those most widely spoken listed first. **Arable land** is given as percentage of country's land area. Pop. of **capitals** and **cities** are projected ests. for urban agglomerations as of mid-2015 unless otherwise noted. **Defense budget** is for 2014, **active troops** for 2015. Selected **industries** are ranked by descending value of annual output. Selected **chief crops** are listed in descending order of importance. Total renewable **water** resources per inhabitant is for 2014. **Crude oil reserves** are as of Jan. 1, 2015; countries without this entry lack reserves. **Electricity prod.** indicates net, not gross, generated in 2012. **Labor force** percentages and **unemployment** (percentage of total labor force actively looking and available for work) are latest available. **Monetary unit** exchange rate is as of Sept. 2015. **GDP** data, for 2014, are based on purchasing power parity calculations; **GDP growth** is year-over-year. **Per capita GDP** is calculated using a country's est. pop. size as of July 1 of given year. Value of **imports** and **exports**, calculated on an exchange rate basis, are from 2014; trade partners—listed in descending order of importance by percentage of total dollar value—are from 2013. **Tourism** is latest available receipts from intl. tourism; data not available for all countries. **Budget** calculated on an exchange rate basis, not purchasing power parity terms, is 2014 expenditures. **Inflation** is measured by the percent change in the consumer price index (or avg. consumer cost for certain goods and services) between 2013 and 2014. Total length of a country's **railway** network is the latest available. **Motor vehicle** statistics, for cars and comm. vehicles in operation based on registrations, are for 2014. The number of **airports** with paved, usable runways are as of 2013. Number of fixed-**telephone** subscriptions; **mobile**-cellular telephone subscriptions offering voice communications; and percentage of pop. accessing the **Internet**, regardless of device used, are for 2014. Wireless-**broadband** subscriptions (the sum of satellite, terrestrial fixed wireless, and mobile-broadband subscriptions to the public Internet) are for 2013. Total **health expend.** (both government and private) is given as a percentage of GDP in 2012. **Life expect.** is in avg. number of years at birth for persons born in 2015. **Infant mortality** measures the probability of a child dying between birth and exact age 1 in 2015. **Undernourished**, or the prevalence of undernourishment, is the probability in 2012-14 that a randomly selected person from the pop. does not consume enough calories for an active, healthy life. **HIV** prevalence is the percentage of a country's pop. of 15- to 49-year-olds living with HIV in 2014. **Education** and **literacy** rate ests. are latest available. Literacy measures the percent of the pop. age 15 and older able to read and write simple statements; some countries define as literate those who have completed certain schooling. **Embassy** addresses are for Wash., DC, area code (202). Current events as of Oct. 1, 2015.

See pages 473-88 for full-color maps and flags of all nations.

Afghanistan

Islamic Republic of Afghanistan

People: Population: 32,564,342. **Age distrib.:** <15: 41.5%; 65+: 2.5%. **Growth:** 2.3%. **Migrants:** 0.3%. **Pop. density:** 129.3 per sq mi, 49.9 per sq km. **Urban:** 26.7%. **Ethnic groups:** Pashtun, Tajik, Hazara, Uzbek, incl. smaller numbers of 10 other constitutionally recognized ethnic groups. **Languages:** Afghan Persian or Dari, Pashto (both official); Turkic langs. (Uzbek, Turkmen); 30 minor langs. (Balochi, Pashai). **Religions:** Sunni Muslim 80%, Shia Muslim 19%.

Geography: Total area: 251,827 sq mi, 652,230 sq km; **Land area:** 251,827 sq mi, 652,230 sq km. **Location:** SW Asia, NW of Indian subcontinent. Pakistan on E, S; Iran on W; Turkmenistan, Tajikistan, Uzbekistan on N. NE tip touches China. **Topography:** Landlocked and mountainous, much of it over 4,000 ft above sea level. The Hindu Kush Mts. tower 16,000 ft above Kabul and reach a height of 25,000 ft to the E. Trade with Pakistan flows through the 35-mi-long Khyber Pass. Dry climate with extreme temperatures; large desert regions. **Arable land:** 11.9%. **Capital:** Kabul, 4,634,875.

Government: Type: Islamic republic. **Head of state and gov.:** Pres. Ashraf Ghani Ahmadzai; in office: Sept. 29, 2014; and Chief Exec. Abdullah Abdullah; in office: Sept. 29, 2014. **Local divisions:** 34 provinces. **Defense budget:** $3.29 bil. **Active troops:** 178,500.

Economy: Industries: small-scale prod. of bricks, textiles, soap, furniture, shoes, fertilizer, apparel, food prods. **Chief crops:** opium, wheat, fruits, nuts. **Natural resources:** nat. gas, petroleum, coal, copper, chromite, talc, barites, sulfur, lead, zinc, iron ore, salt, prec. and semiprec. stones. **Water:** 2,138 cu m per capita. **Electricity prod.:** 884.1 mil kWh. **Labor force:** agric. 78.6%, industry 5.7%, services 15.7%. **Unemployment:** 8%.

Finance: Monetary unit: Afghani (AFN) (63.75 = $1 U.S.). **GDP:** $60.6 bil; **per capita GDP:** $1,900; **GDP growth:** 1.5%. **Imports** (2012): $6.4 bil; Pakistan 28%, U.S. 18.6%, Russia 7.6%, India 6.3%. **Exports** (2012): $2.8 bil (not incl. illicit trade); India 31.9%, Pakistan 28.5%, Tajikistan 7.5%, U.S. 6.2%. **Tourism:** $56 mil. **Budget** (2013 est.): $5 bil. **Inflation:** 4.6%.

Transport: Motor vehicles: 48.5 per 1,000 pop. **Airports:** 23.

Communications: Telephone: 0.3 per 100 pop. **Mobile:** 74.9 per 100 pop. **Broadband:** 2.3 per 100 pop. **Internet:** 6.4%.

Health: Expend.: 8.7%. **Life expect.:** 49.5 male; 52.3 female. **Births:** 38.6 per 1,000 pop. **Deaths:** 13.9 per 1,000 pop. **Infant mortality:** 115.1 per 1,000 live births. **Undernourished:** 24.7%. **HIV:** <0.1%.

Education: Compulsory: ages 7-15. **Literacy:** 38.2%.

Embassy: 2341 Wyoming Ave. NW 20008; 483-6410.

Website: www.president.gov.af

Afghanistan, occupying a favored invasion route since antiquity, has been variously known as Ariana or Bactria (in ancient times) and Khorasan (in the Middle Ages). Foreign empires alternated rule with local emirs and kings until the 18th cent., when a unified kingdom was established. In 1973, a military coup ushered in a republic.

Pro-Soviet leftists took power in a bloody 1978 coup. In Dec. 1979 the USSR began a massive airlift into Kabul and backed a new coup, leading to the installation of a more pro-Soviet leader. Soviet forces fanned out over Afghanistan and waged a protracted guerrilla war with Muslim rebels, in which some 15,000 Soviet troops reportedly died.

A UN-mediated agreement was signed Apr. 14, 1988, providing for withdrawal of Soviet troops, a neutral Afghan state, and repatriation of refugees. Afghan rebels rejected the pact. The Soviets completed their troop withdrawal Feb. 15, 1989; fighting between Afghan rebels and government forces ensued. Communist Pres. Najibullah resigned Apr. 16, 1992, as competing guerrilla forces advanced on Kabul. The rebels achieved power Apr. 28, ending 14 years of Soviet-backed regimes. More than 2 mil Afghans had been killed, and 6 mil had left the country since 1979.

Clashes between moderates and Islamic fundamentalist forces followed the rebel victory. Burhanuddin Rabbani, a guerrilla leader, became president June 28, 1992, but fierce fighting continued around Kabul and elsewhere. The Taliban, an insurgent radical-Islamist faction, captured Kabul in Sept. 1996. The Taliban executed Najibullah and empowered Islamic religious police to enforce strict Islamic codes of dress and behavior. Rabbani and other ousted leaders fled to the north.

Victories in the northern cities of Mazar-e Sharif, Aug. 8, 1998, and Taloqan, Aug. 8-11, gave the Taliban control over more than 90% of the country. On Aug. 20, U.S. cruise missiles struck SE of Kabul, hitting facilities the U.S. said were terrorist training camps run by Osama bin Laden. The UN imposed sanctions Nov. 14, 1999, when Afghanistan refused to turn over bin Laden to the U.S. for prosecution.

After the Sept. 11, 2001, attacks on the World Trade Center and Pentagon, the U.S., blaming bin Laden, demanded that the Taliban surrender him and shut down his al-Qaeda terrorist network. When the Taliban refused, the U.S., with British assistance, began bombing Afghanistan Oct. 7, as part of Operation Enduring Freedom (OEF).

Supported by the U.S., the opposition Northern Alliance recaptured Mazar-e Sharif Nov. 9 and took Kabul 4 days later; Taliban forces abandoned Kandahar, their last stronghold, to southern tribal fighters Dec. 7. A power-sharing agreement signed by 4 anti-Taliban factions, including the Northern Alliance, provided for an interim government headed by Hamid Karzai, a Pashtun tribal leader. The UN authorized a multinational security force Dec. 20, 2001.

Meeting June 13, 2002, in Kabul, a traditional council (*loya jirga*) chose Karzai to head a new transitional government. Although the

U.S. announced the end of major combat operations in Afghanistan, May 1, 2003, resistance continued. NATO officially assumed control of peacekeeping forces—the Intl. Security Assistance Force (ISAF)—Aug. 11.

The most intense fighting in more than 4 years erupted Mar. 2006 with a new wave of attacks and other strikes by Taliban insurgents. Erosion of government authority led to an increase in opium growing; the Taliban, local warlords, and some Karzai associates were accused of profiting from the drug trade.

Operating from sanctuaries in Pakistan, Islamist suicide bombers and Taliban insurgents stepped up their activities, 2007-11. Violence escalated in the run-up to the presidential election Aug. 20, 2009. With Karzai in the lead, a UN-backed commission ordered a recount, citing evidence of fraud; a Nov. runoff election was canceled when Karzai's lone opponent dropped out of the race. Karzai was sworn in for a second term Nov. 19. After a decade-long manhunt, U.S. commandos killed bin Laden shortly after midnight May 2, 2011, in Abbottabad, Pakistan. Insurgents retaliated Aug. 6 by shooting down a helicopter, killing 30 Americans and 8 Afghans. Other violence included attacks Sept. 13, 2011, on the U.S. embassy, NATO headquarters, and other targets in Kabul, as well as the assassination Sept. 20 of former Pres. Rabbani.

Between Jan. 2009 and June 2011, the number of U.S. troops in Afghanistan rose from about 36,000 to 101,000, while the number of allied foreign forces under ISAF increased from nearly 32,000 to more than 42,000. The U.S., June 22, 2011, outlined a timetable for drawing down troops and ending their combat role. Pres. Barack Obama announced, May 27, 2014, that by year's end most U.S. troops would be out of Afghanistan, with a residual force focusing on combating al-Qaeda and training and advising Afghan troops. The UN reported 2,959 civilian deaths from conflict in Afghanistan in 2013 (up 7% from 2012), and 3,699 in 2014 (up 25% from 2013). Almost 2.6 mil Afghan refugees were living outside the country at the end of 2014, and more than 800,000 Afghans were internally displaced. OEF and ISAF officially ended Dec. 28, 2014; since Oct. 2001, 2,215 U.S. and 1,270 allied troops had been killed. The NATO-led Resolute Support mission (RSM) to aid Afghan forces began Jan. 1, 2015. As of June 2015, there were about 13,200 RSM troops in Afghanistan, of which more than 6,800 were from the U.S. Including other counterterrorism forces, total U.S. troop strength was about 9,800.

The first round of elections for a new president was held Apr. 5, 2014. A June 14 runoff between the two top vote-getters—former Foreign Min. Abdullah Abdullah and former Finance Min. Ashraf Ghani Ahmadzai—was marred by allegations of electoral fraud. After an internationally supervised audit of all 8 mil runoff ballots, Ghani was declared the winner Sept. 21. Under a U.S.-brokered power-sharing agreement, he appointed Abdullah chief executive of the government. Fighting between government and Taliban forces continued in 2015, as did terrorist attacks in Kabul and other cities; the conflict killed 1,592 civilians Jan.-June 2015. Amid signs of a leadership struggle, some Taliban officials began preliminary peace talks with government representatives July 7. The government announced, July 29, 2015, that longtime Taliban leader Muhammad Omar had died in 2013; the Taliban, July 30, confirmed his death. An affiliate of the Sunni extremist group ISIS also staged attacks in Afghanistan in 2015 and attracted Taliban defectors. Taliban forces, Sept. 28, 2015, gained control of Kunduz, a provincial capital and the first major city captured by the Taliban in 14 years; a government offensive, assisted by U.S. airstrikes, reportedly retook most of the city by Oct. 1, 2015.

Albania

Republic of Albania

People: Population: 3,029,278. **Age distrib.:** <15: 18.8%; 65+: 11.3%. **Growth:** 0.3%. **Migrants:** 3.1%. **Pop. density:** 286.4 per sq mi, 110.6 per sq km. **Urban:** 57.4%. **Ethnic groups:** Albanian 82.6%. **Languages:** Albanian (official), Greek. **Religions:** Muslim 56.7%, Roman Catholic 10%, Orthodox 6.8%, atheist 2.5%.

Geography: Total area: 11,100 sq mi, 28,748 sq km; **Land area:** 10,578 sq mi, 27,398 sq km. **Location:** SE Europe, on SE coast of Adriatic Sea. Greece on S; Montenegro, Kosovo on N; Macedonia on E. **Topography:** Narrow coastal plain; hills and mountains covered with scrub forest, cut by small E-W rivers. **Arable land:** 22.6%. **Capital:** Tirana, 453,509.

Government: Type: Parliamentary democracy. **Head of state:** Pres. Bujar Nishani; in office: July 24, 2012. **Head of gov.:** Prime Min. Edi Rama; in office: Sept. 10, 2013. **Local divisions:** 12 counties. **Defense budget:** $166 mil. **Active troops:** 8,000.

Economy: Industries: food and tobacco prods., textiles and clothing, lumber. **Chief crops:** wheat, corn, potatoes, vegetables, fruits, sugar beets, grapes. **Natural resources:** petroleum, nat. gas, coal, bauxite, chromite, copper, iron ore, nickel, salt, timber, hydropower. **Water:** 9,518 cu m per capita. **Crude oil reserves:** 168.3 mil bbls. **Electricity prod.:** 4.2 bil kWh. **Labor force:** agric. 41.8%, industry 11.4%, services 46.8%. **Unemployment:** 16%.

Finance: Monetary unit: Lek (ALL) (124.23 = $1 U.S.). **GDP:** $30.7 bil (unreported output may be as large as 50% of official GDP); **per capita GDP:** $11,400; **GDP growth:** 1.9%. **Imports:** $5.3 bil; Italy 36.1%, Greece 9.6%, China 7.2%, Turkey 5.7%. **Exports:** $2.4 bil; Italy 43.5%, China 9.7%, Spain 8.4%, Kosovo 7.5%, India 6.1%. **Tourism:** $1.7 bil. **Budget:** $4.3 bil. **Inflation:** 1.6%.

Transport: Railways: 421 mi. **Airports:** 4.

Communications: Telephone: 7.8 per 100 pop. **Mobile:** 105.5 per 100 pop. **Broadband:** 28.2 per 100 pop. **Internet:** 60.1%.

Health: Expend.: 6%. **Life expect.:** 75.5 male; 81.0 female. **Births:** 12.9 per 1,000 pop. **Deaths:** 6.6 per 1,000 pop. **Infant mortality:** 12.8 per 1,000 live births. **Undernourished:** <5%. **HIV:** NA.

Education: Compulsory: ages 6-14. **Literacy:** 97.6%.

Embassy: 1312 18th St. NW, 4th Fl., 20036; 223-4942.

Website: www.kryeministria.al

Ancient Illyria was conquered by Romans, Slavs, and Turks (15th cent.); the Turks Islamized the population. Independent Albania was proclaimed in 1912; a republic was formed in 1920. King Zog I ruled 1925-39 until Italy invaded.

Communist partisans took over in 1944 and allied Albania with the USSR but broke with the USSR in 1960 over de-Stalinization. Billions of dollars in Chinese financial assistance was cut off in 1978 when Albania attacked China's policies. Large-scale purges of officials occurred during the 1970s.

Enver Hoxha, the nation's ruler for four decades, died Apr. 11, 1985. The new regime introduced some liberalization, including measures in 1990 providing for freedom to travel abroad.

Albania's former Communists were routed in elections Mar. 1992, amid economic collapse and social unrest. Sali Berisha was elected as the first non-Communist president since WWII. Berisha's party claimed a landslide victory in disputed parliamentary elections, May 26 and June 2, 1996. Public protests over the collapse of fraudulent investment schemes in Jan. 1997 led to armed rebellion. The UN Security Council, Mar. 28, authorized a 7,000-member force to restore order. Socialists and their allies won parliamentary elections, June 29 and July 6, and international peacekeepers pulled out by Aug. 11.

During NATO's air war against Yugoslavia, Mar.-June 1999, Albania hosted some 465,000 Kosovar refugees. A pro-Berisha coalition victory in July 3, 2005, elections ended eight years of Socialist rule. Albania became a full member of NATO Apr. 1, 2009. Socialists won June 23, 2013, parliamentary elections, and Edi Rama became the new prime min. The EU granted Albania official candidate status June 27, 2014. Membership negotiations were expected to include EU requests for reforms to reduce organized crime and political corruption. A 2011 UN survey had found that 3 of 10 adults had been involved in bribery of a public official in the previous 12 months. Pope Francis praised "peaceful and fruitful coexistence" between religious communities in Albania during a trip to Tirana, Sept. 21, 2014.

Algeria

People's Democratic Republic of Algeria

People: Population: 39,542,166. **Age distrib.:** <15: 28.7%; 65+: 5.4%. **Growth:** 1.8%. **Migrants:** 0.7%. **Pop. density:** 43 per sq mi, 16.6 per sq km. **Urban:** 70.7%. **Ethnic groups:** Arab-Berber 99%. **Languages:** Arabic (official), French (lingua franca), Berber dialects. **Religions:** Muslim (official; predom. Sunni) 99%.

Geography: Total area: 919,595 sq mi, 2,381,741 sq km; **Land area:** 919,595 sq mi, 2,381,741 sq km. **Location:** NW Africa, from Medit. Sea into Sahara. Morocco, Western Sahara on W; Mauritania, Mali, Niger on S; Libya, Tunisia on E. **Topography:** The Tell, on the coast, comprises fertile plains 50-100 mi wide with a moderate climate and adequate rain. Two major chains of Atlas Mts., running roughly E-W and reaching 7,000 ft, enclose a dry plateau region. Below lies the Sahara. **Arable land:** 3.2%. **Capital:** Algiers, 2,594,112. **Cities:** Oran, 858,272.

Government: Type: Republic. **Head of state:** Pres. Abdelaziz Bouteflika; in office: Apr. 28, 1999. **Head of gov.:** Prime Min. Abdelmalek Sellal; in office: Apr. 28, 2014. **Local divisions:** 48 provinces. **Defense budget:** $12 bil. **Active troops:** 130,000.

Economy: Industries: petroleum, nat. gas, light industries, mining, electrical, petrochemical, food proc. **Chief crops:** wheat, barley, oats, grapes, olives, citrus, fruits. **Natural resources:** petroleum, nat. gas, iron ore, phosphates, uranium, lead, zinc. **Water:** 298 cu m per capita. **Crude oil reserves:** 12.2 bil bbls. **Electricity prod.:** 54 bil kWh. **Labor force:** agric. 14%, industry 13.4%, constr. and public works 10%, trade 14.6%, govt. 32%, other 16%. **Unemployment:** 9.8%.

Finance: Monetary unit: Dinar (DZD) (105.52 = $1 U.S.). **GDP:** $551.8 bil; **per capita GDP:** $14,300; **GDP growth:** 4.1%. **Imports:** $55.4 bil; France 15.1%, China 11.6%, Italy 10.8%, Spain 9.9%. **Exports:** $62.1 bil; Spain 20.2%, France 9.3%, UK 8.8%, U.S. 8.1%, Netherlands 6.9%, Canada 6%, Brazil 5.6%. **Tourism:** $350 mil. **Budget:** $89.2 bil. **Inflation:** 2.9%.

Transport: Railways: 2,469 mi. **Motor vehicles:** 126.3 per 1,000 pop. **Airports:** 64.

Communications: Telephone: 7.7 per 100 pop. **Mobile:** 93.3 per 100 pop. **Broadband:** NA. **Internet:** 18.1%.

Health: Expend.: 5.3%. **Life expect.:** 75.3 male; 78.0 female. **Births:** 23.7 per 1,000 pop. **Deaths:** 4.3 per 1,000 pop. **Infant mortality:** 21.0 per 1,000 live births. **Undernourished:** <5%. **HIV:** <0.1%.

Education: Compulsory: ages 6-16. **Literacy:** 80.2%.

Embassy: 2118 Kalorama Rd. NW 20008; 265-2800.

Website: www.premier-ministre.gov.dz or www.algerianembassy.org

Earliest known inhabitants were ancestors of Berbers, followed by Phoenicians, Romans, Vandals, and Arabs. Turkey ruled 1518-1830, when France took control. Large-scale European immigration followed. Arab nationalists launched a guerrilla war, 1954, that more than 400,000 French troops were unable to suppress. After French Pres. Charles de Gaulle came to power, 1958, colonial rule ended, nearly all Europeans left, and Algeria declared independence July 5, 1962. Ahmed Ben Bella ruled until 1965, when an army coup installed Col. Houari Boumedienne, a former guerrilla leader who held power until his death in 1978.

Hundreds died in antigovernment riots protesting economic hardship, Oct. 1988. In 1989, voters approved a new constitution. The government canceled the Jan. 1992 elections and banned all nonreligious activities at Algeria's 10,000 mosques. Pres. Mohammed Boudiaf was assassinated June 29, 1992. Over the next seven years, Muslim fundamentalists attacked high-ranking officials, security forces, and foreigners; pro-government death squads were active.

Liamine Zeroual won the Nov. 16, 1995, presidential election. A new constitution banning Islamic political parties and increasing the president's powers passed in a Nov. 1996 referendum. Abdelaziz Bouteflika, who became president after a flawed Apr. 15, 1999, election, reconciled with rebels and won approval for an amnesty plan in a referendum, Sept. 16. Some 100 people died and thousands were injured in violent protests Apr.-June 2001, chiefly by Algeria's Berber minority. Bouteflika was reelected Apr. 8, 2004, though opponents charged fraud.

Under a reconciliation plan approved by referendum Sept. 2005, the government in Mar. 2006 began freeing Islamists jailed for their role in the 1990s civil war, which left up to 200,000 people dead and 8,000 "disappeared."

Radical Islamists bombed police stations in Oct. 2006 and Feb. 2007. A group known as al-Qaeda in the Islamic Maghreb (AQIM) carried out several suicide bombings throughout 2007, killing more than 100 people. A surge in AQIM violence in Aug. 2008 left more than 100 people dead.

Parliament, Nov. 12, 2008, amended the constitution to abolish presidential term limits, enabling Bouteflika to run for a 3rd term. He claimed more than 90% of the vote in a 2009 election denounced as fraudulent by opposition parties. During Arab Spring uprisings in early 2011, Bouteflika's government suppressed street protests in Algiers, Feb. 12, and used oil revenues to raise salaries of teachers, police, and other discontented civil servants. The country's governing party, the Natl. Liberation Front, strengthened its hold on power in May 10, 2012, parliamentary elections that opposition groups called fraudulent. The 77-year-old Bouteflika won a fourth term as president with 81.5% of the vote in the Apr. 17, 2014, election, which was boycotted by some opposition parties.

AQIM members protesting France's involvement in Mali seized the In Amenas gas facility Jan. 16, 2013, holding about 40 foreign workers hostage for 4 days and demanding the release of about 100 Islamist prisoners being held in Algeria. In the end, 38 hostages died, including 3 Americans, as well as some 29 militants at the hands of Algerian special forces attempting to liberate the facility. Algerian officials reported that security forces, May 19, 2015, had killed 21 Islamist extremists planning a terrorist attack on Algiers.

Andorra

Principality of Andorra

People: Population: 85,580. **Age distrib.:** <15: 15%; 65+: 14.7%. **Growth:** 0.1%. **Migrants:** 56.9%. **Pop. density:** 473.6 per sq mi, 182.9 per sq km. **Urban:** 85.1%. **Ethnic groups:** Andorran 49%, Spanish 24.6%, Portuguese 14.3%, French 3.9%. **Languages:** Catalan (official), French, Castilian, Portuguese. **Religions:** Catholic (predom.).

Geography: Total area: 181 sq mi, 468 sq km; **Land area:** 181 sq mi, 468 sq km. **Location:** SW Europe, in Pyrenees Mts. Spain on S, France on N. **Topography:** High mountains and narrow valleys across country. **Arable land:** 5.1%. **Capital:** Andorra la Vella, 23,449 (2014).

Government: Type: Parliamentary democracy. **Heads of state:** President of France and Bishop of Urgell (Spain), as co-princes. **Head of gov.:** Antoni Martí Petit; in office: May 12, 2011. **Local divisions:** 7 parishes. **Defense budget/active troops:** NA.

Economy: Industries: tourism (skiing), banking, timber, furniture. **Chief crops:** rye, wheat, barley, oats, vegetables. **Natural resources:** hydropower, mineral water, timber, iron ore, lead. **Water:** 3,995 cu m per capita. **Labor force:** agric. 0.4%, industry 4.7%, services 94.9%. **Unemployment:** NA.

Finance: Monetary unit: Euro (EUR) (0.89 = $1 U.S.). **GDP** (2012): $3.2 bil; **per capita GDP** (2011): $37,200; **GDP growth** (2012): –1.6%. **Imports** (2012): $1.4 bil. **Exports** (2012): $70 mil. **Budget** (2012): $1 bil. **Inflation:** NA.

Transport: NA.

Communications: Telephone: 47.7 per 100 pop. **Mobile:** 82.6 per 100 pop. **Broadband:** 52.3 per 100 pop. **Internet:** 95.9%.

Health: Expend.: 8.3%. **Life expect.:** 80.6 male; 85.0 female. **Births:** 8.1 per 1,000 pop. **Deaths:** 7.0 per 1,000 pop. **Infant mortality:** 3.7 per 1,000 live births. **Undernourished:** <5%. **HIV:** NA.

Education: Compulsory: ages 6-15. **Literacy:** 100%.

Embassy: 2 UN Plz., 27th Fl., New York, NY 10017; (212) 750-8064.

Website: www.govern.ad

France and the bishop of Urgell held joint sovereignty over Andorra from 1278 to 1993. Voters chose to adopt a parliamentary system Mar. 14, 1993, although co-princes remain heads of state. Tourism, especially skiing, is an economic mainstay. For years, Andorra served as a tax haven, but it began reforms in 2008 and was removed by the OECD from its list of uncooperative tax havens, May 27, 2009. In Mar. 2015, the government seized control of Banca Privada d'Andorra (BPA) and arrested its chief executive after U.S. Treasury Dept. accusations that BPA was laundering money for global criminal gangs. Following his party's victory in Mar. 2015 elections, Antoni Martí Petit was reelected by the legislature as head of government.

Angola

Republic of Angola

People: Population: 19,625,353. **Age distrib.:** <15: 42.9%; 65+: 3%. **Growth:** 2.8%. **Migrants:** 0.4%. **Pop. density:** 40.8 per sq mi, 15.7 per sq km. **Urban:** 44%. **Ethnic groups:** Ovimbundu 37%, Kimbundu 25%, Bakongo 13%, mestico (mixed European/native African) 2%. **Languages:** Portuguese (official), Bantu, other African langs. **Religions:** indigenous beliefs 47%, Roman Catholic 38%, Protestant 15%.

Geography: Total area: 481,354 sq mi, 1,246,700 sq km; **Land area:** 481,354 sq mi, 1,246,700 sq km. **Location:** SW Africa on Atlantic coast. Namibia on S, Zambia on E, Dem. Rep. of the Congo on N; Cabinda, an exclave separated from rest of country by short Atlantic coast of Dem. Rep. of the Congo, borders Congo Rep. **Topography:** Mostly plateau 3,000-5,000 ft above sea level, rising from a narrow coastal strip. Temperate highland area in the W-central region, a desert in S, and a tropical rain forest in Cabinda. **Arable land:** 3.9%. **Capital:** Luanda, 5,506,000. **Cities:** Huambo, 1,269,211.

Government: Type: Republic. **Head of state and gov.:** Pres. José Eduardo dos Santos; in office: Sept. 21, 1979. **Local divisions:** 18 provinces. **Defense budget:** $6.85 bil. **Active troops:** 107,000.

Economy: Industries: petroleum; diamonds, mining; cement; metal prods.; fish and food proc. **Chief crops:** bananas, sugarcane, coffee, sisal, corn, cotton, cassava, tobacco. **Natural resources:** petroleum, diamonds, iron ore, phosphates, copper, feldspar, gold, bauxite, uranium. **Water:** 6,911 cu m per capita. **Crude oil reserves:** 9 bil bbls. **Electricity prod.:** 5.5 bil kWh. **Labor force:** agric. 85%, industry and services 15%. **Unemployment:** 6.8%.

Finance: Monetary unit: Kwanza (AOA) (125.60 = $1 U.S.). **GDP:** $175.6 bil; **per capita GDP:** $7,200; **GDP growth:** 4.2%. **Imports:** $28.1 bil; Portugal 19.5%, China 19.1%, U.S. 7%, South Africa 6.9%, Brazil 6.1%, South Korea 6%. **Exports:** $69.5 bil; China 44.7%, U.S. 12.3%, India 9.5%, South Africa 5.1%. **Tourism:** $1.2 mil. **Budget:** $57.7 bil. **Inflation:** 7.3%.

Transport: Railways: 1,772 mi. **Motor vehicles:** 7.1 per 1,000 pop. **Airports:** 31.

Communications: Telephone: 1.3 per 100 pop. **Mobile:** 63.5 per 100 pop. **Broadband:** 12.4 per 100 pop. **Internet:** 21.3%.

Health: Expend.: 3.5%. **Life expect.:** 54.5 male; 56.8 female. **Births:** 38.8 per 1,000 pop. **Deaths:** 11.5 per 1,000 pop. **Infant mortality:** 78.3 per 1,000 live births. **Undernourished:** 18%. **HIV:** 2.4%.

Education: Compulsory: ages 6-11. **Literacy:** 71.1%.

Embassy: 2100-2108 16th St. NW 20009; 785-1156.

Website: www.governo.gov.ao or www.angola.org

From the early centuries CE to 1500, Bantu tribes penetrated most of the region. Portuguese came in 1583, allied with the Bakongo kingdom in the north, and developed the slave trade. Large-scale colonization began in the 20th cent., when 400,000 Portuguese immigrated.

A guerrilla war, 1961-75, ended when Portugal granted independence. Fighting then erupted among 3 rival rebel groups—the

National Front, based in Zaire (now Dem. Rep. of the Congo); the Soviet-backed Popular Movement for the Liberation of Angola (MPLA); and the National Union for the Total Independence of Angola (UNITA), aided by the U.S. and South Africa. Cuban troops and Soviet aid helped the MPLA win control of most of the country by 1976, although fighting continued. The MPLA government and UNITA signed a peace accord May 1, 1991. Elections were held, Sept. 1992, but fighting again broke out, as UNITA rejected the results. UNITA signed a new peace treaty with the government, Nov. 20, 1994, but the rebels were slow to demobilize. The UN Security Council voted, Aug. 28, 1997, to impose sanctions on UNITA. The UN ended its mission in Angola, Mar. 1999, as the civil war continued. The UN estimated that the war with UNITA had claimed some 1 mil lives and left another 2.5 mil people homeless by mid-2001. Government troops killed rebel leader Jonas Savimbi Feb. 22, 2002. UNITA agreed to a truce Apr. 4, 2002, ending the 27-year-long civil war. Separatist rebels in oil-rich Cabinda agreed to a cease-fire July 2006.

With proven petroleum reserves estimated at 9 bil barrels, Angola is among Africa's leading oil producers. Wealth is unevenly distributed. Half the population lacks access to health care, and the country's under-age-5 mortality rate, 157 per 1,000 live births in 2015, was the world's highest. The ruling MPLA claimed victory in voting Sept. 2008, in Angola's first parliamentary elections in 16 years. Parliament approved Jan. 21, 2010, a new constitution augmenting the power of MPLA leader José Eduardo dos Santos, Angola's president since 1979. The MPLA won flawed elections, Aug 31, 2012, giving Dos Santos another 5-year term.

Antigua and Barbuda

People: Population: 92,436. **Age distrib.:** <15: 23.9%; 65+: 7.6%. **Growth:** 1.2%. **Migrants:** 31.9%. **Pop. density:** 540.4 per sq mi, 208.8 per sq km. **Urban:** 23.8%. **Ethnic groups:** black 87.3%, mixed 4.7%, hispanic 2.7%. **Languages:** English (official), Antiguan creole. **Religions:** Protestant 68.3% (incl. Anglican 17.6%, Seventh-day Adventist 12.4%, Pentecostal 12.2%, Moravian 8.3%), Roman Catholic 8.2%, none 5.9%.

Geography: Total area: 171 sq mi, 443 sq km (Antigua, 108 sq mi, 280 sq km; Barbuda, 62 sq mi, 161 sq km); **Land area:** 171 sq mi, 443 sq km. **Location:** E Caribbean. St. Kitts and Nevis to W, Guadeloupe (Fr.) to S. **Topography:** Mostly low-lying and limestone coral islands. Antigua is mostly hilly with an indented coast; Barbuda is a flat island with a large lagoon on W. **Arable land:** 9.1%. **Capital:** St. John's, 21,989 (2014).

Government: Type: Constitutional monarchy with parliamentary system of govt. **Head of state:** Queen Elizabeth II, rep. by Gov.-Gen. Sir Rodney Williams; in office: Aug. 14, 2014. **Head of gov.:** Prime Min. Gaston Browne; in office: June 13, 2014. **Local divisions:** 6 parishes, 2 dependencies. **Defense budget:** $27 mil. **Active troops:** 180.

Economy: Industries: tourism, constr., light mfg. **Chief crops:** cotton, fruits, vegetables, bananas, coconuts. **Natural resources:** negligible. **Water:** 578 cu m per capita. **Electricity prod.:** 315 mil kWh. **Labor force:** agric. 7%, industry 11%, services 82%. **Unemployment:** NA.

Finance: Monetary unit: East Caribbean Dollar (XCD) (2.70 = $1 U.S.). **GDP:** $2 bil; **per capita GDP:** $22,600; **GDP growth:** 2.4%. **Imports:** $313.1 mil. **Exports:** $56.5 mil. **Tourism:** $330 mil. **Budget:** $206.7 mil. **Inflation:** 1.1%.

Transport: Airports: 2.

Communications: Telephone: 35.6 per 100 pop. **Mobile:** 120 per 100 pop. **Broadband:** 47.5 per 100 pop. **Internet:** 64%.

Health: Expend.: 5.2%. **Life expect.:** 74.2 male; 78.5 female. **Births:** 15.9 per 1,000 pop. **Deaths:** 5.7 per 1,000 pop. **Infant mortality:** 12.9 per 1,000 live births. **Undernourished:** NA. **HIV:** NA.

Education: Compulsory: ages 5-15. **Literacy:** 99%.

Embassy: 3216 New Mexico Ave. NW 20016; 362-5122.

Website: www.ab.gov.ag

Christopher Columbus landed on Antigua in 1493. The British colonized it in 1632. The British-associated state of Antigua achieved independence as Antigua and Barbuda on Nov. 1, 1981. Tourism accounts for almost 60% of GDP. The worldwide recession caused the economy to shrink in 2009-11. The economy also suffered after Robert Allen Stanford, a Texas businessman, was charged by U.S. authorities Feb. 17, 2009, with employing his Antigua-based Stanford Intl. Bank to conduct a fraudulent $7-bil investment scheme. He was convicted Mar. 6, 2012. With the economy still weak in 2014, the opposition Antigua and Barbuda Labour Party (ABLP) won an overwhelming victory in June 12 elections for the lower house of parliament, and ABLP leader Gaston Browne became prime minister.

Argentina

Argentine Republic

People: Population: 43,431,886. **Age distrib.:** <15: 24.7%; 65+: 11.6%. **Growth:** 0.9%. **Migrants:** 4.5%. **Pop. density:** 41.1 per sq mi, 15.9 per sq km. **Urban:** 91.8%. **Ethnic groups:** white (mostly Spanish and Italian) 97%; mestizo (mixed white/Amerindian), Amerindian, other non-white groups 3%. **Languages:** Spanish (official), Italian, English, German, French, indigenous (Mapudungun, Quechua). **Religions:** nominally Roman Catholic 92%, Protestant 2%, Jewish 2%.

Geography: Total area: 1,073,518 sq mi, 2,780,400 sq km; **Land area:** 1,056,642 sq mi, 2,736,690 sq km. **Location:** Occupies most of southern S America. Chile on W; Bolivia, Paraguay on N; Brazil, Uruguay on NE. **Topography:** Andean, Central, Misiones, and Southern mountain ranges in W. Aconcagua (22,835 ft) is highest peak in Western Hemisphere. Heavily wooded plains called the Gran Chaco are E of Andes in the N; fertile, treeless Pampas in the central region. Patagonia, in S, is bleak and arid. Rio de la Plata, an estuary in NE, 170 by 140 mi, is mostly freshwater, from 2,485-mi Parana and 1,000-mi Uruguay Rivers. **Arable land:** 14.4%. **Capital:** Buenos Aires, 15,180,176. **Cities:** Córdoba, 1,510,913; Rosario, 1,380,918; Mendoza, 1,009,400.

Government: Type: Republic. **Head of state and gov.:** Pres. Cristina Fernández de Kirchner; in office: Dec. 10, 2007. **Local divisions:** 23 provinces, 1 autonomous city. **Defense budget:** $4.27 bil. **Active troops:** 74,400.

Economy: Industries: food proc., motor vehicles, consumer durables, textiles, chemicals and petrochemicals. **Chief crops:** sunflower seeds, lemons, soybeans, grapes, corn. **Natural resources:** lead, zinc, tin, copper, iron ore, manganese, petroleum, uranium. **Water:** 21,141 cu m per capita. **Crude oil reserves:** 2.4 bil bbls. **Electricity prod.:** 127.9 bil kWh. **Labor force:** agric. 5%, industry 23%, services 72%. **Unemployment:** 7.5%.

Finance: Monetary unit: Peso (ARS) (9.30 = $1 U.S.). **GDP:** $947.6 bil; **per capita GDP:** $22,600; **GDP growth:** 0.5%. **Imports:** $65.9 bil; Brazil 27.9%, U.S. 14.5%, China 12.4%. **Exports:** $76.5 bil; Brazil 21%, China 7.1%, U.S. 5.5%. **Tourism:** $4.6 bil. **Budget:** $130.5 bil. **Inflation** (2012-13): 10.6%.

Transport: Railways: 22,939 mi. **Motor vehicles:** 308.7 per 1,000 pop. **Airports:** 161.

Communications: Telephone: 22.6 per 100 pop. **Mobile:** 158.7 per 100 pop. **Broadband:** 32.2 per 100 pop. **Internet:** 64.7%.

Health: Expend.: 8.5%. **Life expect.:** 74.5 male; 81.1 female. **Births:** 16.6 per 1,000 pop. **Deaths:** 7.3 per 1,000 pop. **Infant mortality:** 9.7 per 1,000 live births. **Undernourished:** <5%. **HIV:** 0.5%.

Education: Compulsory: ages 5-17. **Literacy:** 98.1%.

Embassy: 1600 New Hampshire Ave. NW 20009; 238-6400.

Website: www.argentina.ar

Nomadic Indians roamed the Pampas when Spaniards arrived, 1515-16, led by Juan Díaz de Solís. Nearly all the Indians were killed by the late 19th cent. The colonists won independence, 1816. A long period of disorder ended in a strong centralized government.

Large-scale Italian, German, and Spanish immigration in the decades after 1880 spurred modernization. Social reforms were enacted in the 1920s, but military coups prevailed, 1930-46, until Gen. Juan Perón was elected president.

Perón, with his wife, Eva Duarte (d. 1952), introduced labor reforms but suppressed speech and press freedoms, closed religious schools, and ran the country into debt. A 1955 coup exiled Perón. A series of military and civilian regimes followed. Perón returned in 1973 and was again elected president. He died 10 months later. His wife Isabel, who had been elected vice president, succeeded him, becoming the first woman head of state in the Western Hemisphere.

A military junta ousted Perón in 1976 amid charges of corruption. Under a continuing state of siege, the army conducted a "dirty war" against guerrillas and leftists. An estimated 30,000 people "disappeared."

Argentine troops seized control of the British-held Falkland Islands (Islas Malvinas) on Apr. 2, 1982. The British imposed an air and sea blockade around the Falklands. Fighting began May 1. British troops landed on East Falkland May 21. Argentine troops surrendered, June 14.

Democratic rule returned in 1983. On Dec. 9, 1985, five former junta members were found guilty of murder and human rights abuses during the "dirty war" period. Buenos Aires Mayor Fernando de la Rúa won the presidential election Oct. 24, 1999, but resigned in 2001 after a prolonged recession resulted in a debt of more than $130 bil.

Congress, Jan. 1, 2002, chose a Peronist, Eduardo Alberto Duhalde, to finish de la Rúa's term after 2 weeks of mass protests. Further economic decline and renewed protests led Duhalde, July 2, to schedule an early presidential election for Mar. 2003; another Peronist, Néstor Kirchner, took office May 25, 2003. A new IMF aid deal, approved Sept. 10, 2003, rescued Argentina from default.

The supreme court, June 14, 2005, overturned amnesty laws that had barred prosecution for "dirty war" crimes committed while the military ruled Argentina. Economic growth, 2004-05, allowed Argentina to repay its $9.57-bil debt to the IMF, Jan. 3, 2006.

Cristina Fernández de Kirchner ran as the Peronist candidate after her husband and was elected president Oct. 28, 2007. A candidate slate led by Néstor Kirchner was defeated in legislative elections June 2009, and the Peronists lost control of both houses of congress. Argentina became the first Latin American country to extend full marriage rights to same-sex couples in July 2010.

Néstor Kirchner died Oct. 27, 2010. Cristina Fernández de Kirchner was reelected Oct. 23, 2011. She was the first woman to win reelection in Latin America. An inflation rate of 25% prompted a general strike by farmers, bank workers, and train operators among others on Nov. 20, 2012. Meanwhile, the nation's Jewish population charged the government with anti-Semitism for attempting to ease relations with Iran in Nov. On May 29, 2013, Argentine special prosecutor Alberto Nisman claimed that Iran was plotting to carry out terrorist attacks throughout Latin America, directly and through the Lebanese militant group Hezbollah. Nisman accused Cristina Kirchner of interfering with his investigation of Iranian involvement in a 1994 Jewish community center bombing in Buenos Aires that killed 85 people. Nisman was found dead in his home from a gunshot to the head Jan. 18, 2015, and the accusations against Cristina Kirchner were formally dropped May 12, 2015. Former Pres. Carlos Saúl Menem, who had been convicted Mar. 8, 2013, of weapons smuggling during his 1989-99 term, went on trial, Aug. 6, 2015, on charges of interfering with the 1994 bombing investigation. Buenos Aires Archbishop Jorge Mario Bergoglio was elected pope Mar. 13, 2013; he was the first Jesuit pope and the first pope from the Americas. He took the name Francis after advocate for the poor St. Francis of Assisi.

Armenia

Republic of Armenia

People: Population: 3,056,382. **Age distrib.:** <15: 19.1%; 65+: 10.7%. **Growth:** –0.2%. **Migrants:** 10.6%. **Pop. density:** 280.7 per sq mi, 108.4 per sq km. **Urban:** 62.7%. **Ethnic groups:** Armenian 98.1%, Yezidi (Kurd) 1.1%. **Languages:** Armenian (official), Kurdish. **Religions:** Armenian Apostolic 92.6%.

Geography: Total area: 11,484 sq mi, 29,743 sq km; **Land area:** 10,889 sq mi, 28,203 sq km. **Location:** SW Asia. Georgia on N, Azerbaijan on E, Iran on S, Turkey on W. **Topography:** Mountainous with many peaks above 10,000 ft. **Arable land:** 15.7%. **Capital:** Yerevan, 1,044,443.

Government: Type: Republic. **Head of state:** Pres. Serzh Sargsyan; in office: Apr. 9, 2008. **Head of gov.:** Prime Min. Hovik Abrahamyan; in office: Apr. 13, 2014. **Local divisions:** 11 provinces. **Defense budget:** $470 mil. **Active troops:** 44,800.

Economy: Industries: diamond proc., metal-cutting machine tools, forging and pressing machines, elec. motors, knitted wear. **Chief crops:** fruits (espec. grapes), vegetables. **Natural resources:** gold, copper, molybdenum, zinc, bauxite. **Water:** 2,610 cu m per capita. **Electricity prod.:** 7.6 bil kWh. **Labor force:** agric. 39%, industry 17%, services 44%. **Unemployment:** 16.2%.

Finance: Monetary unit: Dram (AMD) (483.09 = $1 U.S.). **GDP:** $24.3 bil; **per capita GDP:** $7,400; **GDP growth:** 3.4%. **Imports:** $4.4 bil; Russia 24.8%, China 8.6%, Germany 6.3%, Ukraine 5.1%. **Exports:** $1.5 bil; Russia 22.6%, Bulgaria 10.3%, Belgium 8.9%, Iran 6.5%, U.S. 6%, Canada 5.9%, Georgia 5.8%, Germany 5.8%. **Tourism:** $978 mil. **Budget:** $3 bil. **Inflation:** 3%.

Transport: Railways: 485 mi (only partly operational). **Airports:** 10.

Communications: Telephone: 18.9 per 100 pop. **Mobile:** 115.9 per 100 pop. **Broadband:** 31.3 per 100 pop. **Internet:** 46.3%.

Health: Expend.: 4.5%. **Life expect.:** 71.1 male; 78.0 female. **Births:** 13.6 per 1,000 pop. **Deaths:** 9.3 per 1,000 pop. **Infant mortality:** 13.5 per 1,000 live births. **Undernourished:** 5.7%. **HIV:** 0.2%.

Education: Compulsory: ages 6-16. **Literacy:** 99.7%.

Embassy: 2225 R St. NW 20008; 319-1976.

Website: www.gov.am

Ancient Armenia extended into parts of what are now Turkey and Iran. Present-day Armenia was set up as a Soviet republic Apr. 2, 1921. It joined Georgian and Azerbaijan SSRs Mar. 12, 1922, to form the Transcaucasian SFSR, which became part of the USSR Dec. 30, 1922. Armenia became a constituent republic of the USSR Dec. 5, 1936. An earthquake struck Armenia Dec. 7, 1988; approximately 25,000 were killed.

Armenia declared independence Sept. 23, 1991, and became an independent state when the USSR disbanded Dec. 26, 1991. Nagorno-Karabakh, an enclave in Azerbaijan with an ethnic Armenian majority, seceded from Azerbaijan in 1988. A 1992-94 war that cost 30,000 lives ended in a cease-fire with Armenian forces in control. Voters in the breakaway region approved a pro-independence constitution Dec. 10, 2006, that was rejected by the EU and OSCE. Deadly clashes between Armenian and Azerbaijani forces occurred in 2015 in and near Nagorno-Karabakh.

Voters approved, July 5, 1995, a new constitution increasing presidential powers. Pres. Levon Ter-Petrosian won reelection Sept. 22, 1996, amid claims of fraud; he resigned Feb. 3, 1998, in a conflict over Nagorno-Karabakh. Robert Kocharian, a nationalist born in the disputed region, won the presidency Mar. 30, 1998. Gunmen stormed Parliament Oct. 27, 1999, killing Prime Min. Vazgen Sarkissian and 7 others. Kocharian won a second term Mar. 5, 2003, in a runoff vote that opposition groups and Western observers viewed as flawed.

Prime Min. Andranik Margaryan died of a heart attack Mar. 25, 2007, and was replaced by Def. Min. Serzh Sargsyan. He defeated Ter-Petrosian in a Feb. 19, 2008, presidential election criticized as flawed. Pres. Sargsyan's party won May 6, 2012, parliamentary elections that the OSCE called "open and peaceful" in spite of lingering shortcomings, and Sargsyan won reelection Feb. 18, 2013, with 59% of the vote.

Armenia did not ratify an Oct. 2009 treaty it had approved with Turkey over the 1915-18 killing of more than 1 mil Armenians by Ottoman Turks due to renewed friction between the countries in 2010. On Jan. 2, 2015, Armenia joined the new Russian-led Eurasian Economic Union.

Australia

Commonwealth of Australia

People: Population: 22,751,014. **Age distrib.:** <15: 17.9%; 65+: 15.5%. **Growth:** 1.1%. **Migrants:** 27.7%. **Pop. density:** 7.7 per sq mi, 3 per sq km. **Urban:** 89.4%. **Ethnic groups:** English 25.9%, Australian 25.4%, Irish 7.5%, Scottish 6.4%, Italian 3.3%, German 3.2%, Chinese 3.1%. **Languages:** English, Chinese, Italian, Arabic, Greek, Vietnamese. **Religions:** Protestant 30.1% (incl. Anglican 17.1%), Catholic 25.3%, other Christian 2.9%, Orthodox 2.8%, none 22.3%.

Geography: Total area: 2,988,902 sq mi, 7,741,220 sq km; **Land area:** 2,966,153 sq mi, 7,682,300 sq km. **Location:** SE of Asia. Surrounded by Indian O. on W and S, Pacific O. (Coral, Tasman Seas) in E. Tasmania lies 150 mi S of Victoria state, across Bass Strait. Nearest are Indonesia, Papua New Guinea on N; Solomons, Fiji, and New Zealand on E. **Topography:** An island continent. The Great Dividing Range along the E coast has Mt. Kosciusko (7,310 ft). The Western Plateau rises to 2,000 ft, with arid areas in the Great Sandy and Great Victoria Deserts. The NW part of Western Australia and Northern Terr. are arid and hot. The NE has heavy rainfall. Jungles in Cape York Peninsula. **Arable land:** 6.1%. **Capital:** Canberra, 422,674. **Cities:** Sydney, 4,505,341; Melbourne, 4,203,416; Brisbane, 2,201,930; Perth, 1,861,108; Adelaide, 1,255,516.

Government: Type: Federal parliamentary democracy. **Head of state:** Queen Elizabeth II, rep. by Gov.-Gen. Sir Peter Cosgrove; in office: Mar. 28, 2014. **Head of gov.:** Prime Min. Malcolm Turnbull; in office: Sept. 15, 2015. **Local divisions:** 6 states, 2 territories. **Defense budget:** $22.51 bil. **Active troops:** 56,750.

Economy: Industries: mining, industrial and transp. equip., food proc., chemicals, steel. **Chief crops:** wheat, barley, sugarcane, fruits. **Natural resources:** bauxite, coal, iron ore, copper, tin, gold, silver, uranium, nickel, tungsten, rare earth elements, mineral sands, lead, zinc, diamonds, nat. gas, petroleum. **Water:** 21,077 cu m per capita. **Crude oil reserves:** 1.2 bil bbls. **Other resources:** Wool (world's leading producer), beef. **Electricity prod.:** 235.2 bil kWh. **Labor force:** agric. 3.6%, industry 21.1%, services 75%. **Unemployment:** 5.7%.

Finance: Monetary unit: Dollar (AUD) (1.42 = $1 U.S.). **GDP:** $1.1 tril; **per capita GDP:** $46,400; **GDP growth:** 2.7%. **Imports:** $245.9 bil; China 19.5%, U.S. 10.4%, Japan 7.8%, Singapore 5.4%. **Exports:** $250.8 bil; China 36.1%, Japan 18%, South Korea 7.3%. **Tourism:** $32 bil. **Budget:** $521.3 bil. **Inflation:** 2.5%.

Transport: Railways: 22,971 mi. **Motor vehicles:** 746.3 per 1,000 pop. **Airports:** 349.

Communications: Telephone: 38.9 per 100 pop. **Mobile:** 131.2 per 100 pop. **Broadband:** 111.1 per 100 pop. **Internet:** 84.6%.

Health: Expend.: 9.1%. **Life expect.:** 79.7 male; 84.7 female. **Births:** 12.2 per 1,000 pop. **Deaths:** 7.1 per 1,000 pop. **Infant mortality:** 4.4 per 1,000 live births. **Undernourished:** <5%. **HIV:** NA.

Education: Compulsory: ages 6-15. **Literacy:** 99%.

Embassy: 1601 Massachusetts Ave. NW 20036; 797-3000.

Website: www.australia.gov.au

Australia harbors many plant and animal species not found elsewhere, including kangaroos, koalas, platypuses, dingoes (wild dogs), Tasmanian devils, wombats, and barking and frilled lizards.

Capt. James Cook explored the eastern coast in 1770, when the continent and offshore islands were inhabited by Aborigines and other indigenous peoples. The first European settlers, beginning in 1788, were mostly convicts, soldiers, and government officials. By 1830, Britain had claimed the entire continent, and the immigration of free settlers accelerated. The Commonwealth was proclaimed Jan. 1, 1901. Northern Terr. was granted limited self-rule July 1, 1978.

State/territory, capital	Tot. area (sq mi)	Population (2014 est.)
New South Wales, Sydney	309,130	7,565,500
Victoria, Melbourne	87,806	5,886,400
Queensland, Brisbane	668,207	4,750,500
Western Australia, Perth	976,790	2,581,300
South Australia, Adelaide	379,725	1,691,500
Tasmania, Hobart	26,410	515,200
Australian Capital Terr., Canberra	910	387,600
Northern Terr., Darwin	520,902	244,300

Note: Pop. est. as of Dec. 31. (Source: Australian Bureau of Statistics.)

In a 1967 referendum, Australians voted to change parts of the country's constitution that had discriminated against Aborigines. Racially discriminatory immigration policies ended in 1973, after 3 mil Europeans (half British) had entered since 1945.

Australia is among the top exporters of beef, lamb, wool, and wheat. Major mineral deposits have been developed, largely for export.

The Labor Party won a majority in Feb. 1983 general elections and was reelected in 1984, 1987, 1990, and 1993. Conservatives swept into power in Mar. 2, 1996 after an election that focused mainly on economic issues. Incumbent Prime Min. John Howard retained power in the 1998, 2001, and 2004 elections.

Australia led an international peacekeeping force into Timor in Sept. 1999. In a referendum Nov. 6, voters rejected a proposal that would have made Australia a republic.

Australian troops fought in U.S.-led military operations in Afghanistan (2001) and Iraq (2003). Some 2,000 Australian peacekeepers began arriving in the Solomon Isls., July 24, 2003; nearly all were withdrawn by mid-2005. In race riots in Sydney suburbs, Dec. 11-12, 2005, thousands of youths assaulted people of Middle Eastern ancestry, who then retaliated. Australian troops were dispatched, 2006, to suppress disorder in the Solomon Isls. in Apr. and Timor in May. The last Australian troops in Timor returned home on Mar. 27, 2013. The last Australian combat forces in Afghanistan left Dec. 15, 2013. Australian warplanes, Oct. 1, 2014, joined the U.S.-led air campaign in Iraq against the Sunni extremist group ISIS. The government, in late 2014 and early 2015, sent about 500 military advisers to train and assist Iraqi armed forces. In Sept. 2015, Australia joined the U.S.-led air campaign against ISIS in Syria.

Kevin Rudd led the Labor Party to victory in parliamentary elections Nov. 24, 2007. After a series of policy missteps eroded his popularity and alienated his Labor supporters, Rudd was forced out June 24, 2010, by his deputy, Julia Gillard, who became Australia's first female prime minister. Inconclusive parliamentary elections Aug. 21 led to the formation of a minority government headed by Gillard. Downpours from Cyclone Tasha and other storms flooded Queensland in late Dec. 2010 and early Jan. 2011, with three-fourths of the state declared a disaster zone.

Prime Min. Gillard, Mar. 20, 2013, officially apologized for Australia's forced adoption policy (in effect late 1950s-70s), in which the state took the babies of single, teenage, or unfit mothers, often under duress, and gave them to childless married couples. Gillard resigned June 26 after being voted out as party leader. Former Prime Min. Rudd, who engineered Gillard's ouster, became premier once again. The conservatives won Sept. 7, 2013, elections, and Tony Abbott, the party leader, became prime min. The Abbott government intensified efforts to intercept migrants from Asia attempting to reach Australia by boat. Abbott announced, Sept. 9, 2015, that Australia would accept 12,000 refugees from the conflicts in Syria and Iraq. Malcolm Turnbull replaced Abbott as prime min., Sept. 15, after defeating him, Sept. 14, in an election for Liberal Party leader.

Australian External Territories

Norfolk Isl., area 14 sq mi, pop. (2014 est.) 2,210, was taken over, 1914. The soil is very fertile, suitable for citrus, bananas, and coffee. Many of the inhabitants are descended from Pitcairn Islanders who moved to Norfolk in 1856. Australia offered the island limited home rule in 1978. **Website:** www.norfolkisland.gov.nf

The only inhabitants of **Coral Sea Isls.**, area <1.2 sq mi, are meteorological staff on Willis Isl.

Ashmore and Cartier Isls., area 1.9 sq mi, in the Indian O., came under Australian authority in 1934. **Heard Isl. and McDonald Isls.**, area 159 sq mi, are administered by the Australian Antarctic Division.

Cocos (Keeling) Isls. are 27 coral islands in the Indian O. about 1,833 mi NW of Australia. Area 5.4 sq mi; pop. (2014 est.) 596. The residents voted to become part of Australia, Apr. 1984.

Christmas Isl., area 52 sq mi, pop. (2014 est.) 1,530; 230 mi S of Java, was transferred by Britain in 1958. Its phosphate deposits are nearly depleted.

Australian Antarctic Territory was claimed by the UK and then transferred to Australian sovereignty in 1933. It comprises some 2.2 mil sq mi of territory S of 60th parallel S lat. between 45°E and 160°E (not incl. France's Adelie Coast) and between 136°E and 142°E.

Austria
Republic of Austria

People: Population: 8,665,550. **Age distrib.:** <15: 14%; 65+: 18.9%. **Growth:** 0.6%. **Migrants:** 15.7%. **Pop. density:** 272.2 per sq mi, 105.1 per sq km. **Urban:** 66%. **Ethnic groups:** Austrian 91.1%, former Yugoslav (incl. Croatians, Slovenes, Serbs, Bosniaks) 4%. **Languages:** German (official), Turkish, Serbian, Croatian (official in one state). **Religions:** Catholic 73.8%, Protestant 4.9%, Muslim 4.2%, none 12%.

Geography: Total area: 32,383 sq mi, 83,871 sq km; **Land area:** 31,832 sq mi, 82,445 sq km. **Location:** S Central Europe. Switzerland, Liechtenstein on W; Germany, Czech Rep. on N; Slovakia, Hungary on E; Slovenia, Italy on S. **Topography:** Primarily mountainous, with the Alps and foothills covering the western and southern provinces. The eastern provinces and Vienna are located in the Danube River Basin. **Arable land:** 16.4%. **Capital:** Vienna, 1,752,845.

Government: Type: Federal republic. **Head of state:** Pres. Heinz Fischer; in office: July 8, 2004. **Head of gov.:** Chancellor Werner Faymann; in office: Dec. 2, 2008. **Local divisions:** 9 states. **Defense budget:** $3.33 bil. **Active troops:** 22,500.

Economy: Industries: constr., machinery, vehicles and parts, food, metals, chemicals, lumber and wood, paper and paperboard. **Chief crops:** grains, potatoes, wine, fruit. **Natural resources:** oil, coal, lignite, timber, iron ore, copper, zinc, antimony, magnesite, tungsten, graphite, salt, hydropower. **Water:** 9,147 cu m per capita. **Crude oil reserves:** 47.5 mil bbls. **Electricity prod.:** 64.9 bil kWh. **Labor force:** agric. 5.5%, industry 26%, services 68.5%. **Unemployment:** 4.9%.

Finance: Monetary unit: Euro (EUR) (0.89 = $1 U.S.). **GDP:** $395.5 bil; **per capita GDP:** $46,400; **GDP growth:** 0.3%. **Imports:** $172.5 bil; Germany 41.7%, Italy 6.4%. **Exports:** $170.1 bil; Germany 30.7%, Italy 6.6%. **Tourism:** $20.6 bil. **Budget:** $228.6 bil. **Inflation:** 1.6%.

Transport: Railways: 3,273 mi. **Motor vehicles:** 625 per 1,000 pop. **Airports:** 24.

Communications: Telephone: 38.3 per 100 pop. **Mobile:** 151.9 per 100 pop. **Broadband:** 64.5 per 100 pop. **Internet:** 81%.

Health: Expend.: 11.5%. **Life expect.:** 78.8 male; 84.2 female. **Births:** 9.4 per 1,000 pop. **Deaths:** 9.4 per 1,000 pop. **Infant mortality:** 3.5 per 1,000 live births. **Undernourished:** <5%. **HIV:** NA.

Education: Compulsory: ages 6-14. **Literacy:** 98%.

Embassy: 3524 International Ct. NW 20008; 895-6700.

Website: www.austria.gv.at

Rome conquered Austrian lands from Celtic tribes around 15 BCE. In 788 the territory was incorporated into Charlemagne's empire. By 1300, the House of Hapsburg had gained control; they added vast territories in all parts of Europe to their realm in the next few hundred years.

Austrian dominance of Germany was undermined in the 18th cent. and ended by Prussia by 1866. But the Congress of Vienna, 1815, confirmed Austrian control of a large empire in southeast Europe consisting of Germans, Hungarians, Slavs, Italians, and others. The dual Austro-Hungarian monarchy was established in 1867, giving autonomy to Hungary and almost 50 years of peace.

World War I, which started after the June 28, 1914, assassination of Archduke Franz Ferdinand, the Hapsburg heir, by a Serbian nationalist, destroyed the empire. By 1918 Austria was reduced to a small republic, with the borders it has today.

Nazi Germany, ruled by the Austrian-born Adolf Hitler, annexed Austria Mar. 13, 1938. The republic was reestablished in 1945, under Allied occupation. Full independence and neutrality were restored in 1955. Austria joined the EU Jan. 1, 1995.

The right-wing, anti-immigrant Austrian Freedom Party (FPO) challenged the dominance of the Social Democratic Party in the late 1990s and joined the cabinet, Feb. 4, 2000. The Social Democrats won parliamentary elections Oct. 2006. They held onto their plurality in elections Sept. 2008 and Sept. 2013; the FPO won more than 21% of the vote in 2013. Tens of thousands of migrants fleeing war and hardship in Syria and elsewhere entered Austria in 2015, many trying to reach Germany or other destinations in Northern Europe; 71 were found dead in an abandoned truck near Vienna, Aug. 27. By Aug. 1, 2015, the government had detained almost 300 people suspected of involvement in human trafficking.

Azerbaijan
Republic of Azerbaijan

People: Population: 9,780,780. **Age distrib.:** <15: 22.7%; 65+ 6.4%. **Growth:** 1%. **Migrants:** 3.4%. **Pop. density:** 306.6 per sq mi, 118.4 per sq km. **Urban:** 54.6%. **Ethnic groups:** Azerbaijan 91.6%, Lezgian 2%. **Languages:** Azerbaijani (Azeri) (official)

Russian, Armenian. **Religions:** Muslim 93.4%, Russian Orthodox 2.5%, Armenian Orthodox 2.3%.

Geography: Total area: 33,436 sq mi, 86,600 sq km; **Land area:** 31,903 sq mi, 82,629 sq km. **Location:** SW Asia. Russia, Georgia on N; Iran on S; Armenia on W; Caspian Sea on E. **Topography:** The Great Caucasus Mts. in N, Karabakh Upland in W border the Kur-Abas lowland. Arid climate except in subtropical SE. **Arable land:** 22.9%. **Capital:** Baku, 2,373,633.

Government: Type: Republic. **Head of state:** Pres. Ilham Aliyev; in office: Oct. 31, 2003. **Head of gov.:** Prime Min. Artur Rasizade; in office: Nov. 4, 2003. **Local division:** 66 rayons, 11 cities. **Defense budget:** $2.11 bil. **Active troops:** 66,950.

Economy: Industries: petroleum and petroleum prods., nat. gas, oil field equip.; steel, iron ore; cement. **Chief crops:** fruit, vegetables, grain, rice. **Natural resources:** petroleum, nat. gas, iron ore, nonferrous metals, bauxite. **Water:** 3,684 cu m per capita. **Crude oil reserves:** 7 bil bbls. **Electricity prod.:** 21.7 bil kWh. **Labor force:** agric. 38.3%, industry 12.1%, services 49.6%. **Unemployment:** 5.5%.

Finance: Monetary unit: New Manat (AZN) (1.05 = $1 U.S.). **GDP:** $165.3 bil; **per capita GDP:** $17,600; **GDP growth:** 2.8%. **Imports:** $10.7 bil; Turkey 15.8%, Russia 14.1%, UK 11.1%, Germany 7.8%, China 6%, Ukraine 5.5%. **Exports:** $30.9 bil; Italy 25.6%, Indonesia 11.1%, Thailand 7.4%, Germany 6.1%, France 5.5%. **Tourism:** $2.4 bil. **Budget:** $25.2 bil. **Inflation** (2012-13): 2.4%.

Transport: Railways: 1,285 mi. **Motor vehicles:** 135.2 per 1,000 pop. **Airports:** 30.

Communications: Telephone: 18.9 per 100 pop. **Mobile:** 110.9 per 100 pop. **Broadband:** 45.1 per 100 pop. **Internet:** 61%.

Health: Expend.: 5.4%. **Life expect.:** 69.2 male; 75.5 female. **Births:** 16.6 per 1,000 pop. **Deaths:** 7.1 per 1,000 pop. **Infant mortality:** 25.7 per 1,000 live births. **Undernourished:** <5%. **HIV:** 0.1%.

Education: Compulsory: ages 6-14. **Literacy:** 99.8%.

Embassy: 2741 34th St. NW 20008; 337-3500.

Website: www.president.az

Azerbaijan was home to Scythian tribes and part of the Roman Empire. Overrun by Turks in the 11th cent. and conquered by Russia in 1806 and 1813, it joined the USSR Dec. 30, 1922, and became a constituent republic in 1936. Azerbaijan gained independence when the Soviet Union disbanded Dec. 26, 1991.

Nagorno-Karabakh, an enclave with a majority population of ethnic Armenians, seceded from Azerbaijan in 1988, triggering a war between mostly Muslim Azerbaijan and mostly Christian Armenia, 1992-94, in which 30,000 lives were lost.

Voters approved a new constitution expanding presidential powers, Nov. 12, 1995. Pres. Haydar Aliyev, a pro-Russian former Communist, was reelected Oct. 11, 1998, but international monitors called the vote seriously flawed.

The dying Pres. Aliyev named his son Ilham prime min. Aug. 4, 2003. The younger Aliyev won the Oct. 15, 2003, presidential election. International observers called the vote fraudulent. He responded to violent protests Oct. 16 by arresting hundreds of opposition leaders and their supporters. Serious abuses also marred parliamentary elections, Nov. 6, 2005, won by parties loyal to Aliyev. The opening May 25, 2005, of the Baku-Tbilisi-Ceyhan pipeline, providing an outlet for Azerbaijan's vast Caspian oil reserves, transformed the nation's economy. Construction began in 2014 on the second phase of a series of pipelines to carry natural gas from Caspian Sea deposits in Azerbaijan to Georgia, Turkey, Greece, Albania, and Italy.

Pres. Ilham Aliyev won a second term Oct. 15, 2008, but main opposition parties boycotted the election. A constitutional amendment abolishing presidential term limits was approved by referendum Mar. 18, 2009. Aliyev won a third term Oct. 9, 2013, in an election the OSCE said did not meet international standards.

The first European Games, organized by the European Olympic Committee, were held in Baku June 12-28, 2015—amid international criticism of the selection of the host city because of Azerbaijan's poor human rights record.

The Bahamas

Commonwealth of The Bahamas

People: Population: 324,597. **Age distrib.:** <15: 23%; 65+: 7.2%. **Growth:** 0.9%. **Migrants:** 16.3%. **Pop. density:** 84 per sq mi, 32.4 per sq km. **Urban:** 82.9%. **Ethnic groups:** black 90.6%, white 4.7%, black and white 2.1%. **Languages:** English (official), Creole (among Haitian immigrants). **Religions:** Protestant 69.9% (incl. Baptist 34.9%, Anglican 13.7%, Pentecostal 8.9%), Roman Catholic 12%, other Christian 13%.

Geography: Total area: 5,359 sq mi, 13,880 sq km; **Land area:** 3,865 sq mi, 10,010 sq km. **Location:** In Atlantic O., E of Florida. U.S. is on W, Cuba to S. **Topography:** Nearly 700 islands (29 inhabited) and over 2,000 islets in the W Atlantic O. extend 760 mi NW to SE. **Arable land:** 0.8%. **Capital:** Nassau, 266,765 (2014).

Government: Type: Constitutional parliamentary democracy. **Head of state:** Queen Elizabeth II, rep. by Gov.-Gen. Dame Marguerite Pindling; in office: July 8, 2014. **Head of gov.:** Prime Min. Perry Christie; in office: May 8, 2012. **Local divisions:** 31 districts. **Defense budget:** $87 mil. **Active troops:** 1,300.

Economy: Industries: tourism, banking, oil bunkering, maritime industries, transshipment, salt, rum. **Chief crops:** citrus, vegetables. **Natural resources:** salt, aragonite, timber. **Water:** 1,857 cu m per capita. **Electricity prod.:** 1.8 bil kWh. **Labor force:** agric. 3%, industry 11%, tourism 49%, other services 37%. **Unemployment:** 13.6%.

Finance: Monetary unit: Dollar (BSD) (1.00 = $1 U.S.). **GDP:** $9 bil; **per capita GDP:** $25,000; **GDP growth:** 1.3%. **Imports:** $3.1 bil; U.S. 36.6%, South Korea 10%, Singapore 9.7%, India 8%, Colombia 5.8%, Japan 5.7%. **Exports:** $960 mil; Côte d'Ivoire 25.6%, U.S. 21.5%, Dominican Republic 18%. **Tourism:** $2.3 bil. **Budget:** $2.1 bil. **Inflation:** 1.2%.

Transport: Motor vehicles: 406.4 per 1,000 pop. **Airports:** 24.

Communications: Telephone: 36 per 100 pop. **Mobile:** 71.4 per 100 pop. **Broadband:** 7.7 per 100 pop. **Internet:** 76.9%.

Health: Expend.: 7.5%. **Life expect.:** 69.8 male; 74.7 female. **Births:** 15.5 per 1,000 pop. **Deaths:** 7.1 per 1,000 pop. **Infant mortality:** 11.9 per 1,000 live births. **Undernourished:** NA. **HIV:** NA.

Education: Compulsory: ages 5-16. **Literacy:** NA.

Embassy: 2220 Massachusetts Ave. NW 20008; 319-2660.

Website: www.bahamas.gov.bs

Christopher Columbus first set foot in the New World on San Salvador (Watling Isl.) in 1492, when Arawak Indians inhabited the islands. British settlement began in 1647; the islands became a British colony in 1783. Internal self-government was granted in 1964; full independence within the Commonwealth was attained July 10, 1973. International banking and investment management have become major industries alongside tourism. The Progressive Liberal Party's Perry Christie, who was prime min. 2002-07, returned to the post after May 7, 2012, parliamentary elections, which saw the defeat of the Free Natl. Movement as the majority party.

Bahrain

Kingdom of Bahrain

People: Population: 1,346,613. **Age distrib.:** <15: 19.5%; 65+: 2.8%. **Growth:** 2.4%. **Migrants:** 54.7%. **Pop. density:** 4,589.1 per sq mi, 1,771.9 per sq km. **Urban:** 88.8%. **Ethnic groups:** Bahraini 46%, Asian 45.5%, other Arab 4.7%. **Languages:** Arabic (official), English, Farsi, Urdu. **Religions:** Muslim 70.3%, Christian 14.5%, Hindu 9.8%.

Geography: Total area: 293 sq mi, 760 sq km; **Land area:** 293 sq mi, 760 sq km. **Location:** SW Asia, in Persian Gulf. Saudi Arabia on W, Qatar on E. **Topography:** Bahrain Island and several adjacent, smaller islands, are flat, hot, and humid with little rain. **Arable land:** 2.1%. **Capital:** Manama, 411,162.

Government: Type: Constitutional monarchy. **Head of state:** King Hamad bin Isa al-Khalifa; in office: as emir Mar. 6, 1999; as king Feb. 14, 2002. **Head of gov.:** Prime Min. Khalifa bin Salman al-Khalifa; in office: 1971. **Local divisions:** 4 governorates. **Defense budget:** $1.34 bil. **Active troops:** 8,200.

Economy: Industries: petroleum proc. and refining, aluminum smelting, iron pelletization, fertilizers, Islamic and offshore banking. **Chief crops:** fruit, vegetables. **Natural resources:** oil, nat. gas, fish, pearls. **Water:** 87 cu m per capita. **Crude oil reserves:** 124.6 mil bbls. **Electricity prod.:** 13.3 bil kWh. **Labor force:** agric. 1%, industry 32%, services 67%. **Unemployment:** 7.4%.

Finance: Monetary unit: Dinar (BHD) (0.38 = $1 U.S.). **GDP:** $61.9 bil; **per capita GDP:** $51,700; **GDP growth:** 4.7%. **Imports:** $14.3 bil; Saudi Arabia 28%, China 10.1%, U.S. 8.3%, Japan 6.2%, India 5.5%, Australia 5.2%. **Exports:** $22 bil; Saudi Arabia 3.2%, UAE 2.1%, Qatar 1.8%. **Tourism:** $1.2 bil. **Budget** (2013 est.): $8.9 bil. **Inflation:** 2.8%.

Transport: Motor vehicles: 427.1 per 1,000 pop. **Airports:** 4.

Communications: Telephone: 21.2 per 100 pop. **Mobile:** 173.3 per 100 pop. **Broadband:** 119.3 per 100 pop. **Internet:** 91%.

Health: Expend.: 3.9%. **Life expect.:** 76.5 male; 81.0 female. **Births:** 13.7 per 1,000 pop. **Deaths:** 2.7 per 1,000 pop. **Infant mortality:** 9.4 per 1,000 live births. **Undernourished:** NA. **HIV:** NA.

Education: Compulsory: ages 6-14. **Literacy:** 95.7%.

Embassy: 3502 International Dr. NW 20008; 342-1111.

Website: www.bahrain.bh

Long ruled by the Khalifa family, Bahrain was a British protectorate from 1861 to Aug. 15, 1971, when it regained independence. Pearls, shrimp, fruits, and vegetables were the mainstays of the economy until oil was discovered in 1932. Crude oil production has declined since the 1970s, but natural gas output has grown, and international banking has thrived.

Emir Hamad bin Isa al-Khalifa proclaimed himself king Feb. 14, 2002. Local elections in May 2002 marked the first time Bahraini women were allowed to vote and run for office. The first female judge was appointed June 6, 2006. The monarchy suppressed Arab Spring demonstrations Feb.-Mar. 2011; to bolster security, a Gulf Cooperation Council force of 1,600, led by Saudi Arabia, entered Bahrain Mar. 14, and the government recruited former soldiers and police from Pakistan. Protests, however, continued in 2012-15, largely by members of the country's Shiite majority against the mostly Sunni ruling elite. The government arrested opposition leaders. Forced labor and sexual exploitation of immigrants—many from S and SE Asia and from Africa—has gained international attention. Beginning Sept. 23, 2014, Bahrain took part in U.S.-led airstrikes against Sunni extremist forces in Syria. A U.S. ban on military aid to Bahrain, imposed after suppression of Arab Spring protests, was lifted June 29, 2015.

Bangladesh

People's Republic of Bangladesh

People: Population: 168,957,745. **Age distrib.:** <15: 31.6%; 65+: 5.1%. **Growth:** 1.6%. **Migrants:** 0.9%. **Pop. density:** 3,361.8 per sq mi, 1,298 per sq km. **Urban:** 34.3%. **Ethnic groups:** Bengali 98%+. **Languages:** Bangla or Bengali (official). **Religions:** Muslim 89.5%, Hindu 9.6%.

Geography: Total area: 57,321 sq mi, 148,460 sq km; **Land area:** 50,259 sq mi, 130,170 sq km. **Location:** S Asia, on N bend of Bay of Bengal. India nearly surrounds country on W, N, E; Myanmar on SE. **Topography:** Mostly a low plain cut by the Ganges and Brahmaputra Rivers and their delta. Alluvial and marshy along the coast. Hilly only in the extreme SE and NE. Its tropical monsoon climate makes country among the rainiest in the world. **Arable land:** 59%. **Capital:** Dhaka, 17,598,228. **Cities:** Chittagong, 4,539,393; Khulna, 1,021,903.

Government: Type: Parliamentary democracy. **Head of state:** Pres. Abdul Hamid; in office: Apr. 24, 2013. **Head of gov.:** Prime Min. Sheikh Hasina; in office: Jan. 6, 2009. **Local divisions:** 7 divisions. **Defense budget:** $1.96 bil. **Active troops:** 157,050.

Economy: Industries: jute, cotton, garments, paper, leather, fertilizer, iron and steel, cement, petroleum prods., tobacco, pharmaceuticals. **Chief crops:** rice, jute, tea, wheat, sugarcane, potatoes, tobacco, pulses, oilseeds, spices. **Natural resources:** nat. gas, timber, coal. **Water:** 7,835 cu m per capita. **Crude oil reserves:** 28 mil bbls. **Electricity prod.:** 47.3 bil kWh. **Labor force:** agric. 47%, industry 13%, services 40%. **Unemployment:** 4.3%.

Finance: Monetary unit: Taka (BDT) (77.73 = $1 U.S.). **GDP:** $533.7 bil; **per capita GDP:** $3,400; **GDP growth:** 6.1%. **Imports:** $38.5 bil; China 21.9%, India 14%, Singapore 5.8%, Malaysia 5.3%. **Exports:** $31.2 bil; U.S. 16.3%, Germany 11.8%, UK 7.8%. **Tourism:** $128 mil. **Budget:** $24.3 bil. **Inflation:** 7%.

Transport: Railways: 1,529 mi. **Motor vehicles:** 3.8 per 1,000 pop. **Airports:** 16.

Communications: Telephone: 0.7 per 100 pop. **Mobile:** 75.9 per 100 pop. **Broadband:** 1.9 per 100 pop. **Internet:** 9.6%.

Health: Expend.: 3.6%. **Life expect.:** 69.0 male; 72.9 female. **Births:** 21.1 per 1,000 pop. **Deaths:** 5.6 per 1,000 pop. **Infant mortality:** 44.1 per 1,000 live births. **Undernourished:** 16.7%. **HIV:** <0.1%.

Education: Compulsory: ages 6-10. **Literacy:** 61.5%.

Embassy: 3510 International Dr. NW 20008; 244-0183.

Website: www.bangladesh.gov.bd

Muslim invaders conquered the formerly Hindu area in the 12th cent. British rule lasted from the 18th cent. to 1947, when East Bengal became part of Pakistan.

Opposing domination by West Pakistan, the Awami League, based in the East, won control of the National Assembly in 1971. Assembly sessions were postponed; riots broke out. Pakistani troops attacked, Mar. 25; Bangladesh independence was proclaimed the next day. In the ensuing civil war, 1 mil died and 10 mil fled to India. War between India and Pakistan broke out Dec. 3, 1971. Pakistan surrendered in the East on Dec. 16. Mujibur Rahman, known as Sheikh Mujib, became prime min.; he was killed in a coup Aug. 15, 1975.

Army rivals killed Pres. Ziaur Rahman in an unsuccessful coup attempt, May 1981. Vice Pres. Abdus Sattar assumed the presidency but was ousted in a coup led by army chief of staff Gen. H. M. Ershad, Mar. 1982. Ershad declared Bangladesh an Islamic Republic in 1988; a parliamentary system of government was adopted in 1991. A cyclone, Apr. 1991, killed over 131,000 people.

Political turmoil led to the resignation, Mar. 1996, of Prime Min. Khaleda Zia, the widow of Ziaur Rahman. Sheikh Mujib's daughter, known as Sheikh Hasina, led the country after the June 1996 election. Khaleda Zia returned to power following parliamentary elections, Oct. 1, 2001. Militant Islamists set off more than 400 small bombs in more than 50 cities and towns, Aug. 17, 2005, killing 3. Another wave of jihadist bombings killed 22, Nov. 29-Dec. 8, 2005. Bangladeshi economist Muhammad Yunus won the 2006 Nobel Peace Prize for using very small loans (microcredit) to help alleviate the nation's severe poverty.

Escalating political violence led Pres. Iajuddin Ahmed to declare a state of emergency Jan. 11, 2007. A military-backed caretaker government filed criminal charges against Khaleda Zia and Sheikh Hasina but failed to force the two former prime ministers into exile. Cyclone Sidr struck Nov. 15, 2007, damaging more than 1.5 mil homes and leaving about 3,400 dead.

The Awami League triumphed in parliamentary elections Dec. 2008, and Sheikh Hasina was sworn in as prime min. Jan. 6, 2009, ending two years of emergency rule. She remained in office when her party won Jan. 5, 2014, elections marred by violence and low turnout.

A fire in a crowded residential area of Dhaka June 3, 2010, killed at least 117. The UN Intl. Tribunal for the Law of the Sea ruled in favor of Bangladesh in its maritime dispute with Myanmar Mar. 14, 2012, granting its claim to 200 nautical mi in the oil-rich Bay of Bengal and beyond. A garment factory fire Nov. 24, 2012, outside Dhaka killed 112 workers. Rana Plaza, a building that housed 5 garment factories, collapsed Apr. 24, 2013, due to poor construction and unsafe practices, killing more than 1,100 workers in the deadliest garment-factory disaster in world history. The owner of Rana Plaza and factory owners were among 41 people charged, June 1, 2015, with murder in connection with the disaster. Security forces in Dhaka, July 1-2, 2015, arrested 12 people said to be affiliated with al-Qaeda, including a man who had claimed responsibility for the Feb. killing of a Bangladeshi-American blogger who had criticized Islamist extremists. Three other so-called secular bloggers had been killed by Aug. 2015.

Barbados

People: Population: 290,604. **Age distrib.:** <15: 18.3%; 65+: 10.9%. **Growth:** 0.3%. **Migrants:** 11.3%. **Pop. density:** 1,750.4 per sq mi, 675.8 per sq km. **Urban:** 31.5%. **Ethnic groups:** black 92.4%, mixed 3.1%, white 2.7%. **Languages:** English (official), Bajan (English-based creole). **Religions:** Protestant 66.3% (incl. Anglican 23.9%, other Pentecostal 19.5%), Roman Catholic 3.8%, none 20.6%.

Geography: Total area: 166 sq mi, 430 sq km; **Land area:** 166 sq mi, 430 sq km. **Location:** In Atlantic O., farthest E of West Indies. Nearest neighbors are St. Lucia and St. Vincent and the Grenadines to the W. **Topography:** The island lies alone in the Atlantic almost completely surrounded by coral reefs. Highest point is Mt. Hillaby (1,115 ft). **Arable land:** 25.6%. **Capital:** Bridgetown, 90,265 (2014).

Government: Type: Parliamentary democracy. **Head of state:** Queen Elizabeth II, rep. by Gov.-Gen. Sir Elliot Belgrave; in office: June 1, 2012. **Head of gov.:** Prime Min. Freundel Stuart; in office: Oct. 23, 2010. **Local divisions:** 11 parishes, 1 city. **Defense budget:** $33 mil. **Active troops:** 610.

Economy: Industries: tourism, sugar, light mfg., component assembly for export. **Chief crops:** sugarcane, vegetables, cotton. **Natural resources:** petroleum, fish, nat. gas. **Water:** 281 cu m per capita. **Crude oil reserves:** 2.5 mil bbls. **Other resources:** Fish. **Electricity prod.:** 981 mil kWh. **Labor force:** agric. 10%, industry 15%, services 75%. **Unemployment:** 12.2%.

Finance: Monetary unit: Dollar (BBD) (2.00 = $1 U.S.). **GDP:** $4.5 bil; **per capita GDP:** $16,200; **GDP growth:** –0.3%. **Imports:** $1.7 bil; Trinidad and Tobago 35%, U.S. 24.6%, Canada 8%. **Exports:** $774.9 mil; Trinidad and Tobago 20.7%, U.S. 11.2%, St. Lucia 9.6%, St. Vincent and the Grenadines 6%, Jamaica 5.5%. **Tourism:** $947 mil. **Budget:** $1.5 bil. **Inflation:** 1.9%.

Transport: Motor vehicles: 370.4 per 1,000 pop. **Airports:** 1.

Communications: Telephone: 52.9 per 100 pop. **Mobile:** 106.8 per 100 pop. **Broadband:** 41.5 per 100 pop. **Internet:** 76.7%.

Health: Expend.: 6.3%. **Life expect.:** 72.8 male; 77.6 female. **Births:** 11.9 per 1,000 pop. **Deaths:** 8.4 per 1,000 pop. **Infant mortality:** 10.4 per 1,000 live births. **Undernourished:** <5%. **HIV:** NA.

Education: Compulsory: ages 5-15. **Literacy:** NA.

Embassy: 2144 Wyoming Ave. NW 20008; 939-9200.

Website: www.gov.bb

Barbados was probably named by Portuguese sailors in reference to bearded fig trees. An English ship visited in 1605, and British settled on the uninhabited island in 1627. Slaves worked the sugar plantations until slavery was abolished in 1834. Self-rule came gradually, with full independence proclaimed Nov. 30, 1966. Tourism, banking, and manufacturing have surpassed the sugar trade in economic importance since the 1990s. The country signed an Economic and Technical Agreement with China Aug. 24, 2012, to strengthen the two countries' growing ties.

Airline baggage handler and Barbados native Victor Bourne was convicted and sentenced to life in prison Oct. 2012 after a trial in Brooklyn, NY, for leading a drug-smuggling ring that brought drugs from Barbados to New York in commercial jets.

Belarus

Republic of Belarus

People: Population: 9,589,689. **Age distrib.:** <15: 15.5%; 65+: 14.4%. **Growth:** –0.2%. **Migrants:** 11.6%. **Pop. density:** 122.4 per sq mi, 47.3 per sq km. **Urban:** 76.7%. **Ethnic groups:** Belarusian 83.7%, Russian 8.3%, Polish 3.1%. **Languages:** Russian,

Belarusian (both official). **Religions:** Eastern Orthodox 80%, other (incl. Roman Catholic, Protestant, Jewish, Muslim) 20%.

Geography: Total area: 80,155 sq mi, 207,600 sq km; **Land area:** 78,340 sq mi, 202,900 sq km. **Location:** Eastern Europe. Poland on W; Latvia, Lithuania on N; Russia on E; Ukraine on S. **Topography:** Landlocked country consisting mostly of hilly lowland with significant marsh areas in S. **Arable land:** 27.2%. **Capital:** Minsk, 1,915,396.

Government: Type: Republic in name. **Head of state:** Pres. Aleksandr Lukashenko; in office: July 20,1994. **Head of gov.:** Prime Min. Andrei Kobyakov; in office: Dec. 27, 2014. **Local divisions:** 6 provinces, 1 municipality. **Defense budget** (2012): $552 mil. **Active troops:** 48,000.

Economy: Industries: metal-cutting machine tools, tractors, trucks, earthmovers. **Chief crops:** grain, potatoes, vegetables, sugar beets, flax. **Natural resources:** timber, peat, oil, nat. gas, granite, dolomitic limestone, marl, chalk, sand, gravel, clay. **Water:** 6,199 cu m per capita. **Crude oil reserves:** 198 mil bbls. **Electricity prod.:** 29.1 bil kWh. **Labor force:** agric. 9.3%, industry 32.7%, services 58%. **Unemployment:** 5.8%.

Finance: Monetary unit: Ruble (BYR) (17,485.00 = $1 U.S.). **GDP:** $172.3 bil; **per capita GDP:** $18,200; **GDP growth:** 1.6%. **Imports:** $40.5 bil; Russia 53.2%, Germany 7.1%, China 6.6%. **Exports:** $37.9 bil; Russia 45.3%, Ukraine 11.3%, Netherlands 9%. **Tourism:** $822 mil. **Budget:** $26.7 bil. **Inflation:** 18.1%.

Transport: Railways: 3,435 mi. **Motor vehicles:** 354.2 per 1,000 pop. **Airports:** 33.

Communications: Telephone: 48.5 per 100 pop. **Mobile:** 122.5 per 100 pop. **Broadband:** 46 per 100 pop. **Internet:** 59%.

Health: Expend.: 5%. **Life expect.:** 66.9 male; 78.4 female. **Births:** 10.7 per 1,000 pop. **Deaths:** 13.4 per 1,000 pop. **Infant mortality:** 3.6 per 1,000 live births. **Undernourished:** <5%. **HIV:** 0.5%.

Education: Compulsory: ages 6-14. **Literacy:** 99.7%.

Embassy: 1619 New Hampshire Ave. NW 20009; 986-1604.

Website: www.president.gov.by

Belarus became a constituent republic of the USSR in 1922. Overrun by German armies in 1941, Belarus was recaptured by Soviet troops in 1944. Following WWII, Belarus increased in area through Soviet annexation of part of NE Poland. Belarus declared independence Aug. 25, 1991, and became independent when the Soviet Union disbanded Dec. 26, 1991.

After a new constitution was adopted, Mar. 15, 1994, Aleksandr Lukashenko was elected president. Russia and Belarus signed a pact, Apr. 2, 1996, linking their political and economic systems. An authoritarian constitution enacted in Nov. gave Pres. Lukashenko vast new powers. Subsequently, Lukashenko and his supporters retained power in elections criticized as seriously flawed by Western observers.

The IMF agreed Jan. 2009 to extend $2.5 bil in credits to help Belarus weather the global economic downturn. Lukashenko crushed protests that followed the Dec. 19, 2010, presidential election in which he claimed nearly 80% of the vote; the U.S. and EU imposed sanctions on Lukashenko and other Belarus officials Jan. 31, 2011. New sanctions imposed Feb. 28, 2012, prompted Lukashenko to expel the EU and Polish ambassadors from Belarus and recall its own envoys. In Sept. 23, 2012, parliamentary elections that many observers considered fraudulent, Lukashenko's supporters won every seat. Belarus, Russia, and Kazakhstan signed an agreement, May 29, 2014, to create a Eurasian Economic Union (EEU). The EEU came into existence Jan. 1, 2015, and Armenia and Kyrgyzstan joined in Jan. and May, respectively.

Belgium

Kingdom of Belgium

People: Population: 11,323,973. **Age distrib.:** <15: 17.1%; 65+: 18.2%. **Growth:** 0.8%. **Migrants:** 10.4%. **Pop. density:** 968.7 per sq mi, 374 per sq km. **Urban:** 97.9%. **Ethnic groups:** Fleming 58%, Walloon 31%, mixed or other 11%. **Languages:** Dutch, French, German (all official). **Religions:** Roman Catholic 75%, other (incl. Protestant) 25%.

Geography: Total area: 11,787 sq mi, 30,528 sq km; **Land area:** 11,690 sq mi, 30,278 sq km. **Location:** Western Europe, on North Sea. France on W and S, Luxembourg on SE, Germany on E, Netherlands on N. **Topography:** Mostly flat; trisected by the Scheldt and Meuse, major commercial rivers. The land becomes hilly and forested in the Ardennes region to the SE. **Arable land:** 26.5%. **Capital:** Brussels, 2,044,993. **Cities:** Antwerp, 993,511.

Government: Type: Federal parliamentary democracy under constitutional monarchy. **Head of state:** King Philippe; in office: July 21, 2013. **Head of gov.:** Prime Min. Charles Michel; in office: Oct. 11, 2014. **Local divisions:** 3 regions. **Defense budget:** $5.04 bil. **Active troops:** 30,700.

Economy: Industries: engineering and metal prods., motor vehicle assembly, transp. equip., scientific instruments, processed food and beverages. **Chief crops:** sugar beets, vegetables, fruits, grain, tobacco. **Natural resources:** constr. materials, silica sand, carbonates. **Water:** 1,648 cu m per capita. **Electricity prod.:** 76.1 bil kWh. **Labor force:** agric. 1.3%, industry 18.6%, services 80.1%. **Unemployment:** 8.4%.

Finance: Monetary unit: Euro (EUR) (0.89 = $1 U.S.). **GDP:** $481.5 bil; **per capita GDP:** $43,000; **GDP growth:** 1%. **Imports:** $340.2 bil; Netherlands 20.7%, Germany 13.6%, France 10.6%, U.S. 6.8%, UK 5.3%. **Exports:** $323.4 bil; Germany 17.5%, France 16.2%, Netherlands 12.7%, UK 7.8%. **Tourism:** $14.3 bil. **Budget:** $280.8 bil. **Inflation:** 0.3%.

Transport: Railways: 2,232 mi. **Motor vehicles:** 611.3 per 1,000 pop. **Airports:** 26.

Communications: Telephone: 42.1 per 100 pop. **Mobile:** 114.3 per 100 pop. **Broadband:** 46.1 per 100 pop. **Internet:** 85%.

Health: Expend.: 10.8%. **Life expect.:** 78.3 male; 83.6 female. **Births:** 11.4 per 1,000 pop. **Deaths:** 9.6 per 1,000 pop. **Infant mortality:** 3.4 per 1,000 live births. **Undernourished:** <5%. **HIV:** NA.

Education: Compulsory: ages 6-17. **Literacy:** 99%.

Embassy: 3330 Garfield St. NW 20008; 333-6900.

Website: www.belgium.be

Belgium derives its name from the Belgae, the first recorded inhabitants, probably Celts. The land was ruled for 1800 years by conquerors, including Rome, the Franks, Burgundy, Spain, Austria, and France. After 1815, Belgium was made a part of the Netherlands but became an independent constitutional monarchy in 1830.

King Leopold III surrendered to Germany, May 28, 1940. After WWII, he was forced to abdicate in favor of his son, King Baudouin. Baudouin was succeeded by his brother, Albert II, Aug. 9, 1993. Albert's son Philippe became king July 21, 2013.

The Flemings of northern Belgium speak Dutch, while the Walloons in the south speak French. The language difference has been a perennial source of controversy between the 2 groups. Parliament has passed measures aimed at transferring power from the central government to 3 regions—Wallonia, Flanders, and Brussels. Constitutional changes in 1993 made Belgium a federal state.

After elections June 2007, rivalries between Flemings and Walloons led to a 9-month political stalemate. June 2010 elections led to a prolonged political deadlock that ended when Elio Di Rupo became prime min. Dec. 2011. After May 25, 2014, elections in which Flemish nationalist parties made gains, Charles Michel was sworn in as prime min. Oct. 11, heading a center-right coalition government.

An Oct. 2014 government report stated that 350 Belgians had traveled to Syria to fight with Islamist extremists. Two suspects were killed Jan. 15, 2015, in a series of police raids—in Verviers, Brussels, and other locations—on alleged Islamist extremists said to be plotting terrorist attacks in Belgium.

Belize

People: Population: 347,369. **Age distrib.:** <15: 34.9%; 65+: 3.7%. **Growth:** 1.9%. **Migrants:** 15.3%. **Pop. density:** 39.4 per sq mi, 15.2 per sq km. **Urban:** 44%. **Ethnic groups:** mestizo 52.9%, Creole 25.9%, Maya 11.3%, Garifuna 6.1%, E Indian 3.9%, Mennonite 3.6%. **Languages:** English (official), Spanish, Creole, Maya, German, Garifuna. **Religions:** Roman Catholic 40.1%, Protestant 31.5% (incl. Pentecostal 8.4%, Seventh-day Adventist 5.4%), other (incl. Baha'i, Buddhist, Hindu, Morman, Muslim, Rastafarian) 10.5%, none 15.5%.

Geography: Total area: 8,867 sq mi, 22,966 sq km; **Land area:** 8,805 sq mi, 22,806 sq km. **Location:** Eastern coast of Central America. Mexico on N, Guatemala on W and S. **Topography:** Swampy lowlands in N, Maya Mts. in S, coral reefs and cays near coast. Tropical climate. **Arable land:** 3.4%. **Capital:** Belmopan, 16,921.

Government: Type: Parliamentary democracy. **Head of state:** Queen Elizabeth II, rep. by Gov.-Gen. Sir Colville Young; in office: Nov. 17, 1993. **Head of gov.:** Prime Min. Dean Barrow; in office: Feb. 8, 2008. **Local divisions:** 6 districts. **Defense budget:** $18 mil. **Active troops:** 1,050.

Economy: Industries: garment prod., food proc., tourism, constr. **Chief crops:** bananas, cacao, citrus, sugar. **Natural resources:** timber, fish, hydropower. **Water:** 65,452 cu m per capita. **Crude oil reserves:** 6.7 mil bbls. **Electricity prod.:** 423 mil kWh. **Labor force:** agric. 10.2%, industry 18.1%, services 71.7%. **Unemployment:** 14.6%.

Finance: Monetary unit: Dollar (BZD) (1.98 = $1 U.S.). **GDP:** $2.9 bil; **per capita GDP:** $8,200; **GDP growth:** 3.4%. **Imports:** $922.7 mil; U.S. 23.3%, Mexico 14.1%, China 11.8%, Cuba 9.6%, Guatemala 5.5%. **Exports:** $640.9 mil; U.S. 26%, UK 22.2%, Nigeria 5.8%. **Tourism:** $351 mil. **Budget:** $500 mil. **Inflation:** 0.9%.

Transport: Motor vehicles: 105 per 1,000 pop. **Airports:** 6.

Communications: Telephone: 6.7 per 100 pop. **Mobile:** 50.7 per 100 pop. **Broadband:** 2.3 per 100 pop. **Internet:** 38.7%.

Health: Expend.: 5.8%. **Life expect.:** 67.0 male; 70.3 female. **Births:** 24.7 per 1,000 pop. **Deaths:** 6.0 per 1,000 pop. **Infant**

mortality: 19.8 per 1,000 live births. **Undernourished:** 6.5%. **HIV:** 1.2%.

Education: Compulsory: ages 5-14. **Literacy:** 70.3%.

Embassy: 2535 Massachusetts Ave. NW 20008; 332-9636.

Website: www.belize.gov.bz

Belize (formerly British Honduras) was Britain's last colony on the American mainland; independence was achieved Sept. 21, 1981. Relations with neighboring Guatemala, which claims the southern half of Belize and its islands as its own territory, have improved in recent years. Belize has become a center for drug trafficking between Colombia and the U.S.

Benin

Republic of Benin

People: Population: 10,448,647. **Age distrib.:** <15: 43.4%; 65+: 2.8%. **Growth:** 2.8%. **Migrants:** 2.3%. **Pop. density:** 244.6 per sq mi, 94.5 per sq km. **Urban:** 44%. **Ethnic groups:** Fon and related 39.2%, Adja/related 15.2%, Yoruba/related 12.3%, Bariba/related 9.2%, Peulh/related 7%, Ottamari/related 6.1%, Yoa-Lokpa/related 4%, Dendi/related 2.5%. **Languages:** French (official), Fon, Yoruba, tribal langs. **Religions:** Catholic 27.1%, Muslim 24.4%, Vodoun 17.3%, Protestant 10.4%.

Geography: Total area: 43,484 sq mi, 112,622 sq km; **Land area:** 42,711 sq mi, 110,622 sq km. **Location:** W Africa on Gulf of Guinea. Togo on W; Burkina Faso, Niger on N; Nigeria on E. **Topography:** Mostly flat and covered with dense vegetation. The coast is hot, humid, and rainy. **Arable land:** 23.9%. **Capital:** Porto-Novo (official), 268,057 (2014); Cotonou (seat), 682,459.

Government: Type: Republic. **Head of state and gov.:** Pres. Boni Yayi; in office: Apr. 6, 2006. **Local divisions:** 12 departments. **Defense budget:** $89 mil. **Active troops:** 6,950.

Economy: Industries: textiles, food proc., constr. materials, cement. **Chief crops:** cotton, corn, cassava, yams, beans. **Natural resources:** offshore oil, limestone, marble, timber. **Water:** 2,556 cu m per capita. **Crude oil reserves:** 8 mil bbls. **Electricity prod.:** 154 mil kWh. **Labor force:** NA. **Unemployment:** 1%.

Finance: Monetary unit: CFA Franc (XOF) (584.11 = $1 U.S.). **GDP:** $19.8 bil; **per capita GDP:** $1,900; **GDP growth:** 5.5%. **Imports:** $2.9 bil; China 37.1%, India 10.3%, U.S. 7.5%, Malaysia 6.7%, Thailand 6.1%. **Exports:** $2 bil; Lebanon 21.7%, China 21.6%, India 18.5%. **Tourism:** $189 mil. **Budget:** $2.1 bil. **Inflation:** –1.1%.

Transport: Railways: 272 mi. **Motor vehicles:** 3.4 per 1,000 pop. **Airports:** 1.

Communications: Telephone: 1.8 per 100 pop. **Mobile:** 101.7 per 100 pop. **Broadband:** 1.9 per 100 pop. **Internet:** 5.3%.

Health: Expend.: 4.5%. **Life expect.:** 60.1 male; 62.9 female. **Births:** 36.0 per 1,000 pop. **Deaths:** 8.2 per 1,000 pop. **Infant mortality:** 55.7 per 1,000 live births. **Undernourished:** 9.7%. **HIV:** 1.1%.

Education: Compulsory: ages 6-11. **Literacy:** 38.4%.

Embassy: 2124 Kalorama Rd. NW 20008; 232-6656.

Website: www.gouv.bj

The Kingdom of Abomey, rising to power in wars with neighboring kingdoms in the 17th cent., came under French domination in the late 19th cent., and was incorporated into French West Africa by 1904. Under the name Dahomey, the country gained independence Aug. 1, 1960; it became Benin in 1975. In the fifth coup since independence Col. Ahmed Kerekou took power in 1972; two years later he declared a socialist state with a Marxist-Leninist philosophy. In Dec. 1989, Kerekou announced Marxism-Leninism would no longer be the state ideology.

In Mar. 1991, Kerekou lost Benin's first free presidential election in 30 years to Nicéphore Soglo. Kerekou defeated Soglo in Mar. 1996 to reclaim the presidency. He won reelection in a runoff Mar. 22, 2001. Boni Yayi, an economist, won a presidential runoff vote, Mar. 19, 2006.

In 2006, Benin signed a 5-year, $307-mil aid deal with the U.S. Pres. Yayi won reelection to a second 5-year term Mar. 13, 2011. In June 2015, Benin agreed to join Nigeria, Chad, Cameroon, and Niger in contributing troops to a multinational force to fight the Islamist extremist group Boko Haram in northern Nigeria.

Bhutan

Kingdom of Bhutan

People: Population: 741,919. **Age distrib.:** <15: 26.8%; 65+: 6.1%. **Growth:** 1.1%. **Migrants:** 6.7%. **Pop. density:** 50 per sq mi, 19.3 per sq km. **Urban:** 38.6%. **Ethnic groups:** Ngalop or Bhote 50%, ethnic Nepalese (incl. Lhotsampas) 35%, indigenous or migrant tribes 15%. **Languages:** Sharchhopka, Dzongkha (official), Lhotshamkha. **Religions:** Lamaistic Buddhist 75.3%, Indian- and Nepalese-influenced Hinduism 22.1%.

Geography: Total area: 14,824 sq mi, 38,394 sq km; **Land area:** 14,824 sq mi, 38,394 sq km. **Location:** S Asia, in eastern Himalayan Mts. India (Sikkim state) on W and S, China on N. **Topography:** Very high mountains in the N, fertile valleys in the center, and thick forests in the Duar Plain in the S. **Arable land:** 2.6%. **Capital:** Thimphu, 152,398 (2014).

Government: Type: Constitutional monarchy. **Head of state:** King Jigme Khesar Namgyel Wangchuk; in office: Dec. 14, 2006. **Head of gov.:** Prime Min. Tshering Tobgay; in office: July 29, 2013. **Local divisions:** 20 districts. **Defense budget/active troops:** NA.

Economy: Industries: cement, wood prods., processed fruits, alcoholic beverages, calcium carbide, tourism. **Chief crops:** rice, corn, root crops, citrus. **Natural resources:** timber, hydropower, gypsum, calcium carbonate. **Water:** 103,448 cu m per capita. **Electricity prod.:** 6.7 bil kWh. **Labor force:** agric. 56%, industry 22%, services 22%. **Unemployment:** 2.1%.

Finance: Monetary unit: Ngultrum (BTN) (66.20 = $1 U.S.). **GDP:** $5.9 bil; **per capita GDP:** $7,600; **GDP growth:** 6.4%. **Imports:** $980.6 mil; India 72.3%, South Korea 6%. **Exports:** $650.3 mil; (2013) India 83.8%, Hong Kong 10.8%. **Tourism:** $89 mil. **Budget:** $614 mil (nearly one-quarter financed by India's govt.). **Inflation:** 8.2%.

Transport: Airports: 2.

Communications: Telephone: 3.1 per 100 pop. **Mobile:** 82.1 per 100 pop. **Broadband:** 15.6 per 100 pop. **Internet:** 34.4%.

Health: Expend.: 3.8%. **Life expect.:** 68.6 male; 70.5 female. **Births:** 17.8 per 1,000 pop. **Deaths:** 6.7 per 1,000 pop. **Infant mortality:** 35.9 per 1,000 live births. **Undernourished:** NA. **HIV:** NA.

Education: Compulsory: NA. **Literacy:** 64.9%.

Permanent UN mission: 343 E. 43rd St., New York, NY 10017; (212) 661-0551.

Website: www.bhutan.gov.bt

The region came under Tibetan rule in the 16th cent. British influence grew in the 19th cent. A Buddhist monarchy was set up in 1907. After a 1910 treaty, Britain guided Bhutan's external affairs, while the country remained internally self-governing. Upon independence the treaty was revised, 1949, to allow India to assume Britain's role.

Isolated for much of its history, Bhutan has taken steps toward modernization. King Jigme Singye Wangchuk, in power since 1972, stepped down Dec. 14, 2006, in favor of his son, Jigme Khesar Namgyel Wangchuk. Multiparty parliamentary elections took place Mar. 24, 2008, and a new constitution was ratified July 18, making Bhutan a democratic constitutional monarchy. Namgay Peldon became the first woman elected governor in the Mar. 2008 election, and Tashi Chhozom became the first woman appointed to the country's supreme court Aug. 3, 2012. The ruling party was defeated in July 13, 2013, parliamentary elections, with the opposition People's Democratic Party (PDP) winning 32 out of 47 seats.

Bolivia

Plurinational State of Bolivia

People: Population: 10,800,882. **Age distrib.:** <15: 32.8%; 65+: 5.1%. **Growth:** 1.6%. **Migrants:** 1.4%. **Pop. density:** 25.8 per sq mi, 10 per sq km. **Urban:** 68.5%. **Ethnic groups:** mestizo (mixed white/Amerindian) 68%, indigenous 20%, white 5%, cholo/chola 2%. **Languages:** Spanish, Quechua, Aymara, Guarani (all official). **Religions:** Roman Catholic 76.8%, Evangelical and Pentecostal 8.1%, Protestant 7.9%, none 5.5%.

Geography: Total area: 424,164 sq mi, 1,098,581 sq km; **Land area:** 418,265 sq mi, 1,083,301 sq km. **Location:** W central South America, in the Andes Mts. (It is one of two landlocked countries in South America.) Peru, Chile on W; Argentina, Paraguay on S; Brazil on E and N. **Topography:** The great central plateau, more than 500 mi long at an elevation of 12,000 ft, lies between 2 great cordilleras having 3 of the highest peaks in S America. Lake Titicaca, on Peruvian border, is world's highest lake (12,500 ft) navigable by large boats. The E central region has semitropical forests; the llanos, or Amazon-Chaco lowlands, are in E. **Arable land:** 4%. **Capital:** La Paz (admin.), 1,816,453; Sucre (constitutional), 371,933. **Cities:** Santa Cruz, 2,106,682; Cochabamba, 1,240,363.

Government: Type: Republic. **Head of state and gov.:** Pres. Juan Evo Morales Ayma; in office: Jan. 22, 2006. **Local divisions:** 9 departments. **Defense budget:** $405 mil. **Active troops:** 46,100.

Economy: Industries: mining, smelting, petroleum, food and beverages, tobacco, handicrafts, clothing. **Chief crops:** soybeans, quinoa, Brazil nuts, sugarcane, coffee, corn, rice, potatoes. **Natural resources:** tin, nat. gas, petroleum, zinc, tungsten, antimony, silver, iron, lead, gold, timber, hydropower. **Water:** 53,791 cu m per capita. **Crude oil reserves:** 209.8 mil bbls. **Other resources:** Timber. **Electricity prod.:** 7.3 bil kWh. **Labor force:** agric. 32%, industry 20%, services 47.9%. **Unemployment:** 2.6%.

Finance: Monetary unit: Boliviano (BOB) (6.86 = $1 U.S.). **GDP:** $70 bil; **per capita GDP:** $6,200; **GDP growth:** 5.4%. **Imports:** $9.5 bil; Brazil 17.1%, China 13.5%, U.S. 12.6%, Argentina 10.8%, Peru 6.5%, Chile 6.2%, Japan 5%. **Exports:** $12.3 bil; Brazil 33.5%, Argentina 20.3%, U.S. 10.1%, Colombia 5.4%, Peru 5.1%. **Tourism:** $573 mil. **Budget:** $16.8 bil. **Inflation:** 5.8%.

Transport: Railways: 2,177 mi. **Motor vehicles:** 67.4 per 1,000 pop. **Airports:** 21.

Communications: Telephone: 8.1 per 100 pop. **Mobile:** 96.3 per 100 pop. **Broadband:** 14 per 100 pop. **Internet:** 39%.

Health: Expend.: 5.8%. **Life expect.:** 66.1 male; 71.8 female. **Births:** 22.8 per 1,000 pop. **Deaths:** 6.5 per 1,000 pop. **Infant mortality:** 37.5 per 1,000 live births. **Undernourished:** 19.5%. **HIV:** 0.3%.

Education: Compulsory: ages 4-17. **Literacy:** 95.7%.

Embassy: 3014 Massachusetts Ave. NW 20008; 483-4410.

Website: www.bolivia.gob.bo

The Incas conquered the region's earlier Indian inhabitants in the 13th cent. Spanish colonial rule began in the 1530s and lasted until Aug. 6, 1825. The country is named after independence fighter Simón Bolívar. In a series of wars, Bolivia lost its Pacific coast to Chile, the oil-bearing Chaco to Paraguay, and rubber-growing areas to Brazil, 1879-1935.

Economic unrest, especially among militant mine workers, led to continuing political instability. A reformist government under Victor Paz Estenssoro, 1951-64, nationalized tin mines and attempted to improve conditions for the Indian majority but was overthrown by a military junta. A series of coups and countercoups continued until constitutional government was restored in 1982.

U.S. pressure on the government to reduce production of coca, the raw material for cocaine, led to clashes between police and growers and increased anti-U.S. feeling in Bolivia, where chewing coca leaves is fairly common. Gen. Hugo Banzer Suárez, who ruled as a dictator, 1971-78, later governed as president, 1997-2001.

After an inconclusive presidential election June 2002, Congress chose Gonzalo Sánchez de Lozada, a U.S.-educated mining executive, as head of state. He quit Oct. 17, 2003, after indigenous Bolivians staged a month of antigovernment protests in which over 70 people died. His successor, Vice Pres. Carlos D. Mesa Gisbert, was embroiled in controversies over energy policy.

Juan Evo Morales Ayma, a leftist and coca-farmer advocate, won the presidential election, Dec. 2005. He nationalized the hydrocarbon sector, launched a land-redistribution program to benefit poor farmers, and tightened ties with Venezuela and Cuba. He faced resistance and demands for autonomy from leaders of Bolivia's relatively prosperous lowland provinces. Voters, Jan. 25, 2009, approved a new constitution strengthening the rights of Bolivia's indigenous majority and increasing federal control over the country's natural resources. Morales won a second term Dec. 6, 2009. His government nationalized major utility companies in 2012. Morales won reelection Oct. 12, 2014. Pope Francis visited Bolivia in July 2015 and apologized for the Catholic Church's role in "grave sins" against Latin America's native peoples during the colonial period.

Bosnia and Herzegovina

People: Population: 3,867,055. **Age distrib.:** <15: 13.5%; 65+: 13.7%. **Growth:** –0.1%. **Migrants:** 0.6%. **Pop. density:** 195.7 per sq mi, 75.5 per sq km. **Urban:** 39.8%. **Ethnic groups:** Bosniak 48.4%, Serb 32.7%, Croat 14.6%. **Languages:** Bosnian, Croatian, Serbian (all official). **Religions:** Muslim 40%, Orthodox 31%, Roman Catholic 15%.

Geography: Total area: 19,767 sq mi, 51,197 sq km; **Land area:** 19,763 sq mi, 51,187 sq km. **Location:** Balkan Peninsula in SE Europe. Serbia, Montenegro on E and SE; Croatia on N and W. **Topography:** Hilly with some mountains. **Arable land:** 19.7%. **Capital:** Sarajevo, 318,447.

Government: Type: Federal democratic republic. **Heads of state:** Collective presidency with rotating leadership every 8 months. **Head of gov.:** Chairman of the Council of Ministers Denis Zvizdic; in office: Feb. 11, 2015. **Local divisions:** 2 first-order admin. divisions, 1 internationally supervised district. **Defense budget:** $227 mil. **Active troops:** 10,500.

Economy: Industries: steel, coal, mining, motor vehicle assembly, textiles, tobacco prods., wooden furniture, ammunition, domestic appliances, oil refining. **Chief crops:** wheat, corn, fruits, vegetables. **Natural resources:** coal, iron ore, bauxite, copper, lead, zinc, chromite, cobalt, manganese, nickel, clay, gypsum, salt, sand, timber, hydropower. **Water:** 9,794 cu m per capita. **Electricity prod.:** 13.4 bil kWh. **Labor force:** agric. 19%, industry 30%, services 51%. **Unemployment:** 28.4%.

Finance: Monetary unit: Convertible Marka (BAM) (1.74 = $1 U.S.). **GDP:** $38.1 bil; **per capita GDP:** $9,800; **GDP growth:** 0.8%. **Imports:** $11 bil; Croatia 20.5%, Germany 13%, Slovenia 12.3%, Italy 10.1%, Russia 8%, Austria 6.2%, Hungary 5.4%. **Exports:** $5.9 bil; Slovenia 17.3%, Croatia 15.6%, Italy 14.8%, Germany 13.1%, Austria 12%. **Tourism:** $707 mil. **Budget:** $9.4 bil. **Inflation:** –0.9%.

Transport: Railways: 600 mi. **Airports:** 7.

Communications: Telephone: 22.2 per 100 pop. **Mobile:** 91.3 per 100 pop. **Broadband:** 24 per 100 pop. **Internet:** 60.8%.

Health: Expend.: 9.9%. **Life expect.:** 73.5 male; 79.8 female. **Births:** 8.9 per 1,000 pop. **Deaths:** 9.8 per 1,000 pop. **Infant mortality:** 5.7 per 1,000 live births. **Undernourished:** <5%. **HIV:** NA.

Education: Compulsory: ages 6-14. **Literacy:** 98.5%.

Embassy: 2109 E St. NW 20037; 337-1500.

Website: www.fbihvlada.gov.ba

Bosnia was ruled by Croatian kings c. 958 CE, and by Hungary 1000-1200. It became organized c. 1200 and later took control of Herzegovina. The kingdom disintegrated after 1391, with the southern part becoming the independent duchy of Herzegovina. It was conquered by Turks in 1463 and made a Turkish province. The area was placed under control of Austria-Hungary in 1878 and made part of the province of Bosnia and Herzegovina, which was formally annexed to Austria-Hungary, 1908. Bosnia became a province of Yugoslavia in 1918. It was reunited with Herzegovina as a federated republic under the 1946 Yugoslav constitution.

Bosnia and Herzegovina declared sovereignty Oct. 15, 1991. A referendum for independence was passed Feb. 29, 1992. Ethnic Serbs' opposition to the referendum spurred violent clashes and bombings. The U.S. and EU recognized the republic Apr. 7. Fierce three-way fighting continued between Bosnia's Serbs, Muslims, and Croats. Serb forces massacred thousands of Bosnian Muslims (Bosniaks) and engaged in ethnic cleansing, expelling Muslims and other non-Serbs from areas under Bosnian Serb control. The capital, Sarajevo, was surrounded and besieged by Bosnian Serb forces. Muslims and Croats in Bosnia began a cease-fire Feb. 23, 1994, and signed an accord, Mar. 18, to create a Muslim-Croat confederation in Bosnia. However, by mid-1994, Bosnian Serbs controlled over 70% of the country.

As fighting continued in 1995, the balance of power shifted toward the Muslim-Croat alliance. Massive NATO airstrikes at Bosnian Serb targets beginning Aug. 30 triggered a new round of peace talks, and the siege of Sarajevo was lifted Sept. 15. The new talks produced an agreement to create autonomous regions within Bosnia, with the Serb region (Republika Srpska) constituting 49% of the country. A Croat-Muslim offensive in Sept. recaptured significant territory, leaving Bosnian Serbs in control of approximately half that percentage.

A Nov. 1995 peace agreement was signed in Paris, Dec. 14, 1995, by leaders of Bosnia, Croatia, and Serbia. Some 60,000 NATO troops (about 20,000 from the U.S.) moved in to police the accord. Meanwhile, a UN tribunal began bringing charges against suspected war criminals. Elections were held Sept. 14, 1996, for a 3-person collective presidency, for seats in a federal parliament, and for regional offices. In Dec. a revamped NATO Stabilization Force (SFOR) of over 30,000 members (more than 8,000 from the U.S.) received an 18-month mandate, which was later extended.

The UN tribunal found Radislav Krstic, a Bosnian Serb general, guilty Aug. 2, 2001, in connection with the genocide of thousands of Muslims at Srebrenica in 1995. An EU peacekeeping force (EUFOR), with 7,000 members, assumed responsibility from SFOR, Dec. 2, 2004. Accused of complicity in the Sarajevo and Srebrenica atrocities, former Bosnian Serb leader Radovan Karadzic was arrested in Serbia, July 21, 2008, and handed over to the UN tribunal at The Hague, Netherlands. He was charged with 10 counts of genocide, war crimes, and crimes against humanity; his trial ended Oct. 7, 2014, with a verdict expected by late 2015. Also extradited to The Hague was Gen. Ratko Mladic, the former Bosnian Serb military commander accused of directing the Srebrenica massacre, who was arrested in Serbia May 26, 2011. He faced 11 counts of war crimes and crimes against humanity, 2 of them for genocide, in a trial that began May 16, 2012. On Dec. 12, 2012, Mladic's close associate Zdravko Tolimir was convicted of genocide and sentenced to life in prison. Serbian police, Mar. 18, 2015, arrested 8 men accused of killing more than 1,000 people during the Srebrenica massacre. EUFOR strength in Bosnia was about 600 troops in mid-2015.

Violent protests occurred in Feb. 2014 in Sarajevo and other areas, triggered by high unemployment and alleged government corruption and inefficiency.

Botswana

Republic of Botswana

People: Population: 2,182,719. **Age distrib.:** <15: 32.7%; 65+: 4.1%. **Growth:** 1.2%. **Migrants:** 7.2%. **Pop. density:** 10 per sq mi, 3.9 per sq km. **Urban:** 57.4%. **Ethnic groups:** Tswana or Setswana 79%, Kalanga 11%, Basarwa 3%, other (incl. Kgalagadi, white) 7%. **Languages:** Setswana, Kalanga, Sekgalagadi, English (official). **Religions:** Christian 71.6%, Badimo 6%, none 20.6%.

Geography: Total area: 224,607 sq mi, 581,730 sq km; **Land area:** 218,816 sq mi, 566,730 sq km. **Location:** Southern Africa. Namibia on N and W, South Africa on S, Zimbabwe on NE. Botswana claims border with Zambia on N. **Topography:** The Kalahari Desert, supporting nomadic Bushmen (also known as the Basarwa or San people) and wildlife, spreads over SW. Swamplands and farming areas in N; rolling plains in E where livestock are grazed. **Arable land:** 0.5%. **Capital:** Gaborone, 246,562 (2014).

Government: Type: Parliamentary republic. **Head of state and gov.:** Pres. Seretse Khama Ian Khama; in office: Apr. 1, 2008. **Local divisions:** 10 districts, 6 town councils. **Defense budget:** $346 mil. **Active troops:** 9,000.

Economy: Industries: diamonds, mining; livestock processing; textiles. **Chief crops:** sorghum, maize, millet, beans, sunflowers, groundnuts. **Natural resources:** diamonds, copper, nickel, salt, soda ash, potash, coal, iron ore, silver. **Water:** 6,056 cu m per capita. **Electricity prod.:** 235 mil kWh. **Labor force:** NA. **Unemployment:** 18.4%.

Finance: Monetary unit: Pula (BWP) (10.40 = $1 U.S.). **GDP:** $33.7 bil; **per capita GDP:** $16,000; **GDP growth:** 4.9%. **Imports:** $7.1 bil. **Exports:** $7.5 bil. **Tourism:** $45 mil. **Budget:** $5.2 bil. **Inflation:** 4.4%.

Transport: Railways: 552 mi. **Motor vehicles:** 182.4 per 1,000 pop. **Airports:** 10.

Communications: Telephone: 8.3 per 100 pop. **Mobile:** 167.3 per 100 pop. **Broadband:** 74.3 per 100 pop. **Internet:** 18.5%.

Health: Expend.: 5.3%. **Life expect.:** 56.0 male; 52.3 female. **Births:** 21.0 per 1,000 pop. **Deaths:** 13.4 per 1,000 pop. **Infant mortality:** 8.9 per 1,000 live births. **Undernourished:** 26.6%. **HIV:** 25.2%.

Education: Compulsory: NA. **Literacy:** 88.5%.

Embassy: 1531-1533 New Hampshire Ave. NW 20036; 244-4990.

Website: www.gov.bw

First inhabited by Bushmen, then Bantus, the region became the British protectorate of Bechuanaland in 1886. The country became fully independent Sept. 30, 1966. Cattle raising and mining (diamonds, copper, nickel) have contributed to economic growth. Pres. Festus Mogae transferred power Apr. 1, 2008, to Seretse Khama Ian Khama, son of Botswana's independence leader and first president (1966-80), Sir Seretse Khama. In power since independence, the Botswana Democratic Party won legislative elections in 2009 and 2014, and each new National Assembly elected Ian Khama to a full 5-year term as president. The government outlawed commercial hunting in 2014, but poaching of big-game animals remained a problem.

Brazil

Federative Republic of Brazil

People: Population: 204,259,812. **Age distrib.:** <15: 23.3%; 65+: 7.8%. **Growth:** 0.8%. **Migrants:** 0.3%. **Pop. density:** 62.5 per sq mi, 24.1 per sq km. **Urban:** 85.7%. **Ethnic groups:** white 47.7%, mulatto (mixed white/black) 43.1%, black 7.6%. **Languages:** Portuguese (official). **Religions:** Roman Catholic 64.6%, Protestant 22.2% (incl. Adventist 6.5%), none 8%.

Geography: Total area: 3,287,957 sq mi, 8,515,770 sq km; **Land area:** 3,227,096 sq mi, 8,358,140 sq km. **Location:** Occupies E half of South America. French Guiana, Suriname, Guyana, Venezuela on N; Colombia, Peru, Bolivia, Paraguay, on W; Argentina, Uruguay on S. **Topography:** Atlantic coastline stretches 4,603 mi. Heavily wooded Amazon basin covers N half of country. Its network of rivers is navigable for 15,814 mi. The Amazon itself flows 2,093 mi in Brazil. The NE region is semiarid scrubland, heavily settled and poor. Almost half of pop. resides in S central region. Most of the major cities are in the narrow coastal belt. Almost the entire country has a tropical or semitropical climate. **Arable land:** 8.7%. **Capital:** Brasília, 4,155,476. **Cities:** São Paulo, 21,066,245; Rio de Janeiro, 12,902,306; Belo Horizonte, 5,716,422.

Government: Type: Federal republic. **Head of state and gov.:** Pres. Dilma Rousseff; in office: Jan. 1, 2011. **Local divisions:** 26 states, 1 federal district. **Defense budget:** $31.93 bil. **Active troops:** 318,500.

Economy: Industries: textiles, shoes, chemicals, cement, lumber, iron ore, tin, steel, aircraft, motor vehicles and parts. **Chief crops:** coffee, soybeans, wheat, rice, corn, sugarcane, cocoa, citrus. **Natural resources:** bauxite, gold, iron ore, manganese, nickel, phosphates, platinum, tin, rare earth elements, uranium, petroleum hydropower, timber. **Water:** 43,157 cu m per capita. **Crude oil reserves:** 15.3 bil bbls. **Electricity prod.:** 537.6 bil kWh. **Labor force:** agric. 15.7%, industry 13.3%, services 71%. **Unemployment:** 5.9%.

Finance: Monetary unit: Real (BRL) (3.76 = $1 U.S.). **GDP:** $3.3 tril; **per capita GDP:** $16,100; **GDP growth:** 0.1%. **Imports:** $241.9 bil; China 15.6%, U.S. 15.1%, Argentina 6.9%, Germany 6.3%. **Exports:** $242.7 bil; China 19%, U.S. 10.3%, Argentina 8.1%, Netherlands 7.2%. **Tourism:** $6.8 bil. **Budget:** $834.4 bil. **Inflation:** 6.3%.

Transport: Railways: 17,733 mi. **Motor vehicles:** 206 per 1,000 pop. **Airports:** 698.

Communications: Telephone: 21.8 per 100 pop. **Mobile:** 139 per 100 pop. **Broadband:** 52 per 100 pop. **Internet:** 57.6%.

Health: Expend.: 9.3%. **Life expect.:** 70.0 male; 77.3 female. **Births:** 14.5 per 1,000 pop. **Deaths:** 6.6 per 1,000 pop. **Infant mortality:** 18.6 per 1,000 live births. **Undernourished:** <5%. **HIV:** 0.6%.

Education: Compulsory: ages 4-17. **Literacy:** 92.6%.

Embassy: 3006 Massachusetts Ave. NW 20008; 238-2700.

Website: www.brasil.gov.br

Pedro Álvares Cabral, a Portuguese navigator, is generally credited as the first European to reach Brazil, in 1500. The country was thinly settled by various Indian tribes. Only a few survive today, mostly in the Amazon Basin.

In the next centuries, Portuguese colonists gradually pushed inland, bringing along large numbers of African slaves. (Slavery was not abolished until 1888.) The king of Portugal, fleeing Napoleon's army, moved the seat of government to Brazil in 1808. Brazil thereupon became a kingdom under Dom Joao VI. After Joao VI returned to Portugal, his son Pedro proclaimed Brazil's independence, Sept. 7, 1822, and was crowned emperor. The second emperor, Dom Pedro II, was deposed in 1889, and a republic proclaimed, called the United States of Brazil. It was renamed the Federative Republic of Brazil in 1967.

A military junta took control in 1930; Getulio Vargas assumed dictatorial power. The military forced him out in 1945. A democratic regime prevailed 1945-64, during which time the capital was moved from Rio de Janeiro to Brasília. Military-backed governments ruled Brazil for the next 20 years. Censorship was imposed, and the opposition was suppressed.

Brazil became the leading industrial power of Latin America by the 1970s, while agricultural output soared. By the 1990s, Brazil had one of the world's largest economies. Income is poorly distributed, however, and about one-fifth of Brazilians live in poverty. Despite protective environmental legislation, development has destroyed much of the Amazon ecosystem.

Democratic presidential elections held in 1985 brought back civilian rule. Fernando Collor de Mello was elected president, Dec. 1989. In Sept. 1992, Collor was impeached for corruption. He resigned as his trial was beginning, and acting Pres. Itamar Franco was officially sworn in. Fernando Henrique Cardoso won Oct. 1994 and 1998 elections; he guided Brazil through a series of financial crises.

A new civil code guaranteeing legal equality for women was enacted Aug. 15, 2001. With Brazil's debt exceeding $260 bil, the IMF approved a $30-bil loan Aug. 2002. Luiz Inácio Lula da Silva, a union leader and reformer, won a presidential runoff, Oct. 2002. Brazil's space program launched its first rocket into space Oct. 23, 2004.

A top aide to Pres. Lula resigned June 16, 2005, amid allegations the ruling party bribed legislators for votes; he and two others involved in the scandal were found guilty and sentenced to upwards of 40 years in prison Oct.-Nov. 2012. Despite this and other scandals, Lula won a second presidential term, Oct. 2006. The nation reported huge offshore oil finds in 2007-08. Lula's former chief of staff, Dilma Rousseff, won a runoff election Oct. 31, 2010, and took office as Brazil's first woman president Jan. 1, 2011. She narrowly won reelection in an Oct. 26, 2014, runoff.

Brazilian police raided Rocinha, Rio de Janeiro's largest slum, Nov. 13, 2011, as part of an effort to bring law to the entire city as it prepared to host the men's soccer World Cup in 2014 and the Olympic Games in 2016. After 10 months of sporadic demonstrations over planned increases in the cost of public transportation, fares were raised June 1, 2013. Demonstrations began in São Paulo June 6 and quickly spread to other cities (fares were lowered June 20). Demonstrators also protested a lack of public services and government corruption, and criticized the $52-mil price tag of Pope Francis's July 2013 visit. A $3-bil bribery and corruption scandal involving Petrobras (the national oil company), Pres. Rousseff's Workers' Party, and high-level government officials led to the resignations of Petrobras's top executives in Feb. 2015 and to arrests, in Nov. 2014 and June 2015, of business executives whose companies were Petrobras subcontractors. The Workers' Party's former treasurer was convicted of bribery and sentenced, Sept. 21, 2015, to more than 15 years in prison; a former Petrobras manager received a 20+-year sentence. A similar scandal at Electrobras, the government's electric utility company, led to the arrest on bribery charges of 2 company executives, July 28, 2015.

Brunei

Brunei Darussalam

People: Population: 429,646. **Age distrib.:** <15: 23.8%; 65+: 4.3%. **Growth:** 1.6%. **Migrants:** 49.3%. **Pop. density:** 211.4 per sq mi, 81.6 per sq km. **Urban:** 77.2%. **Ethnic groups:** Malay 65.7%, Chinese 10.3%, other indigenous 3.4%. **Languages:** Malay (official), English, Chinese. **Religions:** Muslim (official) 78.8%, Christian 8.7%, Buddhist 7.8%, other (incl. indigenous beliefs) 4.7%.

Geography: Total area: 2,226 sq mi, 5,765 sq km; **Land area:** 2,033 sq mi, 5,265 sq km. **Location:** SE Asia, on the N coast of the island of Borneo. It is surrounded on its landward side by the Malaysian state of Sarawak. **Topography:** Narrow coastal plain with mountains in E, hilly lowlands in W. Swamps in W and NE. Tropical climate. **Arable land:** 0.8%. **Capital:** Bandar Seri Begawan, 14,025 (2014).

Government: Type: Constitutional sultanate. **Head of state and gov.:** Sultan and Prime Min. Sir Hassanal Bolkiah Mu'izzaddin

Waddaulah; in office: Jan. 1, 1984 (sultan since Oct. 5, 1967). **Local divisions:** 4 districts. **Defense budget:** $573 mil. **Active troops:** 7,000.

Economy: Industries: petroleum, petroleum refining, liquefied nat. gas, constr. **Chief crops:** rice, vegetables, fruits. **Natural resources:** petroleum, nat. gas, timber. **Water:** 20,335 cu m per capita. **Crude oil reserves:** 1.1 bil bbls. **Electricity prod.:** 3.7 bil kWh. **Labor force:** agric. 4.2%, industry 62.8%, services 33%. **Unemployment:** 3.8%.

Finance: Monetary unit: Dollar (BND) (1.42 = $1 U.S.). **GDP:** $30.2 bil; **per capita GDP:** $73,200. **GDP growth:** –0.7%. **Imports:** $4.3 bil; Singapore 28.6%, China 22.1%, UK 18.9%, Malaysia 10.8%, U.S. 7.2%. **Exports:** $11.4 bil; Japan 41.9%, South Korea 17%, Australia 8.2%, India 6.8%, Indonesia 5.7%, Vietnam 5.7%. **Tourism:** $92 mil. **Budget:** $6.3 bil. **Inflation:** –0.2%.

Transport: Motor vehicles: 628.6 per 1,000 pop. **Airports:** 1.

Communications: Telephone: 11.4 per 100 pop. **Mobile:** 110.1 per 100 pop. **Broadband:** 6.5 per 100 pop. **Internet:** 68.8%.

Health: Expend.: 2.3%. **Life expect.:** 74.6 male; 79.4 female. **Births:** 17.3 per 1,000 pop. **Deaths:** 3.5 per 1,000 pop. **Infant mortality:** 10.2 per 1,000 live births. **Undernourished:** <5%. **HIV:** NA.

Education: Compulsory: ages 6-14. **Literacy:** 96%.

Embassy: 3520 International Ct. NW 20008; 237-1838.

Website: www.brunei.gov.bn

The Sultanate of Brunei was a powerful state in the early 16th cent., with authority over all of the island of Borneo as well as parts of the Sulu Islands and the Philippines. In 1888, a treaty placed the state under the protection of Great Britain.

Brunei became a fully sovereign and independent state on Jan. 1, 1984. The country fielded female athletes for the first time at the 2012 Summer Olympic Games. Brunei began enacting, May 1, 2014, a new penal code based on Islamic law. If fully implemented in future years, the code would make theft punishable by whipping or limb amputation, and adultery and gay sex would become capital crimes.

Bulgaria

Republic of Bulgaria

People: Population: 7,186,893. **Age distrib.:** <15: 14.5%; 65+: 18.7%. **Growth:** –0.6%. **Migrants:** 1.2%. **Pop. density:** 171.6 per sq mi, 66.2 per sq km. **Urban:** 73.9%. **Ethnic groups:** Bulgarian 76.9%, Turkish 8%, Roma 4.4%. **Languages:** Bulgarian (official), Turkish, Roma. **Religions:** Eastern Orthodox 59.4%, Muslim 7.8%.

Geography: Total area: 42,811 sq mi, 110,879 sq km; **Land area:** 41,888 sq mi, 108,489 sq km. **Location:** SE Europe, in E Balkan Peninsula on Black Sea. Romania on N; Serbia, Macedonia on W; Greece, Turkey on S. **Topography:** The Stara Planina (Balkan) Mts. stretch E-W across the center of country, with the Danubian plain on N, the Rhodope Mts. on SW, and Thracian Plain on SE. **Arable land:** 30.6%. **Capital:** Sofia, 1,226,155.

Government: Type: Parliamentary democracy. **Head of state:** Pres. Rosen Plevneliev; in office: Jan. 22, 2012. **Head of gov.:** Prime Min. Boyko Borisov; in office: Nov. 7, 2014. **Local divisions:** 28 provinces. **Defense budget:** $736 mil. **Active troops:** 31,300.

Economy: Industries: electricity, utilities; food, beverages, tobacco; machinery and equip. **Chief crops:** vegetables, fruits, tobacco, wine, wheat, barley, sunflowers, sugar beets. **Natural resources:** bauxite, copper, lead, zinc, coal, timber. **Water:** 2,949 cu m per capita. **Crude oil reserves:** 15 mil bbls. **Electricity prod.:** 43.7 bil kWh. **Labor force:** agric. 6.7%, industry 30.2%, services 63.1%. **Unemployment:** 12.9%.

Finance: Monetary unit: Lev (BGN) (1.74 = $1 U.S.). **GDP:** $128.6 bil; **per capita GDP:** $17,900; **GDP growth:** 1.7%. **Imports:** $33.6 bil; Russia 18.6%, Germany 10.9%, Italy 7.5%, Romania 6.7%, Turkey 5.7%, Greece 5.6%, Spain 5.3%. **Exports:** $29.3 bil; Germany 12.6%, Italy 8.8%, Turkey 8.6%, Romania 7.9%, Greece 7.1%. **Tourism:** $4.1 bil. **Budget:** $21.3 bil. **Inflation:** –1.4%.

Transport: Railways: 3,178 mi. **Motor vehicles:** 499.2 per 1,000 pop. **Airports:** 57.

Communications: Telephone: 25.3 per 100 pop. **Mobile:** 137.7 per 100 pop. **Broadband:** 58.5 per 100 pop. **Internet:** 55.5%.

Health: Expend.: 7.4%. **Life expect.:** 71.1 male; 77.9 female. **Births:** 8.9 per 1,000 pop. **Deaths:** 14.4 per 1,000 pop. **Infant mortality:** 8.7 per 1,000 live births. **Undernourished:** <5%. **HIV:** NA.

Education: Compulsory: ages 7-14. **Literacy:** 98.4%.

Embassy: 1621 22nd St. NW 20008; 387-0174.

Website: www.government.bg

Bulgaria was settled by Slavs in the 6th cent. Turkic Bulgars arrived in the 7th cent., merged with the Slavs, became Christians by the 9th cent., and set up powerful empires in the 10th and 12th cents. Ottomans took over in 1396 and ruled for nearly 500 years.

An 1876 revolt led to an independent kingdom in 1908. Bulgaria expanded after the first Balkan War but lost its Aegean coastline in WWI, when it sided with Germany. Bulgaria joined the Axis in WWII but withdrew in 1944. Communists took power with Soviet aid; the monarchy was abolished Sept. 8, 1946.

On Nov. 10, 1989, Communist Party leader and head of state Todor Zhivkov resigned after 35 years. In Jan. 1990, Parliament voted to revoke the constitutionally guaranteed dominant role of the Communist Party. A new constitution took effect July 13, 1991.

Bulgaria became a full member of NATO, Apr. 2, 2004, and entered the EU, Jan. 1, 2007. Restrictions on Bulgarians' right to work in 9 other EU nations ended Jan. 1, 2014.

A terrorist blew up a bus carrying Israeli tourists, July 18, 2012, leaving 5 Israelis, the Bulgarian bus driver, and the bomber dead. An investigation ending Feb. 5, 2013, blamed the attack on the Muslim militant group Hezbollah, which denied involvement. The identity of the bomber, a Lebanese-French citizen, was determined by DNA evidence in July 2014.

Worsening economic conditions in 2012-13 inspired protests that led Prime Min. Boyko Borisov to submit his government's resignation Feb. 20, 2013. No clear winner emerged from May 12 elections. Parliament elected Plamen Oresharski, with no party affiliation, prime min. May 29. Amid a banking crisis that began in June 2014, Oresharski resigned July 23. After Oct. 5 elections, Borisov again became prime min., Nov. 7, 2014. Construction began in 2015 on the second phase of a security fence along the Turkish border, intended to stop Middle Eastern, SW Asian, and African migrants from entering Bulgaria. The U.S. announced, June 25, 2015, that it would send 155 Marines, with tanks and other equipment, to Bulgaria as part of an effort to deter Russian aggression.

Burkina Faso

People: Population: 18,931,686. **Age distrib.:** <15: 45.2%; 65+: 2.5%. **Growth:** 3%. **Migrants:** 4.1%. **Pop. density:** 179.1 per sq mi, 69.1 per sq km. **Urban:** 29.9%. **Ethnic groups:** Mossi 40%+, other (incl. Gurunsi, Senufo, Lobi, Bobo, Mande, Fulani) 60%. **Languages:** French (official), native African Sudanic-family langs. **Religions:** Muslim 60.5%, Catholic 19%, animist 15.3%, Protestant 4.2%.

Geography: Total area: 105,869 sq mi, 274,200 sq km; **Land area:** 105,715 sq mi, 273,800 sq km. **Location:** W Africa, S of the Sahara. Mali on NW; Niger on NE; Benin, Togo, Ghana, Côte d'Ivoire on S. **Topography:** Landlocked in the savanna region of W Africa. The N is arid, hot, and thinly populated. **Arable land:** 21.9%. **Capital:** Ouagadougou, 2,741,128.

Government: Type: Parliamentary republic. **Head of state:** Interim Pres. Michel Kafando; in office: Nov. 18, 2014. **Head of gov.:** Prime Min. Yacouba Issac Zida; in office: Nov. 19, 2014. **Local divisions:** 13 regions. **Defense budget** $164 mil. **Active troops:** 11,200.

Economy: Industries: cotton lint, beverages, agric. proc., soap, cigarettes, textiles. **Chief crops:** cotton, peanuts, shea nuts, sesame, sorghum, millet. **Natural resources:** manganese, limestone, marble, gold, phosphates, pumice, salt. **Water:** 797 cu m per capita. **Electricity prod.:** 522 mil kWh. **Labor force:** agric. 90%, industry and services 10%. **Unemployment:** 3.1%.

Finance: Monetary unit: CFA Franc (XOF) (584.11 = $1 U.S.). **GDP:** $29.3 bil; **per capita GDP:** $1,700; **GDP growth:** 4%. **Imports:** $3.1 bil; Côte d'Ivoire 18.9%, France 18.1%. **Exports:** $2.3 bil; China 25.9%, Indonesia 12%, Japan 5.7%, Thailand 5.6%, Turkey 5.1%. **Tourism:** $153 mil. **Budget:** $3.7 bil. **Inflation:** –0.3%.

Transport: Railways: 386 mi. **Motor vehicles:** 11.3 per 1,000 pop. **Airports:** 2.

Communications: Telephone: 0.7 per 100 pop. **Mobile:** 71.7 per 100 pop. **Broadband:** 9 per 100 pop. **Internet:** 9.4%.

Health: Expend.: 6.2%. **Life expect.:** 53.1 male; 57.2 female. **Births:** 42.0 per 1,000 pop. **Deaths:** 11.7 per 1,000 pop. **Infant mortality:** 75.3 per 1,000 live births. **Undernourished:** 20.7%. **HIV:** 0.9%.

Education: Compulsory: ages 6-15. **Literacy:** 36%.

Embassy: 2340 Massachusetts Ave. NW 20008; 332-5577.

Website: www.gouvernement.gov.bf or burkina-usa.org

The Mossi people entered Burkina Faso in the 11th-13th cents. Their kingdoms ruled until they were defeated by the Mali and Songhai empires. French control came by 1896, but Upper Volta (renamed Burkina Faso on Aug. 4, 1984) was not established as a separate territory until 1947. Independence came Aug. 5, 1960; a pro-French government was elected. The military seized power in 1980. A 1987 coup brought to power military officers including Blaise Compaoré, who became sole ruler by 1989. A multiparty system was instituted in the early 1990s. Pres. Compaoré most recently won reelection Nov. 21, 2010. Violent protests in 2014 against economic hardship and attempts to amend the constitution to allow Compaoré to run again led to the president's resignation Oct. 31. Civilian Michel Kafando became interim president Nov. 18, 2014, heading a government in which the military controlled key cabinet positions. The Presidential Security Regiment (RSP), loyal to Compaoré, ousted Kafando, Sept. 16, 2015. An agreement negotiated by the Econ. Community of West African States restored Kafando, Sept. 23, and called for Nov. 2015 elections. Military units supporting Kafando subdued the last RSP resistance Sept. 29.

Burma

***See* Myanmar.**

Burundi

Republic of Burundi

People: Population: 10,742,276. **Age distrib.:** <15: 45.6%; 65+: 2.5%. **Growth:** 3.3%. **Migrants:** 2.5%. **Pop. density:** 1,083.4 per sq mi, 418.3 per sq km. **Urban:** 12.1%. **Ethnic groups:** Hutu (Bantu) 85%, Tutsi (Hamitic) 14%. **Languages:** Kirundi, French (both official). **Religions:** Catholic 62.1%, Protestant 23.9%, Muslim 2.5%.

Geography: Total area: 10,745 sq mi, 27,830 sq km; **Land area:** 9,915 sq mi, 25,680 sq km. **Location:** Central Africa. Rwanda on N, Dem. Rep. of the Congo on W, Tanzania on E and S. **Topography:** Much of country is grassy highland, with mountains reaching 8,900 ft. The southernmost source of the White Nile is located in Burundi. Lake Tanganyika is the second deepest lake in the world (max. depth 4,823 ft). **Arable land:** 42.8%. **Capital:** Bujumbura, 750,862.

Government: Type: Republic. **Head of state and gov.:** Pres. Pierre Nkurunziza; in office: Aug. 26, 2005. **Local divisions:** 17 provinces. **Defense budget:** $61 mil. **Active troops:** 20,000.

Economy: Industries: light consumer goods, assembly of imported components, public works constr., food proc. **Chief crops:** coffee, cotton, tea, corn, sorghum, sweet potatoes, bananas, cassava. **Natural resources:** nickel, uranium, rare earth oxides, peat, cobalt, copper, platinum, vanadium, hydropower, niobium, tantalum, gold, tin, tungsten, kaolin, limestone. **Water:** 1,234 cu m per capita. **Electricity prod.:** 202 mil kWh. **Labor force:** agric. 93.6%, industry 2.3%, services 4.1%. **Unemployment:** 6.9%.

Finance: Monetary unit: Franc (BIF) (1,534.00 = $1 U.S.). **GDP:** $8.4 bil; **per capita GDP:** $900; **GDP growth:** 4.7%. **Imports:** $873 mil; Saudi Arabia 13.3%, China 8.8%, Tanzania 8%, Belgium 7.6%, Kenya 7.5%, Uganda 7%, Zambia 5.7%, India 5.2%. **Exports:** $113.6 mil; Germany 11.4%, Pakistan 9.3%, Dem. Rep. of the Congo 9.2%, Sweden 8.2%, China 7.5%, Uganda 7%, Egypt 5.9%. **Tourism:** $2 mil. **Budget:** $933.2 mil. **Inflation:** 4.4%.

Transport: Motor vehicles: 6.3 per 1,000 pop. **Airports:** 1.

Communications: Telephone: 0.2 per 100 pop. **Mobile:** 30.5 per 100 pop. **Broadband:** 0.01 per 100 pop. **Internet:** 1.4%.

Health: Expend.: 8.1%. **Life expect.:** 58.5 male; 61.8 female. **Births:** 42.0 per 1,000 pop. **Deaths:** 9.3 per 1,000 pop. **Infant mortality:** 61.9 per 1,000 live births. **Undernourished:** NA. **HIV:** 1.1%.

Education: Compulsory: NA. **Literacy:** 85.6%.

Embassy: 2233 Wisconsin Ave. NW, Ste. 408, 20007; 342-2574.

Website: www.burundi-gov.bi or www.burundiembassydc-usa.org

The pygmy Twa were the first inhabitants, followed by Bantu Hutus, who were conquered in the 16th cent. by the Tutsi (Watusi), probably from Ethiopia. Germany gained control in 1899. Belgium took over in 1916, successively exercising a League of Nations mandate and UN trusteeship over Ruanda-Urundi (now the two countries of Rwanda and Burundi). Burundi became independent July 1, 1962.

An unsuccessful Hutu rebellion in 1972-73 left 10,000 Tutsi and 150,000 Hutu dead. Over 100,000 Hutu fled to Tanzania and Zaire (now Dem. Rep. of the Congo). In the 1980s, Burundi's Tutsi-dominated regime pledged itself to ethnic reconciliation and democratic reform. In the nation's first democratic presidential election, June 1993, a Hutu, Melchior Ndadaye, was elected. He was killed in an attempted coup, Oct. 21, 1993. At least 150,000 Burundians died in ethnic conflicts over the next 3 years. Pres. Cyprien Ntaryamira, elected Jan. 1994, and the president of Rwanda were killed when missiles shot down their plane, Apr. 6. The incident sparked massive carnage in Rwanda; violence in Burundi, initially far more limited, intensified in 1995. Ethnic strife continued after a military coup, July 25, 1996. Most warring groups signed a draft peace treaty, Aug. 2000. Two coup attempts were suppressed in 2001. A power-sharing government headed by Pierre Buyoya was sworn in Nov. 1, 2001, but clashes with rebels continued.

Domitien Ndayizeye, a Hutu, became president Apr. 2003. The UN Security Council authorized, May 2004, a peacekeeping force (ONUB) for Burundi. Approval of a power-sharing constitution by referendum, Feb. 28, 2005, paved the way for local and parliamentary elections. Chosen by parliament, Pierre Nkurunziza, former leader of a Hutu rebel group, became president Aug. 2005. ONUB was succeeded by the UN Integrated Office in Burundi (BINUB), 2007-10, and by the UN Office in Burundi (BNUB), 2011-14, both intended to assist with political transition. Under a reconciliation accord reached Dec. 4, 2008, remaining Hutu rebels began to demobilize. Candidates opposing Nkurunziza dropped out of the June 2010 presidential election, claiming the vote was rigged. The government was accused of ordering extrajudicial killings, 2010-11.

Violent protests against Nkurunziza's seeking reelection led to a postponement of 2015 presidential elections from June 26 to July 21. More than 100 people were killed, Apr.-July, and a May 13 attempted military coup was put down; at least 150,000 fled the country. Several opposition parties boycotted the election, won by Nkurunziza and criticized as not credible by the UN, U.S., and UK.

Cabo Verde

Republic of Cabo Verde

People: Population: 545,993. **Age distrib.:** <15: 30.1%; 65+: 5.1%. **Growth:** 1.4%. **Migrants:** 3%. **Pop. density:** 350.6 per sq mi, 135.4 per sq km. **Urban:** 65.5%. **Ethnic groups:** Creole (mulatto) 71%, African 28%. **Languages:** Portuguese (official), Crioulo (blend of Portuguese and W African words). **Religions:** Roman Catholic 77.3%, Protestant 3.7%, none 10.8%.

Geography: Total area: 1,557 sq mi, 4,033 sq km; **Land area:** 1,557 sq mi, 4,033 sq km. **Location:** In Atlantic O., off W tip of Africa. Nearest neighbors are Mauritania, Senegal to E. **Topography:** 15 Cabo Verde islands, volcanic in origin (active crater on Fogo). Landscape is eroded and stark, with vegetation mostly in interior valleys. **Arable land:** 11.7%. **Capital:** Praia, 144,648 (2014).

Government: Type: Republic. **Head of state:** Pres. Jorge Carlos Fonseca; in office: Sept. 9, 2011. **Head of gov.:** Prime Min. José Maria Neves; in office: Feb. 1, 2001. **Local divisions:** 22 municipalities. **Defense budget** $12 mil. **Active troops:** 1,200.

Economy: Industries: food and beverages, fish proc., shoes and garments, salt mining, ship repair. **Chief crops:** bananas, corn, beans, sweet potatoes, sugarcane, coffee, peanuts. **Natural resources:** salt, basalt rock, limestone, kaolin, fish, clay, gypsum. **Water:** 601 cu m per capita. **Labor force:** NA. **Unemployment:** 7%.

Finance: Monetary unit: Escudo (CVE) (97.95 = $1 U.S.). **GDP:** $3.3 bil; **per capita GDP:** $6,300; **GDP growth:** 1%. **Imports:** $888.2 mil; Portugal 33.5%, Netherlands 25.2%, China 7.7%, Spain 6.4%, Belgium 5.6%. **Exports:** $189.8 mil; Spain 56%, Portugal 19.4%, India 5.3%. **Tourism:** $418 mil. **Budget:** $617.6 mil. **Inflation:** –0.2%.

Transport: Airports: 9.

Communications: Telephone: 11.6 per 100 pop. **Mobile:** 121.8 per 100 pop. **Broadband:** 42.6 per 100 pop. **Internet:** 40.3%.

Health: Expend.: 3.9%. **Life expect.:** 69.6 male; 74.2 female. **Births:** 20.3 per 1,000 pop. **Deaths:** 6.1 per 1,000 pop. **Infant mortality:** 23.5 per 1,000 live births. **Undernourished:** 9.9%. **HIV:** 1.1%.

Education: Compulsory: ages 6-13. **Literacy:** 87.6%.

Embassy: 3415 Massachusetts Ave. NW 20007; 965-6820.

Website: www.governo.cv

The first Portuguese colonists landed in 1462; African slaves were brought soon after, and most Cabo Verdeans descend from both groups. Cabo Verde independence came July 5, 1975. Antonio Mascarenhas Monteiro won the nation's first free presidential election Feb. 17, 1991; he was reelected without opposition 5 years later. After Pres. Pedro Pires retired after serving two 5-year terms, 2001-11, Jorge Carlos Fonseca won a presidential runoff election Aug. 21, 2011. Remittances from Cabo Verdean emigrants are a major source of income. Japan announced June 3, 2013, that it would help fund the construction of water and energy projects in Cabo Verde. In Oct. 2013, the government announced that the country would no longer be known by the name Cape Verde.

Cambodia

Kingdom of Cambodia

People: Population: 15,708,756. **Age distrib.:** <15: 31.4%; 65+: 4%. **Growth:** 1.6%. **Migrants:** 0.5%. **Pop. density:** 230.5 per sq mi, 89 per sq km. **Urban:** 20.7%. **Ethnic groups:** Khmer 90%, Vietnamese 5%. **Language:** Khmer (official). **Religions:** Buddhist (official) 96.9%, Muslim 1.9%.

Geography: Total area: 69,898 sq mi, 181,035 sq km; **Land area:** 68,153 sq mi, 176,515 sq km. **Location:** SE Asia, on Indochina Peninsula. Thailand on W and N, Laos on NE, Vietnam on E. **Topography:** The central area, formed by the Mekong R. basin and Tonle Sap Lake, is level. Hills and mountains in SE; long escarpment in NW separates the country from Thailand. **Arable land:** 23.2%. **Capital:** Phnom Penh, 1,731,286.

Government: Type: Multiparty democracy under constitutional monarchy. **Head of state:** King Norodom Sihamoni; in office: Oct. 29, 2004. **Head of gov.:** Prime Min. Hun Sen; in office: Jan. 14, 1985. **Local divisions:** 24 provinces, 1 municipality. **Defense budget:** $445 mil. **Active troops:** 124,300.

Economy: Industries: tourism, garments, constr., rice milling, fishing, wood and wood prods., rubber, cement, gem mining, textiles. **Chief crops:** rice, rubber, corn, vegetables, cashews, cassava. **Natural resources:** oil and gas, timber, gemstones, iron ore, manganese, phosphates. **Water:** 31,457 cu m per capita. **Electricity prod.:** 1.4 bil kWh. **Labor force:** agric. 48.7%, industry 19.9%, services 31.5%. **Unemployment:** 0.3%.

Finance: Monetary unit: Riel (KHR) (4,098.00 = $1 U.S.). **GDP:** $50 bil; **per capita GDP:** $3,300; **GDP growth:** 7%. **Imports:** $10.6 bil; Thailand 27%, China 22%, Vietnam 19.3%, Singapore 7.2%, Hong Kong 6.1%. **Exports:** $7.6 bil; U.S. 28.6%, UK 8.8%, Germany 8.5%, Canada 7.6%, Japan 5.9%, Vietnam 5.2%. **Tourism:** $3 bil. **Budget:** $3.4 bil. **Inflation:** 3.9%.

Transport: Railways: 399 mi (under restoration). **Airports:** 6.

Communications: Telephone: 2.8 per 100 pop. **Mobile:** 155.1 per 100 pop. **Broadband:** 10.1 per 100 pop. **Internet:** 9%.

Health: Expend.: 5.4%. **Life expect.:** 61.7 male; 66.7 female. **Births:** 23.8 per 1,000 pop. **Deaths:** 7.7 per 1,000 pop. **Infant mortality:** 50.0 per 1,000 live births. **Undernourished:** 16.1%. **HIV:** 0.6%.

Education: Compulsory: NA. **Literacy:** 77.2%.

Embassy: 4530 16th St. NW 20011; 726-7742.

Website: cnv.org.kh

Early kingdoms dating from that of Funan in the 1st cent. CE culminated in the great Khmer empire that flourished from the 9th cent. to the 13th, encompassing present-day Thailand, Cambodia, Laos, and southern Vietnam. The peripheral areas were lost to invading Siamese and Vietnamese. France established a protectorate in 1863. Independence came in 1953.

Prince Norodom Sihanouk, king (1941-55) and head of state from 1960, tried to maintain neutrality during the Vietnam War. The U.S. bombed Cambodia, 1969-73, targeting suspected border sanctuaries of Vietnamese insurgents.

In 1970, pro-U.S. Prem. Lon Nol seized power, demanded removal of 40,000 North Vietnamese troops, and abolished the monarchy. Sihanouk formed a government-in-exile in Beijing. Open war began between Nol's government and Communist Khmer Rouge guerrillas supported by Vietnam and China. The U.S. provided Nol with heavy military and economic aid.

Khmer Rouge forces captured Phnom Penh Apr. 17, 1975. Cities were depopulated and their residents executed or condemned to forced labor. An estimated 1.7 mil people died in "killing fields" or from other hardships under Khmer Rouge rule, 1975-79.

Severe border fighting broke out with Vietnam in 1978 and developed into a full-fledged Vietnamese invasion. Formation of a Vietnamese-backed government was announced, Jan. 8, 1979, one day after Phnom Penh was seized. Thousands of refugees fled to Thailand, and widespread starvation was reported. Vietnamese troops remained in Cambodia during the 1980s, meeting resistance from Khmer Rouge guerrillas. Vietnam withdrew nearly all its troops by Sept. 1989.

Following 1993 UN-sponsored elections in Cambodia, two leading parties agreed to share power in an interim government. On Sept. 21, the National Assembly adopted a constitution reestablishing a monarchy, and Sihanouk became king. The Khmer Rouge boycotted the elections and opposed the new government. The insurgency had weakened and splintered by 1996.

Co-Prime Min. Hun Sen staged a coup July 5, 1997, ousting his rival, Prince Norodom Ranariddh. Pol Pot, the Khmer Rouge leader during the late 1970s, was denounced by his former comrades at a show trial, July 25, 1997, and sentenced to house arrest; he died Apr. 15, 1998. Sihanouk abdicated because of poor health and was succeeded, Oct. 2004, by his son Norodom Sihamoni.

Hun Sen's party retained power through a series of flawed elections. A UN-backed war crimes tribunal convicted a former prison warden known as Duch July 2010 for overseeing the killing and torture of more than 14,000 inmates under the Khmer Rouge. Two Khmer Rouge leaders were convicted of murder, crimes against humanity, and other charges, Aug. 7, 2014, and sentenced to life in prison.

Unsafe working conditions led to two factory collapses May 16, 2013, outside of Phnom Penh and in Tream Tbal that killed 4 workers. In June 2014, as many as 200,000 Cambodians working in Thailand repatriated after a Thai military coup raised fears of a crackdown on illegal migrants. In a deal with Australia, Sept. 26, 2014, Cambodia agreed to accept for resettlement, in exchange for foreign aid, migrants held in Nauru detention centers after being intercepted trying to enter Australia; the first migrants arrived June 4, 2015.

Cameroon

Republic of Cameroon

People: Population: 23,739,218. **Age distrib.:** <15: 42.8%; 65+: 3.2%. **Growth:** 2.6%. **Migrants:** 1.3%. **Pop. density:** 130.1 per sq mi, 50.2 per sq km. **Urban:** 54.4%. **Ethnic groups:** Cameroon Highlander 31%, Equatorial Bantu 19%, Kirdi 11%, Fulani 10%, Northwestern Bantu 8%, Eastern Nigritic 7%. **Languages:** 24 major African lang. groups; English, French (both official). **Religions:** indigenous beliefs 40%, Christian 40%, Muslim 20%.

Geography: Total area: 183,568 sq mi, 475,440 sq km; **Land area:** 182,514 sq mi, 472,710 sq km. **Location:** Between W and central Africa. Nigeria on NW; Chad, Central African Republic on E; Congo Rep., Gabon, Equatorial Guinea on S. **Topography:** Low coastal plain with rain forests in S; plateaus in center lead to forested mountains in W, including Mt. Cameroon (13,435 ft). Grasslands in N, marshes around Lake Chad. **Arable land:** 13.1%. **Capital:** Yaoundé, 3,065,692. **Cities:** Douala, 2,943,318.

Government: Type: Republic. **Head of state:** Pres. Paul Biya; in office: Nov. 6, 1982. **Head of gov.:** Prime Min. Philemon Yang; in office: June 30, 2009. **Local divisions:** 10 regions. **Defense budget:** $410 mil. **Active troops:** 14,200.

Economy: Industries: petroleum prod. and refining, aluminum prod., food proc., light consumer goods, textiles, lumber. **Chief crops:** coffee, cocoa, cotton, rubber, bananas, oilseed, grains, cassava. **Natural resources:** petroleum, bauxite, iron ore, timber, hydropower. **Water:** 12,721 cu m per capita. **Crude oil reserves:** 200 mil bbls. **Electricity prod.:** 6.2 bil kWh. **Labor force:** agric. 70%, industry 13%, services 17%. **Unemployment:** 4%.

Finance: Monetary unit: Central African CFA Franc (XAF) (584.11 = $1 U.S.). **GDP:** $67.2 bil; **per capita GDP:** $3,000; **GDP growth:** 5.1%. **Imports:** $6.9 bil; China 23.2%, France 14%, Nigeria 10.8%, Belgium 5.6%, U.S. 5.1%. **Exports:** $6.4 bil; Portugal 18.5%, Spain 10%, Netherlands 8.4%, U.S. 6.4%, China 6.3%, India 5.1%. **Tourism:** $576 mil. **Budget:** $6.9 bil. **Inflation** (2012-13): 1.9%.

Transport: Railways: 613 mi. **Motor vehicles:** 15.2 per 1,000 pop. **Airports:** 11.

Communications: Telephone: 4.6 per 100 pop. **Mobile:** 75.7 per 100 pop. **Broadband:** 1.7 per 100 pop. **Internet:** 11%.

Health: Expend.: 5.1%. **Life expect.:** 56.6 male; 59.3 female. **Births:** 36.2 per 1,000 pop. **Deaths:** 10.1 per 1,000 pop. **Infant mortality:** 53.6 per 1,000 live births. **Undernourished:** 10.5%. **HIV:** 4.8%.

Education: Compulsory: ages 6-11. **Literacy:** 75%.

Embassy: 3400 International Dr. NW, Ste. 5L, 20008; 265-8790.

Website: www.spm.gov.cm

Portuguese sailors were the first Europeans to reach Cameroon, in the 15th cent. The European and American slave trade was very active in the area. German control lasted from 1884 to 1916, when France and Britain divided the territory, for which they later received League of Nations mandates and UN trusteeships. French Cameroon became independent Jan. 1, 1960; one part of British Cameroon joined Nigeria in 1961 while the other part joined Cameroon. Pres. Paul Biya has retained power since 1982 in a series of elections that were boycotted by opposition parties or disputed as fraudulent. Rising food and fuel costs and discontent with Biya's continued rule sparked antigovernment riots Feb. 23-29, 2008. The legislature, controlled by Biya loyalists, voted Apr. 2008 to abolish presidential term limits introduced in 1996.

More than a dozen French citizens were kidnapped during 2013, allegedly in retaliation for France's intervention in Mali, and taken to Nigeria by the Nigerian-based jihadist group Boko Haram. Kidnappings and attacks by Boko Haram in Cameroon continued in 2014-15. In 2015, Cameroon troops fought in Nigeria against Boko Haram forces.

Canada

People: Population: 35,099,836. **Age distrib.:** <15: 15.5%; 65+: 17.7%. **Growth:** 0.8%. **Migrants:** 20.7%. **Pop. density:** 10 per sq mi, 3.9 per sq km. **Urban:** 81.8%. **Ethnic groups:** Canadian 32.2%, English 19.8%, French 15.5%, Scottish 14.4%, Irish 13.8%, German 9.8%, Italian 4.5%, Chinese 4.5%, N Amer. Indian 4.2%. **Languages:** English, French (both official). **Religions:** Catholic 40.6%, Protestant 20.3%, Muslim 3.2%, none 23.9%.

Geography: Total area: 3,855,103 sq mi, 9,984,670 sq km; **Land area:** 3,511,023 sq mi, 9,093,507 sq km. The largest country in land size in the Western Hemisphere. **Location:** Extends 3,426 mi E-W and S from the North Pole to the U.S. **Topography:** Its seacoast includes 36,356 mi of mainland and 115,133 mi of islands, including the Arctic islands almost from Greenland to near the Alaskan border. Generally temperate, though varies from freezing winter cold to blistering summer heat. **Arable land:** 5%. **Capital:** Ottawa, 1,325,846 (figure is for Ottawa-Gatineau metro area). **Cities:** Toronto, 5,992,739; Montréal, 3,980,708; Vancouver, 2,485,173; Calgary, 1,337,106; Edmonton, 1,272,069; Québec City, 805,113; Winnipeg, 759,365; Halifax, 404,748; Victoria, 356,552.

Government: Type: Constitutional monarchy with federal system of parliamentary democracy. **Head of state:** Queen Elizabeth II, rep. by Gov.-Gen. David Johnston; in office: Oct. 1, 2010. **Head of gov.:** Prime Min. Stephen Harper; in office: Feb. 6, 2006. **Local divisions:** 10 provinces, 3 territories. **Defense budget:** $15.93 bil. **Active troops:** 66,000.

Economy: Industries: transp. equip., chemicals, minerals, food prods., wood and paper prods., fish prods. **Chief crops:** wheat, barley, oilseed, tobacco, fruits, vegetables. **Natural resources:** iron ore, nickel, zinc, copper, gold, lead, rare earth elements, molybdenum, potash, diamonds, silver, fish, timber, wildlife, coal, petroleum, nat. gas, hydropower. **Water:** 82,485 cu m per capita. **Crude oil reserves:** 172.5 bil bbls. **Electricity prod.:** 616.2 bil kWh. **Labor force:** agric. 2%, mfg. 13%, constr. 6%, services 76%, other 3%. **Unemployment:** 7.1%.

Finance: Monetary unit: Dollar (CAD) (1.33 = $1 U.S.). **GDP:** $1.6 tril; **per capita GDP:** $44,800; **GDP growth:** 2.5%. **Imports:** $482.1 bil; U.S. 52.1%, China 11.1%, Mexico 5.6%. **Exports:** $465.1 bil; U.S. 75.8%. **Tourism:** $17.4 bil. **Budget:** $717.1 bil. **Inflation:** 1.9%.

Transport: Railways: 48,425 mi. **Motor vehicles:** 655.9 per 1,000 pop. **Airports:** 523.

Communications: Telephone: 46.6 per 100 pop. **Mobile:** 83 per 100 pop. **Broadband:** 51.2 per 100 pop. **Internet:** 87.1%.

Health: Expend.: 10.9%. **Life expect.:** 79.2 male; 84.5 female. **Births:** 10.3 per 1,000 pop. **Deaths:** 8.4 per 1,000 pop. **Infant mortality:** 4.7 per 1,000 live births. **Undernourished:** <5%. **HIV:** NA.

Education: Compulsory: ages 6-15. **Literacy:** 99%.

Embassy: 501 Pennsylvania Ave. NW 20001; 682-1740.

Website: www.canada.ca

French explorer Jacques Cartier, who reached the Gulf of St. Lawrence in 1534, is generally regarded as Canada's founder. But English seaman John Cabot sighted Newfoundland in 1497, and Vikings are believed to have reached the Atlantic coast centuries before either explorer. The French pioneered Canadian settlement, establishing Quebec City (1608) and Montréal (1642) and declaring New France a colony in 1663.

Britain acquired Acadia (later Nova Scotia) in 1717 and defeated French forces in Canada to gain control of Quebec (1759) and the rest of New France in 1763. The French, through the Quebec Act of 1774, retained rights to their language, religion, and civil law. The British presence in Canada increased during the American Revolution when many colonials, calling themselves United Empire Loyalists, moved north to Canada. Fur traders and explorers led Canadians westward across the continent. Sir Alexander Mackenzie reached the Pacific in 1793 and scrawled on a rock, "From Canada by land."

In Upper and Lower Canada (later called Ontario and Quebec) and in the Maritimes, legislative assemblies were formed in the 18th cent. Upper Canada was involved in the War of 1812, a conflict between Great Britain and the U.S. that ended in a stalemate in 1814.

In 1837 political agitation for more democratic government culminated in rebellions in Upper and Lower Canada and the union of the two into the colony of Canada in 1839. The union lasted until the 1867 British North America Act (now known as the Constitution Act, 1867) launched the Dominion of Canada, consisting of Ontario, Quebec, and the former colonies of Nova Scotia and New Brunswick.

The British North America Act, which was the basis for the country's written constitution, established a federal system of government modeled on the British parliament and cabinet structure under the crown. Canada was proclaimed a self-governing dominion within the British Empire in 1931. The Constitution Act, 1982, gave Canada the right to amend its constitution, thereby severing its last legislative link with Britain.

Failure in 1990 of the so-called Meech Lake Accord, which would have assured constitutional protection for Quebec's efforts to preserve its French language and culture, sparked a separatist revival in Quebec. The Charlottetown agreement, calling for constitutional changes, such as recognition of Quebec as a "distinct society" within the Canadian confederation, was defeated by a national referendum Oct. 1992.

The North American Free Trade Agreement among Canada, Mexico, and the U.S. went into effect Jan. 1, 1994. A Quebec referendum on secession held Oct. 1995 was defeated. On Jan. 7, 1998, the government apologized to indigenous peoples for 150 years of mistreatment and pledged to set up a "healing fund." Nunavut ("Our Land"), carved from the Northwest Territories as a homeland for the Inuit, was established Apr. 1, 1999.

Victory by the Liberals in national elections Nov. 27, 2000, made Jean Chrétien the first Canadian prime min. in over 50 years to head a third successive majority government. Canada sent troops and warships to aid the U.S.-led coalition in Afghanistan beginning Oct. 2001; 157 Canadian troops had been killed in Afghanistan by the time Canada's combat mission ended July 7, 2011.

Chrétien retired Dec. 12, 2003, and Paul Martin became prime min. Weakened by a corruption scandal, the Liberals won only 135 of 308 seats in parliamentary elections June 28, 2004. Martin became head of a minority government. Same-sex marriage (already permitted in 8 of 10 provinces) became legal throughout the country July 2005.

Twelve years of Liberal Party rule ended when Conservatives won 124 seats to the Liberals' 103 in parliamentary elections, Jan. 23, 2006. Conservative leader Stephen Harper took office Feb. 6 as head of a minority government. Police and intelligence officials in the Toronto area, June 2-3, 2006, arrested and charged 17 people with plotting terrorist attacks in Canada. The supreme court, Feb. 23, 2007, unanimously struck down a law under which foreign-born terrorism suspects had been indefinitely detained without charge.

Prime Min. Harper remained the head of a minority government after 2008 elections. A no-confidence vote Mar. 25, 2011, led to federal elections May 2, in which Harper's Conservatives gained a parliamentary majority of 166 seats. The New Democratic Party, with 103 seats, became the official opposition.

In a bid to open up the Canadian oil market to international buyers, the government approved Dec. 7, 2012, a $15-bil takeover of the energy company Nexen by China Natl. Offshore Oil and the acquisition of Progress Energy Resources of Canada by the Malaysian state-owned oil-and-gas company Petronas. Improved technology has facilitated extracting oil from tar sands, large deposits of which are found in Alberta. The Canadian government gave conditional approval June 17, 2014, for construction of a pipeline from Alberta to a new port in British Columbia, but U.S. approval for a section of the Keystone XL pipeline to carry Alberta tar-sands oil to the Gulf of Mexico was pending in mid-2015.

On Oct. 22, 2014, a terrorist gunman in Ottawa, apparently inspired by the Islamist extremist group ISIS, killed a soldier at the Canadian War Memorial and opened fire in the Parliament building before being shot to death. Two days earlier in Montréal, a terrorist with apparently similar motivation ran down two soldiers with his car, killing one, before being fatally shot. Canada joined the U.S.-led campaign of airstrikes against ISIS forces in Iraq (first Canadian airstrike Nov. 2, 2014) and Syria (Apr. 8, 2015).

Central African Republic

People: Population: 5,391,539. **Age distrib.:** <15: 40.4%; 65+: 3.5%. **Growth:** 2.1%. **Migrants:** 2.9%. **Pop. density:** 22.4 per sq mi, 8.7 per sq km. **Urban:** 40%. **Ethnic groups:** Baya 33%, Banda 27%, Mandjia 13%, Sara 10%, Mboum 7%, M'Baka 4%, Yakoma 4%. **Languages:** French (official), Sangho (lingua franca and national lang.), tribal langs. **Religions:** indigenous beliefs 35%, Protestant 25%, Roman Catholic 25%, Muslim 15%.

Geography: Total area: 240,535 sq mi, 622,984 sq km; **Land area:** 240,535 sq mi, 622,984 sq km. **Location:** Central Africa. Chad on N, Cameroon on W, Congo Republic and Dem. Rep. of the Congo on S, Sudan on E. **Topography:** Mostly rolling plateau, average elevation 2,000 ft, with rivers draining S to the Congo and N to Lake Chad. Open, well-watered savanna covers most of area,

Canada's Provinces and Territories

Provinces/territories	Joined confed.	Tot. area (sq mi)	Population (2014 est.)	Capital	Premier	Party	In office
Alberta	1905	255,541	4,121,692	Edmonton	Rachel Notley	New Democratic	2015
British Columbia	1871	364,764	4,631,302	Victoria	Christy Clark	Liberal	2011
Manitoba	1870	250,116	1,282,043	Winnipeg	Greg Selinger	New Democratic	2009
New Brunswick	1867	28,150	753,914	Fredericton	Brian Gallant	Liberal	2014
Newfoundland and Labrador	1949	156,453	526,977	St. John's	Paul Davis	Prog. Cons.	2014
Nova Scotia	1867	21,345	942,668	Halifax	Stephen McNeil	Liberal	2013
Ontario	1867	415,598	13,678,740	Toronto	Kathleen Wynne	Liberal	2013
Prince Edward Island	1873	2,185	146,283	Charlottetown	Wade MacLauchlan	Liberal	2015
Québec	1867	595,391	8,214,672	Québec	Philippe Couillard	Liberal	2014
Saskatchewan	1905	251,366	1,125,410	Regina	Brad Wall	Saskatchewan	2007
Northwest Territories[1]	1871	519,734	43,623	Yellowknife	Bob McLeod	Nonpartisan	2011
Nunavut[1,2]	1999	808,185	36,585	Iqaluit	Peter Taptuna	Independent	2013
Yukon[1]	1898	186,272	36,510	Whitehorse	Darrell Pasloski	Yukon	2011

Note: Pop. est. as of July 1. (Source: Statistics Canada.) (1) Territories also have federally appointed commissioners to represent federal interests. (2) Territory created in 1999 from eastern portion of Northwest Territories.

with an arid area in NE and tropical rain forest in SW. **Arable land:** 2.9%. **Capital:** Bangui, 794,022.

Government: Type: Republic. **Head of state:** Interim Pres. Catherine Samba-Panza; in office: Jan. 20, 2014. **Head of gov.:** Interim Prime Min. Mahamat Kamoun; in office: Aug. 10, 2014. **Local divisions:** 14 prefectures, 2 economic prefectures, 1 commune. **Defense budget** (2012): $50 mil. **Active troops:** 7,150.

Economy: Industries: gold, diamond mining; logging; brewing; sugar refining. **Chief crops:** cotton, coffee, tobacco, cassava, yams, millet, corn, bananas. **Natural resources:** diamonds, uranium, timber, gold, oil, hydropower. **Water:** 30,546 cu m per capita. **Electricity prod.:** 181 mil kWh. **Labor force:** NA. **Unemployment:** 7.6%.

Finance: Monetary unit: Central African CFA Franc (XAF) (584.11 = $1 U.S.). **GDP:** $2.9 bil; **per capita GDP:** $600; **GDP growth:** 1%. **Imports:** $216.7 mil; South Korea 17.4%, Netherlands 12.9%, Singapore 9%, Cameroon 8.5%, France 6.2%. **Exports:** $102.4 mil; China 30.3%, Belgium 18.9%, Dem. Rep. of the Congo 10.7%, Indonesia 9.6%, Morocco 5.2%. **Tourism:** $11 mil. **Budget:** $205.4 mil. **Inflation** (2012-13): 1.5%.

Transport: Motor vehicles: 0.9 per 1,000 pop. **Airports:** 2.

Communications: Telephone: 0.02 per 100 pop. **Mobile:** 31.4 per 100 pop. **Broadband:** 0.1 per 100 pop. **Internet:** 4%.

Health: Expend.: 3.8%. **Life expect.:** 50.5 male; 53.2 female. **Births:** 35.1 per 1,000 pop. **Deaths:** 13.8 per 1,000 pop. **Infant mortality:** 90.6 per 1,000 live births. **Undernourished:** 37.6%. **HIV:** 4.3%.

Education: Compulsory: NA. **Literacy:** 36.8%.

Embassy: 2704 Ontario Rd. 20009; 483-7800.

Website: www.rcawashington.org or www.state.gov/p/af/ci/car/

Various Bantu peoples migrated through the region for centuries before French control was asserted in the late 19th cent., when the region was named Ubangi-Shari. Independence was attained Aug. 13, 1960.

Pres. Jean-Bedel Bokassa, who seized power in a 1965 military coup, proclaimed himself constitutional emperor of the renamed Central African Empire Dec. 1976. Bokassa's rule was characterized by ruthless authoritarianism and human rights violations. He was ousted in a bloodless coup aided by the French government, Sept. 20, 1979. In 1981, Gen. André Kolingba became head of state in another bloodless coup. Elections, held in Aug. and Sept. 1993, led to civilian rule under Pres. Ange-Félix Patassé.

Patassé was ousted Mar. 15, 2003, by rebels under former army chief François Bozizé. Bozizé won a presidential runoff election May 8, 2005, but insurgent activity by Patassé loyalists and others continued in the north. A national peace conference, Dec. 8-20, 2008, enabled the installation of a unity government Jan. 19, 2009. Pres. Bozizé won reelection Jan. 23, 2011, but was ousted when the largely Muslim rebel group Seleka, led by Michel Djotodia, seized the capital Mar. 24, 2013. Djotodia declared himself president. Bozizé supporters and Christian militias clashed with pro-Djotodia and Muslim fighters, resulting in thousands of deaths and more than 850,000 internally displaced persons and refugees by the end of 2014. A National Transitional Council elected Catherine Samba-Panza interim pres. Jan. 20, 2014, and other African nations, France, and the EU sent peacekeeping troops. A UN peacekeeping force (MINUSCA) was authorized Apr. 10, 2014, and almost 11,000 MINUSCA uniformed personnel were in the country as of June 30, 2015. More than a dozen allegations of sexual abuse by French or UN peacekeeping troops had been made by the end of Aug. 2015. Muslim-Christian violence in Bangui in Sept. left dozens of people dead.

Chad

Republic of Chad

People: Population: 11,631,456. **Age distrib.:** <15: 44.2%; 65+: 3%. **Growth:** 1.9%. **Migrants:** 3.4%. **Pop. density:** 23.9 per sq mi, 9.2 per sq km. **Urban:** 22.5%. **Ethnic groups:** Sara 27.7%, Arab 12.3%, Mayo-Kebbi 11.5%, Kanem-Bornou 9%, Ouaddai 8.7%, Hadjarai 6.7%, Tandjile 6.5%, Gorane 6.3%, Fitri-Batha 4.7%. **Languages:** French, Arabic (both official); Sara; 120+ langs. and dialects. **Religions:** Muslim 53.1%, Catholic 20.1%, Protestant 14.2%, animist 7.3%, atheist 3.1%.

Geography: Total area: 495,755 sq mi, 1,284,000 sq km; **Land area:** 486,180 sq mi, 1,259,200 sq km. **Location:** Central N Africa. Libya on N; Niger, Nigeria, Cameroon on W; Central African Republic on S; Sudan on E. **Topography:** Wooded savanna, steppe, and desert in the S; part of the Sahara in the N. Southern rivers flow N to Lake Chad, surrounded by marshland. **Arable land:** 3.9%. **Capital:** N'Djaména, 1,260,146.

Government: Type: Republic. **Head of state:** Pres. Idriss Déby Itno; in office: Dec. 4, 1990. **Head of gov.:** Prime Min. Kalzeube Pahimi Deubet; in office: Nov. 21, 2013. **Local divisions:** 23 regions. **Defense budget** (2012): $202 mil. **Active troops:** 25,350.

Economy: Industries: oil, cotton textiles, brewing, natron (sodium carbonate), soap, cigarettes, constr. materials. **Chief crops:** cotton, sorghum, millet, peanuts, sesame, corn, rice, potatoes, cassava. **Natural resources:** petroleum, uranium, natron, kaolin, fish, gold, limestone, sand and gravel, salt. **Water:** 3,563 cu m per capita. **Crude oil reserves:** 1.5 bil bbls. **Electricity prod.:** 205 mil kWh. **Labor force:** agric. 80%, industry and services 20%. **Unemployment:** 7%.

Finance: Monetary unit: Central African CFA Franc (XAF) (584.11 = $1 U.S.). **GDP:** $29.5 bil; **per capita GDP:** $2,600; **GDP growth:** 6.9%. **Imports:** $3.5 bil; China 31%, Cameroon 13.2%, France 11.6%, Belgium 5.4%. **Exports:** $4.9 bil; U.S. 80.7%, Japan 5.9%. **Budget:** $3.7 bil. **Inflation** (2012-13): 0.1%.

Transport: Airports: 9.

Communications: Telephone: 0.2 per 100 pop. **Mobile:** 39.8 per 100 pop. **Broadband:** NA. **Internet:** 2.5%.

Health: Expend.: 2.8%. **Life expect.:** 48.6 male; 51.0 female. **Births:** 36.6 per 1,000 pop. **Deaths:** 14.3 per 1,000 pop. **Infant mortality:** 88.7 per 1,000 live births. **Undernourished:** 34.8%. **HIV:** 2.5%.

Education: Compulsory: ages 6-15. **Literacy:** 40.2%.

Embassy: 2401 Massachusetts Ave. NW 20008; 652-1312.

Website: www.gouvernementdutchad.org or www.state.gov/p/af/ci/cd/

Chad was the site of Paleolithic and Neolithic cultures before the Sahara Desert formed. A succession of kingdoms and Arab slave traders dominated Chad until France took control around 1900. Independence came Aug. 11, 1960. Northern Muslim rebels fought animist and Christian southern government and French troops from 1966.

Rebel forces, led by Hissène Habré, captured the capital and forced Pres. Goukouni Oueddei to flee the country in June 1982. In Dec. 1990, a Libyan-supported insurgent group, the Patriotic Salvation Movement, overthrew Habré. After approval of a new constitution Mar. 1996, Chad's first multiparty presidential election was held in June and July.

Oil began flowing July 15, 2003, through a 665-mi pipeline that allows landlocked Chad to export via Cameroon. Pres. Idriss Déby Itno won a third term, May 3, 2006, in an election boycotted by major opposition groups. Violence along the Sudan border escalated during the year, as Sudanese *janjaweed* militias and Chadian rebels attacked civilians, and Darfur rebels preyed on refugee camps. Between 140 and 700 civilians died in N'Djaména, Feb. 2-5, 2008, as more than 2,000 Chadian rebels stormed the capital and clashed with government troops in a failed coup attempt.

On Jan. 15, 2010, Chad and Sudan signed an accord aimed at normalizing relations and suppressing cross-border activities by rebel groups. Established in 2007, a UN peacekeeping force (MINURCAT) completed its mandate Dec. 31, 2010. More than 368,000 Sudanese refugees were living in Chad in early 2015. Pres. Déby won reelection Apr. 25, 2011, in a vote boycotted by major opposition groups.

After Islamist groups took over northern Mali and imposed a repressive regime in late 2012, Chad contributed roughly 2,000 soldiers to aid French, Malian, and other African forces in a military intervention. On Apr. 15, 2013, the Chadian government announced it would begin pulling its troops out of Mali. Chadian troops in 2015 fought Boko Haram Islamist extremists in Nigeria. Boko Haram fighters staged attacks in Chad, and suicide bombings blamed on Boko Haram killed at least 27 people in N'Djaména, June 15, 2015.

Former Pres. Habré, accused of killing and torturing thousands of opponents in the 1980s, was arrested in Senegal June 30, 2013. The Extraordinary African Chambers charged Habré with crimes against humanity, torture, and war crimes July 2, 2013; his trial began July 20, 2015.

Chile

Republic of Chile

People: Population: 17,508,260. **Age distrib.:** <15: 20.5%; 65+: 10.2%. **Growth:** 0.8%. **Migrants:** 2.3%. **Pop. density:** 61 per sq mi, 23.5 per sq km. **Urban:** 89.5%. **Ethnic groups:** white and non-indigenous 88.9%, Mapuche 9.1%. **Languages:** Spanish (official), English, indigenous. **Religions:** Roman Catholic 66.7%, Evangelical or Protestant 16.4%, none 11.5%.

Geography: Total area: 291,933 sq mi, 756,102 sq km; **Land area:** 287,187 sq mi, 743,812 sq km. **Location:** W coast of southern S America. Peru on N, Bolivia on NE, Argentina on E. **Topography:** Andes Mts., with some of world's highest peaks, on E border; on W is 2,650-mi Pacific coast. Width varies 100-250 mi. Atacama Desert in N. **Arable land:** 1.8%. **Capital:** Santiago, 6,507,400. **Cities:** Valparaíso, 906,967 (seat of natl. legislature).

Government: Type: Republic. **Head of state and gov.:** Pres. Michelle Bachelet Jeria; in office: Mar. 11, 2014. **Local divisions:** 15 regions. **Defense budget:** $3.88 bil. **Active troops:** 61,400.

Economy: Industries: copper, lithium, other minerals; foodstuffs, fish proc.; iron and steel; wood and wood prods.; transp. equip.; cement; textiles. **Chief crops:** grapes, apples, pears, onions, wheat, corn, oats, peaches, garlic, asparagus, beans.

Natural resources: copper, timber, iron ore, nitrates, prec. metals, molybdenum, hydropower. **Water:** 52,389 cu m per capita. **Crude oil reserves:** 150 mil bbls. **Electricity prod.:** 66.9 bil kWh. **Labor force:** agric. 13.2%, industry 23%, services 63.9%. **Unemployment:** 6%.

Finance: Monetary unit: Peso (CLP) (689.69 = $1 U.S.). **GDP:** $409.3 bil; **per capita GDP:** $23,000; **GDP growth:** 1.8%. **Imports:** $70.7 bil; U.S. 20.3%, China 19.7%, Brazil 6.5%, Argentina 5%. **Exports:** $77 bil; China 24.9%, U.S. 12.8%, Japan 9.9%, Brazil 5.8%, South Korea 5.5%. **Tourism:** $2.3 bil. **Budget:** $56.3 bil. **Inflation:** 4.4%.

Transport: Railways: 4,525 mi. **Motor vehicles:** 237.8 per 1,000 pop. **Airports:** 90.

Communications: Telephone: 19.2 per 100 pop. **Mobile:** 133.3 per 100 pop. **Broadband:** 35.7 per 100 pop. **Internet:** 72.4%.

Health: Expend.: 7.2%. **Life expect.:** 75.6 male; 81.8 female. **Births:** 13.8 per 1,000 pop. **Deaths:** 6.0 per 1,000 pop. **Infant mortality:** 6.9 per 1,000 live births. **Undernourished:** <5%. **HIV:** 0.3%.

Education: Compulsory: ages 6-17. **Literacy:** 97.5%.

Embassy: 1732 Massachusetts Ave. NW 20036; 785-1746.

Website: www.gob.cl

Northern Chile was under Inca rule before the Spanish conquest, 1536-40. The southern Araucanian Indians resisted until the late 19th cent. Independence was gained 1810-18 under José de San Martin and Bernardo O'Higgins; the latter, as supreme director 1817-23, sought social and economic reforms until deposed. Chile defeated Peru and Bolivia in 1836-39 and 1879-84, gaining mineral-rich northern land.

In 1970, Salvador Allende Gossens, a Marxist, became president with a narrow plurality of the popular vote. His government improved conditions for the poor, but property seizures by left-wing extremists, poorly planned socialist economic programs, and a destabilization campaign backed by the U.S. led to political and financial chaos. A military junta seized power Sept. 11, 1973. With the presidential palace under attack, Allende refused to surrender; a 2011 autopsy confirmed police reports that he killed himself. The junta, headed by Gen. Augusto Pinochet Ugarte, implemented plans to privatize the economy and "exterminate Marxism." Repression continued into the 1980s.

In Dec. 1989 voters elected a civilian president, although Pinochet continued to head the army until Mar. 10, 1998. In Mar. 1994, a Chilean human rights group estimated that human rights violations had claimed more than 3,100 lives during Pinochet's rule. Efforts to prosecute him failed when courts in Britain and Chile declared him mentally unfit to stand trial.

Ricardo Lagos Escobar, Chile's first Socialist president since the 1973 coup, took office Mar. 11, 2000. Chile and the U.S. signed a free trade accord June 6, 2003. Michelle Bachelet Jeria, also a Socialist, won a runoff election Jan. 2006 and took office in Mar. as Chile's first woman president. Pinochet died Dec. 10, 2006.

Billionaire businessman Sebastián Piñera Echenique, a conservative, won a presidential runoff election Jan. 2010 and took office in Mar. In the interim, a powerful earthquake and the tsunami that followed it Feb. 27, 2010, off the coast of central Chile killed at least 521 people and caused up to $30 bil in property damage. Chile successfully rescued 33 miners trapped for 10 weeks 2,300 ft underground after a cave-in at the San José Mine Aug. 5, 2010. A prison fire Dec. 8 in Santiago killed at least 81 inmates. Chile's economy was growing at a 6.6% annual rate in mid-2011, but lagging wages sparked labor protests against the Piñera government that continued into 2012 and spread to the student population. Bachelet won a presidential runoff election Dec. 15, 2013, and returned to office Mar. 11, 2014. She made major cabinet changes in May 2015 in the wake of an economic slowdown and a series of corruption scandals.

Tierra del Fuego is the largest (18,800 sq mi) island in the archipelago of the same name at the southern tip of S America, an area of majestic mountains, tortuous channels, and high winds. It was visited 1520 by Magellan and named Land of Fire because of its many Indian bonfires. Part of the island is in Chile, part in Argentina. Punta Arenas, on a mainland peninsula, is a center of sheep raising and the world's southernmost city; Puerto Williams is the southernmost settlement.

China

People's Republic of China

(Statistical data do not include Hong Kong or Macao.)

People: Population: 1,367,485,388. **Age distrib.:** <15: 17.1%; 65+: 10%. **Growth:** 0.5%. **Migrants:** 0.1%. **Pop. density:** 379.8 per sq mi, 146.6 per sq km. **Urban:** 55.6%. **Ethnic groups:** Han Chinese 91.6%, other (incl. Hui, Manchu, Uighur, Miao, Yi, Tujia, Tibetan, Mongol, Dong, Buyei, Yao, Bai, Korean, Hani, Li, Kazakh, Dai) 7.1%. **Languages:** Standard Chinese or Mandarin (official; Putonghua, based on Beijing dialect), Yue (Cantonese), Wu (Shanghainese), Minbei (Fuzhou), Minnan (Hokkien-Taiwanese), Xiang, Gan. **Religions:** officially atheist; Buddhist 18.2%, Christian 5.1%, folk religion 21.9%, unaffiliated 52.2%.

Geography: Total area: 3,705,407 sq mi, 9,596,960 sq km; **Land area:** 3,600,947 sq mi, 9,326,410 sq km. **Location:** Occupies most of the habitable mainland of E Asia. Mongolia on N; Russia on NE and NW; Afghanistan, Pakistan, Tajikistan, Kyrgyzstan, Kazakhstan on W; India, Nepal, Bhutan, Myanmar, Laos, Vietnam on S; North Korea on NE. **Topography:** Two-thirds of territory is mountainous or desert; only one-tenth is cultivated. The Da Xing'an Ling Mts. in N separate Manchuria and Mongolia. Other ranges incl. the Tien Shan in Xinjiang and the Himalayan and Kunlun Mts. in the SW and in Tibet. The eastern half of China is one of the world's best-watered lands with three great river systems: the Chang (Yangtze), Huang (Yellow), and Xi. **Arable land:** 11.3%. **Capital:** Beijing, 20,383,994. **Cities:** Shanghai, 23,740,778; Chongqing, 13,331,579; Guangzhou, Guangdong, 12,458,130; Tianjin, 11,210,329; Shenzhen, 10,749,473; Wuhan, 7,905,572; Chengdu, 7,555,705; Dongguan, 7,434,935; Nanjing, Jiangsu, 7,369,157; Foshan, 7,035,945.

Government: Type: Communist state. **Head of state:** Pres. Xi Jinping; in office: Mar. 14, 2013 (gen. sec. of Communist Party since Nov. 15, 2012). **Head of gov.:** Prem. Li Keqiang; in office: Mar. 16, 2013. **Local divisions:** 22 provinces (not incl. Taiwan), 5 autonomous regions, 4 municipalities, plus the special administrative regions of Hong Kong (as of July 1, 1997) and Macao (as of Dec. 20, 1999). **Defense budget:** $129.41 bil. **Active troops:** 2,333,000.

Economy: Industries: mining and ore proc., iron, steel, aluminum, other metals, coal; machine building; armaments; textiles and apparel; petroleum; cement; chemicals; fertilizers; consumer prods.; food proc.; transp. equip.; telecom equip. **Chief crops:** rice, wheat, potatoes, corn, peanuts, tea, millet, barley, apples, cotton, oilseed. **Natural resources:** coal, iron ore, petroleum, nat. gas, mercury, tin, tungsten, antimony, manganese, molybdenum, vanadium, magnetite, aluminum, lead, zinc, rare earth elements, uranium. **Water:** 2,005 cu m per capita. **Crude oil reserves:** 24.6 bil bbls. **Electricity prod.:** 4.8 tril kWh. **Labor force:** agric. 33.6%, industry 30.3%, services 36.1%. **Unemployment:** 4.6%.

Finance: Monetary unit: Yuan Renminbi (CNY) (6.36 = $1 U.S.). **GDP:** $17.6 tril; **per capita GDP:** $12,900; **GDP growth:** 7.4%. **Imports:** $2 tril; (2014) South Korea 9.7%, Japan 8.3%, U.S. 8.1%, Taiwan 7.8%, Germany 5.4%, Australia 5%. **Exports:** $2.3 tril; (2014) U.S. 16.9%, Hong Kong 15.5%, Japan 6.4%. **Tourism:** $56.9 bil. **Budget:** $2.5 tril. **Inflation:** 2%.

Transport: Railways: 118,850 mi. **Motor vehicles:** 105.4 per 1,000 pop. **Airports:** 463.

Communications: Telephone: 17.9 per 100 pop. **Mobile:** 92.3 per 100 pop. **Broadband:** 21.4 per 100 pop. **Internet:** 49.3%.

Health: Expend.: 5.4%. **Life expect.:** 73.4 male; 77.7 female. **Births:** 12.5 per 1,000 pop. **Deaths:** 7.5 per 1,000 pop. **Infant mortality:** 12.4 per 1,000 live births. **Undernourished:** 10.6%. **HIV:** NA.

Education: Compulsory: ages 6-14. **Literacy:** 96.4%.

Embassy: 3505 International Pl. NW 20008; 495-2000.

Website: www.gov.cn

Remains of various humanlike creatures who lived as early as several hundred thousand years ago have been found in many parts of China. Neolithic agricultural settlements dotted the Huang (Yellow) R. basin from about 5000 BCE. Their language, religion, and art were the sources of later Chinese civilization.

Bronze metallurgy reached a peak and Chinese pictographic writing, similar to today's, was in use in the more developed culture of the Shang Dynasty (c. 1500 BCE-c. 1000 BCE), which ruled much of North China.

A succession of dynasties and interdynastic warring kingdoms ruled China for the next 3,000 years. They expanded Chinese political and cultural domination to the south and west, and developed a technologically and culturally advanced society that was unaffected by foreign rule (Mongols in the Yuan Dynasty, 1279-1368, and Manchus in the Qing Dynasty, 1644-1912).

Rebellions in the 19th cent. left tens of millions dead. Russia, Japan, Britain, and other powers exercised political and economic control in large parts of the country. China became a republic Jan. 1, 1912, following the Wuchang Uprising inspired by Dr. Sun Yat-sen, founder of the Kuomintang (Nationalist) party. By 1928, the Kuomintang, led by Chiang Kai-shek, succeeded in nominal reunification of China. About the same time, a bloody purge of Communists from the ranks of the Kuomintang fomented hostilities.

For over 50 years, 1894-1945, China was involved in conflicts with Japan. In 1895, China ceded Korea, Taiwan, and other areas. On Sept. 18, 1931, Japan seized the Northeastern Provinces (Manchuria) and set up a puppet state called Manchukuo. Taking advantage of Chinese dissension, Japan invaded China proper July 7, 1937. On Nov. 20 the retreating Nationalist government moved its capital to Chongqing (Chungking) from Nanking (Nanjing), which Japanese troops then ravaged Dec. 13.

From 1939 the Sino-Japanese War (1937-45) became part of the broader world conflict. After its defeat in World War II, Japan relinquished China. Within China, conflicts involving the Kuomintang, Communists, and other factions resumed. China came under the domination of Communist armies, 1949-50. The Kuomintang government fled to Taiwan, Dec. 8, 1949.

The People's Republic of China was proclaimed in Beijing (Peking) Oct. 1, 1949, under Mao Zedong. China and the USSR signed a 30-year treaty of "friendship, alliance, and mutual assistance," Feb. 15, 1950. The U.S. refused to recognize the new regime. On Nov. 26, 1950, the People's Republic sent armies into Korea against U.S. troops and forced a stalemate in the Korean War.

Frequent drastic changes in policy and violent factionalism 1949-52 interfered with economic development. In 1957, Mao admitted an estimated 800,000 people had been executed 1949-54; opponents claimed much higher figures. The Great Leap Forward, 1958-60, tried to accelerate economic development through intensive labor on huge new rural communes and emphasis on ideological purity. The program caused resistance and was largely abandoned.

By the 1960s, relations with the USSR deteriorated over disagreements on borders, ideology, and leadership of world Communism. The USSR canceled aid accords. The Great Proletarian Cultural Revolution, 1965, an attempt to instruct a new generation in revolutionary principles, resulted in massive purges. Millions of urban teenagers were relocated to rural areas. By 1968 the movement had run its course; many purged officials returned to office in subsequent years, and several ideological reforms were gradually weakened.

On Oct. 25, 1971, the UN General Assembly ousted the Taiwan government from the UN and seated the People's Republic in its place. The U.S. had supported the mainland's admission but opposed Taiwan's expulsion.

U.S. Pres. Richard Nixon visited China Feb. 21-28, 1972, on invitation from Prem. Zhou Enlai, ending years of antipathy between the two nations. China and the U.S. opened liaison offices in each other's capitals, May-June 1973. The U.S., Dec. 15, 1978, formally recognized the People's Republic of China as the sole legal government of China; diplomatic relations between the two were established, Jan. 1, 1979.

Mao died Sept. 9, 1976. By 1978, Vice Prem. Deng Xiaoping had consolidated power, succeeding Mao as "paramount leader" of China. The new ruling group modified Maoist policies in education, culture, and industry, and sought better ties with non-Communist countries. By the mid-1980s, China had enacted far-reaching economic reforms, deemphasizing centralized planning and incorporating market-oriented incentives.

Some 100,000 students and workers marched in Beijing to demand political reforms, May 4, 1989. As the unrest spread, martial law was imposed, May 20. Troops entered Beijing, June 3-4, and crushed the pro-democracy protests, as tanks and armored personnel carriers rolled through Tiananmen Square. It is estimated that hundreds died and thousands were injured, and hundreds of students and workers were arrested.

Deng Xiaoping died Feb. 19, 1997, leaving Jiang Zemin in control as president. Hong Kong reverted to Chinese sovereignty July 1, 1997. Portugal returned Macao to China Dec. 20, 1999.

Hu Jintao was named Communist Party general secretary at the 16th party congress, Nov. 2002, and elected president by the 10th National People's Congress, Mar. 2003. With the successful launch and recovery, Oct. 15-16, 2003, of the *Shenzhou 5* spacecraft, China became the third nation (after the U.S. and USSR) to send a person into space. In Dec. 2013, China became the third nation to reach the Moon with a spacecraft that made a soft landing.

China's industries, exports, and oil demand have increased rapidly since the 1980s. China became the world's largest producer and consumer of coal. In part to diversify energy production, China completed construction in 2006 of the Three Gorges Dam on the Yangtze R., the world's largest hydroelectric dam. However, the burning of fossil fuels has caused severe air pollution in many areas. After negotiations with the U.S. on reducing CO_2 emissions, China pledged, Nov. 11, 2014, that its emissions would peak and then begin to decline no later than 2030 and that 20% of its energy would come from non-fossil fuel sources by that year.

The National People's Congress Mar. 15-16, 2008, reelected Pres. Hu Jintao and Prem. Wen Jiabao. A powerful earthquake rocked Sichuan prov. May 12, leaving 69,226 people dead and 17,923 missing. China reportedly spent $43 bil preparing for the Summer Olympics, held in Beijing Aug. 8-24, 2008. The Chinese government reacted angrily when the Nobel Peace Prize was awarded Oct. 8, 2010, to Liu Xiaobo, a human rights activist who had received an 11-year prison sentence in 2009. Xi Jinping was chosen Communist Party general secretary and China's new leader, and Li Keqiang the country's prime min. Nov. 15, 2012.

Western computer security experts Jan.-Feb. 2010 blamed hackers at two Chinese schools for Internet attacks on Google and at least 30 other firms. Hackers in China were suspected in two attacks on U.S. government computer systems in 2015 in which personal data on tens of millions of people, including federal employees, was stolen. At a White House meeting, Sept. 25, 2015, Xi and U.S. Pres. Barack Obama reached a general agreement on refraining from cybertheft.

Rapid growth during 2009-10 made China the world's second-largest economy, ranking behind the U.S. China's economy subsequently slowed. GDP growth was under 8% annually 2012-14, compared to double-digit gains for most years since the 1980s. After a run-up in prices, shares on China's two largest stock exchanges (Shanghai and Shenzhen) plunged, losing about one-third of their value June 12-July 31, 2015. To boost the economy, China devalued its currency, Aug. 2015. When stocks dropped sharply again, the central bank lowered interest rates, Aug. 25, the fifth such cut since Nov. 2014. Beijing was selected, July 31, 2015, to host the 2022 Winter Olympics. Massive explosions, Aug. 12, at a warehouse storing hazardous chemicals in Tianjin killed at least 173, injured hundreds, and caused widespread destruction.

Autonomous Regions

Guangxi Zhuang is in SE China, bounded on the N by Guizhou and Hunan provinces, E and S by Guangdong, on the SW by Vietnam, and on the W by Yunnan. It produces rice in the river valleys and has valuable forest products. Pop. (2010): 46,026,629. Capital: Nanning.

Inner Mongolia was organized by the People's Republic in 1947. Its boundaries have undergone frequent changes, reaching its greatest extent in 1956 (and restored in 1979), with an area of 454,600 sq mi, allegedly in order to dilute the minority Mongol population. Chinese settlers outnumber the Mongols more than 10 to 1. Pop. (2010) 24,706,321. Capital: Hohhot.

Ningxia Hui, in north-central China, is about 60,000 sq mi. Pop. (2010) 6,301,350. Capital: Yinchuan. The climate is mostly semiarid, with desert areas in the N. The Huang He (Yellow R.) flows across the N, furnishing water for irrigation. Coal is mined in the E. The majority of the population is Han; the Hui (Chinese Muslims) constitute about one-third of the population. The region experienced a significant population boom, 1950-80.

Xinjiang Uighur, in Central Asia, is 635,900 sq mi, pop. (2010) 21,813,334 (75% Uighurs, a Turkic Muslim group, with a heavy Han Chinese increase in recent years). Capital: Urumqi. It is China's richest region in strategic minerals. China has moved to suppress Uighur cultural and religious practices and to crack down on Uighur separatists, whom Beijing regards as terrorists. A protest march July 5, 2009, by Uighurs in Urumqi led to violent clashes with Han Chinese; at least 197 people (mostly Han) were killed in riots. Unrest and domestic terrorist attacks continued, including truck bombings in Urumqi May 22, 2014, that killed more than 40 people. The government's crackdown included the June 16 execution of 13 people convicted of terrorism-related crimes. Violence in Yarkand July 28 left almost 100 people dead. A clash between armed Uighurs and police in Kashgar overnight June 22-23, 2015, resulted in at least 18 deaths.

Tibet, 471,700 sq mi, is a thinly populated region of high plateaus and massive mountains, the Himalayas on the S, the Kunluns on the N. High passes connect with India and Nepal; roads lead into China proper. Capital: Lhasa. Avg. elevation is 15,000 ft. Jiachan, 15,870 ft, is believed to be the highest inhabited town on Earth. Agriculture is primitive. Pop. (2010) 3,002,166 (of whom about 500,000 are Chinese). Another 4 mil Tibetans form the majority of the population of vast adjacent areas that have long been incorporated into China.

China ruled all of Tibet from the 18th cent. Independence came in 1911, but China reasserted control in 1951, and a Communist government was installed in 1953. Serfdom was abolished, but all land remained collectivized.

A Tibetan uprising within China in 1956 spread to Lhasa in 1959. The rebellion was crushed by Chinese troops, and Buddhism was almost totally suppressed. The Dalai Lama and 100,000 Tibetans fled to India. Efforts by Chinese authorities to halt peaceful demonstrations by Tibetan monks led to anti-Chinese riots in Lhasa, Mar. 14, 2008; the Chinese government sent troops into Tibet to crush dissent, sparking international protests. Protests (including self-immolations) and government repression of dissent continued in subsequent years.

Hong Kong

Hong Kong (Xianggang), located at the mouth of the Zhu Jiang (Pearl R.) in SE China, 90 mi S of Guangzhou, was a British dependency from 1842 until July 1, 1997, when it became a Special Administrative Region of China. Its nucleus is Hong Kong Isl., 31 sq mi, occupied by the British in 1841 and formally ceded to them in 1842, on which is located the seat of government. Opposite is Kowloon Peninsula, 3 sq mi, and Stonecutters Isl., added to the territory in 1860. An additional 355 sq mi known as the New Territories, a mainland area and islands, were leased from China, 1898, for 99 years. Area 428 sq mi (total); 414 sq mi (land); pop. (2015 est.) 7,141,106. **Website:** www.gov.hk

Hong Kong is a major trade and banking center. Per capita GDP, $54,700 (2014 est.), is among the highest in the world. Principal industries are textiles and apparel, tourism, electronics, shipbuilding, iron and steel, fishing, cement, and small manufactures. Tourism receipts in 2014 were $38.4 bil. Hong Kong's spinning mills are among the best in the world. Outside of the public sector, the labor force is engaged in the following sectors: wholesale and retail trade, restaurants, and hotels 53.3%; community and social services 17.1%; financing, insurance, and real estate 12.5%; transp. and communications 10.1%; manufacturing 3.8%; and construction 2.8%.

Hong Kong harbor was long an important British naval station and one of the world's great transshipment ports. The colony often provided refuge for exiles from mainland China. It was occupied by Japan during WWII.

From 1949 to 1962, Hong Kong absorbed more than 1 mil refugees fleeing Communist China. Starting in the 1950s, cheap labor led to a boom in light manufacturing, while liberal tax policies attracted foreign investment. Hong Kong became one of the wealthiest, most productive areas in the Far East.

With the end of the 99-year lease on the New Territories drawing near, Britain and China signed an agreement, Dec. 19, 1984, under which all of Hong Kong was to be returned to China in 1997; under this agreement Hong Kong was to be allowed to keep its capitalist system for 50 years. Following the transfer of government, Hong Kong retained its street names and its currency, the Hong Kong dollar, but without the queen's picture. Cantonese (a Chinese dialect) and English remained official languages.

Hundreds of thousands of Hong Kong residents protested July 1, 2003, a proposed anti-subversion law; the bill was withdrawn Sept. 5. Another mass march, July 1, 2004, protested Beijing's refusal to allow greater freedom. Leung Chun-ying, whose close ties to China became an issue during the campaign, was elected chief executive Mar. 2012 by a committee of 1,200 members. Large pro-democracy protests took place July-Dec. 2014, opposing Chinese plans to restrict candidate selection for a proposed direct election of the chief executive in 2017. Hong Kong's Legislative Council, June 18, 2015, rejected the direct-election plan because of limitations on the openness of candidate selection. Several of the 2014 protest leaders where charged, Aug. 2015, with unlawful assembly and other offenses.

Macao

Macao, area of 11 sq mi, is a peninsula and two small islands at the mouth of the Xi (Pearl) R. in China. It was established as a Portuguese trading colony in 1557. In 1849, Portugal claimed sovereignty over the territory; this claim was accepted by China in an 1887 treaty. Portugal granted broad autonomy in 1976. Under a 1987 agreement, Macao reverted to China Dec. 20, 1999. As in the case of Hong Kong, the Chinese government guaranteed Macao it would not interfere in its way of life and capitalist system for a period of 50 years. Tourism is the fastest-growing economic sector. Tourism receipts in 2014 were $50.8 bil. Per capita GDP was $88,700 (2013 est.). The labor force is occupied in the following areas: gambling 25.9%, restaurants and hotels 15%, wholesale and retail trade 12.4%, construction 9.8%, public sector 7.1%, transp. and communications 4.4%, manufacturing 2.5%, and financial services 2.6%. Pop. (2015 est.) 592,731. **Website:** portal.gov.mo

Colombia

Republic of Colombia

People: Population: 46,736,728. **Age distrib.:** <15: 24.9%; 65+: 6.9%. **Growth:** 1%. **Migrants:** 0.3%. **Pop. density:** 116.5 per sq mi, 45 per sq km. **Urban:** 76.4%. **Ethnic groups:** mestizo and white 84.2%, Afro-Colombian (incl. mulatto, Raizal, Palenquero) 10.4%, Amerindian 3.4%. **Language:** Spanish (official). **Religions:** Roman Catholic 90%.

Geography: Total area: 439,736 sq mi, 1,138,910 sq km; **Land area:** 401,044 sq mi, 1,038,700 sq km. **Location:** NW corner of S America. Panama on NW, Ecuador and Peru on S, Brazil and Venezuela on E. **Topography:** Three Andes ranges—Western, Central, and Eastern Cordilleras—run N-S through the country. The eastern range consists mostly of high tablelands. The Magdalena R. rises in the Andes, flows N to Caribbean through a rich alluvial plain. Sparsely settled plains in E are drained by Orinoco and Amazon systems. **Arable land:** 1.4%. **Capital:** Bogotá, 9,764,769. **Cities:** Medellín, 3,910,989; Cali, 2,645,941; Barranquilla, 1,991,158.

Government: Type: Republic. **Head of state and gov.:** Pres. Juan Manuel Santos Calderón; in office: Aug. 7, 2010. **Local divisions:** 32 departments, 1 capital district. **Defense budget:** $13.44 bil. **Active troops:** 296,750.

Economy: Industries: textiles, food proc., oil, clothing and footwear, beverages, chemicals, cement. **Chief crops:** coffee, cut flowers, bananas, rice, tobacco, corn, sugarcane, cocoa beans, oilseed, vegetables. **Natural resources:** petroleum, nat. gas, coal, iron ore, nickel, gold, copper, emeralds, hydropower. **Water:** 48,840 cu m per capita. **Crude oil reserves:** 2.4 bil bbls. **Electricity prod.:** 57.8 bil kWh. **Labor force:** agric. 17%, industry 21%, services 62%. **Unemployment:** 10.5%.

Finance: Monetary unit: Peso (COP) (3,081.00 = $1 U.S.). **GDP:** $640.1 bil; **per capita GDP:** $13,400; **GDP growth:** 4.6%. **Imports:** $56.8 bil; U.S. 27.7%, China 17.5%, Mexico 9.3%. **Exports:** $55 bil; U.S. 31.8%, China 8.7%, Panama 5.7%, India 5.1%. **Tourism:** $3.9 bil. **Budget:** $120.2 bil. **Inflation:** 2.9%.

Transport: Railways: 543 mi. **Motor vehicles:** 92.7 per 1,000 pop. **Airports:** 121.

Communications: Telephone: 14.7 per 100 pop. **Mobile:** 113.1 per 100 pop. **Broadband:** 25.1 per 100 pop. **Internet:** 52.6%.

Health: Expend.: 6.8%. **Life expect.:** 72.3 male; 78.8 female. **Births:** 16.5 per 1,000 pop. **Deaths:** 5.4 per 1,000 pop. **Infant mortality:** 14.6 per 1,000 live births. **Undernourished:** 11.4%. **HIV:** 0.4%.

Education: Compulsory: ages 5-14. **Literacy:** 94.7%.

Embassy: 2118 Leroy Pl. NW 20008; 387-8338.

Website: wp.presidencia.gov.co

Spain subdued the local Indian kingdoms (Funza, Tunja) by the 1530s and ruled Colombia and neighboring areas as New Granada for 300 years. Independence was won by 1819. Venezuela and Ecuador broke away in 1829-30, and Panama withdrew in 1903.

Colombia has been plagued by rural and urban violence. "La Violencia" of 1948-58 claimed 200,000 lives; since 1989, political killings, kidnappings, and "disappearances" have victimized many thousands of civilians, and the internally displaced population was estimated by UNHCR at more than 6 mil as of the end of 2014. Government activity against local drug traffickers has sparked retaliation killings of politicians and judges.

Right-wing paramilitaries launched a campaign Dec. 22, 2000, against suspected left-wing guerrillas. Álvaro Uribe Vélez, a hardliner whose father had been killed by leftist rebels in 1983, won a presidential election May 2002. A wave of guerrilla violence as he took office led Uribe to declare a state of unrest Aug. 12, and police powers were increased as part of a new government offensive. The constitution was amended, Nov. 2004, to allow the president to seek a second consecutive term; Uribe easily won reelection May 2006. Key political figures, including major allies of Uribe, were arrested in 2007 on charges of colluding with paramilitary death squads. Former Defense Min. Juan Manuel Santos Calderón, a conservative ally of Uribe, won a presidential runoff election June 2010; he was reelected June 15, 2014. Peace talks with rebel groups began in Norway Oct. 2012 and shifted to Havana, Cuba, where, May 2013, an agreement to provide equal access to rural land for people of all economic levels was reached. Guerrilla violence continued, however. The government and the FARC rebel group announced a breakthrough in negotiations, Sept. 23, 2015, and pledged to complete a peace agreement in 6 months.

Since 2000, the U.S. has provided billions of dollars to Colombia to reduce farming of coca (used to make cocaine) and combat the drug trade. The Colombian government, May 14, 2015, halted a U.S.-backed program of aerial spraying of coca crops because of concerns the herbicide used could cause cancer.

Pope Francis, May 12, 2013, canonized Colombia's first saint, Laura of St. Catherine of Siena Montoya y Upegui, a 20th-cent. nun and spiritual adviser for the country's indigenous population.

Comoros

Union of the Comoros

People: Population: 780,971. **Age distrib.:** <15: 40.8%; 65+: 3.8%. **Growth:** 1.8%. **Migrants:** 1.7%. **Pop. density:** 905 per sq mi, 349.4 per sq km. **Urban:** 28.3%. **Ethnic groups:** Antalote, Cafre, Makoa, Oimatsaha, Sakalava. **Languages:** Arabic, French, Shikomoro (blend of Swahili and Arabic) (all official). **Religions:** Sunni Muslim 98%, Roman Catholic 2%.

Geography: Total area: 863 sq mi, 2,235 sq km; **Land area:** 863 sq mi, 2,235 sq km. **Location:** 3 islands—Grande Comore (Njazidja), Anjouan (Nzwani), and Moheli (Mwali)—in the Mozambique Channel between NW Madagascar and SE Africa. Nearest neighbor is Mozambique on W. **Topography:** Of volcanic origin; an active volcano on Grande Comore. **Arable land:** 47.3%. **Capital:** Moroni, 55,872 (2014).

Government: Type: Republic. **Head of state and gov.:** Pres. Ikililou Dhoinine; in office: May 26, 2011. **Local divisions:** 3 islands, 4 municipalities. **Defense budget/active troops:** NA.

Economy: Industries: fishing, tourism, perfume distillation. **Chief crops:** vanilla, cloves, ylang-ylang, coconuts, bananas, cassava. **Natural resources:** fish. **Water:** 1,633 cu m per capita. **Electricity prod.:** 43 mil kWh. **Labor force:** agric. 80%, industry and services 20%. **Unemployment:** 6.5%.

Finance: Monetary unit: Franc (KMF) (438.08 = $1 U.S.). **GDP:** $1.2 bil; **per capita GDP:** $1,500; **GDP growth:** 3.3%.

Imports: $235.8 mil; France 16.9%, Pakistan 15.8%, China 12.8%, UAE 11%, India 6.7%, Kenya 6.1%. **Exports:** $24.3 mil; India 15.1%, Singapore 15%, France 14.9%, Netherlands 12.9%, Turkey 11.9%, U.S. 5.7%, Saudi Arabia 5.4%. **Tourism:** $39 mil. **Budget:** $183.3 mil. **Inflation** (2012-13): 2.3%.

Transport: Airports: 4.

Communications: Telephone: 3.1 per 100 pop. **Mobile:** 50.9 per 100 pop. **Broadband:** 1.5 per 100 pop. **Internet:** 7%.

Health: Expend.: 4.5%. **Life expect.:** 61.6 male; 66.2 female. **Births:** 27.8 per 1,000 pop. **Deaths:** 7.6 per 1,000 pop. **Infant mortality:** 63.6 per 1,000 live births. **Undernourished:** NA. **HIV:** NA.

Education: Compulsory: ages 6-11. **Literacy:** 77.8%.

Permanent UN Mission: 866 UN Plz., Ste. 418, New York, NY 10017; (212) 750-1637.

Website: www.beit-salam.km

France acquired the islands from Muslim sultans, 1841-1909. The islands became a French overseas territory in 1947. In a 1974 referendum, all islands favored independence except Mayotte. The French National Assembly decided to allow each island to decide its own fate. The Comore Chamber of Deputies declared independence July 6, 1975, with Ahmed Abdallah as president. In a 1976 referendum, Mayotte voted to remain French.

A leftist regime that seized power from Abdallah in 1975 was deposed in a pro-French 1978 coup in which he regained the presidency. In Nov. 1989, Pres. Abdallah was assassinated; soon after, a multiparty system was instituted. A Sept. 1995 military coup, assisted by French mercenaries, ousted Pres. Said Mohamed Djohar. French troops invaded, Oct. 4, and forced coup leaders to surrender.

Anjouan and Moheli seceded from the Comoros in 1997. Unrest on Grande Comore culminated in a military coup, Apr. 1999. Anjouan endorsed secession in a disputed vote Jan. 2000. A constitution adopted in a referendum Dec. 2001 that went into effect the following year reunited Anjouan and Moheli with Grande Comore, granting each a semi-autonomous status and its own president.

Irregularities marred the Apr. 2002 runoff election for national president, won by Azali Assoumani, who led the 1999 coup. Ahmed Abdallah Mohamed Sambi won a presidential runoff vote, May 2006. After each of the 3 islands elected its own president in 2007, Col. Mohamed Bacar refused to relinquish power in Anjouan when the central government ruled his election illegal; he fled when Comorian and African Union troops took control of the island, Mar. 2008. Sambi's Vice Pres. Ikililou Dhoinine won a runoff election for national president Dec. 2010.

The heaviest rains in decades devastated some of the country's poorest areas Apr. 20-25, 2012, forcing government officials to request $19 mil in aid to facilitate recovery for some 65,000 people who were displaced and affected with waterborne diseases.

Congo

Democratic Republic of the Congo

(Congo, officially Democratic Republic of the Congo, is also known as Congo-Kinshasa. The Republic of the Congo, commonly called Congo Republic, is also known as Congo-Brazzaville.)

People: Population: 79,375,136. **Age distrib.:** <15: 42.7%; 65+: 2.6%. **Growth:** 2.5%. **Migrants:** 0.7%. **Pop. density:** 90.7 per sq mi, 35 per sq km. **Urban:** 42.5%. **Ethnic groups:** 200+ groups, majority Bantu. Four largest tribes (Mongo, Luba, Kongo [all Bantu], and Mangbetu-Azande [Hamitic]) 45% of pop. **Languages:** French (official), Lingala (lingua franca), Kingwana (Kiswahili or Swahili dialect), Kikongo, Tshiluba. **Religions:** Roman Catholic 50%, Protestant 20%, Kimbanguist 10%, Muslim 10%, other (incl. syncretic sects and indigenous beliefs) 10%.

Geography: Total area: 905,355 sq mi, 2,344,858 sq km; **Land area:** 875,312 sq mi, 2,267,048 sq km. **Location:** Central Africa. Republic of the Congo on W; Central African Republic, Sudan on N; Uganda, Rwanda, Burundi, Tanzania on E; Zambia, Angola on S. **Topography:** Includes the bulk of the Congo R. basin. Central region is a low-lying plateau covered by rain forest. Mountainous terraces in the W, savannas in the S and SE, grasslands toward the N, and Ruwenzori Mts. on the E. A short strip of territory borders the Atlantic O. **Arable land:** 3.1%. **Capital:** Kinshasa, 11,586,914. **Cities:** Lubumbashi, 2,015,091; Mbuji-Mayi, 2,006,641.

Government: Type: Republic. **Head of state:** Pres. Joseph Kabila; in office: Jan. 17, 2001. **Head of gov.:** Prime Min. Augustin Matata Ponyo Mapon; in office: Apr. 18, 2012. **Local divisions:** 10 provinces, 1 city. **Defense budget:** $456 mil. **Active troops:** 134,250.

Economy: Industries: mining, mineral proc., consumer prods., metal prods., processed foods and beverages, timber, cement. **Chief crops:** coffee, sugar, palm oil, rubber, tea, cotton, cocoa, quinine, cassava, bananas, plantains, peanuts, root crops, corn, fruits. **Natural resources:** cobalt, copper, niobium, tantalum, petroleum, diamonds, gold, silver, zinc, manganese, tin, uranium, coal, hydropower, timber. **Water:** 19,003 cu m per capita. **Crude oil reserves:** 180 mil bbls. **Electricity prod.:** 7.9 bil kWh. **Labor force:** NA. **Unemployment:** 8%.

Finance: Monetary unit: Franc (CDF) (916.00 = $1 U.S.). **GDP:** $55.8 bil; **per capita GDP:** $700; **GDP growth:** 9.1%. **Imports:** $9.8 bil; South Africa 20.7%, China 15.4%, Zambia 12.3%, Belgium 7.2%, Zimbabwe 5.2%. **Exports:** $10.1 bil; China 43.7%, Zambia 21.1%, Italy 11%. **Tourism:** $1 mil. **Budget:** $4.8 bil. **Inflation** (2012-13): 1.6%.

Transport: Railways: 2,490 mi. **Motor vehicles:** 23.9 per 1,000 pop. **Airports:** 26.

Communications: Telephone (2012): 0.1 per 100 pop. **Mobile:** 53.5 per 100 pop. **Broadband:** 3.2 per 100 pop. **Internet:** 3%.

Health: Expend.: 5.6%. **Life expect.:** 55.4 male; 58.5 female. **Births:** 34.9 per 1,000 pop. **Deaths:** 10.1 per 1,000 pop. **Infant mortality:** 71.5 per 1,000 live births. **Undernourished:** NA. **HIV:** 1.0%.

Education: Compulsory: ages 6-11. **Literacy:** 63.8%.

Embassy: 1726 M St. NW, Ste. 601, 20036; 234-7690.

Website: www.presidentrdc.cd

The earliest inhabitants of Congo may have been the pygmies, followed by Bantus from the east and Nilotic tribes from the north. The large Bantu Bakongo kingdom ruled much of Congo and Angola when Portuguese explorers visited in the 15th cent.

Leopold II, king of the Belgians, formed an international group to exploit the Congo region in 1876. In 1877, British explorer Henry M. Stanley traveled the Congo R, and in 1878 he returned to organize the region and win over the indigenous leaders. The Conference of Berlin, 1884-85, established the Congo Free State with Leopold as king and chief owner. The colony became known as the Belgian Congo in 1908. Millions of Congolese rubber plantation workers were exploited and others died under brutal European rule between 1880 and 1920.

Belgian and Congolese leaders agreed Jan. 27, 1960, that Congo would become independent in June. In the first general elections, May 31, Patrice Lumumba's party won a plurality in the National Assembly. The Republic of the Congo was proclaimed June 30. Europeans and others fled widespread violence. The UN Security Council, Aug. 9, called on Belgium to withdraw its troops and sent a UN contingent. Lumumba was dismissed as premier in Sept. and murdered Jan. 17, 1961. The last UN troops left the Congo June 30, 1964.

In late 1965, Gen. Joseph D. Mobutu was named president. He later changed his name to Mobutu Sese Seko and ruled as a dictator. The country became the Democratic Republic of the Congo (1966) and the Republic of Zaire (1971). Under Mobutu, economic decline and government corruption plagued the country. He retained power despite mounting international pressure and internal opposition.

During 1994, Zaire was inundated with refugees from the massive ethnic bloodshed in Rwanda. Ethnic violence spread to eastern Zaire in 1996. In Oct., militant Hutus, who dominated in the refugee camps, fought rebels (mostly Tutsis) in Zaire, precipitating intervention by government troops. As a result of the fighting, Rwandan refugees abandoned the camps; hundreds of thousands returned to Rwanda, while hundreds of thousands more were dispersed throughout eastern Zaire. The rebels, led by Gen. Laurent Kabila—a former Marxist and longtime opponent of Mobutu—began to move west across Zaire. On May 17, 1997, Kabila's troops entered Kinshasa, and Mobutu went into exile. The country again became the Dem. Rep. of the Congo. Mobutu died Sept. 7 in Morocco.

Kabila, who ruled by decree, alienated UN officials, international aid donors, and former allies. Rebels assisted by Rwanda and Uganda threatened Kinshasa in Aug. 1998 but were turned back with help from Angola, Namibia, and Zimbabwe. Rebel groups agreed to a cease-fire, Aug. 31, 1999, but the truce was widely violated. Kabila was assassinated Jan. 16, 2001, and was succeeded by his son Joseph.

The estimated death toll from the civil war and related causes was 3.3 mil through Nov. 2002. By then, Rwanda and Uganda had agreed to pull out their remaining troops. A power-sharing accord signed Apr. 2, 2003, led to the installation of a new Congolese government in July. A new constitution won legislative approval May 13, 2005. A UN peacekeeping force (MONUC), established in 1999, oversaw July 2006 elections, the nation's first multiparty vote since 1960. Kabila defeated former rebel leader Jean-Pierre Bemba in a presidential runoff election, Oct. 2006.

Hundreds reportedly died in Kinshasa, Mar. 22-23, 2007, in clashes between security forces and a militia loyal to Bemba, who fled to Europe. He was arrested in Belgium May 24, 2008, on war crimes charges; his trial at the Intl. Criminal Court (ICC) at The Hague was ongoing in Sept. 2015. A second trial, for witness tampering, began Sept. 29, 2015. A peace deal with militia groups in eastern Congo, including one led by Tutsi rebel Gen. Laurent Nkunda, was signed Jan. 23, 2008, but Nkunda launched a new offensive Aug. 28; Rwandan authorities arrested him Jan. 2009.

A June 2011 study published by the *American Journal of Public Health* estimated that more than 1,000 women were raped in

Congo every day. The ICC convicted Congolese warlord Thomas Lubanga Dyilo Mar. 2012 of war crimes for conscripting child soldiers during the country's civil war. The ICC, May 23, 2014, sentenced rebel leader Germain Katanga to 12 years in prison in connection with a 2003 massacre of more than 200 villagers.

The MONUC peacekeeping mission, reconstituted and renamed MONUSCO as of July 1, 2010, included almost 20,000 uniformed personnel on June 30, 2015. Eleven African nations signed a peace plan Feb. 24, 2013, designed to end the violence in Congo. Rebel leader Bosco Ntaganda turned himself in at the U.S. embassy in Rwanda Mar. 18, 2013, to face charges of war crimes and crimes against humanity; his trial at the ICC began Sept. 2, 2015. A peace agreement with the M23 militia group was reached in Dec. 2013. About 8,000 rebels laid down their arms by mid-Jan. 2014, but other fighters remained active.

An apparent outbreak of Ebola virus in northern Congo, reported to WHO Aug. 24, 2014, was not related to the Ebola epidemic then occurring in W Africa. By the time WHO declared the Congo outbreak ended Nov. 20, 2014, there had been 66 cases and 49 deaths.

Congo Republic

Republic of the Congo

(Congo Republic, officially Republic of the Congo, is also known as Congo-Brazzaville. The Democratic Republic of the Congo [formerly Zaire], now commonly called Congo or DRC, is also known as Congo-Kinshasa.)

People: Population: 4,755,097. **Age distrib.:** <15: 41.3%; 65+: 3%. **Growth:** 2%. **Migrants:** 9.7%. **Pop. density:** 36.1 per sq mi, 13.9 per sq km. **Urban:** 65.4%. **Ethnic groups:** Kongo 48%, Sangha 20%, M'Bochi 12%, Teke 17%, European, other 3%. **Languages:** French (official); Lingala, Monokutuba (lingua francas); many local langs., dialects (Kikongo most widespread). **Religions:** Roman Catholic 33.1%, Awakening Churches/Christian Revival 22.3%, Protestant 19.9%, none 11.3%.

Geography: Total area: 132,047 sq mi, 342,000 sq km; **Land area:** 131,854 sq mi, 341,500 sq km. **Location:** W central Africa. Gabon and Cameroon on W, Central African Republic on N, Dem. Rep. of the Congo on E, Angola on SW. **Topography:** Thick forests across much of country. A coastal plain leads to the fertile Niari Valley. The Congo R. basin consists of flood plains in the lower portion and savanna in the upper. **Arable land:** 1.6%. **Capital:** Brazzaville, 1,887,625.

Government: Type: Republic. **Head of state and gov.:** Pres. Denis Sassou-Nguesso; in office: Oct. 25, 1997. **Local divisions:** 12 departments. **Defense budget:** $720 mil. **Active troops:** 10,000.

Economy: Industries: petroleum extraction, cement, lumber, brewing, sugar, palm oil. **Chief crops:** cassava, sugar, rice, corn, peanuts, vegetables, coffee, cocoa. **Natural resources:** petroleum, timber, potash, lead, zinc, uranium, copper, phosphates, gold, magnesium, nat. gas, hydropower. **Water:** 187,050 cu m per capita. **Crude oil reserves:** 1.6 bil bbls. **Electricity prod.:** 1.3 bil kWh. **Labor force:** NA. **Unemployment:** 6.5%.

Finance: Monetary unit: Central African CFA Franc (XAF) (584.11 = $1 U.S.). **GDP:** $28 bil; **per capita GDP:** $6,600; **GDP growth:** 6%. **Imports:** $4.4 bil; China 19%, France 18.7%, Italy 6.2%, U.S. 5.5%, India 5.1%. **Exports:** $9 bil; China 53.8%, U.S. 11.1%, Australia 9.4%, France 5.3%. **Budget:** $6 bil. **Inflation** (2012-13): 6%.

Transport: Railways: 317 mi. **Motor vehicles:** 16.4 per 1,000 pop. **Airports:** 8.

Communications: Telephone: 0.4 per 100 pop. **Mobile:** 108.1 per 100 pop. **Broadband:** 10.5 per 100 pop. **Internet:** 7.1%.

Health: Expend.: 3.2%. **Life expect.:** 57.6 male; 60.0 female. **Births:** 35.9 per 1,000 pop. **Deaths:** 10.0 per 1,000 pop. **Infant mortality:** 57.9 per 1,000 live births. **Undernourished:** 31.5%. **HIV:** 2.8%.

Education: Compulsory: ages 6-15. **Literacy:** 79.3%.

Embassy: 1720 16th St. NW 20009; 726-5500.

Website: www.presidence.cg

The Loango kingdom flourished in the 15th cent., as did the Anzico kingdom of the Batekes; by the late 17th cent. they had weakened. By 1885, France controlled the region, then called the Middle Congo. The Republic of the Congo gained independence Aug. 15, 1960.

After trade unions sparked a 1963 coup, the country adopted a Marxist-Leninist stance, with the USSR and China vying for influence. France remained a dominant trade partner and source of technical assistance, and French-owned private enterprise retained a major economic role. In 1970, the country was renamed People's Republic of the Congo. Since the 1980s, oil has dominated the economy.

In 1990, Marxism was renounced and opposition parties were legalized. In 1991 the country's name was changed back to Rep. of the Congo, and a new constitution was approved. A democratically elected government came into office in 1992. Factional fighting broke out in Brazzaville, June 1997, and intensified during the summer, devastating the capital. Troops loyal to former Marxist dictator Denis Sassou-Nguesso took control of the city Oct. 15, 1997; he claimed lopsided victories in 2002 and 2009 presidential elections. His party won an absolute majority in the country's National Assembly, Aug. 5, 2012.

Costa Rica

Republic of Costa Rica

People: Population: 4,814,144. **Age distrib.:** <15: 23.1%; 65+: 7.3%. **Growth:** 1.2%. **Migrants:** 8.6%. **Pop. density:** 244.2 per sq mi, 94.3 per sq km. **Urban:** 76.8%. **Ethnic groups:** white or mestizo 83.6%, mulato 6.7%, indigenous 2.4%. **Languages:** Spanish (official), English. **Religions:** Roman Catholic 76.3%, Evangelical 13.7%, none 3.2%.

Geography: Total area: 19,730 sq mi, 51,100 sq km; **Land area:** 19,714 sq mi, 51,060 sq km. **Location:** Central America. Nicaragua on N, Panama on S. **Topography:** Tropical lowlands by the Caribbean. The interior plateau, at an elevation of about 4,000 ft, is temperate. **Arable land:** 4.8%. **Capital:** San José, 1,170,188.

Government: Type: Democratic republic. **Head of state and gov.:** Pres. Luis Guillermo Solís Rivera; in office: May 8, 2014. **Local divisions:** 7 provinces. **Defense budget:** $420 mil (paramilitary budget). **Active troops:** No armed forces. 9,800 paramilitary only.

Economy: Industries: medical equip., food proc., textiles and clothing, constr. materials, fertilizer, plastic prods. **Chief crops:** bananas, pineapples, coffee, melons, ornamental plants, sugar, corn, rice, beans, potatoes. **Natural resources:** hydropower. **Water:** 23,194 cu m per capita. **Electricity prod.:** 10.1 bil kWh. **Labor force:** agric. 14%, industry 22%, services 64%. **Unemployment:** 7.6%.

Finance: Monetary unit: Colon (CRC) (529.35 = $1 U.S.). **GDP:** $71 bil; **per capita GDP:** $14,900; **GDP growth:** 3.5%. **Imports:** $17.9 bil; U.S. 47.6%, Mexico 6.4%, China 6.1%, Japan 5.2%. **Exports:** $11.8 bil; U.S. 31.9%, China 12.6%, Mexico 9.3%, UK 8.6%, Hong Kong 5.2%, Netherlands 5.1%. **Tourism:** $2.9 bil. **Budget:** $9.7 bil. **Inflation:** 4.5%.

Transport: Railways: 173 mi (not in current use though some sections rehabilitated). **Motor vehicles:** 216.4 per 1,000 pop. **Airports:** 47.

Communications: Telephone: 17.8 per 100 pop. **Mobile:** 143.8 per 100 pop. **Broadband:** 72.9 per 100 pop. **Internet:** 49.4%.

Health: Expend.: 10.1%. **Life expect.:** 75.8 male; 81.2 female. **Births:** 15.9 per 1,000 pop. **Deaths:** 4.6 per 1,000 pop. **Infant mortality:** 8.5 per 1,000 live births. **Undernourished:** 5.9%. **HIV:** 0.3%.

Education: Compulsory: ages 5-14. **Literacy:** 97.8%.

Embassy: 2114 S St. NW 20008; 234-2945.

Website: presidencia.go.cr

Guaymi Indians inhabited the area when Spaniards arrived, 1502. Independence came in 1821. Costa Rica seceded from the Central American Federation in 1838. Since the civil war of 1948-49, free political institutions have been preserved.

Costa Rica, still a largely agricultural country, has achieved a relatively high standard of living, and land ownership is widespread. Tourism is an important source of revenue. Nobel Peace Prize-winner Óscar Arias Sánchez, president 1986-90, won a second term in a close election, Feb. 5, 2006. An election victory Feb. 7, 2010, made ruling party candidate Laura Chinchilla Miranda the nation's first female president. Luis Guillermo Solís Rivera of the opposition Citizen Action Party won an Apr. 6, 2014, runoff election and was sworn in as president May 8, 2014.

Côte d'Ivoire

Republic of Côte d'Ivoire

People: Population: 23,295,302. **Age distrib.:** <15: 37.9%; 65+: 3.3%. **Growth:** 1.9%. **Migrants:** 12%. **Pop. density:** 189.7 per sq mi, 73.3 per sq km. **Urban:** 54.2%. **Ethnic groups:** Akan 42.1%, Voltaique or Gur 17.6%, Northern Mande 16.5%, Krou 11%, Southern Mande 10%, other (incl. Lebanese, French) 2.8%. **Languages:** French (official), 60 native dialects (Dioula most widely spoken). **Religions:** Muslim 38.6%, Christian 32.8%, indigenous 11.9%, none 16.7%.

Geography: Total area: 124,504 sq mi, 322,463 sq km; **Land area:** 122,782 sq mi, 318,003 sq km. **Location:** S coast of W Africa. Liberia, Guinea on W; Mali, Burkina Faso on N; Ghana on E. **Topography:** Forests cover W half of country. A sparse inland plain leads to low mountains in NW. **Arable land:** 9.1%. **Capital:** Yamoussoukro (official), 258,962 (2014); Abidjan (de facto), 4,859,798.

Government: Type: Republic. **Head of state:** Pres. Alassane Ouattara; in office: Apr. 11, 2011 (sworn in Dec. 4, 2010). **Head of gov.:** Prime Min. Daniel Kablan Duncan; in office: Nov. 21, 2012. **Local divisions:** 12 districts, 2 autonomous districts. **Defense budget:** $812 mil. **Active troops:** 40,000 (target).

Economy: Industries: foodstuffs, beverages, wood prods., oil refining, gold mining, truck and bus assembly, textiles, fertilizer. **Chief crops:** coffee, cocoa beans, bananas, palm kernels, corn, rice, cassava, sweet potatoes, sugar, cotton, rubber. **Natural resources:** petroleum, nat. gas, diamonds, manganese, iron ore, cobalt, bauxite, copper, gold, nickel, tantalum, silica sand, clay, cocoa beans, coffee, palm oil, hydropower. **Water:** 4,142 cu m per capita. **Crude oil reserves:** 100 mil bbls. **Electricity prod.:** 6.7 bil kWh. **Labor force:** agric. 68%. **Unemployment:** 4%.

Finance: Monetary unit: CFA Franc (XOF) (584.11 = $1 U.S.). **GDP:** $71.1 bil; **per capita GDP:** $3,100; **GDP growth:** 7.5%. **Imports:** $9.8 bil; Nigeria 23.1%, France 12.1%, China 8.7%, Bahamas 6.4%. **Exports:** $14.6 bil; Ghana 8.8%, Netherlands 8.5%, Nigeria 8.4%, U.S. 6.8%, Germany 6.1%, Gabon 5.7%, France 5.1%. **Tourism:** $201 mil. **Budget:** $8.2 bil. **Inflation:** 0.5%.

Transport: Railways: 410 mi. **Motor vehicles:** 24.4 per 1,000 pop. **Airports:** 7.

Communications: Telephone: 1.2 per 100 pop. **Mobile:** 106.2 per 100 pop. **Broadband:** 1.7 per 100 pop. **Internet:** 14.6%.

Health: Expend.: 7.1%. **Life expect.:** 57.2 male; 59.5 female. **Births:** 28.7 per 1,000 pop. **Deaths:** 9.6 per 1,000 pop. **Infant mortality:** 58.7 per 1,000 live births. **Undernourished:** 14.7%. **HIV:** 3.5%.

Education: Compulsory: NA. **Literacy:** 43.1%.

Embassy: 2424 Massachusetts Ave. NW 20008; 797-0300.

Website: www.gouv.ci

A French protectorate from 1842, Côte d'Ivoire became independent in 1960. The name was officially changed from Ivory Coast, Oct. 1985.

Students and workers protested, Feb. 1990, demanding the ouster of longtime Pres. Félix Houphouët-Boigny. Côte d'Ivoire held its first multiparty presidential election Oct. 1990, which Houphouët-Boigny won. He died Dec. 7, 1993. The National Assembly named as successor Henri Konan Bédié. He was reelected Oct. 1995 but was ousted in a military coup Dec. 24, 1999. The coup leader, Robert Guéi, lost a presidential vote Oct. 2000 but claimed victory anyway. After mass protests, he fled, and Laurent Gbagbo became president. Guéi was killed in Abidjan Sept. 19, 2002.

Agreement on power sharing was reached in Mar. 2003, and Gbagbo and former rebel leaders declared an end to the war July 5. The country remained divided, however. Rebels held the north and government forces controlled the south. Under a new accord reached Mar. 2007, rebel leader Guillaume Soro became prime min.

Both Gbagbo and his main challenger, former Prime Min. Alassane Ouattara, claimed victory after a presidential runoff election Nov. 2010. Gbagbo clung to power, although the UN and much of the international community recognized Ouattara as the legitimate winner. A violent power struggle followed, claiming an estimated 1,500 lives and displacing at least 1 mil people. With support from French and UN forces, Ouattara loyalists captured Gbagbo in Abidjan, Apr. 2011. Human Rights Watch reported June 2 that after taking power, Ouattara's troops killed at least 149 suspected Gbagbo supporters. In 2013 and 2014 reports, Amnesty Intl. accused the army and its allies of killing and torturing Gbagbo loyalists. A UN peacekeeping mission (UNOCI), authorized since 2004, had almost 7,000 uniformed personnel in Côte d'Ivoire as of June 30, 2015. The ICC, June 12, 2014, ordered Gbagbo to stand trial for crimes against humanity; his trial was scheduled to begin Nov. 10, 2015. His wife, Simone Gbagbo, was sentenced, Mar. 10, 2015, by a Côte d'Ivoire court to 20 years in prison for her role in violence that followed elections in 2010.

Croatia

Republic of Croatia

People: Population: 4,464,844. **Age distrib.:** <15: 14.4%; 65+: 18.2%. **Growth:** –0.1%. **Migrants:** 17.6%. **Pop. density:** 206.6 per sq mi, 79.8 per sq km. **Urban:** 59%. **Ethnic groups:** Croat 90.4%, Serb 4.4%, other (incl. Bosniak, Hungarian, Slovene, Czech, Roma) 4.4%. **Languages:** Croatian (official), Serbian. **Religions:** Roman Catholic 86.3%, Orthodox 4.4%, not religious or atheist 3.8%.

Geography: Total area: 21,851 sq mi, 56,594 sq km; **Land area:** 21,612 sq mi, 55,974 sq km. **Location:** SE Europe, on the Balkan Peninsula. Slovenia, Hungary on N; Bosnia and Herzegovina, Serbia, Montenegro on E. **Topography:** Flat plains in NE; highlands, low mts. along Adriatic. **Arable land:** 16.1%. **Capital:** Zagreb, 686,902.

Government: Type: Parliamentary democracy. **Head of state:** Pres. Kolinda Grabar-Kitarovic; in office: Feb. 19, 2015. **Head of gov.:** Prime Min. Zoran Milanovic; in office: Dec. 23, 2011. **Local divisions:** 20 counties, 1 city with special county status. **Defense budget:** $774 mil. **Active troops:** 16,550.

Economy: Industries: chemicals and plastics, machine tools, fabricated metal, electronics. **Chief crops:** wheat, corn, barley, sugar beets, sunflower seeds, rapeseeds, alfalfa, clover, vegetables, fruits, grapes for wine. **Natural resources:** oil, coal, bauxite, iron ore, calcium, gypsum, nat. asphalt, silica, mica, clays, salt, hydropower. **Water:** 24,592 cu m per capita. **Crude oil reserves:** 71 mil bbls. **Electricity prod.:** 10 bil kWh. **Labor force:** agric. 1.9%, industry 27.6%, services 70.4%. **Unemployment:** 17.7%.

Finance: Monetary unit: Kuna (HRK) (6.72 = $1 U.S.). **GDP:** $88.5 bil; **per capita GDP:** $20,900; **GDP growth:** –0.4%. **Imports:** $22.7 bil; Italy 14.3%, Germany 13.6%, Slovenia 7.5%, Russia 7.1%, Austria 6.4%, China 6%. **Exports:** $13.8 bil; Italy 14.1%, Bosnia and Herzegovina 13.3%, Germany 11%, Slovenia 10.1%, Austria 6.2%. **Tourism:** $9.9 bil. **Budget:** $22.3 bil. **Inflation:** –0.2%.

Transport: Railways: 1,691 mi. **Motor vehicles:** 362.4 per 1,000 pop. **Airports:** 24.

Communications: Telephone: 36.7 per 100 pop. **Mobile:** 104.4 per 100 pop. **Broadband:** 66.1 per 100 pop. **Internet:** 68.6%.

Health: Expend.: 6.8%. **Life expect.:** 73.0 male; 80.4 female. **Births:** 9.5 per 1,000 pop. **Deaths:** 12.2 per 1,000 pop. **Infant mortality:** 5.8 per 1,000 live births. **Undernourished:** <5%. **HIV:** NA.

Education: Compulsory: ages 7-14. **Literacy:** 99.3%.

Embassy: 2343 Massachusetts Ave. NW 20008; 588-5899.

Website: www.vlada.hr

From the 7th cent. the area was inhabited by Croats, a south Slavic people. It was formed into a kingdom under Tomislav in 924, and joined with Hungary in 1102. The Croats became westernized and separated from Slavs under Austro-Hungarian influence. Croatia united with other Yugoslav areas to proclaim the Kingdom of Serbs, Croats, and Slovenes in 1918. A nominally independent state between 1941 and 1945, it became a constituent republic of Yugoslavia in the 1946 constitution.

On June 25, 1991, Croatia declared independence from Yugoslavia. Fighting began between ethnic Serbs and Croats. The Serbs gained control of some Croatian territory, but Croatian troops recaptured most of the Serb-held territory Aug. 1995. A peace accord was signed in Dec. The last Serb-held enclave, E Slavonia, was returned to Croatia in 1998. Croatia became a full NATO member Apr. 1, 2009, and joined the EU July 1, 2013.

Former Croatian Gen. Ante Gotovina was convicted by a UN tribunal Apr. 2011 and sentenced to 24 years in prison for war crimes committed in the mid-1990s. A UN tribunal convicted 6 Croats May 29, 2013, for ethnic cleansing of Bosnians during the 1990s. Conservative Kolinda Grabar-Kitarovic narrowly won a runoff election, Jan. 11, 2015, to become Croatia's first woman president. In Sept. 2015, tens of thousands of migrants and refugees—most trying to reach Northern Europe—began entering Croatia from Serbia, after Hungary tightened Serbian border controls Sept. 15.

Cuba

Republic of Cuba

People: Population: 11,031,433. **Age distrib.:** <15: 16%; 65+: 12.9%. **Growth:** –0.2%. **Migrants:** 0.1%. **Pop. density:** 260.2 per sq mi, 100.5 per sq km. **Urban:** 77.1%. **Ethnic groups:** white 64.1%, mestizo 26.6%, black 9.3%. **Languages:** Spanish (official). **Religions:** Roman Catholic (nominally, prior to 1959 revolution) 85%.

Geography: Total area: 42,803 sq mi, 110,860 sq km; **Land area:** 42,402 sq mi, 109,820 sq km. **Location:** In Caribbean, westernmost of West Indies. The Bahamas, U.S. to N; Mexico to W; Jamaica to S; Haiti to E. **Topography:** Coastline is about 2,500 mi. The N coast is steep and rocky, the S coast low and marshy. Low hills and fertile valleys cover more than half the country. Three mountain ranges. **Arable land:** 30.1%. **Capital:** Havana, 2,137,097.

Government: Type: Communist state. **Head of state and gov.:** Pres. Raúl Castro Ruz; in office: Feb. 24, 2008 (acting from July 31, 2006). **Local divisions:** 15 provinces, 1 special municipality. **Defense budget:** NA. **Active troops:** 49,000.

Economy: Industries: petroleum, nickel, cobalt, pharmaceuticals, tobacco, constr., steel, cement, agric. machinery, sugar. **Chief crops:** sugar, tobacco, citrus, coffee, rice, potatoes, beans. **Natural resources:** cobalt, nickel, iron ore, chromium, copper, salt, timber, silica, petroleum. **Water:** 3,384 cu m per capita. **Crude oil reserves:** 124 mil bbls. **Electricity prod.:** 17.4 bil kWh. **Labor force:** agric. 18%, industry 10%, services 72%. **Unemployment:** 3.2%.

Finance: Monetary unit: Peso (CUP) (26.50 = $1 U.S.). **GDP:** $128.5 bil; **per capita GDP** (2010): $10,200; **GDP growth:** 1.3%. **Imports:** $14.7 bil; Venezuela 37.4%, China 12.3%, Spain 9.4%. **Exports:** $5.6 bil; Canada 16%, China 15.2%, Venezuela 14.2%, Spain 7.5%, Netherlands 5.6%. **Tourism:** $2.3 bil. **Budget** (2013 est.): $2 bil. **Inflation:** NA.

Transport: Railways: 5,148 mi. **Motor vehicles:** 42.8 per 1,000 pop. **Airports:** 64.

Communications: Telephone: 11.2 per 100 pop. **Mobile:** 22.5 per 100 pop. **Broadband:** NA. **Internet:** 30%.

Health: Expend.: 8.6%. **Life expect.:** 76.1 male; 80.8 female. **Births:** 9.9 per 1,000 pop. **Deaths:** 7.7 per 1,000 pop. **Infant mortality:** 4.6 per 1,000 live births. **Undernourished:** <5%. **HIV:** 0.3%.

Education: Compulsory: ages 6-14. **Literacy:** 99.8%.

Embassy: 2630 16th St. NW 20009; 797-8518.

Website: www.cubagob.cu

Some 50,000 indigenous people lived in Cuba when Christopher Columbus reached it in 1492. Its name derives from the Indian word Cubanacan. Except for British occupation of Havana, 1762-63, Cuba remained Spanish until 1898. A slave-based sugar plantation economy developed from the 18th cent. Sugar remains a leading agricultural product. Spain failed to deliver on rights guaranteed in 1878, prompting a full-scale liberation movement under Jose Martí in 1895.

The Spanish-American War began Apr. 1898 with the sinking of the USS *Maine* in Havana harbor. Spain lost the war and gave up all claims to Cuba. U.S. troops withdrew in 1902, but under 1903 and 1934 agreements, the U.S. continued to lease a site at Guantánamo Bay in the SE as a naval base. U.S. and other foreign investors dominated the economy. In 1952, former Pres. Fulgencio Batista established a dictatorship, which grew increasingly harsh and corrupt. Fidel Castro began a rebellion in 1956. Batista fled Jan. 1, 1959, and Castro took power, becoming premier Feb. 16.

Government-instituted economic and social changes failed to restore promised liberties. Opponents were imprisoned or executed. Some 700,000 Cubans emigrated in the first years after Castro's takeover, mostly to the U.S. By 1960, all banks and industrial companies had been nationalized, including over $1-bil worth of U.S.-owned properties, mostly without compensation. U.S. economic sanctions became a complete trade embargo under legislation passed by Congress in 1961. The U.S. broke diplomatic relations with Cuba in Jan. 1961.

In Apr. 1961, some 1,400 Cubans, trained and backed by the U.S. Central Intelligence Agency, unsuccessfully tried to overthrow the regime. On Oct. 22, 1962, U.S. Pres. John F. Kennedy ordered a naval blockade around Cuba and demanded that Soviet-installed nuclear missiles be withdrawn. The crisis ended Oct. 28 when Soviet Prem. Nikita S. Khrushchev agreed to withdraw the missiles; the U.S. ended the blockade, pledged not to invade Cuba, and removed its own missiles from Turkey.

In 1977, Cuba and the U.S. agreed to exchange diplomats without restoring full ties. In 1978 and 1980, the U.S. agreed to accept political prisoners released by Cuba, some of whom were criminals and mental patients. A 1987 agreement provided for 20,000 Cubans to emigrate to the U.S. each year; Cuba agreed to take back some 2,500 jailed in the U.S. since 1980. Cuba's support for left-wing regimes and liberation movements in Central America, Africa, and the Caribbean contributed to poor relations with the U.S.

Cuba's economy, hobbled by U.S. sanctions and dependent on aid from other Communist countries, was shaken by the collapse of the Communist bloc in the late 1980s. Stiffer trade sanctions enacted by the U.S. in 1992 made things worse. Antigovernment demonstrations in Aug. 1994 prompted Castro to loosen emigration restrictions. A new U.S.-Cuba accord in Sept. ended the exodus of "boat people" after more than 30,000 had left Cuba. The U.S. also announced May 1995 it would admit 20,000 Cuban refugees held at Guantánamo but would return additional refugees to Cuba.

The U.S. imposed additional sanctions after Cuba, Feb. 1996, shot down two aircraft operated by anti-Castro exiles. Cuba blamed exile groups for bombings at Havana tourist hotels, July-Sept. 1997.

On July 31, 2006, the ailing Fidel Castro yielded power to his 75-year-old brother Raúl, who served as acting president until formally succeeding Feb. 24, 2008.

The U.S. in 2009 eased restrictions on remittances and family travel to the island but retained its trade embargo. The Cuban government announced, Sept. 2010, economic restructuring plans involving cutting more than 500,000 workers from the public payroll. A Communist Party conference, Apr. 2011, confirmed Raúl Castro as first secretary and approved economic reforms, including an expansion of private property rights and private ownership of some small businesses.

The U.S., Jan. 11, 2002, began using its naval base at Guantánamo Bay to detain prisoners captured in Afghanistan. The indefinite detention and aggressive interrogation of Guantánamo prisoners were criticized by human rights groups. U.S. Pres. Barack Obama signed, Jan. 2009, an executive order calling for the closure of the Guantánamo detention center within a year; as of Sept. 30, 2015, however, 114 detainees were still held there.

Landmark migration rules were enacted Jan. 14, 2013, allowing Cubans to remain overseas—including in the U.S.—longer without forfeiting their Cuban residency. Legislation to encourage foreign investment, in part by lowering taxes and allowing investment in more economic sectors, was adopted in Mar. 2014. Pres. Obama announced, Dec. 17, 2014, that the U.S. would restore full diplomatic relations with Cuba. Following the announcement, some travel and economic restrictions were eased. Relations were formally resumed July 20, 2015.

Cyprus

Republic of Cyprus

People: Population: 1,189,197. **Age distrib.:** <15: 15.6%; 65+: 11.5%. **Growth:** 1.4%. **Migrants:** 18.2%. **Pop. density:** 333.3 per sq mi, 128.7 per sq km. **Urban:** 66.9%. **Ethnic groups:** Greek 77%, Turkish 18%. **Languages:** Greek, Turkish (both official); English; Romanian; Russian; Bulgarian. **Religions:** Orthodox Christian 89.1%, Roman Catholic 2.9%, Protestant/Anglican 2%.

Geography: Total area: 3,572 sq mi, 9,251 sq km; **Land area:** 3,568 sq mi, 9,241 sq km. **Location:** Eastern Mediterranean Sea, off Turkish coast. Nearest neighbors are Turkey on N, Syria and Lebanon on E. **Topography:** Two mountain ranges run E-W, separated by a wide, fertile plain. **Arable land:** 9.9%. **Capital:** Nicosia (Lefkosia), 251,142 (2014).

Government: Type: Republic. **Head of state and gov.:** Pres. Nicos Anastasiades; in office: Feb. 28, 2013. **Local divisions:** 6 districts. **Defense budget:** $432 mil. **Active troops:** 12,000 (3,500 in territory where govt. does not exercise effective control).

Economy: Industries: tourism, food and beverage proc., cement and gypsum, ship repair and refurb., textiles, light chemicals, metal prods. **Chief crops:** citrus, vegetables, barley, grapes, olives, vegetables. **Natural resources:** copper, pyrites, asbestos, gypsum, timber, salt, marble, clay earth pigment. **Water:** 684 cu m per capita. **Electricity prod.:** 4.4 bil kWh. **Labor force:** agric. 3.9%, industry 16%, services 80.1%. **Unemployment:** 15.8%.

Finance: Monetary unit: Euro (EUR) (0.89 = $1 U.S.). **GDP:** $27.4 bil; **per capita GDP:** $30,800; **GDP growth:** –2.3%. **Imports:** $6.8 bil; Greece 23.6%, Israel 13.7%, Italy 7.1%, Germany 6.6%, UK 6.5%, France 6.4%, Netherlands 6.2%. **Exports:** $1.9 bil; Greece 17.6%, UK 14.6%. **Tourism:** $2.8 bil. **Budget:** $9.4 bil. **Inflation:** –1.4%.

Transport: Motor vehicles: 577.4 per 1,000 pop. **Airports:** 13.

Communications: Telephone: 28.4 per 100 pop. **Mobile:** 96.3 per 100 pop. **Broadband:** 32.3 per 100 pop. **Internet:** 69.3%.

Health: Expend.: 7.3%. **Life expect.:** 75.7 male; 81.5 female. **Births:** 11.4 per 1,000 pop. **Deaths:** 6.6 per 1,000 pop. **Infant mortality:** 8.4 per 1,000 live births. **Undernourished:** <5%. **HIV:** NA.

Education: Compulsory: ages 6-14. **Literacy:** 99.1%.

Embassy: 2211 R St. NW 20008; 462-5772.

Website: www.cyprus.gov.cy

The Ottoman Empire held Cyprus, 1571-1878, until it yielded control to Britain. Agitation for *enosis* (union) with Greece, which the Turkish minority opposed, increased after WWII and led to violence in 1955-56. In 1959, Britain, Greece, Turkey, and Cypriot leaders approved a plan for an independent republic, with constitutional guarantees for the Turkish minority and permanent division of offices on an ethnic basis.

Archbishop Makarios III was elected president, and full independence became final Aug. 16, 1960. Communal strife led the UN to send a peacekeeping force (UNFICYP) in 1964; its mandate was repeatedly renewed, and more than 900 UNFICYP uniformed personnel were in Cyprus as of June 30, 2015.

The Cypriot National Guard, led by officers from the Greek army, seized the government July 15, 1974. On July 20, Turkey invaded the island; Greece mobilized its forces but did not intervene. By Aug. 16, Turkish forces had occupied the northeastern 40% of the island.

Turkish Cyprus opened its border with Greek Cyprus Apr. 23, 2003, for the first time since partition. In separate referendums Apr. 2004, 65% of Turkish Cypriot voters accepted a UN-sponsored reunification plan, but 76% of Greek Cypriots rejected it. Still divided, Cyprus became a full member of the EU on May 1, 2004. It began using the euro as its currency in 2008. Dimitris Christofias won a 2008 runoff election, becoming the country's first Communist president. In a runoff election Feb. 24, 2013, the conservative candidate and head of the Democratic Rally party, Nicos Anastasiades, was voted Cyprus's new president.

In part because Cypriot banks held large amounts of Greek bonds, Cyprus suffered a banking crisis in 2013. The outline of a Cyprus bailout package was agreed upon Mar. 5, 2013, by the Intl. Monetary Fund, the European Central Bank, and eurozone countries. In exchange for $13 bil in IMF and EU assistance, Cyprus agreed to stringent banking reforms and economic austerity measures. Those with deposits of more than 100,000 euros in Cypriot banks lost some or all the money above that amount to help finance the restructuring of the banking system. Cyprus's GDP shrank in 2012, 2013, and 2014, and the 2014 unemployment rate was 16%. The economy showed some signs of improvement but remained stagnant in 2015.

Turkish Republic of Northern Cyprus

A declaration of independence was announced by Turkish-Cypriot leader Rauf Denktash, Nov. 15, 1983. The state is not internationally recognized but has trade relations with some countries. Denktash was succeeded as president by Mehmet Ali Talat (2005-10) and Dervis Eroglu (2010-15). Political moderate Mustafa Akinci defeated Eroglu in an Apr. 26, 2015, presidential runoff election. Akinci and Anastasiades met in May, and a new round of UN-sponsored reunification talks began in June. Area 1,295 sq mi; pop. (2011 census) 286,257, nearly all Turkish. Capital: Nicosia (Lefkosia). Local divisions: 5 districts. Active troops: 3,500. **Website:** www.kktcb.org

Czech Republic

People: Population: 10,644,842. **Age distrib.:** <15: 15%; 65+: 18%. **Growth:** 0.2%. **Migrants:** 4%. **Pop. density:** 356.9 per sq mi, 137.8 per sq km. **Urban:** 73%. **Ethnic groups:** Czech 64.3%, Moravian 5%. **Languages:** Czech (official), Slovak. **Religions:** Roman Catholic 10.4%, none 34.5%.

Geography: Total area: 30,451 sq mi, 78,867 sq km; **Land area:** 29,825 sq mi, 77,247 sq km. **Location:** E central Europe. Poland on N, Germany on N and W, Austria on S, Slovakia on E and SE. **Topography:** Bohemia, in W, is a plateau surrounded by mountains; Moravia is hilly. **Arable land:** 40.9%. **Capital:** Prague, 1,313,557.

Government: Type: Parliamentary democracy. **Head of state:** Pres. Milos Zeman; in office: Mar. 8, 2013. **Head of gov.:** Prime Min. Bohuslav Sobotka; in office: Jan. 29, 2014. **Local divisions:** 13 regions, 1 capital city. **Defense budget:** $2.09 bil. **Active troops:** 21,000.

Economy: Industries: motor vehicles, metallurgy, machinery and equip., glass, armaments. **Chief crops:** wheat, potatoes, sugar beets, hops, fruit. **Natural resources:** coal, kaolin, clay, graphite, timber. **Water:** 1,229 cu m per capita. **Crude oil reserves:** 15 mil bbls. **Electricity prod.:** 81.9 bil kWh. **Labor force:** agric. 2.6%, industry 37.4%, services 60%. **Unemployment:** 6.9%.

Finance: Monetary unit: Koruna (CZK) (24.07 = $1 U.S.). **GDP:** $314.6 bil; **per capita GDP:** $29,900; **GDP growth:** 2%. **Imports:** $135.1 bil; Germany 30.3%, Poland 8.2%, Slovakia 7.2%, China 5.8%, Netherlands 5.5%, Russia 5.1%. **Exports:** $147.3 bil; Germany 31.7%, Slovakia 9%, Poland 6%, France 5%. **Tourism:** $6.7 bil. **Budget:** $85.3 bil. **Inflation:** 0.3%.

Transport: Railways: 5,979 mi. **Motor vehicles:** 527.5 per 1,000 pop. **Airports:** 41.

Communications: Telephone: 17.6 per 100 pop. **Mobile:** 130 per 100 pop. **Broadband:** 62 per 100 pop. **Internet:** 79.7%.

Health: Expend.: 7.7%. **Life expect.:** 75.5 male; 81.6 female. **Births:** 9.6 per 1,000 pop. **Deaths:** 10.3 per 1,000 pop. **Infant mortality:** 2.6 per 1,000 live births. **Undernourished:** <5%. **HIV:** NA.

Education: Compulsory: ages 6-14. **Literacy:** 99%.

Embassy: 3900 Spring of Freedom St. NW 20008; 274-9100.

Website: www.czech.cz

Bohemia and Moravia were part of the Great Moravian Empire in the 9th cent. and later became part of the Holy Roman Empire. Under the kings of Bohemia, Prague in the 14th cent. was the cultural center of Central Europe. Bohemia and Hungary became part of Austria-Hungary.

In 1914-18, Thomas G. Masaryk and Eduard Benes formed a provisional government with the support of Slovak leaders, including Milan Stefanik. They proclaimed the Republic of Czechoslovakia Oct. 28, 1918.

By 1938, Nazi Germany had generated disaffection among German-speaking citizens in Sudetenland and demanded its cession. British Prime Min. Neville Chamberlain signed with Adolf Hitler at Munich, Sept. 30, 1938, an agreement to the cession, with a guarantee of peace by Hitler and Italian dictator Benito Mussolini. Germany occupied Sudetenland Oct. 1-2. Hitler on Mar. 15, 1939, dissolved Czechoslovakia, made protectorates of Bohemia and Moravia, and supported the autonomy of Slovakia, proclaimed independent Mar. 14, 1939.

Soviet troops with some Czechoslovak contingents entered eastern Czechoslovakia in 1944 and reached Prague in May 1945; Benes returned as president. In May 1946 elections, the Communist Party won 38% of the votes. In Feb. 1948, the Communists seized power in advance of scheduled elections. The country was renamed the Czechoslovak Socialist Republic. A harsh Stalinist period followed; all opposition was suppressed.

In Jan. 1968 a liberalization movement spread through Czechoslovakia. Long-time Stalinist ruler Antonin Novotny was deposed; the democrat Slovak Alexander Dubcek succeeded him. In July, the USSR and 4 Warsaw Pact nations demanded an end to liberalization. On Aug. 20, the Soviet, Polish, East German, Hungarian, and Bulgarian armies invaded Czechoslovakia. Despite demonstrations and riots by students and workers, press censorship was imposed and liberal leaders were ousted. On Apr. 17, 1969, Dubcek resigned as Communist Party leader and was succeeded by Gustav Husak. Censorship was tightened, and the Communist Party expelled a third of its members.

More than 700 leading Czechoslovak intellectuals and former party leaders signed a human rights manifesto in 1977, called Charter 77, prompting a renewed crackdown by the regime.

The police crushed a massive protest in Prague, Nov. 17, 1989. As protesters demanded free elections, the Communist Party leadership resigned Nov. 24; millions went on strike Nov. 27.

On Dec. 10, 1989, the first cabinet in 41 years without a Communist majority took power; Vaclav Havel, playwright and human rights campaigner, was chosen president, Dec. 29. In Mar. 1990 the country was officially renamed the Czech and Slovak Federal Republic. A Slovak-led coalition blocked Havel's bid to win reelection July 1992.

Slovakia declared sovereignty, July 17, 1992. Czech and Slovak leaders agreed, July 23, on a plan for a peaceful division of Czechoslovakia. It split into two separate states—the Czech Republic and Slovakia—Jan. 1, 1993. Havel was elected president of the Czech Republic on Jan. 26. The country became a full member of NATO in 1999.

Vaclav Klaus replaced the retiring Havel, 2003. The nation became a full EU member May 1, 2004. Inconclusive parliamentary elections, June 2006, led to a political deadlock, after which a minority center-right government took office Sept. 2006. Center-right parties made a strong showing in May 2010 parliamentary elections. In the country's first direct presidential election, former Social Democrat prime min. Milos Zeman was elected with more than 55% of the vote in a runoff election Jan. 26, 2013.

Heavy rains in early June 2013 caused massive flooding throughout central Europe, crippling Prague, where the Vitava R. overflowed its banks, submerging parts of the city. On June 4, the prime min. declared a state of emergency throughout the country.

A corruption scandal erupted June 13, 2013, with a police raid on government offices and the arrests of 7 parliamentarians, including the prime min.'s closest aide, causing Prime Min. Petr Necas to resign June 17. After Oct. 2013 elections, Social Democrat Bohuslav Sobotka, who had campaigned on increasing government spending to boost the economy, became prime min. Jan. 29, 2014.

Denmark

Kingdom of Denmark

People: Population: 5,581,503. **Age distrib.:** <15: 16.8%; 65+: 18.7%. **Growth:** 0.2%. **Migrants:** 9.9%. **Pop. density:** 340.7 per sq mi, 131.5 per sq km. **Urban:** 87.7%. **Ethnic groups:** Scandinavian, Inuit, Faroese, German, Turkish, Iranian, Somali. **Languages:** Danish, Faroese, Greenlandic, English (predominant second lang.). **Religions:** Evangelical Lutheran (official) 80%, Muslim 4%.

Geography: Total area: 16,639 sq mi, 43,094 sq km; **Land area:** 16,384 sq mi, 42,434 sq km. **Location:** Northern Europe, separating North and Baltic Seas. Germany on S, Norway on NW, Sweden on NE. **Topography:** Consists of the Jutland Peninsula and about 500 islands, 100 inhabited. Land is flat or gently rolling. **Arable land:** 57%. **Capital:** Copenhagen, 1,268,052.

Government: Type: Constitutional monarchy. **Head of state:** Queen Margretne II; in office: Jan. 14, 1972. **Head of gov.:** Prime Min. Helle Thorning-Schmidt; in office: Oct. 3, 2011. **Local divisions:** 5 regions. **Defense budget:** $4.81 bil. **Active troops:** 17,200.

Economy: Industries: iron, steel, nonferrous metals, chemicals, food proc., machinery and transp. equip., textiles and clothing, electronics, constr., furniture and other wood prods. **Chief crops:** barley, wheat, potatoes, sugar beets. **Natural resources:** petroleum, nat. gas, fish, salt, limestone, chalk, stone, gravel and sand. **Water:** 1,068 cu m per capita. **Crude oil reserves:** 611 mil bbls. **Electricity prod.:** 28.9 bil kWh. **Labor force:** agric. 2.6%, industry 20.3%, services 77.1%. **Unemployment:** 7%.

Finance: Monetary unit: Krone (DKK) (6.65 = $1 U.S.). **GDP:** $249.5 bil; **per capita GDP:** $44,300; **GDP growth:** 1%. **Imports:** $101.6 bil; Germany 21.3%, Sweden 13.2%, Netherlands 7.8%, Norway 6.8%, China 6%, UK 5.4%. **Exports:** $108.8 bil; Germany 17.3%, Sweden 12.4%, UK 8.9%, U.S. 6.2%, Norway 6.2%. **Tourism:** $7.3 bil. **Budget:** $197.5 bil. **Inflation:** 0.6%.

Transport: Railways: 1,500 mi. **Motor vehicles:** 499.6 per 1,000 pop. **Airports:** 28.

Communications: Telephone: 33.3 per 100 pop. **Mobile:** 126 per 100 pop. **Broadband:** 104 per 100 pop. **Internet:** 96%.

Health: Expend.: 11.2%. **Life expect.:** 76.8 male; 81.8 female. **Births:** 10.3 per 1,000 pop. **Deaths:** 10.3 per 1,000 pop. **Infant mortality:** 4.1 per 1,000 live births. **Undernourished:** <5%. **HIV:** 0.2%.

Education: Compulsory: ages 6-15. **Literacy:** 99%.

Embassy: 3200 Whitehaven St. NW 20008; 234-4300.

Website: www.denmark.dk

Most of the Viking raiders in the early Middle Ages were Danes. The Danish kingdom was a major power until the 17th cent., when it lost its land in southern Sweden. Norway was separated in 1815, and Schleswig-Holstein in 1864. Northern Schleswig was returned in 1920. Nazi Germany occupied Denmark, Apr. 1940-May 1945, but Danes helped more than 7,200 Jews escape to safety in Sweden, Sept. 1943. Voters ratified the Maastricht Treaty, enabling Denmark to join the EU, in May 1993.

The Danish newspaper *Jyllands-Posten* published, Sept. 30, 2005, cartoon images of the prophet Muhammad, offensive to Muslims; the caricatures, republished elsewhere, triggered violent protests and a boycott of Danish products in Islamic countries in early 2006. Danish police raids broke up alleged Islamist bomb plots Sept. 2006 and Sept. 2007. A car bomb blast linked to al-Qaeda killed 8 people outside Denmark's embassy in Islamabad, Pakistan, June 2, 2008.

A left-wing coalition won Sept. 2011 parliamentary elections, and Helle Thorning-Schmidt, a Social Democrat, became Denmark's first female prime min. Oct. 3. A bill granting marriage rights to same-sex couples was voted into law, June 7, 2012. A Danish man of Middle Eastern ancestry suspected of terrorist shootings that left two dead in Copenhagen, Feb. 14, 2015, was killed in a shootout with police Feb. 15. A center-right coalition returned to power in June 2015 elections in which the anti-immigration Danish People's Party won 21% of the vote.

The **Faroe Islands** in the N Atlantic, about 300 mi NW of the Shetlands, and 850 mi from Denmark proper, 18 inhabited, have an area of 538 sq mi and pop. (2014 est.) of 49,947. They are an administrative division of Denmark, self-governing in most matters. Capital: Torshavn; pop. (2014 est.) 20,646. Fish is a primary export. **Website:** www.government.fo

Greenland (Kalaallit Nunaat)

Greenland, an island between the North Atlantic and the Polar Sea, is separated from the North American continent by Davis Strait and Baffin Bay. Total area is 836,330 sq mi, about 80% of which is ice-capped. Most of the island is a lofty plateau 9,000-10,000 ft in elevation. The average thickness of the cap is 1,000 ft. Scientists point to accelerated melting of Greenland's ice sheet in recent years as evidence of global warming. The pop. (2015 est.) is 57,733. About 88% of the pop. in 2010 were Inuit. Under the 1953 Danish constitution the colony became an integral part of the realm with representatives in the Folketing (Danish legislature). The Danish parliament, 1978, approved home rule for Greenland, effective May 1, 1979. With home rule, Greenlandic place names came into official use. The technically correct name for Greenland is Kalaallit Nunaat. The official name for its capital is Nuuk (2014 est. pop., 16,911), rather than Godthab. The labor force is distributed as follows: agric. 13.9%, industry 19.2%, services 67%. Fish is the principal export (about 89% of exports in 2010). Other natural resources include coal, iron ore, lead, zinc, molybdenum, diamonds, gold, and platinum. **Website:** naalakkersuisut.gl

Djibouti

Republic of Djibouti

People: Population: 828,324. **Age distrib.:** <15: 32.3%; 65+: 3.6%. **Growth:** 2.2%. **Migrants:** 14.2%. **Pop. density:** 92.6 per sq mi, 35.7 per sq km. **Urban:** 77.3%. **Ethnic groups:** Somali 60%, Afar 35%, other (incl. French, Arab, Ethiopian, Italian) 5%. **Languages:** French, Arabic (both official); Somali; Afar. **Religions:** Muslim 94%, Christian 6%.

Geography: Total area: 8,958 sq mi, 23,200 sq km; **Land area:** 8,950 sq mi, 23,180 sq km. **Location:** E coast of Africa, separated from Arabian Peninsula by strategically vital strait of Bab el-Mandeb. Ethiopia on W and SW, Eritrea on NW, Somalia on SE. **Topography:** Low coastal plain with mountains behind and an interior plateau. Arid, sandy, and desolate. Hot and dry climate. **Arable land:** 0.1%. **Capital:** Djibouti, 528,627.

Government: Type: Republic. **Head of state:** Pres. Ismail Omar Guelleh; in office: May 8, 1999. **Head of gov.:** Prime Min. Abdoulkader Kamil Mohamed; in office: Apr. 1, 2013. **Local divisions:** 6 districts. **Defense budget** (2013): $10 mil. **Active troops:** 10,450.

Economy: Industries: constr., agric. proc., shipping. **Chief crops:** fruits, vegetables. **Natural resources:** potential geothermal power, gold, clay, granite, limestone, marble, salt, diatomite, gypsum, pumice, petroleum. **Water:** 344 cu m per capita. **Electricity prod.:** 335 mil kWh. **Labor force:** NA. **Unemployment:** NA.

Finance: Monetary unit: Franc (DJF) (177.00 = $1 U.S.). **GDP:** $2.9 bil; **per capita GDP:** $3,100; **GDP growth:** 6%. **Imports:** $612.1 mil; China 27.3%, Saudi Arabia 16.4%, India 9.7%, Indonesia 7.7%. **Exports:** $119.5 mil; Somalia 81.2%. **Tourism:** $22 mil. **Budget:** $647.7 mil. **Inflation** (2012-13): 2.4%.

Transport: Railways: 62 mi (largely inoperable; Djibouti segment of railway jointly controlled with Ethiopia). **Airports:** 3.

Communications: Telephone: 2.5 per 100 pop. **Mobile:** 32.4 per 100 pop. **Broadband:** NA. **Internet:** 10.7%.

Health: Expend.: 8.8%. **Life expect.:** 60.3 male; 65.4 female. **Births:** 23.7 per 1,000 pop. **Deaths:** 7.7 per 1,000 pop. **Infant mortality:** 48.7 per 1,000 live births. **Undernourished:** 18.9%. **HIV:** 1.6%.

Education: Compulsory: ages 6-15. **Literacy:** NA.

Embassy: 1156 15th St. NW, Ste. 515, 20005; 331-0270.

Website: www.presidence.dj

France gained control of the territory in stages between 1862 and 1900. As French Somaliland, it became an overseas French territory in 1945; in 1967 it was renamed the French Territory of the Afars and the Issas. Ethiopia and Somalia renounced their claims to the area, but each accused the other of trying to gain control. There were clashes between Afars (ethnically related to Ethiopians) and Issas (related to Somalis) in 1976. Immigrants from both countries continued to enter Djibouti until independence on June 27, 1977.

Post-independence economic support has come from France, Arab countries, the U.S., and China. A peace accord Dec. 1994 ended a 3-year Afar rebel uprising. Drought in 2007-11 devastated crops and livestock. Protests associated with the Arab Spring broke out in late Jan. 2011 demanding the resignation of Pres. Ismail Omar Guelleh. Authorities suppressed the protests, and Guelleh won a third term in an Apr. 2011 election boycotted by the main opposition. The U.S. announced, May 5, 2014, the signing of a new 20-year lease for its military base in Djibouti, used for anti-terrorism and other military operations in the Middle East and Africa. Guelleh stated, May 2015, that his government was negotiating with China for the establishment of a Chinese naval base in Djibouti.

Dominica

Commonwealth of Dominica

People: Population: 73,607. **Age distrib.:** <15: 22%; 65+: 10.7%. **Growth:** 0.2%. **Migrants:** 8.9%. **Pop. density:** 253.8 per sq mi, 98 per sq km. **Urban:** 69.5%. **Ethnic groups:** black 86.6%, mixed 9.1%, indigenous 2.9%. **Languages:** English (official), French patois. **Religions:** Roman Catholic 61.4%, Protestant 20.6% (incl. Evangelical 6.7%, Seventh-day Adventist 6.1%), none 6.1%.

Geography: Total area: 290 sq mi, 751 sq km; **Land area:** 290 sq mi, 751 sq km. **Location:** E Caribbean, most northerly Windward Isl. Guadeloupe to N, Martinique to S (both French terr.). **Topography:** Central ridge runs N-S, terminating in cliffs. Volcanic in origin, with numerous thermal springs. **Arable land:** 8%. **Capital:** Roseau, 14,994 (2014).

Government: Type: Parliamentary democracy. **Head of state:** Pres. Charles A. Savarin; in office: Oct. 2, 2013. **Head of gov.:** Prime Min. Roosevelt Skerrit; in office: Jan. 8, 2004. **Local divisions:** 10 parishes. **Defense budget/active troops:** NA.

Economy: Industries: soap, coconut oil, tourism, copra, furniture, cement blocks, shoes. **Chief crops:** bananas, citrus, mangoes, root crops, coconuts, cocoa. **Natural resources:** timber, hydropower. **Water:** 2,778 cu m per capita. **Electricity prod.:** 96.5 mil kWh. **Labor force:** agric. 40%, industry 32%, services 28%. **Unemployment:** NA.

Finance: Monetary unit: East Caribbean Dollar (XCD) (2.70 = $1 U.S.). **GDP:** $764 mil; **per capita GDP:** $10,800; **GDP growth:** 1.1%. **Imports:** $186.9 mil; Japan 36.3%, U.S. 16.7%, Trinidad and Tobago 15.4%. **Exports:** $38.6 mil; Japan 41.6%, Jamaica 9.4%, Antigua and Barbuda 8.7%, Guyana 7.3%. **Tourism:** $75 mil. **Budget** (2013 est.): $185.2 mil. **Inflation:** 0.8%.

Transport: Airports: 2.

Communications: Telephone: 24.3 per 100 pop. **Mobile:** 127.5 per 100 pop. **Broadband:** NA. **Internet:** 62.9%.

Health: Expend.: 5.9%. **Life expect.:** 73.8 male; 79.9 female. **Births:** 15.4 per 1,000 pop. **Deaths:** 7.9 per 1,000 pop. **Infant mortality:** 11.3 per 1,000 live births. **Undernourished:** NA. **HIV:** NA.

Education: Compulsory: ages 5-16. **Literacy:** NA.

Embassy: 3216 New Mexico Ave. NW 20016; 364-6781.

Website: www.dominica.gov.dm

A British colony since 1805, Dominica was granted self-government in 1967. Independence was achieved Nov. 3, 1978.

Hurricane David struck, Aug. 30, 1979, devastating the island and destroying the banana plantations, Dominica's economic mainstay. Coups were attempted in 1980 and 1981. Prime Min. Pierre Charles died Jan. 6, 2004, and was succeeded by Roosevelt Skerrit. Charles A. Savarin was sworn in as Dominica's eighth pres., Oct. 2, 2013. Tropical storm Erika, Aug. 27, 2015, killed at least 31 and caused widespread damage.

Dominican Republic

People: Population: 10,478,756. **Age distrib.:** <15: 27.5%; 65+: 7.2%. **Growth:** 1.2%. **Migrants:** 3.9%. **Pop. density:** 561.7 per sq mi, 216.9 per sq km. **Urban:** 79%. **Ethnic groups:** mixed 73%, white 16%, black 11%. **Languages:** Spanish (official). **Religions:** Roman Catholic 95%.

Geography: Total area: 18,792 sq mi, 48,670 sq km; **Land area:** 18,656 sq mi, 48,320 sq km. **Location:** W Indies, sharing isl. of Hispaniola with Haiti on W., Puerto Rico (U.S.) to E. **Topography:** The Cordillera Central range crosses center, rising to over 10,000 ft, highest in the Caribbean. Cibao Valley to N. **Arable land:** 16.6%. **Capital:** Santo Domingo, 2,945,353.

Government: Type: Democratic republic. **Head of state and gov.:** Pres. Danilo Medina Sánchez; in office: Aug. 16, 2012. **Local divisions:** 10 regions. **Defense budget:** $397 mil. **Active troops:** 46,000.

Economy: Industries: tourism, sugar proc., gold mining, textiles, cement, tobacco. **Chief crops:** cocoa, tobacco, sugarcane, coffee, cotton, rice, beans, potatoes, corn, bananas. **Natural resources:** nickel, bauxite, gold, silver. **Water:** 2,259 cu m per capita. **Electricity prod.:** 13.9 bil kWh. **Labor force:** agric. 14.4%, industry 20.8%, services 64.7%. **Unemployment:** 14.9%.

Finance: Monetary unit: Peso (DOP) (44.90 = $1 U.S.). **GDP:** $138 bil; **per capita GDP:** $13,000; **GDP growth:** 7.3%. **Imports:** $17 bil; U.S. 44.7%, Venezuela 7.8%, China 6.5%, Mexico 6.3%. **Exports:** $10.1 bil; U.S. 38.9%, Haiti 16%, Canada 11.9%. **Tourism:** $5.6 bil. **Budget:** $11.8 bil. **Inflation:** 3%.

Transport: Railways: 308 mi. **Motor vehicles:** 147.8 per 1,000 pop. **Airports:** 16.

Communications: Telephone: 11.6 per 100 pop. **Mobile:** 78.9 per 100 pop. **Broadband:** 25.8 per 100 pop. **Internet:** 49.6%.

Health: Expend.: 5.4%. **Life expect.:** 75.8 male; 80.3 female. **Births:** 18.7 per 1,000 pop. **Deaths:** 4.6 per 1,000 pop. **Infant mortality:** 18.8 per 1,000 live births. **Undernourished:** 14.7%. **HIV:** 1.0%.

Education: Compulsory: ages 5-13. **Literacy:** 91.8%.

Embassy: 1715 22nd St. NW 20008; 332-6280.

Website: www.presidencia.gov.do

Carib and Arawak Indians inhabited the island of Hispaniola when Christopher Columbus landed in 1492. The city of Santo Domingo, founded 1496, is the oldest European settlement in the Western Hemisphere.

France took over the western third of the island (now Haiti) in 1697 and Santo Domingo in 1795. Spain returned intermittently 1803-21, as several native republics came and went. Haiti ruled again, 1822-44; Spanish occupation occurred 1861-63. U.S. Marines occupied the country 1916-24.

In 1930, Gen. Rafael Leonidas Trujillo Molina was elected president. The brutal Trujillo era ended with his assassination in 1961. Pres. Joaquín Balaguer, appointed by Trujillo in 1960, resigned under pressure in 1962.

Juan Bosch, elected president in the first free elections in 38 years, was overthrown in 1963. On Apr. 24, 1965, Bosch's followers and others, including a few Communists, launched a revolt. Four days later U.S. Marines intervened against pro-Bosch forces. A provisional government supervised a June 1966 election in which Balaguer defeated Bosch. Balaguer remained in office for most of the next 28 years, but his May 1994 reelection was widely denounced as fraudulent. He called for new elections but did not run, and Leonel Fernández Reyna was elected June 1996.

The leftist candidate, Hipólito Mejía, won a presidential vote in 2000. With the nation reeling from a banking scandal and soaring inflation, Fernández defeated Mejía in 2004, and he was reelected in 2008. Danilo Medina Sánchez, Fernández's ally, was elected in 2012.

The Constitutional Court ruled, Sept. 23, 2013, that people born in the Dominican Republic after 1929 whose parents were undocumented immigrants were not entitled to Dominican citizenship. The decision affected perhaps 200,000 people or more, most of Haitian descent. May 2014 legislation provided a path to citizenship for such people if they completed an application process by June 17, 2015; most did not. In 2015, the government also required undocumented immigrants—estimated at more than 500,000, most of them Haitian—to register by June 17 or face deportation; about half had not registered by the deadline. The government said it was not immediately beginning large-scale deportations, but in the weeks after the deadline, tens of thousands of Haitians left the country.

East Timor

See Timor-Leste.

Ecuador

Republic of Ecuador

People: Population: 15,868,396. **Age distrib.:** <15: 28%; 65+: 7.1%. **Growth:** 1.4%. **Migrants:** 2.3%. **Pop. density:** 148.5 per sq mi, 57.3 per sq km. **Urban:** 63.7%. **Ethnic groups:** mestizo (mixed Amerindian/white) 71.9%, Montubio 7.4%, Amerindian 7%, white 6.1%, Afroecuadorian 4.3%. **Languages:** Spanish or Castilian (official), Quechua. **Religions:** Roman Catholic 74%, Evangelical 10.4%, atheist 7.9%.

Geography: Total area: 109,484 sq mi, 283,561 sq km; **Land area:** 106,889 sq mi, 276,841 sq km. **Location:** NW S America, on Pacific coast, astride the equator. Colombia on N, Peru on E and S. **Topography:** Two ranges of Andes run N-S, splitting country into 3 zones: hot, humid lowlands on coast; temperate highlands between ranges; and rainy, tropical lowlands to E. **Arable land:** 4.6%. **Capital:** Quito, 1,726,075. **Cities:** Guayaquil, 2,709,329.

Government: Type: Republic. **Head of state and gov.:** Pres. Rafael Correa; in office: Jan. 15, 2007. **Local divisions:** 24 provinces. **Defense budget:** $1.7 bil. **Active troops:** 58,000.

Economy: Industries: petroleum, food proc., textiles, wood prods., chemicals. **Chief crops:** bananas, coffee, cocoa, rice, potatoes, cassava, plantains, sugarcane. **Natural resources:** petroleum, fish, timber, hydropower. **Water:** 29,063 cu m per capita. **Crude oil reserves:** 8.8 bil bbls. **Electricity prod.:** 22.1 bil kWh. **Labor force:** agric. 27.8%, industry 17.8%, services 54.4%. **Unemployment:** 4.2%.

Finance: Monetary unit: U.S. Dollar (USD). **GDP:** $180.2 bil; **per capita GDP:** $11,200; **GDP growth:** 3.6%. **Imports:** $26.4 bil; U.S. 29.2%, China 12.9%, Colombia 8.5%, Panama 6.8%. **Exports:** $27.3 bil; U.S. 44.6%, Chile 9.9%, Peru 7.5%. **Tourism:** $1.5 bil. **Budget:** $44.7 bil. **Inflation:** 3.6%.

Transport: Railways: 600 mi. **Motor vehicles:** 92.6 per 1,000 pop. **Airports:** 104.

Communications: Telephone: 15.3 per 100 pop. **Mobile:** 103.9 per 100 pop. **Broadband:** 26.7 per 100 pop. **Internet:** 43%.

Health: Expend.: 6.4%. **Life expect.:** 73.6 male; 79.7 female. **Births:** 18.5 per 1,000 pop. **Deaths:** 5.1 per 1,000 pop. **Infant mortality:** 17.4 per 1,000 live births. **Undernourished:** 11.2%. **HIV:** 0.3%.

Education: Compulsory: ages 3-17. **Literacy:** 94.5%.

Embassy: 2535 15th St. NW 20009; 234-7200.

Website: www.presidencia.gob.ec

The region, which was the northern Inca empire, was conquered by Spain in 1533. Liberation forces defeated the Spanish May 24, 1822, near Quito. Ecuador became part of the Great Colombia Republic but seceded, May 13, 1830.

Ecuadoran indigenous peoples, demanding greater rights, staged protests in the 1990s. A border war with Peru flared Jan. 26-Mar. 1, 1995. Elected president, July 1996, Abdalá Bucaram—a populist known as El Loco, or "The Crazy One"—imposed stiff price increases and other austerity measures. His rising unpopularity and erratic behavior led the National Congress, Feb. 1997, to dismiss him for "mental incapacity."

Jamil Mahuad Witt won a presidential runoff election July 1998. In Sept. 1998 and Mar. 1999 he imposed emergency measures to cope with a continuing economic crisis. Opposed by Indian groups and military leaders, he was ousted Jan. 2000, and succeeded by Vice Pres. Gustavo Noboa Bejarano. Noboa enacted a plan introduced by Mahuad to replace the sucre with the U.S. dollar as Ecuador's currency. Lucio Gutiérrez Borbúa, a leader in the 2000 coup, won a presidential runoff Nov. 2002. Noboa, under investigation for financial mismanagement, went into exile Aug. 2003.

Gutiérrez imposed economic austerity measures, purged opponents from the supreme court, Dec. 2004, and then dissolved the court, Apr. 15, 2005. With street protests rising, Congress ousted Gutiérrez Apr. 20, and Vice Pres. Alfredo Palacio González became president. The U.S. suspended free-trade talks after Ecuador, May 2006, took over oil assets belonging to U.S.-based Occidental Petroleum.

Rafael Correa, a left-wing economist, won a presidential runoff vote Nov. 2006. He won voter approval, Apr. 2007, to convene an assembly to rewrite the constitution. The revised constitution was approved in a national referendum Sept. 2008. Early in his term, when oil revenues were high, he boosted development spending and aid to poor families; later, as oil prices dropped, he restricted imports to prevent an outflow of dollars and, Dec. 2008, allowed Ecuador to default on part of its $10 bil foreign debt.

Correa, reelected Apr. 2009, pressured foreign oil companies in 2010 to renegotiate contracts to increase the government's share of mineral revenues. A confrontation Sept. 30, 2010, between Correa and rebellious police officers led to a shootout between government troops and police; 5 people were killed and at least 38 wounded. An Ecuadoran judge Feb. 14, 2011, ordered Chevron (which had absorbed Texaco in 2001) to pay $9.5 bil to clean up oil pollution from Texaco operations in Ecuador, 1965-92; Chevron disputed the ruling and opposed collection efforts in courts in various countries. Ecuador granted asylum, Aug. 16, 2012, to Julian Assange, the founder of WikiLeaks. Assange had been in Ecuador's UK embassy in London since June 19, avoiding extradition to Sweden from Britain. He remained in the embassy as of mid-2015.

Correa was reelected Feb. 17, 2013, becoming Ecuador's longest-serving president. Beginning in 2013, his government encouraged new exploration for oil and other mineral resources in the Amazon. During a July 2015 visit to Ecuador, Pope Francis called for increased protection of the Amazon and the region's indigenous peoples.

The **Galápagos Islands**, pop. (2008 est.) 30,000, about 600 mi to the W, are the home of huge tortoises and other unusual animals. The oil tanker *Jessica* ran aground Jan. 16, 2001, off San Cristóbal Isl., spilling some 185,000 gallons of fuel.

Egypt

Arab Republic of Egypt

People: Population: 88,487,396. **Age distrib.:** <15: 31.9%; 65+: 5.2%. **Growth:** 1.8%. **Migrants:** 0.4%. **Pop. density:** 230.2 per sq mi, 88.9 per sq km. **Urban:** 43.1%. **Ethnic groups:** Egyptian 99.6%. **Languages:** Arabic (official), English and French widely understood by educated classes. **Religions:** Muslim (predom. Sunni) 90%, Christian (most Coptic Orthodox) 10%.

Geography: Total area: 386,662 sq mi, 1,001,450 sq km; **Land area:** 384,345 sq mi, 995,450 sq km. **Location:** NE corner of Africa. Libya on W; Sudan on S; Israel, Gaza Strip on E. **Topography:** Almost entirely desolate and barren with hills and mountains in E and along Nile. Most people live in 550-mi-long Nile Valley. **Arable land:** 2.8%. **Capital:** Cairo, 18,771,769. **Cities:** Alexandria, 4,777,677.

Government: Type: Republic. **Head of state:** Pres. Abdel Fattah al-Sisi; in office: June 8, 2014. **Head of gov.:** Prime Min. Sherif Ismail; in office: Sept. 19, 2015. **Local divisions:** 27 governorates. **Defense budget:** $5.45 bil. **Active troops:** 438,500.

Economy: Industries: textiles, food proc., tourism, chemicals, pharmaceuticals, hydrocarbons, constr., cement, metals, light manufactures. **Chief crops:** cotton, rice, corn, wheat, beans, fruits, vegetables. **Natural resources:** petroleum, nat. gas, iron ore, phosphates, manganese, limestone, gypsum, talc, asbestos, lead, rare earth elements, zinc. **Water:** 711 cu m per capita. **Crude oil reserves:** 4.4 bil bbls. **Electricity prod.:** 155.3 bil kWh. **Labor force:** agric. 29%, industry 24%, services 47%. **Unemployment:** 12.7%.

Finance: Monetary unit: Pound (EGP) (7.83 = $1 U.S.). **GDP:** $943.1 bil; **per capita GDP:** $10,900; **GDP growth:** 2.2%. **Imports:** $55.3 bil; China 12.5%, U.S. 7.8%, Italy 5.4%, Ukraine 5.1%. **Exports:** $27.2 bil; Italy 6.7%, India 6.5%, Saudi Arabia 6.1%, China 5%. **Tourism:** $7.2 bil. **Budget:** $99.1 bil. **Inflation:** 10.2%.

Transport: Railways: 3,160 mi. **Motor vehicles:** 55.4 per 1,000 pop. **Airports:** 72.

Communications: Telephone: 7.6 per 100 pop. **Mobile:** 114.3 per 100 pop. **Broadband:** 31.1 per 100 pop. **Internet:** 31.7%.

Health: Expend.: 5%. **Life expect.:** 71.1 male; 76.5 female. **Births:** 22.9 per 1,000 pop. **Deaths:** 4.8 per 1,000 pop. **Infant mortality:** 21.6 per 1,000 live births. **Undernourished:** <5%. **HIV:** <0.1%.

Education: Compulsory: ages 6-14. **Literacy:** 73.8%.

Embassy: 3521 International Ct. NW 20008; 895-5400.

Website: www.egypt.gov.eg

Archaeological records of ancient Egyptian civilization date back to 4000 BCE. A unified kingdom arose around 3200 BCE and extended south into Nubia and as far north as Syria. A high culture of rulers and priests was built on an economic base of serfdom, fertile soil, and annual flooding of the Nile.

Imperial decline facilitated conquest by Asian invaders (Hyksos, Assyrians). The last native dynasty fell in 341 BCE to the Persians, who were in turn replaced by Greeks (Alexander and the Ptolemies), Romans, Byzantines, and Arabs, who introduced Islam and the Arabic language. The ancient Egyptian language is preserved only in Coptic Christian liturgy.

Egypt was ruled as part of larger Islamic empires for many centuries. Britain intervened in Egypt in 1882 and ruled the country as a protectorate, 1914-22. A 1936 treaty strengthened Egyptian autonomy, but Britain retained bases in Egypt and a condominium over Sudan. When the state of Israel was proclaimed in 1948, Egypt joined other Arab nations invading Israel and was defeated. In 1951 Egypt abrogated the 1936 treaty; Sudan became independent in 1956.

A July 1952 uprising overthrew King Farouk and established a republic. Lt. Col. Gamal Abdel Nasser rose to power, becoming premier in 1954 and president in 1956. Nasser pushed construction of Egypt's Aswan High Dam, completed in 1970.

After guerrilla raids across its border, Israel invaded Egypt's Sinai Peninsula, Oct. 29, 1956. Egypt rejected a cease-fire demand by Britain and France; on Oct. 31 the two nations dropped bombs and on Nov. 5-6 landed forces. Egypt and Israel accepted a UN cease-fire; fighting ended Nov. 7. Subsequently, a UN Emergency Force guarded the border. Full-scale war with Israel broke out again, June 5, 1967; before it ended under a UN cease-fire June 10, Israel had captured Gaza and the Sinai Peninsula and taken control of the E bank of the Suez Canal.

Nasser died Sept. 28, 1970, and was replaced by Vice Pres. Anwar Sadat. In a surprise attack Oct. 6, 1973, Egyptian forces crossed the Suez Canal into the Sinai. (At the same time, Syrian forces attacked Israelis on the Golan Heights.) Israel counterattacked, crossed the canal, and surrounded Suez City. A UN cease-fire took effect Oct. 24. Under an agreement signed Jan. 1974, Israeli forces withdrew from the canal's W bank; limited numbers of Egyptian forces occupied a strip along the E bank. A second accord was signed in 1975, with Israel yielding Sinai oil fields.

Pres. Sadat's surprise visit to Jerusalem, Nov. 1977, opened the prospect of peace with Israel. On Mar. 26, 1979, Egypt and Israel signed a formal peace treaty, ending 30 years of war and establishing diplomatic relations. On Oct. 6, 1981, Muslim extremists within the army assassinated Pres. Sadat, who was succeeded by Hosni Mubarak. Israel returned control of the Sinai to Egypt in Apr. 1982.

Egyptian security forces battled Islamist violence in the 1990s. Pres. Mubarak escaped assassination in Ethiopia, June 26, 1995. On Nov. 17, 1997, near Luxor, Muslim extremists killed 58 foreign tourists and 4 Egyptians. Bombs Oct. 7, 2004, in and near Taba, a Sinai tourist site popular with Israelis, killed at least 35 people. Another 88 people were killed in bombings July 23, 2005, at Sharm el Sheikh, a Red Sea resort city.

Mubarak easily won reelection in Sept. 2005. Suicide bombings at the Sinai resort town of Dahab, Apr. 24, 2006, killed at least 18 people; security forces May 9 killed Nasser Khamis al-Mallahi, leader of the group blamed for the Taba, Sharm el Sheikh, and Dahab attacks. Constitutional amendments expanding presidential powers and barring religiously based political parties were approved Mar. 2007.

Following 18 days of mass protests in which at least 846 people died in clashes between Arab Spring dissidents and Mubarak loyalists, Mubarak surrendered power Feb. 11, 2011. A transitional military regime prepared for elections and charged Mubarak and associates with corruption and abuse of power. Mubarak was convicted June 2, 2012, in connection with the 2011 deaths of protesters and sentenced to life in prison. The verdict was overturned on appeal Jan. 13, 2013, and the charges were dismissed Nov. 29, 2014. However, a judge ordered, June 4, 2015, that Mubarak stand trial again. Mubarak had been convicted of separate corruption charges, May 21, 2014; after that conviction was overturned, Mubarak was re-tried, convicted May 9, 2015, and sentenced to 3 years in prison.

Islamist candidate Mohammed Morsi of the Muslim Brotherhood was declared winner of the presidential election, June 2012. Morsi overhauled the country's military leadership Aug. 12. On Oct. 8, 2012, he pardoned select political prisoners detained during the Arab Spring uprising. At least 110 people were injured in violent clashes between Morsi supporters and opponents Oct. 12, and additional conflicts erupted Nov. 23 after Morsi announced an edict interpreted as a power-grab. The proposal of a new Islamist constitution prompted demonstrations throughout Dec.; it passed Dec. 23, 2012.

Violent clashes, Jan. 25, 2013, killed 9 demonstrators and injured more than 400. Protesters firebombed the Muslim Brotherhood headquarters June 30 demanding Morsi's ouster. The military forced Morsi out of office July 3. Morsi's supporters protested continuously in Cairo and other cities. The military cracked down violently on these encampments Aug. 14. More than 600 protesters and at least 40 police officers died in confrontations. The military outlawed the Muslim Brotherhood as a terrorist organization Dec. 25, 2013. Under a new constitution approved in a Jan. 2014 referendum, former Gen. Abdel Fattah al-Sisi, one of the leaders in ousting Morsi, won a May presidential election. Violence between Morsi supporters and security forces continued, causing hundreds of deaths on both sides. Muslim Brotherhood leader Mohamed Badie was sentenced to death June 21, 2014, in connection with July 2013 violence; the sentence was reduced to life in prison Aug. 30, 2014. In a separate case, Morsi and Badie were sentenced to death May 16, 2015. Morsi had been sentenced to 20 years in prison, Apr. 21, 2015, in a trial related to Dec. 2012 street violence. In 2013-15, Islamist militants battled security forces and seized territory in the northern Sinai. Terrorist attacks occurred at major tourist sites in Luxor and Giza in June 2015. Egypt's top prosecutor was killed in Cairo in a terrorist bombing June 29, one of several terrorist attacks there during the summer.

The Suez Canal, 103 mi long, links the Mediterranean and Red Seas. It was built by a French corporation 1859-69, but Britain obtained controlling interest in 1875. On July 26, 1956, Egypt nationalized the canal. A new side channel and expansion of the main channel to increase the canal's capacity were completed Aug. 6, 2015.

El Salvador

Republic of El Salvador

People: Population: 6,141,350. **Age distrib.:** <15: 27.3%; 65+: 7.1%. **Growth:** 0.3%. **Migrants:** 0.7%. **Pop. density:** 767.6 per sq mi, 296.4 per sq km. **Urban:** 66.7%. **Ethnic groups:** mestizo 86.3%, white 12.7%. **Languages:** Spanish (official), Nahua. **Religions:** Roman Catholic 57.1%, Protestant 21.2%, none 16.8%.

Geography: Total area: 8,124 sq mi, 21,041 sq km; **Land area:** 8,000 sq mi, 20,721 sq km. **Location:** Central America. Guatemala on W, Honduras on N. **Topography:** A hot Pacific coastal plain in S rises to a cooler plateau and valley region, densely populated. The N is mountainous with many volcanoes. **Arable land:** 34%. **Capital:** San Salvador, 1,098,494.

Government: Type: Republic. **Head of state and gov.:** Pres. Salvador Sánchez Cerén; in office: June 1, 2014. **Local divisions:** 14 departments. **Defense budget:** $150 mil. **Active troops:** 15,300.

Economy: Industries: food proc., beverages, petroleum, chemicals, fertilizer, textiles, furniture, light metals. **Chief crops:** coffee, sugar, corn, rice, beans, oilseed, cotton, sorghum. **Natural resources:** hydropower, geothermal power, petroleum. **Water:** 4,144 cu m per capita. **Electricity prod.:** 6.2 bil kWh. **Labor force:** agric. 21%, industry 20%, services 58%. **Unemployment:** 6.3%.

Finance: Monetary unit: Colon (SVC) (8.75 = $1 U.S.). **GDP:** $50.9 bil; **per capita GDP:** $8,000; **GDP growth:** 2%. **Imports:**

$10.1 bil; U.S. 38.2%, Guatemala 8.7%, Mexico 6.8%, China 6.1%, Honduras 5.2%. **Exports:** $4.5 bil; U.S. 43.6%, Honduras 14.5%, Guatemala 13%, Nicaragua 6%. **Tourism:** $822 mil. **Budget:** $6 bil. **Inflation:** 1.1%.

Transport: Railways: 8 mi. **Motor vehicles:** 40.6 per 1,000 pop. **Airports:** 5.

Communications: Telephone: 14.9 per 100 pop. **Mobile:** 144 per 100 pop. **Broadband:** 7.5 per 100 pop. **Internet:** 29.7%.

Health: Expend.: 6.7%. **Life expect.:** 71.1 male; 77.9 female. **Births:** 16.5 per 1,000 pop. **Deaths:** 5.7 per 1,000 pop. **Infant mortality:** 17.9 per 1,000 live births. **Undernourished:** 13.5%. **HIV:** 0.5%.

Education: Compulsory: ages 7-15. **Literacy:** 88%.

Embassy: 1400 16th St. NW, Ste. 100, 20036; 265-9671.

Website: www.presidencia.gob.sv

El Salvador became independent of Spain in 1821, and of the Central American Federation in 1839.

A military coup overthrew the government of Pres. Carlos Humberto Romero in 1979, but the ruling military-civilian junta failed to quell a rebellion by leftist insurgents, armed by Cuba and Nicaragua. Extreme right-wing death squads organized to eliminate suspected leftists killed thousands in the 1980s. The Reagan administration supported the government with military aid. After taking the lives of some 75,000 people (with thousands more "disappeared"), the 12-year civil war ended Jan. 16, 1992, as the government and leftist rebels signed a formal peace treaty. Rightist legislators in the National Assembly passed a sweeping amnesty Mar. 20, 1993, for civil war atrocities.

Members of the right-wing ARENA party held the presidency from 1989 to 2009. Mauricio Funes, a leftist, won the 2009 presidential election. His vice pres., Salvador Sánchez Cerén, a former rebel commander, narrowly won the 2014 election. In late 2013 and the first half of 2014, thousands of undocumented immigrants from El Salvador were caught trying to enter the U.S. from Mexico; most were unaccompanied children or children with their mothers, fleeing drug violence and other hardships. Gang violence and deadly clashes between gang members and security forces increased in 2015.

Equatorial Guinea

Republic of Equatorial Guinea

People: Population: 740,743. **Age distrib.:** <15: 40.5%; 65+: 4%. **Growth:** 2.5%. **Migrants:** 1.3%. **Pop. density:** 68.4 per sq mi, 26.4 per sq km. **Urban:** 39.9%. **Ethnic groups:** Fang 85.7%, Bubi 6.5%, Mdowe 3.6%. **Languages:** Spanish, French (both official); Fang; Bubi. **Religions:** nominally Christian and predom. Roman Catholic, pagan practices.

Geography: Total area: 10,831 sq mi, 28,051 sq km; **Land area:** 10,831 sq mi, 28,051 sq km. **Location:** Bioko Isl. off W Africa coast in Gulf of Guinea, and Rio Muni, mainland enclave. Gabon on S, Cameroon on E and N. **Topography:** Bioko Isl. consists of 2 volcanic mountains and connecting valley. Rio Muni, with over 90% of area, has coastal plain and low hills. **Arable land:** 4.3%. **Capital:** Malabo, 145,077 (2014).

Government: Type: Republic. **Head of state:** Pres. Teodoro Obiang Nguema Mbasogo; in office: Aug. 3, 1979. **Head of gov.:** Prime Min. Vicente Ehate Tomi; in office: May 22, 2012. **Local divisions:** 7 provinces. **Defense budget** (2012): $7 mil. **Active troops:** 1,320.

Economy: Industries: petroleum, nat. gas, sawmilling. **Chief crops:** coffee, cocoa, rice, yams, cassava, bananas, palm oil nuts. **Natural resources:** petroleum, nat. gas, timber, gold, bauxite, diamonds, tantalum, sand and gravel, clay. **Water:** 34,346 cu m per capita. **Crude oil reserves:** 1.1 bil bbls. **Electricity prod.:** 100 mil kWh. **Labor force:** NA. **Unemployment:** 8%.

Finance: Monetary unit: Central African CFA Franc (XAF) (584.11 = $1 U.S.). **GDP:** $25.1 bil; **per capita GDP:** $32,300; **GDP growth:** –3.1%. **Imports:** $6.4 bil; U.S. 28%, Spain 16.5%, China 13.2%, France 5.7%, Italy 5.1%. **Exports:** $13.3 bil; China 18%, Japan 14.9%, UK 13.6%, France 11.1%, Brazil 7.8%, Spain 7.8%, U.S. 6.7%. **Budget:** $6.3 bil. **Inflation** (2012-13): 6.4%.

Transport: Airports: 6.

Communications: Telephone: 1.9 per 100 pop. **Mobile:** 66.4 per 100 pop. **Broadband:** NA. **Internet:** 18.9%.

Health: Expend.: 4.7%. **Life expect.:** 62.8 male; 65.0 female. **Births:** 33.3 per 1,000 pop. **Deaths:** 8.2 per 1,000 pop. **Infant mortality:** 69.2 per 1,000 live births. **Undernourished:** NA. **HIV:** 6.2%.

Education: Compulsory: ages 7-12. **Literacy:** 95.3%.

Embassy: 2020 16th St. NW 20009; 518-5700.

Website: www.guineaecuatorialpress.com or www.state.gov/p/af/ci/ek/

Fernando Po (now Bioko) Island was reached by Portugal in the late 15th cent. and ceded to Spain in 1778. Independence came Oct. 12, 1968. Anti-Spanish riots erupted in 1969 in Rio Muni province on the mainland.

Masie Nguema Biyogo, a mainlander, became president for life in 1972. His reign, among the most brutal in Africa, left the nation bankrupt; most of the nation's 7,000 Europeans emigrated. He was ousted in a military coup, Aug. 1979. Teodoro Obiang Nguema Mbasogo, leader of the coup, became president. Multiparty presidential elections held in 1996, 2002, and 2009 were seriously flawed.

The economy is heavily dependent on oil exports. There have been allegations of government misuse of oil revenue, and poverty remains widespread. Human Rights Watch (HRW) reported in 2012 that the Obiang regime "regularly tortures and arbitrarily detains" suspected dissidents. A referendum on constitutional reforms was overwhelmingly approved Nov. 2011, but HRW reported voter fraud and intimidation. The government planned to move its capital to a newly built city, Oyala, financing construction with oil sales.

Eritrea

State of Eritrea

People: Population: 6,527,689. **Age distrib.:** <15: 40.2%; 65+: 3.7%. **Growth:** 2.3%. **Migrants:** 0.2%. **Pop. density:** 167.4 per sq mi, 64.6 per sq km. **Urban:** 22.6%. **Ethnic groups:** Tigrinya 55%, Tigre 30%, Saho 4%, Kunama 2%, Rashaida 2%, Bilen 2%, other (Afar, Beni Amir, Nera) 5%. **Languages:** Tigrinya, Arabic, English (all official); Tigre; Kunama; Afar. **Religions:** Muslim, Coptic Christian, Roman Catholic, Protestant.

Geography: Total area: 45,406 sq mi, 117,600 sq km; **Land area:** 38,996 sq mi, 101,000 sq km. **Location:** E Africa, on SW coast of Red Sea. Ethiopia on S, Djibouti on SE, Sudan on W. **Topography:** Includes many islands of the Dahlak Archipelago. Low coastal plains in S, mountain range with peaks to 9,000 ft in N. **Arable land:** 6.8%. **Capital:** Asmara, 803,791.

Government: Type: Authoritarian presidential regime. **Head of state and gov.:** Pres. Isaias Afworki; in office: June 8, 1993. **Local divisions:** 6 regions. **Defense budget** (2012): $78 mil. **Active troops:** 201,750.

Economy: Industries: food proc., beverages, clothing and textiles, light mfg. **Chief crops:** sorghum, lentils, vegetables, corn, cotton, tobacco, sisal. **Natural resources:** gold, potash, zinc, copper, salt, fish. **Water:** 1,155 cu m per capita. **Electricity prod.:** 338 mil kWh. **Labor force:** agric. 80%, industry and services 20%. **Unemployment:** 7.2%.

Finance: Monetary unit: Nakfa (ERN) (10.47 = $1 U.S.). **GDP:** $7.8 bil; **per capita GDP:** $1,200; **GDP growth:** 1.7%. **Imports:** $1.2 bil. **Exports:** $573.5 mil. **Budget:** $1.6 bil. **Inflation:** NA.

Transport: Railways: 190 mi. **Airports:** 4.

Communications: Telephone: 1 per 100 pop. **Mobile:** 6.4 per 100 pop. **Broadband:** NA. **Internet:** 1%.

Health: Expend.: 2.6%. **Life expect.:** 61.7 male; 66.0 female. **Births:** 30.0 per 1,000 pop. **Deaths:** 7.5 per 1,000 pop. **Infant mortality:** 37.5 per 1,000 live births. **Undernourished:** NA. **HIV:** 0.7%.

Education: Compulsory: NA. **Literacy:** 73.8%.

Embassy: 1708 New Hampshire Ave. NW 20009; 319-1991.

Website: www.shabait.com or www.state.gov/p/af/ci/er/

Eritrea was part of the Ethiopian kingdom of Aksum. It was an Italian colony from 1890 to 1941, when it was captured by the British. Following a period of British and UN supervision, Eritrea was awarded to Ethiopia as part of a federation in 1952. Ethiopia annexed Eritrea as a province in 1962. After a 31-year struggle, Eritrea formally declared its independence May 24, 1993. A constitution was ratified in 1997 but not implemented.

A border war with Ethiopia that erupted in June 1998 intensified in May 2000, as Ethiopian troops plunged into western Eritrea; a cease-fire signed June 18 provided for a UN peacekeeping force (UNMEE) to patrol a buffer zone on Eritrean territory. A peace treaty was signed Dec. 12, 2000.

A 2007 UN report accused Eritrea of aiding an Islamic insurgency in Somalia. Citing Eritrean obstruction of UNMEE activities, the UN Security Council ended the peacekeeping mission July 2008. Many thousands have fled repressive conditions in Eritrea, including defections by the national soccer team during tournaments in Kenya, Dec. 2009, and Uganda, Dec. 2012. Four Eritrean athletes sought asylum in the UK during the 2012 Summer Olympics in London. A coup attempt against Pres. Isaias Afworki failed, Jan. 21, 2013. A UN commission concluded, June 2015, that the government was committing widespread human rights violations. Thousands of Eritrean children traveling alone were among migrants reaching Southern Europe by boat 2014-15.

Estonia

Republic of Estonia

People: Population: 1,265,420. **Age distrib.:** <15: 16%; 65+: 19.1%. **Growth:** –0.6%. **Migrants:** 16.3%. **Pop. density:** 77.3 per sq mi, 29.9 per sq km. **Urban:** 67.5%. **Ethnic groups:** Estonian

68.7%, Russian 24.8%. **Languages:** Estonian (official), Russian. **Religions:** Orthodox 16.2%, Lutheran 9.9%, none 54.1%.

Geography: Total area: 17,463 sq mi, 45,228 sq km; **Land area:** 16,366 sq mi, 42,388 sq km. **Location:** Eastern Europe, bordering Baltic Sea and Gulf of Finland. Russia on E, Latvia on S. **Topography:** Marshy lowland with numerous lakes and swamps. Elongated hills show evidence of former glaciation. More than 800 islands on Baltic coast. **Arable land:** 14.6%. **Capital:** Tallinn, 391,111.

Government: Type: Parliamentary republic. **Head of state:** Pres. Toomas Hendrik Ilves; in office: Oct. 9, 2006. **Head of gov.:** Prime Min. Taavi Rõivas; in office: Mar. 26, 2014. **Local divisions:** 15 counties. **Defense budget:** $520 mil. **Active troops:** 5,750.

Economy: Industries: engineering, electronics, wood and wood prods., textiles, information tech., telecom. **Chief crops:** grain, potatoes, vegetables. **Natural resources:** oil shale, peat, rare earth elements, phosphorite, clay, limestone, sand, dolomite, sea mud. **Water:** 9,953 cu m per capita. **Electricity prod.:** 11.3 bil kWh. **Labor force:** agric. 3.9%, industry 28.4%, services 67.7%. **Unemployment:** 8.8%.

Finance: Monetary unit: Euro (EUR) (0.89 = $1 U.S.). **GDP:** $35.6 bil; **per capita GDP:** $27,000; **GDP growth:** 2.1%. **Imports:** $17.1 bil; Finland 15.1%, Germany 10.8%, Sweden 10.4%, Latvia 9.5%, Lithuania 8.9%, Poland 8.2%. **Exports:** $15.8 bil; Sweden 17.4%, Finland 16.6%, Russia 11.7%, Latvia 10.7%, Lithuania 6%. **Tourism:** $1.4 bil. **Budget:** $9.9 bil. **Inflation:** –0.1%.

Transport: Railways: 743 mi. **Airports:** 13.

Communications: Telephone: 31.7 per 100 pop. **Mobile:** 160.7 per 100 pop. **Broadband:** 78.9 per 100 pop. **Internet:** 84.2%.

Health: Expend.: 5.9%. **Life expect.:** 71.6 male; 81.5 female. **Births:** 10.5 per 1,000 pop. **Deaths:** 12.4 per 1,000 pop. **Infant mortality:** 3.9 per 1,000 live births. **Undernourished:** <5%. **HIV:** NA.

Education: Compulsory: ages 7-15. **Literacy:** 99.8%.

Embassy: 2131 Massachusetts Ave. NW 20008; 588-0101.

Website: www.eesti.ee

Estonia, a province of imperial Russia before World War I, was independent between World Wars I and II. The USSR conquered it in 1940 and incorporated it as the Estonian SSR. During an abortive Soviet coup, Estonia, Aug. 20, 1991, declared immediate full independence, which the Soviet Union recognized Sept. 1991. The first free elections in over 50 years were held Sept. 20, 1992. The last occupying Russian troops departed Aug. 31, 1994.

Estonia became a full member of the EU and NATO in 2004. The government accused Russia of orchestrating a cyber attack against Estonia's computer network in Apr.-May 2007. Estonia adopted the euro Jan. 1, 2011. Amid growing discontent over austerity policies, Prime Min. Andrus Ansip was replaced, Mar. 26, 2014, by Taavi Rõivas, who formed a center-left government. After his Reform Party won the most votes in Mar. 1, 2015, elections, Rõivas formed a new center-left coalition.

Ethiopia

Federal Democratic Republic of Ethiopia

People: Population: 99,465,819. **Age distrib.:** <15: 43.9%; 65+: 2.9%. **Growth:** 2.9%. **Migrants:** 0.8%. **Pop. density:** 257.6 per sq mi, 99.5 per sq km. **Urban:** 19.5%. **Ethnic groups:** Oromo 34.4%, Amhara 27%, Somali 6.2%, Tigray 6.1%, Sidama 4%, Gurage 2.5%, Welaita 2.3%. **Languages:** Oromo (official in one state), Amharic (official nationally), Somali (official in one state), Tigrigna (official in one state); Sidamo; Wolaytta; Gurage. **Religions:** Ethiopian Orthodox 43.5%, Muslim 33.9%, Protestant 18.5%, traditional 2.7%.

Geography: Total area: 426,373 sq mi, 1,104,300 sq km; **Land area:** 386,102 sq mi, 1,000,000 sq km. **Location:** E Africa. Sudan on W; Kenya on S; Somalia, Djibouti on E; Eritrea on N. **Topography:** A central plateau, 6,000-10,000 ft high, rises to mountains near the Great Rift Valley, cutting in from SW. Blue Nile and other rivers cross the plateau, which descends to plains on W and SE. **Arable land:** 15.3%. **Capital:** Addis Ababa, 3,237,525.

Government: Type: Federal republic. **Head of state:** Pres. Mulatu Teshome Wirtu; in office: Oct. 7, 2013. **Head of gov.:** Prime Min. Hailemariam Desalegn; in office: Sept. 21, 2012. **Local divisions:** 9 states (ethnically based), 2 self-governing administrations. **Defense budget:** $375 mil. **Active troops:** 138,000.

Economy: Industries: food proc., beverages, textiles, leather, chemicals, metals proc., cement. **Chief crops:** cereals, pulses, coffee, oilseed, cotton, sugarcane, vegetables, khat, cut flowers. **Natural resources:** gold, platinum, copper, potash, nat. gas, hydropower. **Water:** 1,296 cu m per capita. **Crude oil reserves:** 430 bbls. **Electricity prod.:** 6.6 bil kWh. **Labor force:** agric. 85%, industry 5%, services 10%. **Unemployment:** 5.7%.

Finance: Monetary unit: Birr (ETB) (20.85 = $1 U.S.). **GDP:** $144.6 bil; **per capita GDP:** $1,600; **GDP growth:** 10.3%. **Imports:** $12.1 bil; China 15.3%, Saudi Arabia 8.1%, India 7.2%, U.S. 5.6%. **Exports:** $4.1 bil; China 13%, Saudi Arabia 8.3%, Germany 8.3%, U.S. 8.1%, Belgium 7.1%. **Tourism:** $350 mil. **Budget:** $9 bil. **Inflation:** 7.4%.

Transport: Railways: 423 mi (Ethiopian segment of Addis Ababa-Djibouti railroad). **Motor vehicles:** 1.6 per 1,000 pop. **Airports:** 17.

Communications: Telephone: 0.8 per 100 pop. **Mobile:** 31.6 per 100 pop. **Broadband:** 4.9 per 100 pop. **Internet:** 2.9%.

Health: Expend.: 3.8%. **Life expect.:** 59.1 male; 63.9 female. **Births:** 37.3 per 1,000 pop. **Deaths:** 8.2 per 1,000 pop. **Infant mortality:** 53.4 per 1,000 live births. **Undernourished:** 35%. **HIV:** 1.2%.

Education: Compulsory: NA. **Literacy:** 49.1%.

Embassy: 3506 International Dr. NW 20008; 364-1200.

Website: www.ethiopia.gov.et

Ethiopian culture was influenced by Egypt and Greece. Italy invaded the region in 1880, but Ethiopia maintained its independence until the Italian invasion of 1936. British forces freed the country in 1941.

A series of droughts in the 1970s killed hundreds of thousands. An army mutiny, strikes, and student demonstrations led to the 1974 dethronement of Ethiopia's last emperor, Haile Selassie I, ending his 58-year reign; he died a prisoner of the ruling junta, known as the Dergue, 1975. The junta dissolved parliament, abolished the monarchy, established a socialist state, redistributed land, curbed the influence of the Coptic Church, and violently suppressed opposition.

The regime, torn by bloody coups, faced uprisings by tribal and political groups aided in part by Sudan and Somalia. Ties with the U.S., once a major ally, deteriorated, while cooperation accords were signed with the USSR in 1977. In 1978, Soviet advisers and Cuban troops helped defeat Somali forces. Ethiopia and Somalia signed a peace agreement in 1988.

A worldwide relief effort began in 1984, as an extended drought precipitated famine; up to 1 mil people died as a result.

The Ethiopian People's Revolutionary Democratic Front (EPRDF), an umbrella group of six rebel armies, launched a major push against government forces in 1991, prompting Pres. Mengistu Haile Mariam's resignation. The EPRDF set up a transitional government. Ethiopia's first multiparty general elections were held in 1995.

Eritrea, a province on the Red Sea, declared its independence May 24, 1993. Fighting along the border with Eritrea, which erupted in 1998, intensified in May 2000, as Ethiopian forces entered Eritrean territory; a peace treaty was signed Dec. 12. The war displaced 350,000 Ethiopians.

The ruling EPRDF won parliamentary elections May 2005. In July 2006, Ethiopia sent troops into Somalia in response to advances by Islamist militias there. Tried in absentia, former Pres. Mengistu was convicted of genocide Dec. 12, 2006. Drought and other food supply disruptions occurred 2008-09. Ethiopia withdrew troops from Somalia Jan. 2009. The EPRDF dominated 2010 parliamentary elections, though the opposition contested the results. When Prime Min. Meles Zenawi died Aug. 2012, the EPRDF's Hailemariam Desalegn became prime min. Ethiopian troops joined an African Union peacekeeping force in Somalia in Jan. 2014. As of the end of 2014, Ethiopia housed more than 650,000 refugees, the largest numbers being from Somalia and South Sudan. The EPRDF won every seat in May 24, 2015, parliamentary elections. Pres. Barack Obama visited Ethiopia July 2015, the first sitting U.S. president to do so.

Ethiopia began construction, Apr. 2, 2013, of the Grand Renaissance Dam (Hidase) across the Blue Nile. The dam, which will be Africa's largest when completed (scheduled for 2017), raised concerns in Egypt and Sudan over loss of water resources. The three nations signed an agreement in principle, Mar. 23, 2015, on sharing Nile R. water.

Fiji

Republic of Fiji

People: Population: 909,389. **Age distrib.:** <15: 28%; 65+: 6.1%. **Growth:** 0.7%. **Migrants:** 2.6%. **Pop. density:** 128.9 per sq mi, 49.8 per sq km. **Urban:** 53.7%. **Ethnic groups:** iTaukei (predom. Melanesian with Polynesian admixture) 56.8%, Indian 37.5%, other (European, part European, other Pac. Islanders, Chinese) 4.5%. **Languages:** English, Fijian (both official); Hindustani. **Religions:** Protestant 45% (incl. Methodist 34.6%), Hindu 27.9%, Roman Catholic 9.1%, Muslim 6.3%.

Geography: Total area: 7,056 sq mi, 18,274 sq km; **Land area:** 7,056 sq mi, 18,274 sq km. Viti Levu, largest island of group, has over half the total land area. **Location:** Western S Pacific O. Nearest neighbors are Vanuatu to W, Tonga to E. **Topography:** 322 isls. (106 inhabited), many mountainous, with tropical forests and large fertile areas. **Arable land:** 9%. **Capital:** Suva, 176,397 (2014).

Government: Type: Republic. **Head of state:** Pres. Ratu Epeli Nailatikau; in office: Nov. 5, 2009 (acting from July 30). **Head of gov.:** Prime Min. Voreqe "Frank" Bainimarama; in office: Sept. 22, 2014. **Local divisions:** 14 provinces, 1 dependency. **Defense budget:** $50 mil. **Active troops:** 3,500.

Economy: Industries: tourism, sugar, clothing, copra. **Chief crops:** sugarcane, coconuts, cassava, rice, sweet potatoes, bananas. **Natural resources:** timber, fish, gold, copper, hydropower. **Water:** 32,406 cu m per capita. **Electricity prod.:** 836.1 mil kWh. **Labor force:** agric. 70%, industry and services 30%. **Unemployment:** 8.1%.

Finance: Monetary unit: Dollar (FJD) (2.18 = $1 U.S.). **GDP:** $7.3 bil; **per capita GDP:** $8,200; **GDP growth:** 4.1%. **Imports:** $2.2 bil; Singapore 17.5%, France 16.1%, New Zealand 13.6%, Australia 12%, China 10.1%, Malaysia 9.8%. **Exports:** $1.2 bil; U.S. 12.4%, Australia 11.3%, Samoa 6.1%, Tonga 5.4%, UK 5.2%. **Tourism:** $751 mil. **Budget:** $1.5 bil. **Inflation:** 0.5%.

Transport: Railways: 371 mi. **Motor vehicles:** 188.7 per 1,000 pop. **Airports:** 4.

Communications: Telephone: 8.4 per 100 pop. **Mobile:** 98.8 per 100 pop. **Broadband:** 53.5 per 100 pop. **Internet:** 41.8%.

Health: Expend.: 4%. **Life expect.:** 69.8 male; 75.2 female. **Births:** 19.4 per 1,000 pop. **Deaths:** 6.0 per 1,000 pop. **Infant mortality:** 9.9 per 1,000 live births. **Undernourished:** <5%. **HIV:** 0.1%.

Education: Compulsory: NA. **Literacy:** NA.

Embassy: 2000 M St. NW, Ste. 710, 20036; 466-8320.

Website: www.fiji.gov.fj

A British colony since 1874, Fiji became independent Oct. 10, 1970. Cultural differences between the Indian community (mostly descendants of contract laborers brought to the islands in the 19th cent.) and indigenous Fijians have led to political tensions. More than 100,000 Indians left Fiji after a 1987 coup deposed an Indian-majority government.

Fiji's first Indian prime minister, Mahendra Chaudhry, and other government officials were taken captive May 19, 2000, by indigenous Fijian gunmen led by George Speight, culminating in a military takeover, May 29, led by Frank Bainimarama. Release of the last remaining hostages in July 2000 coincided with the installation of an interim military-backed government. Speight was convicted of treason and sentenced to life in prison in 2002. Prime Min. Laisenia Qarase headed an elected civilian government, 2001-06, but was ousted in a military coup Dec. 5, 2006. Bainimarama took office as interim prime min. After a court ruled in 2009 that the 2006 coup was illegal, Pres. Ratu Josefa Iloilo abrogated the constitution, dissolved the judiciary, and reappointed Interim Prime Min. Bainimarama. In July, Bainimarama promised a new constitution and legislative elections; he also named Vice Pres. Ratu Epeli Nailatikau to replace the retiring Pres. Iloilo. Bainimarama accepted a draft constitution released Mar. 22, 2013, and he retained office in democratic elections Sept. 17, 2014. The Commonwealth, Sept. 26, 2014, reinstated Fiji's membership, which had been suspended since the 2006 coup; U.S. sanctions were lifted Oct. 2014. Bainimarama announced, Feb. 3, 2015, that the Union Jack would be removed from Fiji's flag, with the new flag scheduled to debut at independence day ceremonies in Oct. 2015.

Finland

Republic of Finland

People: Population: 5,476,922. **Age distrib.:** <15: 16.4%; 65+: 20.2%. **Growth:** 0.4%. **Migrants:** 5.4%. **Pop. density:** 46.7 per sq mi, 18 per sq km. **Urban:** 84.2%. **Ethnic groups:** Finn 93.4%, Swede 5.6%. **Languages:** Finnish, Swedish (both official). **Religions:** Lutheran 78.4%, none 19.2%.

Geography: Total area: 130,559 sq mi, 338,145 sq km; **Land area:** 117,304 sq mi, 303,815 sq km. **Location:** Northern Europe. Norway on N, Sweden on W, Russia on E. **Topography:** Flat with low hills and many lakes in S and center. The N has mountainous areas, 3,000-4,000 ft above sea level. **Arable land:** 7.4%. **Capital:** Helsinki, 1,179,916.

Government: Type: Republic. **Head of state:** Pres. Sauli Niinistö; in office: Mar. 1, 2012. **Head of gov.:** Prime Min. Juha Sipilä; in office: May 29, 2015. **Local divisions:** 19 regions. **Defense budget:** $3.73 bil. **Active troops:** 22,200.

Economy: Industries: metals and metal prods., electronics, machinery and scientific instruments, shipbuilding, pulp and paper, foodstuffs. **Chief crops:** barley, wheat, sugar beets, potatoes. **Natural resources:** timber, iron ore, copper, lead, zinc, chromite, nickel, gold, silver, limestone. **Water:** 20,273 cu m per capita. **Electricity prod.:** 67.5 bil kWh. **Labor force:** agric. and forestry 4.4%; industry 15.5%; constr. 7.1%; commerce 21.3%; finance, insurance, and business services 13.3%; transp. and communications 9.9%; public services 28.5%. **Unemployment:** 8.2%.

Finance: Monetary unit: Euro (EUR) (0.89 = $1 U.S.). **GDP:** $221 bil; **per capita GDP:** $40,300; **GDP growth:** –0.1%. **Imports:** $73 bil; Russia 18%, Sweden 16.1%, Germany 14.1%, Netherlands 8.3%. **Exports:** $78 bil; Sweden 11.6%, Germany 9.8%, Russia 9.5%, Netherlands 6.3%, U.S. 6.2%, UK 5.3%. **Tourism:** $4.1 bil. **Budget:** $156.1 bil (central govt. budget). **Inflation:** 1%.

Transport: Railways: 3,678 mi. **Motor vehicles:** 707.3 per 1,000 pop. **Airports:** 74.

Communications: Telephone: 11.7 per 100 pop. **Mobile:** 139.7 per 100 pop. **Broadband:** 123.6 per 100 pop. **Internet:** 92.4%.

Health: Expend.: 9.2%. **Life expect.:** 77.8 male; 83.9 female. **Births:** 10.7 per 1,000 pop. **Deaths:** 9.8 per 1,000 pop. **Infant mortality:** 2.5 per 1,000 live births. **Undernourished:** <5%. **HIV:** NA.

Education: Compulsory: ages 7-16. **Literacy:** 100%.

Embassy: 3301 Massachusetts Ave. NW 20008; 298-5800.

Website: valtioneuvosto.fi

Early Finns may have migrated from the Ural region and other areas about 6,000 years ago. Swedish settlers brought the country into Sweden, 1154 to 1809, when Finland became an autonomous grand duchy of the Russian Empire. Russian exactions created a strong national spirit; on Dec. 6, 1917, Finland declared its independence, and in 1919 it became a republic.

On Nov. 30, 1939, the Soviet Union invaded, and the Finns were forced to cede 16,173 sq mi of territory. After World War II, further cessions were exacted. In 1948, Finland signed a treaty of mutual assistance with the USSR that was renegotiated in Jan. 1992.

Following approval by Finnish voters in a 1994 advisory referendum, Finland entered the EU Jan. 1, 1995. Former Pres. Martti Ahtisaari was awarded the Nobel Peace Prize, Oct. 10, 2008, for his efforts in mediating international conflicts. The conservative Sauli Niinistö won the 2012 presidential election. Former CEO Juha Sipilä's Center Party won the largest bloc of seats in Apr. 19, 2015, parliamentary elections, and Sipilä formed a center-right government.

Aland, or Ahvenanmaa, an autonomous, Swedish-speaking province, is a group of small islands, 590 sq mi, in the Gulf of Bothnia, 25 mi from Sweden, 15 mi from Finland. Mariehamn is the chief port and seat of government. **Website:** www.aland.ax

France

French Republic

People: Population: 66,553,766. **Age distrib.:** <15: 18.7%; 65+: 18.7%. **Growth:** 0.4%. **Migrants:** 11.6%. **Pop. density:** 269.2 per sq mi, 103.9 per sq km. **Urban:** 79.5%. **Ethnic groups:** Celtic and Latin with Teutonic, Slavic, N African, Indochinese, Basque minorities. **Languages:** French (official); rapidly declining regional dialects and langs. (Provençal, Breton, Alsatian, Corsican, Catalan, Basque, Flemish). **Religions:** Christian (overwhelmingly Roman Catholic) 63%-66%, Muslim 7%-9%, none 23%-28%.

Geography: Total area: 248,573 sq mi, 643,801 sq km; **Land area:** 247,270 sq mi, 640,427 sq km. **Location:** Western Europe, between Atlantic O. and Medit. Sea. Spain, Andorra, Monaco on S; Italy, Switzerland, Germany on E; Luxembourg, Belgium on N. **Topography:** A wide plain covers more than half of the country, in N and W, drained to W by Seine, Loire, Garonne Rivers. The Alps (Mt. Blanc is tallest in W Europe at 15,781 ft), the lower Jura range, and forested Vosges are in E. The Rhone flows from Lake Geneva to Mediterranean. Pyrenees are on SW border. **Arable land:** 33.4%. **Capital:** Paris, 10,843,285. **Cities:** Lyon, 1,608,712; Marseille-Aix-en-Provence, 1,605,046; Lille, 1,027,178.

Government: Type: Republic. **Head of state:** Pres. François Hollande; in office: May 15, 2012. **Head of gov.:** Prime Min. Manuel Valls; in office: Mar. 31, 2014. **Local divisions:** 22 metropolitan regions, 5 overseas regions. **Defense budget:** $53.08 bil. **Active troops:** 215,000.

Economy: Industries: machinery, chemicals, automobiles, metallurgy, aircraft, electronics, textiles, food proc., tourism. **Chief crops:** wheat, cereals, sugar beets, potatoes, wine grapes. **Natural resources:** coal, iron ore, bauxite, zinc, uranium, antimony, arsenic, potash, feldspar, fluorspar, gypsum, timber, fish. **Water:** 3,282 cu m per capita. **Crude oil reserves:** 84.1 mil bbls. **Other resources:** Timber, dairy. **Electricity prod.:** 533.3 bil kWh. **Labor force:** agric. 3%, industry 21.3%, services 75.7%. **Unemployment:** 10.4%.

Finance: Monetary unit: Euro (EUR) (0.89 = $1 U.S.). **GDP:** $2.6 tril; **per capita GDP:** $40,400; **GDP growth:** 0.4%. **Imports:** $678.1 bil; (2014) Germany 19.4%, Belgium 11.1%, Italy 7.6%, Netherlands 7.5%, Spain 6.6%, U.S. 5%, China 5%. **Exports:** $582.5 bil; (2014) Germany 16.4%, Belgium 7.3%, Italy 7.1%, Spain 7%, UK 7%, U.S. 6.2%. **Tourism:** $55.4 bil. **Budget:** $1.6 tril. **Inflation:** 0.5%.

Transport: Railways: 18,417 mi. **Motor vehicles:** 574.7 per 1,000 pop. **Airports:** 294.

Communications: Telephone: 60 per 100 pop. **Mobile:** 100.4 per 100 pop. **Broadband:** 57.1 per 100 pop. **Internet:** 83.8%.

Health: Expend.: 11.8%. **Life expect.:** 78.7 male; 85.0 female. **Births:** 12.4 per 1,000 pop. **Deaths:** 9.2 per 1,000 pop. **Infant mortality:** 3.3 per 1,000 live births. **Undernourished:** <5%. **HIV:** NA.

Education: Compulsory: ages 6-16. **Literacy:** 99%.

Embassy: 4101 Reservoir Rd. NW 20007; 944-6000.

Website: www.gouvernement.fr

Julius Caesar conquered Celtic Gaul 58-51 BCE; Romans ruled for 500 years. Under Charlemagne, Frankish rule extended over much of Europe. After his death, France emerged as one of the successor kingdoms.

The monarchy was overthrown in the French Revolution (1789-93) and succeeded by the First Republic, followed by the First Empire under Napoleon (1804-15), a monarchy (1814-48), the Second Republic (1848-52), the Second Empire (1852-70), the Third Republic (1871-1946), the Fourth Republic (1946-58), and the Fifth Republic (1958-present).

France suffered severe losses in people and wealth in WWI (1914-18) when it was invaded by Germany. By the Treaty of Versailles, 1919, France exacted return of Alsace and Lorraine, provinces seized by Germany in 1871 after it defeated France in the Franco-Prussian War. During WWII (1939-45), Germany invaded France in May 1940 and signed an armistice with a government based in Vichy. After the Allies liberated France in 1944, Gen. Charles de Gaulle became head of the provisional government, serving until 1946. De Gaulle again became premier in 1958, during a crisis over Algeria, and obtained voter approval for a new constitution, ushering in the Fifth Republic. He then became president.

France withdrew from Indochina in 1954 and from Morocco and Tunisia in 1956. Most of its remaining African territories, including Algeria, were freed 1958-62.

In May 1968, students in Paris and other centers rioted, battled police, and were joined by workers who launched nationwide strikes. De Gaulle resigned from office in Apr. 1969, after losing a nationwide referendum on constitutional reform. Georges Pompidou was elected to succeed him. After Pompidou's death, in 1974, Valery Giscard d'Estaing was elected president; he continued his predecessors' conservative policies.

In 1981, France elected François Mitterrand, a Socialist, president. Under Mitterrand the government nationalized five major industries and most private banks. After 1986, however, when rightists won a narrow victory in the National Assembly, Mitterrand chose conservative Jacques Chirac as premier. During a two-year period of "cohabitation," France pursued a privatization program, selling many state-owned companies. During Mitterrand's second 7-year term starting in 1988, he appointed first a Socialist as premier, then a conservative after the center-right won a large majority in 1993 legislative elections.

Chirac won the 1995 presidency in a runoff election. He cut government spending to meet budgetary goals for the introduction of the euro. With unemployment at nearly 13%, leftist parties won a decisive victory in 1997 legislative elections, resulting in a new period of cohabitation. Chirac easily won the 2002 presidential election in a runoff, and his center-right allies won parliamentary elections. Parliament gave final approval in 2004 to a law barring the wearing of Islamic head scarves and other religious symbols in public schools.

Displeased with sluggish economic growth, high unemployment, and budget cuts in entitlement programs, voters rejected, 2005, a proposed EU constitution supported by the Chirac government. A state of emergency was declared Nov. 8 after 12 days of riots that began in Paris and spread to some 300 French cities and towns; rioters were mainly young immigrants from N and W Africa.

The conservative Nicolas Sarkozy won the 2007 presidential runoff election. Sarkozy responded to the global recession, Dec. 2008, with a $33-bil economic stimulus plan focused on infrastructure development; measures announced Feb. 2009, following labor protests, added $3.3 bil in aid for lower-income people. Sarkozy's policy of shutting Roma (Gypsy) encampments and expelling thousands to Romania and Bulgaria drew public rebukes from EU allies, Sept. 2010. With France's economy still struggling, the Socialist François Hollande won a presidential runoff over Sarkozy in 2012, and the Socialist Party won an absolute majority in parliamentary elections. Hollande, May 18, 2013, signed a bill that legalized same-sex marriage and allowed gay couples to adopt children. After a weak showing by Socialists in Mar. 2014 municipal elections and with the economy still sluggish, Prime Min. Jean-Marc Ayrault resigned and was replaced by centrist Socialist Manuel Valls. In European Parliament elections May 25, 2014, the far-right National Front was the largest vote-getter, with 25%.

France, a founding NATO member, formally returned to the alliance's military command structure Apr. 2009 after 43 years. In Dec. 2014, France withdrew its last troops deployed with NATO forces in Afghanistan. France participated in military operations that ousted Libyan leader Muammar al-Qaddafi, Aug. 23, 2011. In 2014-15, France took part in the U.S.-led campaign of airstrikes in Iraq against the Sunni extremist group ISIS. Pres. Hollande announced, Sept. 27, 2015, that France had begun airstrikes against ISIS targets in Syria. French troops entered the conflict between government forces in Mali and Islamist militants Jan. 11, 2013; they pushed the militants out of most seized territory. As fighting continued in 2015, France maintained a regional force of 3,000 troops, based in Mali and Chad.

On Jan. 7, 2015, 2 French gunmen of Algerian descent attacked the Paris offices of the magazine *Charlie Hebdo*, which had published satirical images of Muhammad. The gunmen, who claimed affiliation with al-Qaeda in the Arabian Peninsula, killed 12 people, including magazine staff and police officers, before fleeing. They were killed in a shootout with police at a printing plant outside Paris, Jan. 9. In coordinated attacks in Paris, a third gunman, who claimed loyalty to ISIS, fatally shot a police officer Jan. 8 and killed 4 people and took hostages at a kosher supermarket Jan. 9, before being killed by police. Near Lyon, June 26, a French Islamist extremist beheaded his boss and attempted to set fire to a liquid gas storage facility before being captured. An attempted attack, Aug. 21, by a heavily armed Moroccan man on an Amsterdam-Paris train was foiled by passengers, including 2 U.S. servicemen.

The island of **Corsica**, in the Mediterranean W of Italy and N of Sardinia, is a territorial collectivity and region of France comprising two departments. It elects 2 senators and 3 deputies to the French Parliament. Area 3,369 sq mi; pop. (2014 est.) 323,092. The capital is Ajaccio, birthplace of Napoleon I. Violence by Corsican separatist groups, especially in the 1980s and 1990s, hurt tourism, a leading industry. Corsicans rejected, 51%-49%, a limited autonomy plan in a referendum July 6, 2003. Violence by criminal gangs has been widespread in recent years.

French Overseas Departments

French Guiana is on the NE coast of South America with Suriname on the W and Brazil on the E and S. Its area is 35,135 sq mi (total), 34,421 sq mi (land); pop. (2014 est.) 250,377. Guiana sends one senator and two deputies to the French Parliament. Guiana is administered by a prefect and has a Council General of 16 elected members; capital is Cayenne.

The famous penal colony, Devil's Island, was phased out between 1938 and 1951. The European Space Agency maintains a satellite-launching center (established by France in 1964) in the city of Kourou.

Immense forests of rich timber cover 88% of the land. Fishing (especially shrimp), forestry, and gold mining are the most important industries. Natural resources include petroleum, kaolin, niobium, tantalum, and clay.

Guadeloupe, in the West Indies' Leeward Islands, consists of two large islands, Basse-Terre and Grande-Terre, separated by the Salt R., plus Marie Galante and the Saintes group to the S and, to the N, Desirade. A French possession since 1635, the department is represented in the French Parliament; administration consists of a prefect (governor) as well as an elected general and regional councils.

Area of the islands is 525 sq mi; pop. (2014 est., incl. St. Barthélemy and St. Martin) 403,750, mainly descendants of slaves; capital is Basse-Terre (2014 est. pop: 55,295) on Basse-Terre Island. The land is fertile; sugar, rum, and bananas are exported. Tourism is an important industry. International tourism receipts in 2013 were $671 mil.

Martinique, the northernmost of the Windward Islands, in the West Indies, has been a possession since 1635, and a department since Mar. 1946. It is represented in the French Parliament by 2 senators and 4 deputies. The island was the birthplace of Napoleon's first wife, Empress Josephine.

It has an area of 425 sq mi (total), 409 sq mi (land); pop. (2014 est.) 381,326, mostly descendants of slaves. The capital is Fort-de-France; pop. (2014 est.) 85,817. It is a popular tourist stop; 2014 international tourism receipts were $483 mil. The chief exports are rum, bananas, and petroleum products. **Website:** www.region-martinique.mq

Mayotte, claimed by Comoros and administered by France, voted in 1976 to become a territorial collectivity of France. An island NW of Madagascar, area is 144 sq mi, pop. (2012 est.) 216,000. The capital is Mamoudzou; pop. (2014 est.) 5,715. In a Mar. 29, 2009, referendum, 95% of voters endorsed a plan under which Mayotte became an overseas department of France as of Mar. 31, 2011.

Réunion is a volcanic island in the Indian O. about 420 mi E of Madagascar, and has belonged to France since 1665. Area, 972 sq mi (total), 968 sq mi (land); pop. (2014 est.) 844,994, 30% of French extraction. Capital: Saint-Denis; pop. (2014 est.) 143,617. The chief export is sugar. It elects 5 deputies, 3 senators to the French Parliament. **Website:** www.regionreunion.com

French Overseas Territorial Collectivities

French Polynesia, comprises 130 islands widely scattered among 5 archipelagos in the S Pacific; administered by a Council of Ministers (headed by a president). Territorial Assembly and the Council have headquarters at Papeete, on Tahiti, one of the Society Islands (which include the Windward Isls. and Leeward Isls.). Two deputies and a senator are elected to the French Parliament.

Other groups are the Marquesas Isls.; the Tuamotu Archipelago; the Gambier Isls.; and the Austral, or Tubuai, Isls.

Total area of the islands administered from Tahiti is 1,609 sq mi (total), 1,478 sq mi (land); pop. (2015 est.) 282,703. Tahiti is mountainous with a productive coastline bearing coconuts, citrus, pineapples, and vanilla. Cultured pearls are also produced.

Tahiti was visited by Capt. James Cook in 1769 and by Capt. Bligh in the *Bounty*, 1788-89. Its beauty impressed Herman Melville, Paul Gauguin, and Charles Darwin. A coalition favoring independence for French Polynesia within 20 years gained control of the territorial assembly after elections May 23, 2004. An anti-independence party won May 5, 2013, territorial assembly elections. A UN General Assembly resolution on May 17, 2013, called on France to grant French Polynesia independence.

St. Pierre and Miquelon became a territorial collectivity in 1985. It consists of two groups of rocky islands near the SW coast of Newfoundland, inhabited by fishermen. Fish products are the chief export. The St. Pierre group has an area of 10 sq mi; Miquelon, 83 sq mi. Total pop. (2015 est.) 5,657. Capital: Saint-Pierre; pop. (2014 est.) 5,459. Both Mayotte and St. Pierre and Miquelon elect a deputy and a senator to the French Parliament.

St. Barthélemy and **St. Martin**, both formerly part of Guadeloupe, voted for secession in 2003 and became overseas territorial collectivities in 2007. Total pop. (2015 est.) was 7,237 and 31,754 respectively.

The territorial collectivity of **Wallis and Futuna** comprises two island groups in the SW Pacific S of Tuvalu, N of Fiji, and W of Western Samoa. It became an overseas territory July 29, 1961. The islands have a total area of 55 sq mi and pop. (2015 est.) of 15,613. Alofi, attached to Futuna, is uninhabited. Capital: Mata-Utu; pop. (2014 est.) 1,064. Chief exports are copra, chemicals, and construction materials. A senator and a deputy are elected to the French Parliament.

Overseas Territory and Special Collectivity

The territory of the **French Southern and Antarctic Lands** comprises island groups in the Indian O. Area: 2,991 sq mi (total), 2,960 sq mi (land).

The U.S. does not recognize French claim to Adelie Land, an area of about 193,051 sq mi on Antarctica. Adelie, reached 1840, has a 185-mi coastline and tapers 1,240 mi inland to the S Pole. It has a research station. There are two glaciers: Ninnis, 22 mi wide, 99 mi long, and Mentz, 11 mi by 140 mi.

The Indian O. groups are as follows: Kerguelen Archipelago, visited 1772, consists of one large and 300 small islands. The chief is 87 mi long, 74 mi wide, and has Mt. Ross (6,429 ft). Principal research station is Port-aux-Français. There are seals, blue whales, coal, peat, semiprecious stones. Crozet Archipelago, reached 1772, covers 136 sq mi. Eastern Island rises to 6,560 ft. Saint Paul, in southern Indian O., has warm springs with earth at places heating to 120° to 390°F. Amsterdam Island is nearby; both produce cod and rock lobster. Military garrisons and meteorological stations are located on the Scattered Isls.

The special collectivity of **New Caledonia** and Dependencies is a group of islands in the Pacific O. about 1,115 mi E of Australia and approx. the same distance NW of New Zealand. Dependencies are the Loyalty Isls., Isle of Pines, Belep Archipelago, and Huon Isls.

The largest island, New Caledonia, is 6,530 sq mi. Total area of the territory is 7,172 sq mi (total), 7,056 sq mi (land); pop. (2015 est.) 271,615. The group was acquired by France in 1853.

The territory is administered by a High Commissioner. There is a popularly elected Territorial Congress. Two deputies and a senator are elected to the French Parliament. Capital: Nouméa; pop. (2014 est.) 181,002.

Mining is the chief industry. New Caledonia is one of the world's largest nickel producers. Chrome, iron, cobalt, manganese, silver, gold, lead, and copper are also found. Agric. products include yams, sweet potatoes, potatoes, manioc, corn, and coconuts.

In 1987, New Caledonian voters chose by referendum to remain within the Republic. French and Melanesians (Kanaks) clashed in 1988. An agreement Apr. 21, 1998, between France and rival New Caledonian factions specified a 15- to 20-year period of shared sovereignty and a referendum on independence no later than 2018. Parties favoring remaining part of France won a majority in May 11, 2014, Territorial Congress elections. **Website:** www.gouv.nc

Gabon

Gabonese Republic

People: Population: 1,705,336. **Age distrib.:** <15: 42.1%; 65+: 3.8%. **Growth:** 1.9%. **Migrants:** 23.6%. **Pop. density:** 17.1 per sq mi, 6.6 per sq km. **Urban:** 87.2%. **Ethnic groups:** Bantu tribes, incl. four major tribal groupings (Fang, Bapounou, Nzebi, Obamba). **Languages:** French (official), Fang, Myene, Nzebi, Bapounou/Eschira, Bandjabi. **Religions:** Christian 55%-75%, animist.

Geography: Total area: 103,347 sq mi, 267,667 sq km; **Land area:** 99,486 sq mi, 257,667 sq km. **Location:** Atlantic coast of W central Africa. Equatorial Guinea, Cameroon on N; Congo on E and S. **Topography:** Heavily forested, consisting of coastal lowlands; plateaus in N, E, and S; mountains in N, SE, and center. The Ogooue R. system covers most of Gabon. **Arable land:** 1.3%. **Capital:** Libreville, 707,225.

Government: Type: Republic. **Head of state:** Pres. Ali Bongo Ondimba; in office: Oct. 16, 2009. **Head of gov.:** Prime Min. Daniel Ona Ondo; in office: Jan. 27, 2014. **Local divisions:** 9 provinces. **Defense budget:** $183 mil. **Active troops:** 4,700.

Economy: Industries: petroleum extraction and refining; manganese, gold; chemicals, ship repair, food and beverages. **Chief crops:** cocoa, coffee, sugar, palm oil, rubber. **Natural resources:** petroleum, nat. gas, diamonds, niobium, manganese, uranium, gold, timber, iron ore, hydropower. **Water:** 99,282 cu m per capita. **Crude oil reserves:** 2 bil bbls. **Electricity prod.:** 2.1 bil kWh. **Labor force:** agric. 60%, industry 15%, services 25%. **Unemployment:** 19.6%.

Finance: Monetary unit: Central African CFA Franc (XAF) (584.11 = $1 U.S.). **GDP:** $36.4 bil; **per capita GDP:** $22,900; **GDP growth:** 5.1%. **Imports:** $4.8 bil; France 21.8%, Côte d'Ivoire 16.6%, China 10%, Belgium 5.6%, U.S. 5.5%, Netherlands 5.1%. **Exports:** $8.4 bil; Japan 21.7%, U.S. 10.7%, Australia 9.7%, India 8.8%, China 8.5%, Spain 6.3%. **Budget:** $5.9 bil. **Inflation** (2012-13): 0.5%.

Transport: Railways: 403 mi. **Airports:** 14.

Communications: Telephone: 1 per 100 pop. **Mobile:** 210.4 per 100 pop. **Broadband:** 0.5 per 100 pop. **Internet:** 9.8%.

Health: Expend.: 3.5%. **Life expect.:** 51.6 male; 52.5 female. **Births:** 34.5 per 1,000 pop. **Deaths:** 13.1 per 1,000 pop. **Infant mortality:** 46.1 per 1,000 live births. **Undernourished:** <5%. **HIV:** 3.9%.

Education: Compulsory: ages 6-15. **Literacy:** 83.2%.

Embassy: 2034 20th St. NW 20009; 797-1000.

Website: www.gouvernement.ga or www.state.gov/p/af/ci/gb/

France established control over the region in the second half of the 19th cent. Gabon became independent Aug. 17, 1960. Backed by France, Pres. Albert-Bernard Bongo (later Omar Bongo Ondimba) ruled the country 1967-2009, greatly enriching himself and his family. A multiparty political system was introduced in 1990; a new constitution was enacted in 1991. Bongo's reelection victories in 1993, 1998, and 2003 were faulted by international observers. After he died June 8, 2009, his son Ali Bongo Ondimba, Gabon's defense minister 1999-2009, claimed victory in the disputed 2009 presidential election.

Gabon has abundant natural resources (including oil) and is one of the most prosperous African countries, although there is extreme income inequality. Elephant poaching in game reserves for illegal ivory sales has become a major problem in recent years.

The Gambia

Republic of The Gambia

People: Population: 1,967,709. **Age distrib.:** <15: 38.3%; 65+: 3.4%. **Growth:** 2.2%. **Migrants:** 8.8%. **Pop. density:** 509.6 per sq mi, 196.8 per sq km. **Urban:** 59.6%. **Ethnic groups:** Mandinka 42%, Fula 18%, Wolof 16%, Jola 10%, Serahuli 9%. **Languages:** English (official), Mandinka, Wolof, Fula, other indigenous vernaculars. **Religions:** Muslim 90%, Christian 8%.

Geography: Total area: 4,363 sq mi, 11,300 sq km; **Land area:** 3,907 sq mi, 10,120 sq km. **Location:** Atlantic coast near W tip of Africa. Surrounded on 3 sides by Senegal. **Topography:** Narrow strip of land on each side of lower Gambia R. **Arable land:** 43.5%. **Capital:** Banjul, 503,648.

Government: Type: Republic. **Head of state and gov.:** Pres. Yahya Jammeh; in office: Oct. 18, 1996. **Local divisions:** 5 divisions, 1 city. **Defense budget** (2012): $6 mil. **Active troops:** 800.

Economy: Industries: peanuts, fish, hides, tourism, beverages, agric. machinery assembly. **Chief crops:** rice, millet, sorghum, peanuts, corn, sesame, cassava, palm kernels. **Natural resources:** fish, clay, silica sand, titanium, tin, zircon. **Water:** 4,327 cu m per capita. **Electricity prod.:** 235 mil kWh. **Labor force:** agric. 75%, industry 19%, services 6%. **Unemployment:** 7%.

Finance: Monetary unit: Dalasi (GMD) (39.25 = $1 U.S.). **GDP:** $3.1 bil; **per capita GDP:** $1,600; **GDP growth:** –0.2%. **Imports:** $353.1 mil; China 30.3%, Senegal 9.1%, Brazil 8.2%, India 6.7%. **Exports:** $107.4 mil; China 57%, India 23.2%. **Tourism:** $88 mil. **Budget:** $242.6 mil. **Inflation:** 5.9%.

Transport: Airports: 1.

Communications: Telephone: 2.9 per 100 pop. **Mobile:** 119.6 per 100 pop. **Broadband:** 1.4 per 100 pop. **Internet:** 15.6%.

Health: Expend.: 5%. **Life expect.:** 62.3 male; 67.0 female. **Births:** 30.9 per 1,000 pop. **Deaths:** 7.2 per 1,000 pop. **Infant mortality:** 63.9 per 1,000 live births. **Undernourished:** 6%. **HIV:** 1.8%.

Education: Compulsory: ages 7-15. **Literacy:** 55.5%.

Embassy: 2233 Wisconsin Ave. NW, Ste. 240, 20007; 785-1399.

Website: www.gambia.gm

The peoples of The Gambia were at one time associated with the West African empires of Ghana, Mali, and Songhai. The area became Britain's first African possession in 1588.

Independence came Feb. 18, 1965; republic status within the Commonwealth was achieved in 1970. The country suffered from severe famine in the 1970s. Senegambia, a confederation with Senegal, lasted from 1982 to 1989.

On July 22, 1994, after 24 years in power, Pres. Dawda K. Jawara was deposed in a bloodless coup by a military officer, Yahya Jammeh. Jammeh barred political activity, detained potential opponents, and governed by decree. Despite a nominal return to constitutional government in 1996, Jammeh retained a tight grip on power. Security forces suppressed an alleged coup plot by army officers Mar. 2006. Pres. Jammeh won a fourth 5-year term in 2011. An attempted coup, apparently aided by at least three U.S. citizens, was foiled Dec. 30, 2014. With per capita GDP of less than $2,000 in 2014, The Gambia is one of the world's poorest countries.

Georgia

People: Population: 4,931,226. **Age distrib.:** <15: 17.7%; 65+: 15.5%. **Growth:** –0.1%. **Migrants:** 4.4%. **Pop. density:** 183.2 per sq mi, 70.7 per sq km. **Urban:** 53.6%. **Ethnic groups:** Georgian 83.8%, Azeri 6.5%, Armenian 5.7%. **Languages:** Georgian (official), Russian, Armenian, Azeri, Abkhaz (official in Abkhazia). **Religions:** Orthodox Christian (official) 83.9%, Muslim 9.9%, Armenian-Gregorian 3.9%.

Geography: Total area: 26,911 sq mi, 69,700 sq km; **Land area:** 26,911 sq mi, 69,700 sq km. **Location:** SW Asia, on E coast of Black Sea. Russia on N and NE, Turkey and Armenia on S, Azerbaijan on SE. **Topography:** Main range of Caucasus Mts. on NE separates country from Russia. **Arable land:** 5.8%. **Capital:** Tbilisi, 1,147,486.

Government: Type: Republic. **Head of state:** Pres. Giorgi Margvelashvili; in office: Nov. 17, 2013. **Head of gov.:** Prime Min. Irakli Garibashvili; in office: Nov. 20, 2013. **Local divisions:** 9 regions, 1 city, 2 autonomous republics. **Defense budget:** $393 mil. **Active troops:** 20,650.

Economy: Industries: steel, machine tools, elec. appliances, mining, chemicals, wood prods., wine. **Chief crops:** citrus, grapes, tea, hazelnuts, vegetables. **Natural resources:** timber, hydropower, manganese, iron ore, copper, minor coal and oil deposits. **Water:** 14,589 cu m per capita. **Crude oil reserves:** 35 mil bbls. **Electricity prod.:** 9.5 bil kWh. **Labor force:** agric. 55.6%, industry 8.9%, services 35.5%. **Unemployment:** 14.3%.

Finance: Monetary unit: Lari (GEL) (2.36 = $1 U.S.). **GDP:** $34.2 bil; **per capita GDP:** $7,700; **GDP growth:** 4.7%. **Imports:** $8.3 bil; Turkey 16%, China 8.3%, Ukraine 7.7%, Azerbaijan 7.3%, Russia 6.7%, Germany 5.6%. **Exports:** $4.5 bil; Azerbaijan 24.3%, Armenia 9%, Turkey 7%, Ukraine 6.3%, Bulgaria 5.6%, U.S. 5.1%. **Tourism:** $1.8 bil. **Budget:** $5 bil. **Inflation:** 3.1%.

Transport: Railways: 847 mi. **Airports:** 18.

Communications: Telephone: 25.4 per 100 pop. **Mobile:** 124.9 per 100 pop. **Broadband:** 17.5 per 100 pop. **Internet:** 48.9%.

Health: Expend.: 9.2%. **Life expect.:** 71.9 male; 80.4 female. **Births:** 12.7 per 1,000 pop. **Deaths:** 10.8 per 1,000 pop. **Infant mortality:** 16.2 per 1,000 live births. **Undernourished:** 9.8%. **HIV:** 0.3%.

Education: Compulsory: ages 6-14. **Literacy:** 99.8%.

Embassy: 2209 Massachusetts Ave. NW 20007; 387-2390.

Website: www.gov.ge

The region, which contained the ancient kingdoms of Colchis and Iberia, was Christianized in the 4th cent. and conquered by Arabs in the 8th cent. Annexed by Russia in 1801, Georgia was forcibly incorporated into the USSR in 1922.

Georgia declared independence Apr. 9, 1991, and became an independent country when the Soviet Union disbanded Dec. 26. After a power struggle, former Soviet Foreign Min. Eduard A. Shevardnadze became president. He survived several coup attempts and won reelection in 1995 and 2000. Parliamentary elections Nov. 2, 2003, denounced as fraudulent by opposition groups and international observers, sparked massive antigovernment protests, causing Shevardnadze to resign Nov. 23. Opposition leader Mikhail Saakashvili won the 2004 presidential election. He survived an apparent assassination attempt along with U.S. Pres. George W. Bush in Tbilisi May 10, 2005. He suppressed an alleged coup plot Sept. 6, 2006, and cracked down violently on antigovernment protests and imposed a state of emergency, Nov. 7-16, 2007. He called early elections, Jan. 2008, which he won. Giorgi Margvelashvili of the recently formed Georgian Dream coalition, which won 2012 parliamentary elections, was elected president Oct. 27, 2013. Irakli Garibashvili of Georgian Dream became prime min., Nov. 20, 2013, a post with greatly increased powers under constitutional revisions. Georgia signed an economic cooperation agreement with the EU, June 27, 2014. Saakashvili (then living in the U.S.) was charged, July 28, 2014, with abuse of power in connection with the suppression of the Nov. 2007 protests.

Since independence, secessionist movements in the enclaves of South Ossetia and Abkhazia, supported by Russia, have rejected the Tbilisi government. Open warfare between Georgia and Russia erupted when Saakashvili sent troops, Aug. 7, 2008, to suppress insurgent activity in Tskhinvali, the South Ossetian capital. Russia, Aug. 8-9, dispatched forces to South Ossetia and Abkhazia and attacked key Georgian cities. A cease-fire signed Aug. 15-16 called for withdrawal of Russian forces from Georgia proper, but allowed thousands of Russian troops to remain in the breakaway regions. Russia, Aug. 2008, formally recognized South Ossetia and Abkhazia's independence; almost all other nations have not extended recognition. South Ossetia Pres. Leonid Tibilov, who won a runoff election in Apr. 2012, signed a military cooperation treaty with Russia, Mar. 18, 2015. Raul Khajimba won an Aug. 2014 presidential election in Abkhazia; he signed a new cooperation agreement with Russia, Nov. 24, 2014.

Heavy rains, June 2015, caused the worst flooding in Tbilisi in half a century, in which at least 17 people died, including 1 killed by a tiger after dozens of zoo animals escaped during the flooding.

Germany

Federal Republic of Germany

People: Population: 80,854,408. **Age distrib.:** <15: 12.9%; 65+: 21.5%. **Growth:** –0.2%. **Migrants:** 11.9%. **Pop. density:** 600.6 per sq mi, 231.9 per sq km. **Urban:** 75.3%. **Ethnic groups:** German 91.5%, Turkish 2.4%, other (incl. Greek, Italian, Polish, Russian, Serbo-Croatian, Spanish) 6.1%. **Languages:** German (official); Danish, Frisian, Sorbian, Romany (official minority langs.). **Religions:** Protestant 34%, Roman Catholic 34%, Muslim 3.7%.

Geography: Total area: 137,847 sq mi, 357,022 sq km; **Land area:** 134,623 sq mi, 348,672 sq km. **Location:** Central Europe. Denmark on N; Netherlands, Belgium, Luxembourg, France on W; Switzerland, Austria on S; Czech Rep., Poland on E. **Topography:** Flat in N, hilly in center and W, and mountainous in Bavaria in the S. Chief rivers are Elbe, Weser, Ems, Rhine, and Main, all flowing toward North Sea, and Danube, flowing toward Black Sea. **Arable land:** 34%. **Capital:** Berlin, 3,563,194. **Cities:** Hamburg, 1,830,673; Munich, 1,437,900; Cologne, 1,036,771.

Government: Type: Federal republic. **Head of state:** Pres. Joachim Gauck; in office: Mar. 23, 2012. **Head of gov.:** Chancellor Angela Merkel; in office: Nov. 22, 2005. **Local divisions:** 16 states. **Defense budget:** $43.9 bil. **Active troops:** 181,550.

Economy: Industries: iron, steel, coal, cement, chemicals, machinery, vehicles, machine tools, electronics, automobiles, food and beverages. **Chief crops:** potatoes, wheat, barley, sugar beets, fruit, cabbages. **Natural resources:** coal, lignite, nat. gas, iron ore, copper, nickel, uranium, potash, salt, constr. materials, timber. **Water:** 1,862 cu m per capita. **Crude oil reserves:** 226.8 mil bbls. **Electricity prod.:** 585.2 bil kWh. **Labor force:** agric. 1.6%, industry 24.6%, services 73.8%. **Unemployment:** 5.3%.

Finance: Monetary unit: Euro (EUR) (0.89 = $1 U.S.). **GDP:** $3.7 tril; **per capita GDP:** $45,900; **GDP growth:** 1.6%. **Imports:** $1.3 tril; Netherlands 14.2%, France 7.7%, Belgium 6.4%, China 6.4%, Italy 5.4%. **Exports:** $1.5 tril; France 9.8%, UK 7.4%, Netherlands 6.9%, U.S. 6.4%, Austria 5.5%, China 5.4%, Italy 5.2%. **Tourism:** $43.3 bil. **Budget:** $1.7 tril. **Inflation:** 0.9%.

Transport: Railways: 27,010 mi. **Motor vehicles:** 588.3 per 1,000 pop. **Airports:** 318.

Communications: Telephone: 56.9 per 100 pop. **Mobile:** 120.4 per 100 pop. **Broadband:** 44.8 per 100 pop. **Internet:** 86.2%.

Health: Expend.: 11.3%. **Life expect.:** 78.3 male; 83.0 female. **Births:** 8.5 per 1,000 pop. **Deaths:** 11.4 per 1,000 pop. **Infant mortality:** 3.4 per 1,000 live births. **Undernourished:** <5%. **HIV:** NA.

Education: Compulsory: ages 6-18. **Literacy:** 99%.

Embassy: 2300 M St. NW, Ste. 300, 20037; 298-4000.

Website: www.deutschland.de

Julius Caesar defeated Germanic tribes, 55 and 53 BCE, but Roman expansion north of the Rhine was stopped in 9 CE. Charlemagne, ruler of the Franks, consolidated Saxon, Bavarian, Rhenish, Frankish, and other lands; after him the eastern part became the German Empire. The Thirty Years' War, 1618-48, split Germany into small principalities and kingdoms.

Otto von Bismarck, Prussian chancellor, formed the North German Confederation, 1867. In 1870 Bismarck maneuvered Napoleon III into declaring war. After the quick defeat of France, Bismarck formed the German Empire and on Jan. 18, 1871, in Versailles, proclaimed King Wilhelm I of Prussia the German emperor (Deutscher kaiser).

The German Empire reached its peak before WWI in 1914, with 208,780 sq mi, plus overseas colonies. After losing the war in 1918, Germany ceded Alsace-Lorraine to France, West Prussia and Posen (Poznan) province to Poland, and part of Schleswig to Denmark. It lost all colonies and the ports of Memel and Danzig.

Republic of Germany, 1919-33, adopted the Weimar constitution; met reparation payments and elected Friedrich Ebert and Gen. Paul von Hindenburg presidents.

Third Reich, 1933-45: Adolf Hitler led the National Socialist German Workers' (Nazi) party after WWI. Pres. von Hindenburg named Hitler chancellor in 1933; on Aug. 3, 1934, the day after Hindenburg's death, the cabinet joined the offices of president and chancellor and made Hitler *fuehrer* (leader). Hitler abolished freedom of speech and assembly, and began a long series of persecutions culminating in the murder of millions of Jews and others.

He repudiated the Versailles treaty and reparations agreements, remilitarized the Rhineland (1936), and annexed Austria (Anschluss, 1938). At Munich he made an agreement with British Prime Min. Neville Chamberlain, which permitted Germany to annex part of Czechoslovakia. He signed a nonaggression treaty with the USSR, 1939, and declared war on Poland Sept. 1, 1939, precipitating WWII. With total defeat near, Hitler committed suicide in Berlin Apr. 1945. The victorious Allies voided all acts and annexations of Hitler's Reich.

Germany was sectioned into 4 zones of occupation, administered by the Allied Powers (U.S., USSR, UK, and France). The USSR took control of many E German states. The territory E of the so-called Oder-Neisse line was assigned to, and later annexed by, Poland. The USSR annexed Northern East Prussia (now Kaliningrad). Greater Berlin, within but not part of the Soviet zone, was administered by the 4 occupying powers under the Allied Command. In 1948 the USSR withdrew, established its single command in East Berlin, and cut off supplies. The Western Allies utilized a gigantic airlift to bring food to West Berlin, 1948-49.

In 1949, two separate German states were established. In May the zones administered by the Western Allies became West Germany; in Oct. the Soviet sector became East Germany. West Berlin was considered a West German enclave, a status the Soviet bloc disputed.

East Germany. The German Democratic Republic (East Germany) was proclaimed in the Soviet sector of Berlin Oct. 7, 1949. It was declared fully sovereign in 1954, but Soviet troops remained.

Coincident with the entrance of West Germany into the European defense community in 1952, the East German government decreed a prohibited zone 3 mi deep along its 600-mi border with West Germany and cut Berlin's telephone system in two. Berlin was further divided by erection of a fortified wall in 1961, after over 3 mil East Germans had fled to the West. The oppressive Communist regime maintained control through the state security police, known as the Stasi.

By the early 1970s, the economy of East Germany was highly industrialized, and the nation was credited with the highest standard of living among Warsaw Pact countries. Growth slowed in the late 1970s because of shortages of natural resources and labor and huge debt. Comparison with the lifestyle in the West caused many young people to emigrate.

In the late 1980s the government firmly resisted following the USSR's policy of openness (*glasnost*) but was faced with nationwide demonstrations demanding reform. Pres. Erich Honecker, in office since 1976, was forced to resign Oct. 18, 1989. On Nov. 9, the East German government announced its decision to open the border with the West, signaling the end of the Berlin Wall. On Aug. 23, 1990, the East German parliament agreed to reunite with West Germany.

West Germany. The Federal Republic of Germany (West Germany) was proclaimed May 23, 1949, in Bonn. The occupying powers—the U.S., Britain, and France—restored civil status, Sept. 21. The Western Allies ended the state of war with Germany in 1951, while the USSR did so in 1955. The powers lifted controls, and the republic became fully independent May 5, 1955.

Dr. Konrad Adenauer, a Christian Democrat, was made chancellor 1949 and was reelected 1953, 1957, 1961. Willy Brandt, heading a coalition of Social Democrats and Free Democrats, became chancellor 1969 and pursued a policy of *Ostpolitik*, or rapprochement with East Germany and the USSR. Brandt resigned May 1974 after a spy scandal. Terrorist acts on German soil in the 1970s included activities of the Baader-Meinhof gang, also known as the Red Army Faction, and the murder of Israeli athletes by Palestinian commandos at the Olympic Games in Munich, Sept. 5, 1972.

Helmut Kohl became chancellor in 1982 and led Christian Democrats to victory in 1983 and 1987.

Unified Germany. In May 1990, NATO ministers voted to make the united Germany a full member of NATO and barred the new Germany from having its own nuclear, chemical, or biological weapons. The merger of the two Germanys took place Oct. 3, and the first all-German elections since 1932 were held Dec. 2, with West German Chancellor Helmut Kohl confirmed as leader of the unified nation. Eastern Germany received over $1 tril in public and private funds from western Germany, 1990-95. In 1991, Berlin again became Germany's official capital; the Bundestag (parliament) and parts of the federal executive were relocated from Bonn to Berlin in 1999. Unemployment hit a postwar high of 12.6% in Jan. 1998. The Christian Democrats lost parliamentary elections, Sept. 27, 1998, and Gerhard Schröder, of the Social Democratic Party (SPD), became chancellor. The Christian Democrats, led by Angela Merkel, won a razor-thin plurality in 2005 parliamentary elections, and she became chancellor Nov. 22, heading a "grand coalition" that included the SPD.

Responding to the global recession, the government passed a 50-bil euro economic stimulus plan in early 2009. Merkel led a center-right coalition to victory in 2009 national elections. After an earthquake and tsunami in Japan caused a nuclear disaster, the Merkel government announced May 2011 that it would close Germany's 17 nuclear power plants by 2022. Merkel and then-French Pres. Nicolas Sarkozy led the international response to the European debt crisis involving Greece in late 2009, followed by Ireland, Portugal, Italy, and Spain; debtor nations were required to adopt stern austerity measures in return for aid. Although new recessions in several austerity-bound countries caused some eurozone nations to doubt Germany's strategy, Merkel's government again took a hard line in new debt negotiations with Greece in 2015, requiring further austerity measures in exchange for additional bailout funds.

A report released Jan 19, 2013, contained information from more than 1,100 people describing themselves as victims of child sexual abuse perpetrated by German Catholic priests over the course of several years. The Constitutional Court in Karlsruhe, the nation's highest court, affirmed Feb. 19, 2013, gay couples' right to adopt children.

Merkel's Christian Democrats won a clear-cut victory in Sept. 22, 2013, parliamentary elections but fell short of a majority. She formed a new coalition, including the SPD, in Dec. All 150 people aboard a flight operated by Lufthansa subsidiary Germanwings were killed, Mar. 24, 2015, when the copilot intentionally crashed the plane in the French Alps. Germany was the destination in 2015 for many migrants reaching Europe after fleeing war or hardship in the Middle East, SW Asia, or Africa; it also received large numbers of migrants from the Balkans. More than 500,000 migrants arrived, Jan.-Sept., and the government estimated in Sept. that up to 1 mil refugees and asylum seekers could arrive Jan.-Dec. Germany took a leading role in gaining EU adoption, Sept. 22, of a plan to resettle 120,000 refugees throughout the EU. It provided temporary care and set up expedited procedures for processing asylum applications and began repatriating migrants (perhaps 40% of the total and mostly from Southern Europe) judged to be not true refugees.

Helgoland, an island of 0.66 sq mi in the North Sea, was taken from Denmark by a British naval force in 1807 and ceded to Germany in 1890. The island was surrendered to the UK, May 23, 1945, and returned to then-West Germany, Mar. 1, 1952.

Ghana

Republic of Ghana

People: Population: 26,327,649. **Age distrib.:** <15: 38.4%; 65+: 4.1%. **Growth:** 2.2%. **Migrants:** 1.4%. **Pop. density:** 299.7 per sq mi, 115.7 per sq km. **Urban:** 54%. **Ethnic groups:** Akan 47.5%, Mole-Dagbon 16.6%, Ewe 13.9%, Ga-Dangme 7.4%, Gurma 5.7%, Guan 3.7%, Grusi 2.5%. **Languages:** Asante, Ewe, Fante, Boron, Dagomba, Dangme, Dagarte, Kokomba, Akyem, Ga, English (official). **Religions:** Christian 71.2% (incl. Pentecostal/Charismatic 28.3%, Protestant 18.4%, Catholic 13.1%), Muslim 17.6%, traditional 5.2%, none 5.2%.

Geography: Total area: 92,098 sq mi, 238,533 sq km; **Land area:** 87,851 sq mi, 227,533 sq km. **Location:** S coast of W Africa. Côte d'Ivoire on W, Burkina Faso on N, Togo on E. **Topography:** Mostly low fertile plains and scrubland, cut by rivers and by the artificial Lake Volta. **Arable land:** 20.7%. **Capital:** Accra, 2,277,298. **Cities:** Kumasi, 2,598,789.

Government: Type: Constitutional democracy. **Head of state and gov.:** Pres. John Dramani Mahama; in office: July 24, 2012. **Local divisions:** 10 regions. **Defense budget:** $277 mil. **Active troops:** 15,500.

Economy: Industries: mining, lumbering, light mfg., aluminum smelting, food proc., cement, small comm. shipbuilding. **Chief crops:** cocoa, rice, cassava, peanuts, corn, shea nuts, bananas. **Natural resources:** gold, timber, industrial diamonds, bauxite, manganese, fish, rubber, hydropower, petroleum, silver, salt, limestone. **Water:** 2,169 cu m per capita. **Crude oil reserves:** 660 mil bbls. **Electricity prod.:** 11.7 bil kWh. **Labor force:** agric. 44.7%, industry 14.4%, services 40.9%. **Unemployment:** 4.6%.

Finance: Monetary unit: Cedi (GHS) (3.70 = $1 U.S.). **GDP:** $108.3 bil; **per capita GDP:** $4,100; **GDP growth:** 4.2%. **Imports:** $14.6 bil; China 22.3%, Nigeria 11.8%, Netherlands 6.4%, Côte d'Ivoire 6.3%, U.S. 6%. **Exports:** $13.2 bil; France 12.1%, Italy 9.4%, China 8.2%, Netherlands 7.6%. **Tourism:** $853 mil. **Budget:** $11.6 bil. **Inflation:** 15.5%.

Transport: Railways: 588 mi. **Motor vehicles:** 7.8 per 1,000 pop. **Airports:** 7.

Communications: Telephone: 1 per 100 pop. **Mobile:** 114.8 per 100 pop. **Broadband:** 40.2 per 100 pop. **Internet:** 18.9%.

Health: Expend.: 5.2%. **Life expect.:** 63.8 male; 68.7 female. **Births:** 31.1 per 1,000 pop. **Deaths:** 7.2 per 1,000 pop. **Infant mortality:** 37.4 per 1,000 live births. **Undernourished:** <5%. **HIV:** 1.5%.

Education: Compulsory: ages 4-14. **Literacy:** 76.6%.

Embassy: 3512 International Dr. NW 20008; 686-4520.

Website: www.ghana.gov.gh

Named for an African empire along the Niger R., 400-1240 CE, Ghana was ruled by Britain for 113 years as the Gold Coast. The UN in 1956 approved merger with the British Togoland trust territory. Independence came Mar. 6, 1957, and republic status within the Commonwealth in 1960.

Pres. Kwame Nkrumah built hospitals and schools and promoted development projects but ran the country into debt, jailed opponents, and was accused of corruption. A 1964 referendum gave Nkrumah dictatorial powers and set up a one-party socialist state. A police-army coup overthrew Nkrumah in 1966. Elections were held in 1969, but four further coups occurred in 1972, 1978, 1979, and 1981. A new constitution, allowing multiparty politics, was approved in Apr. 1992. Former coup leader Jerry Rawlings won the 1996 presidential election. Kofi Annan, a career UN diplomat from Ghana, served as UN sec.-gen., 1997-2006.

Opposition leader John Agyekum Kufuor won a 2000 runoff vote and was sworn in Jan. 7, 2001, marking Ghana's first peaceful transfer of power from one elected president to another. He was reelected in 2004. John Atta Mills won a 2008 runoff election. A major offshore oil and gas find was announced June 2007; the Jubilee field, estimated to hold recoverable oil reserves of 1.5 bil barrels, began production Dec. 2010. When Mills died in 2012, Vice Pres. John Dramani Mahama replaced him. Mahama won a full term in Dec. 2012 elections. Heavy rains and flooding in Accra, June 2015, caused more than 150 deaths; most victims died in an explosion at a gas station where people had sought shelter.

Greece

Hellenic Republic

People: Population: 10,775,643. **Age distrib.:** <15: 14%; 65+: 20.5%. **Growth:** 0%. **Migrants:** 8.9%. **Pop. density:** 213.6 per sq mi, 82.5 per sq km. **Urban:** 78%. **Ethnic groups:** Greek 93%, foreign citizen 7%. (Greece does not collect ethnicity data.) **Languages:** Greek (official). **Religions:** Greek Orthodox (official) 98%, Muslim 1.3%.

Geography: Total area: 50,949 sq mi, 131,957 sq km; **Land area:** 50,443 sq mi, 130,647 sq km. **Location:** S end of Balkan Peninsula in SE Europe. Albania, Macedonia, Bulgaria on N; Turkey on E. **Topography:** About three-quarters is non-arable, with mountains in all areas incl. N-S Pindus Mts. Heavily indented coastline is 9,385 mi long. More than 2,000 islands, only 169 inhabited, among them Crete, Rhodes, Milos, Kerkira (Corfu), Chios, Lesbos, Samos, Euboea, Delos, Mykonos. **Arable land:** 19.7%. **Capital:** Athens, 3,051,899. **Cities:** Thessaloniki, 736,628.

Government: Type: Parliamentary republic. **Head of state:** Pres. Karolos Papoulias; in office: Mar. 12, 2005. **Head of gov.:** Prime Min. Alexis Tsipras; in office: Sept. 21, 2015. **Local divisions:** 13 regions, 1 autonomous monastic state. **Defense budget:** $5.64 bil. **Active troops:** 144,950.

Economy: Industries: tourism, food and tobacco proc., textiles, chemicals, metal prods. **Chief crops:** wheat, corn, barley, sugar beets, olives, tomatoes, wine, tobacco, potatoes. **Natural resources:** lignite, petroleum, iron ore, bauxite, lead, zinc, nickel, magnesite, marble, salt. **Water:** 6,147 cu m per capita. **Crude oil reserves:** 10 mil bbls. **Electricity prod.:** 57.6 bil kWh. **Labor force:** agric. 12.9%, industry 14.7%, services 72.4%. **Unemployment:** 27.3%.

Finance: Monetary unit: Euro (EUR) (0.89 = $1 U.S.). **GDP:** $284.3 bil; **per capita GDP:** $25,900; **GDP growth:** 0.8%. **Imports:** $62.8 bil; Russia 14.1%, Germany 9.8%, Italy 8.1%, Iraq 7.8%. **Exports:** $35.8 bil; Turkey 11.8%, Italy 9.1%, Germany 6.7%, Bulgaria 5.4%. **Tourism:** $17.8 bil. **Budget:** $127.9 bil. **Inflation:** –1.3%.

Transport: Railways: 1,583 mi. **Motor vehicles:** 599.1 per 1,000 pop. **Airports:** 68.

Communications: Telephone: 46.9 per 100 pop. **Mobile:** 115 per 100 pop. **Broadband:** 36.1 per 100 pop. **Internet:** 63.2%.

Health: Expend.: 9.3%. **Life expect.:** 77.8 male; 83.2 female. **Births:** 8.7 per 1,000 pop. **Deaths:** 11.1 per 1,000 pop. **Infant mortality:** 4.7 per 1,000 live births. **Undernourished:** <5%. **HIV:** NA.

Education: Compulsory: ages 6-14. **Literacy:** 97.7%.

Embassy: 2217 Massachusetts Ave. NW 20008; 939-1300.

Website: www.primeminister.gov.gr

The achievements of ancient Greece in art, architecture, science, mathematics, philosophy, drama, literature, and democracy became legacies for succeeding ages. Greece reached the height of its power, particularly in the Athenian city-state, in the 5th cent. BCE. Greece fell under Roman rule in the 2nd and 1st cents. BCE. In the 4th cent. CE, it became part of the Byzantine Empire and, after the fall of Constantinople to the Turks in 1453, part of the Ottoman Empire.

Greece won its war of independence from Turkey, 1821-29, and became a kingdom. A republic was established 1924; the monarchy was restored, 1935. In Oct. 1940, Greece rejected an ultimatum from Italy, but the country was defeated and occupied by Germans, Italians, and Bulgarians. By the end of 1944 the invaders withdrew. Communist resistance forces were overcome by Royalist and British troops. A plebiscite restored the monarchy.

Communists waged guerrilla war 1947-49 against the government but were defeated with the aid of the U.S. A period of reconstruction and rapid development followed, mainly with conservative governments under Prem. Constantine Karamanlis. The Center Union, led by Georgios Papandreou, won elections in 1963 and 1964, but King Constantine forced Papandreou to resign. A period of political maneuvers ended with Col. George Papadopoulos's military takeover Apr. 1967. King Constantine tried to reverse the consolidation of the harsh dictatorship Dec. 1967, but failed and fled to Italy. Papadopoulos was ousted Nov. 1973.

Greek army officers serving in the Cyprus National Guard staged a coup on the island July 15, 1974. Turkey invaded Cyprus a week later, precipitating the collapse of the Greek junta. Democratic government returned, and in 1975 the monarchy was abolished.

The 1981 electoral victory of the Panhellenic Socialist Movement (Pasok) of Andreas Papandreou (Georgios's son) substantially changed Greece's internal and external policies. A scandal contributed to the 1989 defeat of the Socialists at the polls. Papandreou, who was acquitted Jan. 1992 of corruption charges, led the Socialists to a comeback victory in 1993 general elections. Costas Simitis replaced the ailing Papandreou as prime minister, Jan. 1996, and led the Socialists to victory in the Sept. 22 election. Socialists retained power by a narrow margin in the 2000 elections.

The conservative New Democracy (ND) party won 2004 parliamentary elections, and Konstantinos (Costas) Karamanlis became prime min. Beset by scandals and an ailing economy, Karamanlis called early elections for Oct. 4, 2009, won by Pasok under the leadership of the U.S.-born George A. Papandreou (Andreas's son). The IMF and eurozone countries agreed in 2010 on a 110-bil euro loan package to prevent Greece from defaulting on its debt; in return, Greek leaders implemented an austerity plan. As the debt crisis continued, parliament passed, amid violent anti-austerity protests, new austerity measures, Feb. 2012, to obtain a second, 130-bil euro bailout in Mar. The conservative, pro-bailout Antonis Samaras of ND became prime min., June 2012. The government agreed on a plan for 13.5 bil euros in budget cuts and austerity measures Sept. 27, touching off renewed violent protests but paving the way for the Intl. Monetary Fund, European Central Bank, and eurozone members (known as the troika) to release 43.7 bil euros in bailout funds Nov. 26. Recession and austerity measures, 2007-13, caused Greece's GDP to shrink by 26%. Campaigning against austerity, the leftist Syriza party won Jan. 25, 2015, elections. Syriza's Alexis Tsipras became prime min. and negotiated with the troika on a third bailout needed by mid-2015 to avert default. Resisting new austerity measures, Tsipras called a July 5 referendum in which Greek voters decisively rejected the austerity terms. Greece failed to make a debt payment to the IMF by June 30. The government closed Greek banks, which were running out of money, June 29-July 20. Negotiations with the troika after the referendum produced an 86-bil euro bailout agreement (final approval came Aug. 19) with tougher austerity terms than previously proposed. The Greek parliament was required to pass a series of measures that included further tax increases and pension cuts, sales of government assets, reduced government control over the economy, and banking system reform. Seeking a renewed mandate, Tsipras resigned Aug. 20 and called new elections for Sept. 20; Syriza won, and Tsipras again became prime min., Sept. 21.

In 2015, Greece became the most common entry point for undocumented migrants from the Middle East, SW Asia, and Africa trying to reach the EU. About 390,000 migrants arrived in Greece, Jan.-Sept.; the leading country of origin was Syria.

Grenada

People: Population: 110,694. **Age distrib.:** <15: 24.4%; 65+: 9.6%. **Growth:** 0.5%. **Migrants:** 10.7%. **Pop. density:** 833.4 per sq mi, 321.8 per sq km. **Urban:** 35.6%. **Ethnic groups:** African descent 89.4%, mixed 8.2%, E Indian 1.6%. **Languages:** English (official), French patois. **Religions:** Roman Catholic 44.6%, Protestant 43.5% (incl. Anglican 11.5%, Pentecostal 11.3%, Seventh-day Adventist 10.5%), none 3.6%.

Geography: Total area: 133 sq mi, 344 sq km; **Land area:** 133 sq mi, 344 sq km. **Location:** In Caribbean, 90 mi N of Venezuela. Trinidad and Tobago to S, St. Vincent and the Grenadines to N. **Topography:** Main island is mountainous. Country also comprised of Carriacou and Petit Martinique Isls. **Arable land:** 8.8%. **Capital:** St. George's, 37,822 (2014).

Government: Type: Parliamentary democracy. **Head of state:** Queen Elizabeth II, rep. by Gov.-Gen. Cecile La Grenade; in office: May 7, 2013. **Head of gov.:** Prime Min. Keith Mitchell; in office: Feb. 20, 2013. **Local divisions:** 6 parishes, 1 dependency. **Defense budget/active troops:** NA.

Economy: Industries: food and beverages, textiles, light assembly operations, tourism, constr. **Chief crops:** bananas, cocoa, nutmeg, mace, citrus, avocados, root crops, sugarcane, corn, vegetables. **Natural resources:** timber. **Water:** 1,887 cu m per capita. **Electricity prod.:** 193 mil kWh. **Labor force:** agric. 11%, industry 20%, services 69%. **Unemployment:** NA.

Finance: Monetary unit: East Caribbean Dollar (XCD) (2.70 = $1 U.S.). **GDP:** $1.3 bil; **per capita GDP:** $12,000; **GDP growth:** 1.5%. **Imports** (2012): $297 mil; Trinidad and Tobago 43.5%, U.S. 20.4%. **Exports** (2012): $40.5 mil; Nigeria 40%, St. Lucia 10.3%, Antigua and Barbuda 7%, U.S. 6.4%, St. Kitts and Nevis 6.3%, Dominica 6.3%, Malaysia 5.9%. **Tourism:** $128 mil. **Budget** (2012 est.): $208.6 mil. **Inflation:** –0.9%.

Transport: Airports: 3.

Communications: Telephone: 26.9 per 100 pop. **Mobile:** 126.5 per 100 pop. **Broadband:** 0.9 per 100 pop. **Internet:** 37.4%.

Health: Expend.: 6.4%. **Life expect.:** 71.5 male; 76.9 female. **Births:** 16.0 per 1,000 pop. **Deaths:** 8.1 per 1,000 pop. **Infant mortality:** 10.2 per 1,000 live births. **Undernourished:** NA. **HIV:** NA.

Education: Compulsory: ages 5-16. **Literacy:** NA.

Embassy: 1701 New Hampshire Ave. NW 20009; 265-2561.

Website: www.gov.gd

Christopher Columbus sighted Grenada in 1498. The first European settlers were French, 1650. The island was held alternately by France and England until final British occupation, 1784. Grenada became fully independent Feb. 7, 1974, during a general strike.

On Oct. 14, 1983, a military coup ousted Prime Min. Maurice Bishop, who was put under house arrest, later freed by supporters, rearrested, and executed Oct. 19. U.S. forces, with a token force from six area nations, invaded Grenada, Oct. 25. Resistance from the Grenadian army and Cuban advisors was quickly overcome, and U.S. troops left Grenada in June 1985.

Hurricane Ivan slammed into Grenada, Sept. 7, 2004, killing 39 people and damaging an estimated 90% of the buildings on the island. Tillman Thomas of the National Democratic Congress became prime min. after 2008 parliamentary elections. The opposition New National Party won all 15 seats available in general elections Feb. 19, 2013, and Keith Mitchell became prime min.

Guatemala

Republic of Guatemala

People: Population: 14,918,999. **Age distrib.:** <15: 35.6%; 65+: 4.3%. **Growth:** 1.8%. **Migrants:** 0.5%. **Pop. density:** 360.6 per sq mi, 139.2 per sq km. **Urban:** 51.6%. **Ethnic groups:** mestizo or Ladino (mixed Amerindian/Spanish) and European 59.4%, K'iche 9.1%, Kaqchikel 8.4%, Mam 7.9%, Q'eqchi 6.3%, other Mayan 8.6%. **Languages:** Spanish (official), Amerindian langs. (23 officially recognized). **Religions:** Roman Catholic, Protestant, indigenous Mayan beliefs.

Geography: Total area: 42,042 sq mi, 108,889 sq km; **Land area:** 41,374 sq mi, 107,159 sq km. **Location:** Central America. Mexico on N and W, El Salvador on S, Honduras and Belize on E. **Topography:** Central highland and mountain areas bordered by a narrow Pacific coast and lowlands and fertile river valleys on the Caribbean. Numerous volcanoes in S, more than half a dozen over 11,000 ft. **Arable land:** 14.3%. **Capital:** Guatemala City, 2,918,337.

Government: Type: Constitutional democratic republic. **Head of state and gov.:** Pres. Alejandro Maldonado; in office: Sept. 3, 2015. **Local divisions:** 22 departments. **Defense budget:** $264 mil. **Active troops:** 17,300.

Economy: Industries: sugar, textiles and clothing, furniture, chemicals, petroleum, metals, rubber, tourism. **Chief crops:** sugarcane, corn, bananas, coffee, beans, cardamom. **Natural resources:** petroleum, nickel, rare woods, fish, chicle, hydropower. **Water:** 8,269 cu m per capita. **Crude oil reserves:** 83.1 mil bbls. **Electricity prod.:** 9.2 bil kWh. **Labor force:** agric. 38%, industry 14%, services 48%. **Unemployment:** 2.8%.

Finance: Monetary unit: Quetzal (GTQ) (7.71 = $1 U.S.). **GDP:** $119.1 bil; **per capita GDP:** $7,500; **GDP growth:** 4%. **Imports:** $17.2 bil; U.S. 36.4%, Mexico 11.4%, China 9.7%. **Exports:** $10.6 bil; U.S. 37.2%, El Salvador 8.7%, Honduras 7.8%, Mexico 5%. **Tourism:** $1.6 bil. **Budget:** $8.1 bil. **Inflation:** 3.4%.

Transport: Railways: 497 mi. **Motor vehicles:** 121.2 per 1,000 pop. **Airports:** 16.

Communications: Telephone: 10.8 per 100 pop. **Mobile:** 106.6 per 100 pop. **Broadband:** 6.2 per 100 pop. **Internet:** 23.4%.

Health: Expend.: 6.7%. **Life expect.:** 70.1 male; 74.1 female. **Births:** 24.9 per 1,000 pop. **Deaths:** 4.8 per 1,000 pop. **Infant mortality:** 22.7 per 1,000 live births. **Undernourished:** 14.3%. **HIV:** 0.5%.

Education: Compulsory: ages 6-15. **Literacy:** 81.5%.

Embassy: 2220 R St. NW 20008; 745-4952.

Website: www.guatemala.gob.gt

A Mayan Indian empire flourished in present-day Guatemala for over 1,000 years before Spaniards came. Guatemala was a Spanish colony 1524-1821. A republic was established in 1839.

The U.S. intervened in Guatemala in 1954 when the Central Intelligence Agency engineered the overthrow of elected Pres. Jacobo Arbenz Guzmán, a left-wing reformer. Since then, the country has experienced a variety of military and civilian governments and periods of insurgency, repression, paramilitary violence, and civil war. After military coups in 1982 and 1983, the nation returned to civilian rule in 1986.

The Guatemalan government and leftist rebels signed a peace accord Dec. 29, 1996. During more than 35 years of armed conflict, some 200,000 people were killed or "disappeared" (and are presumed dead); most casualties were attributed to the government and its paramilitary allies. Former Gen. Otto Pérez Molina won a runoff election Nov. 6, 2011, and took office Jan. 2012.

Gen. Efraín Ríos Montt, dictator for 17 months, 1982-83, was found guilty of genocide and sentenced to 80 years in prison May 10, 2013, but the Constitutional Court overturned his conviction May 20 and ruled that part of his trial had to be repeated. Former Pres. Alfonso Portillo was extradited to the U.S. May 24, 2013, to be tried for money laundering; he pleaded guilty and was sentenced May 22, 2014, to nearly 6 years in prison. Drug trafficking, arms smuggling, police corruption, and one of the world's highest homicide rates pose threats to national stability. Apparently seeking safety from drug-related and other violence, Guatemalans made up a sizable portion of the tens of thousands of undocumented immigrant children—some with their mothers, many traveling unaccompanied—detained trying to enter the U.S. from Mexico in late 2013 and 2014.

Pérez Molina's vice president, Roxana Baldetti, resigned and the president dismissed other officials, May 2015, following bribery and corruption scandals; Baldetti was arrested Aug. 21, 2015. Following large-scale protests, Pérez Molina resigned Sept. 2, was jailed Sept. 3, and was ordered to stand trial on bribery, corruption, and conspiracy charges Sept. 8. After first-round presidential voting Sept. 6, the two top vote-getters—former TV comedian Jimmy Moralez and former first lady Sandra Torres—faced a runoff scheduled for Oct. 25.

Guinea

Republic of Guinea

People: Population: 11,780,162. **Age distrib.:** <15: 41.9%; 65+: 3.6%. **Growth:** 2.6%. **Migrants:** 3.2%. **Pop. density:** 124.2 per sq mi, 47.9 per sq km. **Urban:** 37.2%. **Ethnic groups:** Peuhl 40%, Malinke 30%, Soussou 20%. **Languages:** French (official), ethnic group-specific langs. **Religions:** Muslim 85%, Christian 8%, indigenous beliefs 7%.

Geography: Total area: 94,926 sq mi, 245,857 sq km; **Land area:** 94,872 sq mi, 245,717 sq km. **Location:** Atlantic coast of W Africa. Guinea-Bissau, Senegal, Mali on N; Côte d'Ivoire on E; Liberia, Sierra Leone on S. **Topography:** Narrow coastal belt leads to mountainous middle region, source of the Gambia, Senegal, and Niger Rivers. Upper Guinea, farther inland, is cooler upland. The SE is forested. **Arable land:** 12.2%. **Capital:** Conakry, 1,936,045.

Government: Type: Republic. **Head of state:** Pres. Alpha Condé; in office: Dec. 21, 2010. **Head of gov.:** Prime Min. Mohamed Said Fofana; in office: Dec. 24, 2010. **Local divisions:** 7 regions, 1 governorate. **Defense budget** (2012): $39 mil. **Active troops:** 9,700.

Economy: Industries: bauxite, gold, diamonds, iron; light mfg.; agric. proc. **Chief crops:** rice, coffee, pineapples, mangoes, palm kernels, cocoa, cassava, bananas, potatoes. **Natural resources:** bauxite, iron ore, diamonds, gold, uranium, hydropower, fish, salt. **Water:** 19,242 cu m per capita. **Electricity prod.:** 971 mil kWh. **Labor force:** agric. 76%, industry and services 24%. **Unemployment:** 1.8%.

Finance: Monetary unit: Franc (GNF) (7,395.02 = $1 U.S.). **GDP:** $15 bil; **per capita GDP:** $1,300; **GDP growth:** 0.4%. **Imports:** $2.2 bil; China 15.3%, Netherlands 9.8%. **Exports:** $1.8 bil; India 26.6%, South Korea 7.7%, Spain 7.4%, Ireland 5.5%, Ukraine 5.2%. **Tourism:** $1 mil. **Budget:** $1.8 bil. **Inflation** (2012-13): 11.9%.

Transport: Railways: 411 mi. **Airports:** 4.

Communications: Telephone (2011): 0.2 per 100 pop. **Mobile:** 72.1 per 100 pop. **Broadband:** NA. **Internet:** 1.7%.

Health: Expend.: 6.3%. **Life expect.:** 58.6 male; 61.7 female. **Births:** 35.7 per 1,000 pop. **Deaths:** 9.5 per 1,000 pop. **Infant mortality:** 53.4 per 1,000 live births. **Undernourished:** 18.1%. **HIV:** 1.6%.

Education: Compulsory: ages 7-12. **Literacy:** 30.4%.

Embassy: 2112 Leroy Pl. NW 20008; 986-4300.

Website: www.presidence.gov.gn or www.state.gov/p/af/ci/gv/

Guinea, a French colony, attained independence Oct. 2, 1958. Sékou Touré, Guinea's first president (1958-84), turned to Communist nations for support and set up a one-party state. Thousands of opponents were jailed and tortured, and many were killed in the 1970s after an unsuccessful Portuguese invasion.

The military took control in a bloodless coup after the Mar. 1984 death of Touré. A new constitution was approved in 1991, but movement toward democracy was slow. Gen. Lansana Conté, the incumbent, won a long-awaited presidential election in Dec. 1993, which outside monitors called flawed. Conté suppressed an army mutiny in Conakry, Feb. 2-3, 1996, and won reelection in 1998. Fighting in early 2001 along the border with Liberia and Sierra Leone created a refugee crisis in Guinea; voluntary repatriation of more than 51,000 Liberian refugees was largely completed in 2007.

Major opposition parties boycotted the 2003 presidential election, in which the ailing Conté won 95.6% of the vote. More than 120 died in Jan.-Feb. 2007 strikes and protests that pressured Conté to name a new prime min. from a union-leader approved list; protests followed Prime Min. Lansana Kouyate's ouster by Conté in May 2008. After Conté's death Dec. 22, a military junta took power, calling itself the National Council for Democracy and Development. More than 150 people were reportedly killed Sept. 28, 2009, when Guinean troops fired into a crowd of about 50,000 antigovernment protesters in Conakry. After an assassination attempt Dec. 3, 2009, by a former aide left Pres. Moussa Dadis Camara seriously wounded, Vice Pres. Sékouba Konaté became interim head of state. Presidential elections June-Nov. 2010 brought a civilian government headed by Alpha Condé to power Dec. 21. Postponed legislative elections, held in Sept. 2013, were criticized as flawed. Official results announced Oct. 18 gave a party loyal to Condé a working majority.

The largest known outbreak of Ebola virus disease began in Guinea in Dec. 2013. First identified in Mar. 2014, it spread rapidly to nearby countries. By Sept. 27, 2015, a total of 28,424 cases, including 3,805 in Guinea, had been reported by WHO; 11,311 victims (2,533 in Guinea) had died.

Guinea-Bissau
Republic of Guinea-Bissau

People: Population: 1,726,170. **Age distrib.:** <15: 39.5%; 65+: 3.3%. **Growth:** 1.9%. **Migrants:** 1.1%. **Pop. density:** 159 per sq mi, 61.4 per sq km. **Urban:** 49.3%. **Ethnic groups:** Fula 28.5%, Balanta 22.5%, Mandinga 14.7%, Papel 9.1%, Manjaco 8.3%, Beafada 3.5%, Mancanha 3.1%, Bijago 2.1%. **Languages:** Crioulo, Portuguese (official), French, English. **Religions:** Muslim 45.1%, Christian 22.1%, animist 14.9%.

Geography: Total area: 13,948 sq mi, 36,125 sq km; **Land area:** 10,857 sq mi, 28,120 sq km. **Location:** Atlantic coast of W Africa. Senegal on N, Guinea on E and S. **Topography:** A swampy coastal plain covers most of country. Low savanna region to E. **Arable land:** 10.7%. **Capital:** Bissau, 492,069.

Government: Type: Republic. **Head of state:** Pres. José Mário Vaz; in office: June 23, 2014. **Head of gov.:** Prime Min. Carlos Correia; in office: Sept. 17, 2015. **Local divisions:** 9 regions. **Defense budget** (2012): $26 mil. **Active troops:** 4,450.

Economy: Industries: agric. prods. proc., beer, soft drinks. **Chief crops:** rice, corn, beans, cassava, cashew nuts, peanuts, palm kernels, cotton. **Natural resources:** fish, timber, phosphates, bauxite, clay, granite, limestone, unexploited petroleum deposits. **Water:** 18,427 cu m per capita. **Electricity prod.:** 50 mil kWh. **Labor force:** agric. 82%, industry and services 18%. **Unemployment:** 7.1%.

Finance: Monetary unit: CFA Franc (XOF) (584.11 = $1 U.S.). **GDP:** $2.5 bil; **per capita GDP:** $1,400; **GDP growth:** 2.5%. **Imports:** $236.2 mil; Portugal 27.4%, Senegal 24.1%. **Exports:** $179.9 mil; India 55.6%, Nigeria 28.1%, China 7.1%, Togo 5.8%. **Tourism:** $7 mil. **Budget:** $177.6 mil. **Inflation:** –1%.

Transport: Airports: 2.

Communications: Telephone: 0.3 per 100 pop. **Mobile:** 63.5 per 100 pop. **Broadband:** NA. **Internet:** 3.3%.

Health: Expend.: 5.9%. **Life expect.:** 48.2 male; 52.3 female. **Births:** 33.4 per 1,000 pop. **Deaths:** 14.3 per 1,000 pop. **Infant mortality:** 89.2 per 1,000 live births. **Undernourished:** 17.7%. **HIV:** 3.7%.

Education: Compulsory: ages 6-14. **Literacy:** 59.9%.

Permanent UN Mission: 336 E. 45th St., 13th Fl., New York, NY 10017; (212) 896-8311.

Website: www.gov.gw or www.state.gov/p/af/ci/pu/

Portuguese mariners explored the area in the mid-15th cent.; the slave trade flourished in the 17th and 18th cents., and colonization began in the 19th. Independence came Sept. 10, 1974, ending 13 years of guerrilla warfare against the Portuguese regime.

A Nov. 1980 coup gave army chief João Bernardo Vieira absolute power. Vieira eventually initiated political liberalization; multiparty elections were held in 1994. A 1998 army uprising triggered a civil war, with Senegal and Guinea aiding the Vieira regime. After a peace accord signed Nov. 2 broke down, rebel troops ousted Vieira on May 7, 1999.

Civilian rule returned with 1999-2000 elections, but top military officers staged a coup Sept. 14, 2003. Vieira won a presidential runoff election, July 24, 2005, and returned to power Oct. 1. A group of soldiers murdered Vieira in his presidential palace Mar. 2, 2009. Political violence continued as the 2009 presidential election approached; the ruling party candidate, Malam Bacai Sanhá, won a runoff vote July 26. He died Jan. 9, 2012. A military coup Apr. 12 derailed a runoff election scheduled for Apr. 29. The military appointed Manuel Serifo Nhamadjo to lead a transitional government. Drug trafficking increased substantially in the country with the support of the military. The U.S. arrested and indicted former navy chief Rear Adm. José Américo Bubo Na Tchuto and several others on drug charges Apr. 2013; armed forces head Gen. Antonio Injai was indicted in absentia. Former finance min. José Mário Vaz won 61.9% of the vote in a May 18, 2014, presidential runoff.

Guyana
Cooperative Republic of Guyana

People: Population: 735,222. **Age distrib.:** <15: 28.1%; 65+: 5.5%. **Growth:** 0%. **Migrants:** 1.8%. **Pop. density:** 9.7 per sq mi, 3.7 per sq km. **Urban:** 28.6%. **Ethnic groups:** E Indian 43.5%, black (African) 30.2%, mixed 16.7%, Amerindian 9.1%. **Languages:** English (official), Guyanese Creole, Amerindian langs., Indian langs., Chinese. **Religions:** Protestant 30.5% (incl. Pentecostal 16.9%), Hindu 28.4%, Roman Catholic 8.1%, Muslim 7.2%, none 4.3%.

Geography: Total area: 83,000 sq mi, 214,969 sq km; **Land area:** 76,004 sq mi, 196,849 sq km. **Location:** N coast of S America. Venezuela on W, Brazil on S, Suriname on E. **Topography:** Dense tropical forests cover much of land. A grassy savanna divides it from flat coastal area, where 90% of the pop. lives, with its rich alluvial soil. **Arable land:** 2.1%. **Capital:** Georgetown, 123,852 (2014).

Government: Type: Republic. **Head of state:** Pres. David Arthur Granger; in office: May 16, 2015. **Head of gov.:** Prime Min. Moses Nagamootoo; in office: May 19, 2015. **Local divisions:** 10 regions. **Defense budget:** $37 mil. **Active troops:** 1,100.

Economy: Industries: bauxite, sugar, rice milling, timber, textiles. **Chief crops:** sugarcane, rice, edible oils. **Natural resources:** bauxite, gold, diamonds, timber, shrimp, fish. **Water:** 338,750 cu m per capita. **Electricity prod.:** 800 mil kWh. **Labor force:** NA. **Unemployment:** 11.1%.

Finance: Monetary unit: Dollar (GYD) (203.20 = $1 U.S.). **GDP:** $5.5 bil; **per capita GDP:** $6,900; **GDP growth:** 3.8%. **Imports:** $2 bil; Trinidad and Tobago 23.9%, U.S. 20.2%, China 10.2%, Cuba 6.6%. **Exports:** $1.3 bil; Canada 30.4%, U.S. 27.6%, UK 6.4%. **Tourism:** $77 mil. **Budget:** $874.3 mil. **Inflation:** 1.8%.

Transport: Motor vehicles: 80.6 per 1,000 pop. **Airports:** 11.

Communications: Telephone: 19.9 per 100 pop. **Mobile:** 70.5 per 100 pop. **Broadband:** 0.1 per 100 pop. **Internet:** 37.4%.

Health: Expend.: 6.6%. **Life expect.:** 65.1 male; 71.2 female. **Births:** 15.6 per 1,000 pop. **Deaths:** 7.3 per 1,000 pop. **Infant mortality:** 32.6 per 1,000 live births. **Undernourished:** 10%. **HIV:** 1.8%.

Education: Compulsory: ages 6-14. **Literacy:** 88.5%.

Embassy: 2490 Tracy Pl. NW 20008; 265-6900.

Website: www.gina.gov.gy

Guyana became a Dutch possession in the 17th cent., but sovereignty passed to Britain in 1815. Indentured servants from India soon outnumbered African slaves. Guyana became independent May 26, 1966.

The Port Kaituma ambush of U.S. Rep. Leo J. Ryan and others investigating mistreatment of American followers of the Rev. Jim Jones's Peoples Temple cult triggered a mass suicide-execution of 911 cultists at their commune in Jonestown, Nov. 18, 1978.

The People's National Congress, the party in power since Guyana became independent, was voted out of office with the election of Cheddi Jagan in Oct. 1992. When Pres. Jagan died Mar. 6, 1997, Prime Min. Samuel Hinds succeeded him. Jagan's widow, Janet, became prime min. Mar. 17. She won the presidency in a disputed election Dec. 15. She resigned because of ill health Aug. 1999 and was succeeded by Bharrat Jagdeo. He won reelection in 2001 and 2006. Donald Ramotar, the candidate of Jagdeo's party, was elected president in 2011. Ramotar suspended parliament, Nov. 10, 2014, to prevent a no-confidence vote; an opposition coalition won a 1-seat majority over Ramotar's party in May 11, 2015, elections, and coalition leader David Granger became president, May 16.

Haiti
Republic of Haiti

People: Population: 10,110,019. **Age distrib.:** <15: 33.3%; 65+: 4.2%. **Growth:** 1.2%. **Migrants:** 0.4%. **Pop. density:** 950.1 per sq mi, 366.8 per sq km. **Urban:** 58.6%. **Ethnic groups:** black 95%, mulatto and white 5%. **Languages:** French, Creole (both official). **Religions:** Roman Catholic (official) 54.7%, Protestant 28.5% (incl. Baptist 15.4%), voodoo (official) 2.1%, none 10.2%.

Geography: Total area: 10,714 sq mi, 27,750 sq km; **Land area:** 10,641 sq mi, 27,560 sq km. **Location:** In Caribbean; occupies western third of isl. of Hispaniola. Dominican Republic on E, Cuba to W. **Topography:** About two-thirds is mountainous. Much of rest is semiarid. Coastal areas are warm and moist. **Arable land:** 36.3%. **Capital:** Port-au-Prince, 2,439,775.

Government: Type: Republic. **Head of state:** Pres. Michel Martelly; in office: May 14, 2011. **Head of gov.:** Prime Min. Evans Paul; in office: Jan. 16, 2015. **Local divisions:** 10 departments. **Defense budget:** NA. **Active troops:** 70; UN mission MINUSTAH in country since 2004.

Economy: Industries: textiles, sugar refining, flour milling, cement, light assembly of imported parts. **Chief crops:** coffee, mangoes, cocoa, sugarcane, rice, corn, sorghum. **Natural resources:** bauxite, copper, calcium carbonate, gold, marble, hydropower. **Water:** 1,360 cu m per capita. **Electricity prod.:** 1.1 bil kWh. **Labor force:** agric. 38.1%, industry 11.5%, services 50.4%. **Unemployment:** 7%.

Finance: Monetary unit: Gourde (HTG) (53.20 = $1 U.S.). **GDP:** $18.3 bil; **per capita GDP:** $1,800; **GDP growth:** 2.8%. **Imports:** $3.5 bil; Dominican Republic 35%, U.S. 26.8%, Netherlands Antilles 8.7%, China 7%. **Exports:** $903.1 mil; U.S. 83.5%. **Tourism:** $568 mil. **Budget:** $2.4 bil. **Inflation:** 4.6%.

Transport: Motor vehicles: 8.4 per 1,000 pop. **Airports:** 4.

Communications: Telephone: 0.4 per 100 pop. **Mobile:** 64.7 per 100 pop. **Broadband:** 4.9 per 100 pop. **Internet:** 11.4%.

Health: Expend.: 6.4%. **Life expect.:** 62.1 male; 65.0 female. **Births:** 22.3 per 1,000 pop. **Deaths:** 7.8 per 1,000 pop. **Infant mortality:** 48.0 per 1,000 live births. **Undernourished:** 51.8%. **HIV:** 1.9%.

Education: Compulsory: ages 6-11. **Literacy:** 60.7%.

Embassy: 2311 Massachusetts Ave. NW 20008; 332-4090.

Website: primature.gouv.ht or www.haiti.org

Haiti, visited by Christopher Columbus in 1492 and a French colony from 1697, attained its independence, 1804, following a rebellion led by former slave Toussaint L'Ouverture. After a period of political violence, the U.S. occupied the country 1915-34.

François Duvalier, known as Papa Doc, was elected president in 1957; in 1964 he was named president for life. Upon his death in 1971, he was succeeded by his son, Jean Claude Duvalier, known as Baby Doc. Following weeks of unrest, Jean Claude fled Haiti aboard a U.S. Air Force jet Feb. 7, 1986. His departure ended the Duvalier family's brutal 28-year dictatorship, but political violence, government corruption, poverty, AIDS and other health problems, and deteriorating environmental quality have continued to plague Haiti.

Jean-Bertrand Aristide was elected president in 1990, but the military arrested and expelled him from the country in Sept. 1991. The U.S. Coast Guard intercepted some 35,000 Haitian refugees as they tried to enter the U.S., 1991-92. Most were returned to Haiti. There was a new upsurge of refugees starting in late 1993.

The UN authorized in 1994 an invasion of Haiti by a multinational force. With U.S. troops already en route, a full-scale invasion was averted, Sept. 18, when military leaders agreed to step down. Aristide returned to Haiti and was restored to office Oct. 15. A UN peacekeeping force exercised responsibility in Haiti from 1995 to 1997. Aristide transferred power to his elected successor, René Préval, in 1996.

At least 140 people died and over 160,000 were left homeless when Hurricane Georges struck Haiti Sept. 22, 1998. Aristide won the 2000 presidency in an election boycotted by opposition groups. An armed uprising in early 2004 and pressure from France and the U.S. toppled Aristide, who went into exile Feb. 29. A U.S.-led contingent, sent in after the upheaval, yielded authority June 1, 2004, to a UN stabilization force (MINUSTAH). MINUSTAH uniformed personnel numbered more than 4,500 as of June 30, 2015.

Flooding in late May 2004 killed more than 1,000 people, and more than 2,400 were killed in Tropical Storm Jeanne in Sept. Préval was reelected in 2006. Skyrocketing prices for food imports sparked riots and mass protests in Apr. 2008. A succession of hurricanes and tropical storms (Fay, Gustav, Hanna, Ike), Aug.-Sept. 2008, left more than 550 Haitians dead and up to 1 mil homeless. A school collapse near Port-au-Prince Nov. 7, 2008, killed 91 students and teachers.

An earthquake Jan. 12, 2010, near Port-au-Prince caused cataclysmic damage. More than 220,000 people (including nearly 100 UN peacekeepers) were killed, at least 300,000 were injured, and more than 1.5 mil were left homeless. With the central government paralyzed and the presidential palace and parliament building in ruins, the U.S. and other countries mounted a massive relief effort. Almost 65,000 Haitians were still living in displacement camps as of Mar. 31, 2015. Poor living and sanitation conditions contributed to a cholera epidemic in areas affected by the 2010 earthquake. As of Apr. 2015, almost 9,000 had died, and about 738,000 had been ill with the disease, which may have been brought into the country by UN peacekeepers.

After the first round of presidential balloting Nov. 28, 2010, Michel Martelly, an entertainer, was declared ineligible for the second round. Violent protests by his supporters, allegations of electoral fraud from international observers, and diplomatic pressure from the U.S. and other donor countries gained him a place in the runoff Mar. 20, 2011, which he won. Legislators' terms expired before Martelly and Parliament could agree on electoral legislation; the president began temporarily ruling by executive order, Jan. 13, 2015. When first-round legislative elections were held Aug. 9, they were marred by violence and low turnout; most leading candidates faced a runoff, scheduled for Oct. 25, the same day as first-round presidential voting.

Honduras
Republic of Honduras

People: Population: 8,746,673. **Age distrib.:** <15: 34.2%; 65+: 4.1%. **Growth:** 1.7%. **Migrants:** 0.3%. **Pop. density:** 202.5 per sq mi, 78.2 per sq km. **Urban:** 54.7%. **Ethnic groups:** mestizo (mixed Amerindian/European) 90%, Amerindian 7%, black 2%. **Languages:** Spanish (official), Amerindian dialects. **Religions:** Roman Catholic 97%, Protestant 3%.

Geography: Total area: 43,278 sq mi, 112,090 sq km; **Land area:** 43,201 sq mi, 111,890 sq km. **Location:** Central America. Guatemala on W; El Salvador, Nicaragua on S. **Topography:** Caribbean coast is 500 mi long. Pacific coast, on Gulf of Fonseca, is 40 mi long. Mountainous, with wide fertile valleys and rich forests. **Arable land:** 9.1%. **Capital:** Tegucigalpa, 1,122,523.

Government: Type: Democratic constitutional republic. **Head of state and gov.:** Pres. Juan Orlando Hernandez Alvarado; in office: Jan. 27, 2014. **Local divisions:** 18 departments. **Defense budget:** $216 mil. **Active troops:** 12,000.

Economy: Industries: sugar, coffee, woven and knit apparel, wood prods., cigars. **Chief crops:** bananas, coffee, citrus, corn, African palm. **Natural resources:** timber, gold, silver, copper, lead, zinc, iron ore, antimony, coal, fish, hydropower. **Water:** 11,381 cu m per capita. **Electricity prod.:** 7.3 bil kWh. **Labor force:** agric. 39.2%, industry 20.9%, services 39.8%. **Unemployment:** 4.2%.

Finance: Monetary unit: Lempira (HNL) (21.62 = $1 U.S.). **GDP:** $39.1 bil; **per capita GDP:** $4,700; **GDP growth:** 3.1%. **Imports:** $11.8 bil; U.S. 49.8%, Guatemala 7.4%, El Salvador 6.1%, China 5.8%, Mexico 5.2%. **Exports:** $8.5 bil; U.S. 54.1%, El Salvador 5.8%, Mexico 5.4%. **Tourism:** $630 mil. **Budget:** $4.3 bil. **Inflation:** 6.1%.

Transport: Railways: 434 mi. **Motor vehicles:** 18 per 1,000 pop. **Airports:** 13.

Communications: Telephone: 6.4 per 100 pop. **Mobile:** 93.5 per 100 pop. **Broadband:** 11.7 per 100 pop. **Internet:** 19.1%.

Health: Expend.: 8.6%. **Life expect.:** 69.3 male; 72.7 female. **Births:** 23.1 per 1,000 pop. **Deaths:** 5.2 per 1,000 pop. **Infant mortality:** 18.2 per 1,000 live births. **Undernourished:** 12.1%. **HIV:** 0.4%.

Education: Compulsory: ages 6-14. **Literacy:** 88.5%.

Embassy: 3007 Tilden St. NW, Ste. 4M, 20008; 966-2604.

Website: www.presidencia.gob.hn

Mayan civilization flourished in Honduras in the 1st millennium CE. Columbus arrived in 1502. Honduras became independent after freeing itself from Spain, 1821, and from the Fed. of Central America, 1838.

In 1975, the army ousted Gen. Oswaldo Lopez Arellano, president for most of the time since 1963, over charges of pervasive bribery by United Brands Co. of the U.S. An elected civilian government took power in 1982.

Already one of the poorest countries in the Western Hemisphere, Honduras was devastated in late Oct. 1998 by Hurricane Mitch, which killed at least 5,600 people and caused more than $850 mil in damage to crops and livestock.

Ricardo Maduro, a businessman who pledged to crack down on crime, won the 2001 presidency. He was succeeded by Manuel Zelaya Rosales of the opposition Liberal Party, who won the 2005 presidential election. After the military ousted Zelaya in June 2009, Porfirio "Pepe" Lobo of the conservative National Party defeated Liberal Party nominee Elvin Santos in the Nov. 2009 presidential election and took office Jan. 27, 2010. National Party candidate Juan Orlando Hernández won the Nov. 2013 presidential election.

Northern Honduras has become a major transshipment point for illegal drugs being smuggled from South America to the U.S. Drug-gang violence and other crime apparently contributed to a significant increase in migrants, including thousands of children traveling alone or with their mothers, trying to enter the U.S. along the Mexican border, 2013-14. Demonstrators in Tegucigalpa and other cities, June 2015, protested alleged corruption at a government agency and apparently illicit payments to the National Party.

Hungary

People: Population: 9,897,541. **Age distrib.:** <15: 14.8%; 65+: 18.2%. **Growth:** –0.2%. **Migrants:** 4.7%. **Pop. density:** 286.1 per sq mi, 110.5 per sq km. **Urban:** 71.2%. **Ethnic groups:** Hungarian 85.6%, Roma 3.2%. **Languages:** Hungarian (official), English, German. **Religions:** Roman Catholic 37.2%, Calvinist 11.6%, none 18.2%.

Geography: Total area: 35,918 sq mi, 93,028 sq km; **Land area:** 34,598 sq mi, 89,608 sq km. **Location:** E central Europe. Slovakia, Ukraine on N; Austria on W; Slovenia, Serbia, Croatia on S; Romania on E. **Topography:** Danube R. forms Slovak border in NW, then swings S to bisect the country. Eastern half of Hungary is mainly a great fertile plain, the Alfold. Hilly in W and N. **Arable land:** 48.6%. **Capital:** Budapest, 1,713,903.

Government: Type: Parliamentary democracy. **Head of state:** Pres. János Áder; in office: May 10, 2012. **Head of gov.:** Prime Min. Viktor Orbán; in office: May 29, 2010. **Local divisions:** 19 counties, 23 cities with county rights, 1 capital city. **Defense budget:** $1 bil. **Active troops:** 26,500.

Economy: Industries: mining, metallurgy, constr. materials, processed foods, textiles, chemicals (espec. pharmaceuticals), motor vehicles. **Chief crops:** wheat, corn, sunflower seeds, potatoes, sugar beets. **Natural resources:** bauxite, coal, nat. gas. **Water:** 10,447 cu m per capita. **Crude oil reserves:** 27.2 mil bbls. **Electricity prod.:** 32.5 bil kWh. **Labor force:** agric. 7.1%, industry 29.7%, services 63.2%. **Unemployment:** 10.2%.

Finance: Monetary unit: Forint (HUF) (279.17 = $1 U.S.). **GDP:** $246.4 bil; **per capita GDP:** $24,900; **GDP growth:** 3.6%. **Imports:** $96.8 bil; Germany 25.5%, Russia 8.6%, Austria 6.8%, China 6.7%, Slovakia 5.8%, Poland 5%. **Exports:** $99.5 bil; Germany 26.7%, Romania 5.8%, Austria 5.7%, Slovakia 5.5%. **Tourism:** $5.9 bil. **Budget:** $70.2 bil. **Inflation:** −0.2%.

Transport: Railways: 5,001 mi. **Motor vehicles:** 356.7 per 1,000 pop. **Airports:** 20.

Communications: Telephone: 30.3 per 100 pop. **Mobile:** 118.1 per 100 pop. **Broadband:** 27.5 per 100 pop. **Internet:** 76.1%.

Health: Expend.: 7.8%. **Life expect.:** 72.0 male; 79.6 female. **Births:** 9.2 per 1,000 pop. **Deaths:** 12.7 per 1,000 pop. **Infant mortality:** 5.0 per 1,000 live births. **Undernourished:** <5%. **HIV:** NA.

Education: Compulsory: ages 7-16. **Literacy:** 99.1%.

Embassy: 3910 Shoemaker St. NW 20008; 362-6730.

Website: www.kormany.hu

Earliest settlers, chiefly Slav and Germanic, were overrun by Magyars from the east. Stephen I (997-1038) was made king by Pope Sylvester II in 1000 CE. The country suffered repeated Turkish invasions in the 15th-17th cents. After the Turks were defeated, 1686-97, Austria dominated, but Hungary obtained concessions, and regained internal independence in 1867 under a dual monarchy with the emperor of Austria. Defeated with the Central Powers at the end of WWI in 1918, Hungary lost Transylvania to Romania, Croatia and Bacska to Yugoslavia, and Slovakia and Carpatho-Ruthenia to Czechoslovakia. All had large Hungarian minorities. A republic under Michael Karolyi and a Bolshevist revolt under Bela Kun were followed by a vote for a monarchy in 1920 with Adm. Nicholas Horthy as regent.

Hungary allied with Germany before WWII and was allowed to annex, 1938-41, most of its lost territories. Russian troops captured the country, 1944-45. By terms of an armistice with the Allied powers, Hungary agreed to return to its borders of 1937.

A republic was declared Feb. 1, 1946. In 1947 a hard-line Communist, pro-Soviet government was installed. Demonstrations against Communist rule developed into open revolt in 1956. Soviet forces launched a massive attack Nov. 4 against Budapest. About 200,000 persons fled the country. Thousands were arrested and executed.

Major economic reforms were launched early in 1968, switching from a central planning system to one based on market forces and profit. In 1989 Parliament legalized freedom of assembly and association as Hungary shifted away from Communism. In Oct. the Communist Party was formally dissolved. The last Soviet troops left June 19, 1991. Hungary became a full member of NATO in 1999 and of the EU in 2004.

The IMF, EU, and World Bank agreed Oct. 2008 to extend $25.1 bil to rescue Hungary's economy, battered by a global financial crisis. With the nation still reeling from recession, the center-right Fidesz party ousted the Socialists in 2010 parliamentary elections. Parliament, dominated by Fidesz, approved Apr. 2011 a fiscally and socially conservative constitution that went into force Jan. 1, 2012. Fidesz retained its majority in Apr. 6, 2014, elections. Beginning July 2015, Hungary built security fences along its borders with Serbia and Croatia, intended to keep out migrants from the Balkans, SW Asia, the Middle East, and Africa—mostly people en route to Northern Europe. The EU estimated that more than 155,000 migrants entered Hungary from Serbia Jan.-Aug. 2015. With tens of thousands entering in Sept., despite the fencing, Hungary instituted, Sept. 15, tighter border controls and harsher penalties for coming into the country illegally. Parliamentary action, Sept. 21, gave the army more power to enforce border controls.

Iceland

Republic of Iceland

People: Population: 331,918. **Age distrib.:** <15: 20.4%; 65+: 13.8%. **Growth:** 1.2%. **Migrants:** 10.4%. **Pop. density:** 8.6 per sq mi, 3.3 per sq km. **Urban:** 94.1%. **Ethnic groups:** homogeneous mix of Norse-Celt descendants 94%, pop. of foreign origin 6%. **Languages:** Icelandic, English, Nordic langs., German. **Religions:** Evangelical Lutheran Church of Iceland (official) 73.8%, Roman Catholic 3.6%, Reykjavik Free Church 2.9%, none 5.6%.

Geography: Total area: 39,769 sq mi, 103,000 sq km; **Land area:** 38,707 sq mi, 100,250 sq km. **Location:** Isl. at N end of Atlantic O. Nearest neighbor is Greenland (Den.) to W. **Topography:** Recent volcanic origin. Three-quarters of surface is wasteland: glaciers, lakes, a lava desert, geysers, and hot springs. The climate is moderated by the Gulf Stream. **Arable land:** 1.2%. **Capital:** Reykjavík, 184,171 (2014).

Government: Type: Constitutional republic. **Head of state:** Pres. Olafur Ragnar Grímsson; in office: Aug. 1, 1996. **Head of gov.:** Prime Min. Sigmundur David Gunnlaugsson; in office: May 23, 2013. **Local divisions:** 8 regions. **Defense budget:** $39 mil (Coast Guard budget). **Active troops:** No armed forces; 200 paramilitary. Relies on NATO allies for air policing and defense.

Economy: Industries: fish proc., aluminum smelting, ferrosilicon prod., geothermal power, hydropower, tourism. **Chief crops:** potatoes, green vegetables. **Natural resources:** fish, hydropower, geothermal power, diatomite. **Water:** 515,152 cu m per capita. **Electricity prod.:** 17.4 bil kWh. **Labor force:** agric. 4.8%, industry 22.2%, services 73%. **Unemployment:** 5.6%.

Finance: Monetary unit: Krona (ISK) (128.97 = $1 U.S.). **GDP:** $14.2 bil; **per capita GDP:** $43,600; **GDP growth:** 1.8%. **Imports:** $4.7 bil; Norway 15.6%, U.S. 10%, Germany 8.4%, China 8.2%, Brazil 7.7%, Denmark 6.3%, Netherlands 5.2%. **Exports:** $5 bil; Netherlands 30%, Germany 12.1%, UK 9.5%. **Tourism:** $1.4 bil. **Budget:** $7.3 bil. **Inflation:** 2%.

Transport: Motor vehicles: 785.3 per 1,000 pop. **Airports:** 7.

Communications: Telephone: 51.5 per 100 pop. **Mobile:** 111.1 per 100 pop. **Broadband:** 75.2 per 100 pop. **Internet:** 98.2%.

Health: Expend.: 9.1%. **Life expect.:** 80.8 male; 85.2 female. **Births:** 13.9 per 1,000 pop. **Deaths:** 6.3 per 1,000 pop. **Infant mortality:** 2.1 per 1,000 live births. **Undernourished:** <5%. **HIV:** NA.

Education: Compulsory: ages 6-15. **Literacy:** 99%.

Embassy: 2900 K St. NW, Ste. 509, 20007; 265-6653.

Website: www.iceland.is

Iceland was an independent republic from 930 to 1262, when it joined with Norway. Its language has maintained its purity for 1,000 years. The Althing, or assembly, established in 930, is the world's oldest surviving parliament. Danish rule lasted 1380-1918; the last ties with the Danish crown were severed in 1941.

A 55-year U.S. military presence in Iceland ended with the closure of the Keflavík naval air station in Sept. 2006. Iceland's banking system and currency collapsed amid the global financial crisis in Oct. 2008. More than $10 bil in loans from the IMF and European governments restored financial stability; austerity measures were imposed, and the nation entered a deep recession. Political unrest sparked by soaring inflation and unemployment led to the Feb. 2009 installation of a center-left government, which swept to victory in Apr. 25 elections. A major eruption Apr. 14, 2010, of the Eyjafjallajökull volcano disrupted European air traffic, affecting about 10 mil passengers and 100,000 flights during the next 6 days. The governing coalition lost Apr. 28, 2013, parliamentary elections, in which center-right parties came to power. With the economy recovered in 2015, the government announced plans in June to lift restrictions imposed in 2008 on sending money out of the country.

India

Republic of India

People: Population: 1,251,695,584. **Age distrib.:** <15: 28.1%; 65+: 6%. **Growth:** 1.2%. **Migrants:** 0.4%. **Pop. density:** 1,090.4 per sq mi, 421 per sq km. **Urban:** 32.7%. **Ethnic groups:** Indo-Aryan 72%, Dravidian 25%, Mongoloid and other 3%. **Languages:** Hindi (most widely spoken); 14 other official langs. (incl. Bengali, Telugu, Marathi, Tamil, Urdu, Gujarati); English (subsidiary official lang.; crucial for natl., political, commercial communication); Hindustani (variant of Hindi/Urdu widely spoken throughout N). **Religions:** Hindu 79.8%, Muslim 14.2%.

Geography: Total area: 1,269,219 sq mi, 3,287,263 sq km; **Land area:** 1,147,956 sq mi, 2,973,193 sq km. **Location:** Occupies most of Indian subcontinent in S Asia. Pakistan on W; China, Nepal, Bhutan on N; Myanmar, Bangladesh on E. **Topography:** The Himalayan Mts., highest in world, stretch across northern borders. The Ganges Plain below is among the world's most densely populated regions. The climate varies from tropical heat in S to near-Arctic cold in N. Rajasthan Desert is NW. NE Assam Hills get 400 in. of rain a year. **Arable land:** 52.5%. **Capital:** New Delhi, 25,703,168 (figure is for Delhi National Capital Region). **Cities:** Mumbai (Bombay), 21,042,538; Kolkata (Calcutta), 14,864,919; Bangalore, 10,087,132; Chennai (Madras), 9,890,427; Hyderabad, 8,943,523; Ahmadabad, 7,342,850.

Government: Type: Federal republic. **Head of state:** Pres. Pranab Mukherjee; in office: July 22, 2012. **Head of gov.:** Prime Min. Narendra Modi; in office: May 26, 2014. **Local divisions:** 29 states, 7 union territories. **Defense budget:** $45.21 bil. **Active troops:** 1,346,000.

Economy: Industries: textiles, chemicals, food proc., steel, transp. equip., cement, mining, petroleum, machinery, software, pharmaceuticals. **Chief crops:** rice, wheat, oilseed, cotton, jute, tea, sugarcane, lentils, onions, potatoes. **Natural resources:** coal, iron ore, manganese, mica, bauxite, rare earth elements, titanium ore, chromite, nat. gas, diamonds, petroleum, limestone. **Water:** 1,526 cu m per capita. **Crude oil reserves:** 5.7 bil bbls. **Electricity prod.:** 1.1 tril kWh. **Labor force:** agric. 49%, industry 20%, services 31%. **Unemployment:** 3.6%.

Finance: Monetary unit: Rupee (INR) (66.20 = $1 U.S.). **GDP:** $7.4 tril; **per capita GDP:** $5,900; **GDP growth:** 7.2%. **Imports:** $508.1 bil; China 11%, Saudi Arabia 7.8%, UAE 7.1%, Switzerland 5.5%. **Exports:** $342.5 bil; U.S. 12.4%, UAE 10.2%. **Tourism:** $19.7 bil. **Budget:** $288.8 bil. **Inflation:** 6.4%.

Transport: Railways: 42,579 mi. **Motor vehicles:** 30.8 per 1,000 pop. **Airports:** 253.

Communications: Telephone: 2.1 per 100 pop. **Mobile:** 74.5 per 100 pop. **Broadband:** 3.3 per 100 pop. **Internet:** 18%.

Health: Expend.: 4.1%. **Life expect.:** 67.0 male; 69.4 female. **Births:** 19.6 per 1,000 pop. **Deaths:** 7.3 per 1,000 pop. **Infant mortality:** 41.8 per 1,000 live births. **Undernourished:** 15.2%. **HIV:** NA.

Education: Compulsory: ages 6-13. **Literacy:** 71.2%.

Embassy: 2107 Massachusetts Ave. NW 20008; 939-7000.

Website: india.gov.in

India has one of the oldest civilizations in the world. Excavations trace the Indus Valley civilization back for at least 5,000 years. Paintings in the mountain caves of Ajanta, richly carved temples, the Taj Mahal in Agra, and the Kutab Minar in Delhi are among treasured relics of the past.

Aryan tribes, speaking Sanskrit, invaded from the NW around 1500 BCE. Asoka ruled most of the Indian subcontinent in the 3rd cent. BCE and established Buddhism. But Hinduism revived and eventually predominated. Under the Guptas, 4th-6th cent. CE, science, literature, and the arts enjoyed a golden age. Arab invaders established a Muslim foothold in the west in the 8th cent., and Turkish Muslims gained control of North India by 1200. The Mughal emperors ruled 1526-1857.

Vasco da Gama established Portuguese trading posts 1498-1503. The Dutch followed. The British East India Co. sent Capt. William Hawkins, 1609, to get concessions from the Mughal emperor for spices and textiles. Operating as the East India Co., the British gained control of most of India. The British parliament assumed political direction; under Lord Bentinck, 1828-35, rule by rajahs (princes) was curbed. After the Sepoy troops mutinied, 1857-58, the British supported the native rulers.

Nationalism grew after WWI. The Indian National Congress and the Muslim League demanded constitutional reform. A leader emerged in Mohandas K. Gandhi (called Mahatma, or Great Soul) (b. Oct. 2, 1869), who was assassinated Jan. 30, 1948. He advocated self-rule, nonviolence, and an end to caste discrimination against "untouchables." In 1930 he launched a program of civil disobedience, boycotting British goods and rejecting taxes without representation.

In 1935, Britain gave India a constitution providing a bicameral federal congress. Muhammad Ali Jinnah, head of the Muslim League, sought creation of a Muslim nation, Pakistan.

The British government partitioned British India into the dominions of India and Pakistan. India became a member of the UN in 1945, a self-governing member of the Commonwealth in 1947, and a democratic republic, Jan. 26, 1950. More than 12 mil Hindu and Muslim refugees crossed the India-Pakistan borders in 1947; about 200,000 were killed in communal fighting.

After Pakistan troops began attacks on Bengali separatists in East Pakistan, Mar. 25, 1971, some 10 mil refugees fled to India. India and Pakistan went to war Dec. 3, 1971, on both the east and west fronts. Pakistan troops in the east surrendered Dec. 16; Pakistan agreed to a cease-fire in the west Dec. 17.

Indira Gandhi, India's prime minister since Jan. 1966, invoked emergency powers in June 1975. Thousands of opponents were arrested and press censorship imposed. These and other actions, including population control through forced vasectomies, were widely resented. Opposition parties, united in the Janata coalition, won the 1977 elections.

Gandhi became prime minister for the second time in 1980. She was assassinated by 2 of her Sikh bodyguards Oct. 31, 1984, in response to the government suppression in June 1984 of a Sikh uprising in Punjab, which included an assault on the Golden Temple at Amritsar, the holiest Sikh shrine. Widespread rioting followed the assassination; thousands of Sikhs were killed and some 50,000 left homeless. Rajiv, Indira Gandhi's son, replaced her as prime minister. A gas leak at a Union Carbide chemical plant in Bhopal, Dec. 1984, eventually killed some 14,000 people.

Many died in religious, ethnic, and political conflicts during the late 1980s and early '90s. To suppress the Sikh insurgency in Punjab, Indian government troops attacked the Golden Temple again in 1988. Rajiv Gandhi was swept from office in 1989 amid charges of incompetence and corruption and assassinated May 21, 1991, while campaigning to regain power. Nationwide riots followed the destruction of a 16th-cent. mosque by Hindu militants in Dec. 1992. Ethnic clashes in Assam, in NW India, killed thousands in Feb. 1993. Bombs jolted Mumbai and Kolkata, Mar. 12-19, killing over 300.

India's first president from the lowest caste, K. R. Narayanan, took office July 1997. India conducted a series of nuclear tests in mid-May 1998, raising tensions with Pakistan. India blamed Pakistani-sponsored terrorist groups for an Oct. 1, 2001, suicide attack on the state legislature in Jammu and Kashmir (see below), in which at least 40 people died, and a Dec. 13 assault on the Indian parliament in New Delhi that left 13 people dead. Hindu-Muslim clashes in Gujarat Feb.-Mar. 2002 claimed more than 700 lives. A. P. J. Abdul Kalam, a Muslim scientist who spearheaded India's nuclear weapons program, became president July 25.

Led by Rajiv Gandhi's Italian-born widow, Sonia, the Congress Party won the most seats in 2004 parliamentary elections. When Hindu nationalists objected to her candidacy, she chose not to become prime minister, and Manmohan Singh, a Sikh economist, took office instead.

The Indian Ocean tsunami of Dec. 26, 2004, left more than 10,700 people dead, some 5,600 missing, and over 647,000 displaced. Islamic extremists set off 7 bombs on commuter trains in Mumbai, July 11, 2006, killing some 200 people; 12 men were convicted, Sept. 11, 2015, of murder or other charges in connection with the bombings. The unmanned *Chandrayaan-1*, India's first lunar survey mission, was launched into space Oct. 22, 2008.

Ten Pakistanis linked to the Kashmir militant group Lashkar-e-Taiba stormed luxury hotels, a railway station, a Jewish center, and other sites in Mumbai, Nov. 26, 2008; by the time Indian army commandos took control three days later, the attackers had slaughtered 163 people. Nine of the terrorists were also killed. Convicted of murder and of waging war against India, the lone surviving gunman, Ajmal Kasab, was executed by hanging Nov. 20, 2012.

In 2009 parliamentary elections, Prime Min. Manmohan Singh's United Progressive Alliance, headed by the Congress party, gained a resounding victory. A triple bombing in Mumbai July 13, 2011, killed 26 people and injured about 140; 11 were killed when a bomb exploded Sept. 7 outside the High Court in New Delhi. Electricity blackouts July 30-31, 2012, left 670 mil people without power.

Several rapes in New Delhi in Nov.-Dec. 2012 prompted outrage and large protests for their mishandling by police and government inaction. Tougher laws against sexual violence were passed Feb. 4, 2013. The Hindu nationalist Bharatiya Janata party won a large majority in Apr.-May 2014 parliamentary elections; Narendra Modi became prime min. The Supreme Court, July 9, 2015, ordered the national government to take over the investigation of a large-scale corruption scandal in Madhya Pradesh, involving bribery, cheating, and falsification of results on school admission tests; since 2013, about 2,000 people had been arrested. Police and protester violence left 10 dead, Aug. 2015, in Gujarat, after a large demonstration against the quota system reserving government jobs and public university places for members of the lower castes.

Development of high-tech industries has propelled rapid economic growth since the 1990s; hundreds of millions have emerged from extreme poverty, although distribution of wealth remains highly uneven. Since 2011, India has had the world's third-largest GDP, after the U.S. and China. To combat climate change, the government released a plan, Oct. 1, 2015, for reducing the rate of growth in India's carbon emissions and generating 40% of electricity from non-fossil-fuel sources by 2030.

Sikkim, bordered by Tibet, Bhutan, and Nepal, formerly British protected, became a protectorate of India in 1950. Area 2,740 sq mi; pop. (2011 census) 610,577; capital is Gangtok. In Sept. 1974, India's parliament voted to make Sikkim an associate Indian state, absorbing it into India.

Kashmir is a predominantly Muslim region in the NW that borders India, Pakistan, Afghanistan, and China. Muslim rule of the previously Hindu kingdom began in 1341; after almost 200 years under the Mughals, the area was incorporated into British India in 1846. Fighting broke out in the region between India and Pakistan in 1947 following independence from Britain. A cease-fire was negotiated by the UN Jan. 1, 1949; it gave Pakistan control of one-third of the area as Azad Kashmir, in the W and NW, and India the remaining two-thirds, as the Indian state of Jammu and Kashmir. Area 85,806 sq mi; pop. (2011 census) 12,541,302. Capitals: Srinagar (summer), pop. (2014 est.) 1,393,580; Jammu (winter), pop. (2014 est.) 667,261. Fighting in the area resumed during the 1965 and 1971 wars with Pakistan. China occupied about 14,000 sq mi in the Ladakh district after a war with India in 1962.

In the 1990s, India's decision to impose central government rule triggered clashes between Indian army troops and separatist fighters. India charged Pakistan with aiding the separatists; fighting was especially heavy in May-June 1999.

A cease-fire between Indian and Pakistani troops along the line of control took effect Nov. 2003. Some breaches have occurred, and fighting between Indian forces and Islamic militants has continued. Estimates of conflict-related deaths since 1989 range from 40,000 to over 80,000. A powerful earthquake Oct. 8, 2005, killed about 80,000 and left up to 3 mil homeless in Pakistani-held Kashmir and northern Pakistan.

France, 1952-54, peacefully yielded to India its 5 colonies, former French India: Pondicherry, Karikal, Mahe, and Yanaon were merged to become Pondicherry, now Puducherry, area 185 sq mi; pop. (2011 census) 1,247,953. The colony of Chandernagor was incorporated into the state of West Bengal.

Indonesia

Republic of Indonesia

People: Population: 255,993,674. **Age distrib.:** <15: 25.8%; 65+: 6.6%. **Growth:** 0.9%. **Migrants:** 0.1%. **Pop. density:** 366 per sq mi, 141.3 per sq km. Island of Java is one of the most densely populated areas in the world. **Urban:** 53.7%. **Ethnic groups:** Javanese 40.1%, Sundanese 15.5%, Malay 3.7%, Batak 3.6%, Madurese 3%, Betawi 2.9%, Minangkabau 2.7%, Buginese 2.7%, Bantenese 2%. **Languages:** Bahasa Indonesia (official; modified form of Malay), English, Dutch, local dialects (Javanese most widely spoken). **Religions:** Muslim 87.2%, Christian 7%, Roman Catholic 2.9%.

Geography: Total area: 735,358 sq mi, 1,904,569 sq km; **Land area:** 699,451 sq mi, 1,811,569 sq km. **Location:** Archipelago SE of Asian mainland along the equator. Malaysia on N, Papua New Guinea on E, Timor-Leste on S. **Topography:** Comprises over 13,500 islands (6,000 inhabited), including Java, Sumatra, Kalimantan (most of Borneo), Sulawesi (Celebes), and West Irian (Irian Jaya, the W half of New Guinea). Also Bangka, Billiton, Madura, Bali, Timor. Cooler climate in mountains and plateaus on the major isls; tropical lowlands. **Arable land:** 13%. **Capital:** Jakarta, 10,323,142. **Cities:** Surabaya, 2,853,237; Bandung, 2,543,742; Medan, 2,204,005; Semarang, 1,629,599.

Government: Type: Republic. **Head of state and gov.:** Pres. Joko Widodo; in office: Oct. 20, 2014. **Local divisions:** 31 provinces, 1 autonomous province, 1 special region, 1 national capital district. **Defense budget:** $7.08 bil. **Active troops:** 395,500.

Economy: Industries: petroleum and nat. gas, textiles, automotive, elec. appliances, apparel, footwear, mining, cement, medical instruments and appliances. **Chief crops:** rubber, palm oil, forest prods., cocoa, coffee, medicinal herbs. **Natural resources:** petroleum, tin, nat. gas, nickel, timber, bauxite, copper, coal, gold, silver. **Water:** 8,080 cu m per capita. **Crude oil reserves:** 3.7 bil bbls. **Electricity prod.:** 185.3 bil kWh. **Labor force:** agric. 38.9%, industry 13.2%, services 47.9%. **Unemployment:** 6.3%.

Finance: Monetary unit: Rupiah (IDR) (14,183.00 = $1 U.S.). **GDP:** $2.7 tril; **per capita GDP:** $10,600; **GDP growth:** 5%. **Imports:** $168.4 bil; (2014) China 16%, Singapore 14%, Japan 11%, South Korea 6.9%, Malaysia 6.1%. **Exports:** $175.3 bil; (2014) Japan 15%, China 12%, Singapore 9.1%, U.S. 8.4%, South Korea 7.2%. **Tourism:** $9.8 bil. **Budget:** $155.2 bil. **Inflation:** 6.4%.

Transport: Railways: 5,070 mi (only partly operational). **Motor vehicles:** 82.3 per 1,000 pop. **Airports:** 186.

Communications: Telephone: 11.7 per 100 pop. **Mobile:** 126.2 per 100 pop. **Broadband:** 24.2 per 100 pop. **Internet:** 17.1%.

Health: Expend.: 3%. **Life expect.:** 69.9 male; 75.2 female. **Births:** 16.7 per 1,000 pop. **Deaths:** 6.4 per 1,000 pop. **Infant mortality:** 24.3 per 1,000 live births. **Undernourished:** 8.7%. **HIV:** 0.5%.

Education: Compulsory: ages 7-15. **Literacy:** 93.9%.

Embassy: 2020 Massachusetts Ave. NW 20036; 775-5200.

Website: www.indonesia.go.id

Hindu and Buddhist civilization from India reached Indonesia nearly 2,000 years ago, taking root especially in Java. Islam spread along the maritime trade routes in the 15th cent., and became predominant by the 16th cent. The Dutch replaced the Portuguese as the area's most important European trade power in the 17th cent., securing territorial control over Java by 1750. The outer islands were subdued in the early 20th cent.

Following Japanese occupation, 1942-45, nationalists led by Sukarno and Hatta declared independence. The Netherlands ceded sovereignty in 1949. A republic was declared, Aug. 17, 1950, with Sukarno as president. West Irian, on New Guinea, remained under Dutch control but was transferred by the UN to Indonesia in 1963.

Sukarno suspended parliament in 1960 and was named president for life in 1963. He made close alliances with Communist governments. In Sept. 1965 an attempted coup was successfully put down, but Sukarno was forced to cede power to the army, led by Gen. Suharto, who became acting president in 1967 and ruled Indonesia for the next 31 years. The regime blamed the coup on the Communist Party; more than 300,000 alleged Communists were killed in army-initiated massacres.

Parliament reelected Suharto to a seventh consecutive 5-year term in 1998, as a severe economic downturn focused public anger on nepotism, cronyism, and corruption in the Suharto regime. Price increases in May sparked mass protests and then mob violence in Jakarta and other cities, claiming some 500 lives. Suharto resigned May 21 and was succeeded by his vice president, Bacharuddin Jusuf Habibie. Abdurrahman Wahid, leader of Indonesia's largest Muslim organization, was elected president in 1999. In Aug. 2000, under pressure from the legislature, he agreed to share power with Vice Pres. Megawati Sukarnoputri, the daughter of the late Pres. Sukarno. Charging Wahid with incompetence and corruption, the legislature ousted him July 23, 2001, and Megawati became Indonesia's first woman president.

Clashes between Muslims and Christians in the Maluku (Molucca) Isls., 1999-2002, claimed about 5,000 lives. East Timor, a former Portuguese colony that Indonesia invaded in Dec. 1975 and controlled until Oct. 1999, became a fully independent country May 20, 2002, as Timor-Leste. Separatists in Aceh, NW Sumatra, fought against government troops during the 1980s through early 2000s. A peace agreement granting Aceh greater autonomy was signed Aug. 15, 2005.

Investigators blamed the Islamic terrorist group Jemaah Islamiyah, an al-Qaeda affiliate, for bombings that killed 202 people, mostly foreign tourists, at nightclubs in Bali, Oct. 12, 2002, and 12 people at a Marriott hotel in Jakarta, Aug. 5, 2003. A car bomb attack outside the Australian embassy in Jakarta, Sept. 9, 2004, killed 9 people. Susilo Bambang Yudhoyono, a retired general, defeated Megawati in a 2004 direct presidential runoff vote.

A massive earthquake off northwest Sumatra, Dec. 26, 2004, triggered tsunamis that wreaked havoc in the Indian Ocean region. The death toll in Indonesia alone exceeded 125,000, not counting almost 40,000 missing. Another large quake off northwest Sumatra, Mar. 28, 2005, left at least 1,300 dead. On Java, an earthquake, May 27, 2006, killed 5,800.

Faced with falling oil production, Indonesia left OPEC in 2008. Pres. Yudhoyono won a second 5-year term July 8, 2009. Suicide bombings at two Jakarta hotels July 17 left 9 people dead. Police confirmed Sept. 17 that Noordin Muhammad Top, suspected of plotting the Jakarta attacks and other terrorist bombings, had been killed in a shootout.

Padang, Sumatra, was hit Sept. 30, 2009, by a powerful earthquake, which also triggered mudslides in the region; at least 1,115 people were killed. On Oct. 25, 2010, Mt. Merapi, a volcano near Yogyakarta, Java, began a series of major eruptions that claimed at least 228 lives and displaced 430,500.

The General Elections Commission, July 22, 2014, declared populist Jakarta governor Joko Widodo the presidential election winner over former general Prabowo Subianto. All 162 people aboard an AirAsia Indonesia flight were killed, Dec. 28, 2014, when the plane, en route from Surabaya, Indonesia, to Singapore, crashed into the Java Sea near Borneo. A military aircraft crashed, June 30, 2015, in Medan, Sumatra, killing all 122 on board and more than 20 people on the ground. Indonesia agreed, May 20, 2015, to provide temporary refuge—pending resettlement in another country—for up to 7,000 migrants, mostly ethnic Rohingya from Myanmar and Bangladesh, who were rescued at sea or had landed on Indonesian shores.

Iran

Islamic Republic of Iran

People: Population: 81,824,270. **Age distrib.:** <15: 23.7%; 65+: 5.3%. **Growth:** 1.2%. **Migrants:** 3.4%. **Pop. density:** 138.4 per sq mi, 53.4 per sq km. **Urban:** 73.4%. **Ethnic groups:** Persian, Azeri, Kurd, Lur, Baloch, Arab, Turkmen and Turkic tribes. **Languages:** Persian (official), Azeri Turkic and Turkic dialects, Kurdish, Gilaki and Mazandarani, Luri, Balochi, Arabic. **Religions:** Muslim (official) 99.4% (Shia 90%-95%, Sunni 5%-10%).

Geography: Total area: 636,372 sq mi, 1,648,195 sq km; **Land area:** 591,352 sq mi, 1,531,595 sq km. **Location:** Between the Middle East and S Asia. Turkey, Iraq on W; Armenia, Azerbaijan, Turkmenistan on N; Afghanistan, Pakistan on E. **Topography:** Interior highlands and plains surrounded by high mountains, up to 18,000 ft. Large salt deserts cover much of area, though there are oases and forests. Most of pop. inhabits N and NW. **Arable land:** 10.9%. **Capital:** Tehran, 8,432,196. **Cities:** Mashhad, 3,014,424; Esfahan, 1,879,806; Karaj, 1,807,058; Shiraz, 1,660,545; Tabriz, 1,571,582; Ahvaz, 1,215,782; Qom, 1,204,115.

Government: Type: Theocratic republic. **Religious head:** Ayatollah Sayyed Ali Khamenei; in office: June 4, 1989. **Head of state and gov.:** Pres. Hassan Rouhani; in office: Aug. 4, 2013. **Local divisions:** 31 provinces. **Defense budget:** $15.71 bil. **Active troops:** 523,000.

Economy: Industries: petroleum, petrochemicals, gas, fertilizers, caustic soda, textiles, cement and other constr. materials. **Chief crops:** wheat, rice, other grains, sugar beets, sugarcane, fruits, nuts, cotton. **Natural resources:** petroleum, nat. gas, coal, chromium, copper, iron ore, lead, manganese, zinc, sulfur. **Water:** 1,769 cu m per capita. **Crude oil reserves:** 157.8 bil bbls. **Electricity prod.:** 239.2 bil kWh. **Labor force:** agric. 16.3%, industry 35.1%, services 48.6%. **Unemployment:** 13.2%.

Finance: Monetary unit: Rial (IRR) (29,955.01 = $1 U.S.). **GDP:** $1.3 tril; **per capita GDP:** $17,100; **GDP growth:** 3%. **Imports:** $61.3 bil; UAE 35.8%, China 18.6%, India 6.4%, South

Korea 5.8%, Turkey 5.4%. **Exports:** $95.7 bil; China 26.8%, Turkey 11%, India 10.6%, Japan 7.3%, South Korea 5.9%. **Tourism:** $1.3 bil. **Budget:** $63.3 bil. **Inflation:** 17.2%.

Transport: Railways: 5,271 mi. **Motor vehicles:** 57.2 per 1,000 pop. **Airports:** 140.

Communications: Telephone: 39 per 100 pop. **Mobile:** 87.8 per 100 pop. **Broadband:** 2.5 per 100 pop. **Internet:** 39.4%.

Health: Expend.: 6.7%. **Life expect.:** 69.6 male; 72.8 female. **Births:** 18.0 per 1,000 pop. **Deaths:** 5.9 per 1,000 pop. **Infant mortality:** 38.0 per 1,000 live births. **Undernourished:** <5%. **HIV:** 0.1%.

Education: Compulsory: ages 6-13. **Literacy:** 86.9%.

Permanent UN mission: 622 Third Ave., 34th Fl., New York, NY 10017; (212) 687-2020.

Website: www.president.ir

Ancestors of inhabitants of Iran, formerly known as Persia, came from the east during the second millennium BCE; they were an Indo-European group related to the Aryans of India. In 549 BCE, Cyrus the Great united the Medes and Persians in the Persian Empire; he conquered Babylonia in 538 BCE, and restored Jerusalem to the Jews. Alexander the Great conquered Persia in 333 BCE, but Persians regained independence in the next century under the Parthians, themselves succeeded by Sassanian Persians in 226 CE. Arabs brought Islam to Persia in the 7th cent., replacing the indigenous Zoroastrian faith. After Persian political and cultural autonomy was reasserted in the 9th cent., arts and sciences flourished.

Turks and Mongols ruled Persia in turn from the 11th cent. to 1502, when Ismael I established the Iranian Safavid dynasty and made Shiite Islam the official religion. The dynasty lasted until 1722. The British and Russian empires vied for influence in the 19th cent.; Britain severed Afghanistan from Iran in 1857.

Reza Khan, a military officer, became prime min., 1923, and shah in 1925. He began modernization, curbed foreign influence, and officially changed the country's name from Persia to Iran in 1935. Fearing the shah's Axis sympathies, British and Soviet troops forced him to abdicate, 1941; he was succeeded by his son, Mohammad Reza Pahlavi. The U.S. Central Intelligence Agency had a major role in the ouster, 1953, of Prime Min. Muhammad Mossadegh, who had nationalized the oil industry.

With U.S. backing, the shah brought economic and social change to Iran (White Revolution), but repression of opposition groups grew severe. Violent protests in 1978 eventually forced the shah to depart, Jan. 16, 1979. Shiite leader Ayatollah Ruhollah Khomeini, exiled by the shah in 1963, returned to Tehran, Feb. 1. Pro-Khomeini forces defeated government troops, Feb 11. Khomeini established an Islamic theocracy.

Iranian militants seized the U.S. embassy in Tehran Nov. 4, 1979, and took hostages, including 62 Americans. Despite international condemnations and U.S. efforts, including an abortive Apr. 1980 rescue attempt, the crisis continued. The U.S. broke diplomatic relations with Iran, Apr. 7. The shah died in Egypt, July 27. The hostage drama ended Jan. 20, 1981, when an accord, involving the release of frozen Iranian assets, was reached.

A dispute over the Shatt al-Arab waterway between Iran and Iraq led to a long and costly war between the two countries, 1980-88, killing hundreds of thousands of people. In Nov. 1986 it became known that the U.S., which had generally sided with Iraq during the war, had secretly shipped arms to Iran to gain that country's help in obtaining the release of U.S. hostages held in Lebanon. The revelation sparked a major scandal in the U.S. A U.S. Navy warship shot down an Iranian airliner, July 3, 1988, after mistaking it for an F-14 fighter jet; all 290 aboard died.

An earthquake struck northern Iran June 21, 1990, killing more than 45,000 and leaving 400,000 homeless. Some 1 mil Kurdish refugees fled from Iraq to Iran following the Persian Gulf War of 1991. To curb Iran's alleged support for international terrorism, the U.S. in 1996 authorized sanctions on foreign companies that invested there.

Mohammad Khatami, a moderate Shiite Muslim cleric, was elected president in 1997. During the next three years, hard-line Islamists clashed, sometimes violently, with reformers, who won a majority in 2000 parliamentary elections. Inviting rapprochement with Iran, the U.S. eased some sanctions Mar. 18. Khatami was reelected in 2001 but continued to face resistance from religious conservatives.

An earthquake Dec. 26, 2003, in Bam, SE Iran, killed about 26,000 people. After the Guardian Council, dominated by religious conservatives, disqualified some 2,400 reformist candidates, hardliners won legislative elections Feb. 20, 2004.

The religiously conservative mayor of Tehran, Mahmoud Ahmadinejad, defeated former Pres. Hashemi Rafsanjani in a 2005 runoff election. U.S. Pres. George W. Bush's administration accused Iran of seeking to build nuclear weapons, aiding Shiite militias opposing government forces in the U.S.-led war in Iraq (2003-11), and supplying rockets to Hezbollah fighters in Lebanon for use against Israel.

Seeking to halt Iran's uranium-enrichment program, the UN Security Council imposed sanctions, Dec. 2006, and toughened them, Mar. 2007. After the Guardian Council disqualified about 1,700 reformist candidates, conservative allies of Ahmadinejad won parliamentary elections Mar.-Apr. 2008. Further talks on nuclear enrichment ended in deadlock July 20, and the U.S. imposed additional sanctions Sept. 10.

Ahmadinejad won the 2009 presidential election. His main opponent, former Prime Min. Mir Hussein Moussavi, claimed the vote count was fraudulent. Huge protests by Moussavi supporters in Tehran and other major cities were crushed. Tensions with the U.S. and European governments were heightened in late Sept. 2009 by disclosures that Iran had been secretly enriching uranium at an underground site near Qom, and by Iranian tests of medium-range missiles capable of reaching Israel or U.S. and European bases in the Persian Gulf region. Iran agreed in Oct. to allow international inspection of the Qom site and to other nuclear safeguards.

The UN and U.S. toughened sanctions, June-July 2010, but did not object when loading of uranium fuel began in Aug. at Iran's Russian-built Bushehr nuclear power plant. Iran blamed Israel, the U.S., and other Western powers for carrying out cyberattacks against the country's nuclear facilities and for assassinating Iranian scientists. In Dec. 2010, the U.S. announced new sanctions. Iran announced, Jan. 2012, that it was enriching uranium at its underground Fordo nuclear facility; more international sanctions followed.

Playing a role in regional conflicts, Iran supported the Syrian government with military aid, 2012-15, in its civil war; provided military assistance to Iraqi Shiite militia forces combating ISIS Sunni extremist fighters in Iraq, 2014-15; and aided Houthi rebels in Yemen's civil war, 2014-15.

The moderate cleric Hassan Rouhani was elected president June 14, 2013. Rouhani and U.S. Pres. Barack Obama spoke by phone Sept. 27, 2013—the first time since 1979 that leaders of the two nations directly communicated. An interim agreement was reached Nov. 24, 2013, under which Iran pledged to limit some aspects of its nuclear program and allow wider international inspections in exchange for the temporary lifting of some sanctions. Negotiations toward a longer-term accord produced a 15-year agreement—signed July 14, 2015, by the U.S., UK, France, Germany, Russia, China, Iran, and the EU—for Iran to limit and partly dismantle its nuclear program and submit to international inspections in return for the lifting of sanctions in stages. Critics claimed the accord was too lenient on Iran and would not keep the country from developing nuclear weapons.

Iraq

Republic of Iraq

People: Population: 37,056,169. **Age distrib.:** <15: 40.3%; 65+: 3.3%. **Growth:** 2.9%. **Migrants:** 0.3%. **Pop. density:** 219.4 per sq mi, 84.7 per sq km. **Urban:** 69.5%. **Ethnic groups:** Arab 75%-80%; Kurdish 15%-20%; Turkoman, Assyrian, other 5%. **Languages:** Arabic, Kurdish (both official); Turkmen, Assyrian (both official regionally); Armenian. **Religions:** Muslim (official) 99% (Shia 60%-65%, Sunni 32%-37%).

Geography: Total area: 169,235 sq mi, 438,317 sq km; **Land area:** 168,868 sq mi, 437,367 sq km. **Location:** Middle East, occupying most of historic Mesopotamia. Jordan, Syria on W; Turkey on N; Iran on E; Kuwait, Saudi Arabia on S. **Topography:** Mostly an alluvial plain, including the Tigris and Euphrates Rivers, descending from mountains in N to desert in SW. Persian Gulf region is marshland. **Arable land:** 7.9%. **Capital:** Baghdad, 6,642,848. **Cities:** Mosul, 1,694,284; Erbil, 1,165,714; Basra, 1,019,109; Sulaimaniya, 1,003,782.

Government: Type: Parliamentary democracy. **Head of state:** Pres. Fuad Masum; in office: July 24, 2014. **Head of gov.:** Prime Min. Haider al-Abadi; in office: Sept. 8, 2014. **Local divisions:** 18 governorates, 1 region (Kurdistan Regional Govt.). **Defense budget:** $18.87 bil. **Active troops:** 177,600.

Economy: Industries: petroleum, chemicals, textiles, leather, constr. materials, food proc., fertilizer, metal fabrication/proc. **Chief crops:** wheat, barley, rice, vegetables, dates, cotton. **Natural resources:** petroleum, nat. gas, phosphates, sulfur. **Water:** 2,661 cu m per capita. **Crude oil reserves:** 144.2 bil bbls. **Electricity prod.:** 58.3 bil kWh. **Labor force:** agric. 21.6%, industry 18.7%, services 59.8%. **Unemployment:** 16%.

Finance: Monetary unit: Dinar (IQD) (1,143.00 = $1 U.S.). **GDP:** $522.7 bil; **per capita GDP:** $14,600; **GDP growth:** –2.4%. **Imports:** $62.3 bil; Turkey 25.4%, China 15.6%, Syria 14.3%. **Exports:** $94.4 bil; India 22.2%, China 19.7%, U.S. 14.6%, South Korea 10.1%, Greece 5.2%. **Tourism:** $1.6 bil. **Budget:** $94.6 bil. **Inflation:** 2.2%.

Transport: Railways: 1,412 mi. **Motor vehicles:** 57 per 1,000 pop. **Airports:** 72.

Communications: Telephone: 5.6 per 100 pop. **Mobile:** 94.9 per 100 pop. **Broadband:** NA. **Internet:** 11.3%.

Health: Expend.: 3.6%. **Life expect.:** 72.6 male; 77.2 female. **Births:** 31.5 per 1,000 pop. **Deaths:** 3.8 per 1,000 pop. **Infant mortality:** 37.5 per 1,000 live births. **Undernourished:** 23.5%. **HIV:** NA.

Education: Compulsory: ages 6-15. **Literacy:** 79.7%.

Embassy: 3421 Massachusetts Ave. NW 20007; 742-1600.

Website: www.egov.gov.iq

The Tigris-Euphrates valley, formerly called Mesopotamia, was the site of one of the earliest civilizations in the world. Mesopotamia ceased to be a separate entity after Persian, Greek, and Arab conquests. The Arabs founded Baghdad, from where the caliph ruled a vast Islamic empire in the 8th and 9th cents. Mongol and Turkish conquests led to a decline in the region's population, economy, cultural life, and irrigation system.

Britain secured a League of Nations mandate over Iraq after WWI. Independence under a king came in 1932. Rebellious army officers killed King Faisal II, July 1958, and established a leftist, pan-Arab republic. The Baath Arab Socialist Party increasingly dominated successive regimes. A Baath leader, Saddam Hussein, became president in 1979. He ruled as a dictator for more than two decades, repressing Iraq's Kurds and Shiites. Israeli planes destroyed a nuclear reactor near Baghdad in 1981, claiming it could be used to produce nuclear weapons.

After skirmishing intermittently for 10 months over the sovereignty of the disputed Shatt al-Arab waterway dividing the two countries, Iraq and Iran entered into open warfare on Sept. 22, 1980. Iran repulsed early Iraqi advances, producing a long and costly stalemate; hundreds of thousands of Iraqis lost their lives during the 8-year conflict. Hussein used poison gas against Iraqi Kurds in 1988, killing more than 5,000 people in Halabja, the first mass use of poison gas against civilians since the Holocaust.

Iraq invaded Kuwait in 1990. Backed by the UN, a U.S.-led coalition launched air and missile attacks on Iraq, Jan. 16, 1991, and began a ground attack to retake Kuwait Feb. 23. Iraqi forces showed little resistance and were defeated in 4 days. Some 175,000 Iraqis were taken prisoner, and Iraqi casualties were estimated at over 85,000. As part of the cease-fire agreement, Iraq agreed to scrap all poison gas and germ weapons and allow UN observers to inspect the sites. UN trade sanctions would remain in effect until Iraq complied with all terms.

Iraqi cooperation with UN weapons inspection teams was intermittent throughout the 1990s. Standoffs over inspections led to diplomatic crises 1997-98, culminating in intensive U.S. and British aerial bombardment of Iraqi military targets, Dec. 16-19, 1998. After two years of sporadic activity, U.S. and British warplanes struck sites near Baghdad mid-Feb. 2001.

Despite opposition from some countries, including France, Germany, and Russia, a U.S.-led coalition invaded Iraq Mar. 19, 2003. By Apr. 6 the British controlled Basra and other areas in the south, and the U.S. entered Baghdad Apr. 7. Hussein disappeared, the Iraqi government collapsed, and most of Iraq's armed forces dissolved into the civilian population. On May 1, U.S. Pres. George W. Bush declared the end of major combat. Searches failed to find chemical, biological, or nuclear weapons that the U.S. and other countries claimed Iraq had stockpiled.

The U.S.-led Coalition Provisional Authority was unable to maintain order in the weeks following Hussein's fall. Reconstruction efforts were hampered by guerrilla attacks from Baath remnants, Islamic extremists, and others. Coalition forces succeeded in neutralizing many leaders of the former regime. U.S. troops killed two of Hussein's sons, Uday and Qusay, July 22, 2003, in Mosul. Saddam Hussein was captured in an underground hideout mid-Dec. 2003; tried and convicted for committing crimes against humanity in the 1980s, he was executed Dec. 30, 2006.

Photographs released in Apr. 2004 showed instances of physical abuse and sexual humiliation of Iraqi inmates by U.S. military personnel at Baghdad's Abu Ghraib prison in 2003. The images sparked widespread condemnation and U.S. criminal proceedings against some individuals.

On June 28, 2004, U.S. authorities transferred sovereignty to a transitional Iraqi government. Despite insurgent threats, an estimated 8 mil people in Iraq, mostly Shiites and Kurds, cast ballots Jan. 30, 2005, for a transitional national assembly. The assembly elected Jalal Talabani, a Kurd, as president; Ibrahim al-Jaafari, a Shiite, became prime min. Insurgents launched new waves of attacks. Rumors of a suicide bomber set off a stampede by Shiite pilgrims in northern Baghdad Aug. 31, killing close to 1,000 people. The U.S. blamed Jordanian militant Abu Musab al-Zarqawi, leader of al-Qaeda in Iraq, for directing a series of kidnappings, beheadings, and suicide bombings. He was killed by a U.S. airstrike, June 2006.

A new government elected in legislative elections Dec. 15, 2005, was installed May 20, 2006, headed by Shiite leader Nouri Kamel al-Maliki. The Iraqi civilian death toll averaged more than 2,800 per month in 2006.

A 2007 "surge" elevated U.S. troop strength from 132,000 in Jan. to 171,000 in Oct. U.S. troop deaths in 2007 totaled 899 (the highest for any year since the war began), but military and civilian casualties began dropping after mid-2007. Contributing to the reduction in violence were a cease-fire by Shiite militias and a shift by Sunni clan leaders against al-Qaeda in Iraq.

A Nov. 2008 agreement called for all U.S. forces to leave Iraq by Dec. 31, 2011. Legislative elections in 2010 brought gains by the Iraqi coalition headed by former Prime Min. Iyad Allawi, a Shiite who had campaigned as a secularist to win widespread Sunni support. On Aug. 31, Pres. Barack Obama formally declared an end to the U.S. combat role, and Operation Iraqi Freedom was succeeded by Operation New Dawn. More than 9 months of political deadlock ended when Prime Min. Maliki was sworn in for a second term Dec. 21, heading a unity government that included Shiite, Sunni, and Kurdish factions.

U.S. troops completed their withdrawal from Iraq Dec. 15, 2011. From Mar. 2003 through Dec. 2011, more than 4,486 U.S. service members died in operations in Iraq; another 32,000 were wounded. British troop losses totaled 179; other allies, 139. More than 115,000 Iraqi civilians and over 10,000 police and security forces were killed. U.S. budgeted costs of the Iraq war exceeded $820 bil for the 2003-12 period.

Tensions manifested between Sunnis and Shiites after the U.S. departure. The Sunni-backed Iraqiya began a 6-week boycott of parliament Dec. 17, 2011, and accused Prime Min. Maliki of not sharing power. Maliki issued an arrest warrant for Sunni Vice Pres. Tariq al-Hashemi, Dec. 19, for terrorism. The Sunni insurgent group al-Qaeda in Iraq was blamed for ongoing violence; in periodic assaults throughout 2012, 4,573 civilians were killed. Violence accelerated; the UN reported Jan. 1, 2014, that violent attacks killed 8,868 people in Iraq during 2013, including at least 7,818 civilians. In 2014, 12,282 civilians were killed according to UN estimates, the highest death toll since 2006-07.

In parliamentary elections Apr. 30, 2014, Maliki's coalition won the largest bloc of seats. Parliament elected, July 24, Kurdish politician Fuad Masum as the country's new president. On Aug. 11, Masum named Shiite Haider al-Abadi, of Maliki's Dawa Party, to be prime min.

In Dec. 2013, the Sunni extremist Islamic State in Iraq and Syria (ISIS) began crossing from Syria into Iraq and seizing territory. The ISIS offensive intensified beginning in June 2014. The group took control of large areas of northern and central Iraq, including the cities of Mosul (Iraq's second-largest) and Tikrit. ISIS imposed Islamic law, including harsh punishments, in areas it controlled while suppressing, killing, and sexually assaulting people who were non-Sunni Muslims or members of the Yazidi sect and other religious minorities. The U.S., later joined by European and other allies, began, Aug. 8, airstrikes against ISIS forces, and the U.S. and other nations provided military aid to Kurdish fighters opposing ISIS. A UN effort to aid up to 500,000 refugees of recent fighting in northern Iraq was announced Aug. 19, 2014. Pres. Obama stated Sept. 10 that 475 additional U.S. military advisers would be sent to Iraq, bringing the total to 1,600; further troop increases were announced Nov. 7, 2014, and June 10, 2015, raising the number of U.S. advisers to about 3,500. Forces fighting ISIS in 2015 included government troops, Shiite militias (often backed by Iran), Sunni tribal militias, and Kurdish troops. Kurdish fighters made some gains in northern Iraq, and government and Shiite forces completed recapturing Tikrit, Apr. 1. But ISIS gained control of Ramadi, capital of Anbar province, May 17. Deadly ISIS terrorist bombings occurred in Baghdad and other cities, often targeting Shiite areas.

Ireland

People: Population: 4,892,305. **Age distrib.:** <15: 21.5%; 65+: 12.6%. **Growth:** 1.3%. **Migrants:** 15.9%. **Pop. density:** 183.9 per sq mi, 71 per sq km. **Urban:** 63.2%. **Ethnic groups:** Irish 84.5%, other white 9.8%, Asian 1.9%. **Languages:** English (official; generally used), Irish (Gaelic or Gaeilge) (official; spoken mainly on W coast). **Religions:** Roman Catholic 84.7%, Church of Ireland 2.7%, none 5.7%.

Geography: Total area: 27,133 sq mi, 70,273 sq km; **Land area:** 26,596 sq mi, 68,883 sq km. **Location:** Atlantic O. just W of Great Britain. Northern Ireland (UK) on E. **Topography:** Central plateau surrounded by isolated groups of hills and mountains. Heavily indented Atlantic coastline. **Arable land:** 17%. **Capital:** Dublin, 1,169,371.

Government: Type: Republic; parliamentary democracy. **Head of state:** Pres. Michael D. Higgins; in office: Nov. 11, 2011. **Head of gov.:** Prime Min. Enda Kenny; in office: Mar. 9, 2011. **Local divisions:** 28 counties, 3 cities. **Defense budget:** $1.22 bil. **Active troops:** 9,350.

Economy: Industries: pharmaceuticals, chemicals, computer hardware and software, food prods., beverages and brewing. **Chief crops:** barley, potatoes, wheat. **Natural resources:** nat. gas, peat, copper, lead, zinc, silver, barite, gypsum, limestone, dolomite. **Water:** 11,238 cu m per capita. **Electricity prod.:** 25.9 bil kWh. **Labor force:** agric. 5%, industry 19%, services 76%. **Unemployment:** 13.1%.

Finance: Monetary unit: Euro (EUR) (0.89 = $1 U.S.). **GDP:** $226.8 bil; **per capita GDP:** $49,200; **GDP growth:** 4.8%.

Imports: $66.9 bil; UK 39.8%, U.S. 10%, Germany 8.6%, Netherlands 6.3%. **Exports:** $121.3 bil; U.S. 19.6%, UK 16.9%, Belgium 13.7%, Germany 7.7%, Switzerland 6.3%. **Tourism:** $4.9 bil. **Budget:** $91.9 bil. **Inflation:** 0.2%.

Transport: Railways: 2,011 mi. **Motor vehicles:** 484.6 per 1,000 pop. **Airports:** 16.

Communications: Telephone: 43.2 per 100 pop. **Mobile:** 104.3 per 100 pop. **Broadband:** 68.6 per 100 pop. **Internet:** 79.7%.

Health: Expend.: 8.1%. **Life expect.:** 78.4 male; 83.1 female. **Births:** 14.8 per 1,000 pop. **Deaths:** 6.5 per 1,000 pop. **Infant mortality:** 3.7 per 1,000 live births. **Undernourished:** <5%. **HIV:** 0.3%.

Education: Compulsory: ages 6-15. **Literacy:** 99%.

Embassy: 2234 Massachusetts Ave. NW 20008; 462-3939.

Website: www.gov.ie

Celtic tribes invaded the islands about the 4th cent. BCE; their Gaelic culture and literature flourished in the 5th cent. CE, the same century in which St. Patrick converted the Irish to Christianity. Norse invasions began in the 8th cent., ending with defeat of the Danes by the Irish King Brian Boru in 1014. English invasions started in the 12th cent. For over 700 years the Anglo-Irish struggle continued with bitter rebellions and savage repressions. In the Irish Potato Famine, failure of the staple potato crop, 1845-49, caused 1 mil deaths from starvation and related diseases; up to 2 mil people emigrated, many to the U.S.

The Easter Monday Rebellion in 1916 failed but was followed by guerrilla warfare and harsh reprisals by British troops called the Black and Tans. The Dail Eireann (Irish parliament) reaffirmed independence in Jan. 1919. The British offered dominion status to Ulster (6 counties) and southern Ireland (26 counties) Dec. 1921. The constitution of the Irish Free State, a British dominion, was adopted Dec. 11, 1922. Northern Ireland remained part of the UK (see United Kingdom—Northern Ireland).

A new constitution adopted by plebiscite came into operation Dec. 29, 1937. It declared the name of the state Eire in the Irish language (Ireland in the English) and declared it a sovereign democratic state. On Dec. 21, 1948, the country was declared a republic rather than a dominion and withdrew from the Commonwealth. The British Parliament recognized both actions, 1949, but the six northeastern counties remained in the UK.

Irish governments have favored peaceful unification of all Ireland and cooperated with Britain against terrorist groups. After negotiators in Northern Ireland approved a peace settlement on Good Friday, Apr. 10, 1998, voters in the Irish Republic endorsed the accord, on May 22, and the Irish gave up their constitution's territorial claims on the north.

Expansion of educational opportunities and foreign investment in high-tech industries in the 1990s boosted Ireland's prosperity. Ireland's first woman president, Mary Robinson, resigned Sept. 1997, to become UN high commissioner for human rights, 1997-2002. She was succeeded as president by Mary McAleese, the first person from Northern Ireland to hold the office.

Responding to a growing scandal over abusive Catholic clergy in Ireland, Pope Benedict XVI issued a public apology to victims and their families Mar. 2010.

To aid Ireland's ailing banks and prevent default after a 2008-10 financial crisis, finance ministers from EU member countries approved Nov. 2010 an 85-bil euro ($115-bil) emergency loan package that obligated Ireland to impose unpopular austerity measures. Fianna Fáil, the party that had dominated Irish politics since the 1930s, suffered a crushing defeat in Feb. 2011 elections, and Enda Kenny, leader of the opposition Fine Gael and a critic of the bailout, became prime minister. Lawmakers voted, July 11, 2013, to legalize abortion when a woman's pregnancy is thought to jeopardize her life. In a national referendum, May 22, 2015, voters approved changing the constitution to legalize same-sex marriage.

Israel

State of Israel

People: Population: 8,049,314. **Age distrib.:** <15: 28%; 65+: 10.8%. **Growth:** 1.6%. **Migrants:** 26.5%. **Pop. density:** 1,025.5 per sq mi, 395.9 per sq km. **Urban:** 92.1%. **Ethnic groups:** Jewish (Israel-born 74.4%, Europe/America/Oceania-born 17.4%, Africa-born 5.1%, Asia-born 3.1%) 75%, non-Jewish (mostly Arab) 25%. **Languages:** Hebrew, Arabic (both official); English (most common foreign lang.). **Religions:** Jewish 75%, Muslim 17.5%, Christian 2%.

Geography: Total area: 8,019 sq mi, 20,770 sq km; **Land area:** 7,849 sq mi, 20,330 sq km. **Location:** Middle East, on E end of Mediterranean Sea. Lebanon on N; Syria, West Bank, Jordan on E; Gaza Strip, Egypt on W. **Topography:** The Mediterranean coastal plain is fertile and well-watered. Judean Plateau in center. Semi-desert Negev region extends to apex at head of Gulf of Aqaba. The E border drops sharply into the Jordan Rift Valley, which incl. Lake Tiberias (Sea of Galilee) and the Dead Sea (1,348 ft below sea level), lowest point in Asia. **Arable land:** 13.6%. **Capital:** Jerusalem, 839,077. **Cities:** Tel Aviv-Jaffa, 3,608,265; Haifa, 1,096,669.

Government: Type: Parliamentary democracy. **Head of state:** Pres. Reuven Rivlin; in office: July 27, 2014. **Head of gov.:** Prime Min. Benjamin Netanyahu; in office: Mar. 31, 2009. **Local divisions:** 6 districts. **Defense budget:** $20.14 bil. **Active troops:** 176,500.

Economy: Industries: high-tech prods. (incl. aviation, communications, computer-aided design and manufactures, medical electronics, fiber optics), wood and paper prods. **Chief crops:** citrus, vegetables, cotton. **Natural resources:** timber, potash, copper ore, nat. gas, phosphate rock, magnesium bromide, clays, sand. **Water:** 230 cu m per capita. **Crude oil reserves:** 14 mil bbls. **Electricity prod.:** 59.2 bil kWh. **Labor force:** agric. 1.6%, industry 18.1%, services 80.3%. **Unemployment:** 6.3%.

Finance: Monetary unit: Shekel (ILS) (3.93 = $1 U.S.). **GDP:** $268.5 bil; **per capita GDP:** $32,700; **GDP growth:** 2.8%. **Imports:** $69.7 bil; U.S. 11.3%, China 7.8%, Germany 6.5%, Switzerland 6.1%, Belgium 5.3%. **Exports:** $63.2 bil; U.S. 26.5%, Hong Kong 8.1%, UK 5.9%. **Tourism:** $5.7 bil. **Budget:** $81.8 bil. **Inflation:** 0.5%.

Transport: Railways: 777 mi. **Motor vehicles:** 361.8 per 1,000 pop. **Airports:** 29.

Communications: Telephone: 37.1 per 100 pop. **Mobile:** 121.5 per 100 pop. **Broadband:** 52.5 per 100 pop. **Internet:** 71.5%.

Health: Expend.: 7.5%. **Life expect.:** 80.4 male; 84.2 female. **Births:** 18.5 per 1,000 pop. **Deaths:** 5.2 per 1,000 pop. **Infant mortality:** 3.6 per 1,000 live births. **Undernourished:** <5%. **HIV:** NA.

Education: Compulsory: ages 5-18. **Literacy:** 97.8%.

Embassy: 3514 International Dr. NW 20008; 364-5500.

Website: www.gov.il

Occupying the southwest corner of the ancient Fertile Crescent, Israel contains some of the oldest known evidence of agriculture and of primitive town life. The Hebrews probably arrived early in the 2nd millennium BCE. Under King David and his successors (c. 1000 BCE-597 BCE), Judaism was developed and secured. After conquest by Babylonians, Persians, and Greeks, an independent Jewish kingdom was revived, 168 BCE, but Rome took over in the next century, suppressed Jewish revolts in 70 CE and 135 CE, and renamed Judea Palestine, after the earlier coastal inhabitants, the Philistines.

Arab invaders conquered Palestine in 636. The Arabic language and Islam prevailed within a few centuries, but a Jewish minority remained. The land was ruled from the 11th cent. as a part of non-Arab empires by Seljuks, Mamluks, and Ottomans (with a Crusader interval, 1098-1291).

After 4 centuries of Ottoman rule, the land was taken in 1917 by Britain, which pledged in the Balfour Declaration to support a Jewish homeland there. In 1920 a British Palestine Mandate was recognized; in 1922 the land east of the Jordan R. was detached.

Jewish immigration, begun in the late 19th cent., swelled in the 1930s and 1940s with refugees from Nazi Germany and survivors of the Holocaust; heavy Arab immigration from Syria and Lebanon also occurred. Arab opposition to Jewish immigration turned violent in 1920, 1921, 1929, and 1936. The UN General Assembly voted in 1947 to partition Palestine into an Arab and a Jewish state. Britain withdrew in May 1948.

Israel was declared independent May 14, 1948; Arabs rejected partition. Egypt, Jordan, Syria, Lebanon, Iraq, and Saudi Arabia invaded but failed to destroy the Jewish state, which gained territory. Separate armistices with the Arab nations were signed in 1949; Jordan occupied the West Bank, Egypt occupied Gaza. Neither granted Palestinian autonomy.

After persistent terrorist raids, Israel invaded Egypt's Sinai, Oct. 29, 1956, aided briefly by British and French forces. A UN cease-fire was arranged Nov. 6.

An uneasy truce between Israel and the Arab countries lasted until 1967, when Egypt reoccupied the Gaza Strip and closed the Gulf of Aqaba to Israeli shipping. In the Six-Day War, starting June 5, the Israelis took the Gaza Strip, occupied the Sinai Peninsula to the Suez Canal, and captured East Jerusalem, Syria's Golan Heights, and Jordan's West Bank. Together, the West Bank and Gaza comprise the Palestinian territories, now represented by the Palestinian Authority.

Egypt and Syria attacked Israel, Oct. 6, 1973 (Yom Kippur, the most solemn day in the Jewish calendar). Israel counterattacked, driving the Syrians back, and crossed the Suez Canal. A cease-fire took effect Oct. 24 and a UN peacekeeping force arrived. Under a 1974 disengagement agreement, Israel withdrew from the canal's west bank. Israeli forces raided Entebbe, Uganda, in 1976 and rescued 103 hostages who had been seized by Arab and German terrorists.

Israel's prime ministers, including David Ben-Gurion, Golda Meir, and Yitzhak Rabin, pursued a moderate socialist program, 1948-77. In 1977, the conservative opposition, led by Menachem

Begin, was voted into office for the first time. Egypt's Pres. Anwar al-Sadat visited Jerusalem in 1977, and on Mar. 26, 1979, Egypt and Israel signed a formal peace treaty, ending 30 years of war. Israel returned the Sinai to Egypt in 1982.

Israeli forces invaded Lebanon, June 6, 1982, to destroy Palestine Liberation Organization (PLO) strongholds. After massive Israeli bombing of West Beirut, the PLO agreed to evacuate the city. Israeli troops entered West Beirut after newly elected Lebanese Pres. Bashir Gemayel was assassinated on Sept. 14. Israel drew widespread condemnation when Lebanese Christian forces, Sept. 16, entered two West Beirut refugee camps and slaughtered hundreds of Palestinians.

In 1989, violence escalated over the Israeli military occupation of the West Bank and Gaza Strip. In a series of uprisings known as the first intifada, Palestinian protesters defied Israeli troops, who forcibly retaliated. During the Persian Gulf War, 1991, Iraq fired Scud missiles at Israel.

Ongoing peace talks led to historic agreements between Israel and the PLO, Sept. 1993. The PLO recognized Israel's right to exist; Israel recognized the PLO as the Palestinians' representative. The two sides then signed, Sept. 13, an agreement (known as the Oslo Accord) for limited Palestinian self-rule in the West Bank and Gaza. A follow-up Sept. 1995 agreement (Oslo II) essentially divided the West Bank into areas under Israeli or Palestinian control. Israel and Jordan signed, July 25, 1994, in Washington, DC, a declaration ending their 46-year state of war.

Arab and Jewish extremists repeatedly challenged the peace process. On Nov. 4, 1995, an Orthodox Jewish Israeli assassinated Labor Party Prime Min. Yitzhak Rabin as he left a peace rally in Tel Aviv. Support for Rabin's successor, Shimon Peres, was shaken by a series of suicide bombings and rocket attacks against Israel by Islamic militants. Emphasizing security issues, the candidate of the conservative Likud bloc, Benjamin Netanyahu, was elected prime minister on May 29, 1996.

Under an interim accord brokered by Pres. Bill Clinton and signed by Netanyahu and PLO leader Yasir Arafat at the White House, Oct. 23, 1998, Israel yielded more West Bank territory to the Palestinians, in exchange for new security guarantees. Full implementation did not begin until Sept. 1999. In the interim, Netanyahu lost to the Labor candidate, Ehud Barak, in the May 1999, election.

Israel pulled virtually all its troops out of southern Lebanon in May 2000. Marathon summit talks in the U.S. between Barak and Arafat, July 11-25, failed. A second intifada began in late Sept. in Israel and the Palestinian territories. Barak called new elections for prime minister but lost Feb. 2001 to Ariel Sharon, a hardliner. The bloodshed intensified during the summer, as Palestinian suicide bombers attacked Israeli civilians, and Israel struck at Palestinian-controlled territory attempting to assassinate suspected terrorists.

Israel launched a major West Bank offensive Mar. 29, 2002, two days after a suicide bomber killed 26 Israeli Jews at a Passover celebration in Netanya. A U.S.-sponsored "road map" to Middle East peace, unveiled Apr. 2003, made little headway.

Sharon's decision to pull all Israeli settlers and troops out of Gaza, approved by the cabinet Feb. 2005, led Israeli politics to be realigned. When right-wing Likud members opposed the plan, Sharon and Deputy Prime Min. Ehud Olmert broke with them and formed the centrist Kadima Party. Sharon suffered a massive stroke Jan. 4, 2006. Olmert became prime minister, led Kadima to victory in Mar. elections, and formed a broad coalition government.

Clashes in mid-2006 along the Gaza and Lebanon borders rapidly escalated into full-scale war. By Aug. 14, when a UN-sponsored cease-fire took hold, the estimated death toll from the war included nearly 1,150 Lebanese, almost 200 Gaza Palestinians, and 150 Israelis. Olmert, criticized for leadership failures during the 2006 war and targeted in multiple corruption inquiries, announced his resignation July 30, 2008. (After a four-year trial, he was acquitted of two counts of bribery but convicted of a lesser count of breach of public trust, July 10, 2012.) Early elections were called for Feb. 2009. After a campaign overshadowed by a three-week war between Israel and Hamas in Gaza, both Kadima and Likud fell far short of a majority. On Mar. 31, Netanyahu became prime min. for a second time.

Israel's relations with allies were strained when senior Hamas commander Mahmoud al-Mabhouh was killed Jan. 2010 in Dubai, allegedly by agents of the Israeli spy agency Mossad. Further criticism greeted the Israeli government after its Mar. 2010 announcement that it would proceed to build 1,600 homes in Ramat Shlomo (a Jewish settlement in mostly Arab East Jerusalem), and later in the spring, when Israeli commandos killed 9 pro-Palestinian activists in clashes May 31 on board the *Mavi Marmara*, part of a flotilla that was seeking to break Israel's blockade of Gaza.

Arab Spring uprisings in 2011, which brought to power an Islamist government in neighboring Egypt (until July 2013) and shook other Middle Eastern regimes, unsettled Israeli policy in the region. Egyptian militants Aug. 18, 2011, killed 8 Israelis (6 civilians, 2 soldiers), and Israel killed at least 7 of the attackers, 3 Egyptian security officers, and, according to some reports, several civilians across the border.

Israel clashed with Palestinians in Gaza Oct.-Nov. 2012. In retaliation for the Gaza attacks, the hacker collective Anonymous launched cyberattacks on Israel before a cease-fire was declared Nov. 21, 2012.

Netanyahu's right-wing Likud-Yisrael Beitenu political bloc narrowly won Jan. 22, 2013, parliamentary elections. Likud won the largest bloc of seats in Mar. 17, 2015, elections, and Netanyahu assembled a new coalition government.

Conflict between Israel and Hamas escalated in 2014. Rocket attacks from Gaza into Israel increased beginning in June. Israel blamed Hamas for the June 12 kidnapping and killing of 3 Israeli teenagers in the West Bank. Israel launched air and artillery attacks on targets in Gaza, including suspected missile launch sites, and Hamas intensified rocket attacks on Israel. Israeli ground forces entered Gaza July 17, in part to destroy tunnels used to infiltrate fighters into Israel. Israeli ground and air attacks caused high civilian casualties, for which international criticism mounted. Israel pulled out ground troops Aug. 5. Fighting resumed intermittently (rockets, artillery, airstrikes) when a 3-day cease-fire ended Aug. 8. An Israeli airstrike, Aug. 21, killed 3 top Hamas commanders. A new cease-fire was agreed Aug. 26. By that time, more than 2,100 Palestinians were estimated to have died in the conflict, and Israel reported 64 soldiers and 5 civilians killed.

Tensions between Iran and Israel have grown over Iran's nuclear program, which Israel sees as an existential threat. An agreement to limit Iran's nuclear program, signed July 14, 2015, after U.S.-led negotiations, was criticized by Netanyahu as inadequate to prevent Iran's developing nuclear weapons.

Palestinian Territories

The Palestinian territories comprise the Gaza Strip, often called Gaza, and the West Bank, both occupied by Israel in 1967. Since 1996 the Palestinian Authority has been responsible for civil government in the territories. Elected president Jan. 20, 1996, PLO leader Yasir Arafat headed the Palestinian Authority until his death Nov. 11, 2004. Mahmoud Abbas, who had succeeded Arafat as PLO chairman and leader of the Fatah faction, was elected president Jan. 2005. (Abbas resigned as PLO chairman Aug. 22, 2015.) A victory by Hamas militants in Jan. 2006 legislative elections led to a power struggle with Abbas, who favored a negotiated settlement with Israel. In bitter fighting, Hamas ousted Fatah from Gaza, June 2007, but Abbas retained power in the West Bank. Fatah and Hamas reached a reconciliation agreement Apr. 27, 2011, and announced Feb. 6, 2012, that Abbas would lead an interim unity government. However, Fatah-Hamas tensions increased in 2013. A new reconciliation agreement was completed Apr. 2014; a unity government sworn in June 2, 2014, was unable to exert effective authority in Gaza. In a 2011 UN speech, Abbas sought full UN membership for an independent Palestinian state; the General Assembly voted, Nov. 29, 2012, to make Palestine a non-member observer state. Speaking at the UN Sept. 30, 2015, Abbas said the Palestinian Authority would no longer be bound by the Oslo Accords and other power-sharing agreements with Israel, which he alleged had violated such agreements and was an "occupying power."

The **Gaza Strip** extends NE from the Sinai Peninsula for 25 mi, with the Mediterranean Sea to the W and Israel to the E. The Palestinian Authority is responsible for civil government. Nearly all the inhabitants are Palestinian Arabs, more than 35% of whom live in refugee camps. Area 139 sq mi; pop. (2015 est.) 1,869,055.

Israel captured Gaza from Egypt in the 1967 war. It remained under Israeli occupation until May 1994, when the Israeli Defense Forces withdrew. Agreements between Israel and the PLO in 1993 and 1994 provided for interim self-rule in Gaza, but Israel retained control over security. Israel forcibly evacuated all 9,000 Jewish settlers from Gaza by Aug. 22, 2005, and the last remaining Israeli soldiers pulled out Sept. 12. Israel established a fortified barrier on its Gaza border to block Palestinian infiltrators.

After the Hamas takeover, Israel declared Gaza a "hostile entity," Sept. 19, 2007, and intensified military and economic pressures. Hamas thwarted an Israeli blockade, Jan. 2008, blowing up part of the border wall between Gaza and Egypt. Retaliating for Hamas rocket and mortar attacks, Israel launched an aerial assault and ground offensive in Gaza, Dec. 2008-Jan. 2009. A UN report issued in 2009 found evidence of war crimes committed by both sides. After the *Mavi Marmara* incident, Israel June 2010 eased some restrictions on the flow of goods to Gaza. Egypt's Islamist govt. lifted the blockade along its Gaza border May 28, 2011. However, Egypt's new government re-closed the border in 2013 and sought to destroy tunnels dug by Hamas to bring military and other equipment into Gaza. Egypt briefly reopened the Gaza border several times in 2015, in part to allow in materials for reconstruction after the 2014 conflict.

Members of the Israeli Air Force, Oct. 31, 2012, assassinated Hamas's military chief, Ahmed al-Jabari, in the Gaza Strip.

The **West Bank** is located W of the Jordan R. and Dead Sea, bounded by Jordan on the E and by Israel on the N, W, and S. The Palestinian Authority administers several major cities, but Israel retains control over much land, including Jewish settlements. Total area 2,263 sq mi, land area 2,178 sq mi; pop. (2015 est.) 2,785,366. The Palestinian Authority's National Security Force is a paramilitary organization of about 56,000 that maintains internal security in the West Bank.

In June 2002 the Israeli government began building a controversial security barrier in the West Bank to restrict Palestinian access to Israel and reduce infiltration by suicide bombers. In a nonbinding ruling, July 9, 2004, the World Court said the barrier violated international law. Israel has continued to allow the expansion of Jewish settlements on the West Bank, despite U.S. government calls for a settlement freeze; as of early 2015, more than 350,000 Jewish settlers were living in the West Bank (not including East Jerusalem, which Israel annexed in 1967).

Italy

Italian Republic

People: Population: 61,855,120. **Age distrib.:** <15: 13.7%; 65+: 21.2%. **Growth:** 0.3%. **Migrants:** 9.4%. **Pop. density:** 544.7 per sq mi, 210.3 per sq km. **Urban:** 69%. **Ethnic groups:** Italian (incl. small clusters of German-, French-, and Slovene-Italians in N; Albanian- and Greek-Italians in S). **Languages:** Italian (official), German, French, Slovene. **Religions:** Christian (overwhelmingly Roman Catholic) 80%, atheist and agnostic 20%.

Geography: Total area: 116,348 sq mi, 301,340 sq km; **Land area:** 113,568 sq mi, 294,140 sq km. **Location:** Southern Europe, jutting into Mediterranean Sea. France on W; Switzerland, Austria on N; Slovenia on E. **Topography:** Long boot-shaped peninsula, with Apennine Mts. running its length, extending SE from the Alps into Mediterranean, with islands of Sicily and Sardinia offshore. The alluvial Po Valley drains most of N. Rest of the country is rugged and mountainous, except for intermittent coastal plains like the Campania S of Rome. **Arable land:** 24.2%. **Capital:** Rome, 3,717,956. **Cities:** Milan, 3,098,974; Naples, 2,201,789; Turin, 1,764,868.

Government: Type: Republic. **Head of state:** Pres. Sergio Mattarella; in office: Feb. 3, 2015. **Head of gov.:** Prime Min. Matteo Renzi; in office: Feb. 22, 2014. **Local divisions:** 20 regions (5 autonomous). **Defense budget:** $24.27 bil. **Active troops:** 176,000.

Economy: Industries: tourism, machinery, iron and steel, chemicals, food proc., textiles, motor vehicles, clothing, footwear. **Chief crops:** fruits, vegetables, grapes, potatoes, sugar beets, soybeans, grain, olives. **Natural resources:** coal, mercury, zinc, potash, marble, barite, asbestos, pumice, fluorspar, feldspar, pyrite (sulfur), nat. gas and crude oil reserves, fish. **Water:** 3,137 cu m per capita. **Crude oil reserves:** 544.5 mil bbls. **Electricity prod.:** 281 bil kWh. **Labor force:** agric. 3.9%, industry 28.3%, services 67.8%. **Unemployment:** 12.2%.

Finance: Monetary unit: Euro (EUR) (0.89 = $1 U.S.). **GDP:** $2.1 tril; **per capita GDP:** $35,500; **GDP growth:** –0.4%. **Imports:** $448.3 bil; Germany 15.5%, France 8.9%, China 6.7%, Netherlands 6.1%. **Exports:** $500.3 bil; Germany 12.6%, France 11%, U.S. 6.7%, Switzerland 5.2%, UK 5.1%. **Tourism:** $45.5 bil. **Budget:** $1.1 tril. **Inflation:** 0.2%.

Transport: Railways: 12,540 mi. **Motor vehicles:** 680.1 per 1,000 pop. **Airports:** 98.

Communications: Telephone: 33.7 per 100 pop. **Mobile:** 154.2 per 100 pop. **Broadband:** 62.1 per 100 pop. **Internet:** 62%.

Health: Expend.: 9.2%. **Life expect.:** 79.5 male; 84.9 female. **Births:** 8.7 per 1,000 pop. **Deaths:** 10.2 per 1,000 pop. **Infant mortality:** 3.3 per 1,000 live births. **Undernourished:** <5%. **HIV:** NA.

Education: Compulsory: ages 6-17. **Literacy:** 99.2%.

Embassy: 3000 Whitehaven St. NW 20008; 612-4400.

Website: www.governo.it

Rome emerged as the major power in Italy after 500 BCE, dominating the Etruscans to the north and Greeks to the south. Under the Empire, which lasted until the 5th cent. CE, Rome ruled most of Western Europe, the Balkans, the Middle East, and North Africa. After Rome fell, Italy became a patchwork of kingdoms, principalities, and city-states until reunified, 1870.

The Fascist leader Benito Mussolini came to power, 1922, and aligned Italy with Nazi Germany in WWII. After Fascism was overthrown in 1943, Italy declared war on Germany and Japan and contributed to the Allied victory. It surrendered conquered lands and lost its colonies. Mussolini was killed by partisans Apr. 28, 1945. Victor Emmanuel III abdicated May 9, 1946; his son Humbert II was king until June 10, when Italy became a republic after a referendum, June 2-3. In the postwar decades, Italy had a succession of short-lived governments.

Christian Democratic leader and former prime min. Aldo Moro was abducted and murdered in 1978 by Red Brigade terrorists. The wave of left-wing political violence, including other kidnappings and assassinations, continued into the 1980s.

Political scandals marred the early 1990s, but in Mar. 1994 voting, under reformed election rules, right-wing parties won a majority, dislodging Italy's long-powerful Christian Democratic Party. Italy led a 7,000-member peacekeeping force in Albania, Apr.-Aug. 1997, and contributed 2,000 troops to the NATO-led security force (KFOR) that entered Kosovo in June 1999.

Supporters of Silvio Berlusconi, a multibillionaire media magnate, won the 2001 parliamentary elections. Berlusconi backed American-led military operations in Afghanistan (2001) and Iraq (2003). As of June 2015, about 500 Italian troops were serving with the NATO mission in Afghanistan.

A coalition of center-left parties led by Romano Prodi scored a narrow win over Berlusconi in 2008 parliamentary voting; Berlusconi returned at the head of a center-right coalition. An earthquake in the Abruzzo region of central Italy Apr. 6, 2009, battered the town of L'Aquila, killing more than 300 people. Sluggish economic growth and rising public debt (equal to about 120% of GDP in mid-2011) raised investors' concerns about Italy's financial stability. Berlusconi resigned Nov. 12, 2011, and Mario Monti, an economist, succeeded him Nov. 16. Italy's economic problems worsened, and its public debt reached nearly 2 tril euros ($2.5 tril) by Aug. 30, 2012. Monti announced Dec. 8, 2012, that he would resign the premiership. Elections Feb. 25, 2013, initially produced a deadlock. A coalition government was announced Apr. 27, 2013, with Enrico Letta as prime minister. After leading an intra-party revolt, Matteo Renzi replaced Letta, Feb. 22, 2014, promising political reforms and initiatives to revive the economy.

A Milan court, June 24, 2013, found Berlusconi guilty of paying for sex with a minor and using his office to cover it up. An appeals court overturned the verdict, July 18, 2014, a decision upheld by the Supreme Court, Mar. 10, 2015. Berlusconi was sentenced, Apr. 15, 2014, to community service, following a 2012 conviction for tax fraud. He was convicted, July 8, 2015, of bribing a senator.

An estimated 170,000 African, Middle Eastern, and SW Asian migrants fleeing violence and economic hardship crossed the Mediterranean from Libya to Italy in 2014; more than 130,000 arrived Jan.-Sept. 2015. Thousands died trying to make the crossing, often in unseaworthy boats; Italian Navy and Coast Guard ships, as well other EU vessels, engaged in rescue operations that saved thousands more from drowning.

Sicily, 9,927 sq mi, pop. (2014 est.) 5,094,937, is an island 180 by 120 mi, seat of an autonomous region that embraces the island of Pantelleria, 32 sq mi, and the Lipari group, 44 sq mi, including 2 active volcanoes: Vulcano (1,637 ft) and Stromboli (3,031 ft). From prehistoric times Sicily has been settled by various peoples; a Greek state had its capital at Syracuse. Rome took Sicily from Carthage 215 BCE. Mt. Etna, a 10,925-ft active volcano, is its tallest peak.

Sardinia, 9,301 sq mi, pop. (2014 est.) 1,663,859, lies in the Mediterranean, 115 mi W of Italy and 7½ mi S of Corsica. It is 160 mi long, 68 mi wide, and mountainous, with mining of coal, zinc, lead, copper. In 1720, Sardinia was added to the possessions of the Dukes of Savoy in Piedmont and Savoy to form the Kingdom of Sardinia. Elba, 86 sq mi, lies 6 mi W of Tuscany. Napoleon I lived in exile on Elba 1814-15.

Jamaica

People: Population: 2,950,210. **Age distrib.:** <15: 28%; 65+: 7.9%. **Growth:** 0.7%. **Migrants:** 1.3%. **Pop. density:** 705.5 per sq mi, 272.4 per sq km. **Urban:** 54.8%. **Ethnic groups:** black 92.1%, mixed 6.1%. **Languages:** English, English patois. **Religions:** Protestant 64.8% (incl. Seventh-day Adventist 12%, Pentecostal 11%), none 21.3%.

Geography: Total area: 4,244 sq mi, 10,991 sq km; **Land area:** 4,182 sq mi, 10,831 sq km. **Location:** W Indies. Cuba to N, Haiti to E. **Topography:** Four-fifths of country is covered by mountains. **Arable land:** 11.1%. **Capital:** Kingston, 587,652.

Government: Type: Constitutional parliamentary democracy. **Head of state:** Queen Elizabeth II, rep. by Michaelle Jean; Jan. 5, 2015. **Head of gov.:** Prime Min. Portia Simpson-Miller; in office: Jan. 5, 2012. **Local divisions:** 14 parishes. **Defense budget:** $120 mil. **Active troops:** 2,830.

Economy: Industries: tourism, bauxite/alumina, agric. proc., light manufactures, rum, cement, metal, paper, chem. prods. **Chief crops:** sugarcane, bananas, coffee, citrus, yams, ackees, vegetables. **Natural resources:** bauxite, gypsum, limestone. **Water:** 3,886 cu m per capita. **Electricity prod.:** 4 bil kWh. **Labor force:** agric. 17%, industry 19%, services 64%. **Unemployment:** 15%.

Finance: Monetary unit: Dollar (JMD) (117.30 = $1 U.S.). **GDP:** $24.1 bil; **per capita GDP:** $8,600; **GDP growth:** 0.5%. **Imports:** $5.2 bil; U.S. 33.7%, Venezuela 15.7%, Trinidad and Tobago 11.4%, China 10.6%. **Exports:** $1.5 bil; U.S. 29.4%, Canada 14.8%, Netherlands 7.7%, UK 6%, UAE 5.8%. **Tourism:** $2.1 bil. **Budget:** $4 bil. **Inflation:** 8.3%.

Transport: Motor vehicles: 62.6 per 1,000 pop. **Airports:** 11.

Communications: Telephone: 9.1 per 100 pop. **Mobile:** 102.9 per 100 pop. **Broadband:** 30.8 per 100 pop. **Internet:** 40.5%.

Health: Expend.: 5.9%. **Life expect.:** 71.9 male; 75.2 female. **Births:** 18.2 per 1,000 pop. **Deaths:** 6.7 per 1,000 pop. **Infant mortality:** 13.4 per 1,000 live births. **Undernourished:** 7.9%. **HIV:** 1.6%.

Education: Compulsory: ages 6-11. **Literacy:** 88.7%.

Embassy: 1520 New Hampshire Ave. NW 20036; 452-0660.

Website: www.jis.gov.jm

Jamaica was visited by Christopher Columbus, 1494, and ruled by Spain (under whom Arawak Indians died out) until seized by Britain, 1655. Jamaica won independence Aug. 6, 1962. The island's rich musical innovations include ska and reggae. Rastafarianism is an influential religious movement.

In 1974 Jamaica sought an increase in taxes paid by U.S. and Canadian bauxite mines. The socialist government acquired 50% ownership of the companies' Jamaican interests in 1976. Rudimentary welfare state measures were passed. Relations with the U.S. improved in the 1980s when Jamaican politics entered a more conservative phase.

Portia Simpson-Miller, leader of the People's National Party (PNP), became Jamaica's first female prime min., Mar. 30, 2006. The opposition Jamaica Labour Party (JLP) won the parliamentary elections of Sept. 3, 2007. While trying to arrest an alleged gang leader, Christopher (Dudus) Coke, police and soldiers clashed with residents in the Tivoli Gardens section of Kingston in May 2010, leaving 76 people dead. Coke surrendered June 22, 2010, and was extradited to the U.S.; he pleaded guilty to racketeering charges in 2011. The PNP won Dec. 2011 elections; Simpson-Miller again became prime min. Jan. 2012. Feb. 2015 legislation decriminalized possessing and growing small amounts of marijuana.

Japan

People: Population: 126,919,659. **Age distrib.:** <15: 13.1%; 65+: 26.6%. **Growth:** −0.2%. **Migrants:** 1.9%. **Pop. density:** 901.9 per sq mi, 348.2 per sq km. **Urban:** 93.5%. **Ethnic groups:** Japanese 98.5%, Koreans 0.5%. **Languages:** Japanese. **Religions:** Shintoism 79.2%, Buddhism 66.8% (many people observe both).

Geography: Total area: 145,914 sq mi, 377,915 sq km; **Land area:** 140,728 sq mi, 364,485 sq km. Consists of 4 main islands: Honshu ("mainland"), 87,805 sq mi; Hokkaido, 30,144 sq mi; Kyushu, 14,114 sq mi; Shikoku, 7,049 sq mi. **Location:** Archipelago off E coast of Asia. Russia to N, S. Korea to W. **Topography:** Deeply indented coast. The northern islands are continuation of the Sakhalin Mts. China's Kunlun range continues into southern islands. The ranges meet in Japanese Alps. Group of mostly extinct or inactive volcanoes, incl. Mt. Fuji (Fujiyama) (12,388 ft), cross Honshu E-W in a vast transverse fissure. **Arable land:** 11.6%. **Capital:** Tokyo, 38,001,018 (figure is for Major Metro area). **Cities:** Kinki Major Metro Area (MMA) (Osaka), 20,237,645; Chukyo MMA (Nagoya), 9,406,264; Kitakyushu-Fukuoka MMA, 5,510,478; Shizuoka-Hamamatsu MMA, 3,368,988; Sapporo, 2,571,497; Hiroshima, 2,173,249; Sendai, 2,090,856.

Government: Type: Parliamentary govt. with constitutional monarchy. **Head of state:** Emperor Akihito; in office: Jan. 7, 1989. **Head of gov.:** Prime Min. Shinzo Abe; in office: Dec. 26, 2012. **Local divisions:** 47 prefectures. **Defense budget:** $47.69 bil. **Active troops:** 247,150.

Economy: Industries: motor vehicles, electronic equip., machine tools, steel and nonferrous metals, ships, chemicals. **Chief crops:** vegetables, rice, fruit, flowers, potatoes/taros/yams, sugarcane. **Natural resources:** negligible mineral resources, fish. **Water:** 3,382 cu m per capita. **Crude oil reserves:** 44.1 mil bbls. **Electricity prod.:** 966.4 bil kWh. **Labor force:** agric. 2.9%, industry 26.2%, services 70.9%. **Unemployment:** 4%.

Finance: Monetary unit: Yen (JPY) (120.29 = $1 U.S.). **GDP:** $4.8 tril; **per capita GDP:** $37,400; **GDP growth:** −0.1%. **Imports:** $811.9 bil; China 21.7%, U.S. 8.6%, Australia 6.1%, Saudi Arabia 6%, UAE 5.1%. **Exports:** $710.5 bil; U.S. 18.8%, China 18.1%, South Korea 7.9%, Hong Kong 5.2%, Thailand 5%. **Tourism:** $18.9 bil. **Budget:** $1.8 tril. **Inflation:** 2.7%.

Transport: Railways: 16,873 mi. **Motor vehicles:** 594.2 per 1,000 pop. **Airports:** 142.

Communications: Telephone: 50.1 per 100 pop. **Mobile:** 120.2 per 100 pop. **Broadband:** 120.5 per 100 pop. **Internet:** 90.6%.

Health: Expend.: 10.1%. **Life expect.:** 81.4 male; 88.3 female. **Births:** 7.9 per 1,000 pop. **Deaths:** 9.5 per 1,000 pop. **Infant mortality:** 2.1 per 1,000 live births. **Undernourished:** <5%. **HIV:** NA.

Education: Compulsory: ages 6-14. **Literacy:** 99%.

Embassy: 2520 Massachusetts Ave. NW 20008; 238-6700.

Website: www.kantei.go.jp

According to Japanese legend, the empire was founded by Emperor Jimmu, 660 BCE, but earliest records of a unified Japan date from 1,000 years later. Chinese influence was strong in the formation of Japanese civilization. Buddhism was introduced before the 6th cent. CE.

A feudal system, with locally powerful noble families and their samurai warrior retainers, dominated from 1192. Central power was held by successive families of shoguns (military dictators), 1192-1867, until recovered by Emperor Meiji, 1868. The Portuguese and Dutch had minor trade with Japan in the 16th and 17th cents.; U.S. Commodore Matthew C. Perry opened the country to U.S. trade in a treaty ratified 1854. Industrialization began in the late 19th cent. Military conflicts won Taiwan from China, 1894-95, and the southern half of Sakhalin from Russia, 1904-05. Japan annexed Korea, 1910.

In WWI Japan ousted Germany from Shandong in China and took over German Pacific islands. Japan took Manchuria in 1931 and launched full-scale war in China in 1937. Japan attacked Pearl Harbor Dec. 7, 1941, launching a war with the U.S. The U.S. dropped atomic bombs on Hiroshima, Aug. 6, and Nagasaki, Aug. 9, 1945. Japan surrendered Aug. 14.

In a new constitution adopted May 3, 1947, Japan renounced the right to wage war; the emperor renounced claims to divinity; and the Diet became the sole lawmaking authority. The U.S. and 48 other non-Communist nations signed a peace treaty with Japan on Sept. 8, 1951; on the same day, the U.S. signed a bilateral defense agreement with Japan. The peace treaty restored Japan's sovereignty effective Apr. 28, 1952.

Rebuilding after WWII, Japan emerged as one of the most powerful economies in the world. Japan's controversial import policies allowed it to accumulate huge trade surpluses.

In 1968, the U.S. returned control of the Bonin Isls., Volcano Isls. (including Iwo Jima), and Marcus Isls to Japan. In 1972, the U.S. returned Okinawa, the other Ryukyu Isls., and the Daito Isls., but the U.S. continued to maintain military bases on Okinawa. An agreement was reached in 2012 to reduce the number of U.S. Marines stationed on Okinawa from 19,000 to 10,000.

The Liberal Democratic Party (LDP) governed Japan from the mid-1950s through early 1990s. In 1994, Tomiichi Murayama became Japan's first Socialist premier since 1947-48. With the country mired in a lengthy recession, the LDP regained power in 1996 and led Japan until 2009.

For the first time since WWII, Japan sent troops to an overseas war zone, when about 600 noncombat troops served in Iraq Feb. 2004-July 2006. In a move likely prompted by China's growing military strength, Japan announced, July 1, 2014, a new constitutional interpretation allowing the military to take offensive action to aid an ally, such as the U.S.; legislation to implement the policy won final passage Sept. 19, 2015.

The 2008-09 global recession hit Japan hard, prompting a series of economic stimulus plans. The LDP suffered a crushing defeat in 2009 parliamentary elections, and Yukio Hatoyama of the opposition Democratic Party of Japan (DPJ) became prime min. His public support soon plummeted, and he was replaced June 2010 by former finance min. Naoto Kan.

A magnitude 9.0 earthquake and tsunami in the Pacific Ocean off Japan's east coast Mar. 11, 2011, left at least 18,500 people confirmed dead or listed as missing. Inundated by the tsunami, the Fukushima Daiichi nuclear power plant experienced meltdowns at 3 of the plant's 6 nuclear reactors, spewing radiation over a large area. Criticized for his response to the catastrophe, Prime Min. Kan submitted his resignation Aug. 26, 2011, and was succeeded by Finance Min. Yoshihiko Noda. Following the Fukushima Daiichi meltdowns, Japan began shutting down nuclear reactors for safety tests. Revised nuclear safety guidelines were announced in June 2013. The first power-plant reactor returned to service under the new guidelines was restarted Aug. 11, 2015.

Elections swept LDP candidates into office in Dec. 2012, and former Prime Min. Shinzo Abe became prime minister. Abe's LDP retained its majority in Dec. 14, 2014, elections.

Jordan

Hashemite Kingdom of Jordan

People: Population: 8,117,564. **Age distrib.:** <15: 35.4%; 65+: 3.9%. **Growth:** 0.8%. **Migrants:** 40.2%. **Pop. density:** 236.8 per sq mi, 91.4 per sq km. **Urban:** 83.7%. **Ethnic groups:** Arab 98%, Circassian 1%, Armenian 1%. **Languages:** Arabic (official), English (widely understood among upper and middle classes). **Religions:** Muslim (official; predominantly Sunni) 97.2%, Christian (majority Greek Orthodox) 2.2%.

Geography: Total area: 34,495 sq mi, 89,342 sq km; **Land area:** 34,287 sq mi, 88,802 sq km. **Location:** Middle East. Israel, West Bank on W; Saudi Arabia on S; Iraq on E; Syria on N. **Topography:** About 88% is arid. Fertile areas in W. Only port is on short Aqaba Gulf coast. Country shares Dead Sea (1,348 ft below sea level) with Israel. **Arable land:** 2.4%. **Capital:** Amman, 1,154,670 (excl. Syrian refugees).

Government: Type: Constitutional monarchy. **Head of state:** King Abdullah II; in office: Feb. 7, 1999. **Head of gov.:** Prime Min.

Abdullah Ensour; Oct. 11, 2012. **Local divisions:** 12 governorates. **Defense budget:** $1.27 bil. **Active troops:** 100,500.

Economy: Industries: tourism, information tech., clothing, fertilizers, potash, phosphate mining pharmaceuticals. **Chief crops:** citrus, tomatoes, cucumbers, olives, strawberries, stone fruits. **Natural resources:** phosphates, potash, shale oil. **Water:** 129 cu m per capita. **Crude oil reserves:** 1 mil bbls. **Electricity prod.:** 15.6 bil kWh. **Labor force:** agric. 2%, industry 20%, services 78%. **Unemployment:** 12.6%.

Finance: Monetary unit: Dinar (JOD) (0.71 = $1 U.S.). **GDP:** $79.6 bil; **per capita GDP:** $11,900; **GDP growth:** 3.1%. **Imports:** $22.8 bil; Saudi Arabia 18.5%, China 10.3%, U.S. 6.3%, India 5.1%. **Exports:** $8.6 bil; Iraq 18.4%, U.S. 17.7%, Saudi Arabia 13.6%, India 7.3%. **Tourism:** $4.4 bil. **Budget:** $11.4 bil. **Inflation:** 2.8%.

Transport: Railways: 315 mi. **Motor vehicles:** 168.5 per 1,000 pop. **Airports:** 16.

Communications: Telephone: 5 per 100 pop. **Mobile:** 147.8 per 100 pop. **Broadband:** 17.8 per 100 pop. **Internet:** 44%.

Health: Expend.: 9.8%. **Life expect.:** 73.0 male; 75.8 female. **Births:** 25.4 per 1,000 pop. **Deaths:** 3.8 per 1,000 pop. **Infant mortality:** 15.2 per 1,000 live births. **Undernourished:** <5%. **HIV:** NA.

Education: Compulsory: ages 6-15. **Literacy:** 95.4%.

Embassy: 3504 International Dr. NW 20008; 966-2664.

Website: www.jordan.gov.jo

From ancient times to 1922 the lands to the east of the Jordan R. were culturally and politically united with the lands to the W. Arabs conquered the area in the 7th cent.; the Ottomans took control in the 16th. Britain's 1920 Palestine Mandate covered both sides of the Jordan. In 1921, Abdullah, son of the ruler of Hejaz in Arabia, was installed by Britain as emir of an autonomous Transjordan, covering two-thirds of Palestine. An independent kingdom was proclaimed, 1946.

During the 1948 Arab-Israeli war, the West Bank and East Jerusalem were added to the kingdom, which changed its name to Jordan. These territories were lost to Israel in 1967, which swelled the number of Arab refugees on the East Bank.

Jordan and Israel signed a peace treaty, Oct. 26, 1994. King Hussein died Feb. 7, 1999, ending a nearly 47-year reign; his eldest son assumed the throne as Abdullah II. The king responded to Arab Spring protests, 2011-12, by somewhat liberalizing election laws in advance of Jan. 2013 parliamentary elections.

According to UNHCR estimates, almost 630,000 Syrians fleeing civil war were living in Jordan in Sept. 2015; about 30,000 Iraqi refugees were in Jordan in mid-2015. Jordanian warplanes took part in U.S.-led airstrikes, 2014-15, against ISIS and other Sunni extremist forces in Syria and Iraq; an ISIS video, released Feb. 3, 2015, showed a captured Jordanian pilot being burned alive. The U.S. announced, May 7, 2015, that training had begun in Jordan of Syrian rebel fighters opposed to both ISIS and Syria's government.

Kazakhstan

Republic of Kazakhstan

People: Population: 18,157,122. **Age distrib.:** <15: 25.4%; 65+: 7.2%. **Growth:** 1.1%. **Migrants:** 21.1%. **Pop. density:** 17.4 per sq mi, 6.7 per sq km. **Urban:** 53.2%. **Ethnic groups:** Kazakh or Qazaq 63.1%, Russian 23.7%, Uzbek 2.9%, Ukrainian 2.1%. **Languages:** Kazakh or Qazaq, Russian (both official). **Religions:** Muslim 70.2%, Christian (mainly Russian Orthodox) 26.2%, atheist 2.8%.

Geography: Total area: 1,052,090 sq mi, 2,724,900 sq km; **Land area:** 1,042,360 sq mi, 2,699,700 sq km. **Location:** Central Asia. Russia on N; China on E; Kyrgyzstan, Uzbekistan, Turkmenistan on S. **Topography:** Extends from lower reaches of Volga in Europe to Altay Mts. on Chinese border. **Arable land:** 8.5%. **Capital:** Astana, 758,961. **Cities:** Almaty, 1,522,637.

Government: Type: Republic. **Head of state:** Pres. Nursultan Nazarbayev; in office: Dec. 1, 1991. **Head of gov.:** Prime Min. Karim Massimov; in office: Apr. 2, 2014. **Local divisions:** 14 provinces, 3 cities. **Defense budget:** $2.03 bil. **Active troops:** 39,000.

Economy: Industries: oil, coal, iron ore, manganese, chromite, lead, zinc, copper, titanium, bauxite, gold, silver, phosphates, sulfur, uranium. **Chief crops:** grain (mostly spring wheat, barley), potatoes, vegetables, melons. **Natural resources:** petroleum, nat. gas, coal, iron ore, manganese, chrome ore, nickel, cobalt, copper, molybdenum, lead, zinc, bauxite, gold, uranium. **Water:** 6,593 cu m per capita. **Crude oil reserves:** 30 bil bbls. **Electricity prod.:** 86.1 bil kWh. **Labor force:** agric. 25.8%, industry 11.9%, services 62.3%. **Unemployment:** 5.2%.

Finance: Monetary unit: Tenge (KZT) (240.30 = $1 U.S.). **GDP:** $418.5 bil; **per capita GDP:** $24,000; **GDP growth:** 4.3%. **Imports:** $47.6 bil; China 30.6%, Russia 20.5%, Ukraine 6.8%, Germany 6.2%. **Exports:** $87.3 bil; China 22.7%, France 9.7%, Russia 8%, Germany 7.9%, Italy 6.9%. **Tourism:** $1.3 bil. **Budget:** $45.7 bil. **Inflation:** 6.7%.

Transport: Railways: 8,814 mi. **Airports:** 63.

Communications: Telephone: 26.1 per 100 pop. **Mobile:** 168.6 per 100 pop. **Broadband:** 57.8 per 100 pop. **Internet:** 54.9%.

Health: Expend.: 4.2%. **Life expect.:** 65.3 male; 75.5 female. **Births:** 19.2 per 1,000 pop. **Deaths:** 8.2 per 1,000 pop. **Infant mortality:** 20.9 per 1,000 live births. **Undernourished:** <5%. **HIV:** 0.2%.

Education: Compulsory: ages 7-16. **Literacy:** 99.8%.

Embassy: 1401 16th St. NW 20036; 232-5488.

Website: www.government.kz

The region came under the Mongols' rule in the 13th cent. and gradually came under Russian rule, 1730-1853. It was admitted to the USSR as a constituent republic in 1936.

Kazakhstan's Dec. 16, 1991, declaration of independence became reality when the Soviet Union dissolved Dec. 26, 1991. The Communist Party chief, Nursultan Nazarbayev, was elected president unopposed. Dissent was suppressed. Nazarbayev encouraged Western investment in the oil industry, boosting the economy. Production began, Sept. 2013, at the Kashagan oil field, the largest outside the Middle East, in the Caspian Sea; it was suspended in Oct. 2013 due to gas leaks and was scheduled to resume in 2017.

Kazakhstan agreed, Feb. 1994, to dismantle nuclear missiles. Private land ownership was legalized Dec. 1995. Astana (formerly Akmola) became the nation's new capital, June 9, 1998. Reelected in 1999 and 2005, Pres. Nazarbayev was authorized to run for an unlimited number of terms under a constitutional amendment passed by parliament May 2007; he claimed more than 95% of the vote in the 2011 presidential election, and almost 98% in the 2015 election. Nazarbayev's Nur Otan party won 81% of the vote in 2012 parliamentary elections. With GDP growth sluggish, Nazarbayev named a new prime min., Karim Massimov, Apr. 2, 2014. An agreement to create a limited economic union of Kazakhstan, Russia, and Belarus was signed May 29, 2014 (Armenia and Kyrgyzstan joined in 2015).

Kenya

Republic of Kenya

People: Population: 45,925,301. **Age distrib.:** <15: 41.6%; 65+: 2.9%. **Growth:** 1.9%. **Migrants:** 2.2%. **Pop. density:** 209 per sq mi, 80.7 per sq km. **Urban:** 25.6%. **Ethnic groups:** Kikuyu 22%, Luhya 14%, Luo 13%, Kalenjin 12%, Kamba 11%, Kisii 6%, Meru 6%. **Languages:** English, Kiswahili (both official); numerous indigenous langs. **Religions:** Christian 82.5% (incl. Protestant 47.4%, Catholic 23.3%), Muslim 11.1%.

Geography: Total area: 224,081 sq mi, 580,367 sq km; **Land area:** 219,746 sq mi, 569,140 sq km. **Location:** E Africa, on coast of Indian O. Uganda on W, Tanzania on S, Somalia on E, Ethiopia on N, Sudan on NW. **Topography:** Northern three-fifths of country is arid. A low coastal area and a plateau 3,000-10,000 ft is in S. The Great Rift Valley enters the country N-S, flanked by high mountains. **Arable land:** 9.8%. **Capital:** Nairobi, 3,914,791. **Cities:** Mombasa, 1,103,703.

Government: Type: Republic. **Head of state and gov.:** Pres. Uhuru Kenyatta; in office: Apr. 9, 2013. **Local divisions:** 47 counties. **Defense budget:** $1.04 bil. **Active troops:** 24,120.

Economy: Industries: small-scale consumer goods (plastic, furniture, batteries, textiles, clothing, soap, cigarettes, flour), agric. prods., horticulture, oil refining, aluminum, steel, lead, cement. **Chief crops:** tea, coffee, corn, wheat, sugarcane, fruit, vegetables. **Natural resources:** limestone, soda ash, salt, gems, fluorspar, zinc, diatomite, gypsum, wildlife, hydropower. **Water:** 692 cu m per capita. **Electricity prod.:** 8.1 bil kWh. **Labor force:** agric. 75%, industry and services 25%. **Unemployment:** 9.2%.

Finance: Monetary unit: Shilling (KES) (104.50 = $1 U.S.). **GDP:** $132.4 bil; **per capita GDP:** $3,100; **GDP growth:** 5.3%. **Imports:** $16.5 bil; India 19.9%, China 17.8%, UAE 8.8%, Japan 5%. **Exports:** $6.3 bil; Uganda 13%, Tanzania 8.9%, Netherlands 7.1%, U.S. 6.6%, UK 6.3%, UAE 5.9%. **Tourism:** $798 mil. **Budget:** $15.1 bil. **Inflation:** 6.9%.

Transport: Railways: 2,072 mi. **Motor vehicles:** 27.2 per 1,000 pop. **Airports:** 16.

Communications: Telephone: 0.4 per 100 pop. **Mobile:** 73.8 per 100 pop. **Broadband:** 3.1 per 100 pop. **Internet:** 43.4%.

Health: Expend.: 4.7%. **Life expect.:** 62.3 male; 65.3 female. **Births:** 26.4 per 1,000 pop. **Deaths:** 6.9 per 1,000 pop. **Infant mortality:** 39.4 per 1,000 live births. **Undernourished:** 24.3%. **HIV:** 5.3%.

Education: Compulsory: ages 6-17. **Literacy:** 78%.

Embassy: 2249 R St. NW 20008; 387-6101.

Website: www.president.go.ke

Arab colonies exported spices and slaves from the Kenya coast as early as the 8th cent. Britain obtained control in the 19th cent. Kenya won independence Dec. 12, 1963, 4 years after the end of the violent Mau Mau uprising. Jomo Kenyatta, the country's leader since independence, died Aug. 22, 1978. He was succeeded by his vice president, Daniel arap Moi.

During the first half of the 1990s, Kenya suffered widespread unemployment and high inflation. Tribal clashes in the western provinces claimed thousands of lives and left tens of thousands homeless. Pres. Moi won a fourth term in Dec. 1997, in an election plagued by irregularities. A truck bomb explosion at the U.S. embassy in Nairobi, Aug. 7, 1998, killed more than 200 people and injured about 5,000. The U.S. blamed the attack and a near-simultaneous embassy bombing in Tanzania on al-Qaeda.

Constitutionally barred from seeking another term, Pres. Moi was succeeded, Dec. 2002, by Mwai Kibaki, the candidate of the opposition Democratic Party. After a disputed election Dec. 2007, Kenya's electoral commission declared Kibaki the winner over challenger Raila Odinga. Weeks of factional violence followed, leaving some 1,500 people dead and 600,000 displaced. Under a Feb. 28, 2008, power-sharing agreement, Kibaki remained president and Odinga took the newly created post of prime minister. A new constitution curtailing presidential powers, establishing a senate, and reforming regional government won approval in an Aug. 2010 referendum. The Intl. Criminal Court (ICC), Jan. 2012, charged 4 with crimes against humanity for their roles in the 2007-08 postelection violence. Two of those charged, Deputy Prime Min. Uhuru Kenyatta and former Education Min. William Ruto, were candidates in the Mar. 4, 2013, presidential election, in which Kenyatta was declared the winner Mar. 10 amid accusations of vote-rigging. The trial of Ruto (who became deputy president) began Sept. 10, 2013. The ICC dropped charges against Kenyatta in Dec. 2014. The UNHCR estimated that almost 463,000 Somali refugees were living in Kenya at the beginning of 2015. The Somali Islamist group al-Shabab carried out a series of deadly terrorist attacks in Kenya, 2013-15, including an Apr. 2, 2015, attack on Garissa Univ. College that killed 148 people. In July 2015, Barack Obama became the first sitting U.S. president to visit Kenya.

Kiribati

Republic of Kiribati

People: Population: 105,711. **Age distrib.:** <15: 30.8%; 65+: 4.1%. **Growth:** 1.2%. **Migrants:** 2.6%. **Pop. density:** 337.6 per sq mi, 130.3 per sq km. **Urban:** 44.3%. **Ethnic groups:** I-Kiribati 89.5%, I-Kiribati/mixed 9.7%. **Languages:** I-Kiribati, English (both official). **Religions:** Roman Catholic 55.8%, Kempsville Presbyterian Church 33.5%, Mormon 4.7%.

Geography: Total area: 313 sq mi, 811 sq km; **Land area:** 313 sq mi, 811 sq km. **Location:** 33 atolls (the Gilbert, Line, and Phoenix Isls.) in mid-Pacific scattered over an area of about 1.35 mil sq mi around the point where the International Date Line formerly crossed the Equator. The Date Line was moved in 1997 to follow Kiribati's E border. Nearest neighbors are Nauru to SW, Tuvalu and Tokelau Isls. (N.Z.) to S. **Topography:** Except Banaba (Ocean) Isl., all are low-lying, with soil of coral sand and rock fragments, subject to erratic rainfall. **Arable land:** 2.5%. **Capital:** Tarawa, 45,915 (2014; figure is for Tarawa Isl.).

Government: Type: Republic. **Head of state and gov.:** Pres. Anote Tong; in office: July 10, 2003. **Local divisions:** 3 geographical units. **Defense budget/active troops:** NA.

Economy: Industries: fishing, handicrafts. **Chief crops:** copra, breadfruit. **Natural resources:** phosphate (production discontinued in 1979), fish. **Water:** NA. **Electricity prod.:** 26 mil kWh. **Labor force:** agric. 15%, industry 10%, services 75%. **Unemployment:** NA.

Finance: Monetary unit: Dollar (AUD) (1.42 = $1 U.S.). **GDP:** $188 mil; **per capita GDP:** $1,700; **GDP growth:** 3.8%. **Imports** (2013): $182.2 mil. **Exports** (2013): $84.8 mil. **Budget** (2013 est.): $179.9 mil. **Inflation:** NA.

Transport: Airports: 4.

Communications: Telephone: 8.9 per 100 pop. **Mobile:** 17.4 per 100 pop. **Broadband:** NA. **Internet:** 12.3%.

Health: Expend.: 10.7%. **Life expect.:** 63.4 male; 68.4 female. **Births:** 21.5 per 1,000 pop. **Deaths:** 7.1 per 1,000 pop. **Infant mortality:** 34.3 per 1,000 live births. **Undernourished:** <5%. **HIV:** NA.

Education: Compulsory: ages 6-14. **Literacy:** NA.

Permanent UN mission: 800 Second Ave., Ste. 400A, New York, NY 10017; (212) 867-3310.

Website: www.president.gov.ki

A British protectorate since 1892, the Gilbert and Ellice Islands colony was completed with the inclusion of the Phoenix Islands, 1937. Tarawa Atoll was the scene of some of the bloodiest fighting in the Pacific during WWII.

Self-rule was granted 1971; the Ellice Islands separated from the colony in 1975 and became independent Tuvalu, 1978. Kiribati (pronounced *Kiribass*) independence was attained July 12, 1979. Under a treaty of friendship the U.S. relinquished its claims to several Line and Phoenix islands. Kiribati was admitted to the UN in 1999. Pres. Anote Tong won reelection Oct. 2007. Kiribati's land area is shrinking as a result of rising sea levels, and in 2014, the government began buying land in Fiji to be used for agriculture and fish farming.

Korea, North

Democratic People's Republic of Korea

People: Population: 24,983,205. **Age distrib.:** <15: 21.2%; 65+: 9.9%. **Growth:** 0.5%. **Migrants:** 0.2%. **Pop. density:** 537.4 per sq mi, 207.5 per sq km. **Urban:** 60.9%. **Ethnic groups:** racially homogeneous; small Chinese community, a few ethnic Japanese. **Languages:** Korean. **Religions:** traditionally Buddhist and Confucianist. Autonomous religious activities almost nonexistent.

Geography: Total area: 46,540 sq mi, 120,538 sq km; **Land area:** 46,490 sq mi, 120,408 sq km. **Location:** Northern E Asia. China and Russia on N, S. Korea on S. **Topography:** Mountains and hills cover nearly entire country, with narrow valleys and small plains in between. N and E coasts are most rugged areas. **Arable land:** 19.5%. **Capital:** P'yongyang, 2,862,921.

Government: Type: Communist state. **Head of state:** Kim Jong Un; officially assumed post Dec. 17, 2011. **Head of gov.:** Prem. Pak Pong Ju; in office: Apr. 2, 2013. **Local divisions:** 9 provinces, 2 municipalities. **Defense budget:** NA. **Active troops:** 1,190,000.

Economy: Industries: military prods.; machine building, elec. power, chemicals; mining, metallurgy; textiles, food proc. **Chief crops:** rice, corn, potatoes, soybeans. **Natural resources:** coal, lead, tungsten, zinc, graphite, magnesite, iron ore, copper, gold, pyrites, salt, fluorspar, hydropower. **Water:** 3,099 cu m per capita. **Electricity prod.:** 18.8 bil kWh. **Labor force:** agric. 37%, industry and services 63%. **Unemployment:** 4.6%.

Finance: Monetary unit: Won (KPW) (129.55 = $1 U.S.). **GDP** (2013): $40 bil; **per capita GDP** (2013): $1,800; **GDP growth** (2013): 1.1%. **Imports** (2013): $4.6 bil; (2012) China 78%, South Korea 11%. **Exports** (2013): $3.8 bil; China 76%, South Korea 16%. **Budget** (2007 est.): $3.3 bil. **Inflation:** NA.

Transport: Railways: 4,620 mi. **Airports:** 39.

Communications: Telephone: 4.7 per 100 pop. **Mobile:** 11.2 per 100 pop. **Broadband:** NA. **Internet:** 0%.

Health: Expend.: NA. **Life expect.:** 66.3 male; 74.2 female. **Births:** 14.5 per 1,000 pop. **Deaths:** 9.2 per 1,000 pop. **Infant mortality:** 23.7 per 1,000 live births. **Undernourished:** 37.5%. **HIV:** NA.

Education: Compulsory: ages 6-16. **Literacy:** 100%.

Permanent UN mission: 800 Second Ave., Ste. 400A, New York, NY 10017; (212) 867-3310.

Website: www.korea-dpr.com

The Democratic People's Republic of Korea was founded May 1, 1948, in the zone occupied by Russia after WWII. Its armies tried to conquer the south, 1950. After three years of fighting, with Chinese and U.S. intervention, a cease-fire was proclaimed.

For the next four decades, a hard-line Communist regime headed by Kim Il Sung kept tight control over the nation's political, economic, and cultural life. The nation used its abundant mineral and hydroelectric resources to develop its military strength and heavy industry. By the early 1990s, North Korea was widely believed to be developing nuclear weapons. The U.S. and North Korea signed an agreement, Oct. 21, 1994, providing for phased dismantling of North Korea's nuclear development program in return for U.S. energy aid and improved ties with the U.S.

Kim Il Sung died July 8, 1994. He was succeeded by his son, Kim Jong Il. Defections by high officials, a deteriorating economy, and severe food shortages plagued North Korea in the late 1990s. A first-ever summit conference between North and South Korean leaders was held in P'yongyang, June 13-15, 2000. North Korea and Japan agreed to normalize relations in a Sept. 2002 summit.

In Oct. 2002, North Korea admitted to pursuing a secret nuclear weapons program in violation of past agreements. The U.S. insisted that North Korea end its nuclear weapons program, while P'yongyang demanded a nonaggression treaty and economic aid from the U.S. During 2003-09, as six-nation talks sponsored by China sought to resolve the nuclear dispute, North Korea zigzagged, alternately stopping and resuming its nuclear program in order to win concessions from the U.S.

In Apr.-May 2009, North Korea suspended participation in the six-nation talks, expelled IAEA inspectors, tested multiple missiles, and exploded a nuclear device underground. The UN Security Council June 12 toughened sanctions on North Korea. Tensions between North and South Korea increased after the Mar. 26, 2010, sinking of the South Korean warship *Cheonan* killed 46 sailors; a South Korean panel including international investigators concluded May 20 that the *Cheonan* had been torpedoed by a North Korean submarine.

Kim Jong Il died Dec. 17, 2011. He was succeeded by his son Kim Jong Un. In an apparent move to consolidate his power, Kim Jong Un ordered the execution, Dec. 2013, of his uncle, Jang Song Thaek, who had been considered one of the most powerful political figures in North Korea.

North Korea launched a satellite into space Dec. 12, 2012, demonstrating its rocket capabilities. It conducted a nuclear test Feb. 10, 2013, and threatened to launch a nuclear strike against the U.S., Mar. 7, after additional sanctions were levied against it in response to its nuclear test. North Korea negated, Mar. 11, 2013, the cease-fire agreement with the South that ended the Korean War. It conducted numerous short- and long-range missile tests 2013-15.The U.S. blamed North Korea for cyberattacks on Sony Pictures Entertainment, Nov. 2014, shortly before the studio's scheduled release of a comedy film about an attempt to assassinate Kim Jong Un; the U.S. imposed further economic sanctions, Jan. 2, 2015.

Korea, South

Republic of Korea

People: Population: 49,115,196. **Age distrib.:** <15: 13.7%; 65+: 13%. **Growth:** 0.1%. **Migrants:** 2.5%. **Pop. density:** 1,312.5 per sq mi, 506.8 per sq km. **Urban:** 82.5%. **Ethnic groups:** homogeneous (except for about 20,000 Chinese). **Languages:** Korean, English (widely taught). **Religions:** Christian 31.6% (incl. Protestant 24%), Buddhist 24.2%, none 43.3%.

Geography: Total area: 38,502 sq mi, 99,720 sq km; **Land area:** 37,421 sq mi, 96,920 sq km. **Location:** Northern E Asia. North Korea on N. **Topography:** Mountainous, with a rugged E coast. W and S coasts are deeply indented, with many islands and harbors. **Arable land:** 15.6%. **Capital:** Seoul, 9,773,746; Sejong City (admin. center). **Cities:** Busan, 3,216,298; Incheon, 2,685,238; Daegu, 2,244,086; Daejon, 1,563,706; Gwangju, 1,536,409.

Government: Type: Republic. **Head of state:** Pres. Park Geun Hye; in office: Feb. 25, 2013. **Head of gov.:** Prime Min. Hwang Kyo-ahn; in office: June 18, 2015. **Local divisions:** 9 provinces, 6 metropolitan cities, 1 special city, 1 special self-governing city. **Defense budget:** $34.44 bil. **Active troops:** 655,000.

Economy: Industries: electronics, telecom, auto prod., chemicals, shipbuilding, steel. **Chief crops:** rice, root crops, barley, vegetables, fruit. **Natural resources:** coal, tungsten, graphite, molybdenum, lead. **Water:** 1,415 cu m per capita. **Electricity prod.:** 499.7 bil kWh. **Labor force:** agric. 5.7%, industry 24%, services 70.4%. **Unemployment:** 3.1%.

Finance: Monetary unit: Won (KRW) (1,185.05 = $1 U.S.). **GDP:** $1.8 tril; **per capita GDP:** $35,300; **GDP growth:** 3.3%. **Imports:** $525.5 bil; China 16.1%, Japan 11.6%, U.S. 8.1%, Saudi Arabia 7.3%, Qatar 5%. **Exports:** $572.7 bil; China 26.1%, U.S. 11.1%, Japan 6.2%, Hong Kong 5%. **Tourism:** $18.1 bil. **Budget:** $337.9 bil. **Inflation:** 1.3%.

Transport: Railways: 2,150 mi. **Motor vehicles:** 410.2 per 1,000 pop. **Airports:** 71.

Communications: Telephone: 59.5 per 100 pop. **Mobile:** 115.5 per 100 pop. **Broadband:** 105.3 per 100 pop. **Internet:** 84.3%.

Health: Expend.: 7.5%. **Life expect.:** 77.0 male; 83.3 female. **Births:** 8.2 per 1,000 pop. **Deaths:** 6.8 per 1,000 pop. **Infant mortality:** 3.9 per 1,000 live births. **Undernourished:** <5%. **HIV:** NA.

Education: Compulsory: ages 6-14. **Literacy:** NA.

Embassy: 2450 Massachusetts Ave. NW 20008; 939-5660.

Website: www.korea.net

The recorded history of Korea, once called the Hermit Kingdom, dates back to the 1st cent. BCE. It was united in a kingdom under the Silla Dynasty, 668 CE. It was at times associated with the Chinese empire; the treaty that concluded the Sino-Japanese war of 1894-95 recognized Korea's complete independence. In 1910 Japan forcibly annexed Korea as Chosun.

At the Potsdam conference, July 1945, near the end of WWII, the 38th parallel was designated as the line dividing Soviet and U.S. occupation zones. Russian troops entered Korea Aug. 10, 1945; U.S. troops entered Sept. 8.

The South Koreans formed the Republic of Korea in May 1948 with Seoul as the capital. Dr. Syngman Rhee was chosen president. A separate, Communist regime was formed in the North; its army attacked the south in June 1950, initiating the Korean War. UN troops, under U.S. command, supported South Korea in the war, which ended in an armistice (July 1953) leaving Korea divided by a demilitarized zone (DMZ) along the 38th parallel.

Rhee's authoritarian rule became increasingly unpopular, and a movement spearheaded by college students forced his resignation Apr. 26, 1960. In an army coup May 16, 1961, Gen. Park Chung Hee became chairman of a ruling junta. He was elected president, 1963; a 1972 referendum allowed him to be reelected for an unlimited series of 6-year terms. Park was assassinated by the chief of the Korean CIA, Oct. 26, 1979.

In May 1980, Gen. Chun Doo Hwan, head of military intelligence, ordered the brutal suppression of pro-democracy demonstrations in Kwangju. On July 1, 1987, following weeks of sometimes violent antigovernment protests, Chun agreed to democratic reforms. In Dec., Roh Tae Woo, a longtime ally of Chun's, was elected president. In 1990, the nation's three largest political parties merged; some 100,000 students protested the merger as undemocratic.

Pres. Kim Young Sam took office in 1993. Convicted of mutiny, treason, and corruption, Chun was sentenced to death by a Seoul court, Aug. 26, 1996, for his role in the 1979 coup and 1980 Kwangju massacre; Roh received a 225-year prison sentence. Kim Dae Jung, a longtime dissident, won the presidential election Dec. 18, 1997. Chun and Roh were released and pardoned Dec. 22.

At a summit meeting in P'yongyang, June 13-15, 2000, Pres. Kim Dae Jung and North Korean leader Kim Jong Il agreed to work for reconciliation and eventual reunification of their two countries. On Oct. 13, 2000, Kim Dae Jung was named the winner of the Nobel Peace Prize. Roh Moo Hyun won the 2002 presidential election.

The National Assembly, Mar. 12, 2004, impeached Pres. Roh Moo Hyun for violating political neutrality and urging voters to support the Uri Party; the Constitutional Court May 14 restored Roh to office. The IAEA Sept. 2 said South Korea had acknowledged having secretly processed a small amount of uranium to near weapons-grade level in 2000, violating the Nuclear Non-Proliferation Treaty and a bilateral accord with N. Korea.

Ban Ki-Moon, South Korea's foreign min., 2004-06, became UN sec.-gen. Jan. 1, 2007. Lee Myung Bak, a former construction executive and Seoul mayor, won the presidential election Dec. 19. Former Pres. Roh Moo Hyun, under investigation for corruption, committed suicide May 23, 2009.

Tensions between South Korea and Japan came to the fore after Pres. Lee Myung-bak, Aug. 10, visited Dokdo, a group of small islands administered by South Korea but claimed by Japan. Conservative Park Geun Hye became South Korea's first female president in Dec. 19, 2012, elections.

On Mar. 11, 2013, North Korea declared a negation of the cease-fire agreement with the South that had ended the Korean War; North Korea asserted, Mar. 29, that a state of war existed between it and the South. The U.S., which had about 28,500 troops in South Korea in early 2015, made small increases in its troop strength in 2014 and 2015. The sinking, Apr. 16, 2014, of the ferry *Sewol* off the South Korean coast caused the deaths of more than 300 people, many of them high school students. Unsafe practices by the ferry company were blamed for the disaster. U.S. ambassador Mark Lippert was wounded, Mar. 5, 2015, in a knife attack in Seoul by a Korean nationalist. Prime Min. Lee Wan Koo resigned, Apr. 27, 2015, after being implicated in a bribery scandal; he was indicted July 2.

Kosovo

Republic of Kosovo

People: Population: 1,870,981. **Age distrib.:** <15: 25.8%; 65+: 7%. **Growth:** 0.6%. **Migrants:** NA. **Pop. density:** 445.1 per sq mi, 171.9 per sq km. **Urban:** NA. **Ethnic groups:** Albanian 92.9%, Bosniak 1.6%, Serb 1.5%, Turk 1.1%. **Languages:** Albanian, Serbian (both official); Bosnian. **Religions:** Muslim 95.6%.

Geography: Total area: 4,203 sq mi, 10,887 sq km. **Land area:** 4,203 sq mi, 10,887 sq km. **Location:** SE Europe. Serbia on N, Montenegro on NW, Albania on SW, Macedonia on SE. **Topography:** Low flood basins surrounded by several high mountain ranges. **Arable land:** 27.4%. **Capital:** Pristina.

Government: Type: Republic. **Head of state:** Pres. Atifete Jahjaga; in office: Apr. 7, 2011. **Head of gov.:** Prime Min. Isa Mustafa; in office: Dec. 9, 2014. **Local divisions:** 38 municipalities. **Defense budget/active troops:** NA.

Economy: Industries: mineral mining, constr. materials, base metals, leather, machinery, appliances, foodstuffs and beverages. **Chief crops:** wheat, corn, berries, potatoes, peppers, fruit. **Natural resources:** nickel, lead, zinc, magnesium, lignite, kaolin, chrome, bauxite. **Water:** NA. **Electricity prod.:** 5.6 bil kWh. **Labor force:** agric. 5.9%, industry 16.8%, services 77.3%. **Unemployment:** NA.

Finance: Monetary unit: Euro (EUR) (0.89 = $1 U.S.). **GDP:** $16.9 bil; **per capita GDP:** $8,000; **GDP growth:** 2.7%. **Imports:** $2.7 bil; (2012) Germany 11.9%, Macedonia 11.5%, Serbia 11.1%, Turkey 9%, Italy 8.5%, China 6.4%. **Exports:** $349 mil; (2012) Italy 25.8%, Albania 14.6%, Macedonia 9.6%, China 5.5%, Germany 5.4%, Switzerland 5.4%. **Budget:** $1.6 bil. **Inflation:** 0.4%.

Transport: Railways: 207 mi. **Airports:** 3.

Communications: NA.

Health: Expend.: NA. **Life expect.:** 69.2 male; 73.6 female. **Births:** 17.1 per 1,000 pop. **Deaths:** 7.0 per 1,000 pop. **Infant mortality:** 36.4 per 1,000 live births. **Undernourished:** NA. **HIV:** NA.

Education: Compulsory: NA. **Literacy** (2003): 91.9%.

Embassy: 1101 30th St. NW, Ste. 330/340, 20007; 380-3581.

Website: www.rks-gov.net

Kosovo was part of the Roman and Byzantine empires before Serbs, a Slavic people, took control in the Middle Ages. After Ottoman Turks defeated Serb forces, 1389, Kosovo's population became predominantly Muslim and Kosovar (ethnic Albanian). Serbia regained control in the First Balkan War (1912-13). Kosovo entered the Kingdom of Serbs, Croats, and Slovenes as part of Serbia after World War I and became an autonomous province of Serbia, a constituent republic of Yugoslavia, after World War II.

Revoking provincial autonomy, Serbia began ruling Kosovo by force in 1989. Albanian secessionists proclaimed an independent Republic of Kosovo in July 1990. As Yugoslavia collapsed, the republics of Serbia (incl. Kosovo) and Montenegro proclaimed a new Federal Republic of Yugoslavia, 1992, under Pres. Slobodan Milosevic. Guerrilla attacks by the Kosovo Liberation Army (KLA) in 1997 brought a ferocious counteroffensive by Serbian authorities.

Fearful that the Serbs were employing "ethnic cleansing" tactics, NATO launched an air war against Yugoslavia, Mar.-June 1999; the Serbs retaliated by terrorizing the Kosovars. Hundreds of thousands fled, mostly to Albania and Macedonia. A 50,000-member multinational force (KFOR) entered Kosovo in June, and most refugees returned by Sept. 1, 1999.

From June 1999, Kosovo was administered by a UN mission (UNMIK). Kosovo declared independence, Feb. 17, 2008. More than 100 nations, including the U.S. and most EU members, have recognized Kosovo; Serbia and Russia have not. In a nonbinding ruling, the World Court held July 22, 2010, that Kosovo's independence declaration was legal. Kosovo and Serbia, Apr. 19, 2013, completed negotiating a power-sharing agreement between the northern Kosovo regions with a Serb majority and the Kosovo central government led by ethnic Albanians. As of June 2015, KFOR had about 4,800 troops in Kosovo. An EU special prosecutor reported, July 29, 2014, evidence of "unlawful killings" and other acts of ethnic cleansing against Serbs by the KLA in the late 1990s. Prime Min. Hashim Thaçi, who headed the KLA at that time, had denied any wrongdoing. After June 8, 2014, elections, Thaçi's party was unable to form a new government; conservative Isa Mustafa became prime min., Dec. 9, 2014. Five people believed to have been inspired by the Islamist extremist group ISIS were arrested, July 2015, for allegedly planning to poison Pristina's water supply.

Kuwait

State of Kuwait

People: Population: 2,788,534. **Age distrib.:** <15: 25.3%; 65+: 2.3%. **Growth:** 1.6%. **Migrants:** 60.2%. **Pop. density:** 405.3 per sq mi, 156.5 per sq km. **Urban:** 98.3%. **Ethnic groups:** Kuwaiti 31.3%, other Arab 27.9%, Asian 37.8%, African 1.9%. **Languages:** Arabic (official), English widely spoken. **Religions:** Muslim (official) 76.7%, Christian 17.3%.

Geography: Total area: 6,880 sq mi, 17,818 sq km; **Land area:** 6,880 sq mi, 17,818 sq km. **Location:** Middle East, at N end of Persian Gulf. Iraq on N, Saudi Arabia on S. **Topography:** Flat, very dry, and extremely hot. **Arable land:** 0.6%. **Capital:** Kuwait City, 2,778,724.

Government: Type: Constitutional emirate. **Head of state:** Emir Sheikh Sabah al-Ahmad al-Jabir al-Sabah; in office: Jan. 29, 2006. **Head of gov.:** Prime Min. Sheikh Jaber al-Mubarak al-Hamad al-Sabah; in office: Nov. 30, 2011. **Local divisions:** 6 governorates. **Defense budget:** $4.84 bil. **Active troops:** 15,500.

Economy: Industries: petroleum, petrochemicals, cement, shipbuilding and repair, water desalination, food proc., constr. materials. **Natural resources:** petroleum, fish, shrimp, nat. gas. **Water:** 6 cu m per capita. **Crude oil reserves:** 104 bil bbls (incl. half of Neutral Zone reserves). **Electricity prod.:** 58.9 bil kWh. **Labor force:** NA. **Unemployment:** 3.1%.

Finance: Monetary unit: Dinar (KWD) (0.30 = $1 U.S.). **GDP:** $284 bil; **per capita GDP:** $71,000; **GDP growth:** 1.3%. **Imports:** $26.1 bil; China 10.9%, U.S. 10.6%, Saudi Arabia 7.9%, Japan 7.7%, Germany 5.3%. **Exports:** $109.9 bil; South Korea 17.1%, India 16%, Japan 12.3%, U.S. 11.7%, China 8.8%. **Tourism:** $369 mil. **Budget:** $79.5 bil. **Inflation:** 2.5%.

Transport: Motor vehicles: 676.7 per 1,000 pop. **Airports:** 4.

Communications: Telephone: 14.2 per 100 pop. **Mobile:** 218.4 per 100 pop. **Broadband:** NA. **Internet:** 78.7%.

Health: Expend.: 2.5%. **Life expect.:** 76.5 male; 79.2 female. **Births:** 19.9 per 1,000 pop. **Deaths:** 2.2 per 1,000 pop. **Infant mortality:** 7.3 per 1,000 live births. **Undernourished:** <5%. **HIV:** NA.

Education: Compulsory: ages 6-14. **Literacy:** 96.3%.

Embassy: 2940 Tilden St. NW 20008; 966-0702.

Website: www.pm.gov.kw

Kuwait is ruled by the Sabah dynasty, founded 1759. Britain ran foreign relations and defense from 1899 until independence in 1961. Nearly half the population is non-Kuwaiti, including many Palestinians, and cannot vote.

Oil is the fiscal mainstay, providing most of Kuwait's income. Oil pays for free medical care, education, and social security. There are no taxes, except customs duties.

Kuwait was attacked and overrun by Iraqi forces Aug. 1990. In Operation Desert Storm a U.S.-led coalition, with authorization from the UN Security Council, began bombing Iraq and Iraqi forces in Kuwait, Jan. 1991, then launched a ground assault Feb. 23. By Feb. 27, Iraqi forces were routed and Kuwait liberated.

Political rights were extended to women, May 16, 2005; the first female cabinet member was appointed June 12. Kuwait enacted a $5.2-bil program Mar. 2009 to bail out banks and investment companies battered by the global financial crisis. The moderate Prime Min. Jaber al-Mubarak al-Hamad al-Sabah, first appointed in 2011, remained in office after July 27, 2013, elections; some liberal and marginalized tribal groups won seats, but the majority were won by lawmakers who supported Kuwait's ruling family. A suicide bomber killed 27 worshippers and wounded at least 200 at a Shiite mosque, June 26, 2015; the Sunni extremist group ISIS claimed responsibility.

Kyrgyzstan

Kyrgyz Republic

People: Population: 5,664,939. **Age distrib.:** <15: 29.9%; 65+: 5%. **Growth:** 1.1%. **Migrants:** 4.1%. **Pop. density:** 76.5 per sq mi, 29.5 per sq km. **Urban:** 35.7%. **Ethnic groups:** Kyrgyz 70.9%, Uzbek 14.3%, Russian 7.7%, Dungan 1.1%, other (incl. Uyghur, Tajik, Turk, Kazakh, Tatar, Ukrainian, Korean, German) 5.9%. **Languages:** Kyrgyz, Russian (both official); Uzbek. **Religions:** Muslim 75%, Russian Orthodox 20%.

Geography: Total area: 77,202 sq mi, 199,951 sq km; **Land area:** 74,055 sq mi, 191,801 sq km. **Location:** Central Asia. Kazakhstan on N, China on E, Uzbekistan on W, Tajikistan on S. **Topography:** Landlocked country nearly covered by Tien Shan and Pamir Mts.; avg. elevation 9,020 ft. Issyk-Kul, a large salt lake in NE, is 1 mi above sea level. **Arable land:** 6.7%. **Capital:** Bishkek, 865,193.

Government: Type: Republic. **Head of state:** Pres. Almazbek Atambayev; in office: Dec. 1, 2011. **Head of gov.:** Prime Min. Temir Sariyev; in office: May 1, 2015. **Local divisions:** 7 provinces, 2 cities. **Defense budget:** $95 mil. **Active troops:** 10,900.

Economy: Industries: small machinery, textiles, food proc., cement, shoes, sawn logs, refrigerators, furniture, elec. motors. **Chief crops:** tobacco, cotton, potatoes, vegetables, grapes, fruits and berries. **Natural resources:** hydropower, gold, rare earth metals, coal, oil, nat. gas, nepheline, mercury, bismuth, lead, zinc. **Water:** 4,257 cu m per capita. **Crude oil reserves:** 40 mil bbls. **Electricity prod.:** 15 bil kWh. **Labor force:** agric. 48%, industry 12.5%, services 39.5%. **Unemployment:** 8%.

Finance: Monetary unit: Som (KGS) (64.28 = $1 U.S.). **GDP:** $19.2 bil; **per capita GDP:** $3,400; **GDP growth:** 3.6%. **Imports:** $5.5 bil; China 51.9%, Russia 21.2%, Kazakhstan 7.8%. **Exports:** $2 bil; Kazakhstan 28.2%, Uzbekistan 28%, Russia 11.1%, UAE 6.9%, Afghanistan 5.6%, China 5%. **Tourism:** $530 mil. **Budget:** $2.2 bil. **Inflation:** 7.5%.

Transport: Railways: 292 mi. **Airports:** 18.

Communications: Telephone: 7.9 per 100 pop. **Mobile:** 134.5 per 100 pop. **Broadband** (2012): 19.2 per 100 pop. **Internet:** 28.3%.

Health: Expend.: 7.1%. **Life expect.:** 66.2 male; 74.8 female. **Births:** 23.0 per 1,000 pop. **Deaths:** 6.7 per 1,000 pop. **Infant mortality:** 27.7 per 1,000 live births. **Undernourished:** 6%. **HIV:** 0.3%.

Education: Compulsory: ages 7-15. **Literacy:** 99.5%.

Embassy: 2360 Massachusetts Ave. NW 20008; 449-9823.

Website: www.president.kg

The region was inhabited around the 13th cent. by the Kyrgyz. It was annexed to Russia, 1864, and became a constituent republic of the USSR in 1936. Kyrgyzstan declared independence Aug. 31, 1991, ahead of the USSR disbanding Dec. 26, 1991.

In power since 1990, Pres. Askar Akayev won a third 5-year term in the 2000 election. Fraud by Akayev loyalists in parliamentary elections Feb.-Mar. 2005 sparked protests. Akayev fled the country, Mar. 24, and formally resigned, Apr. 4. His interim successor, former Prime Min. Kurmanbek Bakiyev, a leader of the "tulip revolution," won the 2005 presidential vote and was reelected 2009, when monitors reported numerous irregularities. He was ousted by opposition parties Apr. 7, 2010, after clashes between protesters and government security forces left at least 77 people dead; he left the country and was sentenced in absentia, July 25, 2014, to life in prison for his role in suppressing the protests.

Fighting in mid-June 2010 between majority Kyrgyz and minority Uzbeks in the southern cities of Osh and Jalalabad claimed up to 2,000 lives. A June 2010 referendum on a new constitution received overwhelming approval. After Oct. 2010 elections, Omurbek Babanov became prime min. of a coalition government. Almazbek Atambayev won the 2011 presidential election. Babanov's coalition broke up Aug. 2012, and Jantoro Satybaldiev was sworn in as prime min. on Sept. 5. Three members of the opposition were convicted Mar. 30, 2013, of inciting crowds to assault government offices during an Oct. 2012 demonstration supporting the nationalizing of a gold mine. After a corruption scandal, Joomart Otorbaev became prime min. Apr. 2, 2014. He was replaced by Temir Sariyev, May 1, 2015, after he failed to complete negotiations with a Canadian company over ownership of the country's largest gold mine.

Laos

Lao People's Democratic Republic

People: Population: 6,911,544. **Age distrib.:** <15: 34.1%; 65+: 3.8%. **Growth:** 1.6%. **Migrants:** 0.3%. **Pop. density:** 77.6 per sq mi, 29.9 per sq km. **Urban:** 38.6%. **Ethnic groups:** Lao 54.6%, Khmou 10.9%, Hmong 8%, Tai 3.8%, Phuthai 3.3%, Leu 2.2%, Katang 2.1%, Makong 2.1%. **Languages:** Lao (official), French, English, ethnic langs. **Religions:** Buddhist 66.8%.

Geography: Total area: 91,429 sq mi, 236,800 sq km; **Land area:** 89,112 sq mi, 230,800 sq km. **Location:** Indochina Peninsula in SE Asia. Myanmar, China on N; Vietnam on E; Cambodia on S; Thailand on W. **Topography:** Landlocked, dominated by jungle. Mountains along E border are source of E-W rivers. Mekong R. defines most of W border. **Arable land:** 6.3%. **Capital:** Vientiane, 996,566.

Government: Type: Communist state. **Head of state:** Pres. Choummaly Sayasone; in office: June 8, 2006. **Head of gov.:** Prime Min. Thongsing Thammavong; in office: Dec. 24, 2010. **Local divisions:** 17 provinces, 1 capital city. **Defense budget:** $24 mil. **Active troops:** 29,100.

Economy: Industries: mining, timber, elec. power, agric. proc., rubber, constr., garments. **Chief crops:** sweet potatoes, vegetables, corn, coffee, sugarcane, tobacco, cotton, tea, peanuts, rice, cassava. **Natural resources:** timber, hydropower, gypsum, tin, gold, gems. **Water:** 49,261 cu m per capita. **Electricity prod.:** 12.1 bil kWh. **Labor force:** agric. 73.1%, industry 6.1%, services 20.6%. **Unemployment:** 1.4%.

Finance: Monetary unit: Kip (LAK) (8,149.01 = $1 U.S.). **GDP:** $34.4 bil; **per capita GDP:** $5,000; **GDP growth:** 7.4%. **Imports:** $4.1 bil; Thailand 56%, China 26.1%, Vietnam 6.7%. **Exports:** $2.8 bil; Thailand 33.3%, China 25.1%, Vietnam 11.5%. **Tourism:** $642 mil. **Budget:** $3.3 bil. **Inflation:** 4.1%.

Transport: Airports: 8.

Communications: Telephone: 13.4 per 100 pop. **Mobile:** 67 per 100 pop. **Broadband:** 2.5 per 100 pop. **Internet:** 14.3%.

Health: Expend.: 2.9%. **Life expect.:** 61.9 male; 66.0 female. **Births:** 24.3 per 1,000 pop. **Deaths:** 7.6 per 1,000 pop. **Infant mortality:** 53.0 per 1,000 live births. **Undernourished:** 21.8%. **HIV:** 0.3%.

Education: Compulsory: ages 6-10. **Literacy:** 79.9%.

Embassy: 2222 S St. NW 20008; 332-6416.

Website: www.na.gov.la

Laos became a French protectorate in 1893, but regained independence as a constitutional monarchy July 19, 1949. Conflicts among neutralist, Communist, and conservative factions created a chaotic political situation. Armed conflict increased after 1960.

The three factions formed a coalition government in June 1962 with neutralist Prince Souvanna Phouma as premier. A 14-nation conference in Geneva signed agreements, 1962, guaranteeing independence. By 1964 the leftist Pathet Lao had withdrawn from the coalition, and, with aid from North Vietnamese troops, renewed sporadic attacks. U.S. planes bombed the Ho Chi Minh trail, a supply line from North Vietnam to Communist forces in Laos and South Vietnam.

In 1970 the U.S. stepped up air support and military aid. After Pathet Lao military gains, Souvanna Phouma, May 1975, ordered government troops to cease fighting; the Pathet Lao took control. The Lao People's Democratic Republic was proclaimed Dec. 3, 1975.

From the mid-1970s through the 1980s, Laos relied on Vietnam for military and financial aid. After easing its finance laws in 1988, Laos attracted substantial foreign investment from Thailand, China, Vietnam, the U.S., and other nations. Laos was admitted to the Assn. of SE Asian Nations in 1997. The U.S. Congress approved normalization of trade with Laos in 2004. To spur further investment, Laos opened its first stock exchange Jan. 11, 2011, in Vientiane. Ground was broken Nov. 7, 2012, on the Xayaburi hydroelectric dam on the Mekong R., despite environmentalists' concerns that it will harm the area's wildlife and natural resources. The government planned to build up to 10 more dams on the river.

Latvia

Republic of Latvia

People: Population: 1,986,705. **Age distrib.:** <15: 14.9%; 65+: 19%. **Growth:** –1.1%. **Migrants:** 13.8%. **Pop. density:** 82.7 per sq mi, 31.9 per sq km. **Urban:** 67.4%. **Ethnic groups:** Latvian 61.1%, Russian 26.2%, Belarusian 3.5%, Ukrainian 2.3%, Polish 2.2%. **Languages:** Latvian (official), Russian. **Religions:** Lutheran 19.6%, Orthodox 15.3%.

Geography: Total area: 24,938 sq mi, 64,589 sq km; **Land area:** 24,034 sq mi, 62,249 sq km. **Location:** E Europe, on Baltic Sea. Estonia on N; Lithuania, Belarus on S; Russia on E. **Topography:** Lowland with numerous lakes, marshes, and peat bogs. Principal river is W. Dvina (Daugava). Glacial hills in E. **Arable land:** 18.9%. **Capital:** Riga, 620,847.

Government: Type: Parliamentary democracy. **Head of state:** Pres. Raimonds Vejonis; in office: July 8, 2015. **Head of gov.:** Prime Min. Laimdota Straujuma; in office: Jan. 22, 2014. **Local divisions:** 110 municipalities, 9 cities. **Defense budget** (2013): $210 mil. **Active troops:** 5,310.

Economy: Industries: processed foods, processed wood prods., textiles, processed metals, pharmaceuticals, railroad cars. **Chief crops:** grain, rapeseed, potatoes, vegetables. **Natural resources:** peat, limestone, dolomite, amber, hydropower, timber. **Water:** 17,293 cu m per capita. **Electricity prod.:** 6 bil kWh. **Labor force:** agric. 8.8%, industry 24%, services 67.2%. **Unemployment:** 11.1%.

Finance: Monetary unit: Euro (EUR) (0.89 = $1 U.S.). **GDP:** $48.2 bil; **per capita GDP:** $23,700; **GDP growth:** 2.4%. **Imports:** $16.6 bil; Lithuania 19.3%, Germany 11.3%, Poland 9.4%, Estonia 8.3%, Russia 8.1%. **Exports:** $13.4 bil; Lithuania 16.2%, Russia 16.1%, Estonia 12%, Germany 7%, Poland 6.7%. **Tourism:** $955 mil. **Budget:** $12 bil. **Inflation:** 0.6%.

Transport: Railways: 1,391 mi. **Motor vehicles:** 344.5 per 1,000 pop. **Airports:** 18.

Communications: Telephone: 19 per 100 pop. **Mobile:** 124.2 per 100 pop. **Broadband:** 62.8 per 100 pop. **Internet:** 75.8%.

Health: Expend.: 6%. **Life expect.:** 69.6 male; 79.1 female. **Births:** 10.0 per 1,000 pop. **Deaths:** 14.3 per 1,000 pop. **Infant mortality:** 5.4 per 1,000 live births. **Undernourished:** <5%. **HIV:** NA.

Education: Compulsory: ages 7-15. **Literacy:** 99.9%.

Embassy: 2306 Massachusetts Ave. NW 20008; 328-2840.

Website: www.mk.gov.lv

Prior to 1918, Latvia was occupied by the Russians and Germans. It was an independent republic, 1918-39. The Aug. 1939 Soviet-German agreement assigned Latvia to the Soviet sphere of influence. It was officially absorbed by the USSR in 1940. It was overrun by the German army in 1941, but retaken in 1945.

During an abortive Soviet coup, Latvia declared independence, Aug. 21, 1991. The last Russian troops in Latvia withdrew by Aug. 31, 1994. Responding to international pressure, Latvian voters, 1998, eased citizenship laws that had discriminated against some 500,000 ethnic Russians. Latvia joined the EU and NATO in 2004. It began using the euro as its currency Jan. 1, 2014.

Hit hard by recession, Latvia reached agreement Dec. 2008 on a $10.4-bil emergency loan from the EU, IMF, World Bank, and Nordic countries. Angered by the prolonged economic downturn and the growing influence of wealthy oligarchs, voters approved a July 2011 referendum dissolving parliament. Prime Min. Valdis Dombrovskis's Unity Party came in third in Sept. 2011 elections, but Dombrovskis remained prime min. After more than 50 people died, Nov. 21, 2013, in a Riga supermarket roof collapse blamed on design and construction flaws, Dombrovskis resigned. Laimdota Straujuma became prime min. Jan. 22, 2014. His coalition retained its majority in Oct. 4, 2014, elections. Defense Min. Raimonds Vejonis was elected by parliament as Latvia's president, June 3, 2015.

Lebanon

Lebanese Republic

People: Population: 6,184,701. **Age distrib.:** <15: 25.1%; 65+: 6.6%. **Growth:** 0.9%. **Migrants:** 17.6%. **Pop. density:** 1,565.8 per sq mi, 604.6 per sq km. **Urban:** 87.8%. **Ethnic groups:** Arab 95%, Armenian 4%. Many Christian Lebanese identify not as Arab but as Phoenician. **Languages:** Arabic (official), French, English, Armenian. **Religions:** Muslim 54% (Sunni 27%, Shia 27%), Christian 40.5% (incl. Maronite Catholic 21%), Druze 5.6%.

Geography: Total area: 4,015 sq mi, 10,400 sq km; **Land area:** 3,950 sq mi, 10,230 sq km. **Location:** Middle East, on E end of Mediterranean Sea. Syria on E, Israel on S. **Topography:** Narrow coastal strip. Two N-S mountain ranges enclose the fertile Beqaa Valley. The Litani R. runs S through the valley. **Arable land:** 20.2%. **Capital:** Beirut, 2,226,478 (excl. Syrian refugees).

Government: Type: Republic. **Head of state:** vacant. **Head of gov.:** Prime Min. Tammam Salam; in office: Apr. 6, 2013. **Local divisions:** 6 governorates. **Defense budget** (2012): $1.15 bil. **Active troops:** 60,000.

Economy: Industries: banking, tourism, food proc., wine, jewelry, cement, textiles, mineral and chem. prods., wood and furniture prods. **Chief crops:** citrus, grapes, tomatoes, apples, vegetables, potatoes, olives, tobacco. **Natural resources:** limestone, iron ore, salt, water (surplus in a water-deficit region). **Water:** 934 cu m per capita. **Electricity prod.:** 14 bil kWh. **Labor force:** NA. **Unemployment:** 6.5%.

Finance: Monetary unit: Pound (LBP) (1,504.00 = $1 U.S.). **GDP:** $81.1 bil; **per capita GDP:** $18,000; **GDP growth:** 2.3%. **Imports:** $20.1 bil; China 12.4%, France 8.5%, Italy 8.5%, U.S. 5.1%. **Exports:** $4.1 bil; South Africa 16.9%, Saudi Arabia 9.3%, UAE 9.1%, Syria 7.2%, Switzerland 6.5%, Iraq 5.5%. **Tourism:** $5.9 bil. **Budget:** $14.9 bil. **Inflation:** NA.

Transport: Railways: 249 mi (unusable due to damage from fighting). **Motor vehicles:** 158.8 per 1,000 pop. **Airports:** 5.

Communications: Telephone: 19.4 per 100 pop. **Mobile:** 88.3 per 100 pop. **Broadband:** 43 per 100 pop. **Internet:** 74.7%.

Health: Expend.: 7.3%. **Life expect.:** 76.2 male; 78.7 female. **Births:** 14.6 per 1,000 pop. **Deaths:** 4.9 per 1,000 pop. **Infant mortality:** 7.8 per 1,000 live births. **Undernourished:** <5%. **HIV:** <0.1%.

Education: Compulsory: ages 6-14. **Literacy:** 93.9%.

Embassy: 2560 28th St. NW 20008; 939-6300.

Website: www.pcm.gov.lb or www.presidency.gov.lb

Formed from five former Turkish Empire districts, Lebanon became independent Sept. 1, 1920, and was administered under French mandate 1920-41. French troops withdrew in 1946.

Under the 1943 National Covenant, all public positions were divided among the various religious communities, with Christians in the majority. By the 1970s, Muslims became the majority and demanded a larger political and economic role.

U.S. Marines intervened, May-Oct. 1958, during a Syrian-aided revolt. Continued raids against Israeli civilians, 1970-75, brought Israeli retaliation in southern Lebanon.

An estimated 60,000 were killed in a 1975-76 civil war. Palestinian units and leftist Muslims fought against Maronite militia (the Phalange) and other Christians. Several Arab countries provided support to various factions, while Israel aided Christian forces. Syria, which intervened in 1976 to fight Palestinian groups, largely policed a cease-fire.

Israeli forces invaded Lebanon June 6, 1982, attacking strongholds of the Palestine Liberation Organization (PLO). Israeli and Syrian forces engaged in the Bekaa Valley. On Aug. 21, the PLO evacuated W Beirut after massive Israeli bombings. Israeli troops entered W Beirut following the Sept. 14 assassination of newly elected Lebanese Pres. Bashir Gemayel. On Sept. 16, 1982, Lebanese Christian troops entered the Sabra and Shatila refugee camps and massacred hundreds of Palestinian civilians. An agreement May 17, 1983, between Lebanon, Israel, and the U.S. (but not Syria) provided for the withdrawal of Israeli troops; at least 30,000 Syrian troops remained in Lebanon, and Israel held onto a "security zone" in the south.

In 1983, some 50 people were killed in an explosion at the U.S. embassy, Apr. 18; 241 U.S. service members and 58 French soldiers died in separate Islamist suicide attacks, Oct. 23. The 1980s witnessed kidnappings of U.S., British, French, and Soviet citizens by Islamic militants. All hostages were released by 1992.

A treaty signed May 22, 1991, between Lebanon and Syria recognized Lebanon as a separate state for the first time since 1943.

Israeli forces conducted air raids and artillery strikes against guerrilla bases and villages in southern Lebanon, causing over 200,000 to flee their homes July 25-29, 1993. Some 500,000 civilians fled in Apr. 1996 when Israel struck suspected guerrilla bases in the south. The economy revived in the 1990s, but Syria continued to dominate Lebanon's political affairs. Israel withdrew virtually all its troops from southern Lebanon by May 2000, leaving Hezbollah, an Iranian-backed guerrilla group, in control of much of the region.

Rafik al-Hariri, a former prime min. (1992-98, 2000-04), was killed by a truck bomb, Feb. 14, 2005. Many Lebanese blamed Syria. As anti-Syrian protests mounted, Syrian troops left Lebanon (some intelligence agents may have remained). An anti-Syrian bloc won May and June parliamentary elections. A new cabinet, installed July 2005, was headed by Fouad Siniora and included a Hezbollah member.

A Hezbollah rocket attack and border raid, July 2006, in which 3 Israeli soldiers were killed and 2 captured, triggered a massive escalation of hostilities. Hezbollah bombarded northern Israel with nearly 4,000 rockets, while Israeli air and ground forces assaulted suspected Hezbollah strongholds in southern Lebanon and southern Beirut. By Aug. 14, 2006, when a UN-sponsored cease-fire took hold, the war dead included nearly 1,150 Lebanese. To enforce the truce, thousands of Lebanese troops moved into southern Lebanon, and the small UN force already in Lebanon (UNIFIL) was expanded. As of June 30, 2015, UNIFIL had more than 10,400 uniformed personnel in Lebanon.

At an international conference in Paris, Jan. 2007, donor countries pledged more than $7.6 bil in reconstruction aid. After more than 3 months of fighting in which over 400 people died, Lebanese forces Sept. 2 defeated Islamic militants at the Nahr al-Bared Palestinian refugee camp north of Tripoli. A 2008 power-sharing accord between the Siniora government and Hezbollah eased factional violence and paved the way for Army Chief Gen. Michel Suleiman to become president, ending an 18-month stalemate. A new government headed by Prime Min. Tammam Salam with representatives from Lebanon's various political and communal factions took office. However, factional disputes in parliament led to a lengthy delay in electing a successor when Pres. Suleiman's term expired in May 2014 (the prime min. and cabinet temporarily assumed the duties of the president).

The Syrian civil war spilled over into Lebanon beginning in 2012. In Tripoli, Sunni Muslims and Alawite Muslims took part in firefights, Aug. 21-26, 2012, that left at least 17 dead. A bombing linked to the Syrian civil war took place in Beirut Oct. 19, 2012, killing the anti-Syrian Gen. Wissam al-Hassan. Hezbollah gave military aid to the Syrian government, escalating the conflict on the border and suffering its own casualties. Radical Sunnis fought the Lebanese Army, June 23-24, 2013, in growing sectarian violence. Fighting between Sunni extremists from Syria who seized a border town and Lebanese army units erupted in Aug. 2014. Syrian Sunni extremists fought Hezbollah in northern Lebanon in late 2014 and were apparently responsible for suicide bombings in Tripoli, Jan. 10, 2015, that killed 8. The UNHCR estimated the number of Syrian refugees in Lebanon at more than 1.1 mil as of Aug. 2015.

Lesotho

Kingdom of Lesotho

People: Population: 1,947,701. **Age distrib.:** <15: 32.7%; 65+: 5.4%. **Growth:** 0.3%. **Migrants:** 0.1%. **Pop. density:** 166.2 per sq mi, 64.2 per sq km. **Urban:** 27.3%. **Ethnic groups:** Sotho 99.7%. **Languages:** Sesotho, English (both official); Zulu; Xhosa. **Religions:** Christian 80%, indigenous beliefs 20%.

Geography: Total area: 11,720 sq mi, 30,355 sq km; **Land area:** 11,720 sq mi, 30,355 sq km. **Location:** Southern Africa. Completely surrounded by South Africa. **Topography:** Landlocked and mountainous, 5,000 to 11,000 ft in elevation. **Arable land:** 9.3%. **Capital:** Maseru, 266,580 (2014).

Government: Type: Parliamentary constitutional monarchy. **Head of state:** King Letsie III; in office: Feb. 7, 1996. **Head of gov.:** Prime Min. Pakalitha Mosisili; in office: Mar. 17, 2015. **Local divisions:** 10 districts. **Defense budget:** $54 mil. **Active troops:** 2,000.

Economy: Industries: food, beverages, textiles, apparel assembly, handicrafts, constr., tourism. **Chief crops:** corn, wheat, pulses, sorghum, barley. **Natural resources:** water, diamonds, sand, clay, building stone. **Water:** 1,457 cu m per capita. **Electricity prod.:** 486 mil kWh. **Labor force:** agric. 86% (subsistence), industry and services 14%. Approx. 35% of active male wage earners work in South Africa. **Unemployment:** 24.7%.

Finance: Monetary unit: Loti (LSL) (13.45 = $1 U.S.). **GDP:** $5.3 bil; **per capita GDP:** $2,800; **GDP growth:** 2.2%. **Imports:** $1.9 bil. **Exports:** $824.9 mil. **Tourism:** $39 mil. **Budget:** $1.4 bil. **Inflation:** 5.3%.

Transport: Airports: 3.

Communications: Telephone: 2.4 per 100 pop. **Mobile:** 101.9 per 100 pop. **Broadband:** 11.5 per 100 pop. **Internet:** 11%.

Health: Expend.: 11.6%. **Life expect.:** 52.8 male; 53.0 female. **Births:** 25.5 per 1,000 pop. **Deaths:** 14.9 per 1,000 pop. **Infant mortality:** 49.0 per 1,000 live births. **Undernourished:** 11.5%. **HIV:** 23.4%.

Education: Compulsory: ages 6-12. **Literacy:** 79.4%.

Embassy: 2511 Massachusetts Ave. NW 20008; 797-5533.

Website: www.gov.ls

Lesotho (once called Basutoland) became a British protectorate in 1868. Independence came Oct. 4, 1966. Livestock raising is a major industry; clothing manufactured for sale abroad and diamonds are leading exports. Cultivation of marijuana for smuggling to South Africa is a significant source of income.

In Mar. 1990, King Moshoeshoe was exiled by the military government. Letsie III became king Nov. 12. In Mar. 1993, Ntsu Mokhehle, a civilian, was elected prime minister, ending 23 years of military rule. After a series of violent disturbances, the king dismissed the Mokhehle government Aug. 17, 1994; constitutional rule was restored Sept. 14.

Letsie abdicated and Moshoeshoe was reinstated Jan. 25, 1995. Moshoeshoe died in an automobile accident, Jan. 15, 1996. Letsie returned to power Feb. 7. South Africa and Botswana sent troops Sept. 1998 to help suppress violent antigovernment protests. After parliamentary elections May 26, 2012, the left-leaning Thomas Motsoahae Thabane became prime min. He fled to South Africa, Aug.-Sept. 2014, when units of the military, which backed a political rival, attacked police forces loyal to Thabane. After early elections, Feb. 28, 2015, former Prime Min. Pakalitha Mosisili (1998-2012) formed a coalition govt. and again became prime min.

Liberia

Republic of Liberia

People: Population: 4,195,666. **Age distrib.:** <15: 42.8%; 65+: 3.1%. **Growth:** 2.5%. **Migrants:** 5.3%. **Pop. density:** 112.8 per sq mi, 43.6 per sq km. **Urban:** 49.7%. **Ethnic groups:** Kpelle 20.3%, Bassa 13.4%, Grebo 10%, Gio 8%, Mano 7.9%, Kru 6%, Lorma 5.1%, Kissi 4.8%, Gola 4.4%. **Languages:** English (official), about 20 ethnic-group langs. **Religions:** Christian 85.6%, Muslim 12.2%.

Geography: Total area: 43,000 sq mi, 111,369 sq km; **Land area:** 37,189 sq mi, 96,320 sq km. **Location:** SW coast of W Africa. Sierra Leone on W, Guinea on N, Côte d'Ivoire on E. **Topography:** Marshy Atlantic coastline rises to low mountains and plateaus in forested interior. Six major rivers flow in parallel courses to the ocean. **Arable land:** 5.2%. **Capital:** Monrovia, 1,263,800.

Government: Type: Republic. **Head of state and gov.:** Pres. Ellen Johnson-Sirleaf; in office: Jan. 16, 2006. **Local divisions:** 15 counties. **Defense budget:** $24 mil. **Active troops:** 2,050.

Economy: Industries: mining, rubber and palm oil proc., timber, diamonds. **Chief crops:** rubber, coffee, cocoa, rice, cassava, palm oil, sugarcane, bananas. **Natural resources:** iron ore, timber, diamonds, gold, hydropower. **Water:** 54,029 cu m per capita. **Electricity prod.:** 300 mil kWh. **Labor force:** agric. 70%, industry 8%, services 22%. **Unemployment:** 3.7%.

Finance: Monetary unit: Dollar (LRD) (92.50 = $1 U.S.). **GDP:** $3.7 bil; **per capita GDP:** $900; **GDP growth:** 0.5%. **Imports:** $2.6 bil; Singapore 29.6%, South Korea 26.9%, China 17.9%, Japan 13.8%. **Exports:** $897.9 mil; China 18.9%, U.S. 11.1%, Spain 10.6%, France 8.8%, Algeria 7.9%, Poland 6.8%, Germany 5.6%. **Tourism:** $12 mil. **Budget:** $581.7 mil. **Inflation** (2012-13): 7.6%.

Transport: Railways: 267 mi (most inoperable due to damage from fighting though there is rebuilding). **Motor vehicles:** 14.8 per 1,000 pop. **Airports:** 2.

Communications: Telephone: 0.2 per 100 pop. **Mobile:** 73.4 per 100 pop. **Broadband:** 1.9 per 100 pop. **Internet:** 5.4%.

Health: Expend.: 15.5%. **Life expect.:** 56.9 male; 60.3 female. **Births:** 34.4 per 1,000 pop. **Deaths:** 9.7 per 1,000 pop. **Infant mortality:** 67.5 per 1,000 live births. **Undernourished:** 29.6%. **HIV:** 1.2%.

Education: Compulsory ages: 6-11. **Literacy:** 47.6%.

Embassy: 5201 16th St. NW 20011; 723-0437.

Website: www.emansion.gov.lr

Liberia was founded in 1822 by freed black slaves from the U.S. who settled at Monrovia with the aid of colonization societies. It became a republic July 26, 1847, with a constitution modeled on that of the U.S. Descendants of freed slaves dominated politics for much of the 19th and 20th cents.

Under Pres. William V. S. Tubman, Liberia was a founding member of the UN in 1945. Tubman died in 1971 and was succeeded by his vice president, William R. Tolbert Jr. Charging rampant corruption, an Army Redemption Council of enlisted men staged a bloody predawn coup, Apr. 12, 1980, killing Pres. Tolbert and installing Sgt. Samuel Doe, an indigenous African, as head of state. In 1985, Doe was chosen president in a disputed election.

A civil war began Dec. 1989. In Sept. 1990, Pres. Doe was executed. Despite the introduction of a multinational peacekeeping force, the conflict intensified. Factional fighting devastated Monrovia in Apr. 1996. Ruth Perry became modern Africa's first female head of state Sept. 3, 1996, leading a transitional government. By then, the civil war had claimed more than 150,000 lives.

Former rebel leader Charles Taylor was elected president July 1997, in Liberia's first national election in 12 years. The UN imposed sanctions in 2001, to punish Liberia for aiding the Revolutionary United Front (RUF) insurgency in Sierra Leone. Taylor declared a state of emergency Feb. 8, 2002, after Liberian rebels launched raids near Monrovia.

A UN-sponsored war crimes tribunal indicted Taylor June 2003, for his role in the Sierra Leone conflict. With rebels again threatening Monrovia, Taylor resigned Aug. 11 and went into exile. The UN authorized a 15,000-member peacekeeping force (UNMIL) Sept. 19 to help stabilize the nation. A businessman, Charles Gyude Bryant, was sworn in Oct. 14 to head a power-sharing interim government. Ellen Johnson-Sirleaf won presidential elections in 2005 and 2011, and shared the 2011 Nobel Peace Prize with 2 other women. Captured in 2006 while trying to flee Nigeria, Charles Taylor went to trial at The Hague in 2007. After several delays, he was convicted in 2012 of 11 counts of aiding and abetting war crimes and crimes against humanity, and sentenced to 50 years in prison May 30.

A 2015 UN Security Council resolution set a goal of reducing the UNMIL presence to about 5,100 uniformed personnel by Sept. 2015. UNMIL had more than 5,900 uniformed personnel in Liberia as of June 30, 2015. The Security Council, Sept. 17, extended UNMIL's mandate until Sept. 2016 and set a goal of reducing personnel by some 3,260 by June 2016. Liberia was seriously affected by an Ebola virus epidemic that began in Guinea in Dec. 2013. By the time WHO declared Liberia Ebola-free, Sept. 3, 2015, 10,672 Liberian cases had been reported, and 4,808 had died.

Libya

People: Population: 6,411,776. **Age distrib.:** <15: 26.5%; 65+: 4.1%. **Growth:** 2.2%. **Migrants:** 12.2%. **Pop. density:** 9.4 per sq mi, 3.6 per sq km. **Urban:** 78.6%. **Ethnic groups:** Berber and Arab 97%, other (incl. Greek, Maltese, Italian, Egyptian, Pakistani, Turk, Indian, Tunisian) 3%. **Languages:** Arabic (official), Italian, English, Berber. **Religions:** Muslim (official; virtually all Sunni) 96.6%, Christian 2.7%.

Geography: Total area: 679,362 sq mi, 1,759,540 sq km; **Land area:** 679,362 sq mi, 1,759,540 sq km. **Location:** Mediterranean coast of N Africa. Tunisia, Algeria on W; Niger, Chad on S; Sudan, Egypt on E. **Topography:** Desert and semidesert regions cover 92% of land with low mountains in N, higher mountains in S, and a narrow coastal zone. **Arable land:** 1%. **Capital:** Tarabulus (Tripoli), 1,126,145.

Government: Type: In transition. **Head of state:** Pres. of House of Representatives Agila Saleh Essa Gwaider; in office: Aug. 5, 2014. **Head of gov.:** Prime Min. Abdullah al-Thinni; in office: Mar. 11, 2014. **Local divisions:** 22 districts. **Defense budget** (2013): $4.66 bil. **Active troops:** 7,000.

Economy: Industries: petroleum, petrochemicals, aluminum, iron and steel, food proc., textiles, handicrafts, cement. **Chief crops:** wheat, barley, olives, dates, citrus, vegetables, peanuts, soybeans. **Natural resources:** petroleum, nat. gas, gypsum. **Water:** 113 cu m per capita. **Crude oil reserves:** 48.4 bil bbls. **Electricity prod.:** 31.9 bil kWh. **Labor force:** agric. 17%, industry 23%, services 59%. **Unemployment:** 19.6%.

Finance: Monetary unit: Dinar (LYD) (1.36 = $1 U.S.). **GDP:** $97.6 bil; **per capita GDP:** $15,700; **GDP growth:** –24%. **Imports:** $16.1 bil; Italy 13.1%, China 11.9%, Turkey 11.3%, Egypt 6.8%, Tunisia 5.8%, Germany 5.3%. **Exports:** $17.5 bil; Italy 20.2%, Germany 15.1%, France 10.5%, U.S. 6.3%, Spain 6.3%, Netherlands 5.2%, China 5%. **Tourism:** $60 mil. **Budget:** $25.2 bil. **Inflation** (2012-13): 2.6%.

Transport: Motor vehicles: 414.5 per 1,000 pop. **Airports:** 68.

Communications: Telephone: 11.3 per 100 pop. **Mobile:** 161.1 per 100 pop. **Broadband:** NA. **Internet:** 17.8%.

Health: Expend.: 3.9%. **Life expect.:** 74.5 male; 78.1 female. **Births:** 18.0 per 1,000 pop. **Deaths:** 3.6 per 1,000 pop. **Infant mortality:** 11.5 per 1,000 live births. **Undernourished:** NA. **HIV:** NA.

Education: Compulsory: ages 6-14. **Literacy:** 91%.

Embassy: 2600 Virginia Ave. NW, Ste. 705, 20037; 944-9601.

Website: www.pm.gov.ly or www.embassyoflibyadc.org

First settled by Berbers, Libya was ruled in succession by Carthage, Rome, the Vandals, and the Ottomans. Italy ruled from 1912, and Britain and France after WWII. Libya became an independent constitutional monarchy Jan. 2, 1952. In 1969 a junta led by Col. Muammar al-Qaddafi seized power.

Under Qaddafi's dictatorship, dissent was suppressed and wars were waged with Egypt and Chad. During the 1980s, Libya was accused of promoting terrorism, such as the Apr. 5, 1986, bombing of a West Berlin nightclub, which killed 3, including a U.S. serviceman. The U.S. responded by attacking what it called "terrorist-related targets" in Libya, Apr. 14, including Qaddafi's barracks.

Libyan agents were accused of planting bombs that blew up Pan Am Flight 103 over Lockerbie, Scotland, killing 270 people Dec. 21, 1988, and French UTA Flight 772 over Niger, killing 170 people Sept. 19, 1989. The UN imposed sanctions in 1992 for Libya's failure to cooperate in the Lockerbie and UTA cases.

Libya agreed in 2003 to renounce terrorism and settle compensation cases for the families of the Lockerbie and UTA bombing victims. The UN lifted sanctions in Sept., and in Dec., Libya renounced nuclear, chemical, and biological weapons and long-range missiles. The U.S. ended most economic sanctions Apr. 2004 and restored full diplomatic relations May 2006. Abdel Basset Ali al-Megrahi, a former Libyan agent sentenced to life in prison in 2001 for his role in the Lockerbie bombing, was freed by Scottish authorities on humanitarian grounds Aug. 20, 2009; he died in Tripoli, May 20, 2012.

Arab Spring rebels fought with Qaddafi's forces throughout the spring of 2011. With diplomatic backing from the Arab League and the UN Security Council, NATO forces imposed an arms embargo and no-fly zone against Qaddafi. Aided by NATO, rebels took control of Tripoli Aug. 23, 2011, and began governing. Rebels killed Qaddafi Oct. 20, 2011. Ansar al-Shariah terrorists attacked the U.S. consulate in Benghazi Sept. 11, 2012, killing Ambassador J. Christopher Stephens and three others. The U.S. captured, June 15, 2014, the alleged leader of the attack, Ahmed Abu Khattala; he was charged with conspiracy, June 28, and indicted for murder, Oct. 14, 2014.

Violence between Islamists, rival militia groups, and pro-government forces intensified in 2013-14 and continued in 2015. Fighting in Benghazi, Oct.-Nov. 2014, left an estimated 400 dead. An ISIS-affiliated group seized territory in parts of the country, 2014-15. Parliamentary elections marred by violence were held June 25, 2014. The new parliament met in Tobruk because of militia control of Tripoli, where an Islamist coalition had set up a rival government. Prime Min. Abdullah al-Thinni survived an assassination attempt in Tobruk, May 26, 2015.

Liechtenstein

Principality of Liechtenstein

People: Population: 37,624. **Age distrib.:** <15: 15.5%; 65+: 16.5%. **Growth:** 0.8%. **Migrants:** 33.1%. **Pop. density:** 609 per sq mi, 235.2 per sq km. **Urban:** 14.3%. **Ethnic groups:**

Liechtensteiner 65.6%. **Languages:** German (official). **Religions:** Roman Catholic (official) 75.9%, Protestant Reformed 6.5%, Muslim 5.4%, none 5.4%.

Geography: Total area: 62 sq mi, 160 sq km; **Land area:** 62 sq mi, 160 sq km. **Location:** Central Europe, in Alps. Switzerland on W, Austria on E. **Topography:** Rhine Valley occupies one-third of country, Alps in the rest. **Arable land:** 18.8%. **Capital:** Vaduz, 5,321 (2014).

Government: Type: Hereditary constitutional monarchy. **Head of state:** Prince Hans-Adam II; in office: Nov. 13, 1989. **Head of gov.:** Prime Min. Adrian Hasler; in office: Mar. 27, 2013. **Local divisions:** 11 communes. **Defense budget/active troops:** NA.

Economy: Industries: electronics, metal mfg., dental prods., ceramics, pharmaceuticals, food prods., precision instruments. **Chief crops:** wheat, barley, corn, potatoes. **Natural resources:** hydroelectric potential. **Water:** NA. **Labor force:** agric. 0.8%, industry 39.4%, services 59.9%. **Unemployment:** NA.

Finance: Monetary unit: Franc (CHF) (0.97 = $1 U.S.). **GDP** (2009): $3.2 bil; **per capita GDP** (2009): $89,400; **GDP growth** (2012): 1.8%. **Imports** (2012): $2.1 bil. **Exports** (2012): $3.8 bil. (Trade data excl. trade with Switzerland.) **Budget** (2012 est.): $890.4 mil. **Inflation:** NA.

Transport: Railways: 6 mi (owned by Austrian Railway System).

Communications: Telephone: 48.4 per 100 pop. **Mobile:** 104.3 per 100 pop. **Broadband:** 86.8 per 100 pop. **Internet:** 95.2%.

Health: Expend.: NA. **Life expect.:** 79.6 male; 84.5 female. **Births:** 10.5 per 1,000 pop. **Deaths:** 7.1 per 1,000 pop. **Infant mortality:** 4.3 per 1,000 live births. **Undernourished:** <5%. **HIV:** NA.

Education: Compulsory: ages 6-14. **Literacy:** 100%.

Embassy: 2900 K St. NW, Ste. 602B, 20007; 331-0590.

Website: www.liechtenstein.li

Liechtenstein became sovereign in 1806. It is united with Switzerland by a customs and monetary union. Many workers commute daily from Austria, Switzerland, and Germany.

On Aug. 15, 2004, Prince Hans-Adam II assigned day-to-day responsibilities for running the country to his son, Crown Prince Alois. Long regarded as a tax haven, Liechtenstein took steps, 2008-13, to ease banking secrecy laws that had impeded international tax fraud investigations. A referendum to abolish the prince's power to veto referendums was defeated July 1, 2012.

Lithuania

Republic of Lithuania

People: Population: 2,884,433. **Age distrib.:** <15: 14.9%; 65+: 19.1%. **Growth:** –1%. **Migrants:** 4.9%. **Pop. density:** 119.2 per sq mi, 46 per sq km. **Urban:** 66.5%. **Ethnic groups:** Lithuanian 84.1%, Polish 6.6%, Russian 5.8%. **Languages:** Lithuanian (official), Russian, Polish. **Religions:** Roman Catholic 77.2%, Russian Orthodox 4.1%, none 6.1%.

Geography: Total area: 25,212 sq mi, 65,300 sq km; **Land area:** 24,201 sq mi, 62,680 sq km. **Location:** Eastern Europe, on SE coast of Baltic. Latvia on N; Belarus on E, S; Poland, Russia on W. **Topography:** Lowland with hills in W and S. Many small lakes and rivers with marshes espec. in N and W. **Arable land:** 36.1%. **Capital:** Vilnius, 516,765.

Government: Type: Parliamentary democracy. **Head of state:** Pres. Dalia Grybauskaite; in office: July 12, 2009. **Head of gov.:** Prime Min. Algirdas Butkevicius; in office: Nov. 22, 2012. **Local divisions:** 60 municipalities. **Defense budget:** $436 mil. **Active troops:** 10,950.

Economy: Industries: metal-cutting machine tools, elec. motors, TVs, refrigerators and freezers, petroleum refining, shipbuilding, furniture. **Chief crops:** grain, potatoes, sugar beets, flax, vegetables. **Natural resources:** peat, amber. **Water:** 8,253 cu m per capita. **Crude oil reserves:** 12 mil bbls. **Electricity prod.:** 3.9 bil kWh. **Labor force:** agric. 7.9%, industry 19.6%, services 72.5%. **Unemployment:** 11.8%.

Finance: Monetary unit: Euro (EUR) (0.89 = $1 U.S.). **GDP:** $79.6 bil; **per capita GDP:** $27,100; **GDP growth:** 2.9%. **Imports:** $35.2 bil; Russia 29.4%, Germany 10.4%, Poland 9.5%, Latvia 6.2%, Netherlands 5.2%. **Exports:** $31.6 bil; Russia 20%, Latvia 10.1%, Estonia 7.6%, Poland 7.5%, Germany 7.2%, Belarus 5.2%, UK 5%. **Tourism:** $1.4 bil. **Budget:** $16.6 bil. **Inflation:** 0.1%.

Transport: Railways: 1,099 mi. **Motor vehicles:** 580.8 per 1,000 pop. **Airports:** 22.

Communications: Telephone: 19.5 per 100 pop. **Mobile:** 147 per 100 pop. **Broadband:** 53.9 per 100 pop. **Internet:** 72.1%.

Health: Expend.: 6.7%. **Life expect.:** 69.2 male; 80.5 female. **Births:** 10.1 per 1,000 pop. **Deaths:** 14.3 per 1,000 pop. **Infant mortality:** 3.8 per 1,000 live births. **Undernourished:** <5%. **HIV:** NA.

Education: Compulsory: ages 7-15. **Literacy:** 99.8%.

Embassy: 2622 16th St. NW 20009; 234-5860.

Website: lrvk.lrv.lt

Lithuania, briefly occupied by the German army, 1914-18, was annexed by the Soviet Union until 1919. In 1939 it rejoined the Soviet sphere of influence and was annexed by the USSR Aug. 3, 1940.

Lithuania declared its independence from the Soviet Union Mar. 11, 1990; its independence was ratified by the Soviet Union Sept. 1991. The country became a full member of NATO and the EU in 2004; it began using the euro as its currency, Jan. 1, 2015. A plummeting economy spurred popular discontent and brought a rightward shift in parliamentary and presidential elections, 2008-09. The center-left Social Democrats won Oct. 2012 parliamentary elections. Running as an independent and focusing on national security, Pres. Dalia Grybauskaite won reelection in a May 25, 2014, runoff.

Luxembourg

Grand Duchy of Luxembourg

People: Population: 570,252. **Age distrib.:** <15: 16.9%; 65+: 14.9%. **Growth:** 2.1%. **Migrants:** 43.3%. **Pop. density:** 571.1 per sq mi, 220.5 per sq km. **Urban:** 90.2%. **Ethnic groups:** Luxembourger 57%, Portuguese 16.1%, French 6.1%, Italian 3.5%, Belgian 3.3%, German 2.4%. Groups by citizenship. **Languages:** Luxembourgish (national lang.), French, German (all official admin. langs.); Portuguese. **Religions:** Roman Catholic 87%, other (incl. Protestant, Jewish, Muslim) 13%.

Geography: Total area: 998 sq mi, 2,586 sq km; **Land area:** 998 sq mi, 2,586 sq km. **Location:** Western Europe. Belgium on W, France on S, Germany on E. **Topography:** Heavy forests (Ardennes) cover N. Low, open plateau in S. **Arable land:** 24.2%. **Capital:** Luxembourg, 106,680 (2014).

Government: Type: Constitutional monarchy. **Head of state:** Grand Duke Henri; in office: Oct. 7, 2000. **Head of gov.:** Prime Min. Xavier Bettel; in office: Dec. 4, 2013. **Local divisions:** 12 cantons **Defense budget:** $255 mil. **Active troops:** 900.

Economy: Industries: banking and financial services; constr.; iron, metals, steel; information tech.; telecom; cargo transp. **Chief crops:** grapes, barley, oats, potatoes, wheat, fruits. **Natural resources:** iron ore (no longer exploited). **Water:** 6,604 cu m per capita. **Electricity prod.:** 2.1 bil kWh. **Labor force:** agric. 1.1%, industry 20%, services 78.9%. **Unemployment:** 5.9%.

Finance: Monetary unit: Euro (EUR) (0.89 = $1 U.S.). **GDP:** $51.4 bil; **per capita GDP:** $92,000; **GDP growth:** 2.9%. **Imports:** $27.9 bil; Belgium 31.5%, Germany 24.3%, France 10.9%, U.S. 8.3%, China 6.4%. **Exports:** $18.9 bil; Germany 22.6%, France 15.9%, Belgium 15.8%, Italy 7.3%. **Tourism:** $5.4 bil. **Budget:** $27.8 bil. **Inflation:** 0.6%.

Transport: Railways: 171 mi. **Motor vehicles:** 798.9 per 1,000 pop. **Airports:** 1.

Communications: Telephone: 49.6 per 100 pop. **Mobile:** 148.4 per 100 pop. **Broadband:** 80.6 per 100 pop. **Internet:** 94.7%.

Health: Expend.: 6.9%. **Life expect.:** 79.7 male; 84.8 female. **Births:** 11.4 per 1,000 pop. **Deaths:** 7.2 per 1,000 pop. **Infant mortality:** 3.5 per 1,000 live births. **Undernourished:** <5%. **HIV:** NA.

Education: Compulsory: ages 4-15. **Literacy:** 100%.

Embassy: 2200 Massachusetts Ave. NW 20008; 265-4171.

Website: www.gouvernement.lu

Luxembourg, founded about 963, was ruled by Burgundy, Spain, Austria, and France from 1448 to 1815. It left the Germanic Confederation in 1866. Overrun by Germany in two world wars, Luxembourg ended its neutrality in 1948, when a customs union with Belgium and the Netherlands was adopted.

Luxembourg was one of the 6 founding members (1951) of what became the European Union. Prime Min. Jean-Claude Juncker, in office since 1995, announced July 10, 2013, he would resign, following revelations of abuses by the intelligence service. After Oct. 20 elections, Liberal Party leader Xavier Bettel became prime min. Legislation passed by the Chamber of Deputies, June 18, 2014, legalized same-sex marriage. Prime Min. Bettel, May 15, 2015, became the first EU government head to marry a same-sex partner.

Macedonia

Republic of Macedonia

People: Population: 2,096,015. **Age distrib.:** <15: 17.5%; 65+: 12.7%. **Growth:** 0.2%. **Migrants:** 6.6%. **Pop. density:** 213.4 per sq mi, 82.4 per sq km. **Urban:** 57.1%. **Ethnic groups:** Macedonian 64.2%, Albanian 25.2%, Turkish 3.9%, Roma 2.7%. **Languages:** Macedonian, Albanian (both official); Turkish. **Religions:** Macedonian Orthodox 64.8%, Muslim 33.3%.

Geography: Total area: 9,928 sq mi, 25,713 sq km; **Land area:** 9,820 sq mi, 25,433 sq km. **Location:** SE Europe. Bulgaria on E, Greece on S, Albania on W, Serbia on N. **Topography:** Landlocked, mostly mountainous with deep river valleys, 3 large lakes. Country is bisected by Vardar R. **Arable land:** 16.4%. **Capital:** Skopje, 502,655.

Government: Type: Parliamentary democracy. **Head of state:** Pres. Gjorge Ivanov; in office: May 12, 2009. **Head of gov.:** Prime Min. Nikola Gruevski; in office: Aug. 27, 2006. **Local divisions:** 70 municipalities, 1 city. **Defense budget:** $131 mil. **Active troops:** 8,000.

Economy: Industries: food proc., beverages, textiles, chemicals, iron, steel, cement, energy, pharmaceuticals. **Chief crops:** grapes, tobacco, vegetables, fruits. **Natural resources:** iron ore, copper, lead, zinc, chromite, manganese, nickel, tungsten, gold, silver, asbestos, gypsum, timber. **Water:** 3,037 cu m per capita. **Electricity prod.:** 5.9 bil kWh. **Labor force:** agric. 18.3%, industry 29.1%, services 52.6%. **Unemployment:** 29%.

Finance: Monetary unit: Denar (MKD) (54.55 = $1 U.S.). **GDP:** $27.6 bil (may not reflect country's large informal sector); **per capita GDP:** $13,300; **GDP growth:** 3.8%. **Imports:** $7.3 bil; (2014) UK 12.3%, Germany 11.1%, Greece 9.2%, Serbia 8.2%, Italy 6.2%, China 5.9%, Bulgaria 5.3%, Turkey 5.1%. **Exports:** $4.9 bil; (2014) Germany 41.4%, Bulgaria 6.6%, Italy 6.1%, Serbia 5.2%. **Tourism:** $295 mil. **Budget:** $3.3 bil. **Inflation:** –0.3%.

Transport: Railways: 434 mi. **Airports:** 8.

Communications: Telephone: 18.6 per 100 pop. **Mobile:** 109.1 per 100 pop. **Broadband:** 38.1 per 100 pop. **Internet:** 68.1%.

Health: Expend.: 7.1%. **Life expect.:** 73.4 male; 78.8 female. **Births:** 11.6 per 1,000 pop. **Deaths:** 9.1 per 1,000 pop. **Infant mortality:** 7.7 per 1,000 live births. **Undernourished:** <5%. **HIV:** NA.

Education: Compulsory: ages 6-14. **Literacy:** 97.8%.

Embassy: 2129 Wyoming Ave. NW 20008; 667-0501.

Website: www.vlada.mk

Muslim Turks ruled Macedonia from 1389 to 1912. In 1913, the area was incorporated into Serbia, which in 1918 became part of the Kingdom of Serbs, Croats, and Slovenes (later Yugoslavia). In 1946, Macedonia became a constituent republic of Yugoslavia.

Macedonia declared its independence Sept. 8, 1991, and was admitted to the UN in 1993. Greece, which objected to Macedonia's use of what it considered a Hellenic name, imposed a trade blockade; the countries agreed to normalize relations Sept. 13, 1995. However, Greece continued to block Macedonia's bid to join NATO.

By the end of NATO's air war against Yugoslavia, Mar.-June 1999, Macedonia had a Kosovar refugee population of more than 250,000; over 90% had been repatriated by Sept. 1.

Ethnic Albanian guerrillas launched an offensive Mar. 2001 in NW Macedonia. An accord signed Aug. 13 paved the way for a NATO peacekeeping force. A law broadening the rights of ethnic Albanians was enacted Jan. 2002. Fighting between police and Albanian guerrillas in May 2015 left 8 police officers and 14 rebels dead.

Gjorge Ivanov won a presidential runoff vote Apr. 5, 2009, and was reelected Apr. 27, 2014. After a wiretapping and corruption scandal, Prime Min. Nikola Gruevski agreed, July 15, 2015, to resign by Jan. 15, 2016, to pave the way for early elections in Apr. 2016. Macedonia, Aug. 20, 2015, declared a temporary state of emergency on its borders; tens of thousands of migrants from the Middle East and SW Asia who landed in Greece tried to cross Macedonia in 2015 on their way to Central and Western Europe.

Madagascar

Republic of Madagascar

People: Population: 23,812,681. **Age distrib.:** <15: 40.4%; 65+: 3.2%. **Growth:** 2.6%. **Migrants:** 0.1%. **Pop. density:** 106.1 per sq mi, 40.9 per sq km. **Urban:** 35.1%. **Ethnic groups:** Malayo-Indonesian (Merina and related Betsileo), Cotiers (mixed African/Malayo-Indonesian/Arab ancestry), French, Indian, Creole, Comoran. **Languages:** French, Malagasy (both official); English. **Religions:** indigenous beliefs 52%, Christian 41%, Muslim 7%.

Geography: Total area: 226,658 sq mi, 587,041 sq km; **Land area:** 224,534 sq mi, 581,540 sq km. **Location:** In Indian O., off SE coast of Africa. Comoro Isls. to NW, Mozambique to W. **Topography:** Humid coastal strip in E, fertile valleys in mountainous center plateau region, and a wider coastal strip on W. **Arable land:** 6%. **Capital:** Antananarivo, 2,609,744.

Government: Type: Republic. **Head of state:** Pres. Hery Rajaonarimampianina; in office: Jan. 25, 2014. **Head of gov.:** Prime Min. Jean Ravelonarivo; in office: Jan. 14, 2015. **Local divisions:** 6 provinces. **Defense budget:** $74 mil. **Active troops:** 13,500.

Economy: Industries: meat proc., seafood, soap, beer, leather, sugar, textiles, glassware, cement, auto assembly. **Chief crops:** coffee, vanilla, sugarcane, cloves, cocoa, rice, cassava, beans, bananas, peanuts. **Natural resources:** graphite, chromite, coal, bauxite, rare earth elements, salt, quartz, tar sands, semiprec. stones, mica, fish, hydropower. **Water:** 14,700 cu m per capita. **Electricity prod.:** 2 bil kWh. **Labor force:** NA. **Unemployment:** 3.6%.

Finance: Monetary unit: Ariary (MGA) (3,270.00 = $1 U.S.). **GDP:** $33.9 bil; **per capita GDP:** $1,400; **GDP growth:** 3%. **Imports:** $2.7 bil; China 19.4%, France 11.9%, India 6.4%, South Africa 5.6%. **Exports:** $864.8 mil; France 21.6%, U.S. 8.6%, China 8.2%, Netherlands 5.3%, Germany 5.1%. **Tourism:** $574 mil. **Budget:** $2.7 bil. **Inflation:** 6.1%.

Transport: Railways: 519 mi. **Motor vehicles:** 12.3 per 1,000 pop. **Airports:** 26.

Communications: Telephone: 1.1 per 100 pop. **Mobile:** 38.2 per 100 pop. **Broadband:** 3.2 per 100 pop. **Internet:** 3.7%.

Health: Expend.: 4.1%. **Life expect.:** 64.1 male; 67.1 female. **Births:** 32.6 per 1,000 pop. **Deaths:** 6.8 per 1,000 pop. **Infant mortality:** 43.7 per 1,000 live births. **Undernourished:** 30.5%. **HIV:** 0.3%.

Education: Compulsory: ages 6-10. **Literacy:** 64.7%.

Embassy: 2374 Massachusetts Ave. NW 20008; 265-5525.

Website: www.primature.gov.mg

Madagascar was settled 2,000 years ago by Malayan-Indonesian people, whose descendants still predominate. A unified kingdom ruled in the 18th and 19th cent. The island became a French protectorate, 1885, and a colony, 1896. Independence came June 26, 1960.

Discontent with inflation and French domination led to a coup in 1972. The new regime nationalized French-owned financial interests, closed French bases and a U.S. space-tracking station, and obtained Chinese aid. The government conducted a program of arrests, expulsion of foreigners, and repression of strikes in 1979.

In 1990, Madagascar ended a ban on multiparty politics that had existed since 1975. Albert Zafy won the 1993 presidential election, ending the 17-year rule of Adm. Didier Ratsiraka, but was impeached and removed from office in 1996.

Marc Ravalomanana won a contentious presidential election over Ratsiraka Dec. 2001 and was reelected in 2006. A power struggle between Ravalomanana and the military-backed Andry Rajoelina culminated in Rajoelina's installation as head of a transitional regime, Mar. 17, 2009. The African Union pushed for a power-sharing arrangement, but two accords signed in 2009 were abrogated by Rajoelina. The transitional government suppressed a coup attempt by dissident military officers Nov. 17, 2010. Postponed presidential elections were finally held in late 2013, and won by Hery Rajaonarimampianina. Parliamentary elections were also held Dec. 10, 2013. With economic and living conditions unimproved, Rajaonarimampianina changed prime ministers in Jan. 2015. A vote by parliament, May 26, 2015, to remove Rajaonarimampianina from office was overturned by the constitutional court, June 13.

Malawi

Republic of Malawi

People: Population: 17,964,697. **Age distrib.:** <15: 46.7%; 65+: 2.7%. **Growth:** 3.3%. **Migrants:** 1.3%. **Pop. density:** 494.6 per sq mi, 191 per sq km. **Urban:** 16.3%. **Ethnic groups:** Chewa 32.6%, Lomwe 17.6%, Yao 13.5%, Ngoni 11.5%, Tumbuka 8.8%, Nyanja 5.8%, Sena 3.6%, Tonga 2.1%. **Languages:** English (official), Chichewa (common), Chinyanja, Chiyao, Chitumbuka, Chilomwe, Chinkhonde. **Religions:** Christian 82.6%, Muslim 13%.

Geography: Total area: 45,747 sq mi, 118,484 sq km; **Land area:** 36,324 sq mi, 94,080 sq km. **Location:** SE Africa. Zambia on W, Mozambique on S and E, Tanzania on N. **Topography:** 560 mi N-S along Lake Nyasa (Lake Malawi), most of which belongs to Malawi. High plateaus and mountains line the Rift Valley along length of nation. **Arable land:** 39.8%. **Capital:** Lilongwe, 905,433.

Government: Type: Multiparty democracy. **Head of state and gov.:** Pres. Arthur Peter Mutharika; in office: May 31, 2014. **Local divisions:** 28 districts. **Defense budget:** $42 mil. **Active troops:** 5,300.

Economy: Industries: tobacco, tea, sugar, sawmill prods., cement, consumer goods. **Chief crops:** tobacco, sugarcane, cotton, tea, corn, potatoes, cassava, sorghum, pulses, groundnuts, Macadamia nuts. **Natural resources:** limestone, hydropower, uranium, coal, bauxite. **Water:** 1,056 cu m per capita. **Electricity prod.:** 2.2 bil kWh. **Labor force:** agric. 90%, industry and services 10%. **Unemployment:** 7.6%.

Finance: Monetary unit: Kwacha (MWK) (459.23 = $1 U.S.). **GDP:** $13.7 bil; **per capita GDP:** $800; **GDP growth:** 5.7%. **Imports:** $2.5 bil; South Africa 25.1%, China 12.7%, India 12%, Zambia 11.7%. **Exports:** $1.3 bil; Canada 12.4%, Zimbabwe 9.4%, South Africa 6.7%, U.S. 6.4%, Russia 6.3%, Zambia 6.1%, Germany 6.1%. **Tourism:** $34 mil. **Budget:** $1.6 bil. **Inflation:** 24.4%.

Transport: Railways: 477 mi. **Motor vehicles:** 2 per 1,000 pop. **Airports:** 7.

Communications: Telephone: 0.4 per 100 pop. **Mobile:** 30.5 per 100 pop. **Broadband:** 3.9 per 100 pop. **Internet:** 5.8%.

Health: Expend.: 9.2%. **Life expect.:** 58.7 male; 62.7 female. **Births:** 41.6 per 1,000 pop. **Deaths:** 8.4 per 1,000 pop. **Infant mortality:** 46.3 per 1,000 live births. **Undernourished:** 21.8%. **HIV:** 10.0%.

Education: Compulsory: NA. **Literacy:** 65.8%.
Embassy: 2408 Massachusetts Ave. NW 20008; 721-0270.
Website: www.malawi.gov.mw

Bantus came to the land in the 16th cent., Arab slavers in the 19th. The area became the British protectorate Nyasaland in 1891. It became independent July 6, 1964, and a republic in 1966. After 3 decades as a one-party state under Pres. Hastings Kamuzu Banda, Malawi adopted a new constitution and, in multiparty elections held May 17, 1994, chose a new leader, Bakili Muluzi.

Bingu wa Mutharika, candidate of the ruling United Democratic Front, won a disputed 2004 presidential election. An effort by his former political allies to impeach him was halted by Malawi's Constitutional Court, Oct. 2005. Mutharika won reelection May 2009. Clashes between police and antigovernment protesters July 2011 left at least 19 people dead. Joyce Banda became Malawi's first female pres. after the death of Bingu wa Mutharika Apr. 5, 2012. Banda finished third in May 20-22, 2014, presidential elections. After her attempt to nullify the result was blocked in court, Peter Mutharika was declared the winner. Heavy rains produced widespread flooding in Jan. 2015 that killed hundreds and left more than 200,000 displaced.

Malaysia

People: Population: 30,513,848. **Age distrib.:** <15: 28.5%; 65+: 5.6%. **Growth:** 1.4%. **Migrants:** 8.3%. **Pop. density:** 240.5 per sq mi, 92.8 per sq km. **Urban:** 74.7%. **Ethnic groups:** Malay 50.1%, Chinese 22.6%, indigenous 11.8%, Indian 6.7%, non-citizen 8.2%. **Languages:** Bahasa Malaysia (official), English, Chinese, Tamil, Telugu, Malayalam, Panjabi, Thai. **Religions:** Muslim (official) 61.3%, Buddhist 19.8%, Christian 9.2%, Hindu 6.3%.

Geography: Total area: 127,355 sq mi, 329,847 sq km; **Land area:** 126,895 sq mi, 328,657 sq km. **Location:** SE tip of Asia, plus N coast of the island of Borneo. Thailand, Brunei on N; Indonesia on S. **Topography:** Most of W is covered by tropical jungle, including a central mountain range that runs N-S through the peninsula. Marshy W coast, sandy E coast. Wide swampy coastal plain with interior jungles and mountains in E. **Arable land:** 2.9%. **Capital:** Kuala Lumpur, 6,836,911; Putrajaya (admin. center). **Cities:** Johor Bahru, 911,562.

Government: Type: Constitutional monarchy. **Head of state:** Paramount Ruler Tuanku Abdul Halim Mu'adzam Shah; in office: Apr. 11, 2012. **Head of gov.:** Prime Min. Najib Razak; in office: Apr. 3, 2009. **Local divisions:** 13 states, 1 federal territory. **Defense budget:** $5.03 bil. **Active troops:** 109,000.

Economy: Industries: rubber and palm oil proc. and mfg., petroleum and nat. gas, light mfg., pharmaceuticals, medical tech., logging. **Chief crops:** palm oil, rubber, cocoa, rice, pepper. **Natural resources:** tin, petroleum, timber, copper, iron ore, nat. gas, bauxite. **Water:** 19,517 cu m per capita. **Crude oil reserves:** 4 bil bbls. **Electricity prod.:** 126.8 bil kWh. **Labor force:** agric. 11%, industry 36%, services 53%. **Unemployment:** 3.2%.

Finance: Monetary unit: Ringgit (MYR) (4.21 = $1 U.S.). **GDP:** $746.1 bil; **per capita GDP:** $24,700; **GDP growth:** 6%. **Imports:** $193.6 bil; China 17%, Singapore 13.2%, Japan 8.5%, U.S. 7.6%, Thailand 5.9%. **Exports:** $231.3 bil; China 14.2%, Singapore 13.9%, Japan 10.9%, U.S. 8.2%, Thailand 5.4%. **Tourism:** $21.8 bil. **Budget:** $79.6 bil. **Inflation:** 3.1%.

Transport: Railways: 1,149 mi. **Motor vehicles:** 412 per 1,000 pop. **Airports:** 39.

Communications: Telephone: 14.6 per 100 pop. **Mobile:** 148.8 per 100 pop. **Broadband:** 14.1 per 100 pop. **Internet:** 67.5%.

Health: Expend.: 4%. **Life expect.:** 72.0 male; 77.7 female. **Births:** 19.7 per 1,000 pop. **Deaths:** 5.0 per 1,000 pop. **Infant mortality:** 13.3 per 1,000 live births. **Undernourished:** <5%. **HIV:** 0.5%.

Education: Compulsory: ages 6-11. **Literacy:** 94.6%.
Embassy: 3516 International Ct. NW 20008; 572-9700.
Website: www.malaysia.gov.my

European traders visited in the 16th cent.; Britain established control in 1867. Malaysia was created Sept. 16, 1963. It included Malaya (which gained independence in 1957 after the suppression of Communist rebels), plus the formerly British Singapore, Sabah (N Borneo), and Sarawak (NW Borneo). Singapore was separated in 1965 in order to end tensions between Chinese—the majority in Singapore—and Malays in control of the Malaysian government.

Malaysia has abundant natural resources, though rainforest destruction has become a major environmental problem. Work on a federal administrative center at Putrajaya, south of Kuala Lumpur, was completed in 1999; it is linked by rail with Kuala Lumpur's city center and Cyberjaya, a hub for high-tech manufacturing and research.

The Indian Ocean tsunami of Dec. 26, 2004, left at least 68 people dead in Malaysia. Recession and scandals plagued Malaysia as National Front leader Najib Razak took over the premiership in 2009. Tuanku Abdul Halim Mu'adzam Shah was chosen in 2011 to serve as the paramount ruler for a second 5-year term, more than 40 years after his first (1970-75). In a close election (deemed fraudulent by the opposition), May 5, 2013, the governing coalition was returned to power.

A Malaysia Airlines flight to Beijing, carrying 239 passengers and crew, lost contact with air traffic control Mar. 8, 2014, shortly after takeoff from Kuala Lumpur and was presumed lost in the Indian Ocean. Part of a wing from the plane was found on the French island of Réunion, near Madagascar, in July 2015. On July 17, 2014, a Malaysia Airlines flight from Amsterdam to Kuala Lumpur was shot down by a missile over eastern Ukraine, killing all 298 people onboard; pro-Russian separatists were widely suspected of responsibility for the attack.

In 2015, Malaysian authorities (as well as officials in the U.S. and other countries) investigated possible misappropriation of hundreds of millions of dollars from a development fund, and more than $600 mil in transfers to bank accounts controlled by Prime Min. Najib. The prime min., July 28, dismissed his attorney general, who had been leading a key investigation.

Maldives
Republic of Maldives

People: Population: 393,253. **Age distrib.:** <15: 21.1%; 65+: 4.3%. **Growth:** –0.1%. **Migrants:** 24.4%. **Pop. density:** 3,417.9 per sq mi, 1,319.6 per sq km. **Urban:** 45.5%. **Ethnic groups:** S Indian, Sinhalese, Arab. **Languages:** Dhivehi (official), English (spoken by most govt. officials). **Religions:** Sunni Muslim (official).

Geography: Total area: 115 sq mi, 298 sq km; **Land area:** 115 sq mi, 298 sq km. **Location:** In Indian O. Nearest neighbor is India to NE. **Topography:** 19 atolls with 1,190 islands, 198 inhabited. None of the islands are over 5 sq mi in area; all are nearly flat. **Arable land:** 10%. **Capital:** Male, 156,427 (2014).

Government: Type: Republic. **Head of state and gov.:** Pres. Abdulla Yameen Abdul Gayoom; in office: Nov. 17, 2013. **Local divisions:** 7 provinces, 1 municipality. **Defense budget/active troops:** NA.

Economy: Industries: tourism, fish proc., shipping, boat building, coconut proc., woven mats, rope. **Chief crops:** coconuts, corn, sweet potatoes. **Natural resources:** fish. **Water:** 87 cu m per capita. **Electricity prod.:** 287.2 mil kWh. **Labor force:** agric. 15%, industry 15%, services 70%. **Unemployment:** 11.6%.

Finance: Monetary unit: Rufiyaa (MVR) (14.95 = $1 U.S.). **GDP:** $4.9 bil; **per capita GDP:** $14,400; **GDP growth:** 5%. **Imports** (2013): $1.7 bil; UAE 21.1%, Singapore 17%, India 8.6%, China 7.6%, Thailand 6.2%, Malaysia 6.1%. **Exports** (2013): $166 mil; Thailand 28.1%, France 14.9%, U.S. 9.4%, Sri Lanka 8.2%, UK 8.1%, Italy 6.2%, Germany 5.2%. **Tourism:** $2.7 bil. **Budget** (2013 est.): $876 mil. **Inflation:** 2.1%.

Transport: Airports: 7.

Communications: Telephone: 6.1 per 100 pop. **Mobile:** 189.4 per 100 pop. **Broadband:** 26.2 per 100 pop. **Internet:** 49.3%.

Health: Expend.: 8.5%. **Life expect.:** 73.1 male; 77.8 female. **Births:** 15.8 per 1,000 pop. **Deaths:** 3.9 per 1,000 pop. **Infant mortality:** 23.7 per 1,000 live births. **Undernourished:** 6.2%. **HIV:** NA.

Education: Compulsory: NA. **Literacy:** 99.3%.
Embassy: 800 Second Ave., Ste. 400E, New York, NY 10017; (212) 599-6195.
Website: www.presidencymaldives.gov.mv

A British protectorate since 1887, the nation achieved independence July 26, 1965; long a sultanate, the Maldives became a republic in 1968. Tourism and fishing are the most important sectors of the economy. Rising sea levels threaten the country, which comprises small, low-lying coral islands.

The Indian Ocean tsunami of Dec. 26, 2004, killed at least 82 people and displaced more than 21,600 in the Maldives. Pres. Maumoon Abdul Gayoom, in office 1978-2008, lost a 2008 runoff vote to pro-democracy leader and former political prisoner Mohamed (Anni) Nasheed. Following protests over the arrest of a judge, Nasheed resigned Feb. 2012, and Vice Pres. Mohamed Waheed Hassan Maniku took office. Nasheed ran for president Sept. 7, 2013, and won 45% of the vote, not enough to avoid a runoff. The Supreme Court canceled the runoff Sept. 24. In new elections Nov. 9, 2013, Nasheed won 47% but lost the Nov. 16 runoff to Abdulla Yameen Abdul Gayoom. Nasheed, Mar. 2015, was convicted on terrorism charges and sentenced to 13 years in prison in connection with his 2012 actions against the judge.

Mali
Republic of Mali

People: Population: 16,955,536. **Age distrib.:** <15: 47.4%; 65+: 3%. **Growth:** 3%. **Migrants:** 1.3%. **Pop. density:** 36 per sq mi, 13.9 per sq km. **Urban:** 39.9%. **Ethnic groups:** Mande (Bambara, Malinke, Soninke) 50%, Peul 17%, Voltaic 12%, Songhai 6%, Tuareg and Moor 10%. **Languages:** French (official), Bambara, 12 other national langs. **Religions:** Muslim 94.8%.

Geography: Total area: 478,841 sq mi, 1,240,192 sq km; **Land area:** 471,118 sq mi, 1,220,190 sq km. **Location:** Interior of W Africa. Mauritania, Senegal on W; Guinea, Côte d'Ivoire, Burkina Faso on S; Niger on E; Algeria on N. **Topography:** Landlocked grassy plain in upper basins of the Senegal and Niger Rivers, extending N into the Sahara. **Arable land:** 5.6%. **Capital:** Bamako, 2,515,000.

Government: Type: Republic. **Head of state:** Pres. Ibrahim Boubacar Keita; in office: Sept. 4, 2013. **Head of gov.:** Prime Min. Modibo Keita; in office: Jan. 8, 2015. **Local divisions:** 8 regions, 1 district. **Defense budget:** $365 mil. **Active troops:** 4,000.

Economy: Industries: food proc., constr., phosphate and gold mining. **Chief crops:** cotton, millet, rice, corn, vegetables, peanuts. **Natural resources:** gold, phosphates, kaolin, salt, limestone, uranium, gypsum, granite, hydropower. **Water:** 7,842 cu m per capita. **Electricity prod.:** 949 mil kWh. **Labor force:** agric. 80%, industry and services 20%. **Unemployment:** 8.2%.

Finance: Monetary unit: CFA Franc (XOF) (584.11 = $1 U.S.). **GDP:** $27.3 bil; **per capita GDP:** $1,700; **GDP growth:** 6.8%. **Imports:** $3 bil; France 11.1%, Senegal 10.1%, Côte d'Ivoire 9.2%, China 7.6%. **Exports:** $2.8 bil; China 30.5%, India 15.1%, Indonesia 8.6%, Bangladesh 6.3%, Thailand 5.6%. **Tourism:** $178 mil. **Budget:** $3.3 bil. **Inflation:** 0.9%.

Transport: Railways: 368 mi. **Motor vehicles:** 1.6 per 1,000 pop. **Airports:** 8.

Communications: Telephone: 1 per 100 pop. **Mobile:** 149 per 100 pop. **Broadband:** 1.9 per 100 pop. **Internet:** 7%.

Health: Expend.: 5.8%. **Life expect.:** 53.5 male; 57.3 female. **Births:** 45.0 per 1,000 pop. **Deaths:** 12.9 per 1,000 pop. **Infant mortality:** 102.2 per 1,000 live births. **Undernourished:** <5%. **HIV:** 1.4%.

Education: Compulsory: ages 6-14. **Literacy:** 33.7%.

Embassy: 2130 R St. NW 20008; 332-2249.

Website: www.primature.gov.ml

Until the 15th cent. the area was part of the great Mali Empire. Timbuktu (Tombouctou) was a center of Islamic study. French rule was secured, 1898. The Sudanese Rep. and Senegal became independent as the Mali Federation in 1960, but Senegal withdrew, and the Sudanese Rep. was renamed Mali.

A coup toppled a socialist regime led, 1960-68, by Pres. Modibo Keita. Famine struck in 1973-74, killing as many as 100,000 people. Drought conditions returned in the 1980s.

The military, Mar. 1991, overthrew Pres. Moussa Traoré, who had ruled since 1968. Oumar Konare, a coup leader, was elected president, 1992. The government and a Tuareg rebel group signed a peace accord in 1994, but Taureg separatists remained active in the north. Twice condemned to death for crimes committed in office, Traoré had his sentences commuted to life imprisonment in 1997 and 1999; he was pardoned in 2002.

Amadou Toumani Touré, who led the 1991 coup, was elected president in 2002 and reelected 2007. Amadou Sanogo, an army captain, staged a coup Mar. 2012 and brokered a deal to transfer power Apr. 12 to an interim government led by Pres. Dioncounda Traoré. The coup enabled Islamist rebels, who had allied themselves with the separatists, to seize control of the country's north. France entered the fight against the Islamists Jan. 10, 2013, and West African regional forces joined them Jan 17. The Islamists were pushed out of most of the territory they had seized. The UN Stabilization Mission in Mali (MINUSMA) was approved Apr. 25, 2013; it included more than 10,200 uniformed personnel as of June 30, 2015. Ibrahim Boubacar Keita was elected president Aug. 11, 2013. Attacks by Taureg separatists, as well as fighting against Islamists, continued in 2014 and early 2015. A new peace agreement with separatists was signed June 20, 2015. Islamist extremist attacks continued. France maintained 3,000 troops in the region, based in Mali and Chad, as of Aug. 2015.

Malta

Republic of Malta

People: Population: 413,965. **Age distrib.:** <15: 15%; 65+: 18.5%. **Growth:** 0.3%. **Migrants:** 8%. **Pop. density:** 3,392.9 per sq mi, 1,310 per sq km. **Urban:** 95.4%. **Ethnic groups:** Maltese (descendants of ancient Carthaginians and Phoenicians with Italian, other Mediterranean stock). **Languages:** Maltese, English (both official). **Religions:** Roman Catholic (official) 90%+.

Geography: Total area: 122 sq mi, 316 sq km; **Land area:** 122 sq mi, 316 sq km. Island of Malta is 95 sq mi. Gozo, 26 sq mi, and Comino, 1 sq mi, are other islands in group. **Location:** Center of Mediterranean Sea. Nearest neighbor is Italy on N. **Topography:** Heavily indented coastline. Low hills cover interior. **Arable land:** 28.1%. **Capital:** Valletta, 197,447 (2014).

Government: Type: Republic. **Head of state:** Pres. Marie-Louise Coleiro Preca; in office: Apr. 4, 2014. **Head of gov.:** Prime Min. Joseph Muscat; in office: Mar. 11, 2013. **Local divisions:** 68 localities. **Defense budget:** $61 mil. **Active troops:** 1,950.

Economy: Industries: tourism, electronics, shipbuilding and repair, constr., food and beverages, pharmaceuticals, footwear. **Chief crops:** potatoes, cauliflower, grapes, wheat, barley, tomatoes, citrus, cut flowers, green peppers. **Natural resources:** limestone, salt. **Water:** 118 cu m per capita. **Electricity prod.:** 2.1 bil kWh. **Labor force:** agric. 1.5%, industry 25.7%, services 72.8%. **Unemployment:** 6.5%.

Finance: Monetary unit: Euro (EUR) (0.89 = $1 U.S.). **GDP:** $14.1 bil; **per capita GDP:** $33,200; **GDP growth:** 3.5%. **Imports:** $8.4 bil; (2014) Italy 18.5%, U.S. 9.7%, Turkey 7.2%, UK 6.1%, Germany 5.1%. **Exports:** $4.9 bil; (2014) Egypt 13.3%, Germany 8.2%, Libya 5.6%, France 5.5%, Hong Kong 5.5%, Singapore 5%. **Tourism:** $1.5 bil. **Budget** (2015 est.): $4.9 bil. **Inflation:** 0.3%.

Transport: Motor vehicles: 753.4 per 1,000 pop. **Airports:** 1.

Communications: Telephone: 53.6 per 100 pop. **Mobile:** 127 per 100 pop. **Broadband:** 57.4 per 100 pop. **Internet:** 73.2%.

Health: Expend.: 9.1%. **Life expect.:** 77.9 male; 82.7 female. **Births:** 10.2 per 1,000 pop. **Deaths:** 9.1 per 1,000 pop. **Infant mortality:** 3.6 per 1,000 live births. **Undernourished:** <5%. **HIV:** NA.

Education: Compulsory: ages 5-15. **Literacy:** 94.4%.

Embassy: 2017 Connecticut Ave. NW 20008; 462-3611.

Website: www.gov.mt

Malta was ruled by Phoenicians, Romans, Arabs, Normans, the Knights of Malta, France, and Britain (since 1814). It became independent Sept. 21, 1964. Malta became a republic in 1974. The last British forces withdrew, Apr. 1, 1979.

From 1971 to 1987 and again from 1996 to 1998, Malta was governed by the socialist Labour Party; the Nationalist Party, which pressed for Malta's entry into the EU, held office 1987-96 and won parliamentary elections in 1998, 2003, and 2008. Malta became a full member of the EU May 1, 2004. The Labour Party returned to power as a result of Mar. 9, 2013, elections.

Marshall Islands

Republic of the Marshall Islands

People: Population: 72,191. **Age distrib.:** <15: 36%; 65+: 3.6%. **Growth:** 1.7%. **Migrants:** 3.2%. **Pop. density:** 1,033 per sq mi, 398.8 per sq km. **Urban:** 72.7%. **Ethnic groups:** Marshallese 92.1%, mixed Marshallese 5.9%. **Languages:** Marshallese, English (both official). **Religions:** Protestant 54.8%, Assembly of God 25.8%, Roman Catholic 8.4%, Bukot nan Jesus 2.8%.

Geography: Total area: 70 sq mi, 181 sq km; **Land area:** 70 sq mi, 181 sq km. **Location:** In N Pacific O.; made up of two 800-mi-long parallel chains of coral atolls. Nearest neighbors are Micronesia to W, Nauru and Kiribati to S. **Topography:** Low coral limestone and sand islands. **Arable land:** 11.1%. **Capital:** Majuro, 30,861 (2014).

Government: Type: Constitutional govt. in free association with U.S. **Head of state and gov.:** Pres. Christopher J. Loeak; in office: Jan. 17, 2012. **Local divisions:** 24 municipalities. **Defense budget/active troops:** NA.

Economy: Industries: copra, tuna proc., tourism, craft items. **Chief crops:** coconuts, tomatoes, melons, taro, breadfruit, fruits. **Natural resources:** coconut prods., marine prods., deep-seabed minerals. **Water:** NA. **Labor force:** agric. 11%, industry 16.3%, services 72.7%. **Unemployment:** NA.

Finance: Monetary unit: U.S. Dollar (USD). **GDP:** $181 mil; **per capita GDP:** $3,300; **GDP growth:** 0.5%. **Imports** (2013): $133.7 mil. **Exports** (2013): $53.7 mil. **Budget** (2013 est.): $113.9 mil. **Inflation:** NA.

Transport: Airports: 4.

Communications: Telephone: 4.5 per 100 pop. **Mobile:** 29.4 per 100 pop. **Broadband:** NA. **Internet:** 16.8%.

Health: Expend.: 15.6%. **Life expect.:** 70.7 male; 75.1 female. **Births:** 25.6 per 1,000 pop. **Deaths:** 4.2 per 1,000 pop. **Infant mortality:** 20.7 per 1,000 live births. **Undernourished:** NA. **HIV:** NA.

Education: Compulsory: ages 5-13. **Literacy:** NA.

Embassy: 2433 Massachusetts Ave. NW, 1st Fl., 20008; 234-5414.

Website: www.rmi-op.net

The Marshall Islands were a German possession until WWI and were administered by Japan between the World Wars. After WWII, they were administered by the U.S. as part of the UN Trust Territory of the Pacific Islands. During 1946-58, Bikini and Enewetak Atolls were used as test sites for U.S. nuclear weapons.

The Compact of Free Association, ratified by the U.S. in 1986, gave the islands their independence. In the compact, the U.S. agreed to provide financial aid to the islands, maintain their defense, and compensate victims of nuclear testing; it was renewed Dec. 2003. The Marshall Islands joined the UN in 1991. Severe drought conditions in spring 2013 prompted U.S. Pres. Barack Obama to sign a disaster declaration June 21 for the Marshall Islands, making the country eligible for U.S. federal relief funds. Made up of low-lying atolls, the Marshall Islands is considered one of the world's most vulnerable nations to rising sea levels resulting from climate change.

Mauritania

Islamic Republic of Mauritania

People: Population: 3,596,702. **Age distrib.:** <15: 39.2%; 65+: 3.7%. **Growth:** 2.2%. **Migrants:** 2.3%. **Pop. density:** 9 per sq mi, 3.5 per sq km. **Urban:** 59.9%. **Ethnic groups:** black Moor (Arab-speaking slaves, former slaves, and their descendants, enslaved by white Moors) 40%, white Moor (Arab-Berber descent) 30%, black African (non-Arabic speaking) 30%. **Languages:** Arabic (official and national); Pulaar, Soninke, Wolof (all national); French; Hassaniya. **Religions:** Muslim (official) 100%.

Geography: Total area: 397,955 sq mi, 1,030,700 sq km; **Land area:** 397,955 sq mi, 1,030,700 sq km. **Location:** NW Africa. Western Sahara on N; Algeria, Mali on E; Senegal on S. **Topography:** Fertile Senegal R. valley in S gives way to wide central region of sandy plains and scrub trees. N is arid and extends into the Sahara. **Arable land:** 0.4%. **Capital:** Nouakchott, 967,540.

Government: Type: Presidential republic. **Head of state:** Pres. Mohamed Ould Abdel Aziz; in office: Aug. 5. 2009. **Head of gov.:** Prime Min. Yahya Ould Hademinein; in office: Aug. 21, 2014. **Local divisions:** 13 regions. **Defense budget** (2013): $149 mil. **Active troops:** 15,850.

Economy: Industries: fish proc., oil prod., mining. **Chief crops:** dates, millet, sorghum, rice, corn. **Natural resources:** iron ore, gypsum, copper, phosphate, diamonds, gold, oil, fish. **Water:** 2,931 cu m per capita. **Crude oil reserves:** 20 mil bbls. **Electricity prod.:** 1 bil kWh. **Labor force:** agric. 50%, industry 2%, services 48%. **Unemployment:** 31%.

Finance: Monetary unit: Ouguiya (MRO) (291.50 = $1 U.S.). **GDP:** $15.5 bil; **per capita GDP:** $4,300; **GDP growth:** 6.4%. **Imports:** $3.5 bil; China 15.8%, Netherlands 13.6%, France 7.6%, U.S. 6.5%. **Exports:** $2.6 bil; China 55.4%, Italy 8.1%. **Tourism:** $41 mil. **Budget:** $2 bil. **Inflation:** 3.5%.

Transport: Railways: 452 mi. **Motor vehicles:** 7.5 per 1,000 pop. **Airports:** 9.

Communications: Telephone: 1.3 per 100 pop. **Mobile:** 94.2 per 100 pop. **Broadband:** 5.6 per 100 pop. **Internet:** 10.7%.

Health: Expend.: 6.4%. **Life expect.:** 60.4 male; 65.0 female. **Births:** 31.3 per 1,000 pop. **Deaths:** 8.2 per 1,000 pop. **Infant mortality:** 54.7 per 1,000 live births. **Undernourished:** 6.5%. **HIV:** 0.7%.

Education: Compulsory: ages 6-15. **Literacy:** 52.1%.

Embassy: 2129 Leroy Pl. NW 20008; 232-5700.

Website: www.mauritania.mr

A French protectorate from 1903, Mauritania became independent Nov. 28, 1960. It annexed the south of former Spanish Sahara (now Morocco-claimed Western Sahara) in 1976 but renounced its claim to the region after signing a peace treaty with the Saharan guerrillas of the Polisario Front, 1979.

Maaouiya Ould Sid Ahmed Taya took power in a military coup in 1984. Taya, a U.S. ally, was toppled in a bloodless coup in 2005. During Jan.-June 2006, up to 10,000 people tried to emigrate in handmade boats from Mauritania to Spain's Canary Islands; more than 1,700 died. Civilian rule was restored, 2006-07, but a 2008 military coup toppled the elected government. The coup leader, Gen. Mohamed Ould Abdel Aziz, won disputed presidential elections in 2009 and 2014. Security concerns, including a rising threat from al-Qaeda in the Islamic Maghreb, led the U.S. Peace Corps to remove its volunteers from Mauritania in Aug. 2009. Under a program launched in 2013, U.S. Special Operations troops began providing training and equipment to Mauritanian counterterrorism forces, to help combat Islamic extremists.

Major oil finds have recently been developed. Although slavery has been repeatedly abolished, most recently in 1981, and legislation mandating prison terms for slaveholders was enacted in 2007, more than 155,000 Mauritanians lived under conditions of servitude according to one 2014 estimate.

Mauritius

Republic of Mauritius

People: Population: 1,339,827. **Age distrib.:** <15: 20.7%; 65+: 8.8%. **Growth:** 0.6%. **Migrants:** 3.6%. **Pop. density:** 1,709.4 per sq mi, 660 per sq km. **Urban:** 39.7%. **Ethnic groups:** Indo-Mauritian 68%, Creole 27%, Sino-Mauritian 3%, Franco-Mauritian 2%. **Languages:** Creole, Bhojpuri, French, English (official). **Religions:** Hindu 48.5%, Roman Catholic 26.3%, Muslim 17.3%.

Geography: Total area: 788 sq mi, 2,040 sq km; **Land area:** 784 sq mi, 2,030 sq km. **Location:** In Indian O., 500 mi E of Madagascar, its nearest neighbor. **Topography:** A volcanic island nearly surrounded by coral reefs. A central plateau is encircled by peaks. **Arable land:** 37.4%. **Capital:** Port Louis, 135,496 (2014).

Government: Type: Parliamentary democracy. **Head of state:** Pres. Ameenah Gurib-Fakim; in office: June 5, 2015. **Head of gov.:** Prime Min. Sir Anerood Jugnauth; in office: Dec. 15, 2014. **Local divisions:** 9 districts, 3 dependencies. **Defense budget:** $84 mil. **Active troops:** No standing armed forces; 2,500 paramilitary. Special Mobile Force and coast guard provide security.

Economy: Industries: food proc. (largely sugar milling), textiles, clothing, mining, chemicals, metal prods. **Chief crops:** sugarcane, tea, corn, potatoes, bananas, pulses. **Natural resources:** fish. **Water:** 2,211 cu m per capita. **Electricity prod.:** 2.7 bil kWh. **Labor force:** agric. and fishing 9%; constr. and industry 30%; transp. and communication 7%; trade, restaurants, hotels 22%; finance 6%; other services 25%. **Unemployment:** 8.3%.

Finance: Monetary unit: Rupee (MUR) (34.95 = $1 U.S.). **GDP:** $23.4 bil; **per capita GDP:** $18,600; **GDP growth:** 3.2%. **Imports:** $5.4 bil; India 24.3%, China 14.7%, France 8.2%, South Africa 6.2%. **Exports:** $3.1 bil; UK 16.9%, France 15.1%, U.S. 10.1%, Italy 8.9%, South Africa 8.4%, Madagascar 6.2%, Spain 5.8%. **Tourism:** $1.4 bil. **Budget:** $3.3 bil. **Inflation:** 3.2%.

Transport: Motor vehicles: 165.4 per 1,000 pop. **Airports:** 2.

Communications: Telephone: 29.8 per 100 pop. **Mobile:** 132.2 per 100 pop. **Broadband:** 29.3 per 100 pop. **Internet:** 41.4%.

Health: Expend.: 4.8%. **Life expect.:** 71.9 male; 79.0 female. **Births:** 13.3 per 1,000 pop. **Deaths:** 6.9 per 1,000 pop. **Infant mortality:** 10.3 per 1,000 live births. **Undernourished:** <5%. **HIV:** 0.9%.

Education: Compulsory: ages 5-15. **Literacy:** 90.6%.

Embassy: 1709 N St. NW 20036; 244-1491.

Website: www.govmu.org

Mauritius was uninhabited when settled in 1638 by the Dutch, who introduced sugarcane. France took over in 1721, bringing African slaves. Britain ruled from 1810 to Mar. 12, 1968, bringing Indian workers for the sugar plantations.

Mauritius formally severed its association with the British crown Mar. 12, 1992. Since 2006, Mauritius has topped the Ibrahim Index of African Governance as the best-governed African country.

Mexico

United Mexican States

People: Population: 121,736,809. **Age distrib.:** <15: 27.6%; 65+: 6.8%. **Growth:** 1.2%. **Migrants:** 0.9%. **Pop. density:** 162.2 per sq mi, 62.6 per sq km. **Urban:** 79.2%. **Ethnic groups:** mestizo (Amerindian-Spanish) 62%, predom. Amerindian 21%, Amerindian 7%. **Languages:** Spanish, indigenous langs. (incl. Mayan, Nahuatl). **Religions:** Roman Catholic 82.7%, none 4.7%.

Geography: Total area: 758,449 sq mi, 1,964,375 sq km; **Land area:** 750,561 sq mi, 1,943,945 sq km. **Location:** Southern N America. U.S. on N, Guatemala and Belize on S. **Topography:** The Sierra Madre Occidental Mts. run NW-SE near the W coast; the Sierra Madre Oriental Mts. are near Gulf of Mexico. They join S of Mexico City. In between lies a dry central plateau (5,000-8,000 ft) with temperate vegetation. Coastal lowlands are tropical. About 45% of land is arid. **Arable land:** 11.9%. **Capital:** Mexico City, 20,998,543. **Cities:** Guadalajara, 4,843,241; Monterrey, 4,512,572; Puebla, 2,984,048; Toluca de Lerdo, 2,164,006; Tijuana, 1,986,787; León de los Aldamas, 1,806,862.

Government: Type: Federal republic. **Head of state and gov.:** Pres. Enrique Peña Nieto; in office: Dec. 1, 2012. **Local divisions:** 31 states, 1 federal district. **Defense budget:** $6.55 bil. **Active troops:** 266,550.

Economy: Industries: food and beverages, tobacco, chemicals, iron and steel, petroleum, mining, textiles, clothing, motor vehicles. **Chief crops:** corn, wheat, soybeans, rice, beans, cotton, coffee, fruit, tomatoes. **Natural resources:** petroleum, silver, copper, gold, lead, zinc, nat. gas, timber. **Water:** 3,776 cu m per capita. **Crude oil reserves:** 9.8 bil bbls. **Electricity prod.:** 278.7 bil kWh. **Labor force:** agric. 13.4%, industry 24.1%, services 61.9%. **Unemployment:** 4.9%.

Finance: Monetary unit: Peso (MXN) (16.82 = $1 U.S.). **GDP:** $2.1 tril; **per capita GDP:** $17,900; **GDP growth:** 2.1%. **Imports:** $407.1 bil; U.S. 49.1%, China 16.1%. **Exports:** $406.4 bil; U.S. 78.8%. **Tourism:** $16.3 bil. **Budget:** $348.4 bil. **Inflation:** 4%.

Transport: Railways: 9,562 mi. **Motor vehicles:** 298.4 per 1,000 pop. **Airports:** 243.

Communications: Telephone: 17 per 100 pop. **Mobile:** 82.5 per 100 pop. **Broadband:** 13.8 per 100 pop. **Internet:** 44.4%.

Health: Expend.: 6.2%. **Life expect.:** 72.9 male; 78.6 female. **Births:** 18.8 per 1,000 pop. **Deaths:** 5.3 per 1,000 pop. **Infant mortality:** 12.2 per 1,000 live births. **Undernourished:** <5%. **HIV:** 0.2%.

Education: Compulsory: ages 4-17. **Literacy:** 95.1%.

Embassy: 1911 Pennsylvania Ave. NW 20006; 728-1600.

Website: www.presidencia.gob.mx

Mexico was the site of advanced civilizations. The Mayans, an agricultural people, moved up from Yucatan, built huge stone pyramids and invented a calendar. The Toltecs were overcome by the Aztecs, who founded Tenochtitlan 1325 CE, now Mexico City. Hernán Cortés, Spanish conquistador, destroyed the Aztec empire, 1519-21. After three centuries of Spanish rule the people revolted under Fr. Miguel Hidalgo y Costilla, 1810, Fr. Morelos y Pavón, 1812, and Gen. Agustín Iturbide, who made himself emperor as Agustín I, 1822. A republic was declared in 1823.

Mexican territory extended into the present American SW and California. Texas established a republic in 1836, and Mexico lost lands north of the Rio Grande during the U.S.-Mexican War, 1846-48.

The French supported an Austrian archduke on the Mexican throne as Maximilian I, 1864-67. He was deposed in an uprising led by Benito Juárez. Dictatorial rule by Porfirio Díaz, president 1877-80, 1884-1911, led to a period of rebellion and factional fighting. A new constitution in 1917 brought reform.

The Institutional Revolutionary Party (PRI) dominated politics from 1929 until the late 1990s. Radical opposition, including some guerrilla activity, was contained by strong measures. Gains in agriculture, industry, and social services were achieved, but poverty remained widespread. Vast oil reserves were discovered, 1970s-80s, but inflation and a drop in world oil prices aggravated Mexico's economic problems in the 1980s. Mexico signed the North American Free Trade Agreement (NAFTA) with the U.S. and Canada in 1992; it took effect Jan. 1, 1994.

After guerrillas of the Zapatista National Liberation Army (EZLN) rebelled Jan. 1994, a tentative peace accord was reached Mar. 2. The presidential candidate of the governing PRI, Luis Donaldo Colosio Murrieta, was assassinated at a political rally in Tijuana, Mar. 23. The new PRI candidate, Ernesto Zedillo Ponce de León, won election Aug. 21, 1994.

An austerity plan and pledges of aid from the U.S. saved Mexico's currency from collapse in early 1995. Popular Revolutionary Army guerrillas launched coordinated attacks on government targets in Aug. 1996. In 1997 elections, the PRI lost a congressional majority for the first time since 1929.

In the 2000 presidential election, the PRI lost for the first time in over 7 decades; the winner, Vicente Fox Quesada of the National Action Party (PAN), took office Dec. 1, 2000. The PAN candidate, conservative Felipe Calderón Hinojosa, won the 2006 presidential election. Despite a government crackdown on drug cartels, drug-related violence intensified. The cumulative death toll in the drug war exceeded 47,500, Dec. 2006-Sept. 2012. Enrique Peña Nieto (PRI) won the 2012 presidential election. He continued the policy of using federal troops to combat drug gangs. Notorious drug-gang leader Joaquín Guzmán Loera was captured, Feb. 22, 2014. However, he escaped from Mexico's highest-security prison, July 11, 2015. Peña Nieto passed 2013 constitutional changes intended to bring greater competition to key industries, including oil, telecommunications, and broadcasting. Congress gave final approval to new regulations, Aug. 2014, opening the oil industry (nationalized in 1938) to foreign companies and other private investment. The Supreme Court, June 3, 2015, declared unconstitutional state laws barring gay couples from marrying, in effect legalizing same-sex marriage nationwide.

Micronesia

Federated States of Micronesia

People: Population: 105,216. **Age distrib.:** <15: 31.3%; 65+: 3.5%. **Growth:** –0.5%. **Migrants:** 2.5%. **Pop. density:** 388.2 per sq mi, 149.9 per sq km. **Urban:** 22.4%. **Ethnic groups:** Chuukese/Mortlockese 49.3%, Pohnpeian 29.8%, Kosraean 6.3%, Yapese 5.7%, Yap outer islander 5.1%. **Languages:** English (official), Chuukese, Kosrean, Pohnpeian, Yapese, Ulithian, Woleaian, Nukuoro, Kapingamarangi. **Religions:** Roman Catholic 54.7%, Protestant 41.1% (incl. Congregational 38.5%).

Geography: Total area: 271 sq mi, 702 sq km; **Land area:** 271 sq mi, 702 sq km. **Location:** Consists of 607 islands in W Pacific O. **Topography:** Mountainous islands and coral atolls; volcanic outcroppings on Pohnpei, Kosrae, and Truk. Tropical climate. **Arable land:** 2.9%. **Capital:** Palikir, 6,821 (2014).

Government: Type: Constitutional govt. in free association with U.S. **Head of state and gov.:** Pres. Peter M. Christian; in office: May 11, 2015. **Local divisions:** 4 states. **Defense budget/active troops:** NA.

Economy: Industries: tourism, constr., specialized aquaculture, craft items. **Chief crops:** taro, yams, coconuts, bananas, cassava, kava, Kosraen citrus, betel nuts, black pepper. **Natural resources:** timber, marine prods., deep-seabed minerals, phosphate. **Water:** NA. **Labor force:** agric. 0.9%, industry 5.2%, services 93.9%. Two-thirds of labor force are govt. employees. **Unemployment:** NA.

Finance: Monetary unit: U.S. Dollar (USD). **GDP:** $312 mil (supplemented by grant aid, avg. perhaps $100 mil annually); **per capita GDP:** $3,000; **GDP growth:** 0.1%. **Imports** (2013): $258.5 mil. **Exports** (2013): $88.3 mil. **Tourism:** $24 mil. **Budget** (FY12/13 est.): $192.1 mil. **Inflation:** NA.

Transport: Airports: 6.

Communications: Telephone: 6.8 per 100 pop. **Mobile** (2013): 30.3 per 100 pop. **Broadband:** NA. **Internet:** 29.7%.

Health: Expend.: 12.8%. **Life expect.:** 70.6 male; 74.8 female. **Births:** 20.5 per 1,000 pop. **Deaths:** 4.2 per 1,000 pop. **Infant mortality:** 21.2 per 1,000 live births. **Undernourished:** NA. **HIV:** NA.

Education: Compulsory: NA. **Literacy:** NA.

Embassy: 1725 N St. NW 20036; 223-4383.

Website: micronesia.fm

Micronesia, formerly known as the Caroline Islands, was ruled successively by Spain, Germany, Japan, and the U.S. The nation gained independence under a compact of free association with the U.S., Nov. 1986, and was admitted to the UN in 1991. Micronesian officials have repeatedly warned of the dangers to their country of rising sea levels linked to global climate change.

Moldova

Republic of Moldova

People: Population: 3,546,847. **Age distrib.:** <15: 17.9%; 65+: 11.7%. **Growth:** –1%. **Migrants:** 11.2%. **Pop. density:** 279.3 per sq mi, 107.8 per sq km. **Urban:** 45%. **Ethnic groups:** Moldovan 75.8%, Ukrainian 8.4%, Russian 5.9%, Gagauz 4.4%, Romanian 2.2%. **Languages:** Moldovan (official; virtually the same as Romanian), Romanian, Russian, Ukrainian, Gagauz. **Religions:** Orthodox 93.3%.

Geography: Total area: 13,070 sq mi, 33,851 sq km; **Land area:** 12,699 sq mi, 32,891 sq km. **Location:** Eastern Europe. Romania on W; Ukraine on N, and E, and S. **Topography:** Landlocked; mainly hilly plains with steppelands in S near Black Sea. **Arable land:** 55.2%. **Capital:** Chisëinău, 725,432.

Government: Type: Republic. **Head of state:** Pres. Nicolae Timofti; in office: Mar. 23, 2012. **Head of gov.:** Prime Min. Valeriu Strelet; in office: July 30, 2015. **Local divisions:** 32 raions, 3 municipalities, 2 territorial units (1 autonomous). **Defense budget:** $25 mil. **Active troops:** 5,350.

Economy: Industries: sugar, vegetable oil, food proc., agric. machinery, foundry equip., refrigerators and freezers. **Chief crops:** vegetables, fruits, grapes, grain, sugar beets, sunflower seeds, tobacco. **Natural resources:** lignite, phosphorites, gypsum, limestone. **Water:** 3,341 cu m per capita. **Electricity prod.:** 5.5 bil kWh. **Labor force:** agric. 26.4%, industry 13.2%, services 60.4%. **Unemployment:** 5.1%.

Finance: Monetary unit: Leu (MDL) (19.28 = $1 U.S.). **GDP:** $17.7 bil; **per capita GDP:** $5,000; **GDP growth:** 4.6%. **Imports:** $5.6 bil; Russia 23.3%, Romania 15.1%, Ukraine 14%, Germany 7.6%. **Exports:** $2.6 bil; Russia 18.4%, Romania 16.7%, Turkey 10.1%, Italy 9.6%, Germany 5.6%, Ukraine 5%. **Tourism:** $233 mil. **Budget:** $3.2 bil (natl. public budget). **Inflation:** 5.1%.

Transport: Railways: 728 mi. **Airports:** 5.

Communications: Telephone: 35.2 per 100 pop. **Mobile:** 108 per 100 pop. **Broadband:** 47.3 per 100 pop. **Internet:** 46.6%.

Health: Expend.: 11.7%. **Life expect.:** 66.6 male; 74.5 female. **Births:** 12.0 per 1,000 pop. **Deaths:** 12.6 per 1,000 pop. **Infant mortality:** 12.6 per 1,000 live births. **Undernourished:** <5%. **HIV:** 0.6%.

Education: Compulsory: ages 7-15. **Literacy:** 99.4%.

Embassy: 2101 S St. NW 20008; 667-1130.

Website: www.moldova.md

In 1918, Romania annexed all of Bessarabia that Russia had acquired from Turkey in 1812 by the Treaty of Bucharest. In 1924, the Soviet Union established the Moldavian Autonomous Soviet Socialist Republic on the eastern bank of the Dniester. It was merged with the Romanian-speaking districts of Bessarabia in 1940 to form the Moldavian SSR.

During WWII, Romania, allied with Germany, occupied the area. It was recaptured by the USSR in 1944. Moldova declared independence Aug. 27, 1991, prior to the dissolution of the USSR Dec. 26, 1991.

Fighting erupted Mar. 1992 in the Trans-Dniester region between Moldovan security forces and Slavic separatists—ethnic Russians and ethnic Ukrainians—who feared Moldova's merging with neighboring Romania. In a 1994 plebiscite, voters in Moldova supported independence, without unification with Romania.

Defying the Moldovan government, voters in the breakaway Trans-Dniester region held legislative elections and approved a separatist constitution in 1995. A peace accord with Trans-Dniester separatists was signed in Moscow in 1997. In a 2006 referendum, Trans-Dniester voters overwhelmingly supported independence from Moldova and eventual union with Russia. The Communists gained legislative majorities in 2001 and 2005 but were outpolled by a fragile coalition of pro-Western parties in 2009 and 2010. The pro-Western Nicolae Timofti became president in 2012. Parliament passed a no-confidence motion against Prime Min. Vlad Filat Mar. 5, 2013, forcing his resignation. Iurie Leanca, chosen the new prime min. May 31, supported Timofti's plan for EU integration. Moldova and the EU signed an Association Agreement, June 27, 2014. Pro-Western parties won a narrow majority in Nov. 30, 2014, parliamentary elections. Chiril Gaburici became prime min., Feb. 18, 2015. In the wake of a banking scandal involving the disappearance of hundreds of millions of dollars in bad loans, Gaburici resigned, June 12. Valeriu Strelet became prime min. July 30.

Monaco

Principality of Monaco

People: Population: 30,535. **Age distrib.:** <15: 11.4%; 65+: 30.4%. **Growth:** 0.1%. **Migrants:** 64.2%. **Pop. density:** 39,542.6 per sq mi, 15,267.5 per sq km. **Urban:** 100%. **Ethnic groups:** French (official) 47%, Monegasque 16%, Italian 16%. **Languages:** French (official), English, Italian, Monegasque. **Religions:** Roman Catholic (official) 90%.

Geography: Total area: 0.77 sq mi, 2 sq km; **Land area:** 0.77 sq mi, 2 sq km. **Location:** NW Mediterranean coast. France to W, N, and E. **Topography:** Principality rises from port up to Monaco-Ville on a high promontory. **Arable land:** 0%. **Capital:** Monaco.

Government: Type: Constitutional monarchy. **Head of state:** Prince Albert II; in office: Apr. 6, 2005. **Head of gov.:** Min. of State Michel Roger; in office: Mar. 29, 2010. **Local divisions:** no first-order admin. divisions. **Defense budget/active troops:** NA.

Economy: Industries: banking, insurance, tourism, constr. **Water:** NA. **Labor force:** industry 16.1%, services 83.9%. **Unemployment:** NA.

Finance: Monetary unit: Euro (EUR) (0.89 = $1 U.S.). **GDP** (2013): $6.8 bil; **per capita GDP** (2013): $78,700; **GDP growth** (2013): 9.3%. **Imports** (2011): $1.2 bil; Europe 70.4%, Asia 20.8%. **Exports** (2011): $1.1 bil; Europe 73.2%, Africa 14.6%, America 5.2%. (Full customs integration with France. Also participates in EU market system through customs unions with France.) **Budget** (2011 est.): $1.1 bil. **Inflation:** NA.

Transport: NA

Communications: Telephone: 133 per 100 pop. **Mobile:** 88.5 per 100 pop. **Broadband:** 53.7 per 100 pop. **Internet:** 92.4%.

Health: Expend.: 4.4%. **Life expect.:** 85.6 male; 93.6 female. **Births:** 6.7 per 1,000 pop. **Deaths:** 9.2 per 1,000 pop. **Infant mortality:** 1.8 per 1,000 live births. **Undernourished:** <5%. **HIV:** NA.

Education: Compulsory: ages 6-16. **Literacy:** 99%.

Embassy: 3400 International Dr. NW, Ste. 2K-100, 20008; 234-1530.

Website: www.gouv.mc

An independent principality for over 300 years, Monaco has belonged to the House of Grimaldi since 1297, except during the French Revolution. It was placed under the protectorate of Sardinia in 1815, and under France, 1861. The Prince of Monaco was an absolute ruler until the 1911 constitution. Monaco was admitted to the UN in 1993. Monaco is noted for its mild climate, magnificent scenery, elegant casinos, and Formula One Grand Prix auto race. Prince Rainier III, who ruled Monaco from 1949 and turned it into one of Europe's top tourist spots, died in 2005 and was succeeded by his son, Albert II.

Mongolia

People: Population: 2,992,908. **Age distrib.:** <15: 26.9%; 65+: 4.1%. **Growth:** 1.3%. **Migrants:** 0.6%. **Pop. density:** 5 per sq mi, 1.9 per sq km. **Urban:** 72%. **Ethnic groups:** Khalkh 81.9%, Kazak 3.8%, Dorvod 2.7%, Bayad 2.1%. **Languages:** Khalkha Mongol (official), Turkic, Russian. **Religions:** Buddhist 53%, Muslim 3%, Shamanist 2.9%, none 38.6%.

Geography: Total area: 603,909 sq mi, 1,564,116 sq km; **Land area:** 599,831 sq mi, 1,553,556 sq km. **Location:** E Central Asia. Russia on N, China on E, W, and S. **Topography:** Mostly high plateau with mountains, salt lakes, and vast grasslands. Gobi Desert in S. **Arable land:** 0.4%. **Capital:** Ulaanbaatar, 1,377,308.

Government: Type: Parliamentary. **Head of state:** Pres. Tsakhiagiin Elbegdorj; in office: June 18, 2009. **Head of gov.:** Prime. Min. Chimed Saikhanbileg; in office: Nov. 21, 2014. **Local divisions:** 21 provinces, 1 municipality. **Defense budget:** $105 mil. **Active troops:** 10,000.

Economy: Industries: constr. and constr. materials, mining, oil, food and beverages, animal prods. proc., cashmere and natural fiber mfg. **Chief crops:** wheat, barley, vegetables, forage crops. **Natural resources:** oil, coal, copper, molybdenum, tungsten, phosphates, tin, nickel, zinc, fluorspar, gold, silver, iron. **Water:** 12,258 cu m per capita. **Electricity prod.:** 4.5 bil kWh. **Labor force:** agric. 28.6%, industry 21%, services 50.4%. **Unemployment:** 4.9%.

Finance: Monetary unit: Tughrik (MNT) (1,985.00 = $1 U.S.). **GDP:** $34.8 bil; **per capita GDP:** $11,900; **GDP growth:** 7.8%. **Imports:** $5.2 bil; China 37.8%, Russia 27.6%, South Korea 6.2%. **Exports:** $5.8 bil; China 90%. **Tourism:** $195 mil. **Budget:** $3.7 bil. **Inflation:** 13%.

Transport: Railways: 1,128 mi. **Airports:** 15.

Communications: Telephone: 7.9 per 100 pop. **Mobile:** 105.1 per 100 pop. **Broadband:** 24.7 per 100 pop. **Internet:** 27%.

Health: Expend.: 6.3%. **Life expect.:** 65.0 male; 73.8 female. **Births:** 20.3 per 1,000 pop. **Deaths:** 6.4 per 1,000 pop. **Infant mortality:** 22.4 per 1,000 live births. **Undernourished:** 22.4%. **HIV:** NA.

Education: Compulsory: ages 6-14. **Literacy:** 98.4%.

Embassy: 2833 M St. NW 20007; 333-7117.

Website: www.pmis.gov.mn

One of the world's oldest countries, Mongolia reached the zenith of its power in the 13th cent. when Genghis Khan and his successors conquered all of China and extended their influence as far west as Hungary and Poland. In later centuries, the empire dissolved and Mongolia became a province of China.

With the advent of the 1911 Chinese revolution, Mongolia, with Russian backing, declared its independence. A Communist regime was established, 1921. The Mongolian Communist Party yielded its monopoly on power, 1990. A new constitution took effect, 1992.

Mongolia sent troops to U.S.-led operations in Afghanistan (2001); as of June 2015, 120 remained. Riots followed 2008 parliamentary elections, won by the ruling Mongolian People's Revolutionary Party (MPRP). In 2009 presidential voting, former Prime Min. Tsakhiagiin Elbergdorj (1998, 2004-06), the Democratic Party (DP) candidate, defeated the MPRP's incumbent Pres. Nambaryn Enkhbayar. A 2012 legislative election gave the DP the most seats in parliament, and Norov Altankhuyag became prime min. Aug. 9. Elbergdorj was reelected June 27, 2013. With the economy slumping, Altankhuyag was replaced as prime minister by Chimed Saikhanbileg (also of the DP), Nov. 21, 2014. Rio Tinto mining company concluded an agreement with the government, May 19, 2015, for expansion of a large gold and copper mine.

Montenegro

People: Population: 647,073. **Age distrib.:** <15: 15.2%; 65+: 14.4%. **Growth:** –0.4%. **Migrants:** 8.2%. **Pop. density:** 124.6 per sq mi, 48.1 per sq km. **Urban:** 64%. **Ethnic groups:** Montenegrin 45%, Serbian 28.7%, Bosniak 8.7%, Albanian 4.9%, Muslim 3.3%. **Languages:** Serbian, Montenegrin (official), Bosnian, Albanian, Serbo-Croat. **Religions:** Orthodox 72.1%, Muslim 19.1%, Catholic 3.4%.

Geography: Total area: 5,333 sq mi, 13,812 sq km; **Land area:** 5,194 sq mi, 13,452 sq km. **Location:** Balkan Peninsula in SE Europe. Bosnia and Herzegovina on N and W, Serbia on E, Albania on SE, Croatia on W. **Topography:** Mostly rugged and mountainous, with few arable regions, mostly along the Zeta R. Highly indented narrow coastline. **Arable land:** 12.8%. **Capital:** Podgorica, 164,999 (2014).

Government: Type: Republic. **Head of state:** Pres. Filip Vujanovic; in office: Apr. 6, 2008. **Head of gov.:** Prime. Min. Milo Djukanovic; in office: Dec. 4, 2012. **Local divisions:** 23 municipalities. **Defense budget:** $80 mil. **Active troops:** 2,080.

Economy: Industries: steelmaking, aluminum, agric. proc., consumer goods, tourism. **Chief crops:** tobacco, potatoes, citrus fruits, olives, grapes. **Natural resources:** bauxite, hydroelectricity. **Water:** NA. **Electricity prod.:** 2.7 bil kWh. **Labor force:** agric. 5.3%, industry 17.9%, services 76.8%. **Unemployment:** 19.8%.

Finance: Monetary unit: Euro (EUR) (0.89 = $1 U.S.). **GDP:** $9.4 bil; **per capita GDP:** $15,000; **GDP growth:** 1.1%. **Imports:** $2 bil; (2012) Serbia 29.3%, Greece 8.7%, China 7.1%. **Exports:** $370.2 mil; (2012) Croatia 22.7%, Serbia 22.7%, Slovenia 7.8%. **Tourism:** $906 mil. **Budget:** $1.6 bil. **Inflation:** –0.7%.

Transport: Railways: 155 mi. **Airports:** 5.

Communications: Telephone: 26.5 per 100 pop. **Mobile:** 163 per 100 pop. **Broadband:** 23.1 per 100 pop. **Internet:** 61%.

Health: Expend.: 7.6%. **Life expect.:** 75.5 male; 81.6 female. **Births:** 10.4 per 1,000 pop. **Deaths:** 9.4 per 1,000 pop. **Infant mortality:** 8.7 per 1,000 live births. **Undernourished:** <5%. **HIV:** NA.

Education: Compulsory: ages 6-14. **Literacy:** 98.7%.

Embassy: 1610 New Hampshire Ave. NW 20009; 234-6108.

Website: www.gov.me

Part of the medieval Serbian Kingdom, Montenegro preserved its autonomy for centuries because of its mountainous terrain. After WWI, it was part of the Kingdom of Serbs, Croats, and Slovenes, later renamed Yugoslavia. Italian forces occupied parts of Montenegro during WWII. In 1945, with the establishment of a federal Yugoslavia under Communist rule, Montenegro became one of 6 constituent republics.

In Apr. 1992, after 4 other republics had declared independence, Montenegro and Serbia reconstituted themselves as the Federal Republic of Yugoslavia. Because of its ties with Serbia, Montenegro was a target of NATO airstrikes during the Kosovo war, Mar.-June 1999. The republic sought closer ties with the West, however, and worked to reduce its political and economic dependence on Serbia. A 2006 referendum on independence passed with barely more than the 55% majority required. Montenegro declared independence June 3, 2006, and was admitted as a UN member June 28. It applied, in 2008, to join the EU.

Morocco

Kingdom of Morocco

People: Population: 33,322,699. **Age distrib.:** <15: 26.4%; 65+: 6.4%. **Growth:** 1%. **Migrants:** 0.2%. **Pop. density:** 193.4

per sq mi, 74.7 per sq km. **Urban:** 60.2%. **Ethnic groups:** Arab-Berber 99%. **Languages:** Arabic (official), Berber langs., French (lang. of business, govt., diplomacy). **Religions:** Muslim 99% (official; virtually all Sunni).

Geography: Total area: 172,414 sq mi, 446,550 sq km; **Land area:** 172,317 sq mi, 446,300 sq km. **Location:** NW coast of Africa. Western Sahara on S, Algeria on E, Spain on N. **Topography:** Consists of 5 natural regions: mountain ranges (Riff in N, Middle Atlas, Upper Atlas, and Anti-Atlas); rich plains in W; alluvial plains in SW; well-cultivated plateaus in center; pre-Sahara arid zone extending from SE. **Arable land:** 18%. **Capital:** Rabat, 1,966,802. **Cities:** Dar-el-Beida (Casablanca), 3,514,958; Fès, 1,172,112; Marrakech, 1,133,609.

Government: Type: Constitutional monarchy. **Head of state:** King Mohammed VI; in office: July 30, 1999. **Head of gov.:** Prime Min. Abdelilah Benkirane; in office: Nov. 29, 2011. **Local divisions:** 15 regions (not incl. territory in Western Sahara). **Defense budget:** $3.86 bil. **Active troops:** 195,800.

Economy: Industries: automotive parts, phosphate mining and proc., food proc., aerospace, food proc., leather goods. **Chief crops:** barley, wheat, citrus fruits, grapes, vegetables, olives. **Natural resources:** phosphates, iron ore, manganese, lead, zinc, fish, salt. **Water:** 879 cu m per capita. **Crude oil reserves:** 680 bbls. **Electricity prod.:** 25.4 bil kWh. **Labor force:** agric. 39.1%, industry 20.3%, services 40.5%. **Unemployment:** 9.2%.

Finance: Monetary unit: Dirham (MAD) (9.70 = $1 U.S.). **GDP:** $252.4 bil; **per capita GDP:** $7,600; **GDP growth:** 2.9%. **Imports:** $40 bil; Spain 14%, France 12.7%, China 7.1%, U.S. 6.9%, Saudi Arabia 6.5%, Italy 5.3%. **Exports:** $19.6 bil; France 20.9%, Spain 19.9%, Brazil 5.8%. **Tourism:** $7.1 bil. **Budget:** $35 bil. **Inflation:** 0.4%.

Transport: Railways: 1,284 mi. **Motor vehicles:** 103.4 per 1,000 pop. **Airports:** 31.

Communications: Telephone: 7.4 per 100 pop. **Mobile:** 131.7 per 100 pop. **Broadband:** 15 per 100 pop. **Internet:** 56.8%.

Health: Expend.: 6.4%. **Life expect.:** 73.6 male; 79.9 female. **Births:** 18.2 per 1,000 pop. **Deaths:** 4.8 per 1,000 pop. **Infant mortality:** 23.6 per 1,000 live births. **Undernourished:** <5%. **HIV:** 0.1%.

Education: Compulsory: ages 6-14. **Literacy:** 68.5%.

Embassy: 1601 21st St. NW 20009; 462-7980.

Website: www.maroc.ma

Berbers were the region's original inhabitants, followed by Carthaginians and Romans. Arabs conquered it in 683. In the 11th and 12th cents., a Berber empire ruled all NW Africa and most of Spain from Morocco.

Part of Morocco came under Spanish rule in the 19th cent.; France controlled the rest in the early 20th. Tribal uprisings lasted from 1911 to 1933. Independence was achieved Mar. 2, 1956. Tangier, an internationalized seaport, was incorporated into Morocco, 1956. Ifni, a Spanish enclave, was ceded in 1969. Morocco annexed the disputed territory of Western Sahara during the second half of the 1970s.

King Hassan II assumed the throne in 1961, reigning until his death in 1999; he was succeeded by his eldest son. A bicameral legislature was established in 1997.

Five terrorist attacks in Casablanca May 16, 2003, left 45 people dead, including 12 suicide bombers; the government blamed Salafia Jihadia, an al-Qaeda-linked group. Following a series of suicide bombings in 2007, the government stepped up its campaign against militant Islamists. Following Arab Spring street demonstrations Feb.-Mar. 2011, the monarchy implemented modest constitutional reforms. Throughout 2011, Moroccans staged protests of what they saw as social injustices, including persistent unemployment, unjust detentions, and lack of free speech. The moderate Islamist Justice and Development Party won a plurality in Nov. 25, 2011, parliamentary elections, and Abdelilah Benkirane was named prime min.

Western Sahara

Western Sahara, formerly the protectorate of Spanish Sahara, is bounded on the N by Morocco, the NE by Algeria, the E and S by Mauritania, and the W by the Atlantic O. Phosphates are the major resource. Area 102,703 sq mi; pop. (2015 est.) 570,866. Capital is Laayoune; pop. (2014 est.) 262,360. Half of the labor force is employed in agriculture, the other half in industry and services.

Spain withdrew in Feb. 1976. On Apr. 14, 1976, Morocco annexed over 70,000 sq mi, with the remainder annexed by Mauritania. The Polisario Front guerrilla movement, which proclaimed the region independent Feb. 27, launched attacks with Algerian support. After Mauritania signed a treaty with Polisario Aug. 5, 1979, Morocco occupied Mauritania's portion of Western Sahara.

After years of bitter fighting, Morocco controlled the main urban areas, but Polisario guerrillas moved freely in the vast, sparsely populated deserts. The two sides implemented a cease-fire in 1991, when a UN peacekeeping force (MINURSO) was established with a mandate to prepare for a referendum on self-determination as early as 1992; as of June 30, 2015, MINURSO had 210 uniformed personnel in Western Sahara. A referendum had still not been held.

Mozambique

Republic of Mozambique

People: Population: 25,303,113. **Age distrib.:** <15: 45.1%; 65+: 2.9%. **Growth:** 2.5%. **Migrants:** 0.8%. **Pop. density:** 83.3 per sq mi, 32.2 per sq km. **Urban:** 32.2%. **Ethnic groups:** African (incl. Makhuwa, Tsonga, Lomwe, Sena) 99.66%. **Languages:** Emakhuwa, Portuguese (official), Xichangana, Cisena, Elomwe, other Mozambican langs. **Religions:** Roman Catholic 28.4%, Muslim 17.9%, Zionist Christian 15.5%, Protestant 12.2% (incl. Pentecostal 10.9%), none 18.7%.

Geography: Total area: 308,642 sq mi, 799,380 sq km; **Land area:** 303,623 sq mi, 786,380 sq km. **Location:** SE coast of Africa. Tanzania on N; Malawi, Zambia, Zimbabwe on W; South Africa, Swaziland on S. **Topography:** Coastal lowlands comprise nearly half the country with plateaus rising in steps to mountains along western border. **Arable land:** 7.2%. **Capital:** Maputo, 1,187,214. **Cities:** Matola, 937,176.

Government: Type: Republic. **Head of state:** Pres. Filipe Jacinto Nyusi; in office: Jan. 15, 2015. **Head of gov.:** Prime Min. Carlos Agostinho do Rosario; in office: Jan. 17, 2015. **Local divisions:** 10 provinces, 1 city. **Defense budget:** $35 mil. **Active troops:** 11,200.

Economy: Industries: aluminum, petroleum prods., chemicals, textiles, cement, glass, asbestos, tobacco, food, beverages. **Chief crops:** cotton, cashew nuts, sugarcane, tea, cassava, corn, coconuts, sisal, citrus and tropical fruits, potatoes, sunflowers. **Natural resources:** coal, titanium, nat. gas, hydropower, tantalum, graphite. **Water:** 8,404 cu m per capita. **Electricity prod.:** 15 bil kWh. **Labor force:** agric. 81%, industry 6%, services 13%. **Unemployment:** 8.3%.

Finance: Monetary unit: Metical (MZN) (41.00 = $1 U.S.). **GDP:** $31.1 bil; **per capita GDP:** $1,200; **GDP growth:** 7.4%. **Imports:** $9 bil; South Africa 26%, India 13.9%, China 12.6%. **Exports:** $4.3 bil; South Africa 30.5%, Italy 9.8%, China 9.4%, Belgium 8%, Spain 6.1%, India 5.1%. **Tourism:** $241 mil. **Budget:** $7 bil. **Inflation:** 2.6%.

Transport: Railways: 2,975 mi. **Motor vehicles:** 3.3 per 1,000 pop. **Airports:** 21.

Communications: Telephone: 0.3 per 100 pop. **Mobile:** 69.7 per 100 pop. **Broadband:** 1.7 per 100 pop. **Internet:** 5.9%.

Health: Expend.: 6.4%. **Life expect.:** 52.2 male; 53.7 female. **Births:** 38.6 per 1,000 pop. **Deaths:** 12.1 per 1,000 pop. **Infant mortality:** 70.2 per 1,000 live births. **Undernourished:** 27.9%. **HIV:** 10.6%.

Education: Compulsory: NA. **Literacy:** 58.8%.

Embassy: 1525 New Hampshire Ave. NW 20036; 293-7146.

Website: www.portaldogoverno.gov.mz

The first Portuguese post on the Mozambique coast was established in 1505 on the trade route to Asia. Mozambique became independent June 25, 1975, after a 10-year war against the Portuguese. The 1974 revolution in Portugal paved the way for an orderly transfer of power to Frelimo (Front for the Liberation of Mozambique).

The Frelimo government, headed by Pres. Samora Machel, a former guerrilla commander, gradually transitioned to a Communist system. Most of the country's whites emigrated. In the 1980s, severe drought and civil war caused famine and heavy loss of life. Pres. Machel was killed in a plane crash just inside the South African border, Oct. 19, 1986. Frelimo formally abandoned Marxist-Leninism in 1989, and a new constitution, effective Nov. 30, 1990, established multiparty elections and a free-market economy.

A 1992 peace agreement ended hostilities between the government and the Mozambique National Resistance (MNR). Repatriation of 1.7 mil Mozambican refugees ended June 1995.

In Feb.-Mar. 2000, heavy floods claimed more than 600 lives and devastated the economy. Another flood crisis, Jan.-Mar. 2008, claimed some 700 lives and displaced 650,000 people.

Frelimo retained its hold on power under Pres. Joaquim Chissano (1986-2005) and his successor, Pres. Armando Guebuza, elected in 2004, reelected in 2009. Frelimo candidate Filipe Jacinto Nyusi won the Oct. 15, 2014, presidential election, and the party won almost 60% of the seats in legislative elections the same day. A new penal code, in effect June 29, 2015, decriminalized homosexual sex and abortion.

Abundant energy resources have the potential to increase economic growth. Natural gas reserves were estimated at 100 tril cu ft (third-largest in Africa) as of 2015. Oil exploration continued following initial discoveries of onshore and offshore deposits.

Myanmar

(Burma)

Union of Myanmar

People: Population: 56,320,206. **Age distrib.:** <15: 26.1%; 65+: 5.4%. **Growth:** 1%. **Migrants:** 0.2%. **Pop. density:** 223.2 per sq mi, 86.2 per sq km. **Urban:** 34.1%. **Ethnic groups:** Burman 68%, Shan 9%, Karen 7%, Rakhine 4%, Chinese 3%, Indian 2%, Mon 2%. **Languages:** Burmese (official). **Religions:** Buddhist 89%, Christian 4%, Muslim 4%.

Geography: Total area: 261,228 sq mi, 676,578 sq km; **Land area:** 252,321 sq mi, 653,508 sq km. **Location:** Between S and SE Asia, on Bay of Bengal. Bangladesh, India on W; China, Laos, Thailand on E. **Topography:** Surrounding mountains on W, N, and E. Dense forests cover much of nation. N-S rivers provide habitable valleys, especially the Irrawaddy, navigable for 900 mi. Tropical monsoon climate. **Arable land:** 16.6%. **Capital:** Nay Pyi Taw, 1,029,712. **Cities:** Yangon, 4,801,930; Mandalay, 1,166,906.

Government: Type: Parliamentary govt. took power in Mar. 2011. **Head of state and gov.:** Pres. Thein Sein; in office: Feb. 3, 2011. **Local divisions:** 7 regions, 7 states, 1 union territory. **Defense budget:** $2.43 bil. **Active troops:** 406,000.

Economy: Industries: agric. proc.; wood and wood prods.; copper, tin, tungsten, iron; cement, constr. materials; pharmaceuticals. **Chief crops:** rice, pulses, beans, sesame, groundnuts, sugarcane. **Natural resources:** petroleum, timber, tin, antimony, zinc, copper, tungsten, lead, coal, marble, limestone, prec. stones, nat. gas, hydropower. **Water:** 21,931 cu m per capita. **Crude oil reserves:** 50 mil bbls. **Electricity prod.:** 10.5 bil kWh. **Labor force:** agric. 70%, industry 7%, services 23%. **Unemployment:** 3.4%.

Finance: Monetary unit: Kyat (MMK) (1,273.00 = $1 U.S.). **GDP:** $242 bil; **per capita GDP:** $4,700; **GDP growth:** 7.7%. **Imports:** $12.5 bil; China 40%, Thailand 20.3%, Singapore 12.2%, Japan 5.7%. **Exports:** $10.3 bil; Thailand 35%, China 24.5%, India 12%, Japan 6.6%. (Import/export figures grossly underestimated due to value of goods smuggled into and out of Thailand, China, Malaysia, and India.) **Tourism:** $929 mil. **Budget:** $4.8 bil. **Inflation:** 5.5%.

Transport: Railways: 3,126 mi. **Motor vehicles:** 0.6 per 1,000 pop. **Airports:** 36.

Communications: Telephone: 1 per 100 pop. **Mobile:** 49.5 per 100 pop. **Broadband:** 1 per 100 pop. **Internet:** 2.1%.

Health: Expend.: 1.8%. **Life expect.:** 63.9 male; 68.8 female. **Births:** 18.4 per 1,000 pop. **Deaths:** 8.0 per 1,000 pop. **Infant mortality:** 43.6 per 1,000 live births. **Undernourished:** 16.7%. **HIV:** 0.7%.

Education: Compulsory: ages 5-9. **Literacy:** 93.1%.

Embassy: 2300 S St. NW 20008; 332-3344.

Website: www.president-office.gov.mm

The Burmese arrived from Tibet before the 9th cent., displacing earlier cultures, and a Buddhist monarchy was established by the 11th cent. Burma was conquered by China's Mongol dynasty in 1272, then ruled by the Shan people as a Chinese tributary until the 16th cent. Britain subjugated Burma in three wars, 1824-84, and ruled the country as part of India until 1937, when Burma became self-governing. Full independence was achieved Jan. 4, 1948.

Gen. Ne Win dominated politics from 1962 to 1988, first as military ruler, then as constitutional president, advancing policies that increased economic socialization and international isolation. In 1987, the UN granted Burma, once the richest nation in SE Asia, less-developed status. Ne Win resigned July 1988, following anti-government riots. In Sept., the military seized power, under Gen. Saw Maung. In 1989 the country's name was changed to Myanmar.

Although the main opposition party won a decisive victory in 1990 multiparty elections, the military refused to surrender power. A key opposition leader, Aung San Suu Kyi, was held under house arrest, 1989-95, 2000-02, and 2003-10. The regime's poor human rights record and continued harassment of Suu Kyi and her supporters led to U.S.-imposed sanctions.

In late Sept. 2007, thousands of Buddhist monks led mass protests in Yangon; security forces cracked down by raiding monasteries, arresting monks, and firing on demonstrators. On Sept. 25, the U.S. announced tougher sanctions. Cyclone Nargis, May 2-3, 2008, left at least 84,537 people dead, with an estimated 53,836 missing.

After the military dominated Nov. 2010 parliamentary elections, the ruling council was dissolved and an initially nominal civilian government returned, Mar. 30, 2011. Suu Kyi's National League for Democracy (NLD) won 43 of 45 parliamentary seats in an Apr. 1, 2012, election, and Suu Kyi traveled to Oslo, Norway, to accept the Nobel Peace Prize, which she was awarded in absentia in 1991. The EU, Apr. 23, and U.S., May 17, suspended most sanctions against Myanmar. Myanmar's government announced Aug. 28, 2012, the removal of more than 2,000 names from the country's notorious blacklist of those banned from entering or leaving the country. More than 1,000 political prisoners were granted amnesty between Sept. 2012 and Apr. 2013. However, five journalists received 10-year prison sentences, July 10, 2014, for publishing an article alleging the government was producing chemical weapons. In 2015, Myanmar became the 191st country to sign the Chemical Weapons Convention banning such weapons.

Violence against Rohingya Muslims in the northwest that began in 2012 had killed hundreds and driven hundreds of thousands from their homes by mid-2015. The Rohingya are not recognized as citizens by the government, which as of mid-2015 was confining an estimated 140,000 in camps. Since 2012, more than 100,000 Rohingya have fled by boat, seeking asylum in other SE Asian countries. An estimated 31,000 (including some from neighboring Bangladesh) fled in the first half of 2015; about 370 died at sea. Smugglers reportedly often exploited and abused refugees.

Namibia

Republic of Namibia

People: Population: 2,212,307. **Age distrib.:** <15: 31%; 65+: 4.5%. **Growth:** 0.6%. **Migrants:** 2.2%. **Pop. density:** 7 per sq mi, 2.7 per sq km. **Urban:** 46.7%. **Ethnic groups:** black 87.5%, white 6%, mixed 6.5%. Ovambo tribe about 50% of pop.; Kavangos tribe 9%. **Languages:** Oshiwambo langs., Nama/Damara, Afrikaans (common), Otjiherero langs., Kavango langs., Caprivi langs., English (official). **Religions:** Christian 80%-90% (Lutheran at least 50%), indigenous beliefs 10%-20%.

Geography: Total area: 318,261 sq mi, 824,292 sq km; **Land area:** 317,874 sq mi, 823,290 sq km. **Location:** Southern Africa on Atlantic coast. Angola on N; Botswana, Zambia on E; South Africa on S. **Topography:** Three distinct regions incl. Namib Desert along the Atlantic, a mountainous central plateau with woodland savanna, and Kalahari Desert in E. True forests found in NE. There are 4 rivers but little other surface water. **Arable land:** 1%. **Capital:** Windhoek, 367,987.

Government: Type: Republic. **Head of state:** Pres. Hage Geingob; in office: Mar. 21, 2015. **Head of gov.:** Prime Min. Saara Kuugongelwa-Amadhila; in office: Mar. 21, 2015. **Local divisions:** 14 regions. **Defense budget:** $410 mil. **Active troops:** 9,200.

Economy: Industries: meatpacking, fish proc., dairy prods., pasta, beverages, mining. **Chief crops:** millet, sorghum, peanuts, grapes. **Natural resources:** diamonds, copper, uranium, gold, silver, lead, tin, lithium, cadmium, tungsten, zinc, salt, hydropower, fish. **Water:** 17,330 cu m per capita. **Electricity prod.:** 1.8 bil kWh. **Labor force:** agric. 16.3%, industry 22.4%, services 61.3% (formal sector only). About two-thirds of rural population rely on subsistence agric. **Unemployment:** 16.9%.

Finance: Monetary unit: Dollar (NAD) (13.45 = $1 U.S.). **GDP:** $23.8 bil; **per capita GDP:** $10,800; **GDP growth:** 5.3%. **Imports:** $7.7 bil. **Exports:** $5 bil. **Tourism:** $409 mil. **Budget:** $5.7 bil. **Inflation:** 5.4%.

Transport: Railways: 1,633 mi. **Motor vehicles:** 116.4 per 1,000 pop. **Airports:** 19.

Communications: Telephone: 7.8 per 100 pop. **Mobile:** 113.8 per 100 pop. **Broadband:** 34.3 per 100 pop. **Internet:** 14.8%.

Health: Expend.: 8.4%. **Life expect.:** 52.1 male; 51.2 female. **Births:** 19.8 per 1,000 pop. **Deaths:** 13.9 per 1,000 pop. **Infant mortality:** 45.6 per 1,000 live births. **Undernourished:** 37.2%. **HIV:** 16.0%.

Education: Compulsory: ages 7-13. **Literacy:** 81.9%.

Embassy: 1605 New Hampshire Ave. NW 20009; 986-0540.

Website: www.gov.na

Namibia was declared a German protectorate in 1890 and officially called South-West Africa. South Africa seized the territory in 1915 during WWI; the League of Nations gave South Africa a mandate over the territory in 1920. In 1966, the Marxist South-West Africa People's Organization (SWAPO) launched a guerrilla war for independence. The UN General Assembly named the area Namibia in 1968.

After many years of guerrilla warfare, South Africa, Angola, and Cuba signed a U.S.-mediated agreement Dec. 22, 1988, to end South African administration of Namibia and provide for a cease-fire and transition to independence, in accordance with a 1978 UN plan. A separate accord between Cuba and Angola provided for a phased withdrawal of Cuban troops from Namibia. A constitution providing for multiparty government was adopted Feb. 9, 1990, and Namibia gained independence Mar. 21.

Walvis Bay, the principal deepwater port, had been under South African administration since 1922. South Africa turned control of the port over to Namibia in 1994. Separatist violence flared in the Caprivi Strip in the late 1990s. SWAPO, the leading political group since independence, dominated the presidential and parliamentary elections held Nov. 28, 2014.

SCIENCE

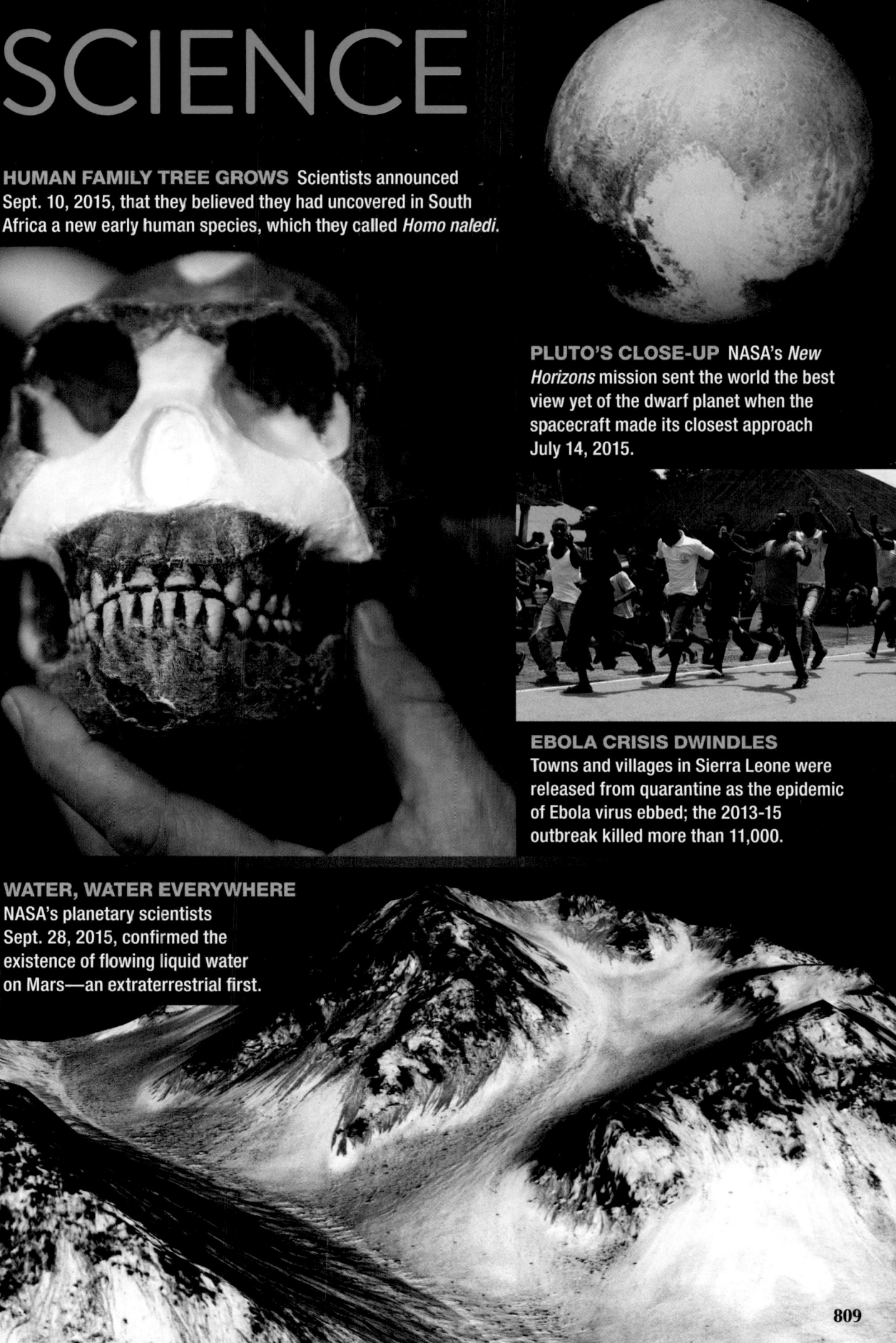

HUMAN FAMILY TREE GROWS Scientists announced Sept. 10, 2015, that they believed they had uncovered in South Africa a new early human species, which they called *Homo naledi*.

PLUTO'S CLOSE-UP NASA's *New Horizons* mission sent the world the best view yet of the dwarf planet when the spacecraft made its closest approach July 14, 2015.

EBOLA CRISIS DWINDLES
Towns and villages in Sierra Leone were released from quarantine as the epidemic of Ebola virus ebbed; the 2013-15 outbreak killed more than 11,000.

WATER, WATER EVERYWHERE
NASA's planetary scientists Sept. 28, 2015, confirmed the existence of flowing liquid water on Mars—an extraterrestrial first.

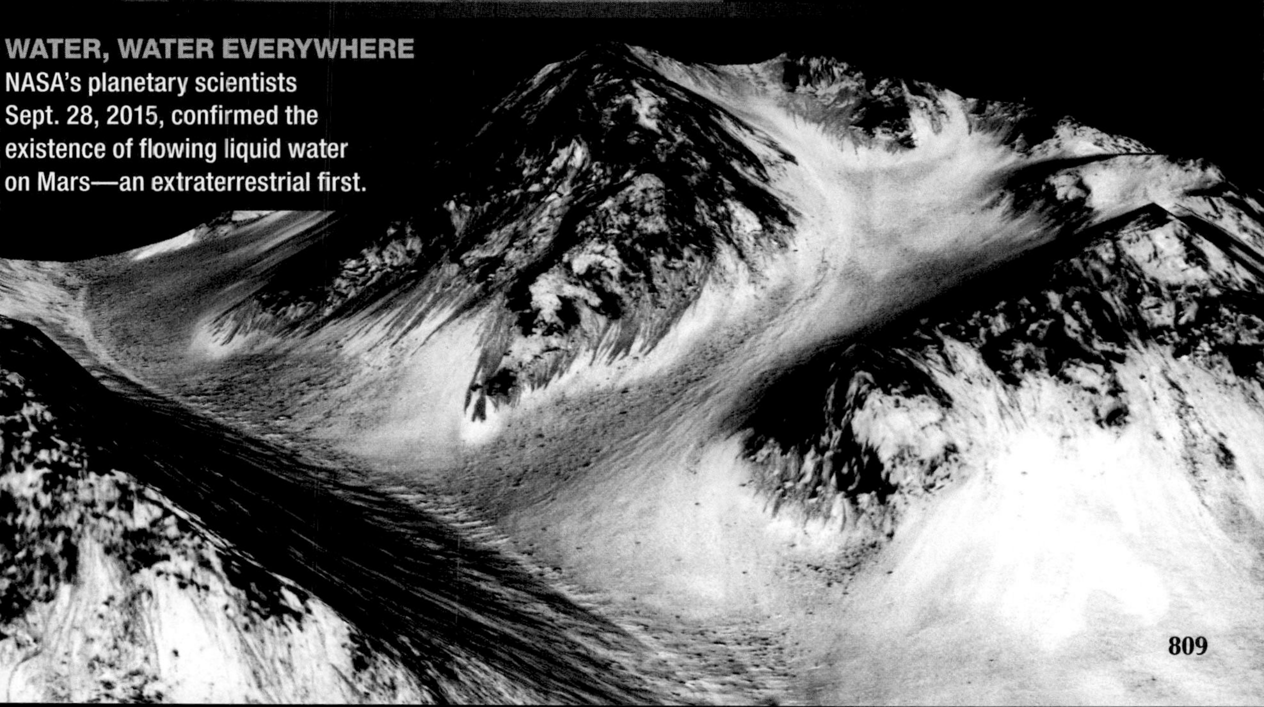

SPORTS

DEFLATEGATE SCANDAL OVERWHELMS Tom Brady and the New England Patriots eked out a win over the defending champion Seattle Seahawks in Super Bowl XLIX Feb. 1, 2015, but the "Deflategate" AFC championship game investigation and legal appeals became ongoing offseason distractions for football fans in 2015.

BUCKS BLOW OUT DUCKS The first-ever College Football Playoff national championship was won by Ezekiel Elliott and the Ohio State Buckeyes, who defeated Oregon Jan. 12, 2015.

CLOSE TO PERFECT Serena Williams won her fourth consecutive Grand Slam event at Wimbledon July 11, 2015, but fell shy of a calendar-year Grand Slam with a semifinal loss at the U.S. Open in Sept.

DUKE DOMINATES The Duke Blue Devils and Coach K defeated Wisconsin Apr. 6, 2015, to take the men's NCAA National Championship, shutting down the Badgers' first chance at the title since 1941.

THREEPEAT UConn's Breanna Stewart was named the Final Four's most outstanding player a record third time Apr. 7, 2015, as the Huskies defeated Notre Dame for the women's national title.

A NEW DYNASTY? Chicago defenseman Duncan Keith scored the game- and Stanley Cup-winning goal over Tampa Bay June 15, 2015, giving the team its third championship in six years.

GOLDEN AGE The Golden State Warriors claimed victory over LeBron James and the Cleveland Cavaliers in Game Six June 16, 2015, to win the team's first NBA championship in four decades.

SPORTS

TIP OF THE HAT Midfielder Carli Lloyd's hat trick July 5, 2015, in the U.S. women's World Cup victory over Japan, achieved in the first 16 minutes of play, was the first ever in a women's World Cup final.

FOOTLOOSE FIFA Protesters at the FIFA congress May 29, 2015, demanded the resignation of FIFA Pres. Sepp Blatter as the organization—responsible for governing world soccer—and affiliated officials were charged with widespread corruption.

TRIPLE CROWN American Pharoah and jockey Victor Espinoza June 6, 2015, achieved the first Triple Crown of thoroughbred racing since 1978.

FIGHT OF THE CENTURY? Floyd Mayweather Jr. emerged triumphant May 2, 2015, in a long-anticipated match-up with Manny Pacquiao; the bout made history as boxing's highest-grossing fight but attracted plenty of criticism.

ARTS

GOOD NIGHT, EVERYBODY David Letterman signed off as the host of CBS's *Late Show* for the last time May 20, 2015; he had hosted the show since 1993.

WORTH THE WAIT? *Go Set a Watchman*, Harper Lee's first published book in 55 years, was greeted upon its July 14, 2015, release by many longtime fans of her classic novel, *To Kill a Mockingbird*.

EN POINTE The American Ballet Theater named Misty Copeland its first African-American principal dancer June 30, 2015.

DAILY NO MORE Pres. Barack Obama July 21, 2015, was among Jon Stewart's final guests as he departed Comedy Central's *The Daily Show*, which Stewart had hosted for 16 years.

PEOPLE

FALLEN STAND-UP In 2005 court filings released July 6, 2015, comedian Bill Cosby admitted to obtaining quaaludes with the intent of giving them to young women; as of Sept. 2015, more than 50 women had publicly accused Cosby of sexual assault.

THE JINX Real estate heir Robert Durst again faced murder charges after participating in a six-part 2015 HBO documentary series about his life and three killings in which he was a suspect.

ANCHOR AWAY *NBC Nightly News* anchor and managing editor Brian Williams (right) was suspended Feb. 10, 2015, when reports surfaced that he had lied about events that transpired during a 2003 helicopter flight in Iraq.

REWRITE HISTORY DNA test results released Aug. 12, 2015, concluded that Pres. Warren Harding had fathered a daughter with Nan Britton, who in 1927 published a book about their six-year affair.

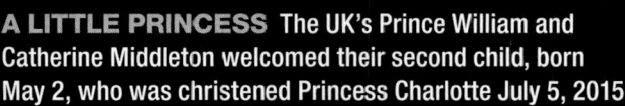

A LITTLE PRINCESS The UK's Prince William and Catherine Middleton welcomed their second child, born May 2, who was christened Princess Charlotte July 5, 2015.

"CALL ME CAITLYN" Caitlyn Jenner—formerly known as Bruce Jenner, a high-profile Olympic athlete and reality-TV star—discussed her life as a transgender woman in a series of interviews (and a new reality show) in 2015.

WOMAN WARRIOR Capt. Kristen Griest was one of the first two women to graduate the U.S. Army's grueling Ranger School at Fort Benning, GA, on Aug. 21, 2015.

GOOD GUESTS French Pres. François Hollande (center) awarded the Legion of Honor Aug. 24, 2015, to British subject Chris Norman and Americans Anthony Sadler, Spencer Stone, and Alek Skarlatos, for thwarting an attack on a high-speed train by a heavily armed gunman.

FAREWELLS

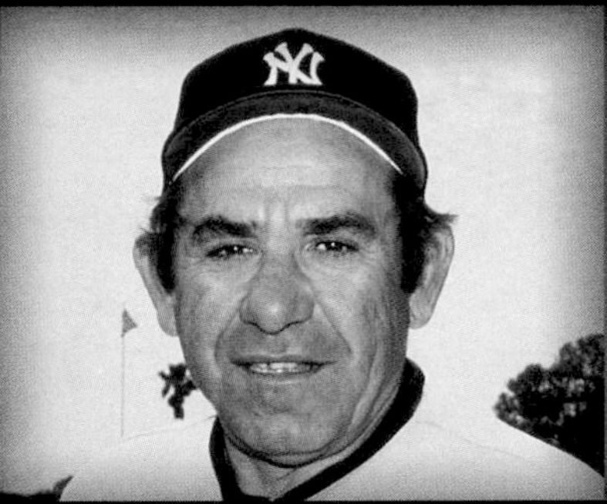

YOGI BERRA
MAY 12, 1925-SEPT. 22, 2015

JULIAN BOND
JAN. 14, 1940-AUG. 15, 2015

MARIO CUOMO
JUNE 15, 1932-JAN. 1, 2015

E. L. DOCTOROW
JAN. 6, 1931-JULY 21, 2015

FRANK GIFFORD
AUG. 16, 1930-AUG. 9, 2015

GÜNTER GRASS
OCT. 16, 1927-APR. 13, 2015

B. B. KING
SEPT. 16, 1925-MAY 14, 2015

ANNE MEARA
SEPT. 20, 1929-MAY 23, 2015

LEONARD NIMOY
MAR. 26, 1931-FEB. 27, 2015

MAUREEN O'HARA
AUG. 17, 1920-OCT. 24, 2015

OLIVER SACKS
JULY 9, 1933-AUG. 30, 2015

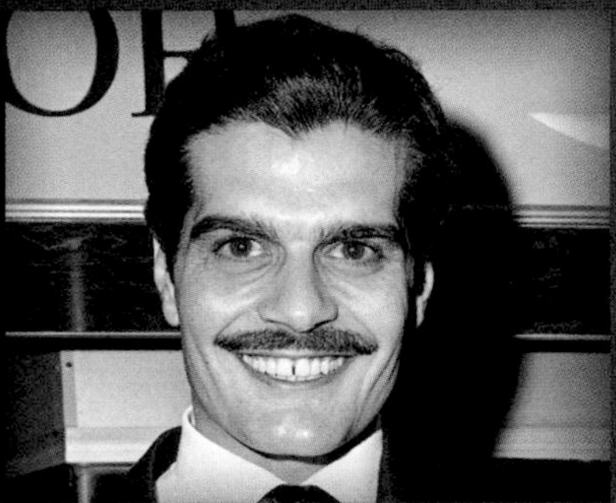

OMAR SHARIF
APR. 10, 1932-JULY 10, 2015

Nauru

Republic of Nauru

People: Population: 9,540. **Age distrib.:** <15: 32.5%; 65+: 2.1%. **Growth:** 0.6%. **Migrants:** 20.6%. **Pop. density:** 1,176.6 per sq mi, 454.3 per sq km. **Urban:** 100%. **Ethnic groups:** Nauruan 58%, other Pac. Islander 26%, Chinese 8%, European 8%. **Languages:** Nauruan (official), English (used in govt. and commerce). **Religions:** Protestant 60.4% (incl. Nauru Congregational 35.7%, Assembly of God 13%), Roman Catholic 33%.

Geography: Total area: 8.1 sq mi, 21 sq km; **Land area:** 8.1 sq mi, 21 sq km. **Location:** In W Pacific O. just S of equator. Nearest neighbor is Kiribati to E. **Topography:** Mostly a plateau bearing high-grade phosphate deposits, surrounded by a sandy shore and coral reef in concentric rings. **Arable land:** 0%. **Capital:** None official; govt. offices in Yaren district.

Government: Type: Republic. **Head of state and gov.:** Pres. Baron Waqa; in office: June 11, 2013. **Local divisions:** 14 districts. **Defense budget/active troops:** NA.

Economy: Industries: phosphate mining, offshore banking, coconut prods. **Chief crops:** coconuts. **Natural resources:** phosphates, fish. **Water:** NA. **Electricity prod.:** 25 mil kWh. **Labor force:** phosphate mining, public admin., education, transportation. **Unemployment:** NA.

Finance: Monetary unit: Australian Dollar (AUD) (1.42 = $1 U.S.). **GDP** (2005): $60 mil; **per capita GDP** (2005): $5,000; **GDP growth:** NA. **Imports** (2013): $143.1 mil. **Exports** (2013): $125 mil. **Budget** (2010 est.): $51.8 mil. **Inflation:** NA.

Transport: Airports: 1.

Communications: Telephone (2009): 18.9 per 100 pop. **Mobile** (2012): 67.8 per 100 pop. **Broadband:** 11.9 per 100 pop. **Internet** (2011): 54%.

Health: Expend.: 7.5%. **Life expect.:** 62.6 male; 70.2 female. **Births:** 25.0 per 1,000 pop. **Deaths:** 5.9 per 1,000 pop. **Infant mortality:** 8.1 per 1,000 live births. **Undernourished:** NA. **HIV:** NA.

Education: Compulsory: ages 4-17. **Literacy:** NA.

Permanent UN mission: 800 2nd Ave., New York, NY 10017; (212) 937-0074.

Website: www.naurugov.nr

The British reached the island in 1798, but it was annexed to the German Empire in 1886. After WWI, Australia administered Nauru under a League of Nations mandate. Japan occupied the island during WWII. In 1947 Nauru was made a UN trust territory, administered by Australia. It became an independent republic Jan. 31, 1968, and was admitted to the UN Sept. 14, 1999.

Phosphate exports provided Nauru with per capita revenues that were among the highest in the Third World. Phosphate reserves, however, are nearly depleted, and environmental damage from strip-mining has been severe. Lax banking practices have made Nauru a haven for money laundering. Rising sea levels linked to global climate change have eroded Nauru's coastline. A Nov. 20, 2012, Amnesty Intl. report found inhumane living conditions at Australia's detention center on Nauru, built to house up to 1,200 people, mostly refugees and undocumented immigrants who had sought to enter Australia by boat. An Australian government report, released Mar. 20, 2015, confirmed allegations of sexual and physical abuse of detainees by staff.

Nepal

Federal Democratic Republic of Nepal

People: Population: 31,551,305. **Age distrib.:** <15: 30.7%; 65+: 4.6%. **Growth:** 1.8%. **Migrants:** 3.5%. **Pop. density:** 570.1 per sq mi, 220.1 per sq km. **Urban:** 18.6%. **Ethnic groups:** Chhettri 16.6%, Brahman-Hill 12.2%, Magar 7.1%, Tharu 6.6%, Tamang 5.8%, Newar 5%, Kami 4.8%, Muslim 4.4%, Yadav 4%, Rai 2.3%, Gurung 2%. **Languages:** Nepali (official), Maithali, Bhojpuri, Tharu, Tamang, Newar, Magar, Bajjika, Urdu. **Religions:** Hindu 81.3%, Buddhist 9%, Muslim 4.4%, Kirant 3.1%.

Geography: Total area: 56,827 sq mi, 147,181 sq km; **Land area:** 55,348 sq mi, 143,351 sq km. **Location:** Astride Himalaya Mts. China on N, India on S. **Topography:** The Himalayas across the N, hill country with fertile valleys across the center. S border region is part of flat, subtropical Ganges Plain. **Arable land:** 14.8%. **Capital:** Kathmandu, 1,182,598.

Government: Type: Federal democratic republic. **Head of state:** Pres. Ram Baran Yadav; in office: July 23, 2008. **Head of gov.:** Prime Min. Sushil Koirala; in office: Feb. 10, 2014. **Local divisions:** 14 zones. **Defense budget:** $311 mil. **Active troops:** 95,750.

Economy: Industries: tourism, carpets, textiles; small rice, jute, sugar, oilseed mills; cigarettes, cement, brick prod. **Chief crops:** pulses, rice, corn, wheat, sugarcane, jute, root crops. **Natural resources:** quartz, water, timber, hydropower, lignite, copper, cobalt, iron ore. **Water:** 7,562 cu m per capita. **Electricity prod.:** 3.5 bil kWh. **Labor force:** agric. 75%, industry 7%, services 18%. **Unemployment:** 2.7%.

Finance: Monetary unit: Rupee (NPR) (105.92 = $1 U.S.). **GDP:** $66.8 bil; **per capita GDP:** $2,400; **GDP growth:** 5.5%. **Imports:** $7.3 bil; India 50.6%, China 35%. **Exports:** $1.1 bil; India 53.7%, U.S. 9.2%, China 5%. **Tourism:** $477 mil. **Budget:** $3.8 bil. **Inflation:** 8.4%.

Transport: Railways: 33 mi. **Airports:** 11.

Communications: Telephone: 3 per 100 pop. **Mobile:** 82.5 per 100 pop. **Broadband** (2012): 10.9 per 100 pop. **Internet:** 15.4%.

Health: Expend.: 5.5%. **Life expect.:** 66.2 male; 68.9 female. **Births:** 20.6 per 1,000 pop. **Deaths:** 6.6 per 1,000 pop. **Infant mortality:** 39.1 per 1,000 live births. **Undernourished:** 13%. **HIV:** 0.2%.

Education: Compulsory: NA. **Literacy:** 63.9%.

Embassy: 2131 Leroy Pl. NW 20008; 667-4550.

Website: nepal.gov.np

Nepal was originally a group of principalities, with the Gurkha principality becoming dominant about 1769. In 1951 King Tribhubana Bir Bikram, member of the Shah family, ended the system of rule by hereditary premiers of the Ranas family, who had kept the kings virtual prisoners, and established a cabinet system of government. Polygamy, child marriage, and the caste system were officially abolished in 1963. Political parties were legalized in 1990.

Nine members of Nepal's royal family, including King Birendra and Queen Aishwarya, died in a June 1, 2001, massacre. The killings were blamed on a 10th family member, Crown Prince Dipendra, who reportedly shot himself that night and died 3 days later, allowing Birendra's brother Gyanendra Bir Bikram Shah Dev to take the throne.

Citing the government's failure to stop a Maoist insurgency, King Gyanendra assumed absolute authority, Feb. 1, 2005. After weeks of pro-democracy demonstrations, the king agreed, Apr. 24, 2006, to reinstate parliament. A new government, led by Prime Min. Girija Prasad Koirala, signed a peace accord with Maoist rebels Nov. 21 ending a decade-long civil war that claimed 13,000 lives.

Under a draft constitution, Maoists joined an interim parliament Jan. 2007 and entered the cabinet Apr. 1. A constituent assembly voted May 2008 to abolish the monarchy and make Nepal a republic. Maoist leader Pushpa Kamal Dahal, popularly known as Prachanda, became prime min. Aug. 18. Prachanda resigned May 4, 2009, when Pres. Ram Baran Yadav overruled his firing of the army chief, who refused orders to integrate former Maoist rebels. Maoist Baburam Bhattarai became prime min. Aug. 29, 2011. Bhattarai dissolved the legislature May 27, 2012, when the deadline for a new constitution passed. Maoists suffered a defeat in Nov. 19, 2013, elections, in which moderate and pro-India parties won the largest blocs.

The new constitution, establishing a federal system with seven states, was adopted Sept. 20, 2015. Protests in Sept., largely by ethnic and religious groups fearing loss of autonomy, left more than 40 people dead.

A magnitude-7.8 earthquake near Kathmandu, Apr. 25, 2015, killed more than 8,000 people and displaced 2.8 mil. Historic temples and other sites were heavily damaged. A second quake, May 12, brought the combined death toll to over 8,600.

Netherlands

Kingdom of the Netherlands

People: Population: 16,947,904. **Age distrib.:** <15: 16.7%; 65+: 18%. **Growth:** 0.4%. **Migrants:** 11.7%. **Pop. density:** 1,295.1 per sq mi, 500 per sq km. **Urban:** 90.5%. **Ethnic groups:** Dutch 80.7%, EU 5%, Indonesian 2.4%, Turkish 2.2%, Surinamese 2%, Moroccan 2%. **Languages:** Dutch (official). **Religions:** Roman Catholic 28%, Protestant 19% (incl. Dutch Reformed 9%, Protestant Church of The Netherlands, 7%), none 42%.

Geography: Total area: 16,040 sq mi, 41,543 sq km; **Land area:** 13,086 sq mi, 33,893 sq km. **Location:** NW Europe on North Sea. Germany on E, Belgium on S. **Topography:** Land is flat with avg. elevation of 37 ft above sea level; much of land reclaimed and protected by some 1,500 mi of dikes. **Arable land:** 30%. **Capital:** Amsterdam, 1,090,772; s-Gravenhage (The Hague) (seat), 649,675. **Cities:** Rotterdam, 993,336.

Government: Type: Constitutional monarchy. **Head of state:** King Willem-Alexander; in office: Apr. 30, 2013. **Head of gov.:** Prime Min. Mark Rutte; in office: Oct. 14, 2010. **Local divisions:** 12 provinces. **Defense budget:** $10.68 bil. **Active troops:** 37,400.

Economy: Industries: agroindustries, metal and engineering prods., elec. machinery and equip., chemicals. **Chief crops:** grains, potatoes, sugar beets, fruits, vegetables. **Natural resources:** nat. gas, petroleum, peat, limestone, salt, sand and gravel. **Water:** 5,430 cu m per capita. **Crude oil reserves:** 144.7 mil bbls. **Electricity prod.:** 94.9 bil kWh. **Labor force:** agric. 1.8%, industry 17%, services 81.2%. **Unemployment:** 6.7%.

Finance: Monetary unit: Euro (EUR) (0.89 = $1 U.S.). **GDP:** $798.6 bil; **per capita GDP:** $47,400; **GDP growth:** 0.8%. **Imports:** $488.8 bil; Germany 14.5%, China 12%, Belgium 8.5%, UK 6.6%, Russia 6.5%, U.S. 6.3%. **Exports:** $552.8 bil; Germany 25.9%, Belgium 13.2%, France 8.8%, UK 8.6%. **Tourism:** $14.7 bil. **Budget:** $437.3 bil. **Inflation:** 1%.

Transport: Railways: 2,003 mi. **Motor vehicles:** 547.3 per 1,000 pop. **Airports:** 23.

Communications: Telephone: 42.4 per 100 pop. **Mobile:** 116.4 per 100 pop. **Broadband:** 62.3 per 100 pop. **Internet:** 93.2%.

Health: Expend.: 12.4%. **Life expect.:** 79.1 male; 83.5 female. **Births:** 10.8 per 1,000 pop. **Deaths:** 8.7 per 1,000 pop. **Infant mortality:** 3.6 per 1,000 live births. **Undernourished:** <5%. **HIV:** NA.

Education: Compulsory: ages 5-16. **Literacy:** 99%.

Embassy: 4200 Linnean Ave. NW 20008; 244-5300.

Website: www.government.nl

Julius Caesar conquered the region in 55 BCE, when it was inhabited by Celtic and Germanic tribes. After the empire of Charlemagne fell apart, the Netherlands (Holland, Belgium, Flanders) split among counts, dukes, and bishops, passed to Burgundy and thence to Spain. William the Silent, prince of Orange, led a confederation of the northern provinces, called Estates, in the Union of Utrecht, 1579; in 1581 they repudiated allegiance to Spain. The rise of the Dutch republic to naval, economic, and artistic eminence came in the 17th cent.

After a period of French hegemony, 1795-1813, the Congress of Vienna in 1815 formed a kingdom of the Netherlands, including Belgium, under William I. In 1830, the Belgians seceded and formed a separate kingdom.

The Netherlands maintained its neutrality in WWI but was invaded during WWII and occupied by Germany, 1940-45. In 1949, after several years of fighting, the Netherlands granted independence to Indonesia.

The murder May 6, 2002, of right-wing populist leader Pim Fortuyn, 9 days before legislative elections, marked the first political assassination in modern Dutch history. Filmmaker Theo van Gogh was killed by an Islamic extremist Nov. 2, 2004. On Apr. 30, 2009, the national Queen's Day holiday, an attempted assassination of Queen Beatrix and other royal family members resulted in the deaths of 7 bystanders and the would-be assassin. The anti-Islamic, right-wing Freedom Party, headed by Geert Wilders, gained in parliamentary elections June 2010. Prime Min. Mark Rutte and his cabinet resigned Apr. 23, 2012, after failing to pass a budget in line with EU requirements. Rutte's government nonetheless remained in a caretaker capacity, and his pro-business Liberal party won a majority of seats in parliamentary elections held Sept. 2012. Queen Beatrix, 75, abdicated the throne to her son, Willem-Alexander, Apr. 30, 2013. A Malaysia Airlines flight from Amsterdam to Kuala Lumpur was shot down over eastern Ukraine, July 17, 2014; nearly 200 Dutch passport holders were among the 298 killed.

Dutch Dependencies

Constitutional changes effective Oct. 10, 2010, dissolved the political entity known as the Netherlands Antilles, which consisted of two island groups in the West Indies. **Curaçao** (area 171 sq mi), near the coast of Venezuela, and **Sint Maarten** (13 sq mi), SE of Puerto Rico., were elevated to the status of autonomous countries. Bonaire, Saba, and St. Eustatius were classified as special municipalities. The northern two-thirds of St. Maarten is a French overseas territorial collectivity (St. Martin). St. Maarten suffered extensive damage from Hurricane Luis, Sept. 1995. Pop. of Curaçao, 148,406 (2015 est.); that of its capital, Willemstad, 144,730 (2014 est.). Sint Maarten, pop. 40,888 (2015 est.); capital is Philipsburg, pop. 46,085 (2014 est.). The principal industry is the refining of crude oil from Venezuela. Tourism and shipbuilding are other important industries. International tourism receipts in 2013 were $583 mil for Curaçao, $857 mil for Sint Maarten. **Websites:** www.gobiernu.cw (Curaçao); www.sintmaartengov.org (St. Maarten)

Aruba, about 26 mi west of Curaçao, was separated from the Netherlands Antilles on Jan. 1, 1986; it is an autonomous component of the Netherlands, with a status similar to Curaçao and St. Maarten. Area: 69 sq mi; pop. (2015 est.) 112,162. Capital: Oranjestad; pop. (2014 est.) 29,041. Chief industries are oil refining and tourism. International tourism receipts in 2014 were $1.6 bil. **Website:** www.kabga.aw

New Zealand

People: Population: 4,438,393. **Age distrib.:** <15: 19.9%; 65+: 14.6%. **Growth:** 0.8%. **Migrants:** 25.1%. **Pop. density:** 42.9 per sq mi, 16.6 per sq km. **Urban:** 86.3%. **Ethnic groups:** European 71.2%, Maori 14.1%, Asian 11.3%, Pacific peoples 7.6%. Respondents could identify more than one ethnic group. **Languages:** English (de facto official), Maori (de jure official), Samoan. **Religions:** Christian 44.3% (incl. Catholic 11.6%, Anglican 10.8%), no religion 38.5%.

Geography: Total area: 103,363 sq mi, 267,710 sq km; **Land area:** 103,363 sq mi, 267,710 sq km. **Location:** SW Pacific O. Nearest neighbors are Australia on W, Fiji and Tonga on N. **Topography:** The 2 main islands (North and South Isls.) are hilly and mountainous. The E coasts consist of fertile plains, incl. Canterbury Plains on South Isl. Volcanic plateau in center of North Isl. Glaciers and 15 peaks over 10,000 ft on South Isl. **Arable land:** 2.2%. **Capital:** Wellington, 382,943. **Cities:** Auckland, 1,344,304.

Government: Type: Parliamentary democracy. **Head of state:** Queen Elizabeth II, rep. by Gov.-Gen. Sir Jeremiah "Jerry" Mateparae; in office: Aug. 31, 2011. **Head of gov.:** Prime Min. John Key; in office: Nov. 19, 2008. **Local divisions:** 16 regions, 1 territory. **Defense budget:** $3.19 bil. **Active troops:** 8,500.

Economy: Industries: agric., forestry, fishing, logs and wood prods., mfg., mining, constr., financial services, real estate services, tourism. **Chief crops:** fruit, vegetables, wine, wheat, barley. **Natural resources:** nat. gas, iron ore, sand, coal, timber, hydropower, gold, limestone. **Water:** 72,570 cu m per capita. **Crude oil reserves:** 67.2 mil bbls. **Electricity prod.:** 43.3 bil kWh. **Labor force:** agric. 7%, industry 19%, services 74%. **Unemployment:** 6.2%.

Finance: Monetary unit: Dollar (NZD) (1.58 = $1 U.S.). **GDP:** $158.9 bil; **per capita GDP:** $35,200; **GDP growth:** 3.2%. **Imports:** $40.7 bil; China 17.5%, Australia 13.3%, U.S. 9.4%, Japan 6.4%. **Exports:** $40.2 bil; China 20.8%, Australia 19%, U.S. 8.5%, Japan 5.9%. **Tourism:** $8.5 bil. **Budget:** $84.4 bil. **Inflation:** 0.8%.

Transport: Railways: 2,565 mi. **Motor vehicles:** 755.4 per 1,000 pop. **Airports:** 39.

Communications: Telephone: 40.6 per 100 pop. **Mobile:** 112.1 per 100 pop. **Broadband:** 81.9 per 100 pop. **Internet:** 85.5%.

Health: Expend.: 10.3%. **Life expect.:** 79.0 male; 83.2 female. **Births:** 13.3 per 1,000 pop. **Deaths:** 7.4 per 1,000 pop. **Infant mortality:** 4.5 per 1,000 live births. **Undernourished:** <5%. **HIV:** NA.

Education: Compulsory: ages 6-15. **Literacy:** 99%.

Embassy: 37 Observatory Cir. NW 20008; 328-4800.

Website: www.govt.nz

New Zealand comprises North Island, 43,911 sq mi; South Island, 58,084 sq mi; Stewart Island, 649 sq mi; Chatham Isls., 373 sq mi; and several groups of smaller islands. The Maori, a Polynesian group from the eastern Pacific, reached New Zealand before and during the 14th cent. The first European to sight New Zealand was Dutch navigator Abel Janszoon Tasman. The Maori refused to allow him to land. British Capt. James Cook explored the coasts, 1769-70.

British sovereignty was proclaimed and Maori land rights were recognized in the Treaty of Waitangi, 1840, with organized settlement beginning in the same year. Representative institutions were granted in 1853. The Maori Wars, or New Zealand Wars, ended in 1870 with British victory. The colony became a dominion in 1907 and gained full independence in 1947.

A progressive tradition in politics began in the 19th cent., when New Zealand was known for social experimentation. Much of the nation's economy has been deregulated since the 1980s. Jenny Shipley of the National Party became the nation's first female prime min., Dec. 8, 1997. The Labour Party, led by Helen Clark, won general elections, Nov. 27, 1999, and July 27, 2002.

Prostitution was legalized June 2003. In July, New Zealand contributed troops to the Australian-led force in the Solomon Islands. A measure establishing a supreme court and ending appeals to the UK Privy Council passed Oct. 14. A major settlement of Maori land claims dating from the 19th cent. was signed June 25, 2008.

An explosion Nov. 19, 2010, at the Pike River coal mine on South Island killed 29 men. A Christchurch earthquake, Feb. 22, 2011, killed 181 people and caused damage estimated at $11 bil to the central business district. Prime Min. John Key's handling of these and other disasters bolstered the National Party's popularity, and it was returned to power in elections Nov. 26, 2011. New Zealand legalized same-sex marriage in a 77-44 parliamentary vote Apr. 17, 2013. Key's National Party won a majority of seats in Sept. 20, 2014, parliamentary elections. Key announced, Feb. 24, 2015, that New Zealand would send 143 troops to Iraq to help train Iraqi forces fighting the Islamist extremist group ISIS.

In 1965, the **Cook Islands** (area: 91 sq mi; 2015 est. pop.: 9,838), halfway between New Zealand and Hawaii, became self-governing. New Zealand retains responsibility for defense and foreign affairs. **Niue** (area: 100 sq mi; 2014 est. pop.: 1,190) attained the same status in 1974; it lies 400 mi W. Cyclone Heta devastated Niue Jan. 6, 2004. **Tokelau** (area: 4.6 sq mi; 2014 est. pop.: 1,337) comprises three atolls 300 mi N of Samoa. Two referendums on Tokelau self-government, held Feb. 13-15, 2006, and Oct. 20-24, 2007, failed to gain the required two-third majority. **Ross Dependency**, administered by New Zealand since 1923, comprises 160,000 sq mi of Antarctic territory.

Nicaragua

Republic of Nicaragua

People: Population: 5,907,881. **Age distrib.:** <15: 28.6%; 65+: 5%. **Growth:** 1%. **Migrants:** 0.7%. **Pop. density:** 127.5 per sq mi, 49.2 per sq km. **Urban:** 58.8%. **Ethnic groups:** mestizo (mixed Amerindian/white) 69%, white 17%, black 9%, Amerindian 5%. **Languages:** Spanish (official), Miskito, English and indigenous langs. **Religions:** Roman Catholic 58.5%, Protestant 23.2% (incl. Evangelical 21.6%), none 15.7%.

Geography: Total area: 50,336 sq mi, 130,370 sq km; **Land area:** 46,328 sq mi, 119,990 sq km. **Location:** Central America. Honduras on N, Costa Rica on S. **Topography:** Both Caribbean and Pacific coasts are over 200 mi long. Cordillera Mts., with many volcanic peaks, run NW-SE through middle of country. **Arable land:** 12.5%. **Capital:** Managua, 956,233.

Government: Type: Republic. **Head of state and gov.:** Pres. Daniel Ortega Saavedra; in office: Jan. 10, 2007. **Local divisions:** 15 departments, 2 autonomous regions. **Defense budget:** $83 mil. **Active troops:** 12,000.

Economy: Industries: food proc., chemicals, machinery and metal prods., knit and woven apparel, petroleum refining and distrib. **Chief crops:** coffee, bananas, sugarcane, rice, corn, tobacco, cotton, sesame, soya, beans. **Natural resources:** gold, silver, copper, tungsten, lead, zinc, timber, fish. **Water:** 27,056 cu m per capita. **Electricity prod.:** 4.2 bil kWh. **Labor force:** agric. 31%, industry 18%, services 50%. **Unemployment:** 7.2%.

Finance: Monetary unit: Cordoba (NIO) (27.48 = $1 U.S.). **GDP:** $29.5 bil; **per capita GDP:** $4,700; **GDP growth:** 4.5%. **Imports:** $6.4 bil; U.S. 17.6%, Venezuela 14.7%, Mexico 13%, Costa Rica 8.8%, China 8.7%, Guatemala 8.3%, El Salvador 5.6%. **Exports:** $4 bil; U.S. 50.1%, Mexico 12.2%, Canada 7.6%, Venezuela 7.4%. **Tourism:** $445 mil. **Budget:** $3.1 bil. **Inflation:** 6%.

Transport: Motor vehicles: 51.1 per 1,000 pop. **Airports:** 12.

Communications: Telephone: 5.5 per 100 pop. **Mobile:** 114.6 per 100 pop. **Broadband:** 1.3 per 100 pop. **Internet:** 17.6%.

Health: Expend.: 8.2%. **Life expect.:** 70.8 male; 75.3 female. **Births:** 18.0 per 1,000 pop. **Deaths:** 5.1 per 1,000 pop. **Infant mortality:** 19.7 per 1,000 live births. **Undernourished:** 16.8%. **HIV:** 0.3%.

Education: Compulsory: ages 6-11. **Literacy:** 82.8%.

Embassy: 1627 New Hampshire Ave. NW 20009; 939-6570.

Website: www.presidencia.gob.ni

Nicaragua, inhabited by various Indian tribes, was conquered by Spain in 1552. After gaining independence from Spain, 1821, Nicaragua was united for a short period with Mexico, then with the United Provinces of Central America, finally becoming an independent republic, 1838. U.S. Marines occupied the country at times in the early 20th cent., the last time from 1926 to 1933.

Gen. Anastasio Somoza Debayle held the presidency 1967-72, 1974-79. Martial law was imposed in Dec. 1974, after officials were kidnapped by Marxist Sandinista guerrillas. Nationwide anti-government strikes touched off a civil war, 1978, which ended when Somoza fled Nicaragua and the Sandinistas took control of Managua, July 1979. Somoza was assassinated in Paraguay, Sept. 17, 1980.

Relations with the U.S. were strained as a result of Nicaragua's aid to leftist guerrillas in El Salvador and U.S. backing of anti-Sandinista contra guerrilla groups, which fought the Sandinista government throughout the 1980s. In 1985 the U.S. House rejected Pres. Ronald Reagan's request for military aid to the contras. The subsequent diversion of funds to the contras from the proceeds of a secret arms sale to Iran caused a major scandal in the U.S.

In a stunning upset, Violeta Barrios de Chamorro defeated Sandinista leader Daniel Ortega Saavedra in national elections, Feb. 25, 1990. The conservative Arnoldo Alemán Lacayo defeated Ortega in the Oct. 1996 presidential election.

Drought and a drop in coffee prices precipitated an economic crisis in 2001. Enrique Bolaños Geyer, a conservative businessman, won the presidency that year. Convicted Dec. 7, 2003, on corruption charges, former Pres. Alemán received a $10-mil fine and a 20-year sentence. Ortega won the Nov. 2006 presidential election and cultivated ties with Venezuela and Iran, which offered Nicaragua financial assistance. He was reelected Nov. 6, 2011. The Sandinista-controlled legislature gave final approval, Jan. 28, 2014, to constitutional changes removing presidential term limits. Amid protests by environmentalists and other opponents of the project, preliminary construction work began, Dec. 2014, on a 170+-mi canal across Nicaragua by a Chinese consortium.

Niger

Republic of Niger

People: Population: 18,045,729. **Age distrib.:** <15: 49.6%; 65+: 2.6%. **Growth:** 3.3%. **Migrants:** 0.7%. **Pop. density:** 36.9 per sq mi, 14.2 per sq km. **Urban:** 18.7%. **Ethnic groups:** Haoussa 55.4%, Djerma Sonrai 21%, Tuareg 9.3%, Peuhl 8.5%, Kanouri Manga 4.7%. **Languages:** French (official), Hausa, Djerma. **Religions:** Muslim 80%, other (incl. indigenous beliefs and Christian) 20%.

Geography: Total area: 489,191 sq mi, 1,267,000 sq km; **Land area:** 489,076 sq mi, 1,266,700 sq km. **Location:** Interior of N Africa. Libya, Algeria on N; Mali, Burkina Faso on W; Benin, Nigeria on S; Chad on E. **Topography:** Mostly arid desert and mountains. Narrow savanna in S and Niger R. basin in the SW. **Arable land:** 12.6%. **Capital:** Niamey, 1,089,589.

Government: Type: Republic. **Head of state:** Pres. Mahamadou Issoufou; in office: Apr. 7, 2011. **Head of gov.:** Prime Min. Brigi Rafini; in office: Apr. 7, 2011. **Local divisions:** 7 regions, 1 capital district. **Defense budget** (2012): $70 mil. **Active troops:** 5,300.

Economy: Industries: uranium mining, petroleum, cement, brick, soap, textiles, food proc., chemicals, slaughterhouses. **Chief crops:** cowpeas, cotton, peanuts, millet, sorghum, cassava, rice. **Natural resources:** uranium, coal, iron ore, tin, phosphates, gold, molybdenum, gypsum, salt, petroleum. **Water:** 1,910 cu m per capita. **Crude oil reserves:** 150 mil bbls. **Electricity prod.:** 355 mil kWh. **Labor force:** agric. 90%, industry 6%, services 4%. **Unemployment:** 5.1%.

Finance: Monetary unit: CFA Franc (XOF) (584.11 = $1 U.S.). **GDP:** $17.9 bil; **per capita GDP:** $1,000; **GDP growth:** 6.9%. **Imports:** $2.3 bil; France 13.7%, China 11.6%, Nigeria 9.1%, French Polynesia 8.6%, Belgium 5.6%, India 5.3%. **Exports:** $1.7 bil; Nigeria 54.2%, South Korea 26.2%, Ghana 6.7%. **Tourism:** $58 mil. **Budget:** $2.8 bil. **Inflation:** –0.9%.

Transport: Motor vehicles: 11.7 per 1,000 pop. **Airports:** 10.

Communications: Telephone: 0.6 per 100 pop. **Mobile:** 44.4 per 100 pop. **Broadband:** 0.9 per 100 pop. **Internet:** 2%.

Health: Expend.: 7.2%. **Life expect.:** 53.9 male; 56.4 female. **Births:** 45.5 per 1,000 pop. **Deaths:** 12.4 per 1,000 pop. **Infant mortality:** 84.6 per 1,000 live births. **Undernourished:** 11.3%. **HIV:** 0.5%.

Education: Compulsory: ages 7-15. **Literacy:** 19.1%.

Embassy: 2204 R St. NW 20008; 483-4224.

Website: www.gouv.ne

Niger was part of ancient and medieval African empires. European explorers reached the area in the late 18th cent. The French colony of Niger was established 1900-22 after the defeat of Tuareg fighters, who had invaded the area from the north a century before. The country became independent Aug. 3, 1960.

In 1993, Niger held its first free and open elections since independence; an opposition leader, Mahamane Ousmane, won the presidency. A peace accord Apr. 24, 1995, ended a Tuareg rebellion that began in 1990. A coup, Jan. 27, 1996, followed by a disputed presidential election in July, left the military in control of Niger. On Apr. 9, 1999, Gen. Ibrahim Bare Mainassara, Niger's president since 1996, was assassinated. Elections were held Oct. 17 and Nov. 24, 1999, under a new constitution, approved by referendum July 18, that restored civilian rule.

One of the world's poorest countries, Niger experienced severe food shortages in 2005 after locusts and drought ruined the grain harvest. Popularly elected in 1999 and 2004, Pres. Mamadou Tandja invoked emergency powers in 2009, seeking to remain in office for a third 5-year term. He was overthrown by a military junta Feb. 18, 2010. Civilian rule returned following Jan.-Mar. 2011 elections. Terrorist attacks in Niger by an al-Qaeda-linked group occurred May 23, 2013; two separate bombings, in Agadez and Arlit, killed 21 soldiers and 5 of the bombers. Beginning in Feb. 2015, the Nigeria-based Islamist extremist group Boko Haram staged attacks in southern Niger. Niger's parliament approved, Feb. 9, sending troops into Nigeria to fight Boko Haram.

Nigeria

Federal Republic of Nigeria

People: Population: 181,562,056. **Age distrib.:** <15: 43%; 65+: 3.1%. **Growth:** 2.5%. **Migrants:** 0.7%. **Pop. density:** 516.3 per sq mi, 199.4 per sq km. **Urban:** 47.8%. **Ethnic groups:** 250+ ethnic groups. Most populous, politically influential: Hausa, Fulani 29%; Yoruba 21%; Igbo (Ibo) 18%; Ijaw 10%; Kanuri 4%; Ibibio 3.5%; Tiv 2.5%. **Languages:** English (official), Hausa, Yoruba, Igbo (Ibo), Fulani, 500+ indigenous langs. **Religions:** Muslim 50%, Christian 40%, indigenous beliefs 10%.

Geography: Total area: 356,669 sq mi, 923,768 sq km; **Land area:** 351,649 sq mi, 910,768 sq km. **Location:** S coast of W Africa. Benin on W, Niger on N, Chad and Cameroon on E. **Topography:** 4 E-W regions: a coastal mangrove swamp, a tropical rain forest, a plateau of savanna and open woodland, and semi-desert in N. **Arable land:** 38.4%. **Capital:** Abuja, 2,440,242. **Cities:** Lagos, 13,122,829; Kano, 3,587,049; Ibadan, 3,160,190; Port Harcourt, 2,343,309.

Government: Type: Federal republic. **Head of state and gov.:** Pres. Muhammadu Buhari; in office: May 29, 2015. **Local divisions:** 36 states, 1 territory. **Defense budget:** $2.25 bil. **Active troops:** 80,000.

Economy: Industries: crude oil, coal, tin, columbite; rubber prods., wood; hides and skins, textiles, cement and other constr. materials. **Chief crops:** cocoa, peanuts, cotton, palm oil, corn, rice, sorghum, millet, cassava, yams, rubber. **Natural resources:** nat. gas, petroleum, tin, iron ore, coal, limestone, niobium, lead, zinc. **Water:** 1,648 cu m per capita. **Crude oil reserves:** 37.1 bil bbls. **Electricity prod.:** 27.3 bil kWh. **Labor force:** agric. 70%, industry 10%, services 20%. **Unemployment:** 7.5%.

Finance: Monetary unit: Naira (NGN) (199.00 = $1 U.S.). **GDP:** $1 tril; **per capita GDP:** $6,000; **GDP growth:** 6.3%. **Imports:** $52.8 bil; China 20.8%, U.S. 11.2%. **Exports:** $93 bil; India 12.8%, U.S. 11.1%, Brazil 10%, Spain 7.1%, Netherlands 7.1%, Germany 5.1%. **Tourism:** $543 mil. **Budget:** $34.6 bil. **Inflation:** 8.1%.

Transport: Railways: 2,360 mi. **Motor vehicles:** 8 per 1,000 pop. **Airports:** 40.

Communications: Telephone: 0.1 per 100 pop. **Mobile:** 77.8 per 100 pop. **Broadband:** 10.1 per 100 pop. **Internet:** 42.7%.

Health: Expend.: 6.1%. **Life expect.:** 52.0 male; 54.1 female. **Births:** 37.6 per 1,000 pop. **Deaths:** 12.9 per 1,000 pop. **Infant mortality:** 72.7 per 1,000 live births. **Undernourished:** 6.4%. **HIV:** 3.2%.

Education: Compulsory: ages 6-14. **Literacy:** 59.6%.

Embassy: 3519 International Ct. NW 20008; 986-8400.

Website: services.gov.ng

Early cultures in Nigeria date back to at least 700 BCE. From the 12th to the 14th cent., more advanced cultures developed in the Yoruba area, at Ife, and in the north, where Muslim influence prevailed. Portuguese and British slavers appeared in the 15th-16th cent. Britain seized Lagos, 1861, and gradually extended control inland until 1900. Nigeria became independent Oct. 1, 1960, and a republic Oct. 1, 1963.

On May 30, 1967, the Eastern Region seceded, proclaiming itself the Republic of Biafra, plunging the country into civil war. Casualties were estimated at over 1 mil, including many Biafrans (mostly Ibos) who died of starvation despite international relief efforts. The secessionists capitulated Jan. 12, 1970.

Nigeria emerged as one of the world's leading oil exporters in the 1970s, but much of the revenue has been squandered through corruption and mismanagement. Oil spills have polluted much of the Niger Delta region.

After 13 years of military rule, the nation made a peaceful return to civilian government Oct. 1979. Military rule resumed Dec. 31, 1983; a second coup came in 1985. Headed by Gen. Ibrahim Babangida, the military regime held elections June 12, 1993, but annulled the vote June 23 when it appeared that Moshood Abiola would win. Babangida resigned and appointed a civilian to head an interim government, Aug. 26, but that government was ousted Nov. 17, 1993, in a coup led by Gen. Sani Abacha. On June 11, 1994, Abiola declared himself president; he was jailed June 23.

Abacha's brutal rule ended June 8, 1998, when he died of an apparent heart attack. Abiola died in prison July 7. Abacha's successor, Gen. Abdulsalam Abubakar, promised elections and a return to civilian rule. Olusegun Obasanjo won the presidential vote Feb. 27, 1999, to lead Nigeria's first civilian government in 15 years.

The imposition of strict Islamic law in northern states led to clashes, Jan.-Mar. 2000, in which at least 800 people died. Fighting between Muslims and Christians Sept. 7-12 and Oct. 13-14, 2001, claimed an estimated 600 lives; another 200 people died when soldiers went on a rampage against civilians in SE Nigeria Oct. 22-24.

At least 1,000 people were killed Jan. 27, 2002, when an army weapons depot in Lagos exploded. Christian militia members massacred about 630 Muslims at Yelwa, central Nigeria, May 2, 2004. Obasanjo's chosen successor, Umaru Musa Yar'Adua, won a presidential election, Apr. 21, 2007, marred by violence and described as "not credible" by international monitors. After prolonged illness, Yar'Adua died May 5, 2010, and was succeeded by Vice Pres. Goodluck Jonathan, a southern Christian. After he won reelection Apr. 16, 2011, over Muhammadu Buhari, a northern-based Muslim, riots in 12 northern provinces left more than 800 people dead.

Boko Haram, a radical Islamist group based in NE Nigeria and seeking to establish an Islamist state, began terrorist attacks in 2009 against government forces and civilian targets. When Islamists gained control of a number of towns, Pres. Jonathan declared a state of emergency in the northeast May 14, 2013. Boko Haram violence and seizures of territory escalated in 2014; attacks continued in 2015. Amnesty Intl. estimated that Boko Haram attacks had killed 17,000 people by June 2015 and displaced more than 1 mil. In a message released Mar. 7, 2015, the group claimed allegiance to ISIS. Vowing tougher action against Boko Haram, Buhari defeated Jonathan in the Mar. 28-29, 2015, presidential election. Boko Haram also staged attacks in neighboring Chad, Cameroon, and Niger, and troops from those countries fought Boko Haram in Nigeria in 2015. UNICEF estimated, Sept. 18, 2015, that Boko Haram violence had displaced more than 1.4 mil children in Nigeria, Chad, Cameroon, and Niger.

Norway

Kingdom of Norway

People: Population: 5,207,689. **Age distrib.:** <15: 18.1%; 65+: 16.3%. **Growth:** 1.1%. **Migrants:** 13.8%. **Pop. density:** 44.3 per sq mi, 17.1 per sq km. **Urban:** 80.5%. **Ethnic groups:** Norwegian (incl. Sami) 94.4%, other European 3.6%. **Languages:** Bokmal Norwegian, Nynorsk Norwegian (both official); Sami (official in 9 municipalities). **Religions:** Church of Norway (Evangelical Lutheran official) 82.1%.

Geography: Total area: 125,021 sq mi, 323,802 sq km; **Land area:** 117,484 sq mi, 304,282 sq km. **Location:** W part of Scandinavian peninsula in NW Europe (extends farther N than any European land). Sweden, Finland, Russia on E. **Topography:** Highly indented coast lined with tens of thousands of islands. Mountains and plateaus cover most of country, which is only 25% forested. **Arable land:** 2.2%. **Capital:** Oslo, 986,093.

Government: Type: Constitutional monarchy. **Head of state:** King Harald V; in office: Jan. 17, 1991. **Head of gov.:** Prime Min. Erna Solberg; in office: Oct. 16, 2013. **Local divisions:** 19 counties. **Defense budget:** $6.98 bil. **Active troops:** 25,800.

Economy: Industries: petroleum and gas, shipping, fishing, aquaculture, food proc., shipbuilding, pulp and paper prods. **Chief crops:** barley, wheat, potatoes. **Natural resources:** petroleum, nat. gas, iron ore, copper, lead, zinc, titanium, pyrites, nickel, fish, timber, hydropower. **Water:** 77,930 cu m per capita. **Crude oil reserves:** 5.5 bil bbls. **Electricity prod.:** 144.6 bil kWh. **Labor force:** agric. 2.2%, industry 20.2%, services 77.6%. **Unemployment:** 3.5%.

Finance: Monetary unit: Krone (NOK) (8.24 = $1 U.S.). **GDP:** $345.2 bil; **per capita GDP:** $66,900; **GDP growth:** 2.2%. **Imports:** $91 bil; Sweden 13.3%, Germany 12.4%, China 9.1%, UK 6.3%, Denmark 6.1%, U.S. 5.9%. **Exports:** $150.2 bil; UK 24.5%, Netherlands 13.1%, Germany 12.9%, France 6.6%, Sweden 5.8%. **Tourism:** $5.6 bil. **Budget:** $230.5 bil. **Inflation:** 2%.

Transport: Railways: 2,641 mi. **Motor vehicles:** 606.9 per 1,000 pop. **Airports:** 67.

Communications: Telephone: 22.7 per 100 pop. **Mobile:** 116.5 per 100 pop. **Broadband:** 91.4 per 100 pop. **Internet:** 96.3%.

Health: Expend.: 9%. **Life expect.:** 79.7 male; 83.8 female. **Births:** 12.1 per 1,000 pop. **Deaths:** 8.1 per 1,000 pop. **Infant mortality:** 2.5 per 1,000 live births. **Undernourished:** <5%. **HIV:** 0.2%.

Education: Compulsory: ages 6-15. **Literacy:** 100%.

Embassy: 2720 34th St. NW 20008; 333-6000.

Website: www.regjeringen.no

The first ruler of Norway was Harald the Fairhaired, who came to power in 872 CE. Between 800 and 1000, Norway's Vikings raided and occupied widely dispersed parts of Europe. The country was united with Denmark, 1381-1814, and with Sweden, 1814-1905. In 1905, the country became independent with Prince Charles of Denmark as king.

Norway remained neutral during WWI. In WWII, Germany attacked Norway Apr. 9, 1940, and held it until liberation May 8, 1945. The country abandoned its neutrality after the war and joined NATO. In a referendum Nov. 28, 1994, Norwegian voters rejected European Union membership.

Abundant hydroelectric resources (accounting for more than 90% of electricity production) have provided a base for industrialization, giving Norway one of the highest living standards in the world. The country is a leading producer and exporter of crude oil, with extensive reserves in the North Sea. Norway has used oil revenue to build up the world's largest sovereign wealth fund (almost $900 bil as of 2015). Amid concern about climate change related to CO_2 emissions, parliament, June 5, 2015, ordered the fund to sell its holdings in companies relying on coal for 30% or more of their business.

A right-wing extremist, Anders Behring Breivik, confessed to killing 8 people with a car bomb in central Oslo and murdering another 69 at an island camp sponsored by the Labor Party's youth wing July 22, 2011. He was sentenced Aug. 24, 2012, to 21 years in prison, the maximum sentence in Norway. Parliament voted June 18, 2013, to make military service compulsory for women as well as men. Rightist parties, including the anti-immigration Progress Party, won the most seats in Sept. 9, 2013, elections; Conservative Party leader Erna Solberg became prime min.

Svalbard is a group of mountainous islands in the Arctic O., area 23,956 sq mi, pop. (2014 est.) 1,872. The largest, Spitsbergen (formerly called West Spitsbergen), 15,060 sq mi, seat of the governor, is about 370 mi N of Norway. By the 1920 Svalbard Treaty (in force 1925), major European powers recognized Norway's sovereignty over the archipelago.

Jan Mayen, area 146 sq mi, is a volcanic island located about 565 mi W-NW of Norway; it was annexed in 1929. The only people on Jan Mayen are military personnel and researchers at a meteorological/radio station.

Oman

Sultanate of Oman

People: Population: 3,286,936. **Age distrib.:** <15: 30.2%; 65+: 3.4%. **Growth:** 2.1%. **Migrants:** 30.6%. **Pop. density:** 27.5 per sq mi, 10.6 per sq km. **Urban:** 77.6%. **Ethnic groups:** Arab, Baluchi, S Asian (Indian, Pakistani, Sri Lankan, Bangladeshi), African. **Languages:** Arabic (official), English, Baluchi, Urdu, Indian dialects. **Religions:** Muslim (official; majority Ibadhi) 85.9%, Christian 6.5%, Hindu 5.5%.

Geography: Total area: 119,499 sq mi, 309,500 sq km; **Land area:** 119,499 sq mi, 309,500 sq km. **Location:** SE coast of Arabian peninsula. United Arab Emirates, Saudi Arabia, Yemen on W. **Topography:** A narrow coastal plain, a range of barren mountains reaching 9,900 ft, and a wide, stony, mostly waterless plateau, avg. elevation 1,000 ft. An exclave at the tip of the Musandam peninsula controls access to the Persian Gulf. **Arable land:** 0.1%. **Capital:** Muscat, 838,019.

Government: Type: Monarchy. **Head of state and gov.:** Sultan Qaboos bin Said al-Said; in office: July 23, 1970 (also prime min. since 1972). **Local divisions:** 11 governorates. **Defense budget:** $9.62 bil. **Active troops:** 42,600.

Economy: Industries: crude oil prod. and refining, nat. and liquefied nat. gas prod., constr., cement, copper, steel, chemicals, optic fiber. **Chief crops:** dates, limes, bananas, alfalfa, vegetables. **Natural resources:** petroleum, copper, asbestos, marble, limestone, chromium, gypsum, nat. gas. **Water:** 386 cu m per capita. **Crude oil reserves:** 5.2 bil bbls. **Electricity prod.:** 23.8 bil kWh. **Labor force:** NA. **Unemployment:** 7.9%.

Finance: Monetary unit: Rial (OMR) (0.38 = $1 U.S.). **GDP:** $162.4 bil; **per capita GDP:** $39,700; **GDP growth:** 2.9%. **Imports:** $34.4 bil; UAE 24.1%, Japan 11%, India 10.4%, China 6.7%, U.S. 5.3%. **Exports:** $58.7 bil; China 38.2%, Japan 10.3%, UAE 10%, South Korea 8.7%, India 5.6%. **Tourism:** $1.2 bil. **Budget:** $37.7 bil. **Inflation:** 1%.

Transport: Motor vehicles: 189.8 per 1,000 pop. **Airports:** 13.

Communications: Telephone: 9.6 per 100 pop. **Mobile:** 157.8 per 100 pop. **Broadband:** 68.9 per 100 pop. **Internet:** 70.2%.

Health: Expend.: 2.6%. **Life expect.:** 73.3 male; 77.2 female. **Births:** 24.4 per 1,000 pop. **Deaths:** 3.4 per 1,000 pop. **Infant mortality:** 13.6 per 1,000 live births. **Undernourished:** NA. **HIV:** 0.2%.

Education: Compulsory: NA. **Literacy:** 91.1%.

Embassy: 2535 Belmont Rd. NW 20008; 387-1980.

Website: www.oman.om

Oman was originally called Muscat and Oman. A long history of rule by other lands, including Portugal in the 16th cent., ended with the ouster of the Persians in 1744. By the early 19th cent., Muscat and Oman controlled much of the Persian and Pakistan coasts.

British influence was confirmed in a 1951 treaty, and Britain helped suppress an uprising by traditionally rebellious interior tribes against control by Muscat in the 1950s.

On July 23, 1970, Sultan Said bin Taimur was overthrown by his son, Sultan Qaboos bin Said al-Said, who changed the nation's name to Sultanate of Oman. Petroleum and natural gas are major sources of income. Oman has strong military and economic ties to the U.S. but also has favorable relations with Iran. Sultan Qaboos shuffled his cabinet after Arab Spring protests Feb. 2011 and expanded the powers of the Majlis al-Shura, the lower house of parliament, Oct. 20, 2011.

Pakistan

Islamic Republic of Pakistan

People: Population: 199,085,847. **Age distrib.:** <15: 32.7%; 65+: 4.3%. **Growth:** 1.5%. **Migrants:** 2.2%. **Pop. density:** 668.9 per sq mi, 258.3 per sq km. **Urban:** 38.8%. **Ethnic groups:** Punjabi 44.68%, Pashtun (Pathan) 15.42%, Sindhi 14.1%, Sariaki 8.38%, Muhajirs 7.57%, Balochi 3.57%. **Languages:** Punjabi, Sindhi, Siraiki, Pashto or Pashtu, Urdu (official), Balochi, Hindko, English (official; lingua franca of elite and most govt. ministries). **Religions:** Muslim (official) 96.4% (Sunni 85%-90%, Shia 10%-15%).

Geography: Total area: 307,374 sq mi, 796,095 sq km; **Land area:** 297,637 sq mi, 770,875 sq km. **Location:** W part of S Asia. Iran on W, Afghanistan and China on N, India on E. **Topography:** The Indus R. rises in the Hindu Kush and Himalaya Mts. in the N, then flows 1,000 mi into Arabian Sea. Thar Desert, Eastern Plains flank Indus Valley. **Arable land:** 27.5%. **Capital:** Islamabad, 1,364,531. **Cities:** Karachi, 16,617,644; Lahore, 8,741,365; Faisalabad, 3,566,952; Rawalpindi, 2,505,889; Gujranwala, 2,122,254; Multan, 1,920,776; Hyderabad, 1,772,143; Peshawar, 1,736,192.

Government: Type: Federal republic. **Head of state:** Pres. Mamnoon Hussain; in office: Sept. 9, 2013. **Head of gov.:** Prime Min. Nawaz Sharif; in office: June 5, 2013. **Local divisions:** 4 provinces, 1 territory, 1 capital territory; 2 admin. entities in Pakistan-administered part of Jammu and Kashmir region. **Defense budget:** $6.01 bil. **Active troops:** 643,800.

Economy: Industries: textiles and apparel, food proc., pharmaceuticals, constr. materials, paper prods., fertilizer, shrimp. **Chief crops:** cotton, wheat, rice, sugarcane, fruits, vegetables. **Natural resources:** nat. gas, limited petroleum, poor quality coal, iron ore, copper, salt, limestone. **Water:** 1,355 cu m per capita. **Crude oil reserves:** 371 mil bbls. **Electricity prod.:** 92.9 bil kWh. **Labor force:** agric. 44%, industry 22%, services 33%. **Unemployment:** 5.1%.

Finance: Monetary unit: Rupee (PKR) (104.15 = $1 U.S.). **GDP:** $882.3 bil; **per capita GDP:** $4,700; **GDP growth:** 4.1%. **Imports:** $45.1 bil; China 22.5%, Saudi Arabia 11.9%, UAE 11.7%, Kuwait 6.1%. **Exports:** $25.1 bil; U.S. 12.9%, China 11%, UAE 9.2%, Afghanistan 8%. **Tourism:** $283 mil. **Budget** (2014 est.): $51 bil. **Inflation:** 7.2%.

Transport: Railways: 4,840 mi. **Motor vehicles:** 15.1 per 1,000 pop. **Airports:** 108.

Communications: Telephone: 2.6 per 100 pop. **Mobile:** 73.3 per 100 pop. **Broadband:** 0.8 per 100 pop. **Internet:** 13.8%.

Health: Expend.: 2.7%. **Life expect.:** 65.5 male; 69.4 female. **Births:** 22.6 per 1,000 pop. **Deaths:** 6.5 per 1,000 pop. **Infant mortality:** 55.7 per 1,000 live births. **Undernourished:** 21.7%. **HIV:** <0.1%.

Education: Compulsory: ages 5-16. **Literacy:** 57.9%.

Embassy: 3517 International Ct. NW 20008; 243-6500.

Website: www.pakistan.gov.pk

Pakistan shares the 5,000-year history of the India-Pakistan subcontinent. At present-day Harappa and Mohenjo Daro, the Indus Valley civilization, with large cities and elaborate irrigation systems, flourished c. 4,000-2,500 BCE. Aryan invaders from the northwest conquered the region around 1,500 BCE, forging the Vedic civilization that dominated the region for over a thousand years. The first Arab invasion, 712 CE, introduced Islam. Present-day Pakistan and India were part of the Mughal Empire from 1526 to 1857. Muslim power faded by the end of the 19th cent. as the British gained control.

Muhammad Ali Jinnah (1876-1948) was the principal architect of Pakistan. When the British withdrew Aug. 14, 1947, India's Islamic majority acquired self-government as Pakistan, with dominion status in the Commonwealth. Pakistan was divided into West Pakistan and East Pakistan, nearly 1,000 mi apart on opposite sides of India. Kashmir, a predominantly Muslim region divided between Pakistan and India, has remained a source of conflict between the two countries.

Rioting and strikes broke out in the East after Pakistan's government, Mar. 1, 1971, postponed the constituent assembly, dominated by supporters of regional autonomy for East Pakistan. Armed conflict between East and West lasted from Mar. to Dec. 1971, with India siding with Easterners, who proclaimed the independent nation of Bangladesh. Thousands were killed, and some 10 mil Easterners fled to India. Full-scale war erupted between India and Pakistan, but Pakistan troops in the East surrendered Dec. 16; Pakistan agreed to a cease-fire in the West Dec. 17. On July 3, 1972, Pakistan and India signed a pact agreeing to troop withdrawals and peaceful conflict resolution.

Dec. 1970 elections brought Zulfikar Ali Bhutto to the presidency Dec. 20, 1971. Bhutto was overthrown in a military coup July 1977. Convicted of complicity in a 1974 political murder, he was executed Apr. 4, 1979. Millions of Afghan refugees flooded into Pakistan after the USSR invaded Afghanistan Dec. 1979; during 2002-10, some 3.6 mil refugees were repatriated, but 1.7 mil remained.

Pres. Mohammad Zia ul-Haq was killed when his plane exploded in Aug. 1988. Following Nov. elections, Benazir Bhutto, daughter of Zulfikar Ali Bhutto, was named prime min., becoming the first woman leader of a Muslim nation. She was accused of corruption and dismissed by the president, Aug. 1990. Bhutto returned to power Oct. 1993 but was dismissed Nov. 1996 amid further corruption charges. Responding to India's nuclear weapons tests, Pakistan conducted its own tests in 1998; the U.S. imposed economic sanctions on both countries.

Prime Min. Nawaz Sharif fired, Oct. 1999, army chief Gen. Pervez Musharraf, whose supporters staged a bloodless coup. Musharraf assumed the presidency June 20, 2001. Following the Sept. 11, 2001, terrorist attacks on the U.S., Pres. Musharraf pledged cooperation with the U.S. in fighting Taliban and al-Qaeda militants within Pakistan and in neighboring Afghanistan. In return, the U.S. waived its 1998 sanctions and offered Pakistan financial aid and debt relief. A referendum Apr. 30, 2002, extended Musharraf's rule for 5 years; many observers called the vote rigged. Musharraf Feb. 5, 2004, pardoned Pakistan's top nuclear scientist, Abdul Qadeer Khan, who admitted to selling atomic secrets to Iran, Libya, and North Korea. An earthquake that rocked Pakistan and the Pakistani-held region of Kashmir Oct. 8, 2005, killed about 80,000 people.

Musharraf's grip weakened in 2007, as his efforts to oust Pakistan's chief justice sparked mass pro-democracy demonstrations. He retained the presidency in an electoral-college vote Oct. 6, 2007, after his main opponents boycotted the election. More than 140 people died Oct. 18 when suicide bombers struck a convoy carrying Benazir Bhutto from the Karachi airport after she spent more than eight years in exile. Musharraf imposed emergency rule Nov. 3 and suspended the constitution while Pakistan's supreme court debated the constitutionality of his reelection. Musharraf gave up his army post Nov. 25, was sworn in as civilian president the next day, and lifted emergency rule Dec. 16. Bhutto was assassinated Dec. 27, 2007, after a rally in Rawalpindi.

Headed by Bhutto's widower, Asif Ali Zardari, the Pakistan Peoples Party led in parliamentary elections Feb. 18, 2008. Musharraf resigned Aug. 18 under threat of impeachment, and Zardari became president Sept. 9. Amid deteriorating security, U.S. and Pakistani forces clashed with the Taliban near the Afghan border, and Islamists carried out new suicide attacks. The government announced Feb. 16, 2009, a truce conceding de facto control of the strategic Swat Valley to the Taliban, but in May, government forces launched an offensive that reclaimed most of the region; the fighting displaced nearly 2 mil civilians. Catastrophic floods and monsoon rains, July-Aug. 2010, inundated one-fifth of Pakistan, leaving more than 1,750 people dead and displacing up to 20 mil.

A decade-long international manhunt came to an end shortly after midnight May 2, 2011, when U.S. commandos killed al-Qaeda leader Osama bin Laden in Abbottabad. The raid, carried out by helicopter from Jalalabad, Afghanistan, was launched without prior warning to Pakistani authorities.

Volunteers attempting to administer polio vaccine to children were attacked and at least 9 were killed, causing a temporary halt to the vaccination campaign Dec. 20, 2012. Polio cases increased in 2013-14, especially in Taliban stronghold North Waziristan; the Taliban attacked health workers to protest U.S. drone strikes and the CIA program that had used vaccination workers as a cover to gather intelligence.

In the worst industrial accident in Pakistan's history, nearly 300 died in a fire that consumed a factory complex in Karachi Sept. 12, 2012. On Oct. 9, 2012, 15-year-old Malala Yousafzai, who advocated for education rights for girls in Pakistan, was shot by the Taliban, sparking worldwide outrage. After treatment at a British hospital, she resumed her work on behalf of children's rights, for which she shared the 2014 Nobel Peace Prize. The Pakistan military announced, Sept. 12, 2014, that 10 people had been arrested in connection with the shooting; 2 were convicted in Apr. 2015.

Musharraf returned to Pakistan Mar. 24, 2013, to attempt a political comeback but was indicted in connection with Benazir Bhutto's assassination Aug. 20, 2013, and charged with treason, Mar. 31, 2014. Amid accusations of vote rigging, former Prime Min. Nawaz Sharif was returned to office with May 11 elections (a judicial commission report, July 23, 2015, rejected voting fraud allegations). Mamnoon Hussain won the presidential election July 30, 2013. In 2014-15, terrorist attacks continued, including an assault on a Peshawar school, Dec. 16, 2014, that left about 150 dead. In 2007-14, an estimated 7,500 people died in terrorist attacks. Conflict also continued in 2014-15 between Islamic extremists and Pakistani forces, sometimes supported by U.S. drone strikes. A major anti-extremist offensive in North Waziristan began in June 2014, displacing more than 1 mil civilians. Fighting between Pakistani forces and extremists resulted in more than 17,000 fatalities, 2007-14.

Palau

Republic of Palau

People: Population: 21,265. **Age distrib.:** <15: 20.3%; 65+: 7.3%. **Growth:** 0.4%. **Migrants:** 26.7%. **Pop. density:** 120 per sq mi, 46.3 per sq km. **Urban:** 87.1%. **Ethnic groups:** Palauan (Micronesian with Malayan/Melanesian admixtures) 72.5%, Filipino 16.3%, other Micronesian 2.4%. **Languages:** Palauan (official on most islands), English (official), Filipino. **Religions:** Roman Catholic 49.4%, Protestant 30.9%, Modekngei (indigenous to Palau) 8.7%.

Geography: Total area: 177 sq mi, 459 sq km; **Land area:** 177 sq mi, 459 sq km. **Location:** Archipelago (26 islands, more than 300 islets) in W Pacific O., about 530 mi SE of the Philippines. Micronesia to E, Indonesia to S. **Topography:** A mountainous main island and low coral atolls, usually fringed with large barrier reefs. **Arable land:** 2.2%. **Capital:** Melekeok.

Government: Type: Constitutional govt. in free association with U.S. **Head of state and gov.:** Pres. Tommy Remengesau; in office: Jan. 17, 2013. **Local divisions:** 16 states. **Defense budget/active troops:** NA.

Economy: Industries: tourism, craft items, constr., garment making. **Chief crops:** coconuts, copra, cassava, sweet potatoes. **Natural resources:** forests, minerals (espec. gold), marine prods., deep-seabed minerals. **Water:** NA. **Labor force:** agric. 20%. **Unemployment:** NA.

Finance: Monetary unit: U.S. Dollar (USD). **GDP:** $288 mil (incl. U.S. subsidy); **per capita GDP:** $16,300; **GDP growth:** 8%. **Imports:** $177.7 mil. **Exports:** $19.1 mil. **Tourism:** $112 mil. **Budget** (2012 est.): $97.5 mil. **Inflation:** NA.

Transport: Airports: 1.

Communications: Telephone: 33.9 per 100 pop. **Mobile:** 90.6 per 100 pop. **Broadband:** NA. **Internet** (2004): 27%.

Health: Expend.: 9.5%. **Life expect.:** 69.7 male; 76.2 female. **Births:** 11.1 per 1,000 pop. **Deaths:** 8.0 per 1,000 pop. **Infant mortality:** 11.2 per 1,000 live births. **Undernourished:** NA. **HIV:** NA.

Education: Compulsory: ages 6-17. **Literacy:** 99.5%.

Embassy: 1701 Pennsylvania Ave. NW, Ste. 300, 20036; 452-6814.

Website: palaugov.org

Spain acquired the Palau Islands, 1886, and sold them to Germany, 1899. Japan seized them in 1914. American forces occupied the islands in 1944; in 1947, they became part of the U.S.-administered UN Trust Territory of the Pacific Islands. In 1981, Palau became an autonomous republic. The republic ratified a compact of free association with the U.S. in 1993 and became an independent nation, Oct. 1, 1994. Palau is threatened by rising sea levels resulting from climate change.

Panama

Republic of Panama

People: Population: 3,657,024. **Age distrib.:** <15: 27.1%; 65+: 8%. **Growth:** 1.3%. **Migrants:** 4.1%. **Pop. density:** 127.4 per sq mi, 49.2 per sq km. **Urban:** 66.6%. **Ethnic groups:** mestizo (mixed Amerindian/white) 65%, Native American (incl. Ngabe 7.6%, Kuna 2.4%) 12.3%, black or African descent 9.2%, mulatto 6.8%, white 6.7%. **Languages:** Spanish (official), indigenous langs. **Religions:** Roman Catholic 85%, Protestant 15%.

Geography: Total area: 29,120 sq mi, 75,420 sq km; **Land area:** 28,703 sq mi, 74,340 sq km. **Location:** Central America. Costa Rica on W, Colombia on E. **Topography:** Two mountain ranges run length of isthmus. Tropical rain forests cover the Caribbean coast and E. **Arable land:** 7.2%. **Capital:** Panama City, 1,672,810.

Government: Type: Constitutional democracy. **Head of state and gov.:** Pres. Juan Carlos Varela; in office: July 1, 2014. **Local divisions:** 10 provinces, 3 indigenous territories. **Defense budget:** $717 mil. **Active troops:** No armed forces. 12,000 paramilitary only.

Economy: Industries: constr., brewing, cement and other constr. materials, sugar milling. **Chief crops:** bananas, rice, corn, coffee, sugarcane, vegetables. **Natural resources:** copper, mahogany forests, shrimp, hydropower. **Water:** 36,051 cu m per capita. **Electricity prod.:** 8.4 bil kWh. **Labor force:** agric. 17%, industry 18.6%, services 64.4%. **Unemployment:** 4.1%.

Finance: Monetary unit: Balboa (PAB) (1.00 = $1 U.S.). **GDP:** $76.4 bil; **per capita GDP:** $19,500; **GDP growth:** 6.2%. **Imports:** $25.7 bil; U.S. 19%, China 14.8%, Singapore 13.1%, Japan 9.5%, Brazil 8.2%, Colombia 5.1%. **Exports:** $18.1 bil; Ecuador 33.9%, U.S. 11.5%, Japan 8.8%. (Import/export figures incl. Colón Free Zone.). **Tourism:** $3.5 bil. **Budget:** $12.7 bil. **Inflation:** 2.6%.

Transport: Railways: 48 mi. **Motor vehicles:** 166 per 1,000 pop. **Airports:** 57.

Communications: Telephone: 15 per 100 pop. **Mobile:** 158.1 per 100 pop. **Broadband:** 25.2 per 100 pop. **Internet:** 44.9%.

Health: Expend.: 7.6%. **Life expect.:** 75.7 male; 81.4 female. **Births:** 18.3 per 1,000 pop. **Deaths:** 4.8 per 1,000 pop. **Infant mortality:** 10.4 per 1,000 live births. **Undernourished:** 10.6%. **HIV:** 0.6%.

Education: Compulsory: ages 6-14. **Literacy:** 95%.

Embassy: 2862 McGill Ter. NW 20007; 483-1407.

Website: www.presidencia.gob.pa

The coast of Panama was sighted by Rodrigo de Bastidas, sailing with Columbus for Spain in 1501, and was visited by Columbus in 1502. Vasco Núñez de Balboa crossed the isthmus and "discovered" the Pacific Ocean, Sept. 13, 1513. Spanish colonies were ravaged by Francis Drake, 1572-95, and Henry Morgan, 1668-71. Morgan destroyed the old city of Panama, which was founded in 1519. Freed from Spain, Panama joined Colombia in 1821.

Panama declared independence from Colombia Nov. 3, 1903, and granted use, occupation, and control of the Canal Zone to the U.S. Feb. 26, 1904. The U.S.-built Panama Canal opened Aug. 15, 1914. A 1978 treaty provided for a gradual takeover by Panama of the canal. The U.S. handed over control Dec. 31, 1999. A $5.3-bil plan to widen the Panama Canal was approved by national referendum Oct. 22, 2006. Construction was more than 90% completed by mid-2015, with completion expected by early 2016.

Pres. Eric Arturo Delvalle was ousted by the National Assembly, Feb. 26, 1988, after he tried to fire Gen. Manuel Antonio Noriega, who was under U.S. federal indictment on drug charges. U.S. troops invaded Panama Dec. 20, 1989, and Noriega surrendered Jan. 3, 1990. Ricardo Martinelli Berrocal, a conservative, was elected president May 3, 2009. After two decades in a U.S. prison, Noriega was extradited to France Apr. 26, 2010, where he was convicted of money laundering July 7 and received a 7-year sentence. France extradited him to Panama, Dec. 11, 2011, to serve a 20-year sentence for human rights violations. In May 4, 2014, presidential elections, Juan Carols Varela defeated the candidate supported by Martinelli.

Papua New Guinea

Independent State of Papua New Guinea

People: Population: 6,672,429. **Age distrib.:** <15: 34.4%; 65+: 4.1%. **Growth:** 1.8%. **Migrants:** 0.3%. **Pop. density:** 38.2 per sq mi, 14.7 per sq km. **Urban:** 13%. **Ethnic groups:** Melanesian, Papuan, Negrito, Micronesian, Polynesian. **Languages:** Tok Pisin, English, Hiri Motu (all official); some 836 indigenous langs. (most spoken by fewer than 1,000). **Religions:** Roman Catholic 27%, Protestant 69.4% (incl. Evangelical Lutheran 19.5%, United Church 11.5%, Seventh-day Adventist 10%).

Geography: Total area: 178,704 sq mi, 462,840 sq km; **Land area:** 174,850 sq mi, 452,860 sq km. **Location:** SE Asia; E half of island of New Guinea and about 600 nearby islands. Indonesia on W, Australia on S. **Topography:** Thickly forested mountains cover much of center, with lowlands along the coasts. Incl. some islands of Bismarck and Solomon groups, such as Admiralty Isls., New Ireland, New Britain, and Bougainville. **Arable land:** 0.7%. **Capital:** Port Moresby, 345,158.

Government: Type: Constitutional parliamentary democracy. **Head of state:** Queen Elizabeth II, rep. by Gov.-Gen. Sir Michael Ogio; in office: Feb. 25, 2011. **Head of gov.:** Prime Min. Peter O'Neill; in office: Aug. 2, 2011. **Local divisions:** 20 provinces, 1 autonomous region, 1 district. **Defense budget:** $99 mil. **Active troops:** 1,900.

Economy: Industries: copra crushing, palm oil proc., plywood prod., wood chip prod., mining, crude oil and petroleum prods. **Chief crops:** coffee, cocoa, copra, palm kernels, tea, sugar, rubber, sweet potatoes. **Natural resources:** gold, copper, silver, nat. gas, timber, oil, fisheries. **Water:** 109,411 cu m per capita. **Crude oil reserves:** 175.2 mil bbls. **Electricity prod.:** 3.4 bil kWh. **Labor force:** agric. 85%. **Unemployment:** 2.1%.

Finance: Monetary unit: Kina (PGK) (2.81 = $1 U.S.). **GDP:** $18.1 bil; **per capita GDP:** $2,400; **GDP growth:** 5.8%. **Imports:** $4.3 bil; Australia 37.9%, Singapore 13.6%, Malaysia 8.8%, China 8.7%. **Exports:** $7.4 bil; Australia 26.2%, Japan 7.2%, China 6.6%. **Tourism:** $2 mil. **Budget:** $5.6 bil. **Inflation** (2012-13): 5%.

Transport: Motor vehicles: 21.5 per 1,000 pop. **Airports:** 21.

Communications: Telephone: 1.9 per 100 pop. **Mobile:** 44.9 per 100 pop. **Broadband:** 6.2 per 100 pop. **Internet:** 9.4%.

Health: Expend.: 5.2%. **Life expect.:** 64.8 male; 69.4 female. **Births:** 24.4 per 1,000 pop. **Deaths:** 6.5 per 1,000 pop. **Infant mortality:** 38.6 per 1,000 live births. **Undernourished:** NA. **HIV:** 0.7%.

Education: Compulsory: NA. **Literacy:** 64.2%.

Embassy: 1779 Massachusetts Ave. NW, Ste. 805, 20036; 745-3680.

Website: www.pm.gov.pg

Human remains dating back at least 10,000 years have been found in the interior of New Guinea. European colonization began in the 19th cent., when the Dutch took control of the island's western half (now part of Indonesia). The southern half of eastern New Guinea was claimed by Britain in 1884 and transferred to Australia in 1905. Germany claimed the northern half in 1884, but Australia captured it in WWI, receiving a League of Nations mandate and later a UN trusteeship. The two territories were administered jointly after 1949; gained self-government Dec. 1, 1973; and became independent Sept. 16, 1975.

Secessionist rebels clashed with government forces on Bougainville 1988-97, claiming some 20,000 lives. A Bougainville autonomy agreement was signed Aug. 30, 2001. Sir Michael Somare, the nation's first prime min. (1975-80, 1982-85), regained the office in 2002 and was reelected by parliament Aug. 13, 2007. Somare took indefinite medical leave Apr. 2011; parliament, Aug. 2, elected Peter O'Neill as permanent replacement. The Supreme Court ruled that election illegal Dec. 12, 2011, and ordered Somare returned to office. O'Neill refused to step aside. The crisis ended after June-July 2012 parliamentary elections; the new parliament elected O'Neill prime min., Aug. 3, 2012. The country's Sorcery Act, which had criminalized the practice, was repealed May 29, 2013; to curb vigilante violence against alleged sorcerers and also violence against women, the death penalty was reinstated for rape, robbery, and murder.

The country has extensive energy resources. After the initial phase of a project to transport natural gas by pipeline was completed, the first shipments of liquefied natural gas through a new processing and shipping facility near Port Moresby were made in May 2014.

Paraguay

Republic of Paraguay

People: Population: 6,783,272. **Age distrib.:** <15: 25.6%; 65+: 6.7%. **Growth:** 1.2%. **Migrants:** 2.7%. **Pop. density:** 44.2 per sq mi, 17.1 per sq km. **Urban:** 59.7%. **Ethnic groups:** mestizo (mixed Spanish/Amerindian) 95%. **Languages:** Spanish, Guaraní (both official). **Religions:** Roman Catholic 89.6%, Protestant 6.2%.

Geography: Total area: 157,048 sq mi, 406,752 sq km; **Land area:** 153,399 sq mi, 397,302 sq km. **Location:** Landlocked country in central S America. Bolivia on N, Argentina on S, Brazil on E. **Topography:** Paraguay R. bisects country. Fertile plains, wooded slopes, grasslands to E. Gran Chaco plain, with marshes and scrub trees, to W. Extreme W is arid. **Arable land:** 11.1%. **Capital:** Asunción, 2,356,174.

Government: Type: Constitutional republic. **Head of state and gov.:** Pres. Horacio Cartes; in office: Aug. 15, 2013. **Local divisions:** 17 departments, 1 capital city. **Defense budget:** $313 mil. **Active troops:** 10,650.

Economy: Industries: sugar, cement, textiles, beverages, wood prods., steel. **Chief crops:** cotton, sugarcane, soybeans, corn, wheat, tobacco, cassava, fruits, vegetables. **Natural resources:** hydropower, timber, iron ore, manganese, limestone. **Water:** 57,013 cu m per capita. **Electricity prod.:** 59.6 bil kWh. **Labor force:** agric. 26.5%, industry 18.5%, services 55%. **Unemployment:** 5.2%.

Finance: Monetary unit: Guarani (PYG) (5,394.01 = $1 U.S.). **GDP:** $58.3 bil; **per capita GDP:** $8,400; **GDP growth:** 4.4%. **Imports:** $12.4 bil; China 28.5%, Brazil 26.5%, Argentina 14.2%, U.S. 6.5%. **Exports:** $14.6 bil; Brazil 30%, Russia 10%, Argentina 9.3%, Chile 5.3%. **Tourism:** $282 mil. **Budget:** $5.7 bil. **Inflation:** 5%.

Transport: Railways: 19 mi. **Motor vehicles:** 67.4 per 1,000 pop. **Airports:** 15.

Communications: Telephone: 5.4 per 100 pop. **Mobile:** 105.6 per 100 pop. **Broadband:** 5.5 per 100 pop. **Internet:** 43%.

Health: Expend.: 10.3%. **Life expect.:** 74.3 male; 79.8 female. **Births:** 16.4 per 1,000 pop. **Deaths:** 4.7 per 1,000 pop. **Infant mortality:** 20.1 per 1,000 live births. **Undernourished:** 11%. **HIV:** 0.4%.

Education: Compulsory: ages 6-14. **Literacy:** 95.6%.

Embassy: 2400 Massachusetts Ave. NW 20008; 483-6960.

Website: www.presidencia.gov.py

Guaraní Indians preceded Europeans in Paraguay, which was visited by Sebastian Cabot in 1527 and became a Spanish possession in 1535. Paraguay gained independence from Spain in 1811. It lost half its population and much of its territory to Brazil, Uruguay, and Argentina in the War of the Triple Alliance, 1865-70. Large areas were won from Bolivia in the Chaco War, 1932-35. Gen. Alfredo Stroessner held the presidency 1954-89, until his ouster in a military coup.

Power struggles ensued between civilian and military leaders, 1993-97. The assassination of Vice Pres. Luis María Argaña, Mar. 23, 1999, was widely attributed to Pres. Raúl Cubas Grau and triggered protests and an impeachment vote; Cubas resigned Mar. 28 and was succeeded by Senate leader Luis Angel González Macchi. An attempted military coup was suppressed May 18, 2000.

Mass protests over the depressed economy led to the proclamation of a state of emergency July 15, 2002. Nicanor Duarte Frutos of the conservative Colorado Party won the presidency, Apr. 27, 2003.

Paraguayan authorities blamed a leftist group for the Sept. 2004 kidnapping and subsequent murder of Cecilia Cubas, daughter of former Pres. Cubas. Fernando Lugo, a former Catholic cleric known as the "bishop of the poor," won a presidential election Apr. 20, 2008, ending over six decades of Colorado rule. On June 22, 2012, Lugo was removed from office after his handling of a dispute between landless peasants and police left 17 dead June 15. Colorado candidate Horacio Cartes, a former tobacco magnate, was elected president Apr. 21, 2013. Pope Francis visited Paraguay, July 10-12, 2015; in public remarks he urged combating corruption and drug trafficking.

Peru

Republic of Peru

People: Population: 30,444,999. **Age distrib.:** <15: 26.9%; 65+: 7%. **Growth:** 1%. **Migrants:** 0.3%. **Pop. density:** 61.6 per sq mi, 23.8 per sq km. **Urban:** 78.6%. **Ethnic groups:** Amerindian 45%; mestizo (mixed Amerindian/white) 37%; white 15%; black, Japanese, Chinese, other 3%. **Languages:** Spanish, Quechua, Aymara (all official). **Religions:** Roman Catholic 81.3%, Evangelical 12.5%, none 2.9%.

Geography: Total area: 496,225 sq mi, 1,285,216 sq km; **Land area:** 494,209 sq mi, 1,279,996 sq km. **Location:** Pacific coast of S America. Ecuador, Colombia on N; Brazil, Bolivia on E; Chile on S. **Topography:** An arid coastal strip, 10-100 mi wide. The Andes cover one-quarter of land area. The uplands are well-watered, as are the eastern slopes reaching the Amazon Basin, which covers half of country. **Arable land:** 3.2%. **Capital:** Lima, 9,897,033. **Cities:** Arequipa, 850,275.

Government: Type: Constitutional republic. **Head of state and gov:** Pres. Ollanta Humala Tasso; in office: July 28, 2011. **Local divisions:** 25 regions, 1 province. **Defense budget:** $2.59 bil. **Active troops:** 115,000.

Economy: Industries: mining, refining of minerals; steel, metal fabrication; petroleum extraction and refining, nat. gas and nat. gas liquefaction; fishing and fish proc., cement, glass, textiles. **Chief crops:** artichokes, asparagus, avocados, blueberries, coffee, cocoa, cotton, sugarcane, rice, potatoes, corn, plantains, grapes, oranges and other fruits, coca, tomatoes, barley, medicinal plants. **Natural resources:** copper, silver, gold, petroleum, timber, fish, iron ore, coal, phosphate, potash, hydropower, nat. gas. **Water:** 62,352 cu m per capita. **Crude oil reserves:** 741.2 mil bbls. **Electricity prod.:** 39.1 bil kWh. **Labor force:** agric. 25.8%, industry 17.4%, services 56.8%. **Unemployment:** 3.9%.

Finance: Monetary unit: Nuevo Sol (PEN) (3.24 = $1 U.S.). **GDP:** $371.3 bil; **per capita GDP:** $11,800; **GDP growth:** 2.4%. **Imports:** $40.3 bil; U.S. 24.8%, China 15.3%, Brazil 5.3%. **Exports:** $36.4 bil; U.S. 18.4%, China 17.8%, Canada 7%, Japan 5.2%. **Tourism:** $3 bil. **Budget:** $64.5 bil. **Inflation:** 3.2%.

Transport: Railways: 1,152 mi. **Motor vehicles:** 65.9 per 1,000 pop. **Airports:** 59.

Communications: Telephone: 9.9 per 100 pop. **Mobile:** 102.9 per 100 pop. **Broadband:** 3 per 100 pop. **Internet:** 40.2%.

Health: Expend.: 5.1%. **Life expect.:** 71.5 male; 75.6 female. **Births:** 18.3 per 1,000 pop. **Deaths:** 6.0 per 1,000 pop. **Infant mortality:** 19.6 per 1,000 live births. **Undernourished:** 8.7%. **HIV:** 0.4%.

Education: Compulsory: ages 5-16. **Literacy:** 94.5%.

Embassy: 1700 Massachusetts Ave. NW 20036; 833-9860.

Website: www.peru.gob.pe

The powerful Inca Empire had its seat at Cuzco in the Andes and covered much of S America. A civil war had weakened the empire when Spaniard Francisco Pizarro began raiding Peru for its wealth, 1532. In 1533 he executed the Inca ruler, Atahualpa, and enslaved the people.

José de San Martin captured Lima from the Spanish in 1821; Simón Bolívar routed Spanish forces in 1824, and for much of the 19th cent., the country was governed by military leaders. Chile defeated Peru in the War of the Pacific, 1879-83. Right-wing groups allied with the military and the leftist APRA party vied for power in the first half of the 20th cent.

Peru returned to democratic leadership in 1980 but was plagued by economic problems and by leftist Shining Path (Sendero Luminoso) guerrillas. Conflict between guerrillas and government troops, 1980-2000, killed more than 69,000 people, mostly Andean Indians.

Elected president in June 1990, Alberto Fujimori, the son of Japanese immigrants, dissolved the National Congress, suspended parts of the constitution, and initiated press censorship, Apr. 1992. The leader of Shining Path was captured Sept. 12. Fujimori won reelection in 1995 and 2000, but his repressive antiterrorism tactics drew international criticism.

Scandals involving top aide and intelligence chief Vladimiro Montesinos led Fujimori to resign Nov. 20, 2000; instead of accepting his resignation, Congress ousted him as "morally unfit." Montesinos was captured in Venezuela June 23, 2001; extradited to Peru, he was convicted in a series of criminal trials. Fujimori was arrested in Chile, Nov. 7, 2005, and extradited to Peru, Sept. 22, 2007. He was convicted in three separate proceedings, 2007-09, on charges that included complicity in a paramilitary death squad's killing of at least 25 people, 1991-92. He was convicted, Jan. 8, 2015, of misusing public funds during his 2000 campaign.

Alan García, whose first term as president, 1985-90, ended with the country facing hyperinflation and guerrilla war, won a presidential runoff election June 4, 2006. In a presidential runoff June 5, 2011, Ollanta Humala Tasso, a leftist former military officer, defeated Keiko Fujimori Higuchi, daughter of jailed former Pres. Fujimori. A maritime border dispute with Chile (with implications for commercial fishing) was settled largely in Peru's favor by the Intl. Court of Justice, Jan. 27, 2014.

Philippines

Republic of the Philippines

People: Population: 100,998,376. **Age distrib.:** <15: 34%; 65+: 4.3%. **Growth:** 1.6%. **Migrants:** 0.2%. **Pop. density:** 877.3 per sq mi, 338.7 per sq km. **Urban:** 44.4%. **Ethnic groups:** Tagalog 28.1%, Cebuano 13.1%, Ilocano 9%, Bisaya/Binisaya 7.6%, Hiligaynon Ilonggo 7.5%, Bikol 6%, Waray 3.4%. **Languages:** Filipino (based on Tagalog), English (both official); 8 major dialects incl. Tagalog. **Religions:** Catholic 82.9% (incl. Roman Catholic 80.9%), Muslim 5%, Evangelical 2.8%, Iglesia ni Kristo 2.3%, other Christian 4.5%.

Geography: Total area: 115,831 sq mi, 300,000 sq km; **Land area:** 115,124 sq mi, 298,170 sq km. **Location:** An archipelago off SE coast of Asia. Malaysia, Indonesia on S; Taiwan on N. **Topography:** The country consists of some 7,100 islands stretching 1,100 mi N-S. About 95% of area and pop. are on 11 largest islands, which are mountainous, except for the heavily indented coastlines and central plain on Luzon. **Arable land:** 18.6%. **Capital:** Manila, 12,946,263 (figure is for natl. capital region). **Cities:** Davao City, 1,629,547; Cebu City, 950,559.

Government: Type: Republic. **Head of state and gov.:** Pres. Benigno "Noynoy" Aquino III; in office: June 30, 2010. **Local divisions:** 80 provinces, 39 chartered cities. **Defense budget:** $2.04 bil. **Active troops:** 125,000.

Economy: Industries: electronics assembly, garments, footwear, pharmaceuticals, chemicals, wood prods., food proc. **Chief crops:** sugarcane, coconuts, rice, corn, bananas, cassava, pineapples, mangoes. **Natural resources:** timber, petroleum, nickel, cobalt, silver, gold, salt, copper. **Water:** 4,868 cu m per capita. **Crude oil reserves:** 138.5 mil bbls. **Electricity prod.:** 69.7 bil kWh. **Labor force:** agric. 30%, industry 16%, services 54%. **Unemployment:** 7.1%.

Finance: Monetary unit: Peso (PHP) (46.70 = $1 U.S.). **GDP:** $692.2 bil; **per capita GDP:** $7,000; **GDP growth:** 6.1%. **Imports:** $63.6 bil; (2014) China 15%, U.S. 8.7%, Japan 8.1%, South Korea 7.8%, Singapore 7%, Taiwan 6.8%, Thailand 5.3%, Saudi Arabia 5%. **Exports:** $47.8 bil; (2014) Japan 22.5%, U.S. 14%, China 12.1%, Hong Kong 9%. **Tourism:** $4.8 bil. **Budget:** $44.6 bil. **Inflation:** 4.1%.

Transport: Railways: 557 mi. **Motor vehicles:** 32.2 per 1,000 pop. **Airports:** 89.

Communications: Telephone: 3.1 per 100 pop. **Mobile:** 111.2 per 100 pop. **Broadband:** 9.1 per 100 pop. **Internet:** 39.7%.

Health: Expend.: 4.6%. **Life expect.:** 65.5 male; 72.6 female. **Births:** 24.3 per 1,000 pop. **Deaths:** 6.1 per 1,000 pop. **Infant mortality:** 22.3 per 1,000 live births. **Undernourished:** 11.5%. **HIV:** <0.1%.

Education: Compulsory: ages 5-17. **Literacy:** 96.3%.

Embassy: 1600 Massachusetts Ave. NW 20036; 467-9300.

Website: www.gov.ph

Originally inhabited by Malay peoples, the archipelago was visited by Magellan, 1521. The Spanish founded Manila, 1571. Spain ceded the islands, named for King Philip II of Spain, to the U.S. for $20 mil, 1898, following the Spanish-American War. U.S. troops suppressed a guerrilla uprising in a brutal war, 1899-1905. Japan attacked the Philippines Dec. 8, 1941, and occupied the islands during WWII. Independence was proclaimed, July 4, 1946. A republic was established.

The repressive and corrupt regime of Pres. Ferdinand Marcos and his wife, Imelda, ruled 1965-86. The assassination of prominent opposition leader Benigno S. Aquino Jr., Aug. 21, 1983, sparked calls for Marcos's resignation. Marcos defeated Corazon Aquino, widow of the slain opposition leader, Feb. 16, 1986, in an allegedly fraudulent election. Mass protests and international pressure forced Marcos to flee the country Feb. 25, and Aquino became president.

Her government was plagued by a weak economy, widespread poverty, Communist and Muslim insurgencies, and lukewarm military support. Rebel troops attempting a coup Dec. 1, 1989, were defeated by government forces and U.S. air support. Fidel Ramos won the May 1992 presidential election. The U.S. vacated the Subic Bay Naval Station in late 1992, ending its long military presence. However, a 2014 agreement gave U.S. forces increased access to Philippines bases. Some Muslim separatist guerrillas refused to abide by a cease-fire agreement signed Jan. 30, 1994, so a new treaty providing for expansion and development of an autonomous Muslim region on Mindanao was signed Sept. 2, 1996; the rebellion had claimed more than 120,000 lives since 1972.

Joseph (Erap) Estrada, a former movie actor, won the presidential election, May 11, 1998, but was impeached on bribery and corruption charges Nov. 13, 2000. Vice Pres. Gloria Macapagal Arroyo became president Jan. 20, 2001.

As part of the post-9/11 war on terror, the U.S. began assisting Filipino troops in combating Abu Sayyaf, an Islamist guerrilla group. The U.S. announced, June 26, 2014, plans to scale back the program. Pres. Arroyo won reelection May 10, 2004. Flooding and mudslides from tropical storms, Nov.-Dec. 2004, killed at least 1,060 people. Former Pres. Estrada was convicted, Sept. 12, 2007, of taking more than $85 mil in bribes and kickbacks while in office; Pres. Arroyo pardoned him Oct. 25. Benigno "NoyNoy" Aquino III, the son of former Pres. Aquino (who died Aug. 1, 2009), defeated Estrada in the May 10, 2010, presidential election.

Former Pres. Arroyo, who was serving in Congress, was arrested Oct. 4, 2012, on corruption charges. The government, Oct. 15, 2012, signed a new peace deal with Muslim rebels on Mindanao; violence had persisted after the 1996 accord. Yet another peace agreement, providing for a large measure of autonomy for Mindanao, was signed by the government and Moro Islamic Liberation Front, Mar. 27, 2014. Abu Sayyaf rejected the accord.

Congress voted, Dec. 17, 2012, to provide free contraceptives at health clinics, despite objections from many of the nation's Catholics; the Supreme Court, Apr. 8, 2014, upheld the law's key provisions. Typhoon Haiyan, with winds up to 195 mph, struck the Philippines Nov. 8, 2013; the storm killed more than 6,200 people and displaced over 4 mil. During a 2015 visit, Pope Francis celebrated an outdoor mass in Manila attended by some 6 mil people, Jan. 18.

Poland

Republic of Poland

People: Population: 38,562,189. **Age distrib.:** <15: 14.7%; 65+: 15.7%. **Growth:** –0.1%. **Migrants:** 1.7%. **Pop. density:** 328.3 per sq mi, 126.7 per sq km. **Urban:** 60.5%. **Ethnic groups:** Polish 96.9%. **Languages:** Polish (official). **Religions:** Catholic 87.2%.

Geography: Total area: 120,728 sq mi, 312,685 sq km; **Land area:** 117,474 sq mi, 304,255 sq km. **Location:** On Baltic Sea in E central Europe. Germany on W; Czech Rep., Slovakia on S; Lithuania, Belarus, Ukraine on E; Russia on N. **Topography:** Mostly lowlands forming part of the Northern European Plain. The Carpathian Mts. along S border rise to 8,200 ft. **Arable land:** 35.7%. **Capital:** Warsaw, 1,722,310. **Cities:** Kraków, 759,557.

Government: Type: Republic. **Head of state:** Pres. Andrzej Duda; in office: Aug. 6, 2015. **Head of gov.:** Prime Min. Ewa Kopacz; in office: Sept. 22, 2014. **Local divisions:** 16 provinces. **Defense budget:** $10.38 bil. **Active troops:** 99,300.

Economy: Industries: machine building, iron and steel, coal mining, chemicals, shipbuilding, food proc., glass, beverages. **Chief crops:** potatoes, fruits, vegetables, wheat. **Natural resources:** coal, sulfur, copper, nat. gas, silver, lead, salt, amber. **Water:** 1,612 cu m per capita. **Crude oil reserves:** 142.4 mil bbls. **Electricity prod.:** 152.7 bil kWh. **Labor force:** agric. 12.9%, industry 30.2%, services 57%. **Unemployment:** 10.4%.

Finance: Monetary unit: Zloty (PLN) (3.77 = $1 U.S.). **GDP:** $954.5 bil; **per capita GDP:** $25,100; **GDP growth:** 3.3%. **Imports:** $217 bil; Germany 27.5%, Russia 10.6%, Netherlands 6%, China 5.7%, Italy 5.3%. **Exports:** $218.9 bil; Germany 26%, UK 6.8%, Czech Republic 6.4%, France 5.8%, Russia 5.3%. **Tourism:** $10.9 bil. **Budget:** $101.5 bil. **Inflation:** 0.1%.

Transport: Railways: 12,326 mi. **Motor vehicles:** 616.3 per 1,000 pop. **Airports:** 87.

Communications: Telephone: 13.2 per 100 pop. **Mobile:** 156.4 per 100 pop. **Broadband:** 62 per 100 pop. **Internet:** 66.6%.

Health: Expend.: 6.7%. **Life expect.:** 73.5 male; 81.5 female. **Births:** 9.7 per 1,000 pop. **Deaths:** 10.2 per 1,000 pop. **Infant mortality:** 4.5 per 1,000 live births. **Undernourished:** <5%. **HIV:** <0.1%.

Education: Compulsory: ages 7-15. **Literacy:** 99.8%.

Embassy: 2640 16th St. NW 20009; 234-3800.

Website: www.premier.gov.pl

Slavic tribes in the area were converted to Latin Christianity in the 10th cent. Poland was a great power from the 14th to the 17th cent. In three partitions (1772, 1793, 1795) it was apportioned among Prussia, Russia, and Austria. Overrun by the Austro-German armies in WWI, it declared its independence on Nov. 11, 1918, and was recognized as independent by the Treaty of Versailles, June 28, 1919. Large territories to the east were taken in a war with Russia, 1921.

Germany and the USSR invaded Poland Sept. 1939 and divided the country. During the war, Nazis killed some 6 mil Polish citizens, half of them Jews. In compensation for territory ceded to the USSR when the war ended, Poland received German territory comprising Silesia, Pomerania, West Prussia, and part of East Prussia. Communists, who aligned themselves with the USSR, dominated the 1947 election.

In 12 years of rule by Stalinists, large estates were abolished, industries nationalized, schools secularized, and Roman Catholic prelates jailed. Farm production fell off. Harsh working conditions caused a riot in Poznan, June 28-29, 1956. A new Politburo, committed to a more independent Polish Communism, was named Oct. 1956, with Wladyslaw Gomulka as first secretary of the party. Collectivization of farms was ended. Gomulka agreed to permit religious liberty and religious publications, provided the church kept out of politics.

In Dec. 1970 workers in port cities rioted because of price rises and new incentive wage rules. On Dec. 20 Gomulka resigned as party leader; he was succeeded by Edward Gierek. The rules were dropped and price rises revoked.

Independent trade union Solidarity grew in popularity and strength throughout the 1980s, organizing strikes and making bold demands. Led by Lech Walesa, who had been arrested along with other Solidarity leaders Dec. 13, 1981, Solidarity helped to win political and economic reforms, including free elections, in an Apr. 5, 1989, accord. Candidates endorsed by Solidarity swept the parliamentary elections, June 4. Lech Walesa became president Dec. 22, 1990.

A radical economic program designed to transform the economy into a free-market system led to inflation, unemployment, and a return to the political left in 1993 parliamentary elections. A former Communist, Aleksander Kwasniewski, defeated Walesa in the 1995 presidential election and was reelected 5 years later. A new constitution was approved by referendum May 25, 1997. Poland became a full member of NATO, Mar. 12, 1999, and entered the European Union May 1, 2004.

Lech Kaczynski, the conservative mayor of Warsaw, won a presidential runoff election Oct. 23, 2005. In July 2006 he appointed his identical twin brother Jaroslaw as prime min. Poland's governing coalition fell apart in 2007, and the center-right Civic Platform party, led by Donald Tusk, won parliamentary elections Oct. 21. Pres. Lech Kaczynski, his wife Maria, and many senior Polish government officials were among the 96 passengers and crew members killed in a plane crash Apr. 10, 2010, near Smolensk, in western Russia. Parliament Speaker Bronislaw Komorowski, an ally of Prime Min. Tusk, became acting president; he won a full term July 4, 2010. Parliament Speaker Ewa Kopacz became prime min. Sept. 22, 2014, when Tusk was selected president of the European Council. Komorowski was narrowly defeated for reelection by conservative Andrzej Duda in a May 24, 2015, runoff.

Portugal

Portuguese Republic

People: Population: 10,825,309. **Age distrib.:** <15: 15.7%; 65+: 18.9%. **Growth:** 0.1%. **Migrants:** 8.4%. **Pop. density:** 306.5 per sq mi, 118.3 per sq km. **Urban:** 63.5%. **Ethnic groups:** homogeneous Mediterranean stock. **Languages:** Portuguese, Mirandese (both official). **Religions:** Roman Catholic 81%, none 6.8%.

Geography: Total area: 35,556 sq mi, 92,090 sq km; **Land area:** 35,317 sq mi, 91,470 sq km. **Location:** SW extreme of Europe. Spain on N, E. **Topography:** Tajus R. bisects country NE-SW. N is cool and rainy, mountainous. S is drier, with warm climate and rolling plains. **Arable land:** 11.9%. **Capital:** Lisbon, 2,884,297. **Cities:** Porto, 1,299,437.

Government: Type: Republic; parliamentary democracy. **Head of state:** Pres. Aníbal Cavaco Silva; in office: Mar. 9, 2006. **Head of gov.:** Prime Min. Pedro Passos Coelho; in office: June 21, 2011. **Local divisions:** 18 districts, 2 autonomous regions. **Defense budget:** $2.63 bil. **Active troops:** 34,600.

Economy: Industries: textiles, clothing, footwear, wood and cork, paper and pulp, chemicals, lubricants, automobiles and auto parts, base metals. **Chief crops:** grain, potatoes, tomatoes, olives, grapes. **Natural resources:** fish, forests (cork), iron ore, copper, zinc, tin, tungsten, silver, gold, uranium, marble, clay, gypsum, salt, hydropower. **Water:** 7,296 cu m per capita. **Electricity prod.:** 43.4 bil kWh. **Labor force:** agric. 8.6%, industry 23.9%, services 67.5%. **Unemployment:** 16.5%.

Finance: Monetary unit: Euro (EUR) (0.89 = $1 U.S.). **GDP:** $280.4 bil; **per capita GDP:** $27,000; **GDP growth:** 0.9%. **Imports:** $76.1 bil; Spain 32.6%, Germany 11.5%, France 6.8%, Italy 5.2%, Netherlands 5%. **Exports:** $66.3 bil; Spain 23.9%, Germany 11.7%, France 11.7%, Angola 6.5%, UK 5.5%. **Tourism:** $13.8 bil. **Budget:** $110.7 bil. **Inflation:** –0.3%.

Transport: Railways: 1,911 mi. **Motor vehicles:** 526.6 per 1,000 pop. **Airports:** 43.

Communications: Telephone: 43.2 per 100 pop. **Mobile:** 111.8 per 100 pop. **Broadband:** 36.8 per 100 pop. **Internet:** 64.6%.

Health: Expend.: 9.5%. **Life expect.:** 75.9 male; 82.6 female. **Births:** 9.3 per 1,000 pop. **Deaths:** 11.0 per 1,000 pop. **Infant mortality:** 4.4 per 1,000 live births. **Undernourished:** <5%. **HIV:** NA.

Education: Compulsory: ages 6-14. **Literacy:** 95.7%.

Embassy: 2012 Massachusetts Ave. NW 20036; 328-8610.

Website: www.portugal.gov.pt

Portugal, an independent state since the 12th cent., was a kingdom until a 1910 revolution drove out King Manoel II and a republic was proclaimed. Beginning in 1932, Prime Min. Antonio de Oliveira Salazar headed a repressive government. Illness forced his retirement in Sept. 1968.

On Apr. 25, 1974, a military junta led by Gen. Antonio de Spinola seized the government; Spinola became president. The new government granted independence to Guinea-Bissau, Mozambique, Cabo Verde, Angola, and São Tomé and Príncipe. Portugal returned Macao to China on Dec. 20, 1999.

With the economy lagging, Socialists led by Jóse Sócrates gained a parliamentary majority in 2005 and held onto a plurality in 2009. The conservative Aníbal Cavaco Silva, a former prime min. (1985-95), won the Jan. 2006 presidential election and was reelected 5 years later. After Portugal was given a 78-bil-euro bailout package from international lenders to avert default, the center-right Social Democratic Party, headed by Pedro Passos Coelho, won parliamentary elections June 2011. Austerity cuts caused widespread protests in Nov. 2012; the Constitutional Court ruled Apr. 5, 2013, that many of the cuts were illegal. Portugal completed loan repayments and exited the bailout program in May 2014.

Azores Isls., in the Atlantic, 740 mi W of Portugal, have an area of 868 sq mi and a pop. (2014 est.) of 246,353. A 1951 agreement gave the U.S. rights to use defense facilities in the Azores. The **Madeira Isls.**, 350 mi off the NW coast of Africa, have an area of 306 sq mi and a pop. (2014 est.) of 258,686. Both groups were offered partial autonomy in 1976.

Qatar

State of Qatar

People: Population: 2,194,817. **Age distrib.:** <15: 12.5%; 65+: 0.9%. **Growth:** 3.1%. **Migrants:** 73.8%. **Pop. density:** 490.6 per sq mi, 189.4 per sq km. **Urban:** 99.2%. **Ethnic groups:** Arab 40%, Indian 18%, Pakistani 18%, Iranian 10%. **Languages:** Arabic (official), English. **Religions:** Muslim 77.5%, Christian 8.5%.

Geography: Total area: 4,473 sq mi, 11,586 sq km; **Land area:** 4,473 sq mi, 11,586 sq km. **Location:** Middle East, occupying peninsula on W coast of Persian Gulf. Saudi Arabia on S. **Topography:** Mostly flat desert with some limestone ridges; scarce vegetation. **Arable land:** 1.1%. **Capital:** Ad-Dawhah (Doha), 717,790.

Government: Type: Emirate. **Head of state:** Emir Sheikh Tamim bin Hamad al-Thani; in office: June 25, 2013. **Head of gov.:** Prime Min. Sheikh Abdullah bin Nasser bin Khalifa al-Thani; in office: June 26, 2013. **Local divisions:** 7 municipalities. **Defense budget** (2012): $3.73 bil. **Active troops:** 11,800.

Economy: Industries: liquefied nat. gas, crude oil prod. and refining, ammonia, fertilizers, petrochemicals, steel reinforcing bars. **Chief crops:** fruits, vegetables. **Natural resources:** petroleum, nat. gas, fish. **Water:** 27 cu m per capita. **Crude oil reserves:** 25.2 bil bbls. **Electricity prod.:** 32.7 bil kWh. **Labor force:** NA. **Unemployment:** 0.5%.

Finance: Monetary unit: Riyal (QAR) (3.64 = $1 U.S.). **GDP:** $320.5 bil; **per capita GDP:** $143,400; **GDP growth:** 6.1%. **Imports:** $39.1 bil; U.S. 18%, UAE 10.3%, Saudi Arabia 7.8%, UK 6.3%, China 6.2%, Germany 5%. **Exports:** $121.2 bil; Japan 27.1%, South Korea 19%, India 10.6%, China 6.2%, Singapore 5.8%. **Tourism:** $4.6 bil. **Budget:** $67.3 bil. **Inflation:** 3%.

Transport: Motor vehicles: 167.7 per 1,000 pop. **Airports:** 4.

Communications: Telephone: 18.4 per 100 pop. **Mobile:** 145.8 per 100 pop. **Broadband:** 76.9 per 100 pop. **Internet:** 91.5%.

Health: Expend.: 2.2%. **Life expect.:** 76.6 male; 80.7 female. **Births:** 9.8 per 1,000 pop. **Deaths:** 1.5 per 1,000 pop. **Infant mortality:** 6.3 per 1,000 live births. **Undernourished:** NA. **HIV:** NA.

Education: Compulsory: ages 6-14. **Literacy:** 97.3%.

Embassy: 2555 M St. NW 20037; 274-1600.

Website: portal.www.gov.qa

Qatar was under Bahrain's control until the Ottoman Turks took power, 1872 to 1915. In a treaty signed 1916, Qatar gave Great Britain responsibility for its defense and foreign relations. Qatar declared itself independent, Sept. 1, 1971. Crown Prince Hamad bin Khalifa al-Thani ousted his father, Emir Khalifa bin Hamad al-Thani, June 27, 1995. In municipal elections held Mar. 8, 1999, women participated for the first time as candidates and voters. Sheikh Hamad bin Khalifa al-Thani abdicated in favor of his son, Sheikh Tamim bin Hamad al-Thani, June 25, 2013.

Qatar, a major oil producer and the world's leading exporter of liquefied natural gas, has experienced rapid economic growth in recent years. Regular flights in and out of Doha's new Hamad Intl. Airport began in May 2014. Military ties with the U.S. have been expanding. Camp As-Sayliyah, a base near Doha, served as a command center for the U.S.-led invasion of Iraq, Mar. 2003. A 10-yr. defense cooperation agreement was signed, Dec. 10, 2013. Qatar provided support for U.S.-led airstrikes, beginning Sept. 2014, against Sunni extremists in Syria. Qatar joined Saudi-led airstrikes, beginning Mar. 2015, against Shiite Houthi rebels in Yemen.

Romania

People: Population: 21,666,350. **Age distrib.:** <15: 14.5%; 65+: 15.7%. **Growth:** –0.3%. **Migrants:** 0.9%. **Pop. density:** 244.1 per sq mi, 94.2 per sq km. **Urban:** 54.6%. **Ethnic groups:** Romanian 83.4%, Hungarian 6.1%, Roma 3.1%. **Languages:** Romanian (official), Hungarian. **Religions:** Eastern Orthodox 81.9%, Protestant 6.4%, Roman Catholic 4.3%.

Geography: Total area: 92,043 sq mi, 238,391 sq km; **Land area:** 88,761 sq mi, 229,891 sq km. **Location:** SE Europe, on the Black Sea. Moldova on E, Ukraine on N, Hungary and Serbia on W, Bulgaria on S. **Topography:** The Carpathian Mts. encase the N central Transylvanian plateau. The lower reaches of the Danube river system flow through plains S and E of the mountains. **Arable land:** 38.2%. **Capital:** Bucharest, 1,867,724.

Government: Type: Republic. **Head of state:** Pres. Klaus Iohannis; in office: Dec. 21, 2014. **Head of gov.:** Prime Min. Victor-Viorel Ponta; in office: May 7, 2012. **Local divisions:** 41 counties, 1 municipality. **Defense budget:** $2.88 bil. **Active troops:** 71,400.

Economy: Industries: elec. machinery and equip., textiles and footwear, light machinery, auto assembly, mining, timber, constr. materials. **Chief crops:** wheat, corn, barley, sugar beets, sunflower seeds, potatoes, grapes. **Natural resources:** petroleum (reserves declining), timber, nat. gas, coal, iron ore, salt, hydropower. **Water:** 9,765 cu m per capita. **Crude oil reserves:** 600 mil bbls. **Electricity prod.:** 56 bil kWh. **Labor force:** agric. 27.9%, industry 28.2%, services 43.9%. **Unemployment:** 7.3%.

Finance: Monetary unit: New Leu (RON) (3.95 = $1 U.S.). **GDP:** $392.8 bil; **per capita GDP:** $19,700; **GDP growth:** 2.9%. **Imports:** $77.2 bil; (2014) Germany 19.1%, Italy 10.8%, Hungary 7.9%, France 5.7%. **Exports:** $69.3 bil; (2014) Germany 19.3%, Italy 11.9%, France 6.8%, Hungary 5.1%. **Tourism:** $1.8 bil. **Budget:** $67.6 bil. **Inflation:** 1.1%.

Transport: Railways: 7,002 mi. **Motor vehicles:** 265.9 per 1,000 pop. **Airports:** 26.

Communications: Telephone: 21.3 per 100 pop. **Mobile:** 105.9 per 100 pop. **Broadband:** 37.7 per 100 pop. **Internet:** 54.1%.

Health: Expend.: 5.1%. **Life expect.:** 71.5 male; 78.6 female. **Births:** 9.1 per 1,000 pop. **Deaths:** 11.9 per 1,000 pop. **Infant mortality:** 9.9 per 1,000 live births. **Undernourished:** <5%. **HIV:** NA.

Education: Compulsory: ages 7-16. **Literacy:** 98.8%.

Embassy: 1607 23rd St. NW 20008; 332-4846.

Website: www.gov.ro

Romania's earliest known people merged with invading Proto-Thracians, preceding by centuries the Dacians. Rome occupied the Dacian kingdom, 106-271 CE; people and language were Romanized. The Turkey-dominated principalities of Wallachia and Moldavia were united in 1859, became Romania in 1861, and gained recognition as an independent kingdom, 1881.

After WWI, Romania acquired Bessarabia, Bukovina, Transylvania, and Banat. In 1940 it ceded Bessarabia and Northern Bukovina to the USSR, part of southern Dobrudja to Bulgaria, and northern Transylvania to Hungary. In 1941, Prem. Marshal Ion Antonescu led Romania in support of Germany against the USSR. He was overthrown in 1944, and Romania joined the Allies. After occupation by Soviet troops, a People's Republic was proclaimed, Dec. 30, 1947.

On Aug. 22, 1965, a new constitution proclaimed Romania a socialist republic. The domestic policies of Pres. Nicolae Ceausescu were repressive. All industry was state-owned, and state farms and cooperatives owned almost all arable land. Ceausescu's security forces fired on antigovernment demonstrators, Dec. 1989, killing hundreds, but when the army sided with the protesters, his regime fell. Charged with genocide and abuse of power, Ceausescu and his wife were executed Dec. 25, 1989.

A new constitution providing for a multiparty system took effect Dec. 8, 1991. Many of Romania's state-owned companies were privatized in 1996. Romania became a full NATO member in 2004. It entered the European Union Jan. 1, 2007; restrictions on Romanians' right to work in 9 other EU countries ended Jan. 1, 2014. The IMF and other donors agreed to provide a $27-bil loan Mar. 25, 2009, to rescue the country from the global recession. Romania, a firm U.S. ally, pulled its remaining troops out of Iraq July 2009. Romanian soldiers served with NATO-led forces in Afghanistan; about 650 remained as of June 2015. Social Democrat Victor-Viorel Ponta became prime min. May 7, 2012. His attempt to remove Pres. Traian Basescu from office for abusing his authority failed. Ponta ran for president in 2014 but lost the Nov. 16 runoff to Klaus Iohannis. While continuing to serve as prime min., Ponta was charged, July 13, 2015, with money laundering, tax evasion, and other offenses while working as a lawyer in 2007-08.

Russia

Russian Federation

People: Population: 142,423,773. **Age distrib.:** <15: 16.7%; 65+: 13.6%. **Growth:** 0%. **Migrants:** 7.7%. **Pop. density:** 22.5 per sq mi, 8.7 per sq km. **Urban:** 74%. **Ethnic groups:** Russian 77.7%, Tatar 3.7%. **Languages:** Russian (official), Dolgang, Tatar. **Religions:** Russian Orthodox 15%-20%, Muslim 10%-15%.

Geography: Total area: 6,601,668 sq mi, 17,098,242 sq km; **Land area:** 6,323,482 sq mi, 16,377,742 sq km, more than 76% of total area of the former USSR and the largest country in the world. **Location:** Stretches from Eastern Europe across N Asia to the Pacific O. Finland, Norway, Estonia, Latvia, Belarus, Ukraine on W; Georgia, Azerbaijan, Kazakhstan, China, Mongolia, N. Korea on S; Kaliningrad exclave bordered by Poland on the S, Lithuania on the N and E. **Topography:** Every type of climate except distinctly tropical. European portion is low plain, grassy in S, wooded in N, with Ural Mts. on E, and Caucasus Mts. on S. Urals stretch N-S for 2,500 mi. Asiatic portion is vast plain, with mountains on S and in E; tundra covers extreme N with forest belt below; plains, marshes in W, desert in SW. **Arable land:** 7.3%. **Capital:** Moscow, 12,165,704. **Cities:** Saint Petersburg, 4,992,991; Novosibirsk, 1,497,164; Yekaterinburg, 1,379,038; Nizhniy Novgorod, 1,211,716; Samara, 1,164,357; Kazan, 1,162,259; Omsk, 1,161,893.

Government: Type: Federation. **Head of state:** Pres. Vladimir Putin; in office: May 7, 2012. **Head of gov.:** Prime Min. Dmitri Medvedev; in office: May 8, 2012. **Local divisions:** 46 provinces, 21 republics, 4 autonomous okrugs, 9 krays, 2 federal cities, 1 autonomous oblast. **Defense budget:** $70.05 bil. **Active troops:** 771,000.

Economy: Industries: coal, oil, gas, chemicals, metals; machine building; defense (incl. radar, missile prod.); shipbuilding; road, rail transp. equip.; communications equip.; agric. machinery, tractors, constr. equip. **Chief crops:** grain, sugar beets, sunflower seeds, vegetables, fruits. **Natural resources:** oil, nat. gas, coal, minerals, rare earth elements, timber. Climate, terrain, and distance are obstacles to exploitation of resources. **Water:** 31,561 cu m per capita. **Crude oil reserves:** 80 bil bbls. **Electricity prod.:** 1 tril kWh. **Labor force:** agric. 9.7%, industry 27.8%, services 62.5%. **Unemployment:** 5.6%.

Finance: Monetary unit: Ruble (RUB) (66.95 = $1 U.S.). **GDP:** $3.6 tril; **per capita GDP:** $24,800; **GDP growth:** 0.6%. **Imports:** $323.9 bil; China 16.5%, Germany 12.5%, Ukraine 5.2%, Belarus 5%. **Exports:** $520.3 bil; Netherlands 10.7%, Germany 8.2%, China 6.8%, Italy 5.5%, Ukraine 5%. **Tourism:** $11.8 bil. **Budget:** $408.3 bil. **Inflation:** 7.8%.

Transport: Railways: 54,157 mi. **Motor vehicles:** 354.5 per 1,000 pop. **Airports:** 594.

Communications: Telephone: 27.7 per 100 pop. **Mobile:** 155.1 per 100 pop. **Broadband:** 60.3 per 100 pop. **Internet:** 70.5%.

Health: Expend.: 6.3%. **Life expect.:** 64.7 male; 76.6 female. **Births:** 11.6 per 1,000 pop. **Deaths:** 13.7 per 1,000 pop. **Infant mortality:** 7.0 per 1,000 live births. **Undernourished:** <5%. **HIV:** NA.

Education: Compulsory: ages 6-15. **Literacy:** 99.7%.

Embassy: 2650 Wisconsin Ave. NW 20007; 298-5700.

Website: www.government.ru

Slavic tribes began migrating into Russia from the W in the 5th cent. The first Russian state, centered in Novgorod and Kiev, was founded by Scandinavian chieftains in the 9th cent. In the 13th cent., Mongols overran the country. It recovered under the grand dukes and princes of Muscovy, or Moscow, and by 1480 freed itself from the Mongols. Ivan the Terrible was proclaimed Tsar, 1547. Peter the Great (1682-1725) extended the domain and, in 1721, founded the Russian empire. Western ideas and the beginnings of modernization spread through the empire in the 19th and early 20th cent.

Military reverses in the 1905 war with Japan and in WWI led to the breakdown of the Tsarist regime. The 1917 Revolution began in Mar. with a series of sporadic strikes for higher wages by factory workers. A provisional democratic government under Prince Georgi Lvov was established but a second provisional government, under Alexander Kerensky, followed in May. Vladimir Ilyich Lenin, Nov. 7, overthrew the Kerensky government and the freely elected Constituent Assembly in a Communist coup.

Soviet Union. Lenin's death Jan. 21, 1924, led to an internal power struggle won by Joseph Stalin. His brutal tactics, including purge trials, mass executions, and exile to work camps, resulted in millions of deaths.

Despite a Germany-USSR non-aggression pact signed in Aug. 1939, Germany invaded the Soviet Union, June 1941. Russian winter counterthrusts, 1941-42 and 1942-43, and resistance to the siege of Leningrad (now St. Petersburg) stopped the German advance. Russians drove the Germans from Eastern Europe and the Balkans in the next two years.

After WWII, Communists took over in countries throughout the region, extending the Soviet sphere of influence. The USSR and the U.S., the world's leading nuclear superpowers, became Cold War rivals. After Stalin died, Mar. 5, 1953, Nikita Khrushchev gained power and denounced Stalin, 1956, beginning "de-Stalinization."

Under Khrushchev the open antagonism of Poles and Hungarians toward Moscow's domination was suppressed in 1956. He aided the Cuban revolution under Fidel Castro but withdrew Soviet missiles from Cuba during a confrontation with U.S. Pres. John Kennedy, Sept.-Oct. 1962. Khrushchev was deposed, Oct. 1964, and replaced by Leonid I. Brezhnev. In Aug. 1968, Soviet forces invaded Czechoslovakia, crushing liberalization there.

Massive Soviet military aid to North Vietnam in the late 1960s and early 1970s helped ensure Communist victories throughout Indochina. In Dec. 1979, Soviet forces entered Afghanistan to support a pro-Soviet regime against U.S.-supported Muslim resistance fighters. In Apr. 1988, the Soviets agreed to withdraw their troops, ending a futile 8-year war.

Mikhail Gorbachev was chosen Communist Party gen. sec., Mar. 1985. In 1987 he initiated a program of political and economic reforms through openness (*glasnost*) and restructuring (*perestroika*). Gorbachev faced economic problems as well as ethnic and nationalist unrest in the republics. A coup by Communist hardliners Aug. 1991 was foiled with help from Russian Republic Pres. Boris Yeltsin. On Aug. 24, Gorbachev resigned as leader of the Communist Party. Several republics declared their independence, including Russia, Ukraine, and Kazakhstan. On Aug. 29, the Soviet Parliament voted to suspend all activities of the Communist Party. The Soviet Union officially broke up Dec. 26, 1991, ending the 74-year domination of the Communist Party.

Russian Federation. Under Pres. Yeltsin, Russia took steps toward privatization, which caused inflation and a severe economic downturn. In June 1992, Yeltsin and U.S. Pres. George H. W. Bush agreed to massive arms reductions. Yeltsin prevailed in a power struggle with the Congress of People's Deputies, which was dominated by former Communists, and in a referendum Dec. 12, 1993, a new constitution was approved. Russian troops fought rebels in the breakaway republic of Chechnya Dec. 1994-Aug. 1996, when a peace accord temporarily ended the conflict. On May 27, 1997, Yeltsin signed a founding act, increasing cooperation with NATO and paving the way for NATO to admit Eastern European nations.

Russia's economic crisis deepened in the late 1990s, heightening tensions between parliament and Pres. Yeltsin, who had been reelected in 1996. An Aug. 1999 operation to suppress Islamic rebels in the republic of Dagestan reignited the war in neighboring Chechnya, where Russia launched a full-scale assault. Yeltsin unexpectedly resigned Dec. 31, 1999, naming Prime Min. Vladimir Putin as his interim successor. Putin won presidential elections Mar. 2000. Putin's allies won legislative elections, Dec. 2003, and the president was reelected Mar. 2004.

A bomb in Grozny, May 9, 2004, killed Chechnya's pro-Moscow president, Akhmad Kadyrov. In another terrorist act linked to the Chechnya conflict, two passenger planes exploded in midair after taking off from Moscow Aug. 24, killing 90 people. Chechen rebels, Sept. 1, 2004, seized control of a school in Beslan, North Ossetia, taking more than 1,100 hostages. Russian troops stormed the school Sept. 3; more than 330 people died, including 186 children. Putin cited the terrorist threat Sept. 13 in proposing a government overhaul that tightened his control over parliament and regional officeholders. Russian forces killed Chechen rebel leader Aslan Maskhadov, Mar. 8, 2005, and Chechen guerrilla leader Shamil Basayev, organizer of the terrorist attack at Beslan, July 10, 2006.

Constitutionally barred from seeking another term, Pres. Putin backed his protégé Prime Min. Dmitri Medvedev, who won the presidential election Mar. 2, 2008. Medvedev named Putin as prime min. A long-simmering conflict with Georgia erupted into open warfare Aug. 7-16. Russia dispatched troops to support secessionists in the enclaves of South Ossetia and Abkhazia and launched assaults on strategic Georgian cities; a cease-fire left thousands of Russian troops in the breakaway regions, which Pres. Medvedev recognized as independent, Aug. 26, 2008.

An economic boom fueled by oil and gas sales stalled in late 2008. The global financial crisis and a drop in oil prices led to turmoil in Russian financial markets.

Russia declared, Apr. 16, 2009, that it had ended counterterrorism operations in Chechnya; from June through Aug., there was an upsurge of insurgent violence in Chechnya and neighboring Dagestan and Ingushetia. Female suicide bombers from Dagestan struck two Moscow subway stations Mar. 29, 2010, killing 40 people. A bombing at a Moscow airport Jan. 24, 2011, killed 37.

With U.S.-Russia relations strained since the 2008 Georgia war, Medvedev and Pres. Barack Obama Apr. 8, 2010, signed a nuclear arms reduction treaty known as New START, which the U.S. Senate ratified Dec. 22. In Dec. 2011 parliamentary elections, Putin's party, United Russia, failed to garner 50% of the vote. In subsequent protests, tens of thousands called for Putin's resignation. Putin nonetheless won 64% of the vote in the Mar. 4, 2012, presidential election, though there were claims of fraud. Medvedev again became prime min. Three members of the anti-Putin punk-protest band Pussy Riot were convicted of hooliganism and sentenced to two years in jail Aug. 17, 2012, despite international criticism; the last two women were released in Dec. 2013.

Putin signed a law banning "homosexual propaganda" June 30, 2013, making it illegal to advocate publicly for gay rights. The Putin administration, disregarding U.S. wishes, granted one-year asylum to National Security Agency whistleblower Edward Snowden Aug. 1, 2013—extended for three years Aug. 1, 2014.

Sochi, Russia, hosted the 2014 Winter Olympics Feb. 7-23, 2014. Although suicide bombings in Volgograd, for which Dagestan separatists claimed responsibility, killed 34, Dec. 29-30, 2013, there were no major security incidents at the Games.

After Ukraine's pro-Russian president was removed from office Feb. 22, 2014, Russia sent troops into Ukraine's Crimean Peninsula and annexed the semi-autonomous republic of Crimea Mar. 18. Russia also apparently provided military equipment and troops to pro-Russian separatists in eastern Ukraine fighting Ukrainian government forces beginning in Apr. 2014. The U.S. and EU imposed several rounds of economic sanctions to protest Russia's Ukraine policies; Russia, Aug. 7, 2014, banned most food imports from the U.S. and EU. Sanctions and low prices for Russian oil exports helped put the economy in recession by the second quarter of 2015.

Opposition leader Boris Nemtsov was shot to death on a Moscow street, Feb. 27, 2015. Five men were arrested in connection with the crime, two of whom, both Chechens, were charged Mar. 8 with murder. A report Nemtsov had been preparing, released May 12, purported to document Russian military involvement and casualties in Ukraine.

Russia supported Pres. Bashar al-Assad in Syria's civil war (2011-). In Sept. 2015, Russia sent combat aircraft, other military equipment, and troops to a base near Latakia, Syria, and began airstrikes against forces fighting the Assad regime Sept. 30.

Rwanda

Republic of Rwanda

People: Population: 12,661,733. **Age distrib.:** <15: 41.8%; 65+: 2.5%. **Growth:** 2.6%. **Migrants:** 3.8%. **Pop. density:** 1,329.4 per sq mi, 513.3 per sq km. **Urban:** 28.8%. **Ethnic groups:** Hutu (Bantu) 84%, Tutsi (Hamitic) 15%. **Languages:** Kinyarwanda (universal Bantu vernacular), French, English (all official). **Religions:** Roman Catholic 49.5%, Protestant 39.4% (incl. Adventist 12.2%, other Protestant 27.2%), other Christian 4.5%, none 3.6%.

Geography: Total area: 10,169 sq mi, 26,338 sq km; **Land area:** 9,524 sq mi, 24,668 sq km. **Location:** E central Africa. Uganda on N, Dem. Rep. of the Congo on W, Burundi on S, Tanzania on E. **Topography:** Grassy uplands and hills cover most of country, with chain of volcanoes in NW. Nile R. source is in headwaters of the Kagera (Akagera) R. **Arable land:** 47.9%. **Capital:** Kigali, 1,256,994.

Government: Type: Republic. **Head of state:** Pres. Paul Kagame; in office: Apr. 22, 2000 (de facto from Mar. 24). **Head of gov.:** Prime Min. Anastase Murekezi; in office: July 24, 2014. **Local divisions:** 4 provinces, 1 city. **Defense budget:** $81 mil. **Active troops:** 33,000.

Economy: Industries: cement, agric. prods., small-scale beverages, soap, furniture, shoes, plastic goods, textiles, cigarettes. **Chief crops:** coffee, tea, pyrethrum (insecticide made from chrysanthemums), bananas, beans, sorghum, potatoes. **Natural resources:** gold, tin ore, tungsten ore, methane, hydropower. **Water:** 1,129 cu m per capita. **Electricity prod.:** 310.2 mil kWh. **Labor force:** agric. 90%, industry and services 10%. **Unemployment:** 0.6%.

Finance: Monetary unit: Franc (RWF) (726.48 = $1 U.S.). **GDP:** $18.8 bil; **per capita GDP:** $1,700; **GDP growth:** 7%. **Imports:** $1.9 bil; Uganda 15.9%, Kenya 15.2%, China 10.4%, UAE 8.6%, India 6.8%, Tanzania 5.1%. **Exports:** $720 mil; China 24.2%, Dem. Rep. of the Congo 17%, Malaysia 13.4%, Swaziland 6.8%, U.S. 5.5%, Pakistan 5.3%. **Tourism:** $305 mil. **Budget:** $2.2 bil. **Inflation:** 1.3%.

Transport: Airports: 4.

Communications: Telephone: 0.4 per 100 pop. **Mobile:** 64 per 100 pop. **Broadband:** 5.9 per 100 pop. **Internet:** 10.6%.

Health: Expend.: 10.7%. **Life expect.:** 58.1 male; 61.3 female. **Births:** 33.8 per 1,000 pop. **Deaths:** 9.0 per 1,000 pop. **Infant mortality:** 58.2 per 1,000 live births. **Undernourished:** 33.8%. **HIV:** 2.8%.

Education: Compulsory: ages 7-12. **Literacy:** 70.5%.

Embassy: 1875 Connecticut Ave. NW, Ste. 418, 20009; 232-2882.

Website: www.gov.rw

For centuries, the Tutsi dominated the Hutu majority. A civil war broke out in 1959 and Tutsi power was ended. Many Tutsi went into exile. Rwanda, which had been part of the Belgian UN trusteeship of Rwanda-Urundi, became independent July 1, 1962.

A large-scale massacre of Tutsi occurred in 1963. Hutu rivalries led to a bloodless coup July 1973 in which Hutu army officer Juvénal Habyarimana took power. After an invasion and coup attempt by Tutsi exiles in 1990, a multiparty democracy was established.

Renewed ethnic strife led to an Aug. 1993 peace accord between the government and rebels of the Tutsi-led Rwandan Patriotic Front (RPF). But after Habyarimana and Burundi Pres. Cyprien Ntaryamira were killed Apr. 6, 1994, in a suspicious plane crash, violence broke out. More than 1 mil May have died in massacres, mostly of Tutsi by Hutu militias, and in civil warfare as the RPF sought power. About 2 mil Tutsi and Hutu fled to camps in Zaire (now Dem. Rep. of the Congo, or DRC) and other countries; many died of disease. French troops under a UN mandate moved into SW Rwanda June 23 to establish a safe zone. The RPF claimed victory, installing a government led by a moderate Hutu president in July. French troops pulled out Aug. 22. A UN peacekeeping mission ended Mar. 8, 1996. More than 1 mil refugees, mostly Hutu, returned to Rwanda in Nov.-Dec. 1996.

Firing squads Apr. 24, 1998, executed 22 people convicted of genocide. Former Prime Min. Jean Kambanda pleaded guilty May 1 before the UN-backed Intl. Criminal Tribunal for Rwanda (ICTR) and received a life sentence Sept. 4, 1998. RPF leader Maj. Gen. Paul Kagame became Rwanda's first Tutsi president Apr. 22, 2000.

Rwandans approved a new constitution, May 26, 2003; reelected Pres. Kagame, Aug. 25; and chose a new parliament, Sept. 29-30. Rwanda cut diplomatic ties with France Nov. 24, 2006, after a French judge linked Kagame and his close aides to the 1994 deaths of Habyarimana and Ntaryamira. The country restored relations with France, Nov. 2009, when Rwanda joined the Commonwealth.

Accused of being one of the architects of the 1994 genocide, Col. Theoneste Bagosora was convicted and sentenced by the ICTR, Dec. 18, 2008, to life in prison (later reduced to 35 years). A Rwandan court Jan. 20, 2009, sentenced former Justice Min. Agnes Ntamabyariro to life in prison for her role in inciting the massacres. Up to 4,000 Rwandan troops fought that month alongside Congolese forces against Hutu militias in eastern DRC. After a campaign criticized as repressive by human rights groups, Pres. Kagame won reelection Aug. 9, 2010.

Steady economic growth beginning in 2003 was accompanied by U.S. funding for military training and the control of HIV/AIDS and malaria. An Oct. 17, 2012, UN report found that the Rwanda military was backing M23 rebel troops in the DRC. The U.S. announced in Oct. 2013 that it was sanctioning Rwanda for its continued support of M23 by withholding military funding. After successful offensives by UN troops in the DRC against M23 and the Hutu militia known as the Democratic Forces for the Liberation of Rwanda (FDLR), some 200 FDLR members laid down their arms in June 2014. More than 70,000 DRC refugees were living in Rwanda as of the end of 2014. Political unrest in Burundi caused tens of thousands to flee to Rwanda Apr.-July 2015.

Saint Kitts and Nevis

Federation of Saint Kitts and Nevis

People: Population: 51,936. **Age distrib.:** <15: 21%; 65+: 8.1%. **Growth:** 0.8%. **Migrants:** 10.5%. **Pop. density:** 515.4 per sq mi, 199 per sq km. **Urban:** 32%. **Ethnic groups:** predominantly black; some British, Portuguese, Lebanese. **Languages:** English (official). **Religions:** Anglican, other Protestant, Roman Catholic.

Geography: Total area: 101 sq mi, 261 sq km; **Land area:** 101 sq mi, 261 sq km. **Location:** In N part of the Leeward group of Lesser Antilles in E Caribbean Sea. Antigua and Barbuda to E. **Topography:** Forested volcanic slopes on St. Kitts; beaches rising to central peak on Nevis. Tropical climate moderated by sea breezes. **Arable land:** 19.2%. **Capital:** Basseterre, 14,149 (2014).

Government: Type: Parliamentary democracy. **Head of state:** Queen Elizabeth II, rep. by Gov.-Gen. Samuel W. T. Seaton; in office: Sept. 2, 2015. **Head of gov.:** Prime Min. Timothy Harris; in office: Feb. 18, 2015. **Local divisions:** 14 parishes. **Defense budget/active troops:** NA.

Economy: Industries: tourism, cotton, salt, copra, clothing, footwear. **Chief crops:** sugarcane, rice, yams, vegetables, bananas. **Water:** 444 cu m per capita. **Electricity prod.:** 140 mil kWh. **Labor force:** NA. **Unemployment:** NA.

Finance: Monetary unit: East Caribbean Dollar (XCD) (2.70 = $1 U.S.). **GDP:** $1.3 bil; **per capita GDP:** $21,100; **GDP growth:** 7%. **Imports:** $189.2 mil; U.S. 28.3%, Germany 16.3%, Trinidad and Tobago 14.4%, Italy 9.7%. **Exports:** $101.5 mil; U.S. 49.8%, Belgium 9.3%, Canada 8.3%. **Tourism:** $104 mil. **Budget:** $222.2 mil. **Inflation:** 1%.

Transport: Railways: 31 mi. **Airports:** 2.

Communications: Telephone: 34.9 per 100 pop. **Mobile:** 139.8 per 100 pop. **Broadband:** 5.5 per 100 pop. **Internet:** 65.4%.

Health: Expend.: 5.9%. **Life expect.:** 73.1 male; 78.0 female. **Births:** 13.5 per 1,000 pop. **Deaths:** 7.1 per 1,000 pop. **Infant mortality:** 8.8 per 1,000 live births. **Undernourished:** NA. **HIV:** NA.

Education: Compulsory: ages 5-16. **Literacy:** NA.

Embassy: 3216 New Mexico Ave. NW 20016; 686-2636.

Website: www.gov.kn

St. Kitts (formerly St. Christopher; known by indigenous peoples as Liamuiga) and Nevis were reached and named by Columbus in 1493. They were settled by Britain in 1623, but ownership was disputed with France until 1713. The colony achieved self-government as an Associated State of the UK in 1967, becoming independent, Sept. 19, 1983. A secession referendum on Nevis, Aug. 10, 1998, fell short of the two-thirds majority required. Twenty years of Labour Party governments ended when an opposition coalition won a majority of seats in Feb. 16, 2015, legislative elections.

Saint Lucia

People: Population: 163,922. **Age distrib.:** <15: 20.7%; 65+: 10.8%. **Growth:** 0.3%. **Migrants:** 6.7%. **Pop. density:** 700.6 per sq mi, 270.5 per sq km. **Urban:** 18.5%. **Ethnic groups:** black/African descent 85.3%, mixed 10.9%, E Indian 2.2%. **Languages:** English (official), French patois. **Religions:** Roman Catholic 61.5%, Protestant 25.5% (incl. Seventh-day Adventist 10.4%), none 5.9%.

Geography: Total area: 238 sq mi, 616 sq km; **Land area:** 234 sq mi, 606 sq km. **Location:** E Caribbean, 2nd largest of Windward Isls. Martinique (Fr.) to N, St. Vincent to S. **Topography:** Mountainous, volcanic in origin; Soufrière Volcanic Centre in S. Wooded mountains run N-S. **Arable land:** 4.9%. **Capital:** Castries, 22,186 (2014).

Government: Type: Parliamentary democracy. **Head of state:** Queen Elizabeth II, rep. by Gov.-Gen. Dame Pearlette Louisy; in office: Sept. 17, 1997. **Head of gov.:** Prime Min. Kenny Davis Anthony; in office: Nov. 30, 2011. **Local divisions:** 10 districts. **Defense budget/active troops:** NA.

Economy: Industries: tourism, clothing, electronic components assembly, beverages, corrugated cardboard boxes, lime proc. **Chief crops:** bananas, coconuts, vegetables, citrus, root crops, cocoa. **Natural resources:** forests, beaches, pumice, mineral springs. **Water:** 1,648 cu m per capita. **Electricity prod.:** 361.7 mil kWh. **Labor force:** agric. 21.7%, industry 24.7%, services 53.6%. **Unemployment:** NA.

Finance: Monetary unit: East Caribbean Dollar (XCD) (2.70 = $1 U.S.). **GDP:** $2 bil; **per capita GDP:** $11,600; **GDP growth:** –1.1%. **Imports:** $558.8 mil; U.S. 47.5%, Trinidad and Tobago 14.9%, Argentina 9.1%, Brazil 7.2%. **Exports:** $203.3 mil; Dominican Republic 29.6%, U.S. 10.5%, UK 7.5%, Peru 7.5%, Antigua and Barbuda 7.2%, Dominica 7%, Barbados 6.3%, Trinidad and Tobago 5.8%. **Tourism:** $360 mil. **Budget** (2011 est.): $222.2 mil. **Inflation:** 3.5%.

Transport: Airports: 2.

Communications: Telephone: 17.9 per 100 pop. **Mobile:** 102.6 per 100 pop. **Broadband:** 32.7 per 100 pop. **Internet:** 51%.

Health: Expend.: 8.5%. **Life expect.:** 74.9 male; 80.5 female. **Births:** 13.7 per 1,000 pop. **Deaths:** 7.4 per 1,000 pop. **Infant mortality:** 11.5 per 1,000 live births. **Undernourished:** NA. **HIV:** NA.

Education: Compulsory: ages 5-14. **Literacy:** NA.

Embassy: 3216 New Mexico Ave. NW 20016; 364-6792.

Website: www.govt.lc

St. Lucia was ceded to Britain by France with the Treaty of Paris, 1814. Independence was attained Feb. 22, 1979. Investigation results announced Mar. 8, 2015, by Prime Min. Kenny Anthony found that 12 people deemed criminals and put on a "death list" had been killed by police in 2010-11 and crime-scene evidence then falsified.

Saint Vincent and the Grenadines

People: Population: 102,627. **Age distrib.:** <15: 22.3%; 65+: 8.8%. **Growth:** –0.3%. **Migrants:** 9.4%. **Pop. density:** 683.3 per sq mi, 263.8 per sq km. **Urban:** 50.6%. **Ethnic groups:** black 66%, mixed 19%, E Indian 6%, European 4%, Carib Amerindian 2%. **Languages:** English, French patois. **Religions:** Protestant 75% (Anglican 47%, Methodist 28%), Roman Catholic 13%, other (incl. Hindu, Seventh-day Adventist, other Protestant) 12%.

Geography: Total area: 150 sq mi, 389 sq km; **Land area:** 150 sq mi, 389 sq km. **Location:** E Caribbean; St. Vincent (133 sq mi) and the northern islets of the Grenadines form a part of Windward chain. St. Lucia to N, Barbados to E, Grenada to S. **Topography:** St. Vincent is volcanic, with a ridge of thickly wooded mountains running its length. **Arable land:** 12.8%. **Capital:** Kingstown, 27,314 (2014).

Government: Type: Parliamentary democracy. **Head of state:** Queen Elizabeth II, rep. by Gov.-Gen. Sir Frederick Ballantyne; in office: Sept. 2, 2002. **Head of gov.:** Prime Min. Ralph Gonsalves; in office: Mar. 29, 2001. **Local divisions:** 6 parishes. **Defense budget/active troops:** NA.

Economy: Industries: tourism, food proc., cement, furniture, clothing, starch. **Chief crops:** bananas, coconuts, sweet potatoes, spices. **Natural resources:** hydropower. **Water:** 917 cu m per capita. **Electricity prod.:** 137 mil kWh. **Labor force:** agric. 26%, industry 17%, services 57%. **Unemployment:** NA.

Finance: Monetary unit: East Caribbean Dollar (XCD) (2.70 = $1 U.S.). **GDP:** $1.2 bil; **per capita GDP:** $10,800; **GDP growth:** 1.1%. **Imports:** $313.6 mil; Trinidad and Tobago 20.8%, Singapore 17.4%, U.S. 15.7%, Denmark 10.9%. **Exports:** $48.2 mil; Trinidad and Tobago 13.4%, St. Lucia 11.9%, Turkey 10%, Barbados 9.9%, Dominica 7.8%, Grenada 7.5%, Antigua and Barbuda 6.7%, Greece 5.6%, Switzerland 5.6%. **Tourism:** $101 mil. **Budget:** $185.2 mil. **Inflation:** 0.2%.

Transport: Airports: 5.

Communications: Telephone: 21.9 per 100 pop. **Mobile:** 105.2 per 100 pop. **Broadband:** NA. **Internet:** 56.5%.

Health: Expend.: 5.2%. **Life expect.:** 73.1 male; 77.1 female. **Births:** 13.6 per 1,000 pop. **Deaths:** 7.2 per 1,000 pop. **Infant mortality:** 12.7 per 1,000 live births. **Undernourished:** 5.7%. **HIV:** NA.

Education: Compulsory: ages 5-16. **Literacy:** NA.

Embassy: 3216 New Mexico Ave. NW 20016; 364-6730.

Website: www.gov.vc

Columbus landed on St. Vincent on Jan. 22, 1498 (St. Vincent's Day). Britain and France both laid claim to the island in the 17th and 18th cent.; the Treaty of Versailles, 1783, ceded it to Britain. Associated State status was granted 1969; independence was attained Oct. 27, 1979.

Samoa

Independent State of Samoa

People: Population: 197,773. **Age distrib.:** <15: 32.7%; 65+: 5.5%. **Growth:** 0.6%. **Migrants:** 3%. **Pop. density:** 181.6 per sq mi, 70.1 per sq km. **Urban:** 19.1%. **Ethnic groups:** Samoan 92.6%, Euronesians (European/Polynesian) 7%. **Languages:** Samoan (Polynesian) (official), English. **Religions:** Protestant 57.4% (incl. Congregationalist 31.8%, Methodist 13.7%), Roman Catholic 19.4%, Mormon 15.2%.

Geography: Total area: 1,093 sq mi, 2,831 sq km; **Land area:** 1,089 sq mi, 2,821 sq km. **Location:** S Pacific O. Nearest neighbors are Fiji to SW, Tonga to S. **Topography:** Main islands, Savaii (659 sq mi) and Upolu (432 sq mi), both ruggedly mountainous. Small islands of Manono and Apolima. **Arable land:** 2.8%. **Capital:** Apia, 36,946 (2014).

Government: Type: Parliamentary democracy. **Head of state:** Tuiatua Tupua Tamasese Efi; in office: June 20, 2007. **Head of gov.:** Prime Min. Tuilaepa Sailele Malielegaoi; in office: Nov. 23, 1998. **Local divisions:** 11 districts. **Defense budget/active troops:** NA.

Economy: Industries: food proc., building materials, auto parts. **Chief crops:** coconuts, nonu, bananas, taro, yams, coffee, cocoa. **Natural resources:** hardwood forests, fish, hydropower. **Water:** NA. **Electricity prod.:** 97.2 mil kWh. **Labor force:** agric. 65%. **Unemployment:** NA.

Finance: Monetary unit: Tala (WST) (2.71 = $1 U.S.). **GDP:** $994 mil; **per capita GDP:** $5,200; **GDP growth:** 1.9%. **Imports** (2012): $308.4 mil; New Zealand 21.6%, Fiji 19.5%, Singapore 15%, China 12.6%, U.S. 6.5%, Australia 5.7%. **Exports** (2012): $31.2 mil; American Samoa 42.4%, Australia 19.1%. **Tourism:** $145 mil. **Budget:** $257.6 mil. **Inflation:** –0.4%.

Transport: Airports: 1.

Communications: Telephone: 6.1 per 100 pop. **Mobile:** 55.5 per 100 pop. **Broadband:** NA. **Internet:** 21.2%.

Health: Expend.: 6.8%. **Life expect.:** 70.6 male; 76.5 female. **Births:** 20.9 per 1,000 pop. **Deaths:** 5.3 per 1,000 pop. **Infant mortality:** 19.6 per 1,000 live births. **Undernourished:** <5%. **HIV:** NA.

Education: Compulsory: ages 5-12. **Literacy:** 99%.

Embassy: 800 Second Ave., 4th Fl., New York, NY 10017; (212) 599-6196.

Website: www.samoagovt.ws

Samoa (formerly known as Western Samoa) was a German colony, 1899 to 1914, when New Zealand landed troops and took over. It became a New Zealand mandate under the League of Nations and, in 1945, a New Zealand UN Trusteeship.

An elected local government took office in Oct. 1959, and the country became fully independent Jan. 1, 1962. Malietoa Tanumafili II, Samoa's head of state since independence, was succeeded by Tuiatua Tupua Tamasese Efi. At the end of the day on Dec. 29, 2011, Samoa moved west of the Intl. Date Line to reduce time differences and simplify trade with Australia and New Zealand.

San Marino

Republic of San Marino

People: Population: 33,020. **Age distrib.:** <15: 15.7%; 65+: 19.1%. **Growth:** 0.8%. **Migrants:** 15.4%. **Pop. density:** 1,402 per sq mi, 541.3 per sq km. **Urban:** 94.2%. **Ethnic groups:** Sammarinese, Italian. **Languages:** Italian. **Religions:** Roman Catholic.

Geography: Total area: 24 sq mi, 61 sq km; **Land area:** 24 sq mi, 61 sq km. **Location:** Completely surrounded by Italy, in N center of that country, near Adriatic coast. **Topography:** On slopes of Mt. Titano. **Arable land:** 16.7%. **Capital:** San Marino, 4,197 (2014).

Government: Type: Republic. **Heads of state:** Two captains regent, elected by parliament from among its members, to 6-month term. **Head of gov.:** Sec. of State for Foreign and Political Affairs Pasquale Valentini; in office: Dec. 5, 2012. **Local divisions:** 9 municipalities. **Defense budget/active troops:** NA.

Economy: Industries: tourism, banking, textiles, electronics, ceramics, cement, wine. **Chief crops:** wheat, grapes, corn, olives. **Natural resources:** building stone. **Water:** NA. **Labor force:** agric. 0.2%, industry 33.5%, services 66.3%. **Unemployment:** NA.

Finance: Monetary unit: Euro (EUR) (0.89 = $1 U.S.). **GDP:** $1.9 bil; **per capita GDP:** $60,700; **GDP growth:** –1%. **Imports** (2011): $2.6 bil; (2012) Italy 81.8%. **Exports** (2011): $3.8 bil; (2012) Italy 82.3%. **Budget** (2011 est.): $719.5 mil. **Inflation:** 1.1%.

Transport: NA.

Communications: Telephone: 58.8 per 100 pop. **Mobile:** 118.8 per 100 pop. **Broadband:** 11.1 per 100 pop. **Internet** (2011): 49.6%.

Health: Expend.: 6.5%. **Life expect.:** 80.7 male; 86.0 female. **Births:** 8.6 per 1,000 pop. **Deaths:** 8.5 per 1,000 pop. **Infant mortality:** 4.5 per 1,000 live births. **Undernourished:** <5%. **HIV:** NA.

Education: Compulsory: ages 6-15. **Literacy:** 96%.

Embassy: 1711 N St. NW, 2nd Fl., 20036; 250-1535.

Website: www.sanmarino.sm

San Marino claims to be the world's oldest republic, having been founded in the 4th cent. It has had a treaty of friendship with Italy since 1862. A Communist-led coalition ruled 1947-57; a similar coalition ruled 1978-86. The broad-based San Marino Common Good coalition won parliamentary elections Nov. 11, 2012.

São Tomé and Príncipe

Democratic Republic of São Tomé and Príncipe

People: Population: 194,006. **Age distrib.:** <15: 43%; 65+: 2.9%. **Growth:** 1.8%. **Migrants:** 3.3%. **Pop. density:** 521.2 per sq mi, 201.3 per sq km. **Urban:** 65.1%. **Ethnic groups:** mestico, angolares (descendants of Angolan slaves), forros (descendants of freed slaves), servicais (contract laborers fr. Angola, Mozambique, Cabo Verde), tongas (children of servicais born on islands), Europeans (primarily Portuguese), Asians (mostly Chinese). **Languages:** Portuguese (official), Forro, Cabo Verdian, French, Angolar, English. **Religions:** Catholic 55.7%, Adventist 4.1%, Assembly of God 3.4%, New Apostolic 2.9%, none 21.2%.

Geography: Total area: 372 sq mi, 964 sq km; **Land area:** 372 sq mi, 964 sq km. **Location:** Gulf of Guinea about 125 mi off W central Africa. Gabon, Equatorial Guinea to E. **Topography:** Part of an extinct volcano chain; lush forests and croplands. **Arable land:** 9.1%. **Capital:** São Tomé, 71,294 (2014).

Government: Type: Republic. **Head of state:** Pres. Manuel Pinto da Costa; in office: Sept. 3, 2011. **Head of gov.:** Prime Min. Patrice Emery Trovoada; in office: Nov. 25, 2014. **Local divisions:** 2 provinces. **Defense budget/active troops:** NA.

Economy: Industries: light constr., textiles, soap, beer, fish proc., timber. **Chief crops:** cocoa, coconuts, palm kernels, copra, cinnamon, pepper, coffee, bananas, papayas, beans. **Natural resources:** fish, hydropower. **Water:** 11,295 cu m per capita. **Electricity prod.:** 65 mil kWh. **Labor force:** Pop. mainly engaged in subsistence agric. and fishing; shortage of skilled workers. **Unemployment:** NA.

Finance: Monetary unit: Dobra (STD) (21,785.01 = $1 U.S.). **GDP:** $624 mil; **per capita GDP:** $3,200; **GDP growth:** 4.5%. **Imports:** $126.2 mil; Portugal 67.2%, Gabon 5.6%, China 5.2%. **Exports:** $12.6 mil; Netherlands 30.5%, Belgium 20.4%, Spain 9.8%, Nigeria 7.4%, Turkey 7.3%. **Tourism:** $13 mil. **Budget:** $135.2 mil. **Inflation:** 6.4%.

Transport: Airports: 2.

Communications: Telephone: 3.4 per 100 pop. **Mobile:** 64.9 per 100 pop. **Broadband:** 7.1 per 100 pop. **Internet:** 24.4%.

Health: Expend.: 7.9%. **Life expect.:** 63.3 male; 65.9 female. **Births:** 34.2 per 1,000 pop. **Deaths:** 7.2 per 1,000 pop. **Infant mortality:** 47.9 per 1,000 live births. **Undernourished:** 6.8%. **HIV:** 0.8%.

Education: Compulsory: ages 6-11. **Literacy:** 74.9%.

Permanent UN mission: 675 Third Ave., Ste. 1807, New York, NY 10017; (212) 651-8116.

Website: www.gov.st

The Portuguese discovered the islands in 1471 and brought the first inhabitants—convicts and exiled Jews. Sugarcane planting was replaced by the slave trade as the chief economic activity until coffee and cocoa were introduced in the 19th cent.

Portugal agreed, 1974, to turn the colony over to the Gabon-based Movement for the Liberation of São Tomé and Príncipe; its East German-trained leader, Manuel Pinto da Costa, became the country's first president. Independence came July 12, 1975. Democratic reforms were instituted in 1987. In 1991, Miguel Trovoada won the first free presidential election. Trovoada defeated Pinto da Costa in a presidential runoff election July 21, 1996.

Fradique de Menezes, a wealthy cocoa exporter, beat Pinto da Costa in July 29, 2001, presidential elections. The government was ousted in a military coup July 16, 2003, but was restored to power a week later and reelected July 30, 2006. After the opposition party Independent Democratic Action (ADI) won parliamentary elections Aug. 1, 2010, Patrice Trovoada (son of the former president) was chosen to head the new government. Pinto da Costa returned to power after a presidential runoff vote Aug. 7, 2011. The National Assembly elected Gabriel Arcanjo Ferreira da Costa prime min. Dec. 2012, but Trovoada again became prime min. after ADI won Oct. 12, 2014, legislative elections. The country, long one of the world's poorest, has sought to develop oil deposits in the Gulf of Guinea.

Saudi Arabia

Kingdom of Saudi Arabia

People: Population: 27,752,316. **Age distrib.:** <15: 27.1%; 65+: 3.2%. **Growth:** 1.5%. **Migrants:** 31.4%. **Pop. density:** 33.4 per sq mi, 12.9 per sq km. **Urban:** 83.1%. **Ethnic groups:** Arab 90%, Afro-Asian 10%. **Languages:** Arabic (official). **Religions:** Muslim (official). Citizens are 85%-90% Sunni and 10%-15% Shia; non-Muslims are not allowed Saudi citizenship.

Geography: Total area: 830,000 sq mi, 2,149,690 sq km; **Land area:** 830,000 sq mi, 2,149,690 sq km. **Location:** Occupies most of Arabian Peninsula in Middle East. Kuwait, Iraq, Jordan on N; Yemen, Oman on S; UAE, Qatar on E. **Topography:** Bordered by Red Sea on W. Highlands in W slope as barren desert to the Persian Gulf on E. **Arable land:** 1.5%. **Capital:** Riyadh, 6,369,710. **Cities:** Jiddah, 4,075,803; Mecca, 1,770,600; Medina, 1,280,248; Ad-Dammam, 1,064,418.

Government: Type: Monarchy. **Head of state and gov.:** King Salman bin Abdul Aziz; in office: Jan. 23, 2015. **Local divisions:** 13 provinces. **Defense budget:** $80.76 bil. **Active troops:** 227,000.

Economy: Industries: crude oil prod., petroleum refining, basic petrochemicals, ammonia, industrial gases, caustic soda, cement, fertilizer. **Chief crops:** wheat, barley, tomatoes, melons, dates, citrus. **Natural resources:** petroleum, nat. gas, iron ore, gold, copper. **Water:** 83 cu m per capita. **Crude oil reserves:** 268.3 bil bbls (incl. half of Neutral Zone reserves). **Electricity prod.:** 255.4 bil kWh. **Labor force:** agric. 6.7%, industry 21.4%, services 71.9%. **Unemployment:** 5.7%.

Finance: Monetary unit: Riyal (SAR) (3.75 = $1 U.S.). **GDP:** $1.6 tril; **per capita GDP:** $52,200; **GDP growth:** 3.6%. **Imports:** $162.2 bil; U.S. 13.1%, China 12.9%, India 8.1%, Germany 7.4%, South Korea 6.1%. **Exports:** $359.4 bil; China 13.9%, U.S. 13.6%, Japan 13%, South Korea 9.8%, India 9.5%. **Tourism:** $8.2 bil. **Budget:** $293.3 bil. **Inflation:** 2.7%.

Transport: Railways: 856 mi. **Motor vehicles:** 235.1 per 1,000 pop. **Airports:** 82.

Communications: Telephone: 13.4 per 100 pop. **Mobile:** 179.6 per 100 pop. **Broadband:** 87.9 per 100 pop. **Internet:** 63.7%.

Health: Expend.: 3.2%. **Life expect.:** 73.0 male; 77.2 female. **Births:** 18.5 per 1,000 pop. **Deaths:** 3.3 per 1,000 pop. **Infant mortality:** 14.1 per 1,000 live births. **Undernourished:** <5%. **HIV:** NA.

Education: Compulsory: ages 6-14. **Literacy:** 94.7%.

Embassy: 601 New Hampshire Ave. NW 20037; 342-3800.

Website: www.saudi.gov.sa

Before Muhammad, Arabia was divided among numerous warring tribes and small kingdoms. Muhammad united it in the early 7th cent. His successors conquered the entire Near East and North Africa, bringing Islam and the Arabic language. But Arabia soon returned to its former status.

Nejd, in central Arabia, long an independent state and center of the Wahhabi sect, fell under Turkish rule in the 18th cent. Ibn Saud, founder of the Saudi dynasty, overthrew the Turks, 1913. He captured Hasa, a Turkish province in eastern Arabia, also 1913; the Hejaz region in western Arabia, 1925; and most of Asir, in SW Arabia, by 1926. The discovery of oil in the 1930s transformed the nation. The Hejaz contains the holy cities of Islam—Medina and Mecca. About 2-3 mil Muslims make the *hajj* (pilgrimage) to Mecca annually.

Ibn Saud reigned until his death, Nov. 1953. Subsequent kings have been his sons. The king exercises authority with a Council of Ministers. The Islamic religious code is the law of the land. Alcohol and public entertainments are restricted; women have an inferior legal status.

Saudi Arabia has often allied itself with and purchased arms from the U.S. and other Western nations. Saudi units, nevertheless, fought against Western ally Israel in the 1948 and 1973 Arab-Israeli wars. Beginning with the 1967 Arab-Israeli war, Saudi Arabia gave large annual financial gifts to Egypt, Syria, Jordan, and Palestinian groups. Saudi Arabia played a leading role in the 1973-74 Arab oil embargo against the U.S. and other nations.

After Iraq invaded Kuwait, Aug. 2, 1990, Saudi Arabia accepted the Kuwait royal family and more than 400,000 Kuwaiti refugees. Western and Arab troops also deployed on Saudi soil before and during the 1991 Persian Gulf War.

When 15 of the 19 al-Qaeda hijackers who carried out the Sept. 11, 2001, attacks on the U.S. were found to be Saudi, some in the U.S. blamed the Saudi government for allowing Muslim extremism to flourish in Saudi Arabia. Alarmed at guerrilla attacks that killed more than 100 people, mostly foreigners, in Saudi Arabia, 2003-04, the Saudis worked with the U.S. to increase antiterrorist activities. The U.S. completed a pullout of its combat forces from Saudi Arabia, Sept. 2003.

Islamist candidates on a "golden list" circulated by conservative clerics fared well in Feb.-Apr. 2005, municipal council elections, the country's first since 1963; women were barred from voting. Just before male-only Sept. 2011 municipal elections, King Abdullah announced that women would be allowed to vote and run for office in future elections, beginning in 2015. In 2012, Saudi women athletes competed in the Olympics for the first time. King Abdullah decreed, Jan. 11, 2013, that women would be permitted to hold 30 of the 150 seats on the government's advisory Shura council. Abdullah died, Jan. 23, 2015, and was succeeded by his half-brother Salman.

Cases of Middle East Respiratory Syndrome (MERS), a viral disease first recognized in Saudi Arabia in 2012, increased in subsequent years. As of Sept. 30, 2015, the Saudi Ministry of Health reported 1,250 total cases since the outbreak began; 536 had died. MERS had spread to 25 other countries by mid-2015.

Hoping to contain the wave of Arab Spring uprisings, a Saudi-led Gulf Cooperation Council force suppressed protests in Bahrain Mar. 14, 2011, and sent financial assistance to Egypt after the military's 2013 ouster of Islamist Pres. Mohammed Morsi. Saudi Arabia supplied weapons to anti-government rebels in Syria's civil war. Beginning Sept. 23, 2014, Saudi warplanes participated in U.S.-led airstrikes against ISIS and other Sunni extremists in Syria. ISIS claimed responsibility for terrorist attacks inside Saudi Arabia in 2015, and the government arrested hundreds of alleged ISIS supporters. Saudi Arabia led a 10-nation Sunni coalition that began an intensive campaign of airstrikes, Mar. 25, 2015, against Shiite Houthi rebels who had gained control of large areas of Yemen; the bombing campaign caused high civilian casualties.

A construction crane collapsed, Sept. 11, 2015, at Mecca's Grand Mosque, killing more than 100 people. A stampede Sept. 24 by pilgrims in Mecca attending the 2015 hajj left at least 769 dead according to Saudi government figures (1,426 according to an Associated Press tally).

Senegal

Republic of Senegal

People: Population: 13,975,834. **Age distrib.:** <15: 42.2%; 65+: 2.9%. **Growth:** 2.5%. **Migrants:** 1.5%. **Pop. density:** 188 per sq mi, 72.6 per sq km. **Urban:** 43.7%. **Ethnic groups:** Wolof 43.3%, Pular 23.8%, Serer 14.7%, Jola 3.7%, Mandinka 3%. **Languages:** French (official), Wolof, Pulaar, Jola, Mandinka. **Religions:** Muslim (mostly four Sufi brotherhoods) 94%, Christian (most Roman Catholic) 5%.

Geography: Total area: 75,955 sq mi, 196,722 sq km; **Land area:** 74,336 sq mi, 192,530 sq km. **Location:** W extreme of Africa. Mauritania on N, Mali on E, Guinea and Guinea-Bissau on S; surrounds The Gambia on three sides. **Topography:** Mostly low rolling plains, rising somewhat in SE. Swamp and jungles in SW. **Arable land:** 17.4%. **Capital:** Dakar, 3,520,215.

Government: Type: Republic. **Head of state:** Pres. Macky Sall; in office: Apr. 2, 2012. **Head of gov.:** Prime Min. Mohammed Abdallah Boun Dionne; in office: July 4, 2014. **Local divisions:** 14 regions. **Defense budget:** $254 mil. **Active troops:** 13,600.

Economy: Industries: agric. and fish proc., phosphate mining, fertilizer prod., petroleum refining, mining, constr. materials, ship constr. and repair. **Chief crops:** peanuts, millet, corn, sorghum, rice, cotton, tomatoes, green vegetables. **Natural resources:** fish, phosphates, iron ore. **Water:** 2,757 cu m per capita. **Electricity prod.:** 3.1 bil kWh. **Labor force:** agric. 77.5%, industry and services 22.5%. **Unemployment:** 10.3%.

Finance: Monetary unit: CFA Franc (XOF) (584.11 = $1 U.S.). **GDP:** $33.6 bil; **per capita GDP:** $2,300; **GDP growth:** 4.5%. **Imports:** $5.5 bil; France 17.7%, Nigeria 11.7%, China 8.2%, Netherlands 5.8%, India 5.5%. **Exports:** $2.5 bil; Mali 14.9%, Switzerland 9.6%, India 7.9%. **Tourism:** $407 mil. **Budget:** $4.7 bil. **Inflation:** –1.1%.

Transport: Railways: 563 mi. **Airports:** 9.

Communications: Telephone: 2.1 per 100 pop. **Mobile:** 98.8 per 100 pop. **Broadband:** 16.2 per 100 pop. **Internet:** 17.7%.

Health: Expend.: 5%. **Life expect.:** 59.3 male; 63.4 female. **Births:** 34.5 per 1,000 pop. **Deaths:** 8.5 per 1,000 pop. **Infant mortality:** 51.5 per 1,000 live births. **Undernourished:** 16.7%. **HIV:** 0.5%.

Education: Compulsory: ages 6-16. **Literacy:** 57.7%.

Embassy: 2215 M St. NW 20007; 234-0540.

Website: www.gouv.sn

Portuguese settlers arrived in the 15th cent., but French control grew from the 17th cent. The last independent Muslim state was subdued in 1893. Senegal became an independent republic Aug. 20, 1960, but French political and economic influence remained strong. Senegambia, a loose confederation of Senegal and The Gambia, was established in 1982 but dissolved seven years later.

Forty years of Socialist Party rule ended when Abdoulaye Wade, leader of the Senegalese Democratic Party, won a presidential runoff election, Mar. 19, 2000. A Senegalese ferry capsized off the coast of The Gambia Sept. 26, 2002, killing at least 1,863 people. A peace accord signed Dec. 30, 2004, with separatists in Cassamance Province, S Senegal, sought to end a 22-year insurgency. Pres. Wade was reelected Feb. 25, 2007, but lost his bid for a third term Mar. 26, 2012, to Macky Sall, his former prime min. Former Chad Pres. Hissène Habré, accused of killing and torturing thousands in the 1980s, was arrested June 30, 2013, in Senegal. His trial by the Extraordinary African Chambers, created within the Senegalese courts in Dakar, for war crimes and crimes against humanity began July 20, 2015.

Serbia

Republic of Serbia

People: Population: 7,176,794. **Age distrib.:** <15: 14.7%; 65+: 17.6%. **Growth:** –0.5%. **Migrants:** 5.6% (incl. Kosovo). **Pop. density:** 239.9 per sq mi, 92.6 per sq km. **Urban:** 55.6% (incl. Kosovo). **Ethnic groups:** Serb 83.3%, Hungarian 3.5%, Romany 2.1%, Bosniak 2%. **Languages:** Serbian (official), Hungarian. **Religions:** Serbian Orthodox 84.6%, Catholic 5%, Muslim 3.1%.

Geography: Total area: 29,913 sq mi, 77,474 sq km; **Land area:** 29,913 sq mi, 77,474 sq km. **Location:** Balkan Peninsula in SE Europe. Croatia, Bosnia and Herzegovina on W; Hungary on N; Romania, Bulgaria on E; Montenegro, Albania, Macedonia on S. **Topography:** Terrain varies widely, with fertile plains drained by Danube and other rivers in N, limestone basins in E, ancient mountains and hills in SE. **Arable land:** 37.5%. **Capital:** Belgrade, 1,181,810.

Government: Type: Republic. **Head of state:** Pres. Tomislav Nikolic; in office: May 31, 2012. **Head of gov.:** Prime Min. Aleksandar Vucic; in office: Apr. 22, 2014. **Local divisions:** 122 municipalities, 23 cities. **Defense budget:** $711 mil. **Active troops:** 28,150.

Economy: Industries: automobiles, base metals, furniture, food proc., machinery, chemicals, sugar, tires. **Chief crops:** wheat, maize, sunflowers, sugar beets, grapes/wine, fruits (raspberries, apples, sour cherries), vegetables. **Natural resources:** oil, gas, coal, iron ore, copper, zinc, antimony, chromite, gold, silver, magnesium, pyrite, limestone, marble, salt. **Water:** 17,054 cu m per capita. **Crude oil reserves:** 77.5 mil bbls. **Electricity prod.:** 31.8 bil kWh. **Labor force:** agric. 21.9%, industry 15.6%, services 62.5%. **Unemployment:** 22.2%.

Finance: Monetary unit: Dinar (RSD) (107.32 = $1 U.S.). **GDP:** $95.5 bil; **per capita GDP:** $13,300; **GDP growth:** –1.8%. **Imports:** $20.7 bil. **Exports:** $14.8 bil; Italy 16.2%, Germany 11.9%, Bosnia and Herzegovina 8.1%, Russia 7.2%, Romania 5.7%. **Tourism:** $1.1 bil. **Budget:** $19.3 bil (consolidated; central and local govt. budgets). **Inflation:** 2.1%.

Transport: Railways: 2,366 mi. **Airports:** 10.

Communications: Telephone: 37.3 per 100 pop. **Mobile:** 122.1 per 100 pop. **Broadband:** 55.7 per 100 pop. **Internet:** 53.5%.

Health: Expend.: 10.5%. **Life expect.:** 72.4 male; 78.3 female. **Births:** 9.1 per 1,000 pop. **Deaths:** 13.7 per 1,000 pop. **Infant mortality:** 6.1 per 1,000 live births. **Undernourished:** <5%. **HIV:** NA.

Education: Compulsory: ages 7-14. **Literacy:** 98.1%.

Embassy: 2134 Kalorama Rd. NW 20008; 332-0333.

Website: www.srbija.gov.rs

Serbia was a vassal principality of Turkey from 1389 to 1878, when the Treaty of Berlin established it as an independent kingdom. After the Balkan wars, Serbia annexed Old Serbia and Macedonia, 1913.

When the Austro-Hungarian empire collapsed after WWI, the Kingdom of Serbs, Croats, and Slovenes—Yugoslavia after 1929—was formed from the provinces of Croatia, Dalmatia, Bosnia, Herzegovina, Slovenia, Vojvodina, and the independent state of Montenegro.

After Nazi Germany's occupation 1941-45, Yugoslavia became a federal republic, headed by Josip Broz, a Communist, known as Marshal Tito. He rejected Stalin's dictatorship and accepted economic and military aid from the West. After Tito died in 1980, Yugoslavia held together for a decade before breaking apart. During 1991-95, Serbia, under Pres. Slobodan Milosevic, supported ethnic Serb fighters in Croatia and in Bosnia and Herzegovina, which had declared independence. The republics of Serbia and Montenegro proclaimed a new Federal Republic of Yugoslavia, Apr. 17, 1992. The UN imposed sanctions on the newly reconstituted Yugoslavia to end the bloodshed in Bosnia.

A peace agreement was reached in 1995. A UN-backed war crimes tribunal began in May 1996 to try suspects from the former Yugoslavia. Mass protests erupted when Milosevic refused to accept opposition victories in local elections, Nov. 17; non-Communist governments took office in Belgrade and other cities, Feb. 1997. Barred from running for a third term as Serbian president, Milosevic had himself inaugurated as president of Yugoslavia, July 23, 1997.

Serbian efforts to suppress a secessionist movement in Kosovo led in Mar.-June 1999 to a war with the U.S. and its NATO allies; they accused Milosevic of pursuing a policy of ethnic cleansing against the predominantly Muslim Kosovars (ethnic Albanians). NATO stationed a multinational force in Kosovo, which was placed under UN administration.

Milosevic initially refused to accept defeat by opposition leader Vojislav Kostunica in a 2000 presidential election but resigned Oct. 6 after mass demonstrations. Kostunica was sworn in the next day. Charged with corruption and abuse of power, Milosevic surrendered to Serbian authorities Apr. 1, 2001. He was extradited June 28 to The Hague, Netherlands, where a UN tribunal had indicted him for war crimes. His trial began Feb. 12, 2002. He was found dead in prison Mar. 11, 2006, before a verdict was reached.

A pact to reconstitute Yugoslavia as a new union of Serbia and Montenegro took effect Feb. 4, 2003. Zoran Djindjic, premier of the Republic of Serbia, was assassinated Mar. 12 in Belgrade, triggering a roundup of more than 4,500 people associated with organized crime and the Milosevic regime. Serbia's union with Montenegro disintegrated in 2006. Montenegrins voted for separation in a referendum May 21, and Montenegro became an independent republic June 3.

Kosovo declared independence from Serbia Feb. 17, 2008, but Serbia refused to recognize the new country. Following parliamentary elections in Serbia May 11, a pro-Western government under Mirko Cvetkovic took office July 7. To meet a requirement for EU membership, Serbia arrested, in 2008, former Bosnian Serb leader Radovan Karadzic, who was extradited to the Intl. Criminal Court in The Hague on charges of genocide and crimes against humanity. Serbia's parliament passed a resolution Mar. 31, 2010, apologizing for the 1995 massacre of thousands of Muslims by Bosnian Serbs at Srebrenica. In a further effort to deal with wartime atrocities, Serbian prosecutors, Sept. 2010, indicted 9 former members of the Jackals paramilitary unit for allegedly killing 43 ethnic Albanian civilians during the 1999 Kosovo conflict. Ratko Mladic, the former Bosnian Serb military commander accused of directing the 1995 massacre of 8,000 Bosnian Muslims (Bosniaks) in Srebrenica, was arrested in Serbia, May 2011, and sent to The Hague. His trial began May 16, 2012. Serbia attained EU candidate status, Mar. 1, 2012. Tomislav Nikolic, an advocate for EU membership, was elected president May 20. Zdravko Tolimir, a former commander in the Bosnian Serb Army, was convicted of genocide Dec. 12 for his role in the July 1995 killings of thousands of prisoners near Srebrenica. After reaching an EU-brokered power-sharing deal with Kosovo Apr. 19, 2013, Serbia began accession negotiations for EU membership Jan. 21, 2014. Aleksandar Vucic, who favors EU membership, became prime min. following Mar. 16, 2014, elections.

Vojvodina (8,304 sq mi) is a nominally autonomous province in northern Serbia with a pop. (2011 census) of 1,931,809, mostly Serbian. The capital is Novi Sad. **Website:** www.vojvodina.gov.rs.

Seychelles

Republic of Seychelles

People: Population: 92,430. **Age distrib.:** <15: 20.5%; 65+: 7.4%. **Growth:** 0.8%. **Migrants:** 13%. **Pop. density:** 526.1 per sq mi, 203.1 per sq km. **Urban:** 53.9%. **Ethnic groups:** mixed French, African, Indian, Chinese, and Arab. **Languages:** Seychellois Creole, English, French (all official). **Religions:** Roman Catholic 76.2%, Protestant 10.6%.

Geography: Total area: 176 sq mi, 455 sq km; **Land area:** 176 sq mi, 455 sq km. **Location:** In Indian O. 700 mi NE of Madagascar. Nearest neighbors are Madagascar and Somalia on NW. **Topography:** A group of 86 islands, about half of them composed of coral, the other half granite, the latter predominantly mountainous. **Arable land:** 2.2%. **Capital:** Victoria, 26,062 (2014).

Government: Type: Republic. **Head of state and gov.:** Pres. James Michel; in office: Apr. 14, 2004. **Local divisions:** 25 admin. districts. **Defense budget** (2013): $13 mil. **Active troops:** 420.

Economy: Industries: fishing, tourism, beverages. **Chief crops:** coconuts, cinnamon, vanilla, sweet potatoes, cassava, copra, bananas. **Natural resources:** fish, cinnamon trees. **Water:** NA. **Electricity prod.:** 316 mil kWh. **Labor force:** agric. 3%, industry 23%, services 74%. **Unemployment:** NA.

Finance: Monetary unit: Rupee (SCR) (12.92 = $1 U.S.). **GDP:** $2.4 bil; **per capita GDP:** $25,600; **GDP growth:** 2.9%. **Imports:** $1.1 bil; Saudi Arabia 21.9%, Spain 11.8%, France 7.4%. **Exports:** $525.1 mil; France 27%, UK 19.1%, Italy 11%, Japan 9.1%, Mauritius 7.7%. **Tourism:** $398 mil. **Budget:** $474.3 mil. **Inflation:** 1.4%.

Transport: Airports: 7.

Communications: Telephone: 22.7 per 100 pop. **Mobile:** 162.2 per 100 pop. **Broadband:** 10.3 per 100 pop. **Internet:** 54.3%.

Health: Expend.: 4.7%. **Life expect.:** 69.9 male; 79.2 female. **Births:** 14.2 per 1,000 pop. **Deaths:** 6.9 per 1,000 pop. **Infant mortality:** 10.5 per 1,000 live births. **Undernourished:** NA. **HIV:** NA.

Education: Compulsory: ages 6-16. **Literacy:** 91.8%.

Permanent UN mission: 800 Second Ave., Ste. 400C, New York, NY 10017; (212) 972-1785.

Website: www.egov.sc

The islands were occupied by France in 1768 and seized by Britain in 1794. Ruled as part of Mauritius from 1814, Seychelles became a separate colony in 1903 and declared independence June 29, 1976. The tourism industry, which employs 30% of workers, has been a major driver of rapid economic growth since independence. The country's first president was ousted in a 1977 coup by socialist leader France Albert René. A new constitution, approved June 1993, provided for a multiparty state. René resigned Apr. 14, 2004, and Vice Pres. James Michel succeeded him. Michel won 5-year terms in 2006 and 2011 elections.

Sierra Leone
Republic of Sierra Leone

People: Population: 5,879,098. **Age distrib.:** <15: 41.9%; 65+: 3.7%. **Growth:** 2.4%. **Migrants:** 1.6%. **Pop. density:** 212.6 per sq mi, 82.1 per sq km. **Urban:** 39.9%. **Ethnic groups:** Temne 35%, Mende 31%, Limba 8%, Kono 5%, Kriole or Krio (descendants of freed Jamaican slaves) 2%, Mandingo 2%, Loko 2%, other (incl. Liberian refugees; small numbers of Europeans, Lebanese, Pakistanis, Indians) 15%. **Languages:** English (official), Mende (principal vernacular in S), Temne (principal vernacular in N), Krio (English-based Creole, a lingua franca). **Religions:** Muslim 60%, indigenous beliefs 30%, Christian 10%.

Geography: Total area: 27,699 sq mi, 71,740 sq km; **Land area:** 27,653 sq mi, 71,620 sq km. **Location:** W coast of W Africa. Guinea on N and E, Liberia on S. **Topography:** Mangrove swamps in heavily indented, 210-mi coastline. Wooded hills rise to a plateau and mountains in E. **Arable land:** 24%. **Capital:** Freetown, 1,007,140.

Government: Type: Constitutional democracy. **Head of state and gov.:** Pres. Ernest Bai Koroma; in office: Sept. 17, 2007. **Local divisions:** 3 provinces, 1 area. **Defense budget:** $15 mil. **Active troops:** 10,500.

Economy: Industries: diamond mining, iron ore, rutile and bauxite mining, small-scale mfg. (beverages, textiles), petroleum refining. **Chief crops:** rice, coffee, cocoa, palm kernels, palm oil, peanuts. **Natural resources:** diamonds, titanium ore, bauxite, iron ore, gold, chromite. **Water:** 26,264 cu m per capita. **Electricity prod.:** 145 mil kWh. **Labor force:** NA. **Unemployment:** 3.2%.

Finance: Monetary unit: Leone (SLL) (4,050.00 = $1 U.S.). **GDP:** $12.6 bil; **per capita GDP:** $2,000; **GDP growth:** 6%. **Imports:** $2.1 bil; China 11.4%, India 9.8%, South Africa 8.5%, UK 8.2%, U.S. 6.2%, Belgium 6.1%. **Exports:** $2.2 bil; China 78.5%, Belgium 8.8%. **Tourism:** $32 mil. **Budget:** $908.8 mil. **Inflation:** 7.3%.

Transport: Motor vehicles: 3.2 per 1,000 pop. **Airports:** 1.

Communications: Telephone: 0.3 per 100 pop. **Mobile:** 76.7 per 100 pop. **Broadband:** NA. **Internet:** 2.1%.

Health: Expend.: 15.1%. **Life expect.:** 55.2 male; 60.4 female. **Births:** 37.0 per 1,000 pop. **Deaths:** 10.8 per 1,000 pop. **Infant mortality:** 71.7 per 1,000 live births. **Undernourished:** 25.5%. **HIV:** 1.4%.

Education: Compulsory: ages 6-14. **Literacy:** 48.1%.

Embassy: 1701 19th St. NW 20009; 939-9261.

Website: www.statehouse.gov.sl

The British founded Freetown, 1787, as a haven for freed slaves. Full independence arrived Apr. 27, 1961. A one-party state was established by referendum in 1978.

Mutinous soldiers ousted Pres. Joseph Momoh, Apr. 30, 1992. A coup, Jan. 16, 1996, paved the way for multiparty elections and a return to civilian rule. A peace accord, signed Nov. 30 with the Revolutionary United Front (RUF), brought a temporary halt to a civil war that had claimed over 10,000 lives in five years.

A coup on May 25, 1997, was met with international opposition. Nigeria's military restored Pres. Ahmad Tejan Kabbah to power on Mar. 10, 1998, but RUF rebels mounted a guerrilla counteroffensive, killing thousands of civilians and mutilating thousands more. A power-sharing agreement between the Kabbah government and the RUF, July 1999, was maintained by a UN mission (UNAMSIL). The accord collapsed in early May 2000, as RUF guerrillas took more than 500 UN peacekeepers hostage. Rebel leader Foday Sankoh was captured in Freetown, May 17. The hostages were freed by the end of May. A UN-sponsored disarmament program in 2001 reduced the level of violence. The Sierra Leone Special Court was created in 2002 to try war crimes that had occurred after Nov. 1996. Government and rebel leaders declared an official end to the war Jan. 18; more than 50,000 people had died in the conflict. Kabbah won the May 14 presidential election.

Sankoh, an indicted war criminal, died in UN custody, July 29, 2003. Opposition leader Ernest Bai Koroma won a presidential runoff vote, Sept. 8, 2007. Three former RUF leaders were convicted of war crimes, Feb. 25, 2009. A cholera epidemic swept through the country in 2012; more than 19,000 cases were reported in Sierra Leone in the first 9 months of the year, killing at least 274. Koroma won reelection Nov. 17, 2012. An Ebola virus epidemic that began in Guinea in Dec. 2013 had caused 13,911 cases of the illness and 3,955 deaths in Sierra Leone by Sept. 27, 2015.

Singapore
Republic of Singapore

People: Population: 5,674,472. **Age distrib.:** <15: 13.1%; 65+: 8.9%. **Growth:** 1.9%. **Migrants:** 42.9%. **Pop. density:** 21,392.7 per sq mi, 8,259.8 per sq km. **Urban:** 100%. **Ethnic groups:** Chinese 74.2%, Malay 13.3%, Indian 9.2%. **Languages:** Mandarin, English, Malay, Tamil (all official); Hokkien; Cantonese; Teochew. **Religions:** Buddhist 33.9%, Muslim 14.3%, Taoist 11.3%, Catholic 7.1%, Hindu 5.2%, none 16.4%.

Geography: Total area: 269 sq mi, 697 sq km; **Land area:** 265 sq mi, 687 sq km. **Location:** Off tip of Malayan Peninsula in SE Asia. Nearest neighbors are Malaysia on N, Indonesia on S. **Topography:** Flat, formerly swampy island with 40 nearby islets. **Arable land:** 0.9%. **Capital:** Singapore, 5,618,866.

Government: Type: Parliamentary republic. **Head of state:** Pres. Tony Tan Keng Yam; in office: Sept. 1, 2011. **Head of gov.:** Prime Min. Lee Hsien Loong; in office: Aug. 12, 2004. **Defense budget:** $10.02 bil. **Active troops:** 72,500.

Economy: Industries: electronics, chemicals, financial services, oil drilling equip., petroleum refining, rubber proc. and rubber prods. **Chief crops:** orchids, vegetables. **Natural resources:** fish. **Water:** 111 cu m per capita. **Electricity prod.:** 44.8 bil kWh. **Labor force** (excl. non-residents): agric. 1.3%, industry 14.8%, services 83.9%. **Unemployment:** 2.8%.

Finance: Monetary unit: Dollar (SGD) (1.42 = $1 U.S.). **GDP:** $445.2 bil; **per capita GDP:** $82,800; **GDP growth:** 2.9%. **Imports:** $366 bil; China 11.7%, Malaysia 10.9%, U.S. 10.4%, South Korea 6.4%, Japan 5.5%, Indonesia 5.2%. **Exports:** $409.5 bil; Malaysia 12.2%, China 11.8%, Hong Kong 11.2%, Indonesia 9.9%, U.S. 5.8%. **Tourism:** $19.2 bil. **Budget** (2015 est.): $50.4 bil (incl. operational and development expenditures). **Inflation:** 1%.

Transport: Motor vehicles: 145.2 per 1,000 pop. **Airports:** 9.

Communications: Telephone: 35.5 per 100 pop. **Mobile:** 158.1 per 100 pop. **Broadband:** 150.9 per 100 pop. **Internet:** 82%.

Health: Expend.: 4.7%. **Life expect.:** 82.1 male; 87.5 female. **Births:** 8.3 per 1,000 pop. **Deaths:** 3.4 per 1,000 pop. **Infant mortality:** 2.5 per 1,000 live births. **Undernourished:** NA. **HIV:** NA.

Education: Compulsory: ages 6-11. **Literacy:** 96.8%.

Embassy: 3501 International Pl. NW 20008; 537-3100.

Website: www.gov.sg

Founded in 1819 by Sir Thomas Stamford Raffles, Singapore was a British colony until 1959, when it became autonomous within the Commonwealth. On Sept. 16, 1963, it joined with Malaya, Sarawak, and Sabah to form the Federation of Malaysia. Tensions between Malayans, dominant in the federation, and ethnic Chinese, dominant in Singapore, led to an accord under which Singapore became a separate nation, Aug. 9, 1965.

Singapore is one of the world's largest ports and a major manufacturing, banking, and commerce center with high standards in health, education, and housing. Immigrant workers from elsewhere in Asia hold many low-paying jobs. The government, dominated by the People's Action Party (PAP), has taken strong actions to keep order and suppress dissent.

Singapore's first prime min., Lee Kuan Yew (in office 1959-90), credited with building the country's strong economy, died Mar. 23, 2015. His son, Lee Hsien Loong, took office as prime min., Aug. 12, 2004. The PAP won a landslide victory in Sept. 11, 2015, parliamentary elections.

Slovakia
Slovak Republic

People: Population: 5,445,027. **Age distrib.:** <15: 15.1%; 65+: 14.4%. **Growth:** 0%. **Migrants:** 2.7%. **Pop. density:** 293.2 per sq mi, 113.2 per sq km. **Urban:** 53.6%. **Ethnic groups:** Slovak 80.7%, Hungarian 8.5%, Roma 2%. **Languages:** Slovak (official), Hungarian, Roma. **Religions:** Roman Catholic 62%, Protestant 8.2%, Greek Catholic 3.8%, none 13.4%.

Geography: Total area: 18,933 sq mi, 49,035 sq km; **Land area:** 18,573 sq mi, 48,105 sq km. **Location:** E central Europe. Poland on N, Hungary on S, Austria and Czech Rep. on W, Ukraine on E. **Topography:** Carpathian Mts. in N, fertile Danube plain in S. **Arable land:** 29%. **Capital:** Bratislava, 400,670.

Government: Type: Parliamentary democracy. **Head of state:** Pres. Andrej Kiska; in office: June 15, 2014. **Head of gov.:** Prime Min. Robert Fico; in office: Apr. 4, 2012. **Local divisions:** 8 regions. **Defense budget:** $1.06 bil. **Active troops:** 15,850.

Economy: Industries: automobiles; metal and metal prods.; electricity, gas, coke, oil, nuclear fuel; chemicals, synthetic fibers, wood and paper prods.; machinery. **Chief crops:** grains, potatoes, sugar beets, hops, fruit. **Natural resources:** lignite, iron ore, copper and manganese ore, salt. **Water:** 9,193 cu m per capita. **Crude oil reserves:** 9 mil bbls. **Electricity prod.:** 26.6 bil kWh. **Labor force:** agric. 3.5%, industry 25.9%, services 70.6%. **Unemployment:** 14.2%.

Finance: Monetary unit: Euro (EUR) (0.89 = $1 U.S.). **GDP:** $152.6 bil; **per capita GDP:** $28,200; **GDP growth:** 2.4%. **Imports:** $79.8 bil; (2014) Germany 14.9%, Czech Republic 10.5%. **Exports:** $85.9 bil; (2014) Germany 22.1%, Czech Republic 12.8%, Poland 8%, Austria 6.1%, Hungary 6.1%, UK 5.2%. **Tourism:** $2.6 bil. **Budget:** $39.4 bil. **Inflation:** –0.1%.

Transport: Railways: 2,252 mi. **Motor vehicles:** 409.8 per 1,000 pop. **Airports:** 21.

Communications: Telephone: 16.8 per 100 pop. **Mobile:** 116.9 per 100 pop. **Broadband:** 54.9 per 100 pop. **Internet:** 80%.

Health: Expend.: 7.8%. **Life expect.:** 73.3 male; 80.7 female. **Births:** 9.9 per 1,000 pop. **Deaths:** 9.7 per 1,000 pop. **Infant mortality:** 5.3 per 1,000 live births. **Undernourished:** <5%. **HIV:** <0.1%.

Education: Compulsory: ages 6-14. **Literacy:** NA.

Embassy: 3523 International Ct. NW 20008; 237-1054.
Website: www.government.gov.sk

Slovakia was originally settled by Illyrian, Celtic, and Germanic tribes and was incorporated into Great Moravia in the 9th cent. It became part of Hungary in the 11th cent. Overrun by Czech Hussites in the 15th cent., it was restored to Hungarian rule in 1526. The Slovaks disassociated themselves from Hungary after WWI and joined the Czechs of Bohemia to form the Republic of Czechoslovakia, Oct. 28, 1918.

Germany invaded Czechoslovakia, 1939, and declared Slovakia independent. Slovakia rejoined Czechoslovakia in 1945. Czechoslovakia split into two separate states—the Czech Republic and Slovakia—on Jan. 1, 1993.

Slovakia joined the EU and NATO in 2004. The country adopted the euro currency Jan. 1, 2009. Its economy, previously one of Europe's fastest growing, was battered in the global recession 2008-09. Slow growth returned beginning in 2010. In Mar. 10, 2012, legislative elections, Robert Fico's social-democratic party, Smer (Direction), won 83 seats, the first time in Slovakia's post-communist history that a single party held the majority. Fico became prime min. Apr. 4, 2012. He ran for president in 2014 but lost a Mar. 29 runoff election to former businessman Andrej Kiska.

Slovenia

Republic of Slovenia

People: Population: 1,983,412. **Age distrib.:** <15: 13.4%; 65+: 18.4%. **Growth:** –0.3%. **Migrants:** 11.3%. **Pop. density:** 254.9 per sq mi, 98.4 per sq km. **Urban:** 49.6%. **Ethnic groups:** Slovene 83.1%, Serb 2%, Croat 1.8%. **Languages:** Slovenian (official), Serbo-Croatian. **Religions:** Catholic 57.8%, none 10.1%.

Geography: Total area: 7,827 sq mi, 20,273 sq km; **Land area:** 7,780 sq mi, 20,151 sq km. **Location:** SE Europe. Italy on W, Austria on N, Hungary on NE, Croatia on SE, S. **Topography:** Mostly hilly; nearly half forested. **Arable land:** 8.5%. **Capital:** Ljubljana, 278,903 (2014).

Government: Type: Parliamentary republic. **Head of state:** Pres. Borut Pahor; in office: Dec. 22, 2012. **Head of gov.:** Prime Min. Miro Cerar; in office: Sept. 18, 2014. **Local divisions:** 200 municipalities, 11 urban municipalities. **Defense budget:** $455 mil. **Active troops:** 7,600.

Economy: Industries: ferrous metallurgy and aluminum prods., lead and zinc smelting, electronics (incl. military), trucks, automobiles, elec. power equip., wood prods. **Chief crops:** potatoes, hops, wheat, sugar beets, corn, grapes. **Natural resources:** lignite, lead, zinc, building stone, hydropower, forests. **Water:** 15,381 cu m per capita. **Electricity prod.:** 14.8 bil kWh. **Labor force:** agric. 2.2%, industry 35%, services 62.8%. **Unemployment:** 10.2%.

Finance: Monetary unit: Euro (EUR) (0.89 = $1 U.S.). **GDP:** $61.1 bil; **per capita GDP:** $29,700; **GDP growth:** 2.6%. **Imports:** $29.4 bil; Germany 16.9%, Italy 13.8%, Austria 10%. **Exports:** $30.5 bil; Germany 19.5%, Italy 11.5%, Austria 8.2%, Croatia 6%. **Tourism:** $2.7 bil. **Budget:** $22 bil. **Inflation:** 0.2%.

Transport: Railways: 764 mi. **Motor vehicles:** 589.8 per 1,000 pop. **Airports:** 7.

Communications: Telephone: 37.1 per 100 pop. **Mobile:** 112.1 per 100 pop. **Broadband:** 42.1 per 100 pop. **Internet:** 71.6%.

Health: Expend.: 8.8%. **Life expect.:** 74.4 male; 81.9 female. **Births:** 8.4 per 1,000 pop. **Deaths:** 11.4 per 1,000 pop. **Infant mortality:** 4.0 per 1,000 live births. **Undernourished:** <5%. **HIV:** <0.1%.

Education: Compulsory: ages 6-14. **Literacy:** 99.7%.
Embassy: 2410 California St. NW 20008; 386-6610.
Website: e-uprava.gov.si

The Slovenes settled in their current territory during the 6th to 8th cent. They fell under German domination in the 9th cent. Modern Slovenian political history began after 1848 when the Slovenes, divided among several Austrian provinces, began their struggle for unification. In 1918 a majority of Slovenes became part of the Kingdom of Serbs, Croats, and Slovenes, later renamed Yugoslavia.

Slovenia declared independence June 25, 1991; joined the UN May 22, 1992; attained full membership in the EU and NATO in 2004; and adopted the euro Jan. 1, 2007. The Positive Slovenia party won the largest bloc of seats in Dec. 2011 parliamentary elections and formed a coalition with Janez Jansa as prime min. Jan. 28, 2012. After corruption charges against Jansa, a new coalition with Alenka Bratusek as prime min. took office in 2013. Bratusek resigned May 5, 2014, after losing her party's leadership. In early elections July 13, a new party headed by Miro Cerar won the most seats; Cerar, Aug. 25, was elected prime min. by the National Assembly.

Solomon Islands

People: Population: 622,469. **Age distrib.:** <15: 35.7%; 65+: 4.1%. **Growth:** 2%. **Migrants:** 1.4%. **Pop. density:** 57.6 per sq mi, 22.2 per sq km. **Urban:** 22.3%. **Ethnic groups:** Melanesian 95.3%, Polynesian 3.1%. **Languages:** Melanesian pidgin (lingua franca in much of country), English (official), 120 indigenous langs. **Religions:** Protestant 73.4% (incl. Church of Melanesia 31.9%, South Sea Evangelical 17.1%, Seventh-day Adventist 11.7%, United Church 10.1%), Roman Catholic 19.6%.

Geography: Total area: 11,157 sq mi, 28,896 sq km; **Land area:** 10,805 sq mi, 27,986 sq km. **Location:** Melanesian Archipelago in W Pacific O. Nearest neighbor is Papua New Guinea to W. **Topography:** 10 large volcanic, rugged islands; 4 groups of smaller islands. **Arable land:** 0.7%. **Capital:** Honiara, 73,302 (2014).

Government: Type: Parliamentary democracy. **Head of state:** Queen Elizabeth II, rep. by Gov.-Gen. Sir Frank Ofagioro Kabui; in office: July 7, 2009. **Head of gov.:** Prime Min. Manasseh Sogavare; in office: Dec. 9, 2014. **Local divisions:** 9 provinces, 1 city. **Defense budget/active troops:** NA.

Economy: Industries: fish (tuna), mining, timber. **Chief crops:** cocoa, coconuts, palm kernels, rice, fruit. **Natural resources:** fish, forests, gold, bauxite, phosphates, lead, zinc, nickel. **Water:** 79,679 cu m per capita. **Electricity prod.:** 85 mil kWh. **Labor force:** agric. 75%, industry 5%, services 20%. **Unemployment:** 3.8%.

Finance: Monetary unit: Dollar (SBD) (7.96 = $1 U.S.). **GDP:** $1.1 bil; **per capita GDP:** $1,900; **GDP growth:** 1.5%. **Imports** (2012): $446 mil; Australia 27.2%, Singapore 24.1%, China 7%. **Exports** (2012): $493.1 mil; China 55.5%, Australia 13.6%. **Tourism:** $55 mil. **Budget:** $450.3 mil. **Inflation** (2012-13): 5.4%.

Transport: Airports: 1.

Communications: Telephone: 1.3 per 100 pop. **Mobile:** 65.8 per 100 pop. **Broadband:** 8 per 100 pop. **Internet:** 9%.

Health: Expend.: 8.1%. **Life expect.:** 72.5 male; 77.9 female. **Births:** 25.8 per 1,000 pop. **Deaths:** 3.9 per 1,000 pop. **Infant mortality:** 15.7 per 1,000 live births. **Undernourished:** 12.5%. **HIV:** NA.

Education: Compulsory: NA. **Literacy:** 84.1%.
Permanent UN Mission: 800 Second Ave., Ste. 400L, New York, NY 10017; (212) 599-6192.
Website: www.pmc.gov.sb

The Solomon Isls. were sighted 1568 by an expedition from Peru. Britain established a protectorate in the 1890s over most of the group, inhabited by Melanesians. The islands saw major WWII battles. They achieved self-government, Jan. 2, 1976, and formal independence, July 7, 1978.

A coup attempt, June 5, 2000, sparked factional fighting in Honiara. To restore order after three years of lawlessness, a 2,225-member intervention force, led by Australia and authorized by the Pacific Isls. Forum, provided security 2003-05.

Following Apr. 2006 elections, parliament's choice of Snyder Rini as prime min. led to two days of rioting in Honiara over alleged influence-buying by the ethnic Chinese business community. Rini resigned Apr. 26, 2006, rather than face a no-confidence vote. Prime Min. Danny Philip, who was elected Aug. 25, 2010, dismissed finance min. Gordon Darcy Lilo and was forced to resign when a number of MPs abandoned the government in protest. The parliament then elected Lilo prime min., Nov. 16, 2011. Former prime min. Manasseh Sogavare (2000-01, 2006-07) again became head of government following Nov. 19, 2014, parliamentary elections.

Somalia

Federal Republic of Somalia

People: Population: 10,616,380. **Age distrib.:** <15: 43.7%; 65+: 2.2%. **Growth:** 1.8%. **Migrants:** 0.2%. **Pop. density:** 43.8 per sq mi, 16.9 per sq km. **Urban:** 39.6%. **Ethnic groups:** Somali 85%; Bantu, other non-Somali 15%. **Languages:** Somali, Arabic (both official); Italian; English. **Religions:** Sunni Muslim (Islam) (official).

Geography: Total area: 246,201 sq mi, 637,657 sq km; **Land area:** 242,216 sq mi, 627,337 sq km. **Location:** Occupies eastern horn of Africa. Djibouti, Ethiopia, Kenya on W. **Topography:** Coastline extends for 1,700 mi. Hills cover the N; center and S are flat. **Arable land:** 1.8%. **Capital:** Mogadishu, 2,137,839.

Government: Type: In transition to federal parliamentary republic. **Head of state:** Pres. Hassan Sheikh Mohamud; in office: Sept. 10, 2012. **Head of gov.:** Prime Min. Omar Abdirashid Ali Sharmarke; in office: Dec. 24, 2014. **Local divisions:** 18 regions. **Defense budget:** NA. **Active troops:** 11,000.

Economy: Industries: light industries incl. sugar refining, textiles, wireless communication. **Chief crops:** bananas, sorghum, corn, coconuts, rice, sugarcane, mangoes, sesame seeds, beans. **Natural resources:** uranium, largely unexploited reserves of iron ore, tin, gypsum, bauxite, copper, salt, nat. gas. **Water:** 1,401 cu m per capita. **Electricity prod.:** 315 mil kWh. **Labor force:** agric. 71%, industry and services 29%. **Unemployment:** 6.9%.

Finance: Monetary unit: Shilling (SOS) (654.87 = $1 U.S.). **GDP** (2010): $5.9 bil. **per capita GDP** (2010): $600; **GDP growth** (2010): 2.6%. **Imports** (2010): $1.3 bil; Djibouti 24.6%, Kenya 12.8%, India 9.6%, China 7.6%, Pakistan 5.8%. **Exports** (2012): $515.8 mil; UAE 50.1%, Yemen 16.5%, Oman 12.6%. **Budget:** NA. **Inflation:** NA.

Transport: Airports: 6.

Communications: Telephone: 0.5 per 100 pop. **Mobile:** 50.9 per 100 pop. **Broadband:** 0.3 per 100 pop. **Internet:** 1.6%.

Health: Expend. (2001): 2.3%. **Life expect.:** 49.9 male; 54.1 female. **Births:** 40.5 per 1,000 pop. **Deaths:** 13.6 per 1,000 pop. **Infant mortality:** 98.4 per 1,000 live births. **Undernourished:** NA. **HIV:** 0.5%.

Education: Compulsory: NA. **Literacy:** NA.

Permanent UN mission: 425 E. 61st St., Ste. 702, New York, NY 10065; (212) 688-9410. (Embassy ceased operation in U.S. in 1991.)

Website: www.villasomalia.gov.so or www.state.gov/p/af/ci/so/

British Somaliland (present-day N Somalia) was formed in the 19th cent., as was Italian Somaliland (now central and S Somalia). Italy lost its African colonies in WWII. British Somaliland gained independence, June 26, 1960, and by prearrangement, merged, July 1, with the UN Trust Territory of Somalia to create the independent Somali Republic.

On Oct. 15, 1969, Somalia's first civilian president, Abdirashid Ali Sharmarke, was assassinated. Six days later, Maj. Gen. Muhammad Siad Barre led a military coup. In 1970, he declared the country a socialist state—the Somali Democratic Republic.

Somalia has laid claim to Ogaden, the huge eastern region of Ethiopia, peopled mostly by Somalis. Some 11,000 Cuban troops with Soviet arms defeated Somali army troops and ethnic Somali rebels in Ethiopia, 1978. As many as 1.5 mil refugees entered Somalia. Guerrilla fighting in Ogaden continued until 1988, when a peace agreement was reached with Ethiopia.

Fighting in Mogadishu led Siad Barre to flee the capital, Jan. 1991. Fighting between rival factions caused 40,000 casualties, 1991-92, and by mid-1992 the civil war, drought, and banditry combined to produce a famine that threatened some 1.5 mil people.

U.S. troops and the UN worked to safeguard food delivery, 1991-93, resulting in significant U.S. and other casualties; a failed mission Oct. 3-4, 1993, left 18 U.S. troops and more than 500 Somalis dead. The U.S. withdrew its peacekeeping forces Mar. 25, 1994.

When the last UN troops pulled out, Mar. 3, 1995, armed factions controlled different regions. A joint police force in the capital could not stop the continued violence and food shortages. A peace deal Jan. 29, 2004, led to the Aug. 22 inauguration of a transitional parliament, Somalia's first legislature in 13 years. Meeting in Nairobi, Kenya, the parliament chose Abdullahi Yusuf Ahmed as president; he was sworn in Oct. 14.

Because Mogadishu was held by his rivals, Pres. Yusuf moved, July 26, 2005, to make his transitional capital at Jowhar; an interim parliament convened Feb. 26, 2006, at Baidoa. On June 5, an Islamist militia took over Mogadishu, defeating U.S.-backed secular warlords. The Islamists, calling themselves the Supreme Islamic Courts Council, held much of the central and southern regions.

With aid from Ethiopian troops, transitional govt. forces recaptured Mogadishu in Dec. 2006. The UN Security Council authorized, Feb. 20, 2007, an African Union peacekeeping mission to Somalia (AMISOM). An upsurge of fighting in Mogadishu, Feb.-Apr., killed hundreds of people and caused 350,000 to flee. Bombings and kidnappings escalated in 2007-08, as a series of cease-fires failed; the increasing violence forced international aid workers to pull out, worsening a humanitarian crisis. Many of the attacks on transitional authorities and their allies were blamed on al-Shabab, an al-Qaeda ally.

After Pres. Yusuf resigned Dec. 29, 2008, the transitional parliament, meeting in Djibouti Jan. 31, 2009, elected a moderate Islamist, Sheikh Sharif Sheikh Ahmed. Meanwhile, pirates carried out more than 200 attacks off the Horn of Africa in 2009. Pirates and Islamist insurgents continued to disrupt famine relief efforts in 2010-11. Pressured by AMISOM forces, al-Shabab pulled out of Mogadishu, Aug. 6, 2011, but continued to control much of southern Somalia. Despite continuing violence, Somali leaders met in Feb. 2012 in Garowe, Somalia, and signed Feb. 18 the Garowe II Principles, which established the conditions to install the caretaker government sworn in Aug. 20. The new parliament elected activist-professor Hassan Sheik Mohamud president Sept. 10, 2012. Bombings and other attacks by al-Shabab, in Mogadishu and elsewhere, continued. The UN, Nov. 12, 2013, authorized a 4,000-troop increase in the AMISOM force, to more than 22,000. In 2014, al-Shabab attacked the parliament building in Mogadishu in May, briefly took over the presidential palace in July, and assassinated several members of parliament. Al-Shabab leader Ahmed Abdi Godane was killed by a U.S. airstrike Sept. 1, 2014, and U.S. drone strikes killed other high-ranking members of the group, 2014-15. AMISOM and Somali forces had pushed al-Shabab out of major towns by mid-2015, but the group's terrorist attacks continued, both in Somalia and Kenya and in other countries providing AMISOM troops.

South Africa

Republic of South Africa

People: Population: 53,675,563. **Age distrib.:** <15: 28.4%; 65+: 5.5%. **Growth:** 1.3%. **Migrants:** 4.5%. **Pop. density:** 114.5 per sq mi, 44.2 per sq km. **Urban:** 64.8%. **Ethnic groups:** black African 80.2%, colored (South African term for persons of mixed-race ancestry) 8.8%, white 8.4%, Indian/Asian 2.5%. **Languages:** IsiZulu, IsiXhosa, Afrikaans, English, Sepedi, Setswana, Sesotho, Xitsonga, siSwati, Tshivenda, isiNdebele (all official). **Religions:** Protestant 36.6% (incl. Zionist Christian 11.1%), Catholic 7.1%, none 15.1%.

Geography: Total area: 470,693 sq mi, 1,219,090 sq km; **Land area:** 468,909 sq mi, 1,214,470 sq km. **Location:** Southern extreme of Africa. Namibia, Botswana, Zimbabwe on N; Mozambique, Swaziland on E; surrounds Lesotho. **Topography:** Large interior plateau reaches close to the country's 1,739-mi coastline. Few major rivers or lakes. Rainfall is sparse in W, more plentiful in E. **Arable land:** 9.9%. **Capital:** Pretoria (admin.), 2,058,789; Cape Town (legis.), 3,660,447; Bloemfontein (judicial), 503,013. **Cities:** Johannesburg, 9,398,698; Durban, 2,900,927; Port Elizabeth, 1,178,729; Vereeniging, 1,155,140.

Government: Type: Republic. **Head of state and gov.:** Pres. Jacob Zuma; in office: May 9, 2009. **Local divisions:** 9 provinces. **Defense budget:** $4.01 bil. **Active troops:** 62,100.

Economy: Industries: mining (platinum, gold, chromium), auto assembly, metalworking, machinery, textiles, iron and steel, chemicals, fertilizer, foodstuffs. **Chief crops:** corn, wheat, sugarcane, fruits, vegetables. **Natural resources:** gold, chromium, antimony, coal, iron ore, manganese, nickel, phosphates, tin, rare earth elements, uranium, gem diamonds, platinum, copper, vanadium, salt, nat. gas. **Water:** 973 cu m per capita. **Crude oil reserves:** 15 mil bbls. **Electricity prod.:** 239 bil kWh. **Labor force:** agric. 4%, industry 18%, services 66%. **Unemployment:** 24.9%.

Finance: Monetary unit: Rand (ZAR) (13.45 = $1 U.S.). **GDP:** $704.5 bil; **per capita GDP:** $13,000; **GDP growth:** 1.5%. **Imports:** $102.2 bil; China 16.2%, Germany 9.5%, Saudi Arabia 8%, U.S. 7%. **Exports:** $97.9 bil; China 32%, U.S. 6.5%, Japan 5%. **Tourism:** $9.3 bil. **Budget:** $102.2 bil. **Inflation:** 5.6%.

Transport: Railways: 13,040 mi. **Motor vehicles:** 199.2 per 1,000 pop. **Airports:** 144.

Communications: Telephone: 8.1 per 100 pop. **Mobile:** 149.7 per 100 pop. **Broadband:** 58.6 per 100 pop. **Internet:** 49%.

Health: Expend.: 8.8%. **Life expect.:** 60.8 male; 63.9 female. **Births:** 20.8 per 1,000 pop. **Deaths:** 9.9 per 1,000 pop. **Infant mortality:** 33.0 per 1,000 live births. **Undernourished:** <5%. **HIV:** 18.9%.

Education: Compulsory: ages 7-15. **Literacy:** 94.3%.

Embassy: 3051 Massachusetts Ave. NW 20008; 232-4400.

Website: www.gov.za

Bushmen and KhoiKhoi were the original inhabitants. Bantus, including Zulu, Xhosa, Swazi, and Sotho, occupied the area from northeastern to southern South Africa before the 17th cent.

The Dutch settled the Cape of Good Hope area, beginning in the 17th cent. Britain seized the Cape, 1806. Many Dutch trekked north and founded two republics, Transvaal and Orange Free State. Diamonds were discovered, 1867, and gold, 1886. The Dutch (Boers) resented encroachments by the British and others; the Anglo-Boer War followed, 1899-1902. Britain won and created, May 31, 1910, the Union of South Africa, incorporating two British colonies (Cape and Natal) with Transvaal and Orange Free State. After a referendum, the Union became the Republic of South Africa, May 31, 1961, and withdrew from the Commonwealth.

Daniel Malan's National Party election in 1948 made the policy of separate development of the races, or apartheid, official. Under apartheid, blacks were severely restricted to certain occupations and paid less than whites for similar work. Only whites could vote or run for public office. Persons of Asian Indian ancestry and those of mixed race ("coloureds") had limited political rights.

Protests against apartheid were suppressed. At Sharpeville on Mar. 21, 1960, government troops killed 69 black protesters. At least 600 persons, mostly Bantus, were killed in 1976 anti-apartheid riots. In 1986, Nobel Peace Prize winner Bishop Desmond Tutu called for Western nations to apply sanctions against South Africa to force an end to apartheid. Pres. P. W. Botha offered blacks an advisory role in government starting in Apr. On May 19, South Africa attacked three neighboring countries—Zimbabwe, Botswana, Zambia—striking at guerrilla strongholds of the anti-apartheid African National Congress (ANC).

Some 2 mil South African black workers staged a strike, June 6-8, 1988. Pres. Botha, head of the government since 1978, resigned Aug. 14, 1989, and was replaced by F. W. de Klerk. In 1990 the government lifted its ban on the ANC. Anti-apartheid leader Nelson Mandela was freed Feb. 11 after more than 27 years in prison. In Feb. 1991, Pres. de Klerk pledged to end apartheid laws.

In 1993 negotiators agreed on basic principles for a new democratic constitution. South Africa's partially self-governing black territories, or "homelands," were incorporated into a national system of 9 provinces. The ANC won elections Apr. 26-29, 1994, making Mandela president. The predominantly-Zulu Inkatha Freedom Party won control of the legislature in a mainly Zulu province. By then, fighting between the ANC and Inkatha (aided, during the apartheid era, by South African defense forces) had killed more than 14,000 people in the Zulu region.

A post-apartheid constitution became law Dec. 10, 1996. The ANC won elections, June 2, 1999, and ANC leader Thabo Mbeki became president. South Africa, Nov. 30, 2006, became the first African country to legalize same-sex marriage.

After Mbeki's former deputy president, Jacob Zuma, defeated him in a power struggle for the ANC leadership, Mbeki resigned his presidency, Sept. 21, 2008. Zuma became president after Apr. 22, 2009, elections. Mandela died Dec. 5, 2013. Despite corruption charges, Zuma was reelected president by the National Assembly, May 21, 2014, following an ANC victory in May 7 parliamentary elections.

Thousands of miners struck for better wages at the Lonmin platinum mine near Marikana, Aug. 10, 2012. Protests at the mine left at least 10 dead before police officers opened fire on protesters Aug. 16, killing 34 and wounding 78. A strike-ending wage agreement was reached Sept. 18. A five-month strike in 2014 against Lonmin, Anglo American Platinum, and Impala Platinum Holdings ended in June with a wage increase for 70,000 union workers. With platinum prices at a 6-year low in July 2015, Lonmin announced plans to close some mine shafts and lay off workers. Anglo American announced, Sept. 9, that it would sell unprofitable platinum mines near Rustenburg.

The government sent troops into parts of Durban and Johannesburg, Apr. 2015, after weeks of violence against immigrants (mainly from other African countries) left at least 7 people dead.

South Sudan

Republic of South Sudan

People: Population: 12,042,910. **Age distrib.:** <15: 45.3%; 65+: 2.1%. **Growth:** 4%. **Migrants:** 5.6%. **Pop. density:** 48.4 per sq mi, 18.7 per sq km. **Urban:** 18.8%. **Ethnic groups:** Dinka 35.8%; Nuer 15.6%; Shilluk, Azande, Bari, Kakwa, Kuku, Murle, Mandari, Didinga, Ndogo, Bviri, Lndi, Anuak, Bongo, Lango, Dungotona, Acholi. **Languages:** English (official), Arabic (incl. Juba, Sudanese variants). **Religions:** animist, Christian.

Geography: Total area: 248,777 sq mi, 644,329 sq km. **Location:** NE Africa. Sudan on N, Uganda and Kenya on S, Ethiopia on E, Central African Rep. and Dem. Rep. of the Congo on W. **Topography:** The White Nile R. flows N through center of country and feeds the Sudd, a swampy area occupying more than 15% of the country's center; it is one of the world's largest wetlands. **Arable land:** NA. **Capital:** Juba, 321,115.

Government: Type: Republic. **Head of state and gov.:** Pres. Salva Kiir Mayardit; in office: July 9, 2011. **Local divisions:** 10 states. **Defense budget:** $1.04 bil. **Active troops:** 185,000.

Economy: Chief crops: sorghum, maize, rice, millet, wheat, gum arabic, sugarcane, fruits, sweet potatoes, sunflower seeds, cotton, sesame seeds, cassava. **Natural resources:** hydropower, gold, diamonds, petroleum, hardwoods, limestone, iron ore, copper, chromium ore, zinc, tungsten, mica, silver. **Water:** 4,382 cu m per capita. **Labor force:** Vast majority of pop. relies on subsistence agriculture. **Unemployment:** NA.

Finance: Monetary unit: Pound (SSP) (3.16 = $1 U.S.). **GDP:** $26 bil; **per capita GDP:** $2,300; **GDP growth:** 5.5%. **Budget** (FY 2013 est.): $2.3 bil. **Inflation:** –3.8%.

Transport: Railways: 154 mi. **Airports:** 3.

Communications: Telephone (2011): 0.02 per 100 pop. **Mobile:** 24.5 per 100 pop. **Broadband:** 1.6 per 100 pop. **Internet:** 15.9%.

Health: Expend.: 2.6%. **Life expect.:** 59.3 male; 62.3 female. **Births:** 36.9 per 1,000 pop. **Deaths:** 8.2 per 1,000 pop. **Infant mortality:** 66.4 per 1,000 live births. **Undernourished:** NA. **HIV:** 2.7%.

Education: Compulsory: ages 6-13. **Literacy:** 27%.

Embassy: 1015 31st St. NW, 3rd Fl., 20007; 293-7940.

Website: www.goss.org

South Sudan was a region of the Republic of the Sudan when that country became independent in 1956. Northerners (mostly Arab Muslims) dominated, while southerners (mostly black Africans who practiced Christianity or traditional religions) were marginalized. Southern Anya Nya rebels waged war against the north, 1955-72, until an agreement was reached offering regional self-government for the south. Oil was discovered in the south in 1978.

Civil war broke out again in 1983, with southern rebels led by the Sudan People's Liberation Movement (SPLM). Fighting and related famine cost an estimated 2 mil lives and displaced millions of southerners. A peace accord was signed in 2005. A power-sharing agreement offered autonomy for southern Sudan and allowed for an independence referendum.

Almost 99% of southern Sudanese who voted in the referendum, Jan. 9-15, 2011, supported secession. The UN Security Council, July 8, authorized a 7,900-personnel peacekeeping force (UNMISS) to the area. South Sudan attained full independence July 9, 2011, and was admitted to the UN, July 14. South Sudan clashed with Sudanese rebels on its northern border and faced challenges of poverty, underdevelopment, and factional conflict.

Violence within South Sudan continued in 2013-15, despite an increase in UNMISS uniformed personnel to more than 12,500 as of June 30, 2015. Pres. Salva Kiir fired his entire cabinet July 23, 2013, including Vice Pres. Riek Machar. Heavy fighting broke out in Juba in Dec. 2013 between government troops and a rebel group led by Machar. Forces of Kiir and Machar (who belong to different ethnic groups) battled throughout the country in 2014-15, killing tens of thousands and displacing more than 2 mil. Kiir and Machar signed a peace accord Aug. 2015, but a number of cease-fire violations occurred in the following weeks.

Spain

Kingdom of Spain

People: Population: 48,146,134. **Age distrib.:** <15: 15.4%; 65+: 17.7%. **Growth:** 0.9%. **Migrants:** 13.8%. **Pop. density:** 249.9 per sq mi, 96.5 per sq km. **Urban:** 79.6%. **Ethnic groups:** mixed Mediterranean/Nordic. **Languages:** Castilian Spanish (official); Catalan, Galician, Basque (all official regionally). **Religions:** Roman Catholic 94%.

Geography: Total area: 195,124 sq mi, 505,370 sq km; **Land area:** 192,657 sq mi, 498,980 sq km. **Location:** SW Europe. Portugal on W; France, Andorra on N; Morocco to S. **Topography:** High, arid plateau broken by mountain ranges and river valleys in interior. The NW is heavily watered, the S has lowlands and a Medit. climate. **Arable land:** 24.9%. **Capital:** Madrid, 6,199,254. **Cities:** Barcelona, 5,258,319.

Government: Type: Parliamentary monarchy. **Head of state:** King Felipe VI; in office: June 19, 2014. **Head of gov.:** Prime Min. Mariano Rajoy; in office: Dec. 20, 2011. **Local divisions:** 17 automonous communities, 2 autonomous cities. **Defense budget:** $15.07 bil. **Active troops:** 133,250.

Economy: Industries: textiles and apparel (incl. footwear), food and beverages, metals and metal manufactures, chemicals, shipbuilding, automobiles, machine tools, tourism. **Chief crops:** grain, vegetables, olives, wine grapes, sugar beets, citrus. **Natural resources:** coal, lignite, iron ore, copper, lead, zinc, uranium, tungsten, mercury, pyrites, magnesite, fluorspar, gypsum, sepiolite, kaolin, potash, hydropower. **Water:** 2,376 cu m per capita. **Crude oil reserves:** 150 mil bbls. **Electricity prod.:** 280 bil kWh. **Labor force:** agric. 2.9%, industry 15%, services 58.4%. **Unemployment:** 26.6%.

Finance: Monetary unit: Euro (EUR) (0.89 = $1 U.S.). **GDP:** $1.6 tril; **per capita GDP:** $33,700; **GDP growth:** 1.4%. **Imports:** $337.9 bil; Germany 12.2%, France 11.8%, Italy 6.3%, China 5.7%, Netherlands 5%. **Exports:** $317.3 bil; France 16.7%, Germany 10.5%, Portugal 7.8%, Italy 7.3%, UK 7%. **Tourism:** $65.2 bil. **Budget:** $608.8 bil. **Inflation:** –0.1%.

Transport: Railways: 10,005 mi. **Motor vehicles:** 571.1 per 1,000 pop. **Airports:** 99.

Communications: Telephone: 40.6 per 100 pop. **Mobile:** 107.8 per 100 pop. **Broadband:** 67.2 per 100 pop. **Internet:** 76.2%.

Health: Expend.: 9.6%. **Life expect.:** 78.6 male; 84.8 female. **Births:** 9.6 per 1,000 pop. **Deaths:** 9.0 per 1,000 pop. **Infant mortality:** 3.3 per 1,000 live births. **Undernourished:** <5%. **HIV:** NA.

Education: Compulsory: ages 6-15. **Literacy:** 98.1%.

Embassy: 2375 Pennsylvania Ave. NW 20037; 452-0100.

Website: www.lamoncloa.gob.es

Settled by Iberians, Basques, and Celts, Spain was successively ruled (wholly or in part) by Carthage, Rome, and the Visigoths. Muslims invaded Iberia from N Africa in 711. Reconquest of the peninsula by Christians from the N laid the foundations of modern Spain. In 1469 the kingdoms of Aragon and Castile were united by the marriage of Ferdinand II and Isabella I. Moorish rule ended with the fall of Granada, 1492, the year Spain's large Jewish community was expelled.

Spain established a colonial empire after Columbus's 1492 "discovery" of America. Cortés conquered Mexico, and Pizarro conquered Peru. Spain also controlled the Netherlands and parts of Italy and Germany. Spain lost its American colonies in the early 19th cent. and Cuba, the Philippines, and Puerto Rico during the Spanish-American War, 1898.

Primo de Rivera became dictator, 1923. King Alfonso XIII revoked the dictatorship, 1930, but was forced into exile in 1931. A republic was proclaimed, which disestablished the church, curtailed its privileges, and secularized education. A Popular Front of socialists, Communists, republicans, and anarchists governed 1936-39.

Army officers under Francisco Franco revolted, 1936. Some 500,000 to 1 mil died before the war's end, Mar. 28, 1939. Franco was named *caudillo*, leader of the nation. Spain was officially neutral in WWII, but its cordial relations with fascist countries prompted its exclusion from the UN until 1955.

After Franco's death, Nov. 20, 1975, Prince Juan Carlos became king. In free elections, June 1977, moderates and democratic socialists won the most votes. The king thwarted a 1981 coup attempt by right-wing military officers. The Socialist Workers' Party, under Felipe González Márquez, won four consecutive general elections, 1982-93, but lost to a coalition of conservative and regional parties, 1996. Conservative Prime Min. José María Aznar, who won a parliamentary majority in the 2000 election, supported the U.S.-led invasion of Iraq, Mar. 2003.

Islamic extremists bombed four commuter trains in central Madrid, Mar. 11, 2004, killing 191 people. The opposition Socialist Workers' Party won elections three days later, and Socialist leader José Luis Rodríguez Zapatero, who became prime min. Apr. 17, removed all 1,300 Spanish troops from Iraq. Spain legalized same-sex marriage in 2005.

Prime Min. Zapatero won a second term in 2008. Spain's banking, building, and tourism industries suffered during the worldwide financial crisis; in May 2010, as the budget deficit mounted, the government introduced austerity measures to reassure international lenders. Mariano Rajoy's conservative Popular Party won Nov. 2011 elections. Spain received a 100-bil-euro EU bailout for its ailing banks in 2012. Spain's unemployment rate surpassed 25% in 2012 and 26% in 2013. GDP grew modestly in 2014, after 5 years of decline, and unemployment dipped slightly, to 23.7%.

An investigation into Luis Bárcenas, former national treasurer of the Popular Party, widened in 2013 to include accusations of illegal financing among other party members. Juan Carlos abdicated in favor of his son, who became King Felipe VI, June 19, 2014. Felipe's sister, Princess Cristina, was indicted, Dec. 22, 2014, for tax fraud in connection with an investigation of alleged embezzlement of public funds by her husband. Anti-austerity and anti-corruption parties made strong showings in May 24, 2015, regional and local elections.

Catalonia and the **Basque Country** were granted autonomy, Jan. 1980, following overwhelming approval in home-rule referendums. But Basque extremists pushed for independence. The Basque separatist group ETA carried out bombings that killed about 830 since 1968. ETA declared a cease-fire effective Mar. 24, 2006, after which Spain agreed to formal peace talks. Negotiations broke down after ETA exploded a car bomb at the Madrid airport, Dec. 30, 2006, killing two. ETA declared a new unilateral cease-fire Oct. 20, 2011. Two top ETA leaders, wanted in Spain on terrorism-related charges, were arrested in France Sept. 22. 2015. In Catalonia, voters approved a plan for expanded home-rule, June 18, 2006. Catalonia held a nonbinding Nov. 9, 2014, referendum on independence. More than 80% of voters favored independence; fewer than half of eligible voters took part. Separatist parties won a majority of seats in Catalonia's regional parliamentary elections Sept. 27, 2015. **Website:** web.gencat.cat

The **Balearic Isls.** in the W Mediterranean, 1,927 sq mi, is an autonomous community of Spain; the islands include Majorca (Mallorca; capital Palma de Mallorca), Minorca, Cabrera, Ibiza, and Formentera. The **Canary Isls.**, 2,807 sq mi, another autonomous community in the Atlantic W of Morocco, includes the islands of Tenerife, Palma, Gomera, Hierro, Grand Canary, Fuerteventura, and Lanzarote; Las Palmas and Santa Cruz are thriving ports. More than 1,700 people died trying to get from Mauritania to the Canary Isls. in rickety boats, Jan.-June 2006.

Ceuta and **Melilla**, small Spanish enclaves on Morocco's Mediterranean coast, gained limited autonomy in Sept. 1994. In 2014 and 2015, thousands of undocumented African migrants seeking to reach European-controlled territory crossed the borders between Morocco and the Spanish enclaves.

Spain has sought the return of Gibraltar, in British hands since 1704.

Sri Lanka

Democratic Socialist Republic of Sri Lanka

People: Population: 22,053,488. **Age distrib.:** <15: 24.6%; 65+: 9%. **Growth:** 0.8%. **Migrants:** 1.5%. **Pop. density:** 883.8 per sq mi, 341.2 per sq km. **Urban:** 18.4%. **Ethnic groups:** Sinhalese 74.9%, Sri Lankan Tamil 11.2%, Sri Lankan Moor 9.2%, Indian Tamil 4.2%. **Languages:** Sinhala (official and national), Tamil (national lang.), English (commonly used in govt.). **Religions:** Buddhist (official) 70.2%, Hindu 12.6%, Muslim 9.7%, Roman Catholic 6.1%.

Geography: Total area: 25,332 sq mi, 65,610 sq km; **Land area:** 24,954 sq mi, 64,630 sq km. **Location:** Indian O. off SE coast of India. **Topography:** Coastal area and N half are flat; S central area is hilly and mountainous. **Arable land:** 19.9%. **Capital:** Colombo, 706,648; Sri Jayewardenepura Kotte (legis.), 127,534 (2014).

Government: Type: Republic. **Head of state and gov.:** Pres. Maithripala Sirisena; in office: Jan. 9, 2015. **Local divisions:** 9 provinces. **Defense budget:** $1.79 bil. **Active troops:** 160,900.

Economy: Industries: rubber, tea, coconuts, tobacco and other agric. commodities proc.; telecom, insurance, banking; tourism, shipping; clothing, textiles; cement, petroleum refining. **Chief crops:** rice, sugarcane, grains, pulses, oilseed, spices, vegetables, fruit, tea, rubber, coconuts. **Natural resources:** limestone, graphite, mineral sands, gems, phosphates, clay, hydropower. **Water:** 2,482 cu m per capita. **Electricity prod.:** 11.4 bil kWh. **Labor force:** agric. 31.8%, industry 25.8%, services 42.4%. **Unemployment:** 4.2%.

Finance: Monetary unit: Rupee (LKR) (134.54 = $1 U.S.). **GDP:** $217.4 bil; **per capita GDP:** $10,400; **GDP growth:** 7.4%. **Imports:** $19.2 bil; India 21.5%, China 17.6%, Singapore 10.1%, UAE 6.1%. **Exports:** $11.9 bil; U.S. 21.8%, UK 8.3%. **Tourism:** $2.4 bil. **Budget:** $14.1 bil. **Inflation:** 3.3%.

Transport: Railways: 899 mi. **Motor vehicles:** 45.2 per 1,000 pop. **Airports:** 15.

Communications: Telephone: 12.5 per 100 pop. **Mobile:** 103.2 per 100 pop. **Broadband:** 7.8 per 100 pop. **Internet:** 25.8%.

Health: Expend.: 3.2%. **Life expect.:** 73.1 male; 80.2 female. **Births:** 15.9 per 1,000 pop. **Deaths:** 6.1 per 1,000 pop. **Infant mortality:** 8.8 per 1,000 live births. **Undernourished:** 24.6%. **HIV:** <0.1%.

Education: Compulsory: ages 5-13. **Literacy:** 92.6%.

Embassy: 2148 Wyoming Ave. NW 20008; 483-4025.

Website: www.president.gov.lk

The island was known to the ancient world as Taprobane (Greek for copper-colored) and later as Serendip (from Arabic). Colonists from N India subdued the indigenous Veddahs about 543 BCE; their descendants, the Buddhist Sinhalese, still form most of the population. Hindu descendants of Tamil immigrants from S India account for about one-fifth of the population.

Parts were occupied by the Portuguese in 1505 and the Dutch in 1658. The British seized the island in 1796. It became an independent member of the Commonwealth as Ceylon in 1948 before changing its name to Sri Lanka May 22, 1972.

Prime Min. Solomon W. R. D. Bandaranaike was assassinated Sept. 25, 1959. His widow, Sirimavo Bandaranaike, served as prime min. 1960-65, 1970-77, 1994-2000. In the 1970s, thousands of ultra-leftists were executed, while massive land reform and nationalization of foreign-owned plantations took place.

Tensions between Sinhalese and Tamil separatists erupted in the early 1980s and turned into a 20-year civil war that killed more than 60,000; another 20,000, mostly young Tamils, "disappeared" while in government custody.

Pres. Ranasinghe Premadasa was assassinated May 1, 1993, by a Tamil rebel. Mrs. Bandaranaike's daughter, Chandrika Bandaranaike Kumaratunga, became prime min. after Aug. 1994 general elections. Elected president Nov. 9, Kumaratunga appointed her mother prime min. Kumaratunga won a second 6-year term Dec. 21, 1999. In failing health, Mrs. Bandaranaike resigned Aug. 10 and died Oct. 10, 2000. A truce intended to bring an end to the civil war was signed Feb. 22, 2002. More than 31,000 died in the Dec. 26, 2004, Indian Ocean tsunami.

Prime Min. Mahinda Rajapaksa of the United People's Freedom Alliance won the 2005 presidential election and was reelected in 2010. Thousands died during three years of fighting among government forces, paramilitary groups, and Tamil rebels beginning in Dec. 2005. About 7,000 noncombatants were killed Jan. 20-May 7, 2009. Tamil leader Vellupillai Prabhakaran was killed May 18-19, 2009, and Pres. Rajapaksa formally declared victory. Maithripala Sirisena defeated Rajapaksa in the Jan. 8, 2015, presidential election. The governing coalition defeated Rajapaksa's coalition in Aug. 17 parliamentary elections. A Sept. 16, 2015, UN report documented numerous human rights violations by both sides during and after Sri Lanka's civil war, including widespread torture of detainees by government security forces; the UN called for a special international court to investigate abuses.

Sudan

Republic of the Sudan

(Pre-2012 data and communications statistics include South Sudan, which became independent July 9, 2011.)

People: Population: 36,108,853. **Age distrib.:** <15: 40.2%; 65+: 3.2%. **Growth:** 1.7%. **Migrants:** 1.2%. **Pop. density:** 50.2 per sq mi, 19.4 per sq km. **Urban:** 33.8%. **Ethnic groups:** Sudanese Arab (approx. 70%), Fur, Beja, Nuba, Fallata. **Languages:** Arabic, English (both official); Nubian; Ta Bedawie; Fur. **Religions:** Sunni Muslim, small Christian minority.

Geography: Total area: 718,723 sq mi, 1,861,484 sq km. **Location:** E end of Sahara desert zone. Egypt on N; Libya, Chad, Central African Republic on W; South Sudan on S; Ethiopia, Eritrea on E. **Topography:** The N consists of Libyan Desert in W and the mountainous Nubia Desert in E, with narrow Nile Valley between. Large rainy areas with fields, pastures, and forests in center. The S has rich soil, heavy rain. **Arable land:** 15.7%. **Capital:** Khartoum, 5,129,358.

Government: Type: Federal republic with strong military influence. **Head of state and gov.:** Pres. Gen. Omar Hassan Ahmad al-Bashir; in office: Oct. 16, 1993 (de facto since June 30, 1989). **Local divisions:** 18 states. **Defense budget** (2013): $1.89 bil. **Active troops:** 244,300.

Economy: Industries: oil, cotton ginning, textiles, cement, edible oils, sugar, soap distilling, shoes, petroleum refining, pharmaceuticals. **Chief crops:** cotton, groundnuts, sorghum, millet, wheat, gum arabic, sugarcane, cassava, mangoes, papayas, bananas, sweet potatoes, sesame seeds. **Natural resources:** petroleum; small reserves of iron ore, copper, chromium ore, zinc, tungsten, mica, silver, gold; hydropower. **Water:** 996 cu m per capita. **Crude oil reserves:** 5 bil bbls (incl. South Sudan). **Electricity prod.:** 9.7 bil kWh (incl. South Sudan). **Labor force:** agric. 80%, industry 7%, services 13%. **Unemployment:** 15.2%.

Finance: Monetary unit: Pound (SDG) (6.08 = $1 U.S.). **GDP:** $159.1 bil; **per capita GDP:** $4,300; **GDP growth:** 3.4%. **Imports:** $9.2 bil; China 25.9%, India 8.5%, Saudi Arabia 7.3%,

Egypt 6.6%. **Exports:** $7.2 bil; UAE 33.6%, China 31.5%, Japan 6.5%. **Tourism:** $967 mil. **Budget:** $9.1 bil. **Inflation:** 36.9%.

Transport: Railways: 4,506 mi. **Motor vehicles:** 3 per 1,000 pop. **Airports:** 16.

Communications: Telephone: 1.1 per 100 pop. **Mobile:** 72.2 per 100 pop. **Broadband:** 26.8 per 100 pop. **Internet:** 24.6%.

Health: Expend.: 7.3%. **Life expect.:** 61.6 male; 65.9 female. **Births:** 29.2 per 1,000 pop. **Deaths:** 7.7 per 1,000 pop. **Infant mortality:** 51.5 per 1,000 live births. **Undernourished:** NA. **HIV:** 0.2%.

Education: Compulsory: 6-13. **Literacy:** 75.9%.

Embassy: 2210 Massachusetts Ave. NW 20008; 338-8565.

Website: www.presidency.gov.sd

Northern Sudan, ancient Nubia, was settled by Egyptians in antiquity. The population was converted to Coptic Christianity in the 6th cent. Arab conquests brought Islam to the area in the 15th cent. In the 1820s, Egypt took over Sudan, defeating the last of the earlier empires, including the Fung. In the 1880s, Muhammad Ahmad, who called himself the Mahdi (leader of the faithful), and his followers, the dervishes, led a revolution. An Anglo-Egyptian force crushed the Mahdi's successors, 1898.

Sudan gained independence Jan. 1, 1956. In 1969, a Revolutionary Council took power, led by authoritarian Pres. Gaafar al-Nimeiry. He was overthrown, Apr. 6, 1985. Sudan held its first democratic parliamentary elections in 18 years in 1986. Brig. Omar Hassan Ahmad al-Bashir staged a bloodless military coup, toppling the elected government, June 30, 1989. He became president in 1993.

During 1955-72 and 1983-2005, rebels in the south (primarily Christians and followers of traditional religions) rebelled against government domination by mostly Arab-Muslim northern Sudan. War and related famine cost an estimated 2 mil lives. An accord ended the rebellion Jan. 9, 2005.

A rebellion in the Darfur region of western Sudan caused a new crisis, 2003-11. Marauding Arab militias, the *janjaweed*, reportedly acting in collusion with Sudanese government troops, looted and burned homes in Darfur and killed many African villagers. More than 7,000 African Union peacekeepers were ineffectual. Rebel and militia activities in Sudan and Chad led to border clashes and further attacks on civilians. By Sept. 2009, the Darfur war had killed about 300,000 people and displaced another 2.7 mil. A joint UN-African Union force of up to 26,000 peacekeepers (UNMIS) was deployed in Aug. 2007, followed by UNMISS upon South Sudan's independence, July 2011.

The Intl. Criminal Court in The Hague, Netherlands, issued two arrest warrants for Pres. Bashir—one in 2009 for war crimes and other crimes against humanity in Darfur, and another in 2010 for genocide, the first time it had ever accused a head of state of genocide. Bashir defied the calls for his arrest. In Apr. 2010 and Apr. 2015, he won new 5-year terms in elections not deemed credible and largely boycotted by the opposition.

After southern Sudanese voted overwhelmingly for secession, Jan. 9-15, 2011, South Sudan attained full independence July 9. Border disputes between Sudan and South Sudan ensued. Conflict in Darfur flared up again in 2014-15, including attacks on civilians by pro-government militias; hundreds of thousands of people were displaced. Government bombings of rebel-held areas in the Nuba Mountains, 2014-15, caused high civilian casualties.

Suriname

Republic of Suriname

People: Population: 579,633. **Age distrib.:** <15: 25.7%; 65+: 5.7%. **Growth:** 1.1%. **Migrants:** 7.7%. **Pop. density:** 9.6 per sq mi, 3.7 per sq km. **Urban:** 66%. **Ethnic groups:** Hindustani or E Indian (descended fr. 19th-cent. emigrants fr. northern India) 37%, Creole (mixed white/black) 31%, Javanese 15%, Maroon (descendants of escaped African slaves) 10%, Amerindian 2%, Chinese 2%. **Languages:** Dutch (official), English (widely spoken), Sranang Tongo (Surinamese), Caribbean Hindustani, Javanese. **Religions:** Hindu 27.4%, Protestant (predom. Moravian) 25.2%, Roman Catholic 22.8%, Muslim 19.6%, indigenous beliefs 5%.

Geography: Total area: 63,251 sq mi, 163,820 sq km; **Land area:** 60,232 sq mi, 156,000 sq km. **Location:** N shore of S America. Guyana on W, Brazil on S, French Guiana on E. **Topography:** Flat Atlantic coast, where dikes permit agriculture. Inland is forest belt. To S, hills cover three-fourths of country. **Arable land:** 0.4%. **Capital:** Paramaribo, 234,483 (2014).

Government: Type: Constitutional democracy. **Head of state and gov.:** Pres. Désire Delano Bouterse; in office: Aug. 12, 2010. **Local divisions:** 10 districts. **Defense budget** (2013): $41 mil. **Active troops:** 1,840.

Economy: Industries: bauxite and gold mining, alumina prod., oil, lumber, food proc., fishing. **Chief crops:** rice, bananas, palm kernels, coconuts, plantains, peanuts. **Natural resources:** timber, hydropower, fish, kaolin, shrimp, bauxite, gold; small amounts of nickel, copper, platinum, iron ore. **Water:** 183,673 cu m per capita. **Crude oil reserves:** 89 mil bbls. **Electricity prod.:** 1.8 bil kWh. **Labor force:** agric. 11.2%, industry 19.5%, services 69.3%. **Unemployment:** 7.8%.

Finance: Monetary unit: Dollar (SRD) (3.24 = $1 U.S.). **GDP:** $9.2 bil; **per capita GDP:** $16,600; **GDP growth** (2013): 4.1%. **Imports:** $2.1 bil; U.S. 21.6%, Netherlands 13.6%, Italy 8.6%, China 8.3%, UAE 7.5%, Antigua and Barbuda 6.5%. **Exports:** $2.5 bil; U.S. 25.5%, Belgium 16.7%, UAE 13%, Canada 10.6%, Guyana 6.2%, France 5.4%. **Tourism:** $95 mil. **Budget:** $1.4 bil. **Inflation:** 3.3%.

Transport: Motor vehicles: 237 per 1,000 pop. **Airports:** 6.

Communications: Telephone: 15.6 per 100 pop. **Mobile:** 170.6 per 100 pop. **Broadband:** 13.1 per 100 pop. **Internet:** 40.1%.

Health: Expend.: 5.9%. **Life expect.:** 69.6 male; 74.5 female. **Births:** 16.3 per 1,000 pop. **Deaths:** 6.1 per 1,000 pop. **Infant mortality:** 26.2 per 1,000 live births. **Undernourished:** 8.4%. **HIV:** 1.0%.

Education: Compulsory: ages 7-12. **Literacy:** 95.6%.

Embassy: 4301 Connecticut Ave. NW, Ste. 460, 20008; 244-7488.

Website: www.gov.sr or www.surinameembassy.org

The Netherlands acquired Suriname in 1667 from Britain. The 1954 Dutch constitution raised the colony to a level of equality with the Netherlands and the Netherlands Antilles. Independence was granted Nov. 25, 1975. Some 40% of the population (mostly E Indians, who opposed independence) immigrated to the Netherlands before independence.

Désire "Dési" Bouterse, who masterminded coups in 1982 and 1990, was elected president by parliament, July 19, 2010. Bouterse had been convicted in absentia in the Netherlands, 1999, for drug trafficking. Named by the U.S. as a transshipment point for cocaine, Suriname signed the UN-supported Container Control Programme (CCP), Aug. 23, 2012, to improve inspection of shipping containers in its ports. Bouterse's son Dino, arrested in Panama in a sting operation and extradited to the U.S. in 2013, pleaded guilty, Aug. 29, 2014, to drug trafficking and to terrorism charges related to his seeking a $2-mil bribe to allow Hezbollah to establish a base in Suriname; he was sentenced, Mar. 10, 2015, to 16 years in prison. Bouterse was elected by parliament to a new 5-year term as president, July 14, 2015.

Swaziland

Kingdom of Swaziland

People: Population: 1,435,613. **Age distrib.:** <15: 36%; 65+: 3.8%. **Growth:** 1.1%. **Migrants:** 2%. **Pop. density:** 216.1 per sq mi, 83.4 per sq km. **Urban:** 21.3%. **Ethnic groups:** African 97%, European 3%. **Languages:** English (used in govt.), siSwati (both official). **Religions:** Zionist (blend of Christianity and indigenous ancestral worship) 40%, Roman Catholic 20%, Muslim 10%, other 30%.

Geography: Total area: 6,704 sq mi, 17,364 sq km; **Land area:** 6,643 sq mi, 17,204 sq km. **Location:** Southern Africa, near Indian O. coast. South Africa on N, W, S; Mozambique on E. **Topography:** Descends W-E in broad belts, becoming more arid in low veld region, then rising to plateau in E. **Arable land:** 10.2%. **Capital:** Mbabane (admin.), 65,990 (2014); Lobamba (legis.).

Government: Type: Monarchy. **Head of state:** King Mswati III; in office: Apr. 25, 1986. **Head of gov.:** Prime Min. Barnabas Sibusiso Dlamini; in office: Oct. 23, 2008. **Local divisions:** 4 districts. **Defense budget/active troops:** NA.

Economy: Industries: coal, forestry, sugar, soft drink concentrates, textiles and apparel. **Chief crops:** sugarcane, cotton, corn, tobacco, rice, citrus, pineapples, sorghum, peanuts. **Natural resources:** asbestos, coal, clay, cassiterite, hydropower, forests, small gold and diamond deposits, quarry stone, talc. **Water:** 3,608 cu m per capita. **Electricity prod.:** 425 mil kWh. **Labor force:** agric. 70%. **Unemployment:** 22.5%.

Finance: Monetary unit: Lilangeni (SZL) (13.45 = $1 U.S.). **GDP:** $8.6 bil; **per capita GDP:** $7,800; **GDP growth:** 1.7%. **Imports:** $2.1 bil. **Exports:** $2.2 bil. **Tourism:** $13 mil. **Budget:** $1.4 bil. **Inflation** (2012-13): 5.6%.

Transport: Railways: 187 mi. **Airports:** 2.

Communications: Telephone: 3.5 per 100 pop. **Mobile:** 72.3 per 100 pop. **Broadband:** 4.4 per 100 pop. **Internet:** 27.1%.

Health: Expend.: 8.5%. **Life expect.:** 51.6 male; 50.5 female. **Births:** 24.7 per 1,000 pop. **Deaths:** 13.6 per 1,000 pop. **Infant mortality:** 52.6 per 1,000 live births. **Undernourished:** 26.1%. **HIV:** 27.7%.

Education: Compulsory: ages 6-12. **Literacy:** 87.5%.

Embassy: 1712 New Hampshire Ave. NW 20009; 234-5002.

Website: www.gov.sz

The royal house of Swaziland traces back 400 years. The Zulus drove the Swazis, a Bantu people, to Swaziland from lands to the N, 1820. Britain and Transvaal (later part of South Africa) later guaranteed their autonomy, and Britain assumed control after 1903. Independence came Sept. 6, 1968. In 1973, the king repealed the constitution and assumed full powers.

A new constitution banning political parties took effect Oct. 13, 1978. Under a revised constitution effective Feb. 8, 2006, nonpartisan parliamentary elections were permitted. An attempt failed in 2012 to unite pro-democracy groups under the banner of the People's United Democratic Movement (PUDEMO), which had been outlawed as a terrorist group in 2008. The AIDS crisis and the huge gap between rich and poor have fueled student and labor unrest in recent years, but the UN reported July 30, 2013, that AIDS-related deaths in Swaziland had fallen drastically due to the use of antiretroviral therapy. PUDEMO leader Mario Masuku, arrested on terrorism charges May 1, 2014, was released on bail July 14, 2015.

Sweden

Kingdom of Sweden

People: Population: 9,801,616. **Age distrib.:** <15: 17.1%; 65+: 20%. **Growth:** 0.8%. **Migrants:** 15.9%. **Pop. density:** 61.9 per sq mi, 23.9 per sq km. **Urban:** 85.8%. **Ethnic groups:** Swedes with Finnish and Sami minorities. Foreign-born or first-gen. immigrants: Finn, Yugoslav, Dane, Norwegian, Greek, Turk. **Languages:** Swedish (official). **Religions:** Lutheran 87%.

Geography: Total area: 173,860 sq mi, 450,295 sq km; **Land area:** 158,431 sq mi, 410,335 sq km. **Location:** Scandinavian Peninsula in N Europe. Norway on W, Denmark on S (across Kattegat), Finland on E. **Topography:** Mountains along NW border cover 25% of Sweden. Flat or rolling terrain with several large lakes across central and southern areas. **Arable land:** 6.4%. **Capital:** Stockholm, 1,485,680.

Government: Type: Constitutional monarchy. **Head of state:** King Carl XVI Gustaf; in office: Sept. 19, 1973. **Head of gov.:** Prime Min. Stefan Löfven; in office: Oct. 3, 2014. **Local divisions:** 21 counties. **Defense budget:** $6.69 bil. **Active troops:** 15,300.

Economy: Industries: iron and steel, precision equip. (bearings, radio and phone parts, armaments), wood pulp and paper prods., processed foods, motor vehicles. **Chief crops:** barley, wheat, sugar beets. **Natural resources:** iron ore, copper, lead, zinc, gold, silver, tungsten, uranium, arsenic, feldspar, timber, hydropower. **Water:** 18,180 cu m per capita. **Electricity prod.:** 161 bil kWh. **Labor force:** agric. 2%, industry 12%, services 86%. **Unemployment:** 8.1%.

Finance: Monetary unit: Krona (SEK) (8.43 = $1 U.S.). **GDP:** $448.2 bil; **per capita GDP:** $46,000; **GDP growth:** 2.1%. **Imports:** $163.8 bil; Germany 17.6%, Norway 8.2%, Denmark 8.1%, Netherlands 7.6%, UK 6%, Finland 5.6%, China 5.1%. **Exports:** $184.1 bil; Norway 10.6%, Germany 10.5%, Finland 7.4%, Denmark 7.1%, UK 6.9%, Netherlands 5.6%, U.S. 5.5%, Belgium 5.3%. **Tourism:** $12.7 bil. **Budget:** $304 bil. **Inflation:** –0.2%.

Transport: Railways: 7,404 mi. **Motor vehicles:** 531.3 per 1,000 pop. **Airports:** 149.

Communications: Telephone: 39.7 per 100 pop. **Mobile:** 127.8 per 100 pop. **Broadband:** 110.3 per 100 pop. **Internet:** 92.5%.

Health: Expend.: 9.6%. **Life expect.:** 80.1 male; 84.0 female. **Births:** 12.0 per 1,000 pop. **Deaths:** 9.4 per 1,000 pop. **Infant mortality:** 2.6 per 1,000 live births. **Undernourished:** <5%. **HIV:** 0.2%.

Education: Compulsory: ages 7-15. **Literacy:** 99%.

Embassy: 2900 K St. NW 20007; 467-2600.

Website: sweden.se

The Swedes have lived in present-day Sweden for at least 5,000 years, longer than nearly any other European people have lived in their present-day homelands. Gothic tribes from Sweden played a major role in the disintegration of the Roman Empire. Other Swedes helped create the first Russian state in the 9th cent.

The Swedes were Christianized from the 11th cent., and a strong centralized monarchy developed. The Riksdag, the first European parliament to represent all classes of society, was first called in 1435.

A revolt led by Gustavus I in 1521-23 freed Sweden from Danish rule (dating from 1397); he built up the government and military and established the Lutheran Church. In the 17th cent. Sweden was a major European power, gaining most of the Baltic seacoast. The Napoleonic wars, 1799-1815, in which Sweden acquired Norway (it became independent 1905), were the last in which Sweden participated. Armed neutrality was maintained in both world wars.

The Social Democratic Party (SAP) has governed Sweden for most of the period since World War II. Prime Min. Olof Palme was shot to death in Stockholm, Feb. 28, 1986, and Christer Pettersson was found guilty in 1988. He was sentenced to life in prison, but his conviction was overturned on appeal in 1989 for lack of evidence.

Sweden entered the EU, Jan. 1, 1995. A center-right alliance led by Fredrik Reinfeldt defeated the Social Democrats in Sept. 2006 elections. Parliament voted Apr. 1, 2009, to legalize same-sex marriage. Reinfeldt's center-right bloc won a renewed mandate in Sept. 2010 parliamentary elections. The SAP won the largest bloc of seats in Sept. 14, 2014, parliamentary elections, in which the anti-immigration Sweden Democrats won 13% of the vote and 49 seats. The SAP's Stefan Löfven became prime minister, heading a center-left minority government, Oct. 3. Early elections sought by the Sweden Democrats were averted when the SAP and opposition center-right parties reached a budget agreement, Dec. 27, 2014.

Switzerland

Swiss Confederation

People: Population: 8,121,830. **Age distrib.:** <15: 15.1%; 65+: 17.8%. **Growth:** 0.7%. **Migrants:** 28.9%. **Pop. density:** 525.9 per sq mi, 203.1 per sq km. **Urban:** 73.9%. **Ethnic groups:** German 65%, French 18%, Italian 10%. **Languages:** German, French, Italian (all official); English; Portuguese; Albanian; Serbo-Croatian; Spanish; Romansch (official). **Religions:** Roman Catholic 38.2%, Protestant 26.9%, Muslim 4.9%, none 21.4%.

Geography: Total area: 15,937 sq mi, 41,277 sq km; **Land area:** 15,443 sq mi, 39,997 sq km. **Location:** In Alps Mts. in central Europe. France on W; Italy on S; Liechtenstein, Austria on E; Germany on N. **Topography:** The Alps cover 60% of land area; the Jura, near France, 10%. The midlands run NE-SW in-between. **Arable land:** 10.2%. **Capital:** Bern, 358,481. **Cities:** Zürich, 1,246,199; Geneva, 557,806.

Government: Type: Federal republic in structure (formally a confederation). **Head of state and gov.:** President chosen on rotating basis from among 7-member Federal Council for 1-year term. **Local divisions:** 26 cantons. **Defense budget:** $5.26 bil. **Active troops:** 21,250.

Economy: Industries: machinery, chemicals, watches, textiles, precision instruments, tourism, banking, insurance. **Chief crops:** grains, fruits, vegetables. **Natural resources:** timber, salt. **Water:** 6,623 cu m per capita. **Electricity prod.:** 64.8 bil kWh. **Labor force:** agric. 3.4%, industry 23.4%, services 73.2%. **Unemployment:** 4.4%.

Finance: Monetary unit: Franc (CHF) (0.97 = $1 U.S.). **GDP:** $472.8 bil; **per capita GDP:** $58,100; **GDP growth:** 2%. **Imports:** $333.8 bil; Germany 28.2%, Italy 10.1%, France 8.2%, China 6.2%, U.S. 6.1%. **Exports:** $388.9 bil; Germany 18.5%, U.S. 11.7%, Italy 7.1%, France 7%, UK 5.2%. **Tourism:** $17.4 bil. **Budget:** $226 bil (federal, cantonal, and municipal). **Inflation:** –0.01%.

Transport: Railways: 3,512 mi. **Motor vehicles:** 599 per 1,000 pop. **Airports:** 40.

Communications: Telephone: 53.6 per 100 pop. **Mobile:** 140.5 per 100 pop. **Broadband:** 63.4 per 100 pop. **Internet:** 87%.

Health: Expend.: 11.3%. **Life expect.:** 80.2 male; 84.9 female. **Births:** 10.5 per 1,000 pop. **Deaths:** 8.1 per 1,000 pop. **Infant mortality:** 3.7 per 1,000 live births. **Undernourished:** <5%. **HIV:** NA.

Education: Compulsory: ages 4-15. **Literacy:** 99%.

Embassy: 2900 Cathedral Ave. NW 20008; 745-7900.

Website: www.ch.ch

Switzerland, the former Roman province of Helvetia, traces its modern history to 1291, when three cantons created a defensive league. Other cantons were subsequently admitted to the Swiss Confederation, which obtained its independence from the Holy Roman Empire through the Peace of Westphalia (1648). The cantons were joined under a federal constitution in 1848.

Switzerland has maintained an armed neutrality since 1815 and has not been involved in a foreign war since 1515. It is the seat of many UN and other international agencies but only became a full UN member on Sept. 10, 2002.

Switzerland is a world banking center. The government announced, Mar. 1997, a $4.7-bil fund to compensate victims of the Nazi Holocaust and other catastrophes. Swiss banks agreed Aug. 12, 1998, to pay $1.25 bil in reparations. A June 2002 referendum decriminalized abortion. Two more referendums in 2005 harmonized travel, asylum, law enforcement, and labor policies with the EU; more rights for same-sex couples were also endorsed June 5, 2005.

The Swiss government bailed out the troubled banking giant UBS during the international financial crisis in Oct. 2008. U.S. tax authorities pressured UBS Jan. 2009 to close some 19,000 hidden offshore accounts and to disclose in Aug. data on accounts for over 4,400 U.S. clients. In a Nov. 2009 referendum reflecting rising anti-Muslim sentiment, voters approved a constitutional ban on construction of new minarets on mosques. In a Feb. 9, 2014, referendum, voters narrowly approved a measure requiring government quotas limiting immigration within three years. However, another referendum proposal, to set a very low specific quota, was defeated, Nov. 30, 2014.

Syria

Syrian Arab Republic

People: Population: 17,064,854. **Age distrib.:** <15: 32.5%; 65+: 4%. **Growth:** –0.2%. **Migrants:** 6.4%. **Pop. density:** 240.7 per sq mi, 92.9 per sq km. **Urban:** 57.7%. **Ethnic groups:** Arab 90.3%; Kurd, Armenian, other 9.7%. **Languages:** Arabic (official), Kurdish, Armenian, Aramaic, Circassian (widely understood). **Religions:** Muslim 87% (official; incl. Sunni 74%; Alawi, Ismaili, Shia 13%), Christian 10%, Druze 3%.

Geography: Total area: 71,498 sq mi, 185,180 sq km; **Land area:** 70,900 sq mi, 183,630 sq km. (500 sq mi of area is occupied by Israel.) **Location:** Middle East, at E end of Medit. Sea. Lebanon, Israel on W; Jordan on S; Iraq on E; Turkey on N. **Topography:** A short Medit. coastline stretches E and S with fertile lowlands and plains, alternating with mountains and large desert areas. **Arable land:** 25.4%. **Capital:** Dimashq (Damascus), 2,565,670 (excl. refugees and internally displaced persons). **Cities:** Halab (Aleppo), 3,561,796; Hims (Homs), 1,641,298; Hamah, 1,236,537. (Figures for Hims and Hamah excl. refugees and internally displaced persons.)

Government: Type: Republic under authoritarian regime. **Head of state:** Pres. Bashar al-Assad; in office: July 17, 2000.

Head of gov.: Prime Min. Wael al-Halqi; in office: Aug. 9, 2012. **Local divisions:** 14 provinces. **Defense budget:** NA. **Active troops:** 178,000.

Economy: Industries: petroleum, textiles, food proc., beverages, tobacco, phosphate rock mining, cement. **Chief crops:** wheat, barley, cotton, lentils, chickpeas, olives, sugar beets. **Natural resources:** petroleum, phosphates, chrome and manganese ores, asphalt, iron ore, rock salt, marble, gypsum, hydropower. **Water:** 767 cu m per capita. **Crude oil reserves:** 2.5 bil bbls. **Electricity prod.:** 29.5 bil kWh. **Labor force:** agric. 17%, industry 16%, services 67%. **Unemployment:** 10.8%.

Finance: Monetary unit: Pound (SYP) (188.82 = $1 U.S.). **GDP** (2011): $107.6 bil; **per capita GDP** (2011): $5,100; **GDP growth** (2011): –2.3%. **Imports:** $7.7 bil; Saudi Arabia 24.6%, UAE 12.1%, Iran 8.9%, Iraq 7.3%, Turkey 6%. **Exports:** $2 bil; Iraq 59.9%, Saudi Arabia 10%, Kuwait 6.5%, UAE 5.6%. **Tourism:** $6.2 bil. **Budget:** $5.5 bil. **Inflation** (2011-12): 36.7%.

Transport: Railways: 1,275 mi. **Motor vehicles:** 90.1 per 1,000 pop. **Airports:** 29.

Communications: Telephone: 18.1 per 100 pop. **Mobile:** 70.9 per 100 pop. **Broadband:** 3.2 per 100 pop. **Internet:** 28.1%.

Health: Expend.: 3.4%. **Life expect.:** 72.3 male; 77.2 female. **Births:** 22.2 per 1,000 pop. **Deaths:** 4.0 per 1,000 pop. **Infant mortality:** 15.6 per 1,000 live births. **Undernourished:** NA. **HIV:** <0.1%.

Education: Compulsory: ages 6-14. **Literacy:** 86.4%.

Embassy: 2215 Wyoming Ave. NW 20008; 232-6313.

Website: www.egov.sy

Syria was the center of the Seleucid Empire but later was absorbed into the Roman and Arab empires. Ottoman rule prevailed for four cents., until the end of WWI.

The state of Syria was formed from former Turkish districts, separated by the Treaty of Sevres, 1920, and divided into the states of Syria and Greater Lebanon. Both were administered under a French League of Nations mandate, 1920-41. The occupying French proclaimed Syria a republic Sept. 16, 1941; independence came Apr. 17, 1946. Syria joined the Arab invasion of Israel in 1948.

Syria belonged to the United Arab Republic from Feb. 1958 to Sept. 1961. The Socialist Baath party seized power Mar. 1963 and became the only legal party. The Alawite minority has dominated the government.

In the June 1967 Arab-Israeli war, Israel seized and occupied the Golan Heights, from which Syria had shelled Israeli settlements. On Oct. 6, 1973, Syria and Egypt attacked Israel but failed to recapture the Golan Heights. Syrian troops entered Lebanon in 1976, during the Lebanese civil war, and remained a strong presence in the country. They fought Palestinian guerrillas and, later, Christian militiamen. Syria sided with Iran during the Iran-Iraq War, 1980-88.

Thousands died in the city of Hama Feb. 1982 when government forces crushed a Muslim Brotherhood uprising. Following Israel's invasion of Lebanon, June 6, 1982, Israeli planes destroyed 17 Syrian antiaircraft missile batteries in the Bekaa Valley, June 9, and some 25 Syrian planes. Israel and Syria agreed to a cease-fire June 11. Syria condemned the Aug. 1990 Iraqi invasion of Kuwait and sent troops to help Allied forces in the Gulf War.

Hafez al-Assad, president of Syria since 1971, died June 10, 2000, and was succeeded by his son Bashar al-Assad. Israeli planes hit an alleged terrorist camp near Damascus Oct. 4, 2003. The U.S. imposed limited sanctions on Syria, May 11, 2004.

Syria denied responsibility for a truck bomb that killed former Lebanese Prime Min. Rafik al-Hariri in Beirut in Feb. 2005. Syria aided Hezbollah fighters in their conflict with Israel and gave about 180,000 Lebanese temporary refuge when Israeli forces targeted Hezbollah in Lebanon, July-Aug. 2006.

On Sept. 6, 2007, Israel bombed a secret site in N Syria where the Israelis believed Syria and North Korea were developing a nuclear facility; both countries denied the claim. The Assad regime used troops and tanks to enforce control during Arab Spring demonstrations in Mar. 2011, but the conflict escalated into outright rebellion. The Intl. Committee of the Red Cross declared the conflict a civil war, July 15, 2012. Various armed opposition groups fought Assad's forces and each other for control of territory. The Natl. Coalition for Syrian Revolutionary and Opposition Forces, including a number of opposition groups, was formed Nov. 11, 2012, and gained international support.

On Jan. 30, 2013, Israel bombed a convoy in Damascus allegedly carrying missiles to Hezbollah forces in Lebanon, which backed Assad. Fighting between government and rebel forces continued throughout 2013. International intelligence communities announced in May 2013 that there was increasing evidence that Assad's forces had used chemical and biological weapons. The EU May 28 lifted an arms embargo prohibiting weapons shipments to rebel fighters. Findings that Assad was using chemical weapons led to U.S. Pres. Barack Obama's June 13 decision to supply military support to rebel groups. A chemical attack on an opposition-controlled Damascus suburb Aug. 21, 2013, killed more than 1,400. Assad and the rebels accused each other of the attack. Russian and U.S. negotiators reached an agreement with Syria requiring the Assad government to relinquish its chemical weapons; the agreement was reinforced by a UN Security Council resolution Sept. 27, 2013. Inspectors arrived in Syria Oct. 1 and the last known chemical weapons were believed to have been removed June 23, 2014. However, the Security Council received allegations that Assad's forces had used chemical weapons in Mar. 2015.

Heavy fighting continued in 2014-15. By summer 2014, the Sunni extremist group ISIS (Islamic State in Iraq and Syria) controlled large areas in eastern and northern Syria. Pres. Obama announced Sept. 10, 2014, that the U.S. would train rebel groups fighting both government forces and ISIS. Beginning the night of Sept. 22-23, 2014, the U.S. conducted air and cruise missile strikes against ISIS and other Islamist extremist groups in Syria, supported by several Middle East countries and later by Canada, Turkey, Australia, and France (as of Sept. 30, 2015). Russia, which had been supporting the Assad regime, sent warplanes to Syria in Sept. 2015 and began its own air campaign, Sept. 30, against anti-government forces. Syrian Kurdish forces, with U.S. air support, had retaken some territory in northern Syria from ISIS as of mid-2015. ISIS destroyed—or sold to fund its operation—antiquities at numerous historic sites, including Palmyra, captured in May 2015. In June 2015, the death toll in Syria's civil war since Mar. 2011 was estimated by the Syrian Observatory for Human Rights to have passed 320,000. The UNHCR reported the number of Syrian refugees at more than 4 mil as of Oct. 1, 2015; an estimated 7.6 mil were displaced within Syria as of midyear.

Taiwan

People: Population: 23,415,126. **Age distrib.:** <15: 13.5%; 65+: 12.5%. **Growth:** 0.2%. **Migrants:** NA. **Pop. density:** 1,879.9 per sq mi, 725.8 per sq km. **Urban:** NA. **Ethnic groups:** Taiwanese (incl. Hakka) 84%, mainland Chinese 14%, indigenous 2%. **Languages:** Mandarin Chinese (official), Taiwanese (Min), Hakka dialects. **Religions:** mixture of Buddhist and Taoist 93%, Christian 4.5%.

Geography: Total area: 13,892 sq mi, 35,980 sq km; **Land area:** 12,456 sq mi, 32,260 sq km. **Location:** Off SE coast of China, between E and S China Seas. **Topography:** A mountain range forms backbone of island. The eastern half is very steep and craggy; western slope is flat, fertile, and well cultivated. **Arable land:** 16.9%. **Capital:** Taipei, 2,665,656. **Cities:** Kaohsiung, 1,522,779; Taichung, 1,224,935.

Government: Type: Multiparty democracy. **Head of state:** Pres. Ma Ying-jeou; in office: May 20, 2008. **Head of gov.:** Prem. Mao Chi-kuo; in office: Dec. 8, 2014. **Local divisions:** 13 counties, 3 cities, 6 special municipalities. **Defense budget:** $10.13 bil. **Active troops:** 290,000.

Economy: Industries: electronics, communications and information tech. prods., petroleum refining, chemicals, textiles, iron and steel, machinery, cement, food proc. **Chief crops:** rice, vegetables, fruit, tea, flowers. **Natural resources:** small deposits of coal, nat. gas, limestone, marble, asbestos. **Water:** NA. **Crude oil reserves:** 2.4 mil bbls. **Electricity prod.:** 233.7 bil kWh. **Labor force:** agric. 5%, industry 36.1%, services 58.9%. **Unemployment:** 4.2%.

Finance: Monetary unit: New Dollar (TWD) (32.48 = $1 U.S.). **GDP:** $1.1 tril; **per capita GDP:** $45,900; **GDP growth:** 3.7%. **Imports:** $277.5 bil; (2012) Japan 17.6%, China 16.1%, U.S. 9.5%. **Exports:** $318 bil; (2012) China 27.1%, Hong Kong 13.2%, U.S. 10.3%, Japan 6.4%. **Tourism:** $14.7 bil. **Budget:** $91.7 bil. **Inflation:** NA.

Transport: Railways: 992 mi. **Motor vehicles:** 320.8 per 1,000 pop. **Airports:** 35.

Communications: Telephone: 60.2 per 100 pop. **Mobile:** 130.2 per 100 pop. **Broadband:** 63.1 per 100 pop. **Internet:** 84%.

Health: Expend.: NA. **Life expect.:** 76.9 male; 83.3 female. **Births:** 8.5 per 1,000 pop. **Deaths:** 7.1 per 1,000 pop. **Infant mortality:** 4.4 per 1,000 live births. **Undernourished:** NA. **HIV:** NA.

Education: Compulsory: ages 6-17. **Literacy:** 96.1%.

Taipei Economic and Cultural Representative Office: 4201 Wisconsin Ave. NW 20016; 895-1800.

Website: www.taiwan.gov.tw

Large-scale immigration from China began in the 17th cent. The island came under mainland control after an interval of Dutch rule, 1620-62. Japan ruled Taiwan (also called Formosa), 1895-1945. The Kuomintang (Chinese Nationalist Party) government fled to Taiwan in 1949 and established the Republic of China under Chiang Kai-shek, who ruled until his death in 1975. The U.S. provided military aid to deter a Communist invasion.

In 1971, the UN expelled Taiwan as a member and recognized the mainland government. The U.S. acknowledged the People's Republic of China, Dec. 15, 1978, and severed ties with Taiwan. However, the U.S. and Taiwan have continued a strong trading relationship and maintain contact via quasi-official agencies.

Land reform, government planning, U.S. aid and investment, and free universal education brought advances in industry, agriculture, and living standards. In 1987 martial law was lifted after 38 years, and in 1991 the 43 years of emergency rule ended. Taiwan held its first direct presidential election Mar. 23, 1996. An earthquake on Sept. 21, 1999, killed more than 2,300 people.

Five decades of Kuomintang rule ended when Chen Shui-bian, leader of the pro-independence Democratic Progressive Party, won the Mar. 2000 presidential election. Chen was wounded in an apparent assassination attempt Mar. 19, 2004, one day before he won a second term as president. Promising increased cooperation with China, Kuomintang candidate Ma Ying-jeou won the presidential election, Mar. 22, 2008, and was reelected Jan. 14, 2012.

Former Pres. Chen was convicted of corruption and sentenced to life in prison, Sept. 11, 2009. Former Pres. Lee Teng-hui, who introduced democratic reforms 1988-2000, was found not guilty of embezzling $7.8 mil while in office, Nov. 15, 2013.

Since 1949, the People's Republic has considered Taiwan a rebel province of the mainland; in 1991, the Kuomintang dropped its claim to be the sole government of both. The first formal talks (focused largely on economic matters) between representatives of Taiwan and China were held Feb. 11, 2014. Concern over recent Kuomintang pro-China policies apparently contributed to a sweeping defeat for the party in Nov. 29, 2014, local elections.

The **Penghu Isls.** (Pescadores), 49 sq mi, pop. (2011 est.) 96,597, lie between Taiwan and the mainland. Kinmen, fmr. Quemoy, pop. (2011 est.) 99,691, and Matsu, pop. (2011 est.) 10,106, lie just off the mainland.

Tajikistan

Republic of Tajikistan

People: Population: 8,191,958. **Age distrib.:** <15: 32.7%; 65+: 3.2%. **Growth:** 1.7%. **Migrants:** 3.4%. **Pop. density:** 149.9 per sq mi, 57.9 per sq km. **Urban:** 26.8%. **Ethnic groups:** Tajik 84.3%, Uzbek (incl. Lakai, Kongrat, Katagan, Barlos, Yuz) 13.8%, other (incl. Kyrgyz, Russian, Turkmen, Tatar, Arab) 2%. **Languages:** Tajik (official), Russian (widely used in govt. and business). **Religions:** Sunni Muslim 85%, Shia Muslim 5%.

Geography: Total area: 55,637 sq mi, 144,100 sq km; **Land area:** 54,637 sq mi, 141,510 sq km. **Location:** Central Asia. Uzbekistan on N and W, Kyrgyzstan on N, China on E, Afghanistan on S. **Topography:** Mountainous; contains the Pamirs, Trans-Alai mountain system. **Arable land:** 6.1%. **Capital:** Dushanbe, 822,331.

Government: Type: Republic. **Head of state:** Pres. Imomali Rakhmon; in office: Nov. 6, 1994. **Head of gov.:** Prime Min. Qohir Rasulzoda; in office: Nov. 23, 2013. **Local divisions:** 2 provinces, 1 autonomous province, 1 capital region, 1 district under republic admin. **Defense budget:** $186 mil. **Active troops:** 8,800.

Economy: Industries: aluminum, cement, vegetable oil. **Chief crops:** cotton, grain, fruits, grapes, vegetables. **Natural resources:** hydropower, petroleum, uranium, mercury, brown coal, lead, zinc, antimony, tungsten, silver, gold. **Water:** 2,669 cu m per capita. **Crude oil reserves:** 12 mil bbls. **Electricity prod.:** 17.5 bil kWh. **Labor force:** agric. 46.5%, industry 10.7%, services 42.8%. **Unemployment:** 10.7%.

Finance: Monetary unit: Somoni (TJS) (6.33 = $1 U.S.). **GDP:** $22.3 bil; **per capita GDP:** $2,700; **GDP growth:** 6.7%. **Imports:** $4.3 bil; China 41.3%, Russia 15.8%, Kazakhstan 12.5%, Turkey 6.1%. **Exports:** $654.8 mil; Turkey 35.3%, Iran 9%, China 8.4%, Bangladesh 6.9%, Kazakhstan 6.8%, Afghanistan 6.7%, Russia 5.9%. **Budget:** $2.9 bil. **Inflation:** 6.1%.

Transport: Railways: 423 mi. **Airports:** 17.

Communications: Telephone: 5.2 per 100 pop. **Mobile:** 95.1 per 100 pop. **Broadband:** NA. **Internet:** 17.5%.

Health: Expend.: 5.8%. **Life expect.:** 64.3 male; 70.7 female. **Births:** 24.4 per 1,000 pop. **Deaths:** 6.2 per 1,000 pop. **Infant mortality:** 33.9 per 1,000 live births. **Undernourished:** 32.3%. **HIV:** 0.4%.

Education: Compulsory: ages 7-15. **Literacy:** 99.8%.

Embassy: 1005 New Hampshire Ave. NW 20037; 223-6090.

Website: www.president.tj

Societies were settled in the region from about 3000 BCE. Invaders have included Iranians, Arabs (who converted the population to Islam), Mongols, Uzbeks, Afghans, and Russians. The USSR gained control 1918-25, making the region a part of the Uzbek SSR until the Tajik SSR was proclaimed, 1929.

Tajikistan declared independence Sept. 9, 1991. Factional fighting led to the installation of a pro-Communist regime, Jan. 1993. A new constitution establishing a presidential system was approved by referendum in 1994.

An estimated 55,000 died in clashes between Muslim rebels and loyalist troops (supported by Russia) by mid-1997, despite a series of peace accords. Constitutional changes including legalization of Islamic political parties were approved by referendum in 1999. Pres. Imomali Rakhmonov, first elected in 1994, won a Nov. 1999 election called a farce by human-rights observers. Voter-approved constitutional changes in 2003 gave Rakhmonov the right to serve as president until 2020. Leading opposition groups boycotted the Nov. 2006 election, again won by Rakhmonov (who changed his name to Rakhmon in 2007). He won the Nov. 2013 election with 84% of the vote.

Poverty and corruption are widespread. Much of the nation's income is supplied by international donors and by remittances from Tajiks working in Kazakhstan and Russia, though a new Russian law in 2015 restricted the ability of Tajiks to work in Russia. After rebels murdered a Tajik general in the semiautonomous province of Gorno-Badakhshan, July 21, 2012, the army attacked and killed about 30 militants July 24; 17 government troops died. A former warlord surrendered Aug. 13, 2012, in exchange for a troop withdrawal from the region.

Tanzania

United Republic of Tanzania

People: Population: 51,045,882. **Age distrib.:** <15: 44.3%; 65+: 3%. **Growth:** 2.8%. **Migrants:** 0.6%. **Pop. density:** 149.3 per sq mi, 57.6 per sq km. **Urban:** 31.6%. **Ethnic groups:** African 99% (of which 95% are Bantu consisting of 130+ tribes). **Languages:** Kiswahili or Swahili, English (primary lang. of commerce, admin., higher ed.) (both official); Arabic (widely spoken in Zanzibar). **Religions:** Muslim 35%, indigenous beliefs 35%, Christian 30%; 99%+ Muslim on Zanzibar.

Geography: Total area: 365,755 sq mi, 947,300 sq km; **Land area:** 342,009 sq mi, 885,800 sq km. **Location:** Coast of E Africa. Kenya, Uganda on N; Rwanda, Burundi, Dem. Rep. of the Congo on W; Zambia, Malawi, Mozambique on S. **Topography:** Hot, arid central plateau surrounded by lake region in W. Temperate highlands in N and S; coastal plains. Mt. Kilimanjaro (19,341 ft) is highest in Africa. **Arable land:** 16.4%. **Capital:** Dodoma (official; National Assembly meets here), 227,762 (2014). **Cities:** Dar es Salaam (exec. branch offices), 5,115,670.

Government: Type: Republic. **Head of state and gov.:** Pres. Jakaya Mrisho Kikwete; in office: Dec. 21, 2005. **Local divisions:** 30 regions. **Defense budget:** $396 mil. **Active troops:** 27,000.

Economy: Industries: agric. proc.; mining; salt, soda ash; cement, oil refining, shoes, apparel. **Chief crops:** coffee, sisal, tea, cotton, pyrethrum (insecticide made from chrysanthemums), cashews, tobacco, cloves, corn, wheat. **Natural resources:** hydropower, tin, phosphates, iron ore, coal, diamonds, gems, gold, nat. gas, nickel. **Water:** 1,955 cu m per capita. **Electricity prod.:** 5.5 bil kWh. **Labor force:** agric. 80%, industry and services 20%. **Unemployment:** 3.5%.

Finance: Monetary unit: Shilling (TZS) (2,145.00 = $1 U.S.). **GDP:** $127.1 bil; **per capita GDP:** $2,700; **GDP growth:** 7.2%. **Imports:** $12 bil; India 25%, China 24.6%, South Africa 5.1%. **Exports:** $6.1 bil; India 20%, China 13.3%. **Tourism:** $2 bil. **Budget:** $8.6 bil. **Inflation:** 6.1%.

Transport: Railways: 2,838 mi. **Motor vehicles:** 1.8 per 1,000 pop. **Airports:** 10.

Communications: Telephone: 0.3 per 100 pop. **Mobile:** 62.8 per 100 pop. **Broadband:** 2.7 per 100 pop. **Internet:** 4.9%.

Health: Expend.: 7%. **Life expect.:** 60.3 male; 63.1 female. **Births:** 36.4 per 1,000 pop. **Deaths:** 8.0 per 1,000 pop. **Infant mortality:** 42.4 per 1,000 live births. **Undernourished:** 34.6%. **HIV:** 5.3%.

Education: Compulsory: ages 7-13. **Literacy:** 70.6%.

Embassy: 1232 22nd St. NW 20037; 939-6125.

Website: www.tanzania.go.tz

Arab colonization and slaving in Tanganyika began in the 8th cent.; Portuguese sailors explored the coast around 1500. Other Europeans followed.

In 1885 Germany established German East Africa, of which Tanganyika formed the bulk. Under Britain, it became a League of Nations mandate and after 1946, a UN trust territory. It became independent, Dec. 9, 1961, and a republic within the Commonwealth a year later.

Zanzibar, the Isle of Cloves, has an area of 640 sq mi and lies 23 mi off mainland Tanzania. The island of Pemba, area 380 sq mi, is 25 mi to the NE. Ethnic groups in Zanzibar include Arabs and Africans. Zanzibar and Pemba produce most of the world's supply of cloves and clove oil.

Zanzibar was for centuries the center for Arab slave traders. Portugal ruled the region for two centuries until ousted by Arabs around 1700. Zanzibar became a British Protectorate in 1890; independence came Dec. 10, 1963. Revolutionary forces overthrew the Sultan, Jan. 12, 1964. The new government ousted Western diplomats and journalists, slaughtered thousands of Arabs, and nationalized farms. Union with Tanganyika followed.

The Republic of Tanganyika in E Africa and the island Republic of Zanzibar, off Tanganyika's coast, both of which had recently gained independence, joined to form the United Republic of Tanzania, Apr. 26, 1964. Zanzibar retains internal self-government.

Until resigning as president in 1985, Julius K. Nyerere, a former Tanganyikan independence leader, dominated Tanzania's single-party government, which emphasized government planning and economic control. A multiparty system was established in 1992, and the economy was privatized in the 1990s.

A bomb at the U.S. embassy in Dar es Salaam, Aug. 7, 1998, killed 11 people and injured at least 70 others. The U.S. blamed the attack and a near-simultaneous embassy bombing in Kenya on Islamic terrorists associated with Osama bin Laden.

Jakaya Mrisho Kikwete of the ruling Chama Cha Mapinduzi (Party of the Revolution) won the Dec. 2005, presidential election; he was reelected to a second 5-year term Oct. 2010. Large offshore natural gas deposits have been discovered in recent years; the government estimated total recoverable gas reserves in 2015 at 55 tril cubic ft. Kikwete made major cabinet changes in Jan. 2015 after high-ranking officials were allegedly involved in misappropriation of $180 mil from a government bank account.

Thailand

Kingdom of Thailand

People: Population: 67,976,405. **Age distrib.:** <15: 17.4%; 65+: 9.9%. **Growth:** 0.3%. **Migrants:** 5.6%. **Pop. density:** 344.6 per sq mi, 133.1 per sq km. **Urban:** 50.4%. **Ethnic groups:** Thai 95.9%, Burmese 2%. **Languages:** Thai (official), English (secondary lang. of elite). **Religions:** Buddhist (official) 93.6%, Muslim 4.9%.

Geography: Total area: 198,117 sq mi, 513,120 sq km; **Land area:** 197,256 sq mi, 510,890 sq km. **Location:** On Indochinese and Malayan peninsulas in SE Asia. Myanmar on W and N, Laos on N, Cambodia on E, Malaysia on S. **Topography:** A plateau dominates NE third of Thailand, dropping to fertile alluvial valley of Chao Phraya R. in center. Forested mountains with narrow fertile valleys are in N. Rain forests cover S peninsula region. **Arable land:** 32.4%. **Capital:** Krung Thep (Bangkok), 9,269,823. **Cities:** Samut Prakan, 1,814,046.

Government: Type: Constitutional monarchy. **Head of state:** King Bhumibol Adulyadej; in office: June 9, 1946. **Head of gov.:** Prime Min. Prayuth Chan-ocha; in office: Aug. 24, 2014. **Local divisions:** 76 provinces, 1 municipality. **Defense budget:** $5.69 bil. **Active troops:** 360,850.

Economy: Industries: tourism, textiles and garments, agric. proc., beverages, tobacco, cement, light mfg. (jewelry, elec. appliances, computers and parts, integrated circuits, furniture). **Chief crops:** rice, cassava, rubber, corn, sugarcane, coconuts, palm oil, pineapples. **Natural resources:** tin, rubber, nat. gas, tungsten, tantalum, timber, lead, fish, gypsum, lignite, fluorite. **Water:** 6,545 cu m per capita. **Crude oil reserves:** 461 mil bbls. **Electricity prod.:** 156.4 bil kWh. **Labor force:** agric. 32.2%, industry 16.7%, services 51.1%. **Unemployment:** 0.7%.

Finance: Monetary unit: Baht (THB) (35.76 = $1 U.S.). **GDP:** $985.5 bil; **per capita GDP:** $14,400; **GDP growth:** 0.7%. **Imports:** $200.2 bil; Japan 16.4%, China 15%, UAE 6.9%, U.S. 5.9%, Malaysia 5.3%. **Exports:** $224.8 bil; China 11.9%, U.S. 10.1%, Japan 9.7%, Hong Kong 5.8%, Malaysia 5.7%. **Tourism:** $38.4 bil. **Budget:** $84.8 bil. **Inflation:** 1.9%.

Transport: Railways: 2,529 mi. **Motor vehicles:** 230.4 per 1,000 pop. **Airports:** 63.

Communication: Telephone: 8.5 per 100 pop. **Mobile:** 144.4 per 100 pop. **Broadband:** 52.3 per 100 pop. **Internet:** 34.9%.

Health: Expend.: 3.9%. **Life expect.:** 71.2 male; 77.8 female. **Births:** 11.2 per 1,000 pop. **Deaths:** 7.8 per 1,000 pop. **Infant mortality:** 9.6 per 1,000 live births. **Undernourished:** 6.8%. **HIV:** 1.1%.

Education: Compulsory: ages 6-14. **Literacy:** 96.7%.

Embassy: 1024 Wisconsin Ave. NW 20007; 944-3600.

Website: www.thaigov.go.th

Thais began migrating from southern China during the 11th cent. and established a unified Thai kingdom, 1350. Known as Siam until 1939, Thailand is the only country in SE Asia never colonized by Europeans. King Mongkut and his son King Chulalongkorn, ruling successively from 1851 to 1910, modernized the country and signed trade treaties with Britain and France. A bloodless revolution in 1932 limited the monarchy. Thailand was an ally of Japan during WWII and of the U.S. during the postwar period. For decades, the military had a dominant role in governing the country.

An economic downturn forced Thailand to seek more than $15 bil in emergency international loans, Aug. 1997. A new constitution won legislative approval Sept. 27. By the end of the 1990s, according to UN estimates, more than 750,000 people in Thailand had HIV/AIDS, with 143,000 new infections in 1991 alone. A nationwide prevention campaign reduced the number of new HIV infections; in 2014 about 450,000 people were living with HIV/AIDS.

Following elections in Jan. 2001, Thaksin Shinawatra became prime min. Feb. 2005 elections gave Thaksin's party a huge parliamentary majority. Facing rising opposition and accused of benefiting improperly from the sale of his family's telecom business, Thaksin called snap elections for Apr. 2006; the vote, which major parties boycotted, was later ruled unconstitutional. A military junta took power in a bloodless coup Sept. 19.

Thaksin supporters won Dec. 2007 elections, and Samak Sundaravej became prime min. after civilian rule was restored Jan. 22, 2008. Thailand's Constitutional Court ousted Samak in Sept., and Thaksin's brother-in-law Somchai Wongsawat became prime min. Sept. 18. But a Constitutional Court ruling, Dec. 2, barred him from politics and dissolved his People Power Party because of electoral fraud.

Mass protests by Thaksin supporters, known as Red Shirts, led the government to declare a state of emergency in Bangkok, Apr. 12-24, 2009. Meanwhile, about 60,000 security forces in southern Thailand suppressed a Muslim insurgency; from Jan. 2004 to Sept. 2009, more than 3,500 people, mostly civilians, died in the fighting.

On Feb. 26, 2010, Thailand's Supreme Court ordered the seizure of about $1.4 bil of Thaksin's family assets. Thaksin supporters staged mass rallies in Bangkok. After the Red Shirts began to build a fortified compound in Bangkok, a crackdown by Thai security forces May 14-19, 2010, left more than 90 people dead and some 470 injured. Thaksin's sister, Yingluck Shinawatra, became Thailand's first female prime min. after parliamentary elections July 3, 2011. Monsoon season brought floods beginning July 25, 2011, that covered two-thirds of the country by Oct. 12. Insurgents in the southern region continued to attack government forces in 2013-15. Mass protests against Yingluck began in Nov. 2013. On May 7, 2014, she was removed from office by the Constitutional Court, and the military seized power in a May 22 coup. An interim legislature, with a majority of military members, was appointed July 31; it named coup leader Gen. Prayuth Chan-ocha as prime min. Aug. 21. A 2015 investigation resulted in charges against dozens, including government and military officials, for involvement in human trafficking; the charges related to smuggling by boat, abusing, holding for ransom, and selling as slave laborers migrants from Myanmar and Bangladesh. A bombing at the Erawan shrine in Bangkok, Aug. 17, 2015, killed 20 and injured more than 100; Thai police arrested 2 suspects, Aug. 29 and Sept. 1, including the alleged bomber.

Timor-Leste

(East Timor)

Democratic Republic of Timor-Leste

People: Population: 1,231,116. **Age distrib.:** <15: 41.8%; 65+: 3.7%. **Growth:** 2.4%. **Migrants:** 1%. **Pop. density:** 214.4 per sq mi, 82.8 per sq km. **Urban:** 32.8%. **Ethnic groups:** Austronesian (Malayo-Polynesian), Papuan, small Chinese minority. **Languages:** Tetum, Portuguese (both official); Indonesian; English; about 16 indigenous langs. **Religions:** Roman Catholic 96.9%.

Geography: Total area: 5,743 sq mi, 14,874 sq km. **Land area:** 5,743 sq mi, 14,874 sq km. **Location:** E half of Timor Isl. in SW Pacific O. Indonesia on W half of island. **Topography:** Terrain is rugged, rising to 9,721 ft at Mt. Ramelau. **Arable land:** 10.8%. **Capital:** Dili, 228,136 (2014).

Government: Type: Republic. **Head of state:** Pres. Taur Matan Ruak; in office: May 20, 2012. **Head of gov.:** Prime Min. Rui Maria de Araújo; in office: Feb. 11, 2015. **Local divisions:** 13 admin. districts. **Defense budget:** $69 mil. **Active troops:** 1,330.

Economy: Industries: printing, soap mfg., handicrafts, woven cloth. **Chief crops:** coffee, rice, corn, cassava, sweet potatoes, soybeans. **Natural resources:** gold, petroleum, nat. gas, manganese, marble. **Water:** 7,251 cu m per capita. **Labor force:** agric. 64%, industry 10%, services 26%. **Unemployment:** 4.4%.

Finance: Monetary unit: U.S. Dollar (USD). **GDP:** $6.1 bil; **per capita GDP:** $4,900; **GDP growth:** 6.6%. **Imports** (2013): $696.2 mil. **Exports** (2012): $154 mil. **Tourism:** $35 mil. **Budget:** $1.8 bil. **Inflation:** 0.4%.

Transport: Airports: 2.

Communication: Telephone: 0.3 per 100 pop. **Mobile:** 58.7 per 100 pop. **Broadband:** 0.4 per 100 pop. **Internet:** 1.1%.

Health: Expend.: 4.3%. **Life expect.:** 66.2 male; 69.4 female. **Births:** 34.2 per 1,000 pop. **Deaths:** 6.1 per 1,000 pop. **Infant mortality:** 37.5 per 1,000 live births. **Undernourished:** 28.8%. **HIV:** NA.

Education: Compulsory: ages 6-14. **Literacy:** 67.5%.

Embassy: 4201 Connecticut Ave. NW, Ste. 504, 20008; 966-3202.

Website: timor-leste.gov.tl

The collapse of Portuguese rule in East Timor led to factional fighting, Aug. 1975, and an invasion by Indonesia in Dec. Indonesia annexed East Timor as a 27th province in 1976. In over two decades, some 200,000 Timorese died due to civil war, famine, and persecution by Indonesian authorities. In a referendum held Aug. 1999 under UN auspices, Timorese voted overwhelmingly for independence but were then terrorized by pro-Indonesian militias. An international peacekeeping force entered in Sept.; a UN interim administration formally took command Oct. 26, 1999. Pro-independence forces won elections for a constituent assembly Aug. 2001. Xanana Gusmão, a former guerrilla leader, won the presidential election Apr. 2002. As Timor-Leste, the territory became independent May 20 and entered the UN Sept. 27.

José Ramos-Horta, a Nobel Peace Prize laureate, won a presidential runoff vote May 2007. After inconclusive parliamentary elections June 30, Ramos-Horta chose Gusmão as prime min. The Gusmão-supported independent candidate, Taur Matan Ruak, became president in a May 2012 runoff election. Gusmão's party won a majority of seats in the July parliamentary election, and he became prime min. of a coalition government in Aug. The UN peacekeeping mission ended Dec. 31, 2012. Beginning in 2005, much of East Timor's budget consisted of revenue from offshore oil and natural gas deposits. Lower oil prices in 2014-15 and indications that gas reserves could be less than previously estimated, even as the government tapped the energy-revenue fund for infrastructure and other projects, were troubling signs for the country's struggling economy. Gusmão resigned Feb. 6, 2015, to pave the way for restructuring; he was replaced as prime min. 5 days later by opposition figure Rui Maria de Araújo.

Togo

Togolese Republic

People: Population: 7,552,318. **Age distrib.:** <15: 40.6%; 65+: 3.3%. **Growth:** 2.7%. **Migrants:** 3%. **Pop. density:** 359.7 per sq mi, 138.9 per sq km. **Urban:** 40%. **Ethnic groups:** African (37 tribes; largest and most important are Ewe, Mina, Kabre) 99%. **Languages:** French (official, lang. of commerce), Ewe and Mina (in S), Kabye and Dagomba (in N). **Religions:** indigenous beliefs 51%, Christian 29%, Muslim 20%.

Geography: Total area: 21,925 sq mi, 56,785 sq km; **Land area:** 20,998 sq mi, 54,385 sq km. **Location:** S coast of W Africa. Ghana on W, Burkina Faso on N, Benin on E. **Topography:** Hills running SW-NE split Togo into 2 savanna plains regions. **Arable land:** 48.7%. **Capital:** Lomé, 956,332.

Government: Type: Republic in transition to multiparty democratic rule. **Head of state:** Pres. Faure Gnassingbé; in office: May 4, 2005. **Head of gov.:** Prime Min. Komi Klassou; in office: June 5, 2015. **Local divisions:** 5 regions. **Defense budget:** $89 mil. **Active troops:** 8,550.

Economy: Industries: phosphate mining, agric. proc., cement, handicrafts, textiles, beverages. **Chief crops:** coffee, cocoa, cotton, yams, cassava, corn, beans, rice, millet, sorghum. **Natural resources:** phosphates, limestone, marble. **Water:** 2,156 cu m per capita. **Electricity prod.:** 109 mil kWh. **Labor force:** agric. 65%, industry 5%, services 30%. **Unemployment:** 6.9%.

Finance: Monetary unit: CFA Franc (XOF) (584.11 = $1 U.S.). **GDP:** $10.1 bil; **per capita GDP:** $1,400; **GDP growth:** 5.2%. **Imports:** $2.3 bil; China 29.4%, Belgium 12.8%, U.S. 11.5%, France 6.2%, Netherlands 6.1%, India 5.6%. **Exports:** $1.4 bil; Lebanon 11.7%, India 10.7%, China 9%, Burkina Faso 8.5%, Benin 8.3%, Belgium 6.5%, Niger 6.4%. **Tourism:** $111 mil. **Budget:** $1.3 bil. **Inflation:** 0.01%.

Transport: Railways: 353 mi. **Motor vehicles:** 25 per 1,000 pop. **Airports:** 2.

Communications: Telephone: 0.9 per 100 pop. **Mobile:** 69 per 100 pop. **Broadband:** 2.8 per 100 pop. **Internet:** 5.7%.

Health: Expend.: 8.6%. **Life expect.:** 61.9 male; 67.2 female. **Births:** 34.1 per 1,000 pop. **Deaths:** 7.3 per 1,000 pop. **Infant mortality:** 45.2 per 1,000 live births. **Undernourished:** 15.3%. **HIV:** 2.4%.

Education: Compulsory: ages 6-15. **Literacy:** 66.5%.

Embassy: 2208 Massachusetts Ave. NW 20008; 234-4212.

Website: www.primature.gouv.tg or www.state.gov/p/af/ci/to/

Togoland was administered by Germany and then by France and Britain. The French sector became the republic of Togo Apr. 27, 1960. In office since 1967, Pres. Gnassingbé Eyadéma was Africa's longest-serving head of state until his death Feb. 5, 2005. His son, Faure Gnassingbé, was installed as president, but African leaders pressured Togo to hold an election, which Gnassingbé won Apr. 24. Opposition parties disputed the result, and protests led to violent clashes in Lomé.

After a shootout at his home Apr. 12, 2009, former Defense Min. Kpatcha Gnassingbé, the president's brother, was arrested and accused of plotting a coup. Pres. Gnassingbé won reelection Mar. 4, 2010, to a second 5-year term. Weeks of antigovernment protest led Prime Min. Gilbert Fossoun Houngbo to resign, July 13, 2012, and a new government was formed. Legislative elections were held July 25, 2013, with the ruling party maintaining its majority and the opposition claiming voting irregularities. Pres. Gnassingbé won a third term in Apr. 25, 2015, elections; the opposition disputed the result. Gnassingbé appointed a new prime min., former Education Min. Komi Klassou, June 5, 2015.

Tonga

Kingdom of Tonga

People: Population: 106,501. **Age distrib.:** <15: 35.1%; 65+: 6.3%. **Growth:** 0%. **Migrants:** 5.2%. **Pop. density:** 384.7 per sq mi, 148.5 per sq km. **Urban:** 23.7%. **Ethnic groups:** Tongan 96.6%. **Languages:** Tongan, English (both official). **Religions:** Protestant 64.9% (incl. Free Wesleyan Church 37.3%, Free Church of Tonga 11.4%), Mormon 16.8%, Roman Catholic 15.6%.

Geography: Total area: 288 sq mi, 747 sq km; **Land area:** 277 sq mi, 717 sq km. **Location:** Western S Pacific O. Nearest neighbors are Fiji to NW, Samoa to NE. **Topography:** Comprises 170 volcanic and coral islands, 36 inhabited. **Arable land:** 22.2%. **Capital:** Nuku'alofa, 24,998 (2014).

Government: Type: Constitutional monarchy. **Head of state:** King Tupou VI; in office: Mar. 18, 2012. **Head of gov.:** Prime Min. 'Akilisi Pohiva; in office: Dec. 30, 2014. **Local divisions:** 5 island divisions. **Defense budget/active troops:** NA.

Economy: Industries: tourism, constr., fishing. **Chief crops:** squash, coconuts, copra, bananas, vanilla beans, cocoa, coffee, sweet potatoes, cassava. **Natural resources:** fish. **Water:** NA. **Electricity prod.:** 48 mil kWh. **Labor force:** agric. 27.5%, industry 27.5%, services 45.1%. **Unemployment:** NA.

Finance: Monetary unit: Pa'anga (TOP) (2.12 = $1 U.S.). **GDP:** $500 mil; **per capita GDP:** $4,900; **GDP growth:** 2.3%. **Imports:** $204.1 mil; Fiji 34%, New Zealand 18.9%, China 17.6%, U.S. 8.8%. **Exports:** $23.4 mil; New Zealand 17.7%, South Korea 16.1%, U.S. 12.1%, Fiji 11.3%, Samoa 9.5%, Japan 9.2%, Australia 9%, American Samoa 6%. **Tourism:** $41 mil. **Budget** (FY13/14 est.): $146.5 mil. **Inflation:** 2.5%.

Transport: Airports: 1.

Communications: Telephone: 11.3 per 100 pop. **Mobile:** 64.3 per 100 pop. **Broadband** (2012): 0.1 per 100 pop. **Internet:** 40%.

Health: Expend.: 5.4%. **Life expect.:** 74.5 male; 77.6 female. **Births:** 23.0 per 1,000 pop. **Deaths:** 4.9 per 1,000 pop. **Infant mortality:** 12.0 per 1,000 live births. **Undernourished:** NA. **HIV:** NA.

Education: Compulsory: ages 4-18. **Literacy:** 99.4%.

Permanent UN mission: 250 E. 51st St., New York, NY 10022; (917) 369-1025.

Website: www.tongaportal.gov.to

The Dutch first visited the islands in the early 17th cent. A series of civil wars ended, 1845, with establishment of the Tupou dynasty. In 1900, Tonga became a British protectorate. Tonga gained independence June 1970 and joined the Commonwealth. It joined the UN in 1999. George Tupou VI became king Mar. 18, 2012, following the death of his brother, who had introduced reforms. Elections in Nov. 2010 gave the country its first democratically elected parliament, taking the monarch's executive powers and reducing his role to that of an adviser. With the economy sluggish, almost two-thirds of directly elected members were voted out of office in Nov. 27, 2014, elections.

Trinidad and Tobago

Republic of Trinidad and Tobago

People: Population: 1,222,363. **Age distrib.:** <15: 19.4%; 65+: 9.8%. **Growth:** –0.1%. **Migrants:** 2.4%. **Pop. density:** 617.4 per sq mi, 238.4 per sq km. **Urban:** 8.4%. **Ethnic groups:** E Indian 35.4%, African 34.2%, mixed-other 15.3%, mixed African/E Indian 7.7%. **Languages:** English (official), Caribbean Hindustani, French, Spanish, Chinese. **Religions:** Protestant 32.1% (incl. Pentecostal/Evangelical/Full Gospel 12%), Roman Catholic 21.6%, Hindu 18.2%, Muslim 5%.

Geography: Total area: 1,980 sq mi, 5,128 sq km; **Land area:** 1,980 sq mi, 5,128 sq km. **Location:** In Caribbean, off E coast of Venezuela. **Topography:** Three low mountain ranges cross Trinidad E-W, with a well-watered plain between N and central ranges. Parts of E and W coasts are swamps. Tobago, 116 sq mi, lies 20 mi NE. **Arable land:** 4.9%. **Capital:** Port of Spain, 34,387 (2014).

Government: Type: Parliamentary democracy. **Head of state:** Pres. Anthony Carmona; in office: Mar. 18, 2013. **Head of gov.:** Prime Min. Keith Rowley; in office: Sept. 9, 2015. **Local divisions:** 9 regions, 3 boroughs, 2 cities, 1 ward. **Defense budget:** $436 mil. **Active troops:** 4,050.

Economy: Industries: petroleum and petroleum prods., liquefied nat. gas, methanol, ammonia, urea, steel prods., beverages. **Chief crops:** cocoa, rice, citrus, coffee, sugar. **Natural resources:** petroleum, nat. gas, asphalt. **Water:** 2,864 cu m per capita. **Crude oil reserves:** 728.3 mil bbls. **Electricity prod.:** 8.6 bil kWh. **Labor force:** agric. 3.8%; mfg., mining, and quarrying 12.8%; constr. and utilities 20.4%; services 62.9%. **Unemployment:** 5.8%.

Finance: Monetary unit: Dollar (TTD) (6.33 = $1 U.S.). **GDP:** $43.4 bil; **per capita GDP:** $32,100; **GDP growth:** 1.1%. **Imports:** $9.1 bil; U.S. 31.6%, Brazil 6.3%, Colombia 5.9%, Gabon 5.3%, Russia 5%. **Exports:** $12.6 bil; U.S. 31.8%, Argentina 9.6%, Brazil 8%, Netherlands 5.1%, Chile 5%. **Tourism:** $450 mil. **Budget:** $9.5 bil. **Inflation:** 5.7%.

Transport: Motor vehicles: 313.5 per 1,000 pop. **Airports:** 2.

Communications: Telephone: 21.4 per 100 pop. **Mobile:** 147.3 per 100 pop. **Broadband:** 20.2 per 100 pop. **Internet:** 65.1%.

Health: Expend.: 5.4%. **Life expect.:** 69.7 male; 75.6 female. **Births:** 13.5 per 1,000 pop. **Deaths:** 8.6 per 1,000 pop. **Infant mortality:** 23.9 per 1,000 live births. **Undernourished:** 9%. **HIV:** NA.

Education: Compulsory: ages 6-11. **Literacy:** 99%.

Embassy: 1708 Massachusetts Ave. NW 20036; 467-6490.

Website: www.ttconnect.gov.tt

Christopher Columbus sighted Trinidad in 1498. It became a British possession in 1802; in the 1800s tens of thousands of indentured servants and their families were brought from India to work in agriculture. Trinidad and Tobago won independence Aug. 31, 1962. It became a republic in 1976.

The nation, among the most prosperous in the Caribbean, produces oil and natural gas; it also refines and exports Middle Eastern oil.

In July 1990, some 120 Muslim extremists captured the Parliament building and TV station and took about 50 hostages, including Prime Min. Arthur N. R. Robinson. After a six-day siege, the rebels surrendered.

Basdeo Panday, in office 1995-2001, was the nation's first prime min. of Indian ancestry. The country's first female prime min., Kamla Persad-Bissessar, leader of the People's Partnership coalition, took office May 26, 2010. After her coalition lost Sept. 7, 2015, elections, Keith Rowley of the People's National Movement became prime min., Sept. 9.

Tunisia

Republic of Tunisia

People: Population: 11,037,225. **Age distrib.:** <15: 23%; 65+: 8%. **Growth:** 0.9%. **Migrants:** 0.3%. **Pop. density:** 184 per sq mi, 71 per sq km. **Urban:** 66.8%. **Ethnic groups:** Arab 98%. **Languages:** Arabic (official), French (used in commerce), Berber (Tamazight). **Religions:** Muslim (official; Sunni) 99.1%.

Geography: Total area: 63,170 sq mi, 163,610 sq km; **Land area:** 59,985 sq mi, 155,360 sq km. **Location:** N coast of Africa. Algeria on W, Libya on E. **Topography:** The N is wooded and fertile. Grazing lands and orchards are in central coastal plains. The S is arid, approaching Sahara Desert. **Arable land:** 18.3%. **Capital:** Tunis, 1,993,487.

Government: Type: Republic. **Head of state:** Pres. Béji Caïd Essebsi; in office: Dec. 31, 2014. **Head of gov.:** Prime Min. Habib Essid; in office: Feb. 6, 2015. **Local divisions:** 24 governorates. **Defense budget:** $911 mil. **Active troops:** 35,800.

Economy: Industries: petroleum, mining, tourism, textiles, footwear, agribusiness, beverages. **Chief crops:** olives, olive oil, grain, tomatoes, citrus, sugar beets, dates, almonds. **Natural resources:** petroleum, phosphates, iron ore, lead, zinc, salt. **Water:** 420 cu m per capita. **Crude oil reserves:** 425 mil bbls. **Electricity prod.:** 16.1 bil kWh. **Labor force:** agric. 14.8%, industry 33.2%, services 51.7%. **Unemployment:** 13.3%.

Finance: Monetary unit: Dinar (TND) (1.95 = $1 U.S.). **GDP:** $124.3 bil; **per capita GDP:** $11,300; **GDP growth:** 2.3%. **Imports:** $23.4 bil; France 20.7%, Italy 18.1%, Germany 7.4%, China 5.4%, Spain 5.1%. **Exports:** $16.6 bil; France 25.4%, Italy 16%, Germany 9.6%, Libya 8.1%. **Tourism:** $2.3 bil. **Budget:** $15.5 bil. **Inflation:** 4.9%.

Transport: Railways: 1,350 mi (only partly operational). **Motor vehicles:** 130.6 per 1,000 pop. **Airports:** 15.

Communications: Telephone: 8.5 per 100 pop. **Mobile:** 128.5 per 100 pop. **Broadband:** 30.9 per 100 pop. **Internet:** 46.2%.

Health: Expend.: 7%. **Life expect.:** 73.8 male; 78.1 female. **Births:** 16.6 per 1,000 pop. **Deaths:** 6.0 per 1,000 pop. **Infant mortality:** 22.4 per 1,000 live births. **Undernourished:** <5%. **HIV:** <0.1%.

Education: Compulsory: ages 6-16. **Literacy:** 81.8%.

Embassy: 1515 Massachusetts Ave. NW 20005; 862-1850.

Website: www.tunisie.gov.tn

Site of ancient Carthage and a former Barbary state under the suzerainty of Turkey, Tunisia became a protectorate of France, May 12, 1881. The nation became independent Mar. 20, 1956, and ended the monarchy the following year. Habib Bourguiba, an independence leader, served as president until 1987, when he was deposed by his prime min., Zine al-Abidine Ben Ali, who then won five presidential elections, 1989-2009, all tightly controlled.

Arab Spring protests, which began Dec. 2010, ousted Ben Ali, Jan. 14, 2011. Subsequent protests also forced the removal of Prime Min. Mohamed Ghannouchi. Moncef Marzouki of the secular center-left Congress for the Republic party was appointed interim president and took office Dec. 13, 2011, but real power lay with Prime Min. Hamadi Jebali, an Islamist leader of the moderate Ennahda party, which won Oct. 2011 elections. Jebali resigned Feb. 19, 2013, after failing to institute promised reforms. The Islamist-dominated Assembly voted Ali Laarayedh his replacement. On July 29, 65 members of the Assembly withdrew; political parties agreed, Dec. 14, 2013, on a caretaker prime min. After a new constitution was approved, Jan. 26, 2014, the secular Nida Tunis party won the most seats in Oct. 26, 2014, legislative elections; independent Habib Essid became prime min. Nida Tunis leader Beji Caid Essebsi was elected pres., Dec. 21, 2014. Deadly clashes occurred between Islamist extremists and security forces, 2014-15. Three extremist gunmen attacked a museum in Tunis, Mar. 18, 2015, killing 22. A gunman killed 38 foreign tourists at a resort hotel in Sousse, June 26; Sunni extremist group ISIS claimed responsibility.

Turkey

Republic of Turkey

People: Population: 79,414,269. **Age distrib.:** <15: 25.4%; 65+: 7.1%. **Growth:** 1.3%. **Migrants:** 2.5%. **Pop. density:** 267.2 per sq mi, 103.2 per sq km. **Urban:** 73.4%. **Ethnic groups:** Turkish 70%-75%, Kurdish 18%. **Languages:** Turkish (official), Kurdish. **Religions:** Muslim (mostly Sunni) 99.8%.

Geography: Total area: 302,535 sq mi, 783,562 sq km; **Land area:** 297,157 sq mi, 769,632 sq km. **Location:** Occupies Asia Minor, stretching into continental Europe; borders on Medit. and Black Seas. Bulgaria, Greece on W; Georgia, Armenia on N; Iran on E; Iraq, Syria on S. **Topography:** Center has wide plateaus with hot, dry summers and cold winters. High mountains ring the interior on all but W, with more than 20 peaks over 10,000 ft. Rolling plains in W; mild, fertile coastal plains in S and W. **Arable land:** 26.7%. **Capital:** Ankara, 4,749,968. **Cities:** Istanbul, 14,163,989; Izmir, 3,040,416; Bursa, 1,922,517; Adana, 1,829,555; Gaziantep, 1,528,366.

Government: Type: Republican parliamentary democracy. **Head of state:** Pres. Recep Tayyip Erdogan; in office: Aug. 28, 2014. **Head of gov.:** Prime Min. Ahmet Davutoglu; in office: Aug. 28, 2014. **Local divisions:** 81 provinces. **Defense budget:** $10.05 bil. **Active troops:** 510,600.

Economy: Industries: textiles, food proc., autos, electronics, mining, steel, petroleum, constr., lumber, paper. **Chief crops:** tobacco, cotton, grain, olives, sugar beets, hazelnuts, pulses, citrus. **Natural resources:** coal, iron ore, copper, chromium, antimony, mercury, gold, barite, borate, strontium, emery, feldspar, limestone, magnesite, marble, perlite, pumice, pyrites (sulfur), clay, hydropower. **Water:** 2,824 cu m per capita. **Crude oil reserves:** 296 mil bbls. **Electricity prod.:** 228.3 bil kWh. **Labor force:** agric. 25.5%, industry 26.2%, services 48.4%. **Unemployment:** 10%.

Finance: Monetary unit: Lira (TRY) (2.94 = $1 U.S.). **GDP:** $1.5 tril; **per capita GDP:** $19,600; **GDP growth:** 2.9%. **Imports:** $240.4 bil; Russia 10%, China 9.8%, Germany 9.6%, Italy 5.1%, U.S. 5%. **Exports:** $176.6 bil; Germany 9%, Iraq 7.6%, UK 5.7%. **Tourism:** $29.6 bil. **Budget:** $209.7 bil. **Inflation:** 8.9%.

Transport: Railways: 7,461 mi. **Motor vehicles:** 175.6 per 1,000 pop. **Airports:** 91.

Communications: Telephone: 16.5 per 100 pop. **Mobile:** 94.8 per 100 pop. **Broadband:** 32.3 per 100 pop. **Internet:** 51%.

Health: Expend.: 6.3%. **Life expect.:** 72.3 male; 77.0 female. **Births:** 16.3 per 1,000 pop. **Deaths:** 5.9 per 1,000 pop. **Infant mortality:** 18.9 per 1,000 live births. **Undernourished:** <5%. **HIV:** NA.

Education: Compulsory: ages 6-17. **Literacy:** 95%.

Embassy: 2525 Massachusetts Ave. NW 20008; 612-6700.

Website: www.tccb.gov.tr

Ancient inhabitants of Turkey were among the world's first agriculturalists. Such civilizations as the Hittite, Phrygian, and Lydian flourished in Asiatic Turkey (Asia Minor), as did much of Greek civilization. After the fall of Rome in the 5th cent., Constantinople (now Istanbul) was the capital of the Byzantine Empire for 1,000 years. It fell in 1453 to Ottoman Turks, who ruled a vast empire for over 400 years.

Just before WWI, Turkey, or the Ottoman Empire, ruled what is now Syria, Lebanon, Iraq, Jordan, Israel, Saudi Arabia, Yemen, and islands in the Aegean Sea. Turkey joined Germany and Austria in WWI, and its defeat resulted in the loss of territory and the fall of the sultanate. A secular republic was established Oct. 29, 1923. The first pres., Mustafa Kemal (later Kemal Ataturk), led Turkey until his death in 1938.

Turkey kept neutral during most of WWII. The country became a full member of NATO in 1952 and remained a Western ally despite domestic political instability. Military coups overthrew civilian governments in 1960 and 1980. Turkey invaded nearby Cyprus July 20, 1974, to prevent that country from uniting with Greece, and Cyprus was divided into Greek and Turkish zones.

In recent decades, Kurdish separatists and Islamic militants have challenged Turkish governments. Turkey joined the U.S.-led force that ousted Iraq from Kuwait, 1991. Millions of Iraqi Kurdish refugees fled to Turkey's border after the war. Turkish offensives in Kurdish areas of Turkey caused heavy casualties among separatist guerrillas and civilians. Kurdish militants raided Turkish diplomatic missions in some 25 Western European cities, June 24, 1993.

Tansu Ciller became Turkey's first woman prime min. July 5, 1993. The Islamic Welfare Party gained strength in the 1990s, and in June 1996, a coalition with Ciller's True Path Party was formed. The pro-Islamic government resigned June 18, 1997, under pressure from the military, which stepped up its campaign against Islamic fundamentalism in 1998.

Kurdish rebel leader Abdullah Öcalan was captured Feb. 15, 1999, and convicted of terrorism June 29. His organization, the Kurdistan Workers' Party (PKK), announced in 1999 that it would abandon its 14-year-old insurgency. Violence continued at a lower level, however, including attacks by both the PKK and Turkish forces.

Earthquakes in Apr. and Nov. 1999 killed over 17,000 people. The Islamic Justice and Development Party (AKP) led by Recep Tayyip Erdogan won Nov. 3, 2002, parliamentary elections. Erdogan became prime min., May 14, 2003. Suicide bombings by Islamic extremists, Nov. 15-20, 2003, killed 58 people and wounded more than 750 in Istanbul. After Erdogan's party scored a landslide win in 2007 elections, parliament chose an Islamic politician, Abdullah Gül, as president. Secularists failed to ban the ruling AKP in Turkey's Constitutional Court in 2008. Turkish voters in 2010 gave resounding approval to constitutional changes favored by the Islamic government.

The AKP gained a third consecutive general election victory in June 2011, while dozens of military officers were detained for allegedly plotting to seize power. After the nation's four top military commanders resigned en masse, July 29, 2011, Pres. Gül appointed their replacements Aug. 4, breaking with the tradition of the military promoting its own leaders.

Turkey has long sought full membership in the European Union, but the EU has deferred talks on accession until economic, human rights, and immigration issues are resolved. Turkey's ties with Islamic countries soured relations with Israel, a former ally.

Demonstrations in Istanbul's Taksim Square in 2013 over plans to replace Gezi Park became protests against Prime Min. Erdogan. Force was used, June 15, to clear Gezi Park, and protests began to die down at the beginning of July. A coal mine explosion in Soma, May 13, 2014, killed 301 and prompted protests over mismanagement and a seeming lack of government concern. Erdogan nevertheless won an Aug. 10 election to become Turkey's first popularly elected president. Foreign Min. Ahmet Davutoglu, an Erdogan ally, replaced him as prime min. The AKP failed to win a majority of seats in June 7, 2015, elections. After Davutoglu was unable to form a coalition government, Erdogan called new parliamentary elections for Nov. 1.

During the Syrian civil war (2011-), Turkey became a haven for refugees (more than 1.9 mil as of Aug. 2015, according to UNHCR). Attacks beginning in Sept. 2014 by the Sunni extremist group ISIS against Kurdish areas in N Syria sent tens of thousands of Kurdish refugees across the border into Turkey. Kurdish forces, including some apparently affiliated with the PKK, retook territory in N Syria in 2015. ISIS staged terrorist attacks in Turkey in 2015; an apparently ISIS-inspired suicide bombing killed 32 people, July 20, in Suruc. Turkey launched its first artillery and airstrikes against ISIS forces in N Syria, July 23-24, 2015. It also began airstrikes, July 24, against PKK strongholds in N Iraq and SE Turkey (as well as stepping up other military action in Kurdish areas of SE Turkey). Turkey agreed, July 2015, to allow U.S. warplanes to use bases in Turkey to attack ISIS targets in Syria, and it officially joined the U.S.-led air campaign against ISIS in Syria, Aug. 28.

Turkmenistan

People: Population: 5,231,422. **Age distrib.:** <15: 26.1%; 65+: 4.4%. **Growth:** 1.1%. **Migrants:** 4.3%. **Pop. density:** 28.8 per sq mi, 11.1 per sq km. **Urban:** 50%. **Ethnic groups:** Turkmen 85%, Uzbek 5%, Russian 4%. **Languages:** Turkmen (official), Russian, Uzbek. **Religions:** Muslim 89%, Eastern Orthodox 9%.

Geography: Total area: 188,456 sq mi, 488,100 sq km; **Land area:** 181,441 sq mi, 469,930 sq km. **Location:** Central Asia. Kazakhstan on N; Uzbekistan on N and E; Afghanistan, Iran on S. **Topography:** Kara Kum Desert occupies 80% of country. Bordered on W by Caspian Sea. **Arable land:** 4.1%. **Capital:** Ashgabat, 745,961.

Government: Type: Republic by definition although authoritarian presidential rule in actuality. **Head of state and gov.:** Pres. Gurbanguly Berdymukhammedov; in office: Feb. 14, 2007 (acting from Dec. 21, 2006). **Local divisions:** 5 provinces, 1 independent city. **Defense budget** (2012): $539 mil. **Active troops:** 22,000.

Economy: Industries: nat. gas, oil, petroleum prods., textiles, food proc. **Chief crops:** cotton, grain, melons. **Natural resources:** petroleum, nat. gas, sulfur, salt. **Water:** 4,727 cu m per capita. **Crude oil reserves:** 600 mil bbls. **Electricity prod.:** 16.7 bil kWh. **Labor force:** agric. 48.2%, industry 14%, services 37.8%. **Unemployment:** 10.6%.

Finance: Monetary unit: Manat (TMT) (3.50 = $1 U.S.). **GDP:** $82.1 bil; **per capita GDP:** $14,200; **GDP growth:** 10.3%. **Imports:** $16.6 bil; Turkey 22.3%, Russia 15.3%, China 13%, UAE 6.8%, Ukraine 6.4%, Germany 6%. **Exports:** $19.8 bil; China 68.3%, Turkey 5%. **Budget:** $6.7 bil. **Inflation:** NA.

Transport: Railways: 1,852 mi. **Airports:** 21.

Communications: Telephone: 11.8 per 100 pop. **Mobile:** 135.8 per 100 pop. **Broadband:** NA. **Internet:** 12.2%.

Health: Expend.: 2%. **Life expect.:** 66.8 male; 72.9 female. **Births:** 19.4 per 1,000 pop. **Deaths:** 6.1 per 1,000 pop. **Infant mortality:** 36.8 per 1,000 live births. **Undernourished:** <5%. **HIV:** NA.

Education: Compulsory: ages 6-17. **Literacy:** 99.7%.

Embassy: 2207 Massachusetts Ave. NW 20008; 588-1500.

Website: www.turkmenistan.gov.tm

The region has been inhabited by Turkic tribes since the 10th cent. It became part of Russian Turkestan in 1881, and a constituent republic of the USSR in 1925. Turkmenistan declared independence Oct. 27, 1991, and became an independent state when the USSR disbanded Dec. 26, 1991.

Turkmenistan has extensive natural gas reserves and also oil reserves. Political power centers on the former Communist Party apparatus and authoritarian leadership. Gurbanguly Berdymukhammedov won the Feb. 2007 presidential election, considered fraudulent by international observers. He was reelected with 97% of the vote, Feb. 12, 2012. In a small gesture toward democracy, the country's one-party system officially ended, Aug. 21, 2012, permitting a second political party, the Party of Industrialists and Entrepreneurs of Turkmenistan, to be founded.

Tuvalu

People: Population: 10,869. **Age distrib.:** <15: 29.4%; 65+: 5.6%. **Growth:** 0.8%. **Migrants:** 1.5%. **Pop. density:** 1,082.7 per sq mi, 418 per sq km. **Urban:** 59.7%. **Ethnic groups:** Polynesian 96%, Micronesian 4%. **Languages:** Tuvaluan, English (both official); Samoan. **Religions:** Protestant 98.4% (Church of Tuvalu [Congregationalist] 97%).

Geography: Total area: 10 sq mi, 26 sq km; **Land area:** 10 sq mi, 26 sq km. **Location:** 9 islands forming NW-SE chain 360 mi long in SW Pacific O. Nearest neighbors are Kiribati to NE, Fiji to S. **Topography:** The islands are all low-lying atolls, no more than 15 ft above sea level, composed of coral reefs. **Arable land:** 0%. **Capital:** Funafuti, 5,816 (2014).

Government: Type: Parliamentary democracy. **Head of state:** Queen Elizabeth II, rep. by Gov.-Gen. Sir Iakoba Taeia Italeli; in office: Apr. 16, 2010. **Head of gov.:** Prime Min. Enele Sopoaga; in office: Aug. 5, 2013. **Local divisions:** 7 island councils, 1 town council. **Defense budget/active troops:** NA.

Economy: Industries: fishing. **Chief crops:** coconuts. **Natural resources:** fish. **Water:** NA. **Labor force:** Pop. makes living mainly through exploitation of the sea, reefs, and atolls and from wages sent home by those abroad (mostly phosphate industry workers and sailors). **Unemployment:** NA.

Finance: Monetary unit: Dollar (TVD) (1.42 = $1 U.S.). **GDP:** $35 mil; **per capita GDP:** $3,300; **GDP growth:** 2.2%. **Imports** (2013): $136.5 mil. **Exports** (2010): $600,000. **Tourism:** $2 mil. **Budget** (2013 est.): $32.5 mil. **Inflation:** NA.

Transport: NA.

Communications: Telephone: 15.2 per 100 pop. **Mobile:** 38.4 per 100 pop. **Broadband:** NA. **Internet** (2013): 37%.

Health: Expend.: 15.4%. **Life expect.:** 64.0 male; 68.4 female. **Births:** 23.7 per 1,000 pop. **Deaths:** 8.7 per 1,000 pop. **Infant mortality:** 30.8 per 1,000 live births. **Undernourished:** NA. **HIV:** NA.

Education: Compulsory: ages 7-14. **Literacy:** NA.

Permanent UN Mission: 800 Second Ave., Ste. 400D, New York, NY 10017; (212) 490-0534.

Website: www.state.gov/p/eap/ci/tv/

The Ellice Islands separated from the British Gilbert and Ellice Islands Colony in 1975 and became Tuvalu; independence came Oct. 1, 1978. In 2000, Tuvalu joined the United Nations. A major drought that began in Nov. 2010 obliged the government to declare a state of emergency Sept. 28, 2011. Prime Min. Enele Sopoaga, in office since Aug. 5, 2013, formed a new government after Mar. 31, 2015, elections. Rising sea levels due to climate change are threatening to submerge the tiny island nation.

Uganda

Republic of Uganda

People: Population: 37,101,745. **Age distrib.:** <15: 48.5%; 65+: 2%. **Growth:** 3.2%. **Migrants:** 1.4%. **Pop. density:** 487.5 per sq mi, 188.2 per sq km. **Urban:** 16.1%. **Ethnic groups:** Baganda 16.9%, Banyankole 9.5%, Basoga 8.4%, Bakiga 6.9%, Iteso 6.4%, Langi 6.1%, Acholi 4.7%, Bagisu 4.6%, Lugbara 4.2%, Bunyoro 2.7%. **Languages:** English (official), Ganda or Luganda (most widely used Niger-Congo lang.). **Religions:** Protestant 42% (incl. Anglican 35.9%), Roman Catholic 41.9%, Muslim 12.1%.

Geography: Total area: 93,065 sq mi, 241,038 sq km; **Land area:** 76,101 sq mi, 197,100 sq km. **Location:** E Central Africa. South Sudan on N, Dem. Rep. of the Congo on W, Rwanda and Tanzania on S, Kenya on E. **Topography:** Mostly high plateau 3,000-6,000 ft high, with Ruwenzori Range in W (Mt. Margherita, 16,763 ft), volcanoes in SW. NE is arid, W and SW rainy. Lakes Victoria, Edward, Albert form much of borders. **Arable land:** 34.5%. **Capital:** Kampala, 1,935,654.

Government: Type: Republic. **Head of state and gov.:** Pres. Yoweri Kaguta Museveni; in office: Jan. 26, 1986. **Local divisions:** 111 districts, 1 capital city. **Defense budget:** $405 mil. **Active troops:** 45,000.

Economy: Industries: sugar, brewing, tobacco, cotton textiles, cement, steel prod. **Chief crops:** coffee, tea, cotton, tobacco, cassava, potatoes, corn, millet, pulses, cut flowers. **Natural resources:** copper, cobalt, hydropower, limestone, salt, gold. **Water:** 1,599 cu m per capita. **Crude oil reserves:** 2.5 bil bbls. **Electricity prod.:** 3 bil kWh. **Labor force:** agric. 82%, industry 5%, services 13%. **Unemployment:** 3.8%.

Finance: Monetary unit: Shilling (UGX) (3,665.00 = $1 U.S.). **GDP:** $76.9 bil; **per capita GDP:** $2,000; **GDP growth:** 4.9%. **Imports:** $4.7 bil; Kenya 19.4%, UAE 14.1%, India 12.2%, China 10.7%. **Exports:** $2.7 bil; UAE 10.9%, Rwanda 10.3%, Kenya 9.4%, Dem. Rep. of the Congo 9.4%, Germany 6.1%, Netherlands 5.4%. **Tourism:** $1.4 bil. **Budget:** $4.4 bil. **Inflation:** 4.3%.

Transport: Railways: 773 mi. **Motor vehicles:** 10.6 per 1,000 pop. **Airports:** 5.

Communications: Telephone: 0.8 per 100 pop. **Mobile:** 52.4 per 100 pop. **Broadband:** 8.6 per 100 pop. **Internet:** 17.7%.

Health: Expend.: 8%. **Life expect.:** 53.5 male; 56.4 female. **Births:** 43.8 per 1,000 pop. **Deaths:** 10.7 per 1,000 pop. **Infant mortality:** 59.2 per 1,000 live births. **Undernourished:** 25.7%. **HIV:** 7.3%.

Education: Compulsory: ages 6-12. **Literacy:** 78.4%.

Embassy: 5911 16th St. NW 20011; 726-0416.
Website: www.statehouse.go.ug

Britain obtained a protectorate over Uganda in 1894. The country became independent Oct. 9, 1962, and a republic within the Commonwealth a year later. In 1967, the traditional kingdoms, including the powerful Buganda state, were abolished.

Gen. Idi Amin seized power from Prime Min. Milton Obote in 1971. During his 8-year dictatorship, he was responsible for the deaths of up to 300,000 of his opponents. In 1972 he expelled nearly all of Uganda's 45,000 Asians. Tanzanian troops and Ugandan exiles and rebels ousted Amin, Apr. 11, 1979.

Obote, president from Dec. 1980, was ousted in a military coup July 1985. Guerrilla war and rampant human rights abuses had plagued Uganda under Obote's regime.

Conditions improved after Yoweri Museveni took power in Jan. 1986. In 1993 the Buganda and other traditional monarchies were restored for ceremonial purposes. Uganda helped Laurent Kabila seize power in the Dem. Rep. of the Congo (formerly Zaire) in 1997 but sent troops in 1998 to aid insurgents seeking his ouster. A withdrawal accord was signed Sept. 2002.

Pres. Museveni won reelection in 2001 and 2006; opponents disputed the latter result. Museveni won a 2011 presidential election that European observers considered flawed.

The rebel Lord's Resistance Army (LRA) began an insurgency agains the Museveni government in 1986 and abducted tens of thousands of children to serve as soldiers and sex slaves. According to UN estimates, the LRA, 1987-2012, killed more than 100,000 people and displaced some 2.5 mil in Uganda and neighboring countries. Peace talks brokered by Sudan began July 2006; as talks continued through 2007, LRA violence in Uganda diminished. A cease-fire accord was signed Feb. 23, 2008, but Ugandan and Congolese troops (with U.S. aid) launched a new offensive against the LRA in late 2008. Suicide bombings July 11, 2010, killed 76 people watching a World Cup soccer match on outdoor video screens in Kampala. Al-Shabab, a Somali al-Qaeda-linked Islamist group, claimed responsibility. An Ebola outbreak in summer 2012 took 176 lives before doctors contained it.

An online campaign to capture the LRA's leader, Joseph Kony, was boosted by the film *Kony 2012*. On Apr. 3, 2013, the U.S. offered a $5 mil reward for information leading to his capture. The UNHCR estimated that more than 172,000 refugees from conflicts in the Dem. Rep. of the Congo were living in Uganda at the beginning of 2014; some later returned home. More than 100,000 refugees from South Sudan's civil war were in Uganda in 2015. An Anti-Homosexuality Act, signed by Museveni Feb. 24, 2014, and making some gay behavior punishable by life in prison, was struck down on technical grounds by a Uganda court Aug. 1, 2014.

Ukraine

People: Population: 44,429,471. **Age distrib.:** <15: 15.2%; 65+: 15.8%. **Growth:** –0.6%. **Migrants:** 11.4%. **Pop. density:** 198.6 per sq mi, 76.7 per sq km. **Urban:** 69.7%. **Ethnic groups:** Ukrainian 77.8%, Russian 17.3%. **Languages:** Ukrainian (official), Russian. **Religions:** Orthodox (incl. Ukrainian Orthodox-Kyiv Patriarchate, Ukrainian Orthodox-Moscow Patriarchate, Ukrainian Greek Catholic).

Geography: Total area: 233,032 sq mi, 603,550 sq km; **Land area:** 223,681 sq mi, 579,330 sq km. **Location:** Eastern Europe. Belarus on N; Russia on NE and E; Moldova, Romania on SW; Hungary, Slovakia, Poland on W. **Topography:** Part of E European plain with arable black soil. Carpathians in the SW, Crimean chain in the S. **Arable land:** 56.1%. **Capital:** Kiev, 2,941,864. **Cities:** Kharkiv, 1,440,839; Odesa, 1,010,475.

Government: Type: Republic. **Head of state:** Pres. Petro Poroshenko; in office: June 7, 2014. **Head of gov.:** Prime Min. Arseniy Yatsenyuk; in office: Feb. 27, 2014. **Local divisions:** 24 provinces, 2 municipalities, 1 autonomous republic. **Defense budget:** $3.59 bil. **Active troops:** 121,500.

Economy: Industries: coal, elec. power, metals, machinery and transp. equip., chemicals, food proc. **Chief crops:** grain, sugar beets, sunflower seeds, vegetables. **Natural resources:** iron ore, coal, manganese, nat. gas, petroleum, salt, sulfur, graphite, titanium, magnesium, kaolin, nickel, mercury, timber. **Water:** 3,086 cu m per capita. **Crude oil reserves:** 395 mil bbls. **Electricity prod.:** 187.1 bil kWh. **Labor force:** agric. 5.6%, industry 26%, services 68.4%. **Unemployment:** 7.9%.

Finance: Monetary unit: Hryvnia (UAH) (22.10 = $1 U.S.). **GDP:** $370.8 bil; **per capita GDP:** $8,700; **GDP growth:** –6.8%. **Imports:** $60.4 bil; Russia 29.6%, China 9.8%, Germany 8.4%, Poland 6.9%, Belarus 5.3%. **Exports:** $52.5 bil; Russia 24.2%, Turkey 6%. **Tourism:** $1.6 bil. **Budget:** $45.9 bil (planned and consolidated). **Inflation:** 12.2%.

Transport: Railways: 13,504 mi. **Motor vehicles:** 215.3 per 1,000 pop. **Airports:** 108.

Communications: Telephone: 24.6 per 100 pop. **Mobile:** 144.1 per 100 pop. **Broadband:** 6.7 per 100 pop. **Internet:** 43.4%.

Health: Expend.: 7.6%. **Life expect.:** 66.8 male; 76.6 female. **Births:** 10.7 per 1,000 pop. **Deaths:** 14.5 per 1,000 pop. **Infant mortality:** 8.1 per 1,000 live births. **Undernourished:** <5%. **HIV:** NA.

Education: Compulsory: ages 6-16. **Literacy:** 99.8%.

Embassy: 3350 M St. NW 20007; 349-2920.
Website: www.kmu.gov.ua

Ukrainians' Slavic ancestors inhabited the region well before the 1st cent. CE. In the 9th cent., the princes of Kiev established a strong state called Kievan Rus, which included much of present-day Ukraine. Internal conflicts led to the disintegration of the Ukrainian state by the 13th cent. Mongol rule was supplanted by Poland and Lithuania in the 14th and 15th cent. The N Black Sea coast and Crimea came under Turkish control in 1478. Ukrainian Cossacks, starting in the late 16th cent., rebelled against the occupiers of Ukraine: Russia, Poland, and Turkey.

An independent Ukrainian National Republic was proclaimed on Jan. 22, 1918. But in 1921, Ukraine's neighbors occupied and divided Ukrainian territory. In 1922, Ukraine became a constituent republic of the USSR. In 1932-33, the Soviet government engineered a famine in eastern Ukraine, and 6-7 mil Ukrainians died. During WWII the Ukrainian nationalist underground fought Nazi and Soviet forces. Over 5 mil Ukrainians died in the war. The reoccupation of Ukraine by Soviet troops in 1944 brought a renewed wave of repression.

The world's worst nuclear power plant disaster occurred in Chernobyl, Ukraine, in Apr. 1986; many thousands were killed or disabled as a result of the radiation leak.

Ukrainian independence was restored, Dec. 1991, with the Soviet Union's dissolution. Following a 1994 accord with Russia and the U.S., Ukraine's large nuclear arsenal was transferred to Russia for destruction.

President since 1994, Leonid Kuchma attempted to engineer the 2004 election of his handpicked successor, the Russian-backed Prime Min. Viktor Yanukovych. When Yanukovych was declared the winner in Nov., supporters of his main challenger, former Prime Min. Viktor Yushchenko, called the election fraudulent and staged massive protests (the Orange Revolution); the vote was annulled. An election rerun Dec. 26 gave Yushchenko the victory. Yushchenko's party fared poorly in Mar. 2006 parliamentary elections, and Yanukovych returned as prime min. in Aug.

Following Sept. 2007 elections, Yulia Tymoshenko, a former Orange Revolution ally of Yushchenko, became prime min. but lost the presidential election to Yanukovych in Feb. 2010. Tymoshenko went on trial in June 2011 for abusing her powers as prime min. She was convicted and sentenced to seven years in prison in Oct. but was released in Feb. 2014.

Large anti-Yanukovych protests began in Nov. 2013, following his decision not to sign a free trade pact with the EU. After dozens were killed in violent protests in Kiev, Feb. 18-20, 2014, parliament removed Yanukovych from office, Feb. 22. Pro-EU candidate Petro Poroshenko won a May 25, 2014, presidential election. Signing and ratification of the EU agreement were completed June 27 and Sept. 16, with most implementation delayed until 2016 to appease Russian opposition. Pro-EU parties won a majority of seats in parliamentary elections, Oct. 26, 2014.

Aiding pro-Russian separatists, Russian forces entered Crimea in Mar., and Russia annexed the region Mar. 18, 2014. Fighting began in Apr. 2014 in eastern Ukraine between Ukrainian forces and pro-Russian separatists, widely reported to be aided by Russian military equipment and troops. Separatists apparently shot down a Malaysia Airlines commercial flight over eastern Ukraine, July 17, 2014, killing all 298 on board. The UN reported that as of Aug. 15, 2015, the death toll in Ukraine's civil war was at least 7,883. UNHCR estimated that by Sept. 2015, more than 2 mil people were internally displaced or had become refugees. A cease-fire, Sept. 5, 2014, failed to hold. A new Feb. 12, 2015, agreement reduced violence but clashes continued as of Sept. 30, 2015.

United Arab Emirates

People: Population: 5,779,760. **Age distrib.:** <15: 20.9%; 65+: 1%. **Growth:** 2.6%. **Migrants:** 83.7%. **Pop. density:** 179.1 per sq mi, 69.1 per sq km. **Urban:** 85.5%. **Ethnic groups:** Emirati 19%, other Arab and Iranian 23%, S Asian 50%, other expatriates (incl. Westerners, E Asians) 8%. Less than 20% of pop. are UAE citizens. **Languages:** Arabic (official), Persian, English, Hindi, Urdu. **Religions:** Muslim (Islam; official) 76%, Christian 9%.

Geography: Total area: 32,278 sq mi, 83,600 sq km; **Land area:** 32,278 sq mi, 83,600 sq km. **Location:** Middle East, on S shore of the Persian Gulf. Saudi Arabia on W and S, Oman on E. **Topography:** A barren, flat coastal plain gives way to uninhabited sand dunes on S. Hajar Mts. in E. **Arable land:** 0.6%. **Capital:** Abu Dhabi, 1,144,933. **Cities:** Dubai, 2,414,591; Sharjah, 1,279,360.

Government: Type: Federation of emirates. **Head of state:** Pres. Sheikh Khalifa ibn Zaid an-Nahayan; in office: Nov. 3, 2004. **Head of gov.:** Prime Min. Sheikh Muhammad ibn Rashid al-Maktum; in office: Jan. 5, 2006. **Local divisions:** 7 emirates: Abu Dhabi, Ajman, Dubai, Fujaira, Ras al-Khaimah, Sharjah, Umm al-Qaiwain. **Defense budget** (2013): $13.9 bil. **Active troops:** 63,000.

Economy: Industries: petroleum and petrochemicals, fishing, aluminum, cement, fertilizers, commercial ship repair, constr. materials. **Chief crops:** dates, vegetables, watermelons. **Natural resources:** petroleum, nat. gas. **Water:** 16 cu m per capita. **Crude oil reserves:** 97.8 bil bbls. **Electricity prod.:** 100.5

bil kWh. **Labor force:** agric. 7%, industry 15%, services 78%. **Unemployment:** 3.8%.

Finance: Monetary unit: Dirham (AED) (3.67 = $1 U.S.). **GDP:** $599.8 bil; **per capita GDP:** $64,500; **GDP growth:** 3.6%. **Imports:** $271.7 bil; China 14.7%, India 14%, U.S. 10.8%, UK 6%, Germany 5.2%. **Exports:** $404.7 bil; Japan 14.6%, India 11.4%, Iran 10.5%, South Korea 6.2%, Thailand 5.9%, Singapore 5.7%. **Tourism:** $11.6 bil. **Budget:** $116 bil (not incl. emirate-level spending in Abu Dhabi and Dubai). **Inflation:** 2.3%.

Transport: Motor vehicles: 423.2 per 1,000 pop. **Airports:** 25.

Communications: Telephone: 22.3 per 100 pop. **Mobile:** 178.1 per 100 pop. **Broadband:** 89.1 per 100 pop. **Internet:** 90.4%.

Health: Expend.: 2.8%. **Life expect.:** 74.7 male; 80.0 female. **Births:** 15.4 per 1,000 pop. **Deaths:** 2.0 per 1,000 pop. **Infant mortality:** 10.6 per 1,000 live births. **Undernourished:** <5%. **HIV:** NA.

Education: Compulsory: ages 6-11. **Literacy:** 93.8%.

Embassy: 3522 International Ct. NW 20008; 243-2400.

Website: www.government.ae

The 7 "Trucial Sheikdoms" gave Britain control of defense and foreign relations in the 19th cent. They merged to become an independent state Dec. 2, 1971. Oil revenues have made the UAE one of the world's wealthiest countries. Foreigners make up most of the work force.

International banking, investment, and construction boomed during the late 1990s and early 2000s. But Dubai, hurt by the global recession beginning in 2008, accepted up to $9.5 bil in government loans to help a state-controlled investment company avoid default. On July 2, 2013, 68 members of the Islamist group Islah were convicted of conspiring to overthrow the government. Beginning in Sept. 2014, UAE warplanes took part in U.S.-led airstrikes against Sunni extremist forces in Syria. The UAE was part of a Saudi-led coalition conducting airstrikes, beginning Mar. 25, 2015, against Shiite Houthi rebels in Yemen. UAE ground troops were reported, Aug. 3, to be fighting in Yemen.

United Kingdom

United Kingdom of Great Britain and Northern Ireland

People: Population: 64,088,222. **Age distrib.:** <15: 17.4%; 65+: 17.7%. **Growth:** 0.5%. **Migrants:** 12.4%. **Pop. density:** 686.1 per sq mi, 264.9 per sq km. **Urban:** 82.6%. **Ethnic groups:** white 87.2%, black/African/Caribbean/black British 3%, Asian/Asian British: Indian 2.3%. **Languages:** English; Scots, Scottish Gaelic, Welsh, Irish (all recognized regional langs.). **Religions:** Christian (incl. Anglican, Roman Catholic, Presbyterian, Methodist) 59.5%, Muslim 4.4%, none 25.7%.

Geography: Total area: 94,058 sq mi, 243,610 sq km; **Land area:** 93,410 sq mi, 241,930 sq km. **Location:** Off NW coast of Europe, across English Channel, Strait of Dover, North Sea. Ireland to W, France to SE. **Topography:** England is mostly rolling land, rising to Uplands of southern Scotland. Lowlands in center of Scotland, granite highlands in N. British Isles have milder climate than N Europe due to Gulf Stream and ample rainfall. Severn, 220 mi, and Thames, 215 mi, are longest rivers. **Arable land:** 25.7%. **Capital:** London, 10,313,307. **Cities:** Manchester, 2,645,598; Birmingham (West Midlands), 2,514,596; West Yorkshire, 1,912,493.

Government: Type: Constitutional monarchy. **Head of state:** Queen Elizabeth II; in office: Feb. 6, 1952. **Head of gov.:** Prime Min. David Cameron; in office: May 11, 2010. **Local divisions:** 232 local authorities (England: 152; Wales: 22; Scotland: 32; Northern Ireland: 11; 15 other dependent areas.). **Defense budget:** $61.82 bil. **Active troops:** 159,150.

Economy: Industries: machine tools, elec. power equip., automation equip., railroad equip., shipbuilding, aircraft, motor vehicles and parts, electronics and communications equip. **Chief crops:** cereals, oilseed, potatoes, vegetables. **Natural resources:** coal, petroleum, nat. gas, iron ore, lead, zinc, gold, tin, limestone, salt, clay, chalk, gypsum, potash, silica sand, slate. **Water:** 2,319 cu m per capita. **Crude oil reserves:** 3 bil bbls. **Electricity prod.:** 335.7 bil kWh. **Labor force:** agric. 1.3%, industry 15.2%, services 83.5%. **Unemployment:** 7.5%.

Finance: Monetary unit: Pound (GBP) (0.65 = $1 U.S.). **GDP:** $2.5 tril; **per capita GDP:** $39,500; **GDP growth:** 2.6%. **Imports:** $802.1 bil; Germany 13.9%, China 8.5%, Netherlands 8.5%, France 6%, U.S. 5.6%, Belgium 5%. **Exports:** $503.4 bil; Switzerland 13.8%, Germany 9%, U.S. 8.8%, Netherlands 7.6%, France 6.4%, Ireland 5.7%. **Tourism:** $45.3 bil. **Budget:** $1.1 tril. **Inflation:** 1.5%.

Transport: Railways: 19,175 mi. **Motor vehicles:** 582.2 per 1,000 pop. **Airports:** 271.

Communications: Telephone: 52.4 per 100 pop. **Mobile:** 123.6 per 100 pop. **Broadband:** 87.2 per 100 pop. **Internet:** 91.6%.

Health: Expend.: 9.4%. **Life expect.:** 78.4 male; 82.8 female. **Births:** 12.2 per 1,000 pop. **Deaths:** 9.4 per 1,000 pop. **Infant mortality:** 4.4 per 1,000 live births. **Undernourished:** <5%. **HIV:** NA.

Education: Compulsory: ages 5-15. **Literacy:** 99%.

Embassy: 3100 Massachusetts Ave. NW 20008; 588-6500.

Website: www.gov.uk

The United Kingdom of Great Britain and Northern Ireland comprises England, Wales, Scotland, and Northern Ireland.

Queen and Royal Family. The ruling sovereign is Elizabeth II of the House of Windsor, elder daughter of King George VI. She succeeded to the throne Feb. 6, 1952, and was crowned June 2, 1953. She was married Nov. 20, 1947, to Lt. Philip Mountbatten (b. June 10, 1921), former Prince of Greece. He was created Duke of Edinburgh, and given the title H.R.H., Nov. 19, 1947; he was named Prince of the United Kingdom and Northern Ireland Feb. 22, 1957. Prince Charles Philip Arthur George (b. Nov. 14, 1948) is the Prince of Wales and heir apparent. His first son, William Philip Arthur Louis (b. June 21, 1982), is second in line to the throne. William's son, George Alexander Louis (b. July 22, 2013), is third in line; William's daughter, Charlotte Elizabeth Diana (b. May 2, 2015), is fourth in line.

Parliament is the UK's legislative body, with certain powers over dependent units. It consists of two houses. The House of Commons has 650 members, elected by direct ballot and divided as follows: England, 533; Wales, 40; Scotland, 59; Northern Ireland, 18. The House of Lords (Sept. 2015) comprised 775 members: 86 hereditary peers, 663 life peers, and 26 archbishops and bishops of the Church of England.

Resources and Industries. Great Britain is a major global trade and financial services center. As of 2014, service industries accounted for 78.8% of GDP; industry, 20.6%; agriculture, 0.6%. Manufacturing, historically important since the Industrial Revolution, has declined in economic significance, while finance, centered in London, has grown in importance. Coal production, also historically important, has declined by more than 90% since 1970. Large oil and gas fields have been found in the North Sea, and commercial oil production began in 1975. However, proved reserves are declining, and the country has been a net energy importer since 2005.

Religion and Education. The Church of England is Protestant Episcopal. The queen is its temporal head, with rights of appointments to archbishoprics, bishoprics, and other offices. There are two provinces, Canterbury and York, each headed by an archbishop. Westminster Abbey (1050-1760) is the site of coronations and the tombs of Elizabeth I, Mary, Queen of Scots, kings, poets, and the Unknown Warrior. Celebrated British universities Oxford and Cambridge each date to the 13th cent.

History. Recent research indicates that Britain was separated from the European continent at least 200,000 years ago by a catastrophic flood that created the English Channel. Migrants across the Channel included the Celts, who arrived 2,500 to 3,000 years ago. Their language survives in Welsh and Gaelic enclaves.

England was part of the Roman Empire 43-410 CE, after which waves of Jutes, Angles, and Saxons arrived from German lands, followed by Danish raiders from the 8th through 11th cent. French-speaking Normans invaded in 1066, uniting the country with their dominions in France.

Opposition by nobles to royal authority forced King John to agree to the Magna Carta in 1215, a guarantee of rights and the rule of law. In the ensuing decades, the foundations of the parliamentary system were laid.

English dynastic claims to large parts of France led to the Hundred Years War, 1338-1453, an unsuccessful campaign. A long civil war, the War of the Roses, 1455-85, ended with the establishment of the Tudor monarchy. The economy prospered over long periods of domestic peace unmatched in continental Europe. The Church of England separated from the authority of the pope, 1534.

During the reign of Queen Elizabeth I, 1558-1603, England became a major naval power, leading to the founding of colonies in the New World and the expansion of trade with Europe and Asia. Scotland and England shared a single monarch after James VI of Scotland was crowned James I of England in 1603.

A struggle between Parliament and the Stuart kings led to a civil war, 1642-49, and the establishment of a republic under the Puritan Oliver Cromwell. The monarchy was restored in 1660, but the Glorious Revolution of 1688 confirmed the sovereignty of Parliament: a Bill of Rights was granted 1689. Scotland was united with England after the ratification of the Articles of Union of Scotland and England, May 1707.

Technological and entrepreneurial innovations led to the Industrial Revolution in the 18th cent. The 13 N American colonies were lost but replaced by growing empires in Canada, India, Australia, and elsewhere. Britain's role in the defeat of Napoleon, 1815, strengthened its position as the leading world power.

The limited extension of voting rights in 1832, 1867, and 1884; the formation of trade unions; and the development of universal public education were among the social changes that accompanied the spread of industrialization and urbanization in the 19th cent. (Men gained full voting rights in 1918 and women in 1928.) Large parts of Africa and Asia were added to the empire during the reign of Queen Victoria, 1837-1901.

Though victorious in WWI, Britain suffered huge casualties and economic dislocation. Ireland became independent in 1921, and independence movements became active in India and other colonies. The country suffered major bombing damage in WWII but rallied behind Prime Min. Winston Churchill and held off Germany until Allied victory was achieved, 1945.

Industrial growth continued in the postwar period, but Britain lost its leadership position to other powers. Labour governments passed socialist programs nationalizing some basic industries and expanding social security. Prime Min. Margaret Thatcher's Conservative governments, 1979-90, fostered private enterprise and began denationalization of key industries. Her Conservative successor, John Major, held power 1990-97. The UK sent military forces to the Persian Gulf War, 1991. The Channel Tunnel linking Britain to the Continent was opened May 6, 1994.

The 1997 victory by the Labour Party made Tony Blair, 43, Britain's youngest prime min. since 1812. Diana, Princess of Wales, died in a car crash in Paris, Aug. 31. Britain played a leading role in the NATO air war against Yugoslavia, Mar.-June 1999, and contributed 12,000 troops to the multinational Kosovo security force.

After the Sept. 11 attacks on the U.S., the UK participated, beginning in 2001, in the Afghanistan war, maintaining as many as 9,500 troops in the country. About 470 remained as of June 2015, and British troops had suffered more than 450 fatalities since the war started. Blair, who won a landslide election victory June 2001, committed British troops to the U.S.-led invasion of Iraq, Mar.-Apr. 2003, despite dissent within his own cabinet. UK forces, which numbered 46,000 at the height of combat operations, almost entirely pulled out by mid-2009; 179 had died. Following an offensive in Iraq by the Sunni extremist group ISIS, beginning in June 2014, Parliament approved, Sept. 26, British airstrikes against ISIS forces in Iraq. The Defense Ministry confirmed, July 17, 2015, that British forces were also aiding U.S.-led airstrikes against ISIS in Syria. Thirty British tourists were among 38 killed in a June 26, 2015, terrorist attack in Tunisia for which ISIS claimed responsibility.

In May 2005 elections, Blair became the first Labour prime min. to win 3 consecutive terms. Suicide bombings on 3 London underground trains and a bus, July 7, 2005, left 56 people dead and hundreds injured; police identified the bombers as 4 British Muslim men (3 of Pakistani origin).

Blair was succeeded by Gordon Brown, June 2007. Responding Oct. 13, 2008, to the worldwide financial crisis, Prime Min. Brown initiated a plan to partially nationalize three of Britain's largest banks and support them with a capital infusion of up to $63 bil.

In the wake of Britain's deepest recession since WWII, voters rejected the Labour Party in May 2010 parliamentary elections. Conservatives and Liberal Democrats formed a coalition government; Conservative leader David Cameron became prime min. Cameron responded to the fiscal crisis with austerity measures meant to rein in debt. The government reported Oct. 25, 2012, that London's hosting of the Olympics, July 27-Aug. 12, 2012, had helped the economy to recover from its double-dip recession during the third quarter of 2012. Justin Welby was installed Feb. 4, 2013, as the new Archbishop of Canterbury, the head of the Church of England. Parliament voted in favor of same-sex marriage July 16, 2013. The Conservatives won a House of Commons majority (331 seats) in May 7, 2015, elections. The pro-independence Scottish National Party (SNP) won almost all seats in Scotland (56). Tens of thousands of undocumented migrants reaching Europe from Africa, the Middle East, and SW Asia in 2015 tried to enter Britain; more than 37,000 were intercepted, Jan.-July, trying to cross via the Channel Tunnel. Britain and France agreed, Aug. 20, on increased security measures at the French end of the tunnel near Calais, where thousands of migrants were camped. Cameron announced Sept. 7 that the UK would admit, over 5 years, 20,000 Syrian refugees from UNHCR camps near Syria. The UK declined to participate in an EU plan, approved Sept. 22, to resettle 120,000 migrants already in Europe.

Wales

The Principality of Wales in western Britain has an area of 8,019 sq mi and a population (2014 est.) of 3,092,036. Cardiff is the capital, pop. (2014 est., city proper) 354,300.

A 1979 referendum rejected, 4-1, the creation of an elected Welsh assembly; a similar proposal passed by a thin margin on Sept. 18, 1997. Elections for the 60-seat assembly were held in 1997, 2003, 2007, and 2011.

Early Anglo-Saxon invaders drove Celtic peoples into the mountains of Wales, where they developed a distinct nationality. Members of the ruling house of Gwynedd in the 13th cent. fought England but were crushed, 1283. Edward of Caernarvon, son of Edward I of England, was created Prince of Wales, 1301. **Website:** gov.wales

Scotland

Scotland occupies the northern 37% of the main British island, and the Hebrides, Orkney, Shetland, and smaller islands. Length 275 mi, breadth approx. 150 mi, area 30,414 sq mi, pop. (2014 est.) 5,347,600.

The Lowlands, a belt of land approx. 60 mi wide from the Firth of Clyde to the Firth of Forth, divide the farming region of the Southern Uplands from the granite Highlands of the N; they contain 75% of the population and most of the industry. The Highlands, famous for hunting and fishing, have been opened to industry by many hydroelectric power stations.

Edinburgh, pop. (2014 est., city proper) 492,680, is the capital. Glasgow, pop. (2014 est., city proper) 599,650, is Scotland's greatest commercial city. It is a major port and shipbuilding center and has developed a services-based economy in the 21st cent., including financial services, healthcare, and engineering. Aberdeen, pop. (2014 est., city proper) 228,990, NE of Edinburgh, is a major port, center of granite industry, fish-processing, and North Sea oil exploration. Dundee, pop. (2014 est., city proper) 148,260, NE of Edinburgh, is an industrial and fish-processing center.

History. Scotland was called Caledonia by the Romans who battled early Celtic tribes and occupied southern areas from the 1st to the 4th cent. Missionaries from Britain introduced Christianity in the 4th cent.; St. Columba, an Irish monk, converted most of Scotland in the 6th cent.

The Kingdom of Scotland was founded in 1018. William Wallace and Robert Bruce both defeated English armies 1297 and 1314, respectively. In 1603, James VI of Scotland, son of Mary, Queen of Scots, succeeded to the English throne as James I, and effected the Union of the Crowns. In 1707 Scotland received representation in the British Parliament, resulting from the union of formerly separate Parliaments. A 1997 proposal to create a regional legislature with limited taxing authority passed by a landslide. In 2011 elections for the 129-seat parliament, SNP candidates won a majority. However, in a referendum on independence Sept. 18, 2014, 55% of Scottish voters opposed separating from the UK.

Memorials of Robert Burns, Sir Walter Scott, John Knox, and Mary, Queen of Scots, draw many tourists, as do the beauties of the Trossachs, Loch Katrine, Loch Lomond, and abbey ruins.

Industries. Engineering products are a key industry, with growing emphasis on office machinery, autos, electronics, and other consumer goods. Oil discoveries offshore in the North Sea stimulated onshore support industries.

Scotland produces fine woolens, worsteds, tweeds, silks, fine linens, and jute. It is known for its special breeds of cattle and sheep. Commercial fishing is an important industry. Whisky is a major export.

The Hebrides are a group of about 500 islands, 100 inhabited, off the W coast. The **Inner Hebrides** include Skye, Mull, and Iona, the last famous for the arrival of St. Columba, 563 CE. The **Outer Hebrides** include Lewis and Harris. Industries include sheep raising and weaving. The approx. 70 **Orkney Isls.** are to the NE. The capital is Kirkwall, on Pomona Isl. Fish curing, sheep raising, and weaving are occupations. NE of the Orkneys are the 200 **Shetland Isls.**, 24 inhabited, home of Shetland ponies. The Orkneys and Shetlands are centers for the North Sea oil industry. **Website:** www.gov.scot

Northern Ireland

Northern Ireland was constituted in 1920 from 6 of the 9 counties of Ulster, the NE corner of Ireland. Area 5,452 sq mi, pop. (2014 est.) 1,840,500. Capital and chief industrial center, Belfast, pop. (2014 est., local govt. dist.) 336,800.

Industries. Shipbuilding, including large tankers, has long been an important industry, centered in Belfast, the largest port. Linen is manufactured, along with apparel, rope, and twine. Growing diversification has added engineering products, synthetic fibers, and electronics. Major farm products include livestock, poultry, potatoes, and dairy foods.

Government and History. An act of the British Parliament, 1920, divided Northern from Southern Ireland, each with a parliament and government. When Ireland became a dominion, 1921, and later a republic, Northern Ireland chose to remain a part of the UK.

During 1968-69, Roman Catholics, a minority comprising about one-third of the population, claimed discrimination against them in voting rights, housing, and employment. Violence and terrorism intensified, involving branches of the Irish Republican Army (IRA; outlawed in the Irish Republic), Protestant groups, police, and British troops. Between 1969 and 2001, more than 3,500 were killed in sectarian violence in Northern Ireland, Ireland, England, and elsewhere. For most of this period, the Northern Ireland parliament was suspended, and Britain imposed direct rule.

A settlement reached on Good Friday, Apr. 10, 1998, and approved May 22 by voters in Northern Ireland and the Irish Republic, restored home rule and election of a 108-member assembly with safeguards for minority rights. Both Ireland and Great Britain agreed to relinquish constitutional claims on Northern Ireland. Elections to the assembly were held June 25. IRA dissidents seeking to derail the agreement detonated a bomb at Omagh Aug. 15 that killed 29 people and injured over 330.

London transferred authority to a Northern Ireland power-sharing government in 1999. Delays in IRA disarmament led to several suspensions of self-government. The IRA July 2005 renounced violence and ordered all units to disarm. The British responded by reducing their military presence in the region. On Sept. 26, an international monitoring group reported that the IRA had apparently scrapped its entire arsenal. The Northern Ireland legislature, suspended for 3½ years, reconvened May 15, 2006. Elections were held in 2007 and 2011.

Religion and Education. Northern Ireland is about 58% Protestant, 42% Roman Catholic. Education is compulsory between the ages of 5 and 16 years. **Website:** www.northernireland.gov.uk

Channel Islands

The Channel Islands, area 75 sq mi, off the NW coast of France, the only parts of the one-time Dukedom of Normandy belonging to England, are Jersey, Guernsey, and the dependencies of Guernsey—Alderney, Brechou, Great Sark, Little Sark, Herm, Jethou, and Lihou. **Jersey**, area 45 sq mi, pop. (2015 est.) 97,294, and **Guernsey**, area 30 sq mi, pop. (2015 est.) 66,080, have separate legal existences and lieutenant governors named by the Crown. The islands were the only British soil occupied by German troops in WWII. **Websites:** www.gov.je (Jersey); www.gov.gg (Guernsey)

Isle of Man

The Isle of Man, area 221 sq mi, pop. (2015 est.) 87,545, is in the Irish Sea, 20 mi from Scotland, 30 mi from Cumberland. It is rich in lead and iron. The island has its own laws and a lieutenant governor appointed by the Crown. The Tynwald (legislature) consists of the Legislative Council, partly elected, and House of Keys, elected. Capital: Douglas; pop. (2011 census, city proper) 27,938. Farming, tourism, and fishing (kippers, scallops) are chief occupations. Man is famous for the Manx tailless cat. **Website:** www.gov.im

Gibraltar

A dependency on the S coast of Spain, Gibraltar guards the entrance to the Mediterranean. The Rock of Gibraltar has been in British possession since 1704. It is 2.5 mi long, 0.75 of a mi wide, and 1,396 ft in height, with a total area of 2.5 sq mi; a narrow isthmus connects it with the mainland. Pop. (2015 est.) 29,258.

Gibraltar has historically been an object of contention between Britain and Spain. In 1967, residents voted almost unanimously to remain under British rule. A new constitution, May 30, 1969, increased Gibraltarian control of domestic affairs (the UK continues to handle defense and internal security matters). The border, closed by Spain in 1969, was fully reopened in Feb. 1985. A UN General Assembly resolution requested Britain to end Gibraltar's colonial status by Oct. 1, 1996. Gibraltar voters rejected a plan for the UK and Spain to share sovereignty, Nov. 7, 2002. Residents approved a new constitution Nov. 30, 2006. Nevertheless, tensions flared again between the two countries in Aug. 2013 over the question of territorial control. **Website:** www.gibraltar.gov.gi

British West Indies

Swinging in a vast arc from the coast of Venezuela NE, then N and NW toward Puerto Rico are the Leeward Isls., forming a coral and volcanic barrier sheltering the Caribbean from the open Atlantic. Many of the islands are self-governing British possessions. Universal suffrage was instituted 1951-54; ministerial systems were set up 1956-60.

The Leeward Isls. still associated with the UK are **Montserrat**, area 39 sq mi, pop. (2015 est.) 5,241, capital Plymouth; the **British Virgin Isls.**, 58 sq mi, pop. (2015 est.) 33,454, capital Road Town (2014 est. pop., 13,102); and **Anguilla**, the most northerly of Leeward Isls., 35 sq mi, pop. (2015 est.) 16,418, capital The Valley (2014 est. pop., 1,039). Montserrat has been devastated by the Soufrière Hills volcano, which began erupting July 18, 1995.

The three **Cayman Isls.**, a dependency, lie S of Cuba, NW of Jamaica. Pop. (2015 est.) 56,092, most of it on Grand Cayman. It is a free port; in the 1970s Grand Cayman became a tax-free refuge for foreign funds and branches of many Western banks were opened there. Total area 102 sq mi. Capital: George Town; pop. (2014 est.) 30,603.

The **Turks and Caicos Isls.** are a dependency at the SE end of the Bahama Islands. Of about 40 islands, only 8 are inhabited; area 366 sq mi, pop. (2015 est.) 50,280; capital Grand Turk. Salt, shellfish, and conch shells are the main exports.

Bermuda

Bermuda is a British dependency governed by a royal governor and an assembly, dating from 1620, the oldest legislative body among British dependencies. Capital: Hamilton; pop. (2014 est.) 10,334. It is a group of about 150 small islands of coral formation, 20 inhabited, comprising 21 sq mi in the western Atlantic, 580 mi E of N. Carolina. Pop. (2015 est.) 70,196 (about 54% of African descent). Pop. density is high.

Tourism is the major industry; tourism receipts in 2013 were $439 mil. Bermuda is also a haven for the offshore insurance industry. Exports include petroleum products, medicine. In a referendum Aug. 15, 1995, voters rejected independence by nearly a 3-to-1 majority. Hurricane Fabian, the most potent storm to reach Bermuda in 50 years, struck Sept. 5, 2003; four people were missing and presumed dead, and damage was estimated at over $300 mil. **Website:** www.gov.bm

South Atlantic Territories

The **Falkland Isls.**, a dependency, lie 300 mi E of the Strait of Magellan at the southern end of S America.

The Falklands, or Islas Malvinas, include 2 large islands and about 200 smaller ones, area 4,700 sq mi, pop. (2014) 3,361, capital Stanley. The licensing of foreign fishing vessels has become the major source of revenue. Sheep-grazing is a main industry; wool is the principal export. There are indications of large oil and gas deposits. The islands are also claimed by Argentina, though 97% of inhabitants are of British origin. Argentina invaded the islands Apr. 2, 1982. The British responded by sending a task force to the area, landing their main force on the Falklands, May 21, and forcing an Argentine surrender at Port Stanley, June 14. A pact resuming commercial air service with Argentina was signed July 14, 1999. **Website:** www.falklands.gov.fk

British Antarctic Territory, S of 60° S lat., formerly a dependency of the Falkland Isls., was made a separate colony in 1962 and includes the South Shetland Isls., the South Orkneys, and the Antarctic Peninsula. A chain of meteorological stations is maintained.

South Georgia and the **South Sandwich Isls.**, formerly administered by the Falklands Isls., became a separate dependency in 1985. Total area of 1,507 sq mi. South Georgia, with no permanent population, is about 800 mi SE of the Falklands; the South Sandwich Isls. are uninhabited, about 470 mi SE of South Georgia.

St. Helena, an island 1,200 mi off the W coast of Africa and 1,800 mi E of S America, 47 sq mi and pop. (2015 est.) 7,795. Flax, lace, and rope-making are the chief industries. After Napoleon Bonaparte was defeated at Waterloo the Allies exiled him to St. Helena, where he lived from Oct. 16, 1815, to his death, May 5, 1821. Capital: Jamestown; pop. (2014 est.) 638. **Website:** www.sainthelena.gov.sh

Tristan da Cunha is the principal island in a group of islands of volcanic origin, total area 38 sq mi, halfway between the Cape of Good Hope and S America. A volcanic peak 6,760 ft high erupted in 1961. The 262 inhabitants were removed to England, but most returned in 1963. The islands are dependencies of St. Helena. Pop. (2010 est.): 265.

Ascension is an island of volcanic origin, 34 sq mi in area, 700 mi NW of St. Helena, through which it is administered. It is a communications relay center for Britain, and has a U.S. satellite tracking center. Pop. (2010) was 884, half of them communications workers. The island is noted for sea turtles. **Website:** www.ascension-island.gov.ac

British Indian Ocean Territory (BIOT)

Formed Nov. 1965, with islands formerly dependencies of Mauritius or Seychelles: the Chagos Archipelago (including Diego Garcia), Aldabra, Farquhar, and Des Roches. The latter three were transferred to Seychelles, which became independent in 1976. Total area 21,004 sq mi, land area 23 sq mi. The Chagos civilian population was removed by the UK in the 1970s to make way for expansion of the U.S. military base on Diego Garcia. A UN tribunal ruled, Mar. 2015, that the UK acted illegally in creating a BIOT marine protected area without adequately consulting with Mauritius.

Pacific Ocean Territories

Pitcairn Isl. is in the Pacific, halfway between S America and Australia. The island was discovered in 1767 by Philip Carteret but was not inhabited until 23 years later when the mutineers of the *Bounty* landed there. Pop. (2014 est.) 48; descendants of mutineers and their Tahitian wives. It is administered by a British High Commissioner in New Zealand and a local Council. The uninhabited islands of Henderson, Ducie, and Oeno are in the Pitcairn group, area 18 sq mi. **Website:** www.government.pn

United States

United States of America

People: Population: 321,368,864. 50 states and DC. (Note: U.S. pop. figures may differ elsewhere in *The World Almanac*.) **Age distrib.:** <15: 19%; 65+: 14.9%. **Growth:** 0.8%. **Migrants:** 14.3%. **Pop. density:** 91 per sq mi, 35.1 per sq km. **Urban:** 81.6%. **Ethnic groups:** white 79.96%, black 12.85%, Asian 4.43%. About 15.1% of pop. is Hispanic (any race). **Languages:** English, Spanish, other Indo-European langs., Asian and Pacific island langs. **Religions:** Protestant 51.3%, Roman Catholic 23.9%, unaffiliated 12.1%, none 4%.

Geography: Total area: 3,794,100 sq mi, 9,826,675 sq km; **Land area:** 3,537,455 sq mi, 9,161,966 sq km. (Area is for 50 states and DC only.) **Location:** Primarily N America. Canada on N, Mexico on S; Pacific on W, Atlantic on E. **Topography:** Vast central plain, mountains in W, hills and low mountains in E. **Arable land:** 17%. **Capital:** Washington, DC, 4,955,139.

Government: Type: Constitution-based federal republic. **Head of state and gov.:** Pres. Barack Obama; in office: Jan. 20, 2009. **Local divisions:** 50 states, 1 district. **Defense budget:** $613.6 bil. **Active troops:** 1,433,150.

Economy: Industries: petroleum, steel, motor vehicles, aerospace, telecom, chemicals, electronics, food proc., consumer goods, lumber, mining. **Chief crops:** wheat, corn, other grains, fruits, vegetables, cotton. **Natural resources:** coal, copper, lead, molybdenum, phosphates, rare earth elements, uranium, bauxite, gold, iron, mercury, nickel, potash, silver, tungsten, zinc, petroleum, nat. gas, timber. **Water:** 9,589 cu m per capita. **Crude oil reserves** (2014): 36.5 bil bbls. **Electricity prod.:** 4 tril kWh. **Labor force** (excl. unemployed): farming, forestry, fishing 0.7%; mfg., extraction, transp., crafts 20.3%; managerial, professional, technical 37.3%; sales and office 24.2%; other services 17.6%. **Unemployment:** 7.4%.

Finance: Monetary unit: Dollar (USD). **GDP:** $17.4 tril; **per capita GDP:** $54,600; **GDP growth:** 2.4%. **Imports:** $2.3 tril; China 19.6%, Canada 14.6%, Mexico 12.3%, Japan 6.1%, Germany 5%. **Exports:** $1.6 tril; Canada 19%, Mexico 14.3%, China 7.7%. **Tourism:** $177 bil. **Budget:** $3.5 tril (excl. approx. $2.3 tril of social benefits). **Inflation:** 1.6%.

Transport: Railways: 182,412 mi. **Motor vehicles:** 809.1 per 1,000 pop. **Airports:** 5,054.

Communications: Telephone: 40.1 per 100 pop. **Mobile:** 98.4 per 100 pop. **Broadband:** 98.9 per 100 pop. **Internet:** 87.4%.

Health: Expend.: 17.9%. **Life expect.:** 77.3 male; 82.0 female. **Births:** 12.5 per 1,000 pop. **Deaths:** 8.2 per 1,000 pop. **Infant mortality:** 5.9 per 1,000 live births. **Undernourished:** <5%. **HIV:** NA.

Education: Compulsory: ages 6-17. **Literacy:** 99%.

Website: www.usa.gov

See also U.S. History chapter; Chronology of the Year's Events.

Uruguay

Oriental Republic of Uruguay

People: Population: 3,341,893. **Age distrib.:** <15: 20.7%; 65+: 14%. **Growth:** 0.3%. **Migrants:** 2.2%. **Pop. density:** 49.5 per sq mi, 19.1 per sq km. **Urban:** 95.3%. **Ethnic groups:** white 88%, mestizo 8%, black 4%. **Languages:** Spanish (official), Portunol, Brazilero. **Religions:** Roman Catholic 47.1%, nondenominational 23.2%, atheist or agnostic 17.2%, non-Catholic Christians 11.1%.

Geography: Total area: 68,037 sq mi, 176,215 sq km; **Land area:** 67,574 sq mi, 175,015 sq km. **Location:** Southern S America, on Atlantic O. Argentina on W, Brazil on N. **Topography:** Rolling, grassy plains and hills, well-watered by rivers flowing W to Uruguay R. **Arable land:** 10%. **Capital:** Montevideo, 1,706,831.

Government: Type: Constitutional republic. **Head of state and gov.:** Pres. Tabaré Vázquez; in office: Mar. 1, 2015. **Local divisions:** 19 departments. **Defense budget:** $427 mil. **Active troops:** 24,650.

Economy: Industries: food proc., elec. machinery, transp. equip., petroleum prods., textiles, chemicals, beverages. **Chief crops:** soybeans, rice, wheat. **Natural resources:** hydropower, minor minerals, fish. **Water:** 50,543 cu m per capita. **Electricity prod.:** 10.3 bil kWh. **Labor force:** agric. 13%, industry 14%, services 73%. **Unemployment:** 6.6%.

Finance: Monetary unit: Peso (UYU) (28.60 = $1 U.S.). **GDP:** $70 bil; **per capita GDP:** $20,600; **GDP growth:** 3.3%. **Imports:** $12.1 bil; China 16.4%, Brazil 14.6%, Argentina 14%, U.S. 12.4%. **Exports:** $11 bil; China 21.9%, Brazil 17.3%. **Tourism:** $1.8 bil. **Budget:** $18.7 bil. **Inflation:** 8.9%.

Transport: Railways: 1,020 mi. **Motor vehicles:** 269.1 per 1,000 pop. **Airports:** 11.

Communications: Telephone: 31.7 per 100 pop. **Mobile:** 160.8 per 100 pop. **Broadband:** 46 per 100 pop. **Internet:** 61.5%.

Health: Expend.: 9%. **Life expect.:** 73.9 male; 80.3 female. **Births:** 13.1 per 1,000 pop. **Deaths:** 9.5 per 1,000 pop. **Infant mortality:** 8.7 per 1,000 live births. **Undernourished:** <5%. **HIV:** 0.7%.

Education: Compulsory: ages 4-17. **Literacy:** 98.5%.

Embassy: 1913 I St. NW 20006; 331-1313.

Website: portal.gub.uy

Spanish settlers began to supplant the indigenous Charrua Indians in 1624. Portuguese from Brazil arrived later, but Uruguay was attached to the Spanish Viceroyalty of Rio de la Plata in the 18th cent. Rebels fought against Spain beginning in 1810, with independence declared Aug. 25, 1825. To suppress Tupamaro guerrilla activities, a repressive military regime took power in 1973. Constitutional government was restored in 1985.

José (Pepe) Mujica, a former guerrilla who transformed his Marxist Tupamaro movement into a mainstream political party, won a presidential runoff election Nov. 2009. Legislation legalizing same-sex marriage was signed into law May 3, 2013. A law passed in Dec. 2013 made Uruguay the first country to legalize marijuana nationwide. Former Pres. (2005-10) Tabaré Vázquez, the candidate of Mujica's Broad Front coalition, won a presidential runoff election, Nov. 30, 2014.

Uzbekistan

Republic of Uzbekistan

People: Population: 29,199,942. **Age distrib.:** <15: 24.6%; 65+: 4.9%. **Growth:** 0.9%. **Migrants:** 4.4%. **Pop. density:** 177.8 per sq mi, 68.6 per sq km. **Urban:** 36.4%. **Ethnic groups:** Uzbek 80%, Russian 5.5%, Tajik 5%, Kazakh 3%, Karakalpak 2.5%. **Languages:** Uzbek (official), Russian, Tajik. **Religions:** Muslim (mostly Sunni) 88%, Eastern Orthodox 9%.

Geography: Total area: 172,742 sq mi, 447,400 sq km; **Land area:** 164,248 sq mi, 425,400 sq km. **Location:** Central Asia. Kazakhstan on N and W; Kyrgyzstan, Tajikistan on E; Afghanistan, Turkmenistan on S. **Topography:** Mostly plains and desert. **Arable land:** 10.2%. **Capital:** Tashkent, 2,251,156.

Government: Type: Republic with authoritarian presidential rule. **Head of state:** Pres. Islam A. Karimov; in office: Mar. 24, 1990. **Head of gov.:** Prime Min. Shavkat Mirziyaev; in office: Dec. 11, 2003. **Local divisions:** 12 provinces, 1 autonomous republic, 1 city. **Defense budget** (2012): $1.46 bil. **Active troops:** 48,000.

Economy: Industries: textiles, food proc., machine building, metallurgy, mining, hydrocarbon extraction, chemicals. **Chief crops:** cotton, vegetables, fruits, grain. **Natural resources:** nat. gas, petroleum, coal, gold, uranium, silver, copper, lead, zinc, tungsten, molybdenum. **Water:** 1,689 cu m per capita. **Crude oil reserves:** 594 mil bbls. **Electricity prod.:** 49.9 bil kWh. **Labor force:** agric. 25.9%, industry 13.2%, services 60.9%. **Unemployment:** 10.7%.

Finance: Monetary unit: Som (UZS) (2,601.05 = $1 U.S.). **GDP:** $171.7 bil; **per capita GDP:** $5,600; **GDP growth:** 8.1%. **Imports:** $12.5 bil; China 20.5%, Russia 20%, South Korea 15.4%, Kazakhstan 11.1%. **Exports:** $13.3 bil; China 28%, Russia 19.4%, Kazakhstan 12.6%, Turkey 11.9%, Bangladesh 8.2%. **Tourism:** $121 mil. **Budget:** $19.3 bil. **Inflation:** NA.

Transport: Railways: 2,265 mi. **Motor vehicles:** 74.7 per 1,000 pop. **Airports:** 33.

Communications: Telephone: 8.6 per 100 pop. **Mobile:** 73.8 per 100 pop. **Broadband:** 22.9 per 100 pop. **Internet:** 43.6%.

Health: Expend.: 5.9%. **Life expect.:** 70.5 male; 76.8 female. **Births:** 17.0 per 1,000 pop. **Deaths:** 5.3 per 1,000 pop. **Infant mortality:** 19.2 per 1,000 live births. **Undernourished:** 5.8%. **HIV:** 0.2%.

Education: Compulsory: ages 7-17. **Literacy:** 99.6%.

Embassy: 1746 Massachusetts Ave. NW 20036; 293-6803.

Website: www.gov.uz

The region was overrun by the Mongols under Genghis Khan in 1220. In the 14th cent., Uzbekistan became the center of a native Timurid empire. In later centuries Muslim feudal states emerged. Russian military conquest began in the 19th cent. Uzbek SSR became a Soviet republic in 1925.

Uzbekistan gained independence when the Soviet Union disbanded Dec. 26, 1991, and has been led by the authoritarian government of a former Communist, Islam A. Karimov.

Attacks by Islamic militants, Mar.-July 2004, killed more than 50 people. In June 2004, Russia's OAO Lukoil signed a $1 bil deal to develop Uzbekistan's natural gas fields. Militants bombed the U.S. and Israeli embassies in Tashkent, July 30.

After armed dissidents at Andizhan, east Uzbekistan, attacked government buildings and freed hundreds of prisoners, May 2005, Uzbek security forces killed many rebels and unarmed demonstrators. Karimov then launched a general crackdown on human rights activists. Irritated by U.S. human rights pressures, Karimov ordered the U.S. to vacate an airbase used to support operations in Afghanistan; the U.S. pullout was completed Nov. 21. Meeting in Moscow a week earlier, Karimov and Russian Pres. Vladimir Putin signed a military cooperation agreement.

Karimov remained in office following the formal expiration of his presidential term Jan. 22, 2007; despite a two-term limit under the constitution, he ran for a third term Dec. 23 and won with an 88.1% majority. Sanctions imposed by the EU on Uzbek officials after the 2005 Andizhan shootings were lifted Oct. 13, 2008. Karimov won a fourth term, with 90.4% of the vote, Mar. 29, 2015.

Vanuatu

Republic of Vanuatu

People: Population: 272,264. **Age distrib.:** <15: 36.7%; 65+: 3.8%. **Growth:** 2%. **Migrants:** 1.2%. **Pop. density:** 57.9 per sq mi, 22.3 per sq km. **Urban:** 26.1%. **Ethnic groups:** Ni-Vanuatu 97.6%. **Languages:** local langs. (100+); Bislama (creole), English, French (all official). **Religions:** Protestant 70% (incl. Presbyterian 27.9%, Anglican 15.1%, Seventh-day Adventist 12.5%), Roman Catholic 12.4%.

Geography: Total area: 4,706 sq mi, 12,189 sq km; **Land area:** 4,706 sq mi, 12,189 sq km. **Location:** SW Pacific, 1,200 mi NE of Brisbane, Australia. Fiji to E, Solomon Isls. to NW. **Topography:** Dense forest with narrow coastal strips of cultivated land. **Arable land:** 1.6%. **Capital:** Port-Vila, 52,542 (2014).

Government: Type: Parliamentary republic. **Head of state:** Pres. Baldwin Lonsdale; in office: Sept. 22, 2014. **Head of gov.:** Prime Min. Sato Kilman; in office: June 11, 2015. **Local divisions:** 6 provinces. **Defense budget/active troops:** NA.

Economy: Industries: food and fish freezing, wood proc., meat canning. **Chief crops:** copra, coconuts, cocoa, coffee, taro, yams, fruits, vegetables. **Natural resources:** manganese, hardwood forests, fish. **Water:** NA. **Electricity prod.:** 53 mil kWh. **Labor force:** agric. 65%, industry 5%, services 30%. **Unemployment:** NA.

Finance: Monetary unit: Vatu (VUV) (108.25 = $1 U.S.). **GDP:** $685 mil; **per capita GDP:** $2,600; **GDP growth:** 2.9%. **Imports:** $290 mil; China 43.5%, Japan 17.1%, Singapore 7.9%, Australia 7.4%. **Exports:** $44 mil; Thailand 68.2%, Japan 15.7%. **Tourism:** $265 mil. **Budget:** $175.2 mil. **Inflation:** 0.8%.

Transport: Motor vehicles: 58.1 per 1,000 pop. **Airports:** 3.

Communications: Telephone: 2.2 per 100 pop. **Mobile:** 60.4 per 100 pop. **Broadband:** 8.9 per 100 pop. **Internet:** 18.8%.

Health: Expend.: 3.6%. **Life expect.:** 71.5 male; 74.7 female. **Births:** 25.0 per 1,000 pop. **Deaths:** 4.1 per 1,000 pop. **Infant mortality:** 15.7 per 1,000 live births. **Undernourished:** 7.2%. **HIV:** NA.

Education: Compulsory: NA. **Literacy:** 85.2%.

Permanent UN mission: 800 Second Ave., Ste. 400C, New York, NY 10017; (212) 661-4303.

Website: governmentofvanuatu.gov.vu

The Anglo-French condominium of the New Hebrides, administered jointly by France and Great Britain since 1906, became the independent Republic of Vanuatu on July 30, 1980. Vanuatu is located in the Ring of Fire, a zone with frequent earthquakes and volcanic eruptions. The nation joined the World Trade Organization Aug. 24, 2012. Cyclone Pam battered Vanuatu, Mar. 13, 2015, destroying 96% of the country's crops and leaving 267,000 people in need of emergency shelter; the official death toll was 11.

Vatican City

The Holy See (Vatican City State)

People: Population (2014): 842. **Migrants:** 100%. **Pop. density** (2014): 4,956.3 per sq mi, 1,913.6 per sq km. **Urban:** 100%. **Ethnic groups:** Italians, Swiss, other. **Languages:** Italian, Latin, French. **Religions:** Roman Catholic.

Geography: Total area: 0.17 sq mi, 0.44 sq km; **Land area:** 0.17 sq mi, 0.44 sq km. **Location:** Within the city of Rome, completely surrounded by Italy. **Arable land:** 0%.

Economy: Industries: printing; coins, medals, postage stamps prod.; mosaics, staff uniforms; worldwide banking, financial activities. **Water:** NA. **Labor force:** Essentially services with small amount of industry; nearly all dignitaries, priests, nuns, guards, and approx. 3,000 lay workers live outside the Vatican.

Finance: Monetary unit: Euro (EUR) (0.89 = $1 U.S.). **Budget** (2011): $326.4 mil. **Inflation:** NA.

Health: Undernourished: <5%.

Apostolic Nunciature: 3339 Massachusetts Ave. NW 20008; 333-7121.

Website: www.vatican.va

The popes for many centuries, with brief interruptions, held temporal sovereignty over mid-Italy (the so-called Papal States), comprising an area of some 16,000 sq mi, with a population in the 19th cent. of more than 3 mil. This territory was incorporated in the new Kingdom of Italy (1861), the sovereignty of the pope being confined to the palaces of the Vatican and the Lateran in Rome and the villa of Castel Gandolfo, by an Italian law, May 13, 1871.

A Treaty of Conciliation, a concordat, and a financial convention were signed Feb. 11, 1929, by Cardinal Gasparri and Prem. Mussolini. The documents established the independent state of Vatican City and gave the Roman Catholic Church special status in Italy. The treaty (Lateran Agreement) was incorporated into Italy's Constitution (Article 7) in 1947. Italy and the Vatican signed an agreement in 1984 eliminating Roman Catholicism as the state religion and ending required religious education in Italian schools.

Vatican City includes the Basilica of Saint Peter, the Vatican Palace and Museum covering over 13 acres, the Vatican gardens, and neighboring buildings between Viale Vaticano and the church. Thirteen buildings in Rome, outside the boundaries, which house congregations or officers necessary for the administration of the Holy See, enjoy extraterritorial rights.

The legal system is based on the code of canon law, the apostolic constitutions, and laws especially promulgated for Vatican City by the pope.

Citing health problems, Pope Benedict XVI, elected Apr. 19, 2005, announced he would resign Feb. 11, 2013, the first pontiff to do so since 1415. He became Pope Emeritus Feb. 28. Cardinal Jorge Mario Bergoglio, from Argentina, was elected Mar. 13, taking the name of Francis. Pope Francis became the first Latin American and the first Jesuit pope. In an encyclical issued June 18, 2015, Francis called for action to stem environmental destruction and climate change. The Vatican signed a treaty June 26, 2015, formalizing its recognition of Palestine as a state.

Venezuela

Bolivarian Republic of Venezuela

People: Population: 29,275,460. **Age distrib.:** <15: 27.8%; 65+: 6.1%. **Growth:** 1.4%. **Migrants:** 3.9%. **Pop. density:** 86 per sq mi, 33.2 per sq km. **Urban:** 89%. **Ethnic groups:** Spanish, Italian, Portuguese, Arab, German, African, indigenous. **Languages:** Spanish (official), indigenous dialects. **Religions:** nominally Roman Catholic 96%.

Geography: Total area: 352,144 sq mi, 912,050 sq km; **Land area:** 340,561 sq mi, 882,050 sq km. **Location:** Carib. coast of S America. Colombia on W, Brazil on S, Guyana on E. **Topography:** Plains, called llanos, extend between Andes Mts. and Orinoco Delta. Orinoco stretches 1,600 mi and drains 80% of country. **Arable land:** 3.1%. **Capital:** Caracas, 2,916,183. **Cities:** Maracaibo, 2,196,435; Valencia, 1,733,641; Maracay, 1,165,922; Barquisimeto, 1,038,556.

Government: Type: Federal republic. **Head of state and gov.:** Pres. Nicolás Maduro Moros; in office: Apr. 19, 2013. **Local divisions:** 23 states, 1 capital district, 1 federal dependency consisting of 11 federally controlled island groups. **Defense budget:** $4.66 bil. **Active troops:** 115,000.

Economy: Industries: agric. prods., livestock, raw materials, machinery and equip., transp. equip., constr. materials, medical equip., pharmaceuticals. **Chief crops:** corn, sorghum, sugarcane, rice, bananas, vegetables, coffee. **Natural resources:** petroleum, nat. gas, iron ore, gold, bauxite, hydropower, diamonds. **Water:** 43,578 cu m per capita. **Crude oil reserves:** 298.4 bil bbls. **Electricity prod.:** 123 bil kWh. **Labor force:** agric. 7.3%, industry 21.8%, services 70.9%. **Unemployment:** 7.5%.

Finance: Monetary unit: Bolivar (VEF) (6.28 = $1 U.S.). **GDP:** $538.9 bil; **per capita GDP:** $17,700; **GDP growth:** –4%. **Imports:** $50.3 bil; U.S. 27.4%, China 12.6%, Brazil 10%, Russia 7.1%, Argentina 5.1%. **Exports:** $83.2 bil; U.S. 34.3%, India 15.9%, China 14%, Netherlands Antilles 8.4%, Singapore 6%. **Tourism:** $858 mil. **Budget:** $204 bil. **Inflation:** 62.2%.

Transport: Railways: 278 mi. **Motor vehicles:** 118.9 per 1,000 pop. **Airports:** 127.

Communications: Telephone: 25.3 per 100 pop. **Mobile:** 99 per 100 pop. **Broadband:** 41 per 100 pop. **Internet:** 57%.

Health: Expend.: 4.7%. **Life expect.:** 71.4 male; 77.8 female. **Births:** 19.2 per 1,000 pop. **Deaths:** 5.3 per 1,000 pop. **Infant mortality:** 18.9 per 1,000 live births. **Undernourished:** <5%. **HIV:** 0.6%.

Education: Compulsory: ages 3-16. **Literacy:** 96.3%.

Embassy: 1099 30th St. NW 20007; 342-2214.

Website: www.presidencia.gob.ve or eeuu.embajada.gob.ve

Columbus first set foot on the South American continent on the peninsula of Paria, Aug. 1498. Alonso de Ojeda, 1499, called the land Venezuela, or Little Venice, because the Indians had houses on stilts. Spanish colonialists dominated Venezuela until Simón Bolívar's victory near Carabobo in June 1821. The republic was formed after secession from the Colombian Federation in 1830. Military strongmen ruled Venezuela for much of its history. Since 1959, the country has had democratically elected governments.

Venezuela has the world's largest crude oil reserves, and oil accounts for more than 95% of export earnings and about 40% of government revenues. The government, Jan. 1, 1976, nationalized the oil industry. Attempts to reduce dependence on the hydrocarbon sector have met with limited success. The country has large reserves of natural gas.

Two attempted coups were thwarted by loyalist troops in Feb. and Nov. 1992. Pres. Carlos Andrés Pérez was removed from office on corruption charges, May 1993, and convicted, May 1996, of mismanaging a $17-mil secret government fund.

A 1992 coup leader, Hugo Chávez, who ran as a populist, was elected president Dec. 1998. That month, voters approved a new constitution greatly increasing his powers.

Popular among the poor, Chávez alienated middle- and upper-class Venezuelans with economic and political reforms, and his foreign policy antagonized the U.S. Gunfire erupted at a mass protest Apr. 11, 2002, in Caracas, killing at least 17 people. Chávez was forced to relinquish power, but when an interim government suspended democratic institutions, Chávez loyalists rebelled, and the president reclaimed his office Apr. 14. Chávez opponents organized strikes and recall efforts, 2003-04, but failed to oust him.

Chávez countered U.S. attempts to isolate him by solidifying ties with Latin American leftist leaders and with Iran and Russia. With the economy surging, he won the Dec. 2006 presidential election. On Jan. 31, 2007, the legislature granted him the power to rule by decree. Venezuelan voters approved constitutional changes abolishing presidential term limits Feb. 15, 2009. Suffering from cancer, Chávez won a tough reelection campaign, Oct. 7, 2012. He died Mar. 5, 2013, before he could be sworn in. Vice Pres. Nicolás Maduro Moros became interim president and won a narrow victory in Apr. 14, 2013, elections. With the economy hurt by low oil prices and tight currency controls, GDP declined 4% in 2014, inflation was 68.4%, and shortages of food and other goods were widespread. Large anti-Maduro protests, Feb.-June 2014, were met with a harsh crackdown by security forces; more than 40 people, mostly protesters, were killed. The Maduro govt. arrested a number of opposition figures in 2014-15, including Caracas Mayor Antonio Ledezma, Feb. 19, 2015, accused of plotting a coup. Opposition leader Leopoldo López was convicted, Sept. 10, 2015, of inciting violence and sentenced to more than 13 years in prison. A continued decline in oil prices led to further cuts in food imports in 2015. The government, Aug. 2015, closed border crossings with Colombia and began expelling Colombian immigrants, in part to crack down on smuggling.

Vietnam
Socialist Republic of Vietnam

People: Population: 94,348,835. **Age distrib.:** <15: 24.1%; 65+: 5.8%. **Growth:** 1%. **Migrants:** 0.1%. **Pop. density:** 788.1 per sq mi, 304.3 per sq km. **Urban:** 33.6%. **Ethnic groups:** Kinh (Viet) 85.7%. **Languages:** Vietnamese (official), English (as second lang.), French, Chinese, Khmer. **Religions:** Buddhist 9.3%, Catholic 6.7%, none 80.8%.

Geography: Total area: 127,881 sq mi, 331,210 sq km; **Land area:** 119,719 sq mi, 310,070 sq km. **Location:** SE Asia, on E coast of Indochinese Peninsula. China on N; Laos, Cambodia on W. **Topography:** Long and narrow, with 1,400-mi coast. Densely settled Red R. Valley in N; narrow coastal plains in center; wide, often marshy Mekong R. Delta in S. Semi-arid plateaus and barren mountains, with some stretches of tropical rain forest, in rest of country. **Arable land:** 20.6%. **Capital:** Hà Noi, 3,629,493. **Cities:** Ho Chi Minh City, 7,297,780; Can Tho, 1,174,693; Hai Phòng, 1,075,499.

Government: Type: Communist state. **Head of state:** Pres. Truong Tan Sang; in office: July 25, 2011. **Head of gov.:** Prime Min. Nguyen Tan Dung; in office: June 27, 2006. **Local divisions:** 58 provinces, 5 municipalities. **Defense budget:** $4.25 bil. **Active troops:** 482,000.

Economy: Industries: food proc., garments, shoes, machine-building, mining, coal, steel, cement, chemical fertilizer. **Chief crops:** rice, coffee, rubber, tea, pepper, soybeans, cashews, sugarcane, peanuts, bananas. **Natural resources:** phosphates, coal, manganese, rare earth elements, bauxite, chromate, offshore oil and gas deposits, timber, hydropower. **Water:** 9,643 cu m per capita. **Crude oil reserves:** 4.4 bil bbls. **Electricity prod.:** 118.2 bil kWh. **Labor force:** agric. 48%, industry 21%, services 31%. **Unemployment:** 2%.

Finance: Monetary unit: Dong (VND) (22,475.00 = $1 U.S.). **GDP:** $510.7 bil; **per capita GDP:** $5,600; **GDP growth:** 6%. **Imports:** $138.6 bil; China 32%, South Korea 13.9%, Singapore 7.2%, Japan 6.9%, Hong Kong 5%. **Exports:** $147 bil; U.S. 17.6%, China 11.8%, Japan 9.9%, South Korea 5%. **Tourism:** $7.3 bil. **Budget:** $51.9 bil. **Inflation:** 4.1%.

Transport: Railways: 1,616 mi. **Motor vehicles:** 4.4 per 1,000 pop. **Airports:** 38.

Communications: Telephone: 6 per 100 pop. **Mobile:** 147.1 per 100 pop. **Broadband:** 21.8 per 100 pop. **Internet:** 48.3%.

Health: Expend.: 6.6%. **Life expect.:** 70.7 male; 75.9 female. **Births:** 16.0 per 1,000 pop. **Deaths:** 5.9 per 1,000 pop. **Infant mortality:** 18.4 per 1,000 live births. **Undernourished:** 12.9%. **HIV:** 0.5%.

Education: Compulsory: ages 5-14. **Literacy:** 94.5%.

Embassy: 1233 20th St. NW, Ste. 400, 20036; 861-0737.

Website: vietnam.gov.vn

Settled by Viets from central China, Vietnam was held by China, 111 BCE-939 CE, and was a vassal state during subsequent periods. Conquest by France began in 1858 and ended in 1884 with the protectorates of Tonkin and Annam in the N and the colony of Cochin-China in the S.

Japan occupied Vietnam in 1940. Several groups formed the Vietminh (Independence) League, headed by Communist guerrilla leader Ho Chi Minh. In Aug. 1945, the Vietminh forced out Bao Dai, former emperor of Annam and head of a Japan-sponsored regime. France, seeking to reestablish colonial control, unsuccessfully battled Communist and nationalist forces, 1946-54.

Separate states formed in N. and S. Vietnam, with Communists under Ho Chi Minh (backed by Russia and China) controlling N. Vietnam and a non-Communist government (backed by the U.S.) controlling S. Vietnam. N. Vietnam aided Vietcong guerrillas who sought to take over S. Vietnam. U.S. troops and the S. Vietnamese army fought N. Vietnamese and Vietcong forces, including in border areas of Laos and Cambodia. Casualties of the war were as follows—combat deaths: U.S. 47,434 (Aug. 4, 1964-Jan. 27, 1973); S. Vietnam more than 200,000; other allied forces 5,225. Total U.S. fatalities numbered more than 58,000. Vietnamese civilian casualties were more than 1 mil. The war displaced more than 6.5 mil in S. Vietnam.

A never-implemented cease-fire agreement was signed in Paris Jan. 27, 1973, by the U.S., N. and S. Vietnam, and the Vietcong. The last U.S. troops left Vietnam Mar. 27, 1973. S. Vietnam surrendered Apr. 30, 1975. N. Vietnam assumed control. The country was officially reunited July 2, 1976.

Among the unstable conditions that persisted in the region, heavy fighting with Cambodia took place, 1977-80. China cut off economic aid when 140,000 ethnic Chinese fled discrimination in Vietnam. Reacting to Vietnam's 1979 invasion of Cambodia, China attacked four Vietnamese border provinces, Feb. 1979.

Vietnam announced reforms aimed at reducing central control of the economy in 1987. Citing Hanoi's cooperation in returning remains of U.S. soldiers killed in the Vietnam War, the U.S. ended, Feb. 1994, a 19-year U.S. embargo on trade with Vietnam. The U.S. extended full diplomatic recognition to Vietnam July 11, 1995. In Aug. 2012, the U.S. began cleaning up the herbicide Agent Orange, used to clear forests during the Vietnam War. In a move apparently aimed at countering China's growing power in the South China Sea region, the U.S., Oct. 2, 2014, eased its embargo on lethal arms sales to allow Vietnam to obtain naval matériel. Communist Party head Nguyen Phu Trong met with U.S. Pres. Barack Obama at the White House, July 7, 2015, for talks on trade and other topics.

Yemen
Republic of Yemen

People: Population: 26,737,317. **Age distrib.:** <15: 41.1%; 65+: 2.7%. **Growth:** 2.5%. **Migrants:** 1.3%. **Pop. density:** 131.2 per sq mi, 50.6 per sq km. **Urban:** 34.6%. **Ethnic groups:** predominantly Arab; Afro-Arab, S Asian, European. **Languages:** Arabic (official). **Religions:** Muslim 99.1% (official; Sunni 65%, Shia 35%).

Geography: Total area: 203,850 sq mi, 527,968 sq km; **Land area:** 203,850 sq mi, 527,968 sq km. **Location:** Middle East, on S coast of the Arabian Peninsula. Saudi Arabia on N, Oman on E. **Topography:** Sandy coastal strip; well-watered fertile mountains in interior. **Arable land:** 2.4%. **Capital:** Sanaa, 2,961,934. **Cities:** Aden, 881,540.

Government: Type: Republic. **Head of state:** Pres. Abd Rabbuh Mansur Hadi; in office: Feb. 25, 2012. **Head of gov.:** Prime Min. Khaled Bahah; in office: Oct. 13, 2014. **Local divisions:** 21 governorates, 1 municipality. **Defense budget:** $1.89 bil. **Active troops:** 66,700.

Economy: Industries: crude oil prod. and petroleum refining, small-scale prod. of cotton textiles and leather goods, food proc. **Chief crops:** grains, fruits, vegetables, pulses, khat, coffee, cotton. **Natural resources:** petroleum; fish; rock salt; marble; small deposits of coal, gold, lead, nickel, copper. **Water:** 86 cu m per capita. **Crude oil reserves:** 3 bil bbls. **Electricity prod.:** 6.2 bil kWh. **Labor force:** Most people employed in agric. and herding; services, constr., industry, and commerce account for less than one-fourth of labor force. **Unemployment:** 17.4%.

Finance: Monetary unit: Rial (YER) (214.85 = $1 U.S.). **GDP:** $103.6 bil; **per capita GDP:** $3,800; **GDP growth:** –0.2%. **Imports:** $10.4 bil; China 15.5%, UAE 13.4%, India 9.5%, Saudi Arabia 6.3%. **Exports:** $7 bil; China 29.4%, South Korea 16%, Thailand 14.7%, India 8.8%, Japan 6.2%, UAE 5%. **Tourism:** $940 mil. **Budget:** $14.3 bil. **Inflation** (2012-13): 11%.

Transport: Motor vehicles: 28.6 per 1,000 pop. **Airports:** 17.

Communications: Telephone: 4.7 per 100 pop. **Mobile:** 68.5 per 100 pop. **Broadband:** 0.3 per 100 pop. **Internet:** 22.6%.

Health: Expend.: 5.5%. **Life expect.:** 63.1 male; 67.4 female. **Births:** 30.0 per 1,000 pop. **Deaths:** 6.3 per 1,000 pop. **Infant mortality:** 48.9 per 1,000 live births. **Undernourished:** 25.7%. **HIV:** <0.1%.

Education: Compulsory: ages 6-14. **Literacy:** 70.1%.

Embassy: 2319 Wyoming Ave. NW 20008; 965-4760.

Website: www.yemen.gov.ye or www.yemenembassy.org

Yemen's territory once was part of the ancient biblical Kingdom of Sheba, or Saba. Yemen became independent in 1918, after centuries of Ottoman Turkish rule.

Imam Yahya ibn Muhammad ruled, 1904-48, and after his assassination was succeeded by his son, Imam Ahmed, 1948-62. Army officers headed by Brig. Gen. Abdullah al-Salal declared the country the Yemen Arab Republic, Sept. 1962. Ahmed's heir, the Imam Mohamad al-Badr, fled to the mountains where tribesmen joined royalist forces, aided by the Saudi monarchy. Fighting between royalists and republicans killed about 150,000 people until hostilities ended in 1970.

South Yemen, formed from the British colony of Aden and the British protectorate of South Arabia, became independent Nov. 1967. A Marxist state and a Soviet ally, it took the name People's Democratic Republic of Yemen in 1970. More than 300,000 Yemenis fled from the S to the N after independence, contributing to two decades of hostility between the two states.

The two countries were formally united May 21, 1990, but regional clan-based rivalries led to full-scale civil war in 1994. Secessionists declared a breakaway state in South Yemen, May 21, 1994, but northern troops captured the former southern capital of Aden in July. A new constitution was approved Sept. 28.

While on a refueling stop in Aden, Oct. 12, 2000, the destroyer U.S.S. *Cole* was bombed, killing 17 Americans and injuring more than three dozen; the U.S. government blamed the attack on terrorists associated with al-Qaeda leader Osama bin Laden.

Clashes beginning in June 2004 between Yemeni government forces and Shiite rebels led by an anti-U.S. cleric, Hussein al-Houthi, left more than 200 people dead. The government announced Sept. 10 that Yemeni troops had killed al-Houthi.

During 2007-10, Shiite rebels in the northwest, secessionists in the south, Sunni militants in the east affiliated with al-Qaeda in the Arabian Peninsula (AQAP), and pirates in coastal waters challenged Yemeni government authority. In 2011, Arab Spring demonstrators demanded Pres. Ali Abdullah Saleh's resignation. Saleh was severely wounded June 3 in a rocket attack on the presidential compound in Sanaa. Vice Pres. Abd Rabbuh Mansur Hadi became acting president. After a 2-year manhunt, Anwar al-Awlaki, a U.S. citizen and radical Muslim cleric linked to several plots against the U.S., was killed Sept. 30, 2011, by a U.S. missile in northern Yemen. Saleh effectively ceded power

Nov. 23, 2011. Hadi officially became president in uncontested Feb. 2012 elections but failed to stabilize the country. The U.S. continued air attacks against AQAP; a drone strike June 9, 2015, killed the group's leader, Nasser al-Wuhayshi. The Sunni extremist group ISIS staged deadly terrorist bombings against Shiite targets in 2015. After heavy fighting, Shiite rebels known as Houthis took over Sanaa in Sept. 2014, and fierce fighting for control of Aden and other areas occurred in 2015. Hadi fled to Saudi Arabia in Mar. 2015, and a Saudi-led coalition of Sunni nations began, Mar. 25, airstrikes against Houthi forces, who were aided by Iran and joined by Yemeni military units loyal to Saleh. AQAP and southern secessionist militias were loosely allied with pro-Hadi forces. Airstrikes and other fighting caused high civilian casualties; an airstrike on a wedding party, Sept. 28, 2015, apparently killed 130 or more. The UN reported, Sept. 29, that 2,355 civilians had been killed since fighting intensified in Mar. About 1.4 mil people were internally displaced.

Zambia

Republic of Zambia

People: Population: 15,066,266. **Age distrib.:** <15: 46.1%; 65+: 2.4%. **Growth:** 2.9%. **Migrants:** 0.7%. **Pop. density:** 52.5 per sq mi, 20.3 per sq km. **Urban:** 40.9%. **Ethnic groups:** Bemba 21%, Tonga 13.6%, Chewa 7.4%, Lozi 5.7%, Nsenga 5.3%, Tumbuka 4.4%, Ngoni 4%, Lala 3.1%, Kaonde 2.9%, Namwanga 2.8%, Lunda (N Western) 2.6%, Mambwe 2.5%, Luvale 2.2%, Lamba 2.1%. **Languages:** Bantu langs. (incl. Bembe, Nyanja, Tonga, Lozi, Chewa, Nsenga, Tumbuka); English (official). **Religions:** Protestant 75.3%, Roman Catholic 20.2%.

Geography: Total area: 290,587 sq mi, 752,618 sq km; **Land area:** 287,028 sq mi, 743,398 sq km. **Location:** S central Africa. Dem. Rep. of the Congo on N; Tanzania, Malawi, Mozambique on E; Zimbabwe, Namibia on S; Angola on W. **Topography:** Mostly high plateau with thick forests, drained by several important rivers, including the Zambezi. **Arable land:** 5.1%. **Capital:** Lusaka, 2,179,470.

Government: Type: Republic. **Head of state and gov.:** Pres. Edgar Lungu; in office: Jan. 25, 2015. **Local divisions:** 10 provinces. **Defense budget:** $422 mil. **Active troops:** 15,100.

Economy: Industries: copper mining and proc., emerald mining, constr., foodstuffs, beverages, chemicals, textiles, fertilizer, horticulture. **Chief crops:** corn, sorghum, rice, peanuts, sunflower seeds, vegetables, flowers, tobacco, cotton, sugarcane, cassava, coffee. **Natural resources:** copper, cobalt, zinc, lead, coal, emeralds, gold, silver, uranium, hydropower. **Water:** 7,208 cu m per capita. **Electricity prod.:** 11.7 bil kWh. **Labor force:** agric. 85%, industry 6%, services 9%. **Unemployment:** 13.3%.

Finance: Monetary unit: Kwacha (ZMW) (9.38 = $1 U.S.). **GDP:** $61.1 bil; **per capita GDP:** $4,100; **GDP growth:** 5.4%. **Imports:** $8.1 bil; South Africa 36.1%, Dem. Rep. of the Congo 15.7%, China 9.5%, Kuwait 6.5%. **Exports:** $9.2 bil; China 38.7%, South Africa 11.6%, Dem. Rep. of the Congo 10.5%, Zimbabwe 6.2%. **Tourism:** $224 mil. **Budget:** $6.8 bil. **Inflation:** 7.8%.

Transport: Railways: 1,942 mi (incl. 1,156 mi of Tanzania-Zambia Railway Authority). **Motor vehicles:** 21.7 per 1,000 pop. **Airports:** 8.

Communications: Telephone: 0.8 per 100 pop. **Mobile:** 67.3 per 100 pop. **Broadband:** 0.8 per 100 pop. **Internet:** 17.3%.

Health: Expend.: 6.5%. **Life expect.:** 50.5 male; 53.8 female. **Births:** 42.1 per 1,000 pop. **Deaths:** 12.7 per 1,000 pop. **Infant mortality:** 64.7 per 1,000 live births. **Undernourished:** 48.3%. **HIV:** 12.4%.

Education: Compulsory: NA. **Literacy:** 63.4%.

Embassy: 2419 Massachusetts Ave. NW 20008; 265-9717.

Website: www.zambia.gov.zm

Ruled by the British as Northern Rhodesia, the country became the independent republic of Zambia within the Commonwealth Oct. 24, 1964. Independence leader Kenneth Kaunda governed as president, 1964-91. A Zambian government corporation in 1970 took over 51% of two foreign-owned copper-mining companies. Privately held land and other enterprises were nationalized in 1975. In the 1980s and 1990s, lowered copper prices hurt the economy and severe drought caused famine.

Food riots erupted in June 1990. Oct. 1991 elections brought an end to Kaunda's one-party rule. The new government sought to sell state enterprises, including the copper industry. Pres. Frederick Chiluba won reelection Nov. 1996. Unable to change the constitution to allow himself a third term, Chiluba endorsed Levy Patrick Mwanawasa, who won a disputed election Dec. 2001. Food shortages threatened more than 2 mil Zambians in 2002; the government refused to distribute shipments of U.S. grain because it was genetically modified. In a hard-fought 2006 election, Mwanawasa won a second term. Accused of embezzling state funds as president, Chiluba was ordered to pay $58 mil by a British court, June 2007; he was acquitted by a Zambian court, Aug. 2009, of misusing $500,000 in public money.

Pres. Mwanawasa suffered a stroke June 29, 2008, and died Aug. 19. Vice Pres. Rupiah Banda became acting pres. He won the presidency by a narrow margin in the Oct. 2008 election but lost to opposition leader Michael Sata Sept. 2011. Sata died in office, Oct. 28, 2014. Edgar Lungu of Sata's Patriotic Front party narrowly won a Jan. 2015 special election.

The country has made progress in treating HIV/AIDS, but the disease afflicted up to 1.2 mil Zambians as of 2014.

Zimbabwe

Republic of Zimbabwe

People: Population: 14,229,541. **Age distrib.:** <15: 37.9%; 65+: 3.5%. **Growth:** 2.2%. **Migrants:** 2.6%. **Pop. density:** 95.3 per sq mi, 36.8 per sq km. **Urban:** 32.4%. **Ethnic groups:** African (predom. Shona; Ndebele is second-largest ethnic group) 99.4%. **Languages:** Shona, Ndebele (both official and most widely spoken); English (official, used in business), 13 official minority langs. **Religions:** Protestant 75.9% (incl. Apostolic 38%, Pentecostal 21.1%), Roman Catholic 8.4%, none 6.1%.

Geography: Total area: 150,872 sq mi, 390,757 sq km; **Land area:** 149,362 sq mi, 386,847 sq km. **Location:** Southern Africa. Zambia on N, Botswana on W, South Africa on S, Mozambique on E. **Topography:** High plateau rising to mountains on E border, sloping down on other borders. **Arable land:** 10.3%. **Capital:** Harare, 1,501,363.

Government: Type: Parliamentary democracy. **Head of state and gov.:** Pres. Robert Gabriel Mugabe; in office: Dec. 31, 1987. **Local divisions:** 8 provinces, 2 cities with provincial status. **Defense budget:** $368 mil. **Active troops:** 29,000.

Economy: Industries: mining, steel, wood prods., cement, chemicals, fertilizer, clothing and footwear, foodstuffs. **Chief crops:** tobacco, corn, cotton, wheat, coffee, sugarcane, peanuts. **Natural resources:** coal, chromium ore, asbestos, gold, nickel, copper, iron ore, vanadium, lithium, tin, platinum group metals. **Water:** 1,413 cu m per capita. **Electricity prod.:** 7.7 bil kWh. **Labor force:** agric. 66%, industry 10%, services 24%. **Unemployment:** 5.4%.

Finance: Monetary unit: Dollar (ZWD) (361.90 = $1 U.S.). **GDP:** $27.1 bil; **per capita GDP:** $2,000; **GDP growth:** 3.2%. **Imports:** $5.1 bil; South Africa 49.1%, Zambia 9.6%, China 8.7%. **Exports:** $3.3 bil; China 23.4%, South Africa 14.5%, Dem. Rep. of the Congo 12%, Botswana 10.7%. **Tourism:** $827 mil. **Budget** (2014): $4.6 bil. **Inflation** (2012-13): 1.6%.

Transport: Railways: 2,129 mi. **Motor vehicles:** 40 per 1,000 pop. **Airports:** 17.

Communications: Telephone: 2.3 per 100 pop. **Mobile:** 80.8 per 100 pop. **Broadband:** 37.8 per 100 pop. **Internet:** 19.9%.

Health: Expend.: NA. **Life expect.:** 56.5 male; 57.6 female. **Births:** 32.3 per 1,000 pop. **Deaths:** 10.1 per 1,000 pop. **Infant mortality:** 26.1 per 1,000 live births. **Undernourished:** 31.8%. **HIV:** 16.7%.

Education: Compulsory: ages 6-12. **Literacy:** 86.5%.

Embassy: 1608 New Hampshire Ave. NW 20009; 332-7100.

Website: www.zim.gov.zw

Britain took over the area as Southern Rhodesia in 1923 from the British South Africa Co. (which, under Cecil Rhodes, had conquered it by 1897) and granted internal self-government. A 1961 constitution restricted voting to keep whites in power.

On Nov. 11, 1965, Prime Min. Ian D. Smith unilaterally declared independence. Britain termed the act illegal and demanded that the country (known as Rhodesia until 1980) enfranchise the black African majority. The UN imposed sanctions and, in May 1968, a trade embargo, as black nationalists launched guerrilla attacks.

After the country held its first universal-franchise election, Apr. 21, 1979, all parties accepted a cease-fire, Dec. 5. The country changed its name to Zimbabwe upon independence, Apr. 18, 1980. Robert Mugabe, the nation's first prime min., became executive president in 1987.

From the late 1990s, Mugabe's rule became increasingly repressive. A land redistribution campaign triggered violent attacks in Apr. 2000 against some white farmers. (Whites made up less than 1% of the population but had held 70% of the land.) Production of corn, the nation's food staple, subsequently declined sharply. Mugabe, relying on fraud and intimidation, international observers claimed, won the Mar. 9-11, 2002, presidential election. The EU and U.S. imposed sanctions; EU sanctions were eased Feb. 2015. In May 2005, Mugabe launched Operation Murambatsvina ("Drive out rubbish"), razing shanty dwellings and illegal street markets in urban areas and leaving some 700,000 people homeless. During 2006-08, inflation soared to a yearly rate of more than 100,000%.

Mugabe clung to power after a widely discredited 2008 presidential election and runoff. Opposition groups, Jan. 18, 2013, condemned an increasing crackdown on Mugabe's critics. In the July 31, 2013, presidential election, Mugabe was once again declared the winner.

The July 2015 killing of a lion named Cecil sparked international outrage. Cecil was allegedly lured out of a national park so that he could be shot in an unprotected area. The Zimbabwean guide, who denied wrongdoing, was charged with failing to prevent an illegal hunt.

SPORTS

Sports Highlights, 2015 853
Editors' Picks: Memorable Super Bowls. 854
Olympics. 855
College Sports 877
Football. 890
Baseball 907
Basketball. 933
Hockey 943
Soccer 948
Golf. 952
Tennis. 955
Auto Racing 959
Boxing. 962
Thoroughbred and Harness Racing 966
Bowling. 971
Chess 971
Figure Skating 972
Alpine Skiing 972
Cycling 973
Swimming 974
Track and Field 975
Dogs 976
Marathons and Triathlon. 976
Sullivan Award. 978
Yachting 979
Rifle and Pistol. 979
Rodeo 979
Sports Organizations, Directory of 419
Sports Personalities. 202
Sports Photos, 2015. 810

Sports Highlights, 2015

It was a year of milestones and near-misses in 2015, as fans witnessed unprecedented feats, several that hadn't been achieved in decades, and some that fell just short of historic.

Ohio State erased any doubt that they belonged in the first-ever FBS College Football Playoff, upsetting top-ranked Alabama, 42-35, on Jan. 2, and toppling second-ranked Oregon, 42-40, to win the **NCAA National Championship** Jan. 12, at AT&T Stadium in Arlington, TX. Sophomore running back Ezekiel Elliott rushed for 246 yards and four touchdowns.

Tom Brady and the New England Patriots won their fourth championship in thrilling fashion in **Super Bowl XLIX**, Feb. 1 at Univ. of Phoenix Stadium in Glendale, AZ. Down by 10 points in the final quarter, the veteran quarterback rallied his team on consecutive drives of 68 and 64 yds to take a 28-24 lead. The Patriots left just enough time on the clock for Russell Wilson and the Seattle Seahawks to stage a comeback of their own. An astounding catch by Jermaine Kearse put the Seahawks at the New England 5-yd line with 1:06 left in the game. But on second and goal, Seattle coach Pete Carroll called for a pass over the middle, and New England's Malcolm Butler blocked intended receiver Ricardo Lockette to deny Seattle its second straight Super Bowl win. Brady, the game's MVP, spent the summer appealing a four-game suspension by NFL Commissioner Roger Goodell for his alleged involvement in **"Deflategate,"** in which the Patriots were accused of deliberately underinflating balls in the AFC championship game. A U.S. federal court judge ruled in Sept. that Goodell had overstepped his bounds in issuing the suspension, which was overturned.

Duke Univ. outlasted the Univ. of Wisconsin 68-63 to win the **NCAA men's basketball championship**, Apr. 6, at Lucas Oil Stadium in Indianapolis, IN. It was the fifth title for the Blue Devils and for coach Mike Krzyzewski. Freshman Tyus Jones led all scorers with 23 points, 19 of them in the second half, to win the tournament's most outstanding player award. Two nights earlier, the Badgers spoiled Kentucky's bid to finish the season undefeated, beating the top-ranked Wildcats, 71-64. UConn cruised to its third straight **NCAA women's basketball championship**, defeating Notre Dame, 63-53, at Amalie Arena in Tampa, FL, Apr. 7. The win gave coach Geno Auriemma his 10th title, tying him with UCLA's legendary John Wooden for most ever. Junior forward Breanna Stewart notched 8 points and 15 rebounds to win her third consecutive most outstanding player award.

American Pharoah became the first horse since Affirmed in 1978 to capture thoroughbred racing's Triple Crown. Trained by Bob Baffert, the Kentucky colt narrowly defeated Firing Line and Dortmund to win the **Kentucky Derby** at Churchill Downs in Louisville, KY, May 2. Two weeks later, he took the **Preakness Stakes** by seven lengths at Pimlico in Baltimore, MD. And on June 6, jockey Victor Espinoza rode American Pharoah to a wire-to-wire victory in the **Belmont Stakes** in Elmont, NY.

The Chicago Blackhawks won their third **Stanley Cup championship** in six years, defeating the Tampa Bay Lightning in six games June 15 at the United Center. It was the first time Chicago won the Cup on home ice since 1938. Defenseman Duncan Keith, who scored the game-clinching goal, won the Conn Smythe Trophy, awarded to the playoff MVP.

The Golden State Warriors won their first **NBA Championship** in 40 years by defeating the Cleveland Cavaliers in six games June 16 at Quicken Loans Arena in Cleveland, OH. Cleveland's LeBron James, who returned to his hometown after a four-year detour to Miami, led all scorers with 35.8 points per game, but he had little help from a Cavalier roster beset by injuries. Stephen Curry led the Golden State offense with 26 points per game, while forward (and series MVP) Andre Iguodala held James to a shooting percentage of less than 40 percent.

Jordan Spieth captured the first two of golf's four major championships, unloosing dreams of the sport's first grand slam since 1930. The 21-year-old Texan tied Tiger Woods's course record of 270 to win the **Masters Championship** in Augusta, GA, Apr. 12. A 25-ft birdie putt on the 16th hole propelled him to victory at the **U.S. Open**, June 21, at Chambers Bay in University Place, WA. But he fell one stroke short of a four-way playoff at the **British Open**, July 20, at the Old Course at St. Andrews in Fife, Scotland. Fellow American Zach Johnson outlasted South Africa's Louis Oosthuizen and Australian Marc Leishman to win the Claret Jug. Spieth also just missed the **PGA Championship**, Aug. 16, at Whistling Straits in Kohler, WI, where he finished three strokes behind Australia's Jason Day.

Serena Williams fell a U.S. Open win shy of achieving a calendar-year Grand Slam. Williams defeated Maria Sharapova in straight sets to take the **Australian Open** in Melbourne, Jan. 31. She dropped a tiebreaker set to Lucie Safarova of the Czech Republic before ultimately winning the **French Open**, June 6 at Roland Garros. She claimed another straight-set victory over Spain's Garbiñe Muguruza at **Wimbledon**, July 11, at the All England Club in London. Those three victories, combined with her 2014 win at the U.S. Open, gave her a Grand Slam, albeit not in the same calendar year. At the **U.S. Open** in Flushing Meadows, NY, she lost in the semifinals, Sept. 11, to unseeded Roberta Vinci of Italy. Vinci lost in the finals Sept. 12 to her countrywoman Flavia Pennetta.

Serbia's Novak Djokovic also won three of the four major tournaments. Djokovic bested Great Britain's Andy Murray at the **Australian Open**, Feb. 1, but lost in four sets to No. 8-seed Stan Wawrinka of Switzerland at the **French Open**, June 7. Djokovic and No. 2-seed Roger Federer traded tiebreakers in the first two sets of their finals match at **Wimbledon**, July 12, before Djokovic went on to take the final two sets. The two men squared off in a rematch at the **U.S. Open**, Sept. 13, with Djokovic again winning in four sets.

The U.S. won its first **Women's World Cup** since 1999, routing Japan, 5-2, in the final game July 5 at BC Place Stadium in Vancouver, BC, Canada. More Americans watched the telecast than any other soccer game in history. Midfielder Carli Lloyd scored six goals in the tournament, including three in the final game that seemed to settle the contest early in the first half.

Major League Baseball's July 31 trading deadline saw several teams making deals that helped to propel them to playoff spots. The Toronto Blue Jays acquired shortstop Troy Tulowitzki and pitcher David Price to take the AL East crown. The Texas Rangers added pitcher Cole Hamels to capture the AL West title, passing the upstart Houston Astros in the final month. Kansas City easily won the AL Central. The NY Mets climbed past the Washington Nationals, who had been widely expected to win the NL East. The injury-plagued St. Louis Cardinals won the NL Central, and the L.A. Dodgers took their third straight NL West crown. The wild-card game pitted the Pittsburgh Pirates against the Chicago Cubs, two Central teams with the second- and third-best records in the NL. In the first **World Series** match-up of expansion teams, Kansas City beat the NY Mets in five games. The season featured a record-tying seven no-hitters, including two by Washington's Max Scherzer. In Scherzer's second, against the NY Mets, he struck out 17 batters and didn't walk any; only a throwing error prevented it from being a perfect game.

WORLD ALMANAC EDITORS' PICKS: MEMORABLE SUPER BOWLS

For all the annual buildup, the ultra-hyped Super Bowl—which turns 50 in 2016—has often failed to deliver. The first four contests were pretty one-sided affairs, but Super Bowl Sunday eventually amassed some truly memorable on-field moments—and we're not referring to the halftime shows or wardrobe malfunctions. Here are our favorites, in chronological order.

Super Bowl III: Jan. 12, 1969

New York Jets 16, Baltimore Colts 7

This game was memorable for what it signified: the ability of the upstart American Football League to compete with the more established National Football League. The NFL champion Green Bay Packers handily defeated their AFL opponents in the first two Super Bowls, and the Colts were heavy favorites to do likewise to the Jets. Undaunted, Joe Namath issued a bold prediction, guaranteeing victory three days before the game. He delivered, completing 17 of 28 passes for 206 yards. Matt Snell rushed for 121 yards and a touchdown, and Jim Turner kicked three field goals. Baltimore's only points came late in the fourth quarter after Johnny Unitas replaced Earl Morrall, who threw three interceptions in the first half.

Super Bowl VII: Jan. 14, 1973

Miami Dolphins 14, Washington Redskins 7

The lowest-scoring game in Super Bowl history wasn't as close as the final score might make it appear. The Miami defense had propelled the Dolphins to the first (and so far only) undefeated season in NFL history, and Washington's only score came in the fourth quarter on a blocked Miami field goal. Dolphins' kicker Garo Yepremian—one of the first foreign-born soccer players to join the NFL—attempted a forward pass, which Washington's Mike Bass caught and ran 49 yards for a touchdown. Miami safety Jake Scott was named MVP, making him first among equals on the Dolphins' heralded "no-name" defense. Members of the 1972 Miami squad still celebrate each season when the last undefeated team loses its first game, ensuring that Miami's accomplishment remains unmatched.

Super Bowl XIII: Jan. 21, 1979

Pittsburgh Steelers 35, Dallas Cowboys 31

Cowboys fans remember this as the "what-if" game, as in "what if Jackie Smith had caught that wide open pass?" Smith, a normally sure-handed future Hall of Famer, dropped a 10-yard touchdown pass that could have allowed the Cowboys to tie the game at 21 late in the third quarter. Instead, Dallas settled for a field goal, cutting their deficit to four points, the final margin of victory. Pittsburgh scored two touchdowns in a 19-second stretch to take a seemingly insurmountable lead. But the Cowboys rallied with two touchdown passes by Roger Staubach in the game's final three minutes to make Smith's muff all the more heartbreaking. The victory made the Steelers the first team and Terry Bradshaw the first quarterback to win three Super Bowls.

Super Bowl XXIII: Jan. 22, 1989

San Francisco 49ers 20, Cincinnati Bengals 16

This rematch of Super Bowl XVI reproduced the final result of the first meeting, in even more thrilling fashion. San Francisco outgained the Bengals, 453 total yards to 229, but trailed late in the fourth quarter after a Jim Breech field goal gave Cincinnati a 16-13 lead. Always steady under pressure, quarterback Joe Montana led the 49ers on an 11-play, 92-yard drive culminating in a 10-yard touchdown pass to John Taylor with 34 seconds left. San Francisco became the first NFC team to win three Super Bowls. The victory was a swan song for 49ers head coach Bill Walsh, who announced his retirement several days later.

Super Bowl XXV: Jan. 27, 1991

New York Giants 20, Buffalo Bills 19

This game had many firsts: first decided on the final play, and first—and so far only—to feature a one-point margin of victory. It was also the first of four consecutive Super Bowl losses by the Bills. Jim Kelly quarterbacked Buffalo's high-flying offense, which averaged a league-leading 26.8 points per game, but the Giants boasted the league's best defense, led by Lawrence Taylor and Carl Banks. Giants quarterback Jeff Hostetler, filling in for the injured Phil Simms, combined short passes and a steady stream of handoffs to Ottis Anderson to keep the ball away from the Bills, maintaining possession for an unprecedented 40:33. Matt Bahr's field goal gave New York the lead with 7:40 left in the game, leaving plenty of time for Buffalo to drive to New York's 29-yard line, from which Buffalo kicker Scott Norwood's field goal attempt sailed wide right.

Super Bowl XXXIV: Jan. 30, 2000

St. Louis Rams 23, Tennessee Titans 16

Just a few years earlier, Rams quarterback Kurt Warner was playing for the Arena Football League and bagging groceries. But his MVP 1999 season brought the Rams and coach Dick Vermeil their first Super Bowl trophy. Warner completed just 24 of 45 passes, but several of them went for big gains, including a 73-yard pass to wide receiver Isaac Bruce and a 52-yard completion to Marshall Faulk out of the backfield. In all, Warner passed for 414 yards, still a Super Bowl record. St. Louis jumped out to a 16-0 lead in the third, but Tennessee clawed back behind the rushing of halfback Eddie George and quarterback Steve McNair. Rams linebacker Mike Jones tackled Kevin Dyson at the St. Louis 1-yard line, preventing a touchdown that could have altered the outcome.

Super Bowl XXXVI: Feb. 3, 2002

New England Patriots 20, St. Louis Rams 17

The Rams and their "Greatest Show on Turf" offense were 14-point favorites, but they were stymied throughout the game by New England's smothering defense. The Patriots scored three times off turnovers (two interceptions and a fumble) to take a 17-3 lead at the end of the third quarter. The Rams finally got in gear in the fourth quarter, scoring on a quarterback sneak and then tying the game on a 26-yard pass from QB Kurt Warner to Ricky Proehl with 90 seconds left. Starting deep in their own territory, the Patriots could have taken their chances in overtime. But quarterback Tom Brady, who inherited the starting job in week two when Drew Bledsoe was injured, drove the offense to the 30-yard line and set up Adam Vinatieri's game-winning field goal as time expired.

Super Bowl XLII: Feb. 3, 2008

New York Giants 17, New England Patriots 14

New England beat the New York Giants in the last week of the regular season to become the first undefeated team since the 1972 Miami Dolphins. By the Super Bowl, the Giants were the only team standing between the Patriots and a complete, undefeated season. After a defensive battle, the Patriots led 7-3 at the beginning of the fourth quarter, which featured a relative explosion of offense and three lead changes. Eli Manning's touchdown pass to Plaxico Burress provided the margin of victory, but the most memorable play was Manning's 32-yard pass on third-and-five to keep the drive going. Manning somehow extricated himself from two New England defenders and threw to David Tyree, who pinned the ball to his helmet.

Super Bowl XLIII: Feb. 1, 2009

Pittsburgh Steelers 27, Arizona Cardinals 23

Pittsburgh linebacker James Harrison intercepted a pass by Arizona's Kurt Warner in the end zone and rumbled down the field for a record 100-yard touchdown as the first half ended. That play was the prelude to a rollicking second half capped by two lead changes in the game's last three minutes. Pittsburgh led 20-7 as the fourth quarter began, but Warner rallied with a touchdown pass to Larry Fitzgerald. A holding penalty in Pittsburgh's end zone resulted in an Arizona safety and cut the Steelers' lead to 20-16 with under three minutes left. Warner hit Fitzgerald again for a 64-yard pass that gave Arizona its first lead on the ensuing drive. But quarterback Ben Roethlisberger orchestrated a 78-yard drive to the 6-yard line, then hit Santonio Holmes, who landed in the end zone with the game-winning TD.

Super Bowl XLIX: Feb. 1, 2015

New England Patriots 28, Seattle Seahawks 24

Patriots quarterback Tom Brady threw four touchdowns to win his fourth Super Bowl and third MVP award, in spite of trailing by 10 at the beginning of the fourth quarter. But it was the team's defense that preserved the victory as it was slipping away in the final seconds. Seattle had the ball at the New England 1-yard line with 26 seconds left. Instead of handing the ball to running back Marshawn Lynch, Seahawks head coach Pete Carroll called for a pass to wide receiver Ricardo Lockette, and Patriots safety Malcolm Butler, who had been beaten two plays earlier, intercepted the pass at the goal line.

OLYMPIC GAMES

2016 Summer Olympic Games

Rio de Janeiro, Brazil, Aug. 5-21, 2016

An estimated 10,500 athletes from 206 nations were expected to meet in Rio de Janeiro, Brazil, to compete for medals in 306 events in the XXXI Olympiad Aug. 5-21, 2016. South America was hosting the Games for the first time. The Games will take place at 32 venues, with Rio's Maracanã stadium (originally constructed for the 1950 World Cup soccer tournament and renovated for the 2014 World Cup) hosting the opening and closing ceremonies.

Nations will face off in 28 sports, including golf and rugby, which were returning after decades-long absences.

General Olympic Information

The modern Olympic Games, first held in Athens, Greece, in 1896, were the result of efforts by Baron Pierre de Coubertin, a French educator, to promote interest in education and culture and to foster better international understanding through love of athletics. His inspiration was the ancient Greek Olympic Games, most notable of the four Panhellenic celebrations. The games were combined patriotic, religious, and athletic festivals held every four years. The first such recorded festival was held in 776 BCE, when the Greeks began to keep their calendar by "Olympiads," or four-year spans between the games.

Coubertin enlisted 14 nations to send athletes to the first modern Olympics. Now athletes from more than 200 nations and territories compete in the Summer Olympics. The Winter Olympic Games, started in 1924, draw competitors from about 80 countries and territories.

Symbol: Five rings or circles, linked to represent the sporting friendship of all peoples. They also symbolize five geographic areas—Africa, America, Asia, Australia, and Europe. Each ring is a different color—blue, yellow, black, green, and red—which, with the color white, represent the colors of the world's flags.

Flag: The five-ring symbol on a plain white background.

Creed: "The most important thing in the Olympic Games is not to win but to take part, just as the most important thing in life is not the triumph but the struggle. The essential thing is not to have conquered but to have fought well."

Motto: Citius, Altius, Fortius. ("Faster, higher, stronger" in Latin)

Oath: "In the name of all the competitors I promise that we shall take part in these Olympic Games, respecting and abiding by the rules which govern them, committing ourselves to a sport without doping and without drugs, in the true spirit of sportsmanship, for the glory of sport and the honor of our teams."

Flame: The modern version of the flame was adopted in 1936. The torch used to kindle it is first lit by the sun's rays in Olympia, Greece, then carried to the site of the Games by relays of runners. Ships and planes are used when necessary.

Winter Olympic Games Sites, 1924-2022

1924 Chamonix, France
1928 St. Moritz, Switzerland
1932 Lake Placid, NY, U.S.
1936 Garmisch-Partenkirchen, Germany
1948 St. Moritz, Switzerland
1952 Oslo, Norway
1956 Cortina d'Ampezzo, Italy
1960 Squaw Valley, CA, U.S.
1964 Innsbruck, Austria
1968 Grenoble, France
1972 Sapporo, Japan
1976 Innsbruck, Austria
1980 Lake Placid, NY, U.S.
1984 Sarajevo, Yugoslavia
1988 Calgary, AB, Canada
1992 Albertville, France
1994 Lillehammer, Norway
1998 Nagano, Japan
2002 Salt Lake City, UT, U.S.
2006 Turin, Italy
2010 Vancouver, BC, Canada
2014 Sochi, Russia
2018 PyeongChang, South Korea
2022 Beijing, China

Summer Olympic Games Sites, 1896-2020

1896 Athens, Greece
1900 Paris, France
1904 St. Louis, MO, U.S.
1906 Athens, Greece*
1908 London, England, UK
1912 Stockholm, Sweden
1920 Antwerp, Belgium
1924 Paris, France
1928 Amsterdam, Netherlands
1932 Los Angeles, CA, U.S.
1936 Berlin, Germany
1948 London, England, UK
1952 Helsinki, Finland
1956 Melbourne, Australia
1960 Rome, Italy
1964 Tokyo, Japan
1968 Mexico City, Mexico
1972 Munich, W. Germany
1976 Montreal, QC, Canada
1980 Moscow, USSR
1984 Los Angeles, CA, U.S.
1988 Seoul, South Korea
1992 Barcelona, Spain
1996 Atlanta, GA, U.S.
2000 Sydney, Australia
2004 Athens, Greece
2008 Beijing, China
2012 London, England, UK
2016 Rio de Janeiro, Brazil
2020 Tokyo, Japan

*Games not recognized by International Olympic Committee. **Note:** Games VI (1916), XII (1940), and XIII (1944) were not celebrated.

2014 Winter Olympic Games

Sochi, Russia, Feb. 7-23, 2014

More than 2,800 athletes from 88 nations met in Sochi, Russia, to compete in a record 98 events in the XXII Olympic Winter Games Feb. 7-23, 2014. Host nation Russia won 33 medals, including 13 gold, to top the final medal count, followed by the United States, Norway, and Canada.

Meryl Davis and Charlie White became the first Americans ever to win gold in ice dancing, but the figure skating events were mostly dominated by Russia, which claimed gold in the women's, pairs, and team events. Russia's former Olympic champion Yevgeny Plushenko bowed out of the men's competition just before the short program, citing a back injury, and Yuzuru Hanyu of Japan won men's gold.

Eighteen-year-old American Mikaela Shiffrin became the youngest Olympian ever to win a gold medal in slalom. Canada won both ice hockey events, with the Canadian women defeating the U.S. in dramatic overtime fashion for the gold.

Twelve new medal events debuted at the Sochi Games, including a figure skating mixed team event, women's ski jumping, ski slopestyle and halfpipe, and snowboard slopestyle and parallel slalom.

2014 Winter Olympic Games: Final Medal Standings

Country	Gold	Silver	Bronze	Total
Russia	13	11	9	33
United States	9	7	12	28
Norway	11	5	10	26
Canada	10	10	5	25
Netherlands	8	7	9	24
Germany	8	6	5	19
Austria	4	8	5	17
France	4	4	7	15
Sweden	2	7	6	15
Switzerland	6	3	2	11
China	3	4	2	9
South Korea	3	3	2	8
Czech Republic	2	4	2	8
Slovenia	2	2	4	8
Japan	1	4	3	8
Italy	0	2	6	8
Belarus	5	0	1	6
Poland	4	1	1	6
Finland	1	3	1	5
Great Britain	1	1	2	4
Latvia	0	2	2	4
Australia	0	2	1	3
Ukraine	1	0	1	2
Slovakia	1	0	0	1
Croatia	0	1	0	1
Kazakhstan	0	0	1	1
Total	**99**	**97**	**99**	**295**

Winter Olympic Games Champions, 1924-2014

The 1980 games were boycotted by 62 nations, including the U.S. The 1984 games were boycotted by the USSR and most Eastern bloc nations. East and West Germany competed separately, 1968-88. In 1992, the Unified Team represented the former Soviet republics of Russia, Ukraine, Belarus, Kazakhstan, and Uzbekistan. Times are shown in hour:minute:sec.

Alpine Skiing

	Men's Downhill	Time
1948	Henri Oreiller, France	2:55.0
1952	Zeno Colo, Italy	2:30.8
1956	Toni Sailer, Austria	2:52.2
1960	Jean Vuarnet, France	2:06.0
1964	Egon Zimmermann, Austria	2:18.16
1968	Jean-Claude Killy, France	1:59.85
1972	Bernhard Russi, Switzerland	1:51.43
1976	Franz Klammer, Austria	1:45.73
1980	Leonhard Stock, Austria	1:45.50
1984	Bill Johnson, United States	1:45.49
1988	Pirmin Zurbriggen, Switzerland	1:59.63
1992	Patrick Ortlieb, Austria	1:50.37
1994	Tommy Moe, United States	1:45.75
1998	Jean-Luc Cretier, France	1:50.11
2002	Fritz Strobl, Austria	1:39.13
2006	Antoine Deneriaz, France	1:48.80
2010	Didier Defago, Switzerland	1:54.31
2014	Matthias Mayer, Austria	2:06.23

	Men's Giant Slalom	Time
1952	Stein Eriksen, Norway	2:25.0
1956	Toni Sailer, Austria	3:00.1
1960	Roger Staub, Switzerland	1:48.3
1964	Francois Bonlieu, France	1:46.71
1968	Jean-Claude Killy, France	3:29.28
1972	Gustavo Thoeni, Italy	3:09.62
1976	Heini Hemmi, Switzerland	3:26.97
1980	Ingemar Stenmark, Sweden	2:40.74
1984	Max Julen, Switzerland	2:41.18
1988	Alberto Tomba, Italy	2:06.37
1992	Alberto Tomba, Italy	2:06.98
1994	Markus Wasmeier, Germany	2:52.46
1998	Hermann Maier, Austria	2:38.51
2002	Stephan Eberharter, Austria	2:23.28
2006	Benjamin Raich, Austria	2:35.00
2010	Carlo Janka, Switzerland	2:37.83
2014	Ted Ligety, United States	2:45.29

	Men's Slalom	Time
1948	Edi Reinalter, Switzerland	2:10.3
1952	Othmar Schneider, Austria	2:00.0
1956	Toni Sailer, Austria	3:14.7
1960	Ernst Hinterseer, Austria	2:08.9
1964	Josef Stiegler, Austria	2:11.13
1968	Jean-Claude Killy, France	1:39.73
1972	Francisco Fernandez-Ochoa, Spain	1:49.27
1976	Piero Gros, Italy	2:03.29
1980	Ingemar Stenmark, Sweden	1:44.26
1984	Phil Mahre, United States	1:39.41
1988	Alberto Tomba, Italy	1:39.47
1992	Finn Christian Jagge, Norway	1:44.39
1994	Thomas Stangassinger, Austria	2:02.02
1998	Hans-Petter Buraas, Norway	1:49.31
2002	Jean-Pierre Vidal, France	1:41.06
2006	Benjamin Raich, Austria	1:43.14
2010	Giuliano Razzoli, Italy	1:39.32
2014	Mario Matt, Austria	1:41.84

	Men's Super Combined	Time
1936	Franz-Pfnuer, Germany	99.25 (pts.)
1948	Henri Oreiller, France	3.27 (pts.)
1988	Hubert Strolz, Austria	36.55 (pts.)
1992	Josef Polig, Italy	14.58 (pts.)
1994	Lasse Kjus, Norway	3:17.53
1998	Mario Reiter, Austria	3:08.06
2002	Kjetil Andre Aamodt, Norway	3:17.56
2006	Ted Ligety, United States	3:09.35
2010	Bode Miller, United States	2:44.92
2014	Sandro Viletta, Switzerland	2:45.20

Note: In 2010, a one-day super combined event replaced the traditional two-day combined event.

	Men's Super Giant Slalom	Time
1988	Franck Piccard, France	1:39.66
1992	Kjetil Andre Aamodt, Norway	1:13.04
1994	Markus Wasmeier, Germany	1:32.53
1998	Hermann Maier, Austria	1:34.82
2002	Kjetil Andre Aamodt, Norway	1:21.58
2006	Kjetil Andre Aamodt, Norway	1:30.65
2010	Aksel Lund Svindal, Norway	1:30.34
2014	Kjetil Jansrud, Norway	1:18.14

	Women's Downhill	Time
1948	Hedi Schlunegger, Switzerland	2:28.3
1952	Trude Beiser-Jochum, Austria	1:47.1
1956	Madeleine Berthod, Switzerland	1:40.7
1960	Heidi Biebl, Germany	1:37.6
1964	Christl Haas, Austria	1:55.39
1968	Olga Pall, Austria	1:40.87
1972	Marie-Theres Nadig, Switzerland	1:36.68
1976	Rosi Mittermaier, W. Germany	1:46.16
1980	Annemarie Moser-Proell, Austria	1:37.52
1984	Michela Figini, Switzerland	1:13.36
1988	Marina Kiehl, W. Germany	1:25.86
1992	Kerrin Lee-Gartner, Canada	1:52.55
1994	Katja Seizinger, Germany	1:35.93
1998	Katja Seizinger, Germany	1:28.89
2002	Carole Montillet, France	1:39.56
2006	Michaela Dorfmeister, Austria	1:56.49
2010	Lindsey Vonn, United States	1:44.19
2014	Tina Maze, Slovenia	1:41.57
	Dominique Gisin, Switzerland (tie)	1:41.57

	Women's Giant Slalom[1]	Time
1952	Andrea Mead Lawrence, United States	2:06.8
1956	Ossi Reichert, Germany	1:56.5
1960	Yvonne Ruegg, Switzerland	1:39.9
1964	Marielle Goitschel, France	1:52.24
1968	Nancy Greene, Canada	1:51.97
1972	Marie-Theres Nadig, Switzerland	1:29.90
1976	Kathy Kreiner, Canada	1:29.13
1980	Hanni Wenzel, Liechtenstein	2:41.66
1984	Debbie Armstrong, United States	2:20.98
1988	Vreni Schneider, Switzerland	2:06.49
1992	Pernilla Wiberg, Sweden	2:12.74
1994	Deborah Compagnoni, Italy	2:30.97
1998	Deborah Compagnoni, Italy	2:50.59
2002	Janica Kostelic, Croatia	2:30.01
2006	Julia Mancuso, United States	2:09.19
2010	Viktoria Rebensburg, Germany	2:27.11
2014	Tina Maze, Slovenia	2:36.87

(1) Beginning in 1980, the event time combined two runs.

	Women's Slalom	Time
1948	Gretchen Fraser, United States	1:57.2
1952	Andrea Mead Lawrence, United States	2:10.6
1956	Renee Colliard, Switzerland	1:52.3
1960	Anne Heggtveit, Canada	1:49.6
1964	Christine Goitschel, France	1:29.86
1968	Marielle Goitschel, France	1:25.86
1972	Barbara Ann Cochran, United States	1:31.24
1976	Rosi Mittermaier, W. Germany	1:30.54
1980	Hanni Wenzel, Liechtenstein	1:25.09
1984	Paoletta Magoni, Italy	1:36.47
1988	Vreni Schneider, Switzerland	1:36.69
1992	Petra Kronberger, Austria	1:32.68
1994	Vreni Schneider, Switzerland	1:56.01
1998	Hilde Gerg, Germany	1:32.40
2002	Janica Kostelic, Croatia	1:46.10
2006	Anja Paerson, Sweden	1:29.04
2010	Maria Riesch, Germany	1:42.89
2014	Mikaela Shiffrin, United States	1:44.54

	Women's Super Combined	Time
1936	Christl Cranz, Germany	97.06 (pts.)
1948	Trude Beiser-Jochum, Austria	6.58 (pts.)
1988	Anita Wachter, Austria	29.25 (pts.)
1992	Petra Kronberger, Austria	2.55 (pts.)
1994	Pernilla Wiberg, Sweden	3:05.16
1998	Katja Seizinger, Germany	2:40.74
2002	Janica Kostelic, Croatia	2:43.28
2006	Janica Kostelic, Croatia	2:51.08
2010	Maria Riesch, Germany	2:09.14
2014	Maria Hoefl-Riesch, Germany	2:34.62

Note: In 2010, a one-day super combined event replaced the traditional two-day combined event.

	Women's Super Giant Slalom	Time
1988	Sigrid Wolf, Austria	1:19.03
1992	Deborah Compagnoni, Italy	1:21.22
1994	Diann Roffe (Steinrotter), United States	1:22.15
1998	Picabo Street, United States	1:18.02
2002	Daniela Ceccarelli, Italy	1:13.59
2006	Michaela Dorfmeister, Austria	1:32.47
2010	Andrea Fischbacher, Austria	1:20.14
2014	Anna Fenninger, Austria	1:25.52

Biathlon

	Mixed 2x6-Kilometer and 2x7.5-Kilometer Relay	Time
2014	Norway, Czech Republic, Italy	1:09:17.0

	Men's 10-Kilometer Sprint	Time
1980	Frank Ullrich, E. Germany	32:10.69
1984	Eirik Kvalfoss, Norway	30:53.80
1988	Frank-Peter Roetsch, E. Germany	25:08.10
1992	Mark Kirchner, Germany	26:02.30
1994	Serguei Tchepikov, Russia	28:07.00
1998	Ole Einar Bjoerndalen, Norway	27:16.20
2002	Ole Einar Bjoerndalen, Norway	24:51.30
2006	Sven Fischer, Germany	26:11.6
2010	Vincent Jay, France	24:07.8
2014	Ole Einar Bjoerndalen, Norway	24:33.5

	Men's 12.5-Kilometer Pursuit	Time
2002	Ole Einar Bjoerndalen, Norway	32:34.6
2006	Vincent Defrasne, France	35:20.2
2010	Bjorn Ferry, Sweden	33:38.4
2014	Martin Fourcade, France	33:48.6

	Men's 15-Kilometer Mass Start	Time
2006	Michael Greis, Germany	47:20.0
2010	Evgeny Ustyugov, Russia	35.35.7
2014	Emil Hegle Svendsen, Norway	42:29.1

	Men's 20-Kilometer Individual	Time
1960	Klas Lestander, Sweden	1:33:21.6
1964	Vladimir Melanin, USSR	1:20:26.8
1968	Magnar Solberg, Norway	1:13:45.9
1972	Magnar Solberg, Norway	1:15:55.50
1976	Nikolai Kruglov, USSR	1:14:12.26
1980	Anatoly Aljabiev, USSR	1:08:16.31
1984	Peter Angerer, W. Germany	1:11:52.7
1988	Frank-Peter Roetsch, E. Germany	0:56:33.33
1992	Yevgeny Redkine, Unified Team	0:57:34.4
1994	Serguei Tarasov, Russia	0:57:25.3
1998	Halvard Hanevold, Norway	0:56:16.4
2002	Ole Einar Bjoerndalen, Norway	0:51:03.03
2006	Michael Greis, Germany	0:54:23.0
2010	Emil Hegle Svendsen, Norway	0:48:22.5
2014	Martin Fourcade, France	0:49:31.7

	Men's 4x7.5-Kilometer Relay	Time
1968	USSR, Norway, Sweden (40 km)	2:13:02.4
1972	USSR, Finland, E. Germany (40 km)	1:51:44.92
1976	USSR, Finland, E. Germany (40 km)	1:57:55.64
1980	USSR, E. Germany, W. Germany	1:34:03.27
1984	USSR, Norway, W. Germany	1:38:51.70
1988	USSR, W. Germany, Italy	1:22:30.00
1992	Germany, Unified Team, Sweden	1:24:43.50
1994	Germany, Russia, France	1:30:22.1
1998	Germany, Norway, Russia	1:19:43.3
2002	Norway, Germany, France	1:23:42.3
2006	Germany, Russia, France	1:21:51.5
2010	Norway, Austria, Russia	1:21:38.1
2014	Russia, Germany, Austria	1:12:15.9

	Women's 7.5-Kilometer Sprint	Time
1992	Anfissa Restsova, Unified Team	24:29.2
1994	Myriam Bedard, Canada	26:08.8
1998	Galina Koukleva, Russia	23:08.0
2002	Kati Wilhelm, Germany	20:41.4
2006	Florence Baverel-Robert, France	22:31.4
2010	Anastasiya Kuzmina, Slovakia	19:55.6
2014	Anastasiya Kuzmina, Slovakia	21:06.8

	Women's 10-Kilometer Pursuit	Time
2002	Olga Pyleva, Russia	31:07.7
2006	Kati Wilhelm, Germany	36:43.6
2010	Magdalena Neuner, Germany	30:16.0
2014	Darya Domracheva, Belarus	29:30.7

	Women's 12.5-Kilometer Mass Start	Time
2006	Anna Carin Olofsson, Sweden	40:36.5
2010	Magdalena Neuner, Germany	35:19.6
2014	Darya Domracheva, Belarus	35:25.6

	Women's 15-Kilometer Individual	Time
1992	Antje Misersky, Germany	51:47.2
1994	Myriam Bedard, Canada	52:06.6
1998	Ekaterina Dafovska, Bulgaria	54:52.0
2002	Andrea Henkel, Germany	47:30.0
2006	Svetlana Ishmouratova, Russia	49:24.1
2010	Tora Berger, Norway	40:52.8
2014	Darya Domracheva, Belarus	43:19.6

	Women's 4x6-Kilometer Relay	Time
1992	France, Germany, Unified Team (22.5 km)	1:15:55.6
1994	Russia, Germany, France (30 km)	1:47:19.5
1998	Germany, Russia, Norway (30 km)	1:40:13.6
2002	Germany, Norway, Russia (30 km)	1:27:55.0
2006	Russia, Germany, France	1:16:12.5
2010	Russia, France, Germany	1:09:36.3
2014	Ukraine, Russia, Norway	1:10:02.5

Bobsledding

(Driver in parentheses.)

	2-Man Bobsled	Time
1932	United States (Hubert Stevens)	8:14.74
1936	United States (Ivan Brown)	5:29.29
1948	Switzerland (Felix Endrich)	5:29.20
1952	Germany (Andreas Ostler)	5:24.54
1956	Italy (Dalla Costa)	5:30.14
1964	Great Britain (Anthony Nash)	4:21.90
1968	Italy (Eugenio Monti)	4:41.54
1972	W. Germany (Wolfgang Zimmerer)	4:57.07
1976	E. Germany (Meinhard Nehmer)	3:44.42
1980	Switzerland (Erich Schaerer)	4:09.36
1984	E. Germany (Wolfgang Hoppe)	3:25.56
1988	USSR (Janis Kipours)	3:54.19
1992	Switzerland (Gustav Weber)	4:03.26
1994	Switzerland (Gustav Weber)	3:30.81
1998	Canada (Pierre Lueders)	3:37.24
	Italy (Guenther Huber) (tie)	3:37.24
2002	Germany II (Christoph Langen)	3:10.11
2006	Germany (Andre Lange)	3:43.38
2010	Germany (Andre Lange)	3:26.65
2014	Russia (Alexander Zubkov)	3:45.39

	4-Man Bobsled	Time
1924	Switzerland (Eduard Scherrer)	5:45.54
1928	United States (William Fiske) (5-man)	3:20.50
1932	United States (William Fiske)	7:53.68
1936	Switzerland (Pierre Musy)	5:19.85
1948	United States (Francis Tyler)	5:20.10
1952	Germany (Andreas Ostler)	5:07.84
1956	Switzerland (Franz Kapus)	5:10.44
1964	Canada (Victor Emery)	4:14.46
1968	Italy (Eugenio Monti) (2 heats)	2:17.39
1972	Switzerland (Jean Wicki)	4:43.07
1976	E. Germany (Meinhard Nehmer)	3:40.43
1980	E. Germany (Meinhard Nehmer)	3:59.92
1984	E. Germany (Wolfgang Hoppe)	3:20.22
1988	Switzerland (Ekkehard Fasser)	3:47.51
1992	Austria (Ingo Appelt)	3:53.90
1994	Germany (Wolfgang Hoppe)	3:27.28
1998	Germany II (Christoph Langen)	2:39.41
2002	Germany II (Andre Lange)	3:07.51
2006	Germany (Andre Lange)	3:40.42
2010	United States (Steven Holcomb)	3:24.46
2014	Russia (Alexander Zubkov)	3:40.60

	2-Woman Bobsled	Time
2002	United States II (Jill Bakken)	1:37.76
2006	Germany (Sandra Kiriasis)	3:49.98
2010	Canada (Kaillie Humphries)	3:32.28
2014	Canada (Kaillie Humphries)	3:50.61

Cross-Country Skiing

	Men's Individual Sprint	Time
2002	Tor Arne Hetland, Norway (1.5 km)	2:56.9
2006	Bjoern Lind, Sweden (1.3 km)	2:26.5
2010	Nikita Kriukov, Russia	3:36.3
2014	Ola Vigen Hattestad, Norway	3:38.39

Men's 10 Kilometers		Time
1992	Vegard Ulvang, Norway	27:36.0
1994	Bjoern Daehlie, Norway	24:20.1
1998	Bjoern Daehlie, Norway	27:24.5
2002	Thomas Alsgaard, Norway	49:48.9
	Frode Estil, Norway (tie)[1]	49:48.9

(1) Both awarded gold after Johann Muehlegg of Spain was stripped of gold for a drug offense.

Men's 15 Kilometers		Time
1924	Thorleif Haug, Norway	1:14:31
1928	Johan Grottumsbraaten, Norway	1:37:01
1932	Sven Utterstrom, Sweden	1:23:07
1936	Erik-August Larsson, Sweden	1:14:38
1948	Martin Lundstrom, Sweden	1:13:50
1952	Hallgeir Brenden, Norway	1:01:34
1956	Hallgeir Brenden, Norway	0:49:39.0
1960	Haakon Brusveen, Norway	0:51:55.5
1964	Eero Maentyranta, Finland	0:50:54.1
1968	Harald Groenningen, Norway	0:47:54.2
1972	Sven-Ake Lundback, Sweden	0:45:28.24
1976	Nikolai Balukov, USSR	0:43:58.47
1980	Thomas Wassberg, Sweden	0:41:57.63
1984	Gunde Svan, Sweden	0:41:25.6
1988	Mikhail Deviatiarov, USSR	0:41:18.9
1992	Bjoern Daehlie, Norway	0:38:01.9
1994	Bjoern Daehlie, Norway	0:35:48.8
1998	Thomas Alsgaard, Norway	1:07:01.7
2002	Andrus Veerpalu, Estonia	0:37:07.4
2006	Andrus Veerpalu, Estonia	0:38:01.3
2010	Dario Cologna, Switzerland	0:33:36.3
2014	Dario Cologna, Switzerland	0:38:29.7

Note: Approx. 18-km course 1924-52.

Men's 30-Kilometer Pursuit		Time
1956	Veikko Hakulinen, Finland	1:44:06.0
1964	Eero Maentyranta, Finland	1:30:50.7
1968	Franco Nones, Italy	1:35:39.2
1972	Vyacheslav Vedenine, USSR	1:36:31.15
1976	Sergei Saveliev, USSR	1:30:29.38
1980	Nikolai Zimyatov, USSR	1:27:02.80
1984	Nikolai Zimyatov, USSR	1:28:56.3
1988	Aleksei Prokourorov, USSR	1:24:26.3
1992	Vegard Ulvang, Norway	1:22:27.8
1994	Thomas Alsgaard, Norway	1:12:26.4
1998	Mika Myllylae, Finland	1:33:55.8
2002	Christian Hoffmann, Austria[1]	1:11:31.0
2006	Eugeni Dementiev, Russia	1:17:00.8
2010	Marcus Hellner, Sweden	1:15:11.4

(1) Awarded gold after Johann Muehlegg of Spain was stripped of gold for a drug offense.

Men's Skiathlon		Time
2014	Dario Cologna, Switzerland	1:08:15.4

Men's 50-Kilometer Mass Start		Time
1924	Thorleif Haug, Norway	3:44:32.0
1928	Per Erik Hedlund, Sweden	4:52:03.0
1932	Veli Saarinen, Finland	4:28:00.0
1936	Elis Wiklund, Sweden	3:30:11.0
1948	Nils Karlsson, Sweden	3:47:48.0
1952	Veikko Hakulinen, Finland	3:33:33.0
1956	Sixten Jernberg, Sweden	2:50:27.0
1960	Kalevi Hamalainen, Finland	2:59:06.3
1964	Sixten Jernberg, Sweden	2:43:52.6
1968	Ole Ellefsaeter, Norway	2:28:45.8
1972	Paal Tyldum, Norway	2:43:14.75
1976	Ivar Formo, Norway	2:37:30.05
1980	Nikolai Zimyatov, USSR	2:27:24.60
1984	Thomas Wassberg, Sweden	2:15:55.8
1988	Gunde Svan, Sweden	2:04:30.9
1992	Bjoern Daehlie, Norway	2:03:41.5
1994	Vladimir Smirnov, Kazakhstan	2:07:20.3
1998	Bjoern Daehlie, Norway	2:05:08.2
2002	Mikhail Ivanov, Russia	2:06:20.8
2006	Giorgio di Centa, Italy	2:06:11.8
2010	Petter Northug, Norway	2:05:35.5
2014	Alexander Legkov, Russia	1:46:55.2

Men's 4x10-Kilometer Relay		Time
1936	Finland, Norway, Sweden	2:41:33.0
1948	Sweden, Finland, Norway	2:32:08.0
1952	Finland, Norway, Sweden	2:20:16.0
1956	USSR, Finland, Sweden	2:15:30.0
1960	Finland, Norway, USSR	2:18:45.6
1964	Sweden, Finland, USSR	2:18:34.6
1968	Norway, Sweden, Finland	2:08:33.5
1972	USSR, Norway, Switzerland	2:04:47.94
1976	Finland, Norway, USSR	2:07:59.72
1980	USSR, Norway, Finland	1:57:03.46
1984	Sweden, USSR, Finland	1:55:06.30
1988	Sweden, USSR, Czechoslovakia	1:43:58.60
1992	Norway, Italy, Finland	1:39:26.00
1994	Italy, Norway, Finland	1:41:15.00
1998	Norway, Italy, Finland	1:40:55.70
2002	Norway, Italy, Germany	1:32:45.5
2006	Italy, Germany, Sweden	1:43:45.7
2010	Sweden, Norway, Czech Republic	1:45:05.4
2014	Sweden, Russia, France	1:28:42.0

Men's Team Sprint		Time
2006	Bjoern Lind & Thobias Fredriksson, Sweden	17:02.9
2010	Oeystein Pettersen & Petter Northug, Norway	19:01.0
2014	Sami Jauhojaervi & Iivo Niskanen, Finland	23:14.89

Women's Individual Sprint		Time
2002	Julia Tchepalova, Russia (1.5 km)	3:10.6
2006	Chandra Crawford, Canada (1.1 km)	2:12.3
2010	Marit Bjoergen, Norway	3:39.2
2014	Maiken Caspersen Falla, Norway	2:35.49

Women's 5 Kilometers		Time
1964	Claudia Boyarskikh, USSR	17:50.5
1968	Toini Gustafsson, Sweden	16:45.2
1972	Galina Koulacova, USSR	17:00.50
1976	Helena Takalo, Finland	15:48.69
1980	Raisa Smetanina, USSR	15:06.92
1984	Marja-Liisa Haemaelainen, Finland	17:04.0
1988	Marjo Matikainen, Finland	15:04.0
1992	Marjut Lukkarinen, Finland	14:13.8
1994	Ljubov Egorova, Russia	14:08.8
1998	Larissa Lazutina, Russia	17:37.9
2002	Beckie Scott, Canada[1]	25:09.9

(1) Awarded gold after Olga Danilova of Russia was stripped of gold and Larissa Lazutina of Russia was stripped of silver for drug offenses.

Women's 10 Kilometers		Time
1952	Lydia Wideman, Finland	41:40.0
1956	Lyubov Kosyreva, USSR	38:11.0
1960	Maria Gusakova, USSR	39:46.6
1964	Claudia Boyarskikh, USSR	40:24.3
1968	Toini Gustafsson, Sweden	36:46.5
1972	Galina Koulacova, USSR	34:17.82
1976	Raisa Smetanina, USSR	30:13.41
1980	Barbara Petzold, E. Germany	30:31.54
1984	Marja-Liisa Haemaelainen, Finland	31:44.2
1988	Vida Ventsene, USSR	30:08.3
1992	Lyubov Egorova, Unified Team	25:53.7
1994	Lyubov Egorova, Russia	27:30.1
1998	Larissa Lazutina, Russia	46.06.9
2002	Bente Skari, Norway	28:05.6
2006	Kristina Smigun, Estonia	27:51.4
2010	Charlotte Kalla, Sweden	24:58.4
2014	Justyna Kowalczyk, Poland	28:17.8

Women's 15-Kilometer Pursuit		Time
1992	Lyubov Egorova, Unified Team	42:20.8
1994	Manuela Di Centa, Italy	39:44.5
1998	Olga Danilova, Russia	46:55.4
2002	Stefania Belmondo, Italy	39:54.4
2006	Kristina Smigun, Estonia	42:48.7
2010	Marit Bjoergen, Norway	39:58.1

Women's Skiathlon		Time
2014	Marit Bjoergen, Norway	38:33.6

Women's 30-Kilometer Mass Start		Time
1992	Stefania Belmondo, Italy	1:22:30.1
1994	Manuela Di Centa, Italy	1:25:41.6
1998	Julija Tchepalova, Russia	1:22:01.5
2002	Gabriella Paruzzi, Italy	1:30:57.1
2006	Katerina Neumannova, Czech Republic	1:22:25.4
2010	Justyna Kowalczyk, Poland	1:30:33.7
2014	Marit Bjoergen, Norway	1:11:05.2

Women's 4x5-Kilometer Relay

		Time
1956	Finland, USSR, Sweden (15 km)	1:09:01.0
1960	Sweden, USSR, Finland (15 km)	1:04:21.4
1964	USSR, Sweden, Finland (15 km)	0:59:20.2
1968	Norway, Sweden, USSR (15 km)	0:57:30.0
1972	USSR, Finland, Norway (15 km)	0:48:46.15
1976	USSR, Finland, E. Germany	1:07:49.75
1980	E. Germany, USSR, Norway	1:02:11.1
1984	Norway, Czechoslovakia, Finland	1:06:49.7
1988	USSR, Norway, Finland	0:59:51.1
1992	United Team, Norway, Italy	0:59:34.8
1994	Russia, Norway, Italy	0:57:12.5
1998	Russia, Norway, Italy	0:55:13.5
2002	Germany, Norway, Switzerland	0:49:30.6
2006	Russia, Germany, Italy	0:54:47.7
2010	Norway, Germany, Finland	0:55:19.5
2014	Sweden, Finland, Germany	0:53:02.7

Women's Team Sprint

		Time
2006	Lina Andersson & Anna Dahlberg, Sweden	16:36.9
2010	Evi Sachenbacher-Stehle & Claudia Nystad, Germany	18:03.7
2014	Marit Bjoergen & Ingvild Flugstad Oestberg, Norway	16:04.05

Curling

Men

1998 Switzerland, Canada, Norway
2002 Norway, Canada, Switzerland
2006 Canada, Finland, United States
2010 Canada, Norway, Switzerland
2014 Canada, Great Britain, Sweden

Women

1998 Canada, Denmark, Sweden
2002 Britain, Switzerland, Canada
2006 Sweden, Switzerland, Canada
2010 Sweden, Canada, China
2014 Canada, Sweden, Great Britain

Figure Skating

Men's Singles

1908[1] Ulrich Salchow, Sweden
1920[1] Gillis Grafstrom, Sweden
1924 Gillis Grafstrom, Sweden
1928 Gillis Grafstrom, Sweden
1932 Karl Schaefer, Austria
1936 Karl Schaefer, Austria
1948 Richard Button, United States
1952 Richard Button, United States
1956 Hayes Alan Jenkins, United States
1960 David W. Jenkins, United States
1964 Manfred Schnelldorfer, Germany
1968 Wolfgang Schwartz, Austria
1972 Ondrej Nepela, Czechoslovakia
1976 John Curry, Great Britain
1980 Robin Cousins, Great Britain
1984 Scott Hamilton, United States
1988 Brian Boitano, United States
1992 Viktor Petrenko, Unified Team
1994 Aleksei Urmanov, Russia
1998 Ilya Kulik, Russia
2002 Alexei Yagudin, Russia
2006 Yevgeny Plushenko, Russia
2010 Evan Lysacek, United States
2014 Yuzuru Hanyu, Japan
(1) Event held during Summer Olympic Games.

Women's Singles

1908[1] Madge Syers, Great Britain
1920[1] Magda Julin-Mauroy, Sweden
1924 Herma von Szabo-Planck, Austria
1928 Sonja Henie, Norway
1932 Sonja Henie, Norway
1936 Sonja Henie, Norway
1948 Barbara Ann Scott, Canada
1952 Jeanette Altwegg, Great Britain
1956 Tenley Albright, United States
1960 Carol Heiss, United States
1964 Sjoukje Dijkstra, Netherlands
1968 Peggy Fleming, United States
1972 Beatrix Schuba, Austria
1976 Dorothy Hamill, United States
1980 Anett Poetzsch, E. Germany
1984 Katarina Witt, E. Germany
1988 Katarina Witt, E. Germany
1992 Kristi Yamaguchi, United States
1994 Oksana Baiul, Ukraine
1998 Tara Lipinski, United States
2002 Sarah Hughes, United States
2006 Shizuka Arakawa, Japan
2010 Kim Yu-Na, South Korea
2014 Adelina Sotnikova, Russia
(1) Event held during Summer Olympic Games.

Pairs

1908[1] Anna Hubler & Heinrich Burger, Germany
1920[1] Ludovika Jakobsson & Walter Jakobsson, Finland
1924 Helene Engelman & Alfred Berger, Austria
1928 Andree Joly & Pierre Brunet, France
1932 Andree Joly & Pierre Brunet, France
1936 Maxi Herber & Ernst Baier, Germany
1948 Micheline Lannoy & Pierre Baugniet, Belgium
1952 Ria Falk & Paul Falk, Germany
1956 Elisabeth Schwartz & Kurt Oppelt, Austria
1964 Ludmila Beloussova & Oleg Protopopov, USSR
1968 Ludmila Beloussova & Oleg Protopopov, USSR
1972 Irina Rodnina & Alexei Ulanov, USSR
1976 Irina Rodnina & Aleksandr Zaitzev, USSR
1980 Irina Rodnina & Aleksandr Zaitzev, USSR
1984 Elena Valova & Oleg Vassiliev, USSR
1988 Ekaterina Gordeeva & Sergei Grinkov, USSR
1992 Natalia Mishkutienok & Artur Dimitriev, Unified Team
1994 Ekaterina Gordeeva & Sergei Grinkov, Russia
1998 Oksana Kazakova & Artur Dmitriev, Russia
2002 Elena Berezhnaya & Anton Sikharulidze, Russia; Jamie Sale & David Pelletier, Canada (tie)
2006 Tatyana Totmianina & Maxim Marinin, Russia
2010 Shen Xue & Zhao Hongbo, China
2014 Tatiana Volosozhar & Maxim Trankov, Russia
(1) Event held during Summer Olympic Games.

Ice Dancing

1976 Ludmila Pakhomova & Aleksandr Gorschkov, USSR
1980 Natalya Linichuk & Gennadi Karponosov, USSR
1984 Jayne Torvill & Christopher Dean, Great Britain
1988 Natalia Bestemianova & Andrei Bukin, USSR
1992 Marina Klimova & Sergei Ponomarenko, Unified Team
1994 Pasha Grishuk & Evgeny Platov, Russia
1998 Pasha Grishuk & Evgeny Platov, Russia
2002 Marina Anissina & Gwendal Peizerat, France
2006 Tatyana Navka & Roman Kostomarov, Russia
2010 Tessa Virtue & Scott Moir, Canada
2014 Meryl Davis & Charlie White, United States

Mixed Team

2014 Russia, Canada, United States

Freestyle Skiing

Men's Aerials

		Points
1994	Andreas Schoenbaechler, Switzerland	234.67
1998	Eric Bergoust, United States	255.64
2002	Ales Valenta, Czech Republic	257.02
2006	Xiaopeng Han, China	250.77
2010	Alexei Grishin, Belarus	248.41
2014	Anton Kushnir, Belarus	134.50

Men's Moguls

		Points
1992	Edgar Grospiron, France	25.81
1994	Jean-Luc Brassard, Canada	27.24
1998	Jonny Moseley, United States	26.93
2002	Janne Lahtela, Finland	27.97
2006	Dale Begg-Smith, Australia	26.77
2010	Alex Bilodeau, Canada	26.75
2014	Alex Bilodeau, Canada	26.31

Men's Ski Cross

2010 Michael Schmid, Switzerland
2014 Jean Frederic Chapuis, France

Men's Ski Halfpipe

		Points
2014	David Wise, United States	92.00

Men's Ski Slopestyle

		Points
2014	Joss Christensen, United States	95.80

Women's Aerials		Points
1994	Lina Tcherjazova, Uzbekistan	166.84
1998	Nikki Stone, United States	193.00
2002	Alisa Camplin, Australia	193.47
2006	Evelyne Leu, Switzerland	202.55
2010	Lydia Lassila, Australia	214.74
2014	Alla Tsuper, Belarus	98.01

Women's Moguls		Points
1992	Donna Weinbrecht, United States	23.69
1994	Stine Lise Hattestad, Norway	25.97
1998	Tae Satoya, Japan	25.06
2002	Kari Traa, Norway	25.94
2006	Jennifer Heil, Canada	26.50
2010	Hannah Kearney, United States	26.63
2014	Justine Dufour-Lapointe, Canada	22.44

Women's Ski Cross

2010 Ashleigh McIvor, Canada
2014 Marielle Thompson, Canada

Women's Ski Halfpipe		Points
2014	Maddie Bowman, United States	89.00

Women's Ski Slopestyle		Points
2014	Dara Howell, Canada	94.20

Ice Hockey

Men

1920[1] Canada, United States, Czechoslovakia
1924 Canada, United States, Great Britain
1928 Canada, Sweden, Switzerland
1932 Canada, United States, Germany
1936 Great Britain, Canada, United States
1948 Canada, Czechoslovakia, Switzerland
1952 Canada, United States, Sweden
1956 USSR, United States, Canada
1960 United States, Canada, USSR
1964 USSR, Sweden, Czechoslovakia
1968 USSR, Czechoslovakia, Canada
1972 USSR, United States, Czechoslovakia
1976 USSR, Czechoslovakia, W. Germany
1980 United States, USSR, Sweden
1984 USSR, Czechoslovakia, Sweden
1988 USSR, Finland, Sweden
1992 Unified Team, Canada, Czechoslovakia
1994 Sweden, Canada, Finland
1998 Czech Republic, Russia, Finland
2002 Canada, United States, Russia
2006 Sweden, Finland, Czech Republic
2010 Canada, United States, Finland
2014 Canada, Sweden, Finland

(1) Event held during Summer Olympic Games.

Women

1998 United States, Canada, Finland
2002 Canada, United States, Sweden
2006 Canada, Sweden, United States
2010 Canada, United States, Finland
2014 Canada, United States, Switzerland

Luge

Men's Singles		Time
1964	Thomas Keohler, E. Germany	3:27.77
1968	Manfred Schmid, Austria	2:52.48
1972	Wolfgang Scheidel, E. Germany	3:27.58
1976	Detlef Guenther, E. Germany	3:27.688
1980	Bernhard Glass, E. Germany	2:54.796
1984	Paul Hildgartner, Italy	3:04.258
1988	Jens Mueller, E. Germany	3:05.548
1992	Georg Hackl, Germany	3:02.363
1994	Georg Hackl, Germany	3:21.571
1998	Georg Hackl, Germany	3:18.436
2002	Armin Zoeggeler, Italy	2:57.941
2006	Armin Zoeggeler, Italy	3:26.088
2010	Felix Loch, Germany	3:13.085
2014	Felix Loch, Germany	3:27.526

Men's Doubles		Time
1964	Austria	1:41.62
1968	E. Germany	1:35.85
1972	Italy, E. Germany (tie)	1:28.35
1976	E. Germany	1:25.604
1980	E. Germany	1:19.331
1984	W. Germany	1:23.620
1988	E. Germany	1:31.940
1992	Germany	1:32.053
1994	Italy	1:36.720
1998	Germany	1:41.105
2002	Germany	1:26.082
2006	Austria	1:34.497
2010	Austria	1:22.705
2014	Germany	1:38.933

Women's Singles		Time
1964	Ortun Enderlein, Germany	3:24.67
1968	Erica Lechner, Italy	2:28.66
1972	Anna M. Muller, E. Germany	2:59.18
1976	Margit Schumann, E. Germany	2:50.621
1980	Vera Zozulya, USSR	2:36.537
1984	Steffi Martin, E. Germany	2:46.570
1988	Steffi Walter, E. Germany	3:03.973
1992	Doris Neuner, Austria	3:06.696
1994	Gerda Weissensteiner, Italy	3:15.517
1998	Silke Kraushaar, Germany	3:23.779
2002	Sylke Otto, Germany	2:52.464
2006	Sylke Otto, Germany	3:07.979
2010	Tatjana Huefner, Germany	2:46.524
2014	Natalie Geisenberger, Germany	3:19.768

Mixed Team Relay		Time
2014	Germany, Russia, Latvia	2:45.649

Nordic Combined

Men's Individual

1924 Thorleif Haug, Norway
1928 Johan Grottumsbraaten, Norway
1932 Johan Grottumsbraaten, Norway
1936 Oddbjorn Hagen, Norway
1948 Heikki Hasu, Finland
1952 Simon Slattvik, Norway
1956 Sverre Stenersen, Norway
1960 Georg Thoma, W. Germany
1964 Tormod Knutsen, Norway
1968 Franz Keller, W. Germany
1972 Ulrich Wehling, E. Germany
1976 Ulrich Wehling, E. Germany
1980 Ulrich Wehling, E. Germany
1984 Tom Sandberg, Norway
1988 Hippolyt Kempf, Switzerland
1992 Fabrice Guy, France
1994 Fred Barre Lundberg, Norway
1998 Bjarte Engen Vik, Norway
2002 Samppa Lajunen, Finland
2006 Georg Hettich, Germany

Men's 10-Kilometer Large Hill

2010 Bill Demong, United States
2014 Joergen Graabak, Norway

Men's 10-Kilometer Normal Hill

2010 Jason Lamy Chappuis, France
2014 Eric Frenzel, Germany

Men's Team 4x5-Kilometer Relay

1988 W. Germany, Switzerland, Austria
1992 Japan, Norway, Austria
1994 Japan, Norway, Switzerland
1998 Norway, Finland, France
2002 Finland, Germany, Austria
2006 Austria, Germany, Finland
2010 Austria, United States, Germany
2014 Norway, Germany, Austria

Skeleton

Men		Time
1928	Jennison Heaton, United States	3:01.8
1948	Nino Bibbia, Italy	5:23.2
2002	Jim Shea, United States	1:41.96
2006	Duff Gibson, Canada	1:55.88
2010	Jon Montgomery, Canada	3:29.73
2014	Alexander Tretiakov, Russia	3:44.29

Women		Time
2002	Tristan Gale, United States	1:45.11
2006	Maya Pedersen, Switzerland	1:59.83
2010	Amy Williams, Great Britain	3:35.64
2014	Elizabeth Yarnold, Great Britain	3:52.89

Ski Jumping

	Men's Normal Hill	Points
1964	Veikko Kankkonen, Finland	229.9
1968	Jiri Raska, Czechoslovakia	216.5
1972	Yukio Kasaya, Japan	244.2
1976	Hans-Georg Aschenbach, E. Germany	252.0
1980	Toni Innauer, Austria	266.3
1984	Jens Weissflog, E. Germany	215.2
1988	Matti Nykaenen, Finland	230.5
1992	Ernst Vettori, Austria	222.8
1994	Espen Bredesen, Norway	282.0
1998	Jani Soininen, Finland	234.5
2002	Simon Ammann, Switzerland	269.0
2006	Lars Bystoel, Norway	266.5
2010	Simon Ammann, Switzerland	276.5
2014	Kamil Stoch, Poland	278.0

	Men's Large Hill	Points
1924	Jacob Tullin Thams, Norway	18.960
1928	Alfred Andersen, Norway	19.208
1932	Birger Ruud, Norway	228.1
1936	Birger Ruud, Norway	232.0
1948	Petter Hugsted, Norway	228.1
1952	Arnfinn Bergmann, Norway	226.0
1956	Antti Hyvarinen, Finland	227.0
1960	Helmut Recknagel, E. Germany	227.2
1964	Toralf Engan, Norway	230.7
1968	Vladimir Beloussov, USSR	231.3
1972	Wojciech Fortuna, Poland	219.9
1976	Karl Schnabl, Austria	234.8
1980	Jouko Tormanen, Finland	271.0
1984	Matti Nykaenen, Finland	231.2
1988	Matti Nykaenen, Finland	224.0
1992	Toni Nieminen, Finland	239.5
1994	Jens Weissflog, Germany	274.5
1998	Kazuyoshi Funaki, Japan	272.3
2002	Simon Ammann, Switzerland	281.4
2006	Thomas Morgenstern, Austria	276.9
2010	Simon Ammann, Switzerland	283.6
2014	Kamil Stoch, Poland	278.7

	Men's Team	Points
1988	Finland, Yugoslavia, Norway	634.4
1992	Finland, Austria, Czechoslovakia	644.4
1994	Germany, Japan, Austria	970.1
1998	Japan, Germany, Austria	933.0
2002	Germany, Finland, Slovenia	974.1
2006	Austria, Finland, Norway	984.0
2010	Austria, Germany, Norway	1,107.9
2014	Germany, Austria, Japan	1,041.1

	Women's Normal Hill	Points
2014	Carina Vogt, Germany	247.4

Snowboarding

	Men's Halfpipe	Points
1998	Gian Simmen, Switzerland	85.2
2002	Ross Powers, United States	46.1
2006	Shaun White, United States	46.8
2010	Shaun White, United States	48.4
2014	Iouri Podladtchikov, Switzerland	94.75

	Men's Parallel Giant Slalom
1998	Ross Rebagliati, Canada
2002	Philipp Schoch, Switzerland
2006	Philipp Schoch, Switzerland
2010	Jasey Jay Anderson, Canada
2014	Vic Wild, Russia

Note: In 2002, the Giant Slalom became the Parallel Giant Slalom.

	Men's Parallel Slalom
2014	Vic Wild, Russia

	Men's Slopestyle	Points
2014	Sage Kotsenburg, United States	93.50

	Men's Snowboard Cross
2006	Seth Wescott, United States
2010	Seth Wescott, United States
2014	Pierre Vaultier, France

	Women's Halfpipe	Points
1998	Nicola Thost, Germany	74.6
2002	Kelly Clark, United States	47.9
2006	Hannah Teter, United States	46.4
2010	Torah Bright, Australia	45.0
2014	Kaitlyn Farrington, United States	91.75

	Women's Parallel Giant Slalom
1998	Karine Ruby, France
2002	Isabelle Blanc, France
2006	Daniela Meuli, Switzerland
2010	Nicolien Sauerbreij, Netherlands
2014	Patrizia Kummer, Switzerland

Note: In 2002, the Giant Slalom became the Parallel Giant Slalom.

	Women's Parallel Slalom
2014	Julia Dujmovits, Austria

	Women's Slopestyle	Points
2014	Jamie Anderson, United States	95.25

	Women's Snowboard Cross
2006	Tanja Frieden, Switzerland
2010	Maelle Ricker, Canada
2014	Eva Samkova, Czech Republic

Speed Skating

*Olympic record

	Men's 500 Meters	Time
1924	Charles Jewtraw, United States	0:44.0
1928	C. Thunberg, Finland; B. Evensen, Norway (tie)	0:43.4
1932	John A. Shea, United States	0:43.4
1936	Ivar Ballangrud, Norway	0:43.4
1948	Finn Helgesen, Norway	0:43.1
1952	Kenneth Henry, United States	0:43.2
1956	Evgeniy Grishin, USSR	0:40.2
1960	Evgeniy Grishin, USSR	0:40.2
1964	Terry McDermott, United States	0:40.1
1968	Erhard Keller, W. Germany	0:40.3
1972	Erhard Keller, W. Germany	0:39.44
1976	Evgeny Kulikov, USSR	0:39.17
1980	Eric Heiden, United States	0:38.03
1984	Sergei Fokichev, USSR	0:38.19
1988	Uwe-Jens Mey, E. Germany	0:36.45
1992	Uwe-Jens Mey, Germany	0:37.14
1994	Aleksandr Golubev, Russia	0:36.33
1998	Hiroyasu Shimizu, Japan	0:35.59
2002	Casey FitzRandolph, United States	0:34.42*
2006	Joey Cheek, United States	0:34.82
2010	Mo Tae-Bum, S. Korea	0:34.906
2014	Michel Mulder, Netherlands	0:69.312

Note: In 2014, results include the total of two 500-km race times.

	Men's 1,000 Meters	Time
1976	Peter Mueller, United States	1:19.32
1980	Eric Heiden, United States	1:15.18
1984	Gaetan Boucher, Canada	1:15.80
1988	Nikolai Guiliaev, USSR	1:13.03
1992	Olaf Zinke, Germany	1:14.85
1994	Dan Jansen, United States	1:12.43
1998	Ids Postma, Netherlands	1:10.64
2002	Gerard van Velde, Netherlands	1:07.18*
2006	Shani Davis, United States	1:08.89
2010	Shani Davis, United States	1:08.94
2014	Stefan Groothuis, Netherlands	1:08.39

	Men's 1,500 Meters	Time
1924	Clas Thunberg, Finland	2:20.8
1928	Clas Thunberg, Finland	2:21.1
1932	John A. Shea, United States	2:57.5
1936	Charles Mathiesen, Norway	2:19.2
1948	Sverre Farstad, Norway	2:17.6
1952	Hjalmar Andersen, Norway	2:20.4
1956	Y. Grishin, USSR; Y. Mikhailov, USSR (tie)	2:08.6
1960	R. Aas, Norway; Y. Grishin, USSR (tie)	2:10.4
1964	Ants Anston, USSR	2:10.3
1968	Cornetis Verkerk, Netherlands	2:03.4
1972	Ard Schenk, Netherlands	2:02.96
1976	Jan Egil Storholt, Norway	1:59.38
1980	Eric Heiden, United States	1:55.44
1984	Gaetan Boucher, Canada	1:58.36
1988	Andre Hoffmann, E. Germany	1:52.06

	Men's 1,500 Meters	Time
1992	Johann Koss, Norway	1:54.81
1994	Johann Koss, Norway	1:51.29
1998	Aadne Sondral, Norway	1:47.87
2002	Derek Parra, United States	1:43.95*
2006	Enrico Fabris, Italy	1:45.97
2010	Mark Tuitert, Netherlands	1:45.57
2014	Zbigniew Brodka, Poland	1:45.006

	Men's 5,000 Meters	Time
1924	Clas Thunberg, Finland	8:39.0
1928	Ivar Ballangrud, Norway	8:50.5
1932	Irving Jaffee, United States	9:40.8
1936	Ivar Ballangrud, Norway	8:19.6
1948	Reidar Liaklev, Norway	8:29.4
1952	Hjalmar Andersen, Norway	8:10.6
1956	Boris Shilkov, USSR	7:48.7
1960	Viktor Kosichkin, USSR	7:51.3
1964	Knut Johannesen, Norway	7:38.4
1968	F. Anton Maier, Norway	7:22.4
1972	Ard Schenk, Netherlands	7:23.61
1976	Sten Stensen, Norway	7:24.48
1980	Eric Heiden, United States	7:02.29
1984	Tomas Gustafson, Sweden	7:12.28
1988	Tomas Gustafson, Sweden	6:44.63
1992	Geir Karlstad, Norway	6:59.97
1994	Johann Koss, Norway	6:34.96
1998	Gianni Romme, Netherlands	6:22.20
2002	Jochem Uytdehaage, Netherlands	6:14.66
2006	Chad Hedrick, United States	6:14.68
2010	Sven Kramer, Netherlands	6:14.60
2014	Sven Kramer, Netherlands	6:10.76*

	Men's 10,000 Meters	Time
1924	Julius Skutnabb, Finland	18:04.8
1928	Event not held because of thawing of ice	
1932	Irving Jaffee, United States	19:13.6
1936	Ivar Ballangrud, Norway	17:24.3
1948	Ake Seyffarth, Sweden	17:26.3
1952	Hjalmar Andersen, Norway	16:45.8
1956	Sigvard Ericsson, Sweden	16:35.9
1960	Knut Johannesen, Norway	15:46.6
1964	Jonny Nilsson, Sweden	15:50.1
1968	Jonny Hoeglin, Sweden	15:23.6
1972	Ard Schenk, Netherlands	15:01.35
1976	Piet Kleine, Netherlands	14:50.59
1980	Eric Heiden, United States	14:28.13
1984	Igor Malkov, USSR	14:39.90
1988	Tomas Gustafson, Sweden	13:48.20
1992	Bart Veldkamp, Netherlands	14:12.12
1994	Johann Koss, Norway	13:30.55
1998	Gianni Romme, Netherlands	13:15.33
2002	Jochem Uytdehaage, Netherlands	12:58.92
2006	Bob de Jong, Netherlands	13:01.57
2010	Lee Seung-Hoon, S. Korea	12:58.55
2014	Jorrit Bergsma, Netherlands	12:44.45*

	Men's Team Pursuit	Time
2006	Italy, Canada, Netherlands	3:44.46
2010	Canada, United States, Netherlands	3:41.37
2014	Netherlands, South Korea, Poland	3:37.71*

	Women's 500 Meters	Time
1960	Helga Haase, Germany	0:45.9
1964	Lydia Skoblikova, USSR	0:45.0
1968	Ludmila Titova, USSR	0:46.1
1972	Anne Henning, United States	0:43.33
1976	Sheila Young, United States	0:42.76
1980	Karin Enke, E. Germany	0:41.78
1984	Christa Rothenburger, E. Germany	0:41.02
1988	Bonnie Blair, United States	0:39.10
1992	Bonnie Blair, United States	0:40.33
1994	Bonnie Blair, United States	0:39.25
1998	Catriona Le May-Doan, Canada	0:38.21
2002	Catriona Le May Doan, Canada	0:37.30
2006	Svetlana Zhurova, Russia	0:38.23
2010	Lee Sang-Hwa, S. Korea	0:37.850
2014	Lee Sang-Hwa, S. Korea	0:74.70*

Note: In 2014, results include the total of two 500-km race times.

	Women's 1,000 Meters	Time
1960	Klara Guseva, USSR	1:34.1
1964	Lydia Skoblikova, USSR	1:33.2
1968	Carolina Geijssen, Netherlands	1:32.6
1972	Monika Pflug, W. Germany	1:31.40
1976	Tatiana Averina, USSR	1:28.43
1980	Natalya Petruseva, USSR	1:24.10
1984	Karin Enke, E. Germany	1:21.61
1988	Christa Rothenburger, E. Germany	1:17.65
1992	Bonnie Blair, United States	1:21.90
1994	Bonnie Blair, United States	1:18.74
1998	Marianne Timmer, Netherlands	1:16.51
2002	Chris Witty, United States	1:13.83*
2006	Marianne Timmer, Netherlands	1:16.05
2010	Christine Nesbitt, Canada	1:16.56
2014	Zhang Hong, China	1:14.02

	Women's 1,500 Meters	Time
1960	Lydia Skoblikova, USSR	2:52.2
1964	Lydia Skoblikova, USSR	2:22.6
1968	Kaija Mustonen, Finland	2:22.4
1972	Dianne Holum, United States	2:20.85
1976	Galina Stepanskaya, USSR	2:16.58
1980	Anne Borckink, Netherlands	2:10.95
1984	Karin Enke, E. Germany	2:03.42
1988	Yvonne van Gennip, Netherlands	2:00.68
1992	Jacqueline Boerner, Germany	2:05.87
1994	Emese Hunyady, Austria	2:02.19
1998	Marianne Timmer, Netherlands	1:57.58
2002	Anni Friesinger, Germany	1:54.02
2006	Cindy Klassen, Canada	1:55.27
2010	Ireen Wust, Netherlands	1:56.89
2014	Jorien Ter Mors, Netherlands	1:53.51*

	Women's 3,000 Meters	Time
1960	Lydia Skoblikova, USSR	5:14.3
1964	Lydia Skoblikova, USSR	5:14.9
1968	Johanna Schut, Netherlands	4:56.2
1972	Christina Baas-Kaiser, Netherlands	4:52.14
1976	Tatiana Averina, USSR	4:45.19
1980	Bjoerg Eva Jensen, Norway	4:32.13
1984	Andrea Schoene, E. Germany	4:24.79
1988	Yvonne van Gennip, Netherlands	4:11.94
1992	Gunda Niemann, Germany	4:19.90
1994	Svetlana Bazhanova, Russia	4:17.43
1998	Gunda Niemann-Stirnemann, Germany	4:07.29
2002	Claudia Pechstein, Germany	3:57.70*
2006	Ireen Wust, Netherlands	4:02.43
2010	Martina Sablikova, Czech Republic	4:02.53
2014	Ireen Wust, Netherlands	4:00.34

	Women's 5,000 Meters	Time
1988	Yvonne van Gennip, Netherlands	7:14.13
1992	Gunda Niemann, Germany	7:31.57
1994	Claudia Pechstein, Germany	7:14.37
1998	Claudia Pechstein, Germany	6:59.61
2002	Claudia Pechstein, Germany	6:46.91*
2006	Clara Hughes, Canada	6:59.07
2010	Martina Sablikova, Czech Republic	6:50.91
2014	Martina Sablikova, Czech Republic	6:51.54

	Women's Team Pursuit	Time
2006	Germany, Canada, Russia	3:01.25
2010	Germany, Japan, Poland	3:02.82
2014	Netherlands, Poland, Russia	2:58.05*

Speed Skating (Short Track)

*Olympic record

	Men's 500 Meters	Time
1998	Takafumi Nishitani, Japan	0:42.862
2002	Marc Gagnon, Canada	0:41.802
2006	Apolo Anton Ohno, United States	0:41.935
2010	Charles Hamelin, Canada	0:40.981
2014	Victor An, Russia	0:41.312

	Men's 1,000 Meters	Time
1992	Kim Ki-Hoon, S. Korea	1:30.76
1994	Kim Ki-Hoon, S. Korea	1:34.57
1998	Kim Dong-Sung, S. Korea	1:32.375
2002	Steven Bradbury, Australia	1:29.109
2006	Ahn Hyun-Soo, S. Korea	1:26.739
2010	Lee Jung-Su, S. Korea	1:23.747*
2014	Victor An, Russia	1:25.325

	Men's 1,500 Meters	Time
2002	Apolo Anton Ohno, United States	2:18.541
2006	Ahn Hyun-Soo, S. Korea	2:25.341
2010	Lee Jung-Su, S. Korea	2:17.611
2014	Charles Hamelin, Canada	2:14.985

	Men's 5,000-Meter Relay	Time
1992	S. Korea, Canada, Japan	7:14.02
1994	Italy, United States, Australia	7:11.74
1998	Canada, S. Korea, China	7:06.075
2002	Canada, Italy, China	6:51.579
2006	S. Korea, Canada, United States	6:43.376*
2010	Canada, S. Korea, United States	6:44.224
2014	Russia, United States, China	6:42.100*

	Women's 500 Meters	Time
1992	Cathy Turner, United States	0:47.04
1994	Cathy Turner, United States	0:45.98
1998	Annie Perreault, Canada	0:46.568
2002	Yang Yang (A), China	0:44.187
2006	Wang Meng, China	0:44.345
2010	Wang Meng, China	0:43.048
2014	Li Jianrou, China	0:45.263

	Women's 1,000 Meters	Time
1998	Chun Lee-Kyung, S. Korea	1:42.776
2002	Yang Yang (A), China	1:36.391
2006	Jin Sun-Yu, S. Korea	1:32.859
2010	Wang Meng, China	1:29.213
2014	Park Seung-Hi, S. Korea	1:30.761

	Women's 1,500 Meters	Time
2002	Ko Gi-Hyun, S. Korea	2:31.581
2006	Jin Sun-Yu, S. Korea	2:23.494
2010	Zhou Yang, China	2:16.993*
2014	Zhou Yang, China	2:19.140

	Women's 3,000-Meter Relay	Time
1992	Canada, United States, Unified Team	4:36.62
1994	S. Korea, Canada, United States	4:26.64
1998	S. Korea, China, Canada	4:16.26
2002	S. Korea, China, Canada	4:12.793
2006	S. Korea, Canada, Italy	4:17.040
2010	China, Canada, United States	4:06.610*
2014	S. Korea, Canada, Italy	4:09.498

Paralympic Games

The first Olympic Games for athletes with an impairment were held in Rome after the 1960 Summer Olympics; use of the name "paralympic" began with the 1964 games in Tokyo. The Paralympics are held by the Olympic host country in the same year and usually the same city and venue or venues. In 1976, the first Winter Paralympics were held in Ornskoldsvik, Sweden.

A record 4,350 athletes from 178 countries were expected to meet Sept. 7-18, 2016, in Rio de Janeiro, Brazil, to compete in the XV Paralympic Summer Games. Athletes will compete in 528 medal events spread across 23 sports, including canoe and triathlon for the first time.

The XI Paralympic Winter Games were held Mar. 7-16, 2014, in Sochi, Russia. More than 500 athletes from 45 nations competed in five sports. Russia dominated the total medal count with 80, followed by Ukraine, with 25 medals, and the U.S., with 18.

2012 Summer Olympic Games

London, England, UK, July 27-Aug. 12, 2012

London welcomed more than 11,000 athletes from 204 nations and territories at the Summer Olympic Games, July 27-Aug. 12, 2012. The XXX Summer Olympiad marked the first time in history that each nation or territory's delegation included women athletes. The U.S. was ahead of all countries with 46 gold medals and 104 overall. Michael Phelps topped all athletes at the Summer Games with six medals and became the all-time most decorated Olympian with 22 career medals. Fellow U.S. swimmers Missy Franklin, Ryan Lochte, and Allison Schmitt each collected five medals. For the first time since 1996, the U.S. women won the gymnastics team all-around gold, and American gymnasts Gabby Douglas and Aly Raisman captured individual gold medals.

London hosted the Olympic Games for the third time and Britain's athletes recorded the country's best performance in over a century, winning 65 medals. Among the British gold medalists were track-and-field stars Mo Farah (men's 5,000-m and 10,000-m) and Jessica Ennis (heptathlon), while Andy Murray earned tennis gold when he defeated Switzerland's Roger Federer in the final in straight sets. Jamaica's Usain Bolt won gold in both the men's 100-m and 200-m sprints, as he did in Beijing, and was part of the team that won the 4x100-m relay in world-record time (36.84 sec.). South African sprinter Oscar Pistorius became the first double-amputee to compete in the Olympics, reaching the semifinals in the men's 400-m race and running in the 4x400-m relay.

2012 Summer Olympic Games: Final Medal Standings

Country	G	S	B	T
United States	46	29	29	104
China	38	27	23	88
Russia	24	26	32	82
Great Britain	29	17	19	65
Germany	11	19	14	44
Japan	7	14	17	38
Australia	7	16	12	35
France	11	11	12	34
South Korea	13	8	7	28
Italy	8	9	11	28
Netherlands	6	6	8	20
Ukraine	6	5	9	20
Canada	1	5	12	18
Hungary	8	4	5	17
Spain	3	10	4	17
Brazil	3	5	9	17
Cuba	5	3	6	14
Kazakhstan	7	1	5	13
New Zealand	6	2	5	13
Iran	4	5	3	12
Jamaica	4	4	4	12
Belarus	2	5	5	12
Kenya	2	4	5	11
Czech Republic	4	3	3	10
Azerbaijan	2	2	6	10
Poland	2	2	6	10
Romania	2	5	2	9
Denmark	2	4	3	9
Sweden	1	4	3	8
Colombia	1	3	4	8
Ethiopia	3	1	3	7
Georgia	1	3	3	7
Mexico	1	3	3	7
North Korea	4	0	2	6
South Africa	3	2	1	6
Croatia	3	1	2	6
India	0	2	4	6
Turkey	2	2	1	5
Lithuania	2	1	2	5
Ireland	1	1	3	5
Mongolia	0	2	3	5
Switzerland	2	2	0	4
Norway	2	1	1	4
Argentina	1	1	2	4
Serbia	1	1	2	4
Slovenia	1	1	2	4
Trinidad and Tobago	1	0	3	4
Uzbekistan	1	0	3	4
Slovakia	0	1	3	4
Tunisia	1	1	1	3
Thailand	0	2	1	3
Armenia	0	1	2	3
Belgium	0	1	2	3
Finland	0	1	2	3
Dominican Republic	1	1	0	2
Latvia	1	0	1	2
Egypt	0	2	0	2
Bulgaria	0	1	1	2
Estonia	0	1	1	2
Indonesia	0	1	1	2
Malaysia	0	1	1	2
Puerto Rico	0	1	1	2
Taiwan	0	1	1	2
Greece	0	0	2	2
Moldova	0	0	2	2
Qatar	0	0	2	2
Singapore	0	0	2	2
Algeria	1	0	0	1
The Bahamas	1	0	0	1
Grenada	1	0	0	1
Uganda	1	0	0	1
Venezuela	1	0	0	1
Botswana	0	1	0	1
Cyprus	0	1	0	1
Gabon	0	1	0	1
Guatemala	0	1	0	1
Montenegro	0	1	0	1
Portugal	0	1	0	1
Afghanistan	0	0	1	1
Bahrain	0	0	1	1
Hong Kong	0	0	1	1
Kuwait	0	0	1	1
Morocco	0	0	1	1
Saudi Arabia	0	0	1	1
Tajikistan	0	0	1	1
Total	**302**	**304**	**356**	**962**

Summer Olympic Games Champions, 1896-2012

* = Olympic record; (w) wind-aided; times are shown in hour:minute:sec.

The 1980 games were boycotted by 62 nations, including the U.S. The 1984 games were boycotted by the USSR and most Eastern bloc nations. East and West Germany competed separately, 1968-88. The 1992 Unified Team consisted of 12 former Soviet republics. The 1992 Independent Olympic Participants (IOP) were from Serbia, Montenegro, and Macedonia.

Not all sports are listed here, and many events are omitted, even within listed sports, particularly if the event has not been held in more recent Games. Point systems for scoring events have changed many times. Points shown are those under the point system in use at the time.

Boxing—Men

Weight class limits have changed many times since the first Olympic boxing events were held in 1904. The limits shown were used in the 2012 Olympic Games. The Super Heavyweight class was known as Heavyweight 1904-80.

Lt. Flyweight (49 kg/108 lbs)

1968 Francisco Rodriguez, Venezuela
1972 Gyorgy Gedo, Hungary
1976 Jorge Hernandez, Cuba
1980 Shamil Sabyrov, USSR
1984 Paul Gonzalez, United States
1988 Ivailo Hristov, Bulgaria
1992 Rogelio Marcelo, Cuba
1996 Daniel Petrov, Bulgaria
2000 Brahim Asloum, France
2004 Yan Bhartelemy Varela, Cuba
2008 Zou Shiming, China
2012 Zou Shiming, China

Flyweight (52 kg/114 lbs)

1904 George Finnegan, United States
1920 Frank Di Gennara, United States
1924 Fidel LaBarba, United States
1928 Antal Kocsis, Hungary
1932 Istvan Enekes, Hungary
1936 Willi Kaiser, Germany
1948 Pascual Perez, Argentina
1952 Nathan Brooks, United States
1956 Terence Spinks, Great Britain
1960 Gyula Török, Hungary
1964 Fernando Atzori, Italy
1968 Ricardo Delgado, Mexico
1972 Georgi Kostadinov, Bulgaria
1976 Leo Randolph, United States
1980 Peter Lesov, Bulgaria
1984 Steve McCrory, United States
1988 Kim Kwang Sun, S. Korea
1992 Choi Chol-Su, N. Korea
1996 Maikro Romero, Cuba
2000 Wijan Ponlid, Thailand
2004 Yuriorkis Gamboa Toledano, Cuba
2008 Somjit Jongjohor, Thailand
2012 Robeisy Ramírez, Cuba

Bantamweight (56 kg/123 lbs)

1904 Oliver Kirk, United States
1908 A. Henry Thomas, Great Britain
1920 Clarence Walker, South Africa
1924 William Smith, South Africa
1928 Vittorio Tamagnini, Italy
1932 Horace Gwynne, Canada
1936 Ulderico Sergo, Italy
1948 Tibor Csik, Hungary
1952 Pentti Hamalainen, Finland
1956 Wolfgang Behrendt, E. Germany
1960 Oleg Grigoryev, USSR
1964 Takao Sakurai, Japan
1968 Valery Sokolov, USSR
1972 Orlando Martinez, Cuba
1976 Yong-Jo Gu, N. Korea
1980 Juan Hernandez, Cuba
1984 Maurizio Stecca, Italy
1988 Kennedy McKinney, United States
1992 Joel Casamayor, Cuba
1996 Istvan Kovacs, Hungary
2000 Guillermo Rigondeaux, Cuba
2004 Guillermo Rigondeaux, Cuba
2008 Badar-Uugan Enkhbat, Mongolia
2012 Luke Campbell, Great Britain

Featherweight (57 kg/125 lbs)

1904 Oliver Kirk, United States
1908 Richard Gunn, Great Britain
1920 Paul Fritsch, France
1924 John Fields, United States
1928 Lambertus van Klaveren, Netherlands
1932 Carmelo Robledo, Argentina
1936 Oscar Casanovas, Argentina
1948 Ernesto Formenti, Italy
1952 Jan Zachara, Czechoslovakia

Featherweight (57 kg/125 lbs)

1956 Vladimir Safronov, USSR
1960 Francesco Musso, Italy
1964 Stanislav Stephashkin, USSR
1968 Antonio Roldan, Mexico
1972 Boris Kousnetsov, USSR
1976 Angel Herrera, Cuba
1980 Rudi Fink, E. Germany
1984 Meldrick Taylor, United States
1988 Giovanni Parisi, Italy
1992 Andreas Tews, Germany
1996 Somluck Kamsing, Thailand
2000 Bekzat Sattarkhanov, Kazakhstan
2004 Alexei Tichtchenko, Russia
2008 Vasyl Lomachenko, Ukraine

Lightweight (60 kg/132 lbs)

1904 Harry Spanger, United States
1908 Frederick Grace, Great Britain
1920 Samuel Mosberg, United States
1924 Hans Nielsen, Denmark
1928 Carlo Orlandi, Italy
1932 Lawrence Stevens, South Africa
1936 Imre Harangi, Hungary
1948 Gerald Dreyer, South Africa
1952 Aureliano Bolognesi, Italy
1956 Richard McTaggart, Great Britain
1960 Kazimierz Pazdzior, Poland
1964 Jozef Grudzien, Poland
1968 Ronald Harris, United States
1972 Jan Szczepanski, Poland
1976 Howard Davis, United States
1980 Angel Herrera, Cuba
1984 Pernell Whitaker, United States
1988 Andreas Zülow, E. Germany
1992 Oscar De La Hoya, United States
1996 Hocine Soltani, Algeria
2000 Mario Kindelan, Cuba
2004 Mario Kindelan, Cuba
2008 Alexey Tishchenko, Russia
2012 Vasyl Lomachenko, Ukraine

Lt. Welterweight (64 kg/141 lbs)

1952 Charles Adkins, United States
1956 Vladimir Yengibaryan, USSR
1960 Bohumil Nemecek, Czechoslovakia
1964 Jerzy Kulej, Poland
1968 Jerzy Kulej, Poland
1972 Ray Seales, United States
1976 Ray Leonard, United States
1980 Patrizio Oliva, Italy
1984 Jerry Page, United States
1988 Viatcheslav Janovski, USSR
1992 Hector Vinent, Cuba
1996 Hector Vinent, Cuba
2000 Mahamadkadyz Abdullaev, Uzbekistan
2004 Manus Boonjumnong, Thailand
2008 Felix Diaz, Dominican Republic
2012 Rosniel Iglesias, Cuba

Welterweight (69 kg/152 lbs)

1904 Albert Young, United States
1920 Albert Schneider, Canada
1924 Jean Delarge, Belgium
1928 Edward Morgan, New Zealand
1932 Edward Flynn, United States
1936 Sten Suvio, Finland
1948 Julius Torma, Czechoslovakia
1952 Zygmunt Chychia, Poland
1956 Nicolae Linca, Romania
1960 Giovanni Benvenuti, Italy
1964 Marian Kasprzyk, Poland
1968 Manfred Wolke, E. Germany
1972 Emilio Correa, Cuba
1976 Jochen Bachfeld, E. Germany
1980 Andres Aldama, Cuba

Welterweight (69 kg/152 lbs)

1984 Mark Breland, United States
1988 Robert Wangila, Kenya
1992 Michael Carruth, Ireland
1996 Oleg Saitov, Russia
2000 Oleg Saitov, Russia
2004 Artayev Bakhtiyar, Kazakhstan
2008 Bakhyt Sarsekbayev, Kazakhstan
2012 Serik Sapiyev, Kazakhstan

Lt. Middleweight (71 kg/156 lbs)

1952 Laszlo Papp, Hungary
1956 Laszlo Papp, Hungary
1960 Wilbert McClure, United States
1964 Boris Lagutin, USSR
1968 Boris Lagutin, USSR
1972 Dieter Kottysch, W. Germany
1976 Jerzy Rybicki, Poland
1980 Armando Martinez, Cuba
1984 Frank Tate, United States
1988 Park Si Hun, S. Korea
1992 Juan Lemus, Cuba
1996 David Reid, United States
2000 Yermakhan Ibraimov, Kazakhstan

Middleweight (75 kg/165 lbs)

1904 Charles Mayer, United States
1908 John Douglas, Great Britain
1920 Harry Mallin, Great Britain
1924 Harry Mallin, Great Britain
1928 Piero Toscani, Italy
1932 Carmen Barth, United States
1936 Jean Despeaux, France
1948 Laszlo Papp, Hungary
1952 Floyd Patterson, United States
1956 Gennady Schatkov, USSR
1960 Edward Crook, United States
1964 Valery Popenchenko, USSR
1968 Christopher Finnegan, Great Britain
1972 Vyacheslav Lemechev, USSR
1976 Michael Spinks, United States
1980 Jose Gomez, Cuba
1984 Joon-Sup Shin, S. Korea
1988 Henry Maske, E. Germany
1992 Ariel Hernandez, Cuba
1996 Ariel Hernandez, Cuba
2000 Jorge Gutierrez, Cuba
2004 Gaydarbek Gaydarbekov, Russia
2008 James Degale, Great Britain
2012 Ryota Murata, Japan

Lt. Heavyweight (81 kg/178 lbs)

1920 Edward Eagan, United States
1924 Harry Mitchell, Great Britain
1928 Victor Avendaño, Argentina
1932 David Carstens, South Africa
1936 Roger Michelot, France
1948 George Hunter, South Africa
1952 Norvel Lee, United States
1956 James Boyd, United States
1960 Cassius Clay, United States
1964 Cosimo Pinto, Italy
1968 Dan Poznyak, USSR
1972 Mate Parlov, Yugoslavia
1976 Leon Spinks, United States
1980 Slobodan Kacar, Yugoslavia
1984 Anton Josipovic, Yugoslavia
1988 Andrew Maynard, United States
1992 Torsten May, Germany
1996 Vassili Jirov, Kazakhstan
2000 Alexander Lebziak, Russia
2004 Andre Ward, United States
2008 Zhang Xiaoping, China
2012 Yegor Mekhontsev, Russia

Heavyweight (91 kg/201 lbs)

1984 Henry Tillman, United States
1988 Ray Mercer, United States
1992 Felix Savon, Cuba

Heavyweight (91 kg/201 lbs)

1996 Felix Savon, Cuba
2000 Felix Savon, Cuba
2004 Odlanier Solis Fonte, Cuba
2008 Rakhim Chakhkiev, Russia
2012 Oleksandr Usik, Ukraine

Super Heavyweight (91+ kg/201+ lbs)

1904 Samuel Berger, United States
1908 Albert Oldham, Great Britain
1920 Ronald Rawson, Great Britain
1924 Otto von Porat, Norway
1928 Arturo Rodriguez Jurado, Argentina
1932 Santiago Lovell, Argentina
1936 Herbert Runge, Germany
1948 Rafael Iglesias, Argentina
1952 H. Edward Sanders, United States
1956 T. Peter Rademacher, United States
1960 Franco De Piccoli, Italy
1964 Joe Frazier, United States
1968 George Foreman, United States
1972 Teofilo Stevenson, Cuba
1976 Teofilo Stevenson, Cuba
1980 Teofilo Stevenson, Cuba
1984 Tyrell Biggs, United States
1988 Lennox Lewis, Canada
1992 Roberto Balado, Cuba
1996 Vladimir Klitchko, Ukraine
2000 Audley Harrison, Great Britain
2004 Alexander Povetkin, Russia
2008 Roberto Cammarelle, Italy
2012 Anthony Joshua, Great Britain

Boxing—Women

Flyweight (51 kg/112 lbs)

2012 Nicola Adams, Great Britain

Lightweight (60 kg/132 lbs)

2012 Katie Taylor, Ireland

Middleweight (75 kg/165 lbs)

2012 Claressa Shields, United States

Gymnastics—Men

Floor Exercise

1932 István Pelle, Hungary
1936 Georges Miez, Switzerland
1948 Ferenc Pataki, Hungary
1952 William Thoresson, Sweden
1956 Valentin Muratov, USSR
1960 Nobuyuki Aihara, Japan
1964 Franco Menichelli, Italy
1968 Sawao Kato, Japan
1972 Nikolay Andrianov, USSR
1976 Nikolay Andrianov, USSR
1980 Roland Brückner, E. Germany
1984 Li Ning, China
1988 Serguei Kharikov, USSR
1992 Li Xiaoshuang, China
1996 Ioannis Melissanidis, Greece
2000 Igors Vihrovs, Latvia
2004 Kyle Shewfelt, Canada
2008 Zou Kai, China
2012 Zou Kai, China

Horizontal Bar

1896 Hermann Weingärtner, Germany
1904 Anton Heida, United States; Edward Hennig, United States (tie)
1924 Leon Stukelj, Yugoslavia
1928 Georges Miez, Switzerland
1932 Dallas Denver Bixler, United States
1936 Aleksanteri Saarvala, Finland
1948 Josef Stadler, Switzerland
1952 Jakob "Jack" Günthard, Switzerland
1956 Takashi Ono, Japan
1960 Takashi Ono, Japan
1964 Boris Shakhlin, USSR
1968 Akinori Nakayama, Japan; Mikhail Voronin, USSR (tie)
1972 Mitsuo Tsukahara, Japan
1976 Mitsuo Tsukahara, Japan
1980 Stoyan Deltchev, Bulgaria
1984 Shinji Morisue, Japan
1988 Vladimir Artemov, USSR; Valeri Lioukine, USSR (tie)
1992 Trent Dimas, United States
1996 Andreas Wecker, Germany
2000 Alexei Nemov, Russia
2004 Igor Cassina, Italy
2008 Zou Kai, China
2012 Epke Zonderland, Netherlands

Individual All-Around

1900 Gustave Sandras, France
1904 Julius Lenhart, United States
1908 G. Alberto Braglia, Italy
1912 G. Alberto Braglia, Italy
1920 Giorgio Zampori, Italy
1924 Leon Stukelj, Yugoslavia
1928 Georges Miez, Switzerland
1932 Romeo Neri, Italy
1936 Karl-Alfred Schwarzmann, Germany
1948 Veikko Huhtanen, Finland
1952 Viktor Ivanovich Chukarin, USSR
1956 Viktor Ivanovich Chukarin, USSR
1960 Boris Shakhlin, USSR
1964 Yukio Endo, Japan
1968 Sawao Kato, Japan
1972 Sawao Kato, Japan
1976 Nikolay Andrianov, USSR
1980 Aleksandr Dityatin, USSR
1984 Koji Gushiken, Japan
1988 Vladimir Artemov, USSR
1992 Vitaly Scherbo, Unified Team (Belarus)
1996 Li Xiaoshuang, China
2000 Alexei Nemov, Russia
2004 Paul Hamm, United States
2008 Yang Wei, China
2012 Kohei Uchimura, Japan

Parallel Bars

1896 Alfred Flatow, Germany
1904 George Eyser, United States
1924 August Güttinger, Switzerland
1928 Ladislav Vacha, Czechoslovakia
1932 Romeo Neri, Italy
1936 Konrad Frey, Germany
1948 Michael Reusch, Switzerland
1952 Hans Eugster, Switzerland
1956 Viktor Ivanovich Chukarin, USSR
1960 Boris Shakhlin, USSR
1964 Yukio Endo, Japan
1968 Akinori Nakayama, Japan
1972 Sawao Kato, Japan
1976 Sawao Kato, Japan
1980 Aleksandr Tkachev, USSR
1984 Bart Conner, United States
1988 Vladimir Artemov, USSR
1992 Vitaly Scherbo, Unified Team (Belarus)
1996 Roustam Sharipov, Ukraine
2000 Li Xiaopeng, China
2004 Valeri Goncharov, Ukraine
2008 Li Xiaopeng, China
2012 Feng Zhe, China

Pommel Horse

1896 Louis Zutter, Switzerland
1904 Anton Heida, United States
1924 Josef Wilhelm, Switzerland
1928 Hermann Hänggi, Switzerland
1932 István Pelle, Hungary
1936 Konrad Frey, Germany
1948 Paavo Johannes Aaltonen, Finland; Veikko Huhtanen, Finland; Heikki Savolainen, Finland (tie)
1952 Viktor Ivanovich Chukarin, USSR
1956 Boris Shakhlin, USSR
1960 Eugen Georg Oskar Ekman, Finland; Boris Shakhlin, USSR (tie)
1964 Miroslav Cerar, Yugoslavia
1968 Miroslav Cerar, Yugoslavia
1972 Viktor Klimenko, USSR
1976 Zoltan Magyar, Hungary
1980 Zoltan Magyar, Hungary
1984 Li Ning, China; Peter Glen Vidmar, United States (tie)
1988 Dmitri Bilozerchev, USSR; Zsolt Borkai, Hungary; Lubomir Geraskov, Bulgaria (tie)
1992 Pae Gil-Su, N. Korea; Vitaly Scherbo, Unified Team (Belarus) (tie)
1996 Li Donghua, Switzerland
2000 Marius Daniel Urzica, Romania
2004 Teng Haibin, China
2008 Xiao Qin, China
2012 Krisztián Berki, Hungary

Rings

1896 Ioannis Mitropoulos, Greece
1904 Hermann Glass, United States
1924 Francesco Martino, Italy
1928 Leon Stukelj, Yugoslavia
1932 George Julius Gulack, United States
1936 Alois Hudec, Czechoslovakia
1948 Karl Frei, Switzerland
1952 Grant Shaginyan, USSR
1956 Albert Azaryan, USSR
1960 Albert Azaryan, USSR
1964 Takuji Hayata, Japan
1968 Akinori Nakayama, Japan
1972 Akinori Nakayama, Japan
1976 Nikolay Andrianov, USSR
1980 Aleksandr Dityatin, USSR
1984 Koji Gushiken, Japan; Li Ning, China (tie)
1988 Holger Behrendt, E. Germany; Dmitri Bilozerchev, USSR (tie)
1992 Vitaly Scherbo, Unified Team (Belarus)
1996 Juri Chechi, Italy
2000 Szilveszter Csollany, Hungary
2004 Dimosthenis Tampakos, Greece
2008 Chen Yibing, China
2012 Arthur Zanetti, Brazil

Team Competition

1904 United States, United States, United States
1908 Sweden, Norway, Finland
1912 Italy, Hungary, Great Britain
1920 Italy, Belgium, France
1924 Italy, France, Switzerland
1928 Switzerland, Czechoslovakia, Yugoslavia
1932 Italy, United States, Finland
1936 Germany, Switzerland, Finland
1948 Finland, Switzerland, Hungary
1952 USSR, Switzerland, Finland
1956 USSR, Japan, Finland
1960 Japan, USSR, Italy
1964 Japan, USSR, Unified Team of Germany
1968 Japan, USSR, E. Germany
1972 Japan, USSR, E. Germany
1976 Japan, USSR, E. Germany
1980 USSR, E. Germany, Hungary
1984 United States, China, Japan
1988 USSR, E. Germany, Japan
1992 Unified Team, China, Japan
1996 Russia, China, Ukraine
2000 China, Ukraine, Russia
2004 Japan, United States, Romania

Team Competition

2008 China, Japan, United States
2012 China, Japan, Great Britain

Vault

1896 Carl Schumann, Germany
1904 George Eyser, United States; Anton Heida, United States (tie)
1924 Frank Kriz, United States
1928 Eugen Mack, Switzerland
1932 Savino Guglielmetti, Italy
1936 Karl-Alfred Schwarzmann, Germany
1948 Paavo Johannes Aaltonen, Finland
1952 Viktor Ivanovich Chukarin, USSR
1956 Helmut Bantz, Unified Team of Germany; Valentin Muratov, USSR (tie)
1960 Takashi Ono, Japan; Boris Shakhlin, USSR (tie)
1964 Haruhiro Yamashita, Japan
1968 Mikhail Voronin, USSR
1972 Klaus Köste, E. Germany
1976 Nikolay Andrianov, USSR
1980 Nikolay Andrianov, USSR
1984 Lou Yun, China
1988 Lou Yun, China
1992 Vitaly Scherbo, Unified Team (Belarus)
1996 Alexei Nemov, Russia
2000 Gervasio Deferr, Spain
2004 Gervasio Deferr, Spain
2008 Leszek Blanik, Poland
2012 Yang Hak-Seon, South Korea

Gymnastics—Women

Balance Beam

1952 Nina Bocharova, USSR
1956 Agnes Keleti, Hungary
1960 Eva Vechtova-Bosakova, Czechoslovakia
1964 Vera Caslavska, Czechoslovakia
1968 Natalya Kuchinskaya, USSR
1972 Olga Korbut, USSR
1976 Nadia Comaneci, Romania
1980 Nadia Comaneci, Romania
1984 Ecaterina Szabo, Romania; Simona Pauca, Romania (tie)
1988 Daniela Silivas, Romania
1992 Tatiana Lyssenko, Unified Team (Ukraine)
1996 Shannon Miller, United States
2000 Liu Xuan, China
2004 Catalina Ponor, Romania
2008 Shawn Johnson, United States
2012 Deng Linlin, China

Floor Exercise

1952 Agnes Keleti, Hungary
1956 Agnes Keleti, Hungary; Larisa Latynina, USSR (tie)
1960 Larisa Latynina, USSR
1964 Larisa Latynina, USSR
1968 Vera Caslavska, Czechoslovakia; Larisa Petrik, USSR (tie)
1972 Olga Korbut, USSR
1976 Nelli Kim, USSR
1980 Nelli Kim, USSR; Nadia Comaneci, Romania (tie)
1984 Ecaterina Szabo, Romania
1988 Daniela Silivas, Romania
1992 Lavinia Corina Milosovici, Romania
1996 Lilia Podkopayeva, Ukraine
2000 Elena Zamolodchikova, Russia
2004 Catalina Ponor, Romania
2008 Sandra Izbasa, Romania
2012 Aly Raisman, United States

Individual All-Around

1952 Mariya Gorokhovskaya, USSR
1956 Larisa Latynina, USSR
1960 Larisa Latynina, USSR
1964 Vera Caslavska, Czechoslovakia
1968 Vera Caslavska, Czechoslovakia
1972 Lyudmila Turischeva, USSR
1976 Nadia Comaneci, Romania
1980 Elena Davydova, USSR
1984 Mary-Lou Retton, United States
1988 Elena Shushunova, USSR
1992 Tatiana Goutsou, Unified Team (Ukraine)
1996 Lilia Podkopayeva, Ukraine
2000 Simona Amanar, Romania
2004 Carly Patterson, United States
2008 Nastia Liukin, United States
2012 Gabby Douglas, United States

Team Competition

1928 Netherlands, Italy, Great Britain
1936 Germany, Czechoslovakia, Hungary
1948 Czechoslovakia, Hungary, United States
1952 USSR, Hungary, Czechoslovakia
1956 USSR, Hungary, Romania
1960 USSR, Czechoslovakia, Romania
1964 USSR, Czechoslovakia, Japan
1968 USSR, Czechoslovakia, E. Germany
1972 USSR, E. Germany, Hungary
1976 USSR, Romania, E. Germany
1980 USSR, Romania, E. Germany
1984 Romania, United States, China
1988 USSR, Romania, E. Germany
1992 Unified Team, Romania, United States
1996 United States, Russia, Romania
2000 Romania, Russia, United States
2004 Romania, United States, Russia
2008 China, United States, Romania
2012 United States, Russia, Romania

Uneven Bars

1952 Margit Korondi, Hungary
1956 Agnes Keleti, Hungary
1960 Polina Astakhova, USSR
1964 Polina Astakhova, USSR
1968 Vera Caslavska, Czechoslovakia
1972 Karin Janz, E. Germany
1976 Nadia Comaneci, Romania
1980 Maxi Gnauck, E. Germany
1984 Julianne McNamara, United States; Yan-Hong Ma, China (tie)
1988 Daniela Silivas, Romania
1992 Lu Li, China
1996 Svetlana Khorkina, Russia
2000 Svetlana Khorkina, Russia
2004 Emilie LePennec, France
2008 He Kexin, China
2012 Aliya Mustafina, Russia

Vault

1952 Ekaterina Kalinchuk, USSR
1956 Larisa Latynina, USSR
1960 Margarita Nikolaeva, USSR
1964 Vera Caslavska, Czechoslovakia
1968 Vera Caslavska, Czechoslovakia
1972 Karin Janz, E. Germany
1976 Nelli Kim, USSR
1980 Natalia Shaposhnikova, USSR
1984 Ecaterina Szabo, Romania
1988 Svetlana Boginskaya, USSR
1992 Henrietta Onodi, Hungary; Lavinia Milosovici, Romania (tie)
1996 Simona Amanar, Romania
2000 Elena Zamolodchikova, Russia
2004 Monica Rosu, Romania
2008 Hong Un Jong, N. Korea
2012 Sandra Izbaşa, Romania

Soccer

Men

1900 Great Britain, France, Belgium
1904 Canada, United States, United States
1908 Great Britain, Denmark, Netherlands
1912 Great Britain, Denmark, Netherlands
1920 Belgium, Spain, Netherlands
1924 Uruguay, Switzerland, Sweden
1928 Uruguay, Argentina, Italy
1936 Italy, Austria, Norway
1948 Sweden, Yugoslavia, Denmark
1952 Hungary, Yugoslavia, Sweden
1956 USSR, Yugoslavia, Bulgaria
1960 Yugoslavia, Denmark, Hungary
1964 Hungary, Czechoslovakia, Unified Team of Germany
1968 Hungary, Bulgaria, Japan
1972 Poland; Hungary; USSR, E. Germany (tie for bronze)
1976 E. Germany, Poland, USSR
1980 Czechoslovakia, E. Germany, USSR
1984 France, Brazil, Yugoslavia
1988 USSR, Brazil, W. Germany
1992 Spain, Poland, Ghana
1996 Nigeria, Argentina, Brazil
2000 Cameroon, Spain, Chile
2004 Argentina, Paraguay, Italy
2008 Argentina, Nigeria, Brazil
2012 Mexico, Brazil, South Korea

Women

1996 United States, China, Norway
2000 Norway, United States, Germany
2004 United States, Brazil, Germany
2008 United States, Brazil, Germany
2012 United States, Japan, Canada

Swimming and Diving—Men

	50-Meter Freestyle	Time
1988	Matt Biondi, United States	0:22.14
1992	Aleksandr Popov, Unified Team	0:21.91
1996	Aleksandr Popov, Russia	0:22.13
2000	Anthony Ervin, United States	0:21.98
	Gary Hall Jr., United States (tie)	0:21.98
2004	Gary Hall Jr., United States	0:21.93
2008	Cesar Cielo Filho, Brazil	0:21.30*
2012	Florent Manaudou, France	0:21.34

	100-Meter Freestyle	Time
1896	Alfred Hajos, Hungary	1:22.2
1904	Zoltan de Halmay, Hungary (100 yds)	1:02.8
1908	Charles Daniels, United States	1:05.6
1912	Duke P. Kahanamoku, United States	1:03.4
1920	Duke P. Kahanamoku, United States	1:01.4
1924	Johnny Weissmuller, United States	0:59.0
1928	Johnny Weissmuller, United States	0:58.6
1932	Yasuji Miyazaki, Japan	0:58.2
1936	Ferenc Csik, Hungary	0:57.6
1948	Wally Ris, United States	0:57.3
1952	Clark Scholes, United States	0:57.4
1956	Jon Henricks, Australia	0:55.4
1960	John Devitt, Australia	0:55.2
1964	Don Schollander, United States	0:53.4
1968	Mike Wenden, Australia	0:52.2
1972	Mark Spitz, United States	0:51.22
1976	Jim Montgomery, United States	0:49.99

	100-Meter Freestyle	Time
1980	Jorg Woithe, E. Germany	0:50.40
1984	Ambrose "Rowdy" Gaines, United States	0:49.80
1988	Matt Biondi, United States	0:48.63
1992	Aleksandr Popov, Unified Team	0:49.02
1996	Aleksandr Popov, Russia	0:48.74
2000	Pieter van den Hoogenband, Netherlands	0:48.30
2004	Pieter van den Hoogenband, Netherlands	0:48.17
2008	Alain Bernard, France	0:47.21
2012	Nathan Adrian, United States	0:47.52

	200-Meter Freestyle	Time
1968	Mike Wenden, Australia	1:55.2
1972	Mark Spitz, United States	1:52.78
1976	Bruce Furniss, United States	1:50.29
1980	Sergei Kopliakov, USSR	1:49.81
1984	Michael Gross, W. Germany	1:47.44
1988	Duncan Armstrong, Australia	1:47.25
1992	Yevgeny Sadovyi, Unified Team	1:46.70
1996	Danyon Loader, New Zealand	1:47.63
2000	Pieter van den Hoogenband, Netherlands	1:45.35
2004	Ian Thorpe, Australia	1:44.71
2008	Michael Phelps, United States	1:42.96*
2012	Yannick Agnel, France	1:43.14

	400-Meter Freestyle	Time
1904	C. M. Daniels, United States (440 yds)	6:16.2
1908	Henry Taylor, Great Britain	5:36.8
1912	George Hodgson, Canada	5:24.4
1920	Norman Ross, United States	5:26.8
1924	Johnny Weissmuller, United States	5:04.2
1928	Albert Zorilla, Argentina	5:01.6
1932	Clarence Crabbe, United States	4:48.4
1936	Jack Medica, United States	4:44.5
1948	William Smith, United States	4:41.0
1952	Jean Boiteux, France	4:30.7
1956	Murray Rose, Australia	4:27.3
1960	Murray Rose, Australia	4:18.3
1964	Don Schollander, United States	4:12.2
1968	Mike Burton, United States	4:09.0
1972	Brad Cooper, Australia	4:00.27
1976	Brian Goodell, United States	3:51.93
1980	Vladimir Salnikov, USSR	3:51.31
1984	George DiCarlo, United States	3:51.23
1988	Ewe Dassler, E. Germany	3:46.95
1992	Yevgeny Sadovyi, Unified Team	3:45.00
1996	Danyon Loader, New Zealand	3:47.97
2000	Ian Thorpe, Australia	3:40.59
2004	Ian Thorpe, Australia	3:43.10
2008	Park Taehwan, S. Korea	3:41.86
2012	Sun Yang, China	3:40.14*

	1,500-Meter Freestyle	Time
1908	Henry Taylor, Great Britain	22:48.4
1912	George Hodgson, Canada	22:00.0
1920	Norman Ross, United States	22:23.2
1924	Johnny Charlton, Australia	20:06.6
1928	Arne Borg, Sweden	19:51.8
1932	Kusuo Kitamura, Japan	19:12.4
1936	Noboru Terada, Japan	19:13.7
1948	James McLane, United States	19:18.5
1952	Ford Konno, United States	18:30.3
1956	Murray Rose, Australia	17:58.9
1960	Jon Konrads, Australia	17:19.6
1964	Robert Windle, Australia	17:01.7
1968	Mike Burton, United States	16:38.9
1972	Mike Burton, United States	15:52.58
1976	Brian Goodell, United States	15:02.40
1980	Vladimir Salnikov, USSR	14:58.27
1984	Michael O'Brien, United States	15:05.20
1988	Vladimir Salnikov, USSR	15:00.40
1992	Kieren Perkins, Australia	14:43.48
1996	Kieren Perkins, Australia	14:56.40
2000	Grant Hackett, Australia	14:48.33
2004	Grant Hackett, Australia	14:43.40
2008	Oussama Mellouli, Tunisia	14:40.84
2012	Sun Yang, China	14:31.02*

	100-Meter Backstroke	Time
1904	Walter Brack, Germany (100 yds)	1:16.8
1908	Arno Bieberstein, Germany	1:24.6
1912	Harry Hebner, United States	1:21.2
1920	Warren Kealoha, United States	1:15.2
1924	Warren Kealoha, United States	1:13.2
1928	George Kojac, United States	1:08.2
1932	Masaji Kiyokawa, Japan	1:08.6
1936	Adolph Kiefer, United States	1:05.9
1948	Allen Stack, United States	1:06.4
1952	Yoshi Oyakawa, United States	1:05.4
1956	David Thiele, Australia	1:02.2
1960	David Thiele, Australia	1:01.9
1968	Roland Matthes, E. Germany	0:58.7
1972	Roland Matthes, E. Germany	0:56.58
1976	John Naber, United States	0:55.49
1980	Bengt Baron, Sweden	0:56.33
1984	Rick Carey, United States	0:55.79
1988	Daichi Suzuki, Japan	0:55.05
1992	Mark Tewksbury, Canada	0:53.98
1996	Jeff Rouse, United States	0:54.10
2000	Lenny Krayzelburg, United States	0:53.72
2004	Aaron Peirsol, United States	0:54.06
2008	Aaron Peirsol, United States	0:52.54
2012	Matt Grevers, United States	0:52.16*

	200-Meter Backstroke	Time
1964	Jed Graef, United States	2:10.3
1968	Roland Matthes, E. Germany	2:09.6
1972	Roland Matthes, E. Germany	2:02.82
1976	John Naber, United States	1:59.19
1980	Sandor Wladar, Hungary	2:01.93
1984	Rick Carey, United States	2:00.23
1988	Igor Polianski, USSR	1:59.37
1992	Martin Lopez-Zubero, Spain	1:58.47
1996	Brad Bridgewater, United States	1:58.54
2000	Lenny Krayzelburg, United States	1:56.76
2004	Aaron Peirsol, United States	1:54.95
2008	Ryan Lochte, United States	1:53.94
2012	Tyler Clary, United States	1:53.41*

	100-Meter Breaststroke	Time
1968	Don McKenzie, United States	1:07.79
1972	Nobutaka Taguchi, Japan	1:04.94
1976	John Hencken, United States	1:03.11
1980	Duncan Goodhew, Great Britain	1:03.44
1984	Steve Lundquist, United States	1:01.65
1988	Adrian Moorhouse, Great Britain	1:02.04
1992	Nelson Diebel, United States	1:01.50
1996	Fred Deburghgraeve, Belgium	1:00.60
2000	Domenico Fioravanti, Italy	1:00.46
2004	Kosuke Kitajima, Japan	1:00.08
2008	Kosuke Kitajima, Japan	0:58.91
2012	Cameron van der Burgh, South Africa	0:58.46*

	200-Meter Breaststroke	Time
1908	Frederick Holman, Great Britain	3:09.2
1912	Walter Bathe, Germany	3:01.8
1920	Haken Malmroth, Sweden	3:04.4
1924	Robert Skelton, United States	2:56.6
1928	Yoshiyuki Tsuruta, Japan	2:48.8
1932	Yoshiyuki Tsuruta, Japan	2:45.4
1936	Tetsuo Hamuro, Japan	2:41.5
1948	Joseph Verdeur, United States	2:39.3
1952	John Davies, Australia	2:34.4
1956	Masura Furukawa, Japan	2:34.7
1960	William Mulliken, United States	2:37.4
1964	Ian O'Brien, Australia	2:27.8
1968	Felipe Munoz, Mexico	2:28.7
1972	John Hencken, United States	2:21.55
1976	David Wilkie, Great Britain	2:15.11
1980	Robertas Zhulpa, USSR	2:15.85
1984	Victor Davis, Canada	2:13.34
1988	Jozsef Szabo, Hungary	2:13.52
1992	Mike Barrowman, United States	2:10.16
1996	Norbert Rozsa, Hungary	2:12.57
2000	Domenico Fioravanti, Italy	2:10.87
2004	Kosuke Kitajima, Japan	2:09.44
2008	Kosuke Kitajima, Japan	2:07.64
2012	Dániel Gyurta, Hungary	2:07.28*

	100-Meter Butterfly	Time
1968	Doug Russell, United States	0:55.9
1972	Mark Spitz, United States	0:54.27
1976	Matt Vogel, United States	0:54.35
1980	Par Arvidsson, Sweden	0:54.92
1984	Michael Gross, W. Germany	0:53.08
1988	Anthony Nesty, Suriname	0:53.00
1992	Pablo Morales, United States	0:53.32
1996	Denis Pankratov, Russia	0:52.27
2000	Lars Froelander, Sweden	0:52.00
2004	Michael Phelps, United States	0:51.25
2008	Michael Phelps, United States	0:50.58*
2012	Michael Phelps, United States	0:51.21

	200-Meter Butterfly	Time
1956	William Yorzyk, United States	2:19.3
1960	Michael Troy, United States	2:12.8
1964	Kevin J. Berry, Australia	2:06.6
1968	Carl Robie, United States	2:08.7
1972	Mark Spitz, United States	2:00.70
1976	Mike Bruner, United States	1:59.23
1980	Sergei Fesenko, USSR	1:59.76
1984	Jon Sieben, Australia	1:57.04
1988	Michael Gross, W. Germany	1:56.94

	200-Meter Butterfly	Time
1992	Mel Stewart, United States	1:56.26
1996	Denis Pankratov, Russia	1:56.51
2000	Tom Malchow, United States	1:55.35
2004	Michael Phelps, United States	1:54.04
2008	Michael Phelps, United States	1:52.03*
2012	Chad le Clos, South Africa	1:52.96

	200-Meter Individual Medley	Time
1968	Charles Hickcox, United States	2:12.0
1972	Gunnar Larsson, Sweden	2:07.17
1984	Alex Baumann, Canada	2:01.42
1988	Tamas Darnyi, Hungary	2:00.17
1992	Tamas Darnyi, Hungary	2:00.76
1996	Attila Czene, Hungary	1:59.91
2000	Massimiliano Rosolino, Italy	1:58.98
2004	Michael Phelps, United States	1:57.14
2008	Michael Phelps, United States	1:54.23*
2012	Michael Phelps, United States	1:54.27

	400-Meter Individual Medley	Time
1964	Dick Roth, United States	4:45.4
1968	Charles Hickcox, United States	4:48.4
1972	Gunnar Larsson, Sweden	4:31.98
1976	Rod Strachan, United States	4:23.68
1980	Aleksandr Sidorenko, USSR	4:22.89
1984	Alex Baumann, Canada	4:17.41
1988	Tamas Darnyi, Hungary	4:14.75
1992	Tamas Darnyi, Hungary	4:14.23
1996	Tom Dolan, United States	4:14.90
2000	Tom Dolan, United States	4:11.76
2004	Michael Phelps, United States	4:08.26
2008	Michael Phelps, United States	4:03.84*
2012	Ryan Lochte, United States	4:05.18

	4x100-Meter Freestyle Relay	Time
1964	United States	3:31.2
1968	United States	3:31.7
1972	United States	3:26.42
1984	United States	3:19.03
1988	United States	3:16.53
1992	United States	3:16.74
1996	United States	3:15.41
2000	Australia	3:13.67
2004	South Africa	3:13.17
2008	United States	3:08.24*
2012	France	3:09.93

	4x200-Meter Freestyle Relay	Time
1908	Great Britain	10:55.6
1912	Australasia (Australia and New Zealand)	10:11.6
1920	United States	10:04.4
1924	United States	9:53.4
1928	United States	9:36.2
1932	Japan	8:58.4
1936	Japan	8:51.5
1948	United States	8:46.0
1952	United States	8:31.1
1956	Australia	8:23.6
1960	United States	8:10.2
1964	United States	7:52.1
1968	United States	7:52.33
1972	United States	7:35.78
1976	United States	7:23.22
1980	USSR	7:23.50
1984	United States	7:15.69
1988	United States	7:12.51
1992	Unified Team	7:11.95
1996	United States	7:14.84
2000	Australia	7:07.05
2004	United States	7:07.33
2008	United States	6:58.56*
2012	United States	6:59.70

	4x100-Meter Medley Relay	Time
1960	United States	4:05.4
1964	United States	3:58.4
1968	United States	3:54.9
1972	United States	3:48.16
1976	United States	3:42.22
1980	Australia	3:45.70
1984	United States	3:39.30
1988	United States	3:36.93
1992	United States	3:36.93
1996	United States	3:34.84
2000	United States	3:33.73
2004	United States	3:30.68
2008	United States	3:29.34*
2012	United States	3:29.35

	10-Kilometer Marathon	Time
2008	Maarten van der Weijden, Netherlands	1:51:51.6
2012	Oussama Mellouli, Tunisia	1:49:55.1

	Platform Diving	Points
1904	Dr. G. E. Sheldon, United States	112.75
1908	Hjalmar Johansson, Sweden	183.75
1912	Erik Adlerz, Sweden	73.94
1920	Clarence Pinkston, United States	100.67
1924	Albert White, United States	97.46
1928	Pete Desjardins, United States	98.74
1932	Harold Smith, United States	124.80
1936	Marshall Wayne, United States	113.58
1948	Sammy Lee, United States	130.05
1952	Sammy Lee, United States	156.28
1956	Joaquin Capilla, Mexico	152.44
1960	Robert Webster, United States	165.56
1964	Robert Webster, United States	148.58
1968	Klaus Dibiasi, Italy	164.18
1972	Klaus Dibiasi, Italy	504.12
1976	Klaus Dibiasi, Italy	600.51
1980	Falk Hoffmann, E. Germany	835.65
1984	Greg Louganis, United States	710.91
1988	Greg Louganis, United States	638.61
1992	Sun Shuwei, China	677.31
1996	Dmitri Sautin, Russia	692.34
2000	Tian Liang, China	724.53
2004	Hu Jia, China	748.08
2008	Matthew Mitcham, Australia	537.95
2012	David Boudia, United States	568.65

	Springboard Diving	Points
1908	Albert Zurner, Germany	85.50
1912	Paul Guenther, Germany	79.23
1920	Louis Kuehn, United States	675.40
1924	Albert White, United States	97.46
1928	Pete Desjardins, United States	185.04
1932	Michael Galitzen, United States	161.38
1936	Richard Degener, United States	163.57
1948	Bruce Harlan, United States	163.64
1952	David Browning, United States	205.29
1956	Robert Clotworthy, United States	159.56
1960	Gary Tobian, United States	170.00
1964	Kenneth Sitzberger, United States	159.90
1968	Bernie Wrightson, United States	170.15
1972	Vladimir Vasin, USSR	594.09
1976	Phil Boggs, United States	619.52
1980	Aleksandr Portnov, USSR	905.02
1984	Greg Louganis, United States	754.41
1988	Greg Louganis, United States	730.80
1992	Mark Lenzi, United States	676.53
1996	Xiong Ni, China	701.46
2000	Xiong Ni, China	708.72
2004	Peng Bo, China	787.30
2008	He Chong, China	572.90
2012	Ilya Zakharov, Russia	555.90

	Synchronized Platform Diving	Points
2004	Tian Liang and Yang Jinghui, China	383.88
2008	Lin Yue and Huo Liang, China	468.18
2012	Cao Yuan and Zhang Yanquan, China	486.78

	Synchronized Springboard Diving	Points
2004	Nikolaos Siranidis and Thomas Bimis, Greece	353.34
2008	Wang Feng and Qin Kai, China	469.08
2012	Luo Yutong and Qin Kai, China	477.00

Swimming and Diving—Women

	50-Meter Freestyle	Time
1988	Kristin Otto, E. Germany	0:25.49
1992	Yang Wenyi, China	0:24.76
1996	Amy Van Dyken, United States	0:24.87
2000	Inge de Bruijn, Netherlands	0:24.32
2004	Inge de Bruijn, Netherlands	0:24.58
2008	Britta Steffen, Germany	0:24.06
2012	Ranomi Kromowidjojo, Netherlands	0:24.05*

	100-Meter Freestyle	Time
1912	Fanny Durack, Australia	1:22.2
1920	Ethelda Bleibtrey, United States	1:13.6
1924	Ethel Lackie, United States	1:12.4
1928	Albina Osipowich, United States	1:11.0
1932	Helene Madison, United States	1:06.8
1936	Hendrika Mastenbroek, Netherlands	1:05.9
1948	Greta Andersen, Denmark	1:06.3
1952	Katalin Szoke, Hungary	1:06.8
1956	Dawn Fraser, Australia	1:02.0
1960	Dawn Fraser, Australia	1:01.2
1964	Dawn Fraser, Australia	0:59.5
1968	Jan Henne, United States	1:00.0

	100-Meter Freestyle	Time
1972	Sandra Neilson, United States	0:58.59
1976	Kornelia Ender, E. Germany	0:55.65
1980	Barbara Krause, E. Germany	0:54.79
1984	Carrie Steinseifer, United States	0:55.92
	Nancy Hogshead, United States (tie)	0:55.92
1988	Kristin Otto, E. Germany	0:54.93
1992	Zhuang Yong, China	0:54.64
1996	Li Jingyi, China	0:54.50
2000	Inge de Bruijn, Netherlands	0:53.83
2004	Jodie Henry, Australia	0:53.84
2008	Britta Steffen, Germany	0:53.12
2012	Ranomi Kromowidjojo, Netherlands	0:53.00*

	200-Meter Freestyle	Time
1968	Debbie Meyer, United States	2:10.5
1972	Shane Gould, Australia	2:03.56
1976	Kornelia Ender, E. Germany	1:59.26
1980	Barbara Krause, E. Germany	1:58.33
1984	Mary Wayte, United States	1:59.23
1988	Heike Friedrich, E. Germany	1:57.65
1992	Nicole Haislett, United States	1:57.90
1996	Claudia Poll, Costa Rica	1:58.16
2000	Susan O'Neill, Australia	1:58.24
2004	Camelia Potec, Romania	1:58.03
2008	Federica Pellegrini, Italy	1:54.82
2012	Allison Schmitt, United States	1:53.61*

	400-Meter Freestyle	Time
1924	Martha Norelius, United States	6:02.2
1928	Martha Norelius, United States	5:42.8
1932	Helene Madison, United States	5:28.5
1936	Hendrika Mastenbroek, Netherlands	5:26.4
1948	Ann Curtis, United States	5:17.8
1952	Valerie Gyenge, Hungary	5:12.1
1956	Lorraine Crapp, Australia	4:54.6
1960	Chris von Saltza, United States	4:50.6
1964	Virginia Duenkel, United States	4:43.3
1968	Debbie Meyer, United States	4:31.8
1972	Shane Gould, Australia	4:19.44
1976	Petra Thuemer, E. Germany	4:09.89
1980	Ines Diers, E. Germany	4:08.76
1984	Tiffany Cohen, United States	4:07.10
1988	Janet Evans, United States	4:03.85
1992	Dagmar Hase, Germany	4:07.18
1996	Michelle Smith, Ireland	4:07.25
2000	Brooke Bennett, United States	4:05.80
2004	Laure Manaudou, France	4:05.34
2008	Rebecca Adlington, Great Britain	4:03.22
2012	Camille Muffat, France	4:01.45*

	800-Meter Freestyle	Time
1968	Debbie Meyer, United States	9:24.0
1972	Keena Rothhammer, United States	8:53.68
1976	Petra Thuemer, E. Germany	8:37.14
1980	Michelle Ford, Australia	8:28.90
1984	Tiffany Cohen, United States	8:24.95
1988	Janet Evans, United States	8:20.20
1992	Janet Evans, United States	8:25.52
1996	Brooke Bennett, United States	8:27.89
2000	Brooke Bennett, United States	8:19.67
2004	Ai Shibata, Japan	8:24.54
2008	Rebecca Adlington, Great Britain	8:14.10*
2012	Katie Ledecky, United States	8:14.63

	100-Meter Backstroke	Time
1924	Sybil Bauer, United States	1:23.2
1928	Marie Braun, Netherlands	1:22.0
1932	Eleanor Holm, United States	1:19.4
1936	Dina Senff, Netherlands	1:18.9
1948	Karen Harup, Denmark	1:14.4
1952	Joan Harrison, South Africa	1:14.3
1956	Judy Grinham, Great Britain	1:12.9
1960	Lynn Burke, United States	1:09.3
1964	Cathy Ferguson, United States	1:07.7
1968	Kaye Hall, United States	1:06.2
1972	Melissa Belote, United States	1:05.78
1976	Ulrike Richter, E. Germany	1:01.83
1980	Rica Reinisch, E. Germany	1:00.86
1984	Theresa Andrews, United States	1:02.55
1988	Kristin Otto, E. Germany	1:00.89
1992	Krisztina Egerszegi, Hungary	1:00.68
1996	Beth Botsford, United States	1:01.19
2000	Diana Mocanu, Romania	1:00.21
2004	Natalie Coughlin, United States	1:00.37
2008	Natalie Coughlin, United States	0:58.96
2012	Missy Franklin, United States	0:58.33

	200-Meter Backstroke	Time
1968	Pokey Watson, United States	2:24.8
1972	Melissa Belote, United States	2:19.19
1976	Ulrike Richter, E. Germany	2:13.43
1980	Rica Reinisch, E. Germany	2:11.77
1984	Jolanda De Rover, Netherlands	2:12.38
1988	Krisztina Egerszegi, Hungary	2:09.29
1992	Krisztina Egerszegi, Hungary	2:07.06
1996	Krisztina Egerszegi, Hungary	2:07.83
2000	Diana Mocanu, Romania	2:08.16
2004	Kirsty Coventry, Zimbabwe	2:09.19
2008	Kirsty Coventry, Zimbabwe	2:05.24
2012	Missy Franklin, United States	2:04.06*

	100-Meter Breaststroke	Time
1968	Djurdjica Bjedov, Yugoslavia	1:15.8
1972	Cathy Carr, United States	1:13.58
1976	Hannelore Anke, E. Germany	1:11.16
1980	Ute Geweniger, E. Germany	1:10.22
1984	Petra Van Staveren, Netherlands	1:09.88
1988	Tania Dangalakova, Bulgaria	1:07.95
1992	Yelena Rudkovskaya, Unified Team	1:08.00
1996	Penny Heyns, South Africa	1:07.73
2000	Megan Quann, United States	1:07.05
2004	Luo Xuejuan, China	1:06.64
2008	Leisel Jones, Australia	1:05.17*
2012	Rūta Meilutytė, Lithuania	1:05.47

	200-Meter Breaststroke	Time
1924	Lucy Morton, Great Britain	3:33.2
1928	Hilde Schrader, Germany	3:12.6
1932	Clare Dennis, Australia	3:06.3
1936	Hideko Maehata, Japan	3:03.6
1948	Nelly Van Vliet, Netherlands	2:57.2
1952	Eva Szekely, Hungary	2:51.7
1956	Ursula Happe, Germany	2:53.1
1960	Anita Lonsbrough, Great Britain	2:49.5
1964	Galina Prozumenschikova, USSR	2:46.4
1968	Sharon Wichman, United States	2:44.4
1972	Beverly Whitfield, Australia	2:41.71
1976	Marina Koshevaia, USSR	2:33.35
1980	Lina Kachushite, USSR	2:29.54
1984	Anne Ottenbrite, Canada	2:30.38
1988	Silke Hoerner, E. Germany	2:26.71
1992	Kyoko Iwasaki, Japan	2:26.65
1996	Penny Heyns, South Africa	2:25.41
2000	Agnes Kovacs, Hungary	2:24.35
2004	Amanda Beard, United States	2:23.37
2008	Rebecca Soni, United States	2:20.22
2012	Rebecca Soni, United States	2:19.59*

	100-Meter Butterfly	Time
1956	Shelley Mann, United States	1:11.0
1960	Carolyn Schuler, United States	1:09.5
1964	Sharon Stouder, United States	1:04.7
1968	Lynn McClements, Australia	1:05.5
1972	Mayumi Aoki, Japan	1:03.34
1976	Kornelia Ender, E. Germany	1:00.13
1980	Caren Metschuck, E. Germany	1:00.42
1984	Mary T. Meagher, United States	0:59.26
1988	Kristin Otto, E. Germany	0:59.00
1992	Qian Hong, China	0:58.62
1996	Amy Van Dyken, United States	0:59.13
2000	Inge de Bruijn, Netherlands	0:56.61
2004	Petria Thomas, Australia	0:57.72
2008	Lisbeth Trickett, Australia	0:56.73
2012	Dana Vollmer, United States	0:55.98*

	200-Meter Butterfly	Time
1968	Ada Kok, Netherlands	2:24.7
1972	Karen Moe, United States	2:15.57
1976	Andrea Pollack, E. Germany	2:11.41
1980	Ines Geissler, E. Germany	2:10.44
1984	Mary T. Meagher, United States	2:06.90
1988	Kathleen Nord, E. Germany	2:09.51
1992	Summer Sanders, United States	2:08.67
1996	Susan O'Neill, Australia	2:07.76
2000	Misty Hyman, United States	2:05.88
2004	Otylia Jedrzejczak, Poland	2:06.05
2008	Liu Zige, China	2:04.18
2012	Jiao Liuyang, China	2:04.06*

	200-Meter Individual Medley	Time
1968	Claudia Kolb, United States	2:24.7
1972	Shane Gould, Australia	2:23.07
1984	Tracy Caulkins, United States	2:12.64
1988	Daniela Hunger, E. Germany	2:12.59
1992	Lin Li, China	2:11.65
1996	Michelle Smith, Ireland	2:13.93
2000	Yana Klochkova, Ukraine	2:10.68
2004	Yana Klochkova, Ukraine	2:11.14
2008	Stephanie Rice, Australia	2:08.45
2012	Ye Shiwen, China	2:07.57*

	400-Meter Individual Medley	Time
1964	Donna de Varona, United States	5:18.7
1968	Claudia Kolb, United States	5:08.5
1972	Gail Neall, Australia	5:02.97
1976	Ulrike Tauber, E. Germany	4:42.77
1980	Petra Schneider, E. Germany	4:36.29
1984	Tracy Caulkins, United States	4:39.24
1988	Janet Evans, United States	4:37.76
1992	Krisztina Egerszegi, Hungary	4:36.54
1996	Michelle Smith, Ireland	4:39.18
2000	Yana Klochkova, Ukraine	4:33.59
2004	Yana Klochkova, Ukraine	4:34.83
2008	Stephanie Rice, Australia	4:29.45
2012	Ye Shiwen, China	4:28.43*

	4x100-Meter Freestyle Relay	Time
1912	Great Britain	5:52.8
1920	United States	5:11.6
1924	United States	4:58.8
1928	United States	4:47.6
1932	United States	4:38.0
1936	Netherlands	4:36.0
1948	United States	4:29.2
1952	Hungary	4:24.4
1956	Australia	4:17.1
1960	United States	4:08.9
1964	United States	4:03.8
1968	United States	4:02.5
1972	United States	3:55.19
1976	United States	3:44.82
1980	East Germany	3:42.71
1984	United States	3:43.43
1988	East Germany	3:40.63
1992	United States	3:39.46
1996	United States	3:39.29
2000	United States	3:36.61
2004	Australia	3:35.94
2008	Netherlands	3:33.76
2012	Australia	3:33.15*

	4x200-Meter Freestyle Relay	Time
1996	United States	7:59.87
2000	United States	7:57.80
2004	United States	7:53.42
2008	Australia	7:44.31
2012	United States	7:42.92*

	4x100-Meter Medley Relay	Time
1960	United States	4:41.1
1964	United States	4:33.9
1968	United States	4:28.3
1972	United States	4:20.75
1976	East Germany	4:07.95
1980	East Germany	4:06.67
1984	United States	4:08.34
1988	East Germany	4:03.74
1992	United States	4:02.54
1996	United States	4:02.88
2000	United States	3:58.30
2004	Australia	3:57.32
2008	Australia	3:52.69
2012	United States	3:52.05*

	10-Kilometer Marathon	Time
2008	Larisa Ilchenko, Russia	1:59:27.7
2012	Éva Risztov, Hungary	1:57:38.2

	Platform Diving	Points
1912	Greta Johansson, Sweden	39.90
1920	Stefani Fryland-Clausen, Denmark	34.60
1924	Caroline Smith, United States	33.20
1928	Elizabeth B. Pinkston, United States	31.60
1932	Dorothy Poynton, United States	40.26
1936	Dorothy Poynton Hill, United States	33.93
1948	Victoria M. Draves, United States	68.87
1952	Patricia McCormick, United States	79.37
1956	Patricia McCormick, United States	84.85
1960	Ingrid Kramer, Germany	91.28
1964	Lesley Bush, United States	99.80
1968	Milena Duchkova, Czechoslovakia	109.59
1972	Ulrika Knape, Sweden	390.00
1976	Elena Vaytsekhouskaya, USSR	406.59
1980	Martina Jaschke, E. Germany	596.25
1984	Zhou Jihong, China	435.51
1988	Xu Yanmei, China	445.20
1992	Fu Mingxia, China	461.43
1996	Fu Mingxia, China	521.58
2000	Laura Wilkinson, United States	543.75
2004	Chantelle Newbery, Australia	590.31
2008	Chen Ruolin, China	447.70
2012	Chen Ruolin, China	422.30

	Springboard Diving	Points
1920	Aileen Riggin, United States	539.90
1924	Elizabeth Becker, United States	474.50
1928	Helen Meany, United States	78.62
1932	Georgia Coleman United States	87.52
1936	Marjorie Gestring, United States	89.27
1948	Victoria M. Draves, United States	108.74
1952	Patricia McCormick, United States	147.30
1956	Patricia McCormick, United States	142.36
1960	Ingrid Kramer, Germany	155.81
1964	Ingrid Engel-Kramer, Germany	145.00
1968	Sue Gossick, United States	150.77
1972	Micki King, United States	450.03
1976	Jenni Chandler, United States	506.19
1980	Irina Kalinina, USSR	725.91
1984	Sylvie Bernier, Canada	530.70
1988	Gao Min, China	580.23
1992	Gao Min, China	572.40
1996	Fu Mingxia, China	547.68
2000	Fu Mingxia, China	609.42
2004	Guo Jingjing, China	633.15
2008	Guo Jingjing, China	415.35
2012	Wu Minxia, China	414.00

	Synchronized Platform Diving	Points
2004	Lao Lishi and Li Ting, China	352.14
2008	Wang Xin and Chen Ruolin, China	363.54
2012	Chen Ruolin and Wang Hao, China	368.40

	Synchronized Springboard Diving	Points
2004	Wu Minxia and Guo Jingjing, China	336.90
2008	Guo Jingjing and Wu Minxia, China	343.50
2012	He Zi and Wu Minxia, China	346.20

Tennis

Men's Singles

- **1896** John Boland, Great Britain
- **1900** Hugh Lawrence Doherty, Great Britain
- **1904** Beals Coleman Wright, United States
- **1908** Josiah George Ritchie, Great Britain
- **1912** Charles Lyndhurst Winslow, South Africa
- **1920** Louis Raymond, South Africa
- **1924** Vincent Richards, United States
- **1988** Miloslav Mecir, Czechoslovakia
- **1992** Marc Rosset, Switzerland
- **1996** Andre Agassi, United States
- **2000** Eugueni Kafelnikov, Russia
- **2004** Nicolas Massu, Chile
- **2008** Rafael Nadal, Spain
- **2012** Andy Murray, Great Britain

Men's Doubles

- **1896** John Boland, Great Britain & Friedrick Traun, Germany
- **1900** Hugh Lawrence Doherty & Reginald Frank Doherty, Great Britain
- **1904** Edgar Welch Leonard & Beals Coleman Wright, U.S.
- **1908** George Whiteside Hillyard & Reginald Frank Doherty, Great Britain
- **1912** Harry Austin Kitson & Charles Lyndhurst Winslow, South Africa
- **1920** Oswald Graham Noel Turnbull & Maxwell Woosnam, Great Britain
- **1924** Vincent Richards & Francis Townsend Hunter, U.S.
- **1988** Kenneth Flach & Robert A. Seguso, United States
- **1992** Boris Becker & Michael Stich, Germany
- **1996** Mark Woodforde & Todd Woodbridge, Australia
- **2000** Sebastien Lareau & Daniel Nestor, Canada
- **2004** Fernando Gonzales & Nicolas Massu, Chile
- **2008** Roger Federer & Stanislas Wawrinka, Switzerland
- **2012** Mike Bryan & Bob Bryan, United States

Women's Singles

- **1900** Charlotte Cooper, Great Britain
- **1908** Dorothy Katherine Chambers, Great Britain
- **1912** Marguerite Broquedis, France
- **1920** Suzanne Lenglen, France
- **1924** Helen Wills, United States
- **1988** Steffi Graf, W. Germany
- **1992** Jennifer Capriati, United States
- **1996** Lindsay Davenport, United States

Women's Singles

2000	Venus Williams, United States
2004	Justine Henin-Hardenne, Belgium
2008	Elena Dementieva, Russia
2012	Serena Williams, United States

Women's Doubles

1920	Winifred Margaret McNair & Kathleen McKane, Great Britain
1924	Hazel Virginia Wightman & Helen Wills, United States
1988	Pam Shriver & Zina Garrison, United States
1992	Gigi Fernandez & Mary Joe Fernandez, United States
1996	Gigi Fernandez & Mary Joe Fernandez, United States
2000	Venus Williams & Serena Williams, United States
2004	Ting Li & Tian Tian Sun, China
2008	Serena Williams & Venus Williams, United States
2012	Serena Williams & Venus Williams, United States

Mixed Doubles

2012	Victoria Azarenka & Max Mirnyi, Belarus

Track and Field—Men

	100-Meter Run	Time
1896	Thomas Burke, United States	0:12.0
1900	Francis Jarvis, United States	0:11.0
1904	Archie Hahn, United States	0:11.0
1908	Reginald Walker, South Africa	0:10.8
1912	Ralph Craig, United States	0:10.8
1920	Charles Paddock, United States	0:10.8
1924	Harold Abrahams, Great Britain	0:10.6
1928	Percy Williams, Canada	0:10.8
1932	Eddie Tolan, United States	0:10.3
1936	Jesse Owens, United States	0:10.3
1948	Harrison Dillard, United States	0:10.3
1952	Lindy Remigino, United States	0:10.4
1956	Bobby Morrow, United States	0:10.5
1960	Armin Hary, Germany	0:10.2
1964	Bob Hayes, United States	0:10.0
1968	Jim Hines, United States	0:09.95
1972	Valery Borzov, USSR	0:10.14
1976	Hasely Crawford, Trinidad	0:10.06
1980	Allan Wells, Great Britain	0:10.25
1984	Carl Lewis, United States	0:09.99
1988	Carl Lewis, United States	0:09.92
1992	Linford Christie, Great Britain	0:09.96
1996	Donovan Bailey, Canada	0:09.84
2000	Maurice Greene, United States	0:09.87
2004	Justin Gatlin, United States	0:09.85
2008	Usain Bolt, Jamaica	0:09.69
2012	Usain Bolt, Jamaica	0:09.63*

	200-Meter Run	Time
1900	Walter Tewksbury, United States	0:22.2
1904	Archie Hahn, United States	0:21.6
1908	Robert Kerr, Canada	0:22.6
1912	Ralph Craig, United States	0:21.7
1920	Allan Woodring, United States	0:22.0
1924	Jackson Scholz, United States	0:21.6
1928	Percy Williams, Canada	0:21.8
1932	Eddie Tolan, United States	0:21.2
1936	Jesse Owens, United States	0:20.7
1948	Mel Patton, United States	0:21.1
1952	Andrew Stanfield, United States	0:20.7
1956	Bobby Morrow, United States	0:20.6
1960	Livio Berruti, Italy	0:20.5
1964	Henry Carr, United States	0:20.3
1968	Tommie Smith, United States	0:19.83
1972	Valery Borzov, USSR	0:20.00
1976	Donald Quarrie, Jamaica	0:20.23
1980	Pietro Mennea, Italy	0:20.19
1984	Carl Lewis, United States	0:19.80
1988	Joe DeLoach, United States	0:19.75
1992	Mike Marsh, United States	0:20.01
1996	Michael Johnson, United States	0:19.32
2000	Konstantinos Kenteris, Greece	0:20.09
2004	Shawn Crawford, United States	0:19.79
2008	Usain Bolt, Jamaica	0:19.30*
2012	Usain Bolt, Jamaica	0:19.32

	400-Meter Run	Time
1896	Thomas Burke, United States	0:54.2
1900	Maxwell Long, United States	0:49.4
1904	Harry Hillman, United States	0:49.2
1908	Wyndham Halswelle, Gr. Brit. (walkover)	0:50.0
1912	Charles Reidpath, United States	0:48.2
1920	Bevil Rudd, South Africa	0:49.6
1924	Eric Liddell, Great Britain	0:47.6
1928	Ray Barbuti, United States	0:47.8
1932	William Carr, United States	0:46.2
1936	Archie Williams, United States	0:46.5
1948	Arthur Wint, Jamaica	0:46.2
1952	George Rhoden, Jamaica	0:45.9
1956	Charles Jenkins, United States	0:46.7
1960	Otis Davis, United States	0:44.9
1964	Michael Larrabee, United States	0:45.1
1968	Lee Evans, United States	0:43.86
1972	Vincent Matthews, United States	0:44.66
1976	Alberto Juantorena, Cuba	0:44.26
1980	Viktor Markin, USSR	0:44.60
1984	Alonzo Babers, United States	0:44.27
1988	Steve Lewis, United States	0:43.87
1992	Quincy Watts, United States	0:43.50
1996	Michael Johnson, United States	0:43.49*
2000	Michael Johnson, United States	0:43.84
2004	Jeremy Wariner, United States	0:44.00
2008	LaShawn Merritt, United States	0:43.75
2012	Kirani James, Grenada	0:43.94

	800-Meter Run	Time
1896	Edwin Flack, Australia	2:11.0
1900	Alfred Tysoe, Great Britain	2:01.2
1904	James Lightbody, United States	1:56.0
1908	Mel Sheppard, United States	1:52.8
1912	James "Ted" Meredith, United States	1:51.9
1920	Albert Hill, Great Britain	1:53.4
1924	Douglas Lowe, Great Britain	1:52.4
1928	Douglas Lowe, Great Britain	1:51.8
1932	Thomas Hampson, Great Britain	1:49.8
1936	John Woodruff, United States	1:52.9
1948	Mal Whitfield, United States	1:49.2
1952	Mal Whitfield, United States	1:49.2
1956	Tom Courtney, United States	1:47.7
1960	Peter Snell, New Zealand	1:46.3
1964	Peter Snell, New Zealand	1:45.1
1968	Ralph Doubell, Australia	1:44.3
1972	Dave Wottle, United States	1:45.9
1976	Alberto Juantorena, Cuba	1:43.50
1980	Steve Ovett, Great Britain	1:45.40
1984	Joaquim Cruz, Brazil	1:43.00
1988	Paul Ereng, Kenya	1:43.45
1992	William Tanui, Kenya	1:43.66
1996	Vebjørn Rodal, Norway	1:42.58
2000	Nils Schumann, Germany	1:45.08
2004	Yuriy Borzakovskiy, Russia	1:44.45
2008	Wilfred Bungei, Kenya	1:44.65
2012	David Lekuta Rudisha, Kenya	1:40.91*

	1,500-Meter Run	Time
1896	Edwin Flack, Australia	4:33.2
1900	Charles Bennett, Great Britain	4:06.2
1904	James Lightbody, United States	4:05.4
1908	Mel Sheppard, United States	4:03.4
1912	Arnold Jackson, Great Britain	3:56.8
1920	Albert Hill, Great Britain	4:01.8
1924	Paavo Nurmi, Finland	3:53.6
1928	Harry Larva, Finland	3:53.2
1932	Luigi Beccali, Italy	3:51.2
1936	Jack Lovelock, New Zealand	3:47.8
1948	Henry Eriksson, Sweden	3:49.8
1952	Joseph Barthel, Luxembourg	3:45.2
1956	Ron Delany, Ireland	3:41.2
1960	Herb Elliott, Australia	3:35.6
1964	Peter Snell, New Zealand	3:38.1
1968	Kipchoge Keino, Kenya	3:34.91
1972	Pekka Vasala, Finland	3:36.33
1976	John Walker, New Zealand	3:39.17
1980	Sebastian Coe, Great Britain	3:38.4
1984	Sebastian Coe, Great Britain	3:32.53
1988	Peter Rono, Kenya	3:35.96
1992	Fermin Cacho Ruiz, Spain	3:40.12
1996	Noureddine Morceli, Algeria	3:35.78
2000	Noah Ngeny, Kenya	3:32.07*
2004	Hicham El Guerrouj, Morocco	3:34.18
2008	Asbel Kiprop, Kenya[1]	3:33.11
2012	Taoufik Makhloufi, Algeria	3:34.08

(1) Originally won by Rashid Ramzi, Bahrain, who was stripped of the gold in 2009 due to doping.

	3,000-Meter Steeplechase	Time
1920	Percy Hodge, Great Britain	10:00.4
1924	Ville Ritola, Finland	9:33.6
1928	Toivo Loukola, Finland	9:21.8
1932	Volmari Iso-Hollo, Finland (about 3,450 m; extra lap by error)	10:33.4
1936	Volmari Iso-Hollo, Finland	9:03.8
1948	Tore Sjöstrand, Sweden	9:04.6
1952	Horace Ashenfelter, United States	8:45.4
1956	Chris Brasher, Great Britain	8:41.2
1960	Zdzislaw Krzyszkowiak, Poland	8:34.2
1964	Gaston Roelants, Belgium	8:30.8
1968	Amos Biwott, Kenya	8:51.0
1972	Kipchoge Keino, Kenya	8:23.64
1976	Anders Garderud, Sweden	8:08.02
1980	Bronislaw Malinowski, Poland	8:09.7
1984	Julius Korir, Kenya	8:11.80
1988	Julius Kariuki, Kenya	8:05.51*
1992	Matthew Birir, Kenya	8:08.84
1996	Joseph Keter, Kenya	8:07.12
2000	Reuben Kosgei, Kenya	8:21.43
2004	Ezekiel Kemboi, Kenya	8:05.81
2008	Brimin Kiprop Kirpruto, Kenya	8:10.34
2012	Ezekiel Kemboi, Kenya	8:18.56

	5,000-Meter Run	Time
1912	Hannes Kolehmainen, Finland	14:36.6
1920	Joseph Guillemot, France	14:55.6
1924	Paavo Nurmi, Finland	14:31.2
1928	Ville Ritola, Finland	14:38.0
1932	Lauri Lehtinen, Finland	14:30.0
1936	Gunnar Höckert, Finland	14:22.2
1948	Gaston Reiff, Belgium	14:17.6
1952	Emil Zatopek, Czechoslovakia	14:06.6
1956	Vladimir Kuts, USSR	13:39.6
1960	Murray Halberg, New Zealand	13:43.4
1964	Bob Schul, United States	13:48.8
1968	Mohamed Gammoudi, Tunisia	14:05.0
1972	Lasse Viren, Finland	13:26.4
1976	Lasse Viren, Finland	13:24.76
1980	Miruts Yifter, Ethiopia	13:20.91
1984	Said Aouita, Morocco	13:05.59
1988	John Ngugi, Kenya	13:11.70
1992	Dieter Baumann, Germany	13:12.52
1996	Venuste Niyongabo, Burundi	13:07.96
2000	Millon Wolde, Ethiopia	13:35.49
2004	Hicham El Guerrouj, Morocco	13:14.39
2008	Kenenisa Bekele, Ethiopia	12:57.82*
2012	Mo Farah, Great Britain	13:41.66

	10,000-Meter Run	Time
1912	Hannes Kolehmainen, Finland	31:20.8
1920	Paavo Nurmi, Finland	31:45.8
1924	Ville Ritola, Finland	30:23.2
1928	Paavo Nurmi, Finland	30:18.8
1932	Janusz Kusocinski, Poland	30:11.4
1936	Ilmari Salminen, Finland	30:15.4
1948	Emil Zatopek, Czechoslovakia	29:59.6
1952	Emil Zatopek, Czechoslovakia	29:17.0
1956	Vladimir Kuts, USSR	28:45.6
1960	Pyotr Bolotnikov, USSR	28:32.2
1964	Billy Mills, United States	28:24.4
1968	Naftali Temu, Kenya	29:27.4
1972	Lasse Viren, Finland	27:38.4
1976	Lasse Viren, Finland	27:40.38
1980	Miruts Yifter, Ethiopia	27:42.7
1984	Alberto Cova, Italy	27:47.54
1988	Brahim Boutayeb, Morocco	27:21.46
1992	Khalid Skah, Morocco	27:46.70
1996	Haile Gebrselassie, Ethiopia	27:07.34
2000	Haile Gebrselassie, Ethiopia	27:18.20
2004	Kenenisa Bekele, Ethiopia	27:05.10
2008	Kenenisa Bekele, Ethiopia	27:01.17*
2012	Mo Farah, Great Britain	27:30.42

	Marathon	Time
1896	Spyridon Louis, Greece	2:58:50
1900	Michel Theato, France	2:59:45.0
1904	Thomas Hicks, United States	3:28:53.0
1908	John Hayes, United States	2:55:18.4
1912	Kenneth McArthur, South Africa	2:36:54.8
1920	Hannes Kolehmainen, Finland	2:32:35.8
1924	Albin Stenroos, Finland	2:41:22.6
1928	Boughera El Ouafi, France	2:32.57
1932	Juan Zabala, Argentina	2:31:36
1936	Kee-chung Sohn, Japan[1]	2:29:19.2
1948	Delfo Cabrera, Argentina	2:34:51.6
1952	Emil Zatopek, Czechoslovakia	2:23:03.2
1956	Alain Mimoun, France	2:25:00.0
1960	Abebe Bikila, Ethiopia	2:15:16.2
1964	Abebe Bikila, Ethiopia	2:12:11.2
1968	Mamo Wolde, Ethiopia	2:20:26.4
1972	Frank Shorter, United States	2:12:19.8
1976	Waldemar Cierpinski, E. Germany	2:09:55.0
1980	Waldemar Cierpinski, E. Germany	2:11:03.0
1984	Carlos Lopes, Portugal	2:09:21
1988	Gelindo Bordin, Italy	2:10:32
1992	Hwang Young-Cho, S. Korea	2:13:23
1996	Josia Thugwane, South Africa	2:12:36
2000	Gezahegne Abera, Ethiopia	2:10:11
2004	Stefano Baldini, Italy	2:10:55
2008	Samuel Kamau Wansiru, Kenya	2:06:32*
2012	Stephen Kiprotich, Uganda	2:08:01

(1) Korean runner who competed under Japanese name Kitei Son.

	4x100-Meter Relay	Time
1912	Great Britain	0:42.4
1920	United States	0:42.2
1924	United States	0:41.0
1928	United States	0:41.0
1932	United States	0:40.0
1936	United States	0:39.8
1948	United States	0:40.6
1952	United States	0:40.1
1956	United States	0:39.5
1960	Germany (U.S. disqualified)	0:39.5
1964	United States	0:39.0
1968	United States	0:38.24
1972	United States	0:38.19
1976	United States	0:38.33
1980	USSR	0:38.26
1984	United States	0:37.83
1988	USSR (U.S. disqualified)	0:38.19
1992	United States	0:37.40
1996	Canada	0:37.69
2000	United States	0:37.61
2004	Great Britain	0:38.07
2008	Jamaica	0:37.10
2012	Jamaica	0:36.84*

	4x400-Meter Relay	Time
1908	United States	3:29.4
1912	United States	3:16.6
1920	Great Britain	3:22.2
1924	United States	3:16.0
1928	United States	3:14.2
1932	United States	3:08.2
1936	Great Britain	3:09.0
1948	United States	3:10.4
1952	Jamaica	3:03.9
1956	United States	3:04.8
1960	United States	3:02.2
1964	United States	3:00.7
1968	United States	2:56.16
1972	Kenya	2:59.8
1976	United States	2:58.65
1980	USSR	3:01.1
1984	United States	2:57.91
1988	United States	2:56.16
1992	United States	2:55.74
1996	United States	2:55.99
2000	Nigeria[1]	2:58.68
2004	United States	2:55.91
2008	United States	2:55.39*
2012	The Bahamas	2:56.72

(1) Originally won by the U.S. but awarded to Nigeria in 2012 after U.S. team member Antonio Pettigrew admitted to doping.

	20-Kilometer Walk	Time
1956	Leonid Spirin, USSR	1:31:27.4
1960	Vladimir Golubnichy, USSR	1:34:07.2
1964	Kenneth Matthews, Great Britain	1:29:34.0
1968	Vladimir Golubnichy, USSR	1:33:58.4
1972	Peter Frenkel, E. Germany	1:26:42.4
1976	Daniel Bautista, Mexico	1:24:40.6
1980	Maurizio Damilano, Italy	1:23:35.5
1984	Ernesto Canto, Mexico	1:23:13
1988	Jozef Pribilinec, Czechoslovakia	1:19.57
1992	Daniel Plaza Montero, Spain	1:21:45
1996	Jefferson Perez, Ecuador	1:20:07
2000	Robert Korzeniowski, Poland	1:18:59
2004	Ivano Brugnetti, Italy	1:19:40

	20-Kilometer Walk	Time
2008	Valeriy Borchin, Russia	1:19:01
2012	Chen Ding, China	1:18.46*

	50-Kilometer Walk	Time
1932	Thomas "Tommy" Green, Great Britain	4:50.10
1936	Harold Whitlock, Great Britain	4:30:41.4
1948	John Ljunggren, Sweden	4:41.52
1952	Giuseppe Dordoni, Italy	4:28:07.8
1956	Norman Read, New Zealand	4:30:42.8
1960	Donald Thompson, Great Britain	4:25:30
1964	Abdon Pamich, Italy	4:11:12.4
1968	Christoph Höhne, E. Germany	4:20:13.6
1972	Bernd Kannenberg, W. Germany	3:56:11.6
1980	Hartwig Gauder, E. Germany	3:49:24.0
1984	Raul Gonzalez, Mexico	3:47:26
1988	Vyacheslav Ivanenko, USSR	3:38.29
1992	Andrey Perlov, Unified Team	3:50:13
1996	Robert Korzeniowski, Poland	3:43:30
2000	Robert Korzeniowski, Poland	3:42:22
2004	Robert Korzeniowski, Poland	3:38:46
2008	Alex Schwazer, Italy	3:37:09
2012	Sergey Kirdyapkin, Russia	3:35:59*

	110-Meter Hurdles	Time
1896	Thomas Curtis, United States	0:17.6
1900	Alvin Kraenzlein, United States	0:15.4
1904	Frederick Schule, United States	0:16.0
1908	Forrest Smithson, United States	0:15.0
1912	Frederick Kelly, United States	0:15.1
1920	Earl Thomson, Canada	0:14.8
1924	Daniel Kinsey, United States	0:15.0
1928	Sydney Atkinson, South Africa	0:14.8
1932	George Saling, United States	0:14.6
1936	Forrest Towns, United States	0:14.2
1948	William Porter, United States	0:13.9
1952	Harrison Dillard, United States	0:13.7
1956	Lee Calhoun, United States	0:13.5
1960	Lee Calhoun, United States	0:13.8
1964	Hayes Jones, United States	0:13.6
1968	Willie Davenport, United States	0:13.33
1972	Rod Milburn, United States	0:13.24
1976	Guy Drut, France	0:13:30
1980	Thomas Munkelt, E. Germany	0:13.39
1984	Roger Kingdom, United States	0:13.20
1988	Roger Kingdom, United States	0:12.98
1992	Mark McKoy, Canada	0:13.12
1996	Allen Johnson, United States	0:12.95
2000	Anier Garcia, Cuba	0:13.00
2004	Liu Xiang, China	0:12.91*
2008	Dayron Robles, Cuba	0:12.93
2012	Aries Merritt, United States	0:12.92

	400-Meter Hurdles	Time
1900	Walter Tewksbury, United States	0:57.6
1904	Harry Hillman, United States	0:53.0
1908	Charles Bacon, United States	0:55.0
1920	Frank Loomis, United States	0:54.0
1924	F. Morgan Taylor, United States	0:52.6
1928	Lord Burghley, Great Britain	0:53.4
1932	Bob Tisdall, Ireland	0:51.7
1936	Glenn Hardin, United States	0:52.4
1948	Roy Cochran, United States	0:51.1
1952	Charles Moore, United States	0:50.8
1956	Glenn Davis, United States	0:50.1
1960	Glenn Davis, United States	0:49.3
1964	Rex Cawley, United States	0:49.6
1968	David Hemery, Great Britain	0:48.12
1972	John Akii-Bua, Uganda	0:47.82
1976	Edwin Moses, United States	0:47.64
1980	Volker Beck, E. Germany	0:48.70
1984	Edwin Moses, United States	0:47.75
1988	Andre Phillips, United States	0:47.19
1992	Kevin Young, United States	0:46.78
1996	Derrick Adkins, United States	0:47.54
2000	Angelo Taylor, United States	0:47.50
2004	Félix Sánchez, Dominican Republic	0:47.63
2008	Angelo Taylor, United States	0:47.25
2012	Félix Sánchez, Dominican Republic	0:47.63

Note: Event not held in 1912.

	Discus Throw	Dist.	
1896	Robert Garrett, United States	29.15m	(95' 7")
1900	Rudolf Bauer, Hungary	36.04m	(118' 3")
1904	Martin Sheridan, United States	39.28m	(128' 10")
1908	Martin Sheridan, United States	40.89m	(134' 1")
1912	Armas Taipale, Finland	45.21m	(148' 3")
1920	Elmer Niklander, Finland	44.68m	(146' 7")
1924	Clarence "Bud" Houser, U.S.	46.15m	(151' 4")
1928	Clarence "Bud" Houser, U.S.	47.32m	(155' 3")
1932	John Anderson, United States	49.49m	(162' 4")
1936	Ken Carpenter, United States	50.48m	(165' 7")
1948	Adolfo Consolini, Italy	52.78m	(173' 2")
1952	Sim Iness, United States	55.03m	(180' 6")
1956	Al Oerter, United States	56.36m	(184' 11")
1960	Al Oerter, United States	59.18m	(194' 2")
1964	Al Oerter, United States	61.00m	(200' 1")
1968	Al Oerter, United States	64.78m	(212' 6")
1972	Ludvik Danek, Czechoslovakia	64.40m	(211' 3")
1976	Mac Wilkins, United States	67.50m	(221' 5")
1980	Viktor Rashchupkin, USSR	66.64m	(218' 8")
1984	Rolf Dannenberg, W. Germany	66.60m	(218' 6")
1988	Jürgen Schult, E. Germany	68.82m	(225' 9")
1992	Romas Ubartas, Lithuania	65.12m	(213' 8")
1996	Lars Riedel, Germany	69.40m	(227' 8")
2000	Virgilijus Alekna, Lithuania	69.30m	(227' 4")
2004	Virgilijus Alekna, Lithuania	69.89m	(228' 9¾")*
2008	Gerd Kanter, Estonia	68.82m	(225' 9½")
2012	Robert Harting, Germany	68.27m	(224')

	Hammer Throw	Dist.	
1900	John Flanagan, United States	49.73m	(163' 1")
1904	John Flanagan, United States	51.23m	(168' 1")
1908	John Flanagan, United States	51.92m	(170' 4")
1912	Matt McGrath, United States	54.74m	(179' 7")
1920	Pat Ryan, United States	52.875m	(173' 5¾")
1924	Fred Tootell, United States	53.295m	(174' 10")
1928	Patrick O'Callaghan, Ireland	51.39m	(168' 7")
1932	Patrick O'Callaghan, Ireland	53.92m	(176' 11")
1936	Karl Hein, Germany	56.49m	(185' 4")
1948	Imre Németh, Hungary	56.07m	(183' 11½")
1952	József Csérmák, Hungary	60.34m	(197' 11")
1956	Harold Connolly, United States	63.19m	(207' 3")
1960	Vasily Rudenkov, USSR	67.10m	(202' 0")
1964	Romuald Klim, USSR	69.74m	(228' 10")
1968	Gyula Zsivótzky, Hungary	73.36m	(240' 8")
1972	Anatoly Bondarchuk, USSR	75.50m	(247' 8")
1976	Yuri Sedykh, USSR	77.52m	(254' 4")
1980	Yuri Sedykh, USSR	81.80m	(268' 4")
1984	Juha Tiainen, Finland	78.08m	(256' 2")
1988	Sergei Litvinov, USSR	84.80m	(278' 2")*
1992	Andrey Abduvaliyev, Unified Team	82.54m	(270' 9")
1996	Balázs Kiss, Hungary	81.24m	(266' 6")
2000	Szymon Ziolkowski, Poland	80.02m	(262' 6")
2004	Koji Murofushi, Japan	82.91m	(272')
2008	Primoz Kozmus, Slovenia	82.02m	(269' 1")
2012	Krisztián Pars, Hungary	80.59m	(264' 5")

	High Jump	Height	
1896	Ellery Clark, United States	1.81m	(5' 11¼")
1900	Irving Baxter, United States	1.90m	(6' 2¾")
1904	Samuel Jones, United States	1.80m	(5' 11")
1908	Harry Porter, United States	1.90m	(6' 2¾")
1912	Alma Richards, United States	1.93m	(6' 4")
1920	Richmond Landon, United States	1.94m	(6' 4¼")
1924	Harold Osborn, United States	1.98m	(6' 6")
1928	Robert "Bob" King, United States	1.94m	(6' 4¼")
1932	Duncan McNaughton, Canada	1.97m	(6' 5½")
1936	Cornelius Johnson, United States	2.03m	(6' 8")
1948	John Winter, Australia	1.98m	(6' 6")
1952	Walter Davis, United States	2.04m	(6' 8¼")
1956	Charles Dumas, United States	2.12m	(6' 11½")
1960	Robert Shavlakadze, USSR	2.16m	(7' 1")
1964	Valery Brumel, USSR	2.18m	(7' 1¾")
1968	Dick Fosbury, United States	2.24m	(7' 4¼")
1972	Jüri Tarmak, USSR	2.23m	(7' 3¾")
1976	Jacek Wszola, Poland	2.25m	(7' 4½")
1980	Gerd Wessig, E. Germany	2.36m	(7' 8¾")
1984	Dietmar Mögenburg, W. Germany	2.35m	(7' 8½")
1988	Gennadi Avdeyenko, USSR	2.38m	(7' 9¾")
1992	Javier Sotomayor, Cuba	2.34m	(7' 8")
1996	Charles Austin, United States	2.39m	(7' 10")*
2000	Sergey Kliugin, Russia	2.35m	(7' 8½")
2004	Stefan Holm, Sweden	2.36m	(7' 8¾")
2008	Andrey Silnov, Russia	2.36m	(7' 8¾")
2012	Ivan Ukhov, Russia	2.38m	(7' 9¾")

	Javelin Throw	Dist.	
1908	Eric Lemming, Sweden	54.82m	(179' 10")
1912	Eric Lemming, Sweden	60.64m	(198' 11")
1920	Jonni Myyrä, Finland	65.78m	(215' 9¾")
1924	Jonni Myyrä, Finland	62.96m	(206' 7")

	Javelin Throw	Dist.	
1928	Erik Lundkvist, Sweden	66.60m	(218' 6")
1932	Matti Järvinen, Finland	72.71m	(238' 6½")
1936	Gerhard Stöck, Germany	71.84m	(235' 8")
1948	Kaj Tapio Rautavaara, Finland	69.77m	(228' 11")
1952	Cy Young, United States	73.78m	(242' 1")
1956	Egil Danielsen, Norway	85.71m	(281' 2½")
1960	Viktor Tsybulenko, USSR	84.64m	(277' 8")
1964	Pauli Nevala, Finland	82.66m	(271' 2")
1968	Janis Lusis, USSR	90.10m	(295' 7")
1972	Klaus Wolfermann, W. Germany	90.48m	(296' 10")
1976	Miklós Németh, Hungary	94.58m	(310' 4")
1980	Dainis Kula, USSR	91.20m	(299' 2")
1984	Arto Härkönen, Finland	86.76m	(284' 8")
1988	Tapio Korjus, Finland	84.28m	(276' 6")
1992	Jan Zelezny, Czechoslovakia	89.66m	(294' 2")
1996	Jan Zelezny, Czech Republic	88.16m	(289' 3")
2000	Jan Zelezny, Czech Republic	90.17m	(295' 9½")
2004	Andreas Thorkildsen, Norway	86.50m	(283' 10")
2008	Andreas Thorkildsen, Norway	90.57m	(297' 1¾")
2012	Keshorn Walcott, Trinidad & Tobago	84.58m	(277' 6")

	Long Jump	Dist.	
1896	Ellery Clark, United States	6.35m	(20' 10")
1900	Alvin Kraenzlein, United States	7.18m	(23' 6¾")
1904	Meyer Prinstein, United States	7.34m	(24' 1")
1908	Frank Irons, United States	7.48m	(24' 6½")
1912	Albert Gutterson, United States	7.60m	(24' 11¼")
1920	William Petersson, Sweden	7.15m	(23' 5½")
1924	William DeHart Hubbard, U.S.	7.45m	(24' 5¼")
1928	Ed Hamm, United States	7.73m	(25' 4½")
1932	Edward Gordon, United States	7.64m	(25' ¾")
1936	Jesse Owens, United States	8.06m	(26' 5½")
1948	Willie Steele, United States	7.82m	(25' 8")
1952	Jerome Biffle, United States	7.57m	(24' 10")
1956	Gregory Bell, United States	7.83m	(25' 8¼")
1960	Ralph Boston, United States	8.12m	(26' 7¾")
1964	Lynn Davies, Great Britain	8.07m	(26' 5¾")
1968	Bob Beamon, United States	8.90m	(29' 2½")*
1972	Randy Williams, United States	8.24m	(27' ½")
1976	Arnie Robinson, United States	8.35m	(27' 4¾")
1980	Lutz Dombrowski, E. Germany	8.54m	(28' ¼")
1984	Carl Lewis, United States	8.54m	(28' ¼")
1988	Carl Lewis, United States	8.72m	(28' 7½")
1992	Carl Lewis, United States	8.67m	(28' 5½")
1996	Carl Lewis, United States	8.50m	(27' 10¾")
2000	Ivan Pedroso, Cuba	8.55m	(28' ¾")
2004	Dwight Phillips, United States	8.59m	(28' 2¼")
2008	Irving Jahir Saladino Aranda, Panama	8.34m	(27' 4¼")
2012	Greg Rutherford, Great Britain	8.31m	(27' 3¼")

	Pole Vault	Height	
1896	William Welles Hoyt, United States	3.30m	(10' 10")
1900	Irving Baxter, United States	3.30m	(10' 10")
1904	Charles Dvorak, United States	3.50m	(11' 6")
1908	Edward Cooke, United States	3.71m	(12' 2")
	Alfred Gilbert, United States (tie)	3.71m	(12' 2")
1912	Harry Stoddard Babcock, U.S.	3.95m	(12' 11½")
1920	Frank Foss, United States	4.09m	(13' 5")
1924	Lee Barnes, United States	3.95m	(12' 11½")
1928	Sabin Carr, United States	4.20m	(13' 9¼")
1932	Bill Miller, United States	4.31m	(14' 1¾")
1936	Earle Meadows, United States	4.35m	(14' 3¼")
1948	Guinn Smith, United States	4.30m	(14' 1¼")
1952	Robert Richards, United States	4.55m	(14' 11¼")
1956	Robert Richards, United States	4.56m	(14' 11½")
1960	Don Bragg, United States	4.70m	(15' 5")
1964	Fred Hansen, United States	5.10m	(16' 8¾")
1968	Bob Seagren, United States	5.40m	(17' 8½")
1972	Wolfgang Nordwig, E. Germany	5.50m	(18' ½")
1976	Tadeusz Slusarski, Poland	5.50m	(18' ½")
1980	Wladyslaw Kozakiewicz, Poland	5.78m	(18' 11½")
1984	Pierre Quinon, France	5.75m	(18' 10¼")
1988	Sergei Bubka, USSR	5.90m	(19' 4¼")
1992	Maksim Tarasov, Unified Team	5.80m	(19' ¼")
1996	Jean Galfione, France	5.92m	(19' 5")
2000	Nick Hysong, United States	5.90m	(19' 4¼")
2004	Timothy Mack, United States	5.95m	(19' 6¼")
2008	Steve Hooker, Australia	5.96m	(19' 6¾")
2012	Renaud Lavillenie, France	5.97m	(19' 7")*

	Shot Put	Dist.	
1896	Robert Garrett, United States	11.22m	(36' 9¾")
1900	Richard Sheldon, United States	14.10m	(46' 3¼")
1904	Ralph Rose, United States	14.81m	(48' 7")
1908	Ralph Rose, United States	14.21m	(46' 7½")
1912	Pat McDonald, United States	15.34m	(50' 4")
1920	Ville Pörhölä, Finland	14.81m	(48' 7¼")
1924	Clarence "Bud" Houser, United States	14.99m	(49' 2¼")
1928	John Kuck, United States	15.87m	(52' ¾")
1932	Leo Sexton, United States	16.00m	(52' 6")
1936	Hans Woellke, Germany	16.20m	(53' 1¾")
1948	Wilbur Thompson, United States	17.12m	(56' 2")
1952	W. Parry O'Brien, United States	17.41m	(57' 1½")
1956	W. Parry O'Brien, United States	18.57m	(60' 11¼")
1960	Bill Nieder, United States	19.68m	(64' 6¾")
1964	Dallas Long, United States	20.33m	(66' 8½")
1968	Randy Matson, United States	20.54m	(67' 4¾")
1972	Wladyslaw Komar, Poland	21.18m	(69' 6")
1976	Udo Beyer, E. Germany	21.05m	(69' ¾")
1980	Vladimir Kiselyov, USSR	21.35m	(70' ½")
1984	Alessandro Andrei, Italy	21.26m	(69' 9")
1988	Ulf Timmermann, E. Germany	22.47m	(73' 8¾")*
1992	Michael Stulce, United States	21.70m	(71' 2½")
1996	Randy Barnes, United States	21.62m	(70' 11¼")
2000	Arsi Harju, Finland	21.29m	(69' 10¼")
2004	Adam Nelson, United States[1]	21.16m	(69' 5¼")
2008	Tomasz Majewski, Poland	21.51m	(70' 6¾")
2012	Tomasz Majewski, Poland	21.89m	(71' 9¾")

(1) Originally won by Yuriy Bilonog, Ukraine, who was stripped of the gold in 2012 due to doping.

	Triple Jump	Dist.	
1896	James Connolly, United States	13.71m	(44' 11¾")
1900	Meyer Prinstein, United States	14.47m	(47' 5¾")
1904	Meyer Prinstein, United States	14.35m	(47' 1")
1908	Tim Ahearne, Gr. Brit.-Ireland	14.92m	(48' 11½")
1912	Gustaf Lindblom, Sweden	14.76m	(48' 5")
1920	Vilho Tuulos, Finland	14.505m	(47' 7")
1924	Anthony Winter, Australia	15.525m	(50' 11¼")
1928	Mikio Oda, Japan	15.21m	(49' 11")
1932	Chuhei Nambu, Japan	15.72m	(51' 7")
1936	Naoto Tajima, Japan	16.00m	(52' 6")
1948	Arne Ahman, Sweden	15.40m	(50' 6¼")
1952	Adhemar Ferreira da Silva, Brazil	16.22m	(53' 2¾")
1956	Adhemar Ferreira da Silva, Brazil	16.35m	(53' 7¾")
1960	Jozef Schmidt, Poland	16.81m	(55' 1½")
1964	Jozef Schmidt, Poland	16.85m	(55' 3½")
1968	Viktor Saneyev, USSR	17.39m	(57' ¾")
1972	Viktor Saneyev, USSR	17.35m	(56' 11¼")
1976	Viktor Saneyev, USSR	17.29m	(56' 8¾")
1980	Jaak Uudmäe, USSR	17.35m	(56' 11")
1984	Al Joyner, United States	17.26m	(56' 7½")
1988	Khristo Markov, Bulgaria	17.61m	(57' 9½")
1992	Mike Conley, United States	18.17m	(59' 7½")(w)
1996	Kenny Harrison, United States	18.09m	(59' 4¼")*
2000	Jonathan Edwards, Britain	17.71m	(58' 1¼")
2004	Christian Olsson, Sweden	17.79m	(58' 4½")
2008	Nelson Evora, Portugal	17.67m	(57' 11¾")
2012	Christian Taylor, United States	17.81m	(58' 5¼")

	Decathlon	Points
1904	Thomas F. Kiely, Ireland	6,036
1912	Jim Thorpe, United States[1]	8,412.995
1920	Helge Lovland, Norway	6,804.355
1924	Harold Osborn, United States	7,710.775
1928	Paavo Yrjölä, Finland	8,053.29
1932	James Bausch, United States	8,462.23
1936	Glenn Morris, United States	7,900
1948	Robert Mathias, United States	7,139
1952	Robert Mathias, United States	7,887
1956	Milton Campbell, United States	7,937
1960	Rafer Johnson, United States	8,392
1964	Willi Holdorf, Germany	7,887
1968	Bill Toomey, United States	8,193
1972	Nikolai Avilov, USSR	8,454
1976	Bruce Jenner, United States	8,618
1980	Daley Thompson, Great Britain	8,495
1984	Daley Thompson, Great Britain	8,797
1988	Christian Schenk, E. Germany	8,488
1992	Robert Zmelik, Czechoslovakia	8,611
1996	Dan O'Brien, United States	8,824
2000	Erki Nool, Estonia	8,641
2004	Roman Sebrle, Czech Republic	8,893*
2008	Bryan Clay, United States	8,791
2012	Ashton Eaton, United States	8,869

Note: Event not held in 1908. (1) Thorpe had been stripped of his medal for playing pro baseball prior to the Olympics. The Intl. Olympic Committee in 1982 posthumously restored his decathlon and pentathlon gold medals.

Track and Field—Women

	100-Meter Run	Time
1928	Elizabeth Robinson, United States	0:12.2
1932	Stella Walsh, Poland[1]	0:11.9
1936	Helen Stephens, United States	0:11.5
1948	Fanny Blankers-Koen, Netherlands	0:11.9
1952	Marjorie Jackson, Australia	0:11.5
1956	Betty Cuthbert, Australia	0:11.5
1960	Wilma Rudolph, United States	0:11.0
1964	Wyomia Tyus, United States	0:11.4
1968	Wyomia Tyus, United States	0:11.08
1972	Renate Stecher, E. Germany	0:11.07
1976	Annegret Richter, W. Germany	0:11.08
1980	Lyudmila Kondratyeva, USSR	0:11.06
1984	Evelyn Ashford, United States	0:10:97
1988	Florence Griffith-Joyner, United States	0:10.54*
1992	Gail Devers, United States	0:10.82
1996	Gail Devers, United States	0:10.94
2000	No winner[2]	NA
2004	Yuliya Nesterenko, Belarus	0:10.93
2008	Shelly-Ann Fraser, Jamaica	0:10.78
2012	Shelly-Ann Fraser-Pryce, Jamaica	0:10.75

(1) Born Stanislawa Walasiewicz. Postmortem testing revealed Walsh possessed both male and female chromosomes. (2) Marion Jones, U.S., was stripped of her gold medal in 2007 due to doping; the Intl. Olympic Committee declined to award the medal to the runner-up, who was also suspected of doping.

	200-Meter Run	Time
1948	Fanny Blankers-Koen, Netherlands	0:24.4
1952	Marjorie Jackson, Australia	0:23.7
1956	Betty Cuthbert, Australia	0:23.4
1960	Wilma Rudolph, United States	0:24.0
1964	Edith McGuire, United States	0:23.0
1968	Irena Szewinska, Poland	0:22.5
1972	Renate Stecher, E. Germany	0:22.40
1976	Bärbel Eckert, E. Germany	0:22.37
1980	Bärbel Wöckel, E. Germany	0:22.03
1984	Valerie Brisco-Hooks, United States	0:21.81
1988	Florence Griffith-Joyner, United States	0:21.34*
1992	Gwen Torrence, United States	0:21.81
1996	Marie-Jose Perec, France	0:22.12
2000	Pauline Davis-Thompson, The Bahamas[1]	0:22.27
2004	Veronica Campbell, Jamaica	0:22.05
2008	Veronica Campbell-Brown, Jamaica	0:21.74
2012	Allyson Felix, United States	0:21.88

(1) Originally won by Marion Jones, U.S., who was stripped of the gold in 2007 due to doping.

	400-Meter Run	Time
1964	Betty Cuthbert, Australia	0:52.0
1968	Colette Besson, France	0:52.0
1972	Monika Zehrt, E. Germany	0:51.08
1976	Irena Szewinska, Poland	0:49.29
1980	Marita Koch, E. Germany	0:48.88
1984	Valerie Brisco-Hooks, United States	0:48.83
1988	Olga Bryzgina, USSR	0:48.65
1992	Marie-Jose Perec, France	0:48.83
1996	Marie-Jose Perec, France	0:48.25*
2000	Cathy Freeman, Australia	0:49.11
2004	Tonique Williams-Darling, The Bahamas	0:49.41
2008	Christine Ohuruogu, Great Britain	0:49.62
2012	Sanya Richards-Ross, United States	0:49.55

	800-Meter Run	Time
1928	Lina Radke, Germany	2:16.8
1960	Lyudmila Shevtsova, USSR	2:04.3
1964	Ann Packer, Great Britain	2:01.1
1968	Madeline Manning, United States	2:00.9
1972	Hildegard Falck, W. Germany	1:58.55
1976	Tatyana Kazankina, USSR	1:54.94
1980	Nadezhda Olizarenko, USSR	1:53.43*
1984	Doina Melinte, Romania	1:57.60
1988	Sigrun Wodars, E. Germany	1:56.10
1992	Ellen Van Langen, Netherlands	1:55.54
1996	Svetlana Masterkova, Russia	1:57.73
2000	Maria Mutola, Mozambique	1:56.15
2004	Kelly Holmes, Great Britain	1:56.38
2008	Pamela Jelimo, Kenya	1:54.87
2012	Mariya Savinova, Russia	1:56.19

	1,500-Meter Run	Time
1972	Lyudmila Bragina, USSR	4:01.04
1976	Tatyana Kazankina, USSR	4:05.48
1980	Tatyana Kazankina, USSR	3:56.06
1984	Gabriella Dorio, Italy	4:03.25
1988	Paula Ivan, Romania	3:53.96*
1992	Hassiba Boulmerka, Algeria	3:55.30
1996	Svetlana Masterkova, Russia	4:00.83
2000	Nouria Merah-Benida, Algeria	4:05.10
2004	Kelly Holmes, Great Britain	3:57.90
2008	Nancy Jebet Langat, Kenya	4:00.23
2012	Asli Cakir Alptekin, Turkey	4:10.23

	3,000-Meter Run	Time
1984	Maricica Puica, Romania	8:35.96
1988	Tatyana Samolenko, USSR	8:26.53*
1992	Elena Romanova, Unified Team	8:46.04

	3,000-Meter Steeplechase	Time
2008	Gulnara Galkina-Samitova, Russia	8:58.81*
2012	Yuliya Zaripova, Russia	9:06.72

	5,000-Meter Run	Time
1996	Wang Junxia, China	14:59.88
2000	Gabriela Szabo, Romania	14:40.79*
2004	Meseret Defar, Ethiopia	14:45.65
2008	Tirunesh Dibaba, Ethiopia	15:41.40
2012	Meseret Defar, Ethiopia	15:04.25

	10,000-Meter Run	Time
1988	Olga Boldarenko, USSR	31:05.21
1992	Derartu Tulu, Ethiopia	31:06.02
1996	Fernanda Ribeiro, Portugal	31:01.63
2000	Derartu Tulu, Ethiopia	30:17.49
2004	Xing Huina, China	30:24.36
2008	Tirunesh Dibaba, Ethiopia	29:54.66*
2012	Tirunesh Dibaba, Ethiopia	30:20.75

	Marathon	Time
1984	Joan Benoit, United States	2:24:52
1988	Rosa Mota, Portugal	2:25:40
1992	Valentina Yegorova, Unified Team	2:32:41
1996	Fatuma Roba, Ethiopia	2:26:05
2000	Naoko Takahashi, Japan	2:23:14
2004	Mizuki Noguchi, Japan	2:26:20
2008	Constantina Tomescu, Romania	2:26:44
2012	Tiki Gelana, Ethiopia	2:23:07*

	4x100-Meter Relay	Time
1928	Canada	0:48.4
1932	United States	0:46.9
1936	United States	0:46.9
1948	Netherlands	0:47.5
1952	United States	0:45.9
1956	Australia	0:44.5
1960	United States	0:44.5
1964	Poland	0:43.6
1968	United States	0:42.8
1972	West Germany	0:42.81
1976	East Germany	0:42.55
1980	East Germany	0:41.60
1984	United States	0:41.65
1988	United States	0:41.98
1992	United States	0:42.11
1996	United States	0:41.95
2000	The Bahamas	0:41.95
2004	Jamaica	0:41.73
2008	Russia	0:42.31
2012	United States	0:40.82*

	4x400-Meter Relay	Time
1972	East Germany	3:23.0
1976	East Germany	3:19.23
1980	USSR	3:20.2
1984	United States	3:18.29
1988	USSR	3:15.18*
1992	Unified Team	3:20.20
1996	United States	3:20.91
2000	United States[1]	3:22.62
2004	United States[2]	3:19.01
2008	United States	3:18.54
2012	United States	3:16.87

(1) Due to team member Marion Jones's doping, the U.S. was stripped of the victory in 2008, but Jones's teammates won an appeal in 2010 to have their medals restored. (2) Team member Crystal Cox was stripped of her gold medal due to doping.

	20-Kilometer Walk	Time
2000	Wang Liping, China	1:29:05
2004	Athanasia Tsoumeleka, Greece	1:29:12
2008	Olga Kaniskina, Russia	1:26:31
2012	Elena Lashmanova, Russia	1:25:02*

	100-Meter Hurdles	Time
1972	Annelie Ehrhardt, E. Germany	0:12.59
1976	Johanna Schaller, E. Germany	0:12.77
1980	Vera Komisova, USSR	0:12.56
1984	Benita Fitzgerald-Brown, United States	0:12.84
1988	Yordanka Donkova, Bulgaria	0:12.38
1992	Paraskevi Patoulidou, Greece	0:12.64
1996	Ludmila Engquist, Sweden	0:12.58
2000	Olga Shishigina, Kazakhstan	0:12.65
2004	Joanna Hayes, United States	0:12.37
2008	Dawn Harper, United States	0:12.54
2012	Sally Pearson, Australia	0:12.35*

	400-Meter Hurdles	Time
1984	Nawal El Moutawakel, Morocco	0:54.61
1988	Debra Flintoff-King, Australia	0:53.17
1992	Sally Gunnell, Great Britain	0:53.23
1996	Deon Hemmings, Jamaica	0:52.82
2000	Irina Privalova, Russia	0:53.02
2004	Faní Halkia, Greece	0:52.82
2008	Melaine Walker, Jamaica	0:52.64*
2012	Natalya Antyukh, Russia	0:52.70

	Discus Throw	Dist.	
1928	Halina Konopacka, Poland	39.62m	(130' 0")
1932	Lillian Copeland, United States	40.58m	(133' 2")
1936	Gisela Mauermayer, Germany	47.63m	(156' 3")
1948	Micheline Ostermeyer, France	41.92m	(137' 6")
1952	Nina Ponomareva, USSR	51.42m	(168' 8")
1956	Olga Fikotová, Czechoslovakia	53.69m	(176' 1¾")
1960	Nina Ponomareva, USSR	55.10m	(180' 9")
1964	Tamara Press, USSR	57.27m	(187' 10¾")
1968	Lia Manoliu, Romania	58.28m	(191' 2")
1972	Faina Melnik, USSR	66.62m	(218' 7")
1976	Evelin Jahl, E. Germany	69.00m	(226' 4")
1980	Evelin Jahl, E. Germany	69.96m	(229' 6")
1984	Ria Stalman, Netherlands	65.36m	(214' 5")
1988	Martina Hellmann, E. Germany	72.30m	(237' 2")*
1992	Maritza Martén, Cuba	70.06m	(229' 10")
1996	Ilke Wyludda, Germany	69.66m	(228' 6")
2000	Ellina Zvereva, Belarus	68.40m	(224' 5")
2004	Natalya Sadova, Russia	67.02m	(219' 8¾")
2008	Stephanie Brown Trafton, U.S.	64.74m	(212' 4¾")
2012	Sandra Perkoviç, Croatia	69.11m	(226' 9")

	Hammer Throw	Dist.	
2000	Kamila Skolimowska, Poland	71.16m	(233' 5¾")
2004	Olga Kuzenkova, Russia	75.02m	(246' 1")
2008	Aksana Miankova, Belarus	76.34m	(250' 5½")
2012	Tatyana Lysenko, Russia	78.18m	(256' 6")*

	High Jump	Height	
1928	Ethel Catherwood, Canada	1.59m	(5' 2½")
1932	Jean Shiley, United States	1.67m	(5' 5½")
1936	Ibolya Csák, Hungary	1.60m	(5' 3")
1948	Alice Coachman, United States	1.68m	(5' 6")
1952	Esther Brand, South Africa	1.67m	(5' 5¾")
1956	Mildred McDaniel, United States	1.76m	(5' 9¼")
1960	Iolanda Balas, Romania	1.85m	(6' ¾")
1964	Iolanda Balas, Romania	1.90m	(6' 2¾")
1968	Miloslava Rezková, Czech.	1.82m	(5' 11½")
1972	Ulrike Meyfarth, W. Germany	1.92m	(6' 3½")
1976	Rosemarie Ackermann, E. Germany	1.93m	(6' 4")
1980	Sara Simeoni, Italy	1.97m	(6' 5½")
1984	Ulrike Meyfarth, W. Germany	2.02m	(6' 7½")
1988	Louise Ritter, United States	2.03m	(6' 8")
1992	Heike Henkel, Germany	2.02m	(6' 7½")
1996	Stefka Kostadinova, Bulgaria	2.05m	(6' 8¾")
2000	Yelena Yelesina, Russia	2.01m	(6' 7")
2004	Yelena Slesarenko, Russia	2.06m	(6' 9")*
2008	Tia Hellebaut, Belgium	2.05m	(6' 8¾")
2012	Anna Chicherova, Russia	2.05m	(6' 8¾")

	Javelin Throw	Dist.	
1932	"Babe" Didrikson, United States	43.68m	(143' 4")
1936	Tilly Fleischer, Germany	45.18m	(148' 3")
1948	Herma Bauma, Austria	45.57m	(149' 6")
1952	Dana Zátopková, Czechoslovakia	50.47m	(165' 7")
1956	Inese Jaunzeme, USSR	53.86m	(176' 8")
1960	Elvira Ozolina, USSR	55.98m	(183' 8")
1964	Mihaela Penes, Romania	60.54m	(198' 7")
1968	Angéla Németh, Hungary	60.36m	(198' 0")
1972	Ruth Fuchs, E. Germany	63.88m	(209' 7")
1976	Ruth Fuchs, E. Germany	65.94m	(216' 4")
1980	Maria Colón, Cuba	68.40m	(224' 5")
1984	Tessa Sanderson, Great Britain	69.56m	(228' 2")
1988	Petra Felke, E. Germany	74.68m	(245' 0")
1992	Silke Renk, Germany	68.34m	(224' 2")
1996	Heli Rantanen, Finland	67.94m	(222' 11")
2000	Trine Hattestad, Norway	68.91m	(226' 1")
2004	Osleidys Menendez, Cuba	71.53m	(234' 8")*
2008	Barbora Špotáková, Czech Republic	71.42m	(234' ¾")
2012	Barbora Špotáková, Czech Republic	69.55m	(228' 2¼")

Note: New records were kept after javelin was modified in 1999.

	Long Jump	Dist.	
1948	Olga Gyarmati, Hungary	5.69m	(18' 8")
1952	Yvette Williams, New Zealand	6.24m	(20' 5¼")
1956	Elzbieta Krzesinska, Poland	6.35m	(20' 10")
1960	Vera Krepkina, USSR	6.37m	(20' 10¾")
1964	Mary Rand, Great Britain	6.76m	(22' 2¼")
1968	Viorica Viscopoleanu, Romania	6.82m	(22' 4½")
1972	Heidemarie Rosendahl, W. Germany	6.78m	(22' 3")
1976	Angela Voigt, E. Germany	6.72m	(22' ¾")
1980	Tatyana Kolpakova, USSR	7.06m	(23' 2")
1984	Anisoara Cusmir-Stanciu, Romania	6.96m	(22' 10")
1988	Jackie Joyner-Kersee, United States	7.40m	(24' 3½")*
1992	Heike Drechsler, Germany	7.14m	(23' 5¼")
1996	Chioma Ajunwa, Nigeria	7.12m	(23' 4¼")
2000	Heike Drechsler, Germany	6.99m	(22' 11¼")
2004	Tatyana Lebedeva, Russia	7.07m	(23' 2½")
2008	Maurren Higa Maggi, Brazil	7.04m	(23' 1¼")
2012	Brittney Reese, United States	7.12m	(23' 4¼")

	Pole Vault	Height	
2000	Stacy Dragila, United States	4.60m	(15' 1")
2004	Elena Isinbaeva, Russia	4.91m	(16' 1¼')
2008	Elena Isinbaeva, Russia	5.05m	(16' 6¾")
2012	Jennifer Suhr, United States	4.75m	(15' 7")

	Shot Put	Dist.	
1948	Micheline Ostermeyer, France	13.75m	(45' 1½")
1952	Galina Zybina, USSR	15.28m	(50' 1½")
1956	Tamara Tyshkevich, USSR	16.59m	(54' 5¼")
1960	Tamara Press, USSR	17.32m	(56' 10")
1964	Tamara Press, USSR	18.14m	(59' 6¼")
1968	Margitta Gummel, E. Germany	19.61m	(64' 4")
1972	Nadezhda Chizhova, USSR	21.03m	(69' 0")
1976	Ivanka Khristova, Bulgaria	21.16m	(69' 5¼")
1980	Ilona Slupianek, E. Germany	22.41m	(73' 6¼")*
1984	Claudia Losch, W. Germany	20.48m	(67' 2")
1988	Natalya Lisovskaya, USSR	22.24m	(72' 11¾")
1992	Svetlana Krivelyova, Unified Team	21.06m	(69' 1¼")
1996	Astrid Kumbernuss, Germany	20.56m	(67' 5½")
2000	Yanina Karolchik, Belarus	20.56m	(67' 5½")
2004	Yumileidi Cumbá, Cuba	19.59m	(64' 3¼")
2008	Valerie Vili, New Zealand	20.56m	(67' 5½")
2012	Valerie Adams, New Zealand	20.70m	(67' 11")

	Triple Jump	Dist.	
1996	Inessa Kravets, Ukraine	15.33m	(50' 3½")
2000	Tereza Marinova, Bulgaria	15.20m	(49' 10½")
2004	Francoise Mbango Etone, Cameroon	15.30m	(50' 2¼")
2008	Francoise Mbango Etone, Cameroon	15.39m	(50' 6")*
2012	Olga Rypakova, Kazakhstan	14.98m	(49' 1¾")

	Heptathlon	Points
1984	Glynis Nunn, Australia	6,390
1988	Jackie Joyner-Kersee, United States	7,291*
1992	Jackie Joyner-Kersee, United States	7,044
1996	Ghada Shouaa, Syria	6,780
2000	Denise Lewis, Great Britain	6,584
2004	Carolina Kluft, Sweden	6,952
2008	Nataliia Dobrynska, Ukraine	6,733
2012	Jessica Ennis, Great Britain	6,955

COLLEGE FOOTBALL

Ohio State Wins Inaugural College Football Playoff

Ohio State defeated Oregon, 42-20, in the first national championship game of the playoff era Jan. 12, 2015, in Arlington, TX. Buckeye sophomore Ezekiel Elliott ran for 246 yards and four touchdowns and head coach Urban Meyer claimed his third career national title just three seasons into his tenure with Ohio State. Oregon's 2014 Heisman-winning quarterback Marcus Mariota passed for 333 yards and two touchdowns, but the Ducks were held to their lowest final score of the season.

No. 4-ranked Ohio State defeated No. 1 Alabama in the College Football Playoff (CFP) semifinal Sugar Bowl, 42-35, to reach the national title game. No. 2-ranked Oregon reached the CFP championship with a 59-20 semifinal Rose Bowl victory over No. 3 Florida State.

The NCAA Football Bowl Subdivision (FBS) College Football Playoff replaced the Bowl Championship Series (BCS) at the end of the 2014 regular season. The four-team CFP consists of a semifinal round (rotating among the following six bowl games: Sugar, Rose, Orange, Cotton, Peach, and Fiesta) and a championship game played on a Monday night. A committee selects and ranks 25 teams for the playoffs and selected other bowl games at the end of the regular season, using guidelines that include strength of schedule, head-to-head results, and won-loss records; preference is given to conference champions.

National College Football Champions, 1936-2014

The Bowl Championship Series (BCS) National Championship game (BCS No. 1 vs. BCS No. 2) determined the NCAA's Football Bowl Subdivision (Div. I-A) official champion in 1998-2013. A four-team College Football Playoff determined the champion beginning with the 2014 season. Years preceding 1998 show the unofficial champion(s), as selected by the AP poll of writers and a separate poll of coaches. Where the polls disagreed, both teams are listed with AP winner first. The AP poll started in 1936, the coaches poll in 1950.

Year	Champion(s)	Year	Champion(s)	Year	Champion(s)	Year	Champion(s)	Year	Champion(s)
1936	Minnesota	1952	Michigan St.	1968	Ohio St.	1983	Miami (FL)	1999	Florida St.
1937	Pittsburgh	1953	Maryland	1969	Texas	1984	Brigham Young	2000	Oklahoma
1938	Texas Christian	1954	Ohio St./UCLA	1970	Nebraska/Texas	1985	Oklahoma	2001	Miami (FL)
1939	Texas A&M	1955	Oklahoma	1971	Nebraska	1986	Penn St.	2002	Ohio St.
1940	Minnesota	1956	Oklahoma	1972	USC	1987	Miami (FL)	2003	LSU/USC
1941	Minnesota	1957	Auburn/Ohio St.	1973	Notre Dame/ Alabama	1988	Notre Dame	2004	Vacated[1]
1942	Ohio St.	1958	LSU			1989	Miami (FL)	2005	Texas
1943	Notre Dame	1959	Syracuse	1974	Oklahoma/USC	1990	Colorado/GA Tech	2006	Florida
1944	Army	1960	Minnesota	1975	Oklahoma	1991	Miami (FL)/Wash.	2007	LSU
1945	Army	1961	Alabama	1976	Pittsburgh	1992	Alabama	2008	Florida
1946	Notre Dame	1962	USC	1977	Notre Dame	1993	Florida St.	2009	Alabama
1947	Notre Dame	1963	Texas	1978	Alabama/USC	1994	Nebraska	2010	Auburn
1948	Michigan	1964	Alabama	1979	Alabama	1995	Nebraska	2011	Alabama
1949	Notre Dame	1965	Alabama/Mich. St.	1980	Georgia	1996	Florida	2012	Alabama
1950	Oklahoma	1966	Notre Dame	1981	Clemson	1997	Mich./Nebraska	2013	Florida St.
1951	Tennessee	1967	USC	1982	Penn St.	1998	Tennessee	2014	Ohio St.

(1) The BCS's Presidential Oversight Committee vacated USC's 2004 championship due to rules violations.

2014 Final Rankings

College Football Playoff Rankings

Rank, team	Rank, team
1. Alabama	13. Georgia
2. Oregon	14. UCLA
3. Florida State	15. Arizona State
4. Ohio State	16. Missouri
5. Baylor	17. Clemson
6. TCU	18. Wisconsin
7. Mississippi State	19. Auburn
8. Michigan State	20. Boise State
9. Mississippi	21. Louisville
10. Arizona	22. Utah
11. Kansas State	23. LSU
12. Georgia Tech	24. USC
	25. Minnesota

Associated Press Poll

Rank, team	Rank, team
1. Ohio State	13. Wisconsin
2. Oregon	14. Missouri
3. TCU	15. Clemson
4. Alabama	16. Boise State
5. Michigan State	17. Mississippi
6. Florida State	18. Kansas State
7. Baylor	19. Arizona
8. Georgia Tech	20. USC
9. Georgia	21. Utah
10. UCLA	22. Auburn
11. Mississippi State	23. Marshall
12. Arizona State	24. Louisville
	25. Memphis

USA Today Coaches Poll

Rank, team	Rank, team
1. Ohio State	14. Arizona State
2. Oregon	15. Clemson
3. TCU	16. Boise State
4. Alabama	17. Arizona
5. Michigan State	18. Kansas State
6. Florida State	19. Mississippi
7. Georgia Tech	20. Utah
8. Baylor	21. USC
9. Georgia	22. Marshall
10. UCLA	23. Auburn
11. Missouri	24. Louisville
12. Mississippi State	25. Memphis
13. Wisconsin	

Note: College Football Playoff ranking is as of Dec. 7, 2014, prior to bowl games and playoffs. Final AP and USA Today polls are as of Jan. 13, 2015 (after all bowls and championship game).

Annual Results of Major Bowl Games

Date indicates year the game was played; bowl games are generally played in late Dec. or early Jan. CFP = College Football Playoff semifinal game.

Rose Bowl Results, 1902-2015

1902	(Jan.) Michigan 49, Stanford 0	1933	USC 35, Pittsburgh 0	1951	Michigan 14, California 6
1916	Washington St. 14, Brown 0	1934	Columbia 7, Stanford 0	1952	Illinois 40, Stanford 7
1917	Oregon 14, Pennsylvania 0	1935	(Jan.) Alabama 29, Stanford 13	1953	USC 7, Wisconsin 0
1918-19	Service teams	1936	Stanford 7, SMU 0	1954	Michigan St. 28, UCLA 20
1920	Harvard 7, Oregon 6	1937	Pittsburgh 21, Washington 0	1955	Ohio St. 20, USC 7
1921	California 28, Ohio St. 0	1938	California 13, Alabama 0	1956	Michigan St. 17, UCLA 14
1922	Washington & Jefferson 0, California 0	1939	USC 7, Duke 3	1957	Iowa 35, Oregon St. 19
		1940	USC 14, Tennessee 0	1958	Ohio St. 10, Oregon 7
1923	USC 14, Penn St. 3	1941	Stanford 21, Nebraska 13	1959	Iowa 38, California 12
1924	Navy 14, Washington 14	1942	Oregon St. 20, Duke 16	1960	Washington 44, Wisconsin 8
1925	Notre Dame 27, Stanford 10	1943	Georgia 9, UCLA 0	1961	Washington 17, Minnesota 7
1926	Alabama 20, Washington 19	1944	USC 29, Washington 0	1962	Minnesota 21, UCLA 3
1927	Alabama 7, Stanford 7	1945	USC 25, Tennessee 0	1963	USC 42, Wisconsin 37
1928	Stanford 7, Pittsburgh 6	1946	Alabama 34, USC 14	1964	Illinois 17, Washington 7
1929	Georgia Tech 8, California 7	1947	Illinois 45, UCLA 14	1965	Michigan 34, Oregon St. 7
1930	USC 47, Pittsburgh 14	1948	Michigan 49, USC 0	1966	UCLA 14, Michigan St. 12
1931	Alabama 24, Washington St. 0	1949	Northwestern 20, California 14	1967	Purdue 14, USC 13
1932	USC 21, Tulane 12	1950	Ohio St. 17, California 14	1968	USC 14, Indiana 3

1969	Ohio St. 27, USC 16
1970	USC 10, Michigan 3
1971	Stanford 27, Ohio St. 17
1972	Stanford 13, Michigan 12
1973	USC 42, Ohio St. 17
1974	Ohio St. 42, USC 21
1975	USC 18, Ohio St. 17
1976	UCLA 23, Ohio St. 10
1977	USC 14, Michigan 6
1978	Washington 27, Michigan 20
1979	USC 17, Michigan 10
1980	USC 17, Ohio St. 16
1981	Michigan 23, Washington 6
1982	Washington 28, Iowa 0
1983	UCLA 24, Michigan 14
1984	UCLA 45, Illinois 9
1985	USC 20, Ohio St. 17
1986	UCLA 45, Iowa 28
1987	Arizona St. 22, Michigan 15
1988	Michigan St. 20, USC 17
1989	Michigan 22, USC 14
1990	USC 17, Michigan 10
1991	Washington 46, Iowa 34
1992	Washington 34, Michigan 14
1993	Michigan 38, Washington 31
1994	Wisconsin 21, UCLA 16
1995	Penn St. 38, Oregon 20
1996	USC 41, Northwestern 32
1997	Ohio St. 20, Arizona St. 17
1998	Michigan 21, Washington St. 16
1999	Wisconsin 38, UCLA 31
2000	Wisconsin 17, Stanford 9
2001	Washington 34, Purdue 24
2002	Miami (FL) 37, Nebraska 14
2003	Oklahoma 34, Washington St. 14
2004	USC 28, Michigan 14
2005	Texas 38, Michigan 37
2006	Texas 41, USC 38
2007	USC 32, Michigan 18
2008	USC 49, Illinois 17
2009	USC 38, Penn St. 24
2010	Ohio St. 26, Oregon 17
2011	TCU 21, Wisconsin 19
2012	Oregon 45, Wisconsin 38
2013	Stanford 20, Wisconsin 14
2014	Michigan St. 24, Stanford 20
2015	Oregon 59, Florida St. 20 (CFP)

Orange Bowl Results, 1935-2015

1935	(Jan.) Bucknell 26, Miami (FL) 0
1936	Catholic U. 20, Mississippi 19
1937	Duquesne 13, Mississippi St. 12
1938	Auburn 6, Michigan St. 0
1939	Tennessee 17, Oklahoma 0
1940	Georgia Tech 21, Missouri 7
1941	Mississippi St. 14, Georgetown 7
1942	Georgia 40, TCU 26
1943	Alabama 37, Boston College 21
1944	LSU 19, Texas A&M 14
1945	Tulsa 26, Georgia Tech 12
1946	Miami (FL) 13, Holy Cross 6
1947	Rice 8, Tennessee 0
1948	Georgia Tech 20, Kansas 14
1949	Texas 41, Georgia 28
1950	Santa Clara 21, Kentucky 13
1951	Clemson 15, Miami (FL) 14
1952	Georgia Tech 17, Baylor 14
1953	Alabama 61, Syracuse 6
1954	Oklahoma 7, Maryland 0
1955	Duke 34, Nebraska 7
1956	Oklahoma 20, Maryland 6
1957	Colorado 27, Clemson 21
1958	Oklahoma 48, Duke 21
1959	Oklahoma 21, Syracuse 6
1960	Georgia 14, Missouri 0
1961	Missouri 21, Navy 14
1962	LSU 25, Colorado 7
1963	Alabama 17, Oklahoma 0
1964	Nebraska 13, Auburn 7
1965	Texas 21, Alabama 17
1966	Alabama 39, Nebraska 28
1967	Florida 27, Georgia Tech 12
1968	Oklahoma 26, Tennessee 24
1969	Penn St. 15, Kansas 14
1970	Penn St. 10, Missouri 3
1971	Nebraska 17, LSU 12
1972	Nebraska 38, Alabama 6
1973	Nebraska 40, Notre Dame 6
1974	Penn St. 16, LSU 9
1975	Notre Dame 13, Alabama 11
1976	Oklahoma 14, Michigan 6
1977	Ohio St. 27, Colorado 10
1978	Arkansas 31, Oklahoma 6
1979	Oklahoma 31, Nebraska 24
1980	Oklahoma 24, Florida St. 7
1981	Oklahoma 18, Florida St. 17
1982	Clemson 22, Nebraska 15
1983	Nebraska 21, LSU 20
1984	Miami (FL) 31, Nebraska 30
1985	Washington 28, Oklahoma 17
1986	Oklahoma 25, Penn St. 10
1987	Oklahoma 42, Arkansas 8
1988	Miami (FL) 20, Oklahoma 14
1989	Miami (FL) 23, Nebraska 3
1990	Notre Dame 21, Colorado 6
1991	Colorado 10, Notre Dame 9
1992	Miami (FL) 22, Nebraska 0
1993	Florida St. 27, Nebraska 14
1994	Florida St. 18, Nebraska 16
1995	Nebraska 24, Miami (FL) 17
1996	Florida St. 31, Notre Dame 26
1996	(Dec.) Nebraska 41, Virginia Tech 21
1998	(Jan.) Nebraska 42, Tennessee 17
1999	Florida 31, Syracuse 10
2000	Michigan 35, Alabama 34 (OT)
2001	Oklahoma 13, Florida St. 2
2002	Florida 56, Maryland 23
2003	USC 38, Iowa 17
2004	Miami (FL) 16, Florida St. 14
2005	USC 55, Oklahoma 19
2006	Penn St. 26, Florida St. 23 (3 OT)
2007	Louisville 24, Wake Forest 13
2008	Kansas 24, Virginia Tech 21
2009	Virginia Tech 20, Cincinnati 7
2010	Iowa 24, Georgia Tech 14
2011	Stanford 40, Virginia Tech 12
2012	West Virginia 70, Clemson 33
2013	Florida St. 31, Northern Illinois 10
2014	Clemson 40, Ohio St. 35
2015	(Dec.) Georgia Tech 49, Mississippi St. 34

Sugar Bowl Results, 1935-2015

1935	(Jan.) Tulane 20, Temple 14
1936	TCU 3, LSU 2
1937	Santa Clara 21, LSU 14
1938	Santa Clara 6, LSU 0
1939	TCU 15, Carnegie Tech 7
1940	Texas A&M 14, Tulane 13
1941	Boston College 19, Tennessee 13
1942	Fordham 2, Missouri 0
1943	Tennessee 14, Tulsa 7
1944	Georgia Tech 20, Tulsa 18
1945	Duke 29, Alabama 26
1946	Oklahoma A&M 33, St. Mary's (CA) 13
1947	Georgia 20, N. Carolina 10
1948	Texas 27, Alabama 7
1949	Oklahoma 14, N. Carolina 6
1950	Oklahoma 35, LSU 0
1951	Kentucky 13, Oklahoma 7
1952	Maryland 28, Tennessee 13
1953	Georgia Tech 24, Mississippi 7
1954	Georgia Tech 42, West Virginia 19
1955	Navy 21, Mississippi 0
1956	Georgia Tech 7, Pittsburgh 0
1957	Baylor 13, Tennessee 7
1958	Mississippi 39, Texas 7
1959	LSU 7, Clemson 0
1960	Mississippi 21, LSU 0
1961	Mississippi 14, Rice 6
1962	Alabama 10, Arkansas 3
1963	Mississippi 17, Arkansas 13
1964	Alabama 12, Mississippi 7
1965	LSU 13, Syracuse 10
1966	Missouri 20, Florida 18
1967	Alabama 34, Nebraska 7
1968	LSU 20, Wyoming 13
1969	Arkansas 16, Georgia 2
1970	Mississippi 27, Arkansas 22
1971	Tennessee 34, Air Force 13
1972	Oklahoma 40, Auburn 22
1972	(Dec.) Oklahoma 14, Penn St. 0
1973	Notre Dame 24, Alabama 23
1974	Nebraska 13, Florida 10
1975	Alabama 13, Penn St. 6
1977	(Jan.) Pittsburgh 27, Georgia 3
1978	Alabama 35, Ohio St. 6
1979	Alabama 14, Penn St. 7
1980	Alabama 24, Arkansas 9
1981	Georgia 17, Notre Dame 10
1982	Pittsburgh 24, Georgia 20
1983	Penn St. 27, Georgia 23
1984	Auburn 9, Michigan 7
1985	Nebraska 28, LSU 10
1986	Tennessee 35, Miami (FL) 7
1987	Nebraska 30, LSU 15
1988	Syracuse 16, Auburn 16
1989	Florida St. 13, Auburn 7
1990	Miami (FL) 33, Alabama 25
1991	Tennessee 23, Virginia 22
1992	Notre Dame 39, Florida 28
1993	Alabama 34, Miami (FL) 13
1994	Florida 41, West Virginia 7
1995	Florida St. 23, Florida 17
1995	(Dec.) Virginia Tech 28, Texas 10
1997	(Jan.) Florida 52, Florida St. 20
1998	Florida St. 31, Ohio St. 14
1999	Ohio St. 24, Texas A&M 14
2000	Florida St. 46, Virginia Tech 29
2001	Miami (FL) 37, Florida 20
2002	LSU 47, Illinois 34
2003	Georgia 26, Florida St. 13
2004	LSU 21, Oklahoma 14
2005	Auburn 16, Virginia Tech 13
2006	West Virginia 38, Georgia 35
2007	LSU 41, Notre Dame 14
2008	Georgia 41, Hawaii 10
2009	Utah 31, Alabama 17
2010	Florida 51, Cincinnati 24
2011	Ohio St. 31, Arkansas 26
2012	Michigan 23, Virginia Tech 20
2013	Louisville 33, Florida 23
2014	Oklahoma 45, Alabama 31
2015	Ohio St. 42, Alabama 35 (CFP)

Other Bowl Results, Dec. 2014-Jan. 2015

Alamo Bowl, San Antonio, TX: UCLA 40, Kansas St. 35

Armed Forces Bowl, Ft. Worth, TX: Houston 35, Pittsburgh 34

Bahamas Bowl, Nassau, Bahamas: Western Kentucky 49, Central Michigan 48

Belk Bowl, Charlotte, NC: Georgia 37, Louisville 14

Birmingham Bowl, Birmingham, AL: Florida 28, East Carolina 20

Boca Raton Bowl, Boca Raton, FL: Marshall 52, Northern Illinois 23

Cactus Bowl, Tempe, AZ: Oklahoma St. 30, Washington 22

Camellia Bowl, Montgomery, AL: Bowling Green 33, South Alabama 28

Citrus Bowl, Orlando FL: Missouri 33, Minnesota 17

Cotton Bowl, Arlington, TX: Michigan St. 42, Baylor 41

Famous Idaho Potato Bowl, Boise, ID: Air Force 38, Western Michigan 24

Fiesta Bowl, Glendale, AZ: Boise St. 38, Arizona 30

Foster Farms Bowl, Santa Clara, CA: Stanford 45, Maryland 21

Gator Bowl, Jacksonville, FL: Tennessee 45, Iowa 28

GoDaddy Bowl, Mobile, AL: Toledo 63, Arkansas St. 44

Hawaii Bowl, Honolulu, HI: Rice 30, Fresno St. 6
Heart of Dallas Bowl, Dallas, TX: Louisiana Tech 35, Illinois 18
Holiday Bowl, San Diego, CA: USC 45, Nebraska 42
Independence Bowl, Shreveport, LA: South Carolina 24, Miami (FL) 21
Las Vegas Bowl, Las Vegas, NV: Utah 45, Colorado St. 10
Liberty Bowl, Memphis, TN: Texas A&M 45, West Virginia 37
Miami Beach Bowl, Miami, FL: Memphis 55, BYU 48 (2OT)
Military Bowl, Annapolis, MD: Virginia Tech 33, Cincinnati 17
Music City Bowl, Nashville, TN: Notre Dame 31, LSU 28
New Mexico Bowl, Albuquerque, NM: Utah St. 21, UTEP 6
New Orleans Bowl, New Orleans, LA: LA-Lafayette 16, Nevada 3
Outback Bowl, Tampa, FL: Wisconsin 34, Auburn 31 (OT)
Peach Bowl, Atlanta, GA: TCU 42, Mississippi 3
Pinstripe Bowl, Bronx, NY: Penn St. 31, Boston Coll. 30 (OT)
Poinsettia Bowl, San Diego, CA: Navy 17, San Diego St. 16
Quick Lane Bowl, Detroit, MI: Rutgers 40, North Carolina 21
Russell Athletic Bowl, Orlando, FL: Clemson 40, Oklahoma 6
St. Petersburg Bowl, St. Petersburg, FL: NC State 34, Central Florida 27
Sun Bowl, El Paso, TX: Arizona St. 36, Duke 31
Texas Bowl, Houston, TX: Arkansas 31, Texas 7

All-Time NCAA Bowl Subdivision (FBS) Statistical Leaders

Career Rushing Yards

Player, team	Yrs	Carries	Yds	Avg
Ron Dayne, Wisconsin	1996-99	1,115	6,397	5.74
Ricky Williams, Texas	1995-98	1,011	6,279	6.21
Tony Dorsett, Pittsburgh	1973-76	1,074	6,082	5.66
DeAngelo Williams, Memphis	2002-05	969	6,026	6.22
Charles White, USC	1976-79	1,023	5,598	5.47

Career Rushing Yards/Game (min. 2,500 yds)

Player, team	Yrs	Carries	Yds	Avg/game
Ed Marinaro, Cornell	1969-71	918	4,715	174.6
O. J. Simpson, USC	1967-68	621	3,214	164.4
Herschel Walker, Georgia	1980-82	994	5,259	159.4
Garrett Wolfe, N. Illinois	2004-06	807	5,164	156.5
LeShon Johnson, N. Illinois	1992-93	592	3,314	150.6

Career Passing Yards

Player, team	Yrs	Comp/att	Yds
Case Keenum, Houston	2007-11	1,546/2,229	19,217
Timmy Chang, Hawaii	2000-04	1,388/2,436	17,072
Landry Jones, Oklahoma	2009-12	1,388/2,183	16,646
Graham Harrell, Texas Tech	2005-08	1,403/2,010	15,793
Ty Detmer, BYU	1988-91	958/1,530	15,031

Career Receiving Yards

Player, team	Yrs	Rec	Yds	Avg
Trevor Insley, Nevada	1996-99	298	5,005	16.8
Ryan Broyles, Oklahoma	2008-11	349	4,586	13.1
Justin Hardy, E. Carolina	2011-15	387	4,541	11.7
Marcus Harris, Wyoming	1993-96	259	4,518	17.4
Rashaun Woods, Oklahoma St.	2000-03	293	4,414	15.1

Note: As of end of 2014 season. Prior to 2002, postseason games were not included in NCAA final football statistics or records. All postseason games were included for the 2002 season and thereafter. Career rushing yards per game rankings do not include active players.

All-Time NCAA Bowl Subdivision (FBS) Team Won-Lost Records

Team	Yrs	W	L	T	Games	Pct.
Notre Dame	126	882	310	42	1,234	0.732
Michigan	135	915	328	36	1,279	0.729
Boise St. (1996)	47	408	155	2	565	0.724
Ohio St.[1]	125	863	319	53	1,235	0.720
Oklahoma	120	850	317	53	1,220	0.718
Alabama[1]	120	850	325	43	1,218	0.716
Texas	122	881	346	33	1,260	0.712
USC[1]	122	805	327	54	1,186	0.702
Nebraska	125	874	361	40	1,275	0.701
Penn St.	128	849	376	42	1,267	0.687
Tennessee	118	811	367	53	1,231	0.680
Florida St.[1]	68	512	238	17	767	0.679
Georgia Southern (2014)	51	364	195	10	569	0.649
LSU	121	761	401	47	1,209	0.649
Georgia	121	777	410	54	1,241	0.648
Appalachian St. (2014)	85	576	324	29	929	0.636
Miami (FL)	89	596	342	19	957	0.633
Auburn	122	734	421	47	1,202	0.630
Florida	108	691	400	40	1,131	0.629
Arizona St.	102	589	368	24	981	0.613

Note: As of end of 2014 season. Includes records as senior college only. Bowl and playoff games are included, and each tie game is computed as half won and half lost. Team listed with year in parentheses indicates reclassification to Bowl Subdivision (FBS), formerly Division I-A. The year in parentheses is the first year of FBS membership. Tiebreaker rule began with 1996 season. (1) Record adjusted by action of the NCAA Committee on Infractions.

Heisman Trophy Winners, 1935-2014

The Heisman Memorial Trophy is awarded annually to the nation's outstanding college football player by the Downtown Athletic Club.

Year	Winner, school, position
1935	Jay Berwanger, Chicago, HB
1936	Larry Kelley, Yale, E
1937	Clinton Frank, Yale, HB
1938	David O'Brien, Texas Christian, QB
1939	Nile Kinnick, Iowa, HB
1940	Tom Harmon, Michigan, HB
1941	Bruce Smith, Minnesota, HB
1942	Frank Sinkwich, Georgia, HB
1943	Angelo Bertelli, Notre Dame, QB
1944	Leslie Horvath, Ohio St., QB
1945	Felix Blanchard, Army, FB
1946	Glenn Davis, Army, HB
1947	John Lujack, Notre Dame, QB
1948	Doak Walker, SMU, HB
1949	Leon Hart, Notre Dame, E
1950	Vic Janowicz, Ohio St., HB
1951	Richard Kazmaier, Princeton, HB
1952	Billy Vessels, Oklahoma, HB
1953	John Lattner, Notre Dame, HB
1954	Alan Ameche, Wisconsin, FB
1955	Howard Cassady, Ohio St., HB
1956	Paul Hornung, Notre Dame, QB
1957	John Crow, Texas A&M, HB
1958	Pete Dawkins, Army, HB
1959	Billy Cannon, LSU, HB
1960	Joe Bellino, Navy, HB
1961	Ernest Davis, Syracuse, HB
1962	Terry Baker, Oregon St., QB
1963	Roger Staubach, Navy, QB
1964	John Huarte, Notre Dame, QB
1965	Mike Garrett, USC, HB
1966	Steve Spurrier, Florida, QB
1967	Gary Beban, UCLA, QB
1968	O. J. Simpson, USC, RB
1969	Steve Owens, Oklahoma, RB
1970	Jim Plunkett, Stanford, QB
1971	Pat Sullivan, Auburn, QB
1972	Johnny Rodgers, Nebraska, RB-WR
1973	John Cappelletti, Penn St., RB
1974	Archie Griffin, Ohio St., RB
1975	Archie Griffin, Ohio St., RB
1976	Tony Dorsett, Pittsburgh, RB
1977	Earl Campbell, Texas, RB
1978	Billy Sims, Oklahoma, RB
1979	Charles White, USC, RB
1980	George Rogers, S. Carolina, RB
1981	Marcus Allen, USC, RB
1982	Herschel Walker, Georgia, RB
1983	Mike Rozier, Nebraska, RB
1984	Doug Flutie, Boston College, QB
1985	Bo Jackson, Auburn, RB
1986	Vinny Testaverde, Miami (FL), QB
1987	Tim Brown, Notre Dame, WR
1988	Barry Sanders, Oklahoma St., RB
1989	Andre Ware, Houston, QB
1990	Ty Detmer, BYU, QB
1991	Desmond Howard, Michigan, WR
1992	Gino Torretta, Miami (FL), QB
1993	Charlie Ward, Florida St., QB
1994	Rashaan Salaam, Colorado, RB
1995	Eddie George, Ohio St., RB
1996	Danny Wuerffel, Florida, QB
1997	Charles Woodson, Michigan, CB
1998	Ricky Williams, Texas, RB
1999	Ron Dayne, Wisconsin, RB
2000	Chris Weinke, Florida St., QB
2001	Eric Crouch, Nebraska, QB
2002	Carson Palmer, USC, QB
2003	Jason White, Oklahoma, QB
2004	Matt Leinart, USC, QB
2005	Reggie Bush, USC, RB[1]
2006	Troy Smith, Ohio St., QB
2007	Tim Tebow, Florida, QB
2008	Sam Bradford, Oklahoma, QB
2009	Mark Ingram, Alabama, RB
2010	Cam Newton, Auburn, QB
2011	Robert Griffin III, Baylor, QB
2012	Johnny Manziel, Texas A&M, QB
2013	Jameis Winston, Florida St., QB
2014	Marcus Mariota, Oregon, QB

(1) Bush forfeited the trophy voluntarily Sept. 14, 2010, following revelations of NCAA rules violations while Bush was at USC.

All-Time Bowl Subdivision (FBS) Coaching Victories

Joe Paterno	409	Bo Schembechler	234	Vince Dooley	201	John Heisman	186
Bobby Bowden	377	Chris Ault	233	Jim Sweeney	200	Johnny Majors	185
Glenn "Pop" Warner	336	Hayden Fry	232	Dana X. Bible	198	Darrell Royal	184
Paul "Bear" Bryant	323	Jim Tressel	229	Fielding Yost	198	Dick Tomey	183
Amos Alonzo Stagg	314	**Steve Spurrier**	226	Dan McGugin	197	Gil Dobie	181
Frank Beamer	273	**Brian Kelly**	216	Howard Jones	194	Jackie Sherrill	180
LaVell Edwards	257	**Dennis Franchione**	210	John Cooper	192	Carl Snavely	180
Tom Osborne	255	Jess Neely	207	John Vaught	190	Jerry Claiborne	179
Lou Holtz	249	Warren Woodson	203	George Welsh	189	Carmen Cozza	179
Mack Brown	244	Don Nehlen	202	**Bill Snyder**	187	Dennis Erickson	179
Woody Hayes	238	Eddie Anderson	201	**Gary Pinkel**	186	Ben Schwartzwalder	178

Note: Coaches active in 2015 shown in bold. Total victories through Jan. 12, 2015, including bowl games; coaches must have at least 10 seasons coaching FBS schools to be eligible.

College Football Coach of the Year, 1935-2014

The Coach of the Year has been selected by the American Football Coaches Assn. (AFCA) since 1935 as well as the Football Writers Assn. of America (FWAA) since 1957. When polls disagree, both winners are indicated.

1935 Lynn Waldorf, Northwestern
1936 Dick Harlow, Harvard
1937 Edward Mylin, Lafayette
1938 Bill Kern, Carnegie Tech
1939 Eddie Anderson, Iowa
1940 Clark Shaughnessy, Stanford
1941 Frank Leahy, Notre Dame
1942 Bill Alexander, Georgia Tech
1943 Amos Alonzo Stagg, Pacific (CA)
1944 Carroll Widdoes, Ohio St.
1945 Bo McMillin, Indiana
1946 Earl "Red" Blaik, Army
1947 Fritz Crisler, Michigan
1948 Bennie Oosterbaan, Michigan
1949 Bud Wilkinson, Oklahoma
1950 Charlie Caldwell, Princeton
1951 Chuck Taylor, Stanford
1952 Biggie Munn, Michigan St.
1953 Jim Tatum, Maryland
1954 Henry "Red" Sanders, UCLA
1955 Duffy Daugherty, Michigan St.
1956 Bowden Wyatt, Tennessee
1957 Woody Hayes, Ohio St.
1958 Paul Dietzel, LSU
1959 Ben Schwartzwalder, Syracuse
1960 Murray Warmath, Minnesota
1961 Paul "Bear" Bryant, Alabama (AFCA); Darrell Royal, Texas (FWAA)
1962 John McKay, USC
1963 Darrell Royal, Texas
1964 Ara Parseghian, Notre Dame & Frank Broyles, Arkansas (AFCA); Ara Parseghian, Notre Dame (FWAA)
1965 Tommy Prothro, UCLA (AFCA); Duffy Daugherty, Mich. St. (FWAA)
1966 Tom Cahill, Army
1967 John Pont, Indiana
1968 Joe Paterno, Penn St. (AFCA); Woody Hayes, Ohio St. (FWAA)
1969 Bo Schembechler, Michigan
1970 Charles McClendon, LSU & Darrell Royal, Texas (AFCA); Alex Agase, Northwestern (FWAA)
1971 Paul "Bear" Bryant, Alabama (AFCA); Bob Devaney, Nebraska (FWAA)
1972 John McKay, USC
1973 Paul "Bear" Bryant, Alabama (AFCA); Johnny Majors, Pittsburgh (FWAA)
1974 Grant Teaff, Baylor
1975 Frank Kush, Arizona St. (AFCA); Woody Hayes, Ohio St. (FWAA)
1976 Johnny Majors, Pittsburgh
1977 Don James, Washington (AFCA); Lou Holtz, Arkansas (FWAA)
1978 Joe Paterno, Penn St.
1979 Earle Bruce, Ohio St.
1980 Vince Dooley, Georgia
1981 Danny Ford, Clemson
1982 Joe Paterno, Penn St.
1983 Ken Hatfield, Air Force (AFCA); Howard Schnellenberger, Miami (FL) (FWAA)
1984 LaVell Edwards, Brigham Young
1985 Fisher De Berry, Air Force
1986 Joe Paterno, Penn St.
1987 Dick MacPherson, Syracuse
1988 Don Nehlen, W. Virginia (AFCA); Lou Holtz, Notre Dame (FWAA)
1989 Bill McCartney, Colorado
1990 Bobby Ross, Georgia Tech
1991 Don James, Washington
1992 Gene Stallings, Alabama
1993 Barry Alvarez, Wisconsin (AFCA); Terry Bowden, Auburn (FWAA)
1994 Tom Osborne, Nebraska (AFCA); Rich Brooks, Oregon (FWAA)
1995 Gary Barnett, Northwestern
1996 Bruce Snyder, Arizona St.
1997 Mike Price, Washington St.
1998 Phillip Fulmer, Tennessee
1999 Frank Beamer, Virginia Tech
2000 Bob Stoops, Oklahoma
2001 Larry Coker, Miami (FL) & Ralph Friedgen, Maryland (AFCA); Ralph Friedgen, Maryland (FWAA)
2002 Jim Tressel, Ohio St.
2003 Pete Carroll, USC (AFCA); Nick Saban, LSU (FWAA)
2004 Tommy Tuberville, Auburn (AFCA); Urban Meyer, Utah (FWAA)
2005 Joe Paterno, Penn St. (AFCA); Charlie Weis, Notre Dame (FWAA)
2006 Jim Grobe, Wake Forest (AFCA); Greg Schiano, Rutgers (FWAA)
2007 Mark Mangino, Kansas
2008 Kyle Whittingham, Utah (AFCA); Nick Saban, Alabama (FWAA)
2009 Gary Patterson, TCU
2010 Chip Kelly, Oregon
2011 Les Miles, LSU (AFCA); Mike Gundy, Oklahoma St. (FWAA)
2012 Brian Kelly, Notre Dame
2013 David Cutcliffe, Duke (AFCA); Gus Malzahn, Auburn (FWAA)
2014 Gary Patterson, TCU

NCAA Div. I-A (FBS) Football Conference Champions, 1995-2014

American Athletic
2013 UCF
2014 UCF, Cincinnati, Memphis

Atlantic Coast
1995 Virginia, Florida St.
1996 Florida St.
1997 Florida St.
1998 Florida St., Georgia Tech
1999 Florida St.
2000 Florida St.
2001 Maryland
2002 Florida St.
2003 Florida St.
2004 Virginia Tech
2005 Florida St.
2006 Wake Forest
2007 Virginia Tech
2008 Virginia Tech
2009 Georgia Tech
2010 Virginia Tech
2011 Clemson
2012 Florida St.
2013 Florida St.
2014 Florida St.

Big Ten
1995 Northwestern
1996 Northwestern, Ohio St.
1997 Michigan
1998 Michigan, Ohio St., Wisconsin
1999 Wisconsin
2000 Michigan, Northwestern, Purdue
2001 Illinois
2002 Iowa, Ohio St.
2003 Michigan
2004 Iowa, Michigan
2005 Ohio St., Penn St.
2006 Ohio St.
2007 Ohio St.
2008 Ohio St., Penn St.
2009 Ohio St.
2010 Michigan St., Ohio St., Wisconsin
2011 Wisconsin
2012 Wisconsin
2013 Michigan St.
2014 Ohio St.

Big 12
1996 Texas
1997 Nebraska
1998 Texas A&M
1999 Nebraska
2000 Oklahoma
2001 Colorado
2002 Oklahoma
2003 Kansas St.
2004 Oklahoma
2005 Texas
2006 Oklahoma
2007 Oklahoma
2008 Oklahoma
2009 Texas
2010 Oklahoma
2011 Oklahoma St.
2012 Kansas St.
2013 Baylor
2014 Baylor, TCU

Conference USA
1996 Houston, Southern Miss
1997 Southern Miss
1998 Tulane
1999 Southern Miss
2000 Louisville
2001 Louisville
2002 Cincinnati, TCU
2003 Southern Miss
2004 Louisville
2005 Tulsa
2006 Houston
2007 UCF
2008 East Carolina
2009 East Carolina
2010 UCF
2011 Southern Miss
2012 Tulsa
2013 Rice
2014 Marshall

Mid-American
1995 Toledo
1996 Ball St.
1997 Marshall
1998 Marshall
1999 Marshall
2000 Marshall
2001 Toledo
2002 Marshall
2003 Miami (OH)
2004 Toledo
2005 Akron
2006 Central Michigan
2007 Central Michigan
2008 Buffalo
2009 Central Michigan
2010 Miami (OH)
2011 Northern Illinois
2012 Northern Illinois
2013 Bowling Green
2014 Northern Illinois

Mountain West
1999 BYU, Colorado St., Utah
2000 Colorado St.
2001 BYU
2002 Colorado St.
2003 Utah
2004 Utah
2005 TCU
2006 BYU, TCU
2007 BYU
2008 Utah
2009 TCU
2010 TCU
2011 TCU
2012 Boise St., Fresno St., San Diego St.
2013 Fresno St.
2014 Boise St.

Pac-12
1995 USC, Washington
1996 Arizona St.
1997 UCLA, Washington St.
1998 UCLA
1999 Stanford
2000 Oregon, Oregon St., Washington
2001 Oregon
2002 USC, Washington St.
2003 USC
2004 USC
2005 USC
2006 California, USC
2007 Arizona St., USC
2008 USC
2009 Oregon
2010 Oregon
2011 Oregon
2012 Stanford
2013 Stanford
2014 Oregon

Southeastern
1995 Florida
1996 Florida
1997 Tennessee
1998 Tennessee
1999 Alabama
2000 Florida
2001 LSU
2002 Georgia
2003 LSU
2004 Auburn
2005 Georgia
2006 Florida
2007 LSU
2008 Florida
2009 Alabama
2010 Auburn
2011 LSU
2012 Alabama
2013 Auburn
2014 Alabama

Sun Belt
2001 Mid. Tenn. St., North Texas
2002 North Texas
2003 North Texas
2004 North Texas
2005 Arkansas St., LA-Lafayette, LA-Monroe
2006 Mid. Tenn. St., Troy
2007 Florida Atlantic, Troy
2008 Troy
2009 Troy
2010 Florida Intl., Troy
2011 Arkansas St.
2012 Arkansas St.
2013 Arkansas St., LA-Lafayette
2014 Georgia Southern

Note: Includes conferences active in 2014.

NCAA Div. I-AA (FCS) Football Conference Champions, 1995-2014

Big Sky
1995 Montana
1996 Montana
1997 Eastern Wash.
1998 Montana
1999 Montana
2000 Montana
2001 Montana
2002 Idaho St., Montana, Montana St.
2003 Montana, Montana St., N. Arizona
2004 Eastern Wash., Montana
2005 Eastern Wash., Montana, Montana St.
2006 Montana
2007 Montana
2008 Montana, Weber St.
2009 Montana
2010 Eastern Wash., Montana St.
2011 Montana, Montana St.
2012 Eastern Wash., Montana St., Cal Poly
2013 Eastern Wash.
2014 Eastern Wash.

Big South
2002 Gardner-Webb
2003 Gardner-Webb
2004 Coastal Carolina
2005 Charleston Southern, Coastal Carolina
2006 Coastal Carolina
2007 Liberty
2008 Liberty
2009 Liberty, Stony Brook
2010 Coastal Carolina, Liberty, Stony Brook
2011 Stony Brook
2012 Coastal Carolina, Liberty, Stony Brook
2013 Coastal Carolina, Liberty
2014 Coastal Carolina, Liberty

Colonial Athletic
2007 Massachusetts, Richmond
2008 James Madison
2009 Richmond, Villanova
2010 Delaware, William & Mary
2011 Towson
2012 New Hampshire, Richmond, Villanova, Towson
2013 Maine
2014 New Hampshire

Ivy League
1995 Princeton
1996 Dartmouth
1997 Harvard
1998 Pennsylvania
1999 Brown, Yale
2000 Pennsylvania
2001 Harvard
2002 Pennsylvania
2003 Pennsylvania
2004 Harvard
2005 Brown
2006 Princeton, Yale
2007 Harvard
2008 Harvard, Brown
2009 Pennsylvania
2010 Pennsylvania
2011 Harvard
2012 Pennsylvania
2013 Harvard, Princeton
2014 Harvard

Mid-Eastern Athletic
1995 Florida A&M
1996 Florida A&M
1997 Hampton
1998 Florida A&M, Hampton
1999 North Carolina A&T
2000 Florida A&M
2001 Florida A&M
2002 Bethune-Cookman
2003 North Carolina A&T
2004 Hampton, South Carolina St.
2005 Hampton
2006 Hampton
2007 Delaware St.
2008 South Carolina St.
2009 South Carolina St.
2010 Bethune-Cookman, Florida A&M, South Carolina St.
2011 Norfolk St.
2012 Bethune-Cookman
2013 Bethune-Cookman, South Carolina St.
2014 Bethune-Cookman, Morgan St., N. Carolina A&T, N. Carolina Central, South Carolina St.

Missouri Valley
1995 Eastern Illinois, Northern Iowa
1996 Northern Iowa
1997 Western Illinois
1998 Western Illinois
1999 Illinois St.
2000 Western Illinois
2001 Northern Iowa
2002 W. Illinois, W. Kentucky
2003 N. Iowa, S. Illinois
2004 Southern Illinois
2005 N. Iowa, S. Illinois, Youngstown St.
2006 Youngstown St.
2007 Northern Iowa
2008 N. Iowa, S. Illinois
2009 Southern Illinois
2010 Northern Iowa
2011 North Dakota St., Northern Iowa
2012 North Dakota St.
2013 North Dakota St.
2014 Illinois St., North Dakota St.

Northeast
1996 Monmouth, Robert Morris
1997 Robert Morris
1998 Monmouth, Robert Morris
1999 Robert Morris
2000 Robert Morris
2001 Sacred Heart
2002 Albany
2003 Albany, Monmouth
2004 Central Conn. St., Monmouth
2005 Central Conn. St., Stony Brook
2006 Monmouth
2007 Albany
2008 Albany
2009 Central Conn. St.
2010 Central Conn. St., Robert Morris
2011 Albany, Duquesne
2012 Albany, Wagner
2013 Duquesne, Sacred Heart
2014 Sacred Heart, Wagner

Ohio Valley
1995 Murray St.
1996 Murray St.
1997 Eastern Kentucky
1998 Tennessee St.
1999 Tennessee St.
2000 Western Kentucky
2001 Eastern Illinois
2002 Eastern Illinois, Murray St.
2003 Jacksonville St.
2004 Jacksonville St.
2005 Eastern Illinois
2006 Eastern Illinois, Tenn.-Martin
2007 Eastern Kentucky
2008 Eastern Kentucky
2009 Eastern Illinois
2010 SE Missouri St.
2011 Eastern Kentucky, Jacksonville St., Tennessee Tech
2012 Eastern Illinois
2013 Eastern Illinois
2014 Jacksonville St.

Patriot
1995 Lehigh
1996 Bucknell
1997 Colgate
1998 Lehigh
1999 Colgate, Lehigh
2000 Lehigh
2001 Lehigh
2002 Colgate, Fordham
2003 Colgate
2004 Lafayette, Lehigh
2005 Colgate, Lafayette
2006 Colgate, Lafayette, Lehigh
2007 Fordham
2008 Colgate
2009 Holy Cross
2010 Lehigh
2011 Lehigh
2012 Colgate
2013 Lafayette
2014 Fordham

Pioneer
1995 Drake
1996 Dayton
1997 Dayton
1998 Drake
1999 Dayton
2000 Dayton, Drake, Valparaiso
2001 Dayton
2002 Dayton
2003 Valparaiso
2004 Drake
2005 San Diego
2006 San Diego
2007 Dayton, San Diego
2008 Jacksonville
2009 Butler, Dayton
2010 Dayton, Jacksonville
2011 Drake, San Diego
2012 Butler, Drake, San Diego
2013 Butler, Marist
2014 San Diego

Southern
1995 Appalachian St.
1996 Marshall
1997 Georgia Southern
1998 Georgia Southern
1999 Appalachian St., Furman, Georgia Southern
2000 Georgia Southern
2001 Furman, Southern
2002 Georgia Southern
2003 Wofford
2004 Furman, Georgia Southern
2005 Appalachian St.
2006 Appalachian St.
2007 Appalachian St., Wofford
2008 Appalachian St.
2009 Appalachian St.
2010 Appalachian St., Wofford
2011 Georgia Southern
2012 Appalachian St., Georgia Southern, Wofford
2013 Chattanooga, Furman, Samford
2014 Chattanooga

Southland
1995 McNeese St.
1996 Troy St.
1997 McNeese St., Northwestern St.
1998 Northwestern St.
1999 Stephen F. Austin, Troy
2000 Troy
2001 McNeese St., Sam Houston St.
2002 McNeese St.
2003 McNeese St.
2004 Northwestern St., Sam Houston St.
2005 Nicholls St., Texas St.
2006 McNeese St.
2007 McNeese St.
2008 Texas St.
2009 McNeese St., Stephen F. Austin
2010 Stephen F. Austin
2011 Sam Houston St.
2012 Central Arkansas, Sam Houston St.
2013 Southeastern LA
2014 Sam Houston St., Southeastern LA

Southwestern Athletic
1995 Jackson St.
1996 Jackson St.
1997 Southern
1998 Southern
1999 Southern
2000 Grambling St.
2001 Grambling St.
2002 Grambling St.
2003 Southern
2004 Alabama St.
2005 Grambling St.
2006 Alabama A&M
2007 Jackson St.
2008 Grambling St.
2009 Prairie View A&M
2010 Texas Southern
2011 Grambling St.
2012 Arkansas-Pine Bluff
2013 Southern
2014 Alcorn St.

Note: Missouri Valley Conference was known as Gateway Football Conference, 1992-2007.

Selected NCAA Division I Teams

(Conferences and coaches listed are as of June 2015.)

Team	Nickname	Team colors	Conference	Basketball coach	Football coach
Air Force	Falcons	Blue & silver	Mountain West	Dave Pilipovich	Troy Calhoun
Akron	Zips	Blue & gold	Mid-American	Keith Dambrot	Terry Bowden
Alabama	Crimson Tide	Crimson & white	Southeastern	Avery Johnson	Nick Saban
Appalachian State	Mountaineers	Black & gold	Sun Belt	Jim Fox	Scott Satterfield
Arizona	Wildcats	Cardinal & navy	Pac-12	Sean Miller	Rich Rodriguez
Arizona State	Sun Devils	Maroon & gold	Pac-12	Bobby Hurley	Todd Graham
Arkansas	Razorbacks	Cardinal & white	Southeastern	Mike Anderson	Bret Bielema
Arkansas State	Red Wolves	Scarlet & black	Sun Belt	John Brady	Blake Anderson
Army	Black Knights	Black, gold, & gray	Independent#	Zach Spiker	Jeff Monken
Auburn	Tigers	Burnt orange & navy blue	Southeastern	Bruce Pearl	Gus Malzahn
Ball State	Cardinals	Cardinal & white	Mid-American	James Whitford	Pete Lembo
Baylor	Bears	Green & gold	Big 12	Scott Drew	Art Briles
Boise State	Broncos	Blue & orange	Mountain West	Leon Rice	Bryan Harsin
Boston College	Eagles	Maroon & gold	Atlantic Coast	Jim Christian	Steve Addazio
Bowling Green	Falcons	Orange & brown	Mid-American	Michael Huger	Dino Babers
Brigham Young (BYU)	Cougars	Dark blue & white	Independent#	Dave Rose	Bronco Mendenh
Brown*	Bears	Brown, red, & white	Ivy League	Mike Martin	Phil Estes
Butler	Bulldogs	Blue & white	Pioneer League#	Chris Holtmann	Jeff Voris
California	Golden Bears	Blue & gold	Pac-12	Cuonzo Martin	Sonny Dykes
Central Michigan	Chippewas	Maroon & gold	Mid-American	Keno Davis	John Bonamego
Cincinnati	Bearcats	Red & black	American Athletic	Mick Cronin	Tommy Tuberville
Citadel*	Bulldogs	Citadel blue & white	Southern	Duggar Baucom	Mike Houston
Clemson	Tigers	Clemson orange & regalia	Atlantic Coast	Brad Brownell	Dabo Swinney
Colgate*	Raiders	Maroon & white	Patriot League	Matt Langel	Dan Hunt
Colorado	Buffaloes	Silver, gold, & black	Pac-12	Tad Boyle	Mike MacIntyre
Colorado State	Rams	Green & gold	Mountain West	Larry Eustachy	Mike Bobo
Columbia*	Lions	Columbia blue & white	Ivy League	Kyle Smith	Al Bagnoli
Connecticut	Huskies	National flag blue & white	American Athletic	Kevin Ollie	Bob Diaco
Cornell*	Big Red	Carnelian red & white	Ivy League	Bill Courtney	David Archer
Dartmouth*	Big Green	Dartmouth green & white	Ivy League	Paul Cormier	Buddy Teevens
Delaware*	Fightin' Blue Hens	Blue & gold	Colonial Athletic	Monté Ross	Dave Brock
Duke	Blue Devils	Duke blue & white	Atlantic Coast	Mike Krzyzewski	David Cutcliffe
East Carolina	Pirates	Purple & gold	American Athletic	Jeff Lebo	Ruffin McNeill
Eastern Illinois*	Panthers	Blue & gray	Ohio Valley	Jay Spoonhour	Kim Dameron
Eastern Kentucky*	Colonels	Maroon & white	Ohio Valley	Dan McHale	Dean Hood
Eastern Michigan	Eagles	Green & white	Mid-American	Rob Murphy	Chris Creighton
Eastern Washington*	Eagles	Red & white	Big Sky	Jim Hayford	Beau Baldwin
Florida	Gators	Orange & blue	Southeastern	Michael White	Jim McElwain
Florida A&M*	Rattlers	Orange & green	Mid-Eastern Athletic	Byron Samuels	Alex Wood
Florida State	Seminoles	Garnet & gold	Atlantic Coast	Leonard Hamilton	Jimbo Fisher
Fresno State	Bulldogs	Red & blue	Mountain West	Rodney Terry	Tim DeRuyter
Furman*	Paladins	Purple & white	Southern	Niko Medved	Bruce Fowler
Georgia	Bulldogs	Red & black	Southeastern	Mark Fox	Mark Richt
Georgia Southern	Eagles	Blue & white	Sun Belt	Mark Byington	Willie Fritz
Georgia Tech	Yellow Jackets	Old gold & white	Atlantic Coast	Brian Gregory	Paul Johnson
Harvard*	Crimson	Crimson, black, & white	Ivy League	Tommy Amaker	Tim Murphy
Hawaii	Rainbow Warriors	Green, black, white, silver	Mountain West#	Eran Ganot	Norm Chow
Holy Cross*	Crusaders	Royal purple	Patriot League	Bill Carmody	Tom Gilmore
Houston	Cougars	Scarlet & white	American Athletic	Kelvin Sampson	Tom Herman
Howard*	Bison	Blue & white	Mid-Eastern Athletic	Kevin Nickelberry	Gary Harrell
Idaho	Vandals	Silver & vandal gold	Sun Belt	Don Verlin	Paul Petrino
Illinois	Fighting Illini	Orange & blue	Big Ten	John Groce	Bill Cubit
Illinois State*	Redbirds	Red & white	Missouri Valley	Dan Muller	Brock Spack
Indiana	Hoosiers	Cream & crimson	Big Ten	Tom Crean	Kevin Wilson
Indiana State*	Sycamores	Royal blue & white	Missouri Valley	Greg Lansing	Mike Sanford
Iowa	Hawkeyes	Black & gold	Big Ten	Fran McCaffery	Kirk Ferentz
Iowa State	Cyclones	Cardinal & gold	Big 12	Steve Prohm	Paul Rhoads
Jackson State*	Tigers	Blue & white	Southwestern Athletic	Wayne Brent	Harold Jackson
James Madison*	Dukes	Purple & gold	Colonial Athletic	Matt Brady	Everett Withers
Kansas	Jayhawks	Crimson & blue	Big 12	Bill Self	David Beaty
Kansas State	Wildcats	Purple & white	Big 12	Bruce Weber	Bill Snyder
Kent State	Golden Flashes	Navy blue & gold	Mid-American	Rob Senderoff	Paul Haynes
Kentucky	Wildcats	Blue & white	Southeastern	John Calipari	Mark Stoops
Lafayette*	Leopards	Maroon & white	Patriot League	Fran O'Hanlon	Frank Tavani
Lehigh*	Mountain Hawks	Brown & white	Patriot League	Brett Reed	Andy Coen
Liberty*	Flames	Red, white, & blue	Big South	Ritchie McKay	Turner Gill
Louisiana State (LSU)	Fighting Tigers	Purple & gold	Southeastern	Johnny Jones	Les Miles
Louisiana Tech	Bulldogs	Red & blue	Conference USA	Eric Konkol	Skip Holtz
Louisiana-Lafayette	Ragin' Cajuns	Vermilion & white	Sun Belt	Bob Marlin	Mark Hudspeth
Louisiana-Monroe	Warhawks	Maroon & gold	Sun Belt	Keith Richard	Todd Berry
Louisville	Cardinals	Red & black	Atlantic Coast	Rick Pitino	Bobby Petrino
Maine*	Black Bears	Blue & white	Colonial Athletic#	Bob Walsh	Jack Cosgrove
Marshall	Thundering Herd	Green & white	Conference USA	Dan D'Antoni	Doc Holliday
Maryland	Terrapins	Red, white, black, gold	Big Ten	Mark Turgeon	Randy Edsall
Massachusetts	Minutemen	Maroon & white	Mid-American#	Derek Kellogg	Mark Whipple
Memphis	Tigers	Blue & gray	American Athletic	Josh Pastner	Justin Fuente
Miami (Florida)	Hurricanes	Orange & green	Atlantic Coast	Jim Larranaga	Al Golden
Miami (Ohio)	RedHawks	Red & white	Mid-American	John Cooper	Chuck Martin
Michigan	Wolverines	Maize & blue	Big Ten	John Beilein	Jim Harbaugh
Michigan State	Spartans	Green & white	Big Ten	Tom Izzo	Mark Dantonio
Mid. Tennessee State	Blue Raiders	Royal blue & white	Conference USA	Kermit Davis	Rick Stockstill
Minnesota	Golden Gophers	Maroon & gold	Big Ten	Richard Pitino	Jerry Kill
Mississippi	Rebels	Cardinal red & navy blue	Southeastern	Andy Kennedy	Hugh Freeze
Mississippi State	Bulldogs	Maroon & white	Southeastern	Ben Howland	Dan Mullen

Team	Nickname	Team colors	Conference	Basketball coach	Football coach
Missouri	Tigers	Old gold & black	Southeastern	Kim Anderson	Gary Pinkel
Montana*	Grizzlies	Maroon & silver	Big Sky	Travis DeCuire	Bob Stitt
Montana State*	Bobcats	Blue & gold	Big Sky	Brian Fish	Rob Ash
Morgan State*	Bears	Blue & orange	Mid-Eastern Athletic	Todd Bozeman	Lee Hull
Murray State*	Racers	Navy & gold	Ohio Valley	Matt McMahon	Mitch Stewart
Navy	Midshipmen	Navy blue & gold	Independent#	Ed DeChellis	Ken Niumatalolo
Nebraska	Cornhuskers	Scarlet & cream	Big Ten	Tim Miles	Mike Riley
Nevada	Wolf Pack	Silver & blue	Mountain West	Eric Musselman	Brian Polian
Nevada-Las Vegas (UNLV)	Rebels	Scarlet & gray	Mountain West	Dave Rice	Tony Sanchez
New Hampshire*	Wildcats	Blue & white	Colonial Athletic#	Bill Herrion	Sean McDonnell
New Mexico	Lobos	Cherry & silver	Mountain West	Craig Neal	Bob Davie
New Mexico State	Aggies	Crimson & white	Western Athletic	Marvin Menzies	Doug Martin
Nicholls State*	Colonels	Red & gray	Southland	J. P. Piper	Tim Rebowe
North Carolina	Tar Heels	Carolina blue & white	Atlantic Coast	Roy Williams	Larry Fedora
North Carolina State	Wolfpack	Red & white	Atlantic Coast	Mark Gottfried	Dave Doeren
North Texas	Mean Green	Green & white	Conference USA	Tony Benford	Dan McCarney
Northern Illinois	Huskies	Cardinal & black	Mid-American	Mark Montgomery	Rod Carey
Northern Iowa*	Panthers	Purple & old gold	Missouri Valley	Ben Jacobson	Mark Farley
Northwestern	Wildcats	Purple & white	Big Ten	Chris Collins	Pat Fitzgerald
Northwestern State*	Demons	Purple, white, & orange	Southland	Mike McConathy	Jay Thomas
Notre Dame	Fighting Irish	Blue & gold	Independent#	Mike Brey	Brian Kelly
Ohio	Bobcats	Hunter green & white	Mid-American	Saul Phillips	Frank Solich
Ohio State	Buckeyes	Scarlet & gray	Big Ten	Thad Matta	Urban Meyer
Oklahoma	Sooners	Crimson & cream	Big 12	Lon Kruger	Bob Stoops
Oklahoma State	Cowboys	Orange & black	Big 12	Travis Ford	Mike Gundy
Oregon	Ducks	Green & yellow	Pac-12	Dana Altman	Mark Helfrich
Oregon State	Beavers	Orange & black	Pac-12	Wayne Tinkle	Gary Andersen
Penn State	Nittany Lions	Blue & white	Big Ten	Patrick Chambers	James Franklin
Pennsylvania*	Quakers	Red & blue	Ivy League	Steve Donahue	Ray Priore
Pittsburgh	Panthers	Gold & blue	Atlantic Coast	Jamie Dixon	Paul Chryst
Princeton*	Tigers	Orange & black	Ivy League	Mitch Henderson	Bob Surace
Purdue	Boilermakers	Old gold & black	Big Ten	Matt Painter	Darrell Hazell
Rhode Island*	Rams	Keaney blue, dark blue, white	Colonial Athletic#	Dan Hurley	Jim Fleming
Rice	Owls	Blue & gray	Conference USA	Mike Rhoades	David Bailiff
Richmond*	Spiders	Red & blue	Colonial Athletic#	Chris Mooney	Danny Rocco
Rutgers	Scarlet Knights	Scarlet	Big Ten	Eddie Jordan	Kyle Flood
Sam Houston State*	Bearkats	Orange & white	Southland	Jason Hooten	K. C. Keeler
San Diego State	Aztecs	Scarlet & black	Mountain West	Steve Fisher	Rocky Long
San Jose State	Spartans	Gold, white, & blue	Mountain West	Dave Wojcik	Ron Caragher
South Carolina	Gamecocks	Garnet & black	Southeastern	Frank Martin	Steve Spurrier
South Carolina State*	Bulldogs	Garnet & blue	Mid-Eastern Athletic	Murray Garvin	Oliver Pough
South Florida	Bulls	Green & gold	American Athletic	Orlando Antigua	Willie Taggart
Southeast Missouri State*	Redhawks	Red, black, & white	Ohio Valley	Rick Ray	Tom Matukewicz
Southern California (USC)	Trojans	Cardinal & gold	Pac-12	Andy Enfield	Steve Sarkisian
Southern Illinois*	Salukis	Maroon & white	Missouri Valley	Barry Hinson	Dale Lennon
Southern Methodist (SMU)	Mustangs	Red & blue	American Athletic	Larry Brown	Chad Morris
Southern Mississippi	Golden Eagles	Black & gold	Conference USA	Doc Sadler	Todd Monken
Stanford	Cardinal	Cardinal & white	Pac-12	Johnny Dawkins	David Shaw
Stephen F. Austin*	Lumberjacks	Purple & white	Southland	Brad Underwood	Clint Conque
Syracuse	Orange	Orange	Atlantic Coast	Jim Boeheim	Scott Shafer
Temple	Owls	Cherry & white	American Athletic	Fran Dunphy	Matt Rhule
Tennessee	Volunteers	Orange & white	Southeastern	Rick Barnes	Butch Jones
Tennessee State*	Tigers	Reflex blue & white	Ohio Valley	Dana Ford	Rod Reed
Tennessee Tech*	Golden Eagles	Purple & gold	Ohio Valley	Steve Payne	Watson Brown
Texas	Longhorns	Burnt orange & white	Big 12	Shaka Smart	Charlie Strong
Texas A&M	Aggies	Maroon & white	Southeastern	Billy Kennedy	Kevin Sumlin
Texas Christian (TCU)	Horned Frogs	Purple & white	Big 12	Trent Johnson	Gary Patterson
Texas Southern*	Tigers	Maroon & gray	Southwestern Athletic	Mike Davis	Darrell Asberry
Texas State*	Bobcats	Maroon & gold	Sun Belt	Danny Kaspar	Dennis Franchione
Texas Tech	Red Raiders	Scarlet & black	Big 12	Tubby Smith	Kliff Kingsbury
Toledo	Rockets	Midnight blue & gold	Mid-American	Tod Kowalczyk	Matt Campbell
Troy	Trojans	Cardinal, silver, & black	Sun Belt	Phil Cunningham	Neal Brown
Tulane	Green Wave	Olive green & sky blue	American Athletic	Ed Conroy	Curtis Johnson
Tulsa	Golden Hurricane	Old gold, royal blue, & crimson	American Athletic	Frank Haith	Philip Montgomery
UCLA	Bruins	Blue & gold	Pac-12	Steve Alford	Jim Mora
Utah	Utes	Crimson & white	Pac-12	Larry Krystkowiak	Kyle Whittingham
Utah State	Aggies	Navy blue & white	Mountain West	Tim Duryea	Matt Wells
UTEP (Texas-El Paso)	Miners	Dark blue, orange, & silver	Conference USA	Tim Floyd	Sean Kugler
Vanderbilt	Commodores	Black & gold	Southeastern	Kevin Stallings	Derek Mason
Villanova*	Wildcats	Blue & white	Colonial Athletic#	Jay Wright	Andy Talley
Virginia	Cavaliers	Orange & blue	Atlantic Coast	Tony Bennett	Mike London
Virginia Tech	Hokies	Burnt orange & Chicago maroon	Atlantic Coast	Buzz Williams	Frank Beamer
Wake Forest	Demon Deacons	Old gold & black	Atlantic Coast	Danny Manning	Dave Clawson
Washington	Huskies	Purple & gold	Pac-12	Lorenzo Romar	Chris Peterson
Washington State	Cougars	Crimson & gray	Pac-12	Ernie Kent	Mike Leach
Weber State*	Wildcats	Royal purple & white	Big Sky	Randy Rahe	Jay Hill
West Virginia	Mountaineers	Old gold & blue	Big 12	Bob Huggins	Dana Holgorsen
Western Illinois*	Leathernecks	Purple & gold	Missouri Valley#	Billy Wright	Bob Nielson
Western Kentucky	Hilltoppers	Red & white	Conference USA	Ray Harper	Jeff Brohm
Western Michigan	Broncos	Brown & gold	Mid-American	Steve Hawkins	P. J. Fleck
Wisconsin	Badgers	Cardinal & white	Big Ten	Bo Ryan	Paul Chryst
Wyoming	Cowboys	Brown & gold	Mountain West	Larry Shyatt	Craig Bohl
Yale*	Bulldogs, Elis	Yale blue & white	Ivy League	James Jones	Tony Reno
Youngstown State*	Penguins	Red & white	Missouri Valley#	Jerry Slocum	Bo Pelini

* = Football Championship Subdivision (FCS) team (formerly known as I-AA). # = Team competes in conference listed in football but not in basketball.

COLLEGE BASKETBALL

2015 Men's NCAA Tournament: Duke Defeats Wisconsin

The Duke Univ. Blue Devils beat the Univ. of Wisconsin Badgers, 68-63, at Lucas Oil Stadium in Indianapolis, IN, to claim the NCAA Men's Division I national basketball title Apr. 6, 2015. Duke head coach Mike Krzyzewski took his 12th trip to the Final Four and claimed his fifth national championship, placing him second all-time among Division I coaches. All four Blue Devil freshman starters scored in the double digits. Duke freshman point guard Tyus Jones had 23 points—all but 4 scored in the second half—and was named the Final Four's most outstanding player.

NCAA Men's Basketball Division I Champions, 1943-2015

Year	Champion	Winning coach	Final opponent	Score	Most outstanding player	Site
1943	Wyoming	Everett Shelton	Georgetown	46-34	Ken Sailors, Wyoming	New York, NY
1944	Utah	Vadal Peterson	Dartmouth	42-40(1)	Arnold Ferrin, Utah	New York, NY
1945	Oklahoma St.(2)	Henry Iba	NYU	49-45	Bob Kurland, Oklahoma St.	New York, NY
1946	Oklahoma St.(2)	Henry Iba	North Carolina	43-40	Bob Kurland, Oklahoma St.	New York, NY
1947	Holy Cross	Alvin Julian	Oklahoma	58-47	George Kaftan, Holy Cross	New York, NY
1948	Kentucky	Adolph Rupp	Baylor	58-42	Alex Groza, Kentucky	New York, NY
1949	Kentucky	Adolph Rupp	Oklahoma St.	46-36	Alex Groza, Kentucky	Seattle, WA
1950	CCNY	Nat Holman	Bradley	71-68	Irwin Dambrot, CCNY	New York, NY
1951	Kentucky	Adolph Rupp	Kansas St.	68-58	Bill Spivey, Kentucky	Minneapolis, MN
1952	Kansas	Forrest Allen	St. John's (NY)	80-63	Clyde Lovellette, Kansas	Seattle, WA
1953	Indiana	Branch McCracken	Kansas	69-68	B. H. Born, Kansas	Kansas City, MO
1954	La Salle	Kenneth Loeffler	Bradley	92-76	Tom Gola, La Salle	Kansas City, MO
1955	San Francisco	Phil Woolpert	La Salle	77-63	Bill Russell, San Francisco	Kansas City, MO
1956	San Francisco	Phil Woolpert	Iowa	83-71	Hal Lear, Temple	Evanston, IL
1957	North Carolina	Frank McGuire	Kansas	54-53(1)	Wilt Chamberlain, Kansas	Kansas City, MO
1958	Kentucky	Adolph Rupp	Seattle	84-72	Elgin Baylor, Seattle	Louisville, KY
1959	California	Pete Newell	West Virginia	71-70	Jerry West, West Virginia	Louisville, KY
1960	Ohio St.	Fred Taylor	California	75-55	Jerry Lucas, Ohio St.	San Francisco, CA
1961	Cincinnati	Edwin Jucker	Ohio St.	70-65(1)	Jerry Lucas, Ohio St.	Kansas City, MO
1962	Cincinnati	Edwin Jucker	Ohio St.	71-59	Paul Hogue, Cincinnati	Louisville, KY
1963	Loyola (IL)	George Ireland	Cincinnati	60-58(1)	Art Heyman, Duke	Louisville, KY
1964	UCLA	John Wooden	Duke	98-83	Walt Hazzard, UCLA	Kansas City, MO
1965	UCLA	John Wooden	Michigan	91-80	Bill Bradley, Princeton	Portland, OR
1966	UTEP(3)	Don Haskins	Kentucky	72-65	Jerry Chambers, Utah	College Park, MD
1967	UCLA	John Wooden	Dayton	79-64	Lew Alcindor(4), UCLA	Louisville, KY
1968	UCLA	John Wooden	North Carolina	78-55	Lew Alcindor(4), UCLA	Los Angeles, CA
1969	UCLA	John Wooden	Purdue	92-72	Lew Alcindor(4), UCLA	Louisville, KY
1970	UCLA	John Wooden	Jacksonville	80-69	Sidney Wicks, UCLA	College Park, MD
1971	UCLA	John Wooden	Villanova*	68-62	Howard Porter, Villanova*	Houston, TX
1972	UCLA	John Wooden	Florida St.	81-76	Bill Walton, UCLA	Los Angeles, CA
1973	UCLA	John Wooden	Memphis(5)	87-66	Bill Walton, UCLA	St. Louis, MO
1974	North Carolina St.	Norm Sloan	Marquette	76-64	David Thompson, NC State	Greensboro, NC
1975	UCLA	John Wooden	Kentucky	92-85	Richard Washington, UCLA	San Diego, CA
1976	Indiana	Bob Knight	Michigan	86-68	Kent Benson, Indiana	Philadelphia, PA
1977	Marquette	Al McGuire	North Carolina	67-59	Butch Lee, Marquette	Atlanta, GA
1978	Kentucky	Joe Hall	Duke	94-88	Jack Givens, Kentucky	St. Louis, MO
1979	Michigan St.	Jud Heathcote	Indiana St.	75-64	Magic Johnson, Michigan St.	Salt Lake City, UT
1980	Louisville	Denny Crum	UCLA*	59-54	Darrell Griffith, Louisville	Indianapolis, IN
1981	Indiana	Bob Knight	North Carolina	63-50	Isiah Thomas, Indiana	Philadelphia, PA
1982	North Carolina	Dean Smith	Georgetown	63-62	James Worthy, N. Carolina	New Orleans, LA
1983	North Carolina St.	Jim Valvano	Houston	54-52	Hakeem Olajuwon, Houston	Albuquerque, NM
1984	Georgetown	John Thompson	Houston	84-75	Patrick Ewing, Georgetown	Seattle, WA
1985	Villanova	Rollie Massimino	Georgetown	66-64	Ed Pinckney, Villanova	Lexington, KY
1986	Louisville	Denny Crum	Duke	72-69	Pervis Ellison, Louisville	Dallas, TX
1987	Indiana	Bob Knight	Syracuse	74-73	Keith Smart, Indiana	New Orleans, LA
1988	Kansas	Larry Brown	Oklahoma	83-79	Danny Manning, Kansas	Kansas City, MO
1989	Michigan	Steve Fisher	Seton Hall	80-79(1)	Glen Rice, Michigan	Seattle, WA
1990	UNLV	Jerry Tarkanian	Duke	103-73	Anderson Hunt, UNLV	Denver, CO
1991	Duke	Mike Krzyzewski	Kansas	72-65	Christian Laettner, Duke	Indianapolis, IN
1992	Duke	Mike Krzyzewski	Michigan	71-51	Bobby Hurley, Duke	Minneapolis, MN
1993	North Carolina	Dean Smith	Michigan	77-71	Donald Williams, N. Carolina	New Orleans, LA
1994	Arkansas	Nolan Richardson	Duke	76-72	Corliss Williamson, Arkansas	Charlotte, NC
1995	UCLA	Jim Harrick	Arkansas	89-78	Ed O'Bannon, UCLA	Seattle, WA
1996	Kentucky	Rick Pitino	Syracuse	76-67	Tony Delk, Kentucky	E. Rutherford, NJ
1997	Arizona	Lute Olson	Kentucky	84-79(1)	Miles Simon, Arizona	Indianapolis, IN
1998	Kentucky	Tubby Smith	Utah	78-69	Jeff Sheppard, Kentucky	San Antonio, TX
1999	Connecticut	Jim Calhoun	Duke	77-74	Richard Hamilton, Connecticut	St. Petersburg, FL
2000	Michigan St.	Tom Izzo	Florida	89-76	Mateen Cleaves, Michigan St.	Indianapolis, IN
2001	Duke	Mike Krzyzewski	Arizona	82-72	Shane Battier, Duke	Minneapolis, MN
2002	Maryland	Gary Williams	Indiana	64-52	Juan Dixon, Maryland	Atlanta, GA
2003	Syracuse	Jim Boeheim	Kansas	81-78	Carmelo Anthony, Syracuse	New Orleans, LA
2004	Connecticut	Jim Calhoun	Georgia Tech	82-73	Emeka Okafor, Connecticut	San Antonio, TX
2005	North Carolina	Roy Williams	Illinois	75-70	Sean May, N. Carolina	St. Louis, MO
2006	Florida	Billy Donovan	UCLA	73-57	Joakim Noah, Florida	Indianapolis, IN
2007	Florida	Billy Donovan	Ohio St.	84-75	Corey Brewer, Florida	Atlanta, GA
2008	Kansas	Bill Self	Memphis	75-68(1)	Mario Chalmers, Kansas	San Antonio, TX
2009	North Carolina	Roy Williams	Michigan St.	89-72	Wayne Ellington, N. Carolina	Detroit, MI
2010	Duke	Mike Krzyzewski	Butler	61-59	Kyle Singler, Duke	Indianapolis, IN
2011	Connecticut	Jim Calhoun	Butler	53-41	Kemba Walker, Connecticut	Houston, TX
2012	Kentucky	John Calipari	Kansas	67-59	Anthony Davis, Kentucky	New Orleans, LA
2013	Louisville	Rick Pitino	Michigan	82-76	Luke Hancock, Louisville	Atlanta, GA
2014	Connecticut	Kevin Ollie	Kentucky	60-54	Shabazz Napier, Connecticut	Arlington, TX
2015	Duke	Mike Krzyzewski	Wisconsin	68-63	Tyus Jones, Duke	Indianapolis, IN

*Declared ineligible after the tournament. (1) Overtime. (2) Then known as Oklahoma A&M. (3) Then known as Texas Western. (4) Changed name to Kareem Abdul-Jabbar in 1971. (5) Then known as Memphis State.

2015 Men's NCAA Basketball Tournament

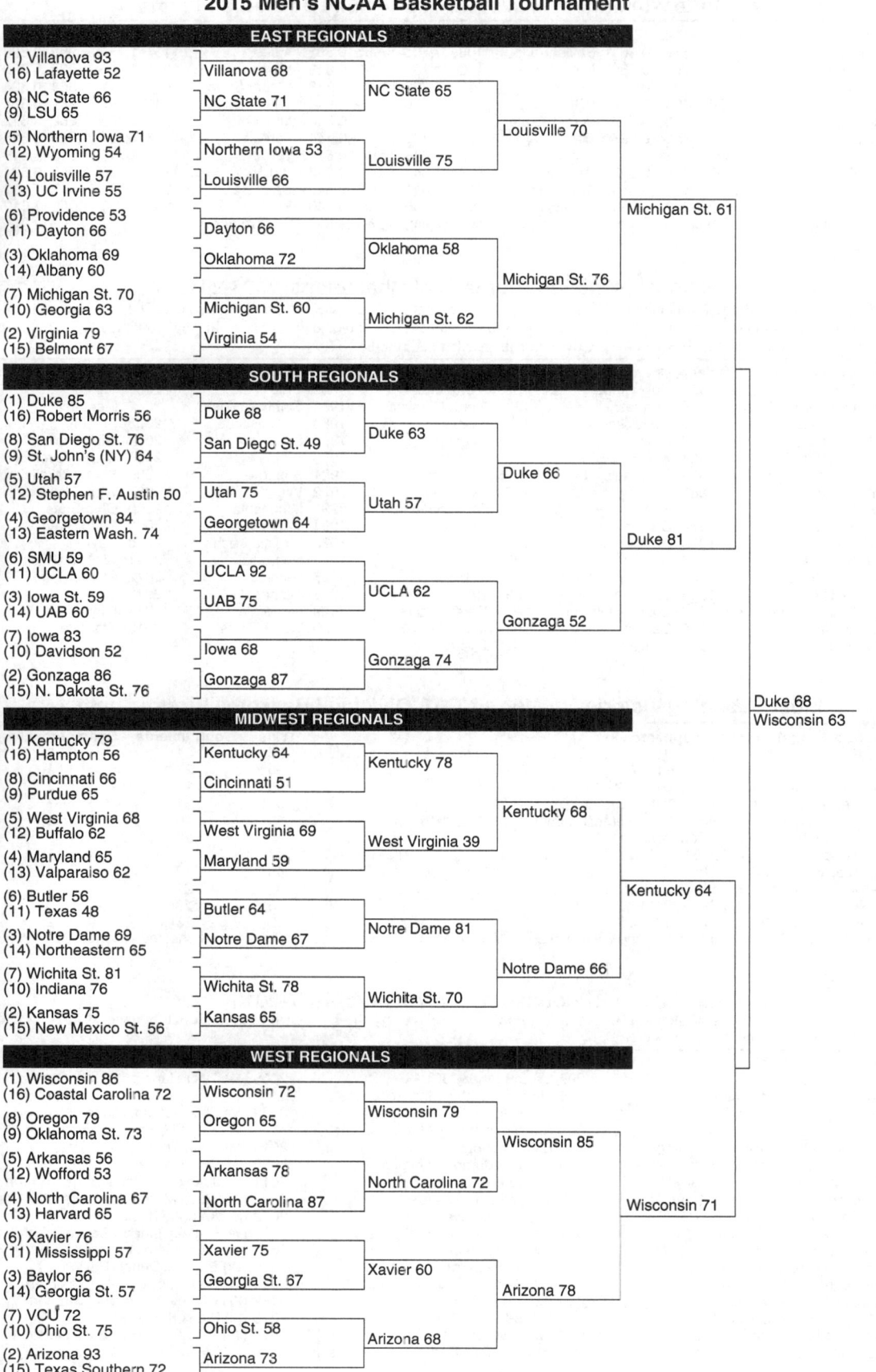

EAST REGIONALS

First round:
- (1) Villanova 93, (16) Lafayette 52
- (8) NC State 66, (9) LSU 65
- (5) Northern Iowa 71, (12) Wyoming 54
- (4) Louisville 57, (13) UC Irvine 55
- (6) Providence 53, (11) Dayton 66
- (3) Oklahoma 69, (14) Albany 60
- (7) Michigan St. 70, (10) Georgia 63
- (2) Virginia 79, (15) Belmont 67

Second round:
- Villanova 68, NC State 71
- Northern Iowa 53, Louisville 66
- Dayton 66, Oklahoma 72
- Michigan St. 60, Virginia 54

Regional semifinals:
- NC State 65, Louisville 75
- Oklahoma 58, Michigan St. 62

Regional final:
- Louisville 70, Michigan St. 76

SOUTH REGIONALS

First round:
- (1) Duke 85, (16) Robert Morris 56
- (8) San Diego St. 76, (9) St. John's (NY) 64
- (5) Utah 57, (12) Stephen F. Austin 50
- (4) Georgetown 84, (13) Eastern Wash. 74
- (6) SMU 59, (11) UCLA 60
- (3) Iowa St. 59, (14) UAB 60
- (7) Iowa 83, (10) Davidson 52
- (2) Gonzaga 86, (15) N. Dakota St. 76

Second round:
- Duke 68, San Diego St. 49
- Utah 75, Georgetown 64
- UCLA 92, UAB 75
- Iowa 68, Gonzaga 87

Regional semifinals:
- Duke 63, Utah 57
- UCLA 62, Gonzaga 74

Regional final:
- Duke 66, Gonzaga 52

MIDWEST REGIONALS

First round:
- (1) Kentucky 79, (16) Hampton 56
- (8) Cincinnati 66, (9) Purdue 65
- (5) West Virginia 68, (12) Buffalo 62
- (4) Maryland 65, (13) Valparaiso 62
- (6) Butler 56, (11) Texas 48
- (3) Notre Dame 69, (14) Northeastern 65
- (7) Wichita St. 81, (10) Indiana 76
- (2) Kansas 75, (15) New Mexico St. 56

Second round:
- Kentucky 64, Cincinnati 51
- West Virginia 69, Maryland 59
- Butler 64, Notre Dame 67
- Wichita St. 78, Kansas 65

Regional semifinals:
- Kentucky 78, West Virginia 39
- Notre Dame 81, Wichita St. 70

Regional final:
- Kentucky 68, Notre Dame 66

WEST REGIONALS

First round:
- (1) Wisconsin 86, (16) Coastal Carolina 72
- (8) Oregon 79, (9) Oklahoma St. 73
- (5) Arkansas 56, (12) Wofford 53
- (4) North Carolina 67, (13) Harvard 65
- (6) Xavier 76, (11) Mississippi 57
- (3) Baylor 56, (14) Georgia St. 57
- (7) VCU 72, (10) Ohio St. 75
- (2) Arizona 93, (15) Texas Southern 72

Second round:
- Wisconsin 72, Oregon 65
- Arkansas 78, North Carolina 87
- Xavier 75, Georgia St. 67
- Ohio St. 58, Arizona 73

Regional semifinals:
- Wisconsin 79, North Carolina 72
- Xavier 60, Arizona 68

Regional final:
- Wisconsin 85, Arizona 78

FINAL FOUR

Semifinals:
- Michigan St. 61, Duke 81
- Kentucky 64, Wisconsin 71

Championship:
- Duke 68, Wisconsin 63

All-Time Winningest Men's NCAA Division I Basketball Teams

Team	Yrs	Won	Lost	Pct.	Team	Yrs	Won	Lost	Pct.	Team	Yrs	Won	Lost	Pct.
Kentucky	112	2,178	673	0.764	St. John's (NY)	108	1,795	956	0.652	Indiana	115	1,756	995	0.638
N. Carolina	105	2,140	767	0.736	Notre Dame	110	1,795	972	0.649	Missouri State	103	1,606	925	0.635
Kansas	117	2,153	831	0.722	Illinois	110	1,729	939	0.648	Weber State	53	977	564	0.634
UNLV	57	1,196	494	0.708	VCU	45	870	474	0.647	Cincinnati	114	1,696	981	0.634
Duke	110	2,062	853	0.707	Murray State	90	1,553	852	0.646	Memphis	94	1,483	862	0.632
Syracuse	114	1,920	851	0.693	Utah	107	1,732	957	0.644	Purdue	117	1,694	1,002	0.628
UCLA	96	1,803	802	0.692	Villanova	95	1,646	911	0.644	Texas	109	1,719	1,019	0.628
Louisville	101	1,755	884	0.665	Temple	119	1,849	1,025	0.643	BYU	113	1,738	1,048	0.624
W. Kentucky	96	1,715	868	0.664	Connecticut	112	1,641	911	0.643	UAB	37	733	447	0.621
Arizona	110	1,712	909	0.653	Arkansas	92	1,605	901	0.640	Penn	115	1,723	1,059	0.619

Note: Through 2014-15 season; winningest teams by percentage. Minimum 25 years as Div. I program.

National Invitation Tournament Champions, 1938-2015

The National Invitation Tournament (NIT), first played in 1938, is the oldest U.S. basketball tournament. The first National Collegiate Athletic Association (NCAA) national championship tournament was played one year later. In Aug. 2005, the NCAA agreed to purchase the NIT from the five New York City-area colleges that had run the NIT.

Year	Champion	Year	Champion	Year	Champion	Year	Champion	Year	Champion
1938	Temple	1954	Holy Cross	1970	Marquette	1986	Ohio State	2001	Tulsa
1939	Long Island Univ.	1955	Duquesne	1971	North Carolina	1987	Southern Miss	2002	Memphis
1940	Colorado	1956	Louisville	1972	Maryland	1988	Connecticut	2003	St. John's (NY)
1941	Long Island Univ.	1957	Bradley	1973	Virginia Tech	1989	St. John's (NY)	2004	Michigan
1942	West Virginia	1958	Xavier (OH)	1974	Purdue	1990	Vanderbilt	2005	South Carolina
1943	St. John's (NY)	1959	St. John's (NY)	1975	Princeton	1991	Stanford	2006	South Carolina
1944	St. John's (NY)	1960	Bradley	1976	Kentucky	1992	Virginia	2007	West Virginia
1945	DePaul	1961	Providence	1977	St. Bonaventure	1993	Minnesota	2008	Ohio State
1946	Kentucky	1962	Dayton	1978	Texas	1994	Villanova	2009	Penn State
1947	Utah	1963	Providence	1979	Indiana	1995	Virginia Tech	2010	Dayton
1948	St. Louis	1964	Bradley	1980	Virginia	1996	Nebraska	2011	Wichita State
1949	San Francisco	1965	St. John's (NY)	1981	Tulsa	1997	Michigan	2012	Stanford
1950	CCNY	1966	Brigham Young	1982	Bradley	1998	Minnesota	2013	Baylor
1951	Brigham Young	1967	Southern Illinois	1983	Fresno State	1999	California	2014	Minnesota
1952	La Salle	1968	Dayton	1984	Michigan	2000	Wake Forest	2015	Stanford
1953	Seton Hall	1969	Temple	1985	UCLA				

Most Coaching Victories in Men's NCAA Division I Basketball Tournament

Coach, school(s), first/latest appearance	Wins	Tournaments	Championships
Mike Krzyzewski, Duke, 1984/2015	88	31	5
Dean Smith, North Carolina, 1967/1997	65	27	2
Roy Williams; Kansas, North Carolina; 1990/2015	65	25	2
Jim Boeheim, Syracuse, 1977/2014	53	31	1
Rick Pitino; Boston Univ., Providence, Kentucky, Louisville; 1983/2015	53	20	2
Jim Calhoun; Northeastern, Connecticut; 1981/2012	49	22	3
John Wooden, UCLA, 1950/1975	47	16	10
Tom Izzo, Michigan St., 1998/2015	46	18	1
Lute Olson; Iowa, Arizona; 1979/2007	46	27	1
Bob Knight; Indiana, Texas Tech; 1973/2007	45	28	3
Denny Crum, Louisville, 1972/2000	42	23	2

Note: Through 2015 tournament. Coaches active in 2014-15 season in bold. Some records adjusted for vacated victories.

John R. Wooden Award Winners, 1977-2015

Awarded to the nation's outstanding men's college basketball player by the Los Angeles Athletic Club since 1977; awarded under the same name to women since 2004.

Year	Player, school
1977	Marques Johnson, UCLA
1978	Phil Ford, North Carolina
1979	Larry Bird, Indiana State
1980	Darrell Griffith, Louisville
1981	Danny Ainge, Brigham Young
1982	Ralph Sampson, Virginia
1983	Ralph Sampson, Virginia
1984	Michael Jordan, North Carolina
1985	Chris Mullin, St. John's (NY)
1986	Walter Berry, St. John's (NY)
1987	David Robinson, Navy
1988	Danny Manning, Kansas
1989	Sean Elliott, Arizona
1990	Lionel Simmons, La Salle
1991	Larry Johnson, UNLV
1992	Christian Laettner, Duke
1993	Calbert Cheaney, Indiana
1994	Glenn Robinson, Purdue
1995	Ed O'Bannon, UCLA
1996	Marcus Camby, Massachusetts
1997	Tim Duncan, Wake Forest
1998	Antawn Jamison, North Carolina
1999	Elton Brand, Duke
2000	Kenyon Martin, Cincinnati
2001	Shane Battier, Duke
2002	Jay Williams, Duke
2003	T. J. Ford, Texas
2004	(M) Jameer Nelson, St. Joseph's
	(W) Alana Beard, Duke
2005	(M) Andrew Bogut, Utah
	(W) Seimone Augustus, LSU
2006	(M) J. J. Redick, Duke
	(W) Seimone Augustus, LSU
2007	(M) Kevin Durant, Texas
	(W) Candace Parker, Tennessee
2008	(M) Tyler Hansbrough, N. Carolina
	(W) Candace Parker, Tennessee
2009	(M) Blake Griffin, Oklahoma
	(W) Maya Moore, Connecticut
2010	(M) Evan Turner, Ohio State
	(W) Tina Charles, Connecticut
2011	(M) Jimmer Fredette, Brigham Young
	(W) Maya Moore, Connecticut
2012	(M) Anthony Davis, Kentucky
	(W) Brittney Griner, Baylor
2013	(M) Trey Burke, Michigan
	(W) Brittney Griner, Baylor
2014	(M) Doug McDermott, Creighton
	(W) Chiney Ogwumike, Stanford
2015	(M) Frank Kaminsky, Wisconsin
	(W) Breanna Stewart, Connecticut

2015 Women's NCAA Basketball Tournament

ALBANY REGIONAL

First Round
- (1) Connecticut 89, (16) St. Francis (NY) 33
- (8) Rutgers 79, (9) Seton Hall 66
- (5) Texas 66, (12) W. Kentucky 64
- (4) California 78, (13) Wichita St. 66
- (6) S. Florida 73, (11) LSU 64
- (3) Louisville 86, (14) BYU 53
- (7) Dayton 78, (10) Iowa St. 66
- (2) Kentucky 97, (15) Tennessee St. 52

Second Round
- Connecticut 91, Rutgers 55
- Texas 73, California 70
- S. Florida 52, Louisville 60
- Dayton 99, Kentucky 94

Regional Semifinals
- Connecticut 105, Texas 54
- Louisville 66, Dayton 82

Regional Final
- Connecticut 91, Dayton 70

SPOKANE REGIONAL

First Round
- (1) Maryland 75, (16) New Mexico St. 57
- (8) Princeton 80, (9) Green Bay 70
- (5) Mississippi St. 57, (12) Tulane 47
- (4) Duke 54, (13) Albany (NY) 52
- (6) George Washington 69, (11) Gonzaga 82
- (3) Oregon St. 74, (14) S. Dakota St. 62
- (7) Chattanooga 40, (10) Pittsburgh 51
- (2) Tennessee 72, (15) Boise St. 61

Second Round
- Maryland 85, Princeton 70
- Mississippi St. 56, Duke 64
- Gonzaga 76, Oregon St. 64
- Pittsburgh 67, Tennessee 77

Regional Semifinals
- Maryland 65, Duke 55
- Gonzaga 69, Tennessee 73 (OT)

Regional Final
- Maryland 58, Tennessee 48

OKLAHOMA CITY REGIONAL

First Round
- (1) Notre Dame 77, (16) Montana 43
- (8) Minnesota 72, (9) DePaul 79
- (5) Oklahoma 111, (12) Quinnipiac 84
- (4) Stanford 73, (13) Cal. St. Northridge 60
- (6) Washington 80, (11) Miami (FL) 86
- (3) Iowa 75, (14) American 67
- (7) Northwestern 55, (10) Arkansas 57
- (2) Baylor 77, (15) Northwestern St. 36

Second Round
- Notre Dame 79, DePaul 67
- Oklahoma 76, Stanford 86
- Miami (FL) 70, Iowa 88
- Arkansas 44, Baylor 73

Regional Semifinals
- Notre Dame 81, Stanford 60
- Iowa 66, Baylor 81

Regional Final
- Notre Dame 77, Baylor 68

GREENSBORO REGIONAL

First Round
- (1) South Carolina 81, (16) Savannah St. 48
- (8) Syracuse 72, (9) Nebraska 69
- (5) Ohio St. 90, (12) James Madison 80
- (4) North Carolina 71, (13) Liberty 65
- (6) Texas A&M 60, (11) Arkansas-Little Rock 69
- (3) Arizona St. 74, (14) Ohio 55
- (7) Florida-Gulf Coast 75, (10) Oklahoma St. 67
- (2) Florida St. 91, (15) Alabama St. 49

Second Round
- South Carolina 97, Syracuse 68
- Ohio St. 84, North Carolina 86
- Arkansas-Little Rock 54, Arizona St. 57
- Florida-Gulf Coast 47, Florida St. 65

Regional Semifinals
- South Carolina 67, North Carolina 65
- Arizona St. 65, Florida St. 66

Regional Final
- South Carolina 80, Florida St. 74

National Semifinals
- Connecticut 81, Maryland 58
- Notre Dame 66, South Carolina 65

Championship
- Connecticut 63, Notre Dame 53

2015 Women's NCAA Tournament: UConn and Stewart Threepeat

The Univ. of Connecticut Huskies Apr. 7, 2015, overtook the Notre Dame Fighting Irish in a 63-53 victory in Tampa, FL, to claim the Women's Division I basketball title. Head coach Geno Auriemma, who has never lost a national title game, claimed his tenth championship with UConn, tying UCLA coaching legend John Wooden's NCAA record. Junior Breanna Stewart scored 8 points with 15 rebounds against the Irish and was named the Final Four's most outstanding player for the third year in a row.

NCAA Women's Basketball Division I Champions, 1982-2015

Year	Champion	Winning coach	Final opponent	Score	Most outstanding player	Site
1982	Louisiana Tech	Sonja Hogg	Cheyney	76-62	Janice Lawrence, LA Tech	Norfolk, VA
1983	USC	Linda Sharp	Louisiana Tech	69-67	Cheryl Miller, USC	Norfolk, VA
1984	USC	Linda Sharp	Tennessee	72-61	Cheryl Miller, USC	Los Angeles, CA
1985	Old Dominion	Marianne Stanley	Georgia	70-65	Tracy Claxton, Old Dominion	Austin, TX
1986	Texas	Jody Conradt	USC	97-81	Clarissa Davis, Texas	Lexington, KY
1987	Tennessee	Pat Summitt	Louisiana Tech	67-44	Tonya Edwards, Tennessee	Austin, TX
1988	Louisiana Tech	Leon Barmore	Auburn	56-54	Erica Westbrooks, LA Tech	Tacoma, WA
1989	Tennessee	Pat Summitt	Auburn	76-60	Bridgette Gordon, Tennessee	Tacoma, WA
1990	Stanford	Tara VanDerveer	Auburn	88-81	Jennifer Azzi, Stanford	Knoxville, TN
1991	Tennessee	Pat Summitt	Virginia	70-67 (OT)	Dawn Staley, Virginia	New Orleans, LA
1992	Stanford	Tara VanDerveer	W. Kentucky	78-62	Molly Goodenbour, Stanford	Los Angeles, CA
1993	Texas Tech	Marsha Sharp	Ohio St.	84-82	Sheryl Swoopes, Texas Tech	Atlanta, GA
1994	North Carolina	Sylvia Hatchell	Louisiana Tech	60-59	Charlotte Smith, North Carolina	Richmond, VA
1995	Connecticut	Geno Auriemma	Tennessee	70-64	Rebecca Lobo, Connecticut	Minneapolis, MN
1996	Tennessee	Pat Summitt	Georgia	83-65	Michelle Marciniak, Tennessee	Charlotte, NC
1997	Tennessee	Pat Summitt	Old Dominion	68-59	Chamique Holdsclaw, Tennessee	Cincinnati, OH
1998	Tennessee	Pat Summitt	Louisiana Tech	93-75	Chamique Holdsclaw, Tennessee	Kansas City, MO
1999	Purdue	Carolyn Peck	Duke	62-45	Ukari Figgs, Purdue	San Jose, CA
2000	Connecticut	Geno Auriemma	Tennessee	71-52	Shea Ralph, Connecticut	Philadelphia, PA
2001	Notre Dame	Muffet McGraw	Purdue	68-66	Ruth Riley, Notre Dame	St. Louis, MO
2002	Connecticut	Geno Auriemma	Oklahoma	82-70	Swin Cash, Connecticut	San Antonio, TX
2003	Connecticut	Geno Auriemma	Tennessee	73-68	Diana Taurasi, Connecticut	Atlanta, GA
2004	Connecticut	Geno Auriemma	Tennessee	70-61	Diana Taurasi, Connecticut	New Orleans, LA
2005	Baylor	Kim Mulkey-Robertson	Michigan State	84-62	Sophia Young, Baylor	Indianapolis, IN
2006	Maryland	Brenda Frese	Duke	78-75 (OT)	Laura Harper, Maryland	Boston, MA
2007	Tennessee	Pat Summitt	Rutgers	59-46	Candace Parker, Tennessee	Cleveland, OH
2008	Tennessee	Pat Summitt	Stanford	64-48	Candace Parker, Tennessee	Tampa Bay, FL
2009	Connecticut	Geno Auriemma	Louisville	76-54	Tina Charles, Connecticut	St. Louis, MO
2010	Connecticut	Geno Auriemma	Stanford	53-47	Maya Moore, Connecticut	San Antonio, TX
2011	Texas A&M	Gary Blair	Notre Dame	76-70	Danielle Adams, Texas A&M	Indianapolis, IN
2012	Baylor	Kim Mulkey	Notre Dame	80-61	Brittney Griner, Baylor	Denver, CO
2013	Connecticut	Geno Auriemma	Louisville	93-60	Breanna Stewart, Connecticut	New Orleans, LA
2014	Connecticut	Geno Auriemma	Notre Dame	79-58	Breanna Stewart, Connecticut	Nashville, TN
2015	Connecticut	Geno Auriemma	Notre Dame	63-53	Breanna Stewart, Connecticut	Tampa, FL

Wade Trophy Winners, 1978-2015

Awarded by the National Assn. for Girls and Women in Sport and the Women's Basketball Coaches Assn. (WBCA) for character, leadership, and player performance.

Year	Player, school
1978	Carol Blazejowski, Montclair St.
1979	Nancy Lieberman, Old Dominion
1980	Nancy Lieberman, Old Dominion
1981	Lynette Woodard, Kansas
1982	Pam Kelly, Louisiana Tech
1983	LaTaunya Pollard, Long Beach St.
1984	Janice Lawrence, Louisiana Tech
1985	Cheryl Miller, USC
1986	Kamie Ethridge, Texas
1987	Shelly Pennefeather, Villanova
1988	Teresa Weatherspoon, Louisiana Tech
1989	Clarissa Davis, Texas
1990	Jennifer Azzi, Stanford
1991	Daedra Charles, Tennessee
1992	Susan Robinson, Penn St.
1993	Karen Jennings, Nebraska
1994	Carol Ann Shudlick, Minnesota
1995	Rebecca Lobo, Connecticut
1996	Jennifer Rizzotti, Connecticut
1997	DeLisha Milton, Florida
1998	Ticha Penicheiro, Old Dominion
1999	Stephanie White-McCarty, Purdue
2000	Edwina Brown, Texas
2001	Jackie Stiles, SW Missouri St.
2002	Sue Bird, Connecticut
2003	Diana Taurasi, Connecticut
2004	Alana Beard, Duke
2005	Seimone Augustus, LSU
2006	Seimone Augustus, LSU
2007	Candace Parker, Tennessee
2008	Candice Wiggins, Stanford
2009	Maya Moore, Connecticut
2010	Maya Moore, Connecticut
2011	Maya Moore, Connecticut
2012	Brittney Griner, Baylor
2013	Brittney Griner, Baylor
2014	Odyssey Sims, Baylor
2015	Breanna Stewart, Connecticut

NCAA Men's Baseball Division I Champions, 1947-2015

Year	Champion
1947	California
1948	USC
1949	Texas
1950	Texas
1951	Oklahoma
1952	Holy Cross
1953	Michigan
1954	Missouri
1955	Wake Forest
1956	Minnesota
1957	California
1958	USC
1959	Oklahoma St.
1960	Minnesota
1961	USC
1962	Michigan
1963	USC
1964	Minnesota
1965	Arizona St.
1966	Ohio St.
1967	Arizona St.
1968	USC
1969	Arizona St.
1970	USC
1971	USC
1972	USC
1973	USC
1974	USC
1975	Texas
1976	Arizona
1977	Arizona St.
1978	USC
1979	Cal St. Fullerton
1980	Arizona
1981	Arizona St.
1982	Miami (FL)
1983	Texas
1984	Cal St. Fullerton
1985	Miami (FL)
1986	Arizona
1987	Stanford
1988	Stanford
1989	Wichita St.
1990	Georgia
1991	LSU
1992	Pepperdine
1993	LSU
1994	Oklahoma
1995	Cal St. Fullerton
1996	LSU
1997	LSU
1998	USC
1999	Miami (FL)
2000	LSU
2001	Miami (FL)
2002	Texas
2003	Rice
2004	Cal St. Fullerton
2005	Texas
2006	Oregon St.
2007	Oregon St.
2008	Fresno St.
2009	LSU
2010	South Carolina
2011	South Carolina
2012	Arizona
2013	UCLA
2014	Vanderbilt
2015	Virginia

NCAA Women's Softball Division I Champions, 1982-2015

Year	Champion	Year	Champion	Year	Champion	Year	Champion	Year	Champion
1982	UCLA	1989	UCLA	1996	Arizona	2003	UCLA	2010	UCLA
1983	Texas A&M	1990	UCLA	1997	Arizona	2004	UCLA	2011	Arizona St.
1984	UCLA	1991	Arizona	1998	Fresno St.	2005	Michigan	2012	Alabama
1985	UCLA	1992	UCLA	1999	UCLA	2006	Arizona	2013	Oklahoma
1986	Cal St. Fullerton	1993	Arizona	2000	Oklahoma	2007	Arizona	2014	Florida
1987	Texas A&M	1994	Arizona	2001	Arizona	2008	Arizona St.	2015	Florida
1988	UCLA	1995	UCLA	2002	California	2009	Washington		

NCAA Men's Hockey Division I Champions, 1948-2015

Year	Champion	Year	Champion	Year	Champion	Year	Champion	Year	Champion
1948	Michigan	1962	Michigan Tech	1976	Minnesota	1990	Wisconsin	2003	Minnesota
1949	Boston College	1963	North Dakota	1977	Wisconsin	1991	North Michigan	2004	Denver
1950	Colorado College	1964	Michigan	1978	Boston Univ.	1992	Lake Superior St.	2005	Denver
1951	Michigan	1965	Michigan Tech	1979	Minnesota	1993	Maine	2006	Wisconsin
1952	Michigan	1966	Michigan St.	1980	North Dakota	1994	Lake Superior St.	2007	Michigan St.
1953	Michigan	1967	Cornell	1981	Wisconsin	1995	Boston Univ.	2008	Boston College
1954	Rensselaer	1968	Denver	1982	North Dakota	1996	Michigan	2009	Boston Univ.
1955	Michigan	1969	Denver	1983	Wisconsin	1997	North Dakota	2010	Boston College
1956	Michigan	1970	Cornell	1984	Bowling Green	1998	Michigan	2011	Minnesota-Duluth
1957	Colorado College	1971	Boston Univ.	1985	Rensselaer	1999	Maine	2012	Boston College
1958	Denver	1972	Boston Univ.	1986	Michigan St.	2000	North Dakota	2013	Yale
1959	North Dakota	1973	Wisconsin	1987	North Dakota	2001	Boston College	2014	Union College
1960	Denver	1974	Minnesota	1988	Lake Superior St.	2002	Minnesota	2015	Providence
1961	Denver	1975	Michigan Tech	1989	Harvard				

NCAA Women's Hockey Champions, 2001-15

Year	Champion	Year	Champion	Year	Champion	Year	Champion	Year	Champion
2001	Minnesota-Duluth	2004	Minnesota	2007	Wisconsin	2010	Minnesota-Duluth	2013	Minnesota
2002	Minnesota-Duluth	2005	Minnesota	2008	Minnesota-Duluth	2011	Wisconsin	2014	Clarkson Univ.
2003	Minnesota-Duluth	2006	Wisconsin	2009	Wisconsin	2012	Minnesota	2015	Minnesota

NCAA Division I Lacrosse Champions, 1982-2015

Year[1]	Men	Women	Year[1]	Men	Women	Year[1]	Men	Women
1982	North Carolina	Massachusetts	1994	Princeton	Princeton	2005	Johns Hopkins	Northwestern
1983	Syracuse	Delaware	1995	Syracuse	Maryland	2006	Virginia	Northwestern
1984	Johns Hopkins	Temple	1996	Princeton	Maryland	2007	Johns Hopkins	Northwestern
1985	Johns Hopkins	New Hampshire	1997	Princeton	Maryland	2008	Syracuse	Northwestern
1986	North Carolina	Maryland	1998	Princeton	Maryland	2009	Syracuse	Northwestern
1987	Johns Hopkins	Penn St.	1999	Virginia	Maryland	2010	Duke	Maryland
1988	Syracuse	Temple	2000	Syracuse	Maryland	2011	Virginia	Northwestern
1989	Syracuse	Penn St.	2001	Princeton	Maryland	2012	Loyola (MD)	Northwestern
1990	Syracuse[2]	Harvard	2002	Syracuse	Princeton	2013	Duke	North Carolina
1991	North Carolina	Virginia	2003	Virginia	Princeton	2014	Duke	Maryland
1992	Princeton	Maryland	2004	Syracuse	Virginia	2015	Denver	Maryland
1993	Syracuse	Virginia						

(1) NCAA Championships began in 1971 for men, in 1982 for women. (2) Vacated due to an NCAA rules violation.

NCAA Division I Soccer Champions, 1982-2014

Year[1]	Men	Women	Year[1]	Men	Women	Year[1]	Men	Women
1982	Indiana	North Carolina	1993	Virginia	North Carolina	2005	Maryland	Portland
1983	Indiana	North Carolina	1994	Virginia	North Carolina	2006	UC Santa Barbara	North Carolina
1984	Clemson	North Carolina	1995	Wisconsin	Notre Dame			
1985	UCLA	George Mason	1996	St. John's (NY)	North Carolina	2007	Wake Forest	USC
1986	Duke	North Carolina	1997	UCLA	North Carolina	2008	Maryland	North Carolina
1987	Clemson	North Carolina	1998	Indiana	Florida	2009	Virginia	North Carolina
1988	Indiana	North Carolina	1999	Indiana	North Carolina	2010	Akron	Notre Dame
1989	Santa Clara; Virginia (tie)	North Carolina	2000	Connecticut	North Carolina	2011	North Carolina	Stanford
			2001	North Carolina	Santa Clara	2012	Indiana	North Carolina
1990	UCLA	North Carolina	2002	UCLA	Portland	2013	Notre Dame	UCLA
1991	Virginia	North Carolina	2003	Indiana	North Carolina	2014	Virginia	Florida St.
1992	Virginia	North Carolina	2004	Indiana	Notre Dame			

(1) NCAA Championships began in 1959 for men, in 1982 for women.

NCAA Division I Wrestling Champions, 1964-2015

Year	Champion	Year	Champion	Year	Champion	Year	Champion	Year	Champion
1964	Oklahoma St.	1975	Iowa	1986	Iowa	1996	Iowa	2006	Oklahoma St.
1965	Iowa St.	1976	Iowa	1987	Iowa St.	1997	Iowa	2007	Minnesota
1966	Oklahoma St.	1977	Iowa St.	1988	Arizona St.	1998	Iowa	2008	Iowa
1967	Michigan St.	1978	Iowa	1989	Oklahoma St.	1999	Iowa	2009	Iowa
1968	Oklahoma St.	1979	Iowa	1990	Oklahoma St.	2000	Iowa	2010	Iowa
1969	Iowa St.	1980	Iowa	1991	Iowa	2001	Minnesota	2011	Penn St.
1970	Iowa St.	1981	Iowa	1992	Iowa	2002	Minnesota	2012	Penn St.
1971	Oklahoma St.	1982	Iowa	1993	Iowa	2003	Oklahoma St.	2013	Penn St.
1972	Iowa St.	1983	Iowa	1994	Oklahoma St.	2004	Oklahoma St.	2014	Penn St.
1973	Iowa St.	1984	Iowa	1995	Iowa	2005	Oklahoma St.	2015	Ohio St.
1974	Oklahoma	1985	Iowa						

FOOTBALL

NFL 2014: Patriots Triumph in Controversy-Plagued Season

Before their fourth Super Bowl victory capped a scandal-plagued season, the New England Patriots won their sixth consecutive AFC East division title amidst controversy. Following New England's 45-7 rout of the Indianapolis Colts in the AFC championship game Jan. 18, 2015, at Gillette Stadium in Foxborough, MA, the NFL found that 11 of the 12 footballs the Patriots provided for the game were underinflated. Patriots quarterback Tom Brady and head coach Bill Belichick denied any deliberate wrongdoing in "Deflategate," but the NFL fined the franchise and suspended Brady for four games following an investigation completed in May 2015. Patriots owner Robert Kraft chose not to appeal the team's sanctions, but a federal judge Sept. 3 nullified Brady's suspension after the quarterback appealed.

The 2013 champion Seattle Seahawks returned to the Super Bowl with a dramatic 28-22 overtime win over Green Bay in the NFC title game Jan. 18, 2015, at CenturyLink Field in Seattle. The Packers, led by 2014 NFL MVP Aaron Rodgers, forced an extra period on a 48-yard field goal, but Seattle clinched a ticket to Super Bowl XLIX when Russell Wilson connected with Jermaine Kearse on a 35-yard TD pass 3:19 into overtime.

New Orleans QB Drew Brees tied Pittsburgh's Ben Roethlisberger for the league lead with 4,952 passing yards. Roethlisberger's favorite target was Steelers wide receiver Antonio Brown, who led the NFL with 129 receptions. Indianapolis QB Andrew Luck led the league with 40 touchdown passes, just one more than Denver's Peyton Manning, who ended the season with 530 career touchdown passes, breaking Brett Favre's record for most touchdown passes (508) in NFL history.

The NFL's season highlights were overshadowed by the league's off-the-field disciplinary issues, primarily involving Ray Rice and Adrian Peterson. Rice and his then-fiancée (now wife), Janay Palmer, were arrested Feb. 15, 2014, for an altercation at an Atlantic City, NJ, casino. Surveillance footage showed Rice dragging an unconscious Palmer out of a casino elevator. The Baltimore running back was accepted into a pre-trial intervention program for first-time offenders and avoided prosecution. The NFL, July 24, suspended Rice for two games but faced criticism when a second video surfaced, in Sept., of Rice punching Palmer in the face inside the elevator. The Ravens released Rice, and the NFL suspended him indefinitely. Rice won his appeal Nov. 28, leaving him free to sign with any team. Minnesota running back Peterson was indicted Sept. 12, 2014, on child abuse charges for allegedly hitting his four-year-old son with a switch. Peterson eventually pleaded no contest to a misdemeanor reckless assault charge. The league suspended him, Nov. 18, through at least Apr. 15, 2015. The suspension was overturned Feb. 26 on a legal challenge brought by the NFL Players Association, and Peterson was free to rejoin the league.

NFL Final Standings, 2014

(playoff seeding in parentheses)

AMERICAN FOOTBALL CONFERENCE

	W	L	T	Pct	PF	PA	Div
East Division							
New England (1)	12	4	0	.750	468	313	4-2
Buffalo	9	7	0	.563	343	289	4-2
Miami	8	8	0	.500	388	373	3-3
NY Jets	4	12	0	.250	283	401	1-5
North Division							
Pittsburgh (3)	11	5	0	.688	436	368	4-2
*Cincinnati (5)	10	5	1	.656	365	344	3-3
*Baltimore (6)	10	6	0	.625	409	302	3-3
Cleveland	7	9	0	.438	299	337	2-4
South Division							
Indianapolis (4)	11	5	0	.688	458	369	6-0
Houston	9	7	0	.563	372	307	4-2
Jacksonville	3	13	0	.188	249	412	1-5
Tennessee	2	14	0	.125	254	438	1-5
West Division							
Denver (2)	12	4	0	.750	482	354	6-0
Kansas City	9	7	0	.563	353	281	3-3
San Diego	9	7	0	.563	348	348	2-4
Oakland	3	13	0	.188	253	452	1-5

*Wild card qualifier for playoffs. **Note:** New England wins tiebreaker over Denver for no. 1 seed based on head-to-head win percentage; Pittsburgh wins tiebreaker over Indianapolis for no. 3 seed based on head-to-head win percentage.

NATIONAL FOOTBALL CONFERENCE

	W	L	T	Pct	PF	PA	Div
East Division							
Dallas (3)	12	4	0	.750	467	352	4-2
Philadelphia	10	6	0	.625	474	400	4-2
NY Giants	6	10	0	.375	380	400	2-4
Washington	4	12	0	.250	301	438	2-4
North Division							
Green Bay (2)	12	4	0	.750	486	348	5-1
*Detroit (6)	11	5	0	.688	321	282	5-1
Minnesota	7	9	0	.438	325	343	1-5
Chicago	5	11	0	.313	319	442	1-5
South Division							
Carolina (4)	7	8	1	.469	339	374	4-2
New Orleans	7	9	0	.438	401	424	3-3
Atlanta	6	10	0	.375	381	417	5-1
Tampa Bay	2	14	0	.125	277	410	0-6
West Division							
Seattle (1)	12	4	0	.750	394	254	5-1
*Arizona (5)	11	5	0	.688	310	299	3-3
San Francisco	8	8	0	.500	306	340	2-4
St. Louis	6	10	0	.375	324	354	2-4

*Wild card qualifier for playoffs. **Note:** Seattle wins tiebreaker over Green Bay and Dallas for no. 1-seed based on better conference record; Green Bay wins tiebreaker over Dallas for no. 2 seed based on better conference record; Arizona wins tiebreaker over Detroit for no. 5 seed based on head-to-head win percentage.

NFL Playoffs, 2014

AFC Wild Card Games: Baltimore 30, Pittsburgh 17; Indianapolis 26, Cincinnati 10
NFC Wild Card Games: Carolina 27, Arizona 16; Dallas 24, Detroit 20
AFC Divisional Playoff Games: New England 35, Baltimore 31; Indianapolis 24, Denver 13
NFC Divisional Playoff Games: Seattle 31, Carolina 17; Green Bay 26, Dallas 21
AFC Championship Game: New England 45, Indianapolis 7
NFC Championship Game: Seattle 28, Green Bay 22 (OT)
Super Bowl XLIX: New England 28, Seattle 24

Super Bowl XLIX: New England 28, Seattle 24

Stellar defense late in the fourth quarter lifted the New England Patriots to a 28-24 victory over the defending champion Seattle Seahawks in Super Bowl XLIX, Feb. 1, 2015, at Univ. of Phoenix Stadium in Glendale, AZ. New England won its fourth Super Bowl in franchise history; head coach Bill Belichick led the team to all four championships.

Patriots quarterback Tom Brady, who was voted Super Bowl MVP for the third time, passed for 328 yards and 4 TDs, surpassing Joe Montana's record (11) for career Super Bowl touchdown passes with 13.

Despite a mutually scoreless first quarter, the teams scored two touchdowns each by the end of the first half. Steven Hauschka gave Seattle the lead with a 27-yard field goal in the third quarter. Seattle quarterback Russell Wilson extended it to 24-14 with a 3-yard touchdown pass to Doug Baldwin.

The Patriots—scoreless in the third quarter—orchestrated a pair of fourth-quarter scoring drives to overcome the 10-point deficit, though Seattle nearly pulled off a dramatic comeback late in the fourth quarter. New England ran out the clock but not before a near brawl erupted that resulted in the ejection of Seahawks linebacker Bruce Irvin; he was the first player ever to be ejected from a Super Bowl game.

Super Bowl XLIX: Box Score

Team	Quarters 1	2	3	4	Final
New England	0	14	0	14	28
Seattle	0	14	10	0	24

Total attendance: 70,288
Game length: 3:36

Super Bowl XLIX: Scoring

New England: Brandon LaFell, 11-yard pass from Tom Brady (Stephen Gostkowski PAT)
Seattle: Marshawn Lynch, 3-yard run (Steven Hauschka PAT)
New England: Ron Gronkowski, 22-yard pass from Brady (Gostkowski PAT)
Seattle: Chris Matthews, 11-yard pass from Russell Wilson (Hauschka PAT)
Seattle: Hauschka, 27-yard field goal
Seattle: Doug Baldwin, 3-yard pass from Wilson (Hauschka PAT)
New England: Danny Amendola, 4-yard pass from Brady (Gostkowski PAT)
New England: Julian Edelman, 3-yard pass from Brady (Gostkowski PAT)

Super Bowl XLIX: Team Statistics

	Patriots	Seahawks
First downs	25	20
Total net yards	377	396
Rushes-yards	21-57	29-162
Passing yards, net	320	234
Punt returns-yards	3-27	2-6
Kickoff returns-yards	3-49	0-0
Interception returns-yards	1-3	2-14
Field goals made-attempts	0-0	1-1
Pass attempts-completions-interceptions	50-37-2	21-12-1
Sacked-yards lost	1-8	3-13
Punts-average	4-49.0	6-44.8
Fumbles-lost	0-0	0-0
Penalties-yards	5-36	7-70
Time of possession	33:46	26:14

NFL Individual Leaders: American Football Conference, 2014

(* = rookie)

PASSING

Player, team	Att	Comp	Pct comp	Yds	Yds/Att	Long	TD	Pct TD	Int	Rating
Ben Roethlisberger, Pittsburgh	608	408	67.1	4,952	8.1	94T	32	5.3	9	103.3
Peyton Manning, Denver	597	395	66.2	4,727	7.9	86T	39	6.5	15	101.5
Tom Brady, New England	582	373	64.1	4,109	7.1	69T	33	5.7	9	97.4
Andrew Luck, Indianapolis	616	380	61.7	4,761	7.7	80	40	6.5	16	96.5
Ryan Fitzpatrick, Houston	312	197	63.1	2,483	8.0	76T	17	5.4	8	95.3
Philip Rivers, San Diego	570	379	66.5	4,286	7.5	59	31	5.4	18	93.8
Alex Smith, Kansas City	464	303	65.3	3,265	7.0	70T	18	3.9	6	93.4
Ryan Tannehill, Miami	590	392	66.4	4,045	6.9	50	27	4.6	12	92.8
Joe Flacco, Baltimore	554	344	62.1	3,986	7.2	80T	27	4.9	12	91.0
Kyle Orton, Buffalo	447	287	64.2	3,018	6.8	84	18	4.0	10	87.8
Andy Dalton, Cincinnati	481	309	64.2	3,398	7.1	81T	19	4.0	17	83.5
Geno Smith, NY Jets	367	219	59.7	2,525	6.9	74T	13	3.5	13	77.5
*Derek Carr, Oakland	599	348	58.1	3,270	5.5	77T	21	3.5	12	76.6

RUSHING YARDS

Player, team	Yds	Att	Avg	Long	TD
Le'Veon Bell, Pittsburgh	1,361	290	4.7	81	8
Justin Forsett, Baltimore	1,266	235	5.4	52	8
Arian Foster, Houston	1,246	260	4.8	51	8
*Jeremy Hill, Cincinnati	1,124	222	5.1	85T	9
Lamar Miller, Miami	1,099	216	5.1	97T	8
Jamaal Charles, Kansas City	1,033	206	5.0	63T	9
C.J. Anderson, Denver	849	179	4.7	27	8
Chris Ivory, NY Jets	821	198	4.1	71T	6
Giovani Bernard, Cincinnati	680	168	4.0	89T	5
*Terrance West, Cleveland	673	171	3.9	36	4

RECEPTIONS

Player, team	Rec	Yds	Avg	Long	TD
Antonio Brown, Pittsburgh	129	1,698	13.2	63T	13
Demaryius Thomas, Denver	111	1,619	14.6	86T	11
Emmanuel Sanders, Denver	101	1,404	13.9	48	9
Julian Edelman, New England	92	972	10.6	69T	4
Andre Johnson, Houston	85	936	11.0	35	3
*Jarvis Landry, Miami	84	758	9.0	25	5
Le'Veon Bell, Pittsburgh	83	854	10.3	48	3
Rob Gronkowski, New England	82	1,124	13.7	46T	12
T.Y. Hilton, Indianapolis	82	1,345	16.4	73T	7
Steve Smith, Baltimore	79	1,065	13.5	80T	6

INTERCEPTIONS

Player, team	No.	Yds	Avg	Long	TD
Tashaun Gipson, Cleveland	6	158	26.3	62T	1
Mike Adams, Indianapolis	5	24	4.8	10	0
Brent Grimes, Miami	5	80	16.0	32	1
Vontae Davis, Indianapolis	4	72	18.0	42	0
Leodis McKelvin, Buffalo	4	10	2.5	9	0
Rahim Moore, Denver	4	36	9.0	19	0
Reggie Nelson, Cincinnati	4	30	7.5	31	0
Buster Skrine, Cleveland	4	34	8.5	30	0
Aqib Talib, Denver	4	62	15.5	33T	2
Charles Woodson, Oakland	4	35	8.8	30	0

SCORING—KICKERS

Player, team	PAT	FG	Long	Pts
Stephen Gostkowski, New England	51/51	35/37	53	156
Adam Vinatieri, Indianapolis	50/50	30/31	53	140
Dan Carpenter, Buffalo	31/32	34/38	58	133
Shaun Suisham, Pittsburgh	45/45	29/32	53	132
Randy Bullock, Houston	40/40	30/35	55	130
Justin Tucker, Baltimore	42/42	29/34	55	129

SCORING—NON-KICKERS

Player, team (position)	TD	Rush	Rec	2-Pt	Pts
Antonio Brown, Pittsburgh (WR)[1]	14	1	13	1	86
Jamaal Charles, Kansas City (RB)	14	9	5	0	84
Arian Foster, Houston (RB)	13	8	5	0	78
Antonio Gates, San Diego (TE)	12	0	12	0	72
Rob Gronkowski, New England (TE)	12	0	12	0	72
Julius Thomas, Denver (TE)	12	0	12	0	72
Demaryius Thomas, Denver (WR)	11	0	11	1	68

(1) Punt return.

KICKOFF RETURNS

Player, team	No.	Yds	Avg	Long	TD
Adam Jones, Cincinnati	27	844	31.3	97	0
Jacoby Jones, Baltimore	32	978	30.6	108T	1
Knile Davis, Kansas City	29	829	28.6	99T	1
*Jarvis Landry, Miami	34	954	28.1	74	0
Jordan Todman, Jacksonville	38	972	25.6	40	0
Markus Wheaton, Pittsburgh	20	494	24.7	41	0

PUNTING

Player, team	No.	Yds	Long	Avg
Bryan Anger, Jacksonville	94	4,464	69	47.5
Sam Koch, Baltimore	60	2,841	73	47.4
Kevin Huber, Cincinnati	73	3,419	69	46.8
Brett Kern, Tennessee	88	4,118	79	46.8
Pat McAfee, Indianapolis	69	3,221	61	46.7
Ryan Allen, New England	66	3,060	67	46.4

PUNT RETURNS

Player, team	No.	Yds	Avg	Long	TD
Julian Edelman, New England	25	299	12.0	84T	1
Adam Jones, Cincinnati	22	265	12.0	47	0
*De'Anthony Thomas, Kansas City	34	405	11.9	81T	1
Antonio Brown, Pittsburgh	30	319	10.6	71T	1
Jacoby Jones, Baltimore	30	275	9.2	45	0
Leodis McKelvin, Buffalo	21	183	8.7	24	0

SACKS

Player, team	No.
Justin Houston, Kansas City	22.0
J.J. Watt, Houston	20.5
Elvis Dumervil, Baltimore	17.0
Mario Williams, Buffalo	14.5
Von Miller, Denver	14.0
Terrell Suggs, Baltimore	12.0
Cameron Wake, Miami	11.5
Paul Kruger, Cleveland	11.0
Marcell Dareus, Buffalo	10.0
Jerry Hughes, Buffalo	10.0
DeMarcus Ware, Denver	10.0

NFL Individual Leaders: National Football Conference, 2014

(* = rookie)

PASSING

Player, team	Att	Comp	Pct comp	Yds	Yds/Att	Long	TD	Pct TD	Int	Rating
Tony Romo, Dallas	435	304	69.9	3,705	8.5	68T	34	7.8	9	113.2
Aaron Rodgers, Green Bay	520	341	65.6	4,381	8.4	80T	38	7.3	5	112.2
Drew Brees, New Orleans	659	456	69.2	4,952	7.5	69T	33	5.0	17	97.0
Carson Palmer, Arizona	224	141	62.9	1,626	7.3	80T	11	4.9	3	95.6
Russell Wilson, Seattle	452	285	63.1	3,475	7.7	80T	20	4.4	7	95.0
Matt Ryan, Atlanta	628	415	66.1	4,694	7.5	79	28	4.5	14	93.9
Eli Manning, NY Giants	601	379	63.1	4,410	7.3	80T	30	5.0	14	92.1
Jay Cutler, Chicago	561	370	66.0	3,812	6.8	74	28	5.0	18	88.6
Mark Sanchez, Philadelphia	309	198	64.1	2,418	7.8	72	14	4.5	11	88.4
Colin Kaepernick, San Francisco	478	289	60.5	3,369	7.0	80T	19	4.0	10	86.4
Matthew Stafford, Detroit	602	363	60.3	4,257	7.1	73T	22	3.7	12	85.7
*Teddy Bridgewater, Minnesota	402	259	64.4	2,919	7.3	87T	14	3.5	12	85.2
Austin Davis, St. Louis	284	180	63.4	2,001	7.0	59T	12	4.2	9	85.1
Shaun Hill, St. Louis	229	145	63.3	1,657	7.2	63T	8	3.5	7	83.9

RUSHING YARDS

Player, team	Yds	Att	Avg	Long	TD
DeMarco Murray, Dallas	1,845	392	4.7	51	13
LeSean McCoy, Philadelphia	1,319	312	4.2	53	5
Marshawn Lynch, Seattle	1,306	280	4.7	79T	13
Eddie Lacy, Green Bay	1,139	246	4.6	44T	9
Frank Gore, San Francisco	1,106	255	4.3	52T	4
Alfred Morris, Washington	1,074	265	4.1	30	8
Matt Forte, Chicago	1,038	266	3.9	32	6
Mark Ingram, New Orleans	964	226	4.3	31	9
Joique Bell, Detroit	860	223	3.9	57	7
Russell Wilson, Seattle	849	118	7.2	55	6

RECEPTIONS

Player, team	Rec	Yds	Avg	Long	TD
Julio Jones, Atlanta	104	1,593	15.3	79	6
Matt Forte, Chicago	102	808	7.9	56	4
Golden Tate, Detroit	99	1,331	13.4	73T	4
Jordy Nelson, Green Bay	98	1,519	15.5	80T	13
*Odell Beckham, NY Giants	91	1,305	14.3	80T	12
Randall Cobb, Green Bay	91	1,287	14.1	70T	12
Martellus Bennett, Chicago	90	916	10.2	37	6
Dez Bryant, Dallas	88	1,320	15.0	68T	16
Jimmy Graham, New Orleans	85	889	10.5	29	10
Alshon Jeffery, Chicago	85	1,133	13.3	74	10
Jeremy Maclin, Philadelphia	85	1,318	15.5	72	10

INTERCEPTIONS

Player, team	No.	Yds	Avg	Long	TD
Glover Quin, Detroit	7	117	16.7	56	0
Bruce Carter, Dallas	5	72	14.4	35	1
Perrish Cox, San Francisco	5	12	2.4	10	0
Harrison Smith, Minnesota	5	150	30.0	81T	1
12 players (incl. 1 rookie) tied with	4				

SCORING—KICKERS

Player, team	PAT	FG	Long	Pts
*Cody Parkey, Philadelphia	54/54	32/36	54	150
Mason Crosby, Green Bay	53/55	27/33	55	134
Steven Hauschka, Seattle	41/41	31/37	58	134
Dan Bailey, Dallas	56/56	25/29	56	131
Matt Bryant, Atlanta	40/40	29/32	54	127
Graham Gano, Carolina	34/34	29/35	53	121

SCORING—NON-KICKERS

Player, team (position)	TD	Rush	Rec	2-Pt	Pts
Marshawn Lynch, Seattle (RB)	17	13	4	0	102
Dez Bryant, Dallas (WR)	16	0	16	0	96
Eddie Lacy, Green Bay (RB)	13	9	4	0	78
DeMarco Murray, Dallas (RB)	13	13	0	0	78
Jordy Nelson, Green Bay (WR)	13	0	13	0	78
Randall Cobb, Green Bay (WR)	12	0	12	1	74

KICKOFF RETURNS

Player, team	No.	Yds	Avg	Long	TD
Benny Cunningham, St. Louis	35	963	27.5	75	0
Cordarrelle Patterson, Minnesota	34	871	25.6	51	0
*Bruce Ellington, San Francisco	24	614	25.6	38	0
Marc Mariani, Chicago	20	510	25.5	67	0
Jeremy Ross, Detroit	23	584	25.4	41	0
Devin Hester, Atlanta	45	1,128	25.1	66	0

PUNTING

Player, team	No.	Yds	Long	Avg
Tress Way, Washington	77	3,659	77	47.5
Andy Lee, San Francisco	72	3,369	71	46.8
Johnny Hekker, St. Louis	80	3,721	61	46.5
Thomas Morstead, New Orleans	58	2,690	63	46.4
Sam Martin, Detroit	68	3,138	71	46.1
Matt Bosher, Atlanta	67	3,063	66	45.7
Steve Weatherford, NY Giants	80	3,640	71	45.5

PUNT RETURNS

Player, team	No.	Yds	Avg	Long	TD
Darren Sproles, Philadelphia	39	506	13.0	82T	2
Tavon Austin, St. Louis	35	391	11.2	78T	1
Marcus Sherels, Minnesota	27	297	11.0	35	0
Ted Ginn, Arizona	26	277	10.7	71T	1
Dwayne Harris, Dallas	30	275	9.2	38	0
Jeremy Ross, Detroit	32	284	8.9	28	0
*Bruce Ellington, San Francisco	23	188	8.2	23	0

SACKS

Player, team	No.
Connor Barwin, Philadelphia	14.5
Ryan Kerrigan, Washington	13.5
Jason Pierre-Paul, NY Giants	12.5
Everson Griffen, Minnesota	12.0
Clay Matthews, Green Bay	11.0
Robert Quinn, St. Louis	10.5
Junior Galette, New Orleans	10.0
Willie Young, Chicago	10.0
Vinny Curry, Philadelphia	9.0
*Aaron Donald, St. Louis	9.0

Super Bowl, 1967-2015

The Super Bowl was created as a condition of the merger between the American Football League (AFL, formed in 1959) and National Football League (NFL, formed in 1920). Announced June 8, 1966, the merger agreement stipulated that the leagues would play separate regular season schedules through the 1969 season but meet after each in an AFL-NFL Championship Game, unofficially dubbed the Super Bowl (the name became official with the second game). The first Super Bowl, played at the Memorial Coliseum in Los Angeles on Jan. 15, 1967, did not sell out, unlike every Super Bowl game since. Each player on the victorious Green Bay Packers earned $15,000 for the win; the defeated Kansas City Chiefs each collected $7,500.

No.	Year	Winner	Opponent	Winning coach	Site
I	1967	*Green Bay Packers, 35	Kansas City Chiefs, 10	Vince Lombardi	Memorial Coliseum, Los Angeles, CA
II	1968	Green Bay Packers, 33	*Oakland Raiders, 14	Vince Lombardi	Orange Bowl, Miami, FL
III	1969	*NY Jets, 16	Baltimore Colts, 7	Weeb Ewbank	Orange Bowl, Miami, FL
IV	1970	Kansas City Chiefs, 23	*Minnesota Vikings, 7	Hank Stram	Tulane Stadium, New Orleans, LA
V	1971	Baltimore Colts, 16	*Dallas Cowboys, 13	Don McCafferty	Orange Bowl, Miami, FL
VI	1972	Dallas Cowboys, 24	*Miami Dolphins, 3	Tom Landry	Tulane Stadium, New Orleans, LA
VII	1973	*Miami Dolphins, 14	Washington Redskins, 7	Don Shula	Memorial Coliseum, Los Angeles, CA
VIII	1974	*Miami Dolphins, 24	Minnesota Vikings, 7	Don Shula	Rice Stadium, Houston, TX
IX	1975	*Pittsburgh Steelers, 16	Minnesota Vikings, 6	Chuck Noll	Tulane Stadium, New Orleans, LA
X	1976	Pittsburgh Steelers, 21	*Dallas Cowboys, 17	Chuck Noll	Orange Bowl, Miami, FL
XI	1977	*Oakland Raiders, 32	Minnesota Vikings, 14	John Madden	Rose Bowl, Pasadena, CA
XII	1978	*Dallas Cowboys, 27	Denver Broncos, 10	Tom Landry	Superdome, New Orleans, LA
XIII	1979	Pittsburgh Steelers, 35	*Dallas Cowboys, 31	Chuck Noll	Orange Bowl, Miami, FL
XIV	1980	Pittsburgh Steelers, 31	*L.A. Rams, 19	Chuck Noll	Rose Bowl, Pasadena, CA
XV	1981	Oakland Raiders, 27	*Philadelphia Eagles, 10	Tom Flores	Superdome, New Orleans, LA
XVI	1982	*San Francisco 49ers, 26	Cincinnati Bengals, 21	Bill Walsh	Silverdome, Pontiac, MI
XVII	1983	Washington Redskins, 27	*Miami Dolphins, 17	Joe Gibbs	Rose Bowl, Pasadena, CA
XVIII	1984	*L.A. Raiders, 38	Washington Redskins, 9	Tom Flores	Tampa Stadium, Tampa, FL
XIX	1985	*San Francisco 49ers, 38	Miami Dolphins, 16	Bill Walsh	Stanford Stadium, Stanford, CA
XX	1986	*Chicago Bears, 46	New England Patriots, 10	Mike Ditka	Superdome, New Orleans, LA
XXI	1987	NY Giants, 39	*Denver Broncos, 20	Bill Parcells	Rose Bowl, Pasadena, CA
XXII	1988	*Washington Redskins, 42	Denver Broncos, 10	Joe Gibbs	Jack Murphy Stadium, San Diego, CA
XXIII	1989	*San Francisco 49ers, 20	Cincinnati Bengals, 16	Bill Walsh	Joe Robbie Stadium, Miami, FL
XXIV	1990	San Francisco 49ers, 55	*Denver Broncos, 10	George Seifert	Superdome, New Orleans, LA
XXV	1991	NY Giants, 20	*Buffalo Bills, 19	Bill Parcells	Tampa Stadium, Tampa, FL
XXVI	1992	*Washington Redskins, 37	Buffalo Bills, 24	Joe Gibbs	Metrodome, Minneapolis, MN
XXVII	1993	Dallas Cowboys, 52	*Buffalo Bills, 17	Jimmy Johnson	Rose Bowl, Pasadena, CA
XXVIII	1994	*Dallas Cowboys, 30	Buffalo Bills, 13	Jimmy Johnson	Georgia Dome, Atlanta, GA
XXIX	1995	*San Francisco 49ers, 49	San Diego Chargers, 26	George Seifert	Joe Robbie Stadium, Miami, FL
XXX	1996	*Dallas Cowboys, 27	Pittsburgh Steelers, 17	Barry Switzer	Sun Devil Stadium, Tempe, AZ
XXXI	1997	Green Bay Packers, 35	*New England Patriots, 21	Mike Holmgren	Superdome, New Orleans, LA
XXXII	1998	Denver Broncos, 31	*Green Bay Packers, 24	Mike Shanahan	Qualcomm Stadium, San Diego, CA
XXXIII	1999	Denver Broncos, 34	*Atlanta Falcons, 19	Mike Shanahan	Pro Player Stadium, Miami, FL
XXXIV	2000	*St. Louis Rams, 23	Tennessee Titans, 16	Dick Vermeil	Georgia Dome, Atlanta, GA
XXXV	2001	Baltimore Ravens, 34	*NY Giants, 7	Brian Billick	Raymond James Stadium, Tampa, FL
XXXVI	2002	New England Patriots, 20	*St. Louis Rams, 17	Bill Belichick	Superdome, New Orleans, LA
XXXVII	2003	*Tampa Bay Buccaneers, 48	Oakland Raiders, 21	Jon Gruden	Qualcomm Stadium, San Diego, CA
XXXVIII	2004	New England Patriots, 32	*Carolina Panthers, 29	Bill Belichick	Reliant Stadium, Houston, TX
XXXIX	2005	New England Patriots, 24	*Philadelphia Eagles, 21	Bill Belichick	Alltel Stadium, Jacksonville, FL
XL	2006	Pittsburgh Steelers, 21	*Seattle Seahawks, 10	Bill Cowher	Ford Field, Detroit, MI
XLI	2007	Indianapolis Colts, 29	*Chicago Bears, 17	Tony Dungy	Dolphin Stadium, Miami Gardens, FL
XLII	2008	*NY Giants, 17	New England Patriots, 14	Tom Coughlin	Univ. of Phoenix Stadium, Glendale, AZ
XLIII	2009	Pittsburgh Steelers, 27	**Arizona Cardinals, 23	Mike Tomlin	Raymond James Stadium, Tampa, FL
XLIV	2010	*New Orleans Saints, 31	Indianapolis Colts, 17	Sean Payton	Sun Life Stadium, Miami Gardens, FL
XLV	2011	**Green Bay Packers, 31	Pittsburgh Steelers, 25	Mike McCarthy	Cowboys Stadium, Arlington, TX
XLVI	2012	NY Giants, 21	**New England Patriots, 17	Tom Coughlin	Lucas Oil Stadium, Indianapolis, IN
XLVII	2013	**Baltimore Ravens, 34	San Francisco 49ers, 31	John Harbaugh	Mercedes-Benz Superdome, New Orleans, LA
XLVIII	2014	**Seattle Seahawks, 43	Denver Broncos, 8	Pete Carroll	MetLife Stadium, East Rutherford, NJ
XLIX	2015	New England Patriots, 28	**Seattle Seahawks, 24	Bill Belichick	Univ. of Phoenix Stadium, Glendale, AZ

* = Team won the coin toss and elected to receive. ** = Team won the coin toss and elected to receive in the second half.

Super Bowl Sites, 2016-18

No.	Site	Date	No.	Site	Date
50 (L)	Levi's Stadium, Santa Clara, CA	Feb. 7, 2016	LII	U.S. Bank Stadium, Minneapolis, MN	Feb. 2018
LI	NRG Stadium, Houston, TX	Feb. 5, 2017			

Super Bowl MVPs, 1967-2015

Year	Most valuable player, team	Year	Most valuable player, team	Year	Most valuable player, team
1967	Bart Starr, Green Bay	1984	Marcus Allen, L.A. Raiders	2000	Kurt Warner, St. Louis
1968	Bart Starr, Green Bay	1985	Joe Montana, San Francisco	2001	Ray Lewis, Baltimore
1969	Joe Namath, NY Jets	1986	Richard Dent, Chicago	2002	Tom Brady, New England
1970	Len Dawson, Kansas City	1987	Phil Simms, NY Giants	2003	Dexter Jackson, Tampa Bay
1971	Chuck Howley, Dallas	1988	Doug Williams, Washington	2004	Tom Brady, New England
1972	Roger Staubach, Dallas	1989	Jerry Rice, San Francisco	2005	Deion Branch, New England
1973	Jake Scott, Miami	1990	Joe Montana, San Francisco	2006	Hines Ward, Pittsburgh
1974	Larry Csonka, Miami	1991	Ottis Anderson, NY Giants	2007	Peyton Manning, Indianapolis
1975	Franco Harris, Pittsburgh	1992	Mark Rypien, Washington	2008	Eli Manning, NY Giants
1976	Lynn Swann, Pittsburgh	1993	Troy Aikman, Dallas	2009	Santonio Holmes, Pittsburgh
1977	Fred Biletnikoff, Oakland	1994	Emmitt Smith, Dallas	2010	Drew Brees, New Orleans
1978	Randy White, Harvey Martin; Dallas	1995	Steve Young, San Francisco	2011	Aaron Rodgers, Green Bay
1979	Terry Bradshaw, Pittsburgh	1996	Larry Brown, Dallas	2012	Eli Manning, NY Giants
1980	Terry Bradshaw, Pittsburgh	1997	Desmond Howard, Green Bay	2013	Joe Flacco, Baltimore
1981	Jim Plunkett, Oakland	1998	Terrell Davis, Denver	2014	Malcolm Smith, Seattle
1982	Joe Montana, San Francisco	1999	John Elway, Denver	2015	Tom Brady, New England
1983	John Riggins, Washington				

Super Bowl Single-Game Statistical Leaders

PASSING YARDS

Player, team	Year	Att/comp	Yds	TD
Kurt Warner, St. Louis	2000	45/24	414	2
Kurt Warner, Arizona	2009	43/31	377	3
Kurt Warner, St. Louis	2002	44/28	365	1
Donovon McNabb, Philadelphia	2005	51/30	357	3
Joe Montana, San Francisco	1989	36/23	357	2

RECEIVING YARDS

Player, team	Year	Rec	Yds	TD
Jerry Rice, San Francisco	1989	11	215	1
Ricky Sanders, Washington	1988	9	193	2
Isaac Bruce, St. Louis	2000	6	162	1

RUSHING YARDS

Player, team	Year	Att	Yds	TD
Timmy Smith, Washington	1988	22	204	2
Marcus Allen, L.A. Raiders	1984	20	191	2
John Riggins, Washington	1983	38	166	1

PASSING TOUCHDOWNS

Player, team	Year	Att/comp	Yds	TD
Steve Young, San Francisco	1995	36/24	325	6
Joe Montana, San Francisco	1990	29/22	297	5
Tom Brady, New England	2015	50/37	328	4
Troy Aikman, Dallas	1993	30/22	273	4
Doug Williams, Washington	1988	29/18	340	4
Terry Bradshaw, Pittsburgh	1979	30/17	318	4

SCORING

Player, team	Year	Pts	
Terrell Davis, Denver	1998	18	(3 TDs)
Jerry Rice, San Francisco	1995	18	(3 TDs)
Ricky Watters, San Francisco	1995	18	(3 TDs)
Jerry Rice, San Francisco	1990	18	(3 TDs)
Roger Craig, San Francisco	1985	18	(3 TDs)
Don Chandler, Green Bay	1968	15	(4 FGs, 3 PATs)
Kevin Butler, Chicago Bears	1986	14	(3 FGs, 5 PATs)
Ray Wersching, San Francisco	1982	14	(4 FGs, 2 PATs)

First-Round Selections in the 2015 NFL Draft

Held Apr. 30-May 2, 2015.

	Team	Player	Pos.	College
1.	Tampa Bay	Jameis Winston	QB	Florida St.
2.	Tennessee	Marcus Mariota	QB	Oregon
3.	Jacksonville	Dante Fowler Jr.	LB	Florida
4.	Oakland	Amari Cooper	WR	Alabama
5.	Washington	Brandon Scherff	G	Iowa
6.	NY Jets	Leonard Williams	DE	USC
7.	Chicago	Kevin White	WR	West Virginia
8.	Atlanta	Vic Beasley	LB	Clemson
9.	NY Giants	Ereck Flowers	G	Miami
10.	St. Louis	Todd Gurley	RB	Georgia
11.	Minnesota	Trae Waynes	CB	Michigan St.
12.	Cleveland	Danny Shelton	NT	Washington
13.	New Orleans	Andrus Peat	OT	Stanford
14.	Miami	DeVante Parker	WR	Louisville
15.	San Diego[1]	Melvin Gordon	RB	Wisconsin
16.	Houston	Kevin Johnson	CB	Lake Forest
17.	San Francisco[2]	Arik Armstead	DT	Oregon
18.	Kansas City	Marcus Peters	CB	Washington
19.	Cleveland[3]	Cameron Erving	C	Florida St.
20.	Philadelphia	Nelson Agholor	WR	USC
21.	Cincinnati	Cedric Ogbuehi	OT	Texas A&M
22.	Pittsburgh	Bud Dupree	LB	Kentucky
23.	Denver[4]	Shane Ray	DE	Missouri
24.	Arizona	D. J. Humphries	OT	Florida
25.	Carolina	Shaq Thompson	LB	Washington
26.	Baltimore	Breshad Perriman	WR	Central Florida
27.	Dallas	Byron Jones	CB	Connecticut
28.	Detroit[5]	Laken Tomlinson	OG	Duke
29.	Indianapolis	Phillip Dorsett	WR	Miami (FL)
30.	Green Bay	Damarious Randall	S	Arizona St.
31.	New Orleans[6]	Stephone Anthony	LB	Clemson
32.	New England	Malcom Brown	DT	Texas

(1) From 49ers. (2) From Chargers. (3) From Bills. (4) From Lions. (5) From Broncos. (6) From Seahawks.

Number One NFL Draft Choices, 1960-2015

Year	Team	Player, pos., college
1960	L.A. Rams	Billy Cannon, HB, LSU
1961	Minnesota	Tommy Mason, HB, Tulane
1962	Washington	Ernie Davis, HB, Syracuse
1963	L.A. Rams	Terry Baker, QB, Oregon St.
1964	San Francisco	Dave Parks, E, Texas Tech
1965	NY Giants	Tucker Frederickson, RB, Auburn
1966	Atlanta	Tommy Nobis, LB, Texas
1967	Baltimore Colts	Bubba Smith, DE, Michigan St.
1968	Minnesota	Ron Yary, OT, USC
1969	Buffalo	O. J. Simpson, RB, USC
1970	Pittsburgh	Terry Bradshaw, QB, LA Tech
1971	New England	Jim Plunkett, QB, Stanford
1972	Buffalo	Walt Patulski, DE, Notre Dame
1973	Houston	John Matuszak, DE, Tampa

Year	Team	Player, pos., college
1974	Dallas	Ed "Too Tall" Jones, DE, Tenn. St.
1975	Atlanta	Steve Bartkowski, QB, California
1976	Tampa Bay	Lee Roy Selmon, DE, Oklahoma
1977	Tampa Bay	Ricky Bell, RB, USC
1978	Houston	Earl Campbell, RB, Texas
1979	Buffalo	Tom Cousineau, LB, Ohio St.
1980	Detroit	Billy Sims, RB, Oklahoma
1981	New Orleans	George Rogers, RB, S. Carolina
1982	New England	Kenneth Sims, DT, Texas
1983	Baltimore Colts	John Elway, QB, Stanford
1984	New England	Irving Fryar, WR, Nebraska
1985	Buffalo	Bruce Smith, DE, Virginia Tech
1986	Tampa Bay	Bo Jackson, RB, Auburn
1987	Tampa Bay	Vinny Testaverde, QB, Miami (FL)
1988	Atlanta	Aundray Bruce, LB, Auburn
1989	Dallas	Troy Aikman, QB, UCLA
1990	Indianapolis	Jeff George, QB, Illinois
1991	Dallas	Russell Maryland, DL, Miami (FL)
1992	Indianapolis	Steve Emtman, DL, Washington
1993	New England	Drew Bledsoe, QB, Washington St.
1994	Cincinnati	Dan Wilkinson, DT, Ohio St.
1995	Cincinnati	Ki-Jana Carter, RB, Penn State
1996	NY Jets	Keyshawn Johnson, WR, USC
1997	St. Louis	Orlando Pace, OT, Ohio St.
1998	Indianapolis	Peyton Manning, QB, Tennessee
1999	Cleveland	Tim Couch, QB, Kentucky
2000	Cleveland	Courtney Brown, DE, Penn State
2001	Atlanta	Michael Vick, QB, Virginia Tech
2002	Houston	David Carr, QB, Fresno St.
2003	Cincinnati	Carson Palmer, QB, USC
2004	San Diego	Eli Manning, QB, Mississippi
2005	San Francisco	Alex D. Smith, QB, Utah
2006	Houston	Mario Williams, DE, NC State
2007	Oakland	JaMarcus Russell, QB, LSU
2008	Miami	Jake Long, OT, Michigan
2009	Detroit	Matthew Stafford, QB, Georgia
2010	St. Louis	Sam Bradford, QB, Oklahoma
2011	Carolina	Cam Newton, QB, Auburn
2012	Indianapolis	Andrew Luck, QB, Stanford
2013	Kansas City	Eric Fisher, OT, Central Michigan
2014	Houston	Jadeveon Clowney, DE, S. Carolina
2015	Tampa Bay	Jameis Winston, QB, Florida St.

American Football League Champions, 1960-69

Year	Eastern (W-L-T)	Western (W-L-T)	Championship
1960	Houston Oilers (10-4-0)	L.A. Chargers (10-4-0)	Houston 24, L.A. 16
1961	Houston Oilers (10-3-1)	San Diego Chargers (12-2-0)	Houston 10, San Diego 3
1962	Houston Oilers (11-3-0)	Dallas Texans (11-3-0)	Dallas 20, Houston 17 (2 OT)
1963	Boston Patriots (7-6-1)[1]	San Diego Chargers (11-3-0)	San Diego 51, Boston 10
1964	Buffalo Bills (12-2-0)	San Diego Chargers (8-5-1)	Buffalo 20, San Diego 7
1965	Buffalo Bills (10-3-1)	San Diego Chargers (9-2-3)	Buffalo 23, San Diego 0
1966	Buffalo Bills (9-4-1)	Kansas City Chiefs (11-2-1)	Kansas City 31, Buffalo 7
1967	Houston Oilers (9-4-1)	Oakland Raiders (13-1-0)	Oakland 40, Houston 7
1968	NY Jets (11-3-0)	Oakland Raiders (12-2-0)[2]	NY Jets 27, Oakland 23
1969	NY Jets (10-4-0)	Oakland Raiders (12-1-1)	Kansas City 17, Oakland 7[3]

(1) Defeated conference champion Buffalo Bills in divisional playoff. (2) Defeated conference champion Kansas City Chiefs in divisional playoff. (3) Kansas City Chiefs defeated NY Jets, and Oakland Raiders defeated Houston Oilers in divisional playoffs.

National Football League Champions, 1933-69

Year	Eastern (W-L-T)	Western (W-L-T)	Championship
1933	NY Giants (11-3-0)	Chicago Bears (10-2-1)	Chicago Bears 23, NY Giants 21
1934	NY Giants (8-5-0)	Chicago Bears (13-0-0)	NY Giants 30, Chicago Bears 13
1935	NY Giants (9-3-0)	Detroit Lions (7-3-2)	Detroit 26, NY Giants 7
1936	Boston Redskins (7-5-0)	Green Bay Packers (10-1-1)	Green Bay 21, Boston 6
1937	Washington Redskins (8-3-0)	Chicago Bears (9-1-1)	Washington 28, Chicago Bears 21
1938	NY Giants (8-2-1)	Green Bay Packers (8-3-0)	NY Giants 23, Green Bay 17
1939	NY Giants (9-1-1)	Green Bay Packers (9-2-0)	Green Bay 27, NY Giants 0
1940	Washington Redskins (9-2-0)	Chicago Bears (8-3-0)	Chicago Bears 73, Washington 0
1941	NY Giants (8-3-0)	Chicago Bears (10-1-0)[1]	Chicago Bears 37, NY Giants 9
1942	Washington Redskins (10-1-0)	Chicago Bears (11-0-0)	Washington 14, Chicago Bears 6
1943	Washington Redskins (6-3-1)[1]	Chicago Bears (8-1-1)	Chicago Bears, 41, Washington 21
1944	NY Giants (8-1-1)	Green Bay Packers (8-2-0)	Green Bay 14, NY Giants 7
1945	Washington Redskins (8-2-0)	Cleveland Rams (9-1-0)	Cleveland Rams 15, Washington 14
1946	NY Giants (7-3-1)	Chicago Bears (8-2-1)	Chicago Bears 24, NY Giants 14
1947	Philadelphia Eagles (8-4-0)[1]	Chicago Cardinals (9-3-0)	Chicago Cardinals 28, Philadelphia 21
1948	Philadelphia Eagles (9-2-1)	Chicago Cardinals (11-1-0)	Philadelphia 7, Chicago Cardinals 0
1949	Philadelphia Eagles (11-1-0)	L.A. Rams (8-2-2)	Philadelphia 14, L.A. Rams 0
1950	Cleveland Browns (10-2-0)[1]	L.A. Rams (9-3-0)[1]	Cleveland 30, L.A. Rams 28
1951	Cleveland Browns (11-1-0)	L.A. Rams (8-4-0)	L.A. Rams 24, Cleveland Browns 17
1952	Cleveland Browns (8-4-0)	Detroit Lions (9-3-0)[1]	Detroit 17, Cleveland Browns 7
1953	Cleveland Browns (11-1-0)	Detroit Lions (10-2-0)	Detroit 17, Cleveland Browns 16
1954	Cleveland Browns (9-3-0)	Detroit Lions (9-2-1)	Cleveland Browns 56, Detroit 10
1955	Cleveland Browns (9-2-1)	L.A. Rams (8-3-1)	Cleveland Browns 38, L.A. Rams 14
1956	NY Giants (8-3-1)	Chicago Bears (9-2-1)	NY Giants 47, Chicago Bears 7
1957	Cleveland Browns (9-2-1)	Detroit Lions (8-4-0)[1]	Detroit 59, Cleveland Browns 14
1958	NY Giants (9-3-0)[1]	Baltimore Colts (9-3-0)	Baltimore 23, NY Giants 17[2]
1959	NY Giants (10-2-0)	Baltimore Colts (9-3-0)	Baltimore 31, NY Giants 16
1960	Philadelphia Eagles (10-2-0)	Green Bay Packers (8-4-0)	Philadelphia 17, Green Bay 13
1961	NY Giants (10-3-1)	Green Bay Packers (11-3-0)	Green Bay 37, NY Giants 0
1962	NY Giants (12-2-0)	Green Bay Packers (13-1-0)	Green Bay 16, NY Giants 7
1963	NY Giants (11-3-0)	Chicago Bears (11-1-2)	Chicago 14, NY Giants 10
1964	Cleveland Browns (10-3-1)	Baltimore Colts (12-2-0)	Cleveland Browns 27, Baltimore 0
1965	Cleveland Browns (11-3-0)	Green Bay Packers (10-3-1)[1]	Green Bay 23, Cleveland Browns 12
1966	Dallas Cowboys (10-3-1)	Green Bay Packers (12-2-0)	Green Bay 34, Dallas 27
1967	Dallas Cowboys (9-5-0)	Green Bay Packers (9-4-1)	Green Bay 21, Dallas 17
1968	Cleveland Browns (10-4-0)	Baltimore Colts (13-1-0)	Baltimore 34, Cleveland Browns 0
1969	Cleveland Browns (10-3-1)	Minnesota Vikings (12-2-0)	Minnesota 27, Cleveland Browns 7

Note: Conference title games preceded NFL Championship from 1967-69. (1) Won divisional or conference playoff. (2) Won at 8:15 of sudden death overtime period.

NFL Divisional Champions and Wild Cards, 1970-95

The American Football League and National Football League officially merged in 1966. At the beginning of the 1970 season, the two leagues became the AFC and NFC conferences in the new NFL. Regular-season (W-L-T) records are in parentheses.

AMERICAN FOOTBALL CONFERENCE

Year	Eastern	Central	Western	Wild card
1970	Baltimore Colts (11-2-1)	Cincinnati Bengals (8-6-0)	Oakland Raiders (8-4-2)	Miami Dolphins (10-4-0)
1971	Miami Dolphins (10-3-1)	Cleveland Browns (9-5-0)	Kansas City Chiefs (10-3-1)	Baltimore Colts (10-4-0)
1972	Miami Dolphins (14-0-0)	Pittsburgh Steelers (11-3-0)	Oakland Raiders (10-3-1)	Cleveland Browns (10-4-0)
1973	Miami Dolphins (12-2-0)	Cincinnati Bengals (10-4-0)	Oakland Raiders (9-4-1)	Pittsburgh Steelers (10-4-0)
1974	Miami Dolphins (11-3-0)	Pittsburgh Steelers (10-3-1)	Oakland Raiders (12-2-0)	Buffalo Bills (9-5-0)
1975	Baltimore Colts (10-4-0)	Pittsburgh Steelers (12-2-0)	Oakland Raiders (11-3-0)	Cincinnati Bengals (11-3-0)
1976	Baltimore Colts (11-3-0)	Pittsburgh Steelers (10-4-0)	Oakland Raiders (13-1-0)	New England Patriots (11-3-0)
1977	Baltimore Colts (10-4-0)	Pittsburgh Steelers (9-5-0)	Denver Broncos (12-2-0)	Oakland Raiders (11-3-0)
1978	New England Patriots (11-5-0)	Pittsburgh Steelers (14-2-0)	Denver Broncos (10-6-0)	Houston Oilers (10-6-0) Miami Dolphins (11-5-0)
1979	Miami Dolphins (10-6-0)	Pittsburgh Steelers (12-4-0)	San Diego Chargers (12-4-0)	Houston Oilers (11-5-0) Denver Broncos (10-6-0)
1980	Buffalo Bills (11-5-0)	Cleveland Browns (11-5-0)	San Diego Chargers (11-5-0)	Houston Oilers (11-5-0) Oakland Raiders (11-5-0)
1981	Miami Dolphins (11-4-1)	Cincinnati Bengals (12-4-0)	San Diego Chargers (10-6-0)	Buffalo Bills (10-6-0) NY Jets (10-5-1)
1982	Strike abbreviated season. See note.			
1983	Miami Dolphins (12-4-0)	Pittsburgh Steelers (10-6-0)	L.A. Raiders (12-4-0)	Denver Broncos (9-7-0) Seattle Seahawks (9-7-0)
1984	Miami Dolphins (14-2-0)	Pittsburgh Steelers (9-7-0)	Denver Broncos (13-3-0)	L.A. Raiders (11-5-0) Seattle Seahawks (12-4-0)
1985	Miami Dolphins (12-4-0)	Cleveland Browns (8-8-0)	L.A. Raiders (12-4-0)	New England Patriots (11-5-0) NY Jets (11-5-0)
1986	New England Patriots (11-5-0)	Cleveland Browns (12-4-0)	Denver Broncos (11-5-0)	Kansas City Chiefs (10-6-0) NY Jets (10-6-0)
1987	Indianapolis Colts (9-6-0)	Cleveland Browns (10-5-0)	Denver Broncos (10-4-1)	Houston Oilers (9-6-0) Seattle Seahawks (9-6-0)
1988	Buffalo Bills (12-4-0)	Cincinnati Bengals (12-4-0)	Seattle Seahawks (9-7-0)	Cleveland Browns (10-6-0) Houston Oilers (10-6-0)
1989	Buffalo Bills (9-7-0)	Cleveland Browns (9-6-1)	Denver Broncos (11-5-0)	Houston Oilers (9-7-0) Pittsburgh Steelers (9-7-0)
1990	Buffalo Bills (13-3-0)	Cincinnati Bengals (9-7-0)	L.A. Raiders (12-4-0)	Houston Oilers (9-7-0) Kansas City Chiefs (10-6-0) Miami Dolphins (12-4-0)
1991	Buffalo Bills (13-3-0)	Houston Oilers (11-5-0)	Denver Broncos (12-4-0)	Kansas City Chiefs (10-6-0) L.A. Raiders (9-7-0) NY Jets (8-8-0)
1992	Miami Dolphins (11-5-0)	Pittsburgh Steelers (11-5-0)	San Diego Chargers (11-5-0)	Buffalo Bills (11-5-0) Houston Oilers (10-6-0) Kansas City Chiefs (10-6-0)
1993	Buffalo Bills (12-4-0)	Houston Oilers (12-4-0)	Kansas City Chiefs (11-5-0)	Denver Broncos (9-7-0) L.A. Raiders (10-6-0) Pittsburgh Steelers (9-7-0)
1994	Miami Dolphins (10-6-0)	Pittsburgh Steelers (12-4-0)	San Diego Chargers (11-5-0)	Cleveland Browns (11-5-0) Kansas City Chiefs (9-7-0) New England Patriots (10-6-0)
1995	Buffalo Bills (10-6-0)	Pittsburgh Steelers (11-5-0)	Kansas City Chiefs (13-3-0)	Miami Dolphins (9-7-0) Indianapolis Colts (9-7-0) San Diego Chargers (9-7-0)

NATIONAL FOOTBALL CONFERENCE

Year	Eastern	Central	Western	Wild card
1970	Dallas Cowboys (10-4-0)	Minnesota Vikings (12-2-0)	San Francisco 49ers (10-3-1)	Detroit Lions (10-4-0)
1971	Dallas Cowboys (11-3-0)	Minnesota Vikings (11-3-0)	San Francisco 49ers (9-5-0)	Washington Redskins (9-4-1)
1972	Washington Redskins (11-3-0)	Green Bay Packers (10-4-0)	San Francisco 49ers (8-5-1)	Dallas Cowboys (10-4-0)
1973	Dallas Cowboys (10-4-0)	Minnesota Vikings (12-2-0)	L.A. Rams (12-2-0)	Washington Redskins (10-4-0)
1974	St. Louis Cardinals (10-4-0)	Minnesota Vikings (10-4-0)	L.A. Rams (10-4-0)	Washington Redskins (10-4-0)
1975	St. Louis Cardinals (11-3-0)	Minnesota Vikings (12-2-0)	L.A. Rams (12-2-0)	Dallas Cowboys (10-4-0)
1976	Dallas Cowboys (11-3-0)	Minnesota Vikings (11-2-1)	L.A. Rams (10-3-1)	Washington Redskins (10-4-0)
1977	Dallas Cowboys (12-2-0)	Minnesota Vikings (9-5-0)	L.A. Rams (10-4-0)	Chicago Bears (9-5-0)
1978	Dallas Cowboys (12-4-0)	Minnesota Vikings (8-7-1)	L.A. Rams (12-4-0)	Atlanta Falcons (9-7-0) Philadelphia Eagles (9-7-0)
1979	Dallas Cowboys (11-5-0)	Tampa Bay Buccaneers (10-6-0)	L.A. Rams (9-7-0)	Chicago Bears (10-6-0) Philadelphia Eagles (11-5-0)
1980	Philadelphia Eagles (12-4-0)	Minnesota Vikings (9-7-0)	Atlanta Falcons (12-4-0)	Dallas Cowboys (12-4-0) L.A. Rams (11-5-0)
1981	Dallas Cowboys (12-4-0)	Tampa Bay Buccaneers (9-7-0)	San Francisco 49ers (13-3-0)	NY Giants (9-7-0) Philadelphia Eagles (10-6-0)
1982	Strike abbreviated season. See note.			
1983	Washington Redskins (14-2-0)	Detroit Lions (9-7-0)	San Francisco 49ers (10-6-0)	Dallas Cowboys (12-4-0) L.A. Rams (9-7-0)
1984	Washington Redskins (11-5-0)	Chicago Bears (10-6-0)	San Francisco 49ers (15-1-0)	L.A. Rams (10-6-0) NY Giants (9-7-0)
1985	Dallas Cowboys (10-6-0)	Chicago Bears (15-1-0)	L.A. Rams (11-5-0)	NY Giants (10-6-0) San Francisco 49ers (10-6-0)
1986	NY Giants (14-2-0)	Chicago Bears (14-2-0)	San Francisco 49ers (10-5-1)	L.A. Rams (10-6-0) Washington Redskins (12-4-0)

1987	Washington Redskins (11-4-0)	Chicago Bears (11-4-0)	San Francisco 49ers (13-2-0)	Minnesota Vikings (8-7-0) New Orleans Saints (12-3-0)
1988	Philadelphia Eagles (10-6-0)	Chicago Bears (12-4-0)	San Francisco 49ers (10-6-0)	L.A. Rams (10-6-0) Minnesota Vikings (11-5-0)
1989	NY Giants (12-4-0)	Minnesota Vikings (10-6-0)	San Francisco 49ers (14-2-0)	L.A. Rams (11-5-0) Philadelphia Eagles (11-5-0)
1990	NY Giants (13-3-0)	Chicago Bears (11-5-0)	San Francisco 49ers (14-2-0)	New Orleans Saints (8-8-0) Philadelphia Eagles (10-6-0) Washington Redskins (10-6-0)
1991	Washington Redskins (14-2-0)	Detroit Lions (12-4-0)	New Orleans Saints (11-5-0)	Atlanta Falcons (10-6-0) Chicago Bears (11-5-0) Dallas Cowboys (11-5-0)
1992	Dallas Cowboys (13-3-0)	Minnesota Vikings (11-5-0)	San Francisco 49ers (14-2-0)	New Orleans Saints (12-4-0) Philadelphia Eagles (11-5-0) Washington Redskins (9-7-0)
1993	Dallas Cowboys (12-4-0)	Detroit Lions (10-6-0)	San Francisco 49ers (10-6-0)	Green Bay Packers (9-7-0) Minnesota Vikings (9-7-0) NY Giants (11-5-0)
1994	Dallas Cowboys (12-4-0)	Minnesota Vikings (10-6-0)	San Francisco 49ers (13-3-0)	Chicago Bears (9-7-0) Detroit Lions (9-7-0) Green Bay Packers (9-7-0)
1995	Dallas Cowboys (12-4-0)	Green Bay Packers (11-5-0)	San Francisco 49ers (11-5-0)	Philadelphia Eagles (10-6-0) Detroit Lions (10-6-0) Atlanta Falcons (9-7-0)

Note: A strike shortened the 1982 season from 16 to 9 games. The top eight teams in each conference played in a tournament to determine the conference champion.

NFL Playoff Results, 1996-2014

Year	Conference	Division	Winner (W-L-T)	Playoffs[1]	Year
1996	American	Eastern	New England Patriots (11-5-0)	Jacksonville* 30, Denver 27	1996
		Central	Pittsburgh Steelers (10-6-0)	New England 28, Pittsburgh 3	
		Western	Denver Broncos (13-3-0)	New England 20, Jacksonville* 6	
	National	Eastern	Dallas Cowboys (10-6-0)	Green Bay 35, San Francisco* 14	
		Central	Green Bay Packers (13-3-0)	Carolina 26, Dallas 17	
		Western	Carolina Panthers (12-4-0)	Green Bay 30, Carolina 13	
1997	American	Eastern	New England Patriots (10-6-0)	Pittsburgh 7, New England 6	1997
		Central	Pittsburgh Steelers (11-5-0)	Denver* 14, Kansas City 10	
		Western	Kansas City Chiefs (13-3-0)	Denver* 24, Pittsburgh 21	
	National	Eastern	NY Giants (10-5-1)	San Francisco 38, Minnesota* 22	
		Central	Green Bay Packers (13-3-0)	Green Bay 21, Tampa Bay* 7	
		Western	San Francisco 49ers (13-3-0)	Green Bay 23, San Francisco 10	
1998	American	Eastern	NY Jets (12-4-0)	Denver 38, Miami* 3	1998
		Central	Jacksonville Jaguars (11-5-0)	NY Jets 34, Jacksonville 24	
		Western	Denver Broncos (14-2-0)	Denver 23, NY Jets 10	
	National	Eastern	Dallas Cowboys (10-6-0)	Atlanta 20, San Francisco* 18	
		Central	Minnesota Vikings (15-1-0)	Minnesota 41, Arizona* 21	
		Western	Atlanta Falcons (14-2-0)	Atlanta 30, Minnesota 27 (OT)	
1999	American	Eastern	Indianapolis Colts (13-3-0)	Jacksonville 62, Miami* 7	1999
		Central	Jacksonville Jaguars (14-2-0)	Tennessee* 19, Indianapolis 16	
		Western	Seattle Seahawks (9-7-0)	Tennessee* 33, Jacksonville 14	
	National	Eastern	Washington Redskins (10-6-0)	Tampa Bay 14, Washington 13	
		Central	Tampa Bay Buccaneers (11-5-0)	St. Louis 49, Minnesota* 37	
		Western	St. Louis Rams (13-3-0)	St. Louis 11, Tampa Bay 6	
2000	American	Eastern	Miami Dolphins (11-5-0)	Oakland 27, Miami 0	2000
		Central	Tennessee Titans (13-3-0)	Baltimore* 24, Tennessee 10	
		Western	Oakland Raiders (12-4-0)	Baltimore* 16, Oakland 3	
	National	Eastern	NY Giants (12-4-0)	Minnesota 34, New Orleans 16	
		Central	Minnesota Vikings (11-5-0)	NY Giants 20, Philadelphia* 10	
		Western	New Orleans Saints (10-6-0)	NY Giants 41, Minnesota 0	
2001	American	Eastern	New England Patriots (11-5-0)	New England 16, Oakland 13 (OT)	2001
		Central	Pittsburgh Steelers (13-3-0)	Pittsburgh 27, Baltimore* 10	
		Western	Oakland Raiders (10-6-0)	New England 24, Pittsburgh 17	
	National	Eastern	Philadelphia Eagles (11-5-0)	Philadelphia 33, Chicago 19	
		Central	Chicago Bears (13-3-0)	St. Louis 45, Green Bay* 17	
		Western	St. Louis Rams (14-2-0)	St. Louis 29, Philadelphia 24	
2002	American	East	NY Jets (9-7-0)		2002
		North	Pittsburgh Steelers (10-5-1)	Oakland 30, NY Jets 10	
		South	Tennessee Titans (11-5-0)	Tennessee 34, Pittsburgh 31 (OT)	
		West	Oakland Raiders (11-5-0)	Oakland 41, Tennessee 24	
	National	East	Philadelphia Eagles (12-4-0)		
		North	Green Bay Packers (12-4-0)	Philadelphia 20, Atlanta* 6	
		South	Tampa Bay Buccaneers (12-4-0)	Tampa Bay 31, San Francisco 6	
		West	San Francisco 49ers (10-6-0)	Tampa Bay 27, Philadelphia 10	

Year	Conference	Division	Winner (W-L-T)	Playoffs[1]	Year
2003	American	East	New England Patriots (14-2-0)		2003
		North	Baltimore Ravens (10-6-0)	Indianapolis 38, Kansas City 31	
		South	Indianapolis Colts (12-4-0)	New England 17, Tennessee* 14	
		West	Kansas City Chiefs (13-3-0)	New England 24, Indianapolis 14	
	National	East	Philadelphia Eagles (12-4-0)		
		North	Green Bay Packers (10-6-0)	Carolina 29, St. Louis 23 (2 OT)	
		South	Carolina Panthers (11-5-0)	Philadelphia 20, Green Bay 17 (OT)	
		West	St. Louis Rams (12-4-0)	Carolina 14, Philadelphia 3	
2004	American	East	New England Patriots (14-2-0)		2004
		North	Pittsburgh Steelers (15-1-0)	Pittsburgh 20, NY Jets* 17 (OT)	
		South	Indianapolis Colts (12-4-0)	New England 20, Indianapolis 3	
		West	San Diego Chargers (12-4-0)	New England 41, Pittsburgh 27	
	National	East	Philadelphia Eagles (13-3-0)		
		North	Green Bay Packers (10-6-0)	Atlanta 47, St. Louis* 17	
		South	Atlanta Falcons (11-5-0)	Philadelphia 27, Minnesota* 14	
		West	Seattle Seahawks (9-7-0)	Philadelphia 27, Atlanta 10	
2005	American	East	New England Patriots (10-6-0)		2005
		North	Cincinnati Bengals (11-5-0)	Denver 27, New England 13	
		South	Indianapolis Colts (14-2-0)	Pittsburgh* 21, Indianapolis 18	
		West	Denver Broncos (13-3-0)	Pittsburgh* 34, Denver 17	
	National	East	NY Giants (11-5-0)		
		North	Chicago Bears (11-5-0)	Seattle 20, Washington* 10	
		South	Tampa Bay Buccaneers (11-5-0)	Carolina* 29, Chicago 21	
		West	Seattle Seahawks (13-3-0)	Seattle 34, Carolina* 14	
2006	American	East	New England Patriots (12-4-0)		2006
		North	Baltimore Ravens (13-3-0)	Indianapolis 15, Baltimore 6	
		South	Indianapolis Colts (12-4-0)	New England 24, San Diego 21	
		West	San Diego Chargers (14-2-0)	Indianapolis 38, New England 34	
	National	East	Philadelphia Eagles (10-6-0)		
		North	Chicago Bears (13-3-0)	New Orleans 27, Philadelphia 24	
		South	New Orleans Saints (10-6-0)	Chicago 27, Seattle 24 (OT)	
		West	Seattle Seahawks (9-7-0)	Chicago 39, New Orleans 14	
2007	American	East	New England Patriots (16-0-0)		2007
		North	Pittsburgh Steelers (10-6-0)	New England 31, Jacksonville* 20	
		South	Indianapolis Colts (13-3-0)	San Diego 28, Indianapolis 24	
		West	San Diego Chargers (11-5-0)	New England 21, San Diego 12	
	National	East	Dallas Cowboys (13-3-0)		
		North	Green Bay Packers (13-3-0)	Green Bay 42, Seattle 20	
		South	Tampa Bay Buccaneers (9-7-0)	NY Giants* 21, Dallas 17	
		West	Seattle Seahawks (10-6-0)	NY Giants* 23, Green Bay 20 (OT)	
2008	American	East	Miami Dolphins (11-5-0)		2008
		North	Pittsburgh Steelers (12-4-0)	Baltimore* 13, Tennessee 10	
		South	Tennessee Titans (13-3-0)	Pittsburgh 35, San Diego 24	
		West	San Diego Chargers (8-8-0)	Pittsburgh 23, Baltimore* 14	
	National	East	NY Giants (12-4-0)		
		North	Minnesota Vikings (10-6-0)	Arizona 33, Carolina 13	
		South	Carolina Panthers (12-4-0)	Philadelphia* 23, NY Giants 11	
		West	Arizona Cardinals (9-7-0)	Arizona 32, Philadelphia* 25	
2009	American	East	New England Patriots (10-6-0)		2009
		North	Cincinnati Bengals (10-6-0)	Indianapolis 20, Baltimore* 3	
		South	Indianapolis Colts (14-2-0)	NY Jets* 17, San Diego 14	
		West	San Diego Chargers (13-3-0)	Indianapolis 30, NY Jets* 17	
	National	East	Dallas Cowboys (11-5-0)		
		North	Minnesota Vikings (12-4-0)	New Orleans 45, Arizona 14	
		South	New Orleans Saints (13-3-0)	Minnesota 34, Dallas 3	
		West	Arizona Cardinals (10-6-0)	New Orleans 31, Minnesota 28 (OT)	
2010	American	East	New England Patriots (14-2-0)		2010
		North	Pittsburgh Steelers (12-4-0)	Pittsburgh 31, Baltimore* 24	
		South	Indianapolis Colts (10-6-0)	NY Jets* 28, New England 21	
		West	Kansas City Chiefs (10-6-0)	Pittsburgh 24, NY Jets* 19	
	National	East	Philadelphia Eagles (10-6-0)		
		North	Chicago Bears (11-5-0)	Green Bay* 48, Atlanta 21	
		South	Atlanta Falcons (13-3-0)	Chicago 35, Seattle 24	
		West	Seattle Seahawks (7-9-0)	Green Bay* 21, Chicago 14	
2011	American	East	New England Patriots (13-3-0)		2011
		North	Baltimore Ravens (12-4-0)	New England 45, Denver 10	
		South	Houston Texans (10-6-0)	Baltimore 20, Houston 13	
		West	Denver Broncos (8-8-0)	New England 23, Baltimore 20	
	National	East	NY Giants (9-7-0)		
		North	Green Bay Packers (15-1-0)	San Francisco 36, New Orleans 32	
		South	New Orleans (13-3-0)	NY Giants 37, Green Bay 20	
		West	San Francisco (13-3-0)	NY Giants 20, San Francisco 17 (OT)	

Year	Conference	Division	Winner (W-L-T)	Playoffs[1]	Year
2012	American	East	New England Patriots (12-4-0)		2012
		North	Baltimore Ravens (10-6-0)	Baltimore 38, Denver 35 (2 OT)	
		South	Houston Texans (12-4-0)	New England 41, Houston 28	
		West	Denver Broncos (13-3-0)	Baltimore 28, New England 13	
	National	East	Washington Redskins (10-6-0)		
		North	Green Bay Packers (11-5-0)	San Francisco 45, Green Bay 31	
		South	Atlanta Falcons (13-3-0)	Atlanta 30, Seattle* 28	
		West	San Francisco 49ers (11-4-1)	San Francisco 28, Atlanta 24	
2013	American	East	New England Patriots (12-4-0)		2013
		North	Cincinnati Bengals (11-5-0)	New England 43, Indianapolis 22	
		South	Indianapolis Colts (11-5-0)	Denver 24, San Diego* 17	
		West	Denver Broncos (13-3-0)	Denver 26, New England 16	
	National	East	Philadelphia Eagles (10-6-0)		
		North	Green Bay Packers (8-7-1)	Seattle 23, New Orleans* 15	
		South	Carolina Panthers (12-4-0)	San Francisco* 23, Carolina 10	
		West	Seattle Seahawks (13-3-0)	Seattle 23, San Francisco* 17	
2014	American	East	New England Patriots (12-4-0)		2014
		North	Pittsburgh Steelers (11-5-0)	New England 35, Baltimore* 31	
		South	Indianapolis Colts (11-5-0)	Indianapolis 24, Denver 13	
		West	Denver Broncos (12-4-0)	New England 45, Indianapolis 7	
	National	East	Dallas Cowboys (12-4-0)		
		North	Green Bay Packers (12-4-0)	Seattle 31, Carolina 17	
		South	Carolina Panthers (7-8-1)	Green Bay 26, Dallas 21	
		West	Seattle Seahawks (12-4-0)	Seattle 28, Green Bay 22 (OT)	

*Wild card team. (1) Only the final two conference playoff rounds are shown.

American Football Conference Leaders, 1960-2014

(American Football League, 1960-69)

PASSING (BASED ON QB RATING POINTS)							RECEPTIONS			
Player, team	Rating	Att	Comp	Yds	TD	Year	Player, team	Rec	Yds	TD
Jack Kemp, L.A. Chargers	NA	406	211	3,018	20	**1960**	Lionel Taylor, Denver	92	1,235	12
George Blanda, Houston	NA	362	187	3,330	36	**1961**	Lionel Taylor, Denver	100	1,176	4
Len Dawson, Dallas Texans	NA	310	189	2,759	29	**1962**	Lionel Taylor, Denver	77	908	4
Tobin Rote, San Diego	NA	286	170	2,510	20	**1963**	Lionel Taylor, Denver	78	1,101	10
Len Dawson, Kansas City	NA	354	199	2,879	30	**1964**	Charley Hennigan, Houston	101	1,546	8
John Hadl, San Diego	NA	348	174	2,798	20	**1965**	Lionel Taylor, Denver	85	1,131	6
Len Dawson, Kansas City	NA	284	159	2,527	26	**1966**	Lance Alworth, San Diego	73	1,383	13
Daryle Lamonica, Oakland	NA	425	220	3,228	30	**1967**	George Sauer, NY Jets	75	1,189	6
Len Dawson, Kansas City	NA	224	131	2,109	17	**1968**	Lance Alworth, San Diego	68	1,312	10
Greg Cook, Cincinnati	NA	197	106	1,854	15	**1969**	Lance Alworth, San Diego	64	1,003	4
Daryle Lamonica, Oakland	NA	356	179	2,516	22	**1970**	Marlin Briscoe, Buffalo	57	1,036	8
Bob Griese, Miami	NA	263	145	2,089	19	**1971**	Fred Biletnikoff, Oakland	61	929	9
Earl Morrall, Miami	NA	150	83	1,360	11	**1972**	Fred Biletnikoff, Oakland	58	802	7
Ken Stabler, Oakland	88.3	260	163	1,997	14	**1973**	Fred Willis, Houston	57	371	1
Ken Anderson, Cincinnati	95.7	328	213	2,667	18	**1974**	Lydell Mitchell, Baltimore Colts	72	544	2
Ken Anderson, Cincinnati	93.9	377	228	3,169	21	**1975**	Reggie Rucker, Cleveland	60	770	3
							Lydell Mitchell, Baltimore Colts	60	554	4
Ken Stabler, Oakland	103.4	291	194	2,737	27	**1976**	MacArthur Lane, Kansas City	66	686	1
Bob Griese, Miami	87.8	307	180	2,252	22	**1977**	Lydell Mitchell, Baltimore Colts	71	620	4
Terry Bradshaw, Pittsburgh	84.7	368	207	2,915	28	**1978**	Steve Largent, Seattle	71	1,168	8
Dan Fouts, San Diego	82.6	530	332	4,082	24	**1979**	Joe Washington, Baltimore Colts	82	750	3
Brian Sipe, Cleveland	91.4	554	337	4,132	30	**1980**	Kellen Winslow, San Diego	89	1,290	9
Ken Anderson, Cincinnati	98.4	479	300	3,754	29	**1981**	Kellen Winslow, San Diego	88	1,075	10
Ken Anderson, Cincinnati	95.3	309	218	2,495	12	**1982**	Kellen Winslow, San Diego	54	721	6
Dan Marino, Miami	96.0	296	173	2,210	20	**1983**	Todd Christensen, L.A. Raiders	92	1,247	12
Dan Marino, Miami	108.9	564	362	5,084	48	**1984**	Ozzie Newsome, Cleveland	89	1,001	5
Ken O'Brien, NY Jets	96.2	488	297	3,888	25	**1985**	Lionel James, San Diego	86	1,027	6
Dan Marino, Miami	92.5	623	378	4,746	44	**1986**	Todd Christensen, L.A. Raiders	95	1,153	8
Bernie Kosar, Cleveland	95.4	389	241	3,033	22	**1987**	Al Toon, NY Jets	68	976	5
Boomer Esiason, Cincinnati	97.4	388	223	3,572	28	**1988**	Al Toon, NY Jets	93	1,067	5
Boomer Esiason, Cincinnati	92.1	455	258	3,525	28	**1989**	Andre Reed, Buffalo	88	1,312	9
Jim Kelly, Buffalo	101.2	346	219	2,829	24	**1990**	Haywood Jeffires, Houston	74	1,048	8
							Drew Hill, Houston	74	1,019	5
Jim Kelly, Buffalo	97.6	474	304	3,844	33	**1991**	Haywood Jeffires, Houston	100	1,181	7
Warren Moon, Houston	89.3	346	224	2,521	18	**1992**	Haywood Jeffires, Houston	90	913	9
John Elway, Denver	92.8	551	348	4,030	25	**1993**	Reggie Langhorne, Indianapolis	85	1,038	3
Dan Marino, Miami	89.2	615	385	4,453	30	**1994**	Ben Coates, New England	96	1,174	7
Jim Harbaugh, Indianapolis	100.7	314	200	2,575	17	**1995**	Carl Pickens, Cincinnati	99	1,234	17
John Elway, Denver	89.2	466	287	3,328	26	**1996**	Carl Pickens, Cincinnati	100	1,180	12
Mark Brunell, Jacksonville	91.2	435	264	3,281	18	**1997**	Tim Brown, Oakland	104	1,408	5
Vinny Testaverde, NY Jets	101.6	421	259	3,256	29	**1998**	O. J. McDuffie, Miami	90	1,050	7
Peyton Manning, Indianapolis	90.7	533	331	4,135	26	**1999**	Jimmy Smith, Jacksonville	116	1,636	6
Brian Griese, Denver	102.9	336	216	2,688	19	**2000**	Marvin Harrison, Indianapolis	102	1,413	14
Rich Gannon, Oakland	95.5	549	361	3,828	27	**2001**	Rod Smith, Denver	113	1,343	11
Chad Pennington, NY Jets	104.2	399	275	3,120	22	**2002**	Marvin Harrison, Indianapolis	143	1,722	11

PASSING (BASED ON QB RATING POINTS) / **RECEPTIONS**

Player, team	Rating	Att	Comp	Yds	TD	Year	Player, team	Rec	Yds	TD
Steve McNair, Tennessee	100.4	400	250	3,215	24	**2003**	LaDainian Tomlinson, San Diego	100	725	4
Peyton Manning, Indianapolis	121.1	497	336	4,557	49	**2004**	Tony Gonzalez, Kansas City	102	1,258	7
Peyton Manning, Indianapolis	104.1	453	305	3,747	28	**2005**	Chad Johnson, Cincinnati	97	1,432	9
Peyton Manning, Indianapolis	101.0	557	362	4,397	31	**2006**	Andre Johnson, Houston	103	1,147	5
Tom Brady, New England	117.2	578	398	4,806	50	**2007**	Wes Welker, New England	112	1,175	8
							T.J. Houshmandzadeh, Cincinnati	112	1,143	12
Philip Rivers, San Diego	105.5	478	312	4,009	34	**2008**	Andre Johnson, Houston	115	1,575	8
Philip Rivers, San Diego	104.4	486	317	4,254	28	**2009**	Wes Walker, New England	123	1,348	4
Tom Brady, New England	111.0	492	324	3,900	36	**2010**	Reggie Wayne, Indianapolis	111	1,355	6
Tom Brady, New England	105.6	611	401	5,235	39	**2011**	Wes Welker, New England	122	1,569	9
Peyton Manning, Denver	105.8	583	400	4,659	37	**2012**	Wes Welker, New England	118	1,354	6
Peyton Manning, Denver	115.1	659	450	5,477	55	**2013**	Antonio Brown, Pittsburgh	110	1,499	8
Ben Roethlisberger, Pittsburgh	103.3	608	408	4,952	32	**2014**	Antonio Brown, Pittsburgh	129	1,698	13

SCORING / **RUSHING YARDS**

Player, team	TD	XPM	FGM	Pts	Year	Player, team	Yds	Att	TD
Gene Mingo, Denver	6	33	18	123	**1960**	Abner Haynes, Dallas Texans	875	156	9
Gino Cappelletti, Boston	8	48	17	147	**1961**	Billy Cannon, Houston	948	200	6
Gene Mingo, Denver	4	32	27	137	**1962**	Cookie Gilchrist, Buffalo	1,096	214	13
Gino Cappelletti, Boston	2	35	22	113	**1963**	Clem Daniels, Oakland	1,099	215	3
Gino Cappelletti, Boston	7	36	25	155	**1964**	Cookie Gilchrist, Buffalo	981	230	6
Gino Cappelletti, Boston	9	27	17	132	**1965**	Paul Lowe, San Diego	1,121	222	7
Gino Cappelletti, Boston	6	35	16	119	**1966**	Jim Nance, Boston	1,458	299	11
George Blanda, Oakland	0	56	20	116	**1967**	Jim Nance, Boston	1,216	269	7
Jim Turner, NY Jets	0	43	34	145	**1968**	Paul Robinson, Cincinnati	1,023	238	8
Jim Turner, NY Jets	0	33	32	129	**1969**	Dickie Post, San Diego	873	182	6
Jan Stenerud, Kansas City	0	26	30	116	**1970**	Floyd Little, Denver	901	209	3
Garo Yepremian, Miami	0	33	28	117	**1971**	Floyd Little, Denver	1,133	284	6
Bobby Howfield, NY Jets	0	40	27	121	**1972**	O. J. Simpson, Buffalo	1,251	292	6
Roy Gerela, Pittsburgh	0	36	29	123	**1973**	O. J. Simpson, Buffalo	2,003	332	12
Roy Gerela, Pittsburgh	0	33	20	93	**1974**	Otis Armstrong, Denver	1,407	263	9
O. J. Simpson, Buffalo	23	0	0	138	**1975**	O. J. Simpson, Buffalo	1,817	329	16
Toni Linhart, Baltimore Colts	0	49	20	109	**1976**	O. J. Simpson, Buffalo	1,503	290	8
Errol Mann, Oakland	0	39	20	99	**1977**	Mark van Eeghen, Oakland	1,273	324	7
Pat Leahy, NY Jets	0	41	22	107	**1978**	Earl Campbell, Houston	1,450	302	13
John Smith, New England	0	46	23	115	**1979**	Earl Campbell, Houston	1,697	368	19
John Smith, New England	0	51	26	129	**1980**	Earl Campbell, Houston	1,934	373	13
Jim Breech, Cincinnati	0	49	22	115	**1981**	Earl Campbell, Houston	1,376	361	10
Nick Lowery, Kansas City	0	37	26	115					
Marcus Allen, L.A. Raiders	14	0	0	84	**1982**	Freeman McNeil, NY Jets	786	151	6
Gary Anderson, Pittsburgh	0	38	27	119	**1983**	Curt Warner, Seattle	1,449	335	13
Gary Anderson, Pittsburgh	0	45	24	117	**1984**	Earnest Jackson, San Diego	1,179	296	8
Gary Anderson, Pittsburgh	0	40	33	139	**1985**	Marcus Allen, L.A. Raiders	1,759	380	11
Tony Franklin, New England	0	44	32	140	**1986**	Curt Warner, Seattle	1,481	319	13
Jim Breech, Cincinnati	0	25	24	97	**1987**	Eric Dickerson, L.A. Rams-Ind.	1,288*	283	6
Scott Norwood, Buffalo	0	33	32	129	**1988**	Eric Dickerson, Indianapolis	1,659	388	14
David Treadwell, Denver	0	39	27	120	**1989**	Christian Okoye, Kansas City	1,480	370	12
Nick Lowery, Kansas City	0	37	34	139	**1990**	Thurman Thomas, Buffalo	1,297	271	11
Pete Stoyanovich, Miami	0	28	31	121	**1991**	Thurman Thomas, Buffalo	1,407	288	7
Pete Stoyanovich, Miami	0	34	30	124	**1992**	Barry Foster, Pittsburgh	1,690	390	11
Jeff Jaeger, L.A. Raiders	0	27	35	132	**1993**	Thurman Thomas, Buffalo	1,315	355	6
John Carney, San Diego	0	33	34	135	**1994**	Chris Warren, Seattle	1,545	333	9
Norm Johnson, Pittsburgh	0	39	34	141	**1995**	Curtis Martin, New England	1,487	368	14
Cary Blanchard, Indianapolis	0	27	36	135	**1996**	Terrell Davis, Denver	1,538	345	13
Mike Hollis, Jacksonville	0	41	31	134	**1997**	Terrell Davis, Denver	1,750	369	15
Steve Christie, Buffalo	0	41	33	140	**1998**	Terrell Davis, Denver	2,008	392	21
Mike Vanderjagt, Indianapolis	0	43	34	145	**1999**	Edgerrin James, Indianapolis	1,553	369	13
Matt Stover, Baltimore	0	30	35	135	**2000**	Edgerrin James, Indianapolis	1,709	387	13
Mike Vanderjagt, Indianapolis	0	41	28	125	**2001**	Priest Holmes, Kansas City	1,555	327	8
Priest Holmes, Kansas City	24	0	0	144	**2002**	Ricky Williams, Miami	1,853	383	16
Priest Holmes, Kansas City	27	0	0	162	**2003**	Jamal Lewis, Baltimore	2,066	387	14
Adam Vinatieri, New England	0	48	31	141	**2004**	Curtis Martin, NY Jets	1,697	371	12
Shayne Graham, Cincinnati	0	47	28	131	**2005**	Larry Johnson, Kansas City	1,750	336	20
LaDainian Tomlinson, San Diego	31	0	0	186	**2006**	LaDainian Tomlinson, San Diego	1,815	348	28
Randy Moss, New England	23	0	0	138	**2007**	LaDainian Tomlinson, San Diego	1,474	315	15
Stephen Gostkowski, New England	0	40	36	148	**2008**	Thomas Jones, NY Jets	1,312	290	13
Nate Kaeding, San Diego	0	50	32	146	**2009**	Chris Johnson, Tennessee	2,006	358	14
Sebastian Janikowski, Oakland	0	43	33	142	**2010**	Arian Foster, Houston	1,616	327	16
Stephen Gostkowski, New England	0	59	28	143	**2011**	Maurice Jones-Drew, Jacksonville	1,606	343	8
Stephen Gostkowski, New England	0	66	29	153	**2012**	Jamaal Charles, Kansas City	1,509	285	5
Stephen Gostkowski, New England	0	44	38	158	**2013**	Jamaal Charles, Kansas City	1,287	259	12
Stephen Gostkowski, New England	0	51	35	156	**2014**	Le'Veon Bell, Pittsburgh	1,361	290	8

*Includes 277 yards after being traded to NFC; 1,011 yards led AFC. NA = Not applicable/available. **Note:** Passer ratings for years prior to 1973 were determined by different measures and are not directly comparable to current passer ratings.

National Football Conference Leaders, 1960-2014

(National Football League, 1960-69)

PASSING (BASED ON QB RATING POINTS) / RECEPTIONS

Player, team	Rating	Att	Comp	Yds	TD	Year	Player, team	Rec	Yds	TD
Milt Plum, Cleveland	NA	250	151	2,297	21	**1960**	Raymond Berry, Baltimore Colts	74	1,298	10
Milt Plum, Cleveland	NA	302	177	2,416	18	**1961**	Jim Phillips, L.A. Rams	78	1,092	5
Bart Starr, Green Bay	NA	285	178	2,438	12	**1962**	Bobby Mitchell, Washington	72	1,384	11
Y. A. Tittle, NY Giants	NA	367	221	3,145	36	**1963**	Bobby Joe Conrad, St. Louis Cardinals	73	967	10
Bart Starr, Green Bay	NA	272	163	2,144	15	**1964**	Johnny Morris, Chicago	93	1,200	10
Rudy Bukich, Chicago	NA	312	176	2,641	20	**1965**	Dave Parks, San Francisco	80	1,344	12
Bart Starr, Green Bay	NA	251	156	2,257	14	**1966**	Charley Taylor, Washington	72	1,119	12
Sonny Jurgensen, Washington	NA	508	288	3,747	31	**1967**	Charley Taylor, Washington	70	990	9
Earl Morrall, Baltimore Colts	NA	317	182	2,909	26	**1968**	Clifton McNeil, San Francisco	71	994	7
Sonny Jurgensen, Washington	NA	442	274	3,102	22	**1969**	Dan Abramowicz, New Orleans	73	1,015	7
John Brodie, San Francisco	NA	378	223	2,941	24	**1970**	Dick Gordon, Chicago	71	1,026	13
Roger Staubach, Dallas	NA	211	126	1,882	15	**1971**	Bob Tucker, NY Giants	59	791	4
Norm Snead, NY Giants	NA	325	196	2,307	17	**1972**	Harold Jackson, Philadelphia	62	1,048	4
Roger Staubach, Dallas	94.6	286	179	2,428	23	**1973**	Harold Carmichael, Philadelphia	67	1,116	9
Sonny Jurgensen, Washington	94.5	167	107	1,185	11	**1974**	Charles Young, Philadelphia	63	696	3
Fran Tarkenton, Minnesota	91.8	425	273	2,994	25	**1975**	Chuck Foreman, Minnesota	73	691	9
James Harris, L.A. Rams	89.6	158	91	1,460	8	**1976**	Drew Pearson, Dallas	58	806	6
Roger Staubach, Dallas	87.0	361	210	2,620	18	**1977**	Ahmad Rashad, Minnesota	51	681	2
Roger Staubach, Dallas	84.9	413	231	3,190	25	**1978**	Rickey Young, Minnesota	88	704	5
Roger Staubach, Dallas	92.3	461	267	3,586	27	**1979**	Ahmad Rashad, Minnesota	80	1,156	9
Ron Jaworski, Philadelphia	91.0	451	257	3,529	27	**1980**	Earl Cooper, San Francisco	83	567	4
Joe Montana, San Francisco	88.4	488	311	3,565	19	**1981**	Dwight Clark, San Francisco	85	1,105	4
Joe Theismann, Washington	91.3	252	161	2,033	13	**1982**	Dwight Clark, San Francisco	60	913	5
Steve Bartkowski, Atlanta	97.6	432	274	3,167	22	**1983**	Roy Green, St. Louis Cardinals	78	1,227	14
							Charlie Brown, Washington	78	1,225	8
							Earnest Gray, NY Giants	78	1,139	5
Joe Montana, San Francisco	102.9	432	279	3,630	28	**1984**	Art Monk, Washington	106	1,372	7
Joe Montana, San Francisco	91.3	494	303	3,653	27	**1985**	Roger Craig, San Francisco	92	1,016	6
Tommy Kramer, Minnesota	92.6	372	208	3,000	24	**1986**	Jerry Rice, San Francisco	86	1,570	15
Joe Montana, San Francisco	102.1	398	266	3,054	31	**1987**	J. T. Smith, St. Louis Cardinals	91	1,117	8
Wade Wilson, Minnesota	91.5	332	204	2,746	15	**1988**	Henry Ellard, L.A. Rams	86	1,414	10
Joe Montana, San Francisco	112.4	386	271	3,521	26	**1989**	Sterling Sharpe, Green Bay	90	1,423	12
Phil Simms, NY Giants	92.7	311	184	2,284	15	**1990**	Jerry Rice, San Francisco	100	1,502	13
Steve Young, San Francisco	101.8	279	180	2,517	17	**1991**	Michael Irvin, Dallas	93	1,523	8
Steve Young, San Francisco	107.0	402	268	3,465	25	**1992**	Sterling Sharpe, Green Bay	108	1,461	13
Steve Young, San Francisco	101.5	462	314	4,023	29	**1993**	Sterling Sharpe, Green Bay	112	1,274	11
Steve Young, San Francisco	112.8	461	324	3,969	35	**1994**	Cris Carter, Minnesota	122	1,256	7
Brett Favre, Green Bay	99.5	570	359	4,413	38	**1995**	Herman Moore, Detroit	123	1,686	14
Steve Young, San Francisco	97.2	316	214	2,410	14	**1996**	Jerry Rice, San Francisco	108	1,254	8
Steve Young, San Francisco	104.7	356	241	3,029	19	**1997**	Herman Moore, Detroit	104	1,293	8
Randall Cunningham, Minnesota	106.0	425	259	3,704	34	**1998**	Frank Sanders, Arizona	89	1,145	3
Kurt Warner, St. Louis	109.2	499	325	4,353	41	**1999**	Muhsin Muhammad, Carolina	96	1,253	8
Trent Green, St. Louis	101.8	240	145	2,063	16	**2000**	Muhsin Muhammad, Carolina	102	1,183	6
Kurt Warner, St. Louis	101.4	546	375	4,830	36	**2001**	Keyshawn Johnson, Tampa Bay	106	1,266	1
Brad Johnson, Tampa Bay	92.9	451	281	3,049	22	**2002**	Randy Moss, Minnesota	106	1,347	7
Daunte Culpepper, Minnesota	96.4	454	295	3,479	25	**2003**	Torry Holt, St. Louis	117	1,696	12
Daunte Culpepper, Minnesota	110.9	548	379	4,717	39	**2004**	Joe Horn, New Orleans	94	1,399	11
							Torry Holt, St. Louis	94	1,372	10
Matt Hasselbeck, Seattle	98.2	449	294	3,459	24	**2005**	Steve Smith, Carolina	103	1,563	12
							Larry Fitzgerald, Arizona	103	1,409	10
Drew Brees, New Orleans	96.2	554	356	4,418	26	**2006**	Mike Furrey, Detroit	98	1,086	6
Tony Romo, Dallas	97.4	520	335	4,211	36	**2007**	Larry Fitzgerald, Arizona	100	1,409	10
Kurt Warner, Arizona	96.9	598	401	4,583	30	**2008**	Larry Fitzgerald, Arizona	96	1,431	12
Drew Brees, New Orleans	109.6	514	363	4,388	34	**2009**	Steve Smith, NY Giants	107	1,220	7
Aaron Rodgers, Green Bay	101.2	475	312	3,922	28	**2010**	Roddy White, Atlanta	115	1,389	10
Aaron Rodgers, Green Bay	122.5	502	343	4,643	45	**2011**	Roddy White, Atlanta	100	1,296	8
Aaron Rodgers, Green Bay	108.0	552	371	4,295	39	**2012**	Calvin Johnson, Detroit	122	1,964	5
Nick Foles, Philadelphia	119.2	317	203	2,891	27	**2013**	Pierre Garcon, Washington	113	1,346	5
Tony Romo, Dallas	113.2	435	304	3,705	34	**2014**	Julio Jones, Atlanta	104	1,593	6

SCORING / RUSHING YARDS

Player, team	TD	XPM	FGM	Pts	Year	Player, team	Yds	Att	TD
Paul Hornung, Green Bay	15	41	15	176	**1960**	Jim Brown, Cleveland	1,257	215	9
Paul Hornung, Green Bay	10	41	15	146	**1961**	Jim Brown, Cleveland	1,408	305	8
Jim Taylor, Green Bay	19	0	0	114	**1962**	Jim Taylor, Green Bay	1,474	272	19
Don Chandler, NY Giants	0	52	18	106	**1963**	Jim Brown, Cleveland	1,863	291	12
Lenny Moore, Baltimore Colts	20	0	0	120	**1964**	Jim Brown, Cleveland	1,446	280	7
Gale Sayers, Chicago	22	0	0	132	**1965**	Jim Brown, Cleveland	1,544	289	17
Bruce Gossett, L.A. Rams	0	29	28	113	**1966**	Gale Sayers, Chicago	1,231	229	8
Jim Bakken, St. Louis Cardinals	0	36	27	117	**1967**	Leroy Kelly, Cleveland	1,205	235	11
Leroy Kelly, Cleveland	20	0	0	120	**1968**	Leroy Kelly, Cleveland	1,239	248	16
Fred Cox, Minnesota	0	43	26	121	**1969**	Gale Sayers, Chicago	1,032	236	8
Fred Cox, Minnesota	0	35	30	125	**1970**	Larry Brown, Washington	1,125	237	5
Curt Knight, Washington	0	27	29	114	**1971**	John Brockington, Green Bay	1,105	216	4
Chester Marcol, Green Bay	0	29	33	128	**1972**	Larry Brown, Washington	1,216	285	8

SCORING						RUSHING YARDS			
Player, team	TD	XPM	FGM	Pts	Year	Player, team	Yds	Att	TD
David Ray, L.A. Rams	0	40	30	130	**1973**	John Brockington, Green Bay	1,144	265	3
Chester Marcol, Green Bay	0	19	25	94	**1974**	Lawrence McCutcheon, L.A. Rams	1,109	236	3
Chuck Foreman, Minnesota	22	0	0	132	**1975**	Jim Otis, St. Louis Cardinals	1,076	269	5
Mark Moseley, Washington	0	31	22	97	**1976**	Walter Payton, Chicago	1,390	311	13
Walter Payton, Chicago	16	0	0	96	**1977**	Walter Payton, Chicago	1,852	339	14
Frank Corral, L.A. Rams	0	31	29	118	**1978**	Walter Payton, Chicago	1,395	333	11
Mark Moseley, Washington	0	39	25	114	**1979**	Walter Payton, Chicago	1,610	369	14
Ed Murray, Detroit	0	35	27	116	**1980**	Walter Payton, Chicago	1,460	317	6
Ed Murray, Detroit	0	46	25	121	**1981**	George Rogers, New Orleans	1,674	378	13
Rafael Septien, Dallas	0	40	27	121					
Wendell Tyler, L.A. Rams	13	0	0	78	**1982**	Tony Dorsett, Dallas	745	177	5
Mark Moseley, Washington	0	62	33	161	**1983**	Eric Dickerson, L.A. Rams	1,808	390	18
Ray Wersching, San Francisco	0	56	25	131	**1984**	Eric Dickerson, L.A. Rams	2,105	379	14
Kevin Butler, Chicago	0	51	31	144	**1985**	Gerald Riggs, Atlanta	1,719	397	10
Kevin Butler, Chicago	0	36	28	120	**1986**	Eric Dickerson, L.A. Rams	1,821	404	11
Jerry Rice, San Francisco	23	0	0	138	**1987**	Charles White, L.A. Rams	1,374	324	11
Mike Cofer, San Francisco	0	40	27	121	**1988**	Herschel Walker, Dallas	1,514	361	5
Mike Cofer, San Francisco	0	49	29	136	**1989**	Barry Sanders, Detroit	1,470	280	14
Chip Lohmiller, Washington	0	41	30	131	**1990**	Barry Sanders, Detroit	1,304	255	13
Chip Lohmiller, Washington	0	56	31	149	**1991**	Emmitt Smith, Dallas	1,563	365	12
Morten Andersen, New Orleans	0	33	29	120	**1992**	Emmitt Smith, Dallas	1,713	373	18
Chip Lohmiller, Washington	0	30	30	120					
Jason Hanson, Detroit	0	28	34	130	**1993**	Emmitt Smith, Dallas	1,486	283	9
Fuad Reveiz, Minnesota	0	30	34	132	**1994**	Barry Sanders, Detroit	1,883	331	7
Emmitt Smith, Dallas	22	0	0	132					
Emmitt Smith, Dallas	25	0	0	150	**1995**	Emmitt Smith, Dallas	1,773	377	25
John Kasay, Carolina	0	34	37	145	**1996**	Barry Sanders, Detroit	1,553	307	11
Richie Cunningham, Dallas	0	24	34	126	**1997**	Barry Sanders, Detroit	2,053	335	11
Gary Anderson, Minnesota	0	59	35	164	**1998**	Jamal Anderson, Atlanta	1,846	410	14
Jeff Wilkins, St. Louis	0	64	20	124	**1999**	Stephen Davis, Washington	1,405	290	17
Marshall Faulk, St. Louis	26	0	0	160	**2000**	Robert Smith, Minnesota	1,521	295	7
Marshall Faulk, St. Louis	21	0	0	128	**2001**	Stephen Davis, Washington	1,432	356	5
Jay Feely, Atlanta	0	42	32	138	**2002**	Deuce McAllister, New Orleans	1,388	325	13
Jeff Wilkins, St. Louis	0	46	39	163	**2003**	Ahman Green, Green Bay	1,883	355	15
David Akers, Philadelphia	0	41	27	122	**2004**	Shaun Alexander, Seattle	1,696	353	16
Shaun Alexander, Seattle	28	0	0	168	**2005**	Shaun Alexander, Seattle	1,880	370	27
Robbie Gould, Chicago	0	47	32	143	**2006**	Frank Gore, San Francisco	1,695	312	8
Mason Crosby, Green Bay	0	48	31	141	**2007**	Adrian Peterson, Minnesota	1,341	238	12
David Akers, Philadelphia	0	45	33	144	**2008**	Adrian Peterson, Minnesota	1,760	363	10
David Akers, Philadelphia	0	43	32	139	**2009**	Steven Jackson, St. Louis	1,416	324	4
David Akers, Philadelphia	0	47	32	143	**2010**	Michael Turner, Atlanta	1,371	334	12
David Akers, San Francisco	0	34	44	166	**2011**	Michael Turner, Atlanta	1,340	301	11
Lawrence Tynes, NY Giants	0	46	33	145	**2012**	Adrian Peterson, Minnesota	2,097	348	12
Steven Hauschka, Seattle	0	44	33	143	**2013**	LeSean McCoy, Philadelphia	1,607	314	9
Cody Parkey, Philadelphia	0	54	32	150	**2014**	DeMarco Murray, Dallas	1,845	392	13

Note: Passer ratings for years prior to 1973 were determined by different measures and are not directly comparable to current passer ratings.

NFL MVP and Rookies of the Year, 1957-2014

The Most Valuable Player, Offensive Rookie of the Year, and Defensive Rookie of the Year are a few of the many awards given out annually by the Associated Press according to the results of balloting by a nationwide panel of media. Many other organizations give out annual awards honoring the NFL's best players.

Year	NFL Most Valuable Player	Offensive Rookie of the Year	Defensive Rookie of the Year
1957	Jim Brown, Cleveland	NA	NA
1958	Jim Brown, Cleveland	NA	NA
1959	Charley Conerly, NY Giants	NA	NA
1960	Norm Van Brocklin, Philadelphia	NA	NA
1961	Paul Hornung, Green Bay	NA	NA
1962	Jim Taylor, Green Bay	NA	NA
1963	Y. A. Tittle, NY Giants	NA	NA
1964	Johnny Unitas, Baltimore	NA	NA
1965	Jim Brown, Cleveland	NA	NA
1966	Bart Starr, Green Bay	NA	NA
1967	Johnny Unitas, Baltimore	Mel Farr, Detroit	Lem Barney, Detroit
1968	Earl Morrall, Baltimore	Earl McCullouch, Detroit	Claude Humphrey, Atlanta
1969	Roman Gabriel, Los Angeles	Calvin Hill, Dallas	Joe Greene, Pittsburgh
1970	John Brodie, San Francisco	Dennis Shaw, Buffalo	Bruce Taylor, San Francisco
1971	Alan Page, Minnesota	John Brockington, Green Bay	Isiah Robertson, Los Angeles
1972	Larry Brown, Washington	Franco Harris, Pittsburgh	Willie Buchanon, Green Bay
1973	O. J. Simpson, Buffalo	Chuck Foreman, Minnesota	Wally Chambers, Chicago
1974	Ken Stabler, Oakland	Don Woods, San Diego	Jack Lambert, Pittsburgh
1975	Fran Tarkenton, Minnesota	Mike Thomas, Washington	Robert Brazile, Houston
1976	Bert Jones, Baltimore	Sammy White, Minnesota	Mike Haynes, New England
1977	Walter Payton, Chicago	Tony Dorsett, Dallas	A. J. Duhe, Miami
1978	Terry Bradshaw, Pittsburgh	Earl Campbell, Houston	Al Baker, Detroit

Year	NFL Most Valuable Player	Offensive Rookie of the Year	Defensive Rookie of the Year
1979	Earl Campbell, Houston	Ottis Anderson, St. Louis	Jim Haslett, Buffalo
1980	Brian Sipe, Cleveland	Billy Sims, Detroit	Buddy Curry, Atlanta; Al Richardson, Atlanta
1981	Ken Anderson, Cincinnati	George Rogers, New Orleans	Lawrence Taylor, NY Giants
1982	Mark Moseley, Washington	Marcus Allen, Los Angeles	Chip Banks, Cleveland
1983	Joe Theismann, Washington	Eric Dickerson, Los Angeles	Vernon Maxwell, Baltimore
1984	Dan Marino, Miami	Louis Lipps, Pittsburgh	Bill Maas, Kansas City
1985	Marcus Allen, Los Angeles	Eddie Brown, Cincinnati	Duane Bickett, Indianapolis
1986	Lawrence Taylor, NY Giants	Rueben Mayes, New Orleans	Leslie O'Neal, San Diego
1987	John Elway, Denver	Troy Stradford, Miami	Shane Conlan, Buffalo
1988	Boomer Esiason, Cincinnati	John Stephens, New England	Erik McMillan, NY Jets
1989	Joe Montana, San Francisco	Barry Sanders, Detroit	Derrick Thomas, Kansas City
1990	Joe Montana, San Francisco	Emmitt Smith, Dallas	Mark Carrier, Chicago
1991	Thurman Thomas, Buffalo	Leonard Russell, New England	Mike Croel, Denver
1992	Steve Young, San Francisco	Carl Pickens, Cincinnati	Dale Carter, Kansas City
1993	Emmitt Smith, Dallas	Jerome Bettis, Los Angeles	Dana Stubblefield, San Francisco
1994	Steve Young, San Francisco	Marshall Faulk, Indianapolis	Tim Bowens, Miami
1995	Brett Favre, Green Bay	Curtis Martin, New England	Hugh Douglas, NY Jets
1996	Brett Favre, Green Bay	Eddie George, Houston	Simeon Rice, Arizona
1997	Brett Favre, Green Bay; Barry Sanders, Detroit	Warrick Dunn, Tampa Bay	Peter Boulware, Baltimore
1998	Terrell Davis, Denver	Randy Moss, Minnesota	Charles Woodson, Oakland
1999	Kurt Warner, St. Louis	Edgerrin James, Indianapolis	Jevon Kearse, Tennessee
2000	Marshall Faulk, St. Louis	Mike Anderson, Denver	Brian Urlacher, Chicago
2001	Kurt Warner, St. Louis	Anthony Thomas, Chicago	Kendrell Bell, Pittsburgh
2002	Rich Gannon, Oakland	Clinton Portis, Denver	Julius Peppers, Carolina
2003	Peyton Manning, Indianapolis; Steve McNair, Tennessee	Anquan Boldin, Arizona	Terrell Suggs, Baltimore
2004	Peyton Manning, Indianapolis	Ben Roethlisberger, Pittsburgh	Jonathan Vilma, NY Jets
2005	Shaun Alexander, Seattle	Cadillac Williams, Tampa Bay	Shawne Merriman, San Diego
2006	LaDainian Tomlinson, San Diego	Vince Young, Tennessee	DeMeco Ryans, Houston
2007	Tom Brady, New England	Adrian Peterson, Minnesota	Patrick Willis, San Francisco
2008	Peyton Manning, Indianapolis	Matt Ryan, Atlanta	Jerod Mayo, New England
2009	Peyton Manning, Indianapolis	Percy Harvin, Minnesota	Brian Cushing, Houston
2010	Tom Brady, New England	Sam Bradford, St. Louis	Ndamukong Suh, Detroit
2011	Aaron Rodgers, Green Bay	Cam Newton, Carolina	Von Miller, Denver
2012	Adrian Peterson, Minnesota	Robert Griffin III, Washington	Luke Kuechly, Carolina
2013	Peyton Manning, Denver	Eddie Lacy, Green Bay	Sheldon Richardson, NY Jets
2014	Aaron Rodgers, Green Bay	Odell Beckham Jr., NY Giants	Aaron Donald, St. Louis

All-Time Professional (NFL and AFL) Football Records

(at end of 2014 season; * = active in 2014; (a) includes AFL statistics; ** = 2-pt conversions scored)

All-Time Scoring Leaders by Points

Player	Yrs	TD	PAT	FG	Total
Morten Andersen	25	0	849	565	2,544
Gary Anderson	23	0	820	538	2,434
Jason Hanson	21	0	665	495	2,150
Adam Vinatieri*	19	0	710**	478	2,146
John Carney	23	0	628	478	2,062
Matt Stover	19	0	591	471	2,004
George Blanda (a)	26	9	943	335	2,002
Jason Elam	17	0	675	436	1,983
John Kasay	20	0	587	461	1,970
Norm Johnson	18	0	638	366	1,736
David Akers	16	0	563	386	1,721
Nick Lowery	18	0	562	383	1,711
Jan Stenerud (a)	19	0	580	373	1,699
Ryan Longwell	15	0	604	361	1,687
Eddie Murray	19	0	538	352	1,594
Al Del Greco	17	0	543	347	1,584

All-Time Scoring Leaders by Touchdowns

Player	Yrs	Rush	Rec	Ret	TD
Jerry Rice	20	10	197	1	208
Emmitt Smith	15	164	11	0	175
LaDainian Tomlinson	11	145	17	0	162
Randy Moss	14	0	156	1	157
Terrell Owens	15	3	153	0	156
Marcus Allen	16	123	21	1	145
Marshall Faulk	12	100	36	0	136
Cris Carter	16	0	130	1	131
Marvin Harrison	13	0	128	0	128
Jim Brown	9	106	20	0	126
Walter Payton	13	110	15	0	125
John Riggins	14	104	12	0	116
Lenny Moore	12	63	48	2	113
Shaun Alexander	9	100	12	0	112
Tony Gonzalez	17	0	111	0	111
Barry Sanders	10	99	10	0	109

Points, season: 186, LaDainian Tomlinson, San Diego, 2006 (31 TDs).
Points, game: 40, Ernie Nevers, Chicago Cardinals vs. Chicago Bears, Nov. 28, 1929 (6 TDs, 4 PATs).
Touchdowns, season: 31, LaDainian Tomlinson, San Diego, 2006.
Touchdowns, game: 6; Ernie Nevers, Chicago Cardinals vs. Chicago Bears, Nov. 28, 1929 (6 rushing);
Dub Jones, Cleveland Browns vs. Chicago Bears, Nov. 25, 1951 (4 rushing, 2 pass receptions);
Gale Sayers, Chicago Bears vs. San Francisco, Dec. 12, 1965 (4 rushing, 1 pass reception, 1 punt return).
Points after TD, season: 75, Matt Prater, Denver, 2013.
Consecutive points after TD: 422, Matt Stover, Baltimore Ravens-Indianapolis, 1996-2009.
Field goals, career: 565, Morten Andersen, New Orleans-Atlanta-NY Giants-Kansas City-Minnesota-Atlanta, 1982-2007.
Field goals, season: 44, David Akers, San Francisco, 2011.
Field goals, game: 8, Rob Bironas, Tennessee vs. Houston, Oct. 21, 2007.
Longest field goal: 64 yards, Matt Prater, Denver vs. Tennesee, Dec. 8, 2013.

All-Time Defensive Leaders

Interceptions, career: 81, Paul Krause, Washington-Minnesota, 1964-79.
Interceptions, season: 14, Dick "Night Train" Lane, L.A. Rams, 1952.
Interception touchdowns, career: 12, Rod Woodson, Pittsburgh-San Francisco-Baltimore Ravens-Oakland, 1987-2003.
Interception touchdowns, season: 4; Ken Houston, Houston, 1971; Jim Kearney, Kansas City, 1972; Eric Allen, Philadelphia, 1993.
Sacks, career (since 1982): 200.0, Bruce Smith, Buffalo-Washington, 1985-2003.
Sacks, season (since 1982): 22.5, Michael Strahan, NY Giants, 2001.

All-Time Rushing Leaders

(ranked by rushing yards; * = active in 2014)

Player	Yrs	Att	Yds	Avg	Long	TD
Emmitt Smith	15	4,409	18,355	4.2	75T	164
Walter Payton	13	3,838	16,726	4.4	76	110
Barry Sanders	10	3,062	15,269	5.0	85	99
Curtis Martin	11	3,518	14,101	4.0	70T	90
LaDainian Tomlinson	11	3,174	13,684	4.3	85T	145
Jerome Bettis	13	3,479	13,662	3.9	71T	91
Eric Dickerson	11	2,996	13,259	4.4	85T	90
Tony Dorsett	12	2,936	12,739	4.3	99T	77
Jim Brown	9	2,359	12,312	5.2	80T	106
Marshall Faulk	12	2,836	12,279	4.3	71T	100
Edgerrin James	11	3,028	12,246	4.0	72	80
Marcus Allen	16	3,022	12,243	4.1	61T	123
Franco Harris	13	2,949	12,120	4.1	75T	91
Thurman Thomas	13	2,877	12,074	4.2	80T	65
Fred Taylor	13	2,534	11,695	4.6	80T	66
Steven Jackson*	11	2,743	11,388	4.2	59T	68
John Riggins	14	2,916	11,352	3.9	66T	104
Corey Dillon	10	2,618	11,241	4.3	96T	82
O. J. Simpson	11	2,404	11,236	4.7	94T	61
Frank Gore*	10	2,442	11,073	4.5	80	11

Yards gained, season: 2,105, Eric Dickerson, L.A. Rams, 1984.
Yards gained, game: 296, Adrian Peterson, Minnesota vs. San Diego, Nov. 4, 2007.
Rushing TDs, career: 164, Emmitt Smith, Dallas-Arizona, 1990-2004.
Rushing TDs, season: 28, LaDainian Tomlinson, San Diego, 2006.
Rushing TDs, game: 6, Ernie Nevers, Chicago Cardinals vs. Chicago Bears, Nov. 28, 1929.
Rushing attempts, game: 45, Jamie Morris, Washington vs. Cincinnati, Dec. 17, 1988 (OT).
Longest run from scrimmage: 99 yards (TD), Tony Dorsett, Dallas vs. Minnesota, Jan. 3, 1983.

All-Time Receiving Leaders

(ranked by number of receptions; * = active in 2014)

Player	Yrs	No.	Yds	Avg	Long	TD
Jerry Rice	20	1,549	22,895	14.8	96T	197
Tony Gonzalez	17	1,325	15,127	11.4	73T	111
Marvin Harrison	13	1,102	14,580	13.2	80T	128
Cris Carter	16	1,101	13,899	12.6	80T	130
Tim Brown	17	1,094	14,934	13.7	80T	100
Terrell Owens	15	1,078	15,934	14.8	98T	153
Reggie Wayne*	14	1,070	14,345	13.4	80	82
Isaac Bruce	16	1,024	15,208	14.9	80T	91
Andre Johnson*	12	1,012	13,597	13.4	77T	64
Hines Ward	14	1,000	12,083	12.1	85T	85
Randy Moss	14	982	15,292	15.6	82T	156
Andre Reed	16	951	13,198	13.9	83T	87
Derrick Mason	15	943	12,061	12.8	79T	66
Jason Witten*	12	943	10,502	11.1	69	57
Anquan Boldin*	12	940	12,406	13.2	79T	70
Art Monk	16	940	12,721	13.5	79T	68
Torry Holt	11	920	13,382	14.5	85T	74
Steve Smith*	14	915	13,262	14.5	80T	73
Larry Fitzgerald*	11	909	12,151	13.4	80T	89
Wes Welker*	11	890	9,822	11.0	99T	50

Yards gained, career: 22,895, Jerry Rice, San Francisco-Oakland-Seattle, 1985-2004.
Yards gained, season: 1,964, Calvin Johnson, Detroit, 2012.
Yards gained, game: 336, Willie "Flipper" Anderson, L.A. Rams vs. New Orleans, Nov. 26, 1989 (OT).
Pass receptions, season: 143, Marvin Harrison, Indianapolis, 2002.
Pass receptions, game: 21, Brandon Marshall, Denver vs. Indianapolis, Dec. 13, 2009.
Touchdown receptions, career: 197, Jerry Rice, San Francisco-Oakland-Seattle, 1985-2004.
Touchdown receptions, season: 23, Randy Moss, New England, 2007.
Touchdown receptions, game: 5; Bob Shaw, Chicago Cardinals vs. Baltimore Colts, Oct. 2, 1950; Kellen Winslow, San Diego vs. Oakland, Nov. 22, 1981; Jerry Rice, San Francisco vs. Atlanta, Oct. 14, 1990.

All-Time Passing Leaders

(minimum 1,500 attempts; ranked by quarterback rating points; * = active in 2014)

Player	Yrs	Att	Comp	Yds	TD	Int	Pts[1]
Aaron Rodgers*	10	3,475	2,286	28,578	226	57	106.0
Tony Romo*	11	4,210	2,743	33,270	242	110	97.6
Peyton Manning*	16	9,049	5,927	69,691	530	234	97.5
Steve Young	15	4,149	2,667	33,124	232	107	96.8
Tom Brady*	15	7,168	4,551	53,258	392	143	95.9
Philip Rivers*	11	4,678	3,025	36,655	252	122	95.7
Drew Brees*	14	7,458	4,937	56,033	396	194	95.4
Ben Roethlisberger*	11	4,954	3,157	39,057	251	131	93.9
Kurt Warner	12	4,070	2,666	32,344	208	128	93.7
Joe Montana	15	5,391	3,409	40,551	273	139	92.3
Matt Ryan*	7	3,916	2,508	28,166	181	91	91.1
Chad Pennington	11	2,471	1,632	17,823	102	64	90.1
Matt Schaub*	11	3,191	2,040	24,311	130	86	89.5
Daunte Culpepper	11	3,199	2,016	24,153	149	106	87.8
Jeff Garcia	11	3,676	2,264	25,537	161	83	87.5
Andrew Luck*	3	1,813	1,062	12,957	86	43	86.6
Dan Marino	17	8,358	4,967	61,361	420	252	86.4
Carson Palmer*	11	4,906	3,071	35,365	224	155	86.3
Brett Favre	20	10,169	6,300	71,838	508	336	86.0
Trent Green	11	3,740	2,266	28,475	162	114	86.0

(1) Rating points based on performances in the following categories: percentage of completions, percentage of touchdown passes, percentage of interceptions, and average gain per pass attempt.

Yards gained, career: 71,838, Brett Favre, Atlanta-Green Bay-NY Jets-Minnesota, 1991-2010.
Yards gained, season: 5,477, Peyton Manning, Denver, 2013.
Yards gained, game: 554, Norm Van Brocklin, L.A. Rams vs. NY Yanks, Sept. 28, 1951 (27 completions in 41 attempts).
Passing touchdowns, career: 530, Peyton Manning, Indianapolis-Denver, 1998-2014.
Passing touchdowns, season: 55, Peyton Manning, Denver, 2013.
Passing touchdowns, game: 7; Sid Luckman, Chicago Bears vs. NY Giants, Nov. 14, 1943; Adrian Burk, Philadelphia vs. Washington, Oct. 17, 1954; George Blanda, Houston vs. NY Titans, Nov. 19, 1961; Y. A. Tittle, NY Giants vs. Washington, Oct. 28, 1962; Joe Kapp, Minnesota vs. Baltimore Colts, Sept. 28, 1969; Peyton Manning, Denver vs. Baltimore, Sept. 5, 2013; Nick Foles, Philadelphia vs. Oakland, Nov. 3, 2013.
Passes completed, career: 6,300, Brett Favre, Atlanta-Green Bay-NY Jets-Minnesota, 1991-2010.
Passes completed, season: 468, Drew Brees, New Orleans, 2011.
Passes completed, game: 45, Drew Bledsoe, New England vs. Minnesota, Nov. 13, 1994 (OT).

National Football League Franchise Origins

(Team: founding year, league. Home stadium location; subsequent history.)

Arizona Cardinals: 1920, American Professional Football Association (APFA)[1]. Chicago, 1920-59; St. Louis, 1960-87; Tempe, AZ, 1988-2005; Glendale, AZ, 2006-present.
Atlanta Falcons: 1966, NFL. Atlanta, 1966-present.
Baltimore Ravens: 1996, NFL. Baltimore, 1996-present.
Buffalo Bills: 1960, American Football League (AFL)[2]. Buffalo, 1960-72; Orchard Park, NY, 1973-present.
Carolina Panthers: 1995, NFL. Clemson, SC, 1995; Charlotte, NC, 1996-present.
Chicago Bears: 1920, APFA. Decatur, IL, 1920; Chicago, 1921-present.
Cincinnati Bengals: 1968, AFL. Cincinnati, 1968-present.
Cleveland Browns: 1946, All-America Football Conference (AAFC)[3]. Cleveland, 1946-95; 1999-present.
Dallas Cowboys: 1960, NFL. Dallas, 1960-70; Irving, TX, 1971-2008; Arlington, TX, 2009-present.
Denver Broncos: 1960, AFL. Denver, 1960-present.
Detroit Lions: 1930, NFL. Portsmouth, OH, 1930-33; Detroit, 1934-74; Pontiac, MI, 1975-2001; Detroit, 2002-present.
Green Bay Packers: 1921, APFA. Green Bay, WI, 1921-present.
Houston Texans: 2002, NFL. Houston, 2002-present.
Indianapolis Colts: 1953, NFL[3]. Baltimore, 1953-83; Indianapolis, 1984-present.
Jacksonville Jaguars: 1995, NFL. Jacksonville, FL, 1995-present.
Kansas City Chiefs: 1960, AFL. Dallas, 1960-62; Kansas City, MO, 1963-present.
Miami Dolphins: 1966, AFL. Miami, 1966-2002; Miami Gardens, FL, 2003-present.
Minnesota Vikings: 1961, NFL. Bloomington, MN, 1961-81; Minneapolis, 1982-present.
New England Patriots: 1960, AFL. Boston, 1960-70; Foxborough, MA, 1971-present.
New Orleans Saints: 1967, NFL. New Orleans, 1967-2004; Baton Rouge and San Antonio, 2005; New Orleans, 2006-present.
NY Giants: 1925, NFL. New York, NY, 1925-73, 1975; New Haven, CT, 1973-74; E. Rutherford, NJ, 1976-present.
NY Jets: 1960, AFL. New York, NY, 1960-83; E. Rutherford, NJ, 1984-present.
Oakland Raiders: 1960, AFL. San Francisco, 1960-61; Oakland, CA, 1962-81; Los Angeles, 1982-94; Oakland, CA, 1995-present.
Philadelphia Eagles: 1933, NFL. Philadelphia, 1933-present.
Pittsburgh Steelers: 1933, NFL. Pittsburgh, 1933-present.
St. Louis Rams: 1937, NFL. Cleveland, 1936-45; Los Angeles, 1946-79; Anaheim, CA, 1980-94; St. Louis, 1995-present.
San Diego Chargers: 1960, AFL. Los Angeles, 1960; San Diego, 1961-present.
San Francisco 49ers: 1946, AAFC. San Francisco, 1946-present.
Seattle Seahawks: 1976, NFL. Seattle, 1976-present.
Tampa Bay Buccaneers: 1976, NFL. Tampa, 1976-present.
Tennessee Titans: 1960, AFL. Houston, 1960-96; Memphis, 1997; Nashville, 1998-present.
Washington Redskins: 1932, NFL. Boston, 1932-36; Washington, DC, 1937-96; Landover, MD, 1997-present.

(1) The American Professional Football Association (APFA) was formed in 1920 to standardize the rules of professional football. In 1922, the name was changed to the National Football League (NFL). (2) The most successful of four leagues called the American Football League, or AFL (1926; 1936-37; 1940-41; 1960-69). Congress approved an NFL/AFL merger in 1966. Baltimore, Cleveland, and Pittsburgh agreed to join the 10 incoming AFL teams to form the American Football Conference. The NFL began play in 1970 with 26 teams. (3) The All-America Football Conference (AAFC), 1946-49. In 1950, three of its teams joined the NFL (Baltimore, Cleveland, and San Francisco). The Baltimore franchise failed, but the NFL awarded the city a second one, also called the Colts, in 1953.

NFL Stadiums, 2014

(**A** = A-Turf Titan, **D** = DD Grassmaster (grass), **F** = FieldTurf, **G** = Grass, **N** = Natural grass, **S** = Synthetic, **SM** = Sportexe Momentum, **SS** = Sportfield Softtop)

Team: stadium, location, surface (year built)	Capacity[1]
Bears: Soldier Field[2], Chicago, IL, N (1924)	61,500
Bengals: Paul Brown Stadium, Cincinnati, OH, S (2000)	65,515
Bills: Ralph Wilson Stadium, Orchard Park, NY, A (1973)	72,169
Broncos: Sports Authority Field at Mile High[3], Denver, CO, D (2001)	76,125
Browns: FirstEnergy Stadium[4], Cleveland, OH, G (1999)	68,000
Buccaneers: Raymond James Stadium, Tampa, FL, G (1998)	65,908
Cardinals: University of Phoenix Stadium, Glendale, AZ, G (2006)	65,000
Chargers: Qualcomm Stadium[5], San Diego, CA, G (1967)	70,000
Chiefs: Arrowhead Stadium, Kansas City, MO, G (1972; fully renovated 2010)	76,416
Colts: Lucas Oil Stadium, Indianapolis, IN, F (2008)	63,000
Cowboys: AT&T Stadium[6], Arlington, TX, SS (2009)	80,000
Dolphins: Sun Life Stadium[7], Miami Gardens, FL, G (1987)	75,192
Eagles: Lincoln Financial Field, Philadelphia, PA, N (2003)	69,144
Falcons: Georgia Dome, Atlanta, GA, F (1992)	71,228
49ers: Levi's Stadium, Santa Clara, CA, N (2014)	68,500
Giants: MetLife Stadium[8], E. Rutherford, NJ, F (2010)	82,500
Jaguars: EverBank Field[9], Jacksonville, FL, G (1995)	67,297
Jets: MetLife Stadium[8], E. Rutherford, NJ, F (2010)	82,500
Lions: Ford Field, Detroit, MI, F (2002)	64,500
Packers: Lambeau Field[10], Green Bay, WI, D (1957)	80,735
Panthers: Bank of America Stadium[11], Charlotte, NC, G (1996)	73,778
Patriots: Gillette Stadium, Foxborough, MA, F (2002)	68,756
Raiders: O.co Coliseum[12], Oakland, CA, G (1966)	53,286
Rams: Edward Jones Dome[13], St. Louis, MO, F (1995)	66,000
Ravens: M&T Bank Stadium[14], Baltimore, MD, SM (1998)	71,008
Redskins: FedExField[15], Landover, MD, N (1997)	85,000
Saints: Mercedes-Benz Superdome[16], New Orleans, LA, S (1975)	73,000
Seahawks: CenturyLink Field[17], Seattle, WA, F (2002)	67,000
Steelers: Heinz Field, Pittsburgh, PA, N (2001)	65,500
Texans: NRG Stadium[18], Houston, TX, G (2002)	71,054
Titans: LP Field[19], Nashville, TN, N (1999)	69,143
Vikings: TCF Bank Stadium[20], Minneapolis, MN, F (2009)	52,000

(1) As of the start of the 2014 season. (2) Renovation in 2002 replaced interior of stadium. (3) Formerly INVESCO Field at Mile High (2001-11). (4) Formerly Cleveland Browns Stadium (1999-2012). (5) Formerly San Diego Stadium (1967-80); San Diego Jack Murphy Stadium (1981-97). (6) Formerly Cowboys Stadium (2009-12). (7) Formerly Joe Robbie Stadium (1987-96); Pro Player Stadium (1996-2005); Land Shark Stadium (2009). (8) Formerly New Meadowlands Stadium (2010-11). (9) Formerly ALLTEL Stadium (1997-2007); Jacksonville Municipal Stadium (1946-97, 2007-09). (10) Formerly City Stadium (1957-65). Renovation completed in 2003 added 11,625 seats. (11) Formerly Ericsson Stadium (1996-2003). (12) Formerly Oakland-Alameda County Coliseum (1966-98); Network Associates Coliseum (1998-2004); McAfee Stadium (2004-08); Oakland Coliseum (2008-11). (13) Formerly Trans World Dome (1995-2001). (14) Formerly PSINet Stadium (1998-2002); Ravens Stadium (2002-03). (15) Formerly Jack Kent Cooke Stadium (1997-99). (16) Formerly Louisiana Superdome (1975-2011). (17) Formerly Seahawks Stadium (2002-04); Qwest Field (2004-11). (18) Formerly Reliant Stadium (2002-13). (19) Formerly Adelphia Coliseum (1999-2002). (20) The Vikings play at the Univ. of Minnesota's TCF Bank Stadium until their new football stadium is built (scheduled for completion in 2016).

Pro Football Hall of Fame, Canton, OH

(Asterisk indicates member elected in Jan. 2015 and inducted Aug. 8, 2015.)

Herb Adderley
Troy Aikman
George Allen
Larry Allen
Marcus Allen
Lance Alworth
Doug Atkins
Morris "Red" Badgro
Lem Barney
Cliff Battles
Sammy Baugh
Chuck Bednarik
Bert Bell
Bobby Bell
Raymond Berry
Elvin Bethea
*Jerome Bettis
Charles Bidwill
Fred Biletnikoff
George Blanda
Mel Blount
Terry Bradshaw
Derrick Brooks
Bob Brown
Jim Brown
Paul Brown
Roosevelt Brown
*Tim Brown
Willie Brown
Junious "Buck" Buchanan
Nick Buoniconti
Dick Butkus
Jack Butler
Earl Campbell
Tony Canadeo
Joe Carr
Harry Carson
Cris Carter
Dave Casper
Guy Chamberlin
Jack Christiansen
Earl "Dutch" Clark
George Connor
Jim Conzelman
Lou Creekmur
Larry Csonka
Curley Culp
Al Davis
Willie Davis
Dermontti Dawson
Len Dawson
Fred Dean
Joe DeLamielleure
Richard Dent
Eric Dickerson
Dan Dierdorf
Mike Ditka
Chris Doleman
Art Donovan
Tony Dorsett
John "Paddy" Driscoll
Bill Dudley
Glen "Turk" Edwards
Carl Eller
John Elway
Weeb Ewbank
Marshall Faulk
Tom Fears
Jim Finks
Ray Flaherty
Len Ford
Dr. Daniel Fortmann
Dan Fouts
Benny Friedman
Frank Gatski
Bill George
Joe Gibbs
Frank Gifford
Sid Gillman
Otto Graham
Harold "Red" Grange
Bud Grant
Darrell Green
Joe Greene
Forrest Gregg
Bob Griese
Russ Grimm
Lou Groza
Ray Guy
Joe Guyon
George Halas
*Charles Haley
Jack Ham
Dan Hampton
Chris Hanburger
John Hannah
Bob Hayes
Mike Haynes
Mel Hein
Ted Hendricks
Wilbur "Pete" Henry
Arnold Herber
Bill Hewitt
Gene Hickerson
Clarke Hinkle
Elroy "Crazylegs" Hirsch
Paul Hornung
Ken Houston
Robert "Cal" Hubbard
Sam Huff
Claude Humphrey
Lamar Hunt
Don Hutson
Michael Irvin
Rickey Jackson
Jimmy Johnson
John Henry Johnson
Charlie Joiner
David "Deacon" Jones
Stan Jones
Walter Jones
Henry Jordan
Sonny Jurgensen
Jim Kelly
Leroy Kelly
Cortez Kennedy
Walt Kiesling
Frank "Bruiser" Kinard
Paul Krause
Earl "Curly" Lambeau
Jack Lambert
Tom Landry
Dick "Night Train" Lane
Jim Langer
Willie Lanier
Steve Largent
Yale Lary
Dante Lavelli
Bobby Layne
Dick LeBeau
Alphonse "Tuffy" Leemans
Marv Levy
Bob Lilly
Floyd Little
Larry Little
James Lofton
Vince Lombardi
Howie Long
Ronnie Lott
Sid Luckman
Roy "Link" Lyman
Tom Mack
John Mackey
John Madden
Tim Mara
Wellington Mara
Gino Marchetti
Dan Marino
George Preston Marshall
Curtis Martin
Bruce Mathews
Ollie Matson
Don Maynard
George McAfee
Mike McCormack
Randall McDaniel
Tommy McDonald
Hugh McElhenny
Johnny "Blood" McNally
Mike Michalske
Wayne Millner
Bobby Mitchell
Ron Mix
Art Monk
Joe Montana
Warren Moon
Lenny Moore
Marion Motley
Mike Munchak
Anthony Muñoz
George Musso
Bronko Nagurski
Joe Namath
Earle "Greasy" Neale
Ernie Nevers
Ozzie Newsome
Ray Nitschke
Chuck Noll
Leo Nomellini
Jonathan Ogden
Merlin Olsen
Jim Otto
Steve Owen
Alan Page
Bill Parcells
Clarence "Ace" Parker
Jim Parker
Walter Payton
Joe Perry
Pete Pihos
*Bill Polian
Fritz Pollard
John Randle
Hugh "Shorty" Ray
Andre Reed
Dan Reeves
Mel Renfro
Jerry Rice
Les Richter
John Riggins
Jim Ringo
Willie Roaf
Dave Robinson
Andy Robustelli
Art Rooney
Dan Rooney
Pete Rozelle
Ed Sabol
Bob St. Clair
Barry Sanders
Charlie Sanders
Deion Sanders
Warren Sapp
Gale Sayers
Joe Schmidt
Tex Schramm
*Junior Seau
Lee Roy Selmon
Shannon Sharpe
Billy Shaw
Art Shell
*Will Shields
Don Shula
O. J. Simpson
Mike Singletary
Jackie Slater
Bruce Smith
Emmitt Smith
Jackie Smith
John Stallworth
Bart Starr
Roger Staubach
Ernie Stautner
Jan Stenerud
Dwight Stephenson
Michael Strahan
Hank Stram
Ken Strong
Joe Stydahar
Lynn Swann
Fran Tarkenton
Charley Taylor
Jim Taylor
Lawrence "LT" Taylor
Derrick Thomas
Emmitt Thomas
Thurman Thomas
Jim Thorpe
*Mick Tingelhoff
Andre Tippett
Y. A. Tittle
George Trafton
Charley Trippi
Emlen Tunnell
Clyde "Bulldog" Turner
Johnny Unitas
Gene Upshaw
Norm Van Brocklin
Steve Van Buren
Doak Walker
Bill Walsh
Paul Warfield
Bob Waterfield
Mike Webster
Randy White
Reggie White
Dave Wilcox
Aeneas Williams
Bill Willis
Larry Wilson
Ralph Wilson Jr.
Kellen Winslow
Alex Wojciechowicz
*Ron Wolf
Willie Wood
Rod Woodson
Rayfield Wright
Ron Yary
Steve Young
Jack Youngblood
Gary Zimmerman

All-Time NFL Coaching Victories

(at end of 2014 season; ranked by overall career wins; * = active in 2014)

			Regular Season				Overall			
Coach	**Team**	**Yrs**	**W**	**L**	**T**	**Pct**	**W**	**L**	**T**	**Pct**
Don Shula	Baltimore Colts, Dolphins	33	328	156	6	.677	347	173	6	.666
George Halas	Bears	40	318	148	31	.682	324	151	31	.682
Tom Landry	Cowboys	29	250	162	6	.607	270	178	6	.603
Bill Belichick*	Browns, Patriots	20	211	109	0	.659	233	118	0	.664
Earl "Curly" Lambeau	Packers, Chicago Cardinals, Redskins	33	226	132	22	.631	229	134	22	.631
Chuck Noll	Steelers	23	193	148	1	.566	209	156	1	.572
Marty Schottenheimer	Browns, Chiefs, Redskins, Chargers	21	200	126	1	.613	205	139	1	.596
Dan Reeves	Broncos, Giants, Falcons	23	190	165	2	.535	201	174	2	.536
Chuck Knox	L.A. Rams, Bills, Seahawks	22	186	147	1	.558	193	158	1	.550
Bill Parcells	Giants, Patriots, Jets, Cowboys	19	172	130	1	.569	183	138	1	.570
Mike Shanahan	L.A. Raiders, Broncos, Redskins	20	170	138	0	.552	178	144	0	.553
Tom Coughlin*	Jaguars, Giants	19	164	140	0	.539	176	147	0	.545
Mike Holmgren	Packers, Seahawks	17	161	111	0	.592	174	122	0	.588
Joe Gibbs	Redskins	16	154	94	0	.621	171	101	0	.629
Paul Brown	Browns, Bengals	21	166	100	6	.624	170	108	6	.612
Bud Grant	Vikings	18	158	96	5	.621	168	108	5	.608
Jeff Fisher*	Houston/Tennessee Oilers, Titans, St. Louis Rams	20	162	147	1	.524	167	153	1	.522
Bill Cowher	Steelers	15	149	90	1	.623	161	99	1	.619
Andy Reid*	Eagles, Chiefs	16	150	105	1	.588	160	115	1	.582

Note: Official NFL records do not include All-America Football Conference statistics.

BASEBALL

Playoff Results, 2015

American League

American League Wild Card Game: Houston defeated NY Yankees, 3-0.

American League Division Series (ALDS): Kansas City defeated Houston, 3 games to 2; Toronto defeated Texas, 3 games to 2.

American League Championship Series (ALCS): Kansas City defeated Toronto, 4 games to 2.

National League

National League Wild Card Game: Chicago Cubs defeated Pittsburgh, 4-0.

National League Division Series (NLDS): Chicago Cubs defeated St. Louis, 3 games to 1; NY Mets defeated L.A. Dodgers, 3 games to 2.

National League Championship Series (NLCS): NY Mets defeated Chicago Cubs, 4 games to 0.

World Series, 2015

Kansas City Royals Defeat the New York Mets in Five Games

The Kansas City Royals defeated the New York Mets in five games to win the 2015 World Series and their first MLB championship since 1985. All four Royals wins were come-from-behind victories, including the 7-2, extra-inning Game 5 series clincher on Nov. 1, 2015, at Citi Field in New York.

In the first-ever World Series matchup of expansion teams, the Royals claimed a Game 1 victory over the Mets at Kauffman Stadium in Kansas City. Shortstop Alcides Escobar led off with an inside-the-park home run off the first pitch in the home first inning. Outfielder Alex Gordon hit a game-tying solo homer in the bottom of the ninth off Mets closer Jeurys Familia; infielder Eric Hosmer delivered a sacrifice fly in the bottom of the 14th that scored Escobar for a 5-4 Royals win. Kansas City starting pitcher Johnny Cueto went the distance in Game 2, allowing only two hits in a complete game, 7-1 victory over the Mets Oct. 28. Escobar and Hosmer led a balanced attack, with two hits and two RBIs each.

The Mets got back into the series in Game 3 Oct. 30 at Citi Field as veteran third baseman David Wright homered and drove in four runs for a 9-3 Mets victory. Mets rookie outfielder Michael Conforto hit two home runs in Game 4 and the Mets took a 3-2 lead through seven innings. But the Royals went ahead in the eighth after Ben Zobrist scored the game-tying run on an error by Mets second baseman Daniel Murphy.

Mets starting pitcher Matt Harvey held the Royals scoreless until the ninth inning of Game 5, when outfielder Lorenzo Cain led off with a walk and scored on Hosmer's RBI double. Familia relieved Harvey, but Hosmer scored later in the inning on a wide throw to home, tying the game 2-2. Royals catcher Salvador Pérez started the Royals' five-run outburst in the 12th inning with a leadoff single, and pinch runner Jarrod Dyson scored the go-ahead run on a single by pinch hitter Christian Colon. Cain capped the rally with a bases-clearing, three-run double. Pérez, who batted .364 with eight hits, two doubles, and two RBIs, was voted World Series MVP.

Game 1

Oct. 27 at Kauffman Stadium, Kansas City, MO

	1	2	3	4	5	6	7	8	9	10	11	12	13	14	R	H	E
New York Mets	0	0	0	1	1	1	0	1	0	0	0	0	0	0	4	11	1
Kansas City Royals	1	0	0	0	0	2	0	0	1	0	0	0	0	1	5	11	1

Winning Pitcher: Chris Young
Losing Pitcher: Bartolo Colon
Attendance: 40,320

Game 2

Oct. 28 at Kauffman Stadium, Kansas City, MO

	1	2	3	4	5	6	7	8	9	R	H	E
New York Mets	0	0	0	1	0	0	0	0	0	1	2	1
Kansas City Royals	0	0	0	0	4	0	0	3	X	7	10	0

Winning Pitcher: Johnny Cueto
Losing Pitcher: Jacob deGrom
Attendance: 40,410

Game 3

Oct. 30 at Citi Field, New York, NY

	1	2	3	4	5	6	7	8	9	R	H	E
Kansas City Royals	1	2	0	0	0	0	0	0	0	3	7	0
New York Mets	2	0	2	1	0	4	0	0	X	9	12	0

Winning Pitcher: Noah Syndergaard
Losing Pitcher: Yordano Ventura
Attendance: 44,781

Game 4

Oct. 31 at Citi Field, New York, NY

	1	2	3	4	5	6	7	8	9	R	H	E
Kansas City Royals	0	0	0	0	1	1	0	3	0	5	9	0
New York Mets	0	0	2	0	1	0	0	0	0	3	6	2

Winning Pitcher: Ryan Madson
Losing Pitcher: Tyler Clippard
Save: Wade Davis
Attendance: 44,815

Game 5

Nov. 1 at Citi Field, New York, NY

	1	2	3	4	5	6	7	8	9	10	11	12	R	H	E
Kansas City Royals	0	0	0	0	0	0	0	0	2	0	0	5	7	10	1
New York Mets	1	0	0	0	0	1	0	0	0	0	0	0	2	4	2

Winning Pitcher: Luke Hochevar
Losing Pitcher: Addison Reed
Attendance: 44,859

Major League Baseball, 2015: Perennial Also-Rans Take the Postseason

The Kansas City Royals led the American League with 95 wins to earn the Central Division crown, their first division title in 30 years. Kansas City achieved an ALDS win over the wild-card Houston Astros, then faced the formidable Toronto Blue Jays, who led the majors with 232 home runs, in the ALCS. Josh Donaldson (41 home runs), Jose Bautista (40), and Edwin Encarnacion (39) had led a Toronto offense that carried Toronto to its first AL East title since 1993 and defeated the AL West champion Texas Rangers in the ALDS. Toronto acquired veteran left-hander David Price July 30; he went 9-1 for the Jays down the stretch. In the deciding Game 6 of the ALCS, an 8th-inning RBI single by Royals first baseman Eric Hosmer lifted KC to a 4-3 win over the Blue Jays Oct. 23, 2015, at Kauffman Stadium in Kansas City, MO. Royals shortstop Alcides Escobar batted .478 in the ALCS and earned the ALCS Most Valuable Player award.

A young pitching staff and late-season fireworks from outfielder Yoenis Cespedes (17 homers in 57 games after a July 31 trade) lifted the NY Mets to their first National League East title since 2006 and first NL pennant in 15 years. The Mets overcame outstanding pitching from the L.A. Dodgers, who won the NL West for the third straight year, to win the NLDS. New York infielder Daniel Murphy's solo home run off Zack Greinke—who led the majors with a 1.66 ERA—in the sixth inning of Game 5 was the difference in New York's 3-2 win Oct. 15, 2015, at Dodger Stadium in Los Angeles. Murphy continued his power onslaught in a four-game sweep of the Chicago Cubs in the NL Championship Series. Murphy batted .529 in the series to win NLCS MVP and set a major league postseason record with home runs in six consecutive playoff games.

The Cubs (97-65) beat Pittsburgh in the NL wild-card game, then dispatched the 100-win St. Louis Cardinals in four games in the NLDS. Cubs right-hander Jake Arrieta (22-6, 1.77 ERA) topped the MLB in wins, including a 2-0 no-hitter (one of seven league-wide in 2015) over the L.A. Dodgers Aug. 30, 2015, at Dodger Stadium. Washington's Max Scherzer became the first pitcher since Nolan Ryan in 1973 to pitch two no-hitters in a single regular season.

Detroit first baseman Miguel Cabrera (.338) won his fourth American League batting title in the past five seasons. Miami's Dee Gordon led the NL in batting (.333) and stolen bases (58), becoming the first NL player to lead the league in both categories in the same season since Jackie Robinson in 1949. Onetime superstar Alex Rodriguez rejoined the NY Yankees in 2015 following a one-year PED suspension and moved past Willie Mays for fourth-place on the all-time career home run list when he belted his 661st on May 7 at Yankee Stadium. New York lost the AL wild-card game, 3-0, to Houston on Oct. 6, 2015, at Yankee Stadium. The Astros reached the postseason for the first time since moving to the AL in 2013 on the strength of All-Star pitcher Dallas Keuchel (20-8, 2.48 ERA) and an offense that hit 230 home runs, second-most in the majors.

National League Final Standings, 2015

(* = wild card)

Eastern Division

Team	W	L	PCT	GB	Home	Road	vs. East	vs. Central	vs. West	vs. AL
NY Mets	90	72	.556	—	49-32	41-40	47-29	13-20	21-12	9-11
Washington	83	79	.512	7	46-35	37-44	44-32	14-19	17-16	8-12
Miami	71	91	.438	19	41-40	30-51	35-41	13-19	16-18	7-13
Atlanta	67	95	.414	23	42-39	25-56	34-42	15-18	12-21	6-14
Philadelphia	63	99	.389	27	37-44	26-55	30-46	11-23	14-18	8-12

Central Division

Team	W	L	PCT	GB	Home	Road	vs. East	vs. Central	vs. West	vs. AL
St. Louis	100	62	.617	—	55-26	45-36	20-12	46-30	23-11	11-9
Pittsburgh*	98	64	.605	2	53-28	45-36	24-9	34-42	27-6	13-7
Chicago Cubs*	97	65	.599	3	49-32	48-33	22-12	46-30	19-13	10-10
Milwaukee	68	94	.420	32	34-47	34-47	17-16	31-45	12-21	8-12
Cincinnati	64	98	.395	36	34-47	30-51	16-17	33-43	8-25	7-13

Western Division

Team	W	L	PCT	GB	Home	Road	vs. East	vs. Central	vs. West	vs. AL
L.A. Dodgers	92	70	.568	—	55-26	37-44	19-13	17-17	46-30	10-10
San Francisco	84	78	.519	8	47-34	37-44	18-15	15-18	38-38	13-7
Arizona	79	83	.488	13	39-42	40-41	15-18	14-19	39-37	11-9
San Diego	74	88	.457	18	39-42	35-46	17-16	15-18	35-41	7-13
Colorado	68	94	.420	24	36-45	32-49	16-18	15-17	32-44	5-15

American League Final Standings, 2015

(* = wild card)

Eastern Division

Team	W	L	PCT	GB	Home	Road	vs. East	vs. Central	vs. West	vs. NL
Toronto	93	69	.574	—	53-28	40-41	42-34	20-14	19-13	12-8
NY Yankees*	87	75	.537	6	45-36	42-39	38-38	21-12	17-16	11-9
Baltimore	81	81	.500	12	47-31	34-50	39-37	15-18	15-18	12-8
Tampa Bay	80	82	.494	13	42-42	38-40	36-40	13-19	17-17	14-6
Boston	78	84	.481	15	43-38	35-46	35-41	15-18	15-18	13-7

Central Division

Team	W	L	PCT	GB	Home	Road	vs. East	vs. Central	vs. West	vs. NL
Kansas City	95	67	.586	—	51-30	44-37	18-16	44-32	20-12	13-7
Minnesota	83	79	.512	12	46-35	37-44	19-14	40-36	16-17	8-12
Cleveland	81	80	.503	13.5	39-41	42-39	18-15	32-43	19-14	12-8
Chicago White Sox	76	86	.469	19	40-41	36-45	14-19	32-44	21-12	9-11
Detroit	74	87	.460	20.5	38-43	36-44	12-20	41-34	12-22	9-11

Western Division

Team	W	L	PCT	GB	Home	Road	vs. East	vs. Central	vs. West	vs. NL
Texas	88	74	.543	—	43-38	45-36	23-11	18-14	36-40	11-9
Houston*	86	76	.531	2	53-28	33-48	18-16	14-18	38-38	16-4
L.A. Angels	85	77	.525	3	49-32	36-45	16-16	17-17	44-32	8-12
Seattle	76	86	.469	12	36-45	40-41	15-17	14-20	39-37	8-12
Oakland	68	94	.420	20	34-47	34-47	10-23	14-19	33-43	11-9

National League Statistics, 2015

Individual statistics. Players recording fewer than 150 at-bats (batters) or fewer than 70 innings or 10 saves (pitchers) are not listed here. * = changed teams within NL during season; entry includes statistics for more than one team. # = changed teams to or from AL during season; entry includes only NL statistics. Team Batting and Team Pitching include players not shown separately.

Team Batting

Team	AVG	AB	R	H	HR	RBI
San Francisco Giants	.267	5,565	696	1,486	136	663
Colorado Rockies	.265	5,572	737	1,479	186	702
Arizona Diamondbacks	.264	5,649	720	1,494	154	680
Miami Marlins	.260	5,463	613	1,420	120	575
Pittsburgh Pirates	.260	5,631	697	1,462	140	661
St. Louis Cardinals	.253	5,484	647	1,386	137	619
Milwaukee Brewers	.251	5,480	655	1,378	145	624
Atlanta Braves	.251	5,420	573	1,361	100	548
Washington Nationals	.251	5,428	703	1,363	177	665
Los Angeles Dodgers	.250	5,385	667	1,346	187	638
Philadelphia Phillies	.249	5,529	626	1,374	130	586
Cincinnati Reds	.248	5,571	640	1,382	167	613
New York Mets	.244	5,527	683	1,351	177	654
Chicago Cubs	.244	5,491	689	1,341	171	657
San Diego Padres	.243	5,457	650	1,324	148	623

Team Pitching

Team	ERA	IP	H	BB	SO	SV
St. Louis Cardinals	2.94	1,464.2	1,359	477	1,329	62
Pittsburgh Pirates	3.21	1,489.2	1,392	453	1,338	54
Chicago Cubs	3.36	1,461.1	1,276	407	1,431	48
New York Mets	3.43	1,462.2	1,341	383	1,337	50
Los Angeles Dodgers	3.44	1,445.2	1,317	395	1,396	47
Washington Nationals	3.62	1,434.2	1,366	364	1,342	41
San Francisco Giants	3.72	1,444.1	1,344	431	1,165	41
Miami Marlins	4.02	1,427.0	1,374	508	1,152	35
Arizona Diamondbacks	4.04	1,466.2	1,450	500	1,215	44
San Diego Padres	4.09	1,440.1	1,371	516	1,393	41
Milwaukee Brewers	4.28	1,435.0	1,432	517	1,260	40
Cincinnati Reds	4.33	1,453.1	1,436	544	1,252	35
Atlanta Braves	4.41	1,425.1	1,462	550	1,148	44
Philadelphia Phillies	4.69	1,436.1	1,592	488	1,153	35
Colorado Rockies	5.04	1,426.1	1,579	579	1,112	36

Arizona Diamondbacks

Batters	AVG	AB	R	H	HR	RBI	SO	SB
Paul Goldschmidt	.321	567	103	182	33	110	151	21
A. J. Pollock	.315	609	111	192	20	76	89	39
David Peralta	.312	462	61	144	17	78	107	9
Ender Inciarte	.303	524	73	159	6	45	58	21
Yasmany Tomas	.273	406	40	111	9	48	110	5
Jake Lamb	.263	350	38	92	6	34	97	3
Mark Trumbo#	.259	174	23	45	9	23	39	0
Welington Castillo#	.243	317	39	77	19	55	87	0
Aaron Hill	.230	313	32	72	6	39	54	7
Chris Owings	.227	515	59	117	4	43	144	16
Nick Ahmed	.226	421	49	95	9	34	81	4
Jarrod Saltalamacchia*	.225	200	26	45	9	24	69	0

Pitchers	ERA	W	L	IP	H	BB	SO	SV
Brad Ziegler	1.85	0	3	68.0	48	17	36	30
Andrew Chafin	2.76	5	1	75.0	56	30	58	2
Randall Delgado	3.25	8	4	72.0	63	33	73	1
Robbie Ray	3.52	5	12	127.2	121	49	119	0
Patrick Corbin	3.60	6	5	85.0	91	17	78	0
Josh Collmenter	3.79	4	6	121.0	129	24	63	1
Chase Anderson	4.30	6	6	152.2	158	40	111	0
Jeremy Hellickson	4.62	9	12	146.0	151	43	121	0
Rubby De La Rosa	4.67	14	9	188.2	193	63	150	0

Manager: Chip Hale

Atlanta Braves

Batters	AVG	AB	R	H	HR	RBI	SO	SB
A. J. Pierzynski	.300	407	38	122	9	49	37	0
Nick Markakis	.296	612	73	181	3	53	83	2
Adonis Garcia	.277	191	20	53	10	26	35	0
Freddie Freeman	.276	416	62	115	18	66	98	3
Cameron Maybin	.267	505	65	135	10	59	102	23
Kelly Johnson*	.265	310	38	82	14	47	81	2
Andrelton Simmons	.265	535	60	142	4	44	48	5
Juan Uribe*	.253	360	40	91	14	43	80	2
Jace Peterson	.239	528	55	126	6	52	120	12
Chris Johnson#	.235	153	12	36	2	11	49	2
Alberto Callaspo*	.235	230	20	54	1	15	34	0
Jonny Gomes#	.221	195	27	43	7	22	67	1
Christian Bethancourt	.200	155	16	31	2	12	33	1

Pitchers	ERA	W	L	IP	H	BB	SO	SV
Jason Grilli	2.94	3	4	33.2	28	10	45	24
Shelby Miller	3.02	6	17	205.1	183	73	171	0
Alex Wood*	3.84	12	12	189.2	198	59	139	0
Julio Teheran	4.04	11	8	200.2	189	73	171	0
Jim Johnson*	4.46	2	6	66.2	77	20	50	10
Matt Wisler	4.71	8	8	109.0	119	40	72	0
Williams Perez	4.78	7	6	116.2	130	51	73	1
Mike Foltynewicz	5.71	4	6	86.2	112	29	77	0

Manager: Fredi González

Chicago Cubs

Batters	AVG	AB	R	H	HR	RBI	SO	SB
Anthony Rizzo	.278	586	94	163	31	101	105	17
Kris Bryant	.275	559	87	154	26	99	199	13
Chris Denorfia	.269	212	18	57	3	18	56	0
Starlin Castro	.265	547	52	145	11	69	91	5
Jorge Soler	.262	366	39	96	10	47	121	3
Dexter Fowler	.250	596	102	149	17	46	154	20
Chris Coghlan	.250	440	64	110	16	41	94	11
Miguel Montero	.248	347	36	86	15	53	103	1
Kyle Schwarber	.246	232	52	57	16	43	77	3
Welington Castillo#	.243	317	39	77	19	55	87	0
Addison Russell	.242	475	60	115	13	54	149	4
David Ross	.176	159	6	28	1	9	61	1

Pitchers	ERA	W	L	IP	H	BB	SO	SV
Hector Rondon	1.67	6	4	70.0	55	15	69	30
Jake Arrieta	1.77	22	6	229.0	150	48	236	0
Jon Lester	3.34	11	12	205.0	183	47	207	0
Dan Haren*	3.60	11	9	187.1	174	38	132	0
Jason Hammel	3.74	10	7	170.2	158	40	172	0
Travis Wood	3.84	5	4	100.2	86	39	118	4
Kyle Hendricks	3.95	8	7	180.0	166	43	167	0

Manager: Joe Maddon

Cincinnati Reds

Batters	AVG	AB	R	H	HR	RBI	SO	SB
Joey Votto	.314	545	95	171	29	80	135	11
Brandon Phillips	.294	588	69	173	12	70	68	23
Eugenio Suarez	.280	372	42	104	13	48	94	4
Brayan Pena	.273	333	17	91	0	18	34	2
Zack Cozart	.258	194	28	50	9	28	29	3
Todd Frazier	.255	619	82	158	35	89	137	13
Tucker Barnhart	.252	242	23	61	3	18	45	0
Marlon Byrd*	.247	506	58	125	23	73	145	2
Ivan De Jesus	.244	201	15	49	4	28	55	0
Skip Schumaker	.242	244	23	59	1	21	51	2
Jason Bourgeois	.240	196	28	47	3	14	33	3
Jay Bruce	.226	580	72	131	26	87	145	9
Billy Hamilton	.226	412	56	93	4	28	75	57

Pitchers	ERA	W	L	IP	H	BB	SO	SV
Aroldis Chapman	1.63	4	4	66.1	43	33	116	33
Johnny Cueto#	2.62	7	6	130.2	93	29	120	0
Mike Leake*	3.70	11	10	192.0	174	49	119	0
Anthony DeSclafani	4.05	9	13	184.2	194	55	151	0
Raisel Iglesias	4.15	3	7	95.1	81	28	104	0
Michael Lorenzen	5.40	4	9	113.1	131	57	83	0

Manager: Bryan Price

Colorado Rockies

Batters	AVG	AB	R	H	HR	RBI	SO	SB
Justin Morneau	.310	168	19	52	3	15	25	0
Corey Dickerson	.304	224	30	68	10	31	56	0

Batters	AVG	AB	R	H	HR	RBI	SO	SB
DJ LeMahieu	.301	564	85	170	6	61	107	23
Nick Hundley	.301	366	45	110	10	43	76	5
Troy Tulowitzki#	.300	323	46	97	12	53	72	0
Nolan Arenado	.287	616	97	177	42	130	110	2
Charlie Blackmon	.287	614	93	176	17	58	112	43
Ben Paulsen	.277	325	42	90	11	49	92	1
Carlos Gonzalez	.271	554	87	150	40	97	133	2
Wilin Rosario	.268	231	22	62	6	29	56	2
Jose Reyes#	.259	193	21	50	3	19	24	8
Brandon Barnes	.251	255	30	64	2	17	67	4
Daniel Descalso	.205	185	22	38	5	22	45	1

Pitchers	ERA	W	L	IP	H	BB	SO	SV
Jorge De La Rosa	4.17	9	7	149.0	137	65	134	0
John Axford	4.20	4	5	55.2	56	32	62	25
Chad Bettis	4.23	8	6	115.0	120	42	98	0
Chris Rusin	5.33	6	10	131.2	170	41	86	0
Eddie Butler	5.90	3	10	79.1	102	42	44	0
David Hale	6.09	5	5	78.1	95	20	61	0
Kyle Kendrick	6.32	7	13	142.1	172	45	80	0

Manager: Walt Weiss

Los Angeles Dodgers

Batters	AVG	AB	R	H	HR	RBI	SO	SB
Enrique Hernandez	.307	202	24	62	7	22	46	0
Howie Kendrick	.295	464	64	137	9	54	82	6
Andre Ethier	.294	395	54	116	14	53	75	2
Justin Turner	.294	385	55	113	16	60	71	5
Adrian Gonzalez	.275	571	76	157	28	90	107	0
Carl Crawford	.265	181	19	48	4	16	41	10
Yasiel Puig	.255	282	30	72	11	38	66	3
Juan Uribe*	.253	360	40	91	14	43	80	2
Scott Van Slyke	.239	222	19	53	6	30	62	3
A. J. Ellis	.238	181	24	43	7	21	38	0
Alberto Callaspo*	.235	230	20	54	1	15	34	0
Yasmani Grandal	.234	355	43	83	16	47	92	0
Alex Guerrero	.233	219	25	51	11	36	57	1
Jimmy Rollins	.224	517	71	116	13	41	86	12
Chase Utley*	.212	373	37	79	8	39	64	4
Joc Pederson	.210	480	67	101	26	54	170	4

Pitchers	ERA	W	L	IP	H	BB	SO	SV
Zack Greinke	1.66	19	3	222.2	148	40	200	0
Clayton Kershaw	2.13	16	7	232.2	163	42	301	0
Kenley Jansen	2.41	2	1	52.1	33	8	80	36
Mike Bolsinger	3.62	6	6	109.1	104	45	98	0
Brett Anderson	3.69	10	9	180.1	194	46	116	0
Alex Wood*	3.84	12	12	189.2	198	59	139	0
Carlos Frias	4.06	5	5	77.2	88	26	43	0
Jim Johnson*	4.46	2	6	66.2	77	20	50	10
Mat Latos#	4.95	4	10	112.2	116	31	97	0

Manager: Don Mattingly

Miami Marlins

Batters	AVG	AB	R	H	HR	RBI	SO	SB
Dee Gordon	.333	615	88	205	4	46	91	58
Christian Yelich	.300	476	63	143	7	44	101	16
Martin Prado	.288	500	52	144	9	63	68	1
Adeiny Hechavarria	.281	470	54	132	5	48	78	7
Giancarlo Stanton	.265	279	47	74	27	67	95	4
Justin Bour	.262	409	42	107	23	73	101	0
Marcell Ozuna	.259	459	47	119	10	44	110	2
J. T. Realmuto	.259	441	49	114	10	47	70	8
Derek Dietrich	.256	250	38	64	10	24	65	0
Michael Morse*	.231	229	14	53	5	19	76	0
Ichiro Suzuki	.229	398	45	91	1	21	51	11
Jarrod Saltalamacchia*	.225	200	26	45	9	24	69	0
Casey McGehee*	.198	237	14	47	2	20	50	1

Pitchers	ERA	W	L	IP	H	BB	SO	SV
A. J. Ramos	2.30	2	4	70.1	45	26	87	32
Dan Haren*	3.60	11	9	187.1	174	38	132	0
Justin Nicolino	4.01	5	4	74.0	72	20	23	0
Tom Koehler	4.08	11	14	187.1	180	77	137	0
David Phelps	4.50	4	8	112.0	119	33	77	0
Mat Latos#	4.95	4	10	112.2	116	31	97	0
Brad Hand	5.30	4	7	93.1	107	32	67	0

Managers: Mike Redmond, Dan Jennings

Milwaukee Brewers

Batters	AVG	AB	R	H	HR	RBI	SO	SB
Gerardo Parra#	.328	323	53	106	9	31	57	9
Jason Rogers	.296	152	22	45	4	16	34	0
Ryan Braun	.285	506	87	144	25	84	115	24
Adam Lind	.277	502	72	139	20	87	100	0
Hernan Perez#	.270	230	13	62	1	21	48	4
Jonathan Lucroy	.264	371	51	98	7	43	64	1
Scooter Gennett	.264	375	42	99	6	29	68	1
Carlos Gomez#	.262	286	42	75	8	43	70	7
Shane Peterson	.259	201	22	52	2	16	55	0
Jean Segura	.257	560	57	144	6	50	93	25
Khris Davis	.247	392	54	97	27	66	122	6
Aramis Ramirez*	.246	475	43	117	17	75	68	1
Elian Herrera	.242	256	29	62	7	33	72	3
Martin Maldonado	.210	229	19	48	4	22	65	0

Pitchers	ERA	W	L	IP	H	BB	SO	SV
Francisco Rodriguez	2.21	1	3	57.0	38	11	62	38
Taylor Jungmann	3.77	9	8	119.1	106	47	107	0
Mike Fiers#	3.89	5	9	118.0	117	43	121	0
Jimmy Nelson	4.11	11	13	177.1	163	65	148	0
Wily Peralta	4.72	5	10	108.2	130	37	60	0
Matt Garza	5.63	6	14	148.2	176	57	104	0
Kyle Lohse	5.85	5	13	152.1	180	43	108	2

Managers: Ron Roenicke, Craig Counsell

New York Mets

Batters	AVG	AB	R	H	HR	RBI	SO	SB
David Wright	.289	152	24	44	5	17	36	2
Yoenis Cespedes#	.287	230	39	66	17	44	54	4
Daniel Murphy	.281	499	56	140	14	73	38	2
Michael Conforto	.270	174	30	47	9	26	39	0
Travis d'Arnaud	.268	239	31	64	12	41	49	0
Kelly Johnson*	.265	310	38	82	14	47	81	2
Wilmer Flores	.263	483	55	127	16	59	63	0
Ruben Tejada	.261	360	36	94	3	28	70	2
Curtis Granderson	.259	580	98	150	26	70	151	11
Michael Cuddyer	.259	379	44	98	10	41	88	2
Juan Lagares	.259	441	47	114	6	41	87	7
Juan Uribe*	.253	360	40	91	14	43	80	2
Lucas Duda	.244	471	67	115	27	73	138	0
Kevin Plawecki	.219	233	18	51	3	21	60	0
Eric Campbell	.197	173	28	34	3	19	37	5

Pitchers	ERA	W	L	IP	H	BB	SO	SV
Jeurys Familia	1.85	2	2	78.0	59	19	86	43
Jacob deGrom	2.54	14	8	191.0	149	38	205	0
Matt Harvey	2.71	13	8	189.1	156	37	188	0
Noah Syndergaard	3.24	9	7	150.0	126	31	166	0
Jonathon Niese	4.13	9	10	176.2	192	55	113	0
Bartolo Colon	4.16	14	13	194.2	217	24	136	0

Manager: Terry Collins

Philadelphia Phillies

Batters	AVG	AB	R	H	HR	RBI	SO	SB
Ben Revere#	.298	366	49	109	1	26	36	24
Odubel Herrera	.297	495	64	147	8	41	129	16
Andres Blanco	.292	233	32	68	7	25	44	1
Maikel Franco	.280	304	45	85	14	50	52	1
Cesar Hernandez	.272	405	57	110	1	35	86	19
Freddy Galvis	.263	559	63	147	7	50	103	10
Jeff Francoeur	.258	326	34	84	13	45	77	0
Cody Asche	.245	425	41	104	12	39	111	1

Batters	AVG	AB	R	H	HR	RBI	SO	SB
Darin Ruf	.235	268	30	63	12	39	69	1
Cameron Rupp	.233	270	24	63	9	28	71	0
Ryan Howard	.229	467	53	107	23	77	138	0
Domonic Brown	.228	189	19	43	5	25	36	3
Chase Utley*	.212	373	37	79	8	39	64	4
Carlos Ruiz	.211	284	23	60	2	22	43	1

Pitchers	ERA	W	L	IP	H	BB	SO	SV
Ken Giles	1.80	6	3	70.0	59	25	87	15
Jonathan Papelbon*	2.13	4	3	63.1	53	12	56	24
Jeanmar Gomez	3.01	2	3	74.2	82	17	50	0
Aaron Nola	3.59	6	2	77.2	74	19	68	0
Cole Hamels#	3.64	6	7	128.2	113	39	137	0
Adam Morgan	4.48	5	7	84.1	88	17	49	0
Aaron Harang	4.86	6	15	172.1	189	51	108	0
Justin De Fratus	5.51	0	2	80.0	92	32	68	0
Jerome Williams	5.80	4	12	121.0	161	34	74	1
Sean O'Sullivan	6.08	1	6	71.0	94	20	35	0
David Buchanan	6.99	2	9	74.2	109	29	44	0

Managers: Ryne Sandberg, Pete Mackanin

Pittsburgh Pirates

Batters	AVG	AB	R	H	HR	RBI	SO	SB
Francisco Cervelli	.295	451	56	133	7	43	94	1
Andrew McCutchen	.292	566	91	165	23	96	133	11
Chris Stewart	.289	159	9	46	0	15	29	0
Jung Ho Kang	.287	421	60	121	15	58	99	5
Josh Harrison	.287	418	57	120	4	28	71	10
Starling Marte	.287	579	84	166	19	81	123	30
Neil Walker	.269	543	69	146	16	71	110	4
Gregory Polanco	.256	593	83	152	9	52	121	27
Sean Rodriguez	.246	224	25	55	4	17	63	2
Aramis Ramirez*	.246	475	43	117	17	75	68	1
Jordy Mercer	.244	394	34	96	3	34	73	3
Pedro Alvarez	.243	437	60	106	27	77	131	2
Michael Morse*	.231	229	14	53	5	19	76	0

Pitchers	ERA	W	L	IP	H	BB	SO	SV
Tony Watson	1.91	4	1	75.1	55	17	62	1
Mark Melancon	2.23	3	2	76.2	57	14	62	51
Gerrit Cole	2.60	19	8	208.0	183	44	202	0
A. J. Burnett	3.18	9	7	164.0	174	49	143	0
Francisco Liriano	3.38	12	7	186.2	155	70	205	0
Arquimedes Caminero	3.62	5	1	74.2	63	29	73	0
Vance Worley	4.02	4	6	71.2	81	21	49	0
Jeff Locke	4.49	8	11	168.1	179	60	129	0
Charlie Morton	4.81	9	9	129.0	137	41	96	0

Manager: Clint Hurdle

St. Louis Cardinals

Batters	AVG	AB	R	H	HR	RBI	SO	SB
Stephen Piscotty	.305	233	29	71	7	39	56	2
Jason Heyward	.293	547	79	160	13	60	90	23
Matt Holliday	.279	229	24	64	4	35	49	2
Randal Grichuk	.276	323	49	89	17	47	110	4
Jhonny Peralta	.275	579	64	159	17	71	111	1
Matt Carpenter	.272	574	101	156	28	84	151	4
Yadier Molina	.270	488	34	132	4	61	59	3
Thomas Pham	.268	153	28	41	5	18	41	2
Kolten Wong	.262	557	71	146	11	61	95	15
Matt Adams	.240	175	14	42	5	24	41	1
Mark Reynolds	.230	382	35	88	13	48	121	2
Jon Jay	.210	210	25	44	1	10	36	0
Peter Bourjos	.200	195	32	39	4	13	59	5

Pitchers	ERA	W	L	IP	H	BB	SO	SV
Trevor Rosenthal	2.10	2	4	68.2	62	25	83	48
Kevin Siegrist	2.17	7	1	74.2	53	34	90	6
Jaime Garcia	2.43	10	6	129.2	106	30	97	0
John Lackey	2.77	13	10	218.0	211	53	175	0
Carlos Martinez	3.01	14	7	179.2	168	63	184	0
Lance Lynn	3.03	12	11	175.1	172	68	167	0
Michael Wacha	3.38	17	7	181.1	162	58	153	0

Manager: Mike Matheny

San Diego Padres

Batters	AVG	AB	R	H	HR	RBI	SO	SB
Yonder Alonso	.282	354	50	100	5	31	48	2
Cory Spangenberg	.271	303	38	82	4	21	75	9
Yangervis Solarte	.270	526	63	142	14	63	56	1
Matt Kemp	.265	596	80	158	23	100	147	12
Melvin Upton Jr.	.259	205	23	53	5	17	62	9
Will Venable#	.258	283	34	73	6	30	73	11
Wil Myers	.253	225	40	57	8	29	55	5
Justin Upton	.251	542	85	136	26	81	159	19
Derek Norris	.250	515	65	129	14	62	131	4
Jedd Gyorko	.247	421	34	104	16	57	107	0
Clint Barmes	.232	207	24	48	3	16	55	0
Will Middlebrooks	.212	255	23	54	9	29	60	2
Alexi Amarista	.204	324	28	66	3	30	55	5

Pitchers	ERA	W	L	IP	H	BB	SO	SV
Craig Kimbrel	2.58	4	2	59.1	40	22	87	39
Tyson Ross	3.26	10	12	196.0	172	84	212	0
James Shields	3.91	13	7	202.1	189	81	216	0
Ian Kennedy	4.28	9	15	168.1	166	52	174	0
Andrew Cashner	4.34	6	16	184.2	200	66	165	0
Odrisamer Despaigne	5.80	5	9	125.2	142	32	69	0

Managers: Bud Black, Dave Roberts, Pat Murphy

San Francisco Giants

Batters	AVG	AB	R	H	HR	RBI	SO	SB
Buster Posey	.318	557	74	177	19	95	52	2
Joe Panik	.312	382	59	119	8	37	42	3
Kelby Tomlinson	.303	178	23	54	2	20	40	5
Matt Duffy	.295	573	77	169	12	77	96	12
Gregor Blanco	.291	327	59	95	5	26	59	13
Nori Aoki	.287	355	42	102	5	26	25	14
Brandon Belt	.280	492	73	138	18	68	147	9
Hunter Pence	.275	207	30	57	9	40	48	4
Angel Pagan	.262	512	55	134	3	37	93	12
Brandon Crawford	.256	507	65	130	21	84	119	6
Marlon Byrd*	.247	506	58	125	23	73	145	2
Justin Maxwell	.209	249	26	52	7	26	76	2
Casey McGehee*	.198	237	14	47	2	20	50	1

Pitchers	ERA	W	L	IP	H	BB	SO	SV
George Kontos	2.33	4	4	73.1	57	12	44	0
Santiago Casilla	2.79	4	2	58.0	51	23	62	38
Madison Bumgarner	2.93	18	9	218.1	181	39	234	0
Jake Peavy	3.58	8	6	110.2	99	25	78	0
Yusmeiro Petit	3.67	1	1	76.0	75	15	59	1
Mike Leake*	3.70	11	10	192.0	174	49	119	0
Chris Heston	3.95	12	11	177.2	169	64	141	0
Tim Lincecum	4.13	7	4	76.1	75	38	60	0
Tim Hudson	4.44	8	9	123.2	134	37	64	0
Ryan Vogelsong	4.67	9	11	135.0	140	58	108	0

Manager: Bruce Bochy

Washington Nationals

Batters	AVG	AB	R	H	HR	RBI	SO	SB
Bryce Harper	.330	521	118	172	42	99	131	6
Yunel Escobar	.314	535	75	168	9	56	70	2
Denard Span	.301	246	38	74	5	22	26	11
Clint Robinson	.272	309	44	84	10	34	52	0
Anthony Rendon	.264	311	43	82	5	25	70	1
Ryan Zimmerman	.249	346	43	86	16	73	79	1
Danny Espinosa	.240	367	59	88	13	37	106	5
Ian Desmond	.233	583	69	136	19	62	187	13
Wilson Ramos	.229	475	41	109	15	68	101	0
Michael Taylor	.229	472	49	108	14	63	158	16
Jayson Werth	.221	331	51	73	12	42	84	0
Tyler Moore	.203	187	14	38	6	27	45	0

Pitchers	ERA	W	L	IP	H	BB	SO	SV
Jonathan Papelbon*	2.13	4	3	63.1	53	12	56	24
Max Scherzer	2.79	14	12	228.2	176	34	276	0
Drew Storen	3.44	2	2	55.0	45	16	67	29
Stephen Strasburg	3.46	11	7	127.1	115	26	155	0
Joe Ross	3.64	5	5	76.2	64	21	69	0
Jordan Zimmermann	3.66	13	10	201.2	204	39	164	0
Gio Gonzalez	3.79	11	8	175.2	181	69	169	0
Doug Fister	4.19	5	7	103.0	120	24	63	1
Tanner Roark	4.38	4	7	111.0	119	26	70	1

Manager: Matt Williams

American League Statistics, 2015

Individual statistics. Players recording fewer than 150 at-bats (batters) or fewer than 70 innings or 10 saves (pitchers) are not listed here. * = Changed teams within AL during season; entry includes statistics for more than one team. # = Changed teams to or from NL during season; entry includes only AL statistics. Team Batting and Team Pitching include players not shown separately.

Team Batting

Team	AVG	AB	R	H	HR	RBI
Detroit Tigers	.270	5,605	689	1,515	151	660
Toronto Blue Jays	.269	5,509	891	1,480	232	852
Kansas City Royals	.269	5,575	724	1,497	139	689
Boston Red Sox	.265	5,640	748	1,496	161	706
Texas Rangers	.257	5,511	751	1,419	172	707
Cleveland Indians	.256	5,439	669	1,395	141	640
Tampa Bay Rays	.252	5,485	644	1,383	167	612
New York Yankees	.251	5,567	764	1,397	212	737
Oakland Athletics	.251	5,600	694	1,405	146	661
Baltimore Orioles	.250	5,485	713	1,370	217	686
Houston Astros	.250	5,459	729	1,363	230	691
Chicago White Sox	.250	5,533	622	1,381	136	595
Seattle Mariners	.249	5,544	656	1,379	198	624
Minnesota Twins	.247	5,467	696	1,349	156	661
Los Angeles Angels	.246	5,417	661	1,331	176	621

Team Pitching

Team	ERA	IP	H	BB	SO	SV
Houston Astros	3.57	1,441.0	1,308	423	1,280	39
Cleveland Indians	3.67	1,432.2	1,274	425	1,407	38
Kansas City Royals	3.73	1,452.0	1,372	489	1,160	56
Tampa Bay Rays	3.74	1,453.1	1,314	477	1,355	60
Toronto Blue Jays	3.80	1,441.0	1,353	397	1,117	34
Los Angeles Angels	3.94	1,440.2	1,355	466	1,221	46
Chicago White Sox	3.98	1,452.2	1,443	474	1,359	37
New York Yankees	4.05	1,457.2	1,417	474	1,370	48
Baltimore Orioles	4.05	1,434.2	1,406	483	1,233	43
Minnesota Twins	4.07	1,443.0	1,506	413	1,046	45
Oakland Athletics	4.14	1,444.2	1,402	474	1,179	28
Seattle Mariners	4.16	1,463.0	1,430	491	1,283	45
Texas Rangers	4.24	1,442.2	1,459	508	1,095	45
Boston Red Sox	4.31	1,448.1	1,486	478	1,218	40
Detroit Tigers	4.64	1,447.0	1,491	489	1,100	35

Baltimore Orioles

Batters	AVG	AB	R	H	HR	RBI	SO	SB
Manny Machado	.286	633	102	181	35	86	111	20
Jonathan Schoop	.279	305	34	85	15	39	79	2
Jimmy Paredes	.275	363	46	100	10	42	111	4
Delmon Young	.270	174	20	47	2	16	29	0
Adam Jones	.269	546	74	147	27	82	102	3
Matt Wieters	.267	258	24	69	8	25	67	0
Chris Davis	.262	573	100	150	47	117	208	2
Alejandro De Aza#	.261	264	39	69	7	32	70	5
Nolan Reimold	.247	170	24	42	6	20	47	0
Travis Snider#	.237	211	23	50	3	20	56	1
Gerardo Parra#	.237	224	30	53	5	20	35	5
Caleb Joseph	.234	320	38	75	11	49	72	0
J. J. Hardy	.219	411	45	90	8	37	88	0
Steve Pearce	.218	294	42	64	15	40	69	1
Ryan Flaherty	.202	267	34	54	9	31	81	0

Pitchers	ERA	W	L	IP	H	BB	SO	SV
Zach Britton	1.92	4	1	65.2	51	14	79	36
Brad Brach	2.72	5	3	79.1	57	38	89	1
Wei-Yin Chen	3.34	11	8	191.1	192	41	153	0
Ubaldo Jimenez	4.11	12	10	184.0	182	68	168	0
Kevin Gausman	4.25	4	7	112.1	109	29	103	0
Miguel Gonzalez	4.91	9	12	144.2	151	51	109	0
Chris Tillman	4.99	11	11	173.0	176	64	120	0

Manager: Buck Showalter

Boston Red Sox

Batters	AVG	AB	R	H	HR	RBI	SO	SB
Xander Bogaerts	.320	613	84	196	7	81	101	10
Mookie Betts	.291	597	92	174	18	77	82	21
Dustin Pedroia	.291	381	46	111	12	42	51	2
Brock Holt	.280	454	56	127	2	45	97	8
Travis Shaw	.274	226	31	62	13	36	57	0
Blake Swihart	.274	288	47	79	5	31	77	4
David Ortiz	.273	528	73	144	37	108	95	0
Alejandro De Aza#	.261	264	39	69	7	32	70	5
Rusney Castillo	.253	273	35	69	5	29	54	4
Hanley Ramirez	.249	401	59	100	19	53	71	6
Jackie Bradley Jr.	.249	221	43	55	10	43	69	3
Ryan Hanigan	.247	174	28	43	2	16	39	0
Pablo Sandoval	.245	470	43	115	10	47	73	0
Shane Victorino*	.230	178	19	41	1	7	32	7
Mike Napoli*	.224	407	46	91	18	50	118	3

Pitchers	ERA	W	L	IP	H	BB	SO	SV
Koji Uehara	2.23	2	4	40.1	28	9	47	25
Clay Buchholz	3.26	7	7	113.1	114	23	107	0
Eduardo Rodriguez	3.85	10	6	121.2	120	37	98	0
Steven Wright	4.09	5	4	72.2	67	27	52	0
Wade Miley	4.46	11	11	193.2	201	64	147	0
Joe Kelly	4.82	10	6	134.1	145	49	110	0
Rick Porcello	4.92	9	15	172.0	196	38	149	0

Manager: John Farrell

Chicago White Sox

Batters	AVG	AB	R	H	HR	RBI	SO	SB
Jose Abreu	.290	613	88	178	30	101	140	0
Adam Eaton	.287	610	98	175	14	56	131	18
Melky Cabrera	.273	629	70	172	12	77	88	3
Avisail Garcia	.257	553	66	142	13	59	141	7
Alexei Ramirez	.249	583	54	145	10	62	68	17
Tyler Flowers	.239	331	21	79	9	39	104	0
Conor Gillaspie*	.228	237	14	54	4	24	47	0
Tyler Saladino	.225	236	33	53	4	20	51	8
Carlos Sanchez	.224	389	40	87	5	31	81	2
Geovany Soto	.219	187	20	41	9	21	63	0
Gordon Beckham	.209	211	24	44	6	20	43	0
Adam LaRoche	.207	429	41	89	12	44	133	0

Pitchers	ERA	W	L	IP	H	BB	SO	SV
Jose Quintana	3.36	9	10	206.1	218	44	177	0
Chris Sale	3.41	13	11	208.2	185	42	274	0
David Robertson	3.41	6	5	63.1	46	13	86	34
Carlos Rodon	3.75	9	6	139.1	130	71	139	0
John Danks	4.71	7	15	177.2	195	56	124	0
Jeff Samardzija	4.96	11	13	214.0	228	49	163	0

Manager: Robin Ventura

Cleveland Indians

Batters	AVG	AB	R	H	HR	RBI	SO	SB
Francisco Lindor	.313	390	50	122	12	51	69	12
Michael Brantley	.310	529	68	164	15	84	51	15
Jason Kipnis	.303	565	86	171	9	52	107	12
Ryan Raburn	.301	173	22	52	8	29	44	0
David Murphy*	.283	361	38	102	10	50	49	0
Abraham Almonte#	.264	178	30	47	5	20	33	6
Lonnie Chisenhall	.246	333	38	82	7	44	69	4
Michael Bourn#	.246	289	29	71	0	19	76	13
Yan Gomes	.231	363	38	84	12	45	104	0
Mike Aviles	.231	290	37	67	5	17	38	3
Carlos Santana	.231	550	72	127	19	85	122	11
Roberto Perez	.228	184	30	42	7	21	64	0
Giovanny Urshela	.225	267	25	60	6	21	58	0
Jose Ramirez	.219	315	50	69	6	27	39	10
Brandon Moss#	.217	337	36	73	15	50	106	0

Pitchers	ERA	W	L	IP	H	BB	SO	SV
Cody Allen	2.99	2	5	69.1	56	25	99	34
Cody Anderson	3.05	7	3	91.1	77	24	44	0
Danny Salazar	3.45	14	10	185.0	156	53	195	0
Corey Kluber	3.49	9	16	222.0	189	45	245	0
Carlos Carrasco	3.63	14	12	183.2	154	43	216	0
Trevor Bauer	4.55	11	12	176.0	152	79	170	0

Manager: Terry Francona

Detroit Tigers

Batters	AVG	AB	R	H	HR	RBI	SO	SB
Miguel Cabrera	.338	429	64	145	18	76	82	1
Jose Iglesias	.300	416	44	125	2	23	44	11
Ian Kinsler	.296	624	94	185	11	73	80	10
Yoenis Cespedes#	.293	403	62	118	18	61	87	3
J. D. Martinez	.282	596	93	168	38	102	178	3
Tyler Collins	.266	192	18	51	4	25	43	2
James McCann	.264	401	32	106	7	41	90	0
Rajai Davis	.258	341	55	88	8	30	76	18
Andrew Romine	.255	184	25	47	2	15	46	10
Nick Castellanos	.255	549	42	140	15	73	152	0
Anthony Gose	.254	485	73	123	5	26	145	23
Victor Martinez	.245	440	39	108	11	64	52	0
Alex Avila	.191	178	21	34	4	13	66	0

Pitchers	ERA	W	L	IP	H	BB	SO	SV
Alex Wilson	2.19	3	3	70.0	61	11	38	2
David Price*	2.45	18	5	220.1	190	47	225	0
Joakim Soria#	2.85	3	1	41.0	32	11	36	23
Justin Verlander	3.38	5	8	133.1	113	32	113	0
Anibal Sanchez	4.99	10	10	157.0	152	49	138	0
Alfredo Simon	5.05	13	12	187.0	201	68	117	0
Neftali Feliz*	6.38	3	4	48.0	57	18	39	10
Shane Greene	6.88	4	8	83.2	103	27	50	0

Manager: Brad Ausmus

Houston Astros

Batters	AVG	AB	R	H	HR	RBI	SO	SB
Jose Altuve	.313	638	86	200	15	66	67	38
Carlos Correa	.279	387	52	108	22	68	78	14
Marwin Gonzalez	.279	344	44	96	12	34	74	4
George Springer	.276	388	59	107	16	41	109	16
Evan Gattis	.246	566	66	139	27	88	119	0
Preston Tucker	.243	300	35	73	13	33	68	0
Colby Rasmus	.238	432	67	103	25	61	154	2
Jake Marisnick	.236	339	46	80	9	36	105	24
Hank Conger	.229	201	25	46	11	33	63	0
Luis Valbuena	.224	434	62	97	25	56	106	1
Jed Lowrie	.222	230	35	51	9	30	43	1
Jason Castro	.211	337	38	71	11	31	115	0
Chris Carter	.199	391	50	78	24	64	151	1

Pitchers	ERA	W	L	IP	H	BB	SO	SV
Will Harris	1.90	5	5	71.0	42	22	68	2
Dallas Keuchel	2.48	20	8	232.0	185	51	216	0
Luke Gregerson	3.10	7	3	61.0	48	10	59	31
Scott Kazmir*	3.10	7	11	183.0	162	59	155	0
Lance McCullers	3.22	6	7	125.2	106	43	129	0
Collin McHugh	3.89	19	7	203.2	207	53	171	0
Scott Feldman	3.90	5	5	108.1	115	27	61	0
Roberto Hernandez	4.36	3	5	84.2	90	26	42	0

Manager: A. J. Hinch

Kansas City Royals

Batters	AVG	AB	R	H	HR	RBI	SO	SB
Lorenzo Cain	.307	551	101	169	16	72	98	28
Eric Hosmer	.297	599	98	178	18	93	108	7
Kendrys Morales	.290	569	81	165	22	106	103	0
Mike Moustakas	.284	549	73	156	22	82	76	1
Ben Zobrist*	.276	467	76	129	13	56	56	3
Alex Gordon	.271	354	40	96	13	48	92	2
Salvador Perez	.260	531	52	138	21	70	82	1
Alcides Escobar	.257	612	76	157	3	47	75	17
Alex Rios	.255	385	40	98	4	32	67	9
Jarrod Dyson	.250	200	31	50	2	18	37	26
Paulo Orlando	.249	241	31	60	7	27	53	3
Omar Infante	.220	440	39	97	2	44	69	2

Pitchers	ERA	W	L	IP	H	BB	SO	SV
Wade Davis	0.94	8	1	67.1	33	20	78	17
Chris Young	3.06	11	6	123.1	91	43	83	0
Edinson Volquez	3.55	13	9	200.1	190	72	155	0
Greg Holland	3.83	3	2	44.2	39	26	49	32
Yordano Ventura	4.08	13	8	163.1	154	58	156	0
Danny Duffy	4.08	7	8	136.2	137	53	102	1
Johnny Cueto#	4.76	4	7	81.1	101	17	56	0
Jeremy Guthrie	5.95	8	8	148.1	186	44	84	0

Manager: Ned Yost

Los Angeles Angels

Batters	AVG	AB	R	H	HR	RBI	SO	SB
Mike Trout	.299	575	104	172	41	90	158	11
David Murphy*	.283	361	38	102	10	50	49	0
Johnny Giavotella	.272	453	51	123	4	49	59	2
Erick Aybar	.270	597	74	161	3	44	73	15
C. J. Cron	.262	378	37	99	16	51	82	3
David Freese	.257	424	53	109	14	56	107	1
Kole Calhoun	.256	630	78	161	26	83	164	4
Carlos Perez	.250	260	20	65	4	21	49	2
Albert Pujols	.244	602	85	147	40	95	72	5
David DeJesus*	.233	288	27	67	5	30	52	3
Shane Victorino*	.230	178	19	41	1	7	32	7
Conor Gillaspie*	.228	237	14	54	4	24	47	0
Chris Iannetta	.188	272	28	51	10	34	83	0
Matt Joyce	.174	247	17	43	5	21	67	0
Taylor Featherston	.162	154	23	25	2	9	46	4

Pitchers	ERA	W	L	IP	H	BB	SO	SV
Huston Street	3.18	3	3	62.1	52	20	57	40
Andrew Heaney	3.49	6	4	105.2	99	28	78	0
Hector Santiago	3.59	9	9	180.2	156	71	162	0
Garrett Richards	3.65	15	12	207.1	181	76	176	0
C. J. Wilson	3.89	8	8	132.0	118	46	110	0
Matt Shoemaker	4.46	7	10	135.1	135	35	116	0
Jered Weaver	4.64	7	12	159.0	163	33	90	0

Manager: Mike Scioscia

Minnesota Twins

Batters	AVG	AB	R	H	HR	RBI	SO	SB
Eduardo Nunez	.282	188	23	53	4	20	29	8
Miguel Sano	.269	279	46	75	18	52	119	1
Eddie Rosario	.267	453	60	121	13	50	118	11
Joe Mauer	.265	592	69	157	10	66	112	2
Eduardo Escobar	.262	409	48	107	12	58	86	2
Aaron Hicks	.256	352	48	90	11	33	66	13
Shane Robinson	.250	180	28	45	0	16	29	6
Trevor Plouffe	.244	573	74	140	22	86	124	2
Kurt Suzuki	.240	433	36	104	5	50	59	0
Kennys Vargas	.240	175	18	42	5	17	54	0
Torii Hunter	.240	521	67	125	22	81	105	2
Brian Dozier	.236	628	101	148	28	77	148	12
Danny Santana	.215	261	30	56	0	21	68	8

Pitchers	ERA	W	L	IP	H	BB	SO	SV
Kevin Jepsen*	2.33	3	6	69.2	52	27	59	15
Glen Perkins	3.32	3	5	57.0	58	10	54	32
Kyle Gibson	3.84	11	11	194.2	186	65	145	0
Tommy Milone	3.92	9	5	128.2	128	36	91	1
Ervin Santana	4.00	7	5	108.0	104	36	82	0
Trevor May	4.00	8	9	114.2	127	26	110	0
Mike Pelfrey	4.26	6	11	164.2	198	45	86	0
Phil Hughes	4.40	11	9	155.1	184	16	94	0

Manager: Paul Molitor

New York Yankees

Batters	AVG	AB	R	H	HR	RBI	SO	SB
John Ryan Murphy	.277	155	21	43	3	14	43	0
Carlos Beltran	.276	478	57	132	19	67	85	0
Didi Gregorius	.265	525	57	139	9	56	85	5
Greg Bird	.261	157	26	41	11	31	53	0
Brett Gardner	.259	571	94	148	16	66	135	20
Chase Headley	.259	580	74	150	11	62	135	0
Jacoby Ellsbury	.257	452	66	116	7	33	86	21
Mark Teixeira	.255	392	57	100	31	79	85	2
Chris Young	.252	318	53	80	14	42	73	3

Batters	AVG	AB	R	H	HR	RBI	SO	SB
Alex Rodriguez	.250	523	83	131	33	86	145	4
Brian McCann	.232	465	68	108	26	94	97	0
Dustin Ackley*	.231	238	28	55	10	30	45	2
Stephen Drew	.201	383	43	77	17	44	71	0

Pitchers	ERA	W	L	IP	H	BB	SO	SV
Dellin Betances	1.50	6	4	84.0	45	40	131	9
Andrew Miller	2.04	3	2	61.2	33	20	100	36
Adam Warren	3.29	7	7	131.1	114	39	104	1
Masahiro Tanaka	3.51	12	7	154.0	126	27	139	0
Nathan Eovaldi	4.20	14	3	154.1	175	49	121	0
Michael Pineda	4.37	12	10	160.2	176	21	156	0
CC Sabathia	4.73	6	10	167.1	188	50	137	0
Ivan Nova	5.07	6	11	94.0	99	33	63	0

Manager: Joe Girardi

Oakland Athletics

Batters	AVG	AB	R	H	HR	RBI	SO	SB
Billy Burns	.294	520	70	153	5	42	81	26
Danny Valencia*	.290	345	59	100	18	66	80	2
Ben Zobrist*	.276	467	76	129	13	56	56	3
Josh Reddick	.272	526	67	143	20	77	65	10
Stephen Vogt	.261	445	58	116	18	71	97	0
Brett Lawrie	.260	562	64	146	16	60	144	5
Marcus Semien	.257	556	65	143	15	45	132	11
Mark Canha	.254	441	61	112	16	70	96	7
Billy Butler	.251	538	63	135	15	65	101	0
Josh Phegley	.249	225	27	56	9	34	51	0
Eric Sogard	.247	372	40	92	1	37	50	6
Ike Davis	.229	214	19	49	3	20	44	0
Sam Fuld	.197	290	34	57	2	22	55	9
Jake Smolinski*	.193	166	24	32	6	26	39	1

Pitchers	ERA	W	L	IP	H	BB	SO	SV
Sonny Gray	2.73	14	7	208.0	166	59	169	0
Tyler Clippard#	2.79	1	3	38.2	25	21	38	17
Scott Kazmir*	3.10	7	11	183.0	162	59	155	0
Jesse Hahn	3.35	6	6	96.2	88	25	64	0
Chris Bassitt	3.56	1	8	86.0	78	30	64	0
Drew Pomeranz	3.66	5	6	86.0	71	31	82	3
Kendall Graveman	4.05	6	9	115.2	126	38	77	0
Jesse Chavez	4.18	7	15	157.0	164	48	136	1
Felix Doubront*	5.50	3	3	75.1	87	26	56	1

Manager: Bob Melvin

Seattle Mariners

Batters	AVG	AB	R	H	HR	RBI	SO	SB
Nelson Cruz	.302	590	90	178	44	93	164	3
Franklin Gutierrez	.292	171	27	50	15	35	54	0
Robinson Cano	.287	624	82	179	21	79	107	2
Ketel Marte	.283	219	25	62	2	17	43	8
Austin Jackson#	.272	419	46	114	8	38	107	15
Kyle Seager	.266	623	85	166	26	74	98	6
Mark Trumbo#	.263	334	39	88	13	41	93	0
Brad Miller	.258	438	44	113	11	46	101	13
Seth Smith	.248	395	54	98	12	42	99	0
Dustin Ackley*	.231	238	28	55	10	30	45	2
Logan Morrison	.225	457	47	103	17	54	81	8
Mike Zunino	.174	350	28	61	11	28	132	0

Pitchers	ERA	W	L	IP	H	BB	SO	SV
Carson Smith	2.31	2	5	70.0	49	22	92	13
Tom Wilhelmsen	3.19	2	2	62.0	56	29	60	13
Felix Hernandez	3.53	18	9	201.2	180	58	191	0
Hisashi Iwakuma	3.54	9	5	129.2	117	21	111	0
Vidal Nuno#	4.10	1	4	74.2	80	17	62	0
Roenis Elias	4.14	5	8	115.1	106	44	97	0
Taijuan Walker	4.56	11	8	169.2	163	40	157	0
Mike Montgomery	4.60	4	6	90.0	92	37	64	0
J. A. Happ#	4.64	4	6	108.2	121	32	82	0
Fernando Rodney#	5.68	5	5	50.2	51	25	43	16

Manager: Lloyd McClendon

Tampa Bay Rays

Batters	AVG	AB	R	H	HR	RBI	SO	SB
John Jaso	.286	185	23	53	5	22	39	1
Logan Forsythe	.281	540	69	152	17	68	111	9
James Loney	.280	361	25	101	4	32	34	2
Joey Butler	.276	257	30	71	8	30	82	5
Evan Longoria	.270	604	74	163	21	73	132	3
Asdrubal Cabrera	.265	505	66	134	15	58	107	6
Brandon Guyer	.265	332	51	88	8	28	61	10
Kevin Kiermaier	.263	505	62	133	10	40	95	18
Grady Sizemore#	.257	175	20	45	6	27	37	3
David DeJesus*	.233	288	27	67	5	30	52	3
Steven Souza Jr.	.225	373	59	84	16	40	144	12
Tim Beckham	.222	203	24	45	9	37	69	3
Rene Rivera	.178	298	16	53	5	26	86	0

Pitchers	ERA	W	L	IP	H	BB	SO	SV
Kevin Jepsen*	2.33	3	6	69.2	52	27	59	15
Chris Archer	3.23	12	13	212.0	175	66	252	0
Jake Odorizzi	3.35	9	9	169.1	149	46	150	0
Nathan Karns	3.67	7	5	147.0	132	56	145	0
Brad Boxberger	3.71	4	10	63.0	54	32	74	41
Erasmo Ramirez	3.75	11	6	163.1	145	40	126	0
Alex Colome	3.94	8	5	109.2	112	31	88	0

Manager: Kevin Cash

Texas Rangers

Batters	AVG	AB	R	H	HR	RBI	SO	SB
Prince Fielder	.305	613	78	187	23	98	88	0
Adrian Beltre	.287	567	83	163	18	83	65	1
Mitch Moreland	.278	471	51	131	23	85	112	1
Shin-Soo Choo	.276	555	94	153	22	82	147	4
Delino DeShields	.261	425	83	111	2	37	101	25
Rougned Odor	.261	426	54	111	16	61	79	6
Elvis Andrus	.258	596	69	154	7	62	78	25
Josh Hamilton	.253	170	22	43	8	25	52	0
Robinson Chirinos	.232	233	33	54	10	34	62	0
Mike Napoli*	.224	407	46	91	18	50	118	3
Leonys Martin	.219	288	26	63	5	25	69	14
Jake Smolinski*	.193	166	24	32	6	26	39	1

Pitchers	ERA	W	L	IP	H	BB	SO	SV
Shawn Tolleson	2.99	6	4	72.1	66	17	76	35
Yovani Gallardo	3.42	13	11	184.1	193	68	121	0
Cole Hamels#	3.66	7	1	83.2	77	23	78	0
Nick Martinez	3.96	7	7	125.0	135	46	77	0
Martin Perez	4.46	3	6	78.2	88	24	48	0
Colby Lewis	4.66	17	9	204.2	211	42	142	0
Wandy Rodriguez	4.90	6	4	86.1	99	36	72	0
Neftali Feliz*	6.38	3	4	48.0	57	18	39	10

Manager: Jeff Banister

Toronto Blue Jays

Batters	AVG	AB	R	H	HR	RBI	SO	SB
Chris Colabello	.321	333	55	107	15	54	96	2
Ben Revere#	.319	226	35	72	1	19	28	7
Devon Travis	.304	217	38	66	8	35	43	3
Josh Donaldson	.297	620	122	184	41	123	133	6
Danny Valencia*	.290	345	59	100	18	66	80	2
Jose Reyes#	.285	288	36	82	4	34	38	16
Kevin Pillar	.278	586	76	163	12	56	85	25
Edwin Encarnacion	.277	528	94	146	39	111	98	3
Ezequiel Carrera	.273	172	27	47	3	26	45	2
Jose Bautista	.250	543	108	136	40	114	106	8
Ryan Goins	.250	376	52	94	5	45	83	2
Dioner Navarro	.246	171	17	42	5	20	29	0
Russell Martin	.240	441	76	106	23	77	106	4
Troy Tulowitzki#	.239	163	31	39	5	17	42	1
Justin Smoak	.226	296	44	67	18	59	86	0

Pitchers	ERA	W	L	IP	H	BB	SO	SV
David Price*	2.45	18	5	220.1	190	47	225	0
Roberto Osuna	2.58	1	6	69.2	48	16	75	20
Marco Estrada	3.13	13	8	181.0	134	55	131	0
Aaron Sanchez	3.22	7	6	92.1	74	44	61	0
Mark Buehrle	3.81	15	8	198.2	214	33	91	0
R. A. Dickey	3.91	11	11	214.1	195	61	126	0
Felix Doubront*	5.50	3	3	75.1	87	26	56	1
Drew Hutchison	5.57	13	5	150.1	179	44	129	0

Manager: John Gibbons

Major League Leaders, 2015

National League

Batting Average: Dee Gordon, Miami, .333; Bryce Harper, Washington, .330; Paul Goldschmidt, Arizona, .321; Buster Posey, San Francisco, .318; A. J. Pollock, Arizona, .315.

Runs Scored: Bryce Harper, Washington, 118; A. J. Pollock, Arizona, 111; Paul Goldschmidt, Arizona, 103; Dexter Fowler, Chicago Cubs, 102; Matt Carpenter, St. Louis, 101.

Runs Batted In: Nolan Arenado, Colorado, 130; Paul Goldschmidt, Arizona, 110; Anthony Rizzo, Chicago Cubs, 101; Matt Kemp, San Diego, 100; Bryce Harper, Washington, 99; Kris Bryant, Chicago Cubs, 99.

Hits: Dee Gordon, Miami, 205; A. J. Pollock, Arizona, 192; Paul Goldschmidt, Arizona, 182; Nick Markakis, Atlanta, 181; Nolan Arenado, Colorado, 177; Buster Posey, San Francisco, 177.

Doubles: Matt Carpenter, St. Louis, 44; Nolan Arenado, Colorado, 43; Todd Frazier, Cincinnati, 43; A. J. Pollock, Arizona, 39; Paul Goldschmidt, Arizona, 38; Bryce Harper, Washington, 38; Nick Markakis, Atlanta, 38; Daniel Murphy, NY Mets, 38; Anthony Rizzo, Chicago Cubs, 38.

Triples: David Peralta, Arizona, 10; Charlie Blackmon, Colorado, 9; Dexter Fowler, Chicago Cubs, 8; Dee Gordon, Miami, 8; Andre Ethier, L.A. Dodgers, 7; Randal Grichuk, St. Louis, 7; J. T. Realmuto, Miami, 7.

Home Runs: Nolan Arenado, Colorado, 42; Bryce Harper, Washington, 42; Carlos Gonzalez, Colorado, 40; Todd Frazier, Cincinnati, 35; Paul Goldschmidt, Arizona, 33.

Stolen Bases: Dee Gordon, Miami, 58; Billy Hamilton, Cincinnati, 57; Charlie Blackmon, Colorado, 43; A. J. Pollock, Arizona, 39; Starling Marte, Pittsburgh, 30.

Pitching Wins: Jake Arrieta, Chicago Cubs, 22; Gerrit Cole, Pittsburgh, 19; Zack Greinke, L.A. Dodgers, 19; Madison Bumgarner, San Francisco, 18; Michael Wacha, St. Louis, 17.

Earned Run Average: Zack Greinke, L.A. Dodgers, 1.66; Jake Arrieta, Chicago Cubs, 1.77, Clayton Kershaw, L.A. Dodgers, 2.13; Jacob deGrom, NY Mets, 2.54; Gerrit Cole, Pittsburgh, 2.60.

Strikeouts: Clayton Kershaw, L.A. Dodgers, 301; Max Scherzer, Washington, 276; Jake Arrieta, Chicago Cubs, 236; Madison Bumgarner, San Francisco, 234; James Shields, San Diego, 216.

Saves: Mark Melancon, Pittsburgh, 51; Trevor Rosenthal, St. Louis, 48; Jeurys Familia, NY Mets, 43; Craig Kimbrel, San Diego, 39; Santiago Casilla, San Francisco, 38; Francisco Rodriguez, Milwaukee, 38.

American League

Batting Average: Miguel Cabrera, Detroit, .338; Xander Bogaerts, Boston, .320; Jose Altuve, Houston, .313; Michael Brantley, Cleveland, .310; Lorenzo Cain, Kansas City, .307.

Runs Scored: Josh Donaldson, Toronto, 122; Jose Bautista, Toronto, 108; Mike Trout, L.A. Angels, 104; Manny Machado, Baltimore, 102; Lorenzo Cain, Kansas City, 101; Brian Dozier, Minnesota, 101.

Runs Batted In: Josh Donaldson, Toronto, 123; Chris Davis, Baltimore, 117; Jose Bautista, Toronto, 114; Edwin Encarnacion, Toronto, 111; David Ortiz, Boston, 108.

Hits: Jose Altuve, Houston, 200; Xander Bogaerts, Boston, 196; Prince Fielder, Texas, 187; Ian Kinsler, Detroit, 185; Josh Donaldson, Toronto, 184.

Doubles: Michael Brantley, Cleveland, 45; Jason Kipnis, Cleveland, 43; Mookie Betts, Boston, 42; Josh Donaldson, Toronto, 41; Kendrys Morales, Kansas City, 41.

Triples: Eddie Rosario, Minnesota, 15; Kevin Kiermaier, Tampa Bay, 12; Rajai Davis, Detroit, 11; Evan Gattis, Houston, 11, Delino DeShields, Texas, 10.

Home Runs: Chris Davis, Baltimore, 47; Nelson Cruz, Seattle, 44; Josh Donaldson, Toronto, 41; Mike Trout, L.A. Angels, 41; Jose Bautista, Toronto, 40; Albert Pujols, L.A. Angels, 40.

Stolen Bases: Jose Altuve, Houston, 38; Lorenzo Cain, Kansas City, 28; Billy Burns, Oakland, 26; Jarrod Dyson, Kansas City, 26; Elvis Andrus, Texas, 25; Delino DeShields, Texas, 25; Kevin Pillar, Toronto, 25.

Pitching Wins: Dallas Keuchel, Houston, 20; Collin McHugh, Houston, 19; Felix Hernandez, Seattle, 18; David Price, Detroit/Toronto, 18; Colby Lewis, Texas, 17.

Earned Run Average: David Price, Detroit/Toronto, 2.45; Dallas Keuchel, Houston, 2.48; Sonny Gray, Oakland, 2.73; Scott Kazmir, Oakland/Houston, 3.10; Marco Estrada, Toronto, 3.13.

Strikeouts: Chris Sale, Chicago White Sox, 274; Chris Archer, Tampa Bay, 252; Corey Kluber, Cleveland, 245; David Price, Detroit/Toronto, 225; Carlos Carrasco, Cleveland, 216; Dallas Keuchel, Houston, 216.

Saves: Brad Boxberger, Tampa Bay, 41; Huston Street, L.A. Angels, 40; Zach Britton, Baltimore, 36; Andrew Miller, NY Yankees, 36; Shawn Tolleson, Texas, 35.

All-Time Major League Single-Season Leaders

Source: www.mlb.com; * = Active in 2015 season; records for "modern" era beginning in 1901.

Home Runs

Barry Bonds (2001)	73
Mark McGwire (1998)	70
Sammy Sosa (1998)	66
Mark McGwire (1999)	65
Sammy Sosa (2001)	64

Runs Scored

Babe Ruth (1921)	177
Lou Gehrig (1936)	167
Lou Gehrig (1931)	163
Babe Ruth (1928)	163
Chuck Klein (1930)	158
Babe Ruth (1920, 1927)	158

Hits

Ichiro Suzuki* (2004)	262
George Sisler (1920)	257
Lefty O'Doul (1929)	254
Bill Terry (1930)	254
Al Simmons (1925)	253
Rogers Hornsby (1922)	250
Chuck Klein (1930)	250

Runs Batted In

Hack Wilson (1930)	191
Lou Gehrig (1931)	184
Hank Greenberg (1937)	183
Jimmie Foxx (1938)	175
Lou Gehrig (1927)	175

Batting Average

Rogers Hornsby (1924)	.424
Napoleon Lajoie (1901)	.421
George Sisler (1922)	.420
Ty Cobb (1911)	.420
Ty Cobb (1912)	.410

Stolen Bases

Rickey Henderson (1982)	130
Lou Brock (1974)	118
Vince Coleman (1985)	110
Vince Coleman (1987)	109
Rickey Henderson (1983)	108

Walks (Batter)

Barry Bonds (2004)	232
Barry Bonds (2002)	198
Barry Bonds (2001)	177
Babe Ruth (1923)	170
Mark McGwire (1998)	162
Ted Williams (1947, 1949)	162

Strikeouts (Batter)

Mark Reynolds* (2009)	223
Adam Dunn (2012)	222
Chris Carter* (2013)	212
Mark Reynolds* (2010)	211
Chris Davis* (2015)	208

Earned Run Average

Dutch Leonard (1914)	0.96
Mordecai "Three Finger" Brown (1906)	1.04
Bob Gibson (1968)	1.12
Christy Mathewson (1909)	1.14
Walter Johnson (1913)	1.14

Wins

Jack Chesbro (1904)	41
Ed Walsh (1908)	40
Christy Mathewson (1908)	37
Walter Johnson (1913)	36
Joe McGinnity (1904)	35

Strikeouts

Nolan Ryan (1973)	383
Sandy Koufax (1965)	382
Randy Johnson (2001)	372
Nolan Ryan (1974)	367
Randy Johnson (1999)	364

Saves

Francisco Rodriguez* (2008)	62
Bobby Thigpen (1990)	57
Eric Gagne (2003)	55
John Smoltz (2002)	55
Trevor Hoffman (1998)	53
Randy Myers (1993)	53
Mariano Rivera (2004)	53

All-Time Major League Leaders

Source: www.mlb.com; * = Active in 2015 season; career records for players in "modern" era beginning in 1901 may include statistics from preceding years.

Games	
Pete Rose	3,562
Carl Yastrzemski	3,308
Hank Aaron	3,298
Rickey Henderson	3,081
Ty Cobb	3,035
Eddie Murray	3,026
Stan Musial	3,026
Cal Ripken Jr.	3,001
Willie Mays	2,992
Barry Bonds	2,986

Stolen Bases	
Rickey Henderson	1,406
Lou Brock	938
Billy Hamilton	912
Ty Cobb	892
Tim Raines	808
Vince Coleman	752
Eddie Collins	745
Arlie Latham	739
Max Carey	738
Honus Wagner	722

Strikeouts	
Nolan Ryan	5,714
Randy Johnson	4,875
Roger Clemens	4,672
Steve Carlton	4,136
Bert Blyleven	3,701
Tom Seaver	3,640
Don Sutton	3,574
Gaylord Perry	3,534
Walter Johnson	3,508
Greg Maddux	3,371

At Bats	
Pete Rose	14,053
Hank Aaron	12,364
Carl Yastrzemski	11,988
Cal Ripken Jr.	11,551
Ty Cobb	11,429
Eddie Murray	11,336
Derek Jeter	11,195
Robin Yount	11,008
Dave Winfield	11,003
Stan Musial	10,972

Triples	
Sam Crawford	309
Ty Cobb	297
Honus Wagner	252
Jake Beckley	243
Roger Connor	233
Tris Speaker	222
Fred Clarke	220
Dan Brouthers	205
Joe Kelley	194
Paul Waner	191

Saves	
Mariano Rivera	652
Trevor Hoffman	601
Lee Smith	478
John Franco	424
Billy Wagner	422
Dennis Eckersley	390
Francisco Rodriguez*	386
Joe Nathan*	377
Jeff Reardon	367
Troy Percival	358

Runs Batted In	
Hank Aaron	2,297
Babe Ruth	2,213
Alex Rodriguez*	2,055
Barry Bonds	1,996
Lou Gehrig	1,995
Stan Musial	1,951
Ty Cobb	1,938
Jimmie Foxx	1,922
Eddie Murray	1,917
Willie Mays	1,903

Batting Average	
Ty Cobb	.367
Rogers Hornsby	.358
Joe Jackson	.356
Ed Delahanty	.346
Tris Speaker	.345
Ted Williams	.344
Billy Hamilton	.344
Dan Brouthers	.342
Babe Ruth	.342
Harry Heilmann	.342

Shutouts	
Walter Johnson	110
Grover Alexander	90
Christy Mathewson	79
Cy Young	76
Eddie Plank	69
Warren Spahn	63
Nolan Ryan	61
Tom Seaver	61
Bert Blyleven	60
Don Sutton	58

Runs	
Rickey Henderson	2,295
Ty Cobb	2,246
Barry Bonds	2,227
Hank Aaron	2,174
Babe Ruth	2,174
Pete Rose	2,165
Willie Mays	2,062
Alex Rodriguez*	2,002
Stan Musial	1,949
Derek Jeter	1,923

Walks (Batter)	
Barry Bonds	2,558
Rickey Henderson	2,190
Babe Ruth	2,062
Ted Williams	2,019
Joe Morgan	1,865
Carl Yastrzemski	1,845
Jim Thome	1,747
Mickey Mantle	1,733
Mel Ott	1,708
Frank Thomas	1,667

Losses	
Cy Young	316
Nolan Ryan	292
Walter Johnson	279
Phil Niekro	274
Gaylord Perry	265
Don Sutton	256
Jack Powell	254
Eppa Rixey	251
Bert Blyleven	250
Robin Roberts	245
Warren Spahn	245

All-Time Home Run Leaders

Source: www.mlb.com; * = Active in 2015 season.

Player	HR
Barry Bonds	762
Hank Aaron	755
Babe Ruth	714
Alex Rodriguez*	687
Willie Mays	660
Ken Griffey Jr.	630
Jim Thome	612
Sammy Sosa	609
Frank Robinson	586
Mark McGwire	583
Harmon Killebrew	573
Rafael Palmeiro	569
Reggie Jackson	563
Albert Pujols*	560
Manny Ramirez	555
Mike Schmidt	548
Mickey Mantle	536
Jimmie Foxx	534
Willie McCovey	521
Frank Thomas	521
Ted Williams	521
Ernie Banks	512
Eddie Mathews	512
Mel Ott	511
Gary Sheffield	509
Eddie Murray	504
David Ortiz*	503
Lou Gehrig	493
Fred McGriff	493
Stan Musial	475
Willie Stargell	475
Carlos Delgado	473
Chipper Jones	468
Dave Winfield	465
Jose Canseco	462
Adam Dunn	462
Carl Yastrzemski	452
Jeff Bagwell	449
Vladimir Guerrero	449
Dave Kingman	442
Jason Giambi	440
Paul Konerko	439
Andre Dawson	438
Juan Gonzalez	434
Andruw Jones	434
Cal Ripken Jr.	431
Mike Piazza	427
Billy Williams	426
Darrell Evans	414
Adrian Beltre*	413
Alfonso Soriano	412
Miguel Cabrera*	408
Duke Snider	407
Andres Galarraga	399
Al Kaline	399
Dale Murphy	398

Players With 3,000 Major League Hits

Source: www.mlb.com; * = Active in 2015 season.

Player	Hits
Pete Rose	4,256
Ty Cobb	4,191
Hank Aaron	3,771
Stan Musial	3,630
Tris Speaker	3,515
Derek Jeter	3,465
Honus Wagner	3,430
Carl Yastrzemski	3,419
Paul Molitor	3,319
Eddie Collins	3,314
Willie Mays	3,283
Eddie Murray	3,255
Napoleon Lajoie	3,252
Cal Ripken Jr.	3,184
George Brett	3,154
Paul Waner	3,152
Robin Yount	3,142
Tony Gwynn	3,141
Dave Winfield	3,110
Alex Rodriguez*	3,070
Craig Biggio	3,060
Rickey Henderson	3,055
Rod Carew	3,053
Lou Brock	3,023
Rafael Palmeiro	3,020
Cap Anson	3,011
Wade Boggs	3,010
Al Kaline	3,007
Roberto Clemente	3,000

50 Home Run Club

Only Barry Bonds and Mark McGwire hit 70 or more home runs in a season. Five players—including Babe Ruth and Roger Maris—hit 60 or more, a feat Sammy Sosa accomplished for the third time in 2001.

HR	Player, team	Year
73	Barry Bonds, San Francisco Giants	2001
70	Mark McGwire, St. Louis Cardinals	1998
66	Sammy Sosa, Chicago Cubs	1998
65	Mark McGwire, St. Louis Cardinals	1999
64	Sammy Sosa, Chicago Cubs	2001
63	Sammy Sosa, Chicago Cubs	1999
61	Roger Maris, NY Yankees	1961
60	Babe Ruth, NY Yankees	1927
59	Babe Ruth, NY Yankees	1921
58	Jimmie Foxx, Philadelphia Athletics	1932
58	Hank Greenberg, Detroit Tigers	1938
58	Ryan Howard, Philadelphia Phillies	2006
58	Mark McGwire, Oakland A's/St. Louis Cardinals	1997
57	Luis Gonzalez, Arizona Diamondbacks	2001
57	Alex Rodriguez, Texas Rangers	2002
56	Ken Griffey Jr., Seattle Mariners	1997
56	Ken Griffey Jr., Seattle Mariners	1998
56	Hack Wilson, Chicago Cubs	1930
54	Jose Bautista, Toronto Blue Jays	2010
54	Ralph Kiner, Pittsburgh Pirates	1949
54	Mickey Mantle, NY Yankees	1961
54	David Ortiz, Boston Red Sox	2006
54	Alex Rodriguez, NY Yankees	2007
54	Babe Ruth, NY Yankees	1920
54	Babe Ruth, NY Yankees	1928
53	Chris Davis, Baltimore Orioles	2013
52	George Foster, Cincinnati Reds	1977
52	Mickey Mantle, NY Yankees	1956
52	Willie Mays, San Francisco Giants	1965
52	Mark McGwire, Oakland A's	1996
52	Alex Rodriguez, Texas Rangers	2001
52	Jim Thome, Cleveland Indians	2002
51	Cecil Fielder, Detroit Tigers	1990
51	Andruw Jones, Atlanta Braves	2005
51	Ralph Kiner, Pittsburgh Pirates	1947
51	Willie Mays, NY Giants	1955
51	Johnny Mize, NY Giants	1947
50	Brady Anderson, Baltimore Orioles	1996
50	Albert Belle, Cleveland Indians	1995
50	Prince Fielder, Milwaukee Brewers	2007
50	Jimmie Foxx, Boston Red Sox	1938
50	Sammy Sosa, Chicago Cubs	2000
50	Greg Vaughn, San Diego Padres	1998

Pitchers With 300 Major League Wins

Source: www.mlb.com

Pitcher	Wins	Pitcher	Wins	Pitcher	Wins	Pitcher	Wins
Cy Young	511	Charles "Kid" Nichols	361	Eddie Plank	326	Charley Radbourn	309
Walter Johnson	417	Greg Maddux	355	Nolan Ryan	324	Mickey Welch	307
Grover Alexander	373	Roger Clemens	354	Don Sutton	324	Tom Glavine	305
Christy Mathewson	373	Tim Keefe	342	Phil Niekro	318	Randy Johnson	303
Warren Spahn	363	Steve Carlton	329	Gaylord Perry	314	Robert "Lefty" Grove	300
James "Pud" Galvin	361	John Clarkson	328	Tom Seaver	311	Early "Gus" Wynn	300

Official Major League Perfect Games Since 1901

Date	Pitcher	Teams
5/5/1904	Cy Young	Boston 3 vs. Phil. 0 (AL)
10/2/1908	Addie Joss	Clev. 1 vs. Chicago 0 (AL)
4/30/1922	Charlie Robertson	Chicago 2 vs. Detroit 0 (AL)
10/8/1956	Don Larsen	NY 2 (AL) vs. Brooklyn 0* (NL)
6/21/1964	Jim Bunning	Phil. 6 vs. NY 0 (NL)
9/9/1965	Sandy Koufax	L.A. 1 vs. Chicago 0 (NL)
5/8/1968	Jim "Catfish" Hunter	Oakland 4 vs. Minn. 0 (AL)
5/15/1981	Len Barker	Clev. 3 vs. Toronto 0 (AL)
9/30/1984	Mike Witt	California 1 vs. Texas 0 (AL)
9/16/1988	Tom Browning	Cincinnati 1 vs. L.A. 0 (NL)
7/28/1991	Dennis Martinez	Montréal 2 vs. L.A. 0 (NL)
7/28/1994	Kenny Rogers	Texas 4 vs. California 0 (AL)
5/17/1998	David Wells	NY 4 vs. Minn. 0 (AL)
7/18/1999	David Cone	NY 6 vs. Montréal 0 (AL)
5/18/2004	Randy Johnson	Arizona 2 vs. Atlanta 0 (NL)
7/23/2009	Mark Buehrle	Chicago 5 vs. Tampa Bay 0 (AL)
5/9/2010	Dallas Braden	Oakland 4 vs. Tampa Bay 0 (AL)
5/29/2010	Roy Halladay	Phil. 1 vs. Florida 0 (NL)
4/21/2012	Philip Humber	Chicago 4 vs. Seattle 0 (AL)
6/13/2012	Matt Cain	S.F. 10 vs. Houston 0 (NL)
8/15/2012	Felix Hernandez	Seattle 1 vs. Tampa Bay 0 (AL)

* = World Series game. **Note:** Two pre-1901 National League pitchers are also credited with perfect games. Within one week in 1880, Lee Richmond (June 12, Worcester 1, Cleveland 0) and John "Monte" Ward (June 17, Providence 5, Buffalo 0) each threw a perfect game.

Most Career Major League No-Hitters

No.	Pitcher
7	Nolan Ryan
4	Sandy Koufax
3	Larry Corcoran, Bob Feller, Cy Young
2	Homer Bailey, Mark Buehrle, Jim Bunning, Steve Busby, Carl Erskine, Bob Forsch, Pud Galvin, Roy Halladay, Ken Holtzman, Randy Johnson, Addie Joss, Dutch Leonard, Tim Lincecum, Jim Maloney, Christy Mathewson, Hideo Nomo, Allie Reynolds, Max Scherzer, Frank Smith, Warren Spahn, Bill Stoneman, Virgil Trucks, Johnny Vander Meer, Justin Verlander, Ed Walsh, Don Wilson

Home Run Leaders by Season, 1901-2015

* = All-time single-season record for league since beginning of "modern" era in 1901.

National League			American League		
Year	Player, team	HR	Year	Player, team	HR
1901	Sam Crawford, Cincinnati	16	1901	Napoleon Lajoie, Philadelphia	14
1902	Thomas Leach, Pittsburgh	6	1902	Socks Seybold, Philadelphia	16
1903	James Sheckard, Brooklyn	9	1903	Buck Freeman, Boston	13
1904	Harry Lumley, Brooklyn	9	1904	Harry Davis, Philadelphia	10
1905	Fred Odwell, Cincinnati	9	1905	Harry Davis, Philadelphia	8
1906	Timothy Jordan, Brooklyn	12	1906	Harry Davis, Philadelphia	12
1907	David Brain, Boston	10	1907	Harry Davis, Philadelphia	8
1908	Timothy Jordan, Brooklyn	12	1908	Sam Crawford, Detroit	7
1909	Red Murray, New York	7	1909	Ty Cobb, Detroit	9
1910	Fred Beck, Boston; Frank Schulte, Chicago	10	1910	Jake Stahl, Boston	10
1911	Frank Schulte, Chicago	21	1911	J. Franklin Baker, Philadelphia	11
1912	Henry Zimmerman, Chicago	14	1912	J. Franklin Baker, Phil.; Tris Speaker, Boston	10
1913	Gavvy Cravath, Philadelphia	19	1913	J. Franklin Baker, Philadelphia	12
1914	Gavvy Cravath, Philadelphia	19	1914	J. Franklin Baker, Philadelphia	9
1915	Gavvy Cravath, Philadelphia	24	1915	Robert Roth, Chicago-Cleveland	7
1916	Dave Robertson, NY; Fred "Cy" Williams, Chi.	12	1916	Wally Pipp, New York	12
1917	Gavvy Cravath, Phil.; Dave Robertson, NY	12	1917	Wally Pipp, New York	9

National League

Year	Player, team	HR
1918	Gavvy Cravath, Philadelphia	8
1919	Gavvy Cravath, Philadelphia	12
1920	Cy Williams, Philadelphia	15
1921	George Kelly, New York	23
1922	Rogers Hornsby, St. Louis	42
1923	Cy Williams, Philadelphia	41
1924	Jacques Fournier, Brooklyn	27
1925	Rogers Hornsby, St. Louis	39
1926	Hack Wilson, Chicago	21
1927	Hack Wilson, Chicago; Cy Williams, Philadelphia	30
1928	Hack Wilson, Chicago; Jim Bottomley, St. Louis	31
1929	Chuck Klein, Philadelphia	43
1930	Hack Wilson, Chicago	56
1931	Chuck Klein, Philadelphia	31
1932	Chuck Klein, Philadelphia; Mel Ott, New York	38
1933	Chuck Klein, Philadelphia	28
1934	Rip Collins, St. Louis; Mel Ott, New York	35
1935	Walter Berger, Boston	34
1936	Mel Ott, New York	33
1937	Joe Medwick, St. Louis; Mel Ott, New York	31
1938	Mel Ott, New York	36
1939	John Mize, St. Louis	28
1940	John Mize, St. Louis	43
1941	Dolph Camilli, Brooklyn	34
1942	Mel Ott, New York	30
1943	Bill Nicholson, Chicago	29
1944	Bill Nicholson, Chicago	33
1945	Tommy Holmes, Boston	28
1946	Ralph Kiner, Pittsburgh	23
1947	Ralph Kiner, Pittsburgh; John Mize, New York	51
1948	Ralph Kiner, Pittsburgh; John Mize, New York	40
1949	Ralph Kiner, Pittsburgh	54
1950	Ralph Kiner, Pittsburgh	47
1951	Ralph Kiner, Pittsburgh	42
1952	Ralph Kiner, Pittsburgh; Hank Sauer, Chicago	37
1953	Ed Mathews, Milwaukee	47
1954	Ted Kluszewski, Cincinnati	49
1955	Willie Mays, New York	51
1956	Duke Snider, Brooklyn	43
1957	Hank Aaron, Milwaukee	44
1958	Ernie Banks, Chicago	47
1959	Ed Mathews, Milwaukee	46
1960	Ernie Banks, Chicago	41
1961	Orlando Cepeda, San Francisco	46
1962	Willie Mays, San Francisco	49
1963	Hank Aaron, Milwaukee; Willie McCovey, S.F.	44
1964	Willie Mays, San Francisco	47
1965	Willie Mays, San Francisco	52
1966	Hank Aaron, Atlanta	44
1967	Hank Aaron, Atlanta	39
1968	Willie McCovey, San Francisco	36
1969	Willie McCovey, San Francisco	45
1970	Johnny Bench, Cincinnati	45
1971	Willie Stargell, Pittsburgh	48
1972	Johnny Bench, Cincinnati	40
1973	Willie Stargell, Pittsburgh	44
1974	Mike Schmidt, Philadelphia	36
1975	Mike Schmidt, Philadelphia	38
1976	Mike Schmidt, Philadelphia	38
1977	George Foster, Cincinnati	52
1978	George Foster, Cincinnati	40
1979	Dave Kingman, Chicago	48
1980	Mike Schmidt, Philadelphia	48
1981	Mike Schmidt, Philadelphia	31
1982	Dave Kingman, New York	37
1983	Mike Schmidt, Philadelphia	40
1984	Dale Murphy, Atlanta; Mike Schmidt, Philadelphia	36
1985	Dale Murphy, Atlanta	37
1986	Mike Schmidt, Philadelphia	37
1987	Andre Dawson, Chicago	49
1988	Darryl Strawberry, New York	39
1989	Kevin Mitchell, San Francisco	47
1990	Ryne Sandberg, Chicago	40
1991	Howard Johnson, New York	38
1992	Fred McGriff, San Diego	35
1993	Barry Bonds, San Francisco	46
1994	Matt Williams, San Francisco	43
1995	Dante Bichette, Colorado	40
1996	Andres Galarraga, Colorado	47
1997[1]	Larry Walker, Colorado	49
1998	Mark McGwire, St. Louis	70
1999	Mark McGwire, St. Louis	65
2000	Sammy Sosa, Chicago	50
2001	Barry Bonds, San Francisco	73*
2002	Sammy Sosa, Chicago	49
2003	Jim Thome, Philadelphia	47
2004	Adrian Beltre, Los Angeles	48

American League

Year	Player, team	HR
1918	Babe Ruth, Boston; Tilly Walker, Philadelphia	11
1919	Babe Ruth, Boston	29
1920	Babe Ruth, New York	54
1921	Babe Ruth, New York	59
1922	Ken Williams, St. Louis	39
1923	Babe Ruth, New York	41
1924	Babe Ruth, New York	46
1925	Bob Meusel, New York	33
1926	Babe Ruth, New York	47
1927	Babe Ruth, New York	60
1928	Babe Ruth, New York	54
1929	Babe Ruth, New York	46
1930	Babe Ruth, New York	49
1931	Lou Gehrig, New York; Babe Ruth, New York	46
1932	Jimmie Foxx, Philadelphia	58
1933	Jimmie Foxx, Philadelphia	48
1934	Lou Gehrig, New York	49
1935	Jimmie Foxx, Phil.; Hank Greenberg, Detroit	36
1936	Lou Gehrig, New York	49
1937	Joe DiMaggio, New York	46
1938	Hank Greenberg, Detroit	58
1939	Jimmie Foxx, Boston	35
1940	Hank Greenberg, Detroit	41
1941	Ted Williams, Boston	37
1942	Ted Williams, Boston	36
1943	Rudy York, Detroit	34
1944	Nick Etten, New York	22
1945	Vern Stephens, St. Louis	24
1946	Hank Greenberg, Detroit	44
1947	Ted Williams, Boston	32
1948	Joe DiMaggio, New York	39
1949	Ted Williams, Boston	43
1950	Al Rosen, Cleveland	37
1951	Gus Zernial, Chicago-Philadelphia	33
1952	Larry Doby, Cleveland	32
1953	Al Rosen, Cleveland	43
1954	Larry Doby, Cleveland	32
1955	Mickey Mantle, New York	37
1956	Mickey Mantle, New York	52
1957	Roy Sievers, Washington	42
1958	Mickey Mantle, New York	42
1959	Rocky Colavito, Clev.; Harmon Killebrew, Wash.	42
1960	Mickey Mantle, New York	40
1961	Roger Maris, New York	61*
1962	Harmon Killebrew, Minnesota	48
1963	Harmon Killebrew, Minnesota	45
1964	Harmon Killebrew, Minnesota	49
1965	Tony Conigliaro, Boston	32
1966	Frank Robinson, Baltimore	49
1967	Harmon Killebrew, Minn.; Carl Yastrzemski, Boston	44
1968	Frank Howard, Washington	44
1969	Harmon Killebrew, Minnesota	49
1970	Frank Howard, Washington	44
1971	Bill Melton, Chicago	33
1972	Dick Allen, Chicago	37
1973	Reggie Jackson, Oakland	32
1974	Dick Allen, Chicago	32
1975	Reggie Jackson, Oak.; George Scott, Milw.	36
1976	Graig Nettles, New York	32
1977	Jim Rice, Boston	39
1978	Jim Rice, Boston	46
1979	Gorman Thomas, Milwaukee	45
1980	Reggie Jackson, New York; Ben Oglivie, Milw.	41
1981	Tony Armas, Oakland; Dwight Evans, Boston; Bobby Grich, Cal.; Eddie Murray, Baltimore	22
1982	Gorman Thomas, Milw.; Reggie Jackson, Cal.	39
1983	Jim Rice, Boston	39
1984	Tony Armas, Boston	43
1985	Darrell Evans, Detroit	40
1986	Jesse Barfield, Toronto	40
1987	Mark McGwire, Oakland	49
1988	Jose Canseco, Oakland	42
1989	Fred McGriff, Toronto	36
1990	Cecil Fielder, Detroit	51
1991	Jose Canseco, Oakland; Cecil Fielder, Detroit	44
1992	Juan Gonzalez, Texas	43
1993	Juan Gonzalez, Texas	46
1994	Ken Griffey Jr., Seattle	40
1995	Albert Belle, Cleveland	50
1996	Mark McGwire, Oakland	52
1997[1]	Ken Griffey Jr., Seattle	56
1998	Ken Griffey Jr., Seattle	56
1999	Ken Griffey Jr., Seattle	48
2000	Troy Glaus, Anaheim	47
2001	Alex Rodriguez, Texas	52
2002	Alex Rodriguez, Texas	57
2003	Alex Rodriguez, Texas	47
2004	Manny Ramirez, Boston	43

National League			American League		
Year	Player, team	HR	Year	Player, team	HR
2005	Andruw Jones, Atlanta	51	2005	Alex Rodriguez, New York	48
2006	Ryan Howard, Philadelphia	58	2006	David Ortiz, Boston	54
2007	Prince Fielder, Milwaukee	50	2007	Alex Rodriguez, New York	54
2008	Ryan Howard, Philadelphia	48	2008	Miguel Cabrera, Detroit	37
2009	Albert Pujols, St. Louis	47	2009	Carlos Pena, Tampa Bay; Mark Teixeira, New York	39
2010	Albert Pujols, St. Louis	42	2010	Jose Bautista, Toronto	54
2011	Matt Kemp, Los Angeles	39	2011	Jose Bautista, Toronto	43
2012	Ryan Braun, Milwaukee	41	2012	Miguel Cabrera, Detroit	44
2013	Pedro Alvarez, Pitt.; Paul Goldschmidt, Arizona	36	2013	Chris Davis, Baltimore	53
2014	Giancarlo Stanton, Miami	37	2014	Nelson Cruz, Baltimore	40
2015	Nolan Arenado, Colorado; Bryce Harper, Washington	42	2015	Chris Davis, Baltimore	47

(1) In 1997, Mark McGwire hit 58 home runs, 34 with the Oakland Athletics (AL) and 24 with the St. Louis Cardinals (NL).

Batting Champions by Season, 1901-2015

* = All-time single-season record for league since beginning of "modern" era in 1901.

National League			American League		
Year	Player, team	AVG	Year	Player, team	AVG
1901	Jesse C. Burkett, St. Louis	.376	1901[1]	Napoleon Lajoie, Philadelphia	.426*
1902	Clarence Beaumont, Pittsburgh	.357	1902	Ed Delahanty, Washington	.376
1903	Honus Wagner, Pittsburgh	.355	1903	Napoleon Lajoie, Cleveland	.357
1904	Honus Wagner, Pittsburgh	.349	1904	Napoleon Lajoie, Cleveland	.382
1905	James Seymour, Cincinnati	.377	1905	Elmer Flick, Cleveland	.308
1906	Honus Wagner, Pittsburgh	.339	1906	George Stone, St. Louis	.358
1907	Honus Wagner, Pittsburgh	.350	1907	Ty Cobb, Detroit	.350
1908	Honus Wagner, Pittsburgh	.354	1908	Ty Cobb, Detroit	.324
1909	Honus Wagner, Pittsburgh	.339	1909	Ty Cobb, Detroit	.377
1910	Sherwood Magee, Philadelphia	.331	1910[2]	Ty Cobb, Detroit	.385
1911	Honus Wagner, Pittsburgh	.334	1911	Ty Cobb, Detroit	.420
1912	Henry Zimmerman, Chicago	.372	1912	Ty Cobb, Detroit	.410
1913	Jacob Daubert, Brooklyn	.350	1913	Ty Cobb, Detroit	.390
1914	Jacob Daubert, Brooklyn	.329	1914	Ty Cobb, Detroit	.368
1915	Larry Doyle, New York	.320	1915	Ty Cobb, Detroit	.369
1916	Hal Chase, Cincinnati	.339	1916	Tris Speaker, Cleveland	.386
1917	Edd Roush, Cincinnati	.341	1917	Ty Cobb, Detroit	.383
1918	Zach Wheat, Brooklyn	.335	1918	Ty Cobb, Detroit	.382
1919	Edd Roush, Cincinnati	.321	1919	Ty Cobb, Detroit	.384
1920	Rogers Hornsby, St. Louis	.370	1920	George Sisler, St. Louis	.407
1921	Rogers Hornsby, St. Louis	.397	1921	Harry Heilmann, Detroit	.394
1922	Rogers Hornsby, St. Louis	.401	1922	George Sisler, St. Louis	.420
1923	Rogers Hornsby, St. Louis	.384	1923	Harry Heilmann, Detroit	.403
1924	Rogers Hornsby, St. Louis	.424*	1924	Babe Ruth, New York	.378
1925	Rogers Hornsby, St. Louis	.403	1925	Harry Heilmann, Detroit	.393
1926	Eugene Hargrave, Cincinnati	.353	1926	Henry Manush, Detroit	.378
1927	Paul Waner, Pittsburgh	.380	1927	Harry Heilmann, Detroit	.398
1928	Rogers Hornsby, Boston	.387	1928	Goose Goslin, Washington	.379
1929	Lefty O'Doul, Philadelphia	.398	1929	Lew Fonseca, Cleveland	.369
1930	Bill Terry, New York	.401	1930	Al Simmons, Philadelphia	.381
1931	Chick Hafey, St. Louis	.349	1931	Al Simmons, Philadelphia	.390
1932	Lefty O'Doul, Brooklyn	.368	1932	Dale Alexander, Detroit-Boston	.367
1933	Chuck Klein, Philadelphia	.368	1933	Jimmie Foxx, Philadelphia	.356
1934	Paul Waner, Pittsburgh	.362	1934	Lou Gehrig, New York	.363
1935	Arky Vaughan, Pittsburgh	.385	1935	Buddy Myer, Washington	.349
1936	Paul Waner, Pittsburgh	.373	1936	Luke Appling, Chicago	.388
1937	Joe Medwick, St. Louis	.374	1937	Charlie Gehringer, Detroit	.371
1938	Ernie Lombardi, Cincinnati	.342	1938	Jimmie Foxx, Boston	.349
1939	John Mize, St. Louis	.349	1939	Joe DiMaggio, New York	.381
1940	Debs Garms, Pittsburgh	.355	1940	Joe DiMaggio, New York	.352
1941	Pete Reiser, Brooklyn	.343	1941	Ted Williams, Boston	.406
1942	Ernie Lombardi, Boston	.330	1942	Ted Williams, Boston	.356
1943	Stan Musial, St. Louis	.357	1943	Luke Appling, Chicago	.328
1944	Dixie Walker, Brooklyn	.357	1944	Lou Boudreau, Cleveland	.327
1945	Phil Cavarretta, Chicago	.355	1945	George Stirnweiss, New York	.309
1946	Stan Musial, St. Louis	.365	1946	Mickey Vernon, Washington	.353
1947	Harry Walker, St. Louis-Phil.	.363	1947	Ted Williams, Boston	.343
1948	Stan Musial, St. Louis	.376	1948	Ted Williams, Boston	.369
1949	Jackie Robinson, Brooklyn	.342	1949	George Kell, Detroit	.343
1950	Stan Musial, St. Louis	.346	1950	Billy Goodman, Boston	.354
1951	Stan Musial, St. Louis	.355	1951	Ferris Fain, Philadelphia	.344
1952	Stan Musial, St. Louis	.336	1952	Ferris Fain, Philadelphia	.327
1953	Carl Furillo, Brooklyn	.344	1953	Mickey Vernon, Washington	.337
1954	Willie Mays, New York	.345	1954	Roberto Avila, Cleveland	.341
1955	Richie Ashburn, Philadelphia	.338	1955	Al Kaline, Detroit	.340
1956	Hank Aaron, Milwaukee	.328	1956	Mickey Mantle, New York	.353
1957	Stan Musial, St. Louis	.351	1957	Ted Williams, Boston	.388
1958	Richie Ashburn, Philadelphia	.350	1958	Ted Williams, Boston	.328
1959	Hank Aaron, Milwaukee	.355	1959	Harvey Kuenn, Detroit	.353
1960	Dick Groat, Pittsburgh	.325	1960	Pete Runnels, Boston	.320
1961	Roberto Clemente, Pittsburgh	.351	1961	Norm Cash, Detroit	.361
1962	Tommy Davis, Los Angeles	.346	1962	Pete Runnels, Boston	.326
1963	Tommy Davis, Los Angeles	.326	1963	Carl Yastrzemski, Boston	.321
1964	Roberto Clemente, Pittsburgh	.339	1964	Tony Oliva, Minnesota	.323
1965	Roberto Clemente, Pittsburgh	.329	1965	Tony Oliva, Minnesota	.321
1966	Matty Alou, Pittsburgh	.342	1966	Frank Robinson, Baltimore	.316
1967	Roberto Clemente, Pittsburgh	.357	1967	Carl Yastrzemski, Boston	.326
1968	Pete Rose, Cincinnati	.335	1968	Carl Yastrzemski, Boston	.301
1969	Pete Rose, Cincinnati	.348	1969	Rod Carew, Minnesota	.332
1970	Rico Carty, Atlanta	.366	1970	Alex Johnson, California	.329

National League			American League		
Year	**Player, team**	**AVG**	**Year**	**Player, team**	**AVG**
1971	Joe Torre, St. Louis	.363	1971	Tony Oliva, Minnesota	.337
1972	Billy Williams, Chicago	.333	1972	Rod Carew, Minnesota	.318
1973	Pete Rose, Cincinnati	.338	1973	Rod Carew, Minnesota	.350
1974	Ralph Garr, Atlanta	.353	1974	Rod Carew, Minnesota	.364
1975	Bill Madlock, Chicago	.354	1975	Rod Carew, Minnesota	.359
1976	Bill Madlock, Chicago	.339	1976	George Brett, Kansas City	.333
1977	Dave Parker, Pittsburgh	.338	1977	Rod Carew, Minnesota	.388
1978	Dave Parker, Pittsburgh	.334	1978	Rod Carew, Minnesota	.333
1979	Keith Hernandez, St. Louis	.344	1979	Fred Lynn, Boston	.333
1980	Bill Buckner, Chicago	.324	1980	George Brett, Kansas City	.390
1981	Bill Madlock, Pittsburgh	.341	1981	Carney Lansford, Boston	.336
1982	Al Oliver, Montréal	.331	1982	Willie Wilson, Kansas City	.332
1983	Bill Madlock, Pittsburgh	.323	1983	Wade Boggs, Boston	.361
1984	Tony Gwynn, San Diego	.351	1984	Don Mattingly, New York	.343
1985	Willie McGee, St. Louis	.353	1985	Wade Boggs, Boston	.368
1986	Tim Raines, Montréal	.334	1986	Wade Boggs, Boston	.357
1987	Tony Gwynn, San Diego	.370	1987	Wade Boggs, Boston	.363
1988	Tony Gwynn, San Diego	.313	1988	Wade Boggs, Boston	.366
1989	Tony Gwynn, San Diego	.336	1989	Kirby Puckett, Minnesota	.339
1990	Willie McGee, St. Louis	.335	1990	George Brett, Kansas City	.329
1991	Terry Pendleton, Atlanta	.319	1991	Julio Franco, Texas	.341
1992	Gary Sheffield, San Diego	.330	1992	Edgar Martinez, Seattle	.343
1993	Andres Galarraga, Colorado	.370	1993	John Olerud, Toronto	.363
1994	Tony Gwynn, San Diego	.394	1994	Paul O'Neill, New York	.359
1995	Tony Gwynn, San Diego	.368	1995	Edgar Martinez, Seattle	.356
1996	Tony Gwynn, San Diego	.353	1996	Alex Rodriguez, Seattle	.358
1997	Tony Gwynn, San Diego	.372	1997	Frank Thomas, Chicago	.347
1998	Larry Walker, Colorado	.363	1998	Bernie Williams, New York	.339
1999	Larry Walker, Colorado	.379	1999	Nomar Garciaparra, Boston	.357
2000	Todd Helton, Colorado	.372	2000	Nomar Garciaparra, Boston	.372
2001	Larry Walker, Colorado	.350	2001	Ichiro Suzuki, Seattle	.350
2002	Barry Bonds, San Francisco	.370	2002	Manny Ramirez, Boston	.349
2003	Albert Pujols, St. Louis	.359	2003	Bill Mueller, Boston	.326
2004	Barry Bonds, San Francisco	.362	2004	Ichiro Suzuki, Seattle	.372
2005	Derrek Lee, Chicago	.335	2005	Michael Young, Texas	.331
2006	Freddy Sanchez, Pittsburgh	.344	2006	Joe Mauer, Minnesota	.347
2007	Matt Holliday, Colorado	.340	2007	Magglio Ordonez, Detroit	.363
2008	Chipper Jones, Atlanta	.364	2008	Joe Mauer, Minnesota	.328
2009	Hanley Ramirez, Florida	.342	2009	Joe Mauer, Minnesota	.365
2010	Carlos Gonzalez, Colorado	.337	2010	Josh Hamilton, Texas	.359
2011	Jose Reyes, New York	.337	2011	Miguel Cabrera, Detroit	.344
2012	Buster Posey, San Francisco	.336	2012	Miguel Cabrera, Detroit	.330
2013	Michael Cuddyer, Colorado	.331	2013	Miguel Cabrera, Detroit	.348
2014	Justin Morneau, Colorado	.319	2014	Jose Altuve, Houston	.341
2015	Dee Gordon, Miami	.333	2015	Miguel Cabrera, Detroit	.338

(1) Napoleon Lajoie's 1901 batting average varies in historical records from .421 to .426. (2) Some baseball researchers have concluded that Ty Cobb actually hit .382 in 1910 while Napoleon Lajoie, Cleveland, hit .383.

Earned Run Average Leaders by Season, 1977-2015

National League					American League				
Year	**Pitcher, team**	**G**	**IP**	**ERA**	**Year**	**Pitcher, team**	**G**	**IP**	**ERA**
1977	John Candelaria, Pittsburgh	33	230.2	2.34	1977	Frank Tanana, California	31	241.1	2.54
1978	Craig Swan, New York	29	207.1	2.43	1978	Ron Guidry, New York	35	273.2	1.74
1979	J. R. Richard, Houston	38	292.1	2.71	1979	Ron Guidry, New York	33	236.1	2.78
1980	Don Sutton, Los Angeles	32	212.1	2.20	1980	Rudy May, New York	41	175.1	2.46
1981	Nolan Ryan, Houston	21	149.0	1.69	1981	Sammy Stewart, Baltimore	29	112.1	2.32
1982	Steve Rogers, Montréal	35	277.0	2.40	1982	Rick Sutcliffe, Cleveland	34	216.0	2.96
1983	Atlee Hammaker, San Francisco	23	172.1	2.25	1983	Rick Honeycutt, Texas	25	174.2	2.42
1984	Alejandro Pena, Los Angeles	28	199.1	2.48	1984	Mike Boddicker, Baltimore	34	261.1	2.79
1985	Dwight Gooden, New York	35	276.2	1.53	1985	Dave Stieb, Toronto	36	265.0	2.48
1986	Mike Scott, Houston	37	275.1	2.22	1986	Roger Clemens, Boston	33	254.0	2.48
1987	Nolan Ryan, Houston	34	211.2	2.76	1987	Jimmy Key, Toronto	36	261.0	2.76
1988	Joe Magrane, St. Louis	24	165.1	2.18	1988	Allan Anderson, Minnesota	30	202.1	2.45
1989	Scott Garrelts, San Francisco	30	193.1	2.28	1989	Bret Saberhagen, Kansas City	36	262.1	2.16
1990	Danny Darwin, Houston	48	162.2	2.21	1990	Roger Clemens, Boston	31	228.1	1.93
1991	Dennis Martinez, Montréal	31	222.0	2.39	1991	Roger Clemens, Boston	35	271.1	2.62
1992	Bill Swift, San Francisco	30	164.2	2.08	1992	Roger Clemens, Boston	32	246.2	2.41
1993	Greg Maddux, Atlanta	36	267.0	2.36	1993	Kevin Appier, Kansas City	34	238.2	2.56
1994	Greg Maddux, Atlanta	25	202.0	1.56	1994	Steve Ontiveros, Oakland	27	115.1	2.65
1995	Greg Maddux, Atlanta	28	209.2	1.63	1995	Randy Johnson, Seattle	30	214.1	2.48
1996	Kevin Brown, Florida	32	233.0	1.89	1996	Juan Guzman, Toronto	27	187.2	2.93
1997	Pedro Martinez, Montréal	31	241.1	1.90	1997	Roger Clemens, Toronto	34	264.0	2.05
1998	Greg Maddux, Atlanta	34	251.0	2.22	1998	Roger Clemens, Toronto	33	234.2	2.65
1999	Randy Johnson, Arizona	35	271.2	2.48	1999	Pedro Martinez, Boston	31	213.1	2.07
2000	Kevin Brown, Los Angeles	33	230.0	2.58	2000	Pedro Martinez, Boston	29	217.0	1.74
2001	Randy Johnson, Arizona	35	249.2	2.49	2001	Freddy Garcia, Seattle	34	238.2	3.05
2002	Randy Johnson, Arizona	35	260.0	2.32	2002	Pedro Martinez, Boston	30	199.1	2.26
2003	Jason Schmidt, San Francisco	29	207.2	2.34	2003	Pedro Martinez, Boston	29	186.2	2.22
2004	Jake Peavy, San Diego	27	166.1	2.27	2004	Johan Santana, Minnesota	34	228.0	2.61
2005	Roger Clemens, Houston	32	211.1	1.87	2005	Kevin Millwood, Cleveland	30	192.0	2.86
2006	Roy Oswalt, Houston	33	220.2	2.98	2006	Johan Santana, Minnesota	34	233.2	2.77
2007	Jake Peavy, San Diego	34	223.1	2.54	2007	John Lackey, Los Angeles	33	224.0	3.01
2008	Johan Santana, New York	34	234.1	2.53	2008	Cliff Lee, Cleveland	31	223.1	2.54
2009	Chris Carpenter, St. Louis	28	192.2	2.24	2009	Zack Greinke, Kansas City	33	229.1	2.16
2010	Josh Johnson, Florida	28	183.2	2.30	2010	Felix Hernandez, Seattle	34	249.2	2.27
2011	Clayton Kershaw, Los Angeles	33	233.1	2.28	2011	Justin Verlander, Detroit	34	251.0	2.40
2012	Clayton Kershaw, Los Angeles	33	227.2	2.53	2012	David Price, Tampa Bay	31	211.0	2.56
2013	Clayton Kershaw, Los Angeles	33	236.0	1.83	2013	Anibal Sanchez, Detroit	29	182.0	2.57
2014	Clayton Kershaw, Los Angeles	27	198.1	1.77	2014	Felix Hernandez, Seattle	34	236.0	2.14
2015	Zack Greinke, Los Angeles	32	222.2	1.66	2015	David Price, Detroit-Toronto	32	220.1	2.45

Strikeout Leaders by Season, 1901-2015

* = All-time single-season record for league since beginning of "modern" era in 1901.

National League			American League		
Year	Pitcher, team	SO	Year	Pitcher, team	SO
1901	Noodles Hahn, Cincinnati	239	1901	Cy Young, Boston	158
1902	Vic Willis, Boston	225	1902	Rube Waddell, Philadelphia	210
1903	Christy Mathewson, New York	267	1903	Rube Waddell, Philadelphia	302
1904	Christy Mathewson, New York	212	1904	Rube Waddell, Philadelphia	349
1905	Christy Mathewson, New York	206	1905	Rube Waddell, Philadelphia	287
1906	Fred Beebe, Chicago-St. Louis	171	1906	Rube Waddell, Philadelphia	196
1907	Christy Mathewson, New York	178	1907	Rube Waddell, Philadelphia	232
1908	Christy Mathewson, New York	259	1908	Ed Walsh, Chicago	269
1909	Orval Overall, Chicago	205	1909	Frank Smith, Chicago	177
1910	Earl Moore, Philadelphia	185	1910	Walter Johnson, Washington	313
1911	Rube Marquard, New York	237	1911	Ed Walsh, Chicago	255
1912	Grover Alexander, Philadelphia	195	1912	Walter Johnson, Washington	303
1913	Tom Seaton, Philadelphia	168	1913	Walter Johnson, Washington	243
1914	Grover Alexander, Philadelphia	214	1914	Walter Johnson, Washington	225
1915	Grover Alexander, Philadelphia	241	1915	Walter Johnson, Washington	203
1916	Grover Alexander, Philadelphia	167	1916	Walter Johnson, Washington	228
1917	Grover Alexander, Philadelphia	200	1917	Walter Johnson, Washington	188
1918	Hippo Vaughn, Chicago	148	1918	Walter Johnson, Washington	162
1919	Hippo Vaughn, Chicago	141	1919	Walter Johnson, Washington	147
1920	Grover Alexander, Chicago	173	1920	Stan Coveleski, Cleveland	133
1921	Burleigh Grimes, Brooklyn	136	1921	Walter Johnson, Washington	143
1922	Dazzy Vance, Brooklyn	134	1922	Urban Shocker, St. Louis	149
1923	Dazzy Vance, Brooklyn	197	1923	Walter Johnson, Washington	130
1924	Dazzy Vance, Brooklyn	262	1924	Walter Johnson, Washington	158
1925	Dazzy Vance, Brooklyn	221	1925	Lefty Grove, Philadelphia	116
1926	Dazzy Vance, Brooklyn	140	1926	Lefty Grove, Philadelphia	194
1927	Dazzy Vance, Brooklyn	184	1927	Lefty Grove, Philadelphia	174
1928	Dazzy Vance, Brooklyn	200	1928	Lefty Grove, Philadelphia	183
1929	Pat Malone, Chicago	166	1929	Lefty Grove, Philadelphia	170
1930	Bill Hallahan, St. Louis	177	1930	Lefty Grove, Philadelphia	209
1931	Bill Hallahan, St. Louis	159	1931	Lefty Grove, Philadelphia	175
1932	Dizzy Dean, St. Louis	191	1932	Red Ruffing, New York	190
1933	Dizzy Dean, St. Louis	199	1933	Lefty Gomez, New York	163
1934	Dizzy Dean, St. Louis	195	1934	Lefty Gomez, New York	158
1935	Dizzy Dean, St. Louis	190	1935	Tommy Bridges, Detroit	163
1936	Van Lingle Mungo, Brooklyn	238	1936	Tommy Bridges, Detroit	175
1937	Carl Hubbell, New York	159	1937	Lefty Gomez, New York	194
1938	Clay Bryant, Chicago	135	1938	Bob Feller, Cleveland	240
1939	Claude Passeau, Philadelphia-Chicago; Bucky Walters, Cincinnati	137	1939	Bob Feller, Cleveland	246
1940	Kirby Higbe, Philadelphia	137	1940	Bob Feller, Cleveland	261
1941	John Vander Meer, Cincinnati	202	1941	Bob Feller, Cleveland	260
1942	John Vander Meer, Cincinnati	186	1942	Tex Hughson, Boston; Bobo Newsom, Washington	113
1943	John Vander Meer, Cincinnati	174	1943	Allie Reynolds, Cleveland	151
1944	Bill Voiselle, New York	161	1944	Hal Newhouser, Detroit	187
1945	Preacher Roe, Pittsburgh	148	1945	Hal Newhouser, Detroit	212
1946	Johnny Schmitz, Cincinnati	135	1946	Bob Feller, Cleveland	348
1947	Ewell Blackwell, Cincinnati	193	1947	Bob Feller, Cleveland	196
1948	Harry Brecheen, St. Louis	149	1948	Bob Feller, Cleveland	164
1949	Warren Spahn, Boston	151	1949	Virgil Trucks, Detroit	153
1950	Warren Spahn, Boston	191	1950	Bob Lemon, Cleveland	170
1951	Warren Spahn, Boston; Don Newcombe, Brooklyn	164	1951	Vic Raschi, New York	164
1952	Warren Spahn, Boston	183	1952	Allie Reynolds, New York	160
1953	Robin Roberts, Philadelphia	198	1953	Billy Pierce, Chicago	186
1954	Robin Roberts, Philadelphia	185	1954	Bob Turley, Baltimore	185
1955	Sam Jones, Chicago	198	1955	Herb Score, Cleveland	245
1956	Sam Jones, Chicago	176	1956	Herb Score, Cleveland	263
1957	Jack Sanford, Philadelphia	188	1957	Early Wynn, Cleveland	184
1958	Sam Jones, St. Louis	225	1958	Early Wynn, Chicago	179
1959	Don Drysdale, Los Angeles	242	1959	Jim Bunning, Detroit	201
1960	Don Drysdale, Los Angeles	246	1960	Jim Bunning, Detroit	201
1961	Sandy Koufax, Los Angeles	269	1961	Camilo Pascual, Minnesota	221
1962	Don Drysdale, Los Angeles	232	1962	Camilo Pascual, Minnesota	206
1963	Sandy Koufax, Los Angeles	306	1963	Camilo Pascual, Minnesota	202
1964	Bob Veale, Pittsburgh	250	1964	Al Downing, New York	217
1965	Sandy Koufax, Los Angeles	382*	1965	Sam McDowell, Cleveland	325
1966	Sandy Koufax, Los Angeles	317	1966	Sam McDowell, Cleveland	225
1967	Jim Bunning, Philadelphia	253	1967	Jim Lonborg, Boston	246
1968	Bob Gibson, St. Louis	268	1968	Sam McDowell, Cleveland	283
1969	Ferguson Jenkins, Chicago	273	1969	Sam McDowell, Cleveland	279
1970	Tom Seaver, New York	283	1970	Sam McDowell, Cleveland	304
1971	Tom Seaver, New York	289	1971	Mickey Lolich, Detroit	308
1972	Steve Carlton, Philadelphia	310	1972	Nolan Ryan, California	329
1973	Tom Seaver, New York	251	1973	Nolan Ryan, California	383*
1974	Steve Carlton, Philadelphia	240	1974	Nolan Ryan, California	367
1975	Tom Seaver, New York	243	1975	Frank Tanana, California	269
1976	Tom Seaver, New York	235	1976	Nolan Ryan, California	327
1977	Phil Niekro, Atlanta	262	1977	Nolan Ryan, California	341
1978	J. R. Richard, Houston	303	1978	Nolan Ryan, California	260

National League			American League		
Year	Pitcher, team	SO	Year	Pitcher, team	SO
1979	J. R. Richard, Houston	313	1979	Nolan Ryan, California	223
1980	Steve Carlton, Philadelphia	286	1980	Len Barker, Cleveland	187
1981	Fernando Valenzuela, Los Angeles	180	1981	Len Barker, Cleveland	127
1982	Steve Carlton, Philadelphia	286	1982	Floyd Bannister, Seattle	209
1983	Steve Carlton, Philadelphia	275	1983	Jack Morris, Detroit	232
1984	Dwight Gooden, New York	276	1984	Mark Langston, Seattle	204
1985	Dwight Gooden, New York	268	1985	Bert Blyleven, Cleveland-Minnesota	206
1986	Mike Scott, Houston	306	1986	Mark Langston, Seattle	245
1987	Nolan Ryan, Houston	270	1987	Mark Langston, Seattle	262
1988	Nolan Ryan, Houston	228	1988	Roger Clemens, Boston	291
1989	Jose DeLeon, St. Louis	201	1989	Nolan Ryan, Texas	301
1990	David Cone, New York	233	1990	Nolan Ryan, Texas	232
1991	David Cone, New York	241	1991	Roger Clemens, Boston	241
1992	John Smoltz, Atlanta	215	1992	Randy Johnson, Seattle	241
1993	Jose Rijo, Cincinnati	227	1993	Randy Johnson, Seattle	308
1994	Andy Benes, San Diego	189	1994	Randy Johnson, Seattle	204
1995	Hideo Nomo, Los Angeles	236	1995	Randy Johnson, Seattle	294
1996	John Smoltz, Atlanta	276	1996	Roger Clemens, Boston	257
1997	Curt Schilling, Philadelphia	319	1997	Roger Clemens, Toronto	292
1998	Curt Schilling, Philadelphia	300	1998	Roger Clemens, Toronto	271
1999	Randy Johnson, Arizona	364	1999	Pedro Martinez, Boston	313
2000	Randy Johnson, Arizona	347	2000	Pedro Martinez, Boston	284
2001	Randy Johnson, Arizona	372	2001	Hideo Nomo, Boston	220
2002	Randy Johnson, Arizona	334	2002	Pedro Martinez, Boston	239
2003	Kerry Wood, Chicago	266	2003	Esteban Loaiza, Chicago	207
2004	Randy Johnson, Arizona	290	2004	Johan Santana, Minnesota	265
2005	Jake Peavy, San Diego	216	2005	Johan Santana, Minnesota	238
2006	Aaron Harang, Cincinnati	216	2006	Johan Santana, Minnesota	245
2007	Jake Peavy, San Diego	240	2007	Scott Kazmir, Tampa Bay	239
2008	Tim Lincecum, San Francisco	265	2008	A. J. Burnett, Toronto	231
2009	Tim Lincecum, San Francisco	261	2009	Justin Verlander, Detroit	269
2010	Tim Lincecum, San Francisco	231	2010	Jered Weaver, Los Angeles	233
2011	Clayton Kershaw, Los Angeles	248	2011	Justin Verlander, Detroit	250
2012	R. A. Dickey, New York	230	2012	Justin Verlander, Detroit	239
2013	Clayton Kershaw, Los Angeles	232	2013	Yu Darvish, Texas	277
2014	Johnny Cueto, Cincinnati; Stephen Strasburg, Washington	242	2014	David Price, Tampa Bay-Detroit	271
2015	Clayton Kershaw, Los Angeles	301	2015	Chris Sale, Chicago	274

Victory Leaders by Season, 1901-2015

* = All-time single-season record for league since beginning of "modern" era in 1901.

National League			American League		
Year	Pitcher, team	Wins	Year	Pitcher, team	Wins
1901	Bill Donovan, Brooklyn	25	1901	Cy Young, Boston	33
1902	Jack Chesbro, Pittsburgh	28	1902	Cy Young, Boston	32
1903	Joe McGinnity, New York	31	1903	Cy Young, Boston	28
1904	Joe McGinnity, New York	35	1904	Jack Chesbro, New York	41*
1905	Christy Mathewson, New York	31	1905	Rube Waddell, Philadelphia	27
1906	Joe McGinnity, New York	27	1906	Al Orth, New York	27
1907	Christy Mathewson, New York	24	1907	Addie Joss, Cleveland; Doc White, Chicago	27
1908	Christy Mathewson, New York	37*	1908	Ed Walsh, Chicago	40
1909	Mordecai Brown, Chicago	27	1909	George Mullin, Detroit	29
1910	Christy Mathewson, New York	27	1910	Jack Coombs, Philadelphia	31
1911	Grover Alexander, Chicago	28	1911	Jack Coombs, Philadelphia	28
1912	Larry Cheney, Chicago; Rube Marquard, New York	26	1912	Joe Wood, Boston	34
1913	Tom Seaton, Philadelphia	27	1913	Walter Johnson, Washington	36
1914	Grover Alexander, Philadelphia	27	1914	Walter Johnson, Washington	28
1915	Grover Alexander, Philadelphia	31	1915	Walter Johnson, Washington	27
1916	Grover Alexander, Philadelphia	33	1916	Walter Johnson, Washington	25
1917	Grover Alexander, Philadelphia	30	1917	Eddie Cicotte, Chicago	28
1918	Hippo Vaughn, Chicago	22	1918	Walter Johnson, Washington	23
1919	Jesse Barnes, New York	25	1919	Eddie Cicotte, Chicago	29
1920	Grover Alexander, Philadelphia	27	1920	Jim Bagby, Cleveland	31
1921	Wilbur Cooper, Pitt.; Burleigh Grimes, Brooklyn	22	1921	Carl Mays, New York; Urban Shocker, St. Louis	27
1922	Eppa Rixey, Cincinnati	25	1922	Eddie Rommel, Philadelphia	27
1923	Dolf Luque, Cincinnati	27	1923	George Uhle, Cleveland	26
1924	Dazzy Vance, Brooklyn	28	1924	Walter Johnson, Washington	23
1925	Dazzy Vance, Brooklyn	22	1925	Ted Lyons, Chicago; Eddie Rommel, Philadelphia	21
1926	Pete Donohue, Cincinnati; Remy Kremer, Pitt.; Lee Meadows, Pitt.; Flint Rhem, St. Louis	20	1926	George Uhle, Cleveland	27
1927	Charlie Root, Chicago	26	1927	Waite Hoyt, New York; Ted Lyons, Chicago	22
1928	Burleigh Grimes, Pittsburgh; Larry Benton, NY	25	1928	Lefty Grove, Philadelphia; George Pipgras, NY	24
1929	Pat Malone, Chicago	22	1929	George Earnshaw, Philadelphia	24
1930	Pat Malone, Chicago; Remy Kremer, Pitt.	20	1930	Lefty Grove, Philadelphia	28
1931	Jumbo Elliott, Phil.; Bill Hallahan, St. Louis; Heinie Meine, Pittsburgh	19	1931	Lefty Grove, Philadelphia	31
1932	Lon Warneke, Chicago	22	1932	Alvin Crowder, Washington	26
1933	Carl Hubbell, New York	23	1933	Alvin Crowder, Wash.; Lefty Grove, Phila.	24
1934	Dizzy Dean, St. Louis	30	1934	Lefty Gomez, New York	26
1935	Dizzy Dean, St. Louis	28	1935	Wes Ferrell, Boston	25
1936	Carl Hubbell, New York	26	1936	Tommy Bridges, Detroit	23
1937	Carl Hubbell, New York	22	1937	Lefty Gomez, New York	21
1938	Bill Lee, Chicago	22	1938	Red Ruffing, New York	21
1939	Bucky Walters, Cincinnati	27	1939	Bob Feller, Cleveland	24
1940	Bucky Walters, Cincinnati	22	1940	Bob Feller, Cleveland	27

National League

Year	Pitcher, team	Wins
1941	Kirby Higbe, Brooklyn; Whit Wyatt, Brooklyn	22
1942	Mort Cooper, St. Louis	22
1943	Mort Cooper, St. Louis; Elmer Riddle, Cincinnati; Rip Sewell, Pittsburgh	21
1944	Bucky Walters, Cincinnati	23
1945	Red Barrett, Boston-St. Louis	23
1946	Howie Pollet, St. Louis	21
1947	Ewell Blackwell, Cincinnati	22
1948	Johnny Sain, Boston	24
1949	Warren Spahn, Boston	21
1950	Warren Spahn, Boston	21
1951	Larry Jansen, New York; Sal Maglie, New York	23
1952	Robin Roberts, Philadelphia	28
1953	Robin Roberts, Phil.; Warren Spahn, Milwaukee	23
1954	Robin Roberts, Philadelphia	23
1955	Robin Roberts, Philadelphia	23
1956	Don Newcombe, Brooklyn	27
1957	Warren Spahn, Milwaukee	21
1958	Bob Friend, Pitt.; Warren Spahn, Milwaukee	22
1959	Lew Burdette, Warren Spahn, Milwaukee; Sam Jones, New York	21
1960	Ernie Broglio, St. Louis; Warren Spahn, Milwaukee	21
1961	Joey Jay, Cincinnati; Warren Spahn, Milwaukee	21
1962	Don Drysdale, Los Angeles	25
1963	Sandy Koufax, L.A.; Juan Marichal, San Francisco	25
1964	Larry Jackson, Chicago	24
1965	Sandy Koufax, Los Angeles	26
1966	Sandy Koufax, Los Angeles	27
1967	Mike McCormick, San Francisco	22
1968	Juan Marichal, San Francisco	26
1969	Tom Seaver, New York	25
1970	Bob Gibson, St. Louis; Gaylord Perry, San Francisco	23
1971	Ferguson Jenkins, Chicago	24
1972	Steve Carlton, Philadelphia	27
1973	Ron Bryant, San Francisco	24
1974	Andy Messersmith, L.A.; Phil Niekro, Atlanta	20
1975	Tom Seaver, New York	22
1976	Randy Jones, San Diego	22
1977	Steve Carlton, Philadelphia	23
1978	Gaylord Perry, San Diego	21
1979	Joe Niekro, Houston; Phil Niekro, Atlanta	21
1980	Steve Carlton, Philadelphia	24
1981	Tom Seaver, Cincinnati	14
1982	Steve Carlton, Philadelphia	23
1983	John Denny, Philadelphia	19
1984	Joaquin Andujar, St. Louis	20
1985	Dwight Gooden, New York	24
1986	Fernando Valenzuela, Los Angeles	21
1987	Rick Sutcliffe, Chicago	18
1988	Orel Hershiser, L.A.; Danny Jackson, Cincinnati	23
1989	Mike Scott, Houston	20
1990	Doug Drabek, Pittsburgh	22
1991	Tom Glavine, Atlanta; John Smiley, Pittsburgh	20
1992	Tom Glavine, Atlanta; Greg Maddux, Chicago	20
1993	John Burkett, San Francisco; Tom Glavine, Atlanta	22
1994	Ken Hill, Montréal; Greg Maddux, Atlanta	16
1995	Greg Maddux, Atlanta	19
1996	John Smoltz, Atlanta	24
1997	Denny Neagle, Atlanta	20
1998	Tom Glavine, Atlanta	20
1999	Mike Hampton, Houston	22
2000	Tom Glavine, Atlanta	21
2001	Matt Morris, St. Louis; Curt Schilling, Arizona	22
2002	Randy Johnson, Arizona	24
2003	Russ Ortiz, Atlanta	21
2004	Roy Oswalt, Houston	20
2005	Dontrelle Willis, Florida	22
2006	Aaron Harang, Cincinnati; Derek Lowe, L.A.; Brad Penny, L.A.; John Smoltz, Atlanta; Brandon Webb, Arizona; Carlos Zambrano, Chicago	16
2007	Jake Peavy, San Diego	19
2008	Brandon Webb, Arizona	22
2009	Adam Wainwright, St. Louis	19
2010	Roy Halladay, Philadelphia	21
2011	Ian Kennedy, Arizona; Clayton Kershaw, L.A.	21
2012	Gio Gonzalez, Washington	21
2013	Adam Wainwright, St. Louis; Jordan Zimmermann, Washington	19
2014	Clayton Kershaw, Los Angeles	21
2015	Jake Arrieta, Chicago	22

American League

Year	Pitcher, team	Wins
1941	Bob Feller, Cleveland	25
1942	Tex Hughson, Boston	22
1943	Spurgeon "Spud" Chandler, New York; Dizzy Trout, Detroit	20
1944	Hal Newhouser, Detroit	29
1945	Hal Newhouser, Detroit	25
1946	Bob Feller, Cleveland; Hal Newhouser, Detroit	26
1947	Bob Feller, Cleveland	20
1948	Hal Newhouser, Detroit	21
1949	Mel Parnell, Boston	25
1950	Bob Lemon, Cleveland	23
1951	Bob Feller, Cleveland	22
1952	Bobby Shantz, Philadelphia	24
1953	Bob Porterfield, Washington	22
1954	Bob Lemon, Early Wynn, Cleveland	23
1955	Whitey Ford, New York; Bob Lemon, Cleveland; Frank Sullivan, Boston	18
1956	Frank Lary, Detroit	21
1957	Jim Bunning, Detroit; Billy Pierce, Chicago	20
1958	Bob Turley, New York	21
1959	Early Wynn, Chicago	22
1960	Chuck Estrada, Baltimore; Jim Perry, Cleveland	18
1961	Whitey Ford, New York	25
1962	Ralph Terry, New York	23
1963	Whitey Ford, New York	24
1964	Dean Chance, Los Angeles; Gary Peters, Chicago	20
1965	Jim "Mudcat" Grant, Minnesota	21
1966	Jim Kaat, Minnesota	25
1967	Jim Lonborg, Boston; Earl Wilson, Detroit	22
1968	Denny McLain, Detroit	31
1969	Denny McLain, Detroit	24
1970	Mike Cuellar, Baltimore; Dave McNally, Baltimore; Jim Perry, Minnesota	24
1971	Mickey Lolich, Detroit	25
1972	Gaylord Perry, Cleveland; Wilbur Wood, Chicago	24
1973	Wilbur Wood, Chicago	24
1974	Jim "Catfish" Hunter, Oak.; Ferguson Jenkins, Tex.	25
1975	Jim "Catfish" Hunter, NY; Jim Palmer, Baltimore	23
1976	Jim Palmer, Baltimore	22
1977	Dave Goltz, Minnesota; Dennis Leonard, Kansas City; Jim Palmer, Baltimore	20
1978	Ron Guidry, New York	25
1979	Mike Flanagan, Baltimore	23
1980	Steve Stone, Baltimore	25
1981	Dennis Martinez, Balt.; Steve McCatty, Oakland; Jack Morris, Detroit; Pete Vuckovich, Milwaukee	14
1982	LaMarr Hoyt, Chicago	19
1983	LaMarr Hoyt, Chicago	24
1984	Mike Boddicker, Baltimore	20
1985	Ron Guidry, New York	22
1986	Roger Clemens, Boston	24
1987	Roger Clemens, Boston; Dave Stewart, Oakland	20
1988	Frank Viola, Minnesota	24
1989	Bret Saberhagen, Kansas City	23
1990	Bob Welch, Oakland	27
1991	Scott Erickson, Minnesota; Bill Gullickson, Detroit	20
1992	Kevin Brown, Texas; Jack Morris, Toronto	21
1993	Jack McDowell, Chicago	22
1994	Jimmy Key, New York	17
1995	Mike Mussina, Baltimore	19
1996	Andy Pettitte, New York	21
1997	Roger Clemens, Toronto	21
1998	Roger Clemens, Toronto; David Cone, New York; Rick Helling, Texas	20
1999	Pedro Martinez, Boston	23
2000	Tim Hudson, Oakland; David Wells, Toronto	20
2001	Mark Mulder, Oakland	21
2002	Barry Zito, Oakland	23
2003	Roy Halladay, Toronto	22
2004	Curt Schilling, Boston	21
2005	Bartolo Colon, Los Angeles	21
2006	Johan Santana, Minnesota; Chien-Ming Wang, New York	19
2007	Josh Beckett, Boston	20
2008	Cliff Lee, Cleveland	22
2009	Felix Hernandez, Seattle; CC Sabathia, New York; Justin Verlander, Detroit	19
2010	CC Sabathia, New York	21
2011	Justin Verlander, Detroit	24
2012	David Price, Tampa Bay; Jered Weaver, L.A.	20
2013	Max Scherzer, Detroit	21
2014	Corey Kluber, Cleveland; Max Scherzer, Detroit; Jered Weaver, Los Angeles	18
2015	Dallas Keuchel, Houston	20

Cy Young Award Winners, 1956-2014

Year	Pitcher, team
1956	Don Newcombe, Brooklyn
1957	Warren Spahn, Milwaukee
1958	Bob Turley, NY Yankees
1959	Early Wynn, Chicago White Sox
1960	Vernon Law, Pittsburgh
1961	Whitey Ford, NY Yankees
1962	Don Drysdale, L.A. Dodgers
1963	Sandy Koufax, L.A. Angels
1964	Dean Chance, L.A. Dodgers
1965	Sandy Koufax, L.A. Dodgers
1966	Sandy Koufax, L.A. Dodgers
1967	(NL) Mike McCormick, S.F.
	(AL) Jim Lonborg, Boston
1968	(NL) Bob Gibson, St. Louis
	(AL) Denny McLain, Detroit
1969	(NL) Tom Seaver, NY
	(AL) (tie) Denny McLain, Detroit; Mike Cuellar, Baltimore
1970	(NL) Bob Gibson, St. Louis
	(AL) Jim Perry, Minnesota
1971	(NL) Ferguson Jenkins, Chicago
	(AL) Vida Blue, Oakland
1972	(NL) Steve Carlton, Philadelphia
	(AL) Gaylord Perry, Cleveland
1973	(NL) Tom Seaver, NY
	(AL) Jim Palmer, Baltimore
1974	(NL) Mike Marshall, L.A.
	(AL) Jim "Catfish" Hunter, Oakland
1975	(NL) Tom Seaver, NY
	(AL) Jim Palmer, Baltimore
1976	(NL) Randy Jones, San Diego
	(AL) Jim Palmer, Baltimore
1977	(NL) Steve Carlton, Philadelphia
	(AL) Sparky Lyle, NY
1978	(NL) Gaylord Perry, San Diego
	(AL) Ron Guidry, NY
1979	(NL) Bruce Sutter, Chicago
	(AL) Mike Flanagan, Baltimore
1980	(NL) Steve Carlton, Philadelphia
	(AL) Steve Stone, Baltimore
1981	(NL) Fernando Valenzuela, L.A.
	(AL) Rollie Fingers, Milwaukee
1982	(NL) Steve Carlton, Philadelphia
	(AL) Pete Vuckovich, Milwaukee
1983	(NL) John Denny, Philadelphia
	(AL) LaMarr Hoyt, Chicago
1984	(NL) Rick Sutcliffe, Chicago
	(AL) Willie Hernandez, Detroit
1985	(NL) Dwight Gooden, NY
	(AL) Bret Saberhagen, Kansas City
1986	(NL) Mike Scott, Houston
	(AL) Roger Clemens, Boston
1987	(NL) Steve Bedrosian, Phil.
	(AL) Roger Clemens, Boston
1988	(NL) Orel Hershiser, L.A.
	(AL) Frank Viola, Minnesota
1989	(NL) Mark Davis, San Diego
	(AL) Bret Saberhagen, Kansas City
1990	(NL) Doug Drabek, Pittsburgh
	(AL) Bob Welch, Oakland
1991	(NL) Tom Glavine, Atlanta
	(AL) Roger Clemens, Boston
1992	(NL) Greg Maddux, Chicago
	(AL) Dennis Eckersley, Oakland
1993	(NL) Greg Maddux, Atlanta
	(AL) Jack McDowell, Chicago
1994	(NL) Greg Maddux, Atlanta
	(AL) David Cone, Kansas City
1995	(NL) Greg Maddux, Atlanta
	(AL) Randy Johnson, Seattle
1996	(NL) John Smoltz, Atlanta
	(AL) Pat Hentgen, Toronto
1997	(NL) Pedro Martinez, Montréal
	(AL) Roger Clemens, Toronto
1998	(NL) Tom Glavine, Atlanta
	(AL) Roger Clemens, Toronto
1999	(NL) Randy Johnson, Arizona
	(AL) Pedro Martinez, Boston
2000	(NL) Randy Johnson, Arizona
	(AL) Pedro Martinez, Boston
2001	(NL) Randy Johnson, Arizona
	(AL) Roger Clemens, NY
2002	(NL) Randy Johnson, Arizona
	(AL) Barry Zito, Oakland
2003	(NL) Eric Gagne, L.A.
	(AL) Roy Halladay, Toronto
2004	(NL) Roger Clemens, Houston
	(AL) Johan Santana, Minnesota
2005	(NL) Chris Carpenter, St. Louis
	(AL) Bartolo Colon, L.A.
2006	(NL) Brandon Webb, Arizona
	(AL) Johan Santana, Minnesota
2007	(NL) Jake Peavy, San Diego
	(AL) CC Sabathia, Cleveland
2008	(NL) Tim Lincecum, S.F.
	(AL) Cliff Lee, Cleveland
2009	(NL) Tim Lincecum, S.F.
	(AL) Zack Greinke, Kansas City
2010	(NL) Roy Halladay, Philadelphia
	(AL) Felix Hernandez, Seattle
2011	(NL) Clayton Kershaw, L.A.
	(AL) Justin Verlander, Detroit
2012	(NL) R. A. Dickey, NY
	(AL) David Price, Tampa Bay
2013	(NL) Clayton Kershaw, L.A.
	(AL) Max Scherzer, Detroit
2014	(NL) Clayton Kershaw, L.A.
	(AL) Corey Kluber, Cleveland

Most Valuable Players, 1931-2014

As selected by the Baseball Writers' Assn. of America. Prior to 1931, MVP honors were named by various sources.

National League

Year	Player, team
1931	Frank Frisch, St. Louis
1932	Chuck Klein, Philadelphia
1933	Carl Hubbell, New York
1934	Dizzy Dean, St. Louis
1935	Gabby Hartnett, Chicago
1936	Carl Hubbell, New York
1937	Joe Medwick, St. Louis
1938	Ernie Lombardi, Cincinnati
1939	Bucky Walters, Cincinnati
1940	Frank McCormick, Cincinnati
1941	Dolph Camilli, Brooklyn
1942	Mort Cooper, St. Louis
1943	Stan Musial, St. Louis
1944	Martin Marion, St. Louis
1945	Phil Cavarretta, Chicago
1946	Stan Musial, St. Louis
1947	Bob Elliott, Boston
1948	Stan Musial, St. Louis
1949	Jackie Robinson, Brooklyn
1950	Jim Konstanty, Philadelphia
1951	Roy Campanella, Brooklyn
1952	Hank Sauer, Chicago
1953	Roy Campanella, Brooklyn
1954	Willie Mays, New York
1955	Roy Campanella, Brooklyn
1956	Don Newcombe, Brooklyn
1957	Hank Aaron, Milwaukee
1958	Ernie Banks, Chicago
1959	Ernie Banks, Chicago
1960	Dick Groat, Pittsburgh
1961	Frank Robinson, Cincinnati
1962	Maury Wills, Los Angeles
1963	Sandy Koufax, Los Angeles
1964	Ken Boyer, St. Louis
1965	Willie Mays, San Francisco
1966	Roberto Clemente, Pittsburgh
1967	Orlando Cepeda, St. Louis
1968	Bob Gibson, St. Louis
1969	Willie McCovey, San Francisco
1970	Johnny Bench, Cincinnati
1971	Joe Torre, St. Louis
1972	Johnny Bench, Cincinnati
1973	Pete Rose, Cincinnati
1974	Steve Garvey, Los Angeles
1975	Joe Morgan, Cincinnati
1976	Joe Morgan, Cincinnati
1977	George Foster, Cincinnati
1978	Dave Parker, Pittsburgh
1979	(tie) Keith Hernandez, St. Louis; Willie Stargell, Pittsburgh
1980	Mike Schmidt, Philadelphia
1981	Mike Schmidt, Philadelphia
1982	Dale Murphy, Atlanta
1983	Dale Murphy, Atlanta
1984	Ryne Sandberg, Chicago
1985	Willie McGee, St. Louis
1986	Mike Schmidt, Philadelphia
1987	Andre Dawson, Chicago
1988	Kirk Gibson, Los Angeles
1989	Kevin Mitchell, San Francisco
1990	Barry Bonds, Pittsburgh
1991	Terry Pendleton, Atlanta
1992	Barry Bonds, Pittsburgh
1993	Barry Bonds, San Francisco
1994	Jeff Bagwell, Houston
1995	Barry Larkin, Cincinnati
1996	Ken Caminiti, San Diego
1997	Larry Walker, Colorado
1998	Sammy Sosa, Chicago
1999	Chipper Jones, Atlanta
2000	Jeff Kent, San Francisco
2001	Barry Bonds, San Francisco
2002	Barry Bonds, San Francisco
2003	Barry Bonds, San Francisco
2004	Barry Bonds, San Francisco
2005	Albert Pujols, St. Louis
2006	Ryan Howard, Philadelphia
2007	Jimmy Rollins, Philadelphia
2008	Albert Pujols, St. Louis
2009	Albert Pujols, St. Louis
2010	Joey Votto, Cincinnati
2011	Ryan Braun, Milwaukee
2012	Buster Posey, San Francisco
2013	Andrew McCutchen, Pittsburgh
2014	Clayton Kershaw, Los Angeles

American League

Year	Player, team
1931	Lefty Grove, Philadelphia
1932	Jimmie Foxx, Philadelphia
1933	Jimmie Foxx, Philadelphia
1934	Mickey Cochrane, Detroit
1935	Hank Greenberg, Detroit
1936	Lou Gehrig, New York
1937	Charlie Gehringer, Detroit
1938	Jimmie Foxx, Boston
1939	Joe DiMaggio, New York

Year	Player, team
1940	Hank Greenberg, Detroit
1941	Joe DiMaggio, New York
1942	Joe Gordon, New York
1943	Spurgeon "Spud" Chandler, New York
1944	Hal Newhouser, Detroit
1945	Hal Newhouser, Detroit
1946	Ted Williams, Boston
1947	Joe DiMaggio, New York
1948	Lou Boudreau, Cleveland
1949	Ted Williams, Boston
1950	Phil Rizzuto, New York
1951	Yogi Berra, New York
1952	Bobby Shantz, Philadelphia
1953	Al Rosen, Cleveland
1954	Yogi Berra, New York
1955	Yogi Berra, New York
1956	Mickey Mantle, New York
1957	Mickey Mantle, New York
1958	Jackie Jensen, Boston
1959	Nellie Fox, Chicago
1960	Roger Maris, New York
1961	Roger Maris, New York
1962	Mickey Mantle, New York
1963	Elston Howard, New York
1964	Brooks Robinson, Baltimore
1965	Zoilo Versalles, Minnesota
1966	Frank Robinson, Baltimore
1967	Carl Yastrzemski, Boston
1968	Denny McLain, Detroit
1969	Harmon Killebrew, Minnesota
1970	John "Boog" Powell, Baltimore
1971	Vida Blue, Oakland
1972	Dick Allen, Chicago
1973	Reggie Jackson, Oakland
1974	Jeff Burroughs, Texas
1975	Fred Lynn, Boston
1976	Thurman Munson, New York
1977	Rod Carew, Minnesota
1978	Jim Rice, Boston
1979	Don Baylor, California
1980	George Brett, Kansas City
1981	Rollie Fingers, Milwaukee
1982	Robin Yount, Milwaukee
1983	Cal Ripken Jr., Baltimore
1984	Willie Hernandez, Detroit
1985	Don Mattingly, New York
1986	Roger Clemens, Boston
1987	George Bell, Toronto
1988	Jose Canseco, Oakland
1989	Robin Yount, Milwaukee
1990	Rickey Henderson, Oakland
1991	Cal Ripken Jr., Baltimore
1992	Dennis Eckersley, Oakland
1993	Frank Thomas, Chicago
1994	Frank Thomas, Chicago
1995	Mo Vaughn, Boston
1996	Juan Gonzalez, Texas
1997	Ken Griffey Jr., Seattle
1998	Juan Gonzalez, Texas
1999	Ivan Rodriguez, Texas
2000	Jason Giambi, Oakland
2001	Ichiro Suzuki, Seattle
2002	Miguel Tejada, Oakland
2003	Alex Rodriguez, Texas
2004	Vladimir Guerrero, Anaheim
2005	Alex Rodriguez, New York
2006	Justin Morneau, Minnesota
2007	Alex Rodriguez, New York
2008	Dustin Pedroia, Boston
2009	Joe Mauer, Minnesota
2010	Josh Hamilton, Texas
2011	Justin Verlander, Detroit
2012	Miguel Cabrera, Detroit
2013	Miguel Cabrera, Detroit
2014	Mike Trout, Los Angeles

Rookie of the Year, 1949-2014

(as selected by the Baseball Writers' Assn. of America)

1947: Jackie Robinson, Brooklyn, 1B (combined selection); 1948: Alvin Dark, Boston (NL), SS (combined selection).

National League

Year	Player, team, position
1949	Don Newcombe, Brooklyn, P
1950	Sam Jethroe, Boston, OF
1951	Willie Mays, NY, OF
1952	Joe Black, Brooklyn, P
1953	Jim Gilliam, Brooklyn, 2B
1954	Wally Moon, St. Louis, OF
1955	Bill Virdon, St. Louis, OF
1956	Frank Robinson, Cincinnati, OF
1957	Jack Sanford, Philadelphia, P
1958	Orlando Cepeda, San Francisco, 1B
1959	Willie McCovey, San Francisco, 1B
1960	Frank Howard, L.A., OF
1961	Billy Williams, Chicago, OF
1962	Ken Hubbs, Chicago, 2B
1963	Pete Rose, Cincinnati, 2B
1964	Richie Allen, Philadelphia, 3B
1965	Jim Lefebvre, L.A., 2B
1966	Tommy Helms, Cincinnati, 2B
1967	Tom Seaver, NY, P
1968	Johnny Bench, Cincinnati, C
1969	Ted Sizemore, L.A., 2B
1970	Carl Morton, Montréal, P
1971	Earl Williams, Atlanta, C
1972	Jon Matlack, NY, P
1973	Gary Matthews, San Francisco, OF
1974	Bake McBride, St. Louis, OF
1975	John Montefusco, San Francisco, P
1976	(tie) Butch Metzger, San Diego, P; Pat Zachry, Cincinnati, P
1977	Andre Dawson, Montréal, OF
1978	Bob Horner, Atlanta, 3B
1979	Rick Sutcliffe, L.A., P
1980	Steve Howe, L.A., P
1981	Fernando Valenzuela, L.A., P
1982	Steve Sax, L.A., 2B
1983	Darryl Strawberry, NY, OF
1984	Dwight Gooden, NY, P
1985	Vince Coleman, St. Louis, OF
1986	Todd Worrell, St. Louis, P
1987	Benito Santiago, San Diego, C
1988	Chris Sabo, Cincinnati, 3B
1989	Jerome Walton, Chicago, OF
1990	Dave Justice, Atlanta, 1B
1991	Jeff Bagwell, Houston, 1B
1992	Eric Karros, L.A., 1B
1993	Mike Piazza, L.A., C
1994	Raul Mondesi, L.A., OF
1995	Hideo Nomo, L.A., P
1996	Todd Hollandsworth, L.A., OF
1997	Scott Rolen, Philadelphia, 3B
1998	Kerry Wood, Chicago, P
1999	Scott Williamson, Cincinnati, P
2000	Rafael Furcal, Atlanta, SS
2001	Albert Pujols, St. Louis, OF
2002	Jason Jennings, Colorado, P
2003	Dontrelle Willis, Florida, P
2004	Jason Bay, Pittsburgh, OF
2005	Ryan Howard, Philadelphia, 1B
2006	Hanley Ramirez, Florida, SS
2007	Ryan Braun, Milwaukee, 3B
2008	Geovany Soto, Chicago, C
2009	Chris Coghlan, Florida, OF
2010	Buster Posey, San Francisco, C
2011	Craig Kimbrel, Atlanta, P
2012	Bryce Harper, Washington, OF
2013	Jose Fernandez, Miami, P
2014	Jacob deGrom, NY, P

American League

Year	Player, team, position
1949	Roy Sievers, St. Louis, OF
1950	Walt Dropo, Boston, 1B
1951	Gil McDougald, NY, 3B
1952	Harry Byrd, Philadelphia, P
1953	Harvey Kuenn, Detroit, SS
1954	Bob Grim, NY, P
1955	Herb Score, Cleveland, P
1956	Luis Aparicio, Chicago, SS
1957	Tony Kubek, NY, IF-OF
1958	Albie Pearson, Washington, OF
1959	Bob Allison, Washington, OF
1960	Ron Hansen, Baltimore, SS
1961	Don Schwall, Boston, P
1962	Tom Tresh, NY, IF-OF
1963	Gary Peters, Chicago, P
1964	Tony Oliva, Minnesota, OF
1965	Curt Blefary, Baltimore, OF
1966	Tommie Agee, Chicago, OF
1967	Rod Carew, Minnesota, 2B
1968	Stan Bahnsen, NY, P
1969	Lou Piniella, Kansas City, OF
1970	Thurman Munson, NY, C
1971	Chris Chambliss, Cleveland, 1B
1972	Carlton Fisk, Boston, C
1973	Al Bumbry, Baltimore, OF
1974	Mike Hargrove, Texas, 1B
1975	Fred Lynn, Boston, OF
1976	Mark Fidrych, Detroit, P
1977	Eddie Murray, Baltimore, DH
1978	Lou Whitaker, Detroit, 2B
1979	(tie) John Castino, Minnesota, 3B; Alfredo Griffin, Toronto, SS
1980	Joe Charboneau, Cleveland, OF
1981	Dave Righetti, NY, P
1982	Cal Ripken Jr., Baltimore, SS
1983	Ron Kittle, Chicago, OF
1984	Alvin Davis, Seattle, 1B
1985	Ozzie Guillen, Chicago, SS
1986	Jose Canseco, Oakland, OF
1987	Mark McGwire, Oakland, 1B
1988	Walt Weiss, Oakland, SS
1989	Gregg Olson, Baltimore, P
1990	Sandy Alomar Jr., Cleveland, C
1991	Chuck Knoblauch, Minnesota, 2B
1992	Pat Listach, Milwaukee, SS
1993	Tim Salmon, California, OF
1994	Bob Hamelin, Kansas City, DH
1995	Marty Cordova, Minnesota, OF
1996	Derek Jeter, NY, SS
1997	Nomar Garciaparra, Boston, SS
1998	Ben Grieve, Oakland, OF
1999	Carlos Beltran, Kansas City, OF
2000	Kazuhiro Sasaki, Seattle, P
2001	Ichiro Suzuki, Seattle, OF
2002	Eric Hinske, Toronto, 3B
2003	Angel Berroa, Kansas City, SS
2004	Bobby Crosby, Oakland, SS
2005	Huston Street, Oakland, P
2006	Justin Verlander, Detroit, P
2007	Dustin Pedroia, Boston, 2B
2008	Evan Longoria, Tampa Bay, 3B
2009	Andrew Bailey, Oakland, P
2010	Neftali Feliz, Texas, P
2011	Jeremy Hellickson, Tampa Bay, P
2012	Mike Trout, L.A., OF
2013	Wil Myers, Tampa Bay, OF
2014	Jose Abreu, Chicago, 1B

Major League Pennant Winners, 1901-75

National League						American League					
Year	Winner	W	L	PCT	Manager	Year	Winner	W	L	PCT	Manager
1901	Pittsburgh	90	49	.647	Clarke	1901	Chicago	83	53	.610	Griffith
1902	Pittsburgh	103	36	.741	Clarke	1902	Philadelphia	83	53	.610	Mack
1903	Pittsburgh	91	49	.650	Clarke	1903	Boston	91	47	.659	Collins
1904	New York	106	47	.693	McGraw	1904	Boston	95	59	.617	Collins
1905	New York	105	48	.686	McGraw	1905	Philadelphia	92	56	.622	Mack
1906	Chicago	116	36	.763	Chance	1906	Chicago	93	58	.616	Jones
1907	Chicago	107	45	.704	Chance	1907	Detroit	92	58	.613	Jennings
1908	Chicago	99	55	.643	Chance	1908	Detroit	90	63	.588	Jennings
1909	Pittsburgh	110	42	.724	Clarke	1909	Detroit	98	54	.645	Jennings
1910	Chicago	104	50	.675	Chance	1910	Philadelphia	102	48	.680	Mack
1911	New York	99	54	.647	McGraw	1911	Philadelphia	101	50	.669	Mack
1912	New York	103	48	.682	McGraw	1912	Boston	105	47	.691	Stahl
1913	New York	101	51	.664	McGraw	1913	Philadelphia	96	57	.627	Mack
1914	Boston	94	59	.614	Stallings	1914	Philadelphia	99	53	.651	Mack
1915	Philadelphia	90	62	.592	Moran	1915	Boston	101	50	.669	Carrigan
1916	Brooklyn	94	60	.610	Robinson	1916	Boston	91	63	.591	Carrigan
1917	New York	98	56	.636	McGraw	1917	Chicago	100	54	.649	Rowland
1918	Chicago	84	45	.651	Mitchell	1918	Boston	75	51	.595	Barrow
1919	Cincinnati	96	44	.686	Moran	1919	Chicago	88	52	.629	Gleason
1920	Brooklyn	93	61	.604	Robinson	1920	Cleveland	98	56	.636	Speaker
1921	New York	94	59	.614	McGraw	1921	New York	98	55	.641	Huggins
1922	New York	93	61	.604	McGraw	1922	New York	94	60	.610	Huggins
1923	New York	95	58	.621	McGraw	1923	New York	98	54	.645	Huggins
1924	New York	93	60	.608	McGraw	1924	Washington	92	62	.597	Harris
1925	Pittsburgh	95	58	.621	McKechnie	1925	Washington	96	55	.636	Harris
1926	St. Louis	89	65	.578	Hornsby	1926	New York	91	63	.591	Huggins
1927	Pittsburgh	94	60	.610	Bush	1927	New York	110	44	.714	Huggins
1928	St. Louis	95	59	.617	McKechnie	1928	New York	101	53	.656	Huggins
1929	Chicago	98	54	.645	McCarthy	1929	Philadelphia	104	46	.693	Mack
1930	St. Louis	92	62	.597	Street	1930	Philadelphia	102	52	.662	Mack
1931	St. Louis	101	53	.656	Street	1931	Philadelphia	107	45	.704	Mack
1932	Chicago	90	64	.584	Hornsby, Grimm	1932	New York	107	47	.695	McCarthy
1933	New York	91	61	.599	Terry	1933	Washington	99	53	.651	Cronin
1934	St. Louis	95	58	.621	Frisch	1934	Detroit	101	53	.656	Cochrane
1935	Chicago	100	54	.649	Grimm	1935	Detroit	93	58	.616	Cochrane
1936	New York	92	62	.597	Terry	1936	New York	102	51	.667	McCarthy
1937	New York	95	57	.625	Terry	1937	New York	102	52	.662	McCarthy
1938	Chicago	89	63	.586	Grimm, Hartnett	1938	New York	99	53	.651	McCarthy
1939	Cincinnati	97	57	.630	McKechnie	1939	New York	106	45	.702	McCarthy
1940	Cincinnati	100	53	.654	McKechnie	1940	Detroit	90	64	.584	Baker
1941	Brooklyn	100	54	.649	Durocher	1941	New York	101	53	.656	McCarthy
1942	St. Louis	106	48	.688	Southworth	1942	New York	103	51	.669	McCarthy
1943	St. Louis	105	49	.682	Southworth	1943	New York	98	56	.636	McCarthy
1944	St. Louis	105	49	.682	Southworth	1944	St. Louis	89	65	.578	Sewell
1945	Chicago	98	56	.636	Grimm	1945	Detroit	88	65	.575	O'Neill
1946	St. Louis	98	58	.628	Dyer	1946	Boston	104	50	.675	Cronin
1947	Brooklyn	94	60	.610	Shotton	1947	New York	97	57	.630	Harris
1948	Boston	91	62	.595	Southworth	1948	Cleveland	97	58	.626	Boudreau
1949	Brooklyn	97	57	.630	Shotton	1949	New York	97	57	.630	Stengel
1950	Philadelphia	91	63	.591	Sawyer	1950	New York	98	56	.636	Stengel
1951	New York	98	59	.624	Durocher	1951	New York	98	56	.636	Stengel
1952	Brooklyn	96	57	.627	Dressen	1952	New York	95	59	.617	Stengel
1953	Brooklyn	105	49	.682	Dressen	1953	New York	99	52	.656	Stengel
1954	New York	97	57	.630	Durocher	1954	Cleveland	111	43	.721	Lopez
1955	Brooklyn	98	55	.641	Alston	1955	New York	96	58	.623	Stengel
1956	Brooklyn	93	61	.604	Alston	1956	New York	97	57	.630	Stengel
1957	Milwaukee	95	59	.617	Haney	1957	New York	98	56	.636	Stengel
1958	Milwaukee	92	62	.597	Haney	1958	New York	92	62	.597	Stengel
1959	Los Angeles	88	68	.564	Alston	1959	Chicago	94	60	.610	Lopez
1960	Pittsburgh	95	59	.617	Murtaugh	1960	New York	97	57	.630	Stengel
1961	Cincinnati	93	61	.604	Hutchinson	1961	New York	109	53	.673	Houk
1962	San Francisco	103	62	.624	Dark	1962	New York	96	66	.593	Houk
1963	Los Angeles	99	63	.611	Alston	1963	New York	104	57	.646	Houk
1964	St. Louis	93	69	.574	Keane	1964	New York	99	63	.611	Berra
1965	Los Angeles	97	65	.599	Alston	1965	Minnesota	102	60	.630	Mele
1966	Los Angeles	95	67	.586	Alston	1966	Baltimore	97	63	.606	Bauer
1967	St. Louis	101	60	.627	Schoendienst	1967	Boston	92	70	.568	Williams
1968	St. Louis	97	65	.599	Schoendienst	1968	Detroit	103	59	.636	Smith
1969	New York	100	62	.617	Hodges	1969	Baltimore	109	53	.673	Weaver
1970	Cincinnati	102	60	.630	Anderson	1970	Baltimore	108	54	.667	Weaver
1971	Pittsburgh	97	65	.599	Murtaugh	1971	Baltimore	101	57	.639	Weaver
1972	Cincinnati	95	59	.617	Anderson	1972	Oakland	93	62	.600	Williams
1973	New York	82	79	.509	Berra	1973	Oakland	94	68	.580	Williams
1974	Los Angeles	102	60	.630	Alston	1974	Oakland	90	72	.556	Dark
1975	Cincinnati	108	54	.667	Anderson	1975	Boston	95	65	.594	Johnson

Major League Pennant Winners, 1976-2015

National League

Year	East winner	W	L	PCT	Manager	West winner	W	L	PCT	Manager	Pennant winner
1976	Philadelphia	101	61	.623	Ozark	Cincinnati	102	60	.630	Anderson	Cincinnati
1977	Philadelphia	101	61	.623	Ozark	Los Angeles	98	64	.605	Lasorda	Los Angeles
1978	Philadelphia	90	72	.556	Ozark	Los Angeles	95	67	.586	Lasorda	Los Angeles
1979	Pittsburgh	98	64	.605	Tanner	Cincinnati	90	71	.559	McNamara	Pittsburgh

National League

Year	East winner	W	L	PCT	Manager	West winner	W	L	PCT	Manager	Pennant winner
1980	Philadelphia	91	71	.562	Green	Houston	93	70	.571	Virdon	Philadelphia
1981(a)	Philadelphia	34	21	.618	Green	Los Angeles	36	21	.632	Lasorda	(c)
1981(b)	Montréal	30	23	.566	Williams, Fanning	Houston	33	20	.623	Virdon	Los Angeles
1982	St. Louis	92	70	.568	Herzog	Atlanta	89	73	.549	Torre	St. Louis
1983	Philadelphia	90	72	.556	Corrales, Owens	Los Angeles	91	71	.562	Lasorda	Philadelphia
1984	Chicago	96	65	.596	Frey	San Diego	92	70	.568	Williams	San Diego
1985	St. Louis	101	61	.623	Herzog	Los Angeles	95	67	.586	Lasorda	St. Louis
1986	New York	108	54	.667	Johnson	Houston	96	66	.593	Lanier	New York
1987	St. Louis	95	67	.586	Herzog	San Francisco	90	72	.556	Craig	St. Louis
1988	New York	100	60	.625	Johnson	Los Angeles	94	67	.584	Lasorda	Los Angeles
1989	Chicago	93	69	.574	Zimmer	San Francisco	92	70	.568	Craig	San Francisco
1990	Pittsburgh	95	67	.586	Leyland	Cincinnati	91	71	.562	Piniella	Cincinnati
1991	Pittsburgh	98	64	.605	Leyland	Atlanta	94	68	.580	Cox	Atlanta
1992	Pittsburgh	96	66	.593	Leyland	Atlanta	98	64	.605	Cox	Atlanta
1993	Philadelphia	97	65	.599	Fregosi	Atlanta	104	58	.642	Cox	Philadelphia

Year	Division	Winner	W	L	PCT	Manager	Playoffs	Pennant winner
1994(d)	East	Montréal	74	40	.649	Alou	—	—
	Central	Cincinnati	66	48	.579	Johnson		
	West	Los Angeles	58	56	.509	Lasorda		
1995	East	Atlanta	90	54	.625	Cox	Atlanta 3, Colorado* 1	Atlanta
	Central	Cincinnati	85	59	.590	Johnson	Cincinnati 3, Los Angeles 0	
	West	Los Angeles	78	66	.542	Lasorda	Atlanta 4, Cincinnati 0	
1996	East	Atlanta	96	66	.593	Cox	Atlanta 3, Los Angeles* 0	Atlanta
	Central	St. Louis	88	74	.543	La Russa	St. Louis 3, San Diego 0	
	West	San Diego	91	71	.562	Bochy	Atlanta 4, St. Louis 3	
1997	East	Atlanta	101	61	.623	Cox	Atlanta 3, Houston 0	Florida*
	Central	Houston	84	78	.519	Dierker	Florida* 3, San Francisco 0	(Leyland)
	West	San Francisco	90	72	.556	Baker	Florida* 4, Atlanta 2	
1998	East	Atlanta	106	56	.654	Cox	Atlanta 3, Chicago* 0	San Diego
	Central	Houston	102	60	.630	Dierker	San Diego 3, Houston 1	
	West	San Diego	98	64	.605	Bochy	San Diego 4, Atlanta 2	
1999	East	Atlanta	103	59	.636	Cox	Atlanta 3, Houston 1	Atlanta
	Central	Houston	97	65	.599	Dierker, Galante	New York* 3, Arizona 1	
	West	Arizona	100	62	.617	Showalter	Atlanta 4, New York* 2	
2000	East	Atlanta	95	67	.586	Cox	St. Louis 3, Atlanta 0	New York*
	Central	St. Louis	95	67	.586	La Russa	New York* 3, San Francisco 1	(Valentine)
	West	San Francisco	97	65	.599	Baker	New York* 4, St. Louis 1	
2001	East	Atlanta	88	74	.543	Cox	Atlanta 3, Houston 0	Arizona
	Central	Houston	93	69	.574	Dierker	Arizona 3, St. Louis* 2	
	West	Arizona	92	70	.568	Brenly	Arizona 4, Atlanta 1	
2002	East	Atlanta	101	59	.631	Cox	St. Louis 3, Arizona 0	San Francisco*
	Central	St. Louis	97	65	.599	La Russa	San Francisco* 3, Atlanta 2	(Baker)
	West	Arizona	98	64	.605	Brenly	San Francisco* 4, St. Louis 1	
2003	East	Atlanta	101	61	.623	Cox	Chicago 3, Atlanta 2	Florida*
	Central	Chicago	88	74	.543	Baker	Florida* 3, San Francisco 1	(McKeon)
	West	San Francisco	100	61	.621	Alou	Florida* 4, Chicago 3	
2004	East	Atlanta	96	66	.593	Cox	Houston* 3, Atlanta 2	St. Louis
	Central	St. Louis	105	57	.648	La Russa	St. Louis 3, Los Angeles 1	
	West	Los Angeles	93	69	.574	Tracy	St. Louis 4, Houston* 3	
2005	East	Atlanta	90	72	.556	Cox	St. Louis 3, San Diego 0	Houston*
	Central	St. Louis	100	62	.617	La Russa	Houston* 3, Atlanta 1	(Garner)
	West	San Diego	82	80	.506	Bochy	Houston* 4, St. Louis 2	
2006	East	New York	97	65	.599	Randolph	New York 3, Los Angeles* 0	St. Louis
	Central	St. Louis	83	78	.516	La Russa	St. Louis 3, San Diego 1	
	West	San Diego	88	74	.543	Bochy	St. Louis 4, New York 3	
2007	East	Philadelphia	89	73	.549	Manuel	Colorado* 3, Philadelphia 0	Colorado*
	Central	Chicago	85	77	.525	Piniella	Arizona 3, Chicago 0	(Hurdle)
	West	Arizona	90	72	.556	Melvin	Colorado* 4, Arizona 0	
2008	East	Philadelphia	92	70	.568	Manuel	Philadelphia 3, Milwaukee* 1	Philadelphia
	Central	Chicago	97	64	.602	Piniella	Los Angeles 3, Chicago 0	
	West	Los Angeles	84	78	.519	Torre	Philadelphia 4, Los Angeles 1	
2009	East	Philadelphia	93	69	.574	Manuel	Philadelphia 3, Colorado* 1	Philadelphia
	Central	St. Louis	91	71	.562	La Russa	Los Angeles 3, St. Louis 0	
	West	Los Angeles	95	67	.586	Torre	Philadelphia 4, Los Angeles 1	
2010	East	Philadelphia	97	65	.599	Manuel	San Francisco 3, Atlanta* 1	San Francisco
	Central	Cincinnati	91	71	.562	Baker	Philadelphia 3, Cincinnati 0	
	West	San Francisco	92	70	.568	Bochy	San Francisco 4, Philadelphia 2	
2011	East	Philadelphia	102	60	.630	Manuel	Milwaukee 3, Arizona 2	St. Louis*
	Central	Milwaukee	96	66	.593	Roenicke	St. Louis* 3, Philadelphia 2	(La Russa)
	West	Arizona	94	68	.580	Gibson	St. Louis* 4, Milwaukee 2	
2012	East	Washington	98	64	.605	Johnson	#St. Louis* 6, Atlanta* 3	San Francisco
	Central	Cincinnati	97	65	.599	Baker	St. Louis* 3, Washington 2	
	West	San Francisco	94	68	.580	Bochy	San Francisco 3, Cincinnati 2	
							San Francisco 4, St. Louis* 3	
2013	East	Atlanta	96	66	.593	González	#Pittsburgh* 6, Cincinnati* 2	St. Louis
	Central	St. Louis	97	65	.599	Matheny	St. Louis 3, Pittsburgh* 2	
	West	Los Angeles	92	70	.568	Mattingly	Los Angeles 3, Atlanta 1	
							St. Louis 4, Los Angeles 2	
2014	East	Washington	96	66	.593	Williams	#San Francisco* 8, Pittsburgh* 0	San Francisco*
	Central	St. Louis	90	72	.556	Matheny	San Francisco* 3, Washington 1	(Bochy)
	West	Los Angeles	94	68	.580	Mattingly	St. Louis 3, Los Angeles 1	
							San Francisco* 4, St. Louis 1	
2015	East	New York	90	72	.556	Collins	#Chicago* 4, Pittsburgh* 0	New York
	Central	St. Louis	100	62	.617	Matheny	Chicago* 3, St. Louis 1	
	West	Los Angeles	92	70	.568	Mattingly	New York 3, Los Angeles 2	
							New York 4, Chicago* 0	

American League

Year	East winner	W	L	PCT	Manager	West winner	W	L	PCT	Manager	Pennant winner
1976	New York	97	62	.610	Martin	Kansas City	90	72	.556	Herzog	New York
1977	New York	100	62	.617	Martin	Kansas City	102	60	.630	Herzog	New York
1978	New York	100	63	.613	Martin, Lemon	Kansas City	92	70	.568	Herzog	New York

Year	East winner	W	L	PCT	Manager	West winner	W	L	PCT	Manager	Pennant winner
1979	Baltimore	102	57	.642	Weaver	California	88	74	.543	Fregosi	Baltimore
1980	New York	103	59	.636	Howser	Kansas City	97	65	.599	Frey	Kansas City
1981(a)	New York	34	22	.607	Michael	Oakland	37	23	.617	Martin	(c)
1981(b)	Milwaukee	31	22	.585	Rodgers	Kansas City	30	23	.566	Frey, Howser	New York
1982	Milwaukee	95	67	.586	Rodgers, Kuenn	California	93	69	.574	Mauch	Milwaukee
1983	Baltimore	98	64	.605	Altobelli	Chicago	99	63	.611	La Russa	Baltimore
1984	Detroit	104	58	.642	Anderson	Kansas City	84	78	.519	Howser	Detroit
1985	Toronto	99	62	.615	Cox	Kansas City	91	71	.562	Howser	Kansas City
1986	Boston	95	66	.590	McNamara	California	92	70	.568	Mauch	Boston
1987	Detroit	98	64	.605	Anderson	Minnesota	85	77	.525	Kelly	Minnesota
1988	Boston	89	73	.549	McNamara, Morgan	Oakland	104	58	.642	La Russa	Oakland
1989	Toronto	89	73	.549	Williams, Gaston	Oakland	99	63	.611	La Russa	Oakland
1990	Boston	88	74	.543	Morgan	Oakland	103	59	.636	La Russa	Oakland
1991	Toronto	91	71	.562	Gaston, Tenace	Minnesota	95	67	.586	Kelly	Minnesota
1992	Toronto	96	66	.593	Gaston	Oakland	96	66	.593	La Russa	Toronto
1993	Toronto	95	67	.586	Gaston	Chicago	94	68	.580	Lamont	Toronto

Year	Division	Winner	W	L	PCT	Manager	Playoffs	Pennant winner
1994(d)	East	New York	70	43	.619	Showalter	—	—
	Central	Chicago	67	46	.593	Lamont		
	West	Texas	52	62	.456	Kennedy		
1995	East	Boston	86	58	.597	Kennedy	Cleveland 3, Boston 0	Cleveland
	Central	Cleveland	100	44	.694	Hargrove	Seattle 3, New York* 2	
	West	Seattle	79	66	.545	Piniella	Cleveland 4, Seattle 2	
1996	East	New York	92	70	.568	Torre	Baltimore* 3, Cleveland 1	New York
	Central	Cleveland	99	62	.615	Hargrove	New York 3, Texas 1	
	West	Texas	90	72	.556	Oates	New York 4, Baltimore* 1	
1997	East	Baltimore	98	64	.605	Johnson	Baltimore 3, Seattle 1	Cleveland
	Central	Cleveland	86	75	.534	Hargrove	Cleveland 3, New York* 2	
	West	Seattle	90	72	.556	Piniella	Cleveland 4, Baltimore 2	
1998	East	New York	114	48	.704	Torre	New York 3, Texas 0	New York
	Central	Cleveland	89	73	.549	Hargrove	Cleveland 3, Boston* 1	
	West	Texas	88	74	.543	Oates	New York 4, Cleveland 2	
1999	East	New York	98	64	.605	Torre	New York 3, Texas 0	New York
	Central	Cleveland	97	65	.599	Hargrove	Boston* 3, Cleveland 2	
	West	Texas	95	67	.586	Oates	New York 4, Boston* 1	
2000	East	New York	87	74	.540	Torre	New York 3, Oakland 2	New York
	Central	Chicago	95	67	.586	Manuel	Seattle* 3, Chicago 0	
	West	Oakland	91	70	.565	Howe	New York 4, Seattle* 2	
2001	East	New York	95	65	.594	Torre	Seattle 3, Cleveland 2	New York
	Central	Cleveland	91	71	.562	Manuel	New York 3, Oakland* 2	
	West	Seattle	116	46	.716	Piniella	New York 4, Seattle 1	
2002	East	New York	103	58	.640	Torre	Anaheim* 3, New York 1	Anaheim* (Scioscia)
	Central	Minnesota	94	67	.584	Gardenhire	Minnesota 3, Oakland 2	
	West	Oakland	103	59	.636	Howe	Anaheim* 4, Minnesota 1	
2003	East	New York	101	61	.623	Torre	New York 3, Minnesota 1	New York
	Central	Minnesota	90	72	.556	Gardenhire	Boston* 3, Oakland 2	
	West	Oakland	96	66	.593	Macha	New York 4, Boston* 3	
2004	East	New York	101	61	.623	Torre	New York 3, Minnesota 1	Boston* (Francona)
	Central	Minnesota	92	70	.568	Gardenhire	Boston* 3, Anaheim 0	
	West	Anaheim	92	70	.568	Scioscia	Boston* 4, New York 3	
2005	East	New York	95	67	.586	Torre	Chicago 3, Boston* 0	Chicago
	Central	Chicago	99	63	.611	Guillen	Los Angeles 3, New York 2	
	West	Los Angeles	95	67	.586	Scioscia	Chicago 4, Los Angeles 1	
2006	East	New York	97	65	.599	Torre	Oakland 3, Minnesota 0	Detroit* (Leyland)
	Central	Minnesota	96	66	.593	Gardenhire	Detroit* 3, New York 1	
	West	Oakland	93	69	.574	Macha	Detroit* 4, Oakland 0	
2007	East	Boston	96	66	.593	Francona	Boston 3, Los Angeles 0	Boston
	Central	Cleveland	96	66	.593	Wedge	Cleveland 3, New York* 1	
	West	Los Angeles	94	68	.580	Scioscia	Boston 4, Cleveland 3	
2008	East	Tampa Bay	97	65	.599	Maddon	Tampa Bay 3, Chicago 1	Tampa Bay
	Central	Chicago	89	74	.546	Guillen	Boston* 3, Los Angeles 1	
	West	Los Angeles	100	62	.617	Scioscia	Tampa Bay 4, Boston* 3	
2009	East	New York	103	59	.636	Girardi	New York 3, Minnesota 0	New York
	Central	Minnesota	87	76	.534	Gardenhire	Los Angeles 3, Boston* 0	
	West	Los Angeles	97	65	.599	Scioscia	New York 4, Los Angeles 2	
2010	East	Tampa Bay	96	66	.593	Maddon	New York* 3, Minnesota 0	Texas
	Central	Minnesota	94	68	.580	Gardenhire	Texas 3, Tampa Bay 2	
	West	Texas	90	72	.556	Washington	Texas 4, New York* 2	
2011	East	New York	97	65	.599	Girardi	Detroit 3, New York 2	Texas
	Central	Detroit	95	67	.586	Leyland	Texas 3, Tampa Bay* 1	
	West	Texas	96	66	.593	Washington	Texas 4, Detroit 2	
2012	East	New York	95	67	.586	Girardi	#Baltimore* 5, Texas* 1	Detroit
	Central	Detroit	88	74	.543	Leyland	New York 3, Baltimore* 2	
	West	Oakland	94	68	.580	Melvin	Detroit 3, Oakland 2	
							Detroit 4, New York 0	
2013	East	Boston	97	65	.599	Farrell	#Tampa Bay* 4, Cleveland* 0	Boston
	Central	Detroit	93	69	.574	Leyland	Boston 3, Tampa Bay* 1	
	West	Oakland	96	66	.593	Melvin	Detroit 3, Oakland 2	
							Boston 4, Detroit 2	
2014	East	Baltimore	96	66	.593	Showalter	#Kansas City* 9, Oakland* 8	Kansas City* (Yost)
	Central	Detroit	90	72	.556	Ausmus	Kansas City* 3, Los Angeles 0	
	West	Los Angeles	98	64	.605	Scioscia	Baltimore 3, Detroit 0	
							Kansas City* 4, Baltimore 0	
2015	East	Toronto	93	69	.574	Gibbons	#Houston* 3, New York* 0	Kansas City
	Central	Kansas City	95	67	.586	Yost	Kansas City 3, Houston* 2	
	West	Texas	88	74	.543	Banister	Toronto 3, Texas 2	
							Kansas City 4, Toronto 2	

* = Wild-card team. If pennant winner is wild-card team, manager's name is given in parentheses. # = Single-game wild card playoff (debuted in 2012). (a) First half. (b) Second half. (c) Montréal, L.A., NY Yankees, and Oakland won the divisional playoffs. (d) In Aug. 1994, a players' strike began that caused the cancellation of the remainder of the season, the playoffs, and the World Series. Teams listed as division "winners" for 1994 were leading their divisions at the time of the strike.

World Series Results, 1903-2015

1903 Boston AL 5, Pittsburgh NL 3
1904 No series
1905 New York NL 4, Philadelphia AL 1
1906 Chicago AL 4, Chicago NL 2
1907 Chicago NL 4, Detroit AL 0, 1 tie
1908 Chicago NL 4, Detroit AL 1
1909 Pittsburgh NL 4, Detroit AL 3
1910 Philadelphia AL 4, Chicago NL 1
1911 Philadelphia AL 4, New York NL 2
1912 Boston AL 4, New York NL 3, 1 tie
1913 Philadelphia AL 4, New York NL 1
1914 Boston NL 4, Philadelphia AL 0
1915 Boston AL 4, Philadelphia NL 1
1916 Boston AL 4, Brooklyn NL 1
1917 Chicago AL 4, New York NL 2
1918 Boston AL 4, Chicago NL 2
1919 Cincinnati NL 5, Chicago AL 3
1920 Cleveland AL 5, Brooklyn NL 2
1921 New York NL 5, New York AL 3
1922 New York NL 4, New York AL 0, 1 tie
1923 New York AL 4, New York NL 2
1924 Washington AL 4, New York NL 3
1925 Pittsburgh NL 4, Washington AL 3
1926 St. Louis NL 4, New York AL 3
1927 New York AL 4, Pittsburgh NL 0
1928 New York AL 4, St. Louis NL 0
1929 Philadelphia AL 4, Chicago NL 1
1930 Philadelphia AL 4, St. Louis NL 2
1931 St. Louis NL 4, Philadelphia AL 3
1932 New York AL 4, Chicago NL 0
1933 New York NL 4, Washington AL 1
1934 St. Louis NL 4, Detroit AL 3
1935 Detroit AL 4, Chicago NL 2
1936 New York AL 4, New York NL 2
1937 New York AL 4, New York NL 1
1938 New York AL 4, Chicago NL 0
1939 New York AL 4, Cincinnati NL 0
1940 Cincinnati NL 4, Detroit AL 3
1941 New York AL 4, Brooklyn NL 1
1942 St. Louis NL 4, New York AL 1
1943 New York AL 4, St. Louis NL 1
1944 St. Louis NL 4, St. Louis AL 2
1945 Detroit AL 4, Chicago NL 3
1946 St. Louis NL 4, Boston AL 3
1947 New York AL 4, Brooklyn NL 3
1948 Cleveland AL 4, Boston NL 2
1949 New York AL 4, Brooklyn NL 1
1950 New York AL 4, Philadelphia NL 0
1951 New York AL 4, New York NL 2
1952 New York AL 4, Brooklyn NL 3
1953 New York AL 4, Brooklyn NL 2
1954 New York NL 4, Cleveland AL 0
1955 Brooklyn NL 4, New York AL 3
1956 New York AL 4, Brooklyn NL 3
1957 Milwaukee NL 4, New York AL 3
1958 New York AL 4, Milwaukee NL 3
1959 Los Angeles NL 4, Chicago AL 2
1960 Pittsburgh NL 4, New York AL 3
1961 New York AL 4, Cincinnati NL 1
1962 New York AL 4, San Francisco NL 3
1963 Los Angeles NL 4, New York AL 0
1964 St. Louis NL 4, New York AL 3
1965 Los Angeles NL 4, Minnesota AL 3
1966 Baltimore AL 4, Los Angeles NL 0
1967 St. Louis NL 4, Boston AL 3
1968 Detroit AL 4, St. Louis NL 3
1969 New York NL 4, Baltimore AL 1
1970 Baltimore AL 4, Cincinnati NL 1
1971 Pittsburgh NL 4, Baltimore AL 3
1972 Oakland AL 4, Cincinnati NL 3
1973 Oakland AL 4, New York NL 3
1974 Oakland AL 4, Los Angeles NL 1
1975 Cincinnati NL 4, Boston AL 3
1976 Cincinnati NL 4, New York AL 0
1977 New York AL 4, Los Angeles NL 2
1978 New York AL 4, Los Angeles NL 2
1979 Pittsburgh NL 4, Baltimore AL 3
1980 Philadelphia NL 4, Kansas City AL 2
1981 Los Angeles NL 4, New York AL 2
1982 St. Louis NL 4, Milwaukee AL 3
1983 Baltimore AL 4, Philadelphia NL 1
1984 Detroit AL 4, San Diego NL 1
1985 Kansas City AL 4, St. Louis NL 3
1986 New York NL 4, Boston AL 3
1987 Minnesota AL 4, St. Louis NL 3
1988 Los Angeles NL 4, Oakland AL 1
1989 Oakland AL 4, San Francisco NL 0
1990 Cincinnati NL 4, Oakland AL 0
1991 Minnesota AL 4, Atlanta NL 3
1992 Toronto AL 4, Atlanta NL 2
1993 Toronto AL 4, Philadelphia NL 2
1994 No series due to strike
1995 Atlanta NL 4, Cleveland AL 2
1996 New York AL 4, Atlanta NL 2
1997 Florida NL 4, Cleveland AL 3
1998 New York AL 4, San Diego NL 0
1999 New York AL 4, Atlanta NL 0
2000 New York AL 4, New York NL 1
2001 Arizona NL 4, New York AL 3
2002 Anaheim AL 4, San Francisco NL 3
2003 Florida NL 4, New York AL 2
2004 Boston AL 4, St. Louis NL 0
2005 Chicago AL 4, Houston NL 0
2006 St. Louis NL 4, Detroit AL 1
2007 Boston AL 4, Colorado NL 0
2008 Philadelphia NL 4, Tampa Bay AL 1
2009 New York AL 4, Philadelphia NL 2
2010 San Francisco NL 4, Texas AL 1
2011 St. Louis NL 4, Texas AL 3
2012 San Francisco NL 4, Detroit AL 0
2013 Boston AL 4, St. Louis NL 2
2014 San Fran. NL 4, Kansas City AL 3
2015 Kansas City AL 4, New York NL 1

World Series Most Valuable Player, 1955-2015

Year	Player, position, team
1955	Johnny Podres, P, Brooklyn
1956	Don Larsen, P, NY (AL)
1957	Lew Burdette, P, Milwaukee (NL)
1958	Bob Turley, P, NY (AL)
1959	Larry Sherry, P, Los Angeles (NL)
1960[1]	Bobby Richardson, 2B, NY (AL)
1961	Whitey Ford, P, NY (AL)
1962	Ralph Terry, P, NY (AL)
1963	Sandy Koufax, P, Los Angeles (NL)
1964	Bob Gibson, P, St. Louis
1965	Sandy Koufax, P, Los Angeles (NL)
1966	Frank Robinson, OF, Baltimore
1967	Bob Gibson, P, St. Louis
1968	Mickey Lolich, P, Detroit
1969	Donn Clendenon, 1B, NY (NL)
1970	Brooks Robinson, 3B, Baltimore
1971	Roberto Clemente, OF, Pittsburgh
1972	Gene Tenace, C, Oakland
1973	Reggie Jackson, OF, Oakland
1974	Rollie Fingers, P, Oakland
1975	Pete Rose, 3B, Cincinnati
1976	Johnny Bench, C, Cincinnati
1977	Reggie Jackson, OF, NY (AL)
1978	Bucky Dent, SS, NY (AL)
1979	Willie Stargell, 1B, Pittsburgh
1980	Mike Schmidt, 3B, Philadelphia
1981	Ron Cey, 3B, Los Angeles (NL); Pedro Guerrero, OF, Los Angeles; Steve Yeager, C, Los Angeles
1982	Darrell Porter, C, St. Louis
1983	Rick Dempsey, C, Baltimore
1984	Alan Trammell, SS, Detroit
1985	Bret Saberhagen, P, Kansas City
1986	Ray Knight, 3B, NY (NL)
1987	Frank Viola, P, Minnesota
1988	Orel Hershiser, P, Los Angeles (NL)
1989	Dave Stewart, P, Oakland
1990	Jose Rijo, P, Cincinnati
1991	Jack Morris, P, Minnesota
1992	Pat Borders, C, Toronto
1993	Paul Molitor, DH, Toronto
1994	No series due to strike
1995	Tom Glavine, P, Atlanta
1996	John Wetteland, P, NY (AL)
1997	Livan Hernandez, P, Florida
1998	Scott Brosius, 3B, NY (AL)
1999	Mariano Rivera, P, NY (AL)
2000	Derek Jeter, SS, NY (AL)
2001	Curt Schilling, P, Arizona; Randy Johnson, P, Arizona
2002	Troy Glaus, 3B, Anaheim
2003	Josh Beckett, P, Florida
2004	Manny Ramirez, OF, Boston
2005	Jermaine Dye, OF, Chicago (AL)
2006	David Eckstein, SS, St. Louis
2007	Mike Lowell, 3B, Boston
2008	Cole Hamels, P, Philadelphia
2009	Hideki Matsui, DH, NY (AL)
2010	Edgar Renteria, SS, San Francisco
2011	David Freese, 3B, St. Louis
2012	Pablo Sandoval, 3B, San Francisco
2013	David Ortiz, DH, Boston
2014	Madison Bumgarner, P, San Francisco
2015	Salvador Pérez, C, Kansas City

Note: World Series cancelled in 1994 due to strike. (1) Richardson won the MVP although Pittsburgh beat New York.

World Series Won-Lost Records, by Franchise

Since beginning of "modern" era in 1901. Figures represent overall Series wins, not individual games.

Team	Wins	Losses
New York Yankees	27	13
St. Louis Cardinals	11	8
Philadelphia/Kansas City/Oakland A's	9	5
Boston Red Sox	8	4
New York/San Francisco Giants	8	12
Brooklyn/Los Angeles Dodgers	6	12
Pittsburgh Pirates	5	2
Cincinnati Reds	5	4
Detroit Tigers	4	7
Chicago White Sox	3	2
Washington Senators/Minnesota Twins	3	3
St. Louis Browns/Baltimore Orioles	3	4
Boston/Milwaukee/Atlanta Braves	3	6
Florida Marlins	2	0
Toronto Blue Jays	2	0
Kansas City Royals	2	2
Cleveland Indians	2	3
New York Mets	2	3
Philadelphia Phillies	2	5
Chicago Cubs	2	8
Arizona Diamondbacks	1	0
L.A./California/Anaheim/L.A. Angels	1	0
Colorado Rockies	0	1
Houston Astros	0	1
Seattle Pilots/Milwaukee Brewers	0	1
Tampa Bay Rays	0	1
San Diego Padres	0	2
Texas Rangers	0	2

All-Time World Series Career Leaders

(through 2015)

Batting Leaders

Batter (min. 50 PA)	H	AB	AVG	Batter (min. 50 PA)	H	AB	AVG
1. David Ortiz	20	44	.455	6. Hal McRae	18	45	.400
2. Pablo Sandoval	20	47	.426	7. Lou Brock	34	87	.391
3. Johnny "Pepper" Martin	23	55	.418	8. Marquis Grissom	30	77	.390
4. Paul Molitor	23	55	.418	9. Thurman Munson	25	67	.373
5. Lance Berkman	16	39	.410	10. George Brett	19	51	.373

Games Played

Yogi Berra	75
Mickey Mantle	65
Elston Howard	54
Hank Bauer	53
Gil McDougald	53
Phil Rizzuto	52
Joe DiMaggio	51
Frankie Frisch	50
Pee Wee Reese	44
Roger Maris	41
Babe Ruth	41

Runs Batted In

Mickey Mantle	40
Yogi Berra	39
Lou Gehrig	35
Babe Ruth	33
Joe DiMaggio	30
Bill Skowron	29
Duke Snider	26

Hits

Yogi Berra	71
Mickey Mantle	59
Frankie Frisch	58
Joe DiMaggio	54
Derek Jeter	50
Hank Bauer	46
Pee Wee Reese	46
Gil McDougald	45
Phil Rizzuto	45
Lou Gehrig	43

Home Runs

Mickey Mantle	18
Babe Ruth	15
Yogi Berra	12
Duke Snider	11
Lou Gehrig	10
Reggie Jackson	10
Joe DiMaggio	8
Frank Robinson	8
Bill Skowron	8

Runs

Mickey Mantle	42
Yogi Berra	41
Babe Ruth	37
Derek Jeter	32
Lou Gehrig	30
Joe DiMaggio	27
Roger Maris	26
Elston Howard	25
Gil McDougald	23
Jackie Robinson	22

Stolen Bases

Lou Brock	14
Eddie Collins	14
Frank Chance	10
Dave Lopes	10
Phil Rizzuto	10
Frankie Frisch	9
Kenny Lofton	9
Honus Wagner	9
Johnny Evers	8

Pitching Leaders

Games Pitched

Mariano Rivera	24
Whitey Ford	22
Mike Stanton	20
Rollie Fingers	16
Jeff Nelson	16
Allie Reynolds	15
Bob Turley	15
Clay Carroll	14
Clem Labine	13
Andy Pettitte	13
Mark Wohlers	13
Jeremy Affeldt	12
Waite Hoyt	12
Catfish Hunter	12
Art Nehf	12

Wins

Whitey Ford	10
Bob Gibson	7
Allie Reynolds	7
Red Ruffing	7
Chief Bender	6
Lefty Gomez	6
Waite Hoyt	6
Three Finger Brown	5
Jack Coombs	5
Catfish Hunter	5
Christy Mathewson	5
Herb Pennock	5
Andy Pettitte	5
Vic Raschi	5

Strikeouts

Whitey Ford	94
Bob Gibson	92
Allie Reynolds	62
Sandy Koufax	61
Red Ruffing	61
Chief Bender	59
George Earnshaw	56
Andy Pettitte	56
John Smoltz	52
Roger Clemens	49
Waite Hoyt	49
Christy Mathewson	48
Bob Turley	46

Saves

Mariano Rivera	11
Rollie Fingers	6
Johnny Murphy	4
Robb Nen	4
Allie Reynolds	4
John Wetteland	4
Roy Face	3
Neftali Feliz	3
Firpo Marberry	3
Will McEnaney	3
Tug McGraw	3
Jonathan Papelbon	3
Herb Pennock	3
Troy Percival	3
Sergio Romo	3
Kent Tekulve	3
Todd Worrell	3

All-Star Baseball Games, 1933-2015

Year	Winner, score	Host team
1933*	American, 4-2	Chicago (AL)
1934*	American, 9-7	New York (NL)
1935*	American, 4-1	Cleveland
1936*	National, 4-3	Boston (NL)
1937*	American, 8-3	Washington
1938*	National, 4-1	Cincinnati
1939*	American, 3-1	New York (AL)
1940*	National, 4-0	St. Louis (NL)
1941*	American, 7-5	Detroit
1942	American, 3-1	New York (NL)
1943	American, 5-3	Philadelphia (AL)
1944	National, 7-1	Pittsburgh
1945	Not played	
1946*	American, 12-0	Boston (AL)
1947*	American, 2-1	Chicago (NL)
1948*	American, 5-2	St. Louis (AL)
1949*	American, 11-7	Brooklyn
1950*	National, 4-3(1)	Chicago (AL)
1951*	National, 8-3	Detroit
1952*	National, 3-2	Philadelphia (NL)
1953*	National, 5-1	Cincinnati
1954*	American, 11-9	Cleveland
1955*	National, 6-5(2)	Milwaukee
1956*	National, 7-3	Washington
1957*	American, 6-5	St. Louis
1958*	American, 4-3	Baltimore
1959*	National, 5-4	Pittsburgh
1959*	American, 5-3	Los Angeles (NL)
1960*	National, 5-3	Kansas City
1960*	National, 6-0	New York (AL)
1961*	National, 5-4(3)	San Francisco
1961*	Called–rain, 1-1	Boston
1962*	National, 3-1	Washington
1962*	American, 9-4	Chicago (NL)
1963*	National, 5-3	Cleveland
1964*	National, 7-4	New York (NL)
1965*	National, 6-5	Minnesota
1966*	National, 2-1(3)	St. Louis
1967*	National, 2-1(4)	California
1968	National, 1-0	Houston
1969*	National, 9-3	Washington
1970	National, 5-4(2)	Cincinnati
1971	American, 6-4	Detroit
1972	National, 4-3(3)	Atlanta
1973	National, 7-1	Kansas City
1974	National, 7-2	Pittsburgh
1975	National, 6-3	Milwaukee
1976	National, 7-1	Philadelphia
1977	National, 7-5	New York (AL)
1978	National, 7-3	San Diego
1979	National, 7-6	Seattle
1980	National, 4-2	Los Angeles (NL)
1981	National, 5-4	Cleveland
1982	National, 4-1	Montréal
1983	American, 13-3	Chicago (AL)
1984	National, 3-1	San Francisco
1985	National, 6-1	Minnesota
1986	American, 3-2	Houston
1987	National, 2-0(5)	Oakland
1988	American, 2-1	Cincinnati
1989	American, 5-3	California
1990	American, 2-0	Chicago (NL)
1991	American, 4-2	Toronto
1992	American, 13-6	San Diego
1993	American, 9-3	Baltimore
1994	National, 8-7(3)	Pittsburgh
1995	National, 3-2	Texas
1996	National, 6-0	Philadelphia
1997	American, 3-1	Cleveland
1998	American, 13-8	Colorado
1999	American, 4-1	Boston
2000	American, 6-3	Atlanta
2001	American, 4-1	Seattle
2002	Tie, 7-7(6)	Milwaukee
2003	American, 7-6(7)	Chicago (AL)
2004	American, 9-4	Houston
2005	American, 7-5	Detroit
2006	American, 3-2	Pittsburgh
2007	American, 5-4	San Francisco
2008	American, 4-3(4)	New York (AL)
2009	American, 4-3	St. Louis
2010	National, 3-1	Los Angeles (AL)
2011	National, 5-1	Arizona
2012	National, 8-0	Kansas City
2013	American, 3-0	New York (NL)
2014	American, 5-3	Minnesota
2015	American, 6-3	Cincinnati

* = Day game. **Note:** Two all-star games played 1959-62 to help increase players' pension fund. (1) 14 innings. (2) 12 innings. (3) 10 innings. (4) 15 innings. (5) 13 innings. (6) Commissioner's decision—game called in 11th inning when both teams ran out of pitchers. (7) Under rule change beginning in 2003, league winning All-Star game earned World Series home-field advantage.

MLB Stadiums, 2015

Team	Stadium (year opened)	Surface	Distances (ft) LF	Center	RF	Seating capacity[1]
Arizona Diamondbacks	Chase Field (1998)	Grass	330	407	335	48,519
Atlanta Braves	Turner Field (1997)	Grass	335	400	330	49,393
Chicago Cubs	Wrigley Field (1914)	Grass	355	400	353	41,072
Cincinnati Reds	Great American Ball Park (2003)	Grass	328	404	325	42,319
Colorado Rockies	Coors Field (1995)	Grass	347	415	350	50,480
Los Angeles Dodgers	Dodger Stadium (1962)	Grass	330	395	330	56,000
Miami Marlins	Marlins Park (2012)	Grass	344	418	335	37,422
Milwaukee Brewers	Miller Park (2001)	Grass	344	400	345	41,900
New York Mets	Citi Field (2009)	Grass	335	408	330	41,922
Philadelphia Phillies	Citizens Bank Park (2004)	Grass	329	401	330	43,651
Pittsburgh Pirates	PNC Park at North Shore (2001)	Grass	325	399	320	38,362
St. Louis Cardinals	Busch Stadium (2006)	Grass	336	400	335	45,582
San Diego Padres	Petco Park (2004)	Grass	336	396	322	41,164
San Francisco Giants	AT&T Park (2000)	Grass	339	399	309	41,915
Washington Nationals	Nationals Park (2008)	Grass	336	402	335	41,506
Baltimore Orioles	Oriole Park at Camden Yards (1992)	Grass	333	400	318	45,971
Boston Red Sox	Fenway Park (1912)	Grass	310	390	302	37,221[2]
Chicago White Sox	U.S. Cellular Field (1991)	Grass	330	400	335	40,615
Cleveland Indians	Progressive Field (1994)	Grass	325	405	325	36,856
Detroit Tigers	Comerica Park (2000)	Grass	345	420	330	41,681
Houston Astros	Minute Maid Park (2000)	Grass	315	435	326	42,060
Kansas City Royals	Kauffman Stadium (1973)	Grass	330	410	330	37,903
Los Angeles Angels	Angel Stadium of Anaheim (1966)	Grass	347	396	348	45,493
Minnesota Twins	Target Field (2010)	Grass	339	404	328	39,029
New York Yankees	Yankee Stadium (2009)	Grass	318	408	314	49,638
Oakland Athletics	O.co Coliseum (1968)	Grass	330	400	330	35,067
Seattle Mariners	Safeco Field (1999)	Grass	331	401	326	47,591
Tampa Bay Rays	Tropicana Field (1990)	Astroturf	315	404	322	31,042
Texas Rangers	Globe Life Park in Arlington (1994)	Grass	332	400	325	48,114
Toronto Blue Jays	Rogers Centre (1989)	Astroturf	328	400	328	49,282

(1) As of 2015 season. (2) For day games; night game capacity is 37,673.

Major League Franchise Shifts and Additions

1953: Boston Braves (NL) became Milwaukee Braves.
1954: St. Louis Browns (AL) became Baltimore Orioles.
1955: Philadelphia Athletics (AL) became Kansas City Athletics.
1958: New York Giants (NL) became San Francisco Giants.
1958: Brooklyn Dodgers (NL) became L.A. Dodgers.
1961: Washington Senators (AL) became Minnesota Twins.
1961: L.A. Angels enfranchised by the AL.
1961: Washington Senators enfranchised by the AL, replacing the former Washington club, whose franchise moved to Minneapolis-St. Paul.
1962: Houston Colt .45's enfranchised by the NL.
1962: New York Mets enfranchised by the NL.
1966: Milwaukee Braves (NL) became Atlanta Braves.
1968: Kansas City Athletics (AL) became Oakland Athletics.
1969: Kansas City Royals and Seattle Pilots enfranchised by the AL; Montréal Expos and San Diego Padres enfranchised by the NL.
1970: Seattle Pilots (AL) became Milwaukee Brewers.
1971: Washington Senators (AL) became Texas Rangers (Dallas-Fort Worth area).
1977: Toronto Blue Jays and Seattle Mariners enfranchised by the AL.
1993: Colorado Rockies (Denver) and Florida Marlins (Miami) enfranchised by the NL.
1998: Tampa Bay Devil Rays began play in the AL; Arizona Diamondbacks (Phoenix) began play in the NL (both teams enfranchised in 1995). Milwaukee Brewers moved from the AL to the NL.
2005: Montréal Expos (NL) became Washington Nationals.
2013: Houston Astros moved from the NL to the AL.

Little League World Series, 1950-2015

The Little League World Series is played annually in Williamsport, PA.

Year	Winning team; opponent	Score
1950	Houston, TX; Bridgeport, CT	2-1
1951	Stamford, CT; Austin, TX	3-0
1952	Norwalk, CT; Monongahela, PA	4-3
1953	Birmingham, AL; Schenectady, NY	1-0
1954	Schenectady, NY; Colton, CA	7-5
1955	Morrisville, PA; Merchantville, NJ	4-3
1956	Roswell, NM; Delaware, NJ	3-1
1957	Mexico; La Mesa, CA	4-0
1958	Mexico; Kankakee, IL	10-1
1959	Hamtramck, MI; Auburn, CA	12-0
1960	Levittown, PA; Ft. Worth, TX	5-0
1961	El Cajon, CA; El Campo, TX	4-2
1962	San Jose, CA; Kankakee, IL	3-0
1963	Granada Hills, CA; Stratford, CT	2-1
1964	Staten Island, NY; Mexico	4-0
1965	Windsor Locks, CT; Stoney Creek, ON, Canada	3-1
1966	Houston, TX; W. New York, NJ	8-2
1967	Tokyo, Japan; Chicago, IL	4-1
1968	Osaka, Japan; Richmond, VA	1-0
1969	Taiwan; Santa Clara, CA	5-0
1970	Wayne, NJ; Campbell, CA	2-0
1971	Taiwan; Gary, IN	12-3
1972	Taiwan; Hammond, IN	6-0
1973	Taiwan; Tucson, AZ	12-0
1974	Taiwan; Red Bluff, CA	12-1
1975	Lakewood, NJ; Tampa, FL	4-3
1976	Tokyo, Japan; Campbell, CA	10-3
1977	Taiwan; El Cajon, CA	7-2
1978	Taiwan; Danville, CA	11-1
1979	Taiwan; Campbell, CA	2-1
1980	Taiwan; Tampa, FL	4-3
1981	Taiwan; Tampa, FL	4-2
1982	Kirkland, WA; Taiwan	6-0
1983	Marietta, GA; Dominican Republic	3-1
1984	South Korea; Altamonte Springs, FL	6-2
1985	South Korea; Mexico	7-1
1986	Tainan Park, Taiwan; Tucson, AZ	12-0
1987	Hualien, Taiwan; Irvine, CA	21-1
1988	Taichung, Taiwan; Pearl City, HI	10-0
1989	Trumbull, CT; Kaohsiung, Taiwan	5-2
1990	Tainan County, Taiwan; Shippensburg, PA	9-0
1991	Taichung, Taiwan; Danville, CA	11-0
1992	Long Beach, CA; Mindanao, Philippines	6-0[1]
1993	Long Beach, CA; David, Panama	3-2
1994	Maracaibo, Venezuela; Northridge, CA	4-3
1995	Tainan, Taiwan; Spring, TX	17-3
1996	Kaohsiung, Taiwan; Cranston, RI	13-3
1997	Guadalupe, Mexico; Mission Viejo, CA	5-4
1998	Toms River, NJ; Kashima, Japan	12-9
1999	Osaka, Japan; Phenix City, AL	5-0
2000	Maracaibo, Venezuela; Bellaire, TX	3-2
2001	Tokyo, Japan; Apopka, FL	2-1
2002	Louisville, KY; Sendai, Japan	1-0
2003	Tokyo, Japan; Boynton Beach, FL	10-1
2004	Willemstad, Curaçao; Thousand Oaks, CA	5-2
2005	Ewa Beach, HI; Willemstad, Curaçao	7-6
2006	Columbus, GA; Kawaguchi City, Japan	2-1
2007	Warner Robins, GA; Tokyo, Japan	3-2
2008	Waipahu, HI; Matamoros, Mexico	12-3
2009	Chula Vista, CA; Taoyuan, Taiwan	6-3
2010	Tokyo, Japan; Waipahu, HI	4-1
2011	Huntington Beach, CA; Hamamatsu, Japan	2-1
2012	Tokyo, Japan; Goodlettsville, TN	12-2
2013	Tokyo, Japan; Chula Vista, CA	6-4
2014	Seoul, South Korea; Chicago, IL	8-4
2015	Tokyo, Japan; Lewisberry, PA	18-11

(1) Philippines won 15-4 but was disqualified for using ineligible players. Long Beach was awarded title by forfeit 6-0 (1 run per inning).

Manager of the Year, 1986-2014

1986 (NL) Hal Lanier, Houston
(AL) John McNamara, Boston
1987 (NL) Buck Rodgers, Montréal
(AL) Sparky Anderson, Detroit
1988 (NL) Tommy Lasorda, L.A.
(AL) Tony La Russa, Oakland
1989 (NL) Don Zimmer, Chicago
(AL) Frank Robinson, Baltimore
1990 (NL) Jim Leyland, Pittsburgh
(AL) Jeff Torborg, Chicago
1991 (NL) Bobby Cox, Atlanta
(AL) Tom Kelly, Minnesota
1992 (NL) Jim Leyland, Pittsburgh
(AL) Tony La Russa, Oakland
1993 (NL) Dusty Baker, San Francisco
(AL) Gene Lamont, Chicago
1994 (NL) Felipe Alou, Montréal
(AL) Buck Showalter, NY
1995 (NL) Don Baylor, Colorado
(AL) Lou Piniella, Seattle
1996 (NL) Bruce Bochy, San Diego
(AL) (tie) Joe Torre, NY;
Johnny Oates, Texas
1997 (NL) Dusty Baker, San Francisco
(AL) Davey Johnson, Baltimore
1998 (NL) Larry Dierker, Houston
(AL) Joe Torre, NY
1999 (NL) Jack McKeon, Cincinnati
(AL) Jimy Williams, Boston
2000 (NL) Dusty Baker, San Francisco
(AL) Jerry Manuel, Chicago
2001 (NL) Larry Bowa, Philadelphia
(AL) Lou Piniella, Seattle
2002 (NL) Tony La Russa, St. Louis
(AL) Mike Scioscia, Anaheim
2003 (NL) Jack McKeon, Florida
(AL) Tony Pena, Kansas City
2004 (NL) Bobby Cox, Atlanta
(AL) Buck Showalter, Texas
2005 (NL) Bobby Cox, Atlanta
(AL) Ozzie Guillen, Chicago
2006 (NL) Joe Girardi, Florida
(AL) Jim Leyland, Detroit
2007 (NL) Bob Melvin, Arizona
(AL) Eric Wedge, Cleveland
2008 (NL) Lou Piniella, Chicago
(AL) Joe Maddon, Tampa Bay
2009 (NL) Jim Tracy, Colorado
(AL) Mike Scioscia, L.A.
2010 (NL) Bud Black, San Diego
(AL) Ron Gardenhire, Minnesota
2011 (NL) Kirk Gibson, Arizona
(AL) Joe Maddon, Tampa Bay
2012 (NL) Davey Johnson, Washington
(AL) Bob Melvin, Oakland
2013 (NL) Clint Hurdle, Pittsburgh
(AL) Terry Francona, Cleveland
2014 (NL) Matt Williams, Washington
(AL) Buck Showalter, Baltimore

National Baseball Hall of Fame and Museum, Cooperstown, NY

= Player chosen in first year of eligibility (five seasons after retirement) or earlier. * = 2015 inductee.

#Aaron, Hank
Alexander, Grover
Alomar, Roberto
Alston, Walt
Anderson, George
Anson, Cap
Aparicio, Luis
Appling, Luke
Ashburn, Richie
Averill, Earl
Baker, Frank "Home Run"
Bancroft, Dave
#Banks, Ernie
Barlick, Al
Barrow, Edward G.
Beckley, Jake
Bell, James "Cool Papa"
#Bench, Johnny
Bender, Charles "Chief"
Berra, Lawrence "Yogi"
*Biggio, Craig
Blyleven, Bert
#Boggs, Wade
Bottomley, Jim
Boudreau, Lou
Bresnahan, Roger
#Brett, George
#Brock, Lou
Brouthers, Dan
Brown, Mordecai
Brown, Ray
Brown, Willard
Bulkeley, Morgan C.
Bunning, Jim
Burkett, Jesse C.
Campanella, Roy
#Carew, Rod
Carey, Max
#Carlton, Steve
Carter, Gary
Cartwright, Alexander
Cepeda, Orlando
Chadwick, Henry
Chance, Frank
Chandler, Albert "Happy"
Charleston, Oscar
Chesbro, John
Chylak, Nestor
Clarke, Fred
Clarkson, John
#Clemente, Roberto
Cobb, Ty[1]
Cochrane, Mickey
Collins, Eddie
Collins, James
Combs, Earle
Comiskey, Charles A.
Conlan, John "Jocko"
Connolly, Thomas H.
Connor, Roger
Cooper, Andy
Coveleski, Stan
Cox, Bobby
Crawford, Sam
Cronin, Joe
Cummings, W. A.
Cuyler, Hazen "Kiki"
Dandridge, Ray
Davis, George
Dawson, Andre
Day, Leon
Dean, Jay Hanna "Dizzy"
Delahanty, Ed
Dickey, Bill
Dihigo, Martín
#DiMaggio, Joe
#Doby, Larry
Doerr, Bobby
Dreyfuss, Barney
Drysdale, Don
Duffy, Hugh
Durocher, Leo
#Eckersley, Dennis
Evans, Billy
Evers, John
Ewing, Buck
Faber, Urban "Red"
#Feller, Bob
Ferrell, Rick
Fingers, Rollie
Fisk, Carlton
Flick, Elmer H.
Ford, Whitey
Foster, Andrew "Rube"
Foster, Bill
Fox, Nellie
Foxx, Jimmie
Frick, Ford
Frisch, Frank
Galvin, James "Pud"
#Gehrig, Lou
Gehringer, Charles
#Gibson, Bob
Gibson, Josh
Giles, Warren
Gillick, Pat
#Glavine, Tom
Gomez, Lefty
Gordon, Joe
Goslin, Leon "Goose"
Gossage, Rich
Grant, Frank
Greenberg, Hank
Griffith, Clark
Grimes, Burleigh
Grove, Lefty
#Gwynn, Tony
Hafey, Charles "Chick"
Haines, Jesee
Hamilton, Bill
Hanlon, Ned
Harridge, Will
Harris, Bucky
Hartnett, Gabby
Harvey, Doug
Heilmann, Harry
#Henderson, Rickey
Herman, Billy
Herzog, Whitey
Hill, Pete
Hooper, Harry
Hornsby, Rogers
Hoyt, Waite
Hubbard, Cal
Hubbell, Carl
Huggins, Miller
Hulbert, William
Hunter, James "Catfish"
Irvin, Monte
#Jackson, Reggie
Jackson, Travis
Jenkins, Ferguson
Jennings, Hugh
Johnson, Byron "Ban"
*#Johnson, Randy
Johnson, Walter[1]
Johnson, William "Judy"
Joss, Addie
#Kaline, Al
Keefe, Timothy
Keeler, William
Kell, George
Kelley, Joe
Kelly, George
Kelly, King
Killebrew, Harmon
Kiner, Ralph
Klein, Chuck
Klem, Bill
#Koufax, Sandy
Kubek, Tony
Kuhn, Bowie
La Russa, Tony
Lajoie, Napoleon
Landis, Kenesaw M.
Larkin, Barry
Lasorda, Tom
Lazzeri, Tony
Lemon, Bob
Leonard, Buck
Lindstrom, Fred
Lloyd, Pop
Lombardi, Ernie
Lopez, Al
Lyons, Ted
Mack, Connie
Mackey, James "Biz"
MacPhail, Larry
MacPhail, Lee
Madden, Bill
#Maddux, Greg
Manley, Effa
#Mantle, Mickey
Manush, Henry
Maranville, Walter
Marichal, Juan
Marquard, Rube
*#Martinez, Pedro
Mathews, Eddie
Mathewson, Christy[1]
#Mays, Willie
Mazeroski, Bill
McCarthy, Joe
McCarthy, Thomas
#McCovey, Willie
McGinnity, Joe
McGowan, Bill
McGraw, John
McKechnie, Bill
McPhee, John "Bid"
Medwick, Joe
Mendez, Jose
Mize, Johnny
#Molitor, Paul
#Morgan, Joe
#Murray, Eddie
#Musial, Stan
Newhouser, Hal
Nichols, Kid
Niekro, Phil
O'Day, Hank
O'Malley, Walter
O'Rourke, Jim
Ott, Mel
Paige, Satchel
#Palmer, Jim
Pennock, Herb
Perez, Tony
Perry, Gaylord
Plank, Ed
Pompez, Alex
Posey, Cum(berland)
#Puckett, Kirby
Radbourn, Charlie
Reese, Pee Wee
Rice, Jim
Rice, Sam
Rickey, Branch
#Ripken, Cal, Jr.
Rixey, Eppa
Rizzuto, Phil "Scooter"
Roberts, Robin
#Robinson, Brooks
#Robinson, Frank
#Robinson, Jackie
Robinson, Wilbert
Rogan, Joe "Bullet"
Roush, Edd
Ruffing, Red
Ruppert, Jacob
Rusie, Amos
#Ruth, Babe[1]
#Ryan, Nolan
Sandberg, Ryne
Santo, Ron
Santop, Louis
Schalk, Ray
#Schmidt, Mike
Schoendienst, Red
#Seaver, Tom
Selee, Frank
Sewell, Joe
Simmons, Al
Sisler, George
Slaughter, Enos
Smith, Hilton
#Smith, Ozzie
*#Smoltz, John
Snider, Duke
Southworth, Billy
#Spahn, Warren
Spalding, Albert
Speaker, Tris
#Stargell, Willie
Stearnes, Norman
Stengel, Casey
Sutter, Bruce
Suttles, George "Mule"
Sutton, Don
Taylor, Ben
Terry, Bill
#Thomas, Frank
Thompson, Sam
Tinker, Joe
Torre, Joe
Torriente, Cristobal
Traynor, Harold J. "Pie"
Vance, Arthur "Dazzy"
Vaughan, Joseph "Arky"
Veeck, Bill
Waddell, Rube
Wagner, Honus[1]
Wallace, Roderick
Walsh, Ed
Waner, Lloyd
Waner, Paul
Ward, John
Weaver, Earl
Weiss, George
Welch, Mickey
Wells, Willie
Wheat, Zach
White, Deacon
White, Sol
Wilhelm, Hoyt
Wilkinson, J. L.
Williams, Billy
Williams, Dick
Williams, Joe
#Williams, Ted
Willis, Vic
Wilson, Hack
Wilson, Jud
#Winfield, Dave
Wright, George
Wright, Harry
Wynn, Early
#Yastrzemski, Carl
Yawkey, Tom
Young, Cy
Youngs, Ross
#Yount, Robin

(1) Player inducted in 1936, the year the Hall of Fame began.

BASKETBALL

Golden State Beats Cleveland and Prodigal LeBron in 2015 Finals

The Golden State Warriors capped their best regular season in franchise history by defeating the Cleveland Cavaliers, four games to two, to win the 2015 NBA championship. Golden State's Stephen Curry and Andre Iguodala each scored 25 points in their team's decisive Game 6 win, 105-97, June 16, 2015, at Quicken Loans Arena in Cleveland, OH, as the Warriors captured their first title since 1975.

Iguodala, in the starting lineup only from Game 4 on, averaged 16.3 points, 5.8 rebounds, and 4 assists in the Finals and was voted Most Valuable Player, despite massive scoring efforts in the series from Curry (26 points per game) and Cleveland's LeBron James (35.8 ppg). James, who played the first seven seasons of his career with the Cavaliers and returned to the club after four years in Miami, made his fifth consecutive appearance in the NBA Finals.

Curry set a single-season record with 286 three-point field goals and averaged 23.8 ppg as he won his first season MVP award. First-year head coach Steve Kerr led Golden State to a franchise-record 67 wins. The Warriors' season included winning streaks of 16 and 12 games, but both fell short of the Atlanta Hawks' 19-game win streak that began with a 90-85 victory in Milwaukee Dec. 27, 2014, and ended with a 115-100 loss to the New Orleans Pelicans Feb. 2 at Smoothie King Center in New Orleans.

The Hawks finished with a franchise-record 60-22 mark and were the top seed in the Eastern Conference playoffs for the first time since the 1993-94 season. Atlanta was swept in its four-game conference final series against Cleveland, and Golden State eliminated the second-seed Houston Rockets in five games in the Western Conference finals. Houston's James Harden (27.4 ppg) finished second in scoring behind Oklahoma City guard Russell Westbrook, who topped the league with 28.1 ppg.

L.A. Clippers center DeAndre Jordan led the league in rebounding (15.0 rebounds per game) and his 71.0 field goal percentage was the second highest season total in league history behind the 72.7% that Wilt Chamberlain recorded in 1972-73. The L.A. Lakers (21-61) endured their worst season in franchise history, but Lakers veteran Kobe Bryant moved past Michael Jordan into third place on the all-time NBA scoring list (32,482 points).

NBA Final Standings, 2014-15

(playoff seeding in parentheses)

Eastern Conference

Atlantic Division	W	L	PCT	GB
Toronto Raptors (4)	49	33	.598	—
Boston Celtics (7)	40	42	.488	9
Brooklyn Nets (8)	38	44	.463	11
Philadelphia 76ers	18	64	.220	31
NY Knicks	17	65	.207	32

Central Division	W	L	PCT	GB
Cleveland Cavaliers (2)	53	29	.646	—
Chicago Bulls (3)	50	32	.610	3
Milwaukee Bucks (6)	41	41	.500	12
Indiana Pacers	38	44	.463	15
Detroit Pistons	32	50	.390	21

Southeast Division	W	L	PCT	GB
Atlanta Hawks (1)	60	22	.732	—
Washington Wizards (5)	46	36	.561	14
Miami Heat	37	45	.451	23
Charlotte Hornets	33	49	.402	27
Orlando Magic	25	57	.305	35

Western Conference

Northwest Division	W	L	PCT	GB
Portland Trail Blazers (4)	51	31	.622	—
Oklahoma City Thunder	45	37	.549	6
Utah Jazz	38	44	.463	13
Denver Nuggets	30	52	.366	21
Minnesota Timberwolves	16	66	.195	35

Pacific Division	W	L	PCT	GB
Golden State Warriors (1)	67	15	.817	—
L.A. Clippers (3)	56	26	.683	11
Phoenix Suns	39	43	.476	28
Sacramento Kings	29	53	.354	38
L.A. Lakers	21	61	.256	46

Southwest Division	W	L	PCT	GB
Houston Rockets (2)	56	26	.683	—
Memphis Grizzlies (5)	55	27	.671	1
San Antonio Spurs (6)	55	27	.671	1
Dallas Mavericks (7)	50	32	.610	6
New Orleans Pelicans (8)	45	37	.549	11

Note: The Brooklyn Nets earned the No. 8 seed over Indiana in the East due to a better head-to-head record (2-1); the Memphis Grizzlies earned the No. 5 seed over San Antonio in the West due to a better record against Southwest Division opponents (9-7 vs. 8-8); the New Orleans Pelicans earned the No. 8 seed over Oklahoma City due to a better head-to-head record (3-1).

NBA Playoff Results, 2015

Eastern Conference

Atlanta defeated Brooklyn, 4 games to 2
Washington defeated Toronto, 4 games to 0
Chicago defeated Milwaukee, 4 games to 2
Cleveland defeated Boston, 4 games to 0
Atlanta defeated Washington, 4 games to 2
Cleveland defeated Chicago, 4 games to 2
Cleveland defeated Atlanta, 4 games to 0

Western Conference

Golden State defeated New Orleans, 4 games to 0
Memphis defeated Portland, 4 games to 1
L.A. Clippers defeated San Antonio, 4 games to 3
Houston defeated Dallas, 4 games to 1
Golden State defeated Memphis, 4 games to 2
Houston defeated the L.A. Clippers, 4 games to 3
Golden State defeated Houston, 4 games to 1

Championship

Golden State defeated Cleveland, 4 games to 2 (108-100 [OT], 93-95 [OT], 91-96, 103-82, 104-91, 105-97)

NBA Regular Season Individual Highs, 2014-15

Minutes, game: 55, Khris Middleton, Milwaukee v. Brooklyn, Mar. 20 (3 OT)
Points, game: 57, Kyrie Irving, Cleveland v. San Antonio, Mar. 12 (OT)
Field goals, game: 21, Russell Westbrook, Oklahoma City v. Indiana, Apr. 12
Field goal attempts, game: 43, Russell Westbrook, Oklahoma City v. Indiana, Apr. 12
3-pointers, game: 11, Klay Thompson, Golden State v. Sacramento, Jan. 23; Kyrie Irving, Cleveland v. Portland, Jan. 28
3-pt. attempts, game: 19, Kyrie Irving, Cleveland v. Portland, Jan. 28
Free throws, game: 22, James Harden, Houston v. Denver, Mar. 19
Free throw attempts, game: 28, DeAndre Jordan, L.A. Clippers v. San Antonio, Feb. 19
Rebounds, game: 27, DeAndre Jordan, L.A. Clippers v. Dallas, Feb. 9
Assists, game: 21, Brandon Jennings, Detroit v. Orlando, Jan. 21
Steals, game: 8, Mario Chalmers, Miami v. New York, Feb. 20
Blocks, game: 12, Hassan Whiteside, Miami v. Chicago, Jan. 25
Minutes played, season: 2,981, James Harden, Houston
Off. rebounds, season: 437, Andre Drummond, Detroit
Def. rebounds, season: 829, DeAndre Jordan, L.A. Clippers
Personal fouls, season: 285, Andre Drummond, Detroit

NBA Finals MVP, 1969-2015

Year	Player, team	Year	Player, team	Year	Player, team
1969	Jerry West, L.A. Lakers	1985	Kareem Abdul-Jabbar, L.A. Lakers	2000	Shaquille O'Neal, L.A. Lakers
1970	Willis Reed, New York	1986	Larry Bird, Boston	2001	Shaquille O'Neal, L.A. Lakers
1971	Lew Alcindor (Kareem Abdul-Jabbar), Milwaukee	1987	Magic Johnson, L.A. Lakers	2002	Shaquille O'Neal, L.A. Lakers
1972	Wilt Chamberlain, L.A. Lakers	1988	James Worthy, L.A. Lakers	2003	Tim Duncan, San Antonio
1973	Willis Reed, New York	1989	Joe Dumars, Detroit	2004	Chauncey Billups, Detroit
1974	John Havlicek, Boston	1990	Isiah Thomas, Detroit	2005	Tim Duncan, San Antonio
1975	Rick Barry, Golden State	1991	Michael Jordan, Chicago	2006	Dwyane Wade, Miami
1976	Jo Jo White, Boston	1992	Michael Jordan, Chicago	2007	Tony Parker, San Antonio
1977	Bill Walton, Portland	1993	Michael Jordan, Chicago	2008	Paul Pierce, Boston
1978	Wes Unseld, Washington	1994	Hakeem Olajuwon, Houston	2009	Kobe Bryant, L.A. Lakers
1979	Dennis Johnson, Seattle	1995	Hakeem Olajuwon, Houston	2010	Kobe Bryant, L.A. Lakers
1980	Magic Johnson, L.A. Lakers	1996	Michael Jordan, Chicago	2011	Dirk Nowitzki, Dallas
1981	Cedric Maxwell, Boston	1997	Michael Jordan, Chicago	2012	LeBron James, Miami
1982	Magic Johnson, L.A. Lakers	1998	Michael Jordan, Chicago	2013	LeBron James, Miami
1983	Moses Malone, Philadelphia	1999	Tim Duncan, San Antonio	2014	Kawhi Leonard, San Antonio
1984	Larry Bird, Boston			2015	Andre Iguodala, Golden State

NBA Finals All-Time Statistical Leaders

(At the end of the 2015 NBA Finals. * = Active in 2014-15 season. Minimum 10 games played.)

Scoring average leader	GP	FG	FT	PTS	AVG
Rick Barry	10	138	87	363	36.3
Michael Jordan	35	438	258	1,176	33.6
Jerry West	55	612	455	1,679	30.5
Shaquille O'Neal	30	340	185	865	28.8
Bob Pettit	25	241	227	709	28.4
Hakeem Olajuwon	17	187	91	467	27.5
*LeBron James	33	323	170	871	26.4
Elgin Baylor	44	442	227	1,161	26.4
Julius Erving	22	216	128	561	25.5
*Kobe Bryant	37	333	223	937	25.3

Games Played

Bill Russell	70
Sam Jones	64
Kareem Abdul-Jabbar	56
Jerry West	55
Tom Heinsohn	52

Rebounds

Bill Russell	1,718
Wilt Chamberlain	862
Elgin Baylor	593
Kareem Abdul-Jabbar	507
Tom Heinsohn	473

Assists

Magic Johnson	584
Bob Cousy	400
Bill Russell	315
Jerry West	306
Dennis Johnson	228

NBA Most Valuable Player, 1956-2015

Year	Player, team	Year	Player, team	Year	Player, team
1956	Bob Pettit, St. Louis	1976	Kareem Abdul-Jabbar, L.A. Lakers	1996	Michael Jordan, Chicago
1957	Bob Cousy, Boston	1977	Kareem Abdul-Jabbar, L.A. Lakers	1997	Karl Malone, Utah
1958	Bill Russell, Boston	1978	Bill Walton, Portland	1998	Michael Jordan, Chicago
1959	Bob Pettit, St. Louis	1979	Moses Malone, Houston	1999	Karl Malone, Utah
1960	Wilt Chamberlain, Philadelphia	1980	Kareem Abdul-Jabbar, L.A. Lakers	2000	Shaquille O'Neal, L.A. Lakers
1961	Bill Russell, Boston	1981	Julius Erving, Philadelphia	2001	Allen Iverson, Philadelphia
1962	Bill Russell, Boston	1982	Moses Malone, Houston	2002	Tim Duncan, San Antonio
1963	Bill Russell, Boston	1983	Moses Malone, Philadelphia	2003	Tim Duncan, San Antonio
1964	Oscar Robertson, Cincinnati	1984	Larry Bird, Boston	2004	Kevin Garnett, Minnesota
1965	Bill Russell, Boston	1985	Larry Bird, Boston	2005	Steve Nash, Phoenix
1966	Wilt Chamberlain, Philadelphia	1986	Larry Bird, Boston	2006	Steve Nash, Phoenix
1967	Wilt Chamberlain, Philadelphia	1987	Magic Johnson, L.A. Lakers	2007	Dirk Nowitzki, Dallas
1968	Wilt Chamberlain, Philadelphia	1988	Michael Jordan, Chicago	2008	Kobe Bryant, L.A. Lakers
1969	Wes Unseld, Baltimore	1989	Magic Johnson, L.A. Lakers	2009	LeBron James, Cleveland
1970	Willis Reed, New York	1990	Magic Johnson, L.A. Lakers	2010	LeBron James, Cleveland
1971	Lew Alcindor (Abdul-Jabbar), Milw.	1991	Michael Jordan, Chicago	2011	Derrick Rose, Chicago
1972	Kareem Abdul-Jabbar, Milwaukee	1992	Michael Jordan, Chicago	2012	LeBron James, Miami
1973	Dave Cowens, Boston	1993	Charles Barkley, Phoenix	2013	LeBron James, Miami
1974	Kareem Abdul-Jabbar, Milwaukee	1994	Hakeem Olajuwon, Houston	2014	Kevin Durant, Oklahoma City
1975	Bob McAdoo, Buffalo	1995	David Robinson, San Antonio	2015	Stephen Curry, Golden State

NBA Scoring Leaders, 1947-2015

(Average points per game; 58 games minimum in 2014-15; prior season minimums vary.)

Year	Player, team	PTS	AVG
1947	Joe Fulks, Philadelphia	1,389	23.2
1948	Max Zaslofsky, Chicago	1,007	21.0
1949	George Mikan, Minneapolis	1,698	28.3
1950	George Mikan, Minneapolis	1,865	27.4
1951	George Mikan, Minneapolis	1,932	28.4
1952	Paul Arizin, Philadelphia	1,674	25.4
1953	Neil Johnston, Philadelphia	1,564	22.3
1954	Neil Johnston, Philadelphia	1,759	24.4
1955	Neil Johnston, Philadelphia	1,631	22.7
1956	Bob Pettit, St. Louis	1,849	25.7
1957	Paul Arizin, Philadelphia	1,817	25.6
1958	George Yardley, Detroit	2,001	27.8
1959	Bob Pettit, St. Louis	2,105	29.2
1960	Wilt Chamberlain, Philadelphia	2,707	37.6
1961	Wilt Chamberlain, Philadelphia	3,033	38.4
1962	Wilt Chamberlain, Philadelphia	4,029	50.4
1963	Wilt Chamberlain, San Francisco	3,586	44.8
1964	Wilt Chamberlain, San Francisco	2,948	36.9
1965	Wilt Chamberlain, San Francisco-Phil.	2,534	34.7
1966	Wilt Chamberlain, Philadelphia	2,649	33.5
1967	Rick Barry, San Francisco	2,775	35.6
1968	Dave Bing, Detroit	2,142	27.1
1969	Elvin Hayes, San Diego	2,327	28.4
1970	Jerry West, L.A. Lakers	2,309	31.2
1971	Lew Alcindor (Kareem Abdul-Jabbar), Milw.	2,596	31.7
1972	Kareem Abdul-Jabbar, Milwaukee	2,822	34.8
1973	Nate Archibald, Kansas City-Omaha	2,719	34.0
1974	Bob McAdoo, Buffalo	2,261	30.6
1975	Bob McAdoo, Buffalo	2,831	34.5
1976	Bob McAdoo, Buffalo	2,427	31.1
1977	Pete Maravich, New Orleans	2,273	31.1
1978	George Gervin, San Antonio	2,232	27.2
1979	George Gervin, San Antonio	2,365	29.6
1980	George Gervin, San Antonio	2,585	33.1
1981	Adrian Dantley, Utah	2,452	30.7
1982	George Gervin, San Antonio	2,551	32.3
1983	Alex English, Denver	2,326	28.4
1984	Adrian Dantley, Utah	2,418	30.6
1985	Bernard King, New York	1,809	32.9
1986	Dominique Wilkins, Atlanta	2,366	30.3
1987	Michael Jordan, Chicago	3,041	37.1
1988	Michael Jordan, Chicago	2,868	35.0

Year	Player, team	PTS	AVG
1989	Michael Jordan, Chicago	2,633	32.5
1990	Michael Jordan, Chicago	2,753	33.6
1991	Michael Jordan, Chicago	2,580	31.5
1992	Michael Jordan, Chicago	2,404	30.1
1993	Michael Jordan, Chicago	2,541	32.6
1994	David Robinson, San Antonio	2,383	29.8
1995	Shaquille O'Neal, Orlando	2,315	29.3
1996	Michael Jordan, Chicago	2,491	30.4
1997	Michael Jordan, Chicago	2,431	29.6
1998	Michael Jordan, Chicago	2,357	28.7
1999	Allen Iverson, Philadelphia	1,284	26.8
2000	Shaquille O'Neal, L.A. Lakers	2,344	29.7
2001	Allen Iverson, Philadelphia	2,207	31.1
2002	Allen Iverson, Philadelphia	1,883	31.4
2003	Tracy McGrady, Orlando	2,407	32.1
2004	Tracy McGrady, Orlando	1,878	28.0
2005	Allen Iverson, Philadelphia	2,302	30.7
2006	Kobe Bryant, L.A. Lakers	2,832	35.4
2007	Kobe Bryant, L.A. Lakers	2,430	31.6
2008	LeBron James, Cleveland	2,250	30.0
2009	Dwyane Wade, Miami	2,386	30.2
2010	Kevin Durant, Oklahoma City	2,472	30.1
2011	Kevin Durant, Oklahoma City	2,161	27.7
2012	Kevin Durant, Oklahoma City	1,850	28.0
2013	Carmelo Anthony, New York	1,920	28.7
2014	Kevin Durant, Oklahoma City	2,593	32.0
2015	Russell Westbrook, Oklahoma City	1,886	28.1

NBA Champions, 1947-2015

	Regular season		Playoffs		
Year	Eastern champion	Western champion	Champion	Winning coach	Opponent
1947	Washington Capitols	Chicago Stags	Philadelphia	Ed Gottlieb	Chicago
1948	Philadelphia Warriors	St. Louis Bombers	Baltimore	Buddy Jeannette	Philadelphia
1949	Washington Capitols	Rochester	Minneapolis	John Kundla	Washington
1950[1]	Syracuse	Indianapolis	Minneapolis	John Kundla	Syracuse
1951	Philadelphia Warriors	Minneapolis	Rochester	Lester Harrison	New York
1952	Syracuse	Rochester	Minneapolis	John Kundla	New York
1953	New York	Minneapolis	Minneapolis	John Kundla	New York
1954	New York	Minneapolis	Minneapolis	John Kundla	Syracuse
1955	Syracuse	Ft. Wayne	Syracuse	Al Cervi	Ft. Wayne
1956	Philadelphia Warriors	Ft. Wayne	Philadelphia	George Senesky	Ft. Wayne
1957	Boston	St. Louis	Boston	Red Auerbach	St. Louis
1958	Boston	St. Louis	St. Louis	Alex Hannum	Boston
1959	Boston	St. Louis	Boston	Red Auerbach	Minneapolis
1960	Boston	St. Louis	Boston	Red Auerbach	St. Louis
1961	Boston	St. Louis	Boston	Red Auerbach	St. Louis
1962	Boston	L.A. Lakers	Boston	Red Auerbach	L.A. Lakers
1963	Boston	L.A. Lakers	Boston	Red Auerbach	L.A. Lakers
1964	Boston	San Francisco	Boston	Red Auerbach	San Francisco
1965	Boston	L.A. Lakers	Boston	Red Auerbach	L.A. Lakers
1966	Philadelphia	L.A. Lakers	Boston	Red Auerbach	L.A. Lakers
1967	Philadelphia	San Francisco	Philadelphia	Alex Hannum	San Francisco
1968	Philadelphia	St. Louis	Boston	Bill Russell	L.A. Lakers
1969	Baltimore	L.A. Lakers	Boston	Bill Russell	L.A. Lakers
1970	New York	Atlanta	New York	Red Holzman	L.A. Lakers

Year	Atlantic	Central	Midwest	Pacific	Champion	Winning coach	Opponent
1971	New York	Baltimore	Milwaukee	L.A. Lakers	Milwaukee	Larry Costello	Baltimore
1972	Boston	Baltimore	Milwaukee	L.A. Lakers	L.A. Lakers	Bill Sharman	New York
1973	Boston	Baltimore	Milwaukee	L.A. Lakers	New York	Red Holzman	L.A. Lakers
1974	Boston	Capital	Milwaukee	L.A. Lakers	Boston	Tom Heinsohn	Milwaukee
1975	Boston	Washington	Chicago	Golden State	Golden State	Al Attles	Washington
1976	Boston	Cleveland	Milwaukee	Golden State	Boston	Tom Heinsohn	Phoenix
1977	Philadelphia	Houston	Denver	L.A. Lakers	Portland	Jack Ramsay	Philadelphia
1978	Philadelphia	San Antonio	Denver	Portland	Washington	Dick Motta	Seattle
1979	Washington	San Antonio	Kansas City	Seattle	Seattle	Len Wilkens	Washington
1980	Boston	Atlanta	Milwaukee	L.A. Lakers	L.A. Lakers	Paul Westhead	Philadelphia
1981	Boston	Milwaukee	San Antonio	Phoenix	Boston	Bill Fitch	Houston
1982	Boston	Milwaukee	San Antonio	L.A. Lakers	L.A. Lakers	Pat Riley	Philadelphia
1983	Philadelphia	Milwaukee	San Antonio	L.A. Lakers	Philadelphia	Billy Cunningham	L.A. Lakers
1984	Boston	Milwaukee	Utah	L.A. Lakers	Boston	K. C. Jones	L.A. Lakers
1985	Boston	Milwaukee	Denver	L.A. Lakers	L.A. Lakers	Pat Riley	Boston
1986	Boston	Milwaukee	Houston	L.A. Lakers	Boston	K. C. Jones	Houston
1987	Boston	Atlanta	Dallas	L.A. Lakers	L.A. Lakers	Pat Riley	Boston
1988	Boston	Detroit	Denver	L.A. Lakers	L.A. Lakers	Pat Riley	Detroit
1989	New York	Detroit	Utah	L.A. Lakers	Detroit	Chuck Daly	L.A. Lakers
1990	Philadelphia	Detroit	San Antonio	L.A. Lakers	Detroit	Chuck Daly	Portland
1991	Boston	Chicago	San Antonio	Portland	Chicago	Phil Jackson	L.A. Lakers
1992	Boston	Chicago	Utah	Portland	Chicago	Phil Jackson	Portland
1993	New York	Chicago	Houston	Phoenix	Chicago	Phil Jackson	Phoenix
1994	New York	Atlanta	Houston	Seattle	Houston	Rudy Tomjanovich	New York
1995	Orlando	Indiana	San Antonio	Phoenix	Houston	Rudy Tomjanovich	Orlando
1996	Orlando	Chicago	San Antonio	Seattle	Chicago	Phil Jackson	Seattle
1997	Miami	Chicago	Utah	Seattle	Chicago	Phil Jackson	Utah
1998	Miami	Chicago	Utah	L.A. Lakers	Chicago	Phil Jackson	Utah
1999	Miami	Indiana	San Antonio	Portland	San Antonio	Gregg Popovich	New York
2000	Miami	Indiana	Utah	L.A. Lakers	L.A. Lakers	Phil Jackson	Indiana
2001	Philadelphia	Milwaukee	San Antonio	L.A. Lakers	L.A. Lakers	Phil Jackson	Philadelphia
2002	New Jersey	Detroit	San Antonio	Sacramento	L.A. Lakers	Phil Jackson	New Jersey
2003	New Jersey	Detroit	San Antonio	Sacramento	San Antonio	Gregg Popovich	New Jersey
2004	New Jersey	Indiana	Minnesota	L.A. Lakers	Detroit	Larry Brown	L.A. Lakers

Year	Atlantic	Central	Southeast	Northwest	Pacific	Southwest	Champion	Winning coach	Opponent
2005	Boston	Detroit	Miami	Seattle	Phoenix	San Antonio	San Antonio	Gregg Popovich	Detroit
2006	New Jersey	Detroit	Miami	Denver	Phoenix	San Antonio	Miami	Pat Riley	Dallas
2007	Toronto	Detroit	Miami	Utah	Phoenix	Dallas	San Antonio	Gregg Popovich	Cleveland
2008	Boston	Detroit	Orlando	Utah	L.A. Lakers	New Orleans	Boston	Glenn "Doc" Rivers	L.A. Lakers
2009	Boston	Cleveland	Orlando	Denver	L.A. Lakers	San Antonio	L.A. Lakers	Phil Jackson	Orlando
2010	Boston	Cleveland	Orlando	Denver	L.A. Lakers	Dallas	L.A. Lakers	Phil Jackson	Boston
2011	Boston	Chicago	Miami	OK City	L.A. Lakers	San Antonio	Dallas	Rick Carlisle	Miami
2012	Boston	Chicago	Miami	OK City	L.A. Lakers	San Antonio	Miami	Erik Spoelstra	OK City
2013	New York	Indiana	Miami	OK City	L.A. Clippers	San Antonio	Miami	Erik Spoelstra	San Antonio
2014	Toronto	Indiana	Miami	OK City	L.A. Clippers	San Antonio	San Antonio	Gregg Popovich	Miami
2015	Toronto	Cleveland	Atlanta	Portland	Golden State	Houston	Golden State	Steve Kerr	Cleveland

(1) The newly formed NBA combined the 11-team BAA (Basketball Assn. of Amer.) and six NBL (Natl. Basketball League) teams in the 1949-50 season and had three divisions for one year. The Minneapolis Lakers were co-champions of the soon-defunct Central Division.

All-NBA and All-Defensive Teams, 2014-15

All-NBA Team

First Team	Second Team
LeBron James, Cleveland	LaMarcus Aldridge, Portland
Anthony Davis, New Orleans	DeMarcus Cousins, Sacramento
Marc Gasol, Memphis	Pau Gasol, Chicago
Stephen Curry, Golden State	Russell Westbrook, Oklahoma City
James Harden, Houston	Chris Paul, L.A. Clippers

All-Defensive Team

Position	First Team	Second Team
Forward	Kawhi Leonard, San Antonio	Anthony Davis, New Orleans
Forward	Draymond Green, Golden State	Tim Duncan, San Antonio
Center	DeAndre Jordan, L.A. Clippers	Andrew Bogut, Golden State
Guard	Tony Allen, Memphis	Jimmy Butler, Chicago
Guard	Chris Paul, L.A. Clippers	John Wall, Washington

NBA Statistical Leaders, 2014-15

(* = rookie)

To qualify for averaged categories, player must be on pace to play 58 games in an 82-game season.

Scoring Average

Player, team	GP	FG	FT	PTS	AVG
Russell Westbrook, Oklahoma City	67	627	546	1,886	28.1
James Harden, Houston	81	647	715	2,217	27.4
LeBron James, Cleveland	69	624	375	1,743	25.3
Anthony Davis, New Orleans	68	642	371	1,656	24.4
DeMarcus Cousins, Sacramento	59	498	423	1,421	24.1
Stephen Curry, Golden State	80	653	308	1,900	23.8
LaMarcus Aldridge, Portland	71	659	306	1,661	23.4
Blake Griffin, L.A. Clippers	67	574	311	1,469	21.9
Kyrie Irving, Cleveland	75	578	315	1,628	21.7
Klay Thompson, Golden State	77	602	225	1,668	21.7

3-Point Field Goal Percentage (Minimum 82 3-point field goals made)

Player, team	3-FGM	3-FGA	PCT
Kyle Korver, Atlanta	221	449	.492
Eric Gordon, New Orleans	141	315	.448
Stephen Curry, Golden State	286	646	.443
Klay Thompson, Golden State	239	545	.439
J.J. Redick, L.A. Clippers	200	458	.437
Anthony Morrow, Oklahoma City	141	325	.434
Danny Green, San Antonio	191	457	.418
Kyrie Irving, Cleveland	157	378	.415
Bradley Beal, Washington	106	259	.409
Mike Dunleavy, Chicago	107	263	.407
Khris Middleton, Milwaukee	109	268	.407

Field Goal Percentage (Minimum 300 field goals made)

Player, team	FGM	FGA	PCT
DeAndre Jordan, L.A. Clippers	379	534	.710
Jonas Valanciunas, Toronto	373	652	.572
Marcin Gortat, Washington	439	775	.566
Timofey Mozgov, Denver-Cleveland	314	566	.555
Tyler Zeller, Boston	340	619	.549
Al Horford, Atlanta	519	965	.538
Anthony Davis, New Orleans	642	1,199	.535
Derrick Favors, Utah	482	918	.525
Nikola Vucevic, Orlando	631	1,206	.523
Enes Kanter, Utah-Oklahoma City	482	928	.519

Free Throw Percentage (Minimum 125 free throws made)

Player, team	FTM	FTA	PCT
Stephen Curry, Golden State	308	337	.914
Jodie Meeks, Detroit	145	160	.906
J.J. Redick, L.A. Clippers	183	203	.901
Jamal Crawford, L.A. Clippers	227	252	.901
Chris Paul, L.A. Clippers	289	321	.900
Danilo Gallinari, Denver	171	191	.895
Nick Young, L.A. Lakers	132	148	.892
Dirk Nowitzki, Dallas	255	289	.882
Jarrett Jack, Brooklyn	200	227	.881
Kevin Martin, Minnesota	170	193	.881

Rebounds per Game

Player, team	GP	OFF	DEF	TOT	AVG
DeAndre Jordan. L.A. Clippers	82	397	829	1,226	15.0
Andre Drummond, Detroit	82	437	667	1,104	13.5
DeMarcus Cousins, Sacramento	59	185	562	747	12.7
Pau Gasol, Chicago	78	220	699	919	11.8
Tyson Chandler, Dallas	75	294	570	864	11.5
Nikola Vucevic, Orlando	74	238	572	810	10.9
Zach Randolph, Memphis	71	225	522	747	10.5
Anthony Davis, New Orleans	68	173	523	696	10.2
LaMarcus Aldridge, Portland	71	177	549	726	10.2
Greg Monroe, Detroit	69	229	475	704	10.2

Assists per Game

Player, team	GP	AST	APG
Chris Paul, L.A. Clippers	82	838	10.2
John Wall, Washington	79	792	10.0
Ty Lawson, Denver	75	720	9.6
Russell Westbrook, Oklahoma City	67	574	8.6
Rajon Rondo, Boston-Dallas	68	538	7.9
Stephen Curry, Golden State	80	619	7.7
LeBron James, Cleveland	69	511	7.4
Jeff Teague, Atlanta	73	513	7.0
James Harden, Houston	81	565	7.0
Kyle Lowry, Toronto	70	473	6.8

Steals per Game

Player, team	GP	STL	AVG
Kawhi Leonard, San Antonio	64	148	2.31
Russell Westbrook, Oklahoma City	67	140	2.09
Tony Allen, Memphis	63	129	2.05
Stephen Curry, Golden State	80	163	2.04
Chris Paul, L.A. Clippers	82	156	1.90
James Harden, Houston	81	154	1.90
Trevor Ariza, Houston	82	152	1.85
Monta Ellis, Dallas	80	148	1.85
Paul Millsap, Atlanta	73	130	1.78
*Nerlens Noel, Philadelphia	75	133	1.77

Blocked Shots per Game

Player, team	GP	BLK	AVG
Anthony Davis, New Orleans	68	200	2.94
Serge Ibaka, Oklahoma City	64	155	2.42
Rudy Gobert, Utah	82	189	2.30
DeAndre Jordan, L.A. Clippers	82	183	2.23
John Henson, Milwaukee	67	135	2.01
Tim Duncan, San Antonio	77	151	1.96
*Nerlens Noel, Philadelphia	75	142	1.89
Pau Gasol, Chicago	78	147	1.88
Andre Drummond, Detroit	82	153	1.87
Brook Lopez, Brooklyn	72	126	1.75
DeMarcus Cousins, Sacramento	59	103	1.75

NBA Defensive Player of the Year, 1983-2015

Year	Player, team
1983	Sidney Moncrief, Milwaukee
1984	Sidney Moncrief, Milwaukee
1985	Mark Eaton, Utah
1986	Alvin Robertson, San Antonio
1987	Michael Cooper, L.A. Lakers
1988	Michael Jordan, Chicago
1989	Mark Eaton, Utah
1990	Dennis Rodman, Detroit
1991	Dennis Rodman, Detroit
1992	David Robinson, San Antonio
1993	Hakeem Olajuwon, Houston
1994	Hakeem Olajuwon, Houston
1995	Dikembe Mutombo, Denver
1996	Gary Payton, Seattle
1997	Dikembe Mutombo, Atlanta
1998	Dikembe Mutombo, Atlanta
1999	Alonzo Mourning, Miami
2000	Alonzo Mourning, Miami
2001	Dikembe Mutombo, Philadelphia-Atlanta
2002	Ben Wallace, Detroit
2003	Ben Wallace, Detroit
2004	Ron Artest, Indiana
2005	Ben Wallace, Detroit
2006	Ben Wallace, Detroit
2007	Marcus Camby, Denver
2008	Kevin Garnett, Boston
2009	Dwight Howard, Orlando
2010	Dwight Howard, Orlando
2011	Dwight Howard, Orlando
2012	Tyson Chandler, New York
2013	Marc Gasol, Memphis
2014	Joakim Noah, Chicago
2015	Kawhi Leonard, San Antonio

NBA Rookie of the Year, 1953-2015

Year	Player, team	Year	Player, team	Year	Player, team
1953	Don Meineke, Ft. Wayne	1974	Ernie DiGregorio, Buffalo	1996	Damon Stoudamire, Toronto
1954	Ray Felix, Baltimore	1975	Jamaal Wilkes, Golden State	1997	Allen Iverson, Philadelphia
1955	Bob Pettit, Milwaukee	1976	Alvan Adams, Phoenix	1998	Tim Duncan, San Antonio
1956	Maurice Stokes, Rochester	1977	Adrian Dantley, Buffalo	1999	Vince Carter, Toronto
1957	Tom Heinsohn, Boston	1978	Walter Davis, Phoenix	2000	Elton Brand, Chicago; Steve Francis, Houston
1958	Woody Sauldsberry, Philadelphia	1979	Phil Ford, Kansas City	2001	Mike Miller, Orlando
1959	Elgin Baylor, Minneapolis	1980	Larry Bird, Boston	2002	Pau Gasol, Memphis
1960	Wilt Chamberlain, Philadelphia	1981	Darrell Griffith, Utah	2003	Amar'e Stoudemire, Phoenix
1961	Oscar Robertson, Cincinnati	1982	Buck Williams, New Jersey	2004	LeBron James, Cleveland
1962	Walt Bellamy, Chicago	1983	Terry Cummings, San Diego	2005	Emeka Okafor, Charlotte
1963	Terry Dischinger, Chicago	1984	Ralph Sampson, Houston	2006	Chris Paul, New Orl./OK City
1964	Jerry Lucas, Cincinnati	1985	Michael Jordan, Chicago	2007	Brandon Roy, Portland
1965	Willis Reed, New York	1986	Patrick Ewing, New York	2008	Kevin Durant, Seattle
1966	Rick Barry, San Francisco	1987	Chuck Person, Indiana	2009	Derrick Rose, Chicago
1967	Dave Bing, Detroit	1988	Mark Jackson, New York	2010	Tyreke Evans, Sacramento
1968	Earl Monroe, Baltimore	1989	Mitch Richmond, Golden State	2011	Blake Griffin, L.A. Clippers
1969	Wes Unseld, Baltimore	1990	David Robinson, San Antonio	2012	Kyrie Irving, Cleveland
1970	Lew Alcindor (Abdul-Jabbar), Milwaukee	1991	Derrick Coleman, New Jersey	2013	Damian Lillard, Portland
1971	Dave Cowens, Boston; Geoff Petrie, Portland	1992	Larry Johnson, Charlotte	2014	Michael Carter-Williams, Philadelphia
1972	Sidney Wicks, Portland	1993	Shaquille O'Neal, Orlando	2015	Andrew Wiggins, Minnesota
1973	Bob McAdoo, Buffalo	1994	Chris Webber, Golden State		
		1995	Grant Hill, Detroit; Jason Kidd, Dallas		

NBA Sixth Man Award, 1983-2015

Year	Player, team	Year	Player, team	Year	Player, team
1983	Bobby Jones, Philadelphia	1994	Dell Curry, Charlotte	2005	Ben Gordon, Chicago
1984	Kevin McHale, Boston	1995	Anthony Mason, New York	2006	Mike Miller, Memphis
1985	Kevin McHale, Boston	1996	Toni Kukoc, Chicago	2007	Leandro Barbosa, Phoenix
1986	Bill Walton, Boston	1997	John Starks, New York	2008	Manu Ginobili, San Antonio
1987	Ricky Pierce, Milwaukee	1998	Danny Manning, Phoenix	2009	Jason Terry, Dallas
1988	Roy Tarpley, Dallas	1999	Darrell Armstrong, Orlando	2010	Jamal Crawford, Atlanta
1989	Eddie Johnson, Phoenix	2000	Rodney Rogers, Phoenix	2011	Lamar Odom, L.A. Lakers
1990	Ricky Pierce, Milwaukee	2001	Aaron McKie, Philadelphia	2012	James Harden, Oklahoma City
1991	Detlef Schrempf, Indiana	2002	Corliss Williamson, Detroit	2013	J.R. Smith, New York
1992	Detlef Schrempf, Indiana	2003	Bobby Jackson, Sacramento	2014	Jamal Crawford, L.A. Clippers
1993	Clifford Robinson, Portland	2004	Antawn Jamison, Dallas	2015	Lou Williams, Toronto

NBA Player Draft First-Round Picks, 2015

(June 25, 2015)

Team	Player, position, school/team	Team	Player, position, school/team
1. Minnesota	Karl-Anthony Towns, Center, Kentucky	16. Boston	Terry Rozier, Guard, Louisville
2. L.A. Lakers	D'Angelo Russell, Guard, Ohio State	17. Milwaukee	Rashad Vaughn, Guard, UNLV
3. Philadelphia	Jahlil Okafor, Center, Duke	18. Houston[3]	Sam Dekker, Forward, Wisconsin
4. New York	Kristaps Porzingis, Forward, Sevilla (Spain)	19. Washington	Jerian Grant, Guard, Notre Dame[4]
5. Orlando	Mario Hezonja, Guard, Barcelona (Spain)	20. Toronto	Delon Wright, Guard, Utah
6. Sacramento	Willie Cauley-Stein, Center, Kentucky	21. Dallas	Justin Anderson, Guard, Virginia
7. Denver	Emmanuel Mudiay, Guard, Guangdong (China)	22. Chicago	Bobby Portis, Forward, Arkansas
8. Detroit	Stanley Johnson, Forward, Arizona	23. Portland	Rondae Hollis-Jefferson, Forward, Arizona[5]
9. Charlotte	Frank Kaminsky, Forward, Wisconsin	24. Cleveland	Tyus Jones, Guard, Duke[6]
10. Miami	Justise Winslow, Guard, Duke	25. Memphis	Jarell Martin, Forward, LSU
11. Indiana	Myles Turner, Forward, Texas	26. San Antonio	Nikola Milutinov, Center, Partizan (Serbia)
12. Utah	Trey Lyles, Forward, Kentucky	27. L.A. Lakers[7]	Larry Nance Jr., Forward, Wyoming
13. Phoenix	Devin Booker, Guard, Kentucky	28. Boston[8]	R.J. Hunter, Guard, Georgia State
14. Oklahoma City	Cameron Payne, Guard, Murray State	29. Brooklyn[9]	Chris McCullough, Forward, Syracuse
15. Atlanta[1]	Kelly Oubre, Forward, Kansas[2]	30. Golden State	Kevon Looney, Forward, UCLA

(1) From Brooklyn. (2) Rights traded to Washington. (3) From New Orleans. (4) Rights traded to New York. (5) Rights traded to Brooklyn. (6) Rights traded to Minnesota. (7) From Houston. (8) From L.A. Clippers. (9) From Atlanta.

Number-One First-Round NBA Draft Picks, 1966-2015

Year	Team	Player, school/team	Year	Team	Player, school/team
1966	New York	Cazzie Russell, Michigan	1984	Houston	Hakeem Olajuwon, Houston
1967	Detroit	Jimmy Walker, Providence	1985	New York	Patrick Ewing, Georgetown
1968	San Diego	Elvin Hayes, Houston	1986	Cleveland	Brad Daugherty, North Carolina
1969	Milwaukee	Lew Alcindor (Kareem Abdul-Jabbar), UCLA	1987	San Antonio	David Robinson, Navy
			1988	L.A. Clippers	Danny Manning, Kansas
1970	Detroit	Bob Lanier, St. Bonaventure	1989	Sacramento	Pervis Ellison, Louisville
1971	Cleveland	Austin Carr, Notre Dame	1990	New Jersey	Derrick Coleman, Syracuse
1972	Portland	LaRue Martin, Loyola-Chicago	1991	Charlotte	Larry Johnson, UNLV
1973	Philadelphia	Doug Collins, Illinois State	1992	Orlando	Shaquille O'Neal, LSU
1974	Portland	Bill Walton, UCLA	1993	Orlando	Chris Webber[2], Michigan
1975	Atlanta	David Thompson[1], NC State	1994	Milwaukee	Glenn Robinson, Purdue
1976	Houston	John Lucas, Maryland	1995	Golden State	Joe Smith, Maryland
1977	Milwaukee	Kent Benson, Indiana	1996	Philadelphia	Allen Iverson, Georgetown
1978	Portland	Mychal Thompson, Minnesota	1997	San Antonio	Tim Duncan, Wake Forest
1979	L.A. Lakers	Earvin "Magic" Johnson, Michigan State	1998	L.A. Clippers	Michael Olowokandi, Pacific (CA)
1980	Golden State	Joe Barry Carroll, Purdue	1999	Chicago	Elton Brand, Duke
1981	Dallas	Mark Aguirre, DePaul	2000	New Jersey	Kenyon Martin, Cincinnati
1982	L.A. Lakers	James Worthy, North Carolina	2001	Washington	Kwame Brown, Glynn Academy (HS)
1983	Houston	Ralph Sampson, Virginia	2002	Houston	Yao Ming, Shanghai Sharks (China)

Year	Team	Player, school/team
2003	Cleveland	LeBron James, St. Vincent-St. Mary (HS)
2004	Orlando	Dwight Howard, Southwest Atlanta Christian Academy (HS)
2005	Milwaukee	Andrew Bogut, Utah
2006	Toronto	Andrea Bargnani, Benetton Treviso (Italy)
2007	Portland	Greg Oden, Ohio State
2008	Chicago	Derrick Rose, Memphis
2009	L.A. Clippers	Blake Griffin, Oklahoma
2010	Washington	John Wall, Kentucky
2011	Cleveland	Kyrie Irving, Duke
2012	New Orleans	Anthony Davis, Kentucky
2013	Cleveland	Anthony Bennett, UNLV
2014	Cleveland	Andrew Wiggins, Kansas
2015	Minnesota	Karl-Anthony Towns, Kentucky

HS = High school. (1) Signed with Denver of the American Basketball Association (ABA). (2) Traded to Golden State for rights to Anfernee Hardaway and three future first-round draft choices.

All-Time NBA Statistical Leaders

(At the end of the 2014-15 season. * = Active in 2014-15 season.)

Scoring Average
(Minimum 400 games or 10,000 points)

	GP	PTS	AVG
Michael Jordan	1,072	32,292	30.1
Wilt Chamberlain	1,045	31,419	30.1
Elgin Baylor	846	23,149	27.4
*LeBron James	911	24,913	27.3
*Kevin Durant	569	15,537	27.3
Jerry West	932	25,192	27.0
Allen Iverson	914	24,368	26.7
Bob Pettit	792	20,880	26.4
George Gervin	791	20,708	26.2
Oscar Robertson	1,040	26,710	25.7

Field Goal Percentage
(Minimum 2,000 field goals made)

	FGM	FGA	PCT
Artis Gilmore	5,732	9,570	.599
*Tyson Chandler	3,026	5,118	.591
Shaquille O'Neal	11,330	19,457	.582
Mark West	2,528	4,356	.580
*Dwight Howard	5,228	9,024	.579
Darryl Dawkins	3,477	6,079	.572
Steve Johnson	2,841	4,965	.572
James Donaldson	3,105	5,442	.571
Bo Outlaw	2,005	3,534	.567
Jeff Ruland	2,105	3,734	.564

Free Throw Percentage
(Minimum 1,200 free throws made)

	FTM	FTA	PCT
Steve Nash	3,060	3,384	.904
Mark Price	2,135	2,362	.904
Rick Barry	3,818	4,243	.900
*Stephen Curry	1,305	1,450	.900
Peja Stojakovic	2,237	2,500	.895
Chauncey Billups	4,496	5,029	.894
Ray Allen	4,398	4,920	.894
Calvin Murphy	3,445	3,864	.892
Scott Skiles	1,548	1,741	.889
Reggie Miller	6,237	7,026	.888

3-Point Field Goal Percentage
(Minimum 250 3-point field goals made)

	3-FGM	3-FGA	PCT
Steve Kerr	726	1,599	.454
Hubert Davis	728	1,651	.441
*Stephen Curry	1,191	2,704	.440
Drazen Petrovic	255	583	.437
Jason Kapono	457	1,054	.434
*Kyle Korver	1,729	3,998	.432
*Steve Novak	567	1,316	.431
Tim Legler	260	603	.431
*Anthony Morrow	687	1,600	.429
Steve Nash	1,685	3,939	.428

Minutes Played

Kareem Abdul-Jabbar	57,446
Karl Malone	54,852
Jason Kidd	50,111
Elvin Hayes	50,000
*Kevin Garnett	49,862
Wilt Chamberlain	47,859
John Stockton	47,764
Reggie Miller	47,619
Gary Payton	47,117
*Kobe Bryant	46,774

Field Goals Attempted

Kareem Abdul-Jabbar	28,307
Karl Malone	26,210
*Kobe Bryant	25,087
Michael Jordan	24,537
Elvin Hayes	24,272
John Havlicek	23,930
Wilt Chamberlain	23,497
Dominique Wilkins	21,589
Alex English	21,036
*Kevin Garnett	21,027

Points

Kareem Abdul-Jabbar	38,387
Karl Malone	36,928
*Kobe Bryant	32,482
Michael Jordan	32,292
Wilt Chamberlain	31,419
Shaquille O'Neal	28,596
*Dirk Nowitzki	28,119
Moses Malone	27,409
Elvin Hayes	27,313
Hakeem Olajuwon	26,946

Games Played

Robert Parish	1,611
Kareem Abdul-Jabbar	1,560
John Stockton	1,504
Karl Malone	1,476
*Kevin Garnett	1,424
Kevin Willis	1,424
Jason Kidd	1,391
Reggie Miller	1,389
Clifford Robinson	1,380
Gary Payton	1,335

Field Goals Made

Kareem Abdul-Jabbar	15,837
Karl Malone	13,528
Wilt Chamberlain	12,681
Michael Jordan	12,192
Shaquille O'Neal	11,330
*Kobe Bryant	11,321
Elvin Hayes	10,976
Hakeem Olajuwon	10,749
Alex English	10,659
John Havlicek	10,513

Rebounds

Wilt Chamberlain	23,924
Bill Russell	21,620
Kareem Abdul-Jabbar	17,440
Elvin Hayes	16,279
Moses Malone	16,212
Karl Malone	14,968
Robert Parish	14,715
*Tim Duncan	14,644
*Kevin Garnett	14,512
Nate Thurmond	14,464

Personal Fouls

Kareem Abdul-Jabbar	4,657
Karl Malone	4,578
Robert Parish	4,443
Charles Oakley	4,421
Hakeem Olajuwon	4,383
Buck Williams	4,267
Elvin Hayes	4,193
Clifford Robinson	4,175
Kevin Willis	4,172
Shaquille O'Neal	4,146
Otis Thorpe	4,146

3-Point Field Goals Attempted

Ray Allen	7,429
Reggie Miller	6,486
Jason Kidd	5,701
*Paul Pierce	5,531
*Jason Terry	5,463
*Jamal Crawford	5,195
*Kobe Bryant	5,079
*Vince Carter	5,020
Chauncey Billups	4,725
Rashard Lewis	4,625

Assists

John Stockton	15,806
Jason Kidd	12,091
Steve Nash	10,335
Mark Jackson	10,334
Magic Johnson	10,141
Oscar Robertson	9,887
Isiah Thomas	9,061
Gary Payton	8,966
*Andre Miller	8,437
Rod Strickland	7,987

Blocked Shots

Hakeem Olajuwon	3,830
Dikembe Mutombo	3,289
Kareem Abdul-Jabbar	3,189
Mark Eaton	3,064
David Robinson	2,954
*Tim Duncan	2,942
Patrick Ewing	2,894
Shaquille O'Neal	2,732
Tree Rollins	2,542
Robert Parish	2,361

3-Point Field Goals Made

Ray Allen	2,973
Reggie Miller	2,560
*Jason Terry	2,076
*Paul Pierce	2,053
Jason Kidd	1,988
*Vince Carter	1,878
Chauncey Billups	1,830
*Jamal Crawford	1,816
Rashard Lewis	1,787
Peja Stojakovic	1,760

Steals

John Stockton	3,265
Jason Kidd	2,684
Michael Jordan	2,514
Gary Payton	2,445
Maurice Cheeks	2,310
Scottie Pippen	2,307
Clyde Drexler	2,207
Hakeem Olajuwon	2,162
Alvin Robertson	2,112
Karl Malone	2,085

NBA Coach of the Year, 1963-2015

Year	Coach, team	Year	Coach, team	Year	Coach, team
1963	Harry Gallatin, St. Louis	1981	Jack McKinney, Indiana	1999	Mike Dunleavy, Portland
1964	Alex Hannum, San Francisco	1982	Gene Shue, Washington	2000	Glenn "Doc" Rivers, Orlando
1965	Red Auerbach, Boston	1983	Don Nelson, Milwaukee	2001	Larry Brown, Philadelphia
1966	Dolph Schayes, Philadelphia	1984	Frank Layden, Utah	2002	Rick Carlisle, Detroit
1967	Johnny Kerr, Chicago	1985	Don Nelson, Milwaukee	2003	Gregg Popovich, San Antonio
1968	Richie Guerin, St. Louis	1986	Mike Fratello, Atlanta	2004	Hubie Brown, Memphis
1969	Gene Shue, Baltimore	1987	Mike Schuler, Portland	2005	Mike D'Antoni, Phoenix
1970	Red Holzman, New York	1988	Doug Moe, Denver	2006	Avery Johnson, Dallas
1971	Dick Motta, Chicago	1989	Cotton Fitzsimmons, Phoenix	2007	Sam Mitchell, Toronto
1972	Bill Sharman, L.A. Lakers	1990	Pat Riley, L.A. Lakers	2008	Byron Scott, New Orleans
1973	Tom Heinsohn, Boston	1991	Don Chaney, Houston	2009	Mike Brown, Cleveland
1974	Ray Scott, Detroit	1992	Don Nelson, Golden State	2010	Scott Brooks, Oklahoma City
1975	Phil Johnson, Kansas City-Omaha	1993	Pat Riley, New York	2011	Tom Thibodeau, Chicago
1976	Bill Fitch, Cleveland	1994	Lenny Wilkens, Atlanta	2012	Gregg Popovich, San Antonio
1977	Tom Nissalke, Houston	1995	Del Harris, L.A. Lakers	2013	George Karl, Denver
1978	Hubie Brown, Atlanta	1996	Phil Jackson, Chicago	2014	Gregg Popovich, San Antonio
1979	Cotton Fitzsimmons, Kansas City	1997	Pat Riley, Miami	2015	Mike Budenholzer, Atlanta
1980	Bill Fitch, Boston	1998	Larry Bird, Indiana		

National Basketball Association Franchise Origins

Team, founding year (in NBA, BAA, or ABA), location, and subsequent history. Neutral sites and arena sites in the same metropolitan area not listed separately.

Atlanta Hawks: 1949, NBA, as Tri-Cities Blackhawks, 1949-51, Moline, IL. Milwaukee Hawks, 1951-55; St. Louis Hawks, 1955-68; Atlanta Hawks, 1968-present.
Boston Celtics: 1946, BAA, Boston, 1946-present.
Brooklyn Nets: 1967, ABA, as New Jersey Americans, 1967-68, Teaneck, NJ. New York Nets, 1968-77; New Jersey Nets, 1977-2012; Brooklyn Nets, 2012-present.
Charlotte Hornets: 2004, NBA, as Charlotte Bobcats, 2004-14, Charlotte, NC. Charlotte Hornets, 2014-present.
Chicago Bulls: 1966, NBA, Chicago, 1966-present.
Cleveland Cavaliers: 1970, NBA, Cleveland, OH, 1970-present.
Dallas Mavericks: 1980, NBA, Dallas, TX, 1980-present.
Denver Nuggets: 1967, ABA, as Denver Rockets, 1967-74, Denver, CO. Denver Nuggets, 1974-present.
Detroit Pistons: 1948, BAA, as Ft. Wayne Pistons, 1948-57, Ft. Wayne, IN. Detroit Pistons, 1957-present.
Golden State Warriors: 1946, BAA, as Philadelphia Warriors, 1946-62, Philadelphia, PA. San Francisco Warriors, 1962-71; Golden State Warriors, 1971-present, Oakland, CA.
Houston Rockets: 1967, NBA, as San Diego Rockets, 1967-71, San Diego, CA. Houston Rockets, 1971-present.
Indiana Pacers: 1967, ABA, Indianapolis, IN, 1974-present.
L.A. Clippers: 1970, NBA, as Buffalo Braves, 1970-78, Buffalo, NY. San Diego Clippers, 1978-84; L.A. Clippers, 1984-present.
L.A. Lakers: 1948, BAA, as Minneapolis Lakers, 1948-60, Minneapolis, MN. L.A. Lakers, 1960-present.
Memphis Grizzlies: 1995, NBA, as Vancouver Grizzlies, 1995-2001, Vancouver, BC, Canada. Memphis Grizzlies, 2001-present.
Miami Heat: 1988, NBA, Miami, FL, 1988-present.
Milwaukee Bucks: 1968, NBA, Milwaukee, WI, 1968-present.
Minnesota Timberwolves: 1989, NBA, Minneapolis, MN, 1989-present.
New Orleans Pelicans: 1988, NBA, as Charlotte Hornets, 1988-2002, Charlotte, NC. New Orleans Hornets, 2002-13 (Hornets played most home games in Oklahoma City, 2005-07, as city repaired Hurricane Katrina damage); New Orleans Pelicans, 2013-present.
New York Knicks: 1946, BAA, New York, 1946-present.
Oklahoma City Thunder: 1967, NBA, as Seattle SuperSonics, 1967-2008, Seattle, WA. Oklahoma City Thunder, 2008-present.
Orlando Magic: 1989, NBA, Orlando, FL, 1989-present.
Philadelphia 76ers: 1949, NBA, as Syracuse Nationals, 1949-63, Syracuse, NY. Philadelphia 76ers, 1963-present.
Phoenix Suns: 1968, NBA, Phoenix, AZ, 1968-present.
Portland Trail Blazers: 1970, NBA, Portland, OR, 1970-present.
Sacramento Kings: 1948, BAA, as Rochester Royals, 1948-57, Rochester, NY. Cincinnati Royals, 1957-72; Kansas City-Omaha Kings, 1972-75; Kansas City Kings, 1975-85; Sacramento Kings, 1985-present.
San Antonio Spurs: ABA, as Dallas Chaparrals, 1967-73, Dallas, TX. San Antonio Spurs, 1973-present.
Toronto Raptors: 1995, NBA, Toronto, ON, Canada, 1995-present.
Utah Jazz: 1974, NBA, as New Orleans Jazz, 1974-79, New Orleans, LA. Utah Jazz, 1979-present, Salt Lake City.
Washington Wizards: 1961, NBA, as Chicago Packers, 1961-62, Chicago. Chicago Zephyrs, 1962-63; Baltimore Bullets, 1963-73; Capital Bullets, 1973-74, Landover, MD; Washington Bullets, 1974-97; Washington Wizards, 1997-present.

NBA Home Courts

Team	Name (year built)	Capacity[1]	Team	Name (year built)	Capacity[1]
Atlanta	Philips Arena (1999)	18,118	Miami	AmericanAirlines Arena (1999)	19,600
Boston	TD Garden[2] (1995)	18,624	Milwaukee	BMO Harris Bradley Center[6] (1988)	18,717
Brooklyn	Barclays Center[3] (2012)	17,732	Minnesota	Target Center (1990)	19,356
Charlotte	Time Warner Cable Arena (2005)	19,077	New Orleans	Smoothie King Center[7] (1999)	16,867
Chicago	United Center (1994)	20,917	New York	Madison Square Garden (IV) (1968)	19,812
Cleveland	Quicken Loans Arena (1994)	20,562	Oklahoma City	Chesapeake Energy Arena[8] (2002)	18,203
Dallas	American Airlines Center (2001)	19,200	Orlando	Amway Center (2010)	18,846
Denver	Pepsi Center (1999)	19,155	Philadelphia	Wells Fargo Center[9] (1996)	20,328
Detroit	The Palace of Auburn Hills (1988)	21,165	Phoenix	US Airways Center[10] (1992)	18,422
Golden State	ORACLE Arena[4] (1966)	19,596	Portland	Moda Center[11] (1995)	19,980
Houston	Toyota Center (2003)	18,055	Sacramento	Sleep Train Arena[12] (1988)	17,317
Indiana	Bankers Life Fieldhouse[5] (1999)	18,165	San Antonio	AT&T Center[13] (2002)	18,581
L.A. Clippers	STAPLES Center (1999)	19,060	Toronto	Air Canada Centre (1999)	19,800
L.A. Lakers	STAPLES Center (1999)	18,997	Utah	EnergySolutions Arena[14] (1991)	19,911
Memphis	FedExForum (2004)	18,119	Washington	Verizon Center[15] (1997)	20,356

(1) At the end of the 2014-15 season. (2) FleetCenter, 1995-2005; TD Banknorth Garden, 2005-09. (3) The New Jersey Nets relocated to Brooklyn prior to the 2012-13 season. (4) Oakland Coliseum Arena, 1966-96; Arena in Oakland, 1997-2006. (5) Conseco Fieldhouse, 1999-2011. (6) Bradley Center, 1988-2012. (7) New Orleans Arena, 1999-2014; because of damage to New Orleans Arena due to Hurricane Katrina, the Hornets played 35 games in the Ford Center in Oklahoma City, OK, 3 games in New Orleans Arena, and 3 games at other locations during the 2005-06 season; in 2006-07, the Hornets played 35 games at the Ford Center and 6 games in New Orleans Arena. (8) Ford Center, 2008-11; the Seattle SuperSonics relocated to Oklahoma City prior to the 2008-09 season. (9) CoreStates Center, 1996-98; First Union Center, 1998-2003; Wachovia Center, 2003-10. (10) America West Arena, 1992-2006. (11) The Rose Garden, 1995-2013. (12) ARCO Arena, 1988-2011; Power Balance Pavilion, 2011-12. (13) SBC Center, 2002-06. (14) Delta Center, 1991-2006. (15) MCI Center, 1997-2006.

All-Time NBA Regular Season Coaching Victories

(At the end of the 2014-15 season, ranked by wins. * = Active in 2014-15 season.)

Coach	W	L	PCT	Coach	W	L	PCT	Coach	W	L	PCT
Don Nelson	1,335	1,063	.557	*Gregg Popovich	1,022	470	.685	*Glenn "Doc" Rivers	700	524	.572
Lenny Wilkens	1,332	1,155	.536	Bill Fitch	944	1,106	.460	Red Holzman	696	604	.535
Jerry Sloan	1,221	803	.603	Red Auerbach	938	479	.662	Mike Fratello	667	548	.549
Pat Riley	1,210	694	.636	Dick Motta	935	1,017	.479	*Flip Saunders	654	592	.525
Phil Jackson	1,155	485	.704	Jack Ramsay	864	783	.525	Chuck Daly	638	437	.593
*George Karl	1,142	775	.596	Cotton Fitzsimmons	832	775	.518	Doug Moe	628	529	.543
Larry Brown	1,098	904	.548	Gene Shue	784	861	.477	*Rick Carlisle	619	431	.590
Rick Adelman	1,042	749	.582	John MacLeod	707	657	.518	Mike Dunleavy	613	716	.461

Naismith Memorial Basketball Hall of Fame

(Located in Springfield, MA. * = 2015 inductee. + = Enshrined as both a player and coach.)

Players

Abdul-Jabbar, Kareem
Archibald, Nate
Arizin, Paul
Barkley, Charles
Barlow, Thomas
Barry, Rick
Baylor, Elgin
Beckman, John
Bellamy, Walt
Belov, Sergei
Bing, Dave
Bird, Larry
Blazejowski, Carol
Borgmann, Bennie
Bradley, Bill
Brennan, Joseph
Brown, Roger
Cervi, Al
Chamberlain, Wilt
Cooper, Charles
Cooper, Cynthia
Cosic, Kresimir
Cousy, Bob
Cowens, Dave
Crawford, Joan
Cunningham, Billy
Curry, Denise
Dalipagic, Drazen
*Dampier, Louis
Daniels, Mel
Dantley, Adrian
Davies, Bob
DeBernardi, Forrest
DeBusschere, Dave
Dehnert, Henry "Dutch"
Donovan, Anne
Drexler, Clyde
Dumars, Joe
Edwards, Teresa
Endacott, Paul
English, Alex
Erving, Julius
Ewing, Patrick
Foster, Bud
Frazier, Walt
Friedman, Max
Fulks, Joe
Gale, Lauren
Gallatin, Harry
Gates, William "Pop"
Gervin, George
Gilmore, Artis
Gola, Tom
Goodrich, Gail
Greer, Hal
Gruenig, Robert "Ace"
Guerin, Richard
Hagan, Cliff
Hanson, Victor
Harris-Stewart, Lusia
Havlicek, John
Hawkins, Cornelius "Connie"
Hayes, Elvin
Haynes, Marques
*Haywood, Spencer
*+Heinsohn, Tom
Holman, Nat
Houbregs, Bob
Howell, Bailey
Hyatt, Chuck
*Isaacs, John
Issel, Dan
Jeannette, Harry "Buddy"
Johnson, Dennis
Johnson, Earvin "Magic"
Johnson, Gus
Johnson, William
Johnston, Neil
Jones, K. C.
Jones, Sam
Jordan, Michael
King, Bernard
Krause, Ed "Moose"
Kurland, Bob
Lanier, Bob
Lapchick, Joe
*Leslie, Lisa
Lieberman, Nancy
Lovellette, Clyde
Lucas, Jerry
Luisetti, Angelo "Hank"
Macauley, Ed
Malone, Karl
Malone, Moses
Maravich, Pete
Marcari, Hortencia
Marciulionis, Sarunas
Martin, Slater
McAdoo, Bob
McClain, Katrina
McCracken, Emmett "Branch"
McCracken, Jack
McDermott, Bobby
McGuire, Dick
McHale, Kevin
Meneghin, Dino
Meyers, Ann
Mikan, George
Mikkelsen, Vern
Miller, Cheryl
Miller, Reggie
Monroe, Earl
Mourning, Alonzo
Mullin, Chris
Murphy, Calvin
Murphy, Charles "Stretch"
*Mutombo, Dikembe
Olajuwon, Hakeem
Page, Harlan "Pat"
Parish, Robert
Payton, Gary
Pereira, Maciel "Ubiratan"
Petrovic, Drazen
Pettit, Bob
Phillip, Andy
Pippen, Scottie
Pollard, Jim
Ramsey, Frank
Reed, Willis
Richmond, Mitch
Risen, Arnie
Robertson, Oscar
Robinson, David
Rodgers, Guy
Rodman, Dennis
Roosma, John
Russell, Bill
Russell, John "Honey"
Sabonis, Arvydas
Sampson, Ralph
Sanders, Tom "Satch"
Schayes, Adolph
Schmidt, Ernest
Schmidt, Oscar
Schommer, John
Sedran, Barney
Semjonova, Uljana
+Sharman, Bill
Staley, Dawn
Steinmetz, Chris
Stockton, John
Stokes, Maurice
Tatum, Reece "Goose"
Thomas, Isiah
Thompson, David
Thompson, John
Thurmond, Nate
Twyman, Jack
Unseld, Wes
Vandivier, Robert "Fuzzy"
Wachter, Ed
Walker, Chet
Walton, Bill
Wanzer, Bobby
West, Jerry
*White, Jo Jo
White, Nera
+Wilkens, Lenny
Wilkes, Jamaal
Wilkins, Dominique
Woodard, Lynette
+Wooden, John
Worthy, James
Yardley, George

Coaches

Alexeeva, Lidia
Allen, Forrest C. "Phog"
Anderson, Harold
Auerbach, Arnold "Red"
Auriemma, Geno
Barmore, Leon
Barry, Justin "Sam"
Blood, Ernest
Boeheim, Jim
Brown, Larry
Calhoun, Jim
*Calipari, John
Cann, Howard
Carlson, Clifford
Carnesecca, Lou
Carnevale, Ben
Carril, Pete
Case, Everett
Chancellor, Van
Chaney, John
Conradt, Jody
Crum, Denzil "Denny"
Daly, Chuck
Dean, Everett
Diaz-Miguel, Antonio
Diddle, Edgar
Drake, Bruce
Ferrandiz, Pedro
Gaines, Clarence
Gamba, Sandro
Gardner, James "Jack"
*Gaze, Lindsay
Gill, Amory "Slats"
Gomelsky, Aleksandr
Gunter, Sue
Hannum, Alex
Harshman, Marv
Haskins, Don
Hatchell, Sylvia
*+Heinsohn, Tom
Hickey, Edgar
Hobson, Howard
Holzman, William "Red"
Hurley, Bob, Sr.
Iba, Hank
Jackson, Phil
Julian, Alvin
Keaney, Frank
Keogan, George
Knight, Bob
Krzyzewski, Mike
Kundla, John
Lambert, Ward
Leonard, Bob
Lewis, Guy V.
Litwack, Harry
Loeffler, Kenneth
Lonborg, Arthur "Dutch"
Magee, Herb
McCutchan, Arad
McGuire, Al
McGuire, Frank
McLendon, John
Meanwell, Dr. Walter
Meyer, Ray
Miller, Ralph
Moore, Billie
Nelson, Don
Newell, Pete
Nikolic, Aleksandar
Novosel, Mirko
Olson, Robert "Lute"
Pitino, Rick
Ramsay, John "Jack"
Richardson, Nolan
Riley, Pat
Rubini, Cesare
Rupp, Adolph
Rush, Cathy
Sachs, Leonard
+Sharman, Bill
Shelton, Everett
Sloan, Jerry
Smith, Dean
Stringer, C. Vivian
Summitt, Pat
Tarkanian, Jerry
Taylor, Fred
Thompson, John R.
VanDerveer, Tara
Wade, Margaret
Watts, Stan
+Wilkens, Lenny
Williams, Gary
Williams, Roy
Winter, Tex
+Wooden, John
Woolpert, Phil
Wootten, Morgan
Yow, Kay

Teams

1960 USA Men's Olympic Team
1992 USA Men's Olympic "Dream Team"
All American Red Heads
Buffalo Germans
First Team
Harlem Globetrotters
Immaculata University
New York Renaissance
Original Celtics
Texas Western

Referees

*Bavetta, Dick
Enright, James
Hepbron, George
Hoyt, George
Kennedy, Matthew
Leith, Lloyd
Mihalik, Zigmund "Red"
Nichols, Hank
Nucatola, John
Quigley, Ernest
Rudolph, Marvin "Mendy"
Shirley, J. Dallas
Strom, Earl
Tobey, David
Walsh, David

Contributors

Abbott, Senda Berenson
Barksdale, Don
Bee, Clair
Biasone, Danny
Brown, Hubert "Hubie"
Brown, Walter
Bunn, John
Buss, Jerry
Clifton, Nat
Colangelo, Jerry
Davidson, Bill
Douglas, Bob
Duer, Al
Embry, Wayne
Fagan, Cliff
Fisher, Harry
Fleisher, Larry
Gavitt, David
Gottlieb, Edward
Granik, Russ
Gulick, Dr. Luther
Harrison, Lester
Hearn, Francis "Chick"
Henderson, E. B.
Hepp, Dr. Ferenc
Hickox, Edward
Hinkle, Tony
Irish, Edward "Ned"
Jones, R. William
Kennedy, Walter
Knight, Phil
Lemon, Meadowlark
Liston, Emil
Lloyd, Earl
Mokray, Bill
Morgan, Ralph
Morgenweck, Frank
Naismith, Dr. James
Newton, C. M.
O'Brien, John
O'Brien, Larry
Olsen, Harold
Podoloff, Maurice
Porter, Henry V.
*Raveling, George
Reid, William
Ripley, Elmer
St. John, Lynn
Saperstein, Abe
Schabinger, Arthur
Stagg, Alonzo
Stankovic, Boris
Steitz, Edward
Stern, David
Taylor, Chuck
Teague, Bertha
Tower, Oswald
Trester, Arthur
Wells, Clifford
Wilke, Lou
Zollner, Fred

Fowles Leads Minnesota Lynx to 2015 WNBA Title

The Minnesota Lynx became WNBA champions for the third time in five seasons, all with head coach Cheryl Reeve at the helm. Sylvia Fowles scored 20 points with 11 rebounds in Minnesota's 69-52 series-clinching victory over the Indiana Fever in Game 5 of the WNBA Finals, Oct. 14, 2015, at Target Center in Minneapolis, MN. Fowles, who joined the Lynx in a midseason trade, averaged 15.6 points per game in the playoffs and was named WNBA Finals MVP.

The Lynx swept the Phoenix Mercury in the Western Conference finals, and Indiana advanced by defeating the top-seeded NY Liberty in three games in the Eastern Conference finals. Chicago's Elena Delle Donne averaged 23.4 points and 8.4 rebounds per game and won the league's MVP award.

WNBA Final Standings, 2015

(playoff seeding in parentheses; conference winner automatically gets top seed)

Eastern Conference

	W	L	PCT	GB
NY Liberty (1)	23	11	.676	—
Chicago Sky (2)	21	13	.618	2
Indiana Fever (3)	20	14	.588	3
Washington Mystics (4)	18	16	.529	5
Atlanta Dream	15	19	.441	8
Connecticut Sun	15	19	.441	8

Western Conference

	W	L	PCT	GB
Minnesota Lynx (1)	22	12	.647	—
Phoenix Mercury (2)	20	14	.588	2
Tulsa Shock (3)	18	16	.529	4
L.A. Sparks (4)	14	20	.412	8
Seattle Storm	10	24	.294	12
San Antonio Stars	8	26	.235	14

WNBA Playoff Results, 2015

Eastern Conference

(1) New York defeated (4) Washington, 2 games to 1
(3) Indiana defeated (2) Chicago, 2 games to 1
(3) Indiana defeated (1) New York, 2 games to 1

Western Conference

(1) Minnesota defeated (4) Los Angeles, 2 games to 1
(2) Phoenix defeated (3) Tulsa, 2 games to 0
(1) Minnesota defeated (2) Phoenix, 2 games to 0

WNBA Championship, 2015

Minnesota defeated Indiana, 3 games to 2 (69-75, 77-71, 80-77, 69-75, 69-52), in the best-of-five series.

All-WNBA Teams, 2015

First team	Position	Second team	Position
Elena Delle Donne, Chicago	Forward	Candace Parker, Los Angeles	Forward
Maya Moore, Minnesota	Forward	Tamika Catchings, Indiana	Forward
Tina Charles, New York	Center	Brittney Griner, Phoenix	Center
DeWanna Bonner, Phoenix	Guard	Epiphanny Prince, New York	Guard
Angel McCoughtry, Atlanta	Guard	Courtney Vandersloot, Chicago	Guard

WNBA Statistical Leaders, 2015

Minutes played: 1,148, Jantel Lavender, Los Angeles
Total points: 725, Elena Delle Donne, Chicago
Points per game: 23.4, Elena Delle Donne, Chicago
Field goal pct.: .565, Brittney Griner, Phoenix
3-point field goal pct.: .431, Briann January, Indiana
Free throw pct.: .950, Elena Delle Donne, Chicago
Rebounds: 317, Courtney Paris, Tulsa
Assists: 198, Courtney Vandersloot, Chicago
Steals: 72, Angel McCoughtry, Atlanta
Blocks: 105, Brittney Griner, Phoenix

WNBA Champions, 1997-2015

	Regular Season		Playoffs		
Year	Eastern champion	Western champion	Champion	Winning coach	Opponent
1997	Houston Comets	Phoenix Mercury	Houston	Van Chancellor	New York
1998	Cleveland Rockers	Houston Comets	Houston	Van Chancellor	Phoenix
1999	New York Liberty	Houston Comets	Houston	Van Chancellor	New York
2000	New York Liberty	Los Angeles Sparks	Houston	Van Chancellor	New York
2001	Cleveland Rockers	Los Angeles Sparks	Los Angeles	Michael Cooper	Charlotte
2002	New York Liberty	Los Angeles Sparks	Los Angeles	Michael Cooper	New York
2003	Detroit Shock	Los Angeles Sparks	Detroit	Bill Laimbeer	Los Angeles
2004	Connecticut Sun	Los Angeles Sparks	Seattle	Anne Donovan	Connecticut
2005	Connecticut Sun	Sacramento Monarchs	Sacramento	John Whisenant	Connecticut
2006	Connecticut Sun	Los Angeles Sparks	Detroit	Bill Laimbeer	Sacramento
2007	Detroit Shock	Phoenix Mercury	Phoenix	Paul Westhead	Detroit
2008	Detroit Shock	San Antonio Silver Stars	Detroit	Bill Laimbeer	San Antonio
2009	Indiana Fever	Phoenix Mercury	Phoenix	Corey Gaines	Indiana
2010	Washington Mystics	Seattle Storm	Seattle	Brian Agler	Atlanta
2011	Indiana Fever	Minnesota Lynx	Minnesota	Cheryl Reeve	Atlanta
2012	Connecticut Sun	Minnesota Lynx	Indiana	Lin Dunn	Minnesota
2013	Chicago Sky	Minnesota Lynx	Minnesota	Cheryl Reeve	Atlanta
2014	Atlanta Dream	Phoenix Mercury	Phoenix	Sandy Brondello	Chicago
2015	New York Liberty	Minnesota Lynx	Minnesota	Cheryl Reeve	Indiana

WNBA Finals MVP, 1997-2015

Year	Player, team	Year	Player, team	Year	Player, team
1997	Cynthia Cooper, Houston	2004	Betty Lennox, Seattle	2010	Lauren Jackson, Seattle
1998	Cynthia Cooper, Houston	2005	Yolanda Griffith, Sacramento	2011	Seimone Augustus, Minnesota
1999	Cynthia Cooper, Houston	2006	Deanna Nolan, Detroit	2012	Tamika Catchings, Indiana
2000	Cynthia Cooper, Houston	2007	Cappie Pondexter, Phoenix	2013	Maya Moore, Minnesota
2001	Lisa Leslie, Los Angeles	2008	Katie Smith, Detroit	2014	Diana Taurasi, Phoenix
2002	Lisa Leslie, Los Angeles	2009	Diana Taurasi, Phoenix	2015	Sylvia Fowles, Minnesota
2003	Ruth Riley, Detroit				

WNBA Most Valuable Player, 1997-2015

Year	Player, team	Year	Player, team	Year	Player, team
1997	Cynthia Cooper, Houston	2004	Lisa Leslie, Los Angeles	2010	Lauren Jackson, Seattle
1998	Cynthia Cooper, Houston	2005	Sheryl Swoopes, Houston	2011	Tamika Catchings, Indiana
1999	Yolanda Griffith, Sacramento	2006	Lisa Leslie, Los Angeles	2012	Tina Charles, Connecticut
2000	Sheryl Swoopes, Houston	2007	Lauren Jackson, Seattle	2013	Candace Parker, Los Angeles
2001	Lisa Leslie, Los Angeles	2008	Candace Parker, Los Angeles	2014	Maya Moore, Minnesota
2002	Sheryl Swoopes, Houston	2009	Diana Taurasi, Phoenix	2015	Elena Delle Donne, Chicago
2003	Lauren Jackson, Seattle				

WNBA Rookie of the Year, 1997-2015

Year	Player, team	Year	Player, team	Year	Player, team
1997	No award	2004	Diana Taurasi, Phoenix	2010	Tina Charles, Connecticut
1998	Tracy Reid, Charlotte	2005	Temeka Johnson, Washington	2011	Maya Moore, Minnesota
1999	Chamique Holdsclaw, Washington	2006	Seimone Augustus, Minnesota	2012	Nneka Ogwumike, Los Angeles
2000	Betty Lennox, Minnesota	2007	Armintie Price, Chicago	2013	Elena Delle Donne, Chicago
2001	Jackie Stiles, Portland	2008	Candace Parker, Los Angeles	2014	Chiney Ogwumike, Connecticut
2002	Tamika Catchings, Indiana	2009	Angel McCoughtry, Atlanta	2015	Jewell Loyd, Seattle
2003	Cheryl Ford, Detroit				

WNBA Scoring Leaders, 1997-2015

(Average points per game; 24 games or 480 point minimum in 2015; prior season minimums vary.)

Year	Player, team	PTS	AVG	Year	Player, team	PTS	AVG
1997	Cynthia Cooper, Houston	621	22.2	2007	Lauren Jackson, Seattle	739	23.8
1998	Cynthia Cooper, Houston	680	22.7	2008	Diana Taurasi, Phoenix	820	24.1
1999	Cynthia Cooper, Houston	686	22.1	2009	Diana Taurasi, Phoenix	631	20.4
2000	Sheryl Swoopes, Houston	643	20.7	2010	Diana Taurasi, Phoenix	702	22.6
2001	Katie Smith, Minnesota	739	23.1	2011	Diana Taurasi, Phoenix	692	21.6
2002	Chamique Holdsclaw, Washington	397	19.9	2012	Angel McCoughtry, Atlanta	514	21.4
2003	Lauren Jackson, Seattle	698	21.2	2013	Angel McCoughtry, Atlanta	711	21.5
2004	Lauren Jackson, Seattle	634	20.5	2014	Maya Moore, Minnesota	812	23.9
2005	Sheryl Swoopes, Houston	614	18.6	2015	Elena Delle Donne, Chicago	725	23.4
2006	Diana Taurasi, Phoenix	860	25.3				

WNBA Rebounding Leaders, 1997-2015

(Average rebounds per game; 24 games or 240 rebounds minimum in 2015; prior season minimums vary.)

Year	Player, team	REB	RPG	Year	Player, team	REB	RPG
1997	Lisa Leslie, Los Angeles	266	9.5	2007	Lauren Jackson, Seattle	300	9.7
1998	Lisa Leslie, Los Angeles	285	10.2	2008	Candace Parker, Los Angeles	313	9.5
1999	Yolanda Griffith, Sacramento	329	11.3	2009	Candace Parker, Los Angeles	244	9.8
2000	Natalie Williams, Utah	336	11.6	2010	Tina Charles, Connecticut	398	11.7
2001	Yolanda Griffith, Sacramento	357	11.2	2011	Tina Charles, Connecticut	374	11.0
2002	Chamique Holdsclaw, Washington	232	11.6	2012	Tina Charles, Connecticut	345	10.5
2003	Chamique Holdsclaw, Washington	294	10.9	2013	Sylvia Fowles, Chicago	369	11.5
2004	Lisa Leslie, Los Angeles	336	9.9	2014	Courtney Paris, Tulsa	347	10.2
2005	Cheryl Ford, Detroit	322	9.8	2015	Courtney Paris, Tulsa	317	9.3
2006	Cheryl Ford, Detroit	363	11.3				

WNBA Assist Leaders, 1997-2015

(Average assists per game; 24 games or 140 assists minimum in 2015; prior season minimums vary.)

Year	Player, team	AST	APG	Year	Player, team	AST	APG
1997	Teresa Weatherspoon, New York	172	6.1	2007	Becky Hammon, San Antonio	140	5.0
1998	Ticha Penicheiro, Sacramento	224	7.5	2008	Lindsay Whalen, Connecticut	166	5.4
1999	Ticha Penicheiro, Sacramento	226	7.1	2009	Sue Bird, Seattle	179	5.8
2000	Ticha Penicheiro, Sacramento	236	7.9	2010	Ticha Penicheiro, Los Angeles	220	6.9
2001	Ticha Penicheiro, Sacramento	172	7.5	2011	Lindsay Whalen, Minnesota	199	5.9
2002	Ticha Penicheiro, Sacramento	192	8.0	2012	Lindsay Whalen, Minnesota	178	5.4
2003	Ticha Penicheiro, Sacramento	229	6.7	2013	Danielle Robinson, San Antonio	168	6.7
2004	Nikki Teasley, Los Angeles	207	6.1	2014	Diana Taurasi, Phoenix	185	5.6
2005	Sue Bird, Seattle	176	5.9	2015	Courtney Vandersloot, Chicago	198	5.8
2006	Nikki Teasley, Washington	183	5.4				

All-Time WNBA Statistical Leaders

(At the end of the 2015 season. * = Active in 2015 season.)

Scoring Average (minimum 100 games)

Player	G	PTS	AVG	Player	G	PTS	AVG
Cynthia Cooper	124	2,601	21.0	*Seimone Augustus	264	4,805	18.2
Diana Taurasi	334	6,722	20.1	*Cappie Pondexter	324	5,887	18.2
*Angel McCoughtry	223	4,347	19.5	*Candace Parker	195	3,480	17.8
Lauren Jackson	317	6,007	18.9	Lisa Leslie	363	6,263	17.3
*Maya Moore	169	3,128	18.5	*Tina Charles	198	3,413	17.2

Points

Player	Points
Tina Thompson	7,488
*Tamika Catchings	6,947
Diana Taurasi	6,722
Katie Smith	6,452
Lisa Leslie	6,263
Lauren Jackson	6,007
*Cappie Pondexter	5,887
Becky Hammon	5,841
*DeLisha Milton-Jones	5,571
Katie Douglas	5,563

Rebounds

Player	Rebounds
Lisa Leslie	3,307
*Tamika Catchings	3,153
Tina Thompson	3,070
Taj McWilliams-Franklin	3,013
*Rebekkah Brunson	2,746
*DeLisha Milton-Jones	2,574
*Michelle Snow	2,482
Lauren Jackson	2,447
Yolanda Griffith	2,444
*Swin Cash	2,416

Assists

Player	Assists
Ticha Penicheiro	2,599
*Sue Bird	2,215
*Lindsay Whalen	2,036
Becky Hammon	1,708
Diana Taurasi	1,448
Shannon Johnson	1,424
*Tamika Catchings	1,422
*Temeka Johnson	1,382
Teresa Weatherspoon	1,338
Dawn Staley	1,337

3-Point Field Goals Made

Katie Smith	906
Becky Hammon	829
Diana Taurasi	811
Tina Thompson	748
Katie Douglas	727
*Sue Bird	664
*Kara Lawson	584
Nicole Powell	580
*Tamika Catchings	571
*Ivory Latta	460

Steals

Player	Steals
*Tamika Catchings	1,012
Ticha Penicheiro	764
Sheryl Swoopes	657
Katie Douglas	623
*DeLisha Milton-Jones	619
Taj McWilliams-Franklin	580
Tully Bevilaqua	573
*Jia Perkins	566
*Sue Bird	547
Yolanda Griffith	529

Blocked Shots

Margo Dydek	877
Lisa Leslie	822
Lauren Jackson	586
Tangela Smith	557
Tammy Sutton-Brown	555
Ruth Riley	505
Taj McWilliams-Franklin	443
*Sylvia Fowles	404
*Michelle Snow	403
Candace Parker	380

HOCKEY

Chicago Blackhawks Claim Third Stanley Cup in Six Years

The Chicago Blackhawks won their third championship in the last six seasons after beating the Tampa Bay Lightning, four games to two, in the 2015 NHL Stanley Cup Final. Chicago clinched its latest title in front of hometown fans with a 2-0 victory over the Lightning June 15, 2015, at the United Center. Blackhawks defenseman Duncan Keith broke a scoreless tie in Game 6 with a second-period goal and earned the Conn Smythe award as playoff MVP.

The Blackhawks reached the Final by winning the last two games of their seven-game Western Conference Final series over the Anaheim Ducks. Tampa Bay advanced with a seven-game Eastern Conference Final victory over the New York Rangers, who won the Presidents' Trophy with the league's best overall record in the regular season and set franchise records in wins (53) and points (113).

Washington's Alex Ovechkin topped the league with 53 goals to win his third straight Maurice Richard Trophy. Ovechkin tallied one of those goals outdoors in the Capitals' 3-2 win over Chicago in the NHL Winter Classic Jan. 1, 2015, at Nationals Park in Washington, DC. Montréal Canadiens goaltender Carey Price led the NHL in wins (44), goals-against average (1.96), and save percentage (.933).

Final NHL Standings, 2014-15

(* = clinched playoff berth)

Standings are determined by total points, then by the greater number of games won, excluding games won in a shootout. This figure is reflected in the ROW column. Teams tied at the end of regulation time are each awarded one point. An additional point is awarded to the overtime or shootout winner.

The top three finishers in each division qualify for the first 12 playoff seeds. Two additional wild card playoff spots are awarded in each conference to the next two highest-placed finishers, regardless of division.

Eastern Conference

Atlantic Division	W	L	OT	GF	GA	PTS	ROW
*Montréal Canadiens	50	22	10	221	189	110	43
*Tampa Bay Lightning	50	24	8	262	211	108	47
*Detroit Red Wings	43	25	14	235	221	100	39
*Ottawa Senators	43	26	13	238	215	99	37
Boston Bruins	41	27	14	213	211	96	37
Florida Panthers	38	29	15	206	223	91	30
Toronto Maple Leafs	30	44	8	211	262	68	25
Buffalo Sabres	23	51	8	161	274	54	15

Metropolitan Division	W	L	OT	GF	GA	PTS	ROW
*New York Rangers	53	22	7	252	192	113	49
*Washington Capitals	45	26	11	242	203	101	40
*New York Islanders	47	28	7	252	230	101	40
*Pittsburgh Penguins	43	27	12	221	210	98	39
Columbus Blue Jackets	42	35	5	236	250	89	33
Philadelphia Flyers	33	31	18	215	234	84	30
New Jersey Devils	32	36	14	181	216	78	27
Carolina Hurricanes	30	41	11	188	226	71	25

Western Conference

Central Division	W	L	OT	GF	GA	PTS	ROW
*St. Louis Blues	51	24	7	248	201	109	42
*Nashville Predators	47	25	10	232	208	104	41
*Chicago Blackhawks	48	28	6	229	189	102	39
*Minnesota Wild	46	28	8	231	201	100	42
*Winnipeg Jets	43	26	13	230	210	99	36
Dallas Stars	41	31	10	261	260	92	37
Colorado Avalanche	39	31	12	219	227	90	29

Pacific Division	W	L	OT	GF	GA	PTS	ROW
*Anaheim Ducks	51	24	7	236	226	109	43
*Vancouver Canucks	48	29	5	242	222	101	42
*Calgary Flames	45	30	7	241	216	97	41
Los Angeles Kings	40	27	15	220	205	95	38
San Jose Sharks	40	33	9	228	232	89	36
Edmonton Oilers	24	44	14	198	283	62	19
Arizona Coyotes	24	50	8	170	272	56	19

Stanley Cup Playoff Results, 2015

Eastern Conference

NY Rangers defeated Pittsburgh, 4 games to 1
Montréal defeated Ottawa, 4 games to 2
Tampa Bay defeated Detroit, 4 games to 3
Washington defeated NY Islanders, 4 games to 3
NY Rangers defeated Washington, 4 games to 3
Tampa Bay defeated Montréal, 4 games to 2
Tampa Bay defeated NY Rangers, 4 games to 3

Western Conference

Anaheim defeated Winnipeg, 4 games to 0
Minnesota defeated St. Louis, 4 games to 2
Chicago defeated Nashville, 4 games to 2
Calgary defeated Vancouver, 4 games to 2
Anaheim defeated Calgary, 4 games to 1
Chicago defeated Minnesota, 4 games to 0
Chicago defeated Anaheim, 4 games to 3

Stanley Cup Final

Chicago defeated Tampa Bay, 4 games to 2 (2-1, 3-4, 2-3, 2-1, 2-1, 2-0)

Stanley Cup Champions, 1927-2015

Year	Champion	Coach	Final opponent
1927	Ottawa	Dave Gill	Boston
1928	NY Rangers	Lester Patrick	Montréal Maroons
1929	Boston	Cy Denneny	NY Rangers
1930	Montréal Canadiens	Cecil Hart	Boston
1931	Montréal Canadiens	Cecil Hart	Chicago
1932	Toronto	Dick Irvin	NY Rangers
1933	NY Rangers	Lester Patrick	Toronto
1934	Chicago	Tommy Gorman	Detroit
1935	Montréal Maroons	Tommy Gorman	Toronto
1936	Detroit	Jack Adams	Toronto
1937	Detroit	Jack Adams	NY Rangers
1938	Chicago	Bill Stewart	Toronto
1939	Boston	Art Ross	Toronto
1940	NY Rangers	Frank Boucher	Toronto
1941	Boston	Cooney Weiland	Detroit
1942	Toronto	Hap Day	Detroit
1943	Detroit	Jack Adams	Boston
1944	Montréal	Dick Irvin	Chicago
1945	Toronto	Hap Day	Detroit
1946	Montréal	Dick Irvin	Boston
1947	Toronto	Hap Day	Montréal
1948	Toronto	Hap Day	Detroit
1949	Toronto	Hap Day	Detroit
1950	Detroit	Tommy Ivan	NY Rangers
1951	Toronto	Joe Primeau	Montréal
1952	Detroit	Tommy Ivan	Montréal
1953	Montréal	Dick Irvin	Boston
1954	Detroit	Tommy Ivan	Montréal
1955	Detroit	Jimmy Skinner	Montréal
1956	Montréal	Toe Blake	Detroit
1957	Montréal	Toe Blake	Boston
1958	Montréal	Toe Blake	Boston
1959	Montréal	Toe Blake	Toronto
1960	Montréal	Toe Blake	Toronto
1961	Chicago	Rudy Pilous	Detroit
1962	Toronto	Punch Imlach	Chicago
1963	Toronto	Punch Imlach	Detroit
1964	Toronto	Punch Imlach	Detroit
1965	Montréal	Toe Blake	Chicago
1966	Montréal	Toe Blake	Detroit
1967	Toronto	Punch Imlach	Montréal
1968	Montréal	Toe Blake	St. Louis
1969	Montréal	Claude Ruel	St. Louis
1970	Boston	Harry Sinden	St. Louis
1971	Montréal	Al MacNeil	Chicago
1972	Boston	Tom Johnson	NY Rangers
1973	Montréal	Scotty Bowman	Chicago
1974	Philadelphia	Fred Shero	Boston
1975	Philadelphia	Fred Shero	Buffalo
1976	Montréal	Scotty Bowman	Philadelphia
1977	Montréal	Scotty Bowman	Boston
1978	Montréal	Scotty Bowman	Boston
1979	Montréal	Scotty Bowman	NY Rangers
1980	NY Islanders	Al Arbour	Philadelphia
1981	NY Islanders	Al Arbour	Minnesota
1982	NY Islanders	Al Arbour	Vancouver
1983	NY Islanders	Al Arbour	Edmonton
1984	Edmonton	Glen Sather	NY Islanders
1985	Edmonton	Glen Sather	Philadelphia

Year	Champion	Coach	Final opponent	Year	Champion	Coach	Final opponent
1986	Montréal	Jean Perron	Calgary	2001	Colorado	Bob Hartley	New Jersey
1987	Edmonton	Glen Sather	Philadelphia	2002	Detroit	Scotty Bowman	Carolina
1988	Edmonton	Glen Sather	Boston	2003	New Jersey	Pat Burns	Anaheim
1989	Calgary	Terry Crisp	Montréal	2004	Tampa Bay	John Tortorella	Calgary
1990	Edmonton	John Muckler	Boston	2005	No competition (labor dispute; season cancelled)		
1991	Pittsburgh	Bob Johnson	Minnesota	2006	Carolina	Peter Laviolette	Edmonton
1992	Pittsburgh	Scotty Bowman	Chicago	2007	Anaheim	Randy Carlyle	Ottawa
1993	Montréal	Jacques Demers	Los Angeles	2008	Detroit	Mike Babcock	Pittsburgh
1994	NY Rangers	Mike Keenan	Vancouver	2009	Pittsburgh	Dan Bylsma	Detroit
1995	New Jersey	Jacques Lemaire	Detroit	2010	Chicago	Joel Quenneville	Philadelphia
1996	Colorado	Marc Crawford	Florida	2011	Boston	Claude Julien	Vancouver
1997	Detroit	Scotty Bowman	Philadelphia	2012	Los Angeles	Darryl Sutter	New Jersey
1998	Detroit	Scotty Bowman	Washington	2013	Chicago	Joel Quenneville	Boston
1999	Dallas	Ken Hitchcock	Buffalo	2014	Los Angeles	Darryl Sutter	NY Rangers
2000	New Jersey	Larry Robinson	Dallas	2015	Chicago	Joel Quenneville	Tampa Bay

Most NHL Goals in a Season

Player	Team	Season	Goals	Player	Team	Season	Goals
Wayne Gretzky	Edmonton	1981-82	92	Jari Kurri	Edmonton	1984-85	71
Wayne Gretzky	Edmonton	1983-84	87	Mario Lemieux	Pittsburgh	1987-88	70
Brett Hull	St. Louis	1990-91	86	Bernie Nicholls	Los Angeles	1988-89	70
Mario Lemieux	Pittsburgh	1988-89	85	Brett Hull	St. Louis	1991-92	70
Phil Esposito	Boston	1970-71	76	Mike Bossy	NY Islanders	1978-79	69
Alexander Mogilny	Buffalo	1992-93	76	Mario Lemieux	Pittsburgh	1992-93	69
Teemu Selanne	Winnipeg	1992-93	76	Mario Lemieux	Pittsburgh	1995-96	69
Wayne Gretzky	Edmonton	1984-85	73	Phil Esposito	Boston	1973-74	68
Brett Hull	St. Louis	1989-90	72	Mike Bossy	NY Islanders	1980-81	68
Wayne Gretzky	Edmonton	1982-83	71	Jari Kurri	Edmonton	1985-86	68

All-Time Regular Season Scoring Leaders

(Through end of 2014-15 season. * = active in 2014-15 season.)

Player	Goals	Assists	Points	Player	Goals	Assists	Points	Player	Goals	Assists	Points
Wayne Gretzky	894	1,963	2,857	Mario Lemieux	690	1,033	1,723	Teemu Selanne	684	773	1,457
Mark Messier	694	1,193	1,887	Joe Sakic	625	1,016	1,641	Bryan Trottier	524	901	1,425
Gordie Howe	801	1,049	1,850	Phil Esposito	717	873	1,590	Adam Oates	341	1,079	1,420
*Jaromir Jagr	722	1,080	1,802	Ray Bourque	410	1,169	1,579	Doug Gilmour	450	964	1,414
Ron Francis	549	1,249	1,798	Mark Recchi	577	956	1,533	Dale Hawerchuk	518	891	1,409
Marcel Dionne	731	1,040	1,771	Paul Coffey	396	1,135	1,531	Jari Kurri	601	797	1,398
Steve Yzerman	692	1,063	1,755	Stan Mikita	541	926	1,467	Luc Robitaille	668	726	1,394

Hart Memorial Trophy (MVP), 1927-2015

Year	Player, team
1927	Herb Gardiner, Montréal Canadiens
1928	Howie Morenz, Montréal Canadiens
1929	Roy Worters, NY Americans
1930	Nels Stewart, Montréal Maroons
1931	Howie Morenz, Montréal Canadiens
1932	Howie Morenz, Montréal Canadiens
1933	Eddie Shore, Boston
1934	Aurel Joliat, Montréal Canadiens
1935	Eddie Shore, Boston
1936	Eddie Shore, Boston
1937	Babe Siebert, Montréal Canadiens
1938	Eddie Shore, Boston
1939	Toe Blake, Montréal
1940	Ebbie Goodfellow, Detroit
1941	Bill Cowley, Boston
1942	Tom Anderson, Brooklyn Americans
1943	Bill Cowley, Boston
1944	Babe Pratt, Toronto
1945	Elmer Lach, Montréal
1946	Max Bentley, Chicago
1947	Maurice Richard, Montréal
1948	Buddy O'Connor, NY Rangers
1949	Sid Abel, Detroit
1950	Chuck Rayner, NY Rangers
1951	Milt Schmidt, Boston
1952	Gordie Howe, Detroit
1953	Gordie Howe, Detroit
1954	Al Rollins, Chicago
1955	Ted Kennedy, Toronto
1956	Jean Beliveau, Montréal
1957	Gordie Howe, Detroit
1958	Gordie Howe, Detroit
1959	Andy Bathgate, NY Rangers
1960	Gordie Howe, Detroit
1961	Bernie Geoffrion, Montréal
1962	Jacques Plante, Montréal
1963	Gordie Howe, Detroit
1964	Jean Beliveau, Montréal
1965	Bobby Hull, Chicago
1966	Bobby Hull, Chicago
1967	Stan Mikita, Chicago
1968	Stan Mikita, Chicago
1969	Phil Esposito, Boston
1970	Bobby Orr, Boston
1971	Bobby Orr, Boston
1972	Bobby Orr, Boston
1973	Bobby Clarke, Philadelphia
1974	Phil Esposito, Boston
1975	Bobby Clarke, Philadelphia
1976	Bobby Clarke, Philadelphia
1977	Guy Lafleur, Montréal
1978	Guy Lafleur, Montréal
1979	Bryan Trottier, NY Islanders
1980	Wayne Gretzky, Edmonton
1981	Wayne Gretzky, Edmonton
1982	Wayne Gretzky, Edmonton
1983	Wayne Gretzky, Edmonton
1984	Wayne Gretzky, Edmonton
1985	Wayne Gretzky, Edmonton
1986	Wayne Gretzky, Edmonton
1987	Wayne Gretzky, Edmonton
1988	Mario Lemieux, Pittsburgh
1989	Wayne Gretzky, Los Angeles
1990	Mark Messier, Edmonton
1991	Brett Hull, St. Louis
1992	Mark Messier, NY Rangers
1993	Mario Lemieux, Pittsburgh
1994	Sergei Fedorov, Detroit
1995	Eric Lindros, Philadelphia
1996	Mario Lemieux, Pittsburgh
1997	Dominik Hasek, Buffalo
1998	Dominik Hasek, Buffalo
1999	Jaromir Jagr, Pittsburgh
2000	Chris Pronger, St. Louis
2001	Joe Sakic, Colorado
2002	Jose Theodore, Montréal
2003	Peter Forsberg, Colorado
2004	Martin St. Louis, Tampa Bay
2006	Joe Thornton, San Jose
2007	Sidney Crosby, Pittsburgh
2008	Alexander Ovechkin, Washington
2009	Alexander Ovechkin, Washington
2010	Henrik Sedin, Vancouver
2011	Corey Perry, Anaheim
2012	Evgeni Malkin, Pittsburgh
2013	Alexander Ovechkin, Washington
2014	Sidney Crosby, Pittsburgh
2015	Carey Price, Montréal

Conn Smythe Trophy (MVP in Playoffs), 1965-2015

Year	Player, team
1965	Jean Beliveau, Montréal
1966	Roger Crozier, Detroit
1967	Dave Keon, Toronto
1968	Glenn Hall, St. Louis
1969	Serge Savard, Montréal
1970	Bobby Orr, Boston
1971	Ken Dryden, Montréal
1972	Bobby Orr, Boston
1973	Yvan Cournoyer, Montréal
1974	Bernie Parent, Philadelphia
1975	Bernie Parent, Philadelphia
1976	Reggie Leach, Philadelphia
1977	Guy Lafleur, Montréal
1978	Larry Robinson, Montréal
1979	Bob Gainey, Montréal
1980	Bryan Trottier, NY Islanders
1981	Butch Goring, NY Islanders
1982	Mike Bossy, NY Islanders
1983	Billy Smith, NY Islanders
1984	Mark Messier, Edmonton
1985	Wayne Gretzky, Edmonton
1986	Patrick Roy, Montréal
1987	Ron Hextall, Philadelphia
1988	Wayne Gretzky, Edmonton
1989	Al MacInnis, Calgary
1990	Bill Ranford, Edmonton
1991	Mario Lemieux, Pittsburgh
1992	Mario Lemieux, Pittsburgh
1993	Patrick Roy, Montréal
1994	Brian Leetch, NY Rangers
1995	Claude Lemieux, New Jersey
1996	Joe Sakic, Colorado
1997	Mike Vernon, Detroit
1998	Steve Yzerman, Detroit
1999	Joe Nieuwendyk, Dallas
2000	Scott Stevens, New Jersey

Year	Player, team
2001	Patrick Roy, Colorado
2002	Nicklas Lidstrom, Detroit
2003	Jean-Sebastien Giguere, Anaheim
2004	Brad Richards, Tampa Bay
2006	Cam Ward, Carolina
2007	Scott Niedermayer, Anaheim
2008	Henrik Zetterberg, Detroit
2009	Evgeni Malkin, Pittsburgh
2010	Jonathan Toews, Chicago
2011	Tim Thomas, Boston
2012	Jonathan Quick, Los Angeles
2013	Patrick Kane, Chicago
2014	Justin Williams, Los Angeles
2015	Duncan Keith, Chicago

Calder Memorial Trophy (Rookie of the Year), 1933-2015

Year	Player, team
1933	Carl Voss, Detroit
1934	Russ Blinco, Montréal Maroons
1935	Dave Schriner, NY Americans
1936	Mike Karakas, Chicago
1937	Syl Apps, Toronto
1938	Cully Dahlstrom, Chicago
1939	Frank Brimsek, Boston
1940	Kilby MacDonald, NY Rangers
1941	John Quilty, Montréal
1942	Grant Warwick, NY Rangers
1943	Gaye Stewart, Toronto
1944	Gus Bodnar, Toronto
1945	Frank McCool, Toronto
1946	Edgar Laprade, NY Rangers
1947	Howie Meeker, Toronto
1948	Jim McFadden, Detroit
1949	Pentti Lund, NY Rangers
1950	Jack Gelineau, Boston
1951	Terry Sawchuk, Detroit
1952	Bernie Geoffrion, Montréal
1953	Gump Worsley, NY Rangers
1954	Camille Henry, NY Rangers
1955	Ed Litzenberger, Chicago
1956	Glenn Hall, Detroit
1957	Larry Regan, Boston
1958	Frank Mahovlich, Toronto
1959	Ralph Backstrom, Montréal
1960	Bill Hay, Chicago
1961	Dave Keon, Toronto
1962	Bobby Rousseau, Montréal
1963	Kent Douglas, Toronto
1964	Jacques Laperrière, Montréal
1965	Roger Crozier, Detroit
1966	Brit Selby, Toronto
1967	Bobby Orr, Boston
1968	Derek Sanderson, Boston
1969	Danny Grant, Minnesota
1970	Tony Esposito, Chicago
1971	Gilbert Perreault, Buffalo
1972	Ken Dryden, Montréal
1973	Steve Vickers, NY Rangers
1974	Denis Potvin, NY Islanders
1975	Eric Vail, Atlanta
1976	Bryan Trottier, NY Islanders
1977	Willi Plett, Atlanta
1978	Mike Bossy, NY Islanders
1979	Bobby Smith, Minnesota
1980	Ray Bourque, Boston
1981	Peter Stastny, Quebec
1982	Dale Hawerchuk, Winnipeg
1983	Steve Larmer, Chicago
1984	Tom Barrasso, Buffalo
1985	Mario Lemieux, Pittsburgh
1986	Gary Suter, Calgary
1987	Luc Robitaille, Los Angeles
1988	Joe Nieuwendyk, Calgary
1989	Brian Leetch, NY Rangers
1990	Sergei Makarov, Calgary
1991	Ed Belfour, Chicago
1992	Pavel Bure, Vancouver
1993	Teemu Selanne, Winnipeg
1994	Martin Brodeur, New Jersey
1995	Peter Forsberg, Quebec
1996	Daniel Alfredsson, Ottawa
1997	Bryan Berard, NY Islanders
1998	Sergei Samsonov, Boston
1999	Chris Drury, Colorado
2000	Scott Gomez, New Jersey
2001	Evgeni Nabokov, San Jose
2002	Dany Heatley, Atlanta
2003	Barret Jackman, St. Louis
2004	Andrew Raycroft, Boston
2006	Alexander Ovechkin, Washington
2007	Evgeni Malkin, Pittsburgh
2008	Patrick Kane, Chicago
2009	Steve Mason, Columbus
2010	Tyler Myers, Buffalo
2011	Jeff Skinner, Carolina
2012	Gabriel Landeskog, Colorado
2013	Jonathan Huberdeau, Florida
2014	Nathan MacKinnon, Colorado
2015	Aaron Ekblad, Florida

Lady Byng Memorial Trophy (Most Gentlemanly Player), 1925-2015

Year	Player, team
1925	Frank Nighbor, Ottawa
1926	Frank Nighbor, Ottawa
1927	Billy Burch, NY Americans
1928	Frank Boucher, NY Rangers
1929	Frank Boucher, NY Rangers
1930	Frank Boucher, NY Rangers
1931	Frank Boucher, NY Rangers
1932	Joe Primeau, Toronto
1933	Frank Boucher, NY Rangers
1934	Frank Boucher, NY Rangers
1935	Frank Boucher, NY Rangers
1936	Doc Romnes, Chicago
1937	Marty Barry, Detroit
1938	Gordie Drillon, Toronto
1939	Clint Smith, NY Rangers
1940	Bobby Bauer, Boston
1941	Bobby Bauer, Boston
1942	Syl Apps, Toronto
1943	Max Bentley, Chicago
1944	Clint Smith, Chicago
1945	Bill Mosienko, Chicago
1946	Toe Blake, Montréal
1947	Bobby Bauer, Boston
1948	Buddy O'Connor, NY Rangers
1949	Bill Quackenbush, Detroit
1950	Edgar Laprade, NY Rangers
1951	Red Kelly, Detroit
1952	Sid Smith, Toronto
1953	Red Kelly, Detroit
1954	Red Kelly, Detroit
1955	Sid Smith, Toronto
1956	Earl Reibel, Detroit
1957	Andy Hebenton, NY Rangers
1958	Camille Henry, NY Rangers
1959	Alex Delvecchio, Detroit
1960	Don McKenney, Boston
1961	Red Kelly, Toronto
1962	Dave Keon, Toronto
1963	Dave Keon, Toronto
1964	Ken Wharram, Chicago
1965	Bobby Hull, Chicago
1966	Alex Delvecchio, Detroit
1967	Stan Mikita, Chicago
1968	Stan Mikita, Chicago
1969	Alex Delvecchio, Detroit
1970	Phil Goyette, St. Louis
1971	John Bucyk, Boston
1972	Jean Ratelle, NY Rangers
1973	Gil Perreault, Buffalo
1974	John Bucyk, Boston
1975	Marcel Dionne, Detroit
1976	Jean Ratelle, NYR-Boston
1977	Marcel Dionne, Los Angeles
1978	Butch Goring, Los Angeles
1979	Bob MacMillan, Atlanta
1980	Wayne Gretzky, Edmonton
1981	Rick Kehoe, Pittsburgh
1982	Rick Middleton, Boston
1983	Mike Bossy, NY Islanders
1984	Mike Bossy, NY Islanders
1985	Jari Kurri, Edmonton
1986	Mike Bossy, NY Islanders
1987	Joe Mullen, Calgary
1988	Mats Naslund, Montréal
1989	Joe Mullen, Calgary
1990	Brett Hull, St. Louis
1991	Wayne Gretzky, Los Angeles
1992	Wayne Gretzky, Los Angeles
1993	Pierre Turgeon, NY Islanders
1994	Wayne Gretzky, Los Angeles
1995	Ron Francis, Pittsburgh
1996	Paul Kariya, Anaheim
1997	Paul Kariya, Anaheim
1998	Ron Francis, Pittsburgh
1999	Wayne Gretzky, NY Rangers
2000	Pavol Demitra, St. Louis
2001	Joe Sakic, Colorado
2002	Ron Francis, Carolina
2003	Alexander Mogilny, Toronto
2004	Brad Richards, Tampa Bay
2006	Pavel Datsyuk, Detroit
2007	Pavel Datsyuk, Detroit
2008	Pavel Datsyuk, Detroit
2009	Pavel Datsyuk, Detroit
2010	Martin St. Louis, Tampa Bay
2011	Martin St. Louis, Tampa Bay
2012	Brian Campbell, Florida
2013	Martin St. Louis, Tampa Bay
2014	Ryan O'Reilly, Colorado
2015	Jiri Hudler, Calgary

James Norris Memorial Trophy (Outstanding Defenseman), 1954-2015

Year	Player, team
1954	Red Kelly, Detroit
1955	Doug Harvey, Montréal
1956	Doug Harvey, Montréal
1957	Doug Harvey, Montréal
1958	Doug Harvey, Montréal
1959	Tom Johnson, Montréal
1960	Doug Harvey, Montréal
1961	Doug Harvey, Montréal
1962	Doug Harvey, NY Rangers
1963	Pierre Pilote, Chicago
1964	Pierre Pilote, Chicago
1965	Pierre Pilote, Chicago
1966	Jacques Laperrière, Montréal
1967	Harry Howell, NY Rangers
1968	Bobby Orr, Boston
1969	Bobby Orr, Boston
1970	Bobby Orr, Boston
1971	Bobby Orr, Boston
1972	Bobby Orr, Boston
1973	Bobby Orr, Boston
1974	Bobby Orr, Boston
1975	Bobby Orr, Boston
1976	Denis Potvin, NY Islanders
1977	Larry Robinson, Montréal
1978	Denis Potvin, NY Islanders
1979	Denis Potvin, NY Islanders
1980	Larry Robinson, Montréal
1981	Randy Carlyle, Pittsburgh
1982	Doug Wilson, Chicago
1983	Rod Langway, Washington
1984	Rod Langway, Washington
1985	Paul Coffey, Edmonton
1986	Paul Coffey, Edmonton
1987	Ray Bourque, Boston
1988	Ray Bourque, Boston
1989	Chris Chelios, Montréal
1990	Ray Bourque, Boston
1991	Ray Bourque, Boston
1992	Brian Leetch, NY Rangers
1993	Chris Chelios, Chicago
1994	Ray Bourque, Boston
1995	Paul Coffey, Detroit
1996	Chris Chelios, Chicago
1997	Brian Leetch, NY Rangers
1998	Rob Blake, Los Angeles
1999	Al MacInnis, St. Louis
2000	Chris Pronger, St. Louis
2001	Nicklas Lidstrom, Detroit
2002	Nicklas Lidstrom, Detroit
2003	Nicklas Lidstrom, Detroit
2004	Scott Niedermayer, New Jersey
2006	Nicklas Lidstrom, Detroit
2007	Nicklas Lidstrom, Detroit
2008	Nicklas Lidstrom, Detroit
2009	Zdeno Chara, Boston
2010	Duncan Keith, Chicago
2011	Nicklas Lidstrom, Detroit
2012	Erik Karlsson, Ottawa
2013	P. K. Subban, Montréal
2014	Duncan Keith, Chicago
2015	Erik Karlsson, Ottawa

Art Ross Trophy (Point-Scoring Leader), 1947-2015

Year	Player, team
1947	Max Bentley, Chicago
1948	Elmer Lach, Montréal
1949	Roy Conacher, Chicago
1950	Ted Lindsay, Detroit
1951	Gordie Howe, Detroit
1952	Gordie Howe, Detroit
1953	Gordie Howe, Detroit
1954	Gordie Howe, Detroit
1955	Bernie Geoffrion, Montréal
1956	Jean Beliveau, Montréal
1957	Gordie Howe, Detroit
1958	Dickie Moore, Montréal
1959	Dickie Moore, Montréal
1960	Bobby Hull, Chicago
1961	Bernie Geoffrion, Montréal
1962	Bobby Hull, Chicago
1963	Gordie Howe, Detroit
1964	Stan Mikita, Chicago
1965	Stan Mikita, Chicago
1966	Bobby Hull, Chicago
1967	Stan Mikita, Chicago
1968	Stan Mikita, Chicago
1969	Phil Esposito, Boston
1970	Bobby Orr, Boston
1971	Phil Esposito, Boston
1972	Phil Esposito, Boston
1973	Phil Esposito, Boston
1974	Phil Esposito, Boston
1975	Bobby Orr, Boston
1976	Guy Lafleur, Montréal
1977	Guy Lafleur, Montréal
1978	Guy Lafleur, Montréal
1979	Bryan Trottier, NY Islanders
1980	Marcel Dionne, Los Angeles
1981	Wayne Gretzky, Edmonton
1982	Wayne Gretzky, Edmonton
1983	Wayne Gretzky, Edmonton
1984	Wayne Gretzky, Edmonton
1985	Wayne Gretzky, Edmonton
1986	Wayne Gretzky, Edmonton
1987	Wayne Gretzky, Edmonton
1988	Mario Lemieux, Pittsburgh
1989	Mario Lemieux, Pittsburgh
1990	Wayne Gretzky, Los Angeles
1991	Wayne Gretzky, Los Angeles
1992	Mario Lemieux, Pittsburgh
1993	Mario Lemieux, Pittsburgh
1994	Wayne Gretzky, Los Angeles
1995	Jaromir Jagr, Pittsburgh
1996	Mario Lemieux, Pittsburgh
1997	Mario Lemieux, Pittsburgh
1998	Jaromir Jagr, Pittsburgh
1999	Jaromir Jagr, Pittsburgh
2000	Jaromir Jagr, Pittsburgh
2001	Jaromir Jagr, Pittsburgh
2002	Jarome Iginla, Calgary
2003	Peter Forsberg, Colorado
2004	Martin St. Louis, Tampa Bay
2006	Joe Thornton, San Jose
2007	Sidney Crosby, Pittsburgh
2008	Alexander Ovechkin, Washington
2009	Evgeni Malkin, Pittsburgh
2010	Henrik Sedin, Vancouver
2011	Daniel Sedin, Vancouver
2012	Evgeni Malkin, Pittsburgh
2013	Martin St. Louis, Tampa Bay
2014	Sidney Crosby, Pittsburgh
2015	Jamie Benn, Dallas

Vezina Trophy (Outstanding Goalie), 1927-2015

Before 1982, awarded to the goalie or goalies who played a minimum of 25 games for the team that allowed the fewest goals; since 1982, awarded to the most outstanding goalie, as determined by a vote of NHL general managers.

Year	Player, team
1927	George Hainsworth, Montréal Canadiens
1928	George Hainsworth, Montréal Canadiens
1929	George Hainsworth, Montréal Canadiens
1930	Tiny Thompson, Boston
1931	Roy Worters, NY Americans
1932	Charlie Gardiner, Chicago
1933	Tiny Thompson, Boston
1934	Charlie Gardiner, Chicago
1935	Lorne Chabot, Chicago
1936	Tiny Thompson, Boston
1937	Normie Smith, Detroit
1938	Tiny Thompson, Boston
1939	Frank Brimsek, Boston
1940	Dave Kerr, NY Rangers
1941	Turk Broda, Toronto
1942	Frank Brimsek, Boston
1943	Johnny Mowers, Detroit
1944	Bill Durnan, Montréal
1945	Bill Durnan, Montréal
1946	Bill Durnan, Montréal
1947	Bill Durnan, Montréal
1948	Turk Broda, Toronto
1949	Bill Durnan, Montréal
1950	Bill Durnan, Montréal
1951	Al Rollins, Toronto
1952	Terry Sawchuk, Detroit
1953	Terry Sawchuk, Detroit
1954	Harry Lumley, Toronto
1955	Terry Sawchuk, Detroit
1956	Jacques Plante, Montréal
1957	Jacques Plante, Montréal
1958	Jacques Plante, Montréal
1959	Jacques Plante, Montréal
1960	Jacques Plante, Montréal
1961	Johnny Bower, Toronto
1962	Jacques Plante, Montréal
1963	Glenn Hall, Chicago
1964	Charlie Hodge, Montréal
1965	Sawchuk, Bower; Toronto
1966	Worsley, Hodge; Montréal
1967	Hall, DeJordy; Chicago
1968	Worsley, Vachon; Montréal
1969	Hall, Plante; St. Louis
1970	Tony Esposito, Chicago
1971	Giacomin, Villemure; NY Rangers
1972	Esposito, Smith; Chicago
1973	Ken Dryden, Montréal
1974	Bernie Parent, Philadelphia; Tony Esposito, Chicago
1975	Bernie Parent, Philadelphia
1976	Ken Dryden, Montréal
1977	Dryden, Larocque; Montréal
1978	Dryden, Larocque; Montréal
1979	Dryden, Larocque; Montréal
1980	Sauve, Edwards; Buffalo
1981	Sevigny, Larocque, Herron; Montréal
1982	Bill Smith, NY Islanders
1983	Pete Peeters, Boston
1984	Tom Barrasso, Buffalo
1985	Pelle Lindbergh, Philadelphia
1986	John Vanbiesbrouck, NY Rangers
1987	Ron Hextall, Philadelphia
1988	Grant Fuhr, Edmonton
1989	Patrick Roy, Montréal
1990	Patrick Roy, Montréal
1991	Ed Belfour, Chicago
1992	Patrick Roy, Montréal
1993	Ed Belfour, Chicago
1994	Dominik Hasek, Buffalo
1995	Dominik Hasek, Buffalo
1996	Jim Carey, Washington
1997	Dominik Hasek, Buffalo
1998	Dominik Hasek, Buffalo
1999	Dominik Hasek, Buffalo
2000	Olaf Kolzig, Washington
2001	Dominik Hasek, Buffalo
2002	Jose Theodore, Montréal
2003	Martin Brodeur, New Jersey
2004	Martin Brodeur, New Jersey
2006	Miikka Kiprusoff, Calgary
2007	Martin Brodeur, New Jersey
2008	Martin Brodeur, New Jersey
2009	Tim Thomas, Boston
2010	Ryan Miller, Buffalo
2011	Tim Thomas, Boston
2012	Henrik Lundqvist, NY Rangers
2013	Sergei Bobrovsky, Columbus
2014	Tuukka Rask, Boston
2015	Carey Price, Montréal

NHL Home Ice

Team	Name (year built)	Capacity[1]
Anaheim	Honda Center[2] (1993)	17,174
Arizona*	Gila River Arena[3] (2003)	17,125
Boston	TD Garden[4] (1995)	17,565
Buffalo	First Niagara Center[5] (1996)	19,070
Calgary	Scotiabank Saddledome[6] (1983)	19,289
Carolina	PNC Arena[7] (1999)	18,680
Chicago	United Center (1994)	19,717
Colorado	Pepsi Center (1999)	18,007
Columbus	Nationwide Arena (2000)	18,144
Dallas	American Airlines Center (2001)	18,532
Detroit	Joe Louis Arena (1979)	20,027
Edmonton	Rexall Place[8] (1974)	16,839
Florida	BB&T Center[9] (1998)	15,720
Los Angeles	STAPLES Center (1999)	18,230
Minnesota	Xcel Energy Center (2000)	17,954
Montréal	Le Centre Bell[10] (1996)	21,273
Nashville	Bridgestone Arena[11] (1997)	17,113
New Jersey	Prudential Center (2007)	16,592
NY Islanders	Nassau Veterans Memorial Coliseum[12] (1972)	16,170
NY Rangers	Madison Square Garden (1968)	18,006
Ottawa	Canadian Tire Centre[13] (1996)	19,153
Philadelphia	Wells Fargo Center[14] (1996)	19,541
Pittsburgh	CONSOL Energy Center (2010)	18,387
St. Louis	Scottrade Center[15] (1994)	19,150
San Jose	SAP Center at San Jose[16] (1993)	17,562
Tampa Bay	Amalie Arena[17] (1996)	19,204
Toronto	Air Canada Centre (1999)	18,819
Vancouver	Rogers Arena[18] (1995)	18,910
Washington	Verizon Center[19] (1997)	18,506
Winnipeg	MTS Centre (2004)	15,004

* = The Phoenix Coyotes officially changed their name to the Arizona Coyotes prior to the 2014-15 NHL season. (1) At the end of the 2014-15 season. (2) The Arrowhead Pond of Anaheim, 1993-2006. (3) Glendale Arena, 2003-06; Jobing.com Arena, 2006-14. (4) FleetCenter, 1995-2005; TD Banknorth Garden, 2005-09. (5) Marine Midland Arena, 1996-99; HSBC Arena, 1999-2011. (6) Olympic Saddledome, 1983-96; Canadian Airlines Saddledome, 1996-2000; Pengrowth Saddledome, 2000-10. (7) Raleigh Entertainment and Sports Arena, 1999-2002; RBC Center, 2002-11. (8) Northlands Coliseum, 1974-79; Edmonton Col., 1979-98; Skyreach Centre, 1998-2003. (9) National Car Rental Center, 1998-2002; Office Depot Center, 2002-05; BankAtlantic Center, 2005-12. (10) Le Centre Molson, 1996-2002. (11) Nashville Arena, 1997-99; Gaylord Entertainment Center, 1999-2007; Sommet Center, 2007-10. (12) Barclays Center in Brooklyn, NY, beginning with 2015-16 season. (13) Corel Centre, 1996-2006; Scotiabank Place, 2006-13. (14) CoreStates Center, 1996-98; First Union Center, 1998-2003; Wachovia Center, 2003-10. (15) Kiel Center, 1994-2000; Savvis Center, 2000-06. (16) San Jose Arena, 1993-2001; Compaq Center, 2001-02; HP Pavilion at San Jose, 2002-13. (17) Ice Palace, 1996-2002; St. Pete Times Forum, 2002-12; Tampa Bay Times Forum, 2012-14. (18) General Motors Place, 1995-2010. (19) MCI Center, 1997-2006.

Hockey Hall of Fame

(Located in Toronto, ON, Canada. * = 2015 inductee.)

Players

Abel, Sid
Adams, Jack
Anderson, Glenn
Apps, Syl
Armstrong, George
Bailey, Irvine "Ace"
Bain, Dan
Baker, Hobey
Barber, Bill
Barry, Marty
Bathgate, Andy
Bauer, Bobby
Belfour, Ed
Beliveau, Jean
Benedict, Clint
Bentley, Doug
Bentley, Max
Blake, Hector "Toe"
Blake, Rob
Boivin, Leo
Boon, Dickie
Bossy, Mike
Bouchard, Butch
Boucher, Frank
Boucher, George
Bourque, Ray
Bower, Johnny
Bowie, Russell "Dubbie"
Brimsek, Frank
Broadbent, Harry L. "Punch"
Broda, Turk
Bucyk, John
Burch, Billy
Bure, Pavel
Cameron, Harry
Cheevers, Gerry
Chelios, Chris
Ciccarelli, Dino
Clancy, King
Clapper, Aubrey "Dit"
Clarke, Bobby
Cleghorn, Sprague
Coffey, Paul
Colville, Neil
Conacher, Charlie
Conacher, Lionel
Conacher, Roy
Connell, Alex
Cook, Bill
Cook, Frederick "Bun"
Coulter, Art
Cournoyer, Yvan
Cowley, Bill
Crawford, Rusty
Darragh, Jack
Davidson, Scotty
Day, Clarence "Hap"
Delvecchio, Alex
Denneny, Cy
Dionne, Marcel
Drillon, Gordie
Drinkwater, Graham
Dryden, Ken
Duff, Terrance "Dick"
Dumart, Woody
Dunderdale, Tommy
Durnan, Bill
Dutton, Mervyn "Red"
Dye, Babe
Esposito, Phil
Esposito, Tony
Farrel, Arthur
Federko, Bernie
*Fedorov, Sergei
Fetisov, Viacheslav
Flaman, Fernie
Forsberg, Peter
Foyston, Frank
Francis, Ron
Fredrickson, Frank
Fuhr, Grant
Gadsby, Bill
Gainey, Bob
Gardiner, Chuck
Gardiner, Herb
Gardiner, Jimmy
Gartner, Mike
Geoffrion, Bernie
Gerard, Eddie
Giacomin, Eddie
Gilbert, Rod
Gillies, Clark
Gilmour, Billy
Gilmour, Doug
Goheen, Frank "Moose"
Goodfellow, Ebbie
Goulet, Michel
Granato, Cammi
Grant, Mike
Green, Wilfred "Shorty"
Gretzky, Wayne
Griffis, Si
Hainsworth, George
Hall, Glenn
Hall, Joe
Harvey, Doug
Hasek, Dominik
Hawerchuk, Dale
Hay, George
Heaney, Geraldine
Hern, Riley
Hextall, Bryan
Holmes, Hap
Hooper, Tom
Horner, Red
Horton, Tim
*Housley, Phil
Howe, Gordie
Howe, Mark
Howe, Syd
Howell, Harry
Hull, Bobby
Hull, Brett
Hutton, John "Bouse"
Hyland, Harry
Irvin, Dick
Jackson, Harvey "Busher"
James, Angela
Johnson, Ching
Johnson, Ernie
Johnson, Tom
Joliat, Aurel
Keats, Duke
Kelly, Red
Kennedy, Ted
Keon, Dave
Kharlamov, Valeri
Kurri, Jari
Lach, Elmer
Lafleur, Guy
LaFontaine, Pat
Lalonde, Newsy
Langway, Rod
Laperrière, Jacques
Lapointe, Guy
Laprade, Edgar
Larionov, Igor
Laviolette, Jack
Leetch, Brian
Lehman, Hughie
Lemaire, Jacques
Lemieux, Mario
LeSueur, Percy
Lewis, Herbie
*Lidstrom, Nicklas
Lindsay, Ted
Lumley, Harry
MacInnis, Al
MacKay, Mickey
Mahovlich, Frank
Malone, Joe
Mantha, Sylvio
Marshall, Jack
Maxwell, Fred
McDonald, Lanny
McGee, Frank
McGimsie, Billy
McNamara, George
Messier, Mark
Mikita, Stan
Modano, Mike
Moore, Dickie
Moran, Paddy
Morenz, Howie
Mosienko, Bill
Mullen, Joe
Murphy, Larry
Neely, Cam
Niedermayer, Scott
Nieuwendyk, Joe
Nighbor, Frank
Noble, Reg
Oates, Adam
O'Connor, Buddy
Oliver, Harry
Olmstead, Bert
Orr, Bobby
Parent, Bernie
Park, Brad
Patrick, Lester
Patrick, Lynn
Perreault, Gilbert
Phillips, Tom
Pilote, Pierre
Pitre, Didier
Plante, Jacques
Potvin, Denis
Pratt, Babe
Primeau, Joe
*Pronger, Chris
Pronovost, Marcel
Pulford, Bob
Pulford, Harvey
Quackenbush, Bill
Rankin, Frank
Ratelle, Jean
Rayner, Chuck
Reardon, Kenny
Richard, Henri
Richard, Maurice
Richardson, George
Roberts, Gordie
Robinson, Larry
Robitaille, Luc
Ross, Art
Roy, Patrick
*Ruggiero, Angela
Russel, Blair
Russell, Ernie
Ruttan, Jack
Sakic, Joe
Salming, Börje
Savard, Denis
Savard, Serge
Sawchuk, Terry
Scanlan, Fred
Schmidt, Milt
Schriner, Sweeney
Seibert, Earl
Seibert, Oliver
Shanahan, Brendan
Shore, Eddie
Shutt, Steve
Siebert, Babe
Simpson, Joe "Bullet"
Sittler, Darryl
Smith, Alf
Smith, Billy
Smith, Clint
Smith, Hooley
Smith, Tommy
Stanley, Allan
Stanley, Barney
Stastny, Peter
Stevens, Ronald Scott
Stewart, Jack
Stewart, Nels
Stuart, Bruce
Stuart, Hod
Sundin, Mats
Taylor, Frederick "Cyclone"
Thompson, Cecil "Tiny"
Tretiak, Vladislav
Trihey, Harry
Trottier, Bryan
Ullman, Norm
Vezina, Georges
Walker, Jack
Walsh, Marty
Watson, Harry "Moose"
Watson, Harry Percival
Weiland, Cooney
Westwick, Harry
Whitcroft, Fred
Wilson, Gordon Allan "Phat"
Worsley, Gump
Worters, Roy
Yzerman, Steve

Builders

Adams, Charles
Adams, Weston
Ahearn, Frank
Ahearn, John "Bunny"
Allan, Sir Montagu
Allen, Keith
Arbour, Al
Ballard, Harold
Bauer, Father David
Bickell, J. P.
Bowman, Scotty
Brooks, Herbert
Brown, George
Brown, Walter
Buckland, Frank
Burns, Pat
Bush, Walter, Jr.
Butterfield, Jack
Calder, Frank
Campbell, Angus
Campbell, Clarence
Cattarinich, Joseph
Chynoweth, Ed
Costello, Murray
Dandurand, Leo
Devellano, Jim
Dilio, Frank
Dudley, George
Dunn, James
Fletcher, Cliff
Francis, Emile
Gibson, Jack
Gorman, Tommy
Gregory, Jim
Griffiths, Frank
Hanley, Bill
*Hay, Bill
Hay, Charles
Hendy, Jim
Hewitt, Foster
Hewitt, William
Hotchkiss, Harley
Hume, Fred
Ilitch, Mike
Imlach, Harry "Punch"
Ivan, Tommy
Jennings, William
Johnson, Bob
Juckes, Gordon
*Karmanos, Peter, Jr.
Kilpatrick, John
Kilrea, Brian
Knox, Seymour
Lamoriello, Lou
Leader, Al
LeBel, Robert
Lockhart, Thomas
Loicq, Paul
Mariucci, John
Mathers, Frank
McLaughlin, Frederic
Milford, Jake
Molson, Sen. Hartland
Morrison, Ian "Scotty"
Murray, Athol "Père"
Neilson, Roger
Nelson, Francis
Norris, Bruce
Norris, James
Norris, James, Sr.
Northey, William
O'Brien, J. Ambrose
O'Neill, Brian Francis
Page, Frederick
Patrick, Craig
Patrick, Frank
Pickard, Allan
Pilous, Rudy
Poile, Bud
Pollock, Sam
Raymond, Sen. Donat
Robertson, John Ross
Robinson, Claude
Ross, Phillip
Sabetzki, Gunther
Sather, Glen
Seaman, Daryl "Doc"
Selke, Frank
Shero, Fred
Sinden, Harry
Smith, Frank
Smythe, Conn
Snider, Ed
Stanley, Lord (of Preston)
Sutherland, Capt. James T.
Tarasov, Anatoli
Torrey, Bill
Turner, Lloyd
Tutt, William
Voss, Carl
Waghorne, Fred
Wirtz, Arthur
Wirtz, Bill
Ziegler, John A., Jr.

Referees and Linesmen

Armstrong, Neil
Ashley, John
Chadwick, Bill
D'Amico, John
Elliott, Edwin "Chaucer"
Hayes, George
Hewiston, Bobby
Ion, Mickey
McCreary, Bill
Pavelich, Matt
Rodden, Mike
Scapinello, Ray
Smeaton, Cooper
Storey, Red
Udvari, Frank
Van Hellemond, Andy

U.S. Wins 2015 World Cup in Japan Rematch

The U.S. women's soccer team won the 2015 World Cup with a 5-2 victory over Japan July 5, 2015, at BC Place Stadium in Vancouver, BC, Canada. Veteran midfielder Carli Lloyd scored three goals in the first 16 minutes—the first-ever hat trick in a women's FIFA World Cup final match—as the U.S. captured its third World Cup title and first since 1999. Lloyd, who won the Golden Ball award as the tournament's top player, complemented a strong U.S. defense that allowed only three goals; U.S. goalkeeper Hope Solo won the Golden Glove as best goalie. Lloyd tied Germany's Celia Sasic with six goals and one assist in the tournament, but Sasic won the Golden Boot award as top scorer based on fewer minutes played.

Canada served as host of the 2015 tournament, which was contested in six venues throughout the country. The Canadian squad won Group A and beat Switzerland, 1-0, in a Round of 16 game on June 21 in Vancouver before falling to England six days later, 2-1. All of the stadiums featured artificial turf, the first time that all Women's World Cup matches were played on such surfaces. Prior to the tournament, a group of players concerned over gender equity, increased injury risk, and excessive heat while playing on turf filed but eventually dropped a lawsuit against FIFA and the Canadian Soccer Assn.

Women's World Cup Results, 2015

Round of 16

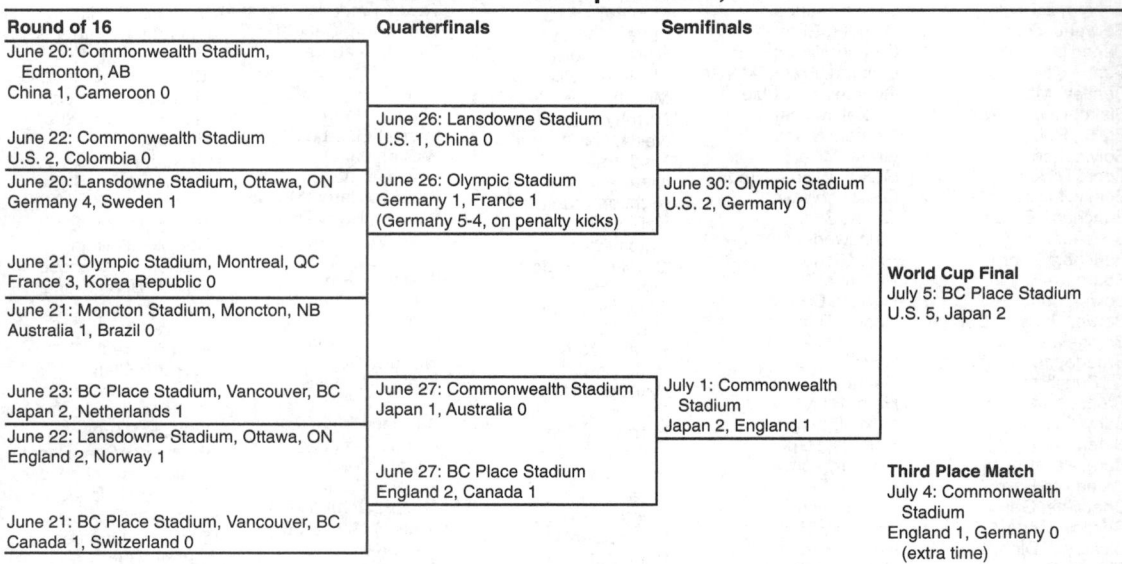

June 20: Commonwealth Stadium, Edmonton, AB
China 1, Cameroon 0

June 22: Commonwealth Stadium
U.S. 2, Colombia 0

June 20: Lansdowne Stadium, Ottawa, ON
Germany 4, Sweden 1

June 21: Olympic Stadium, Montreal, QC
France 3, Korea Republic 0

June 21: Moncton Stadium, Moncton, NB
Australia 1, Brazil 0

June 23: BC Place Stadium, Vancouver, BC
Japan 2, Netherlands 1

June 22: Lansdowne Stadium, Ottawa, ON
England 2, Norway 1

June 21: BC Place Stadium, Vancouver, BC
Canada 1, Switzerland 0

Quarterfinals

June 26: Lansdowne Stadium
U.S. 1, China 0

June 26: Olympic Stadium
Germany 1, France 1
(Germany 5-4, on penalty kicks)

June 27: Commonwealth Stadium
Japan 1, Australia 0

June 27: BC Place Stadium
England 2, Canada 1

Semifinals

June 30: Olympic Stadium
U.S. 2, Germany 0

July 1: Commonwealth Stadium
Japan 2, England 1

World Cup Final
July 5: BC Place Stadium
U.S. 5, Japan 2

Third Place Match
July 4: Commonwealth Stadium
England 1, Germany 0 (extra time)

Women's World Cup Results, 1991-2015

Year	Winner	Final opponent	Score	Site
1991	U.S.	Norway	2-1	China
1995	Norway	Germany	2-0	Sweden
1999	U.S.	China	0-0 (5-4)*	Pasadena, CA, U.S.
2003	Germany	Sweden	2-1#	Carson, CA, U.S.
2007	Germany	Brazil	2-0	China
2011	Japan	U.S.	2-2 (3-1)*	Germany
2015	U.S.	Japan	5-2	Canada

* = Match decided in penalty kicks (shootout score in parentheses). # = Match decided in extra time.

FC Kansas City Wins 2015 NWSL Title

FC Kansas City won the National Women's Soccer League Championship for the second straight year with a 1-0 victory over Seattle Reign FC, Oct. 1, 2015, at Providence Park in Portland, OR. Amy Rodriguez scored the lone goal in the 78th minute and was named MVP. FC Kansas City led the league with nine shutouts during the season, and advanced to the final with a 3-0 road win over the Chicago Red Stars in the playoff semifinals on Sept. 13. Seattle Reign FC finished atop the 2015 NWSL standings and reached the title game with a 3-0 playoff win over the Washington Spirit Sept. 13.

Women's Professional Soccer Champions

Year	Winner	Final opponent	Score	Site	MVP
		Women's United Soccer Association champions			
2001	Bay Area CyberRays	Atlanta Beat	3-3 (4-2)*	Foxborough, MA	Julie Murray
2002	Carolina Courage	Washington Freedom	3-2	Atlanta, GA	Birgit Prinz
2003	Washington Freedom	Atlanta Beat	2-1	San Diego, CA	Abby Wambach
		Women's Professional Soccer champions			
2009	Sky Blue FC	Los Angeles Sol	1-0	Carson, CA	Heather O'Reilly
2010	FC Gold Pride	Philadelphia Independence	4-0	Hayward, CA	Marta
2011	Western New York Flash	Philadelphia Independence	1-1 (5-4)*	Rochester, NY	Christine Sinclair
		National Women's Soccer League champions			
2013	Portland Thorns FC	Western New York Flash	2-0	Rochester, NY	Tobin Heath
2014	FC Kansas City	Seattle Reign FC	2-1	Tukwila, WA	Lauren Holiday
2015	FC Kansas City	Seattle Reign FC	1-0	Portland, OR	Amy Rodriguez

*= Match decided on penalty kicks (shootout score in parentheses). **Note:** The Women's United Soccer Association (WUSA) folded in 2003. Women's Professional Soccer (WPS) began play in 2009 but stopped operating in 2012, suspending its fourth season. In Apr. 2013, the new National Women's Soccer League (NWSL) began play with eight teams competing: Boston Breakers, Chicago Red Stars, FC Kansas City, Portland Thorns FC, Seattle Reign FC, Sky Blue FC (New York/New Jersey), Washington Spirit, and Western New York Flash. The Houston Dash began play as an NWSL expansion team for the 2014 season; a 10th team, Orlando Pride, was expected to join the league for the 2016 season.

Germany Defeats Argentina for 2014 Men's World Cup Title

Germany won its fourth FIFA World Cup title July 13, 2014, with a dramatic goal in extra time, defeating Argentina, 1-0, at the Estádio do Maracanã in Rio de Janeiro, Brazil. Mario Götze, who entered the match for Germany in the 88th min., scored in the 113th min. Thomas Müller led Germany with five goals in the tournament, and teammate Manuel Neuer won the Golden Glove as the tournament's top goalkeeper. Argentina's Lionel Messi earned the Golden Ball as the competition's best player, and James Rodriguez of Colombia won the Golden Boot as top scorer with six goals in five games. After exceeding expectations somewhat in the so-called "Group of Death," the U.S. team fell July 1, 2-1, to Belgium in the Round of 16.

Men's World Cup Results, 2014

Round of 16

June 28: Estádio Mineirão, Belo Horizonte
Brazil 1, Chile 1
(Brazil won, 3-2, on penalties)

June 28: Estádio do Maracanã, Rio de Janeiro
Colombia 2, Uruguay 0

June 30: Estádio Nacional, Brasília
France 2, Nigeria 0

June 30: Estádio Beira-Rio, Porto Alegre
Germany 2, Algeria 1 (extra time)

June 29: Estádio Castelão, Fortaleza
Netherlands 2, Mexico 1

June 29: Arena Pernambuco, Recife
Costa Rica 1, Greece 1
(Costa Rica won, 5-3, on penalties)

July 1: Arena de São Paulo, São Paulo
Argentina 1, Switzerland 0 (extra time)

July 1: Arena Fonte Nova, Salvador
Belgium 2, U.S. 1 (extra time)

Quarterfinals

July 4: Estádio Castelão
Brazil 2, Colombia 1

July 4: Estádio do Maracanã
Germany 1, France 0

July 5: Arena Fonte Nova
Netherlands 0, Costa Rica 0
(Netherlands won, 4-3, on penalties)

July 5: Estádio Nacional
Argentina 1, Belgium 0

Semifinals

July 8: Estádio Mineirão
Germany 7, Brazil 1

July 9: Arena de São Paulo
Argentina 0, Netherlands 0
(Argentina won, 4-2, on penalties)

World Cup Final
July 13: Estádio do Maracanã
Germany 1, Argentina 0
(extra time)

Third Place Match
July 12: Estádio Nacional
Netherlands 3, Brazil 0

Men's World Cup Results, 1930-2014

Year	Winner	Final opponent	Score	Site
1930	Uruguay	Argentina	4-2	Uruguay
1934	Italy	Czechoslovakia	2-1#	Italy
1938	Italy	Hungary	4-2	France
1950	Uruguay	Brazil	2-1	Brazil
1954	W. Germany	Hungary	3-2	Switzerland
1958	Brazil	Sweden	5-2	Sweden
1962	Brazil	Czechoslovakia	3-1	Chile
1966	England	W. Germany	4-2#	England
1970	Brazil	Italy	4-1	Mexico
1974	W. Germany	Netherlands	2-1	W. Germany
1978	Argentina	Netherlands	3-1#	Argentina
1982	Italy	W. Germany	3-1	Spain
1986	Argentina	W. Germany	3-2	Mexico
1990	W. Germany	Argentina	1-0	Italy
1994	Brazil	Italy	0-0 (3-2)*	U.S.
1998	France	Brazil	3-0	France
2002	Brazil	Germany	2-0	Japan/S. Korea
2006	Italy	France	1-1 (5-3)*	Germany
2010	Spain	Netherlands	1-0#	South Africa
2014	Germany	Argentina	1-0#	Brazil

* = Match decided in penalty kicks (shootout score in parentheses). # = Match decided in extra time.

Los Angeles Captures 2014 MLS Cup as Donovan Departs

The Los Angeles Galaxy won their fifth MLS Cup in franchise history with a 2-1 overtime victory over the New England Revolution Dec. 7, 2014, at StubHub Center in Carson, CA. Robbie Keane scored for L.A. in the 111th minute and earned the game's Most Valuable Player award. Keane was also voted regular-season MVP with a career-high 19 goals and 14 assists.

Veteran Galaxy forward Landon Donovan, the all-time MLS leading scorer, retired at the end of the 2014 season. MLS announced in 2015 that the league's MVP award would be named after Donovan, a six-time MLS champion, from 2015 on.

In the Western Conference final, L.A. defeated Seattle, which led the MLS in 2014 with 20 wins and 64 points, to reach the MLS Cup. New England overcame New York in the Eastern Conference final but continued the franchise's losing streak in the MLS Cup. MLS took a two-week break during the 2014 season to allow some of its players to compete in the FIFA World Cup soccer tournament.

Major League Soccer (MLS) Cup Results, 1996-2014

Year	Winner	Final opponent	Score	Site	MVP
1996	DC United	Los Angeles Galaxy	3-2 (OT)	Foxborough, MA	Marco Etcheverry
1997	DC United	Colorado Rapids	2-1	Washington, DC	Jaime Moreno
1998	Chicago Fire	DC United	2-0	Pasadena, CA	Peter Nowak
1999	DC United	Los Angeles Galaxy	2-0	Foxborough, MA	Ben Olsen
2000	Kansas City Wizards	Chicago Fire	1-0	Washington, DC	Tony Meola
2001	San Jose Earthquakes	Los Angeles Galaxy	2-1 (OT)	Columbus, OH	Dwayne De Rosario
2002	Los Angeles Galaxy	New England Revolution	1-0 (OT)	Foxborough, MA	Carlos Ruiz
2003	San Jose Earthquakes	Chicago Fire	4-2	Carson, CA	Landon Donovan
2004	DC United	Kansas City Wizards	3-2	Carson, CA	Alecko Eskandarian
2005	Los Angeles Galaxy	New England Revolution	1-0 (OT)	Frisco, TX	Guillermo Ramírez
2006	Houston Dynamo	New England Revolution	1-1 (4-3)*	Frisco, TX	Brian Ching
2007	Houston Dynamo	New England Revolution	2-1	Washington, DC	Dwayne De Rosario
2008	Columbus Crew	New York Red Bulls	3-1	Carson, CA	Guillermo Barros Schelotto
2009	Real Salt Lake	Los Angeles Galaxy	1-1 (5-4)*	Seattle, WA	Nick Rimando
2010	Colorado Rapids	FC Dallas	2-1 (OT)	Toronto, ON, Canada	Conor Casey
2011	Los Angeles Galaxy	Houston Dynamo	1-0	Carson, CA	Landon Donovan
2012	Los Angeles Galaxy	Houston Dynamo	3-1	Carson, CA	Omar Gonzalez
2013	Sporting Kansas City	Real Salt Lake	1-1 (7-6)*	Kansas City, KS	Aurelien Collin
2014	Los Angeles Galaxy	New England Revolution	2-1 (OT)	Carson, CA	Robbie Keane

* = Match decided in penalty kicks (shootout score in parentheses). OT = Overtime.

Major League Soccer Final Standings, 2014

(Does not include playoff games.)

Eastern Conference	W	L	T	PTS	GF	GA	GD
D.C. United	17	9	8	59	52	37	15
New England Revolution	17	13	4	55	51	46	5
Columbus Crew SC.	14	10	10	52	52	42	10
New York Red Bulls.	13	10	11	50	55	50	5
Sporting Kansas City	14	13	7	49	48	41	7
Philadelphia Union	10	12	12	42	51	51	0
Toronto FC	11	15	8	41	44	54	–10
Houston Dynamo	11	17	6	39	39	58	–19
Chicago Fire	6	10	18	36	41	51	–10
Montréal Impact	6	18	10	28	38	58	–20

Western Conference	W	L	T	PTS	GF	GA	GD
Seattle Sounders FC	20	10	4	64	65	50	15
L.A. Galaxy	17	7	10	61	69	37	32
Real Salt Lake	15	8	11	56	54	39	15
FC Dallas	16	12	6	54	55	45	10
Vancouver Whitecaps	12	8	14	50	42	40	2
Portland Timbers	12	9	13	49	61	52	9
Chivas USA	9	19	6	33	29	61	–32
Colorado Rapids	8	18	8	32	43	62	–19
San Jose Earthquakes	6	16	12	30	35	50	–15

Major League Soccer Scoring Leaders, 2014

Player	Club	GP	Goals
Bradley Wright-Phillips	New York	32	27
Dom Dwyer	Kansas City	33	22
Robbie Keane	Los Angeles	29	19
Lee Nguyen	New England	32	18
Obafemi Martins	Seattle	31	17
Gyasi Zardes	Los Angeles	32	16
Clint Dempsey	Seattle	26	15
Erick Torres	Chivas USA	29	15
Chris Wondolowski	San Jose	26	14
Joao Plata	Real Salt Lake	26	13

UEFA Champions League Results, 1956-2015

Year	Winner	Final opponent	Score
1956	Real Madrid	Reims	4-3
1957	Real Madrid	Fiorentina	2-0
1958	Real Madrid	AC Milan	3-2#
1959	Real Madrid	Reims	2-0
1960	Real Madrid	Eintracht Frankfurt	7-3
1961	Benfica	FC Barcelona	3-2
1962	Benfica	Real Madrid	5-3
1963	AC Milan	Benfica	2-1
1964	Inter Milan	Real Madrid	3-1
1965	Inter Milan	Benfica	1-0
1966	Real Madrid	Partizan	2-1
1967	Celtic	Inter Milan	2-1
1968	Manchester United	Benfica	4-1#
1969	AC Milan	Ajax	4-1
1970	Feyenoord	Celtic	2-1#
1971	Ajax	Panathinaikos	2-0
1972	Ajax	Inter Milan	2-0
1973	Ajax	Juventus	1-0
1974	Bayern Munich	Atlético Madrid	5-1[1]
1975	Bayern Munich	Leeds United	2-0
1976	Bayern Munich	St-Étienne	1-0
1977	Liverpool	Borussia Mönchengladbach	3-1
1978	Liverpool	Club Brugge	1-0
1979	Nottingham Forest	Malmö	1-0
1980	Nottingham Forest	Hamburg SV	1-0
1981	Liverpool	Real Madrid	1-0
1982	Aston Villa	Bayern Munich	1-0
1983	Hamburg SV	Juventus	1-0
1984	Liverpool	AS Roma	1-1 (4-2)*
1985	Juventus	Liverpool	1-0
1986	Steaua	FC Barcelona	0-0 (2-0)*
1987	Porto	Bayern Munich	2-1
1988	PSV	Benfica	0-0 (6-5)*
1989	AC Milan	Steaua	4-0
1990	AC Milan	Benfica	1-0
1991	Crvena Zvezda	Marseille	0-0 (5-3)*
1992	FC Barcelona	Sampdoria	1-0#
1993	Marseille	AC Milan	1-0
1994	AC Milan	FC Barcelona	4-0
1995	Ajax	AC Milan	1-0
1996	Juventus	Ajax	1-1 (4-2)*
1997	Borussia Dortmund	Juventus	3-1
1998	Real Madrid	Juventus	1-0
1999	Manchester United	Bayern Munich	2-1
2000	Real Madrid	Valencia	3-0
2001	Bayern Munich	Valencia	1-1 (5-4)*
2002	Real Madrid	Leverkusen	2-1
2003	AC Milan	Juventus	0-0 (3-2)*
2004	Porto	Monaco	3-0
2005	Liverpool	AC Milan	3-3 (3-2)*
2006	FC Barcelona	Arsenal	2-1
2007	AC Milan	Liverpool	2-1
2008	Manchester United	Chelsea	1-1 (6-5)*
2009	FC Barcelona	Manchester United	2-0
2010	Inter Milan	Bayern Munich	2-0
2011	FC Barcelona	Manchester United	3-1
2012	Chelsea	Bayern Munich	1-1 (4-3)*
2013	Bayern Munich	Borussia Dortmund	2-1
2014	Real Madrid	Atlético Madrid	4-1#
2015	FC Barcelona	Juventus	3-1

* = Match decided in penalty kicks (shootout score in parentheses). # = Match decided in extra time. (1) Aggregate score. First game 1-1; second, 4-0.

UEFA European Football Championships, 1960-2012

The final rounds of the 2012 Union of European Football Associations (UEFA) European Championships were jointly hosted by Poland and Ukraine and opened June 8, 2012, in Warsaw and Wroclawa, Poland, with the final match at Olympic Stadium in Kiev, Ukraine, on July 1, 2012.

Year	Winner	Final opponent	Score	Site
1960	USSR	Yugoslavia	2-1#	France
1964	Spain	USSR	2-1	Spain
1968	Italy	Yugoslavia	2-0	Italy
1972	W. Germany	USSR	3-0	Belgium
1976	Czechoslovakia	W. Germany	2-2 (5-3)*	Yugoslavia
1980	W. Germany	Belgium	2-1	Italy
1984	France	Spain	2-0	France
1988	Netherlands	USSR	2-0	W. Germany
1992	Denmark	Germany	2-0	Sweden
1996	Germany	Czech Rep.	2-1#	England
2000	France	Italy	2-1#	Belgium/Neth.
2004	Greece	Portugal	1-0	Portugal
2008	Spain	Germany	1-0	Austria/Switz.
2012	Spain	Italy	4-0	Poland/Ukr.

* = Match decided in penalty kicks (shootout score in parentheses). # = Match decided in extra time.

Selected European Soccer League Champions, 1950-2015

Season	England: Premier League[1]	Spain: La Liga	Italy: Serie A	Germany: Bundesliga[2]
1949-50	Portsmouth FC	Atlético Madrid	Juventus	VfB Stuttgart
1950-51	Tottenham Hotspur	Atlético Madrid	AC Milan	Kaiserslautern
1951-52	Manchester United	FC Barcelona	Juventus	VfB Stuttgart
1952-53	Arsenal	FC Barcelona	Inter Milan	Kaiserslautern
1953-54	Wolverhampton Wanderers	Real Madrid	Inter Milan	Hannoverscher SV 96
1954-55	Chelsea	Real Madrid	AC Milan	Rot-Weiss Essen
1955-56	Manchester United	Athletic Bilbao	Fiorentina	Borussia Dortmund
1956-57	Manchester United	Real Madrid	AC Milan	Borussia Dortmund
1957-58	Wolverhampton Wanderers	Real Madrid	Juventus	Schalke 04
1958-59	Wolverhampton Wanderers	FC Barcelona	AC Milan	Eintracht Frankfurt
1959-60	Burnley FC	FC Barcelona	Juventus	Hamburg SV
1960-61	Tottenham Hotspur	Real Madrid	Juventus	FC Nuremberg
1961-62	Ipswich Town	Real Madrid	AC Milan	FC Cologne
1962-63	Everton	Real Madrid	Inter Milan	Borussia Dortmund
1963-64	Liverpool	Real Madrid	Bologna	FC Cologne
1964-65	Manchester United	Real Madrid	Inter Milan	Werder Bremen
1965-66	Liverpool	Atlético Madrid	Inter Milan	TSV 1860 Munich
1966-67	Manchester United	Real Madrid	Juventus	Eintracht Braunschweig
1967-68	Manchester City	Real Madrid	AC Milan	FC Nuremberg
1968-69	Leeds United	Real Madrid	Fiorentina	Bayern Munich
1969-70	Everton	Atlético Madrid	Cagliari	Borussia Mönchengladbach
1970-71	Arsenal	Valencia	Inter Milan	Borussia Mönchengladbach
1971-72	Derby County	Real Madrid	Juventus	Bayern Munich
1972-73	Liverpool	Atlético Madrid	Juventus	Bayern Munich
1973-74	Leeds United	FC Barcelona	Lazio	Bayern Munich
1974-75	Derby County	Real Madrid	Juventus	Borussia Mönchengladbach
1975-76	Liverpool	Real Madrid	Torino	Borussia Mönchengladbach
1976-77	Liverpool	Atlético Madrid	Juventus	Borussia Mönchengladbach
1977-78	Nottingham Forest	Real Madrid	Juventus	FC Cologne
1978-79	Liverpool	Real Madrid	AC Milan	Hamburg SV
1979-80	Liverpool	Real Madrid	Inter Milan	Bayern Munich
1980-81	Aston Villa	Real Sociedad	Juventus	Bayern Munich
1981-82	Liverpool	Real Sociedad	Juventus	Hamburg SV
1982-83	Liverpool	Athletic Bilbao	AS Roma	Hamburg SV
1983-84	Liverpool	Athletic Bilbao	Juventus	VfB Stuttgart
1984-85	Everton	FC Barcelona	Verona	Bayern Munich
1985-86	Liverpool	Real Madrid	Juventus	Bayern Munich
1986-87	Everton	Real Madrid	Napoli	Bayern Munich
1987-88	Liverpool	Real Madrid	AC Milan	Werder Bremen
1988-89	Arsenal	Real Madrid	Inter Milan	Bayern Munich
1989-90	Liverpool	Real Madrid	Napoli	Bayern Munich
1990-91	Arsenal	FC Barcelona	Sampdoria	FC Kaiserslautern
1991-92	Leeds United	FC Barcelona	AC Milan	VfB Stuttgart
1992-93	Manchester United	FC Barcelona	AC Milan	Werder Bremen
1993-94	Manchester United	FC Barcelona	AC Milan	Bayern Munich
1994-95	Blackburn Rovers	Real Madrid	Juventus	Borussia Dortmund
1995-96	Manchester United	Atlético Madrid	AC Milan	Borussia Dortmund
1996-97	Manchester United	Real Madrid	Juventus	Bayern Munich
1997-98	Arsenal	FC Barcelona	Juventus	FC Kaiserslautern
1998-99	Manchester United	FC Barcelona	AC Milan	Bayern Munich
1999-2000	Manchester United	Deportivo Coruña	Lazio	Bayern Munich
2000-01	Manchester United	Real Madrid	AS Roma	Bayern Munich
2001-02	Arsenal	Valencia	Juventus	Borussia Dortmund
2002-03	Manchester United	Real Madrid	Juventus	Bayern Munich
2003-04	Arsenal	Valencia	AC Milan	Werder Bremen
2004-05	Chelsea	FC Barcelona	None[3]	Bayern Munich
2005-06	Chelsea	FC Barcelona	Inter Milan[3]	Bayern Munich
2006-07	Manchester United	Real Madrid	Inter Milan	VfB Stuttgart
2007-08	Manchester United	Real Madrid	Inter Milan	Bayern Munich
2008-09	Manchester United	FC Barcelona	Inter Milan	VfL Wolfsburg
2009-10	Chelsea	FC Barcelona	Inter Milan	Bayern Munich
2010-11	Manchester United	FC Barcelona	AC Milan	Borussia Dortmund
2011-12	Manchester City	Real Madrid	Juventus	Borussia Dortmund
2012-13	Manchester United	FC Barcelona	Juventus	Bayern Munich
2013-14	Manchester City	Atlético Madrid	Juventus	Bayern Munich
2014-15	Chelsea	FC Barcelona	Juventus	Bayern Munich

(1) Football League champions are listed prior to 1992-93 season, when the Premier League formed. (2) Regional champions are listed prior to 1963-64 season, when National Bundesliga formed. (3) Juventus was stripped of two titles in 2006 because of match-fixing.

FIFA Confederations Cup, 2013

Brazil won its third straight Confederations Cup title with a 3-0 victory over Spain June 30, 2013, at Maracanã Stadium in Rio de Janeiro, Brazil. Fred scored twice in the championship and Neymar, who won the Golden Ball as the tournament's top player, added his fourth goal of the tournament in the 44th minute. Brazil advanced to the championship game with a 2-1 victory over Uruguay June 26 on a goal by Paulinho in the 86th minute at Mineirão Stadium in Belo Horizonte. Spain and Italy played to a 0-0 draw in the semifinals June 27 at Castelão Stadium in Fortaleza, but Spain advanced with a 7-6 win on penalty kicks.

FIFA Confederations Cup Results, 1997-2013

The FIFA Confederations Cup, now held every four years, is a tournament contested by six continental champions, the World Cup winner, and the host country.

Year	Winner	Final opponent	Score	Third place	Fourth place	Site
1997	Brazil	Australia	6-0	Czech Republic	Uruguay	Saudi Arabia
1999	Mexico	Brazil	4-3	U.S.	Saudi Arabia	Mexico
2001	France	Japan	1-0	Australia	Brazil	S. Korea/Japan
2003	France	Cameroon	1-0	Turkey	Colombia	France
2005	Brazil	Argentina	4-1	Germany	Mexico	Germany
2009	Brazil	U.S.	3-2	Spain	South Africa	South Africa
2013	Brazil	Spain	3-0	Italy	Uruguay	Brazil

GOLF

Men's All-Time Major Professional Championship Leaders

Through Sept. 2015. * = Active PGA player in 2015; (a) = amateur.

Player	Masters	U.S. Open	British Open	PGA	Total
Jack Nicklaus	1963, '65-'66, '72, '75, '86	1962, '67, '72, '80	1966, '70, '78	1963, '71, '73, '75, '80	18
Tiger Woods*	1997, 2001-02, '05	2000, '02, '08	2000, '05-'06	1999-2000, '06-'07	14
Walter Hagen	—	1914, '19	1922, '24, '28-'29	1921, '24-'27	11
Ben Hogan	1951, '53	1948, '50-'51, '53	1953	1946, '48	9
Gary Player	1961, '74, '78	1965	1959, '68, '74	1962, '72	9
Tom Watson	1977, '81	1982	1975, '77, '80, '82-'83	—	8
Bobby Jones (a)	—	1923, '26, '29-'30	1926-27, '30	—	7
Arnold Palmer	1958, '60, '62, '64	1960	1961-62	—	7
Gene Sarazen	1935	1922, '32	1932	1922-23, '33	7
Sam Snead	1949, '52, '54	—	1946	1942, '49, '51	7
Harry Vardon	—	1900	1896, '98-'99, 1903, '11, '14	—	7
Nick Faldo	1989-90, '96	—	1987, '90, '92	—	6
Lee Trevino	—	1968, '71	1971-72	1974, '84	6

Professional Golfers' Association Leading Money Winners, 1946-2015

Year	Player	Earnings
1946	Ben Hogan	$42,556
1947	Jimmy Demaret	27,936
1948	Ben Hogan	32,112
1949	Sam Snead	31,593
1950	Sam Snead	35,758
1951	Lloyd Mangrum	26,088
1952	Julius Boros	37,032
1953	Lew Worsham	34,002
1954	Bob Toski	65,819
1955	Julius Boros	63,121
1956	Ted Kroll	72,835
1957	Dick Mayer	65,835
1958	Arnold Palmer	42,607
1959	Art Wall Jr.	53,167
1960	Arnold Palmer	75,262
1961	Gary Player	64,540
1962	Arnold Palmer	81,448
1963	Arnold Palmer	128,230
1964	Jack Nicklaus	113,284
1965	Jack Nicklaus	140,752
1966	Billy Casper	121,944
1967	Jack Nicklaus	188,998
1968	Billy Casper	205,168
1969	Frank Beard	164,707
1970	Lee Trevino	$157,037
1971	Jack Nicklaus	244,490
1972	Jack Nicklaus	320,542
1973	Jack Nicklaus	308,362
1974	Johnny Miller	353,201
1975	Jack Nicklaus	298,149
1976	Jack Nicklaus	266,438
1977	Tom Watson	310,653
1978	Tom Watson	362,429
1979	Tom Watson	462,636
1980	Tom Watson	530,808
1981	Tom Kite	375,699
1982	Craig Stadler	446,462
1983	Hal Sutton	426,668
1984	Tom Watson	476,260
1985	Curtis Strange	542,321
1986	Greg Norman	653,296
1987	Curtis Strange	925,941
1988	Curtis Strange	1,147,644
1989	Tom Kite	1,395,278
1990	Greg Norman	1,165,477
1991	Corey Pavin	979,430
1992	Fred Couples	1,344,188
1993	Nick Price	$1,478,557
1994	Nick Price	1,499,927
1995	Greg Norman	1,654,959
1996	Tom Lehman	1,780,159
1997	Tiger Woods	2,066,833
1998	David Duval	2,591,031
1999	Tiger Woods	6,616,585
2000	Tiger Woods	9,188,321
2001	Tiger Woods	5,687,777
2002	Tiger Woods	6,912,625
2003	Vijay Singh	7,573,907
2004	Vijay Singh	10,905,166
2005	Tiger Woods	10,628,024
2006	Tiger Woods	9,941,563
2007	Tiger Woods	10,867,052
2008	Vijay Singh	6,601,094
2009	Tiger Woods	10,508,163
2010	Matt Kuchar	4,910,477
2011	Luke Donald	6,683,214
2012	Rory McIlroy	8,047,952
2013	Tiger Woods	8,553,439
2014	Rory McIlroy	8,280,096
2015	Jordan Spieth	12,030,465

Note: The PGA tour introduced a new split season format in Oct. 2013, which concluded with the FedEx Cup in Sept. 2014. From 2014 on, year shown is the one in which season ended.

Masters Golf Tournament Winners, 1940-2015

First contested in 1934 as Augusta National Invitation Tournament (name changed in 1939); not played, 1943-45.

Year	Winner
1940	Jimmy Demaret
1941	Craig Wood
1942	Byron Nelson
1946	Herman Keiser
1947	Jimmy Demaret
1948	Claude Harmon
1949	Sam Snead
1950	Jimmy Demaret
1951	Ben Hogan
1952	Sam Snead
1953	Ben Hogan
1954	Sam Snead
1955	Cary Middlecoff
1956	Jack Burke
1957	Doug Ford
1958	Arnold Palmer
1959	Art Wall Jr.
1960	Arnold Palmer
1961	Gary Player
1962	Arnold Palmer
1963	Jack Nicklaus
1964	Arnold Palmer
1965	Jack Nicklaus
1966	Jack Nicklaus
1967	Gay Brewer Jr.
1968	Bob Goalby
1969	George Archer
1970	Billy Casper
1971	Charles Coody
1972	Jack Nicklaus
1973	Tommy Aaron
1974	Gary Player
1975	Jack Nicklaus
1976	Ray Floyd
1977	Tom Watson
1978	Gary Player
1979	Fuzzy Zoeller
1980	Seve Ballesteros
1981	Tom Watson
1982	Craig Stadler
1983	Seve Ballesteros
1984	Ben Crenshaw
1985	Bernhard Langer
1986	Jack Nicklaus
1987	Larry Mize
1988	Sandy Lyle
1989	Nick Faldo
1990	Nick Faldo
1991	Ian Woosnam
1992	Fred Couples
1993	Bernhard Langer
1994	José María Olazábal
1995	Ben Crenshaw
1996	Nick Faldo
1997	Tiger Woods
1998	Mark O'Meara
1999	José María Olazábal
2000	Vijay Singh
2001	Tiger Woods
2002	Tiger Woods
2003	Mike Weir
2004	Phil Mickelson
2005	Tiger Woods
2006	Phil Mickelson
2007	Zach Johnson
2008	Trevor Immelman
2009	Angel Cabrera
2010	Phil Mickelson
2011	Charl Schwartzel
2012	Bubba Watson
2013	Adam Scott
2014	Bubba Watson
2015	Jordan Spieth

U.S. Open Winners, 1940-2015

First contested in 1895; not played, 1942-45.

Year	Winner
1940	Lawson Little
1941	Craig Wood
1946	Lloyd Mangrum
1947	Lew Worsham
1948	Ben Hogan
1949	Cary Middlecoff
1950	Ben Hogan
1951	Ben Hogan
1952	Julius Boros
1953	Ben Hogan
1954	Ed Furgol
1955	Jack Fleck
1956	Cary Middlecoff
1957	Dick Mayer
1958	Tommy Bolt
1959	Billy Casper
1960	Arnold Palmer
1961	Gene Littler
1962	Jack Nicklaus
1963	Julius Boros
1964	Ken Venturi
1965	Gary Player
1966	Billy Casper
1967	Jack Nicklaus
1968	Lee Trevino
1969	Orville Moody
1970	Tony Jacklin
1971	Lee Trevino
1972	Jack Nicklaus
1973	Johnny Miller
1974	Hale Irwin
1975	Lou Graham
1976	Jerry Pate
1977	Hubert Green
1978	Andy North
1979	Hale Irwin
1980	Jack Nicklaus
1981	David Graham
1982	Tom Watson
1983	Larry Nelson
1984	Fuzzy Zoeller
1985	Andy North
1986	Ray Floyd
1987	Scott Simpson
1988	Curtis Strange
1989	Curtis Strange
1990	Hale Irwin
1991	Payne Stewart
1992	Tom Kite
1993	Lee Janzen
1994	Ernie Els
1995	Corey Pavin
1996	Steve Jones
1997	Ernie Els
1998	Lee Janzen
1999	Payne Stewart
2000	Tiger Woods
2001	Retief Goosen
2002	Tiger Woods
2003	Jim Furyk
2004	Retief Goosen
2005	Michael Campbell
2006	Geoff Ogilvy
2007	Angel Cabrera
2008	Tiger Woods
2009	Lucas Glover
2010	Graeme McDowell
2011	Rory McIlroy
2012	Webb Simpson
2013	Justin Rose
2014	Martin Kaymer
2015	Jordan Spieth

British Open Winners, 1946-2015

Officially called the Open Championship. First contested in 1860; not played, 1940-45.

Year	Winner	Year	Winner	Year	Winner	Year	Winner	Year	Winner
1946	Sam Snead	1960	Kel Nagle	1974	Gary Player	1988	Seve Ballesteros	2002	Ernie Els
1947	Fred Daly	1961	Arnold Palmer	1975	Tom Watson	1989	Mark Calcavecchia	2003	Ben Curtis
1948	Henry Cotton	1962	Arnold Palmer	1976	Johnny Miller	1990	Nick Faldo	2004	Todd Hamilton
1949	Bobby Locke	1963	Bob Charles	1977	Tom Watson	1991	Ian Baker-Finch	2005	Tiger Woods
1950	Bobby Locke	1964	Tony Lema	1978	Jack Nicklaus	1992	Nick Faldo	2006	Tiger Woods
1951	Max Faulkner	1965	Peter Thomson	1979	Seve Ballesteros	1993	Greg Norman	2007	Padraig Harrington
1952	Bobby Locke	1966	Jack Nicklaus	1980	Tom Watson	1994	Nick Price	2008	Padraig Harrington
1953	Ben Hogan	1967	Roberto de Vicenzo	1981	Bill Rogers	1995	John Daly	2009	Stewart Cink
1954	Peter Thomson	1968	Gary Player	1982	Tom Watson	1996	Tom Lehman	2010	Louis Oosthuizen
1955	Peter Thomson	1969	Tony Jacklin	1983	Tom Watson	1997	Justin Leonard	2011	Darren Clarke
1956	Peter Thomson	1970	Jack Nicklaus	1984	Seve Ballesteros	1998	Mark O'Meara	2012	Ernie Els
1957	Bobby Locke	1971	Lee Trevino	1985	Sandy Lyle	1999	Paul Lawrie	2013	Phil Mickelson
1958	Peter Thomson	1972	Lee Trevino	1986	Greg Norman	2000	Tiger Woods	2014	Rory McIlroy
1959	Gary Player	1973	Tom Weiskopf	1987	Nick Faldo	2001	David Duval	2015	Zach Johnson

PGA Championship Winners, 1940-2015

First contested in 1916; not played, 1943.

Year	Winner	Year	Winner	Year	Winner	Year	Winner	Year	Winner
1940	Byron Nelson	1956	Jack Burke	1971	Jack Nicklaus	1986	Bob Tway	2001	David Toms
1941	Victor Ghezzi	1957	Lionel Hebert	1972	Gary Player	1987	Larry Nelson	2002	Rich Beem
1942	Sam Snead	1958	Dow Finsterwald	1973	Jack Nicklaus	1988	Jeff Sluman	2003	Shaun Micheel
1944	Bob Hamilton	1959	Bob Rosburg	1974	Lee Trevino	1989	Payne Stewart	2004	Vijay Singh
1945	Byron Nelson	1960	Jay Hebert	1975	Jack Nicklaus	1990	Wayne Grady	2005	Phil Mickelson
1946	Ben Hogan	1961	Jerry Barber	1976	Dave Stockton	1991	John Daly	2006	Tiger Woods
1947	Jim Ferrier	1962	Gary Player	1977	Lanny Wadkins	1992	Nick Price	2007	Tiger Woods
1948	Ben Hogan	1963	Jack Nicklaus	1978	John Mahaffey	1993	Paul Azinger	2008	Padraig Harrington
1949	Sam Snead	1964	Bob Nichols	1979	David Graham	1994	Nick Price	2009	Y.E. Yang
1950	Chandler Harper	1965	Dave Marr	1980	Jack Nicklaus	1995	Steve Elkington	2010	Martin Kaymer
1951	Sam Snead	1966	Al Geiberger	1981	Larry Nelson	1996	Mark Brooks	2011	Keegan Bradley
1952	James Turnesa	1967	Don January	1982	Ray Floyd	1997	Davis Love III	2012	Rory McIlroy
1953	Walter Burkemo	1968	Julius Boros	1983	Hal Sutton	1998	Vijay Singh	2013	Jason Dufner
1954	Melvin Harbert	1969	Ray Floyd	1984	Lee Trevino	1999	Tiger Woods	2014	Rory McIlroy
1955	Doug Ford	1970	Dave Stockton	1985	Hubert Green	2000	Tiger Woods	2015	Jason Day

FedEx Cup Winners, 2007-15

The FedEx Cup, a season-long, $10-mil competition with points awarded by finishing rank in each tournament, divides the PGA Tour into a regular season consisting of 43 events, combined with a 4-event playoff that ends with the Tour Championship.

Year	Winner	Year	Winner	Year	Winner	Year	Winner	Year	Winner
2007	Tiger Woods	2009	Tiger Woods	2011	Bill Haas	2013	Henrik Stenson	2015	Jordan Spieth
2008	Vijay Singh	2010	Jim Furyk	2012	Brandt Snedeker	2014	Billy Horschel		

Women's All-Time Major Professional Championship Leaders

Through Oct. 2015. * = Active in 2015 LPGA season.

Player	ANA Inspiration[1]	KPMG Women's PGA[2]	U.S. Women's Open	Women's British Open[3]	Titleholders[4]	Western Open[5]	Total
Patty Berg	—	—	1946	—	1937-39, '48, '53, '55, '57	1941, '43, '48, '51, '55, '57-'58	15
Mickey Wright	—	1958, '60-'61, '63	1958-59, '61, '64	—	1961-62	1962-63, '66	13
Louise Suggs	—	1957	1949, '52	—	1946, '54, '56, '59	1946-47, '49, '53	11
Annika Sorenstam	2001-02, '05	2003-05	1995-96, 2006	2003	—	—	10
Babe Zaharias	—	—	1948, '50, '54	—	1947, '50, '52	1940, '44-'45, '50	10
Betsy Rawls	—	1959, '69	1951, '53, '57, '60	—	—	1952, '59	8
Juli Inkster*	1984, '89	1999-2000	1999, 2002	1984	—	—	7
Karrie Webb*	2000, '06	2001	2000-01	1999, 2002	—	—	7
Inbee Park*	2013	2013-15	2008, '13	2015	—	—	7

(1) Formerly the Nabisco Dinah Shore (1982-99), the Nabisco Championship (2000-01), and the Kraft Nabisco Championship (2002-14); designated major in 1983. (2) Formerly the LPGA Championship (1955-2014). (3) In 2001, the British Open replaced the du Maurier Classic as the LPGA's fourth major; wins in column prior to 2001 are for the Peter Jackson (1979-82) or du Maurier (1983-2000) Classic. (4) Titleholders Championship was a major, 1937-72. (5) Western Open was a major, 1930-67.

Ladies Professional Golf Association Leading Money Winners, 1954-2014

Year	Player	Earnings	Year	Player	Earnings	Year	Player	Earnings
1954	Patty Berg	$16,011	1975	Sandra Palmer	$76,374	1995	Annika Sorenstam	$666,533
1955	Patty Berg	16,492	1976	Judy Rankin	150,734	1996	Karrie Webb	1,002,000
1956	Marlene Hagge	20,235	1977	Judy Rankin	122,890	1997	Annika Sorenstam	1,236,789
1957	Patty Berg	16,272	1978	Nancy Lopez	189,814	1998	Annika Sorenstam	1,092,748
1958	Beverly Hanson	12,639	1979	Nancy Lopez	197,489	1999	Karrie Webb	1,591,959
1959	Betsy Rawls	26,774	1980	Beth Daniel	231,000	2000	Karrie Webb	1,876,853
1960	Louise Suggs	16,892	1981	Beth Daniel	206,998	2001	Annika Sorenstam	2,105,868
1961	Mickey Wright	22,236	1982	JoAnne Carner	310,400	2002	Annika Sorenstam	2,863,904
1962	Mickey Wright	21,641	1983	JoAnne Carner	291,404	2003	Annika Sorenstam	2,029,506
1963	Mickey Wright	31,269	1984	Betsy King	266,771	2004	Annika Sorenstam	2,544,707
1964	Mickey Wright	29,800	1985	Nancy Lopez	416,472	2005	Annika Sorenstam	2,588,240
1965	Kathy Whitworth	28,658	1986	Pat Bradley	492,021	2006	Lorena Ochoa	2,592,872
1966	Kathy Whitworth	33,517	1987	Ayako Okamoto	466,034	2007	Lorena Ochoa	4,364,994
1967	Kathy Whitworth	32,937	1988	Sherri Turner	350,851	2008	Lorena Ochoa	2,763,193
1968	Kathy Whitworth	48,379	1989	Betsy King	654,132	2009	Jiyai Shin	1,807,334
1969	Carol Mann	49,152	1990	Beth Daniel	863,578	2010	Na Yeon Choi	1,871,166
1970	Kathy Whitworth	30,235	1991	Pat Bradley	763,118	2011	Yani Tseng	2,921,713
1971	Kathy Whitworth	41,181	1992	Dottie Mochrie	693,335	2012	Inbee Park	2,287,080
1972	Kathy Whitworth	65,063	1993	Betsy King	595,992	2013	Inbee Park	2,456,619
1973	Kathy Whitworth	82,864	1994	Laura Davies	687,201	2014	Stacy Lewis	2,539,039
1974	JoAnne Carner	87,094						

ANA Inspiration Winners, 1983-2015

Formerly the Colgate Dinah Shore (1972-81), the Nabisco Dinah Shore (1982-99), the Nabisco Championship (2000-01), and the Kraft Nabisco Championship (2002-14). Designated as a major championship in 1983.

Year	Winner	Year	Winner	Year	Winner	Year	Winner	Year	Winner
1983	Amy Alcott	1990	Betsy King	1997	Betsy King	2004	Grace Park	2010	Yani Tseng
1984	Juli Inkster	1991	Amy Alcott	1998	Pat Hurst	2005	Annika Sorenstam	2011	Stacy Lewis
1985	Alice Miller	1992	Dottie Pepper	1999	Dottie Pepper	2006	Karrie Webb	2012	Sun Young Yoo
1986	Pat Bradley	1993	Helen Alfredsson	2000	Karrie Webb	2007	Morgan Pressel	2013	Inbee Park
1987	Betsy King	1994	Donna Andrews	2001	Annika Sorenstam	2008	Lorena Ochoa	2014	Lexi Thompson
1988	Amy Alcott	1995	Nanci Bowen	2002	Annika Sorenstam	2009	Brittany Lincicome	2015	Brittany Lincicome
1989	Juli Inkster	1996	Patty Sheehan	2003	P. Meunier-Lebouc				

KPMG Women's PGA Championship Winners, 1955-2015

Formerly LPGA Championship (1955-2014).

Year	Winner	Year	Winner	Year	Winner	Year	Winner	Year	Winner
1955	Beverly Hanson	1968	Sandra Post	1980	Sally Little	1992	Betsy King	2004	Annika Sorenstam
1956	Marlene Hagge	1969	Betsy Rawls	1981	Donna Caponi	1993	Patty Sheehan	2005	Annika Sorenstam
1957	Louise Suggs	1970	Shirley Englehorn	1982	Jan Stephenson	1994	Laura Davies	2006	Se Ri Pak
1958	Mickey Wright	1971	Kathy Whitworth	1983	Patty Sheehan	1995	Kelly Robbins	2007	Suzann Pettersen
1959	Betsy Rawls	1972	Kathy Ahern	1984	Patty Sheehan	1996	Laura Davies	2008	Yani Tseng
1960	Mickey Wright	1973	Mary Mills	1985	Nancy Lopez	1997	Christa Johnson	2009	Anna Nordqvist
1961	Mickey Wright	1974	Sandra Haynie	1986	Pat Bradley	1998	Se Ri Pak	2010	Cristie Kerr
1962	Judy Kimball	1975	Kathy Whitworth	1987	Jane Geddes	1999	Juli Inkster	2011	Yani Tseng
1963	Mickey Wright	1976	Betty Burfeindt	1988	Sherri Turner	2000	Juli Inkster	2012	Shanshan Feng
1964	Mary Mills	1977	Chako Higuchi	1989	Nancy Lopez	2001	Karrie Webb	2013	Inbee Park
1965	Sandra Haynie	1978	Nancy Lopez	1990	Beth Daniel	2002	Se Ri Pak	2014	Inbee Park
1966	Gloria Ehret	1979	Donna Caponi	1991	Meg Mallon	2003	Annika Sorenstam	2015	Inbee Park
1967	Kathy Whitworth								

U.S. Women's Open Winners, 1946-2015

Year	Winner	Year	Winner	Year	Winner	Year	Winner	Year	Winner
1946	Patty Berg	1960	Betsy Rawls	1974	Sandra Haynie	1988	Liselotte Neumann	2002	Juli Inkster
1947	Betty Jameson	1961	Mickey Wright	1975	Sandra Palmer	1989	Betsy King	2003	Hilary Lunke
1948	Babe Zaharias	1962	Murle Lindstrom	1976	JoAnne Carner	1990	Betsy King	2004	Meg Mallon
1949	Louise Suggs	1963	Mary Mills	1977	Hollis Stacy	1991	Meg Mallon	2005	Birdie Kim
1950	Babe Zaharias	1964	Mickey Wright	1978	Hollis Stacy	1992	Patty Sheehan	2006	Annika Sorenstam
1951	Betsy Rawls	1965	Carol Mann	1979	Jerilyn Britz	1993	Lauri Merten	2007	Cristie Kerr
1952	Louise Suggs	1966	Sandra Spuzich	1980	Amy Alcott	1994	Patty Sheehan	2008	Inbee Park
1953	Betsy Rawls	1967	Catherine Lacoste	1981	Pat Bradley	1995	Annika Sorenstam	2009	Eun-Hee Ji
1954	Babe Zaharias	1968	Susie Berning	1982	Janet Alex	1996	Annika Sorenstam	2010	Paula Creamer
1955	Fay Crocker	1969	Donna Caponi	1983	Jan Stephenson	1997	Alison Nicholas	2011	So Yeon Ryu
1956	Kathy Cornelius	1970	Donna Caponi	1984	Hollis Stacy	1998	Se Ri Pak	2012	Na Yeon Choi
1957	Betsy Rawls	1971	JoAnne Carner	1985	Kathy Baker	1999	Juli Inkster	2013	Inbee Park
1958	Mickey Wright	1972	Susie Berning	1986	Jane Geddes	2000	Karrie Webb	2014	Michelle Wie
1959	Mickey Wright	1973	Susie Berning	1987	Laura Davies	2001	Karrie Webb	2015	In Gee Chun

Women's British Open Winners, 1979-2015

First contested as the Ladies' British Open in 1976; became the LPGA's fourth major championship in 2001, replacing the du Maurier Classic. Winners listed are for the Peter Jackson (1979-82) and du Maurier (1983-2000) Classic.

Year	Winner	Year	Winner	Year	Winner	Year	Winner	Year	Winner
1979	Amy Alcott	1987	Jody Rosenthal	1995	Jenny Lidback	2002	Karrie Webb	2009	Catriona Matthew
1980	Pat Bradley	1988	Sally Little	1996	Laura Davies	2003	Annika Sorenstam	2010	Yani Tseng
1981	Jan Stephenson	1989	Tammie Green	1997	Colleen Walker	2004	Karen Stupples	2011	Yani Tseng
1982	Sandra Haynie	1990	Cathy Johnston	1998	Brandie Burton	2005	Jeong Jang	2012	Jiyai Shin
1983	Hollis Stacy	1991	Nancy Scranton	1999	Karrie Webb	2006	Sherri Steinhauer	2013	Stacy Lewis
1984	Juli Inkster	1992	Sherri Steinhauer	2000	Meg Mallon	2007	Lorena Ochoa	2014	Mo Martin
1985	Pat Bradley	1993	Brandie Burton	2001	Se Ri Pak	2008	Jiyai Shin	2015	Inbee Park
1986	Pat Bradley	1994	Martha Nause						

Evian Championship

Became an LPGA major tournament in 2013, when it was won by Suzann Pettersen. Hyo Joo Kim won in 2014, Lydia Ko in 2015.

Ryder Cup, 1927-2014

The Ryder Cup began in 1927 as a biennial team competition between pro male golfers from the U.S. and Great Britain. The British team was expanded in 1973 to include players from Ireland and in 1979 to golfers from the rest of Europe.

Year	Winner, score	Year	Winner, score	Year	Winner, score	Year	Winner, score
1927	U.S., 9½-2½	1955	U.S., 8-4	1975	U.S., 21-11	1995	Europe, 14½-13½
1929	Britain-Ireland, 7-5	1957	Britain-Ireland, 7½-4½	1977	U.S., 12½-7½	1997	Europe, 14½-13½
1931	U.S., 9-3	1959	U.S., 8½-3½	1979	U.S., 17-11	1999	U.S., 14½-13½
1933	Britain, 6½-5½	1961	U.S., 14½-9½	1981	U.S., 18½-9½	2002	Europe, 15½-12½
1935	U.S., 9-3	1963	U.S., 23-9	1983	U.S., 14½-13½	2004	Europe, 18½-9½
1937	U.S., 8-4	1965	U.S., 19½-12½	1985	Europe, 16½-11½	2006	Europe, 18½-9½
1947	U.S., 11-1	1967	U.S., 23½-8½	1987	Europe, 15-13	2008	U.S., 16½-11½
1949	U.S., 7-5	1969	Draw, 16-16	1989	Draw, 14-14	2010	Europe, 14½-13½
1951	U.S., 9½-2½	1971	U.S., 18½-13½	1991	U.S., 14½-13½	2012	Europe, 14½-13½
1953	U.S., 6½-5½	1973	U.S., 19-13	1993	U.S., 15-13	2014	Europe, 16½-11½

Solheim Cup, 1990-2015

The Solheim Cup began in 1990 as a biennial team competition between pro women golfers from the U.S. and Europe.

Year	Winner, score	Year	Winner, score	Year	Winner, score	Year	Winner, score
1990	U.S., 11½-4½	1998	U.S., 16-12	2005	U.S., 15½-12½	2011	Europe, 15-13
1992	Europe, 11½-6½	2000	Europe, 14½-11½	2007	U.S., 16-12	2013	Europe, 18-10
1994	U.S., 13-7	2002	U.S., 15½-12½	2009	U.S., 16-12	2015	U.S., 14½-13½
1996	U.S., 17-11	2003	Europe, 17½-10½				

Australian Open Champions, 1969-2015

First contested 1905 for men, 1922 for women. Became an open championship in 1969. Two tournaments held in 1977, in Jan. and Dec. No tournament held in 1986.

Men's Singles

Year	Champion	Final opponent
1969	Rod Laver	Andrés Gimeno
1970	Arthur Ashe	Dick Crealy
1971	Ken Rosewall	Arthur Ashe
1972	Ken Rosewall	Mal Anderson
1973	John Newcombe	Onny Parun
1974	Jimmy Connors	Phil Dent
1975	John Newcombe	Jimmy Connors
1976	Mark Edmondson	John Newcombe
1977	Roscoe Tanner	Guillermo Vilas
	Vitas Gerulaitis	John Lloyd
1978	Guillermo Vilas	John Marks
1979	Guillermo Vilas	John Sadri
1980	Brian Teacher	Kim Warwick
1981	Johan Kriek	Steve Denton
1982	Johan Kriek	Steve Denton
1983	Mats Wilander	Ivan Lendl
1984	Mats Wilander	Kevin Curren
1985	Stefan Edberg	Mats Wilander
1987	Stefan Edberg	Pat Cash
1988	Mats Wilander	Pat Cash
1989	Ivan Lendl	Miloslav Mecir
1990	Ivan Lendl	Stefan Edberg
1991	Boris Becker	Ivan Lendl
1992	Jim Courier	Stefan Edberg
1993	Jim Courier	Stefan Edberg
1994	Pete Sampras	Todd Martin
1995	Andre Agassi	Pete Sampras
1996	Boris Becker	Michael Chang
1997	Pete Sampras	Carlos Moya
1998	Petr Korda	Marcelo Rios
1999	Yevgeny Kafelnikov	Thomas Enqvist
2000	Andre Agassi	Yevgeny Kafelnikov
2001	Andre Agassi	Arnaud Clement
2002	Thomas Johansson	Marat Safin
2003	Andre Agassi	Rainer Schuettler
2004	Roger Federer	Marat Safin
2005	Marat Safin	Lleyton Hewitt
2006	Roger Federer	Marcos Baghdatis
2007	Roger Federer	Fernando Gonzalez
2008	Novak Djokovic	Jo-Wilfried Tsonga
2009	Rafael Nadal	Roger Federer
2010	Roger Federer	Andy Murray
2011	Novak Djokovic	Andy Murray
2012	Novak Djokovic	Rafael Nadal
2013	Novak Djokovic	Andy Murray
2014	Stanislas Wawrinka	Rafael Nadal
2015	Novak Djokovic	Andy Murray

Women's Singles

Year	Champion	Final opponent
1969	Margaret Smith Court	Billie Jean King
1970	Margaret Smith Court	Kerry Melville Reid
1971	Margaret Smith Court	Evonne Goolagong
1972	Virginia Wade	Evonne Goolagong
1973	Margaret Smith Court	Evonne Goolagong
1974	Evonne Goolagong	Chris Evert
1975	Evonne Goolagong	Martina Navratilova
1976	Evonne Goolagong Cawley	Renata Tomanova
1977	Kerry Reid	Dianne Balestrat
	Evonne Goolagong Cawley	Helen Gourlay
1978	Chris O'Neil	Betsy Nagelsen
1979	Barbara Jordan	Sharon Walsh
1980	Hana Mandlikova	Wendy Turnbull
1981	Martina Navratilova	Chris Evert Lloyd
1982	Chris Evert Lloyd	Martina Navratilova
1983	Martina Navratilova	Kathy Jordan
1984	Chris Evert Lloyd	Helena Sukova
1985	Martina Navratilova	Chris Evert Lloyd
1987	Hana Mandlikova	Martina Navratilova
1988	Steffi Graf	Chris Evert
1989	Steffi Graf	Helena Sukova
1990	Steffi Graf	Mary Joe Fernandez
1991	Monica Seles	Jana Novotna
1992	Monica Seles	Mary Joe Fernandez
1993	Monica Seles	Steffi Graf
1994	Steffi Graf	Arantxa Sánchez Vicario
1995	Mary Pierce	Arantxa Sánchez Vicario
1996	Monica Seles	Anke Huber
1997	Martina Hingis	Mary Pierce
1998	Martina Hingis	Conchita Martínez
1999	Martina Hingis	Amélie Mauresmo
2000	Lindsay Davenport	Martina Hingis
2001	Jennifer Capriati	Martina Hingis
2002	Jennifer Capriati	Martina Hingis
2003	Serena Williams	Venus Williams
2004	Justine Henin-Hardenne	Kim Clijsters
2005	Serena Williams	Lindsay Davenport
2006	Amélie Mauresmo	Justine Henin-Hardenne
2007	Serena Williams	Maria Sharapova
2008	Maria Sharapova	Ana Ivanovic
2009	Serena Williams	Dinara Safina
2010	Serena Williams	Justine Henin
2011	Kim Clijsters	Li Na
2012	Victoria Azarenka	Maria Sharapova
2013	Victoria Azarenka	Li Na
2014	Li Na	Dominika Cibulkova
2015	Serena Williams	Maria Sharapova

French Open (Roland Garros) Champions, 1968-2015

First contested 1891 for men, 1897 for women. Became an open championship in 1968.

Men's Singles

Year	Champion	Final opponent
1968	Ken Rosewall	Rod Laver
1969	Rod Laver	Ken Rosewall
1970	Jan Kodes	Zeljko Franulovic
1971	Jan Kodes	Ilie Nastase
1972	Andrés Gimeno	Patrick Proisy
1973	Ilie Nastase	Nikki Pilic
1974	Björn Borg	Manuel Orantes
1975	Björn Borg	Guillermo Vilas
1976	Adriano Panatta	Harold Solomon
1977	Guillermo Vilas	Brian Gottfried
1978	Björn Borg	Guillermo Vilas
1979	Björn Borg	Victor Pecci
1980	Björn Borg	Vitas Gerulaitis
1981	Björn Borg	Ivan Lendl
1982	Mats Wilander	Guillermo Vilas
1983	Yannick Noah	Mats Wilander
1984	Ivan Lendl	John McEnroe
1985	Mats Wilander	Ivan Lendl
1986	Ivan Lendl	Mikael Pernfors
1987	Ivan Lendl	Mats Wilander
1988	Mats Wilander	Henri Leconte
1989	Michael Chang	Stefan Edberg
1990	Andres Gomez	Andre Agassi
1991	Jim Courier	Andre Agassi
1992	Jim Courier	Petr Korda
1993	Sergi Bruguera	Jim Courier
1994	Sergi Bruguera	Alberto Berasategui
1995	Thomas Muster	Michael Chang
1996	Yevgeny Kafelnikov	Michael Stich
1997	Gustavo Kuerten	Sergi Bruguera
1998	Carlos Moya	Alex Corretja
1999	Andre Agassi	Andrei Medvedev
2000	Gustavo Kuerten	Magnus Norman
2001	Gustavo Kuerten	Alex Corretja
2002	Albert Costa	Juan Carlos Ferrero
2003	Juan Carlos Ferrero	Martin Verkerk
2004	Gaston Gaudio	Guillermo Coria
2005	Rafael Nadal	Mariano Puerta
2006	Rafael Nadal	Roger Federer
2007	Rafael Nadal	Roger Federer
2008	Rafael Nadal	Roger Federer
2009	Roger Federer	Robin Soderling
2010	Rafael Nadal	Robin Soderling
2011	Rafael Nadal	Roger Federer
2012	Rafael Nadal	Novak Djokovic
2013	Rafael Nadal	David Ferrer
2014	Rafael Nadal	Novak Djokovic
2015	Stan Wawrinka	Novak Djokovic

Women's Singles

Year	Champion	Final opponent
1968	Nancy Richey	Ann Jones
1969	Margaret Smith Court	Ann Jones
1970	Margaret Smith Court	Helga Niessen
1971	Evonne Goolagong	Helen Gourlay
1972	Billie Jean King	Evonne Goolagong
1973	Margaret Smith Court	Chris Evert
1974	Chris Evert	Olga Morozova
1975	Chris Evert	Martina Navratilova
1976	Sue Barker	Renata Tomanova
1977	Mima Jausovec	Florenta Mihai
1978	Virginia Ruzici	Mima Jausovec
1979	Chris Evert Lloyd	Wendy Turnbull
1980	Chris Evert Lloyd	Virginia Ruzici
1981	Hana Mandlikova	Sylvia Hanika
1982	Martina Navratilova	Andrea Jaeger

Year	Champion	Final opponent
1983	Chris Evert Lloyd	Mima Jausovec
1984	Martina Navratilova	Chris Evert Lloyd
1985	Chris Evert Lloyd	Martina Navratilova
1986	Chris Evert Lloyd	Martina Navratilova
1987	Steffi Graf	Martina Navratilova
1988	Steffi Graf	Natalia Zvereva
1989	Arantxa Sánchez Vicario	Steffi Graf
1990	Monica Seles	Steffi Graf
1991	Monica Seles	Arantxa Sánchez Vicario
1992	Monica Seles	Steffi Graf
1993	Steffi Graf	Mary Joe Fernandez
1994	Arantxa Sánchez Vicario	Mary Pierce
1995	Steffi Graf	Arantxa Sánchez Vicario
1996	Steffi Graf	Arantxa Sánchez Vicario
1997	Iva Majoli	Martina Hingis
1998	Arantxa Sánchez Vicario	Monica Seles
1999	Steffi Graf	Martina Hingis
2000	Mary Pierce	Conchita Martínez
2001	Jennifer Capriati	Kim Clijsters
2002	Serena Williams	Venus Williams
2003	Justine Henin-Hardenne	Kim Clijsters
2004	Anastasia Myskina	Elena Dementieva
2005	Justine Henin-Hardenne	Mary Pierce
2006	Justine Henin-Hardenne	Svetlana Kuznetsova
2007	Justine Henin	Ana Ivanovic
2008	Ana Ivanovic	Dinara Safina
2009	Svetlana Kuznetsova	Dinara Safina
2010	Francesca Schiavone	Samantha Stosur
2011	Li Na	Francesca Schiavone
2012	Maria Sharapova	Sara Errani
2013	Serena Williams	Maria Sharapova
2014	Maria Sharapova	Simona Halep
2015	Serena Williams	Lucie Safarova

Wimbledon Champions, 1925-2015

First contested 1877 for men, 1884 for women. Became an open championship in 1968. Not held 1940-45.

Men's Singles

Year	Champion	Final opponent
1925	René Lacoste	Jean Borotra
1926	Jean Borotra	Howard Kinsey
1927	Henri Cochet	Jean Borotra
1928	René Lacoste	Henri Cochet
1929	Henri Cochet	Jean Borotra
1930	Bill Tilden	Wilmer Allison
1931	Sidney B. Wood	Francis X. Shields
1932	Ellsworth Vines	Henry Austin
1933	Jack Crawford	Ellsworth Vines
1934	Fred Perry	Jack Crawford
1935	Fred Perry	Gottfried von Cramm
1936	Fred Perry	Gottfried von Cramm
1937	Donald Budge	Gottfried von Cramm
1938	Donald Budge	Henry Austin
1939	Bobby Riggs	Elwood Cooke
1946	Yvon Petra	Geoff E. Brown
1947	Jack Kramer	Tom P. Brown
1948	Bob Falkenburg	John Bromwich
1949	Ted Schroeder	Jaroslav Drobny
1950	Budge Patty	Frank Sedgman
1951	Dick Savitt	Ken McGregor
1952	Frank Sedgman	Jaroslav Drobny
1953	Vic Seixas	Kurt Nielsen
1954	Jaroslav Drobny	Ken Rosewall
1955	Tony Trabert	Kurt Nielsen
1956	Lew Hoad	Ken Rosewall
1957	Lew Hoad	Ashley Cooper
1958	Ashley Cooper	Neale Fraser
1959	Alex Olmedo	Rod Laver
1960	Neale Fraser	Rod Laver
1961	Rod Laver	Chuck McKinley
1962	Rod Laver	Martin Mulligan
1963	Chuck McKinley	Fred Stolle
1964	Roy Emerson	Fred Stolle
1965	Roy Emerson	Fred Stolle
1966	Manuel Santana	Dennis Ralston
1967	John Newcombe	Wilhelm Bungert
1968	Rod Laver	Tony Roche
1969	Rod Laver	John Newcombe
1970	John Newcombe	Ken Rosewall
1971	John Newcombe	Stan Smith
1972	Stan Smith	Ilie Nastase
1973	Jan Kodes	Alex Metreveli
1974	Jimmy Connors	Ken Rosewall
1975	Arthur Ashe	Jimmy Connors
1976	Björn Borg	Ilie Nastase
1977	Björn Borg	Jimmy Connors
1978	Björn Borg	Jimmy Connors
1979	Björn Borg	Roscoe Tanner
1980	Björn Borg	John McEnroe
1981	John McEnroe	Björn Borg
1982	Jimmy Connors	John McEnroe
1983	John McEnroe	Chris Lewis
1984	John McEnroe	Jimmy Connors
1985	Boris Becker	Kevin Curren
1986	Boris Becker	Ivan Lendl
1987	Pat Cash	Ivan Lendl
1988	Stefan Edberg	Boris Becker
1989	Boris Becker	Stefan Edberg
1990	Stefan Edberg	Boris Becker
1991	Michael Stich	Boris Becker
1992	Andre Agassi	Goran Ivanisevic
1993	Pete Sampras	Jim Courier
1994	Pete Sampras	Goran Ivanisevic
1995	Pete Sampras	Boris Becker
1996	Richard Krajicek	MaliVai "Mai" Washington
1997	Pete Sampras	Cedric Pioline
1998	Pete Sampras	Goran Ivanisevic
1999	Pete Sampras	Andre Agassi
2000	Pete Sampras	Patrick Rafter
2001	Goran Ivanisevic	Patrick Rafter
2002	Lleyton Hewitt	David Nalbandian
2003	Roger Federer	Mark Philippoussis
2004	Roger Federer	Andy Roddick
2005	Roger Federer	Andy Roddick
2006	Roger Federer	Rafael Nadal
2007	Roger Federer	Rafael Nadal
2008	Rafael Nadal	Roger Federer
2009	Roger Federer	Andy Roddick
2010	Rafael Nadal	Tomas Berdych
2011	Novak Djokovic	Rafael Nadal
2012	Roger Federer	Andy Murray
2013	Andy Murray	Novak Djokovic
2014	Novak Djokovic	Roger Federer
2015	Novak Djokovic	Roger Federer

Women's Singles

Year	Champion	Final opponent
1925	Suzanne Lenglen	Joan Fry
1926	Kathleen McKane Godfree	Lili de Alvarez
1927	Helen Wills	Lili de Alvarez
1928	Helen Wills	Lili de Alvarez
1929	Helen Wills	Helen H. Jacobs
1930	Helen Wills Moody	Elizabeth Ryan
1931	Cilly Aussem	Hilde Krahwinkel
1932	Helen Wills Moody	Helen H. Jacobs
1933	Helen Wills Moody	Dorothy Round
1934	Dorothy Round	Helen H. Jacobs
1935	Helen Wills Moody	Helen H. Jacobs
1936	Helen H. Jacobs	Hilde Krahwinkel Sperling
1937	Dorothy Round	Jadwiga Jedrzejowska
1938	Helen Wills Moody	Helen H. Jacobs
1939	Alice Marble	Kay Stammers
1946	Pauline Betz	Louise Brough
1947	Margaret Osborne	Doris Hart
1948	Louise Brough	Doris Hart
1949	Louise Brough	Margaret Osborne duPont
1950	Louise Brough	Margaret Osborne duPont
1951	Doris Hart	Shirley Fry
1952	Maureen Connolly	Louise Brough
1953	Maureen Connolly	Doris Hart
1954	Maureen Connolly	Louise Brough
1955	Louise Brough	Beverly Fleitz
1956	Shirley Fry	Angela Buxton
1957	Althea Gibson	Darlene Hard
1958	Althea Gibson	Angela Mortimer
1959	Maria Bueno	Darlene Hard
1960	Maria Bueno	Sandra Reynolds
1961	Angela Mortimer	Christine Truman
1962	Karen Hantze-Susman	Vera Sukova
1963	Margaret Smith	Billie Jean Moffitt
1964	Maria Bueno	Margaret Smith
1965	Margaret Smith	Maria Bueno
1966	Billie Jean King	Maria Bueno
1967	Billie Jean King	Ann Haydon Jones
1968	Billie Jean King	Judy Tegart
1969	Ann Haydon Jones	Billie Jean King
1970	Margaret Smith Court	Billie Jean King
1971	Evonne Goolagong	Margaret Smith Court
1972	Billie Jean King	Evonne Goolagong
1973	Billie Jean King	Chris Evert
1974	Chris Evert	Olga Morozova
1975	Billie Jean King	Evonne Goolagong Cawley

Year	Champion	Final opponent
1976	Chris Evert	Evonne Goolagong Cawley
1977	Virginia Wade	Betty Stove
1978	Martina Navratilova	Chris Evert
1979	Martina Navratilova	Chris Evert Lloyd
1980	Evonne Goolagong Cawley	Chris Evert Lloyd
1981	Chris Evert Lloyd	Hana Mandlikova
1982	Martina Navratilova	Chris Evert Lloyd
1983	Martina Navratilova	Andrea Jaeger
1984	Martina Navratilova	Chris Evert Lloyd
1985	Martina Navratilova	Chris Evert Lloyd
1986	Martina Navratilova	Hana Mandlikova
1987	Martina Navratilova	Steffi Graf
1988	Steffi Graf	Martina Navratilova
1989	Steffi Graf	Martina Navratilova
1990	Martina Navratilova	Zina Garrison
1991	Steffi Graf	Gabriela Sabatini
1992	Steffi Graf	Monica Seles
1993	Steffi Graf	Jana Novotna
1994	Conchita Martínez	Martina Navratilova
1995	Steffi Graf	Arantxa Sánchez Vicario
1996	Steffi Graf	Arantxa Sánchez Vicario
1997	Martina Hingis	Jana Novotna
1998	Jana Novotna	Nathalie Tauziat
1999	Lindsay Davenport	Steffi Graf
2000	Venus Williams	Lindsay Davenport
2001	Venus Williams	Justine Henin
2002	Serena Williams	Venus Williams
2003	Serena Williams	Venus Williams
2004	Maria Sharapova	Serena Williams
2005	Venus Williams	Lindsay Davenport
2006	Amélie Mauresmo	Justine Henin-Hardenne
2007	Venus Williams	Marion Bartoli
2008	Venus Williams	Serena Williams
2009	Serena Williams	Venus Williams
2010	Serena Williams	Vera Zvonareva
2011	Petra Kvitova	Maria Sharapova
2012	Serena Williams	Agnieszka Radwanska
2013	Marion Bartoli	Sabine Lisicki
2014	Petra Kvitova	Eugenie Bouchard
2015	Serena Williams	Garbiñe Muguruza

U.S. Open Champions, 1925-2015

First contested 1881 for men, 1887 for women. The former U.S. National Championship became an open championship in 1968.

Men's Singles

Year	Champion	Final opponent
1925	Bill Tilden	William Johnston
1926	René Lacoste	Jean Borotra
1927	René Lacoste	Bill Tilden
1928	Henri Cochet	Francis Hunter
1929	Bill Tilden	Francis Hunter
1930	John Doeg	Francis X. Shields
1931	Ellsworth Vines	George Lott
1932	Ellsworth Vines	Henri Cochet
1933	Fred Perry	John Crawford
1934	Fred Perry	Wilmer Allison
1935	Wilmer Allison	Sidney Wood
1936	Fred Perry	Don Budge
1937	Don Budge	Gottfried von Cramm
1938	Don Budge	C. Gene Mako
1939	Bobby Riggs	S. Welby Van Horn
1940	Don McNeill	Bobby Riggs
1941	Bobby Riggs	F. L. Kovacs
1942	F. R. Schroeder Jr.	Frank Parker
1943	Joseph Hunt	Jack Kramer
1944	Frank Parker	Bill Talbert
1945	Frank Parker	Bill Talbert
1946	Jack Kramer	Tom Brown Jr.
1947	Jack Kramer	Frank Parker
1948	Pancho Gonzales	Eric Sturgess
1949	Pancho Gonzales	F. R. Schroeder Jr.
1950	Arthur Larsen	Herbert Flam
1951	Frank Sedgman	E. Victor Seixas Jr.
1952	Frank Sedgman	Gardnar Mulloy
1953	Tony Trabert	E. Victor Seixas Jr.
1954	E. Victor Seixas Jr.	Rex Hartwig
1955	Tony Trabert	Ken Rosewall
1956	Ken Rosewall	Lewis Hoad
1957	Malcolm Anderson	Ashley Cooper
1958	Ashley Cooper	Malcolm Anderson
1959	Neale A. Fraser	Alejandro Olmedo
1960	Neale A. Fraser	Rod Laver
1961	Roy Emerson	Rod Laver
1962	Rod Laver	Roy Emerson
1963	Rafael Osuna	F. A. Froehling III
1964	Roy Emerson	Fred Stolle
1965	Manuel Santana	Cliff Drysdale
1966	Fred Stolle	John Newcombe
1967	John Newcombe	Clark Graebner
1968	Arthur Ashe	Tom Okker
1969	Rod Laver	Tony Roche
1970	Ken Rosewall	Tony Roche
1971	Stan Smith	Jan Kodes
1972	Ilie Nastase	Arthur Ashe
1973	John Newcombe	Jan Kodes
1974	Jimmy Connors	Ken Rosewall
1975	Manuel Orantes	Jimmy Connors
1976	Jimmy Connors	Björn Borg
1977	Guillermo Vilas	Jimmy Connors
1978	Jimmy Connors	Björn Borg
1979	John McEnroe	Vitas Gerulaitis
1980	John McEnroe	Björn Borg
1981	John McEnroe	Björn Borg
1982	Jimmy Connors	Ivan Lendl
1983	Jimmy Connors	Ivan Lendl
1984	John McEnroe	Ivan Lendl
1985	Ivan Lendl	John McEnroe
1986	Ivan Lendl	Miloslav Mecir
1987	Ivan Lendl	Mats Wilander
1988	Mats Wilander	Ivan Lendl
1989	Boris Becker	Ivan Lendl
1990	Pete Sampras	Andre Agassi
1991	Stefan Edberg	Jim Courier
1992	Stefan Edberg	Pete Sampras
1993	Pete Sampras	Cedric Pioline
1994	Andre Agassi	Michael Stich
1995	Pete Sampras	Andre Agassi
1996	Pete Sampras	Michael Chang
1997	Patrick Rafter	Greg Rusedski
1998	Patrick Rafter	Mark Philippoussis
1999	Andre Agassi	Todd Martin
2000	Marat Safin	Pete Sampras
2001	Lleyton Hewitt	Pete Sampras
2002	Pete Sampras	Andre Agassi
2003	Andy Roddick	Juan Carlos Ferrero
2004	Roger Federer	Lleyton Hewitt
2005	Roger Federer	Andre Agassi
2006	Roger Federer	Andy Roddick
2007	Roger Federer	Novak Djokovic
2008	Roger Federer	Andy Murray
2009	Juan Martin del Potro	Roger Federer
2010	Rafael Nadal	Novak Djokovic
2011	Novak Djokovic	Rafael Nadal
2012	Andy Murray	Novak Djokovic
2013	Rafael Nadal	Novak Djokovic
2014	Marin Cilic	Kei Nishikori
2015	Novak Djokovic	Roger Federer

Women's Singles

Year	Champion	Final opponent
1925	Helen Willis	Kathleen McKane
1926	Molla B. Mallory	Elizabeth Ryan
1927	Helen Wills	Betty Nuthall
1928	Helen Wills	Helen H. Jacobs
1929	Helen Wills	Phoebe Holcroft-Watson
1930	Betty Nuthall	Anna McCune Harper
1931	Helen Wills Moody	E. B. Whittingstall
1932	Helen H. Jacobs	Carolin A. Babcock
1933	Helen H. Jacobs	Helen Wills Moody
1934	Helen H. Jacobs	Sarah H. Palfrey
1935	Helen H. Jacobs	Sarah Palfrey Fabyan
1936	Alice Marble	Helen H. Jacobs
1937	Anita Lizana	Jadwiga Jedrzejowska
1938	Alice Marble	Nancye Wynne
1939	Alice Marble	Helen H. Jacobs
1940	Alice Marble	Helen H. Jacobs
1941	Sarah Palfrey Cooke	Pauline Betz
1942	Pauline Betz	Louise Brough
1943	Pauline Betz	Louise Brough
1944	Pauline Betz	Margaret Osborne
1945	Sarah Palfrey Cooke	Pauline Betz
1946	Pauline Betz	Patricia Canning
1947	Louise Brough	Margaret Osborne
1948	Margaret Osborne duPont	Louise Brough
1949	Margaret Osborne duPont	Doris Hart
1950	Margaret Osborne duPont	Doris Hart
1951	Maureen Connolly	Shirley Fry
1952	Maureen Connolly	Doris Hart
1953	Maureen Connolly	Doris Hart

Year	Champion	Final opponent
1954	Doris Hart	Louise Brough
1955	Doris Hart	Patricia Ward
1956	Shirley Fry	Althea Gibson
1957	Althea Gibson	Louise Brough
1958	Althea Gibson	Darlene Hard
1959	Maria Bueno	Christine Truman
1960	Darlene Hard	Maria Bueno
1961	Darlene Hard	Ann Haydon
1962	Margaret Smith	Darlene Hard
1963	Maria Bueno	Margaret Smith
1964	Maria Bueno	Carole Graebner
1965	Margaret Smith	Billie Jean Moffitt
1966	Maria Bueno	Nancy Richey
1967	Billie Jean King	Ann Haydon Jones
1968	Virginia Wade	Billie Jean King
1969	Margaret Smith Court	Nancy Richey
1970	Margaret Smith Court	Rosemary Casals
1971	Billie Jean King	Rosemary Casals
1972	Billie Jean King	Kerry Melville
1973	Margaret Smith Court	Evonne Goolagong
1974	Billie Jean King	Evonne Goolagong
1975	Chris Evert	Evonne Goolagong Cawley
1976	Chris Evert	Evonne Goolagong Cawley
1977	Chris Evert	Wendy Turnbull
1978	Chris Evert	Pam Shriver
1979	Tracy Austin	Chris Evert Lloyd
1980	Chris Evert Lloyd	Hana Mandlikova
1981	Tracy Austin	Martina Navratilova
1982	Chris Evert Lloyd	Hana Mandlikova
1983	Martina Navratilova	Chris Evert Lloyd
1984	Martina Navratilova	Chris Evert Lloyd
1985	Hana Mandlikova	Martina Navratilova
1986	Martina Navratilova	Helena Sukova
1987	Martina Navratilova	Steffi Graf
1988	Steffi Graf	Gabriela Sabatini
1989	Steffi Graf	Martina Navratilova
1990	Gabriela Sabatini	Steffi Graf
1991	Monica Seles	Martina Navratilova
1992	Monica Seles	Arantxa Sánchez Vicario
1993	Steffi Graf	Helena Sukova
1994	Arantxa Sánchez Vicario	Steffi Graf
1995	Steffi Graf	Monica Seles
1996	Steffi Graf	Monica Seles
1997	Martina Hingis	Venus Williams
1998	Lindsay Davenport	Martina Hingis
1999	Serena Williams	Martina Hingis
2000	Venus Williams	Lindsay Davenport
2001	Venus Williams	Serena Williams
2002	Serena Williams	Venus Williams
2003	Justine Henin-Hardenne	Kim Clijsters
2004	Svetlana Kuznetsova	Elena Dementieva
2005	Kim Clijsters	Mary Pierce
2006	Maria Sharapova	Justine Henin-Hardenne
2007	Justine Henin	Svetlana Kuznetsova
2008	Serena Williams	Jelena Jankovic
2009	Kim Clijsters	Caroline Wozniacki
2010	Kim Clijsters	Vera Zvonareva
2011	Samantha Stosur	Serena Williams
2012	Serena Williams	Victoria Azarenka
2013	Serena Williams	Victoria Azarenka
2014	Serena Williams	Caroline Wozniacki
2015	Flavia Pennetta	Roberta Vinci

Davis Cup, 1950-2014

The Davis Cup began in 1900 as a competition between the U.S. and Great Britain and later expanded to include other countries.

Year	Result
1950	Australia 4, U.S. 1
1951	Australia 3, U.S. 2
1952	Australia 4, U.S. 1
1953	Australia 3, U.S. 2
1954	U.S. 3, Australia 2
1955	Australia 5, U.S. 0
1956	Australia 5, U.S. 0
1957	Australia 3, U.S. 2
1958	U.S. 3, Australia 2
1959	Australia 3, U.S. 2
1960	Australia 4, Italy 1
1961	Australia 5, Italy 0
1962	Australia 5, Mexico 0
1963	U.S. 3, Australia 2
1964	Australia 3, U.S. 2
1965	Australia 4, Spain 1
1966	Australia 4, India 1
1967	Australia 4, Spain 1
1968	U.S. 4, Australia 1
1969	U.S. 5, Romania 0
1970	U.S. 5, W. Germany 0
1971	U.S. 3, Romania 2
1972	U.S. 3, Romania 2
1973	Australia 5, U.S. 0
1974	South Africa (default by India)
1975	Sweden 3, Czechoslovakia 2
1976	Italy 4, Chile 1
1977	Australia 3, Italy 1
1978	U.S. 4, Great Britain 1
1979	U.S. 5, Italy 0
1980	Czechoslovakia 4, Italy 1
1981	U.S. 3, Argentina 1
1982	U.S. 4, France, 1
1983	Australia 3, Sweden 2
1984	Sweden 4, U.S. 1
1985	Sweden 3, W. Germany 2
1986	Australia 3, Sweden 2
1987	Sweden 5, India 0
1988	W. Germany 4, Sweden 1
1989	W. Germany 3, Sweden 2
1990	U.S. 3, Australia 2
1991	France 3, U.S. 1
1992	U.S. 3, Switzerland 1
1993	Germany 4, Australia 1
1994	Sweden 4, Russia 1
1995	U.S. 3, Russia 2
1996	France 3, Sweden 2
1997	Sweden 5, U.S. 0
1998	Sweden 4, Italy 1
1999	Australia 3, France 2
2000	Spain 3, Australia 1
2001	France 3, Australia 2
2002	Russia 3, France 2
2003	Australia 3, Spain 1
2004	Spain 3, U.S. 2
2005	Croatia 3, Slovakia 2
2006	Russia 3, Argentina 2
2007	U.S. 4, Russia 1
2008	Spain 3, Argentina 1
2009	Spain 3, Czech Republic 0
2010	Serbia 3, France 2
2011	Spain 3, Argentina 1
2012	Czech Republic 3, Spain 2
2013	Czech Republic 3, Serbia 2
2014	Switzerland 3, France 1

Note: The challenge round format, which guaranteed the previous year's winner a spot in the finals at home, was eliminated in 1972.

All-Time Grand Slam Singles Titles Leaders

Men	Australian Open	French Open[1]	Wimbledon	U.S. Open	Total
Roger Federer	2004, '06-'07, '10	2009	2003-07, '09, '12	2004-08	17
Rafael Nadal	2009	2005-08, '10-'14	2008, '10	2010, '13	14
Pete Sampras	1994, '97	—	1993-95, 1997-2000	1990, '93, '95-'96, 2002	14
Roy Emerson	1961, '63-'67	1963, '67	1964-65	1961, '64	12
Björn Borg	—	1974-75, '78-'81	1976-80	—	11
Rod Laver	1960, '62, '69	1962, '69	1961-62, '68-'69	1962, '69	11
Bill Tilden	—	—	1920-21, '30	1920-25, '29	10
Novak Djokovic	2008, '11-'13, '15	—	2011, '14-'15	2011, '15	10
Andre Agassi	1995, 2000, '01, '03	1999	1992	1994, '99	8
Jimmy Connors	1974	—	1974, '82	1974, '76, '78, '82-'83	8
Ivan Lendl	1989-90	1984, '86-'87	—	1985-87	8
Fred Perry	1934	1935	1934-36	1933-34, '36	8
Ken Rosewall	1953, '55, '71-'72	1953, '68	—	1956, '70	8
Women	**Australian Open**	**French Open[1]**	**Wimbledon**	**U.S. Open**	**Total**
Margaret Smith Court	1960-66, '69-'71, '73	1962, '64, '69-'70, '73	1963, '65, '70	1962, '65, '69-'70, '73	24
Steffi Graf	1988-90, '94	1987-88, '93, '95-'96, '99	1988-89, '91-'93, '95-'96	1988-89, '93, '95-'96	22
Serena Williams	2003, '05, '07, '09-'10, '15	2002, '13, '15	2002-03, '09-'10, '12, '15	1999, 2002, '08, '12-'14	21
Helen Wills Moody	—	1928-30, '32	1927-30, '32-'33, '35, '38	1923-25, '27-'29, '31	19
Chris Evert	1982, '84	1974-75, '79-'80, '83, '85-'86	1974, '76, '81	1975-78, '80, '82	18
Martina Navratilova	1981, '83, '85	1982, '84	1978-79, '82-'87, '90	1983-84, '86-'87	18
Billie Jean King	1968	1972	1966-68, '72-'73, '75	1967, '71-'72, '74	12
Suzanne Lenglen	—	1920-23, '25-'26	1919-23, '25	—	12
Maureen Connolly	1953	1953-54	1952-54	1951-53	9
Monica Seles	1991-93, '96	1990-92	—	1991-92	9

Note: Players active in 2015 are in bold. (1) Prior to 1925, French Open entry was limited to members of French clubs.

Indianapolis 500 Winners, 1911-2015

At Indianapolis Motor Speedway in Indianapolis, IN. Not held 1917-18, 1942-45. * = Race record.

Year	Driver(s), car[1]	Avg. mph
1911	Ray Harroun, Marmon	74.602
1912	Joe Dawson, National	78.719
1913	Jules Goux, Peugeot	75.933
1914	Rene Thomas, Delage	82.474
1915	Ralph DePalma, Mercedes	89.840
1916	Dario Resta, Peugeot	84.001
1919	Howdy Wilcox, Peugeot	88.050
1920	Gaston Chevrolet, Frontenac	88.618
1921	Tommy Milton, Frontenac	89.621
1922	Jimmy Murphy, Duesenberg-Miller	94.484
1923	Tommy Milton, Miller	90.954
1924	L. L. Corum/Joe Boyer, Duesenberg	98.234
1925	Peter DePaolo, Duesenberg	101.127
1926	Frank Lockhart, Miller	95.904
1927	George Souders, Duesenberg	97.545
1928	Louis Meyer, Miller	99.482
1929	Ray Keech, Miller	97.585
1930	Billy Arnold, Summers-Miller	100.448
1931	Louis Schneider, Stevens-Miller	96.629
1932	Fred Frame, Wetteroth-Miller	104.144
1933	Louis Meyer, Miller	104.162
1934	Bill Cummings, Miller	104.863
1935	Kelly Petillo, Wetteroth-Offy	106.240
1936	Louis Meyer, Stevens-Miller	109.069
1937	Wilbur Shaw, Shaw-Offy	113.580
1938	Floyd Roberts, Wetteroth-Miller	117.200
1939	Wilbur Shaw, Maserati	115.035
1940	Wilbur Shaw, Maserati	114.277
1941	Floyd Davis/Mauri Rose, Wetteroth-Offy	115.117
1946	George Robson, Adams-Sparks	114.820
1947	Mauri Rose, Deidt-Offy	116.338
1948	Mauri Rose, Deidt-Offy	119.814
1949	Bill Holland, Deidt-Offy	121.327
1950	Johnnie Parsons, Kurtis-Offy	124.002
1951	Lee Wallard, Kurtis-Offy	126.244
1952	Troy Ruttman, Kuzma-Offy	128.922
1953	Bill Vukovich, KK500A-Offy	127.740
1954	Bill Vukovich, KK500A-Offy	130.840
1955	Bob Sweikert, KK500C-Offy	128.213
1956	Pat Flaherty, Watson-Offy	128.490
1957	Sam Hanks, Salih-Offy	135.601
1958	Jimmy Bryan, Salih-Offy	133.791
1959	Rodger Ward, Watson-Offy	135.857
1960	Jim Rathmann, Watson-Offy	138.767
1961	A. J. Foyt, Trevis-Offy	139.130
1962	Rodger Ward, Watson-Offy	140.293
1963	Parnelli Jones, Watson-Offy	143.137
1964	A. J. Foyt, Watson-Offy	147.350
1965	Jim Clark, Lotus-Ford	150.686
1966	Graham Hill, Lola-Ford	144.317
1967	A. J. Foyt, Coyote-Ford	151.207
1968	Bobby Unser, Eagle-Offy	152.882
1969	Mario Andretti, Hawk-Ford	156.867
1970	Al Unser, P.J. Colt-Ford	155.749
1971	Al Unser, P.J. Colt-Ford	157.735
1972	Mark Donohue, McLaren-Offy	162.962
1973	Gordon Johncock, Eagle-Offy	159.036
1974	Johnny Rutherford, McLaren-Offy	158.589
1975	Bobby Unser, Eagle-Offy	149.213
1976	Johnny Rutherford, McLaren-Offy	148.725
1977	A. J. Foyt, Coyote-Foyt	161.331
1978	Al Unser, Lola-Cosworth	161.363
1979	Rick Mears, Penske-Cosworth	158.899
1980	Johnny Rutherford, Chaparral-Cosworth	142.862
1981	Bobby Unser, Penske-Cosworth	139.084
1982	Gordon Johncock, Wildcat-Cosworth	162.029
1983	Tom Sneva, March-Cosworth	162.117
1984	Rick Mears, March-Cosworth	163.612
1985	Danny Sullivan, March-Cosworth	152.982
1986	Bobby Rahal, March-Cosworth	170.722
1987	Al Unser, March-Cosworth	162.175
1988	Rick Mears, Penske-Chevy Indy V8	144.809
1989	Emerson Fittipaldi, Penske-Chevy Indy V8	167.581
1990	Arie Luyendyk, Lola-Chevy Indy V8	185.981
1991	Rick Mears, Penske-Chevy Indy V8	176.457
1992	Al Unser Jr., Galmer-Chevy Indy V8A	134.477
1993	Emerson Fittipaldi, Penske-Chevy Indy V8C	157.207
1994	Al Unser Jr., Penske-Mercedes Benz	160.872
1995	Jacques Villeneuve, Reynard-Ford Cosworth XB	153.616
1996	Buddy Lazier, Reynard-Ford Cosworth XB	147.956
1997	Arie Luyendyk, G Force-Aurora	145.827
1998	Eddie Cheever Jr., Dallara-Aurora	145.155
1999	Kenny Brack, Dallara-Aurora	153.176
2000	Juan Pablo Montoya, G Force-Oldsmobile	167.607
2001	Helio Castroneves, Dallara-Oldsmobile	141.574
2002	Helio Castroneves, Dallara-Chevrolet	166.499
2003	Gil de Ferran, G Force-Toyota	156.291
2004	Buddy Rice, G Force-Honda	138.518
2005	Dan Wheldon, Dallara-Honda	157.603
2006	Sam Hornish Jr., Dallara-Honda	157.085
2007	Dario Franchitti, Dallara-Honda	151.774
2008	Scott Dixon, Dallara-Honda	143.567
2009	Helio Castroneves, Dallara-Honda	150.318
2010	Dario Franchitti, Dallara-Honda	161.623
2011	Dan Wheldon, Dallara-Honda	170.265
2012	Dario Franchitti, Dallara-Honda	167.734
2013	Tony Kanaan, Dallara-Chevrolet	187.433*
2014	Ryan Hunter-Reay, Dallara-Honda	186.563
2015	Juan Pablo Montoya, Dallara-Chevrolet	161.341

Note: The race was less than 500 mi in the following years: 1916 (300 mi), 1926 (400 mi), 1950 (345 mi), 1973 (332.5 mi), 1975 (435 mi), 1976 (255 mi), 2004 (450 mi), 2007 (415 mi). (1) Chassis-engine.

IndyCar Series Champions, 1996-2015

A breakaway group of Championship Auto Racing Teams (CART) drivers began the Indy Racing League (IRL) in 1994; it awarded its first championship in 1996. Known as the IndyCar Series in 2003-11 and as IndyCar from 2011 on. Merged with Champ Car World Series, 2008.

Year	Driver
1996	Scott Sharp; Buzz Calkins (tie)
1997	Tony Stewart
1998	Kenny Brack
1999	Greg Ray
2000	Buddy Lazier
2001	Sam Hornish Jr.
2002	Sam Hornish Jr.
2003	Scott Dixon
2004	Tony Kanaan
2005	Dan Wheldon
2006	Sam Hornish Jr.
2007	Dario Franchitti
2008	Scott Dixon
2009	Dario Franchitti
2010	Dario Franchitti
2011	Dario Franchitti
2012	Ryan Hunter-Reay
2013	Scott Dixon
2014	Will Power
2015	Scott Dixon

Champ Car World Series Winners, 1959-2007

Known as U.S. Auto Club, 1959-78; Championship Auto Racing Teams (CART), 1979-2003; Champ Car World Series, 2004-07. The Vanderbilt Cup became the series championship trophy in 2000. Merged with Indy Racing League (now IndyCar) in 2008.

Year	Driver
1959	Rodger Ward
1960	A. J. Foyt
1961	A. J. Foyt
1962	Rodger Ward
1963	A. J. Foyt
1964	A. J. Foyt
1965	Mario Andretti
1966	Mario Andretti
1967	A. J. Foyt
1968	Bobby Unser
1969	Mario Andretti
1970	Al Unser
1971	Joe Leonard
1972	Joe Leonard
1973	Roger McCluskey
1974	Bobby Unser
1975	A. J. Foyt
1976	Gordon Johncock
1977	Tom Sneva
1978	Tom Sneva
1979	Rick Mears
1980	Johnny Rutherford
1981	Rick Mears
1982	Rick Mears
1983	Al Unser
1984	Mario Andretti
1985	Al Unser
1986	Bobby Rahal
1987	Bobby Rahal
1988	Danny Sullivan
1989	Emerson Fittipaldi
1990	Al Unser Jr.
1991	Michael Andretti
1992	Bobby Rahal
1993	Nigel Mansell
1994	Al Unser Jr.
1995	Jacques Villeneuve
1996	Jimmy Vasser
1997	Alex Zanardi
1998	Alex Zanardi
1999	Juan Montoya
2000	Gil de Ferran
2001	Gil de Ferran
2002	Cristiano da Matta
2003	Paul Tracy
2004	Sébastien Bourdais
2005	Sébastien Bourdais
2006	Sébastien Bourdais
2007	Sébastien Bourdais

NASCAR Sprint Cup Series Champions, 1949-2014

Known as Strictly Stock, 1949; Grand National, 1950-70; Winston Cup, 1971-2003; and Sprint Cup, 2004-present.

Year	Driver
1949	Red Byron
1950	Bill Rexford
1951	Herb Thomas
1952	Tim Flock
1953	Herb Thomas
1954	Lee Petty
1955	Tim Flock
1956	Buck Baker
1957	Buck Baker
1958	Lee Petty
1959	Lee Petty
1960	Rex White
1961	Ned Jarrett
1962	Joe Weatherly
1963	Joe Weatherly
1964	Richard Petty
1965	Ned Jarrett
1966	David Pearson
1967	Richard Petty
1968	David Pearson
1969	David Pearson
1970	Bobby Isaac
1971	Richard Petty
1972	Richard Petty
1973	Benny Parsons
1974	Richard Petty
1975	Richard Petty
1976	Cale Yarborough
1977	Cale Yarborough
1978	Cale Yarborough
1979	Richard Petty
1980	Dale Earnhardt
1981	Darrell Waltrip
1982	Darrell Waltrip
1983	Bobby Allison
1984	Terry Labonte
1985	Darrell Waltrip
1986	Dale Earnhardt
1987	Dale Earnhardt
1988	Bill Elliott
1989	Rusty Wallace
1990	Dale Earnhardt
1991	Dale Earnhardt
1992	Alan Kulwicki
1993	Dale Earnhardt
1994	Dale Earnhardt
1995	Jeff Gordon
1996	Terry Labonte
1997	Jeff Gordon
1998	Jeff Gordon
1999	Dale Jarrett
2000	Bobby Labonte
2001	Jeff Gordon
2002	Tony Stewart
2003	Matt Kenseth
2004	Kurt Busch
2005	Tony Stewart
2006	Jimmie Johnson
2007	Jimmie Johnson
2008	Jimmie Johnson
2009	Jimmie Johnson
2010	Jimmie Johnson
2011	Tony Stewart
2012	Brad Keselowski
2013	Jimmie Johnson
2014	Kevin Harvick

NASCAR Sprint Cup Series Rookie of the Year, 1958-2014

Year	Driver
1958	Shorty Rollins
1959	Richard Petty
1960	David Pearson
1961	Woodie Wilson
1962	Tom Cox
1963	Billy Wade
1964	Doug Cooper
1965	Sam McQuagg
1966	James Hylton
1967	Donnie Allison
1968	Pete Hamilton
1969	Dick Brooks
1970	Bill Dennis
1971	Walter Ballard
1972	Larry Smith
1973	Lennie Pond
1974	Earl Ross
1975	Bruce Hill
1976	Skip Manning
1977	Ricky Rudd
1978	Ronnie Thomas
1979	Dale Earnhardt
1980	Jody Riley
1981	Ron Bouchard
1982	Geoff Bodine
1983	Sterling Marlin
1984	Rusty Wallace
1985	Ken Schrader
1986	Alan Kulwicki
1987	Davey Allison
1988	Ken Bouchard
1989	Dick Trickle
1990	Rob Moroso
1991	Bobby Hamilton
1992	Jimmy Hensley
1993	Jeff Gordon
1994	Jeff Burton
1995	Ricky Craven
1996	Johnny Benson
1997	Mike Skinner
1998	Kenny Irwin
1999	Tony Stewart
2000	Matt Kenseth
2001	Kevin Harvick
2002	Ryan Newman
2003	Jamie McMurray
2004	Kasey Kahne
2005	Kyle Busch
2006	Denny Hamlin
2007	Juan Montoya
2008	Regan Smith
2009	Joey Logano
2010	Kevin Conway
2011	Andy Lally
2012	Stephen Leicht
2013	Ricky Stenhouse Jr.
2014	Kyle Larson

Daytona 500 Winners, 1959-2015

At Daytona International Speedway in Daytona Beach, FL.

Year	Driver, car	Avg. mph
1959	Lee Petty, Oldsmobile	135.521
1960	Junior Johnson, Chevrolet	124.740
1961	Marvin Panch, Pontiac	149.601
1962	Fireball Roberts, Pontiac	152.529
1963	Tiny Lund, Ford	151.566
1964	Richard Petty, Plymouth	154.334
1965	Fred Lorenzen, Ford	141.539
1966	Richard Petty, Plymouth	160.627
1967	Mario Andretti, Ford	146.926
1968	Cale Yarborough, Mercury	143.251
1969	LeeRoy Yarbrough, Ford	157.950
1970	Pete Hamilton, Plymouth	149.601
1971	Richard Petty, Plymouth	144.462
1972	A. J. Foyt, Mercury	161.550
1973	Richard Petty, Dodge	157.205
1974	Richard Petty, Dodge	140.894
1975	Benny Parsons, Chevrolet	153.649
1976	David Pearson, Mercury	152.181
1977	Cale Yarborough, Chevrolet	153.218
1978	Bobby Allison, Ford	159.730
1979	Richard Petty, Oldsmobile	143.977
1980	Buddy Baker, Oldsmobile	177.602
1981	Richard Petty, Buick	169.651
1982	Bobby Allison, Buick	153.991
1983	Cale Yarborough, Pontiac	155.979
1984	Cale Yarborough, Chevrolet	150.994
1985	Bill Elliott, Ford	172.265
1986	Geoff Bodine, Chevrolet	148.124
1987	Bill Elliott, Ford	176.263
1988	Bobby Allison, Buick	137.531
1989	Darrell Waltrip, Chevrolet	148.466
1990	Derrike Cope, Chevrolet	165.761
1991	Ernie Irvan, Chevrolet	148.148
1992	Davey Allison, Ford	160.256
1993	Dale Jarrett, Chevrolet	154.972
1994	Sterling Marlin, Chevrolet	156.931
1995	Sterling Marlin, Chevrolet	141.710
1996	Dale Jarrett, Ford	154.308
1997	Jeff Gordon, Chevrolet	148.295
1998	Dale Earnhardt, Chevrolet	172.712
1999	Jeff Gordon, Chevrolet	161.551
2000	Dale Jarrett, Ford	155.669
2001	Michael Waltrip, Chevrolet	161.783
2002	Ward Burton, Dodge	142.971
2003	Michael Waltrip, Chevrolet	133.870
2004	Dale Earnhardt Jr., Chevrolet	156.345
2005	Jeff Gordon, Chevrolet	135.173
2006	Jimmie Johnson, Chevrolet	142.667
2007	Kevin Harvick, Chevrolet	149.335
2008	Ryan Newman, Dodge	152.672
2009	Matt Kenseth, Ford	132.816
2010	Jamie McMurray, Chevrolet	137.284
2011	Trevor Bayne, Ford	130.326
2012	Matt Kenseth, Ford	140.256
2013	Jimmie Johnson, Chevrolet	159.250
2014	Dale Earnhardt Jr., Chevrolet	145.290
2015	Joey Logano, Ford	161.939

Note: The race was less than 500 mi in the following years: 1965 (322.5 mi), 1966 (495 mi), 1974 (450 mi), 2003 (272.5 mi), 2009 (380 mi).

Coca-Cola 600 Winners, 1960-2015

At Charlotte Motor Speedway in Concord, NC. Known as the World 600, 1960-85. * = Rain-shortened.

Year	Driver, car	Avg. mph
1960	Joe Lee Johnson, Chevrolet	107.735
1961	David Pearson, Pontiac	111.633
1962	Nelson Stacy, Ford	125.552
1963	Fred Lorenzen, Ford	132.418
1964	Jim Paschal, Plymouth	125.772
1965	Fred Lorenzen, Ford	121.722
1966	Marvin Panch, Plymouth	135.042
1967	Jim Paschal, Plymouth	135.832
1968	Buddy Baker, Dodge	104.207*
1969	LeeRoy Yarbrough, Mercury	134.361
1970	Donnie Allison, Ford	129.680
1971	Bobby Allison, Mercury	140.422
1972	Buddy Baker, Dodge	142.255
1973	Buddy Baker, Dodge	134.890
1974	David Pearson, Mercury	135.720
1975	Richard Petty, Dodge	145.327
1976	David Pearson, Mercury	137.352
1977	Richard Petty, Dodge	137.676
1978	Darrell Waltrip, Chevrolet	138.355
1979	Darrell Waltrip, Chevrolet	136.674
1980	Benny Parsons, Chevrolet	119.265
1981	Bobby Allison, Buick	129.326
1982	Neil Bonnett, Ford	130.058
1983	Neil Bonnett, Chevrolet	140.707
1984	Bobby Allison, Buick	129.233
1985	Darrell Waltrip, Chevrolet	141.807
1986	Dale Earnhardt, Chevrolet	140.406
1987	Kyle Petty, Ford	131.483
1988	Darrell Waltrip, Chevrolet	124.460
1989	Darrell Waltrip, Chevrolet	144.077
1990	Rusty Wallace, Pontiac	137.650
1991	Davey Allison, Ford	138.951
1992	Dale Earnhardt, Chevrolet	132.980
1993	Dale Earnhardt, Chevrolet	145.504
1994	Jeff Gordon, Chevrolet	139.445
1995	Bobby Labonte, Chevrolet	151.952
1996	Dale Jarrett, Ford	147.581
1997	Jeff Gordon, Chevrolet	136.745*
1998	Jeff Gordon, Chevrolet	136.424
1999	Jeff Burton, Ford	151.367
2000	Matt Kenseth, Ford	142.640
2001	Jeff Burton, Ford	138.107
2002	Mark Martin, Ford	137.729
2003	Jimmie Johnson, Chevrolet	126.198*
2004	Jimmie Johnson, Chevrolet	142.763
2005	Jimmie Johnson, Chevrolet	114.698
2006	Kasey Kahne, Dodge	128.840
2007	Casey Mears, Chevrolet	130.222
2008	Kasey Kahne, Dodge	135.772
2009	David Reutimann, Toyota	120.899*
2010	Kurt Busch, Dodge	144.966
2011	Kevin Harvick, Chevrolet	132.414
2012	Kasey Kahne, Chevrolet	155.687
2013	Kevin Harvick, Chevrolet	130.521
2014	Jimmie Johnson, Chevrolet	145.484
2015	Carl Edwards, Toyota	147.803

Brickyard 400 Winners, 1994-2015

At Indianapolis Motor Speedway in Indianapolis, IN.

Year	Driver, car	Avg. mph
1994	Jeff Gordon, Chevrolet	131.977
1995	Dale Earnhardt, Chevrolet	155.206
1996	Dale Jarrett, Ford	139.508
1997	Ricky Rudd, Ford	130.814
1998	Jeff Gordon, Chevrolet	126.772
1999	Dale Jarrett, Ford	148.194
2000	Bobby Labonte, Pontiac	155.912
2001	Jeff Gordon, Chevrolet	130.790
2002	Bill Elliott, Dodge	125.033
2003	Kevin Harvick, Chevrolet	134.554
2004	Jeff Gordon, Chevrolet	115.037
2005	Tony Stewart, Chevrolet	118.782
2006	Jimmie Johnson, Chevrolet	137.182
2007	Tony Stewart, Chevrolet	117.379
2008	Jimmie Johnson, Chevrolet	115.117
2009	Jimmie Johnson, Chevrolet	145.882
2010	Jamie McMurray, Chevrolet	136.054
2011	Paul Menard, Chevrolet	140.762
2012	Jimmie Johnson, Chevrolet	137.680
2013	Ryan Newman, Chevrolet	153.485
2014	Jeff Gordon, Chevrolet	150.297
2015	Kyle Busch, Toyota	131.656

Irwin Tools Night Race Winners, 1961-2015

At Bristol Motor Speedway in Bristol, TN. Known as the Volunteer 500, 1961-75, '78-'79; Volunteer 400, 1976-77; Busch 500, 1980-90; Bud 500, 1991-93; Goody's 500, 1994-99; goracing.com 500, 2000; Sharpie 500, 2001-09. * = Rain-shortened.

Year	Driver, car	Avg. mph
1961	Jack Smith, Pontiac	68.373
1962	Bobby Johns, Pontiac	73.320
1963	Fred Lorenzen, Ford	74.844
1964	Fred Lorenzen, Ford	78.044
1965	Ned Jarrett, Ford	61.826
1966	Paul Goldsmith, Plymouth	77.963
1967	Richard Petty, Plymouth	78.705
1968	David Pearson, Ford	76.310
1969	David Pearson, Ford	79.737
1970	Bobby Allison, Dodge	84.880
1971	Charlie Glotzbach, Chevrolet	101.074
1972	Bobby Allison, Chevrolet	92.735
1973	Benny Parsons, Chevrolet	91.342
1974	Cale Yarborough, Chevrolet	75.430
1975	Richard Petty, Dodge	97.016
1976	Cale Yarborough, Chevrolet	99.175
1977	Cale Yarborough, Chevrolet	79.726
1978	Cale Yarborough, Olds.	88.628
1979	Darrell Waltrip, Chevrolet	91.493
1980	Cale Yarborough, Chevrolet	86.973
1981	Darrell Waltrip, Buick	84.723
1982	Darrell Waltrip, Buick	94.318
1983	Darrell Waltrip, Chevrolet	89.430*
1984	Terry Labonte, Chevrolet	85.365
1985	Dale Earnhardt, Chevrolet	81.388
1986	Darrell Waltrip, Chevrolet	86.934
1987	Dale Earnhardt, Chevrolet	90.373
1988	Dale Earnhardt, Chevrolet	78.775
1989	Darrell Waltrip, Chevrolet	85.554
1990	Ernie Irvan, Chevrolet	91.782
1991	Alan Kulwicki, Ford	82.028
1992	Darrell Waltrip, Chevrolet	91.198
1993	Mark Martin, Ford	88.172
1994	Rusty Wallace, Ford	91.363
1995	Terry Labonte, Chevrolet	81.979
1996	Rusty Wallace, Ford	91.267
1997	Dale Jarrett, Ford	80.013
1998	Mark Martin, Ford	86.949
1999	Dale Earnhardt, Chevrolet	91.276
2000	Rusty Wallace, Ford	85.394
2001	Tony Stewart, Pontiac	85.106
2002	Jeff Gordon, Chevrolet	77.097
2003	Kurt Busch, Ford	77.421
2004	Dale Earnhardt Jr., Chevrolet	88.538
2005	Matt Kenseth, Ford	84.678
2006	Matt Kenseth, Ford	90.025
2007	Carl Edwards, Ford	89.006
2008	Carl Edwards, Ford	91.581
2009	Kyle Busch, Toyota	84.820
2010	Kyle Busch, Toyota	99.071
2011	Brad Keselowski, Dodge	96.753
2012	Denny Hamlin, Toyota	84.402
2013	Matt Kenseth, Toyota	90.279
2014	Joey Logano, Ford	92.965
2015	Joey Logano, Ford	96.890

NASCAR Sprint All-Star Race Winners, 1985-2015

At Charlotte Motor Speedway in Concord, NC. Known as The Winston, 1985-93, 1997-2003; The Winston Select, 1994-96; and Nextel All-Star Challenge, 2004-07.

Year	Driver, car
1985	Darrell Waltrip, Chevrolet
1986	Bill Elliott, Ford
1987	Dale Earnhardt, Chevrolet
1988	Terry Labonte, Chevrolet
1989	Rusty Wallace, Pontiac
1990	Dale Earnhardt, Chevrolet
1991	Davey Allison, Ford
1992	Davey Allison, Ford
1993	Dale Earnhardt, Chevrolet
1994	Geoffrey Bodine, Ford
1995	Jeff Gordon, Chevrolet
1996	Michael Waltrip, Ford
1997	Jeff Gordon, Chevrolet
1998	Mark Martin, Ford
1999	Terry Labonte, Chevrolet
2000	Dale Earnhardt Jr., Chevrolet
2001	Jeff Gordon, Chevrolet
2002	Ryan Newman, Ford
2003	Jimmie Johnson, Chevrolet
2004	Matt Kenseth, Ford
2005	Mark Martin, Ford
2006	Jimmie Johnson, Chevrolet
2007	Kevin Harvick, Chevrolet
2008	Kasey Kahne, Dodge
2009	Tony Stewart, Chevrolet
2010	Kurt Busch, Dodge
2011	Carl Edwards, Ford
2012	Jimmie Johnson, Chevrolet
2013	Jimmie Johnson, Chevrolet
2014	Jamie McMurray, Chevrolet
2015	Denny Hamlin, Toyota

Formula One World Drivers' Champions, 1950-2014

Awarded by the Fédération Internationale de l'Automobile (FIA); champions determined through a series of Grand Prix races.

Year	Driver, country
1950	Giuseppe "Nino" Farina, Italy
1951	Juan Manuel Fangio, Argentina
1952	Alberto Ascari, Italy
1953	Alberto Ascari, Italy
1954	Juan Manuel Fangio, Argentina
1955	Juan Manuel Fangio, Argentina
1956	Juan Manuel Fangio, Argentina
1957	Juan Manuel Fangio, Argentina
1958	Mike Hawthorn, England, UK
1959	Jack Brabham, Australia
1960	Jack Brabham, Australia
1961	Phil Hill, United States
1962	Graham Hill, England, UK
1963	Jim Clark, Scotland, UK
1964	John Surtees, England, UK
1965	Jim Clark, Scotland, UK
1966	Jack Brabham, Australia
1967	Denis Hulme, New Zealand
1968	Graham Hill, England, UK
1969	Jackie Stewart, Scotland, UK
1970	Jochen Rindt, Austria
1971	Jackie Stewart, Scotland, UK
1972	Emerson Fittipaldi, Brazil
1973	Jackie Stewart, Scotland, UK
1974	Emerson Fittipaldi, Brazil
1975	Niki Lauda, Austria
1976	James Hunt, England, UK
1977	Niki Lauda, Austria
1978	Mario Andretti, United States
1979	Jody Scheckter, South Africa
1980	Alan Jones, Australia
1981	Nelson Piquet, Brazil
1982	Keke Rosberg, Finland
1983	Nelson Piquet, Brazil
1984	Niki Lauda, Austria
1985	Alain Prost, France
1986	Alain Prost, France
1987	Nelson Piquet, Brazil
1988	Ayrton Senna, Brazil
1989	Alain Prost, France
1990	Ayrton Senna, Brazil
1991	Ayrton Senna, Brazil
1992	Nigel Mansell, England, UK
1993	Alain Prost, France
1994	Michael Schumacher, Germany
1995	Michael Schumacher, Germany
1996	Damon Hill, England, UK
1997	Jacques Villeneuve, Canada
1998	Mika Hakkinen, Finland
1999	Mika Hakkinen, Finland
2000	Michael Schumacher, Germany
2001	Michael Schumacher, Germany
2002	Michael Schumacher, Germany
2003	Michael Schumacher, Germany
2004	Michael Schumacher, Germany
2005	Fernando Alonso, Spain
2006	Fernando Alonso, Spain
2007	Kimi Raikkonen, Finland
2008	Lewis Hamilton, England, UK
2009	Jenson Button, England, UK
2010	Sebastian Vettel, Germany
2011	Sebastian Vettel, Germany
2012	Sebastian Vettel, Germany
2013	Sebastian Vettel, Germany
2014	Lewis Hamilton, England, UK

24 Hours of Le Mans Race, 2015

Porsche won the 24 Hours of Le Mans at Circuit de la Sarthe in Le Mans, France, June 13-14, 2015, ending Audi's five-year winning streak. The team of Germany's Nico Hulkenberg (currently active on the Formula One circuit), Earl Bamber of New Zealand, and the UK's Nick Tandy completed 395 laps in the No. 19 Porsche 919 Hybrid to bring Porsche its record 17th victory in the endurance race. Porsche also took second place in the 83rd running of the race with its No. 17 car. The 2014 championship team of Switzerland's Marcel Fassler, Andre Lotterer of Germany, and France's Benoit Treluyer finished third in the No. 7 Audi R18 e-tron quattro. Audi had won seven of the previous eight events.

BOXING

There are many boxing governing bodies, including the World Boxing Assn. (WBA; known as the National Boxing Assn. [NBA] until 1962), World Boxing Council (WBC), International Boxing Fed. (IBF), World Boxing Org., U.S. Boxing Assn., N. American Boxing Fed., and European Boxing Union. All have their own champions and divisions.

Boxing Champions by Class

Class (weight limit)	WBA Champion	WBC Champion	IBF Champion
Heavyweight (none)	Wladimir Klitschko, Ukraine[1] Ruslan Chagaev, Uzbekistan[2]	Deontay Wilder, U.S.	Wladimir Klitschko, Ukraine
Cruiserweight (200 lbs)	Denis Lebedev, Russia Beibut Shumenov, Kazakhstan[3]	Grigory Drozd, Russia	Yoan Pablo Hernandez, Germany Victor Emilio Ramirez, Argentina[3]
Light Heavyweight (175 lbs)	Sergey Kovalev, Russia Juergen Braehmer, Germany[2] Felix Valera, Dominican Republic[3]	Adonis Stevenson, Canada	Sergey Kovalev, Russia
Super Middleweight (168 lbs)	Andre Ward, U.S.[1] Fedor Chudinov, Russia[2] Vincent Feigenbutz, Germany[3]	Badou Jack, Sweden	James DeGale, UK
Middleweight (160 lbs)	Gennady Golovkin, Kazakhstan[1] Daniel Jacobs, U.S.[2] Chris Eubank Jr., UK[3]	Miguel Cotto, Puerto Rico Gennady Golovkin, Kazakhstan[3]	David Lemieux, Canada
Super Welterweight/ Jr. Middleweight (154 lbs)	Floyd Mayweather Jr., U.S.[1] Erislandy Lara, Cuba[2] Jack Culcay, Germany[3]	Floyd Mayweather Jr., U.S.	Jermall Charlo, U.S.
Welterweight (147 lbs)	Floyd Mayweather Jr., U.S. Keith Thurman, U.S.[2] Andre Berto, U.S.[3]	Floyd Mayweather Jr., U.S.	Kell Brook, UK
Super Lightweight/ Jr. Welterweight (140 lbs)	Jose Benavidez Jr., U.S.[3]	Vacant	Cesar Cuenca, Argentina
Lightweight (135 lbs)	Darleys Perez, Colombia	Jorge Linares, Venezuela	Vacant
Super Featherweight/ Jr. Lightweight (130 lbs)	Takashi Uchiyama, Japan[1] Javier Fortuna, Dominican Republic[2]	Takashi Miura, Japan	Jose Pedraza, U.S.
Featherweight (126 lbs)	Leo Santa Cruz, Mexico[1] Jesus Andres Cuellar, Argentina	Gary Russell Jr., U.S.	Lee Selby, Wales
Super Bantamweight/ Jr. Featherweight (122 lbs)	Guillermo Rigondeaux, Cuba Scott Quigg, UK[2]	Leo Santa Cruz, Mexico Julio Cesar Ceja, Mexico[3]	Carl Frampton, Northern Ireland
Bantamweight (118 lbs)	Juan Carlos Payano, Dominican Republic Jamie McDonnell, UK[2]	Shinsuke Yamanaka, Japan	Randy Caballero, U.S. Lee Haskins, UK[3]
Super Flyweight/ Jr. Bantamweight (115 lbs)	Kohei Kono, Japan	Carlos Cuadras, Mexico	McJoe Arroyo, Puerto Rico
Flyweight (112 lbs)	Juan Francisco Estrada, Mexico Kazuto Ioka, Japan[2]	Roman Gonzalez, Nicaragua	Amnat Ruenroeng, Thailand
Jr. Flyweight (108 lbs)	Ryoichi Taguchi, Japan	Pedro Guevara, Mexico	Javier Mendoza, Mexico
Strawweight/ Mini Flyweight (105 lbs)	Hekkie Budler, South Africa	Wanheng Menayothin, Thailand	Katsunari Takayama, Japan

Note: As of Sept. 21, 2015. Interim champions for WBA classes below 135 lbs are not shown. (1) Super champion (holds title of two or more WBA-recognized orgs.). (2) Regular champion. (3) Interim champion.

Ring Champions by Years

* = Abandoned/relinquished the title or was stripped of it. IBF champions listed only for heavyweight division. International Boxing Hall of Fame inductees in *italics*. For years with multiple champions, boxers are listed according to date of earliest title bout.

Heavyweights

1882-92	*John L. Sullivan*[1]
1892-97	*James J. Corbett*[2]
1897-99	*Bob Fitzsimmons*
1899-1905	*James J. Jeffries**[3]
1905-06	Marvin Hart
1906-08	*Tommy Burns*
1908-15	*Jack Johnson*
1915-19	*Jess Willard*
1919-26	*Jack Dempsey*
1926-28	*Gene Tunney**
1928-30	Vacant
1930-32	*Max Schmeling*
1932-33	*Jack Sharkey*
1933-34	Primo Carnera
1934-35	*Max Baer*
1935-37	*James J. Braddock*
1937-49	*Joe Louis**
1949-51	*Ezzard Charles*
1951-52	*Joe Walcott*
1952-56	*Rocky Marciano**
1956-59	*Floyd Patterson*
1959-60	*Ingemar Johansson*
1960-62	*Floyd Patterson*
1962-64	*Sonny Liston*
1964-67	*Cassius Clay (Muhammad Ali)**[4]
1968-70	Jimmy Ellis[4]
1970-73	*Joe Frazier*
1973-74	*George Foreman*
1974-78	*Muhammad Ali*
1978	Leon Spinks (WBA/WBC*)[5]; *Ken Norton* (WBC)
1978-79	*Muhammad Ali* (WBA*)[5]
1978-83	*Larry Holmes* (WBC*)[6]
1979-80	John Tate (WBA)
1980-82	Mike Weaver (WBA)
1982-83	Michael Dokes (WBA)
1983-84	Gerrie Coetzee (WBA)
1983-85	*Larry Holmes* (IBF)[6]
1984	Tim Witherspoon (WBC)
1984-86	Pinklon Thomas (WBC)
1984-85	Greg Page (WBA)
1985-86	Tony Tubbs (WBA)
1985-87	*Michael Spinks* (IBF*)
1986	Tim Witherspoon (WBA); Trevor Berbick (WBC)
1986-87	*Mike Tyson* (WBC); James "Bonecrusher" Smith (WBA)
1987	Tony Tucker (IBF)
1987-90	*Mike Tyson* (WBA/WBC/IBF)
1990	James "Buster" Douglas (WBA/WBC/IBF)
1990-92	Evander Holyfield (WBA/WBC/IBF)
1992-93	*Riddick Bowe* (WBA/WBC*/IBF)
1992-94	*Lennox Lewis* (WBC)
1993-94	Evander Holyfield (WBA/IBF)
1994	Michael Moorer (WBA/IBF)
1994-95	Oliver McCall (WBC); *George Foreman* (WBA*/IBF*)
1995-96	Bruce Seldon (WBA); Frank Bruno (WBC)
1995	Frans Botha (IBF*)
1996	*Mike Tyson* (WBA/WBC*)
1996-97	Michael Moorer (IBF)
1996-99	Evander Holyfield (WBA/IBF)
1997-99	*Lennox Lewis* (WBC)
1999-2001	*Lennox Lewis* (WBA*/WBC/IBF)
2000-01	Evander Holyfield (WBA)
2001-03	John Ruiz (WBA)
2001	Hasim Rahman (WBC/IBF)
2001-02	*Lennox Lewis* (IBF*)
2001-04	*Lennox Lewis* (WBC)
2002-06	Chris Byrd (IBF)
2003	Roy Jones Jr. (WBA*)
2004-05	John Ruiz (WBA)[7]; Vitali Klitschko (WBC*)
2005-06	Hasim Rahman (WBC)
2005-07	Nicolai Valuev (WBA)
2006-	Wladimir Klitschko (IBF)
2006-08	Oleg Maskaev (WBC)
2007-08	Ruslan Chagaev (WBA)
2008	Samuel Peter (WBC)
2008-09	Nikolai Valuev (WBA)
2008-13	Vitali Klitschko (WBC)
2009-11	David Haye (WBA)
2011-	Wladimir Klitschko (WBA)
2014-15	Bermane Stiverne (WBC)
2015-	Deontay Wilder (WBC)

(1) London Prize Ring (bare-knuckle champion). (2) First Marquis of Queensberry champion. (3) Jeffries vacated title (1905) and designated Marvin Hart and Jack Root as logical contenders. Hart def. Root in 12 rounds (1905); in turn was def. by Tommy Burns (1906), who claimed the title. Jack Johnson def. Burns (1908) and was recognized as champ. Johnson won the title by defeating Jeffries in the latter's attempted comeback (1910). (4) Title declared vacant by the WBA and others in 1967 after Ali refused military induction for religious reasons during the Vietnam War. Joe Frazier recognized as champ by six states, Mexico, and S. America. Jimmy Ellis won a tournament for the WBA title. (5) After Spinks def. Ali for the WBA title, the WBC recognized Ken Norton as champ. Ali def. Spinks in 1978 rematch for WBA title and retired in 1979. (6) Relinquished WBC title in Dec. 1983 to fight as champ of the new IBF. (7) James Toney def. Ruiz Apr. 30, 2005, to claim the title, but it was rescinded when Toney tested positive for steroids.

Light Heavyweights

1903	*Jack Root*; George Gardner
1903-05	*Bob Fitzsimmons*
1905-12	*Philadelphia Jack O'Brien**
1912-16	*Jack Dillon*
1916-20	*Battling Levinsky*
1920-22	*Georges Carpentier*
1922-23	Battling Siki
1923-25	Mike McTigue
1925-26	*Paul Berlenbach*
1926-27	*Jack Delaney**
1927-29	*Tommy Loughran**
1930-34	*Maxie Rosenbloom*
1934-35	Bob Olin
1935-39	*John Henry Lewis**
1939	Melio Bettina
1939-41	*Billy Conn**
1941	Anton Christoforidis (NBA)
1941-48	Gus Lesnevich
1948-50	Freddie Mills
1950-52	*Joey Maxim*
1952-62	*Archie Moore*
1962-63	*Harold Johnson*
1963-65	*Willie Pastrano*
1965-66	*Jose Torres*
1966-68	*Dick Tiger*
1968-74	*Bob Foster**
1974-77	John Conteh (WBC)
1974-78	*Victor Galindez* (WBA)
1977-78	Miguel Cuello (WBC)
1978	Mate Parlov (WBC)
1978-79	Mike Rossman (WBA); Marvin Johnson (WBC)
1979	*Victor Galindez* (WBA)
1979-81	*Matthew Saad Muhammad* (WBC)
1979-80	Marvin Johnson (WBA)
1980-81	Eddie Mustafa Muhammad (WBA)
1981-85	*Michael Spinks* (WBA)
1981-83	*Dwight Muhammed-Qawi Braxton* (WBC)
1983-85	*Michael Spinks* (WBC*)
1985-86	J. B. Williamson (WBC)
1986-87	Marvin Johnson (WBA); Dennis Andries (WBC)
1987	*Thomas Hearns* (WBC*)
1987	Leslie Stewart (WBA)
1987-91	*Virgil Hill* (WBA)
1987-88	Don Lalonde (WBC)
1988	*Sugar Ray Leonard* (WBC*)
1989	Dennis Andries (WBC)
1989-90	Jeff Harding (WBC)
1990-91	Dennis Andries (WBC)
1991-92	*Thomas Hearns* (WBA)
1991-94	Jeff Harding (WBC)
1992	Iran Barkley (WBA*)
1992-97	*Virgil Hill* (WBA)
1994-95	*Mike McCallum* (WBC)
1995-96	Fabrice Tiozzo (WBC*)
1996-97	Roy Jones Jr. (WBC)
1997	Montell Griffin (WBC); Darius Michalczewski (WBA*); Roy Jones Jr. (WBC)
1997-98	Lou Del Valle (WBA)
1998-2003	Roy Jones Jr. (WBA*/WBC*)
2003	Mehdi Sahnoune (WBA); Silvio Branco (WBA); Antonio Tarver (WBC)
2003-04	Roy Jones Jr. (WBA/WBC*)
2004	Antonio Tarver (WBA/WBC*)
2004-06	Fabrice Tiozzo (WBA)
2005-07	Tomasz Adamek (WBC)
2006-07	Silvio Branco (WBA)
2007-08	Chad Dawson (WBC)
2007	Stipe Drews (WBA); Danny Green (WBA)
2008-09	Hugo Hernan Garay (WBA); Adrian Diaconu (WBC)
2009-11	Jean Pascal (WBC)
2009-10	Gabriel Campillo (WBA)
2010-14	Beibut Shumenov (WBA)
2011-12	Bernard Hopkins (WBC)
2012-13	Chad Dawson (WBC)
2013-	Adonis Stevenson (WBC)
2014	Bernard Hopkins (WBA)
2014-	Sergey Kovalev (WBA)

Middleweights

1884-91	*Jack "Nonpareil" Dempsey*
1891-97	*Bob Fitzsimmons**
1897-1907	*Tommy Ryan**
1907-08	*Stanley Ketchel*; *Billy Papke*
1908-10	*Stanley Ketchel*
1911-13	Vacant
1913	Frank Klaus; George Chip
1914-17	Al McCoy
1917-20	*Mike O'Dowd*
1920-23	Johnny Wilson
1923-26	*Harry Greb*
1926	*Theodore "Tiger" Flowers*
1926-31	*Mickey Walker*
1931-32	*William "Gorilla" Jones* (NBA)
1932-37	*Marcel Thil*
1938	Al Hostak (NBA); Solly Krieger (NBA)
1939-40	Al Hostak (NBA)
1940-47	*Tony Zale*
1947-48	*Rocky Graziano*
1948	*Tony Zale*; *Marcel Cerdan*
1949-51	*Jake LaMotta*
1951	*"Sugar" Ray Robinson*; *Randy Turpin*; *"Sugar" Ray Robinson**
1953-55	*Carl "Bobo" Olson*
1955-57	*"Sugar" Ray Robinson*
1957	*Gene Fullmer*; *"Sugar" Ray Robinson*
1957-58	*Carmen Basilio*
1958	*"Sugar" Ray Robinson*
1959	*Gene Fullmer* (NBA); *"Sugar" Ray Robinson* (NY)
1960	*Gene Fullmer* (NBA); Paul Pender (NY/MA)
1961	*Gene Fullmer* (NBA); Terry Downes (NY/MA/Europe)
1962	*Gene Fullmer*; Paul Pender (NY/MA*); *Dick Tiger* (NBA)
1963	*Dick Tiger* (universal)
1963-65	*Joey Giardello*
1965-66	*Dick Tiger*
1966-67	*Emile Griffith*
1967	*Nino Benvenuti*
1967-68	*Emile Griffith*
1968-70	*Nino Benvenuti*
1970-77	*Carlos Monzon**
1977-78	Rodrigo Valdez
1978-79	Hugo Corro
1979-80	Vito Antuofermo
1980	Alan Minter
1980-87	*"Marvelous" Marvin Hagler*
1987	*Sugar Ray Leonard* (WBC*)
1987-89	Sumbu Kalambay (WBA)
1987-88	*Thomas Hearns* (WBC)
1988-89	Iran Barkley (WBC)
1989-90	*Roberto Duran* (WBC*)
1989-91	*Mike McCallum* (WBA)
1990-93	Julian Jackson (WBC)
1992-93	Reggie Johnson (WBA)
1993-95	Gerald McClellan (WBC*)
1993-94	John David Jackson (WBA)
1994-97	Jorge Castro (WBA)
1995	Julian Jackson (WBC)
1995-96	Quincy Taylor (WBC); Shinji Takehara (WBA)
1996-98	Keith Holmes (WBC)
1996-97	William Joppy (WBA)
1997	Julio Cesar Green (WBA)
1998-2001	William Joppy (WBA)
1998-99	Hassine Cherifi (WBC)
1999-2001	Keith Holmes (WBC)
2001	*Felix Trinidad* (WBA)
2001-05	Bernard Hopkins (WBC/WBA)
2005-06	Jermain Taylor (WBA)
2005-07	Jermain Taylor (WBC)
2006-07	Javier Castillejo (WBA)[1]
2007-12	Felix Sturm (WBA)
2007-10	Kelly Pavlik (WBC)
2009-11	Sebastian Zbik (WBC)
2010	Sergio Martinez (WBC)
2011-12	Julio Cesar Chavez Jr. (WBC)
2012	Daniel Geale (WBA*)
2012-14	Sergio Martinez (WBC)
2012-	Gennady Golovkin (WBA)
2014-	Miguel Cotto (WBC)

(1) Castillejo lost title to Mariano Carrera Dec. 2, 2006, but regained it Feb. 23, 2007, after Carrera tested positive for steroids.

Welterweights

1892-94	*"Mysterious" Billy Smith*
1894-96	*Tommy Ryan*
1896	*Kid McCoy**
1900	Rube Ferns; Matty Matthews
1901	Rube Ferns
1901-04	*Joe Walcott*
1904-06	*Dixie Kid*; *Joe Walcott*
1906	William "Honey" Mellody
1907-11	Mike Sullivan
1911-15	Vacant
1915-19	*Ted Lewis*
1919-22	*Jack Britton*
1922-26	*Mickey Walker*
1926-27	Pete Latzo
1927-29	Joe Dundee
1929-30	Jackie Fields
1930	Jack Thompson; Tommy Freeman
1931	Tommy Freeman; Jack Thompson; *Lou Brouillard*
1932	*Jackie Fields*
1933	*Young Corbett III*; *Jimmy McLarnin*
1934	*Barney Ross*; *Jimmy McLarnin*
1935-38	*Barney Ross*
1938-40	*Henry Armstrong*
1940-41	*Fritzie Zivic*
1941-46	Fred Cochrane
1946	Marty Servo*
1946-51	*"Sugar" Ray Robinson**[1]
1951	Johnny Bratton (NBA)
1951-54	*Kid Gavilan*
1954-55	Johnny Saxton
1955	Tony De Marco
1955-56	*Carmen Basilio*
1956	Johnny Saxton
1956-57	*Carmen Basilio**
1958	Virgil Akins
1958-60	Don Jordan
1960-61	Benny Paret
1961	*Emile Griffith*
1961-62	Benny Paret
1962-63	*Emile Griffith*
1963	*Luis Rodriguez*
1963-66	*Emile Griffith**
1966-69	*Curtis Cokes*
1969-70	*Jose Napoles*
1970-71	Billy Backus
1971-75	*Jose Napoles*
1975-76	Angel Espada (WBA); John Stracey (WBC)
1976-79	*Carlos Palomino* (WBC)
1976-80	*Jose "Pipino" Cuevas* (WBA)
1979	*Wilfred Benitez* (WBC)
1979-80	*Sugar Ray Leonard* (WBC)
1980	*Roberto Duran* (WBC)
1980-81	*Thomas Hearns* (WBA)
1980-82	*Sugar Ray Leonard* (WBC*/WBA*)
1983-85	Donald Curry (WBA); Milton McCrory (WBC)
1985-86	Donald Curry (WBC)
1986-87	Lloyd Honeyghan (WBC)
1987	Mark Breland (WBA)
1987-88	Marlon Starling (WBA); Jorge Vaca (WBC)
1988-89	Tomas Molinares (WBA*); Lloyd Honeyghan (WBC)

1989-90	Marlon Starling (WBC); Mark Breland (WBA)
1990-91	Maurice Blocker (WBC); Aaron Davis (WBA)
1991-92	Meldrick Taylor (WBA)
1991	Simon Brown (WBC)
1991-93	Buddy McGirt (WBC)
1992-94	Crisanto Espana (WBA)
1993-97	_Pernell Whitaker_ (WBC)
1994-98	Ike Quartey (WBA*)
1997-99	_Oscar De La Hoya_ (WBC*)
1998-2000	James Page (WBA*)
1999-2000	_Felix Trinidad_ (WBC*)
2000	_Oscar De La Hoya_ (WBC*)
2000-02	Shane Mosley (WBC)
2001-02	Andrew Lewis (WBA)
2002-03	Vernon Forrest (WBC)
2002	Ricardo Mayorga (WBA)
2003	Ricardo Mayorga (WBA/WBC)
2003-05	Cory Spinks (WBA/WBC)
2005-06	Zab Judah (WBA/WBC)
2006	Carlos Baldomir (WBC); Ricky Hatton (WBA)
2006-08	Floyd Mayweather Jr. (WBC); Miguel Cotto (WBA)
2008	Antonio Margarito (WBA)
2008-11	Andre Berto (WBC)
2009	Shane Mosley (WBA)
2009-12	Vyacheslav Senchenko (WBA)
2011	Victor Ortiz (WBC)
2011-	Floyd Mayweather Jr. (WBC)
2012-13	Paulie Malignaggi (WBA)
2013	Adrien Broner (WBA); Marcos Maidana (WBA)
2014-	Floyd Mayweather Jr. (WBA)

(1) Robinson gained the title by defeating Tommy Bell in an elimination agreed to by the New York Commission and the National Boxing Association. Both claimed Robinson waived his title when he won the middleweight crown from Jake LaMotta in 1951.

Lightweights

1896-99	_George "Kid" Lavigne_
1899-1902	Frank Erne
1902-08	_Joe Gans_
1908-10	_Oscar "Battling" Nelson_
1910-12	_Ad Wolgast_
1912-14	_Willie Ritchie_
1914-17	_Freddie Welsh_
1917-25	_Benny Leonard_*
1925	Jimmy Goodrich; _Rocky Kansas_
1926-30	_Sammy Mandell_
1930	_Al Singer_; _Tony Canzoneri_
1930-33	_Tony Canzoneri_
1933-35	_Barney Ross_*
1935-36	_Tony Canzoneri_
1936-38	_Lou Ambers_
1938	_Henry Armstrong_
1939	_Lou Ambers_
1940	_Lew Jenkins_
1941-43	_Sammy Angott_
1944	_Sammy Angott_ (NBA); Juan Zurita (NBA)
1945-51	_Ike Williams_ (NBA; later universal)
1951-52	_James Carter_
1952	Lauro Salas; _James Carter_
1953-54	_James Carter_
1954	Paddy De Marco; _James Carter_
1955	_James Carter_; Bud Smith
1956	Bud Smith; _Joe Brown_
1956-62	_Joe Brown_
1962-65	_Carlos Ortiz_
1965	_Ismael Laguna_
1965-68	_Carlos Ortiz_
1968-69	Teo Cruz
1969-70	Mando Ramos
1970	_Ismael Laguna_
1970-72	_Ken Buchanan_ (WBA)
1971-72	Pedro Carrasco (WBC)
1972	Mando Ramos (WBC)
1972-79	_Roberto Duran_ (WBA*)
1972	Chango Carmona (WBC)
1972-74	Rodolfo Gonzalez (WBC)
1974-76	Ishimatsu Suzuki (WBC)
1976-78	Esteban De Jesus (WBC)
1979-81	Jim Watt (WBC)
1979-80	Ernesto Espana (WBA)
1980-81	Hilmer Kenty (WBA)
1981	Sean O'Grady (WBA); Claude Noel (WBA)
1981-83	_Alexis Arguello_ (WBC*)
1981-82	Arturo Frias (WBA)
1982-84	_Ray Mancini_ (WBA)
1983-84	_Edwin Rosario_ (WBC)
1984-86	Livingstone Bramble (WBA)
1984-85	Jose Luis Ramirez (WBC)
1985-86	Hector "Macho" Camacho (WBC)
1986-87	_Edwin Rosario_ (WBA)
1987-88	_Julio Cesar Chavez_ (WBA); Jose Luis Ramirez (WBC)
1988-89	_Julio Cesar Chavez_ (WBA/WBC)
1989-90	_Edwin Rosario_ (WBA); _Pernell Whitaker_ (WBC)
1990	Juan Nazario (WBA)
1990-92	_Pernell Whitaker_ (WBC*/WBA*)
1992	Joey Gamache (WBA)
1992-96	Miguel Angel Gonzalez (WBC*)
1992-93	Tony Lopez (WBA)
1993	Dingaan Thobela (WBA)
1993-98	Orzubek Nazarov (WBA)
1996-97	Jean-Baptiste Mendy (WBC)
1997-98	Steve Johnston (WBC)
1998-99	Jean-Baptiste Mendy (WBA); Cesar Bazan (WBC)
1999-2000	Steve Johnston (WBC)
1999	Julian Lorcy (WBA); Stefano Zoff (WBA)
1999-2000	Gilberto Serrano (WBA)
2000-01	Takanori Hatakeyama (WBA)
2000-02	Jose Luis Castillo (WBC)
2001	Julien Lorcy (WBA)
2001-02	Raul Balbi (WBA)
2002-03	Leonard Dorin (WBA)
2002-04	Floyd Mayweather Jr. (WBC)
2004	Lakva Sim (WBA)
2004-05	Jose Luis Castillo (WBC)
2004-08	Juan Diaz (WBA)
2005-06	Diego Corrales (WBC)
2006	Joel Casamayor (WBC)
2006-08	David Diaz (WBC)
2008	Nate Campbell (WBA); Manny Pacquiao (WBC)
2009-12	Juan Manuel Marquez (WBA*)
2009-10	Edwin Valero (WBC)
2010-11	Humberto Soto (WBC*)
2011-12	Antonio DeMarco (WBC)
2012-14	Adrien Broner (WBC*)
2013-15	Richard Abril (WBA*)
2014	Omar Figueroa (WBC*)
2014-	Jorge Linares (WBC)
2015-	Darleys Perez (WBA)

Featherweights

1892-1900	_George Dixon_ (disputed)
1900-01	_Terry McGovern_; _Young Corbett II_*
1901-12	_Abe Attell_
1912-23	_Johnny Kilbane_
1923	_Eugene Criqui_
1923-25	_Johnny Dundee_*
1925-27	_Louis "Kid" Kaplan_*
1927-28	_Benny Bass_; _Tony Canzoneri_
1928-29	Andre Routis
1929-32	_Battling Battalino_*
1932-34	Tommy Paul (NBA)
1933-36	_Freddie Miller_
1936-37	Petey Sarron
1937-38	_Henry Armstrong_*
1938-40	Joey Archibald
1940-41	Harry Jeffra
1942-48	_Willie Pep_
1948-49	_Sandy Saddler_
1949-50	_Willie Pep_
1950-57	_Sandy Saddler_*
1957-59	Hogan "Kid" Bassey
1959-63	Davey Moore
1963-64	_Ultiminio "Sugar" Ramos_
1964-67	_Vicente Saldivar_*
1968	Raul Rojas (WBA)
1968-69	Jose Legra (WBC)
1968-71	Shozo Saijyo (WBA)
1969-70	Johnny Famechon (WBC)
1970	_Vicente Saldivar_ (WBC)
1970-72	Kuniaki Shibata (WBC)
1971-72	Antonio Gomez (WBA)
1972	Clemente Sanchez (WBC*)
1972-74	Ernesto Marcel (WBA*)
1972-73	Jose Legra (WBC)
1973-74	_Eder Jofre_ (WBC*)
1974	_Ruben Olivares_ (WBA)
1974-75	_Bobby Chacon_ (WBC)
1974-76	_Alexis Arguello_ (WBA*)
1975	_Ruben Olivares_ (WBC)
1975-76	David Kotey (WBC)
1976-80	_Danny "Little Red" Lopez_ (WBC)
1977	Rafael Ortega (WBA)
1977-78	Cecilio Lastra (WBA)
1978-85	_Eusebio Pedroza_ (WBA)
1980-82	_Salvador Sanchez_ (WBC)
1982-84	Juan LaPorte (WBC)
1984	_Wilfredo Gomez_ (WBC)
1984-88	_Azumah Nelson_ (WBC)
1985-86	_Barry McGuigan_ (WBA)
1986-87	Steve Cruz (WBA)
1987-91	Antonio Esparragoza (WBA)
1988-90	_Jeff Fenech_ (WBC*)
1990-91	Marcos Villasana (WBC)
1991-93	Park Yung Kyun (WBA); Paul Hodkinson (WBC)
1993	Goyo Vargas (WBC)
1993-95	Kevin Kelley (WBC)
1993-96	Eloy Rojas (WBA)
1995	Alejandro Gonzalez (WBC); Manuel Medina (WBC)
1995-99	Luisito Espinosa (WBC)
1996-98	Wilfredo Vasquez (WBA*)
1998	Freddie Norwood (WBA)
1998-99	Antonio Cermeno (WBA)
1999	Cesar Soto (WBC)
1999-2000	Freddie Norwood (WBA)
1999	_Naseem Hamed_ (WBC*)
2000-01	Guty Espadas (WBC)
2000-03	Derrick Gainer (WBA)
2001-04	Erik Morales (WBC)[1]
2003-05	Juan Manuel Marquez (WBA*)
2004-06	In-Jin Chi (WBC)
2005-13	Chris John (WBA)
2006	Takashi Koshimoto (WBC); Rodolfo Lopez (WBC)
2006-07	In-Jin Chi (WBC)
2007-08	Jorge Linares (WBC*)
2008	Oscar Larios (WBC)
2009	Takahiro Ao (WBC)
2009-10	Elio Rojas (WBC)
2010-11	Hozumi Hasegawa (WBC)
2011-12	Jhonny Gonzalez (WBC)
2012-13	Daniel Ponce de León (WBC)
2013	Abner Mares (WBC)
2013-15	Jhonny Gonzalez (WBC)
2013-14	Simpiwe Vetyeka (WBA)
2014	Nonito Donaire (WBA)
2014-15	Nicholas Walters (WBA*)
2015-	Gary Russell Jr. (WBC)
2015-	Jesus Andres Cuellar (WBA)

(1) Marco Antonio Barrera won unanimous decision over Morales, June 22, 2002, but refused WBC title. Morales regained WBC title with unanimous decision over Paulie Ayala, Nov. 16, 2002. Morales moved up to Jr. Lightweight div. in 2004.

International Boxing Hall of Fame Inductees, 2015

Source: International Boxing Hall of Fame, 1 Hall of Fame Dr., Canastota, NY 13032. www.ibhof.com

Modern	Riddick Bowe, 43-1 (33 KO)	Naseem Hamed, 36-1 (31 KO)	Ray Mancini, 29-5 (23 KO)
Old-Timer	Yoko Gushiken, 23-1 (15 KO)	Masao Ohba, 35-2-1 (16 KO)	Ken Overlin, 135-19-9-2 (23 KO)
Pioneer	none inducted in this category in 2015		
Non-Participant	John F.X. Condon, publicist, president, MSG Boxing	Rafael Mendoza, agent/manager	Steve Smoger, referee
Observer	Nigel Collins, journalist	Jim Lampley, broadcaster	

Title-Changing Heavyweight Championship Bouts, 1889-2015

1889: July 8, John L. Sullivan def. Jake Kilrain, 75, Richburg, MS.

1892: Sept. 7, James J. Corbett def. John L. Sullivan, 21, New Orleans.

1897: Mar. 17, Bob Fitzsimmons def. James J. Corbett, 14, Carson City, NV.

1899: June 9, James J. Jeffries def. Bob Fitzsimmons, 11, Coney Island, NY. (Jeffries retired as champion in 1905.)

1905: July 3, Marvin Hart KOd Jack Root, 12, Reno, NV. (James J. Jeffries refereed, gave title to Hart. Jack O'Brien also claimed the title.)

1906: Feb. 23, Tommy Burns def. Marvin Hart, 20, Los Angeles.

1908: Dec. 26, Jack Johnson KOd Tommy Burns, 14, Sydney, Australia. (Police halted contest.)

1915: Apr. 5, Jess Willard KOd Jack Johnson, 26, Havana, Cuba.

1919: July 4, Jack Dempsey KOd Jess Willard, Toledo, OH. (Willard failed to answer bell for 4th round.)

1926: Sept. 23, Gene Tunney def. Jack Dempsey, 10, Philadelphia. (Tunney retired as champion in 1928.)

1930: June 12, Max Schmeling def. Jack Sharkey on a foul, 4, New York City. (Resulted in the election of a successor to Gene Tunney.)

1932: June 21, Jack Sharkey def. Max Schmeling, 15, NYC.

1933: June 29, Primo Carnera KOd Jack Sharkey, 6, NYC.

1934: June 14, Max Baer KOd Primo Carnera, 11, NYC.

1935: June 13, James J. Braddock def. Max Baer, 15, NYC.

1937: June 22, Joe Louis KOd James J. Braddock, 8, Chicago. (Louis retired as champion in 1949.)

1949: June 22, Ezzard Charles def. Joe Walcott, 15, Chicago; NBA recognition only.

1951: July 18, Joe Walcott KOd Ezzard Charles, 7, Pittsburgh.

1952: Sept. 23, Rocky Marciano KOd Joe Walcott, 13, Philadelphia. (Marciano retired as champion in 1956.)

1956: Nov. 30, Floyd Patterson KOd Archie Moore, 5, Chicago.

1959: June 26, Ingemar Johansson KOd Floyd Patterson, 3, NYC.

1960: June 20, Floyd Patterson KOd Ingemar Johansson, 5, NYC.

1962: Sept. 25, Sonny Liston KOd Floyd Patterson, 1, Chicago.

1964: Feb. 25, Cassius Clay (Muhammad Ali) KOd Sonny Liston, 7, Miami Beach, FL. (In 1967, Ali was stripped of his title by the WBA and others for refusing military service.)

1970: Feb. 16, Joe Frazier KOd Jimmy Ellis, 5, NYC. (Frazier def. Ali, 15, NYC, on Mar. 8, 1971, in "Fight of the Century.")

1973: Jan. 22, George Foreman KOd Joe Frazier, 2, Kingston, Jamaica.

1974: Oct. 30, Muhammad Ali KOd George Foreman, 8, Kinshasa, Zaire (billed as the "Rumble in the Jungle").

1978: Feb. 15, Leon Spinks def. Muhammad Ali, 15, Las Vegas (WBC recognized Ken Norton as champion after Spinks refused to fight him before his rematch with Ali); June 9, (WBC) Larry Holmes def. Ken Norton, 15, Las Vegas; Sept. 15, (WBA) Muhammad Ali def. Leon Spinks, 15, New Orleans. (Ali retired as champion in 1979.)

1979: Oct. 20, (WBA) John Tate def. Gerrie Coetzee, 15, Pretoria, South Africa.

1980: Mar. 31, (WBA) Mike Weaver KOd John Tate, 15, Knoxville, TN.

1982: Dec. 10, (WBA) Michael Dokes KOd Mike Weaver, 1, Las Vegas.

1983: Sept. 23, (WBA) Gerrie Coetzee KOd Michael Dokes, 10, Richfield, OH; in Dec., Larry Holmes relinquished the WBC title and was named champion of the newly formed IBF.

1984: Mar. 9, (WBC) Tim Witherspoon def. Greg Page, 12, Las Vegas; Aug. 31, (WBC) Pinklon Thomas def. Tim Witherspoon, 12, Las Vegas; Dec. 1, (WBA) Greg Page KOd Gerrie Coetzee, 8, Sun City, Bophuthatswana, South Africa.

1985: Apr. 29, (WBA) Tony Tubbs def. Greg Page, 15, Buffalo, NY; Sept. 21, (IBF) Michael Spinks def. Larry Holmes, 15, Las Vegas (Spinks relinquished title in Feb. 1987).

1986: Jan. 17, (WBA) Tim Witherspoon def. Tony Tubbs, 15, Atlanta; Mar. 22, (WBC) Trevor Berbick def. Pinklon Thomas, 12, Miami; Nov. 22, (WBC) Mike Tyson KOd Trevor Berbick, 2, Las Vegas; Dec. 12, (WBA) James "Bonecrusher" Smith KOd Tim Witherspoon, 1, NYC.

1987: Mar. 7, (WBA) Mike Tyson def. James "Bonecrusher" Smith, 12, Las Vegas; May 30, (IBF) Tony Tucker KOd James "Buster" Douglas, 10, Las Vegas; Aug. 1, (IBF) Mike Tyson def. Tony Tucker, 12, Las Vegas. (Tyson became undisputed champion.)

1990: Feb. 11, (WBA/WBC/IBF) James "Buster" Douglas KOd Mike Tyson, 10, Tokyo, Japan; Oct. 25, (WBA/WBC/IBF) Evander Holyfield KOd James "Buster" Douglas, 3, Las Vegas.

1992: Nov. 13, (WBA/WBC/IBF) Riddick Bowe def. Evander Holyfield, 12, Las Vegas; in Dec., Lennox Lewis was named WBC champion after Bowe relinquished the WBC title rather than fight Lewis.

1993: Nov. 6, (WBA/IBF) Evander Holyfield def. Riddick Bowe, 12, Las Vegas.

1994: Apr. 22, (WBA/IBF) Michael Moorer def. Evander Holyfield, 12, Las Vegas; Sept. 24, (WBC) Oliver McCall KOd Lennox Lewis, 2, London, Eng.; Nov. 5, (WBA/IBF) George Foreman KOd Michael Moorer, 10, Las Vegas.

1995: In Mar., George Foreman was stripped of his WBA title for refusing to fight challenger Tony Tucker; in June, Foreman relinquished his IBF title rather than submit to a rematch with Axel Schulz; Sept. 2, (WBC) Frank Bruno def. Oliver McCall, 12, London, Eng.; Dec. 9, (IBF) Frans Botha def. Axel Schulz, 12, Stuttgart, Germany (Botha was subsequently stripped of title after testing positive for a steroid).

1996: Mar. 16, (WBC) Mike Tyson KOd Frank Bruno, 3, Las Vegas; June 22, (IBF) Michael Moorer def. Axel Schulz, 12, Dortmund, Germany; Sept. 7, (WBA) Mike Tyson KOd Bruce Seldon, 1, Las Vegas (Tyson was subsequently stripped of WBC title after refusing to fight Lennox Lewis); Nov. 9, (WBA) Evander Holyfield KOd Mike Tyson, 11, Las Vegas.

1997: Feb. 7, (WBC) Lennox Lewis TKOd Oliver McCall, 5, Las Vegas; Nov. 8, (IBF) Evander Holyfield def. Michael Moorer, 8, Las Vegas.

1999: Nov. 13, (IBF) Lennox Lewis def. Evander Holyfield, 12, Las Vegas. (Lewis became undisputed champion.)

2000: In Apr., Lennox Lewis was stripped of his WBA title after refusing to fight challenger John Ruiz; Aug. 12, (WBA) Evander Holyfield def. John Ruiz, 12, Las Vegas.

2001: Mar. 3, (WBA) John Ruiz def. Evander Holyfield, 12, Las Vegas; Apr. 21, (WBC/IBF) Hasim Rahman KOd Lennox Lewis, 5, Brakpan, South Africa; Nov. 17, (WBC/IBF) Lennox Lewis KOd Hasim Rahman, 4, Las Vegas.

2002: In Sept., Lennox Lewis relinquished his IBF title; Dec. 14, (IBF) Chris Byrd def. Evander Holyfield, 12, Atlantic City, NJ.

2003: Mar. 1, (WBA) Roy Jones Jr. def. John Ruiz, 12, Las Vegas.

2004: Feb. 20, (WBA) John Ruiz gained title when Roy Jones Jr. relinquished it; Apr. 24, (WBC) Vitali Klitschko TKOd Corrie Sanders, 8, Los Angeles, to win title vacated by retirement of Lennox Lewis in Feb.

2005: Apr. 30, (WBA) James Toney def. John Ruiz, 12, NYC (title was returned to Ruiz after Toney tested positive for steroids); Nov. 9, (WBC) Hasim Rahman gained title when Vitali Klitschko retired due to an injury; Dec. 17, (WBA) Nikolai Valuev def. John Ruiz, 12, Berlin, Germany.

2006: Apr. 22, (IBF) Wladimir Klitschko TKOd Chris Byrd, 7, Mannheim, Germany; Aug. 12, (WBC) Oleg Maskaev TKOd Hasim Rahman, 12, Las Vegas.

2007: Apr. 14, (WBA) Ruslan Chagaev def. Nikolai Valuev, 12, Stuttgart, Germany. (An injured Chagaev was named champion in recess, July 2008.)

2008: Mar. 8, (WBC) Samuel Peter TKOd Oleg Maskaev, 6, Cancun, Mexico; Aug. 30, (WBA) Nikolai Valuev def. John Ruiz, 12, Berlin, Germany. Oct. 11, (WBC) Vitali Klitschko TKOd Samuel Peter, 8, Berlin, Germany.

2009: Nov. 7, (WBA) David Haye def. Nikolai Valuev, 12, Nuremberg, Germany.

2011: July 2, (WBA) Wladimir Klitschko def. David Haye, 12, Hamburg, Germany.

2014: May 10, (WBC) Bermane Stiverne TKOd Chris Arreola, 6, Los Angeles, to win title vacated by Vitali Klitschko in Dec. 2013.

2015: Jan. 17, (WBC) Deontay Wilder def. Bermane Stiverne, 12, Las Vegas.

THOROUGHBRED RACING

Triple Crown Winners

The Kentucky Derby, Preakness Stakes, and Belmont Stakes make up the Triple Crown. Since 1920, colts have carried 126 lbs in Triple Crown events; fillies, 121 lbs.

Year	Horse	Jockey	Trainer
1919	Sir Barton	J. Loftus	H. G. Bedwell
1930	Gallant Fox	E. Sande	J. Fitzsimmons
1935	Omaha	W. Sanders	J. Fitzsimmons
1937	War Admiral	C. Kurtsinger	G. Conway
1941	Whirlaway	E. Arcaro	B. A. Jones
1943	Count Fleet	J. Longden	G. D. Cameron
1946	Assault	W. Mehrtens	M. Hirsch
1948	Citation	E. Arcaro	H. A. Jones
1973	Secretariat	R. Turcotte	L. Laurin
1977	Seattle Slew	J. Cruguet	W. H. Turner Jr.
1978	Affirmed	S. Cauthen	L. S. Barrera
2015	American Pharoah	V. Espinoza	B. Baffert

Kentucky Derby Winners, 1875-2015

Churchill Downs, Louisville, KY; inaug. 1875. Distance: 1-1/4 mi; 1-1/2 mi until 1896. 3-year-olds. Best time: 1:59 2/5, Secretariat (1973); 2015 time: 2:03.02. (Until 2001, times were measured in fifths of a second.)

Year	Horse	Jockey
1875	Aristides	O. Lewis
1876	Vagrant	R. Swim
1877	Baden Baden	W. Walker
1878	Day Star	J. Carter
1879	Lord Murphy	C. Schauer
1880	Fonso	G. Lewis
1881	Hindoo	J. McLaughlin
1882	Apollo	B. Hurd
1883	Leonatus	W. Donohue
1884	Buchanan	I. Murphy
1885	Joe Cotton	E. Henderson
1886	Ben Ali	P. Duffy
1887	Montrose	I. Lewis
1888	Macbeth II	G. Covington
1889	Spokane	T. Kiley
1890	Riley	I. Murphy
1891	Kingman	I. Murphy
1892	Azra	A. Clayton
1893	Lookout	E. Kunze
1894	Chant	F. Goodale
1895	Halma	J. Perkins
1896	Ben Brush	W. Simms
1897	Typhoon II	F. Garner
1898	Plaudit	W. Simms
1899	Manuel	F. Taral
1900	Lieut. Gibson	J. Boland
1901	His Eminence	J. Winkfield
1902	Alan-a-Dale	J. Winkfield
1903	Judge Himes	H. Booker
1904	Elwood	F. Prior
1905	Agile	J. Martin
1906	Sir Huon	R. Troxler
1907	Pink Star	A. Minder
1908	Stone Street	A. Pickens
1909	Wintergreen	V. Powers
1910	Donau	F. Herbert
1911	Meridian	G. Archibald
1912	Worth	C. Shilling
1913	Donerail	R. Goose
1914	Old Rosebud	J. McCabe
1915	Regret[1]	J. Notter
1916	George Smith	J. Loftus
1917	Omar Khayyam	C. Borel
1918	Exterminator	W. Knapp
1919	Sir Barton	J. Loftus
1920	Paul Jones	T. Rice
1921	Behave Yourself	C. Thompson
1922	Morvich	A. Johnson
1923	Zev	E. Sande
1924	Black Gold	J. D. Mooney
1925	Flying Ebony	E. Sande
1926	Bubbling Over	A. Johnson
1927	Whiskery	L. McAtee
1928	Reigh Count	C. Lang
1929	Clyde Van Dusen	L. McAtee
1930	Gallant Fox	E. Sande
1931	Twenty Grand	C. Kurtsinger
1932	Burgoo King	E. James
1933	Brokers Tip	D. Meade
1934	Cavalcade	M. Garner
1935	Omaha	W. Saunders
1936	Bold Venture	I. Hanford
1937	War Admiral	C. Kurtsinger
1938	Lawrin	E. Arcaro
1939	Johnstown	J. Stout
1940	Gallahadion	C. Bierman
1941	Whirlaway	E. Arcaro
1942	Shut Out	W. Wright
1943	Count Fleet	J. Longden
1944	Pensive	C. McCreary
1945	Hoop Jr.	E. Arcaro
1946	Assault	W. Mehrtens
1947	Jet Pilot	E. Guerin
1948	Citation	E. Arcaro
1949	Ponder	S. Brooks
1950	Middleground	W. Boland
1951	Count Turf	C. McCreary
1952	Hill Gail	E. Arcaro
1953	Dark Star	H. Moreno
1954	Determine	R. York
1955	Swaps	W. Shoemaker
1956	Needles	D. Erb
1957	Iron Liege	W. Hartack
1958	Tim Tam	I. Valenzuela
1959	Tomy Lee	W. Shoemaker
1960	Venetian Way	W. Hartack
1961	Carry Back	J. Sellers
1962	Decidedly	W. Hartack
1963	Chateaugay	B. Baeza
1964	Northern Dancer	W. Hartack
1965	Lucky Debonair	W. Shoemaker
1966	Kauai King	D. Brumfield
1967	Proud Clarion	R. Ussery
1968	Forward Pass[2]	I. Valenzuela
1969	Majestic Prince	W. Hartack
1970	Dust Commander	M. Manganello
1971	Canonero II	G. Avila
1972	Riva Ridge	R. Turcotte
1973	Secretariat	R. Turcotte
1974	Cannonade	A. Cordero
1975	Foolish Pleasure	J. Vasquez
1976	Bold Forbes	A. Cordero
1977	Seattle Slew	J. Cruguet
1978	Affirmed	S. Cauthen
1979	Spectacular Bid	R. Franklin
1980	Genuine Risk[1]	J. Vasquez
1981	Pleasant Colony	J. Velasquez
1982	Gato del Sol	E. Delahoussaye
1983	Sunny's Halo	E. Delahoussaye
1984	Swale	L. Pincay
1985	Spend a Buck	A. Cordero
1986	Ferdinand	W. Shoemaker
1987	Alysheba	C. McCarron
1988	Winning Colors[1]	G. Stevens
1989	Sunday Silence	P. Valenzuela
1990	Unbridled	C. Perret
1991	Strike the Gold	C. Antley
1992	Lil E. Tee	P. Day
1993	Sea Hero	J. Bailey
1994	Go for Gin	C. McCarron
1995	Thunder Gulch	G. Stevens
1996	Grindstone	J. Bailey
1997	Silver Charm	G. Stevens
1998	Real Quiet	K. Desormeaux
1999	Charismatic	C. Antley
2000	Fusaichi Pegasus	K. Desormeaux
2001	Monarchos	J. Chavez
2002	War Emblem	V. Espinoza
2003	Funny Cide	J. Santos
2004	Smarty Jones	S. Elliot
2005	Giacomo	M. Smith
2006	Barbaro	E. Prado
2007	Street Sense	C. Borel
2008	Big Brown	K. Desormeaux
2009	Mine That Bird	C. Borel
2010	Super Saver	C. Borel
2011	Animal Kingdom	J. Velazquez
2012	I'll Have Another	M. Gutierrez
2013	Orb	J. Rosario
2014	California Chrome	V. Espinoza
2015	American Pharoah	V. Espinoza

Only two jockeys have won the Kentucky Derby five times: Eddie Arcaro (1938, 1941, 1945, 1948, 1952) and Bill Hartack (1957, 1960, 1962, 1964, 1969). Willie Shoemaker won four times (1955, 1959, 1965, 1986). Seven jockeys won three times: Isaac Murphy (1884, 1890, 1891); Earle Sande (1923, 1925, 1930); Angel Cordero (1974, 1976, 1985); Gary Stevens (1988, 1995, 1997); Kent Desormeaux (1998, 2000, 2008); Calvin Borel (2007, 2009, 2010); and Victor Espinoza (2002, 2014, 2015). (1) Regret, Genuine Risk, and Winning Colors are the only fillies to have won the Derby. (2) Dancer's Image came in first but was disqualified after tests disclosed that the horse had run with a prohibited painkilling drug in his system. All wagers were paid on Dancer's Image, but Forward Pass was awarded the first-place money.

Fastest Winning Times for the Kentucky Derby

Until 2001, Kentucky Derby times were measured in fifths of a second.

Time	Horse	Jockey	Year
1 min., 59-2/5 s.	Secretariat	Ron Turcotte	1973
1 min., 59.97 s.	Monarchos	Jorge Chavez	2001
2 min.	Northern Dancer	Bill Hartack	1964
2 min., 1/5 s.	Spend a Buck	Angel Cordero Jr.	1985
2 min., 2/5 s.	Decidedly	Bill Hartack	1962
2 min., 3/5 s.	Proud Clarion	Robert Ussery	1967
2 min., 1 s.	Fusaichi Pegasus	Kent Desormeaux	2000
	Grindstone	Jerry Bailey	1996
2 min., 1.13 s.	War Emblem	Victor Espinoza	2002
2 min., 1.19 s.	Funny Cide	Jose Santos	2003
2 min., 1-1/5 s.	Thunder Gulch	Gary Stevens	1995
	Affirmed	Steve Cauthen	1978
	Lucky Debonair	Bill Shoemaker	1965
2 min., 1-2/5 s.	Barbaro	Edgar Prado	2006
	Whirlaway	Eddie Arcaro	1941
2 min., 1-3/5 s.	Bold Forbes	Angel Cordero Jr.	1976
	Hill Gail	Eddie Arcaro	1952
	Middleground	William Boland	1950

Preakness Stakes Winners, 1873-2015

Pimlico Race Course, Baltimore, MD; inaug. 1873. Distance: 1-3/16 mi. 3-year-olds. * = Horses ran in two divisions. Best time: 1:53, Secretariat (1973); 2015 time: 1:58.46.

Year	Horse	Jockey
1873	Survivor	G. Barbee
1874	Culpepper	M. Donohue
1875	Tom Ochiltree	L. Hughes
1876	Shirley	G. Barbee
1877	Cloverbrook	C. Holloway
1878	Duke of Magenta	C. Holloway
1879	Harold	L. Hughes
1880	Grenada	L. Hughes
1881	Saunterer	W. Costello
1882	Vanguard	W. Costello
1883	Jacobus	G. Barbee
1884	Knight of Ellerslie	S. Fisher
1885	Tecumseh	J. McLaughlin
1886	The Bard	S. Fisher
1887	Dunboyne	W. Donohue
1888	Refund	F. Littlefield
1889	Buddhist	G. Anderson
1890	Montague	W. Martin
1894	Assignee	F. Taral
1895	Belmar	F. Taral
1896	Margrave	H. Griffin
1897	Paul Kauvar	C. Thorpe
1898	Sly Fox	W. Simms
1899	Half Time	R. Clawson
1900	Hindus	H. Spencer
1901	The Parader	F. Landry
1902	Old England	L. Jackson
1903	Flocarline	W. Gannon
1904	Bryn Mawr	E. Hildebrand
1905	Cairngorm	W. Davis
1906	Whimsical	W. Miller
1907	Don Enrique	G. Mountain
1908	Royal Tourist	E. Dugan
1909	Effendi	W. Doyle
1910	Layminster	R. Estep
1911	Watervale	E. Dugan
1912	Colonel Holloway	C. Turner
1913	Buskin	J. Butwell
1914	Holiday	A. Schuttinger
1915	Rhine Maiden	D. Hoffman
1916	Damrosch	L. McAtee
1917	Kalitan	E. Haynes
1918*	War Cloud	J. Loftus
	Jack Hare Jr.	C. Peak
1919	Sir Barton	J. Loftus
1920	Man o' War	C. Kummer
1921	Broomspun	F. Coltiletti
1922	Pillory	L. Morris
1923	Vigil	B. Marinelli
1924	Nellie Morse	J. Merimee
1925	Coventry	C. Kummer
1926	Display	J. Malben
1927	Bostonian	A. Abel
1928	Victorian	R. Workman
1929	Dr. Freeland	L. Schaefer
1930	Gallant Fox	E. Sande
1931	Mate	G. Ellis
1932	Burgoo King	E. James
1933	Head Play	C. Kurtsinger
1934	High Quest	R. Jones
1935	Omaha	W. Saunders
1936	Bold Venture	G. Woolf
1937	War Admiral	C. Kurtsinger
1938	Dauber	M. Peters
1939	Challedon	G. Seabo
1940	Bimelech	F. A. Smith
1941	Whirlaway	E. Arcaro
1942	Alsab	B. James
1943	Count Fleet	J. Longden
1944	Pensive	C. McCreary
1945	Polynesian	W. D. Wright
1946	Assault	W. Mehrtens
1947	Faultless	D. Dodson
1948	Citation	E. Arcaro
1949	Capot	T. Atkinson
1950	Hill Prince	E. Arcaro
1951	Bold	E. Arcaro
1952	Blue Man	C. McCreary
1953	Native Dancer	E. Guerin
1954	Hasty Road	J. Adams
1955	Nashua	E. Arcaro
1956	Fabius	W. Hartack
1957	Bold Ruler	E. Arcaro
1958	Tim Tam	I. Valenzuela
1959	Royal Orbit	W. Harmatz
1960	Bally Ache	R. Ussery
1961	Carry Back	J. Sellers
1962	Greek Money	J. L. Rotz
1963	Candy Spots	W. Shoemaker
1964	Northern Dancer	W. Hartack
1965	Tom Rolfe	R. Turcotte
1966	Kauai King	D. Brumfield
1967	Damascus	W. Shoemaker
1968	Forward Pass	I. Valenzuela
1969	Majestic Prince	W. Hartack
1970	Personality	E. Belmonte
1971	Canonero II	G. Avila
1972	Bee Bee Bee	E. Nelson
1973	Secretariat	R. Turcotte
1974	Little Current	M. Rivera
1975	Master Derby	D. McHargue
1976	Elocutionist	J. Lively
1977	Seattle Slew	J. Cruguet
1978	Affirmed	S. Cauthen
1979	Spectacular Bid	R. Franklin
1980	Codex	A. Cordero
1981	Pleasant Colony	J. Velasquez
1982	Aloma's Ruler	J. Kaenel
1983	Deputed Testamony	D. Miller
1984	Gate Dancer	A. Cordero
1985	Tank's Prospect	P. Day
1986	Snow Chief	A. Solis
1987	Alysheba	C. McCarron
1988	Risen Star	E. Delahoussaye
1989	Sunday Silence	P. Valenzuela
1990	Summer Squall	P. Day
1991	Hansel	J. Bailey
1992	Pine Bluff	C. McCarron
1993	Prairie Bayou	M. Smith
1994	Tabasco Cat	P. Day
1995	Timber Country	P. Day
1996	Louis Quatorze	P. Day
1997	Silver Charm	G. Stevens
1998	Real Quiet	K. Desormeaux
1999	Charismatic	C. Antley
2000	Red Bullet	J. Bailey
2001	Point Given	G. Stevens
2002	War Emblem	V. Espinoza
2003	Funny Cide	J. Santos
2004	Smarty Jones	S. Elliot
2005	Afleet Alex	J. Rose
2006	Bernardini	J. Castellano
2007	Curlin	R. Albarado
2008	Big Brown	K. Desormeaux
2009	Rachel Alexandra	C. Borel
2010	Lookin At Lucky	M. Garcia
2011	Shackleford	J. Castanon
2012	I'll Have Another	M. Gutierrez
2013	Oxbow	G. Stevens
2014	California Chrome	V. Espinoza
2015	American Pharoah	V. Espinoza

Belmont Stakes Winners, 1867-2015

Belmont Park, Elmont, NY; inaug. 1867. Distance: 1-1/2 mi. 3-year-olds. Best time: 2:24, Secretariat (1973); 2015 time: 2:26.65.

Year	Horse	Jockey
1867	Ruthless	J. Gilpatrick
1868	General Duke	R. Swim
1869	Fenian	C. Miller
1870	Kingfisher	W. Dick
1871	Harry Bassett	W. Miller
1872	Joe Daniels	J. Rowe
1873	Springbok	J. Rowe
1874	Saxon	G. Barbee
1875	Calvin	R. Swim
1876	Algerine	W. Donohue
1877	Cloverbrook	C. Holloway
1878	Duke of Magenta	L. Hughes
1879	Spendthrift	S. Evans
1880	Grenada	L. Hughes
1881	Saunterer	T. Costello
1882	Forester	J. McLaughlin
1883	George Kinney	J. McLaughlin
1884	Panique	J. McLaughlin
1885	Tyrant	P. Duffy
1886	Inspector B.	J. McLaughlin
1887	Hanover	J. McLaughlin
1888	Sir Dixon	J. McLaughlin
1889	Eric	W. Hayward
1890	Burlington	S. Barnes
1891	Foxford	E. Garrison
1892	Patron	W. Hayward
1893	Comanche	W. Simms
1894	Henry of Navarre	W. Simms
1895	Belmar	F. Taral
1896	Hastings	H. Griffin
1897	Scottish Chieftain	J. Scherrer
1898	Bowling Brook	F. Littlefield
1899	Jean Bereaud	R. R. Clawson
1900	Ildrim	N. Turner
1901	Commando	H. Spencer
1902	Masterman	J. Bullman
1903	Africander	J. Bullman
1904	Delhi	G. Odom
1905	Tanya	E. Hildebrand
1906	Burgomaster	L. Lyne
1907	Peter Pan	G. Mountain
1908	Colin	J. Notter
1909	Joe Madden	E. Dugan
1910	Sweep	J. Butwell
1913	Prince Eugene	R. Troxler
1914	Luke McLuke	M. Buxton
1915	The Finn	G. Byrne
1916	Friar Rock	E. Haynes
1917	Hourless	J. Butwell
1918	Johren	F. Robinson
1919	Sir Barton	J. Loftus
1920	Man o' War	C. Kummer
1921	Grey Lag	E. Sande
1922	Pillory	C. H. Miller
1923	Zev	E. Sande
1924	Mad Play	E. Sande
1925	American Flag	A. Johnson
1926	Crusader	A. Johnson
1927	Chance Shot	E. Sande
1928	Vito	C. Kummer
1929	Blue Larkspur	M. Garner
1930	Gallant Fox	E. Sande
1931	Twenty Grand	C. Kurtsinger
1932	Faireno	T. Malley
1933	Hurryoff	M. Garner
1934	Peace Chance	W. D. Wright
1935	Omaha	W. Saunders
1936	Granville	J. Stout
1937	War Admiral	C. Kurtsinger
1938	Pasteurized	J. Stout
1939	Johnstown	J. Stout
1940	Bimelech	F. A. Smith
1941	Whirlaway	E. Arcaro
1942	Shut Out	E. Arcaro
1943	Count Fleet	J. Longden
1944	Bounding Home	G. L. Smith
1945	Pavot	E. Arcaro
1946	Assault	W. Mehrtens
1947	Phalanx	R. Donoso
1948	Citation	E. Arcaro
1949	Capot	T. Atkinson
1950	Middleground	W. Boland
1951	Counterpoint	D. Gorman
1952	One Count	E. Arcaro
1953	Native Dancer	E. Guerin
1954	High Gun	E. Guerin
1955	Nashua	E. Arcaro
1956	Needles	D. Erb
1957	Gallant Man	W. Shoemaker
1958	Cavan	P. Anderson
1959	Sword Dancer	W. Shoemaker
1960	Celtic Ash	W. Hartack
1961	Sherluck	B. Baeza
1962	Jaipur	W. Shoemaker
1963	Chateaugay	B. Baeza
1964	Quadrangle	M. Ycaza
1965	Hail to All	J. Sellers
1966	Amberoid	W. Boland
1967	Damascus	W. Shoemaker

Year	Horse	Jockey	Year	Horse	Jockey	Year	Horse	Jockey
1968	Stage Door Johnny	H. Gustines	1984	Swale	L. Pincay	2000	Commendable	P. Day
1969	Arts and Letters	B. Baeza	1985	Creme Fraiche	E. Maple	2001	Point Given	G. Stevens
1970	High Echelon	J. L. Rotz	1986	Danzig Connection	C. McCarron	2002	Sarava	E. Prado
1971	Pass Catcher	W. Blum	1987	Bet Twice	C. Perret	2003	Empire Maker	J. Bailey
1972	Riva Ridge	R. Turcotte	1988	Risen Star	E. Delahoussaye	2004	Birdstone	E. Prado
1973	Secretariat	R. Turcotte	1989	Easy Goer	P. Day	2005	Afleet Alex	J. Rose
1974	Little Current	M. Rivera	1990	Go and Go	M. Kinane	2006	Jazil	F. Jara
1975	Avatar	W. Shoemaker	1991	Hansel	J. Bailey	2007	Rags to Riches	J. Velazquez
1976	Bold Forbes	A. Cordero	1992	A.P. Indy	E. Delahoussaye	2008	Da' Tara	A. Garcia
1977	Seattle Slew	J. Cruguet	1993	Colonial Affair	J. Krone	2009	Summer Bird	K. Desormeaux
1978	Affirmed	S. Cauthen	1994	Tabasco Cat	P. Day	2010	Drosselmeyer	M. Smith
1979	Coastal	R. Hernandez	1995	Thunder Gulch	G. Stevens	2011	Ruler On Ice	J. Valdivia Jr.
1980	Temperence Hill	E. Maple	1996	Editor's Note	R. Douglas	2012	Union Rags	J. Velazquez
1981	Summing	G. Martens	1997	Touch Gold	C. McCarron	2013	Palace Malice	M. Smith
1982	Conquistador Cielo	L. Pincay	1998	Victory Gallop	G. Stevens	2014	Tonalist	J. Rosario
1983	Caveat	L. Pincay	1999	Lemon Drop Kid	J. Santos	2015	American Pharoah	V. Espinoza

Annual Leading Jockey by Earnings, 1957-2014

Total purses earned by all horses that jockey raced in year listed; does not reflect what jockey earned.

Year	Jockey	Earnings	Year	Jockey	Earnings	Year	Jockey	Earnings
1957	Bill Hartack	$3,060,501	1977	Steve Cauthen	$6,151,750	1996	Jerry D. Bailey	$19,465,376
1958	Willie Shoemaker	2,961,693	1978	Darrel McHargue	6,029,885	1997	Jerry D. Bailey	18,320,743
1959	Willie Shoemaker	2,843,133	1979	Laffit Pincay Jr.	8,193,535	1998	Gary Stevens	19,622,855
1960	Willie Shoemaker	2,123,961	1980	Chris McCarron	7,663,300	1999	Pat Day	18,092,845
1961	Willie Shoemaker	2,690,819	1981	Chris McCarron	8,397,604	2000	Pat Day	17,479,838
1962	Willie Shoemaker	2,916,844	1982	Angel Cordero Jr.	9,483,590	2001	Jerry D. Bailey	22,597,720
1963	Willie Shoemaker	2,526,925	1983	Angel Cordero Jr.	10,116,697	2002	Jerry D. Bailey	19,271,814
1964	Willie Shoemaker	2,649,553	1984	Chris McCarron	12,045,813	2003	Jerry D. Bailey	23,354,960
1965	Braulio Baeza	2,582,702	1985	Laffit Pincay Jr.	13,353,299	2004	John R. Velazquez	22,220,261
1966	Braulio Baeza	2,951,022	1986	Jose Santos	11,329,297	2005	John R. Velazquez	20,799,923
1967	Braulio Baeza	3,088,888	1987	Jose Santos	12,375,433	2006	Garrett K. Gomez	20,122,592
1968	Braulio Baeza	2,835,108	1988	Jose Santos	14,877,298	2007	Garrett K. Gomez	22,800,074
1969	Jorge Velasquez	2,542,315	1989	Jose Santos	13,838,389	2008	Garrett K. Gomez	23,344,351
1970	Laffit Pincay Jr.	2,626,526	1990	Gary Stevens	13,881,198	2009	Garrett K. Gomez	18,536,105
1971	Laffit Pincay Jr.	3,784,377	1991	Chris McCarron	14,441,083	2010	Ramon A. Dominguez	16,911,880
1972	Laffit Pincay Jr.	3,225,827	1992	Kent Desormeaux	14,193,006	2011	Ramon A. Dominguez	20,267,032
1973	Laffit Pincay Jr.	4,093,492	1993	Mike Smith	14,024,815	2012	Ramon A. Dominguez	25,584,852
1974	Laffit Pincay Jr.	4,251,060	1994	Mike Smith	15,979,820	2013	Javier Castellano	26,214,007
1975	Braulio Baeza	3,695,198	1995	Jerry D. Bailey	16,311,876	2014	Javier Castellano	25,056,464
1976	Angel Cordero Jr.	4,709,500						

Breeders' Cup World Thoroughbred Championships, 1984-2015

The Breeders' Cup began in 1984 and through 2006, consisted of seven races at one track on one day. In 2007, it expanded to two days, and three new races debuted: Filly and Mare Sprint, Juvenile Turf, and Dirt. In 2008, a "Ladies' Day" for fillies and several more races debuted: Turf Sprint, Marathon (eliminated in 2014), and Juvenile Fillies Turf. In 2011, the Juvenile Sprint debuted; it was eliminated in 2013.

Classic

Distance: 1-1/4 mi.

Year	Horse	Jockey	Year	Horse	Jockey	Year	Horse	Jockey
1984	Wild Again	P. Day	1995	Cigar	J. Bailey	2006	Invasor	F. Jara
1985	Proud Truth	J. Velasquez	1996	Alphabet Soup	C. McCarron	2007	Curlin	R. Albarado
1986	Skywalker	L. Pincay Jr.	1997	Skip Away	M. Smith	2008	Raven's Pass	F. Dettori
1987	Ferdinand	W. Shoemaker	1998	Awesome Again	P. Day	2009	Zenyatta	M. Smith
1988	Alysheba	C. McCarron	1999	Cat Thief	P. Day	2010	Blame	G. Gomez
1989	Sunday Silence	C. McCarron	2000	Tiznow	C. McCarron	2011	Drosselmeyer	M. Smith
1990	Unbridled	P. Day	2001	Tiznow	C. McCarron	2012	Fort Larned	B. Hernandez
1991	Black Tie Affair	J. Bailey	2002	Volponi	J. Santos	2013	Mucho Macho Man	G. Stevens
1992	A.P. Indy	E. Delahoussaye	2003	Pleasantly Perfect	A. Solis	2014	Bayern	M. Garcia
1993	Arcangues	J. Bailey	2004	Ghostzapper	J. Castellano	2015	American Pharoah	V. Espinoza
1994	Concern	J. Bailey	2005	Saint Liam	J. Bailey			

Juvenile

Distance: 1-1/16 mi, 1986 and since 1988; 1 mi, 1984-85, 1987.

Year	Horse	Jockey	Year	Horse	Jockey	Year	Horse	Jockey
1984	Chief's Crown	D. MacBeth	1995	Unbridled's Song	M. Smith	2006	Street Sense	C. Borel
1985	Tasso	L. Pincay Jr.	1996	Boston Harbor	J. Bailey	2007	War Pass	C. Velasquez
1986	Capote	L. Pincay Jr.	1997	Favorite Trick	P. Day	2008	Midshipman	G. Gomez
1987	Success Express	J. Santos	1998	Answer Lively	J. Bailey	2009	Vale of York	A. Ajtebi
1988	Is It True	L. Pincay Jr.	1999	Anees	G. Stevens	2010	Uncle Mo	J. Velazquez
1989	Rhythm	C. Perret	2000	Macho Uno	J. Bailey	2011	Hansen	R. Dominguez
1990	Fly So Free	J. Santos	2001	Johannesburg	M. Kinane	2012	Shanghai Bobby	R. Napravnik
1991	Arazi	P. Valenzuela	2002	Vindication	M. Smith	2013	New Year's Day	M. Garcia
1992	Gilded Time	C. McCarron	2003	Action This Day	D. Flores	2014	Texas Red	K. Desormeaux
1993	Brocco	G. Stevens	2004	Wilko	F. Dettori	2015	Nyquist	M. Gutierrez
1994	Timber Country	P. Day	2005	Stevie Wonderboy	G. Gomez			

Juvenile Fillies

Distance: 1-1/16 mi, 1986 and since 1988; 1 mi, 1984-85, 1987. Outstandingly won the 1984 race by disqualification.

Year	Horse	Jockey	Year	Horse	Jockey	Year	Horse	Jockey
1984	Outstandingly	W. Guerra	1995	My Flag	J. Bailey	2006	Dreaming of Anna	R. Douglas
1985	Twilight Ridge	J. Velasquez	1996	Storm Song	C. Perret	2007	Indian Blessing	G. Gomez
1986	Brave Raj	P. Valenzuela	1997	Countess Diana	S. Sellers	2008	Stardom Bound	M. Smith
1987	Epitome	P. Day	1998	Silverbulletday	G. Stevens	2009	She Be Wild	J. Leparoux
1988	Open Mind	A. Cordero Jr.	1999	Cash Run	J. Bailey	2010	Awesome Feather	J. Sanchez
1989	Go for Wand	R. Romero	2000	Caressing	J. Velazquez	2011	My Miss Aurelia	C. Nakatani
1990	Meadow Star	J. Santos	2001	Tempera	D. Flores	2012	Beholder	G. Gomez
1991	Pleasant Stage	E. Delahoussaye	2002	Storm Flag Flying	J. Velazquez	2013	Ria Antonia	J. Castellano
1992	Eliza	P. Valenzuela	2003	Halfbridled	J. Krone	2014	Take Charge Brandi	V. Espinoza
1993	Phone Chatter	L. Pincay Jr.	2004	Sweet Catomine	C. Nakatani			
1994	Flanders	P. Day	2005	Folklore	E. Prado	2015	Songbird	M. Smith

Sprint

Distance: 6 furlongs.

Year	Horse	Jockey
1984	Eillo	C. Perret
1985	Precisionist	C. McCarron
1986	Smile	J. Vasquez
1987	Very Subtle	P. Valenzuela
1988	Gulch	A. Cordero Jr.
1989	Dancing Spree	A. Cordero Jr.
1990	Safely Kept	C. Perret
1991	Sheikh Albadou	P. Eddery
1992	Thirty Slews	E. Delahoussaye
1993	Cardmania	E. Delahoussaye
1994	Cherokee Run	M. Smith
1995	Desert Stormer	K. Desormeaux
1996	Lit de Justice	C. Nakatani
1997	Elmhurst	C. Nakatani
1998	Reraise	C. Nakatani
1999	Artax	J. Chaves
2000	Kona Gold	A. Solis
2001	Squirtle Squirt	J. Bailey
2002	Orientate	J. Bailey
2003	Cajun Beat	C. Velasquez
2004	Speightstown	J. Velazquez
2005	Silver Train	E. Prado
2006	Thor's Echo	C. Nakatani
2007	Midnight Lute	G. Gomez
2008	Midnight Lute	G. Gomez
2009	Dancing in Silks	J. Rosario
2010	Big Drama	E. Coa
2011	Amazombie	M. Smith
2012	Trinniberg	W. Martinez
2013	Secret Circle	M. Garcia
2014	Work All Week	F. Geroux
2015	Runhappy	E. Prado

Mile

Year	Horse	Jockey
1984	Royal Heroine	F. Toro
1985	Cozzene	W. Guerra
1986	Last Tycoon	Y. St.-Martin
1987	Miesque	F. Head
1988	Miesque	F. Head
1989	Steinlen	J. Santos
1990	Royal Academy	L. Piggott
1991	Opening Verse	P. Valenzuela
1992	Lure	M. Smith
1993	Lure	M. Smith
1994	Barathea	F. Dettori
1995	Ridgewood Pearl	J. Murtagh
1996	Da Hoss	G. Stevens
1997	Spinning World	C. Asmussan
1998	Da Hoss	J. Velazquez
1999	Silic	C. Nakatani
2000	War Chant	G. Stevens
2001	Val Royal	J. Valdivia Jr.
2002	Domedriver	T. Thulliez
2003	Six Perfections	J. Bailey
2004	Singletary	D. Flores
2005	Artie Schiller	G. Gomez
2006	Miesque's Approval	E. Castro
2007	Kip Deville	C. Velasquez
2008	Goldikova	O. Peslier
2009	Goldikova	O. Peslier
2010	Goldikova	O. Peslier
2011	Court Vision	R. Albarado
2012	Wise Dan	J. Velazquez
2013	Wise Dan	J. Lezcano
2014	Karakatonie	S. Pasquier
2015	Tepin	J. Leparoux

Filly and Mare Turf

Distance: 1-3/16 mi; 1-3/8 mi, 1999-2000, 2004, 2006-07; 1-1/4 mi, 2001-03, 2005, 2008-14.

Year	Horse	Jockey
1999	Soaring Softly	J. Bailey
2000	Perfect Sting	J. Bailey
2001	Banks Hill	O. Peslier
2002	Starine	J. Velazquez
2003	Islington	K. Fallon
2004	Ouija Board	K. Fallon
2005	Intercontinental	R. Bejarano
2006	Ouija Board	F. Dettori
2007	Lahudood	A. Garcia
2008	Forever Together	J. Leparoux
2009	Midday	T. Queally
2010	Shared Account	E. Prado
2011	Perfect Shirl	J. Velazquez
2012	Zagora	J. Castellano
2013	Dank	R. Moore
2014	Dayatthespa	J. Castellano
2015	Stephanie's Kitten	I. Ortiz Jr.

Distaff

Distance: 1-1/8 mi since 1988; 1-1/4 mi, 1984-87; race known as Ladies' Classic, 2008-12.

Year	Horse	Jockey
1984	Princess Rooney	E. Delahoussaye
1985	Life's Magic	A. Cordero Jr.
1986	Lady's Secret	P. Day
1987	Sacahuista	R. Romero
1988	Personal Ensign	R. Romero
1989	Bayakoa	L. Pincay Jr.
1990	Bayakoa	L. Pincay Jr.
1991	Dance Smartly	P. Day
1992	Paseana	C. McCarron
1993	Hollywood Wildcat	E. Delahoussaye
1994	One Dreamer	G. Stevens
1995	Inside Information	M. Smith
1996	Jewel Princess	C. Nakatani
1997	Ajina	M. Smith
1998	Escena	G. Stevens
1999	Beautiful Pleasure	J. Chaves
2000	Spain	V. Espinoza
2001	Unbridled Elaine	P. Day
2002	Azeri	M. Smith
2003	Adoration	P. Valenzuela
2004	Ashado	J. Velazquez
2005	Pleasant Home	C. Velasquez
2006	Round Pond	E. Prado
2007	Ginger Punch	R. Bejarano
2008	Zenyatta	M. Smith
2009	Life Is Sweet	G. Gomez
2010	Unrivaled Belle	K. Desormeaux
2011	Royal Delta	J. Lezcano
2012	Royal Delta	M. Smith
2013	Beholder	G. Stevens
2014	Untapable	R. Napravnik
2015	Stopchargingmaria	J. Castellano

Turf

Distance: 1-1/2 mi.

Year	Horse	Jockey
1984	Lashkari	Y. St.-Martin
1985	Pebbles	P. Eddery
1986	Manila	J. Santos
1987	Theatrical	P. Day
1988	Great Communicator	R. Sibille
1989	Prized	E. Delahoussaye
1990	In the Wings	G. Stevens
1991	Miss Alleged	E. Legrix
1992	Fraise	P. Valenzuela
1993	Kotashaan	K. Desormeaux
1994	Tikkanen	M. Smith
1995	Northern Spur	C. McCarron
1996	Pilsudski	W. Swinburn
1997	Chief Bearhart	J. Santos
1998	Buck's Boy	S. Sellers
1999	Daylami	F. Dettori
2000	Kalanisi	J. Murtagh
2001	Fantastic Light	F. Dettori
2002	High Chaparral	M. Kinane
2003	(tie) High Chaparral	M. Kinane
	Johar	A. Solis
2004	Better Talk Now	R. Dominguez
2005	Shirocco	C. Soumillon
2006	Red Rocks	F. Dettori
2007	English Channel	J. Velasquez
2008	Conduit	R. Moore
2009	Conduit	R. Moore
2010	Dangerous Midge	F. Dettori
2011	St Nicholas Abbey	J. O'Brien
2012	Little Mike	R. Dominguez
2013	Magician	R. Moore
2014	Main Sequence	J. Velazquez
2015	Found	R. Moore

Filly and Mare Sprint

Distance: 6 furlongs, 2007; 7 furlongs since 2008.

Year	Horse	Jockey
2007	Maryfield	E. Trujillo
2008	Ventura	G. Gomez
2009	Informed Decision	J. Leparoux
2010	Dubai Majesty	J. Theriot
2011	Musical Romance	J. Leyva
2012	Groupie Doll	R. Maragh
2013	Groupie Doll	R. Maragh
2014	Judy the Beauty	M. Smith
2015	Wavell Avenue	J. Rosario

Juvenile Turf

Distance: 1 mi.

Year	Horse	Jockey
2007	Nownownow	J. Leparoux
2008	Donativum	F. Dettori
2009	Pounced	F. Dettori
2010	Pluck	G. Gomez
2011	Wrote	R. Moore
2012	George Vancouver	R. Moore
2013	Outstrip	M. Smith
2014	Hootenanny	F. Dettori
2015	Hit It a Bomb	R. Moore

Dirt Mile

Year	Horse	Jockey
2007	Corinthian	K. Desormeaux
2008	Albertus Maximus	G. Gomez
2009	Furthest Land	J. Leparoux
2010	Dakota Phone	J. Rosario
2011	Caleb's Posse	R. Maragh
2012	Tapizar	C. Nakatani
2013	Goldencents	R. Bejarano
2014	Goldencents	R. Bejarano
2015	Liam's Map	J. Castellano

Turf Sprint

Distance: 5-1/2 furlongs; 6-1/2 furlongs, 2008-09, 2012-14; 5 furlongs, 2010-11.

Year	Horse	Jockey
2008	Desert Code	R. Migliore
2009	California Flag	J. Talamo
2010	Chamberlain Bridge	J. Theriot
2011	Regally Ready	C. Nakatani
2012	Mizdirection	M. Smith
2013	Mizdirection	M. Smith
2014	Bobby's Kitten	J. Rosario
2015	Mongolian Saturday	F. Geroux

Juvenile Fillies Turf

Distance: 1 mi.

Year	Horse	Jockey
2008	Maram	J. Lezcano
2009	Tapitsfly	R. Albarado
2010	More Than Real	G. Gomez
2011	Stephanie's Kitten	J. Velazquez
2012	Flotilla	C. Lemaire
2013	Chriselliam	R. Hughes
2014	Lady Eli	I. Ortiz Jr.
2015	Catch a Glimpse	F. Geroux

Eclipse Awards

The Eclipse Awards, honoring the Horse of the Year and other champions of thoroughbred racing, began in 1971 and are sponsored by the *Daily Racing Form*, the National Thoroughbred Racing Association, and the National Turf Writers Assn. Prior to 1971, the *DRF* (1936-70) and the NTRA (1950-70) issued separate selections for Horse of the Year.

Eclipse Awards, 2014

Horse of the Year: California Chrome
2-year-old male: American Pharoah
2-year-old female: Take Charge Brandi
3-year-old male: California Chrome
3-year-old female: Untapable
Older male (4+ years old): Main Sequence
Older female (4+ years old): Close Hatches
Male sprinter: Work All Week
Female sprinter: Judy the Beauty
Male turf horse: Main Sequence
Female turf horse: Dayatthespa
Steeplechase horse: Demonstrative
Trainer: Todd Pletcher
Jockey: Javier Castellano
Apprentice jockey: Drayden Van Dyke
Breeder: Ken and Sarah Ramsey
Owner: Ken and Sarah Ramsey
Handicapper: Jose Arias

Horse of the Year, 1936-2014

Year	Horse
1936	Granville
1937	War Admiral
1938	Seabiscuit
1939	Challedon
1940	Challedon
1941	Whirlaway
1942	Whirlaway
1943	Count Fleet
1944	Twilight Tear
1945	Busher
1946	Assault
1947	Armed
1948	Citation
1949	Capot
1950	Hill Prince
1951	Counterpoint
1952	One Count (DRF); Native Dancer (NTRA)
1953	Tom Fool
1954	Native Dancer
1955	Nashua
1956	Swaps
1957	Bold Ruler (DRF); Dedicate (NTRA)
1958	Round Table
1959	Sword Dancer
1960	Kelso
1961	Kelso
1962	Kelso
1963	Kelso
1964	Kelso
1965	Roman Brother (DRF); Moccasin (NTRA)
1966	Buckpasser
1967	Damascus
1968	Dr. Fager
1969	Arts and Letters
1970	Fort Marcy (DRF); Personality (NTRA)
1971	Ack Ack
1972	Secretariat
1973	Secretariat
1974	Forego
1975	Forego
1976	Forego
1977	Seattle Slew
1978	Affirmed
1979	Affirmed
1980	Spectacular Bid
1981	John Henry
1982	Conquistador Cielo
1983	All Along
1984	John Henry
1985	Spend a Buck
1986	Lady's Secret
1987	Ferdinand
1988	Alysheba
1989	Sunday Silence
1990	Criminal Type
1991	Black Tie Affair
1992	A.P. Indy
1993	Kotashaan
1994	Holy Bull
1995	Cigar
1996	Cigar
1997	Favorite Trick
1998	Skip Away
1999	Charismatic
2000	Tiznow
2001	Point Given
2002	Azeri
2003	Mineshaft
2004	Ghostzapper
2005	Saint Liam
2006	Invasor
2007	Curlin
2008	Curlin
2009	Rachel Alexandra
2010	Zenyatta
2011	Havre de Grace
2012	Wise Dan
2013	Wise Dan
2014	California Chrome

HARNESS RACING

Harness Horse of the Year, 1947-2014

Chosen by the U.S. Trotting Assn. and the U.S. Harness Writers Assn.

Year	Horse
1947	Victory Song
1948	Rodney
1949	Good Time
1950	Proximity
1951	Pronto Don
1952	Good Time
1953	Hi Lo's Forbes
1954	Stenographer
1955	Scott Frost
1956	Scott Frost
1957	Torpid
1958	Emily's Pride
1959	Bye Bye Byrd
1960	Adios Butler
1961	Adios Butler
1962	Su Mac Lad
1963	Speedy Scot
1964	Bret Hanover
1965	Bret Hanover
1966	Bret Hanover
1967	Nevele Pride
1968	Nevele Pride
1969	Nevele Pride
1970	Fresh Yankee
1971	Albatross
1972	Albatross
1973	Sir Dalrae
1974	Delmonica Hanover
1975	Savoir
1976	Keystone Ore
1977	Green Speed
1978	Abercrombie
1979	Niatross
1980	Niatross
1981	Fan Hanover
1982	Cam Fella
1983	Cam Fella
1984	Fancy Crown
1985	Nihilator
1986	Forrest Skipper
1987	Mack Lobell
1988	Mack Lobell
1989	Matt's Scooter
1990	Beach Towel
1991	Precious Bunny
1992	Artsplace
1993	Staying Together
1994	Cam's Card Shark
1995	CR Kay Suzie
1996	Continental Victory
1997	Malabar Man
1998	Moni Maker
1999	Moni Maker
2000	Gallo Blue Chip
2001	Bunny Lake
2002	Real Desire
2003	No Pan Intended
2004	Rainbow Blue
2005	Rocknroll Hanover
2006	Glidemaster
2007	Donato Hanover
2008	Somebeachsomewhere
2009	Muscle Hill
2010	Rock N Roll Heaven
2011	San Pail
2012	Chapter Seven
2013	Bee a Magician
2014	JK She'salady

The Hambletonian Winners (3-year-old trotters), 1965-2015

Year	Horse	Driver
1965	Egyptian Candor	Del Cameron
1966	Kerry Way	Frank Ervin
1967	Speedy Streak	Del Cameron
1968	Nevele Pride	Stanley Dancer
1969	Lindy's Pride	Howard Beissinger
1970	Timothy T	John Simpson Sr.
1971	Speedy Crown	Howard Beissinger
1972	Super Bowl	Stanley Dancer
1973	Flirth	Ralph Baldwin
1974	Christopher T	Bill Haughton
1975	Bonefish	Stanley Dancer
1976	Steve Lobell	Bill Haughton
1977	Green Speed	Bill Haughton
1978	Speedy Somolli	Howard Beissinger
1979	Legend Hanover	George Sholty
1980	Burgomeister	Bill Haughton
1981	Shiaway St. Pat	Ray Remmen
1982	Speed Bowl	Tommy Haughton
1983	Duenna	Stanley Dancer
1984	Historic Freight	Ben Webster
1985	Prakas	Bill O'Donnell
1986	Nuclear Kosmos	Ulf Thoresen
1987	Mack Lobell	John Campbell
1988	Armbro Goal	John Campbell

Year	Horse	Driver	Year	Horse	Driver
1989	Park Avenue Joe	Ron Waples	2003	Amigo Hall	Mike Lachance
1990	Harmonious	John Campbell	2004	Windsong's Legacy	Trond Smedshammer
1991	Giant Victory	Jack Moiseyev	2005	Vivid Photo	Roger Hammer
1992	Alf Palema	Mickey McNicholl	2006	Glidemaster	John Campbell
1993	American Winner	Ron Pierce	2007	Donato Hanover	Ron Pierce
1994	Victory Dream	Michel Lachance	2008	Deweycheatumnhowe	Ray Schnittker
1995	Tagliabue	John Campbell	2009	Muscle Hill	Brian Sears
1996	Continental Victory	Michel Lachance	2010	Muscle Massive	Ron Pierce
1997	Malabar Man	Malvern Burroughs	2011	Broad Bahn	George Brennan
1998	Muscles Yankee	John Campbell	2012	Market Share	Tim Tetrick
1999	Self Possessed	Mike Lachance	2013	Royalty For Life	Brian Sears
2000	Yankee Paco	Trevor Ritchie	2014	Trixton	Jimmy Takter
2001	Scarlet Knight	Stefan Melander	2015	Pinkman	Brian Sears
2002	Chip Chip Hooray	Eric Ledford			

BOWLING

Professional Bowlers Association Tournament of Champions, 1965-2015

Year	Winner	Year	Winner	Year	Winner	Year	Winner
1965	Billy Hardwick	1977	Mike Berlin	1989	Del Ballard Jr.	2003	Patrick Healey Jr.
1966	Wayne Zahn	1978	Earl Anthony	1990	Dave Ferraro	2005	Steve Jaros
1967	Jim Stefanich	1979	George Pappas	1991	David Ozio	2006	Chris Barnes
1968	Dave Davis	1980	Wayne Webb	1992	Marc McDowell	2007	Tommy Jones
1969	Jim Godman	1981	Steve Cook	1993	George Branham III	2008	Michael Haugen Jr.
1970	Don Johnson	1982	Mike Durbin	1994	Norm Duke	2009	Patrick Allen
1971	Johnny Petraglia	1983	Joe Berardi	1996	Dave D'Entremont	2010	Kelly Kulick
1972	Mike Durbin	1984	Mike Durbin	1997	John Gant	2011	Mika Koivuniemi
1973	Jim Godman	1985	Mark Williams	1998	Bryan Goebel	2012	Sean Rash
1974	Earl Anthony	1986	Marshall Holman	1999	Jason Couch	2013	Pete Weber
1975	Dave Davis	1987	Pete Weber	2000	Jason Couch	2014	Jason Belmonte
1976	Marshall Holman	1988	Mark Williams	2002	Jason Couch	2015	Jason Belmonte

Note: No tournament held in 2001 or 2004.

Professional Bowlers Association Leading Money Winners, 1962-2015

Total winnings from tournaments only. For 2000-13, year shown is year the PBA season ended. As of Sept. 18, 2015.

Year	Bowler	Earnings	Year	Bowler	Earnings	Year	Bowler	Earnings
1962	Don Carter	$49,972	1980	Wayne Webb	$116,700	1998	Walter Ray Williams Jr.	$238,225
1963	Dick Weber	46,333	1981	Earl Anthony	164,735	1999	Parker Bohn III	240,912
1964	Bob Strampe	33,592	1982	Earl Anthony	134,760	2000	Norm Duke	143,325
1965	Dick Weber	47,674	1983	Earl Anthony	135,605	2002	Parker Bohn III	245,200
1966	Wayne Zahn	54,720	1984	Mark Roth	158,712	2003	Walter Ray Williams Jr.	419,700
1967	Dave Davis	54,165	1985	Mike Aulby	201,200	2004	Mika Koivuniemi	238,590
1968	Jim Stefanich	67,377	1986	Walter Ray Williams Jr.	145,550	2005	Patrick Allen	350,740
1969	Billy Hardwick	64,160	1987	Pete Weber	175,491	2006	Tommy Jones	301,700
1970	Mike McGrath	52,049	1988	Brian Voss	225,485	2007	Doug Kent	200,530
1971	Johnny Petraglia	85,065	1989	Mike Aulby	298,237	2008	Norm Duke	176,855
1972	Don Johnson	56,648	1990	Amleto Monacelli	204,775	2009	Norm Duke	199,130
1973	Don McCune	69,000	1991	David Ozio	225,585	2010	Walter Ray Williams Jr.	152,670
1974	Earl Anthony	99,585	1992	Marc McDowell	174,215	2011	Mika Koivuniemi	333,040
1975	Earl Anthony	107,585	1993	Walter Ray Williams Jr.	296,370	2012	Sean Rash	140,250
1976	Earl Anthony	110,833	1994	Norm Duke	273,753	2013	Sean Rash	248,317
1977	Mark Roth	105,583	1995	Mike Aulby	219,792	2014	Jason Belmonte	163,778
1978	Mark Roth	134,500	1996	Walter Ray Williams Jr.	241,330	2015	Jason Belmonte	170,042
1979	Mark Roth	124,517	1997	Walter Ray Williams Jr.	240,544			

World Chess Champions, 1886-2015

Source: U.S. Chess Federation, International Chess Federation (FIDE)

Official world champions since the title was first used.

Years	Champion, country	Years	Champion, country
1886-94	Wilhelm Steinitz, Austria	**1972-75**	Bobby Fischer, U.S.[2]
1894-1921	Emanuel Lasker, Germany	**1975-85**	Anatoly Karpov, USSR
1921-27	Jose R. Capablanca, Cuba	**1985-2000**	Garry Kasparov, USSR/Russia[3]
1927-35	Alexander Alekhine, France	**1993-99**	Anatoly Karpov, Russia (FIDE)[3]
1935-37	Max Euwe, Netherlands	**1999-2000**	Alexander Khalifman, Russia (FIDE)
1937-46	Alexander Alekhine, France[1]	**2000-02**	Viswanathan Anand, India (FIDE)
1948-57	Mikhail Botvinnik, USSR	**2000-06**	Vladimir Kramnik, Russia (classical)[4]
1957-58	Vassily Smyslov, USSR	**2002-04**	Ruslan Ponomariov, Ukraine (FIDE)
1958-59	Mikhail Botvinnik, USSR	**2004-05**	Rustam Kasimdzhanov, Uzbekistan (FIDE)
1960-61	Mikhail Tal, USSR	**2005-06**	Veselin Topalov, Bulgaria (FIDE)[5]
1961-63	Mikhail Botvinnik, USSR	**2006-07**	Vladimir Kramnik, Russia[5]
1963-69	Tigran Petrosian, USSR	**2007-13**	Viswanathan Anand, India
1969-72	Boris Spassky, USSR	**2013-**	Magnus Carlsen, Norway

(1) After Alekhine died in 1946, the title was vacant until 1948, when Botvinnik won the first world championship event sanctioned by FIDE. (2) Defaulted championship after refusing to accept FIDE rules for a championship match, Apr. 1975. (3) Kasparov broke with FIDE, Feb. 26, 1993. FIDE stripped Kasparov of his FIDE title Mar. 23. Kasparov defeated Nigel Short (UK) in a world championship match played Sept.-Oct. 1993 under the auspices of the Professional Chess Association (PCA), a new organization the two had founded. FIDE held a championship match between Anatoly Karpov (Russia) and Jan Timman (Netherlands), which Karpov won in Nov. 1993. The PCA folded in 1995, but Kasparov was still considered the "classical" world champion. (That is, he defended his title against challengers; FIDE matches are arranged differently.) (4) In Nov. 2000, Kramnik defeated Kasparov for the classical world championship title. (5) Kramnik, the classical world champion since 2000, unified the chess titles by defeating Topalov on Oct. 13, 2006, at a world championship match.

U.S. and World Figure Skating Championships, 1952-2015

U.S. Champions			World Champions	
Men's winner	**Women's winner**	**Year**	**Men's winner, country**	**Women's winner, country**
Dick Button	Tenley Albright	**1952**	Dick Button, U.S.	Jacqueline du Bief, France
Hayes Jenkins	Tenley Albright	**1953**	Hayes Jenkins, U.S.	Tenley Albright, U.S.
Hayes Jenkins	Tenley Albright	**1954**	Hayes Jenkins, U.S.	Gundi Busch, W. Germany
Hayes Jenkins	Tenley Albright	**1955**	Hayes Jenkins, U.S.	Tenley Albright, U.S.
Hayes Jenkins	Tenley Albright	**1956**	Hayes Jenkins, U.S.	Carol Heiss, U.S.
David Jenkins	Carol Heiss	**1957**	David Jenkins, U.S.	Carol Heiss, U.S.
David Jenkins	Carol Heiss	**1958**	David Jenkins, U.S.	Carol Heiss, U.S.
David Jenkins	Carol Heiss	**1959**	David Jenkins, U.S.	Carol Heiss, U.S.
David Jenkins	Carol Heiss	**1960**	Alain Giletti, France	Carol Heiss, U.S.
Bradley Lord	Laurence Owen	**1961**	No competition[1]	No competition[1]
Monty Hoyt	Barbara Roles Pursley	**1962**	Don Jackson, Canada	Sjoukje Dijkstra, Netherlands
Tommy Litz	Lorraine Hanlon	**1963**	Don McPherson, Canada	Sjoukje Dijkstra, Netherlands
Scott Allen	Peggy Fleming	**1964**	Manfred Schnelldorfer, W. Germany	Sjoukje Dijkstra, Netherlands
Gary Visconti	Peggy Fleming	**1965**	Alain Calmat, France	Petra Burka, Canada
Scott Allen	Peggy Fleming	**1966**	Emmerich Danzer, Austria	Peggy Fleming, U.S.
Gary Visconti	Peggy Fleming	**1967**	Emmerich Danzer, Austria	Peggy Fleming, U.S.
Tim Wood	Peggy Fleming	**1968**	Emmerich Danzer, Austria	Peggy Fleming, U.S.
Tim Wood	Janet Lynn	**1969**	Tim Wood, U.S.	Gabriele Seyfert, E. Germany
Tim Wood	Janet Lynn	**1970**	Tim Wood, U.S.	Gabriele Seyfert, E. Germany
John Misha Petkevich	Janet Lynn	**1971**	Ondrej Nepela, Czechoslovakia	Beatrix Schuba, Austria
Ken Shelley	Janet Lynn	**1972**	Ondrej Nepela, Czechoslovakia	Beatrix Schuba, Austria
Gordon McKellen Jr.	Janet Lynn	**1973**	Ondrej Nepela, Czechoslovakia	Karen Magnussen, Canada
Gordon McKellen Jr.	Dorothy Hamill	**1974**	Jan Hoffmann, E. Germany	Christine Errath, E. Germany
Gordon McKellen Jr.	Dorothy Hamill	**1975**	Sergei Volkov, USSR	Dianne de Leeuw, Neth.
Terry Kubicka	Dorothy Hamill	**1976**	John Curry, UK	Dorothy Hamill, U.S.
Charles Tickner	Linda Fratianne	**1977**	Vladimir Kovalev, USSR	Linda Fratianne, U.S.
Charles Tickner	Linda Fratianne	**1978**	Charles Tickner, U.S.	Anett Poetzsch, E. Germany
Charles Tickner	Linda Fratianne	**1979**	Vladimir Kovalev, USSR	Linda Fratianne, U.S.
Charles Tickner	Linda Fratianne	**1980**	Jan Hoffmann, E. Germany	Anett Poetzsch, E. Germany
Scott Hamilton	Elaine Zayak	**1981**	Scott Hamilton, U.S.	Denise Biellmann, Switzerland
Scott Hamilton	Rosalynn Sumners	**1982**	Scott Hamilton, U.S.	Elaine Zayak, U.S.
Scott Hamilton	Rosalynn Sumners	**1983**	Scott Hamilton, U.S.	Rosalynn Sumners, U.S.
Scott Hamilton	Rosalynn Sumners	**1984**	Scott Hamilton, U.S.	Katarina Witt, E. Germany
Brian Boitano	Tiffany Chin	**1985**	Aleksandr Fadeev, USSR	Katarina Witt, E. Germany
Brian Boitano	Debi Thomas	**1986**	Brian Boitano, U.S.	Debi Thomas, U.S.
Brian Boitano	Jill Trenary	**1987**	Brian Orser, Canada	Katarina Witt, E. Germany
Brian Boitano	Debi Thomas	**1988**	Brian Boitano, U.S.	Katarina Witt, E. Germany
Christopher Bowman	Jill Trenary	**1989**	Kurt Browning, Canada	Midori Ito, Japan
Todd Eldredge	Jill Trenary	**1990**	Kurt Browning, Canada	Jill Trenary, U.S.
Todd Eldredge	Tonya Harding	**1991**	Kurt Browning, Canada	Kristi Yamaguchi, U.S.
Christopher Bowman	Kristi Yamaguchi	**1992**	Viktor Petrenko, Ukraine	Kristi Yamaguchi, U.S.
Scott Davis	Nancy Kerrigan	**1993**	Kurt Browning, Canada	Oksana Baiul, Ukraine
Scott Davis	Vacant[2]	**1994**	Elvis Stojko, Canada	Yuka Sato, Japan
Todd Eldredge	Nicole Bobek	**1995**	Elvis Stojko, Canada	Chen Lu, China
Rudy Galindo	Michelle Kwan	**1996**	Todd Eldredge, U.S.	Michelle Kwan, U.S.
Todd Eldredge	Tara Lipinski	**1997**	Elvis Stojko, Canada	Tara Lipinski, U.S.
Todd Eldredge	Michelle Kwan	**1998**	Alexei Yagudin, Russia	Michelle Kwan, U.S.
Michael Weiss	Michelle Kwan	**1999**	Alexei Yagudin, Russia	Maria Butyrskaya, Russia
Michael Weiss	Michelle Kwan	**2000**	Alexei Yagudin, Russia	Michelle Kwan, U.S.
Timothy Goebel	Michelle Kwan	**2001**	Yevgeny Plushenko, Russia	Michelle Kwan, U.S.
Todd Eldredge	Michelle Kwan	**2002**	Alexei Yagudin, Russia	Irina Slutskaya, Russia
Michael Weiss	Michelle Kwan	**2003**	Yevgeny Plushenko, Russia	Michelle Kwan, U.S.
Johnny Weir	Michelle Kwan	**2004**	Yevgeny Plushenko, Russia	Shizuka Arakawa, Japan
Johnny Weir	Michelle Kwan	**2005**	Stephane Lambiel, Switzerland	Irina Slutskaya, Russia
Johnny Weir	Sasha Cohen	**2006**	Stephane Lambiel, Switzerland	Kimmie Meissner, U.S.
Evan Lysacek	Kimmie Meissner	**2007**	Brian Joubert, France	Miki Ando, Japan
Evan Lysacek	Mirai Nagasu	**2008**	Jeffrey Buttle, Canada	Mao Asada, Japan
Jeremy Abbott	Alissa Czisny	**2009**	Evan Lysacek, U.S.	Yuna Kim, South Korea
Jeremy Abbott	Rachael Flatt	**2010**	Daisuke Takahashi, Japan	Mao Asada, Japan
Ryan Bradley	Alissa Czisny	**2011**	Patrick Chan, Canada	Miki Ando, Japan
Jeremy Abbott	Ashley Wagner	**2012**	Patrick Chan, Canada	Carolina Kostner, Italy
Max Aaron	Ashley Wagner	**2013**	Patrick Chan, Canada	Yuna Kim, South Korea
Jeremy Abbott	Gracie Gold	**2014**	Yuzuru Hanyu, Japan	Mao Asada, Japan
Jason Brown	Ashley Wagner	**2015**	Javier Fernandez, Spain	Elizaveta Tuktamysheva, Russia

(1) Competition canceled after 18-member U.S. team died in plane crash en route. (2) Tonya Harding was stripped of the title for her involvement in an attack on rival Nancy Kerrigan.

Alpine Skiing Men's World Cup Champions, 1967-2015

Year	Champion, country	Year	Champion, country	Year	Champion, country
1967	Jean Claude Killy, France	1984	Pirmin Zurbriggen, Switzerland	2000	Hermann Maier, Austria
1968	Jean Claude Killy, France	1985	Marc Girardelli, Luxembourg	2001	Hermann Maier, Austria
1969	Karl Schranz, Austria	1986	Marc Girardelli, Luxembourg	2002	Stephan Eberharter, Austria
1970	Karl Schranz, Austria	1987	Pirmin Zurbriggen, Switzerland	2003	Stephan Eberharter, Austria
1971	Gustavo Thoeni, Italy	1988	Pirmin Zurbriggen, Switzerland	2004	Hermann Maier, Austria
1972	Gustavo Thoeni, Italy	1989	Marc Girardelli, Luxembourg	2005	Bode Miller, U.S.
1973	Gustavo Thoeni, Italy	1990	Pirmin Zurbriggen, Switzerland	2006	Benjamin Raich, Austria
1974	Piero Gros, Italy	1991	Marc Girardelli, Luxembourg	2007	Aksel Lund Svindal, Norway
1975	Gustavo Thoeni, Italy	1992	Paul Accola, Switzerland	2008	Bode Miller, U.S.
1976	Ingemar Stenmark, Sweden	1993	Marc Girardelli, Luxembourg	2009	Aksel Lund Svindal, Norway
1977	Ingemar Stenmark, Sweden	1994	Kjetil Andre Aamodt, Norway	2010	Carlo Janka, Switzerland
1978	Ingemar Stenmark, Sweden	1995	Alberto Tomba, Italy	2011	Ivica Kostelic, Croatia
1979	Peter Luescher, Switzerland	1996	Lasse Kjus, Norway	2012	Marcel Hirscher, Austria
1980	Andreas Wenzel, Liechtenstein	1997	Luc Alphand, France	2013	Marcel Hirscher, Austria
1981	Phil Mahre, U.S.	1998	Hermann Maier, Austria	2014	Marcel Hirscher, Austria
1982	Phil Mahre, U.S.	1999	Lasse Kjus, Norway	2015	Marcel Hirscher, Austria
1983	Phil Mahre, U.S.				

Alpine Skiing Women's World Cup Champions, 1967-2015

Year	Champion, country	Year	Champion, country	Year	Champion, country
1967	Nancy Greene, Canada	1984	Erika Hess, Switzerland	2000	Renate Goetschl, Austria
1968	Nancy Greene, Canada	1985	Michela Figini, Switzerland	2001	Janica Kostelic, Croatia
1969	Gertrud Gabl, Austria	1986	Maria Walliser, Switzerland	2002	Michaela Dorfmeister, Austria
1970	Michele Jacot, France	1987	Maria Walliser, Switzerland	2003	Janica Kostelic, Croatia
1971	Annemarie Proell, Austria	1988	Michela Figini, Switzerland	2004	Anja Paerson, Sweden
1972	Annemarie Proell, Austria	1989	Vreni Schneider, Switzerland	2005	Anja Paerson, Sweden
1973	Annemarie Proell, Austria	1990	Petra Kronberger, Austria	2006	Janica Kostelic, Croatia
1974	Annemarie Proell, Austria	1991	Petra Kronberger, Austria	2007	Nicole Hosp, Austria
1975	Annemarie Proell, Austria	1992	Petra Kronberger, Austria	2008	Lindsey Vonn, U.S.
1976	Rose Mittermaier, W. Germany	1993	Anita Wachter, Austria	2009	Lindsey Vonn, U.S.
1977	Lise-Marie Morerod, Switzerland	1994	Vreni Schneider, Switzerland	2010	Lindsey Vonn, U.S.
1978	Hanni Wenzel, Liechtenstein	1995	Vreni Schneider, Switzerland	2011	Maria Höfl-Riesch, Germany
1979	Annemarie Proell Moser, Austria	1996	Katja Seizinger, Germany	2012	Lindsey Vonn, U.S.
1980	Hanni Wenzel, Liechtenstein	1997	Pernilla Wiberg, Sweden	2013	Tina Maze, Slovenia
1981	Marie-Theres Nadig, Switzerland	1998	Katja Seizinger, Germany	2014	Anna Fenninger, Austria
1982	Erika Hess, Switzerland	1999	Alexandra Meissnitzer, Austria	2015	Anna Fenninger, Austria
1983	Tamara McKinney, U.S.				

Tour de France, 2015

The UK's Chris Froome won the Tour de France for the second time in three years in the 102nd edition of cycling's premier race July 26, 2015. The first stage of the 2,088-mi (3,360-km) Tour de France began July 4 in Utrecht, Netherlands. The final and 21st stage concluded on the streets of Paris, where Froome claimed victory in 84 hr., 46 min., 14 sec., followed by Colombia's Nairo Alexander Quintana Rojas, 1 min., 12 sec. behind, and Spain's Alejandro Valverde Belmonte, 5 min., 25 sec. behind. Quintana Rojas won the white jersey as the best rider under age 25 in the Tour de France, and Froome won the polka dot jersey as the best climber. Slovakian Peter Sagan won the green jersey as the points leader for the fourth straight year.

The 2016 Tour de France is scheduled to be held July 2-24. Its route will take cyclists from Mont-Saint-Michel, France, to Paris.

Tour de France Winners, 1903-2015

The Tour de France was first held in 1903. Sixty cyclists began the 1,509-mi (2,428-km) race at Montgeron, a suburb of Paris, and 21 cyclists finished the six-stage race 17 days later in Paris. The race route changes every year. Race not held, 1915-18; 1940-46.

Year	Winner, country	Year	Winner, country	Year	Winner, country
1903	Maurice Garin, France	1948	Gino Bartali, Italy	1982	Bernard Hinault, France
1904	Henri Cornet, France	1949	Fausto Coppi, Italy	1983	Laurent Fignon, France
1905	Louis Trousselier, France	1950	Ferdi Kübler, Switzerland	1984	Laurent Fignon, France
1906	René Pottier, France	1951	Hugo Koblet, Switzerland	1985	Bernard Hinault, France
1907	Lucien Petit-Breton, France	1952	Fausto Coppi, Italy	1986	Greg LeMond, U.S.
1908	Lucien Petit-Breton, France	1953	Louison Bobet, France	1987	Stephen Roche, Ireland
1909	François Faber, Luxembourg	1954	Louison Bobet, France	1988	Pedro Delgado, Spain
1910	Octave Lapize, France	1955	Louison Bobet, France	1989	Greg LeMond, U.S.
1911	Gustave Garrigou, France	1956	Roger Walkowiak, France	1990	Greg LeMond, U.S.
1912	Odile Defraye, Belgium	1957	Jacques Anquetil, France	1991	Miguel Indurain, Spain
1913	Philippe Thys, Belgium	1958	Charly Gaul, Luxembourg	1992	Miguel Indurain, Spain
1914	Philippe Thys, Belgium	1959	Federico Bahamontes, Spain	1993	Miguel Indurain, Spain
1919	Firmin Lambot, Belgium	1960	Gastone Nencini, Italy	1994	Miguel Indurain, Spain
1920	Philippe Thys, Belgium	1961	Jacques Anquetil, France	1995	Miguel Indurain, Spain
1921	Léon Scieur, Belgium	1962	Jacques Anquetil, France	1996	Bjarne Riis, Denmark
1922	Firmin Lambot, Belgium	1963	Jacques Anquetil, France	1997	Jan Ullrich, Germany
1923	Henri Pélissier, France	1964	Jacques Anquetil, France	1998	Marco Pantani, Italy
1924	Ottavio Bottecchia, Italy	1965	Felice Gimondi, Italy	1999	Vacant[1]
1925	Ottavio Bottecchia, Italy	1966	Lucien Aimar, France	2000	Vacant[1]
1926	Lucien Buysse, Belgium	1967	Roger Pingeon, France	2001	Vacant[1]
1927	Nicolas Frantz, Luxembourg	1968	Jan Janssen, Netherlands	2002	Vacant[1]
1928	Nicolas Frantz, Luxembourg	1969	Eddy Merckx, Belgium	2003	Vacant[1]
1929	Maurice Dewaele, Belgium	1970	Eddy Merckx, Belgium	2004	Vacant[1]
1930	André Leducq, France	1971	Eddy Merckx, Belgium	2005	Vacant[1]
1931	Antonin Magne, France	1972	Eddy Merckx, Belgium	2006	Óscar Pereiro, Spain[2]
1932	André Leducq, France	1973	Luis Ocana, Spain	2007	Alberto Contador, Spain
1933	Georges Speicher, France	1974	Eddy Merckx, Belgium	2008	Carlos Sastre, Spain
1934	Antonin Magne, France	1975	Bernard Thévenet, France	2009	Alberto Contador, Spain
1935	Romain Maes, Belgium	1976	Lucien Van Impe, Belgium	2010	Andy Schleck, Luxembourg[3]
1936	Sylvère Maes, Belgium	1977	Bernard Thévenet, France	2011	Cadel Evans, Australia
1937	Roger Lapépie, France	1978	Bernard Hinault, France	2012	Bradley Wiggins, UK
1938	Gino Bartali, Italy	1979	Bernard Hinault, France	2013	Chris Froome, UK
1939	Sylvère Maes, Belgium	1980	Joop Zoetemelk, Netherlands	2014	Vincenzo Nibali, Italy
1947	Jean Robic, France	1981	Bernard Hinault, France	2015	Chris Froome, UK

(1) Lance Armstrong, U.S., was stripped of his seven Tour titles Oct. 22, 2012, in accordance with World Anti-Doping Code; Armstrong had dropped his fight against doping charges Aug. 23, 2012. (2) Floyd Landis, U.S., was stripped of the 2006 title, Sept. 20, 2007, for doping. Landis lost a final appeal of the ruling June 30, 2008. (3) Alberto Contador, Spain, was stripped of the 2010 title, Feb. 6, 2012, for doping.

Swimming World Records

Long course (50-m pools only) records, as of Sept. 2015. All times in minutes:seconds. * = Record pending ratification.

Men's Records

Freestyle

Distance	Record	Holder	Nationality	Location	Date
50 meters	**0:20.91**	César Cielo Filho	Brazil	São Paulo, Brazil	Dec. 18, 2009
100 meters	**0:46.91**	César Cielo Filho	Brazil	Rome, Italy	July 30, 2009
200 meters	**1:42.00**	Paul Biedermann	Germany	Rome, Italy	July 28, 2009
400 meters	**3:40.07**	Paul Biedermann	Germany	Rome, Italy	July 26, 2009
800 meters	**7:32.12**	Zhang Lin	China	Rome, Italy	July 29, 2009
1,500 meters	**14:31.02**	Yang Sun	China	London, England, UK	Aug. 4, 2012

Backstroke

Distance	Record	Holder	Nationality	Location	Date
50 meters	**0:24.04**	Liam Tancock	UK	Rome, Italy	Aug. 2, 2009
100 meters	**0:51.94**	Aaron Peirsol	U.S.	Indianapolis, IN	July 8, 2009
200 meters	**1:51.92**	Aaron Peirsol	U.S.	Rome, Italy	July 31, 2009

Breaststroke

Distance	Record	Holder	Nationality	Location	Date
50 meters	**0:26.42***	Adam Peaty	UK	Kazan, Russia	Aug. 4, 2015
100 meters	**0:57.92**	Adam Peaty	UK	London, England, UK	Apr. 17, 2015
200 meters	**2:07.01**	Akihiro Yamaguchi	Japan	Gifu, Japan	Sept. 15, 2012

Butterfly

Distance	Record	Holder	Nationality	Location	Date
50 meters	**0:22.43**	Rafael Muñoz	Spain	Malaga, Spain	Apr. 5, 2009
100 meters	**0:49.82**	Michael Phelps	U.S.	Rome, Italy	Aug. 1, 2009
200 meters	**1:51.51**	Michael Phelps	U.S.	Rome, Italy	July 29, 2009

Individual medley

Distance	Record	Holder	Nationality	Location	Date
200 meters	**1:54.00**	Ryan Lochte	U.S.	Shanghai, China	July 28, 2011
400 meters	**4:03.84**	Michael Phelps	U.S.	Beijing, China	Aug. 10, 2008

Freestyle relay

Distance	Record	Holder	Nationality	Location	Date
400 m (4×100)	**3:08.24**	Phelps, Weber-Gale, Jones, Lezak	U.S.	Beijing, China	Aug. 11, 2008
800 m (4×200)	**6:58.55**	Phelps, Berens, Walters, Lochte	U.S.	Rome, Italy	July 31, 2009

Medley relay

Distance	Record	Holder	Nationality	Location	Date
400 m (4×100)	**3:27.28**	Peirsol, Shanteau, Phelps, Walters	U.S.	Rome, Italy	Aug. 2, 2009

Women's Records

Freestyle

Distance	Record	Holder	Nationality	Location	Date
50 meters	**0:23.73**	Britta Steffen	Germany	Rome, Italy	Aug. 2, 2009
100 meters	**0:52.07**	Britta Steffen	Germany	Rome, Italy	July 31, 2009
200 meters	**1:52.98**	Federica Pellegrini	Italy	Rome, Italy	July 29, 2009
400 meters	**3:58.37**	Katie Ledecky	U.S.	Gold Coast, Australia	Aug. 23, 2014
800 meters	**8:07.39***	Katie Ledecky	U.S.	Kazan, Russia	Aug. 8, 2015
1,500 meters	**15:25.48***	Katie Ledecky	U.S.	Kazan, Russia	Aug. 4, 2015

Backstroke

Distance	Record	Holder	Nationality	Location	Date
50 meters	**0:27.06**	Zhao Jing	China	Rome, Italy	July 30, 2009
100 meters	**0:58.12**	Gemma Spofforth	UK	Rome, Italy	July 28, 2009
200 meters	**2:04.06**	Missy Franklin	U.S.	London, England, UK	Aug. 3, 2012

Breaststroke

Distance	Record	Holder	Nationality	Location	Date
50 meters	**0:29.48**	Ruta Meilutyte	Lithuania	Barcelona, Spain	Aug. 3, 2013
100 meters	**1:04.35**	Ruta Meilutyte	Lithuania	Barcelona, Spain	July 29, 2013
200 meters	**2:19.11**	Rikke Moller Pedersen	Denmark	Barcelona, Spain	Aug. 1, 2013

Butterfly

Distance	Record	Holder	Nationality	Location	Date
50 meters	**0:24.43**	Sarah Sjostrom	Sweden	Boras, Sweden	July 5, 2014
100 meters	**0:55.64***	Sarah Sjostrom	Sweden	Kazan, Russia	Aug. 3, 2015
200 meters	**2:01.81**	Liu Zige	China	Jinan, China	Oct. 21, 2009

Individual medley

Distance	Record	Holder	Nationality	Location	Date
200 meters	**2:06.12***	Katinka Hosszu	Hungary	Kazan, Russia	Aug. 3, 2015
400 meters	**4:28.43**	Ye Shiwen	China	London, England, UK	July 28, 2012

Freestyle relay

Distance	Record	Holder	Nationality	Location	Date
400 m (4×100)	**3:30.98**	Campbell, Schlanger, McKeon, Campbell	Australia	Glasgow, Scotland, UK	July 24, 2014
800 m (4×200)	**7:42.08**	Yang, Zhu, Liu, Pang	China	Rome, Italy	July 30, 2009

Medley relay

Distance	Record	Holder	Nationality	Location	Date
400 m (4×100)	**3:52.05**	Franklin, Soni, Vollmer, Schmitt	U.S.	London, England, UK	Aug. 4, 2012

World Track and Field Outdoor Records

The International Association of Athletics Federations (IAAF), the world body of track and field, recognizes only records in metric distances, except for the mile. As of Sept. 2015.

Men's Records

Running

Event	Record	Holder	Nationality	Location	Date
100 meters	**9.58 s.**	Usain Bolt	Jamaica	Berlin, Germany	Aug. 16, 2009
200 meters	**19.19 s.**	Usain Bolt	Jamaica	Berlin, Germany	Aug. 20, 2009
400 meters	**43.18 s.**	Michael Johnson	U.S.	Seville, Spain	Aug. 26, 1999
800 meters	**1 min., 40.91 s.**	David Lekuta Rudisha	Kenya	London, England, UK	Aug. 9, 2012
1,000 meters	**2 min., 11.96 s.**	Noah Ngeny	Kenya	Rieti, Italy	Sept. 5, 1999
1,500 meters	**3 min., 26.00 s.**	Hicham El Guerrouj	Morocco	Rome, Italy	July 14, 1998
1 mile	**3 min., 43.13 s.**	Hicham El Guerrouj	Morocco	Rome, Italy	July 7, 1999
2,000 meters	**4 min., 44.79 s.**	Hicham El Guerrouj	Morocco	Berlin, Germany	Sept. 7, 1999
3,000 meters	**7 min., 20.67 s.**	Daniel Komen	Kenya	Rieti, Italy	Sept. 1, 1996
3,000-meter stpl.	**7 min., 53.63 s.**	Saif Saaeed Shaheen	Qatar	Brussels, Belgium	Sept. 3, 2004
5,000 meters	**12 min., 37.35 s.**	Kenenisa Bekele	Ethiopia	Hengelo, Netherlands	May 31, 2004
10,000 meters	**26 min., 17.53 s.**	Kenenisa Bekele	Ethiopia	Brussels, Belgium	Aug. 26, 2005
20,000 meters	**56 min., 26.00 s.**	Haile Gebrselassie	Ethiopia	Ostrava, Czech Rep.	June 27, 2007
25,000 meters	**1 hr., 12 min., 25.4 s.**	Moses Cheruiyot Mosop	Kenya	Eugene, OR	June 3, 2011
Marathon	**2 hr., 2 min., 57 s.**	Dennis Kimetto	Kenya	Berlin, Germany	Sept. 28, 2014
110-meter hurdles	**12.80 s.**	Aries Merritt	U.S.	Brussels, Belgium	Sept. 7, 2012
400-meter hurdles	**46.78 s.**	Kevin Young	U.S.	Barcelona, Spain	Aug. 6, 1992
400 m (4x100)	**36.84 s.**	Carter, Frater, Blake, Bolt	Jamaica	London, England, UK	Aug. 11, 2012
800 m (4x200)	**1 min., 18.63 s.**	Ashmeade, Weir, Brown, Blake	Jamaica	Nassau, The Bahamas	May 24, 2014
1,600 m (4x400)	**2 min., 54.29 s.**	Valmon, Watts, Reynolds, Johnson	U.S.	Stuttgart, Germany	Aug. 22, 1993
3,200 m (4x800)	**7 min., 2.43 s.**	Mutua, Yiampoy, Kombich, Bungei	Kenya	Brussels, Belgium	Aug. 25, 2006

Field Events

Event	Record	Holder	Nationality	Location	Date
High jump	**2.45 m** (8' ½")	Javier Sotomayor	Cuba	Salamanca, Spain	July 27, 1993
Long jump	**8.95 m** (29' 4½")	Mike Powell	U.S.	Tokyo, Japan	Aug. 30, 1991
Triple jump	**18.29 m** (60' ¼")	Jonathan Edwards	UK	Gothenburg, Sweden	Aug. 7, 1995
Pole vault	**6.14 m** (20' 1¾")	Sergey Bubka	Ukraine	Sestriere, Italy	July 31, 1994
Discus	**74.08 m** (243' 0")	Jürgen Schult	E. Germany	Neubrandenburg, E. Germany	June 6, 1986
Hammer	**86.74 m** (284' 7")	Yuriy Sedykh	USSR	Stuttgart, W. Germany	Aug. 30, 1986
Javelin	**98.48 m** (323' 1")	Jan Zelezný	Czech Rep.	Jena, W. Germany	May 25, 1996
Shot put	**23.12 m** (75' 10¼")	Randy Barnes	U.S.	Westwood, CA	May 20, 1990
Decathlon	**9,045 pts.**	Ashton Eaton	U.S.	Beijing, China	Aug. 29, 2015

Women's Records

Running

Event	Record	Holder	Nationality	Location	Date
100 meters	**10.49 s.**	Florence Griffith-Joyner	U.S.	Indianapolis, IN.	July 16, 1988
200 meters	**21.34 s.**	Florence Griffith-Joyner	U.S.	Seoul, S. Korea	Sept. 29, 1988
400 meters	**47.60 s.**	Marita Koch	E. Germany	Canberra, Australia	Oct. 6, 1985
800 meters	**1 min., 53.28 s.**	Jarmila Kratochvílová	Czechoslovakia	Munich, W. Germany	July 26, 1983
1,000 meters	**2 min., 28.98 s.**	Svetlana Masterkova	Russia	Brussels, Belgium	Aug. 23, 1996
1,500 meters	**3 min., 50.07 s.**	Genzebe Dibaba	Ethiopia	Fontvieille, Monaco	July 17, 2015
1 mile	**4 min., 12.56 s.**	Svetlana Masterkova	Russia	Zürich, Switzerland	Aug. 14, 1996
2,000 meters	**5 min., 25.36 s.**	Sonia O'Sullivan	Ireland	Edinburgh, Scotland, UK	July 8, 1994
3,000 meters	**8 min., 6.11 s.**	Wang Junxia	China	Beijing, China	Sept. 13, 1993
3,000-meter stpl.	**8 min., 58.81 s.**	Gulnara Galkina-Samitova	Russia	Beijing, China	Aug. 17, 2008
5,000 meters	**14 min., 11.15 s.**	Tirunesh Dibaba	Ethiopia	Oslo, Norway	June 6, 2008
10,000 meters	**29 min., 31.78 s.**	Wang Junxia	China	Beijing, China	Sept. 8, 1993
20,000 meters	**1 hr., 5 min., 26.6 s.**	Tegla Loroupe	Kenya	Borgholzhausen, Germany	Sept. 3, 2000
Marathon	**2 hr., 15 min., 25.0 s.**	Paula Radcliffe	UK	London, England, UK	Apr. 13, 2003
100-meter hurdles	**12.21 s.**	Yordanka Donkova	Bulgaria	Stara Zagora, Bulgaria	Aug. 20, 1988
400-meter hurdles	**52.34 s.**	Yuliya Pechenkina	Russia	Tula, Russia	Aug. 8, 2003
400 m (4x100)	**40.82 s.**	Madison, Felix, Knight, Jeter	U.S.	London, England, UK	Aug. 10, 2012
800 m (4x200)	**1 min., 27.46 s.**	Jenkins, Colander, Perry, Jones	U.S.	Philadelphia, PA	Apr. 29, 2000
1,600 m (4x400)	**3 min., 15.17 s.**	Ledovskaya, Nazarova, Pinigina, Bryzgina	USSR	Seoul, S. Korea	Oct. 1, 1988
3,200 m (4x800)	**7 min., 50.17 s.**	Olizarenko, Gurina, Borisova, Podyalovskaya	USSR	Moscow, USSR	Aug. 5, 1984

Field Events

Event	Record	Holder	Nationality	Location	Date
High jump	**2.09 m** (6' 10¼")	Stefka Kostadinova	Bulgaria	Rome, Italy	Aug. 30, 1987
Long jump	**7.52 m** (24' 8¼")	Galina Chistyakova	USSR	Leningrad, Russia	June 11, 1988
Triple jump	**15.50 m** (50' 10¼")	Inessa Kravets	Ukraine	Gothenburg, Sweden	Aug. 10, 1995
Pole vault	**5.06 m** (16' 7¾")	Yelena Isinbaeva	Russia	Zürich, Switzerland	Aug. 28, 2009
Discus	**76.80 m** (252' 0")	Gabriele Reinsch	E. Germany	Neubrandenburg, E. Germany	July 9, 1988
Hammer	**81.08** (266')	Anita Wlodarczyk	Poland	Cetniewo, Poland	Aug. 1, 2015
Javelin	**72.28 m** (237' 1¾")	Barbora Spotáková	Czech Rep.	Stuttgart, Germany	Sept. 13, 2008
Shot put	**22.63 m** (74' 3")	Natalya Lisovskaya	USSR	Moscow, Russia	June 7, 1987
Heptathlon	**7,291 pts.**	Jackie Joyner-Kersee	U.S.	Seoul, S. Korea	Sept. 24, 1988

Iditarod Trail Sled Dog Race, 2015

Dallas Seavey won the 43rd annual Iditarod Trail Sled Dog Race to Nome, AK, Mar. 18, 2015. It was the third victory in four years for the 28-year-old Seavey, who finished the 998-mi course along the Fairbanks route to Nome. The Fairbanks route—named for the location of the race's restart Mar. 9 after the ceremonial start Mar. 7 in Anchorage—was used for just the second time in race history due to poor snow conditions in the Alaska range.

The 2016 race is scheduled to begin Mar. 5 in Anchorage and follow the 975-mi northern route to Nome.

Westminster Kennel Club Best-In-Show Dogs, 1985-2015

Year	Best-in-Show winner, breed	Year	Best-in-Show winner, breed
1985	Ch. Braeburn's Close Encounter, Scottish Terrier	2001	Ch. Special Times Just Right, Bichon Frise
1986	Ch. Marjetta's National Acclaim, Pointer	2002	Ch. Surrey Spice Girl, Poodle (Miniature)
1987	Ch. Covy Tucker Hill's Manhattan, German Shepherd Dog	2003	Ch. Torums Scarf Michael, Kerry Blue Terrier
1988	Ch. Great Elms Prince Charming II, Pomeranian	2004	Ch. Darbydale's All Rise PouCh. Cove, Newfoundland
1989	Ch. Royal Tudor's Wild As The Wind, Doberman Pinscher	2005	Ch. Kan-Point's VJK Autumn Roses, Pointer (German Shorthaired)
1990	Ch. Wendessa Crown Prince, Pekingese	2006	Ch. Rocky Top's Sundance Kid, Bull Terrier (Colored)
1991	Ch. Whisperwind On A Carousel, Poodle (Standard)	2007	Ch. Felicity's Diamond Jim, Spaniel (English Springer)
1992	Ch. Registry's Lonesome Dove, Fox Terrier (Wire)	2008	Ch. K-Run's Park Me In First, Beagle (15 Inch)
1993	Ch. Salilyn's Condor, Spaniel (English Springer)	2009	Ch. Clussexx Three D Grinchy Glee, Spaniel (Sussex)
1994	Ch. Chidley Willum The Conqueror, Norwich Terrier	2010	Ch. Roundtown Mercedes Of Maryscot, Scottish Terrier
1995	Ch. Gaelforce Post Script, Scottish Terrier	2011	GCh. Foxcliffe Hickory Wind, Scottish Deerhound
1996	Ch. Clussexx Country Sunrise, Spaniel (Clumber)	2012	GCh. Palacegarden Malachy, Pekingese
1997	Ch. Parsifal Di Casa Netzer, Standard Schnauzer	2013	GCh. Banana Joe V Tani Kazari, Affenpinscher
1998	Ch. Fairewood Frolic, Norwich Terrier	2014	GCh. Afterall Painting The Sky, Fox Terrier (Wire)
1999	Ch. Loteki Supernatural Being, Papillon	2015	Ch. Tashtins Lookin For Trouble, Beagle (15 Inch)
2000	Ch. Salilyn 'N Erin's Shameless, Spaniel (English Springer)		

MARATHONS

World Marathon Majors, 2006-14

Five of the world's leading marathons (Berlin, Boston, Chicago, London, and New York) agreed Jan. 23, 2006, to form a series called the World Marathon Majors. Tokyo joined the series in 2013. Marathon runners are awarded points relative to their finish in each race in the series and in Olympic and the Intl. Assn. of Athletics Federations World Championships marathons. The male and female runners with the most points at the end of each two-year cycle win $500,000.

Cycle	Men's winner, country	Women's winner, country
2006-07	Robert Kipkoech Cheruiyot, Kenya	Gete Wami, Ethiopia
2007-08	Martin Lel, Kenya	Gete Wami, Ethiopia
2008-09	Samuel Wanjiru, Kenya	Irina Mikitenko, Germany
2009-10	Samuel Wanjiru, Kenya	Liliya Shobukhova, Russia
2010-11	Emmanuel Mutai, Kenya	Liliya Shobukhova, Russia
2011-12	Geoffrey Mutai, Kenya	Mary Keitany, Kenya
2012-13	Tsegaye Kebede, Ethiopia	Priscah Jeptoo, Kenya
2013-14	Wilson Kipsang, Kenya	Not available[1]

(1) Kenya's Rita Jeptoo ended the 2013-14 season ranked first but tested positive for a banned substance in Sept. 2014. Final women's WMM results are pending.

Boston Marathon Winners, 1972-2015

All times in hour:minute:second format. * = Course record.

Men's winner, country	Time	Year	Women's winner, country	Time
Olavi Suomalainen, Finland	2:15:39	1972	Nina Kuscsik, U.S.	3:10:26
Jon Anderson, U.S.	2:16:03	1973	Jacqueline Hansen, U.S.	3:05:59
Neil Cusack, Ireland	2:13:39	1974	Michiko Gorman, U.S.	2:47:11
Bill Rodgers, U.S.	2:09:55	1975	Liane Winter, West Germany	2:42:24
Jack Fultz, U.S.	2:20:19	1976	Kim Merritt, U.S.	2:47:10
Jerome Drayton, Canada	2:14:46	1977	Michiko Gorman, U.S.	2:48:33
Bill Rodgers, U.S.	2:10:13	1978	Gayle S. Barron, U.S.	2:44:52
Bill Rodgers, U.S.	2:09:27	1979	Joan Benoit, U.S.	2:35:15
Bill Rodgers, U.S.	2:12:11	1980	Jacqueline Gareau, Canada	2:34:28
Toshihiko Seko, Japan	2:09:26	1981	Allison Roe, New Zealand	2:26:46
Alberto Salazar, U.S.	2:08:52	1982	Charlotte Teske, West Germany	2:29:33
Greg Meyer, U.S.	2:09:00	1983	Joan Benoit, U.S.	2:22:43
Geoff Smith, England, UK	2:10:34	1984	Lorraine Moller, New Zealand	2:29:28
Geoff Smith, England, UK	2:14:05	1985	Lisa Larsen Weidenbach, U.S.	2:34:06
Robert de Castella, Australia	2:07:51	1986	Ingrid Kristiansen, Norway	2:24:55
Toshihiko Seko, Japan	2:11:50	1987	Rosa Mota, Portugal	2:25:21
Ibrahim Hussein, Kenya	2:08:43	1988	Rosa Mota, Portugal	2:24:30
Abebe Mekonnen, Ethiopia	2:09:06	1989	Ingrid Kristiansen, Norway	2:24:33
Gelindo Bordin, Italy	2:08:19	1990	Rosa Mota, Portugal	2:25:24
Ibrahim Hussein, Kenya	2:11:06	1991	Wanda Panfil, Poland	2:24:18
Ibrahim Hussein, Kenya	2:08:14	1992	Olga Markova, Russia	2:23:43
Cosmas Ndeti, Kenya	2:09:33	1993	Olga Markova, Russia	2:25:27
Cosmas Ndeti, Kenya	2:07:15	1994	Uta Pippig, Germany	2:21:45
Cosmas Ndeti, Kenya	2:09:22	1995	Uta Pippig, Germany	2:25:11
Moses Tanui, Kenya	2:09:15	1996	Uta Pippig, Germany	2:27:12
Lameck Aguta, Kenya	2:10:34	1997	Fatuma Roba, Ethiopia	2:26:23
Moses Tanui, Kenya	2:07:34	1998	Fatuma Roba, Ethiopia	2:23:21
Joseh Chebet, Kenya	2:09:52	1999	Fatuma Roba, Ethiopia	2:23:25
Elijah Lagat, Kenya	2:09:47	2000	Catherine Ndereba, Kenya	2:26:11
Lee Bong-ju, South Korea	2:09:43	2001	Catherine Ndereba, Kenya	2:23:53
Rodgers Rop, Kenya	2:09:02	2002	Margaret Okayo, Kenya	2:20:43
Robert Kipkoech Cheruiyot, Kenya	2:10:11	2003	Svetlana Zakharova, Russia	2:25:20
Timothy Cherigat, Kenya	2:10:37	2004	Catherine Ndereba, Kenya	2:24:27
Hailu Negussie, Ethiopia	2:11:45	2005	Catherine Ndereba, Kenya	2:25:13
Robert Kipkoech Cheruiyot, Kenya	2:07:14	2006	Rita Jeptoo, Kenya	2:23:38
Robert Kipkoech Cheruiyot, Kenya	2:14:13	2007	Lidiya Grigoryeva, Russia	2:29:18
Robert Kipkoech Cheruiyot, Kenya	2:07:46	2008	Dire Tune, Ethiopia	2:25:25
Deriba Merga, Ethiopia	2:08:42	2009	Salina Kosgei, Kenya	2:32:16
Robert Kiprono Cheruiyot, Kenya	2:05:52	2010	Teyba Erkesso, Ethiopia	2:26:11
Geoffrey Mutai, Kenya	2:03:02*	2011	Caroline Kilel, Kenya	2:22:36
Wesley Korir, Kenya	2:12:40	2012	Sharon Cherop, Kenya	2:31:50
Lelisa Desisa, Ethiopia	2:10:22	2013	Rita Jeptoo, Kenya	2:26:25
Meb Keflezighi, U.S.	2:08:37	2014	Rita Jeptoo, Kenya	2:18:57*
Lelisa Desisa, Ethiopia	2:09:17	2015	Caroline Rotich, Kenya	2:24:55

Boston Marathon Winners, 1897-1971

The first Boston Marathon was held in 1897. Women were officially accepted into the race in 1972. Times in hr.:min.:sec. format.

Year	Winner, state/country	Time
1897	John J. McDermott, New York	2:55:10
1898	Ronald J. MacDonald, Canada	2:42:00
1899	Lawrence Brignolia, Massachusetts	2:54:38
1900	John Caffery, Canada	2:39:44
1901	John Caffery, Canada	2:29:23
1902	Sammy Mellor, New York	2:43:12
1903	John Lorden, Massachusetts	2:41:29
1904	Michael Spring, New York	2:38:04
1905	Frederick Lorz, New York	2:38:25
1906	Tim Ford, Massachusetts	2:45:45
1907	Thomas Longboat, Canada	2:24:24
1908	Thomas Morrissey, New York	2:25:43
1909	Henri Renaud, New Hampshire	2:53:36
1910	Fred Cameron, Canada	2:28:52
1911	Clarence DeMar, Massachusetts	2:21:39
1912	Michael Ryan, New York	2:21:18
1913	Fritz Carlson, Minnesota	2:25:14
1914	James Duffy, Canada	2:25:14
1915	Edouard Fabre, Canada	2:31:41
1916	Arthur Roth, Massachusetts	2:27:16
1917	Bill Kennedy, New York	2:28:37
1918	Military relay, Camp Devens	2:29:53
1919	Carl Linder, Massachusetts	2:29:13
1920	Peter Trivoulides, New York	2:29:31
1921	Frank Zuna, New York	2:18:57
1922	Clarence DeMar, Massachusetts	2:18:10
1923	Clarence DeMar, Massachusetts	2:23:47
1924	Clarence DeMar, Massachusetts	2:29:40
1925	Charles Mellor, Illinois	2:33:00
1926	John C. Miles, Canada	2:25:40
1927	Clarence DeMar, Massachusetts	2:40:22
1928	Clarence DeMar, Massachusetts	2:37:07
1929	John C. Miles, Canada	2:33:08
1930	Clarence DeMar, Massachusetts	2:34:48
1931	James P. Henigan, Massachusetts	2:46:45
1932	Paul DeBruyn, Germany	2:33:36
1933	Leslie S. Pawson, Rhode Island	2:31:01
1934	Dave Komonen, Canada	2:32:53
1935	John A. Kelley, Massachusetts	2:32:07
1936	Ellison M. Brown, Rhode Island	2:33:40
1937	Walter Young, Canada	2:33:20
1938	Leslie S. Pawson, Rhode Island	2:35:34
1939	Ellison M. Brown, Rhode Island	2:28:51
1940	Gerard Cote, Canada	2:28:28
1941	Leslie S. Pawson, Rhode Island	2:30:38
1942	Joe Smith, Massachusetts	2:26:51
1943	Gerard Cote, Canada	2:28:25
1944	Gerard Cote, Canada	2:31:50
1945	John A. Kelley, Massachusetts	2:30:40
1946	Stylianos Kyriakides, Greece	2:29:27
1947	Yun Bok Suh, Korea	2:25:39
1948	Gerard Cote, Canada	2:31:02
1949	Karl Leandersson, Sweden	2:31:50
1950	Kee Yong Ham, Korea	2:32:39
1951	Shigeki Tanaka, Japan	2:27:45
1952	Doroteo Flores, Guatamela	2:31:53
1953	Keizo Yamada, Japan	2:18:51
1954	Veikko Karvonen, Finland	2:20:39
1955	Hideo Hamamura, Japan	2:18:22
1956	Antti Viskari, Finland	2:14:14
1957	John J. Kelley, Connecticut	2:20:05
1958	Franjo Mihalic, Yugoslavia	2:25:54
1959	Eino Oksanen, Finland	2:22:42
1960	Paavo Kotila, Finland	2:20:54
1961	Eino Oksanen, Finland	2:23:39
1962	Eino Oksanen, Finland	2:23:48
1963	Aurele Vandendriessche, Belgium	2:18:58
1964	Aurele Vandendriessche, Belgium	2:19:59
1965	Morio Shigematsu, Japan	2:16:33
1966	Kenji Kemihara, Japan	2:17:11
1967	David McKenzie, New Zealand	2:15:45
1968	Amby Burfoot, Connecticut	2:22:17
1969	Yoshiaki Unetani, Japan	2:13:49
1970	Ron Hill, England, UK	2:10:30
1971	Alvaro Mejia, Colombia	2:18:45

New York City Marathon Winners, 1970-2015

All times in hour:minute:second format. * = Course record. Race not held, 2012.

Men's winner, country	Time	Year	Women's winner, country	Time
Gary Muhrcke, U.S.	2:31:38	**1970**	No finisher	—
Norman Higgins, U.S.	2:22:54	**1971**	Beth Bonner, U.S.	2:55:22
Sheldon Karlin, U.S.	2:27:52	**1972**	Nina Kuscsik, U.S.	3:08:41
Tom Fleming, U.S.	2:19:25	**1973**	Nina Kuscsik, U.S.	2:57:07
Norbert Sander, U.S.	2:26:30	**1974**	Katherine Switzer, U.S.	3:07:29
Tom Fleming, U.S.	2:19:27	**1975**	Kim Merritt, U.S.	2:46:14
Bill Rodgers, U.S.	2:10:10	**1976**	Miki Gorman, U.S.	2:39:11
Bill Rodgers, U.S.	2:11:28	**1977**	Miki Gorman, U.S.	2:43:10
Bill Rodgers, U.S.	2:12:12	**1978**	Grete Waitz, Norway	2:32:30
Bill Rodgers, U.S.	2:11:42	**1979**	Grete Waitz, Norway	2:27:33
Alberto Salazar, U.S.	2:09:41	**1980**	Grete Waitz, Norway	2:25:42
Alberto Salazar, U.S.	2:08:13	**1981**	Allison Roe, New Zealand	2:25:29
Alberto Salazar, U.S.	2:09:29	**1982**	Grete Waitz, Norway	2:27:14
Rod Dixon, New Zealand	2:08:59	**1983**	Grete Waitz, Norway	2:27:00
Orlando Pizzolato, Italy	2:14:53	**1984**	Grete Waitz, Norway	2:29:30
Orlando Pizzolato, Italy	2:11:34	**1985**	Grete Waitz, Norway	2:28:34
Gianni Poli, Italy	2:11:06	**1986**	Grete Waitz, Norway	2:28:06
Ibrahim Hussein, Kenya	2:11:01	**1987**	Priscilla Welch, England, UK	2:30:17
Steve Jones, Wales, UK	2:08:20	**1988**	Grete Waitz, Norway	2:28:07
Juma Ikangaa, Tanzania	2:08:01	**1989**	Ingrid Kristiansen, Norway	2:25:30
Douglas Wakiihuri, Kenya	2:12:39	**1990**	Wanda Panfil, Poland	2:30:45
Salvador Garcia, Mexico	2:09:28	**1991**	Liz McColgan, Scotland, UK	2:27:32
Willie Mtolo, South Africa	2:09:29	**1992**	Lisa Ondieki, Australia	2:24:40
Andres Espinosa, Mexico	2:10:04	**1993**	Uta Pippig, Germany	2:26:24
German Silva, Mexico	2:11:21	**1994**	Tegla Loroupe, Kenya	2:27:37
German Silva, Mexico	2:11:00	**1995**	Tegla Loroupe, Kenya	2:28:06
Giacomo Leone, Italy	2:09:54	**1996**	Anuta Catuna, Romania	2:28:43
John Kagwe, Kenya	2:08:12	**1997**	F. Rochat-Moser, Switzerland	2:28:43
John Kagwe, Kenya	2:08:45	**1998**	Franca Fiacconi, Italy	2:25:17
Joseph Chebet, Kenya	2:09:14	**1999**	Adriana Fernandez, Mexico	2:25:06
Abdelkader El Mouaziz, Morocco	2:10:09	**2000**	Ludmila Petrova, Russia	2:25:45
Tesfaye Jifar, Ethiopia	2:07:43	**2001**	Margaret Okayo, Kenya	2:24:21
Rodgers Rop, Kenya	2:08:07	**2002**	Joyce Chepchumba, Kenya	2:25:56
Martin Lel, Kenya	2:10:30	**2003**	Margaret Okayo, Kenya	2:22:31*
Hendrik Ramaala, South Africa	2:09:28	**2004**	Paula Radcliffe, England, UK	2:23:10
Paul Tergat, Kenya	2:09:30	**2005**	Jelena Prokopcuka, Latvia	2:24:41
Marilson Gomes dos Santos, Brazil	2:09:58	**2006**	Jelena Prokopcuka, Latvia	2:25:05
Martin Lel, Kenya	2:09:04	**2007**	Paula Radcliffe, England, UK	2:23:09
Marilson Gomes dos Santos, Brazil	2:08:43	**2008**	Paula Radcliffe, England, UK	2:23:56
Meb Keflezighi, U.S.	2:09:15	**2009**	Derartu Tulu, Ethiopia	2:28:52
Gebre Gebrmariam, Ethiopia	2:08:14	**2010**	Edna Kiplagat, Kenya	2:28:20
Geoffrey Mutai, Kenya	2:05:06*	**2011**	Firehiwot Dado, Ethiopia	2:23:15
Geoffrey Mutai, Kenya	2:08:24	**2013**	Priscah Jeptoo, Kenya	2:25:07
Wilson Kipsang, Kenya	2:10:59	**2014**	Mary Keitany, Kenya	2:25:07
Stanley Biwott, Kenya	2:10:34	**2015**	Mary Keitany, Kenya	2:24:25

Other Marathon Results, 2015

Tokyo Marathon: Feb. 22. Men: Endeshaw Negesse, Ethiopia, 2:06:00. Women: Birhane Dibaba, Ethiopia, 2:23:15.
Los Angeles Marathon: Mar. 15. Men: Daniel Kiprop Limo, Kenya, 2:10:36. Women: Ogla Jerono Kimaiyo, Kenya, 2:34:10.
Paris Marathon: Apr. 12. Men: Mark Korir, Kenya, 2:05:48. Women: Meseret Mengistu, Ethiopia, 2:23:26.
Rotterdam Marathon: Apr. 12. Men: Abera Kuma, Ethiopia, 2:06:47. Women: Asami Kato, Japan, 2:26:30.
London Marathon: Apr. 26. Men: Eliud Kipchoge, Kenya, 2:04:42. Women: Tigist Tufa, Ethiopia, 2:23:22.
Berlin Marathon: Sept. 27. Men: Eliud Kipchoge, Kenya, 2:04:00. Women: Gladys Cherono, Kenya, 2:19:25.
Chicago Marathon: Oct. 11. Men: Dickson Chumba, Kenya, 2:09:25. Women: Florence Kiplagat, Kenya, 2:23:33.

Ironman Triathlon World Championships, 1978-2015

The Ironman Triathlon World Championship—a 2.4-mi ocean swim, 112-mi bike ride, and 26.2-mi run—is held annually in Kailua-Kona, HI. All times in hour:minute:second format. * = Course record.

Men's winner, country	Time	Year	Women's winner, country	Time
Gordon Haller, U.S.	11:46:58	**1978**	No finisher	—
Tom Warren, U.S.	11:15:56	**1979**	Lyn Lemaire, U.S.	12:55:00
Dave Scott, U.S.	9:24:33	**1980**	Robin Beck, U.S.	11:21:24
John Howard, U.S.	9:38:29	**1981**	Linda Sweeney, U.S.	12:00:32
Dave Scott, U.S.	9:08:23	**1982**	Julie Leach, U.S.	10:54:08
Dave Scott, U.S.	9:05:57	**1983**	Sylviane Puntous, Canada	10:43:36
Dave Scott, U.S	8:54:20	**1984**	Sylviane Puntous, Canada	10:25:13
Scott Tinley, U.S.	8:50:54	**1985**	Joanne Ernst, U.S.	10:25:22
Dave Scott, U.S.	8:28:37	**1986**	Paula Newby-Fraser, Zimbabwe	9:49:14
Dave Scott, U.S.	8:34:13	**1987**	Erin Baker, New Zealand	9:35:25
Scott Molina, U.S.	8:31:00	**1988**	Paula Newby-Fraser, Zimbabwe	9:01:01
Mark Allen, U.S.	8:09:15	**1989**	Paula Newby-Fraser, Zimbabwe	9:00:56
Mark Allen, U.S.	8:28:17	**1990**	Erin Baker, New Zealand	9:13:42
Mark Allen, U.S.	8:18:32	**1991**	Paula Newby-Fraser, Zimbabwe	9:07:52
Mark Allen, U.S.	8:09:08	**1992**	Paula Newby-Fraser, Zimbabwe	8:55:28
Mark Allen, U.S.	8:07:45	**1993**	Paula Newby-Fraser, Zimbabwe	8:58:23
Greg Welch, Australia	8:20:27	**1994**	Paula Newby-Fraser, Zimbabwe	9:20:14
Mark Allen, U.S.	8:20:34	**1995**	Karen Smyers, U.S.	9:16:46
Luc Van Lierde, Belgium	8:04:08	**1996**	Paula Newby-Fraser, Zimbabwe	9:06:49
Thomas Hellriegel, Germany	8:33:01	**1997**	Heather Fuhr, Canada	9:31:43
Peter Reid, Canada	8:24:20	**1998**	Natascha Badmann, Switzerland	9:24:16
Luc Van Lierde, Belgium	8:17:17	**1999**	Lori Bowden, U.S.	9:13:02
Peter Reid, Canada	8:21:01	**2000**	Natascha Badmann, Switzerland	9:26:16
Timothy Deboom, U.S.	8:31:18	**2001**	Natascha Badmann, Switzerland	9:28:37
Timothy Deboom, U.S.	8:29:56	**2002**	Natascha Badmann, Switzerland	9:07:54
Peter Reid, Canada	8:22:35	**2003**	Lori Bowden, Canada	9:11:55
Normann Stadler, Germany	8:33:29	**2004**	Natascha Badmann, Switzerland[1]	9:50:04
Faris al-Sultan, Germany	8:14:17	**2005**	Natascha Badmann, Switzerland	9:09:30
Normann Stadler, Germany	8:11:56	**2006**	Michellie Jones, Australia	9:18:31
Chris McCormack, Australia	8:15:34	**2007**	Chrissie Wellington, UK	9:08:45
Craig Alexander, Australia	8:17:45	**2008**	Chrissie Wellington, UK	9:06:23
Craig Alexander, Australia	8:20:21	**2009**	Chrissie Wellington, UK	8:54:02
Chris McCormack, Australia	8:10:37	**2010**	Mirinda Carfrae, Australia	8:58:36
Craig Alexander, Australia	8:03:56*	**2011**	Chrissie Wellington, UK	8:55:08
Pete Jacobs, Australia	8:18:37	**2012**	Leanda Cave, U.S.	9:15:54
Frederik Van Lierde, Belgium	8:12:29	**2013**	Mirinda Carfrae, Australia	8:52:14*
Sebastian Kienle, Germany	8:14:18	**2014**	Mirinda Carfrae, Australia	9:00:55
Jan Frodeno, Germany	8:14:40	**2015**	Daniela Ryf, Switzerland	8:57:57

(1) First-place finisher Nina Kraft, Germany, admitted to using performance-enhancing drugs and was disqualified, Nov. 15, 2004.

James E. Sullivan Award Winners, 1930-2014

The James E. Sullivan Award, named after the former president of the Amateur Athletic Union (AAU), is given annually by the AAU to the American athlete who "by his or her performance, example, and influence as an amateur, has done the most during the year to advance the cause of sportsmanship."

Year	Winner	Sport
1930	Bobby Jones	Golf
1931	Barney Berlinger	Track
1932	Jim Bausch	Track
1933	Glenn Cunningham	Track
1934	Bill Bonthron	Track
1935	Lawson Little	Golf
1936	Glenn Morris	Track
1937	Don Budge	Tennis
1938	Don Lash	Track
1939	Joe Burk	Rowing
1940	Greg Rice	Track
1941	Leslie MacMitchell	Track
1942	Cornelius Warmerdam	Track
1943	Gilbert Dodds	Track
1944	Ann Curtis	Swimming
1945	Doc Blanchard	Football
1946	Arnold Tucker	Football
1947	John Kelly Jr.	Rowing
1948	Robert Mathias	Track
1949	Dick Button	Skating
1950	Fred Wilt	Track
1951	Rev. Robert Richards	Track
1952	Horace Ashenfelter	Track
1953	Dr. Sammy Lee	Diving
1954	Mal Whitfield	Track
1955	Harrison Dillard	Track
1956	Patricia McCormick	Diving
1957	Bobby Joe Morrow	Track
1958	Glenn Davis	Track
1959	Parry O'Brien	Track
1960	Rafer Johnson	Track
1961	Wilma Rudolph Ward	Track
1962	James Beatty	Track
1963	John Pennel	Track
1964	Don Schollander	Swimming
1965	Bill Bradley	Basketball
1966	Jim Ryun	Track
1967	Randy Matson	Track
1968	Debbie Meyer	Swimming
1969	Bill Toomey	Track
1970	John Kinsella	Swimming
1971	Mark Spitz	Swimming
1972	Frank Shorter	Track
1973	Bill Walton	Basketball
1974	Rick Wohlhutter	Track
1975	Tim Shaw	Swimming
1976	Bruce Jenner	Track
1977	John Naber	Swimming
1978	Tracy Caulkins	Swimming
1979	Kurt Thomas	Gymnastics
1980	Eric Heiden	Speed skating
1981	Carl Lewis	Track
1982	Mary Decker	Track
1983	Edwin Moses	Track
1984	Greg Louganis	Diving
1985	Joan Benoit Samuelson	Marathon
1986	Jackie Joyner-Kersee	Track
1987	Jim Abbott	Baseball
1988	Florence Griffith Joyner	Track
1989	Janet Evans	Swimming
1990	John Smith	Wrestling
1991	Mike Powell	Track
1992	Bonnie Blair	Speed skating
1993	Charlie Ward	Football, basketball
1994	Dan Jansen	Speed skating
1995	Bruce Baumgartner	Wrestling
1996	Michael Johnson	Track
1997	Peyton Manning	Football
1998	Chamique Holdsclaw	Basketball
1999	Coco Miller and Kelly Miller	Basketball
2000	Rulon Gardner	Wrestling
2001	Michelle Kwan	Figure skating
2002	Sarah Hughes	Figure skating
2003	Michael Phelps	Swimming
2004	Paul Hamm	Gymnastics
2005	J. J. Redick	Basketball
2006	Jessica Long	Swimming (paralympics)
2007	Tim Tebow	Football
2008	Shawn Johnson	Gymnastics
2009	Amy Palmiero-Winters	Ultra-marathon
2010	Evan Lysacek	Figure skating
2011	Andrew Rodriguez	Football
2012	Missy Franklin	Swimming
2013	John Urschel	Football
2014	Ezekiel Elliott	Football

America's Cup Yacht Race, 1851-2013

Competition for the America's Cup grew out of a yachting race during the London Exposition of 1851. The race covered an approximately 60-mi course around the Isle of Wight. The prize was a cup donated by the Royal Yacht Squadron of England. It became known as the America's Cup after the New York Yacht Club won the race with the ship *America*. Prior to 1983, all yachts are American unless otherwise noted.

Year	Result (score)
1851	America
1870	Magic defeated Cambria, England (1-0)
1871	Columbia (first three races) and Sappho (last two races) defeated Livonia, England (4-1)
1876	Madeline defeated Countess of Dufferin, Canada (2-0)
1881	Mischief defeated Atalanta, Canada (2-0)
1885	Puritan defeated Genesta, England (2-0)
1886	Mayflower defeated Galatea, England (2-0)
1887	Volunteer defeated Thistle, Scotland (2-0)
1893	Vigilant defeated Valkyrie II, England (3-0)
1895	Defender defeated Valkyrie III, England (3-0)
1899	Columbia defeated Shamrock, England (3-0)
1901	Columbia defeated Shamrock II, England (3-0)
1903	Reliance defeated Shamrock III, England (3-0)
1920	Resolute defeated Shamrock IV, England (3-2)
1930	Enterprise defeated Shamrock V, England (4-0)
1934	Rainbow defeated Endeavour, England (4-2)
1937	Ranger defeated Endeavour II, England (4-0)
1958	Columbia defeated Sceptre, England (4-0)
1962	Weatherly defeated Gretel, Australia (4-1)
1964	Constellation defeated Sovereign, England (4-0)
1967	Intrepid defeated Dame Pattie, Australia (4-0)
1970	Intrepid defeated Gretel II, Australia (4-1)
1974	Courageous defeated Southern Cross, Australia (4-0)
1977	Courageous defeated Australia, Australia (4-0)
1980	Freedom defeated Australia, Australia (4-1)
1983	Australia II, Australia, defeated Liberty, U.S. (4-3)
1987	Stars & Stripes, U.S., defeated Kookaburra III, Aust. (4-0)
1988	Stars & Stripes, U.S., defeated New Zealand, NZ (2-0)
1992	America^3, U.S., defeated Il Moro di Venezia, Italy (4-1)
1995	Team New Zealand, NZ, defeated Young America, U.S. (5-0)
2000	Team New Zealand, NZ, defeated Luna Rossa, Italy (5-0)
2003	Alinghi, Switzerland, defeated Team New Zealand, NZ (5-0)
2007	Alinghi, Switzerland, defeated Emirates Team New Zealand, NZ (5-2)
2010	BMW Oracle Racing, U.S., defeated Alinghi 5, Switzerland (2-0)
2013	Oracle Team USA, U.S., defeated Emirates Team New Zealand, NZ (9-8)

Rifle and Pistol Championships, 2015

Source: National Rifle Association (NRA)

NRA Bianchi Cup National Action Pistol Championship

Action Pistol: Doug Koenig, Hamburg, PA, 1920-180X
Woman Action Pistol: Anita Mackiewicz, Australia, 1916-166X
Junior Action Pistol: Tim Yackley, Portage, WI, 1898-125X

National Outdoor Rifle and Pistol Championships

Pistol: SFC Keith A. Sanderson, USA Res., Colorado Springs, CO, 2655-122X
Civilian Pistol: Brian H. Zins, Girard, OH, 2641-127X
Woman Pistol: Kimberly L. Hobart, New Philadelphia, OH, 2593-74X
Smallbore Rifle Prone: Kevin Nevius, Gibsonburg, OH, 4793
Woman Smallbore Rifle Prone: Nancy Tompkins, Prescott, AZ, 4785
Smallbore Rifle Metric Position: Virginia Thrasher, Springfield, VA, 2305
Woman Smallbore Rifle Metric Position: Virginia Thrasher, Springfield, VA, 2305
High Power Rifle: SFC Brandon Green, USA Reg., Box Springs, GA, 2387-140X
Civilian High Power Rifle: Norman Houle, Warwick, RI, 2380-126X
Woman High Power Rifle: Holly Stowe, Portsmouth, RI, 2367-95X
High Power Rifle Long Range: Nancy Tompkins, Prescott, AZ, 1242-58X
Woman High Power Rifle Long Range: Nancy Tompkins, Prescott, AZ, 1242-58X

National Indoor Rifle and Pistol Championships

Smallbore Rifle Conventional Position: Casey Lutz, Meridian, ID, 799-58X
Woman Smallbore Rifle Conventional Position: Sylvia Dreistadt, Washington, PA, 792-59X
Smallbore Rifle Metric Position: Timothy Sherry, Highlands Ranch, CO, 1170
Woman Smallbore Rifle Metric Position: Lisette Grunwell-Lacey, Old Lyme, CT, 1158
Air Rifle: Alec Patajo, Puyallup, WA, 590
Woman Air Rifle: Randi Loudin, Post Falls, ID, 583
Conventional Pistol: David Lange, Glen Rock, NJ, 885-37X
Woman Conventional Pistol: Brenda Martin-Silva, Snowflake, AZ, 878-28X
International Free Pistol: Nick Mowrer, Colorado Springs, CO, 555
Woman International Free Pistol: Marilyn Mumby, Golden, CO, 468
International Standard Pistol: David Lange, Glen Rock, NJ, 571
Woman International Standard Pistol: Nicole Yim, Los Angeles, CA, 519
Air Pistol: Will Brown, Twin Falls, ID, 584
Woman Air Pistol: Lydia Paterson, Kansas City, KS, 564

Pro Rodeo Cowboys Association All-Around Champions, 1977-2014

Year	Winner, hometown	Earnings
1977	Tom Ferguson, Miami, OK	$76,730
1978	Tom Ferguson, Miami, OK	103,734
1979	Tom Ferguson, Miami, OK	96,272
1980	Paul Tierney, Rapid City, SD	105,568
1981	Jimmie Cooper, Monument, NM	105,862
1982	Chris Lybbert, Coyote, CA	123,709
1983	Roy Cooper, Durant, OK	153,391
1984	Dee Pickett, Caldwell, ID	122,618
1985	Lewis Feild, Elk Ridge, UT	130,347
1986	Lewis Feild, Elk Ridge, UT	166,042
1987	Lewis Feild, Elk Ridge, UT	144,335
1988	Dave Appleton, Arlington, TX	121,546
1989	Ty Murray, Odessa, TX	134,806
1990	Ty Murray, Stephenville, TX	213,772
1991	Ty Murray, Stephenville, TX	244,230
1992	Ty Murray, Stephenville, TX	225,992
1993	Ty Murray, Stephenville, TX	297,896
1994	Ty Murray, Stephenville, TX	246,170
1995	Joe Beaver, Huntsville, TX	141,753
1996	Joe Beaver, Huntsville, TX	$166,103
1997	Dan Mortensen, Manhattan, MT	184,559
1998	Ty Murray, Stephenville, TX	264,673
1999	Fred Whitfield, Hockley, TX	217,819
2000	Joe Beaver, Huntsville, TX	225,396
2001	Cody Ohl, Stephensville, TX	296,419
2002	Trevor Brazile, Anson, TX	273,997
2003	Trevor Brazile, Anson, TX	294,839
2004	Trevor Brazile, Decatur, TX	253,170
2005	Ryan Jarrett, Summerville, GA	263,665
2006	Trevor Brazile, Decatur, TX	329,924
2007	Trevor Brazile, Decatur, TX	425,115
2008	Trevor Brazile, Decatur, TX	419,868
2009	Trevor Brazile, Decatur, TX	346,779
2010	Trevor Brazile, Decatur, TX	507,921
2011	Trevor Brazile, Decatur, TX	337,601
2012	Trevor Brazile, Decatur, TX	298,626
2013	Trevor Brazile, Decatur, TX	426,010
2014	Trevor Brazile, Decatur, TX	494,369

GENERAL INDEX

Note: Page numbers in boldface indicate key reference. Page numbers in italics indicate photo or illustration captions.

A

Aaron, Hank 448
Abbas, Mahmoud 670
Abbasid Empire 650, 651
Abbreviations
- Common 710-11
- International organizations 739-40
- Postal 367
- UN agencies 741-42

ABM Treaty, U.S. withdrawal (2001) 452, 739
Abortion
- Catholic forgiveness of 31
- Criminal violence 454
- Legalized (1973) 448, 561
- Partial birth abortion ban (2007) 453
- RU-486 marketing approval (2000) 452
- U.S. data (1970-2011) 167

Abramoff, Jack 453
Abu Ghraib prison (Iraq) 453
Academy Awards (Oscars) 19, 274-76
Accidents and disasters **317-28**
- Aviation 15, 19, 21, 30, 33, 87, *196*, 317-19
- Bridge collapse 453
- Droughts *198*, 328, 668
- Earthquakes 22-23, 33, *196*, *324*, 325, *442*
- Explosions 29, *196*, 327, 454, 455
- Fires 326, 436, 438, 441, 442
- Floods 17, 24, 33, 324, 441, 451, 453, *453*
- Marine 26, 320-21, 442
- Mining 322
- Miscellaneous 328
- Mortality statistics 171
- Motor vehicle 105, 169-70, 171
- Mudslides 33
- Nuclear 328, 449
- Occupational 105
- Oil spills 328, 450, 454, 455
- Railroad 23, 321-22, *321*
- Space exploration 330, 332, 447, 450, 452, 671
- Storms 21, 322-23, 450, 453, *453*, 455, 456
- Tidal waves 324
- Tsunamis 671
- Volcanic eruptions 449, 685-86

***Achille Lauro* incident (1985)** 450, 668
Acquired Immune Deficiency Syndrome. *See* HIV/AIDS
Acronyms 710-11
ACT scores 389
Activists, noted past 201-02
Actors, actresses
- Academy Awards (Oscars) 274-76
- Noted past 235-41
- Noted present 222-34
- Original names 241-42

Adams, John 438, 439, 491, **493**, *493*, 503, 504, 508
Adams, John Quincy 439, 491, **494**, *494*, 503, 504, 508
ADHD 150
Admirals, USN 128, 135
Adoptions 166, 375, 618
Adultery stigma eased (1782) 438
Aerospace. *See* Aviation; Space exploration
Affordable Care Act 4, 25, 143, 454, 455, 456, 457, 562
Afghanistan **745-46**
- Agriculture 98, 99
- Area, population 731, 745
- Drinking water 737
- Flag, map 473, 484
- Foreign aid to 738
- Fossil fuel reserves 112
- Health expenditures 142
- Internally displaced persons 736
- Languages 714, 745
- Military strength 133
- Muslim population 706
- Refugees from/in 735
- Soviet invasion (1979) 667
- Taliban 28, 31, 32, 452, 455, 669, 670, 672
- U.S. military financing 134
- U.S. troops in 129
- (*see also* Operation Enduring Freedom-Afghanistan)

AFL-CIO 417, 441, 445
Africa
- Agriculture 97, 98, 99
- AIDS crisis 668, 669
- Area, population 730
- Elevations (highest, lowest) 695
- Floods (2015) 17
- Fossil fuel reserves 112
- History 649, 651, 653, 659, 664, 668
- HIV/AIDS cases 737
- Lakes 694
- Languages 714-15
- Map 486-87
- Mountain peaks 687
- Religious adherents 698
- Rivers 691
- Sanitation/drinking water 737
- Temperature/precipitation extremes 315
- Trade 73
- Travel and tourism 87
- U.S. ancestral claims 621
- U.S. investment 78
- U.S. military financing 134
- U.S. troops in 129
- Volcanoes 686
- Waterfalls 695
- (*see also* specific countries)

African Americans. *See* Blacks
African Union (AU) 739
Age and aging. *See* Elderly
Agent Orange settlement (1984) 449
Agnew, Spiro T. 448
Agnosticism 123, 697, 698
Agriculture **92-100**
- Acreage, number of farms 92
- Employment/unemployment 102, 103, 106, 369
- Exports, imports 74, 98
- Government subsidies 93-94, 457
- Grange (1867) 441
- Land grants (1862) 440
- Legislation (1916) 443
- Organic 95
- Prices received 96-97
- U.S. expenditures 58
- U.S. national income 44
- (*see also* Food; specific foods)

Agriculture, Department of 106, **544**
Ahmadinejad, Mahmoud 671
AIDS (Acquired Immune Deficiency Syndrome). *See* HIV/AIDS
AIG (American International Group) 454
Air Commerce Act 443
Air Force, U.S. Department of the
- Academy 136
- Address for information 137
- Flights, notable 336
- Generals (active duty) 128
- Insignia 137
- Personnel, active duty 130
- Salutes, honors 135
- Units 129

Air mail 336
Air Medal 136
Air pollution 303-04
- Clean air legislation (1970, 1990) 447, 450

Aircraft. *See* Aviation
Airlines 87-88, 90
Airports, busiest 88
Akkadians 647
Alabama **563**
- Agriculture 92, 93
- Coastline 423
- Congressional representation 551, 552, 609
- Crime, prisons, death penalty 117, 119, 120
- Education 380-83, 389-90
- Elevations (high, low) 423
- Energy consumption 111
- Finances 60
- Governor 37
- Hazardous waste 305
- Health insurance coverage 142
- Immigrant admissions 619
- Motor vehicles 83, 84
- Name origin, nickname 426, 563
- Oil production 111
- Population 563, 605, 606-07, 608, 611, 612, 622
- Poverty rates 49
- Taxes 84, 378
- Unemployment 101
- Weather 312
- ZIP and area codes 622

Alamo, Siege of the (1836) 439
Aland (Ahvenanmaa) 775
Alarcón, Hernando de 436, 683
Alaska **563-64**
- Accession (1867) 427, 441
- Agriculture 92, 93
- Coastline 423
- Congressional representation 551, 552, 609
- Crime, prisons, death penalty 117, 119
- Education 380-83, 389-90
- Elevations (high, low) 423
- Energy consumption 111
- Finances 60
- Governor 37
- Hazardous waste 305
- Health insurance coverage 142
- Immigrant admissions 619
- Map 478
- Motor vehicles 83, 84
- Name origin, nickname 426, 563
- Native Alaskans 122, 123, 148, 166, 371, 384, 610, 611, 612, 621
- Oil production 111
- Population 563, 594, 605, 606-07, 608, 611, 612, 622
- Poverty rates 49
- Taxes 84
- Unemployment 101
- U.S. troops in 129
- Weather 312
- ZIP and area codes 622

al-Awlaki, Anwar 455
Albania 112, 383, 473, 483, 714, 731, **746**
Albany Congress (1754) 437
al-Bashir, Omar Hassan Ahmad 671
Albright, Madeleine 451
Albuquerque, NM 71, 309-11, 313, **594**, 614, 696
Alcoholic beverages. *See* Liquor
Alcott, Louisa May 441
Aldrin, Edward "Buzz" 447, *448*
Aleutian Islands 689
Alexander the Great 649
Alger, Horatio 441
Algeria **746-47**
- Area, population 731, 746
- Flag, map 473, 486
- Fossil fuel reserves, exports 112, 113
- Health expenditures 142
- Languages 714, 746
- Muslim population 706
- Piracy (1795, 1815) 438, 439
- Prison population 121
- Refugees in 735
- Unrest (1990s) 669

Alien and Sedition Acts (1798) 438
Aliens. *See* Immigration and immigrants
Alito, Samuel A., Jr. 38, 453, 559
Allergies 149, 421
al-Maliki, Nouri 670, 672
Alps 688
al-Qaeda 4, 452, 670, 672
Alzheimer's disease 149, 171, 421
Amazon River 692
Ambassadors and envoys, salutes to 135
"America, the Beautiful" 442
American Anti-Slavery Society 439
American College Testing (ACT) program 389
American Colonization Society (1816) 439
American Federation of Labor. *See* AFL-CIO
American Indians
- Arrest records 122
- Education 384, 621
- Geronimo surrender (1886) 441
- Gold discovery impact (1835) 439
- Hate crime victims 123
- HIV/AIDS cases 148
- Indian Removal Act (1830) 439
- Indian wars (1800s) 439, 440, 441
- New England uprisings (1676, 1704) 436, 437
- Nonmarital childbearing 166
- Population 610, 611, 612, 621
- Social Security 371
- Trail of Tears (1838) 439
- Tribes 612
- U.S. citizenship (1924) 443

American International Group (AIG) 454
American Kennel Club 293
American League. *See* Baseball
American Manual Alphabet 713
American Pharoah 24, *812*, 966-68
American Red Cross (1881) 441
American Revolution (1775-83) 139, 656
- Articles of Confederation (1777) 437, 460
- Battles 437
- Black troops 132
- Casualties, numbers serving 138

American Samoa **591**
- Accession (1900) 427
- Area, population 591, 689
- Congressional delegate 558
- Education 382
- Elevations (high, low) 423
- Governor 37
- Map 488
- Population 731

America's Cup (yachting) 979
Amnesty Act (1872) 441
Amputations 154
Amusement parks 89
Anaheim, CA 71, 118, **594**, 614
Anchorage, AK 46, 309-11, 313, **594**, 614, 696
Ancient civilizations 363, 647-50, 674
Andaman Sea 690
Anderson, Marian 444
Andorra 297, 473, 482, 731, **747**
Andros, Sir Edmund 436
Anesthesia (1842) 439
Angkor complex *652*
Angola **747-48**
- Area, population 731, 747
- Drinking water 737
- Flag, map 473, 487
- Forests 306
- Fossil fuel reserves, exports 112, 113
- History 667, 669, 671
- Languages 714, 747
- Mortality rate by cause 736

Anguilla . . . 731, 848
Animals
American Kennel Club . . . 293
Associations and organizations . . . 407
Cat breeds . . . 293
Classification . . . 291
Dog breeds . . . 293
Endangered species . . . 307
Gestation, incubation, longevity . . . 291
Livestock . . . 74, 75, 95, 96-97
Names for offspring/collectives . . . 709-10
Speeds . . . 292
Venomous . . . 291-92
Annapolis (MD) (Naval Academy) . . . 136
Antarctica
Area, population . . . 730
Australian Territory . . . 750
British Territory . . . 848
Desert condition . . . 690
Elevations (highest, lowest) . . . 695
Exploration . . . 684-85
French Territory . . . 777
Islands . . . 689
Map . . . 481
Mountain peaks . . . 688
Temperature/precipitation extremes . . . 315
Volcanoes . . . 686
Anthrax . . . 452
Antietam, Battle of . . . 440
Antigonids . . . 649
Antigua and Barbuda . . . 77, 473, 479, 689, 731, 733, **748**
Anti-Semitism
Holocaust . . . 664, 744
19th-century . . . 659
U.S. hate crimes . . . 123
Antoinette Perry Awards (Tonys) . . . 272
AOL Time Warner . . . 452
Apartheid . . . 668, 669, 834
Aphelion, perihelion . . . 337
Apogee of moon . . . 337, 353
Apollo space missions . . . 329-30, 447
Apple Computer Company . . . 294
Apportionment, congressional . . . 609
Aquaculture . . . 100
Aquino, Corazon . . . 668
Arab League . . . 740
Arab Spring protests . . . 672
Arab-Israeli conflict
Camp David accord (1978) . . . 449
Egypt-Israel peace treaty (1979) . . . 667
Jordanian peace treaty (1994) . . . 669, 790
1920s . . . 662
1950s . . . 665
October War (1973) . . . 667, 772, 789, 830
Palestinian militancy, uprisings (1987, 2002, 2015) . . . 33, 667, 670
Peace talks (2013-14) . . . 672
PLO peace accord (1993) . . . 669
Six-Day War (1967) . . . 666, 772, 789, 830
Arafat, Yasir . . . 669, 670
Archimedes . . . 649
Architecture
Architects, noted past . . . 177-78
Gothic . . . 652, 658
Timeline . . . 727-29
Archives, National . . . 435, 547
Arctic exploration . . . 684
Arctic Ocean . . . 423, 689, 690
Area codes, telephone . . . 622-45
Arenas. *See* Stadiums and arenas
Argentina . . . **748-49**
Agriculture . . . 97, 98, 99
Area, population . . . 730, 731, 748
Cell phone use . . . 300
Education . . . 383
Flag, map . . . 473, 481
Forests . . . 306
Fossil fuel reserves, exports . . . 112, 113
Health expenditures . . . 142
History . . . 665, 667, 670, 671
Languages . . . 748
Motor vehicle production . . . 79
News (2015) . . . 18
Nuclear arms abandonment . . . 738
Nuclear power . . . 114
Travel and tourism . . . 85, 86
U.S. investment . . . 78
Wages, hourly . . . 734
Aristide, Jean-Bertrand . . . 669-70, 671
Aristotle . . . 648
Arizona . . . **564**
Agriculture . . . 92, 93
Congressional redistricting . . . 38
Congressional representation . . . 551, 552-53, 609
Crime, prisons, death penalty . . . 117, 119, 120
Education . . . 380-83, 389-90
Elevations (high, low) . . . 423
Energy consumption . . . 111
Finances . . . 60
Governor . . . 37
Hazardous waste . . . 305
Health insurance coverage . . . 142
Immigrants . . . 455, 619
Motor vehicles . . . 83, 84
Name origin, nickname . . . 426, 564
Oil production . . . 111
Population . . . 564, 595, 597, 600, 601, 603, 604, 605, 606-07, 608, 611, 612, 622
Poverty rates . . . 49
Taxes . . . 84, 378
Unemployment . . . 101
Weather . . . 312
ZIP and area codes . . . 622
Arkansas . . . **564-65**
Agriculture . . . 92, 93
Congressional representation 551, 553, 609
Crime, prisons, death penalty 117, 119, 120
Desegregation (1957) . . . 446
Education . . . 380-83, 389-90
Elevations (high, low) . . . 423
Energy consumption . . . 111
Finances . . . 60
Governor . . . 37
Hazardous waste . . . 305
Health insurance coverage . . . 142
Immigrant admissions . . . 619
Motor vehicles . . . 83, 84
Name origin, nickname . . . 426, 564
Oil production . . . 111
Population . . . 564, 605, 606-07, 608, 611, 612, 622-23
Poverty rates . . . 49
Taxes . . . 84, 378
Unemployment . . . 101
Weather . . . 312
ZIP and area codes . . . 622-23
Arkansas River . . . 692
Arlington National Cemetery (VA) . . . 434
Arlington, TX . . . 71, 304, **594**, 614, 619
Armed forces, U.S. . . . **128-40**
Academies . . . 136
Addresses for information . . . 137
Associations and organizations . . . 408-09
Awards . . . 135-36
Black troops . . . 132
Budget for war on terror . . . 133
Casualties in principal wars . . . 138
Commands . . . 128
Defense contracts . . . 134
"Don't Ask, Don't Tell" policy . . . 451, 455
Expenditures . . . 58
Generals . . . 128
Insignia . . . 137
Joint Chiefs of Staff . . . 128
Leaders, noted past . . . 186-87
Pay scales . . . 131
Personnel . . . 129-31
Salutes . . . 135
Time, 24-hour . . . 360
Troop strength . . . 133
Units . . . 129
Veterans . . . 131-32
Women . . . 130, 434, 447, *815*
(*see also* Military affairs; specific branches)
Armenia . . . 112, 114, 473, 484, 714, 731, 736, **749**
Armenians, Turkish expulsion of . . . 662
Arms contracts/sales . . . 133, 134
Arms control
ABM Treaty U.S. withdrawal (2001) . . . 452, 739
Comprehensive Test Ban Treaty . . . 451, 739
INF treaty (1987) . . . 450, 667, 739
Iran accord (2015) . . . 27, 30
Limitations of Armaments Conf. (1921) 443
Naval Reduction Treaty (1930) . . . 443
Nuclear Non-Proliferation Treaty . . . 738, 739
Pacifist pacts (1920s) . . . 662
Partial Test Ban Treaty (1963) . . . 446, 739
SALT (1972, 1979) . . . 448, 667, 739
SORT Moscow Treaty . . . 452, 739
START (1991, 1996, 2010) . . 451, 454, 739
Threshold Test Ban Treaty . . . 739
Armstrong, Lance . . . 456
Armstrong, Neil . . . 447
Army Commendation award . . . 136
Army, U.S. Department of the . . . 443
Academy (West Point) . . . 136
Address for information . . . 137
Generals . . . 128
First women (1970) . . . 447
Insignia . . . 137
Personnel, active duty . . . 129
Salutes, honors . . . 135
Units . . . 129
Arnold, Benedict . . . 437
Arson . . . 122, 170
Art
Abstract . . . 662, 663
Abstract expressionism . . . 664
Artists, noted past . . . 178-81
Auction records (2015) . . . 24
Baroque . . . 655
Beaux Arts . . . 659
Cubism . . . 660
Impressionist . . . 659
Museums . . . 247-48
Neoclassical . . . 656
NY Armory Show (1913) . . . 442
Pop . . . 666
Postimpressionist . . . 659
Renaissance . . . 653, 654
Rococo . . . 656
Romanesque . . . 652
Romanticism . . . 657-58
Arthritis . . . 150, 421
Arthur, Chester A. . . . 491, **496-97**, *496*, 504
Articles of Confederation (1777) . . . 437, 460
Artillery salutes . . . 135
Aruba . . . 689, 731, 818
Aryans . . . 647
Ascension Island . . . 689, 848
Ash Wednesday . . . 699, 700
Ashmore and Cartier Islands . . . 750
Asia
Agriculture . . . 97, 98, 99
Area, population . . . 730
Elevations (highest, lowest) . . . 695
Festivals . . . 355
Fossil fuel reserves . . . 112
HIV/AIDS cases . . . 737
Lakes . . . 694
Languages . . . 714-15
Map . . . 484-85
Mountain peaks . . . 687, 688
Religious adherents . . . 698
Rivers . . . 691
Sanitation/drinking water . . . 737
Temperature/precipitation extremes . . . 315
Trade . . . 73
Travel and tourism . . . 87
U.S. investment . . . 78
U.S. military financing . . . 134
U.S. troops in . . . 129
Volcanoes . . . 685, 686
Waterfalls . . . 695
(*see also* specific countries)
Asian Americans
Arrest records . . . 122
Education . . . 384, 621
Hate crime victims . . . 123
Health insurance coverage . . . 142
HIV/AIDS cases . . . 148
Incomes, wages . . . 47, 107
Internet use . . . 299
Nonmarital childbearing . . . 166
Population . . . 610, 611, 621
Poverty rates . . . 48
Social Security . . . 371
Unemployment . . . 103
Asia-Pacific Economic Cooperation (APEC) . . . 73, 739
Assassinations (and attempts) . . . 123-25
Assault . . . 116-18, 121, 122
Association of Southeast Asian Nations (ASEAN) . . . 73, 739
Associations and organizations . . . **407-21**
Asteroids . . . 350
Asthma . . . 149, 421
Astrological signs . . . 355
Astronauts and cosmonauts . . . **329-33**
Deaths . . . 447, 450, 452
First on moon (1969) . . . 329, 447, 666
First orbit (1962) . . . 446
First woman (1983) . . . 449
Astronomy . . . **337-53**
Celestial highlights (2016) . . . 337-40
Constants . . . 337
Eclipses . . . 337, 343
Moon phases (2016) . . . 353
Ataturk, Kemal . . . 662
Atheism . . . 123, 409, 697, 698
Atlanta, GA . . . **594**
Air quality . . . 304
Airport traffic . . . 88
Buildings, tall . . . 717
Consumer Price Index . . . 46
Crime rates . . . 118
Geography . . . 696
Housing . . . 71, 72
Immigrant admissions . . . 619
Population . . . 614, 615
Weather . . . 309-11, 313
Atlantic cable, first (1858) . . . 440
Atlantic Charter (1941) . . . 444
Atlantic City, NJ . . . 46, 71, 309-11, 441, 722
Atlantic Ocean
Area, depth . . . 690
Crossings, notable (1819, 1919) . . 336, 439
Fishing . . . 100
Islands . . . 689
Ports, U.S. . . . 76
U.S. coastline . . . 423
***Atlantis* (space shuttle)** . . . 330-32, 333, 451, 455, 670, 673
Atmosphere
Composition/temperature/density . . . 351-52
Pressure . . . 365
Atolls . . . 593
Atomic bomb (1945) . . . 444, 445, 663, *664*
Atomic clock . . . 352
Atomic numbers/weights . . . 282-83

Attention Deficit Hyperactivity Disorder (ADHD) 150
Attorneys general, U.S. 22, **542-43**
Attucks, Crispus 437
Aung San Suu Kyi 673
Aunu'u Island 591
Aurora, CO 71, 72, 118, 304, **594**, 614, 615
Austin, TX 71, 72, **594**, 614, 615, 619, 696, 717
Austral (Tubuai) Islands 776
Australia **749-50**
Agriculture 97, 98, 99
Area, population 731, 749
Arms purchases 133
Budget deficits 59
Carbon dioxide emissions 302
Commonwealth creation 660
Computer use 294
Education 383, 385
Elevations (highest, lowest) 695
Energy production 109
First female prime minister 673
Flag, map 473, 488
Foreign aid from 738
Foreign exchange rates 75
Forests 306
Fossil fuel reserves, exports 112
Gasoline prices 110
Gold production 68
Gross domestic product 733
Health expenditures 142
Lakes 694
Languages 749
Motor vehicle production 79
Mountain peaks 687
Rivers 691
Securities held by U.S. 64
Taxes 734
Temperature/precipitation extremes 315
Territories 750
Terrorism 15
Trade 73
Travel and tourism 85, 86
Unemployment rates 734
U.S. investment 78
U.S. troops in 129
Vacation days 89
Wages, hourly 734
Australian Open (tennis) 17, 853, 955
Austria **750**
Area, population 731, 750
Budget deficits 59
Education 383, 385
Flag, map 473, 482
Foreign aid from 738
Foreign exchange rates 75
Gross domestic product 733
History 661
Languages 714, 750
Mortality rate by cause 736
Motor vehicle production 79
Refugees in 735
Rulers 656, 678
Taxes 734
Travel and tourism 85
U.S. immigrants from 620
U.S. investment 78
Vacation days 89
Wages, hourly 734
Austrian Succession, War of the (1740-48) 139
Authors, noted. *See* Writers, noted
Autism 421
Auto racing 19, 24, **959-61**
Automobiles, motor vehicles
Accidents, deaths 105, 169-70, 171
Colors, most popular 82
Drivers 83, 84
Exports, imports 74, 79
Fuel consumption/efficiency 82, 84
Fuel economy standards 453, 454
Gasoline prices 110, 453
History 442, 660
Hybrid and electric 81
Industry bailout 62, 454
Leading U.S. companies 52
News (2015) 15, 23, 30
Personal expenditures 51
Phone/texting device laws 83
Production 79-80
Registration 82
Safety belt laws, U.S. 84
Sales 80-82
Speed limits (1995) 451
Theft 116-18, 121, 122
Truck sales 82
Autumn, Autumnal Equinox 339, 352
Avant garde music 214-15
Aviation **335-36**
Air mileage, between world cities 91
Airlines 87-88, 90
Airmen/aircraft statistics 335
Disasters 15, 19, 21, 30, 33, *196*, 317-19
Leading companies 52
Milestones 336, 442, 443, 445, 446
Occupational fatalities 105
Safety record (1985-2014) 87
Traffic 88
Wright brothers (1903) 336, 442, 660
Awards, prizes **259-78**
Azerbaijan 112, 113, 121, 473, 484, 714, 731, 736, **750-51**
Azores 689, **825**
Aztecs 655, 804

B

Bacon, Francis 437
Bacon, Nathaniel 436
Baha'i Faith 409, 697, 698, **706-07**
Bahamas 77, 78, 473, 479, 689, 731, **751**
Bahrain 112, 129, 134, 297, 306, 473, 484, 689, 731, 733, **751-52**
Baker Island 593
Bakersfield, CA 304, **594-95**, 614
Balance of trade 73, 74
Balearic Islands 689, 836
Bales, Robert 456
Bali 670, 689
Ballet 219
Balloons and ballooning 336
Baltic Sea 689, 690
Baltimore, MD **595**
Air quality 304
Airport traffic 88
Buildings, tall 722
Consumer Price Index 46
Crime rates 118
Geography 696
Housing 71, 72
Immigrant admissions 619
Population 614
Port traffic 76
Protests (2015) *199*
Tides 316
Weather 309-11, 313
Bangladesh **752**
Agriculture 98, 99
Area, population 730, 731, 752
Cell phone use 300
Fishing, aquaculture 100
Flag, map 473, 484
Fossil fuel reserves 112
Health expenditures 142
Independence 666
Internally displaced persons 736
Languages 714, 752
Muslim population 706
Refugees in 735
Bank of America 62, 454, 455, 457
Banks
Bailout 62, 454
Charters (1781, 1791, 1816) 437, 438, 439
Closed (1933) 443
Deposits, U.S. 61
Failures (1934-2015) 62
Gold reserves (world) 733
Insurance 61
International 23, 742
Leading U.S. 52, 62
Mortgages 70
Number, U.S. 61
Savings and loan crisis (1989, 1996) 450
Baptist churches 409, 697, 704-05
Barbados 78, 121, 473, 479, 689, 731, **752**
Barley 96, 97
Barton, Clara 441
Baseball **907-32**
Addresses, team 419
AL final standings/team statistics 908, 912-14
All-Star games (1933-2015) 930
All-time leaders 915-16
Awards and honors (1931-2014) 924-25, 929
Batting champions 919-20
Black Sox scandal (1921) 443
Franchise shifts, additions 931
Gehrig farewell (1939) 444
Hall of Fame 17, 444, 932
Home run leaders 917-19
Little League 931
Managers of the year (1983-2014) 932
NCAA champions 888
NL final standings/team statistics 908-11
PED scandals 453, 455
Pennant, division winners 926-28
Pitchers, leading 917, 920-23
Players' strike (1994-95) 451
Racial integration (1947) 445
Rose banning (1989) 450
Season highlights (2015) 853, 907
Stadiums 931
World Series 442, 443, 445-46, 450, 907, 929-30
Basketball
NBA **933-40**
Addresses, team 419-20
All-NBA/All-defensive teams 936
Arenas 939
Awards and honors 934, 936-37
Champions (1947-2015) 935
Coaches 939, 940
Final standings (2014-15) 933
Franchise origins 939
Hall of Fame 940
Player draft picks 937-38
Scoring leaders (1947-2015) 934-35
Season highlights (2014-15) 26, *811*, 853, 933
Statistical leaders 934, 938
NCAA **884-88**
Awards 886
Coaches 886
Men's all-time winningest teams 886
Men's tournament champions 22, *811*, 853, 884-85
Women's tournament champions 23, *811*, 853, 887-88
WNBA 33, **941-42**
Baton Rouge, LA 71, 76, 304, **595**, 615, 696
Battlefields, national 429-30
Beans 96
Beatles, The 446, 666
Beauty pageants 271
Beef 94, 95, 96-97, 99
Begin, Menachem 449, 667
Belarus 112, 473, 483, 668, 714, 731, **752-53**
Belep Archipelago 777
Belgium **753**
Agriculture 97
Area, population 731, 753
Education 383, 385
Flag, map 473, 482
Foreign aid from 738
Foreign exchange rates 75
History 657
Languages 753
Merchant fleet 77
Motor vehicle production 79
Nuclear power 114
Rulers, royal family 680
Taxes 734
Trade 73
Travel and tourism 85
U.S. investment 78
U.S. troops in 129
Vacation days 89
Wages, hourly 734
Belize 473, 479, 731, **753-54**
Bell, Alexander Graham 441
Belmont Stakes 853, 967-68
Benin 473, 486, 731, 737, **754**
Bergdahl, Bowe 457
Bering Sea 690
Bering, Vitus 437, 683
Berlin, Germany
Blockade, airlift (1948) 445
Wall built, leveled (1961, 1989) 666, 667, *667*
Bermuda 64, 77, 78, 689, 731, **848**
Bernhardt, Sarah 441
Berra, Yogi 34, *816*
Beverages
Consumption statistics 94
Exports, imports 74, 75
Leading U.S. companies 52
Price indexes 45, 46
Bhutan 306, 473, 484, 731, **754**
Bhutto, Benazir 668, 671
Biathlon 857
Bible
Biblical figures 703
Books of 703
First printed in colonial America (1661) 436
Measures 363
Ten Commandments 702
Biden, Joe 7, 32, 39, 454, 539
Big Bang 344
Biker gang violence 24
Bill of Rights 438, 466
bin Laden, Osama 452, 455, 670, 672
Biology
Animal, plant classification 291
Discoveries 285-86
Glossary 280
Biomass 109, 115
Birth control 168, 446. 457
Birth statistics 164, 165, 166
Birthdays, milestone (2016) 5
Birthstones 360
Black Death 654
Black Friday (1869) 441
Black Hawk War (1832) 439
Black Sea 690
Blacks
Africa return by (1816, 1820) 439
Arrest records 122
Bus boycott (1955) 445
Cancer rates 153
Cigarette use 146
Civil rights legislation (1875, 1957, 1960, 1964) 441, 446, 665
Coretta Scott King Award 270
Education 380, 384, 389, 621
First cabinet member (1966) 447

First governor (1989) . . . 450
First in colonies (1619) . . . 436
First in Congress . . . 550
First Joint Chiefs chairman (1989) . . . 450
First major league baseball player (1947) . . . 445
First mayors of major cities . . . 447, 449
First Supreme Court justice (1967) . . . 447
First U.S. president . . . 454
Hate crime victims . . . 25, 123
Health insurance coverage . . . 141, 142
HIV/AIDS cases . . . 148
Home ownership rates . . . 70
Households . . . 618
Incomes, wages . . . 47, 107
Infant mortality . . . 172
Internet use . . . 299
Jim Crow laws (1875) . . . 441
Life expectancy . . . 172
March on Washington (1963) . . . 446
Million Man March (1995) . . . 451
NAACP founding (1909) . . . 442
Nonmarital childbearing . . . 166
Police shootings, protests . . 4, 12, 19, 21-22, 27, 28, 29, *199*, 457, *457*
Population . . . 610, 611, 621
Poverty rates . . . 48, 49
Prison inmates . . . 120, 121
Race riots (1908, 1943, 1965, 1967, 1992) . . . 442, 444, 447, 450
"Separate but equal" doctrine (1896) . . . 442
Sexual activity . . . 167
Sit-ins (1960) . . . 446
Slave/"free colored" census data . . . 609
Social Security . . . 371
Spingarn Medal . . . 271
Unemployment . . . 103
Voting rights (1870, 1957, 1965) . . . 441, 447, 467
War service . . . 132

Blackwater convictions . . . 21, 457
Blagojevich, Rod . . . 454, 455
Blair, Tony . . . 671
Blindness . . . 154, 421
Blizzards . . . 308, 323, 441
Blois, House of . . . 675
Blood disorders . . . 421
Blood pressure . . . 155
Blood vessels. *See* Heart, blood vessels
Blues artists, noted . . . 216-17
Boat racing . . . 979
Bobsledding . . . 857
Body mass index . . . 161
Body weight . . . 151, 155, 161-62
Boehner, John . . . 4, 30, 39, *198*, 455
Boer War (1899-1902) . . . 659, 834
Boesky, Ivan . . . 450
Boiling points . . . 362
Boise, ID . . . 71, 309-11, 313, **595**, 615, 696
Bolivia . . . 112, 306, 473, 480, 665, 667, 671, 714, 731, **754-55**
Bollingen Prize in Poetry . . . 270
Bombings. *See* Terrorism
Bonaire . . . 818
Bond, Julian . . . 34, *816*
Bonds . . . 16, 66
Bonds, Barry . . . 453, 455
Bonus March (1932) . . . 443
Booker Prize (Man Booker Prize) . . . 267
Books
Best-selling (2014) . . . 250
Children's . . . 249-50, 267-68
First American printing (1640) . . . 436
Most challenged (2014) . . . 249
Notable (2015) . . . 249-50
(*see also* Literature; Writers, noted)
Border fence . . . 453
Border Protection . . . 547
Borneo . . . 639
Bosnia and Herzegovina . . . **755**
Area, population . . . 731, 755
Dayton accord (1995) . . . 451
Flag, map . . . 473, 482
Fossil fuel reserves . . . 112
History . . . 668
Internally displaced persons . . . 736
Languages . . . 755
U.S. military financing . . . 134
Boston, MA . . . **595**
Air quality . . . 304
Airport traffic . . . 88
Brinks robbery (1950) . . . 445
Buildings, tall . . . 717
Consumer Price Index . . . 46
Crime rates . . . 118
Geography . . . 696
History, early . . . 436-37
Housing . . . 71
Immigrant admissions . . . 619
Marathon . . . 442, 976-77
Marathon bombing . . . 23, 456, *456*, 672
Police strike (1919) . . . 443
Population . . . 614
Port traffic . . . 76
Tides . . . 316
Weather . . . 309-11, 313

Botanical classification . . . 291
Botha, P. W. . . . 668
Botswana . . . 121, 473, 487, 714, 731, **755-56**
Boundary lines, U.S. . . . 425
Bourbon, House of . . . 677
Bowling . . . **971**
Boxer Rebellion (1900) . . . 442
Boxing . . . 24, 441, 444, *812*, 864-65, **962-65**
Boy Scouts . . . 407, 442, 456
Bradford, William . . . 436
Bradstreet, Anne . . . 436
Brady Bill (1993) . . . 451
Brady, James . . . 449
Brady, Tom . . . 24, 31, 39, *810*, 853
Branch Davidians . . . 450-51
Brand names . . . 68-70
Brat, David . . . 457
Brazil . . . **756**
Agriculture . . . 97, 98, 99
Aquaculture . . . 100
Area, population . . . 730, 731, 756
Budget deficits . . . 59
Carbon dioxide emissions . . . 302
Cell phone use . . . 300
Computer/Internet use . . . 294, 297
Education . . . 383
Elections . . . 673
Energy production, consumption . . . 109
Flag, map . . . 473, 480-81
Foreign exchange rates . . . 75
Forests . . . 306
Fossil fuel reserves, exports . . . 112, 113
Gold production . . . 68
Gross domestic product . . . 733
Health expenditures . . . 142
History . . . 658, 670, 671
Languages . . . 714, 756
Military strength . . . 133
Motor vehicle production . . . 79
Nuclear arms abandonment . . . 738
Nuclear power . . . 114
Securities held by U.S. . . . 64
Trade . . . 73
Travel and tourism . . . 85, 86
U.S. investment . . . 78
Wages, hourly . . . 734
Breast cancer . . . 150-51, 152
Breeders' Cup . . . 13, 968-70
Brennan, William . . . 450
Breyer, Stephen G. . . . 38, 559
Brezhnev, Leonid . . . 667, 681
Bridge (card game) . . . 362
Bridgegate . . . 456
Bridges . . . 422, 441, 444, 447, 453, **722-25**
Britain. *See* United Kingdom
Britain, Battle of . . . 663
British Indian Ocean Territory . . . 848
British Open . . . 28, 853, 953, 954
British Virgin Islands . . . 848
Broadcasting. *See* Radio; Television
Broadway. *See* Theater
Bronze Star . . . 136
Brooke, Edward . . . 447
Brown, Jerry . . . 39
Brown, John . . . 440
Brown, Michael . . . 457, *457*
Brown, Scott . . . 454
Brown v. Board of Education . . . 561
Brownie camera (1900) . . . 442
Brunei . . . 112, 473, 485, 731, 733, **756-57**
Bryan, William Jennings . . . 442
Bubonic plague . . . 654
Buchanan, James . . . 491, **495**, *495*, 503, 504, 507, 508
Buck, Pearl . . . 443
Buddhism . . . **707**
Adherents (U.S., world) . . . 697, 698
Headquarters (U.S.) . . . 409
History . . . 648, 649, 654
Budget
Deficits for selected countries . . . 59
Federal . . . 57-59
Budget control measures (2011) . . . 455
Deficit reduction legislation (1993) . . . 451
Disputes and government shutdown (2012-13) . . . 456
Fiscal 2015 . . . 14, 17, 30, 457
Surplus reported (1998) . . . 452
State finances . . . 60-61
Buffalo, NY . . . 71, 72, 309-11, 313, **595**, 614, 696, 722
Buhari, Muhammadu . . . *197*
Buildings, tall . . . 13, 422, **716-22**
Bulgaria . . . 85, 98, 112, 114, 134, 166, 383, 473, 483, 667, 714, 731, **757**
Bulge, Battle of the . . . 444
Bulger, James "Whitey" . . . 456
Bull Run, Battle of (1861) . . . 440
Bullying . . . 382
Bunker Hill, Battle of (1775) . . . 437
Burger, Warren . . . 447
Burgesses, House of (1619) . . . 436
Burglary . . . 116-18, 121, 122
Burj Khalifa . . . 716
Burkina Faso . . . 31, 473, 486, 673, 714, 731, 733, 737, **757-58**

Burma. *See* Myanmar
Burns . . . 163
Burr, Aaron . . . 438
Burundi . . . 473, 487, 669, 714, 731, 733, 735, 736, **758**
Burwell, Sylvia Mathews . . . 457
Bush, George H.W. . . . 450, 491, **501**, *501*, 503, 507, 508, 509-38
Bush, George W. . . . 452, 453, 454, 491, **501-02**, *501*, 503, 507, 508, 509-38
Bush, Jeb . . . 6, 7, 39, *198*
Business
Antitrust legislation (1890, 1914) . . 441, 442
Companies directory . . . 410-17
Corporate tax rates . . . 66
Franchises, top U.S. . . . 55
International transactions, U.S. . . . 77
Leaders, noted past . . . 181-82
Leading companies . . . 52-54
Patents granted . . . 289
Professional organizations . . . 418-19
Rotary club, first (1905) . . . 442
U.S. investments abroad . . . 78
(*see also* Banks; Corporations; Economics; Industries, U.S.; Stocks)
Byzantine Empire . . . 651, 728

C

Cabeza de Vaca, Alvar Nuñez . . . 683
Cabinet, U.S. . . . **539-47**
First black member (1966) . . . 447
First woman (1933) . . . 443
Obama administration . . . 539
Personal salutes, honors . . . 135
Cable television . . . 254, 255
Cabo Verde (Cape Verde) . . 473, 689, 731, **758**
Cabot, John . . . 683
Cabrera Island . . . 836
Cabrini, Mother Frances Xavier . . . 445
Caicos Island . . . 732, 848
Calcium (dietary) . . . 159, 160
Caldecott Medal . . . 268
Calderón, Felipe . . . 671
Calendars . . . **354-60**
Celestial (2016) . . . 337-40
Chinese (lunar) . . . 355
Gregorian . . . 354
Julian . . . 354-55
Leap years . . . 354
Perpetual . . . 356-57
Religious . . . 699-700
Year 2016 . . . 358
California . . . **565-66**
Agriculture . . . 92, 93
Bear flag raised (1846) . . . 440
Coastline . . . 423
Congressional representation . . 551, 553, 609
Crime, prisons, death penalty . . 117, 119, 120
Drought . . . 21, *198*
Education . . . 380-83, 389-90
Elevations (high, low) . . . 423
Energy consumption . . . 111
Finances . . . 60
Governor . . . 37
Gubernatorial recall election (2003) . . . 452
Hazardous waste . . . 305
Health insurance coverage . . . 142
Immigrant admissions . . . 619
Motor vehicles . . . 83, 84
Name origin, nickname . . . 426, 565
Oil production . . . 111
Population . . . 565, 594-604, 605, 606-07, 608, 611, 612, 623-25
Poverty rates . . . 49
Taxes . . . 84, 378, 449
Traveler spending . . . 86
Unemployment . . . 101
Weather . . . 312
Wildfires (2015) . . . 31-32
ZIP and area codes . . . 623-25
California, Gulf of . . . 690
Calley, William L., Jr. . . . 448
Calories (dietary) . . . 158, 159, 161
Calvin, John . . . 654
Cambodia . . 98, 473, 485, 665, 667, 714, 731, 735, **758-59**
Cameron, David . . . 673
Cameroon . . . 306, 473, 486-87, 731, 735, 736, **759**
Canada . . . **759-60**
Agriculture . . . 97, 98, 99
Area, population . . . 731, 759
Budget deficits . . . 59
Buildings, tall . . . 717, 720, 722
Carbon dioxide emissions . . . 302
Computer/Internet use . . . 294, 297, 298
Consumer price changes . . . 733
Dominion of Canada (1867) . . . 659
Education . . . 383, 385
Elections (2006, 2011, 2015) . . . 32-33, 671, 673
Energy production, consumption . . . 109
Flag, map . . . 473, 478
Foreign aid from . . . 738
Foreign exchange rates . . . 75

Forests . . . 306
Fossil fuel reserves, exports . . . 112, 113
French and Indian War (1754-63) . . . 437
Gasoline prices . . . 110
Gold production, reserves . . . 68, 733
Gross domestic product . . . 733
Health expenditures . . . 142
Islands . . . 689
Languages . . . 759
Latitudes, longitudes, elevations . . . 696
Mortality rate by cause . . . 736
Motor vehicle production, exports . . . 79
Newspaper circulation . . . 252
Nuclear power . . . 114
Nunavut creation . . . 669
Postal information . . . 367
Prime ministers . . . 676
Provinces, territories . . . 367, 760
Refugees in . . . 735
Rivers . . . 692-93
Securities held by U.S. . . . 64
Spaceflight . . . 333
Taxes . . . 734
Terrorism . . . 672
Trade . . . 73, 75, 76
Travel and tourism . . . 85, 86, 87
Unemployment rates . . . 734
U.S. ancestral claims . . . 621
U.S. immigrants from . . . 9, 620
U.S. investment . . . 78
U.S. troops in . . . 129
Vacation days . . . 89
Wages, hourly . . . 734
Water supply . . . 306

Canary Islands . . . 689, 836
Cancer . . . **150-53**, 171, 421
Cantor, Eric . . . 457
Capetian dynasty . . . 677
Capital punishment. *See* Death penalty
Capitol, U.S. . . . 434, 439
Capone, Al . . . 443
Carbohydrates . . . 158
Carbon dioxide emissions . . . 302, 303, 457
Carbon monoxide emissions . . . 303
Cárdenas, García López de . . . 436, 683
Cardinals, Roman Catholic . . . 702
Cardiovascular disease . . . 155
Cardoso, Henrique . . . 670
Cards, playing (odds) . . . 362
Caribbean Community and Common Market (CARICOM) . . . 739
Caribbean region . . . **87**, 479, 735, 737
Caribbean Sea
Area, depth . . . 690
Islands . . . 592-93, 689
Maps . . . 479
Carnegie Hall . . . 441
Carolingian dynasty . . . 677, 678
Cars. *See* Automobiles, motor vehicles
Carson, Ben . . . 6, 7, *198*
Carson, Rachel . . . 446
Carter, Ashton . . . 17, 457
Carter, Jimmy . . . 39, 449, 491, **500**, *500*, 503, 507, 508, 509-38
Cartoonists . . . 182, 262
Castro, Fidel . . . 665, 671, 768
Castro, Raúl . . . 457
Cat breeds . . . 293
Catalonia . . . 836
Catherine the Great . . . 657
Catholic churches . . . 697, 698
(*see also* Roman Catholicism)
Cattle. *See* Beef; Livestock
Caucasus Mountains . . . 688
Cayman Islands . . . 64, 731, 848
Celebes . . . 689
Celebrities. *See* Noted personalities; specific fields; specific names
Celestial events (2016) . . . 337-40
Cell phones . . . 300-01
Celsius scale . . . 361
Celts . . . 651
Cemeteries
Arlington National (VA) . . . 434
Presidential burial sites . . . 504
Census
Authorized (1790) . . . 438
Figures . . . 606-07, 622-45
Origins and methods . . . 605
Permanent Bureau established . . . 442
Slave/"free colored" census data . . . 609
Third (1810) . . . 439
Centers for Disease Control . . . 421
Central African Republic . . . 306, 473, 486, 731, 733, 735, 736, 737, 742, **760-61**
Central America
Agriculture . . . 97, 98, 99
Fossil fuel reserves . . . 112
Maps . . . 479
Mayan culture . . . 649, 652
Trade . . . 73
Travel and tourism . . . 87
Volcanoes . . . 685, 686
(*see also* specific countries)
Central Intelligence Agency (CIA)
Directors . . . 128
Illegal operations report (1974) . . . 448
Internet address . . . 547
Interrogation tactics . . . 13-14, 454, 457
Reform bill signed (2004) . . . 453
Reorganization (2015) . . . 19
Spy cases (1994, 1997) . . . 451
Cerebral palsy . . . 421
Cerebrovascular diseases. *See* Strokes
Ceres (dwarf planet) . . . 279, 344, 345, **348-49**
Ceuta . . . 836
Ceylon. *See* Sri Lanka
Chad . . . 113, 473, 486, 667, 731, 735, 736, 737, **761**
***Challenger* (space shuttle)** . . . 330, 332, 450
Champlain, Samuel de . . . 436, 683
Chandler, AZ . . . **595**, 614, 615
Channel Islands . . . 689, **848**
Chaplin, Charlie . . . 443
Charlemagne . . . 651, 677, 678
Charles Martel . . . 650
Charleston, SC . . . 4, *199*, 436
Charlotte (Princess of Cambridge) . . . 24, *815*
Charlotte, NC . . . 71, 72, 88, **595**, 614, 615, 619, 696, 717
Chatham Islands . . . 689, 818
Chávez, Hugo . . . 670, 671, 673
Chechnya . . . 668
Chemical weapons . . . 12
Chemicals
Exports, imports . . . 74, 75
Leading U.S. companies . . . 52
Toxic . . . 449
Chemistry
Discoveries . . . 285-86
Glossary . . . 280
Nobel Prizes . . . 259, 260
Periodic table of elements . . . 283
Chesapeake, VA . . . **595**, 615
Chess . . . 971
Chiang Kai-shek . . . 662
Chicago Board of Trade. *See* CME Group
Chicago, IL . . . **595-96**
Air mileage to other cities . . . 91
Air quality . . . 304
Airport traffic . . . 88
Buildings, tall . . . 717-18
Consumer Price Index . . . 46
Crime rates . . . 118
Fire (1871) . . . 441
First black mayor . . . 449
Geography . . . 696
Housing . . . 71, 72
Immigrant admissions . . . 619
Marathon . . . 978
Population . . . 614
Port traffic . . . 76
Weather . . . 309-11, 313
Chicken. *See* Poultry products
Chicken pox . . . 156
Children
Associations and organizations . . . 407-08
Child care arrangements . . . 168
Health insurance coverage . . . 141, 142
Help organizations . . . 421
HIV/AIDS cases . . . 148
Living arrangements . . . 618
Obesity in . . . 162
Population . . . 617
Risk behavior . . . 145-47, 169
Social Security benefits . . . 369, 372
(*see also* Education)
Children's books . . . 249-50, 267-68
Chile . . . **761-62**
Agriculture . . . 97
Area, population . . . 731, 761
Education . . . 383
Fishing, aquaculture . . . 100
Flag, map . . . 473, 480-81
Forests . . . 306
Fossil fuel reserves . . . 112
History . . . 667, 668, 671, 681
Languages . . . 761
Taxes . . . 734
U.S. investment . . . 78
China, Dynastic
Architecture . . . 727, 728
Boxer Rebellion (1900) . . . 442
European powers and . . . 659
Great Wall . . . 648, *648*
Open Door Policy (1899) . . . 442, 659
Opium War (1839-42) . . . 658
Revolution (1911) . . . 661
Ruling dynasties . . . 647-48, 649, 652, 654, 656, 682
U.S. immigrants from . . . 620
China, People's Republic of . . . **762-64**
Agriculture . . . 97, 98, 99
Area, population . . . 730, 731, 762
Arms sales . . . 134
Autonomous regions . . . 763
Budget deficits . . . 59
Carbon dioxide emissions . . . 302
Cell phone use . . . 300
Computer/Internet use . . . 294, 297
Consumer price changes . . . 733
Cultural Revolution . . . 665-66
Earthquakes (2008, 2010, 2014) . . . 325
Education . . . 383
Energy production, consumption . . . 109
Fishing, aquaculture . . . 100
Flag, map . . . 473, 484-85
Foreign exchange rates . . . 75
Forests . . . 306
Fossil fuel reserves . . . 112
Gasoline prices . . . 110
Gold production . . . 68
Gold reserves . . . 733
Gross domestic product . . . 733
Health expenditures . . . 142
History . . . 662, 663, 664, 665, 666, 668, *668*, 669, 762-63
Languages . . . 714, 762
Leaders . . . 666, 682, 762-63
Merchant fleet . . . 77
Military strength . . . 133
Mortality rate by cause . . . 736
Motor vehicle production . . . 79
Muslim population . . . 706
News (2014-15) . . . 13, 15, 28-29, *196*
Nixon visit (1972) . . . 448
Nuclear arms . . . 738
Nuclear power . . . 114
Refugees from/in . . . 735
Securities held by U.S. . . . 64
Spaceflight . . . 333, 671, 673
Trade . . . 73, 75, 76, 448
Travel and tourism . . . 85, 86, 87
U.S. adoptions from . . . 166
U.S. immigrants from . . . 9, 619, 620
U.S. investment . . . 78
U.S. spy plane dispute (2001) . . . 452
China, Republic of. *See* Taiwan
Chinese calendar . . . 355
Chinese Exclusion Act (1882) . . . 441
Chinese folk religionists . . . 697, 698
Chlamydia . . . 156
Choking . . . 163
Cholera . . . 673
Cholesterol . . . 155, 159
Choreographers, noted . . . 219
Christ (Jesus Christ) . . . 650
Christian Church (Disciples of Christ) . . . 409, 697, 704-05
Christianity
Adherents, world . . . 697-98
Denominations . . . 409-10, 704-05
History . . . 650, 652, 654, 655, 667
Christie, Chris . . . 6, 7, *198*, 456
Christmas Day . . . 358
Christmas Island . . . 689, 750
Chromium . . . 160
Chrysler Corporation . . . 62, 454
Chula Vista, CA . . . **596**, 614
Church of Christ . . . 409, 697
Church of England . . . 437, 846
Churches. *See* Religion
Churchill, Winston . . . 664
CIA. *See* Central Intelligence Agency
Cigarettes. *See* Smoking
Cincinnati, OH . . . 46, 71, 72, 75, 118, 304, **596**, 614, 619, 696, 722
Cinema. *See* Movies
Circumnavigation . . . 336
CIS (Commonwealth of Independent States) . . . 668, 739
Cities, U.S. . . . **594-604**
Air quality . . . 304
Airport traffic . . . 88
Buildings, tall . . . 717-22
Consumer Price Indexes . . . 46
Farthest east, north, south, west . . . 422
Housing prices . . . 71
Immigrant admissions . . . 619
Latitudes, longitudes, elevations . . . 696
Museums . . . 247-48
Population . . . 614-15, 622-45
Ports . . . 76
Weather . . . 309-11, 313
Cities, world
Air mileage between . . . 91
Air pollution . . . 304
Airport traffic . . . 88
Buildings . . . 716
Latitudes, longitudes . . . 695
Population . . . 730
Time differences . . . 359
Weather . . . 313
Civil rights
Activism (1955, 1960, 1963, 1965) 446, 447
Disabilities Act (1990) . . . 450
Legislation (1875, 1957, 1960, 1964) . . 441, 446, 665
U.S. Commission on . . . 547
(*see also* Desegregation; Voting rights *under* Elections; Women)
Civil service reform (1883) . . . 441
Civil War, U.S. (1861-65) . . . 140, 440
Amnesty Act (1872) . . . 441
Black troops . . . 132
Casualties, numbers serving . . . 138

Gettysburg Address (1863) 470
Lee's surrender 440
Lincoln Prize 270
Military awards 136
Secession 470
Clancy, Joseph 17
Classical music 214-15
Clayton Antitrust Act (1914) 442
Cleveland, Grover ... 491, **497**, *497*, 503, 504, 507, 508
Cleveland, OH **596**
Air quality 304
Buildings, tall 718
Consumer Price Index 46
Geography 696
Housing 71, 72
Immigrant admissions 619
Population 614
Port traffic 76
Weather 309-11, 313
Climate. *See* Global warming; Weather
Clinton, Bill 491, **501**, *501*, 503
Impeachment, acquittal 452, 669
Presidential elections (1992, 1996) ... 450, 451, 507, 508, 509-38
Whitewater report (2002) 452
Clinton, Hillary Rodham 6, 7, 21, 32, 39, *198*, 453, 454, 456
Cloning 670
Clothing
Exports, imports 74
Personal expenditures 51
Price index 45, 46
CME Group 67
Coal
Exports, imports 74, 109
Mining strikes (1922, 1946) 443, 444
Production, consumption 109, 110, 113
Reserves 112
Coast Guard, U.S.
Academy 136
Address for information 137, 547
Commandants 128
Insignia 137
Personnel, active duty 130
Coastlines, U.S. 423
Coca-Cola (1886, 1985) 441, 450
Cocos (Keeling) Islands 750
Cody, Buffalo Bill 441
Coffee 74, 94
Coins 55, 57
Cold War 444-45, 664-65, 667
Colds and flu. *See* Common cold; Influenza
***Cole* bombing (2000)** 452, 670
Colleges and universities
Bachelor's degrees conferred 388
Coeducation, first (1833) 439
College, first (1636) 436
Desegregation (1962) 446
Endowment assets 387
Enrollment 386
Faculty salaries 389
Financial aid for 386, 388
Four-year institutions 391-406
Fraternity misconduct (2015) 20-21
Land Grant Act (1862) 440
Nicknames, colors 882-83
Sports 877-89
State university, first (1795) 438
Tuition and costs 387, 391-406
Women's, first (1821) 439
Collins, Michael 447
Colombia **764**
Agriculture 97, 98
Area, population 731, 764
Education 383
Flag, map 473, 480
Foreign aid to 738
Forests 306
Fossil fuel reserves, exports 112, 113
Health expenditures 142
Internally displaced persons 736
Language 764
Liberation of 681
Military strength 133
Prison population 121
Refugees from 735
Trade 73
Travel and tourism 86
U.S. adoptions from 166
U.S. investment 78
U.S. military financing 134
U.S. troops in 129
Color spectrum 285
Colorado **566**
Agriculture 92, 93
Congressional representation 551, 553, 609
Crime, prisons, death penalty 117, 119, 120
Education 380-83, 389-90
Elevations (high, low) 423
Energy consumption 111
Finances 60
Governor 37
Hazardous waste 305
Health insurance coverage 142
Immigrant admissions 619
Motor vehicles 83, 84
Name origin, nickname 426, 566
Oil production 111
Population 566, 594, 596, 605, 606-07, 608, 611, 612, 625-26
Poverty rates 49
Taxes 84, 378
Unemployment 101
Weather 312
ZIP and area codes 625-26
Colorado River 683, 692
Colorado Springs, CO 71, **596**, 614, 696
Colorectal cancer 152
***Columbia* (space shuttle)** ... 330-32, 449, 452, 671
Columbia River 692
Columbian Exposition (1893) 441
Columbine High School (Littleton, CO) .. 452
Columbus, Christopher 436, 654, 683
Columbus Day 358
Columbus, OH .. 71, 72, 309-11, **596**, 614, 619, 696, 718
Comets 350
Commerce. *See* Exports, imports; Ships and shipping; Trade
Commerce, Department of **544**
Commercial revolution 655
Commission on Civil Rights 547
Common cold 156
***Common Sense* (Paine pamphlet) (1776)** 437
Commonwealth (British) 739
Commonwealth of Independent States (CIS) 668, 739
Communications. *See* Telecommunications
Communism
Post-World War II 664-65
Russian revolution (1917) 661
Soviet Bloc breakup (1991) 668
U.S. 443, 445
Comoros 473, 487, 731, 733, **764-65**
Composers, noted 214-16
Comprehensive Test Ban Treaty (1996) . 451, 739
Compromise of 1850 440
Computers **294-99**
Access/usage 294
Fastest supercomputers 295
Hardware sales and household penetration 295
Leading U.S. companies 54
Milestones 294, 671
Top operating systems 297
(*see also* Internet)
Concentration camps. *See* Holocaust
Concerts, top-grossing (1985-2014) 254
Confederate States of America
Amnesty Act (1872) 441
Civil War (1861-65) 138, 440
Flags 25, *199*, 470
Secession, government 470
Confederations Cup (soccer) 951
Confucianism 648, 698
Congo, Democratic Republic of the .. **765-66**
Area, population 730, 731, 765
Flag, map 473, 487
Foreign aid to 738
Forests 306
Fossil fuel reserves 112
Gross domestic product 733
Health expenditures 142
History *665*, 666, 667, 669, 671
Internally displaced persons 736
Languages 714, 765
Mortality rate by cause 736
Refugees from/in 735
Sanitation/drinking water 737
UN peacekeeping mission 742
U.S. adoptions from 166
Congo, Republic of the 98, 99, 112, 113, 306, 473, 487, 731, 735, 736, **766**
Congo River 691
Congress of Industrial Organizations. *See* AFL-CIO
Congress of Vienna (1814-15) 657
Congress, U.S. 15, **548-58**
Activity (1947-2014) 550
Apportionment 609
Bill-into-law process 469
Firsts and milestones 438, 550
House of Representatives
Bank closure (1991) 450
Members 552-58
Salaries, term 552
Speakers 32, 548
Nonvoting members 558
Political divisions (1901-2015) 548-49
Presidential vetoes (1789-2015) 549
Salutes, honors 135
Senate
Floor leaders 548
Members 551-52
Salaries, term 551
Visitors, admission of 434
Conjunction (astronomical position) 337
Connecticut **566-67**
Agriculture 92, 93
Congressional representation .. 551, 553-54, 609
Crime, prisons, death penalty 117, 119
Education 380-83, 389-90
Elevations (high, low) 423
Energy consumption 111
Finances 60
Governor 37
Hazardous waste 305
Health insurance coverage 142
Immigrant admissions 619
Motor vehicles 83, 84
Name origin, nickname 426, 566
Population 566, 605, 606-07, 608, 611, 612, 626
Poverty rates 49
Shoreline 423
Taxes 84, 378
Unemployment 101
Weather 312
ZIP and area codes 626
Conservation. *See* Environment
Constantine 650, 651
Constantinople 651
Constellations 342
Constitution, U.S. **461-69**, *461*
Adopted (1788) 438
Amendments 466-69
Bill of Rights 466
Preamble 461
Ratification (1787) 438, 461
200th anniversary 450
Constitutional Convention (1787) 438, 460-61
Construction
Employment/unemployment 102, 103
Leading companies 52
Median earnings 106
Occupational injuries, illnesses 105
U.S. national income 44
Consumer Price Indexes (CPI) 44-46
Consumer Product Safety Commission .. 547
Continental Congress
Articles of Confederation (1777) ... 437, 460
Declaration of Independence (1776) .. 437, 458-60, *459*
First (1774) 437
Great Seal of the U.S. 471, *471*
Stars and Stripes (1777) 437, 471
Continental Divide 424, 439
Continents
Agriculture 97, 98, 99
Area, population 730
Carbon dioxide emissions 302
Elevations (highest, lowest) 695
Exploration 683-85
Fossil fuel reserves 112
Lakes 694
Maps 477-88
Mountain peaks 687-88
Rivers 691-93
Temperature/precipitation extremes 315
Volcanoes 686
Waterfalls 695
(*see also* specific continents)
Contract With America (1995) 451
Cook Islands 488, 731, 818
Coolidge, Calvin . 491, **498**, *498*, 504, 507, 508
Cooper, James Fenimore 439
Copeland, Misty *813*
Copernicus, Nicolaus 655
Copper 68, 160
Copyrights. *See* Patents and copyrights
Coral Sea Islands 750
Coretta Scott King Award 270
Corn 96-99
Coronado, Francisco de 436, 683
Corporations
Bond yields 66
Brand ownership 69-70
Business directory 410-17
Leading U.S. 52-54
Patents received (2014) 289
Tax rates 66
World's largest 54
Corpus Christi, TX 71, 76, **596**, 614, 696
Corsica 482, 689, 776
Cortés, Hernán 655, 683
Cosby, Bill 13, 39, *814*
Cosmic background radiation 344
Cosmonauts. *See* Astronauts and cosmonauts
Costa Book Awards 270
Costa Rica ... 78, 121, 383, 473, 479, 731, **766**
Côte d'Ivoire (Ivory Coast) 473, 486, 671, 714, 731, 736, 737, 742, **766-67**
Cotton 96, 97
Cotton gin (1793) 438, *438*
Counties, U.S.
Highest weekly wages 104
Largest, by population 615
Largest, smallest 422
Country music 218, 277
Courts. *See* Supreme Court, U.S.; World Court
Cox, Archibald 448

Coxey, Jacob S. 441
CPI (Consumer Price Indexes) 44-46
Crane, Stephen 442
Crater Lake 422, 685
Craxi, Bettino 668
Credit, consumer 47
Creek Indian War (1813-14) 439
Crime **116-27**
Arrests, by race 122
Hate crimes 123
Law enforcement officers 121
Rates of 116-18
(*see also* Gun violence; Murder)
Crimean War (1853-56) 140, 659
Croatia 85, 383, 473, 482, 668, 714, 731, **767**
Cromwell, Oliver 655
Crozet Archipelago 777
Crude oil. *See* Petroleum
Crusades 139, 652
Cruz, Ted 6, 7, *198*
Crystal Palace 658
Cuba **767-68**
Agriculture 98, 99
Area, population 689, 731, 767
Bay of Pigs (1961) 446, 665
Castro resignation 671
Flag, map 473, 479
Fossil fuel reserves 112
Independence (1901) 442
Language 767
Missile crisis (1962) 446
Revolution (1959) 665, 768
Travel restrictions eased (2009) 454
U.S. immigrants from 620
U.S. relations restored 14-15, 22, 27, *197*, 457, 673
U.S. troops in 129
(*see also* Guantánamo Bay)
Cumberland Road (1811) 439
Cuneiform 647
Cuomo, Mario 34, *816*
Curaçao 64, 78, 689, 731, 818
Curling 859
Currency, U.S.
Circulation, amount in 57
Denominations, portraits on 56
Dollar bill 56, *56*
Engraving, printing 56, 434
Foreign exchange rates 75
Gold Standard dropped (1933) 443
Mint, U.S. 55, 438
Custer, George A. 441
Customs, U.S. 547
Cy Young Award 924
Cyberbullying 382
Cycles, chronological 359
Cycling 28, 456, 973
Cyclones 21, 308, 312, 323
Cyprus 77, 383, 473, 484, 673, 689, 731, 736, 742, **768-69**
Cyrus the Great 649
Cystic fibrosis 421
Czech Republic 621, **769**
Area, population 731, 769
Budget deficits 59
Education 383, 385
Flag, map 473, 482
Foreign aid from 738
Formation of (1993) 669
Fossil fuel reserves 112
Languages 714, 769
Motor vehicle production 79
NATO treaty 669
Nuclear power 114
Taxes 734
Travel and tourism 85
U.S. investment 78
U.S. military financing 134
U.S. missiles in 453-54
Wages, hourly 734
Czechoslovakia 620, 662, 663, 667, 669, 769

D

Da Vinci, Leonardo 653
Dada movement 662
Daguerre, Louis *658*, 659
Dairy products, livestock 74, 95, 96-97
Dallas, TX **596**
Air quality 304
Airport traffic 88
Buildings, tall 718
Consumer Price Index 46
Crime rates 118
Geography 696
Housing 71, 72
Immigrant admissions 619
Population 614
Weather 309-11, 313
Dams, major 422, 444, **726-27**
Dance 219, 660, *813*
Danes 675
Daoism 649, 698
Dare, Virginia 436
Darfur 671, 742, 744
Darius 649
Dark energy 344
Dark matter 344
Darwin, Charles 658
Davis Cup (tennis) 958
Davis, Kim 30, 39, *200*
Davis, Viola 39
Dawes, William 437
Day, Jason 29-30
Daylight Saving Time 360
Days, length of 352
Daytona 500 (auto race) 19, 960
De Blasio, Bill 456
de Klerk, F. W. 668, 669
De Soto, Hernando 436, 683
Deafness. *See* Hearing disorders
Death penalty
Abolition, reinstatement (1972, 1976) 448, 449
Illinois commutations (2003) 452
New Jersey repeal 453
State statutes 119
Supreme Court rulings 25, 38
Deaths
Accidental 171
Cancer 152
HIV/AIDS 148, 737
Infant rates, causes 166, 172
Leading causes 171
Occupational 105
Rates 164, 736
Suicides 170
Survivor benefits 369
(*see also* Accidents and disasters; Murder)
Debt
Consumer 47
National/state 60
Decibels 365
Decimals 363
Declaration of Independence 437, 458-60, *459*
Deep Throat 453
Deepwater Horizon explosion 15, 26, 328, 454, 455
Defense contractors 52, 134
Defense, national. *See* Armed forces, U.S.; Military affairs; Nuclear arms
Defense, U.S. Department of **541**
Budget, expenditures 58, 133, 134
Employees 106
Pentagon 435
Personal salutes, honors 135
Secretaries 17, 541
Delaware **567**
Agriculture 92, 93
Coastline 423
Congressional representation 551, 554, 609
Crime, prisons, death penalty 117, 119, 120
Education 380-83, 389-90
Elevations (high, low) 423
Energy consumption 111
Finances 60
Governor 37
Hazardous waste 305
Health insurance coverage 142
Immigrant admissions 619
Motor vehicles 83, 84
Name origin, nickname 426, 567
Population 567, 605, 606-07, 608, 611, 612, 626
Poverty rates 49
Taxes 84, 378
Unemployment 101
Weather 312
ZIP and area codes 626
DeLay, Tom 453
Democratic Party
Congressional members 548-49
Presidential, vice presidential candidates (1856-2012) 507
Denali (formerly Mt. McKinley) 422, 423, 687, 695
Deng Xiaoping 668, 682, 763
Denmark **769-70**
Agriculture 97
Area, population 731, 769
Budget deficits 59
Computer/Internet use 297
Education 383, 385
Flag, map 473, 482
Foreign aid from 738
Foreign exchange rates 75
Languages 714, 769
Merchant fleet 77
Rulers, royal family 680
Taxes 734
Travel and tourism 85
U.S. investment 78
Vacation days 89
Wages, hourly 734
Denominations, religious 704-05
Denver, CO **596**
Air quality 304
Airport traffic 88
Buildings, tall 718
Consumer Price Index 46
Crime rates 118
Geography 696
Housing 71, 72
Immigrant admissions 619
Population 614, 615
Weather 309-11, 313
Department stores 52
Depression, economic
Panics (1873, 1893, 1907) 441, 442
Stock market crash (1929) 443, *444*, 662
Depression, mental 153, 421
Descartes, René 655, 656
Desegregation 445, 446, *446*, 561
Deserts, world 690
Detroit, MI **596-97**
Air quality 304
Airport traffic 88
Bankruptcy declared (2013) 456
Buildings, tall 718
Consumer Price Index 46
Crime rates 118
Geography 696
Housing 71, 72
Immigrant admissions 619
Population 614
Port traffic 76
Riots (1943, 1967) 444, 447
Weather 309-11, 313
Dewey, John 442
Diabetes 154, 155, 171
Dice 362
Dickinson, Emily 441
Diego Garcia 129
Diet. *See* Nutrition
Directory **407-21**
Dirigibles 336
Disabled people
Anti-discrimination act (1990) 450
Hate crime victims 123
Olympics for 863
Population, by age 617
School programs 381
Social Security benefits 369, 372
Veterans 132
Disarmament. *See* Arms control
Disasters. *See* Accidents and disasters
***Discovery* (space shuttle)** 330-32, 333
Diseases. *See* Health and medicine; specific diseases
Distinguished Flying Cross 136
Distinguished Service Cross 136
District of Columbia. *See* Washington, DC
Diving. *See* Swimming and diving
Divorce 164
Djibouti 134, 473, 486, 667, 731, **770**
Djokovic, Novak 17, 28, 31, 853
Doctorow, E. L. 34, *816*
Dogs
American Kennel Club 293
Iditarod sled race 976
Therapy dogs 421
Westminster Kennel Club 976
Dole, Robert 509-38
Dollar bill, U.S. 56, *56*
Dominica 473, 479, 689, 731, 733, **770**
Dominican Republic **770-71**
Area, population 731, 770
Flag, map 473, 479
Languages 770
Travel and tourism 85, 87
U.S. immigrants from 9, 620
U.S. investment 78
U.S. involvement in (1916, 1965) 443, 447
Dow Jones Industrial Average 64-65
Draft, U.S.
NYC riots (1863) 440
Peacetime, first (1940) 444
Selective Service System 547
Vietnam-era (1973, 1977) 448, 449
World War I 443
Drake, Sir Francis 436, 683
Drama. *See* Theater
Dred Scott decision (1857) 440, 560
Drone strikes 21, 455, 670, 671
Droughts 21, *198*, 328, 668
Drownings 171
Drug abuse
Help organizations 421
Prevalence 145
Prison population 121
Sports PED scandals 453, 456
Drug cartels 28, 671
Drug stores 52
Drugs, therapeutic
Consumer protection (1906) 442
Discoveries 285-86
Leading U.S. companies 53
Medicare coverage 370
Most frequently mentioned 144
Dubai. *See* United Arab Emirates
Dukakis, Michael 450, 509-38
Dumbarton Oaks (1944) 444
Durham, NC 71, **597**, 615, 696
Durst, Robert 21, 39, *814*
DVDs 246
Dwarf planets 279, 344, 345, **348-50**

E

Earhart, Amelia 336, 443, 444
Early humans 20, 279, *809*
Earth 344, 345, **351-53**
Earthquakes, major 22-23, 33, *196*, *324*, **325**, *442*
East China Sea 690
East Germany. *See* Germany
East Indies 689
East Timor. *See* Timor-Leste
Easter Sunday 699, 700
Eastern Orthodox churches 704-05
 Church calendar 699
 Membership 697, 698
Eating disorders 154, 421
Ebla civilization 647
Ebola 24, 457, 673, *809*
Eclipse Awards 970
Eclipses 337, 343
Ecology. *See* Environment
Economic Stimulus Acts (2008, 2009) 453
Economics **43-72**
 Banking statistics 61-62
 Budget, U.S. 57-59
 Consumer price changes 733
 Consumer Price Indexes 44-46
 Credit rating downgrade 455
 Crisis and recovery efforts (2008-11) 453, 454, 455, 670
 Economists, noted past 184-84
 GDP, GNP 43, 733
 Income, national 44
 Nobel Prizes 259, 262
 Recent developments (2014-15) 14, 15-16, 17-18, 19-20, 21, 23, 25, 26, 27, 29
 State finances 60-61
 (*see also* Depression, economic; Stocks)
Ecuador 78, 100, 112, 113, 473, 480, 619, 731, 735, **771**
Edgar Awards 270
Edison, Thomas A. 441
Education **380-406**
 Associations and organizations 407
 Bullying and fighting 382
 Charter schools 384
 Common Core State Standards 385
 Educational attainment, U.S. 621
 Educators, noted past 183-84
 Employment correlation 106
 Enrollment 380, 381, 384
 Food program costs 92
 History 436, 438, 439, 653
 Homeschooling 384
 Nursing school, first (1873) 441
 Personal expenditures 51
 Price index 45
 Racial integration 445, 446
 Revenues and expenditures, public schools 380, 382
 Student drug and alcohol use 145-47
 Tax credits 375
 Test scores 383, 389-90
 U.S. expenditures 58
 (*see also* Colleges and universities; High schools)
Education, Department of 106, **546**
Eggs 96-97
Egypt **771-72**
 Agriculture 97, 98, 99
 Ancient 647, *647*, 727
 Aquaculture 100
 Area, population 730, 731, 771
 Arms purchases 133
 Artifacts 662, *662*
 Cell phone use 300
 Flag, map 473, 486
 Fossil fuel reserves 112
 Health expenditures 142
 Languages 714, 771
 Military coup (2013) 672
 Military strength 133
 Motor vehicle production 79
 Muslim population 706
 News (2014) 13
 Protests (2008, 2011, 2013) 670, 672
 Refugees from/in 735
 Religious unrest (1970s) 667
 Travel and tourism 85
 UN peacekeeping mission 742
 U.S. investment 78
 U.S. military financing 134
 U.S. troops in 129
 Water supply 306
Egypt-Israel peace treaty 667
Einstein, Albert 284, 444, 661
Eisenhower, Dwight D. 491, **499**, *499*, 503, 504, 507, 508
El Niño 316
El Paso, TX 71, **597**, 614, 619, 696
El Salvador 121, 134, 473, 479, 619, 620, 667, 731, 735, 736, **772-73**
Elba 689, 791
Elderly
 Alzheimer's disease 149, 171
 Disability status 617
 Employment, U.S. 108
 Help organizations 421
 HIV/AIDS cases 148
 Home ownership rates 70
 Median income 107, 108
 Medicare, health insurance 142, 370, 374, 447, 450, 453
 Population 617
 Poverty level 49
 Social Security 368-74
 Tax considerations 376
Election Day 358
Elections, U.S.
 Campaign finance 6, 7, 452, 562
 Midterm (2014) 12, 457
 Presidential (*See* Presidential elections)
 Primary voting system, first (1903) 442
 Voting rights
  Blacks (1870, 1957, 1965) 441, 447, 467
  Discriminatory laws (2015) 28
  Minimum age lowered (1971) 448, 469
  Motor-voter bill 451
  Supreme Court rulings (2013) 456
  Women (1869, 1920) 441, 443, 468
Electoral College 467, 506
Electric power
 Blackouts (1965, 2003) 447, 452
 Hydroelectric plants 727
 Leading U.S. utilities 52
 Physics of 284
 Production, consumption 109, 114
 Renewable sources 109, 110, 115
 Unit measurements 365
Electronics industry 52, 54
Elements, chemical 282-83
Eliot, T(homas) S(tearns) 443
Elizabeth I, Queen of England 654, *654*, 655
Elliott, Ezekiel 853
Ellis Island 441, **490**, *661*
Ellison, Ralph 445
Email 298
Emancipation Proclamation (1863) 440
Embargo Act (1807) 438
Embryo research. *See* Stem-cell research
Emerson, Ralph Waldo 439
Emmy Awards 31, 272-73
Empire State Building (NYC) 443, 444, 716
Employment, U.S. **101-08**
 Cities (selected) 594-604
 Displaced workers 102
 Education correlation 106
 Elderly 108
 Fair practices (1941) 444
 Government 106
 Military 129-31
 Occupational injuries, illnesses 105
 Occupations and gender 103
 Projections 104
 Rates (1900-2014) 101
 Social Security benefits 368-74
Endangered species 307
***Endeavour* (space shuttle)** 332, 333
Energy **109-15**
 Expenditures 51, 58
 Exports, imports 74, 109, 112, 113
 Leading companies 52
 Price indexes 46
 Production, consumption 109-10, 111, 113-15
 Renewable sources 109, 110, 115
 Tax credits 376
 (*see also* specific countries, sources, types)
Energy, Department of 449, **545-46**
England. *See* United Kingdom
English Civil Wars (1638-60) 139
Engraving and Printing, Bureau of 56 434
Enlightenment (18th century) 656
Enron Corp. 452
Entente Cordiale 660
Entertainers
 Noted past 235-41
 Noted present 222-34
 Original names 241-42
Environment **302-07**
 Associations and organizations 407
 Cancer link 151
 Earth Day, first (1970) 447
 Endangered species 307
 Greenhouse-gas accord 454
 News (2015) 28
 U.S. expenditures 58
 (*see also* Global warming; Pollution)
Environmental Protection Agency (EPA)
 Gorsuch contempt citation (1982) 449
 Mailing, Internet addresses 547
 News (2015) 28
Envoys and ambassadors, salutes to 135
EPA. *See* Environmental Protection Agency
Epicureans 649
Episcopal Church 410, 452, 697, 699, 704-05
Eponyms 712
Equal Employment Opportunity Commission 547
Equal Rights Amendment (ERA) 448, 449
Equatorial Guinea 113, 473, 487, 731, 737, **773**
Equinoxes 338, 339, 352
ERA (Equal Rights Amendment) 448, 449
Ericson, Leif 652, 683
Erie Canal (1825) 439
Erie, Lake 694
Eris (dwarf planet) 344, 345, **350**
Eritrea 133, 473, 486, 671, 731, 733, 735, 736, 737, **773**
Essenes 650
Estonia 59, 121, 383, 385, 474, 483, 668, 731, 734, **773-74**
Eta Aquarids meteor shower 337
Ethiopia **774**
 Agriculture 98
 Area, population 732, 773
 Drinking water 737
 Flag, map 474, 486
 Foreign aid to 738
 Gross domestic product 733
 Health expenditures 142
 History 667
 Internally displaced persons 736
 Languages 714, 774
 Muslim population 706
 Peace treaty 671
 Refugees from/in 735
 U.S. adoptions from 166
Ethnoreligionists 697, 698
Etna, Mount 791
Etruscans 649
EU. *See* European Union
Euclid 649
Europe
 Agriculture 97, 98, 99
 Area, population 730
 Elevations (highest, lowest) 695
 Fossil fuel reserves 112
 HIV/AIDS cases 737
 Islands 689
 Lakes 694
 Languages 714-15
 Map 482-83
 Migrant crisis (2015) 4, 22, 31, 33, *194*
 Motor vehicle production, exports 79
 Mountain peaks 688
 Religious adherents 698
 Rivers 691-92
 Rulers, royal families 674-80
 Temperature/precipitation extremes 315
 Trade 73
 Travel and tourism 87
 U.S. investment 78
 U.S. military financing 134
 U.S. troops in 129
 Volcanoes 685, 686
 Waterfalls 695
 (*see also* specific countries)
European Free Trade Assn. (EFTA) 740
European Space Agency 333
European Union (EU) 73, 78, 669, 671, 740
Evening stars (2016) 341
Everest, Mount 688, 695
Evers, Medgar 446, 451
Evolution theory 443, 658
Exchange rates, foreign 75
Executions, U.S. *See* Death penalty
Executive agencies, U.S. 106, 539
Exercise 151, 155, 161
Existentialism 664
Explorations, expeditions
 Arctic/Antarctic 684-85
 Western Hemisphere 654, 683
Explosions 29, 105, *196*, 327, 454, 455
 (*see also* Terrorism)
Exports, imports 73-77
 Agricultural 74, 98
 Automobiles 79
 Balance of trade 73, 74
 Commodities 74, 75
 Energy 74, 109, 112, 113
 International transactions, U.S. 77
 Manufactured goods 74
 Petroleum 74, 109, 112, 113

F

Facebook 298, 456
Fahrenheit scale 361
Falkland Islands 689, 848
Families. *See* Households
Famine 668
Famous people. *See* Noted personalities; specific fields
Fannie Mae, Freddie Mac bailout 454
FAO (Food and Agriculture Org.) 741
Farms. *See* Agriculture
Faroe Islands 689, 732, 770
Fats and oils 74, 158, 159
Faulkner, William 443
FBI 434
FCC (Federal Communications Commission) 547

FDIC (Federal Deposit Insurance Corporation) 61, 547
Federal agencies 547
(*see also* specific agencies)
Federal Bureau of Investigation (FBI) 434
Federal Communications Commission (FCC) 547
Federal Deposit Insurance Corporation (FDIC) 61, 547
Federal Emergency Management Agency (FEMA) 547
Federal government. *See* Government, U.S.
Federal Reserve System **63**, 442, 547
Federal taxes. *See* Income taxes, federal
Federal Trade Commission (FTC) 547
Federalist Papers (1787) 438
FedEx Cup 953
Feminism 665
Ferdinand, Franz 661
Ferguson, Miriam (Ma) 443
Ferguson, MO 12, 19, 28, 457, *457*
Ferraro, Geraldine 449
Fertility rates 165
Fiber (dietary) 158-59
Figure skating. *See* Skating
Fiji 474, 488, 689, 732, **774-75**
Fillmore, Millard 491, **495**, *495*, 504
Films. *See* Movies
Finance. *See* Banks; Business; Economics; Stocks
Finland **775**
Area, population 732, 775
Budget deficits 59
Computer/Internet use 297
Education 383, 385
Flag, map 474, 483
Foreign aid from 738
Forests 306
Languages 714, 775
Motor vehicle production 79
Nuclear power 114
Taxes 734
U.S. investment 78
Vacation days 89
Wages, hourly 734
Fiorina, Carly 6, 7, 39
Fire engines, first in colonies 436
Firearms
Brady Bill (1993) 451
Deaths involving 171
Gun gauge, caliber 365
Operation Fast and Furious 455
(*see also* Gun violence; Shooting (sport))
Fires
Arson arrests 122
Deaths 170, 171, 326
Major 30, 31-32, **326**, 436, 438, 441, 442
Occupational fatalities 105
Property damage, loss 170
First aid 163
First ladies 504
Fish and fishing
Commercial 100
Consumption, U.S. 95
Exports, imports 74
First warm-blooded species 279
U.S. national income 44
Venomous species 292
World catch figures 100
Fitzgerald, F. Scott 443
Flags
Confederate 25, *199*, 470
Olympic 855
21-gun-salute to 135
United States 437, 471-72, *471*, *476*
World (color) 473-76
Flaxseed production 96
Fleets, merchant 77
Flights. *See* Aviation
Floods
Characteristics 308
Notable 17, 24, 33, 324, 441, 451, 453, *453*
Florida **567-68**
Accession (1819) 427, 439
Agriculture 92, 93
Coastline 423
Congressional representation 551, 554, 609
Crime, prisons, death penalty 117, 119, 120
Education 380-83, 389-90
Elevations (high, low) 423
Energy consumption 111
Finances 60
Governor 37
Hazardous waste 305
Health insurance coverage 142
Immigrant admissions 619
Motor vehicles 83, 84
Name origin, nickname 426, 567
Oil production 111
Population 567, 598, 600, 601, 603, 604, 606-07, 608, 611, 612, 627-28
Poverty rates 49
Taxes 84
Traveler spending 86
Unemployment 101
Weather 312
ZIP and area codes 627-28
Fluoride (dietary) 160
Foley, James 457
Folger Shakespeare Library (DC) 434
Food
Consumption statistics 94-95, 98-99
Cost of food 93
Eating disorders 154, 421
Exports, imports 74, 75
Federal assistance programs 92
Label claims 159
Leading U.S. companies 52
Nutrition 158-61
Personal expenditures 51
Price indexes 45, 46
Pure Food and Drug Act (1906) 442
(*see also* Agriculture; specific foods)
Food and Agriculture Org. (FAO) 741
Food stamp program (SNAP) 92
Football
NCAA **877-81**
Banned (1822) 439
Bowl games 877-79
Coaches 880
Conference champions 880-81
Heisman Trophy 879
National champions 17, *810*, 853, 877
Poll leaders, final standings (2014) 877
Sandusky scandal 456
Statistical leaders 879
Team winning percentage leaders 879
NFL 23, **890-906**
Addresses, teams 420
All-time records 903-04
Awards and honors (1957-2014) 902-03
Champions 895-99
Coaching victories, all-time 906
"Deflategate" 24, 31, 39, *810*, 853
Final standings (2014) 890
Franchise origins 905
Hall of Fame 17, 906
Leading players 891-92, 899-902
Player draft 894-95
Season highlights (2014) 890
Stadiums 905
Strike (1982) 449
Super Bowl 18-19, 447, *810*, 853, 854, 890-91, 893-94
Force, measures of 365
Ford, Gerald R. 448, 491, **500**, *500*, 503, 504, 509-38
Ford, Henry 442
Ford Motor Co. 442, 660
Foreign aid 738
Foreign trade. *See* Exports, imports; Trade
Foreign words, phrases 709
Forest Reserve Act (1891) 441
Forests 306
Formentera 836
Formula One Racing 961
Fort Hood shootings 454
Fort Wayne, IN **597**, 614, 696
Fort Worth, TX 46, 71, 88, 118, 304, 309-11, 313, **597**, 614, 615, 696, 718
Fossil fuel reserves 112
Fossils 15, 20, 279, 646, *646*, *809*
Foster, Stephen 440
Four Freedoms (1941) 444
Fox, Vicente 671
Fraction-to-decimal conversions 363
France **775-76**
Agriculture 97, 98, 99
Area, population 730, 775
Arms sales 134
Budget deficits 59
Carbon dioxide emissions 302
Cell phone use 300
Computer/Internet use 294, 297, 298
Consumer price changes 733
Departments, territories 776-77
Education 383, 385
Energy consumption 109
Flag, map 474, 482
Foreign aid from 738
Foreign exchange rates 75
Forests 306
Gasoline prices 110
Gold reserves 733
Gross domestic product 733
Health expenditures 142
History 653, 655-56, 657, 661, 663, 664, 668, 671
American Revolution role 437, 438
French and Indian War (1754-63) 437
New World claims, colonies (1562, 1682) 436
Languages 714, 775
Merchant fleet 77
Military strength 133
Mortality rate by cause 736
Motor vehicle production, exports 79
Nuclear arms 738
Nuclear power 114
Refugees in 735
Rulers/presidents 657, 673, 677
Securities held by U.S. 64
Spaceflight 333
Taxes 734
Terrorism 16, 26, *195*, 672
Trade 73
Travel and tourism 85, 86, 87
Unemployment rates 734
U.S. ancestral claims 621
U.S. immigrants from 9, 620
U.S. investment 78
Vacation days 89
Wages, hourly 734
Franchises, top U.S. 55
Francis, Pope 17, 26, 30, 39, *197*, 673, *673*, 700, 701
Franco, Francisco 663
Franco-Prussian War (1870-71) 140
Franklin, Benjamin 437, 656
Fraternal organizations 408
Frederick the Great 656
Free speech 38
"Freedom Rides" 446
Freedom Statue (U.S. Capitol) 434
Freemen 451
Freezing point, water 362
Fremont, CA 71, 304, **597**, 615
French and Indian War (1754-63) 437
French Guiana 480, 776
French Open (tennis) 26, 853, 955-56
French Polynesia 488, 732, 776
French Revolution (1789) 139, 657
Fresno, CA 304, 309, 311, **597**, 614, 619
Freud, Sigmund 659
Friedan, Betty 446
Froome, Chirs 28, 973
Fruit 94, 96, 97
FTC (Federal Trade Commission) 547
Fuel. *See* Energy; specific kinds
Fuel cells 115
Fujimori, Alberto 670
Fulton, Robert 438
Furniture 51, 74

G

G-7 25
G-8 740
Gabon 113, 306, 474, 487, 732, **777**
Gadsden Purchase (1854) 427, 440
Galapagos Islands 689, 771
Galaxies 344
Galileo Galilei 655
Gambia 474, 486, 732, 733, **777-78**
Gambier Islands 776
Gandhi, Indira 668
Gandhi, Mahatma 661, 663, 664
Garfield, James A. 441, 491, **496**, *496*, 503, 504, 507, 508
Garland, TX **597**, 615
Garner, Eric 457
Gas, natural. *See* Natural gas
Gasoline
Arab embargo (1973) 448, 830
Automobile consumption 84
Personal expenditures 51
Prices, retail 110, 453
Taxes (by state) 84
GATT (General Agreement on Tariffs and Trade) 665
(*see also* World Trade Org.)
Gays. *See* LGBT
Gaza Strip 670, 672, 732, 738, **790**
GDP. *See* Gross domestic product
Gehrig, Lou 444
Geithner, Timothy 454
Geminids meteor shower 340
General Motors 62, 454, 457
General Services Administration 547
Generals, U.S. **128**
Insignia 137
Pay scale 131
Personal salutes, honors 135
Women, first (1970) 447
Genetics and genetic engineering 452, 670
Geneva Conventions 658, 744
Genghis Khan 653
Genocide 671, 744
Geography 422-24, **683-96**
Geology 281, 290
Geometry 362
George, Henry 441
Georgia (state) **568**
Agriculture 92, 93
Charter (1732) 437
Coastline 423
Congressional representation 551, 554, 609
Crime, prisons, death penalty 117, 119, 120
Education 380-83, 389-90
Elevations (high, low) 423
Energy consumption 111
Finances 60
Governor 37
Hazardous waste 305
Health insurance coverage 142
Immigrant admissions 619

Motor vehicles 83, 84
Name origin, nickname 426, 568
Population 568, 594, 605, 606-07, 608, 611, 612, 628-29
Poverty rates 49
Taxes 84, 378
Traveler spending 86
Unemployment 101
Weather 312
ZIP and area codes 628-29
Georgia, Republic of 112, 134, 474, 484, 714, 732, 736, **778**
Geothermal energy 109, 115
Germany **778-79**
Agriculture 97, 98, 99
Area, population 732, 778
Arms sales 134
Berlin Wall 666, 667, *667*
Budget deficits 59
Carbon dioxide emissions 302
Cell phone use 300
Computer/Internet use 294, 297, 298
Consumer price changes 733
Education 383, 385
Energy consumption 109
Flag, map 474, 482
Foreign aid from 738
Foreign exchange rates 75
Fossil fuel reserves 112
Gasoline prices 110
Gold reserves 733
Gross domestic product 733
Health expenditures 142
History 652, 654, 656, 659, 667, 671
New World colonies (1683) 436
Reunification (1990) 669
Third Reich 662, 678, 778-79
Weimar Republic 662
World War I 661
World War II 663-64
Language 714, 778
Merchant fleet 77
Military strength 133
Mortality rate by cause 736
Motor vehicle production, exports 79
Nuclear power 114
Refugees in 735
Rulers 652, 654, 678-79
Securities held by U.S. 64
Spaceflight 333
Taxes 734
Terrorism 666
Trade 73, 75, 76
Travel and tourism 85, 86, 87
Unemployment rates 734
U.S. ancestral claims 621
U.S. immigrants from 9, 620
U.S. investment 78
U.S. troops in 129
Vacation days 89
Wages, hourly 734
Geronimo 441
Gershwin, George 443
Gettysburg Address (1863) 440, *440*, 470
Ghana **779-80**
Area, population 732, 779
Flag, map 474, 486
Gold production 68
Health expenditures 142
History 651, 664, 666
Languages 714, 779
Sanitation 737
GI Bill of Rights (1944) 444
Gibraltar 732, 848
Gifford, Frank 34, *816*
Giffords, Gabrielle 125, 455
Gilbert, AZ **597**, 615
Gillard, Julia 673
Gingrich, Newt 451
Ginsburg, Ruth Bader 38, 39, 451, 559
Girl Scouts 408, 442
GLBT. *See* LGBT
Glendale, AZ **597**, 615, 619
Glenn, John H., Jr. 446
Global warming 13, 17, 303, 671, 673
Globalization 668
Glorious Revolution 655
GNP (gross national product, U.S.) 43
Goetz, Bernhard 450
Gold
Black Friday (1869) 441
Discovered, U.S. (1835, 1848) 439, 440
Dropped as U.S. standard (1933) 443
Fineness measure 365
Klondike gold rush 442
Production, reserves 67-68, 733
Golden Globe Awards 273
Golden Kite Awards 270
Goldman Sachs 455
Goldwater, Barry 447, 509-38
Golf 22, 26, 28, 29-30, 452, 853, **952-54**
Gonorrhea 156
Gonzales, Alberto 453
Gonzalez, Elian 452
Good Friday 699
Google 21
Gorbachev, Mikhail 667, 668, 681
Gore, Al 452, 509-38
Government, U.S. **539-62**
Agencies 547
Branches 539
Cabinet-level departments, officers 539-47
Employees 106
Obama administration 539
Receipts and outlays (2000-14) 57-59
Shutdowns (1995, 2013) 451, 456
Governors, state **37**
Grains 96-99
Grammy Awards 19, 277-78
Grandma Moses 444
Grange, National (1867) 441
Grant, Ulysses S. 491, **496**, *496*, 504, 507, 508
Grass, Günter 35, *816*
Gravity 284
Great Awakening (1726, 1741) 437
Great Britain. *See* United Kingdom
Great Lakes 100, 694
Great Seal of the U.S. 471, *471*
Great Society 447, 665
Great Wall of China 648, *648*
Great White Fleet (1907) 442
Greece **780**
Area, population 732, 780
Arms purchases 133
Budget deficits 59
Education 383, 385
Elections (2015) 17, 29
Financial crisis (2010-15) 4, 27, 29, *195*, 673
Flag, map 474, 483
Foreign aid from 738
Foreign exchange rates 75
Fossil fuel reserves 112
History 657, 666
Language 714, 780
Merchant fleet 77
Taxes 734
Travel and tourism 85
U.S. investment 78
U.S. troops in 129
Vacation days 89
Wages, hourly 734
Greece, ancient
Architecture 728
City-states 648
Hellenistic Era 649
Historical figures 674
Measures 363
Minoan civilization 647
Parthenon 648
Philosophers 648
Greek Orthodox Church. *See* Eastern Orthodox churches
Greenhouse gas emissions 302, 303, 454, 672
Greenland 112, 129, 315, 478, 689, 732, **770**
Greensboro, NC 71, **597-98**, 614, 696
Greenwich meridian 360, 476
Greenwich sidereal time (2015) 341
Gregorian calendar 354
Grenada 449, 474, 479, 732, 733, **780-81**
Grenadines. *See* St. Vincent and the Grenadines
Gross domestic product
International 745-808, 817-52
Budget deficits as percent of 59
Highest/lowest rates 733
U.S. 43
Gross national product, U.S. 43
Group of Eight (G-8) 740
Guadalcanal 444, 663, 689
Guadeloupe 689, 776
Guam **591-92**
Accession (1898) 427, 442
Area, population 591, 689, 732
Congressional delegate 558
Education 382
Elevations (high, low) 423
Governor 37
Hazardous waste 305
Immigrant admissions 619
U.S. troops in 129
Guangxi Zhuang 763
Guantánamo Bay 129, 452, 453, 454, 768 (*see also* Cuba)
Guatemala 33, 474, 479, 619, 620, 732, 735, 736, **780**
Guernsey 732, 848
Guinea, Republic of 474, 486, 714, 732, 733, **735**, 737, **781-82**
Guinea-Bissau 474, 486, 672, 673, 732, 733, 736, 737, **782**
Gulf Coast 423
Gulf War. *See* Persian Gulf Wars
Gun violence
Homicide statistics 122
Mass shootings 454, 455, 456
Recent events 4, 12, 14, 19, 21-22, 25, 27, 28, 30, 33, *199*
School shootings 447, 452, 453, 456
Sniper attack (2003) 452-53
Guns. *See* Firearms; Shooting (sport)
Guyana 121, 306, 474, 480, 731, 732, **782**
Guzmán, Joaquín "El Chapo" 28
Gymnastics 865-66

H

Habsburg dynasty 654, 658, 678
Hagel, Chuck 12, 17, 456
Hague Conference 660
Haiku 656
Haiti **782-83**
Area, population 732, 782
Drinking water 737
Earthquake (2010) 325, 673
Flag, map 474, 479
Foreign aid to 738
Languages 714, 782
Peacekeeping efforts (1995) 451
Political unrest (1990s) 669-70
Protests (2008) 670
Refugees from 735
Regime change (2004) 671
Rule by decree (2015) 16
Slave revolt 658
UN peacekeeping mission 742
U.S. adoptions from 166
U.S. occupation (1915, 1934) 442, 443
U.S. troops in 129
Hale, Nathan 437
Hall of Fame
Baseball 17, 444, 932
Basketball 940
Boxing 965
Football, pro 17, 906
Hockey 947
Rock and Roll 220-22
Hambletonian 970-71
Hammett, Dashiell 443
Hammurabi 647
Hannibal 649
Hanover, House of 675
Hanssen, Robert 452
Hapsburg dynasty. *See* Habsburg dynasty
Harbors 76
Harding, Warren G. 491, **498**, *498*, 503, 504, 507, 508, *814*
Hardness 282
Harness racing 970-71
Harpers Ferry (1859) 440
Harrison, Benjamin 491, **497**, *497*, 503, 504, 507, 508
Harrison, William Henry 491, **494**, *494*, 504, 508
Hart Memorial Trophy 944
Hartford, CT 718
Harun al-Rashid 651
Harvard College (1636) 436
Harvest moon 353
Hastert, Dennis 23
Hate crimes 19, 25, 123
Haumea (dwarf planet) 344, 345, **349**
Hawaii **568-69**
Accession (1898) 427, 442
Agriculture 92, 93
Area 689
Coastline 423
Congressional representation 551, 554, 609
Crime, prisons, death penalty 117, 119, 120
Education 380-83, 389-90
Elevations (high, low) 423
Energy consumption 111
Finances 60
Fishing 100
Governor 37
Hazardous waste 305
Health insurance coverage 142
Immigrant admissions 619
Maps 477, 488
Motor vehicles 83, 84
Name origin, nickname 426, 568
Native Hawaiians 148, 371, 610, 611, 621
Population 568, 598, 605, 606-07, 608, 611, 612, 629
Poverty rates 49
Taxes 84, 378
Unemployment 101
U.S. troops in 129
Weather 312
Wettest spot (U.S.) 422
ZIP and area codes 629
Hawley-Smoot Tariff (1930) 443
Hawthorne, Nathaniel 440
Hay 96, 97
Hayes, Rutherford B. 441, 491, **496**, *496*, 503, 504, 507, 508
Haymarket riot (1886) 441
Hazardous waste sites 305
Health and Human Services, Department of **546**
Health and medicine **141-63**
Body weight guidelines 161

Drug and alcohol abuse . . . 145, 147
Exercise . . . 151, 155, 161
Expenditures (U.S., global) . . . 141, 142
First aid . . . 163
Help organizations . . . 421
Hospital emergency room visits . . . 144
Immunization and vaccination . . 18, 90, *200*
Leading U.S. companies . . . 52-53
Medical discoveries . . . 285-86
Mortality rates by cause . . . 736
Nobel Prizes . . . 259, 260-61
Nutrition . . . 158-61
Occupational injuries, illnesses . . . 105
Outpatient visits . . . 144
Patient characteristics . . . 143
Personal expenditures . . . 51
Price Indexes . . . 45, 46
Sanitation/drinking water . . . 737
Smoking . . . 146
Transplants . . . 144
U.S. expenditures . . . 58
(*see also* Drugs, therapeutic; specific diseases)
Health insurance
Coverage . . . 141
Hacking incident (2015) . . . 17
Insurance marketplace . . . 143, 456, 457
Medicaid . . . 141
Medicare . . . 370, 374, 447, 450, 453
Population without . . . 142
Reform legislation (2010) . . . 454, 455
Supreme Court rulings . . 4, 25, 38, 456, 562
Heard Island . . . 750
Hearing disorders
Deaf education (1817) . . . 439
Help organizations . . . 421
Manual alphabet . . . 713
Hearst, Patty . . . 126, 449
Heart, blood vessels
Diseases of . . . 154, 155, 171
First artificial heart (1982) . . . 449
Heart attack warning signs . . . 155
Help organizations . . . 421
Heat index . . . 314
Heat stroke . . . 163
Heaven's Gate (religious cult) . . . 451
Hebrews. *See* Judaism
Hebrides . . . 689, 847
Heisman Trophy . . . 879
Helgoland . . . 779
Hemingway, Ernest . . . 443, 445
Henderson, NV . . . **72**, 118, **598**, 614, 615
Henry VIII . . . 654
Henry, Patrick . . . 437, 458
Henson, Matthew . . . 442
Hepatitis . . . 156
Herzegovina. *See* Bosnia and Herzegovina
Hialeah, FL . . . **598**, 615
Hieroglyphic writing . . . 647
High blood pressure . . . 155
High schools
ACT, SAT scores . . . 389-90
Dropout rates . . . 380
Enrollment . . . 380
First public tax-supported (1827) . . . 439
Graduation rates . . . 380
Risk behaviors . . . 145-47, 169
Sexual activity . . . 169
Highways. *See* Roads
Hijackings . . . 317-19
Hinckley, John W., Jr. . . . 449
***Hindenburg* airship** . . . 444
Hinduism . . . **707**
Adherents (U.S., world) . . . 697, 698
Festivals . . . 700
Hiroshima bombing (1945) . . . 444, 663, *664*
Hispanics
Cigarette use . . . 146
Education . . . 380, 384, 389, 621
First attorney general (2005) . . . 453
First Supreme Court justice . . . 454
Hate crime victims . . . 123
Health insurance coverage . . . 141, 142
HIV/AIDS cases . . . 148
Home ownership rates . . . 70
Households . . . 618
Incomes, wages . . . 47, 107
Internet use . . . 299
Nonmarital childbearing . . . 166
Population . . . 610, 611, 621
Poverty rates . . . 48
Prison inmates . . . 120, 121
Sexual activity . . . 167
Social Security . . . 371
Unemployment . . . 103
Hiss, Alger . . . 445
Historic sites and parks, national . . . 429-31, 489-90
Historical societies . . . 408
History . . . **436-57, 646-73**
Anniversaries . . . 41-42
Historians, noted past . . . 183-84
Historical figures . . . 674-82
Pulitzer Prizes . . . 264
U.S. chronology . . . 436-57
World chronology . . . 646-73
Hitchcock, Alfred . . . 446
Hitler, Adolf . . . 662-63, *663*, 678, 778-79
HIV/AIDS . . . **147-48**
African crisis . . . 668, 669
AZT approval (1987) . . . 450
Cases worldwide (2014) . . . 736-37
Early report on (1981) . . . 449
Help organizations . . . 421
"Hobbit" skull . . . *646*
Hockey
NCAA champions . . . 889
NHL . . . **943-47**
Addresses, teams . . . 420
Hall of Fame . . . 947
Season highlights (2015) . . 26, *811*, 853, 943
Stadiums . . . 946
Olympic champions (1920-2014) . . . 860
Hogs . . . 95, 96-97
Holidays
International, selected . . . 358
Legal, public (U.S.) . . . 358
Flag display . . . 472
Religious . . . 699-700
Vacation days (selected countries) . . . 89
Holland. *See* Netherlands
Hollande, François . . . 673, *815*
Holocaust . . . 664, 744
Holocaust Memorial Museum . . . 434
Holy Roman Empire . . . 652
Homeland Security, Department of . . 18, 106, 452, **546-47**
Homer . . . 648
Homes. *See* Housing
Homeschooling . . . 384
Homestead Act (1862) . . . 440
Honduras . . . 78, 129, 474, 479, 619, 671, 732, 736, **783**
Honduras, British. *See* Belize
Hong Kong . . . **763-64**
Area . . . 689
China regains (1997) . . . 669
Education . . . 383
Foreign exchange rates . . . 75
Merchant fleet . . . 77
Population/projections . . . 732
Protests (2014) . . . 14, 673
Securities held by U.S. . . . 64
Trade . . . 73
Travel and tourism . . . 85
U.S. immigrants from . . . 9, 620
U.S. investment . . . 78
Honolulu, HI . . . **598**
Air mileage to other cities . . . 91
Consumer Price Index . . . 46
Geography . . . 696
Housing . . . 71, 72
Immigrant admissions . . . 619
Population . . . 614
Port traffic . . . 76
Tides . . . 316
Weather . . . 309-11, 313
Hoover Dam . . . 444
Hoover, Herbert . . . 443, 491, **498**, *498*, 503, 504, 507, 508
Horne, Jenny . . . 39
Horse racing . . . 4, 13, 24, 26, 441, 444, 448, *812*, 853, **966-71**
Horsepower . . . 365
Hospices . . . 421
Hospital emergency room visits . . . 144
House of Representatives. *See* Congress, U.S.
Households
Financial assets . . . 48
Poverty rates, thresholds . . . 49
Size, types . . . 616, 617, 618
Housing
Characteristics of U.S. . . . 72
Home ownership rates . . . 70
Personal expenditures . . . 51
Price Indexes . . . 45, 46, 70
Prices, affordability (1990-15) . . . 70-71
Rents, fair market . . . 72
Supreme Court ruling . . . 38
Housing and Urban Development, Department of . . . **545**
Houston, Sam . . . 439
Houston, TX . . . **598**
Air quality . . . 304
Airport traffic . . . 88
Buildings, tall . . . 718
Consumer Price Index . . . 46
Crime rates . . . 118
Geography . . . 696
Housing . . . 71
Immigrant admissions . . . 619
Population . . . 614
Port traffic . . . 76
Weather . . . 309-11, 313
Howland Island . . . 593
HPV infection . . . 151, 156
Hu Jintao . . . 671, 673, 682, 763
Hubble Space Telescope . . . 330-32, 341, 670
Huckabee, Mike . . . 6, 7, *198*
HUD. *See* Housing and Urban Development
Hudson Bay . . . 690
Hudson, Henry . . . 436, 683
Hudson River . . . 692
Hudson River School (1823) . . . 439
Hugo Awards . . . 270
Human genome . . . 452
Humanitarians, noted past . . . 201-02
Hume, David . . . 656
Humphrey, Hubert . . . 448, 509-38
Hundred Years War (1337-1453) . . . 139, 653
Hungary . . . **783-84**
Agriculture . . . 98
Area, population . . . 732, 783
Budget deficits . . . 59
Education . . . 383, 385
Flag, map . . . 474, 482-83
Fossil fuel reserves . . . 112
History . . . 652, 658, 661, 665, 667, 669
Languages . . . 714, 783
Motor vehicle production . . . 79
Nuclear power . . . 114
Rulers . . . 678, 679
Taxes . . . 734
Travel and tourism . . . 85
U.S. ancestral claims . . . 621
U.S. immigrants from . . . 620
U.S. investment . . . 78
Wages, hourly . . . 734
Huns . . . 651
Hunter's moon . . . 353
Huon Islands . . . 777
Huron, Lake . . . 694
Hurricanes
Characteristics, classifications . . . 308
Notable . . . 323, 450, 453, *453*, 456
Hussein, Saddam . . . 452, 670
Hydroelectric plants . . . 109, 115, 727
Hydrogen bomb (1950, 1952) . . . 445
Hydrogen fuel cells . . . 115
Hypertension . . . 155

I

IAEA (International Atomic Energy Agency) . . . 741
Ibiza . . . 836
Ice hockey. *See* Hockey
Ice skating. *See* Skating
Iceland . . . 689, **784**
Area, population . . . 731, 732, 784
Budget deficits . . . 59
Computer/Internet use . . . 297
Education . . . 383, 385
Financial crisis (2008) . . . 670
Fishing . . . 100
Flag, map . . . 474, 482
Foreign aid from . . . 738
Languages . . . 784
Taxes . . . 734
Water supply . . . 306
Idaho . . . **569**
Agriculture . . . 92, 93
Congressional representation . . 551, 554, 609
Crime, prisons, death penalty . . 117, 119, 120
Education . . . 380-83, 389-90
Elevations (high, low) . . . 423
Energy consumption . . . 111
Finances . . . 60
Governor . . . 37
Hazardous waste . . . 305
Health insurance coverage . . . 142
Immigrant admissions . . . 619
Motor vehicles . . . 83, 84
Name origin, nickname . . . 426, 569
Population . . . 569, 595, 605, 606-07, 608, 611, 612, 629
Poverty rates . . . 49
Ruby Ridge siege (1992) . . . 450
Taxes . . . 84, 378
Unemployment . . . 101
Weather . . . 312
ZIP and area codes . . . 629
Iditarod dog race . . . 976
Illinois . . . **569-70**
Agriculture . . . 92, 93
Congressional representation 551, 554, 609
Crime, prisons, death penalty 117, 119, 120
Education . . . 380-83, 389-90
Elevations (high, low) . . . 423
Energy consumption . . . 111
Finances . . . 60
Governor . . . 37
Hazardous waste . . . 305
Health insurance coverage . . . 142
Immigrant admissions . . . 619
Motor vehicles . . . 83, 84
Name origin, nickname . . . 426, 569
Oil production . . . 111
Population . . . 569, 595, 605, 606-07, 608, 611, 612, 629-30
Poverty rates . . . 49
Taxes . . . 84, 378
Traveler spending . . . 86

Unemployment 101
Weather 312
ZIP and area codes 629-30
IMF (International Monetary Fund) 742
Immigration and immigrants
Chinese Exclusion Act 441
Country of origin 9, 620
Ellis Island 441
Executive action (2014) 12, 18, 457
History 8-9, 660, *660*
Legislation (1952, 1987, 2010, 2012, 2013) . . 11, 445, 450, 455, 456
Quota system (1921, 1965) 443, 447
State, area of residence 619
Unauthorized population 10-11, 619
Immigration and Naturalization Act (1952) 445
Immunization and vaccination 18, 90, 156-57, *200*
Impeachment
Clinton impeachment 452, 669
Johnson trial (1868) 441
Nixon hearings (1974) 448
Overview 503
Imports. *See* Exports, imports
Inaugural ball, first 438
Inca Empire 655, *655*
Income
Average hours and earnings 107
Highest wages by county 104
International 734
Median 47, 106, 107, 108
Military pay scale 131
National, U.S. 44
Personal, U.S. 45
Poverty levels 48-49
Teachers' salaries 381, 389
(*see also* Minimum wage, U.S.)
Income taxes **375-79**
Federal 375-77
Amendment authorizing 442, 467
Audits 376
Bush-era cuts 452, 455, 456
Corporate rates 66
Individual rates (2015) 375
Paycheck withholding (1943) 444
Reagan cuts 449
Revenues 57, 377
Social Security 368
Tax credits 375-76
Foreign 734
State 377-79
Independence Day 358
India **784-86**
Agriculture 97, 98, 99
Area, population 730, 731, 732, 784
Budget deficits 59
Carbon dioxide emissions 302
Cell phone use 300
Computer/Internet use 294, 297
Elections (2014) 673
Energy production, consumption 109
Fishing, aquaculture 100
Flag, map 474, 484
Foreign exchange rates 75
Forests 306
Fossil fuel reserves 112
Gold reserves 733
Gross domestic product 733
Health expenditures 142
Heat waves (2015) 26, *197*
History 647, 648, 649, 653, 657, 659, 660, 661, 663, 664, 667, 671
Internally displaced persons 736
Languages 714-15, 784
Merchant fleet 77
Military strength 133
Motor vehicle production 79
Muslim population 706
Nuclear arms 738
Nuclear power 114
Refugees in 735
Securities held by U.S. 64
Spaceflight 333
Terrorist bombings 670
Trade 73
Travel and tourism 85, 86, 87
UN peacekeeping mission 742
U.S. immigrants from 9, 619, 620
U.S. investment 78
Indian Ocean 689, 690
Indian Removal Act (1830) 439
Indiana **570-71**
Agriculture 92, 93
Congressional representation . . 551, 554, 609
Crime, prisons, death penalty . . 117, 119, 120
Education 380-83, 389-90
Elevations (high, low) 423
Energy consumption 111
Finances 60
Governor 37
Hazardous waste 305
Health insurance coverage 142
Immigrant admissions 619
Motor vehicles 83, 84
Name origin, nickname 426, 570
Oil production 111
Population 570, 597, 598, 605, 606-07, 608, 611, 612, 630-31
Poverty rates 49
Taxes 84, 378
Unemployment 101
Weather 312
ZIP and area codes 630-31
Indianapolis 500 (auto race) 24, 959
Indianapolis, IN 71, 72, 304, 309-11, 313, **598**, 614, 619, 696, 718
Individual Retirement Accounts 375
Indochina. *See* Cambodia; Laos; Vietnam
Indochina War (1946-54) 664
Indonesia **786**
Agriculture 97, 98, 99
Area, population 730, 731, 732, 786
Budget deficits 59
Carbon dioxide emissions 302
Cell phone use 300
Computer/Internet use 297
Education 383
Energy production 109
Fishing, aquaculture 100
Flag, map 474, 485
Forests 306
Fossil fuel reserves, exports 112, 113
Gold production 68
Gross domestic product 733
Health expenditures 142
History 664, 666, 669
Internally displaced persons 736
Languages 715, 786
Merchant marine 77
Military strength 133
Motor vehicle production 79
Muslim population 706
Travel and tourism 85
U.S. investment 78
U.S. military financing 134
Industrial Revolution 656, *656*, 658
Industrial Workers of the World 442
Industries, U.S.
Associations and organizations 408
Business directory 410-17
Employment/unemployment 102, 103
Median income by gender 106
National income 44
Occupational injuries, illnesses 105
(*see also* Business; specific types)
INF treaty (1987) 450, 667, 739
Infant mortality 166, 172
Infectious diseases 156-57
Infertility services 165
Inflation. *See* Consumer Price Indexes
Influenza 156, 171
Epidemics (1733, 1918) 437, 443
Swine flu pandemic 454, 672
Inner Mongolia 763
Inquisition 655
Insects 163, 292
Insurance
Bank deposits 61
Leading U.S. companies 53
(*see also* Health insurance)
Interest (discount) rates 63
Interior, Department of the 106, **543**
Internal Revenue Service 376, 456, **540**
(*see also* Income taxes)
Internally displaced persons 735, 736
International Atomic Energy Agency (IAEA) 741
International Bank for Reconstruction and Development (IBRD) 742
International boundary lines, U.S. 425
International Center for the Settlement of Investment Disputes (ICSID) . . . 742
International Civil Aviation Org. (ICAO) . . . 741
International Court of Justice 741
International Criminal Court 744
International Criminal Police Org. 740
International Date Line 360, 476
International Development Assn. (IDA) . . 742
International Finance Corp. (IFC) 742
International Fund for Agricultural Development (IFAD) 741
International Labor Org. (ILO) 741
International Ladies' Garment Workers Union (1900) 442
International Maritime Org. (IMO) 741
International Monetary Fund (IMF) 742
International organizations **739-40**
International Space Station 333, 670
International System of Units 361
International Telecommunication Union (ITU) 742
Internet **295-99**
Access/usage 297-99, 671-72
Cyberbullying 382
Domain names 296
History 295-96, 668, 670
Net neutrality 18
Personal expenditures 51
Presidential chat, first 503
Security and data breaches 17, 26-27, 296
Social networking 298
Top browsers 297
Websites 89, 245, 252, 297, 298
INTERPOL 740
Interstate Commerce Act (1887) 441
Intolerable Acts (1774) 437
Inventions 286-89
Investiture Controversy 652
Iodine 160
Iowa **571**
Agriculture 92, 93
Congressional representation . . 551, 554, 609
Crime, prisons, death penalty . . 117, 119, 120
Education 380-83, 389-90
Elevations (high, low) 423
Energy consumption 111
Finances 60
Governor 37
Hazardous waste 305
Health insurance coverage 142
Immigrant admissions 619
Motor vehicles 83, 84
Name origin, nickname 426, 571
Population 571, 605, 606-07, 608, 611, 612, 631
Poverty rates 49
Taxes 84, 378
Unemployment 101
Weather 312
ZIP and area codes 631
IRA. *See* Individual Retirement Accounts
Iran **786-87**
Agriculture 97, 98, 99
Aquaculture 100
Area, population 732, 786
Carbon dioxide emissions 302
Cell phone use 300
Elections (2013) 673
Energy production 109
Flag, map 474, 484
Fossil fuel reserves 112
Gross domestic product 733
Health expenditures 142
Languages 715, 786
Military strength 133
Motor vehicle production 79
Muslim population 706
Nuclear arms 4, 22, 27, 30, *195*, 671
Nuclear power 114, 738
Persia 649, 653, 654, 662, 728
Refugees from/in 735
Revolution (1979-80) . . . 666, 667, 668, 787
Spaceflight 333
Travel and tourism 85
U.S. embassy occupation (1979-81) . . 449, 668
Iran-Contra affair (1986, 1987, 1989) 450, 667
Iran-Iraq War (1980-88) 667, 787
Iraq **787-88**
Agriculture 98, 99
Area, population 732, 787
Arms purchases 133
Flag, map 474, 484
Foreign aid to 738
Fossil fuel reserves, exports 112, 113
Government overhaul 29
Gulf War (1991) 450, 669, 788
Health expenditures 142
Internally displaced persons 736
ISIS offensive 672, *672*
Kuwait invasion (1990) 450, 669, 788
Languages 715, 787
Military strength 133
Missile attack on U.S. frigate (1987) 450
Muslim population 706
Refugees from/in 735
U.S. invasion of (2003) 452, 670
U.S. troops in 129
(*see also* Operation Iraqi Freedom/New Dawn)
Ireland, Northern . . 482, 667, 669, 689, **847-48**
Ireland, Republic of **788-89**
Agriculture 97
Area, population 689, 732, 788
Budget deficits 59
Education 383, 385
Financial crisis (2010) 673
Flag, map 474, 482
Foreign aid from 738
Foreign exchange rates 75
Gross domestic product 733
History 651, 661
Languages 788
Securities held by U.S. 64
Taxes 734
Trade 73
Travel and tourism 85
U.S. ancestral claims 621
U.S. immigrants from 9, 620
U.S. investment 78
Vacation days 89
Wages, hourly 734
Irish Republican Army (IRA). *See* Ireland, Northern

Iron (dietary) 159, 160
Iron ore 74
Ironman Triathlon 978
IRS. *See* Internal Revenue Service
Irvine, California 71, **598**, 615
Irving, TX **598**, 615
Irving, Washington 439
ISIS (Islamic State in Iraq and Syria) . . 4, 12, 18, 20, 24, 25-26, 27, *194*, 456, 457, 672, *672*
Islam **706**
Adherents (U.S., world) 697, 698, 706
Architecture 728
Hajj stampede 32
Hate crime victims 19, 123
Headquarters (U.S.) 410
History 650, 653, 666-67
Holy days 700
Muhammad caricatures 23, 671
Islands 689
(*see also* specific islands)
Isle of Man 77, 689, 732, 848
Isle of Pines 777
Israel **789-91**
Agriculture 98, 99
Area, population 732, 789
Arms purchases 133
Budget deficits 59
Education 383, 385
Elections (2015) 20
Flag, map 474, 484
Formed (1948) 664
Fossil fuel reserves 112
Labor Party ousted (1977) 667
Languages 715, 789
Military strength 133
Nuclear arms 738
Spaceflight 333
Taxes 734
Trade 73
Travel and tourism 85
UN peacekeeping mission 742
U.S. investment 78
U.S. military financing 134
Wages, hourly 734
Water supply 306
Israeli-Arab wars. *See* Arab-Israeli conflict
Italy **791**
Agriculture 97, 98, 99
Area, population 732, 791
Arms sales 134
Budget deficits 59
Carbon dioxide emissions 302
Cell phone use 300
Computer/Internet use 294, 297, 298
Consumer price changes 733
Education 383, 385
Flag, map 474, 482
Foreign aid from 738
Foreign exchange rates 75
Fossil fuel reserves 112
Gasoline prices 110
Gold reserves 733
Gross domestic product 733
Health expenditures 142
History 653, 659, 662, 663, 668
Languages 715, 791
Merchant fleet 77
Mortality rate by cause 736
Motor vehicle production, exports 79
Refugees in 735
Rulers/Prime Ministers 680
Securities held by U.S. 64
Taxes 734
Trade 73
Travel and tourism 85, 86, 87
Unemployment rates 734
U.S. ancestral claims 621
U.S. immigrants from 9, 620
U.S. investment 78
U.S. troops in 129
Vacation days 89
Wages, hourly 734
Ivory Coast. *See* Côte d'Ivoire
Iwo Jima landing (1945) 444, 663
Memorial (statue) 434

J

Jackson, Andrew . . . 439, 491, **494**, *494*, 503, 504, 508
Jackson, Helen Hunt 441
Jackson, Michael 449
Jacksonville, FL 71, 72, 76, 309-11, 313, **598**, 614, 619, 696, 722
Jainism 697, 698
Jamaica . . 87, 474, 479, 689, 715, 732, **791-92**
James, Henry 442
James, Jesse 441
Jamestown, VA (1607-19) 436
Jan Mayen Island 820
Japan **792**
Agriculture 97, 98, 99
Area, population 730, 731, 732, 792
Arms purchases 133
Budget deficits 59
Carbon dioxide emissions 302
Cell phone use 300
Computer/Internet use 294, 297, 298
Consumer price changes 733
Disasters (2011) 325, 328, 673
Education 383
Energy consumption 109
Fishing, aquaculture 100
Flag, map 474, 485
Foreign aid from 738
Foreign exchange rates 75
Forests 306
Fossil fuel reserves 112
Gasoline prices 110
Gold reserves 733
Gross domestic product 733
Health expenditures 142
History 651, 654, 656, 659, 663, 667, 668, 669, 671, 682
Treaties (1853, 1951) 440, 445, 792
World War II 444, 663, 664, *664*
Islands, areas 689
Language 715, 792
Merchant fleet 77
Military strength 27, 133
Mortality rate by cause 736
Motor vehicle production, exports 79
Nuclear power 114
Securities held by U.S. 64
Spaceflight 333
Taxes 734
Trade 73, 75, 76
Travel and tourism 85, 86
Unemployment rates 734
U.S. investment 78
U.S. troops in 129
Vacation days 89
Wages, hourly 734
Japan, Sea of 690
Japanese-American detentions (1942-45) 444
Jarvis Island 593
Java 652, 689, 786
Jay, John 438
Jazz artists, noted 216-17
Jefferson Memorial (DC) 434
Jefferson, Thomas . . 438, 439, 491, **493**, *493*, 503, 504, 508
Jeffords, James 452
Jehovah's Witnesses 410, 697, 704-05
Jenner, Caitlyn 39, *815*
Jersey (British Isle) 689, 732, 848
Jersey City, NJ . . 118, **598-99**, 614, 696, 718-19
Jesus Christ 650
(*see also* Christianity)
Jewish people. *See* Anti-Semitism; Judaism
Jiang Zemin 669
Jobs. *See* Employment, U.S.
Jockeys, leading 968
Johnson, Andrew . . . 440, 441, 491, **496**, *496*, 503, 504
Johnson, Gary 505, 509-38
Johnson, Lyndon B. 446, 447, 491, **499-500**, *499*, 503, 504, 507, 508, 665
Johnson, Zach 28
Johnston Atoll 488
Johnstown (PA) flood (1889) 441
Joint Chiefs of Staff 128, 135
Jolliet, Louis 436, 683
Jones, John Paul 437
Jones, Paula 452
Jordan **792-93**
Area, population 732, 792
Education 383
Flag, map 474, 484
Foreign aid to 738
Israeli peace treaty (1994) 669
Languages 715, 792
Refugees in 735
UN peacekeeping mission 742
U.S. military financing 134
Water supply 306
Journalism awards 262, 270
Journalists, noted past 184-85
Judaism **707**
Adherents (U.S., world) 697, 698
Ancient Hebrews 363, 648
Headquarters (U.S.) 410
History 650
Holy days 699
(*see also* Anti-Semitism)
Judiciary, U.S. *See* Supreme Court, U.S.; World Court
Julian calendar 354-55
Julius Caesar 649
Jupiter (planet) 344, 345, **346-47**
Morning, evening stars 341
Position by month 337-40
Justice, Department of **542**
Attorneys general 542-43
First Hispanic (2005) 453
First woman (1993) 451
Employees 106
Justinian 651

K

Kaczynski, Theodore 452
Kagan, Elena 38, 455, 559
Kalaallit Nunaat (Greenland) . . 112, 129, 315, 478, 689, 732, **770**
Kansas **571-72**
Agriculture 92, 93
Congressional representation . . 551, 555, 609
Crime, prisons, death penalty . . 117, 119, 120
Education 380-83, 389-90
Elevations (high, low) 423
Energy consumption 111
Finances 60
Governor 37
Hazardous waste 305
Health insurance coverage 142
Immigrant admissions 619
Motor vehicles 83, 84
Name origin, nickname 426, 571
Oil production 111
Population 571, 604, 605, 606-07, 608, 611, 612, 631
Poverty rates 49
Taxes 84, 378
Unemployment 101
Weather 312
ZIP and area codes 631
Kansas City, MO 46, 71, 118, 304, 309-11, **599**, 614, 619, 696, 722
Kansas-Nebraska Act (1854) 440
Kant, Immanuel 656
Karadzic, Radovan 671
Karami, Rashid 668
Kardashian, Kim 39
Karzai, Hamid 670
Kasa-Vubu, Joseph *665*
Kashmir 669, 785
Kasich, John 6, 7, *198*
Kassig, Peter 457
Katrina (hurricane) 453, *453*
Kazakhstan **793**
Agriculture 98
Area, population 731, 732, 793
Education 383
Flag, map 474, 484
Fossil fuel reserves 112
Languages 715, 793
Prison population 121
Kefauver, Estes 445
Keith, Duncan *811*
Keller, Helen 442
Kellogg-Briand Pact (1928) 662
Kennedy, Anthony M. 38, 39, 559
Kennedy Center for the Performing Arts, John F. (DC) 435
Kennedy, Edward M. "Ted" 454
Kennedy, John F. 491, **499**, *499*, 503, 504, 665
Assassination (1963) 124, 446, 449
Presidential election 446, 507, 508, 509-38
Kennedy, John F., Jr. 452
Kennedy, Robert F. 447
Kent State University unrest (1970) 447
Kentucky **572**
Agriculture 92, 93
Congressional representation 551, 555, 609
Crime, prisons, death penalty 117, 119, 120
Education 380-83, 389-90
Elevations (high, low) 423
Energy consumption 111
Finances 60
Governor 37
Hazardous waste 305
Health insurance coverage 142
Immigrant admissions 619
Motor vehicles 83, 84
Name origin, nickname 426, 572
Oil production 111
Population 572, 599, 605, 606-07, 608, 611, 612, 631
Poverty rates 49
Taxes 84, 378
Unemployment 101
Weather 312
ZIP and area codes 631
Kentucky Derby 24, 441, 853, 966
Kenya **793-94**
Agriculture 99
Area, population 732, 793
Drinking water 737
Elections (2008, 2013) 671
Flag, map 474, 487
Foreign aid to 738
Health expenditures 142
Internally displaced persons 736
Languages 715, 793
Refugees in 735
Terrorism 22, *196*, 452, 670, 672
Kepler, Johannes 655
Kerguelen Archipelago 777
Kerouac, Jack 446
Kerry, John *195*, 456, 509-38
Kevorkian, Jack 452
Kharijites. *See* Islam
Khmer Empire 652, *652*, 728

Khomeini, Ayatollah Ruhollah 666
Khrushchev, Nikita 446, 665, 681
Kidd, William 437
Kidnappings 13, **125-26**, 443, 449
Kidney disease 154, 171
Kim Jong Il 669, 673
Kim Jong Un 457, 673
Kindergarten (1856) 440
King, (Riley) B. B. 35, *816*
King, Billie Jean 448
King, Coretta Scott 270
King George's War (1744-48) 437
King, Martin Luther, Jr.
Alabama march (1965) 447
Assassination (1968) 124, 447, 665
Birthday (legal holiday) 358, 450
March on Washington (1963) 446
Memorial 435
Montgomery bus boycott (1955) 445
King, Rodney 450, 451
Kingman Reef 593
Kinmen (Quemoy) 840
Kinsey Report (1948) 445
Kiribati 474, 488, 732, 733, **794**
Knights of Labor (1869) 441
Koran. *See* Quran
Korea, North (Democratic People's Republic of) **794-95**
Agriculture 98, 99
Area, population 732, 794
Axe Murder incident (1976) 449
Flag, map 474, 485
Fossil fuel reserves 112
History 660, 664, 669
Interview, The 15, 457
Language 794
Leaders 673
Military strength 133
Nuclear arms 452, 669, 671, 673, 738
Pueblo incident (1968) 447
Spaceflight 333
U.S. immigrants from 619, 620
Korea, South (Republic of) **795**
Agriculture 97, 98, 99
Area, population 732, 795
Arms purchases 133
Budget deficits 59
Carbon dioxide emissions 302
Computer/Internet use 294, 297
Economic crisis (1997) 669
Education 383, 385
Energy consumption 109
Established 665
Fishing, aquaculture 100
Flag, map 474, 485
Foreign aid from 738
Foreign exchange rates 75
Fossil fuel reserves 112
Gasoline prices 110
Gross domestic product 733
Health expenditures 142
History 669
Invaded by North Korea (1950) . . . 445, 665
Languages 715, 795
Merchant fleet 77
Military strength 133
Motor vehicle production, exports 79
Nuclear power 114
Securities held by U.S. 64
Spaceflight 333
Taxes 734
Trade 73
Travel and tourism 85, 86
U.S. adoptions from 166
U.S. immigrants from 619, 620
U.S. investment 78
U.S. troops in 129
Wages, hourly 734
Korean War (1950-53) 140, 445
Black troops 132
Casualties, U.S. forces 138
Military awards 136
Veteran population 131
Veterans Memorial (DC) 435
Kosovo . . . 474, 668, 671, 732, 735, 736, 742, **795-96**, 831
Krakatau volcano 685
Ku Klux Klan 441, 443
Kublai Khan 653
Kuiper Belt 345, 350
Kush 649
Kuwait **796**
Area, population 732, 796
Flag, map 474, 484
Fossil fuel reserves, exports 112, 113
Gross domestic product 733
Gulf War (1991) 450, 796
Iraqi invasion (1990) 450, 669, 796
Languages 715, 796
Terrorism 26
Water supply 306
Kyoto Protocol 668, 672
Kyrgyzstan 112, 474, 484, 671, 673, 715, 732, **796**

L

La Follette, Robert M. 507
La Niña 316
La Salle, René-Robert Cavelier Sieur de 436, 683
Labor. *See* Employment, U.S.; Labor unions
Labor Day 358
Labor, Department of **544-45**
Labor unions
AFL formed (1886) 441
AFL-CIO merger (1955) 445
Associations and organizations 417-18
CIO formed (1935) 444
Haymarket riot (1886) 441
ILGWU founded (1900) 442
IWW founded (1905) 442
Knights of Labor (1869) 441
Membership (1930-2014) 108
Rise of 658
Salaries/wages for members of 108
Taft-Hartley Act (1947) 445
Wisconsin bargaining limits 455
(*see also* Strikes)
Lacrosse 889
Lake Champlain, Battle of (1814) 439
Lakes 422, 694
Lamb, mutton 94, 95, 96-97
Lancaster, House of 675
Land, public
Forest Service administered 333
Homestead, Land Grant Acts (1862) . . . 440
Language **708-15**
Abbreviations and acronyms 710-11
Commonly misspelled words 709
Foreign words, phrases 709
New words, English 708
Words about words 708
World languages 620, 714-15
Laos **797**
Agriculture 98
Area, population 732, 797
Flag, map 474, 485
Forests 306
Fossil fuel reserves 112
History 665, 667
Internally displaced persons 736
Languages 715, 797
Refugees from 735
U.S. involvement in 446
Laredo, TX **599**, 614, 696
Las Vegas, NV 71, 72, 88, 118, 304, **599**, 614, 619, 696, 719
Latin America 730
HIV/AIDS cases 737
Religious adherents 698
Sanitation/drinking water 737
Trade 73
U.S. investment 78
(*see also* Central America; South America)
Latinos. *See* Hispanics
Latitude
Cities (U.S., world) 695-96
Position, reckoning 352
Latter-Day Saints (Mormons) . . . 440, 704-05
Headquarters 409
History 439, 440, 441
Membership 697
Latvia 121, 383, 474, 483, 668, 732, **797**
Law enforcement officers 121
Lead (metal) 68
League of Arab States 740
League of Nations (1920) 443, 661
League of Women Voters (1920) 443
Leap years 354
Lebanon **797-98**
Area, population 732, 797
Flag, map 474, 484
Internally displaced persons 736
Israeli invasion 667
Israeli-Palestinian conflicts . . . 670, 790, 798
Languages 797
Refugees in 735
Religious warfare 667
Terrorism 449, 668, 798
Travel and tourism 85
UN peacekeeping mission 742
U.S. military financing 134
U.S. military intervention (1958) 446
Lee, Harper *813*
Lee, Robert E. 440
Leeward Islands 848
Legion of Merit 136
Legionnaires' disease (1976) 449
Lehman Brothers 454
Leibniz, Gottfried von 655
LeMans race 961
Lend-Lease Act (1941) 444
Lenin, Vladimir 661
Lennon, John 449
Lent 699
Leonid meteor shower 340
Lesbians. *See* LGBT
Lesotho 474, 487, 715, 732, 736, **798**
Letterman, David 39, *813*
Lewinsky scandal 451-52
Lewis and Clark expedition (1804) . . 438, 683
Lewis, Sinclair 443
Lexington, KY 71, 309-11, **599**, 614, 696
Leyte Gulf, Battle of (1944) 663
LGBT (Lesbian, Gay, Bisexual, Transgender)
Boy Scouts policies 456
Caitlyn Jenner *815*
Civil unions 452
Discrimination against (2015) 21, *200*
Gay rights movement (1969) 447
Hate crime victims 123
Marriage . . 4, 24, 25, 30, 38, *200*, 451, 453, 454, 455, *455*, 456
Military policy 451, 455
NH bishop election (2003) 452
Shepard murder trial (1999) 452
Supreme Court rulings (2000, 2011, 2013) 562
Li Keqiang 682, 763
Libby, I. Lewis "Scooter" 453
Liberia **798-99**
Area, population 732, 798
Civil war 671
Flag, map 474, 486
Gross domestic product 733
History 669
Internally displaced persons 736
Languages 798
Merchant fleet 77
Sanitation 737
UN peacekeeping mission 742
U.S. military financing 134
Liberty Bell 437, 439, **489**
Libraries
America's first circulating (1731) 437
Presidential 503
Public 385
Library of Congress 435
Libya **799**
Area, population 731
Flag, map 474, 486
Fossil fuel reserves, exports 112, 113
History 667
Internally displaced persons 736
Languages 715, 799
Political unrest (2011, 2014) 13, 672
Population 731, 732, 799
U.S. consulate attack 32, 456, 457, 672
Liechtenstein . . 121, 297, 383, 474, 482, 731, 732, 733, **799-800**
Life expectancy
Animals 291
Humans 172
Light
Spectrum 285
Speed of 337
Lightning 315
Limitation of Armaments Conference 443
Lincoln, Abraham 491, **495-96**, *495*, 503, 504, 507, 508
Assassination (1865) 123, 440
Emancipation Proclamation (1863) 440
Gettysburg Address (1863) . . 440, *440*, 470
Memorial (DC) 435
Lincoln, NE 71, **599**, 614, 696
Lincoln Prize 270
Lindbergh, Charles A. 125, 336, 443
Line-Item Veto Act (1996) 451
Lipari Islands 791
Liquor
Alcoholics Anonymous 421
Cancer link 151
Drinking age legislation 450
Measures 365
Prohibition (1919, 1933) 443, *443*, 468
Temperance movement (1874, 1900) 441, 442
Underage drinking 147
Lisbon, Treaty of 671
Literature
Awards 259, 261, 263-66, 267-70
Best-selling books (2014) 250
Notable (2015) 249-50
(*see also* Writers, noted)
Lithuania 121, 383, 474, 483, 668, 715, 732, **800**
Little Big Horn, Battle of (1876) 441
Little League baseball 931
Livestock 74, 75, 95, 96-97
(*see also* Meat)
Lizards, venomous 292
Lloyd, Carli *812*
Loans. *See* Credit, consumer; Mortgages
Lobo, Porfirio (Pepe) 671
Locke, John 655, 656
Lockerbie crash (1988) 450
Lockjaw (tetanus) 157
Long Beach, CA . . . 71, 72, 76, 118, 304, **599**, 614, 619
Long, Huey 444
Long Island, Battle of (1776) 437
Longevity. *See* Life expectancy

Longfellow, Henry Wadsworth 440
Longitude
Cities (U.S., world) 695-96
Position, reckoning 352
Los Angeles, CA **599**
Air mileage to other cities 91
Air quality 304
Airport traffic 88
Buildings, tall 719
Consumer Price Index 46
Crime rates 118
Earthquake (1994) 325, 451
Geography 696
Housing 71, 72
Immigrant admissions 619
Marathon 978
Population 614
Port traffic 76
Riots (1965, 1992) 447, 450
Tides 316
Weather 309-11, 313
Lott, Trent 452
Louis, Joe 444
Louisiana **572-73**
Agriculture 92, 93
Coastline 423
Congressional representation . . 551, 555, 609
Crime, prisons, death penalty . . 117, 119, 120
Education 380-83, 389-90
Elevations (high, low) 423
Energy consumption 111
Finances 60
Governor 37
Hazardous waste 305
Health insurance coverage 142
Immigrant admissions 619
Motor vehicles 83, 84
Name origin, nickname 426, 572
Oil production 111
Population 572, 595, 600, 605, 606-07, 608, 611, 612, 632
Poverty rates 49
Taxes 84, 378
Unemployment 101
Weather 312
ZIP and area codes 632
Louisiana Purchase (1803) 427, 438, 658
Louisville, KY . . 71, 72, 309-11, 313, **599**, 614, 696, 722
Loyalty Islands 777
LPGA (Ladies Professional Golf) . . . 953, 954
Lubbock, TX **599**, 615
Luge (sledding) 860
Lumumba, Patrice *665*, 666
Lunar calendar 355
Lung disease 152, 446
***Lusitania* sinking** 442
Luther, Martin 654, 704
Lutheran churches 410, 697, 698, 704-05
Luxembourg **800**
Area, population 732, 800
Budget deficits 59
Computer/Internet use 297
Education 383, 385
Flag, map 474, 482
Foreign aid from 738
Gross domestic product 733
Languages 800
Securities held by U.S. 64
Taxes 734
Travel and tourism 85
U.S. investment 78
Lyme disease 156
Lynch, Loretta 22
Lyricists, noted 216

M

Macao 85, 121, 383, 654, 669, 732, **764**
MacArthur, Douglas 444, 445
Macedonia 112, 134, 474, 483, 668, 732, 736, **800-801**
Machu Picchu *655*
Madagascar 98, 306, 474, 487, 689, 715, 732, 733, 737, **801**
Madeira Islands 689, **825**
Madison, James 491, **493**, *493*, 503, 504, 508
Madison, WI 71, **600**, 615, 696
Madoff, Bernard 454
Madura 689
Maduro Moros, Nicolás 673, 850
Magazines
Best-selling (2015) 248
Journalism awards 270
Journalists, noted past 184-85
Magna Carta (1215) 653
Magnesium (dietary) 160
Magnetic fields 351
Magnetic poles 352
Mahabharata 648
Mail service **366-67**
Maine **573**
Agriculture 92, 93
Coastline 423
Congressional representation . . 551, 555, 609
Crime, prisons, death penalty . . 117, 119, 120
Education 380-83, 389-90
Elevations (high, low) 423
Energy consumption 111
Finances 60
Governor 37
Hazardous waste 305
Health insurance coverage 142
Immigrant admissions 619
Motor vehicles 83, 84
Name origin, nickname 426, 573
Population 573, 605, 606-07, 608, 611, 612, 632
Poverty rates 49
Taxes 84, 378
Unemployment 101
Weather 312
ZIP and area codes 632
Major, John 669, *669*
Major League Baseball. *See* Baseball
Major League Soccer. *See* Soccer
Majorca 836
Makemake (dwarf planet) . . . 344, 345, **349-50**
Malaria 156
Malawi 474, 487, 715, 732, 733, **801-02**
Malaysia 77, **802**
Agriculture 97, 98
Area, population 732, 802
Education 383
Fishing, aquaculture 100
Flag, map 474, 485
Foreign exchange rates 75
Forests 306
Fossil fuel reserves 112
Health expenditures 142
Languages 715, 802
Motor vehicle production 79
Muslim population 706
Refugees in 735
Trade 73
Travel and tourism 85
U.S. investment 78
Maldives 306, 474, 484, 731, 732, **802**
Mali . . . 474, 486, 673, 715, 732, 733, 735, 736, 742, **802-03**
Malta 77, 474, 482, 689, 731, 732, **803**
Man Booker Prize 267
Mandela, Nelson *668*, 669, 834-35
Manganese 160
Manhattan Island purchase 436
Manifest destiny 440
Manning, Chelsea 456
Manson, Charles 448
Manu'a Islands 591
Manual alphabet, American 713
Manufacturing
Exports, imports 74, 75
Median earnings 106
Unemployment 102, 103
U.S. national income 44
Wages, hourly 734
(*see also* specific industries)
Mao Zedong (Mao Tse-tung) . . . 665, 682, 763
Maps, world 476-88
Marathons 872, 976-78
Marcos, Ferdinand 668
Mariana Islands. *See* Northern Mariana Islands
Marijuana legalization 456
Marine Corps, U.S.
Address for information 137
Generals (active duty) 128
Insignia 137
Personnel, active duty 130
War memorial 434
Marine life 292
Marine warnings, advisories 308
Marquesas Islands 488, 689, 776
Marquette, Jacques 436, 683
Marriage
Defense of Marriage Act (DOMA) 451, 455, 456
Rates, patterns 164
Same-sex 4, 24, 25, 30, 38, *200*, 453, 454, *455*, 456, 673
Social Security benefits 369, 372
U.S. data 618
Wedding anniversaries 359
Mars (planet) 344, 345, **346**
Landings/exploration 32, 333-34, 449, 456, 671, 673, *809*
Morning, evening stars 341
Position by month 337-40
Marshall Islands 77, 474, 488, 689, 731, 732, 733, **803**
Marshall, John 438, 439
Marshall Plan (1947-51) 445, 664
Marshall, Thurgood 447, 450
Martin, Trayvon 456
Martinique 689, 776
Marx, Karl 658
Maryland **573-74**
Agriculture 92, 93
Coastline 423
Congressional representation 551, 555, 609
Crime, prisons, death penalty 117, 119
Education 380-83, 389-90
Elevations (high, low) 423
Energy consumption 111
Finances 60
Founded (1634) 436
Governor 37
Hazardous waste 305
Health insurance coverage 142
Immigrant admissions 619
Motor vehicles 83, 84
Name origin, nickname 426, 573
Population 573, 595, 605, 606-07, 608, 611, 612, 632-33
Poverty rates 49
Religious legislation (1702) 437
Taxes 84, 378
Unemployment 101
Weather 312
ZIP and area codes 632-33
Mass extinctions 279
Mass shootings. *See* Gun violence
Massachusetts **574**
Agriculture 92, 93
Coastline 423
Congressional representation 551, 555, 609
Crime, prisons, death penalty 117, 119, 120
Education 380-83, 389-90, 436
Elevations (high, low) 423
Energy consumption 111
Finances 60
Governor 37
Hazardous waste 305
Health insurance coverage 142
Immigrant admissions 619
Motor vehicles 83, 84
Name origin, nickname 426, 574
Population 574, 595, 605, 606-07, 608, 611, 612, 633-34
Poverty rates 49
Slavery outlawed (1783) 438
Taxes 84, 378
Unemployment 101
Weather 312
ZIP and area codes 633-34
Masters (golf) 22, 853, 952
Mathematics
Formulas 362
Fractions, decimals 363
Mathematicians, noted past 192, 201
Test scores 383
Matsu 840
Mauritania 475, 486, 667, 715, 731, 732, 735, 737, **804**
Mauritius 475, 689, 731, 732, **804**
Mayans 649, 652, 727
Mayflower Compact 436, *436*
***Mayflower* pilgrimage (1620)** 436
Mayotte 776
Mayweather, Floyd, Jr. 24, *812*
McAuliffe, Terry 456
McCain, John 453, 454, 505, 509-38
McCarthy, Joseph 445
McCarthy, Kevin 457
McDonald Islands 750
McDonald, Robert 457
McDonnell, Bob 15
McGovern, George 509-38
McKinley, Mount. *See* Denali
McKinley, William . . . 442, 491, **497**, *497*, 503, 504, 507, 508
McVeigh, Timothy 451
Mean solar time 352
Meara, Anne 35, *816*
Measles 18, 156, *200*
Measures. *See* Weights and measures
Meat 74, 94-97, 99
Meat Inspection Act (1906) 442
Medal of Honor 135
Media 53
(*see also* Cable television; Magazines; Newspapers; Radio; Television)
Medicaid 141
Medicare
Enacted (1965) 447
Expanded (1988, 2003) 450, 453
Income/disbursements 58, 374
Program summary 370
Medicine. *See* Health and medicine
Mediterranean Sea 689, 690
Medvedev, Dmitri 671, 681
Melilla 836
Melville, Herman 440
Memorial Day 358
Memorials, national 430, 434-35
Memphis, TN 71, 72, 76, 304, 309-11, **600**, 614, 696
Men
Cancer 151, 152
Cigarette use 146

Education 380, 384, 386, 390
Employment, unemployment 103, 108
HIV/AIDS cases 148
Income, wages 47, 106
Life expectancy. 172
Population. 610, 617
Poverty rates 49
Prison inmates 120
Sexual activity. 167, 168
Single-parent families. 618
Suicide rates. 170
Mencius 648
Mental health. 153, 421
Mercantilism 655
Merchant Marine. 77, 136
Mercury (planet) 344, **345**
Morning, evening stars 341
Position by month. 337-40
Transit. 337
Meredith, James 446
Mergers
Labor unions (1955) 445
Recent announcements (2015) . . 23, 27, 32
Sherman Antitrust Act (1890) 441
Merkel, Angela *195*, 671
Merrill Lynch 454
Mesa, AZ 46, 71, 72, 304, **600**, 614, 619
Mesopotamia. 647, 727
Metals
Exports, imports 74
Leading U.S. companies 53
News (2015) 279
Production, prices. 68
Meteorology. *See* Weather
Meteors, meteorites, meteoroids . . . 337, 340
Methodist churches . . . 410, 697, 698, 704-05
Metric system 361, 363
Metropolitan areas, U.S.
Air quality 304
Crime rates. 118
Housing 71
Immigrants' areas of residence 619
Population (2000-14) 613
Mexican War (1846-48). 138, 440
Mexico **804-05**
Agriculture 97, 98, 99
Ancient architecture 727
Area, population 730, 732, 804
Buildings, tall 719-20, 722
Carbon dioxide emissions 302
Cell phone use 300
Cession to U.S. (1848) 427
Computer/Internet use 294, 297
Drug cartels, violence. 671
Education 383, 385
Elections (2012) 673
Fishing 100
Flag, maps 475, 479
Foreign exchange rates 75
Forests 306
Fossil fuel reserves, exports 112, 113
Gasoline prices. 110
Gold production 68
Gross domestic product 733
Health expenditures 142
History 648, 657, 669, 671, 683
U.S. military interventions
(1914, 1916) 442, 443
Internally displaced persons. 736
Kidnappings (2014) 13
Languages 804
Mayan culture 652
Military strength 133
Motor vehicle production, exports. 79
Nuclear power 114
Prison population 121
Refugees from 735
Revolution (1910) 661
Securities held by U.S. 64
Taxes 734
Trade 73, 75, 76
Travel and tourism 85, 86, 87
U.S. border fence 453
U.S. emergency aid (1995). 451
U.S. immigrants from 9, 619, 620
U.S. investment 78
U.S. military financing. 134
Wages, hourly. 734
Mexico, Gulf of 690
Miami, FL. **600**
Air quality 304
Airport traffic 88
Buildings, tall 719, 722
Consumer Price Index 46
Crime rates. 118
Geography 696
Housing 71, 72
Immigrant admissions. 619
Population. 614, 615
Tides. 316
Weather 309-11, 313
Michelangelo. 655
Michigan **574-75**
Agriculture 92, 93
Congressional representation 551, 555, 609
Crime, prisons, death penalty 117, 119, 120
Education 380-83, 389-90
Elevations (high, low) 423
Energy consumption. 111
Finances 60
Governor. 37
Hazardous waste 305
Health insurance coverage 142
Immigrant admissions. 619
Motor vehicles 83, 84
Name origin, nickname. 426, 574
Oil production 111
Population. 574, 596, 605, 606-07, 608,
611, 612, 634
Poverty rates 49
Taxes 84, 378
Unemployment 101
Weather 312
ZIP and area codes 634
Michigan, Lake 694
Micronesia. 475, 488, 689, 732, 733, **805**
Microsoft Corp. 294
Midway Atoll 593
Midway, Battle of (1942). 444, 663
Migrant crisis (2015). . . . 4, 22, 24, 31, 33, *194*
Military Academy, U.S. (West Point, NY) . 136
Military affairs **128-40**
Arms contracts/sales 133, 134
Financing 134
Geneva Conventions 744
Leaders, noted past 186-87
Major wars since 1066 139-40
(*see also* Armed forces, U.S.)
Military parks, U.S. 430
Military time (24-hour) 360
Milken, Michael. 450
Millennium, arrival of 452
Miller, Arthur. 445
Million Man March (1995). 451
Milosevic, Slobodan. 671
Milwaukee, WI. . . 46, 71, 72, 309-11, 313, **600**,
614, 619, 696, 719
Minerals (dietary) 159, 160
Minimum wage, U.S.
Enacted (1938). 444
Hourly rates (1938-2009) 105
Increases 445, 453, 457
Mining
Disasters. 322
Leading U.S. companies 53
Molly Maguires (1877) 441
Strikes (coal miners, 1922, 1946). . 443, 444
Unemployment. 102, 103
U.S. national income 44
Minneapolis, MN. **600**
Air quality 304
Airport traffic 88
Bridge disaster 453
Buildings, tall 719
Consumer Price Index 46
Crime rates. 118
Geography 696
Housing 71
Immigrant admissions. 619
Population. 614
Weather 309-11, 313
Minnesota **575**
Agriculture 92, 93
Congressional representation 551, 555, 609
Crime, prisons, death penalty 117, 119, 120
Education 380-83, 389-90
Elevations (high, low) 423
Energy consumption. 111
Finances. 60
Governor. 37
Hazardous waste 305
Health insurance coverage. 142
Immigrant admissions. 619
Motor vehicles 83, 84
Name origin, nickname. 426, 575
Population. 575, 600, 602, 605, 606-07,
608, 611, 612, 634-35
Poverty rates 49
Taxes 84, 378
Unemployment 101
Weather 312
ZIP and area codes 634-35
Minoans. 647, 727
Minorca 836
Mint, U.S.. . . . . 55, 438
Miquelon Island 777
***Mir* (space station)** 330-31, 451, 670
Miss America (beauty pageant). 271
Missiles, rockets. *See* Arms control; Space
exploration
Mississippi **576**
Agriculture 92, 93
Civil rights slayings (1964) 446
Coastline. 423
Congressional representation . .551, 555, 609
Crime, prisons, death penalty . .117, 119, 120
Education 380-83, 389-90
Elevations (high, low) 423
Energy consumption. 111
Finances. 60
Governor. 37
Hazardous waste 305
Health insurance coverage. 142
Immigrant admissions. 619
Motor vehicles 83, 84
Name origin, nickname. 426, 576
Oil production 111
Population. 576, 605, 606-07, 608, 611,
612, 635
Poverty rates 49
Taxes 84, 378
Unemployment 101
Weather 312
ZIP and area codes 635
Mississippi River
Exploration 683
First railroad crossing (1855) 440
Length. 422, 693
Missouri. **576-77**
Agriculture 92, 93
Congressional representation 551, 555, 609
Crime, prisons, death penalty 117, 119, 120
Education 380-83, 389-90
Elevations (high, low) 423
Energy consumption. 111
Ferguson protests. 12, 19, 29, 457, *457*
Finances. 60
Governor. 37
Hazardous waste 305
Health insurance coverage. 142
Immigrant admissions. 619
Motor vehicles 83, 84
Name origin, nickname. 426, 576
Oil production 111
Population. 576, 599, 602, 605, 606-07,
608, 611, 612, 635-36
Poverty rates 49
Taxes 84, 378
Unemployment 101
Weather 312
ZIP and area codes 635-36
Missouri Compromise (1820) 439
Missouri River. 693
Mitchell, Margaret. 444
Mitterrand, François. 668
Mobility, in U.S. 616
Mohammed. *See* Muhammad
Mohs scale 282
Moldova. 14, 475, 483, 732, **805**
Moluccas. 689
Molybdenum 160
Monaco 297, 475, 482, 731, 732, 733, **806**
Mondale, Walter 449, 509-38
Money. *See* Currency, U.S.; Income
Mongolia 112, 121, 134, 475, 484-85, 715,
731, 732, 737, **806**
Mongolia, Inner. 763
Mongols. 653
Monroe Doctrine (1823) 439
Monroe, James . . 491, **494**, *494*, 503, 504, 508
Montana. **577**
Agriculture 92, 93
Congressional representation 551, 556, 609
Crime, prisons, death penalty 117, 119, 120
Education 380-83, 389-90
Elevations (high, low) 423
Energy consumption. 111
Finances. 60
Governor. 37
Hazardous waste 305
Health insurance coverage. 142
Immigrant admissions. 619
Motor vehicles 83, 84
Name origin, nickname. 426, 577
Oil production 111
Population. 577, 605, 606-07, 608, 611,
612, 636
Poverty rates 49
Taxes 84, 379
Unemployment 101
Weather 312
ZIP and area codes 636
Montenegro 112, 383, 475, 483, 668, 732, **806**
Montoya, Juan Pablo 24
Montserrat. 732, 848
Monuments, national. *See* National parks/
monuments
Moon 345, **353**
Apollo, exploratory missions. 329-30,
333-34, 447
Chinese calendar 355
Conjunctions. 337-40
Eclipses (2016). 337, 343
First humans on (1969) 329, 447, *448*, 666
Occultations 337-40
Phases (2016) 353
Position by month. 337-40
Tides, effects on. 316
Morales, Evo 671
Mormons. *See* Latter-Day Saints
Morning stars (2016) 341
Morocco. **806-07**

Agriculture 98
Area, population 732, **806-07**
Fishing 100
Flag, map 475, 486
Foreign aid to 738
Health expenditures 142
Languages 715, 807
Military strength 133
Muslim population 706
Travel and tourism 85
U.S. military financing 134
Morsi, Mohammed 25, 772
Mortgages 17, 19, 70
Motion, laws of 284
Motor vehicles. *See* Automobiles, motor vehicles
Mott, Lucretia 440
Motto, U.S. 470
Mount Vernon (VA) 435
Mountains 422, 423, **687-88**
Volcanoes 449, 685-86
Moussaoui, Zacarias 452
MOVE radical group 450
Movies **243-46**
Awards 19, 273, 274-76
Best all time 245
Content ratings 246
DVDs, most popular (2014) 246
Film websites 245
Kinetoscope (1894) 441
Most pirated 244
National Film Registry (2014) 245
Notable past 442-43, 444, 446, 448, 449, 451, 453
Notable present (2014-15) 15, 19, 243, 457
Pioneering (1903, 1915, 1923, 1927) 442, 443
Stars, directors (2014-15) 243
Theater statistics 245
Top grossing 244
Mozambique 112, 142, 306, 475, 487, 715, 732, 733, 736, 737, 738, **807-08**
MTV Music Video Awards 278
Mubarak, Hosni 13
Mughals 654
Muhammad 650, 671, 700, 706
Multilateral Investment Guarantee Agency (MIGA) 742
Multiple births 166
Multiple sclerosis 421
Mumps 156-57
Municipal bonds 66
Municipal solid waste 305
Murder
Arrests, by race 122
Assassinations 123-25
Firearm use 122
News (2015) 21, 39, *814*
Prison population 121
Rates of 116-18
Workplace 105
Muscular dystrophy 421
Museums **247-48**, 435, 437
Musharraf, Pervez 671, 821-22
Music and musicians
Awards 253, 266-67, 273, 277-78
Classical, avant garde 214-15
Concerts, top-grossing (1985-2014) 254
Country music 218
Jazz, blues 216-17
Opera 219-20, 246, 444
Original names 241-42
Rap 220-22
Recordings 252-54, 660
Rhythm and blues 220-22
Rock and roll 220-22, 450
Theater, popular 215-16
Videos 254
Muslims. *See* Islam
Mussolini, Benito 662, *663*
Mutual funds 66-67
My Lai massacre 447, 448
Myanmar (Burma) **808**
Agriculture 97, 98
Area, population 732, 808
Cyclone (2008) 671
Elections (2010, 2012) 673
Fishing, aquaculture 100
Flag, map 475, 484-85
Forests 306
Fossil fuel reserves 112
Health expenditures 142
Internally displaced persons 736
Languages 715, 808
Military strength 133
Protests (2007) 671
Refugees from 735

N

NAACP (National Assn. for the Advancement of Colored People) 442
Nabokov, Vladimir 445
Nader, Ralph 505, 509-38
NAFTA (North American Free Trade Agreement) 79, 450, 669
Nagasaki bombing (1945) 444, 663, *664*
Names
Popular given 711-12
Pseudonyms 241-42
Namibia 112, 475, 487, 669, 731, 732, **808**
Nantes, Edict of 654
Napoleon Bonaparte 139, 657
NASA (National Aeronautics and Space Administration) 547
NASCAR (auto racing) 960-61
Nasdaq Stock Market 65
Nashville, TN 71, 72, 304, 309-11, 313, **600**, 614, 619, 696, 722
Nation, Carry 442
National Aeronautics and Space Administration (NASA) 547
National anthem, U.S. 439, 489
National Archives 435, 547
National Assn. for the Advancement of Colored People (NAACP) 442
National Basketball Assn. (NBA). *See* Basketball
National Book Awards 269-70
National Book Critics Circle Awards 270
National Collegiate Athletic Assn. (NCAA)
Baseball 888
Basketball 884-88
Football 877-81
Misc. sports 889
Team nicknames, colors 882-83
National debt 60
National Film Registry (2014) 245
National Football League (NFL). *See* Football
National Forest System 433
National Gallery of Art (DC) 435
National Heritage Areas 434
National Hockey League. *See* Hockey
National income, U.S. 44
National Invitational Tournament (NIT) 886
National League. *See* Baseball
National Magazine Awards 270
National monuments. *See* National parks/monuments
National Org. for Women (NOW) 665
National Park Service 427, 428
National parks/monuments **428-35**, 441, 489-90
National recreation areas 333, 432
National Rifle Assn. 441, 979
National Science Foundation 547
National Security Agency 21, 24-25, 453, 456
National Trails System 433
Nations of the World **745-808, 817-52**
Agriculture 97-99
Cell phone use 300
Computer/Internet use 294, 297
Daylight Saving Time 360
Energy production, consumption 109, 114
Fishing, aquaculture 100
Flags 473-76
Gasoline prices 110
Gross domestic product 733
Health expenditures 142
Internally displaced persons 735
Maps 477-88
Merchant fleets 77
Military strength 133
Motor vehicle production 79
Population/projections 731-34
Prison population 121
Refugees 735
Trade 73
Native Americans. *See* American Indians
NATO. *See* North Atlantic Treaty Org.
Natural gas
Exports, imports 74, 109
Fracking 111
Leading U.S. companies 53
Production, consumption 109, 110, 111
Resources, reserves 111, 112
Shortage (1977) 449
Naturalization Act (1790) 438
Nauru 475, 488, 731, 732, 733, **817**
Nautilus (nuclear submarine) 445, 446
Naval Academy, U.S. (Annapolis, MD) 136
Naval leaders, noted past 186-87
Naval Reduction Treaty (1930) 443
Navassa Island 593
Navigation Act (1660) 436
Navy, U.S. Department of the
Academy (Annapolis, MD) 136
Address for information 137
Admirals (active duty) 128
China spy plane dispute (2001) 452
Insignia 137
Personnel, active duty 130
Salutes, honors 135
Secretaries 542
Nazis 664, 778-79
NBA (National Basketball Assn.). *See* Basketball
NCAA. *See* National Collegiate Athletic Assn.
Nebraska **577-78**
Agriculture 92, 93
Congressional representation 551, 556, 609
Crime, prisons, death penalty 117, 119, 120
Education 380-83, 389-90
Elevations (high, low) 423
Energy consumption 111
Finances 60
Governor 37
Hazardous waste 305
Health insurance coverage 142
Immigrant admissions 619
Motor vehicles 83, 84
Name origin, nickname 426, 577
Oil production 111
Population 577, 599, 601, 605, 606-07, 608, 611, 612, 636
Poverty rates 49
Taxes 84, 379
Unemployment 101
Weather 312
ZIP and area codes 636
Nebula Awards 270
Nemtsov, Boris *195*
Nepal 22-23, 98, 142, *196*, *324*, 325, 475, 484, 715, 732, 735, 736, **817**
Neptune (planet) 344, 345, **348**
Morning, evening stars 341
Position by month 337-40
Netanyahu, Benjamin 20, 39, *195*, 669, 671, 672
Netherlands **817-18**
Agriculture 97
Area, population 732, 817
Budget deficits 59
Computer/Internet use 297
Dutch dependencies 818
Education 383, 385
Flag, map 475, 482
Foreign aid from 738
Foreign exchange rates 75
Fossil fuel reserves 112
Gold reserves 733
Gross domestic product 733
History 655
Languages 715, 817
Merchant fleet 77
Motor vehicle production 79
New World colonization (1624-64) 436
Nuclear power 114
Refugees in 735
Rulers, royal family 680
Securities held by U.S. 64
Taxes 734
Trade 73
Travel and tourism 85, 86
Unemployment rates 734
U.S. ancestral claims 621
U.S. investment 78
U.S. troops in 129
Vacation days 89
Wages, hourly 734
Netherlands Antilles 64, 818
Nevada **578**
Agriculture 92, 93
Congressional representation 551, 556, 609
Crime, prisons, death penalty 117, 119
Education 380-83, 389-90
Elevations (high, low) 423
Energy consumption 111
Finances 60
Governor 37
Hazardous waste 305
Health insurance coverage 142
Immigrant admissions 619
Motor vehicles 83, 84
Name origin, nickname 426, 578
Oil production 111
Population 578, 598, 599, 601, 602, 605, 606-07, 608, 611, 612, 636
Poverty rates 49
Taxes 84
Traveler spending 86
Unemployment 101
Weather 312
ZIP and area codes 636
New Amsterdam (1626, 1664) 436
New Britain 689
New Caledonia 488, 689, 732, 777
New Deal (1933) 443, 663
New Guinea. *See* Papua New Guinea
New Hampshire **578-79**
Agriculture 92, 93
Coastline 423
Congressional representation 551-52, 556, 609
Crime, prisons, death penalty 117, 119, 120
Education 380-83, 389-90
Elevations (high, low) 423
Energy consumption 111
Finances 60
Governor 37
Hazardous waste 305
Health insurance coverage 142
Immigrant admissions 619
Motor vehicles 83, 84

Name origin, nickname . . . 426, 578
Population . . . 578, 605, 606-07, 608, 611, 612, 636
Poverty rates . . . 49
Taxes . . . 84, 379
Unemployment . . . 101
Weather . . . 312
ZIP and area codes . . . 636
New Ireland . . . 689
New Jersey . . . **579**
Agriculture . . . 92, 93
Coastline . . . 423
Congressional representation 552, 556, 609
Crime, prisons, death penalty 117, 119, 120
Death penalty repeal . . . 453
Education . . . 380-83, 389-90
Elevations (high, low) . . . 423
Energy consumption . . . 111
Finances . . . 60
Governor . . . 37
Hazardous waste . . . 305
Health insurance coverage . . . 142
Immigrants (2013) . . . 619
Motor vehicles . . . 83, 84
Name origin, nickname . . . 426, 579
Population . . . 579, 598, 601, 605, 606-07, 608, 611, 612, 636-37
Poverty rates . . . 49
Taxes . . . 84, 379
Unemployment . . . 101
Weather . . . 312
ZIP and area codes . . . 636-37
New Mexico . . . **579-80**
Agriculture . . . 92, 93
Congressional representation 552, 556, 609
Crime, prisons, death penalty 117, 119, 120
Education . . . 380-83, 389-90
Elevations (high, low) . . . 423
Energy consumption . . . 111
Finances . . . 60
Governor . . . 37
Hazardous waste . . . 305
Health insurance coverage . . . 142
Immigrant admissions . . . 619
Motor vehicles . . . 83, 84
Name origin, nickname . . . 426, 579
Oil production . . . 111
Population . . . 579, 594, 605, 606-07, 608, 611, 612, 637
Poverty rates . . . 49
Taxes . . . 84, 379
Unemployment . . . 101
Weather . . . 312
ZIP and area codes . . . 637
New Netherland (1624, 1664) . . . 436
New Orleans, LA . . . **600**
Air quality . . . 304
Buildings, tall . . . 720
Fires (1788) . . . 438
Geography . . . 696
Housing . . . 71, 72
Hurricane Katrina . . . 453, *453*
Population . . . 614, 615
Port traffic . . . 76
Weather . . . 309-11, 313
New religionists . . . 697, 698
New Testament . . . 703
New Year
Chinese . . . 355
Jewish . . . 699
New Year's Day . . . 358
Tet . . . 355
New York (state) . . . **580**
Agriculture . . . 92, 93
Coastline . . . 423
Congressional representation 552, 556, 609
Crime, prisons, death penalty 117, 119, 120
Education . . . 380-83, 389-90
Elevations (high, low) . . . 423
Energy consumption . . . 111
Finances . . . 60
Governor . . . 37
Hazardous waste . . . 305
Health insurance coverage . . . 142
Immigrant admissions . . . 619
Motor vehicles . . . 83, 84
Name origin, nickname . . . 426, 580
Oil production . . . 111
Population . . . 580, 595, 600, 605, 606-07, 608, 611, 612, 637-38
Poverty rates . . . 49
Taxes . . . 84, 379
Traveler spending . . . 86
Unemployment . . . 101
Weather . . . 312
ZIP and area codes . . . 637-38
New York City . . . **600**
Air mileage to other cities . . . 91
Air pollution . . . 304
Airport traffic . . . 88
Buildings, tall . . . 720-21
Consumer Price Index . . . 46
Crime rates . . . 118
Geography . . . 696
Housing . . . 71, 72
Immigrant admissions . . . 619
Marathon . . . 977
Nursing school, first (1873) . . . 441
Population . . . 614, 730
Port traffic . . . 76
Riots (1863, 1943) . . . 440, 444
Roller coaster (1884) . . . 441
Subway debut (1904) . . . 442
Tides . . . 316
Tweed convicted (1873) . . . 441
United Nations . . . 741
Wall Street bombing (1920) . . . 443
Weather . . . 309-11, 313
World Trade Center (1993, 2001) . . . 450, 452, 670
World's Fair . . . 440, 444
New York Stock Exchange. *See* Dow Jones Industrial Average
New Zealand . . . **818**
Agriculture . . . 97, 99
Area, population . . . 732, 818
Budget deficits . . . 59
Computer/Internet use . . . 297
Dominion status . . . 660
Education . . . 383, 385
Flag, map . . . 475, 488
Foreign aid from . . . 738
Fossil fuel reserves . . . 112
Islands, areas . . . 689
Languages . . . 818
Mountain peaks . . . 687
Taxes . . . 734
Travel and tourism . . . 85
U.S. investment . . . 78
Vacation days . . . 89
Wages, hourly . . . 734
Water supply . . . 306
Newark, NJ . . . 88, 118, 309, 311, 313, 447, **601**, 614, 696
Newbery Medal . . . 267-68
Newfoundland . . . 9, 689
News
Chronology of events (2013-14) . . . 12-33
Notable quotes . . . 39
Offbeat . . . 40
Photos . . . *193-200, 809-16*
Top 10 topics (2015) . . . 4
Top websites (2015) . . . 252
Newspapers
Abolitionist (1831) . . . 439
Advertising revenues . . . 251
Circulation . . . 251
First U.S. (1690, 1704, 1783) 436, 437, 438
Journalism awards . . . 262, 270
Journalists, noted past . . . 184-85
Muckrakers . . . 660
U.S., Canadian dailies . . . 251, 252
Websites . . . 252
Newton, Sir Isaac . . . 264, 655, 656
NFL. *See* Football
Ngo Dinh Diem . . . 446
Niagara Falls . . . 695
Nicaragua . . . 442, 475, 479, 667, 670, 732, **818-19**
Nicholas II . . . 660, 661
Nietzsche, Friedrich . . . 659
Niger . . . 112, 475, 486, 673, 732, 733, 735, 736, 737, **819**
Nigeria . . . **819-20**
Agriculture . . . 98, 99
Aquaculture . . . 100
Area, population . . . 730, 731, 732, 819
Boko Haram . . . 13, 16, 20, 27, 672
Cell phone use . . . 300
Elections (2015) . . . 20, *197*, 673
Flag, map . . . 475, 486
Foreign aid to . . . 738
Fossil fuel reserves, exports . . . 112, 113
Gross domestic product . . . 733
Health expenditures . . . 142
History . . . 649, 664, 669
Internally displaced persons . . . 736
Languages . . . 715, 819
Muslim population . . . 706
Refugees from . . . 735
U.S. investment . . . 78
Nile River . . . 691
Nimoy, Leonard . . . 35, *816*
Ningxia Hui . . . 763
Nitrogen oxide emissions . . . 303
Niue Island . . . 488, 818
Nixon, Richard M. . . . 445, 446, 491, **500**, *500*, 503, 504
China visit (1972) . . . 448
Impeachment hearings (1974) . . . 448
Library . . . 503
Moscow summit (1972) . . . 448
Presidential elections . . . 447, 448, 507, 508, 509-38
Resignation (1974) . . . 448
Watergate (1973, 1974) . . . 448
No hitters (baseball) . . . 917
Nobel Prizes . . . **259-62**
Nordic combined . . . 860
Norfolk Island . . . 750
Norfolk, VA . . . 71, 76, 309-11, **601**, 615
Noriega, Manuel . . . 450, 670
Norman, Chris . . . *815*
Norman Conquest . . . 139, 652
Normandy, House of . . . 675
Normandy invasion (1944) . . . 444, 664
North America
Agriculture . . . 97, 98, 99
Area, population . . . 730
Bridges . . . 723-25
Buildings, tall . . . 717-22
Cities . . . 594-604, 614-15, 695-96
Elevations (highest, lowest) . . . 695
Explorations . . . 654, 683
Fossil fuel reserves . . . 112
HIV/AIDS cases . . . 737
Lakes . . . 694
Maps . . . 478-79
Mountain peaks . . . 687
Religious adherents . . . 698
Rivers . . . 692-93
Temperature/precipitation extremes . . . 315
Trade . . . 73
Tunnels . . . 725-26
Volcanoes . . . 449, 685, 686
Waterfalls . . . 695
(*see also* specific countries)
North American Free Trade Agreement (NAFTA) . . . 79, 450, 669
North Atlantic Treaty Org. (NATO) . . . **740**
Eastward expansion (1997) . . . 669
Established (1949) . . . 445, 664
International commands . . . 128
Trade with U.S. allies in . . . 73
North Carolina . . . **580-81**
Agriculture . . . 92, 93
Coastline . . . 423
Congressional representation 552, 556, 609
Crime, prisons, death penalty 117, 119, 120
Education . . . 380-83, 389-90
Elevations (high, low) . . . 423
Energy consumption . . . 111
Finances . . . 60
Governor . . . 37
Hazardous waste . . . 305
Health insurance coverage . . . 142
Immigrant admissions . . . 619
Motor vehicles . . . 83, 84
Name origin, nickname . . . 426, 580
Population . . . 580, 595, 597-98, 602, 604, 605, 606-07, 608, 611, 612, 638-39
Poverty rates . . . 49
Taxes . . . 84, 379
Traveler spending . . . 86
Unemployment . . . 101
Weather . . . 312
ZIP and area codes . . . 638-39
North Dakota . . . **581-82**
Agriculture . . . 92, 93
Congressional representation . . . 552, 556, 609
Crime, prisons, death penalty . . . 117, 119, 120
Education . . . 380-83, 389-90
Elevations (high, low) . . . 423
Energy consumption . . . 111
Finances . . . 60
Governor . . . 37
Hazardous waste . . . 305
Health insurance coverage . . . 142
Immigrant admissions . . . 619
Motor vehicles . . . 83, 84
Name origin, nickname . . . 426, 581
Oil production . . . 111
Population . . . 581, 605, 606-07, 608, 611, 612, 639
Poverty rates . . . 49
Taxes . . . 84, 379
Unemployment . . . 101
Weather . . . 312
ZIP and area codes . . . 639
North Korea. *See* Korea, North
North Las Vegas, NV . . . **601**, 615
North, Oliver . . . 450
North Pole . . . 352, 442, 446, 684
North Sea . . . 690
Northern Cyprus, Turkish Republic of **768-69**
Northern Ireland. *See* Ireland, Northern
Northern Mariana Islands . . . 37, 382, 427, 488, 558, **592**, 689, 732
Northwest Ordinance (1787) . . . 438
Northwest Territory, U.S. (1787, 1795) . . . 425, 438
Norway . . . **820**
Area, population . . . 732, 820
Budget deficits . . . 59
Computer/Internet use . . . 297
Education . . . 383, 385
Fishing, aquaculture . . . 100
Flag, map . . . 475, 482
Foreign aid from . . . 738
Foreign exchange rates . . . 75

Fossil fuel reserves, exports 112, 113
Gross domestic product 733
Languages 715, 820
Merchant fleet. 77
Rulers, royal family. 680
Taxes 734
Terrorism 672
Travel and tourism 85
U.S. ancestral claims 621
U.S. immigrants from 620
U.S. investment 78
Vacation days. 89
Wages, hourly. 734
Water supply. 306
Noted personalities 5, **173-92, 201-42**
NOW (National Org. for Women). 665
NPT Treaty (1968). 738, 739
Nuclear arms
A-bomb. 444, 445, 663, *664*
Countries with. 738
H-bomb (1950, 1952) 445
Nautilus submarine (1954) 446
Treaties, negotiations (1963-2010). . . . 446, 450, 454, 739
Nuclear energy
Accidents, major. 328, 449
First chain reaction (1942) 444
Production, consumption 109, 110, 114-15
Nuclear Regulatory Commission 547
Nullification (1828) 439
Numbers, large and prime 362
Nuremberg Laws (1935). 662
Nuremberg Tribunal (1946) 664, 744
Nursing school, first (1873). 441
Nutrition. **158-61**
Cancer prevention 151
Dietary guidelines, requirements 158
Federal program costs 92
Food labels. 159
Nutrients 158-60
Nuts 96, 97

O

Oakland, CA 46, 71, 76, 118, 304, **601**, 614, 619
Oats 96, 97
Obama, Barack . . 454, 456, **502**, *502*, 503, *813*
Administration. 539
Birth date, place 491
Cabinet 539
Health care reform 454, 455, 456
Immigration action 12, 18, 457
Library. 503
Presidential elections (2008, 2012) . . . 453, 454, 456, 505, 506, 507, 508, 509-38
Recent actions (2015) 16, 18, 39
Salary 539
Obama, Michelle. 504
Obamacare. *See* Affordable Care Act
Oberlin College (1833) 439
Obesity 151, 155, 161, 162
Obituaries (2014-15). 34-36, *816*
Occultation (astronomical position). 337
Occupy Wall Street protests 455
Oceania
Agriculture 97, 98, 99
Area, population 730
Fossil fuel reserves. 112
Religious adherents 698
Sanitation/drinking water 737
Travel and tourism 87
Volcanoes. 685, 686
Waterfalls 695
(*see also* specific countries)
Oceanography 316
Oceans and seas
Areas, depths. 690
Crossings, notable 336
Energy from 115
Fishing 100
Islands 689
Marine warnings, advisories. 308
Territorial extent, U.S. 427
O'Connor, Sandra Day 449, *449*
Offbeat news stories 40
Office of the United Nations High Commissioner for Refugees (UNHCR) . . 742
O'Hara, Maureen. 35, *816*
Ofu Island 591
Ohio **582**
Agriculture 92, 94
Congressional representation. . 552, 556-57, 609
Crime, prisons, death penalty 117, 119, 120
Education 380-83, 389-90
Elevations (high, low) 423
Energy consumption. 111
Finances. 60
Governor. 37
Hazardous waste 305
Health insurance coverage. 142
Immigrant admissions. 619
Motor vehicles 83, 84
Name origin, nickname. 426, 582
Oil production 111
Population. 582, 596, 604, 605, 606-07, 608, 611, 612, 639-40
Poverty rates 49
Taxes 84, 379
Unemployment 101
Weather 312
ZIP and area codes 639-40
Ohio River 693
Oil and oil spills. *See* Petroleum
OK Corral gun battle (1881). 441
Okhotsk, Sea of 690
Okinawa Island 663, 689
Oklahoma **582-83**
Agriculture 92, 94
Congressional representation 552, 557, 609
Crime, prisons, death penalty 117, 119, 120
Education 380-83, 389-90
Elevations (high, low) 423
Energy consumption. 111
Finances. 60
Governor. 37
Hazardous waste 305
Health insurance coverage. 142
Immigrant admissions. 619
Land rush (1889) 441
Motor vehicles 83, 84
Name origin, nickname. 426, 582
Oil production 111
Population. 582, 601, 604, 605, 606-07, 608, 611, 612, 640
Poverty rates 49
Taxes 84, 379
Unemployment 101
Weather 312
ZIP and area codes 640
Oklahoma City, OK. **601**
Bombing and aftermath (1995, 1997, 2001) 451, *451*, 670
Buildings, tall 722
Geography 696
Housing 71, 72
Population. 614
Weather 309-11, 313
Old Ironsides (1797). 438
Old Testament. 703
Olmecs. 648, 727
Olmert, Ehud. 670
Olney-Pauncefote Treaty (1897) 442
Olosega Island 591
Olympic Games **855-76**
Game sites 855
History, symbolism 442, 855
Summer
Boycotts. 449
Champions (1896-2012) 864-76
Highlights, medal standings (2012) . . 863
Terrorism (1972, 1996). 451, 666
Winter
Champions (1924-2014) 856-63
Highlights, medal standings (2014) . . 855
(*see also* Paralympics; specific sports)
Omaha, NE 71, 309, 310, 313, **601**, 614, 615, 696, 722
Oman 112, 134, 475, 484, 732, **820-21**
One World Trade Center 13, 457, 716
O'Neill, Eugene. 446
Ontario, Lake. 694
Oort Cloud. 350
OPEC (Organization of Petroleum Exporting Countries) 73, 78, 113, 740
Open Door Policy (1899) 442, 659
Opera. 219-20, 246, 444
Operation Anaconda (2002). 452
Operation Enduring Freedom
Budget, funding 133, 453
Civilian casualties. 32, 454
End of combat 15, 457, 672
Military awards 136
U.S. troop deployments, casualties 132, 454
Operation Fast and Furious. 455
Operation Iraqi Freedom/New Dawn
Budget, funding 133, 453
Chemical weapons. 12
End declared 452, 455
Military awards 136
Overview. 140, 787
U.S., coalition troop withdrawal . . 454, 455, 672
U.S. troop deployments, casualties . . . 132, 138, 453, 455, 670
Opium War 658
Opposition (astronomical position) 337
Orange Bowl 878
Oregon. **583**
Accession (1846) 427
Agriculture 92, 94
Coastline. 423
Congressional representation 552, 557, 609
Crime, prisons, death penalty 117, 119, 120
Education 380-83, 389-90
Elevations (high, low) 423
Energy consumption. 111
Finances. 60
Governor. 18, 37
Hazardous waste 305
Health insurance coverage. 142
Immigrant admissions. 619
Motor vehicles 83, 84
Name origin, nickname. 426, 583
Population. 583, 602, 605, 606-07, 608, 611, 612, 640
Poverty rates 49
Taxes 84, 379
Unemployment 101
Weather 312
ZIP and area codes 640
Oregon Trail (1843). 440
Organ donation. 421
Organic agriculture 95
Organic food labels 159
Organization for Economic Cooperation and Development (OECD) . . . 59, 73, 740
Organization for Security and Cooperation in Europe (OSCE) 740
Organization of American States (OAS) 445, 740
Organization of Petroleum Exporting Countries (OPEC) . . 73, 78, 113, 740
Organizations. *See* Associations and organizations; International organizations
Orinoco River 692
Orionids meteor shower 340
Orkney Islands 689, 847
Orlando, FL 71, 72, 88, 118, **601**, 614, 615
Ortega, Daniel. 670
Orthodox churches. *See* Eastern Orthodox churches
Oscars (Academy Awards) 19, 274-76
Osteoporosis 421
Oswald, Lee Harvey 446
Ottoman Empire 439, 653, 659, 660
Outlying areas, U.S. 591-93
(*see also* specific areas)
Owens, Jesse 444

P

Pacific Islanders. *See* Asian Americans
Pacific Ocean
Area, depth. 690
Crossings, notable 336
Discovery 683
Fishing 100
Islands 591-92, 593, 689
Map. 488
Ports, U.S. 76
U.S. coastline 423
Pacific/Remote Islands National Wildlife Refuge Complex 593
Padilla, José 453
Pain relief 421
Paine, Thomas 437
Painters, noted past. 178-81
Pakistan. **821-22**
Agriculture 97, 98, 99
Area, population 730, 731, 732, 821
Cell phone use 300
Flag, map 475, 484
Floods (2010, 2014) 673
Foreign aid to 738
Fossil fuel reserves. 112
Health expenditures 142
Heat waves (2015) 26, *197*
History 664, 666, 668, 669, 671
Internally displaced persons. 736
Languages 715, 821
Military strength 133
Muslim population. 706
Nuclear arms 738
Nuclear power 114
Refugees from/in 735
Taliban 14
Terrorism 672
UN peacekeeping mission 742
U.S. drone strikes. 21
U.S. military financing. 134
Palau 475, 488, 689, 731, 732, 733, **822**
Palestinian Territories **790-91**
Drinking water. 737
Internally displaced persons. 736
Peace accord with Israel (1993). 669
Refugees from 735
UN status 672
(*see also* Arab-Israeli conflict)
Palin, Sarah. 454
Palm Sunday. 699
Palmyra Atoll. 593
Pan Am Flight 103 bombing (1988). 450
Panama **822**
Area, population 732, 822
Flag, map 475, 479
Languages 822
Merchant fleet. 77
Treaties, U.S. (1903, 1978) . . 442, 449, 822
U.S. invasion (1989). 450, 670, 822
U.S. investment 78
U.S. relations suspended (1964) 446
Panama Canal. 442, 449, 503, 670, **822**

Panetta, Leon . . . 455
Pantelleria Island . . . 791
Paper
Exports, imports . . . 74
Invention . . . 649
Leading U.S. companies . . . 52
Measures . . . 365
Papua New Guinea . . 306, 475, 488, 689, 732, 736, 737, **822-23**
Paraguay 121, 306, 475, 480-81, 715, 732, **823**
Paralympics . . . 863
Paris Peace Conference (1919) . . . 661
Park, Inbee . . . 28
Parkinson's disease . . . 421
Parks. *See* Amusement parks; National parks/monuments
Parks, Rosa . . . 445, *446*
Parthenon . . . 648
Parthians . . . 649
Partial Test Ban Treaty . . . 446, 739
Passport regulations, U.S. . . . 38, 90
Pasteur, Louis . . . 658
Patents and copyrights . . . 289
Patient Protection and Affordable Care Act (PPACA). *See* Affordable Care Act
Patrick, Saint . . . 651
Patriot Act . . . 452, 455
Paul, Rand . . . 6, 7, 39, *198*
Peabody Awards . . . 270
Peace Corps, U.S. . . . 446, 547
Peace Prize, Nobel . . . 259, 261-62
Peale Atoll . . . 593
Peanuts . . . 96, 97
Pearl Harbor (1941) . . . 444, 663
Peary, Robert E. . . . 442, 684
Peas . . . 96
Peloponnesian Wars . . . 648
Pelosi, Nancy . . . 453
Pemba . . . 689, 840
Pendleton Act (1883) . . . 441
PEN/Faulkner Award . . . 270
Penghu Islands (Pescadores) . . . 840
Pennetta, Flavia . . . 31
Pennsylvania . . . **583-84**
Agriculture . . . 92, 94
Congressional representation 552, 557, 609
Crime, prisons, death penalty 117, 119, 120
Education . . . 380-83, 389-90
Elevations (high, low) . . . 423
Energy consumption . . . 111
Finances . . . 60
Governor . . . 37
Hazardous waste . . . 305
Health insurance coverage . . . 142
History (1683) . . . 436
Immigrant admissions . . . 619
Motor vehicles . . . 83, 84
Name origin, nickname . . . 426, 583
Oil production . . . 111
Population . . . 583, 601-02, 605, 606-07, 608, 611, 612, 640-41
Poverty rates . . . 49
Shoreline . . . 423
Taxes . . . 84, 379
Traveler spending . . . 86
Unemployment . . . 101
Weather . . . 312
ZIP and area codes . . . 640-41
Pennsylvania Academy of Fine Arts (1801) . . . 438
Pentagon Building . . . 435, 452, 670
Pentagon Papers (1971) . . . 448
Pentecostal churches . . . 697, 698, 704-05
People's Choice Awards . . . 273
Peptic ulcers . . . 157
Peres, Shimon . . . 669
Perfect games (baseball) . . . 917
Perigee of moon . . . 337, 353
Perihelion . . . 337
Periodic table of elements . . . 283
Perkins, Frances . . . 443
Perón, Juan . . . 665
Perot, H. Ross . . . 507, 509-38
Perpetual calendar . . . 356-57
Perry, Rick . . . 7
Perseids meteor shower . . . 337, 340
Pershing, John J. . . . 443
Persia. *See* Iran
Persian Gulf . . . 484, 689, 690
Persian Gulf Wars (1991, 2003-10) . . 140, 450, 669, 670
Black troops . . . 132
Casualties, U.S. forces . . . 138
Military awards . . . 136
Veteran population . . . 131
(*see also* Operation Iraqi Freedom/New Dawn)
Personal consumption, U.S. . . . 51
Personal income, U.S. *See* Income
Personalities, noted. *See* Noted personalities
Pertussis . . . 157
Peru . . . 715, **823-24**
Agriculture . . . 97, 98
Ancient civilizations . . . 649
Area, population . . . 730, 732, 823
Education . . . 383
Fishing . . . 100
Flag, map . . . 475, 480
Forests . . . 306
Fossil fuel reserves, exports . . . 112, 113
Gold production . . . 68
Health expenditures . . . 142
History . . . 667, 670
Internally displaced persons . . . 736
Languages . . . 823
Liberation of . . . 681
Prison population . . . 121
U.S. investment . . . 78
Pescadores (Penghu Islands) . . . 840
Peter the Great . . . 656, 657
Petraeus, David . . . 19, 453, 455, 456
Petroleum
Arab embargo (1973) . . . 448, 830
Crude oil prices (2014-15) . . . 14, 16
Exports, imports . . . 74, 109, 112, 113
First well (PA) (1859) . . . 440
Keystone Pipeline . . . 18
Leading U.S. companies . . . 53
Oil spills . . . 328, 450, 454, 455
Production, consumption, U.S. 109, 110, 111
Resources, reserves . . . 111, 112
Standard Oil dissolved (1911) . . . 442
Texas strike (1901) . . . 442
(*see also* Gasoline; OPEC)
PGA Championship . . . 29-30, 853, 953
Pharisees . . . 650
Pharmaceuticals. *See* Drugs, therapeutic
Philadelphia, PA . . . **601**
Air quality . . . 304
Airport traffic . . . 88
Buildings, tall . . . 721
Capital of U.S. (1790) . . . 438
Consumer Price Index . . . 46
Crime rates . . . 118
Geography . . . 696
Housing . . . 71, 72
Immigrant admissions . . . 619
Liberty Bell . . . 437, 439, 489
Library (1731) . . . 437
Newspaper (1783) . . . 438
Population . . . 614
Port traffic . . . 76
Streetlights (1757) . . . 437
Tides . . . 316
Weather . . . 309-11, 313
Philanthropists, noted past . . . 181-82
Philippines, Republic of the . . . **824**
Accession, U.S. (1898) . . . 442
Agriculture . . . 97, 98, 99
Area, population . . . 730, 732, 824
Cell phone use . . . 300
Fishing, aquaculture . . . 100
Flag, maps . . . 475, 485
Fossil fuel reserves . . . 112
Health expenditures . . . 142
Independence . . . 445, 664
Insurrection (1899) . . . 442
Internally displaced persons . . . 736
Islands, areas . . . 689
Languages . . . 715, 824
Muslim rebellion (1970s) . . . 667
Revolt (1986) . . . 668
Travel and tourism . . . 85
U.S. adoptions from . . . 166
U.S. immigrants from . . . 9, 619, 620
U.S. investment . . . 78
U.S. military financing . . . 134
U.S. troops in . . . 129
Wages, hourly . . . 734
Philosophers, noted . . . 187-88, 648, 657
Phoenicians . . . 647, 648
Phoenix, AZ . . . **601**
Air quality . . . 304
Airport traffic . . . 88
Consumer Price Index . . . 46
Geography . . . 696
Housing . . . 71, 72
Immigrant admissions . . . 619
Population . . . 614
Weather . . . 309-11, 313
Phosphorus (dietary) . . . 159, 160
Photography
Brownie camera (1900) . . . 442
Early example . . . *658*
Photographers, noted past . . . 178-81
Pulitzer Prizes . . . 262
Year in Pictures (2015) . . . *193-200, 809-16*
Physics . . . 259, 281, 284, 285-86
Physiology (Nobel prizes) . . . 260-61
Pierce, Franklin . . . 491, **495**, *495*, 504, 508
Pinochet, Augusto . . . 668, 670
Pirates . . . 438, 439
PISA scores . . . 383
Pistol champions (2015) . . . 979
Pitcairn Island . . . 848
Pittsburgh, PA . . . 46, 71, 72, 76, 118, 304, 309-11, 313, **601-02**, 614, 619, 696, 721
Pizarro, Francisco . . . 655, 683
Planets . . . **345-50**
Configurations . . . 337-40
Exploration of . . . 333-34
Extrasolar . . . 351
Morning, evening stars . . . 341
New definition of . . . 345
Superlatives . . . 344
(*see also* Space exploration)
Plano, TX . . . **602**, 614
Plantagenet, House of . . . 675
Plants . . . 291
Plastic surgery . . . 421
Platinum . . . 68
Plato . . . 648
Playing cards (odds) . . . 362
Plays. *See* Theater
Pledge of Allegiance . . . 472
PLO. *See* Palestinian Territories
Pluto (dwarf planet) . . 28, 279, 344, 345, **349**, *809*
Plymouth colony (1620) . . . 436
Poe, Edgar Allan . . . 439, 440
Poetry
Awards . . . 269, 270
Bradstreet book published (1678) . . . 436
Haiku invention . . . 656
Poets Laureate . . . 214, 450
Pulitzer prizes . . . 265-66
Poisons and poisoning
Animals, venomous . . . 291-92
Death rates . . . 171
First aid . . . 163
Poker odds . . . 362
Pol Pot . . . 667, 744
Poland . . . **824-25**
Agriculture . . . 97, 98
Area, population . . . 732, 824
Arms purchases . . . 133
Budget deficits . . . 59
Cell phone use . . . 300
Education . . . 383, 385
Flag, map . . . 475, 482-83
Foreign aid from . . . 738
Fossil fuel reserves . . . 112
Health expenditures . . . 142
History . . . 652, 656, 657, 669, 825
Languages . . . 715, 824
Motor vehicle production . . . 79
Prison population . . . 121
Rulers/presidents . . . 673, 679
Solidarity . . . 667
Taxes . . . 734
Travel and tourism . . . 85
U.S. ancestral claims . . . 621
U.S. immigrants from . . . 620
U.S. investment . . . 78
U.S. military financing . . . 134
U.S. missiles in . . . 453-54
Wages, hourly . . . 734
Polar exploration . . . 684-85
Poles of the earth . . . 352
Police shootings 4, 12, 14, 19, 21-22, 27, *199*
Polio . . . 421
Political leaders, noted past . . . 188-91
Political organizations . . . 409
Polk, James K. . . . 491, **495**, *495*, 504, 508
Pollution . . . 303-05, 447, 450
Ponce de León, Juan . . . 436, 683
Pony Express (1860) . . . 440
Ponzi schemes . . . 454
***Poor Richard's Almanack* (1732)** . . . 437
Popes . . . 17, 26, 30, 39, *197*, 671, 673, *673*, 700, 701
Population, U.S. . . . **605-45**
Age distribution . . . 610, 617
Ancestral roots . . . 621
Births, deaths . . . 164
Census (1790-2010) . . . 606-07
Census Act (1790) . . . 438
Center of (1790-2010) . . . 607
Children . . . 618
Cities . . . 614-15
Colonies (1630-1780) . . . 606
Congressional apportionment . . . 609
Counties . . . 615
Density (by state) . . . 608
Disability status, by age . . . 617
Drug and alcohol abuse . . . 145, 147
Educational attainment . . . 621
Ethnic, racial distribution . . . 610-12, 621
Foreign-born . . . 620
Gender distribution . . . 610, 617
Household size, type . . . 616, 617, 618
Immigrants . . . 619-20
Languages spoken at home . . . 620
Marriage, divorce . . . 164, 618
Metropolitan Statistical Areas . . . 613
Mobility . . . 616
Outlying areas . . . 591-93
Poverty rates . . . 48-49
Projections . . . 617
Regions . . . 605
Religious groups . . . 697-98

States 563-93, 605-08, 622-45
Urban/rural 616
Population, world **730-32**
Pork 94, 95, 97, 99
Pororshenko, Petro 673
Portland, OR 46, 71, 72, 76, 118, 309-11, 313, **602**, 614, 619, 696, 721
Ports, busiest U.S., world 76
Portugal **825**
Area, population 732, 825
Budget deficits 59
Education 383, 385
Financial crisis (2011) 673
Flag, map 475, 482
Foreign aid from 738
Foreign exchange rates 75
History 661, 662, 666
Languages 715, 825
Motor vehicle production 79
Taxes 734
Travel and tourism 85
U.S. ancestral claims 621
U.S. investment 78
U.S. troops in 129
Vacation days 89
Wages, hourly 734
Possessions, U.S. 591-93
Postage stamps 440
Postal cards (1873) 441
Postal Service, U.S. **366-67**, 436, 437, 447, 547, 622-45
Potatoes 96, 97
Potsdam Conference (1945) 444
Poultry products 94, 95, 96-97, 99
Poverty 48-49, 447
Powell, Colin 450
Preakness Stakes 24, 853, 967
Precipitation
Global 313, 315
U.S. 309-11
Wettest spots 315, 422
(*see also* Blizzards)
Pregnancy and childbirth. *See* Births
Prehistory 279, **646-47**
Presbyterian churches 410, 697-98, 704-05
Prescott, Samuel 437
Presidential elections **505-38**
Campaign-finance reform (2002, 2010) 452
Election 2012 6-7, 456
Election 2016 4, 21, 23, 25, 32, *198*
Electoral College 506
Party nominees (1856-2012) 507
Popular, electoral vote (1789-2012) 508
Returns (2008, 2012) 505, 509-38
Third-party/independent candidates 507
Voter turnout (1932-2012) 506
Presidents, U.S. **491-504**
Biographies 493-502
Birth, death dates 491
Burial sites 504
Cabinets 539-58
Children, number of 504
Congresses 491-92
Impeachments 503
Miscellaneous facts 503
Oath of office 469
Salary 539
Salutes, honors 135
Succession law 447, 469-70
Term limits 468
Vetoes 549
Vice presidents 491-92
Wives 504
(*see also* specific names)
Press. *See* Magazines; Newspapers
Pressure, measures of 365
Prices. *See* Consumer Price Indexes
Prime Meridian 360, 476
Prime numbers 362
Printer's measures 365
Prison population 119-21
Prisoners of war
Geneva Conventions 744
Prizes. *See* Awards, prizes
Professional organizations 418-19
Program for International Student Assessment (PISA) 383
Prohibition (1919, 1933) 443, *443*, 468
Prostate cancer 151, 152
Protein 158
Protestant churches **704-05**
Books of the Bible 703
Hate crime victims 123
Headquarters 409-10
Membership 697-98
Reformation 654
(*see also* specific denominations)
Providence, RI (1636) 436
Prussia. *See* Germany
Pseudonyms 241-42
Ptolemies 649
Ptolemy 649
Public debt 60
Public libraries. *See* Libraries
Public schools. *See* Education
Public-Private Investment Program (PPIP) 454
Puducherry Union Territory 786
Pueblo incident (1968) 447
Puerto Rico **592-93**
Accession (1898) 427, 442
Area 592, 689
Commonwealth balloting (1952, 1993) 445, 451
Congressional delegate 558
Crime rates 117, 118
Education 382
Elevations (high, low) 423
Governor 37
Hazardous waste 305
Immigrant admissions 619
Jones Act (1917) 443
Name origin, nickname 426
Nationalist movement violence 445
Population/projections 592, 732
Unemployment 101
U.S. troops in 129
Pulitzer Prizes 262-67
Pullman strike (1894) 441-42
Punic Wars 649
Pure Food and Drug Act (1906) 442
Purple Heart 136
Putin, Vladimir 668, 671, 673, 681, 827
Pyramids 647
Pyrenees 688

Q

Qatar 112, 129, 297, 306, 383, 475, 484, 732, 733, **825-26**
Quadrature (astronomical position) 337
Quantum physics 284
Quartering Act (1765) 437
Queen Anne's War (1702-13) 437
Quemoy (Kinmen) 689, 840
Quotes, notable 39
Quran 650, *650*, 706

R

Rabin, Yitzhak 669
Racism, pseudoscientific 659
Radio
Awards 270
Broadcast, first (1920) 443
Commercial stations 253
Journalists, noted past 184-85
Presidential broadcast, first (1922) 503
Transatlantic transmission, first (1901) 660
War of the Worlds scare (1938) 444
Ragtime (1899) 442
Railroads, U.S.
Accidents, deaths 23, 105, 321-22, *321*
Busiest Amtrak stations 88
Freight/mileage 77
Labor unrest (1877, 1894, 1950) 441-42, 445
Leading companies 53
Milestones 439, 440, 441
Railroads, world 321-22, 725
Rainfall. *See* Precipitation
Raleigh, NC 71, 309-11, **602**, 614, 615, 619, 696, 722
Raleigh, Sir Walter 436, 683
Ramayana 648
Rankin, Jeannette 443
Rap music 220-22
Rape 116-18, 121, 122
Reading tests 383
Reagan, Ronald *449*, 450, 491, **500-501**, *501*, 503, 504, 667
Presidential elections 449, 507, 508, 509-38
Real estate. *See* Housing
Realism 663
Reality TV 255
Reconstruction Era 441, 467
Reconstruction Finance Corp. (1932) 443
Recreation
Areas, national 432, 433
Personal expenditures 51
Prices indexes 45, 46
Recycling 305
Red Sea 690
Reform Party. *See* Perot, H. Ross
Reformation, Protestant 654
Refugees, world 4, 22, 24, 31, *194*, 735
Rehnquist, William 450, 453, 559
Reid, Richard 452
Religion **697-707**
Adherents, members 697-98
Associations and organizations 409-10
Bible 702, 703
Christian denominations 704-05
Great Awakening (1726, 1741) 437
History 650
Holy days 699-700
Major world 706-07
Religious figures 187-88
School prayer banned (1963) 446
Supreme Court ruling (2015) 38
(*see also* specific faiths, denominations)
Rembrandt 655
Renaissance 653-54, 728
Renewable energy 109, 110, 115
Reno, Janet 451
Reno, NV 71, 309-11, **602**, 615, 696
Republican Party
Congressional members 548-49
First presidential nominee (1856) 440
Formed (1854) 440
Midterm elections (2014) 12, 457
Presidential, V.P. candidates (1856-2012) 507
(*see also* specific candidates)
Reservoirs, major **726-27**
Réunion Island 689, 776
Revere, Paul 437
Revolutionary War. *See* American Revolution
Rhode Island **584**
Agriculture 92, 94
Coastline 423
Congressional representation 552, 557, 609
Constitution (1647) 436
Crime, prisons, death penalty 117, 119, 120
Education 380-83, 389-90
Elevations (high, low) 423
Energy consumption 111
Finances 60
Governor 37
Hazardous waste 305
Health insurance coverage 142
Immigrant admissions 619
Motor vehicles 83, 84
Name origin, nickname 426, 584
Population 584, 605, 606-07, 608, 611, 612, 641
Poverty rates 49
Slavery outlawed (1774) 437
Taxes 84, 379
Unemployment 101
Weather 312
ZIP and area codes 641
Rhythm and blues 220-22
Rice 96-99
Rice, Condoleezza 453
Richest individuals 48
Richmond, VA 71, 72, 309-11, **602**, 615, 696
Ride, Sally 449
Riesman, David 445
Rig Veda 647
Right ascension (astronomical position) 337
Right to die cases 449, 452, 453
Riis, Jacob 441, *441*
Ring of Fire volcanoes 685
Rio Grande 693
Riots
Detroit (1943, 1967) 444, 447
Ferguson (MO) (2014-15) 12, 28, 457, *457*
Haymarket (1886) 441
Los Angeles (1965, 1992) 447, 450
New York City (1863, 1943) 440, 444
Newark (NJ) (1967) 447
Springfield (1908) 442
Rivers 422, 432, **691-93**
(*see also* Mississippi River)
Riverside, CA 46, 71, 72, 118, 304, **602**, 614, 619
Roads
Interstate system (1956) 445
Speed limits (1995) 451
Roanoke Island "lost colony" (1585-90) 436
Robbery 116-18, 121, 122
Roberts, John G., Jr. 38, 39, 453, 559
Robinson, Jackie 445
Rock and roll
Concerts, top-grossing (1985-2014) 254
Hall of Fame 220-22
Live Aid (1985) 450
Noted artists 220-22
Rockefeller, Nelson 448
Rodeo 979
***Roe v. Wade* (1973)** 448, 561
Rogers, Will 444
Roller coasters 89, 441
Roman Catholicism 704-05
Adherents (U.S., world) 697, 698
Books of the Bible 703
Cardinals 702
Hate crime victims 123
Headquarters (U.S.) 409
Hierarchy 700
Liberalization 665
Popes 17, 26, 30, 39, *197*, 671, 673, *673*, 700, 701
Saints 445
Sexual abuse scandal 26, 452, 671
Vatican City 476, 850
Roman numerals 363
Romania **826**
Agriculture 98
Area, population 732, 826
Education 383
Flag, map 475, 483
Fossil fuel reserves 112
History 662, 667

Languages . . . 715, 826
Motor vehicle production . . . 79
Nuclear power . . . 114
U.S. military financing . . . 134
Romans, ancient
Architecture . . . 728
Fall of Rome . . . 651
Gods and goddesses . . . 650
Historical figures/rulers . . . 674
Leading figures/rulers . . . 649
Measures . . . 363
Rome founded . . . 649
Romanticism . . . 657-58
Romney, Mitt . . . 456, 505, 506, 509-38
Roosevelt, Franklin D. . . . 491, **498-99**, *498*, 503, 504, 507, 508, 664
Elections . . . 443, 444
Memorial (DC) . . . 435
New Deal (1933) . . . 443, 663
World War II (1939, 1941, 1945) . . . 444
Roosevelt, Theodore . . . 442, 491, **497**, *497*, 503, 504, 507, 508
Rose Bowl . . . 877-78
Rose Island . . . 591
Rosenberg, Julius and Ethel . . . 445
Ross, Betsy . . . 471
Ross Dependency . . . 818
Ross, Nellie Tayloe . . . 443
Rotary Club (1905) . . . 442
Rouhani, Hassan . . . 673
Rousseau, Jean-Jacques . . . 656, 657
Royalty . . . 24, **674-82**, *815*, 846
Rubio, Marco . . . 6, 7, 39, *198*
Ruby, Jack . . . 446
Ruby Ridge siege (1992) . . . 450
Rumsfeld, Donald . . . 453
Rural Credits Act (1916) . . . 443
Russia . . . **826-27**
Agriculture . . . 97, 98, 99
Area, population . . . 730, 731, 732, 826
Arms sales . . . 134
Budget deficits . . . 59
Carbon dioxide emissions . . . 302
Cell phone use . . . 300
Chechnya revolt . . . 668
Computer/Internet use . . . 294, 297
Crimea annexation . . . 673
Education . . . 383
Energy production, consumption . . . 109
Fishing . . . 100
Flag, map . . . 475, 483, 484-85
Forests . . . 306
Fossil fuel reserves, exports . . . 112, 113
Gold production . . . 68
Gold reserves . . . 733
Gross domestic product . . . 733
Health expenditures . . . 142
History . . . 826-27
Internally displaced persons . . . 736
Islands, areas . . . 689
Languages . . . 715, 826
Leaders . . . 673, 681
Military strength . . . 133
Mortality rate by cause . . . 736
Motor vehicle production . . . 79
NATO treaty . . . 669
Nemtsov death (2015) . . . *195*
Nuclear arms . . . 454, 738
Nuclear power . . . 114
Prison population . . . 121
Refugees from/in . . . 735
Soviet Union breakup . . . 668
Spaceflight . . . 329-32, 333
Spy swap with U.S. (2010) . . . 455
Terrorist bombings (2004, 2010, 2013) 670
Travel and tourism . . . 85
U.S. ancestral claims . . . 621
U.S. investment . . . 78
(*see also* Soviet Union)
Russian Empire (pre-1917)
Alaska (1741, 1867) . . . 437, 441
Congress of Vienna . . . 657
Crimean War (1853-56) . . . 659
Russian Revolution (1905-06) . . . 660
Russian Revolution (1917) . . . 661
Tsars and rulers . . . 653, 656, 657, 661, 681
U.S. immigrants from . . . 9
Russian Federation. *See* Russia
Russian Orthodox churches. *See* Eastern Orthodox churches
Russian Revolution (1917) . . . 661
Rwanda . . . 475, 487, 669, 715, 732, 733, 735, **827-28**
Ryan, Paul . . . 4, 32, 455, 456
Ryder Cup . . . 954
Rye production . . . 96

S

Saba Island . . . 818
Sacco-Vanzetti case (1920) . . . 443
Sacks, Oliver . . . 36, *816*
Sacramento, CA . . . 71, 72, 118, 304, **602**, 614, 619, 696
Sadat, Anwar . . . 449, 667, 668
Sadducees . . . 650
Sadler, Anthony . . . *815*
Safavids . . . 654
St. Augustine, FL (1565) . . . 436
St. Barthélemy . . . 732, 777
St. Croix Island . . . **593**
St. Eustatius Island . . . 818
St. Helena Island . . . 689, 732, 848
St. John Island . . . **593**
St. Kitts and Nevis . . . 475, 479, 731, 732, 733, **828**
St. Lawrence Seaway (1959) . . . 446
St. Louis, MO . . . **602**
Buildings, tall . . . 721
Consumer Price Index . . . 46
Crime rates . . . 118
Geography . . . 696
Housing . . . 71, 72
Immigrant admissions . . . 619
Population . . . 614
Port traffic . . . 76
Weather . . . 309-11, 313
St. Lucia . . . 475, 479, 732, 733, **828**
St. Martin . . . 732, 777
St. Paul, MN . . . 46, 71, 72, 88, 118, 304, **602-03**, 614, 619, 696
St. Petersburg, FL . . . 46, 71, 72, 118, 316, **603**, 614, 619
St. Pierre and Miquelon . . . 732, 777
St. Thomas Island . . . **593**
St. Valentine's Day Massacre (1929) . . . 443
St. Vincent and the Grenadines . . . 475, 479, 732, 733, **828-29**
Saints. *See* specific names in inverted form
Saladin . . . 652
Salem (MA) witchcraft trials (1674, 1691) 436
Salem (MA) witchcraft trials (1674, 1692) . . . 437, *437*
Salinger, J.D. . . . 445
Salmonella . . . 157
SALT (1972, 1979) . . . 448, 667, 739
Same-sex marriage. *See* Marriage
Samoa . . . 475, 488, 689, 732, 733, **829**
Samoa, American. *See* American Samoa
San Antonio, TX . . . 71, 72, 118, 309, 311, **603**, 614, 615, 619, 696, 722
San Bernardino, CA . . . 71, 72, 118, 304, **603**, 615, 619
San Diego, CA . . . **603**
Buildings, tall . . . 722
Consumer Price Index . . . 46
Crime rate . . . 118
Geography . . . 696
Housing . . . 71, 72
Immigrant admissions . . . 619
Population . . . 614
Tides . . . 316
Weather . . . 309, 311
San Francisco, CA . . . **603**
Air mileage to other cities . . . 91
Air quality . . . 304
Airport traffic . . . 88
Buildings, tall . . . 721
Consumer Price Index . . . 46
Crime rates . . . 118
Earthquakes (1906, 1989) . . . 325, 442, *442*, 450
Geography . . . 696
Housing . . . 71, 72
Immigrant admissions . . . 619
Population . . . 614
Preparedness Day parade bombing (1916) . . . 443
Tides . . . 316
Weather . . . 309-11, 313
San Jose, CA . . . 46, 71, 72, **603**, 614, 619, 696
San Marino . . . 475, 482, 731, 732, 733, **829**
San Miguel de Guadalupe (1526) . . . 436
Sand Creek Massacre (1864) . . . 440
Sanders, Bernie . . . 6, 7, 39, *198*
Sandusky, Jerry . . . 456
Sandy (hurricane) . . . 456
Sandy Hook Elementary School . . . 456
Santa Ana, CA . . . 71, 304, **603**, 614, 619
São Tomé and Principe . . . 475, 487, 732, 733, **829**
Sardinia . . . 482, 673, 689, 791
Sarkozy, Nicolas . . . 671, 673
Sassanians . . . 649
SAT scores . . . 390
Satellites, space. *See* Space exploration
Saturn (planet) . . . 344, 345, **347**
Morning, evening stars . . . 341
Position by month . . . 337-40
Saudi Arabia . . . **830**
Agriculture . . . 99
Area, population . . . 732, 830
Arms purchases . . . 133
Carbon dioxide emissions . . . 302
Energy production . . . 109
Flag, map . . . 475, 484
Fossil fuel reserves, exports . . . 112, 113
Gross domestic product . . . 733
Health expenditures . . . 142
History . . . 666
Language . . . 715, 830
Military strength . . . 133
Muslim population . . . 706
News (2015) . . . 16
Persian Gulf War (1991) . . . 830
Trade . . . 73
Travel and tourism . . . 85
U.S. installation bombings . . . 451
U.S. investment . . . 78
U.S. troops in . . . 129
Water supply . . . 306
Savings and loan crisis (1989) . . . 450
Savings bonds, U.S. . . . 66
Saxe-Coburg and Gotha, House of . . . 675
Saxons . . . 675
Scalia, Antonin . . . 38, 450, 559
Scandinavia . . . 652
(*see also* Denmark; Norway; Sweden)
Schiavo, Terri . . . 453
Scholastic Aptitude Testing (SAT) Program . . . 390
School shootings, attacks. *See* Gun violence
Schools. *See* Colleges and universities; Education; High schools
Schwarzenegger, Arnold . . . 452
Science and technology . . . **279-93**
Awards . . . 259-61
Glossary . . . 280-81
Inventions, discoveries . . . 279, 285-89
News (2015) . . . 279, *809*
Patents . . . 289
Scientific Revolution (1500-1700) . . . 655
Scientists, noted past . . . 192, 201
Test scores . . . 383
Scleroderma . . . 421
Scopes trial (1925) . . . 443
Scorpions, venomous . . . 292
Scotland . . . 482, 621, 669, 676, **847**
Scottsdale, AZ . . . 71, 72, 304, **603**, 615
Scripps Howard Awards . . . 270
Sculptors, noted past . . . 178-81
Seabiscuit . . . 444
Seas. *See* Oceans and seas
Seashores, national . . . 432
Seasons . . . 352
Seattle, WA . . . **603-06**
Air quality . . . 304
Airport traffic . . . 88
Buildings, tall . . . 721
Consumer Price Index . . . 46
Crime rates . . . 118
Geography . . . 696
Housing . . . 71, 72
Immigrant admissions . . . 619
Minimum wage increase . . . 457
Population . . . 614, 615
Port traffic . . . 76
Tides . . . 316
Weather . . . 309-11, 313
Sebelius, Kathleen . . . 457
Secret Service, U.S. . . . 17, 19, 457, 547
Secretariat . . . 448
Securities. *See* Bonds; Stocks
Securities and Exchange Commission . . . 443, 547
Security breaches. *See under* Internet
Segregation. *See* Desegregation
Selective Service System. *See* Draft, U.S.
Selenium (dietary) . . . 160
Seleucids . . . 649
Self-employment, Social Security benefits . . . 369
Seminole War (1835) . . . 439
Senate. *See* Congress, U.S.
Senegal . . . 475, 486, 715, 732, 736, **830**
September 11, 2001, terrorist attacks . . . 452, 670
Serbia . . . **831**
Agriculture . . . 98
Area, population . . . 732, 831
Education . . . 383
Flag, map . . . 475, 483
Fossil fuel reserves . . . 112
History . . . 668
Internally displaced persons . . . 736
Languages . . . 715, 831
Motor vehicle production . . . 79
Refugees from . . . 735
(*see also* Kosovo)
Seven Years' War . . . 139
Sewing machine (1846) . . . 440
Sexual behavior . . . 167-68, 169, 445
Seychelles . . . 475, 689, 732, 733, **831**
Shakespeare Library, Folger (DC) . . . 434
Sharif, Omar . . . 36, *816*
Shays's Rebellion (1787) . . . 438
Sheep . . . 95, 96-97
Shepard, Matthew . . . 452
Sherman Antitrust Act (1890) . . . 441
Sherman, William Tecumseh . . . 440
Shetland Islands . . . 689, 847
Shigellosis . . . 157
Shiites. *See* Islam

Shinseki, Eric . . . 457
Shintoism . . . 698
Ships and shipping
Busiest ports (U.S., world) . . . 76
Disasters. . . . 26, 320-21, 442
Merchant fleets. . . . 77
Speed measurement . . . 365
Shooting (sport) . . . 979
Siam . . . 660
(*see also* Thailand)
Sicily . . . 482, 689, 791
Sidereal day, year, time . . . 341, 352
SIDS (Sudden Infant Death Syndrome) . . 421
Sierra Leone . . . 475, 486, 732, 736, 737, **832**
Sign language . . . 713
Signs and symbols
Chemical elements . . . 282-83
Manual alphabet . . . 713
Zodiac . . . 355
Sikhism . . . 654, 698, **707**
Sikkim . . . 785
Silver . . . 68
Silver Star . . . 136
Simpson, O. J. . . . 451
Sinclair, Upton . . . 442
Singapore . . . **832**
Area, population . . . 731, 732, 832
Education . . . 383
Flag, map . . . 475, 485
Foreign exchange rates . . . 75
Gross domestic product . . . 733
Languages . . . 832
Merchant fleet . . . 77
Prison population . . . 121
Trade . . . 73
Travel and tourism . . . 85
U.S. investment . . . 78
U.S. troops in . . . 129
Wages, hourly . . . 734
Single-parent households . . . 618
Sino-Japanese War . . . 659
Sint Maarten . . . 732, 818
Sioux Indian War (1876) . . . 441
Sjögren's syndrome . . . 421
Skarlatos, Alek . . . *815*
Skating
Figure . . . 859, 972
Speed . . . 861-63
Skeleton (sledding) . . . 860
Skiing
Alpine World Cup . . . 972-73
Olympics . . . 856-60, 861
Skin diseases . . . 151, 421
Skye, Isle of . . . 689
Skylab . . . 330, 448
Slavery
Abolished
Illinois (1824) . . . 439
New England (1774, 1783) . . . 437, 438
13th Amendment (1865) . . . 440, 467
Abolitionist raids (1856, 1859) . . . 440
Ban defeated (1784) . . . 438
Census data . . . 609
Compromise of 1850 . . . 440
Dred Scott decision (1857) . . . 440, 560
Emancipation Proclamation (1863) . . . 440
Importation outlawed (1808) . . . 439
Introduced into America (1619) . . . 436
Kansas-Nebraska Act (1854) . . . 440
Missouri Compromise (1820) . . . 439
New World presence . . . 655
Rebellions (1712, 1739, 1811, 1831) . . 437, 439
Slavic states . . . 652
Slovakia . . . **832-33**
Area, population . . . 732, 832
Budget deficits . . . 59
Education . . . 383, 385
Flag, map . . . 475, 483
Foreign aid from . . . 738
Formation of (1993) . . . 669
Fossil fuel reserves . . . 112
Languages . . . 715, 832
Motor vehicle production . . . 79
Nuclear power . . . 114
Taxes . . . 734
Travel and tourism . . . 85
Wages, hourly . . . 734
Slovenia . . . 59, 79, 112, 114, 383, 385, 475, 482, 668, 732, 734, 738, **833**
Small Business Administration . . . 547
Small solar system bodies . . . 345, 350
Smart, Elizabeth . . . 126
Smith, John . . . 436, 683
Smith, Sam . . . 19
Smithsonian Institution . . . 435
Smoking
Cancer link . . . 151
Heart disease . . . 155
Prevalence . . . 146
Tobacco industry settlement (1998) . . . 452
U.S. government reports (1957, 1988) 446, 450
Smythe Trophy . . . 944-45
Snakes, venomous . . . 163, 291-92
SNAP (Supplemental Nutritional Assistance Program) . . . 92
Snowboarding . . . 861
Snowden, Edward . . . 456
Snowfall (blizzards) . . . 308, 323, 441
Sobell, Morton . . . 445
Soccer . . . 4, 15, 26, 28, *812*, 853, 866, 889, **948-51**
Social Darwinism . . . 659
Social networking . . . 298
Social reformers, noted past . . . 201-02
Social scientists, noted past . . . 183-84
Social Security . . . **368-74**
Act passed (1935) . . . 444
Administration . . . 547
Bankruptcy rescue (1983) . . . 449
Benefits . . . 368-74, 376
Domestic workers . . . 370
Expenditures . . . 58
Tax revenues . . . 57, 371, 734
(*see also* Medicare)
Social service organizations . . . 407-08
Socialism . . . 658, 666
Societies. *See* Associations and organizations
Society Islands . . . 488, 776
Socrates . . . 648
Sodium (dietary) . . . 159
Softball . . . 889
Software, computer . . . 53-54
Solar day . . . 352
Solar energy . . . 109, 115, 336
Solar system . . . **344-51**
(*see also* Planets)
Soldier's Medal . . . 136
Solheim Cup . . . 954
Solid waste generation, recycling . . . 305
Solidarity (Poland) . . . 667, 825
Solomon Islands 306, 475, 488, 732, 733, **833**
Solstices . . . 339, 340, 352
Somalia . . . **833-34**
Area, population . . . 732, 833
Flag, map . . . 475, 486-87
Gross domestic product . . . 733
Internally displaced persons . . . 736
Languages . . . 715, 833
Mortality rate by cause . . . 736
Peacekeeping operation (1992-94) . . . 450, 451, 669
Refugees from . . . 735
Somerset Island . . . 689
Sorghum . . . 96, 97
SORT (Moscow Treaty) . . . 452, 739
Sotloff, Steven . . . 457
Sotomayor, Sonia . . . 38, 454, 559
Sound . . . 285, 365
Sousa, John Philip . . . 442
Souter, David . . . 450, 454
South Africa . . . **834-35**
Agriculture . . . 97, 98, 99
Apartheid . . . 668, 669, 834
Area, population . . . 732, 834
Boer War (1899-1902) . . . 834
Budget deficits . . . 59
Carbon dioxide emissions . . . 302
Cell phone use . . . 300
Flag, map . . . 475, 487
Foreign aid to . . . 738
Fossil fuel reserves . . . 112
Gasoline prices . . . 110
Gold production . . . 68
Health expenditures . . . 142
Languages . . . 715, 834
Motor vehicle production . . . 79
Nuclear arms abandonment . . . 738
Nuclear power . . . 114
Refugees in . . . 735
Securities held by U.S. . . . 64
Self-government (1910) . . . 660
Travel and tourism . . . 85
U.S. investment . . . 78
U.S. sanctions (1986) . . . 450
U.S. troops in . . . 129
South America
Agriculture . . . 97, 98, 99
Elevations (highest, lowest) . . . 695
Explorations . . . 683
Fossil fuel reserves . . . 112
Lakes . . . 694
Liberation wars, leaders . . . 681
Map . . . 480-81
Mountain peaks . . . 687
Pre-Inca culture . . . 652
Rivers . . . 692
Temperature/precipitation extremes . . . 315
Trade . . . 73
Travel and tourism . . . 87
Volcanoes . . . 685, 686
Waterfalls . . . 695
(*see also* Latin America; specific countries)
South Carolina . . . **584-85**
Agriculture . . . 92, 94
Coastline . . . 423
Congressional representation 552, 557, 609
Crime, prisons, death penalty 117, 119, 120
Education . . . 380-83, 389-90
Elevations (high, low) . . . 423
Energy consumption . . . 111
Finances . . . 60
Governor . . . 37
Hazardous waste . . . 305
Health insurance coverage . . . 142
Immigrant admissions . . . 619
Motor vehicles . . . 83, 84
Name origin, nickname . . . 426, 584
Nullification (1828) . . . 439
Population . . . 584, 605, 606-07, 608, 611, 612, 641
Poverty rates . . . 49
Taxes . . . 84, 379
Unemployment . . . 101
Weather . . . 312
ZIP and area codes . . . 641
South China Sea . . . 690
South Dakota . . . **585**
Agriculture . . . 92, 94
Congressional representation 552, 557, 609
Crime, prisons, death penalty 117, 119, 120
Education . . . 380-83, 389-90
Elevations (high, low) . . . 423
Energy consumption . . . 111
Finances . . . 60
Governor . . . 37
Hazardous waste . . . 305
Health insurance coverage . . . 142
Immigrant admissions . . . 619
Motor vehicles . . . 83, 84
Name origin, nickname . . . 426, 585
Oil production . . . 111
Population . . . 585, 605, 606-07, 608, 611, 612, 641
Poverty rates . . . 49
Taxes . . . 84
Unemployment . . . 101
Weather . . . 312
ZIP and area codes . . . 641
South Georgia Islands . . . 848
South Korea. *See* Korea, South
South Pole . . . 352, 684-85
South Sandwich Islands . . . 848
South Sudan . . . 29, 133, 475, 486, 673, 732, 735, 736, 737, 738, 742, **835**
South Yemen. *See* Yemen
Southern Ocean . . . 690
Soviet Union . . . **826-27**
Berlin blockade (1948) . . . 445
Breakup (1991) . . . 668
Chernobyl disaster (1986) . . . 328
Cold War . . . 444-45, 664
Cuban missile crisis (1962) . . . 446
Glasnost and perestroika . . . 667
History . . . 662, 663, 667, 826-27
Hungarian revolt (1956) . . . 665
Leaders . . . 681
Nixon visit (1972) . . . 448
Space exploration . . . 665
Spaceflight . . . 329-32
Summit talks (1972, 1985) . . . 448, 450
U-2 incident . . . 446
U.S. immigrants from . . . 620
World War II . . . 444, 663
(*see also* Arms control; Russia; Russian Empire; specific former republics)
Soybeans . . . 96, 97
Space exploration . . . **329-34**
Hubble Telescope . . . 330-32, 341, 670
Human spaceflight . . . 329-33, 446, 449
International Space Station . . . 333, 670
Lunar/planetary science missions (U.S.) . . . 279, 333-34
Mars missions (1976, 2008, 2012) . . . 449, 456, 671, 673
Moonwalk, U.S. (1969) . . 329, 447, *448*, 666
Privatization . . . 333, 336
Recent news (2014-15) . . . 13, 28, 32, *809*
Skylab . . . 448
Space shuttle disasters (1986, 2003) . . 330, 332, 447, 450, 452, 671
Space shuttle retirement . . . 333, 455, 673
Sputnik (1957) . . . 665
U.S. expenditures . . . 58
U.S. policy shift . . . 333, 454
U.S.-Russian space linkup (1995) 451, 670
Spain . . . **835-36**
Agriculture . . . 97, 98
Area, population . . . 732, 835
Budget deficits . . . 59
Carbon dioxide emissions . . . 302
Computer/Internet use . . . 294, 297
Consumer price changes . . . 733
Education . . . 383, 385
Financial crisis (2012) . . . 673
Fishing . . . 100
Flag, map . . . 475, 482
Foreign aid from . . . 738

Foreign exchange rates, 75
Forests, 306
Fossil fuel reserves, 112
Gasoline prices, 110
Gross domestic product, 733
Health expenditures, 142
History, 436, 437, 652, 654, 663, 666
Languages, 715, 835
Motor vehicle production, 79
Nuclear power, 114
Rulers, royal family, 680-81
Securities held by U.S., 64
Taxes, 734
Terrorist bombings (2004), 670
Travel and tourism, 85, 86, 87
U.S. investment, 78
U.S. troops in, 129
Vacation days, 89
Wages, hourly, 734
Spanish Civil War (1936-39), 663
Spanish Sahara, 667
Spanish Succession, War of the (1701-14), 139
Spanish-American War (1898), 138, 140, 442, 659
Spectrum, colors of, 285
Speech disorders, 421
Speed skating. *See* Skating
Spelling, 709
Spelling Bee, National, 708
Sphinx, Great (Egypt), *647*
Spiders, venomous, 292
Spieth, Jordan, 22, 26, 853
Spinal cord injuries, 421
Spingarn Medal, 271
Spinning jenny, 656
Spinoza, Baruch de, 656
Spiritism, 698
Spitz, Mark, 448
Sports, **853-979**
Directory, 419-20
Highlights (2015), *810-12*, 853
Memorable Super Bowls, 854
PED scandals, 453, 455, 456
Personalities, noted, 202-07
(*see also* specific sports)
Spring (season), 338, 352
Sprint Cup (auto racing), 960
Sputnik (1957), 665
Sri Lanka, 16, 98, 475, 484, 669, 671, 689, 715, 732, 735, 736, **836**
SSI (Supplemental Security Income), 371
Stadiums and arenas
Baseball, 931
Basketball, 939
Football, 905
Hockey, 946
Stagecoaches (1785), 438
Stalin, Joseph, 662, 664, 681
Stamp Act (1765), 437
Stamps. *See* Postage stamps
Standard Oil Co. (1911), 442
Standard & Poor's 500 Index, 64
Standard time, 359, 360
Stanley Cup, 26, *811*, 853, 943-44
Stanton, Elizabeth Cady, 440
Stars
Constellations, 342
Morning, evening, 341
"Star-Spangled Banner", 439, 489
START (1991, 1996, 2010), 451, 454, 739
State, Department of, **540**
Created, 438
First woman secretary, 451
Stateless persons, 735
States, U.S., **563-93**
Abbreviations, postal, 367
Agriculture, 92, 93-94
Area codes, telephone, 622-45
Area, rank, 422, 424
Capitals, 424
Coastline, in miles, 423
Congressional representation, 551-58, 609
Counties, largest, 615
Crime, prisons, death penalty 117, 119, 120
Divorce rates, 164
Education, 380-83, 389-90
Electoral votes, 505, 506
Elevations (high, low), 423
Energy consumption, production, 111
Famous natives, 563-93
Finances, 60-61
Geographic centers, 425
Geographic superlatives, 422
Governors, 37
Hazardous waste, 305
Health insurance coverage, 142
Immigrant admissions, 619
Inland water area, 424
Motor vehicles, 83-84
Name origins, 426
Nicknames, 563-93
Original thirteen, 424
Population, 563-93, 605-08, 611, 612, 622-45
Poverty rates, 49
Presidential elections, 505-38
Settlement dates, 424
Statehood dates, 424, 425
Taxes, 84, 377-79
Tourist attractions, 563-93
Traveler spending, 86
Unemployment insurance, 101
Weather, 312
ZIP codes, 622-45
Statue of Liberty, 441, 450, **490**
Steamships (1807, 1819), 438
Steel
Exports, imports, 74
Strikes (1892, 1946, 1952, 1959), 441, 444, 445, 446
Steinbeck, John, 444
Stem-cell research, 452, 453
Stepchildren, 618
Stevens, John Paul, 455
Stewart, Breanna, *811*
Stewart Island, 689, 818
Stewart, Jon, *813*
Stocks
Leading U.S. companies, 52
Market crashes (1929, 1987, 2011), 443, 450, 662, 667
Mutual funds, 66-67
Trading scandals (1986, 1988), 450
U.S. markets, 64-65
(*see also* Dow Jones Industrial Average)
Stockton, CA, **604**, 614
Stoics, 649
Stone, Spencer, 39, *815*
Storms
Classifications, names, 308, 312
Notable, 21, 322-23, *453*
Watches, warnings, advisories, 308
Stowe, Harriet Beecher, 440
Strategic Arms Limitation Talks (SALT), 448, 667, 739
Strikes
Air traffic controllers (1981), 449
Baseball players (1994-95), 451
Boston police (1919), 443
Coal miners (1922, 1946), 443, 444
NFL (1982), 449
Number, days idle (1950-2014), 108
Railroad workers (1877, 1894, 1950), 441-42, 445
Shoeworkers (1860), 440
Steel workers (1892, 1946, 1952, 1959), 441, 444, 445, 446
Women weavers (1824), 439
Strokes
Deaths, 171
Diabetes-related, 154
Help organizations, 421
Warning signs, 155
Stuart, House of, 675
Students. *See* Colleges and universities; Education; High schools
Submarines
Nautilus (1954, 1958), 445, 446
Warfare (1917), 443, 661
Sub-Saharan Africa. *See* Africa
Sudan, **836-37**
Area, population, 732, 836
Flag, map, 475, 486
Foreign aid to, 738
Fossil fuel reserves, 112
Health expenditures, 142
History, 671
Internally displaced persons, 736
Languages, 715, 836
Military strength, 133
Muslim population, 706
Refugees from/in, 735
UN peacekeeping mission, 742
Sudden Infant Death Syndrome (SIDS), 421
Suez Canal, 658, 659, 772
Suffrage
Men's (1818-21), 439
Women's (1869, 1920), 441, 443, 468
Sufism, 651, 653, 706
Sugar
Exports, imports, 74
Food label claims, 159
Production, 96
Sugar Act (1764), 437
Sugar Bowl, 878
Suicide, 170, 171
Suicide bombings. *See* Terrorism
Sulfur dioxide emissions, 303
Sullivan Trophy, 978
Sumatra, 689
Sumerians, 647
Summer Solstice, 339, 352
Sun, 345, **350-51**
Eclipses (2016-35), 337, 343
Solar energy, 109, 115, 336
Ultraviolet index, 314
Sun Yat-sen, 660
Sunnis. *See* Islam
Sunny Isles Beaches, FL, 721
Sunspots, 351
Super Bowl, 18-19, 447, *810*, 853, 854, 890-91, 893-94
Superior, Lake, 694
Superlative statistics, U.S., 422
Supplemental Nutritional Assistance Program (SNAP), 92
Supplemental Security Income (SSI), 371
Supreme Court, U.S., **559-62**
Created (1789), 438
Decisions, notable, 560-62
2014-15 term, 4, 25, 38, *200*
History, 560
Justices, 559-60
Packing plan defeated (1937), 444
Surgical transplants, 144
Suriname, 306, 476, 480, 731, 732, **837**
Surrealism, 662
Surveillance programs, 24-25, 453, 454, 456
Svalbard Islands, 689, 820
Swains Island, 591
Swaziland, 112, 476, 487, 732, 736, **837-38**
Sweden, **838**
Area, population, 732, 838
Budget deficits, 59
Computer/Internet use, 297
Consumer price changes, 733
Education, 383, 385
Flag, map, 476, 482-83
Foreign aid from, 738
Foreign exchange rates, 75
Forests, 306
Gross domestic product, 733
History, 656
Languages, 715, 838
Motor vehicle production, exports, 79
Nuclear power, 114
Refugees in, 735
Rulers, royal family, 680
Securities held by U.S., 64
Taxes, 734
Travel and tourism, 85, 86
Unemployment rates, 734
U.S. ancestral claims, 621
U.S. immigrants from, 620
U.S. investment, 78
Vacation days, 89
Wages, hourly, 734
Sweet potato production, 96
Swimming and diving, 448, 866-70, 974
Switzerland, **838**
Alps, 688
Area, population, 732, 838
Budget deficits, 59
Computer/Internet use, 297
Consumer price changes, 733
Education, 383, 385
Flag, map, 476, 482
Foreign aid from, 738
Foreign exchange rates, 75
Gold reserves, 733
Gross domestic product, 733
Languages, 715, 838
Nuclear power, 114
Refugees in, 735
Securities held by U.S., 64
Taxes, 734
Trade, 73
Travel and tourism, 85, 86
U.S. immigrants from, 620
U.S. investment, 78
Vacation days, 89
Wages, hourly, 734
Symbols. *See* Signs and symbols
Syphilis, 157
Syria, **838-39**
Area, population, 732, 838
Civil war, 4, 29, 31, 33, 672
Flag, map, 476, 484
Foreign aid to, 738
Fossil fuel reserves, 112
Internally displaced persons, 736
ISIS, 4, 672-73
Languages, 715, 838
Military strength, 133
Muslim population, 706
Refugees from/in, 735
UN peacekeeping mission, 742

T

Taft, William Howard, 491, **497-98**, *497*, 503, 504, 507, 508
Taft-Hartley Act (1947), 445
Tahiti, 488, 689, 776-77
Taiwan, **839-40**
Agriculture, 97
Aquaculture, 100
Area, population, 689, 731, 732, 839
Arms purchases, 133

Carbon dioxide emissions 302
Education 383
Elections (2014) 13
Flag, map 476, 485
Foreign exchange rates 75
Gasoline prices. 110
Languages 839
Military strength 133
Motor vehicle production 79
Nuclear power 114
Securities held by U.S. 64
Trade 73
Travel and tourism 85, 86
U.S. immigrants from 620
U.S. investment 78
Wages, hourly. 734
Taj Mahal 654
Tajikistan 112, 476, 484, 715, 732, **840**
Talmud 650
Tambora, Mount 685
Tampa, FL 46, 71, 72, 76, 118, 309, 311, **604**, 614, 619, 696, 722
TANF (Temporary Assistance to Needy Families) 50
Tanganyika 840
Tanzania **840-41**
Area, population 732, 840
Flag, map 476, 487
Foreign aid to 738
Forests 306
Fossil fuel reserves. 112
Health expenditures 142
Languages 715, 840
Merchant fleet. 77
Refugees in 735
Sanitation/drinking water 737
U.S. embassy bombing (1998) 452, 670
Taoism 698
Tarbell, Ida 442
Tariffs. *See* Customs, U.S.
TARP (Troubled Assets Relief Program) 454, 455
Ta'u Island 591
Taurids meteor shower 337
Tax Court, U.S. 376
Taxes, federal. *See* Income taxes, federal
Taxes, state
California reduction (1978) 449
Gasoline 84
Income tax rates. 378-79
Revenues 60, 377
Taylor, Zachary 491, **495**, *495*, 504, 508
Teachers
College, university 389
Noted past 183-84
Public school 381
Teapot Dome (1929) 443
Technology. *See* Science and technology
Telecommunications **300-301**
Area codes, domestic. 622-45
AT&T breakup (1982, 1984) 449
Cell phones. 83, 300-301
Leading U.S. companies 52, 53
Milestones 300
First long-distance phone call (1884) 441
First telephone exchange (1878) 441, 658
Transatlantic telephone cable (1956) 445
Transcontinental telephone call, first (1915) 442
White House first telephone. 503
Telegraph, historic events 440, 658
Telephones. *See* Telecommunications
Telescopes 330-32, 341, 670
Television
Awards 32, 270, 272-73
Cable 254, 255
Content ratings 246
Journalists, noted past 184-85
Presidential appearance, first. 503
Program ratings, most watched 256-58
Quiz show scandal (1959) 446
Reality show winners 255
Set ownership. 254
Time spent viewing. 256
Transcontinental broadcast, first (1951) 445
Temperance movement (1874, 1900) 441, 442
Temperature
Boiling, freezing points 362
Celsius-Fahrenheit conversion 361
Extremes 312, 315
Global averages 303, 313
Heat index 314
U.S. normal, highs, lows. 309-12
Temporary Assistance to Needy Families (TANF) 50
Ten Commandments 702
Tennessee **586**
Agriculture 92, 94
Congressional representation 552, 557, 609
Crime, prisons, death penalty 117, 119, 120
Education 380-83, 389-90
Elevations (high, low) 423
Energy consumption. 111
Finances. 60
Governor. 37
Hazardous waste 305
Health insurance coverage. 142
Immigrant admissions. 619
Motor vehicles 83, 84
Name origin, nickname. 426, 586
Oil production 111
Population. 586, 600, 605, 606-07, 608, 611, 612, 641-42
Poverty rates 49
Taxes 84, 379
Unemployment 101
Weather 312
ZIP and area codes 641-42
Tennessee Valley Authority (TVA) . . 443, 547
Tennis 4, 17, 26, 28, 31, 448, *810*, 853, 870-71, **955-58**
Territorial sea, U.S. 427
Territories, U.S.
Accessions 427
Areas, population 591-93
Elevations (high, low) 423
Governors. 37
Statehood 425
Terrorism
African embassy bombings (1998) 452, 670
Boston Marathon bombing . . . 23, 456, *456*, 672
Budget for war on 133
Cole bombing (2000) 452, 670
Detainees 453, 454
Foiled plots 30, 451, 453, 454, 455, *815*
Lebanon 449, 668, 797
Libya, U.S. consulate attack (2012) . . . 456, 457, 672
Notable incidents since 1971 126-27
Oklahoma City bombing (1995) . . 451, *451*, 670
Olympic Games (1972, 1996). 451, 666
Recent events (2014-15) 4, 12, 15, 16, 20, 22, 26, 29, *196*
World Trade Center (1993, 2001). 450, 451, 452, 670
Tet New Year 355
Tetanus 157
Texas **586-87**
Accession (1845) 427, 439
Agriculture 92, 94
Coastline. 423
Congressional representation. . 552, 557-58, 609
Crime, prisons, death penalty 117, 119, 120
Education 380-83, 389-90
Elevations (high, low) 423
Energy consumption. 111
Finances. 60
Governor. 37
Hazardous waste 305
Health insurance coverage. 142
History (1682, 1821). 436, 439
Immigrant admissions. 619
Motor vehicles 83, 84
Name origin, nickname. 426, 586
Oil production 111
Population. 586, 594, 596, 597, 598, 599, 602, 603, 605, 606-07, 608, 611, 612, 642-43
Poverty rates 49
Taxes 84
Traveler spending. 86
Unemployment 101
Weather 312
ZIP and area codes 642-43
Textile trade 74
Thailand **841**
Agriculture 97, 98, 99
Area, population 732, 841
Cell phone use 300
Economic crisis (1997) 669
Education 383
Fishing, aquaculture 100
Flag, map 476, 485
Foreign exchange rates 75
Forests 306
Fossil fuel reserves, exports 112, 113
Gasoline prices. 110
Health expenditures 142
Internally displaced persons. 735
Languages 715, 841
Military coups, protests. 673
Military strength 133
Motor vehicle production 79
Refugees in 735
Terrorism (2015). 29
Trade 73
Travel and tourism 85
U.S. investment 78
U.S. troops in 129
Thames River 692
Thanksgiving Day. 358, 440
Thatcher, Margaret 668, 669, *669*
Theater
Awards, prizes 263-64, 272
Broadway statistics. 247
Composers 215-16
First in colonies (1716) 437
Notable openings . . 443, 444, 445, 446, 450
Theft. 116-18, 121, 122
Theme parks 89
Thermodynamics, laws of 284
Third Reich. *See* Germany
Thirty Years War (1618-48) 139, 655
Thomas, Clarence. 38, 450, 559
Thoreau, Henry David 440
Thoroughbred racing. *See* Horse racing
Three Mile Island disaster (1979) 449
Threshold Test Ban Treaty 739
Thunderstorm characteristics. 308
Thurmond, Strom 507
Tiananmen Square protest 668, *668*
Tibet. 763
Ticonderoga, Fort. 437
Tidal waves 324
Tides 316
Tierra del Fuego 689, 762
Tilden, Samuel J. 441
Timbuktu 653
Time
Cities. 359
Daylight Saving. 360
Earth's rotation 352
Geologic scale 290
Greenwich 341, 360
International Date Line 360, 476
Military (24-hour) 360
Sidereal 341, 352
Solar. 352
Standard. 359, 360
Zones (map). 476
Time capsule (2015) 42
Timelines
Architecture 727-29
War. 139-40
Timor-Leste (East Timor) 476, 485, 488, 669, 689, 732, 736, **841-42**
Tin 68
Tippecanoe, Battle of (1811) 439
Tobacco
Exports, imports 74, 75
Leading U.S. companies 54
Production 96
(*see also* Smoking)
Tobago. *See* Trinidad and Tobago
Togo. 476, 486, 732, 733, 736, 737, **842**
Tokelau Island. 488, 818
Toledo, OH 71, **604**, 614
Tonga. 476, 488, 732, 733, **842**
Tonkin Resolution (1964). 447
Tony Awards. 272
Top 10 News Topics of 2015 4
Tornadoes. 308, 322, 455
Tour de France 28, 973
Tourette syndrome. 421
Tourism. *See* Travel and tourism
Toussaint L'Ouverture, François . . . *657*, 658
Towers, free-standing 716
Townshend Acts (1767). 437
Track and field 871-76, 975
(*see also* Marathons)
Trade 32, **73-78**
(*see also* Exports, imports)
Trademarks. *See* Patents and copyrights
Trail of Tears (1838) 439
Trails, national scenic 433
Trains. *See* Railroads, U.S.; Railroads, world
Transcendentalism (1836) 439
Transgender. *See* LGBT
Transplants, surgical 144
Transportation **79-91**
Employment 102, 103, 106
Expenditures, consumer. 51
History 442, 445, 660
Leading U.S. companies 53
Occupational injuries, illnesses 105
Ports 76
Price Indexes 45, 46
U.S. expenditures. 58
U.S. national income 44
(*see also* Travel and tourism; specific types)
Transportation, Department of **545**
Created (1966) 447
Employees 106
Secretaries 545
Transportation Safety Board, National. . . 547
Travel and tourism **85-91**
Air distances between world cities 91
Air travel regulations. 90
Associations and organizations 408
Destination rankings. 85
Health regulations. 90
International visitors to U.S. 86
Leading U.S. companies 54
National parks/monuments. . 428-35, 489-90
Passports, visas 90
Receipts, global 85
States, territories 563-93
Top websites 89
Travel warnings 90

Traveler spending . . . 86
TSA regulations . . . 90
U.S. domestic travel . . . 86
U.S. resident travel abroad . . . 87
Washington (DC) sites . . . 434-35
Treasury, Department of the . . . **540-41**
Bonds and securities . . . 66
Created . . . 438
Employees . . . 106
Secretaries . . . 540-41
Treaties. *See* Arms control; specific treaties
Trees . . . 306
Triangle Shirtwaist Co. fire (1911) . . . 442
Triathlon . . . 978
Trinidad and Tobago 112, 113, 121, 476, 479, 689, 732, **842-43**
Triple Alliance . . . 660
Triple Crown (horse racing) . . . 4, 26, *812*, 966
Tripoli (1801, 1805, 1815) . . . 438, 439
Tristan da Cunha . . . 689, 848
Tropical storms . . . 308, 312, 323
Troubled Assets Relief Program (TARP) . . . 454, 455
Trucks. *See* Automobiles, motor vehicles
Trudeau, Garry . . . 447
Truman Doctrine . . . 445, 664
Truman, Harry S. . . . 444, 445, 491, **499**, *499*, 503, 504, 507, 508
Trump, Donald . . . 6, 7, 25, 39, *198*
Tsars, Russian . . . 653, 681
Tsunami . . . 308, 671
Tuamotu Archipelago . . . 776
Tuberculosis . . . 157
Tubuai (Astral) Islands . . . 776
Tucson, AZ . . . 71, 304, **604**, 614, 696
Tudor, House of . . . 653, 675
Tulsa, OK . . . 71, **604**, 614, 696, 722
Tunisia . . . 20, 26, 85, 134, 383, 439, 476, 486, 672, 715, 732, **843**
Tunnels . . . **725-26**
Turkey . . . **843-44**
Agriculture . . . 97, 98, 99
Area, population . . . 730, 732, 843
Cell phone use . . . 300
Computer/Internet use . . . 297
Education . . . 383, 385
Election (2015) . . . 25
Flag, map . . . 476, 484
Fossil fuel reserves . . . 112
Gross domestic product . . . 733
Health expenditures . . . 142
History . . . 653, 662, 666
Internally displaced persons . . . 736
Languages . . . 715, 843
Merchant fleet . . . 77
Military strength . . . 133
Motor vehicle production . . . 79
Muslim population . . . 706
Prison population . . . 121
Refugees from/in . . . 735
Separatist movement (2015) . . . 31, 32
Taxes . . . 734
Travel and tourism . . . 85
U.S. investment . . . 78
U.S. military financing . . . 134
U.S. troops in . . . 129
Turkeys. *See* Poultry products
Turkmenistan . . . 112, 476, 484, 715, 732, 736, **844**
Turks and Caicos Islands . . . 732, 848
Turner, Nat . . . 439
Tutankhamen, tomb of . . . 662, *662*
Tutuila Island . . . 591
Tuvalu . . . 476, 488, 731, 732, 733, **844**
TV. *See* Television
TVA (Tennessee Valley Authority) . . . 443, 547
Twain, Mark . . . 441
Tweed, William "Boss" . . . 441
21-gun salute . . . 135
24-hour time . . . 360
Twins. *See* Multiple births
Twitter . . . 298
Tyler, John . . . 491, **494**, *494*, 504
Typhoons . . . 308, 323

U

Uganda . . . 142, 166, 476, 487, 672, 715, 732, 735, 736, 737, 738, **844-45**
Ukraine . . . **845**
Agriculture . . . 97, 98, 99
Area, population . . . 732, 845
Cell phone use . . . 300
Flag, map . . . 476, 483
Fossil fuel reserves . . . 112
Health expenditures . . . 142
Internally displaced persons . . . 736
Languages . . . 715, 845
Motor vehicle production . . . 79
Nuclear power . . . 114
Political crisis . . . 17, 18, 28, 30, 32, 34, 36, 37-38, 39, 41, 674
Presidential elections (2004, 2010) 671, 673
Soviet Union breakup . . . 668
Spaceflight . . . 333
Travel and tourism . . . 85
U.S. adoptions from . . . 166
U.S. military financing . . . 134
Ulcers. *See* Peptic ulcers
Ulster. *See* Ireland, Northern
Ultraviolet (UV) index . . . 314
Umayyad dynasty . . . 650
Unabomber case . . . 452
Underwear bomber . . . 454
Unemployment insurance . . . 101, 454, 455
Unemployment rates . . . 12, 19, 101-03, 106, 454, 734
UNESCO . . . 742
UNICEF . . . 742
Union of Soviet Socialist Republics. *See* Soviet Union
Unions. *See* Labor unions
United Arab Emirates . . . **845-46**
Agriculture . . . 99
Area, population . . . 732, 845
Computer/Internet use . . . 297
Dubai debt crisis . . . 670
Education . . . 383
Flag, map . . . 476, 484
Fossil fuel reserves . . . 112
Gross domestic product . . . 733
Languages . . . 845
Travel and tourism . . . 85
U.S. investment . . . 78
U.S. troops in . . . 129
Water supply . . . 306
United Church of Christ . . . 698, 704-05
United Kingdom . . . **846-48**
Agriculture . . . 97, 98, 99
Area, population . . . 730, 732, 846
Arms purchases/sales . . . 133, 134
Budget deficits . . . 59
Carbon dioxide emissions . . . 302
Cell phone use . . . 300
Commonwealth . . . 739
Computer/Internet use . . . 294, 297, 298
Consumer price changes . . . 733
Education . . . 383, 385
Flag, map . . . 476, 482
Foreign aid from . . . 738
Foreign exchange rates . . . 75
Fossil fuel reserves, exports . . . 112, 113
Gasoline prices . . . 110
Gold reserves . . . 733
Gross domestic product . . . 733
Health expenditures . . . 142
History . . . 846-47
American Revolution . . . 437-38
Industrial Revolution . . . 656, *656*, 658
Iraq war . . . 670
Post-Cold war . . . 668, 669
Pre-1800 . . . 139, 653-54, 655
Urbanization . . . 659
War of 1812 . . . 439
World War I and aftermath . . . 661, 662
World War II . . . 444, 664
Hong Kong handover (1997) . . . 669
Islands, areas . . . 689
Languages . . . 715, 846
Merchant fleet . . . 77
Mortality rate by cause . . . 736
Motor vehicle production, exports . . . 79
News (2015) . . . 23-24, *815*
Nuclear arms . . . 738
Nuclear power . . . 114
Prime ministers . . . 676
Refugees in . . . 735
Rulers and royal family . . . 675-76, 846
Securities held by U.S. . . . 64
Spaceflight . . . 333
Taxes . . . 734
Terrorist bombings (2005) . . . 670
Trade . . . 73
Travel and tourism . . . 85, 86, 87
Unemployment rates . . . 734
U.S. ancestral claims . . . 621
U.S. immigrants from . . . 9, 620
U.S. investment . . . 78
U.S. troops in . . . 129
Vacation days . . . 89
Wages, hourly . . . 734
(*see also* specific countries)
United Nations . . . **741-43**
Agencies . . . 741-42
Charter (1945) . . . 664, 741
Dumbarton Oaks conference (1944) . . . 444
Headquarters . . . 741
Members . . . 743
Peacekeeping efforts . . . 451, 742
Secretaries General . . . 741
U.S. ambassadors to . . . 743
United Nations High Commissioner for Refugees (UNHCR) . . . 742
United Nations Industrial Development Org. (UNIDO) . . . 742
United States of America . . . **848-49**
Abortions . . . 167
Accessions . . . 427
Agencies, government . . . 547
Agriculture . . . 92-100
Anthem, national . . . 439, 489
Area codes, telephone . . . 622-45
Areas . . . 422, 424, 608, 848
Banks . . . 61-62
Boundaries . . . 425
Budget . . . 57-59
Cabinets, presidential . . . 539-47
Cell phone use . . . 300, 301
Cities . . . 594-604, 614-15
Coastline (by states) . . . 423
Computer/Internet use . . . 294, 297, 298
Congress . . . 548-58
Constitution . . . 450, 461-69, *461*
Consumer prices . . . 44-46, 733
Continental Divide . . . 424
Currency . . . 55-57
Debt, national . . . 60
Elevations (highest, lowest) . . . 423
Energy production/consumption . . . 109-15
Fishing, aquaculture . . . 100
Flag . . . 437, 471-72, *471*, *476*
Foreign aid from . . . 738
Foreign investment in . . . 78
Forest Service administered areas . . . 333
Forests . . . 306
Gasoline prices . . . 110
Geographic centers . . . 425
Geographic superlatives . . . 422
Gold production, reserves . . . 67-68, 733
Government . . . 539-62
Greenhouse gas/carbon dioxide emissions . . . 302, 303
Gross domestic/national products . . . 43
Gross national/domestic products . . . 733
History . . . 436-57
Holidays . . . 358
Immigration . . . 619-20
Income, national . . . 44
Income taxes . . . 375-79, 734
Investments abroad . . . 78
Labor force . . . 101-08
Languages . . . 848
Maps . . . 477
Merchant fleet . . . 77
Military affairs . . . 128-40
Mortality rate by cause . . . 736
Motor vehicle production, exports/imports . . . 79-80
Motto, national . . . 470
National parks/monuments . . 428-35, 489-90
Nuclear arms, treaties . . . 738, 739
Outlying areas . . . 591-93
Population . . . 605-45, 730, 731, 732, 848
Postal information . . . **366-67**
Presidential elections . . . 505-38
Presidents . . . 491-504
Recreation areas . . . 333, 432
Refugees in . . . 735
Religions . . . 697-98
Seal . . . 471, *471*
Social Security . . . 368-74, 734
Space program . . . 329-34
State profiles . . . 563-93
Statehood dates . . . 424, 425
Trade . . . 73-78
Travel and tourism . . . 85, 86-87
Unemployment . . . 12, 20, 101-03, 106, 454, 734
Vice presidents . . . 491-92
Vital statistics . . . 164-72
Wages, hourly . . . 734
War casualties . . . 138
Water area . . . 424, 608
ZIP codes . . . 622-45
Universal Postal Union (UPU) . . . 742
Universe, early . . . 344
Universities. *See* Colleges and universities
Unknowns, Tomb of the . . . 434
Unmarried partner households . . . 618
Upanishads . . . 648, 707
UPU (Universal Postal Union) . . . 742
Uranus (planet) . . . 344, 345, **347-48**
Morning, evening stars . . . 341
Position by month . . . 337-40
Urban areas. *See* Cities, U.S.; Cities, world; Metropolitan areas, U.S.
Urinary incontinence . . . 421
Uruguay . . . 121, 383, 476, 481, 732, **849**
U.S. Open (golf) . . . 26, 853, 952, 954
U.S. Open (tennis) . . . 31, 957-58
USSR. *See* Soviet Union
Utah . . . **587**
Agriculture . . . 92, 94
Congressional representation 552, 558, 609
Crime, prisons, death penalty 117, 119, 120
Education . . . 380-83, 389-90
Elevations (high, low) . . . 423
Energy consumption . . . 111
Finances . . . 60
Governor . . . 37
Hazardous waste . . . 305
Health insurance coverage . . . 142
Immigrant admissions . . . 619

Motor vehicles 83, 84
Name origin, nickname 426, 587
Oil production 111
Population 587, 605, 606-07, 608, 611, 612, 643
Poverty rates 49
Taxes 84, 379
Unemployment 101
Weather 312
ZIP and area codes 643
Utilities, gas and electric 46, 51, 52
U-2 incident (1960) 446
Uzbekistan **849**
Agriculture 97, 98
Area, population 732, 849
Flag, map 476, 484
Fossil fuel reserves 112
Gold production 68
Health expenditures 142
Internally displaced persons 736
Languages 715, 849
Motor vehicle production 79
Muslim population 706

V

Vacations. *See* Holidays
Vaccination. *See* Immunization and vaccination
Valcour Island, Battle of 437
Valois, House of 677
Van Buren, Martin 491, **494**, *494*, 503, 504, 508
Vanuatu 21, 476, 488, 689, 732, 733, **849-50**
Varangians 652
Vatican City (Holy See) 476, 731, 732, **850**
Veal 94, 96-97
Veda 648, 707
Vegetables production, consumption 94
Venezuela **850**
Agriculture 97, 99
Area, population 732, 850
Coup (2002) 671
Elections (2012, 2013) 673
Flag, map 476, 480
Forests 306
Fossil fuel reserves, exports 112, 113
Health expenditures 142
Languages 850
Liberation of 681
Presidents 670
Refugees from/in 735
Trade 73
Travel and tourism 86
U.S. investment 78
Venomous animals 291-92
Venus (planet) 344, **345-46**
Morning, evening stars 341
Position by month 337-40
Vermont **587-88**
Agriculture 92, 94
Congressional representation 552, 558, 609
Crime, prisons, death penalty 117, 119, 120
Education 380-83, 389-90
Elevations (high, low) 423
Energy consumption 111
Finances 60
Governor 37
Hazardous waste 305
Health insurance coverage 142
Immigrant admissions 619
Motor vehicles 83, 84
Name origin, nickname 426, 587
Population 587, 605, 606-07, 608, 611, 612, 643-44
Poverty rates 49
Taxes 84, 379
Unemployment 101
Weather 312
ZIP and area codes 643-44
Vernal Equinox 338, 352
Verrazano, Giovanni da 436, 683
Versailles, Treaty of (1919) 661
Vespucci, Amerigo 683
Vesuvius, Mount 685
Veterans Affairs, Department of 106, **546**
Veterans' Day 358
Veterans, U.S.
Agent Orange suit (1984) 449
Associations and organizations 408-09
Disabled 132
GI Bill 444
Health administration 132
Numbers, compensation 131, 132
U.S. expenditures 58
Vetoes, presidential 549
Vice presidents, U.S. **491-92**
Nominees (1856-2012) 507
Presidential succession 447, 469-70
Salary 539
Salutes, honors 135
Video games 246
Videos/DVDs
Movies, most popular (2014) 246
Music 254, 278
(*see also* Movies)
Vietnam **851**
Agriculture 97, 98, 99
Area, population 732, 851
Cell phone use 300
Division (1954) 665
Education 383
Fishing, aquaculture 100
Flag, map 476, 485
Forests 306
Fossil fuel reserves, exports 112, 113
Health expenditures 142
Indochina War (1946-54) 665
Languages 715, 851
Merchant fleet 77
Military strength 133
Nam-Viet Kingdom 652
Refugees from 449, 735
Tet New Year 355
Travel and tourism 85
U.S. immigrants from 619, 620
U.S. trade ban lifted/relations normalized (1994, 1995) 451
Vietnam War 140, 665, 666
Agent Orange settlement (1984) 449
Black troops 132
Bombings (1965, 1966, 1971, 1972) 447, 448
Casualties, U.S. forces 138
Chicago 7 trial (1970) 447
Demonstrations against 447, *447*, 665
End (1975) 448-49, 666, *666*
Military awards 136
My Lai massacre 447, 448
Peace talks, pacts (1969, 1973) 447
Tet offensive (1968) 447
Tonkin Resolution (1964) 447
Troop withdrawal (1973) 448
Veteran population 131
Veterans Memorial (DC) 435
Vikings 652, 683
Virgin Islands, British 689, 732, 848
Virgin Islands, U.S. **593**
Accession (1917) 427, 443
Area, capital, population 593, 689, 732
Congressional delegate 558
Education 382
Elevations (high, low) 423
Governor 37
Hazardous waste 305
Virginia **588**
Agriculture 92, 94
Coastline 423
Congressional representation 552, 558, 609
Crime, prisons, death penalty 117, 119, 120
Education 380-83, 389-90
Elevations (high, low) 423
Energy consumption 111
Finances 60
Governor 37
Hazardous waste 305
Health insurance coverage 142
Immigrant admissions 619
Memorials, monuments 434-35
Motor vehicles 83, 84
Name origin, nickname 426, 588
Oil production 111
Population 588, 595, 601, 602, 604, 605, 606-07, 608, 611, 612, 644
Poverty rates 49
Taxes 84, 379
Traveler spending 86
Unemployment 101
Weather 312
ZIP and area codes 644
Virginia Beach, VA 71, **604**, 614, 722
Virginia Tech shooting 453
Visas 90
Vital statistics **164-72**
Vitamins 159, 160
Vojvodina 831
Volcanoes 279, 449, 685-86
Volga River 692
Voltaire 656
Vonnegut, Kurt, Jr. 447
Voting rights. *See* Elections
Voting Rights Act (1965) 447, 456

W

Wade Trophy 888
Wake Atoll 488, 593
Wales 621, 669, **847**
Walesa, Lech 669, 825
Walker, Scott 6, 7, 39, *198*, 455, 456
Wall Street. *See* Stocks
Wallace, George 448, 507, 509-38
Wallis and Futuna Islands 488, 732, 777
Walter Reed Army Medical Center 453
War crimes
Geneva Conventions 744
Milosevic trial 671
My Lai massacre (1969) 447, 448
Nuremberg trials (1946) 664
War, Department of 438, 541-42
War of 1812 (1812-15) 138, 439
War of the Austrian Succession (1740-48) 139
War of the Spanish Succession (1701-14) 139
***War of the Worlds* (radio broadcast) (1938)** 444
War timeline 139-40
(*see also* Military affairs; specific wars)
Warehouse Act (1916) 443
Warren Commission (1964) 447
Wars of the Roses (1455-85) 139, 653
Washington (state) **588-89**
Agriculture 92, 94
Coastline 423
Congressional representation 552, 558, 609
Crime, prisons, death penalty 117, 119, 120
Education 380-83, 389-90
Elevations (high, low) 423
Energy consumption 111
Finances 60
Governor 37
Hazardous waste 305
Health insurance coverage 142
Immigrant admissions 619
Motor vehicles 84
Name origin, nickname 426, 588
Population 588, 603, 605, 606-07, 608, 611, 612, 644-45
Poverty rates 49
Taxes 84
Unemployment 101
Weather 312
Wildfires (2015) 30
ZIP and area codes 644-45
Washington, Booker T. 441, 442
Washington, DC **591, 604**
Air mileage to other cities 91
Air quality 304
Airport traffic 88
British burning of (1814) 439
Buildings, tall 722
Congressional delegate 558
Consumer Price Index 46
Crime rates 118
Education 380-83, 389-90
Elevations (high, low) 423
Energy consumption 111
Geography 696
Hazardous waste 305
Health insurance coverage 142
Housing 71, 72
Immigrant admissions 619
Marches and protests
Antiwar (1967) 447
Black civil rights (1963) 446
Million Man (1995) 451
Motor vehicles 84
Name origin, nickname 426
Population 591, 604, 605, 608, 611, 614, 615, 626
Poverty rates 49
Sniper case (2002-03) 452-53
Taxes 84, 378
Tides 316
Tourist attractions 434-35
Unemployment 101
Voting rights 468
Weather 309, 311, 313
Wilson burial place 503
ZIP and area code 626
Washington, George 491, **493**, *493*, 504
Birthday (legal holiday) 358
Commander-in-chief (1775) 437
Constitutional convention (1787) 438
Delaware crossing (1776) 437
Farewell address (1796) 438
Long Island battle (1776) 437
Mount Vernon 435
President (1789, 1793) 438, 508
Princeton battle (1777) 437
Washington Monument (DC) 435, 441
Water
Area (U.S.) 424, 608
Boiling, freezing points 362
Dams, reservoirs 726-27
Drinking water sources 737
Energy from 109, 115, 727
Health, nutrition 159
Lakes 694
Oceans, seas, gulfs 690
Renewable resources 306
Rivers 691-93
Waterfalls 422, 695
Watergate scandal (1972-75) 448, 453, 666
Waterloo, Battle of (1815) 657
Wawrinka, Stanislas 26
Wayne, "Mad" Anthony 438
Wealthiest individuals 48
Weapons. *See* Arms contracts/sales; Firearms; Nuclear arms
Weather **308-16**
Blizzards 308, 323, 441
Cities and states (U.S.) 309-12
Cities, world 313
Cyclones 21, 308, 312, 323

Floods. 17, 25, 33, 308, 324, 441, 451, 453, *453*
Global 315
Heat index 314
Heat waves (2015) 26, *197*
Hurricanes . . . 308, 323, 450, 453, *453*, 456
Lightning 315
Marine warnings, advisories 308
Precipitation 309-11, 313, 315, 422
Storm classifications, names 308, 312
Temperatures 17, 303, 309-13, 315
Thunderstorms 308
Tornadoes 308, 322, 455
Typhoons 308, 323
Ultraviolet index 314
Watches, warnings 308
Wind chill 314
Wind speed 313
Weather Bureau, founded 441
Weaver, James B. 507
Websites. *See* Internet
Webster, Daniel 439
Webster, Noah 439
Webster-Ashburton Treaty (1842) 439
Wedding anniversaries 359
Weight, body 151, 155, 161-62
Weights and measures **361-65**
Welfare
Federal food programs 92
Reform legislation (1996) 451
Supplemental Security Income 371
Temporary Assistance to Needy Families (by state) 50
Wen Jiabao 682, 763
West Bank 33, 670, 732, 738, **791**
West Germany. *See* Germany
West Indies 621, 686
West Indies, British 848
West Point Military Academy 136, 438
West Virginia **589**
Agriculture 92, 94
Congressional representation 552, 558, 609
Crime, prisons, death penalty 117, 119
Education 380-83, 389-90
Elevations (high, low) 423
Energy consumption 111
Finances 60
Governor 37
Hazardous waste 305
Health insurance coverage 142
Immigrant admissions 619
Motor vehicles 83, 84
Name origin, nickname 426, 589
Oil production 111
Population 589, 605, 606-07, 608, 645
Poverty rates 49
Taxes 84, 379
Unemployment 101
Weather 312
ZIP and area codes 645
Western Sahara 732, 735, 742, **807**
Westminster Kennel Club 976
Wheat 96-99
Whiskey Rebellion (1794) 438
Whitbread Award (Costa Book Awards) . . 270
White House
History (1792, 1814, 1889) . . . 438, 439, 441
Security breaches 19
Staff 539
Tourist attraction 435
Whitewater scandal 451, 452
Whitman, Walt 440
Whitney, Eli 438, *438*
WHO (World Health Org.) 742
Whooping cough 157
Wichita, KS 71, 313, **604**, 614, 696
WikiLeaks 455, 456, 673
Wilder, L. Douglas 451
Wilder, Thornton 444
Wilkes Atoll 593
William the Conqueror 652, 675
Williams, Brian 19, *814*
Williams, Serena 4, 17, 26, 28, *810*, 853
Wilson, Woodrow . . . 491, **498**, *498*, 503, 504, 507, 508
Wimbledon 28, 853, 956-57
Wind
Chill factor 314
Energy from 109, 115
Solar 351
Speeds (U.S.) 313
Windsor, House of 676, 846
Windward Islands. *See* Dominica; St. Lucia; St. Vincent and the Grenadines
Winston-Salem, NC 71, 304, **604**, 615
Winter Solstice 340, 352
Wisconsin **590**
Agriculture 92, 94
Collective bargaining limits 455
Congressional representation 552, 558, 609
Crime, prisons, death penalty 117, 119, 120
Education 380-83, 389-90
Elevations (high, low) 423
Energy consumption 111
Finances 60
Governor 37
Hazardous waste 305
Health insurance coverage 142
Immigrant admissions 619
Motor vehicles 83, 84
Name origin, nickname 426, 590
Population 590, 600, 605, 606-07, 608, 611, 612, 645
Poverty rates 49
Primary voting (1903) 442
Taxes 84, 379
Unemployment 101
Weather 312
ZIP and area codes 645
Women
Armed forces 130, 434, 447, *815*
Cancer 150-51, 152
Cardiovascular disease 155
Cigarette use 146
Colleges, first (1821) 439
Education 380, 384, 386, 390
Employment, unemployment 103, 108
Equal Rights Amendment 448, 449
Feminist revival (1960s) 665
First attorney general (1993) 451
First cabinet member (1933) 443
First congresswoman (1916) 443
First Federal Reserve chair 456
First governor (1924) 443
First House leader (2007) 453
First in space 449
First ladies 504
First secretary of state (1997) 451
Health information 421
HIV/AIDS cases 148
Income, wages 47, 106
Life expectancy 172
Population 610, 617
Poverty rates 49
Prison inmates 120
Rights convention (1848) 440
Sexual activity 167, 168
Single-parent households 618
Strikers, first (1824) 439
Suicide rates 170
Supreme Court justices (1981, 1993) . . 449, *449*, 451
Vice-presidential nominees (1984, 2008) 449, 454
Voting rights (1869, 1920) . . . 441, 443, 468
World leaders 668, 671, 673
Women's Christian Temperance Union (1874) 441
Women's National Basketball Assn. (WNBA) 33, 941-42
Women's World Cup (soccer) 4, 28, *812*, 853, 948
Wooden Award, John R. 886
Woods, Tiger 452
Woodstock music festival (1969) . . . 447, 666
Wool 96-97
Woolworth's Five and Dime (1879) 441
Workers. *See* Employment, U.S.
Works Progress Administration (WPA) (1935) 443
***World Almanac*, first (1868)** 441
World Bank 742
World Court 741
World Cup (soccer) 949
World Health Org. (WHO) 742
World history
Chronology 646-73
Historical figures 674-82
World Intellectual Property Org. (WIPO) 742
World Meteorological Org. (WMO) 742
World Series
Black Sox scandal (1921) 443
Earthquake during (1989) 450
First (1903) 442
Perfect game pitched (1956) 445-46
Recent (2015) 907
Results (1903-2014) 929
World Tourism Org. (UNWTO) 742
World Trade Center
Bombing (1993) 450, 451, 670
Destruction (2001) 452, 670
(*see also* One World Trade Center)
World Trade Org. (WTO) 74, 742
World War I (1914-18) 140, 443, 661, *661*
Black troops 132
Casualties, U.S. forces 138
Military awards 136
U.S. neutrality (1914) 442
Versailles, Treaty of (1919) 661
World War II (1939-45) . . 140, 444, *445*, 663-64
Atomic bombs (1945) 444, 663, *664*
Black troops 132
Casualties, U.S. forces 138
Military awards 136
National memorial (DC) 435
Peace treaties, Japan (1951) 445
Pearl Harbor attack (1941) 444, 663
U.S. neutrality (1939) 444
Veteran population 131
WorldCom Inc. 452
Wounded Knee, Battle of (1890) 441
WPA (Works Progress Administration) . . 443
Wrangell-St. Elias National Park 422
Wrestling 889
Wright brothers (1903) 336, 442, 660
Wright, Jeremiah 453
Wright, Richard 444
Writers, noted **208-14**
Lyricists 216
Nobel Prizes 259, 261
Poets laureate 214
WTO (World Trade Org.) 74, 742
Wyoming **590**
Agriculture 92, 94
Congressional representation 552, 558, 609
Crime, prisons, death penalty 117, 119, 120
Education 380-83, 389-90
Elevations (high, low) 423
Energy consumption 111
Finances 60
Governor 37
Hazardous waste 305
Health insurance coverage 142
Immigrant admissions 619
Motor vehicles 83, 84
Name origin, nickname 426, 590
Oil production 111
Population 590, 605, 606-07, 608, 611, 612, 645
Poverty rates 49
Taxes 84
Unemployment 101
Weather 312
ZIP and area codes 645

X

Xi Jinping 457, 673, 682, 763
Xinjiang Uighur 763

Y

Yacht racing 979
Yalta Conference (1945) 444, 664
Year
Calendar, perpetual 356-57
Chronology of events (2013-14) 12-33
Holidays 358
In pictures (2015) *193-200, 809-16*
Sidereal, tropical 341, 352
Yellen, Janet 456
Yellow fever 157
Yellow Sea 690
Yellowstone National Park 279, 422, 441
Yeltsin, Boris 668, 681, 827
Yemen **851-52**
al-Queda 671, 672
Area, population 732
Flag, map 476, 484
Fossil fuel reserves 112
Health expenditures 142
Internally displaced persons 736
Languages 715
Muslim population 706
News (2015) 16, 18, 20, 22, 27-28, 29, *194*
Refugees in 735
U.S. military financing 134
Water supply 306
(*see also* Arab Spring protests)
York, House of 675
Y2K 452
Yugoslavia 662, 668
(*see also* Montenegro; Serbia)
Yukon River 693

Z

Zaire. *See* Congo
Zambia 306, 476, 487, 715, 732, 738, **852**
Zanzibar 689, **840**
Zelaya, Manuel 671
Zen Buddhism 654
(*see also* Buddhism)
Zenger, John Peter 437
Ziggurats 647
Zimbabwe **852**
Area, population 732, 852
Elections (2008, 2013) 671
Flag, map 476, 487
Forests 306
Fossil fuel reserves 112
Independence 667
Languages 715, 852
Refugees from 735, 736
Zimmerman, George 456
Zinc 68, 160
ZIP codes 622-45
Zodiac signs 355
Zoological hierarchy 291
Zoos, first 441
Zoroaster 649
Zoroastrianism 649, 698

QUICK REFERENCE INDEX

ACADEMY AWARDS ... 19, 274-76
ACTORS, ACTRESSES ... 222-42
AEROSPACE ... 329-36
AGRICULTURE ... 92-100
ANIMALS ... 291-93, 709-10
AREA CODES, U.S. ... 622-45
ARTISTS, PHOTOGRAPHERS, AND SCULPTORS ... 178-81
ARTS AND MEDIA ... 243-58
ASSASSINATIONS ... 123-25
ASSOCIATIONS AND ORGANIZATIONS ... 407-21
ASTRONOMY ... 337-53
AUTO RACING ... 959-61
AWARDS, MEDALS, PRIZES ... 259-78
BASEBALL ... 888, 907-32
BASKETBALL ... 882-88, 933-42
BIBLICAL FIGURES ... 703
BOOKS ... 249-50, 263-70
BOXING ... 962-65
BUILDINGS, BRIDGES, AND TUNNELS ... 716-29
BUSINESSES AND CORPORATIONS ... 52-55, 68-70, 410-17
CABINETS, U.S. ... 539-47
CALENDARS ... 354-60
CHEMICAL ELEMENTS ... 282-83
CHRONOLOGY (2014-15) ... 12-33
CITIES OF THE U.S. ... 594-604, 614-15
COLLEGES AND UNIVERSITIES ... 391-406, 877-89
COMPUTERS AND TELECOMMUNICATIONS ... 294-301
CONGRESS, U.S. ... 548-58
CONSTITUTION, U.S. ... 461-69
CRIME ... 116-27
DEFENSE, NATIONAL ... 128-40
DIRECTORY ... 407-21
DISASTERS ... 317-28
ECONOMICS ... 43-72
EDUCATION ... 380-406
ELECTIONS, U.S. ... 6-7, 505-38
EMPLOYMENT ... 101-08
ENERGY ... 109-15
ENTERTAINERS ... 222-42
ENVIRONMENT ... 302-07
EXPLORATION AND GEOGRAPHY ... 683-96
FAMOUS PEOPLE ... 173-92, 201-42
FIRST AID ... 163
FIRST LADIES ... 504
FLAGS OF THE WORLD (COLOR) ... 473-76
FOOD AND NUTRITION ... 158-61
FOOTBALL ... 854, 877-83, 890-906
GEOGRAPHICAL DATA ... 422-27, 683-96
GOLF ... 952-54
GOVERNMENT, U.S. ... 539-62
GOVERNORS, U.S. ... 37
GRAMMY AWARDS ... 19, 277-78
HEADS OF STATE ... 745-808, 817-52
HEALTH ... 141-63
HEALTH ORGANIZATIONS ... 421
HISTORICAL ANNIVERSARIES ... 41-42
HISTORICAL FIGURES ... 674-82
HOCKEY ... 889, 943-47
HOLIDAYS ... 358, 699-700
HOUSE OF REPRESENTATIVES, U.S. ... 548-50, 552-58
IMMIGRATION ... 8-11
INTERNET ... 295-99
INVENTIONS AND DISCOVERIES ... 285-89
LABOR UNION DIRECTORY ... 417-18
LANGUAGE ... 708-15
LATITUDE, LONGITUDE, AND ELEVATION OF CITIES 695-96
MAPS (COLOR) ... 476-88
METEOROLOGY ... 308-16
METRIC SYSTEM ... 361, 363-65
MILEAGE BETWEEN CITIES ... 91
MILITARY ... 128-40
MOUNTAINS ... 687-88
MOVIES ... 243-46, 273-77
MUSIC ... 214-18, 252-54
NAMES, POPULAR ... 711-12
NATIONAL PARKS AND MONUMENTS ... 428-35
NATIONS OF THE WORLD ... 745-808, 817-52
NEWS EVENTS (2014-15) ... 12-33
NEWS TOPICS, TOP 10 (2015) ... 4
NOBEL PRIZES ... 259-62
NUCLEAR POWERS ... 738
OBAMA ADMINISTRATION ... 539
OBITUARIES ... 34-36, 816
OFFBEAT NEWS STORIES (2015) ... 40
PERIODIC TABLE ... 283
PERSONALITIES ... 173-92, 201-42
PICTURES, YEAR IN (COLOR) ... 193-200, 809-16
PLANETS ... 345-50
POPULATION, U.S. ... 605-45
POPULATION, U.S. PLACES OF 10,000+ ... 622-45
POPULATION, WORLD ... 730-32
POSTAL INFORMATION ... 366-67, 622-45
PRESIDENTIAL ELECTIONS, U.S. ... 6-7, 505-38
PRESIDENTS, U.S. ... 491-504
RELIGION ... 697-707
RELIGIOUS LEADERS ... 187-88
RELIGIOUS ORGANIZATIONS ... 409-10, 697-98, 704-05
RENEWABLE ENERGY ... 115
RIVERS ... 432, 691-93
SCIENCE AND TECHNOLOGY ... 279-93
SCIENCE NEWS (2015) ... 279
SENATE, U.S. ... 548, 551-52
SOCCER ... 889, 948-51
SOCIAL SECURITY AND MEDICARE ... 368-74
SPACE FLIGHTS, NOTABLE ... 329-33
SPORTS ... 853-979
STATE GOVERNORS ... 37
STATES, KEY DATA ... 422-26
STATES OF THE UNION ... 563-93
SUPREME COURT, U.S. ... 38, 559-62
TAXES ... 375-79
TELECOMMUNICATIONS ... 300-01
TELEVISION ... 254-58, 272-73
TENNIS ... 955-58
TERRORISM ... 126-27
TIME CAPSULE (2015) ... 42
TIME DIFFERENCES ... 359, 476
TRADE ... 73-78
TRANSPORTATION AND TRAVEL ... 79-91
UNITED NATIONS ... 741-43
U.S. FACTS ... 422-35
U.S. FLAG ... 471-72
U.S. GOVERNMENT ... 539-62
U.S. HISTORY ... 436-57
VETERANS ... 131-32
VICE PRESIDENTS, U.S. ... 491-92
VIDEO GAMES ... 246
VITAL STATISTICS ... 164-72
WEATHER ... 308-16
WEIGHTS AND MEASURES ... 361-65
WORLD AT A GLANCE ... 5
WORLD HISTORY ... 646-73
WORLD PERSONALITIES ... 176-77
WRITERS ... 208-14, 261-70
ZODIAC SIGNS ... 355

For complete index, see pages 980-1007.

[redacted]